FICTION CORE COLLECTION

TWENTIETH EDITION

CORE COLLECTION SERIES

FORMERLY
STANDARD CATALOG SERIES

SHAUNA GRIFFIN, MLS

CHILDREN'S CORE COLLECTION
MIDDLE AND JUNIOR HIGH CORE COLLECTION
SENIOR HIGH CORE COLLECTION
FICTION CORE COLLECTION
PUBLIC LIBRARY CORE COLLECTION: NONFICTION
GRAPHIC NOVELS CORE COLLECTION
YOUNG ADULT FICTION CORE COLLECTION

FICTION CORE COLLECTION

TWENTIETH EDITION

EDITED BY

KENDAL SPIRES

H. W. Wilson
A Division of EBSCO Information Service, Inc.
Ipswich, Massachusetts
2020

GREY HOUSE PUBLISHING

ISBN 978-1-64265-316-8

Abridged Dewey Decimal Classification and Relative Index, Edition 15 is © 2004-2012 OCLC Online Computer Library Center, Inc. Used with Permission. DDC, Dewey, Dewey Decimal Classification, and WebDewey are registered trademarks of OCLC.

Fiction Core Collection, 2020, published by Grey House Publishing, Inc., Amenia, NY, under exclusive license from EBSCO Information Services, Inc.

A catalog record for this title is available from the Library of Congress.

PRINTED IN CANADA

TABLE OF CONTENTS

PREFACE

FICTION CORE COLLECTION is a curated list of essential and recommended classic and contemporary works of adult fiction either written in or translated to English. Developed by a team of skilled librarians, this list of recommended titles will be helpful to all libraries to develop their collection serving general adult readers. This volume is designed to assist with collection development and maintenance, help locate curriculum and programming materials, provide helpful purchasing and bibliographic information, and assist in readers' advisory support. It is drawn from the database of the same name available from EBSCO Information Services, which has an additional two recommendation levels, Lexile measures, and book reviews and articles.

What's in this Edition?

This 20th edition of the FICTION CORE COLLECTION emphasizes equity, diversity, and inclusion, representing and reflecting a varied community in which many voices can be heard. Our team of librarians has provided a significant review of titles to ensure that older, outdated books have been removed in favor of more relevant recommendations. The result is more than 8,100 fiction titles in all genres, as well as short story collections, anthologies, and classics. Also new to this edition is an increased coverage of urban fiction titles.

For the first time ever, book records in FICTION CORE COLLECTION will include subject headings. New metadata includes precise genres and subgenres, and subject headings that consistently include both location and time period where appropriate. Books will be much easier to find through the index, and the metadata associated with each record offers better insight into the contents of the book.

Additionally, beginning with this volume, we have increased the number of awards and short lists; all entries for titles in series will also include the name of that series.

As always, a star (*) at the start of an entry indicates that a book is an Essential title, our highest recommendation level. These titles are the essential books in a given category or on a given subject; while there are often a number of recommended titles, this designation helps users who want only a small selection. Non-starred entries represent Recommended titles, which provide a fuller list of recommended books.

History

The first appearance of fiction selections for adults was in 1923, with the publication of the Fiction Section. This was followed by supplements in 1928 and 1931, but fiction was omitted from the first edition of the complete "Standard Catalog" in 1934, which contained only recommendations for adult nonfiction. A new expanded edition of the Fiction Section was published as FICTION CATALOG in 1942. In its preface, that catalog was referred to as "a companion volume to the Standard Catalog for Public Libraries."

The collection subsequently evolved, along with other Core Collections, into an online resource called WilsonWeb. EBSCO Information Services acquired H.W. Wilson in 2011, and the collections became EBSCOhost databases in 2012. In 2020, the readers' advisory experts at NoveList applied their expertise: while Core Collections continues to provide impartial collection development guidance by experts in their fields, this marriage of readers advisory and collection development expertise strengthened the application of genre and subject headings, expanded awards content, and improved search and browse capabilities in the online Core Collections databases.

Scope

The items in the FICTION CORE COLLECTION are considered appropriate for libraries serving adult readers and have been selected by collection development specialists with expertise in fiction, using guidance from review sources and the advice of librarian advisors. FICTION CORE COLLECTION includes novels deemed to have lasting value to readers as well as new literary and genre titles. Both classic novels that remain significant achievements and perennially popular titles appear here, as do those that that appeal to readers from a variety of backgrounds and with a variety of reading interests. The Core Collection excludes non-English-language materials; however, there are many works of translation in this volume.

FICTION CORE COLLECTION is a guide to works of fiction only. Users who seek literary criticism, literary history, biographies of authors, and books on the writing of fiction should instead use the companion publication PUBLIC LIBRARY CORE COLLECTIONS: NONFICTION. At this time, graphic novels are not included; users who wish to find recommendations on graphic novels should use GRAPHIC NOVELS CORE COLLECTION.

Books are listed with an ISBN – most frequently for a hardcover edition published in the United States, or published in Canada or the United Kingdom and distributed in the U.S. Out-of-print titles are retained in the belief that good books are not obsolete simply because they happen to go out of print.

The Database

This Core Collection is derived from the database available from EBSCO Information Services. Metadata for the titles in this volume is provided by the metadata librarians at NoveList, who manage and apply a controlled vocabulary that adapts as terms come in and out of style, or as events require new ones. There are additional, browsable access points, plus full-text book reviews and articles, full-color cover art, Lexile measures, and all of the Supplementary book recommendations and Weeded titles. It is updated weekly. For more information or for a free trial, contact your EBSCO or NoveList sales rep, or visit https://www.ebscohost.com/novelist/our-products/core-collections. EBSCO also invites feedback from Core Collections customers at novelist@ebsco.com.

Preparation

Books included in Core Collections are selected by experienced librarians representing public library systems, school libraries, and academic libraries across the United States and Canada, as well as NoveList staff. These librarians also act as a committee of advisors on library policy, trends, and special projects. The names of participating librarians and their affiliations are listed in the Acknowledgements. EBSCO invites feedback from Core Collections customers at novelist@ebsco.com.

Core Collections Products

For recommendations for children's books, librarians are encouraged to investigate the following databases and their associated print versions:

CHILDREN'S CORE COLLECTION

MIDDLE AND JUNIOR HIGH CORE COLLECTION

SENIOR HIGH CORE COLLECTION

For adult nonfiction for the general reader, try the database NONFICTION CORE COLLECTION or the associated print volume PUBLIC LIBRARY CORE COLLECTION: NONFICTION. For fiction, please use FICTION CORE COLLECTION, either as a database or the associated print version.

For Graphic Novels for all ages, try the GRAPHIC NOVEL CORE COLLECTION in print or database form, which includes both fiction and nonfiction recommendations.

PURPOSE AND ORGANIZATION

PURPOSE

CORE COLLECTIONS is designed to serve a number of purposes:

As an aid in purchasing. Core Collections assists in the selection and ordering of titles. Summaries and evaluative excerpts are provided for each title along with information regarding the publisher, ISBN, page count, and publication year. In evaluating the suitability of a work, each library will want to consider the needs of the unique patron base it serves.

As an aid in verification of information. For this purpose, bibliographical information is provided in the Classified List of Works. Entries also include recommended subject headings based on NoveList's proprietary subject vocabulary. Notes may describe editions available and other content; for the most up-to-date metadata, please consult the EBSCO-host database.

As an aid in curriculum or programming support. The classified approach, subject indexing, annotations, and evaluative excerpts are helpful in identifying materials appropriate for classroom support, for book discussions, and other programming.

As an aid in collection maintenance. Information about titles available on a subject facilitates decisions to rebind, replace, or discard items. If a book has been demoted to the Supplementary or Weeded recommendation levels and therefore no longer appears in the print abridgement of the database, that demotion is not intended as a sign that the book is no longer valuable or that it should necessarily be weeded from your library's collection.

As an aid in professional development or instruction. The Core Collection is useful in courses or professional training that deal with collection development and readers' advisory; it may also be used in courses that deal with literature and book selection, especially in the creation of bibliographies and reading lists.

As an aid to readers' advisory. Every title in this Core Collection is a recommended work and can be given with confidence to a user who expresses a need based on topic, genre, etc. Readers' advisory and user service are further aided by series and awards information, by the descriptive summaries and evaluative excerpts from trusted review sources, and by the subject headings in the Title and Subject Index applied by professional metadata librarians at NoveList.

ORGANIZATION

This Core Collection is organized into two parts: a List of Fictional Works and the Indexes.

Part 1. Classified List of Works

Part 1 lists works of fiction in alphabetical order by last name of the author or by title, if the title is the main entry.

Each listing consists of a bibliographical description. Entries include, where relevant, series names and publication history. Whenever possible, a summary and an evaluative excerpt from a quoted source are also included. The following is an example of a typical entry and a description of its components.

Jones, Tayari

★ An **American** Marriage / Tayari Jones. Algonquin Books of Chapel Hill, 2018. 308 p.
ISBN 978-1-6162-0134-0
1. Marriage 2. African American families 3. False imprisonment 4. Husband and wife 5. Life change events 6. Atlanta, Georgia 7. Louisiana 8. Literary fiction 9. Southern fiction 10. Domestic fiction.
LC 2011-33996

ALA Notable Book, 2019
Women's Prize for Fiction, 2019.
BCALA Literary Award for Fiction, 2019.
LibraryReads Favorites, 2018.
Library Journal Best Books, 2018.
New York Times Notable Book, 2018
    When her new husband is arrested and imprisoned for a crime she knows he did not commit, a rising artist takes comfort in a longtime friendship, only to encounter unexpected challenges in resuming her life when her husband's sentence is suddenly overturned.
    "Jones crafts an affecting tale that explores marriage, family, regret, and other feelings made all the more resonant by her well-drawn characters and their intricate conflicts of heart and mind." Booklist

The name of the author, Tayari Jones, is given in conformity with NoveList author authorities. The star at the start of the title indicates that this is an Essential title. The title of the book is An American Marriage. The book was published by Algonquin Books of Chapel Hill in 2018.

The book has 308 pages. If it were part of a series, the series name would follow the page count.

An ISBN (International Standard Book Number) is included to facilitate ordering; however, there will often be many editions and formats of a given title; due to space constraints these ISBNs are not provided in the print edition, though many can be found in the corresponding database. The Library of Congress control number is provided when available.

Next are the awards this title has won, as well as the international and national short lists and best lists the book has appeared on that are tracked by NoveList staff. These are followed by a brief summary, provided in most cases by the publisher, and an excerpt from a critical reviewing source, in this case Booklist, that provides a reviewer's perspective on the book. Such summaries and excerpts are useful in evaluating books for selection and in determining which of several books on the same subject is best suited for the individual reader or purchasing library. Notes are also made to describe special features, such as publication history, film adaptations, or series order.

Part 2. Indexes

The title and subject index is a single alphabetical list of all the books entered in the Core Collection. Each book can be found under their title entry, which is followed by the name of the author under which the book can be found in Part 1. Books are also listed under their main subjects, as well as under headings for genre. Subject headings are printed in capital letters.

The following are examples of index entries for the book cited above:

Title   An **American** marriage. Jones, Tayari

Subject   **LITERARY FICTION**
                        Jones, Tayari. An American Marriage

The Name Index is a list of names and pseudonyms used by authors. This list in included as a separate index for ease of reference, readers' advisory, and display creation.

ACKNOWLEDGMENTS

H.W. Wilson, NoveList, and EBSCO Information Services express special gratitude to the following librarians who both advised in editorial matters and assisted in the selection and weeding of titles for this Core Collection.

Tracy Babiasz
Acquisitions and Collections Manager
Chapel Hill Public Library
Chapel Hill, NC

Robin Bradford
Collection Development Librarian
Pierce County Library System
Pierce County, WA

Heather Cover
Special Projects Librarian
Homewood Public Library
Homewood, AL

Gail de Vos
Storyteller & Adjunct Instructor, SLIS
University of Alberta
Alberta, Canada

Brian Flota
Humanities Librarian
James Madison University
Harrisonburg, VA

Francisca Goldsmith
Library and Media Consultant
Worcester, MA

Mary Griffin
Library Administrator
Omaha Public Library (retired)
Omaha, NE

Lauren Havens
Project Manager for Digital Collections
University of Michigan
Ann Arbor, MI

John Meier
Head, STEM for Engagement and Outreach
Penn State University Libraries
State College, PA

Liza Oldham
Director of the Annenberg Center for Learning and Research
The Chapin School
New York, NY

Natalie Romano
Librarian, Decker Branch
Denver Public Library
Denver, CO

James Stubbs
Reference Instructional Librarian
Florence County Library System
Florence, SC

Rebecca Vargha
Head, SILS Library
UNC Chapel Hill
Chapel Hill, NC

Linda Ward-Callaghan
Youth Services Manager (retired)
Joliet Public Library
Joliet, IL

The editors would also like to thank NoveList Readers' Advisory Librarians Ashley Lyons, Dawn Towery, Gillian Speace, Kaitlin Conner, and Lindsey Dunn, and Metadata Librarian Elizabeth Coleman for their help in creating this collection, along with Digital Content Integration Managers Christine Wells and Halle Eisenman. Lastly, Collection Development Coordinator Lisa Schimmer was instrumental in the creation of this collection.

FICTION CORE COLLECTION
TWENTIETH EDITION

A

Aalborg, Gordon
  River of porcupines / G. K. Aalborg. Five Star, 2018. 217 p.
  ISBN 9781432838157
  1. Hudson's Bay Company. 2. North West Company. 3. 19th century 4. Fur industry and trade 5. Metis 6. Competition 7. Corporations 8. Voyages and travels 9. Courage in women 10. Interethnic romance 11. Wilderness survival 12. Interpersonal attraction 13. Men/women relations 14. Canada -- History -- 19th century 15. Historical fiction
  LC 2018014288
  Spur Awards, Best Western Historical Novel, 2019.
  In the Rocky Mountain fur trade of the early 1800s, the intense rivalry between the powerful Hudson's Bay Company and the North-West Company is complicated by the arrival of Ilona Baptiste--a lovely and much-desired Metis maiden who could become the catalyst for a bloody trade war between two companies.

Aaronovitch, Ben, 1964-
  Broken homes / Ben Aaronovitch. DAW Books, 2014, c2013. 320 p. Rivers of London
  ISBN 9780756409609
  1. Wizards 2. Murder investigation 3. Detectives 4. Police -- Great Britain 5. Stolen property recovery 6. Supernatural 7. London, England 8. Urban fantasy 9. Fantasy mysteries
  Sworn to enforce the Queen's Peace, Constable Peter Grant, a magician and keeper of the flame, must discover if a mutilated body found in Crawley is the work of a common serial killer or an associate of the evil wizard known as the Faceless Man.

Aaronovitch, Ben, 1964-
  Midnight riot / Ben Aaronovitch. Del Rey, 2011. 336 p. Rivers of London
  ISBN 9780345524256
  1. Murder investigation 2. Ghosts 3. Witnesses 4. Police -- Great Britain 5. Wizards 6. Detectives 7. Magic 8. Multiracial men 9. London, England 10. Urban fantasy 11. Fantasy mysteries
  Originally published in the UK under the title, Rivers of London.
  When his ability to speak with the lingering dead brings him to the attention of Detective Chief Inspector Thomas Nightingale, who investigates paranormal crimes, Probationary Constable Peter Grant is drawn into a world where an ancient evil is making a comeback on a rising tide of murder and dark magic.

Aaronovitch, Ben, 1964-
  Moon over Soho / Ben Aaronovitch. Del Rey, 2011. 352 p. Rivers of London
  ISBN 9780345524591
  1. Jazz musicians 2. Magic 3. Supernatural 4. Detectives 5. Police -- Great Britain 6. Murder investigation 7. Detectives 8. London,
England 9. Urban fantasy 10. Fantasy mysteries
  After the death of a part-time jazz drummer, London constable and sorcerer's apprentice Peter Grant investigates a series of supernatural deaths in and around Soho that are linked to Peter's dad--a talented trumpet player named Richard "Lord" Grant.

Aaronovitch, Ben, 1964-
  Whispers under ground / Ben Aaronovitch. Del Rey, 2012. 352 p. Rivers of London
  ISBN 9780345524614
  1. Americans in England 2. Wizards 3. Murder investigation 4. Wizards 5. Detectives 6. Police -- Great Britain 7. Women FBI agents 8. Born again Christians 9. Supernatural 10. Urban fantasy 11. Fantasy mysteries
  To solve a perplexing murder case, Peter Grant, London constable and sorcerer's apprentice, must plumb the haunted depths of the oldest, largest, and deadliest subway system in the world.

Abani, Christopher
  GraceLand / Chris Abani. Farrar, Straus, and Giroux, 2004. 368 p.
  ISBN 0374165890
  1. 1970s 2. 1980s 3. Elvis Presley impersonators 4. Teenage boys 5. Teenage boys -- Friendship 6. Teenage abuse victims 7. Poor teenagers 8. Children of widowers 9. Fathers and sons 10. Ghettoes -- Lagos, Nigeria 11. Redemption 12. Nigeria -- Social life and customs 13. Lagos, Nigeria 14. Domestic fiction 15. Coming-of-age stories
  LC 2003012705
  Hemingway Foundation/PEN Award, 2005.
  Hurston/Wright Legacy Award: Debut Fiction, 2005.
  Shortlisted for the International IMPAC Dublin Literary Award, 2006
  Born into poverty in the chaotic capital city of Nigeria, Elvis is tempted by the underworld and enters a life of crime, encountering beggers, musicians, and American pop culture as he tries to survive in postcolonial Nigeria.
  "This book works brilliantly in two ways. As a convincing and unpatronizing record of life in a poor Nigerian slum, and as a frighteningly honest insight into a world skewed by casual violence, it's wonderful." New York Times Book Review.

Abani, Christopher
  The **secret** history of Las Vegas : a novel / Chris Abani. Penguin Books, 2014. 304 p.
  ISBN 9780143124955
  1. Psychiatrists 2. Betrayal 3. Redemption 4. Conjoined twins 5. Psychopaths 6. Immigrants -- United States 7. Misfits (Persons) 8. Detectives 9. Police 10. Serial murder investigation 11. Secrets 12. Apartheid 13. Las Vegas, Nevada 14. Mysteries
  LC 2013033496
  Edgar Allan Poe Award for Best Paperback Original Mystery, 2015.

A detective on the brink of retirement and a psychiatrist with a guilty burden are brought together by a series of deaths in Las Vegas.

"[A]n intricate braid of story strands, enriched by vivid descriptions, intriguingly dysfunctional characters, and abundant metaphors." Booklist.

Abbott, Jeff

Blame / Jeff Abbott. Grand Central Pub., 2017. 400 p.

ISBN 9781455558438

1. Traffic accidents 2. Amnesia 3. Teenage girls 4. Murder suspects 5. Suicide notes 6. Frameups 7. Guilt 8. Texas 9. Austin, Texas 10. Thrillers and suspense

Two years after a car crash killed her friend and left her with amnesia, Jane Norton receives an online message from someone claiming to know what really happened that night, but her search for the truth puts many lives in danger.

"The unconventional plot, the constant surprises, and above all the psychological depth of the characters all make this a first-rate crime novel." Kirkus.

Abbott, Jeff

The **three** Beths / Jeff Abbott. Grand Central Pub., 2018 400 p.

ISBN 9781538728697

1. Missing women 2. Teenage girls 3. Suspicion 4. Missing persons investigation 5. Mothers and daughters 6. Mother-separated girls 7. Names, Personal 8. Psychological suspense

Glimpsing the devoted mother who went missing and was presumed dead two years earlier, Mariah discovers that two other women who share her mother's name have also disappeared.

Abbott, Megan E., 1971-

Bury me deep / Megan Abbott. Simon & Schuster, 2009. 224 p.

ISBN 9781416599098

1. 1930s 2. Physicians' spouses 3. Extramarital affairs 4. Nurses 5. Gender role 6. Murder 7. Friendship 8. Phoenix, Arizona 9. Noir fiction 10. Historical fiction

LC 2008030676

In the wake of a double murder in which the victims' bodies are concealed in trunks aboard a Los Angeles-bound train, suspicion falls upon a young blonde woman whose guilt becomes subject to her gender, class, and ill-advised passion.

"But for all the classic-noir simplicity, such as the use of repetition rather than elaboration for emphasis, her prose carries an urgency that brings hardboiled crime fiction kicking and screaming into the modern age." Kirkus.

Abbott, Megan E., 1971-

The **fever** / Megan Abbott. Little Brown & Co, 2014. 240 p.

ISBN 9780316231053

1. High school students 2. Communicable diseases 3. Teenage girls -- Sexuality 4. Rumor 5. Communities 6. Insecurity (Psychology) 7. Hysteria (Social psychology) 8. Convulsions 9. Suburban life 10. Family relationships 11. Secrets 12. Thrillers and suspense

Thriller Award for Best Novel, 2015.

A small town becomes unraveled after a young teen has a scary, unexplained seizure in her high school class and rumors of a hazardous illness quickly move through the school and the community, spreading hysteria and destroying friendships and families.

"Once again, Abbott makes an unforgettable inquiry into the emotional lives of young people, this time balanced with parents own fears

and failings. Its also a powerful portrait of community, with interesting echoes of The Crucible." Booklist.

Abbott, Megan E., 1971-

* **Give** me your hand / Megan Abbott. Little Brown & Co., 2018. 352 p.

ISBN 9780316547185

1. Scientists 2. Competition 3. Academic rivalry 4. Secrets 5. Research 6. Competition 7. Best friends 8. Psychological suspense

Distancing herself from an intense best friend who inspired her scientific ambitions before divulging a life-changing secret, Kit competes for a dream research job and finds herself in a dangerous game of cat and mouse.

Abbott, Megan E., 1971-

Queenpin : a novel / Megan Abbott. Simon & Schuster Paperbacks, 2007. 192 p.

ISBN 1416534288

1. 20th century 2. Organized crime 3. Gangsters 4. Young women 5. Women criminals 6. Gender role 7. Casinos 8. Power (Social sciences) 9. Gambling industry and trade 10. Crime bosses 11. Noir fiction 12. Crime fiction

LC 2006052299

First appeared in the anthology Damn Near Dead (2006)

Edgar Allan Poe Award for Best Paperback Original, 2008.

Taken under the wing of an infamous mob luminary who reigned during the golden era of such figures as Bugsy Siegel and Lucky Luciano, a bookkeeper from a seedy nightclub finds herself seduced by the lucrative lifestyle of the underworld.

Abbott, Megan E., 1971-

* **You** will know me : a novel / Megan Abbott. Little, Brown and Company, 2016. 352 p.

ISBN 9780316231077

1. Gymnasts 2. Gymnastics 3. Hit-and-run victims 4. Murder 5. Suspicion 6. Teenage athletes 7. Fifteen-year-old girls 8. Hit-and-run accidents 9. Athletes with disabilities 10. Ambition in teenage girls 11. Thrillers and suspense

LC 2015026542

When a violent death rocks her close-knit gymnastics community weeks before an important competition, the mother of an Olympics hopeful works frantically to hold her family together in spite of being irresistibly drawn to the crime.

"It's vivid, troubling, and powerful--and Abbott totally sticks the landing." Booklist.

Abbott, Patricia

Concrete angel / Patricia Abbott. Polis Books, 2015. 320 p.

ISBN 9781940610382

1. 1970s 2. Compulsive behavior 3. Mothers and daughters 4. Children of people with mental illnesses 5. Murder 6. Deception 7. Dishonesty 8. Criminal behavior 9. Women with mental illnesses 10. Brothers and sisters 11. Dysfunctional families 12. Psychological fiction

Eve Moran will do anything to get the things she wants, disregarding how her actions impact those closest to her, but when she begins to use her three year-old son for personal gain, her daughter Christine vows to stop her.

Abbott, Shirley

The **future** of love : a novel / Shirley Abbott. Algonquin Books of Chapel Hill, 2008. 352 p.

ISBN 9781565125674

1. 2000s (Decade) 2. Fathers 3. Publishers and publishing 4. Sexuality 5. Devotedness 6. Betrayal 7. Interpersonal relations 8. Men/women relations 9. Marriage 10. Families 11. Extramarital affairs 12. September 11 Terrorist Attacks, 2001 13. New York City 14. Manhattan, New York City 15. Psychological fiction

LC 2007046035

Eight New Yorkers are forced to confront their tangled lives, loves, and affairs after the terrorist attacks on September 11, 2001.

Abdul-Jabbar, Kareem, 1947-

The **empty** birdcage / Kareem Abdul-Jabbar and Anna Waterhouse. Titan Books, 2019. 336 p. Mycroft Holmes novels (Kareem Abdul-Jabbar)

ISBN 9781785659300

1. 1870s 2. Serial murder investigation 3. Serial murders 4. Missing persons investigation 5. Missing persons 6. Greed 7. Interracial friendship 8. Chinese in Great Britain 9. London, England -- History -- 19th century 10. Historical mysteries 11. Mysteries 12. Adaptations, retellings, and spin-offs 13. African American fiction

A latest collaboration by the NBA All-Star and the co-creator of On the Shoulders of Giants finds the Holmes brothers on the trail of a killer who leaves victims unmarked, a case that is complicated by a loved one's disappearance.

Abdul-Jabbar, Kareem, 1947-

Mycroft and Sherlock / Kareem Abdul-Jabbar and Anna Waterhouse. Titan Books, 2018 359 p. Mycroft Holmes novels (Kareem Abdul-Jabbar)

ISBN 9781785659256

1. 1870s 2. Orphanages 3. Opium smuggling 4. Serial murder investigation 5. Race relations 6. Serial murders 7. Interracial friendship 8. Chinese in Great Britain 9. Violence against minorities 10. West Indians in Great Britain 11. London, England -- History -- 19th century 12. Trinidad and Tobago -- History -- 19th century 13. Historical mysteries 14. Mysteries 15. Adaptations, retellings, and spin-offs 16. African American fiction

Rising War Office star Mycroft Holmes persuades his brother, Sherlock, to volunteer at a best friend's orphanage, where the suspicious death of a street urchin and a mysterious Chinese woman lead the brothers into the London opium trade's dark underside.

"Abdul-Jabbar and Waterhouse again nail the historical ambience, the dialogue, and the plotting, effectively paying tribute to Arthur Conan Doyle but also adding large dollops of humor and romance. This is a wonderful mystery in what one hopes will be a long-running series." Booklist.

Abdul-Jabbar, Kareem, 1947-

* **Mycroft** Holmes / Kareem Abdul-Jabbar and Anna Waterhouse. Titan Books, 2015. 336 p. Mycroft Holmes novels (Kareem Abdul-Jabbar)

ISBN 9781783291533

1. 1870s 2. Crimes against children 3. Murder investigation 4. Secrets 5. Race relations 6. Young men 7. Engaged persons 8. Interracial friendship 9. London, England -- History -- 19th century 10. Trinidad and Tobago -- History -- 19th century 11. Historical mysteries 12. Mysteries 13. Adaptations, retellings, and spin-offs 14. African American fiction

"The authors hit all the right notes here, combining fascinating historical detail (on Trinidadian culture and folklore, on tobacco importation in London, even on the development of the Gatling gun) with rousing adventure, including some cleverly choreographed fight scenes and a pair of protagonists whose rich biracial friendship, while presented realistically, given the era (Douglas must sometimes pose as a butler), is the highlight of the book." Booklist.

Abe, Kobo, 1924-1993

* The **woman** in the dunes / Kobo Abe ; translated from the Japanese by E. Dale Saunders ; with drawings by Machi Abe. Knopf Publishing Group, 1991, c1964. 239 p..

ISBN 0679733787

1. Women teachers 2. Widows 3. Entomologists 4. Scientists 5. Imprisonment 6. Futility (Psychology) 7. Frustration 8. Tradition (Philosophy) 9. Change (Psychology) 10. Alienation (Social psychology) 11. Helpfulness in men 12. Self-acceptance 13. Sand 14. Coastal towns 15. Villages 16. Allegories 17. Translations -- Japanese to English

Kobo Abe is a pseudonym of Kimifusa Abe.

The inhabitants of a remote seaside village imprison a Japanese biologist in a deep sand pit.

Aboulela, Leila, 1964-

Elsewhere, home / Leila Aboulela. Black Cat, 2019. 224 p.

ISBN 9780802129130

1. Identity (Psychology) 2. Muslim women 3. Alienation (Social psychology) 4. Stereotypes (Social psychology) 5. Cultural differences 6. Khartoum, Sudan 7. Great Britain 8. Short stories 9. Literary fiction

LC 2018047042

A collection of short stories celebrates life as an immigrant abroad and the challenges of navigating assimilation and difference.

Abraham, Tola Rotimi

Black Sunday / Tola Rotimi Abraham. Catapult, 2020. 240 p.

ISBN 9781948226561

1. 1990s 2. Twin sisters 3. Self-discovery in women 4. Family problems 5. Poverty 6. Separated friends, relatives, etc 7. Brothers and sisters 8. Sexual violence 9. Swindlers and swindling 10. Churches 11. Lagos, Nigeria 12. Nigeria 13. Literary fiction 14. Domestic fiction

Joining a new church in 1996 Lagos in the face of impoverishing losses, twins Bibike and Riyike find their bond challenged by wrenching hardships, a father's reckless choice and their respective views on independence.

"The novel's strength lies in its lush, unflinching scenes, as when a seemingly simple infection leads gradually but inexorably to a life-threatening condition, revealing the dynamics of the family and community along the way. Abraham mightily captures a sense of the stresses of daily life in a family, city, and culture that always seems on the edge of self-destruction." Publishers Weekly.

Abramowitz, Andy

Thank you, goodnight : a novel / Andy Abramowitz. Simon & Schuster, 2015. 352 p.

ISBN 9781476791777

1. Rock groups 2. Middle aged men 3. Musicians 4. Fame 5. Singers 6. Lawyers 7. Midlife crisis 8. Fans (Persons) 9. Second chances 10. Singers 11. Interpersonal relations 12. Switzerland 13. Mainstream

fiction 14. Humorous stories

LC 2014041615

"A Touchstone Book."

Teddy Tremble, the former lead singer of a one-hit-wonder 90s band, gets a chance to rekindle is past fame when he gets a reason to reunite the band--but first he has to convince his estranged band members that getting back together is a good idea.

Abrams, David (David Mark)

Fobbit / David Abrams. Black Cat, 2012. 384 p.
ISBN 9780802120328

1. United States. Army Public relations. 2. Iraq War, 2003-2011 3. Military bases, American 4. War correspondents 5. Military journalism -- 21st century 6. Spin control (Public relations) 7. War and society 8. Mass media 9. Iraq 10. War stories 11. Satirical fiction

LC bl2012016566

At Foreward Operating Base Triumph, a combat-avoiding staff sergeant named Chance Gooding spends his time composing press releases that spin grim events into statements more palatable to the public.

Abrams, Melanie

Meadowlark / Melanie Abrams. Little A, 2020. 240 p.
ISBN 9781542007351

1. Reunions 2. Psychic trauma 3. Childhood friends 4. Memories 5. Secrets 6. Synesthesia 7. Deception 8. Communes 9. Thrillers and suspense

Returning to Meadowlark, the spiritual compound in which she grew up that is home to children with unusual abilities, to document its story, photojournalist Simrin finds herself caught in a desperate situation when a conflict with the authorities escalates.

Abu-Jaber, Diana

Birds of paradise : a novel / Diana Abu-Jaber. W. W. Norton & Co., 2011. 384 p.
ISBN 9780393064612

1. Runaway teenagers 2. Family secrets 3. Dysfunctional families 4. Teenage girls 5. Family problems 6. Parent and teenager 7. Brothers and sisters 8. Miami, Florida 9. Psychological fiction 10. Domestic fiction

LC 2011014575

In Miami, Avis and Brian Muir are still haunted by the disappearance of their beautiful daughter, Felice, who ran away when she was thirteen. Now, after five years of skateboarding, clubbing, and squatting, Felice is about to turn eighteen. Her family will be forced to confront their anguish, loss, and sense of betrayal. Meanwhile, Felice must reckon with the guilty secret that drove her away, and must face her fear of losing her family and her sense of self forever.

" Abu-Jaber . . . employs her descriptive talents in bringing Miami to steamy, pulsing life, but it is Birds of Paradise's neither predictable nor merely haphazard momentum and its rich cast of characters that make us feel we're in deliciously capable hands." Elle

Abu-Jaber, Diana

Crescent / Diana Abu-Jaber. W.W. Norton & Co., 2003. 352 p.
ISBN 039305747X

1. Arab American women 2. Cooking, Lebanese 3. College teachers 4. Women cooks 5. Men/women relations 6. Immigrant families 7. Arab Americans 8. Race relations 9. Restaurants 10. Los Angeles, California 11. Literary fiction

LC 2002152907

An Arab-American Chocolat--a sensual blend of food, love and longing. Populated by colorful and memorable characters--the lovely Sirine; the handsome Han; Sirine's story-telling uncle, whose fantasic fables are woven into the novel; a poet named Aziz; Nadia and her daughter Mireille--Crescent explores the universal themes of love and loyalty to countries old and new, to those left behind, and to tradition.

"Abu-Jaber's language is miraculous, whether describing the texture of Han's skin or Sirine's way with an onion. It is not possible to stop reading." Booklist.

Abu-Jaber, Diana

Origin : a novel / Diana Abu-Jaber. W. W. Norton & Co., 2007. 384 p.
ISBN 9780393064551

1. Women forensic scientists 2. Identity (Psychology) 3. Infanticide 4. Serial murders 5. Forensic sciences 6. Violence against children 7. Memories 8. Forensic scientists 9. Serial murderers 10. New York (State) 11. Syracuse, New York 12. Mysteries 13. Literary fiction

LC 2007004963

New York-based fingerprint expert Lena investigates a series of crib deaths that may actually be the work of a serial killer, a case that reminds Lena of the mystery surrounding her own childhood, marked by her orphaned status and her intuitive talents.

"For all its internal chill, the drama that unfolds around fingerprint expert Lena Dawson is a struggle toward spring and the light. Haunting and compelling, Origin combines the traditions of the crime novel with an examination of Lena's unusual upbringing. It's a little film noir, a bit independent-woman-detective thriller, and winningly fresh in its approach." PopMatters.

Abulhawa, Susan

The **blue** between sky and water / Susan Abulhawa. Bloomsbury, 2015 304 p.
ISBN 9781632862211

1. Palestinians 2. Military occupation 3. Life after death 4. Refugees 5. Families 6. Refugee camps 7. Israel 8. Family sagas

While in a refugee camp in Gaza, the women of a Palestinian family are left behind as their men join the resistance and Nazmiyeh -- the matriarch and center of a household of sisters, daughters and granddaughters who has a large heart and a zest for life that heals -- will do anything to keep them all together.

Acampora, Lauren

The **paper** wasp : a novel / Lauren Acampora. Grove Press, 2019 240 p.
ISBN 9780802129413

1. Childhood friends 2. Obsession 3. Ambition in women 4. Creativity in women 5. Women artists 6. Loneliness 7. Actors and actresses 8. Secrets 9. Female friendship 10. Los Angeles, California 11. Michigan 12. Literary fiction 13. Second person narratives

LC 2018058112

Traces the dark friendship of twisted ambition shared between a failed artist and a rising star in contemporary Hollywood.

Acampora, Lauren

The **wonder** garden / Lauren Acampora. Grove Press, 2015. 288 p.
ISBN 9780802123558

1. Suburban life 2. Connecticut 3. Literary fiction 4. Short stories

Shares the myriad and bizarre secrets of a Connecticut suburb, including a young soon-to-be mother who watches her husband walk away from a fifteen-year career in advertising at the urging of his spirit animal.

"Acampora not only meticulously conveys the allure of an outwardly paradisiacal suburban community, with its perfectly restored Victorian homes and well-tended lawns; she also clearly captures the inner turmoil of its residents, homing in on their darkest impulses and beliefs. Some of the stories' starring characters make cameos in others, adding considerable complexity to the whole." Booklist.

Acevedo, Chantel

The **distant** marvels / Chantel Acevedo. Europa Editions, 2015. 304 p.

ISBN 9781609452520

1. 1960s 2. Hurricanes 3. Storytelling 4. Courage in women 5. Memory 6. Rebels 7. Families 8. Women -- Psychology 9. Interpersonal relations 10. Cuba 11. Political fiction

A professional storyteller imparts the incredible tale of her youth during the Third War of Independence to eight women who need hope to survive Hurricane Flora in 1963 Cuba.

"This extraordinary narrative tells, from these womens perspectives, how war brings lovers together and tears families apart. This is a major, uniquely powerful, and startlingly beautiful novel that should bring Acevedos name to the top echelon of this generations writers." Booklist.

Achebe, Chinua

* **Things** fall apart / Chinua Achebe. Anchor Books, 1994. 209 p.

ISBN 0385474547

1. Culture conflict 2. Social structure 3. Igbo (African people) 4. Exiles -- Nigeria 5. Colonialism -- Nigeria 6. Villages -- Nigeria 7. British in Nigeria 8. Race relations 9. Religion and culture 10. Christianity and culture 11. Christianity and indigenous peoples 12. Nigeria -- Colonization 13. Nigeria -- History 14. Historical fiction 15. Modern classics 16. Literary fiction

LC 94013429

Originally published: London : Heinemann, 1958.

Traces the growing friction between village leaders and Europeans determined to save the heathen souls of Africa. But its hero, a noble man who is driven by destructive forces, speaks a universal tongue.

Aciman, Andre

Call me by your name / Andre Aciman. Farrar, Straus and Giroux, 2007. 256 p.

ISBN 9780374299217

1. First loves 2. Self-discovery in teenage boys 3. Graduate students 4. Summer 5. Gay teenagers 6. Teenage boys -- Sexuality 7. Jews 8. Homosexuality 9. Men/men relations 10. Italy 11. LGBTQIA fiction 12. Literary fiction 13. Coming-of-age stories

LC 2006011720

Sequel: Find me.

Lambda Literary Award for Gay Men's Fiction, 2007.

The sudden and powerful attraction between a teenage boy and a summer guest at his parents' house on the Italian Riviera has a profound and lasting influence that will mark them both for a lifetime.

Aciman, Andre

Enigma variations : a novel / Andre Aciman. Farrar, Straus and Giroux, 2017. 272 p.

ISBN 9780374148430

1. Desire (Philosophy) 2. Self-awareness 3. Bisexual men 4. First loves 5. Lovers 6. Men -- Psychology 7. Memories 8. Bisexuality 9. Men/men relations 10. Men/women relations 11. Italy 12. New York City 13. Psychological fiction 14. Literary fiction 15. LGBTQIA fiction

LC 2016020262

Five interconnected tales exploring the contradictory power of love follow the romantic endeavors of Paul, who experiences consuming pas-

sion for a girl he meets repeatedly through the years while enduring a spectrum of hopes, denials, fears and regrets.

"Aciman's sensuous, subtle language supports not only his marvelous descriptive power but also how deeply and resonantly he constructs his fondly and fully conceived characters." Booklist.

Aciman, Andre

* **Find** me / Andre Aciman. Farrar, Straus and Giroux, 2019. 224 p.

ISBN 9780374155018

1. Regret 2. Self-discovery in men 3. Homosexuality 4. Fathers and sons 5. Young women -- Relations with older men 6. Young men -- Relations with older men 7. Jews 8. Gay men 9. Sexuality 10. First loves 11. Men/men relations 12. LGBTQIA fiction 13. Literary fiction

LC 2019020195

Sequel to: Call me by your name.

Elio's father, Samuel, has a chance encounter on the train with a beautiful young woman that upends Sami's plans and changes his life forever. Elio soon moves to Paris, where he, too, has a consequential affair, while Oliver, now a New England college professor with a family, suddenly finds himself contemplating a return trip across the Atlantic.

Aciman, Andre

Harvard square / Andre Aciman. W. W. Norton & Co., 2013. 304 p.

ISBN 9780393088601

1. Harvard University 2. 1970s 3. Immigrants 4. Male friendship 5. Graduate students 6. Taxicab drivers 7. Assimilation (Sociology) 8. Jewish men 9. Muslim men 10. Universities and colleges 11. Men/women relations 12. Cambridge, Massachusetts 13. Literary fiction

An Egyptian-Jewish Harvard graduate student trying to assimilate into American culture in 1977 befriends an impetuous, loud Arab cab driver and must choose between his dream or his friend.

Acker, Jennifer

* The **limits** of the world / Jennifer Acker. Delphinium, 2019. 225 p.

ISBN 9781883285777

1. Immigration and emigration 2. Family secrets 3. Immigrant families 4. Intergenerational communication 5. Family relationships 6. Life change events 7. Interethnic romance 8. Couples 9. Cultural relations 10. Cultural differences 11. Ethics 12. United States 13. Nairobi, Kenya 14. Kenya 15. India 16. Family sagas

"Acker's debut novel about multigeneration migrations from India to Kenya to the U.S. is ambitious in geographical scope and philosophical engagement." Booklist

Ackerman, Elliot

Dark at the crossing / Elliot Ackerman. Alfred A. Knopf, 2017. 272 p.

ISBN 9781101947371

1. Idealism 2. Refugees 3. Civil war 4. Arab Americans 5. Americans in Turkey 6. Loss (Psychology) 7. Missing girls 8. Veterans 9. Translators 10. War -- Psychological aspects 11. Interpersonal relations 12. Men/women relations 13. Turkey 14. Literary fiction

National Book Award for Fiction finalist, 2017

Presents a contemporary love story set on the Turkish border of Syria, where an Arab American with a conflicted past attempts to join the fight against Bashar al-Assad's regime before the plight of his host family reshapes his loyalties.

"Here is a thriller, psychological fiction, political intrigue, and even a love story all wrapped into a stunningly realistic and sometimes horrifying package." Library Journal.

Ackerman, Elliot

* **Waiting** for Eden : a novel / Elliot Ackerman. Alfred A. Knopf, 2018. 192 p.

ISBN 9781101947395

1. Veterans 2. Consciousness 3. Burn victims 4. War -- Psychological aspects 5. Dead 6. Male friendship 7. Husband and wife 8. Communication 9. Marital conflict 10. Secrets 11. Flashbacks 12. Literary fiction

LC 2017055697

ALA Notable Book, 2019.

A veteran enduring life trapped in his own mind begins to find a way to communicate before troubling realities about his marriage come to the surface.

Ackroyd, Peter, 1949-

The **trial** of Elizabeth Cree : a novel of the Limehouse murders / Peter Ackroyd. N. A. Talese, 1995, c1994. 261 p.

ISBN 9780385477079

1. Marx, Karl, 1818-1883 2. Victorian era (1837-1901) 3. Trials (Murder) 4. Victorian mysteries 5. Historical mysteries

LC 94037348

In 1880, with London's poverty-stricken Limehouse district being terrorized by a series of brutal murders, Elizabeth Cree is on trial for the poisoning of her husband, but she may also be the one person who knows the truth about the killings.

"Mr. Ackroyd's methods are both subtle and outrageous. Everything and everyone in this novel is so intimately connected that one reads with a sense of the world becoming progressively smaller and tighter; a kind of anguished claustrophobia sets in. The tone is agitated and compelling, by turns macabre and inventive." New York Times Book Review

Adam, Claire

Golden child : a novel / Claire Adam. SJP for Hogarth, 2019. 281 p.

ISBN 9780525572992

1. Fathers and sons 2. Rural life 3. Missing teenage boys 4. Poor families 5. Twins 6. Problem youth 7. Teenage boys 8. Decision-making 9. Family relationships 10. Trinidad and Tobago 11. Literary fiction

Working exhausting hours in their rural Trinidad home, the family of a petroleum plant worker is shattered by the disappearance of a troubled twin son whose fate forces his father to make a devastating choice.

"Throughout this stunning portrait of Trinidad's multicultural diversity, and one family's sacrifices, soaring hopes and ultimate despair, Adam weaves a poetic lightness and beauty that will transfix readers." Publishers Weekly.

Adams, Alice, 1926-1999

A **southern** exposure : a novel / Alice Adams. A. A. Knopf, 1995. 305 p.

ISBN 0679444521

1. College towns -- Southern States 2. Depressions -- 1929-1941 -- Southern States 3. Families -- Southern States 4. Moving to a new state 5. North Carolina 6. Literary fiction 7. Southern fiction

LC 95016109

Sequel: After the war.

Escaping from a poor job and a brush with adultery, the Bairds move to South Carolina during the Depression in the hopes of regaining their lost innocence, but their new home changes them in unexpected ways

"Though this plot teeters on the edge of soap opera, it never slips into the slush, thanks in part to the sobering imminence of war, which casts an air of gravity over all these amorous proceedings. Ms. Adams's breezy, wistful lyricism perfectly captures this lovely place and golden time, just before things got so damn serious forever." New York Times Book Review.

Adams, Alice, 1926-1999

The **stories** of Alice Adams Knopf, 2002. 624 p.

ISBN 0375412859

1. United States -- Social life and customs -- 20th century 2. Short stories

LC 2002070940

A collection of fifty-three short stories reveals the author's evocative explorations into the mysteries of human relationships in "Verlie I Say Unto You," "Berkeley House," "Greyhound People," and other notable works.

"Taken together, these stories betray the changing mores of the past half-century; taken in sequence, they trace the changes in the American short story over the past 40 years, some of those changes wrought by Adams herself." Publishers Weekly.

Adams, Douglas, 1952-2001

Dirk Gently's holistic detective agency / Douglas Adams. Simon and Schuster, 1987. 247 p. Dirk Gently

ISBN 9780671625825

1. Time travel 2. Private investigators 3. Lost animals 4. Misadventures 5. Science fiction mysteries 6. Science fiction 7. Humorous stories

LC 879464

Adapted into a television series on BBC America in 2016.

There is a long tradition of Great Detectives, and Dirk Gently does not belong to it. But his search for a missing cat uncovers a ghost, a time traveler, and the devastating secret of humankind! Detective Gently's bill for saving the human race from extinction: no charge.

"That Adams manages to bring together his various scenarios and round up his wandering characters shows his skill as a writer. His insightful commentary on the human condition is the hot fudge on this literary banana split." Booklist.

Adams, Douglas, 1952-2001

* The **hitchhiker's** guide to the galaxy / Douglas Adams. Harmony Books, 1980, c1979. 215 p. Hitchhiker series

ISBN 9780517542095

1. Misadventures 2. Meaning (Psychology) 3. Life on other planets 4. Aliens (Humanoid) 5. Space flight 6. Science fiction 7. Humorous stories

LC 80014572

10th anniversary printing includes introduction by author.

Chronicles the off-beat and occasionally extraterrestrial journeys, notions, and acquaintances of galactic traveler Arthur Dent.

Adams, Douglas, 1952-2001

Life, the universe, and everything / Douglas Adams. Harmony Books, 1982. 232 p. Hitchhiker series

ISBN 9780795328343

1. Misadventures 2. Time travel (Past) 3. Aliens (Humanoid) 4. Conflict resolution 5. Science fiction 6. Humorous stories

Arthur Dent is transported from a prehistoric Earth to a cricket match at Lords' Cricket Ground, two days before the Earth is to be demolished by the Vogens.

"Arthur Dent and his motley crew do tie up most of the loose ends and manage to prevent the destruction of the universe, but the first two novels . . . 'must' be read to understand the situation, and even then it's confusing." Library Journal.

Adams, Douglas, 1952-2001

The **restaurant** at the end of the universe / Douglas Adams. Harmony Books, 1980. 245 p. Hitchhiker series
ISBN 9780517545355
1. Misadventures 2. Life on other planets 3. Conspiracies 4. Restaurants 5. Aliens (Humanoid) 6. Space flight 7. Science fiction 8. Humorous stories

Arthur Dent and Ford Prefect join with Zaphod Beeblebrox, the two-headed former president of the galaxy, in a search for the current ruler of the universe.

"Poor uprooted Arthur Dent finds himself swept along in the wake of Zaphod Beeblebrox, former President of the Galaxy, as Zaphod searches for the man who rules the Universe. They and their companions tumble from one scrape into another, with the erratic aid of Zaphod's dead great-grandfather and Marvin, their perpetually depressed robot. Adams's live-ly sense of the ridiculous has concocted many hilarious episodes, though the inspired lunacy of the first book has become rather uneven here. Still, this is one of the best pieces of sf humor available." Library Journal.

Adams, Ellery

The **secret,** book & scone society / Ellery Adams. Kens-ington Books, 2017. 290 p. Secret, book & scone society
ISBN 9781496718563
1. Small town life 2. Female friendship 3. Women amateur detectives 4. Small towns 5. Murder suspects 6. Amateur detectives 7. Murder investigation 8. Books and reading 9. Secret societies 10. Bookstores 11. Secrets 12. North Carolina 13. Cozy mysteries

When a visiting businessman reaches out to Nora of Miracle Books for advice on the perfect novel to read, she knows exactly which ones will help, but before he can keep their appointment, he's found dead on the train tracks.

"Four women with hidden secrets form a group to combat deceit and solve murders. The ladies of Miracle Springs work in mysterious ways." Kirkus.

Adams, Henry, 1838-1918

* **Democracy** : an American novel / Henry Adams. H. Holt & Co., 1908 374 p., 18 cm.
ISBN 037576058X
1. Political fiction

LC 08010432

Variously attributed by different authorities to Henry Adams, John Hay and Clarence King. cf. W. R. Thayer, Life of John Hay, 1915, v. 2, p. 58-59. The authorship of Adams is affirmed by the publisher Henry Holt in the Unpartizan review, no. 29, Jan.-Mar. 1921, p. 156; and Literary review, Dec. 24, 1920.

While fighting each other for power, Senate member Silas Ratcliffe actively pursues society widow and government newcomer Mrs. Light-foot Lee in 1870s Washington, D.C.

Adams, Lyssa Kay

The **bromance** book club / Lyssa Kay Adams. Jove, 2019. 352 p. Bromance book club
ISBN 9781984806093
1. Professional baseball players 2. Marital conflict 3. Book clubs 4. Romantic love 5. Male friendship 6. Books and reading 7. Advice 8. Orgasm 9. Sexuality 10. Romance book clubs 11. Secret societies 12. Men/women relations 13. Nashville, Tennessee 14. Romantic comedies 15. Sports romances 16. Contemporary romances

LC 2019006240

Nashville Legends second baseman Gavin Scott's marriage is in ma-jor league trouble. Distraught and desperate, Gavin finds help from an unlikely source: a secret romance book club made up of Nashville's top alpha men. With the help of their current read, a steamy Regency titled Courting the Countess, the guys coach Gavin on saving his marriage.

Adams, Richard, 1920-2016

Watership Down / Richard Adams. Macmillan, 1974, c1972. 448 p. Rabbit tales
ISBN 0027000303
1. Rabbits 2. Survival 3. Safety 4. Peace 5. Nature 6. Ethics 7. Freedom 8. Personal conduct 9. Land development 10. Fantasy fiction 11. Classics

LC 73006044

Sequel: Tales from Watership Down.
Includes "Lapine glossary."
Originally published: 1972.
California Young Reader Medal, Young Adult, 1977.
Carnegie Medal, 1972.

In a constant struggle against oppression, a group of rabbits search for peaceful co-existence. Chronicles the adventures of a group of rab-bits searching for a safe place to establish a new warren where they can live in peace.

Adamson, Gil, 1961-

The **outlander** / Gil Adamson. Ecco, 2008, c2007. 389 p.
ISBN 9780061491252
1. 1900s (Decade) 2. Widows 3. Grief in women 4. Murder 5. Voyages and travels 6. Brothers 7. Revenge in men 8. Landslides 9. Disasters 10. Coal mines and mining 11. Supernatural 12. Frank, Alberta 13. Alberta -- History -- 20th century 14. Canada -- History -- 1867-1914 15. Canada -- History -- 20th century 16. Historical fiction

LC 200741062

"Originally published in Canada in 2007 by House of Anansi Press"-
-T.p. verso.
Books in Canada First Novel Award, 2007.

After killing her husband, Mary Boulton races toward the mountains while being tormented by visions of the cold-blooded brothers-in-law who pursue her, forcing her to retreat deeper into the wilds of the West and her own imagination.

"Of course, the Girl Being Chased is one of the most enduring fig-ures of chivalric and chauvinistic literature, a staple of television dramas and horror films. . . . But Gil is short for Gillian, and her strange and complicated heroine has nothing in common with Hollywood's wornout damsels in distress. . . there are pages here you can't read slowly enough to catch every word." Washington Post Book World.

Adebayo, Ayobami, 1988-

* **Stay** with me / Ayobami Adebayo. Alfred A. Knopf, 2017. 288 p.
ISBN 9780451494603
1. 21st century 2. Husband and wife 3. Infertility 4. Marriage 5. Married women 6. Polygamy 7. Motherhood 8. Family relationships 9. Gender role 10. Social pressure 11. Nigeria 12. Literary fiction 13. Domestic fiction
Originally published: Edinburgh : Canongate, 2017.
ALA Notable Book, 2018.
Shortlisted for The Baileys Women's Prize for Fiction, 2017.

Despite cultural pressures for her husband to take a second wife, Yejide trusts that Akin would never do so... until, after four years of fail-ing to conceive a child, he does. Under constant scrutiny to conceive and keeping secrets from one other, the couple struggles while their marriage falters and the country's political system crumbles. Alternating chapters told from each characters' perspective capture both the agony of would-be parents struggling with infertility, and the broader turmoil in Nigeria during the late 1980s. -- Description by Shauna Griffin

". . . Adebayo's novel captures how the turmoil of Nigerian life in the 1980s and '90s seeps into the most personal of decisions--to fight for, and protect, one's family. Adebayo's debut marks the emergence of a fine young writer." Kirkus.

Adelman, Michelle

Piece of mind : a novel / Michelle Adelman. W. W. Norton & Company, 2016. 304 p.

ISBN 9780393245707

1. Women with disabilities 2. Brothers and sisters 3. Life change events 4. Self-doubt 5. Self-fulfillment in women 6. Women with brain injuries 7. Twenties (Age) 8. Fathers -- Death 9. Human/animal relationships 10. Women artists 11. Family relationships 12. New York City 13. Mainstream fiction

LC 2015032331

Unable to relate to people or hold a job after suffering a head injury in early childhood, talented artist Lucy is forced out of her protective Jewish home and into a New York City studio apartment with her college-age brother, where she struggles to adapt to life without a safety net.

Adichie, Chimamanda Ngozi, 1977-

* **Americanah** : a novel / Chimamanda Ngozi Adichie. Alfred A. Knopf, 2013. 352 p.

ISBN 9780307271082

1. Immigrants 2. Refugees 3. Nigerians in England 4. Nigerians in the United States 5. Men/women relations 6. Race relations 7. Nigeria 8. England 9. United States 10. Political fiction 11. Love stories 12. Literary fiction

LC 2012043875

ALA Notable Book, 2014

National Book Critics Circle Award for Fiction, 2013.

Andrew Carnegie Medal for Excellence in Fiction finalist, 2014.

Shortlisted for the International Dublin Literary Award, 2015

Shortlisted for The Baileys Women's Prize for Fiction, 2014

Separated by respective ambitions after falling in love in occupied Nigeria, beautiful Ifemelu experiences triumph and defeat in America while exploring new concepts of race, while Obinze endures an undocumented status in London until the pair is reunited in their homeland 15 years later, where they face the toughest decisions of their lives.

"Witty, wry, and observant, Adichie is a marvelous storyteller who writes passionately about the difficulty of assimilation and the love that binds a man, a woman, and their homeland." Library Journal.

Adichie, Chimamanda Ngozi, 1977-

Half of a yellow sun / Chimamanda Ngozi Adichie. Alfred A. Knopf, 2006. 448 p.

ISBN 1400044162

1. 1960s 2. Civil war 3. Political corruption 4. Postcolonialism 5. Igbo (African people) 6. Thirteen-year-old boys 7. Twin sisters 8. Families 9. Murder 10. Genocide 11. Teenagers and war 12. Sexuality 13. British in Nigeria 14. Peasantry -- Nigeria 15. Rich families 16. Loss (Psychology) 17. Nigeria -- History -- Civil War, 1967-1970 18. Biafra (1967-1970) 19. Historical fiction 20. Political fiction 21. Literary fiction

LC 2005057784

First published: Great Britain: Fourth Estate, 2006.

Film tie-in.

Orange Prize for Fiction, 2007.

Shortlisted for the James Tait Black Memorial Prize for Fiction, 2006

National Book Critics Circle Award for Fiction finalist, 2006

"The author has a gift for capturing the rhythms of African middle-class life: not just its political awareness but the aspirations and cultural imperatives that lend it its varied character. . . . For its portrayal of Nigeria's political and cultural past, [this book] is a welcome addition to the corpus of African letters." Times Literary Supplement.

Adichie, Chimamanda Ngozi, 1977-

The **thing** around your neck / Chimamanda Ngozi Adichie. Alfred A. Knopf, 2009. 240 p.

ISBN 9780307271075

1. Nigerians in the United States 2. Men/women relations 3. Culture conflict 4. Immigrants 5. Nigeria 6. Short stories 7. Literary fiction

A collection of twelve stories includes the tale of a medical student in hiding with a poor Muslim woman, and a woman who discovers a devastating secret about her brother's death.

"The stories are set both in the United States and in Nigeria, where things continue to fall apart. . . . Adichie, a brilliant writer whose characters stay with you for a long time, deserves to be more widely known." Library Journal.

Adiga, Aravind

* **Amnesty** / Aravind Adiga. Scribner, 2020. 288 p.

ISBN 9781982127244

1. Undocumented immigrants 2. Household employees 3. Options, alternatives, choices 4. Murderers 5. Witnesses 6. Ethics 7. Murder 8. Sri Lankans 9. Immigration and emigration 10. Sydney, New South Wales 11. Literary fiction

A young illegal immigrant in Sydney, Australia is forced to choose between risking deportation and reporting the murder of a female client.

"Best-selling Adiga's smart, funny, and timely tale with a crime spin of an undocumented immigrant will catalyze readers." Booklist.

Adiga, Aravind

* **Last** man in tower : a novel / Aravind Adiga. Alfred A. Knopf, 2011. 368 p.

ISBN 9780307594099

1. Apartment houses 2. Real estate developers 3. Social conflict 4. Teachers 5. India -- Social life and customs 6. Mumbai, India 7. Literary fiction

LC 2011003406

Refusing to leave his home when a powerful real-estate developer offers to buy out the residents of a crumbling apartment complex near the infamous Dharavi slums, a retired schoolteacher becomes a target of violence by the developer and his own neighbors.

"[Adiga] maps out, in luminous prose, India's ambivalence toward its accelerated growth, while creating an engaging protagonist in the stubborn resident: a man whose ambition and independence have been tempered with an understanding of the important, if almost imperceptible, difference between development and progress." Entertainment Weekly.

Adiga, Aravind

Selection day / Aravind Adiga. Scribner, 2017, c2016. 304 p.

ISBN 9781501150838

1. Cricket (Sports) 2. Sports 3. Fathers and sons 4. Social classes 5. Brothers 6. Competition 7. Family relationships 8. India 9. Literary fiction

Two brothers growing up in a Mumbai slum are raised by an obsessive father to become cricket stars only to have their relationship, future and senses of self threatened by unexpected dynamics that shape their coming-of-age.

"A master class in integrating character and landscape, Adiga's novel also portrays Mumbai as alternatively stifling and liberating." Booklist.

Adiga, Aravind

* The **white** tiger : a novel / Aravind Adiga. Free Press, 2008. 288 p.

ISBN 9781416562597

1. Social classes 2. Racism 3. Class conflict 4. Automobile drivers 5. Political corruption 6. Ambition 7. Murder 8. Personal conduct 9. Ethics 10. Revenge 11. Poverty 12. India -- Social life and customs 13. Bangalore, India 14. Literary fiction 15. Epistolary novels 16. Satirical fiction

LC 2007045527

Man Booker Prize, 2008.

When he relocates to New Delhi to take a new job, Balram Halwai is disillusioned by the city's materialism and technology-spawned violence, a circumstance that forces him to question his loyalties, ambitions, and past

"In this darkly comic debut novel set in India, Balram, a chauffeur, murders his employer, justifying his crime as the act of a social entrepreneur. ... Adiga's message isn't subtle or novel, but Balram's appealingly sardonic voice and acute observations of the social order are both winning and unsettling." The New Yorker.

Adimi, Kaouther, 1986-

Our riches / Kaouther Adimi ; translated from the French by Chris Andrews. New Directions Publishing, 2020, c2017. 160 p.

ISBN 9780811228152

1. Charlot, Edmond, 1915-2004 2. Second World War era (1939-1945) 3. Publishers and publishing 4. Bookstores 5. Archives 6. War 7. Generosity 8. Algiers, Algeria 9. Algeria 10. Biographical fiction 11. Historical fiction 12. Translations -- French to English 13. Parallel narratives

Originally published: Paris : Editions du Seuil, 2017.

Our Riches celebrates quixotic devotion and the love of books in the person of Edmond Charlot, who at the age of twenty founded Les Vraies Richesses (Our True Wealth), the famous Algerian bookstore/publishing house/lending library.

"This is a moving tribute to the enduring power of literature." Publishers Weekly.

Adjei-Brenyah, Nana Kwame

Friday black : stories / Nana Kwame Adjei-Brenyah. Mariner Books, 2018. 194 p.

ISBN 9781328911247

1. African Americans 2. Racism 3. Race relations 4. United States 5. Literary fiction 6. Afrofuturism and Afrofantasy 7. Satirical fiction 8. Short stories

LC 2017061489

ALA Notable Book, 2019.

A piercingly raw debut story collection from a young writer with an explosive voice; a treacherously surreal, and, at times, heartbreakingly satirical look at what it's like to be young and black in America.

Adkins, Mary

When you read this / Mary Adkins. Harper, 2019 376 p.
ISBN 9780062834676

1. Women with terminal illnesses 2. Friends' death 3. Bereavement 4. Public relations consultants 5. Last words 6. Sisters 7. Blogs 8. Grief 9. Epistolary novels 10. Mainstream fiction

After his friend, Iris, dies from a terminal illness at age 33, PR genius Smith Simonyi teams up with Iris's sister, Jade, to make Iris's final request--to get her blog posts published as a book--a reality.

"Debut novelist Adkins brilliantly captures the rhythms and cadences of the epistolary format in the digital age through a delightful cast of quirky, imperfect characters, both dead and alive. Tart, sweet, poignant, and rich with humor; completely irresistible." Library Journal.

Adler-Olsen, Jussi

The **absent** one / Jussi Adler-Olsen ; translated from the Danish by K.E. Semmel. Dutton, 2012. 400 p. Department Q

ISBN 9780525952893

1. Cold cases (Criminal investigation) 2. Brothers and sisters -- Death 3. Police -- Copenhagen, Denmark 4. Innocence (Law) 5. Murder investigation -- Copenhagen, Denmark 6. Homeless women 7. Copenhagen, Denmark 8. Denmark 9. Thrillers and suspense 10. Psychological suspense 11. Translations -- Danish to English 12. Scandinavian crime fiction

English translation originally published under the title Disgrace : London : Michael Joseph, 2012.

Detective Carl Mørck investigates the twenty-year-old murders of a brother and sister whose confessed killer may actually be innocent, a case with ties to a homeless woman and powerful adversaries.

Adler-Olsen, Jussi

A **conspiracy** of faith / Jussi Adler-Olsen ; translated from the Danish by Martin Aitken. Dutton, 2013. 384 p. Department Q

ISBN 9780525954002

1. Cold cases (Criminal investigation) 2. Arson investigation 3. Abused women 4. Ocean bottles 5. Brothers 6. Marital conflict 7. Police -- Copenhagen, Denmark 8. Kidnapping 9. Missing persons 10. Murder investigation 11. Copenhagen, Denmark 12. Denmark 13. Thrillers and suspense 14. Translations -- Danish to English 15. Scandinavian crime fiction

Receiving a sealed bottle with a years-old plea for help by two young victims imprisoned in a boathouse by the sea, Detective Carl Mørck follows leads to a desperate woman trapped in a brutal marriage to a man who keeps her in isolation and hides deadly secrets.

Adler-Olsen, Jussi

The **hanging** girl / Jussi Adler-Olsen ; translated from the Danish by William Frost. E.P. Dutton, 2015. 432 p. Department Q

ISBN 9780525954941

1. Cold cases (Criminal investigation) 2. Cults 3. Missing women 4. Islands 5. Teenage girls -- Death 6. Murder 7. Suicide 8. Denmark 9. Scandinavian crime fiction 10. Thrillers and suspense 11. Translations -- Danish to English

Translation from the Danish of: Den grænselose.

Originally published: Copenhagen : Politikens Forlag, 2014.

Forced to investigate the cold case murder of a 17-year-old girl, Department Q head Carl Mørck and his enigmatic assistants infiltrate a sun-worshipping cult to stop a string of new killings.

Adler-Olsen, Jussi

The **keeper** of lost causes / Jussi Adler-Olsen ; translated from the Danish by Lisa Hartford. Dutton, 2011, c2007. 400 p. Department Q

ISBN 9780525952480

1. Cold cases (Criminal investigation) 2. Missing women 3. Police 4. Missing persons investigation 5. Conspiracies 6. Politicians 7.

Copenhagen, Denmark 8. Denmark 9. Thrillers and suspense 10. Psychological suspense 11. Translations -- Danish to English 12. Scandinavian crime fiction

LC 2011014873

"Originally published with the title Mercy in Great Britain by Penguin Books."

Originally published in Danish as Kvinden i buret: Kbh. : Politiken, 2007.

Chief detective Carl Mørck, recovering from what he thought was a career-destroying gunshot wound, is relegated to cold cases and becomes immersed in the five-year disappearance of a politician.

Adler-Olsen, Jussi

The **Marco** effect : a Department Q novel / Jussi Adler-Olsen ; translated from the Danish by Martin Aitken. Dutton, 2014, c2012. 480 p. Department Q

ISBN 9780525954026

1. Missing persons investigation 2. Thieves 3. Teenage boys 4. Romanies 5. Criminals 6. Crime 7. Police 8. Denmark 9. Scandinavian crime fiction 10. Thrillers and suspense 11. Translations -- Danish to English

LC 2014014674

Translation from the Danish of: Marco Effekten.

Also published in Great Britain under the title Buried.

Originally published: Copenhagen : Politiken, 2012.

Denied Danish citizenship and an education by his oppressive gypsy clan leader, 15-year-old Marco is forced to beg and steal before fleeing in the wake of a murderous act, which is investigated by Detective Carl Mørck for its ties to petty crime rings, embezzlers and child soldiers.

Adler-Olsen, Jussi

The **purity** of vengeance : a Department Q novel / Jussi Adler-Olsen ; translated from the Danish by Martin Aitken. Dutton Adult, 2014 400 p. Department Q

ISBN 9780525954019

1. Cold cases (Criminal investigation) 2. Missing persons 3. Police -- Copenhagen, Denmark 4. Kidnapping 5. Missing persons investigation 6. Murder investigation 7. Copenhagen, Denmark 8. Denmark 9. Thrillers and suspense 10. Translations -- Danish to English 11. Scandinavian crime fiction

LC 2013033253

Previously published as Journal 64 with a variant title of Journal fireogtreds in Danish.

After new evidence surfaces, Detective Carl Mørck and his assistants look into the case of a brothel owner who went missing in the 1980s and discover that numerous other people went missing around the same time.

Adler-Olsen, Jussi

The **scarred** woman / Jussi Adler-Olsen ; translated from the Danish by Willam Frost. Dutton, 2017. 432 p. Department Q

ISBN 9780525954958

1. Violence against women 2. Women murderers 3. Violence in women 4. Cold cases (Criminal investigation) 5. Missing women 6. Detectives 7. Murder 8. Murder investigation 9. Coworkers 10. Denmark 11. Scandinavian crime fiction 12. Thrillers and suspense 13. Translations -- Danish to English

LC 2017013668

Unable to determine links between a Copenhagen park murder and another unsolved case that is unsettlingly similar, Detective Carl Mørck of Department Q finds his job and division on the line at the same time

the team investigates a possible crime that a struggling Rose has brought to light.

Adler-Olsen, Jussi

* **Victim** 2117 / Jussi Adler-Olsen ; translated from the Danish by William Frost. Dutton, 2020. 468 p. Department Q

ISBN 9781524742553

1. Refugees 2. International intrigue 3. Police 4. Secrets 5. Terrorists 6. Memories 7. Families 8. Terrorism -- Prevention 9. Denmark 10. Scandinavian crime fiction 11. Thrillers and suspense 12. Translations -- Danish to English

Originally published in Denmark, 2019.

The death of a seemingly random refugee in the Mediterranean Sea triggers powerful reverberations in a teen with murderous impulses, an Abu Ghraib terrorist and Department Q's Assad, who uncovers links to a family he assumed was long dead.

"In a feat of unparalleled storytelling, this eighth Department Q episode brings the full team back together as Adler-Olsen weaves el-Assad's heart-wrenching story into a pair of relentless manhunts." Booklist.

Afrika, Tatamkulu

Bitter Eden : a novel / Tatamkhulu Afrika. Picador, 2014. 352 p.

ISBN 9781250043665

1. Second World War era (1939-1945) 2. Prisoners of war, American 3. Male friendship 4. Sexual attraction 5. Men -- Psychology 6. World War II -- Prisoners and prisons 7. War stories 8. Autobiographical fiction 9. LGBTQIA fiction

LC 2013038598

Originally published: 2002.

A U.S. release of a modern classic is based on the author's real experiences and follows the story of three prisoners of war who must negotiate the complex emotions and belief-challenging intimacies of survival in a male-only prison camp.

"First published in Britain in 2002 (and written years earlier), this sole novel from Egyptian-born, South African-raised Afrika is based on his experiences in Italian and German prisoner-of-war camps in World War II...Afrika focuses on aspects of prison camp life that have been little explored. While the novel's theme of repressed desire might have had more power and perhaps a bit of shock value had it been published at the time it was written, it's still notable for its compelling depiction of an individual's struggle to maintain some measure of humanity and tenderness under the most inhuman of conditions." Library Journal.

Afshar, Tessa,

Thief of Corinth / Tessa Afshar. Tyndale House Publishers, 2018 400 p.

ISBN 9781496428653

1. Paul,, the Apostle, Saint 2. Roman Empire (27 BCE-476 CE) 3. Ancient Greece (800 BCE-640 CE) 4. Thieves 5. Redemption 6. Forgiveness 7. Fathers and daughters 8. Corruption 9. Secrets 10. Hope 11. Courage 12. Healing 13. Faith 14. Corinth, Greece 15. Christian historical fiction

LC 2018007681

Young Ariadne flees her mother's home to live with her father in ancient Corinth, only to find that the man is secretly an infamous thief, but when she and her father meet a Jewish rabbi named Paul their lives are profoundly changed.

Agee, James, 1909-1955

* A **death** in the family / James Agee. Vintage Books, 1998, c1957. ix, 310 p.

ISBN 9780375701238

1. Traffic accident victims 2. Fathers and sons 3. Grief 4. Family and death 5. Literary fiction 6. Coming-of-age stories 7. Southern fiction

LC 57012114

Originally published: New York : McDowell, Obolensky, 1957
Pulitzer Prize for Fiction, 1958.

On a sultry summer night in 1915, Jay Follet leaves his house in Knoxville, Tennessee, to tend to his father, whom he believes is dying. The summons turns out to be a false alarm, but on his way back to his family, Jay has a car accident and is killed instantly. From this situation, Agee weaves a story of the complex ways that people deal with life, love, and loss.

Agee, Jonis

The **bones** of paradise / Jonis Agee. William Morrow, 2016. 432 p.

ISBN 9780062413475

1. 1900s (Decade) 2. Families 3. Race relations 4. Indians of North America 5. Nebraska -- History 6. Historical fiction

LC 2015037302

A decade after the Wounded Knee Massacre, when the U.S. 7th Cavalry regiment gunned down over 200 Lakota, white rancher J.B. Bennett and Sioux woman Star are found dead on Bennett's land. As Bennett's estranged wife, Dulcinea, returns to the ranch and gathers the remaining family members, Star's sister, Rose, vows to find Star's killer and avenge her death. Set in the Nebraska Sandhills at the dawn of the 20th century,?The Bones of Paradise?is a haunting multi-generational family saga that explores a tragedy with deep historical roots through the eyes of flawed and fully fleshed-out characters. -- Description by Gillian Speace.

"The storys several partsgritty Western, family saga, mystery-work together for a memorable tale of heartbreak and redemption." Publishers Weekly.

Agnon, Shmuel Yosef, 1888-1970

* **Only** yesterday / S.Y. Agnon ; translated from the Hebrew by Barbara Harshav. Princeton University Press, 2000. 652 p.

ISBN 0691009724

1. Zionists 2. Israel -- Immigration and emigration 3. Palestine 4. Translations -- Hebrew to English 5. Allegories

LC 00021147

Follows an idealistic man as he emigrates to Palestine in the early part of the century, determined to revive Hebrew culture and build a homeland for Jews.

"Though Agnon would go on to write much of compelling interest during his remaining 25 years, this would be his masterpiece--a novel that deserves comparison with Kafka's The Trial, Mann's The Magic Mountain and Hermann Broch's The Sleepwalkers as a deployment of the resources of fiction for plumbing those abysses of cultural and personal crisis that haunted so many imaginations in the modernist period." Los Angeles Times Book Review.

Aguilar Camin, Hector, 1946-

Death in Veracruz / Hector Aguilar Camin. Schaffner Press, 2015. 212 p.

ISBN 9781936182923

1. 1970s 2. Friends' death 3. Oil industry and trade -- Corrupt practices 4. Men/women relations 5. Police misconduct 6. Villages -- Mexico 7. Labor leaders 8. Corruption 9. Escapes 10. Widows 11. Secrets 12. Mexico 13. Noir fiction 14. Translations -- Spanish to English

"While Camin's style recalls Robert Stone more than it does the noir fiction of three decades ago, he obviously possesses an intimate knowledge of the Mexican sociopolitical landscape, and this is a revealing time capsule." Publishers Weekly.

Ahava, Selja, 1974-

Things that fall from the sky / Selja Ahava ; translated from the Finnish by Emily Jeremiah and Fleur Jeremiah. Oneworld, 2019, c2015. 230 p.

ISBN 9781786075413

1. Families 2. Life change events 3. Mothers -- Death 4. Lottery winners 5. Lightning 6. Mainstream fiction 7. Translations -- Finnish to English

Originally published: Finland : Gummerus Publishers, 2015.

Exploring the unexpected and inexplicable nature of reality, this meditation on the passing of time, the endurance of love and the pain of loss follows three people whose lives are forever changed by a series of events.

"[A] whimsical and thoughtful rumination on the terrifying randomness that dictates the course of a life." Booklist.

Ahern, Cecelia, 1981-

Roar / Cecelia Ahern. Grand Central Publishing, 2019, c2018. 288 p.

ISBN 9781538730966

1. Women 2. Feminism 3. Self-perception in women 4. Self-discovery 5. Self-acceptance 6. Women's role 7. Gender role 8. Emotions in women 9. Short stories 10. Allegories

Originally published : London : HarperCollins, 2018.

Cecelia Ahern gives us thirty stories, all titled 'The Woman Who...', that capture the different facets of women's lives. Humorous, moving and poignant, the stories capture the moments the characters are overwhelmed by guilt, confusion, frustration, intimidation, exhaustion the private moments when they feel the need to roar.--Provided by publisher.

Ahlborn, Ania

The **devil** crept in / Ania Ahlborn. Gallery Books, 2017. 374 p.

ISBN 9781476783758

1. Small towns 2. Missing boys 3. Missing persons investigation 4. Boys 5. Police 6. Forests 7. Secrets 8. Cousins 9. Best friends 10. Supernatural 11. Cold cases (Criminal investigation) 12. Oregon 13. Horror

LC 2016037375

The residents of Deer Valley, Oregon have worried for years about the mysterious deaths and disappearances of animals, and -- even more disturbing -- the death of a young boy. Now 12-year-old Jude Brighton has also gone missing, and his ten-year-old cousin Stevie Clark fears that the woods harbor a monster. Jude suddenly returns, but Stevie senses that he's changed beyond recognition. Author Ania Ahlborn sensitively portrays her characters' emotions while deftly escalating the dread that emanates from the forest. -- Description by Katherine Bradley Johnson

Ahmad, Jamil

The **wandering** falcon / Jamil Ahmad. Riverhead Books, 2011. 256 p.

ISBN 9781594488276

1. Nomads 2. Borderlands 3. Exile (Punishment) 4. Refugees 5. Belonging 6. Desert life 7. Shepherds 8. Extremism 9. Place (Philosophy) 10. Kinship-based society 11. Wanderers and wandering 12. Pakistan 13. Afghanistan 14. Iran 15. Literary fiction

First published: Hamish Hamilton : Penguin Books India, 2011. Simultaneously published: Great Britain : Hamish Hamilton, 2011.

A debut novel set in the Federally Administered Tribal Lands at the intersection of Iran, Pakistan and Afghanistan follows the story of banished refugees' son Tor Baz, who travels throughout the region while considering his prestigious lineage and witnessing the effects of extreme culture and geography on the lives of those he encounters.

"A gripping book, as important for illuminating the current state of this region as it is timeless in its beautiful imagery and rhythmic prose." Publishers Weekly.

Aira, Cesar, 1949-

The **seamstress** and the wind / Cesar Aira ; translated from the Spanish by Rosalie Knecht. New Directions Books, 2011. 144 p.

ISBN 9780811219129

1. Working class families 2. Misadventures 3. Kidnapping 4. Child kidnapping victims 5. Husband and wife 6. Desire 7. Truck drivers 8. Dressmakers 9. Seamstresses 10. Patagonia (Argentina and Chile) 11. Surrealist fiction 12. Translations -- Spanish to English 13. Literary fiction

LC 2011006006

Originally published by in Argentina as La costurera y el viento, in 1994.

This translation first published: New York : New Directions Books, 2011.

In a small town in Argentina, a seamstress is sewing a wedding dress. All of a sudden she fears that her son has been kidnapped and driven off to Patagonia. Completely unhinged, she calls a local taxi to follow the semi in hot pursuit. When her husband finds out what's happened, he takes off after wife and child. They race to the end of the world where the wild Southern wind falls in love with the seamstress, a monster child takes up with the truck driver, and a man finds a phosphorescent demon attached to him after he violates a pregnant woman.

Airth, Rennie, 1935-

The **decent** inn of death / Rennie George Airth. Penguin, 2019. 368 p. John Madden novels

ISBN 9780143134299

1. Former detectives 2. Manors 3. Winter storms 4. Murder 5. Murder investigation 6. Germans in Great Britain 7. Postwar life 8. Rural life 9. England -- History -- 20th century 10. Historical mysteries

Snowed in at a country manor, former Scotland Yard inspectors John Madden and Angus Sinclair find themselves trapped in the company of a murderer.

"Post-WWII England comes to life in vivid detail, with an atmosphere so rich that readers will feel the cold seeping into their bones. An absorbing winter read for fans of well-crafted British procedurals." Booklist.

Ajvide Lindqvist, John, 1968-

Let the right one in / John Ajvide Lindqvist ; translated from the Swedish by Ebba Segerberg. Thomas Dunne Books, 2007. 472 p.

ISBN 9780312355289

1. Twelve-year-old boys 2. Overweight boys 3. Suburban life 4. Neighbors 5. Teenage murder victims 6. Curiosity in boys 7. Obsession 8. Vampires 9. Revenge 10. Sweden -- Social life and customs -- 20th century 11. Horror 12. Translations -- Swedish to English

LC 2007023510

Later published in English as: Let me in.

Two films have been based on this book: Let the right one in (2008) and Let me in (2010).

Twelve-year-old Oskar is obsessed by the murder that's taken place in his neighborhood. Then he meets the new girl from next door. She's a bit weird, though. And she only comes out at night.

Akhtar, Ayad

American **dervish** : a novel / Ayad Akhtar. Little, Brown and Co., 2012. 320 p.

ISBN 9780316183314

1. Faith 2. Islam 3. Muslim families 4. Pakistani Americans 5. Religion 6. Jealousy 7. Intergenerational relations 8. Antisemitism 9. Coming-of-age stories 10. Psychological fiction

LC 2011019737

A young Pakistani boy, whose parents left the fundamentalists behind when they came to America, finds transformation and a path to happiness through a family friend, Mina, who shows him the beauty and power of the Quran.

Akpan, Uwem

Say you're one of them / Uwem Akpan. Little, Brown and Co., 2008. 240 p.

ISBN 9780316113786

1. Child war victims 2. Social history 3. Genocide -- Rwanda 4. War victims 5. Violence 6. Children -- Africa 7. Sexual slavery 8. Africa 9. Sub-Saharan Africa 10. Literary fiction 11. Short stories

LC 2007041350

Hurston/Wright Legacy Award: Fiction, 2009.

A collection of tales about modern African children in crisis.

"Akpan's prose is beautiful and his stories are insightful and revealing, made even more harrowing because all the horror--and there is much--is seen through the eyes of children." Publishers Weekly.

Akunin, B. (Boris)

The **coronation** : the further adventures of Erast Fandorin / Boris Akunin ; translated by Andrew Bromfield. Weidenfeld & Nicolson, 2009. 311 p. Erast Fandorin mysteries

ISBN 9780802127815

1. Nicholas II,, Emperor of Russia, 1868-1918 2. Romanov Dynasty (1613-1917) 3. 19th century 4. 1890s 5. 19th century 6. Kidnapping 7. Ransom 8. Detectives -- Moscow, Russia 9. Coronations 10. Russia -- History -- 1801-1917 11. Historical mysteries 12. Translations -- Russian to English 13. Mysteries

First published in Russian as Koronaciya by Zakharov Publications, Moscow, Russia and Edizioni Frassinell, Milan, Italy.

Ernst Fandorin and a race against time just before the coronation of Tsar Nicholas II as one of the Grand Duke's children is kidnapped and a ransom note arrives - from Fandorin's nemesis, Doctor Lind.

Akunin, B. (Boris)

Sister Pelagia and the white bulldog : a mystery / Boris Akunin ; translated from the Russian by Andrew Bromfield. Random House Trade Paperbacks, 2007, c2000. 288 p. Sister Pelagia mysteries

ISBN 0812975138

1. Russian Orthodox Church. 2. Romanov Dynasty (1613-1917) 3. 19th century 4. Nuns 5. Women amateur detectives 6. Betrayal 7. Clergy 8. Families 9. Great-aunts 10. Human/animal relationships 11. Greed 12. Pets -- Death 13. Family relationships 14. Men/women relations 15. Heirs and heiresses 16. Inheritance and succession 17. Russia -- History -- 19th century 18. Historical mysteries 19.

Translations -- Russian to English 20. Mysteries

LC 2006050387

Originally published in Russian: Moscow: Izd-vo AST, 2000.

"Set in the late 19th century, this charming, highly unusual whodunit from Russian author Akunin (the pen name of Grigory Chkhartishvili) introduces Sister Pelagia, a young nun in a remote Russian province far removed from the intrigue of the czarist government." Publisher's Weekly.

Al Rawi, Shahad,

The **Baghdad** clock / Shahad al Rawi. Oneworld Publications, 2018. 288 p.

ISBN 9781786073242

1. 1990s 2. Persian Gulf War, 1991 3. Girls 4. Friendship 5. Civil war 6. Growing up 7. Best friends 8. Survival 9. Loss (Psychology) 10. Bombings 11. Coping 12. Iraq -- History -- 20th century 13. Literary fiction 14. Translations -- Arabic to English

Baghdad, 1991. In the midst of the first Gulf War, a young Iraqi girl huddles with her neighbours in an air raid shelter. There, she meets Nadia. The two girls quickly become best friends and together they imagine a world not torn apart by civil war, sharing their dreams, their hopes and their desires, and their first loves. But as they grow older and the bombs continue to fall, the international sanctions bite and friends begin to flee the country, the girls must face the fact that their lives will never be the same again.

Al-Ramli, Muhsin

The **president's** gardens / Muhsin Al-Ramli ; translated from the Arabic by Luke Leafgren. MacLehose Press, 2018. 290 p.

ISBN 9781635060362

1. Male friendship 2. Violence -- Psychological aspects 3. Political persecution 4. War and society 5. Injustice 6. Villages 7. Interpersonal relations 8. Iraq -- Social life and customs -- 20th century 9. Iraq -- Social life and customs -- 21st century 10. Political fiction 11. Literary fiction 12. Translations -- Arabic to English

LC 2017045305

Originally published: 2012.

When the severed head of his son is found, Ibrahim the Fated searches for answers to why this happened, from the battlefields of the Gulf War to what lies behind the locked gates of the president's gardens.

"This powerful, sweeping novel ... is highly recommended. It profoundly humanizes modern Mideast history for Western readers." Library Journal.

Alam, Rumaan

That kind of mother : a novel / Rumaan Alam. Ecco, 2018. 320 p.

ISBN 9780062667601

1. Nannies 2. New mothers 3. Race relations 4. European American women 5. African American women 6. Interracial adoption 7. Interracial families 8. Race awareness 9. Self-awareness 10. Motherhood 11. United States -- Race relations 12. Domestic fiction 13. Literary fiction

LC 2018000165

Overwhelmed by new motherhood in spite of her love for her infant son, Rebecca, a white woman, asks a kind black woman, Priscilla, to become her family's nanny, only to have her perspectives changed about her own life of privilege, a situation that compels her to take on unanticipated challenges in the aftermath of a tragedy.

Alameddine, Rabih

* An **unnecessary** woman / Rabih Alameddine. Grove Press, 2014. 320 p.

ISBN 9780802122148

1. Senior women 2. Books and reading 3. Reminiscing in old age 4. Women translators 5. Female friendship 6. Women's role 7. Lebanon 8. Psychological fiction 9. Literary fiction

National Book Critics Circle Award for Fiction finalist, 2014

National Book Award for Fiction finalist, 2014

A love letter to literature and its power to define who we are, this is a nuanced rendering of one woman's life in the Middle East.

"Alameddine's storytelling is rich with a bookish humor that's accessible without being condescending. A gemlike and surprisingly lively study of an interior life." Kirkus.

Alarcon, Daniel, 1977-

The **king** is always above the people : stories / Daniel Alarcon. Riverhead Books, 2017. 256 p.

ISBN 9781594631726

1. Families 2. Human nature 3. Family and death 4. Death 5. Loss (Psychology) 6. Short stories 7. Literary fiction

LC 2017016056

Longlisted for the National Book Award for Fiction, 2017.

A collection of short stories from the author of At Night We Walk in Circles features tales about people forging into new lands and a man dealing with the mysterious deaths of his blind relatives.

"A smart and understated collection that puts some new twists on old-fashioned identity crises." Kirkus.

Alarcon, Daniel, 1977-

Lost City Radio : a novel / Daniel Alarcon. Harper Collins Publishers, 2007. 224 p.

ISBN 0060594799

1. Boys -- Peru 2. Radio broadcasters 3. Missing persons -- Peru 4. Political prisoners -- Peru 5. Radio stations 6. Radio programs 7. Political violence 8. South America 9. Lima, Peru 10. Peru -- Social life and customs 11. Political fiction

LC 2006046498

Imparting comfort while reading the names of missing people to her war-ravaged listeners, radio host Norma finds her life irrevocably changed when a young boy from a remote jungle village provides a connection to her long-missing husband.

"This is a fable for an entire continent, and is no less pertinent in other parts of the world where different languages are spoken in different climates but where the same ruinous dance is played out." Washington Post Book World.

Alarcon, Daniel, 1977-

At **night** we walk in circles : a novel / Daniel Alarcon. Riverhead Hardcover, 2013. 400 p.

ISBN 9781594631719

1. Actors and actresses 2. Life change events 3. Performing arts 4. Drama 5. Civil war -- Post-war aspects 6. Traveling theater 7. Consequences 8. Memory 9. Interpersonal relations 10. Men/women relations 11. Postwar life 12. South America 13. Psychological fiction 14. Political fiction

LC 2013019446

Feeling unfulfilled in the wake of personal and professional setbacks, South American youth Nelson lands a starring role in a revival of a legendary play by his hero and confronts the realities of civil war while touring unfamiliar landscapes.

"[A] fast-unraveling mystery of role-playing and retribution, told in compelling prose that is smart, subtle, and totally engrossing." Booklist.

Albahari, David, 1948-

Gotz and Meyer / David Albahari ; translated from the Serbian by Ellen Elias-Bursac. Harcourt, 2005. 176 p.

ISBN 0151011419

1. 1940s 2. Jews, Serbian 3. Jews 4. Nazis 5. Truck drivers 6. Teachers 7. College teachers 8. Students 9. Concentration camps 10. Mass murder 11. Genocide 12. Good and evil 13. Holocaust (1933-1945) 14. World War II -- Yugoslavia 15. Yugoslavia -- History -- Axis occupation, 1941-1945 16. Yugoslavia -- History -- 1918-1945 17. Belgrade, Yugoslavia 18. Psychological fiction 19. War stories 20. Translations -- Serbian to English

LC 2005040359

Originally published in Serbian in 1998 as Gec i Majer.

"There are no chapters or even paragraphs, but the spacious text is simple and eloquent, and readers will be drawn into the professor's obsessive first-person narrative in which the horror is in the facts of bureaucratic efficiency and the unimaginable evil in ordinary life." Booklist.

Albert, Elisa, 1978-

After birth / Elisa Albert. Houghton Mifflin Harcourt, 2015. 208 p.

ISBN 9780544273733

1. Motherhood 2. Female friendship 3. Social isolation 4. New mothers 5. Postpartum depression 6. Academics 7. Women poets 8. College teachers 9. Marriage 10. Pregnant women 11. New York State 12. Psychological fiction

LC 2014006756

First published in (hbk.) by Chatto & Windus in 2015. First published in the United States of America by Houghton Mifflin Harcourt in 2015.

Parts of this book have appeared in a different form in Tin house.

In snowy upstate New York, a struggling mother of a one-year-old and a nine-months-pregnant woman who is new to town become comrades-in-arms.

"Irreverent, hilarious, and honest, Alberts newest novel loudly decries the isolation of new mothers in todays world. Her opinionated protagonist is sympathetic, if not entirely likable, and will pull readers along on her journey toward a new normal with great humor and wit." Booklist.

Albert, Elisa, 1978-

The **book** of Dahlia : novel / Elisa Albert. Free Press, 2008. 288 p.

ISBN 9780743291293

1. Women with terminal illnesses 2. Jewish American women 3. Women with cancer 4. Jewish women 5. Young women 6. Strokes 7. Parent and adult child 8. Brothers and sisters 9. Family relationships 10. Failure (Psychology) 11. California 12. Pacific States (United States) 13. Mainstream fiction

LC 2007033839

A young Jewish-American woman learns that she has brain cancer and through a series of flashbacks examines her wasted life.

"Basing her chapters on a self-help book that Dahlia buys (It's Up to You: The Cancer To-Do List), Albert writes with the black humor of Lorrie Moore and a pathos that is uniquely her own, all the more blistering for being slyly invoked." The New Yorker.

Albert, Susan Wittig

Bittersweet / Susan Wittig Albert. Berkley Prime Crime, 2015. 304 p. China Bayles mysteries

ISBN 9780425255629

1. Thanksgiving Day 2. Ranches 3. Heart attack 4. Murder investigation 5. Women amateur detectives 6. Small town life --

Texas 7. Texas 8. Pecan Springs (TX : Imaginary place) 9. Mysteries

Planning to spend the Thanksgiving holiday on her mother's ranch-turned-birdwatcher's retreat, China learns that her mother's divorcee helper has died in a suspicious accident that is tied to the murder of a local veterinarian.

Albert, Susan Wittig

The **Darling** Dahlias and the cucumber tree / Susan Wittig Albert. Berkley Prime Crime, 2010. 290 p. Darling Dahlias mysteries

ISBN 9780425234457

1. Depression era (1929-1941) 2. 1930s 3. Women gardeners 4. Gardening -- Societies, etc 5. Treasure troves 6. Women murder victims 7. Women amateur detectives 8. Murder investigation 9. Depressions -- 1929-1941 -- Alabama 10. Small towns 11. Alabama 12. Cozy mysteries 13. Historical mysteries 14. Hobby mysteries 15. Gentle reads

The Depression-era women of a Darling, Alabama, garden club get to the bottom of a mysterious buried treasure and a young woman's murder.

"Albert brings a small Southern town to life and vividly captures an era and culture--the Depression, segregation, class differences, the role of women in the South--with authentic period details." Library Journal.

Albom, Mitch, 1958-

The **five** people you meet in heaven / Mitch Albom. Hyperion, 2003. 342 p. Five people you meet in Heaven

ISBN 0786868716

1. Life after death 2. Heaven 3. Meaning (Psychology) 4. Death 5. Secrets 6. Memories 7. Accident victims 8. Senior men 9. Repairers 10. Veterans 11. Octogenarians 12. Amusement parks 13. Amusement park rides 14. Psychological fiction

LC 2003047888

Sequel: The next person you meet in Heaven.

Killed in a tragic accident at a seaside amusement park while trying to save a little girl, Eddie, an elderly man who believes that he had lived an uninspired life, awakens in the afterlife, where he discovers that heaven consists of having five people, acquaintances and strangers, explain the meaning of one's life.

Albom, Mitch, 1958-

The **next** person you meet in Heaven / Mitch Albom. Harper, 2018 224 p. Five people you meet in Heaven

ISBN 9780062294449

1. Heaven 2. Life after death 3. Accident victims 4. Amusement parks 5. Amusement rides 6. Senior men 7. Reunions 8. Death 9. Psychological fiction

LC 2018020005

Sequel to: The five people you meet in Heaven.

Fifteen years after Eddie died saving a little girl named Annie, Annie suffers a terrible accident and finds herself reunited with Eddie, one of the five people who will show her how her life mattered in ways she never considered.

Alcott, Kate

A **touch** of stardust / Kate Alcott. Doubleday, 2015. 304 p.

ISBN 9780385539043

1. Gable, Clark, 1901-1960 2. Lombard, Carole, 1908-1942 3. Gone With the Wind (Motion picture) 4. Film actors and actresses 5. Personal assistants 6. Extramarital affairs 7. Scandals 8. Female friendship 9. Hollywood, California 10. Biographical fiction 11. Love stories 12. Historical fiction

LC 2014020972

RUSA Reading List Short List, 2016.

Taking a job at the studio where David O. Selznick is filming Gone with the Wind, Julie Crawford becomes an assistant to Carole Lombard, a rising actress from Julie's hometown who embarks on a scandalous affair with Clark Gable.

"The briskly paced narrative captivates as it lets readers view the creation of silver-screen magic, and its also a terrific tribute to the industry pioneers, like screenwriter Frances Marion, who helped others jump-start their dreams." Booklist.

Alderman, Naomi

* The **power** / Naomi Alderman. Little, Brown and Co., 2017, c2016. ix, 340 p.

ISBN 9780316547611

1. Superhuman abilities 2. Power (Social sciences) 3. Gender role 4. Social change 5. Violence against men 6. Teenage girls 7. Women -- Social conditions 8. Social science fiction 9. Science fiction 10. Literary fiction

Originally published: London : Viking, 2016.

Baileys Women's Prize for Fiction, 2017.

RUSA Reading List Short List, 2018.

When a new force takes hold of the world, people from different areas of life are forced to cross paths in an alternate reality that gives women and teenage girls immense physical power that can cause pain and death.

"Both the main story and the frame narrative ask interesting questions about gender, but this isn't a dry philosophical exercise. It's fast-paced, thrilling, and even funny." Kirkus.

Alenyikov, Michael

Ivan and Misha : stories / Michael Alenyikov. TriQuarterly Books, 2010. 199 p.

ISBN 9780810127180

1. 1990s 2. Twin brothers 3. Immigrants 4. Familial love 5. Fathers and sons 6. Russians in the United States 7. Russian American families 8. Family relationships 9. Men with bipolar disorder 10. Gay men -- Identity 11. Identity (Psychology) 12. Loss (Psychology) 13. New York City 14. Short stories 15. Mainstream fiction

LC 2010024016

"Highly recommended, especially for readers of literary gay fiction, although the themes of exile and familial affection will interest a wider audience." Library Journal.

Alexander, Tamera

* A **note** yet unsung / Tamera Alexander. Bethany House, 2017 352 p. Belmont mansion novels

ISBN 9780764206245

1. Gilded Age (1865-1898) 2. Women musicians 3. Orchestras 4. Conductors (Music) 5. Violinists 6. Sexism 7. Interpersonal attraction 8. Men/women relations 9. Upper class -- Tennessee 10. Southern States -- History -- 1865-1877 11. Nashville, Tennessee 12. Christian historical romances

LC 2016035450

Series complete in 3 volumes.

Christy Award for Historical Romance Category, 2017.

In 1871, 23-year-old violinist Rebekah Carrington unhappily returns home to Nashville. She's been studying in Vienna for ten years, but her money's been cut off by her estranged mother and stepfather since her paternal grandmother unexpectedly (and suspiciously) passed away. Rebekah hopes to play with the newly formed Nashville Philharmonic, but woman aren't allowed. Still, when conductor Nathaniel Tate Whitcomb needs help finishing the symphony that he's writing for his ill father, he calls on Rebekah, to whom he feels a connection. This conclusion to the Belmont Mansion trilogy will be music to the ears of readers who like lyrically told tales with a hint of mystery and note-perfect romances. -- Description by Dawn Towery

Alexander, Tamera

With this pledge / Tamera Alexander. Thomas Nelson, 2019. 352 p. Carnton novels

ISBN 9780718081850

1. American Civil War era (1861-1865) 2. Confederate soldiers 3. Governesses 4. Personal conduct 5. Widowers 6. Hospitals 7. War wounds 8. Engaged persons 9. Faith (Christianity) 10. Interpersonal attraction 11. Men/women relations 12. Tennessee -- History 13. Franklin, Tennessee 14. Christian historical romances

LC 2018037968

Christy Award for Historical Romance Category, 2019.

When her home is converted into a Confederate hospital Lizzie Clouston must be true to her own heart while standing for what she knows is right.

Alexander, V. S.

The **Magdalen** girls / V.S. Alexander. Kensington Books, 2016 304 p.

ISBN 9781496706126

1. 1960s 2. Forced labor 3. Women -- Social conditions 4. Survival (in concentration camps, prisons, etc) 5. Clergy 6. Reputation 7. Prostitution 8. Teenage girls 9. Women's shelters 10. Men/women relations 11. Sexism in the Catholic Church 12. Dublin, Ireland 13. Historical fiction

When her beauty provokes a lustful revelation from a young priest, sixteen-year-old Teagan is sent to one of Dublin's Magdalen Laundries for fallen women, where she befriends two other girls who help her endure the harsh captivity.

Alexander, Victoria

The **Lady** Travelers Guide to larceny with a dashing stranger / Victoria Alexander. HQN Books, 2017. 537 p. Lady Travelers Guide

ISBN 9780373804009

1. Victorian era (1837-1901) 2. Widows 3. Women travelers 4. Art -- Collectors and collecting 5. Interpersonal attraction 6. Voyages and travels 7. Men/women relations 8. Deception 9. Heirlooms 10. Venice, Italy 11. England 12. Victorian romances 13. Historical romances

Includes bonus story: The rise and fall of Reginald Everheart.

In Regency Venice, a desperate widow and a determined bachelor search for a missing masterpiece that will change their lives.

Alexander, Victoria

* The **Lady** Travelers Guide to scoundrels and other gentlemen : / Victoria Alexander. HQN Books, 2017. 384 p. Lady Travelers Guide

ISBN 9780373803989

1. Victorian era (1837-1901) 2. Personal assistants 3. Womanizers 4. Women travelers 5. Heirs and heiresses 6. Missing women 7. Missing persons investigation 8. British in foreign countries 9. Men/women relations 10. Paris, France 11. England 12. Victorian romances 13. Historical romances

Includes bonus story: The Proper Way to Stop a Wedding in Seven Days or Less.

Searching for her aunt, a member of the possibly fraudulent Lady Travelers society, India Prendergast is joined by the nephew of one of the group's members, Derek Saunders, a handsome man with a scandalous reputation.

"Alexander celebrates the spirit of adventure, elevates dubious scheming with good intentions, and advocates for the yielding of judgment and practicality to hedonism and happiness. Readers will savor every page." Publishers Weekly.

Alexander, Victoria

What happens at Christmas / Victoria Alexander. Zebra Books, 2012. 396 p. Millworth Manor

ISBN 9780758255686

1. Victorian era (1837-1901) 2. Deception 3. Engagement 4. Christmas 5. Families 6. Princes 7. Marriage proposals 8. Men/women relations 9. Holiday romances 10. Historical romances 11. Victorian romances

Hiring a troupe of actors to pose as her "conventional" family to secure a long-awaited proposal from a dashing prince, Camille, Lady Lydingham, finds her plans going awry when a man from her past crashes her party, determined to win her hand as well.

Alexie, Sherman, 1966-

Blasphemy : new and selected stories / Sherman Alexie. Grove Press, 2012. 304 p.

ISBN 9780802120397

1. Marriage 2. Racism 3. Addiction 4. Indians of North America 5. Native American men 6. Pacific Northwest 7. Short stories 8. Pacific Northwest fiction 9. Literary fiction

Collects 15 previously published and 15 new short stories.

A collection of thirty-one new and selected short stories by Native American author Sherman Alexie.

Alexie, Sherman, 1966-

Flight / Sherman Alexie. Grove Press, 2007 208 p.

ISBN 0802170374

1. 19th century 2. 21st century 3. Indians of North America 4. Family relationships 5. Identity (Psychology) 6. Teenage boys 7. Time travel (Past) 8. FBI agents 9. Violence 10. Native American teenage boys 11. Violence 12. Orphans 13. Social science fiction 14. Pacific Northwest fiction 15. Science fiction 16. Literary fiction

On the verge of commiting an act of violence, a troubled, orphaned Indian teenager finds himself hurtled through time and into the bodies of a civil rights era FBI agent, an Indian child during the battle at Little Big Horn, a nineteenth- century Indian tracker, and a modern-day airline pilot, before returning to himself, forever altered by his experiences.

"Many of [the] allegorical, action-packed vignettes tread familiar thematic territory--the continuing fight for survival, the anger of racial divides, the absence of fathers--of Mr. Alexie's earlier works. . . . But with 'Flight,' he takes these themes a step further: he skillfully explores both sides of the proverbial war. Zits witnesses brutal violence through the eyes of whites and Indians, fathers and sons, and he begins to understand what it means to be the hero, the villain and the victim." New York Times.

Alexie, Sherman, 1966-

Reservation blues / Sherman Alexie. Atlantic Monthly Press, 1995. 306 p.

ISBN 9780871135940

1. Johnson, Robert, 1911-1938 2. Native American rock musicians 3. Spokane Indian Reservation 4. Spokane Indians -- Washington (State) 5. Indians of North America -- Washington (State) 6. Indians of North America -- Alcoholism 7. Magic guitars 8. Washington (State) 9. Literary fiction 10. Pacific Northwest fiction

LC 94046132

Song lyrics begin each chapter.

Shortlisted for the International IMPAC Dublin Literary Award, 1997

Legendary blues guitarist Robert Johnson appears on an Indian reservation to lead a Catholic rock band.

"Hilarious but poignant, filled with enchantments yet dead-on accurate with regard to modern Indian life, this tour de force will leave readers wondering if Alexie himself hasn't made a deal with the Gentleman in order to do everything so well." Publishers Weekly.

Alexis, Andre, 1957-

Fifteen dogs / Andre Alexis. Coach House Books, 2015. 160 p.

ISBN 9781552453056

1. Dogs 2. Consciousness 3. Happiness 4. Gods and goddesses, Greek 5. Humans and dogs 6. Knowledge 7. Hermes (Greek deity) 8. Apollo (Greek deity) 9. Toronto, Ontario 10. Canada 11. Literary fiction

Rogers Writers' Trust Fiction Prize, 2015.

Scotiabank Giller Prize, 2015.

Gods Apollo and Hermes grant human intelligence and consciousness to fifteen dogs who wrestle with the challenges that arise as the result of their elevated thinking.

Alexis, Andre, 1957-

The **hidden** keys / Andre Alexis Coach House Book, 2016 200 p.

ISBN 9781552453254

1. Thieves 2. Quests 3. Inheritance and succession 4. Treasure hunting 5. Puzzles 6. Bars (Drinking establishments) 7. Heroin addicts 8. Detectives 9. Albinos and albinism 10. Psychopaths 11. Honor 12. Loyalty 13. Literary fiction

Tancred Palmieri, an accomplished and honourable thief is enlisted to help aging heroin addict, Willow Azarian steal the five mysterious objects Willow's wealthy father left to each of his five children that provide clues to the whereabouts of a large inheritance.

Algren, Nelson, 1909-1981

* The **man** with the golden arm : a novel / Nelson Algren. Seven Stories Press, 1999, c1949. viii, 454 p.

ISBN 9781583220078

1. Drug addicts 2. City life 3. Morphine addiction 4. Criminals 5. Gambling 6. Chicago, Illinois 7. Literary fiction 8. Modern classics

Originally published: Garden City, N.Y. : Doubleday, 1949.

National Book Award for Fiction, 1950.

This is the story of "Frankie Machine," a veteran, drug addict, and card-dealer in an illicit poker game being run in Chicago's Near Northwest Side. Frankie has just returned from the federal prison for narcotics addicts in Louisville, Kentucky, where he was exposed to all the pressures, anxieties, and temptations that had put him there in the first place.

Algren, Nelson, 1909-1981

A **walk** on the wild side / Nelson Algren. Farrar, Straus and Giroux, 2001, c1956. xi, 346 p.

ISBN 9780374525323

1. 1930s 2. Prostitutes 3. Bootleggers 4. City life 5. Men/women relations 6. French Quarter (New Orleans, La) 7. New Orleans, Louisiana 8. Literary fiction

Depicts the downtrodden prostitutes, bootleggers, and hustlers of Perdido Street in the old French Quarter of 1930s New Orleans.

"Algren's vivid writing gives this degenerate cast the power to shock or appall, and if a glimmer of compassion leaks through occasionally it is slapped down before it gets out of hand." Library Journal.

Alharthi, Jokha

Celestial bodies / Jokha Alharthi ; translated from the Arabic by Marilyn Booth. Catapult, 2019, c2010. 254 p.
ISBN 9781948226943
1. 20th century 2. Sisters 3. Social change 4. Villages 5. Tradition (Philosophy) 6. Generation gap 7. Families 8. Communities 9. Loss (Psychology) 10. Family relationships 11. Manners and customs 12. Oman 13. Oman -- Social life and customs 14. Family sagas 15. Literary fiction 16. Translations -- Arabic to English
Originally published: Beirut : Dar al-Adab, 2010.
Man Booker International Prize, 2019.
Tells of Oman's coming-of-age through the prism of one family's losses and loves.
"A richly layered, ambitious work that teems with human struggles and contradictions, providing fascinating insight into Omani history and society." Kirkus.

Ali, Monica, 1967-

* **Brick** Lane : a novel / Monica Ali. Scribner, 2003. 369 p.
ISBN 9780743243308
1. 1980s 2. 1990s 3. 2000s (Decade) 4. Self-discovery in women 5. Self-confidence in women 6. Women -- Identity 7. Immigrants 8. Women immigrants 9. Bangladeshis in England 10. Bengali (South Asian people) in England 11. Muslims 12. Women's role 13. Arranged marriage 14. Men/women relations 15. Families 16. London, England 17. Bangladesh 18. Coming-of-age stories 19. Literary fiction
LC 2003042795
ALA Notable Book, 2004.
Shortlisted for the Man Booker Prize, 2003.
National Book Critics Circle Award for Fiction finalist, 2003
Presents the story of two Bangladeshi sisters, one who chooses her destiny by opting for a "love marriage" and one who lets destiny dictate her future when she is married off to an older man and moves with him to a small, claustrophobic London flat.
"Nazeen, a young Bangladeshi woman, moves to London's Bangla Town (around the street of the title) in the mid-nineteen eighties after an arranged marriage with an older man. Seen through Nazeen's eyes, England is at first utterly baffling, but over the seventeen years of the narrative (which takes us into the post-September 11th era), she gradually finds her way, bringing up two daughters and eventually starting an all-female tailoring business. . . . In Ali's subtle narration, Nazeen's mixture of traditionalism, and adaptability, of acceptence and restlessness, emerges as a quiet strength." The New Yorker.

Alison, Jane, 1961-

The **marriage** of the sea / Jane Alison. Farrar, Straus, Giroux, 2003. 262 p.
ISBN 0374199418
1. Husband and wife 2. Married people 3. Architects 4. Lovers 5. Artists 6. Women painters 7. Men/women relations 8. Venice, Italy 9. New Orleans, Louisiana 10. New York City 11. Psychological fiction 12. Love stories
LC 2002033887
"The author wonderfully captures the romantically stymied antics of smart people who lack the emotional grit needed to figure out the relationship they are in before drifting on to the next." Library Journal.

Aliu, Xhenet, 1978-

* **Brass** : a novel / Xhenet Aliu. Random House, 2018 304 p.
ISBN 9780399590245
1. 1990s 2. 2010s 3. Mothers and daughters 4. Immigrants 5. Social classes 6. Goals and objectives 7. Life change events 8. Teenage pregnancy 9. Single mothers 10. Teenage girls 11. Family relationships 12. Men/women relations 13. Connecticut 14. Literary fiction 15. Parallel narratives
LC 2017002763
A fierce debut novel about mothers and daughters, haves and have-nots, and the stark realities behind the American Dream.
"Aliu's riveting, sensitive work shines with warmth, clarity, and a generosity of spirit. Her characters are nuanced and real, capable of taking risks, making mistakes, and growing in unexpected ways." Kirkus.

Allen, Jane

I lost my girlish laughter / Jane Allen. Vintange Books, 2019, c1938. 256 p.
ISBN 9781984897763
1. 1930s 2. Secretaries 3. Film producers and directors 4. Film studios 5. Actors and actresses 6. Film industry and trade 7. Women employees 8. Men/women relations 9. Hollywood, California 10. Satirical fiction 11. Classics
Jane Allen is a peudonym for Silvia Schulman Lardner and Jane Shore.
Originally published: New York : Random House, 1938.
Madge Lawrence, fresh from New York City, lands a job as the personal secretary to the powerful Hollywood producer Sidney Brand (based on the legendary David O. Selznick). In a series of letters home, Western Union telegrams, office memos, Hollywood gossip newspaper items, and personal journal entries, we get served up the inside scoop on all the shenanigans, romances, backroom deals, and betrayals that go into making a movie.

Allen, Sarah Addison

First frost / Sarah Addison Allen. St. Martin's Press, 2015. 304 p. Waverley family novels
ISBN 9781250019837
1. Sisters 2. Magic 3. Autumn 4. Candy 5. Enchantment 6. Small towns -- North Carolina 7. Fathers and daughters 8. Family relationships 9. Men/women relations 10. North Carolina 11. Mainstream fiction 12. Southern fiction 13. Gentle reads
LC 2014032166
Includes a reading group guide.
A tale set 10 years after the events in Garden Spells finds Claire's happy contentment shattered by her father's revelations, which challenge everything she ever believed about herself.
"Fans of Allen (The Peach Keeper; The Sugar Queen) will recognize familiar characters from her 2007 Garden Spells. This novel features charming characters, exploration of the family ties that bind and captivate us, and a touch of the supernatural, which will especially please longtime Allen readers." Library Journal.

Allen, Sarah Addison

Garden spells / Sarah Addison Allen. Bantam Books, 2007. 304 p. Waverley family novels
ISBN 9780553805482
1. Sisters 2. Magic 3. Enchantment 4. Small towns -- North Carolina 5. Gardens 6. Gardening 7. Secrets 8. Plants -- Occult aspects 9. Mothers and daughters 10. North Carolina 11. Mainstream fiction 12. Southern fiction 13. Gentle reads
LC 2007000195

RUSA Reading List, 2008.

A successful caterer in Bascomb, North Carolina, Claire has always remained tied to the legacy of the Waverly family, until her peaceful life is transformed by Tyler Hughes, an art teacher and new next-door neighbor, and by the return of her prodigal sister, Sydney.

"Spellbindingly charming, Allens impressively accomplished debut novel will bewitch fans of Alice Hoffman and Laura Esquivel, as her entrancing brand of magic realism nimbly blends the evanescent desires of hopeless romantics with the inherent wariness of those who have been hurt once too often." Booklist.

Allen, Sarah Addison

* The **girl** who chased the moon : a novel / Sarah Addison Allen. Bantam Books, 2010. 304 p.

ISBN 9780553807219

1. Family secrets 2. Grandfathers 3. Recluses 4. Magic 5. Bakers 6. Mothers -- Death 7. North Carolina 8. Mainstream fiction 9. Family sagas 10. Southern fiction 11. Gentle reads

LC 2009042254

Emily Benedict came to Mullaby, North Carolina, hoping to solve at least some of the riddles surrounding her mother's life. But the moment Emily enters the house where her mother grew up and meets the grandfather she never knew--a reclusive, real-life gentle giant--she realizes that mysteries aren't solved in Mullaby, they're a way of life.

"That it is never too late to change the future and that high school sins can be forgiven--these are wonderful messages, but Allen's warm characters and quirky setting are what will completely open readers' hearts to this story. Nothing in it disappoints." Library Journal.

Allende, Isabel

Daughter of fortune : a novel / Isabel Allende ; translated from the Spanish by Margaret Sayers Peden. Harper Collins, 1999. 399 p.

ISBN 9780060194918

1. 1840s 2. Hispanic American women -- California 3. Gold mines and mining -- California 4. Gold rush -- California 5. Male impersonators 6. Chinese Americans -- California 7. California -- History -- 1846-1850 8. California -- Social life and customs -- 19th century 9. Historical fiction 10. Literary fiction 11. Translations -- Spanish to English 12. Magical realism

LC 99026021

Sequel: Portrait in sepia

The story of a young woman's quest for love and fortune during the California Gold Rush in San Francisco.

"This novel has pretensions, but they are overridden by Allende's riproaring girl's adventure story.... Throughout it all, Allende projects a woman's point of view with confidence, control and an expansive definition of romance as a fact of life." Time.

Allende, Isabel

***Eva** Luna / Isabel Allende ; translated from the Spanish by Margaret Sayers Peden. A. A. Knopf, 1988. 271 p.

ISBN 9780394572734

1. Women -- South America 2. Orphans 3. Storytelling 4. Women -- Interpersonal relations 5. South America 6. Picaresque fiction 7. Magical realism 8. Literary fiction 9. Translations -- Spanish to English

LC 88045272

A servant woman relates the tale of her life and of the landowners, emigres, urchins, guerilla leaders, entertainers, eccentrics, and refugees who instruct and transform her.

"This wonderful novel, crammed with the strange and fantastical, the sensuous and the erotic, also speaks powerfully in the cause of freedom." Publishers Weekly.

Allende, Isabel

*The **house** of the spirits / Isabel Allende ; translated from Spanish by Magda Bogin Bantam Books, 1989, c1985. 368 p.

ISBN 0394539079

1. Culture conflict 2. Family relationships 3. Psychics -- South America 4. Men/women relations 5. South America -- History 6. Chile -- History 7. Family sagas 8. Magical realism 9. Literary fiction 10. Translations -- Spanish to English 11. Modern classics

LC 84048516

Originally published in 1985.

"A strong, absorbing Chilean family chronicle, plushly upholstered--with mystical undercurrents (psychic phenomena) and a measure of leftward political commitment." Kirkus.

Allende, Isabel

In the midst of winter : a novel / Isabel Allende ; translated from the Spanish by Nick Castor and Amanda Hopkinson. Atria Books, 2017, c2017. 352 p.

ISBN 9781501178139

1. 2010s 2. 1970s 3. College teachers 4. Women college teachers 5. Undocumented immigrants 6. Human rights 7. Immigrants 8. Jewish American men 9. Interpersonal relations 10. Life change events 11. Traffic accidents 12. Murder 13. New York City 14. Guatemala 15. Chile 16. Literary fiction 17. Love stories

LC 2017027807

Originally published by Vintage Espanol, 2017.

A minor traffic accident becomes a catalyst for an unexpected bond among a human rights scholar, his Chilean lecturer tenant and an undocumented immigrant from Guatemala, who explore firsthand the difficulties of immigrants and refugees in today's world.

"Filled with Allende's signature lyricism and ingenious plotting, the book delves wonderfully into what it means to respect, protect, and love." Publishers Weekly.

Allende, Isabel

The **Japanese** lover / Isabel Allende. Pocket Books, 2015. 352 p.

ISBN 9781501116971

1. World War II 2. Interracial romance 3. Artists 4. Race relations 5. Aging 6. Senior women 7. Concentration camps 8. San Francisco, California -- Social life and customs 9. Literary fiction

Originally published as El Amante Japones in 2015 in Spain by Penguin Random House Grupo Editorial. First published in the USA by Atria Books, 2015. First published in Great Britain by Scribner, 2015.

"From internationally bestselling author Isabel Allende comes an exquisitely crafted love story and multigenerational epic that sweeps from present-day San Francisco to Poland and the United States during WWII. In 1939, as Poland falls under the shadow of the Nazis and the world goes to war, young Alma Belasco's parents send her away to live in safety with an aunt and uncle in their opulent mansion in San Francisco. There she meets Ichimei Fukuda, the son of the family's Japanese gardener, and between them a tender love blossoms. Following Pearl Harbor, the two are cruelly pulled apart when Ichimei and his family - like thousands of Japanese Americans - are declared enemies by the US government and relocated to internment camps. Throughout their lifetimes, Alma and Ichimei reunite again and again, but theirs is a love they are forever forced to hide from the world. Decades later, Alma is nearing the end of her long and eventful life. Irina Bazili, a care worker struggling to come to terms with her own troubled past, meets the older woman and her grandson, Seth, at Lark House nursing home. As Irina and Seth forge a friendship, they become intrigued by a series of mysterious gifts and letters sent to Alma, and learn about Ichimei and this extraordinary secret passion that has endured for nearly seventy years. "--, Provided by publisher.

"Allende's latest (Maya's Notebook), a glorious family saga, with its rich cast of decent, complex characters caught up in America's struggles with war, prejudice, AIDS, and society's old taboos that are fast disappearing, is a beautiful tribute to devotion." Library Journal.

Allende, Isabel

A **long** petal of the sea : a novel / Isabel Allende ; translated from the Spanish by Nick Caistor and Amanda Hopkinson. Ballantine Books, 2020. 352 p.
  ISBN 9781984820150
  1. Neruda, Pablo, 1904-1973 2. 20th century 3. Refugees 4. Loss (Psychology) 5. Young widows 6. Physicians 7. Marriage 8. War -- Psychological aspects 9. Violence -- Psychological aspects 10. Life change events 11. Voyages and travels 12. Belonging 13. Families 14. Men/women relations 15. Chile -- History -- 20th century 16. Spain -- History -- Civil War, 1936-1939 17. Historical fiction 18. Translations -- Spanish to English
                                          LC 2019037428
  "Originally published in Spain in 2019 as Largo pétalo de mar"--Title page verso.
  Sponsored by the poet Pablo Neruda to flee the violence of the Spanish Civil War, a pregnant widow and an army doctor unite in an arranged marriage, only to be swept up by the early days of World War II.
  "Allende's assured prose vividly evokes her fictional characters, historical figures like Neruda, and decades of complex international history; her imagery makes the suffering of war and displacement palpable yet also does justice to human strength, hope and rebirth." Publishers Weekly.

Allende, Isabel

Of love and shadows / Isabel Allende ; translated from the Spanish by Margaret Sayers Peden A. A. Knopf, 1987. 274 p.
  ISBN 9780394549620
  1. Dictatorship -- Latin America 2. Political refugees 3. Journalists 4. Journalism -- Political aspects 5. Men/women relations 6. Latin America 7. Literary fiction 8. Political fiction 9. Love stories 10. Translations -- Spanish to English 11. Magical realism
                                          LC 86046164
  Soaring Eagle Book Award (Wyoming), 1990.
  Irene Beltran, a reporter for a women's magazine in a Latin American country, and Francisco Leal, a photographer and a clandestine worker in the resistance, uncover a hideous crime that challenges the official terrorism of their country's military dictatorship.
  "Ms. Allende skillfully evokes both the terrors of daily life under military rule and the subtler forms of resistance in the hidden corners and 'shadows' of her title, particularly in the churches or in simple unsung acts of solidarity. At the same time the author ably captures the voices of the regime's apologists--the complex lies and cliches of its proud male foot soldiers and the pat false phrases of its rich lady cheerleaders." New York Times Book Review.

Allende, Isabel

Portrait in sepia : a novel / Isabel Allende ; translated from the Spanish by Margaret Sayers Peden. Harper Collins Publishers, 2001. 304 p.
  ISBN 0066211611
  1. 19th century 2. Family secrets 3. Memories 4. Betrayal 5. Grandmother and child 6. Men/women relations 7. Women

photographers 8. Photography 9. Marriage 10. Death 11. Loss (Psychology) 12. Chile -- History -- 19th century 13. Family sagas 14. Translations -- Spanish to English 15. Literary fiction 16. Historical fiction 17. Magical realism
                                          LC 00054127
  Sequel to: Daughter of fortune.
  With her earliest memories erased by a brutal trauma, Aurora del Valle is raised amid great wealth in Chile by her shrewd, commanding grandmother. But her nights are tormented by a nightmare set in San Francisco's Chinatown. Now, reaching womanhood and thrust into a marriage that quickly leaves her disillusioned, she begins a search for her missing years and unwinds a twisted saga linking three generations of a powerful family to a courageous Chinese physician and Eliza Sommers, a protagonist of Allende's Daughter of Fortune, in a tale that explores the complexity of passion, the power of memory, and a woman's emerging self.
  "Through Aurora, Allende exercises her supreme storytelling abilities, of which strong, passionate characters are paramount." Publishers Weekly.

Allende, Isabel

Ripper : a novel / Isabel Allende ; translated from the Spanish by Oliver Brock and Frank Wynne. Harper, 2014, c2014 478 p.
  ISBN 9780062291400
  1. Children of divorced parents 2. Serial murderers -- San Francisco, California 3. Internet games 4. Murder investigation 5. Teenagers 6. Missing persons 7. San Francisco, California 8. Mysteries 9. Literary fiction 10. Translations -- Spanish to English
                                          LC 2013030359
  Originally published as: El juego de Ripper. Spain : Random House Mondadori, 2014.
  Fascinated by the dark side of human nature, high school senior Amanda Jackson, a natural-born sleuth addicted to an online mystery game called Ripper, launches her own investigation into a string of strange murders across the city that hits too close to home when her mother vanishes.

Allende, Isabel

The **stories** of Eva Luna / Isabel Allende ; translated from the Spanish by Margaret Sayers Peden Atheneum, 1991. 330 p.
  ISBN 0689121024
  1. South America 2. Magical realism 3. Literary fiction 4. Short stories 5. Translations -- Spanish to English
                                          LC 90039615
  23 short stories.
  When her lover asks her to tell him a story, Eva Luna complies with this collection of tales
  "The title character of Allende's Eva Luna returns to frame this collection of stories in a Scheherazade-like fashion. . . . Allende covers familiar territory: social warfare between the rich and the poor, sexual battles between men and women, the dissolution of corrupt politicians and macho military leaders, all set within the landscape of contemporary South America." Booklist.

Allio, Kirstin

Buddhism for Western children : a novel / Kirstin Allio. University of Iowa Press, 2018. 284 p.
  ISBN 9781609385965
  1. 1970s 2. 1980s 3. Cults 4. Spirituality 5. Gurus 6. Life change events 7. Communities 8. Boys 9. Power (Social sciences) 10. Manipulation (Social sciences) 11. Change (Psychology) 12.

Families 13. Maine 14. New Mexico 15. Coming-of-age stories

LC 2018010061

Set on the coast of Maine and in the high desert of New Mexico in the late 1970s through the early 80s, Buddhism for Western Children is a universal and timeless story of a boy who must escape subjugation, tell his story, and reclaim his soul.

Allison, Dorothy

*Bastard out of Carolina / Dorothy Allison. Dutton, 1992. 309 p.

ISBN 9780525934257

1. 1950s 2. Twelve-year-old girls 3. Poor families 4. Stepfathers 5. Child abuse victims 6. Sexually abused children 7. Illegitimacy 8. Prejudice 9. Independence in women 10. South Carolina 11. Coming-of-age stories 12. Southern Gothic 13. Southern fiction

LC 91034607

National Book Award for Fiction finalist, 1992

Tired of being labeled white trash, Ruth Anne Boatwright--a South Carolina bastard who is attached to the indomitable women in her mother's family--longs to escape from her hometown, and especially from Daddy Glen and his meanspirited jealousy

"Set in the rural South, this tale centers around the Boatwright family, a proud and closeknit clan known for their drinking, fighting, and womanizing. Nicknamed Bone by her Uncle Earle, Ruth Anne is the bastard child of Anney Boatwright, who has fought tirelessly to legitimize her child. When she marries Glen, a man from a good family, it appears that her prayers have been answered. However, Anney suffers a miscarriage and Glen begins drifting. He develops a contentious relationship with Bone and then begins taking sexual liberties with her. . . . Unaware of her husband's abusive behavior, Anney stands by her man. Eventually, a violent encounter wrests Bone away from her stepfather." Library Journal.

Alomar, Osama, 1968-

The teeth of the comb & other stories / Osama Alomar ; translated by Osama Alomar and C.J. Collins. New Directions, 2017. 102 p.

ISBN 9780811226073

1. Animals 2. Nature 3. Allegories 4. Short stories 5. Translations -- Arabic to English

LC 2016039664

Personified animals (snakes, wolves, sheep), natural things (a swamp, a lake, a rainbow, trees), mankind's creations (trucks, swords, zeroes) are all characters in The Teeth of the Comb. They aspire, they plot, they hope, they destroy, they fail, they love.

Alther, Lisa

Kinflicks : a novel / Lisa Alther. Knopf, 1976, c1975. 503 p.

ISBN 0394498364

1. 1960s 2. Mothers and daughters 3. Mother and adult daughter 4. Generation gap 5. Women college students 6. Mothers with terminal illnesses 7. Women -- Identity 8. Women -- Sexuality 9. Families 10. Family relationships 11. Intergenerational communication 12. Death 13. Tennessee 14. Vermont 15. Coming-of-age stories 16. Domestic fiction

Returning home to Hullsport, Tennessee, to visit her dying mother, Ginny Babcock reviews the Kinflicks of her life--the home movies her mother used to make--from adolescence to middle-aged limbo, in an effort to discover herself.

"An ambitious, funny, lucid, and unfailingly honest first novel. . . . While a number of excellent writers have covered various parts of the turf covered here . . . no other writer has yet synthesized this material as well as Miss Alther has." The New Yorker.

Altschul, Andrew Foster

Deus ex machina / Andrew Foster Altschul. Counterpoint, 2011. 205 p.

ISBN 9781582436012

1. Television producers and directors 2. Reality television programs 3. Identity (Psychology) 4. Competition 5. Diseases 6. Mass media and culture 7. Satirical fiction

LC 2010031494

On a distant island, reality show contestants battle for bragging rights and a slot on next week's episode. They've perfected their dramatic roles and are prepared to do whatever it takes to win. When real catastrophes strike, the producer finds it harder and harder to navigate his surreal landscape, where boundaries of the real, imagined, and orchestrated have blurred beyond recognition.

"As the camera jumps from character to character, from reality television to real life, Altschul brilliantly blurs fact and fantasy, entertainment and voyeurism, forming a smartly funny and timely montage that challenges the meaning of celebrity." Booklist.

Alvar, Mia, 1978-

In the country : stories / Mia Alvar. Alfred A. Knopf, 2015. 288 p.

ISBN 9780385352819

1. Filipinos 2. Voyages and travels 3. Immigration and emigration 4. Home (Concept) 5. Families 6. Literary fiction 7. Short stories

LC 2014036940

ALA Notable Book, 2016.

"Exploring the universal experience of loss, displacement, and the longing to connect across borders both real and imagined, In the Country speaks to the heart of everyone who has ever searched for a place to call home"--, Provided by publisher.

"Both intrepid readers and armchair tourists eager to explore debut narratives that straddle multiple countries and cultures--à la Violet Kupersmith's The Frangipani Hotel or Rajesh Parameswaran's I Am an Executioner--will be opulently rewarded here." Library Journal.

Alvarez, Julia

* How the Garcia girls lost their accents / Julia Alvarez. Algonquin Books of Chapel Hill, 1991. 290 p.

ISBN 9780945575573

1. 1960s 2. Dominican American families 3. Sisters 4. Immigrants, Hispanic American -- Bronx, New York City 5. Hispanic Americans 6. Immigrant families 7. Child immigrants 8. Immigrants 9. Dominican American women 10. Exiles 11. Immigration and emigration 12. New York City 13. Bronx, New York City 14. Dominican Republic 15. Women's lives and relationships

LC 90048575

Sequel: Yo!

ALA Notable Book, 1992.

Forced to flee their native Caribbean island after an attempted coup, the Garcias--Carlos, Laura, and their four daughters--must learn a new way of life in the Bronx, while trying to cling to the old ways that they loved.

"This is an account of parallel odysseys, as each of the four daughters adapts in her own way, and a large part of Alvarez's accomplishment is the complexity with which these vivid characters are rendered." Publishers Weekly.

Alyan, Hala, 1986-

Salt houses / Hala Alyan. Houghton Mifflin Harcourt, 2017. 336 p.

ISBN 9780544912588

1. Refugees 2. Culture conflict 3. Home (Concept) 4. Palestinians -- Diaspora 5. War -- Psychological aspects 6. Families 7. Generation gap 8. Loss (Psychology) 9. Family relationships 10. Palestine -- History -- 20th century 11. Middle East -- History -- 20th century 12. Family sagas 13. Literary fiction

LC 2016046956

Foreseeing blessings and troubles in the lives of her daughter and grandchildren, Salma endures hardships stemming from the Six-Day War of 1967 in Palestine before rebuilding in Kuwait, before the family is scattered by Saddam Hussein's regime.

"A deeply moving look inside the Palestinian diaspora." Kirkus.

Amado, Jorge, 1912-2001

* Dona Flor and her two husbands : a moral and amorous tale / Jorge Amado ; translated from the Portuguese by Harriet de Onis. Vintage Books, 2006, c1969. 576 p.

ISBN 9780307276643

1. Women -- Brazil 2. Women -- Sexuality 3. Husband and wife -- Brazil 4. Married people 5. Bahia, Brazil 6. Brazil 7. Magical realism 8. Literary fiction 9. Translations -- Portuguese to English

LC 69010710

Originally published in Portuguese as Dona Flor e seus dois maridos by Livraria Martins Editora, Sao Paulo, in 1966.

This translation originally published in (hbk.) by Alfred A. Knopf, Inc. New York, in 1969.

"Dona Flor has such a harridan of a mother (Dona Rozilda) that you would like her to have her cake and eat it, too, and she very nearly does. Dona Flor's first husband, Vadinho, is a scamp, a prevaricator, and a 'shameless lover.' On Carnival Sunday, at the height of the gaiety, filled with rum, he drops dead. Dona Flor is desolate but cuts a handsome figure as a widow. She lives through the wake (a gem of a scene) and her mourning quite well, with memories and her cooking school to sustain her. Then suitors appear. None appeal but Dr. Teodoro Madureira, pharmacist and bassoonist, a pillar of propriety. Dona Rozilda is ecstatic, but the well-rounded Dona Flor has her troubles, for alas, Dr. Teodoro is no lover. Dreams haunt her and strange things begin to happen. Thanks to a Yoruba charm, Vadinho returns to ravish our bewildered heroine, and then the fun begins. Bahia in Brazil is the setting for this delectable rum cake of a novel." Publishers Weekly.

Amado, Jorge, 1912-2001

Gabriela, clove and cinnamon / Jorge Amado ; translated from the Portuguese by James L. Taylor and William L. Grossman Vintage Books, 2006, c1962. 425 p.

ISBN 9780307276650

1. Women cooks 2. Brazil 3. Literary fiction 4. Translations -- Portuguese to English

Gabriela, from Brazil's cacao-growing region, becomes an Arab's cook, mistress, and reluctant wife in an autocratic town with double standards.

Amdahl, Gary, 1956-

I am death : two novellas / Gary Amdahl. Milkweed Editions, 2008. 169 p.

ISBN 9781571310712

1. Ghostwriters 2. Men with paranoia 3. Employees -- Interpersonal relations 4. Gangsters 5. Fear in men 6. Men -- Psychology 7. Job

stress 8. Black humor 9. Psychological fiction

LC 2008000365

A pair of novellas by the Pushcart Prize-winning author of Visigoth includes "I Am Death: Bartleby the Mobster," in which a muckraking journalist finds himself in over his head while ghost writing a mob boss's autobiography, and "Peasants," in which a publishing employee fears he is being targeted by co-workers.

"A writer who inhabits this literary realm risks sacrificing meaning in pursuit of cleverness, but Amdahl stays true to his antiheroes. Jack and Walter don't insult us by saying they're better for their struggles. Instead, they speak another truth, one that's much more difficult to hear: Death, and, at this point only death, will set us free." Los Angeles Times Book Review.

American fantastic tales : terror and the uncanny from Poe to the pulps / [edited by] Peter Straub. Library of America, 2009. xv, 746 p. American fantastic tales

ISBN 9781598530476

1. Supernatural 2. Horror 3. Fantasy fiction 4. Short stories

A first volume in a two-part anthology edited by a leading contemporary author is an authoritative treasury of horror tales from the Edwardian era through the pulp heyday of Weird Tales.

"A valuable collection of excellent, often deeply disturbing stories." Kirkus.

American fantastic tales : terror and the uncanny from the 1940s to now / [edited by] Peter Straub. Library of America, 2009. xv, 713 p. American fantastic tales

ISBN 9781598530483

1. Supernatural 2. Horror 3. Fantasy fiction 4. Short stories

LC 2009927074

A second half of a two-part anthology is a diverse volume of short tales by leading genre authors from the latter half of the twentieth century that includes entries by such names as Shirley Jackson, Ray Bradbury, and Stephen King.

"This volume's contents reflect confused and perturbed reactions to radical changes in people's daily lives and the larger world around them during periods of instability beginning around the time of World War II and extending into the dizzying technological changes of the past quarter-century. . . . A terrific, must-have collection." Kirkus.

American West : twenty new stories / from the Western Writers of America ; edited with an introduction by Loren D. Estleman. Forge, 2001. 367 p.

ISBN 0312873174

1. Mining camps 2. Frontier and pioneer life 3. Outlaws 4. The West (United States) -- Social life and customs 5. Westerns 6. Short stories

LC 00048446

20 short stories.

"Uniformly fine writing makes this a welcome addition to any western collection." Booklist.

Amidon, Stephen

Human capital / Stephen Amidon. Farrar, Strauss and Giroux, 2004. 384 p.

ISBN 0374173508

1. Fatal traffic accidents 2. Disillusionment 3. Suburban life -- Connecticut 4. Real estate agents 5. Women psychologists 6. Divorced fathers 7. Teenagers -- Alcohol use 8. People with bipolar disorder 9. Rich people 10. Fathers and daughters 11. Husband and wife 12. Family relationships 13. Extramarital affairs 14. Investments 15. Hedge funds 16. Inheritance and succession 17. Hit-and-run accidents 18. Connecticut 19. Psychological fiction 20.

Mainstream fiction

LC 2004043985

Drew Hagel's financial decline is halted by his relationship with hedge fund manager Quint Manning, but the relationship between Drew's and Quint's teenage children bears the most fruit when an accident involving the two promises a big payoff.

"It all sounds a bit like Peyton Place, but Amidon's intentions are far more serious. Writing with a sociologist's insight, he crafts a sharp page-turner mined with moments of dark satire. Amidon's previous novels had moments of profundity, but this exceptional novel delves deeper and more passionately into the fractured lives of people whose lives revolve around money." Publishers Weekly.

Amidon, Stephen

Security : a novel / Stephen Amidon. Farrar, Straus and Giroux, 2009. 288 p.

ISBN 9780374257118

1. Private security services 2. Sex crimes 3. Private police 4. Indecent assault 5. Electric alarms 6. Security systems 7. Women college students 8. Young women -- Relations with older men 9. Rich people -- Massachusetts 10. College towns -- Massachusetts 11. New England 12. Massachusetts 13. Satirical fiction

LC 2008013850

Sleepy Stoneleigh, Massachusetts, is turned upside down by a local student's claims that she had been sexually assaulted by a wealthy resident, an accusation that prompts an investigation by security company head Edward Inman.

"The book is part campus tale, part mystery, part police procedural. The proportions are well mixed. Stoneleigh's customary tranquility is stirred when Mary Steckl, a local college student, accuses Doyle Cutler of sexually assaulting her. Cutler rebounds with an accusation that Mary's father, a drunk with a criminal record, is the real perp. The town is divided. . . . For all its plot twists, Security is a book stitched of sensible prose. There are no flourishes, no embroidery." New York Observer

Amirrezvani, Anita

The **blood** of flowers : a novel / Anita Amirrezvani. Little, Brown, 2007. 384 p.

ISBN 0316065765

1. 17th century 2. Forced marriage 3. Teenage girls -- Iran 4. Comets 5. Fathers -- Death 6. Bad luck 7. Rugs 8. Weaving 9. Mate selection 10. Indentured servants 11. Mothers and daughters -- Iran 12. Women's role -- Iran 13. Independence in teenage girls 14. Persian Empire 15. Iran -- Social life and customs -- 17th century 16. Historical fiction

LC 2006023034

After her father dies without leaving her with a dowry, a seventeenth-century Persian teen becomes a servant to her wealthy rug designer uncle in the court of Shah Abbas the Great, where her weaving talents prove both a blessing and curse.

"The author has crafted a lush and sensuous story, where betrayal is common, wealth is unequally distributed, and temporary marriages allow prosperous men to take advantage of impoverished virgins without the burden of a full-time wife. . . . Though the trajectory of this novel seemed sure to lead toward a full marriage in a society where this is expected, Amirrezvani provides more than that: a wonderful man might exist in fairytales, but a woman can be self-sufficient and happy without him." PopMatters.

Amirrezvani, Anita

Equal of the sun / Anita Amirrezvani. Simon & Schuster, 2012 352 p.

ISBN 9781451660463

1. 16th century 2. Princesses -- Iran 3. Secrecy in government -- Iran 4. Eunuchs 5. Courts and courtiers 6. Political intrigue 7. Inheritance and succession 8. Power (Social sciences) 9. Ambition in women 10. Political consultants 11. Iran -- History 12. Historical fiction

When the court of 16th-century Iran is thrown into turmoil by the heirless Shah's death, his daughter, Princess Pari, incites dissent with her efforts to instill order and taps the assistance of a eunuch servant to navigate a Machiavellian power struggle.

Amis, Kingsley

* **Lucky** Jim / Kingsley Amis. Penguin, 1992, c1954. 251 p.

ISBN 9780140186307

1. 1950s 2. College teachers 3. Men's fantasies 4. Drinking 5. Universities and colleges 6. Academic rivalry 7. Interpersonal relations 8. Men/women relations 9. Great Britain -- Social life and customs -- 1945- 10. Literary fiction 11. Satirical fiction 12. Modern classics

LC 93233719

Originally published: London : Gollancz, 1954.
Somerset Maugham Award, 1955.

A young Englishman embarks on a humorous crusade against traditional class structures.

Amis, Martin

Lionel Asbo : state of England / Martin Amis. Alfred A. Knopf, 2012. 320 p.

ISBN 9780307958082

1. Guardian and ward 2. Criminals 3. Lottery winners 4. Multiracial men 5. Popular culture 6. Sexuality 7. Incest 8. Family secrets 9. Crime 10. Teenage boys 11. Dating (Social customs) 12. Family relationships 13. England -- Social life and customs 14. Satirical fiction 15. Literary fiction

A satire of modern society and celebrity culture finds the seemingly simple pursuits of young Desmond Pepperdine hampered by his uncle Lionel's near-criminal habits, which become more prominent when Lionel wins the lottery.

Amis, Martin

London fields : a novel / Martin Amis. Harmony Books, 1989. 470 p.

ISBN 9780886192563

1. 1990s 2. Women psychics 3. Manipulation by women 4. Criminals 5. Rich men 6. Love triangles 7. Men/women relations 8. Murder 9. Precognition 10. Casual sex 11. London, England 12. Mysteries 13. Literary fiction

LC 89049558

"Amis's technical virtuosity is extraordinary. . . . [This is] the most intellectually interesting fiction of the year, and a work beyond the reach of any British contemporary. Amis's figures, like those of Dickens, are caricatures that have their own gigantic reality." London Review of Books.

Amis, Martin

* The **pregnant** widow / Martin Amis. Alfred A. Knopf, 2010. 272 p.

ISBN 9781400044528

1. 1970s 2. College students -- Sexuality 3. Love triangles 4. Men/

women relations 5. British in Italy 6. Memory 7. Sexual revolution 8. Interpersonal relations 9. Vacations 10. Italy 11. London, England 12. Literary fiction

LC 2009041689

The year is 1970, and it's a long, hot summer. In a castle on a mountainside in Italy, half a dozen young lives are afloat on a sea of change, trapped inside the history of the sexual revolution. The girls are acting like boys, the boys are going on acting like boys, and Keith Nearing--twenty years old, a literature student all clogged up with the English novel--is struggling to twist feminism and women's ascendency toward his own ends.

"When Amis shows us the sexual revolution in action and reaction, when he tells us how people dressed and what it meant, when he depicts the effects of women's sexual aggression on men's egos, how women talked about men and vice versa when he is pretending to be a well-behaved comic-naturalist novelist, the book works. But when he philosophises he can sound just like tedious-clever journalism. . . . And the narrative is slowed and blurred by Amis' unwillingness ever to say anything in a simple or straightforward way." The Age.

Amis, Martin
* Time's arrow, or The nature of the offense / Martin Amis. Harmony Books, 1991. 168 p.
ISBN 9780517585153
1. Auschwitz (Concentration camp) 2. Nazi physicians 3. Holocaust (1933-1945) 4. Guilt in men 5. Conscience 6. Physicians 7. Nazi fugitives -- United States 8. Literary fiction

LC   91004144

Shortlisted for the Booker-McConnell Prize, 1991.

Escaping from the body of a dying doctor who had worked in Nazi concentration camps, the doctor's conciousness begins living the doctor's life backward, aware only that he is living the life of a horrible man at a horrible place in time

Amis, Martin
*The zone of interest : a novel / Martin Amis. Knopf, 2014. 288 p.
ISBN 9780385353496
1. Auschwitz (Concentration camp) 2. Second World War era (1939-1945) 3. Holocaust (1933-1945) 4. Concentration camps 5. Personal conduct 6. Courtship 7. Imprisonment 8. Concentration camp inmates 9. Revenge 10. Extramarital affairs 11. Dead 12. Married people 13. Jewish men 14. Nazis 15. World War II 16. Men/women relations 17. Poland -- History -- 1918-1945 18. Germany 19. Psychological fiction 20. Historical fiction 21. Literary fiction

LC 2014011667

Shortlisted for the Walter Scott Prize for Historical Fiction, 2015

A portrait of life and unexpected love in a concentration camp explores the depths and contradictions of the human soul as well as the capacity of individuals who are tested to acknowledge their true selves.

"An audaciously satiric and brilliantly realized tale about personal angst and mass psychosis, and the immolation of self and soul." Booklist.

Ammaniti, Niccolo, 1966-
I'm not scared / Niccolo Ammaniti ; translated from the Italian by Jonathan Hunt. Canongate, 2003, c2001 200 p.
ISBN 9781841952970
1. 1970s 2. Nine-year-old boys 3. Children's secrets 4. Innocence (Personal quality) 5. Italy 6. Psychological fiction 7. Translations -- Italian to English
Originally published: Torino : Einaudi, 2001.

In the summer of 1978 in a small Italian village, nine-year-old Michele Amitrano loses his innocence of childhood when he accidentally uncovers a dark secret being kept by the adults of Acqua Traverse.

"During a piercingly hot summer, a few kilometres from a bone-dry hamlet in rural Tuscany, a shy, nervy, nine-year-old boy called Michele explores a derelict house and discovers, under moldering leaves, a horrifying secret. The novel is saved from sensationalism by Ammaniti's almost cinematic ability to conjure detail." The New Yorker.

Anam, Tahmima, 1975-
The bones of grace / Tahmima Anam. Harper, 2016. 304 p. Haque family trilogy
ISBN 9780061478949
1. Muslims 2. Women's role 3. Forced marriage 4. Islam 5. Loyalty 6. Familial love 7. Social change 8. Fundamentalism 9. Family relationships 10. Bangladeshi families 11. Independence in women 12. Bangladesh 13. Literary fiction
Originally published: Great Britain : Edinburgh, 2016.

Zubaida is torn between an arranged marriage in Bangladesh and her love for Elijah Strong, the American she met while working in Boston.

"In having Zubaida come to terms with her origins and her own contentment, Anam captures two very different cultures in an introspective character study that will mesmerize readers from the very first page." Publishers Weekly.

Anappara, Deepa
Djinn patrol on the purple line : a novel / Deepa Anappara. Random House, 2020. 256 p.
ISBN 9780593129197
1. Missing children 2. Police corruption 3. Friendship 4. Growing up 5. East Indians 6. Muslim children 7. Slums 8. India 9. Mysteries 10. Literary fiction 11. Coming-of-age stories

LC 2019031351

A 9-year-old reality-television enthusiast in India uses crime-show approaches to investigate the disappearance of a classmate, before additional abductions shatter life in his sprawling city home.

"The author has done an excellent job of telling her sometimes sad story in Jai's credible nine-year-old voice, and her treatment of her setting, with its ingrained social inequities, is a model of verisimilitude." Booklist.

Anaya, Rudolfo A.
The man who could fly and other stories / Rudolfo Anaya. University of Oklahoma Press, 2006. 197 p.
ISBN 080613738X
1. Mexican Americans 2. Mexican American women 3. Interpersonal relations 4. Southwest (United States) 5. Mexico -- Social life and customs 6. Short stories

LC 2005051426

Collects 18 short stories.

"The stories showcase 30 years of Anaya's Chicano literary voice, simultaneously innocent and omniscient and always rooted in the landscape, especially the windswept llanos of New Mexico. . . . The characters' passionate force radiates from Anaya's simple prose as they confront ethical dilemmas in varied regional settings." Library Journal.

Anders, Adriana
* Under her skin / Adriana Anders. Sourcebooks, 2017. 352 p. Blank canvas series
ISBN 9781492633846
1. Coping 2. Second chances 3. Abused women 4. Small towns 5. Tattooing 6. Tenderness (Personal quality) 7. Neighbors 8. Compassion in men 9. Blacksmiths 10. Interpersonal attraction 11.

Men/women relations 12. Virginia 13. Contemporary romances

"Old hag in need of live-in helper to abuse. Nothing kinky." Although the job description is far from reassuring, the position is Uma's best option right now. On the run from her monstrously abusive ex-boyfriend, who tortured and then forcibly tattooed her, Uma arrives in Blackwood, Virginia, seeking a fresh start. As she adjusts to the eccentricities of her new employer, the cantankerous Ms. Lloyd, Uma gets to know her neighbor, Ivan, a gentle blacksmith with a troubled past. With its sympathetic characters and emotional intensity, this one will make an indelible impression upon readers. -- Description by Gillian Speace

"An incredibly sexy, heartbreaking, and intense romantic debut." Kirkus.

Anders, Charlie Jane

* **All** the birds in the sky / Charlie Jane Anders. Tor, 2016. 320 p.

ISBN 9780765379948

1. Reunions 2. End of the world 3. Friendship 4. Magic 5. Engineers 6. Trust 7. Near future 8. Cooperation 9. Climate change 10. Environmental degradation 11. San Francisco, California 12. Science fantasy 13. Apocalyptic fiction

LC 2015031481

Locus Award for Fantasy Novel, 2017.

Nebula Award for Best Novel, 2016.

Reunited as adults in the hipster mecca San Francisco as the planet falls apart around them, childhood friends Patricia Delfine, who is magically gifted, and Laurence Armstead, an engineering genius, discover that something bigger than either of them has brought them together to either save the world, or plunge it into a new dark ages.

"Anders clearly has an intimate understanding of how hard it is to find friends when you're perceived as 'different' as well as a sweeping sense of how nice it would be to solve large problems with a single solution (and how infrequently that succeeds)." Kirkus.

Anders, Charlie Jane

* The **city** in the middle of the night / Charlie Jane Anders. Tor Books, 2019. 336 p.

ISBN 9780765379962

1. Exiles 2. Women revolutionaries 3. Human/alien encounters 4. Aliens 5. Survival 6. Dystopias 7. Friendship 8. Revolutionaries 9. Life on other planets 10. Extreme environments 11. Aliens (Non-humanoid) 12. Social science fiction 13. Science fiction

LC 2018022175

A reluctant revolutionary survives exile by forging an unusual, world-changing bond with a family of ice creatures that live outside the human confines of their dying planet.

Anders, Charlie Jane

Rock Manning goes for broke / Charlie Jane Anders. Subterranean Press, 2018. 128 p.

ISBN 9781596068780

1. Filmmakers 2. Near future 3. Stunts 4. Slapstick 5. End of the world 6. Violence 7. Disasters 8. High school students 9. United States 10. Farcical fiction 11. Apocalyptic fiction

"This gonzo vision of an apocalyptic America is a challenging mixture of both farce and tragedy; it makes its point about the influence and responsibility of the media in the weirdest possible way." Booklist.

Andersen, Laura

The **Boleyn** deceit / Laura Andersen. Ballantine Books, 2013. 368 p. Anne Boleyn trilogy

ISBN 9780345534118

1. Anne Boleyn,, Queen, consort of Henry VIII, King of England,

1507-1536 2. Henry VIII,, King of England, 1491-1547 3. 16th century 4. Rulers 5. Political intrigue 6. Conspiracies 7. Heirs and heiresses 8. Courts and courtiers 9. Betrayal 10. Men/women relations 11. Great Britain -- History -- 16th century 12. Alternative histories

Includes reading group guide.

Henry IX, known as William, is the son of Anne Boleyn and now the leader of England, his regency period finally at an end. His newfound power, however, comes with the looming specter of war with the other major powers of Europe, with strategic alliances--that must be forged on both the battlefield and in the bedroom, and with a court, severed by religion, rife with plots to take over the throne. Will trusts only three people: his older sister, Elizabeth; his best friend and loyal counselor, Dominic; and Minuette, a young orphan raised as a royal ward by Anne Boleyn. But as the pressure rises alongside the threat to his life, even William must begin to question--and to fear Provided by publisher.

Andersen, Laura

* The **Boleyn** king / Laura Andersen. Ballantine Books Trade Paperbacks, 2013. 304 p. Anne Boleyn trilogy

ISBN 9780345534095

1. Anne Boleyn,, Queen, consort of Henry VIII, King of England, 1507-1536 2. Henry VIII,, King of England, 1491-1547 3. Tudor period (1485-1603) 4. 16th century 5. Rulers 6. Political intrigue 7. Conspiracies 8. Heirs and heiresses 9. Courts and courtiers 10. Betrayal 11. Love triangles 12. Interpersonal attraction 13. Men/women relations 14. Great Britain -- History -- Henry VIII, 1509-1547 15. England -- History -- 16th century 16. Great Britain -- History -- Tudors, 1485-1603 17. Alternative histories

LC 2013004505

Struggling to prove himself as the French threaten battle and the Catholics plot at home, seventeen-year-old King Henry IX relies on his best friend and loyal counselor, Dominic, until they both fall in love with the same woman.

Andersen, Laura

The **Boleyn** reckoning / Laura Andersen. Ballantine Books, 2014. 400 p. Anne Boleyn trilogy

ISBN 9780345534132

1. Anne Boleyn,, Queen, consort of Henry VIII, King of England, 1507-1536 2. Henry VIII,, King of England, 1491-1547 3. 16th century 4. Rulers 5. Political intrigue 6. Conspiracies 7. Heirs and heiresses 8. Courts and courtiers 9. Betrayal 10. Men/women relations 11. Great Britain -- History -- 16th century 12. Alternative histories

LC 2014012571

A Ballantine Books Trade Paperback Original.

"Elizabeth Tudor is at a crossroads. Though her brother, William, has survived the smallpox, scars linger on the king's body and mind and he marches to the drumbeat of his own desires rather than his country's welfare. Wary, Elizabeth assembles her own shadow court to protect England as best she can. Meanwhile, Minuette and Dominic have married in secret, but the truth cannot stay hidden for long. Faced with betrayal by those he loved most, William's need for vengeance pushes England to the brink of civil war and in the end, Elizabeth must choose: her brother, or her country? Provided by publisher.

Anderson, Alison

The **summer** guest / Alison Anderson. HarperCollins, 2016. 400 p.

ISBN 9780062423368

1. Chekhov, Anton Pavlovich, 1860-1904 2. 1880s 3. 21st century 4. Diary writing 5. Women physicians 6. Blindness 7. Friendship

8. Lost books 9. Women editors 10. Diaries 11. Women translators 12. Women -- Interpersonal relations 13. Ukraine -- History -- 19th century 14. London, England -- History -- 21st century 15. Literary fiction 16. Historical fiction 17. Parallel narratives

After a diary documenting a friendship between a young Ukrainian doctor and author Anton Pavlovich Chekhov is found, Katya Kendall believes it may be the key to saving her struggling publishing house.

Anderson, Catherine (Adeline Catherine)

Mulberry moon / Catherine Anderson. Jove, 2017. 416 p. Mystic Creek novels

ISBN 9780451488022

1. Abused women 2. Ranchers 3. Trust in women 4. Small town life 5. Men/women relations 6. Contemporary romances

Swearing off men, Sissy Sue Bentley, the new owner of the local café, struggles with her growing feelings for cowboy Ben Sterling who keeps showing up whenever she needs help, especially when her past comes back with a vengeance.

Anderson, Kent, 1945-

Green sun : a novel / Kent Anderson. Mulholland Books, 2018. 340 p.

ISBN 9780316466806

1. 1980s 2. Police 3. Vietnam veterans 4. Community policing 5. African American neighborhoods 6. Urban problems 7. Police ethics 8. Police patrol 9. Drug lords 10. Oakland, California 11. California 12. Police procedurals

Moving to 1980s East Oakland, California, to join the mostly black community he serves and protects, Vietnam veteran Hanson befriends a neighborhood boy, pursues a romantic relationship, navigates a tricky relationship with a drug dealer and works diligently to stay honest in spite of the forces of hate and violence that compromise his job.

Anderson, Kevin J., 1962-

Death warmed over / Kevin J. Anderson. Kensington Books., 2012. 304 p. Shamble & Die Investigations

ISBN 9780758277343

1. Zombies 2. Private investigators 3. Undead 4. Supernatural 5. Murder victims 6. Ghosts 7. Murder investigation 8. Vampires 9. New Orleans, Louisiana 10. Humorous stories 11. Mysteries

Zombie P.I. Dan Chambeaux, along with his human partner and ghost girlfriend, tries to juggle his unnatural caseload, including a resurrected mummy who is suing the museum that put him on display, while trying to figure out who killed him.

Anderson, Kevin J., 1962-

The **last** days of Krypton / Kevin J. Anderson. William Morrow, 2007. 432 p.

ISBN 9780061340741

1. Power (Social sciences) 2. Isolationism 3. Natural disasters 4. Greed in men 5. Space flight 6. Parents -- Death 7. Life on other planets 8. Superhero stories 9. Franchise books

LC 2007031174

An account of the tragic destruction of Superman's home planet depicts the lives of his parents, Jor-El and Lara, while giving insight into the political factors that doomed the planet and paved the way for such villains as Brainiac and General Zod.

Anderton, Jo

Debris / Jo Anderton. Angry Robot, 2011. 432 p. Veiled worlds trilogy

ISBN 9780857661548

1. Conspiracies 2. Psychokinesis 3. Brain injury 4. Pariahs 5. Social classes 6. Lovers 7. Sabotage 8. Architects 9. Accidents 10. Technology -- Social aspects 11. Posthumanism 12. Science fiction

Able to control the building blocks of reality with the power of her mind, Tanyana, a gifted engineer, must find out who is trying to destroy her after a horrific disaster causes her to be demoted to the lowest of the low as a debris collector.

"Anderton's debut impressively combines far-future world-building, conspiracies, and a redemption quest. ... Anderton clearly telegraphs the overall plot arc, but keeps it interesting with Tanyana's strong, proud narrative voice and the complex culture built up around the pions and debris." Publishers Weekly.

Andrew, Sally

Recipes for love and murder / Sally Andrew. Ecco Press, 2015. 384 p. Tannie Maria novels

ISBN 9780062397669

1. Women amateur detectives 2. Advice columnists 3. Partner abuse 4. Murder 5. Cooking 6. Wife-killing 7. Food writers 8. Abusive men 9. Abused women 10. Murder suspects 11. Murder investigation 12. Recipes 13. South Africa 14. Culinary mysteries 15. Cozy mysteries 16. Gentle reads

Forced to make the transition from dispensing culinary tips to advice on romance, middle-aged Afrikaans newspaper columnist Tannie Maria discovers her knack for helping others and risks her life to help track down an abusive man who has murdered his wife.

"The mystery takes on the worldwide problem of abused women while revealing both the beauties and problems of South Africa. And the recipes will make you want to drop everything and start cooking." Kirkus.

Andrew, Sally

The **Satanic** mechanic : a Tannie Maria mystery / Sally Andrew. Ecco Press, 2017. 368 p. Tannie Maria novels

ISBN 9780062397690

1. Women amateur detectives 2. Advice columnists 3. Land claims 4. Greed 5. Murder 6. Cooking 7. Food writers 8. San (African people) 9. Murder investigation 10. Business -- Corrupt practices 11. Recipes 12. South Africa 13. Culinary mysteries 14. Cozy mysteries 15. Gentle reads

When Slimkat the Bushman's life is threatened by an unknown adversary, recipe writer-turned-crime fighter Tannie Maria becomes embroiled in a nature-reserve land dispute among Bushmen descendants, diamond miners and cattle companies.

Andrews, Donna

Owl be home for Christmas : a Meg Langslow mystery / Donna Andrews. Minotaur Books, 2019. 304 p. Meg Langslow mysteries

ISBN 9781250305312

1. Christmas 2. Owls 3. Women amateur detectives 4. Inns 5. Professional conferences 6. Extended families 7. Murder 8. Murder investigation 9. Winter storms 10. Small towns 11. Virginia 12. Holiday mysteries 13. Gentle reads 14. Cozy mysteries

LC 2019029130

Snowed in at a hotel during a scientific conference, Meg Langslow assists Chief Burke in identifying which of the guests is responsible for the murder of a visiting ornithologist.

Andrews, Mary Kay, 1954-

Sunset Beach / Mary Kay Andrews. St Martins Press, 2019. 448 p.

ISBN 9781250126108

1. Inheritance and succession 2. Cottages 3. Coastal towns 4. Law firms 5. Beaches 6. Father and adult daughter 7. Father-deserted children 8. Cold cases (Criminal investigation) 9. Men/women relations 10. Women's lives and relationships 11. Mysteries 12. Gentle reads

Reluctantly accepting a job at her estranged father's law firm in the aftermath of her mother's passing, Drue is tangled in a decades-old mystery that threatens everyone she loves.

Andrews, Mesu, 1963-

* **Isaiah's** daughter : a novel of prophets and kings / Mesu Andrews. WaterBrook, 2018. 400 p.

ISBN 9780735290259

1. Isaiah, (Biblical prophet) 2. Rulers 3. Prophets 4. Orphans 5. Loss (Psychology) 6. Trust in God 7. Fate and fatalism -- Religious aspects 8. Prophecies 9. Bible novels

LC 2017032698

Christy Award for Historical Category, 2018.

"The Bible jumps to life in this spellbinding narrative drawn from verses in the books of 2 Kings and Isaiah, bringing the troubled kingdoms that followed Solomon's reign into focus and particularly a young woman being raised by the prophet Isaiah"--, Provided by publisher.

Andrews, Mesu, 1963-

Of fire and lions : a novel / Mesu Andrews. Waterbrook, 2019. 400 p.

ISBN 9780735291867

1. Daniel, (Biblical figure) 2. Bible. Daniel. 3. Bible History of Biblical events. 4. 5th century BCE 5. Faith (Judaism) 6. Prophets 7. Lion 8. Fire 9. Married people 10. Exiles 11. Military occupation 12. Secrets 13. Babylon (Extinct city) 14. Bible novels 15. Christian historical fiction

LC 2018029026

Seventy years ago, the Babylonians ransacked Jerusalem and took captives back to Babylon, including a frightened girl named Belili. Now a confident woman, married to Daniel the prophet, she realizes her need of the God who conquers both fire and lions.

Andric, Ivo, 1892-1975

The **bridge** on the Drina / Ivo Andric ; translated from the Serbo-Croat by Lovett F. Edwards ; with an introduction by William H. McNeill. University of Chicago Press, 1977. 314 p. Yugoslavian trilogy

ISBN 9780226020457

1. Bridges -- Design and construction 2. Small towns 3. Culture conflict 4. Bosnia and Hercegovina 5. Visegrad (Bosnia and Hercegovina : East) 6. Translations -- Serbo-Croatian to English 7. Modern classics 8. Literary fiction

LC 77368170

Translation of Na Drini cuprija.

The life of a bridge near the Bosnian town of Visegrad and the events near it span three and a half centuries of Turkish rule.

Angelo, Megan

Followers / Megan Angelo. Graydon House, 2020. 380 p.

ISBN 9781525836268

1. 21st century 2. Fame 3. Social media 4. Celebrities 5. Deception 6. Surveillance 7. Ambition 8. Technology 9. Popular culture 10. Interpersonal relations 11. Near future 12. United States -- Social life and customs 13. Dystopian fiction

Decades after an ambitious writer and her A-list wannabe roommate abandon their ethics for social-media stardom, a government-appointed celebrity discovers a shattering secret from her past that her corporate sponsors would gladly exploit.

"An edgy, exciting read, a slap-in-the-face cautionary tale, and future thrills that provide au courant shivers." Library Journal.

Anolik, Lili

Dark rooms / Lili Anolik. HarperCollins, 2015 256 p.

ISBN 9780062345868

1. Murder 2. Prep schools 3. Suicide 4. Unrequited love 5. Sisters 6. Murder investigation 7. Revenge 8. New England 9. Mysteries

Unable to come to terms with her wild teen sister's murder, Grace drops out of college and takes a job at the privileged and progressive prep school she once attended to identify and exact revenge on the killer.

"As much as this is a crime drama, it's also a coming-of-age novel. The plot is high-suspense, but it's the strength of the charactersand the strength of Anolik's hypnotic, unfussy prosethat gives the book its lasting force. Wholly absorbing and emotionally rich, this novel dodges Law & Order: Special Victims Unit cliches to deliver something deeply satisfying." Kirkus.

Anshaw, Carol, 1946-

Carry the one / Carol Anshaw. Simon & Schuster, 2012. 304 p.

ISBN 9781451636888

1. Life change events 2. Fatal traffic accidents 3. Interpersonal relations 4. Tragedy 5. Lesbians 6. Women artists 7. Weddings 8. Marital conflict 9. Drug abusers 10. Astronomers 11. Addiction 12. Literary fiction

When a car of inebriated guests from Carmen's wedding hits and kills a girl on a country road, Carmen and the people involved in the accident connect, disconnect and reconnect throughout 25 subsequent years of marriage, parenthood, holidays and tragedies.

Anstruther, Eleanor

A **perfect** explanation / Eleanor Anstruther. Houghton Mifflin Harcourt, 2020, c2019. 256 p.

ISBN 9780358120858

1. Campbell, Enid, 1892-1964 2. Aristocracy 3. Divorce 4. Marital conflict 5. Child custody 6. Married women 7. Women's role 8. Social pressure 9. Dysfunctional families 10. Mothers and daughters 11. Inheritance and succession 12. Postpartum depression 13. Christian science 14. Scotland 15. Biographical fiction 16. Historical fiction 17. Literary fiction 18. Family sagas

LC 2019024925

A debut novel based on true events from the author's grandmother's life follows the experiences of an aristocratic woman who abandons her family and life of privilege in search of something to claim as her own.

"This immersive story about family, inheritance, and motherhood is a good read-alike for Paula McLain's historical fiction." Booklist.

Anthony, Mark, 1973-

Diary of a young girl / Mark Anthony. Urban Books, 2010. 230 p.

ISBN 9781601622211

1. Rape 2. College graduates 3. Malicious accusation 4. Secrets 5. DNA testing 6. Men/women relations 7. African American women 8. African American fiction 9. Drama lit

LC bl2010019464

Shayla finally manages to overcome her troubled adolescence and graduate from college, but a DNA test threatens to unravel her future, reopening the rape case from her past in which she falsely accused the wrong man of the crime.

Antoinette, Ashley, 1985-
Butterfly / Ashley Antoinette. St. Martin's Griffin, 2020. 288 p. Butterfly novels
ISBN 9781250136367
1. Engaged persons 2. Cheating (Interpersonal relations) 3. Loss (Psychology) 4. Life change events 5. Rich men 6. Unhappiness in women 7. Options, alternatives, choices 8. Flint, Michigan 9. London, England 10. Drama lit 11. African American fiction
LC 2019035019
Morgan Atkins has always been a spoiled girl and she tries to have it all, but when she's forced to choose between a good man and a bad boy, someone will end up hurt. Someone just may end up dead.
"Urban-fiction superstar Antoinette (Luxe, 2015) starts Morgan's story at a leisurely pace; the novel is the first in a series, so Antoinette is able to dive deep into Morgan's internal conflict." Booklist.

Antoinette, Ashley, 1985-
* The **Cartel** / Ashley & JaQuavis. Urban, 2008. 278 p. Cartel novels
ISBN 9781601621429
1. Drug traffic 2. Murder for hire 3. Organized crime 4. Family relationships 5. Street life 6. Cocaine traffic 7. Competition 8. Illegitimacy 9. African American men 10. African American men/women relations 11. Miami, Florida 12. Romantic suspense 13. African American fiction 14. Drama lit
Sequel: The Cartel 2.
The most notorious crime family Miami has ever seen.
Also published in the omnibus edition The Cartel: deluxe edition books 1-3, Urban Books, 2018.
When Carter Diamon, the leader of The Cartel, which controls eighty percent of the cocaine industry, dies, his illegitimate son, Carter Jones, takes his place and starts sleeping with the enemy--Miamor, the leader of The Murder Mamas, who wants to take down The Cartel.

Antoinette, Ashley, 1985-
The **Cartel** 2 / Ashley & JaQuavis. Urban Books, 2009. 236 p. Cartel novels
ISBN 9781601622563
1. Drug traffic 2. Murder for hire 3. Organized crime 4. Family relationships 5. Street life 6. Cocaine traffic 7. Competition 8. Illegitimacy 9. African American men 10. African American men/women relations 11. Miami, Florida 12. Romantic suspense 13. African American fiction 14. Drama lit
Sequel to: The Cartel.
Sequel: The Cartel 3.
Tale of the Murder Mamas.
Also published in the omnibus edition The Cartel: deluxe edition books 1-3, Urban Books, 2018.
Street Lit Book Award Medal: Adult Fiction, 2010
Young Carter, after someone in the organization breaks the rules, faces drug kingpin charges due to the betrayal of his best friend, Ace.

Antoinette, Ashley, 1985-
The **Cartel** 3 : the last chapter / Ashley & JaQuavis. Urban Books, 2010. 219 p. Cartel novels
ISBN 9781601622570
1. Drug traffic 2. Murder for hire 3. Organized crime 4. Family relationships 5. Grief 6. Street life 7. Cocaine traffic 8. Competition

9. Illegitimacy 10. African American men 11. African American men/women relations 12. Miami, Florida 13. Romantic suspense 14. African American fiction 15. Drama lit
LC bl2010019310
Sequel to: The Cartel 2.
Also published in the omnibus edition The Cartel: deluxe edition books 1-3, Urban Books, 2018.
Miamor is fighting for her life in the belly of the beast. She's been kidnapped, and she's staring death in the eye. Is the reign over for the head of the Murda Mamas? Carter is in federal custody and leaves the Diamond Empire to Zyir and Mecca. When the past comes back to haunt Mecca and the truth finally comes to light, will The Cartel rise or fall? Breeze is in the clutches of the crazed Ma'tee, and she desperately searches for a way out. Will she escape, or die his love slave?

Antoinette, Ashley, 1985-
* **Murderville** / Ashley & JaQuavis. Simon & Schuster, 2011 256 p. Murderville trilogy
ISBN 9781936399000
1. Women with terminal illnesses 2. Redemption 3. Love 4. Immigrants 5. African American men/women relations 6. Street life 7. Violence 8. African Americans 9. Memories 10. Arranged marriage 11. Drug traffic 12. Detroit, Michigan 13. Los Angeles, California 14. Urban fiction 15. African American fiction
While Liberty dies from a fatal heart condition, she asks A'shai to tell her a story while she waits for her sister, who promised to visit her on her upcoming twenty-fifth birthday. A'shai, who blames himself for not protecting Liberty, retells the story of how they got to this point, from an arranged marriage and child brothels to drug cartels and hustling the streets of Detroit.

Anton, Maggie
Apprentice : a novel of love, the Talmud, and sorcery / Maggie Anton. Plume, 2012. 480 p. Rav Hisda's daughter
ISBN 9780452298095
1. Talmud 2. Jewish women 3. Scholars and academics 4. Fathers and daughters 5. Magicians 6. Rabbis 7. Options, alternatives, choices 8. Arranged marriage 9. Jewish education 10. Babylon (Extinct city) 11. Historical fiction
LC 2012014785
After learning the Torah by heart in third-century Babylonia, Hisdadukh cannot continue with her studies because she is female, so instead she considers practicing sorcery.

Antopol, Molly
The **UnAmericans** / Molly Antopol. W.W. Norton & Co., 2014. 256 p.
ISBN 9780393241136
1. Jews 2. Family relationships 3. Fathers and daughters 4. Actors and actresses 5. Soldiers 6. Women journalists 7. Marriage 8. Jewish Americans 9. Short stories 10. Literary fiction 11. Political fiction
This complex debut collection of short stories traces the experiences of deeply flawed and painfully human characters from a range of backgrounds, including a Czechoslovakian dissident, a McCarthy-era communist/actor, and an Israeli journalist. Exploring themes of estrangement, family, and politics, these stories span much of the 20th century and take place in locations as varied as Maine and Kiev. -- Description by Shauna Griffin.
"Antopol depicts with bold strokes and uncanny intelligence the intimate links between family, history, and politics, never failing to capture the grit and hurt of intergenerational confrontation." Booklist.

Antunes, Antonio Lobo, 1942-

The **return** of the caravels : a novel / Antonio Lobo Antunes ; translated from the Portuguese by Gregory Rabassa. Grove Press, 2002, c1988. 210 p. History of Portugal tetralogy

ISBN 0802117082

1. Gama, Vasco da, 1469-1524 2. 1970s 3. Colonialism -- Africa 4. Poker 5. Lisbon, Portugal 6. Portugal -- Politics and government -- 20th century 7. Portugal -- Social life and customs -- 20th century 8. Literary fiction 9. Translations -- Portuguese to English

LC 2001051236

"Originally published in Portuguese under the title As Naus by Publicacaoes Dom Quixote, Lisbon, 1988" -- t.p. verso

"Antunes has to fight to stop himself from being swept away by the almost appalling energy of his language. You sense that rather than struggling for the next phrase, his art lies in containing words without taming them. Line by line, you get exact physical detail. Antunes makes you see. He's also obsessive, repetitive, entirely preoccupied by memory." New York Times Book Review.

Apelfeld, Aharon

Badenheim 1939 / Aharon Applefeld ; translated from the Hebrew by Dalya Bilu. D. R. Godine, 1980. 148 p.

ISBN 0879233427

1. 1930s 2. Jews, Austrian 3. Literary fiction 4. Translations -- Hebrew to English

LC 80066192

In the summer of 1939, prosperous members of the Jewish middle class flock to the resort town of Badenheim, oblivious of the ominous political and military events that will transform them into de facto prisoners in their familiar resort

"The most shocking thing about this novel is not its satirical humor, but its charm. Appelfeld manages to treat his appalling theme with grace." The New York Review of Books.

Apelfeld, Aharon

Blooms of darkness / Aharon Appelfeld ; translated from the Hebrew by Jeffrey M. Green. Schocken Books, 2010. 272 p.

ISBN 9780805242805

1. Second World War era (1939-1945) 2. Occupations 3. Jewish boys 4. Prostitutes 5. World War II 6. War 7. Ukraine 8. Historical fiction

LC 2009033532

Originally published in Hebrew as Pirkhei ha'hafeilah in Israel: Keter, 2006 .

Hidden in a brothel from the Nazis, smitten 11-year-old Hugo is fiercely protected by an increasingly depressed Mariana, who clashes with visiting soldiers and is wrongly accused of being a Nazi collaborator

"Appelfeld narrates Blooms of Darkness in a taut, terse present-tense voice that refuses the consolations of retrospect. His decision to use the present tense is particularly shrewd since it eliminates--for the reader, as for Hugo--any possibility of a future. . . Like Anne Frank's diary--a work to which it will draw justified comparison--Blooms of Darkness, beautifully translated from the Hebrew by Jeffrey M. Green, records a brutal process of education." New York Times Book Review.

Apelfeld, Aharon

The **man** who never stopped sleeping / Aharon Appelfeld ; translated from the Hebrew by Jeffrey M. Green. Schocken Books, 2017, c2010. 224 p.

ISBN 9780805243192

1. 1940s 2. Holocaust survivors 3. Refugees 4. Sleep 5. Memories 6. Loss (Psychology) 7. Dreams 8. Writing 9. Kibbutz 10. Postwar life

11. Teenage boys 12. Wound healing 13. Jews 14. Europe -- History -- 20th century 15. Israel -- History -- 20th century 16. Literary fiction 17. Historical fiction 18. Translations -- Hebrew to English

Originally published: 2010.

Follows the story of Erwin, a young Holocaust survivor, who travels from a refugee camp to a kibbutz in Haifa to begin a new life while still desperately clinging to his memories of the past.

"Appelfeld's style is never flashy, but the plainness of his writing gives post-Holocaust events both starkness and power." Kirkus.

Apelfeld, Aharon

To the edge of sorrow : a novel / Aharon Appelfeld ; translated from the Hebrew by Stuart Schoffman. Schocken Books, 2020, c2012. 272 p.

ISBN 9780805243420

1. Second World War era (1939-1945) 2. Jews 3. Holocaust (1933-1945) 4. Guerrillas 5. Tradition (Philosophy) 6. Survivor guilt 7. Protectiveness 8. Rescues 9. Atrocities 10. Persecution by Nazis 11. Ukraine 12. Historical fiction 13. Translations -- Hebrew to English

LC 2019011548

Originally published in Israel, 2012.

A group of brave Jewish partisans escapes from a ghetto and establishes a hiding place in the Ukrainian forest to survive World War II, sabotage German forces and rescue Jewish prisoners from trains heading toward concentration camps.

"This powerful tale of lives lived amid the duress and horrors of war is unflinching in its authenticity." Publishers Weekly.

Apostol, Gina

Gun dealers' daughter : a novel / Gina Apostol. W. W. Norton & Co., 2012, c2010. 224 p.

ISBN 9780393062946

1. People with amnesia 2. Women revolutionaries 3. Memories 4. Revolutions -- Philippines 5. Families 6. Men/women relations 7. Rebels 8. Manila, Philippines 9. Philippines -- History -- 1946-1986 10. New York City 11. Coming-of-age stories

LC 2011049404

Originally published: Manila : Anvil Pub., 2010.

A Filipino woman living in New York City recounts her youthful indiscretions as a university student in Manila whose boyfriend turned her into a communist rebel and the fatal act she committed that haunts her to this day.

Apostol, Gina,

Insurrecto / Gina Apostol. Soho Press, 2018. 336 p.

ISBN 9781616959449

1. Women filmmakers 2. Imperialism, American 3. Massacres 4. Philippine-American War, 1896-1902 5. Translators 6. Historiography 7. Storytelling 8. History 9. Philippines 10. Literary fiction

LC 2018027922

While on a road trip in Duterte's Philippines, two women, a Filipino translator and an American filmmaker, both collaborate and clash in the writing of a film script about a massacre during the Philippine-American war.

Araghi, Alireza Taheri

* The **immortals** of Tehran / Ali Araghi. Melville House, 2020. 400 p.

ISBN 9781612198187

1. Extended families 2. Poets 3. Men who are mute 4. Patriarchs 5. Politicians 6. Fathers and daughters 7. Immortality 8. Revolutions 9. Fate and fatalism 10. Loss (Psychology) 11. Tehran, Iran 12. Iran

-- History -- 20th century 13. Historical fiction 14. Magical realism 15. Family sagas

Learning the story of a centuries-old family curse upon his father's death, young Ahmad struggles to protect his loved ones through decades of famine, loss and political turmoil before unexpected life changes converge at the height of the Iranian Revolution.

"A highly recommended literary page-turner worth a second reading; fans of Gabriel Garcia Marquez will delight in this fantastical--and fantastic--work." Library Journal.

Aramburu, Fernando, 1959-

Homeland / Fernando Aramburu ; translated from the Spanish by Alfred MacAdam. Pantheon Books, 2019, c2016. 590 p.
ISBN 9781524747121
1. ETA (Organization) 2. 1980s 3. 1990s 4. 2000s (Decade) 5. 2010s 6. Family and war 7. Loss (Psychology) 8. Family feuds 9. Basque families 10. Terrorism 11. Terrorism victims' families 12. Militants 13. Violence -- Psychological aspects 14. Loyalty 15. Consequences 16. Childhood friends 17. Ethics 18. Translations -- Spanish to English 19. War stories 20. Literary fiction
LC 2018031975
Originally published: Barcelona : Tusquets Editores, 2016.

Describes the story of two Basque families, who were friends for generations, but who became bitter enemies after the father of one is killed by ETA militants during the violent insurgency that plagued the region from the 1980s to 2011.

Archer, Jeffrey, 1940-

Best kept secret / Jeffrey Archer. St. Martin's Press, 2013. 448 p. Clifton Chronicles
ISBN 9781250000989
1. 1940s 2. Inheritance and succession 3. Political culture 4. Heirs and heiresses 5. Family feuds 6. Politicians 7. Adoption 8. Gifted children 9. England 10. New York City 11. Family sagas 12. Historical fiction

Embarking on a shared family life, Harry, Emma, Sebastian, and Jessica find their happiness challenged by Emma's brother's engagement to a fortune-seeker, Sebastian's hedonist pursuits, and a grudge-bearing enemy from the past who would destroy their careers.

Archer, Jeffrey, 1940-

Nothing ventured / Jeffrey Archer. St Martin's Press, 2019. 416 p. William Warwick novels
ISBN 9781250200761
1. 20th century 2. Detectives 3. Criminals 4. Art thefts 5. Independence (Personal quality) 6. Couples 7. Criminal investigation 8. Secrets 9. City life 10. Men/women relations 11. Family relationships 12. London, England 13. Great Britain 14. Literary fiction

This new series introduces William Warwick, a family man and a detective who will battle throughout his career against a powerful criminal nemesis. Through twists, triumph and tragedy, this series will show that William Warwick is destined to become one of Jeffrey Archer's most enduring legacies.

Archer, Jeffrey, 1940-

Only time will tell / Jeffrey Archer. St Martins Pr, 2011. 448 p. Clifton Chronicles
ISBN 9780312539559
1. 1920s 2. 1930s 3. 1940s 4. Fathers -- Death 5. Identity (Psychology) 6. Paternity 7. Working class families 8. World War II 9. Growing up 10. Family secrets 11. England 12. New York City 13. Family sagas 14. Historical fiction
Originally published in the UK.

The epic tale of Harry Clifton's life begins in 1920, with the chilling words, 'I was told that my father was killed in the war'. But it will be another 20 years before Harry discovers how his father really died, which will only lead him to question: who was his father? Is he the son of Arthur Clifton, a stevedore who worked in Bristol docks, or the firstborn son of a scion of West Country society, whose family owns a shipping line? Volume one of the Clifton Chronicles takes us from the ravages of the Great War to the outbreak of the Second World War when Harry must decide whether to take up a place at Oxford or join the navy and go to war with Hitler's Germany.

Archer, Jeffrey, 1940-

The **prodigal** daughter / Jeffrey Archer. Linden Press/Simon and Schuster, 1982. 464 p. Kane and Abel series
ISBN 9780671422295
1. Competition 2. Families 3. Ambition 4. Family feuds 5. Women legislators 6. Polish American women 7. Family sagas
LC 82015310
Sequel to: Kane and Abel.
Sequel: Shall we tell the President?

"Covering their careers from 1964 into the future to 1991, the author manages the labyrinthine British parliamentary system with an adroit hand and generates real suspense in the race. For there can be only one winner, and even in the striving each man pays a price. Fastpaced and satisfying." Library Journal.

Archer, Jeffrey, 1940-

And **thereby** hangs a tale / Jeffrey Archer. St. Martin's Press, 2010. 301 p.
ISBN 9780312539535
1. Short stories
Originally published: London : Macmillan, 2010.

Fifteen short pieces are set in various world regions and include "Members Only," in which a young man's life is transformed by a Christmas cracker.

"Archer assembles 15 more of the clever stories for which he is known. They are split between tales of trickery, as with Stuck on You, where an eager young man is played by a diamond thief, and decidedly sentimental stories, such as Members Only, about a man who wants nothing more than to join a private country club. . . . His trademark twists-sometimes a surprise to the reader, sometimes not--and genial tone will endear these mostly cozy stories to his many fans." Publishers Weekly.

Archer, Jeffrey, 1940-

This was a man / Jeffrey Archer. St Martin's Press, 2016. 403 p. Clifton Chronicles
ISBN 9781250061638
1. Authors 2. Political intrigue 3. Political prisoners 4. Politicians 5. Married people 6. Politicians' spouses 7. International intrigue 8. England 9. London, England 10. Family sagas 11. Historical fiction
Series complete in 7 volumes.

A conclusion to the best-selling saga finds Giles discovering the truth about his wife's identity, Emma receiving a job offer from Margaret Thatcher and Lady Virginia pursuing an opportunity to solve her financial problems before a shocking diagnosis throws all of their lives into turmoil.

"Archer wraps up the Clifton Chronicles with this seventh and final entry in the series. ... All of the trademark Archer storytelling elements are here in abundance:cliff-hanger chapters, mistaken identities, deaths, and one red herring after another. To be sure, they are exactly what his readers expect (and want)." Booklist.

Archer, Zoe

Dangerous seduction / Zoe Archer. St. Martin's Press, 2013. 384 p. Nemesis, Unlimited novels

ISBN 9781250015600

1. Victorian era (1837-1901) 2. 1880s 3. Secret societies 4. Copper mines and mining 5. Miners 6. Revenge 7. Business -- Corrupt practices 8. Sexual attraction 9. Men/women relations 10. Ireland -- Social life and customs -- Victoria, 1837-1901 11. Historical romances 12. Victorian romances

A shadowy group of individuals seeks retribution for the voiceless downtrodden. Alyce Carr, a member of an oppressed mining community, is unexpectedly attracted to a newcomer who would change the fate of the entire town.

Arden, Katherine

* The **bear** and the nightingale / Katherine Arden. Del Rey, 2017 322 p. Winternight trilogy

ISBN 9781101885932

1. Medieval period (476-1492) 2. 14th century 3. Young women 4. Good and evil 5. Immortalism 6. Villages 7. Spirits 8. Social conflict 9. Religion and culture 10. Priests 11. Folktales, Russian 12. Russia 13. Historical fantasy 14. Literary fiction 15. Mythological fiction

"In a village at the edge of the wilderness of northern Russia, where the winds blow cold and the snow falls many months of the year, a stranger with piercing blue eyes presents a new father with a gift - a precious jewel on a delicate chain, intended for his young daughter. Uncertain of its meaning, Pytor hides the gift away and Vasya grows up a wild, willful girl, to the chagrin of her family. But when mysterious forces threaten the happiness of their village, Vasya discovers that, armed only with the necklace, she may be the only one who can keep the darkness at bay"--, Provided by publisher.

"Arden has shaped a world that neatly straddles the seen and the unseen, where readers will hear echoes of stories from childhood while recognizing the imagination that has transformed old material into something fresh." Kirkus.

Arden, Katherine

* The **girl** in the tower / Katherine Arden. Del Rey, 2017 352 p. Winternight trilogy

ISBN 9781101885963

1. 14th century 2. Folktales, Russian 3. Spirits 4. Deception 5. Young women 6. Magic 7. Princes 8. Adventure 9. Political intrigue 10. Brothers and sisters 11. Determination in women 12. Russia 13. Historical fantasy 14. Mythological fiction 15. Literary fiction

Librarians' Choice (Australia), 2018.

The magical adventure begun in The Bear and the Nightingale continues as brave Vasya, now a young woman, is forced to choose between marriage or life in a convent and instead flees her home--but soon finds herself called upon to help defend the city of Moscow when it comes under siege Provided by publisher.

"A masterfully told story of folklore, history, and magic with a spellbinding heroine at the heart of it all." Booklist.

Arden, Katherine,

* The **winter** of the witch / Katherine Arden. Del Rey, 2019. 384 p. Winternight trilogy

ISBN 9781101885994

1. 14th century 2. Folktales, Russian 3. Spirits 4. Political intrigue 5. Deception 6. Young women 7. Fate and fatalism 8. Magic 9. Princes 10. Adventure 11. Brothers and sisters 12. Determination in women 13. Good and evil 14. Russia 15. Historical fantasy 16. Mythological fiction 17. Literary fiction

Vasilisa Petrovna, a girl determined to forge her own path in a world that would rather lock her away, finds herself beset by the Grand Prince of Moscow on one side and a demon determined to spread chaos on the other. With the fate of both worlds resting on her shoulders, Vasya will uncover surprising truths about herself as she desperately tries to save Russia, Morozko, and the magical world she treasures.

"Visceral descriptions of battle, an atmospheric sense of place, and some truly heartbreaking moments of loss make this a gut-wrenching read, but there's ample hope and satisfaction to be found as Vasya chooses her own unique path to triumph." Booklist.

Aridjis, Chloe

Asunder / Chloe Aridjis. Mariner Books, 2013. 192 p.

ISBN 9780544003460

1. National Gallery (Great Britain) 2. Boredom 3. Roommates 4. Museums 5. Guards 6. Art 7. Recluses 8. Voyages and travels 9. Interpersonal relations 10. Men/women relations 11. London, England 12. Paris, France 13. Psychological fiction

When she begins to feel restless in her job as a museum guard, Marie takes a trip to Paris, where, with the arrival of an uninvited guest and an unexpected encounter, her world is torn open.

Arikawa, Hiro, 1972-

The **travelling** cat chronicles / Hiro Arikawa ; translated by Philip Gabriel. Berkley, 2018, c2012. 288 p.

ISBN 9780451491336

1. Cats 2. Pets -- Travel 3. Human/animal relationships 4. Voyages and travels 5. Personal conduct 6. Men and cats 7. Cats as pets 8. Friendship 9. Japan 10. Literary fiction 11. Domestic fiction 12. Translations -- Japanese to English

LC 2018010823

A reissue of the 2017 edition published by Doubleday (London).

"Originally published 2012 in Japanese as Tabineko Ripôto" -- Verso title page.

An ode to kindness, sacrifice, and the power of small things traces the experiences of adventurous Nana the cat and his owner, Satoru, as they embark on a road trip across Japan to visit three old friends.

Arimah, Lesley Nneka

* **What** it means when a man falls from the sky : stories / Lesley Nneka Arimah. Riverhead Books, 2017. 240 p.

ISBN 9780735211025

1. Interpersonal relations 2. Family relationships 3. Human nature 4. Short stories 5. Domestic fiction

LC 2016036303

Kirkus Prize for Fiction, 2017.

"Lesley Arimah emigrated from Nigeria to Louisiana at the age of thirteen, a disorienting transition that left her keenly attuned to the shock waves set in motion by displacement. In these twelve powerful stories that embrace magical-realist elements while deploying a powerfully empathetic understanding of character and circumstance, she explores how parents and children, husbands and wives, lovers and friends, navigate conflicting cultures and struggle to reconcile conflicting desires, wants, and needs."--Provided by the publisher

"This speculative turn joins everything from fabulism to folk tale as Arimah confidently tests out all the tools in her kit while also managing to create a wholly cohesive and original collection." Kirkus.

Armfield, Julia

Salt slow : stories / Julia Armfield. Flatiron Books, 2019. 195 p.

ISBN 9781250224774

1. Feminism 2. Monsters 3. Loss (Psychology) 4. Interpersonal

relations 5. Transformations(Magic) 6. Magical realism 7. Literary fiction 8. Short stories

A collection of short stories that examines women's place in society as seen through their unique body experiences, including a teenager struggling through puberty and a group of fangirls who disrupt a popular band's tour.

Armstrong, Kelley

Alone in the wild / Kelley Armstrong. Minotaur Books, 2020. 368 p. Casey Duncan novels

ISBN 9781250254283

1. Sheriffs 2. Women detectives 3. Murder investigation 4. Infants 5. Wilderness areas 6. Rural life 7. Abandoned infants 8. Yukon Territory 9. Canada 10. Mysteries

LC 2019038492

Discovering a live baby beside its murdered mother in the woods, detective Casey Duncan tries to uncover what happened while struggling to care for the infant in a Rockton community that disapproves of children.

"The prolific Armstrong is an adept storyteller (she's writes horror and fantasy as well as mysteries, for both adults and teens) who makes the rather out-there idea of a small, protected community full of people with things to hide seem not only plausible but entirely believable." Booklist.

Armstrong, Kelley,

Watcher in the woods / Kelley Armstrong. St Martins Pr, 2019 368 p. Casey Duncan novels

ISBN 9781250159915

1. Sheriffs 2. Women detectives 3. Murder investigation 4. United States marshals 5. Wilderness areas 6. Social isolation 7. Murderers 8. Yukon Territory 9. Canada 10. Mysteries

LC 2018049401

When a suspicious U.S. marshal shows up demanding the release of a Rockton resident only to be found murdered hours later, detective Casey and sheriff Dalton race to identify the killer and prevent additional deaths.

Armstrong, Kelley

Wherever she goes / Kelley Armstrong. Minotaur Books, 2019. 400 p.

ISBN 9781250181350

1. Single mothers 2. Child kidnapping victims 3. Skepticism 4. Child custody 5. Secrets 6. Deception 7. Women witnesses 8. Separation (Marital relations) 9. Neighbors 10. Illinois 11. Psychological suspense

LC 2019002288

Witnessing the abduction of a child at the park, Aubrey struggles to find the boy and his missing mother when the police and her neighbors begin to question her sanity.

"Aubrey and Paul's achingly poignant interactions add texture and depth, while clever twists, realistic complications, and a propulsive, present-tense narration catapult the story to a gratifying finish. This is a gripping tale of secrets, lies, and maternal anxieties." Publishers Weekly.

Armstrong, Richard, 1952-

The **don** con / Richard Armstrong. Pace Press, 2019. 250 p.

ISBN 9781610353366

1. Fan conventions 2. Mafia 3. Actors and actresses 4. Former convicts 5. Womanizers 6. Robbery 7. Marital conflict 8. Poor people 9. Revenge 10. Caper novels

LC 2018052703

The Mafia comes to Comic-Con in this fast-paced suspense caper and outrageous pop culture satire.

Arnaldur Indridason, 1961-

Outrage / Arnaldur Indridason ; translated from the Icelandic by Anna Yates. St Martin's Minotaur, 2012, c2008. 288 p. Erlendur Sveinsson mysteries

ISBN 9780312659110

1. Secrets 2. Cold cases (Criminal investigation) 3. Drug traffic 4. Policewomen 5. Murder investigation 6. Police -- Reykjavik, Iceland 7. Middle-aged men 8. Reykjavik, Iceland 9. Iceland 10. Mysteries 11. Translations -- Icelandic to English 12. Scandinavian crime fiction

Translation of: Myrka.

Originally published in Icelandic as: Myrka: Reykjavik : Vaka-Helgafell, 2008.

When Detective Erlender places her in charge during his leave of absence, Elinborg tackles a disturbing serial rapist case that has the local police racing against time to prevent another attack.

Arnaldur Indridason, 1961-

Reykjavik nights : an Inspector Erlendur novel / Arnaldur Indridason ; translated from the Icelandic by Victoria Cribb. Minotaur Books, 2015, c2012. 288 p. Erlendur Sveinsson mysteries

ISBN 9781250048424

1. Police 2. Young men 3. Drowning victims 4. Crime 5. Murder 6. Homeless men 7. Murder investigation 8. Violence against homeless people 9. Reykjavik, Iceland 10. Iceland 11. Mysteries 12. Translations -- Icelandic to English 13. Scandinavian crime fiction

LC 2014044425

This title is a prequel to the Erlendur Sveinsson mysteries, but the recommended reading order is tenth in the series.

Originally published in Icelandic as Reykjavikurnaetur: Reykjavik : Vaka-Helgafell, 2012.

Erlendur is a young, budding detective who is introduced to Reykjavik's dark underworld while investigating the death of a homeless man.

Arnaldur Indridason, 1961-

The **shadow** district : a thriller / Arnaldur Indridason ; translated from the Icelandic by Victoria Cribb. Minotaur Books, 2017. 304 p. Reykjavik wartime mysteries

ISBN 9781250124029

1. Second World War era (1939-1945) 2. 1940s 3. World War II 4. Murder investigation 5. Cold cases (Criminal investigation) 6. Murder 7. Former detectives 8. Retirees 9. Iceland 10. Reykjavik, Iceland 11. Historical mysteries 12. Parallel narratives 13. Scandinavian crime fiction 14. Translations -- Icelandic to English

LC 2017025692

"A Thomas Dunne Book."

First published with the title Skuggasund in Iceland by Vaka-Helgafell in 2013.

Investigating the murder of a 90-year-old man, a retired detective discovers unsettling links between the victim, the World War II case of a strangled woman and a pair of attacks that suggest the wrong man may have been arrested decades earlier.

"With minimalist prose, Indridason skillfully weaves the present-day murder with the past in this classic whodunit that ends with a satisfying and logical resolution." Kirkus.

Arnaldur Indridason, 1961-

Strange shores : an Inspector Erlendur novel / Arnaldur Indridason; translated from the Icelandic by Victoria Cribb. Minotaur Books, 2014, c2010. 304 p. Erlendur Sveinsson mysteries
ISBN 9781250000408

1. Missing persons 2. Cold cases (Criminal investigation) 3. Loss
(Psychology) 4. Detectives 5. Blizzards 6. Camping 7. Seniors
8. Reykjavik, Iceland 9. Iceland 10. Mysteries 11. Translations --
Icelandic to English 12. Scandinavian crime fiction

LC 2014007876

First published with the title Furdustrandir in Iceland by Vaka-Helgafell in 2010.

Decades after a woman disappears from the Icelandic fjords amid a
tempest of lies, betrayal and revenge, Detective Erlendur searches the
same region for his long-lost brother, only to uncover disturbing secrets.

Arnett, Kristen N.

Mostly dead things / Kristen Arnett. Tin House Books,
2019. 354 p.
ISBN 9781947793309

1. Family and suicide 2. Taxidermy 3. Eccentrics and eccentricities
4. Dysfunctional families 5. Family businesses 6. Fathers -- Death
7. Lesbians 8. Identity (Psychology) 9. Grief 10. Mother and adult
daughter 11. Loss (Psychology) 12. Family relationships 13. Florida
14. Psychological fiction

LC 2019005820

Taking over her family's failing taxidermy shop in the wake of her
father's suicide, a grief-stricken woman pursues less-than-legal ways of
generating income while struggling to figure out her place among her
eccentric loved ones.

Arnoult, Darnell, 1955-

Sufficient grace : a novel / Darnell Arnoult. Free Press,
2006. 320 p.
ISBN 074328447X

1. Women with mental illnesses 2. Middle aged women 3. Mother
and adult daughter 4. African American families 5. Daughters-in-law
6. Widows 7. Women with schizophrenia 8. Family relationships 9.
Interracial friendship 10. Female friendship 11. Hallucinations and
illusions 12. Life change events 13. Women -- Identity 14. Women
-- Spiritual life 15. Aging 16. Loss (Psychology) 17. Grief in women
18. Self-discovery in women 19. Southern States 20. Mainstream
fiction 21. Southern fiction

LC 2005058001

Gracie Hollaman finally decides to follow the voices in her head.
She leaves behind her family for the small African-American town of
Rockrun to join Mama Toot and Mattie. Together, the three will learn to
shed their pasts to begin life anew.

"With astute sensitivity, Arnoult bravely endows her formidable
characters with charming candor and perceptive humanity in an elegiac
yet hopeful tale of elegant strength, serene love, and infectious desire."
Booklist.

Arnow, Harriette Louisa Simpson, 1908-1986

The **dollmaker** / Harriette Simpson Arnow Scribner,
2009, c1954. 677 p.
ISBN 9781439154434

1. Moving to a new city 2. Poor families 3. Poverty 4. World War
II 5. Women wood-carvers 6. Women -- Kentucky 7. Mothers 8.
Detroit, Michigan 9. Historical fiction

LC 85040073

Gertie, a naive newcomer from Kentucky, develops a unique defense
against the ugliness and despair of the city.

"It is hard to believe that anyone who opens its pages will soon forget [Gertie] and her sufferings as traced in Harriette Arnow's long, heavily packed masterwork." New York Times Book Review.

Arsenault, Emily

The **broken** teaglass / Emily Arsenault. Bantam Books,
2009. 384 p.
ISBN 9780553807332

1. Lexicographers 2. Cold cases (Criminal investigation) 3. Clues
4. Men/women relations 5. Murder investigation 6. Massachusetts
7. Mysteries

LC 2008039167

Engaging in office flirtation and amateur sleuthing to alleviate the
boredom of their jobs as dictionary updaters, Billy Webb and Mona Minot discover that someone has been lacing their dictionary files with
clues to a long-unsolved murder.

"[This] novel has a delightful premise, crisply drawn characters, and
a subtle sense of humor. Word nerds, too, will enjoy the peeks at the
procedure of making a dictionary." Booklist.

Arsenault, Emily

In search of the Rose notes / Emily Arsenault. William
Morrow & Co., 2011. 304 p.
ISBN 9780062012326

1. Cold cases (Criminal investigation) 2. Murder 3. Babysitters
4. Missing persons 5. Potters 6. Teachers 7. Female friendship 8.
Connecticut 9. Mysteries

Drawn back to her old neighborhood and to her former best friend
Charlotte when the bones of their babysitter Rose are found, Nora
must revisit the events surrounding Rose's disappearance and her own
troubled adolescence.

"Instead of dwelling on fear and pain, Arsenault guides the reader
through grief, compassion, and understanding in this emotionally complex and deeply satisfying read." Publishers Weekly.

Artson, Barbara

Odessa, Odessa / Barbara Artson. She Writes Press, 2018.
264 p.
ISBN 9781631524431

1. 20th century 2. Jewish families 3. Religious persecution 4.
Immigrant families 5. Antisemitism 6. Life change events 7. Jews 8.
Memories 9. Immigrants, Jewish 10. Extended families 11. Family
relationships 12. Ukraine 13. United States 14. Israel 15. Family
sagas

A novel of unforgettable characters about two brothers who emigrate
out of Russia to escape anti-Semitism--one to America and one to Israel-
-Odessa, Odessa gives readers a great story for our time: a younger generation discovering their lost heritage and reuniting a family.

Arudpragasam, Anuk

The **story** of a brief marriage / Anuk Arudpragasam. Flatiron Books, 2016. 224 p.
ISBN 9781250072405

1. Newlyweds 2. Refugee camps 3. War -- Psychological aspects
4. Civil war -- Sri Lanka 5. Loss (Psychology) 6. Young men 7.
Helpfulness in men 8. Bombs 9. Strangers 10. Married people 11.
Men/women relations 12. Sri Lanka 13. Sri Lanka -- History -- Civil
War, 1983-2009 14. Literary fiction 15. War stories

LC 2016020830

Set on a single day towards the end of the Sri Lankan Civil War, a newlywed couple tries to balance love and intimacy in an evacuee camp which is constantly being bombarded by enemy shells.

"Dinesh finds beauty in the worst of situations, which contributes to making this debut deeply moving and hopeful." Publishers Weekly.

Arvin, Reed

Blood of angels : a novel / Reed Arvin. HarperCollins, 2005. 288 p.
> ISBN 9780060596347
> 1. Public prosecutors 2. Lawyers 3. Capital punishment 4. Judicial error 5. Trials (Murder) 6. Murder investigation 7. Protests, demonstrations, vigils, etc 8. Immigrants -- Tennessee 9. Sudanese in the United States 10. Missing persons 11. Women social advocates 12. Men/women relations 13. Nashville, Tennessee 14. Legal thrillers 15. Psychological suspense
> LC 2004060931

Struggling to maintain a sense of purpose in a Tennessee county that has been changed by ten years of immigration, prosecutor Thomas Dennehy tackles a difficult case involving a Sudanese murder suspect and racially charged locals.

Asaro, Catherine

Primary inversion / Catherine Asaro. Tor, 1995. 317 p. Saga of the Skolian Empire
> ISBN 0312857640
> 1. Women psychics 2. Fighter pilots 3. Heirs and heiresses 4. Enemies 5. Women pilots 6. Biotechnology 7. Space vehicles 8. Space flight 9. Space warfare 10. Imaginary empires 11. Science fiction 12. Space opera
> LC 94047207

Sequel: Catch the lightning.

Sauscony Valdoria, linked to the powerful Skolian Web, and the Aristo heir to the evil Trader Empire of Tarnth link minds and fall in love instantly, but to prevent interstellar war, Sauscony must be either his lover or his killer.

"Asaro's sf debut features strong male and female protagonists and a well-realized far-future world. Blending hard science with a familiar tale of star-crossed lovers." Library Journal.

Asch, Sholem, 1880-1957

The **Nazarene** Carroll and Graf, 1984, c1967. 698 p. Biblical series (Sholem Asch)
> ISBN 9780786703791
> 1. Jesus Christ 2. Bible novels

Originally published in 1939.

"Judged purely as a novel, The Nazarene is a superb achievement. Even on the factual side, a work such as Papini's Life is thin beside it. This is because Mr. Asch has taken an infinite amount of trouble to build up an historical background against which the figure of Jesus may move authentically, with that sense of reality which we should expect of fiction as of life." The Atlantic.

Ashe, Katharine

The **duke** / Katharine Ashe. Avon Books, 2017. 398 p. Devil's duke novels
> ISBN 9780062641724
> 1. Georgian era (1714-1837) 2. Recluses 3. Dukes and duchesses 4. Widows 5. Castles 6. Secrets 7. Missionaries 8. Forgiveness 9. Sexual attraction 10. Men/women relations 11. Scotland -- Social life and customs -- 19th century 12. Jamaica -- Social life and customs -- 19th century 13. Georgian romances 14. Historical romances

" Subplots include the development of romances between two appealing interracial couples. Likable lovers, witty dialogue, intriguing supporting characters, and a zippy pace result in a lively page-turner." Publishers Weekly.

Ashe, Katharine

The **earl** / Katharine Ashe. Avon Books, 2016. 384 p. Devil's duke novels
> ISBN 9780062412751
> 1. Regency period (1811-1820) 2. Earls and countesses 3. Women social advocates 4. Secret identity 5. Nobility 6. Engaged persons 7. Missing persons 8. Secret societies 9. Interpersonal attraction 10. Men/women relations 11. Highlands, Scotland 12. Scotland -- Social life and customs -- 19th century 13. Historical romances 14. Regency romances

Determined to unmask Lady Justice, the rabble-rousing pamphleteer, Colin Gray, the new Earl of Egremoor, embarks on a dangerous mission that brings him face-to-face with the smart, big-hearted and passionate woman who vows to teach him a lesson in humility--and love.

Ashe, Katharine

The **prince** / Katharine Ashe. HarperCollins, 2018. 384 p. Devil's duke novels
> ISBN 9780062641748
> 1. Georgian era (1714-1837) 2. Exiles 3. Princes 4. Women surgeons 5. Sexism 6. Portraits 7. Secret identity 8. Portrait painters 9. Sexual attraction 10. Male impersonators 11. Men/women relations 12. Scotland -- Social life and customs -- 19th century 13. Georgian romances 14. Historical romances

Libby Shaw refuses to accept society's dictates. She's determined to become a member of Edinburgh's all-male Royal College of Surgeons. Disguising herself as a man, she attends the surgical theater and fools everyone except the one man who has never forgotten the shape of her exquisitely sensual lips.

"Ashe deftly infuses some fascinating bits of nineteenth-century history into the fourth top-notch addition to her Devils Duke series, while at the same time delivering her trademark captivating characters and heart-melting passion." Booklist.

Asher, Neal L., 1961-

The **skinner** / Neal Asher. Tor, 2004, c2002. 473 p. Spatterjay series
> ISBN 9780765307378
> 1. Terraforming 2. Virus diseases 3. Aliens (Humanoid) 4. Space colonies 5. Voyages and travels 6. Travelers 7. Space flight 8. Death 9. Revenge 10. Quests 11. Hard science fiction 12. Science fiction
> LC bl2004005060

Originally published: London : Macmillan, 2002.

Three unusual travelers arrive on the remote ocean planet of Spatterjay, braving the perils of the world's voracious wildlife as they pursue their individual quests, unaware that their paths are about to converge as the planet threatens to erupt into chaos.

"Asher displays great virtuosity in dramatizing Spatterjay's eat-and-be-eaten ecosystem. . . . Episodes of horrific violence alternate with surprisingly lucid conversations that touch on issues like the psychology of revenge in the aftermath of a holocaust. Asher keeps raising the stakes so that despite the repetitive nature of the violence, it never becomes merely formulaic. You may not relish your stay on Spatterjay. But you won't easily forget it." New York Times Book Review.

Ashford, Jane

* **Heir** to the duke / Jane Ashford. Sourcebooks Casablanca, 2016. 384 p. Duke's sons

ISBN 9781492621560

1. Regency period (1811-1820) 2. Viscounts and viscountesses 3. Arranged marriage 4. Husband and wife 5. Married women 6. Transformations, Personal 7. Nobility 8. Family secrets 9. Men/women relations 10. England 11. Regency romances 12. Historical romances

After marrying Lady Violet Devere, who was oppressed by her family all her life, Nathaniel Gresham, devoted to familial duty, finds his quiet, reserved life forever changed by this spirited beauty who is determined to show him the comparative freedom their married life brings them both in and out of the bedroom.

Ashford, Jane

Lord Sebastian's secret / Jane Ashford. Sourcebooks Casablanca, 2017. 377 p. Duke's sons

ISBN 9781492621621

1. Regency period (1811-1820) 2. Illiterate men 3. Soldiers 4. Engaged persons 5. Nobility 6. Eccentric families 7. Secrets 8. Interpersonal attraction 9. Men/women relations 10. England 11. Great Britain 12. Regency romances 13. Historical romances

Lord Sebastian Gresham is a battle tested soldier and brilliant strategist. Yet all his life he's had to hide his complete failure to decipher letters. In his own mind, he's just stupid. What a miracle it is that he's found the perfect bride. Lady Georgina Stane is beautiful, witty, and brilliantly intelligent. Sebastian is head over heels in love, proud as a peacock, and terrified. If she finds out, he'll lose her love forever.

Ashford, Jane

What the duke doesn't know / Jane Ashford. Sourcebooks Casablanca, 2016. 384 p. Duke's sons

ISBN 9781492621591

1. Great Britain. Royal Navy Officers 2. Regency period (1811-1820) 3. Ship captains 4. Multiracial women 5. Misunderstanding 6. Jewelry theft 7. Independence in women 8. Cultural differences 9. Nobility 10. Women marriage resisters 11. Mate selection 12. Interpersonal attraction 13. Men/women relations 14. England 15. Great Britain 16. Regency romances 17. Historical romances

After making his fortune abroad, Royal Navy Captain James Gresham returns home to find a proper English wife, but instead finds himself drawn to Kawena Benson, who, out to reclaim a cache of stolen jewels, believes he is behind the theft.

"Throw in Ashford's gift for creating intriguingly different characters and her dry sense of humor, and you have a romance worth cherishing." Booklist.

Ashley, Jennifer

Lady Isabella's scandalous marriage / Jennifer Ashley. Berkley Sensation, 2010. 325 p. Highland pleasures

ISBN 9780425235454

1. Victorian era (1837-1901) 2. 1880s 3. Runaway wives, husbands, etc 4. Second chances 5. Scandals 6. Seduction 7. Artists 8. Men/women relations 9. England -- History -- 19th century 10. Historical romances 11. Victorian romances 12. Highland romances

LC bl2010017234

When her husband, Lord Mac Mackenzie, follows her to London, determined to win her back, Lady Isabella Scranton rises to the challenge by tempting him in ways he could have never imagined, but a dangerous enemy waits in the wings to stop them from reuniting--forever.

Ashley, Jennifer

* The **madness** of Lord Ian Mackenzie / Jennifer Ashley. Leisure Books, 2009. 320 p. Highland pleasures

ISBN 9780843960433

1. Victorian era (1837-1901) 2. 1880s 3. Widows 4. Rumor 5. Inheritance and succession 6. Truth 7. Malicious accusation 8. Family relationships 9. Brothers 10. Murder 11. Men/women relations 12. England -- History -- 19th century 13. Historical romances 14. Victorian romances 15. Highland romances

LC bl2009011649

Beth, a young widow, is inexplicably drawn to Ian MacKenzie, a Scottish lord who is rumored to be a murderer and who spent his youth in an asylum, and she is determined to prove to London society that he is perfectly sane.

Asimov, Isaac, 1920-1992

* **Foundation** / Isaac Asimov. Bantam Books, 2004. 244 p. Foundation series

ISBN 0553803719

1. Far future 2. Psychohistory 3. Life on other planets 4. Psychohistorians 5. Mathematicians 6. Space colonies 7. Space flight 8. Space exploration 9. Social forecasting 10. Scientific forecasting 11. Hard science fiction 12. Space opera 13. Science fiction

LC 2003069137

A band of psychologists, under the leadership of psychohistorian Hari Seldon, plant a colony to encourage art, science, and technology in the declining Galactic Empire and to preserve the accumulated knowledge of humankind.

Asimov, Isaac, 1920-1992

Foundation and empire / Isaac Asimov. Bantam Books, 2004. 244 p. Foundation series

ISBN 9780586013557

1. Life on other planets 2. Psychohistory 3. Mind control 4. Psychohistorians 5. Space colonies 6. Space flight 7. Survival 8. Mutants 9. Secrets 10. Chases 11. Individuality 12. Imaginary wars and battles 13. Hard science fiction 14. Space opera 15. Science fiction

LC 2003069136

The Foundation, a colony of psychologists, battles for supreme power in the galaxy, while also struggling to preserve all the accumulated knowledge of humankind in The Foundation, a sanctuary created by Hari Seldon.

Asimov, Isaac, 1920-1992

* **I,** robot / Isaac Asimov. Bantam Books, 2004, c1950. 224 p.

ISBN 0553803700

1. Robots 2. Androids 3. Robotics 4. Artificial intelligence 5. Robots -- Behavior 6. Rules 7. Telepathy 8. Individuality 9. Power (Social sciences) 10. Women scientists 11. Women psychologists 12. Journalists 13. Human/computer interaction 14. Emotions 15. Short stories 16. Hard science fiction 17. Science fiction

LC 2003069139

This title is not a part of the Robot Series according to the author. Originally published: c1950.

Originally published: New York : Gnome Press, 1950.

Asimov chronicles the development of the robot through a series of interlinked stories: from its primitive origins in the present to its ultimate perfection in the not-so-distant future--a future in which humanity itself may be rendered obsolete. Here are stories of robots gone mad, of mind-read robots, and robots with a sense of humor. Of robot politicians, and robots who secretly run the world.

Asimov, Isaac, 1920-1992

Second foundation / Isaac Asimov. Bantam Books, 2004. viii, 241 p. Foundation series

ISBN 0553803735

1. Psychohistory 2. Life on other planets 3. Mind control 4. Mathematicians 5. Psychohistorians 6. Mutants 7. Monsters 8. Fourteen-year-olds 9. Political corruption 10. Traitors 11. Betrayal 12. Conspiracies 13. Hard science fiction 14. Space opera 15. Science fiction

LC 2003069134

"The third volume in the world-famous Foundation saga"--cover.

This is reckoned by Asimov to be the 12th in terms of the chronology of the events covered. (Cf. His 'Prelude to Foundation'. Author's note, p. 9-[10]). Also called the fourth Foundation novel.

Originally published: New York : Gnome Press, 1953.

The Second Foundation meets the threat of a perilous mutant, only to face the challenge of the corrupt First Foundation for control of the galactic empire.

Aslam, Nadeem

* The **blind** man's garden / Nadeem Aslam. Alfred A. Knopf, 2013. 336 p.

ISBN 9780307961716

1. Pakistanis in Afghanistan 2. Brothers 3. Men who are blind 4. September 11 Terrorist Attacks, 2001 5. Muslims 6. Medical students 7. Guilt in men 8. Pakistan 9. Afghanistan 10. Political fiction 11. Literary fiction

LC 2012041083

"THIS IS A BORZOI BOOK."

Set in Pakistan and Afghanistan in the months following 9/11, a story of war, of one family's losses, and of the simplest, most enduring human impulses.

Aslam, Nadeem

* The **golden** legend : a novel / Nadeem Aslam. Alfred A. Knopf, 2017. 304 p.

ISBN 9780451493781

1. Culture conflict 2. Widows 3. Muslim women 4. Secrets 5. Forgiveness 6. Interpersonal relations 7. Resistance to government 8. Pakistan 9. Psychological fiction 10. Literary fiction

LC 2016034887

Longlisted for the Andrew Carnegie Medal for Excellence in Fiction, 2018.

Hiding her past, Nargis feels her life crumbling around her when someone begins broadcasting local people's secrets from the minaret of a local mosque.

"Brooding and beautiful: a mature, assured story of the fragility of the world and of ourselves." Kirkus.

Aslam, Nadeem

Maps for lost lovers / Nadeem Aslam. Knopf, 2005. 384 p.

ISBN 9781400042425

1. Pakistanis in England 2. Immigrants 3. Muslims 4. Muslim men 5. Muslim women 6. Muslim families 7. Married men 8. Married women 9. Families of murder victims 10. Brothers -- Death 11. Honor killings 12. Fundamentalism 13. Culture conflict 14. Assimilation (Sociology) 15. Loss (Psychology) 16. Sexual freedom 17. Cohabitation 18. Men/women relations 19. Islam 20. England 21. Psychological fiction 22. Domestic fiction

LC 2004059428

Kiriyama Prize for Fiction, 2005.

Shortlisted for the International IMPAC Dublin Literary Award, 2006

The disappearance of unmarried lovers Jugnu and Chanda turns tragic when Chanda's brothers are arrested for their murders and the families struggle to reconcile their Islamic faith with their lives in England, the murders, and the crime's devastating impact on the rest of their families, in the lyrical story of a Pakistani family in England.

Aslam, Nadeem

The **wasted** vigil / Nadeem Aslam. Alfred A. Knopf, 2008. 319 p.

ISBN 9780307268426

1. Men/women relations 2. Loss (Psychology) 3. Coping 4. Grief 5. Physicians 6. Interpersonal relations 7. Afghanistan -- Social life and customs 8. Afghanistan 9. Psychological fiction

LC 2008017772

ALA Notable Book, 2009.

In a post-9/11 Afghanistan, the lives and destinies of five very different people intertwine--Marcus, an English doctor whose Afghani wife had been murdered by the Taliban; Lara, a Russian woman probing the fate of her brother who vanished during the Soviet invasion; David, an American former spy; Casa, a young Afghani who hates the West; and James, a rigid Special Forces soldier.

"The prose in The Wasted Vigil is usually so generous with startling perceptions that the reader rarely feels overwhelmed by the social and historical facts that Aslam, writing about a country largely unknown to his readers, has to constantly smuggle into his narrative. . . . Aslam's determination to gaze resolutely at the darkest side of our many cold and hot wars is what gives The Wasted Vigil its depth and power." The New York Review of Books.

Aswani, Alaa, 1957-

Chicago : a modern Arabic novel / Alaa Al Aswany ; translated by Farouk Abdel Wahab. Harper, 2007. 342 p.

ISBN 9780061452567

1. Refugees 2. Egyptians in the United States 3. Fanaticism 4. Hypocrisy 5. Greed in men 6. College teachers 7. African Americans 8. African American women 9. Anarchists 10. Racism 11. Identity (Psychology) 12. Immigrants 13. Sexuality 14. Men/women relations 15. Chicago, Illinois 16. Illinois 17. Psychological fiction 18. Translations -- Arabic to English

Originally published in Arabic in 2007. Originally published in Great Britain by Fourth Estate, 2008.

Post-9/11 Chicago becomes the site of a cultural collision involving a sixties-style anti-establishment professor who is targeted for his relationship with an African-American woman, a veiled Ph.D. candidate whose traditional upbringing is challenged by her American experiences, and an émigré whose western values are countered by questions about his daughter's honor.

Atakora, Afia

* **Conjure** women / Afia Atakora. Random House, 2020. 416 p.

ISBN 9780525511489

1. 19th century 2. Midwives 3. Women healers 4. Plantation life 5. Curses 6. Slavery 7. Mother and child 8. Superstition 9. Secrets 10. Freed slaves 11. African Americans 12. Southern States -- Social life and customs -- 19th century 13. Southern States -- History -- 19th century 14. Historical fiction 15. African American fiction

A midwife and conjurer of curses reflects on her life before and after the Civil War, her relationships with the families she serves and the secrets she has learned about a plantation owner's daughter.

"Atakora effectively handles the before-during-and-after structure, enriching her story. If its center is the vibrant Rue, the entire community finally feels like the main character." Library Journal.

Atilgan, Yusuf

Motherland hotel / Yusuf Atilgan ; translated by Fred Stark. City Lights Books, 2016, c1973. 152 p.

ISBN 9780872867116

1. Hotel owners 2. Obsession in men 3. Mental illness 4. Loneliness 5. Women travelers 6. Hotel workers 7. Men with emotional illnesses 8. Antisocial personality disorders 9. Psychological fiction 10. Literary fiction 11. Translations -- Turkish to English

LC 2016018905

Originally published: Ankara : Bilgi, 1973.

Lonely, middle-aged Zebercet, the last surviving member of a once prosperous Ottoman family, is the owner of the Motherland Hotel, a run-down establishment near the railroad station. One day, a beautiful woman from the capital comes to spend the night and suddenly Zebercet's insular, mechanical existence is dramatically and irrevocably changed.

Atkins, Ace

The **broken** places / Ace Atkins. G. P. Putnam's Sons, 2013. 352 p. Quinn Colson novels

ISBN 9780399161780

1. United States. Army. Rangers 2. Sheriffs 3. Revenge 4. Former convicts 5. Murderers 6. Women deputy police chiefs 7. Mississippi 8. Thrillers and suspense

When an infamous murderer is released from prison and returns to Jericho preaching redemption, skeptical sheriff Quinn Colson is forced to confront the man's vengeance-seeking victims and former partners in crime, a situation that is further complicated by a dangerous tornado.

Atkins, Ace

The **fallen** / Ace Atkins. G.P. Putnam's Sons, 2017. 384 p. Quinn Colson novels

ISBN 9780399576713

1. Sheriffs 2. Bank robberies 3. Criminals 4. Robbery 5. Veterans 6. Secrets 7. Mississippi 8. Thrillers and suspense

Investigating a series of bank robberies that have been orchestrated with skill and precision worthy of a military raid, Mississippi sheriff and former Army Ranger Quinn Colson calls on old allies and new enemies in his effort to outmaneuver a sophisticated band of elite criminals.

Atkins, Ace

The **forsaken** / Ace Atkins. G. P. Putnam's Sons, 2014. 352 p. Quinn Colson novels

ISBN 9780399161797

1. United States. Army. Rangers 2. Sheriffs 3. Lynching 4. Race relations 5. Hate crimes 6. Murderers 7. Women deputy police chiefs 8. Mississippi 9. Thrillers and suspense

LC 2014015440

County sheriff Quinn Colson is determined to find those responsible for lynching an innocent black man in Jericho, Mississippi, 30 years prior.

"The dive into Jerichos dark past makes for great reading as Atkins rolls through a handful of perspectives, propelling the storys threads toward an adrenaline-laced, Wild Weststyle conclusion." Booklist.

Atkins, Ace

The **innocents** / Ace Atkins. G.P. Putnam's Sons, 2016. 384 p. Quinn Colson novels

ISBN 9780399173950

1. Sheriffs 2. Murder investigation 3. Teenage girl murder victims 4. Secrets 5. Mississippi 6. Thrillers and suspense

She was just seventeen, a high school dropout named Milly Jones, found walking down the middle of the highway, engulfed in flames. Even in a tough Mississippi county like Tibbehah, it shatters the community, and it is up to Sheriff Quinn Colson, back on the job after a year away, and his deputy Lillie Virgil, to investigate what happened and why. Before long, however, accusations start to fly, national media and federal authorities descend, and what seemed like a senseless act of violence begins to appear like something even more disturbing?with more victims waiting in the shadows.

Atkins, Ace

The **lost** ones / Ace Atkins. G.P. Putnam's Sons, 2012. 352 p. Quinn Colson novels

ISBN 9780399158766

1. United States. Army. Rangers 2. Sheriffs 3. Drug cartels 4. Adoption racket 5. Gangs 6. Child abuse victims 7. Women deputy police chiefs 8. Drug traffic 9. Veterans 10. Hometowns 11. Mississippi 12. Thrillers and suspense

Newly-elected Tibbehah County sheriff Quinn Colson investigates an old friend's gun sales when stolen military rifles are found in the possession of a Mexican drug gang, a case that is complicated by his discovery of a black market baby adoption ring.

Atkins, Ace

The **ranger** / Ace Atkins. G.P. Putnam's Sons, 2011. 352 p. Quinn Colson novels

ISBN 9780399157486

1. United States. Army Commando troops 2. Drug traffic 3. White supremacists 4. Murder investigation 5. Uncles -- Death 6. Women deputy police chiefs 7. Crimes against police 8. Methamphetamine 9. Corruption investigation 10. Secrets 11. Hometowns 12. Mississippi 13. Thrillers and suspense

LC 2011002785

Returning to what has become his violently corrupt hometown in Mississippi after a tour in Afghanistan, Army Ranger Quinn Colson investigates his uncle's alleged suicide and uncovers shocking personal secrets.

Atkins, Ace

The **redeemers** / Ace Atkins. Penguin Group USA, 2015 352 p. Quinn Colson novels

ISBN 9780399173943

1. Former sheriffs 2. Organized crime 3. Stealing 4. Police murders 5. Thieves 6. Former lovers 7. Summer 8. Secrets 9. Veterans 10. Mississippi 11. Thrillers and suspense

LC 2015015992

"The electrifying new novel in New York Times-bestselling author Ace Atkins's acclaimed series about the real Deep South"--, Provided by publisher.

Atkins, Ace

The **sinners** / Ace Atkins. G. P. Putnam's Sons, 2018. 384 p. Quinn Colson novels

ISBN 9780399576744

1. Sheriffs 2. Revenge 3. Drug dealers 4. Crime 5. Criminals 6. Drug lords 7. Former convicts 8. Mississippi 9. Thrillers and suspense

When the recently released patriarch of a drug-dealing clan begins targeting the family of the man responsible for his long imprisonment, Quinn Colson finds himself relying on new deputies to survive Old West acts of violence.

Atkins, Ace

The **shameless** / Ace Atkins. G.P. Putnam's Sons, 2019. 384 p. Quinn Colson novels

ISBN 9780525539469

1. Suicide investigation 2. Organized crime 3. Sheriffs 4. Cold cases (Criminal investigation) 5. Corruption 6. Newlyweds 7. Podcasts 8. Elections 9. Murder 10. Small towns 11. Mississippi 12. Thrillers and suspense

LC 2019018652

Approached by two New York reporters to reopen a 20-year-old suicide case, Sheriff Quinn Colson finds the investigation complicated by a local crime syndicate's involvement in a gubernatorial election.

Atkins, Ace

Wicked city / Ace Atkins. G. P. Putnam's Sons, 2008. 352 p.

ISBN 9780399154577

1. 1950s 2. Organized crime 3. Lawyers 4. Murder 5. Murder investigation 6. Alabama 7. Southeastern States 8. Thrillers and suspense 9. Noir fiction

LC 2007032774

In the aftermath of an innocent man's murder by powerful mobsters in mid-twentieth-century Alabama, a small group of citizens bands together to fight back against the organized machine that has taken over their city.

"Atkins provides a 3-D view through two narrators, an omniscient teller and Lamar Murphy, an ex-boxer enlisted to help solve Albert Patterson's murder. . . . A character warns that the sweetness of Phenix City moonshine masks the embalming fluid that provides its kick. Atkins has likewise crafted a smart tale of a decadent place; Southern sweetness laced with poison." Paste.

Atkinson, Kate

* **Big** sky / Kate Atkinson. Little, Brown and Co., 2019. 400 p. Jackson Brodie mysteries

ISBN 9780316523097

1. Private investigators 2. Coastal towns 3. Deception 4. Teenage boys 5. Fathers and sons 6. Criminal investigation 7. Secrets 8. England 9. Yorkshire, England 10. Mysteries 11. Literary fiction

Investigating a new client's suspicions about an unfaithful spouse, iconoclastic detective Jackson Brodie is catapulted by a chance encounter into a sinister network of secrets and lies.

Atkinson, Kate

* **Case** histories / Kate Atkinson. Little, Brown and Co., 2004. 312 p. Jackson Brodie mysteries

ISBN 9780316740401

1. Lawyers 2. Private investigators 3. Missing girls 4. Divorced men 5. Fathers and daughters 6. Family relationships 7. Women murderers 8. Grief 9. Fate and fatalism 10. Loss (Psychology) 11. Murder 12. Reconciliation 13. Cambridge, England 14. England 15. Mysteries

LC 2004002379

Private detective Jackson Brodie finds his own need for resolution sparked by three investigations including those of two sisters who discover a shocking clue to the disappearance of their third sister thirty years earlier, a lawyer whose life is turned upside-down when his daughter joins the firm, and a woman whose past mistakes and demanding family life culminate in a violent escape.

"The novel is packed with women whose appetites are large, and Atkinson's prose is correspondingly loose and louche: no single point of view predominates, and everyone's thoughts effortlessly rollick along." New York Times Book Review.

Atkinson, Kate

*A **god** in ruins / Kate Atkinson. Little Brown & Co, 2015. 400 p.

ISBN 9780316176538

1. Great Britain. Royal Air Force Airmen 2. Men 3. Family relationships 4. Aging 5. Bomber pilots 6. Fatherhood 7. Husband and wife 8. Loss (Psychology) 9. Veterans 10. Identity (Psychology) 11. World War II 12. Great Britain -- History -- 20th century 13. Historical fiction 14. Literary fiction

LC 916023580

Sequel to: Life after life.
Companion to: Life after life.
Costa Novel Award, 2015.
Longlisted for the Baileys Women's Prize for Fiction, 2016.

Ursula Todd's brother Teddy is an old man trying to come to grips with his post-War life and with a modern world and family. Switching back and forth in time between memories of his childhood and his present, Teddy is an oblivious husband, a rueful father. He never quite got over the War and part of him never adjusted to having a future. Would-be poet, heroic pilot, husband, father, and grandfather, Teddy navigates the perils and progress of a rapidly changing world; his greatest challenge is living in afuture he never expected to have. --, Source other than Library of Congress.

"As in Life After Life, Atkinson isnt just telling a story: she's deconstructing, taking apart the notion of how we believe stories are told. Using narrative tricks that range from the subtlest sleight of hand to direct address, she makes us feel the power of storytelling not as an intellectual conceit, but as a punch in the gut." Publishers Weekly.

Atkinson, Kate

Human croquet / Kate Atkinson. Picador, 1997. 349 p.

ISBN 0312155506

1. Eccentric families 2. Family relationships 3. Mother-separated children 4. Missing persons 5. Families 6. Curses 7. Time travel 8. Clairvoyance 9. Dysfunctional families 10. Sixteen-year-old girls 11. England 12. Family sagas 13. Magical realism 14. Coming-of-age stories 15. Literary fiction

Once part of a vast expanse where a wealthy Elizabethan family settled and built Fairfax Manor, but now, in the mid 1960s, it has become a disintegrated forest where the destroyed, dysfunctional Fairfax family continues to crumble.

"Human Croquet is peppered with snatches of hilarious nonsensical suburban dialogue; big, exuberant exclamations; savvy rhetorical questions and a knuckle crackingly morbid sense of humor. . . . The narrator's youthful cynicism does not descend into mannerism. Atkinson shows that it is the logical outcome of cruelty and trauma." New Statesman.

Atkinson, Kate

* **Life** after life : a novel / Kate Atkinson. Reagan Arthur Books, 2013. 560 p.

ISBN 9780316176484

1. Reincarnation 2. World War II 3. Options, alternatives, choices 4. Identity (Psychology) 5. Purpose in life 6. Great Britain -- History -- 20th century 7. Alternative histories 8. Literary fiction

LC 2012046158

Sequel: A god in ruins.

ALA Notable Book, 2014

Costa Novel Award, 2013

Goodreads Choice Award, 2013.

Shortlisted for the Walter Scott Prize for Historical Fiction, 2014

Shortlisted for The Women's Prize for Fiction, 2013

Follows the experiences of a woman, who after being born on a snowy night in 1910, repeatedly dies and reincarnates into the same life to correct missteps and ultimately save the world.

Atkinson, Kate

One good turn : a novel / Kate Atkinson. Little, Brown, 2006. 418 p. Jackson Brodie mysteries

ISBN 9780316154840

1. Millionaires 2. Police 3. Extramarital affairs 4. Private investigators 5. Men/women relations 6. Former detectives 7. Witnesses 8. Crime 9. Authors 10. Interpersonal relations 11. Murder 12. Road rage 13. Edinburgh, Scotland 14. Scotland 15. Mysteries

LC 2005031123

In the sequel to Case Histories, millionaire ex-detective Jackson Brodie follows his girlfriend to Edinburgh for the famous arts festival, but when he becomes an eyewitness to a brutal attack on a man during a traffic jam, he becomes caught up in a string of events that draw him and the wife of an unscrupulous tycoon, a timid crime novelist, and female police detective into the heart of deadly conspiracy.

"In the past Ms. Atkinson has played the minor time trick of letting events almost converge and then replaying them from slightly different points of view. She does that here to the same smart, unnerving effect. And she frequently brings up the image of Russian dolls, each hidden inside another, to illustrate how her storytelling tactics work. By the apt ending of One Good Turn a whole series of these dolls has been opened." New York Times.

Atkinson, Kate

Started early, took my dog / Kate Atkinson. Little, Brown, 2011, c2010. 400 p. Jackson Brodie mysteries

ISBN 9780316066730

1. Former police 2. Security consultants 3. Girl orphans 4. Life change events 5. Private investigators 6. Cold cases (Criminal investigation) 7. Police cover-ups 8. Women murder victims 9. Birthparents -- Identification 10. Leeds, England 11. Mysteries

Originally published: London : Doubleday,

Recently retired from the police force, Tracy Waterhouse is enjoying the quiet life. However, when she sees a miserable young child under the care of routine offender Kelly Cross, Tracy decides to bring the child under her wardship. Meanwhile, detective Jackson Brodie adopts an abused dog. It doesn't take long, however, for both Tracy and Brodie to learn that they are both in way over their heads.

"A delight: an intricate construction that assembles itself before the reader's eyes, populated by idiosyncratic, multidimensional characters and written with shrewd, mordant grace. . . . Atkinson's Jackson Brodie books are like high-wire acts in which she is forever defying gravity (in the form of crime fiction's improbable conventions) by making the work fresh, unpredictable and alive." Salon.com.

Atkinson, Kate

* Transcription / Kate Atkinson. Little, Brown and Co., 2018. 343 p.

ISBN 9780316176637

1. M I 5 2. 20th century 3. Espionage 4. Consequences 5. War and society 6. Radio programs 7. Postwar life 8. World War II 9. War -- Psychological aspects 10. Life change events 11. Undercover operations 12. Intrigue 13. Great Britain -- Social life and customs -- 20th century 14. Literary fiction 15. Historical fiction

Juliet Armstrong is a radio producer in a 1950s London that is recovering from the war as much as she is. During World War Two, Juliet transcribed conversations between an MI5 agent and a ring of suspected German sympathizers, which quickly plunged Juliet into a treacherous world of code words and secret meetings. Now her routine is upended by an meeting with a mysterious man from her past. Haunted by the actions of her past and a very real threat in the present, Juliet realizes she cannot escape the repercussions of her work for the government.

Atkinson, Kate

* When will there be good news? : a novel / Kate Atkinson. Little, Brown, 2008. 400 p. Jackson Brodie mysteries

ISBN 9780316154857

1. Missing persons 2. Physicians 3. Women detectives 4. Private investigators 5. Teenage girls 6. Missing women 7. Former convicts 8. Nannies 9. Murderers 10. Edinburgh, Scotland 11. Mysteries

LC 2008014738

Originally published: London: Doubleday,

British Book Award for the Richard & Judy Best Read of the Year, 2009.

On a hot summer day, Joanna Mason's family slowly wanders home along a country lane. A moment later, Joanna's life is changed forever. On a dark night thirty years later, ex-detective Jackson Brodie finds himself on a train that is both crowded and late. Lost in his thoughts, he suddenly hears a shocking sound. At the end of a long day, 16-year-old Reggie is looking forward to watching a little TV. Then a terrifying noise shatters her peaceful evening.

"As always, Atkinson inhabits her characters with fluency, clarity and a good eye and ear for quirks and habits of mind." Times Literary Supplement.

Attenberg, Jami

* All this could be yours / Jami Attenberg. Houghton Mifflin Harcourt, 2019. 240 p.

ISBN 9780544824256

1. Fathers -- Death 2. Dysfunctional families 3. Family secrets 4. Abusive men 5. Consequences 6. Options, alternatives, choices 7. Family relationships 8. Memories 9. New Orleans, Louisiana 10. Domestic fiction

LC 2019002554

Family secrets are revealed in the heat of a New Orleans summer.

Attenberg, Jami

The **Middlesteins** / Jami Attenberg. Grand Central Pub., 2012. 288 p.

ISBN 9781455507214

1. Jewish families 2. Families 3. Food habits 4. Life change events 5. Compulsive behavior in women 6. Obsession 7. Family relationships 8. Overweight women 9. Diet 10. Father-separated families 11. Middle West 12. Mainstream fiction 13. Domestic fiction

LC 2011025990

Two siblings with very different personalities attempt to take control of their mother's food obsession and massive weight gain to save her life after their father walks out and leaves her reeling in the Chicago suburbs.

Atwood, Margaret, 1939-

Alias Grace / Margaret Atwood. Nan A. Talese/Doubleday, 1996 468 p.

ISBN 9780385475716

1. Marks, Grace, b 1826 2. 1840s 3. Trials (Murder) 4. Women murderers 5. Murder 6. Irish Canadians 7. Men/women relations 8. Household employees 9. Women prisoners 10. Housekeepers 11. Canada -- History -- 19th century 12. Historical mysteries 13.

Literary fiction 14. Psychological fiction

ALA Notable Book, 1998.

Giller Prize, 1996.

Shortlisted for the Booker-McConnell Prize, 1996.

Shortlisted for the International IMPAC Dublin Literary Award, 1998

Shortlisted for The Orange Prize for Fiction, 1997

Governor General's Literary Awards, English-language Fiction finalist

Takes readers into the life and mind of Grace Marks, one of the most notorious women of the 1840s, who is serving a life sentence for murders she claims she cannot remember.

"Always a powerful writer, Atwood outdoes herself with compelling prose, expert control of the material, and fine attention to historical detail." Library Journal.

Atwood, Margaret, 1939-

* The **blind** assassin / Margaret Atwood. Nan A. Talese/ Doubleday, 2000. 521 p.

ISBN 9780385475723

1. 1940s 2. Widows 3. Family secrets 4. Sibling rivalry 5. Sisters -- Death 6. Political corruption 7. Betrayal 8. Loss (Psychology) 9. Women authors 10. Family relationships 11. Toronto, Ontario 12. Canada 13. Literary fiction 14. Novels-within-novels

LC 99462109

ALA Notable Book, 2001.

Booker Prize, 2000.

Governor General's Literary Awards, English-language Fiction finalist, 2000.

Shortlisted for the International IMPAC Dublin Literary Award, 2002.

Shortlisted for The Orange Prize for Fiction, 2001.

Iris describes the 1945 death of her sister, who drives her car off a bridge, followed, two years later, by the death of her husband, in a story that features a novel-within-a-novel about two unnamed lovers who meet in a dark backstreet room.

Atwood, Margaret, 1939-

Bluebeard's egg and other stories / Margaret Atwood. Anchor Books, 1983. 244 p.

ISBN 039540424X

1. Family relationships 2. Interpersonal relations 3. Husband and wife 4. Literary fiction 5. Short stories

LC 97-32459

"As Atwood's attitude ranges from the hilarious to the shocking, the reader is introduced to a series of relationships--husband and wife, parent and child, man and woman--in which the characters' inner and outer worlds are beautifully probed, expressed in the author's understated style." Booklist.

Atwood, Margaret, 1939-

* **Cat's** eye / Margaret Atwood. Doubleday, 1989. 446 p.

ISBN 9780385260077

1. Women painters -- Canada 2. Self-discovery in women 3. Female friendship 4. Childhood -- Toronto, Ontario 5. Memories 6. Fathers and daughters 7. Men/women relations 8. Coping in girls 9. Competition in girls 10. Childhood friends 11. Social acceptance 12. Self-acceptance in women 13. Canada 14. Toronto, Ontario 15. Literary fiction 16. Psychological fiction

LC 88024345

ALA Notable Book, 1990.

Toronto Book Awards, 1989.

Shortlisted for the Booker-McConnell Prize, 1989.

Governor General's Literary Awards, English-language Fiction finalist

Years after painter Elaine Risley flees Toronto for Vancouver, she returns to search for long-missing parts of her life and pursue the elusive Cordelia, her best friend and sometimes enemy.

"Atwood's achievement is the decoding of childhood's secrets, and the creation of a flawed and haunting work of art." Time.

Atwood, Margaret, 1939-

* The **handmaid's** tale / Margaret Atwood. Houghton Mifflin, 1986. 311 p. Handmaid's tale

ISBN 9780395404256

1. 21st century 2. Women's role 3. Dystopias 4. Infertility 5. Caste 6. Young women 7. Sexism 8. Theocracy 9. Near future 10. Misogyny 11. Sex discrimination 12. North America 13. Literary fiction 14. Dystopian fiction 15. Science fiction

LC 85021944

Arthur C. Clarke Award, 1987.

Governor General's Literary Award for English-Language Fiction, 1985.

Shortlisted for the Booker-McConnell Prize, 1986.

Offred, a Handmaid, describes life in what was once the United States, now the Republic of Gilead, a shockingly repressive and intolerant monotheocracy, in a satirical tour de force set in the near future.

"A gripping suspense tale, The Handmaid's Tale is an allegory of what results from a politics based on misogyny, racism, and anti-Semitism." Ms.

Atwood, Margaret, 1939-

Life before man / Margaret Atwood. Bantam Books, 1996, c1979. 351 p.

ISBN 0553377825

1. Married people 2. Husband and wife 3. Extramarital affairs 4. Middle-aged women 5. Lovers -- Death 6. Love triangles 7. Men/ women relations 8. Domestic fiction 9. Literary fiction

LC 95032375

Originally published: New York : Simon & Schuster, 1979.

Governor General's Literary Awards, English-language Fiction finalist

"This is a powerful, introspective view of contemporary marriage and the changing roles of the sexes. . . . [This novel] returns to the survival and identity theme of Atwood's early thematic guide to Canadian literature, but at a level that transcends the national. With men and mores rooted in the prehistoric past, Atwood forces us to confront a harrowing present that anticipates an ecologically and culturally doomed future." Choice.

Atwood, Margaret, 1939-

* **Maddaddam** : a novel / Margaret Atwood. Random House Inc., 2013. 352 p. MaddAddam trilogy

ISBN 9780385528788

1. Dystopias 2. New religious movements 3. Religion and science 4. Genetically engineered animals 5. Regression (Civilization) 6. Men/ women relations 7. End of the world 8. Proselytizing 9. Preaching 10. Theology 11. Pacifism 12. Social science fiction 13. Apocalyptic fiction 14. Literary fiction 15. Science fiction

LC 2013018715

Sequel to: The Year of the Flood.

Originally published in Canada by McClelland & Stewart Ltd., Toronto.

Goodreads Choice Award, 2013.

A conclusion to the trilogy finds Toby and Ren returning to the MaddAddamite cob house after rescuing Amanda and assuming the duties of the Craker's religious overseers while Zeb searches for the founder of the pacifist green religion he left years earlier.

Atwood, Margaret, 1939-

Moral disorder / Margaret Atwood. Nan A. Talese, 2006. 240 p.

ISBN 0385503849

1. Women's role 2. Marriage 3. Aging 4. Family relationships 5. Growing up 6. Toronto, Ontario 7. Canada 8. Autobiographical fiction 9. Literary fiction 10. Short stories

LC 2006044589

A collection of short fiction presents eleven stories that capture important moments in the course of a life and in the lives intertwined with it, in a volume that ranges from the 1930s to the 1980s.

"This collection of 11 interconnected short stories opens as a Canadian woman named Nell and her longtime partner, Gilbert (known as Tig), face aging together into an uncertain future. ... The result is alternatively humorous and heart-wrenching, occasionally sardonic and always brutally honest in the depiction of our often contorted relationships with one another, with nature, and with ourselves." Library Journal.

Atwood, Margaret, 1939-

* **Oryx** and Crake / Margaret Eleanor Atwood. Doubleday, 2003. 432 p. MaddAddam trilogy

ISBN 0385503857

1. Ecology 2. Dystopias 3. Environmental degradation 4. Disasters 5. Male friendship 6. Biotechnology 7. Canada 8. Apocalyptic fiction 9. Social science fiction 10. Science fiction 11. Literary fiction

Sequel: The year of the flood.

Governor General's Literary Awards, English-language Fiction finalist, 2003

Shortlisted for the Giller Prize, 2003

Shortlisted for the Man Booker Prize, 2003

Shortlisted for The Orange Prize for Fiction, 2004

A novel of the future explores a world that has been devastated by ecological and scientific disasters.

"Rigorous in its chilling insights and riveting in its fast-paced 'what if' dramatization, Atwood's superb novel is as brillantly provocative as it is profoundly engaging." Booklist.

Atwood, Margaret, 1939-

* **Stone** mattress : nine tales / Margaret Atwood. Nan A. Talese/Doubleday, 2014. 256 p.

ISBN 9780385539128

1. Interpersonal relations 2. Seniors 3. Couples 4. Revenge 5. Literary fiction 6. Short stories

LC 2014013010

Standard print edition originally published: London: Bloomsbury, 2014.

In these nine dazzlingly inventive and rewarding stories, Margaret Atwood's signature dark humour, playfulness, and deadly seriousness are in abundance.

"Most of the nine stories feature women who have been wronged as girls but recover triumphantly as adults. Atwood brings her biting wit to bear on the battle of the sexes." Publishers Weekly.

Atwood, Margaret, 1939-

* The **testaments** : a novel / Margaret Atwood. Nan A. Talese, 2019. 320 p. Handmaid's tale

ISBN 9780385543781

1. 21st century 2. Near future 3. Resistance to government 4. Gender role 5. Political persecution 6. Women -- Interpersonal relations 7. Loss (Psychology) 8. Misogyny 9. Sex discrimination 10. Theocracy

11. North America 12. Literary fiction 13. Dystopian fiction 14. Science fiction

Man Booker Prize, 2019.

Goodreads Choice Award, 2019

In this sequel to The Handmaid's Tale, author Margaret Atwood answers the question that has tantalized readers for decades: What happens to Offred?

"The tone is informative without becoming accusatory; indeed the facts speak clearly on their own." Booklist.

Atwood, Margaret, 1939-

* The **year** of the flood : a novel / Margaret Atwood. Nan A. Talese/Doubleday, 2009. 448 p. MaddAddam trilogy

ISBN 9780385528771

1. Young women 2. End of the world 3. Dystopias 4. Regression (Civilization) 5. Religion and science 6. Environmental disasters 7. Natural disasters 8. Survival (after disaster) 9. Genetically engineered animals 10. Apocalyptic fiction 11. Social science fiction 12. Literary fiction 13. Science fiction

LC 2009005901

Sequel to: Oryx and Crake.

Sequel: MaddAddam.

ALA Notable Book, 2010.

The times and species have been changing at a rapid rate, and the social compact is wearing as thin as environmental stability. Adam One, the kindly leader of the God's Gardeners--a religion devoted to the melding of science and religion, as well as the preservation of all plant and animal life--has long predicted a natural disaster that will alter Earth as we know it. Now it has occurred, obliterating most human life.

"A novel set in the nightmarish future first envisioned in Oryx and Crake. Contrary to expectations, the waterless flood, a biological disaster predicted by a fringe religious group, actually arrives. In its wake, the survivors must rely on their wits to get by, all the while reflecting on what went wrong. Atwood wins major style points here for her framing device, the liturgical year of the God's Gardeners sect." Library Journal.

Auður Ava Ólafsdóttir

Butterflies in November / Auour Ava Olafsdottir ; translated from the Icelandic by Brian FitzGibbon. Black Cat, 2014, c2004. 304 p.

ISBN 9780802123183

1. Thirties (Age) 2. Automobile travel 3. Life change events 4. Self-fulfillment in women 5. Children who are deaf and mute 6. Lottery winners 7. Marital conflict 8. Women translators 9. Four-year-old boys 10. Men/women relations 11. Interpersonal relations 12. Iceland 13. Mainstream fiction 14. Translations -- Icelandic to English

Originally published: Reykjavik : Salka, 2004.

After being dumped and then winning the lottery, a woman in her thirties, along with her best friend's four-year-old deaf-mute son, takes a transformative road trip through Iceland, encountering eccentrics and finding herself.

Auel, Jean M.

* The **clan** of the cave bear : a novel / Jean M. Auel. Crown, 1980. 468 p. Earth's children

ISBN 9780517542026

1. Stone Age 2. Heroes and heroines 3. Prehistoric humans 4. Cave dwellers 5. Ice age (Geology) -- Europe 6. Women -- Europe 7. Europe 8. Historical fiction

LC 80014581

An injured and orphaned infant carries within her the seed and hope of mankind in this epic of survival and destiny set at the dawn of prehistory.

Auslander, Shalom

Hope : a tragedy / Shalom Auslander. Riverhead Books, 2012. 304 p.

ISBN 9781594488382

1. Jewish families 2. Moving, Household 3. Arsonists 4. Mother and adult son 5. Farmhouses 6. Financial crises 7. Holocaust (1933-1945) 8. Satirical fiction

Deliberately relocating his family to an unremarkable rural town in New York in the hopes of starting over, Solomon Kugel finds his efforts challenged by his depressive mother, a local arsonist and the discovery of a believed-dead historical specimen hiding his attic.

Austen, Jane, 1775-1817

* Emma / Jane Austen. Oxford University Press, 2003, c1816. xli, 402 p.

ISBN 9780192802378

1. Young women 2. Villages 3. Matchmakers 4. Mate selection for women 5. Courtship 6. Fathers and daughters 7. England -- Social life and customs -- 19th century 8. Love stories 9. Classics

Emma was the inspiration for the movie Clueless.

Originally published: London : John Murray, 1816.

Emma is young, rich and independent. She has decided not to get married and instead spends her time organising her acquaintances' love affairs. Her plans for the matrimonial success of her new friend Harriet, however, lead her into complications that ultimately test her own detachment from the world of romance.

Austen, Jane, 1775-1817

Mansfield Park / Jane Austen. Knopf, 1992, c1814. xxxvii, 488 p.

ISBN 9780679412694

1. Church of England Clergy 2. 19th century 3. Middle class 4. Families 5. Cousins 6. Sisters 7. Social classes 8. Men/women relations 9. England -- Social life and customs -- 19th century 10. Classics 11. Love stories

First published in 1814.

Includes extra material.

The private and social worlds of three families are revealed through the experiences of the heroine, Fanny Price.

Austen, Jane, 1775-1817

Northanger Abbey / Jane Austen. Modern Library, 2002, c1818. xxvii, 220 p.

ISBN 9780375759178

1. Teenage girls 2. Imagination in teenage girls 3. Mate selection for women 4. Family estates 5. Misunderstanding 6. Clergymen 7. Men/women relations 8. Love triangles 9. Reading -- Psychological aspects 10. England -- Social life and customs -- 18th century 11. Bath, England 12. Classics 13. Satirical fiction 14. Coming-of-age stories

Originally published: London : John Murray, 1818.

When Catherine, a clergyman's daughter, is invited to spend a season in Bath with fashionable high society, little does she imagine the delights and perils that await her. Captivated and disconcerted by what she finds, and introduced to the joys of Gothic novels by her friends, Catherine longs for mystery and romance. When invited to stay with the beguiling Henry Tilney and his family, she expects mystery and intrigue at every turn but the truth turns out to be even stranger than fiction.

Austen, Jane, 1775-1817

* Persuasion / Jane Austen. Knopf, 1992, c1818. xxxvii, 260 p.

ISBN 9780679409861

1. Interclass romance 2. Classism -- 19th century 3. Sisters 4. Men/women relations 5. England -- Social life and customs -- 18th century 6. Love stories 7. Classics

First published posthumously in 1818.

Originally published: London : John Murray, 1818.

The romance between Captain Wentworth and Anne, the daughter of Sir Walter Elliot, seems doomed because of the young man's family connections and lack of wealth.

Austen, Jane, 1775-1817

* Pride and prejudice / Jane Austen. Modern Library, 1995, c1813. 281 p.

ISBN 9780679601685

1. 19th century 2. Sisters 3. Young women 4. Families 5. Mothers and daughters 6. Courtship 7. Marriage 8. Romantic love 9. Men/women relations 10. Aristocracy 11. Social classes 12. England -- Social life and customs -- 19th century 13. Classics 14. Love stories

Originally published: London : T. Egerton, 1813.

Human foibles and early nineteenth-century manners are satirized in this romantic tale of English country family life as Elizabeth Bennet and her four sisters are encouraged to marry well in order to keep the Bennet estate in their family.

Austen, Jane, 1775-1817

* Sense and sensibility / Jane Austen ; edited by James Kinsley ; with an introduction by Margaret Anne Doody ; notes by Claire Lamont. Oxford University Press, 2004, c1811. li, 327 p.

ISBN 9780192804785

1. Young women 2. Sisters 3. Courtship 4. Mate selection 5. Rich families 6. Classism -- 19th century 7. Men/women relations 8. Inheritance and succession 9. Great Britain -- History -- 19th Century 10. England -- Social life and customs -- 19th century 11. Classics 12. Love stories

"Optimized reading formats" -- Cover.

Originally published: London : T. Egerton, 1811.

Two sisters, one practical and conventional and the other emotional and sentimental, set their sights on men who will perfectly match their disparate personalities, with unexpected results.

Auster, Paul, 1947-

4 3 2 1 : a novel / Paul Auster. Henry Holt and Company, 2017. 880 p.

ISBN 9781627794466

1. 20th century 2. Growing up 3. Identity (Psychology) 4. Life change events 5. Jewish men 6. Men -- Psychology 7. Family relationships 8. Men/women relations 9. New Jersey 10. Literary fiction 11. Coming-of-age stories

LC 2016020041

Shortlisted for the Man Booker Prize, 2017.

Longlisted for the Andrew Carnegie Medal for Excellence in Fiction, 2018.

A single child born in 1947 experiences four parallel lifetimes poignantly marked by shifting family fortunes, athletic pursuits, friendships, sex, intellectual passions and the same intriguing woman.

"With this novel, Auster reminds us that not just life, but also narrative is always conditional, that it only appears inevitable after the fact." Kirkus.

Auster, Paul, 1947-

*The **book** of illusions : a novel / Paul Auster. Henry Holt & Co., 2002. 336 p.

ISBN 0805054081

1. Grief in men 2. Film actors and actresses 3. Filmmaking 4. Loss (Psychology) 5. Families of airplane accident victims 6. Missing persons 7. Silent films 8. Biographers 9. Comedians 10. Widowers 11. Senior men 12. Vermont 13. Psychological fiction 14. Literary fiction

LC 2002017218

ALA Notable Book, 2003.

Shortlisted for the International IMPAC Dublin Literary Award, 2004

A Vermont professor, disillusioned with self-pity and grief over his family's death in a plane crash, finds a new purpose when he becomes obsessed with research into the life and art of a silent film comedian who mysteriously disappeared when silent films ended.

"Auster limns Mann's many-layered cinematic and earthly worlds in mesmerizing and voluptuous detail within an artful, poignantly metaphysical, and delectably Hitchcockian tale of mayhem, murder, and myriad illusions within illusions." Booklist.

Auster, Paul, 1947-

The **Brooklyn** follies / Paul Auster. Henry Holt, 2005. 320 p.

ISBN 9780805077148

1. 2000s (Decade) 2. Self-evaluation in men 3. Eccentrics and eccentricities 4. Middle-aged men -- Family relationships 5. Divorced men 6. Forgery 7. Nephews 8. Gay men 9. Former convicts 10. Booksellers 11. Alienation in men 12. Missing women 13. New York City 14. Psychological fiction 15. Literary fiction

LC 2005040201

Retired life insurance salesman Nathan Glass moves to Brooklyn to find anonymity and solitude through his declining years, but a chance meeting with Tom Wood, his long-lost nephew, forces him to come to terms with his past.

"This is a departure for Auster. Instead of tight plotting and theoretical figure work, there is domestic realism. The result is a novel far more passionately American than Auster's previous ones." Times Literary Supplement.

Auster, Paul, 1947-

* **In** the country of last things / Paul Auster. Viking, 1987. 188 p.

ISBN 9780670814459

1. Dystopias 2. Survival 3. Missing persons 4. Death 5. Brothers and sisters 6. Authors 7. Cities and towns 8. Apocalyptic fiction 9. Literary fiction

LC 86040257

Anna Blume, searching for her brother who has disappeared, recounts her wanderings through a modern urban reprise of the Dark Ages where she becomes a member of a scavenger class in search of objects from the past.

"This novel is distinguished by an uncanny grasp of the day-to-day realities of homelessness. This is a scary but highly relevant book." Library Journal.

Auster, Paul, 1947-

Invisible / Paul Auster. Henry Holt and Co., 2009. 320 p.

ISBN 9780805090802

1. 1960s 2. College students 3. Love triangles 4. Poets 5. Campus life 6. Identity (Psychology) 7. Memory 8. New York City 9. Psychological fiction 10. LIterary fiction 11. Coming-of-age stories

12. Second person narratives

LC 2009002237

Poet and student Adam Walker meets the enigmatic Frenchman Rudolf Born and his silent, seductive girlfriend, Margot, sending Adam into a perverse triangle that leads to a shocking act of violence that will alter his life.

"To be blunt, as a writer of sentences, Auster isn't anything special; reading this book after reading Roth or Richard Yates, for example--or, to draw upon a couple of comparisons that are even more unfair, Bellow or Nabokov--one is aware of how neutral and unremarkable, and occasionally even plodding, Auster's prose can be. What Auster is, instead, is a spellbinding storyteller, sometimes thanks to, and other times in spite of, his post-modern narrative trickery. Even more important, he is a writer of high moral seriousness. Indeed, this novel, like some of his others, could best be described as a moral suspense story. As such, it succeeds brilliantly." PopMatters.

Auster, Paul, 1947-

* **Leviathan** / Paul Auster. Viking, 1992. 275 p.

ISBN 9780670846764

1. Anarchists 2. Obsession in men 3. Love triangles 4. Missing persons 5. Vietnam War protesters 6. Bombings 7. Male friendship 8. Betrayal 9. Authors 10. Self-discovery in men 11. Literary fiction

LC 92001282

ALA Notable Book, 1993.

When his closest friend, Benjamin Sachs, accidentally blows himself up on a Wisconsin road, Peter Aaron attempts to piece together the events that led to Ben's tragic demise and determine the reason for his death.

"Mr. Auster may write about coincidence, but there is nothing coincidental about his prose, in which seemingly straightforward information has an allegorical dimension. . . . Thus in the literary looking glass of 'Leviathan,' in which things are not always what they seem, our pleasure in reading the story is enhanced by the challenge of making other connections." New York Times Book Review.

Auster, Paul, 1947-

Oracle night / Paul Auster. H. Holt, 2003. 256 p.

ISBN 9780805073201

1. 1980s 2. Authors 3. Fiction writing 4. Precognition 5. Men who are blind 6. Husband and wife 7. Memories 8. Near-death experience 9. Paranormal phenomena 10. World War II 11. Brooklyn, New York City 12. Psychological fiction 13. Literary fiction 14. Novels-within-novels 15. Noir fiction

LC 2003051063

Recovering from a near-fatal illness, Sidney Orr, a thirty-four-year-old novelist, purchases a mysterious blue notebook from a Brooklyn stationery shop and is drawn into a bizarre world of eerie premonitions and baffling events.

"A novelist writing about a novelist writing about an editor reading a novel: these Russian dolls might come across as merely cute, were it not for the fact that the lucid Mr Auster is a natural storyteller, with a seemingly inexhaustible trove of yarns at his disposal. All of the stories within stories are compelling in their own right." The Economist.

Auster, Paul, 1947-

Sunset Park / Paul Auster. Henry Holt and Co., 2010. 320 p.

ISBN 9780805092868

1. Young adults 2. Fugitives 3. Squatters 4. Intergenerational relations 5. Guilt in men 6. Brooklyn, New York City 7. Sunset Park (New York, NY) 8. Literary fiction

LC 2009045726

"A Frances Coady book."

After falling in love with an underage girl and stirring the wrath of her older sister, New York native Miles Heller flees to Brooklyn and shacks up with a group of artists squatting in the borough's Sunset Park neighborhood.

"The novel is graphically sexual and, more surprisingly, insistently phallic. This is a little bewildering until, as the novel progresses, one comes to accept that, for Auster's characters, the body-- in its fragility and strength-- is one of the only certainties in a time of increasing darkness. In a way, Sunset Park is Auster's most Whitmanesque novel and it's very entertaining." Globe and Mail (Toronto).

Auster, Paul, 1947-

Timbuktu : a novel / Paul Auster. H. Holt, 1999. 181 p.
ISBN 9780805054071
1. Men with mental illnesses 2. Dogs 3. Human/animal relationships 4. Men and dogs 5. Poets 6. Loss (Psychology) 7. Transformations, Personal 8. Death 9. Teacher-student relationships 10. Stories told by animals 11. Picaresque fiction 12. Literary fiction
LC 9846742
Mr. Bones, the canine sidekick of Willy G. Christmas, a brilliant but troubled Brooklyn poet, accompanies his master on a trip to Baltimore, Maryland, to search for Willy's high school teacher and beloved mentor, Bea Swanson, in a novel narrated from the dog's point of view.

"Auster handles the language better than almost anyone else writing today, . . . the first chapter of Timbuktu is one of the finest and most polished to have appeared in any recent novel." The National Review.

Auster, Paul, 1947-

*****Travels** in the scriptorium : a novel / Paul Auster. H. Holt, 2007, c2006. 160 p.
ISBN 0805081453
1. Criminals 2. People with amnesia 3. Memories 4. Senior men 5. Identity (Psychology) 6. Manuscripts 7. Cameras 8. Photographs 9. Fate and fatalism 10. Metaphysics 11. Observation (Psychology) 12. Literary fiction
LC 2005055038
Originally published under the same title: London, England : Faber and Faber, 2006.

An elderly man awakens disoriented in an unfamiliar room, with no memory of who he is or how he got there, and receives visits from a series of people who give him frustrating hints about his identity and his past.

"One of Blank's visitors, an ex-policeman named Flood, exudes an economical malevolence: instead of two shakes of a cat's tail, he speaks of two shakes of a cat. When challenged, he responds, with imperturbably menacing politeness: Just an expression, Mr Blank. No harm intended. But harm intended, this novel wants to say, is not the only kind of harm. . . . Auster sets [the] lyricism of the mundane against an increasingly oppressive atmosphere in which ghosts might come alive from books." New Statesman.

Austin, Lynn N.

All **she** ever wanted / Lynn Austin. Bethany House, 2005. 400 p.
ISBN 9780764228896
1. Alienation in families 2. Forgiveness (Christianity) 3. Family problems 4. Mothers and daughters 5. Women -- Interpersonal relations 6. Family secrets 7. Family relationships 8. Faith (Christianity) 9. Christian fiction 10. Women's lives and relationships
LC 2005018574
The emotion-packed story of three generations of women: Kathleen, her mother, Eleanor, and her grandmother, Fiona. Each woman left

home to escape her family's past and to start a new life. Kathleen has been estranged from her family for 35 years, and she is torn between the need to forgive and the urge to forget. Hoping to find answers that will patch the wounds of her tattered heart and salvage her relationship with her daughter, Kathleen embarks on a journey into her family's mysterious past.

Ausubel, Ramona

Sons and daughters of ease and plenty / Ramona Ausubel. Riverhead Books, 2016. 320 p.
ISBN 9781594634888
1. 1970s 2. 1960s 3. Rich families 4. Life change events 5. Parent-separated children 6. Extramarital affairs 7. Husband and wife 8. Leisure class 9. Bankruptcy 10. Families 11. Coping 12. Martha's Vineyard, Massachusetts 13. Domestic fiction
LC 2016002763
From the award-winning author of No One Is Here Except All of Us, an imaginative novel about a wealthy New England family in the 1960s and '70s that suddenly loses its fortune--and its bearings. Labor Day, 1976, Martha's Vineyard. Summering at the family beach house along this moneyed coast of New England, Fern and Edgar--married with three children--are happily preparing for a family birthday celebration when they learn that the unimaginable has occurred: There is no more money. More specifically, there's no more money in the estate of Fern's recently deceased parents, which, as the sole source of Fern and Edgar's income, had allowed them to live this beautiful, comfortable life despite their professed anti-money ideals. Quickly, the once-charmed family unravels. In distress and confusion, Fern and Edgar are each tempted away on separate adventures: she on a road trip with a stranger, he on an ill-advised sailing voyage with another woman. The three children are left for days with no guardian whatsoever, in an improvised Neverland helmed by the tender, witty, and resourceful Cricket, age nine. Brimming with humanity and wisdom, humor and bite, and imbued with both the whimsical and the profound, Sons and Daughters of Ease and Plenty is a story of American wealth, class, family, and mobility, approached by award-winner Ramona Ausubel with a breadth of imagination and understanding that is fresh, surprising, and exciting Provided by publisher.

Avery, Ellis

The **last** nude / Ellis Avery. Riverhead Books, 2012. 320 p.
ISBN 9781594488139
1. Lempicka, Tamara de, 1898-1980 2. 1920s 3. Women painters 4. Lesbians 5. Artists' models 6. Women and success 7. Interpersonal relations 8. Art -- Exhibitions 9. Young women 10. Americans in Paris, France 11. Desire 12. Paris, France 13. Historical fiction
LC 2011027708
Stonewall Book Award for the Barbara Gittings Literature Award, 2013.
Agreeing to model nude for Art Deco painter Tamara de Lempicka in 1927 Paris, young American Rafaela Fano inspires the artist's most iconic Jazz Age images and becomes her lover while discovering darker truths about Tamara's private life.

Avon, Joy

In peppermint peril : a Book Tea Shop mystery / Joy Avon. Crooked Lane Books, 2018. 304 p. Book Tea Shop novel
ISBN 9781683317937
1. Books and reading 2. Tea 3. Dogs as pets 4. Christmas 5. Boston terriers 6. Wills 7. Heirlooms 8. Small town life 9. Small towns 10. Women amateur detectives 11. Murder investigation 12. Maine 13. Cozy mysteries 14. Holiday mysteries

In the run-up to Christmas Eve, organizer of book-themed tea parties Callie Aspen and her lovable Boston terrier will have to conquer threefold trouble a mysterious will, a missing heirloom and a dead body to restore the festive spirit to their small town.

Aw, Tash

We, the survivors / Tash Aw. Farrar, Straus and Giroux, 2019. 336 p.

ISBN 9780374287245

1. Confession (Law) 2. Murderers 3. Social classes 4. Social change 5. Migrant workers 6. Crimes against immigrants 7. Malaysia 8. Political fiction 9. Literary fiction

A man from a Malaysian fishing village who has completed a sentence for murder and a privileged young journalist whose life has taken an unexpected turn confront the systems of power, race and class that drove the former into violence.

Awad, Mona

* **13** ways of looking at a fat girl / Mona Awad. Penguin Books, 2016. 240 p.

ISBN 9780143128489

1. Female friendship 2. Body image 3. Self-esteem in women 4. Interpersonal relations 5. Dieting 6. Weight control 7. Overweight girls 8. Family relationships 9. Husband and wife 10. Women's lives and relationships

Books in Canada First Novel Award, 2015.

Shortlisted for the Giller Prize, 2016

Follows Lizzie, a young woman growing up in Mississauga, as she fights her way from fat to thin, but who still, even as a married adult woman, sees herself as a fat girl.

"Lizzie's particular sadness is unsettlingly sharp: she gets under your skin, and she stays there. Beautifully constructed; a devastating novel but also a deeply empathetic one." Kirkus.

Awad, Mona

Bunny / Mona Awad. Viking, 2019. 320 p.

ISBN 9780525559733

1. Women graduate students 2. Rites and ceremonies 3. Female friendship 4. Loneliness 5. Belonging 6. Writing 7. Creativity in women 8. Women authors 9. Clubs 10. Universities and colleges 11. Interpersonal relations 12. New England 13. Black humor

LC 2018045360

Invited to join a popular clique at her university, a misfit artist with a dark imagination is drawn into ritualistic activities that transform her perspectives on reality.

Ayatsuji, Yukito, 1960-

The **Decagon** House murders / Yukito Ayatsuji ; translated from the Japanese by Ho-Ling Wong. Locked Room International, 2015, c1987. 228 p.

ISBN 9781508503736

1. College students 2. Murder investigation 3. Student organizations 4. Japan 5. Mysteries 6. Translations -- Japanese to English

Originally published in Japanese by Kodansha, Ltd, Tokyo, in 1987.

"First published in 1987, Ayatsuji's brilliant and richly atmospheric puzzle will appeal to fans of golden age whodunits." Publishers Weekly.

Azzopardi, Trezza

Winterton blue / Trezza Azzopardi. Grove Press, 2007. 288 p.

ISBN 0802118410

1. Middle-aged men 2. Loss (Psychology) 3. Quests 4. Mother and adult daughter 5. Family relationships 6. Men/women relations 7. Love 8. Trust 9. Norfolk, England 10. Romantic suspense

LC 2006049239

Haunted by his brother's death twenty years earlier, tormented Lewis finds solace in a new relationship with Anna, a woman whose memories about her subdued late father prevent her from supporting her septuagenarian mother's daredevil lifestyle.

"Azzopardi portrays with extraordinary empathy characters whose grief and alienation overwhelm their sanity. . . . It was a gamble to isolate her brooding characters to emphasize their feelings of apartness, a limiting approach rectified by the mesmerizing novel's strong undercurrent of suspense." Booklist.

B

Babson, Marian

The **company** of cats / Marian Babson. St. Martin's Press, 1999. 183 p.

ISBN 0312199244

1. Cats 2. Rich men 3. Inheritance and succession 4. Gossiping and gossips 5. Family secrets 6. Interior decorators 7. London, England 8. Cozy mysteries

LC 98-52967

Also published as: The multiple cat.

Gossip-monger Annabel Hinchby-Smythe, mistaken by billionaire Arthur Arbuthnot for his interior decorator, uses his mistake to get inside information about Arthur's extremely odd world, information that proves useful when Arthur is murdered and Annabel and Sally, Arthur's rescued cat, investigate.

"Readers who love cats will enjoy the Annabel/Sally relationship." Booklist.

Baca, Jimmy Santiago, 1952-

The **importance** of a piece of paper / Jimmy Santiago Baca. Grove Press, 2004. 225 p.

ISBN 0802117651

1. Mexican Americans -- Southwest (United States) 2. Mexican American families 3. Poor people 4. American dream 5. Men/women relations 6. Husband and wife 7. Breaking up (Interpersonal relations) 8. Family relationships 9. Brothers and sisters 10. Farmers 11. Inheritance and succession 12. Betrayal 13. Southwest (United States) 14. Short stories 15. Literary fiction

LC 2003057089

In a collection of short stories, a pair of siblings confront a betraying brother and place their community in jeopardy, a long-suffering mother's efforts to reunite her offspring has tragic consequences, and a young orphan cares for a boy whose circumstances are worse than his own.

"The rural Southwest landscape of Baca's short stories is inhabited by outsiders: drug addicts and convicts, absentee mothers and runaways. Baca's first collection of fiction . . . paints a picture of Chicano life that is at once cruel and sweetly redemptive." Publishers Weekly.

Bacigalupi, Paolo

* The **water** knife / Paolo Bacigalupi. Alfred A. Knopf, 2015. 384 p.

ISBN 9780385352871

1. Near future 2. Power (Social sciences) 3. Droughts 4. Water 5. Rivers 6. Assassins 7. Cities and towns 8. Social classes 9. Violence 10. Southwest (United States) 11. Phoenix, Arizona 12. Colorado River 13. Dystopian fiction 14. Science fiction

RUSA Reading List Short List, 2016.

Working as an enforcer for a corrupt developer, Angel Velasquez teams up with a hardened journalist and a street-smart Texan to investigate rumors of California's imminent monopoly on limited water supplies.

"The way the novel's environmental nightmare affects society, as individuals and larger entities--both official and criminal--vie for a limited and essential resource, feels solid, plausible, and disturbingly believable." Kirkus.

Bacigalupi, Paolo

* The **windup** girl / Paolo Bacigalupi. Night Shade, 2009. 359 p.
> ISBN 9781597801577
> 1. Genetically engineered women 2. Biological terrorism 3. Civil war 4. Corporations 5. Agribusiness 6. Terrorism 7. Dystopias 8. Post-apocalypse 9. Posthumanism 10. Bangkok, Thailand 11. Dystopian fiction 12. Science fiction
>
> LC oc2009038816
> Hugo Award for Best Novel, 2010.
> John W. Campbell Memorial Award for Best Science Fiction Novel, 2010.
> Locus Award for First Novel, 2010.
> Nebula Award for Best Novel, 2009.
> RUSA Reading List, 2010.

Living in a future where food is scarce, Anderson Lake tries to find ways to exploit this need, as he comes into conflict with Jaidee, an official of the Environmental Ministry, and encounters Emiko, a engineered windup girl who has been discarded by her creator.

"One of the strengths of The Windup Girl, other than its intriguing characters, is Bacigalupi's world building. You can practically taste this future Thailand he's built." io9.

Backman, Fredrik, 1981-

Britt-Marie was here / Fredrik Backman. Pocket Books, 2016, c2014. 384 p.
> ISBN 9781501142536
> 1. Senior women 2. Small town life 3. Self-discovery in women 4. Mentors 5. Poor people 6. Personality change 7. Self-fulfillment in women 8. Children and senior women 9. Passive-aggressive personality 10. Mainstream fiction 11. Translations -- Swedish to English
> Translated from the Swedish Britt-Marie var har, originally published in 2014.

Walking away from her loveless marriage and taking a job in a derelict, financially devastated town, sixty-three-year-old Britt-Marie uses her fierce organizational skills to become a local soccer coach to a group of lost children.

Backman, Fredrik, 1981-

* **Beartown** : a novel / Fredrik Backman ; translated from the Swedish by Neil Smith. Atria Books, 2017. 336 p. Beartown
> ISBN 9781501160769
> 1. Communities 2. Scandals 3. Sports teams 4. Hockey 5. Sports 6. Small towns 7. Small town life 8. Teenagers 9. Sweden 10. Mainstream fiction 11. Translations -- Swedish to English
>
> LC 2017000377
> Originally published in Swedish in 2016 as Bjornstad. Published in the UK as The Scandal by Michael Joseph, 2017.

In the tiny forest community of Beartown, the possibility that the amateur hockey team might win a junior championship, bringing the hope of revitalization to the fading town, is shattered by the aftermath of a violent act that leaves a young girl traumatized.

"The sentimentally savvy Backman...takes a sobering and solemn look at the ways alienation and acceptance, ethics and emotions nearly destroy a small town." Booklist.

Backman, Fredrik, 1981-

A **man** called Ove / Fredrik Backman ; translation from the Swedish by Henning Koch. Atria Books, 2014, c2012. 352 p.
> ISBN 9781476738017
> 1. Senior men 2. Neighbors 3. Communities 4. Grouches 5. Suicidal behavior 6. Widowers 7. Loss (Psychology) 8. Interpersonal relations 9. Seniors 10. Aging 11. Mainstream fiction 12. Translations -- Swedish to English
> Translation from the Swedish of: En man som heter Ove.
> Originally published: Stockholm : Forum, 2012.

A curmudgeon hides beneath a cranky and short-tempered exterior a terrible personal loss while clashing with new neighbors, a boisterous family whose chattiness and habits lead to unexpected friendship.

Backman, Fredrik, 1981-

* **My** grandmother asked me to tell you she's sorry : a novel / Fredrik Backman ; translated from the Swedish by Henning Koch. Atria Books, 2015. 352 p.
> ISBN 9781501115066
> 1. Seven-year-old girls 2. Grandparent and child 3. Grandmothers -- Death 4. Eccentrics and eccentricities 5. Fairy tales 6. Life change events 7. Letters 8. Individuality 9. Storytelling 10. Neighbors 11. Girls 12. Sweden 13. Mainstream fiction 14. Translations -- Swedish to English
>
> LC 2015000829
> Originally published as: Min mormor halsar och sager forlat. Stockholm : Manpocket, 2013.

Seven-year-old Elsa's grandmother dies and leaves behind a series of letters, sending the girl on a journey that brings to life the world of her grandmother's fairy tales.

"A delectable homage to the power of stories to comfort and heal, Backman's tender tale of the touching relationship between a grandmother and granddaughter is a tribute to the everlasting bonds of deep family ties." Booklist.

Backman, Fredrik, 1981-

Us against you : a novel / Fredrik Backman ; translated by Neil Smith. Atria Books, 2018, c2017. 336 p. Beartown
> ISBN 9781501160790
> 1. Hockey 2. Sports rivalry 3. Small town life 4. Sports 5. Teenagers 6. Small towns 7. Sports teams 8. Consequences 9. Sweden 10. Mainstream fiction 11. Translations -- Swedish to English
> Originally published in 2017 by Bokforlaget Forum.

When the small community of Beartown learns their amateur ice hockey team may be disbanded, the tensions mount, but a surprising new coach offers a chance at a comeback.

Bacon, Charlotte, 1965-

There **is** room for you / Charlotte Bacon. Farrar, Straus and Giroux, 2004. 256 p.
> ISBN 0374281858
> 1. 1990s 2. Mothers and daughters 3. Divorced women 4. Women travelers 5. Americans in India 6. British in India 7. Nannies 8. Loss (Psychology) 9. Fathers -- Death 10. Diaries 11. Memories 12. Childhood 13. New York City 14. India -- Social life and customs -- 20th century 15. Psychological fiction 16. Domestic fiction
>
> LC 2003059579

"Rose's memories bring to Bacon's novel an intensity that Anna's travel-writing persona only sporadically achieves. As she uncovers

Rose's past and stumbles upon its best-kept secrets, Anna's pronouncements on her American life and Indian experience gain coherence." Washington Post.

Bagshawe, Tilly

* Adored / Tilly Bagshawe. Warner Books, 2005. 560 p.

ISBN 0446576883

1. Film actors and actresses 2. Film industry and trade 3. Sexuality 4. Actors and actresses 5. Celebrities 6. Actors and actresses 7. Grandfathers 8. Fashion models 9. Film producers and directors 10. Generation gap 11. Ambition in women 12. Men/women relations 13. Fame 14. Betrayal 15. Family relationships 16. Hollywood, California 17. England 18. Glitz and glamour novels

LC 2004017366

Possessing a magnetic sexuality and a driving ambition to be her generation's most successful actress and model, Siena McMahon embarks on a series of affairs with the wrong men and continues the legacy of her powerful family.

Bahr, Howard, 1946-

The **Judas** Field : a novel of the Civil War / Howard Bahr. H. Holt., 2006. 292 p.

ISBN 0805067396

1. American Civil War era (1861-1865) 2. 1880s 3. Union soldiers 4. People with cancer 5. Cancer 6. Voyages and travels 7. Female friendship 8. Memories 9. Civil War veterans 10. Men/women relations 11. Civil war 12. United States Civil War, 1861-1865 13. United States -- History -- Civil War, 1861-1865 -- Battlefields 14. United States -- History -- Civil War, 1861-1865 15. Southern States 16. Tennessee -- History -- 19th century 17. Historical fiction 18. War stories

LC 2005055011

Michael Shaara Prize for Excellence in Civil War Fiction, 2007

It's been twenty years since Cass Wakefield returned from the Civil War to his hometown in Mississippi, but he is still haunted by battlefield memories. Now he is presented with a chance to literally retrace his steps from the past, as his dying friend Alison urges him to accompany her on a trip to Franklin, Tennessee, to recover the bodies of her father and brother. As they make their way north over the battlefields, they are joined by two of Cass's former brothers-in-arms, and his memories reemerge with overwhelming vividness. Before long the group has assembled on the haunted ground of Franklin, where past and present--the legacy of the war and the narrow hope of redemption--will draw each of them toward a painful confrontation. Moving between harrowing scenes of battle and the novel's present-day quest, author Bahr recreates this era with devastating authority.--From publisher description.

"The author recreates this seminal moment in American history with prose that is vivid, unflinching and often incantatory. The book's pace and detail are wrenching, and it is starkly devoid of romanticism. Within the battlefield scenes, Bahr's accomplishment is magnificent: a fully realized depiction of controlled mass butchery on a field of blood, body parts and utterly obliterated human beings. The reader puts down the book with a sense of shock to find he is not actually inside a level of hell." Washington Post Book World.

Bail, Murray, 1941-

Eucalyptus : a novel / Murray Bail. Farrar, Straus, and Giroux, 1998. 255 p.

ISBN 9780374148577

1. Fathers and daughters -- New South Wales, Australia 2. Courtship 3. Storytellers -- Australia 4. Eucalyptus 5. New South Wales 6. Australia 7. Love stories 8. Magical realism 9. Literary fiction

LC 98-5880

Australian Literature Society Gold Medal, 1999.
Miles Franklin Award, 1999.

A farmer announces that his daughter may only wed the man who can correctly name the species of each and every eucalyptus tree on his property, a decision that is complicated when Ellen chances upon a mysterious young man.

"The novel's categorizations and mysteries become a playful inquiry into the nature of storytelling, with an unpredictable conclusion." The New Yorker.

Bailey, Martine

An **appetite** for violets : a novel / Martine Bailey. Thomas Dunne Books/St. Martin's Press, 2015. 400 p.

ISBN 9781250056917

1. 18th century 2. Cooks 3. Upper class 4. Men/women relations 5. Murder investigation 6. British in Italy 7. Deception 8. Recipes 9. Intrigue 10. Murder 11. England -- Social life and customs -- 18th century 12. Italy -- Social life and customs -- 18th century 13. Historical mysteries 14. Culinary mysteries

LC 2014032365

In 1772, wealthy Sir Geoffrey suddenly marries Lady Carinna, a mysterious woman four decades younger. Would-be tavern keeper Biddy Leigh, a 22-year-old under-cook, finds herself part of a small group accompanying her new mistress on a trip across England, Paris, and Italy. Biddy studies the foreign cuisines as well as her mistress, and suspects that murder is on the menu. A richly detailed debut, which includes authentic 18th-century European recipes, serves up an eclectic mixture of historical novel, Gothic mystery, and culinary adventure along with helpings of romance and melodrama. -- Description by Dawn Towery.

"Though the novel seems to have too many ingredients, everything is kneaded together at the end. This is a delectable dish that will appeal to readers with a taste for historical mysteries as well as fiction about food." Booklist.

Bailey, Paul, 1937-

Chapman's odyssey / Paul Bailey. Bloomsbury USA, 2012. 211 p.

ISBN 9781608198214

1. Hospital patients 2. Characters and characteristics in literature 3. Men with terminal illnesses 4. Dreams 5. Conversation 6. Psychological fiction

LC 2011029642

Enduring a hallucinatory, heavily medicated existence while recovering in the hospital, Harry Chapman imagines he sees famous real and fictional characters intermingling with people from his own life while his story gradually unfolds.

"Readers who have a passion for literature, poetry, and well-rendered characterization will find themselves happily drawn into the world of Harry Chapman." Library Journal.

Bailey, Paul, 1937-

Uncle Rudolf / Paul Bailey. St. Martin's Press, 2004. 192 p.

ISBN 9780312318345

1. 20th century 2. Romanians in foreign countries 3. Parent-separated boys 4. Jewish boys 5. Exiles 6. Jews, Romanian 7. Jewish men 8. Senior men 9. Tenors (Singers) 10. Men opera singers 11. Opera singers 12. Singers 13. Uncles 14. Guardian and ward 15. Uncle and nephew 16. Reminiscing in old age 17. Childhood 18. Love 19. Failure (Psychology) 20. Obsession in men 21. London, England 22. Europe -- History -- 1939-1945 23. Psychological fiction

LC 2003058773

A septuagenarian reflects on his childhood relationship with his eccentric but talented tenor uncle, who took him in and humorously educated him in the ways of a gentleman after fleeing fascist Romania.

"The tale of a young boy's escape from fascist Romania in the late 1930s to England. Now 70, Andrew is writing his memoirs about life in his adopted country with Uncle Rudolf, an internationally acclaimed operetta tenor. This contemplative, retrospective focus heightens the emotional weight of the events he recounts and gives power to this novel of exile and loss. Andrew had spent years wondering about his parents until he learns that his mother was murdered by fascist thugs and that his father committed suicide soon after. He struggles his whole life with guilt about having left them for a life of luxury with his generous, outrageous, internationally beloved uncle. Bailey explores these emotions with considerable skill and sympathy and brings the historical milieu convincingly to life." Library Journal.

Bailey, Tessa

Fix her up / Tessa Bailey. Avon Books, 2019. 384 p.
ISBN 9780062872838
1. Clowns 2. Former professional athletes 3. Transformations, Personal 4. Sexual attraction 5. Men/women relations 6. New York State 7. Contemporary romances 8. Romantic comedies

When her best friend's sister, Georgie, proposes a wild scheme that they pretend to date to shock her family and help him land a new job, for major league baseball player Travis Ford agrees and soon finds himself wanting to make their fake relationship real.

Bainbridge, Beryl, 1932-2010

Every man for himself / Beryl Bainbridge. Carroll & Graf, 1996. 224 p.
ISBN 9780786703494
1. Titanic (Steamship) 2. 1910s 3. Social classes 4. Young men 5. Rich people 6. Shipwrecks -- History -- 20th century 7. Historical fiction 8. Coming-of-age stories

LC 96-32518
Whitbread Book Award for Novel, 1996.
Shortlisted for the Booker-McConnell Prize, 1996.

Recapturing the four crucial days prior to the sinking of the Titanic and the loss of fifteen hundred lives, this story is told from the perspective of Morgan, the American nephew of the owner of the shipping line, and reveals how his destiny is linked to other passengers.

"Bainbridge hits a tremendous pace as her story reaches its climax. In a remarkably concise book, shot through with laconic wit, she establishes complex characters who engage first the reader's curiosity, then affection. The elegiac theme extends far beyond the historical event." New Statesman.

Baker, Chandler

Whisper network : a novel / Chandler Baker. Flatiron Books, 2019. 352 p.
ISBN 9781250319470
1. Sexual harassment 2. Women employees 3. Corporate culture 4. Women lawyers 5. Supervisors 6. Sexism in employment 7. Me Too Movement 8. Secrets 9. Dallas, Texas 10. Thrillers and suspense

LC 2019009104
An adult debut by the author of the High School Horror series follows four women who speak out when their ill-reputed boss is slated to become CEO, a decision that triggers catastrophic shifts throughout every department of their company.

Baker, Dorothy, 1907-1968

* **Young** man with a horn / Dorothy Baker. New York Review of Books, 2012, c1938. 185 p.
ISBN 9781590175774
1. 1920s 2. Self-destructive behavior 3. Jazz musicians 4. Jazz trumpeters 5. Trumpeters 6. Music 7. Gifted men 8. Ambition in men 9. Alcoholic men 10. Young men -- Death 11. United States -- History -- 1919-1933 12. Psychological fiction

Rick Martin loved music and the music loved him. He could pick up a tune so quickly that it didn't matter to the Cotton Club boss that he was underage, or to the guys in the band that he was just a white kid. He started out in the slums of LA with nothing, and he ended up on top of the game in the speakeasies and nightclubs of New York. But while talent and drive are all you need to make it in music, they aren't enough to make it through a life.

Baker, Ellen, 1975-

Keeping the house : a novel / Ellen Baker. Random House, 2007. 544 p.
ISBN 1400066352
1. Rural families 2. Loss (Psychology) 3. Conflict in families 4. Husband and wife 5. Homemakers 6. Men/women relations 7. Marriage 8. Houses 9. Infertility 10. Love 11. Family relationships 12. Wisconsin 13. Family sagas 14. Parallel narratives

LC 2007008236
Lonely, restless, and bored with her life as a housewife in 1950s Pine Rapids, Wisconsin, Dolly Magnuson becomes fascinated by the abandoned grand old house on the hill overlooking the town and sets out to unravel the dark secrets of the family that had once owned it.

"Brimming with luscious details that authenticate the story's various time periods, from early to midtwentieth century, Baker's accomplished, ambitious debut novel is a majestic, vibrant multigenerational saga in the finest tradition of the genre." Booklist.

Baker, Jo

The **body** lies / Jo Baker. Alfred A. Knopf, 2019. 256 p.
ISBN 9780525656111
1. Violence against women 2. Women authors 3. Rural life 4. Universities and colleges 5. Creative writing 6. Married women 7. Psychic trauma 8. Victims of violent crimes 9. England 10. Psychological suspense

LC 2018050099
"This is a Borzoi book."
Moving to an English countryside university after witnessing an assault in London, a young writer supervises an escalating debate about violence against women before one of her male students writes a novel about her horrific murder.

Baker, Jo

* **Longbourn** / Jo Baker. Alfred A. Knopf, 2013. 331 p.
ISBN 9780385351232
1. Regency period (1811-1820) 2. Families 3. Household employees 4. Social classes 5. Intrigue 6. Balls (parties) 7. Housekeepers 8. Working class 9. Family estates 10. Rural life 11. Interpersonal attraction 12. Great Britain -- Social life and customs -- 19th century 13. Great Britain -- History -- Regency, 1811-1820 14. Historical fiction 15. Adaptations, retellings, and spin-offs

LC 2013016430
"Originally published in Great Britain by Transworld, an imprint of the Random House Group Ltd., London."
A reimagining of Jane Austen's "Pride and Prejudice" from the perspectives of its below-stairs servants captures the drama of the Bennet household from the sideline viewpoint of Sarah, an orphaned housemaid.

"British author Baker's second novel after her much lauded The Undertow is densely plotted and achingly romantic. This exquisitely reimagined Pride and Prejudice will appeal to Austen devotees and to anyone who finds the goings-on below the stairs to be at least as compelling as the ones above." Library Journal.

Baker, Jo

The **undertow** / Jo Baker. Knopf, 2012. 336 p.
ISBN 9780307957092
1. Families -- Great Britain 2. Family and war 3. Family secrets 4. Interpersonal relations 5. Family relationships -- Great Britain 6. Great Britain -- Social life and customs -- 20th century 7. Family sagas

LC 2012002079

"Originally published in Great Britain as The Picture Book by Portobello Books, London, in 2011"--T.p. verso.

A multigenerational saga follows the experiences of four family members, including a young factory worker who leaves to fight in World War I and his champion cyclist son, who makes important military contributions on D-Day.

Baker, Kage

The **bird** of the river / Kage Baker. Tor books, 2010. 304 p.
ISBN 9780765322968
1. Teenagers 2. Boats 3. Supernatural 4. Assassins 5. Rivers 6. Quests 7. Pirates 8. Mothers -- Death 9. Fantasy fiction
Set in the world of "The Anvil of the World" and "The House of the Stag."

Sharp-eyed orphan Eliss and her half-brother make a new home on a river barge and clash with a teen assassin amid an escalating series of pirate attacks on riverside cities.

"A vivid setting . . . with minimal fantasy elements, agreeably complemented by solid plotting, mysteries, surprises and characters that grow in the telling. A sparkling farewell from a writer whose illustrious career proved all too brief." Kirkus.

Baker, Kage

The **house** of the stag / Kage Baker. Tor, 2008. 384 p.
ISBN 9780765317452
1. Fate and fatalism 2. Rebels 3. Revenge 4. Wizards 5. Good and evil 6. Magic 7. Resentfulness in men 8. Redemption 9. Fathers 10. Violence 11. Men/women relations 12. Demons 13. Infants 14. Fantasy fiction 15. Coming-of-age stories
Before the Riders came to their remote valley, the Yendri led a tranquil pastoral life. Gard, taken as a slave by powerful mages, has found subtle ways to earn his freedom, and becomes lord and commander of a demon army.

"Baker's fantasy is completely different from her science fiction, but it's just as good. Gently humorous and ironic, Gard is a character readers will pull for as he moves from foundling to outcast to slave to ruler. Baker's worldbuilding is consistently topnotch, and the various supporting characters are just as well drawn as her antihero." Romantic Times.

Baker, Kage

In the garden of Iden : a novel of the Company / Kage Baker. Harcourt, Brace, 1997. 329 p. The Company
ISBN 0151002991
1. 16th century 2. 24th century 3. Time travel (Past) 4. Plants 5. Rare and endangered plants 6. Immortality 7. Women botanists 8. Hypocrisy 9. Xenophobia 10. Dr Zeus Incorporated (Imaginary organization) 11. Eighteen-year-old women 12. Cyborgs 13. Cancer -- Treatment 14. Cancer research 15. Impersonation 16. Inquisition

-- Spain 17. Men/women relations 18. England -- Civilization -- 16th century 19. Science fiction

LC 97-23284

Trained by the Company as a botanist and rendered immortal, Mendoza is sent back amidst the turmoil of Renaissance England with the assignment to safeguard a species of holly that contains properties to cure cancer for future generations.

"Baker's story comments powerfully on religious hypocrisy and xenophobia." Library Journal.

Baker, Nicholson, 1957-

House of holes : a book of raunch / Nicholson Baker. Simon & Schuster, 2011. 288 p.
ISBN 9781439189511
1. Sexuality 2. Resorts 3. Hedonism 4. Desire 5. Sexual fantasies 6. Erotic fiction

LC 2010047433

Presents an explicit new tale of carnal improprieties and comic raunchiness set in a surreal but familiar world of fantasy sex.

"It's a bit repetitive, for sure, and the characters are hard to tell apart, which doesn't really matter, as there is no unifying plot. They are interchangeable bodies, reflecting the theme of mutability in their own stories." Globe and Mail (Toronto)

Baker, Tiffany

The **little** giant of Aberdeen County / Tiffany Baker. Grand Central Pub., 2009. 352 p.
ISBN 9780446194204
1. Tall women 2. Small town life 3. Sisters 4. Family relationships 5. Healing 6. Interpersonal relations 7. Misfits (Persons) 8. Loneliness 9. Eccentrics and eccentricities 10. Mainstream fiction

LC 2008000774

Since her birth, Truly has endured constant embarrassment for her large size. Her sister Serena has always been a timeless beauty. But beauty comes with a price when Serena finds herself mixed up with the wrong guy. When Serena Jane leaves town, Truly is left to care for her nephew, and her life leads her into some unexpected places.

"Baker enters Alice Hoffman territory in this parable about beauty and ugliness, meanness and mercy and magic, and does it with considerable dark humor." Hartford Courant

Bakker, Robert T.

Raptor red / Robert T. Bakker. Bantam Books, 1995. 246 p.
ISBN 0553101242
1. Survival 2. Animal migration 3. Voyages and travels 4. Dinosaurs 5. Utahraptor 6. Paleontology -- Cretaceous 7. Paleontology -- Mesozoic 8. Stories told by animals

LC 95017907

After her mate is killed in an attack on a brontosaurus, a female raptor embarks on a perilous year-long odyssey as she copes with a flash flood, migrates to the ocean, finds a new mate, and produces a family of chicks, in a novel set against the exotic prehistoric background of the early Cretaceous

"Even lacking much polish as a stylist, Mr. Bakker very nearly succeeds in bringing off the illusion that we are seeing the world as Raptor Red might have, an ambitious feat for any writer and one that is undeniably very satisfying to the adolescent dino-fan in all of us." New York Times Book Review.

Bala, Sharon

The **boat** people : a novel / Sharon Bala. Doubleday, 2018 304 p.

ISBN 9780385542296

1. Refugees 2. Fathers and sons 3. Prejudice 4. Asylum, Right of 5. Refugees' rights 6. Lawyers 7. Civil war -- Sri Lanka 8. Terrorists 9. Public safety 10. Flashbacks 11. Interpersonal relations 12. Sri Lanka 13. Vancouver, British Columbia 14. Canada 15. Mainstream fiction

LC 2017020049

Journeying to what he hopes will be a new life with his young son on a rusty cargo ship with 500 fellow refugees from Sri Lanka's civil war, a young father arrives on Vancouver's shores, where the group is thrown into a detention processing center and threatened with deportation amid accusations of terrorism.

Balaskovits, A. A.

Magic for unlucky girls : stories / A.A. Balaskovits. SFWP, 2017 230 p.

ISBN 9781939650665

1. Characters and characteristics in fairy tales 2. Women 3. Girls 4. Adaptations, retellings, and spin-offs 5. Fantasy fiction 6. Short stories

LC 2016033041

The fourteen fantastical stories in Magic For Unlucky Girls take the familiar tropes of fairy tales and twist them into new and surprising shapes.

"In this reimagining and reinventing of traditional, patriarchal fairy tales, Balaskovits creates a safea nd often startling space for girls and women in her book of short stories." Booklist.

Balasubramanyam, Rajeev, 1974-

Professor Chandra follows his bliss : a novel / Rajeev Balasubramanyam. The Dial Press, 2019. 288 p.

ISBN 9780525511380

1. College teachers 2. Success (Concept) 3. Divorced men 4. Senior men 5. East Indian British men 6. Self-awareness 7. Fatherhood 8. Voyages and travels 9. Economists 10. Family relationships 11. England 12. United States 13. Mainstream fiction

LC 2018034477

An internationally renowned curmudgeon economist and divorced father of three survives an accident before whimsically trading in his high-stress Nobel Prize ambitions to pursue elusive happiness.

Baldacci, David

The **fallen** / David Baldacci. Grand Central Pub., 2018. 432 p. Amos Decker novels

ISBN 9781538761397

1. Private investigators 2. Journalists 3. Murder investigation 4. Small towns 5. Pennsylvania 6. Thrillers and suspense

While Amos and his journalist friend Alex visit Alex's sister in Baronville, Pennsylvania, Amos discovers two dead men in a nearby house, but finds the police and unseen forces are stonewalling the investigation.

Baldacci, David

Hell's Corner / David Baldacci. Grand Central Pub, 2010 432 p.   Camel Club novels

ISBN 9780446195522

1. Secret societies 2. Intelligence service 3. Murder 4. National security 5. Camel Club (Imaginary organization) 6. Virginia 7. Political thrillers 8. Thrillers and suspense

Originally published: London : Macmillan, 2010.

A bomb detonates in the White House immediately after the British Prime Minister departs from the State Dinner. Oliver Stone, who witnesses the event, believes the Prime Minister and the President were the targets of a terrorist plot. MI-5 agent Mary Chapman is assigned to assist Stone and his Camel Club with the investigation, which reveals that the bombing may have actually been botched and is part of a darker, deadlier conspiracy.

Baldacci, David

A **minute** to midnight / David Baldacci. Grand Central Pub, 2019 432 p. Atlee Pine novels

ISBN 9781538761601

1. Women FBI agents 2. Families of murder victims 3. Twin sisters 4. Serial murders 5. Serial murder investigation 6. Secrets 7. Loss (Psychology) 8. Georgia 9. Thrillers and suspense

FBI Agent Atlee Pine returns to her Georgia hometown to reopen the investigation of her twin sister's abduction, only to encounter a serial killer beginning a reign of terror, in this page-turning thriller from #1 New York Times bestselling author David Baldacci.

Baldacci, David

Long road to mercy / David Baldacci. Grand Central Pub, 2018 432 p. Atlee Pine novels

ISBN 9781538761571

1. FBI 2. Women FBI agents 3. Missing persons investigation 4. Murder investigation 5. FBI agents 6. Twin sisters 7. Families of murder victims 8. Arizona 9. Grand Canyon 10. Thrillers and suspense

Devoting her life to bringing criminals to justice after her twin is murdered in childhood, FBI agent Atlee Pine investigates a missing-persons case in the Grand Canyon that may be tied to a string of disappearances.

Baldacci, David

* **One** good deed / David Baldacci. Grand Central Pub, 2019. 416 p.

ISBN 9781538750568

1. 1940s 2. World War II veterans 3. Parolees 4. Murder suspects 5. Former convicts 6. Bill collecting 7. Small towns 8. Murder 9. Murder investigation 10. Postwar life 11. Historical mysteries

The best-selling author of The Fallen and The Fix presents a latest thriller introducing straight-talking World War II veteran and recent prison inmate, Aloysius Archer.

"All signs suggest a sequel where he hangs out a shamus shingle. Archer will be a great series character for fans of crime fiction." Kirkus.

Baldacci, David

One summer / David Baldacci. Grand Central Pub., 2011. 288 p.

ISBN 9780446583145

1. Men with terminal illnesses 2. Widowers 3. Fatal traffic accidents 4. Beaches 5. Family relationships 6. Life change events 7. Lighthouses 8. Married women -- Death 9. Single fathers 10. Single-parent families 11. Mothers-in-law 12. South Carolina 13. Ohio 14. Mainstream fiction

Jack, terminally-ill and preparing to say goodbye to his family, has a miraculous recovery after his wife is killed in a car accident and struggles to reunite his family at her childhood home on the South Carolina oceanfront.

"Baldacci's muscle-bound style doesn't do subtle: He is best at choreographing fight scenes, rescues and dire brushes with severe weather, all of which, thankfully, are here in abundance." Kirkus.

Baldacci, David

Redemption / David Baldacci. Grand Central, 2019. 432 p. Amos Decker novels

ISBN 9781538761410

1. Private investigators 2. False imprisonment 3. Former convicts 4. Widowers 5. Judicial error 6. Murderers 7. Memory 8. Murder investigation 9. Former police 10. Overweight men 11. Ohio 12. Thrillers and suspense

Confronted by the first murder suspect of his early career while visiting his hometown, FBI detective Amos Decker reexamines startling connections to another crime that make him question if he arrested the wrong man years earlier.

Baldwin, James, 1924-1987

* **Another** country / James Baldwin. Vintage, 1993, 436 p.

ISBN 9780679744719

1. 1960s 2. Race relations 3. Jazz musicians 4. Identity (Psychology) 5. Racism 6. Love 7. Class conflict 8. Alienation (Social psychology) 9. African Americans 10. African American gay men 11. Gay men 12. Interracial couples 13. Bisexuality 14. Sexuality 15. Suicide 16. Death 17. Friendship 18. Loss (Psychology) 19. New York City 20. Literary fiction 21. African American fiction 22. LGBTQIA fiction 23. Modern classics

Originally published by Dial in 1962.

Presents a graphic portrayal of bisexuality and interracial relations. Rufus Scott, a black jazz musician, commits suicide, impelling his friends to search for the meaning of his death and, consequently, for a deeper understanding of their own identities. Employing a loose, episodic structure, this work traces the affairs--heterosexual and homosexual as well as interracial--among Scott's friends.

Baldwin, James, 1924-1987

* **Early** novels and stories / James Baldwin. Library of America, 1998. 970 p.

ISBN 1883011515

1. African Americans 2. African American gay men 3. Gay men 4. Identity (Psychology) 5. Literary fiction 6. LGBTQIA fiction 7. Autobiographical fiction 8. African American fiction

LC 97023028

A collection of stories penned by one of the greatest African American writers of the postwar era.

Baldwin, James, 1924-1987

* **Giovanni's** room / James Baldwin. Vintage International, 2013. c1956. 248 p.

ISBN 9780345806567

1. 1950s 2. Gay men 3. Identity (Psychology) 4. Alienation (Social psychology) 5. Expatriates 6. Americans in France 7. Sexual orientation 8. Sexuality 9. Love 10. Bisexuals 11. Consequences 12. Paris, France 13. LGBTQIA fiction 14. Literary fiction 15. Psychological fiction 16. African American fiction 17. Modern classics

LC 56012125

Originally published: New York : Dial, 1956.

When David meets the sensual Giovanni in a bohemian bar, he is swept into a passionate love affair. But his girlfriend's return to Paris destroys everything. Unable to admit to the truth, David pretends the liaison never happened - while Giovanni's life descends into tragedy.

Baldwin, James, 1924-1987

* **Go** tell it on the mountain / James Baldwin. Dial Press Trade Paperbacks, 2005, c1953. 226 p.

ISBN 0385334575

1. 1930s 2. African American men 3. Identity (Psychology) 4. Culture conflict 5. Racism 6. Children of clergy 7. African American fathers and sons 8. African American families 9. Familial love 10. Christian men 11. Depressions -- 1929-1941 12. Fundamentalists 13. Christianity 14. Harlem, New York City 15. New York City 16. United States -- Social life and customs -- 20th century 17. Modern classics 18. Literary fiction 19. Coming-of-age stories 20. African American fiction

LC 2005280211

Originally published: 1953.

"Though the religious experiences of these characters may seem sectarian, they are really universal. All of the major characters are trying to build and sustain community in the face of dehumanizing oppression. Their particular version of Christianity is an effective response to being captives in a racist culture. " Magill Book Review.

Baldwin, James, 1924-1987

* **Going** to meet the man / James Baldwin Vintage Books, 1995, c1965. 249 p.

ISBN 9780679761792

1. African Americans 2. Race relations 3. Racism 4. Jazz music 5. Jazz musicians 6. Family relationships 7. Suffering 8. Survival 9. United States -- Social life and customs -- 20th century 10. African American fiction 11. Short stories 12. Literary fiction 13. Modern classics

"There's no way not to suffer. But you try all kinds of ways to keep from drowning in it." The men and women in these eight short fictions grasp this truth on an elemental level, and their stories, as told by James Baldwin, detail the ingenious and often desperate ways in which they try to keep their heads above water.

Baldwin, James, 1924-1987

* **If** Beale Street could talk / James Baldwin. Vintage Books, 2018, c1974. 197 p.

ISBN 9780525566120

1. 1970s 2. Teenage couples 3. Race relations 4. Injustice 5. Innocence (Law) 6. False imprisonment 7. Racism 8. Prisons 9. Teenage pregnancy 10. African American families 11. African American women 12. Nineteen-year-old women 13. New York City 14. Harlem, New York City 15. African American fiction 16. Love stories 17. Literary fiction 18. Modern classics

LC 74001161

Originally published: New York : Dial Press, 1974.

When a pregnant Tish's boyfriend Fonny, a sculptor, is wrongfully jailed for the rape of a Puerto Rican woman, their families unite to prove the charge false.

Baldwin, James, 1924-1987

Just above my head / James Baldwin. Dial Press, 1979. 597 p.

ISBN 9780803747777

1. 1950s 2. 1960s 3. 1970s 4. African American families 5. Loss (Psychology) 6. Brothers 7. Grief in men 8. Race relations 9. Racism 10. Identity (Psychology) 11. Jazz music 12. Gay men 13. Gospel singers 14. Clergywomen 15. New York City 16. Paris, France 17. African American fiction 18. Literary fiction 19. Modern classics

LC 79053577

National Book Award for Fiction finalist, 1980

"Two years after the death of his younger brother Arthur, Hall Montana is finally able to 'stammer out' the story of Arthur's career as a gospel and soul singer, his homosexual love affairs, and his inglorious death in the men's room of a London pub. He also comes to terms with his own more conventional adventures in love." Library Journal.

Baldwin, James, 1924-1987

Tell me how long the train's been gone : a novel / James Baldwin. Vintage Books, 1998, c1968. 496 p.

ISBN 9780375701894

1. African American men 2. Race relations 3. Interracial friendship 4. Racism 5. Interracial dating 6. African American authors 7. Gay men 8. Bisexual men 9. New York City 10. Harlem, New York City 11. African American fiction 12. Modern classics 13. Literary fiction

Leo Proudhammer, an African American actor, reminisces about his past life and loves, while lying in the hospital, recovering from a heart attack

"Leo Proudhammer, a successful black actor has a serious heart attack on stage. Barbara King, his leading lady . . . and in a strange way his inamorata, stays by his side. In a series of flashbacks . . . Leo relives his past from his Harlem boyhood on. Although he learned early to hate 'the man,' Leo's own betrayal as a man and as a human being is not limited to the white man's corruption. It encompasses his painful relationship with his brother, who lures him into homosexuality. Paralleling this story is the tale of Leo's career. The third thread is his bisexual private life in which the two main figures are white Barbara, his true but unattainable love, and black Christopher, worshipful and available." Publishers Weekly.

Baldwin, Joshua

The **Wilshire** sun / Joshua Baldwin. Turtle Point Press, 2011. 104 p.

ISBN 9781933527468

1. Screenwriters 2. Men with mental illnesses 3. Success (Concept) 4. Moving, Household 5. Authors 6. Marching bands 7. Paranoia 8. Goals and objectives 9. Los Angeles, California 10. Psychological fiction

A novella about a whimsical, hapless young Brooklyn writer who moves to Los Angeles to write for the movies.

"Written in the first person and partially in an epistolary style, with a clearly unreliable narrator, the novella bears hallmarks of Nathanael West and seems to knowingly invite comparison. Surreal and paranoid, Jacob's story encapsulates the legend of Los Angeles as told by an outsider. Jacob, a young writer from Brooklyn, lives with his mother and aunt and aspires to move to Los Angeles with a work acquaintance to write screenplays. After a false start lands him back in New York, he finally makes it to L.A. for good. However, life in the city doesn't provide the fecund creative experience he'd anticipated, and his tenuous mental state declines rapidly. The ensuing narrative becomes ever more dreamlike, and the fictional letters he writes to and from imaginary people . . . grow more nonsensical, treating readers to a tantalizing glimpse beyond the edge of sanity." Publishers Weekly.

Ball, Jesse, 1978-

Census / Jesse Ball. Ecco Press, 2018. 241 p.

ISBN 9780062676139

1. Father and adult son 2. People with Down syndrome 3. Voyages and travels 4. Sick fathers 5. Census 6. Widowers 7. Parental love 8. Interpersonal relations 9. Literary fiction

Learning that he does not have long to live and will need to figure out how to provide for his developmentally disabled adult son, a widower signs up as a census taker for a mysterious government bureau

and leaves town with his son on a cross-country journey of memories and revelations.

Ball, Jesse, 1978-

The **way** through doors : a novel / Jesse Ball. Vintage Books, 2009. 240 p.

ISBN 9780307387462

1. Women with amnesia 2. Men/women relations 3. Hit-and-run accidents 4. Impersonators 5. Hit-and-run victims 6. Young women -- Identity 7. Deception 8. Young women 9. Psychological fiction

LC 2008022852

"In an inversion of the Scheherazade legend, the hero of this dizzyingly circuitous novel must tell stories all night to a beautiful amnesiac, to keep her awake and alive. ... It's a thrilling ride through an alternative New York (think Steven Millhauser on acid), where the tallest building extends hundreds of feet below ground and cabbies are paid in gold doubloons." The New Yorker.

Ball, John Dudley, 1911-1988

In the heat of the night / John Ball Harper & Row, 1965. 185 p. Virgil Tibbs mystery novels

ISBN 9780786708833

1. Murder 2. Racism 3. African American police 4. Detectives 5. African American men 6. Police chiefs 7. Race relations 8. North Carolina 9. Southern States 10. Mysteries

This novel was made into a film of the same name in 1967, starring Sidney Poitier, Rod Steiger, and Warren Oates, and directed by Normal Jewison.

First published in the United States of America by Harper & Row, 1965.

Edgar Allan Poe Award for Best First Mystery Novel, 1966.

Virgil Tibbs, an African-American homicide detective from California, arrives in a 1960s Southern town to conduct an unpopular investigation into a local murder, after being picked up by the local police as the prime suspect in the crime.

Ballard, J. G., 1930-2009

* The **complete** stories of J.G. Ballard. / J. G. Ballard. W.W. Norton & Co., 2009. xv, 1199 p.

ISBN 9780393072624

1. Great Britain -- Social life and customs -- 20th century 2. Short stories 3. Social science fiction 4. Science fiction

LC 2009018456

Collects 92 short stories.

Previously published as: The complete short stories.

Collects all ninety-two of the late author's stories--including "Prima Belladonna," "Dead Time," and "The Index"-- which span five decades and explore everything from musical orchids to human cannibalism to the secret history of World War III.

"An astonishing record of a vibrant and vital mind at work. This volume includes 92 stories, most of which are set in some kind of nightmarish future world or alternate visionary present, to use Ballard's phrase from his introduction to the book. The variety of stories here is impressive, even dizzying." Library Journal.

Ballard, J. G., 1930-2009

* The **day** of creation / J.G. Ballard. Picador USA : 2002, c1987. 253 p.

ISBN 0312421281

1. World Health Organization Central African operations 2. Physicians -- Central Africa 3. Rivers -- Central Africa 4. Water supply -- Central Africa 5. Generals -- Central Africa 6. Police chiefs -- Central Africa 7. Guerrillas -- Central Africa 8. Documentary

filmmakers -- Central Africa 9. Twelve-year-olds -- Central Africa 10. Central Africa 11. Sahara 12. Psychological fiction 13. Adventure stories

LC 2002066774

Originally published: London : Gollancz, 1987.

"Had Conrad been more inclined to fantasy, or less to fact and discipline, this is a novel he might have written. A blend of animated reverie, myth and adventure story, The Day of Creation imprints itself on the mind by its acid sweetness." Times Literary Supplement.

Ballard, J. G., 1930-2009

Empire of the sun : a novel / J.G. Ballard. Simon and Schuster, 1984. 279 p.

ISBN 0671530518

1. Ballard, J G, 1930-2009 2. Second World War era (1939-1945) 3. Teenage prisoners -- Shanghai, China 4. Parent-separated boys 5. World War II -- Prisoners and prisons, Japanese 6. Boys 7. World War II -- China 8. Teenage boys -- Shanghai, China 9. Prisoners of war, British 10. Shanghai, China -- History -- 1927-1949 11. China 12. Coming-of-age stories 13. War stories 14. Historical fiction 15. Autobiographical fiction

LC 84010630

Sequel: The kindness of women.
Guardian First Book Award, 1983.
James Tait Black Memorial Prize for Fiction, 1984.
Shortlisted for the Booker-McConnell Prize, 1984.

A young boy living in China at the outbreak of World War II is separated from his wealthy parents, forced to forage for survival in Shanghai's foreign quarter, interned in a Japanese prison camp, and, eventually, reunited with his parents. Ballard's enduring novel of war and deprivation, internment camps and death marches, and starvation and survival is an honest coming-of-age tale set in a world thrown utterly out of joint.

"This novel is much more than the gritty story of a child's miraculous survival in the grimly familiar setting of World War II's concentration camps. There is no nostalgia for a good war here, no sentimentality for the human spirit at extremes. Mr. Ballard is more ambitious than romance usually allows. He aims to render a vision of the apocalypse, and succeeds so well that it can hurt to dwell upon his images." New York Times Book Review.

Ballard, J. G., 1930-2009

The **kindness** of women / J. G. Ballard. Farrar, Straus and Giroux, 1991. 343 p.

ISBN 0374181101

1. Ballard, J G, 1930-2009 2. 20th century 3. Marriage 4. Fatherhood 5. Prisoners of war, British 6. Sexuality 7. Friendship 8. Growing up 9. Men/women relations 10. Men -- Shepperton, London, England 11. World War II -- China 12. Shanghai, China -- History -- 1927-1949 13. Shepperton, London, England 14. Coming-of-age stories 15. Autobiographical fiction

LC 91073730

Sequel to: Empire of the sun.

Continues the story of the boy whose life in Japanese-occupied Shaghai was described so memorably in 'Empire of the Sun'. It sets those traumatic events within the context of a lifetime as we follow the narrator, Jim, to England and suburban Shepperton after the war. Jim tries and fails to find stability as a medical student at Cambridge and a trainee RAF pilot in Canada. Then, after settling happily into family life, his world is ripped apart by domestic tragedy. He plunges into the maelstrom of the 1960s, an instigator and subject of every aspect of cultural, social and sexual revolution. All this and much more, we see as the attempt of a bruised mind to make sense of the upheaval around it.

"For a writer whose inventiveness is so firmly anchored in 20th century-icons . . . Ballard remains firmly ambivalent about our image-led culture. His whole work is a celebration and an excoriation of 'the media landscape' and [this book] comes face to face with the contradictions." New Statesman.

Ballard, J. G., 1930-2009

Kingdom come / J. G. Ballard. W. W. Norton & Co., 2012. 304 p.

ISBN 9780871404039

1. Consumerism 2. Neo-fascism 3. Unemployed persons 4. Advertising executives 5. Shopping malls 6. Gunshot victims 7. Advertising 8. Conspiracies 9. London, England 10. Satirical fiction 11. Science fiction

An unemployed advertising executive investigates why the deranged man who shot his father in a shopping mall was released without being charged.

Ballard, J. G., 1930-2009

Millennium people / J.G. Ballard. W.W. Norton & Co., 2011. 288 p.

ISBN 9780393081770

1. Psychologists 2. Political activists 3. Political violence 4. Protest movements 5. Brainwashing 6. Middle class 7. Terrorism 8. Great Britain 9. Satirical fiction

LC 2010052504

After his ex-wife is killed in a bombing at Heathrow airport, David Markham infiltrates the shadowy protest group responsible and finds himself becoming brainwashed by the group's charismatic leader in this posthumous novel.

"Ballard is a natural surrealist; his is a world where the unthinkable is commonplace and rationality chucked in the towel long ago. . . . Ballard's phrasing is as sure as ever. He writes wonderfully well about London. His characterization is as vivid as it is strange. An extremely unsettling novel. Reading it is like having all the planks that underpin your life removed one by one and being forced to confront the brutality and emptiness that lies below." The Scotsman.

Balogh, Mary

The **arrangement** / Mary Balogh. Delacorte Press, 2013. 336 p. Survivors' Club septet

ISBN 9780345535870

1. Regency period (1811-1820) 2. 19th century 3. Napoleonic Wars veterans 4. Aristocracy 5. Courtship 6. Men who are blind 7. Matchmaking 8. Social classes 9. Men/women relations 10. Rural life 11. England -- History -- 19th century 12. Regency romances 13. Historical romances

LC 2012037711

Sequel to: The Proposal.

Blinded by a cannon blast on the battlefields of Napoleon, Vincent Hunt, Lord Darleigh, struggles to maintain anonymity and escapes his matchmaking mother's interference by entering a marriage of convenience with an unassuming woman with whom he finds unexpected passion.

Balogh, Mary

The **escape** / Mary Balogh. Delacorte Press, 2014. 336 p. Survivors' Club septet

ISBN 9780345536068

1. Regency period (1811-1820) 2. 19th century 3. Napoleonic Wars veterans 4. Widows 5. Soldiers 6. Mate selection 7. Courtship 8. Escapes 9. Men/women relations 10. Rural life 11. England -- History -- 19th century 12. Regency romances 13. Historical romances

Sir Benedict Harper, a wounded veteran of the Napoleonic Wars, finds an unexpected ally in widow Samantha McKay, who is attempting to escape her oppressive in-laws and needs his help in claiming a house she has inherited in Wales.

"As always, Balogh's scarred protagonists find deep wells of strength and generosity within as well as experiencing great sexual tension and forging tender relationships." Booklist.

Balogh, Mary

More than a mistress / Mary Balogh Delacorte Press, 2000. 343 p. Mistress trilogy (Mary Balogh)

ISBN 0385335318

1. Regency period (1811-1820) 2. Dukes and duchesses 3. Mistresses 4. Scandals 5. Men/women relations 6. Nurses 7. Interclass romance 8. England -- Social life and customs -- 19th century 9. Regency romances 10. Historical romances

LC 99462117

Two romantic tales of powerful passions and scandalous liaisons from the Regency era.

"When Jane Ingleby tries to stop a duel, Jocelyn Dudley, Duke of Tresham, is wounded. So it's surprising that she ends up employed as his nurse and ultimately his mistress as well. But as their relationship blossoms, Jocelyn commits the unpardonable sin of falling in love. In this refreshingly unconventional romance, which boasts an outspoken, memorable heroine, the author again pushes the edges of the genre." Library Journal.

Balogh, Mary

Only enchanting / Mary Balogh. Signet, 2014 400 p. Survivors' Club septet

ISBN 9780451469663

1. Regency period (1811-1820) 2. 19th century 3. Jilted men 4. Former lovers 5. Men/women relations 6. Revenge 7. Mate selection 8. Courtship 9. England -- History -- 19th century 10. Regency romances 11. Historical romances

Viscount Ponsonby proposes to young widow Agnes Keeping in order to escape his former fiancée, who deserted him after his return home from the Napoleonic Wars but is now eager to revive their engagement.

Balogh, Mary

The **secret** mistress / Mary Balogh. Delacorte Press, 2011. 320 p. Mistress trilogy (Mary Balogh)

ISBN 9780385343312

1. Regency period (1811-1820) 2. Nobility 3. Mistresses 4. Mate selection for women 5. Secrets 6. Duty 7. Men/women relations 8. England -- Social life and customs -- 19th century 9. Regency romances 10. Historical romances

LC 2010052864

Follows the coming-out of Lady Angeline Dudley, who harbors a secret desire for a simple marriage in spite of expectations that she marry a wealthy, titled man, a situation that is compounded by her unexpected love for an earl who does not return her feelings.

"Balogh pairs a staid young nobleman with a vivacious debutante in this topnotch tale. ... An unusually accurate portrayal of Regency society, laden with colorful period detail, makes a sparkling backdrop, and the supporting characters are delightful." Publishers Weekly.

Balogh, Mary

Someone to hold / Mary Balogh. Jove, 2017. 390 p. Westcott novels

ISBN 9780451477804

1. Regency period (1811-1820) 2. Scandals 3. Illegitimacy 4. Social status 5. Life change events 6. Orphanages 7. Teachers 8. Half-sisters 9. Painters 10. Group identity 11. Interpersonal attraction 12. Men/women relations 13. Bath, England 14. London, England 15. England 16. Regency romances 17. Historical romances

Declared illegitimate and without a title, Camille Westcott leaves London to teach at the Bath orphanage where she meets artist Joel Cunningham with whom she shares a mutual contempt until her sittings with him take a passionate turn.

"Written with an irresistibly wry sense of humor and graced with a cast of unforgettable characters, the second in Baloghs exceptional Westcott series, following Someone to Love (2016), is another gorgeously written love story from the queen of Regency romances." Booklist.

Balogh, Mary

* Simply love / Mary Balogh. Delacorte Press, 2006. 320 p. Simply quartet (Mary Balogh)

ISBN 038533883X

1. Regency period (1811-1820) 2. Single mothers 3. Nobility 4. Women teachers 5. Men with disfigurements 6. Veterans 7. Aristocracy 8. Girls' schools 9. Families 10. Family estates 11. Summer 12. Matchmaking 13. Independence in women 14. Men/women relations 15. England 16. Wales 17. Bath, England 18. Regency romances 19. Historical romances

LC 2005058262

Anne Jewell, a favorite teacher at Miss Martin's School for Girls, is forced to confront the tragedies of the past in order to build a new life for herself and her son after she meets Sydnam Butler, a quiet and gentle hero of the Peninsular Wars.

"Balogh has once again crafted a sensuous tale of two very real people finding love and making each other's lives whole and beautiful." Booklist.

Balogh, Mary

* Someone to love / Mary Balogh. Signet, 2016 400 p. Westcott novels

ISBN 9780451477798

1. Regency period (1811-1820) 2. Orphans 3. Dukes and duchesses 4. Inheritance and succession 5. Life change events 6. Nobility 7. Scandals 8. Heirs and heiresses 9. Family secrets 10. Transformations, Personal 11. Interpersonal attraction 12. Men/women relations 13. London, England 14. England 15. Regency romances 16. Historical romances

Arriving in London to claim an unexpected inheritance from the late Earl of Riverdale, orphan Anna Snow turns to the new earl's guardian, the Duke of Netherby, for help in transforming herself into a lady and navigate the very society that threatens to overwhelm her.

"Fans will be delighted to meet the Westcotts here and anticipate future installments of their series." Publishers Weekly.

Balogh, Mary

* Someone to remember : a Westcott story / Mary Balogh. Berkley, 2019. 272 pges Westcott novels

ISBN 9780593099728

1. Regency period (1811-1820) 2. Independence in single women 3. Aristocracy 4. Second chances 5. Former lovers 6. Courtship 7. Viscounts and viscountesses 8. Determination in men 9. Interpersonal attraction 10. Men/women relations 11. Identity (Psychology) 12. Great Britain -- History -- Regency, 1811-1820 13. England 14. Historical romances 15. Regency romances

LC 2019027613

A noblewoman who has established a solitary life caring for her aging dowager countess mother resists the renewed courtship of a viscount she once loved decades earlier.

Balogh, Mary

Someone to trust / Mary Balogh. Berkley, 2018. 400 p. Westcott novels

ISBN 9780399586101

1. Regency period (1811-1820) 2. Widows 3. Christmas 4. Aristocracy 5. Young men -- Relations with older women 6. Interpersonal attraction 7. Men/women relations 8. Great Britain -- History -- Regency, 1811-1820 9. England 10. Holiday romances 11. Historical romances 12. Regency romances

Widow Elizabeth Overfield and Colin Handrich know there can never be a relationship between them, but an agreement to share a waltz at each ball they attend leaves them questioning what they are willing to sacrifice for love.

Balogh, Mary

Someone to wed / Mary Balogh. Berkley Books, 2017 384 p. Westcott novels

ISBN 9780399586064

1. Regency period (1811-1820) 2. Heirs and heiresses 3. Earls and countesses 4. Businesspeople 5. Interpersonal attraction 6. Men/women relations 7. Rich women 8. Birthmarks 9. Courtship 10. Veils 11. Great Britain -- History -- Regency, 1811-1820 12. London, England 13. England 14. Historical romances 15. Regency romances

When heiress Wren Heyden offers Alexander Westcott, the new Earl of Riverdale, a marriage of convenience, he proposes a proper courtship in hopes that at least a friendship will develop between them.

"With her signature voice and steady pace, Balogh crafts a thoughtful, sweet Regency-era love story to follow Someone to Hold." Publishers Weekly.

Balzac, Honore de, 1799-1850

The **country** doctor / Honore de Balzac ; translated by Ellen Marriage. Roberts brothers, 1887. 3 p.l., 304 p. The Human Comedy

1. Physicians 2. Translations -- French to English 3. Classics

LC 03023174

Balzac, Honore de, 1799-1850

Cousin Bette / Honore de Balzac ; translated from the French by James Waring. Knopf, 1991. xliii, 484 p. The Human Comedy

ISBN 0679406719

1. Social classes -- Paris, France 2. Revenge -- Paris, France 3. Individualism in literature 4. Paris, France -- Social conditions 5. Translations -- French to English 6. Allegories 7. Classics

LC 91052964

Introduction by Michael Tilby.

Balzac, Honore de, 1799-1850

Eugenie Grandet / Honore de Balzac ; translated by Lowell Bair ; with an introduction by Milton Crane. Bantam Books, 1994, c1959. 233 p. The Human Comedy

ISBN 0553214292

1. France -- Social life and customs -- 19th century 2. Allegories 3. Classics 4. Translations -- French to English

"First published in 1833."

The five-foot-high Grandet allows his avaricious passion to thwart his daughter, Eugenie's, love in the classic work of social satire, carnal desire, greed, and obsession.

Bambara, Toni Cade

Gorilla, my love / Toni Cade Bambara. Vintage Books, 1992, 177 p.

ISBN 9780679738985

1. African American women 2. Family relationships 3. Race relations 4. African Americans 5. Social classes 6. City life 7. Small town life 8. Widows 9. Men/women relations 10. Middle-aged women 11. African American girls 12. New York City -- Social life and customs 13. North Carolina 14. Southern States 15. African American fiction 16. Short stories 17. Literary fiction

LC 91058065

Originally published: New York : Random House, 1972.

Fifteen short stories record the author's ideas about the challenge and complexity of contemporary life

Bambara, Toni Cade

* The **salt** eaters / Toni Cade Bambara. Random House, 1980. 295 p.

ISBN 9780394507125

1. African American women 2. Communities 3. Women with depression 4. Social classes 5. African American communities 6. African Americans 7. Healing 8. Healers 9. Faith healers 10. Faith healing 11. Social classes 12. Southern States 13. Georgia 14. Literary fiction 15. African American fiction

LC 79004806

"This novel with its beautiful, difficult prose, is a work at once intensely personal and political that will assure Bambara's place in black American fiction." Library Journal.

Bambara, Toni Cade

Those bones are not my child / Toni Cade Bambara. Pantheon Books, 1999. 676 p.

ISBN 0679442618

1. 1980s 2. Child kidnapping victims 3. African American women 4. African Americans 5. Kidnapping 6. Child murder victims 7. African American single mothers 8. Serial kidnappings 9. Single women 10. Missing children 11. Working class 12. African American communities 13. Racism 14. Race relations 15. Atlanta, Georgia 16. Literary fiction 17. African American fiction

LC 99021534

Presents a fictionalized account of one family's nightmare as they learn their child is a victim of Atlanta serial killer Wayne Williams

"The anger and desperation of the parents is portrayed so vividly that their search for the truth becomes the reader's. Bambara's final work is an honest and passionate tour de force." Library Journal.

Banasky, Carmiel

The **suicide** of Claire Bishop / Carmiel Banasky. Dzanc Books, 2015. 280 p.

ISBN 9781938103087

1. People with mental illnesses 2. Suicide 3. Memory 4. Young women 5. People with schizophrenia 6. Husband and wife 7. Portraits 8. Art thefts 9. Obsession 10. New York City 11. Psychological fiction

LC 2015000623

"Although the novel's structure suggests a chronological approach, its nonlinear sections make story elements more challenging to follow. But a careful reader is rewarded by Banasky's skillful character development, innovative points-of-view technique, and fresh language. The book is full of quotable sentences, including one descriptive of the book itself, 'Here's the truth: we're all connected, but not in a straight line. More like constellations, or islands.'" Booklist.

Bandele, Asha

Daughter : a novel / Asha Bandele. Scribner, 2003. 266 p.
ISBN 0743211847

1. African American women 2. African American widows 3. Single parent families 4. Single mothers 5. African Americans 6. African American families 7. Mothers and daughters 8. Police shootings 9. Police brutality 10. College students 11. Police misconduct 12. Men/women relations 13. Death 14. Loss (Psychology) 15. Fear of intimacy 16. Memories 17. Life change events 18. Self-fulfillment in women 19. Brooklyn, New York City 20. New York City 21. United States -- Race relations 22. African American fiction 23. Psychological fiction 24. Domestic fiction

LC 2003045536

Miriam Rivers tries to give her daughter Aya a good life, but also keeps her at an emotional distance. One tragic night while Aya is taking a jog, she is mistaken for a robber and shot. With her daughter fighting for her life, Miriam must open up and let herself face the feelings of the past and the present.

Bandi, 1950-

The **accusation** : forbidden stories from inside North Korea / Bandi ; translated from the Korean by Deborah Smith. Grove Press, 2017, c2014. vii, 247 p.
ISBN 9780802126207

1. Kim, Chong-il, 1942-2011 2. 21st century 3. 1990s 4. Dictators 5. Totalitarianism 6. Communism -- North Korea 7. Dissenters 8. Censorship 9. Oppression (Psychology) 10. Resistance to government 11. North Korea -- Politics and government 12. Political fiction 13. Literary fiction 14. Short stories 15. Translations -- Korean to English
Originally published in South Korea in 2014.

A work of dissident fiction from North Korea, written by an anonymous author and smuggled out of the country, depicts a powerful portrait of life under the North Korean regime as it impacts a diverse range of people, from a disillusioned war hero to a family man who travels without a permit to visit his critically ill mother.

"With these uncompromising stories, the pseudonymous Bandi gives a rare glimpse of life in the truly fathomless darkness of North Korea." Publishers Weekly.

Bank, Melissa

The **wonder** spot / Melissa Bank. Viking, 2005. 336 p.
ISBN 0670034118

1. Self-discovery in women 2. Family relationships 3. Jewish teenage girls 4. Middle child 5. Young women 6. Misfits (Persons) 7. Female friendship 8. Alienation in families 9. Men/women relations 10. Pennsylvania 11. New York City 12. Chick lit 13. Coming-of-age stories 14. Domestic fiction

LC 2004061189

Novel composed of linked short stories.

Struggling with ambivalent feelings toward the passions and identities that are important to other members of her Jewish Pennsylvania family, Sophie Applebaum makes observations about her family life over the course of twenty years.

Banks, Iain, 1954-2013

Consider Phlebas / Iain M. Banks. St. Martin's Press, 1987. 471 p. Culture Universe series
ISBN 9780312017521

1. Imaginary wars and battles 2. Mercenaries 3. Interplanetary relations 4. Imaginary empires 5. Religious persecution 6. Faith 7. Good and evil 8. Space warfare 9. Space opera 10. Hard science fiction 11. Science fiction

LC 87036718

Horza, a Changer, finds himself at the center of an epic galactic confrontation between the fanatical Idirans and the communistic Culture, made up of humans ruled by the Mind machines that they have created.

Banks, Iain, 1954-2013

The **crow** road / Iain Banks. MacAdam/Cage Pub., 2008. 500 p.
ISBN 9781596923065

1. Families 2. Identity (Psychology) 3. Mortality 4. Missing persons 5. Death 6. Coping 7. Homecomings 8. Love 9. Funerals 10. Scotland 11. Coming-of-age stories

Banks, Iain, 1954-2013

The **hydrogen** sonata / Iain Banks. Little Brown & Co., 2012. 496 p. Culture Universe series
ISBN 9780316212373

1. Aliens (Humanoid) 2. Frameups 3. Innocence (Law) 4. Space flight 5. Dystopias 6. Life on other planets 7. Space opera 8. Hard science fiction 9. Science fiction

Suspected of involvement after the Regimental High Command is destroyed as they prepared to go to a new level of existence called Sublime, Lieutenant Commander Vyr Cossont must find a nine-thousand year old man to clear her name.

Banks, Iain, 1954-2013

Matter / Iain M. Banks. Orbit, 2008. 608 p. Culture Universe series
ISBN 9780316005364

1. Aliens (Humanoid) 2. Technology 3. Cyborgs 4. Princesses 5. Spies 6. Utopias 7. Dystopias 8. Space flight 9. Space warfare 10. Space opera 11. Hard science fiction 12. Science fiction

LC 2007941828

In a distant-future human-machine symbiotic society of seemingly unlimited technological capability, the Culture is threatened by ongoing wars, political upheavals, and alien intruders.

"Beautifully written and filled with memorable characters and startling technology." Publishers Weekly.

Banks, Iain, 1954-2013

The **player** of games / Iain M. Banks. St. Martin's Press, 1989. 309 p. Culture Universe series
ISBN 9780312026301

1. Contests 2. Imaginary wars and battles 3. Interplanetary relations 4. Competition in men 5. Good and evil 6. Science fiction games 7. Imaginary empires 8. Space warfare 9. Space opera 10. Hard science fiction 11. Science fiction

LC 88029899

Bored with his routine successes, game player Jernau Morat Gurgeh of the Culture travels to the Empire of Azad in search of more challenging prospects and finds himself thrust into a high-stakes competition that threatens his survival.

Banks, Iain, 1954-2013

Use of weapons / Iain Banks. Orbit, 1990. 389 p. Culture Universe series
ISBN 9780553292244

1. Spies 2. Robots 3. Imaginary wars and battles 4. Interplanetary relations 5. Good and evil 6. Space warfare 7. Space opera 8. Hard science fiction 9. Science fiction

Called back from early retirement by Special Circumstances, the elite weapon of the Culture's policy of moral espionage, Cheradenine Zakalwe reluctantly returns to work, but his fatal flaw could cost them the battle.

Banks, Maya

Never seduce a Scot / Maya Banks. Ballantine Books, 2012. 352 p. The Montgomerys and Armstrongs

ISBN 9780345533234

1. Medieval period (476-1492) 2. Women who are deaf 3. Warriors 4. Arranged marriage 5. Women who are deaf and mute 6. Secrets 7. Husband and wife 8. Alliances 9. Clans -- Scotland 10. Men/women relations 11. Scotland -- History -- 13th century 12. Highlands, Scotland -- History -- 13th century 13. Medieval romances 14. Highland romances 15. Historical romances

When Eveline Armstrong, who never speaks, is forced into an arranged marriage with Graeme Montgomery, a warrior from a rival clan, love grows between them as clan rivalries and dark forces conspire to keep them apart.

Banks, Russell, 1940-

* **Affliction** / Russell Banks. Harper & Row, 1989. 355 p.

ISBN 9780060161422

1. Violence in men -- New Hampshire 2. Divorced men 3. Cynicism 4. Alcoholic fathers 5. Fathers and daughters 6. Brothers -- New Hampshire 7. Small town life -- New Hampshire 8. Men -- New Hampshire 9. New Hampshire 10. Literary fiction

LC 89094473

A gentle man, the victim of a violent father, is made violent himself by a fellow cop whom he suspects of murdering a local labor official, and an ex-wife who limits contact with their daughter

"This novel is psychological portraiture of a high order, and like all profound portraits it finds in its subject astonishing contradictions." New York Times Book Review.

Banks, Russell, 1940-

Cloudsplitter : a novel / Russell Banks. Harper Flamingo, 1998. 758 p.

ISBN 0060168609

1. Brown, John, 1800-1859 2. Brown, Owen, 1824-1889 3. 19th century 4. Abolitionists 5. Racism 6. Fathers and sons 7. Race relations 8. Rebels 9. Families 10. Guerrillas 11. United States -- History -- 19th century 12. United States -- Race relations -- History -- 19th century 13. Literary fiction 14. Epistolary novels 15. Biographical fiction

LC 9722163

Offers a fictional re-creation of the turbulent landscape of pre-Civil War America and of John Brown's 1859 raid on the federal arsenal at Harpers Ferry, Virginia, as narrated by the enigmatic abolitionist's son, Owen.

"To rise above period costume and stately diction, a historical novel must have a saving tincture of anachronism, a point of forced contact with the unfinished business of the present. Cloudsplitter, is brought alive by Owen's ambivalent, recognizably modern consciousness." The Nation.

Banks, Russell, 1940-

Continental drift / Russell Banks. HarperCollins, 1985. 366 p.

ISBN 9780060153830

1. Materialism 2. Good and evil 3. Shame in men 4. Racism 5. Extramarital affairs 6. Refugees, Haitian 7. Disillusionment in men 8. Haitian Americans 9. Women -- Haiti 10. Smuggling 11. Blue collar workers 12. Miami, Florida 13. Florida 14. Literary fiction

LC 84048137

Pulitzer Prize for Fiction finalist, 1986.

After his ill-fated pursuit of the American dream, Bob Dubois finds employment on a fishing boat off the Florida Keys where he becomes involved in a plot to smuggle two Haitians into Florida.

"There are raw edges to Bank's novel, and a numbing insistence on the powerlessness of its characters, but there's no denying its almost frightening intensity." Library Journal.

Banks, Russell, 1940-

Lost memory of skin / Russell Banks. Ecco Press, 2011. 352 p.

ISBN 9780061857638

1. Misfits (Persons) 2. Sex addicts 3. Pornography 4. Sex offenders 5. College teachers 6. Sociologists 7. Good and evil 8. Homeless persons 9. Psychological fiction 10. Literary fiction

ALA Notable Book, 2012.

Andrew Carnegie Medal for Excellence in Fiction finalist, 2012.

A young outcast known as the Kid who lives with other sex offenders in a makeshift encampment under a south Florida causeway is taken up by a professor of sociology who sees in the Kid a perfect subject for his research. The Kid accepts the counsel and financial assistance of the older man, but when the Professor's past resurfaces and threatens to destroy his carefully constructed world, the balance in the two men's relationship shifts.

"Set in a fictional part of Florida in a time of paranoia (possibly the near future), Lost Memory of Skin is the story of a twentyish sex offender (known simply as the Kid) on parole and the affable but troubled sociology instructor (called the Professor) on a misguided mission to help him become better adjusted. The Kid is a wastrel addicted to Internet porn, with only his pet iguana for company, until an unfortunate series of events beginning with an Internet chat with a underage girl and ending To Catch a Predator-style lands him in prison. Upon his release, he is forced to live with other sex offenders under a causeway because of a law that keeps them 2,500 feet from anywhere children are playing. The Professor, a behemoth in a suit, begins interviewing the Kid for academic research purposes; as he learns more about the Kid's crime, he begins to reveal his own troubled history, which only undermines his efforts to help. Banks inhabits unsympathetic voices well, and it is a pleasure to see his gift turned to big, semisurreal characters. The grand, rambling examination of guilt and blame takes place against a ravishingly bleak backdrop, lyrically described, while each revelation of character is like a quiet explosion." Time Out New York.

Banks, Russell, 1940-

* The **sweet** hereafter / Russell Banks. Harper Collins Publishers, 1991. 257 p.

ISBN 0060167033

1. Children -- Death 2. Bereavement -- Psychological aspects 3. Survival (after automobile, truck, train accidents, etc) 4. Children -- Death -- Psychological aspects 5. Fate and fatalism 6. Redemption 7. School bus accidents 8. Small town life -- New York (State) 9. Adirondack Mountains, New York 10. New York (State) 11. Literary fiction

LC 90056404

ALA Notable Book, 1992.

Four narrators--bus driver Dolores, upright Bill, shrewd Mitchell, and teenaged Nichole--address agonizing questions as they describe an accident that killed fourteen children and the effects of the tragedy on themselves and their town

"Banks handles his dark theme with judicious restraint, empathy and compassion." Publishers Weekly.

Bannalec, Jean-Luc, 1966-

Death in Brittany / Jean-Luc Bannalec ; translated from the German by Sorcha McDonagh. Minotaur, 2015, c2012. 256 p. Georges Dupin novels

ISBN 9781250061744

1. Murder investigation 2. Small towns 3. Police 4. Detectives 5. Seniors 6. Art -- Collectors and collecting 7. Brittany, France 8. Police procedurals 9. Mysteries 10. Translations -- German to English

Originally published as Bretonische Verhaltnisse by Kiepenheuer & Witsch in 2012.

After a hotelier is murdered in a small village on the Breton coast, Commissaire Georges Dupin identifies five possible suspects and un-covers disturbing secrets behind the village's calm exterior.

"Bannalec feeds the reader with intriguing bits of history (for ex-ample, Bretons are descended from the Celts, who fled Britain during the Anglo-Saxon invasions) and culture, along with bracing glimpses of centuries-old stone buildings, river banks, and the sea." Booklist.

Bannalec, Jean-Luc, 1966-

The **killing** tide : a Brittany mystery / Jean-Luc Bannalec ; translated from the German by Peter Millar. Minotaur Books, 2020, c2016. 358 p. Georges Dupin novels

ISBN 9781250173386

1. Islands 2. Smuggling 3. Coastal towns 4. Murder investigation 5. Detectives 6. Fishing villages 7. Dolphins 8. Water -- Pollution 9. Brittany, France 10. France 11. Police procedurals 12. Translations -- German to English

LC 2019036389

Originally published: Cologne : Kiepenheuer & Witsch, 2016.

On an island off the west coast of Brittany shrouded in superstition, Commissaire Dupin and his team follow a puzzling case that pushes them to their very limits.

"Bannalec (the pen name of Jorg Bong) has concocted the perfect blend of police procedural and travelogue." Publishers Weekly.

Banner, Catherine

The **house** at the edge of night : a novel / Catherine Banner. Random House, 2016 416 p.

ISBN 9780812998795

1. 20th century 2. 21st century 3. Bars (Drinking establishments) 4. Island life 5. Family businesses 6. Families 7. Communities 8. Small towns 9. Neighbors 10. Family relationships 11. Interpersonal relations 12. Italy 13. Family sagas 14. Historical fiction

LC 2015023813

Four generations of women on a Mediterranean island fight to safe-guard their family against the forces of history and bitterness that divide them from World War I through the 2008 recession.

"Banner deftly touches on weightier themes while weaving an enchanting narrative, the events of which extend to the present." Publishers Weekly.

Bannister, Jo

Kindred spirits / Jo Bannister. Severn House, 2018. 220 p. Gabriel Ash and Hazel Best mysteries

ISBN 9780727887962

1. Policewomen 2. Detectives 3. Small towns 4. Kidnapping 5. Cold cases (Criminal investigation) 6. Suspicion 7. Great Britain 8. Mysteries

LC bl2018109585

After an attempted kidnapping, Gabriel Ash asks Constable Hazel Best to keep his sons safe, but Hazel's investigation puts her at odds with superiors when she uncovers information about a crime committed seventeen years earlier.

Bannister, Jo

Silent footsteps / Jo Bannister. Severn House, 2019 224 p. Gabriel Ash and Hazel Best mysteries

ISBN 9780727888648

1. Policewomen 2. Stalkers 3. Women stalking victims 4. Murder investigation 5. Obsession 6. Conspiracies 7. Small towns 8. Great Britain 9. Mysteries 10. Police procedurals

Constable Hazel Best attracts a new admirer whose intentions turn sinister after an attack on Hazel's friend; and, with her colleagues tied up, it is up to Hazel to deal with the stalker alone.

Banville, John

Ancient light / John Banville. Alfred A. Knopf, 2012. 304 p. Alexander Cleave trilogy

ISBN 9780307957054

1. Senior men 2. Actors and actresses 3. Reminiscing in old age 4. Loss (Psychology) 5. First loves 6. Memory 7. Psychological fiction 8. Literary fiction

LC 2012019891

"This is a Borzoi book"--T.p. verso.

Sequel to: Shroud.

"Originally published in Great Britain by Picador, an imprint of Pan Macmillan Ltd., London, in 2012"--T.p. verso.

An actor in the twilight of his career reflects on a poignant first love affair at the age of 15 with his best friend's mother and inexplicably lands a role opposite a famous but fragile actress who helps him come to an astonishing realization.

Banville, John

The **blue** guitar / John Banville. Alfred A. Knopf, 2015 304 p.

ISBN 9780385354264

1. Artists 2. Thieves 3. Creativity in men 4. Betrayal 5. Memories 6. Stealing 7. Extramarital affairs 8. Friendship 9. Secrets 10. Men/women relations 11. Psychological fiction 12. Literary fiction

LC 2015006555

A semi-famous artist and petty thief, despairing of limits in his tal-ents, flees when his latest theft is discovered and sequesters himself in his childhood home, where he struggles to understand how he reached his current state.

"Banville delights in descriptions of people and nature, and here he has the added excuse of writing through a painter's gifted eye. The artist Orme is not a pleasant creation to spend several hours with, but in the hands of this gifted Irish writer, even a potbellied, melancholic petty thief and Lothario offers countless delights." Kirkus.

Banville, John

The **book** of evidence / John Banville. C. Scribner's Sons, 1989. 219 p. Evidence trilogy

ISBN 9780684191805

1. Murder 2. Art thefts 3. Guilt in men 4. Good and evil 5. Criminals 6. Thieves 7. Shame in men 8. Confession (Law) 9. Obsession in men 10. Gambling 11. Psychological suspense 12. Literary fiction

LC 89010985

Shortlisted for the Booker-McConnell Prize, 1989.

Returning to Ireland to reclaim a painting that is part of his patri-mony, a thirty-eight-year-old man commits a ghastly and motiveless murder, which he confesses in a novel-length narrative.

"This novel, the inventive testimony of a murderer more interested in making an impression than escaping conviction, is . . . hauntingly beautiful and original. . . . Mr. Banville shows his uncanny ability to make everything he describes seem new and rare, yet instantly recognisable." The Economist.

Banville, John

* **Eclipse** : a novel / John Banville. Alfred A. Knopf :, 2000. 211 p. Alexander Cleave trilogy

ISBN 9780375411298

1. Midlife crisis in men 2. Actors and actresses 3. Family relationships 4. Fathers and daughters 5. Identity (Psychology) 6. Memories 7. Dysfunctional families 8. Selfishness in men 9. Psychological fiction 10. Literary fiction

LC 00062014

Sequel: Shroud.

Originally published: London : Picador, 2000.

Alexander Cleave, a famous actor with a disintegrating career, retreats to his childhood home where he struggles to come to terms with his memories, the unsettling presence of a caretaker and teenage housekeeper, and ghosts of the past.

"Banville's writing is richly descriptive and full of original images. . . . Eclipse is essentially a reflective work. The actual narrative is Cleave's interior journey, not the rather banal series of lived events, and for this reason the magnificent atmospherics, in a way, are the story." The New Leader.

Banville, John

The **infinities** / John Banville. Alfred A. Knopf, 2010, c2009. 272 p.

ISBN 9780307272799

1. People with terminal illnesses -- Family relationships 2. Gods and goddesses 3. Family relationships 4. Fathers and sons 5. Mathematicians 6. Interpersonal relations 7. Ireland 8. Psychological fiction 9. Literary fiction

LC 2009048331

Originally published: London : Picador, 2009.

Attending the deathbed of a renowned mathematician, his second wife and adult children reflect on their personal demons, including the son's pretty wife, who has caught the attention of the mischievous god Zeus.

"Sure, The Infinities will have you looking up invigilate in the dictionary (I'll save you the time: to keep watch) and Googling Amphitryon (a Greek myth dramatized by the 19th century German writer Heinrich von Kleist). But none of this legwork feels like a chore, because The Infinities is constructed as a tantalizing puzzle you're eager to piece together. And Hermes is a delightfully cheeky and amiable narrator, constantly mocking randy old Zeus and guiding us through the multiple worlds of the novel. Moreover, Banville is a glorious stylist whose prose holds sustaining pleasures, both large and small." Newsday.

Banville, John

* The **sea** / John Banville. A. A. Knopf, 2006. 208 p.

ISBN 0307263118

1. Widowers 2. Grief in men 3. Memories 4. Death 5. Identity (Psychology) 6. Middle-aged men 7. Authors 8. Loss (Psychology) 9. Seaside resorts 10. England 11. Psychological fiction 12. Literary fiction

LC 2005050418

Booker Prize, 2005.

Following the death of his wife, Max Morden retreats to the seaside town of his childhood summers, where his own life becomes inextricably entwined with the members of the vacationing Grace family.

"What's strangest about The Sea is that the novel somehow becomes simpler and clearer as it gets more selfconscious: a consequence, I sup-

pose, of its author dropping the pretense of being one kind of writer and giving in to his authentic and much more complicated creative nature. This misshapen but affecting novel turns out to be about something even more familiar than the loss of innocence: it's about grief, the misery and confusion the narrator feels on losing his wife." New York Times Book Review.

Bao, Ninh

The **sorrow** of war : a novel of North Vietnam / Ninh Bao ; translated from the Vietnamese by Phan Thanh Hao ; edited by Frank Palmos. Pantheon Books, 1995. 233 p.

ISBN 0679439617

1. Vietnam War, 1961-1975 2. Vietnam 3. War stories 4. Translations -- Vietnamese to English

LC 94022390 //r952

Originally published 1991 by Writers' Association Publishing House, Hanoi.

Originally published: London: Secker & Warburg, 1993.

Kien's job is to search the Jungle of Screaming Souls for corpses. He knows the area well, this was where, in the dry season of 1969, his battalion was obliterated by American napalm and helicopter gunfire. Kien was one of only ten survivors. This book is his attempt to understand the eleven years of his life he gave to a senseless war.

"The word classic is bandied about with ridiculous laxity, but in this case it is hard not to fall back on it. Nothing else really fits the elemental simplicity of theme and treatment: love, war, death, disillusionment, betrayal." New Statesman.

Barbash, Tom

The **last** good chance / Tom Barbash. Picador USA, 2002. 440 p., 22 cm.

ISBN 0312287968

1. Architects 2. Urban renewal 3. Harbors 4. Hazardous waste sites 5. Brothers 6. Greed 7. Small town life -- New York (State) 8. Business -- Corrupt practices 9. New York (State) 10. Psychological fiction

LC 2002025847

An architectural phenom, Jack Lambeau returns to his hometown to resurrect the dying lakeside village, but a reunion with an old friend is spoiled when Jack's fiancée comes between them.

"Steven Turner is a young journalist exiled at a paper in Lakeland, a decaying port town in rural upstate New York. His best friend, Jack Lambeau, is the Lakeland town planner. An ambitious Ivy League graduate, Lambeau had had difficulty advancing his experimental urban planning ideas in New York City. When Lakeland's mayor, William Hickey, promised him carte blanche for his New Urbaniststyle visions, Lambeau agreed to return to his hometown. With evangelical fervor, he tries to revive Lakeland through a glittering lakefront development project. What he doesn't know, and what the mayor does, is that there are tubs of toxic materials illegally dumped under the lakefront. . . .This is a taut, intricate vision of ambition, corruption and love in the postindustrial era." Publishers Weekly.

Barber, Lizzy

A **girl** named Anna / Lizzy Barber. Harlequin Books, 2019. 368 p.

ISBN 9780778308997

1. Child kidnapping victims 2. Sisters 3. Deception 4. Missing persons investigation 5. Loss (Psychology) 6. Families 7. Consequences 8. Teenage girls 9. England 10. Florida 11. Thrillers and suspense

If your whole life is a lie, who can you trust?

Barbery, Muriel, 1969-

The **elegance** of the hedgehog / Muriel Barbery; translated by Alison Anderson. Europa Editions, 2008, c2006. 336 p..

ISBN 1933372605

1. Pessimism 2. Philosophy 3. Social classes 4. Aesthetics 5. Friendship 6. Widows 7. Japanese in France 8. Secrets 9. Twelve-year-old girls 10. Suicide 11. Women and cats 12. Apartment house life 13. Paris, France 14. Literary fiction 15. Translations -- French to English

Translated from the French: L'elegance du herisson.

First published in 2006 in France as L'elegance du herisson by Editions Gallimard, Paris.

Originally published: Paris, France : Gallimard, 2006.

Shortlisted for the International IMPAC Dublin Literary Award, 2010

The lives of fifty-four-year-old concierge Rene Michel and extremely bright, suicidal twelve-year-old Paloma Josse are transformed by the arrival of a new tenant, Kakuro Ozu.

"Barbery's sly wit, which bestows lightness on the most ponderous cogitations, keeps her tale aloft." The New Yorker.

Barclay, Linwood

Broken promise / Linwood Barclay. New American Library, 2015 464 p. Promise Falls (Linwood Barclay)

ISBN 9780451472670

1. Widowers 2. Single fathers 3. Family secrets 4. Small towns 5. Mothers 6. Murder 7. Murder investigation 8. New York (State) 9. Mysteries

LC 2015000081

First published: London : Orion, 2015.

From the New York Times bestselling author of No Safe House comes an explosive novel about the disturbing secrets of a quiet small town... After his wife's death and the collapse of his newspaper, David Harwood has no choice but to uproot his nine-year-old son and move back into his childhood home in Promise Falls, New York. David believes his life is in free fall, and he can't find a way to stop his descent. Then he comes across a family secret of epic proportions. A year after a devastating miscarriage, David's cousin Marla has continued to struggle. But when David's mother asks him to check on her, he's horrified to discover that she's been secretly raising a child who is not her own-a baby she claims was a gift from an "angel" left on her porch. When the baby's real mother is found murdered, David can't help wanting to piece together what happened-even if it means proving his own cousin's guilt. But as he uncovers each piece of evidence, David realizes that Marla's mysterious child is just the tip of the iceberg. Other strange things are happening. Animals are found ritually slaughtered. An ominous abandoned Ferris wheel seems to stand as a warning that something dark has infected Promise Falls. And someone has decided that the entire town must pay for the sins of its past... in blood Provided by publisher.

Barclay, Linwood

* **Elevator** pitch : a novel / Linwood Barclay. William Morrow, 2019. 464 p.

ISBN 9780062678287

1. Elevators 2. Disasters 3. Fear 4. Sabotage 5. Murder victims 6. Serial murders 7. Detectives 8. Women journalists 9. Mayors 10. Families 11. New York City 12. Thrillers and suspense

LC 2019014755

When an outbreak of fatal elevator crashes in Manhattan coincides with a sinister drop in emergency response services, two seasoned New York detectives and a straight-shooting journalist race against time to find answers.

Barclay, Linwood

Far from true : a novel / Linwood Barclay. New American Library, 2015 464 p. Promise Falls (Linwood Barclay)

ISBN 9780451472700

1. Cold cases (Criminal investigation) 2. Robbery 3. Family secrets 4. Small towns 5. Murder 6. Murder investigation 7. Mysteries

After the screen of a run-down drive-in movie theatre collapses and kills four people, the daughter of one of the victims asks private investigator Cal Weaver to look into a break-in at her father's house. Cal discovers a hidden room where salacious activities have taken place - as well as evidence of missing DVDs. But it may not be the discs the thief was interested in. . . .Meanwhile, Detective Barry Duckworth is still trying to solve two murders he believes are connected, since each featured a similar distinctive wound.

Barclay, Linwood

No safe house / Linwood Barclay. New American Library, 2014. 512 p.

ISBN 9780451414205

1. Crimes against seniors 2. Murder for hire 3. Survival 4. Murder investigation 5. Protectiveness in men 6. Murderers 7. Teenage girls 8. Betrayal 9. Families 10. Thrillers and suspense

LC 2013046120

Features characters previously seen in No Time for Goodbye.

A troubled family accidentally reconnects with the criminal who saved their lives seven years prior and is propelled into another potentially lethal situation.

Barclay, Linwood

A **noise** downstairs : a novel / Linwood Barclay. William Morrow, 2018. 356 p.

ISBN 9780062678256

1. Post-traumatic stress disorder 2. Murder witnesses 3. College teachers 4. Writing 5. Authors 6. Typewriters 7. Spirit possession 8. Murder investigation 9. Murderers 10. Thrillers and suspense

LC 2017048396

Battling PTSD and depression after an accidental stumble into a murder scene, a college professor begins writing his novel on a vintage typewriter that he comes to believe is possessed and somehow linked to the crime he survived.

Barclay, Linwood

Parting shot / Linwood Barclay. Doubleday Canada, 2017. 448 p. Promise Falls (Linwood Barclay)

ISBN 9780385690232

1. Drunk drivers 2. Traffic accidents 3. Private investigators 4. Clues 5. Murder 6. Intrigue 7. Detectives 8. Small towns 9. Murder investigation 10. New York (State) 11. Mysteries

A standalone spin-off from the Promise Falls trilogy finds Cal Weaver investigating threats made against an accused killer's family in spite of local outrage, a case that embroils him in a vicious revenge plot.

Barclay, Linwood

A **tap** on the window / Linwood Barclay. New American Library, 2013. 512 p.

ISBN 9780451414182

1. Drug traffic 2. Runaway children 3. Private investigators 4. Grief 5. Secrets 6. Hitchhikers 7. Sons -- Death 8. Missing teenagers 9. Teenage drug abusers 10. Bereavement in fathers 11. New York (State) 12. Mysteries

LC 2012050861

Still deeply grieving over the loss of his son from a drug overdose, private investigator Cal Weaver decides to give a teenage girl a ride home one night when she taps on his window and gets caught up in exposing the sordid secrets in Griffin, a small town in upstate New York where something seems to be horribly wrong.

Barclay, Linwood

The **twenty-three** : a Promise Falls novel / Linwood Barclay. Berkley Books, 2016. 464 p. Promise Falls (Linwood Barclay)

ISBN 9780451472724

1. Poisoning 2. Epidemics 3. Private investigators 4. Clues 5. Murder 6. Intrigue 7. Detectives 8. Small towns 9. Murder investigation 10. New York (State) 11. Mysteries

LC 2015045543

When hundreds of people are sickened by deliberately contaminated water in a small New York community's water supply, Detective Barry Duckworth scrambles to identify the culprit while investigating the murder of a college student whose crime scene disturbingly resembles those of two other victims.

Barclay, Linwood

Trust your eyes : a thriller / Linwood Barclay. New American Library, 2012. 496 p.

ISBN 9780451237903

1. Murder witnesses 2. Men with schizophrenia 3. Computerized mapping systems 4. Maps 5. Murder 6. Brothers 7. Recluses 8. Caregivers 9. Conspiracies 10. Murder investigation 11. Obsession 12. New York City 13. Thrillers and suspense

LC 2011053176

A schizophrenic, map-obsessed shut-in who tours the world using a computer program witnesses what he believes to be a murder in downtown New York City and enlists his caretaker brother in an effort to investigate.

Bardugo, Leigh

* **Ninth** house / Leigh Bardugo. Flatiron Books, 2019. 448 p.

ISBN 9781250313072

1. Yale University 2. Women college students 3. Secret societies 4. Occultism 5. Magic 6. Universities and colleges 7. Campus life 8. Psychic ability 9. Ghosts 10. Criminal investigation 11. Murder 12. Flashbacks 13. Supernatural 14. New Haven, Connecticut 15. Connecticut 16. Urban fantasy

LC 2019019855

Goodreads Choice Award, 2019

Surviving a horrific multiple homicide, a girl from the wrong side of the tracks is unexpectedly offered a full scholarship to Yale, where her mysterious benefactors task her with monitoring the university's secret societies.

Barker, Clive, 1952-

* **Weaveworld** / Clive Barker. Poseidon Press, 1987. 584 p.

ISBN 9780671612689

1. Parallel universes 2. Magic 3. Rugs 4. Magicians 5. Demons 6. Good and evil 7. Adventure 8. Fantasy fiction

LC 87018602

Susanna, granddaughter of the last caretaker, Calhoun Mooney, and Immacolata, an exiled witch intent on destroying her race, vie for a rug into which the world of Seerkind has been woven.

"Barker creates a fantastic romance of magic and promise that is at once popular fiction and utopian conjuring. . . . There is great wit in the struggle that ensues, and keen attention to the facts of poverty and exile." New York Times Book Review.

Barker, Nicola, 1966-

Darkmans / Nicola Barker. Ecco Press, 2008, c2007. 838 p.

ISBN 9780061575211

1. Fathers and sons 2. Drug dealers 3. Healers 4. Mothers -- Death 5. Neighbors 6. Families 7. Eccentrics and eccentricities 8. Sensitivity (Personal quality) 9. Sensitivity in men 10. Spirits 11. Troublemakers 12. Spirit possession 13. Practical jokes 14. Friendship 15. Literary fiction 16. Humorous stories

LC 2007040012

First published: London : Fourth Estate, 2007.

Hawthornden Prize, 2008.

Shortlisted for the Man Booker Prize, 2007.

If history is just a sick joke which keeps on repeating itself, then who exactly might be telling it, and why?

"[The plot] is twisted and braided with an intricacy so delicate you barely notice the links until the whole web engulfs you." Scotland on Sunday.

Barker, Pat, 1943-

Another world / Pat Barker. Farrar Straus & Giroux, 1999, c1998. 277 p.

ISBN 9780374105259

1. Blended families 2. Family relationships 3. Stepchildren 4. Family secrets 5. World War I veterans 6. Senior men 7. Newcastle upon Tyne, England 8. England 9. Psychological fiction

Originally published: London : Viking, 1998.

Nick tries to keep the peace in his disintegrating family while comforting his grandfather, a proud, intelligent man who lies dying on the other side of town.

"This novel demonstrates the extraordinary immediacy and vigor of expression we have come to expect from Barker." New York Times Book Review.

Barker, Pat, 1943-

* The **eye** in the door / Pat Barker. Dutton, 1994, c1993. 280 p. Regeneration trilogy (Pat Barker)

ISBN 9780525938088

1. Rivers, William, 1864-1922 2. Sassoon, Siegfried, 1886-1967 3. 1910s 4. World War I -- Great Britain 5. Religious persecution 6. Paranoia 7. Scapegoats (Persons) 8. Bisexuals 9. Pacifists 10. Gay men -- Great Britain 11. Homophobia -- Great Britain 12. Poets, English -- 20th century 13. Psychiatrists 14. London, England -- Social conditions -- 20th century 15. Historical fiction 16. War stories 17. Literary fiction

LC 93043833

Originally published: London : Viking, 1993.

Guardian First Book Award, 1993.

Characters from Regeneration return in a tale set after World War I, as Britain undergoes a period of repression and psychiatrist Dr. William Rivers, poet Siegfried Sassoon, and Lieutenant Billy Prior cope with the war's aftermath.

"This work succeeds as both historical fiction and as sequel. Its research and speculation combine to produce a kind of educated imagination that is persuasive and illuminating about this particular place and time. . . . The novel's greatest success, however, has to do with the insight it provides into its central doctor-patient relationships." New York Times Book Review.

Barker, Pat, 1943-

* The **ghost** road / Pat Barker. Dutton, 1996, c1995. 277 p. Regeneration trilogy (Pat Barker)

ISBN 9780525941910

1. Owen, Wilfred, 1893-1918 2. Rivers, William, 1864-1922 3. World War I -- Great Britain 4. Psychiatrists -- Great Britain 5. Poets, English -- 20th century 6. Working class men -- Great Britain 7. Soldiers -- Great Britain -- 20th century 8. Historical fiction 9. War stories 10. Literary fiction

Originally published: London : Viking, 1995.

Booker Prize, 1995.

As World War I winds to a close, two men--Dr. William Rivers, a psychologist whose dedicated healing sends men back to the brutal front, and Billy Prior, a shell-shocked soldier determined to rejoin the final English offensive--are profoundly affected by the events of the era.

"The Ghost Road is a startlingly good novel in its own right. With the other two volumes of the trilogy, it forms one of the richest and most rewarding works of fiction of recent times. Intricately plotted, beautifully written, skillfully assembled, tender, horrifying and funny, it lives on in the imagination, like the war it so imaginatively and so intelligently explores." Times Literary Supplement.

Barker, Pat, 1943-

* **Regeneration** / Pat Barker. Dutton, 1992, c1991. 251p. Regeneration trilogy (Pat Barker)

ISBN 9780525934271

1. Sassoon, Siegfried, 1886-1967 2. Rivers, William, 1864-1922 3. First World War era (1914-1918) 4. G I resistance and revolts 5. Soldiers -- Great Britain 6. Military hospitals 7. Poets, English -- 20th century 8. Psychiatrist and patient 9. Psychiatrists 10. Peace activists 11. World War I 12. Historical fiction 13. War stories

LC 91041264

Originally published: London : Viking, 1991.

Stressed by the war, poet, pacifist, and protestor Siegfried Sassoon is sent to Craiglockhart Hospital, where his views challenge the patriotic vision of Dr. William Rivers, a neurologist assigned to restore the sanity of shell-shocked soldiers.

"Regeneration is an antiwar war novel, in a tradition that is by now an established one, though it tells a part of the whole story of war that is not often told--how war may batter and break men's minds--and so makes the madness of war more than a metaphor, and more awful." New York Times Book Review.

Barker, Pat, 1943-

* The **silence** of the girls : a novel / Pat Barker. Doubleday, 2018. 293 p.

ISBN 9780385544214

1. Ancient Aegean civilizations (3000?1000 BCE) 2. Trojan War 3. Women and war 4. Captives 5. Gender role 6. Warriors 7. Women slaves 8. Violence in men 9. Gods and goddesses 10. Civilization, Ancient 11. Loss (Psychology) 12. Achilles (Greek mythology) 13. Briseis 14. Patroclus (Greek mythology) 15. Agamemnon (Greek mythology) 16. Troy (Extinct city) 17. Mythological fiction 18. War stories 19. Adaptations, retellings, and spin-offs

LC 2018014387

Shortlisted for The Women's Prize for Fiction, 2019.

Reimagines *The Iliad* from the perspectives of the captured women living in the Greek camp in the final weeks of the Trojan War.

Barker, Susan, 1978-

* The **incarnations** : a novel / Susan Barker. Simon & Schuster, 2015, viii, 371 p.

ISBN 9781501106781

1. Reincarnation 2. Soul mates 3. Identity (Psychology) 4. Stalking 5. Obsession 6. Stalkers 7. China -- History 8. Historical fiction 9. Literary fiction

LC 2014043145

"A Touchstone Book "

Originally published: London : Doubleday, 2014.

Kirkus Prize for Fiction finalist, 2015.

Receiving mysterious letters from someone claiming to be his soul-mate, a Beijing taxi driver learns about their shared relationships in numerous past lives before becoming increasingly certain that someone is watching him.

"Barker's historical tour de force is simultaneously sweeping and precise. It would be easy for the novel to teeter into overwrought melodrama; instead, Barker's psychologically nuanced characters and sharp wit turn the bleakness and the gore into something seriously moving." Kirkus.

Barnard, Robert

Death of a literary widow / Robert Barnard. Scribner, 1980, c1979. 192 p.

ISBN 0684166488

1. Widows 2. Authors, English 3. Arson 4. Murder investigation 5. Mysteries

LC 80013128

First published in Great Britain in 1979 under title: Posthumous papers.

"Two elderly women, Viola and Hilda, live in the same house, avoiding each other like the plague. Both have been married to the same man, the late writer Walter Mackin, who is the object of a sudden, intense renewal of interest--articles are written about him, his books are reissued. The great concern of the two wives is who will profit from Mackin's posthumous reputation. One of the old ladies dies in a fire, leaving everyone wondering whether she went out in an accidental blaze or as the result of someone's murderous rage." Booklist.

Barnes, Djuna, 1892-1982

* **Nightwood** / Djuna Barnes. Modern Library, 2000, c1937. xxxii, 169 p.

ISBN 067964024X

1. Americans in Paris, France 2. Extramarital affairs 3. Husband and wife 4. Lesbians 5. Sex addiction 6. Paris, France 7. Psychological fiction 8. Modern classics

LC 99056308

The impassioned monologues of Doctor Dante O'Connor reveal the story of Robin Vote, a young American woman in interwar Paris whose fate is the destruction of all who love her.

Barnes, Jonathan

The **somnambulist** / Jonathan Barnes. William Morrow, 2008. 368 p.

ISBN 0061375381

1. Blake, William, 1757-1827 2. Actors and actresses 3. Murder 4. Murder suspects 5. Sleep-walkers 6. Sleep-walking 7. London, England 8. England 9. Mysteries 10. Historical fantasy

A tale set in Victorian London introduces the characters of stage magician and detective Edward Moon and his silent sidekick, whose fiendish plot to re-create the apocalyptic prophecies of Samuel Taylor Coleridge threaten the British Empire.

"There is much that is strange, magical and darkly hilarious in this book, at least if one savors the sardonic and the bizarre. At various points it recalls Dickens, Alice in Wonderland and Frankenstein, but it remains an original and monumentally inventive piece of work." Washington Post Book World.

Barnes, Julian
  * **England,** England / Julian Barnes. Knopf, 1999, c1998. 275 p.
    ISBN 9780375405822
    1. National characteristics, English 2. Venture capitalists 3. Amusement parks 4. Isle of Wight (England) 5. England -- Civilization 6. Satirical fiction 7. Literary fiction
                                            LC 9846170
    Originally published: London : J. Cape, 1998.
    Shortlisted for the Booker-McConnell Prize, 1998.
    A replica of Britain is created on the Isle of Wight, complete with Robin Hood, Princess Di and replays of the Battle of Britain. It is the idea of a millionaire to show tourists the real Britain, a land with a great past and no future.
    "This tale of a theme-park England created on the Isle of Wight by a hateful entrepreneur--complete with fake Stonehenge and half-size Buckingam Palace--does not disappoint. But it is deepened by the story of Martha Cochrane, an overachiever employed to be the project's official naysayer. Both personally and professionally, Martha is devoted to searching for the authentic: for the missing jigsaw piece that disappeared in her father's pocket when he abandoned her family; for the missing piece in her love for a shy fellow-executive; and for the missing ingredient in success. Her meditations are worth any number of clever entertainments." The New Yorker.

Barnes, Julian
  * **Flaubert's** parrot / Julian Barnes. A. A. Knopf, 1985, c1984. 190 p.
    ISBN 9780394542720
    1. Flaubert, Gustave, 1821-1880 Study and teaching 2. Scholars and academics 3. Literary historians 4. Biographers 5. Parrots 6. Biographical fiction 7. Literary fiction
                                            LC 84048550
    Originally published: London : J. Cape, 1984.
    Shortlisted for the Booker-McConnell Prize, 1984.
    Interwoven with the story of obsessive amateur Flaubert scholar Charles Braithwaite are speculations on life and art and on the difficulty of knowing another person and above--and throughout--all is the brooding presence of Flaubert.
    "A minor classic, and one of the best criticism novels ever, because its critic/narrator has some dignity, because his choice of subject makes emotional sense and because the book has a lively, questioning spirit. . . . [Barnes has] written a modernist text with a nineteenth-century heart, a French novel with English lucidity and tact." The Nation.

Barnes, Julian
  * A **history** of the world in 10 1/ 2 chapters / Knopf, 1989. 307 p., 1 folded leaf of plates
    ISBN 9780394580616
    1. Meduse (Ship) 2. Survival (after airplane accidents, shipwrecks, etc) 3. Shipwrecks 4. Noah's ark 5. History 6. Literary fiction
                                            LC 89045266
    Includes a fold-out color reproduction of Gericault's Scene de naufrage.
    A History of the world in 10 and 1/2 chapters tells a series of apparently unconnected stories ranging from a woodworm's-eye-view of the journey on Noah's Ark to an astronaut's quest for its final resting place. There is pastiche and learned disquisition; there is heart-stopping documentary and heart-lifting revelation. But these stories are not separate.

They are all linked by a complex weave of inquiry into history itself, into love, myth and fabulation.
    "This book shapes up not only as Barnes's funniest novel but also his most richly cargoed and imaginatively designed. . . . As satirist and story-teller he has few equals at present." New Statesman.

Barnes, Julian
  The **noise** of time / Julian Barnes. Alfred A. Knopf, 2016. xi, 201 p.
    ISBN 9781101947241
    1. Shostakovich, Dmitri Dmitrievich, 1906-1975 2. Composers 3. Political persecution 4. Communism 5. Creativity in men 6. Fear in men 7. Communism and art 8. Personal conduct 9. Soviet Union 10. Biographical fiction 11. Literary fiction 12. Historical fiction
                                            LC 2015043444
    Longlisted for the Walter Scott Prize for Historical Fiction, 2017
    1936: Dmitri Shostakovich, just thirty, fears for his livelihood and his life. Stalin, hitherto a distant figure, has taken a sudden interest in his work and denounced his latest opera. Now, certain he will be exiled to Siberia (or, more likely, shot dead on the spot), he reflects on his predicament, his personal history, his parents, various women and wives, his children-- all of those hanging in the balance of his fate. And though a stroke of luck prevents him from becoming yet another casualty of the Great Terror, for years to come he will be held fast under the thumb of despotism: made to represent Soviet values, forced into joining the Party, and compelled, constantly, to weigh appeasing those in power against the integrity of his music.
    "A moody, muted composition about art under the thumb of tyranny." Kirkus.

Barnes, Julian
  The **only** story / Julian Barnes. Knopf, 2018. 253 p.
    ISBN 9780525521211
    1. May-December romance 2. Young men -- Relations with older women 3. Reminiscing in old age 4. Consequences 5. Life change events 6. Married women 7. Families 8. Unhappiness 9. Alcoholic women 10. Growing up 11. Men/women relations 12. London, England 13. England 14. Psychological fiction 15. Literary fiction 16. Second person narratives
                                            LC 2017047844
    "This is Borzoi book."
    A man who ran away as a teen university student with a married woman more than twice his age reflects on how they fell in love, how he freed her from a sterile marriage and how their relationship fell apart as she succumbed to depression.
    "[T]he novel slowly unfurls, and the reader drifts along on Barnes's gorgeous, undulating prose. Focusing on love, memory, nostalgia, and how contemporary Britain came to be, Barnes's latest will enrapture readers from beginning to end." Booklist.

Barnes, Julian
  * The **sense** of an ending / Julian Barnes. Jonathan Cape, 2011. 160 p.
    ISBN 9780224094153
    1. Middle-aged men 2. Male friendship 3. Memories -- Psychological aspects 4. Regret in men 5. Self-deception 6. Survivors of suicide victims 7. England 8. Literary fiction 9. Psychological fiction
    Film tie-in.
    First published in (hbk.) by Jonathan Cape in 2011. First published by Vintage in 2012.
    ALA Notable Book, 2012.
    Man Booker Prize, 2011.

Tony Webster and his clique first met Adrian Finn at school. Maybe Adrian was a little more serious than the others, certainly more intelligent, but they all swore to stay friends for life. Now Tony is in middle age. He's had a career and a single marriage, a calm divorce. He's certainly never tried to hurt anybody. Memory, though, is imperfect. It can always throw up surprises, as a lawyer's letter is about to prove.

"Tony Webster, a contented man settling comfortably into middle age, fondly carries his youth with him until a long-ago first love and an old childhood friend begin to haunt his present, forcing him to question the core of his character. Barnes' latest-- a meditation on memory and aging-- occasionally feels more like a series of wise, underline-worthy insights than a novel. But the many truths he highlights make it worthy of a careful read." Entertainment Weekly.

Barnes, Kim

In the kingdom of men : a novel / Kim Barnes. Alfred A. Knopf, 2012. 320 p.
ISBN 9780307273390
1. 1960s 2. Married women 3. Oil industry and trade 4. Americans in Saudi Arabia 5. Women murder victims 6. Bedouins 7. Oklahoma 8. Saudi Arabia 9. Mainstream fiction
LC 2011045617
Traces the experiences of an impoverished 1960s Oklahoma native who follows her husband to glamorous Saudi Arabia, where the death of a young Bedouin woman causes her to question the decadence and corruption of her new home.

Barnes, Steven, 1952-

Domino Falls / Steven Barnes and Tananarive Due Atria Books, 2013. 371 p. Devil's wake
ISBN 9781451617023
1. Survival (after epidemics) 2. Zombies 3. Cults 4. Epidemics 5. Aliens 6. New Agers 7. Teenagers 8. California 9. Afrofuturism and afrofantasy 10. Horror 11. Science fiction 12. African American fiction
An apocalyptic disease spread by a race of aliens turns its victims into zombies and begins an infection that threatens to overwhelm the Earth.

Barnett, Karen, 1969-

Ever faithful / Karen Barnett. WaterBrook, 2019 352 p. Vintage national parks novels
ISBN 9780735289581
1. Depression era (1929-1941) 2. Illiterate men 3. Single women 4. Civilian Conservation Corps 5. Wilderness areas 6. Forest fires 7. Suspicion 8. Secrets 9. Trust 10. Men/women relations 11. Yellowstone National Park 12. Christian historical romances
LC 2018046955
A man who can't read will never amount to anything--or so Nate Webber believes. But he takes a chance to help his family by signing up for the new Civilian Conservation Corps, skirting the truth about certain "requirements." Elsie Brookes was proud to grow up as a ranger's daughter, but she longs for a future of her own. After four years serving as a maid in the park's hotels, she still hasn't saved enough money for her college tuition. A second job, teaching a crowd of rowdy men in the CCC camp, might be the answer, but when Elsie discovers Nate's secret, it puts his job as camp foreman in jeopardy.

Barnett, LaShonda K. (LaShonda Katrice), 1974-

Jam on the Vine / LaShonda Barnett. Grove Press, 2015. viii, 323 p.
ISBN 9780802123343
1. 1910s 2. African American women 3. Women journalists 4. African American women journalists 5. Lesbians 6. Newspapers 7. African American newspapers 8. Race relations 9. Racism 10. Sexism 11. Family relationships 12. Women/women relations 13. Texas 14. Kansas City, Missouri 15. Paris, France 16. Historical fiction 17. LGBTQIA fiction 18. African American fiction
RUSA Reading List Short List, 2016.
A poor, African-American Muslim girl in rural, racially segregated turn-of-the-century Texas, Ivoe Williams discovers a passion for journalism while pilfering old newspapers from her mother's white employer. Ivoe keeps her eyes on the horizon, first earning a college scholarship and later moving to Kansas City with her former teacher and lover, Ona. Together, the women start Jam! On the Vine, the nation's first female-run Black newspaper. Loosely based on pioneering journalist Ida B. Wells and Charlotta Bass (the first African-American woman to own and operate a newspaper), this dramatic debut should enchant readers who enjoy strong female characters and well-researched, vividly described period detail. -- Description by Gillian Speace.

Barnhill, Kelly Regan

Dreadful young ladies and other stories / Kelly Barnhill. Algonquin Books of Chapel Hill, 2018. 304 p.
ISBN 9781616207977
1. Magic 2. Witches 3. Human behavior 4. Fantasy fiction 5. Short stories
LC 2017039839
A first collection of short stories by the Newbery Medal-winning author of The Girl Who Drank the Moon includes the World Fantasy Award-winning novella, The Unlicensed Magician, in which an invisible girl once left for dead pursues a secret, magical life.

Barr, Mark

Watershed / Mark Barr. Hub City Press, 2019. 304 p.
ISBN 9781938235597
1. Tennessee Valley Authority. 2. 1930s 3. Depression era (1929-1941) 4. Engineers 5. Homemakers 6. Dams -- Design and construction 7. Electricity 8. Depressions -- 1929-1941 9. Ambition in men 10. Self-confidence in women 11. Small towns 12. Secrets 13. Guilt 14. Tennessee 15. Southern States 16. Historical fiction
David J. Langum, Sr. Prize in American Historical Fiction, 2019.
In 1937 rural Tennessee, a small-town housewife, finding her place in the post-Depression South, struggles to balance motherhood and a new-found freedom that awakens ambitions and a sexuality she never knew she possessed.

Barr, Nevada

Destroyer angel : an Anna Pigeon novel / Nevada Barr. Minotaur Books, 2014. 368 p. Anna Pigeon mysteries
ISBN 9780312614584
1. United States. National Park Service Officials and employees. 2. Women park rangers 3. Canoeing 4. Kidnapping 5. Missing persons 6. Mysteries
LC 2013032879
Testing outdoor sporting equipment designed for a disabled companion, U.S. Park Services ranger Anna Pigeon returns from a solo outing to discover that her fellow campers have been abducted.
"Barr's gift for depicting breathtaking scenery elevates the story, as does Anna's complex, ever-evolving personality." Publishers Weekly.

Barr, Nevada

The **rope** : an Anna Pigeon novel / Nevada Barr. Minotaur Books, 2012. 368 p. Anna Pigeon mysteries
ISBN 9780312614577
1. 1990s 2. Imprisonment 3. Escapes 4. Determination in women

5. Attempted murder 6. Deserts 7. Widows 8. Women park rangers 9. Women amateur detectives 10. Temporary employment 11. Glen Canyon 12. Mysteries

LC 2011035837

This novels occurs before the events in Track of the Cat and feature the backstory of Anna Pigeon.

The long-anticipated story of Anna Pigeon's past traces her broken-hearted 1995 relocation from New York City and first days as a Glen Canyon park ranger, a new start that is shattered by her abduction and imprisonment in the bottom of a dry well without supplies.

Barr, Nevada

Track of the cat / Nevada Barr. G. P. Putnam's Sons, 1993. 238 p. Anna Pigeon mysteries

ISBN 0399138242

1. United States. National Park Service Officials and employees. 2. Puma -- West Texas 3. Women park rangers 4. National parks and reserves -- West Texas 5. Women amateur detectives 6. Guadalupe Mountains National Park 7. Texas 8. Mysteries

LC 92029694

Agatha Award for Best First Novel, 1994.
Anthony Award for Best First Novel, 1994.

Fleeing New York to find refuge as a ranger in the remote backcountry of West Texas, Anna Pigeon stumbles into a web of violence and murder when fellow park ranger Sheila Drury is mysteriously killed and another ranger vanishes

Barr, Nevada

What Rose forgot / Nevada Barr. Minotaur Books, 2019. 320 p.

ISBN 9781250207135

1. Grandmothers 2. Amnesia 3. Nursing homes 4. Escapes 5. Threat (Psychology) 6. Sisters 7. Granddaughters 8. Hackers 9. Family secrets 10. North Carolina 11. Charlotte, North Carolina 12. Mysteries

LC 2019012649

Waking up in a nursing-home Alzheimer's Unit with no memory of how she got there, Rose Dennis orchestrates an escape but does not know who to trust.

Barry, Brunonia

The **map** of true places / Brunonia Barry. William Morrow, 2010. 406 p.

ISBN 9780061624780

1. Family secrets 2. Father and adult daughter 3. Women psychotherapists 4. Psychotherapist and patient 5. Suicide 6. Grief in women 7. People with Parkinson's disease 8. Psychological fiction

Zee Finch, a psychotherapist, has come home to Salem to take care of her ailing father and to try to figure out her own life after the suicide of one of her patients, which was made even more difficult by Zee's past--her mother committed suicide herself, in front of her.

"Although marred by unnecessary come-to-realize moments, this woman-in-jeopardy thriller retooled with gothic elements shifting identities, secrets and portents, a deserted cottage and a missing suicide note manages to transcend its component cliches." Kirkus.

Barry, Dave

Insane city / Dave Barry. G. P. Putnam's Sons, 2013. 341 p.

ISBN 9780399158681

1. Misadventures 2. Slackers 3. Engaged persons 4. Lost articles 5. Stripteasers 6. Women lawyers 7. Weddings 8. Humorous stories

LC 2012028009

Astonished by his imminent marriage to a women he believed out of his league, Seth flies to their destination wedding in Florida only to be swept up in a maelstrom of violence involving rioters, Russian gangsters, angry strippers and a desperate python.

Barry, Dave

Lunatics / Dave Barry and Alan Zweibel. G. P. Putnam's Sons, 2012. 309 p.

ISBN 9780399158698

1. Misadventures 2. Bad days 3. Hate 4. Pet shops 5. Voyages and travels 6. Humorous stories

Philip Horkman is a happy man, the owner of a pet store called The Wine Shop, and on Sundays a referee for kids' soccer. Jeffrey Peckerman is the sole sane person in a world filled with goddamned jerks and morons, and he's having a really bad day. The two of them are about to collide in a swiftly escalating series of events that will send them running for their lives, pursued by the police, soldiers, terrorists, subversives, bears, and a man dressed as Chuck E. Cheese.

Barry, Jessica

* **Don't** turn around / Jessica Barry. HarperCollins, 2020. 400 p.

ISBN 9780062874863

1. Young women 2. Secrets 3. Strangers 4. Trust 5. Stalking 6. New Mexico 7. Thrillers and suspense

Cait and Rebecca, each with secrets to protect, find their lives in danger while on a desolate road in the New Mexico desert and must learn to trust one another.

"Barry follows up her attention-grabbing debut, Freefall, with two women, heretofore strangers, pursued on the bleak New Mexican back roads by a truck whose driver clearly means to deliver death." Library Journal.

Barry, Kevin, 1969-

City of Bohane / Kevin Barry. Graywolf Press, 2012, c2011. 277 p.

ISBN 9781555976088

1. 21st century 2. Near future 3. Crime 4. Gangs 5. Gang leaders 6. Power (Social sciences) 7. Violence in gangs 8. Inner city 9. Murder 10. Ireland 11. Dystopian fiction 12. Crime fiction 13. Literary fiction

Originally published: London : Jonathan Cape, 2011.
International IMPAC Dublin Literary Award, 2013.

A tale set in a near-future coastal Ireland finds the long-time rule of dapper godfather Logan Hartnett threatened by the return of an old nemesis, the ambitions of once-trusted henchmen, and his wife's request for him to abandon his life of crime.

Barry, Kevin, 1969-

Night boat to Tangier : a novel / Kevin Barry. Doubleday, 2019. 255 p.

ISBN 9780385540315

1. Criminals 2. Aging 3. Irish 4. Drug smuggling 5. Reminiscing in old age 6. Harbors 7. Ferryboats 8. Daughters 9. Memories 10. Spain 11. Literary fiction

LC 2019016293

Longlisted for the Booker Prize, 2019.

Two Irish drug-smuggling partners reevaluate a career marked by violence, betrayal and exile during a nocturnal vigil in a sketchy Spanish ferry terminal where one of them would reconnect with an estranged daughter.

Barry, Max, 1973-

Lexicon : a novel / Max Barry. The Penguin Press, 2013. 384 p.

ISBN 9781594205385

1. Persuasion (Psychology) 2. Secret societies 3. Wizards 4. Linguists 5. Mind control 6. Conspiracies 7. Power (Social sciences) 8. Satirical fiction 9. Thrillers and suspense 10. Parallel narratives

LC 2012046980

Aurealis Awards, Best Science Fiction Novel, 2013.

Recruited into an exclusive government school where students are taught the science of coercion to support a secretive organization of "poet" world manipulators, orphaned street hustler Emily Ruff becomes the school's most talented prodigy before catastrophically falling in love, while a seemingly innocent young man is rendered a pawn in a dangerous power struggle.

Barry, Sebastian, 1955-

Days without end : a novel / Sebastian Barry. Viking Press, 2017, c2016. 259 p.

ISBN 9780525427360

1. 19th century 2. Immigrants, Irish 3. Soldiers 4. Gender identity 5. Gay men 6. Frontier and pioneer life 7. Nonconformists 8. Native American girls 9. Dakota Indians 10. United States Civil War, 1861-1865 11. Indians of North America -- Wars 12. Protectiveness in men 13. Men/men relations 14. United States -- Social life and customs -- 19th century 15. Historical fiction 16. LGBTQIA fiction 17. Literary fiction

First published in the United Kingdom in 2016 by Faber & Faber Limited.

ALA Notable Book, 2018.

Costa Book of the Year Award, 2016

Costa Novel Award, 2016.

Walter Scott Prize for Historical Fiction, 2017.

Longlisted for the Man Booker Prize, 2017.

Longlisted for the Andrew Carnegie Medal for Excellence in Fiction, 2018.

A survivor of Ireland's Great Famine and a recent immigrant to the United States, 17-year-old Thomas McNulty joins the U.S. Army in 1851 with his best friend and fellow orphan, John Cole. Sent first to the Great Plains to butcher the Sioux, and later, to the battlefields of the Civil War, the young carry out their orders despite their horror of the carnage. Meanwhile, they become lovers and must find a way to build a life together in a society that doesn't recognize or understand romantic relationships between men. -- Description by Gillian Speace

"A lively, richly detailed story of one slice of the Irish immigrant experience in America." Kirkus.

Barry, Sebastian, 1955-

The **secret** scripture : a novel / Sebastian Barry. Viking, 2008. 304 p.

ISBN 9780670019403

1. Psychiatric hospital patients 2. Senior women 3. Physicians 4. Physician and patient 5. Protestants -- Ireland 6. Secrets 7. Manipulation by men 8. Psychiatric hospitals 9. Sligo, Ireland 10. Ireland -- Social conditions -- 20th century 11. Psychological fiction 12. Parallel narratives 13. Literary fiction

LC 2007041716

Costa Novel Award, 2008.

Costa Book of the Year Award, 2008.

James Tait Black Memorial Prize for Fiction, 2008.

Shortlisted for the Man Booker Prize, 2008.

Roseanne McNulty, once one of the most beautiful and beguiling girls in County Sligo, Ireland, is now an elderly patient at Roscommon Regional Mental Hospital. As her hundredth year draws near, she decides to record the events of her life, hiding the manuscript beneath the floorboards. Meanwhile, the hospital is preparing to close and is evaluating its patients to determine whether they can return to society. Dr. Grene, Roseanne's caretaker, takes a special interest in her case. In his research, he discovers a document written by a local priest that tells a very different story of Roseanne's life than what she recalls. As doctor and patient attempt to understand each other, they begin to uncover long-buried secrets about themselves.

"While not a historical novel in the accepted sense, The Secret Scripture uses history's complex relationship with truth to generate momentum and sharpen the definition of character. . . . The reader applauds the wisdom of its heroine in keeping her integrity entire. 'Sligo made me and Sligo undid me', Roseanne remarks, echoing Dante, and in the process of this undoing she finds her greatness." Times Literary Supplement.

Bartels, Erin, 1980-

We hope for better things / Erin Bartels. Revell, 2019. 393 p.

ISBN 9780800734916

1. Women journalists 2. Family secrets 3. Family history 4. Farmhouses 5. Racism 6. Great-aunts 7. Decision-making 8. Faith (Christianity) 9. Families 10. Michigan 11. Christian fiction

In this richly textured debut novel, a disgraced journalist moves into her great aunt's secret-laden farmhouse and discovers that the women in her family were testaments to true love and courage in the face of war, persecution, and racism.

"Bartels successfully weaves American history into a deeply moving story of heartbreak, long-held secrets, and the bonds of family." Publishers Weekly.

Barth, John, 1930-

Chimera / John Barth. Houghton Mifflin, 2001, c1972. 308 p.

ISBN 9780618131709

1. Storytelling 2. Gods and goddesses, Greek 3. Pegasus (Greek mythology) 4. Perseus (Greek mythology) 5. Scheherazade 6. Mythology, Greek 7. Mythological fiction 8. Literary fiction 9. Experimental fiction 10. Metafiction

Originally published: New York: Random House, 1972.

National Book Award for Fiction, 1973.

The comic adventures of Dunyazade, Perseus, and Bellerophon reveal the author's thoughts on the nature of a hero and relationships between men and women.

"The protagonists of these witty confessions are walking psyches, at war with ultimate ambivalence. (Far from clarifying what is ambiguous, Barth deepens it--by retelling familiar stories, deploying their unsettled alternatives so as to virtually insist on their unreality). . . . [He] employs literary devices that multiply confusion [including] . . . the removal of all barriers posed by time and history." Library Journal.

Barth, John, 1930-

* The **end** of the road / John Barth. Doubleday, 1967. 188 p.

1. 1950s 2. Love triangles 3. Mental illness 4. Indecision in men 5. Single men 6. Married people 7. Psychiatrists 8. College teachers 9. Extramarital affairs 10. Maryland 11. Literary fiction

"In the story, at once comic, tragic and satirical, Barth made a frontal attack on the excesses of Sartrean existentialism and existential philosophy popular in the 1950's." Publishers Weekly.

Barth, John, 1930-

* The **floating** opera / John Barth. Doubleday, 1967. 252 p.

ISBN 9780385076302

1. Lawyers 2. Love triangles 3. Suicide 4. Cynicism 5. Sexuality 6. People with heart disease 7. Meaning (Psychology) 8. Fathers and sons 9. Literary fiction 10. Experimental fiction

LC 67012864

"Just as Voltaire's Candide decides to contentedly cultivate his garden after a disillusioning journey, so does Barth's Todd come to terms with life by discovering in time that it is best to choose among the relative values that life offers rather than cynically rejecting all values by way of suicide." New York Times Book Review.

Barth, John, 1930-

* **Giles** Goat-Boy ; or, The revised new syllabus / John Barth. Doubleday, 1966. xxxi, 710 p.

ISBN 0385043996

1. 1960s 2. Universities and colleges 3. College students 4. Campus life 5. Goats 6. United States -- Social life and customs -- 20th century 7. Allegories 8. Literary fiction 9. Satirical fiction 10. Experimental fiction 11. Modern classics

LC 66015666

George Giles encounters new people and ideas as he ascends from a goat farm to the position of Grand Tutor of the human university.

Barth, John, 1930-

The **last** voyage of somebody the sailor / John Barth. Little, Brown, 1991. 573 p.

ISBN 9780316082518

1. Storytelling 2. Time travel (Past) 3. Voyages and travels 4. Authors 5. Shipwrecks 6. Sindbad the Sailor (Legendary character) 7. Baghdad, Iraq 8. Experimental fiction 9. Literary fiction

LC 90044991

While retracing the legendary voyages of Sindbad the Sailor, journalist Simon William Behler finds himself in Sindbad's household in medieval Baghdad and competes with Sindbad in a storytelling marathon in the hopes of finding a way back to the modern world.

"If the setting is sober, the narrator is not. This is John Barth, . . . after all, and his hero is variously exuberant, obnoxious, funny, self-conscious, and, not sober at all, but thoroughly intoxicated with sex, love, and story telling, especially with their commingling." Commonwealth

Barth, John, 1930-

* The **sot-weed** factor / John Barth. Doubleday, 1987, c1967. xii, 756 p.

ISBN 9780385240888

1. Colonial America (1600-1775) 2. 18th century 3. Sexuality 4. Innocence (Personal quality) 5. Voyages and travels 6. Good and evil 7. Pirates 8. Poets 9. Twin brothers and sisters 10. Maryland -- History -- Colonial period, 1600-1775 11. Great Britain -- History -- Stuarts, 1603-1714 12. Picaresque fiction 13. Literary fiction 14. Experimental fiction 15. Satirical fiction

Ebnezer Cooke, his twin sister, and their young tutor go from England to Maryland where they participate in the area's early years.

Barthelme, Donald

Sixty stories / Donald Barthelme. G. P. Putnam's Sons, 1981. 457 p.

ISBN 9780399126598

1. Experimental fiction 2. Short stories 3. Anthologies

LC 818646

National Book Critics Circle Award for Fiction finalist, 1981

"Lots of very good old Barthelme, then, a smidgin of pretty good new Barthelme: a collection without a reason, perhaps, but an expansive sampling for newcomers and a chic bedside book for fans who want to replace their tattered paperbacks." Kirkus.

Barthelme, Frederick, 1943-

Bob the gambler / Frederick Barthelme. Houghton Mifflin, 1997. 213 p.

ISBN 0395809770

1. Compulsive gamblers -- Biloxi, Mississippi 2. Architects -- Biloxi, Mississippi 3. Casinos -- Biloxi, Mississippi 4. Families -- Biloxi, Mississippi 5. Gambling -- Biloxi, Mississippi 6. Husband and wife -- Biloxi, Mississippi 7. Biloxi, Mississippi 8. Mainstream fiction

LC 974363

An architect and his wife living near a casino in Mississippi become hooked on gambling and lose everything they own. They move into his mother's house and embark on a new life, discovering happiness in simplicity and insecurity.

"Paradise, as it happens, is the name of the local casino. The irony in this is obvious enough, but it is Barthelme's peculiar post-modern gift to be able to invert the easy ironies of contemporary life and reveal the truths beneath them." New York Times Book Review.

Barthelme, Frederick, 1943-

Elroy Nights / Frederick Barthelme. Counterpoint, 2003. 224 p.

ISBN 1582431280

1. College teachers 2. Art teachers 3. Middle-aged men 4. Separated men (Marital relations) 5. Midlife crisis 6. Middle-aged men -- Relations with younger women 7. Intergenerational friendship 8. Gulf Coast, Mississippi 9. Mississippi 10. Mainstream fiction

LC 2003007830

A reasonably successful, fiftysomething artist and professor caught between a midlife crisis and the decay of his sixties, Elroy Nights--with his wife's agreement--elects to live separately from his wife and embarks on a journey of discovery with his young students, until an unforeseen tragedy forces him to deal with a world suddenly gone wrong.

"Barthelme's world is vague and unclear. Conversations dead-end, spousal jabs go unanswered, Elroy and Freddie's relationship never evolves into anything defined. Still, currents of hope run through Elroy Nights. Elroy and Clare's relationship contains remarkable moments of kindness-not in showy grand scenes but in small gestures, in bitten tongues, in the silent lowering of expectations." New York Times Book Review.

Barthelme, Frederick, 1943-

Painted desert : a novel / Frederick Barthelme Viking, 1995. 243 p. Del Tribute series

ISBN 0670864692

1. Television news 2. Riots 3. Automobile travel 4. Anarchists 5. Popular culture 6. Mainstream fiction

LC 95006769

A junior college professor and his girlfriend pry themselves from their television and computer screens and take to the road, achieving an epiphany in the Arizona desert.

"Laced with sharp dialogue and wit, this novel suggests that we are what we witness, whether it's the gypsum hills of White Sands or the slaying of a stranger a thousand miles away." The New Yorker.

Bartlett, Neil, 1958-

* The **disappearance** boy / Neil Bartlett. St. Martin's Press, 2014 320 p.

ISBN 9781620407257

1. 1950s 2. Magicians 3. Gay men 4. Orphans 5. Friendship 6. Twenties (Age) 7. Men with disabilities 8. Theater 9. England 10. Coming-of-age stories 11. LGBTQIA fiction

When the show moves to the Brighton Grand, Reggie Rainbow, the magician's behind-the-scenes assistant, begins questioning how much of his own life has been an act and sets out to find somebody who disappeared from his own life years before.

Barton, Fiona

The **child** / Fiona Barton. Berkley, 2017 336 p. Kate Waters novels (Fiona Barton)

ISBN 9781101990483

1. Human remains (Archaeology) 2. Women journalists 3. Baby stealing 4. Kidnapping 5. Secrets 6. Criminal investigation 7. Psychological suspense

LC 2016055096

"You can bury the story... but you can't hide the truth" --Cover.

"The author of the stunning New York Times bestseller The Widow returns with a brand-new novel of twisting psychological suspense. As an old house is demolished in a gentrifying section of London, a workman discovers a tiny skeleton, buried for years. For journalist Kate Waters, it's a story that deserves attention. She cobbles together a piece for her newspaper, but at a loss for answers, she can only pose a question: Who is the Building Site Baby? As Kate investigates, she unearths connections to a crime that rocked the city decades earlier: A newborn baby was stolen from the maternity ward in a local hospital and was never found. Her heartbroken parents were left devastated by the loss. But there is more to the story, and Kate is drawn--house by house--into the pasts of the people who once lived in this neighborhood that has given up its greatest mystery. And she soon finds herself the keeper of unexpected secrets that erupt in the lives of three women--and torn between what she can and cannot tell"--, Provided by publisher.

"Bartons second missing-child story is a gut-wrenching tale of narcissism, cunning predators, and bare-knuckle survival." Booklist.

Barton, Fiona,

The **suspect** / Fiona Barton. Penguin Group USA, 2019 384 p. Kate Waters novels (Fiona Barton)

ISBN 9781101990513

1. Missing teenage girls 2. Women journalists 3. Mothers and sons 4. British in Thailand 5. Suspicion 6. Separated friends, relatives, etc 7. Thailand 8. Psychological suspense

LC 2018048595

Pursuing the story of two British teens who disappeared during a Bangkok hostel fire, journalist Kate Waters struggles to remain objective when her estranged son is declared a main suspect.

Bartz, Andrea

The **herd** : a novel / Andrea Bartz. Ballantine Books, 2020. 336 p.

ISBN 9781984826367

1. Women business owners 2. Missing persons 3. Sisters 4. Women professional employees 5. Women journalists 6. Women publicity agents 7. Missing persons investigation 8. Secrets 9. Psychological suspense

LC 2019038590

When the enigmatic founder of their exclusive New York women's mentorship community goes missing, two sisters search for answers to protect their friends and careers before uncovering dangerous secrets.

"A soapy and fun woman-centric thriller." Kirkus.

Bartz, Andrea

The **lost** night / Andrea Bartz. Crown Pub, 2019. 336 p.

ISBN 9780525574712

1. 2010s 2. Friends' death 3. Suicide victims 4. Murder investigation 5. Survivors of suicide victims 6. Loss of consciousness 7. Suicide investigation 8. Young adults 9. Memories 10. Partying 11. New York City 12. Brooklyn, New York City 13. Psychological suspense

A chance discovery of a 10-year-old video shares disturbing insights into the suicide of a college classmate who may have been murdered on a hazy drunken night, a revelation that compels one woman to determine her own role.

"Bartz calls upon psychology and technology as Lindsay, whose profession is research and fact-checking, uncovers the truth." Booklist.

Barzak, Christopher

One for sorrow / Christopher Barzak. Bantam Dell, 2007. 320 p.

ISBN 9780553384369

1. Teenage boys 2. Ghosts 3. Murder 4. Teenage boys -- Friendship 5. Happiness in teenage boys 6. Self-perception 7. Coming-of-age stories 8. Psychological fiction 9. Domestic fiction

LC 2007015871

This novel was made into film in 2014 under the title, Jamie Marks is Dead, directed by Carter Smith and starring Judy Greer, Liv Tyler, and Cameron Monaghan.

With his family life falling apart after his mother is paralyzed in a drunk-driving accident, Adam McCormik is drawn to the site where the body of a murdered classmate, Jamie Marks, a boy ignored by almost everyone, had been found and finds himself entering into a strange friendship with a ghost.

"The author possesses a remarkable gift for depicting adolescent sexuality in prose that's at once unadorned and unabashedly romantic. He also creates lively, oddball secondary characters. . . . The novel has some problems with pacing, and in a few spots believable characterization and dialogue are ground under the wheels of the plot machine. But One for Sorrow is a considerable achievement, a lyrical ghost story as moving and credible as it is unsettling." Village Voice.

Bassani, Giorgio, 1916-2000

The **garden** of the Finzi-Continis / Giorgio Bassani ; translated from the Italian by Isabel Quigly. Atheneum, 1965. 293 p.

ISBN 9781400044221

1. 1930s 2. Jewish families 3. Holocaust (1933-1945) 4. Innocence (Personal quality) 5. Rich families 6. World War II 7. Antisemitism 8. Italy 9. Coming-of-age stories 10. Translations -- Italian to English 11. Historical fiction

This novel was the basis for the 1970 Italian film of the same name that later went on to win the Academy Award for Best Foreign Language Film in 1971.

Bateman, Kate

This earl of mine / Kate Bateman. St Martins Press, 2019. 320 p. Bow Street bachelors

ISBN 9781250305954

1. Young widows 2. Detectives 3. Independence in women 4. Undercover operations 5. Heirs and heiresses 6. Prisoners 7. Death row prisoners 8. Marriage 9. Courtship 10. Womanizers 11. Spies 12. Investigations 13. Interpersonal attraction 14. Men/women relations 15. Historical romances 16. Regency romances

Marrying a condemned criminal, newly widowed shipping heiress Georgiana Caversteed is stunned to discover her husband very much alive at a social gathering weeks later and finds herself being courted by this well-known rake who was working undercover in Newgate prison.

Bates, H. E. (Herbert Ernest), 1905-1974

Fair stood the wind for France / H. E. Bates. Little, Brown and Company, 1944. 239 p.

1. World War II -- France 2. Pilots -- Great Britain 3. France -- History -- German occupation, 1940-1945 4. Love stories 5. War stories 6. Historical fiction

"An almost unbearable suspense, the romance of the two young people and a true portrait of the little people of France, defenseless but possessed of an enduring power, all these go to make an unforgettable story, beautifully told." Bookmarks Magazine.

Bates, Judy Fong, 1949-

* **Midnight** at the Dragon Cafe / Judy Fong Bates. Counterpoint, 2005, c2004. 317 p.

ISBN 9781582431895

1. 1950s 2. Chinese Canadian girls 3. Girls -- Canada 4. Chinese in Ontario 5. Chinese in Canada 6. Immigrants, Chinese -- Canada 7. Immigrants -- Canada 8. Chinese Canadian families 9. Restaurateurs 10. Restaurants 11. Ethnic restaurants, shops, etc 12. Family secrets 13. Love triangles 14. Extramarital affairs 15. Love 16. Men/women relations 17. Parent and child 18. Small towns -- Canada 19. Social isolation 20. Resentfulness 21. Ontario 22. Canada 23. Domestic fiction

LC 2004381288

Originally published: Toronto: McClelland & Stewart, 2004.
ALA Notable Book, 2006.

Su-Jen Chou, a Chinese immigrant growing up in 1950s Ontario finds herself shouldering the weight of her mother's hopes and dreams as her isolated family attempts to forge a life for themselves in a small town.

Batuman, Elif, 1977-

* The **idiot** / Elif Batuman. Penguin Press, 2017. 480 p.
ISBN 9781594205613

1. Harvard University Students 2. 1990s 3. Women college students 4. Identity (Psychology) 5. Turkish Americans 6. Self-discovery in women 7. Children of immigrants 8. Mathematicians 9. Young women 10. Campus life 11. Email 12. Cambridge, Massachusetts 13. Massachusetts 14. Coming-of-age stories 15. Literary fiction 16. Autobiographical fiction

LC 2016029596

Shortlisted for The Women's Prize for Fiction, 2018.
Pulitzer Prize for Fiction finalist, 2018.

Embarking on her freshman year at Harvard in the early tech days of the 1990s, a young artist and daughter of Turkish immigrants begins a correspondence with an older mathematics student from Hungary while struggling with her changing sense of self, first love and a daunting career prospect.

"A sweetly caustic first novel...Self-aware, cerebral, and delightful." Kirkus.

Bauer, Ann

The **forever** marriage : a novel / Ann Bauer. Overlook Press, 2012. 336 p.
ISBN 9781590207215

1. Widows 2. Marriage 3. Self-fulfillment in women 4. Lovers 5. Women -- Psychology 6. Psychological fiction

LC 2012008053

Unexpectedly falling in love with the late husband she resented throughout their marriage, a grieving Carmen embarks on a series of romantic trysts only to discover that her own life may be in danger, a situation that forces her to reflect on her experiences as a privileged suburban wife, fierce friend and mother of a child with Down syndrome.

Bauer, Belinda, 1962-

The **beautiful** dead / Belinda Bauer. Atlantic Monthly Press, 2017, c2016. 341 p.

ISBN 9780802125330

1. Women television journalists 2. Ambition in women 3. Art -- Exhibitions 4. Women murder victims 5. Serial murderers 6. Serial murders 7. People with dementia -- Care 8. Obsession 9. Police 10. London, England 11. Thrillers and suspense

A television crime reporter desperate to recharge her flagging career becomes an unwitting accomplice to an attention-hungry serial killer at the center of the decade's biggest murder investigation.

Bauer, Belinda, 1962-

Snap / Belinda Bauer. Atlantic Monthly Press, 2018. 352 p.

ISBN 9780802127747

1. Criminal investigations 2. Burglary 3. Detectives 4. Death threats 5. Psychic trauma 6. Murder investigation 7. Fourteen-year-old boys 8. Father-deserted children 9. Children of murder victims 10. England 11. Thrillers and suspense

LC 2018012770

Longlisted for the Man Booker Prize, 2018.

Waking up to discover a knife and sinister note in her bed, a young woman is connected to a string of burglaries and the recent brutal murder of a mother of three.

Bauer, Carlene

* **Frances** and Bernard / Carlene Bauer. Houghton Mifflin Harcourt, 2013. 224 p.

ISBN 9780547858241

1. 1950s 2. Authors 3. Letter writing 4. Catholics 5. Friendship 6. New York City -- Social life and customs -- 20th century 7. Epistolary novels 8. Love stories

LC 2012014028

A tale loosely inspired by Robert Lowell and Flannery O'Connor traces the intense friendship and literary bond shared by two mid-20th-century New York writers through an exchange of letters that explores their respective writing forms and beliefs about faith, passion and the nature of acceptable sacrifice.

Bauermeister, Erica

The **scent** keeper / Erica Bauermeister. St. Martin's Press, 2019. 304 p.

ISBN 9781250200136

1. Fathers and daughters 2. Senses and sensation 3. Family secrets 4. Imaginary machines 5. Gadgets 6. Odors 7. Smell 8. Memories 9. Nature study 10. Island life 11. Life change events 12. Adjustment (Psychology) 13. Identity (Psychology) 14. Growing up 15. Self-discovery 16. Pacific Northwest 17. Literary fiction 18. Coming-of-age stories

LC 2018055448

A young woman raised on a remote island with a father who identifies the scents of the natural world makes illuminating discoveries about her identity and a mysterious cache of fragrances.

Bauermeister, Erica

The **school** of essential ingredients / Erica Bauermeister. G. P. Putnam's Sons, 2009. 256 p.

ISBN 9780399155437

1. Women cooks 2. Cooking schools 3. Restaurants 4. Friendship 5. Interpersonal relations 6. Self-perception 7. Food 8. Hope 9. Pacific Northwest 10. Pacific Northwest fiction 11. Mainstream fiction 12. Gentle reads

LC 2008029728

Sequel: The Lost Art of Mixing

Eight students gather in Lillian's Restaurant every Monday night for cooking class. It soon becomes clear, however, that each one seeks a recipe for something beyond the kitchen as Chef Lillian, a woman whose connection with food is both soulful and exacting, helps them to create dishes whose flavor and techniques expand beyond the restaurant and into the secret corners of her students' lives.

Bauman, Bruce

* **Broken** sleep : an American dream / Bruce Bauman. Other Press, 2015 474 p.

ISBN 9781590514481

1. 20th century 2. 21st century 3. Birthmothers 4. Family secrets 5. Families -- United States 6. Candidates for public office 7. Rock music 8. People with leukemia 9. Adoptive families 10. Rock groups 11. Artists 12. Family sagas 13. Allegories

LC 2015006100

"Diagnosed with an aggressive form of leukemia, Moses Teumer, searching for a donor, hunts down his birth parents and must unravel the intertwined destinies of his adopted and biological families, in a saga about rock music, art, politics and the elusive nature of love. Original."--Provided by publisher.

Baume, Sara

Spill simmer falter wither / Sara Baume. Houghton Mifflin Harcourt, 2016, c2015. 224 p.

ISBN 9780544716193

1. Human-animal relationships 2. Misfits (Persons) 3. Dog owners 4. Dogs 5. Suspicion 6. Small town life 7. Voyages and travels 8. Ireland 9. Literary fiction

LC 2015037012

Originally published: London : Windmill Books, 2015.

Two damaged creatures, a man who has been shunned by his village, and a one-eyed dog, accidentally find each other and form a lasting relationship that transforms their lives as they travel the Irish countryside.

Bausch, Richard, 1945-

Hello to the cannibals : a novel / Richard Bausch. Harper-Collins, 2002. 661 p.

ISBN 006019295X

1. Kingsley, Mary Henrietta, 1862-1900 2. Adult child abuse victims 3. Women dramatists 4. Married women 5. Young women 6. Playwriting 7. Virginia 8. Psychological fiction

LC 2002023270

Pregnant, newly married, and living with her in-laws, Lily Austin writes a play about famed nineteenth-century British explorer Mary Kinglsey and finds inspiration in her subject's writings.

"The novel is ambitious not only in its historical and geographical sweep but also in its author's choice to confine himself, with admirable-conviction and credibility, to the consciousness of two women." New York Times Book Review.

Bausch, Richard, 1945-

* **Rebel** powers / Richard Bausch. Houghton Mifflin, 1993. 390 p.

ISBN 0395595088

1. 1960s 2. Vietnam veterans -- Family relationships 3. Vietnam veterans' spouses 4. Vietnam veterans -- Wyoming 5. Fathers and sons 6. Prisoners' spouses 7. Prisoners -- Wyoming 8. Military dependents 9. Air Force spouses 10. Children of prisoners 11. War stories

LC 93009194

A decorated Air Force officer and former POW returns from Vietnam alive, but faces a dishonorable discharge and a two-year prison term

"The key to the novel's credibility is the unretouched quality of its portraiture. Its characters live in a carefully chronicled American moment when threatening new ideas are beginning to rub up against weighty old certainties." New York Times Book Review.

Bausch, Richard, 1945-

Peace / Richard Bausch. Knopf, 2008. 192 p.

ISBN 9780307268334

1. Second World War era (1939-1945) 2. 1940s 3. Soldiers 4. Personal conduct 5. Ethics 6. Killing (Ethics) 7. Duty 8. Options, alternatives, choices 9. World War II 10. Italy 11. Historical fiction 12. War stories

LC 2007037096

ALA Notable Book, 2009.

W. Y. Boyd Literary Award, 2009.

Italy, near Cassino. The terrible winter of 1944. A dismal icy rain, continuing unabated for days. Guided by a seventy-year-old Italian man in rope-soled shoes, three American soldiers are sent on a reconnaissance mission up the side of a steep hill that they discover, before very long, to be a mountain. And the old man's indeterminate loyalties only add to the terror and confusion that engulf them on that mountain, where they are confronted with the horror of their own time--and then set upon by a sniper.--From publisher description.

"A story cleanly told void of trickery or plot shifting, without the faux drama of point-of-view shifts or uninvited monologue on the state of the cultural landscape well, that's a thing to behold. . . . Bausch, among the most prolific and accomplished story writers of the last two decades, provides a gift to those who like to swallow their stories whole, in one sitting, without digression or narrative handstands." Esquire.

Bausch, Richard, 1945-

The **stories** of Richard Bausch / Richard Bausch. Harper Collins, 2003. 572 p.

ISBN 0060196491

1. United States -- Social life and customs 2. Short stories

LC 2003042318

Includes 42 stories.

In a collection of forty-two short stories, the author explores his fascination with the everyday details of human relationships and considers the dramatic roots of common interactions.

"Failure and its exactions this is Bausch's big subject. These 42 stories test the play of hope and disappointment in the lives of spouses and lovers, of parents and children and siblings. And while Bausch does in several instances write with insight and authority from a woman's perspective, it is the sons, fathers and husbands in their daily trials that he registers most memorably. Indeed, so alive are these characters, with their credible flaws, their complaints and loud excitements, that closing the book feels like pushing the door shut on some clamorous party." New York Times Book Review.

Bawden, Nina, 1925-2012

Family money / Nina Bawden. St. Martin's, 1991. 250 p.

ISBN 0312063512

1. Women with amnesia 2. Greed 4. Mother and adult child 3. Independence in women 4. Middle class families 5. Inheritance and succession 6. Widows 7. Mainstream fiction

LC 91021186

A tough independent woman, Fanny Pye learns to adjust to the crippling events brought on by old age and the selfish interests of her adult children

"Sharply observed and drawn with precision, Fanny's troubles and their eventual resolution make a compelling read." Publishers Weekly.

Baxter, Charles, 1947-

The **feast** of love / Charles Baxter. Pantheon Books, 2000. 308 p.

ISBN 0375410198

1. Community life 2. Lovers 3. Interpersonal relations 4. Men/women relations 5. Neighbors 6. Friendship 7. Ann Arbor, Michigan 8. Michigan 9. Psychological fiction 10. Love stories

LC 99053088

National Book Award for Fiction finalist, 2000

A collection of vignettes set in a coffee shop explores the subtle movements of love between ordinary people.

"An insomniac Mid-western novelist named Charlie Baxter becomes the unwitting audience of a neighbor's midnight confession, and is drawn into a tale of love in its manifold guisesconfused, ecstatic, unrequited. We hear the story of Kathryn, who left her husband for the female shortstop of a local softball team; of Diana, a capricious lawyer who doesn't want anyone to want her too much; and of Chlo, a pierced teenager with a strong sense of justice and a doomed passion for a former drug addict. Baxter's novel is a modern Symposium, unexpectedly hilarious in its attempt to get at the evasive truths of love; unlike Plato's treatise, though, its strength lies in its recognition that such truths aren't universal." The New Yorker.

Baxter, Charles, 1947-

Saul and Patsy / Charles Baxter. Pantheon Books, 2003. 320 p.

ISBN 0375410295

1. Small towns 2. Jewish men 3. Suicide 4. Married people 5. Teenagers 6. High school teachers 7. High school students 8. Newlyweds 9. Interfaith romance 10. Motherhood 11. Obsession 12. Voyeurism 13. Confrontation (Interpersonal relations) 14. Michigan 15. Domestic fiction 16. Psychological fiction

LC 2003042027

A seemingly happy domestic scene is turned upside down by the obsessive attentions of a troubled sixteen-year-old boy.

"The narrative is dense with quotidian detail, precisely charted shifts of consciousness and pitch-perfect moments of emotional truth." Publishers Weekly.

Baxter, Charles, 1947-

There's **something** I want you to do : stories / Charles Baxter. Pantheon Books, 2015. 240 p.

ISBN 9781101870013

1. Virtues 2. Personal conduct 3. Vices 4. Minneapolis, Minnesota 5. Short stories

LC 2014003352

A collection of interrelated stories exploring virtues and vices features characters whose actions are equally divided between hateful and heroic.

"Rooted in Minneapolis, its industrial ruins so poetically rendered, these ravishing, funny, and compassionate stories redefine our perceptions of vice and virtue, delusion and reason, love and loss." Booklist.

Bayard, Louis

The **black** tower : a novel / Louis Bayard. William Morrow, 2008. 368 p.

ISBN 9780061173509

1. Vidocq, Francois Eugene, 1775-1857 2. 1810s 3. 19th century 4. Detectives 5. Murder investigation 6. Disguises 7. Murder 8. Murder suspects 9. Rulers 10. France -- History -- 19th century 11. France -- Rulers 12. Historical mysteries 13. Mysteries

LC 2008005059

Having used his mastery of disguise and surveillance to nab France's most notorious criminals, early nineteenth-century detective Vidocq tracks down the most challenging adversary of his career, a case with ties to the missing son of Marie Antoinette.

"Bayard makes brilliant application of Vidocq in this fanciful adventure. . . . No snatch-and-run researcher, Bayard takes care to capture Vidocq's roguish voice and grandiose affectations, as well as the melodramatic substance of his published memoirs." New York Times Book Review.

Bayard, Louis

The **pale** blue eye : a novel / Louis Bayard. Harper Collins Publishers, 2006. 432 p.

ISBN 0060733977

1. Poe, Edgar Allan, 1809-1849 2. United States Military Academy Cadets. 3. 1830s 4. Former police -- New York (State) 5. Murder investigation 6. Widowers 7. Young men 8. Brothers and sisters 9. Secret societies 10. Human sacrifice 11. Mutilation 12. Men/women relations 13. Revenge 14. Murder 15. Alcoholic men 16. Hazing 17. Friendship 18. West Point, New York 19. New York (State) -- History -- 19th century 20. Historical mysteries 21. Mysteries

LC 2005044741

When a suicide victim's body disappears from the West Point Military Academy, detective Gus Landor gets called in to investigate. When a new cadet, Edgar Allan Poe, approaches Landor with his theory that the man they are looking for is a poet, the duo begins to narrow down suspects all the while dealing with their own personal demons.

"Bayard scatters seeds of Poe's short stories and poems throughout the novel, culminating in a grisly set piece that out-Goths The Fall of the House of Usher. But just when a reader's eyes start rolling, Bayard's ending brilliantly upends the entire novel." Christian Science Monitor.

Beach, Edward L., 1918-

Run silent, run deep / Edward L. Beach ; with an introduction by Edward P. Stafford Naval Institute Press, 1987, c1955. 343 p. Rich Richardson series

ISBN 9780870215575

1. Second World War era (1939-1945) 2. Submarine warfare 3. Submarines, American 4. Naval battles 5. World War II 6. Pacific Ocean 7. Sea stories 8. War stories 9. Historical fiction

LC 85021801

"Originally published in 1955 by Henry Holt."

A narrative with the drama of war, love, and jealousy during submarine service in World War II

"If ever a book has the ring of reality, this is it. From the moment the reader steps aboard a training boat in New London, Conn., to the time when the submarine Walrus dives deeply to avoid the depth charges of the enemy's destroyers, there is awe and respect for the author who created them." New York Times Book Review.

Beagin, Jen

* **Vacuum** in the dark : a novel / Jen Beagin. Scribner, 2019. 224 p.

ISBN 9781501182143

1. Women house cleaners 2. Discontent 3. Extramarital affairs 4. Boyfriends 5. Drug addicts 6. Drug abuse 7. Mothers and daughters 8. Mental illness 9. Adult child sexual abuse victims 10. Self-discovery 11. Men/women relations 12. Interpersonal relations 13. New Mexico 14. Literary fiction

A young house cleaner in New Mexico balances a bad, junkie boyfriend with a bad, unstable boyfriend who happens to be married to one of her clients as she embarks on an eccentric journey of self-discovery and redemption.

"Beagin pulls no punches--this novel is viciously smart and morbidly funny." Publishers Weekly

Beagle, Peter S.

A **fine** and private place / Peter S. Beagle Roc Books, 1992, c1960. 290 p.

ISBN 0451450965

1. Cemeteries 2. Ghosts 3. Romantic love 4. Eccentric men 5. Recluses 6. Alienation in men 7. Loneliness 8. Widows 9. Life after death 10. New York City 11. Love stories 12. Contemporary fantasy
LC 9148054

A kindly raven brings food to and is the companion of a man who has taken refuge in an abandoned mausoleum in a New York City cemetery for nineteen years

Beagle, Peter S.

In Calabria / Peter S. Beagle. Tachyon Publications, 2017. 176 p.

ISBN 9781616962487

1. Farmers 2. Unicorns 3. Life change events 4. Poets 5. Rural life 6. Mass media 7. Social isolation 8. May/December romance 9. Southern Italy 10. Italy 11. Contemporary fantasy

"Claudio Bianchi has lived alone for many years on a hillside in Southern Italy's scenic Calabria. Set in his ways and suspicious of outsiders, Claudio has always resisted change, preferring farming and writing poetry. But one chilly morning, as though from a dream, an impossible visitor appears at the farm. When Claudio comes to her aid, an act of kindness throws his world into chaos."--Provided by the publisher

"This is a pleasant snack of a story about an Italian farmer who encounters a unicorn that changes his life for the better." Booklist.

Beagle, Peter S.

* The **last** unicorn / Peter S. Beagle ; illustrated by Mel Grant. Penguin Books, 1991, c1968 212 p.

ISBN 0451450523

1. Unicorns 2. Magicians 3. Rulers 4. Magic 5. Escapes 6. Carnivals 7. Extinction (Biology) 8. Quests 9. Voyages and travels 10. Mythical creatures 11. Fantasy fiction

LC 90007696

The sequel, Two Hearts, is included in the short story collection, The line between.

"A ROC book."

Originally published: New York : Viking, 1968.

Recounts the quest of the last unicorn, who leaves the protection of the enchanted forest to search for her own kind, and who is joined by Schmedrick the Magician and Molly Grue in her search

Beagle, Peter S.

Summerlong / Peter S. Beagle. Tachyon Publications, 2016. 240 p.

ISBN 9781616962449

1. Waitresses 2. Couples 3. Fate and fatalism 4. Love 5. Independence (Personal quality) 6. Characters and characteristics in mythology 7. Superhuman abilities 8. Families 9. Magic 10. Aging 11. Men/women relations 12. Puget Sound 13. Washington (State) 14. Contemporary fantasy

A complicated family brings a young woman named Lioness Lazos into their lives, and as spring leads into summer, Lioness awakens each family member's long-hidden dreams and desires.

"In his first new novel in more than a decade, Beagle creates an intimate drama between the members of a family who are slowly blindsided by myth and magic spilling into their ordinary world." Kirkus.

Beagle, Peter S.

The **unicorn** sonata / Illustrations by Robert Rodriguez. Turner Publishing, 1996. 154 p.

ISBN 1570362882

1. Thirteen-year-old girls 2. Unicorns 3. Interdimensional travel 4. Teenage girls 5. Mythical creatures 6. Fairies 7. Blindness 8. Greed 9. Gateway fantasy 10. Fantasy fiction

LC 96-16007

In Los Angeles a thirteen-year-old girl follows haunting music across an in invisible border into an enchanted land known as Shei'rah that is inhabited by satyrs, unicorns, and phoenixes.

"The story is slight, but the characterizations are grand, enhanced by graceful prose laced with exquisite detail, and through both literary creativity and folkloric expertise where unicorns are concerned." Publishers Weekly.

Beah, Ishmael, 1980-

Radiance of tomorrow / Ishmael Beah. Farrar, Straus & Giroux, 2014. 256 p.

ISBN 9780374246020

1. Civil war 2. Atrocities 3. Violence 4. Corruption 5. Threat (Psychology) 6. Sierra Leone 7. War stories 8. Literary fiction

A parable about postwar life in Sierra Leone in which two long-time friends return to their ruined home village and struggle to rebuild in the face of violence, scarcity and a corrupt foreign mining company.

Beams, Clare

The **illness** lesson / Clare Beams. Doubleday, 2020. 288 p.
ISBN 9780385544665

1. Gilded Age (1865-1898) 2. 1870s 3. Girls' schools 4. Secrets 5. Women's role 6. Young women 7. Philosophers 8. Fathers and daughters 9. Sexual violence 10. Women teachers 11. Birds 12. Signs and symbols 13. Hysteria (Social psychology) 14. New England 15. Massachusetts 16. Historical fiction 17. Literary fiction

Interpreting a mysterious flock of red birds as an omen to pursue his newest venture, a once-famous philosopher opens a revolutionary school to shape the intellectual development of women, before his students' bizarre symptoms reveal otherworldly secrets.

"This suspenseful and vividly evocative tale expertly explores women's oppression as well as their sexuality through the eyes of a heroine who is sometimes maddening, at other times sympathetic, and always wholly compelling and beautifully rendered." Booklist.

Bear, Elizabeth

All the windwracked stars / Elizabeth Bear. Tor, 2008. 368 p. Edda of burdens

ISBN 9780765318824

1. End of the world 2. Imaginary wars and battles 3. Warriors 4. Valkyries (Norse mythology) 5. Survival 6. Gods and goddesses 7. Magic 8. Shame 9. Guilt 10. Survivor guilt 11. Mythological fiction 12. Fantasy fiction

LC 2008034076

A last surviving member of the ancient Valkyries race returns to the last surviving city on her dying world to reclaim a sword of power owned by her lost brothers and sisters, an effort that is challenged by a hunting Mingan the Wolf.

"The author's ability to create breathtaking variations on ancient themes and make them new and brilliant is, perhaps, unparalleled in the genre." Library Journal.

Bear, Elizabeth

Blood and iron : a novel of the Promethean Age / Elizabeth Bear. ROC, 2005. 448 p. Promethean Age

ISBN 0451460928

1. Fairies 2. Changelings 3. Women college teachers 4. Women rulers 5. Mothers and sons 6. Children 7. Wizards 8. Courts and courtiers 9. Dragons 10. Quests 11. Magic (Occultism) 12. Kidnapping 13. Competition 14. Imaginary kingdoms 15. Prometheus Club (Imaginary organization) 16. Contemporary fantasy 17. Mythological fiction 18. Celtic fantasy

LC 2005033954

"Ancient grudges and ruthless schemes are simply business as usual to the Faerie court in Bear's complex and involving contemporary fantasy. Seeker, formerly Elaine Andraste, is a changeling bound to the Mebd, the queen of the Daoine Sidhe, to find other changelings and bring them to the Faerie court. There, like legendary Tam Lin, and Seeker's own son, Ian, they entertain the queen until she tires of them. Now the queen needs Seeker to find and win the heart of the new Merlin, latest incarnation of a being who, in the hands of the Protheans, could be used to destroy the Fae. Pragmatic college professor Carel Bierce, the first female Merlin, is not easily swayed by Faeor Promethean advances. Long-forgotten rivalries and unsuspected blood ties arise to tug at Seeker's loyalties, even as the queen promises to free Ian when she succeeds." Publishers Weekly.

Bear, Elizabeth

Ink and steel : a novel of the Promethean Age / Elizabeth Bear. Roc, 2008. xii, 427 p. Promethean Age

ISBN 9780451462091

1. Shakespeare, William, 1564-1616 2. Elizabethan era (1558-1603) 3. Tudor period (1485-1603) 4. 16th century 5. Secret societies 6. Magicians 7. Fairies 8. Imaginary wars and battles 9. Imaginary kingdoms 10. Prometheus Club (Imaginary organization) 11. Great Britain -- History -- Elizabeth I, 1558-1603 12. Historical fantasy 13. Mythological fiction

LC 2008000746

With playwright and spy Kit Marley dead, the victim of murder, dramatist William Shakespeare unsuccessfully takes on the Promethean Club's secret battle against sorcerers out to destroy England, until Marley, resurrected by Faerie enchantment, comes to his aid.

"Bear reveals the secret war between fae and the Elizabethan court in this dramatic prequel to Blood and Iron and Whiskey and Water. Framed with the intrigues of queens and courtiers, the story focuses on the mutual respect and growing love of Kit Marley (aka Christopher Marlowe) and Will Shakespeare. As Morgan le Fey rescues Kit from assassins, various factions recruit Will to bolster their political machinations with the magic of poetry. Kit pulls Will into Faerie and both are forced to face their own deepest desires and fears, which cannot be resolved until they deal with a power even higher than mortal Queen Elizabeth or fae Queen Mab. Copious quotes and intelligent speculation about their lives and works mark this sensitive and sensual look at the two supreme playwrights of the English Renaissance." Publishers Weekly.

Bear, Elizabeth

Range of ghosts / Elizabeth Bear. Tor, 2012. 336 p. Eternal sky trilogy

ISBN 9780765327543

1. Civil war 2. Alliances 3. Magic 4. Wizards 5. Exiles 6. Betrayal 7. Epic fantasy 8. Middle Eastern-influenced fantasy 9. Asian-influenced fantasy

LC 2011025171

Going into exile after barely escaping a war waged by his cousin and brother, Temur, the grandson and heir of the Great Khan, teams up against an enemy cult with former princess Samarkar, who after a series of bitter betrayals has pursued a life of magical study.

Bear, Elizabeth

The **red-stained** wings / Elizabeth Bear. Tor Books, 2019. 336 p. Lotus Kingdoms

ISBN 9780765380159

1. Mercenaries 2. Machinery 3. Wizards 4. Rulers 5. Quests 6. Magic 7. Automata 8. Riddles 9. Deserts 10. Imaginary kingdoms 11. Imaginary wars and battles 12. Fantasy fiction 13. Epic fantasy

Despite the Lotus Kingdoms being at war, The Gage and the Dead Man bring a message, disguised as a riddle, to the queen of Sarathai in the second novel of the series following The Stone in the Skull.

Bear, Elizabeth

Shattered pillars / Elizabeth Bear. Tor, 2013. 336 p. Eternal sky trilogy

ISBN 9780765327550

1. Magic 2. Heirs and heiresses 3. Alliances 4. Civil war 5. Wizards 6. Exiles 7. Betrayal 8. Imaginary wars and battles 9. Epic fantasy 10. Middle Eastern-influenced fantasy 11. Asian-influenced fantasy

LC 2012038826

Exiled heir Re-Tamur and his wizard friend Sarmarkar are pitted against dark forces that would conquer the great Empires along the Celedon Road.

Bear, Elizabeth

Steles of the sky / Elizabeth Bear. Tor, 2014. 336 p. Eternal sky trilogy

ISBN 9780765327567

1. Wolves 2. Human/animal relationships 3. Humans and wolves 4. Telepathy 5. Warriors 6. Men/women relations 7. Sexuality 8. Violence 9. Imaginary wars and battles 10. Epic fantasy 11. Middle Eastern-influenced fantasy 12. Asian-influenced fantasy

LC 2013029676

"A Tom Doherty Associates book."

After declaring war against a usurping uncle, Re Tamur makes a final journey to the Dragon Lake to raise an army of his followers, while in the east the city of Asmaracanda has burned and the caliph deposed, and in the south a plague rages in the Rasan empire.

"Battles are fought on both a personal level and a grand scale, with artifacts of obscure ancient civilizations, spirit animals, magical creatures, and poetry and politics. The conclusion is both untelegraphed and completely appropriate." Publishers Weekly.

LIST OF FICTIONAL WORKS

Bear, Elizabeth

The **stone** in the skull / Elizabeth Bear. Tor, 2017. 368 p. Lotus Kingdoms

ISBN 9780765380135

1. Mercenaries 2. Machinery 3. Wizards 4. Rulers 5. Quests 6. Magic 7. Letters 8. Fantasy fiction 9. Epic fantasy

As they brave a perilous journey through the Steles of the Sky and into the Lotus Kingdoms, a pair of mercenaries -- brass automaton Gage and the Dead Man, a former bodyguard for a deposed caliph -- think they're delivering a message from a powerful wizard to a beleaguered rajni (ruler). Little do they know they're wandering into the middle of a dynastic war.?Set in the world of the Eternal Sky trilogy,?The Stone in the Skull?is the first of a new series -- Description by Gillian Speace

"Readers familiar with Bears work will recognize the city of Messaline and the names of the Lotus Kingdoms, but this is the farthest she's delved into this shattered empire. As usual, the setting is wonderfully realized; the characters are possessed of depth, personality, and individuality; the threads of politics that drive the plot are a fascinating knot to try to unravel. This is a promising beginning indeed for an epic; there are many lines of story left to follow, and it will no doubt be a magnificent journey." Booklist.

Bear, Elizabeth

Stone mad / Elizabeth Bear. Tor.com, 2018. 183 p.

ISBN 9781250163837

1. 19th century 2. Imaginary creatures 3. Retirees 4. Spiritualists 5. Kidnapping 6. Supernatural 7. Sisters 8. The West (United States) 9. Steampunk 10. Weird Westerns

Karen and Priya are out for a night on the town, celebrating the purchase of their own little ranch and Karen's retirement from the Hotel Ma Cherie, when they meet the Arcadia Sisters, spiritualists who unexpectedly stir up the tommy-knocker in the basement. The ensuing show could bring down the house, if Karen didn?t rush in to rescue everyone she can.

Bear, Greg, 1951-

Anvil **of** stars / Greg Bear. Warner Books, 1992. 434 p. Forge of God

ISBN 9780446516013

1. Space warfare 2. Survival 3. Revenge 4. Space flight 5. Robots 6. Good and evil 7. Aliens (Non-humanoid) 8. Hard science fiction 9. Science fiction

LC 91050411

Sequel to Forge of God (1987).

Follows the mission of a select group of human survivors as they search in the Ship of Law for the aliens who destroyed their planet

"Bear is superlatively competent in the English language and a master of both technical wizardry and powerful scenes. Throughout the book, he addresses the question of an ethical basis for genocide, leaving the matter sufficiently open to make one wonder whether the story is yet completed." Booklist.

Bear, Greg, 1951-

The **forge** of God / Greg Bear. Tor, 1987. 474p. Forge of God

ISBN 9780312930219

1. Aliens (Non-humanoid) 2. Space warfare 3. Robots 4. Deception 5. Good and evil 6. Helpfulness 7. Earth -- Invasions 8. Hard science fiction 9. Science fiction

LC 87050482

Sequel: Anvil of Stars (1992).

"The battle over Earth is seen through the eyes of a large cast of well-drawn characters, crowned by a climax of enormous power." Booklist.

Bear, Greg, 1951-

The **collected** stories of Greg Bear / Greg Bear. Tor, 2002. 653 p.

ISBN 9780765301604

1. Science fiction 2. Anthologies 3. Short stories

LC 2002020466

A collection of science fiction short stories includes "Blood Music," "Tangents," "Hardfought," and "Petra."

"In addition to Blood music (1985), a novelette where a genetic engineer injects himself with experimental intelligent microorganisms with disasterous results, this volume subsumes Bear's earlier collections, The wind from a burning woman (1983) and Tangents (1989), while also including more recent work." Anatomy of Wonder, 5th edition.

Beaton, M. C., 1936-2019

Agatha Raisin and the quiche of death / M.C. Beaton. Ivy Books, 1993, c1992. 185 p. Agatha Raisin mysteries

ISBN 9780804111638

1. Villages -- Cotswolds, England 2. Cooking contests 3. Poisoning 4. Murder investigation 5. Women detectives 6. Murder suspects 7. England 8. Cotswolds, England 9. Cozy mysteries 10. Gentle reads

LC 92028381

Originally published: New York : St. Martin's Press, c1992.

In order to introduce herself to the picturesque English village where she has just retired, Mrs. Agatha Raisin enters a quiche in a local competition and promptly finds herself a murder suspect when the judge dies from her poisonous pie

"Bored with her early retirement and still on the lookout for romance wherever she can find it, Spunky Agatha Raisin, former owner of a London public-relations firm, welcomes the arrival of veterinarian Paul Bladen to her quiet Cotswold village. When the new vet, whose charming con-man exterior conceals a hatred of dogs and cats, dies from an injection from his own hypodermic syringe, Agatha and her neighbor James Lacey decide that Bladen has been murdered, and line up an extended list of possible suspects." Booklist.

Beaton, M. C., 1936-2019

Death of a macho man / M.C. Beaton. Mysterious Press, 1996. 216 p. Hamish Macbeth mysteries

ISBN 0892965312

1. Villages 2. Murder investigation 3. Former husbands 4. Murder suspects 5. Police -- Scotland 6. Detectives 7. Scotland 8. Cozy mysteries 9. Gentle reads

LC 96-7268

The one-man Scottish police force Hamish Macbeth becomes the prime suspect in the murder of the town ne'er-do-well, Randy "Macho Man" Duggan, whose real killer is surprisingly close at hand.

"Befuddled, earnest and utterly endearing, Hamish makes his triumphs sweetly satisfying." Publishers Weekly.

Beaton, M. C., 1936-2019

Pushing up daisies : an Agatha Raisin mystery / M. C. Beaton. Minotaur Books, 2016. 304 p. Agatha Raisin mysteries

ISBN 9781250057440

1. Women private investigators 2. Murder suspects 3. Murder investigation 4. Widows 5. Villages 6. Secrets 7. Cotswolds, England 8. England 9. Cozy mysteries 10. Gentle reads

LC 2016010568

"A queen of the village mystery"--Cover.

Gloria French was a jolly widow with dyed blonde hair, a raucous laugh and rosy cheeks. When she first moved from London to the charming Cotswolds Hills, she was heartily welcomed. She seemed a do-gooder par excellence, raising funds for the church and caring for the elderly.

But she had a nasty habit of borrowing things and not giving them back, just small things, a teapot here, a set of silverware there. So it's quite the shock when she is found dead, murdered by a poisoned bottle of elderberry wine.

"A twisty plot, a familiar cast of eccentric characters, and a charming English country setting mean that lovers of cozy mysteries will be satisfied indeed." Publishers Weekly.

Beattie, Ann

* **Chilly** scenes of winter Vintage Books, 1991, c1976. 280p.

ISBN 0385116586

1. 1970s 2. Male friendship 3. Men/women relations 4. Mainstream fiction

LC 90050186

Surrounded by family members and friends not appreciably unlike himself, a twenty-seven-year-old government worker longs to recapture his ex-lover Laura, who has recently returned to her husband, step-daughter, and A-frame.

Beattie, Ann

The **doctor's** house : a novel / Ann Beattie. Scribner, 2002. 279 p.

ISBN 0743212649

1. Dysfunctional families 2. Psychic trauma 3. Family secrets 4. Obsession 5. Abusive men 6. Self-deception 7. Despair 8. Brothers and sisters 9. Men -- Sexuality 10. Psychological fiction

Reveals the story of Nina, a reclusive copyeditor who has become obsessed with her brother Andrew's sexual exploits and indiscretions, through the differing viewpoints of Nina, Andrew, and their mother.

Beattie, Ann

* **Picturing** Will / Ann Beattie. Random House, 1989. 230 p.

ISBN 9780394569871

1. Stepfathers 2. Child-rearing 3. Five-year-old boys 4. Single-parent families 5. Women photographers 6. Domestic fiction

LC 89042781

A five-year-old, his photographer mother, and his prepetually unlucky, philandering father populate this novel about the trials and rewards of both being and raising a child.

"Beattie has almost as many narrative voices as characters in this book, yet the result is never confusing. . . . 'Picturing Will' would be admirable for its technique alone; what makes it Beattie's best novel is her new and fearless way with emotional complexity." Newsweek.

Beattie, Ann

The **state** we're in : Maine stories / Ann Beattie. Scribner, 2015. x, 206 p.

ISBN 9781501107818

1. Coastal towns 2. Women 3. Maine 4. Short stories

An award-winning short story master presents a collection of linked tales that impart the diverse perspectives of women orbiting around a disaffected teen who is staying with relatives while attending summer school.

"Some pieces read like sketches with promising characters but little movement: a 77-year-old writer discusses poetry with an IRS agent, a doctor reminisces about her life in New York before moving north, an author interviews a local for a book about people who have negative effects on other people's lives. A full novel on Jocelyn might be more fulfilling, but Beattie clearly enjoys wandering around the neighborhood. An engaging collection of varied characters, if varying degrees of substance." Kirkus.

Beattie, Ann

A **wonderful** stroke of luck : a novel / Ann Beattie. Viking, 2019. 274 p.

ISBN 9780525557340

1. Teacher-student relationships 2. Dishonesty 3. Men -- Psychology 4. Former teachers 5. Personal conduct 6. Boarding schools 7. Secrets 8. Family problems 9. Interpersonal relations 10. Ambivalence 11. Passivity (Psychology) 12. New Hampshire 13. New York (State) 14. New England 15. Psychological fiction 16. Literary fiction

A man who attended a prestigious New England boarding school has his life turned upside down by the reappearance in his life of an enigmatic and brilliant but difficult former teacher that makes him question everything he knows.

"Obvious is one thing Beattie never is. Her elegantly sculpted tale is both wrenchingly sad and ultimately enigmatic: as usual." Kirkus.

Beatty, Paul

* The **sellout** : a novel / Paul Beatty. Farrar, Straus and Giroux, 2015. 288 p.

ISBN 9780374260507

1. Racism 2. Segregation 3. Inner city 4. Race relations 5. African Americans 6. Farmers 7. Slavery 8. Fathers and sons 9. Los Angeles, California 10. Satirical fiction 11. Literary fiction 12. African American fiction

LC 2014027451

ALA Notable Book, 2016.
National Book Critics Circle Award for Fiction, 2015.
Man Booker Prize, 2016

In this satirical take on race, politics, and culture in the U.S., a young black man grows up determined to resegregate a portion of an inner city, aided by a former Little Rascals star who volunteers to be his slave. This illegal activity brings him to the attention of the Supreme Court, who must consider the ramifications of this (and other) race-related cases. Readers who can handle provocative language and racial stereotypes will appreciate the glee that African-American humorist Paul Beatty brings to his critique and questioning of black identity; others will find it incendiary.*-- Description by Shauna Griffin.

"Beatty . . . creates a wicked satire that pokes fun at all that is sacred to life in the United States, from father-son dynamics right up to the Supreme Court. His story is full of the unexpected, resulting in absurd and hilarious drama." Library Journal.

Beatty, Paul

Slumberland : a novel / Paul Beatty. Bloomsbury, 2008. 256 p.

ISBN 9781596912403

1. 1980s 2. African Americans 3. African American men 4. Musicians 5. African Americans in Germany 6. Race relations 7. Avant-garde (Aesthetics) 8. Men/women relations 9. Self-discovery 10. Berlin, Germany -- History -- 1945-1990 11. Picaresque fiction 12. African American fiction

LC 2007045049

Traveling to recently unified Berlin in search of a little-known avant-garde jazzman whom he believes to be a musical kindred spirit, disaffected Los Angeles DJ Darky encounters the dramatic local changes that have transpired after the tearing down of the Berlin Wall and ruminates on a range of cultural, social, and philosophical topics.

"Slumberland is laugh-out-loud funny in many places, and its wit and satire can be burning, regardless of where they are pointed: blackness or whiteness." Los Angeles Times Book Review.

Beauman, Ned

Madness is better than defeat / Ned Beauman. Alfred A. Knopf, 2018, c2017 399 p.

ISBN 9780385352994

1. 20th century 2. Conspiracies 3. Temples 4. Social isolation 5. Competition 6. Enemies 7. Film industry and trade 8. CIA agents 9. Industrialists 10. Intrigue 11. Interpersonal relations 12. Honduras 13. Adventure stories 14. Historical fiction

LC 2017024820

"This is Borzoi Book."

"Originally published in Great Britain by Sceptre, an imprint of Hodder & Stoughton, a Hachette UK company, London, in 2017."

A CIA agent sets out to exploit an ancient temple in the Honduran jungle for his own purposes but discovers the site is the focal point of large conspiracies that began 20 years prior.

Beauvoir, Simone de, 1908-1986

* The **Mandarins** : a novel / Simone de Beauvoir ; translated by Leonard M. Friedman Regnery Gateway, 1979, c1956. 610 p.

ISBN 9780895268983

1. 1940s 2. Intellectual life -- Paris, France 3. Interpersonal relations 4. Desire 5. Philosophy, Modern 6. Social conflict 7. Families 8. Existentialism 9. Paris, France 10. France 11. Translations -- French to English 12. Love stories 13. Psychological fiction

Young French men and women interact in love and politics as they simultaneously create and react to the social, intellectual and political climate of post-war Paris

Beauvoir, Simone de, 1908-1986

The **woman** destroyed / Simone de Beauvoir ; translated from the French by Patrick O'Brian. Pantheon Books, 2013, c1969. 254 p.

ISBN 9780394711034

1. Literary fiction 2. Short stories 3. Translations -- French to English

LC 69015496

Originally published: London : Collins, 1969.

Three women, all past their first youth, face unexpected crises.

Beck, Haylen

Here and gone / Haylen Beck. Crown, 2017. 287 p.

ISBN 9780451499578

1. Child custody 2. Abused women 3. Police corruption 4. Abusive men 5. Missing children 6. Parental kidnapping 7. Malicious accusation 8. Arizona 9. Thrillers and suspense

Wrongly arrested after fleeing her abusive husband's home, a mother desperately fights corrupt authorities to recover her stolen children; while a man across the country hears the story on the news and identifies links to similar events in his own past.

Beck, Haylen

Lost you / Haylen Beck. Crown Pub, 2019. 272 p.

ISBN 9781524759582

1. Single mothers 2. Kidnapping 3. Surrogate mothers 4. Surrogate motherhood -- Psychological aspects 5. Infertility 6. Mothers and sons 7. Vacations 8. Deception 9. Secrets 10. Authors 11. Psychological suspense

After a closing elevator door separates them, a single mother on vacation with her son discovers he has been abducted by another woman who claims she is his mother in the new novel from the author of Here and Gone.

Beckerman, Hannah

If only I could tell you / Hannah Beckerman. William Morrow, 2019. 368 p.

ISBN 9780062952189

1. Sisters 2. Family secrets 3. Family relationships 4. Secrets 5. Families 6. Mother and adult daughter 7. People with terminal illnesses 8. Mothers and daughters 9. Granddaughters 10. Options, alternatives, choices 11. Domestic fiction 12. Mainstream fiction

A novel of mothers and daughters, the bonds of family and the secrets that can sometimes divide us yet also bring us together follows Audrey, who has been dealt more ups and downs than she can handle, as she searches for a way to fix her broken family.

Beckett, L. X.

Gamechanger / L. X. Beckett. Tor books, 2019. 576 p.

ISBN 9781250165268

1. Women defense attorneys 2. Rebels 3. Electronic surveillance 4. Near future 5. Pariahs 6. Social evolution 7. Social control 8. Virtual reality 9. Environmentalism 10. Artificial intelligence 11. Loyalty 12. Options, alternatives, choices 13. Social science fiction

LC 2019948647

After the end of the world, humanity thrives in a new generation raised free of the troubles of the late twenty first century. Rubi is a member of this generation that works as a public defender to help troubled individuals with anti-social behavior. That's how she met Luce, a firebrand, that the governments of the world want to bring into custody. But there's more to him than beind a lightning rod for controversy. The reasons that make Luce hell bent on stopping the recovery of the planet is something that Rubi hopes to find out.

Beckett, Samuel, 1906-1989

* **Murphy** / Samuel Beckett. Grove/Atlantic, 2011, c1938. 170 p.

ISBN 9780802144454

1. Personal conduct 2. Social isolation 3. Men nurses 4. London, England 5. Dublin, Ireland 6. Literary fiction 7. Modern classics

LC 57006939

Originally published: London : Routledge, 1938.

A poor Irishman, seeking his own identity, drifts through worsening stages of despair until his final disintegration.

Begley, Louis

About **Schmidt** / Louis Begley. A. A. Knopf, 1996. 273 p. Albert Schmidt novels

ISBN 9780679450337

1. Widowers 2. Alienation in men 3. May-December romance 4. Lawyers 5. Father and adult daughter 6. Antisemites 7. Senior men 8. Jewish men 9. Grief in men 10. Waitresses 11. Wealth 12. New York City 13. Psychological fiction 14. Literary fiction

LC 96-8244

National Book Critics Circle Award for Fiction finalist, 1996.

Albert Schmidt, a retired WASP lawyer, copes with the boredom of retirement, the devastating loss of his wife, and his Ivy League daughter's new fiance, an ambitious, Jewish drone, until an unexpected new love brings the promise of a new life.

Belfer, Lauren

And **after** the fire : a novel / Lauren Belfer. Harper, 2016. 432 p.

ISBN 9780062428516

1. Bach, Johann Sebastian, 1685-1750 2. 20th century 3. 21st century 4. 18th century 5. Manuscript thefts 6. Family secrets 7.

Americans in Germany 8. Manuscripts 9. Uncle and niece 10. Music -- Manuscripts 11. World War II veterans 12. Determination in women 13. Germany 14. Historical fiction 15. Parallel narratives

LC 2015038472

A tale inspired by historical events traces the experiences of two women, one European and one American, whose lives are transformed by a mysterious Johann Sebastian Bach choral masterpiece.

"Based on impressive research, this remarkable novel spans centuries and continents, touching finally on the Holocaust and serving as a paean to Bachs music while acknowledging the composers expressed hatred of Jews." Booklist.

Belfoure, Charles, 1954-

The **Paris** architect : a novel / Charles Belfoure. Sourcebooks Landmark, 2013. 384 p.

ISBN 9781402284311

1. Second World War era (1939-1945) 2. Architects 3. Hiding-places (Secret chambers, etc) 4. Jews, French 5. Resistance to military occupation 6. World War II 7. French Resistance (World War II) 8. Nazism 9. Religious persecution 10. Nazis 11. Hiding 12. Revenge 13. France -- History -- German occupation, 1940-1945 14. Paris, France -- History -- German occupation, 1940-1944 15. Historical fiction

LC 2013017034

Originally published: 2013.

In 1942 Paris, gifted architect Lucien Bernard accepts a commission that will bring him a great deal of money and maybe get him killed. But if he's clever enough, he'll avoid any trouble. All Lucien has to do is design a secret hiding place for a wealthy Jewish man, a space so invisible that even the most determined German officer won't find it. He sorely needs the money, and outwitting the Nazis who have occupied his beloved city is a challenge he can't resist. But when one of his hiding spaces fails horribly, and the problem of where to hide a Jew becomes personal, Lucien can no longer ignore what's at stake. The Paris Architect asks us to consider what we owe each other, and just how far we'll go to make things right.

Bell, Lenora

For the duke's eyes only / Lenora Bell. Avon Books, 2018. 384 p. School for dukes

ISBN 9780062692498

1. Regency period (1811-1820) 2. Women archaeologists 3. Dukes and duchesses 4. Intrigue 5. Antiquities 6. Art thefts 7. Former lovers 8. Quests 9. Sexual attraction 10. Men/women relations 11. Great Britain -- Social life and customs -- 19th century 12. Historical romances 13. Regency romances

Archaeologist Lady India Rochester, when a priceless relic is stolen from the British Museum, must team up with the Duke of Ravenwood, the man who dared to break her heart, to avoid an international disaster.

Bell, Lenora

* **How** the duke was won / Lenora Bell. Avon Books, 2016. 370 p. Disgraceful dukes

ISBN 9780062397720

1. Regency period (1811-1820) 2. Dukes and duchesses 3. Mate selection 4. Reputation 5. Courtesans 6. Impostors 7. Illegitimacy 8. Single fathers 9. Half-sisters 10. Deception 11. Chocolate industry and trade 12. Sexual attraction 13. Men/women relations 14. England -- Social life and customs -- 19th century 15. Great Britain -- History -- Regency, 1811-1820 16. Regency romances 17. Historical romances

When she is offered a life-changing fortune to pose as her half-sister, Lady Dorothea, and win the Duke of Harland's proposal, Charlene Beck-

ett, the unacknowledged daughter of an earl and a courtesan, falls for the duke and must decide if the promise of a new life is worth risking everything.

"Charlene is smart and tough and easily steals the show with her gutsy nonconformity." Library Journal.

Bell, Lenora

One fine duke / Lenora Bell. Avon, 2019. 256 p. School for dukes

ISBN 9780062913074

1. Regency period (1811-1820) 2. Dukes and duchesses 3. Independence in single women 4. Womanizers 5. Protectiveness in men 6. Brothers 7. Mate selection 8. Aristocracy 9. Sexual attraction 10. Men/women relations 11. Great Britain -- Social life and customs -- 19th century 12. Historical romances 13. Regency romances

This was supposed to be simple. Duke goes to London. Duke selects suitable bride. Love match? Not a chance. But when Drew meets Mina, she complicates everything. How can a lady armed with such beauty and brains fall for his irresponsible degenerate of a brother? Drew vows to save her from heartbreak and ruin, no matter the cost.

Bell, Lenora

* **What** a difference a duke makes / Lenora Bell. HarperCollins, 2018 384 p. School for dukes

ISBN 9780062692481

1. Regency period (1811-1820) 2. 19th century 3. Georgian era (1714-1837) 4. Dukes and duchesses 5. Governesses 6. Single fathers 7. Twins 8. Interclass romance 9. Men/women relations 10. Interpersonal attraction 11. Great Britain -- Social life and customs -- 19th century 12. Historical romances 13. Regency romances

Hiring governess Miss Mari Perkins to keep his unruly twins in line, the Duke of Banksford finds himself drawn to this woman who is strictly off limits until she tempts him into breaking all his rules.

Bell, Madison Smartt

The **color** of night : a novel / Madison Smartt Bell. Vintage Books, 2011. 288 p.

ISBN 9780307741882

1. Card dealers 2. Social marginality 3. Social isolation 4. Sexuality 5. Violence 6. Casinos 7. Former lovers 8. September 11 Terrorist Attacks, 2001 9. Cults 10. Sex crimes 11. Las Vegas, Nevada 12. Psychological fiction

LC 2010019104

"As Bell maps Mae's trajectory of mayhem and death in this brilliantly ferocious novel of abuse and survival, this sinister fable of blood lust and madness, he grapples with timeless equations of predator and prey, the sublime and the demonic, the dark ecstasy of destruction and the hell wrought by catastrophic delusion." Kansas City Star.

Bell, Shelly

At his mercy / Shelly Bell. Forever, 2017. 336 p. Forbidden lovers novels

ISBN 9781455595976

1. Sexual dominance and submission 2. Women college students 3. College teachers 4. Victims of violent crimes 5. Teacher-student relationships 6. Sexual attraction 7. Men/women relations 8. Erotic romances 9. Romantic suspense

LC 2017003017

After a night of no-strings attached passion, Isabella discovers that her new lover Tristan is also her professor.

LIST OF FICTIONAL WORKS

Bell, Shelly

For his pleasure / Shelly Bell. Grand Central Pub, 2019. 384 p. Forbidden lovers novels

ISBN 9781455596034

1. Former convicts 2. Parolees 3. Sexual dominance and submission 4. Women parole officers 5. Judicial error 6. Investigations 7. Victims of violent crimes 8. Widowers 9. Sexual attraction 10. Men/women relations 11. Erotic romances 12. Romantic suspense

The only man she trusts is also the most dangerous.

Bell, Ted

Overkill : an Alex Hawke novel / Ted Bell. William Morrow, 2018 544 p. Alexander Hawke thrillers

ISBN 9780062684516

1. M I 6 2. Spies -- Great Britain 3. High technology weapons 4. Assassination 5. International intrigue 6. Intelligence service 7. Intelligence officers 8. National security 9. Military power 10. Espionage 11. Europe -- Foreign relations -- Russia 12. Russia -- Foreign relations -- Europe 13. Spy fiction 14. Adventure stories

LC 2017053351

"Counterspy Alex Hawke goes all out to rescue his son and takes on Russian President Vladimir Putin in the bargain in the latest action-packed thriller in Ted Bell's New York Times bestselling series"--, Provided by publisher.

Belle, Kimberly

Dear wife / Kimberly Belle. Park Row, 2019. 352 p.

ISBN 9780778309147

1. Abused women 2. Missing women 3. New identities 4. Partner abuse 5. Detectives 6. Missing persons investigation 7. Abusive men 8. Arkansas 9. Oklahoma 10. Psychological suspense

A woman who has changed her identity to escape domestic abuse and a woman who has gone missing under suspicious circumstances find their lives connected in unexpected ways.

Bellow, Saul

* The **adventures** of Augie March / Saul Bellow ; with an introduction by Martin Amis. Knopf, 1995, c1953. xxxvii, 616 p.

ISBN 0679444602

1. Jewish Americans 2. Depressions -- 1929-1941 3. Eccentrics and eccentricities 4. Purpose in life 5. Men/women relations 6. Abortion 7. Chicago, Illinois 8. Literary fiction 9. Coming-of-age stories 10. Picaresque fiction 11. Modern classics

Originally published: New York : Viking Press, 1953.

National Book Award for Fiction, 1954.

Refusing to submit to specialization, Augie March wanders from job to job, experiencing life in its fullness.

Bellow, Saul

The **Bellarosa** connection / Saul Bellow. Penguin Books, 1989. 102 p.

ISBN 9780140126860

1. Rose, Billy, 1899-1966 2. Theatrical producers and directors 3. World War II -- Jews -- Rescue 4. Righteous Gentiles in the Holocaust 5. Refugees, Jewish 6. Jewish Americans 7. Businesspeople 8. Husband and wife 9. Overweight women 10. Literary fiction

LC 89032936

"The end of 'The Bellarosa Connection' is abrupt, matter-of-fact, almost offbeat. It is a conclusion, perhaps, in which nothing is concluded, . . . but it is appropriate to the overall pitch and voice of this cannily resourceful entertainment." New York Times Book Review.

Bellow, Saul

Dangling man / Saul Bellow. Vanguard, 1944. 191 p.

ISBN 9780814900246

1. War -- Moral and ethical aspects 2. Draft 3. Identity (Psychology) 4. Conformity 5. Young men 6. Intellectuals 7. Boredom in men 8. Diary novels 9. Literary fiction

Set during the second World War, Joseph quits his job and prepares for his induction into the army. However a series of mishaps cause a delay in his induction, resulting in a year of idleness Joseph is unprepared for. Seeing war all around him and having no way to cope, Joseph expresses his thoughts into his diary.

"The book is an excellent document on the experience of the non-combatant in time of war. It is well written and never dull--in spite of the dismalness of the Chicago background and the undramatic character of the subject. It is also one of the most honest pieces of testimony on the psychology of a whole generation who have grown up during the depression and the war." The New Yorker.

Bellow, Saul

The **dean's** December : a novel / Saul Bellow. Harper and Row, 1982. 312 p.

ISBN 9780060148492

1. Social problems 2. Mothers-in-law 3. Death 4. College deans 5. Husband and wife 6. Americans in Bucharest 7. Chicago, Illinois 8. Romania 9. Political fiction 10. Literary fiction

LC 80008705

Dean Corde is a man of position and authority at a Chicago university. He accompanies his wife to Bucharest where her mother lies dying in a state hospital. As he tries to help her grapple with an unfeeling bureaucracy, Corde is troubled: at home the centre is not holding firm, in Eastern Europe authority is cruel and dehumanising.

Bellow, Saul

* **Henderson** the rain king : a novel / Saul Bellow Viking, 1959. 341 p.

ISBN 9780670366552

1. Self-discovery in men 2. Rain makers 3. Americans in Africa 4. Millionaires 5. Middle-aged men 6. Discontent in men 7. Purpose in life 8. Africa 9. Literary fiction 10. Satirical fiction 11. Modern classics

A story of a middle-aged American millionaire who, seeking a new, more rewarding life, descends upon an African tribe. Henderson's awesome feats of strength and his unbridled passion for life earns him the admiration of the tribe - but it is his gift for making rain that turns him from mere hero into messiah.

Bellow, Saul

* **Herzog** / Saul Bellow. Penguin Books, 1976, c1964. 341 p.

ISBN 9780380008698

1. Jewish American men 2. Intellectuals 3. College teachers 4. Alienation in men 5. Divorce 6. Marital conflict 7. Letter writing 8. Chicago, Illinois 9. Literary fiction 10. Psychological fiction 11. Modern classics

Originally published: New York : Viking Press, 1964.

National Book Award for Fiction, 1965.

Moses E. Herzog suffers from the breakup of his second marriage, the general failure of his life, and the specter of growing up Jewish in the middle of the 20th century. He responds to his personal crisis by writing a series of letters never to be sent, examining his life and times and asking "the piercing questions."

Bellow, Saul

* **Humboldt's** gift / Saul Bellow. Viking, 1975. 487 p.
ISBN 0670386553
1. Authors, American 2. Best friends -- Death 3. Divorce 4. Crushes in men 5. Mafia 6. Mentors 7. Meaning (Psychology) 8. Middle-aged men 9. Poets, American 10. Literary fiction 11. Modern classics
LC 75012595
Pulitzer Prize for Fiction, 1976.
Charlie Citrine, suffering from steadily worsening troubles with women, career, and life in general, receives unexpected aid and comfort in the form of a belated bequest from his onetime friend and mentor, the poet Von Humboldt Fleisher.

Bellow, Saul

More die of heartbreak / Saul Bellow. W. Morrow, 1987. 335 p.
ISBN 9780688069353
1. Sexuality 2. Uncle and nephew 3. Marital conflict 4. Botanists 5. Family relationships 6. Jewish Americans 7. Literary fiction
LC 87005770
Kenneth Trachtenberg, an expert in Russian history and literature, tries to protect his revered uncle Benn Crader, a world-renowned botanist, from a tangle of family relationships, greed, and the willfulness of the human heart.
"Bellow has always been as enthralled by crooks as by the higher realms of thought. His prose mixes soaring meditation with streetsmart wisecracks. The farcical collisions of ill-prepared idealists with hard-as-nails swindlers and connivers give 'More Die of Heartbreak' its juicy vivacity." Newsweek.

Bellow, Saul

* **Mr.** Sammler's planet / Saul Bellow Penguin Books, 2004, c1970. xxiv, 260 p.
ISBN 0142437832
1. 1960s 2. Jewish American men 3. Holocaust survivors 4. City life 5. Intellectuals 6. Senior men 7. New York City 8. Psychological fiction 9. Literary fiction
Originally appeared in Atlantic monthly in a different form.
Originally published in book form: New York : Viking Press, 1970 .
National Book Award for Fiction, 1971.
Mr Artur Sammler, a lecturer at Columbia University in 1960s New York City, is a "registrar of madness," a refined and civilized being caught among people crazy with the promises of the future (moon landings, endless possibilities). His Cyclopean gaze reflects on the degradations of city life while looking into the sufferings of the human soul.

Bellow, Saul

Novels, 1944-1953 / Saul Bellow. Library of America, 2003. 1029 p.
ISBN 1931082383
1. Jewish Americans 2. Jewish American men 3. Depressions -- 1929-1941 4. Conformity 5. Identity (Psychology) 6. Literary fiction 7. Psychological fiction
LC 2003040144
Celebrates the fiftieth anniversary of "The Adventures of Augie March," and reflects the mid-twentieth-century's psychological turmoil from more inhibited times in a volume that also includes "The Victim" and "Dangling Man."

Bellow, Saul

Ravelstein / Saul Bellow Viking, 2000. 233 p.
ISBN 067084134X
1. Friendship 2. People with AIDS 3. College teachers 4. Americans in France 5. Authors, American 6. Biographers 7. Paris, France 8. Middle West 9. Literary fiction 10. Psychological fiction
LC 99056336
Encouraged by his friend, Chick, to write down his ideas about humankind, university professor Abe Ravelstein receives unexpected acclaim and bounty and invites Chick to join in his success, a situation that sparks a philosophical journey for both.
"This might, like the author's earlier works, be called a novel of ideas, but that is too bloodless a description of Bellow's signature accomplishment. . . . [It] brims with life, thanks to Chick's that is Bellow's comic observations on the passing scene." Time.

Bellow, Saul

* **Seize** the day / Saul Bellow ; with an introduction by Cynthia Ozick. Penguin Books, 1996. xxiv, 118 p.
ISBN 0140189378
1. Middle-aged men 2. Self-esteem 3. Separation (Marital relations) 4. Father and adult son 5. Self-discovery in men 6. Jewish American men 7. Unemployed persons 8. Alienation in men 9. New York City 10. Psychological fiction 11. Literary fiction
LC 96145374
Fading charmer Tommy Wilhelm has reached his day of reckoning and is scared. In his forties, he still retains a boyish impetuousness that has brought him to the brink of chaos: he is separated from his wife and children; at odds with his vain, successful father; failed in his acting career; and in a financial mess. In the course of one climactic day he reviews his past mistakes and spiritual malaise, until a mysterious, philosophizing con man grants him a glorious, illuminating moment of truth and understanding and offers him one last hope.
"Seize the Day gives contemporary literature a story which will be explained, expounded, and argued, but about which a final reckoning can be made only after it ripples out in the imagination of the generations of readers to come. I suspect that it is one of the central stories of our day." The Nation.

Benaron, Naomi, 1951-

* **Running** the rift : a novel / Naomi Benaron. Algonquin Books of Chapel Hill, 2012. 365 p.
ISBN 9781616200428
1. 1990s 2. Runners 3. Genocide -- Rwanda 4. Fathers -- Death 5. Fame 6. Athletes 7. Rwanda 8. Political fiction 9. War stories 10. Coming-of-age stories
LC 2011026349
Also published: Toronto : HarperCollins, 2012.
Bellwether Prize for Fiction, 2010.
Rwandan runner Jean Patrick Nkuba dreams of winning an Olympic gold medal and uniting his ethnically divided country, only to be driven from everyone he loves when the violence starts, after which he must find a way back to a better life.

Benchley, Peter

Jaws / Peter Benchley. Fawcett Crest, 1974. 278 p.
ISBN 0449219631
1. Sheriffs 2. Shark attacks 3. Summer resorts -- New York (State) 4. Sharks 5. Humans and sharks 6. Great white shark 7. Extramarital affairs 8. Violence 9. Police chiefs 10. Seaside resorts 11. Marine biologists 12. Atlantic Ocean 13. New York (State) 14. Horror
LC 73080799
When three people are killed by a great white shark in three different incidents, the police chief of a Long Island resort town is forced to take action.
"This is a story about what happens when a great white shark terrorizes a small Long Island town. . . . A woman swimmer is devoured by

the shark, and Police Chief Martin Brody insists on closing the beaches. But he's overruled by the town fathers who remind him that the community is dependent on summer visitors for economic survival. Two deaths later, the news can no longer be suppressed and Brody, an oceanographer and a fisherman go after the monster in an exciting chase." Publishers Weekly.

Bender, Aimee

The **particular** sadness of lemon cake / Aimee Bender. Doubleday, 2010. 288 p.

ISBN 9780385501125

1. Family relationships 2. Family secrets 3. Food 4. Taste 5. Emotions 6. Empathy 7. Magic 8. Curses 9. Love 10. Magical realism 11. Literary fiction

Discovering in childhood a supernatural ability to taste the emotions of others in their cooking, Rose Edelstein grows up to regard food as a curse when it reveals everyone's secret realities.

"Nine-year-old Rose Edelstein bids adieu to normality after taking a bite of her mother's lemon cake. Immediately, she is overwhelmed by the emptiness of her mother's life. All food has this effect on her. She can taste emotions, particularly those that are hidden or repressed. . . . While the time period is never specified the book appears to open in the 1970s the setting is forever-sunny Los Angeles. Until the emergence of her super sense, Rose had been the unexceptional child of a supposedly unexceptional nuclear family. As we follow her into maturity, however, she discovers she has more in common with her father and her brother Joseph than previously thought. Each of them possesses a special ability as well." Miami Herald.

Bender, Karen E.

Refund : stories / Karen Bender. Counterpoint Press, 2015. 258 p.

ISBN 9781619024557

1. Money 2. Wealth 3. Value 4. Self-esteem 5. Short stories 6. Mainstream fiction

LC 2014034079

National Book Award for Fiction finalist, 2015

We think about it every day, sometimes every hour: Money. Who has it. Who doesn't. How you get it. How you don't. In Refund, Bender creates an award-winning collection of stories that deeply explore the ways in which money and the estimation of value affect the lives of her characters. The stories in Refund reflect our contemporary world-swindlers, reality show creators, desperate artists, siblings, parents - who try to answer the question: What is the real definition of worth?

"Although her tone can veer toward bitterness, Bender excels at characters on the edge of despair, particularly mothers who resent the children they love." Kirkus.

Bender, Tony, 1958-

The **last** ghost dancer / Tony Bender. Thomas Dunne Books, 2010. 256 p.

ISBN 9780312592301

1. 1970s 2. Mechanics 3. Nostalgia 4. Spirituality 5. Lost love 6. Summer 7. Friendship 8. Growing up 9. Middle West 10. Coming-of-age stories

LC 2009047578

A prize-winning columnist presents the story of Midwest mechanic Bones, who remembers a 1970s summer when he worked at a west river town's solitary gas station while forging friendships, losing a love and making a life-changing spiritual discovery.

Benedetti, Mario, 1920-2009

Springtime in a broken mirror / Mario Benedetti ; translated by Nick Caistor. The New Press, 2018. 192 p.

ISBN 9781620974902

1. 1970s 2. Political prisoners 3. Exiles 4. Father-separated families 5. Political persecution 6. Separated couples 7. Husband and wife 8. Nine-year-old girls 9. Fathers-in-law 10. Men/women relations 11. Loneliness 12. Loss (psychology) 13. Uruguay 14. Buenos Aires, Argentina 15. Literary fiction 16. Political fiction 17. Translations -- Spanish to English

LC 2018049329

"Originally published in Uruguay as Primavera con una esquina rota in 1982. First published in Great Britain by Penguin Random House UK, London, 2018."

"Santiago, a political prisoner in Uruguay, was jailed after a brutal military coup that saw many of his comrades flee elsewhere. Santiago, feeling trapped, can do nothing but write letters to his family, and try to stay sane. Far away, his nine-year-old daughter Beatrice wonders at the marvels of 1970s Buenos Aires, but her grandpa and mother--Santiago's beautiful, careworn wife, Graciela--struggle to adjust to a life in exile"--, Provided by publisher.

Benedict, Helen

Wolf season / Helen Benedict. Bellevue Literary Press, 2017. 288 p.

ISBN 9781942658306

1. Post-traumatic stress disorder 2. Psychic trauma 3. Family relationships 4. Iraq War, 2003-2011 5. Family and war 6. Women and war 7. Women veterans 8. Women refugees 9. Families of military personnel 10. Wolves 11. Friendship 12. Small towns 13. New York (State) 14. Mainstream fiction

LC 2017015974

The war comes home in a searingly compassionate story about the wounds inflicted on soldiers, refugees, and their families.

Benedict, Marie

* **Lady** Clementine / Marie Benedict. Sourcebooks Landmark, 2020. 300 p.

ISBN 9781492666905

1. Churchill, Clementine, 1885-1977 2. Churchill, Winston, 1874-1965 3. 20th century 4. Prime ministers' spouses 5. Husband and wife 6. Ambition 7. Romantic love 8. Politicians 9. Political science 10. Protectiveness in women 11. Family relationships 12. Men/women relations 13. Great Britain -- History -- 20th century 14. Historical fiction 15. Biographical fiction

LC 2019010233

Traces Clementine Churchill's unflinching role in protecting the life and wartime agendas of her husband, Winston Churchill.

"Benedict's well-researched, illuminating account of a complex, intelligent woman will undoubtedly be enjoyed by fans of Melanie Benjamin and Nancy Horan." Booklist.

Benedict, Marie

The **only** woman in the room / Marie Benedict. Sourcebooks Landmark, 2019. 288 p.

ISBN 9781492666868

1. Lamarr, Hedy, 1913-2000 2. 20th century 3. Women inventors 4. Women scientists 5. Jewish women 6. Actors and actresses 7. Nazism 8. World War II 9. Information 10. Military secrets 11. Intrigue 12. Vienna, Austria 13. Hollywood, California 14. Biographical fiction 15. Historical fiction

LC 2018009020

A beautiful woman escapes her Austrian arms-dealer husband to become Hollywood legend Hedy Lamarr while hiding a secret double life as a Jewish scientist and sharing vital information about the Third Reich.

"Benedict paints a shining portrait of a complicated woman who knows the astonishing power of her beauty but longs to be recognized for her sharp intellect. Readers will be enthralled." Publishers Weekly.

Benioff, David

City of thieves : a novel / David Benioff. Viking, 2008. 272 p.

ISBN 0670018708

1. Second World War era (1939-1945) 2. Quests 3. Stealing 4. Seventeen-year-old boys 5. Arrest 6. Hunger 7. Death 8. Nazis 9. World War II 10. Survival 11. Male friendship 12. Faustian bargains 13. Teenage boys -- Friendship 14. St Petersburg, Russia -- Siege, 1941-1944 15. Biographical fiction 16. Coming-of-age stories 17. Historical fiction

LC 2007042784

This novel was based on memories of author Benioff's grandfather. ALA Notable Book, 2009.

When a dead German paratrooper lands in his street, Lev is caught looting the body and dragged to jail, fearing for his life. He shares his cell with the charismatic and grandiose Kolya, a handsome young soldier arrested on desertion charges. Instead of the standard bullet in the back of the head, Lev and Kolya are given a shot at saving their own lives by complying with an outrageous directive: secure a dozen eggs for a powerful colonel to use in his daughter's wedding cake. In a city cut off from all supplies and suffering unbelievable deprivation, Lev and Kolya embark on a hunt to find the impossible.

"In contrast to the piety of so many of today's historical novels, Benioff's book lets its characters inhabit the human condition in all of its sometimes compromised versatility. But it's never cavalier, because the author has done his research." New York Times

Benjamin, Chloe

* The **immortalists** : a novel / Chloe Benjamin. G. P. Putnam's Sons, 2018 352 p.

ISBN 9780735213180

1. Brothers and sisters 2. Fortune-tellers 3. Fate and fatalism 4. Families 5. Faith 6. Options, alternatives, choices 7. Interpersonal relations 8. Family relationships 9. Family sagas 10. Literary fiction

LC 2016053641

Wisconsin Library Association Literary Award, 2019.

Sneaking out to get readings from a traveling psychic reputed to be able to tell customers when they will die, four adolescent siblings from New York City's 1969 Lower East Side hide what they learn from each other before embarking on five decades of respective experiences shaped by their determination to control fate.

"Benjamin has created mesmerizing characters and richly suspenseful predicaments in this profound and glimmering novel of deaths ever-shocking inevitability and lifes wondrously persistent whirl of chance and destiny." Booklist.

Benjamin, Melanie, 1962-

Alice I have been / Melanie Benjamin. Delacorte Press, 2010. 368 p.

ISBN 9780385344135

1. Hargreaves, Alice Pleasance Liddell, 1852-1934 2. Carroll, Lewis, 1832-1898 3. 19th century 4. Muses (Persons) 5. Authors 6. Friendship 7. Men/women relations 8. England -- History 9. Oxford, England 10. Biographical fiction 11. Historical fiction 12. Love stories 13. Literary fiction

LC 2009035353

Alice Liddell Hargreaves's life has been a richly woven tapestry. As a young woman, wife, mother, and widow, she's experienced intense passion, great privilege, and greater tragedy. But as she nears her eighty-first birthday, she knows that, to the world around her, she is and will always be only "Alice." Her life was permanently dog-eared at one fateful moment in her tenth year, the golden summer day she urged a grown-up friend to write down one of his fanciful stories.

Benjamin, Melanie, 1962-

* The **aviator's** wife : a novel / Melanie Benjamin. Delacorte Press, 2013. 416 p.

ISBN 9780345528674

1. Lindbergh, Anne Morrow, 1906-2001 2. Lindbergh, Charles A (Charles Augustus), 1902-1974 3. 20th century 4. Independence in women 5. Self-discovery in women 6. Pilots 7. Husband and wife 8. Motherhood 9. Mass media 10. Flight 11. Kidnapping 12. United States -- History -- 20th century 13. Biographical fiction 14. Historical fiction 15. Literary fiction

LC 2012017014

A story inspired by the marriage between Charles and Anne Morrow Lindbergh traces the romance between a handsome young aviator and a shy ambassador's daughter whose relationship is marked by wild international acclaim, history-making flights and the world-shocking abduction of their child.

Benn, James R.

Billy Boyle : a World War Two mystery / James R. Benn. Soho Press, 2006. 304 p. Billy Boyle World War II mysteries

ISBN 1569474338

1. Second World War era (1939-1945) 2. 1940s 3. 20th century 4. Resistance to military occupation 5. World War II 6. Sabotage -- Norway -- History -- German occupation, 1940-1945 7. Soldiers 8. Police 9. Young men 10. Spies 11. Murder 12. Murder investigation 13. International intrigue 14. Men/women relations 15. Loss (Psychology) 16. Consequences 17. London, England 18. Norway 19. Historical mysteries 20. Mysteries

LC 2006042300

"Benn provides historically accurate background and appealing characters, spices the narrative with romance and emotion, and ruminates about the consequences of actions, all in a suitably straightforward prose style. A solid addition to mystery collections." Library Journal.

Bennett, Alan, 1934-

* The **uncommon** reader / Alan Bennett. Farrar, Straus and Giroux, 2007. 128 p.

ISBN 9780374280963

1. Elizabeth II,, Queen of Great Britain, 1926- 2. Traveling libraries 3. Books and reading 4. Happiness in women 5. Libraries 6. Nobility 7. Rulers 8. Bookmobiles 9. Great Britain -- History -- Elizabeth II, 1952- 10. Humorous stories

LC 2007926975

Obliged to borrow a book when her corgis stray into a mobile library, the Queen discovers a passion for reading, setting the palace upon its head and causing the royal head of Great Britain to question her role in the monarchy.

"This modest but sturdy novella is a spoof of two ridiculous holdovers: the British monarchy and high literary values. The first Mr. Bennett deflates, without urgency; the second he defends, without urgency. True wit relaxes, the author argues implicitly; it never overexcites." New York Observer.

Bennett, Anna

First earl I see tonight / Anna Bennett. St Martins Press, 2018. 368 p. Debutante diaries

ISBN 9781250199461

1. Regency period (1811-1820) 2. Jilted men 3. Marriage proposals 4. Aristocracy 5. Family estates 6. Money 7. Extortion 8. Families 9. Sexual attraction 10. Men/women relations 11. Great Britain -- Social life and customs -- 19th century 12. Regency romances 13. Historical romances

To stop a blackmailer from revealing a secret that could ruin her family, Miss Fiona Hartley, in desperate need of a husband to access her huge dowry, proposes marriage to the infuriating Earl of Somerdale who gives her a run for her money.

Bennett, Brit

The **mothers** / Brit Bennett. Riverhead Books, 2016. 272 p.

ISBN 9780399184512

1. Survivors of suicide victims 2. African American communities 3. Teenage pregnancy 4. Abortion 5. Religious communities 6. Best friends 7. Secrets 8. Young women 9. Regret 10. Options, alternatives, choices 11. Men/women relations 12. Self-destructive behavior 13. Southern California 14. Coming-of-age stories 15. Psychological fiction 16. Literary fiction 17. African American fiction

RUSA Reading List Short List, 2017

In a contemporary black community, 17-year-old Nadia Turner mourns the suicide of her mother, leading her to take up with the local's pastor's son; but when she gets pregnant, the pregnancy and the subsequent cover-up will have an impact that goes far beyond their youth.

"Chapel provides further context and an extra layer to an already exquisitely developed story." Publishers Weekly.

Bennett, Jenn

* **Bitter** spirits / Jenn Bennett. Berkley, 2014. 336 p. Roaring twenties

ISBN 9780425269572

1. 1920s 2. Mediums 3. Bootleggers 4. Psychic ability 5. Ghosts 6. Curses 7. Supernatural 8. Men/women relations 9. Interpersonal attraction 10. San Francisco, California 11. Paranormal romances

Despite her star billing at Gris-Gris, Chinatown's notorious speakeasy, San Francisco spirit medium Aida Palmer's stage show is not an act -- she really can conjure (or exorcise) supernatural entities. Her abilities attract the attention of Winter Magnusson (a.k.a. "the Viking Bootlegger"), who's been haunted by the ghost of a murdered prostitute ever since someone put a hex on him. Although Aida easily removes Winter's curse, she soon discovers that she's fallen under the spell of the mysterious man, who's burdened with as many secrets as Aida herself. Bitter Spirits boasts a richly detailed Prohibition-era setting, a supernaturally themed mystery, and complex, well-matched protagonists. -- Description by Gillian Speace.

"The details of the Prohibition era are well researched but not intrusive, providing a solid and tangible backdrop for the developing romance and supernatural mystery." Publishers Weekly.

Bennett, Robert Jackson, 1984-

American elsewhere / Robert Jackson Bennett. Orbit, 2012. 608 p.

ISBN 9780316200202

1. Secrets 2. Small towns 3. Suburban life 4. Former police 5. Inheritance and succession 6. Family secrets 7. Home -- Psychological aspects 8. Supernatural 9. Paranormal phenomena 10.

New Mexico 11. Horror 12. Psychological suspense

LC 2012016166

Shirley Jackson Awards, Novel, 2013.

An ex-cop inherits her mother's home in Wink, New Mexico, and discovers that the residents of the small, quiet town are even stranger than she had imagined.

Bennett, Robert Jackson, 1984-

City of blades : a novel / Robert Jackson Bennett. Broadway Books, 2016. 464 p. Divine cities

ISBN 9780553419719

1. Totalitarianism 2. International relations 3. Gods and goddesses 4. Spies 5. Warriors 6. Assassins 7. Espionage 8. Political intrigue 9. Imaginary wars and battles 10. Fantasy fiction

LC 2015020205

After turning her back on a position most people could only dream of, General Turyin Mulaghesh, one of the most powerful people in all the Saypur empire, is sent to a backwater posting to investigate a discovery only she's qualified to make sense of, one that could change the world--or destroy it.

"Bennett continues his theme of the influence of imperialism on what appears to be a very similar world to ours (albeit one in which gods helped shape the geopolitics), seamlessly melding spycraft and mythology. Turyin, a physically and emotionally wounded warrior who both loathes battle and excels at it, serves as a fascinating character to shoulder the books heavy burden of tragedy." Publishers Weekly.

Bennett, Robert Jackson, 1984-

City of miracles : a novel / Robert Jackson Bennett. Broadway Books, 2017 464 p. Divine cities

ISBN 9780553419733

1. Fugitives 2. Assassination 3. Curses 4. Murder investigation 5. Political intrigue 6. Secrets 7. Exiles 8. Death 9. Gods and goddesses 10. Revenge 11. Fantasy fiction

LC 2016043643

After the assassination of his former friend and ally, Prime Minister Shara Komayd, fugitive and exile Sigrud je Harvaldsson sets out on a mission of revenge.

Bennett, Robert Jackson, 1984-

City of stairs : a novel / Robert Jackson Bennett. Broadway Books, 2014. 448 p. Divine cities

ISBN 9780804137171

1. Gods and goddesses 2. Murder investigation 3. Women spies 4. International relations 5. Political intrigue 6. Totalitarianism 7. Staged deaths 8. Espionage 9. Secrets 10. Fantasy fiction

LC 2013040422

Now that its gods are dead, the once-powerful city of Bulikov is a shadow of its former self -- its history erased, its citizenry subjugated, and its laws enforced by Saypur, its technologically advanced former colony. Posing as a diplomat, intelligence operative Shara Thivani arrives in Bulikov to investigate the murder of Dr. Efrem Pangyui, a controversial scholar whose secret research, if published, could destabilize an entire civilization and change the course of history. -- Description by Gillian Speace.

"The world Bennett . . . has constructed is a complex political landscape of a subjugated people holding onto the memories of their glory days and protective gods and the conquerors reaping revenge for their own previous subjugation. An excellent spy story wrapped in a vivid imaginary world." Library Journal.

Bennett, Robert Jackson, 1984-

Foundryside / Robert Jackson Bennett. Crown Publishing, 2018. 496 p. The founders

ISBN 9781524760366

1. Women thieves 2. Power (Social sciences) 3. City life 4. Magic 5. Technology 6. Rites and ceremonies 7. Alliances 8. Secrets 9. Fantasy fiction

RUSA Reading List, 2019.

A thief in a city controlled by industrialized magic joins forces with a rare honest police officer to stop an ancient evil ritual that endangers thousands of lives.

Bennett, Robert Jackson, 1984-

The **troupe** / Robert Jackson Bennett. Orbit, 2012. 300 p.

ISBN 9780316187527

1. Vaudeville 2. Mysticism 3. Runaway teenagers 4. Pianists 5. Teenage boys 6. Father-separated children 7. Fathers and sons 8. Quartets 9. Good and evil 10. Horror

LC 2011018068

A teenager with an expertise in piano runs away from home and joins the Vaudeville circuit, joining a mysterious troupe run by the enigmatic Silenus and must uncover the group's mysterious true purpose before it's too late.

Benson, E. F. (Edward Frederic), 1867-1940

Make way for Lucia / E. F. Benson. Harper and Row, 1986, c1977. 1119 p.

ISBN 0060156783

1. Gossiping and gossips 2. Women 3. Small town life 4. Social classes 5. England -- Social life and customs -- 20th century 6. Humorous stories

LC 86045639

Six novels and one short story.

Benton, Janet, 1963-

Lilli de Jong : a novel / Janet Benton. Nan A. Talese / Doubleday, 2017. 335 p.

ISBN 9780385541459

1. 1880s 2. Quaker women 3. Single mothers 4. Mother and child 5. Defiance 6. Scandals 7. Women's role 8. Social pressure 9. Christian women 10. Determination in women 11. Self-fulfillment in women 12. Philadelphia, Pennsylvania -- History -- 19th century 13. Pennsylvania -- History -- 19th century 14. Historical fiction

LC 2016012853

Banished from her Quaker home and teaching job after being abandoned by her lover, a pregnant woman gives birth at an institution for unwed mothers in 1883 Philadelphia and refuses to give the child up, braving moral condemnation and poverty in her resolve to support her baby.

Benz, Chanelle

* The **gone** dead / Chanelle Benz. Ecco Press, 2019. 304 p.

ISBN 9780062490698

1. Inheritance and succession 2. Injustice 3. Fathers -- Death 4. Race relations 5. African Americans 6. Poets 7. Racism 8. Investigations 9. Secrets 10. Mississippi 11. Southern States 12. Southern fiction 13. Literary fiction

Returning to her ramshackle home in the Mississippi Delta after 30 years, Billie James investigates the accident that killed her famous poet father as well as rumors that she went missing the day he died.

Berenson, Alex

The **deceivers** / Alex Berenson. G.P. Putnam's Sons, 2018 432 p. John Wells novels

ISBN 9780399176166

1. CIA 2. CIA agents 3. Intelligence service 4. International intrigue 5. Conspiracies 6. Terrorism -- Prevention 7. Thrillers and suspense 8. Spy fiction

LC 2017037135

In the wake of a fatal incident in Dallas that may have been staged to look like a terrorist attack, former CIA agent John Wells is dispatched to Colombia to collect information from an old asset, a mission involving an audacious Russian plot that proves to be the most deadly of his career.

Berenson, Alex

The **faithful** spy : a novel / Alex Berenson. Random House, 2006. 352 p. John Wells novels

ISBN 0345478991

1. Bin Laden, Osama, 1957-2011 2. Qaida (Organization) 3. Undercover operations 4. Conversion to Islam 5. CIA agents 6. Men -- Spiritual life 7. Intelligence officers 8. International intrigue 9. Mass murder 10. Terrorism 11. Fundamentalists 12. Islam 13. Muslims 14. New York (State) 15. Thrillers and suspense 16. Spy fiction

LC 2005044689

Edgar Allan Poe Award for Best First Mystery Novel, 2007.

John Wells, an undercover operative who has infiltrated al Qaeda, is trapped between his terrorist associates and the CIA, which no longer trusts his loyalty, when he becomes a prime suspect in two bombings in Los Angeles.

"If Mr. Berenson remains as much reporter as novelist at this point --a newspaper editor would tell him he had overstuffed his lead, and that he often tended to impart information that was all too well known- -he still has an ingenious narrative to show for it. Uncertain times call for tough examinations, and The Faithful Spy doesn't back away." New York Times.

Berenson, Alex

The **prisoner** / Alex Berenson. G.P. Putnam's Sons, 2017 384 p. John Wells novels

ISBN 9780399176159

1. CIA 2. ISIS (Islamic State of Iraq and Syria) 3. Qaida (Organization) 4. Moles (Spies) 5. Undercover operations 6. CIA agents 7. Espionage 8. Intelligence service 9. Thrillers and suspense 10. Spy fiction

LC 2016041437

Forced to resume an old undercover identity as an al-Qaida jihadi to unmask a CIA mole, John Wells gets close to an ISIS prisoner in a secret Bulgarian prison, where he confronts the profoundly cruel and ambitious plans of increasingly formidable terrorist organizations.

"...Berenson delivers some surprises along the way, focusing in large part on two shockingly complex characters : the mole and an ISIS scientist creating a stash of sarin gas to be deployed in an attack designed to wipe out the CIAs brain trust. Another strong mix of finely tuned suspense and subtle character development." Booklist.

Berg, Elizabeth

The **art** of mending : a novel / Elizabeth Berg. Random House, 2004. 240 p.

ISBN 1400061598

1. 1960s 2. Family reunions 3. Forgiveness in women 4. Adult children of dysfunctional families 5. Brothers and sisters 6. Mother and child 7. Women psychotherapy patients 8. Mothers and daughters 9. Dysfunctional families 10. Family relationships 11. Confrontation

(Interpersonal relations) 12. Repression (Psychology) in women 13. Family secrets 14. Child abuse 15. Minnesota 16. Mainstream fiction 17. Gentle reads

LC 2003066726

"At her annual family reunion, Laura Bartone, a 50-something quilt artist, is forced to confront the secrets that have long haunted her family. Her emotionally unstable sister, Caroline, tells Laura and their brother, Steve, that their mother abused her as a child. As Laura and Steve-whose own childhoods were reasonably happy-struggle to make sense of Caroline's accusations and wonder how they could've been oblivious to or complicit in what happened, their father dies. This could be the stuff of melodrama, but Berg generally manages to avoid it. Her prose is often luminous and buoyant, and her insights can be penetrating." Publishers Weekly.

Berg, Elizabeth

The **confession** club : a novel / Elizabeth Berg. Random House, 2019 272 p. Mason novels

ISBN 9781984855176

1. Clubs 2. Female friendship 3. Secrets 4. Dinners and dining 5. Change (Psychology) 6. Self-fulfillment in women 7. Missouri 8. Mainstream fiction 9. Gentle reads

LC 2019007966

Invited to join a supper club where friends in their community support each other throughout private setbacks, two women enduring difficult relationships discover the power of friendship and sharing their secrets.

Berg, Elizabeth

The **last** time I saw you : a novel / Elizabeth Berg. Random House, 2010. 244 p.

ISBN 9781400068647

1. Class reunions 2. Second chances 3. Middle-aged persons 4. Mainstream fiction

LC 2009040008

Attending a 45th anniversary at the sides of former classmates, Dorothy reconnects with old friends with whom she reevaluates her life, choices and relationships.

"As the narrative moves us toward the main event, we feel sympathy for these people, as much as we would for ourselves, which points up the success of Berg's gentle, but never bowdlerized, renderings of the hopes and desires of this rather large cast of everyday characters." Chicago Tribune.

Berg, Elizabeth

Never change / Elizabeth Berg. Pocket Books, 2001. 224 p.

ISBN 0743411323

1. People with brain tumors 2. Men/women relations 3. Loneliness in women 4. Men with terminal illnesses 5. Independence in single women 6. Middle-aged women 7. Single women 8. Home health care nurses 9. Home nursing 10. Transformations, Personal 11. Feminine beauty (Aesthetics) 12. Mainstream fiction 13. Gentle reads

LC 00069874

Myra Lipinsky, a 51-year old visiting nurse, has been content to be a self-appointed spinster--until a man she adored in high school is struck by an incurable illness and returns to New England to spend what time he has left.

"In an inspiring, well-deserved denouement, Chip's inevitable death forces Myra to embrace the world in all its bittersweet complexity." Publishers Weekly.

Berg, Elizabeth

Night of miracles / Elizabeth Berg. Random House, 2018 288 p. Mason novels

ISBN 9780525509509

1. Baking 2. Senior women 3. Community life 4. Friendship 5. Small town life 6. Intergenerational friendship 7. Missouri 8. Mainstream fiction 9. Gentle reads

Sequel to: The Story of Arthur Truluv.

A baking class instructor, her haunted assistant and a youth reeling from a family tragedy discover the power of community while navigating complicated choices and uncertain futures.

Berg, Elizabeth

Once upon a time, there was you : a novel / Elizabeth Berg. Random House, 2011. 280 p.

ISBN 9781400068654

1. Divorced women 2. Men/women relations 3. Family problems 4. Parent and child 5. Sixteen-year-old girls 6. Marriage 7. Mainstream fiction

Sharing nothing in common except their 16-year-old daughter, divorced parents John and Irene reconnect in the wake of a devastating tragedy and discover things about each other that they had not revealed during their marriage.

"As often happens in a Berg novel, the plot seems momentarily derailed into stereotype at this point. But, once again, Berg manages to restrain the melodrama through a lucky coincidence. . . . Berg's psychological wisdom about love, family, and aging always make her well-paced novels a good read." Providence Journal.

Berg, Elizabeth

* The **story** of Arthur Truluv : a novel / Elizabeth Berg. Random House, 2017 192 p. Mason novels

ISBN 9781400069903

1. Teenage girls 2. Widowers 3. Intergenerational friendship 4. Senior men 5. Interpersonal relations 6. Loneliness 7. Loss (Psychology) 8. Missouri 9. Coming-of-age stories 10. Mainstream fiction 11. Gentle reads

LC 2016047564

Sequel: Night of Miracles.

Making daily visits to the grave of his beloved late wife, Arthur forges unexpected relationships with a nosy neighbor and a troubled teen who dubs him "Truluv" before the trio discovers healing and family together.

"Richly complex characters and clear prose. Redemptive without being maudlin, this story of two misfits lucky to have found one another will tug at readers heartstrings." Booklist.

Berg, Elizabeth

* **We** are all welcome here : a novel / Elizabeth Berg. Random House, 2006. xiii, 187 p.

ISBN 140006161X

1. 1960s 2. People with poliomyelitis 3. Abandoned wives 4. Civil Rights Movement 5. Women with poliomyelitis 6. Women with quadriplegia 7. Single mothers 8. Caregivers 9. Women caregivers 10. African Americans 11. African American women 12. Girls 13. Mothers and daughters 14. Paralysis 15. Race relations 16. Loyalty 17. Mississippi 18. Tupelo, Mississippi 19. Coming-of-age stories 20. Mainstream fiction 21. Domestic fiction 22. Southern fiction

LC 2005048956

It is the summer of 1964. In Tupelo, Mississippi, the town of Elvis's birth, tensions are mounting over civil-rights demonstrations occurring ever more frequently--and violently--across the state. But in Paige Dunn's small, ramshackle house, there are more immediate concerns.

Challenged by the effects of the polio she contracted during her last month of pregnancy, Paige is nonetheless determined to live as normal a life as possible and to raise her daughter, Diana, in the way she sees fit--with the support of her tough-talking black caregiver, Peacie.

"Full of humor, devoid of self-pity, with lively characters that rise above their circumstances, this is the story of an adolescent accepting adult responsibilities, encountering the temptations of boys and booze, and experiencing the tensions between race and class in the 1960s." School Library Journal.

Berg, Gretchen

The **operator** / Gretchen Berg. William Morrow & Co, 2020. 336 p.

ISBN 9780062917188

1. 1950s 2. Telephone operators 3. Eavesdropping 4. Telephone calls 5. Gossiping and gossips 6. Secrets 7. Small town life 8. Ohio 9. Historical fiction

A 1950s Ohio switchboard operator who eavesdrops on her neighbors' conversations uncovers unexpected secrets when she decides to investigate a malicious rumor that threatens to upend her carefully ordered life.

"Berg's storytelling is warm, sympathetic, and witty." Kirkus.

Bergen, David, 1957-

See the child : a novel / David Bergen. Harper Flamingo Canada, 1999. 234 p.

ISBN 0002255219

1. Grief in men 2. Drowning victims 3. Fathers and sons 4. Sons -- Death 5. Small town life -- Manitoba 6. Canada 7. Manitoba 8. Mainstream fiction

LC 99209527

"A Phyllis Bruce book."

"Bergen writes with a precision that reveals every detail, every action, carefully depicting Paul's emotional vulnerability and his need to determine how much he is responsible for his son's death and the fate of his grandson." Publishers Weekly.

Berger, Thomas, 1924-

Being invisible : a novel / Thomas Berger. Little, Brown, 1987. 262 p.

ISBN 0316091588

1. Unhappiness in men 2. Invisibility 3. Authors, American 4. Single men 5. Advertising copywriters 6. Misadventures 7. Ability 8. Satirical fiction

LC 86020897

"There is much in 'Being Invisible' to celebratethe pleasures of invention, humor, surprise, of Mr. Berger's enraged, unforgiving view. That so much of his vision seems neither freakish nor admonitory but rather, oddly tonic, says something about the era in which we live. . . . It is a sign of the times that we feel such affection for Thomas Berger's dogged, cranky courage, and for the denizens of his unwelcoming and chaotic corner of the fictional world." New York Times Book Review.

Berger, Thomas, 1924-

* Little Big Man / Thomas Berger. Delta, 1989, c1964. 440 p.

1. 19th century 2. Little Big Horn, Battle of the, 1876 3. Indians of North America -- Relations with European-Americans 4. Culture conflict 5. Indian captivities 6. Cheyenne Indians 7. European Americans -- Relations with Indians 8. The West (United States) 9. Westerns

Sequel: The return of Little Big Man.

Originally published: New York : Dial Press, 1964.

Western Heritage Award for Outstanding Western Novel, 1965.

The astonishing reminiscences of an ancient and immodest Indian frontiersman form a witty, lusty, and highly impressive epic, a panoramic enlargement of the way of life in the Old West.

Berger, Thomas, 1924-

* Neighbors : a novel / Thomas Berger. Delacorte Press/S. Lawrence, 1980. 275p.

ISBN 0440065569

1. New neighbors 2. Feuds 3. Rudeness 4. Family relationships 5. Fathers and daughters 6. Husband and wife 7. Suburban life 8. Psychological fiction

LC 79020307

"Berger quickly conditions the reader to expect the unexpected but manages to be consistently surprising nevertheless, introducing new twists and outrages that not even the most warped spectator could have foreseen. The novel adopts a formal, almost fussy style to convey lunacy, as if Berger were describing low deeds to a maiden aunt. . . . [The book] is not at all interested in being socially redeeming, and those who read books to gain warm feelings or philosophic nuggets will come away from this one empty-handed and probably angry. . . .What Berger has produced is a tour de force." Time.

Berger, Thomas, 1924-

* Reinhart's women : a novel / Thomas Berger. Delacorte Press/S. Lawrence, 1981. 295 p. Reinhart saga

1. Middle-aged men 2. Father and adult daughter 3. Cooks 4. Television food programs 5. Kindness in men 6. Men 7. Men/women relations 8. Psychological fiction

LC 81003271

"Although the hilarity is occasionally forced, this uniquely happy novel is certainly worth reading for all it attempts to cover and mostly for sheer manic fun." Library Journal.

Berger, Thomas, 1924-

Vital parts / Thomas Berger. R. W. Baron, 1970. 432 p. Reinhart saga

1. Cryonics 2. Middle-aged men 3. Former friends 4. Kindness in men 5. Men 6. United States -- History -- 1945- 7. Psychological fiction

"As Reinhart is pushed further and further into the absurdities he prides himself so successfully on avoiding, the promise of the brilliant opening scenes is not only confirmed but fulfilled by the double takes in plotting and narrative surface." Harper's..

Bergman, Megan Mayhew

Almost **famous** women : stories / Megan Mayhew Bergman. Scribner, 2015. 236 p.

ISBN 9781476786568

1. Fame 2. Women 3. Women celebrities 4. Socialites 5. Women artists 6. Women adventurers 7. Women musicians 8. Women authors 9. Biographical fiction 10. Short stories

This collection of short stories depicts the forgotten lives of women who almost achieved fame and notoriety, including Lord Byron's illegitimate daughter, Oscar Wilde's niece and Edna St. Vincent Milay's sister.

"The author has infused her characters with passion and yearning; they are so lifelike we feel we know them... Writing with brilliant cadence and economy, Bergman is an impressionist who uses her brilliant palette to illuminate facets of the lives of these brave and creative lesser-known strivers." Library Journal.

Bergstrom, Heather Brittain

Steal the north : a novel / Heather Brittain Bergstrom. Viking, 2014. 320 p.

ISBN 9780670786183

1. Single-parent families 2. Faith healing 3. Young women 4. Infertility 5. Aunt and niece 6. Native American teenage boys 7. Teenage boy/girl relations 8. Fundamentalists 9. Mainstream fiction 10. Coming-of-age stories

LC 2013036976

Sent by her fundamentalist mother to help an estranged sister participate in a faith healing ceremony, sheltered 16-year-old Emmy feels instant ties to her sister's eastern Washington home and falls in love with a Native American boy against the apprehensions of her family.

Berkowitz, Ira

Old flame : a Jackson Steeg novel / Ira Berkowitz. Three Rivers Press, 2008. 304 p. Jackson Steeg mysteries

ISBN 9780307408624

1. Former police 2. Gangsters 3. Violence 4. Murder 5. Former wives 6. Police corruption 7. Friendship 8. New York City 9. Hardboiled fiction 10. Mysteries

LC 2008005177

Former NYPD homicide detective Jackson Steeg is finding his retirement anything but peaceful when his ex-wife's new beau is beaten to death outside a trendy restaurant in a killing that may have links to corruption in the awarding of city construction contracts, an old friend is in debt to a vicious Israeli mobster, and a mob war is threatening to erupt.

Berlin, Lucia

* Evening in paradise : more stories / Lucia Berlin. Farrar, Straus and Giroux, 2018. 256 p.

ISBN 9780374279486

1. Human nature 2. Interpersonal relations 3. Family relationships 4. Texas 5. Chile 6. Short stories

LC 2018002535

Collects previously uncompiled selections from the late author's remaining story collection.

"Following the posthumous collection A Manual for Cleaning Women, which received major attention, here is a selection of Berlin's remaining stories proving that she should have been better known." Library Journal.

Berlin, Lucia

* A manual for cleaning women : selected stories / Lucia Berlin ; edited by Stephen Emerson. Farrar, Straus and Giroux, 2015. 403 p.

ISBN 9780374202392

1. Family relationships 2. Interpersonal relations 3. Southwest (United States) 4. Short stories

LC 2014047119

Kirkus Prize for Fiction finalist, 2015.

Taking place in the American Southwest, an anthology of short stories, celebrating the author's trademark blend of humor and melancholy, finds miracles in everyday life and uncovers moments of grace in cafeterias, laundromats, homes of the upper class and hotel dining rooms.

"As characters recur and settings and predicaments vary, Berlin unflinchingly strips bare casual and catastrophic cruelty and injustice. . . . An essential collection of jazzy, jolting, incisive, wryly funny, and keenly compassionate, virtuoso tales." Booklist.

Berne, Lisa

* You may kiss the bride / Lisa Berne. Avon Books, 2017. 373 p. Penhallow dynasty

ISBN 9780062451781

1. Regency period (1811-1820) 2. Rich men 3. Mate selection 4. Women marriage resisters 5. Orphans 6. Poor women 7. Intimacy (Psychology) 8. Interclass romance 9. Men/women relations 10. Interpersonal attraction 11. England 12. Great Britain 13. Regency romances 14. Historical romances

Searching for a biddable bride who can produce an heir and then live separate lives as generations before him, wealthy and arrogant Gabriel Penhallow sets his sights on Livia Stuart who, after provoking him into a kiss, challenges him at every turn and refuses to become his wife.

"Author Berne offers a masterful Regency debut that explores pride and prejudices with a tone that seems much less modern than that of many recent historical releases and two main characters who epitomize traditional Regency sensibilities as they sort through what they want and how to get it. Livia becomes the sun shining in on a stuffy, wounded family whose initial dread at the thought of her joining them transforms into happiness as she turns out to be their salvation. A sheer delight." Kirkus.

Berne, Suzanne

The **dogs** of Littlefield : a novel / Suzanne Berne. Simon & Schuster, 2016, c2013. 275 p.

ISBN 9781476794242

1. Poisoning 2. Sociologists 3. Small town life 4. Sociology 5. Communities 6. Dogs -- Death 7. Girls -- Psychology 8. Murder investigation 9. Interpersonal conflict 10. Middle school students 11. African American women 12. Massachusetts 13. Mysteries

LC 2015017821

Originally published: London : Fig Tree, 2013.

A sociologist studying what makes "a good quality of life," arrives in a seemingly perfect town as someone begins poisoning the local dogs.

Bernhard, Emilia

The **books** of the dead / Emilia Bernhard. Crooked Lane Books, 2019. 309 p. Death in Paris mysteries

ISBN 9781643851570

1. Women amateur detectives 2. Expatriates 3. Married women 4. Libraries 5. Undercover operations 6. Rare books 7. Murder 8. Murder investigation 9. Summer 10. City life 11. Paris, France 12. Cozy mysteries

Parisian summers are for strolls in the park . . . and solving a murder--or two.

Bernhard, Thomas

Frost : a novel / Thomas Bernhard ; translated from the German by Michael Hofmann. Knopf, 2006, c1963. 352 p.

ISBN 9781400040667

1. Young men -- Austria 2. Medical students 3. Senior men -- Austria 4. Brothers 5. Painters -- Austria 6. Eccentric men -- Austria 7. Observation (Psychology) 8. Small town life -- Austria 9. Austria 10. Diary novels 11. Translations -- German to English

LC 2006040886

Originally published: Frankfurt am Main : Insel-Verlag, 1963.

At the behest of his surgical mentor, a young Austrian medical student poses as a law student to journey to a remote mining town in order to observe Strauch, an aging painter and brother of his mentor, without letting Strauch know his true occupation, and becomes caught up in the lives of the mad artist and a colorful assortment of local characters.

"A student's increasingly erratic dispatches over 27 days comprise this obsessive first novel by Bernhard. . . . Bernhard's glorious talent for bleak existential monologues is second only to Beckett's, and seems to have sprung up fully mature in his mesmerizing debut." Publishers Weekly.

Bernhard, Thomas

* The **loser** / Thomas Bernhard ; translated from the German by Jack Dawson ; afterword by Mark M. Anderson. A. A. Knopf, 1991, c1983. 189 p.

ISBN 0394572394

1. Gould, Glenn 2. Pianists 3. Philosophers 4. Autobiographical fiction 5. Translations -- German to English

LC 90045942

Bernhard's imaginary account of a friendship with the pianist Glenn Gould explores the soul of the artist and the world of isolation, solitude, and obsession that often accompanies genius

Bernhard, Thomas

Wittgenstein's nephew : a friendship / Thomas Bernhard ; translated from the German by David McLintock. Knopf, 1989. 99 p.

ISBN 039456376X

1. Bernhard, Thomas 2. Wittgenstein, Paul, 1907- 3. Authors 4. Philosophers 5. Germany 6. Austria 7. Biographical fiction

LC 88045317

"The narrator muses on genius, sickness, madness, and death in the world and wonders why Wittgenstein succumbs while he survives. The translation is excellent." Choice.

Bernhard, Thomas

* **Woodcutters** / Translated from the German by David McLintock A. A. Knopf, 1987. 181 p.

ISBN 9780394551524

1. Dinners and dining 2. Vienna, Austria 3. Satirical fiction 4. Translations -- German to English

LC 87045123

"Mr. Bernhard's portrait of a society in dissolution has a Scandinavian darkness reminiscent of Ibsen and Strindberg, but it is filtered through a minimalist prose of obsessive repetition and ever so slight modulations." New York Times Book Review.

Berry, Connie

A **legacy** of murder / Connie Berry. Crooked Lane Books, 2019. 327 p. Kate Hamilton mystery

ISBN 9781643851549

1. Women amateur detectives 2. Antique dealers 3. Christmas 4. Widows 5. Americans in Great Britain 6. Mothers and daughters 7. Women murder suspects 8. Historic buildings 9. Murder investigation 10. Thieves 11. Secrets 12. Men/women relations 13. England 14. Cozy mysteries 15. Holiday mysteries

American antique dealer Kate Hamilton's Christmastime jaunt to a charming English village leads to an investigation of a missing ruby... and a chain of murders.

Berry, Steve, 1955-

* The **bishop's** pawn / Steve Berry. Minotaur Books, 2018. 340 p. Cotton Malone novels

ISBN 9781250140227

1. King, Martin Luther,, Jr, 1929-1968 Assassination 2. Hoover, J Edgar, 1895-1972 3. Assassination 4. Conspiracies 5. Political intrigue 6. Secret societies 7. Politicians 8. Intelligence service 9. Secrecy in government 10. Political thrillers

LC 2017044458

Former Justice Department agent Cotton Malone uncovers a disturbing link between a case from his past and the assassination of Martin Luther King, Jr. that risks innocent lives and threatens the legacy of the Civil Rights movement's iconic martyr.

Berry, Steve, 1955-

The **lost** order / Steve Berry. Minotaur, 2017. 493 p. Cotton Malone novels

ISBN 9781250056252

1. Treasure troves 2. Secret societies 3. Treasure hunters 4. Political intrigue 5. Politicians 6. Intelligence service 7. Secrecy in government 8. Political thrillers

When rival factions of a dangerous clandestine organization begin a race to find billions in stolen treasure hidden by their progenitors, Justice Department agent Cotton Malone finds the case complicated by his unsuspected ties to the organization and the political schemes of an unscrupulous politician.

"The fusion of contemporary and historical adventure makes this a page-turner of the highest order." Publishers Weekly.

Berry, Steve, 1955-

* The **Malta** exchange : a novel / Steve Berry. Minotaur Books, 2019. 400 p. Cotton Malone novels

ISBN 9781250140265

1. Knights of Malta. 2. Secret societies 3. Intelligence service 4. Secrecy in government 5. Popes -- Elections 6. Letters 7. Power (Social sciences) 8. International intrigue 9. Italy 10. Vatican City 11. Malta 12. Political thrillers

LC 2018050884

Former Justice Department operative Cotton Malone races to Italy to secure a history-changing document with ties to a 900-year-old organization that would manipulate the selection of the next pope.

Berry, Steve, 1955-

* The **Templar** legacy : a novel of suspense / Steve Berry. Ballantine Books, 2006. 496 p. Cotton Malone novels

ISBN 0345476158

1. Knights Templar (Masonic order) 2. Catholic Church 3. United States. Department of Justice Officials and employees 4. Booksellers 5. Treasure hunting 6. Conspiracies 7. Secrets 8. Monasticism and religious orders for men 9. Antiquarian booksellers 10. Christianity -- History 11. Inquisition -- France 12. Amateur detectives 13. France 14. Rennes-le-Chateau, France 15. Southern France 16. Thrillers and suspense

LC 2005053566

Sequel: The Alexandria link.

Cotton Malone, a former covert U.S. Justice Department operative, and his ex-supervisor Stephanie Nelle, follow a labyrinthine trail of danger, treachery, high-level intrigue, and overwhelming ambition across Europe on a quest that leads them to the enigmatic secrets of the Knights Templar.

Berry, Steve, 1955-

* The **Warsaw** protocol / Steve Berry. Minotaur Books, 2020. 400 p. Cotton Malone novels

ISBN 9781250140302

1. Power (Social sciences) 2. International intrigue 3. Christian relics 4. Intelligence service 5. Stealing 6. Auctions 7. Extortion 8. Warsaw, Poland 9. Poland 10. Political thrillers

LC 2019043232

Investigating the thefts of the seven Arma Christi relics from their international sanctuaries, former Justice Department agent Cotton Malone learns that the relics are being demanded by a blackmailer in possession of incriminating evidence against the president of Poland.

Berry, Wendell, 1934-

Jayber Crow : a novel / Wendell Berry. Counterpoint, 2000. 363 p. Port William series

ISBN 1582430292

1. Unrequited love 2. Farm life 3. Small town life 4. Rural families 5. Barbers 6. Orphans 7. Single men 8. Barbers 9. Orphans 10. Family relationships 11. Community life 12. Kentucky 13. Domestic fiction 14. Literary fiction 15. Gentle reads

LC   00035889

"The life story of Jayber Crow, barber, of the Port William Membership, as written by himself" -- cover

In a new novel set in a small-town "Heaven," the rural Kentucky farmer-philosopher returns to his fictional Port William to explore themes of love, suffering, and joy.

"The richly portrayed community unfolds delicately and surely, with the human dramas of its inhabitants revealed from Jayber's perspective. A moving, lyrical work on a small canvas." Library Journal.

Berry, Wendell, 1934-

* **That** distant land : the collected stories of Wendell Berry / Wendell Berry. Shoemaker & Hoard, 2004. 440 p. Port William series

ISBN 1593760272

1. Rural families 2. Farmers 3. Families 4. Small town life 5. Rural life 6. Farm life 7. Community life 8. Family relationships 9. Kentucky -- Social life and customs 10. Short stories 11. Domestic fiction 12. Literary fiction 13. Gentle reads

LC   2003025213

Contains all of the "Port William membership" short stories and arranges them by year of story's setting.

Twenty-three short stories.

"Set in a small Kentucky farming village, this collection of Berry's Port William stories illuminates the evolution of rural American life over the course of the 20th century. In 23 stories, Berry chronicles Port William from the 1880s to the 1980s, evoking the connectedness of the small town's denizens to each other and to the land." Publishers Weekly.

The **best** American mystery stories 2017 / edited by John Sandford ; Otto Penzler, series editor. Mariner Books, 2017. 384 p. Best American mystery stories

ISBN 9780544949089

1. Detectives 2. Crime 3. Private investigators 4. Murder 5. Criminals 6. United States -- Social life and customs -- 21st century 7. Mysteries 8. Short stories 9. Anthologies

Otto Penzler and John Sandford select the best mystery writing of the year.

The **best** American mystery stories 2018 / edited by Louise Penny ; Otto Penzler, series editor. Mariner Books, 2018. 384 p. Best American mystery stories

ISBN 9780544949096

1. Detectives 2. Crime 3. Private investigators 4. Murder 5. Criminals 6. Murder investigation 7. Criminal investigation 8. United States -- Social life and customs -- 21st century 9. Mysteries 10. Short stories 11. Anthologies

An anthology of the best mystery short stories published in 2017 selected by best-selling author Louise Penny.

The **best** American mystery stories 2019 / edited by Jonathan

Lethem, Otto Penzler, series editor. Mariner Books, 2019. 352 p. Best American mystery stories

ISBN 9781328636096

1. Crime 2. Murder 3. Criminals 4. Families 5. Interpersonal relations 6. Criminal investigation 7. Murder investigation 8. Mysteries 9. Psychological suspense 10. Short stories 11. Anthologies

Best-selling author of ten genre-bending novels Jonathan Lethem helms this collection of the year's best mystery short fiction.

The **best** American noir of the century / edited by James Ellroy and Otto Penzler ; with an introduction by James Ellroy. Houghton Mifflin Harcourt, 2010. 752 p.

ISBN 9780547330778

1. Criminals 2. Crime 3. Noir fiction 4. Crime fiction 5. Mysteries 6. Hardboiled fiction 7. Short stories 8. Anthologies

LC 2010017204

"This anthology features noir of the literary kind. For those of you for whom the shot glass is always half empty and the forecast is always grim, you can't do much better this sterling collection of 39 tales from the darkness at the edge of town, full of characters doomed to bad choices and worse luck. You can gripe about the editors' definition of noir or some of their omissions, but they've done a great job here, offering lesser known tales by such expected perpetrators as Cornell Woolrich, Jim Thompson, James M. Cain, Mickey Spillane, Evan Hunter and Patricia Highsmith as well as a few outliers, such as Dorothy B. Hughes, David Rambo Morrell and Lorenzo Sleepers Carcaterra and a few authors even the most devoted noir devotee may not be familiar with. Tod Robbins, anyone?" Mystery Scene.

* The **best** American short stories 2019 / edited by Anthony Doerr and Heidi Pitlor Houghton Mifflin Harcourt, 2019. 320 p. Best American short stories

ISBN 9781328465825

1. Anthologies 2. Short stories

#1 New York Times best-selling, Pulitzer Prize?winning author Anthony Doerr brings his"stunning sense of physical detail and gorgeous metaphors" (San Francisco Chronicle) to selecting The Best American Short Stories 2019. Doerr and the series editor, Heidi Pitlor, winnow down twenty stories out of thousands that represent the best examples of the form published the previous year.

The **best** of the best horror of the year : 10 years of essential short horror fiction / edited by Ellen Datlow. Night Shade Books, 2018. 481 p. Best horror of the year (Ellen Datlow)

ISBN 9781597809832

1. Supernatural 2. Horror 3. Short stories 4. Anthologies

For more than three decades, editor and anthologist Ellen Datlow, winner of multiple Hugo, Bram Stoker, and World Fantasy awards, has had her finger on the pulse of the horror genre, introducing readers to writers whose tales can unnerve, frighten, and terrify. This anniversary volume, which collects the best stories from the first ten years of her annual The Best Horror of the Year anthology series

Betts, Doris

* **Souls** raised from the dead : a novel / Doris Betts. Knopf, 1994. 339 p.

ISBN 0679426213

1. Families 2. Fathers and daughters 3. Children -- Death 4. Southern states 5. Domestic fiction

LC   93030900

ALA Notable Book, 1995.

Members of a Southern family, a young girl, her state trooper father, two sets of grandparents, her runaway mother, and their neighbors and friends struggle to cope with the child's incurable disease.

Beukes, Lauren

Broken monsters / Lauren Beukes. Mulholland Books, 2014. 288 p.

ISBN 9780316216821

1. Women detectives 2. Psychopaths 3. City life 4. Dead 5. Murder 6. Murder investigation 7. Journalists 8. Reality 9. Artists 10. Detroit, Michigan 11. Thrillers and suspense

RUSA Reading List, 2015.

Detective Gabriella Versado investigates after disturbing displays that fuse the bodies of murder victims with those of animals are uncovered in abandoned Detroit buildings.

"Beukes avoids predictability by leading readers to doubt their interpretations of motives and events, blending detection and atmospheric horror to court both hard-boiled mystery and literary-horror fans." Booklist.

Beukes, Lauren

Slipping : stories, essays, & other writing / Lauren Beukes. Tachyon Publications, 2016. 288 p.

ISBN 9781616962401

1. Near future 2. Life on other planets 3. Johannesburg, South Africa 4. Science fiction 5. Literary fiction 6. Short stories 7. Essays 8. Anthologies

A satiric retrospective collection of fiction and nonfiction writings includes pieces about a Punk Lolita fighter pilot who rescues Tokyo from a marauding art installation, corporate recruits who harvest poisonous plants on an inhospitable planet and an inquisitive teen ghost who disrupts an architect's life.

"Whether they're set in modern-day Johannesburg or on a planet circling a distant star, these powerful, beautifully written stories are always about today and the darkness of the human soul." Publishers Weekly.

Beukes, Lauren

Zoo city / Lauren Beukes. Angry Robot, 2011, c2010. 413 p.

ISBN 9780857660558

1. Slums 2. Missing persons investigation 3. Magic (Occultism) -- Africa 4. Criminals 5. Music industry and trade 6. Crime bosses 7. Ghettoes 8. Johannesburg, South Africa 9. Urban fantasy

Originally published: Auckland Park, S.A. : Jacana Media, 2010.

Arthur C. Clarke Award, 2011.

Zinzi searches for a missing pop star in the ghettos of Johannesburg, which is inhabited by former criminals marked by an animal companion for their crimes, while a shaman crime lord sets out to kill anyone who tries to find her.

Beverley, Jo

Devilish / Jo Beverley. Signet, 2000. 372 p. Malloren chronicles

ISBN 0451199979

1. Georgian era (1714-1837) 2. 1760s 3. 18th century 4. Nobility -- History -- 18th century 5. Independence in women 6. Counts and countesses 7. Single women 8. Marquis and marchionesses 9. Men/women relations 10. Family secrets 11. Inheritance and succession 12. Heirs and heiresses 13. Grief 14. London, England 15. Great Britain -- History -- George III, 1760-1820 16. Georgian romances 17. Historical romances

RITA Award for Best Long Historical, 2001.

Ordered by the king to escort the fiery, willful Countess of Arradale to London, Lord Rothgar finds his own famous willpower tested by the lovely temptress.

Beverley, Jo

* **My** lady notorious / Jo Beverley. Avon Books, 1993 380 p. Malloren chronicles

ISBN 9780380767854

1. Georgian era (1714-1837) 2. 1760s 3. 18th century 4. Impersonators 5. Kidnapping 6. Disguises 7. Women impostors 8. Women thieves 9. Rescues 10. Widows 11. Sisters 12. Fathers and daughters 13. Chases 14. Escapes 15. Family secrets 16. Seduction 17. Brothers 18. London, England 19. Great Britain -- History -- George III, 1760-1820 20. Georgian romances 21. Historical romances

Later published under the title Lady notorious: Caerphilly, South Wales : Everlyn, 2009.

RITA Award for Best Long Historical, 1994.

Lady Chastity Ware dresses as a highwayman to help her widowed sister and her infant niece escape a treacherous pursuer, and she accosts the first stagecoach she sees--capturing, among others, a handsome aristocrat eager for adventure

Beverley, Jo

Something wicked / Jo Beverley. Topaz, 1997. 374 p. Malloren chronicles

ISBN 0451407806

1. Georgian era (1714-1837) 2. 1760s 3. 18th century 4. Disguises 5. Single women 6. Twins 7. Brothers and sisters 8. Treason 9. Earls and countesses 10. Seduction 11. Kidnapping 12. Independence in women 13. Risk-taking in women 14. Escapes 15. Boredom in women 16. Great Britain -- History -- George III, 1760-1820 17. London, England 18. Georgian romances 19. Historical romances

Beverley, Jo

* **Tempting** fortune / Jo Beverley. Zebra Books, 1995. 444 p. Malloren chronicles

ISBN 9781420120554

1. Georgian era (1714-1837) 2. 1760s 3. 18th century 4. Rogues 5. Deception 6. Single women 7. Half-brothers 8. Gambling 9. Debtor and creditor 10. Earls and countesses 11. Independence in women 12. Men/women relations 13. Family feuds 14. London, England 15. Great Britain -- History -- George III, 1760-1820 16. Georgian romances 17. Historical romances

Portia St. Claire's brother's gambling has put her in the unenviable plight of having her virtue auctioned off in London's most notorious brothel. Bryght Malloren, who believes he has meet Portia before, is unable to leave her to such a cruel fate and turns the private wager into a public game of seduction, one that confirms his reputation as a shameless rake and keeps all of London society breathless with anticipation.

Beverly, William, 1965-

Dodgers : a novel / Bill Beverly. Crown Publishers, 2016. 290 p.

ISBN 9781101903735

1. Gang members 2. Teenage boys 3. Self-discovery 4. Witnesses 5. Purpose in life 6. Gangs 7. Attempted murder 8. Wisconsin 9. Coming-of-age stories 10. Crime fiction

Gold Dagger Award for Best Crime Novel of the Year, 2016

New Blood Dagger Award, 2016

East, a Los Angeles gang member who works as a lookout, is only 16 when he's sent to Wisconsin as part of a group to kill a witness hiding out there. Along with three other teens (including his younger brother), he must traverse an entirely alien America, where as young black men they stand out far more than they did in L.A. Observant and cautious, East is a complex character, one who is good at what he does but not entirely hardened by his life. -- Description by Shauna Griffin.

"Highly recommended for fans of Richard Price, this is a searing novel about crime, race, and coming-of-age, with characters who live, breathe, and bleed." Booklist.

Beyda, Emily

The **body** double / Emily Beyda. Doubleday, 2020. 304 p.
ISBN 9780385545273

1. Impersonation 2. Celebrities 3. Deception 4. Nervous breakdown 5. Life change events 6. Control (Psychology) 7. Identity (Psychology) 8. Secrets 9. Los Angeles, California 10. Psychological suspense

Hired as the body double of a famous but troubled celebrity, a small-town girl diligently mimics her Hollywood doppelganger in public appearances before encountering sinister questions about the star's mental collapse.

"This auspicious debut will get under the reader's skin and stay there." Publishers Weekly.

Bezmozgis, David, 1973-

The **betrayers** : a novel / David Bezmozgis. Little, Brown and Company, 2014. 225 p.
ISBN 9780316284332

1. Politicians 2. Betrayal 3. Consequences 4. Jewish men 5. Family relationships 6. Forgiveness 7. Reunions 8. Israel 9. Soviet Union 10. Literary fiction 11. Psychological suspense

Edward Lewis Wallant Award, 2014.
National Jewish Book Award for Fiction, 2014.
Shortlisted for the Giller Prize, 2014

Escaping his political opponents in a Crimean resort town, disgraced Israeli politician Baruch Kotler runs into a former friend who had him sent to the gulag 40 years prior and must reconcile with his betrayers and his own poor choices.

"Though the action is fixed largely in one location, Bezmozgis's novel feels vast, its pages heavy with the complicated debts we owe one another, which are impossible to leave behind." Publishers Weekly.

Bhuvaneswar, Chaya, 1971-

White dancing elephants : stories / Chaya Bhuvaneswar. Dzanc Books, 2018. 208 p.
ISBN 9781945814617

1. Love 2. Extramarital affairs 3. Grief 4. Women 5. South Asians 6. Race (Social sciences) 7. Social classes 8. Sexuality 9. Interpersonal relations 10. Family relationships 11. Women's lives and relationships 12. Short stories 13. Mainstream fiction
LC 2018005798

In these remarkable stories, Chaya Bhuvaneswar spotlights diverse women of color--cunning, bold, and resolute--facing sexual harassment and racial violence, and occasionally inflicting that violence on each other. Winner of the 2017 Dzanc Short Story Collection Prize, White Dancing Elephants marks the emergence of a new and original voice in fiction and explores feminist, queer, religious, and immigrant stories with precision, drama, and compassion.

"Bhuvaneswar's compelling stories portray diverse characters grappling with shifts in their lives, the complications of their actions, and the impacts of others. Conflicts play out in various circumstances--strained relationships, failing health, regret--and characters are often poised at crossroads." Booklist.

Bialosky, Jill

House under snow / Jill Bialosky. Harcourt, 2002. 242 p.
ISBN 9780151006854

1. Mothers and daughters -- Ohio 2. Children of widows -- Ohio 3. Grief 4. Fathers -- Death 5. Fiances 6. Sisters -- Ohio 7. Widows -- Ohio 8. Ohio 9. Psychological fiction
LC 2001007435

Anna Crane reflects back on her childhood in Ohio during the 1960s and 1970s with two sisters and a self-destructive mother as she recalls her first love affair with a troubled boy and her betrayal by two important figures in her life.

"Bialosky's haunting first novel aches with the sensitivity of a soulful girl who is discovering love, sexuality, and the pain of unsurpassable betrayal." Booklist.

Bialosky, Jill

The **prize** : a novel / Jill Bialosky. Counterpoint Press, 2015 325 p.
ISBN 9781619025707

1. Artists 2. Greed 3. Ethical problems 4. Marital conflict 5. Art dealers 6. Family relationships 7. Fathers and sons 8. Competition 9. Self-discovery 10. Secrets 11. Psychological fiction
LC 2015023052

Determined not to let ambition, money and power corrode the sanctuary of his domestic and private life, Edward Darby, a partner at an esteemed gallery, finds himself unhinged by his ideals when he is betrayed by one artist and another very different artist awakens his heart and stirs up secrets from his past.

"This fluently sophisticated and exquisitely pleasurable novel is radiant with precise and sensuous descriptions and intricately laced with discerning and affecting insights into the passion and business of art and the meaning and struggles of marriage." Booklist.

The **big** book of science fiction / edited by Ann VanderMeer and Jeff VanderMeer. Vintage Crime/Black Lizard, 2016. 800 p.
ISBN 9781101910092

1. Science fiction 2. Anthologies 3. Short stories
LC 2015042397

Locus Award for Best Anthology, 2017.

Bringing together writers from all over the world who ponder "what if?" about important current topics, an anthology features such authors as Isaac Asimov, Ursula K. Le Guin, H.G. Wells, Margaret St. Clair, and Philip K. Dick.

"A necessity for those wishing to broaden their understanding of science fiction as a genre...or just those looking for some darn good stories." Kirkus.

* The **big** book of Sherlock Holmes stories / edited by Otto Penzler. Vintage Crime/Black Lizard / Vintage Books, 2015. xxii, 789 p.
ISBN 9781101870891

1. Doyle, Arthur Conan,, Sir, 1859-1930 Characters Sherlock Holmes 2. Private investigators 3. Criminal investigation 4. London, England 5. Mysteries 6. Short stories 7. Anthologies 8. Adaptations, retellings, and spin-offs

"Penzler has composed a short history of Holmes and also provides a brief introduction to each tale, which covers the author, the work itself, how it came to be published and why it is included. The pieces are separated into categories, which makes choosing a story more fun for the reader. For example, one can decide to read a famous O. Henry or Stephen King story, or elect to read a parody of Holmes by R.C. Leyman or by Doyle himself." Library Journal.

Biguenet, John

Oyster / John Biguenet Ecco, 2002. 288 p.
ISBN 0060198362

1. Murder -- Louisiana 2. Jealousy 3. Families 4. Family feuds 5. Revenge 6. Bayous -- Louisiana 7. Louisiana 8. Southern Gothic 9. Southern fiction

LC 2001050170

A bitter rivalry between two oyster fishing families in Louisiana during the 1950s leads to tragedy.

"Biguenet's gritty, violent and sometimes melodramatic first novel . . . catches the scents and sounds of the bayou, and his characters bristle with a dark intensity." New York Times Book Review.

Bijan, Donia

The **last** days of Cafe Leila / Donia Bijan. Algonquin Books of Chapel Hill, 2017. 304 p.
ISBN 9781616205850

1. Marital conflict 2. Family businesses 3. Homecomings 4. Iranian American women 5. Restaurants 6. Cooking 7. Food 8. Families 9. Extramarital affairs 10. Family relationships 11. Mothers and daughters 12. Life change events 13. Tehran, Iran 14. Iran -- History -- 20th century 15. Iran -- Social life and customs 16. Literary fiction 17. Coming-of-age stories

A neighborhood cafe in Tehran is at the center of this powerful and transporting story of love, family, friendship, and homecoming told against the backdrop of Iran's rich, yet tragic, history.

"Bijan has crafted a richly layered story of the deep connections within a family, resilient links that survive tragedy and distance." Booklist.

Bilal, Parker

The **burning** gates : a Makana investigation / Parker Bilal. Bloomsbury, 2015. 384 p. Makana mysteries
ISBN 9781620408865

1. Art thefts 2. War criminals 3. Smuggling 4. Violence 5. Private investigators 6. Political intrigue 7. Cairo, Egypt 8. Egypt 9. Mysteries

When a priceless painting goes missing from Baghdad during the U.S. invasion, private investigator Makana tracks it down to the black market of Cairo in what may be his most dangerous case yet.

Bilal, Parker

The **ghost** runner / Parker Bilal. Bloomsbury, 2014. 352 p. Makana mysteries
ISBN 9781620403402

1. Extramarital affairs 2. Honor killings 3. Terrorists 4. Violence 5. Private investigators 6. Political intrigue 7. Former police 8. Sudanese in Egypt 9. Cairo, Egypt 10. Egypt 11. Mysteries

Sudanese investigator Makana travels into the desert heart of Egypt to solve a series of brutal murders and explore the shifting sands of the past.

Bilenchi, Romano, 1909-1989

* The **chill** / Romano Bilenchi ; translated from the Italian by Ann Goldstein. Europa, 2009 120 p.
ISBN 9781933372907

1. 1920s 2. Bereavement 3. Rumor 4. Teenage boys 5. Grandfathers 6. Death 7. Tuscany, Italy -- Social life and customs 8. Translations -- Italian to English 9. Psychological fiction

Translated from the Italian.

A teenage boy becomes increasingly removed from his friends and family after the death of his beloved grandfather, as he becomes more aware of his own mortality and sexuality.

"Most coming-of-age novels illuminate the tumultuous inner world of adolescence; Bilenchi's reveals the brutality of the adulthood that surrounds it." The New Yorker.

Billingham, Mark

* Their **little** secret / Mark Billingham. Atlantic Monthly Press, 2019. 400 p. Tom Thorne novels
ISBN 9780802147363

1. Detectives 2. Suicide investigation 3. Women detectives 4. Swindlers and swindling 5. Murder 6. Murder investigation 7. Deception 8. England 9. Psychological suspense 10. Thrillers and suspense

LC 2019009800

Suspecting foul play while investigating a metro station suicide, Tom Thorne enlists Nicola Tanner to help investigate the activities of a murderous con man before linking the case to a bludgeoning death.

"The twisted plot unfolds gradually, with a maximum of suspense. Billingham never strains credulity in this thoughtful page-turner." Publishers Weekly.

Billingsley, ReShonda Tate

* The **secret** she kept / ReShonda Tate Billingsley. Gallery Books, 2012. 355 p.
ISBN 9781451639650

1. Women with mental illnesses 2. Pregnancy 3. Schizophrenia 4. Businesspeople 5. Men/women relations 6. Married people 7. Mental illness 8. Contemporary romances 9. African American fiction 10. Multicultural romances

LC 2011053379

When his wife Tia begins acting erratically after their wedding, and her pregnancy brings about signs of further instability, executive Lance Kingston urges her to seek medical attention and wonders how he can help her if she refuses to help herself.

Binchy, Maeve

Circle of friends / Maeve Binchy. Delacorte Press, 1991. 565 p.
ISBN 9780385301497

1. Betrayal 2. Women 3. Friendship 4. Loyalty 5. Villages -- Ireland 6. City life 7. Small town life 8. Female friendship 9. Ireland 10. Dublin, Ireland 11. Women's lives and relationships 12. Gentle reads

LC 90003944

Portrays the uneasy association between beautiful, greedy jet-setter Nan Mahon and Benny Hogan and Eve Malone, best friends from a small Irish village

"There is nothing fancy about 'Circle of Friends.' There is no torrid sex, no profound philosophy. There are no stunning metaphors. There is just a wonderfully absorbing story about people worth caring about. And that is a rare pleasure." New York Times Book Review.

Binchy, Maeve

Firefly summer / Maeve Binchy. Delacorte Press, 1988. 601 p.
ISBN 9780440500179

1. 1960s 2. Americans in Ireland 3. Small town life -- Ireland 4. Women with disabilities 5. Rich men 6. Neighbors 7. Ireland 8. Mainstream fiction 9. Gentle reads

LC 88005412

"The careful examination of life and culture in a small Irish town during the 1960s will appeal to many readers." Booklist.

Binchy, Maeve

* **Whitethorn** Woods / Maeve Binchy. Knopf , 2007, c2006. 352 p.

ISBN 0307265781

1. Sacred space 2. Miracles 3. Wishing and wishes 4. Small towns 5. Small town life 6. Economic development 7. Roads -- Design and construction 8. Ireland 9. Mainstream fiction 10. Gentle reads

Originally published: Toronto : McArthur, 2006.

The town of Rossmore is divided when a new motorway threatens Whitethorn Woods and St. Ann's Well where generations have come to make wishes.

"Story by story, voice by voice, Binchy builds the fictional community of Rossmore so that, by the end of the novel, we know Rossmores inhabitants better than our own neighbours .... Few contemporary novelists match Binchys gift for giving us the world through her characters' eyes." The Globe and Mail (Toronto).

Binet, Laurent

* **HHhH** / Laurent Binet ; translated from the French by Sam Taylor. Farrar, Straus and Giroux, 2012, c2010. 336 p.

ISBN 9780374169916

1. Heydrich, Reinhard, 1904-1942 Assassination 2. Second World War era (1939-1945) 3. Assassins 4. Resistance to government 5. Resistance to military occupation 6. World War II 7. Nazis 8. Guerrillas 9. Memories -- Psychological aspects 10. Czechoslovakia 11. Historical fiction 12. Metafiction 13. Translations -- French to English

LC 2011046063

Originally published: Paris : Grasset & Fasquelle, 2010.

National Book Critics Circle Award for Fiction finalist, 2012

Imagines the story of two Czechoslovakian partisans responsible for assassinating the "Butcher of Prague" Reinhard Heydrich, traces their escape from the Nazis and recruitment by the British secret service.

Bing, Stanley

You look nice today : a novel / Stanley Bing. Bloomsbury, 2003. 291 p.

ISBN 1582342806

1. Executives 2. Businesspeople 3. Personal assistants 4. Women with mental illnesses 5. Sexual harassment 6. Corporate culture 7. Business 8. Big business 9. Corporations 10. Suing (Law) 11. Trials 12. Chicago, Illinois 13. Psychological fiction 14. Humorous stories 15. Legal stories

LC 2003060092

"The density of detail makes for slow going early in the novel, but the account of the civil trial that follows is a riveting and often hilarious account of CaroleAnne's fabrications and the corporate legal response." Publishers Weekly.

Birch, Carol, 1951-

Jamrach's menagerie / Carol Birch. Doubleday, 2011. 295 p.

ISBN 9780385534406

1. Victorian era (1837-1901) 2. Poor boys 3. Exotic animals 4. Ocean travel 5. Human behavior 6. Seafaring life 7. Menageries 8. England -- Social life and customs -- 19th century 9. Great Britain -- History -- Victoria, 1837-1901 10. South Pacific Ocean 11. Historical fiction 12. Adventure stories

First published in London : Canongate, 2011.

Shortlisted for the Man Booker Prize, 2011.

Recruited by a famed importer of exotic animals to capture a fabled dragon during a three-year whaling expedition, former street urchin Jaffy Brown and his friend and rival, Tim, successfully capture the beast only to find themselves targeted by superstitious sailors.

"Jaffy's experience could well move the reader as profoundly as it changed the narrator." Kirkus.

Bird, Sarah

Daughter of a daughter of a queen / Sarah Bird. St. Martin's Press, 2018. 398 p.

ISBN 9781250193162

1. Williams, Cathy, b 1844 2. United States. Army African American troops 3. American Westward Expansion (1803-1899) 4. Women soldiers 5. African American women 6. Male impersonators 7. Courage in women 8. Determination in women 9. Freed slaves 10. Gender role 11. Indians of North America -- Wars 12. Families 13. Men/women relations 14. United States -- History -- 19th century 15. Biographical fiction 16. Historical fiction 17. War stories

LC 2018010894

In 1864 Missouri, newly freed slave Cathy Williams makes the difficult decision to fight in the Army disguised as a man with the Buffalo Soldiers.

Bird, Sarah

*The **flamenco** academy : a novel / Sarah Bird. Knopf, 2006. 381 p.

ISBN 9781400040841

1. Grief in families 2. Young women 3. Flamenco dancers 4. Seventeen-year-old girls 5. Czech American women 6. Children of people with cancer 7. Fathers -- Death 8. Guitarists 9. Flamenco dancing 10. Men/women relations 11. Interpersonal relations 12. Family secrets 13. Cults 14. Dancing 15. Love triangles 16. Grief in women 17. New Mexico 18. Albuquerque, New Mexico 19. Coming-of-age stories

LC 2005044418

In Albuquerque, New Mexico, two young women--shy teenager Cyndi Rae Hrncir and Didi Steinberg, the school bad girl--become entranced by young flamenco guitarist Tomas Montenegro and by the hypnotic storytelling of Dona Carlota, Tomas's great aunt, and decide to dedicate themselves to the disciplines and demands of the university's Flamenco Academy.

"In the monolithic culture of flamenco, Bird finds a remarkable landscape for transforming the inaccessible whims of an obsessive, lonely teenager into the epic saga of self-acceptance, loyalty and love to which no one is immune." Austin Chronicle.

Bird, Sarah

The **gap** year : a novel / Sarah Bird. Alfred A. Knopf, 2011. 320 p.

ISBN 9780307592798

1. Mother and teenager 2. Letting go (Psychology) 3. Parenting -- Psychological aspects 4. Former husbands 5. Teenage girls -- Interpersonal relations 6. Domestic fiction 7. Humorous stories

LC 2010051495

Setting aside her rebellious dreams for the sake of her teenage daughter, lactation consultant Cam Lightsey is horrified when her daughter falls in love with a football player, turns secretive and loses interest in college, a situation that is further complicated by a reappearance by Cam's ex, a member of a celebrity cult.

"The title alludes to the break in a mother-daughter relationship during the daughter's senior year of high school. Single mom Camilla feels her daughter, Aubrey, beginning to pull away from her, especially after Aubrey embarks on a romance with classmate Tyler. Add in the sudden reappearance of Aubrey's father, who years ago left the family to join a cultlike religion (it might sound familiar to fans of certain Hollywood types), and gaps in this family open and close at blinding speed. The narrative alternates between Camilla's current perspective over the course of a few days and Aubrey's retelling of the previous year. This technique makes for a compelling read and builds to a satisfying and surprisingly tender conclusion." Library Journal.

Bird, Sarah

The **Yokota** Officers Club : a novel / Sarah Bird. Knopf, 2001. 367 p.

ISBN 037541214X

1. United States. Air Force 2. 1960s 3. Military dependents 4. Dysfunctional families 5. Missing persons 6. Eighteen-year-olds 7. Sisters 8. Women with depression 9. Dance contests 10. Family relationships 11. Secrets 12. Japan 13. Okinawa 14. Tokyo, Japan 15. Psychological fiction 16. Domestic fiction

LC 2001089763

While living at Kadena Air Base on Okinawa, Bernadette "Bernie" Root, hoping to escape her oddball military family, takes a job as second banana to a third-rate comedian touring Japanese military bases, only to be reunited with her family's former maid, Fumiko, and uncovers a painful family secret.

Birmingham, Stephen

The **Auerbach** will / Stephen Birmingham. Little, Brown, 1983. 430 p.

ISBN 0316096466

1. Jewish American women 2. Rich women 3. Jewish families 4. Jewish Americans 5. Immigrant families 6. Russian Americans 7. Mother and child 8. Husband and wife 9. Inheritance and succession 10. New York City 11. Family sagas

LC 83009413

In The Auerbach Will, the novel by America's most renowned chronicler of the rich, ambitious young Essie Litsky defies a rigid upbringing by immigrant Russian Jewish parents to achieve wealth and success. But her children tear Essie and her husband Jack Auerbach's family apart in fights over their fortune, and Essie finds that money will not mend broken lives ...

"Birmingham's deft handling of the fabric of family life and shifting patterns of deception, betrayal and tragedy produces a dramatic narrative. Essie is a wonderfully sympathetic figure, and Birmingham moves her gracefully through her bitter-sweet years from determined young girl to passionate woman to sophisticated grande dame." Publishers Weekly.

Birmingham, Stephen

Carriage trade / Stephen Birmingham. Bantam Books, 1993. 469 p.

ISBN 0553081357

1. Rich men 2. Clothing industry and trade 3. Rich people 4. Retail stores 5. Retail industry and trade 6. Rich families 7. Betrayal 8. Inheritance and succession 9. Fathers and daughters 10. Families 11. Jewish American families 12. Murder 13. Family secrets 14. Corporate acquisitions 15. Secrets 16. New York City 17. Domestic fiction

LC 92039567

When department store founder Silas Tarkington dies, his family--among them, his socialite wife, his pampered daughter, his first wife, his mistress, and his mother--learns of Tarkington's forty-year-old secrets

"This novel tells the tale of one Silas Tarkington, founder of an exclusive Manhattan department store. . . . Tarkington is actually Solomon Tarcher, a Jew from the Lower East Side who once served time for larceny. While retailing was in his blood--Tarkington's grandmother and mother created a successful millinery business back when women wore hats--his brilliant and calculating career was engineered by a nasty shyster named Moe Minskoff. We learn all the dirty secrets of Tarkington's messy life in flashbacks as his spunky daughter, fiesty mother, stunning and resilient wife, and current mistress try to fathom the chaos of the store's financial straits after Tarkington's suspicious death. . . . Birmingham's casting of women as the heroes in this mercantile thriller cum murder mystery is a nice touch." Booklist.

Bishop, Anne

Written in red : a novel of the Others / Anne Bishop. Roc, 2013. 448 p. Courtyards of the Others

ISBN 9780451464965

1. Prophets 2. Shapeshifters 3. Slavery 4. Escapes 5. Actors and actresses 6. Visions 7. Trust 8. Self-discovery in women 9. Men/women relations 10. Urban fantasy 11. Fantasy fiction

LC 2012036432

Blood prophet Meg Corbyn escapes enslavement by Others and teams up with a shape-shifter who employs her as a Human Liaison.

Bisson, Terry

Any day now / Terry Bisson. Overlook Press, 2012. 256 p.

ISBN 9781590207093

1. 1960s 2. Beat culture 3. Radicalism 4. Communes 5. Bombings 6. New York City 7. Kentucky 8. Alternative histories 9. Coming-of-age stories

A tale inspired by the final days of the Beats is set against a backdrop of an emerging radicalized culture of the 1960s throughout the Eastern United States, in a coming-of-age story that serves as a transcendent commentary on the nation as experienced by members of an isolated hippie commune under threat of revolution.

Bittner, Rosanne, 1945-

Logan's lady / Rosanne Bittner. Sourcebooks Casablanca, 2019. 352 p.

ISBN 9781492673491

1. American Westward Expansion (1803-1899) 2. Aristocracy 3. Bounty hunters 4. British in the United States 5. Independence in women 6. Revenge 7. Voyages and travels 8. Murder 9. Frontier and pioneer life 10. Sexual attraction 11. Men/women relations 12. The West (United States) -- Social life and customs -- 19th century 13. Western romances 14. Historical romances

Embarking on an adventure to America after reading penny dreadfuls, wealthy Englishwoman Lady Elizabeth arrives excited to start a new life, only to be swindled by a gentlemanly thief, forcing her to place her trust in a dangerous man who hunts wanted men.

Bivald, Katarina, 1983-

The **readers** of Broken Wheel recommend / Katarina Bivald ; translated from the Swedish by Alice Menzies. Landmark, 2016, c2013. 400 p.

ISBN 9781492623441

1. Small town life -- Iowa 2. Friendship 3. Books and reading 4. Life change events 5. Women booksellers 6. Pen pals 7. Loss (Psychology) 8. Iowa 9. Mainstream fiction 10. Epistolary novels 11. Translations -- Swedish to English

Originally published: Sweden: Forum, 2013.

"Originally published as Lasarna i Broken Wheel rekommenderar in 2013 in Sweden by Bokförlaget Forum. This edition issued based on the (hbk.) edition published in 2015 in the United Kingdom by Chatto & Windus, an imprint of Random House" -- Verso title page.

"Broken Wheel, Iowa, has never seen anyone like Sara, who traveled all the way from Sweden just to meet her pen pal, Amy. When she arrives, however, she finds that Amy's funeral has just ended. Luckily, the townspeople are happy to look after their bewildered tourist--even if they don't understand her peculiar need for books. Marooned in a farm town that's almost beyond repair, Sara starts a bookstore in honor of her friend's memory. All she wants is to share the books she loves with the citizens of Broken Wheel and to convince them that reading is one of the great joys of life. But she makes some unconventional choices that could force a lot of secrets into the open and change things for everyone in town. Reminiscent of The Guernsey Literary and Potato Peel Pie Society, this is a warm, witty book about friendship, stories, and love" --, Provided by publisher.

Black, Benjamin, 1945-
* **Christine** Falls : a novel / Benjamin Black. H. Holt, 2007. 352 p. Quirke mysteries
  ISBN 0805081526
  1. 1950s 2. Religious cover-ups 3. Murder investigation 4. Upper class -- Ireland 5. Catholics 6. Pathologists 7. Conspiracies 8. Criminal evidence tampering 9. Family secrets 10. Classism 11. Organized crime 12. Irish Americans 13. Dublin, Ireland 14. Boston, Massachusetts 15. Psychological fiction 16. Mysteries
  LC 2006043581
Originally published: London: Picador, 2006.
TV tie-in.
Returning to the morgue where he works after an office party, Dublin pathologist Quirke stumbles across a body that should not have been there, as well as his brother-in-law, pediatrician Malachy Griffin, altering a file to cover up the corpse's cause of death.
"As the story moves from Ireland to Boston, the push and pull of the novel's dual existence as literary thriller becomes almost as absorbing as the plot; the tension between the two halves of that troublesome equation regularly rippling the book's surface. . . . At its best, the prose here is every bit as acute as one would expect from John Banville, even Banville in disguise--the baroque flourishes are held in check . . . , but the stern elegance remains, and its marriage to a thriller's momentum can have startling results." Times Literary Supplement.

Black, Benjamin, 1945-
Wolf on a string : a novel / Benjamin Black. Henry Holt & Co., 2017. 320 p.
  ISBN 9781627795173
  1. Holy Roman Empire. Emperor (1576-1612 : Rudolf II) 2. 16th century 3. Murder investigation 4. Courts and courtiers 5. Political intrigue 6. Rulers 7. Murder 8. Scholars and academics 9. Mistresses 10. Alchemists 11. Favorites, Royal 12. Power (Social sciences) 13. Prague, Czech Republic -- History -- 16th century 14. Historical mysteries
  LC 2016029320
Discovering the body of a young woman after arriving in 1599 Prague, an ambitious young scholar and alchemist becomes entangled in the machinations of several ruthless courtiers before attracting the attention of an emperor who would retain the power of the throne.

Black, Benjamin, 1945-
* **The secret** guests : a novel / Benjamin Black. Henry Holt and Company, 2020, c2019. 304 p.
  ISBN 9781250133014
  1. Elizabeth II, Queen of Great Britain, 1926- 2. Margaret, Princess, Countess of Snowdon, 1930-2002 3. Second World War era (1939-1945) 4. Princesses 5. British in Ireland 6. Secrecy 7. Intelligence service 8. Intrigue 9. Suspicion 10. Resentfulness 11. Rural life 12. Ireland -- Social life and customs -- 20th century 13. London (England) -- History -- Bombardment, 1940-1941 14. Historical

thrillers
  LC 2019015981
The secret World War II relocation of the princesses Elizabeth and Margaret to an old estate in Ireland becomes subject to the devastations of the Blitz, the resentments of grieving townspeople and suspicions about the girls' true identities.
"Black's lucid prose is the perfect foil for tangled politics, old hatreds, unsolved crimes, the threat to Irish neutrality, and the possibility of new alliances that seethe underneath." Library Journal.

Black, Cara, 1951-
Murder in the Bastille / Cara Black. Soho Press, 2003. 276 p. Aimee Leduc investigations
  ISBN 1569473242
  1. Bastille. 2. 1990s 3. Mistaken identity 4. Women who are blind 5. Antique dealers 6. Women private investigators 7. Drug traffic 8. Physicians 9. Murder 10. Murder investigation 11. Serial murder investigation 12. Mysteries
  LC 2002042625

Black, Cara, 1951-
Murder in the Marais / Cara Black. Soho, 1999. 354 p. Aimee Leduc investigations
  ISBN 1569471592
  1. Neo-Nazism 2. Little people 3. Jewish women 4. Women private investigators 5. Murder 6. Crimes against Jewish women 7. Murder investigation 8. Jews 9. Paris, France 10. France 11. Mysteries
  LC 98052070
Detective Aimee Leduc goes undercover inside a neo-Nazi group to ferret out a killer in the old Jewish quarter of Paris.

Black, Cara, 1951-
Murder in the rue de Paradis : an Aimee Leduc investigation / Cara Black. Soho Crime, 2008. 312 p. Aimee Leduc investigations
  ISBN 9781569474747
  1. 1990s 2. Loss (Psychology) 3. Assassins 4. Kurds 5. Women private investigators 6. Female friendship 7. Policewomen 8. Murder suspects 9. Murder 10. Murder investigation 11. Shiah Islam 12. Men/women relations 13. Paris, France 14. Mysteries
  LC 2007009194
Thrilled that her former lover Yves Robert has returned to Paris, Aimee Leduc accepts his marriage proposal, but her happiness is short-lived after he is found dead in a doorway in the Rue de Paradis.

Black, Cara, 1951-
* **Three** hours in Paris / Cara Black. Soho Press, 2020. 360 p.
  ISBN 9781641290418
  1. Hitler, Adolf, 1889-1945 2. Second World War era (1939-1945) 3. Women assassins 4. Spies 5. Attempted assassination 6. Shooting 7. Anti-Nazi movement 8. Young widows 9. Americans in France 10. World War II 11. France -- History -- German occupation, 1940-1945 12. Paris, France 13. Historical thrillers 14. Spy fiction 15. Historical fiction
  LC 2019038373
A suspenseful historical tale based on the mystery of Hitler's abrupt departure from newly occupied 1940 Paris follows the mission of a British intelligence markswoman who, while trying to assassinate the Fuhrer, discovers that she has been set up.
"Fans of The Day of the Jackal won't want to miss this heart-stopping thriller." Publishers Weekly.

Black, Lisa, 1963-

Let justice descend / Lisa Black. Kensington Books, 2019. 320 p. Maggie Gardiner and Jack Renner novels

ISBN 9781496722355

1. Women forensic psychologists 2. Vigilantes 3. Politicians 4. Elections 5. Detectives 6. Murder 7. Murder investigation 8. Secrets 9. Ohio 10. Cleveland, Ohio 11. Thrillers and suspense

In a taut, brilliantly twisted new thriller from bestselling author Lisa Black, forensics expert Maggie Gardiner and Cleveland detective Jack Renner investigate the bizarre murder of a senator with secrets to hide.

Black, Lisa, 1963-

Suffer the children / Lisa Black. Kensington, 2018. 320 p. Maggie Gardiner and Jack Renner novels

ISBN 9781496713575

1. Women forensic psychologists 2. Vigilantes 3. Juvenile detention 4. Children -- Death 5. Problem youth 6. Murder investigation 7. Detectives 8. Divorced women 9. Secrets 10. Cleveland, Ohio 11. Ohio 12. Thrillers and suspense

Cleveland forensics expert Maggie Gardiner and her partner, Jack Renner, investigate after two young people turn up dead at a secure facility for juvenile offenders.

Black, Lisa, 1963-

That darkness / Lisa Black. Kensington, 2016. 336 p. Maggie Gardiner and Jack Renner novels

ISBN 9781496701886

1. Forensic scientists 2. Women murder victims 3. Women forensic scientists 4. Murder investigation 5. Cleveland, Ohio 6. Thrillers and suspense

In this tour de force of psychological suspense, bestselling author Lisa Black draws from her experience as a forensic investigator to create two of the most fascinating characters in crime fiction: a killer with a unique sense of justice and a woman in a lifelong relationship with death.

Black, Saul

Anything for you / Saul Black. St. Martin's Press, 2019. 352 p. Valerie Hart novels

ISBN 9781250199911

1. Women detectives 2. Married women 3. Murder victims 4. Secrets 5. Flashbacks 6. Murder investigation 7. San Francisco, California 8. Thrillers and suspense

LC 2019024267

When her next-door neighbor, a San Francisco prosecutor, is brutally murdered, a woman is forced to reckon with her murky past to help the victim's family and the police uncover clues about the killer's identity

Black, Saul

* The **killing** lessons / Saul Black. St. Martin's Press, 2015. 416 p. Valerie Hart novels

ISBN 9781250057341

1. Women detectives 2. Children of murder victims 3. Psychopaths 4. Serial murderers 5. Serial murder investigation 6. Crimes against women 7. Psychic trauma 8. Colorado 9. San Francisco, California 10. Thrillers and suspense

LC 2015017805

RUSA Reading List Short List, 2016.

In this menacing, unnerving novel, which combines nail-biting suspense with all the details of a police procedural, a damaged female detective offers the best hope for justice for the victims of a sadistic killer -- and for preventing more cruel, violent deaths at his hands. Or are there two monsters? Detective Valerie Hart, battling personal and professional

problems, shares narrative duties with both a potential victim desperate to live and the killer himself. Fair warning though -- this series debut is graphic and bloody. -- Description by Shauna Griffin.

"Aficionados may fault Black for allowing the police at least one major oversight, but most readers will likely be too engrossed or happily grossed out to do anything but whip through the pages." Kirkus.

Black, Saul

* **Lovemurder** / Saul Black. St. Martin's Press, 2017, c2016. 320 p. Valerie Hart novels

ISBN 9781250057419

1. Women detectives 2. Psychopaths 3. Crime scenes 4. Children of murder victims 5. Serial murderers 6. Serial murder investigation 7. Copycat murders 8. Colorado 9. San Francisco, California 10. Thrillers and suspense

LC 2017006878

Investigating an eerily familiar crime scene before discovering a note written in the style of a killer she helped put away six years earlier, San Francisco Homicide detective Valerie Hart is forced to ask the imprisoned psychopath to help capture a copycat.

Blackmore, R. D. (Richard Doddridge), 1825-1900

Lorna Doone : a romance of Exmoor / R.D. Blackmore ; edited with an introduction by Sally Shuttleworth. Oxford University Press, 2008, c1869. xxix, 680 p.

ISBN 9780199537594

1. Stuart period (1603-1714) 2. Monmouth's Rebellion, 1685 3. Outlaws 4. Heroes and heroines 5. Families of murder victims 6. Kidnapping 7. Exmoor, England 8. Great Britain -- History -- James II, 1685-1688 9. Historical fiction 10. Love stories 11. Classics

LC 88037446

First published in 1869.

In seventeenth-century England, John Ridd returns home to Exmoor and forms a forbidden but enduring friendship with Lorna Doone, the granddaughter of the head of the outlaw Doone clan responsible for the death of John's father.

Blackstock, Terri, 1957-

Catching Christmas / Terri Blackstock. Thomas Nelson, 2018. 293 p.

ISBN 9780310351726

1. Women lawyers 2. Taxicab drivers 3. Christmas 4. Grandmothers 5. Dementia 6. Cooks 7. Workaholics 8. Interpersonal attraction 9. Men/women relations 10. Holiday romances 11. Christian romances

New York Times bestselling author Terri Blackstock tells the rich and heartwarming story of a cab driver, a young attorney, and the elderly woman who will stop at nothing to give her granddaughter one special gift for Christmas.

"Quirky characters and a wholesome plot will please inspirational readers looking for a heartwarming Christmas story." Publishers Weekly.

Blackstock, Terri, 1957-

Shadow in Serenity / Terri Blackstock. Zondervan, 2011. 352 p.

ISBN 9780310332329

1. Small towns 2. Swindlers and swindling 3. Love-hate relationships 4. Small town life 5. Trust in women 6. Carnivals 7. Selfishness in men 8. Interpersonal attraction 9. Texas 10. Christian romances

Carny Sullivan, suspicious about suave, handsome Logan Brisco and his charming ways, is drawn to him, despite her best intentions and her determination to expose his plans for her quiet Texas town.

Blackstock, Terri, 1957-

Smoke screen / Terri Blackstock. Thomas Nelson, 2019. 352 p.

ISBN 9780310332602

1. Fire fighters 2. Fathers 3. Murder 4. Homecomings 5. Former lovers 6. Child custody 7. Fathers and sons 8. Alcoholic women 9. Family relationships 10. Wildfires 11. Confrontation (Interpersonal relations) 12. Faith (Christianity) 13. Men/women relations 14. Christian suspense

LC bl2019025328

Reluctantly returning to his hometown when his father is released from prison amid murderous accusations, a smoke jumper reconnects with his former love, who is fighting a painful custody battle.

Blackwell, Juliet

Letters from Paris / Juliet Blackwell. Berkley, 2016. 384 p.

ISBN 9780451473707

1. Sculpture 2. Family secrets 3. Grandmother and granddaughter 4. Men/women relations 5. Voyages and travels 6. Accident victims 7. Sculptors 8. Families 9. Secrets 10. Paris, France 11. Chicago, Illinois 12. Louisiana 13. Mainstream fiction

"After surviving the accident that took her mother's life, Claire Broussard worked hard to escape her small Louisiana hometown. At her grandmother's urging, Claire travels to Paris to track down the centuries old mask-making atelier where the sculpture, known only as "L'inconnue"--or the Unknown Woman--was created. With the help of a passionate sculptor, Claire discovers a cache of letters that offer insight into the life of the Belle Epoque woman immortalized in the work of art."--Provided by the publisher.

"Blackwell seamlessly incorporates details about art, cast making, and the City of Light. She also skillfully weaves in chapters from the point of view of Sabine--the poor country girl behind the mystery, who became the muse of an abusive sculptor after a life of poverty. Blackwell does a fantastic job of incorporating recurring themes in this story; for instance, having survived drowning as a child, Claire is wary of rivers, while Sabine is rumored to have met her end in the Seine. Blackwell especially stuns in the aftermath of the main story by unleashing a twist that is both a complete surprise and a point that expertly ties everything together." Publishers Weekly.

Blake, James Carlos

The **house** of Wolfe / James Carlos Blake. The Mysterious Press, 2015. 248 p. Wolfe family novels

ISBN 9780802122469

1. Ransom 2. Kidnapping 3. Gangs 4. Organized crime 5. Mexican-American Border Region 6. Thrillers and suspense 7. Crime fiction

Kidnapped by a small-time gangster with big-time aspirations in Mexico City, Jessie Wolfe knows that her own family of notorious outlaws will come to her rescue.

"Blake excels at ensemble pieces and plays to his strengths here. Like a director with a small army of camera teams at his disposal, he wheels from one location to another, racking the focus with such intensity that, at any moment, the story you're in feels like the only story there is until he cuts away again. A hard-edged, fast-moving thriller that will hold your attention hostage--good luck getting away." Booklist.

Blake, Robin, 1948-

A **dark** anatomy : a mystery / Robin Blake. Minotaur Books, 2012, c2011. 359 p. Preston novels

ISBN 9781250006721

1. 18th century 2. 1740s 3. Murder investigation 4. Superstition 5. Amateur detectives 6. Coroners 7. Small towns 8. Body snatching

9. Lawyers 10. Secrets 11. Murder 12. England -- History -- 18th century 13. Lancashire, England 14. Historical mysteries 15. Mysteries

Originally published: London : Macmillan, 2011.

When a squire's wife is found murdered in lawless 18th-century Lancaster, Coroner Titus Cragg enlists the help of young doctor Luke Fidelis in a case that is challenged by local superstition, corrupt officials and denunciations by the victim's husband.

Blake, Sarah, 1960-

The **guest** book : a novel / Sarah Blake. Flatiron Books, 2019. 486 p.

ISBN 9781250110251

1. 1930s 2. 1950s 3. Rich families 4. Islands 5. Antisemitism 6. Racism 7. Family estates 8. Family secrets 9. Wealth 10. Loss (Psychology) 11. Family relationships 12. Prejudice 13. Interfaith romance 14. Race relations 15. Maine 16. New York City 17. Family sagas 18. Historical fiction

The bereaved matriarch of a powerful early-20th-century American family makes a fateful decision that reverberates throughout two subsequent generations further impacted by racism, reversed circumstances and disturbing revelations.

"This novel sets out to be more than a juicy family saga--it aims to depict the moral evolution of a part of American society. Its convincing characters and muscular narrative succeed on both counts." Kirkus.

Blake, Sarah, 1960-

The **postmistress** / Sarah Blake. Amy Einhorn Books/G.P. Putnam's Sons, 2010. 336 p.

ISBN 9780399156199

1. Second World War era (1939-1945) 2. Postmasters 3. World War II -- Massachusetts 4. Radio 5. War 6. Secrets 7. Small town life 8. World War II -- Radio broadcasting and the war 9. World War II home front 10. London, England -- History -- Bombardment, 1940-1945 11. Historical fiction

LC 2009024532

The stories of a small Cape Cod postmistress and an American radio reporter stationed in London collide on the eve of the United States's entrance into World War II, a meeting that is shaped by a broken promise to deliver a letter.

"Iris, an ungainly 40-year-old with unflattering red lipstick and a crush on the town mechanic, ultimately proves to be the heart of Blake's novel." Entertainment Weekly.

Blatty, William Peter

* The **exorcist** / William Peter Blatty. Harper & Row, 1971. 340 p.

ISBN 0060103655

1. Eleven-year-old girls 2. Demonic possession 3. Exorcism 4. Demons 5. Good and evil 6. Actors and actresses 7. Washington, D.C. 8. Horror

LC 73144189

Sequel: Legion.

Includes unpaged photos from the feature film of the same title.

A Jesuit priest, unable to find plausible explanations for an eleven-year-old's strange behavior, begins to suspect demonic possession.

"Blatty has done his homework. He discourses, a bit bookishly, on the history of possession and the relation of autosuggestion to masked guilt. . . . Blatty maintains headlong thrust, slowly increasing Regan's agony until the reader winces; no more, a part of us says, but of course we want more because Blatty handles the horror so well." Newsweek.

Blau, Jessica Anya

The **summer** of naked swim parties : a novel / Jessica Anya Blau. Perennial, 2008. 320 p.

ISBN 9780061452024

1. 1970s 2. Teenage girls 3. Neighbors 4. Neighborhoods 5. Summer 6. Family relationships 7. Sisters 8. Fourteen-year-old boys 9. Nudism 10. Teenage boy/girl relations 11. Virginity 12. Friendship 13. Betrayal 14. Southern California 15. Coming-of-age stories

LC 2007038064

Over the course of a single summer in 1976 Santa Barbara, California, fourteen-year-old Jamie gains new insights into the confusing world of adolescence, sex, friendship, love, and family, in a poignant coming-of-age tale.

Blau, Jessica Anya

The **Wonder** Bread summer / Jessica Anya Blau. Harper-Perennial, 2013. 320 p.

ISBN 9780062199553

1. 1980s 2. Young women 3. Drug use 4. Cocaine 5. Students 6. Stealing 7. Assassins 8. Sexuality 9. Interpersonal relations 10. Men/women relations 11. California 12. Coming-of-age stories 13. Caper novels

It's 1983 in Berkeley, California. Twenty-year-old Allie Dodgson is a straitlaced college student working part-time at a dress shop to make ends meet. But when the shop turns out to be a front for a dangerous drug-dealing business, Allie finds herself on the lam, speeding toward Los Angeles in her best friend's Prelude with a Wonder Bag full of cocaine riding shotgun and a hit man named Vice Versa on her tail.--From back cover.

Bledsoe, Alex

Gather her round : a novel of the Tufa / Alex Bledsoe. Tor, 2017. 288 p. Tufa novels

ISBN 9780765383341

1. Murder 2. Hunters 3. Rural life 4. Hunting 5. Ethnic groups 6. Magic 7. Curses 8. Secrets 9. Small towns 10. Great Smoky Mountains (NC and Tenn) 11. Tennessee 12. East Tennessee 13. New York City 14. Urban fantasy

In critically-acclaimed Alex Bledsoe's latest Tufa novel, a monster roams the woods of Cloud County, while another kind of evil lurks in the hearts of men.

Bledsoe, Alex

The **hum** and the shiver / Alex Bledsoe. Tor Books, 2011. 304 p. Tufa novels

ISBN 9780765327444

1. Ethnic groups 2. Small towns 3. Magic 4. Music 5. Women veterans 6. Omens 7. Former lovers 8. Iraq War veterans 9. Tennessee 10. East Tennessee 11. Urban fantasy

LC 2011021573

Iraq War veteran Bronwyn Hyatt must reconnect with the Tufa, her people, and their ancient song if she is ever going to stop the death stalking her family.

"Bledsoe turns standard urban fantasy tropes on their head by reimagining modern elves as a tiny, isolated ethnic group unsure of their own origins, like the Lemkos of Poland or the Melungeons of the southern Appalachians. The plot is a bit thin, but the slowly unfolding mystery of the Tufa is a fascinating and absorbing masterpiece of world-building." Publishers Weekly.

Bledsoe, Alex

Long black curl / Alex Bledsoe. Tor Books, 2015. 368 p. Tufa novels

ISBN 9780765376541

1. Ethnic groups 2. Forbidden love 3. Musicians 4. Music 5. Magic 6. Exiles 7. Curses 8. Small towns 9. Great Smoky Mountains (NC and Tenn) 10. Tennessee 11. East Tennessee 12. Urban fantasy

When Bo-Kate Wisby makes her way back to Cloud Country, Tennessee in spite of a curse upon her, she plans to take over both Tufa clans with the help of a rockabilly singer of immense size and strength named Byron Harley.

Bledsoe, Alex

Wisp of a thing / Alex Bledsoe. Tor, 2013. 320 p. Tufa novels

ISBN 9780765334138

1. Lovers -- Death 2. Ethnic groups 3. Musicians 4. Curses 5. Wild children 6. Small towns 7. Magic 8. Music 9. Great Smoky Mountains (NC and Tenn) 10. Tennessee 11. East Tennessee 12. Urban fantasy

LC 2013003720

Musician Rob Quillen searches for an enigmatic Smoky Mountains clan of people whose existence is shrouded in myth, a journey marked by a disappearance, an incomprehensible power play, and a howling feral girl.

Bledsoe, Lucy Jane

* The **big** bang symphony : a novel of Antarctica / Lucy Jane Bledsoe. Terrace Books, 2010. 333 p.

ISBN 9780299235000

1. Loneliness 2. Lesbians 3. Female friendship 4. Women composers 5. Women cooks 6. Women artists 7. Women geologists 8. Interpersonal attraction 9. Antarctica 10. LGBTQIA fiction

LC 2009040630

"Bledsoe digs into themes of individuality and lonesomeness, and the idea of safety in numbers, and though the narrative's introspectiveness can at times be as daunting as the Antarctic's harsh climate, Bledsoe finds the spark of life amid the ice and desolation." Publishers Weekly

Block, Lawrence

All the flowers are dying / Lawrence Block. William Morrow, 2005. 304 p. Matthew Scudder mysteries

ISBN 0060198311

1. Psychologists 2. Death row prisoners 3. Husband and wife 4. Executions and executioners 5. Online romance 6. Recovering alcoholics 7. Private investigators 8. Alcoholic men 9. Former police 10. New York City 11. Mysteries 12. Hardboiled fiction

LC 2004053643

Matthew Scudder, with his eye keenly on retirement, unofficially investigates the suspicious online suitor of an acquaintance, and finds his own life in grave danger.

"Although Scudder's hunt for the killer turns into a companionable tour of colorful neighborhoods, his thoughts on the city run deep and reflect real feelings about its humanity." New York Times Book Review.

Block, Lawrence

The **burglar** in the closet / Lawrence Block. Random House, 1978. 166 p. Bernie Rhodenbarr mysteries

ISBN 0394423747

1. Jewelry theft 2. Women murder victims 3. Dentists 4. Thieves 5. Booksellers 6. Lesbians 7. New York City 8. Cozy mysteries 9.

Caper novels

LC 7857116

Sequel to: Burglars can't be choosers.

"A New York dentist has set Bernie Rhodenbarr up to rob his estranged wife, which he does. Embarrassingly, he gets interrupted and locked in a closet while the woman is stabbed to death and the boodle is stolen. In a temper, the burglar investigates, as does a corrupt policeman who wants half the take. Things are sorted out when a suitcase full of counterfeit money turns up and a couple of suspects conveniently die. Amusing and very easy to read." Library Journal.

Block, Lawrence

* The **burglar** in the library / Lawrence Block. Dutton, 1997. 342 p. Bernie Rhodenbarr mysteries

ISBN 0525943013

1. Book thefts 2. Bed-and-breakfast 3. Murder investigation 4. Blizzards 5. First editions 6. Rare books 7. Murder 8. Thieves 9. Booksellers 10. Lesbians 11. New England 12. New York City 13. Cozy mysteries 14. Caper novels

LC 9637537

For Bernie Rhodenbarr, bookseller and compulsive burglar, a weekend at a country bed & breakfast inn takes an unexpected twist when a valuable book is stolen and a dead body turns up in the library.

"[T]he drollest sendup of a murder-in-a-teacup mystery that you will ever hope to beg, borrow--or steal." New York Times Book Review.

Block, Lawrence

A **drop** of the hard stuff : a Matthew Scudder novel / Lawrence Block. Mulholland Books/Little, Brown and Co., 2011. 336 p. Matthew Scudder mysteries

ISBN 9780316127332

1. 1980s 2. Sobriety 3. Grief in men 4. Alcoholic men 5. Private investigators 6. Former police 7. Murder investigation 8. New York City 9. Mysteries 10. Hardboiled fiction

LC 2010041792

After a childhood friend is shot down while attempting to atone for past sins, Scudder is drawn into a murder investigation that threatens to upset his path toward recovery--and get him killed in the process.

Block, Lawrence

Eight million ways to die / Lawrence Block. William Morrow, 2008, c1982. 318 p. Matthew Scudder mysteries

ISBN 9780061457968

1. Crimes against prostitutes 2. Women murder victims 3. Murder investigation 4. Prostitutes 5. Private investigators 6. Alcoholic men 7. Former police 8. New York City 9. Mysteries 10. Hardboiled fiction

Originally published: New York : Arbor House, 1982.

Shamus Award for Best P.I. Novel, 1983.

Kim was a young hooker who wanted out: a beautiful kid, old before her time, seeking Matthew Scudder's protection. She didn't deserve to die the way she did: slashed to ribbons in the seedy waterfront district. Now the tormented ex-cop-turned-P.I. wants to find her killer.

"This novel is both a rousing private-eye story and an extended meditation on the whimsical ways of death--through freak accident, premeditated murder, and self-destruction. Private eye Matthew Scudder solves murders while he battles his own alcoholism. . . . In [this] tale, a 23-year old prostitute, Kim Dakkinen, wants out of 'the life' and asks Scudder to speak to her pimp, Chance. Scudder does, and a few days later Kim is found stabbed to death. Chance does the unexpected by hiring Scudder to find Kim's murderer, and while Scudder investigates, another one of Chance's prostitutes commits suicide; then another slashing occurs. A magnificently plotted, sensitive portrayal of two kinds of death:the kind that comes as an intruder and the kind that comes as an invited guest." Booklist.

Block, Lawrence

* **Hit** me : a Keller novel / Lawrence Block. Mulholland Books, 2013. 448 p. John Keller novels

ISBN 9780316127356

1. Houses -- Conservation and restoration 2. Stamp collecting 3. Deception 4. Loss (Psychology) 5. Men -- Decision-making 6. Assassins 7. Stamp collecting 8. Murder for hire 9. New York City 10. White Plains, New York 11. Crime fiction

LC 2012019988

With a new wife and a baby on the way, Keller, a.k.a. Nicholas Edwards, is done killing people for money until a phone call from Dot draws him back into the old game, taking him to Dallas to settle a domestic dispute to New York, where people might remember him.

Block, Lawrence

Killing Castro / Lawrence Block. Hard Crime Case, 2008, c1961. 208 p.

ISBN 9780843961133

1. Castro, Fidel, 1926-2016 Attempted assassination 2. 1960s 3. Dictators -- Cuba 4. Assassins 5. Attempted assassination 6. International intrigue 7. Assassins 8. Betrayal 9. Revolutions -- Cuba 10. Attempted murder 11. Cuba -- History -- 20th century 12. Thrillers and suspense

Originally published as Fidel Castro assassinated under the pseudonym Lee Duncan: Derby, Conn. : Monarch Books, 1961.

There were five of them, each prepared to kill, each with his own reasons for accepting what might well be a suicide mission. The pay? $20,000 apiece. The mission? Find a way into Cuba and kill Castro.

"[An] absorbing yarn about five men vying for a $100,000 prize put on Fidel Castro's head by a mysterious guy named Hiraldo...Passages discussing Castro's life and times add depth to this intense, taut thriller, just as good now as it was in 1961." Publishers Weekly.

Block, Lawrence

The **sins** of the fathers / Lawrence Block. Dark Harvest, 1992, c1976. 179p. Matthew Scudder mysteries

ISBN 9780913165669

1. Block, Lawrence Criticism and interpretation 2. Murder investigation 3. Clergymen 4. Fathers and sons 5. Murder 6. Prostitutes 7. Private investigators 8. Alcoholic men 9. Former police 10. New York City 11. Mysteries 12. Hardboiled fiction

LC 90035227

Introduction by Stephen King: "No cats: an appreciation of Lawrence Block and Matthew Scudder."

Originally published: New York : Dell, 1976.

Matthew Scudder, a private detective who had been a cop for fifteen years, investigates the savage murder of a Greenwich Village hooker supposedly killed by her homosexual roommate.

"This novel introduced the then-hard-drinking ex-cop Matt Scudder. This is a fine opportunity to get in on the start of what has become one of the most rewarding PI series currently in progress." Publishers Weekly.

Block, Lawrence

A **ticket** to the boneyard : a Matthew Scudder novel / Lawrence Block. Morrow, 1990. 302 p. Matthew Scudder mysteries

ISBN 0688090702

1. Men with mental illnesses 2. Serial murders 3. Revenge 4. Former convicts 5. Recovering alcoholics 6. Private investigators 7. Alcoholic men 8. Former police 9. New York City 10. Mysteries 11.

Hardboiled fiction

LC 90005710

When ex-policeman and recovering alcoholic Matthew Scudder is stalked by a psychotic killer who murders, one by one, Scudders' friends and acquaintances, his fate hinges on the survival of a glamorous call girl

"The author has a fine nose for the pungencies of New York's after-dark street life, and he gives his hero wonderful opportunities to swap syllables with the city's most articulate riffraff. This is primo stuff, and Scudder doesn't get any sharper than when he's interviewing transvestite hookers, desk clerks in fleabag hotels and bouncers in gay leather bars." New York Times Book Review.

Block, Lawrence

* **When** the sacred ginmill closes / Lawrence Block. Arbor House, 1986. 239 p. Matthew Scudder mysteries
ISBN 0877957746
1. 1970s 2. Women murder victims 3. Robbery 4. Private investigators 5. Alcoholic men 6. Former police 7. New York City 8. Mysteries 9. Hardboiled fiction

LC 85018682

"The writing is realistic in the best sense of the word. There are no artificial heroics, forced lines of dialogue or false moves. Mr. Block knows his New York and the way people speak." New York Times Book Review.

Block, Stefan Merrill

Oliver Loving : a novel / Stefan Merrill Block. Flatiron Books, 2018. 400 p.
ISBN 9781250169730
1. School shootings 2. People in comas 3. Life change events 4. Loss (Psychology) 5. Small town life 6. Dysfunctional families 7. Memories 8. Guilt 9. Secrets 10. Interpersonal relations 11. Mass shootings 12. Texas 13. Mainstream fiction

LC 2017041748

The complicated bonds uniting a family and the members of their community are tested by a devastating school shooting that has left a young man in a coma for nine years, a tragedy that is illuminated by an experimental diagnostic technology that suggests that his mind may still be active and capable of revealing what happened.

Bloom, Amy, 1953-

Lucky us : a novel / Amy Bloom. Random House, 2014. 256 p.
ISBN 9781400067244
1. 1940s 2. Half-sisters 3. Cross-country automobile trips 4. Abandoned children 5. Fathers and daughters 6. Voyages and travels 7. Family relationships 8. Success (Concept) 9. Misfits (Persons) 10. Sisters 11. Ambition 12. Hollywood, California -- History -- 20th century 13. Ohio -- History -- 20th century 14. Historical fiction 15. Farcical fiction 16. Literary fiction

LC 2013017648

Forging a life together after being abandoned by their parents, half sisters Eva and Iris share decades in and out of the spotlight in golden-era Hollywood and mid-20th-century Long Island.

"At its core, this is a novel of resilience. . . . Full of intriguing characters and lots of surprises." Library Journal.

Bloom, Amy, 1953-

* **White** houses : a novel / Amy Bloom. Random House, 2018. 218 p.
ISBN 9780812995664
1. Roosevelt, Eleanor, 1884-1962 2. Hickok, Lorena Alice, 1893- 1968 3. 1930s 4. 1940s 5. 20th century 6. Women journalists 7. Presidents' spouses 8. Women/women relations 9. Romantic love 10. Bisexual women 11. Female friendship 12. Loss (Psychology) 13. Married men -- Death 14. Men/women relations 15. Extramarital affairs 16. Women -- Interpersonal relations 17. Biographical fiction 18. Historical fiction 19. LGBTQIA fiction

LC 2017028296

After meeting the future first lady while covering Franklin Roosevelt's campaign, Lorena Hickock and Eleanor discover a powerful passion between them.

Blum, Jenna

The **lost** family / Jenna Blum. Harper, 2018 417 p.
ISBN 9780062742162
1. 1960s 2. Holocaust survivors 3. Husband and wife 4. Second wives 5. Cooks 6. Marriage 7. Widowers 8. Grief in men 9. Fashion models 10. Parent and child 11. Loss (Psychology) 12. Children of Holocaust survivors 13. Manhattan, New York City 14. New York City 15. Historical fiction 16. Literary fiction

Resigning himself to solitude, chef and Auschwitz survivor, Peter Rashkin, in 1965 Manhattan, devotes himself to running Masha's restaurant, until he meets and marries June, but the horrors of his past soon overshadow him, June and their daughter.

"This exquisitely crafted and compassionate novel offers a lesson in honesty, regardless of how difficult the truth may be. It will offer plenty of discussion for book groups." Library Journal.

Blume, Judy

In the unlikely event / Judy Blume. Alfred A. Knopf, 2015. 432 p.
ISBN 9781101875049
1. 1950s 2. Airplane accidents 3. Intergenerational relations 4. Families 5. Neighbors 6. Friendship 7. First loves 8. Family relationships 9. Interpersonal relations 10. New Jersey -- Social life and customs -- 20th century 11. Family sagas 12. Historical fiction

LC 2015007629

A novel inspired by a series of passenger airplane crashes that occurred in 1951 and 1952 New Jersey reimagines the impact of the tragedies on three generations of families, friends and strangers.

"Maintaining her knack for personal detail, Blume mixes Miri's familiar coming-of-age melodrama with an exploration of how disasters test character, alter relationships, and reveal undercurrents of a seemingly simple world. She evokes '50s music, ethnic neighborhoods, and Las Vegas in the early days." Publishers Weekly.

Blumenfeld, Amy

The **cast** / Amy Blumenfeld. SparkPress, 2018. 310 p.
ISBN 9781943006724
1. Friendship 2. Women cancer survivors 3. Videos 4. Reunions 5. Fourth of July 6. Middle age 7. Life change events 8. Options, alternatives, choices 9. Domestic fiction 10. Mainstream fiction

Twenty-five years after a group of ninth graders produces a Saturday Night Live'style videotape to cheer up their cancer-stricken friend, they reunite to celebrate her good health--but the happy holiday card facades quickly crumble and give way to an unforgettable three days filled with moral dilemmas and life-altering choices.

Blundell, Judy

The **high** season : a novel / Judy Blundell. Random House, 2018. 396 p.
ISBN 9780525508717
1. Houses 2. Rich people 3. Landlord and tenant 4. Women -- Psychology 5. Museum curators 6. Family problems 7. Anger in

women 8. Class conflict 9. Billionaires 10. Long Island, New York 11. Women's lives and relationships

LC 2017037646

RUSA Reading List Short List, 2019.

Forced to rent out her family's beautiful seaside Long Island home every summer just so that they can afford to keep it, Ruthie is forced to go to extreme lengths to protect the life she loves in the wake of a suddenly estranged marriage, greedy co-workers who are threatening her job, the return of an old flame and her teen daughter's destructive relationship.

Bobotis, Andrea

The **last** list of Miss Judith Kratt / Andrea Bobotis. Sourcebooks Landmark, 2019. 320 p.

ISBN 9781492678861

1. Small towns 2. Matriarchs 3. Family secrets 4. Heirlooms 5. Memories 6. Sisters 7. Families -- History 8. Inheritance and succession 9. Brothers -- Death 10. Race relations 11. Families of murder victims 12. South Carolina 13. Southern fiction

LC 2018033669

Judith Kratt inherited all the Kratt family had to offer - the pie safe, the copper clock, the murder that no one talks about - and she knows in her old bones that it's time to make an inventory of her household and its valuables. But she finds that cataloging the family heirlooms can't contain their misfortunes, not when her wayward sister suddenly returns, determined to expose secrets that the Kratts had hoped to take to their grave. Interweaving the present with chilling flashbacks from one fateful evening in 1929, Judith pieces together the influence of her family on their small South Carolina cotton town, learning that the effects of dark family secrets can last for decades. Provided by publisher.

Bock, Charles

Alice & Oliver : a novel / Charles Bock. Random House, 2016. 336 p.

ISBN 9781400068388

1. 1990s 2. Women with cancer 3. Married women 4. Husband and wife 5. People with terminal illnesses 6. Mothers 7. Cancer 8. Medical care 9. Hospitals 10. Family relationships 11. New York City 12. Domestic fiction 13. Literary fiction

LC 2015022303

Alice Culvert is a force: passionate, independent, smart, and gorgeous, she--to her delight--attracts attention wherever she goes, even amid the buzz of mid-90s New York. In knee-high boots, with her newborn daughter, Doe, strapped to her chest, Alice is one of those people who just seem so vividly alive, which makes her cancer diagnosis feel almost incongruous. How could such a being not go on? But all at once, Alice's existence, and that of her husband Oliver, is reduced to a single purpose: survival. As they combat the disease, the couple must also face off against the serpentine healthcare system, the good intentions of loved ones, and the deep, dangerous stressors that threaten to push the two of them apart. With veracity, humor, wisdom, and love, Charles Bock navigates one family's unforgettable story - inspired by his own Provided by publisher.

"The illness doesn't interrupt humanity; humanity grows from the illness, which is a narrative strategy that makes the book one of the most moving in recent memory. A stunning book about Alice and Oliver, yes, but also about the way illness shatters us all." Kirkus.

Bock, Charles

Beautiful children : a novel / Charles Bock. Random House, 2008. 432 p.

ISBN 9781400066506

1. Boys 2. Missing children 3. Deserts 4. Twelve-year-old boys 5. Marital conflict 6. Family relationships 7. Las Vegas, Nevada 8.

Nevada 9. Psychological fiction

LC 2007004166

One Saturday night in Las Vegas, twelve-year-old Newell Ewing goes out with a friend and doesn't come home. In the aftermath of his disappearance, his mother, Lorraine, makes daily pilgrimages to her son's room and tortures herself with memories. Equally distraught, the boy's father, Lincoln, finds himself wanting to comfort his wife even as he yearns for solace, a loving touch, any kind of intimacy. As the Ewings navigate the mystery of what's become of their son, the circumstances surrounding Newell's vanishing and other events on that same night reverberate through the lives of seemingly disconnected strangers: a comic book illustrator in town for a weekend of debauchery; a painfully shy and possibly disturbed young artist; a stripper who imagines moments from her life as if they were movie scenes; a bubbly teenage wiccan anarchist; a dangerous and scheming gutter punk; a band of misfit runaways.

Bognanni, Peter

The **house** of tomorrow / Peter Bognanni. Amy Einhorn Books/G.P. Putnam's Sons, 2010. 304 p.

ISBN 9780399156090

1. Fuller, R Buckminster, 1895-1983 Influence 2. Grandmothers 3. Social isolation 4. Growth (Psychology) 5. Young men 6. Punk rock musicians 7. Family relationships 8. Friendship 9. Music 10. Coming-of-age stories

LC 2009023542

Homeschooled teenager Sebastian Prendergast is forced by his grandmother's stroke to venture out of his geodesic dome habitat and befriends a chain-smoking teen who introduces him to pop culture through the punk band they form together.

"Sebastian's first stumble out of the woods into the sweet and vicious real world may not break any new ground, but it's worthwhile, distracting and delightful. Bognanni . . . captures that breath we take before we jump out into our life." Minneapolis Star Tribune..

Bohjalian, Chris, 1960-

The **buffalo** soldier : a novel / Chris Bohjalian. Shaye Areheart Books, 2002. 404 p.

ISBN 0609608339

1. African American foster children 2. Bereavement in parents 3. Intergenerational friendship 4. Ten-year-old boys 5. Daughters -- Death 6. Extramarital affairs 7. Foster parents 8. Interracial families 9. Neighbors 10. Twin sisters 11. Birthfathers 12. Friendship 13. Small town life 14. Vermont 15. Psychological fiction 16. Mainstream fiction 17. Domestic fiction

LC 2001049042

The devastating loss of their twin daughters in a flash flood turns the lives of Terry and Laura Sheldon upside down as their marriage is tested by grief, Terry's brief love affair, and their growing relationship with their foster child, a ten-year-old African American boy.

"Bohjalian's characters combat their moral and racial confusion with a healthy application of ordinary love and good will, though their basic goodness often makes them feel less complex than the plot itself." New York Times Book Review.

Bohjalian, Chris, 1960-

The **double** bind : a novel / Chris Bohjalian. Shaye Areheart Books, 2007. 384 p.

ISBN 1400047463

1. Shelters for the homeless 2. Obsession 3. Men with mental illnesses 4. Coping in women 5. Women college students 6. Women crime victims 7. Photographers 8. Friendship 9. Men -- Death 10. Family secrets 11. Fear in women 12. Vermont 13. Psychological

fiction

LC 2006015402

"Conflating literary lore, photographic analysis and meditations on homelessness and mental illness, Bohjalian produces his best and most complex fiction yet. Ultra-clever, and moving, too." Kirkus.

Bohjalian, Chris, 1960-

The **flight** attendant : a novel / Chris Bohjalian. Doubleday, 2018. 368 p.

ISBN 9780385542418

1. Flight attendants 2. Deception 3. Addiction 4. Alcoholic women 5. Binge-drinking 6. Murder 7. Assassins 8. Consequences 9. Thrillers and suspense

LC 2017034159

A binge-drinking flight attendant wakes up in an unfamiliar hotel room beside a dead body and sneaks back to her work, telling a series of lies that complicate her ability to figure out what really happened.

Bohjalian, Chris, 1960-

The **night** strangers : a novel / Christopher A. Bohjalian. Crown Publishers, 2011. 400 p.

ISBN 9780307394996

1. Victorian houses 2. Airplane accidents 3. Ghosts 4. Herbalists 5. Families 6. Post-traumatic stress disorder 7. Twin sisters 8. Magic (Occultism) 9. Pilots 10. Men with depression 11. New Hampshire 12. Ghost stories 13. Horror

After he crashes his plane into Lake Champlain, killing most of the passengers, Chip Linton moves into a new home with his wife and twin daughters and soon finds himself being haunted by the dead passengers, all while his wife wonders why the strange herbalist denizens of the town have taken such an interest in her daughters.

"Chip Linton is at the controls of a jet that flies into a flock of birds and goes down in Lake Champlain. Although Linton does everything correctly, an errant wave tips the plane over. Thirty-nine of the 48 people aboard die, and the captain's life, obviously, is changed forever. His lawyer wife, Emily, and their 10-year-old twins decide they need to start over. So they leave Pennsylvania for the small town of Bethel, N.H. But things do not get better. The ghost of several drowned passengers haunts him, particularly Ashley, a young girl, and her dad. They are stuck in purgatory and alone. Linton believes he's responsible, and that Ashley deserves company, and he's prepared to kill his own daughters to provide it. He's crazy, of course-- or is he? The denouement is not only unexpected but is also perfect and true to the story. Bohjalian is a terrific writer and parsimonious in the way he issues information, slowly building an increasing sense of dread and excitement." Minneapolis Star Tribune.

Bohjalian, Chris, 1960-

*The **red** lotus / Chris Bohjalian. Doubleday, 2020. 400 p.

ISBN 9780385544801

1. Women physicians 2. Couples 3. Hospitals -- Emergency service 4. Voyages and travels 5. Bicycling 6. Deception 7. Missing men 8. Vietnam 9. United States 10. Thrillers and suspense

Falling in love with a wounded former patient and accompanying him on a cycling trip to Vietnam, an emergency-room doctor uncovers a bizarre series of deceptions that culminate in her boyfriend's unexplained disappearance.

"Alternating action between Vietnam and New York, along with the dynamic pace, will please suspense fans." Library Journal.

Bohjalian, Chris, 1960-

The **sandcastle** girls / Chris Bohjalian. Doubleday, 2012. 288 p.

ISBN 9780385534796

1. 1910s 2. Americans in the Middle East 3. Armenian genocide, 1915-1923 4. Nurses 5. Engineers 6. Loss (Psychology) 7. Grief in men 8. Men/women relations 9. Mass murder 10. Family secrets 11. Historical fiction 12. Love stories 13. Parallel narratives 14. Family sagas

LC 2011050285

A historical love story inspired by the author's Armenian heritage finds early 20th-century nurse Elizabeth Endicott arriving in Syria to help deliver food and medical aid to genocide refugees, a volunteer service during which she exchanges letters with an Armenian engineer and widower.

"Bohjalian powerfully narrates an intricately nuanced romance with a complicated historical event at the forefront." Library Journal.

Bohjalian, Chris, 1960-

Secrets of Eden : a novel / Chris Bohjalian. Shaye Areheart Books, 2010. 384 p.

ISBN 9780307394972

1. Clergymen 2. Guilt in men 3. Children of murder victims 4. Faith in men 5. Women authors 6. Secrets 7. Murder victims 8. Small-town life 9. Vermont 10. Mysteries

LC 2009023946

Haunted by the final words of a newly baptized congregation member who was subsequently murdered by her husband, the Reverend Stephen Drew abandons his pulpit to spend time with an author who writes best-selling books about angels.

"This novel is engrossing without being cheesy, informative without being didactic, and gripping despite the fact that the ending is quite predictable." Boston Globe.

Bohjalian, Chris, 1960-

Skeletons at the feast : a novel / Chris Bohjalian. Shaye Areheart Books, 2008. 372 p.

ISBN 9780307394958

1. Second World War era (1939-1945) 2. 1940s 3. Jews, German -- History -- 1933-1945 4. Refugees 5. Military pilots 6. Antisemitism 7. World War II -- Germany 8. Concentration camp survivors 9. Jews 10. Racism 11. Jewish women 12. Germany -- History -- 1933-1945 13. War stories 14. Historical fiction 15. Parallel narratives

LC 2007040800

During the final months of World War II, a small group of people make their way westward across a ravaged Europe in a desperate attempt to reach British and American lines.

Bohjalian, Chris, 1960-

The **sleepwalker** / Chris Bohjalian. Doubleday, 2017. 336 p.

ISBN 9780385538916

1. Sleep-walking 2. Missing women 3. Missing persons investigation 4. Men/women relations 5. Family relationships 6. Detectives 7. Secrets 8. Sisters 9. Vermont 10. Mysteries

LC 2016015531

When a sleepwalker who has experienced episodes of near violence while unconscious goes missing, her eldest daughter, Lianna, finds herself drawn to a lead detective who seems to know more than he is revealing.

"Set in Vermont in 2000, this stylish fusion of mystery and domestic thriller from Bohjalian (The Guest Room) explores the aftermath of the inexplicable disappearance of a woman prone to sleepwalking" Publishers Weekly.

Boianjiu, Shani, 1987-

The **people** of forever are not afraid : a novel / Shani Boianjiu. Hogarth, 2012. 352 p.

ISBN 9780307955951

1. Women soldiers -- Israel 2. Female friendship 3. Military education -- Israel 4. Draft 5. Military life 6. Young women 7. Life change events 8. Nationalism -- Israel 9. Men/women relations 10. Interpersonal relations 11. War stories 12. Coming-of-age stories

Three young women in Israel are conscripted into the army and struggle to stay friends as they see their lives change in unpredictable ways.

Bolano, Roberto, 1953-2003

* **2666** / Roberto Bolano ; translated from the Spanish by Natasha Wimmer. Farrar, Straus and Giroux, 2008. 912 p.

ISBN 9780374100148

1. Blue collar workers 2. Missing persons 3. Factories 4. Scholars and academics 5. Authors 6. Critics 7. Violence 8. Violence against women 9. Mexican-American Border Region 10. Literary fiction 11. Translations -- Spanish to English

LC 2008018295

National Book Critics Circle Award for Fiction, 2008.

An American sportswriter, an elusive German novelist, and a teenage student interact in an urban community on the U.S.-Mexico border where hundreds of young factory workers have disappeared.

"More vast and more lurid than his previous novels that have been translated into English, 2666 is not Roberto Bolao's masterpiece but almost a compendium, in individual scenes, of the qualities that made him a great writer. His themes are violence, dislocation, and the sexiness of literature, and here these strands are recombined endlessly, in Europe, Detroit, and Mexico, through multiple narrators and prose styles. The action converges on the Sonoran desert, where Bolao anatomizes, in brutal and eerie detail, the true-life murders of hundreds of women, most of which remain unsolved. By the end, after close to nine hundred pages, the reader will be impressed by the range and power on display but might wish that the novel cohered, rather than merely concluding." The New Yorker.

Bolano, Roberto, 1953-2003

Amulet / Roberto Bolano ; translated from the Spanish by Chris Andrews. New Directions, 2007, c1999. 192 p.

ISBN 0811216640

1. 1960s 2. Latin Americans 3. Revolutionaries -- Latin America 4. College students 5. Women college students 6. Poets, Mexican 7. Women poets 8. Hallucinations and illusions 9. Memories 10. Revolutions -- Latin America -- History -- 20th century 11. Student movements -- Mexico 12. Violence 13. Latin America -- History -- 20th century 14. Mexico -- History -- 20th century 15. Literary fiction 16. Translations -- Spanish to English

LC 2006023507

Originally published as Amuleto: Barcelona : Editorial Anagrama, 1999.

"This is a curiously joyful novel that delights in its storytelling even as it struggles with the question of how art might be sustained under conditions resolutely opposed to it." Harper's.

Bolano, Roberto, 1953-2003

* **By** night in Chile / Roberto Bolano ; translated from the Spanish by Chris Andrews. New Directions Books, 2003. 130 p.

ISBN 0811215474

1. Pinochet Ugarte, Augusto 2. Opus Dei. 3. Catholic Church. 4. Priests 5. Memories 6. Secrets 7. Responsibility 8. Identity (Psychology) 9. Last words 10. Generals 11. Reminiscing in old age 12. Chile -- History -- 1973-1988 13. Literary fiction 14. Translations -- Spanish to English

LC 2003013223

"Postwar Chilean politics and literature infuse this densely learned, richly evocative novel. In Chris Andrews's lucid translation, Bolano's febrile narrative tack and occasional surreal touches bring to mind the classics of Latin American magic realism; his cerebral protagonist and nonfiction borrowings are reminiscent of Thomas Bernhard and W. G. Sebald." New York Times Book Review.

Bolano, Roberto, 1953-2003

* **Distant** star / Roberto Bolano ; translated from the Spanish by Chris Andrews. New Directions, 2004. 149 p.

ISBN 0811215865

1. Dictatorship 2. Poets 3. Universities and colleges 4. Concentration camps 5. Pilots 6. Chile -- History -- Coup d'etat, 1973 7. Political fiction 8. Literary fiction

LC 2004019033

"The melancholy folklore of exile pervades this novel, which describes the divergent paths of three young Chilean poets around the time of Pinochets coup. At university, the unnamed narrator and his friend are fascinated by a mysterious new member of their poetry workshop. Alberto Ruiz-Tagle is serious, well mannered, a clear thinker, but his poems seem false, as if his true work were yet to be revealed. It becomes apparent that this is literally the case when Allende's government falls: as an Air Force officer for the new regime, he becomes famous for writing nationalist slogans in the sky. (The left-wing narrator, now in jail, reads them from his prison yard.) Bolano's spare prose lends his narrators account a chilly precision--as if the detachment of his former classmate had become his country's, and his own." The New Yorker.

Bolano, Roberto, 1953-2003

Last evenings on Earth / Roberto Bolano ; translated from the Spanish by Chris Andrews. New Directions Books, 2006. 256 p.

ISBN 9780811216340

1. Bolano, Roberto, 1953-2003 2. Men 3. Desire 4. Men/women relations 5. Men -- Family relationships 6. Literary fiction 7. Short stories 8. Translations -- Spanish to English

LC 2006003819

"These 14 bleakly luminous stories are all told in the first person by men (usually young) who yearn for something just out of their grasp (fame, talent, love) and who harbor few hopes of attaining what they desire. . . . The stories are similar, in theme and voice (though not in locale), and they are perfectly calibrated: Bolao limns the capacity of a voice to carry despair without shading into bitterness." Publishers Weekly.

Bolano, Roberto, 1953-2003

Monsieur Pain / Roberto Bolano ; translated from the Spanish by Chris Andrews. New Directions, 2010. 192 p.

ISBN 9780811217149

1. Vallejo, Cesar, 1892-1938 2. 1930s 3. Hypnotists 4. Magic 5. Unrequited love 6. Assassination 7. Hypnotism 8. Guilt in men 9. Paris, France 10. Literary fiction 11. Translations -- Spanish to

English

LC 2009037431

Originally published by Anagrama Barcelona Spain, as Monsieur Pain in 1999.

After he accepts a bribe not to treat chronically hiccupping Peruvian poet Csar Vallejo, mesmerist Monsieur Pierre Pain is racked with guilt but is barred from the hospital when he tries to do the right thing, only to discover a rival mesmerist has entered the picture, along with an assassination and a host of other nightmares.

"Bolano draws on actual facts-- the real Vallejo was hospitalized in Paris in 1938, and his wife called in practitioners of occult sciences when doctors failed to cure him --to weave his brilliant, noir-steeped fictional world. As Pain wanders the rainy streets of Paris, convinced of a plot to assassinate Vallejo, haunted by his own complicity and helpless rebellion, we enter a hallucinatory dreamscape flooded with resonant symbols." San Francisco Chronicle.

Bolano, Roberto, 1953-2003

*Nazi literature in the Americas / Roberto Bolano ; translated from the Spanish by Chris Andrews. New Directions, 2008. ix, 227 p.

ISBN 9780811217057

1. Right-wing extremists 2. Fascism 3. Nazis 4. Nazism 5. Authors 6. Poets 7. Journalists 8. White supremacists 9. Parodies 10. Translations -- Spanish to English

"This novel, a wicked, invented encyclopedia of imaginary fascist writers and literary tastemakers, is Bolao playing with sharp, twisting knives. As if he were Borges's wisecracking, sardonic son, Bolao has meticulously created a tightly woven network of far-right litterateurs and purveyors of belles lettres for whom Hitler was beauty, truth and great lost hope. Cross-referenced, complete with bibliography and a biographical list of secondary figures, Nazi Literature is composed of a series of sketches, the compressed life stories of writers in North and South America who never existed, but all too easily could have. Goose-stepping caricatures a la The Producers they are not; instead, they are frighteningly subtle, poignant and plausible." New York Times Book Review.

Bolano, Roberto, 1953-2003

* The savage detectives / Roberto Bolano ; translated from the Spanish by Natasha Wimmer. Farrar, Straus and Giroux, 2007, c1998. 592 p.

ISBN 9780374191481

1. 1970s 2. Poets, Mexican 3. Militants 4. Literary movements 5. Male friendship 6. Quests 7. Missing persons 8. Voyages and travels 9. Self-fulfillment in men 10. Mexico (City) 11. Psychological fiction 12. Literary fiction 13. Translations -- Spanish to English 14. Diary novels

LC 2006022176

Originally published: Barcelona : Editorial Anagrama, 1998.

Chronicles the strange journey of two Latin American poets, Arturo Belano and Ulises Lima, as seen through the eyes of the people whose paths they cross in Central America, Europe, Israel, and West Africa.

"Though the fragmented narrative can be frustrating at times, the late-20th-century panorama emerging from the cacophony is simultaneously frightening and spectacular. At every turn, Bolao examines the individual lives history discards. The result is a large, sprawling and--most of all--sublime novel." Paste.

Bolano, Roberto, 1953-2003

* The Third Reich / Roberto Bolano ; translated from the Spanish by Natasha Wimmer. Farrar Straus & Giroux, 2011. 288 p.

ISBN 9780374275624

1. Germans in Spain 2. War games 3. Violence in men 4. Couples 5. Egotism in men 6. Burn victims 7. Missing persons 8. Literary fiction 9. Translations -- Spanish to English

Originally published: Barcelona : Anagrama, 2010.

While vacationing in Spain, German war-game champion Udo Berger and his girlfriend meet another vacationing German couple, Charly and Hanna, who introduce them to a band of locals. When Charly disappears, the women return to Germany but Udo stays and becomes enmeshed in Third Reich, a World War II strategy game whose consequences may be all too real.

Boll, Heinrich, 1917-1985

* Billiards at half-past nine / Heinrich Boll. Penguin Books, 1994, c1962. 280 p.

ISBN 0140187243

1. Billiards 2. Household activities 3. Germany -- History -- 1945-1955 4. Modern classics 5. Literary fiction 6. Translations -- German to English

Robert Faehmel finds his structured life threatened by an old schoolmate and former Nazi.

Boll, Heinrich, 1917-1985

* The clown / Heinrich Boll ; translated from the German by Leila Vennewitz Penguin Books, 1994, c1963. 247 p.

ISBN 014018726X

1. Germany -- Social conditions -- 1933-1945 2. Modern classics 3. Literary fiction 4. Translations -- German to English

"What Schnier (and the author) seem to be asking is: How can an honest man profess Christianity when Christian culture in the West failed to stop the rise of Nazism . . . and when the Church thrives in a society that worships nothing but the values of the marketplace? Hard questions but embodied in a bitter and brilliant book." New York Times Book Review.

Boll, Heinrich, 1917-1985

The lost honor of Katharina Blum : how violence develops and where it can lead / Heinrich Boll ; translated from the German by Leila Vennewitz. McGraw-Hill, 1975 140 p.

ISBN 0070064253

1. Political surveillance 2. Libel and slander 3. State-sponsored terrorism 4. Journalists 5. Germany 6. Translations -- German to English

LC 74028138

A young woman's association with a hunted man makes her the target of a journalist determined to grab headlines by portraying her as an evil woman. As the attacks on her escalate and she becomes the victim of anonymous threats, Katharina sees only one way out of her nightmare. Turning the mystery genre on its head, the novel begins with the confession of a crime, drawing the reader into a web of sensationalism, character assassination, and the unavoidable eruption of violence.

Boll, Heinrich, 1917-1985

The silent angel / Heinrich Boll ; translated by Breon Mitchell. St. Martin's Press, 1994. 182 p.

ISBN 0312110642

1. World War II 2. Soldiers -- Germany 3. Faith (Christianity) 4. Army towns 5. Germany -- History -- 1933-1945 6. Love stories 7.

Literary fiction 8. Translations -- German to English

LC 94002052

Originally published in Germany as Der Engel schwieg (1992)

Returning to the ruins of post-World War II Cologne, Hans finds his cynicism fading through his healing relationships with the Church and with his new love, Regina

"While the bleakness Boll portrays might have made German publishers wary in 1950, the artistry of his portrayal makes 'The Silent Angel' a rich novel, one still pertinent to our own hunger for the bread of meaning amid the rubble of history. Heinrich Bll's gift to us is the skill with which he captures its first pangs." New York Times Book Review.

Bolton, S. J. (Sharon J.)

The **craftsman** / S.J. Bolton. Minotaur Books, 2018. 418 p.

ISBN 9781250300034

1. Women detectives 2. Small towns 3. Confession (Law) 4. Crimes against children 5. Suspicion 6. Murder investigation 7. Missing children 8. Premature burial 9. Belief and doubt 10. Lancashire, England 11. England 12. Mysteries 13. Gothic fiction

LC 2018020147

When eerily familiar child abductions and murders start recurring in a small Lancashire village, a local cop struggles to figure out if she sent the wrong person to jail decades earlier or if a copycat killer is responsible.

Bolton, S. J. (Sharon J.)

A **dark** and twisted tide / Sharon Bolton. St Martins Pr, 2014 448 p. Lacey Flint novels

ISBN 9781250028587

1. 2000s (Decade) 2. Policewomen 3. Communities 4. Rivers 5. Murder 6. Murder investigation 7. Murderers 8. Houseboats 9. Thames River 10. London, England 11. Psychological suspense

LC 2014003443

Originally published: London: Bantam Press, 2014.

"Now living in a houseboat on the River Thames, Lacey Flint is becoming a part of London's weird and wonderful riverboat community. But at dawn one hot summer morning, Lacey finds the body of a shrouded young woman in the river. She assumes it was chance--after all she's recently joined the marine policing unit--but further investigation leads her team to suspect it was deliberately left for her to find. She is no longer a detective, but as she begins to suspect someone is watching her very closely, she can't help but be drawn into the investigation. Award-winning author Sharon Bolton has once again crafted a tightly-plotted, utterly unpredicatable thriller around one of the most compelling characters in crime fiction today, enigmatic London police officer Lacey Flint"--, Provided by publisher.

Bolton, S. J. (Sharon J.)

Now you see me / S.J. Bolton. Minotaur Books, 2011. 416 p. Lacey Flint novels

ISBN 9780312600525

1. Jack,, the Ripper Influence 2. 2000s (Decade) 3. Women detectives 4. Crimes against women 5. Serial murder investigation 6. Copycat murderers 7. Stalkers 8. Stabbing victims 9. Serial murders 10. Women murder victims 11. Stalking 12. London, England 13. Psychological suspense

LC 2011008751

Stumbling onto a murder scene that a reporter likens to the crimes of Jack the Ripper, young detective constable Lacey Flint races against time to prevent additional deaths and realizes that the killer is taunting her with secrets from her past.

"On the anniversary of the original Ripper's first killing, Det. Constable Lacey Flint is horrified to find a dying woman, her abdomen . . . a mass of scarlet, leaning against the detective's car in a London car park. The guilt-ridden Flint wonders whether different actions on her part might have saved the victim's life or caught the killer. The connection with the 1888 autumn of terror becomes clear after a journalist receives a letter obviously derived from some of the correspondence Scotland Yard received back then, ostensibly from the Ripper himself. By coincidence, Flint is something of a Ripper expert, and her knowledge proves useful in what develops into a multiple murder investigation. Avoiding gratuitous violence, Bolton . . . skillfully plays with the reader's expectations." Publishers Weekly.

Bond, Cynthia, 1961-

Ruby : a novel / Cynthia Bond. Hogarth, 2014 288 p.

ISBN 9780804139090

1. Small town life 2. Discrimination 3. Prostitution 4. African Americans 5. Homecomings 6. First loves 7. Racism 8. Brothers and sisters 9. Violence against women 10. Sexual violence 11. Secrets 12. Sexuality 13. Interpersonal relations 14. Men/women relations 15. Texas 16. Literary fiction 17. Southern Gothic 18. African American fiction 19. Southern fiction

LC 2013033049

Shortlisted for the Baileys Women's Prize for Fiction, 2016.

Loving the beautiful but damaged Ruby all of his life, Ephram is torn between his sister and a chance for a life with Ruby when the latter returns to their small hometown and confronts the forces that traumatized her early years.

Bonnaffons, Amy

The **regrets** / Amy Bonnaffons. Little Brown & Co, 2020. 304 p.

ISBN 9780316516167

1. Spirits 2. Life after death 3. Interpersonal attraction 4. Love triangles 5. Dead 6. Librarians 7. Men/women relations 8. Love 9. Literary fiction 10. Love stories 11. Surrealist fiction

In order to "cross over" to the afterlife, Thomas must complete a 90-day stint on earth during which he is forbidden to get involved with a member of the living until he falls in love with Rachel, setting in motion a series of strange, troubling consequences.

"Bonnaffons (The Wrong Heaven, 2018) has a deft hand for dialogue and character development, which grounds the fantastical nature of her novel in the sharp truths of real-life love and desire." Booklist.

Bonnaffons, Amy

The **wrong** heaven : stories / Amy Bonnaffons. Ecco., 2018. 245 p.

ISBN 9780316516211

1. Literary fiction 2. Short stories

In a collection of revelatory stories, some of which are more grounded in reality than others, anything is possible: bodies can transform, inanimate objects come to life and angels appear and disappear.

Bonner, Cindy, 1953-

Lily : a novel / Cindy Bonner. Algonquin Books of Chapel Hill, 1992. 336 p. McDade cycle

ISBN 9780945575955

1. 1880s 2. Teenage romance 3. Outlaws -- Texas 4. Small towns 5. Love triangles 6. Interpersonal attraction 7. Teenage girls 8. Men/women relations 9. Vigilantes -- Texas 10. Texas -- History -- 1846-1950 11. Western romances 12. Historical romances

LC 91040237

Fifteen-year-old Lily DeLony tells her version of the events of Christmas Eve night 1883, when a vigilante group of citizens--including her father--struck against a gang of outlaws, one of whom was the love of her life

"A fine first novel, making the timeworn theme of a responsible young girl's falling in love with an ne'er-do-well rascal new and fresh. . . . The book's strongest assets are its verisimilitude, fortified by the wonderful use of the vernacular, and the pure, simple clarity of the writing." Library Journal.

Booth, Coe

* Bronxwood / Coe Booth. PUSH, 2011. 320 p.

ISBN 9780439925341

1. Sixteen-year-old boys 2. Children of former convicts 3. Family problems 4. Teenage boy/girl relations 5. African American teenage boys 6. Separated friends, relatives, etc 7. Poverty 8. Disc jockeys 9. City life 10. Bronx, New York City 11. Realistic fiction 12. African American fiction 13. Books for reluctant readers

Tyrell's life is spinning out of control after his father is released from prison, his little brother is placed in foster care, and the drug dealers he's living with are pressuring him to start dealing.

"Action scenes combine with interpersonal exchanges to keep the pace moving forward at a lightning speed, but Booth never sacrifices the street-infused dialogue and emotional authenticity that characterize her works. She has created a compelling tale of a teen still trying to make the right choices despite the painful consequences." School Library Journal.

Booth, Coe

Kendra / Coe Booth. PUSH, 2008. 320 p.

ISBN 9780439925365

1. Mothers and daughters 2. Family problems 3. Teenage mothers 4. African Americans 5. Grandmothers 6. African American teenage girls 7. Inner city 8. Fourteen-year-old girls 9. Teenage boy/girl relations 10. Friendship 11. City life 12. New York City 13. Realistic fiction 14. African American fiction 15. Books for reluctant readers

LC 2008012819

High schooler Kendra longs to live with her mother who, unprepared for motherhood at age fourteen, left Kendra in the care of her grandmother.

"The convoluted but redeeming friendship between Kendra and her best friend and aunt, Adonna, resonates with heartbreak and honesty. Teens will appreciate Kendra's internal justification monologues, especially in relation to her Nana. . . . From Bronx blocks to Harlem hangouts, Booth delivers dynamic characters and an engaging story." School Library Journal.

Bordas, Camille, 1987-

How to behave in a crowd / Camille Bordas. Tim Duggan Books, 2017 336 p.

ISBN 9780451497543

1. Brothers and sisters 2. Small towns 3. Families 4. Family relationships 5. Brothers and sisters 6. Misfits (Persons) 7. Overachievers 8. Grief 9. Boys 10. Empathy 11. Loss (Psychology) 12. France 13. Literary fiction 14. Coming-of-age stories 15. Domestic fiction

LC 2016023941

A misfit youngest child in a large French family of overachievers makes quiet observations about his world and becomes the only family member brave enough to help the others through their grief in the wake of a devastating tragedy.

Borges, Jorge Luis, 1899-1986

* Collected fictions / Jorge Luis Borges ; translated from the Spanish by Andrew Hurley. Viking, 1998. 565 p.

ISBN 9780670849703

1. Immortalism 2. Outlaws 3. Curiosities and wonders 4. Gauchos 5. Labyrinths 6. Literary fiction 7. Short stories 8. Translations -- Spanish to English

LC 98021217

101 short stories

ALA Notable Book, 1999.

The first complete, annotated collection of short stories in English by the twentieth-century Spanish master ranges from his 1935 debut up to his last work, "Shakespeare's Memory," in its first appearance in English

"A Borges invention . . . always takes the reader on a roller-coaster ride into some previously unsuspected dimension. This collection of the great magician's work is a new translation and includes one piece never before put into English." The Atlantic.

Borges, Jorge Luis, 1899-1986

Ficciones / Jorge Luis Borges ; with an introduction by John Sturrock. A. A. Knopf, 1993. 142 p.

ISBN 0679422994

1. Metaphysics 2. Libraries 3. Infinity 4. Labyrinths 5. Short stories 6. Magical realism 7. Literary fiction 8. Translations -- Spanish to English 9. Modern classics

LC 9255353

Stories deal with an unusual garden, an enormous library, authorship, language, memory, philosophy, and the art of writing.

Borjlind, Cecilia, 1961-

Spring tide / Cilla and Rolf Borjlind ; translated from the Swedish by Rod Bradbury. Hesperus Nova, 2014, c2012. 474 p.

ISBN 9781843915157

1. Cold cases (Criminal investigation 2. Violence against homeless people 3. Policewomen 4. Business -- Corrupt practices 5. Sex industry and trade 6. Murder investigation 7. Pregnant women 8. Social problems 9. Social media 10. Detectives 11. Police 12. Sweden -- Social life and customs -- 21st century 13. Scandinavian crime fiction 14. Thrillers and suspense 15. Translations -- Swedish to English

Originally published as Springfloden: [Stockholm] : Norstedts, 2012.

While training to follow in her father's footsteps by joining the police force, Olivia Rönning receives a challenge from her professor to pick a cold case and solve it, unknowingly putting herself in danger.

"Two Swedish scriptwriters (TV series Wallander and Beck) deliver an intense, action-packed first novel. They smoothly transition among the many well-developed characters and set a chilling mood with an excellent evocation of the Swedish landscape. In addition, the authors effortlessly blend two mysteries to create a plot with many twists and turns that will be sure to appeal to fans of Henning Mankell, Maj Sjwall and Per Wahl, and Camilla Lckberg. While the English translation is excellent, the British slang might be off-putting to some U.S. readers." Library Journal.

Borland, Hal, 1900-1978

When the legends die / Hal Borland. Dell Laurel-Leaf, 2001, c1963. 294 p.

ISBN 9780553257380

1. Ute boys 2. Indian reservations 3. Wilderness living 4. Rodeos 5. Discrimination 6. Identity (Psychology) 7. Ute Indians 8. Native

American boys 9. Colorado 10. Coming-of-age stories

Originally published: Philadelphia : Lippincott, 1963.

At the death of his parents, a young Native American boy must enter the world of the white man. When his father killed another brave, Thomas Black Bull and his parents sought refuge in the wilderness. There they took up life as it had been in the old days, hunting and fishing, battling for survival. But an accident claimed the father's life and the grieving mother died shortly afterward....

Boswell, Robert, 1953-

Century's son / Robert Boswell. Alfred A. Knopf, 2002. 307 p.

ISBN 0375412379

1. Women college teachers 2. Garbage collectors 3. Husband and wife 4. Russian Americans 5. Teenage mothers 6. Brothers and sisters 7. Brothers -- Death 8. Fathers 9. Families 10. Family and suicide 11. Grief 12. Loss (Psychology) 13. Forgiveness 14. Secrets 15. Illinois 16. Psychological fiction

In the small college town of Hayden, Illinois, Morgan and Zhenya have settled into a loveless, stagnant marriage. The suicide of their son, Philip, ten years before has left the pair emotionally dead, lacking even the courage to separate from each other. Their surviving child, Emma, has become a teenage mother and refuses to reveal the identity of her child's father. Into this sullen mix marches Peter Ivanovich Kamenev, Zhenya's exasperating father. His arrival, though it tears at the family, also rejuvenates it.

"Morgan, whose first name has fallen away 'from disuse,' was once a fearless labor organizer for his fellow sanitation workers; it was his uncompromising idealism that led Zhenya, his college-professor wife, to fall in love with him. But, ten years later, Morgan has abandoned his activism; he spends his days collecting garbage and contemplating his decline, which began when his son hanged himself, at the age of twelve. As if the Morgan marriage didn't have enough to deal with, Zhenya's father, the famous Russian writer Peter Ivanovich Kamenev, is coming to visit. . . . A moving portrait of a family both torn apart and united by grief." The New Yorker.

Bouchet, Amanda

Breath of fire / Amanda Bouchet. Sourcebooks Casablanca, 2017 416 p. Kingmaker chronicles

ISBN 9781492626046

1. Warlords 2. Women psychics 3. Fate and fatalism 4. Tournaments 5. Magic 6. Gods and goddesses, Greek 7. Imaginary kingdoms 8. Power (Social sciences) 9. Duty 10. Secret identity 11. Men/women relations 12. Fantasy romances

As the realms are descending into all-out war, Cat and Griffin must embrace their fate together.

"With breathtaking storytelling, high-octane action and adventure, intense romance, and threads to ancient Greek mythology . . . Bouchet sets the bar for high-concept fantasy romance." Kirkus.

Bouchet, Amanda

Nightchaser / Amanda Bouchet. Sourcebooks Casablanca, 2019. 352 p. Nightchaser novels

ISBN 9781492667131

1. Women spaceship captains 2. Mechanics 3. Space flight 4. Women thieves 5. Protectiveness in women 6. Helpfulness in men 7. Space vehicles 8. Friendship 9. Enemies 10. Secrets 11. Sexual attraction 12. Men/women relations 13. Space ships 14. Orphanages 15. Secrecy 16. Science fiction 17. Love stories 18. Futuristic romances

"A space rebel with a price on her head discovers she may have the power to alter the balance of power in a galactic struggle--just as she's falling for a sexy trader with dangerous secrets of his own." Kirkus.

Bouchet, Amanda

* A **promise** of fire / Amanda Bouchet. Sourcebooks Casablanca, 2016 352 p. Kingmaker chronicles

ISBN 9781492626015

1. Warlords 2. Women psychics 3. Kidnapping 4. Secret identity 5. Fate and fatalism 6. Magic 7. Gods and goddesses, Greek 8. Imaginary kingdoms 9. Power (Social sciences) 10. Duty 11. Interpersonal attraction 12. Men/women relations 13. Fantasy romances

RUSA Reading List Short List, 2017

Despite her reputation as a Kingmaker, soothsayer Catalia "Cat" Fisa has turned her back on both the magic-wielding elite who use their gifts to oppress their subjects and the non-magical upstarts who would use her powers to further their own political agendas. She succeeds by disguising herself as an elderly fortune teller in a traveling circus until she's captured by Griffin, a warlord who needs Cat's assistance to defend his realm. Dismissing him as yet another power-hungry political player, Cat comes to revise her opinion as he defends her from assassins. -- Description by Gillian Speace.

Boudjedra, Rachid, 1941-

The **Barbary** figs / Rashid Boudjedra ; translated and with an afterword by Andre Naffis-Sahely. Haus Publishing, 2013. 191 p.

ISBN 9781906697426

1. Cousins 2. Reminiscing in old age 3. Revolutions 4. Colonized peoples 5. Conversation 6. Memory 7. Violence 8. Family relationships 9. Algeria -- History -- Revolution, 1954-1962 10. Algeria 11. Psychological fiction 12. Political fiction 13. Translations -- French to English

LC bl2013005674

Translation from the French of Figuiers de Barbarie.

Originally published: Paris : Grasset, c2010.

Two cousins are on a flight from Algiers to Constantine and during the hour long flight old resentments emerge as they examine their past as boys in French Algeria and teenagers fighting in the revolution.

Boulle, Pierre, 1912-1994

The **bridge** over the River Kwai : a novel / Pierre Boulle ; translated from the French by Xan Fielding. Presidio Press, 2007, c1954. 224 p.

ISBN 9780517207413

1. Burma-Siam Railroad 2. Second World War era (1939-1945) 3. Forced labor 4. Prisoners of war, British 5. World War II -- Thailand 6. Bridges 7. Prisoners of war 8. World War II -- Prisoners and prisons, Japanese 9. World War II -- Conscript labor 10. Thailand 11. War stories 12. Historical fiction 13. Translations -- French to English

Originally published in English: New York : Vanguard, 1954.

Originally published in French in 1952.

Re-creates the events surrounding the construction of a Japanese supply bridge over the River Kwai by British prisoners-of-war during World War II.

Bouman, Tom

Dry bones in the valley : a novel / Tom Bouman. W. W. Norton & Company, 2014. 288 p. Henry Farrell novels

ISBN 9780393243024

1. Police -- Pennsylvania 2. Murder investigation 3. Rural life -- Pennsylvania 4. Social conflict 5. Drug dealers 6. Murder 7. Crime 8. Pennsylvania 9. Mysteries

LC 2014002224

Edgar Allan Poe Award for Best First Novel by an American Author, 2015.

The lone police officer in a rural Northern Pennsylvania town finds trouble on the heels of the gas drilling, which has brought money, crime and heroin and meth into the territory and must investigate a murder that tears at old wounds.

"Henry's growth from a grief-stricken widower to a lawman with an inner resolve fuels the brisk plot, as does an evocative look at a changing landscape." Publishers Weekly.

Bourdeaut, Olivier, 1980-

Waiting for Bojangles : a novel / Olivier Bourdeaut ; translated from the French by Regan Kramer. Simon & Schuster, 2019. 176 p.

ISBN 9781501145919

1. People with mental illnesses 2. Familial love 3. Birds as pets 4. Family relationships 5. Mothers and sons 6. Rural life 7. Families 8. Eccentric parents 9. Family and mental illness 10. Children of people with mental illnesses 11. Paris, France 12. Spain 13. Literary fiction 14. Love stories 15. Translations -- French to English

A young boy lives with his madcap parents, Louise and George, and an exotic bird in a Parisian apartment. As his mother, mesmerizing and unpredictable, descends deeper into mental illness, it is up to the boy and his father to keep her safe and, when that fails, happy. Fleeing Paris for a country home in Spain, they come to understand that some of the most radiant people bear the heaviest burdens.

Bourland, Barbara

* **Fake** like me / Barbara Bourland. Grand Central Publishing, 2019. 336 p.

ISBN 9781538759516

1. Women artists 2. Creativity in women 3. Ambition in women 4. Artists' retreats 5. Identity (Psychology) 6. Painting 7. Inspiration 8. Loss (Psychology) 9. Suicide victims 10. Secrets 11. Men/women relations 12. New York City 13. New York (State) 14. Satirical fiction 15. Psychological suspense

LC 2018048057

A satire of the absurdly glamorous New York high art scene, in which a young artist crumbles under unimaginable pressure while at an upstate artists' retreat.

Bourne, Joanna

The **black** hawk / Joanna Bourne. Berkley Sensation, 2011. 336 p. Spymaster series

ISBN 9780425244531

1. Regency period (1811-1820) 2. Women spies 3. Frameups 4. Men/women relations 5. Spies 6. London, England -- History -- 19th century 7. Regency romances 8. Historical romances

RITA Award for Best Historical Romance, 2012.

After a brutal attack leaves her close to death, agent Justine DeCabrillac, known as "Owl," staggers to the door of the one man who can save her--and the one man she hates--Adrian Hawkhurst.

Bourne, Joanna

The **forbidden** rose / Joanna Bourne. Berkley, 2010. 400 p. Spymaster series

ISBN 9780425235614

1. Disguises 2. Men/women relations 3. Spies 4. Revolutions -- History 5. Revenge in men 6. France -- History 7. Historical romances

During the revolution in Paris, Marguerite de Fleurignac, once a wealthy aristocrat, disguises herself as a governess and is rescued from fanatics by a mysterious stranger who, unbeknownst to her, is England's top spy and needs her to settle an old score.

"The author delivers another addictively readable installment in her loosely connected Spymaster novels, a flawless romance in which an espionage-steeped plot is deftly balanced with a lusciously sensual love story." Booklist.

Bourne, Joanna

* **My** lord and spymaster / Joanna Bourne. Berkley, 2008. 336 p. Spymaster series

ISBN 9780425222461

1. Fathers and daughters 2. Rich women 3. Traitors 4. Undercover operations 5. Organized crime 6. Ship captains 7. Secrets 8. Deception 9. Interpersonal attraction 10. Men/women relations 11. Malicious accusation 12. London, England -- History -- 19th century 13. Historical romances

RITA Award for Best Regency, 2009.

"Glimpses of the leads' sordid pasts add depth, and Bourne's consummate way with a story line and an explosive denouement do the rest." Publishers Weekly.

Bourne, Joanna

Rogue spy / Joanna Bourne. Berkley Sensation, 2014. 320 p. Spymaster series

ISBN 9780425260821

1. Women spies 2. Spies -- France 3. Double agents 4. Treason 5. Extortion 6. Loyalty 7. Undercover operations 8. Interpersonal attraction 9. Men/women relations 10. Napoleonic Wars, 1800-1815 11. London, England 12. England -- History -- 19th century 13. Tuscany, Italy 14. Historical romances

To prove his loyalty to the British Crown, Thomas Paxton must renew an old friendship with former French spy Camille Leyland, and as love blossoms between them, he must choose between going rogue from the Service or losing her forever.

"Bourne continues to demonstrate a remarkable flair for deftly mixing danger and desire in an impeccably crafted Regency setting." Booklist.

Bourne, Joanna

* The **spymaster's** lady / Joanna Bourne. Berkley, 2008. 384 p. Spymaster series

ISBN 9780425219607

1. Regency period (1811-1820) 2. Women spies 3. Spies -- France 4. Spies -- Great Britain 5. Prisons 6. Secrets 7. Enemies 8. War 9. Napoleonic Wars, 1800-1815 10. Alliances 11. Interpersonal attraction 12. Men/women relations 13. France -- History -- 19th century 14. England -- History -- 19th century 15. Regency romances 16. Historical romances

RUSA Reading List, 2009.

As the fates of nations hang in the balance, Annique Villiers, an elusive spy known as the Fox Cub, meets her match in British spymaster Robert Grey, when they, captured and thrown into prison, form an uneasy alliance in order to survive.

Bowen, Elizabeth, 1899-1973

The **heat** of the day / Elizabeth Bowen. Penguin Books in association with J. Cape, 1985, c1948. 329 p.

ISBN 9780140018448

1. Second World War era (1939-1945) 2. World War II 3. World War II home front 4. London, England 5. Psychological fiction 6. Modern classics

LC 85204051

In London, at the height of the German bombing during World War II, Stella Rodney finds her world turned upside down when she discovers that her lover, Robert, is suspected of selling secrets to the enemy and that his enigmatic pursuer, Harrison, will exchange his silence for Stella herself.

Bowen, Kelly, (Romance fiction writer)

* Between the devil and the duke / Kelly Bowen. Forever, 2017 336 p. Season for scandal

ISBN 9781455563418

1. Regency period (1811-1820) 2. Casinos 3. Women gamblers 4. Cardsharping 5. Card dealers 6. Scandals 7. Aristocracy 8. Dukes and duchesses 9. Interpersonal attraction 10. Men/women relations 11. England 12. Great Britain 13. Regency romances 14. Historical romances

RITA Award, 2018.

When he catches Angelique Archer counting cards at his vingt-et-un table, club owner Alexander Lavoie gives this blonde beauty an offer she can't refuse--until their business arrangement turns into a game of love that neither of them want to lose.

"Bowen (You're the Earl I Want, 2015) again delivers the goods with this exquisitely written historical romance, whose richly nuanced characters, unexpected flashes of dry wit, and superbly sensual love story will have readers sighing happily in satisfaction." Booklist.

Bowen, Kelly, (Romance fiction writer)

I've got my duke to keep me warm / Kelly Bowen. Forever, 2014. 336 p. The Lords of Worth

ISBN 9781455583812

1. Regency period (1811-1820) 2. Abused women 3. Runaway wives, husbands, etc 4. Nobility 5. Veterans 6. Napoleonic Wars veterans 7. Rescues 8. Sexual attraction 9. Men/women relations 10. England 11. Great Britain 12. Regency romances 13. Historical romances

When the husband who abused her, whom she faked her own death to escape, plans to marry again, Gisele Whitby enlists the aid of the disreputable Jamie Moncrief in order to discredit her husband before he can hurt anyone else.

Bowen, Kelly, (Romance fiction writer)

A **rogue** by night / Kelly Bowen. Forever/Grand Central Publishing, 2019. 368 p. Devils of Dover

ISBN 9781478918622

1. Regency period (1811-1820) 2. Aristocracy 3. Smugglers 4. Interpersonal attraction 5. Physicians 6. Smuggling 7. Men/women relations 8. England 9. Great Britain -- History -- Regency, 1811-1820 10. Regency romances 11. Historical romances

Harland Hayward is living a double life as an aristocrat by day and a criminal by night. As a doctor, Harland has the perfect cover to appear in odd places at all hours, although he's chosen this life to save his family from financial ruin ... Katherine Wright thought she was done smuggling. But her father and brother need her help to fulfill one last contract. Which means working with Hayward, even when her instincts tell her that becoming his ally may be a risk to her heart, as well as her life.

Bowen, Peter, 1945-

Badlands / Peter Bowen. St. Martin's Minotaur, 2003. 250 p. Gabriel Du Pre mysteries

ISBN 9780312262525

1. Cults 2. Serial murder investigation 3. Small towns 4. Sheriffs 5. Police 6. Amateur detectives 7. Metis 8. Fiddlers 9. FBI agents 10. Religious fanatics 11. Serial murders 12. Serial murders 13. Montana -- Social life and customs -- 20th century 14. Pacific

Northwest fiction 15. Mysteries

LC 2002037196

Part-time sheriff and fiddler Gabriel Du Pre's investigates the shooting deaths of seven former members of the Host of Yahweh, a California cult recently relocated to Toussaint, Montana's cattle country.

"Montana sheriff Gabriel Du Pre's suspicions are aroused when the Host of Yahweh immediately destroys the ranch buildings, sells the livestock and erects a makeshift metal chapel for secret rites. Soon, reports of mass murders and suicides bring in cautious FBI agents ever mindful of the Waco debacle. Du Pre's blunt speech and sometimes opaque thought patterns can be hard to follow, but his pursuits of wrongdoers over cliffs, canyons and arid river beds are truly riveting." Publishers Weekly.

Bowen, Rhys

The **victory** garden / Rhys Bowen. Lake Union Publishing, 2019 353 p.

ISBN 9781542040129

1. First World War era (1914-1918) 2. Gardens 3. Women and war 4. World War I -- Women 5. Engaged persons 6. Herbalists 7. Diaries 8. Single mothers 9. Victory gardens 10. Herb gardening 11. Soldiers -- Australia 12. Determination in women 13. Devon, England 14. England -- History -- 20th century 15. Historical fiction 16. Gentle reads

Engaged to an Australian pilot during World War I, Emily volunteers to tend the neglected grounds of a Devonshire estate where she finds inspiration and support in an herbalist's long-forgotten journals.

"Lovers of history will better understand the sacrifices in England during the Great War, while romance fans will revel in the engagement and growth of the characters." Library Journal.

Bowles, David (David O.)

Feathered serpent, dark heart of sky : myths of Mexico / David Bowles. Cinco Puntos Press, 2017. 368 p.

ISBN 9781941026717

1. Indians of Central America -- Religion 2. Aztecs -- Religion 3. Mayas -- Religion 4. Olmecs -- Religion 5. Toltecs -- Religion 6. Indians of Mexico 7. Indian mythology -- Mexico 8. Mythology, Aztec 9. Civilization, Pre-Columbian 10. Creation (Religion) 11. Gods and goddesses, Aztec 12. Gods and goddesses, Mayan 13. Mexico 14. Literary fiction

LC 2017021739

A contemporary retelling of the origin myths of Mexico, crafted as a single concrete narrative.

Bowles, Paul, 1910-1999

* The sheltering sky / Paul Bowles. Vintage International, 1990, c1949. 335 p.

ISBN 0679729798

1. Americans in Morocco 2. Travelers 3. Voyages and travels 4. Culture conflict 5. Culture shock 6. Morocco 7. Sahara 8. Psychological fiction 9. Literary fiction 10. Modern classics

LC 89028905

Three Americans drifting through postwar North Africa encounter the limits of human existence in the form of a land and a people utterly alien to them.

Bowman, Conor

* Horace Winter says goodbye / Conor Bowman. Hachette Books Ireland, 2017. 330 p.

ISBN 9781473641808

1. Bankers 2. Midlife crisis 3. Redemption 4. Banks and banking 5. Senior men 6. Butterflies 7. Moths 8. Psychic trauma 9. Retirement 10. Letter writing 11. People with cancer 12. Family relationships

13. Dublin, Ireland 14. Mainstream fiction

Horace Winter has spent forty-seven years working in a Dublin bank, and doesn't, strictly speaking, have friends. But then he meets Amanda and Max. He discovers a letter his father never posted, and goes on a mission to find its addressee; he gets a man jailed (sort of) and rescues his son (sort of); he learns to fly a model airplane and takes his own first flight abroad, to answer one central question: is Horace Winter a Butterfly? Or is he a Moth?

Bowman, David, 1957-2012

Big bang : a nonfiction novel / David Bowman ; introduction by Jonathan Lethem. Little Brown & Co, 2019. xxiii, 595 p.

ISBN 9780316560238

1. 1950s 2. 1960s 3. Social change 4. Celebrities 5. Historical fiction 6. Literary fiction

Set in the 1950's, this epic, Warholian novel presents a brilliant and wholly original take on the years leading up to the Kennedy assassination.

"Bowman's posthumous novel is a masterpiece, certainly long but never tedious because of the rapid focus changes." Library Journal.

Bowman, Valerie

The **accidental** countess / Valerie Bowman. St Martin's Press, 2014. 312 p. Playful brides

ISBN 9781250042088

1. Regency period (1811-1820) 2. Mistaken identity 3. Love triangles 4. Deception 5. Napoleonic Wars veterans 6. Cousins 7. Unrequited love 8. Interpersonal attraction 9. Men/women relations 10. Aristocracy 11. England -- History -- 19th century 12. Regency romances 13. Historical romances

Returning home from the war and to an unwanted arranged marriage, Captain Julian Swift finds himself falling for Lady Cassandra Monroe, his fiancée cousin who, unbeknownst to him, has been in love with him for years.

"The second in Bowman's thoroughly entertaining, Regency-set Playful Brides series (The Unexpected Duchess, 2014) will delight readers with its madcap plot and buoyant sense of humor." Booklist.

Bowman, Valerie

The **unexpected** duchess / Valerie Bowman. St Martin's Press, 2014. 354 p. Playful brides

ISBN 9781250042071

1. Regency period (1811-1820) 2. Aristocracy 3. Love triangles 4. Female friendship 5. Courtship 6. Promises 7. Veterans 8. Interpersonal attraction 9. Men/women relations 10. London, England -- History -- 19th century 11. Regency romances 12. Historical romances

To help her painfully shy friend discourage an unwanted suitor, sharp-tongued Lady Lucy Upton engages in a battle of wits with Lord Derek Hunt and is shocked to discover that tangling with this tenacious man is the most fun she has had in ages.

"Lucy is the Regency shrew to Hunt's gentle-warrior hero who falls for her quick wit, then recognizes the wounded girl behind the virago mask. A fun, smart comedy of errors and a sexy, satisfying romance." Kirkus.

Bowman, Valerie

Secrets of a wedding night / Valerie Bowman. St. Martins Press, 2012. 352 p. Secret brides

ISBN 9781250008954

1. Regency period (1811-1820) 2. Scandals 3. Counts and countesses 4. Pamphlets 5. Widows 6. Seduction 7. Jilted men 8. Women authors 9. Dissenting opinions 10. Men/women relations 11. Interpersonal attraction 12. Marquis and marchionesses 13. London, England -- History -- 19th century 14. Regency romances 15. Historical romances

To stop an innocent girl from marrying the Marquis of Colton, who had broken her own heart five years earlier, young widow Lily Andrews anonymously writes and distributes a pamphlet entitled "Secrets of a Wedding Night" and garners the ire of the Marquis, who issues a wicked challenge.

Box, C. J.

Badlands / C. J. Box. Minotaur Books, 2015. 400 p.. Cassie Dewell novels

ISBN 9780312583217

1. Police misconduct 2. Greed 3. Murder investigation 4. Detectives 5. Ambition in boys 6. Courage in boys 7. Oil industry and trade 8. Accidents 9. Drugs 10. Gangs 11. Mothers and sons 12. Small towns 13. North Dakota 14. Thrillers and suspense

Thanks to a massive oil discovery, once-dying Grimstad, North Dakota has become a sprawling boom town full of newcomers and new houses -- plus drugs, gangs, and violence. Twelve-year-old paperboy Kyle Westergaard, witnesses a vehicle fatally force another car off the road and snatches up a mysterious bag that falls out of it at the scene. The police say it's a single-car accident -- and Kyle learns that bag is something a lot of people want. Narrated by both Kyle and deputy sheriff Cassie Dewell (readers of The Highway will remember her), this atmospheric novel brims with suspense and action. -- Description by Dawn Towery.

"Cassie arrives just as a series of brutal murders signals a war between drug gangs--although the missing duffle bag the criminals are searching for has accidentally wound up in the hands of a special-needs paperboy, 12-year-old Kyle Westergaard. . . . The story's brisk action is broken into alternating sections as Cassie and Kyle try to figure out what's going on and what they must do. The vulnerable boy's plight gives emotional heft to the criminal investigation, balancing cynicism with warm empathy." Publishers Weekly.

Box, C. J.

* The **bitterroots** : a novel / C.J. Box. Minotaur Books, 2019. 352 p. Cassie Dewell novels

ISBN 9781250051059

1. Women private investigators 2. Former police 3. Single mothers 4. Rape investigation 5. Rape 6. Rich families 7. Corruption 8. Betrayal 9. Secrets 10. Ranches 11. Montana 12. Thrillers and suspense

LC 2019006884

Private investigator Cassie Dewell agrees to take a case involving the assault of a young woman, but as she tries to uncover the truth, Cassie finds herself fighting an influential family as well as ghosts from her own past.

Box, C. J.

Blue heaven / C.J. Box. St. Martin's Minotaur, 2008. 352 p.

ISBN 9780312365707

1. Child witnesses 2. Former police 3. Single mothers 4. Bankers 5. Ranchers 6. Trust in children 7. Missing children 8. Runaway children 9. Game wardens 10. Deception 11. Protectiveness in men 12. Land development 13. Fear in men 14. Resistance to land development 15. Families 16. Idaho 17. Mysteries

LC 2007038728

Edgar Allan Poe Award for Best Novel, 2009.

RUSA Reading List, 2009.

Fleeing the killers whom they witnessed committing murder, twelve-year-old Annie and her younger brother William escape into the woods of northern Idaho, not knowing whom they can trust and pursued by the murderers and a group of dirty cops seeking to prevent the youngsters from revealing what they know.

"Two young kids witness a backwoods execution-style murder in their rural Idaho hamlet. Worse yet, the killers-four retired cops from Los Angeles-see the children and begin a dogged pursuit. Struggling rancher Jess Rawlins is surprised to find Annie and William hiding in his barn, but he's wise enough to believe their lurid tale. He also astutely recognizes the goodness of a stranger in town: Eduardo Villatoro, a retired detective, is determined to put one last unsolved case-a big one-to rest. Villatoro's case is the final nail in the coffin for these bad cops, and it's up to Jess and him to save the children. . . . A quick, satisfying, and straightforwardif fairly transparent read." Library Journal.

Box, C. J.

The **disappeared** / C. J. Box. G.P. Putnam's Sons, 2018. 384 p. Joe Pickett novels

ISBN 9780399176623

1. Game wardens 2. Ranches 3. Missing women 4. Falconers 5. Wilderness areas 6. Missing persons investigation 7. Wyoming 8. Thrillers and suspense

Wyoming game warden Joe Pickett tackles two parallel cases involving the disappearance of a prominent British executive and a group of falconers who are being harassed by the feds, a double assignment that catches the attentions of a dangerous adversary.

Box, C. J.

The **highway** / C.J. Box. Minotaur Books, 2013. 400 p. Cody Hoyt novels

ISBN 9780312583200

1. Serial murder investigation 2. Missing women 3. Sisters 4. Serial murders 5. Missing persons investigation 6. Roads 7. Former police 8. Alcoholic men 9. Women detectives 10. Father and adult son 11. Montana 12. Thrillers and suspense

When two teens go missing during a clandestine car trip, alcoholic investigator Cody Hoyt is convinced by his son and former partner to search for answers before discovering similar disappearances on a remote Montana highway that point to the work of a serial killer.

Box, C. J.

* **Long** range / C. J. Box. G. P. Putnam's Sons, 2020. 384 p. Joe Pickett novels

ISBN 9780525538233

1. Attempted murder 2. Judges 3. Game wardens 4. Rescues 5. Assassins 6. Animal attacks 7. Gunshot victims 8. Grizzly bear 9. Thrillers and suspense

Assisting an investigation into a fatal grizzly attack that is not what it seems, Joe Pickett become embroiled in the case of a prominent judge's wife by a would-be assassin who was shooting from a confoundingly long distance.

"Box remains the gold standard among writers of modern western-mystery blends." Booklist.

Box, C. J.

* **Open** season / C.J. Box. G. P. Putnam's Sons, 2001. 320 p. Joe Pickett novels

ISBN 0399147489

1. Hunters 2. Rare and endangered animals 3. Murder investigation 4. Courage in men 5. Poachers 6. Families 7. Game wardens 8. Fathers and daughters 9. Wyoming 10. Thrillers and suspense

LC 00050992

Anthony Award for Best Novel, 2002.

Macavity Award for Best First Mystery Novel, 2002.

As Wyoming game warden Joe Pickett races against time to save an endangered species, he finds himself plunged into a deadly mystery that soon threatens his family and the life he loves.

Box, C. J.

Paradise Valley / C.J. Box. Minotaur Books, 2017. 352 p. Cassie Dewell novels

ISBN 9781250051042

1. Policewomen 2. Serial murderers 3. Serial murder investigation 4. Missing persons investigation 5. Boys with learning disabilities 6. Determination in women 7. Tracking and trailing 8. Unemployed women 9. Missing boys 10. Captives 11. Montana 12. North Dakota 13. Thrillers and suspense

LC 2017011481

Setting a trap for a serial killer she has hunted for three years, investigator Cassie Dewell is disgraced when the operation goes horribly wrong, a situation that is further complicated by the loss of her job, the disappearance of a troubled youth and her determination to catch the killer at any cost.

Box, C. J.

Savage run / C.J. Box. G.P. Putnam's Sons, 2002. 400 p. Joe Pickett novels

ISBN 0399148876

1. Environmentalists 2. Conspiracies 3. Explosions 4. Criminal investigation 5. Eco-terrorists 6. Game wardens 7. Newlyweds 8. Wyoming 9. Thrillers and suspense

LC 2001057872

While investigating a string of bizarre murders, Wyoming game warden Joe Pickett is forced to flee across treacherous terrain with a deadly tracker on his trail.

Box, C. J.

Trophy hunt : a Joe Pickett novel / C.J. Box. G.P. Putnam's Sons, 2004. 336 p. Joe Pickett novels

ISBN 0399152008

1. Mutilation 2. Murder 3. Families 4. Human/alien encounters 5. Animal mutilations 6. Serial murders 7. Cattle mutilations 8. Game wardens 9. Murder investigation 10. Wyoming 11. Thrillers and suspense

LC 2004044389

"With its credible and sensitively drawn characters, loads of interesting tidbits about the natural world and timely plot, this skillfully crafted page-turner should have wide appeal." Publishers Weekly

Box, C. J.

Vicious circle / C.J. Box. G.P. Putnam's Sons, 2017. 367 p. Joe Pickett novels

ISBN 9780399176616

1. Revenge 2. Game wardens 3. Wilderness areas 4. Fathers and daughters 5. Protectiveness in men 6. Fugitives 7. Murder suspects 8. Rodeo performers 9. Revenge 10. Wyoming 11. Thrillers and suspense

Rescuing his daughters from the violent Cates family, game warden Joe Pickett realizes that his new adversaries have plotted revenge against his entire family before teaming up with his friend, Nate, to take defensive steps.

"Box masterfully tightens the suspense until were caught in a vicious circle of our own and unable to stop reading." Booklist.

Box, C. J.

Winterkill : a novel / C.J. Box. G. P. Putnam's Sons, 2003. 372 p. Joe Pickett novels

ISBN 9780399150456

1. Foster parents 2. Survivalists 3. Government investigators 4. Families 5. Cults 6. Kidnapping 7. Child custody 8. Game wardens 9. Murder 10. Murder investigation 11. Fathers and daughters 12. Blizzards 13. Wyoming 14. Thrillers and suspense

LC 2002037120

The arrow-riddled corpse of Lamar Gardiner, district supervisor for the Twelve Sleep National Forest, and the bodies of seven illegally shot elk start Wyoming game warden Joe Pickett on a pursuit that endangers the life of his beloved foster daughter April.

"As the story begins, Joe Pickett, game warden of Wyoming's Twelve Sleep County, is caught in a mountain blizzard with a dead body beside him in his pick-up truck. The body belongs to a much-hated federal bureaucrat, who may have been killed by a group of survivalists calling themselves the Sovereigns. . . .Box handles this controversial material superbly, showing vividly how government rigidity causes human tragedy in the name of patriotism. Pickett remains an utterly sympathetic, Gary Cooperish hero, but as the series developes he has begun to darken noticeably." Booklist.

Box, C. J.

* **Wolf** pack / C.J. Box. G.P. Putnam'S Sons, 2019. 384 p. Joe Pickett novels

ISBN 9780525538196

1. Game wardens 2. Ranches 3. Assassins 4. Witnesses 5. Drone aircraft 6. Organized crime 7. Wilderness areas 8. Wyoming 9. Thrillers and suspense

"The action-packed final quarter of the book ranks among Joe and Nate's best and bloodiest confrontations. Box is the king of contemporary crime fiction set in the West." Publishers Weekly

Boyden, Joseph, 1966-

Three day road : a novel / Joseph Boyden. Viking, 2005. 351 p.

ISBN 9780670034314

1. First World War era (1914-1918) 2. 1910s 3. Native American men -- Friendship 4. Snipers 5. World War I 6. Trench warfare 7. Military campaigns 8. Cree Indians 9. Canadians in Europe 10. Aunt and nephew 11. Native American women healers 12. Morphine addiction 13. War -- Moral and ethical aspects 14. Family relationships 15. Social marginality 16. Canada 17. Europe 18. War stories 19. Historical fiction 20. Literary fiction

LC 2004066149

Books in Canada First Novel Award, 2005.
Canadian Authors Association Literary Awards, MOSAID Technologies Inc. Award for Fiction, 2006.
CBA Libris Award for Fiction Book of the Year, 2006.
Evergreen Award (Ontario), 2006.
Rogers Writers' Trust Fiction Prize, 2005.
Governor General's Literary Awards, English-language Fiction finalist

The nephew of a Canadian Oji-Cree who is the last of a line of healers and diviners, Cree reserve student Xavier enlists in the military during World War I, a conflict throughout which he and his friend, Elijah, are marginalized for their appearances, their culturally enhanced marksmanship, and their disparate views of the war.

Boyden, Joseph, 1966-

Through black spruce / Joseph Boyden. Viking Press, 2009, c2008. 360 p.

ISBN 9780670020577

1. People in comas 2. Missing women 3. Identity (Psychology) 4. Betrayal 5. Loss (Psychology) 6. Resilience (Personal quality) 7. Secrets 8. Dreams 9. Bush pilots 10. Sisters 11. Uncle and niece 12. Cree Indians 13. Ontario 14. Manhattan, New York City 15. Canada 16. Literary fiction

Originally published: Toronto : Viking, 2008.
CBA Libris Award for Fiction Book of the Year, 2009.
Scotiabank Giller Prize, 2008.

Maintaining a bedside vigil for her comatose uncle, Annie Bird remembers a painful search for her missing model sister; while her uncle Will, a legendary Cree bush pilot, ruminates on a tragic betrayal that cost him his family.

Boylan, Jennifer Finney, 1958-

Long black veil / Jennifer Finney Boylan. Crown Pub., 2017. 272 p.

ISBN 9780451496324

1. Cold cases (Criminal investigation) 2. College students 3. Witnesses 4. Prisons 5. Secrets 6. Criminal evidence 7. Innocence (Law) 8. Murder suspects 9. Staged deaths 10. Transgender persons 11. Philadelphia, Pennsylvania 12. Maine 13. Thrillers and suspense

When the body of a college friend is discovered 20 years after her disappearance, Judith, the only witness who can testify to the innocence of the chief suspect, is forced to confront dark secrets from her past that compromise the healthy life she has built for her family.

Boyle, Elizabeth

Along came a duke / Elizabeth Boyle. Avon, 2012. 384 p. Rhymes with love

ISBN 9780062089069

1. Regency period (1811-1820) 2. Mate selection for women 3. Heirs and heiresses 4. Inheritance and succession 5. Single women 6. Arranged marriage 7. Nobility 8. Love triangles 9. Young women 10. Men/women relations 11. Interpersonal attraction 12. England -- Social life and customs -- 19th century 13. London, England -- Social life and customs -- 19th century 14. Regency romances 15. Historical romances

In order to claim a vast fortune, Tabitha Timmons must marry the respectable Mr. Barkworth, but finds herself torn between the money and her feelings for the Duke of Preston, who vows to save her from a passionless union.

Boyle, Elizabeth

And the miss ran away with the rake / Elizabeth Boyle. Avon Books, 2013. 384 p. Rhymes with love

ISBN 9780062089083

1. Regency period (1811-1820) 2. Mate selection 3. Letter writing 4. Nobility 5. Secret identity 6. Seduction 7. Womanizers 8. Single women 9. Young women 10. Men/women relations 11. Interpersonal attraction 12. England -- Social life and customs -- 19th century 13. London, England -- Social life and customs -- 19th century 14. Regency romances 15. Historical romances

Exchanging romantic letters with a very appropriate suitor, one whom she has yet to meet, Daphne Dale is confused by her feelings when a rakish charmer, who is everything she's vowed to avoid, enters her life, testing her practical sensibilities and resolve.

Boyle, T. Coraghessan

The **harder** they come / T.C. Boyle. Ecco Press, 2015 400 p.

ISBN 9780062349378

1. Father and adult son 2. Violence 3. Anger in men 4. Vietnam veterans 5. People with schizophrenia 6. Paranoia 7. Anarchists 8. Shooting 9. Interpersonal relations 10. California 11. Psychological fiction 12. Literary fiction

First published in Great Britain in 2015.

Set in contemporary Northern California, The Harder They Come explores the volatile connections between three damaged people -- an aging ex-Marine and Vietnam veteran, his psychologically unstable son, and the son's paranoid, much older lover -- as they careen towards an explosive confrontation.

"Boyle remains a master at sustaining narrative momentum as the sense of foreboding darkens and deepens." Kirkus.

Boyle, T. Coraghessan

Outside looking in : a novel / T. C. Boyle. HarperCollins Publishers, 2019. 400 p.

ISBN 9780062882981

1. Leary, Timothy, 1920-1996 2. 1960s 3. Hallucinogenic drugs 4. Graduate students 5. Husband and wife 6. L S D use 7. L S D 8. Drug use 9. Drug culture 10. Counterculture 11. Psychologists 12. Marriage 13. Communes 14. Literary fiction

A novel inspired by the controversial psychedelic drug experiments of Timothy Leary traces the impact of LSD and communal living on a 1960s Harvard grad student and his wife.

Boyle, T. Coraghessan

The **relive** box : and other stories / T.C. Boyle. Ecco, 2017 192 p.

ISBN 9780062673398

1. Human nature 2. Memories 3. Interpersonal relations 4. Eccentrics and eccentricities 5. Short stories 6. Humorous stories

LC bl2017032114

A collection of one dozen short stories includes the title piece, in which a "relive box" allows users to re-experience almost any moment from their past, and "The Five-Pound Burrito," in which a man aspires to make the town's largest burrito.

"Boyle's substantial collection is funny, disarming, and crushing, haunting and beautiful . . . ." Booklist.

Boyle, T. Coraghessan

The **Terranauts** / T. Coraghessan Boyle. Ecco Press, 2016. 528 p.

ISBN 9780062349408

1. Biosphere 2 (Project) 2. 1990s 3. Experiments 4. Biotic communities 5. Scientists 6. Wilderness survival 7. Sustainable communities 8. Human nature 9. Human behavior 10. Interpersonal relations 11. Surveillance 12. Human ecology 13. Closed ecological systems 14. Arizona 15. Psychological fiction

Sealed inside a glass enclosure designed as a prototype for a possible off-earth colony, eight Terranauts in the 1990s Arizona desert test their skills in five biome environments that they must protect from skeptics who would sabotage the mission.

"Beneath the high-tech sheen is a rather old-fashioned theme: how idealistic enterprises can crumble owing to the foibles and fragility of human nature. This is one of Boyle's best--and quite possibly one of the best of the year." Library Journal.

Boyle, T. Coraghessan

* The **tortilla** curtain / T. Coraghessan Boyle. Viking, 1995. 355 p.

ISBN 9780670856046

1. Undocumented immigrants 2. Race relations 3. Rich people 4. Suburban life 5. Undocumented workers 6. Mexicans in California 7. Los Angeles, California 8. Los Angeles County, California -- Race relations 9. Political fiction 10. Mainstream fiction 11. Literary fiction

LC 95-1970

The lives of two very different couples--wealthy Los Angeles liberals Delaney and Kyra Mossbacher, and Candido and America Rincon, a pair of Mexican undocumented immigrants--suddenly collide, in a story that unfolds from the shifting viewpoints of the various characters.

"What Boyle does, and does well, is lay on the line our national cult of hypocrisy. Comically and painfully he details the snug wastefulness of the haves and the vile misery of the have-nots. . . . Americans of every stripe will find themselves rooting for Candido and America, right up to the riproaring deus ex machina ending that screams out that we are all in this together." The Nation.

Boyle, T. Coraghessan

World's end : a novel / T. Coraghessan Boyle. Viking, 1987. 456 p.

ISBN 9780670814893

1. Dutch Americans 2. Families -- History 3. Class struggle 4. Social conflict 5. Betrayal 6. Loyalty 7. Family feuds 8. Father-deserted children 9. Hudson Valley 10. New York (State) -- Social conditions -- 20th century 11. New York (State) -- Social conditions -- 17th century 12. Parallel narratives 13. Family sagas

LC 87040023

PEN-Faulkner Award, 1988.

Walter Van Brunt, woozy with pot, cheap wine, and sex, collides with his own historical roots when he crashes his motorcycle into a historical marker along the highway.

"The themes Mr. Boyle develops as his story shuttles between epochs make us grasp in new terms their connection with the American social and political experiment. His mastery of history is the secret of the accomplishment here. Mr. Boyle has lost none of the qualities that marked him a wit writer before, but now he has challenged his own disengagement; passion, need and belief breathe with striking force and freedom through this smashing good novel." New York Times Book Review.

Boyle, T. Coraghessan

The **women** : a novel / T. Coraghessan Boyle. Viking, 2009. 464 p.

ISBN 9780670020416

1. Wright, Frank Lloyd, 1867-1959 Relations with women 2. 20th century 3. Architects 4. Husband and wife 5. Men/women relations 6. Biographical fiction 7. Historical fiction 8. Literary fiction

LC 2008042462

A tale inspired by the life of Frank Lloyd Wright is presented from the perspectives of four very different women who loved him and offers insight into the eminent architect's enduring struggles against conventional boundaries.

"Boyle's latest novel takes on the architect Frank Lloyd Wright by examining his notoriously tumultuous relationships with four women, each unique in her own histrionic way. Narrated in reverse chronological order by a fictional Japanese apprentice, the book is extremely readable and deftly builds a portrait of the artist as pure egoist. Unfortunately, the novel avoids any sustained consideration of Wright's relationship to his art--a passion arguably more important in forming his genius than any of the women in his life were. Still, it proves an effective showcase for

Boyle's own strengths as a craftsman. His prose is full of vivid descriptions and turns of phrase that pop with a preternatural precision." The New Yorker.

Boyle, T. Coraghessan

When the killing's done : a novel / T. Coraghessan Boyle. Viking, 2011. 369 p.

ISBN 9780670022328

1. Women biologists 2. Invasive species -- Control 3. Environmentalists 4. Social conflict 5. Island life -- California 6. Santa Cruz Island, California 7. Channel Islands, California 8. Mainstream fiction

Alma Boyd Takesue, a National Park Service biologist, is in charge of preserving the Channel Islands' native animals, which means removing the rats and feral pigs from the island chain. However, businessman Dave LaJoy and folksinger Anise Reed staunchly oppose Alma's plans to kill the rats and pigs, and actively work against her.

"The novel never reduces its narrative to polemics--there are no heroes here--while underscoring the difficult decisions that those who consider themselves on the side of the angels must face. Narrative propulsion is laced with delicious irony in this winning novel." Kirkus.

Boyle, William, 1978-

City of margins : a novel / William Boyle. Pegasus Books, 2020. 320 p.

ISBN 9781643133188

1. 1990s 2. City life 3. Organized crime 4. Loss (Psychology) 5. Revenge 6. Neighborhoods 7. Working-class 8. Brooklyn, New York City 9. Noir fiction

The lives of several lost souls intersect in gritty 1990s south Brooklyn, from a disgraced ex-cop with blood on his hands to the grieving mother of a suicide victim.

"Battered by loss and unrealized dreams, Boyle's characters are vividly drawn and painfully real. Fans of literary crime novelists such as George Pelecanos and Richard Price will be highly rewarded." Publishers Weekly.

Boyle, William, 1978-

The lonely witness / William Boyle. Pegasus Books, 2018. 272 p.

ISBN 9781681777955

1. Murder witnesses 2. Murder investigation 3. Women amateur detectives 4. Murderers 5. Volunteers 6. Caregivers 7. City dwellers 8. Young women 9. Lifestyle change 10. Brooklyn, New York City 11. New York City 12. Mysteries

A former party girl who now helps house-bound seniors in the Gravesend neighborhood of Brooklyn agrees to help a woman whose usual caretaker is missing and ends up witnessing a murder that she doesn't report and develops a fascination with the killer.

Boyne, John, 1971-

The absolutist / John Boyne. Other Press, 2012, c2011. 309 p.

ISBN 9781590515525

1. Homosexuality 2. Soldiers 3. Young men 4. Secrets 5. War -- Psychological aspects 6. World War I 7. Military campaigns 8. Western Front (World War I) 9. World War I veterans 10. Trench warfare 11. Male friendship 12. Civil disobedience 13. War stories 14. Historical fiction 15. Literary fiction

LC 2012000433

Originally published : London : Doubleday, c2011.

In September 1919, 21-year-old Tristan Sadler takes a train from London to Norwich to deliver some letters to the sister of a man he fought alongside of during World War I, but the letters are not the real reason for Tristan's visit.

"A thought-provoking and surprising page-turner that for some readers may recall Ian McEwan's Atonement, another novel with themes of war and recrimination." Library Journal.

Boyne, John, 1971-

Crippen : a novel of murder / John Boyne. Thomas Dunne Books, 2006. 352 p.

ISBN 9780312343583

1. Crippen, Hawley Harvey, 1862-1910 2. Edwardian era (1901-1914) 3. Murderers -- Great Britain 4. Physicians 5. Fugitives 6. Ship passengers 7. Wife-killing 8. Crimes against married women 9. Men/women relations 10. Mistresses 11. Women impostors 12. Police 13. Cruise ships 14. Transatlantic voyages 15. Voyages and travels 16. Great Britain -- History -- Edward VII, 1901-1910 17. Historical mysteries 18. Mysteries

LC 2005056011

"Chief Inspector Walter Dew of Scotland Yard did not expect the house to be empty. Nor did he expect to find a body in the cellar. Buried under the flagstones are the remains of Cora Crippen, former music-hall singer and wife of Dr. Hawley Crippen. No one would have thought the quiet, unassuming Dr. Crippen capable of murder, yet the doctor and his mistress have disappeared from London, and now a full-scale hunt for them has begun." -- Jacket.

"Boyne starts with the basic facts. . . but he has altered the story to suit his dramatic needs and authorial whims. The result of his reinvention is a dark comedy that is supremely readable, always suspenseful, sometimes laugh-out-loud funny and, finally, a monumental piece of misogyny. In Boyne's sardonic telling, Cora Crippen was a monster who richly deserved to die, and her long-suffering husband was a man more sinned against than sinning." Washington Post Book World.

Boyne, John, 1971-

A history of loneliness : a novel / John Boyne. Farrar, Straus and Giroux, 2015, c2014. 352 p.

ISBN 9780374171339

1. Priests 2. Child sexual abuse 3. Responsibility 4. Catholic Church and child sexual abuse 5. Clergy 6. Deception 7. Secrets 8. Self-deception 9. Ireland 10. Psychological fiction

LC 2014027629

Originally published: London : Doubleday,

A longtime priest in Ireland witnesses a dark period for the Catholic Church in the face of allegations against his colleagues, a downfall that reopens a wound from his past and forces him to recognize his own complicity.

Boyne, John, 1971-

The house of special purpose / John Boyne. Other Press, 2013, c2009. 480 .

ISBN 9781590515983

1. Romanov, House of 2. Romanov Dynasty (1613-1917) 3. 20th century 4. Reminiscing in old age 5. Courts and courtiers 6. Bodyguards -- Russia 7. Russians in England 8. Memory -- Psychological aspects 9. Homecomings 10. Revolutions -- Russia 11. Russia -- History -- Nicholas II, 1894-1917 12. Russia -- History -- 1914-1917 13. St Petersburg, Russia -- History -- To 1917 14. Parallel narratives 15. Historical fiction

Eighty-year-old Georgy Jachmenev is haunted by his past -- a past of death, suffering, and scandal that will stay with him until the end of his days. Living in England with his beloved wife, Zoya, Georgy prepares to make one final journey back to the Russia he once knew and loved, the Russia that both destroyed and defined him. As Georgy remembers days gone by, we are transported to Saint Petersburg, to the Winter Palace of the tsar, in the early twentieth century -- a time of change, threat, and bloody revolution. As Georgy overturns the most painful stone of all, we uncover the story of the house of special purpose.

Boyne, John, 1971-

The **heart's** invisible furies / John Boyne. Hogarth Press, 2017. 592 p.

ISBN 9781524760786

1. 20th century 2. Single mothers 3. Pariahs 4. Discrimination 5. Growing up 6. Mothers and sons 7. Survival 8. Teenage mothers 9. Gay men 10. Eccentrics and eccentricities 11. Hypocrisy 12. Toleration 13. Ireland -- Social conditions -- 20th century 14. United States -- Social conditions -- 20th century 15. Netherlands -- Social conditions -- 20th century 16. Picaresque fiction 17. Coming-of-age stories 18. Literary fiction

Originally published: London : Doubleday, 2017.

Longlisted for the Andrew Carnegie Medal for Excellence in Fiction, 2018.

In 1945, Cyril Avery was born to an unmarried teenager (the book opens with a dramatic scene in a rural Irish church that sets this up with relish) and adopted by a wealthy if rather eccentric Dublin couple. As readers, we visit Cyril every seven years, as he grows and comes to terms with his homosexuality in a violently repressive Ireland, flees his home country, and falls in love. An absorbing story, this novel offers richly drawn characters, plausibly life-altering choices, and an often humorous writing style. -- Description by Shauna Griffin

"Often quite funny, the story nevertheless has its sadness, sometimes approaching tragedy. Utterly captivating and not to be missed." Booklist.

Boyne, John, 1971-

* A **ladder** to the sky / John Boyne. Hogarth Press, 2018. 362 p.

ISBN 9781984823014

1. 1980s 2. Authors 3. Ambition in men 4. Manipulation by men 5. Fame 6. Writing 7. Secrets 8. Betrayal 9. Plagiarism 10. Publishers and publishing 11. West Berlin, Germany 12. Literary fiction

Aspiring writer Maurice Swift, whose desire for fame exceeds his talent, uses a chance meeting with celebrated novelist Erich Ackermann to obtain secrets about Ackermann's wartime activities, which becomes material for his first novel.

"Boynes fast-paced, white-knuckle plot, accompanied by delightfully sardonic commentary on the ego, insecurities, and pitfalls of those involved in the literary world, makes for a truly engrossing experience." Publishers Weekly.

Bradbury, Jamey

The **wild** inside : a novel / Jamey Bradbury. William Morrow, 2018. 290 p.

ISBN 9780062741998

1. Wilderness areas 2. Violence against women 3. Strangers 4. Women trackers 5. Families 6. Secrets 7. Sled dogs 8. Loss (Psychology) 9. Alaska 10. Coming-of-age stories

LC 2017042752

Spending her days tracking and running with her dogs in the Alaskan wilderness, Iditarod contender Tracy survives a mysterious encounter in the woods and begins to question the agenda of a stranger who she fears may be targeting her family.

Bradbury, Ray, 1920-2012

Bradbury stories : 100 of his most celebrated tales / Ray Bradbury. William Morrow, 2003. 912 p.

ISBN 006054242X

1. Space flight 2. Space exploration 3. Mars (Planet) 4. Science fiction 5. Short stories

LC 2003042189

"100 of his most celebrated tales."

A retrospective collection of one hundred short stories features pieces written after 1943 includes both popular favorites and lesser-known works of distinction.

"This massive retrospective of self-selected Bradbury stories offers a compendium of his eccentrics, misfits, losers, and small-town dreamers, who typically inhabit an uncanny setting or confront a strange, unsettling situation." Library Journal.

Bradbury, Ray, 1920-2012

* **Dandelion** wine : a novel / Ray Bradbury ; with an introduction from the author. Avon Books, 1999. xiv, 267 p.

ISBN 0380977265

1. 1920s 2. Twelve-year-old boys -- Illinois 3. Growing up 4. Families 5. Family relationships 6. Old and new things 7. Dandelions 8. Wine and wine making 9. Life 10. Boys and nature 11. Friendship 12. Loss (Psychology) 13. Summer 14. Self-discovery in boys 15. Small town life -- Illinois 16. Illinois 17. Coming-of-age stories

LC 98093914

Originally published: Garden City, N.Y. : Doubleday,

Sequel: Farewell summer.

A summer in the life of a 12 year old boy in 1928 in the hamlet of Green Town, Ill.

"The writing is beautiful and the characters are wonderful living people. A rare reading experiencehighly recommended to all libraries." Library Journal.

Bradbury, Ray, 1920-2012

* **Fahrenheit** 451 / Ray Bradbury. Simon & Schuster, 1993, c1953. 190 p.

ISBN 9780671870362

1. Censorship 2. Dystopias 3. Totalitarianism 4. Banned books 5. Conformity 6. Reading 7. Book burning 8. Fires 9. Political persecution 10. Mass media 11. Near future 12. Dystopian fiction 13. Social science fiction 14. Science fiction

LC 93010885

Originally published: New York : Ballantine Books, 1953.

A totalitarian regime has ordered all books to be destroyed, but one of the book burners, Guy Montag, suddenly realizes their merit.

Bradbury, Ray, 1920-2012

The **illustrated** man / Ray Bradbury. Avon Books, 1997, c1951. 288 p.

ISBN 0380973847

1. Tattooing 2. Storytelling 3. Magic 4. Technology and civilization 5. Husband and wife 6. Children 7. Space flight 8. Virtual reality 9. Aliens 10. Space colonies 11. Prejudice 12. Earth -- Invasions 13. Mars (Planet) 14. Short stories 15. Horror 16. Science fiction 17. Science fantasy

Short stories originally published between 1948 and 1951.

Originally published: New York : Doubleday, 1951.

Eighteen imaginative science fiction stories--including the title story in which a tattooist's needle creates a canvas that captures humankind's destiny--range from the not-so-ordinary world of middle America to the vast reaches of outer space as they explore themes of love, madness, and death.

Bradbury, Ray, 1920-2012

* The **Martian** chronicles : the fortieth anniversary edition / Ray Bradbury. Doubleday, 1990, c1950. xi, 205 p.

ISBN 0385050607

1. Space colonies 2. Human/alien encounters 3. Martians 4. Space exploration 5. Life on other planets 6. Space flight 7. Culture conflict 8. Loneliness 9. Social isolation 10. Plague 11. Diseases 12. Secrets 13. Prejudice 14. Frontier and pioneer life 15. Small town life 16. Mars (Planet) 17. Social science fiction 18. Science fiction 19. Short stories

LC 90044362

Includes a new foreword, as well as "a story excised from the original book."

Originally published: Garden City, N.Y. : Doubleday, 1950.

Interconnected, chronological stories of Earth's settlement of Mars include tales of human interaction with one another and with the Martians, interplanetary interracial strife, self-doubt, and the metamorphosis of humanity.

Bradbury, Ray, 1920-2012

* **Something** wicked this way comes / Ray Bradbury. Avon Books, 1998. 304 p.

ISBN 0380729407

1. Carnivals -- Illinois 2. Good and evil 3. Thirteen-year-old boys -- Illinois 4. Boys -- Friendship 5. Best friends -- Illinois 6. Fathers and sons -- Illinois 7. Halloween 8. Janitors -- Illinois 9. Secrets 10. Temptation 11. Wishing and wishes 12. Self-discovery in boys 13. Small town life -- Illinois 14. Illinois 15. Horror 16. Coming-of-age stories 17. Fantasy classics

Originally published: New York : Simon and Schuster, 1962.

Story of two young boys who begin to encounter evil secrets when a lightning rod salesman gives them one of his contraptions covered with mystical symbols.

Bradford, Barbara Taylor, 1933-

Just rewards / Barbara Taylor Bradford. St. Martin's Press, 2006. 496 p. Harte Family

ISBN 9780312307066

1. 2000s (Decade) 2. Mothers and daughters 3. Rich families 4. Family relationships 5. Rich women 6. Businesspeople 7. Sisters 8. Divorced women 9. Mothers of kidnapping victims 10. Intergenerational relations 11. Family businesses 12. Kidnapping 13. Women -- Family relationships 14. Women -- Interpersonal relations 15. Men/women relations 16. Family secrets 17. London, England 18. New York City 19. Family sagas

LC 2005052095

Sequel to: Unexpected blessings.

Emma Harte's great-granddaughters find themselves at a crossroads involving family values, traditions, new romance, and business, in the final episode of the Harte family saga.

"Series devotees will take heart at the ending, which hints that Ainsley's evil will survive his death and the struggles will continue offstage even if Bradford lays down her golden pen." Publishers Weekly.

Bradford, Barbara Taylor, 1933-

Master of his fate / Barbara Taylor Bradford. St Martins Pr., 2018. 448 p. House of Falconer

ISBN 9781250187390

1. Victorian era (1837-1901) 2. 1880s 3. Businesspeople 4. Men and success 5. Life change events 6. Ambition in men 7. Business failures 8. Business success 9. Determination in men 10. Self-confidence in men 11. England -- History -- Victoria, 1837-1901 12. Great Britain -- Social life and customs -- Victoria, 1837-1901 13. Historical fiction 14. Family sagas

A charismatic and ambitious businessman in Victorian England faces the tragic ruin of everything he has worked to achieve before a royal summons gives him a chance to prove his talents.

Bradford, Barbara Taylor, 1933-

Power of a woman / Barbara Taylor Bradford. HarperCollins, 1997. 335 p.

ISBN 0060182687

1. Widows 2. Family secrets 3. Revenge 4. Forties (Age) 5. Rich women 6. Mother and child 7. Romantic suspense 8. Glitz and glamour novels

A family tragedy forces successful career woman Stephanie Jardine to come to terms with the secrets of her past and a stormy relationship

Bradford, Barbara Taylor, 1933-

* A **woman** of substance / Barbara Taylor Bradford. Doubleday, 1979. 755 p. Harte Family

ISBN 0385120508

1. Businesspeople 2. Power (Social sciences) 3. Rich women 4. Family relationships 5. Family businesses 6. Family sagas

LC 77009231

Sequel: Hold the dream.

Emma Harte, an enormously wealthy and powerful self-made woman, learns that her four children are plotting to sell the business that she founded, which leads her to summon everyone to her Yorkshire estate for a showdown

Bradley, Anna

A **season** of ruin / Anna Bradley. Berkley Sensation, 2016 294 p. Sutherland scandals

ISBN 9780425282649

1. Regency period (1811-1820) 2. Womanizers 3. Debutantes 4. Scandals 5. Reputation 6. Gossiping and gossips 7. Mate selection 8. Interpersonal attraction 9. Men/women relations 10. London, England 11. England -- Social life and customs -- 19th century 12. Great Britain -- History -- Regency, 1811-1820 13. Regency romances 14. Historical romances

When faced with a scandal that could destroy her hopes of marriage to a respectable gentleman, Lily Somerset must convince Robyn Sutherland to be her escort for the season in an attempt to repair her tattered reputation.

Bradley, Anna

A **wicked** way to win an earl / Anna Bradley. Berkley, 2015 296 p. Sutherland scandals

ISBN 9780425282632

1. Regency period (1811-1820) 2. Earls and countesses 3. Womanizers 4. Enemies 5. Seduction 6. Family feuds 7. Scandals 8. Interpersonal attraction 9. Men/women relations 10. Kent, England 11. England -- Social life and customs -- 19th century 12. Great Britain -- History -- Regency, 1811-1820 13. Regency romances 14. Historical romances

To appease her sister, Della Somerset, who despises the privileged ton, agrees to attend a party at the Sutherland estate, home to the infamous scoundrel Alec Sutherland, and catches the eye of the notorious rogue whose intentions are less than honorable.

Bradley, C. Alan, 1938-

As chimney sweepers come to dust : a Flavia de Luce novel / Alan Bradley. Delacorte Press, 2015. 392 p. Flavia De Luce mysteries

ISBN 9780345539939

1. Girl detectives 2. Boarding schools 3. Murder 4. Girl scientists 5. Intelligence 6. Sisters 7. Eleven-year-old girls 8. Canada 9. Mysteries

LC 2014029962

Young chemist and aspiring detective Flavia de Luce once again uses her knowledge of poisons and her indefatigable spirit to solve a crime, but this time she leaves behind the English countryside and enters the unexpectedly unsavory world of Canadian boarding schools.

"Flavias resourcefulness away from her English village with a whole new set of well-drawn characters is reason to rejoice. Fans of Dorothy Sayers, Gladys Mitchell, and Agatha Christie will delight in this engaging series." Library Journal.

Bradley, C. Alan, 1938-

The **golden** tresses of the dead : a Flavia de Luce novel / Alan Bradley. Delacorte Press, 2019. 400 p. Flavia De Luce mysteries

ISBN 9780345540027

1. 1950s 2. Girl detectives 3. Girl scientists 4. Weddings 5. Wedding cakes 6. Private investigators 7. Investigations 8. Family estates 9. Families 10. England 11. Historical mysteries

LC 2018039374

Setting up shop to solve crimes, 12-year-old Flavia de Luce, aided by trusty gardener Dogger, investigates a grisly discovery in her older sister's wedding cake.

"Bradley, who has few peers at combining fair-play clueing with humor and has fun mocking genre conventions, shows no sign of running out of ideas." Publishers Weekly.

Bradley, C. Alan, 1938-

The **grave's** a fine and private place : a Flavia de Luce novel / Alan Bradley. Delacorte Press, 2018. 432 p. Flavia De Luce mysteries

ISBN 9780345539991

1. 1950s 2. Girl detectives 3. Girl scientists 4. Boating 5. Dead 6. Sisters 7. Murder investigation 8. Loss (Psychology) 9. England 10. Historical mysteries

LC 2017031500

Joining her older sisters for a recuperative boating trip in the aftermath of a devastating tragedy, 12-year-old Flavia de Luce discovers a body in the water near the church of a murderous vicar.

Bradley, C. Alan, 1938-

I am half-sick of shadows : a Flavia de Luce novel / Alan Bradley. Delacorte Press, 2011. 384 p. Flavia De Luce mysteries

ISBN 9780385344012

1. Filmmaking 2. Actors and actresses 3. Murder investigation 4. Film industry and trade 5. Girl detectives 6. Eleven-year-old girls 7. Detectives 8. England 9. Mysteries 10. Christmas stories

After the whole village of Bishop's Lacey descends on Flavia de Luce's family's estate during a raging blizzard to watch the filming of a movie, a person ends up dead, strangled by a length of film, and the 11-year-old budding chemist must find the killer.

Bradley, C. Alan, 1938-

A **red** herring without mustard / Alan Bradley. Delacorte Press, 2011. 384 p. Flavia De Luce mysteries

ISBN 9780385342322

1. Romani women 2. Girl detectives 3. Murder investigation 4. Girl scientists 5. Poisons 6. Missing children 7. Intelligence 8. Eleven-year-old girls 9. England 10. Mysteries

Includes reading group notes.

When a Gypsy woman is wrongly accused of kidnapping a local child, precocious young Flavia de Luce draws on her encyclopedic knowledge of poisons and Gypsy lore to discern what really happened while investigating the mystery of her own mother's fate.

"Think preteen Nancy Drew, only savvier and a lot richer, and you have Flavia de Luce, an 11-year-old sleuth of the English gentry who's morbidly interested in both corpses and poison (she's got a chemistry lab in the attic). When a body turns up on the lawn of the family estate skewered by an heirloom sterling lobster fork she gets to work. Don't be fooled by Flavia's age or the 1950s setting: A Red Herring isn't a dainty tea-and-crumpets sort of mystery. It's shot through with real grit." Entertainment Weekly.

Bradley, C. Alan, 1938-

Speaking from among the bones : a Flavia de Luce novel / Alan Bradley. Delacorte Press, 2013. 400 p. Flavia De Luce mysteries

ISBN 9780385344036

1. Girl detectives 2. Murder investigation 3. Masks 4. Murder 5. Girl scientists 6. Intelligence 7. Sisters 8. Fathers and daughters 9. Eleven-year-old girls 10. England 11. Mysteries

LC 2012028396

When the tomb of Saint Tancred, the patron saint of Bishop's Lacey, is opened on the five-hundredth anniversary of his death and the body of the missing church organist, Mr. Collicutt, is discovered inside, eleven-year-old amateur detective Flavia de Luce launches her own investigation into his death.

Bradley, C. Alan, 1938-

* The **sweetness** at the bottom of the pie / Alan Bradley. Delacorte Press, 2009. 272 p. Flavia De Luce mysteries

ISBN 9780385342308

1. 1950s 2. Girl scientists 3. Girl detectives 4. Murder investigation 5. Intelligence 6. Sisters 7. Fathers and daughters 8. Eleven-year-old girls 9. Stamp collecting 10. Widowers 11. England 12. Mysteries

LC 2008041787

Agatha Award for Best First Novel, 2009.

Amelia Bloomer List, 2010

Arthur Ellis Award for Best First Novel, 2010.

Macavity Award for Best First Mystery Novel, 2010.

Eleven-year-old Flavia de Luce, an aspiring chemist with a passion for poison, begins her adventure when a dead bird is found on the doorstep of her family's mansion in the summer of 1950, thus propelling her into a mystery that involves an investigation into a man's murder where her father is the main suspect.

"Mystery fans, Anglophiles, and science buffs will delight in this book and may come away with a slightly altered view of what is possible for a headstrong girl to achieve." School Library Journal.

Bradley, C. Alan, 1938-

Thrice the brinded cat hath mew'd : a Flavia de Luce novel / Alan Bradley. Delacorte Press, 2016. 331 p. Flavia De Luce mysteries

ISBN 9780345539960

1. Girl detectives 2. Homecomings 3. Murder 4. Girl scientists 5. Intelligence 6. Fathers 7. England 8. Mysteries

LC 2016006913

Excitedly sailing home to England after being ejected from her stuffy young ladies' school, 12-year-old Flavia receives news of her father's serious illness and is surrounded by annoying family members before stumbling onto a murder scene where the only witness is the cat.

Bradley, C. Alan, 1938-

The **weed** that strings the hangman's bag : a Flavia de Luce mystery / Alan Bradley. Delacorte Press, 2010. 364 p. Flavia De Luce mysteries

ISBN 9780385342315

1. 1950s 2. Puppeteers 3. Girl detectives 4. Poisons 5. Murder investigation 6. Eleven-year-old girls 7. Detectives 8. England 9. Mysteries

LC 2009043002

Flavia de Luce applies her skills in the chemistry lab to solving the murder of a master puppeteer, a case that is further complicated by her tormenting sisters.

Braffet, Kelly, 1976-

* **Last** seen leaving : a novel / Kelly Braffet. Houghton Mifflin, 2006. 272 p.

ISBN 9780618441440

1. Mothers and daughters 2. Father-separated girls 3. Family relationships 4. Missing women 5. Women college students 6. Hitchhiking 7. Women drifters 8. Strangers 9. Escapes 10. Missing persons investigation 11. Serial murders 12. Psychological fiction

LC 2005037965

When Miranda, a young drifter, vanishes after being picked up by a passing stranger following a car accident, no one realizes that she is missing for two months or that her highway rescuer could be tied to rumors of a serial killer stalking young women.

"Both Anne and Miranda tell their sides of the story, allowing Braffet to flesh out their strained relationship. It is a story about the fragility of relationships as well as the secrets we keep and the lies we tell ourselves to get us through the pain of love and loss." Booklist.

Bragg, Melvyn, 1939-

A **son** of war / Melvyn Bragg. Sceptre, 2001. 426 p. Soldier's return quartet

ISBN 0340734159

1. 1940s 2. Teenage boys -- Family relationships 3. World War II veterans 4. Husband and wife 5. Children of veterans 6. Eight-year-old boys 7. Eight-year-olds 8. Fathers and sons 9. Piano teachers 10. Brothers and sisters 11. World War II -- Post-war aspects 12. Postwar life 13. England 14. Domestic fiction 15. Coming-of-age stories

LC 2001536049

"A hauntingly evocative slice of postwar life." Booklist.

Bragi Olafsson, 1962-

The **pets** / Bragi Olafsson ; translated from the Icelandic by Janice Balfour. Open Letter, 2008, c2001. 157 p.

ISBN 9781934824016

1. Men -- Psychology 2. Housesitting 3. Misadventures 4. Fear in men 5. Options, alternatives, choices 6. Reykjavik, Iceland 7. Black humor 8. Translations -- Icelandic to English

LC 2008926608

Originally published as Gaeludyrin: Reykjavik : Bjartur, 2001.

When ex-mental patient and former pet-sitter Havard arrives at the doorstep of his apartment, Emil hides under the bed to avoid him but finds himself stuck there as Havard breaks in and throws a raucous party inside.

Braithwaite, Oyinkan

My sister, the serial killer : a novel / Oyinkan Braithwaite. Random House Inc., 2018 160 p.

ISBN 9780385544238

1. Women serial murderers 2. Family relationships 3. Sisters 4. Sisterhood 5. Serial murders 6. Love triangles 7. Men/women relations 8. Nigeria 9. Lagos, Nigeria 10. Satirical fiction 11. Black humor

LC 2018013372

Anthony Award for Best First Novel, 2019.

Shortlisted for The Women's Prize for Fiction, 2019.

Longlisted for the Booker Prize, 2019.

Realizing that her beautiful, beloved younger sister has murdered yet another boyfriend, an embittered Nigerian woman works to direct suspicion away from the family, until a handsome doctor she fancies asks for her sister's number.

Bram, Christopher

Lives of the circus animals : a novel / Christopher Bram. HarperCollins, 2003. 341 p.

ISBN 0060542535

1. Dramatists, American 2. Personal assistants 3. Actors and actresses 4. Gay actors 5. Theater critics 6. Theatrical producers and directors 7. Gay men -- Sexuality 8. Celebrities 9. Brothers and sisters 10. Theater 11. Musicals 12. Theater life 13. Performing arts 14. Unrequited love 15. Gay men and AIDS 16. Birthday parties 17. Sexuality 18. Friendship 19. Broadway, New York City 20. New York City -- Social life and customs 21. Psychological fiction

LC 2002192195

Lambda Literary Award for Gay Men's Fiction, 2003.

A comedy of manners explores themes of love, work, and success in the world behind the scenes of contemporary New York theater.

"Bram has a sophisticated understanding of celebrity and the intersection of gay and straight worlds. His savvy--and his easy familiarity with the New York theater scene--gives edge and nuance to this witty entertainment." Publishers Weekly.

Brand, Max, 1892-1944

Beyond the outposts / Max Brand. Leisure Books, 2001, c1997. 254 p.

ISBN 0843948477

1. Dakota Indians 2. Westerns

Previously published: Unity, Me. : Five Star, c1997.

From pre-Civil War Virginia to the distant prairies of the far West, the epic journey of young Lew Dorsey begins as he searches the frontier for his father--an escaped convict on the run-- but finds much more than he was looking for.

Brand, Max, 1892-1944

Chinook / Max Brand. Leisure Books, 2002. 269 p.

ISBN 0843950579

1. Gold mines and mining -- Alaska 2. Sled dogs -- Alaska 3. Alaska 4. Adventure stories 5. Westerns

Traveling to Alaska with Andrew Steen and his dog team during the gold rush of 1898, Joe Harney befriends Kate Winslow, a woman traveling alone by dogsled to the same destination, and finds himself drawn into the danger and intrigue surrounding her.

Brand, Max, 1892-1944

* The **collected** stories of Max Brand / Edited, with story prefaces by Robert and Jane Easton. Introduction by William Bloodworth University of Nebraska Press, 1994. 342 p.

ISBN 0803212445

1. Short stories 2. Westerns

LC 93043938

Includes eighteen stories taken from different genres.

Collects eighteen short stories by the noted writer of westerns, including "Above the Law," "Outcast Breed," "The Sun Stood Still," "Interns Can't Take Money," and "The Strange Villa"

Brand, Max, 1892-1944

Max Brand's best western stories / edited, with a biographical introduction by William F. Nolan. Dodd, Mead, 1981. 228 p.

ISBN 0396079849

1. Gunfighters 2. Outlaws 3. Frontier and pioneer life 4. The West (United States) -- History -- 19th century 5. Westerns 6. Short stories

Brand, Max, 1892-1944

*The **Stingaree** / Max Brand. R. Bentley, 1981, c1930. 216 p.

ISBN 0837604613

1. The West (Canada) 2. Westerns

Half Indian and half white, Jimmy Green is only 13 when the Stingaree arrives in his French-Canadian town searching for the murderer of his partner.

Brandreth, Benet

The **assassin** of Verona / Benet Brandreth. Pegasus Books, 2019, c2017. 384 p. William Shakespeare novels (Benet Brandreth)

ISBN 9781681778761

1. Shakespeare, William, 1564-1616 2. Renaissance (1300-1600) 3. 16th century 4. Papacy 5. Assassins 6. Intrigue 7. Actors and actresses 8. Espionage 9. Spies 10. Dramatists, English 11. British in Italy 12. London, England -- History -- 16th century 13. Venice, Italy -- History -- 1508-1797 14. Historical mysteries

Originally published: London : Zaffre, c2017.

Venice, 1585. Threatened daily by Papal assassins, William Shakespeare and his friends, Oldcastle and Hemminges, possess a deadly secret - the names of the Catholic spies in England who seek to destroy Queen Elizabeth. Before long the Pope's agents will close in and fleeing the city will be the players' only option. In Verona, a duke's daughter, Aemilia, is struggling to conceal an affair with her cousin. But darker times are ahead as Father Thornhill is determined to seek out any who don't conform to the pope's agenda. Events will converge in the forests around Verona as plots are hatched and discovered, and disguises are adopted and discarded. Can Shakespeare and his friends escape with their secrets and their lives?

Brandreth, Benet

The **spy** of Venice / Benet Brandreth. Pegasus Books, 2018, c2016. xii, 434 p. William Shakespeare novels (Benet Brandreth)

ISBN 9781681777986

1. Shakespeare, William, 1564-1616 2. Renaissance (1300-1600) 3. 16th century 4. Assassins 5. Intrigue 6. Actors and actresses 7. Espionage 8. Spies 9. Dramatists, English 10. British in Italy 11. London, England -- History -- 16th century 12. Venice, Italy -- History -- 1508-1797 13. Historical mysteries

Originally published: London : Twenty7, 2016.

Seeking his fortune in 16th-century London, a talented wordsmith joins a band of players before he is dispatched to Venice on an assignment that renders him the target of Catholic assassins and a shadowy killer.

"As rich in period detail as Rory Clement's John Shakespeare series (about Williams older brother) and C. J. Sansom's Matthew Shardlake novels, also set in the sixteenth century, but a lot more fun. Bravo!" Booklist.

Brandt, Harry, 1949-

The **Whites** : a novel / Harry Brandt. Henry Holt and Company, 2015. 336 p.

ISBN 9780805093995

1. Forties (Age) 2. City life 3. Consequences 4. Murder victims 5. Friendship 6. Detectives 7. Murder 8. Murder investigation 9. New York City 10. Hardboiled fiction 11. Mysteries

LC 2014028457

Forty-two-year-old Sergeant Billy Graves marks time as head of the Manhattan's Night Watch, the motley group of detectives who deal with felonies between 1 a.m. and 8 a.m. Married with two kids, he was an NYPD officer on the rise until a bullet from his gun missed a criminal and hit a kid. Billy and his cadre of fellow gung-ho cops from that time all have a "white" -- that one criminal who escaped justice. Now, the group's whites are turning up dead. This compelling, authentic novel is sure to please fans of police procedurals. -- Description by Dawn Towery.

"In the wake of rage and sorrow, ordinary people respond by going crazy and screwing up. In this far-from-ordinary novel, Price/Brandt explores the hows and whys. Fasten your seat belt." Kirkus.

Brashares, Ann

My name is memory / Ann Brashares. Riverhead Books, 2010. 336 p.

ISBN 9781594487583

1. Soul mates 2. Reincarnation 3. Romantic love 4. Men/women relations 5. Memories 6. Teenagers 7. High school students 8. Teenage boy/girl relations 9. Love stories

LC 2010000276

Sharing multiple lifetimes with the reincarnations of Sophia, Daniel, a soul with a rare ability to remember his past lives, arrives in the present frustrated that their time together has always been cut short and hopeful that Sophia's burgeoning memories can help them overcome past-life challenges.

Braun, Lilian Jackson

The **cat** who ate Danish modern / Lilian Jackson Braun. Dutton, 1967. 192 p. Cat Who mysteries

ISBN 9789997404985

1. Art thefts 2. Murder investigation 3. Women murder victims 4. City life 5. Cat detectives 6. Journalists 7. Journalists 8. Amateur detectives 9. Cat owners 10. Cats 11. Siamese cat 12. Middle West 13. Cozy mysteries 14. Gentle reads

Qwilleran and his cats become embroiled in a mystery while working on an article about interior design.

"The mystery is mild, the satire on interior decorating fads and fancies amusing, and the Siamese cat who helps play detective delightful." Publishers Weekly.

Braun, Lilian Jackson

The **cat** who went underground / Lilian Jackson Braun. G. P. Putnam's Sons, 1989. 223 p. Cat Who mysteries
ISBN 9780399134319
1. Carpenters 2. Serial murders 3. Houses -- Maintenance and repair 4. Murder investigation 5. Cat detectives 6. Journalists 7. Journalists 8. Amateur detectives 9. Cat owners 10. Cats 11. Siamese cat 12. Small town life 13. Middle West 14. Cozy mysteries 15. Gentle reads
LC 88032185

Qwill and his cats vacation in Mooseville, but when the carpenter he hires disappears, he begins to investigate what may be a serial killer's plan to wipe out the area's woodworkers.

"Qwill's saving grace is that he is properly humble before the superior intelligence of his pets, while the author is shrewd enough to balance the cats' amazing antics with many amusing character studies of the Mooseville natives." New York Times Book Review.

Brautigan, Richard, 1935-1984

An **unfortunate** woman : a journey / Richard Brautigan. St. Martin's Press, 2000. 110 p.
ISBN 0312262434
1. Death -- Psychological aspects 2. Diary novels 3. Psychological fiction 4. Pacific Northwest fiction
LC 00024760

Explores the fragile and mysterious shadowland surrounding death and considers the protagonist's ruminations on another person's suicide

"An autobiographical novelette in journal form. The episodic entries, dating from January to June of 1982, at first seem whimsically random, as the narrator recounts a peripatetic six months wandering among Montana, Berkeley, Hawaii, San Francisco, Buffalo, the Midwest, Alaska, Canada and points in between, but soon it's obvious that a preoccupation with death is the dominant theme. . . . Brautigan maintains his ironic humor and his ability to write clear, often crystalline prose, though at time his mannerisms . . . become irritating. Yet the reader cannot help being moved by this candid cri de coeur of a soul in anguish." Publishers Weekly.

Brayden, Melissa

First position / Melissa Brayden. Bold Strokes Books, 2016. 264 p.
ISBN 9781626396029
1. Lesbians 2. Ballet dancers 3. Women/women relations 4. Sexual attraction 5. Women dancers 6. Competition 7. New York City 8. Contemporary romances 9. LGBTQIA romances 10. LGBTQIA fiction

Anastasia Mikhelson is the rising star of the NY City Ballet. Though at the peak of her career, competition from a new and noteworthy dancer puts all she's worked for in jeopardy.

"Brayden ably develops the growing relationship between Ana and Natalie, making the emotional payoff that much sweeter when the two finally admit their lust for each other. Readers will relate to the realism of the romance and the emotional aftermath of serious injuries. This ably plotted, moving offering will earn its place deep in readers hearts." Publishers Weekly.

Brekke, Jorgen, 1968-

The **fifth** element / Jorgen Brekke. Minotaur Books, 2017, c2013. 336 p. Odd Singsaker
ISBN 9781250073914
1. Missing women 2. Detectives 3. Searching 4. Crime 5. Police 6. Captivity 7. Assassins 8. Drug dealers 9. Married people 10. Police corruption 11. Men/women relations 12. Norway 13. Scandinavian crime fiction 14. Parallel narratives 15. Translations -- Norwegian to English

Originally published as Menneskets natur in 2013 by Gyldendal.

"Police Inspector Odd Singsaker has been captured, imprisoned on an island off the Northern coast of Norway. He wakes to find himself holding a shotgun. Next to him is a corpse. But what events led him to this point? And how did he get here?"--Provided by the publisher.

"It's Brekke's prodigious powers of invention, his ability to keep coming up with unforgettable characters and indelible episodes, that lift this above his own earlier work and most of the heavy Nordic competition." Kirkus.

Brennan, Marie

A **natural** history of dragons : a memoir by Lady Trent / Marie Brennan. Tor, 2013. 336 p. Memoirs of Lady Trent
ISBN 9780765331960
1. Women scientists 2. Dragons 3. Natural history 4. Villages 5. Research 6. Adventure 7. Smuggling 8. Naturalists 9. Women's role 10. Married people 11. Imaginary kingdoms 12. Fantasy fiction 13. Illustrated books
LC 2012038819

"A Tom Doherty Associates Book."

Fascinated by dragons since childhood, Lady Isabella Trent devotes her time and considerable energy to the study of natural history, thus defying convention in the alternate Victorian England society in which she lives (where science is not an appropriate study for ladies). Her intellect attracts the notice of famed explorer Lord Hilford, who invites her to join his expedition in search of rock-wyrms, finally giving Lady Isabella the chance to prove herself. Illustrations enhance this artful combination of fantasy and alternate history, with elements of mystery. - Description by Gillian Speace.

Brennan, Marie

The **tropic** of serpents : a memoir by Lady Trent / Marie Brennan. Tor, 2014. 331 p. Memoirs of Lady Trent
ISBN 9780765331977
1. Women scientists 2. Dragons 3. Natural history 4. Villages 5. Research 6. Adventure 7. Smuggling 8. Naturalists 9. Women's role 10. Married people 11. Imaginary kingdoms 12. Fantasy fiction
LC 2013026345

Sequel to: A Natural History of Dragons
Sequel: Voyage of the Basilisk
"A Tom Doherty Associates book."

Lady Trent reflects on the second stage of her illustrious and occasionally scandalous career, during which she visited the war-torn continent of Eriga to observe exotic draconian species.

"Structuring the story like a Victorian memoir is a nice touch, too, allowing Brennan to give us a good, long look at our narrator (a thoroughly likable and spunky woman), while also allowing her to filter the events through the perceptions of the heroine. Gaslamp fantasy is a relatively new subgenre ... and this is a shining example of it." Booklist.

Brennan, Marie

Within the sanctuary of wings : a memoir by Lady Trent / Marie Brennan. Tor, 2017. 352 p. Memoirs of Lady Trent
ISBN 9780765377654
1. Women scientists 2. Natural history 3. Dragons 4. Voyages and travels 5. Imaginary kingdoms 6. Married people 7. Women's role 8. Naturalists 9. Adventure 10. Research 11. Fantasy fiction
Series complete in five volumes.
A dragon naturalist and an explorer prone to igniting scandals, Lady Trent reveals what she discovered in the Sanctuary of Wings, behind the territory of Scirland's enemies.

Brenner, Jamie, 1971-

Drawing home / Jamie Brenner. Little Brown & Co, 2019. 368 p.
ISBN 9780316476799
1. Inheritance and succession 2. Friends' death 3. Teenagers with mental illnesses 4. Artists 5. Women business partners 6. Hotel workers 7. Secrets 8. Contested wills 9. Child-separated fathers 10. Coastal towns 11. Drawing 12. New York (State) 13. Sag Harbor, New York 14. Women's lives and relationships
When Sag Harbor's most famous resident, artist Henry Wyatt, dies suddenly, Emma Mapson finds herself in a battle against Henry's former business partner, Bea Winstead, when they discover that Henry has left his waterfront home to Emma's teenage daughter, Penny.

Brennert, Alan

Daughter of Moloka'i / Alan Brennert. St. Martin's Press, 2019. 320 p.
ISBN 9781250137661
1. 20th century 2. Adopted girls 3. Multiracial girls 4. Adoptive families 5. Birthmothers 6. California 7. Historical fiction 8. Family sagas
Rachel Kalama was quarantined for most of her life at the isolated leprosy settlement of Kalaupapa-- and forced to give up her daughter at birth. Ruth is taken to the Kapi'olani Home for Girls in Honolulu, and adopted by a Japanese couple who raise her on a farm in California. During World War II Ruth and her husband suffer internment at Manzanar Relocation Camp. After the war, she receives a letter from Rachel. As the two meet and come to love one another, Ruth discovers a past she knew nothing about. -- adapted from jacket
"A historically solid, ultimately hopeful novel about injustice, survival, and unbreakable family bonds." Booklist.

Breslin, Jimmy

I don't want to go to jail : a good novel / Jimmy Breslin. Little, Brown, 2001. 306 p.
ISBN 0316118451
1. Italian American families 2. Organized crime 3. Criminals 4. Priests 5. Mafia 6. Families 7. Family relationships 8. Crime 9. Crime bosses 10. New York City 11. Black humor 12. Humorous stories
LC 00058880
Chronicles the fictional life of a mob family trying to survive in modern-day New York.
"Fausti 'The Fist' Dellacava is a gangster's gangster, an old school tough guy and a tyrant who uses his Mafia power to indulge a variety of whims. . . . But his nephew and namesake is cut from a different cloth: when the younger Fausti decides that the threat of jail is a steep price to pay for a mobster's life of leisure, he tries his luck in the real world with decidedly mixed results. The bulk of the novel tracks the Fist's decline and demise in parallel with his nephew's efforts to establish himself beyond the Mob--but the book's real raison d'tre is to give the audacious Breslin an opportunity to tell nonstop stories about the Mafia." Publishers Weekly.

Breslin, Jimmy

Table money / Jimmy Breslin. Ticknor and Fields, 1986. 435 p.
ISBN 9780899193120
1. Blue collar workers 2. Working class women 3. Alcoholic men 4. Family and alcoholism 5. Vietnam veterans 6. Queens, New York City 7. Psychological fiction
LC 85028880
Returned to his Queens home in 1970 after winning a Congressional Medal of Honor in Vietnam, Owney Morrison works at digging tunnels during the day and escapes with drink at night--from everything, including his wife Dolores and their child.
"This saga concerning the Morrisons of Queens, New York--from their late-nineteenth-century arrival in the U.S. to the present day--is painfully stereotypical in its depiction of the men (a long line of hard-drinking, male chauvinistic, and irresponsible tunnel workers) and their beleaguered, long-suffering women. Generation after generation repeats the same mistakes--dying too soon from alcoholism, giving birth too early in life--and even when Owen Morrison, the latter-day lad whose story takes up most of the book, wins the Congressional medal of honor in Vietnam, he finds that his hero's badge is virtually worthless on the gray borough streets and in the perilous tunnel that epitomizes his clan's plight." Booklist.

Brett, Simon

Mrs Pargeter's principle / Simon Brett. Severn House, 2015. 192 p. Mrs. Pargeter mysteries
ISBN 9781780290744
1. Kidnapping 2. Illegal arms transfers 3. Political corruption 4. Politicians 5. Widows 6. Senior women 7. Women amateur detectives 8. England 9. Cozy mysteries 10. Gentle reads
Investigating the connection between her late husband and a wealthy man who has recently passed away, Mrs. Pargeter finds herself in a shady world of gun-runners, shifty politicians and high-profile abductions.
"Brett's customary wit and good humor abound." Publishers Weekly.

Brett, Simon

Murder unprompted / Simon Brett. C. Scribner's Sons, 1982. 160 p. Charles Paris mysteries
ISBN 0684176599
1. Murder investigation 2. Actors and actresses 3. Shooting 4. Detectives 5. Amateur detectives 6. England 7. Mysteries
LC 82005578
In this Charles Paris mystery, the seasoned actor and part-time sleuth gets the part of understudy to the lead in a West End play. But when the lead gets shot on stage on the opening night, it falls to Charles once again to solve the murder.

Brett, Simon

The **torso** in the town : a Fethering mystery / Simon Brett. Berkley Prime Crime, 2002. 340 p. Fethering mysteries
ISBN 0425185028
1. Women detectives 2. Coastal towns 3. Murder investigation 4. Murder 5. Women retirees 6. Female friendship 7. England 8. Cozy mysteries 9. Gentle reads
LC 2002018482
During a boring dinner party at a Fedborough mansion with some stuffy acquaintances, the mummified torso of a woman turns up in the cellar, and Jude and her reluctant neighbor, Carole, find themselves playing detective.

Brin, David

Existence / David Brin. Tor Books, 2012. 480 p.
ISBN 9780765303615

1. Alien artifacts 2. Human/alien encounters 3. Luddites 4. Material culture 5. Plague 6. Autism 7. Aliens 8. Hard science fiction 9. Science fiction

In a future world dominated by a neural-link web where people can tune into live events and revolutions can be instantly sparked, an active alien communication device is discovered in orbit around the Earth, triggering an international upheaval of fear, hope and violence.

Brink, Andre P. (Andre Philippus), 1935-

Philida : a novel / Andre Brink. Vintage Books, 2012. 320 p.
ISBN 9780345805034

1. 19th century 2. 1830s 3. Slavery 4. Betrayal 5. Women slaves 6. Rape victims 7. Lust 8. Interracial romance 9. Independence in women 10. Slaves -- Emancipation 11. South Africa -- History -- 19th century 12. Historical fiction

LC 2012031043

Originally published: London : Harvill Secker, 2012.

Amelia Bloomer List, 2014

When Francois Brink, her children's father and the son of her master, reneges on his promise to grant her freedom, Philida files a complaint against the Brink family in 1830s South Africa, an act that changes her life beyond recognition.

"With alternating present-tense viewpoints, the aching personal drama is set against the history of lechery, power, and violent abuse... [a] stirring novel." Booklist.

Brink, Andre P. (Andre Philippus), 1935-

The **rights** of desire / Andre Brink. Harcourt, 2000. 311 p.
ISBN 0151006547

1. Post-apartheid era 2. Widowers 3. May-December romance 4. Men 5. Ghosts 6. Violence 7. Men/women relations 8. South Africa 9. Love stories 10. Political fiction

LC 00046141

Includes glossary.

Ruben Olivier, a widower who leads an isolated existence in a Cape Town suburb, takes in a younger boarder who transforms his life.

"Although this isn't Brink's best effort, he remains a consummately professional storyteller, and the voice of his narrator, with its subtle wit and vulnerability, is a welcome one." Publishers Weekly.

Brinkley, Jamel

A **lucky** man : stories / Jamel Brinkley. Graywolf Press, 2018. 243 p.
ISBN 9781555978051

1. African American men 2. African American boys 3. Interpersonal relations 4. Ethnic identity 5. New York City 6. African American fiction 7. Literary fiction 8. Short stories

Finalist for the Hurston/Wright Legacy Awards for Fiction, 2019.

National Book Award for Fiction finalist, 2018

Jamel Brinkley's stories, in a debut that announces the arrival of a significant new voice, reflect the tenderness and vulnerability of black men and boys whose hopes sometimes betray them, especially in a world shaped by race, gender, and class;where luck may be the greatest fiction of all.

"The nine stories in Brinkleys promising debut address persistent issues of race, class, and masculinity across three decades of New York City's history, from Manhattan's corporatization in the mid-90s to the outer boroughs' gentrification today." Publishers Weekly.

Brinkman, Kiara

Up high in the trees / Kiara Brinkman. Grove Press, 2007. 240 p.
ISBN 9780802118479

1. Mothers and sons 2. Grief in children 3. Loss (Psychology) 4. Boys with autism 5. Children with autism 6. Nine-year-old boys 7. Grief 8. Coping 9. Fathers and sons 10. Mothers -- Death 11. Loneliness 12. Abandonment (Psychology) 13. Dreams 14. Psychological fiction

LC 2006052161

Struggling to deal with the loss of his mother, nine-year-old Sebby Lane goes with his father to live in the family's summerhouse, but as his father deteriorates in the isolation, Sebby reaches out to a favorite teacher back home and to nearby children.

Brkic, Courtney Angela

The **first** rule of swimming / Courtney Angela Brkic. Little Brown & Co, 2013. 384 p.
ISBN 9780316217385

1. Sisters 2. Family secrets 3. Missing persons 4. Betrayal 5. Families -- History 6. Loss (Psychology) 7. Searching 8. Family relationships 9. Croatia 10. New York City 11. Psychological fiction 12. Family sagas

Traveling to New York from her Croatian island home, Magdelena searches for her missing, free-spirited sister, Jadranka, and uncovers dark family secrets that span three generations.

Brockmeier, Kevin

The **brief** history of the dead / Kevin Brockmeier. Pantheon Books, 2006. 272 p.
ISBN 0375423699

1. Women scientists 2. Dead 3. Soul 4. Husband and wife 5. Parent and adult child 6. Death 7. Epidemics 8. Life after death 9. Bereavement 10. Grief 11. Loss (Psychology) 12. Memories 13. Cities and towns 14. Research institutes -- Anatarctic regions 15. Wilderness survival -- Anatarctic regions 16. Antarctica 17. Literary fiction

LC 2005048882

In an afterlife world inhabited by the recently departed who remain in the memories of the living, Marion and Phillip Byrd fall in love again, while on Earth, their daughter, Laura, is stranded alone in an Antarctic research station.

"Although it never quite lives up to its promising premise, the novel's Borges-like spirit will appeal to select readers." Booklist.

Brockmeier, Kevin

The **illumination** / Kevin Brockmeier. Pantheon Books, 2011. 256 p.
ISBN 9780375425318

1. Suffering 2. Bereavement 3. Death 4. Widowers 5. Love letter writing 6. Traffic accidents 7. Diseases 8. Alienation (Social psychology) 9. Light and darkness 10. Faith 11. Psychological fiction

LC 2010020732

A journal of private love notes written by a husband to his wife in the wake of a fatal car accident passes through the hands of a hospital patient and five other suffering people whose respective experiences connect them to each other in poignant and complex ways.

"For a novel so relentlessly fixed on elucidating human suffering in all its permutations, The Illumination is surprisingly uplifting. This is a testament to Brockmeier's considerable stylistic gifts the man writes exquisite sentences and to the palpable compassion with which he frames each of his characters." Cleveland Plain Dealer.

LIST OF FICTIONAL WORKS

Brockmeier, Kevin

The **truth** about Celia / Kevin Brockmeier. Pantheon Books, 2003. 216 p.

ISBN 9780375421358

1. 1990s 2. Fathers and daughters 3. Parent and child 4. Husband and wife 5. Loss (Psychology) 6. Grief 7. Bereavement 8. Missing children 9. Missing girls 10. Seven-year-old girls 11. Seven-year-olds 12. Missing persons investigation 13. Authors 14. Fantasy fiction writing 15. Police 16. Extramarital affairs 17. Small town life 18. Small towns 19. Psychological fiction

LC 2002035513

A novel about the disappearance of a young girl, narrated from her father's point of view as he struggles to come to terms with her vanishing.

"The fragmented narration may deflect some readers, but others will cherish Brockmeier's seductive turns of phrase and sharp imagination." Publishers Weekly.

Brockway, Connie

The **golden** season / Connie Brockway. Penguin, 2010. 388 p.

ISBN 9780451412836

1. Regency period (1811-1820) 2. 19th century 3. Nobility 4. Financial crises 5. Men/women relations 6. Interpersonal attraction 7. Wealth 8. Deception 9. England -- History -- 1800-1837 10. Historical romances 11. Regency romances

When her fortune suddenly disappears, Lady Lydia Eastlake, the town's most celebrated beauty, must find a wealthy husband and sets her sights on a dashing war hero who, unbeknownst to her, is searching for a rich bride to save his family from a life of poverty.

Brockway, Connie

No place for a dame / Connie Brockway. Montlake Romance, 2013. 278 p.

ISBN 9781477808580

1. Regency period (1811-1820) 2. Ambition in women 3. Disguises 4. Independence in women 5. Rich men 6. Social classes 7. Astronomy 8. Interclass romance 9. Interpersonal attraction 10. Men/women relations 11. Great Britain 12. Regency romances 13. Historical romances

Avery dresses as a man in order to join the Royal Astronomical Society, a plan helped along by Lord Giles, who agrees to take her on as a prodigy in exchange for her help searching for a missing colleague.

"Brockway delivers a unique, engaging historical storyline with fun, intriguing elements and with a delicious arc of two star-crossed misfits who share a deep love and deserve an exceptional future." Kirkus.

Brockway, Connie

So enchanting / Connie Brockway. Onyx, 2009. 421 p.

ISBN 9780451416292

1. 19th century 2. Witches 3. Exile (Punishment) 4. Men/women relations 5. Death threats 6. Female friendship 7. Romantic love 8. Scotland 9. Historical romances

LC bl2009002974

When Lord Greyson Sheffield, the very same man who had ruined her reputation and sent her into exile in the Scottish Highlands, arrives on her doorstep, Francesca Walcott, a mysteriously gifted medium, discovers magic in his arms amidst peril and evil.

Broder, Melissa

The **pisces** : a novel / Melissa Broder. Hogarth Press, 2018 270 p.

ISBN 9781524761554

1. Mermen 2. Men/women relations 3. Breaking up (Interpersonal relations) 4. Sexuality 5. Dog baby sitters 6. Doctoral students 7. Dissertation writing 8. Women -- Sexuality 9. Interspecies romance 10. Self-destructive behavior 11. Los Angeles, California 12. Contemporary fantasy 13. Women's lives and relationships

Longlisted for The Women's Prize for Fiction, 2019.

Bottoming out after a dramatic breakup, a habitual student accepts her sister's invitation to dog-sit on Venice Beach for the summer, where she meets an eerily attractive swimmer one night whose Sirenic identity transforms her understanding of what real love looks like.

Brodesser-Akner, Taffy

Fleishman is in trouble : a novel / Taffy Brodesser-Akner. Random House, 2019. 288 p.

ISBN 9780525510871

1. Divorced fathers 2. Physicians 3. Marital conflict 4. Parenting 5. Middle-aged men 6. Jewish men 7. Online dating 8. Casual sex 9. Former wives 10. Missing persons 11. Former friends 12. Thought and thinking 13. New York (State) 14. Literary fiction

LC 2018054871

Longlisted for the National Book Award for Fiction, 2019.

Divorcing his hostile wife when he concludes he could find genuine happiness elsewhere, a doctor is astonished when his ex abruptly disappears, making him unable to move on without acknowledging painful truths about his marriage.

Broken stars : contemporary Chinese science fiction in translation / translated and edited by Ken Liu. Tor, 2019. 464 p.

ISBN 9781250297662

1. Translations -- Chinese to English 2. Science fiction 3. Anthologies 4. Short stories 5. Essays

LC 2018046025

"A Tom Doherty Associates Book."

Collected, translated and edited, an anthology of Chinese science fiction fetures stories from the Hugo Award-winning author Cixin Liu as well as Chen Qiufan, Bao Shu, Xia Jia, Zhang Ran, Tang Fei and Han Song.

"Rounded out by essays on topics related to Chinese sf, this anthology is a must-read for any genre fan." Booklist.

Bronsky, Alina, 1978-

The **hottest** dishes of the Tartar cuisine / Alina Bronsky ; translated from the German by Tim Mohr. Europa Editions, 2011, c2010. 262 p.

ISBN 9781609450069

1. Teenage pregnancy 2. Dysfunctional families 3. Cruelty in women 4. Family relationships 5. Pregnant teenagers 6. Mothers and daughters 7. Grandmother and granddaughter 8. Soviet Union 9. Literary fiction 10. Translations -- German to English

Originally published in German as Die scharfsten Gerichte der tatarischen Kuche: Cologne : Kiepenheuer & Witsch, 2010.

Rosa's schemes to abort her daughter Sulfia's fetus after learning of the pregnancy, take her granddaughter Aminat after the baby's birth, and move the family out of the Soviet Union eventually lead to tragedy.

Bronte, Anne, 1820-1849

The **tenant** of Wildfell Hall / Anne Bronte. Modern Library, 1997, c1848. xiii, 510 p.

ISBN 0679602798

1. Georgian era (1714-1837) 2. Victorian era (1837-1901) 3. Married women 4. Alcoholic men 5. Women -- Social conditions 6. Husband and wife 7. Women 8. Men/women relations 9. Family and alcoholism 10. England -- Social life and customs -- 19th century 11. Great Britain -- Social life and customs -- Victoria, 1837-1901 12. Great Britain -- Social life and customs -- George III, 1760-1820 13. Great Britain -- Social life and customs -- George IV, 1820-1830 14. Domestic fiction 15. Classics

LC   97014200

Originally published: London : T.C. Newby, 1848.

A nineteenth century novel depicts the unhappy marriage of Helen Graham and her drunken husband, realistically portraying the devastating impact of alcholism.

Bronte, Charlotte, 1816-1855

* **Emma** / Charlotte Bronte and "Another Lady". Everest House, 1980. 201 p.

ISBN 9780896961142

1. Abandoned children 2. Boarding schools 3. Secret identity 4. England -- Social life and customs -- 19th century 5. Gothic fiction 6. Classics

LC   81066096

The last, unfinished work by the author. This fragment (two chapters) was first published in Cornhill magazine, April 1860.

"In the full-blown literary manner and circuitous story-telling characteristic of Charlotte Bronte, . . . an intriguing melodrama unrolls in this tale of wrongs finally righted. ... The author of this Gothic romp is obviously steeped in the period and felicitous style of the brilliant English novelist, providing entertainment on the same grand scale." Publishers Weekly.

Bronte, Charlotte, 1816-1855

* **Jane** Eyre / Charlotte Bronte. Modern Library, 1997, c1847. 682 p.

ISBN 9780679602699

1. 19th century 2. Governesses 3. Young women 4. Rich men 5. Orphans 6. Friendship 7. Integrity 8. Family secrets 9. Young women -- Relations with older men 10. Men/women relations 11. Boarding schools 12. England -- Social life and customs -- 19th century 13. Gothic fiction 14. Classics

Originally published in 1847 under the pseudonym Currer Bell, Jane Eyre is Charlotte Bronte's best-known novel, a Gothic masterpiece of character and emotion.

Originally published 1847.

In early nineteenth-century England, an orphaned young woman accepts employment as a governess and soon finds herself in love with her employer who has a terrible secret.

Bronte, Emily, 1818-1848

* **Wuthering** Heights / Emily Bronte. Puffin Books, 1990. 412 p.

ISBN 9780140366945

1. Interclass romance 2. Jealousy 3. Revenge 4. Inheritance and succession 5. Foster children 6. Classism 7. Obsession in men 8. Men/women relations 9. Ghosts 10. England -- Social life and customs -- 19th century 11. Gothic fiction 12. Classics 13. Love stories

Originally published: Thomas Cautley Newby, 1847.

Heathcliff, an orphan, is raised by Mr Earnshaw as one of his own children. Hindley despises him but wild Cathy becomes his constant companion, and he falls deeply in love with her. When she will not marry him, Heathcliff's terrible vengeance ruins them all - but still his and Cathy's love will not die...

Brookmyre, Christopher, 1968-

Black widow / Christopher Brookmyre. Atlantic Monthly Press, 2016. 422 p. Jack Parlabane novels

ISBN 9780802125736

1. Ambition in women 2. Women murder suspects 3. Newlyweds 4. Journalists 5. Divorced men 6. Bloggers 7. Women surgeons 8. Brothers and sisters 9. Rich families 10. Secrets 11. Scotland 12. Hardboiled fiction

First published: London : Abacus, 2016.

Theakston Old Peculier Crime Novel of the Year Award, 2017

Rogue reporter Jack Parlabane investigates the case of a skilled surgeon and fierce blog activist who endured brutal persecution before her whirlwind romance and marriage to a man who she has been accused of killing.

Brookmyre, Christopher, 1968-

When the devil drives / Christopher Brookmyre. Atlantic Monthly, 2013. 288 p. Jasmine Sharp and Catherine McLeod novels

ISBN 9780802120892

1. Gangs 2. Women detectives 3. Police -- Glasgow, Scotland 4. Street life 5. Drug dealers 6. Murder investigation 7. Private investigators 8. Women private investigators 9. Glasgow, Scotland 10. Mysteries 11. Police procedurals

Actress turned private investigator Jasmine Sharp finds her simple missing persons case turning into a dangerous murder investigation when the disappearance of her client's younger sister is linked to the shooting death of a prominent figure in the Scottish arts community.

Brookmyre, Christopher, 1968-

Where the bodies are buried / Christopher Brookmyre. Atlantic Monthly Press, 2012, c2011. 304 p. Jasmine Sharp and Catherine McLeod novels

ISBN 9780802120250

1. Gangs 2. Women detectives 3. Police -- Glasgow, Scotland 4. Street life 5. Drug dealers 6. Missing men 7. Missing persons 8. Police misconduct 9. Murder investigation 10. Private investigators 11. Women private investigators 12. Glasgow, Scotland 13. Mysteries 14. Police procedurals

Originally published: London : Little, Brown, 2011.

Detective Superintendent Catherine McLeod's investigation into the murder of a small-time heroin dealer is challenged by numerous suspects and an unexpected tie to the disappearance of fledgling private investigator Jasmine Sharpe's mentor uncle.

"Red herrings and plot convolutions abound, but its Brookmyres sense of the city and its no-nuance criminals that makes this one a winner." Booklist.

Brookner, Anita

Brief lives / Anita Brookner. Random House, 1991, c1990. 260 p.

ISBN 0679737332

1. 1940s 2. Loneliness in women 3. Actors and actresses 4. Friendship 5. Widows 6. Female friendship 7. London, England 8. Literary fiction

LC   90038904

Fay Langdon and Julia Morton, two aged entertainers, form a precarious friendship which is tested by disappointment and betrayal.

"This short, subtle, beautifully organised and orchestrated novel positively gains from the deliberate restraint and detachment of the writing." London Review of Books.

Brookner, Anita
Family and friends / Anita Brookner. Pantheon Books, 1985. 187 p.
ISBN 0679781641
1. Single mothers 2. Mother and adult child 3. Widows 4. Rich people 5. Family relationships 6. Families 7. Mother and child 8. London, England 9. Literary fiction
LC 85006373

"Anita Brookner's prose is impeccably elegant and she is unsentimental with it. . . . There is a closeness of atmosphere, almost claustrophobic, in Family and Friends, as if we were alternating between a discreetly perfumed lady's boudoir and the smoking room of a superior gentleman's club. There is no mistaking the originality as well as the skill and consistency with which the novel so beautifully conforms to its genre and its intentions." The New York Review of Books.

Brookner, Anita
* **Hotel** Du Lac / Anita Brookner. Pantheon Books, 1984. 184 p.
ISBN 0394542150
1. Friendship 2. Thought and thinking 3. Hotels -- Switzerland 4. Women authors 5. Romance writers 6. Switzerland 7. Literary fiction
LC 84020641
Originally published: London : Cape, 1984.
Booker Prize, 1984.

Into the rarified atmosphere of the Hotel du Lac timidly walks Edith Hope, romantic novelist and holder of modest dreams. Edith has been exiled from home after embarassing herself and her friends. She has refused to sacrifice her ideals and remains stubbornly single. But among the pampered women and minor nobility Edith finds Mr Neville, and her chance to escape from a life of humilitating spinsterhood is renewed.

"The tone of this novel is oddly detached, very small-scale, faintly humorous. . . . It is by means of this very remoteness that Edith manages to hold our interest throughout this achingly uneventful holiday, with its empty chasms of time, its murmuring respectability, its dining room scattered sparsely with people who mean nothing to her. . . . There are some uncomfortable patches. . . . But generally, the writing is graceful and attractive." New York Times Book Review.

Brooks, Bill, 1943-
Blood storm / Bill Brooks. Five Star, 2012. 344 p. John Henry Cole novels
ISBN 9781594149115
1. 1870s 2. 19th century 3. Outlaws 4. Crimes against prostitutes 5. Gunfighters 6. Frontier and pioneer life 7. Detectives 8. Prostitutes 9. Murder investigation 10. Conspiracies 11. Extortion 12. The West (United States) -- History -- 19th century 13. Dakota Territory 14. Westerns
Sequel: Frontier Justice.
When three young escorts turn up dead in the mining town of Deadwood, John Henry Cole is called in to investigate the murders.

Brooks, Bill, 1943-
Frontier justice / Bill Brooks. Five Star, 2012. 322 p. John Henry Cole novels
ISBN 9781432826079
1. Bounty hunters 2. African American murder suspects 3. Frontier

and pioneer life -- Wyoming 4. Outlaws 5. Revenge 6. Murderers 7. Detectives 8. Prostitutes 9. Friends' death 10. Murder investigation 11. Interpersonal attraction 12. The West (United States) -- History -- 19th century 13. Wyoming -- History -- 19th century 14. Westerns
LC 2012016329
Sequel to: Blood Storm.
"Leavening the action is Brooks' sly humor--for instance, when a near-penniless Cole shops for an ornery, speckled, $30 horse; or when, by the campfire, Cole and Harper discuss Don Quixote." Booklist.

Brooks, Bill, 1943-
Winter kill / Bill Brooks. Five Star, 2013. 262 p. John Henry Cole novels
ISBN 9781432826345
1. Texas Rangers 2. Frontier and pioneer life -- Wyoming 3. Women murder suspects 4. Outlaws 5. Detectives 6. Voyages and travels 7. The West (United States) -- History -- 19th century 8. Wyoming -- History -- 19th century 9. Westerns
LC 2013005469
The winter around Cheyenne, Wyoming that year was devastating, killing both people and livestock. John Henry Cole was three miles out of town on his small ranch, waiting out the storm that was quickly killing his cattle and horses, and starting to feel alittle crazy himself.

Brooks, Geraldine
Caleb's crossing / Geraldine Brooks. Penguin, 2011. 320 p.
ISBN 9780670021048
1. Cheeshahteaumuck, Caleb, ca 1646-1666 2. Harvard University. 3. 1660s 4. 17th century 5. Indians of North America 6. Clergymen's families 7. Spirituality 8. Friendship 9. Household employees 10. Shamans 11. College students 12. Wampanoag Indians 13. Housekeepers 14. Martha's Vineyard, Massachusetts -- History 15. Literary fiction 16. Historical fiction 17. Biographical fiction
Forging a deep friendship with a Wampanoag chieftain's son on the Great Harbor settlement where her minister father is working to convert the tribe, Bethia follows his subsequent ivy league education and efforts to bridge cultures among the colonial elite.

"A historical novel inspired by Caleb Cheeshahteaumauck, the first Native American to graduate from Harvard. Brooks brings the 1660s to life with evocative period detail, intriguing characters, and a compelling story narrated by Bethia Mayfield, the outspoken daughter of a Calvinist preacher. ... [H]er descriptions of 17th-century Cambridge and Harvard are as entertaining as they are enlightening." Publishers Weekly.

Brooks, Geraldine
People of the book / Geraldine Brooks. Viking, 2008. 372 p.
ISBN 9780670018215
1. Aggadah Adaptations 2. Manuscripts 3. Religious persecution 4. Voyages and travels 5. Greed 6. Freedom of religion 7. Toleration 8. History 9. Judaism 10. Books -- Conservation and restoration 11. Sacred books 12. Bosnia and Hercegovina 13. Historical fiction 14. Literary fiction 15. Parallel narratives
LC 2007018082
Australian Book Industry Awards, Book of the Year, 2008.
Australian Book Industry Awards, Literary Fiction Book of the Year, 2008.
Massachusetts Book Awards, Fiction Award, 2009.
In 1996, Hanna Heath, a young Australian book conservator is called to analyze the famed Sarajevo Haggadah, a priceless six-hundred-year-old Jewish prayer book that has been salvaged from a destroyed Bosnian

library. When Hanna discovers a series of artifacts in the centuries' old binding, she unwittingly exposes an international cover up.

"When an Australian rare-book conservator named Hanna Heath finds a butterfly wing, a salt crystal, a white hair, and bloodstains in the recently rediscovered Sarajevo Haggadah, a late-medieval illuminated codex of uncertain provenance, she sets out to solve the mystery of the book's origins. To her disappointment, analysis of the specimens reveals little. . . . Brooks, beginning where science leaves off, uses Hanna's finds as entry points to richly imagined historical landscapes peopled by the Haggadah's creators, protectors, and would-be destroyers a female Muslim slave in Convivencia Spain, a Jewish doctor in fin-de-sicle Vienna, an alcoholic priest in seventeenth-century Venice. Their narratives alternate with Hanna's own, and the final, multilayered effect is complex and moving." The New Yorker.

Brooks, Max

* **World** War Z : an oral history of the zombie war / Max Brooks. Crown, 2006. 320 p.

ISBN 0307346609

1. Oral historians 2. War 3. Undead 4. Zombies 5. Diseases 6. Epidemics 7. Military strategy 8. Oral histories 9. Survival (after epidemics) 10. Post-apocalypse 11. Horror 12. Satirical fiction 13. Apocalyptic fiction

LC 2006009517

In World War Z, life as we know it ends the way many horror fans knew it would: zombies rise up! After the post-war devastation, author Max Brooks "interviews" survivors and records their stories as well as details on what causes zombies, how they spread, what will stop them, and effective strategic warfare methods against them. -- Description by Dawn Towery.

"Brooks tells the story of the world's desperate battle against the zombie threat with a series of first-person accounts as told to the author by various characters around the world. A Chinese doctor encounters one of the earliest zombie cases at a time when the Chinese government is ruthlessly suppressing any information about the outbreak that will soon spread across the globe. The tale then follows the outbreak via testimony of smugglers, intelligence officials, military personnel and many others who struggle to defeat the zombie menace. Despite its implausible premise and choppy delivery, the novel is surprisingly hard to put down." Publishers Weekly.

Broun, Bill

Night of the animals / Bill Broun. Ecco Press, 2016. 592 p.

ISBN 9780062400796

1. 21st century 2. Zoo animals 3. Men with mental illnesses 4. Cults 5. Dystopias 6. Near future 7. Brothers -- Death 8. Zoos 9. London, England 10. Literary fiction 11. Dystopian fiction

In 2052 London a homeless man, who believes he has the magical ability to communicate with animals, sets off on a quest to release all the animals from the zoo before the members of a suicide cult can destroy them.

"Brouns novel is strange, witty, and engrossing, skipping through madness and into the realm of myth." Publishers Weekly.

Brouwer, Sigmund, 1959-

Thief of glory : a novel / Sigmund Brouwer. WaterBrook Press, 2014. 288 p.

ISBN 9780307446497

1. World War II 2. Concentration camps 3. Faith (Christianity) 4. Survival (in concentration camps, prisons, etc) 5. Family secrets 6. Redemption 7. Mothers and sons 8. Indonesia -- History -- Japanese occupation, 1942-1945 9. War stories 10. Christian historical fiction

LC 2014007072

Alberta Readers' Choice Award, 2015.
Christy Award for Historical Romance Category, 2015.
Christy Award for Book of the Year, 2015.

"This WWII drama is both exciting in its revelations and heartrending in its truth about human nature and forgiveness"--, Provided by publisher.

Brown, Dale, 1956-

Flight of the Old Dog : a novel / Dale Brown. D. I. Fine, 1987. 347 p. Patrick McLanahan novels

ISBN 1556110340

1. Space weapons 2. Military aviation 3. Military pilots 4. B-52 bomber 5. Space-based missile defenses -- Soviet Union 6. Strategic defense initiative 7. United States -- Foreign relations -- Soviet Union 8. Soviet Union -- Foreign relations -- United States 9. Adventure stories 10. Techno-thrillers

LC 86046388

"Despite spinning his wheels in the opening portions of the book--labored attempts at developing character, a stumbling stab at establishing a love interest, a series of predictable Soviet low blows that bring the world to the precipice of nuclear war-- Dale Brown finally . . . draws the reader into a tense, compelling adventure tale of the first order." Booklist.

Brown, Dale, 1956-

The **Kremlin** strike / Dale Brown. William Morrow, 2019 464 p. Patrick McLanahan novels

ISBN 9780062843012

1. International intrigue 2. Presidents -- United States 3. Fighter planes 4. Elite operatives 5. Space stations 6. Artificial satellites 7. Technology 8. National security 9. United States -- Foreign relations -- Russia 10. Russia -- Foreign relations -- United States 11. Space 12. Techno-thrillers

LC 2018037551

In this exciting, visionary, and all-too-plausible next chapter in the legendary Dale Brown's techno-warfare series, Brad McLanahan and the Iron Wolf Squadron must fight the Russians on a dangerous, untested battlefield: outer space.

Brown, Dale, 1956-

The **Moscow** offensive : a novel / Dale Brown. William Morrow, 2018. 432 p. Patrick McLanahan novels

ISBN 9780062442017

1. Special operations (Military science) 2. Special forces 3. Terrorism -- Prevention 4. National security 5. High technology 6. Weapons 7. International intrigue 8. Techno-thrillers

LC 2017053352

America's first line of defense--Brad McLanahan and the heroes of the Iron Wolf Squadron--must counter a dangerous Russian strike from within the homeland.

Brown, Dan, 1964-

Angels & demons / Dan Brown. Pocket Books, 2000. 430 p. Robert Langdon novels

ISBN 9780671027353

1. Catholic Church. 2. Secret societies 3. Signs and symbols 4. Popes -- Election 5. Papacy 6. Scientists 7. Cryptographers 8. Bombs 9. Sculpture 10. Art 11. Conspiracies 12. Vatican City 13. Thrillers and suspense

LC 99087852

Illustrated with maps.

The murder of a world-famous physicist raises fear that the Illuminati are operating again after centuries of silence, and religion professor Robert Langdon is called in to assist with the case.

Brown, Dan, 1964-

The **Da** Vinci code / Dan Brown. Doubleday, 2003. 400 p. Robert Langdon novels

ISBN 0385504209

1. Leonardo da Vinci, 1452-1519 Manuscripts 2. Catholic Church 3. Opus Dei. 4. Louvre Museum, Paris, France. 5. Prieure de Sion. 6. Secret societies 7. Relics 8. Conspiracies 9. Artists 10. Painters 11. Painting 12. Museum curators 13. Murder investigation 14. Cryptographers 15. Women cryptographers 16. Codes (Communication) 17. Monks 18. Albinos and albinism 19. Grail 20. Police -- Paris, France 21. Paris, France 22. London, England 23. Europe 24. Thrillers and suspense

LC 2002040918

Book Sense Book of the Year Adult Fiction, 2004.
British Book Award for Book of the Year, 2005.
Iowa High School Book Award, 2006.
Teen Buckeye Book Award (Ohio), 2005.

When an elderly curator of the Louvre turns up murdered, his body surrounded by enigmatic ciphers written in invisible ink, code-breaker Robert Langdon and French cyptologist are called in to unravel the clues to the killing, only to discover that the riddles are linked to the works of Leonardo da Vinci and to a clandestine, ruthless sect within the Catholic Church.

"The story is full of brain-teasing puzzles and fascinating insights into religious history and art." Booklist.

Brown, Dan, 1964-

Inferno / Dan Brown. Doubleday, 2013. 480 p. Robert Langdon novels

ISBN 9780385537858

1. Dante Alighieri, 1265-1321 Inferno 2. Signs and symbols 3. Secret societies 4. Conspiracies 5. Cryptographers 6. Codes (Communication) 7. Washington, D.C. 8. Thrillers and suspense
Adapted into a film in 2016 under the same title.
Goodreads Choice Award, 2013.

In the heart of Italy, Harvard professor of symbology, Robert Langdon, is drawn into a harrowing world centered on one of history's most enduring and mysterious literary masterpieces--Dante's Inferno. Against this backdrop, Langdon battles a chilling adversary and grapples with an ingenious riddle.

Brown, Dan, 1964-

The **lost** symbol / Dan Brown. Doubleday, 2009. 528 p. Robert Langdon novels

ISBN 9780385504225

1. Signs and symbols 2. Secret societies 3. Conspiracies 4. Freemasonry 5. Cryptographers 6. Codes (Communication) 7. Washington, D.C. 8. Thrillers and suspense

The discovery of a mysterious object in the U.S. Capitol building and a subsequent kidnapping lead Harvard symbologist Robert Langdon into a web of mysterious codes, secret locations, and hidden knowledge.

"Brown has never been lauded for his deft handling of the written word. As in his other books, here his prose can be clumsy, flowery and heavyhanded. But, to his credit, he tells an action-packed story filled with fascinating history, myths, math, science, madmen and philosophers." USA Today.

Brown, Dee, 1908-2002

Creek Mary's blood : a novel / Dee Brown. Holt, Rinehart and Winston, 1980. 401 p.

ISBN 0030442818

1. 18th century 2. 19th century 3. Native American men 4. Native American women 5. Creek Indians 6. Cherokee Indians 7. Cheyenne Indians 8. Indians of North America 9. Journalists 10. Trail of Tears, 1838-1839 11. Government relations with indigenous peoples 12. Great Plains (United States) 13. Wounded Knee, South Dakota 14. Historical fiction 15. Family sagas

LC 79009060

Proud and beautiful Creek Mary dominates a saga that spans the years from the American Revolution to the preWorld War I era and portrays such characters as Tecumseh, Andrew Jackson, Crazy Horse, Sitting Bull, and Teddy Roosevelt.

Brown, Dee, 1908-2002

The **way** to Bright Star / Dee Brown. TOR, 1998. 352 p.

ISBN 0312866127

1. Former circus performers 2. Camels 3. Civil war 4. United States Civil War, 1861-1865 5. United States -- History -- Civil War, 1861-1865 6. Coming-of-age stories

LC 98-14621

Presents the story of a boy who makes an adventure-filled journey across Kansas and Missouri to Bright Star, Indiana, during the Civil War

"This picaresque yarn whose main strength rests in its cast of colorful characters, whom readers quickly come to know as individuals and with whom they will want to spend time." Booklist.

Brown, Eleanor, 1973-

The **weird** sisters / Eleanor Brown. Amy Einhorn Books/ G.P. Putnam's Sons, 2011. 336 p.

ISBN 9780399157226

1. Sisters 2. Parents with terminal illnesses 3. Self-discovery 4. Middle-aged women 5. Family relationships 6. Scholars and academics 7. College towns 8. People with cancer 9. Ohio 10. Mainstream fiction 11. Domestic fiction 12. Gentle reads

LC 2010029599

Unwillingly brought together to care for their ailing mother, three sisters who were named after famous Shakespearean characters discover that everything they have been avoiding may prove more worthwhile than expected.

Brown, Joe David

Addie **Pray** : a novel / Joe David Brown. Simon and Schuster, 1971. 313p.

ISBN 9780671209629

1. Depression era (1929-1941) 2. Swindlers and swindling 3. Father figures 4. Depressions -- 1929-1941 5. Door-to-door sales fraud 6. Orphans 7. Girls 8. Poverty 9. Southern States 10. Historical fiction 11. Coming-of-age stories

LC 73154096

Later published as: Paper moon. New York : Four Walls Eight Windows, 2002.

Set in the darkest days of the Great Depression, Addie is left in the questionable hands of a con-man after her mother dies. Together they hustle their way through the Deep South, proving that making money is no fun unless it's with someone you love.

"Brown has a special feeling for the Depression-era South. . . . [Addie's speech] is vulgar, pungent country talk, which adds greatly to the book's easygoing charm. Looking at Long Boy with his floozy, she observes that 'he got that silly, dazed grin like a tom cat being choked to death with cream.' Like that extravagant expression, the book is a long tall, oldtime tale. But as Addie might put it, in the right hands that kind of yarn has a lot of prance left." Time.

Brown, Karen, 1960-

The **clairvoyants** : a novel / Karen Brown. Henry Holt and Co., 2017. 381 p.

ISBN 9781627797054

1. Women psychics 2. Ghosts 3. Sisters 4. Missing women 5. Obsession 6. Women college students 7. College teachers 8. Photographs 9. Campus life 10. Secrets 11. Memories 12. Men/women relations 13. Connecticut 14. Gothic fiction

LC 2016019129

A young woman who wants to escape the challenges of being able to see ghosts pursues a college education and a budding romance before the apparition of a missing young woman prompts her to help.

"Brown's novel is a riveting page-turner. She deftly reveals bits of Martha's and Del's past in tandem with more details about the mystery that Martha is trying to unravel, leaving the reader wondering if Martha might be an unreliable narrator. Though the ending isn?t entirely satisfying, Brown shows an admirable ability to create suspense." Publishers Weekly.

Brown, Karma

The **life** Lucy knew / Karma Brown. Park Row, 2018. 320 p.

ISBN 9780778319344

1. Head injury survivors 2. Amnesia 3. Memory 4. Head injuries 5. False memory syndrome 6. Trust 7. People in comas 8. Decision-making 9. Life 10. Men/women relations 11. Mainstream fiction 12. Love stories

After hitting her head, Lucy Sparks awakens in the hospital to a shocking revelation: she has created false memories of her life over the past four years, and she must make a difficult choice about which life she wants to lead, and who she really is.

Brown, Larry, 1951-2004

Fay : a novel / Larry Brown. Algonquin Books of Chapel Hill, 2000. 487 p.

ISBN 1565121686

1. Children of migrant workers 2. Seventeen-year-old girls 3. Girl hitchhikers 4. Young women -- Relations with older men 5. Mississippi 6. Biloxi, Mississippi 7. Literary fiction 8. Southern Gothic 9. Southern fiction

LC 99088594

Saga of 17-year-old Fay Jones, who leaves her family's squalid home with three dollars to hitchhike to Biloxi, Mississippi. Along the way she is befriended by a variety of people whose lives she affects in unpredictable ways, finally becoming the catalyst in a chain reaction of desire and violence.

"The raw power of this novel, the clear, graphic accounts of both humble and perverted lives (in the bars and strip joints of Biloxi), is a triumph of realism and a humane imagination." Publishers Weekly.

Brown, Larry, 1951-2004

Joe : a novel / Larry Brown Algonquin Books of Chapel Hill, 1991. 345 p.

ISBN 0945575610

1. Small town life -- Mississippi 2. Good and evil 3. Redemption 4. Middle-aged men 5. Fifteen-year-old boys 6. Boys and men 7. Mississippi 8. Rural noir 9. Literary fiction 10. Southern fiction

LC 91012026

ALA Notable Book, 1992.

The lives of two men--Joe Ransom, a drinking, gambling, reckless fifty-year-old, and Gary Jones, a luckless fifteen-year-old raised by an evil father and an insane mother, become intertwined in a novel of good, evil, temptation, and sacrifice.

"Brown is a talented fiction writer in the whiskeyish, rascally Southern tradition of Faulkner and Erskine Caldwell. . . . The new novel is clear, simple and powerful, and it is great, rowdy fun to read." Time.

Brown, Larry, 1951-2004

* **Tiny** love : the complete stories of Larry Brown / Larry Brown ; with a Foreword by Jonathan Miles. Algonquin Books of Chapel Hill, 2019. 320 p.

ISBN 9781616209759

1. Southern States 2. Short stories 3. Southern fiction 4. Literary fiction

LC 2019008852

A career-spanning collection, Tiny Love brings together for the first time the stories of Larry Brown's previous collections along with those never before gathered.

Brown, Pierce, 1988-

Golden son / Pierce Brown. Ballantine Books, 2015. 288 p. Red rising novels

ISBN 9780345539816

1. Resistance to government 2. Dystopias 3. Life on other planets 4. Mines and mineral resources 5. Survival 6. Grief 7. Far future 8. Mars (Planet) 9. Science fiction 10. Dystopian fiction

RUSA Reading List, 2016.

"With shades of The Hunger Games, Ender's Game, and Game of Thrones, debut author Pierce Brown's genre-defying epic Red Rising hit the ground running and wasted no time becoming a sensation. Golden Son continues the stunning saga of Darrow, a rebel forged by tragedy, battling to lead his oppressed people to freedom from the overlords of a brutal elitist future built on lies. Now fully embedded among the Gold ruling class, Darrow continues his work to bring down Society from within. A life-or-death tale of vengeance with an unforgettable hero at its heart, Golden Son guarantees Pierce Brown's continuing status as one of fiction's most exciting new voices.

"The stakes are even higher than they were in Red Rising, and the twists and turns of the story are every bit as exciting. The jaw-dropper of an ending will leave readers hungry for the conclusion to Brown's wholly original, completely thrilling saga." Booklist.

Brown, Pierce, 1988-

Morning star / Pierce Brown. Del Rey, 2016. 288 p. Red rising novels

ISBN 9780345539847

1. Revolutionaries 2. Dystopias 3. Interplanetary relations 4. Exploitation 5. Class conflict 6. Elite (Social sciences) 7. Far future 8. Mars (Planet) 9. Dystopian fiction 10. Science fiction

Goodreads Choice Award, 2016

Darrow emerges from years of hiding among the Golds and declares an open revolution against the overlords who oppress his people and caused the loss of his wife.

"Brown's vivid, first-person prose puts the reader right at the forefront of impassioned speeches, broken families, and engaging battle scenes that don't shy away from the gore as this intrastellar civil war comes to a most satisfying conclusion." Publishers Weekly.

Brown, Pierce, 1988-

Red rising / Pierce Brown. Ballantine Books, 2014 400 p. Red rising novels

ISBN 9780345539786

1. Resistance to government 2. Dystopias 3. Life on other planets 4. Mines and mineral resources 5. Survival 6. Grief 7. Far future 8. Mars (Planet) 9. Science fiction 10. Dystopian fiction

LC 2013020634

Goodreads Choice Award, 2014.

A tale set in a bleak future society torn by class divisions follows the experiences of secret revolutionary Darrow, who after witnessing his wife's execution by an oppressive government joins a revolutionary cell and attempts to infiltrate an elite military academy.

"This is a very ambitious novel, with a fully realized society . . . and a cast of well-drawn characters." Booklist.

Brown, Rita Mae

The **litter** of the law : a Mrs. Murphy mystery / Rita Mae Brown & Sneaky Pie Brown ; Illustrated by Michael Gellatly. Bantam Books, 2013. 288 p. Mrs. Murphy mysteries

ISBN 9780345530486

1. Women amateur detectives 2. Murder 3. Conspiracies 4. Amateur detectives 5. Murder investigation 6. Animal detectives 7. Women cat owners 8. Virginia 9. Cozy mysteries 10. Gentle reads

The discovery of a murdered body disguised as a cornfield scarecrow becomes the first of several disturbing events in a scenic Virginia community, where Harry and her husband prepare for the local Halloween festivities and uncover a lucrative conspiracy.

Brown, Rita Mae

Murder at Monticello, or, Old sins / Rita Mae Brown & Sneaky Pie Brown ; illustrations by Wendy Wray. Bantam Books, 1994. 298 p. Mrs. Murphy mysteries

ISBN 0553081403

1. Excavations (Archaeology) 2. Dead -- Identification 3. Murder investigation 4. Race relations 5. Cat detectives 6. Animal detectives 7. Women cat owners 8. Women detectives 9. Women postmasters 10. Welsh corgis 11. Cats 12. Small town life -- Virginia 13. Murder 14. Anthropomorphism 15. Monticello (Va) 16. Virginia 17. Crozet, Virginia 18. Cozy mysteries 19. Gentle reads

LC 94016711

An old skeleton uncovered beneath the slave quarters of Monticello and a new murder in Crozet, Virginia, bring together tiger-striped Mrs. Murphy and Welsh Corgi Tee Tucker to solve the killing

"An entertaining treat for animal-loving mystery/history fans." Booklist.

Brown, Rita Mae

* **Rubyfruit** jungle / Rita Mae Brown. Bantam Books, 1988, c1973. 246 p.

ISBN 9780553278866

1. Growing up 2. Lesbians -- Sexuality 3. Prejudice 4. Lesbian teenagers 5. Poor people 6. Adopted children 7. Mothers and daughters 8. Sexism 9. Lesbian filmmakers 10. Lesbianism 11. Women/women relations 12. Sex discrimination 13. Southern States 14. Coming-of-age stories 15. Satirical fiction 16. LGBTQIA fiction

First published: 1973.

Born out of wedlock and adopted by a poor, loving family, Molly Bolt finds the South and even bohemian New York a hostile world for a lesbian but manages to thrive and remain confident.

Brown, Rita Mae

Six of one / Rita Mae Brown. Bantam Books, 1999, c1978. 270 p. Julia and Louise novels

ISBN 9780553380378

1. 1980s 2. Sisters 3. Prohibition 4. Lesbians 5. Small town life -- Maryland 6. Widows 7. Senior women 8. Eccentrics and eccentricities 9. Family relationships 10. Family sagas

Locked in an intense love-hate relationship, two sisters--Julia and Louise Hunsenmeir--grow up, marry, raise their families, and enter old age, surrounded by their fellow citizens of a small town on the Pennsylvania-Maryland border.

"The author extols the vitality and variety of women by tracing the lives of two sisters, their families, and cronies. The women are rich and poor, heterosexual (mostly) and lesbian, but they are linked by emotional and physical experiences common to all women. . . . Structurally, the novel intersperses vivid scenes from the past with those from the present (1980 in the book). Despite flaws, the narrative is engrossing, as are the women." Library Journal.

Brown, Rita Mae

Wish you were here / Rita Mae Brown and Sneaky Pie Brown ; illustrations by Wendy Wray. Bantam Books, 1990. 242 p. Mrs. Murphy mysteries

ISBN 9780553058819

1. Dismemberment 2. Death threats 3. Murder investigation 4. Cat detectives 5. Animal detectives 6. Women cat owners 7. Women detectives 8. Women postmasters 9. Welsh corgis 10. Cats 11. Small town life -- Virginia 12. Murder 13. Anthropomorphism 14. Virginia 15. Crozet, Virginia 16. Cozy mysteries 17. Gentle reads

LC 90001071

Mary Minor Haristeen, postmistress of Crozet, Virginia, joins forces with her willful cat, Mrs. Murphy, and her Welsh corgi, Tucker, to investigate a series of bizarre postcards sent to the town's inhabitants that forecast impending death

"Ms. Brown writes with wise, disarming wit about her country-bred characters and their not-always-neighborly ways." New York Times Book Review.

Brown, Rosellen

* **Before** and after / Rosellen Brown. Farrar Straus Giroux, 1992. 354 p.

ISBN 0374109990

1. Teenage murder suspects 2. Parents of criminals 3. Criminal evidence tampering 4. Families 5. Small town life 6. Murder suspects 7. Sculptors 8. Women pediatricians 9. New Hampshire 10. Psychological fiction 11. Mainstream fiction 12. Domestic fiction

LC 92081571

ALA Notable Book, 1993.

When the chief of police comes to question Jacob Reiser about the brutal murder of his teenage girlfriend, it throws the entire family into a feud laced with guilt and questions of loyalty.

"Brown is tenacious in her examination of each major character. Deftly, artfully, she strips away the delicate shelter of conventional relationships." New York Times Book Review.

Brown, Rosellen

Half a heart / Rosellen Brown. Farrar, Straus, and Giroux, 2000. 402 p.

ISBN 0374299870

1. Rich families -- Houston, Texas 2. Multiracial persons 3. Jewish American women -- Relations with African-American men 4. Mothers and daughters 5. Birthmothers 6. Mother-separated children

7. Single mothers 8. Middle-aged women 9. Prejudice 10. Race relations 11. Mainstream fiction

LC 00022926

Miriam Vener, a former civil rights activist, feels trapped in the comfortable white upper-middle-class life she leads with her family in Houston in the 1980's. That life suddenly shatters with the appearance, after almost eighteen years, of Veronica (Ronnee), her biracial daughter, born of Miriam's passionate affair a generation ago with Eijay, a brilliant black professor at a Mississippi college, who raised the child ever since.

"The situation is an intriguing one rendered all the more so by Brown's skillful and sympathetic handling of her two central characters." Time.

Brown, Rosellen

Tender mercies / Rosellen Brown. Delta, 1998, c1978. 273 p.

ISBN 0385333323

1. Accident victims 2. Family relationships 3. Husband and wife 4. Boating accidents 5. Women wheelchair users 6. Guilt in men 7. Caregivers 8. Mainstream fiction

"Remarkable depths of pity, pain, and human complication are plumbed in this sensitive book; the language, like a luminescent wand, lights up areas of emotion normally too devastating to consider." Kirkus.

Brown, Sandra, 1948-

Fat Tuesday / Sandra Brown. Warner Books, 1997. 454 p.
ISBN 0446516325

1. Defense attorneys 2. Men/women relations 3. Murder 4. Police 5. Mardi Gras 6. Former police 7. Lawyers' spouses 8. Revenge 9. Murderers 10. Kidnapping 11. Women kidnapping victims 12. New Orleans, Louisiana 13. French Quarter (New Orleans, La) 14. Romantic suspense

LC 977012

In the French Quarter during Mardi Gras week, New Orleans narcotics cop Burke Basile sets out to avenge the acquittal of the murderer of his partner by kidnapping the sheltered wife of the defense attorney.

Brown, Sandra, 1948-

Mean streak / Sandra Brown. Grand Central Publishing, 2014. 304 p.
ISBN 9781455581122

1. Captives 2. Deception 3. Wilderness areas 4. Wounds and injuries 5. Missing persons 6. Married people 7. Justice 8. Men/women relations 9. North Carolina 10. Romantic suspense

LC 2014017848

After being abducted from a mountain road in North Carolina, a pediatrician and avid runner, Dr. Emory Charbonneau, finds herself held captive by a violent man with a dark past who may ultimately end up being her savior.

Brown, Sandra, 1948-

* Outfox / Sandra Brown. Grand Central Pub, 2019. 300 p.

ISBN 9781455572199

1. FBI agents 2. Swindlers and swindling 3. Rich women 4. Missing women 5. Neighbors 6. Surveillance 7. Undercover operations 8. Impostors 9. Serial murderers 10. Serial murder investigation 11. Robbery suspects 12. Sexual attraction 13. Men/women relations 14. South Carolina 15. Romantic suspense

Sure to keep readers on the edge of their seats, this new novel will feature Brown's signature combination of steamy romance and jaw-dropping plot twists.

Brown, Sandra, 1948-

* Ricochet / Sandra Brown. Simon & Schuster, 2006. 400 p.

ISBN 0743289331

1. Detectives -- Savannah, Georgia 2. Judges -- Savannah, Georgia 3. Trophy wives 4. Drug lords 5. Judicial corruption 6. Gunshot victims 7. Murder victims 8. Women murder suspects 9. Missing women 10. Assassins 11. Criminal investigation 12. Interpersonal attraction 13. Savannah, Georgia 14. Romantic suspense

LC 2006047351

Investigating the shooting of a burglar in the home of a high-profile Savannah district judge, detectives Hatcher and Bowen suspect the judge's dutiful wife's declarations of innocence and find the case complicated by the judge's notorious soft-on-crime tactics.

"Det. Sgt. Duncan Hatcher, a sexy Savannah homicide cop, falls hard for Elise Laird, a dishy damsel-in-distress, the moment he spots her at a police awards dinner. Too bad she's married to Judge Cato Laird, who consistently subverts Hatcher's efforts to bring local drug lord Robert Savich to justice. When Hatcher and his feisty partner, Det. DeeDee Bowen, are called to the Laird home after Elise supposedly shoots an intruder in self-defense, the desperate trophy wife confides to Hatcher that she believes her husband, a secret Savich crony, intended her to be the intruder's victim. Later, as the uncertain Hatcher grapples with his desires, Elise vanishes, leaving behind another dead body. Tight plotting, a hot love story with some nice twists and a credible ending help make this a standout thriller." Publishers Weekly.

Brown, Sandra, 1948-

White hot / Sandra Brown. Simon & Schuster, 2004. 419 p.

ISBN 0743245539

1. Women interior decorators 2. Men/women relations 3. Labor disputes 4. Lawyers 5. Brothers -- Death 6. Foundry workers 7. Brothers and sisters 8. Father and adult daughter 9. Factories 10. Labor unions 11. Occupational health and safety 12. Factory management 13. Family relationships 14. Homecomings 15. Louisiana 16. Romantic suspense

LC 2004052129

When she learns that her younger brother Danny has committed suicide, Sayre Lynch relents from her vow never to return to Destiny, the small Louisiana town in which she grew up. She plans to leave immediately after the funeral, but instead soon finds herself drawn into the web cast by Huff Hoyle, her controlling and tyrannical father, the man who owns the town's sole industry, an iron foundry, and in effect runs the lives of everyone who lives there. As she feared, Sayre learns that nothing has changed. Her father and older brother, Chris, are as devious as ever, and now they have a new partner-in-crime, a canny and disarming lawyer named Beck Merchant, who appears to be their equal in corruption. Soon, Sayre is thrown in closer contact with Beck and becomes convinced that something more sinister is at play than her father's usual need to dominate people and events. As she sets out to learn just what did happen to Danny, she comes to realize that there are many secrets in Destiny--secrets that hide decades of pain and anger, and that threaten at any moment to erupt and destroy not only her father and brother, but perhaps Sayre herself.--From publisher description.

Brown, Sandra, 1948-

The **witness** / Sandra Brown. Warner Books, 1995. 422 p.
ISBN 0446603309

1. Conspiracies 2. Traffic accident victims 3. Women lawyers 4. Mother and child 5. People with amnesia 6. Hate groups 7. Anti-hate group action 8. Women public defenders 9. Men/women relations 10. White supremacy movements 11. White supremacists 12. South

Carolina 13. Romantic suspense

LC 94042733

Kendall Deaton courageously risks her own life and that of her unborn child to testify against her ex-husband, a violent white supremacist, and his father.

Brown, Taylor, 1982-
Fallen land / Taylor Brown St. Martin's Press, 2016. 256 p.
ISBN 9781250077974

1. American Civil War era (1861-1865) 2. Thieves 3. Pregnant women 4. Survival 5. Escapes 6. Hiding 7. Sherman's March to the Sea 8. War and society 9. United States Civil War, 1861-1865 10. Confederate States of America 11. Blue Ridge Mountains Region 12. United States -- History -- Civil War, 1861-1865 13. Historical fiction

A couple races through the destroyed South, relying on the kindness of strangers and foraging from abandoned farms, as they flee a slave hunter, tracking dogs and ex-partisan rangers during the final year of the Civil War.

"Picaresque in style--tracing the couple's wanderings from danger to devastation--with photographic precision and a stunning descriptive style reminiscent of a mournful ballad, this historical novel bleeds sorrow and regret. And the reader cannot look away or forget. Brown uses lovely language to describe the horrific, and dramatizes humanitys best and worst in wartime." Booklist.

Brown, Taylor, 1982-
* **Gods** of Howl Mountain : a novel / Taylor Brown. St. Martin's Press, 2018. 288 p.
ISBN 9781250111777

1. 1950s 2. Bootleggers 3. Women healers 4. Mountain life 5. Korean War veterans 6. Grandmother and grandson 7. Mothers and sons 8. Family secrets 9. Communities 10. Family relationships 11. Men/women relations 12. North Carolina 13. Literary fiction 14. Rural noir 15. Southern fiction 16. Historical fiction

LC 2017043677

Concocting potions and cures for her mountain-dwelling community, a folk healer with a dark past helps her bootleg-whiskey-runner grandson outmaneuver rivals, federal agents, snake charmers and the mystery of his mother's long confinement in a mental hospital.

Browne, S. G. (Scott G.)
Less than hero : a novel / S.G. Browne. Gallery Books, 2015. 384 p.
ISBN 9781476711744

1. Drugs -- Testing 2. Vigilantes 3. Human experimentation in medicine 4. Medical care 5. Drugs -- Side effects 6. Criminals 7. Superhuman abilities 8. New York City 9. Satirical fiction

LC 2014032357

"With the razor-sharp satire that earned him rave reviews for Big Egos and Lucky Bastard, among others, S.G. Browne delivers another irresistible read, about an unlikely band of heroes who use their medical complications to gain fame, confront villains, and bring their own unique brand of justice to New York City. Lloyd Prescott is a professional guinea pig. After nearly a year on unemployment, Lloyd discovered he could make money volunteering for Phase One pharmaceutical drug clinical trials, where drugs are tested for safety by giving them to subjects and studying the side effects. Every month, Lloyd meets up with a group of other guinea pigs to share information on their clinical trials, but soon they learn they're getting a lot more than they bargained for... Convulsions. Memory loss. Hallucinations. Drowsiness. Vomiting. Sudden weight gain. These and other side effects affect them all-

-but rather than simply suffer the consequences, the guinea pigs find they're able to project these side effects onto others. And once they realize this, there's no end to the ruckus they'll cause using their powers for good...or ill. In a winning combination of pitch-perfect humor and biting social commentary, S.G. Browne proves with Less than Hero that he is still"one of America's very best writers" (Jonathan Maberry)"--, Provided by publisher.

Brownmiller, Susan
Waverly Place / Susan Brownmiller. Grove Press, 1989. 294 p.

1. Steinberg, Lisa, 1981-1987 2. Steinberg, Joel Barnet, 1941- 3. Nussbaum, Hedda, 1942- 4. Child abuse 5. Child neglect 6. Abused women 7. Murder 8. Violence against children 9. Greenwich Village, New York City 10. Mainstream fiction

LC 88026072

Inspired by the notorious Lisa Steinberg case, this novel follows a couple as they descend into a nightmarish reality of child abuse and the society that quietly tolerates it.

Brownrigg, Sylvia
* The **delivery** room : a novel / Sylvia Brownrigg. Counterpoint, 2008, c2006. 384 p.
ISBN 9781582434247

1. Women psychotherapists 2. Married people 3. Psychotherapist and patient 4. Interpersonal relations 5. Serbs in England 6. Yugoslav War, 1991-1995 -- Psychological aspects 7. Family and work 8. Family relationships 9. London, England 10. Psychological fiction

LC 2008013102

Originally published: London : Picador, 2006.

"The Delivery Room is, despite its contemporary themes, an old-fashioned novel, one full of texture and detail, in which character and plot are patiently dissected and illuminated so that a larger picture might become apparent." Times Literary Supplement.

Brownrigg, Sylvia
Morality tale : a novel / Sylvia Brownrigg ; drawings by Monica Scott. Counterpoint, 2008. 224 p.
ISBN 9781582434049

1. Second wives 2. Love triangles 3. Self-discovery in women 4. Extramarital affairs 5. Husband and wife 6. Remarriage 7. Stepchildren 8. Marriage 9. Remarried persons 10. California 11. Domestic fiction 12. Love stories

LC 2007043783

Feeling unfulfilled in her life as the second wife of a man with two demanding children and an angry ex, a woman pursues an illicit relationship with a Zen-spouting salesman, a situation that prompts her to let go of past demons.

"Contemplating Sylvia Brownrigg's short new novel, the adjective quirky comes to mind. Bold, dry, eccentric, Morality Tale cries out for a descriptive term that can pinpoint its oddness along with its likability. Quirky it will have to be, for this curious, teasing, idiosyncratic and strangely charming book." San Francisco Chronicle.

Bruen, Ken
Cross / Ken Bruen. St. Martin's Minotaur, 2008, c2007. 288 p. Jack Taylor series
ISBN 9780312341428

1. Murder investigation 2. Revenge 3. Religious fanaticism 4. Former police 5. Detectives 6. Loss (Psychology) 7. Recovering alcoholics 8. Gunshot victims 9. Interpersonal relations 10. Private investigators 11. Crimes against children 12. Crucifixion 13. Galway,

Ireland 14. Ireland 15. Hardboiled fiction 16. Mysteries

LC 2007042421

Originally published: London : Bantam, 2007.

With his surrogate son, Cody, in a hospital in a coma, a troubled Jack Taylor takes the opportunity to assist Ridge, his old friend from the guards, with a horrific case involving the crucifixion slaying of a boy in Galway.

"Bruen riffs on different meanings and implications of the word cross throughout, and his insights into pain, loss and Irishness are unforgettable." Publishers Weekly.

Bruen, Ken

Galway girl : a Jack Taylor novel / Ken Bruen. The Mysterious Press, 2019 288 p. Jack Taylor series

ISBN 9780802147936

1. Private investigators 2. Police murders 3. Psychopaths 4. Former police 5. Loss (Psychology) 6. Murder 7. Murder investigation 8. Galway, Ireland 9. Ireland 10. Hardboiled fiction 11. Mysteries

LC 2019037892

Reeling from a violent family tragedy, private investigator Jack Taylor finds himself on the trail of a psychotic assassin who has been murdering high-profile Galway police officers.

Bruen, Ken

The **guards** / Ken Bruen. St. Martin's Minotaur, 2003, c2001. 291 p. Jack Taylor series

ISBN 0312303556

1. Former police 2. Alcoholic men 3. Murder investigation 4. Mothers of murder victims 5. Teenagers 6. Friendship 7. Despair 8. Men/women relations 9. Bars (Drinking establishments) 10. Private investigators 11. Galway, Ireland 12. Ireland 13. Hardboiled fiction 14. Mysteries

LC 2002035855

Originally published in the UK in 2001.

Shamus Award for Best P.I. Novel, 2004.

Stuck in a rut after his dismissal from the Irish police force and still grieving over the death of his father, Jack Taylor finds renewal when an intriguing woman hires him based on his rumored talent for finding things.

"Bruen's astringent prose and death's-head humor keep this quest for redemption from getting maudlin, just as his 'tapestry of talk' makes somber poetry of the bar-stool laments that serve as dialogue." New York Times Book Review.

Brundage, Elizabeth

* All **things** cease to appear / Elizabeth Brundage. Alfred A. Knopf, 2016. 384 p.

ISBN 9781101875599

1. 1970s 2. Women murder victims 3. Cold cases (Criminal investigation) 4. Farms 5. Suspicion 6. Wife-killing 7. Small towns 8. Marital conflict 9. Murder victims 10. Suicide victims 11. Haunted places 12. New York (State) 13. Psychological suspense 14. Parallel narratives

LC 2015024682

Arriving home to find his wife murdered and their toddler left alone, art history professor George Clare is targeted with suspicion by a relentless police officer as dark community secrets are revealed over a span of decades.

"Succeeding as murder mystery, ghost tale, family drama, and love story, her novel is both tragic and transcendent." Publishers Weekly.

Bruni, Sarah

The **night** Gwen Stacy died / Sarah Bruni. Mariner Books/Houghton Mifflin Harcourt, 2013. 272 p.

ISBN 9780547898162

1. Young women 2. Self-discovery in women 3. Deception 4. Small town life 5. Misfits (Persons) 6. Iowa 7. Love stories 8. Mainstream fiction

LC 2012040352

Dreaming of a life in Paris while working at a small-town Iowa gas station, Sheila stages her own kidnapping to run away with an oddball who shares a superhero's name and who begins to regard her as the character's girlfriend.

Brunkhorst, Alex

The **gilded** Life of Matilda Duplaine / Alex Brunkhorst. Mira, 2015. 320 p.

ISBN 9780778317531

1. Rich people 2. Mansions 3. Actors and actresses 4. Recluses 5. Journalists 6. Young women 7. Secrets 8. Men/women relations 9. Interpersonal attraction 10. Hollywood, California 11. Mainstream fiction

When Thomas Cleary, a young journalist with working class roots, meets Matilda Duplaine, a young woman raised in the lap of luxury, they begin a secret love affair that quickly unravels into a web of secrets and lies that hold the power to destroy their lives and the lives of everyone around them.

Brunt, Carol Rifka

* **Tell** the wolves I'm home : a novel / Carol Rifka Brunt. Dial Press, 2012. 368 p.

ISBN 9780679644194

1. 1980s 2. Teenage girls 3. Loss (Psychology) 4. Friendship 5. AIDS (Disease) 6. Uncles -- Death 7. Fourteen-year-old girls 8. Familial love 9. Intergenerational friendship 10. Grief 11. Family relationships 12. Compassion 13. New York City 14. Coming-of-age stories 15. Mainstream fiction

LC 2011027932

Her world upended by the death of a beloved artist uncle who was the only person who understood her, fourteen-year-old June is mailed a teapot by her uncle's grieving friend, with whom June forges a poignant relationship.

Bryant, Niobia

Christmas with the billionaire / Niobia Bryant Kimani, 2019. 448 p. Passion Grove

ISBN 9781335470997

1. Christmas 2. Rich families 3. Authors 4. Landowners 5. Impersonation 6. Secrets 7. Interpersonal attraction 8. Men/women relations 9. Holiday romances 10. Multicultural romances 11. Contemporary romances 12. African American fiction 13. Category romances

"2 novels : great value" -- cover.

Despite her family's billions, Samira Ansah is climbing the corporate ladder on her own. She needs to buy a lucrative property owned by bestselling author Emerson Lance Miller. The sexy recluse isn't selling, but when he assumes she's his new assistant, Samira plays along to get closer.

Bryant, Niobia

Madam, may I / Niobia Bryant. Dafina, 2019. 276 p.

ISBN 9781496716545

1. Escort services (Prostitution) 2. Madams (Prostitution) 3. African

American women 4. Prostitutes 5. Protectiveness in women 6. Loneliness 7. Adult education 8. Tutors 9. Self-esteem 10. Men/women relations 11. Drama lit 12. African American fiction

A high-class madam pursues an education and a normal life while protecting the women who work for her, particularly Portia, her gorgeous, new protégé who is spinning out of control and putting their whole operation at risk.

Bryant, Niobia

Message from a mistress / Niobia Bryant. Dafina, 2010. 320 p. Mistress novels (Niobia Bryant)

ISBN 9780758238214

1. African Americans 2. Extramarital affairs 3. Betrayal 4. Friendship 5. Marriage 6. Secrets 7. Drama lit 8. African American fiction

Sequel: Mistress no more.

Through good times and bad, longtime friends Jaime, Renee, Aria, and Jessa have shared just about everything. But all hell breaks loose when Jessa texts them a shocking revelation: she's been sharing her bed-with one of their husbands. Worse, she refuses to name which husband. And all three wives believe they have reason to worry.

Buchan, John, 1875-1940

* The **thirty-nine** steps / John Buchan ; edited with an introduction and notes by Christopher Harvie. Oxford University Press, 1999, c1915. 119 p. Richard Hannay adventures

ISBN 0192839314

1. 1910s 2. Spies -- Germany 3. Secrets 4. Conspiracies 5. Mining engineers 6. Murder 7. Frameups 8. Malicious accusation 9. Germans in Great Britain 10. International intrigue 11. Chases 12. Prejudice 13. Antisemitism 14. World War I -- Causes 15. Great Britain 16. Scotland 17. Spy fiction 18. Classics

LC 00267062

Later published in: The four adventures of Richard Hannay (1988)

Originally published: London : William Blackwood and Sons, 1915.

In the days leading up to the First World War, typical everyman Richard Hannay finds himself caught in the middle of an anarchist plot to plunge Europe into chaos by assassinating the Greek Premier. However, when his American contact is murdered, Hannay makes it his duty to elude his enemies and save the Greek leader.

Buchanan, Cathy Marie

* The **painted** girls / Cathy Marie Buchanan. Riverhead Books, 2013. 368 p.

ISBN 9781594486241

1. Degas, Edgar, 1834-1917 2. Belle Epoque (1871-1914) 3. 1870s 4. 19th century 5. Sisters 6. Artists' models -- France 7. Ballet dancers 8. Murder suspects 9. Paris, France 10. Historical fiction

Evergreen Award (Ontario), 2014.

A tale inspired by the real-life model for Degas's Little Dancer Aged Fourteen is set in belle epoque Paris and traces the survival efforts of the Van Goethem sisters after the sudden death of their father, a situation that prompts young Marie's ballet training, introduction to a genius painter and patronage by a wealthy man whose assistance comes with a price.

"Buchanan brings the unglamorous reality of the late-19th-century Parisian demimonde into stark relief while imagining the life of Marie Van Goethem, the actual model for the iconic Degas statue Little Dancer Aged Fourteen... the moving yet unsentimental portrait of family love, of two sisters struggling to survive with dignity, makes this a must-read." Kirkus.

Buchanan, Edna

You only die twice : a Britt Montero mystery / Edna Buchanan. W. Morrow, 2001. 304 p. Britt Montero novels

ISBN 0380976552

1. Secret identity 2. Women journalists 3. Judicial error 4. Police 5. Murder investigation 6. Cuban American women 7. Women amateur detectives 8. Miami, Florida 9. Mysteries

LC 00049543

The perfect, nude corpse of a beautiful woman washes up on a perfect Miami Beach--her body tanned and shapely, her nails elegantly manicured. The problem is the victim, Kaithlin Jordan, was supposedly murdered ten years ago. And her convicted killer--her husband, R. I. Jordan, scion of a wealthy and powerful South Florida family--sits on Death Row, just weeks from his execution. It's up to reporter-detective Britt Montero to make sense of all this.

"A fascinating amalgam of red herrings, misdirection, and guilt by personality. . . . An intelligent, thoroughly entertaining crime novel." Booklist.

Buchman, M. L. (Matthew Lieber)

The **night** is mine / M. L. Buchman. Sourcebooks Casablanca, 2012 384 p. Night Stalkers (M. L. Buchman)

ISBN 9781402258107

1. White House, Washington, D.C. 2. United States. Army. Special Operations Aviation Regiment (Airborne), 160th 3. Undercover operations 4. Bodyguards 5. Helicopter pilots 6. Soldiers 7. Women cooks 8. First loves 9. Romantic suspense

A pilot for the Night Stalkers air squad, Emily develops a forbidden attraction to her commander, Mark, when he gets himself involved in her special assignment as an undercover bodyguard for the First Lady, who has been receiving anonymous threats.

Buchman, M. L. (Matthew Lieber)

Pure heat / M.L. Buchman. Sourcebooks Casablanca, 2014. 352 p. Firehawks

ISBN 9781402286889

1. Fire fighters 2. Terrorism 3. Wildfires 4. Wildfire fighters 5. Pilots 6. Courage 7. Smokejumpers 8. Men/women relations 9. Elite operatives 10. Oregon 11. Romantic suspense

A third-generation forest fire specialist who lost both her father and fiancé to the flames, Carly Thomas copilots a Firehawk with former smokejumper Steve Mercer to battle the worst wildfire in decades--and the blazing attraction between them.

Buck, Pearl S. (Pearl Sydenstricker), 1892-1973

* The **good** Earth / Pearl S. Buck. Washington Square Press, 2004, c1931. 357 p. House of Earth trilogy

ISBN 0743272935

1. Farmers -- China 2. Husband and wife 3. Social classes 4. Men/women relations 5. Families 6. Poor people 7. Gender equity 8. Gender role 9. China 10. Historical fiction 11. Family sagas 12. Literary fiction 13. Modern classics

Originally published: New York : John Day Co., 1931.

Pulitzer Prize for Fiction, 1932.

A Chinese peasant overcomes the forces of nature and the frailties of human nature to become a wealthy landowner.

Buckley, Christopher, 1952-

Supreme Courtship / Christopher Buckley. Twelve, 2008. 304 p.

ISBN 9780446579827

1. United States. Supreme Court 2. Judges 3. Television personalities

4. Presidents -- United States -- Election 5. Interpersonal attraction 6. Men/women relations 7. Washington, D.C. 8. Political fiction 9. Satirical fiction

LC 2008007788

When a television judge ends up on the Supreme Court, romance and the fate of a presidential election take center stage in this comic political satire.

"Christopher Buckley doesn't merely observe the zeitgeist better than anyone else on the planet. He anticipates it. . . . Satire doesn't cut much closer to the bone." The National Review.

Buckley, Fiona

The **doublet** affair : a mystery at Queen Elizabeth I's court / Fiona Buckley. Scribner, 1998. 294 p. Ursula Blanchard mysteries

ISBN 0684838427

1. Elizabeth I, Queen of England, 1533-1603 2. Elizabethan era (1558-1603) 3. Tudor period (1485-1603) 4. 16th century 5. Treason 6. Undercover operations 7. Ladies-in-waiting 8. Women spies 9. Conspiracies 10. Kidnapping 11. Women amateur detectives 12. Widows 13. Great Britain -- Court and courtiers 14. Great Britain -- History -- Elizabeth I, 1558-1603 15. Historical mysteries 16. Mysteries

Lady-in-waiting Ursula Blanchard is sent by Queen Elizabeth I to visit a scholar's home where she was the children's governess. Ostensibly a social call, the trip is to investigate a report of a plot to overthrow the queen.

Buckley, Fiona

The **siren** queen : an Ursula Blanchard mystery at Queen Elizabeth I's court / Fiona Buckley. Scribner, 2004. 288 p. Ursula Blanchard mysteries

ISBN 0743237528

1. Elizabeth I,, Queen of England, 1533-1603 2. Elizabethan era (1558-1603) 3. 16th century 4. Tudor period (1485-1603) 5. Treason 6. Women spies 7. Women detectives 8. Resistance to government 9. Deception 10. Courts and courtiers 11. Women rulers 12. Conspiracies 13. Great Britain -- Court and courtiers 14. Great Britain -- History -- Elizabeth I, 1558-1603 15. Historical mysteries 16. Mysteries

LC 2004045284

When the powerful Duke of Norfolk arranges a marriage between her daughter and an unsuitable man, Ursula Blanchard, a half-sister to Elizabeth I, uncovers a plot to overthrow the queen and begins to spy on one of the conspirators.

Buckley, William F. (William Frank), 1925-2008

* **Mongoose,** R.I.P. : a Blackford Oakes novel / William F. Buckley, Jr. Random House, 1987. 322 p. Blackford Oakes novels

ISBN 0394559312

1. Castro, Fidel, 1926-2016 2. Kennedy, John F (John Fitzgerald), 1917-1963 3. Kennedy, Robert Francis, 1925-1968 4. CIA Cuban operations 5. 1960s 6. Spies -- United States 7. Spy fiction

LC 87028344

"The best of the Blacky books, this is an entertainment of the Graham Greene order that truly entertains, excites, and edifies. . . . The story builds with considerable suspense up to Blackford's horrendous dilemma on the day of JFK's assassination." The National Review.

Buckman, Daniel, 1967-

* **Because** the rain / Daniel Buckman. St. Martin's Press, 2007. 272 p.

ISBN 0312362684

1. Vietnam veterans 2. Vietnamese American women 3. Police 4. Prostitutes 5. Husband and wife 6. Murder 7. Spouses of murder victims 8. Interpersonal relations 9. Chicago, Illinois 10. Psychological fiction

LC 2006051180

"Buckman writes convincingly of Vietnam vets and captures nicely the disillusionment his characters share. It's a bleak but redeeming read." Publishers Weekly.

Buehlman, Christopher

The **Suicide** Motor Club / Christopher Buehlman. Berkley Books, 2016. 360 p.

ISBN 9781101988732

1. Vampires 2. Mothers and sons 3. Revenge in women 4. Vampire slayers 5. Missing boys 6. Automobiles 7. Revenge 8. Widows 9. Murder 10. Nuns 11. Horror

RUSA Reading List Short List, 2017

Two years after killing a man, taking his son and leaving a wife and mother for dead, the ruthless Suicide Motor Club vampires are hunted by a woman whose thirst for vengeance proves more powerful than their hunger for blood.

"Buehlman's latest is gripping the whole way through, with a perfectly poignant ending." Publishers Weekly.

Buffett, Jimmy

A **salty** piece of land / Jimmy Buffett. Little, Brown and Co., 2004. xiv, 462 p.

ISBN 0316908452

1. Travelers 2. Voyages and travels 3. Islands -- Tropics 4. Yucatan Peninsula 5. Caribbean Area 6. Mysteries 7. Short stories

LC 2004016508

Tully Mars finds himself regretting a decision to help find the missing lens belonging to the Cayo Loco lighthouse, in a tequila-inspired adventure featuring such characters as Indian shaman Ix-Nay and boatman Captain Kirk.

"Perhaps it is because Buffett has long been a writer of lyrics that his prose style now seems to flow in a fresh, fanciful, finely imagined fashion. . . . What makes the incredible so credible to the reader, what makes the old lighthouse shine again, is the spiritual savvy Buffett has gleaned from the beach of life as he's wandered in the raw poetry of time." New York Times Book Review.

Bujold, Lois McMaster

* **Shards** of honor / Lois McMaster Bujold. Baen Books, 1986. 239 p. Vorkosigan saga

ISBN 9781476781105

1. Space warfare 2. Nobility 3. Ship captains 4. Interstellar relations 5. Space flight 6. Men/women relations 7. Space opera 8. Science fiction

Shards of Honoris set a year before the birth of Miles Vorkosigan.

Cordelia Naismith, Betan Survey Captain, was expecting the unexpected: hexapods, floating creatures, odd parasites... She was not, however, expecting to find hostile humans on an uninhabited planet. And she wasn't really expecting to fall in love with a 40-plus barbarian known to cosmopolitan galactics as the Butcher of Komarr.

Bujold, Lois McMaster

* The **warrior's** apprentice / Lois McMaster Bujold Baen, 1986. 311 p. Vorkosigan saga

ISBN 067172066X

1. Space warfare 2. Nobility 3. Ship captains 4. Men with disfigurements 5. Interstellar relations 6. Short men 7. Civil war 8. Men/women relations 9. Space flight 10. Space 11. Space opera 12. Science fiction

Takes place 17 years after Miles Vorkosigan's birth.

Discharged from the Barrarayan academy after flunking the physical, a discouraged Miles Vorkosigan takes possession of a jumpship and becomes the leader of a mercenary force that expands to a fleet of treasonous proportions.

Bulawayo, NoViolet

We need new names : a novel / NoViolet Bulawayo. Reagan Arthur Books, 2013. 304 p.

ISBN 9780316230810

1. Girl immigrants 2. Political violence -- Zimbabwe 3. Africans in the United States 4. Families 5. Immigration and emigration 6. Moving to a new country 7. Aunt and niece 8. Zimbabwe 9. United States -- Immigration and emigration 10. Political fiction 11. Literary fiction

LC 2012038068

Hemingway Foundation/PEN Award, 2014.
Hurston/Wright Legacy Award: Fiction, 2014.
Shortlisted for the Man Booker Prize, 2013.

Follows 10-year-old Zimbabwe native, Darling, as she escapes the closed schools and paramilitary police control of her homeland in search of opportunity and freedom with an aunt in America.

Bulgakov, Mikhail, 1891-1940

* The **master** and Margarita / Mikhail Bulgakov ; translated from the Russian by Michael Glenny ; with an introduction by Simon Franklin. Knopf, 1992. xxix, 446 p.

ISBN 9780679410461

1. Jesus Christ Crucifixion 2. Pilate, Pontius, 1st cent 3. 1920s 4. Faustian bargains 5. Devil 6. Authors, Soviet 7. Separated friends, relatives, etc 8. Lovers 9. Psychiatric hospital patients 10. Magicians 11. Communists -- Soviet Union 12. Talking cats 13. Good and evil 14. Manuscripts 15. Murder 16. Black magic 17. Psychiatric clinics 18. Intellectual life 19. Communism 20. Bureaucracy 21. Moscow, Russia 22. Soviet Union -- Social conditions -- 1917-1945 23. Rome -- History -- Empire, 30 BC-96 AD 24. Allegories 25. Literary fiction 26. Novels-within-novels 27. Political fiction 28. Translations -- Russian to English 29. Modern classics

Set in Moscow of the 1920's, this satirical novel recounts the dealings a writer and his mistress have with Satan.

Bump, Gabriel

* **Everywhere** you don't belong : a novel / Gabriel Bump. Algonquin Books of Chapel Hill, 2020. 240 p.

ISBN 9781616208790

1. African American teenage boys 2. High schools 3. Police brutality 4. Growing up 5. Riots 6. Gangs 7. Grandmothers 8. Community organization 9. Civil rights workers 10. Chicago, Illinois 11. Coming-of-age stories 12. African American fiction

LC 2019008323

Raised by a civil-rights activist grandmother on the South Side of Chicago, Claude McKay Love searches for a sense of belonging before a riot compels his departure for college, where he discovers he cannot escape his past.

"With deft writing and rat-a-tat, laugh-until-you-gasp-at-the-implications dialog, Bump delivers a singular sense of growing up black that will resonate with readers." Library Journal.

Bunn, T. Davis, 1952-

Outbreak / Davis Bunn. Bethany House, 2019. 368 p.

ISBN 9780764230011

1. Scientists 2. Epidemics 3. Plague 4. Algae 5. Ocean currents 6. Conspiracies 7. Vaccines 8. Brothers 9. Government cover-ups 10. Christian suspense

LC 2018042273

Along the coast of West Africa, strange algae is growing and mysterious deaths are rising--until suddenly, with the sea currents' shift, the deaths stop. Professor Theo Bishop and biological researcher Avery Madison are the only ones who know the truth. Will the authorities heed their warning before it happens again?

Buntin, Julie

* **Marlena** : a novel / Julie Buntin. Henry Holt and Co., 2017. 288 p.

ISBN 9781627797641

1. Female friendship 2. Influence (Psychology) 3. Teenage girl drug abusers 4. Teenage girls -- Friendship 5. Self-fulfillment in women 6. Life change events 7. Forgiveness 8. Memories 9. Librarians 10. Drug use 11. Coping 12. Michigan 13. New York City 14. Psychological fiction 15. Literary fiction

LC 2016021949

Struggling to adapt to a new home in rural Michigan, 15-year-old Cat bonds with a pill-popping, manic young neighbor with whom she renders their desolate community into a kind of playground until suffering a tragedy that she confronts decades later.

"Jumping between their teenage friendship in Michigan and Cat's adult life in New York City, Buntin creates a world so subtle and nuanced and alive that it imprints like a memory. Devastating; as unforgettable as it is gorgeous." Kirkus.

Bunyan, John, 1628-1688

The **pilgrim's** progress / John Bunyan. Oxford University Press, 2003, c1678. 333 p.

ISBN 9780192803610

1. Pilgrims and pilgrimages, Christian 2. Spiritual journeys 3. Christian life 4. Imaginary journeys 5. Good and evil 6. Faith (Christianity) 7. Voyages and travels 8. Christian fiction 9. Classics 10. Allegories

An allegorical account of Christian's journeys towards the Celestial City from the City of Destruction.

Burdett, John

Bangkok 8 / John Burdett. Alfred A. Knopf, 2003. 352 p. Sonchai Jitpleecheep mysteries

ISBN 1400040442

1. Police -- Bangkok, Thailand 2. Murder investigation 3. Buddhists 4. African American soldiers 5. Marines 6. FBI agents 7. Women FBI agents 8. Snakes 9. Thai Americans 10. Multiracial men 11. Bangkok, Thailand 12. Thailand 13. Mysteries

LC 2002040658

Sequel: Bangkok tattoo.

"The narrator, a Buddhist cop named Sonchai Jitplecheep, finds himself plunged into a dangerous investigation of the deaths of his partner Pichai Apiradee and U. S. Embassy Sgt. William Bradley. Sonchai is an unusual character on several levels, from the mysteries of his violent past to his conversations with the ghost of Pichai. His ambiguous feelings toward Kimberley Jones, an American FBI agent brought in to work the case, reflect his upbringing as the child of a Thai mother and an unknown American father. . . .The mix of detective work, Bangkok street life, the Thai sex trade and drug smuggling forms a powerful mlange of images and insight." Publishers Weekly.

Burdick, Eugene L.

Fail-safe / Eugene Burdick and Harvey Wheeler McGraw-Hill, 1962 286 p.

1. Cold War 2. Nuclear weapons 3. Soviet Union -- Foreign relations -- United States 4. United States -- Foreign relations -- Soviet Union 5. Political fiction

LC 62019642

The question of accidental war is examined in this novel about American planes which fly past the point of recall to drop nuclear bombs on Moscow.

Burdick, Serena

The **girls** with no names / Serena Burdick. Park Row, 2020. 336 p.

ISBN 9780778309994

1. 1910s 2. Sisters 3. Teenage girls 4. Missing girls 5. Family secrets 6. Rescues 7. Imprisonment 8. Psychiatric hospitals 9. New York City 10. Historical fiction

In 1910s New York City, Effie and Luella discover a secret about their father which later leads to Luella's disappearance. Effie suspects their father has sent Luella to the House of Mercy and hatches a plan to get herself committed in order to save her.

"A well-plotted story with an excellent sense of time and place. Readers looking for historical fiction with emotional depth will enjoy." Library Journal.

Burgess, Anthony, 1917-1993

* A **clockwork** orange / Anthony Burgess. Norton, 1986, c1967. 192 p.

ISBN 0939305538

1. Social control 2. Aversion therapy 3. Dystopias 4. Violence 5. Crime 6. Good and evil 7. Criminals 8. Near future 9. Transgressive fiction 10. Modern classics 11. Dystopian fiction 12. Science fiction

LC 86-23843

Includes introduction by author, publisher's note and the "controversial last chapter not previously published in the United States."

Originally published: London : Heinemann, 1962.

Presents Burgess' satire of the present inhumanity of man to man through a futuristic culture where teenagers rule with violence.

"Paradox is at the heart of this book, as this newly restored, fiftieth-anniversary edition makes more clear than ever...a fitting publication of a book that remains...shocking and thought provoking." Booklist.

Burke, Alafair

The **better** sister : a novel / Alafair Burke. Harper, 2019. 336 p.

ISBN 9780062853370

1. Sisters 2. Dysfunctional families 3. Murder suspects 4. Murder 5. Alienation in families 6. Husband and wife 7. Former wives 8. Stepchildren 9. Family secrets 10. False arrest 11. Murder investigation 12. New York City 13. Psychological suspense

LC 2018051071

When a prominent Manhattan lawyer is murdered, two estranged sisters--one the victim's widow, the other his ex?navigate long-standing

resentments to uncover devastating family secrets. By the best-selling author of The Wife.

Burke, James Lee, 1936-

Black cherry blues / James Lee Burke. Little, Brown, 1989. 290 p. Dave Robicheaux novels

ISBN 9780316116992

1. Oil industry and trade 2. Mafia 3. Murder investigation 4. Native American activists 5. Grief in men 6. Vietnam veterans 7. Recovering alcoholics 8. Cajun men 9. Detectives 10. Police 11. New Orleans, Louisiana 12. New Iberia, Louisiana 13. Montana 14. Mysteries 15. Hardboiled fiction 16. Pacific Northwest fiction 17. Police procedurals 18. Southern fiction

LC 89007977

Edgar Allan Poe Award for Best Mystery Novel, 1990.

An ex-New Orleans cop comes up against Indians, oil company roughnecks, and Mafia honchos on the rugged Montana landscape.

"A stunning novel that takes detective fiction into new imaginative realms. . . . All the main characters in this darkly beautiful, lyric saga carry heavy emotional baggage, and Robicheaux's sleuthing is a simultaneous exorcism of demons of grief, loss, fear, rage, vengeance." Publishers Weekly.

Burke, James Lee, 1936-

Heaven's prisoners / James Lee Burke. H. Holt, 1988. 292 p. Dave Robicheaux novels

ISBN 0805006656

1. Drug smugglers 2. Refugees, Salvadoran 3. Revenge 4. Guilt in men 5. Vietnam veterans 6. Recovering alcoholics 7. Cajun men 8. Detectives 9. Police 10. New Orleans, Louisiana 11. New Iberia, Louisiana 12. Mysteries 13. Hardboiled fiction 14. Police procedurals 15. Southern fiction

LC 87026878

"There is a pronounced streak of poetry in Mr. Burke's prose. He has the knack of combining action with reflection; he has pity for the human condition, and even his villains can have some sympathetic and redeeming qualities. Mr. Burke writes in an unhurried manner, but the book never loses tension because he is so wrapped up in his characters and their locale." New York Times Book Review.

Burke, James Lee, 1936-

House of the rising sun : a novel / James Lee Burke. Simon & Schuster, 2015. 448 p. Hackberry Holland novels

ISBN 9781501107108

1. Texas Rangers 2. First World War era (1914-1918) 3. Fathers and sons 4. Voyages and travels 5. Enemies 6. Grail 7. Arms dealers 8. World War I 9. Quests 10. Family relationships 11. Men/women relations 12. Texas 13. Historical thrillers

LC 2015012518

Escaping with a stolen artifact after a violent encounter with Mexican soldiers, a Texas Ranger is pursued by a bloodthirsty Austrian arms dealer, who, believing the artifact to be the Holy Grail, targets the man's estranged son.

"Crisp dialogue highlights this tale of redemption and the bonds of family, and the breathtaking conclusion is one that readers wont soon forget." Publishers Weekly.

Burke, James Lee, 1936-

The **jealous** kind / James Lee Burke. Simon & Schuster, 2016. 383 p. Holland family saga

ISBN 9781501107207

1. 1950s 2. High school students 3. Class conflict 4. Mafia 5. Violence in men 6. Crime 7. Korean War, 1950-1953 8. Police

brutality 9. Teenagers 10. Teenage boy/girl relations 11. Houston, Texas 12. Coming-of-age stories 13. Crime fiction

Intervening when he sees a beautiful, gifted girl fighting with her boyfriend, a young man inadvertently challenges the power of the Mob in his Korean War-era Texas community and must summon the courage of his soldier father in order to stand up for his beliefs.

"Raging teenage hormones, gangster violence, class warfare, and a pink Cadillac stuffed with cash and gold bars set up Burke's latest novel, a mystery set in Houston, Tex. in 1952. Burke has a hit with this dark, atmospheric story of teenagers trying to make it through high school without getting killed by Mafia hitmen, low-life thugs, and greasers with oily ducktails and switchblade knives." Publishers Weekly.

Burke, James Lee, 1936-

* The **New** Iberia blues / James Lee Burke. Simon & Schuster, 2019. 464 p. Dave Robicheaux novels

ISBN 9781501176876

1. Escaped convicts 2. Murder investigation 3. Film industry and trade 4. Mafia 5. Tarot 6. Women murder victims 7. Murder 8. Detectives 9. Father and adult daughter 10. Men/women relations 11. Louisiana 12. New Iberia, Louisiana 13. Police procedurals 14. Southern fiction 15. Hardboiled fiction

The shocking death of a young woman leads detective Dave Robicheaux into the dark corners of Hollywood, the Mafia and the Louisiana backwoods.

"With his lush, visionary prose and timeless literary themes of loss and redemption, Burke is in full command in this outing for his aging but still capable hero." Publishers Weekly.

Burke, James Lee, 1936-

* **Robicheaux** / James Lee Burke. Simon & Schuster, 2018. 448 p. Dave Robicheaux novels

ISBN 9781501176845

1. Murder suspects 2. Post-traumatic stress disorder 3. Widowers 4. Vietnam veterans 5. Loss (Psychology) 6. Murder investigation 7. Murderers 8. Alcoholism 9. Louisiana 10. Police procedurals 11. Hardboiled fiction 12. Southern fiction

Struggling with PTSD, alcoholism and wrenching loss, Dave Robicheaux discovers that he may have committed the homicide he is investigating and endeavors to clear his name and make sense of the killing.

Burke, James Lee, 1936-

Wayfaring stranger : a novel / James Lee Burke. Simon & Schuster, 2014. 544 p. Holland family saga

ISBN 9781476710792

1. 1940s 2. Oil industry and trade 3. Antisemitism 4. Good and evil 5. Jewish women 6. Men/women relations 7. Soldiers 8. Texas 9. Historical fiction

LC 2014000147

A decade after taking a shot at Bonnie and Clyde during one of their notorious armed robberies, a Depression teen-turned-soldier escapes death during the Battle of the Bulge and marries a beautiful young woman with whom he seeks his fortune along the Texas-Louisiana oil coast.

"Burke takes a break from his Dave Robicheaux series to offer an ambitious, deeply satisfying historical thriller that fills in backstory on the author's other fictional family, the Hollands. With two series already in place starring contemporary members of the Holland clan, Burke now steps back in time to tell the story of oilman Weldon Avery Holland and his struggle to carve a life for himself on his own terms." Booklist.

Burke, Marcus

Team seven / Marcus Burke. Doubleday, 2014. 259 p.

ISBN 9780385537797

1. African American teenagers 2. Drug traffic 3. City life 4. Gangs 5. Inner city 6. Street life 7. Basketball 8. Urban problems 9. Family relationships 10. African American families 11. Teenage basketball players 12. Massachusetts 13. Coming-of-age stories 14. African American fiction

LC 2013032242

Follows the experiences of young Andre Battel as he grows away from his Jamaican family, discovers basketball court talents and turns drug dealer for a street gang.

Burke, Sue, 1955-

Semiosis / Sue Burke. Tor Books, 2018. 368 p. Semiosis duology

ISBN 9780765391353

1. Space colonies 2. Human/alien encounters 3. Plants 4. Aliens (Non-humanoid) 5. Communication 6. Life on other planets 7. Hard science fiction 8. Science fiction

LC 2017049645

"A Tom Doherty Associates Book."

Human colonists are forced to survive on limited resources on a planet with an inexplicable environment, where trees offer deliciously addictive fruit one day and poison the next and the ruins of an alien race are discovered within plant roots.

Burnet, Graeme Macrae, 1967-

The **disappearance** of Adele Bedeau : a historical thriller / Graeme Macrae Burnet. Arcade Publishing, 2017, c2014. 256 p. Inspector Gorski novels

ISBN 9781510723092

1. 1980s 2. Loners 3. Obsession 4. Guilt 5. Murder suspects 6. Murderers 7. Missing women 8. Detectives 9. Small towns 10. France 11. Mysteries 12. Literary fiction

LC 2017019827

Originally published: Glasgow : Contraband, 2014.

When an alluring waitress named Adele Bedeau vanishes into thin air, Detective Georges Gorski, haunted by his failure to solve one of his first murder cases, sets his sights on socially awkward loner Manfred Baumann.

"There's more than enough existential dread and guilt to go around in this whip-smart metafictional novel by the author of the acclaimed His Bloody Project, short-listed for 2016's Man Booker Prize. It's a novel best devoured while wearing a trench coat, its collar upturned, and puffing on a Gauloises cigarette." Library Journal.

Burnet, Graeme Macrae, 1967-

His bloody project : documents relating to the case of Roderick Macrae / Graeme Macrae Burnet. Skyhorse Publishing , 2016, c2015. 288 p.

ISBN 9781510719217

1. 1860s 2. Murderers 3. Trials (Murder) 4. Guilt (Law) 5. Motive (Law) 6. Insanity (Law) 7. Violence 8. Seventeen-year-old boys 9. Murder 10. Social classes 11. Poverty 12. Power (Social sciences) 13. Revenge 14. Highlands, Scotland -- History -- 19th century 15. Historical thrillers 16. Legal thrillers 17. Literary fiction

Originally published: Glasgow : Faber Factory, 2015.

Shortlisted for the Man Booker Prize, 2016

A triple murder in a remote northwestern farming community in 1869 leads to the arrest of a young man by the name of Roderick Macrae. There's no question that Macrae is guilty, but the police and courts must uncover what drove him to murder the local village constable and his two children.

"Although Burnet paints a disturbing picture of the hopelessness and hardships of tenant farmers, as well as providing an eye-opening introduction to the fallibility of so-called expert witnesses, this is not a bleak book. Rather, it is sly, poignant, gritty, thought-provoking, and sprinkled with wit." Publishers Weekly.

Burns, Anna, 1962-

Little constructions / Anna Burns. Graywolf Press, 2020. 304 p.

ISBN 9781644450130

1. Organized crime 2. Revenge 3. Chases 4. Families 5. Guns 6. Family violence 7. Violence against women 8. Women criminals 9. Crime fiction 10. Black humor 11. Literary fiction

In the small town of Tiptoe Floorboard, the Doe clan, a close-knit family of criminals and victims, has the run of the place. Yet there are signs that patriarch John Doe's reign may be coming to an end. When Jetty Doe breaks into a gun store and makes off with a Kalashnikov, the stage is set for a violent confrontation. But while Jetty is making her way across town in a taxi, an elusive, chatty narrator takes us on a wild journey, zooming in and out on various members of the Doe clan with long, digressive riffs that chase down the causes and repercussions of Jetty's act.

"Burns' style can make for tough sledding, but the intensity of her material justifies the effort." Kirkus.

Burns, Anna, 1962-

Milkman : a novel / Anna Burns. Graywolf Press, 2018. 352 p.

ISBN 9781644450000

1. 1970s 2. Teenage girls 3. Paramilitary forces 4. Threat (Psychology) 5. Stalkers 6. Sisters 7. Violence in men 8. Terrorism 9. Bombs 10. Gossiping and gossips 11. The Troubles, 1968-1998 12. Northern Ireland -- History -- 1969-1994 13. Ireland -- History -- 20th century 14. Literary fiction

Originally published: London : Faber & Faber, 2018.

Man Booker Prize, 2018.

National Book Critics Circle Award for Fiction, 2018.

Orwell Prize, 2019.

Shortlisted for The Women's Prize for Fiction, 2019.

In Northern Ireland during the Troubles of the 1970s, an unnamed narrator finds herself targeted by a high-ranking dissident known as Milkman.

"Milkman is a uniquely meandering and mesmerizing, wonderful and enigmatic work about borders and barriers, both physical and spiritual, and the cost of survival." Booklist.

Burns, Olive Ann

* **Cold** Sassy tree / Olive Ann Burns. Ticknor & Fields, 1984. 391 p. Cold Sassy series

ISBN 0899193099

1. 1900s (Decade) 2. Widowers 3. Elopement 4. May-December romance 5. Senior men 6. Small town life 7. Teenage boys 8. Family relationships 9. Rural life 10. Georgia 11. Humorous stories 12. Coming-of-age stories 13. Southern fiction

LC 84008570

One thing you could depend on in Cold Sassy, Georgia, was that word got around - fast. On July 5, 1906, things took a scandalous turn. That was the day that E. Rucker Blakeslee, proprietor of the general store and barely three weeks a widower, eloped with Miss Love Simpson - a woman half his age and, worse yet, a Yankee! On that day, fourteen-year-old Will Tweedy's adventures began, and an unimpeachably pious town came to life.

Burns, Olive Ann

Leaving Cold Sassy : the unfinished sequel to Cold Sassy Tree, With a reminiscence by Katrina Kenison Ticknor and Fields, 1992. 290 p. Cold Sassy series

ISBN 0618919805

1. 1910s 2. Engaged persons 3. Teachers 4. Modernization (Social sciences) 5. Small town life 6. Family relationships 7. Rural life 8. Georgia 9. Humorous stories 10. Coming-of-age stories

LC 92005561

Author's unfinished sequel to Cold Sassy Tree.

"Readers should prepare for an interrupted work-in-process, an uneasy sense of a writer's voice about to be stilled." Publishers Weekly

Burns, Rex

Body slam / Rex Burns. Open Road Media, 2014. 311 p. Touchstone agency novels

ISBN 9781480445703

1. Private investigators 2. Fathers and daughters 3. Wrestling 4. Murder 5. Murder investigation 6. Wrestlers 7. Coercion 8. Denver, Colorado 9. Hardboiled fiction

When Otto Lidke got a tryout in pro football, he hired a lawyer friend named Jim Raiford to handle his contract. The negotiations were bungled, forcing both men into a career change. Trying to start a pro wrestling circuit in Denver, Lidke runs afoul of the national federation, which does everything it can, legal and otherwise, to stamp out his new venture. When shady business practices escalate into threats on his life, Lidke calls on Raiford, now a private investigator, to dig up some dirt on the men who are trying to put him out of business. But instead he gets Raiford's daughter, Julie, a whip-smart sleuth looking to prove she's every bit as savvy as her father. As Julie and her dad dig into the vicious world of small-time wrestling, they find that though the fights may be fixed, the danger is all too real.

Burroughs, William S., 1914-1997

* **Naked** lunch : the restored text / William S. Burroughs ; restored text edited by James Grauer holz and Barry Miles. Grove Press, 2009, c1959. vii, 299 p.

ISBN 9780802119261

1. Drug addicts 2. Homosexuality 3. Hallucinations and illusions 4. Gay men 5. Recovering addicts 6. Alienation (Social psychology) 7. Drug withdrawal symptoms 8. Surrealist fiction 9. Transgressive fiction 10. Modern classics 11. Science fiction

LC 91022972

Originally published: Paris : Olympia Press, 1959. Restored text c2001.

An unnerving tale of a narcotics addict unmoored in New York, Tangiers, and ultimately a nightmarish wasteland known as Interzone, its formal innovation, formerly taboo subject matter, and tour de force execution have exerted their influence on the work of authors like Thomas Pynchon, J.G. Ballard, and William Gibson; on the relationship of art and obscenity; and on the shape of music, film, and media generally. This restored text includes many editorial corrections to errors present in previous editions, and incorporates Burroughs' notes on the text, and several essays he wrote over the years about the book.

LIST OF FICTIONAL WORKS

Burrowes, Grace

The **bridegroom** wore plaid / Grace Burrowes. Sourcebooks Casablanca, 2012. 375 p. MacGregor novels

ISBN 9781402268663

1. Victorian era (1837-1901) 2. 19th century 3. Nobility 4. Earls and countesses 5. Duty 6. Heirs and heiresses 7. Love triangles 8. Interpersonal attraction 9. Men/women relations 10. Highlands, Scotland -- Social life and customs -- 19th century 11. Great Britain -- History -- Victoria, 1837-1901 12. Victorian romances 13. Historical romances

Forced to marry for money to save the family estate, the Earl of Balfour devises a strategy to win the heart of Genie Daniels, a rich English heiress, until he meets her poor cousin Augusta, forcing him to choose between family duty and love.

Burrowes, Grace

The **captive** / Grace Burrowes. Sourcebooks, 2014. 384 p. Captive hearts (Grace Burrowes)

ISBN 9781402278785

1. Regency period (1811-1820) 2. Revenge 3. Dukes and duchesses 4. Nobility 5. Single fathers 6. Men/women relations 7. Widows 8. Interpersonal attraction 9. England -- Social life and customs -- 19th century 10. Regency romances 11. Historical romances

Struggling with society life, Christian Severn, who lost his wife, son, and will to live, finds an ally in the Countess of Windmere, who helps him stay strong for his surviving daughter.

Burrowes, Grace

* The **heir** / Grace Burrowes. Sourcebooks Casablanca, 2010. 448 p. Windham novels

ISBN 9781402244346

1. Regency period (1811-1820) 2. Men/women relations 3. Mate selection for men 4. Secrets 5. Earls and countesses 6. Household employees 7. Social classes 8. Heirs and heiresses 9. Inheritance and succession 10. Housekeepers 11. London, England -- Social life and customs -- 19th century 12. Regency romances 13. Historical romances

Follows the Earl of Wyndham as he, trying to avoid the rounds of country houses and matchmaking mamas, decides to spend the summer in London where he meets the woman of his dreams in his beautiful and mysterious housekeeper.

Burrowes, Grace

Lady Sophie's Christmas wish / Grace Burrowes. Sourcebooks Casablanca, 2011 384 p. Windham novels

ISBN 9781402261541

1. Regency period (1811-1820) 2. Abandoned infants 3. Mistaken identity 4. Secrets 5. Solitude 6. Christmas 7. Strangers 8. Interpersonal attraction 9. Rich women 10. Brothers 11. London, England 12. Regency romances 13. Holiday romances 14. Historical romances

During a snowstorm, Lady Sophie Windham, with an abandoned baby on her hands with nobody to help her, takes in a mysterious stranger, Lord Vim Charpentier, who hates the holidays.

Burrowes, Grace

My one and only duke / Grace Burrowes. Forever, 2018. 442 p. Rogues to riches

ISBN 9781538728956

1. Regency period (1811-1820) 2. Heirs and heiresses 3. Revenge 4. Frameups 5. Widows 6. Pregnant women 7. Dukes and duchesses 8. Former convicts 9. Sexual attraction 10. Men/women relations 11. London, England 12. Historical romances 13. Regency romances

Falsely imprisoned Quinn Wentworth marries pregnant widow Jane Winston in order to help her, but when he is saved from execution by the discovery that he is the heir to a dukedom, they must live with their marriage of convenience.

"Burrowes offers a fun and provocative new premise, along with her trademark intelligent heroine and hero, as she kicks off the Rogues to Riches series." Booklist.

Burrowes, Grace

The **soldier** / Grace Burrowes. Sourcebooks Casablanca, 2011. 448 p. Windham novels

ISBN 9781402245671

1. Regency period (1811-1820) 2. Earls and countesses 3. Nobility 4. Men/women relations 5. Family estates 6. Illegitimacy 7. Guardian and ward 8. Psychic trauma 9. Social classes 10. London, England -- Social life and customs -- 19th century 11. Regency romances 12. Historical romances

When Devlin St. Just, the bastard son of a duke, arrives at his new estate, he discovers that he is responsible for the previous owner's illegitimate daughter and her beautiful cousin, which further complicates his life.

Burrowes, Grace

Tremaine's true love / Grace Burrowes. Sourcebooks Inc., 2015 384 p. True gentlemen novels

ISBN 9781492621027

1. Regency period (1811-1820) 2. 19th century 3. Independence in women 4. Rich men 5. Nobility 6. Interpersonal attraction 7. Men/women relations 8. Marriage 9. Determination in men 10. Great Britain -- History -- Regency, 1811-1820 11. Regency romances 12. Historical romances

Living a meaningful life tending to the sick and the poor, practical, reserved Nita Haddonfield wishes to avoid the limitations of marriage, but wealthy busnessman Tremaine St. Michael is determined to win her heart.

"The second installment of Burrowes' (The Duke's Disaster, 2015, etc.) new True Gentlemen series is a tightly woven story that deals with many of the world's timeless moral issuespoverty, domestic violence, professional recognition for women, and animal rights. The characters are complicated and compelling and experience enough personal growth during the course of the novel to keep the reader enthralled. Burrowes is at the top of her game, and this latest offering is not to be missed." Kirkus.

Burrowes, Grace

The **trouble** with dukes / Grace Burrowes. Forever, 2016 384 p. Windham brides

ISBN 9781455569960

1. Dukes and duchesses 2. Scots 3. Napoleonic Wars veterans 4. Redheads 5. Nobility 6. Manners and customs 7. Mate selection 8. Coercion 9. Protectiveness in men 10. Interpersonal attraction 11. Men/women relations 12. London, England 13. England 14. Regency romances 15. Highland romances 16. Historical romances

Hamish McHugh, the new Duke of Murdoch, to make his sisters happy, fights his hardest battle yet-the London Season-and decides to take on any challenge, including learning to waltz and Miss Megan Windham, the only woman who sees him as he truly is.

Burton, Jeffrey B.

The **eulogist** / Jeffrey B. Burton. The Permanent Press, 2017. 360 p. Drew Cady thrillers

ISBN 9781579625023

1. FBI agents 2. Assassination 3. Assassins 4. Politicians -- Death 5. Eulogies 6. Serial murder investigation 7. Drug traffic 8. Washington, D.C. 9. Thrillers and suspense

LC 2017024218

FBI Special Agent Drew Cady is reluctantly drawn into investigating the assassination of a sitting United States senator.

Burton, Jessie, 1982-

The **miniaturist** / Jessie Burton. Ecco Press, 2014. 400 p.

ISBN 9780062306814

1. 17th century 2. Young women 3. Sexuality 4. Husband and wife 5. Obsession 6. Miniature objects 7. Miniaturists 8. Merchants 9. Secrets 10. Social classes 11. Rich men 12. Religion 13. Amsterdam, Netherlands 14. Netherlands 15. Historical fiction

British Book Award for Book of the Year, 2014.

Engaging the services of a miniaturist to furnish a cabinet-sized replica of her new home, 18-year-old Nella Oortman, the wife of an illustrious merchant trader, soon discovers that the artist's tiny creations mirror their real-life counterparts in eerie and unexpected ways.

Burton, Tara Isabella

Social creature / Tara Isabella Burton. Doubleday, 2018. 273 p.

ISBN 9780385543521

1. Young women 2. Female friendship 3. Obsession 4. Envy 5. Compulsive behavior 6. Elite (Social sciences) 7. Social status 8. Manhattan, New York City 9. New York City 10. Psychological suspense 11. Glitz and glamour novels 12. Horror

LC 2017046955

Two aspiring writers, one with wealth and the other underprivileged, spiral into an intense, partially toxic friendship that challenges their goals to see the world before one of them dies under circumstances forged by seduction and obsession.

"Louise and Lavinia are bold, brilliant characters. This devious, satisfying novel perfectly captures a very narrow slice of the Manhattan demimonde." Publishers Weekly.

Bussi, Michel, 1965-

Black water lilies : a novel / Michel Bussi ; translated from the French by Shaun Whiteside Hachette Books, 2017, c2011. 416 p.

ISBN 9780316504997

1. Monet, Claude, 1840-1926 2. Gardens 3. Painting, French 4. Married men -- Death 5. Art 6. Murder 7. Murder investigation 8. Cold cases (Criminal investigation) 9. Detectives 10. Extramarital affairs 11. Villages 12. Small town life 13. Secrets 14. France 15. Giverny, France 16. Mysteries 17. Literary fiction 18. Translations -- French to English

LC 2016037620

"First published in France in 2011 as Nympheas Noirs by Presses de la Cite. Published in the UK as Black Water Lilies by Weidenfeld & Nicolson [2016]" --Verso title page.

Originally published: Paris : Presses de la Cite, 2011.

A man, who is passionate about both women and art, is found dead in the gardens depicted in Monet's Water Lilies.

Butcher, Jim, 1971-

Proven guilty / Jim Butcher. ROC, 2006. 416 p. Dresden files

ISBN 0451460855

1. Supernatural 2. Magic 3. Private investigators 4. Wizards 5. Men/women relations 6. Film industry and trade 7. Monsters 8. Black magic 9. Magicians 10. Executions and executioners 11. Police 12. Chicago, Illinois 13. Hardboiled fiction 14. Urban fantasy 15. Fantasy mysteries

LC 2005030130

The only wizard in the Chicago phone book, Harry is given the task of investigating rumors of black magic in the Windy City, while, at the same time, searching for some malevolent entities that feed on fear who have been set loose on Chicago.

Butland, Stephanie

The **lost** for words bookshop : a novel / Stephanie Butland. Thomas Dunne Books/St. Martin's Press, 2018. 304 p.

ISBN 9781250124531

1. Bookstores 2. Life change events 3. Women -- Psychology 4. Trust 5. Secrecy 6. Cynicism 7. Psychic trauma 8. Poetry 9. Interpersonal relations 10. Self-fulfillment in women 11. York, England 12. England 13. Women's lives and relationships 14. First-person narratives

LC 2017060625

"First published in Great Britain under the title Lost for words by Zaffre Publishing" -- t.p. verso.

A secretly heartbroken woman who prefers books to people finds her world upended by the arrivals of a poet, a lover and three suspicious deliveries that reveal that someone has found out about her mysterious past.

Butler, Gwendoline

Death lives next door / Gwendoline Butler. St. Martin's Press, 1992, c1960. 191 p. John Coffin mysteries

ISBN 0312081758

1. Women anthropologists 2. Women with schizophrenia 3. Police 4. Oxford, England 5. Mysteries

LC 92001581

Also published as: Dine and Be Dead.

Investigating a missing person case, young Scotland Yard Inspector John Coffin discovers that his case is somehow involved with that of respected professor Marion Manning, who is being hounded by a mysterious watcher, and with murder

"Keeping her detective in the wings, [Butler] begins by focusing her narrative on a gang of shabby, bitter academic types in Oxford, at the center of which dysfunctional clique is the famous and slightly mysterious Marion Manning, watched by a man who in time will claim to be her long lost husband. Everything in Marion's past is weird, and as Coffin is drawn out of London into this narrow little world, it is the investigation of this mysterious past that forms the heart of the book. Butler's regulars shouldn't pass up the chance for this peek at Coffin's past." Booklist.

Butler, Halle

The **new** me : a novel / Halle Butler. Penguin Books, 2019 208 p.

ISBN 9780143133605

1. Young women 2. Purpose in life 3. Lifestyle change 4. Temporary employees 5. Growth (Psychology) 6. Self-esteem in women 7. Self-destructive behavior 8. Consumer society 9. Satirical fiction

LC 2018028609

Thirty-year-old Millie just can't pull it together; she spends her days killing time at a thankless temp job until she can return home to her empty apartment, where she fixates on all the ways she might change her life. Then she watches TV until she drops off to sleep, and the cycle begins again. When the possibility of a full-time job offer arises, it seems to bring the better life she's envisioning within reach. But with it also comes the paralyzing realization of just how hollow that vision has become.

"Her darkly hilarious novel vividly captures contemporary American life and will keep readers addicted to the end." Booklist.

Butler, Kirker

Pretty ugly : a novel / Kirker Butler. Thomas Dunne Books, St. Martin's Press, 2015. 294 p.

ISBN 9781250049728

1. Eccentric mothers 2. Beauty contests 3. Beauty contestants 4. Pregnant women 5. Men nurses 6. Drug addiction 7. Cheating (Interpersonal relations) 8. Debt 9. Southern states 10. Satirical fiction

LC 2014037218

A satirical portrait of a dysfunctional family follows the determined woman's mission to render her young daughter a successful child-pageant contestant in spite of the girl's efforts to binge eat her way into preadolescent retirement.

Butler, Marcia

* **Pickle's** progress / Marcia Butler. Central Ave Press, 2019. 384 p.

ISBN 9781771681551

1. Identical twin brothers 2. Husband and wife 3. Self-perception 4. Bereavement in women 5. Police 6. Drinking 7. Life change events 8. Families 9. Secrets 10. Interpersonal relations 11. Men/women relations 12. Interpersonal attraction 13. New York City 14. Psychological fiction

Over the course of five weeks, identical twin brothers, one wife, a dog, and a bereaved young woman collide with each other to comical and sometimes horrifying effect. Everything is questioned and tested as they jockey for position and try to maintain the status quo. Love is the poison, the antidote, the devil and, ultimately, the hero.

Butler, Nickolas

* The **hearts** of men / Nickolas Butler. Ecco Press, 2017. 392 p.

ISBN 9780062469687

1. 1960s 2. Vietnam veterans 3. Summer camps 4. Boy Scouts 5. Altruism 6. Popularity 7. Male friendship 8. Misfits (Persons) 9. Personal conduct 10. Boys -- Friendship 11. Boy Scout leaders 12. Intergenerational relations 13. Wisconsin 14. Coming-of-age stories 15. Psychological fiction 16. Literary fiction

A scarred Vietnam veteran and successful businessman reflects on his teen years as a social outcast and friend to a popular youth during a summer camp reunion marked by selflessness and an unthinkable event involving his friend's family members.

"Butler demonstrates enormous command over the material and sympathy for his flawed characters. This beautiful novel might be his best yet." Publishers Weekly.

Butler, Nickolas

Little faith : a novel / Nickolas Butler. HarperCollins, 2019. 336 p.

ISBN 9780062469717

1. Religious radicals 2. Faith (Christianity) 3. Family relationships 4. Rural life 5. Single mothers 6. Grandfather and grandson 7. Charismatic movement 8. Extended families 9. Women adoptees 10. Parent and child 11. Protectiveness in men 12. Loss (Psychology) 13. Wisconsin 14. Literary fiction 15. Domestic fiction

A Wisconsin family grapples with the power and limitations of faith when an adult daughter falls under the influence of a radical church that threatens a grandchild's safety.

"A beautifully realized meditation on the nature of parenting and living in a perplexing (and often cruel) world. Enthusiastically recommended for parents and fans of literary fiction." Library Journal.

Butler, Octavia E.

Adulthood rites / Octavia E. Butler. Warner Books, 1988. 277 p. Xenogenesis series

ISBN 9780446514224

1. Nuclear holocaust survivors 2. Genetic engineering 3. Aliens (Non-humanoid) 4. Dystopias 5. Human evolution 6. Mother and child 7. Human-alien hybrids 8. Kidnapping 9. Eugenics 10. Posthumanism 11. African American fiction 12. Afrofuturism and afrofantasy 13. Hard science fiction 14. Social science fiction 15. Science fiction

LC 87034620

In the sequel to "Dawn," Akin, the son of Lilith, struggles to cope with his dual human and alien Oankali legacy while preparing for the time of metamorphosis when he will take on the form of future human beings.

Butler, Octavia E.

Bloodchild : and other stories / Octavia E. Butler. Seven Stories Press, 1996. 145 p.

ISBN 1888363363

1. Women 2. Aliens (Non-humanoid) 3. Afrofuturism and afrofantasy 4. Science fiction 5. Short stories 6. African American fiction

LC 96-41587

"Five intense, thought-provoking tales of people caught up in extraordinary situations." School Library Journal

Butler, Octavia E.

* **Dawn** : xenogenesis / Octavia Butler. Warner Books, 1987. 264 p. Xenogenesis series

ISBN 9780446513630

1. Nuclear holocaust survivors 2. Genetic engineering 3. Aliens (Non-humanoid) 4. Human-alien hybrids 5. Eugenics 6. Human evolution 7. Space vehicles 8. Space flight 9. Human/alien encounters 10. Posthumanism 11. Afrofuturism and afrofantasy 12. African American fiction 13. Hard science fiction 14. Social science fiction 15. Science fiction

LC 87006195

The human race, now infertile, fights to maintain its identity when the alien species, Oankali, offers to trade genetic material and bioengineering at the price of metamorphosing a new kind of being.

"Butler is one of the few sf writers who can handle effectively a slow-moving plot that emphasizes characters' emotions. Her command of the language is superior, and her aliens are quite convincing creations." Booklist.

Butler, Octavia E.

Imago / Octavia E. Butler. Warner Books, 1989. 264 p. Xenogenesis series

ISBN 9780446514729

1. Genetic engineering 2. Aliens (Non-humanoid) 3. Human-alien hybrids 4. Human evolution 5. Eugenics 6. Human/alien encounters 7. Posthumanism 8. Afrofuturism and afrofantasy 9. African American fiction 10. Hard science fiction 11. Social science fiction 12. Science fiction

LC 88027975

"The concluding volume of the Xenogenesis trilogy considers a post-holocaust humanity whose only chance for survival is to be absorbed by the alien Oankali. Totally uninterested in domination, this race thrives on a symbiosis that Earthlings find difficult to credit. That distrust hampers the narrator, an ooloi (neuter) named Jodahs, as it tries to find life partners in the same ratio as its five parents: a human couple, an Oankali couple and itself, the essential ooloi who joins all five and melds their genetic legacy. Butler's achievement here is less the abstract reassignment of sexual roles than a warmth and urgency that dramatizes and personalizes these conflicts and transformations." Publishers Weekly.

Butler, Octavia E.

* **Kindred** / Octavia Butler. Beacon Press, 1988, c1979. xxvii, 264 p.

ISBN 9780807083055

1. Time travel (Past) 2. Ancestors 3. Slavery -- Maryland 4. Interracial couples 5. Rescues 6. African American women 7. Slaveholders 8. Maryland -- History -- 19th century 9. Maryland -- History -- 20th century 10. African American fiction 11. Social science fiction 12. Science fiction

Originally published: Garden City, N.Y. : Doubleday,

Dana, a Black woman, finds herself repeatedly transported to the antebellum South, where she must make sure that Rufus, the plantation owner's son, survives to father Dana's ancestor.

"This sometimes painful novel features superb character development." Anatomy of Wonder, 5th edition.

Butler, Octavia E.

* **Parable** of the sower / Octavia E. Butler. Warner Books, 2000, c1993. 299 p.

ISBN 0446675504

1. 21st century 2. Dystopias 3. Women psychics 4. Religion 5. African American women 6. African American mothers and daughters 7. Disasters 8. Violence 9. Quests 10. Post-apocalypse 11. California 12. Afrofuturism and afrofantasy 13. African American fiction 14. Diary novels 15. Dystopian fiction 16. Social science fiction 17. Science fiction

                                          LC 93008703

Sequel: Parable of the Talents.

In 2025 California, an eighteen-year-old African American woman, suffering from a hereditary trait that causes her to feel others' pain as well as her own, flees northward from her small community and its desperate savages.

"The author infuses this tale with an allegorical quality that is part meditation, part warning. Simple, direct, and deeply felt, this should reach both mainstream and sf audiences." Library Journal.

Butler, Octavia E.

Parable of the talents : a novel / Octavia E. Butler. Seven Stories Press, 1998. 365 p.

ISBN 1888363819

1. Dystopias 2. Women psychics 3. Violence 4. African American women 5. African American mothers and daughters 6. Disasters 7. Imaginary wars and battles 8. Fundamentalists 9. Afrofuturism and afrofantasy 10. Dystopian fiction 11. Social science fiction 12. Science fiction 13. African American fiction

                                          LC 9835863

Sequel to: Parable of the sower.

Nebula Award for Best Novel, 1999.

It is 2032 and Lauren Olamina's daughter Larkin narrates the story of her mother's life as she spreads the word of her Earthseed philosophy. As Larkin describes how they attain their goal of reaching the stars, she denounces her mother.

"The narrative is both impassioned and bitter. . . . Lauren, at once loving wife and mother, prophet and fanatic, victim and leader, gains stature as one of the most intense and well-developed protagonists in recent SF." Publishers Weekly.

Butler, Robert Olen

A **good** scent from a strange mountain : stories / Robert Olen Butler. H. Holt, 1992. 249 p.

ISBN 0805019863

1. Vietnamese Americans 2. Vietnamese Americans 3. Vietnam 4. Louisiana 5. Short stories 6. Literary fiction

                                       LC 91031359

Fifteen stories dealing with Vietnam and Vietnamese-Americans in Louisiana.

ALA Notable Book, 1993.

Pulitzer Prize for Fiction, 1993.

A collection of stories about the residents of Saigon as they face love, loss, and despair

"Recommended for all literary fiction collections and essential for libraries seeking to expand Asian American literature collections." Library Journal.

Butler, Robert Olen

Hell : a novel / Robert Olen Butler. Grove Press, 2009. 240 p.

ISBN 9780802119018

1. Television journalists 2. Hell 3. Damned persons 4. Future punishment 5. Free will and determinism 6. Good and evil 7. Devil 8. Satirical fiction 9. Literary fiction

Struggling through Sisyphean tortures in Hell where he lives with Anne Boleyn and regularly encounters late popes and presidents, news presenter Hatcher McCord learns of a possible means of escape that involves exposing Satan as a charlatan.

"Butler's lust for the tabloid romp and his stream of the never-ending punch line both irritates and illuminates. The reader's taste will have to be the final arbiters of worth." Publishers Weekly.

Butler, Robert Olen

The **hot** country / Robert Olen Butler. Grove Press, 2012. 440 p. Christopher Marlowe Cobb novels

ISBN 9780802120465

1. Mexican Revolution (1910-1920) 2. 1910s 3. War correspondents -- United States 4. Civil war 5. Espionage 6. Mexico -- History -- Revolution, 1910-1920 7. Historical thrillers

While covering the Mexican civil war, a newspaper correspondent, Kit, falls in love with a young laundress and enlists the help of a pickpocket to determine who shot a priest.

Butler, Robert Olen

Paris in the dark / Robert Olen Butler. Mysterious Press, 2018. 360 p. Christopher Marlowe Cobb novels

ISBN 9780802128379

1. First World War era (1914-1918) 2. World War I 3. War correspondents 4. Undercover operations 5. Intelligence service 6. Bombings 7. Investigations 8. Americans in France 9. Terrorists 10. Historical thrillers

                                        LC 2018013058

Working undercover for the U.S. government in World War I Paris, reporter Kit Cobb tests the limits of his skills and principles to investigate a string of dynamite bombings possibly linked to a German operative.

LIST OF FICTIONAL WORKS

Butler, Robert Olen

Perfume River / Robert Olen Butler. Atlantic Monthly Press, 2016. 273 p.

ISBN 9780802125750

1. Vietnam veterans 2. Fathers and sons 3. War -- Psychological aspects 4. Vietnam War, 1961-1975 -- Psychological aspects 5. Seniors 6. Homeless persons 7. Brothers 8. Marital conflict 9. College teachers 10. Fathers -- Death 11. Options, alternatives, choices 12. Secrets 13. Family relationships 14. Florida 15. Literary fiction

Presents the story of a single North Florida family shaped and overshadowed by the Vietnam War and the estrangements between the fathers, sons and brothers who supported or protested against it.

"This is thoughtful, introspective fiction of the highest caliber, but it carries a definite edge, thanks to an insistent backbeat that generates suspense with the subtlest of brushstrokes." Booklist.

Butler, Sarah

Ten things I've learnt about love : a novel / Sarah Butler. The Penguin Press, 2013. 258 p.

ISBN 9781594205330

1. Fathers and daughters 2. Families 3. Homecomings 4. Loss (Psychology) 5. Sisters 6. Homeless men 7. Misfits (Persons) 8. London, England 9. Mainstream fiction

LC 2012046987

Drawn to dangerous world regions and unconventional career paths, Alice, the black sheep of her family, rushes to say goodbye when she learns her father is dying; while Daniel, an artist suffering from synesthesia and failing health, clings to thoughts of the daughter he has never been able to find.

Butler, Season

* **Cygnet** / Season Butler. HarperCollins, 2019. 272 p.

ISBN 9780062870919

1. Seniors 2. Abandoned teenagers 3. Social isolation 4. Islands 5. Hostility (Psychology) 6. Memories 7. Communities 8. Weather 9. Teenage girls 10. Growing up 11. New Hampshire 12. Coming-of-age stories

An utterly original coming-of-age tale, marked by wrenching humor and staggering charisma, about a young woman resisting the savagery of adulthood in a community of the elderly rejecting the promise of youth.

Buwalda, Peter, 1971-

* **Bonita** Avenue : a novel / Peter Buwalda ; translated from the Dutch by Jonathan Reeder. Hogarth, 2014, c2010. 480 p.

ISBN 9781908968173

1. College teachers 2. Family relationships 3. Dysfunctional families 4. Dishonesty 5. Revenge 6. Internet pornography 7. Family secrets 8. Parent and child 9. Extortion 10. Netherlands 11. Literary fiction 12. Translations -- Dutch to English

LC 2014009172

"Bonita Avenue first published in Dutch as Bonita Avenue in 2010"--T.p. verso.

Originally published in Dutch: Amsterdam : De Bezige Bij, 2010.

"The rich layer of detail would be impressive when applied to one topic, but Buwalda creates multiple complex worlds around vastly different subjects: the porn industry, mathematics, music, and judo, among others. An outstanding literary suspense story." Library Journal.

Buxbaum, Julie

After you / Julie Buxbaum. Dial Press, 2009. 340 p.

ISBN 9780385341240

1. Families of murder victims 2. Americans in England 3. Grief 4. Best friends 5. Life change events 6. London, England 7. Notting Hill (London, England) 8. England 9. Psychological fiction

LC 2009009634

Rushing to assist the family of her murdered best friend, Ellie consoles reclusive widower Greg and nurtures eight-year-old Lucy, who has stopped speaking.

Buxton, Kira Jane

* **Hollow** kingdom / Kira Jane Buxton. Grand Central Pub, 2019 320 p.

ISBN 9781538745823

1. Crows 2. Zombies 3. Human/animal relationships 4. Dogs 5. Bloodhounds 6. Crows as pets 7. Dogs and birds 8. End of the world 9. Post-apocalypse 10. Environmental degradation 11. Seattle, Washington 12. Stories told by animals 13. Apocalyptic fiction

Sensing something is wrong with his owner, a domesticated crow abandons the only life he ever knew to discover that humans are turning into zombies and must use knowledge gleaned from his TV-viewing to save them.

Byatt, A. S. (Antonia Susan), 1936-

Babel Tower / A. S. Byatt. Random House, 1996. 625 p. Frederica Potter series

ISBN 0679405135

1. 1960s 2. Divorced women 3. Censorship -- History -- 20th century 4. Family violence 5. Single mothers 6. Divorce 7. Trials (Obscenity) 8. Trials (Divorce) 9. Women literature teachers 10. Universities and colleges 11. English language -- Study and teaching 12. Trials (Child custody) 13. England 14. Psychological fiction 15. Literary fiction

LC 95-53210

Frederica Potter becomes disenchanted with her marriage after attending Cambridge and leaves her country home for London where, in the turbulent 1960s, she struggles with single motherhood, politics, ideals, and changing sexual roles in a sequel to Still Life.

"In many ways, this is a book about language, and how it is used to conceal and reveal (there is a wonderfully satirical subplot about a commission examining English educational methods). But it also employs language, brilliantly, to create a large cast of characters whose struggles, anxieties and small triumphs are at once specific to a time and place, and universal." Publishers Weekly.

Byatt, A. S. (Antonia Susan), 1936-

The **biographer's** tale / A.S. Byatt. Alfred A. Knopf, 2001, c2000. 305 p.

ISBN 0375411143

1. Biographers 2. Love triangles 3. Authors 4. Young men 5. Biography 6. Writing 7. Men/women relations 8. Psychological fiction 9. Coming-of-age stories 10. Literary fiction

LC 00062012

Phineas G. Nanson sets out to write a biography of a great biographer, only to discover that the fragmentary facts and bits of information are difficult to put together, a discovery that becomes a metaphor for his own complex life.

"Theory and esoteric allusion dominate the action from start to finish. Byatt remains an author of daunting erudition and precious phrasing." The Atlantic.

Byatt, A. S. (Antonia Susan), 1936-

The **children's** book : a novel / A.S. Byatt. Alfred A. Knopf, 2009. 675 p.

ISBN 9780307272096

1. Female friendship 2. Upper class 3. Family secrets 4. Family relationships 5. Women authors 6. Ambition in girls 7. Parent and

child 8. Change 9. Obsessive-compulsive disorder 10. Marriage 11. Sex offenders 12. World War I 13. Children and adults 14. Runaway children 15. Country homes 16. England -- History -- 19th century 17. England -- History -- 20th century 18. Great Britain -- History -- 20th century 19. Historical fiction 20. Coming-of-age stories 21. Literary fiction

LC 2009016334

James Tait Black Memorial Prize for Fiction, 2009.
Shortlisted for the Man Booker Prize, 2009.

A tale spanning the end of the Victorian era through World War I finds famous children's book author Olive Wellwood taking in a runaway and exposing the boy to dark truths about her family's summer bacchanals at their rambling country house.

"Byatt steps deeper into the realm of writing for special readers, forging onward in creating increasingly complicated fictional narratives. Her new novel can be labeled, at first call, as both historical fiction and a family saga; on second consideration, it can also be seen as a psychological study of social and economic privilege in the high tide of Britain's power: the last decade of the Victorian age, the Edwardian period, and up to World War I." Booklist.

Byatt, A. S. (Antonia Susan), 1936-
* **Possession** : a romance / A.S. Byatt Random House, 1990. 555 p.
ISBN 9780394586236
1. 19th century 2. 1980s 3. Literary historians 4. Women college teachers 5. College teachers 6. Poets, English -- 19th century 7. Women poets 8. Poets 9. Universities and colleges 10. Literary research 11. Romantic love 12. Men/women relations 13. Poetry 14. Extramarital affairs 15. Letter writing 16. Manuscripts -- Collectors and collecting 17. Academic rivalry 18. Ownership 19. London, England 20. Whitby, England 21. France 22. Love stories 23. Literary fiction 24. Parallel narratives

LC 90008374

ALA Notable Book, 1991.
Booker Prize, 1990.

Roland Mitchell has devoted his life to studying the life and works of 19th-century writer Randolph Henry Ash. When Roland discovers a provocative letter to an unnamed woman, he begins a quest for information. Along with fellow academician Maud Bailey, Roland discovers an unconventional love story that echoes through their own modern lives.

"Intelligent, ingenious and humane, [this] bids fair to be looked back upon as one of the most memorable novels of the 1990s." Times Literary Supplement.

Byatt, A. S. (Antonia Susan), 1936-
* **Ragnarok** : the end of the gods / A.S. Byatt. Grove Press, 2012, c2011. 177 p. Myths series
ISBN 9780802129925
1. Second World War era (1939-1945) 2. Child refugees 3. Mythology, Norse 4. Girls 5. End of the world 6. Gods and goddesses, Norse 7. World War II 8. World War II home front 9. England -- History -- 20th century 10. Literary fiction 11. Mythological fiction
First published: Edinburgh : Canongate, 2011.
Presents a retelling of the Norse myth about the end of the world that follows the blitz-era evacuation of a young girl whose worldview is dramatically changed upon reading "Asgard and the Gods."

Byatt, A. S. (Antonia Susan), 1936-
A **whistling** woman / A.S. Byatt. Alfred A. Knopf, 2003. 448 p. Frederica Potter series
ISBN 0375415343
1. 1960s 2. Divorced women 3. Television programs 4. Counterculture 5. Women television personalities 6. Single mothers 7. Television personalities 8. Cults 9. Cult leaders 10. Biological research 11. Men/women relations 12. England -- Social life and customs -- 20th century 13. Psychological fiction 14. Literary fiction

LC 2002072957

In the late 1960s, the world begins to split, while Frederica falls almost by accident into a career in television in London, tumultuous events in her home county of Yorkshire threaten to change her life, and those of the people she loves.

"There is no other writer alive who is as interested as Byatt in creating characters who are thinking women and men while at the same time recognizing the limits of cognition in the face of unreason, or love." New York Times Book Review.

Bybee, Catherine
Staying for good / Catherine Bybee. Montlake Romance, 2017. 320 p. Most likely to
ISBN 9781503939172
1. Homecomings 2. Women cooks 3. Mechanics 4. Former lovers 5. Options, alternatives, choices 6. Families 7. Small town life 8. Interpersonal attraction 9. Men/women relations 10. Oregon 11. Contemporary romances

Zoe Brown didn't just leave, she escaped River Bend, turning her back on the shame of her black-sheep siblings and imprisoned dad. Now a celebrity chef in Dallas, she can afford all the things she never could have growing up. But when she returns, Zoe has to face all that she abandoned -- including Luke, her high school boyfriend.

"Bybees novel will draw the reader in from the very first page. A cast of multidimensional characters brings the story to life and promises enticing future installments." Publishers Weekly.

Bynum, Sarah Shun-lien
Ms. Hempel chronicles / Sarah Shun-lien Bynum. Harcourt, 2008. 224 p.
ISBN 9780151014965
1. Middle school teachers 2. Loss (Psychology) 3. Grief in women 4. Coping 5. Young women 6. Women teachers 7. Self-fulfillment in women 8. Asian Americans 9. Coming-of-age stories 10. Psychological fiction

LC 2008008924

Ms. Beatrice Hempel, new to teaching, new to the school, newly engaged, and newly bereft of her idiosyncratic father, struggles to figure out what is expected of her in life and at work.

"Eight interconnected stories about Beatrice Hempel, a middle school English teacher. Ms. Hempel is the sort of teacher students adore, and despite feeling disenchanted with her job, she regards her students as intelligent, insightful and sometimes fascinating. Bynum . . . weaves stories of the teacher's childhood with the presentreminiscences about Beatrice's now deceased father and her relationship with her younger brother, Calvin--while simultaneously fleshing out the lives of Beatrice's impressionable students." Publishers Weekly.

Byrne, Kerrigan
The **duke** with the dragon tattoo / Kerrigan Byrne. St Martin's Paperbacks, 2018. 336 p. Victorian rebels
ISBN 9781250122568
1. Victorian era (1837-1901) 2. Tattooing 3. Men with amnesia 4. Dukes and duchesses 5. Protectiveness in men 6. Mate selection 7. Sexual attraction 8. Men/women relations 9. Great Britain -- History -- Victoria, 1837-1901 10. Victorian romances 11. Historical romances
The sixth book in the Victorian Rebel series introduces The Rook, a man who wakes up in a mass grave with no memory and a dragon

tattoo on his arm. Years after being rescued and nursed back to health by Lorelei, he returns to claim her heart and avenge those who have wronged her.

Byrne, Kerrigan

How to love a duke in ten days / Kerrigan Byrne. St Martins Pr, 2019. 464 p. Devil you know

ISBN 9781250318848

1. Victorian era (1837-1901) 2. Dukes and duchesses 3. Nobility 4. Women archaeologists 5. Rape victims 6. Murder 7. Extortion 8. Secrets 9. Bankruptcy 10. Rich men 11. Mate selection 12. Revenge 13. Protectiveness in men 14. Historical romances 15. Victorian romances

Famed and brilliant, Lady Alexandra Lane has always known how to look out for to herself. But nobody would ever expect that she has darkness in her past - one that she pays a blackmailer to keep buried. Now, with her family nearing bankruptcy, Alexandra strikes upon a solution: Get married to one of the empire's most wealthy eligible bachelors. Even if he does have the reputation of a devil.

Byrne, Kerrigan

The **hunter** / Kerrigan Byrne. St Martin's Paperbacks, 2016 432 p. Victorian rebels

ISBN 9781250076069

1. Victorian era (1837-1901) 2. Actors and actresses 3. Assassins 4. Loners 5. Protectiveness in men 6. Secrets 7. Men/women relations 8. Sexual attraction 9. London, England 10. Great Britain -- History -- Victoria, 1837-1901 11. Victorian romances 12. Historical romances

When he is hired to kill beautiful actress Millie LeCour, Christopher Argent, London's deadliest hitman, is unable to complete his mission as he becomes overwhelmed by the passion that simmers between them, and vows to keep her safe from her enemies as danger closes in.

Byrne, Trevor

* Ghosts and lightning / Trevor Byrne. Doubleday, 2009. 336 p.

ISBN 9780385531276

1. Bereavement 2. Self-destructive behavior 3. Homecomings 4. Drug use 5. Families 6. Mothers -- Death 7. Violence 8. Young men 9. Ireland 10. Dublin, Ireland -- Social life and customs 11. Picaresque fiction

LC 2009020031

Called back to his native Dublin to attend his mother's funeral, Denny struggles with feelings of powerlessness in the face of death, drug use, and unemployment while spending his empty days with a series of hooligan companions.

"[A] witty and often disturbing portrait of the Irish underclass . . . , and the story is inventively narrated in a thick Irish brogue, saturated with profanities and folkloric allusions." The New Yorker.

C

Ca$h

Thugs cry : a novel / Ca$h Lockdown Pub., 2013. 252 p. Thugs cry novels (Ca$h)

ISBN 9781492717928

1. Gangs 2. Drug traffic 3. African Americans 4. Men/women relations 5. Revenge in men 6. Criminals 7. Organized crime 8. Newark, New Jersey 9. Urban fiction 10. African American fiction

Cam'ron and Raheem hail from the notorious Brick City in Newark New Jersey. The two friends grew up eating noodles off of the same fork, now they are primed to eat off the drug game.

Ca$h

Trust no man / Cash. Authorhouse, 2005. 440 p. Trust no man novels

ISBN 9781420886238

1. African American young men 2. Street life 3. Gangs 4. Robbery 5. Drug addicts 6. Cheating (Interpersonal relations) 7. Inner city 8. Trust 9. Betrayal 10. Options, alternatives, hoices 11. Former convicts 12. African American men/women relations 13. Atlanta, Georgia 14. African American fiction 15. Urban fiction

Ca$h

Trust no man 2 / Ca$h. Wahida Clark Presents, 2009. 209 p. Trust no man novels

ISBN 9780981854526

1. African American young men 2. Street life 3. Gangs 4. Former convicts 5. Options, alternatives, choices 6. African American men/women relations 7. Love triangles 8. Cheating (Interpersonal relations) 9. Inner city 10. Trust 11. Betrayal 12. Robbery 13. Atlanta, Georgia 14. African American fiction 15. Urban fiction

After Youngblood is snatched up and beaten down by unknown thugs he vows fatal revenge on his attackers, but his homie Murder Mike gives him an ultimatum that tests his principles, while Youngblood must also decide between Inez and Juanita and deal with enemies who are closer to him then he realizes.

Ca$h

Trust no man 3 / Ca$h. Wahida Clark Presents, 2009. 267 p. Trust no man novels

ISBN 9780981854595

1. African American young men 2. Street life 3. Gangs 4. Former convicts 5. Options, alternatives, choices 6. African American men/women relations 7. Love triangles 8. Cheating (Interpersonal relations) 9. Inner city 10. Trust 11. Betrayal 12. Robbery 13. Atlanta, Georgia 14. African American fiction 15. Urban fiction

After his father's execution on death row, Trouble sets out to avenge his death by killing anyone who helped bring about the patriarch's downfall, with the help of his loyal girlfriend Kamora and friend Criminal.

Cabot, Meg

No judgments : a novel / Meg Cabot. William Morrow, 2019. 384 p.

ISBN 9780062913579

1. Young women 2. Hurricanes 3. Pets 4. Womanizers 5. Power failures 6. Animal rescue 7. Interpersonal attraction 8. Men/women relations 9. Former boyfriends 10. Emotionally abusive men 11. Florida Keys 12. Contemporary romances

LC 2019010863

Relocating to the Florida Keys after a devastating breakup, Bree refuses to evacuate during a Category 5 hurricane before finding herself scrambling to protect the pets her neighbors were forced to leave behind.

Cain, Chelsea

One Kick : a novel / Chelsea Cain. Simon & Schuster, 2014. 306 p. Kick Lannigan

ISBN 9781476749785

1. Women martial artists 2. Kidnapping victims 3. Post-traumatic stress disorder 4. Child pornography victims 5. Obsession in women 6. Kidnapping 7. Child kidnapping victims 8. Recovered memory 9.

Shooting 10. Psychopaths 11. Obsession 12. Seattle, Washington 13. Thrillers and suspense

LC 2013044441

Kick Lannigan, a famous kidnapping survivor, uses her martial-arts mastery and affiliation with a wealthy patron to find and rescue missing children.

"The subject matter is uncomfortable, even stomach-churning at times, but Cain manages to deal sensitively with her material while still allowing Kick's character to emerge with multifaceted humanity--and even snatches of humor." Booklist.

Caldwell, Erskine, 1903-1987

Tobacco Road / Erskine Caldwell ; foreword by Lewis Nordan. University of Georgia Press, 1995. 184 p.

ISBN 082031661X

1. Sharecroppers 2. Poor families 3. Rural life 4. Depressions -- 1929-1941 5. Rural poor people 6. Farm life 7. Georgia 8. Modern classics 9. Southern Gothic 10. Literary fiction 11. Southern fiction

LC 9413090

The Depression has hit the depleted farmlands of Augusta, Georgia, hard. For the Lester family, grinding poverty has become a way of life. Trapped by ignorance and selfishness, the Lesters are torn between surrendering to their hunger and sexual longings, and the fear that they may be slipping even lower than they already are in society's eyes.

Callaghan, Mary Rose

Billy, come home / Mary Rose Callaghan. Brandon, 2007. 201 p.

ISBN 9780863223662

1. Men with schizophrenia 2. Men with mental illnesses 3. Malicious accusation 4. Murder suspects 5. Brothers and sisters 6. People with schizophrenia -- Family relationships 7. Mental illness -- Social aspects 8. Discrimination in law enforcement 9. Ireland 10. Domestic fiction

"The author gives such a subtle, chilling portrayal of institutional cruelty, parental indifference and government warehousing that readers will want to share her faith." Kirkus

Callanan, Liam

Paris by the book / Liam Callanan. E.P. Dutton, 2018. 368 p.

ISBN 9781101986271

1. Moving to a new country 2. Books and reading 3. Bookstores 4. Authors 5. Missing men 6. Married women 7. Mothers and daughters 8. Women booksellers 9. Family secrets 10. Men/women relations 11. Paris, France 12. Mainstream fiction

When her eccentric novelist husband disappears, leaving behind nothing but a hidden pair of plane tickets to Paris, Leah relocates to France and takes ownership of a small bookstore, where clues she discovers in an unfinished manuscript and in the literary paths of beloved Parisian classics lead to consequential truths for her daughters.

Callender, Kacen

Queen of the conquered / Kheryn Callender. Orbit, 2019. 480 p. Islands of blood and storm

ISBN 9780316454933

1. Orphans 2. Adult children of murder victims 3. Revenge 4. Royal houses 5. Islands 6. Race (Social sciences) 7. Supernatural 8. Telepathy 9. Mind control 10. Magic 11. Slavery 12. Inheritance and succession 13. Power (Social sciences) 14. Corruption 15. Options, alternatives, choices 16. Epic fantasy

LC 2019019777

Sigourney Rose is the only surviving daughter of a noble lineage on the islands of Hans Lollik. When she was a child, her family was murdered by the islands' colonizers, who have massacred and enslaved generations of her people -- and now, Sigourney is ready to exact her revenge. When the childless king of the islands declares that he will choose his successor from amongst eligible noble families, Sigourney uses her ability to read and control minds to manipulate her way onto the royal island and into the ranks of the ruling colonizers. But when she arrives, prepared to fight for control of all the islands, Sigourney finds herself the target of a dangerous, unknown magic.

Callihan, Kristen

* Firelight / Kristen Callihan. Forever, 2012. 384 p. Darkest London

ISBN 9781455508594

1. Victorian era (1837-1901) 2. 19th century 3. Arranged marriage 4. Men with disfigurements 5. Curses 6. Superhuman abilities 7. Nobility 8. Magic 9. Good and evil 10. Redheads 11. Men/women relations 12. Sexual attraction 13. Malicious accusation 14. Serial murders 15. Great Britain -- History -- Victoria, 1837-1901 16. Paranormal romances 17. Historical romances 18. Victorian romances

RUSA Reading List, 2013.

Forced to wed London's most nefarious nobleman to save her family from financial ruin, Miranda Ellis, who is gifted with exceptional abilities, discovers that her new husband is no ordinary man when she must enter a world of dark magic to save his soul.

Calvi, Mary, 1969-

Dear George, Dear Mary : a novel of George Washington's first love / Mary Calvi. St. Martin's Press, 2019. viii, 322 p.

ISBN 9781250162946

1. Washington, George, 1732-1799 2. Philipse, Mary, 1730-1825 3. Colonial America (1600-1775) 4. Soldiers 5. First loves 6. Heirs and heiresses 7. Courtship 8. Unrequited love 9. Men/women relations 10. American Revolution, 1775-1783 11. United States -- Religion -- Colonial period, 1600-1775 12. United States -- History -- Revolution, 1775-1783 13. Biographical fiction 14. Historical fiction

LC 2018037733

Reimagines the unrequited love affair between a young George Washington and controversial New York heiress Mary Philipse as a catalyst for the American Revolution.

"It is ... a fascinating and unique look at pre-Revolutionary War society, with its misunderstandings and simmering resentments, and notable for the author's use of contemporaneous documents." Booklist.

Calvino, Italo

The **baron** in the trees / Italo Calvino ; translated by Archibald Colquhoun. Harcourt Brace Jovanovich, 1977, c1957. 217 p.

ISBN 0156106809

1. 18th century 2. Eccentrics and eccentricities 3. Nobility -- Italy 4. Defiance 5. Tree climbing 6. Tree houses 7. Barons and baronesses -- Italy 8. Adventurers -- Italy 9. Italy -- Social life and customs -- 18th century 10. Magical realism 11. Translations -- Italian to English 12. Modern classics 13. Literary fiction

LC 76039704

A Helen and Kurt Wolff book.

Originally published: Turin : Giulio Einaudi Editore, 1957.

Calvino, Italo

* **If** on a winter's night a traveler / Italo Calvino ; translated from the Italian by William Weaver. Harcourt Brace Jovanovich, 1981, c1979. 260 p.

ISBN 9780151436897

1. Books and reading 2. Writing 3. Men/women relations 4. Magical realism 5. Literary fiction 6. Metafiction 7. Modern classics 8. Experimental fiction 9. Translations -- Italian to English 10. Second person narratives

LC 80008741

A Helen and Kurt Wolff book.

Originally published: Torino : Einaudi, 1979.

Ten different and thoroughly dissimilar novels intertwine as the beginning of each book, interrupted at a critical moment of suspense, leads into yet another novel reflecting yet another literary mode.

Calvino, Italo

Invisible cities / Italo Calvino ; translated from the Italian by William Weaver. Harcourt Brace Jovanovich, 1978, c1972. 165 p.

ISBN 9780156453806

1. Polo, Marco, 1254-1323? 2. Kublai Khan, 1216-1294 3. Storytelling 4. Rulers 5. Cities and towns 6. Manipulation (Social sciences) 7. Survival 8. Literary fiction 9. Magical realism 10. Translations -- Italian to English 11. Modern classics

"A Helen and Kurt Wolff book."

Originally published: Torino : Einaudi, 1972.

In Kublai Khan's garden, at sunset, the young Marco Polo diverts the aged emperor from his obsession with the impending end of his empire with tales of countless cities past, present, and future.

"Italo Calvino is recognized as one of the consummate stylists among writers today, a novelist whose superbly imaginative mind conjures up metaphorical fables of exquisite beauty to transcribe his personal visions of man and the universe." Choice.

Cambias, James L.

A **darkling** sea / James L. Cambias. Tor, 2014. 336 p.

ISBN 9780765336279

1. Underwater cities 2. Interplanetary relations 3. Human/alien encounters 4. Space flight 5. Planets -- Exploration 6. Life on other planets 7. Underwater exploration 8. Death 9. Undersea colonies 10. Space exploration 11. Social science fiction 12. Hard science fiction 13. Science fiction

LC 2013025215

"A Tom Doherty Associates Book."

Ilmatar is an ice-bound planet whose vast sub-surface ocean supports a blind, sentient alien race. Contact with the Ilmatarans is strictly forbidden, due to rules put in place by the six-limbed Sholen, who believe that humanity is too dangerous to be permitted contact with other species. Their concerns are soon justified by the actions of one Earthling, a journalist killed during an illicit attempt to film the Ilmatarans. This incident sets off an inter-galactic diplomatic crisis as well as conflict between human researchers and Sholen regulators. Boasting strong characterizations and extensive, immersive world-building, A Darkling Sea presents a gripping story that also provides a thought-provoking exploration of ethical issues. -- Description by Gillian Speace.

"Cambias makes the Sholen and Ilmataran people and cultures as real as the more familiar human component. Beautifully written, with a story that captures the imagination." Booklist.

Cameron, Cate

Just a summer fling / Cate Cameron. Berkley, 2015 304 p. Sullivan Lake romances

ISBN 9780425282052

1. Vacations 2. Film actors and actresses 3. Cheating (Interpersonal relations) 4. Small towns 5. Fame 6. Trust in men 7. Repairers 8. Interpersonal attraction 9. Men/women relations 10. Contemporary romances

After her boyfriend's affair with a costar, movie star Ashley Carlsen retreats to Vermont with a Hollywood power player and has a summer fling with handyman Josh Sullivan that turns into something much more.

Cameron, Marc

* **Code** of honor / Marc Cameron. Putnam Pub Group, 2019. 592 p. Jack Ryan and John Clark novels

ISBN 9780525541721

1. Elite operatives 2. National security 3. Malicious accusation 4. Friendship 5. International intrigue 6. Intelligence service 7. United States -- Foreign relations 8. Political thrillers 9. Thrillers and suspense

When an old college friend-turned-humanitarian is arrested in Indonesia amid false accusations, President Ryan assigns the Campus team to find answers at the same time he receives an ominous warning.

Cameron, Marc

* **Oath** of office / Marc Cameron. Penguin Group USA, 2018 432 p. Jack Ryan and John Clark novels

ISBN 9780735215955

1. Presidents -- United States 2. Regime change 3. Arms dealers 4. Epidemics 5. National security 6. Intelligence officers 7. Elite operatives 8. United States -- Foreign relations -- Iran 9. Iran -- Foreign relations -- United States 10. Political thrillers 11. Thrillers and suspense

When a change of regimes in Iran presents new opportunities for a balance of power in the region, President Jack Ryan becomes a lone Western voice in urging caution in the wake of an international arms dealer's rise to power.

Cameron, Marc

* **Power** and empire / Marc Cameron. G.P. Putnam's Sons, 2017. 432 p. Jack Ryan and John Clark novels

ISBN 9780735215894

1. Presidents -- United States 2. International intrigue 3. Terrorism -- Prevention 4. Spies 5. Negotiation 6. National security 7. Intelligence service 8. Intelligence officers 9. Elite operatives 10. United States -- Foreign relations -- China 11. China -- Foreign relations -- United States 12. Political thrillers 13. Thrillers and suspense

A newly belligerent Chinese government leaves U.S. President Jack Ryan with only a few desperate options to control a series of attacks designed to sabotage peace negotiations.

Cameron, Peter, 1959-

The **city** of your final destination / Peter Cameron. Farrar, Straus, and Giroux, 2002. 311 p.

ISBN 0374281971

1. Biographers 2. Mistresses 3. Love triangles 4. Authors 5. Americans in Uruguay 6. Iranian Americans 7. Suicide 8. Life change events 9. Gay men 10. Happiness 11. Guilt in women 12. Men/women relations 13. Widows 14. Graduate students 15. Biography 16. Uruguay 17. Kansas 18. Literary fiction

LC 2001051127

This novel was made into film of the same name in 2007, directed by James Ivory and starring Anthony Hopkins, Laura Linney, and Charlotte Gainsbourg.

After receiving a grant to write the biography of recently deceased Latin American author Jules Gund, graduate student Omar Razaghi's request to become Gund's official biogapher is turned down, prompting Omar to travel to Uruguay to try to persuade the author's literary heirs to change their minds.

"The characters discover themselves not through the books they have read (as Omar first believes) or the places they have been (as the title would suggest) but through Cameron's precisely rendered conversations." The New Yorker.

Cameron, W. Bruce

* A **dog's** promise / W. Bruce Cameron. Forge, 2019. 336 p. Dog's purpose

ISBN 9781250163516

1. Reincarnation 2. Purpose in life 3. Promises 4. Human/animal relationships 5. Humans and dogs 6. Helpfulness 7. Stories told by animals

A latest entry in the series that includes, A Dog's Journey, continues the story of Bailey, who is joined by another special dog, Lola, in an effort to fulfill a promise over the course of several lives.

Cameron, W. Bruce

The **dogs** of Christmas / W. Bruce Cameron. Forge Books, 2013. 224 p.

ISBN 9780765330550

1. Single men 2. Abandoned dogs 3. Animal rescue 4. Animal shelter workers 5. Dogs 6. Puppies 7. Human/animal relationships 8. Men/women relations 9. Unconditional love 10. Colorado 11. Mainstream fiction 12. Christmas stories

LC 2013018448

"A Tom Doherty Associates book."

When his neighbor abandons his very pregnant dog Lucy at his Colorado home, Josh Michaels, recovering from a broken heart, learns to care for Lucy's tiny puppies with the help of local animal shelter worker Kerri, a beautiful woman with a quick wit and fierce love for animals.

Cameron, W. Bruce

Repo madness / W. Bruce Cameron. Forge Books, 2016. 368 p. Ruddy McCann novels

ISBN 9780765377500

1. Repossessors 2. Serial murder investigation 3. Women murder victims 4. Auditory hallucinations 5. Men and dogs 6. Amateur detectives 7. Former convicts 8. Engaged persons 9. Ghosts 10. Men/women relations 11. Fathers and daughters 12. Interpersonal attraction 13. Former football players 14. Small town life -- Michigan 15. Michigan 16. Supernatural mysteries

Juggling the possible loss of his job, a romantic estrangement, and court-ordered medication, Michigan repo man Ruddy McCann learns that the tragedy that defined his life may be a lie, a possibility that compels his investigation into a string of local disappearances.

Camp, Bryan

The **city** of lost fortunes / Bryan Camp. John Joseph Adams/Houghton Mifflin Harcourt, 2018. 384 p. Crescent City novels (Bryan Camp)

ISBN 9781328810793

1. 2010s 2. Gods and goddesses 3. Psychic ability 4. Demigods 5. Supernatural 6. Magic 7. Murder 8. Loss (Psychology) 9. Swindlers and swindling 10. Imaginary creatures 11. Secrets 12. City life 13.

New Orleans, Louisiana 14. Urban fantasy

LC 2017045346

Maintaining a low profile in the aftermath of Hurricane Katrina in New Orleans, a street magician who inherited an ability to find lost things from his superhuman father, is drawn back into the world by the murder of a Fortune god to whom he owes a debt, an event that exposes a plot that threatens the city's soul.

Camp, Bryan

Gather the fortunes / Bryan Camp. Houghton Mifflin Harcourt, 2019. 336 p. Crescent City novels (Bryan Camp)

ISBN 9781328876713

1. Spirit guides 2. Missing persons investigation 3. Gods and goddesses 4. Soul 5. Ghosts 6. Death (Personification) 7. Psychic ability 8. Demigods 9. Supernatural 10. Magic 11. Imaginary creatures 12. Secrets 13. City life 14. African American women 15. New Orleans, Louisiana 16. Urban fantasy

LC 2018043604

"A John Joseph Adams book."

Establishing herself among the guides who lead the souls of the dead through the Seven Gates of the Underworld, Renaissance Raines lands at the center of a deity plot involving a boy's escape of his foretold death.

"Full of magic and numerous mythologies but still tied to the lush New Orleans setting, this Crescent City is one readers will not want to leave." Library Journal.

Campbell, Aifric

On the floor / Aifric Campbell. Picador, 2013. 250 p.

ISBN 9781250028396

1. 1990s 2. Women bankers 3. Investment bankers 4. Floor traders (Finance) 5. Self-discovery in women 6. Breaking up (Interpersonal relations) 7. Financial services industry and trade 8. Persian Gulf War, 1991 9. London, England 10. Mainstream fiction

LC 2012043261

Originally published: 2012.

A tale set against a backdrop of the Gulf War finds once-successful investment banker Geri Molloy shaken from a breakup-related malaise by an eccentric hedge fund manager in Hong Kong who embroils Geri in a high-stakes takeover that places her future at risk.

Campbell, Bebe Moore, 1950-2006

Brothers and sisters / Bebe Moore Campbell. G. P. Putnam's Sons, 1994. 476 p.

ISBN 039913929X

1. Women bankers 2. Sexual harassment 3. Interracial friendship 4. Racism 5. African American women 6. Race relations 7. Female friendship 8. Men/women relations 9. Los Angeles, California 10. Psychological fiction 11. African American fiction

LC 94014196

Struggling with her own personal issues after the Los Angeles riots, Esther Jackson, a Black employee at a downtown bank, is heartened when a Black man is hired as senior vice-president, until he sexually harasses her white friend and coworker

"What makes 'Brothers and Sisters' different from the traditional potboiler is Ms. Campbell's genuine attempt to address the complexities of race in the modern age." New York Times Book Review.

Campbell, Bebe Moore, 1950-2006

Your blues ain't like mine / Bebe Moore Campbell. G. P. Putnam's Sons, 1992. 332p.

ISBN 9780345401120

1. 1950s 2. Racism -- Mississippi 3. Hate crimes 4. Civil Rights Movement 5. African American teenage boys -- Mississippi 6. Poor

people -- Mississippi 7. Race relations 8. African American families -- Mississippi 9. Mississippi -- Race relations 10. Coming-of-age stories 11. African American fiction

LC 91045518

The racially motivated deadly beating of a black teenager in a small Mississippi town ripples through generations, changing forever the lives of everyone involved in the incident.

"Written in poetic prose, filled with masterfully drawn and sympathetic characters that a less able hand might have rendered in stereotypes, this first novel blends the irony of Flannery O'Connor's fiction and the poignance of Harper Lee's." Publishers Weekly.

Campbell, Bonnie Jo, 1962-

American salvage : stories / Bonnie Jo Campbell. Wayne State University Press, 2009. 184 p.

ISBN 9780814334126

1. Rural life 2. Michigan 3. United States -- Social life and customs 4. Rural noir 5. Short stories 6. Literary fiction

LC 2008051203

National Book Award for Fiction finalist, 2009.

National Book Critics Circle Award for Fiction finalist, 2009.

In rural Michigan, the American dream, if it ever existed, lies discarded like so much rusty scrap metal. For the inhabitants of Campbell's tales, the real truth of life can be found in industrial accidents, soul-deadening labor, and the comfort of five drinks too many. But even amid the despair of meth labs and empty pocketbooks, Campbell's characters yearn for something, anything, to raise them above it all--and sometimes, impossibly, they find it.

"Campbell's knockout short stories about postindustrial rural Michigan portray damaged, discarded, and busted-broke people rich in yearning, forgiveness, and love." Booklist.

Campbell, Bonnie Jo, 1962-

* **Once** upon a river / Bonnie Jo Campbell. W. W. Norton & Co., 2011. 320 p.

ISBN 9780393079890

1. 1970s 2. Teenage girls 3. Fathers -- Death 4. River life 5. Mothers and daughters 6. Rape 7. Boating 8. Survival skills 9. Voyages and travels 10. Michigan 11. Rural noir 12. Coming-of-age stories 13. Literary fiction

LC 2011001499

Margo Crane, a beautiful and uncanny markswoman takes to the Stark River after being complicit in the death of her father and embarks on an odyssey in search of her vanished mother.

"Celebrates the timeless secrets of life, death, and imaginationand the enduring power of words. Fans, rejoice!" Kirkus.

Campbell, Rick, (Navy Commander)

Treason / Rick Campbell. St. Martin's Press, 2019. 352 p. Trident deception

ISBN 9781250164650

1. United States. Navy. SEALs. 2. Coups d'etat 3. Military occupation 4. International intrigue 5. Armed Forces 6. Nuclear weapons 7. Treaties 8. Rescues 9. Navy SEALs 10. Russia 11. Ukraine 12. United States 13. Techno-thrillers

LC 2018044449

A military coup in Russia leads to a swift invasion of former Soviet territories--while the U.S. has been rendered powerless to respond.

Campisi, Megan

Sin eater / Megan Campisi. Atria Books, 2020. 320 p.

ISBN 9781982124106

1. Elizabethan era (1558-1603) 2. Sin 3. Superstition 4. Punishment 5. Teenage girls 6. Political intrigue 7. Courts and courtiers 8. Rites and ceremonies 9. Murder 10. Blame 11. Social isolation 12. Investigations 13. Misfits (Persons) 14. England -- Social life and customs -- 16th century 15. Historical fantasy

Sentenced to become a Sin Eater for the crime of stealing bread, a 14-year-old orphan in 16th-century England becomes ensnared in a deadly royal plot that helps her discover the power of her subjugated position.

"This spellbinding novel is a treat for fans of feminist speculative fiction." Publishers Weekly.

Camus, Albert, 1913-1960

* The **fall** / Albert Camus ; translated from the French by Justin O'Brien. Vintage Books, 1991, c1956. 147 p.

ISBN 9780679720225

1. Conscience 2. Lawyers 3. Deception 4. Existentialism 5. Strangers 6. Expatriates 7. Social ethics 8. Guilt in men 9. Paris, France 10. Amsterdam, Netherlands 11. Literary fiction 12. Psychological fiction 13. Classics 14. Translations -- French to English

Translation from the French of: La chute.

"First published in the U.S. by Alfred A. Knopf in 1956"--T.p. verso.

A man's confessions reveal his perception of justice and his own downfall.

Camus, Albert, 1913-1960

The **plague** / Albert Camus ; translated from the French by Stuart Gilbert. Vintage Books, 1991, c1947. 308 p.

ISBN 9780679720218

1. Plague 2. Epidemics 3. Social isolation 4. Poverty 5. Physicians 6. Quarantine 7. Meaning (Psychology) 8. Existentialism 9. Algeria 10. Translations -- French to English 11. Literary fiction 12. Modern classics

Translation from the French of: La peste.

This translation first published: Allen Lane The Penguin Press, 2001.

Originally published as La peste, 1947.

Originally published: Paris : Gallimard, 1947.

Chaos prevails when the bubonic plague strikes the Algerian coastal city of Oran.

Camus, Albert, 1913-1960

* The **stranger** / Albert Camus ; translated from the French by Matthew Ward. A. A. Knopf, 1988, c1942. vii, 123 p.

ISBN 9780394533056

1. Trials (Murder) 2. Murderers 3. Conformity 4. Poverty 5. Honesty 6. Death -- Psychological aspects 7. Executions and executioners 8. Existentialism 9. Meaning (Psychology) 10. Algeria 11. Psychological fiction 12. Translations -- French to English 13. Literary fiction 14. Modern classics

LC 83048885

Translation from the French of: L'Etranger.

Also published as: The outsider (1946).

Originally published in French by Librairie Gallimard, Paris in 1942.

When a young Algerian named Meursault kills a man, his subsequent imprisonment and trial are puzzling and absurd. The apparently amoral Meursault--who puts little stock in ideas like love and God--seems to be on trial less for his murderous actions, and more for what the authorities believe is his deficient character.

"The new translation of Camus's classic is a cultural event. . . . With the domestications pruned away from the text, students will be as close to the original as another language will allow." Library Journal.

Cander, Chris

The **weight** of a piano : a novel / Chris Cander. Alfred A Knopf, 2019. 323 p.

ISBN 9780525654674

1. Pianos 2. Family history 3. Loss (Psychology) 4. Music 5. Obsession 6. Life change events 7. Families 8. Interpersonal relations 9. Death Valley 10. California 11. Soviet Union 12. Parallel narratives 13. Literary fiction

An immigrant from the Soviet Union and an orphaned mechanic find their lives fatefully linked across half a century of history by a German Bluthner piano.

"Strong characterization and attention to detail, whether in the manufacture of a piano or in the desolate beauty of Death Valley, elevate Cander's . . . tale about learning to let go of the past." Booklist.

Candlish, Louise

* **Our** house / Louise Candlish. Berkley, 2018. 416 p.

ISBN 9780451489111

1. Divorced parents 2. Coparenting 3. Houses 4. Missing men 5. Missing children 6. Children of divorced parents 7. Social media 8. Secrets 9. London, England 10. Psychological suspense

LC 2017029542

Arriving home to find strangers moving into the prized family home she agreed to share with her ex, Fiona endures a domino effect of horrors as she discovers that her children have gone missing amid terrible revelations.

Candlish, Louise

* **Those** people / Louise Candlish. Berkley, 2019. 416 p.

ISBN 9780451489142

1. Neighborhoods 2. Neighbors 3. Interpersonal conflict 4. Class conflict 5. Suburban life 6. Quarreling 7. Hate 8. Death 9. Perception 10. Thrillers and suspense

LC 2018059466

An idyllic suburban neighborhood is thrown into chaos by the arrival of new neighbors who disrupt the community with rude behavior, loud music and unsightly renovations, until a shattering murder exposes a network of secrets.

"An upscale London neighborhood becomes the setting for escalating class warfare in Candlish's ... acidly funny and disturbing novel of domestic suspense. ... A nicely paced, wryly intelligent novel with sharp insights into human behavior." Kirkus.

Canin, Ethan

America America : a novel / Ethan Canin. Random House, 2008. 464 p.

ISBN 9780679456803

1. Working class men 2. Rich people 3. Upper class women 4. Character 5. College students 6. Men/women relations 7. Love 8. Ethics 9. New York (State) -- Politics and government 10. United States -- Politics and government 11. Political fiction

LC 2008002341

Corey Sifter is befriended by the wealthy Metarey family, a politically powerful dynasty in New York, and becomes an aide to New York senator Henry Bonwiller as he runs for the Democratic presidential nomination during the Nixon era.

"Sifter is, at times, too perfect a lead, and his Saline coming-of-age is an idealized yesteryear, a mythic America encased in amber. But it is so passionately imagined that it is hard to resist Mr. Canin's retreat to simpler times and his vision of those who would forfeit comfort for the possibility of unknown highs (or lows)." New York Sun.

Canin, Ethan

A **doubter's** almanac : a novel / Ethan Canin. Random House, 2016, c2014. xi, 558 p.

ISBN 9781400068265

1. Genius 2. Mathematicians 3. Ambition in men 4. Fathers and sons 5. Drug use 6. Sexuality 7. Addiction 8. Jealousy 9. Family relationships 10. Literary fiction

LC 2014022315

Also known as: The confessions of Milo Andret.

A controversial mathematician pursues hedonist vices in 1970s university environments while coming to terms with the mysteries of his father's outsized life and his own personal legacy.

"A moving, spiritual journey, this poetic novel clocks in at well over 500 pages but begs to be read in one sitting. It will delight literary fiction readers of all stripes with its diverse themes, from coming of age to love, grief, and addiction. But a warning; it's tough to keep a dry eye through this one." Library Journal.

Cannon, Joanna, (Psychiatrist),

Three things about Elsie : a novel / Joanna Cannon. Scribner, 2018. 304 p.

ISBN 9781501187384

1. Nursing home patients 2. Senior women 3. Reminiscing in old age 4. Memories 5. Friendship 6. Childhood 7. Secrets 8. England 9. Psychological fiction

LC 2017061726

Longlisted for The Women's Prize for Fiction, 2018.

Presents the story of an injured woman who meditates on her complicated relationship with a best friend when a man they believed was dead joins her retirement community.

Cantero, Edgar, 1981-

Meddling kids : a novel / Edgar Cantero. Doubleday, 2017. 322 p.

ISBN 9780385541992

1. Reunions 2. Teenage detectives 3. Cold cases (Criminal investigation 4. Amateur detectives 5. Consequences 6. Investigations 7. Occult crime 8. Monsters 9. Ghosts 10. Dogs 11. Oregon 12. New York City 13. Supernatural mysteries 14. Humorous stories 15. Horror

LC 2016040471

In Meddling Kids, Catalonian author Edgar Cantero portrays a reunion of old friends who decide to complete some unfinished business in the resort town where they spent their summers as kids. While pitting good against evil, Cantero pays homage to H.P. Lovecraft's Cthulhu mythos, the bumbling but resourceful gang in Scooby-Doo (yes, there are four kids and a dog), and a full range of road trip, haunted house, and reclusive wizard tropes. This gripping escapade (with touches of quirky humor) will have you rooting for the sympathetic, well-drawn kids -- now adults -- as your knuckles all turn white. -- Description by Katherine Bradley Johnson

"Canteros imagination is vivid, and the story, once it gains speed, continues at a breakneck, roller-coaster pace. He plays with form and style, which makes for an enjoyable romp." Booklist.

Cantor, Melanie

Death and other happy endings : a novel / Melanie Cantor. Pamela Dorman Books, 2019 336 p.

ISBN 9780525562115

1. Women with terminal illnesses 2. Letter writing 3. Truth 4. Divorced women 5. Reconciliation 6. Life change events 7. Diagnosis 8. Mainstream fiction

LC 2018058602

Regretting nothing except the relationships she has lost upon learning she has only three months to live, Jennifer writes cathartic letters to the most significant people in her life before she is confronted by unexpected surprises.

Canty, Kevin

The **underworld** : a novel / Kevin Canty. W. W. Norton & Company, 2017 256 p.

ISBN 9780393293050

1. 1970s 2. Silver mines and mining 3. Survival (after disaster) 4. Mine accidents 5. Fires 6. Miners 7. Rural life 8. Small town life 9. Family relationships 10. Working class families 11. Iowa 12. Literary fiction

LC 2016035694

A tale inspired by true events from an isolated Iowa mining town in the 1970s traces the experiences of a handful of survivors after a disastrous fire and how they struggled to endure wrenching losses while rebuilding and pursuing dreams rendered harder by the tragedy.

"His sculpted, lapidarian cadence deftly navigates the terrain separating numbness and pain, second guesses and second chances, to illuminate the fragility and preciousness of life." Booklist.

Capote, Truman, 1924-1984

* **Breakfast** at Tiffany's / Truman Capote. Random House, 1958. 179 p.

ISBN 9780141037264

1. Misfits (Persons) 2. Organized crime 3. Friendship 4. Prostitution 5. Marriage 6. Single women 7. Young women 8. Socialites 9. Single men 10. Manhattan, New York City 11. Literary fiction 12. Short stories 13. Modern classics

LC 58010956

"A short novel and three stories."

"Breakfast at Tiffany's a novelette and three short stories, is no exception and bears the indelible mark of Capote and an indication of his literary maturation." Kirkus.

Capote, Truman, 1924-1984

* The **complete** stories of Truman Capote / Truman Capote ; introduction by Reynolds Price. Random House, 2004. 320 p.

ISBN 0679643109

1. Short stories 2. Literary fiction

LC 2004046876

Twenty short stories.

Children on their birthdays was released as a movie with the same title.

A complete collection of the author's short stories includes pieces set in locales ranging from the Gothic South to the chic East Coast and offers insight into his cultural influence and mastery of the short story form.

"Now, for the first time, all of Capote's short stories are being published together, an event that signifies a renewed appreciation of his overall contribution to literature, for evidence is presented in this one volume that he should be ranked as a major American short story writer." Booklist.

Capote, Truman, 1924-1984

The **grass** harp : including A tree of night and other stories / Truman Capote. Vintage Books, 1993, c1951. 216 p.

ISBN 9780679745570

1. Misfits (Persons) -- Southern States 2. Small town life -- Southern States 3. Southern States 4. Short stories 5. Literary fiction

Children on their birthdays was released as a movie with the same title.

Originally published: New York : New American Library, 1951.

The protagonists of these nine short stories learn to accept the harsh loneliness of life.

Capri, NeNe

The **pussy** trap / NeNe Capri. Wahida Clark Presents, 2011. 300 p. Pussy trap

ISBN 9780982841488

1. Street life 2. Drug dealers 3. Revenge 4. Drug traffic 5. Sexuality 6. African American women 7. African Americans 8. New York City 9. African American fiction 10. Urban fiction

Sequel: The Pussy Trap Part 2: The Kiss of Death.

Kayson, a New York drug dealer, recruits KoKo, an up-and-coming female gangster, to settle an old score for him, but when their unexpected romance abruptly ends with his murder, she decides to avenge his death.

Caputo, Philip, 1941-

Acts of faith / Philip Caputo. Knopf, 2005. 688 p.

ISBN 9780375411663

1. Humanitarian assistance 2. Americans in Sudan 3. Pilots 4. Women missionaries 5. Missionaries 6. Rebels 7. Warlords 8. Conspiracies 9. Violence 10. Civil war -- Sudan 11. Food relief organizations 12. Illegal arms transfers 13. Ambition in men 14. Charities 15. Slavery 16. Men/women relations 17. Sudan 18. Adventure stories 19. Political fiction

LC 2004048982

A disparate group of men and women confronts their own indivudual moral crises, fears, and physical dangers as they work to alleviate the hardships and suffering caused by civil war and famine in contemporary Sudan.

"Mr. Caputo writes with such authority that he's able to invest events that might seem improbable in another novelist's hands with an uncommon degree of verisimilitude, delineating not only the viewpoints of his Western visitors, but also those of the Sudanese rebels and their Islamic opponents with equally sure-handed drama and psychological ballast." New York Times.

Caputo, Philip, 1941-

Crossers : a novel / Philip Caputo. Alfred A. Knopf, 2009. 464 p.

ISBN 9780375411670

1. Widows 2. Drug traffic 3. Family secrets 4. Borderlands 5. Grief 6. Violence 7. Right and wrong 8. Undocumented immigrants 9. Moving to a new state 10. Arizona 11. Mexican-American Border Region 12. Mexico -- Immigration and emigration 13. Mainstream fiction

LC 2009019096

"This is a Borzoi book"--T.p. verso.

In a tale inspired by the brutality and beauty of life on the Arizona-Mexico border, a September 11 widower finds his efforts to heal challenged by dark truths about his fearsome grandfather and retaliations against an act of kindness.

"This is at once a color-filled action tale; a generational saga with a moral; a touching love story; and a bold lesson in history and its inevitabilities." Dallas Morning News

Carcaterra, Lorenzo

Tin badges : a novel / Lorenzo Carcaterra. Ballantine Books, 2020. 304 p.

ISBN 9780345483928

1. Former detectives 2. Uncle and nephew 3. Criminal investigation 4. Drug traffic investigation 5. Guardian and ward 6. Teenage

orphans 7. Drug dealers 8. Computers 9. Drug lords 10. New York City 11. Thrillers and suspense

LC 2019012582

Retired NYPD detective Tank Rizzo becomes guardian to his orphaned, teenage nephew who reveals an interest in true crime and stunning computer skills and must debate involving his young charge in an effort to take down a notorious drug dealer.

Card, Maisy

* These **ghosts** are family : a novel / Maisy Card. Simon & Schuster, 2020. 224 p.

ISBN 9781982117436

1. Family secrets 2. Life change events 3. Family history 4. New identities 5. Jamaicans in the United States 6. Men with terminal illnesses 7. Colonialism 8. Slavery 9. Violence -- Psychological aspects 10. Immigrants -- Identity 11. Ghosts 12. Racism 13. Families 14. Jamaica 15. New York City 16. Literary fiction 17. Family sagas

LC 2019038809

A man on his deathbed reveals that he stole another man's identity decades earlier, traces the family's history from colonial Jamaica to present-day Harlem and reconnects with the firstborn daughter he never knew.

"Card's clean, readable prose provides an important counterbalance to the dense, heavy problems her broad scope of characters endure. A fantastic debut." Booklist.

Card, Orson Scott

* **Ender's** game / Orson Scott Card. T. Doherty Associates, 1985. 357 p. Ender Wiggin

ISBN 0312932081

1. Gifted children 2. Space warfare 3. Aliens (Humanoid) 4. Brothers and sisters 5. Violence 6. Good and evil 7. Telepathy 8. Politics and culture 9. Life on other planets 10. Imaginary wars and battles 11. Hard science fiction 12. Science fiction

"Part of this novel was published in Analog."

Sequel: Ender's shadow.

According to the author, there is no preferred reading order to the Ender Wiggin series, except that "Xenocide" should be read before "Children of the Mind."

Hugo Award for Best Novel, 1986.

Nebula Award for Best Novel, 1985.

Six-year-old Ender Wiggin and his fellow students at Battle School are being tested and trained to determine whether they possess the abilities to remake the world -- if the world survives an all-out war with an alien enemy.

"The key, of course, is Ender Wiggin himself. Mr. Card never makes the mistake of patronizing or sentimentalizing his hero. Alternately likable and insufferable, he is a convincing little Napoleon in short pants." New York Times Book Review.

Card, Orson Scott

Saints / Orson Scott Card. Forge, 2001, c1984. 604 p.

ISBN 0312876068

1. Mormon women 2. Mormons 3. Frontier and pioneer life 4. Industrialization 5. Polygamy 6. Immigration and emigration 7. Mormon fiction

Originally published in 1984 as A woman of destiny.

This historical novel tells of the early days of the Mormon Church, and the trek of "Saints" to what is now Salt Lake City. One of the Saints was an English woman named Dinah who is convinced that her religious destiny lies in America. The book follows her travels from Manchester to Utah, ending in her spiritual new life in a new land.

Card, Orson Scott

Speaker for the dead / Orson Scott Card. TOR, 1986. 415 p. Ender Wiggin

ISBN 9780312937386

1. Aliens (Non-humanoid) 2. Space warfare 3. Gifted children 4. Dead 5. Aliens (Non-humanoid) 6. Artificial intelligence 7. Hard science fiction 8. Science fiction

LC 85051765

Hugo Award for Best Novel, 1987.

Locus Award for Best Science Fiction Novel, 1987.

Nebula Award for Best Novel, 1986.

Ender Wiggin, the young military genius, discovers that a second alien war is inevitable and that he must dismiss his fears to make peace with humanity's strange new brothers

"This book lacks the sheer dramatic power of Ender's transformation from child into warlord as portrayed in its predecessor. However, it benefits from increased dramatic unity, a well-developed background and supporting cast on the colony planet Lusitania, and the author's customarily stylish writing." Booklist.

Carey, Edward, 1970-

* **Little** : a novel / Edward Carey. Riverhead Books, 2018. 436 p.

ISBN 9780525534327

1. Tussaud, Marie, 1761-1850 2. Revolutionary France (1789-1799) 3. Orphans 4. Waxworks 5. Wax modellers 6. Revolutions 7. Sculptors 8. French Revolution, 1789-1799 9. Paris, France -- History -- Revolution, 1789-1799 10. France -- History -- Revolution, 1789-1799 11. Biographical fiction 12. Historical fiction

LC 2017061111

Follows the story of a Swiss orphan who, apprenticed to an eccentric wax sculptor in the seamy streets of Paris, learns her craft and hones her art to become the famous Madame Tussaud.

Carey, Jacqueline, 1964-

Starless / Jacqueline Carey. Tor, 2018. 587 p.

ISBN 9780765386823

1. Bodyguards 2. Warriors 3. Gods and goddesses 4. Quests 5. Princesses 6. Prophecies 7. Fate and fatalism 8. Fantasy fiction

LC 2017049771

Trained as an elite warrior before learning a profound truth about his identity, Khai navigates the deadly intrigues of court before embarking on a quest to save his soul's twin.

Carey, Lisa

The **stolen** child : a novel / Lisa Carey. HarperPerennial, 2017 400 p.

ISBN 9780062492180

1. 1950s 2. Communities 3. Mothers and sons 4. Islands -- Ireland 5. Curses 6. Miracles 7. Interpersonal relations 8. Superstition 9. Sisters 10. Fairies 11. Inheritance and succession 12. Ireland -- History -- 20th century 13. Clare Island, Ireland 14. Literary fiction 15. Magical realism 16. Historical fiction

LC 2016032315

"A novel about a community living on an enchanted island off the coast of Ireland that explores the town's heady brew of tangled relationships, distrust of strangers, dark magic, and superstition." -- Provided by publisher.

"Magical realism of the best kind, utterly devoid of whimsy." Kirkus.

Carey, M. R., 1959-

Someone like me / M. R. Carey. Little Brown & Co, 2018 400 p.

ISBN 9780316477420

1. Single mothers 2. Control (Psychology) 3. Dissociative identity disorder 4. Women -- Personal conduct 5. Abused women 6. Former captives 7. Family violence 8. Good and evil 9. Psychological suspense

A gentle, devoted mother hides the dark and malicious side of her personality until it takes control, triggering devastating consequences.

Carey, Peter, 1943-

The **chemistry** of tears / Peter Carey. Alfred A. Knopf, 2012. 288 p.

ISBN 9780307592712

1. Mechanical toys 2. Museum employees 3. Notebooks 4. Clock and watch makers 5. Antique toys -- Conservation and restoration 6. Robots 7. Museums 8. Mistresses 9. Lovers -- Death 10. Separated friends, relatives, etc 11. Fathers of sick children 12. British in Germany 13. London, England -- Social life and customs -- 21st century 14. Germany -- Social life and customs -- 19th century 15. Literary fiction 16. Parallel narratives

Forced to hide her grief when her married lover dies unexpectedly, museum curator Catherine Gehrig works in solitude to restore a 19th-century automaton and finds comfort in the journals of its adventurous commissioner.

Carey, Peter, 1943-

His illegal self / Peter Carey. Alfred A. Knopf, 2008. 288 p.

ISBN 9780307263728

1. Seven-year-old boys 2. Communes 3. Kidnapping 4. Grandmother and grandson 5. Children of Sixties' parents 6. Family relationships 7. Hippies 8. Mothers and sons 9. Subcultures 10. Radicals 11. FBI agents 12. Belonging 13. Identity (Psychology) 14. Queensland 15. Australia 16. New York City 17. Literary fiction

LC 2007042862

Brought up in isolated privilege by his New York grandmother, Che, a precocious seven-year-old boy, yearns for his parents, radical activists wanted by the FBI, until one afternoon, a woman claiming to be his mother arrives to help him escape, sending him on a bizarre odyssey that leads him to confront his life, his family, and his identity.

"Hippie communal disintegration has been done before, and better by T.C. Boyle in Drop City, but Carey keeps us reading with his vivid lyricism, his finely tuned sense of the ridiculous and his focus on two very specific characters: a boy aching for mother love and a woman who is trying to make sense of having maternal love thrust upon her. In the end, this is a love story, an unconventional but emotionally compelling one." St. Louis Post-Dispatch.

Carey, Peter, 1943-

A **long** way from home / Peter Carey. Alfred A. Knopf, 2018, c2017. 288 p.

ISBN 9780525520177

1. REDeX Reliability Car Trials (Race) 2. 1950s 3. Automobile racing 4. Identity (Psychology) 5. Voyages and travels 6. Race relations 7. Husband and wife 8. Automobile rallies 9. Sales personnel 10. Motorsports 11. Australia -- History -- 20th century 12. Australian 13. Historical fiction 14. Literary fiction

Originally published: Melbourne, Vic. : Penguin Random House Australia, 2017.

Shortlisted for the Walter Scott Prize for Historical Fiction, 2019.

Irene Bobs, her car salesman husband, and a thrill-seeking quiz-show champion enter a dangerous race that circumnavigates the natural obstacles of 1954 Australia.

Carey, Peter, 1943-

My life as a fake : a novel / Peter Carey. Knopf, 2003. 304 p.

ISBN 0375414983

1. 1950s 2. Literary forgeries and hoaxes 3. Compulsive behavior in women 4. Women editors 5. Poets 6. Characters and characteristics in literature 7. Stalkers 8. British in Australia 9. British in Malaysia 10. Suing (Law) 11. Truth 12. Kidnapping 13. Stalking 14. Australia 15. Malaysia 16. Literary fiction

LC 2003052746

Shortlisted for the Miles Franklin Literary Award, 2004

The editor of a London poetry magazine, Sarah Wode-Douglass accompanies John Slater, an elderly poet who had figured prominently in her parents' marital woes, to Malaysia, where Slater reveals a ruinous decades-old hoax and produces a manuscript whose provenance is marked by exile, kidnapping, and death.

"This work is so confidently brilliant, so economical yet lively in its writing, so tightly fitted and continuously startling in its plot that something, we feel, must be wrong with it. It ends in a bit of a rush, and left several questions dangling in this reader's mind. Unfortunately, to spell out those questions would be to betray too much of an intricate fictional construct where little is as it first seems and fantastic developments unfold like scenes on a fragile paper fan." The New Yorker.

Carey, Peter, 1943-

Parrot and Olivier in America / Peter Carey. Alfred A. Knopf, 2010, c2009. 379 p.

ISBN 9780307592620

1. Cultural differences 2. Social classes 3. Friendship 4. Democracy 5. Spies 6. French in the United States 7. United States -- Social life and customs -- 19th century 8. Historical fiction 9. Picaresque fiction 10. Literary fiction

Originally published: Australia: Penguin, 2009.

Shortlisted for the Man Booker Prize, 2010.

National Book Award for Fiction finalist, 2010

A tale loosely inspired by the life of Alexis de Tocqueville is set in the early nineteenth century and follows an unlikely friendship between a survivor of the French Revolution and an itinerant English engraver's son.

"In short, it's a buddy novel. But what a novel! . . . . Funny, bawdy, brainy and moving, Parrot & Olivier in America is an utter delight." Globe and Mail (Toronto)

Carlino, Renee

Swear on this life / Renee Carlino. Atria Books, 2016. 320 p.

ISBN 9781501105791

1. Women graduate students 2. Books and reading 3. First loves 4. Authors 5. Young women 6. Memories 7. Men/women relations 8. Love stories 9. Novels-within-novels

When a young graduate student discovers she is the romantic inspiration behind a pseudonymously published literary sensation, she embarks on a search for the elusive writer.

Carlson, Melody,

A **Christmas** by the sea / Melody Carlson. Revell, 2018. 176 p.

ISBN 9780800722715

1. Widows 2. Mothers and sons 3. Christmas 4. Single mothers 5.

Cottages 6. Coastal towns 7. Renovation (Architecture 8. Artisans 9. Second chances 10. Small town life 11. Faith (Christianity) 12. Men/women relations 13. Maine 14. Christmas stories 15. Christian fiction 16. Gentle reads

LC 2017053948

Hoping that an inherited beach house will help her recover from debts after her husband's death, a widow moves into the property to renovate and sell it before a local craftsman encourages her to stay.

"This breezy, entertaining read provides the perfect afternoon getaway during a busy holiday season." Publishers Weekly.

Carlson, Ron

Five skies / Ron Carlson. Viking, 2007. 256 p.
ISBN 0670038504

1. Male friendship 2. Construction workers 3. Betrayal 4. Personal conduct 5. Secrets 6. Spirituality 7. Ranchers 8. Anger in men 9. Emotions in men 10. Grief in men 11. Idaho 12. Rocky Mountains 13. Psychological fiction

LC 2006051760

ALA Notable Book, 2008.

Working together on a summer construction project high in the Rocky Mountains, drifter Arthur Key, shiftless Ronnie Panelli, and foreman Darwin Gallegos reveal details about their pasts and beliefs in cautious and profound ways.

Carlson, Steve, 1943-

Almost Graceland / Steve Carlson. Thomas Dunne Books/ St. Martin's Press, 2007. 256 p.
ISBN 9780312373986

1. Presley, Elvis, 1935-1977 2. 1970s 3. Rock musicians 4. Brothers 5. Twin brothers 6. Twins 7. Adoptees 8. Truck drivers 9. Memphis, Tennessee 10. Mainstream fiction

LC 2007027634

Perusing his late mother's journals, Memphis truck driver and Elvis look-alike Ray Johnston learns that he had been adopted from the same hospital as Presley and may actually be his twin brother, a discovery that proves complicated when he meets his famous would-be sibling. A first novel.

Carlyle, Christy

A **duke** changes everything / Christy Carlyle. Avon Impulse, 2018. 384 p. Duke's den
ISBN 9780062853950

1. Victorian era (1837-1901) 2. Inheritance and succession 3. Castles 4. Adult child abuse victims 5. Men with disfigurements 6. Dukes and duchesses 7. Casino owners 8. Stewarts 9. Aristocracy 10. Interpersonal attraction 11. Men/women relations 12. England 13. Great Britain -- Social life and customs -- 19th century 14. Victorian romances 15. Historical romances

When the new heir to the Tremayne dukedom arrives, determined to take away her home and position as steward of the Enderley estate, Mina Thorne must find a way to make him change his mind.

Carlyle, Liz

Never lie to a lady / Liz Carlyle. Simon and Schuster, 2007 432 p. Neville family trilogy
ISBN 1416527141

1. 19th century 2. Men/women relations 3. Smuggling 4. Inheritance and succession 5. Marquis and marchionesses 6. Shipping industry and trade 7. Spies 8. Women's role 9. Sexuality 10. London, England -- Social life and customs -- 19th century 11. Historical romances

One of the Regency's most notorious and scandalous rakes, the Marquis of Nash gets more than he had bargained for when he encounters a mysterious lady, Miss Xanthia Neville, who draws him into a dangerous world of smugglers, intrigue, espionage, and passion.

Carpenter, Emily, 1967-

Every single secret / Emily Carpenter. Lake Union Press, 2018. 316 p.
ISBN 9781503951907

1. Engaged persons 2. Repression (Psychology) 3. Surveillance 4. Memories -- Psychological aspects 5. Secrets 6. Nightmares 7. Social isolation 8. Psychologist and patient 9. Couples -- Psychotherapy 10. Wilderness areas 11. Men/women relations 12. Psychological suspense

In this harrowing psychological thriller, a young couple must save their relationship by doing the unthinkable: sharing their darkest secrets?

Carpenter, Emily, 1967-

Until the day I die / Emily Carpenter. Lake Union Publishing, 2019. 340 p.
ISBN 9781503904217

1. Widows 2. Mothers and daughters 3. Grief in women 4. Married men -- Death 5. Corporations 6. Women executives 7. Women college students 8. Vacations 9. Health resorts 10. Conspiracies 11. Betrayal 12. Business partners 13. Birmingham, Alabama 14. Caribbean Area 15. Thrillers and suspense

If there's a healthy way to grieve, Erin Gaines hasn?t found it. After her husband's sudden death, the runaway success of the tech company they built with their best friends has become overwhelming. Her nerves are frayed, she's disengaged, and her frustrated daughter, Shorie, is pulling away from her. Maybe Erin's friends and family are right. Maybe a few weeks at a spa resort in the Caribbean islands is just what she needs to hit the reset button?

Carpenter, Emily, 1967-

The **weight** of lies / Emily Carpenter. Lake Union Publishing, 2017. 372 p.
ISBN 9781477818435

1. Mothers and daughters 2. Women authors 3. Murderers 4. Deception 5. Best sellers (Books) 6. Fame 7. Murder investigation 8. Islands 9. Secrets 10. Young women 11. New York City 12. Georgia 13. Psychological suspense

Reformed party girl Meg Ashley leads a life of privilege, thanks to a bestselling horror novel her mother wrote decades ago. But Meg knows that the glow of their very public life hides a darker reality of lies, manipulation, and the heartbreak of her own solitary childhood. Desperate to break free of her mother, Meg accepts a proposal to write a scandalous, tell-all memoir. Digging into the past--and her mother's cult classic--draws Meg to Bonny Island, Georgia, and an unusual woman said to be the inspiration for the book. At first island life seems idyllic, but as Meg starts to ask tough questions, disturbing revelations come to light--including some about her mother. Soon Meg's search leads her to question the facts of a decades-old murder. She's warned to leave it alone, but as the lies pile up, Meg knows she's getting close to finding a murderer. When her own life is threatened, Meg realizes the darkness found in her mother's book is nothing compared to the chilling truth that lurks off the page.

Carr, Brian Allen, 1979-

* **Opioid,** Indiana / Brian Allen Carr. Soho, 2019. 224 p.
ISBN 9781641290784

1. Drug abuse 2. Foster teenagers 3. Missing men 4. Small town life 5. Student suspension 6. Teenage employees 7. Uncle and nephew 8. Puppets 9. Racism 10. Indiana 11. Coming-of-age stories 12.

Literary fiction

LC 2019004391

A recently orphaned teen in rural Indiana finds himself suspended from school and searching for both a job and his drug-addled uncle, now his legal guardian, to get the rent paid in five days

"This latest novel presents a fresh twist on today's teenager in a wasteland of drugs and economic hardship." Library Journal.

Carr, Caleb, 1955-

* The **alienist** / Caleb Carr. Random House, 1994. 496 p. Laszlo Kreizler mysteries

ISBN 0679417796

1. Roosevelt, Theodore, 1858-1919 2. Gilded Age (1865-1898) 3. 1890s 4. Journalists 5. Crimes against boys 6. Psychologists 7. Serial murderers 8. Crime 9. Forensic psychology 10. Crimes against male prostitutes 11. Crime bosses 12. New York City 13. Historical mysteries 14. TV tie-ins

LC 9332766

Sequel: The angel of darkness.

Anthony Award for Best Novel, 1995.

The year is 1896, and a serial killer is loose in New York City. His targets are poor young boys working as transvestite prostitutes. While the general public has little interest in the victims, Chief of Police Theodore Roosevelt wants the murderer stopped. He assembles a clandestine group of amateur detectives to track the killer.

"This story boasts a veracious historical feel and a tight plot that keeps open the murderer's identity to the end. An original that fits no established mystery niche." Booklist.

Carr, Caleb, 1955-

The **angel** of darkness / Caleb Carr. Random House, 1997. 629 p. Laszlo Kreizler mysteries

ISBN 0679435328

1. Darrow, Clarence, 1857-1938 2. Stanton, Elizabeth Cady, 1815-1902 3. Gilded Age (1865-1898) 4. 1890s 5. Thirteen-year-old boys 6. Crimes against children 7. Psychologists 8. Nurses 9. Forensic psychology 10. Journalists 11. Crime 12. Diplomats' spouses 13. Kidnapping 14. Infanticide 15. Forensic psychology 16. New York City 17. Historical mysteries

LC 9725063

Sequel to: The alienist.

Dr. Kreizler, the Alienist, returns to investigate the kidnapping of the baby daughter of the wife of a Spanish diplomat, in the process uncovering a fiendish woman who has murdered a number of innocent children.

"Carr is an adept miniaturist, and he succeeds in evoking the wonderful grotesqueries of old New York without straying into sub-Dickensian caricature." New York Times Book Review.

Carr, Robyn

* **Virgin** river / Robyn Carr. Mira, 2007. 416 p. Virgin River

ISBN 0778324907

1. Widows 2. Nurses 3. Abandoned infants 4. Bar owners 5. Former Marines 6. Small towns 7. Small town life 8. Mountain life 9. Moving to a new city 10. Life change events 11. Men/women relations 12. Northern California 13. Contemporary romances

When recently widowed Melinda Monroe accepts a job as nurse practitioner and midwife in the remote mountain town of Virgin River, she thinks she's found the perfect place to start over. The town isn't at all what she expected, though, and she considers leaving, but then a tiny baby, abandoned on a front porch, changes her plans... and a former marine cements them into place.

Carr, Robyn

* The **wanderer** / Robyn Carr. Mira Books, 2013. 384 p. Thunder Point novels

ISBN 9780778314479

1. United States. Coast Guard. 2. Small town life -- Oregon 3. Inheritance and succession 4. Land development 5. Coastal towns 6. Home (Concept) 7. Women pilots 8. Men/women relations 9. Oregon 10. Contemporary romances

When newcomer Hank Cooper inherits beachfront property in Thunder Point, Oregon, he holds the fate of an entire community in his hands as he decides whether this small town of rocky beaches and rugged charm is the place he can finally call home.

Carr, Robyn

What we find / Robyn Carr. Harlequin MIRA, 2016. 384 p. Sullivan's Crossing

ISBN 9780778318859

1. Women surgeons 2. Hikers 3. Life change events 4. Coping 5. Healing 6. Camp sites, facilities, etc 7. Interpersonal attraction 8. Men/women relations 9. Mountain life 10. Colorado 11. Rocky Mountain region 12. Contemporary romances 13. Chick lit

Abandoned by her boyfriend in the aftermath of wrongful malpractice suit, a Denver neurosurgeon relocates to a small rural town named after her ancestor, where she slowly recovers and reconnects with her estranged father while bonding with a mysterious loner.

Carroll, James, 1943-

Fault lines / James Carroll. Little, Brown, 1980. 248 p.

ISBN 9780316130127

1. Draft resisters 2. Men/women relations 3. Child custody 4. Draft resistance 5. Blended families 6. Domestic fiction

LC 80036756

"Mr. Carroll has told his story from all the characters' points of view- which is to say that the narrator's voice jumps from one character's mind to another's even within a single conversation. And by doing so he's made his people too strong and complex to be reduced to mere agents of the action." Books of the Times

Carter, Angela, 1940-1992

* **Burning** your boats : the collected short stories / Angela Carter ; with an introduction by Salman Rushdie. H. Holt, 1996, c1995. xiv, 462 p.

ISBN 0805044620

1. Sexuality 2. Fantasy fiction 3. Short stories 4. Adaptations, retellings, and spin-offs

LC 95-26312

Collects stories written by the late author such as "The Bloody Chamber," "Our Lady of the Massacre," and "Saints and Strangers"

"Gathered from 30 years of Carter's writing life, this collection is arranged chronologically to reveal her evolution as a writer as well as her consistent preoccupation with the Gothic. . . . As her friend Salman Rushdie writes in his moving introduction, Carter is not an easy read, but there are many rewards for the persistent." Library Journal.

Carter, Angela, 1940-1992

Nights at the circus / Angela Carter. Viking, 1985, c1984. 294 p.

ISBN 0670803758

1. 1890s 2. Circus 3. Women trapeze and high-wire performers 4. Magic 5. Circus performers 6. Eccentrics and eccentricities 7. Magical realism 8. Historical fiction 9. Literary fiction

LC 84040459

Originally published: London : Chatto & Windus, 1984.
James Tait Black Memorial Prize for Fiction, 1984.

Sophie Fevvers - the toast of Europe's capitals, courted by the Prince of Wales, painted by Toulouse-Lautrec - is an aerialiste extraordinaire, star of Colonel Kearney's circus. She is also part woman, part swan. Jack Walser, an American journalist, is on a quest to discover Fevvers's true identity. Dazzled by his love for her, and desperate for the scoop of a lifetime, Walser joins the circus on its tour through turn-of-the-nineteenth century London, St. Petersburg, and Siberia.

"Carter describes a locale as exotic to the traditional reader as her women are to Walser and, by implication, all men; and she undercuts accepted Western history as she goes." The New Republic.

Carter, Michaela, 1967-
Further out than you thought : a novel / Michaela Carter. William Morrow Paperbacks, 2014 320 p.
ISBN 9780062292377
1. 1990s 2. Los Angeles Rebellion, April 29-May 2, 1992 3. Stripteasers 4. Identity (philosophical concept) 5. Women poets 6. People with HIV 7. Unplanned pregnancy 8. Los Angeles, California 9. Mainstream fiction
LC 2013033884
Set against the chaos of the 1992 L.A. riots, a taut and erotically charged literary debut that follows an exotic dancer and her two bohemian compatriots on their search for identity and meaning in life, from an award-winning poet and indie bookshop owner.

Carter, Miranda, 1965-
The **strangler** vine / M. J. Carter. G. P. Putnam's Sons, 2015, c2014. 384 p. Avery & Blake novels
ISBN 9780399171673
1. East India Company (English) 2. 1830s 3. British in India 4. Missing persons 5. Cults 6. Intrigue 7. Soldiers 8. Government investigators 9. Voyages and travels 10. Ambition 11. India 12. Calcutta, India 13. Historical mysteries 14. Adventure stories
LC 2014017351
First published in the U.K. in 2014 by Fig Tree.
While tracking down a missing writer who has exposed the true nature of Calcutta society in 1837 India, a young soldier with few prospects, a secret political agent and a master of disguise are drawn into the mysterious Thuggee cult and its even more ominous suppression.

"Making pleasing use of the developing bromance/adventure formula and a wealth of research, Carter delivers an engaging, skeptical, modern take on empire." Kirkus.

Carter, Stephen L., 1954-
New England white : a novel / Stephen L. Carter. Alfred A. Knopf, 2007. 576 p.
ISBN 9780375413629
1. Murder investigation 2. Family secrets 3. Deception 4. African American college teachers 5. Murder 6. Race relations 7. Prejudice 8. African-American college presidents 9. Interpersonal relations 10. Former lovers 11. Scandals 12. New England 13. Mysteries
LC 2006019721
BCALA Literary Award for Fiction, 2008.
In the peaceful New England university town of Elm Harbor, a murder threatens to unravel the thin veneer hiding the racial complications of the town's past, the hidden secrets of a prominent family, and African-American political influence in the United States.

"Carter creates an invigorating and often scathing portrait of the Carlyles' community. He refutes political correctness, preferring to explore the contradictions warring within Julia. . . . [He] is equally intense in his portrayal of the Carlyles' outwardly perfect, inwardly turbulent marriage, a delicate balance of duty and endurance, even love of a sort." PopMatters.

Carter, Stephen L., 1954-
Back channel / Stephen L. Carter. Alfred A. Knopf, 2014. 352 p.
ISBN 9780385349604
1. 1960s 2. International relations 3. College students 4. African Americans 5. World politics 6. Intelligence service 7. Nuclear weapons 8. Historical fiction 9. Political fiction
While the Kennedy administration furiously debates about a response to the Cuban Missile Crisis, 19-year-old black Cornell sophomore Margo Jensen becomes an unwitting pawn in escalating tensions between American and Soviet government forces.

Cartwright, Justin
To heaven by water / Justin Cartwright. Bloomsbury, 2009. 320 p.
ISBN 9781596916210
1. University of Oxford 2. Reminiscing in old age 3. Purpose in life 4. Family secrets 5. Senior men 6. Campus life 7. Family relationships 8. Foreign correspondents 9. Nostalgia 10. Apartheid 11. Men -- South Africa 12. Classism 13. Oxford, England 14. Mainstream fiction
Having lost his wife, Nancy, to illness, and retired from his job as a prominent television news anchor, David Cross is working out at the gym and living an unexpected new life. His children, Ed and Lucy, suspect him of being on the lookout for a new woman. He cannot tell them that he is, in some ways, happier than he was before Nancy died. And when David goes to see his estranged brother in the African desert, he will come to a life-affirming epiphany.

Carty-Williams, Candice, 1989-
* **Queenie** / Candice Carty-Williams. Gallery/Scout Press, 2019. 320 p.
ISBN 9781501196010
1. Race relations 2. Self-discovery in women 3. Dating (Social customs) 4. Female friendship 5. Interracial romance 6. Casual sex 7. British Jamaicans 8. Single women 9. Women journalists 10. Mental illness 11. Black Lives Matter movement 12. London, England 13. Women's lives and relationships 14. Mainstream fiction
LC 2018032717
Constantly compared to her white middle-class peers, a young Jamaican-British woman in London makes a series of questionable decisions in the aftermath of a messy breakup before challenging herself to figure out who she wants to be.

Carver, Raymond, 1938-1988
What we talk about when we talk about love : stories / Raymond Carver. Knopf, 1981. 159 p.
ISBN 9780394516844
1. Failure (Psychology) 2. Violence 3. Marriage 4. Drinking 5. Men/women relations 6. United States -- Social life and customs -- 20th century 7. Short stories 8. Literary fiction
LC 80021752
"In spare, deft, precise prose, whole lives are portrayed in a single second as Carver briefly exposes his doom-ridden characters to one startling flash of agonizing self-recognition. These disturbing images remain long in the memory even after their immediate impression has disappeared." Booklist.

Carver, Tania

The **surrogate** / Tania Carver. Pegasus Books, 2011, c2009. 448 p. Philip Brennan novels

ISBN 9781605982564

1. Detectives 2. Pregnant women -- Death 3. Women psychologists 4. Police 5. Violence against women 6. Gender identity 7. Serial murder investigation 8. Serial murders 9. Criminal profiling 10. Former lovers 11. England 12. Colchester, England 13. Thrillers and suspense

Martyn and Linda Waites writing under the pseudonym Tania Carver. Originally published in the U.K. (London: Sphere, 2009)

Investigating a series of murders in which the victims have been pregnant women, Detective Inspector Philip Brennan sets aside his personal feelings to enlist the aid of his ex, psychologist Marina Esposito, in a harrowing race against time.

"This well-written . . . novel grips the reader from the start, with plenty of violence, gore, and psychological suspense." Library Journal.

Cary, Joyce, 1888-1957

The **horse's** mouth / Joyce Cary ; introduction by Brad Leithauser. New York Review Books, 1999, c1944. 412 p. Art trilogy

ISBN 0940322196

1. Painters 2. Household employees 3. Lawyers 4. Love triangles 5. Housekeepers 6. London, England 7. Psychological fiction

LC 99015898

Originally published: London : Michael Joseph, 1944.

Cash, Wiley

The **last** ballad : a novel / Wiley Cash. William Morrow, 2017. 378 p.

ISBN 9780062313119

1. 1920s 2. Mothers 3. Families 4. Women textile workers 5. Labor movement 6. Murder victims 7. Single mothers 8. Labor leaders 9. Labor unions 10. Textile mills 11. Mill towns 12. Strikes 13. North Carolina -- History -- 20th century 14. Historical fiction 15. Southern fiction

LC 2017007053

ALA Notable Book, 2018.
Sir Walter Raleigh Award for Fiction, 2018.

Inspired by actual events, a tale set in the Appalachian foothills of 1929 North Carolina follows the struggles of an ordinary woman to reclaim her dignity and rights in a labor mill, where she earns a paltry salary before risking her family and future to join a union.

"Although it is initially a bit difficult to keep so many points of view straight, it is satisfying to see them all connect. It's refreshing that Cash highlights the struggles of often forgotten heroes and shows how crucial women and African-Americans were in the fight for workers' rights. A heartbreaking and beautifully written look at the real people involved in the labor movement." Kirkus.

Cash, Wiley

This dark road to mercy : a novel / Wiley Cash. William Morrow, 2014. 232 p.

ISBN 9780062088253

1. Fathers and daughters 2. Sisters 3. Parental kidnapping 4. Life change events 5. Rescues 6. Families 7. Thieves 8. Atonement 9. Revenge 10. North Carolina 11. Southern Gothic 12. Psychological suspense 13. Southern fiction

LC 2013022221

Gold Dagger Award for Best Crime Novel of the Year, 2014.

After their mother dies unexpectedly, 12-year-old Easter and her 6-year-old sister Ruby are kidnapped by their errant father Wade, an ex-minor league baseball player whom they haven't seen in years, while their court appointed guardian races against time to find them before a vengeful killer does.

"A story of family, blood loyalty and making choices that can seem right but end up wrong." Kirkus.

Cassara, Joseph

The **house** of impossible beauties / Joseph Cassara. Ecco, 2018. 400 p.

ISBN 9780062676979

1. Corey, Dorian, 1937-1993 2. 1980s 3. 1990s 4. Runaways 5. Gay culture 6. Gay teenagers 7. Transgender teenage girls 8. Transgender persons 9. Latin Americans 10. Home (Concept) 11. AIDS (Disease) 12. City dwellers 13. Drag queens 14. Homophobia 15. Harlem, New York City 16. New York City 17. LGBTQIA fiction 18. Literary fiction

LC 2017021665

Follows a cast of gay and transgender kids navigating the Harlem ball scene of the 1980s and 1990s.

Castel-Bloom, Orly, 1960-

Textile / Orly Castel-Bloom. The Feminist Press, 2013. 232 p.

ISBN 9781558618251

1. Jewish families 2. Alienation (Social psychology) 3. Plastic surgery 4. Family relationships 5. Women business owners 6. Snipers 7. Mother and adult son 8. Marital conflict 9. Young women -- Relations with older men 10. Israel 11. Tel-Aviv, Israel 12. Psychological fiction

A wealthy Israeli family becomes estranged as war and commerce increasingly define their lives.

Castellani, Christopher, 1972-

All this talk of love : a novel / Christopher Castellani. Algonquin Books of Chapel Hill, 2013. 320 p. Maddalena novels

ISBN 9781616201708

1. Family secrets 2. Extended families 3. Loss (Psychology) 4. Families 5. Immigrants 6. Survivors of suicide victims 7. Italian American families 8. Children of immigrants 9. Nostalgia 10. Family sagas

LC 2012030841

The American-born daughter of an immigrant plots to bring her entire family back to Santa Cecilia, Italy, so that her grandmother can make amends with her estranged sister.

Castellani, Christopher, 1972-

Leading men : a novel / Christopher Castellani. Viking, 2019. 352 p.

ISBN 9780525559054

1. Williams, Tennessee, 1911-1983 2. Merlo, Frank, 1921-1963 3. 1950s 4. 1960s 5. Gay couples 6. Creativity in men 7. Fame 8. Ambition 9. Authors 10. Actors and actresses 11. Memories 12. Art 13. Interpersonal relations 14. Men/men relations 15. Italy 16. New York City 17. Historical fiction 18. LGBTQIA fiction

LC 2018029036

A life-changing encounter among Tennessee Williams, his lover Frank Merlo and a taciturn Swedish beauty at a 1953 Truman Capote party culminates in deathbed revelations about Williams' final play a decade later.

"With imagination and feeling, Castellani reconjures history to reveal the intricate dynamics--loving and passionate, selfless and devastating--among artists and those who nurture them." Booklist.

Castile, Zoey

Flashed / Zoey Castile. Kensington Books, 2019. 304 p. Happy endings

ISBN 9781496715289

1. Wounds and injuries 2. Men recluses 3. Housekeepers 4. Former soccer players 5. Male fashion models 6. Male stripteasers 7. Actors and actresses 8. Women artists 9. Women college students 10. Interpersonal attraction 11. Men/women relations 12. Montana 13. Contemporary romances

When a man makes his living by his looks, he can forget that love - and lust - are more than skin deep. But the right woman can remind him.

Castille, Sarah

In your corner / Sarah Castille. Sourcebooks Casablanca, 2014. 384 p. Redemption novels (Sarah Castille)

ISBN 9781402296239

1. Former lovers 2. Women lawyers 3. Martial artists 4. Mixed martial arts 5. Sexual attraction 6. Men/women relations 7. Erotic romances 8. Contemporary romances 9. Sports romances

LC 2014011625

After breaking up two years earlier, mixed martial artist Jake and high-powered lawyer Amanda have a chance encounter and sparks fly.

Castillo, Elaine

America is not the heart / Elaine Castillo. Viking Press, 2018. 408 p.

ISBN 9780735222410

1. 1980s 2. 1990s 3. Immigrants 4. Identity (Psychology) 5. Culture conflict 6. Extended families 7. Violence against women 8. Loss (Psychology) 9. Generation gap 10. Secrets 11. California 12. Philippines 13. Family sagas

Three generations of women from one immigrant family trying to reconcile the home they left behind with the life they're building in America.

Castillo, Linda

A gathering of secrets / Linda Castillo. Minotaur Books, 2018. 320 p. Kate Burkholder thrillers

ISBN 9781250121318

1. Amish 2. Women detectives 3. Violence against women 4. Fires 5. Secrets 6. Former Amish 7. Murder investigation 8. Ohio 9. Thrillers and suspense

LC 2018004425

A deadly fire resulting in the death of an Amish teen exposes the dark side of the community to which Chief of Police Kate Burkholder once belonged.

Castillo, Linda

Shamed / Linda Castillo. Minotaur Books, 2019. 320 p. Kate Burkholder thrillers

ISBN 9781250142863

1. Amish 2. Women detectives 3. Missing persons investigation 4. Murder investigation 5. Missing girls 6. Murder 7. Family secrets 8. Former Amish 9. Ohio 10. Thrillers and suspense

LC 2019006908

Investigating the kidnapping of a girl and the murder of her grandmother in an Amish community, Chief of Police Kate Burkholder uncovers an isolated Old Order settlement that hides a tragic secret.

Castle, Jayne

Illusion Town / Jayne Castle. Jove, 2016. 352 p. Illusion Town novels

ISBN 9780515155754

1. Marriage 2. Heirs and heiresses 3. Women psychics 4. Psychic ability 5. Magic 6. Memories 7. Far future 8. Catacombs 9. Paranormal phenomena 10. Sexual attraction 11. Men/women relations 12. Paranormal romances 13. Futuristic romances

When they wake up married, with only vague memories of running from something, Hannah West and Elias Coppersmith's investigation into what happened leads to underground catacombs where secrets from their past are revealed.

Castle, Jayne

The **lost** night / Jayne Castle. Jove, 2012. 339 p. Rainshadow novels

ISBN 9780515152845

1. Psychics 2. Misfits (Persons) 3. Lost articles 4. Paranormal phenomena 5. Auras 6. Wilderness areas 7. Island life 8. Interpersonal attraction 9. Good and evil 10. Women booksellers 11. Recovered memory 12. Men/women relations 13. Paranormal romances 14. Romantic suspense

Rachel Blake, who is trained in an exotic form of martial arts and gifted with special abilities, finds her peaceful existence shattered by the arrival of Harry Sebastian, the descendant of a notorious pirate, who needs her help in tracking down the dangerous rogues who have violated the Preserve.

Castro, Joy

Hell or high water : a novel / Joy Castro. Thomas Dunne Books, 2012. 368 p. Nola Cespedes novels

ISBN 9781250004574

1. Women journalists -- New Orleans, Louisiana 2. Self-fulfillment in women 3. Missing persons investigation -- New Orleans, Louisiana 4. Crime -- New Orleans, Louisiana 5. Truth 6. New Orleans, Louisiana 7. Mysteries

LC 2012009377

Hoping she has caught a lucky break when she is assigned to write a full-length feature, ambitious young reporter Nola Cespedes becomes fixated on the search for a missing tourist in New Orleans at the same time questions emerge about her trustworthiness.

Cather, Willa, 1873-1947

* Death comes for the archbishop / Willa Cather ; historical essay and explanatory notes by John J. Murphy ; textual editing by Charles W. Mignon with Frederick M. Link and Kari A. Ronning. University of Nebraska Press, 1999. 614 p.

ISBN 0803214294

1. 1850s 2. Christian missionaries -- New Mexico 3. Faith (Christianity) 4. Priests -- New Mexico 5. Spirituality 6. Christianity 7. Determination (Personal quality) 8. Religion 9. Navajo Indians -- Relations with missionaries, traders, etc 10. Men and nature 11. New Mexico -- History -- 19th century 12. Santa Fe, New Mexico 13. Historical fiction 14. Classics

LC 98026107

Willa Cather's best known novel; a narrative that recounts a life lived simply in the silence of the southwestern desert.

Cather, Willa, 1873-1947

* A lost lady / Willa Cather ; historical essay by Susan J. Rosowski, with Kari A. Ronning ; explanatory notes by Kari A. Ronning ; textual editing by Charles W. Mignon & Frederick

M. Link, with Kari A. Ronning. University of Nebraska Press, 1997, c1923. xii, 371 p.

ISBN 0803214278

1. 1890s 2. Frontier and pioneer life 3. Independence in women 4. Railroads -- Nebraska 5. Technology and civilization 6. May-December romance 7. Loneliness in women 8. Women's role 9. Racism 10. Prejudice 11. Modernization (Social sciences) 12. Small town life -- Nebraska 13. Nebraska 14. Literary fiction 15. Psychological fiction 16. Domestic fiction 17. Coming-of-age stories 18. Classics

LC 96020642

Mrs. Forrester, the resident aristocrat of Sweet Water, a remote railroad town on the Western frontier, is the lone representative of culture and refinement.

Cather, Willa, 1873-1947

* **My** Antonia / Willa Cather ; edited by Charles Mignon with Kari Ronning ; historical essay by James Woodress ; explanatory notes by James Woodress with the assistance of Kari Ronning, Kathleen Danker & Emily Levine. University of Nebraska Press, 1994, c1918. xii, 544 p.

ISBN 9780803214682

1. 19th century 2. Frontier and pioneer life -- Nebraska 3. Pioneer women 4. Independence in women 5. Czech American women 6. Immigrants -- Nebraska 7. Household employees 8. Fathers and daughters 9. Fathers -- Death 10. Elopement 11. Growing up 12. Farmers' spouses 13. Farm life -- Nebraska 14. Housekeepers 15. Nebraska -- History -- 19th century 16. Domestic fiction 17. Coming-of-age stories 18. Historical fiction 19. Classics

LC 93050941

Originally published: New York : Houghton Mifflin Co., 1918.

After the death of her immigrant father, Antonia works as a servant for neighbors in the farmlands of Nebraska. She leaves for an unfortunate affair with an Irish railway conductor, but returns home, eventually marries and raises a large family in true pioneer style.

Cather, Willa, 1873-1947

* **O** pioneers! / Willa Cather ; edited with an introduction and notes by Marilee Lindemann. Oxford University Press, 1999. xxxi, 179 p.

ISBN 9780192832160

1. 19th century 2. Pioneer women 3. Immigrants -- Nebraska 4. Frontier and pioneer life -- Nebraska 5. Swedish American families 6. Brothers and sisters 7. Women immigrants 8. Women farmers 9. Fathers -- Death 10. Men's dreams 11. Determination in women 12. Farm life 13. Nebraska 14. Historical fiction 15. Classics 16. Domestic fiction

LC 98035944

When her father dies, the daughter of Swedish immigrants assumes responsibility for her family and their Nebraska farm.

Cather, Willa, 1873-1947

* The **song** of the lark / Willa Cather. Vintage Books, 1999. 429 p.

ISBN 0375706453

1. Women opera singers 2. Determination in women 3. Self-discovery in women 4. Children of clergy 5. Swedish American families 6. Ambition in women 7. Young women 8. Operas 9. Music 10. Women's dreams 11. Men/women relations 12. Small town life 13. Chicago, Illinois 14. Colorado 15. Literary fiction 16. Coming-of-age stories 17. Domestic fiction 18. Classics

LC 98052932

The daughter of a Swedish minister growing up in Colorado, Thea Kronborg's musical talent sets her apart from her contemporaries. Driven by her determination to satisfy her artistic impulse, she moves to Chicago, where she falls in love with a wealthy married man. The novel follows Thea's growth from provincial Midwesterner to acclaimed international opera singer.

Catton, Eleanor, 1985-

* The **luminaries** : a novel / Eleanor Catton. Little Brown & Co., 2013. 834 p.

ISBN 9780316074315

1. Colonial New Zealand (1841-1907) 2. Gold miners 3. Crime 4. Murder 5. Secrecy 6. Astrology 7. Gold rush 8. Prostitutes 9. Storytelling 10. Criminal investigation 11. Interpersonal relations 12. New Zealand -- History -- 19th century 13. Literary fiction 14. Historical fiction

Originally published: Wellington, N.Z. : Victoria University Press, 2013.

Governor General's Literary Award for English-Language Fiction, 2013.

Man Booker Prize, 2013.

Shortlisted for the Walter Scott Prize for Historical Fiction, 2014

Arriving in New Zealand in 1866 to seek his fortune in the goldfields, Walter Moody finds himself drawn into a series of unsolved crimes and complex mysteries.

Cauwelaert, Didier van, 1960-

One-way : a novel / Didier van Cauwelaert ; translated from the French by Mark Polizzotti. Other Press, 2003. 152 p.

ISBN 1590510860

1. Nineteen-year-old men 2. Orphans 3. Young men -- Friendship 4. Travelers 5. Identity (Psychology) 6. Immigrants, French 7. Immigration and emigration 8. Deportation 9. Dishonesty in men 10. Imagination in men 11. Belonging 12. Morocco 13. France -- Politics and government -- 20th century 14. Translations -- French to English 15. Humorous stories 16. Picaresque fiction

LC 2003010266

Originally published in France in 1994 as "Aller simple."

"Van Cauwelaert's tale of an orphan's quest for cultural identity won the Prix Goncourt when it was published in 1994, the year after France passed laws restricting immigration and the rights of current immigrants." Publishers Weekly

Cavanagh, Steve

Thirteen / Steve Cavanagh. Flatiron Books, 2019, c2018 320 p. Eddie Flynn novels

ISBN 9781250297600

1. Trials (Murder) 2. Jurors 3. Frameups 4. Murder suspects 5. Innocence (Law) 6. Murderers 7. Legal thrillers

"Originally published in Great Britain in 2018 by Orion Books, an imprint of The Orion Publishing Group Ltd."

Theakston Old Peculier Crime Novel of the Year Award, 2019

A defense lawyer and former conman defends his movie-star client in a high profile murder trial and discovers that the actual killer is sitting on the jury.

Celello, Erin

Leaning to stay / Erin Celello. New American Library Accent, 2013. 352 p.

ISBN 9780451236975

1. Marital conflict 2. Post-traumatic stress disorder 3. Iraq War veterans 4. Human/animal relationships 5. Coping 6. Head injuries 7. Marriage 8. Change (Psychology) 9. Women lawyers 10. Husband

and wife 11. Mainstream fiction

LC 2012031699

A dog named Jones helps Elise Sabato understand life's unexpected turns and to accept the changes in her marriage when her husband Brad returns home with a traumatic brain injury after serving in Iraq.

Celine, Louis-Ferdinand, 1894-1961

Journey to the end of the night / Louis-Ferdinand Celine ; translated from the French by Ralph Manheim ; afterword by William T. Vollmann. New Directions Book, 2006, c1932. 468 p.

ISBN 0811216543

1. Soldiers 2. Voyages and travels 3. Veterans 4. Physicians 5. Poor men 6. World War I 7. Fear in men 8. Human nature 9. War 10. Nihilism 11. Picaresque fiction 12. Black humor 13. Modern classics 14. Translations -- French to English

LC 2005036494

Originally published: Boston : Little, Brown, 1934 and in France in 1932.

Originally published to shocked reviews in 1932 France, a scathing literary critique of what the writer believed to be the poor judgment and hypocrisy of society follows the travels of petit-bourgeois anti-hero Bardamu, from the trenches of World War I and the African jungle to America and Paris.

Center, Katherine

How to walk away : a novel / Katherine Center. St. Martin's Press, 2018. 352 p.

ISBN 9781250149060

1. Engaged persons 2. Accident victims 3. Life change events 4. Women -- Interpersonal relations 5. Young women -- Psychology 6. Family relationships 7. Airplane accidents 8. Family secrets 9. Women's lives and relationships

LC 2017060163

RUSA Reading List Short List, 2019.

When an accident on what was supposed to be the happiest day of her life lands her in the hospital with a very uncertain future, Margaret struggles to come to terms with family secrets, heartbreak and starting over before discovering love in an unexpected place.

"Center's characters ... leap off the page with their unique voices, and their relationships evolve slowly and satisfyingly. Although this is largely the story of Margaret learning to make the most of her life, it's also a touching and believable love story with plenty of romantic-comedy flourishes. A story about survival that is heartbreakingly honest and wryly funny, perfect for fans of Jojo Moyes and Elizabeth Berg." Kirkus.

Center, Katherine

Things you save in a fire / Katherine Center. St. Martin's Press, 2019. 352 p.

ISBN 9781250047328

1. Women fire fighters 2. Women -- Psychology 3. Men/women relations 4. Trust 5. Betrayal 6. Fire fighters 7. Competition 8. Coping in women 9. Moving to a new city 10. Sexism in employment 11. Boston, Massachusetts 12. Women's lives and relationships

LC 2018057650

When a family emergency compels her move from Texas to Boston, a skilled firefighter becomes the only woman in her new firehouse and navigates discrimination, low funding and her private edicts about falling in love with another firefighter.

"Center gives readers a sharp and witty exploration of love and forgiveness that is at once insightful, entertaining, and thoroughly addictive." Kirkus.

A **century** of great Western stories : an anthology of Western fiction / edited by John Jakes. Forge, 2000. 525 p.

ISBN 031286986X

1. Frontier and pioneer life -- The West (United States) 2. The West (United States) -- Social life and customs 3. Westerns 4. Short stories

LC 99462096

30 short stories.

"Romance, murder, action, mystery and suspense are mixed with hefty doses of moral dilemma, guilt and redemption in these carefully plotted tales. . . . Many of the stories are appearing here for the first time since they were published in the pulps of the '30s, '40s and '50s, but their appeal is as fresh as ever." Publishers Weekly.

Cervantes Saavedra, Miguel de, 1547-1616

* **Don** Quixote / Miguel de Cervantes ; translated, with a critical text based on the first editions of 1605 and 1615, and with variant readings, variorum notes, and an introduction by Samuel Putnam. Modern Library, 1998. xl, 1239 p.

ISBN 0679602860

1. 16th century 2. Eccentric men 3. Adventurers -- Spain 4. Imagination in men 5. Squires -- Spain 6. Friendship 7. Knights and knighthood 8. Chivalry 9. Integrity 10. Delusions 11. Idealism 12. Quests 13. Right and wrong 14. Spain -- Social life and customs -- 16th century 15. Spain -- History -- 16th century 16. Classics 17. Picaresque fiction 18. Translations -- Spanish to English

LC 97047415

Presents the classic Spanish tale of chivalry and abiding optimism, depicting the exploits of a knight who attempts to bring justice and truth to the world.

Cha, Steph

* **Your** house will pay / Steph Cha. Ecco Press, 2019. 272 p.

ISBN 9780062868855

1. Korean American families 2. African American families 3. Loss (Psychology) 4. Violence -- Psychological aspects 5. Communities 6. City life 7. Children of immigrants 8. Attempted murder 9. Injustice 10. Teenage murder victims 11. Racism 12. Race relations 13. Family secrets 14. Family relationships 15. Los Angeles, California 16. Literary fiction

Two teenagers in Los Angeles, one Korean-American and the other African-American, deal with the ripple effects of a shooting from decades ago after a new incident brings their families? painful memories hurtling back.

Chabon, Michael

The **amazing** adventures of Kavalier & Clay : a novel / Michael Chabon. Random House, 2000. 639 p.

ISBN 0679450041

1. Comic book writing 2. Superheroes 3. Heroes and heroines in mass media 4. Artists 5. Czech Americans 6. Young men 7. Cousins 8. Men/women relations 9. Gay men 10. Jewish men 11. Immigrants 12. Creativity in men 13. New York City -- History -- 20th century 14. Historical fiction 15. Literary fiction

LC 00029063

ALA Notable Book, 2001.

Pulitzer Prize for Fiction, 2001.

National Book Critics Circle Award for Fiction finalist, 2000

In 1939 New York City, Joe Kavalier, a refugee from Hitler's Prague, joins forces with his Brooklyn-born cousin, Sammy Clay, to create comic-book superheroes inspired by their own fantasies, fears, and dreams.

"Themes are masterfully explored, leaving the book's sense of humor intact and characters so highly developed they could walk off the page." Newsweek.

Chabon, Michael
Moonglow / Michael Chabon. HarperCollins, 2016 432 p.
ISBN 9780062225559
1. Last words 2. Family secrets 3. Grandfather and grandson 4. Memories 5. Grandparents 6. Jewish families 7. Former convicts 8. Space programs 9. Mail-order business 10. World War II veterans 11. Women psychiatric hospital patients 12. Philadelphia, Pennsylvania 13. Domestic fiction 14. Psychological fiction 15. Literary fiction
Sophie Brody Medal, 2017.
Andrew Carnegie Medal for Excellence in Fiction Finalist, 2017
National Book Critics Circle Award for Fiction finalist, 2016
A man bears witness to his grandfather's deathbed confessions, which reveal his family's long-buried history and his involvement in a mail-order novelty company, World War II, and the space program.
"As towering a figure as the grandfather is, all of Chabon's characters are complex and commanding." Booklist.

Chabon, Michael
Telegraph Avenue : a novel / Michael Chabon. Harper, 2012. 468 p.
ISBN 9780061493348
1. Friendship 2. Businesspeople 3. Family relationships 4. Records, Phonograph 5. Music stores 6. Birthfathers 7. Business competition 8. Midwives 9. Men 10. Male friendship 11. Oakland, California 12. Berkeley, California 13. Literary fiction
LC 2012001355
When ex-NFL quarterback Gibson Goode, the fifth richest black man in America, decides to open his newest Dogpile megastore on Telegraph Avenue, Nat and Archy, the owners of Brokeland Records, fear for their business until Gibson's endeavor exposes a decades-old secret history.

Chabon, Michael
* **Wonder** boys / Michael Chabon. Villard Books, 1995. 368 p.
ISBN 0679415882
1. Young men 2. Self-destructive behavior in men 3. Creativity in men 4. Creative writing teachers 5. Authors, American 6. Editors 7. Marijuana use 8. Male friendship 9. Pennsylvania 10. Pittsburgh, Pennsylvania 11. Humorous stories 12. Novels-within-novels 13. Literary fiction
LC 94028921
In a story exploring the theme of the artist's isolation, Grady Tripp, an obese, aging writer who has lost his way, and debauched editor Terry Crabtree struggle to rekindle their friendship, a sense of adventure, and purpose in their lives.
"Bright promise gone awry is the theme of this exuberantly comic novel, whose convoluted plot sparkles with inventiveness and wit." Publishers Weekly.

Chabon, Michael
The **Yiddish** Policemen's Union / Michael Chabon. Harper Collins, 2007. 400 p.
ISBN 0007149824
1. 1940s 2. Murder 3. Jewish families 4. Immigrants, Jewish 5. Identity (Religion) 6. Jewish American men 7. Police -- Alaska 8. Detectives 9. Men/women relations 10. Faith (Judaism) 11. Alaska -- History -- 20th century 12. Alternative histories 13. Mysteries 14. Hardboiled fiction 15. Literary fiction
Hugo Award for Best Novel, 2008.

Locus Award for Best Science Fiction Novel, 2008.
Nebula Award for Best Novel, 2007.
Sidewise Awards for Alternate History, 2007.
In a world in which Alaska, rather than Israel, has become the homeland for the Jews following World War II, Detective Meyer Landsman and his half-Tlingit partner Berko investigate the death of a heroin-addicted chess prodigy.
"Though the ultimate secret behind the murder that kick-starts the story involves a religious-political scheme that tips over clumsily into surreal satire, the remainder of the book is so authoritatively and minutely imagined that the reader, absorbed in the plight of [the author's] shambling hero, really doesn't mind. . . . Mr. Chabon has so thoroughly conjured the fictional world of Sitka--its history, culture, geography, its incestuous and byzantine political and sectarian divisions--that the reader comes to take its existence for granted." New York Times.

Chacon, Daniel
And the shadows took him : a novel / Daniel Chacon. Atria Books, 2004. 339 p.
ISBN 9780743466387
1. Mexican American families 2. Ethnicity 3. Gangs 4. Mexican Americans 5. Family relationships 6. Small towns 7. Small town life -- Oregon 8. Growing up 9. Fresno, California 10. California 11. Oregon 12. Coming-of-age stories
LC 2004300040
Moving his family from their barrio neighborhood when he gets a better job, William Molina finds their Latino background proving a challenge in their new community and reacts with a combination of rage and machismo that threatens his family's security.

Chai, May-Lee
Useful phrases for immigrants : stories / May-lee Chai. Blair, 2018 170 p.
ISBN 9780932112767
1. Immigrants, Chinese 2. Immigrants -- Identity 3. Belonging 4. Chinese Americans 5. Asian Americans 6. Home (Concept) 7. China -- Immigration and emigration 8. United States -- Immigration and emigration 9. Short stories 10. Literary fiction
LC 2018035244
Eight innovative, timely stories illuminate the hopes and fears of Chinese immigrants and their descendants.

Chakraborty, S. A.
The **city** of brass / S. A. Chakraborty. Harper Voyager, 2017. 400 p. Daevabad trilogy
ISBN 9780062678102
1. 18th century 2. Genies 3. Women swindlers 4. Magic 5. Princes 6. Warriors 7. Imaginary wars and battles 8. Cairo, Egypt -- History 9. Egypt -- History 10. Historical fantasy 11. Middle Eastern-influenced fantasy
LC 2017020068
RUSA Reading List Short List, 2019.
Nahri, a young con artist, inadvertently summons a mysterious djinn warrior to her side during one of her cons, revealing the existence of true magic before the future of a magical Middle Eastern kingdom falls into her hands.
"There is enough material here--a feisty, independent lead searching for answers, reminiscent of Star Wars's Rey, and a richly imagined alternate world-- to support a potential series." Publishers Weekly.

Chakraborty, S. A.

The **empire** of gold / S. A Chakraborty. Harper Voyager, 2020. 400 p. Daevabad trilogy

ISBN 9780062678164

1. 18th century 2. Genies 3. Women swindlers 4. Magic 5. Rulers 6. Warriors 7. Imaginary kingdoms 8. Imaginary wars and battles 9. Cairo, Egypt -- History 10. Egypt -- History 11. Historical fantasy 12. Middle Eastern-influenced fantasy

In this final installment in the critically acclaimed trilogy, Nahri and Ali are determined to save both their city and their loved ones, but when Ali seeks support in his mother's homeland, he makes a discovery that threatens not only his relationship with Nahri, but his very faith.

Chakraborty, S. A.

The **kingdom** of copper : a novel / S. A. Chakraborty. Harper Voyager, 2019. 640 p. Daevabad trilogy

ISBN 9780062678133

1. Genies 2. Women swindlers 3. Imaginary kingdoms 4. Captivity 5. Rulers 6. Magic 7. Princes 8. Water spirits 9. Warriors 10. Family secrets 11. Cairo, Egypt -- History 12. Egypt -- History 13. Historical fantasy 14. Middle Eastern-influenced fantasy

LC 2018036755

A follow-up to The City of Brass finds a trapped Nahri reluctantly embracing her power to safeguard her tribe, while an exiled Ali accepts help from water spirits who unearth a family secret.

"Chakraborty's deeply thought-out system of race relations and clashing classes mirrors real-world conflicts, making it all the more captivating--and frustrating--as the dream of peace grows more futile. The action scenes--vivid, entrancing, terrifying--will keep readers riveted, especially as enemies shift to allies, allies to friends, friends to enemies." Booklist.

Chambers, Becky

A **closed** and common orbit / Becky Chambers. Harper Voyager, 2017. 367 p. Wayfarers (Becky Chambers)

ISBN 9780062569400

1. Astronauts 2. Hyperspace 3. Space vehicles 4. Interplanetary relations 5. Aliens (Non-humanoid) 6. Interpersonal relations 7. Voyages and travels 8. Space flight 9. Secrets 10. Aliens 11. Space opera 12. Science fiction

Sequel to: The long way to a small, angry planet.

RUSA Reading List Short List, 2018.

A spaceship's artificial intelligence, Lovelace, wakes up in a new body with no memory of her prior existence and must learn to negotiate the universe.

"As with her amazing debut, the power of Chamber's second space opera is in her appealing characters." Library Journal.

Chambers, Becky

* The **long** way to a small, angry planet / Becky Chambers. Harper Voyager, 2016, c2014. 416 p. Wayfarers (Becky Chambers)

ISBN 9780062444134

1. Astronauts 2. Hyperspace 3. Space vehicles 4. Interplanetary relations 5. Aliens (Non-humanoid) 6. Interpersonal relations 7. Voyages and travels 8. Space flight 9. Secrets 10. Aliens 11. Space opera 12. Science fiction

Originally self-published in 2014.

Longlisted for the Baileys Women's Prize for Fiction, 2016.

Joining the crew of the aging Wayfarer, a patched-up ship that has seen better days, loner Rosemary Harper must unexpectedly risk her life when they are offered the job of a lifetime, which teaches her valuable lessons about love and trust, and that having a family isn't the worst thing in the universe.

Chambers, Becky

Record of a spaceborn few / Becky Chambers. Harper Voyager, 2018 400 p. Wayfarers (Becky Chambers)

ISBN 9780062699220

1. Space vehicles 2. Space flight 3. Astronauts 4. Life on other planets 5. Home (Concept) 6. Space colonies 7. Aliens 8. Space opera 9. Science fiction

A young apprentice, an alien academic, a caretaker for the dead, an archivist and others wrestle with profound questions after their evacuation ship, carrying the last humans on Earth, finally reaches its destination.

"The multiple narrators and seemingly unrelated plot lines converge thematically into an intensely powerful and multifaceted meditation on time, history, change, and memory, leavened with a welcome touch of humor. The characters are distinct and lovable, each shedding light on a different facet of the Fleet. Chambers uses the interconnections inevitable in such a small society to provide moments of both horrific pain and soaring grace, and to make it clear that those things are inextricably intermingled. This is a superb work from one of the genres rising stars." Publishers Weekly.

Chambers, Becky

To be taught, if fortunate / Becky Chambers. Harper Voyager, 2019. 144 p.

ISBN 9780062936011

1. Women astronauts 2. Genetically engineered women 3. Home (Concept) 4. Space exploration 5. Planets 6. Galaxies 7. Space and time 8. Options, alternatives, choices 9. Earth 10. Space 11. Hard science fiction

While on a mission to ecologically survey four habitable worlds, Ariadne O'Neill and a team of explorers, shifting through space and time, discover that the culture back on Earth has been transformed and must make a difficult decision.

Chancellor, Bryn

Sycamore : a novel / Bryn Chancellor. Harper, 2017. 320 p.

ISBN 9780062661098

1. Dead 2. Small towns 3. Missing teenage girls 4. Memories 5. Local history 6. Small town life 7. Community life 8. Loss (Psychology) 9. Arizona 10. Literary fiction 11. Parallel narratives

LC 2016042150

"In the tradition of EVERYTHING I NEVER TOLD YOU, and with echoes of OLIVE KITTERIDGE, comes a stunning debut from Bryn Chancellor, an award-winning writer hailed as "amazing, sensitive, and thoughtful" by Kevin Wilson"--, Provided by publisher.

"This is a movingly written, multivoiced novel examining how one tragic circumstance can sow doubt about fundamental things." Publishers Weekly.

Chandler, Raymond, 1888-1959

The **annotated** Big sleep / Raymond Chandler ; annotated and edited, with an introduction, by Owen Hill, Pamela Jackson, and Anthony Dean Rizzuto ; with a foreword by Jonathan Lethem. Vintage Crime/Black Lizard, 2018. xxxiii, 474 p.

ISBN 9780804168885

1. 1930s 2. Extortion 3. Rich people 4. Private investigators 5. Heirs and heiresses 6. Capitalists and financiers 7. Sisters 8. Marlowe, Philip (Fictional character) 9. Los Angeles, California 10. Mysteries

11. Hardboiled fiction 12. Modern classics

Features hundreds of illuminating notes and images alongside the full text of the novel.

Follows Philip Marlowe into an underworld of booze, violence, pornography, and sex, as he searches for the blackmailer of a millionaire's daughter.

Chandler, Raymond, 1888-1959

* The **big** sleep / Raymond Chandler. Vintage Books, 1992, c1939. 231 p. Philip Marlowe mysteries

ISBN 9780394758282

1. 1930s 2. Extortion 3. Rich people 4. Private investigators 5. Heirs and heiresses 6. Capitalists and financiers 7. Sisters 8. Marlowe, Philip (Fictional character) 9. Los Angeles, California 10. Mysteries 11. Hardboiled fiction 12. Modern classics

LC 9150919

Sequel by Robert B. Parker: Perchance to Dream.

Originally published: London: Hamish Hamilton, 1939.

One of the classic detective novels that established the genre, The Big Sleep follows Philip Marlowe into an underworld of booze, violence, pornography, and sex, as he searches for the blackmailer of a millionaire's daughter.

Chandler, Raymond, 1888-1959

The **lady** in the lake / Raymond Chandler. Vintage Books, 1992, c1943. 266 p., 19 cm. Philip Marlowe mysteries

ISBN 9780394758251

1. 1940s 2. Missing persons 3. Murder 4. Police corruption 5. Private investigators 6. Marlowe, Philip (Fictional character) 7. Los Angeles, California 8. Mysteries 9. Hardboiled fiction

Originally published: New York : A.A. Knopf, 1943.

Philip Marlowe, L.A.'s toughest private eye, ventures away from the city's mean streets, to search the mountains outside Los Angeles for a missing woman and unravels a tangled web of murder and deception.

Chandler, Raymond, 1888-1959

The **long** goodbye / Raymond Chandler. Vintage Books, 1992, c1954. 379 p. Philip Marlowe mysteries

ISBN 9780394757681

1. Gangsters 2. Murder 3. Rich people 4. Suicide 5. Private investigators 6. Alcoholic veterans 7. Marlowe, Philip (Fictional character) 8. Los Angeles, California 9. Mysteries 10. Hardboiled fiction 11. Modern classics

The Long Goodbye inspired the film The Long Goodbye in 1973.

Originally published: Boston : Houghton Mifflin, 1954.

Edgar Allan Poe Award for Best Mystery Novel, 1955.

Down-and-out drunk Terry Lennox has a problem: his millionaire wife is dead and he needs to get out of LA fast. So he turns to his only friend in the world: Philip Marlowe, Private Investigator. He's willing to help a man down on his luck, but later, Lennox commits suicide in Mexico and things start to turn nasty.

Chang, Alexandra, 1988-

* **Days** of distraction / Alexandra Chang. Ecco Press, 2020. 320 p.

ISBN 9780062951809

1. Identity (Psychology) 2. Asian American women 3. Interracial romance 4. High technology industry and trade 5. Moving, Household 6. Young adults 7. Self-discovery 8. Race relations 9. Silicon Valley, California 10. Ithaca, New York 11. Coming-of-age stories 12. Literary fiction

A marginalized Silicon Valley staff writer moves with her boyfriend to a quiet upstate New York town where she confronts the challenges of their interracial relationship and the questions it raises about her heritage.

"Chang's humorous, timely observations on race, technology, and relationships lend immediacy to the narrator's chronicle of self-awareness." Publishers Weekly.

Chang, Lan Samantha

All is forgotten, nothing is lost / Lan Samantha Chang. W. W. Norton & Co., 2010. 192 p.

ISBN 9780393063066

1. Poetry writing 2. Teacher-student relationships 3. Success (Concept) 4. Male friendship 5. Poets 6. Resentfulness 7. Psychological fiction

LC 2010017503

At the renowned writing school in Bonneville, every student is simultaneously terrified of and attracted to the charismatic and mysterious poet and professor Miranda Sturgis, whose high standards for art are both intimidating and inspiring. As two students, Roman and Bernard, strive to win her admiration, the lines between mentorship, friendship, and love are blurred.

"Among the many threads Chang elegantly pursuesthe fraught relationships between mentors and students, the value of poetry, the price of ambitionit is her indelible portrait of the loneliness of artistic endeavor that will haunt readers the most in this exquisitely written novel about the poet's lot." Booklist.

Chanter, Catherine

The **well** / Catherine Chanter. Atria Books, 2015. 368 p.

ISBN 9781476772769

1. Droughts 2. Farms 3. Suspicion 4. Husband and wife 5. Cults 6. Women -- Psychology 7. Murder 8. Home confinement (Corrections) 9. Memory 10. Families 11. Great Britain 12. Dystopian fiction

Follows the experiences of an Englishwoman who is targeted by suspicion and superstition when her farm remains lush and her grandson drowns in spite of a widespread drought.

"Combining gripping mystery, nuanced psychological drama, and striking prose, this debut is a mesmerizing read." Publishers Weekly.

Chaon, Dan

Ill will / Dan Chaon. Ballantine Books, 2017. 496 p.

ISBN 9780345476043

1. Psychologists 2. Family relationships 3. Coping 4. Murder suspects 5. DNA 6. Serial murders 7. Widowers 8. Drowning 9. Misconceptions 10. Self-destructive behavior 11. Drug addiction 12. Psychological suspense

"Two sensational unsolved crimes--one in the past, another in the present--are linked by one man's memory and self-deception in this chilling novel of literary suspense from National Book Award finalist Dan Chaon. "We are always telling a story to ourselves, about ourselves," Dustin Tillman likes to say. It's one of the little mantras he shares with his patients, and it's meant to be reassuring. But what if that story is a lie? A psychologist in suburban Cleveland, Dustin is drifting through his fortieswhen he hears the news: His adopted brother, Rusty, is being released from prison. Thirty years ago, Rusty received a life sentence for the massacre of Dustin's parents, aunt, and uncle. The trial came to symbolize the 1980s hysteria over Satanic cults; despite the lack of physical evidence, the jury believed the outlandish accusations Dustin and his cousin made against Rusty. Now, after DNA analysis has overturned the conviction, Dustin braces for a reckoning. Meanwhile, one of Dustin's patients gets him deeply engaged in a string of drowning deaths involving drunk college boys. At first Dustin dismisses talk of a serial killer as paranoid thinking, but as he gets wrapped up in their amateur investigation, Dustin starts to believe that there's more to the deaths than coincidence. Soon he becomes obsessed, crossing all professional boundaries--and putting his own family in harm's way. From one of today's most renowned practitioners of literary suspense, Ill Will is an intimate thriller about the failuresof memory and the perils of self-deception. In Dan Chaon's nimble, chilling prose, the past looms over the present, turning each into a haunted place."--, Provided by publisher

"Chaon has mastered multiple psychologically complex and often fearsome characters. A shadowy narrative that's carried well by the author's command and insight." Kirkus.

Chariandy, David John, 1969-

Brother : a novel / David Chariandy Bloomsbury USA, 2018, c2017. 192 p.
>   ISBN 9781635572049
>   1. 1990s 2. Brothers 3. Children of immigrants 4. Public housing 5. Trinidadians in Canada 6. Dreams 7. Inner city 8. City life 9. Street life 10. Poverty 11. Scarborough, Ontario 12. Ontario 13. Literary fiction 14. Urban fiction
>   Originally published; Toronto : McClelland &Stewart, 2017.
>   BC Book Prizes, Ethel Wilson Fiction Prize, 2018.
>   Rogers Writers' Trust Fiction Prize, 2017.
>   Toronto Book Awards, 2018.

Coming of age during a sweltering summer in their Toronto housing complex, two boys, the sons of Trinidadian immigrants, dare to imagine better lives in the face of a violent shooting and the pulsing beats of 1990s hip-hop culture.

"The tone of this often melancholy story is elegiac, as Michael tells it in his muted, first-person voice. The characters are well drawn, and the setting is beautifully realized. The result is a haunting story that will linger in readers memories." Booklist.

Charles, KJ

Wanted, a gentleman : or, Virtue over-rated / K.J. Charles. Riptide Publishing, 2017. 155 p.
>   ISBN 9781626494725
>   1. 1800s (Decade) 2. Gay men 3. Interracial romance 4. Secrets 5. Personal ads 6. Black British 7. Racism 8. Sexual attraction 9. Revenge 10. London, England -- History -- 19th century 11. Historical romances 12. LGBTQIA romances 13. LGBTQIA fiction

"Charles provides a little gothic plot twist that stretches the imagination, while this historical gay romance remains true to its roots in grand nineteenth-century love stories. Period dialogue coupled with a strong setting make this an affecting, quick read." Booklist

Charlton, Blake

Spellbound / Blake Charlton. Tor, 2011. 416 p. Spellwright trilogy
>   ISBN 9780765317285
>   1. Wizards 2. Spells (Magic) 3. Demons 4. End of the world 5. Epic fantasy
>   LC 2011013451
>   "A Tom Doherty Associates book."

Pursued by the demon who cursed him, Nicodemus must try to avoid spinning the world into chaos with his unique disability, the nasty inclination to misspell magical texts.

"Middle volumes are always tricky, but Charlton succeeds brilliantly here." Kirkus.

Charlton, Blake

Spellbreaker / Blake Charlton. Tor Books, 2016. 464 p. Spellwright trilogy
>   ISBN 9780765317292
>   1. Wizards 2. Spells (Magic) 3. Demons 4. Prophecies 5. Families 6.

Imaginary wars and battles 7. Epic fantasy

While hunting neodemons, Leandra, Warden of Ixos, uncovers a prophecy spell that tells her she will have to murder someone she loves or die herself.

"Vivid, intelligent, and painful in an authentically laudable way." Kirkus.

Charlton, Blake

Spellwright / Blake Charlton. Tor Books, 2010. 352 p. Spellwright trilogy
>   ISBN 9780765317278
>   1. Prophecies 2. Murder 3. Spells (Magic) 4. Magic 5. Wizards 6. Apprentices 7. Epic fantasy

Hampered by his inability to spell in a world where magic must be written in order to work, gifted young wizard Nicodemus experiences disturbing dreams in the wake of an ancient demon's murderous campaign that suggests that Nicodemus's spelling problem may be related to a curse.

"A fantastic first novel, set in an intriguing world of magic based on the written word. Charlton uses his own experiences with dyslexia to create a protagonist, Nicodemus, whose learning disability could unmake the world. Reading Spellwright as a bibliophile is a real treat, and the focus on language, reading, writing and understanding as a wizardly trait is something that seems somewhat new, and honestly, something long overdue in the fantasy realm." io9.

Chase, Loretta Lynda, 1949-

Don't tempt me / Loretta Lynda Chase. Avon, 2009. 384 p. Fallen women
>   ISBN 9780061632662
>   1. Regency period (1811-1820) 2. Young women 3. Kidnapping 4. Men/women relations 5. Scandals 6. Harems 7. Aristocracy 8. Women kidnapping victims 9. Romantic love 10. England -- History -- 19th century 11. Regency romances 12. Historical romances

Returning to England after spending twelve years in the exotic east, Zoe Lexham, who has mastered the art of pleasure, agrees to a marriage of convenience with the Duke of Marchmont who, tired of being the most popular bachelor, can save her reputation.

Chase, Loretta Lynda, 1949-

A duke in shining armor / Loretta Lynda Chase. Avon Books, 2017. 384 p. Difficult dukes
>   ISBN 9780062457387
>   1. Georgian era (1714-1837) 2. 1830s 3. Dukes and duchesses 4. Jilted men 5. Nobility 6. Interpersonal attraction 7. Men/women relations 8. Best friends 9. Books and reading 10. England -- Social life and customs -- 19th century 11. Georgian romances 12. Historical romances

Introduces three less-than-virtuous dukes, the first of whom falls for a bookish lady who is reluctantly engaged to his best friend.

"When it comes to writing unforgettable, superbly crafted historical romances, RITA Awardwinning Chase is the crème de la crème, and A Duke in Shining Armor, which launches her new Disgraceful Dukes series, is another exquisitely sensual, perfectly calibrated masterpiece of frothy wit and flawless characterization." Booklist.

Chase, Loretta Lynda, 1949-

Miss Wonderful / Loretta Lynda Chase. Berkley, 2004. 352 p. Carsington brothers series
>   ISBN 9780425194836
>   1. Regency period (1811-1820) 2. 19th century 3. Canals -- Design and construction 4. Independence in women 5. Single men 6. Single women 7. Men/women relations 8. Great Britain -- History

-- Regency, 1811-1820 9. England -- Social life and customs -- 19th century 10. Derbyshire, England 11. Regency romances 12. Historical romances

The character of Rupert Carsington also appears in the author's Mr. Impossible.

Rather then succumb to temptation with the fairer sex, reformed rake Alistair Carsington journeys to Derbyshire, a secluded country town, to keep out of trouble, but his plans go by the wayside when he meets the infuriatingly irresistible Miss Mirabel Oldridge.

Chase, Loretta Lynda, 1949-

Silk is for seduction / Loretta Chase. Avon Books, 2011. 384 p. Dressmakers

ISBN 9780061632686

1. Georgian era (1714-1837) 2. 19th century 3. 1830s 4. Dressmaking 5. Aristocracy 6. Sisters 7. Men/women relations 8. Interpersonal attraction 9. Ambition in women 10. Georgian romances 11. Historical romances

RUSA Reading List, 2012.

In this first installment in a new series, sisters from a scandalous aristocratic family--and the purveyors of London's most fashionable shop--find love as divine as the gowns they create.

"With a sharp eye for both upper-class society and the cutthroat world of high-class London mantua makers, Chase mixes snappy dialogue, erotic tension, and the fanciful styles of the era into a sparkling love story as Marcelline's strategy ensnares not only Clevedon's patronage but his heart." Publishers Weekly.

Chase, Loretta Lynda, 1949-

Your scandalous ways / Loretta Chase. Avon, 2008. 384 p. Fallen women

ISBN 006123124X

1. Regency period (1811-1820) 2. Loneliness in women 3. Trust 4. Spies 5. Courtesans 6. Extramarital affairs 7. Divorced women 8. Nobility 9. Scandals 10. Men/women relations 11. Sexuality 12. Venice, Italy -- Social life and customs -- 19th century 13. Regency romances 14. Historical romances

Weary of his life as a spy, Jack Cordier wants nothing more than to return to London and his aristocratic lifestyle, but first he is assigned to retrieve some incriminating letters from the notorious Francesca Bonnard, a young woman who has weathered heartbreak, scandal, and the scorn of her peers.

Chatterjee, Upamanyu

English, August : an Indian story / Upamanyu Chatterjee ; introduction by Akhil Sharma. New York Review Books, 2006, 330 p.

ISBN 9781590171790

1. Young men 2. Culture conflict 3. Drug abuse 4. Civil service 5. City life 6. Cities and towns 7. Small town life 8. India 9. Humorous stories 10. Coming-of-age stories

LC 2005022842

"This satiric novel chronicles the reluctant coming of age of a privileged young man who has just entered the prestigious Indian Administrative Service. Posted to a small town deep in the interior, he finds himself a foreigner in his own country, wary of cholera, defenseless against mosquitoes, and shocked by the sight of a tribal woman: They exist, he shrieked silently, outside arty films about tribal exploitation and agrarian reform. In revolt, he sneaks out of meetings, pretends to be the son of Antarctic explorers, and smokes copious amounts of pot. He's an avatar of the Western slacker: overeducated, bored, plagued with doubts, and incapable of action. Still, Chatterjee's story is uniquely Indian, as he plumbs his hero's fear of being just one more urban Indian bewitched by America's hard sell in the Third World." The New Yorker.

Chatwin, Bruce, 1940-1989

On the black hill / Bruce Chatwin. Viking Press, 1983, c1982. 248 p.

ISBN 9780670524921

1. Farm life -- Wales 2. Rural life 3. Twins 4. Brothers 5. Farms 6. Wales 7. Literary fiction

LC 82010923

Originally published: London : Jonathan Cape, 1982.

Whitbread Book Award for First Novel, 1982.

James Tait Black Memorial Prize for Fiction, 1982.

A tale of identical twin brothers who grow up on a farm in rural Wales and never leave home. They till the rough soil and sleep in the same bed, touched only occasionally by the advances of the 20th century. In depicting the lives and their interactions with their small local community the author comments on the questions of human experience.

"This is an odd, somber story, compelling because of Chatwin's compassionate depiction of these characters whose very withdrawal from historical time accentuates its passage." Library Journal.

Chatwin, Bruce, 1940-1989

Utz / Bruce Chatwin. Viking, 1989. 154 p.

ISBN 9780140115765

1. Figurines -- Collectors and collecting 2. Porcelain, German -- Collectors and collecting 3. Human nature 4. Jews, Czech 5. Socialism 6. Art dealers 7. Prague, Czech Republic 8. Satirical fiction

LC 88040310

Shortlisted for the Booker-McConnell Prize, 1988.

In a classic Cold War story, Meissen porcelain collector and Czech citizen Kaspar Utz considers defecting each time he travels abroad, but his precious collection--held hostage by the Communist authorities back home--prevents him.

"The hero of Mr. Chatwin's provocative short novel is a successful survivor. He is part Jewish but has managed to survive Hitler. . . . [Utz is] required to bequeath the collection to the state, and what he does about that insult to his elegant eighteenth-century companions becomes his own peculiar final solution. Mr. Chatwin has created an intriguing propositionthat obedient passivity can amount to successful rebellion." The Atlantic.

Chavez, Heather

No bad deed / Heather Chavez. William Morrow & Co., 2019. 400 p.

ISBN 9780062936172

1. Women veterinarians 2. Stalkers 3. Paranoia 4. Family secrets 5. Missing men 6. Missing persons investigation 7. Assault and battery 8. Criminals 9. California 10. Thrillers and suspense 11. Psychological suspense

After coming to the rescue of a woman left for dead, veterinarian Cassie Larkin becomes the target of a deadly stalker who knows too much about her own dark family history? and who could be linked to the recent disappearance of her husband.

"Chavez is in full command of plot and pacing as the connection between Cassie's roadside confrontation and Sam's disappearance becomes clear. Domestic thriller fans will be well satisfied." Publishers Weekly.

Chayefsky, Paddy, 1923-1981

Altered **states** : a novel / Paddy Chayevsky. Harper and Row, 1978. 184 p.

ISBN 0060107278

1. Scientists 2. Psychological research 3. Altered states of consciousness

LC   77011542

Edward Jessup, a neurophysiologist at the Harvard Medical School, relentlessly seeks the origins of human consciousness and, with the aide of an isolation tank and a hallucinogenic drug, regresses farther and farther into a proto-human state.

Chee, Alexander

The **queen** of the night / Alexander Chee. Houghton Mifflin Harcourt, 2016. 576 p.

ISBN 9780618663026

1. Belle Epoque (1871-1914) 2. Independence in women 3. Change (Psychology) 4. Operas 5. Secrets 6. Sopranos (Singers) 7. Americans in France 8. Intrigue 9. Lovers 10. Paris, France 11. France -- History -- 19th century 12. Historical fiction

LC 2014014409

With her distinctive "falcon" soprano, Lilliet Berne is the uncontested star of the Paris Opera. Only one accolade has thus far eluded her: the chance to originate a leading role, ensuring that she'll never be forgotten. Her wish comes true when she's presented with a libretto that alludes to the secrets of her past. Only four other people know the details of her early life, but which one of them betrayed her? As she tries to solve the mystery, she reflects on the various parts she has played, beginning with her childhood on the Minnesota prairie and encompassing roles as a circus performer, as a servant to Empress?Eugénie, and?as a celebrated courtesan. As lush and dramatic as the theatrical world it depicts, this sweeping novel brings?Belle Époque France to richly detailed life. -- Description by Gillian Speace.

"Richly researched, ornately plotted, this story demands, and repays, close attention." Kirkus.

Cheek, Chip

Cape May / Chip Cheek. Celadon Books, 2019. 256 p.

ISBN 9781250297150

1. 1950s 2. Newlyweds 3. Extramarital affairs 4. Honeymoons 5. Betrayal 6. Lust 7. Men/women relations 8. Marriage 9. Husband and wife 10. Lovers 11. Coastal towns 12. New Jersey 13. Historical fiction 14. Literary fiction

Southern newlyweds honeymooning in 1957 Cape May are pulled into the dramas of a trio of sophisticated New England urbanites who render the deserted beach community an intimate playground of corruptive recklessness.

Cheever, John

Bullet Park : a novel / John Cheever. Knopf, 1969. 245 p.

ISBN 9780394418193

1. 1960s 2. Murder 3. Suburban life 4. Eccentric men 5. Neighbors 6. Good and evil 7. Chemists 8. Fathers and sons 9. Men with depression 10. Psychological fiction 11. Literary fiction

"The author mixes compassion and high comedy brilliantly, holding up to view an America that is fatally schizoid in many of its manifestations. The confrontation that finally comes between Hammer and Nailles is a horrifying dark allegory of our times." Publishers Weekly.

Cheever, John

Falconer / John Cheever. Knopf, 1977. 211 p.

ISBN 9780394410715

1. Prisoners 2. Suburban families 3. Murderers 4. Prisons 5. Drug addicts 6. Closeted gay men 7. Fratricide 8. Sexuality 9. Dysfunctional families 10. Psychological fiction 11. Literary fiction 12. LGBTQIA fiction

LC   76019382

National Book Critics Circle Award for Fiction finalist, 1977

Convicted and imprisoned for having killed his brother, an exceptional middle-aged man enters into a close relationship with a thief and hustler named Jody and experiences an unexpected liberation

Cheever, John

The **Wapshot** chronicle / John Cheever. Harper, 1957. xiv, 352 p.   Wapshot series

1. 20th century 2. Family relationships 3. Small town life 4. Coastal towns 5. Brothers 6. College students 7. Teenage boys 8. Fathers -- Death 9. Aunts 10. Sexuality 11. Extramarital affairs 12. Massachusetts 13. New York City 14. Washington, D.C. 15. Family sagas 16. Literary fiction 17. Modern classics

National Book Award for Fiction, 1958.

"The interludes of Leander's diary and of Honora's disturbances have a tart sting and the whole offers candor and a loving care for men and their concerns in a world tyrannized by women. A rowdy, bawdy, feeling, root-sensed New England gallery, this has its high -- and not quite so high -- moments for an audience which may suffer shock but never shame." Kirkus

Cheever, John

The **Wapshot** scandal / John Cheever. Harper Row, 1964. xiii, 304 p.   Wapshot series

1. 1960s 2. Small town life 3. Brothers 4. Husband and wife 5. Parent and child 6. Septuagenarians 7. Aunts 8. Scientists 9. Extramarital affairs 10. Alcoholics 11. Suburbs 12. Massachusetts 13. New York (State) 14. The West (United States) 15. Family sagas 16. Literary fiction

Continuation of the Wapshot chronicle about small town life in Massachusetts.

"This sequel to The Wapshot chronicle continues the tale of the decline of the fortunes of the Wapshot family and of the mythical New England town of St. Botolphs. The 'scandal' is the discovery that Aunt Honora has never paid her income taxes, and the principal disaster stems from the long-standing oversight. The novel also traces the misfortunes of two Wapshot nephews, Coverly, a public relations man at a missile site, and Moses, an alcoholic. Despite the somberness of the main line of events, the book is not depressing; it is lighted by the high gloss of Mr. Cheever's style, by glints of humor, and especially by the warm glow of human fortitude under stress." Library Journal.

Chekhov, Anton Pavlovich, 1860-1904

Early short stories, 1883-1888 / edited by Shelby Foote ; translated from the Russian by Constance Garnett. Modern Library, 1998. xix, 642 p.

ISBN 9780679603177

1. Short stories 2. Translations -- Russian to English

Tells the stories of a fawning official, a man's search for convictions, a boy's journey across Russia, and ordinary people in situations that reveal a surprising change of emotion.

Chekhov, Anton Pavlovich, 1860-1904

Later short stories, 1888-1903 / edited by Shelby Foote ; translated from the Russian by Constance Garnett. Modern Library, 1998. xvii, 628 p.

ISBN 9780679603160

1. Short stories 2. Translations -- Russian to English

LC 98020048

Tells the stories of a doubting writer, the unexpected results of a love affair, and everyday people facing life's surprises.

Chen, Da, 1962-2019

Brothers : a novel / Da Chen. Shaye Areheart Books, 2006. 432 p.

ISBN 1400097282

1. Chinese Cultural Revolution (1966-1976) 2. 20th century 3. Stepbrothers and stepsisters 4. Social change -- China 5. Abandoned children 6. Orphans 7. Illegitimacy 8. Revenge 9. Family secrets 10. Men/women relations 11. Interpersonal relations 12. Love 13. Love triangles 14. Families 15. Tragedy 16. Revolutions -- China 17. China -- Politics and government 18. China -- History -- Cultural Revolution, 1966-1976 19. Family sagas 20. Historical fiction

LC 2005036267

Asian Pacific American Award for Literature: Adult Fiction, 2007.

"Da Chen has achieved something that sounds simple but is, in fact, close to impossible: he brings the Western reader into the guts of the conflict, the agonies and the revelations of events that shook the world's largest population in the 35 years after 1960, when Shento and his brother were born. Make no mistake, this is not contemporary history retold. This is magnificent fiction. It transcends the events it chronicles and does what fiction at its best should do: it changes our internal landscape." Washington Post Book World.

Chen, Mike

Here and now and then / Mike Chen. MIRA, 2019. 384 p.

ISBN 9780778369042

1. Spies 2. Time travel 3. Families 4. Fathers and daughters 5. Amnesia 6. Protectiveness in men 7. Near future 8. Rescues 9. Family relationships 10. San Francisco, California 11. Science fiction

Stranded for 18 years since the 1990s, time-traveling agent Kin Stewart, suffering from memory loss, has started a new life, but when rescuers from the year 2142 finally arrive, he must choose between his current family and the one he left behind in the future.

"Chen carefully balances heart, humor, and precise world building to bring alive an emotional and genre-bending story that will please fans of Doctor Who." Booklist.

Chen, Qiufan, 1981-

Waste tide / Chen Qiufan ; translated from the Chinese by Ken Liu. Tor Books, 2019, c2013. 304 p.

ISBN 9780765389312

1. Class conflict 2. Recycling (Waste, etc) 3. Near future 4. Migrant workers 5. Clans 6. Toxins 7. Viruses 8. Pollution 9. Technology and civilization 10. Power (Social sciences) 11. Poverty 12. Solid waste disposal 13. China 14. Dystopian fiction 15. Science fiction 16. Translations -- Chinese to English

LC 2018050987

Originally published: Beijing : Changjiang Literature Art Publishing House, 2013.

An exploited lowest-caste factory worker, her ruthless employer, an American corporate representative and his heritage-seeking translator intersect when a dark futuristic virus is unleashed on a major Chinese technological site, triggering a war between the classes.

"Anglophone readers will cherish the opportunity to experience Chen's sweeping, complex, and deeply emotional near-future dystopian vision via this thoughtful rendition by Hugo-winning translator and author Liu that maintains the story's essential Chinese character." Publishers Weekly.

Cheng, Bill

Southern cross the dog / Bill Cheng. Ecco Press, 2013. 336 p.

ISBN 9780062225009

1. 1920s 2. Blues music 3. Floods 4. Curses 5. Voyages and travels 6. Survival (after floods) 7. Eccentrics and eccentricities 8. Southern States 9. Mississippi River 10. Historical fiction

"When I was a baby child, they put the jinx on me," explains Robert Lee Chatham, a young African-American man from rural Mississippi. Everything he's experienced so far in his short life has lead him to believe he's marked by the Devil -- from his mother's mental illness to his brother's lynching at the hands of a mob. Even Robert's first kiss (with a white girl named Dora) comes just before the Great Mississippi Flood of 1927, a disaster that then robs him of everything he holds dear in one fell swoop. In the aftermath of that devastating event, Robert journeys across the deep South, encountering dangers and numerous eccentric characters as he strives to outrun what he's sure is his terrible fate. - Description by Gillian Speace.

Cherryh, C. J.

Foreigner : a novel of first contact / C. J. Cherryh. DAW Books, 1994. 378 p. Foreigner universe. First foreigner sequence

ISBN 9780886775902

1. Space colonies 2. Aliens (Humanoid) -- Sightings and encounters 3. Human/alien encounters 4. Culture conflict 5. Loyalty 6. Attempted assassination 7. Space opera 8. Science fiction

Two hundred years after a group of humans had lost a war to the atevi, Bren Cameron, the only human allowed into the atevi society, realizes he must forge a bond between the two seemingly incompatible species.

"Cherryh plays her strongest suit in this exploration of human/alien contact, producing an incisive study-in-contrast of what it means to be human in a world where trust is nonexistent." Library Journal.

Chevalier, Tracy

* **Girl** with a pearl earring / Tracy Chevalier. Dutton, 1999. 233 p.

ISBN 052594527X

1. Vermeer, Johannes, 1632-1675 2. 17th century 3. Artists -- Netherlands -- History -- 17th century 4. Artists' models -- Netherlands 5. Sixteen-year-old girls -- Netherlands 6. Women domestics -- Netherlands 7. Husband and wife -- Netherlands 8. Mothers and daughters -- Netherlands 9. Mothers-in-law -- Netherlands 10. Jewelry 11. Pearls 12. Catholics -- Netherlands 13. Netherlands -- History -- 17th century 14. Netherlands -- Social life and customs -- 17th century 15. Coming-of-age stories 16. Historical fiction

LC 99032493

In this richly imagined portrait of the young woman who inspired one of Vermeer's most celebrated paintings, history and fiction merge seamlessly in a luminous tale of artistic vision, sensual awakening, and daily life in the Netherlands of the 17th-century.

"The author has done very well in creating the feel of a society with sharp divisions of status and creed. . . . Griet is a memorable character-reserved, wary, observant, and, although she does not know it, afflicted with a serious and ultimately dangerous crush on her employer. The situation makes a fine story, which is exceptionally well told." The Atlantic. Monthly.

Chevalier, Tracy

The **last** runaway / Tracy Chevalier. Dutton, 2013. 320 p. ISBN 9780525952992

1. Antebellum America (1820-1861) 2. 1850s 3. 19th century 4. Underground Railroad 5. Quaker women 6. Quakers 7. Fugitive slaves 8. Ohio -- History 9. Historical fiction

LC 2012034693

Forced to leave England and struggling with illness in the wake of a family tragedy, Quaker Honor Bright is forced to rely on strangers in the harsh landscape of 1850 Ohio and is compelled to join the Underground Railroad network to help runaway slaves escape to freedom.

"Chevalier offers a cast of strong characters wrestling with thorny personalities, the harsh realities of the frontier, and the legal and moral complexities of American slavery." Booklist.

Chevalier, Tracy

A **single** thread / Tracy Chevalier. Viking, 2019 336 p. ISBN 9780525558248

1. Between the Wars (1918-1939) 2. 1930s 3. Young women 4. Loss (Psychology) 5. Needlework 6. Cathedrals 7. Communities 8. Friendship 9. Embroidery 10. Christian church decoration and ornament 11. Rites and ceremonies 12. Self-discovery in women 13. England 14. Historical fiction

LC 2019007094

Facing limited prospects after the loss of her loved ones, a woman joins a circle of embroiderers continuing a centuries-long tradition at the Winchester Cathedral.

Chiang, Ted

* **Exhalation** : stories / Ted Chiang. Alfred A. Knopf, 2019. 350 p.

ISBN 9781101947883

1. Technology and civilization 2. Exploration 3. High technology 4. Human behavior 5. Parallel universes 6. Short stories 7. Hard science fiction 8. Science fiction

"Chiang remains one of the most skilled stylists in sf, and this will appeal to genre and literary-fiction fans alike." Booklist.

Chiang, Ted

The **lifecycle** of software objects / Ted Chiang. Subterranean, 2010. 144 p.

ISBN 9781596063174

1. Artificial intelligence 2. Virtual reality games 3. Cyber-pets 4. Computer software developers 5. Hard science fiction 6. Science fiction

Follows the lives of Ana Alvarado and Derek Brooks as they create and relate to the artificial intelligences they helped design.

"The best science fiction integrates its technology seamlessly, making way for the ideas, and Chiang is fluent in this skill." Time. Out Chicago

Chiang, Ted

* **Stories** of your life and others / Ted Chiang. Tor, 2002. 333 p.

ISBN 076530418X

1. Short stories 2. Hard science fiction 3. Science fiction

LC 2001059658

Locus Award for Best Collection, 2003.

Presents a first collection of seven science fiction short stories, and includes an original tale, "Liking What You See: A Documentary" for this anthology.

"Chiang writes seldom, but his almost unfathomably wonderful stories tick away with the precision of a Swiss watch--and explode in your awareness with shocking, devastating force." Kirkus.

Chiaverini, Jennifer

Mrs. Lincoln's dressmaker : a novel / Jennifer Chiaverini. Dutton, 2013. 352 p.

ISBN 9780525953616

1. Keckley, Elizabeth, ca 1818-1907 2. Lincoln, Mary Todd, 1818-1882 3. 19th century 4. Interracial friendship 5. Dressmakers 6. Female friendship 7. African American women 8. Presidents' spouses -- United States 9. Freed slaves 10. Racism 11. Washington, D C 12. United States -- History -- 19th century 13. Historical fiction 14. Gentle reads

LC 2012036366

Chosen as the personal modiste for Mary Todd Lincoln, freedwoman Elizabeth Keckley is drawn into the intimate life of the Lincoln family as she supports Mary in the loss of her husband from the assassination that stunned the nation and the world.

Chiaverini, Jennifer

Resistance women : a novel / Jennifer Chiaverini. William Morrow, 2019. 384 p.

ISBN 9780062841100

1. Harnack-Fish, Mildred, 1902-1943 2. Kuckhoff, Greta, 1902-1981 3. Dodd, Martha, 1908-1990 4. Rote Kapelle (Resistance group) 5. 1930s 6. 1940s 7. Second World War era (1939-1945) 8. Women spies 9. Anti-Nazi movement 10. Americans in Germany 11. Intellectuals 12. Resistance to government 13. Courage in women 14. Jews, German 15. Anti-Nazis 16. Nazism 17. Espionage 18. Expatriates 19. Berlin, Germany 20. Germany -- Politics and government -- 1933-1945 21. Historical fiction 22. Biographical fiction 23. Gentle reads

LC 2018044622

Resisting the power grabs of an increasingly formidable Nazi Party in 1930s Berlin, the courageous American wife of a German intellectual and her circle of women friends engage in a clandestine battle to sabotage Hitler's regime.

Child, Lee

61 hours : a Reacher novel / Lee Child. Delacorte Press, 2010. 400 p. Jack Reacher novels

ISBN 9780385340588

1. Former military police 2. Witnesses -- Protection 3. Assassins 4. Retired military personnel 5. Winter storms 6. South Dakota 7. Thrillers and suspense

LC 2009052804

Theakston Old Peculier Crime Novel of the Year Award, 2011

Reacher arrives accidentally in a small South Dakota town, where during a dangerous winter storm he is enlisted to protect a lone witness who local police hope can help convict a brutal crime ring.

"Child is a superb craftsman of suspense, juggling several plots and keeping his herrings well-rouged. . . . Best of all, this is a rare series book that reads like a stand-alone. Everything you need to know about Jack Reacher is contained within its pages." Entertainment Weekly.

Child, Lee

The **affair** : a Reacher novel / Lee Child. Delacorte Press, 2011. 304 p. Jack Reacher novels

ISBN 9780385344326

1. Former military police 2. Undercover operations 3. Conspiracies 4. Murder investigation 5. Women murder victims 6. Women sheriffs 7. Military cover-ups 8. Military bases 9. Mississippi 10. Thrillers and suspense

LC 2011017151

A young woman is dead, and solid evidence points to a soldier at a nearby military base. But that soldier has powerful friends in Washington. Reacher is ordered undercover--to find out everything he can, to control the local police, and then to vanish.

"Exciting and suspenseful, with deceit and cover-ups, violence, and sex, this is another great entry in Child's compelling series." Library Journal.

Child, Lee

Bad luck and trouble : a Jack Reacher novel / Lee Child. Delacorte Press, 2007. 384 p. Jack Reacher novels

ISBN 9780385340557

1. Former military police 2. Mercenaries 3. Conspiracies 4. Murder 5. Missing persons 6. Terrorism 7. Terrorists 8. National security -- United States 9. International relations 10. Kidnapping 11. Revenge 12. Thrillers and suspense

LC 2006031931

When a man is killed by being thrown from a helicopter high over the California desert, loner Jack Reacher discovers that someone is targeting his old friends and teammates and launches a personal campaign to end the conspiracy before it claims any more lives.

"Throughout the book, Reacher remains fanatically interested in codes, fractions, cube roots and probabilities. The [author] who devises all this must also be acutely aware of formulas, because he is smart enough to avoid them. . . . In the world of Mr. Child's novels, what matters, and dazzles, is what works on the page." New York Times.

Child, Lee

* **Blue** moon : a Jack Reacher novel / Lee Child. Delacorte Press, 2019. 400 p. Jack Reacher novels

ISBN 9780399593543

1. Veterans 2. Gangs 3. Protectiveness in men 4. Debt 5. Violence in gangs 6. Violence in men 7. Justice 8. Thrillers and suspense

LC 2019029141

Jack Reacher comes to the aid of an elderly couple . . . and confronts his most dangerous opponents yet.

Child, Lee

* **Die** trying / Lee Child. G. P. Putnam's Sons, 1998. 374 p. Jack Reacher novels

ISBN 0399143793

1. Former military police 2. Kidnapping 3. White supremacists 4. Hostages 5. Neo-Nazism 6. Women FBI agents 7. Revenge 8. Montana 9. Chicago, Illinois 10. Thrillers and suspense

LC 9739763

In a plot to overthrow the U.S. government, Montana neo-Nazis abduct the daughter of the nation's top general and her male companion. The companion is Jack Reacher, a former military policeman and he turns the tables on the captors.

Child, Lee

Echo burning / Lee Child. G.P Putnam's Sons, 2001. 354 p. Jack Reacher novels

ISBN 0399147268

1. Former military police 2. Assassins 3. Murder 4. Protectiveness in men 5. Murder investigation -- Texas 6. Family problems 7. Texas 8. Thrillers and suspense

LC 00045910

While hitchhiking through West Texas, former MP Jack Reacher encounters a young woman seeking protection for herself and her little girl from her monstrous husband, due to be released from jail, and his horrible family.

"Reacher is a one-man wrecking crew nourished only by the hunt. For anyone who thinks the hard-boiled genre is growing soft around the edges." Booklist.

Child, Lee

The **enemy** : a Jack Reacher novel / Lee Child. Delacorte Press, 2004. 393 p. Jack Reacher novels

ISBN 9780385336673

1. 1990s 2. Military police 3. Crimes against generals 4. Americans in France 5. Murder investigation 6. Conspiracies 7. Mothers and sons 8. Family secrets 9. France 10. North Carolina 11. Thrillers and suspense

LC 2003065282

Former army cop Jack Reacher finds himself questioning the instincts that made him an elite soldier when his latest case forces him to choose between obeying the law and becoming a renegade.

"Known for his hold-your-breath action scenes, Child proves equally adept at portraying how a criminal investigation uses the smallest of building blocks . . . to construct a compelling circumstantial case." Booklist.

Child, Lee

The **hard** way : a Jack Reacher novel / Lee Child. Delacorte Press, 2006. 384 p. Jack Reacher novels

ISBN 9780385336697

1. Former military police 2. Kidnapping 3. Mercenaries 4. Arms dealers 5. Undercover operations 6. Ransom 7. Revenge 8. Secrets 9. Women kidnapping victims 10. Girl kidnapping victims 11. Assassins 12. New York City 13. Thrillers and suspense

LC 2005051946

Jack Reacher comes to the aid of Edward Lane, the head of an illegal soldiers-for-hire operation, who enlists Reacher's assistance to find and stop a vicious kidnapper who has abducted Lane's wife and child, but Reacher soon discovers that his new employer's dirty secrets could get him killed.

"The imperfections Child adds to his protagonist's character this time out, such as Reacher's not catching onto all of the questionable dealings early on in the novel, give Reacher a much-needed vulnerability. . . . [This is a] breathless, well-paced thriller that will satisfy die-hard fans and newcomers." Denver Post.

Child, Lee

* **Killing** floor / Lee Child. G. P. Putnam's Sons, 1997. 359 p. Jack Reacher novels

ISBN 9780399142536

1. Former military police 2. Murder suspects 3. Conspiracies 4. Brothers -- Death 5. Revenge 6. Murder investigation 7. Frameups 8. Small town life 9. Georgia 10. Thrillers and suspense

LC 96-34452

Anthony Award for Best Novel, 1998.

A discharged soldier is framed for a murder by the chief of police in a small town in Georgia where he has just arrived. When the soldier learns that the murdered man was his brother he breaks out of jail and carries out his own investigation. A first novel.

"Child serves up a big, rangy plot, menace as palpable as a ticking bomb, and enough battered corpses to make an undertaker grin." Kirkus.

Child, Lee

Make me / Lee Child. Random House, 2015. 416 p. Jack Reacher novels

ISBN 9780804178778

1. Missing persons 2. Assassins 3. Conspiracies 4. Fugitives 5. Murder investigation 6. Murder 7. Thrillers and suspense

When he teams up with Michelle Chang, Jack Reacher finds himself involved in a private investigation that has turned lethal.

Child, Lee

* The **midnight** line / Lee Child. Delacorte Press, 2017. 400 p. Jack Reacher novels

ISBN 9780399593482

1. Motorcycle gangs 2. Lost articles 3. Women veterans 4. Rings 5. Missing persons 6. Veterans 7. Wisconsin 8. Thrillers and suspense

Reacher takes a stroll through a small Wisconsin town and sees a class ring in a pawn shop window: West Point 2005. A tough year to graduate: Iraq, then Afghanistan.The ring is tiny, for a woman, and it has her initials engraved on the inside. Reacher wonders what unlucky circumstance made her give up something she earned over four hard years. He decides to find out. And find the woman. And return her ring. Why not? So begins a harrowing journey that takes Reacher through the upper Midwest, from a lowlife bar on the sad side of a small town to a dirt-blown crossroads in the middle of nowhere, encountering bikers, cops, crooks, muscle, and a missing persons PI who wears a suit and a tie in the Wyoming wilderness. The deeper Reacher digs, and the more he learns, the more dangerous the terrain becomes. Turns out the ring was just a small link in a far darker chain. Powerful forces are guarding a vast criminal enterprise. Some lines should never be crossed. But then, neither should Reacher. Praise for #1 bestselling author Lee Child and his Jack Reacher series "There's a reason why Child is considered the best of the best in the thriller genre."--Associated Press

"The identity of the ring's owner is established reasonably quickly, and her backstory (and what Reacher does about it) takes the reader from the wars in Afghanistan to the opioid crisis in America (including a damning thumbnail history of how corporate America has profited from selling heroin in one form or another and a devastating portrait of opioid addiction). As usual, Child makes his narrative entirely credible and compulsively readable." Publishers Weekly.

Child, Lee

Never go back : a Jack Reacher novel / Lee Child. Delacorte Press, 2013. 416 p. Jack Reacher novels

ISBN 9780385344340

1. Former military police 2. Cold cases (Criminal investigation) 3. Missing women 4. Conspiracies 5. Murder investigation 6. Murder 7. Virginia 8. Thrillers and suspense

Jack Reacher arrives in Virginia hoping to contact the woman he spoke with on the phone in "61 Hours," only to be drafted back into the Army, where he confronts life-changing elements from his past.

Child, Lee

Night school : a Jack Reacher novel / Lee Child. Delacorte Press, 2016. 416 p. Jack Reacher novels

ISBN 9780804178808

1. Missing persons 2. Assassins 3. Conspiracies 4. Fugitives 5. Murder investigation 6. Murder 7. Thrillers and suspense

LC 2016018769

A military policeman fresh off a mission in 1996, Jack Reacher is assigned to a covert task force with two government experts to track down an American who is about to make a mysterious sale to Middle Eastern radicals.

"This way- back novel, with its old-school investigating, street-smart tactics, and classic Reacher attitude, is an edge-of-your-seat book readers won't want to put down." Library Journal.

Child, Lee

No middle name : the complete collected Jack Reacher short stories / Lee Child. Random House, 2017. 400 p. Jack Reacher novels

ISBN 9780399593574

1. Assassins 2. Fugitives 3. Murder 4. Wanderers and wandering 5. Short stories 6. Thrillers and suspense

The novella "Too Much Time" leads into Jack Reacher novel #22, The Midnight Line.

Includes excerpt for The midnight line.

A high-action anthology of Jack Reacher stories includes a previously unseen novella and 11 other stories collected for the first time in print, in a volume that complements each story with an original author introduction.

Child, Lee

Nothing to lose / Lee Child. Delacorte Press, 2008. 432 p. Jack Reacher novels

ISBN 9780385340564

1. Former military police 2. Conspiracies 3. Missing persons 4. Police 5. Mercenaries 6. Secrets 7. International relations 8. Colorado 9. Thrillers and suspense

LC 2007043735

Sequel to: Bad luck and trouble.

Arriving in the small town of Despair, Colorado, Jack Reacher finds himself taking on an entire town as he searches for the truths behind its sinister connection to a brutal war that is killing Americans thousands of miles away.

"With his powerful sense of justice, dogged determination and the physical and mental skills to overcome what to most would be overwhelming odds, Jack Reacher makes an irresistible modern knight-errant." Publishers Weekly.

Child, Lee

One shot : a Jack Reacher novel / Lee Child. Delacorte Press, 2005. 376 p. Jack Reacher novels

ISBN 9780385336680

1. Former military police 2. Serial murders 3. Frameups 4. Snipers 5. Women defense attorneys 6. Men with amnesia 7. Serial murder investigation 8. Manipulation (Social sciences) 9. Indiana 10. Middle West 11. Thrillers and suspense

LC 2004058246

This book made into a movie called Jack Reacher, starring Tom Cruise and directed by Christopher McQuarrie.

Ex-military investigator Jack Reacher is called in by James Barr, a man accused of a lethal sniper attack that leaves five people dead, and teams up with a young defense attorney to find an unseen enemy who is manipulating events.

"Mr. Child's idea of heroism has nihilism around the edges but a fierce, fighting spirit at its core. In marked contrast to the brooding figures who otherwise dominate contemporary detective stories, Reacher is not one for self-doubt. His is a two-fisted decency. But Mr. Child also gives him amazing powers of deduction, a serious conscience and the occasional touch of tenderness. It's a wildly improbable mixture, one that can't be beat." New York Times.

Child, Lee

* **Past** tense / Lee Child. Delacorte Press, 2018. 400 p. Jack Reacher novels

ISBN 9780399593512

1. Fathers and sons 2. Family secrets 3. Deception 4. Canadians in the United States 5. Small towns 6. Veterans 7. Thrillers and suspense

LC 2018022559

Detouring to his father's childhood hometown at the beginning of a cross-country hitchhiking tour, Jack uncovers disturbing family revelations at the same time he becomes entangled in a dangerous high-ticket sale.

"Another first-class entry in a series that continues to set the gold standard for aspiring thriller authors." Booklist.

Child, Lee

Personal : a Jack Reacher novel / Lee Child. Random House, 2014. 416 p. Jack Reacher novels

ISBN 9780804178747

1. Assassins 2. Snipers 3. Organized crime 4. Politicians 5. Fugitives 6. Murder investigation 7. Murder 8. Thrillers and suspense

Jack Reacher finds himself working for the State Department and the CIA to track down the American sniper who took a shot at the president of France and is possibly targeting the G-8 summit packed with world leaders.

"Child sets up a thriller premise better than anybody, expertly mixing gun talk, trivia, and tension and, when the time comes, detailing the bloodletting with the care of a connoisseur." Booklist.

Child, Lee

Persuader : a Jack Reacher novel / Lee Child. Delacorte Press, 2003. 352 p. Jack Reacher novels

ISBN 0385336667

1. Former military police 2. Drug traffic 3. Missing persons 4. Government investigators 5. Enemies 6. Drug enforcement agents 7. Women drug enforcement agents 8. Drug dealers 9. Boston, Massachusetts 10. Maine 11. Thrillers and suspense

LC 2002034965

Jack Reacher takes an undercover assignment to investigate the disappearance of a federal agent from the home of a notorious drug dealer, but Reacher soon discovers that the dealer has ties to a man from Reacher's own past.

"What makes the novel really zing, though, is Reacher's narration--a unique mix of the brainy and the brutal, of strategic thinking and explosive action, moral rumination and ruthless force, marking him as one of the most memorable heroes in contemporary thrillerdom." Publishers Weekly.

Child, Lee

A **wanted** man : a Reacher novel / Lee Child. Delacorte Press, 2012. 416 p. Jack Reacher novels

ISBN 9780385344333

1. Former military police 2. Conspiracies 3. Murder investigation 4. Murder 5. Stabbing victims 6. FBI agents 7. Hitchhiking 8. Chicago, Illinois 9. Thrillers and suspense

LC 2012018420

British Book Award for Crime Thriller of the Year, 2012.

Hitching a ride to Virginia in a car with three strangers, Jack Reacher finds himself unwittingly involved in a massive conspiracy that makes him a threat.

Child, Lee

Without fail / Lee Child. G.P. Putnam's Sons, 2002. 374 p. Jack Reacher novels

ISBN 0399148612

1. Former military police 2. Assassination plots 3. Women vice-presidents 4. Assassins 5. Secret service 6. Washington, D.C. 7. Thrillers and suspense

LC 2001048849

Jack Reacher is hired to attempt to assassinate the Vice President of the United States to ensure that his security team is up to scratch, but in the meantime there is a very real and deadly team of assassins that has just put the VP in their sights.

"This novel is a stunner, packed with extraordinary detail regarding executive protection and overlaid with a genuine mystery that will baffle even the most astute armchair crime buffs." Booklist.

Child, Lee

Worth dying for : a Reacher novel / Lee Child. Delacorte Press, 2010. 416 p. Jack Reacher novels

ISBN 9780385344319

1. Cold cases (Criminal investigation) 2. Secrets 3. Criminals 4. Former military police 5. Missing children 6. Nebraska 7. Thrillers and suspense

LC 2010023100

Jack Reacher clashes with an organized crime family that is terrorizing Nebraska corn country in their efforts to supply dangerous international customers, a battle that is complicated by the unsolved case of a missing child.

"Crisp, efficient prose and well-rounded characterizations (at least of the guys in the white hats) raise this beyond other attempts to translate the pulse-pounding feel of the Die Hard films into prose." Publishers Weekly.

Child, Lincoln

Deep storm : a novel / Lincoln Child. Doubleday, 2006. 384 p. Jeremy Logan novels

ISBN 0385515502

1. Research institutes 2. Sick persons 3. Undercover operations 4. Atlantis (Legendary place) 5. Scientists 6. Physicians 7. Excavations (Archaeology) 8. Underwater archaeology 9. Secrets 10. Atlantic Ocean 11. Thrillers and suspense

LC 2006021093

Summoned to a remote oil rig to diagnose a strange medical ailment among the rig workers, ex-Navy physician Peter Crane soon discovers that the condition is linked to the underwater excavation being done at science research station Deep Storm.

"The prose may be a tad rough, but the story is imaginative and filled with wonder." Booklist.

Child, Lincoln

Full wolf moon / Lincoln Child. Random House Inc., 2017. 368 p. Jeremy Logan novels

ISBN 9780385531429

1. Paranormal phenomena investigation 2. Private investigators 3. Writers' retreats 4. Hikers 5. Scientists 6. Murder suspects 7. Murder investigation 8. Werewolves 9. Adirondack Mountains, New York 10. Thrillers and suspense

Traveling to an isolated writers' retreat deep in the Adirondacks, Jeremy Logan, an investigator who specializes in unexplained phenomena, discovers a dead hiker whose wounds suggest an unnatural attack before encountering numerous suspects and a woman scientist struggling with the death of her father.

Childress, Mark

Crazy in Alabama Ballantine Books, 1993. 383 p.
ISBN 9780345389244
1. 1960s 2. Orphans 3. Twelve-year-old boys 4. Racism 5. Eccentric women 6. Alabama 7. Hollywood, California 8. Coming-of-age stories

LC 92038334

In Alabama during the racially restless summer of 1965, an orphan boy comes of age, and his aunt escapes from an unhappy marriage.

"It is a measure of Mr. Childress's skill as a novelist---not to mention a triumphant example of style over content--that he soon had me eating out of his hand. I don't know how he did it but he managed to confront every clich, every convention of the genre head on and pound it into submission, so that his novel seems not only fresh and original but also positively inspired." New York Times Book Review.

Childress, Mark

One Mississippi : a novel / Mark Childress. Little, Brown and Co., 2006. 400 p.
ISBN 0316012114
1. 1970s 2. High school students 3. Small town life 4. Misfits (Persons) 5. Teenage boys -- Friendship 6. Sixteen-year-old boys 7. Violence in teenagers 8. Identity (Psychology) 9. Traffic accidents 10. Race relations 11. New students 12. Secrets 13. Mississippi -- History -- 20th century 14. Southern fiction 15. Coming-of-age stories

LC 2006002337

Struggling with his outsider status after moving to a small Mississippi town at the beginning of his junior year, 1970s teen Daniel Musgrove befriends fellow misfit Tim and becomes embroiled in a devastating chain of events following a car accident.

"The book climaxes in a Columbine-like scene wherein Tim goes berserk with rifles in the school and Daniel attempts to act heroically but is not enough of a hero to save his two closest friends. Serious issues of race, identity, and loyalty are raised, and tragic and violent events occur, but the author retains a surprisingly light touch in this highly engaging read." Library Journal.

Childs, Laura

Lavender blue murder / Laura Childs. Berkley Prime Crime, 2020. 336 p. Tea Shop mysteries (Laura Childs)
ISBN 9780451489661
1. Tearooms 2. Women shopkeepers 3. Hunting 4. Women amateur detectives 5. Murder 6. Arson 7. Murder investigation 8. Money 9. Friendship 10. Couples 11. South Carolina 12. Cozy mysteries 13. Gentle reads 14. Culinary mysteries

LC 2019043266

Attending a traditional English bird hunt, tea-maven Theodosia Browning and her sommelier, Drayton Conneley, stumble on the wounded body of their host before suspicious accidents prompt the organization of a seance to expose the culprit.

"Genteel Southern charm and murderous mayhem mix in a mystery that keeps you guessing." Kirkus.

Chizmar, Richard T.

A **long** December / Richard Chizmar. Subterranean Press, 2016. 519 p.
ISBN 9781596067936
1. Neighbors 2. Secrets 3. Deception 4. Serial murderers 5. Family relationships 6. Suspicion 7. Horror 8. Psychological suspense 9. Short stories

"Chizmar's stories are united by the feelings they produce--dread, anxiety, and suspense--but more remarkable is how they are presented with an underlying poignancy. ... his is a must-read for fans of intense tales where psychological suspense and horror overlap." Booklist.

Cho, Zen

Sorcerer to the crown / Zen Cho. Ace, 2015. 384 p. Sorcerer royal
ISBN 9780425283370
1. 19th century 2. Wizards 3. Class conflict 4. Racism 5. Universities and colleges 6. Freed slaves 7. Slavery 8. Sexism 9. Magic 10. England -- Social conditions -- 19th century 11. Historical fantasy 12. Fantasy fiction

LC 2015007899

Amelia Bloomer List, 2017
RUSA Reading List Short List, 2016.

Born a slave, Zacharias Wythe has just been appointed England's new Sorcerer Royal -- much to the dismay of the socially conservative Royal Society of Unnatural Philosophers, who are already plotting to oust him from his post. But Zacharias has more urgent problems, including a dwindling national supply of magic and strained diplomatic relations with the Faerie realm. Unexpected assistance arrives in the form of fellow outsider Prunella Gentlewoman, an orphaned witch of uncertain origins and immense power. -- Description by Gillian Speace.

"Cho's entertaining, fantastical debut brings past and current issues of diversity and social class to light with charm, wit, and magic." Booklist.

Choi, Ann Y. K.

Kay's lucky coin variety / Ann Choi. Touchstone Books, 2016. 276 p.
ISBN 9781476748054
1. 1980s 2. Families 3. Family relationships 4. Girls 5. Koreans 6. Growing up 7. Mate selection 8. Deception 9. Toronto, Ontario 10. Canada 11. Coming-of-age stories

Mary, a Korean girl growing up with her brother above her parents' convenience store in 1980s Toronto, is caught between the traditional culture of her parents and her desire to be a Canadian.

Choi, Susan, 1969-

My education / Susan Choi. Viking, 2013. 304 p.
ISBN 9780670024902
1. Graduate students 2. College teachers 3. Love triangles 4. Husband and wife 5. Marital conflict 6. Sexuality 7. Homosexuality 8. Lesbianism 9. Errors 10. Lust 11. Psychological fiction 12. LGBTQIA fiction

LC 2013001605

Lambda Literary Award for Bisexual Fiction

Warned about the womanizing activities of Professor Nicholas Brodeur before her arrival at his prestigious university, graduate student Regina Gottlieb is nevertheless captured by his charisma and good looks before falling prey to his volatile wife.

"Choi's talent resides in her densely layered prose and her slowing down the pace to draw readers into the inner worlds of her characters. The result is a deeply human tale of intentional mistakes, love and lust, and the search for a clearer vision of one's self." Library Journal.

Choi, Susan, 1969-

* **Trust** exercise : a novel / Susan Choi. Henry Holt and Company, 2019. 272 p.
ISBN 9781250309884
1. Teenage romance 2. Teacher-student relationships 3. Performing arts schools 4. Theater 5. Theater and teenagers 6. Reunions 7. Teenage boy/girl relations 8. Sexual ethics for teenagers 9. Sexuality 10. Teenagers -- Sexuality 11. Acting teachers 12. Southern States

13. Literary fiction

LC 2018032027

ALA Notable Book, 2020.

National Book Award for Fiction, 2019.

Falling in love while attending a competitive 1980s performing arts high school, David and Sarah rise through the ranks before the realities of their family dynamics and economic statuses trigger a spiral that impacts their adult lives.

"Fiercely intelligent, impeccably written, and observed with searing insight, this novel is destined to be a classic." Publishers Weekly.

Choo, Yangsze

The **ghost** bride : a novel / Yangsze Choo. William Morrow, 2013. 362 p.

ISBN 9780062227324

1. 1890s 2. Life after death 3. Ghosts 4. Dead 5. Marriage 6. Poor women 7. Chinese in Malaysia 8. Men/women relations 9. Malaysia 10. Historical fantasy 11. Asian-influenced fantasy

LC 2013000727

Although Malacca, Malaya's diverse but declining trading port, has endured Portuguese, Dutch, and finally British rule, local traditions persist. To rescue her once-affluent family from poverty, Li Lan agrees to become the ghost bride of Lim Tian Ching, the deceased son of one of the city's wealthiest families. Though dead, Li Lan's bridegroom makes his presence known, visiting her in dreams while hinting that his was an untimely demise. Now, guided by spirits, Li Lan must undertake a journey into the afterlife to discover the truth. - Description by Gillian Speace.

"Choo's clear and charming style creates an alternate reality where the stakes are just as high as in the real world, combining grounded period storytelling with the supernatural." Publishers Weekly.

Choo, Yangsze

* The **night** tiger : a novel / Yangsze Choo. Flatiron Books, 2019. 352 p.

ISBN 9781250175458

1. 1930s 2. Colonialism 3. Superstition 4. Social classes 5. Underclass 6. Shapeshifting 7. Death 8. Identity (Psychology) 9. Malaysia 10. Asian-influenced fantasy 11. Historical fantasy

LC 2018030163

A vivacious dance-hall girl in 1930s colonial Malaysia is drawn into unexpected danger by the discovery of a severed finger that is being sought by a young houseboy who would protect his late master's soul.

"Mythical creatures, conversations with the dead, lucky numbers, Confucian virtues, and forbidden love provide the backdrop for Choos superb murder mystery." Publishers Weekly.

Christie, Agatha, 1890-1976

* The **A** B C murders / Agatha Christie. Dodd, Mead, 1977, c1936. 250 p. Hercule Poirot mysteries

ISBN 9781579126247

1. Serial murders 2. Murder investigation 3. Murderers 4. Letter writing 5. Senior men 6. Private investigators 7. Belgians in England 8. Mysteries

Also published under the title: The alphabet murders.

Originally published in the UK in 1936.

A is for Ascher, cudgeled in Andover. B is for Barnard, strangled in Bexhill. C is for Clarke, struck down in Churston. Beside each body is an A.B.C. Railway guide; before each murder Hercule Poirot is notified. In one of Christie's most twisted tales, the meticulous Belgian sleuth must navigate the eerie maze of a serial killer's mind. D is for Doncaster, where the next victim dies... E is for evidence, ingeniously analyzed.

Christie, Agatha, 1890-1976

* And **then** there were none / Agatha Christie. St. Martin's Griffin, 2004, c1939. 264 p.

ISBN 0312330871

1. Murder victims 2. Millionaires 3. Islands 4. Secrets 5. Strangers 6. Resorts 7. England 8. Devon, England 9. Mysteries

LC 2004041165

Also published as: Ten little Indians.

Book made into a movie called Ten little Indians.

Originally published: New York : Dodd, Mead, 1940.

Ten houseguests, trapped on an isolated island, are the prey of a diabolical killer. A famous nursery rhyme is framed and hung in every room of the mansion: Ten little Indian boys went out to dine; One choked his little self and then there were nine--When they realize that murders are occurring as described in the rhyme, terror mounts. Who has choreographed this dastardly scheme? And who will be left to tell the tale?

Christie, Agatha, 1890-1976

The **body** in the library : a Miss Marple mystery / Agatha Christie. Black Dog & Leventhal Publishers, 2006, c1942. 198 p. Jane Marple murder mysteries

ISBN 9781579126261

1. Murder investigation 2. Senior women 3. Women amateur detectives 4. England 5. Mysteries

LC 2006045983

Originally published: London : Collins, 1942.

When Colonel and Mrs. Bantry find the corpse of a beautiful girl in their library, they rely upon their good friend Miss Marple to solve the crime.

Christie, Agatha, 1890-1976

* **Curtain** / Agatha Christie. Dodd, Mead, 1975. 238 p. Hercule Poirot mysteries

ISBN 9780396071914

1. Murder investigation 2. Murder suspects 3. Belgians in England 4. Senior men 5. Private investigators 6. England 7. Mysteries

LC 75016368

The house guests at Styles seemed perfectly pleasant to Captain Hastings: there was his own daughter Judith, an ornithologist called Norton, dashing Mr Allerton, brittle Miss Cole, Doctor Franklin and his fragile wife Barbara, Nurse Craven, Colonel Luttrell and his wife Daisy, and the charismatic Boyd-Carrington. So Hastings was shocked when Poirot declared that one of them was a five-times murderer. True, the ageing detective was crippled with arthritis, but had his deductive instincts finally deserted him?

Christie, Agatha, 1890-1976

Endless night / Agatha Christie. William Morrow & Co., 2011, c1967. 239 p.

ISBN 9780062073518

1. Rural life 2. Heirs and heiresses 3. Curses 4. Murder 5. Husband and wife 6. England 7. Mysteries

LC 85004390

Originally published: London : Collins Crime Club, 1967.

After marrying an American heiress and fulfilling his dream of building a home in his favorite area, Michael Rogers and his new wife's lives are plagued by a deadly curse that gypsies have placed on the land.

Christie, Agatha, 1890-1976

The **Hollow** / Agatha Christie. G. P. Putnam's Sons, 1992, c1946. 296 p. Hercule Poirot mysteries

ISBN 0399137270

1. Murder investigation 2. Senior men 3. Private investigators 4. Poisoning 5. Murder suspects 6. Belgians in England 7. Mysteries

Also published as: Murder after hours.

Originally published: [London] : Collins, 1946.

"Agatha Christie 125th anniversary 1890-2015" -- Cover.

A weekend party at the Angkatell's estate, The Hollow, is the perfect prescription for physician John Christow. The celebrated doctor longs for a little R & R and a rendezvous with his mistress, Henrietta. But romantic rivalry complicates the country escape as the doctor dodges both his wife and actress Veronica Cray. Famous crime man Hercule Poirot arrives to find Dr. Christow permanently extricated from his affairs by a revolver at close range.

Christie, Agatha, 1890-1976

Mrs. McGinty's Dead / Agatha Christie. G. P. Putnam's Sons, 1993, c1979. 259 p. Hercule Poirot mysteries

ISBN 0399138234

1. Murder investigation 2. Murder suspects 3. Household employees 4. Belgians in England 5. Senior men 6. Private investigators 7. Housekeepers 8. Mysteries

LC 92-32590

Also published as: Blood will tell.

Poirot pays no attention to the sad case of Mrs. McGinty, an old woman apparently struck dead by her lodger for thirty pounds that she kept under a floorboard. When, however, he is asked by the investigating officer to take another look at the case in order to stop an innocent man going to the gallows, he realizes that things may not be as simple as they first appear to be.

Christie, Agatha, 1890-1976

* The **Murder** at the Vicarage / Agatha Christie. Berkley, 1984, c1930. 230 p. Jane Marple murder mysteries

ISBN 9780425067901

1. Murder investigation 2. Murder suspects 3. Gunshot victims 4. Senior women 5. Women amateur detectives 6. Villages 7. England 8. Mysteries

Originally published: London : Collins Crime Club, 1930.

Miss Jane Marple, spinster sleuth extraordinaire, is introduced in this first mystery to feature her brilliant talents. Here she must use all her intuitive powers to solve the murder of the detested Colonel Protheroe when he is found shot in the local vicar's study.

Christie, Agatha, 1890-1976

A **murder** is announced : a Miss Marple mystery / Agatha Christie. Black Dog & Leventhal Publishers, 2006, c1950. 288 p. Jane Marple murder mysteries

ISBN 9781579126292

1. Senior women 2. Women amateur detectives 3. Gunshot victims 4. Murder investigation 5. Newspaper advertising 6. Murder suspects 7. England 8. Mysteries

LC 2006042978

Originally published: London: Collins, 1950.

A notice in the Gazette reads: "A murder is announced and will take place on Friday, October 29, at Little Paddocks." The guests arrive, thinking they have come to a mystery party. When death and chaos ensue, the indomitable Miss Marple sorts it out.

Christie, Agatha, 1890-1976

* The **murder** of Roger Ackroyd : a Hercule Poirot mystery / Agatha Christie. Black Dog & Leventhal, 2006, c1926. 276 p. Hercule Poirot mysteries

ISBN 9781579126278

1. Suicide 2. Extortion 3. Murder investigation 4. Murder suspects 5. Physicians 6. Senior men 7. Private investigators 8. Belgians in England 9. Mysteries

LC 2006042980

A murder in a small English village leads Hercule Poirot into a strange mystery involving a determined, curious spinster, the local doctor, and a wide range of suspects with possible motives and mysterious relationships.

"Roger Ackroyd, a retired business man, is found dead in his study shortly after the suicide of the woman he was to have married. Suspicion and the police point to Ackroyd's adopted son as the murderer, but the outcome of the story is a complete surprise. As in others of Miss Christie's tales, the mystery is solved by . . . M. Poirot." Booklist.

Christie, Agatha, 1890-1976

* **Murder** on the Orient Express / Agatha Christie. G. P. Putnam's Sons, 1960, c1934. 263 p. Hercule Poirot mysteries

ISBN 9780062838629

1. Crimes aboard trains 2. Railroad travel 3. Murder investigation 4. Belgians in England 5. Rich men 6. Orient Express (Train) 7. Senior men 8. Private investigators 9. Mysteries

"Originally published in the U. S. as Murder in the Calais coach."

Originally published: London : Collins, 1934.

On a three-day journey through the snowbound Balkan hills, Hercule Poirot must weed through an array of international suspects to find the passenger who murdered a gangster on the Orient Express.

Christie, Agatha, 1890-1976

* The **pale** horse / Agatha Christie. Dodd, Mead, 1985, c1961. 259 p.

ISBN 0396087051

1. Organized crime 2. Priests 3. Murder investigation 4. Murder suspects 5. Murder 6. England 7. Mysteries

LC 85004368

Book inspired 1996 TV movie with Colin Buchanan as Mark Easterbrook.

Mark Easterbrook investigates the brutal death of Father Gorman, a Catholic priest who had just heard the deathbed confession of longtime town gossip Mrs. Davis. On his body, Father Gorman had a list of names, supposedly related to Mrs. Davis' confession. As Mark delves deep into the mystery, he uncovers a series of startling secrets.

Christie, Agatha, 1890-1976

Three blind mice, and other stories / Agatha Christie. Dodd, Mead, 1985, c1948. 250 p., 20 cm. Jane Marple murder mysteries

ISBN 0396087078

1. Criminal investigation 2. Murder investigation 3. Senior women 4. Women amateur detectives 5. Mysteries 6. Short stories

LC 50003535

Also published under the title: Mousetrap and other stories.

A blinding snowstorm-and a homicidal maniac-traps a small party of friends in an isolated estate. Out of this deceptively simple setup, Agatha Christie fashioned one of her most ingenious puzzlers, which in turn would provide the basis for The Mousetrap.

Christie, Agatha, 1890-1976

Towards zero / Agatha Christie. Dodd, Mead, 1986, c1944 242 p. Superintendent Battle mysteries

ISBN 0396088724

1. Scotland Yard 2. Police 3. Widows 4. Suicide 5. Murder investigation 6. Mysteries

LC 86011494

Originally published: London : Collins Crime Club, 1944.

Reprint. Previously published: Philadelphia : Blakiston, 1944.

"A dashing tennis player named Neville Strange, his current stylish wife, his not-so-stylish ex-wife, plus a distant relative and a few others find their way to a house party. When a murder occurs, Superintendent Battle is nearby and called on to help solve the case. But is the information on hand enough to go by, or go the events leading to the murder begin years in the past?"--Publisher's website.

Christie, Michael, 1976-

* **Greenwood** : a novel / Michael Christie. Hogarth, 2020, c2019. 528 p.

ISBN 9781984822000

1. Lumber industry and trade 2. Trees 3. Forests 4. Family secrets 5. Family businesses 6. Inheritance and succession 7. Crime 8. Survival 9. Interpersonal relations 10. Families 11. Literary fiction 12. Family sagas

LC 2019026891

Originally published: Toronto : McClelland & Stewart, 2019.

A shining, intricate clockwork of a novel, Greenwood is a rain-soaked and sun-dappled story of the bonds and breaking points of money and love, wood and blood--and the hopeful, impossible task of growing toward the light.

"This superb family saga will satisfy fans of Richard Powers's The Overstory while offering a convincing vision of potential ecological destruction." Publishers Weekly.

Christopher, Andie J.

* **Not** the girl you marry / Andie J. Christopher. Berkley Jove, 2019. 336 p.

ISBN 9781984802682

1. Dating (Social customs) 2. Planners 3. Ambition in women 4. Journalists 5. Multiracial women 6. Deception 7. Interracial dating 8. Men/women relations 9. Interpersonal attraction 10. Romantic comedies 11. Contemporary romances

To prove to her boss that she's not scared of feelings, Hannah Mayfield decides Jack Nolan is the perfect man to date for a couple of weeks, but, unbeknownst to her, Jack has chosen her for an article called "How to Lose a Girl."

Chu, Wesley

The **lives** of tao / Wesley Chu. Angry Robot, 2013. 464 p. Lives of Tao

ISBN 9780857663290

1. Imaginary wars and battles 2. Space flight 3. Aliens (Humanoid) 4. Manipulation (Social sciences) 5. Family problems 6. Earth 7. Science fiction

When an alien civil war threatens the entire human race, IT technician Roen, who has a passenger in his brain, must train to become an agent.

"Imagine humans are not Earth's dominant species, and aliens live among us in plain sight. This is the conceit of Chu's hip, wise-cracking military SF debut." Publishers Weekly.

Chung, Catherine

The **tenth** muse : a novel / Catherine Chung. Ecco Press, 2019. 304 p.

ISBN 9780062574060

1. Women mathematicians 2. Identity (Psychology) 3. Family history 4. Women's role 5. Intellectuals 6. Mathematics 7. Hypothesis 8. Self-discovery 9. Interracial families 10. Secrets 11. World War II 12. Reminiscing in old age 13. Historical fiction 14. Mainstream fiction

Determined to conquer the Riemann hypothesis in the face of cultural discrimination against women intellectuals, a genius mathematician uncovers a mysterious theorem's unexpected World War II link to her family.

"A powerful and virtuosically researched story about the mysteries of the head and the heart." Kirkus.

Chung, Maxine Mei-Fung

The **eighth** girl / Maxine Mei-Fung Chung. William Morrow & Co,, 2020. 480 p.

ISBN 9780062931122

1. Dissociative identity disorder 2. Best friends 3. Women photojournalists 4. Psychiatrists 5. City life 6. Secrets 7. Human trafficking 8. Crime 9. Stripteasers 10. Psychotherapy 11. Men/women relations 12. London, England 13. Psychological suspense

A woman with multiple personality disorder finds her other selves becoming assets and vulnerabilities in her effort to rescue her friend, a worker at a London gentlemen's club who has uncovered a dangerous secret.

"Though extremely dark and disturbing, this psychological thriller, told in the voice of multiple unreliable narrators, is filled with surprises until the end, and is a fresh take on the suspense genre." Booklist.

Church, James, 1947-

Bamboo and blood : an Inspector O novel / James Church. Minotaur Books, 2008. 304 p. Inspector O novels

ISBN 9780312372910

1. International intrigue 2. Crimes against women 3. Political corruption 4. Intercontinental ballistic missiles 5. Conspiracies 6. Police 7. Winter 8. Betrayal 9. National security 10. Ballistic missiles 11. Detectives 12. Missiles 13. North Korea 14. Pakistan 15. Mysteries 16. Police procedurals

LC 2008030116

In a late 1990s North Korea, a younger Inspector O is working Pyongyang as the country's nuclear missile program begins to escalate and as the wife of a North Korean diplomat turns up dead in Pakistan under suspicious circumstances, but as Inspector O investigates, he discovers that the woman's death could lead to a larger conspiracy.

Church, James, 1947-

* A **corpse** in the Koryo / James Church. Thomas Dunne Books, 2006. 288 p. Inspector O novels

ISBN 0312352085

1. Police 2. Political corruption 3. Spies 4. Detectives 5. Totalitarianism 6. National security 7. Surveillance 8. Justice 9. North Korea 10. Asia 11. Mysteries 12. Police procedurals

LC 2006045471

A rebellious survivor of North Korea's brutal totalitarian regime, Inspector O, a state security officer, risks his life and career to solve a case that begins innocuously enough when he is asked to photograph a certain vehicle.

Church, James, 1947-

A **drop** of Chinese blood / James Church. Minotaur, 2012. 304 p. Inspector O novels

ISBN 9780312550639

1. Missing persons 2. International intrigue 3. Intelligence officers 4. Uncle and nephew 5. China 6. North Korea 7. Mysteries 8. Police procedurals

When clues link a beautiful woman's disappearance to a sensitive mission to deliver an agent across the North Korean border, Bing, a director of state security in a volatile region of China, receives reluctant help from his uncle, Inspector O, to navigate an increasingly complex investigation.

Church, James, 1947-

Hidden moon : an Inspector O novel / James Church. Thomas Dunne Books/St. Martin's Minotaur, 2007. 288 p. Inspector O novels

ISBN 9780312352097

1. Police 2. Bank robberies 3. Secrecy in government 4. International intrigue 5. Assassination 6. Bureaucracy 7. Totalitarianism 8. Justice 9. Detectives 10. Political corruption 11. North Korea 12. Asia 13. Mysteries 14. Police procedurals

LC 2007024593

Inspector O returns from a mission abroad, only to find himself investigating a bank robbery, the first ever in Pyongyang, in a case that is complicated by a host of suspects, all with their own agendas, and high-level political intrigue.

Ciotta, Beth

Her sky cowboy / Beth Ciotta. Signet Eclipse, 2012. 352 p. Glorious victorious Darcys

ISBN 9780451238474

1. 19th century 2. Airships 3. Interpersonal attraction 4. Reputation 5. Women mechanics 6. Cowboys 7. Men/women relations 8. Quests 9. Nobility 10. Conspiracies 11. Fathers -- Death 12. England 13. Steampunk

After her father dies, Amelia Darcy, to save the family reputation and fortune, must discover an invention of historical importance in honor of Queen Victoria's Golden Jubilee--a quest that takes a romantic turn when her kitecycle crashes into the airship of a scandalous dime novel hero.

Ciotta, Beth

His clockwork canary / Beth Ciotta. Penguin, 2013. 352 p. Glorious victorious Darcys

ISBN 9780451239990

1. 19th century 2. Airships 3. Interpersonal attraction 4. Reputation 5. Women mechanics 6. Cowboys 7. Men/women relations 8. Quests 9. Nobility 10. Conspiracies 11. Fathers -- Death 12. England 13. Steampunk

Simon Darcy works with sensationalist London reporter the Clockwork Canary, whom he loved and lost when he was younger, in order to find a time-travel engine and win Queen Victoria's contest to recover lost inventions.

Cisneros, Sandra

* The **house** on Mango Street / Sandra Cisneros. Alfred A. Knopf, 1984, c1991. 134 p.

ISBN 9780679433354

1. Home (Concept) 2. Mexican American girls 3. Growing up 4. Friendship 5. Family relationships 6. Mexican Americans -- Identity 7. Hispanic Americans 8. Poverty 9. Chicago, Illinois 10. Illinois 11. Coming-of-age stories 12. Novels in verse 13. Classics

LC 93043564

"Originally published, in somewhat different form, by Arte Publico Press in 1984. Reprinted by Vintage Books, a division of Random House, Inc., in 1991"--Title page verso.

For Esperanza, a young girl growing up in the Hispanic quarter of Chicago, life is an endless landscape of concrete and run-down tenements, and she tries to rise above the hopelessness.

"This is a composite of evocative snapshots that manages to passionately recreate the milieu of the poor quarters of Chicago." Commonwealth.

Clancy, Tom, 1947-2013

The **cardinal** of the Kremlin / Tom Clancy. G. P. Putnam's Sons, 1988. 543 p. Jack Ryan and John Clark novels

ISBN 9780399133459

1. CIA Soviet operations 2. Spies -- United States 3. International intrigue 4. Strategic defense initiative 5. Intelligence service -- United States 6. Elite operatives 7. Soviet Union 8. Spy fiction 9. Thrillers and suspense

LC 88005818

Jack Ryan, CIA analyst, must rescue Colonel Filitov, America's highest agent in the Kremlin, from the KGB as the race to build the first Star Wars missile defense system continues.

Clancy, Tom, 1947-2013

Clear and present danger / Tom Clancy G. P. Putnam's Sons, 1989. 656 p. Jack Ryan and John Clark novels

ISBN 9780399134401

1. FBI 2. Drug smugglers -- Colombia 3. Assassination 4. Intelligence service 5. Ambassadors -- United States 6. Drug lords -- Colombia 7. Elite operatives 8. United States -- Covert operations -- Colombia 9. Spy fiction 10. Techno-thrillers 11. Thrillers and suspense

LC 89010287

The assassinations of the U.S. ambassador and the visiting head of the F.B.I. by Colombian drug lords trigger a mysterious covert response and an investigation of U.S. and Colombian actions by Jack Ryan.

"Superior even to his descriptions of tools and techniques, however, is Clancy's analysis of the legal and moral problems of operating in a twilight zone, where the rules are ambiguous and an open society makes secrecy impossible." Publishers Weekly.

Clancy, Tom, 1947-2013

* The **hunt** for Red October / Tom Clancy. Naval Institute Press, 1984. 387 p. Jack Ryan and John Clark novels

ISBN 9780870212857

1. United States. Navy. 2. CIA 3. Submarines, Soviet 4. Nuclear submarines 5. Spies 6. Elite operatives 7. Atlantic Ocean 8. Thrillers and suspense 9. Techno-thrillers 10. Sea stories

LC 84016569

The Soviets' new ballistic-missile submarine is attempting to defect to the United States, but the Soviet Atlantic fleet has been ordered to find and destroy her at all costs. Can Red October reach the U.S. safely?

"Based on a true incident--the attempted defection of a Soviet destroyer in 1975--the plot concerns the defection of the Red October, a Soviet submarine carrying 26 Seahawk missiles able to destroy 200 cities. Russia's fleet is ordered to find and destroy the sub; the U.S. Navy wants to find it and get it to an American port. An 18-day, 4,000-mile hunt across the Atlantic ensues." Booklist.

LIST OF FICTIONAL WORKS

Clancy, Tom, 1947-2013
Patriot games / Tom Clancy. G. P. Putnam's Sons, 1987. 540 p. Jack Ryan and John Clark novels

ISBN 9780399132414

1. Diana,, Princess of Wales, 1961-1997 Attempted assassination 2. William,, Prince, Duke of Cambridge, 1982- Attempted assassination 3. Charles,, Prince of Wales, 1948- Attempted assassination 4. Irish Republican Army 5. CIA European operations 6. Terrorism 7. Military tactics 8. International intrigue 9. Revenge in men 10. Attempted assassination 11. Elite operatives 12. Thrillers and suspense 13. Techno-thrillers

LC 87006910

While vacationing in London, CIA analyst Jack Ryan saves the Prince and Princess of Wales from a terrorist attack and gains the gratitude of a nation and the enmity of its most dangerous men.

"On a visit with his wife and daughter in London, Ryan stumbles onto an attempt by a new Irish revolutionary group to kidnap the Prince and Princess of Wales and their eldest son. Using his Marine Corps training, Ryan saves the royals (which leads to several visits between the Ryans and the residents of Buckingham Palace), but Ryan becomes the target of the surviving terrorists." Publishers Weekly.

Clare, Alys
The **woman** who spoke to spirits / Alys Clare. Severn House, 2019. 234 p. World's End Bureau

ISBN 9780727888686

1. Victorian era (1837-1901) 2. 1880s 3. Women private investigators 4. Women psychics 5. Seances 6. Threat (Psychology) 7. Private investigators 8. Criminal investigation 9. Independence in women 10. Great Britain 11. London, England -- Social life and customs -- 19th century 12. Victorian mysteries 13. Historical mysteries

London, 1880. When accounts clerk Ernest Stibbins approaches the World's End investigation bureau with wild claims that his wife Albertina has been warned by her spirit guides that someone is out to harm her, the bureau's owner Lily Raynor and her new employee Felix Wilbraham are initially sceptical. How are the two private enquiry agents supposed to investigate threats from beyond the grave? But after she attends a seance at the Stibbins family home, Lily comes to realize that Albertina is in terrible danger. And very soon so too is Lily herself.

"A clever plot, two engaging sleuths, plenty of period ambience, and a satisfying ending make this a fine choice for all mystery collections." Booklist.

Clark, Clare
In the full light of the sun / Clare Clark. Houghton Mifflin Harcourt, 2019. 400 p.

ISBN 9780544147577

1. Between the Wars (1918-1939) 2. Art forgeries 3. Art dealers 4. City life 5. Nazism 6. Art 7. Deception 8. Interpersonal relations 9. Berlin, Germany -- History -- 1918-1945 10. Historical fiction

LC 2019001730

Traces the fortunes of three disparate Berliners who against a backdrop of rising Nazi power are caught up in an art scandal involving newly discovered van Goghs.

Clark, Georgia
The **bucket** list / Georgia Clark. Emily Bestler Books/ Atria, 2018. 343 p.

ISBN 9781501173028

1. Young women 2. Body image 3. Breast cancer -- Genetic aspects 4. Female friendship 5. Self-fulfillment in women 6. Forecasting 7. Application software 8. Clothing industry and trade 9. Lists 10. City life 11. Chick lit

LC 2017053609

A young woman with a bustling life discovers she carries the gene for breast cancer and decides to tick off items on a "boob bucket list" before a double mastectomy.

Clark, Marcia
Blood defense / Marcia Clark. Thomas & Mercer, 2016. 398 p. Samantha Brinkman novels

ISBN 9781503936195

1. Women lawyers 2. Trials (Murder) 3. Criminal law 4. Murder 5. Detectives 6. Mass media 7. Psychopaths 8. Secrets 9. Defense attorneys 10. Guilt (Law) 11. Los Angeles, California 12. Legal thrillers

Samantha Brinkman, an ambitious, hard-charging Los Angeles criminal defense attorney, is struggling to make a name for herself and to drag her fledgling practice into the big leagues. Sam lands a high-profile double-murder case in which one of the victims is a beloved TV star, and the defendant is a decorated veteran LAPD detective. It promises to be exactly the kind of media sensation that would establish her as a heavy hitter in the world of criminal law. Though Sam has doubts about his innocence, she and her two associates (her closest childhood friend and a brilliant ex-con) take the case. Notorious for living by her own rules and fearlessly breaking everyone else's, Samantha pulls out all the stops in her quest to uncover evidence that will clear the detective. But when a shocking secret at the core of the case shatters her personal world, Sam realizes that not only has her client been playing her, he might be one of the most dangerous sociopaths she's ever encountered.

Clark, Marcia
Final judgment / Marcia Clark. Thomas & Mercer, 2020. 416 p. Samantha Brinkman novels

ISBN 9781542091176

1. Couples 2. Women lawyers 3. Murder suspects 4. Businesspeople 5. Secrets 6. Defense attorneys 7. Murder 8. Men/women relations 9. Los Angeles, California 10. California 11. Legal thrillers

Breaking her personal rule about avoiding relationships when she falls for an ambitious entrepreneur, defense attorney Samantha Brinkman is challenged to prove her lover's innocence of murder when his alibi and past are thrown into question.

Clark, Martin, 1959-
The **Jezebel** remedy / Martin Clark. Knopf, 2015. 400 p.

ISBN 9780385353595

1. Lawyers 2. Husband and wife 3. Women murder victims 4. Conspiracies 5. Murder 6. Extramarital affairs 7. Marital conflict 8. Drug industry and trade 9. Ethics 10. Secrets 11. Virginia 12. Legal thrillers

When an unpopular local dies in a suspicious accident, the husband-and-wife legal team of Joe and Lisa Stone are entangled in a corporate conspiracy that threatens their lives and Lisa's desperate secret.

Clark, Martin, 1959-
The **substitution** order / Martin Clark. Alfred A. Knopf, 2019. 352 p.

ISBN 9780525656326

1. Law 2. Disbarred lawyers 3. Innocence (Law) 4. Swindlers and swindling 5. Life change events 6. Probation 7. Divorced men 8. Restaurants 9. Rural life 10. Virginia 11. Southern states 12. Legal thrillers

LC 2019003946

A disbarred attorney takes a job in a run-down sandwich shop before an offer by a gang of con artists challenges the extent of his legal savvy.

Clark, Mary Higgins, 1927-2020

Death wears a beauty mask and other stories / Mary Higgins Clark. Simon & Schuster, 2015. 224 p.

ISBN 9781501110993

1. 1970s 2. Fashion 3. Threat (Psychology) 4. Suspicion 5. Murder 6. New York City 7. Mysteries 8. Thrillers and suspense 9. Short stories

This collection of short stories by the "Queen of Suspense" features her first published short story, "Stowaway."

Clark, Mary Higgins, 1927-2020

* **I've** got my eyes on you / Mary Higgins Clark. Simon & Schuster, 2018. 246 p.

ISBN 9781501171680

1. Sisters 2. Drowning victims 3. Murder suspects 4. Families of murder victims 5. Murder 6. Secrets 7. Thrillers and suspense

When an 18-year-old girl is found murdered at the bottom of her family's pool, her older sister, a guidance counselor, rules out the chief suspects and teams up with the Prosecutor's Office to uncover the truth, unaware that doing so is putting her own life at risk.

Clark, Mary Higgins, 1927-2020

* **Kiss** the girls and make them cry / Mary Higgins Clark. Simon & Schuster, 2019. 384 p.

ISBN 9781501171703

1. Women journalists 2. Sexual violence victims 3. Violence in men 4. Rich men 5. Sex crimes 6. Businesspeople 7. Threat (Psychology) 8. Thrillers and suspense

Navigating traumatic memories of an assault in college, a journalist researching the #MeToo movement discovers that her attacker is on the cusp of a merger that will render him a billionaire.

Clark, Mary Higgins, 1927-2020

The **melody** lingers on / Mary Higgins Clark. Simon & Schuster, 2015 320 p.

ISBN 9781476749112

1. Rich families 2. Family secrets 3. Cold cases (Criminal investigation) 4. Staged deaths 5. Suspicion 6. Grandmothers 7. Greed 8. Murder 9. Thrillers and suspense

When interior designer Lane Harmon assists in redecorating the home of the wife of missing disgraced financier Parker Bennett, she finds herself drawn to Bennett's family without realizing that her life is in jeopardy.

Clark, Mary Higgins, 1927-2020

My gal Sunday / Mary Higgins Clark. Simon & Schuster, 1996. 244 p. Henry and Sunday mysteries

ISBN 9780684832296

1. United States. Congress. House 2. Husband-and-wife detectives 3. Murder investigation 4. Criminal investigation 5. Women legislators 6. Murder 7. Former presidents 8. Amateur detectives 9. Women amateur detectives 10. Washington, D.C. 11. Short stories 12. Mysteries

Four stories on Henry and Sandra Britland, husband-and-wife team of sleuths, he a former U.S. president, she a former congresswoman.

"Clark uses every occasion to celebrate her gorgeous newlyweds' delirious happiness and misses no opportunity to cater to those readers who favor a little romance with their mild suspense." Publishers Weekly.

Clark, P. Djeli

The **black** god's drums / P. Djeli Clark. Tor/Forge, 2018. 112 p.

ISBN 9781250294715

1. 1870s 2. Pirates 3. Airships 4. Civil war 5. Weapons 6. Spirits 7. City life 8. New Orleans, Louisiana 9. Steampunk 10. Alternative histories

In an alternate New Orleans caught in the tangle of the American Civil War, the wall-scaling girl named Creeper yearns to escape the streets for the air--in particular, by earning a spot on-board the airship Midnight Robber. Creeper plans to earn the captain's trust with information she discovers about a Haitian scientist and a mysterious weapon he calls The Black God's Drums.

Clark, Wahida

Honor thy thug / Wahida Clark. Cash Money Content, 2013 304 p. Thug novels

ISBN 9781936399390

1. Marital conflict 2. Sexuality 3. Drugs 4. Inner city 5. City life 6. African American women 7. African American criminals 8. Men/women relations 9. African American fiction 10. Urban fiction

Street Lit Book Award Medal: Adult Fiction, 2014

Four friends try to salvage their shattered relationship in the wake of murder, betrayal, and the machinations of a sophisticated and deadly Chinese crime organization.

Clark, Wahida

* **Justify** my thug : a novel / Wahida Clark. Cash Money Content, 2011. 273 p. Thug novels

ISBN 9781451617092

1. Marital conflict 2. Sexuality 3. Drugs 4. Inner city 5. City life 6. African American women 7. African American criminals 8. Men/women relations 9. African American fiction 10. Urban fiction

LC bl2011010649

Includes discussion questions.

In the latest novel of Clark's Thug series, Tasha and Trae try to overcome their troubles and make their marriage work. Meanwhile, Jaz is facing drama of her own.

Clark, Wahida

Payback ain't enough / Wahida Clark. Cash Money Content, 2012 336 p. Payback novels

ISBN 9781936399116

1. Drug traffic 2. Street life 3. Options, alternatives, choices 4. African American women -- Friendship 5. African Americans 6. Love triangles 7. Drug dealers 8. Detroit, Michigan 9. Urban fiction 10. African American fiction

Returns to the hip-hop scene of "Payback with Ya Life," where sexy, dangerous men and fashion-savvy, seductive women navigate psychologically complex games of power and intrigue.

Clark, Wahida

* **Payback** is a mutha / Wahida Clark. Dafina, 2006 227 p. Payback novels

ISBN 0758212534

1. African American women -- Friendship 2. Swindlers and swindling 3. Betrayal 4. Street life 5. Inner city 6. Sexuality 7. Extramarital affairs 8. Urban fiction 9. African American fiction

Sequel: Payback with ya life

Using sex to get cars, expensive clothes, and anything else she desires, Brianna, a spoiled and selfish hustler, must make a tough decision when one of her schemes goes too far and her best friend Shan is caught in the crossfire.

Clark, Wahida

Payback with ya life / Wahida Clark. Grand Central Pub., 2008. 336 p. Payback novels

ISBN 9780446178082

1. Drug traffic 2. Determination in men 3. Options, alternatives, choices 4. Pregnant women 5. African American women -- Friendship 6. Moving to a new city 7. Revenge 8. Brothers and sisters 9. Love triangles 10. Drug dealers 11. Street life 12. Detroit, Michigan 13. Urban fiction 14. African American fiction

LC 2007033395

Sequel to: Payback is a mutha.

A sequel to "Payback is a Mutha" finds a pregnant Shan relocating to Detroit in the aftermath of her best friend's suicide, struggling against a revenge-minded adversary targeting her brother, and witnessing turf wars affecting her brother's efforts to reclaim his position at the top of the drug game.

Clark, Wahida

* **Thug** lovin' / Wahida Clark. Grand Central Pub., 2009. 352 p. Thug novels

ISBN 9780446178099

1. Temptation 2. Drugs 3. Moving to a new state 4. Nightclub owners 5. African American women 6. Men/women relations 7. Street life 8. African American criminals 9. California 10. New York City 11. African American fiction 12. Urban fiction

LC 2008051427

Having relocated to sunny Los Angeles after the events of Thug Matrimony, Tasha and Trae manage a nightclub together and find their relationship further tested by a series of models, shady lawyers, and the temptations of big money.

Clark, Wahida

Thug matrimony / Wahida Clark. Dafina Books, 2007. vii, 277 p. Thug novels

ISBN 9780758212559

1. Weddings 2. Unwanted guests 3. African American women lawyers 4. Men/women relations 5. African American women 6. African American businesspeople 7. Street life 8. Inner city 9. New York City 10. African American fiction 11. Urban fiction

LC bl2007012913

When an unwanted guest from her soon-to-be husband's past crashes her wedding, Angel, finally finding Mr. Right in Kaylin, a former drug dealer turned record producer, realizes that she might never make it to the altar.

Clark, Wahida

Thugs and the women who love them / Wahida Clark. Black Print Pub., 2004. 210 p. Thug novels

ISBN 0972277110

1. Women physical therapists 2. Gangsters 3. Jealousy 4. African American women 5. Street life 6. Inner city 7. Drug abuse 8. Sexuality 9. Revenge 10. Pennsylvania 11. African American fiction 12. Urban fiction

Clark, Walter Van Tilburg, 1909-1971

The **ox-bow** incident / Walter Van Tilburg Clark ; introduction by Wallace Stegner. Modern Library, 2001. xix, 225 p.

ISBN 0375757023

1. Lynching 2. Mobs 3. Nevada 4. Westerns

LC 00064584

Originally published 1940.

The murder of a cowboy sends a vigilante group on a frenzied hunt to track down the killer.

Clarke, Arthur C. (Arthur Charles), 1917-2008

* **2001** : a space odyssey / Arthur C. Clarke New American Library, 1968. 221 p. Space Odyssey series

ISBN 0451457994

1. 21st century 2. Human/computer interaction 3. Artificial intelligence 4. Space exploration 5. Space vehicles 6. Astronauts 7. Space flight 8. Computers 9. Communication 10. Near future 11. Aliens 12. Alien artifacts 13. Saturn (Planet) 14. Moon 15. Hard science fiction 16. Science fiction

LC 68029754

Sequel: 2010: odyssey two.

"Based on a screenplay by Stanley Kubrick and Arthur C. Clarke."

Two astronauts find their journey into space and their very lives jeopardized by the jealousy of an extraordinary computer named Hal.

"By standing the universe on its head, the author makes us see the ordinary universe in a different light. . . . [This novel becomes] a complex allegory about the history of the world." The New Yorker.

Clarke, Arthur C. (Arthur Charles), 1917-2008

* **Childhood's** end / Arthur C. Clarke. Del Rey Impact, 2001, c1953. x, 240 p.

ISBN 9780345444059

1. Aliens (Non-humanoid) 2. Evolution 3. Children 4. Freedom 5. Space vehicles 6. Peace 7. Posthumanism 8. Hard science fiction 9. Science fiction

Originally published: New York : Harcourt, Brace & World, 1953.

The Overlords appeared suddenly over every city-intellectually, technologically, and militarily superior to humankind. Benevolent, they made few demands: unify earth, eliminate poverty, and end war. With little rebellion, humankind agreed, and a golden age began. But at what cost? With the advent of peace, man ceases to strive for creative greatness, and a malaise settles over the human race....

Clarke, Arthur C. (Arthur Charles), 1917-2008

* The **collected** stories of Arthur C. Clarke / Arthur C. Clarke. Tor, 2000. 966 p.

ISBN 0312878214

1. Alien artifacts 2. Anthologies 3. Science fiction 4. Short stories

Introduces readers to the author's shorter works, spanning his entire writing career, including "The Nine Billion Names of God," "Nemesis," "The Sentinel," and "The Songs of Distant Earth."

"Although most of these stories date from between 1946 and 1970, seven earlier tales, rescued from what would now be called fanzines, extend coverage back to 1937, and a few snippets stretch it toward the present. At least two dozen stories bear titles that are household words among sf readers. . . . The stories demonstrate Clarke's dazzling and unique combination of command of the language, scientific and other kinds of erudition, and inimitable wit." Booklist.

Clarke, Arthur C. (Arthur Charles), 1917-2008

Rendezvous with Rama / Arthur C. Clarke. Harcourt Brace Jovanovich, 1973. 243 p. Rama series

ISBN 9780151768356

1. 22nd century 2. Space vehicles 3. Astronauts 4. Space exploration 5. Rama (Imaginary space vehicle) 6. Aerospace technology 7. Aliens (Non-humanoid) 8. Alien artifacts 9. Hard science fiction 10. Science fiction

LC   73003497

Sequel: Rama II.

BSFA Award for Best Novel, 1973.

Hugo Award for Best Novel, 1974.

John W. Campbell Memorial Award for Best Science Fiction Novel, 1974.

Locus Award for Best Science Fiction Novel, 1974.

Nebula Award for Best Novel, 1973.

During the twenty-second century, a space probe's investigation of a mysterious, cylindrical asteroid brings man into contact with an extragalactic civilization.

"This work contains flights of prose where the language fairly purrs. And here too one finds the questioning and probing of man and his place in the cosmos that marks good fiction and good science fiction." Library Journal.

Clarke, Brock

An **arsonist's** guide to writers' homes in New England : a novel / Brock Clarke. Algonquin Books Of Chapel Hill, 2007. 320 p.

ISBN 9781565125513

1. Dickinson, Emily, 1830-1886 Homes and haunts Amherst, Massachusetts 2. Teenage arsonists 3. Accidental death 4. Former convicts 5. Authors, American -- 20th century -- Homes and haunts 6. Arsonists 7. Arson investigation 8. Frameups 9. Quests 10. New England 11. Black humor

LC 2006100732

ALA Notable Book, 2008.

Sam Pulsifer is determined to put his past behind him after serving a prison term for torching an American literary landmark and killing two people in the blaze, but when the homes of notable American writers begin to go up in smoke, his history makes him the prime suspect.

"This straight-faced, postmodern comedy scorches all things literary, from those moldy author museums to the excruciating question-and-answer sessions that follow public readings. There are no survivors here: women's book clubs, literary critics, Harry Potter fans, bookstores, English professors, memoir writers, librarians, Jane Smiley, even the author himself--they're all singed under Clarke's crisp wit." Washington Post Book World.

Clarke, Brock

The **price** of the haircut : stories / Brock Clarke. Workman Publishing, 2018. 224 p.

ISBN 9781616208172

1. Dysfunctional families 2. Race relations 3. Post-traumatic stress disorder 4. Marital conflict 5. Satirical fiction 6. Short stories

Using his trademark social satire, and taking readers on a wild ride of heart-wrenching insight and self-discovery, the acclaimed and original writer presents a new collection of stories that touch on such subjects as racial attitudes in contemporary America, PTSD, the fate of child actors and marital discord.

Clarke, Lucy, 1981-

A **single** breath : a novel / Lucy Clarke. Touchstone, 2014. 320 p.

ISBN 9781476750156

1. Widows 2. Bereavement 3. Deception 4. Midwives 5. Brothers 6. Interpersonal attraction 7. Family secrets 8. Men/women relations 9. Tasmania 10. Mainstream fiction

LC 2013035565

After her husband is swept out to sea, Eva decides to visit his estranged family to grieve, but when she arrives she discovers that her husband was not the man she thought she knew and finds herself falling for his brother, Saul.

Clarke, Maxine Beneba

* **Foreign** soil / Maxine Beneba-Clarke. Hachette Australia, 2014. 267 p.

ISBN 9780733632426

1. Race relations 2. Refugees 3. Racism -- Australia 4. Asylum, Right of 5. Immigration prisons 6. Melbourne, Victoria 7. Sydney, New South Wales 8. Australia 9. Short stories

LC 2013456466

First published in Australia and New Zealand in 2014.

Australian Book Industry Awards, Literary Fiction Book of the Year, 2015.

Shortlisted for the Stella Prize, 2015.

This book is a collection of stories : a desperate asylum seeker is pacing the hallways of Sydney's notorious Villawood detention centre, a seven-year-old Sudanese boy has found solace in a patchwork bike, an enraged black militant is on the warpath through the rebel squats of 1960s Brixton, a Mississippi housewife decides to make the ultimate sacrifice to save her son from small-town ignorance, a young woman leaves rural Jamaica in search of her destiny, and a Sydney schoolgirl loses her way.

"Australian writer and poet Clarkes powerful debut collection of award-winning short stories addresses oppressed, downtrodden, and mistreated outsiders of society." Booklist.

Clarke, Susanna

* **Jonathan** Strange & Mr. Norrell / Susanna Clarke. Bloomsbury, 2004. 800 p.

ISBN 1582344167

1. Georgian era (1714-1837) 2. 19th century 3. Fairies 4. Magicians 5. Recluses 6. Men recluses 7. Aristocracy 8. Magic 9. Political science 10. Teacher-student relationships 11. Napoleonic Wars, 1800-1815 12. England -- History -- 19th century 13. London, England 14. York, England 15. Historical fantasy 16. Literary fiction

LC 2004002402

Book Sense Book of the Year Adult Fiction, 2005.

Hugo Award for Best Novel, 2005.

Locus Award for First Novel, 2005.

Mythopoeic Award for Adult Literature, 2005.

World Fantasy Award, 2005.

In nineteenth-century England, all is going well for rich, reclusive Mr. Norrell, who has regained some of the power of England's magicians from the past, until a rival magician, Jonathan Strange, appears and becomes Mr. Norrell's pupil.

"Clarke's ability to construct a fully imagined world--much of it explained in long, witty footnotes--is impressive." The New Yorker.

Clavell, James, 1924-1994

Shogun / James Clavell. Delacorte Press, 1975. 802 p. Asian saga

ISBN 9780689105654

1. Catholic Church Japan 2. Warlords -- Japan 3. Samurai 4. Honor 5. British in Japan 6. Pilots -- Japan 7. Japan -- History -- Period of Civil Wars, 1480-1603 8. Historical fiction

LC 82019788

Some copies include endpaper maps.

A bold English adventurer; an invincible Japanese warlord; a beautiful woman torn between two ways of life, two ways of love'all brought together in an extraordinary saga of a time and a place aflame with conflict, passion, ambition, lust, and the struggle for power.

"Clavell creates a world: people, customs, settings, needs and desires all become so enveloping that you forget who and where you are. 'Shogun' is history infused with fantasy. It strives for epic dimension and occasionally it approaches that elevated state. It's irresistible, maybe unforgettable." New York Times Book Review.

Clayborn, Kate

Love lettering / Kate Clayborn. Kensington Books, 2019. 320 p.

ISBN 9781496725172

1. Women designers 2. Women business owners 3. Lettering 4. Signs and symbols 5. Pattern perception 6. Inspiration 7. Self-acceptance 8. Sexual attraction 9. Men/women relations 10. City life 11. New York City 12. Romantic comedies

In this warm and witty romance from acclaimed author Kate Clayborn, one little word puts a woman's business - and her heart - in jeopardy . . .

"Reid and Meg are wonderfully unique, and their romance carves a sweet, winding, and sexy path to self-acceptance and mutual affirmation." Kirkus.

Clayton, Meg Waite

The **last** train to London / Meg Waite Clayton. Harper, 2019. 464 p.

ISBN 9780062946935

1. Wijsmuller-Meijer, Truus 2. Between the Wars (1918-1939) 3. 1930s 4. Second World War era (1939-1945) 5. Jewish teenagers 6. Christian women 7. Nazis 8. Anschluss movement, 1918-1938 9. Kindertransports (Rescue operations) 10. Anti-Nazi movement 11. Holocaust (1933-1945) 12. World War II -- Austria 13. Child refugees 14. World War II -- Underground movements 15. World War II -- Women 16. Austria 17. Vienna, Austria 18. Historical fiction

A tale inspired by the Kindertransports of World War II finds a Jewish teen's life shattered by the Nazi takeover before he joins a member of the Dutch resistance in a life-risking effort to escape Germany.

Cleage, Pearl

Some things I never thought I'd do / Pearl Cleage. One World/Ballantine Books, 2003. 256 p.

ISBN 0345456068

1. Recovering women drug abusers 2. Jilted brides 3. Aunt and niece 4. African-American motivational speakers 5. African American women 6. African American men/women relations 7. Visions 8. Reincarnation 9. Family estates 10. September 11 Terrorist Attacks, 2001 11. Paternity 12. Violence 13. Atlanta, Georgia 14. Washington, D.C. 15. Contemporary romances 16. African American fiction

LC 2003051752

Sequel: Baby Brother's Blues.

Taking a job in Atlanta to save the family home, Regina Burns finds herself unable to forgive her new employer for ruining her wedding plans years earlier and finds herself falling for a handsome stranger whom her aunt predicted she would meet.

Cleage, Pearl

What looks like crazy on an ordinary day : a novel / Pearl Cleage. Avon Books, 1997. 244 p.

ISBN 9780380975846

1. 1990s 2. African American women with HIV 3. Children of women cocaine addicts 4. Hairdressers 5. Homecomings 6. African American women 7. African American communities 8. African American sisters 9. African American widows 10. Small town life -- Michigan 11. Michigan 12. Idlewild, Michigan 13. Michigan 14. Women's lives and relationships 15. African American fiction 16. Mainstream fiction 17. Psychological fiction

LC 97-17708

Sequel: I Wish I Had a Red Dress

HIV-positive Ava Johnson returns to the Michigan town where she grew up, and finds that what she thought might be the end is, in fact, a beginning.

"Despite the early bad news, Cleage's funny, irreverent, and hopeful novel is stunningly real and evocative of the conditions behind the high unemployment, aimlessness, and drug culture that permeate the urban landscape and have invaded smaller towns as well." Booklist.

Cleary, Jon, 1917-2010

The **sundowners** / Jon Cleary. Collins, 1979, c1952. 320 p.

ISBN 9780002217798

1. 1920s 2. Fourteen-year-olds 3. Families -- Australia 4. Drifters 5. Growing up 6. Self-reliance 7. Temporary employees 8. Voyages and travels 9. Sheep shearers (Persons) 10. Wilderness areas -- Australia 11. Australia 12. Domestic fiction 13. Coming-of-age stories

Originally published: New York : Scribner's, 1952.

The epic tale of the outback Australian family, the Carmodys. The Carmodys live in the outback, travelling around, shearing, droving, making ends meet and looking for that one special place they can settle down in. Along the way, Paddy, his wife Ida, and their son, Sean, meet some of the most memorable characters in fiction. The Sundowners is a novel filled with kindness and happiness, as well as toughness and danger and is set against the magnificent backdrop of the wild, harsh and beautiful Australian landscape.

Cleave, Chris

* **Gold** / Chris Cleave. Simon & Schuster, 2012. 336 p.

ISBN 9781451672725

1. Female friendship -- Great Britain 2. Olympic games 3. Leukemia 4. Children with cancer 5. Women bicyclists 6. Friendship 7. Competition 8. Great Britain 9. Psychological fiction

LC 2011043699

"Originally published in Great Britain in 2012 by Hodder & Stoughton"--T.p. verso.

Sharing a close friendship and rivalry throughout their Elite training, world-class athletes Zoe and Kate find the limits of their physical and emotional realities tested on the eve of London 2012, where they consider difficult sacrifices and weigh their senses of mortality.

Cleave, Chris

Little Bee / Chris Cleave. Simon & Schuster, 2009, c2008. 271 p.

ISBN 9781416589631

1. Women refugees 2. Nigerians in England 3. Identity (Psychology)

4. Resilience (Personal quality) 5. Immigration and emigration 6. Deportation 7. Young women 8. London, England 9. Mainstream fiction

LC 2008030689

"Originally published in Great Britain in 2008 as The Other Hand, by Sceptre, an imprint of Hodder & Stoughton."

ALA Notable Book, 2010.

Presents a tale of a precarious friendship between an illegal Nigerian refugee and a recent widow from suburban London, a story told from the alternating and disparate perspectives of both women.

Cleave, Paul, 1974-

The **cleaner** : a thriller / Paul Cleave. Atria Books, 2012. 416 p. Christchurch novels

ISBN 9781451677799

1. Serial murders 2. Crimes against women 3. Copycat murderers 4. Serial murderers 5. Murder investigation 6. Police misconduct 7. Frameups 8. Police 9. New Zealand 10. Christchurch, New Zealand 11. Psychological suspense

LC 2012030312

Joe tries to take care of all the women in his life while investigating the copy cat killer who has emulated the Christchurch Carver.

Cleave, Paul, 1974-

Joe Victim : a thriller / Paul Cleave. Atria Books, 2013. 416 p. Christchurch novels

ISBN 9781451677973

1. Serial murderers 2. Death row prisoners 3. Television personalities 4. Capital punishment 5. Despair in men 6. Accomplices 7. Detectives 8. Psychics 9. Christchurch, New Zealand 10. New Zealand 11. Psychological suspense

LC 2013005568

Sequel to: The cleaner.

In this psycho-thriller the infamous serial killer known as the Christchurch Carver is serving time in prison and may face execution. He's also the target of sinister forces inside and outside the prison.

Cleave, Paul, 1974-

A **killer** harvest : a thriller / Paul Cleave. Atria Books, 2017. 386 p.

ISBN 9781501153013

1. Donation of organs, tissues, etc 2. Fathers and sons 3. Police 4. Eye 5. Secrets 6. Murderers 7. Teenage boys 8. Teenagers who are blind 9. Thrillers and suspense

LC 2016037791

A blind teen receives a corneal donation that restores his sight but gives him an eerie capacity to experience the memories of their previous owner, his homicide detective father.

"Starting with a macabre setup, Cleave keeps upping the stakes till any scrap of plausibility is left far behind and only an increasingly effective series of hair-raising thrills remains." Kirkus.

Cleave, Paul, 1974-

Trust no one : a thriller / Paul Cleave. Atria Books, 2015 336 p.

ISBN 9781476779171

1. Authors 2. People with Alzheimer's disease 3. Murder 4. Memory 5. Senior men 6. Reality 7. New Zealand 8. Psychological suspense

First published in New Zealand in 2015 by Upstart Press.

Ngaio Marsh Award for Best Crime Novel, 2016

Jerry Grey is known to most of the world by his crime writing pseudonym, Henry Cutter -- a name that has been keeping readers at the edge of their seats for more than a decade. His books tell stories of brutal murders and of victims finding the darkest forms of justice. Recently diagnosed with early onset Alzheimer's at the age of forty-nine, Jerry's crime writing days are coming to an end. As his dementia begins to break down the wall between his life and the lives of the characters he has created, Jerry confesses his worst secret: The stories are real.

Cleeton, Chanel

Next year in Havana / Chanel Cleeton. Berkley, 2018. 382 p.

ISBN 9780399586682

1. 1950s 2. Cuban American women 3. Family secrets 4. Communist countries 5. Men/women relations 6. Revolutionaries 7. Political persecution 8. Political intrigue 9. Miami, Florida 10. Havana, Cuba 11. Cuba 12. Historical fiction 13. Parallel narratives 14. Love stories

LC 2017027806

Characters from this novel also appear in the author's When we left Cuba.

A freelance writer returns to her grandmother's homeland to fulfill her last wish to have her ashes scattered in Havana and discovers her family history amidst Cuba's tropical beauty and dangerous political environment.

Cleeves, Ann

The **crow** trap / Ann Cleeves. Pan Books, 2010, c1999. 551 p. Vera Stanhope novels

ISBN 9781250122735

1. Women detectives 2. Murder investigation 3. Women murder victims 4. Environmental surveys 5. Betrayal 6. Secrets 7. Northumberland, England 8. Police procedurals 9. Mysteries

Originally published: London : Macmillan, 1999.

Three very different women come together to complete an environmental survey. Three women who, in some way or another, know the meaning of betrayal....For team leader Rachael Lambert the project is the perfect opportunity to rebuild her confidence after a double-betrayal by her lover and boss, Peter Kemp. Botanist Anne Preece, on the other hand, sees it as a chance to indulge in a little deception of her own. And then there is Grace Fulwell, a strange, uncommunicative young woman with plenty of her own secrets to hide... When Rachael arrives at the cottage, however, she is horrified to discover the body of her friend Bella Furness. Bella, it appears, has committed suicide--a verdict Rachael finds impossible to accept. Only when the next death occurs doesa fourth woman enter the picture--the unconventional Detective Inspector Vera Stanhope, who must piece together the truth from these women's tangled lives in The Crow Trap . Ann Cleeves's popular Vera Stanhope books have been made into the hit series "Vera" starring Brenda Blethyn and are available in the U.S.

Cleeves, Ann

The **long** call / Ann Cleeves. Minotaur Books, 2019. 400 p. Two rivers

ISBN 9781250204448

1. Detectives 2. Evangelists 3. Murder 4. Murder investigation 5. Missing women 6. People with Down syndrome 7. Sects 8. Gay husbands 9. Community centers 10. Secrets 11. Fathers -- Death 12. Men/men relations 13. England 14. Devon, England 15. Mysteries

LC 2019018211

When a man with a significant tattoo is found murdered in North Devon, Detective Matthew Venn is forced to return to the strict evangelical community of his childhood to uncover deadly secrets.

Cleeves, Ann

Raven black / Ann Cleeves. Macmillan, 2006. 375 p. Shetland mysteries

ISBN 1405054727

1. Teenage murder victims 2. Detectives 3. Secrets 4. Police 5. Death 6. Loners 7. Crimes against teenage girls 8. Winter 9. Murder 10. Strangling 11. Murder investigation 12. Suspicion 13. Small towns 14. Small town life 15. Islands 16. Shetland Islands -- Social life and customs 17. Scotland -- Social life and customs 18. Mysteries 19. Police procedurals

Duncan Lawrie Dagger, 2006.

When murder strikes a remote hamlet in the Shetland Islands, and the body of a teenage girl turns up in the winter snow, Inspector Jimmy Perez launches an investigation into the killing that takes him into the heart of sinister secrets from the past.

"Cleeves masterfully paints Perez as an empathetic hero and sprinkles the story with a lively cast of supporting characters who help bring the Shetlands alive." Publishers Weekly.

Cleeves, Ann

Thin air / Ann Cleeves. Minotaur Books, 2015. 400 p. Shetland mysteries

ISBN 9781250069948

1. Detectives 2. Small town life 3. Murder investigation 4. Secrets 5. Islands 6. Drowning 7. Cold cases (Criminal investigation) 8. Small towns 9. Scotland -- Social life and customs 10. Shetland Islands 11. Police procedurals

"Now a major BBC drama starring Douglas Henshall" -- Cover. TV tie-in.

When a woman mysteriously disappears, Detectives Jimmy Perez and Willow Reeves are assigned to the case and discover that the victim had an unhealthy and obsessive interest in a cold case involving the drowning of a local child, which just might have been the death of her.

"This nicely detailed procedural and rich character study pairs beautifully with Peter Mays Lewis trilogy." Booklist.

Cleeves, Ann

Wild fire / Ann Cleeves. Minotaur Books, 2018. 400 p. Shetland mysteries

ISBN 9781250124845

1. Resentfulness 2. Threat (Psychology) 3. Fame 4. Fashion designers 5. Lovers 6. Detectives 7. Unplanned pregnancy 8. Murder investigation 9. Families 10. Island life 11. Small town life 12. Scotland -- Social life and customs 13. Shetland Islands 14. Police procedurals 15. TV tie-ins

LC 2018013608

Series complete in 8 volumes.

Finds the Flemings' efforts to start over in a remote northern community challenged by local animosity and a series of anonymous threats.

"Throughout the Shetland Island series, Cleeves lovingly depicts the Scottish island life, and this volume is no exception. Fans may be saddened but certainly not disappointed by this final installment." Library Journal.

Clegg, Bill

* Did you ever have a family / Bill Clegg. Gallery Books, 2015. 304 p.

ISBN 9781476798172

1. Loss (Psychology) 2. Healing 3. Change (Psychology) 4. Grief in women 5. Death 6. Explosions 7. Automobile travel 8. Flashbacks 9. Secrets 10. Families 11. Interpersonal relations 12. Literary fiction

ALA Notable Book, 2016.

Surviving a disaster that kills everyone else in her family, June relocates West and settles into a directionless existence while other people impacted by the tragedy struggle with new circumstances.

"Clegg is both delicately lyrical and emotionally direct in this masterful novel, which strives to show how people make bearable what is unbearable, offering consolation in small but meaningful gestures." Booklist.

Clement, Jennifer

Gun love / Jennifer Clement. Hogarth Press, 2018. 288 p.

ISBN 9781524761684

1. Teenage girls 2. Mothers and daughters 3. Mobile home parks 4. Guns 5. Homeless families 6. Foster care 7. Growing up 8. Florida 9. Coming-of-age stories 10. Literary fiction

Growing up in the front seat of the car she shares with her mother in a lot beside a trailer park, Pearl suffers a terrible tragedy stemming from her mother's gun-toting boyfriend and is forced to survive on her own as she comes of age.

Clement, Jennifer

Prayers for the stolen / Jennifer Clement. Hogarth Press, 2014. 224 p.

ISBN 9780804138789

1. Drug traffic 2. Violence 3. Gangs 4. Mothers and daughters 5. Alcoholic women 6. Women prisoners 7. Villages -- Mexico 8. Mexico 9. Literary fiction 10. Psychological fiction

Originally published: London : Hogarth, 2014.

Born in a rural Mexico region where girls are disguised as boys to avoid the attentions of traffickers, Ladydi dreams of a better life before moving to Mexico City, where she falls in love and ends up in a prison with other women who share her experiences.

"Clements deft first-person narrative style imbues authenticity to her depiction of a world turned upside down by drug cartels, police corruption, and American exploitation." Booklist.

Clements, Rory

Martyr / Rory Clements. Bantam Books, 2009. 400 p. John Shakespeare series

ISBN 9780385342827

1. Shakespeare, John, died 1601 2. Drake, Francis,, Sir, 1540?-1596 Assassination attempts 3. Elizabethan era (1558-1603) 4. 16th century 5. Tudor period (1485-1603) 6. Secret service 7. Conspiracies 8. Spies 9. Assassins 10. Murder 11. Women rulers 12. Great Britain -- History -- Elizabeth I, 1558-1603 13. Historical mysteries 14. Mysteries

LC 2008048057

The year is 1587. One of Queen Elizabeth's cousins is found murdered, her flesh marked with profane symbols. A plot to assassinate Sir Francis Drake, England's most famous sea warrior, is discovered. One man is charged with the desperate task of solving both cases: John Shakespeare.

Clements, Rory

Revenger / Rory Clements. John Murray, 2010. 436 p. John Shakespeare series

ISBN 9781848540835

1. Shakespeare, John, died 1601 2. Salisbury, Robert Cecil, Earl of, 1563-1612 3. Essex, Robert Devereux, Earl of, 1566-1601 4. Elizabethan era (1558-1603) 5. 16th century 6. Tudor period (1485-1603) 7. Intelligence officers 8. Courts and courtiers 9. Conspiracies 10. Colonists 11. Treason 12. Spies 13. Great Britain -- History -- Elizabeth I, 1558-1603 14. Great Britain -- Colonies -- North America 15. Historical mysteries 16. Mysteries

Ellis Peters Historical Dagger Award, 2010.

Clemmons, Zinzi

What we lose / Zinzi Clemmons. Viking Press, 2017. 192 p.

ISBN 9780735221710

1. Multiracial women 2. Belonging 3. Grief in women 4. Identity (Psychology) 5. Loss (Psychology) 6. Race relations 7. Young women 8. Motherhood 9. Families 10. Interpersonal relations 11. Philadelphia, Pennsylvania 12. Johannesburg, South Africa 13. Pennsylvania 14. South Africa 15. Literary fiction 16. African American fiction

Longlisted for the Andrew Carnegie Medal for Excellence in Fiction, 2018.

Raised in America, the multiracial daughter of a mother from Johannesburg struggles with her mother's terminal cancer and her own need to find love and a place to belong, quests shaped by losses, changes in her sense of identity and unexpected motherhood.

"A compelling exploration of race, migration, and womanhood in contemporary America." Kirkus.

Cleveland, Karen

Keep you close : a novel / Karen Cleveland. Ballantine Books, 2019 240 p.

ISBN 9781524797058

1. Single mothers 2. Mothers and sons 3. Domestic terrorism 4. Suspicion 5. FBI agents 6. Conspiracies 7. Innocence (Law) 8. Political intrigue 9. Women FBI agents 10. Parent and teenager 11. Terrorism -- Prevention 12. Political thrillers 13. Thrillers and suspense

LC 2018059380

The mother of a much-loved son on the brink of college discovers a hidden gun in the teen's room before an FBI domestic-terrorism squad arrives, challenging her to confront disturbing secrets and the limits of her own protectiveness.

Clinch, Jon

Finn : a novel / Jon Clinch. Random House, 2007. 320 p.
ISBN 1400065917

1. Fathers and sons 2. Brothers 3. Runaway children 4. Fugitive slaves 5. Women slaves 6. Male friendship 7. Race relations 8. Boys 9. Paternity 10. Dead 11. Murder 12. Mississippi River 13. Missouri 14. Adaptations, retellings, and spin-offs 15. Adventure stories 16. Coming-of-age stories 17. Literary fiction

LC 2006045802

ALA Notable Book, 2008.

A novel inspired by Mark Twain's classic tales explores the mysterious life and strange death of Huckleberry Finn's infamous father, describing Finn's fearsome father, the Judge; his brother, the sickly, sycophantic Will; and young Huck.

"Shocking and charming. Clinch creates a folk-art masterpiece that will delight, beguile and entertain as it does justice to its predecessor. . . . In Finn, Clinch expands the bloodlines and scope of the original story and casts new light on the troubled legacy of our country's infamous past." The New York Post.

Clinch, Jon

Marley : a novel / Jon Clinch. Atria Books, 2019. 288 p.
ISBN 9781982129705

1. 19th century 2. Extortion 3. Deception 4. Ambition in men 5. Greed 6. Slave trade 7. Business partners 8. Betrayal 9. City life 10. London, England 11. England -- History -- 19th century 12. Adaptations, retellings, and spin-offs 13. Historical fiction

LC 2019275079

A reimagining of Charles Dickens? classic A Christmas Carol that explores the twisted relationship between Ebenezer Scrooge and Jacob Marley.

Cline, Emma

The girls : a novel / Emma Cline. Random House, 2016. 368 p.

ISBN 9780812998603

1. 1960s 2. Teenage girls 3. Communes 4. Counterculture 5. Obsession 6. Social acceptance 7. Belonging 8. Self-esteem 9. Interpersonal relations 10. California 11. Psychological fiction 12. Coming-of-age stories

LC 2015012714

Shirley Jackson Awards, Novel, 2016.

Mesmerized by a band of girls in the park she perceives as enjoying a life of free and careless abandon, 1960s teen Evie Boyd becomes obsessed with gaining acceptance into their circle, only to find herself drawn into a cult and seduced by its charismatic leader.

"Cline pushes past the myths, vividly imagining how the darkness crept in and turned a group of idealistic young adults into cold-blooded killers. In her impressive debut, Cline illuminates the darkest truths of a girls coming-of-age, telling a story that is familiar on multiple levels in a unique and compelling way." Booklist.

Cline, Ernest

Ready player one : a novel / Ernest Cline. Crown Publishers, 2011. 352 p.

ISBN 9780307887436

1. 21st century 2. Virtual reality 3. Quests 4. Near future 5. Inheritance and succession 6. Teenage boys 7. Dystopias 8. Puzzles 9. Avatars (Virtual reality) 10. Social networks 11. Locks and keys 12. Geeks (Computer enthusiasts) 13. Popular culture -- History -- 1970-1979 14. Regression (Civilization) 15. Science fiction 16. Coming-of-age stories

LC 2011015247

Nutmeg Children's Book Award, High School category, 2016.

Immersing himself in a mid-twenty-first-century technological virtual utopia to escape an ugly real world of famine, poverty, and disease, Wade Watts joins an increasingly violent effort to solve a series of puzzles by the virtual world's creator.

"Cultural items from VH1's I Love the 80's series and early G4 programming like Icons or Portal cover a basic swath of the material, but Monty Python, John Hughes, Dungeons & Dragons, WarGames, Blade Runner, Pac-Man, Rush, and infinitely more highly regarded geek cultural touchstones appear both as delightful inclusions and ingenious plot devices. Ready Player One lends itself easily to mash-up comparisons, since in its more complicated passages, it amounts to long strings of cultural references pumped through well-worn story arcs. The adventure comedy of Mike Judge's Idiocracy meets South Park's Imaginationland with a dash of Willy Wonka, except all of the cynicism has been replaced by sheer geeky love." A.V. Club.

Cline, Rachel, 1957-

* **My** liar : a novel / Rachel Cline. Random House, 2008. 274 p.

ISBN 9781400062270

1. Women film editors 2. Women film producers and directors 3. Female friendship 4. Film industry and trade 5. Entertainment industry and trade 6. Identity (Psychology) 7. Gender identity 8. Gender role 9. Men/women relations 10. Power (Social sciences)

11. Domestic fiction

LC 2007019601

Working together on a film, two women--Annabeth Jensen, a film editor who prefers to work by herself, and Laura Katz, a sociable and seductive director--form an intense friendship in which both women use each other in ways they do not understand.

Coady, Lynn, 1970-

The **antagonist** / Lynn Coady. House of Anansi Press, 2011. 352 p.

ISBN 9780887842962

1. Misfits (Persons) 2. Fathers and sons 3. Self-hate in men 4. Dysfunctional families 5. College students 6. Memories 7. Violence 8. Family relationships 9. Literary fiction

Shortlisted for the Giller Prize, 2011

Due to his size, but against his true nature, Gordon Rankin ("Rank") has always been cast in the role of enforcer. After tragedy strikes, he disappears. Almost twenty years later, he discovers that an old friend has written a novel mirroring his life. The betrayal leads Rank to finally confront the tragedy he's been running from.

Coake, Christopher

You came back / Christopher Coake. Grand Central Pub., 2012. 432 p.

ISBN 9781455506705

1. Parent and child 2. Children -- Death 3. Grief 4. Loss (Psychology) 5. Families 6. Columbus, Ohio 7. Psychological fiction

Getting his life back together after the death of his young son, Brendan, and his divorce, Mark Fife is jolted when he receives a call from a woman who owns his old house and claims it is haunted by Brendan's ghost.

"A captivating page-turner that examines the mechanics of loss and the seductions of belief, this novel, with its combination of tragedy and hope, has an irresistible appeal, offering quite a ride while still delivering a cold dose of reality." Library Journal.

Coates, Ta-Nehisi

* The **water** dancer : a novel / Ta-Nehisi Coates. One World, 2019. 432 p.

ISBN 9780399590597

1. Antebellum America (1820-1861) 2. Boy slaves 3. Escapes 4. Underground Railroad 5. Slave families 6. Loss (Psychology) 7. Mothers 8. Drowning 9. Superhuman abilities 10. Photographic memory 11. African Americans -- Social conditions -- 19th century 12. Ancestors 13. Fugitive slaves 14. Plantations -- Virginia 15. Plantation owners 16. Racism 17. Slavery 18. Slaves -- United States -- Social conditions 19. Southern States -- Race relations -- History -- 19th century 20. Virginia -- History 21. Northern States 22. Philadelphia, Pennsylvania 23. Historical fiction 24. Magical realism 25. Literary fiction 26. African American fiction

LC 2019011177

ALA Notable Book, 2020.

BCALA Literary Award for First Novelist, 2020.

Andrew Carnegie Medal for Excellence in Fiction finalist, 2020.

A Virginia slave narrowly escapes a drowning death through the intervention of a mysterious force that compels his escape and personal underground war against slavery.

Cobbs Hoffman, Elizabeth

The **Hamilton** affair / Elizabeth Cobbs. Arcade Publishing, 2016. 403 p.

ISBN 9781628727203

1. Hamilton, Alexander, 1757-1804 2. Hamilton, Elizabeth Schuyler, 1757-1854 3. 18th century 4. Politicians 5. Husband and wife 6. American Revolution, 1775-1783 7. Extramarital affairs 8. Betrayal 9. Extortion 10. Burr-Hamilton Duel, Weehawken, NJ, 1804 11. United States -- History -- Revolution, 1775-1783 12. United States -- Social life and customs -- 18th century 13. Biographical fiction 14. Historical fiction

Relates the tumultuous true love story of Alexander Hamilton and Elizabeth Schuyler against the dramatic backdrop of the American Revolution.

"Hamilton's close relationship to George Washington, his friendships and conflicts with his fellow revolutionaries, and the rise and fall of his political star are all detailed, but it is his courtship of and marriage to the beautiful, vivacious Elizabeth Schuyler, a member of one of the oldest and most distinguished colonial families, that serves as the centerpiece of Cobbs page-turning historical novel. Cobbs paints a portrait of a love so deep it was able to survive betrayal and a devastatingly public scandal. The focus alternates between Alexander and Elizabeth as their tempestuous tale unfolds in all its triumph and tragedy. Hamiltons true story is so fantastical, it is amazing that it has taken this long to transform his life and times into a national sensation." Booklist.

Cobbs Hoffman, Elizabeth

The **Tubman** command : a novel / Elizabeth Cobbs. Arcade Publishing, 2019 360 p.

ISBN 9781948924344

1. Tubman, Harriet, 1820?-1913 2. Hunter, David, 1802-1886 3. 1860s 4. American Civil War era (1861-1865) 5. African American soldiers 6. African American women 7. Military missions 8. United States Civil War, 1861-1865 9. Scouting (Reconnaissance) 10. Raids (Military science) 11. Command of troops 12. Freed slaves 13. Slavery 14. South Carolina -- History -- Civil War, 1861-1865 15. United States -- History -- Civil War, 1861-1865 -- African American troops 16. Biographical fiction 17. War stories 18. Historical fiction

Tells the story of Harriet Tubman at the height of her powers, when she devises the largest plantation raid of the Civil War after General David Hunter places her in charge of a team of black scouts even though skeptical of what one woman can accomplish.

"The heroic and brilliant Tubman is brought vividly to life as a flesh-and-blood woman and a strong and cunning leader in this compelling and instructive fictional tribute." Booklist.

Coben, Harlan, 1962-

* The **boy** from the woods / Harlan Coben. Grand Central Publishing, 2020. 400 p.

ISBN 9781538748145

1. Missing teenagers 2. Women lawyers 3. Private investigators 4. Men with amnesia 5. Power (Social sciences) 6. Secrets 7. Communities 8. Celebrities 9. Wilderness areas 10. Wilderness survival 11. Politicians 12. High school students 13. Thrillers and suspense

LC 2019041849

A man with a past shrouded in mystery searches desperately for a missing teenage girl whose disappearance is triggering disastrous consequences throughout her community and the world.

Coben, Harlan, 1962-

* **Don't** let go / Harlan Coben. E.P. Dutton, 2017. 400 p.

ISBN 9780525955115

1. Former lovers 2. Murder 3. Secrets 4. Twins 5. Brothers 6. Detectives 7. Missing persons 8. Murder suspects 9. Fingerprints 10. Deception 11. New Jersey 12. Thrillers and suspense

When he gets a lead on Maura, an ex who left him without explanation fifteen years earlier, Nap Dumas searches for answers and uncovers dark secrets about the woman he once loved and the real reason behind his twin brother's death.

Coben, Harlan, 1962-

Fool me once / Harlan Coben. E.P. Dutton, 2016. 400 p.

ISBN 9780525955092

1. Deception 2. Women veterans 3. Power (Social sciences) 4. Husband and wife 5. Former Special Forces members 6. Murder investigation 7. Death 8. Secrets 9. Thrillers and suspense

Horrified when she spots the husband who was reported dead weeks earlier playing with their toddler on her nanny cam, former special ops pilot Maya confronts deep secrets and deceit in her own past in order to discern the truth.

"Once again, Coben marries his two greatest strengthsmasterfully paced plotting that leads to a climactic string of fireworks and the ability to root all the revelations in deeply felt emotionsin a tale guaranteed to fool even the craftiest readers a lot more than once." Kirkus.

Coben, Harlan, 1962-

Hold tight / Harlan Coben. Dutton, 2008. 400 p.

ISBN 9780525950608

1. Survivors of suicide victims 2. Grief in women 3. Stalking 4. Parent and child 5. Teenage boys 6. Suicide 7. Mothers 8. Sixteen-year-old boys 9. Teenagers 10. Stalkers 11. Thrillers and suspense

LC 2007051582

Just how far parents will go to protect their kids? When their son Adam is implicated in the death of his classmate, Tia and Mike Baye install a sophisticated spy program on Adam's computer, and within days are jolted by a message from an unknown correspondent.

"Coben's style is laid back initially, but it builds into a strong, smart, suspenseful novel including at least five different storylines." Deseret News.

Coben, Harlan, 1962-

Long lost / Harlan Coben. Penguin Group, 2009. 400 p. Myron Bolitar mysteries

ISBN 9780525951056

1. Spouses of murder victims 2. Crime scenes 3. Murder investigation 4. Sports-agents 5. Amateur detectives 6. Americans in Paris, France 7. Former lovers 8. Women murder suspects 9. Professional sports 10. Paris, France 11. United States 12. Hardboiled fiction 13. Mysteries

Contacted by a woman with whom he had an affair years earlier, Myron Bolitar learns how she has been wrongfully accused of murdering her ex-husband, a situation that is further complicated by a long-hidden family secret.

Coben, Harlan, 1962-

* Run away / Harlan Coben. Grand Central Publishing, 2019. 376 p.

ISBN 9781538748466

1. Women drug abusers 2. Father and adult daughter 3. Runaways 4. Protectiveness in men 5. Murder suspects 6. Rich families 7. Missing persons investigation 8. City life 9. New York City 10. Thrillers and suspense

LC 2018037100

After discovering his drug-addicted daughter Paige, who he has not seen in six months, panhandling in Central Park, Simon follows her into a dark and dangerous world he never knew existed that puts his family and his life on the line.

"An absolutely brilliant, taut thriller that begs to be read in one sitting." Library Journal.

Coben, Harlan, 1962-

The **stranger** / Harlan Coben. Dutton, 2015. 400 p.

ISBN 9780525953500

1. Marriage 2. Secrets 3. Conspiracies 4. Husband and wife 5. Strangers 6. Marital conflict 7. Social media 8. Deception 9. Extortion 10. Family relationships 11. Thrillers and suspense

Parents Adam and Hannah Price confront the shocking secret on which their marriage was built, leaving Adam to wonder whether he ever truly knew his wife at all, and soon he stumbles into a dark conspiracy that places lives at risk.

"Coben can always be relied on to generate thrills from the simplest premises, but his finest tales maintain a core of logic throughout the twists. This 100-proof nightmare ranks among his most potent." Kirkus.

Cocco, Giovanni, 1976-

Shadows on the lake : A Stefania Valenti Mystery / Giovanni Cocco and Amneris Magella ; translated from the Italian by Stephen Sartarelli. Penguin Books, 2017, c2013. 304 p. Stefania Valenti novels

ISBN 9780143127253

1. Single mothers 2. Women detectives 3. Cold cases (Criminal investigation) 4. Dead 5. Divorced women 6. Tunnels 7. Rich families 8. World War II 9. Family secrets 10. Italy 11. Lake Como, Italy 12. Police procedurals 13. Translations -- Italian to English

LC 2016012231

Originally published: 2013.

A new Italian mystery novel set in Lake Como, introducing the clever and captivating Inspector Stefania Valenti.

"A well-crafted piece of crime fiction cleverly enhanced by an inviting travel narrative from a husband-and-wife writing team who live in the region." Booklist.

Cocks, Heather

The **royal** we / Heather Cocks, Jessica Morgan. Grand Central Publishing, 2015. 252 p.

ISBN 9781455557103

1. Weddings 2. Americans in England 3. Princes 4. Nobility 5. Sisters 6. Friendship 7. Tabloid newspapers 8. Self-fulfillment 9. Men/women relations 10. England 11. Chick lit

RUSA Reading List Short List, 2016.

"In their first adult novel, authors Heather Cocks and Jessica Morgan take on a story of romance and rivalries inspired by today's most talked-about royal couple: Will and Kate. "If I'm Cinderella today, I dread who they'll think I am tomorrow. I guess it depends on what I do next." American Rebecca Porter was never one for fairy-tales. Her twin sister Lacey was always the romantic, the one who daydreamed of being a princess. But it's adventure-seeking Bex who goes to Oxford and meets dreamy Nick across the hall - and thus Bex who accidentally finds herself in love with the eventual heir to the British throne. Nick is everything she could have imagined, but Prince Nicholas has unimaginable baggage: grasping friends, a thorny family, hysterical tabloids tracking his every move, and a public that expected its future king to marry a native. On the eve of the most talked-about wedding of the century, Bex reflects on what she's sacrificed for love -- and exactly whose heart she may yet have to break.""--, Provided by publisher.

"Parallels to the love story of Prince William and Kate Middleton are obvious, but the authors create their own unique and endearing characters with Bex and Nick--along with an entertaining cast of characters including lovable rogue Prince Freddie, Nick's younger brother; Bex's twin, Lacey; and a bunch of colorful school chums." Publishers Weekly.

Coe, Jonathan

Number 11 / Jonathan Coe. Alfred A. Knopf, 2017. 368 p. Winshaw legacy

ISBN 9780451493361

1. 20th century 2. 21st century 3. Female friendship 4. Social classes 5. Social media 6. Rich families 7. Greed 8. Corruption 9. Consequences 10. Growing up 11. Secrets 12. Interpersonal relations 13. Great Britain -- Social life and customs -- 20th century 14. Great Britain -- Social life and customs -- 21st century 15. Satirical fiction 16. Literary fiction 17. Political fiction

LC 2016019484

"Jonathan Coe finally provides a sequel to The Winshaw Legacy, the 1995 novel that introduced American readers to one of Britain's most exciting new writers -- an acerbic, hilariously dark, and unflinching portrait of modern society."--, Provided by publisher.

Coe, Jonathan

The **rain** before it falls / Jonathan Coe. Alfred A. Knopf, 2008. 336 p.

ISBN 9780307268037

1. Family secrets 2. Reminiscing in old age 3. World War II 4. Memories 5. Cousins 6. Family relationships 7. England 8. Domestic fiction

LC 2007043487

A family saga examines the events and relationships that bind three generations of women, as the elderly Rosamond records her memories of her troubled cousin Beatrix and the tragedy that transformed all of their lives.

"If Rosamond's temperament makes for a somewhat mannered novel, it's nevertheless an absorbing one." Village Voice.

Coe, Jonathan

The **rotters'** club / Jonathan Coe. Alfred A. Knopf :, 2003, c2001. 419 p. Rotters' Club

ISBN 9780375713125

1. 1970s 2. Teenage boys 3. Male friendship 4. Punk rock music 5. Political participation 6. Men 7. Social change 8. Birmingham, England 9. Psychological fiction 10. Political fiction 11. Coming-of-age stories

LC 2001042523

Sequel: The closed circle (2005).

First published: London : Viking, 2001.

Four teenage boys, friends and schoolmates, deal with the hopes, dreams, traumas, and challenges of adolescence as they come of age in industrial Birmingham, a British city that is confronting its own economic crisis, during the upheaval and change of the 1970s.

Coe, Jonathan

The **terrible** privacy of Maxwell Sim / Jonathan Coe. Alfred A. Knopf, 2011. 304 p.

ISBN 9780307594815

1. Losers (Persons) 2. Automobile travel 3. Self-fulfillment 4. Technology 5. Social media 6. Failure (Psychology) 7. Divorced men 8. Middle-aged men 9. Interpersonal relations 10. Picaresque fiction

LC 2010035997

Struggling in vain to make a meaningful connection with his preoccupied family members and friends, Maxwell Sim quits his job to make a promotional sales delivery to the remote Shetland Islands, a car journey that forces him to confront events from his past.

"The author broadly satirizes the disconnectedness of modern life with the story of Maxwell Sim, who has 70 Facebook friends but no one he can turn to when his wife and daughter leave him. After a trip to Australia to reconnect with his estranged father leads nowhere, Trevor, one of Max's few real friends, offers him an unusual gig: drive a Prius to the northernmost tip of the British Isles as part of a promotion for a startup eco-toothbrush company. Max takes a meandering route that allows him to visit his ex-wife, check in on his father's long-empty apartment, and pay a visit to the parents of his childhood friends. He also develops a romantic fixation on the voice coming from his GPS, which he names Emma. . . . Coe has a lot of fun skewering the way technology and social media have become buttresses of society." Publishers Weekly.

Coel, Margaret, 1937-

Blood memory / Margaret Coel. Berkley Prime Crime, 2008. 320 p. Catherine McLeod novels (Margaret Coel)

ISBN 9780425223451

1. Attempted assassination 2. Death threats 3. Women investigative journalists 4. Indians of North America -- Land tenure 5. Conspiracies 6. Secrets 7. Native American women 8. Political corruption 9. Denver, Colorado 10. Thrillers and suspense

LC 2008022197

Investigative reporter Catherine McLeod has been covering the local Arapaho and Cheyenne tribes' case to reclaim 27 million acres of land, but after barely surviving an assassination attempt, she decides to lie low for a while. Yet Catherine's persistence in covering the story soon leads her to uncover a startling conspiracy--and some eye-opening truths about her own heritage.

Coelho, Paulo

* The **alchemist** / Paulo Coelho ; translated by Alan R. Clarke HarperOne, 1993. 177 p.

ISBN 9780062502179

1. Self-discovery 2. Voyages and travels -- Egypt 3. Wisdom 4. Boy shepherds 5. Dreams 6. Imagination in boys 7. Courage in boys 8. Spiritual fiction 9. Allegories 10. Literary fiction 11. Translations -- Portuguese to English

LC 92056413

First published by Editora Rocco Ltd 1988.

A fable about undauntingly following one's dreams, listening to one's heart, and reading life's omens features dialogue between a boy and an unnamed being.

"The story has the comic charm, dramatic tension and psychological intensity of a fairy tale, but it's full of specific wisdom as well, about becoming self-empowered, overcoming depression, and believing in dreams. The cumulative effect is like hearing a wonderful bedtime story from an inspirational psychiatrist. Comparisons to The Little Prince are appropriate; this is a sweetly exotic tale for young and old alike." Publishers Weekly.

Coes, Ben

Bloody Sunday / Ben Coes. St. Martin's Press, 2018. 432 p. Dewey Andreas thrillers

ISBN 9781250140760

1. CIA agents 2. Nuclear weapons 3. National security 4. Poisons 5. Intelligence service 6. Military missions 7. United States -- Politics and government 8. North Korea -- Politics and government 9. Political thrillers 10. Thrillers and suspense

LC 2018006500

CIA top special forces operative Dewey Andreas goes undercover in Macau, where he must foil Iran and North Korea's plot to acquire nuclear and long-range attack capabilities.

Coes, Ben

The **Russian** : a thriller / Ben Coes. St Martins Press, 2019. 400 p. Rob Tacoma novels

ISBN 9781250140791

1. CIA agents 2. Mafia 3. Special operations (Military science) 4. Assassins 5. Russians in the United States 6. Former Navy SEALs 7. Violence in men 8. Organized crime 9. United States 10. Political thrillers

When criminals from the former Soviet Union establish a vicious underworld in the U.S., former Navy SEAL and CIA agent Rob Tacoma conducts a top-secret mission to neutralize the mob boss behind the murder of a CIA Special Ops leader.

Coetzee, J. M., 1940-

Age **of** Iron / J.M. Coetzee. Random House, 1990. 198 p.

ISBN 0394588592

1. Apartheid 2. Race relations 3. Women with terminal illnesses 4. Women with cancer 5. Homeless men 6. Senior women 7. Last days 8. Revenge 9. South Africa 10. South Africa -- Race relations 11. Cape Town, South Africa 12. Epistolary novels 13. Literary fiction

LC 90008310

ALA Notable Book, 1991.

South African professor Mrs. Curren has always been opposed to apartheid's brutality though she has lived isolated from its horrors, but as she nears death from cancer, she confronts a generation of blood and revenge.

"The word 'shame' throbs through the text like a recurrent pain. The principal character thinks she is dying of it. . . . One can, of course, read her death as a metaphor for the doom of liberalism in South Africa. . . . But Age of Iron is about dying as much as it is about apartheid, and that raises it above the level of a political novel or a roman thse, and gives resonance to the political message." The New York Review of Books.

Coetzee, J. M., 1940-

The **childhood** of Jesus / J. M. Coetzee. Viking, 2013. 288 p. Childhood of Jesus

ISBN 9780670014651

1. Refugees 2. Gifted children 3. Guardian and ward 4. Boys 5. Families 6. Motherhood 7. Boys and men 8. Family relationships 9. Nontraditional families 10. Immigration and emigration 11. Overprotectiveness in mothers 12. Literary fiction 13. Coming-of-age stories

Originally published: Melbourne : Text Publishing Company, 2013.

David is a small boy who comes by boat across the ocean to a new country. He has been separated from his parents, and has lost the piece of paper that would have explained everything. On the boat a stranger named Simon takes it upon himself to look after the boy. On arrival they are assigned new names, new birthdates. They know little Spanish, the language of their new country, and nothing about its customs. They have also suffered a kind of forgetting of old attachments and feelings. They are people without a past. Simon's goal is to find the boy's mother. He feels sure he will know her when he sees her. And David? He wants to find his mother too but he also wants to understand where he is and how he fits in. He is a boy who is always asking questions. The Childhood of Jesus is not like any other novel you have read. This beautiful and surprising fable is about childhood, about destiny, about being an outsider. It is a novel about the riddle of experience itself.

Coetzee, J. M., 1940-

* **Disgrace** / J.M. Coetzee. Viking, 1999. 220 p.

ISBN 0670887315

1. Father and adult daughter 2. Sexuality 3. Race relations 4. Middle-aged men 5. Farm life 6. College teachers 7. Men/women relations 8. Teacher-student relationships 9. Family relationships 10. Employees -- Dismissal 11. South Africa -- Social conditions -- 1981- 12. Psychological fiction 13. Literary fiction

LC 99055216

ALA Notable Book, 2001.

Booker Prize, 1999.

National Book Critics Circle Award for Fiction finalist, 1999

In a novel set in post-apartheid South Africa, a fifty-two-year-old college professor who has lost his job for sleeping with a student tries to relate to his daughter, Lucy, who works with an ambitious African farmer.

"A novel that not only works its spell but makes it impossible for us to lay it aside once we've finished reading it. . . . Coetzee's sentences are coiled springs, and the energy they release would take other writers pages to summon." The New Yorker.

Coetzee, J. M., 1940-

Elizabeth Costello / J. M. Coetzee. Viking, 2003. 224 p.

ISBN 0670031305

1. Women authors 2. Awards, prizes, honors, etc 3. Storytelling 4. Writing 5. Mothers 6. Sisters 7. Women missionaries 8. Lovers 9. Poets, African 10. Australians in foreign countries 11. Fame 12. Australia 13. Speeches, addresses, etc 14. Literary fiction

LC 2003060849

Queensland Premier's Literary Awards, Fiction Book Award, 2004.

Shortlisted for the Miles Franklin Literary Award, 2004

Reveals the life of aging Australian novelist Elizabeth Costello through a series of formal addresses that includes an award-acceptance speech at a New England liberal arts college and a lecture on evil in Amsterdam.

"There is no justice in the ability of youth to shame age, and yet it's a fundamental fact of the embodied life. Coetzee's unflinching exploration of this desolate and strangely beautiful terrain represents the cruelest and best use to which literature can be put." New York Times Book Review.

Coetzee, J. M., 1940-

* **Foe** / J. M. Coetzee. Viking, 1986. 157p.

ISBN 9780670813988

1. Widows 2. Islands 3. Survival (after airplane accidents, shipwrecks, etc) 4. Shipwrecks 5. Solitude 6. Castaways 7. Men who are mute 8. Race relations 9. Authors 10. Allegories 11. Literary fiction

LC 86040267

Originally published: London: Secker & Warburg, 1986.

Returning to London after being marooned on an island in the Atlantic, Susan Barton approaches the author Daniel Foe with the story of her adventures with Robinson Cruso and the mute Friday.

"In adding to Defoe's repertory company, Coetzee has introduced urgencies that are neither fresh nor illumined, only brilliantly disguised. Flashing back and forward, scattering allusions, adopting a series of poses and styles, the author is less reminiscent of a prior novelist than of contemporary street mimes who build hints until the audience shouts in recognition." Time.

Coetzee, J. M., 1940-

* **Life** & times of Michael K / J.M. Coetzee. Penguin Books, 1996, c1983. 184 p.

ISBN 9780140074482

1. Men with developmental disabilities 2. War -- South Africa 3. Mothers -- Death 4. Gardeners 5. Prisoners 6. Mother and adult son 7. Voyages and travels 8. Violence 9. Cleft lip 10. South Africa 11. Psychological fiction 12. Literary fiction

Originally published: London : Secker & Warburg, 1983.

Booker Prize, 1983.

Michael K, a young South African, becomes unwillingly and unwittingly involved in a war in South Africa after he loses his gardening job in Capetown and embarks on an odyssey to return his dying mother to her homeland.

Coetzee, J. M., 1940-

Slow man / J. M. Coetzee. Viking, 2005. 208 p.
ISBN 0670034592
1. People who have had amputations 2. Men/women relations 3. Dependency (Psychology) 4. Senior men 5. Traffic accident victims 6. Photographers 7. Nurses 8. Home health care nurses 9. Croats 10. Women immigrants 11. Women authors 12. Independence (Personal quality) 13. Aging 14. Death 15. Love 16. Memories 17. Australia 18. Adelaide, South Australia 19. Psychological fiction 20. Literary fiction
Includes an appearance by the main character of Coetzee's previous novel, Elizabeth Costello.
Shortlisted for the International IMPAC Dublin Literary Award, 2007
Dependent on others after losing his leg in an accident, sixty-year-old Paul Rayment finds himself falling in love with a down-to-earth Croatian nurse and encouraged by a mysterious writer to take an activist role in his own life
"What saves Slow Man from being a sterile, self-referential literary exercise is the vividness of the characters who animate it. Coetzee writes in a degree-zero style, purposely flat and unemphatic-he must be a translator's dream-yet in this book he has found a new access of warmth and humor, and displays a vivifying fondness for his characters. It is his triumph in Slow Man to bring a world into being with a minimum of literary effects." The New Republic.

Coetzee, J. M., 1940-

* **Summertime** : scenes from a provincial life / J. M. Coetzee. Knopf Australia, 2009. 266 p. ; Memoir trilogy
ISBN 9781741669022
1. Coetzee, J M, 1940- 2. 1970s 3. Authors, South African -- 20th century 4. European Africans 5. Biographers 6. Writing 7. Misfits (Persons) 8. Cape Town, South Africa 9. South Africa -- Social life and customs 10. Autobiographies and memoirs 11. Life stories Arts and culture Writing Authors 12. Arts and Entertainment Writing and Publishing
Sequel to: "Boyhood" and "Youth".
Queensland Premier's Literary Awards, Fiction Book Award, 2010.
Western Australian Premier's Book Awards, Fiction category, 2009.
Shortlisted for the Man Booker Prize, 2009.
"At stake is what it means to commit oneself: to a person, a place, a moral imperative. . . . Not since Disgrace has he written with such urgency and feeling." The New Yorker.

Cogburn, Emily Beck

Ava's **place** / Emily Beck Cogburn. Kensington Books, 2017 320 p.
ISBN 9781496700117
1. Single mothers 2. Divorced women 3. Women journalists 4. Parenting 5. Dating (Social customs) 6. Cooks 7. Change (Psychology) 8. Balance (Psychology) 9. Men/women relations 10. Long distance romance 11. Louisiana 12. Mainstream fiction
Divorced mother Ava Olson is trying to balance work and parenting when she encounters cafe owner Ford, who wins her over with his warm smile and delicious po'boy sandwiches.
"Cogburn (Louisiana Saves the Library) writes a sweet, down-to-earth story about pursuing a second chance at love and dreams in the Big Easy." Library Journal.

Cogman, Genevieve

The **burning** page / Genevieve Cogman. Penguin Group, 2017, c2016. 336 p. Invisible library
ISBN 9781101988688
1. Libraries 2. Librarians 3. Interdimensional travel 4. Magic 5. Villains 6. Dragons 7. Betrayal 8. Alliances 9. Librarians 10. Magical books 11. Book thefts 12. Parallel universes 13. London, England 14. Steampunk 15. Fantasy fiction
Originally published by Pan in 2016.
Librarian spy Irene is doing probation in the Invisible Library, but her nemesis, Alberich, is determined to destroy the library and she must gather her allies around her to defeat him, never suspecting that someone close to her may be about to betray her.

Cogman, Genevieve

The **invisible** library / Genevieve Cogman. ROC, 2016, c2015. 328 p. Invisible library
ISBN 9781101988640
1. Libraries 2. Librarians 3. Magical books 4. Magic 5. Secrets 6. Book thefts 7. Secret societies 8. Interdimensional travel 9. London, England 10. Steampunk 11. Fantasy fiction
Originally published: London: Tor, 2015.
"Collecting books can be a dangerous prospect in this fun, time-traveling, fantasy adventure from a spectacular debut author. One thing any Librarian will tell you: the truth is much stranger than fiction... Irene is a professional spy for the mysterious Library, a shadowy organization that collects important works of fiction from all of the different realities. Most recently, she and her enigmatic assistant Kai have been sent to an alternative London. Their mission: Retrieve a particularly dangerous book. The problem: By the time they arrive, it's already been stolen. London's underground factions are prepared to fight to the death to find the tome before Irene and Kai do, a problem compounded by the fact that this world is chaos-infested--the laws of nature bent to allow supernatural creatures and unpredictable magic to run rampant. To make matters worse, Kai is hiding something--secrets that could be just as volatile as the chaos-filled world itself. Now Irene is caught in a puzzling web of deadly danger, conflicting clues, and sinister secret societies. And failure is not an option--because it isn't just Irene's reputation at stake, it's the nature of reality itself..."--, Provided by publisher.
"Intriguing characters and fast-paced action are wrapped up in a spellbinding, well-built world." Library Journal.

Cogman, Genevieve

The **masked** city / Genevieve Cogman. ROC, 2016, c2015. 336 p. Invisible library
ISBN 9781101988664
1. Libraries 2. Librarians 3. Magical books 4. Magic 5. Secrets 6. Book thefts 7. Secret societies 8. Interdimensional travel 9. London, England 10. Steampunk 11. Fantasy fiction
Originally published: London : Tor, 2015.
"Librarian-spy Irene and her apprentice Kai are back in the second in this "dazzling"* book-filled fantasy series from the author of The Invisible Library. The written word is mightier than the sword--most of the time... Working in an alternate version of Victorian London, Librarian-spy Irene has settled into a routine, collecting important fiction for the mysterious Library and blending in nicely with the local culture. But when her apprentice, Kai--a dragon of royal descent--is kidnapped by the Fae, her carefully crafted undercover operation begins to crumble. Kai's abduction could incite a conflict between the forces of chaos and order that would devastate all worlds and all dimensions. To keep humanity from getting caught in the crossfire, Irene will have to team up with a local Fae leader to travel deep into a version of Venice filled with dark magic, strange coincidences, and a perpetual celebration of

Carnival--and save her friend before he becomes the first casualty of a catastrophic war. But navigating the tumultuous landscape of Fae politics will take more than Irene's book-smarts and fast-talking--to ward off Armageddon, she might have to sacrifice everything she holds dear.... INCLUDES AUTHOR INTERVIEW"--, Provided by publisher.

Cogman, Genevieve

The **mortal** word : an invisible library novel / Genevieve Cogman. Berkley, 2018. 368 p. Invisible library

ISBN 9780399587443

1. Librarians 2. Dragons 3. Interdimensional travel 4. Magic 5. Murder 6. Peace conferences 7. Alliances 8. Magical books 9. Book thefts 10. Parallel universes 11. Libraries 12. Secret societies 13. London, England 14. Steampunk 15. Fantasy fiction

LC 2018023853

During a top secret dragon-Fae peace conference in progress that the Library is mediating, the second-in-command dragon has been stabbed to death. Irene is tasked with solving the case, and she and Vale immediately go to 1890s Paris to start their investigation--but was it a dragon, a Fae, or even a Librarian who committed the crime?

Cognetti, Paolo, 1978-

The **eight** mountains : a novel / Paolo Cognetti ; translated by Simon Carnell and Erica Segre. Atria Books, 2018. 224 p.

ISBN 9781501169885

1. Male friendship 2. Interclass friendship 3. Mountain life 4. Vacations 5. City life 6. Family relationships 7. Fathers and sons 8. Italy 9. Dolomite Alps (Italy) 10. Literary fiction 11. Coming-of-age stories 12. Translations -- Italian to English

LC 2017038835

Describes the friendship between two young boys, one from cosmopolitan Milan, the other from the mountains, who spent many summers together exploring the Dolomites and how they try to sustain their connection despite divergent paths in life.

Cohen, Joshua, 1980-

* **Book** of numbers : a novel / Joshua Cohen. Random House, 2015 448 p.

ISBN 9780812996913

1. Rich men 2. Authors 3. Internet 4. High technology industry and trade 5. Autobiography 6. Ghostwriters 7. Voyages and travels 8. Jewish men 9. Identity (Psychology) 10. Cyber-thrillers 11. Literary fiction

LC 2014040735

Hired by a dying tech company tycoon to ghostwrite his memoirs, failed novelist Josh Cohen learns the history of the man's profoundly influential company before being initiated into the high-stakes truth behind the autobiography project.

"A dense, thrilling, and occasionally perplexing work, Cohen's encyclopedic epic is about many things--language, art, divinity, narrative, desire, global politics, surveillance, consumerism, genealogy--but it is above all a standout novel about the Internet, humanity's 'first mutual culture,' in which our identities are increasingly defined by a series of ones and zeroes." Publishers Weekly.

Cohen, Leah Hager

The **grief** of others / Leah Hager Cohen. Riverhead Books, 2011. 384 p.

ISBN 9781594488054

1. Children -- Death 2. Bereavement in families 3. Loss (Psychology) 4. Marital conflict 5. Grief 6. Secrets 7. Domestic fiction

LC 2011009414

Managing their grief by pretending that everything is normal after the tragic loss of a newborn, John and Ricky find themselves confronting long-suppressed uncertainties about their relationship at the same time a terrible secret emerges about the pregnancy.

"Occasionally, the action of Cohen's novel seems forced when it moves outside the family circle, particularly when John goes to his job managing the theatrical scene shop at a community college. Sometimes, too, in shifting the perspective from one character to another, Cohen lets her own voice intrude, breaking the spell she's cast. But those are quibbles about a novel that's otherwise graceful, satisfying, and closely observed." Boston Globe.

Cohen, Tammy

They all fall down / Tammy Cohen. W W Norton & Co Inc, 2018 384 p.

ISBN 9781681776477

1. Psychiatric hospitals 2. Patients 3. Serial murders 4. Married women 5. Suspicion 6. Suicide 7. Psychiatrists 8. Psychiatrist and patient 9. Mothers and daughters 10. Trust 11. Paranoia 12. London, England 13. England 14. Psychological suspense

After Hannah is admitted to a high-risk psychiatric unit, she has a hard time convincing anyone that a serial killer is methodically ending the lives of the other patients in her ward in this new novel by the author of Dying for Christmas.

Cohen, Tish, 1963-

The **summer** we lost her : a novel / Tish Cohen. Gallery Books, 2019. 340 p.

ISBN 9781501199684

1. Husband and wife 2. Vacation homes 3. Missing girls 4. Cabins 5. Lakes 6. Parents of missing children 7. Former lovers 8. Single women 9. Grief 10. Women equestrians 11. Patriarchs 12. Marital conflict 13. Family relationships 14. New York City 15. New York (State) 16. Adirondack Mountains, New York 17. Domestic fiction

Preparing to sell a valuable lakefront cabin that has been in the family for generations, a lawyer and equestrian whose marriage has been strained by ambition encounter the husband's teen crush before their young daughter goes missing.

"A sharp, suspenseful portrait of a family on the verge of collapse." Kirkus.

Coldsmith, Don, 1926-2009

The **long** journey home / Don Coldsmith. Forge, 2001. 400 p.

ISBN 0312876173

1. Thorpe, Jim, 1887-1953 2. 1910s 3. 1920s 4. Native American athletes 5. Olympic games 6. Ambition in men 7. Racism 8. Wild West shows 9. Westerns

LC 00048459

A Native American track star training for the Olympics in the early part of the 1900s meets 1912 gold medal winner Jim Thorpe and Bill Pickett, the black cowboy who invented steer wrestling.

"This well-researched piece of historical fiction interweaves a compelling life story with many of the pivotal events of the early twentieth century." Booklist.

Coldsmith, Don, 1926-2009

Tallgrass : a novel of the Great Plains / Don Coldsmith. Bantam Books, 1997. 454 p. Great Plains saga

ISBN 9780553106329

1. Indians of North America -- Great Plains (United States) 2. Indians of North America -- Relations with European-Americans 3. Frontier and pioneer life -- Great Plains (United States) 4. Prairie

life 5. Kansas -- History 6. Great Plains (United States) -- History 7. Santa Fe, New Mexico 8. Westerns

LC 9619672

A saga set in the Great Plains follows the warriors, priests, trappers, traders, explorers, schemers, and other pioneers of the American West.

"This powerful novel demonstrates the diversity of the Native American culture while treating the tribes and their history with dignity and understanding." Library Journal.

Cole, Alyssa

* A **duke** by default / Alyssa Cole. Avon Books, 2018 384 p. Reluctant royals

ISBN 9780062685568

1. Swordmaking 2. Dukes and duchesses 3. Interracial romance 4. Armorers 5. Apprenticeship 6. African American women 7. Sexual attraction 8. Heirs and heiresses 9. Men/women relations 10. Americans in Scotland 11. Scotland 12. New York City 13. Contemporary romances 14. Multicultural romances 15. African American fiction

When her gruff new boss, Scottish swordmaker Tavish McKenzie, discovers that he is a duke, New York City socialite Portia Hobbs puts her social media skills to good use on Tavish's behalf, despite her growing attraction to him.

"Cole includes just the right amount of sass, sex, and heart to satisfy romance readers." Publishers Weekly.

Cole, Alyssa

*An **extraordinary** union / Alyssa Cole. Kensington Books, 2017 258 p. The Loyal League

ISBN 9781496707444

1. American Civil War era (1861-1865) 2. Spies 3. Freed slaves 4. Undercover operations 5. Interracial romance 6. Detectives 7. Espionage 8. Men/women relations 9. Virginia 10. Historical romances 11. Multicultural romances 12. African American fiction RUSA Reading List, 2018.

Born into slavery, Elle Burns is now a free woman and a spy for the pro-Union Loyalty League. While on assignment in Richmond, Virginia, she encounters another undercover operative: white Pinkerton Detective Malcolm McCall. Their attraction is instantaneous (and mutual), but there are so many reasons they can't be together. Set during the American Civil War, this compelling story of forbidden love and espionage boasts authentic characters and well-researched historical detail that should please fans of Beverly Jenkins' novels. -- Description by Gillian Speace

"Any reader who thinks romance novels are pure fluff will be schooled by Cole's richly drawn characters, who must overcome generations of trauma in order to let themselves love each other. A masterful tale that bodes well for future work from Cole." Kirkus.

Cole, Alyssa

* A **hope** divided / Alyssa Cole. Kensington Books, 2017. 266 p. The Loyal League

ISBN 9781496707468

1. American Civil War era (1861-1865) 2. Spies 3. Union soldiers 4. African American women 5. Underground Railroad 6. Civil War 7. Escaped prisoners of war 8. Multiracial women 9. Civil War veterans 10. Men/women relations 11. Southern States 12. Historical romances 13. Multicultural romances 14. African American fiction

The Civil War has turned neighbor against neighbor, but for scientist-spy and free black woman Marlie Lynch and the philosophical Union soldier she helps to hide, war could bind them together when they must go on the run on the Underground Railroad to escape a common enemy.

"Thoughtfully portrayed characters with deep minds and passionate hearts make this second novel in Coles Loyal League series, following An Extraordinary Union (2017), sparkle." Booklist.

Cole, Alyssa

*A **prince** on paper / Alyssa Cole. Avon Books, 2019. 377 p. Reluctant royals

ISBN 9780062685582

1. Adult children of politicians 2. Dukes and duchesses 3. Interracial romance 4. Women -- Africa 5. Womanizers 6. Stepbrothers 7. Gender nonconformity 8. Fear of intimacy 9. Celebrities 10. Paparazzi 11. Political intrigue 12. Sexual attraction 13. Men/women relations 14. New York City 15. Africa 16. Europe 17. Contemporary romances 18. Multicultural romances 19. African American fiction

Forced into a pretend engagement with real-life celebrity prince Johan von Braustein, whom she loves to hate, Nya Jerami starts falling for him and wonders if they are destined for their own happily ever after.

"In a book by a less skilled writer, a subplot involving a character's emerging nonbinary gender identity might feel unnecessary, but not here. Nya and Johan's swoony sexual tension evolves into a scorching exploration that recognizes Nya's relative inexperience while rendering the pair's matched desire, fulfillment, and power. A gifted writer at the top of her emotional, sexy, romantic, and inclusive game." Kirkus.

Cole, Alyssa

* A **princess** in theory / Alyssa Cole. Avon Books, 2018. 373 p. Reluctant royals

ISBN 9780062685544

1. Princes 2. Women graduate students 3. Engaged persons 4. Women scientists 5. Deception 6. Trust 7. African American women 8. Sexual attraction 9. Men/women relations 10. Contemporary romances 11. Multicultural romances 12. African American fiction RUSA Reading List Short List, 2019.

Mistaken by his betrothed as a pauper instead of a prince, Prince Thabiso, the sole heir to the throne of Thesolo, decides to keep his real identity a secret as he experiences life and love with Naledi Smith--until the truth comes out, which changes everything.

Cole, Alyssa

* An **unconditional** freedom / Alyssa Cole. Kensington Books, 2019. 320 p. The Loyal League

ISBN 9781496707482

1. American Civil War era (1861-1865) 2. Spies 3. Freed slaves 4. Interracial romance 5. Revenge 6. African American men 7. Hispanic American women 8. Civil War 9. Secrets 10. Sexual attraction 11. Men/women relations 12. Ohio 13. Historical romances 14. Multicultural romances 15. African American fiction

An assassination plot that could end the Civil War, and a hidden enemy that could destroy a secret league of unsung heroes.

"A heroine torn by conflicting loyalties and a vengeance-driven hero haunted by the past struggle to come to terms with reality and their feelings in this emotionally compelling, information-rich story." Library Journal.

Cole, Daniel

Hangman / Daniel Cole. Ecco, 2018. 256 p. Fawkes and Baxter novels

ISBN 9780062653987

1. Copycat murders 2. Law enforcement 3. Intelligence service 4. Women detectives 5. Serial murder investigation 6. Secrets 7. Thrillers and suspense

Still recovering from the Ragdoll case and the disappearance of her friend, Detective Emily Baxter delves into yet another gruesome case when a copycat killer emerges in New York City and must shake off the grief and fear that have paralyzed her to stop the murders.

Cole, Daniel

Ragdoll / Daniel Cole. Ecco, 2017. 256 p. Fawkes and Baxter novels

ISBN 9780062653956

1. Divorced men 2. Dismemberment 3. Murder victims 4. Crime scenes 5. Women journalists 6. Women detectives 7. Detectives 8. Serial murderers 9. Serial murder investigation 10. City life 11. Men/women relations 12. London, England 13. England 14. Thrillers and suspense

Reinstated to his post after months of psychological assessment, controversial detective William Fawkes is summoned by his former partner to help investigate a serial killer who has already murdered six victims and may be targeting Fawkes himself.

"With a third-person omniscient narrator, the briskly paced story line allows readers into the mind-sets of the various characters from the multiple detectives to potential victims." Library Journal.

Cole, Kresley

Dreams of a dark warrior / Kresley Cole. Simon & Schuster, 2011. 384 p. Immortals after dark series

ISBN 9781439136805

1. Reincarnation 2. Revenge 3. Fiances -- Death 4. Warriors 5. Immortality 6. Former lovers 7. Memories 8. Witches 9. Secrets 10. Sexual attraction 11. Paranormal romances

When she encounters Celtic soldier Declan, recognizing that he is her beloved Aidan reincarnated, Regin must choose between rekindling memories of their past, which could kill him, or losing the only man she could ever love.

Cole, Teju

Every day is for the thief / Teju Cole. Random House Inc., 2014 176 p.

ISBN 9780812995787

1. City life 2. Homecomings 3. Identity (Psychology) 4. Cities and towns 5. Reconciliation 6. Authors 7. Nigeria 8. Psychological fiction 9. Literary fiction

"Visiting Lagos after many years away, Teju Cole's unnamed narrator rediscovers his hometown as both a foreigner and a local. A young writer uncertain of what he wants to say, the man moves through tableaus of life in one of the most dynamic cities in the world: he hears the muezzin's call to prayer in the early morning light, and listens to John Coltrane during the late afternoon heat. He witnesses teenagers diligently perpetrating e-mail frauds from internet cafes, longs after a woman reading Michael Ondaatje on a public bus, and visits the impoverished National Museum. Along the way, he reconnects with old school friends and his family, who force him to ask himself profound questions of personal and national history. Over long, wandering days, the narrator compares present-day Lagos to the Lagos of his memory, and in doing so reveals changes that have taken place in himself. Just as Open City uses New York to reveal layers of the narrator's soul, in Every Day is for the Thief the complex, beautiful, generous, and corrupt city of Lagos exposes truths about our protagonist, and ourselves"--, Provided by publisher.

"The structure is loose, a collection of observances of daily life in Lagos in which Cole presents the complexities of culture and poverty. In addition, Cole sprinkles dramatic black-and-white photos throughout the book, but it's his willingness to explore so many uncomfortable paradoxes that sears this narrative into our brains." Publishers Weekly.

Cole, Teju

* **Open** city : a novel / Teju Cole. Random House, 2011. 272 p.

ISBN 9781400068098

1. Immigrants 2. Identity (Psychology) 3. Race relations 4. Nigerians in the United States 5. Psychiatrists 6. Loneliness 7. City life 8. New York City 9. Psychological fiction 10. Literary fiction

LC 2010008927

Hemingway Foundation/PEN Award, 2012.

National Book Critics Circle Award for Fiction finalist, 2011

Feeling adrift after ending a relationship, Julius, a young Nigerian doctor living in New York, takes long walks through the city while listening to the stories of fellow immigrants until a shattering truth is revealed.

"Cole's writing is assured, his ideas are well developed, and his imagery is delicious. . . . His readers will be those who understand that all stories are interconnected, that literature is not mere entertainment, and that art is nothing if not an extended conversation spanning eras, nations and languages. The novel's importance lies in its honesty." New York Times Book Review.

Coleman, Reed Farrel, 1956-

What you break / Reed Farrel Coleman. G.P. Putnam's Sons, 2017 368 p. Gus Murphy novels

ISBN 9780399173042

1. Murder investigation 2. Former police 3. Secrets 4. Motive (Law) 5. Police corruption 6. Assassins 7. Long Island, New York 8. Mysteries 9. Hardboiled fiction

LC 2016029299

Former Suffolk County cop Gus Murphy returns to prowl the meaner streets of Long Island's darkest precincts with a Russian mercenary at his back in the stunning second installment of Reed Farrel Coleman's critically acclaimed series.

Coleman, Reed Farrel, 1956-

* **Where** it hurts : a Gus Murphy novel / Reed Farrel Coleman. G. P. Putnam's Sons, 2016 368 p. Gus Murphy novels

ISBN 9780399173035

1. Murder investigation 2. Police corruption 3. Mafia 4. Former police 5. Former convicts 6. Divorced men 7. Grief in men 8. Secrets 9. Long Island, New York 10. Mysteries 11. Hardboiled fiction

LC 2015017115

Shamus Award for Best P.I. Novel, 2017.

Losing everything in a single shattering moment, former Suffolk County cop Gus Murphy reluctantly agrees to help an ex-con who would solve a family member's murder.

"Coleman's moving portrayal of a man in deep, deep pain, a tightly constructed plot, and a gift for making Long Island seem like James Ellroy's L.A. add up to a winner." Publishers Weekly.

Coleridge, Nicholas, 1957-

Godchildren / Nicholas Coleridge. Thomas Dunne Books, 2008, c2002. 560 p.

ISBN 9780312382582

1. Family secrets 2. Godfathers 3. Betrayal 4. Capitalists and financiers 5. Rich men 6. Islands 7. Family relationships 8. Domestic fiction 9. Epic fiction

LC 2008019639

Visiting with their charismatic tycoon godfather on a luxurious island, six adult godchildren unite to confront their own insecurities as well as secrets and betrayals that have been shadowing their lives over the course of thirty years.

"This wickedly enjoyable novel about a venal British billionaire and his godchildren shows a moribund class society being rapidly dismantled by global wealth. ... While the story of who triumphs is predictable, Coleridge dissects the social mores of Cap Ferrat and Lyford Cay with skill, noting sartorial codes with the precision of Tom Wolfe." The New Yorker.

Coleridge, Nicholas, 1957-
A **much** married man / Nicholas Coleridge. Thomas Dunne Books, 2007. 464 p.
ISBN 0312363834
1. Bankers 2. Marriage 3. Husband and wife 4. Upper class 5. Extended families 6. Villages 7. Blended families 8. Family relationships 9. Small town life 10. England 11. Domestic fiction 12. Humorous stories
LC 2007003200
Social satire in the manner of Edith Wharton or Anthony Trollope. A man of wealth and privilege, Anthony Anscombe has everything he could ever want: an exquisite family estate, enviable social standing, and a desirable inheritance. But with all of his money and privilege, Anthony still has an aching desire for one thing: the perfect match. Running headlong into marriage is Anthony's forte--and his greatest weakness. As Anthony surveys Winchford Priory, his beautiful Elizabethan house in the English countryside, he has the distinct feeling that he's under siege. And he's absolutely right. Lurking in the village are more than one or two reminders of his complicated past, including three ex-wives, a mistress, and a legion of children and stepchildren, all dependent on him and all determined to do whatever it takes to get what they want.--From publisher description.
"Anthony Anscombe, scion of a London banking family and heir to Winchford Priory and the village it dominates, might seem a cad to those who know him only through the gossip columns. Instead, he is a kind, unassuming man, genetically predisposed to be forever polite, who slowly gets sucked into a maelstrom created by his several wives, their offspring, and other hangers-on. ... Finely detailed, psychologically astute, and boasting a beautifully rendered cast of characters, this magnificent novel offers an intriguing insider's view of the lives of the gentry." Library Journal.

Colette, 1873-1954
The **collected** stories of Colette / edited, and with an introduction, by Robert Phelps ; translated by Matthew Ward ... [et al.]. Farrar, Straus, Giroux, 1989, c1983. xvi, 605 p.
ISBN 9780374518653
1. France -- Social life and customs 2. Short stories 3. Anthologies 4. Translations -- French to English
LC 83016449
"Includes two novellas that rank as classics, not only in Colette's canon, but in all of 20th century French literature. The Tender Shoot is the story of a singularly nasty middle-aged rou's pursuit of a 15-year-old peasant girl. Upon this squalid tale, Colette lavished her most lyrical language and poetic fancies, heightening the sense of evil. ... As Colette remarked of her writing, her 'great landscape was always the human face.' No work demonstrates this better than The Kepi, the portrait of a doomed 46-year-old French lieutenant." Time.

Colette, 1873-1954
The **complete** Claudine / Colette ; translated from the French by Antonia White ; introduction by Judith Thurman. Farrar, Straus and Giroux, 2001. xviii, 632 p.
ISBN 9780374528034
1. Young women 2. Manners and customs 3. France -- Social life and customs -- 19th century 4. Diary novels 5. Coming-of-age stories 6.

Translations -- French to English
LC 2001033699
All four of the great French writer's Claudine novels present a unified view of the amoral, tender, fun-loving, and savage child-woman and sustained insight into her creator's life.

Colfer, Eoin
Plugged / Eoin Colfer. Overlook, 2011. 288 p. Plugged
ISBN 9781590204634
1. Bouncers 2. Murder -- New Jersey 3. Gangsters 4. Death threats 5. Police corruption 6. Eccentrics and eccentricities 7. Crime bosses 8. New Jersey 9. Caper novels 10. Crime fiction
When his girlfriend and several people close to him are murdered, Daniel McEvoy finds himself targeted by the New Jersey mafia, corrupt cops, and an eccentric neighbor and searches for a hair-plug technician who may hold crucial answers.
"Outrageous characters, ... uproariously funny plot twists, and brutal, nonstop action make this a sure-fire winner." Publishers Weekly.

Colgan, Jenny
* The **endless** beach / Jenny Colgan. William Morrow & Co., 2018. 416 p. Island of Mure novels
ISBN 9780062851116
1. Island life 2. Women restaurateurs 3. Superstition 4. Life change events 5. Communities 6. Families 7. Couples 8. Recipes 9. Small town life 10. Family relationships 11. Men/women relations 12. Scotland 13. Mainstream fiction
Leaving her glum career in London to open a cafe by the sea on the beautiful Scottish island of Mure, Flora is astonished when her adorable if difficult boss, Joel, follows her and initiates a promising new romance that is overshadowed by local superstitions.

Colin, Emily A., 1975-
The **memory** thief : a novel / Emily Colin. Ballantine Books, 2012. 368 p.
ISBN 9780345530394
1. Life change events 2. Love triangles 3. Grief 4. Memory 5. Mothers and sons 6. Self-fulfillment in women 7. Mountaineers 8. Men/women relations 9. Interpersonal attraction 10. Widows 11. Guilt 12. Traffic accident victims 13. Men with amnesia 14. Mainstream fiction
LC 2012020348
Receiving her mountaineer husband's promise that he will return to her after climbing Mount McKinley, Maddie is devastated to learn that her husband has died in an avalanche, a situation that reveals a best friend's longtime love for her before an accident victim across the country becomes haunted by dreams of Maddie and her young son.

Collins, Ciaran, 1977-
The **gamal** / Ciaran Collins. Bloomsbury USA, 2013. 480 p.
ISBN 9781608198757
1. Lovers 2. Small town life 3. Friendship 4. Misfits (Persons) 5. Writing 6. Music 7. Psychotherapy patients 8. Bereavement 9. Loss (Psychology) 10. Young men 11. Secrets 12. Interpersonal relations 13. Men/women relations 14. Ireland 15. Psychological fiction
LC 2012046539
Meet Charlie. People think he's crazy. But he's not. People think he's stupid. But he's not. People think he's innocent...He's the Gamal. Charlie has a story to tell, about his best friends Sinead and James and the bad things that happened. But he can't tell it yet, at least not till he's worked out where the beginning is. Because is the beginning long ago when Sinead first spoke up for him after Charlie got in trouble at school for the

millionth time? Or was it later, when Sinead and James followed the music and found each other? Or was it later still on that terrible night when something unspeakable happened after closing time and someone chose to turn a blind eye? Charlie has promised Dr Quinn he'll write 1,000 words a day, but it's hard to know which words to write. And which secrets to tell...This is the story of the dark heart of an Irish village, of how daring to be different can be dangerous and how there is nothing a person will not do for love. Exhilarating, bitingly funny and unforgettably poignant, this is a story like no other. This is the story of the Gamal.

Collins, Kathleen, 1942-1988

Notes from a black woman's diary : selected works of Kathleen Collins / Kathleen Collins ; introduction by Danielle Evans. Ecco, 2019 464 p.

ISBN 9780062800954

1. African Americans -- Social conditions 2. African American families 3. Civil Rights Movement 4. Sexism 5. Racism 6. Student films 7. Women 8. United States -- Race relations 9. Diaries 10. Short stories 11. African American fiction

LC 2018022069

"A stunning collection of fiction, diary entries, screenplays and scripts by the brilliant African-American artist and filmmaker"--, Provided by publisher.

"While not as eye-opening as Collins's earlier stories, this compilation will add appreciation for a talented writer whose life was cut too short as well as provide hope for the recovery of her previously unpublished work. Recommended for all libraries." Library Journal.

Collins, Kathleen, 1942-1988

* **Whatever** happened to interracial love? : stories / Kathleen Collins. Ecco Press, 2016. 175 p.

ISBN 9780062484154

1. African Americans 2. Race relations 3. Family relationships 4. African American families 5. Civil Rights Movement 6. Literary fiction 7. Short stories 8. African American fiction

A collection of newly found stories by the late playwright and filmmaker explores race, gender, family, and sexuality.

"As the provocative collection title suggests, interracial love is the chief romantic theme Collins explores in stories of varying lengths and complexity, but its not her only focus. She also examines the different types of connections formed within African American family relationships across generations. And a few stories are wholly stream-of-consciousness. Each of Collins stories leaves the reader wanting to know more about the characters and their creator, which makes this an intriguing and bittersweet publication of these stories long awaiting the attention they deserve." Booklist.

Collins, Manda

A **good** rake is hard to find / Manda Collins. St Martin's Paperbacks, 2015. 336 p. Lords of Anarchy novels

ISBN 9781250061065

1. Regency period (1811-1820) 2. Former fiances 3. Men's organizations 4. Brothers -- Death 5. Murder investigation 6. Undercover operations 7. Sexual attraction 8. Men/women relations 9. England -- Social life and customs -- 19th century 10. Great Britain -- History -- Regency, 1811-1820 11. Regency romances 12. Historical romances

"Readers who relish historical romances served up with a generous measure of dangerous intrigue and sizzling sensuality will definitely want to test drive this smartly crafted tale." Booklist

Collins, Manda

Ready set rogue / Manda Collins. St Martin's Paperbacks, 2017. 310 p. Studies in scandal novels

ISBN 9781250109866

1. Regency period (1811-1820) 2. Women scholars and academics 3. Heirs and heiresses 4. Marquis and marchionesses 5. Inheritance and succession 6. Murder investigation 7. Interpersonal attraction 8. Men/women relations 9. England 10. Great Britain 11. Regency romances 12. Historical romances

When her inheritance offers her the independence she craves, bluestocking Miss Ivy Wareham, who is more comfortable discussing the details of ancient Greek literature than the latest fashion, gets involved in a murder mystery at the behest of the Marquess of Kerr who is seeking the truth behind his aunt's death.

Collins, Max Allan

Ask not : Nathan Heller Mystery / Max Allan Collins. Forge Books, 2013. 320 p. Nathan Heller novels

ISBN 9780765336262

1. 1960s 2. Assassination 3. Private investigators 4. Conspiracies 5. Organized crime 6. Witnesses 7. Murder investigation 8. Mafia 9. Former police 10. Los Angeles, California 11. Historical mysteries 12. Hardboiled fiction 13. Mysteries

LC 2013018440

After the assassination of JFK, a suspicious outbreak of suicides, accidental deaths and outright murders decimates assassination witnesses and private detective Nathan Heller, with the blessing of Bobby Kennedy, investigates the increasing wave of violence.

Collins, Max Allan

The **wrong** Quarry / Max Allan Collins. Hard Case Crime, 2014. 256 p. Quarry novels

ISBN 9781781162668

1. Assassins 2. Murder for hire 3. Vietnam veterans 4. Cheerleaders 5. Missing teenagers 6. Murder 7. Hardboiled fiction 8. Pulp fiction

Hitman Quarry, who helps his marked-for-death clients by eliminating the killers sent after them--and finding out who hired them--wonders if he has the wrong target in his sights when he zeroes in on the grieving family of a missing cheerleader.

Collins, Sara

The **confessions** of Frannie Langton / Sara Collins. Harper360, 2019. 375 p.

ISBN 9780062851895

1. 18th century 2. Murder suspects 3. Women prisoners 4. Multiracial women 5. Household employees 6. Social classes 7. Innocence (Law) 8. Trials (Murder) 9. England -- History -- 19th century 10. Jamaica -- History -- 19th century 11. Historical fiction

Costa First Novel Award, 2019.

A servant and former slave enduring a sensational trial for her employers' murders reflects on her Jamaican childhood and her apprenticeship under a debauched scientist whose questionable ethics set the stage for a forbidden affair.

Collins, Wilkie, 1824-1889

* The **moonstone** / Wilkie Collins. Oxford University Press, 2008, c1868. lviii, 502 p.

ISBN 9780199536726

1. Victorian era (1837-1901) 2. 19th century 3. Jewel thieves 4. Jewelry theft 5. Police 6. East Indians in England 7. Detectives 8. Moonstones 9. Diamonds 10. Fortune hunters 11. Greed in men 12. Marriage 13. Birthday parties 14. Brahmins 15. England -- History

-- 19th century 16. Mysteries 17. Victorian mysteries 18. Classics

Originally published as a serialized publication in All the Year Round of 1868, first published as a complete novel by Tinsley Brothers: 1868.

Originally published in 3 volumes: London : Tinsley Brothers, 1868.

Rachel Verrinder receives the stone as a gift and does not realize that it has been passed to her in a sinister form of revenge by John Herncastle who, it transpires, acquired the moonstone by means of murder and theft. The jewel also brings bad luck. The stone disappears on the very night it is given to Rachel, though, and the tale concerns the unveiling of the culprit after the intervention of Sergeant Cuff, a famous London detective.

Collins, Wilkie, 1824-1889

* The **woman** in white / William Wilkie Collins. Knopf, 1991, c1860. xxxvii, 569 p.

ISBN 0679405631

1. Victorian era (1837-1901) 2. Psychiatric hospital patients 3. Deception 4. Nobility 5. Inheritance and succession 6. Love triangles 7. Country homes 8. Sisters 9. Men/women relations 10. England -- Social life and customs -- 19th century 11. Gothic fiction 12. Mysteries 13. Victorian mysteries 14. Classics

LC 91052971

Originally published in 3 volumes: London : Sampson Low, Son & Co., 1860.

The mysterious appearance of a woman dressed in all white leads to the discovery of a complicated plot involving a stolen inheritance.

Colombani, Laetitia, 1976-

The **braid** : a novel / Laetitia Colombani. Atria Paperback, 2019, c2017. 199 p.

ISBN 9781982130039

1. Hair 2. Social status 3. Women's role 4. Mothers and daughters 5. Sick persons 6. Social classes 7. Poverty 8. Refugees 9. Self-fulfillment in women 10. Women with cancer 11. India 12. Sicily, Italy 13. Canada 14. Mainstream fiction 15. Women's lives and relationships 16. Translations -- French to English

Originally published: Paris : Editions Grasset & Fasquelle, 2017.

An Indian "untouchable" who would give her daughter an education, a Sicilian wigmaker who would save her father's business and a Canadian lawyer and single mother with cancer find their lives intertwined by a fateful object.

"This title is perfect for those who enjoy quick reads and conflicts that resolve into satisfying endings." Library Journal.

Colvin, Jeffrey

* Africaville : a novel / Jeffrey Colvin. Amistad, 2019. 384 p.

ISBN 9780062913722

1. 20th century 2. Freed slaves 3. African Americans -- Migrations 4. Black Canadians 5. Racism 6. Mothers and sons 7. Identity (Psychology) 8. Fathers and sons 9. Passing (Identity) 10. Home (Concept) 11. Africville (Halifax, NS) 12. Canada 13. Nova Scotia 14. United States 15. Family sagas

LC 2019017430

Three generations of a family of former slaves, the founders of a small Nova Scotia community, navigate prejudice, harsh weather and estrangements against a backdrop of the historical events of the 20th century.

"Colvin depicts the heartbreaking neglect and ultimate destruction of Africaville by white Canadian governments while also dramatizing the resilience that enabled its residents to survive." Booklist.

Colwin, Laurie, 1944-1992

Goodbye without leaving / Laurie Colwin. Poseidon Press, 1990. 253 p.

ISBN 9780671707064

1. Married women -- Identity 2. Self-perception in women 3. Self-fulfillment in women 4. Memories 5. Marriage 6. Singers 7. Race relations 8. Domestic fiction

LC 90006797

Geraldine Coleshares, former backup singer for Ruby Shakely and the Shakettes, muddles through marriage, motherhood, and employment while struggling to reconcile youth with maturity and expectations with real life.

"The tone here is disarmingly light, the humor intimate, and the plot inventive. A cheerfully irreverent look at an identity crisis and its unexpected resolution." Booklist.

Colwin, Laurie, 1944-1992

Happy all the time : a novel Knopf, 1978. 213 p.

ISBN 039450190X

1. Married people 2. Friendship 3. Dating (Social customs) 4. Manners and customs 5. Mainstream fiction

LC 78002425

The courtship of Vincent Cardworthy and Misty Berkowitz and the marriage of Holly Stergis and Guido Morris are marked by practical concerns, romance, surprises, luck, and no upper hands

"What we, as readers are treated to, however, is one of the most engaging and funniest dual courtships in a long time. The dialogue is sparkling and crisp, the encounter situations perfectly believable and perfectly ridiculous, as these four people, who really are 'happy all the time,' go through the 'angst' of realizing it." Publishers Weekly.

Conde, Maryse

I, Tituba, Black witch of Salem / Maryse Conde ; translated by Richard Philcox ; foreword by Angela Y. Davis ; afterword by Ann Armstrong Scarboro. University Press of Virginia, 1992. xiii, 227 p.

ISBN 0813913985

1. Tituba 2. Witchcraft -- Salem, Massachusetts -- History -- 17th century 3. African West Indian women 4. Women slaves -- History -- 17th century 5. Witch hunting -- Salem, Massachusetts 6. Trials (Witchcraft) 7. Salem, Massachusetts -- History -- Colonial period, 1626-1775 8. Translations -- French to English 9. Historical fiction

LC 92008134

A fictionalized account of the West Indian slave Tituba, who was accused of witchcraft in Salem, Massachusetts in 1692, and was arrested and jailed for two years.

"Part historical novel, part literary fable, part exploration of the clash of irreconcilable cultures, [this] is most of all an affirmation of a courageous and resourceful woman's capacity for survival." New York Times Book Review.

Conde, Maryse

The **story** of the cannibal woman : a novel / Maryse Conde ; translated from the French by Richard Philcox. Atria Books, 2007, c2003. 320 p.

ISBN 0743271289

1. Married women 2. Women psychics 3. Missing men 4. Abandoned women 5. Survival 6. Clairvoyance 7. Murder 8. Multiculturalism 9. Culture conflict 10. Women's role 11. Independence in women 12. Self-reliance in women 13. Post-apartheid era 14. Cape Town, South Africa 15. South Africa 16. Mysteries 17. Translations -- French to

English

LC 2006049155

Originally published: Paris : Mercure de France, 2003.

Rendered frightened and penniless by her husband's mysterious violent death, Rosalie reluctantly taps her clairvoyant skills in order to support herself in post-apartheid South Africa, an endeavor during which she pursues answers for the events in her life.

"Flitting back and forth in time, Conde parcels out the rich texture of Roselie's life in piecemeal fashion, a strategy that invests The Story of the Cannibal Woman with enormous narrative verve. Though written in French, and subject to the occasional awkward construction in translation, it is nonetheless a book of strong narrative juice, its language so rewarding that what is happening in any given passage is almost--but not quite--beside the point." PopMatters.

Conklin, Tara

The **house** girl : a novel / Tara Conklin. William Morrow Paperbacks, 2013. 384 p.

ISBN 9780062207395

1. Women 2. Identity (Psychology) 3. Freedom 4. Fugitive slaves -- Virginia 5. Corporate lawyers 6. Reparations 7. Reparations for historical injustices 8. Slaves 9. Children of slaves 10. Women artists 11. Social justice 12. Virginia -- History -- 19th century 13. New York City -- History -- 21st century 14. Literary fiction 15. Parallel narratives

LC 2012027370

A novel of love, family, and justice follows Lina Sparrow, an ambitious first-year associate in a Manhattan law firm, as she searches for the "perfect plaintiff" to lead a historic class-action lawsuit worth trillions of dollars in reparations for descendants of American slaves.

Conlon, Edward, 1965-

Red on red : a novel / Edward Conlon. Spiegel & Grau, 2011. 464 p.

ISBN 9780385519175

1. Criminal investigation 2. Police 3. Undercover operations 4. Detectives 5. Friendship 6. Gangs 7. Drugs 8. Rape investigation 9. New York City 10. Mysteries

LC 2010017534

NYC detective Nick Meehan takes a special case for Internal Affairs--to investigate a suspected dirty cop. Meehan and his partner then investigate other cases, including one in which gangs slay rival drug dealers.

Connell, Evan S., 1924-2013

Mrs. Bridge : a novel / Evan S. Connell. North Point Press, 1959. 246 p. Bridge series (Evan S. Connell)

1. Married women -- Kansas City, Missouri 2. Families -- Kansas City, Missouri 3. Kansas City, Missouri 4. Literary fiction

LC 81081514

Book Mr. Bridge and book Mrs. Bridge were the inspiration for the movie Mr. & Mrs. Bridge.

Connelly, Michael, 1956-

The **black** ice / Michael Connelly Little, Brown, 1993. 322 p. Harry Bosch mysteries

ISBN 9780316153829

1. Vietnam veterans 2. Murder investigation 3. Drug smuggling 4. Police -- Los Angeles, California 5. Detectives -- Los Angeles, California 6. Murder 7. Police misconduct 8. Mistaken identity 9. Los Angeles, California 10. Mysteries 11. Police procedurals

LC 92033500

L.A.P.D. detective Harry Bosch investigates the mysterious death of a narcotics officer who was reportedly selling a new drug called black ice.

Connelly, Michael, 1956-

The **brass** verdict : a novel / Michael Connelly. Little, Brown, 2008. 432 p. Harry Bosch mysteries

ISBN 9780316166294

1. Crimes against lawyers 2. Trials (Murder) 3. Murder investigation 4. Defense attorneys 5. Police -- Los Angeles, California 6. Detectives -- Los Angeles, California 7. Lawyers 8. Vietnam veterans 9. Los Angeles, California 10. Legal thrillers

LC 2008019374

Harry Bosch from the author's Harry Bosch series is featured as a secondary character in this title.

Anthony Award for Best Novel, 2009.

Hoping to revitalize his career when he inherits a high-profile defense case after a fellow lawyer is murdered, Mickey Haller discovers that he may be the next target and reluctantly teams up with LAPD detective Harry Bosch to find the killer.

"If this were no more than a standard legal thriller, it would still be hard to put down. But for all the glee we might take in watching Mickey in action--psychoanalyzing the jury pool, shredding the credibility of a prosecution witness or faking civility to a powerful judge--The Brass Verdict is not just a conventional legal thriller but also a complicated morality play." New York Times Book Review.

Connelly, Michael, 1956-

The **burning** room / Michael Connelly. Little Brown & Co., 2014. 400 p. Harry Bosch mysteries

ISBN 9780316225939

1. Murder investigation 2. Cold cases (Criminal investigation) 3. Police 4. Detectives 5. Los Angeles, California 6. Police procedurals 7. Mysteries

When the vicitim of a crime succumbs to complications from a bullet wound from nine years ago, Detective Harry Bosch and his new partner, Lucia Soto must find new leads from the past.

"Bosch is very much of the old school in this high-tech world, but his hands-on tenacity serves him and the case well--just as Connelly serves his readers well with his encyclopedic knowledge and gifts as a storyteller." Publishers Weekly.

Connelly, Michael, 1956-

The **crossing** / Michael Connelly. Little Brown & Co., 2015. 400 p. Harry Bosch mysteries

ISBN 9780316225885

1. Murder investigation 2. Innocence (Law) 3. Frameups 4. Police 5. Detectives 6. Los Angeles, California 7. Police procedurals 8. Mysteries

Coming out of retirement to help his defense attorney half-brother prove that a client has been framed for murder, Detective Harry Bosch secretly teams up with former partner Lucy Soto to investigate possible corruption inside the LAPD.

"As always, Connelly's blackboard work is as precise as his finale is exciting." Booklist.

Connelly, Michael, 1956-

Dark sacred night / Michael Connelly. Little, Brown and Co., 2018. 400 p. Renee Ballard novels

ISBN 9780316484800

1. Women detectives 2. Private investigators 3. Cold cases (Criminal investigation) 4. Runaways 5. Crimes against teenage girls 6. Former police 7. Former detectives 8. Murder investigation 9. Hollywood,

California 10. Los Angeles, California 11. Police procedurals 12. Mysteries

LC 2018945140

Teaming up with Harry Bosch to reopen a cold case, LAPD detective Renee Ballard navigates interpersonal differences to pursue justice for a murdered runaway in Hollywood.

Connelly, Michael, 1956-

Echo Park : a novel / Michael Connelly. Little, Brown and Co., 2006. 416 p. Harry Bosch mysteries

ISBN 9780316734950

1. Vietnam veterans 2. Women FBI agents 3. Cold cases (Criminal investigation) 4. Crimes against young women 5. Police -- Los Angeles, California 6. Detectives -- Los Angeles, California 7. Missing persons 8. Serial murderers 9. Conspiracies 10. Forensic sciences 11. Los Angeles, California 12. Police procedurals 13. Mysteries

LC 2006009809

Eleven years after his investigation into the 1995 disappearance of Marie Gesto goes cold, Harry Bosch finally gets a chance to put the case to rest when a man accused of two brutal killings agrees to come clean about several others, including that of Marie Gesto, until Harry discovers that he and his partner had missed a clue in 1995 that could have found the killer and stopped nine other killings.

"What puts Connelly in the top rank of modern procedural writers and, perhaps, into the ranks of the better modern L.A. writers of any genre, is his willingness to accept that there aren't always easy answers in Bosch's life, or sometimes any answers at all. . . . That sense of uncertainty and dread, combined with Bosch's going from middle age to the precipice of old age, informs every page of this novel." Washington Post Book World.

Connelly, Michael, 1956-

The **fifth** witness / Michael Connelly. Little, Brown and Co., 2011. 416 p. Mickey Haller novels

ISBN 9780316069359

1. Attorney and client 2. Trials (Murder) 3. Foreclosure 4. Witnesses 5. Single mothers 6. Defense attorneys 7. Lawyers 8. Los Angeles, California 9. Legal thrillers

LC 2011000576

Mickey Haller must defend a client who is accused of killing the banker involved with her foreclosure, a case that reveals strong suspicions, black-market dealings and a threat to Mickey's own life.

"The story line is compelling, intense, and terrifying while providing an in-depth look at the mortgage crisis that is surprisingly interesting." Library Journal.

Connelly, Michael, 1956-

The **gods** of guilt / Michael Connelly. Little, Brown, 2013. 416 p. Mickey Haller novels

ISBN 9780316069519

1. Attorney and client 2. Trials (Murder) 3. Crimes against prostitutes 4. Defense attorneys 5. Lawyers 6. Los Angeles, California 7. Legal thrillers

Defense attorney Mickey Haller investigates after a former client, a prostitute who had left the life for the straight and narrow, turns up dead.

Connelly, Michael, 1956-

The **late** show / Michael Connelly. Little, Brown & Co., 2017. 400 p. Renee Ballard novels

ISBN 9780316225984

1. Women detectives 2. Crimes against women 3. Murder investigation 4. Nightclubs 5. Sexual harassment 6. Violence against women 7. Hollywood, California 8. Los Angeles, California 9. California 10. Mysteries

Includes an excerpt from Two kinds of truth.

Relegated to the night shift after filing a sexual harassment complaint against a supervisor, a once up-and-coming LAPD detective disobeys orders by refusing to walk away from two cases, including an assault on a prostitute and the death of a young woman in a nightclub shooting.

Connelly, Michael, 1956-

The **Lincoln** lawyer : a novel / Michael Connelly. Little, Brown, 2005. 416 p. Mickey Haller novels

ISBN 0316734934

1. Defense attorneys 2. Attorney and client 3. Innocence (Law) 4. Trials (Assault and battery) 5. Lawyers 6. Rich people 7. Automobiles 8. Integrity 9. Belief and doubt 10. Beverly Hills, California 11. Legal thrillers

LC 2005012863

Originally published: 2005.

Macavity Award for Best Mystery Novel, 2006.

Shamus Award for Best P.I. Novel, 2006.

Mickey Haller, who represents some unsavory characters in his work as a defense lawyer, takes on his first high-paying and possibly innocent client in years, but finds the case complicated by events that suggest a particularly evil perpetrator.

"The book is haunted by Mickey's worst nightmare: the thought of having to defend an innocent man. He starts out without the foggiest idea of what to do with someone like that. But by the end of the story an Honest Abe conscience has begun to kick in. That's when Mickey becomes a Connelly character through and through." New York Times.

Connelly, Michael, 1956-

The **night** fire / Michael Connelly. Little Brown & Co, 2019. 400 p. Renee Ballard novels

ISBN 9780316485616

1. Detectives 2. Cold cases (Criminal investigation) 3. Alliances 4. Women detectives 5. Mentors 6. Secrets 7. Murder investigation 8. Drug dealers 9. Los Angeles, California 10. California 11. Mysteries

Receiving a with details about a 20-year cold case, homicide detective Harry Bosch teams up with LAPD detective Renee Ballard before uncovering disturbing clues about his late mentor.

Connelly, Michael, 1956-

The **scarecrow** : a novel / Michael Connelly. Little, Brown and Co., 2009. 432 p. Jack McEvoy novels

ISBN 9780316166300

1. Serial murder investigation 2. Computer industry and trade 3. Drug dealers 4. Journalists 5. Sixteen-year-old boys 6. Hackers 7. Newspaper publishers and publishing 8. Women FBI agents 9. Los Angeles, California 10. Thrillers and suspense

LC 2009000855

Pursuing a big story in anticipation of his imminent layoff, Los Angeles reporter Jack McEvoy investigates the murder confession of a teen drug dealer and realizes that the youth may be innocent, a discovery that pits him against a killer operating below police radar.

"The Scarecrow is swift and engrossing, and it marks a development that has needed to happen in Connelly's novels for a while." Boston Phoenix.

Connelly, Michael, 1956-

The **wrong** side of goodbye / Michael Connelly. Little Brown & Co., 2016. 400 p. Harry Bosch mysteries

ISBN 9780316225946

1. Rape investigation 2. Private investigators 3. Missing persons

investigation 4. Billionaires 5. Serial rapists 6. Former police 7. Former detectives 8. Heirs and heiresses 9. Murder investigation 10. Los Angeles, California 11. Police procedurals 12. Mysteries

California's newest private investigator, Harry Bosch, searches for a reclusive billionaire's possible heir, a case with odd links to his own past, and volunteers to find a serial rapist for a small cash-strapped police department.

Connolly, John, 1968-

A **book** of bones / John Conolly. Atria Books, 2019. 496 p. Charlie "Bird" Parker novels

ISBN 9781982127510

1. Private investigators 2. Detectives 3. Serial murders 4. Murder investigation 5. Women murder victims 6. Maine 7. Mysteries 8. Supernatural mysteries

Three murders in different regions of England reveal the work of a sinister killer who is sacrificing victims for an evil agenda, compelling Charlie Parker's gripping search for clues in multiple countries.

Connolly, John, 1968-

The **book** of lost things / John Connolly. Atria Books, 2006. 342 p.

ISBN 0743298853

1. Second World War era (1939-1945) 2. Grief in children 3. Imagination in boys 4. Characters and characteristics in fairy tales 5. Twelve-year-old boys 6. Books and reading 7. World War II 8. Quests 9. England -- History -- 20th century 10. Gateway fantasy 11. Fantasy fiction 12. Horror

LC 2006049340

Taking refuge in fairy tales after the loss of his mother, twelve-year-old David finds himself violently propelled into an imaginary land in which the boundaries of fantasy and reality are disturbingly melded.

"A novel about a 12-year-old English boy, David, who is thrust into a realm where eternal stories and fairy tales assume an often gruesome reality. Books are the magic that speak to David, whose mother has died at the start of WWII after a long debilitating illness. His father remarries, and soon his stepmother is pregnant with yet another interloper who will threaten David's place in his father's life. When a portal to another world opens in time-honored fashion, David enters a land of beasts and monsters where he must undertake a quest if he is to earn his way back out. Connolly echoes many great fairy tales and legends (Little Red Riding Hood, Roland, Hansel and Gretel), but cleverly twists them to his own purposes." Library Journal.

Connolly, John, 1968-

The **burning** soul : a thriller / John Connolly. Atria Books, 2011. 352 p. Charlie "Bird" Parker novels

ISBN 9781439165270

1. Extortion 2. Former convicts 3. Kidnapping 4. Secrets 5. Deception 6. Crimes against children 7. Private investigators 8. Criminal investigation 9. Supernatural 10. Small towns 11. Small town life 12. Former police 13. Maine 14. Mysteries 15. Supernatural mysteries

LC 2011021367

Investigating sinister threats against a man hiding a criminal past, detective Charlie Parker stumbles into a web of corruption and deceit involving the FBI, a doomed mobster, and a missing teenage girl.

"An intelligent, plausible thriller, both harrowing and memorable." Kirkus.

Connolly, John, 1968-

The **woman** in the woods / John Connolly. Emily Bestler Books, 2018. 448 p. Charlie "Bird" Parker novels

ISBN 9781501171925

1. Newborn infants 2. Missing persons 3. Private investigators 4. Detectives 5. Small towns 6. Murder investigation 7. Women murder victims 8. Infant kidnapping victims 9. Missing persons investigation 10. Maine 11. Mysteries 12. Supernatural mysteries

LC 2017058422

When the body of a woman--who apparently died in childbirth--is discovered, Parker is hired to track down both her identity and her missing child. In the beautiful Maine woods, a partly preserved body is discovered. Investigators realize that the dead young woman gave birth shortly before her death. But there is no sign of a baby.

Connolly, Sheila

The **lost** traveller / Sheila Connolly. Crooked Lane Books, 2019. 336 p. County Cork mysteries

ISBN 9781683318903

1. Americans in Ireland 2. Women amateur detectives 3. Women bar owners 4. Villages 5. Rural life 6. Murder 7. Murder investigation 8. Options, alternatives, choices 9. Couples 10. Secrets 11. Cork County, Ireland 12. Ireland 13. Cozy mysteries 14. Gentle reads

Danger comes to Cork and it's up to Maura Donovan to find a way to protect all she's worked for.

"Although the mystery is cleverly woven into the story, it's the heroine's slow awakening and the marvelous local color that make this one of the best in a fine series." Kirkus.

Conrad, Joseph, 1857-1924

Complete short fiction of Joseph Conrad: the stories: Joseph Conrad ; edited with an introduction by Samuel Hynes ECCO Press, 1991. 296 p.

ISBN 9780880013079

1. Seafaring life 2. Personal conduct 3. Men/women relations 4. Short stories 5. Classics 6. Literary fiction

LC 91027115

Includes the first 9 of 22 stories published between 1896-1928.

Collects Conrad's short stories and tales, with a chronology and the author's own notes on his shorter fiction.

Conrad, Joseph, 1857-1924

* **Heart** of darkness / Joseph Conrad. Penguin Books, 1999, c1902. 146 p.

ISBN 0140281630

1. Ship captains 2. Colonialism 3. Violence 4. Steamboats 5. Voyages and travels 6. Doppelgangers 7. Congo (Democratic Republic) -- Exploration -- British 8. Psychological fiction 9. Literary fiction 10. Classics

Heart of darkness was first published as The heart of darkness in Blackwood's Magazine in 1899.

Heart of darkness was first published in book form with Youth and The end of the tether in Youth: a narrative, and two other stories in 1902.

Marlowe sails down the Congo in search of Kurtz, a company agent who has, according to rumors, become insane in the jungle isolation.

Conrad, Joseph, 1857-1924

* **Lord** Jim / Joseph Conrad. Penguin, 2007, c1900. 417 p.

ISBN 9780141441610

1. Sailors 2. Young men -- Identity 3. Self-fulfillment in men 4. Shipwrecks 5. Cowardice 6. Self-hate in men 7. Honor in men 8. Europeans in developing countries 9. Alienation in men 10.

Loyalty in men 11. Redemption 12. Guilt in men 13. Wanderers and wandering 14. British in Southeast Asia 15. Psychological fiction 16. Sea stories 17. Classics 18. Literary fiction

Originally published: 1900.

Includes essay: Lord Jim / by Harold Bloom.

A young Englishman branded as a coward seeks personal redemption for an act of selfishness

Conrad, Joseph, 1857-1924

* **Nostromo** : a tale of the seaboard / Joseph Conrad. Penguin, 2007, c1904 532 p.

ISBN 9780141441634

1. Heroes and heroines 2. Revolutions -- South America 3. Sailors 4. Greed 5. Silver mines and mining -- South America 6. Imperialism 7. South America -- History -- 19th century 8. Psychological fiction 9. Classics 10. Literary fiction

LC 91053185

Originally published: 1904.

Set in the fictional South American country of Costaguana, this story of revolution, deception, and self-betrayal centers on Nostromo, a handsome Italian sailor, who, like Costaguana, is being consumed by secret guilt and corruption.

Conrad, Joseph, 1857-1924

Victory : an island tale / Joseph Conrad ; edited with an introduction and notes by Mara Kalnins. Oxford University Press, 2009, 400 p.

ISBN 9780199554058

1. Island life 2. Colonialism 3. Social isolation 4. Alienation in men 5. Europeans in Indonesia 6. Men/women relations 7. Indonesia 8. Psychological fiction 9. Classics 10. Literary fiction

Conroy, Pat

The **prince** of tides / Pat Conroy. Houghton Mifflin, 1986. 567 p.

ISBN 9780395353004

1. Adult child abuse victims 2. People with mental illnesses 3. Women poets -- United States -- 20th century 4. Women 5. Family problems 6. Extramarital affairs 7. Dysfunctional families -- South Carolina 8. Twins 9. Brothers and sisters 10. Suicidal behavior 11. South Carolina 12. New York City 13. Psychological fiction 14. Southern fiction

LC 86010689

Spanning forty years, it is a story about Tom Wingo, his twin sister, Savannah, and the dark and violent past of an extraordinary family into which they were born.

Conroy, Pat

South of Broad : a novel / Pat Conroy. Nan A. Talese/ Doubleday, 2009. 528 p.

ISBN 9780385413053

1. 1960s 2. 1980s 3. Nostalgia 4. Growing up 5. Social classes 6. Teenagers -- Friendship 7. Family relationships 8. Friendship 9. Race relations 10. Men/women relations 11. Charleston, South Carolina 12. San Francisco, California 13. Coming-of-age stories 14. Southern fiction

LC 2008045681

After his brother's suicide, Leopold Bloom King struggles along with the rest of his family in Charleston, South Carolina, until he begins to gather an intimate circle of friends, whose ties endure for two decades until a final, unexpected test of friendship.

"In the great Southern tradition of storytelling, the city of Charleston, S.C. is the principal character in Pat Conroy's new novel. . . . Like the Southern Gothic masters, William Faulkner and Flannery O'Connor, Conroy understands that a compelling sense of place will lend grace to his narrative, inhabiting the minds of his readers like the mournful strains of an old folk song." Boston Globe.

Constantine, K. C.

Blood mud / K. C. Constantine. Mysterious Press, 1999. 375 p. Rocksburg, Pennsylvania novels

ISBN 9780892966479

1. Gun thefts 2. Insurance companies 3. Private investigators 4. Former police 5. Police 6. Pennsylvania 7. Mysteries

LC 98-34909

Private detective Mario Balzic, whose heart is acting up, returns to investigate the disappearance of guns from a local shop and finds himself confronted with a number of dangerous and powerful suspects, including a local politician and a police chief.

"Constantine knows that Faulkner was right: the only subject truly worth writing about is the human heart in conflict with itself. The evocation of Mario's fears and inner conflicts, told through agonizingly wonderful dialogue between husband and wife, raises this latest Balzic novel to the level of the best contemporary literature." Booklist.

Constantine, Liv

The **last** Mrs. Parrish / Liv Constantine. HarperCollins, 2017. 400 p.

ISBN 9780062667571

1. Rich people 2. Manipulation by women 3. Socialites 4. Female friendship 5. Jealousy 6. Married men 7. Deception 8. Secrets 9. Connecticut 10. Psychological suspense

"Some women get everything. Some women get everything they deserve. Amber Patterson is fed up. She's tired of being a nobody: a plain, invisible woman who blends into the background. She deserves more--a life of money and power like the one blond-haired,blue-eyed goddess Daphne Parrish takes for granted. To everyone in the exclusive town of Bishops Harbor, Connecticut, Daphne--a socialite and philanthropist--and her real-estate mogul husband, Jackson, are a couple straight out of a fairy tale. Amber's envy could eat her alive ... if she didn't have a plan. Amber uses Daphne's compassion and caring to insinuate herself into the family's life--the first step in a meticulous scheme to undermine her. Before long, Amber is Daphne's closest confidante, traveling to Europe with the Parrishes and their lovely young daughters, and growing closer to Jackson. But a skeleton from her past may undermine everything that Amber has worked towards, and if it is discovered, her well-laid plan may fall to pieces. With shocking turns and dark secrets that will keep you guessing until the very end, The Last Mrs. Parrish is a fresh, juicy, and utterly addictive thriller from a diabolically imaginative talent."--Provided by publisher.

"A Gone Girl-esque confection with villainy and melodrama galore." Kirkus.

Constantine, Liv

The **last** time I saw you / Liv Constantine. HarperCollins, 2019 320 p.

ISBN 9780062868817

1. Families of murder victims 2. Mothers -- Death 3. Suspicion 4. Murderers 5. Rich people 6. Former friends 7. Childhood friends 8. Heart surgeons 9. Threat (Psychology) 10. Murder investigation 11. Baltimore, Maryland 12. Thrillers and suspense

Supported by her childhood best friend in the aftermath of her mother's murder, a prominent heart surgeon receives threatening taunts from the killer and risks her mental stability in her desperation to solve the case.

"Sisters Lynne and Valerie Constantine, under the pseudonym Liv Constantine (The Last Mrs. Parrish), have crafted another clever whodunit jam-packed with enough twists, turns, and secrets to keep avid thriller readers second-guessing until the bitter end." Library Journal.

Cook, Dave F. (Dave Fuller), 1951-

* **Reservation** nation : a novel / David Fuller Cook. Boaz Pub., 2007. 199 p.

ISBN 9781893448049

1. United States. Bureau of Indian Affairs. 2. American Indian Movement. 3. Indians of North America -- North Carolina 4. Government relations with indigenous peoples 5. Native American boys -- Identity 6. Native American families 7. Indian reservations 8. North Carolina 9. Domestic fiction

In channeling Warren, Cook's beautifully modulated, speechlike cadences give his debut novel a quiet power. Publishers Weekly.

Cook, Robin, 1940-

Cell / Robin Cook. Putnam Adult, 2014. 448 p.

ISBN 9780399166303

1. Physicians 2. Medical technology 3. Murder investigation 4. Technological innovations 5. Diagnosis 6. Physician and patient 7. Engaged persons 8. Medical thrillers

LC 2013037703

Also published: New York : G.P. Putnam's Sons, 2014.

Entering a profession on the brink of radical transformation by a new smartphone technology capable of diagnosing and treating patients, radiology resident George Wilson is horrified when his fiancee and several patients die after beta testing the technology. By the best-selling author of Intervention.

Cook, Robin, 1940-

* **Charlatans** / Robin Cook. G. P. Putnam's Sons, 2017. 416 p.

ISBN 9780735212480

1. Surgeons 2. Medical malpractice 3. Manslaughter 4. Blame 5. Anesthesiologists 6. Surgery 7. Murder suspects 8. Boston, Massachusetts 9. Medical thrillers

Newly minted chief resident at Boston Memorial Hospital Noah Rothauser is swamped in his new position, from managing the surgical schedules to dealing with the fallouts from patient deaths. Known for its medical advances, the famed teaching hospital has fitted several ORs as "hybrid operating rooms of the future"--an improvement that seems positive until an anesthesia error during a routine procedure results in the death of an otherwise healthy man. Noah suspects Dr. William Mason, an egotistical, world-class surgeon, of an error during the operation and of tampering with the patient's record afterward. But Mason is quick to blame anesthesiologist, Dr. Ava London.

Cook, Robin, 1940-

Coma : a novel / Robin Cook. Little, Brown, 1977. 306 p.

ISBN 0316155101

1. Hospital patients 2. Physicians 3. Surgery patients 4. Surgeons 5. Medical students 6. People in comas 7. Donation of organs, tissues, etc 8. Black market 9. Organ and tissue thefts 10. Hospitals 11. Murder 12. Transplantation of organs, tissues, etc 13. Surgery 14. Medicine 15. Boston, Massachusetts 16. Thrillers and suspense 17. Medical thrillers

LC 76052951

Book made into a movie called Coma.

A third-year medical student in a Boston teaching hospital uncovers a medical black market dealing in human organs when she investigates why two young patients have lapsed into comas.

Cook, Robin, 1940-

* **Genesis** / Robin Cook. Putnam Pub Group, 2019. 400 p.

ISBN 9780525542155

1. DNA 2. Genetic genealogy 3. Coroners 4. Pregnant women -- Death 5. Birthfathers 6. Murder 7. Secrets 8. Medical thrillers

New York Times-bestselling author Robin Cook takes on the ripped-from-the-headlines topic of harnessing DNA from ancestry websites to catch a killer in this timely and explosive new medical thriller.

Cook, Robin, 1940-

* **Host** / Robin Cook. G. P. Putnam's Sons, 2015. 416 p.

ISBN 9780399172144

1. Death threats 2. Women medical students 3. Medical malpractice 4. Boyfriends -- Death 5. Surgery 6. Death 7. Hospitals 8. Medical thrillers

Devastated by the death of her boyfriend after a routine surgery, fourth-year medical student Lynn Pierce investigates the accident and discovers a string of suspicious deaths at the hospital.

Cook, Robin, 1940-

Nano / Robin Cook. G. P. Putnam's Sons, 2012 432 p.

ISBN 9780399160820

1. Human experimentation in medicine 2. Nanotechnology 3. Secrets 4. Medical technology 5. Former medical students 6. Business ethics 7. Conspiracies 8. Medical thrillers 9. Thrillers and suspense
Sequel to: Death benefit

Taking a year off from her medical studies and leaving New York City, Pia Grazdani accepts a job at Nano, a nanotechnology institute, where she is quickly warned not to investigate the other work done at the facility and not to ask questions about their source of funding.

Cook, Robin, 1940-

* **Pandemic** / Robin Cook. Penguin Group USA, 2018 400 p. Jack Stapleton and Laurie Montgomery series

ISBN 9780525535331

1. Coroners 2. Epidemics 3. Conspiracies 4. Biotechnology 5. Businesspeople 6. Transplantation of organs, tissues, etc 7. Black market 8. New York City 9. Medical thrillers 10. Thrillers and suspense

LC 2018038076

When a heart-transplant recipient abruptly dies under suspicious circumstances, veteran medical examiner Jack Stapleton follows leads to a gene-editing biotechnology and the unethical requirements of a megalomaniacal businessman.

Cook, Thomas H.

The **Chatham** School affair / Thomas H. Cook. Bantam Books, 1996. 292 p.

ISBN 0553096524

1. 1920s 2. Private schools 3. Extramarital affairs 4. Art teachers 5. Cape Cod, Massachusetts 6. Psychological fiction

LC 96-4021

Edgar Allan Poe Award for Best Mystery Novel, 1997.

When Malcolm Gaines asks his attorney to prepare his will, he resurrects the long-buried secret behind a tragedy at Chatham School, which destroyed lives and shattered a quiet community.

"Cook is a marvelous stylist, gracing his prose with splendid observations about people and the lush, potentially lethal landscape surrounding them. Events accelerate with increasing force, but few readers will be prepared for the surprise that awaits at novel's end." Publishers Weekly.

Cook, Thomas H.

The **crime** of Julian Wells / Thomas H. Cook. Mysterious Press, 2012. 288 p.

ISBN 9780802126030

1. Authors -- Death 2. Suicide investigation 3. Suspicion 4. Questions and answers 5. True crime writers 6. Mysteries

When a famous true-crime writer is found dead in a boat on a Montauk pond, his best friend begins a quest to determine if the author committed suicide and uncovers a darkness amidst a life filled with adventure and achievement.

Cook, Thomas H.

*A **dancer** in the dust / Thomas H. Cook. Grove, 2014. 352 p.

ISBN 9780802122728

1. Murder investigation 2. Identity (Psychology) 3. Former lovers 4. Guilt in men 5. Nonprofit organizations 6. Secrets 7. Humanitarian assistance 8. Murder victims 9. New York City 10. Africa 11. Mysteries

"A Mysterious Press book for Head of Zeus".

Originally published: 2014.

A former aid worker who was stationed in a newly independent African country is distraught when a friend from that period of his life turns up murdered in New York and he must come to terms with the loss.

Cook, Thomas H.

The **fate** of Katherine Carr / Thomas H. Cook. Houghton Mifflin Harcourt, 2009. 288 p.

ISBN 9780151014019

1. Travel writers 2. Missing persons investigation 3. Cold cases (Criminal investigation) 4. Murder 5. Grief 6. Stalking 7. Stalkers 8. Psychological suspense 9. Mysteries

LC 2008049203

Shattered by the unsolved murder of his eight-year-old son, travel writer George Gates is approached by a retired missing-persons detective and given a mysterious story left behind by a woman who disappeared twenty years earlier.

"Adept at merging past and present plot lines, Cook eloquently examines the often cathartic act of storytelling." Publishers Weekly.

Cook, Thomas H.

Instruments of night / Thomas H. Cook. Bantam Books, 1998. 293 p.

ISBN 055310554X

1. Cold cases (Criminal investigation) 2. Mystery story writers 3. Murder 4. Trust 5. Betrayal 6. Brothers and sisters 7. Torture 8. Teenage girl murder victims 9. New York (State) 10. Mysteries 11. Psychological suspense

LC 9752760

Assisting in a murder investigation, a writer is brought face to face with a horrible crime from his own past

"Although it's easy to miss the very real clues that Cook drops so artfully into the story, there's no ignoring his savage imagery, or escaping the airless chambers of his disturbing imagination." New York Times Book Review.

Cook, Thomas H.

Sandrine's case / Thomas H. Cook. Grove, 2013. 352 p.

ISBN 9780802126085

1. Wife killing 2. Trials (Murder) 3. College teachers 4. Love 5. Secrets 6. Suspicion 7. Husband and wife 8. Fathers and daughters 9. Malicious accusation 10. Extramarital affairs 11. Families of murder victims 12. Legal thrillers

Sharing a seemingly tranquil relationship with his brilliant bohemian wife only to find himself on trial for her murder, liberal arts college professor Samuel Madison struggles with a hostile town while reevaluating his marriage.

Cookson, Catherine

The **year** of the virgins : a novel / Catherine Cookson. Simon & Schuster, 1993. 269 p.

ISBN 0671896504

1. Revenge 2. Extramarital affairs 3. Jealousy 4. Husband and wife 5. Brothers 6. Women with mental illnesses 7. Psychological fiction 8. Domestic fiction

LC 94029796

Struggling to maintain a facade of family harmony for the sake of their religious beliefs and three grown children, Winifred and Daniel Coulson begin a legacy in which their youngest son, Donald, must choose between the values of the past and present.

"Cookson adeptly paints a stark, psychologically realistic portrait of the disintegration of the Coulson clan." Publishers Weekly.

Cooley, Martha

The **archivist** : a novel / Martha Cooley. Little, Brown, 1998. 328 p.

ISBN 9780316158725

1. Eliot, T S, 1888-1965 2. Librarians 3. Poets 4. Love letters 5. Men/women relations 6. Alienation in men 7. Husband and wife 8. Women with mental illnesses 9. Epistolary novels

LC 9738385

A battle of wills between Matt, a careful, orderly archivist for a private university, and Roberta, a determined young poet, over a collection of T. S. Eliot's letters, sealed by bequest until 2019, sparks an unusual friendship and reawakens painful memories of the past.

"The novel treats serious questions in a humane and passionate manner, and leaves one thinking about these questions long after one has read the last page. Cooley is an accomplished stylist--there's scarcely a graceless or unintelligent sentence in the book--and a subtle chronicler of the inner life." New York Times Book Review.

Coomer, Joe

One vacant chair / Joe Coomer. Graywolf Press, 2003. 273 p.

ISBN 155597385X

1. Married women 2. Husband and wife 3. Extramarital affairs 4. Grandmother and granddaughter 5. Grandmothers -- Death 6. Aunts 7. Aunt and niece 8. Women artists 9. Secrets 10. Voyages and travels 11. Men who are blind 12. Fort Worth, Texas 13. Scotland 14. Domestic fiction

LC 2003101448

The funeral of her grandmother reunites Sarah with her aunt Edna, a strange woman who has filled her house with paintings of empty chairs.

Cooney, Ellen

The **mountaintop** school for dogs and other second chances / Ellen Cooney. Houghton Mifflin Harcourt, 2014 304 p.

ISBN 9780544236158

1. Dogs -- Training 2. Dog rescue 3. Animal welfare 4. Animal rescue 5. Mainstream fiction

A novel of a young woman who, despite knowing nothing about animals, signs herself up for dog training school at The Sanctuary, where she discovers that rescue can find even the most hopeless among us and that friends come in all shapes, sizes, and breeds.

Coonts, Stephen, 1946-

* The **armageddon** file / Stephen Coonts. Regnery Fiction, 2017. 256 p. Tommy Carmellini novels

ISBN 9781621576594

1. CIA agents 2. Presidents -- United States -- Election 3. Conspiracies 4. Intelligence service 5. Sabotage 6. National security 7. United States 8. Political-thrillers 9. Spy fiction

LC 2017034764

When a new president-elect's chief of staff discovers evidence of vote tampering, the validity of the election is brought into question at the same time the agendas of dangerous adversaries are revealed.

Coonts, Stephen, 1946-

The **art** of war : a novel / Stephen Coonts. St Martins Pr, 2016 368 p. Tommy Carmellini novels

ISBN 9781250041999

1. CIA agents 2. Assassination 3. Nuclear weapons 4. International intrigue 5. Naval power 6. Intelligence service 7. United States -- Foreign relations -- China 8. Techno-thrillers 9. Spy fiction

LC 2015038676

When newly appointed CIA director Jake Grafton hears murmurings of a Chinese plot to attack the US and assassinations of upper level goverment officials occur, he must investigate the threat and stop China.

Coonts, Stephen, 1946-

* **Flight** of the Intruder / Stephen Coonts. Naval Institute Press, 1986. 329 p. Jake Grafton novels

ISBN 9780870212000

1. Vietnam War, 1961-1975 -- Aerial operations, American 2. Carrier pilots 3. Techno-thrillers

LC 86016440

Sequel: Final flight.

During the war in Vietnam, Jack Grafton loves to fly and beat the enemy with his A-6 Intruder.

Coonts, Stephen, 1946-

Liberty's last stand / Stephen Coonts. Regnery Pub., 2016 354 p. Tommy Carmellini novels

ISBN 9781621575078

1. Attempted assassination 2. Elections 3. Conspiracies 4. Candidates for public office 5. Snipers 6. Techno-thrillers 7. Spy fiction

In the wake of an assassination attempt by a decorated sniper on the eve of a presidential election, Jake Grafton and Tommy Carmellini risk everything to uncover a massive conspiracy while helping a new resistance movement rise up against a new enemy.

Coonts, Stephen, 1946-

* The **Russia** account / Stephen Coonts. Regnery Pub, 2019 256 p. Tommy Carmellini novels

ISBN 9781621576600

1. CIA agents 2. Conspiracies 3. International intrigue 4. Assassins 5. National security 6. Financial intrigue 7. Political thrillers 8. Spy fiction

CIA officer Tommy Carmellini navigates an international financial conspiracy that puts CIA head Jake Grafton in the crosshairs of an assassin.

Cooper, Ellison

Buried / Ellison Cooper. Minotaur Books, 2019. 320 p. Agent Sayer Altair novels

ISBN 9781250173867

1. Women FBI agents 2. Women neuroscientists 3. Psychopaths 4.

Dead 5. Cold cases (Criminal investigation) 6. Kidnapping victims 7. Serial murderers 8. Power (Social sciences) 9. Virginia 10. Thrillers and suspense

LC 2018055981

Returning to the field after six months of desk duty, FBI neuroscientist Sayer Altair investigates the grisly discovery of a serial killer's uncovered body-dump site, reopening a decades-old case with ties to a recent abduction.

Cooper, Ellison

Caged / Ellison Cooper. Minotaur Books, 2018. 384 p. Agent Sayer Altair novels

ISBN 9781250173836

1. Women FBI agents 2. Women neuroscientists 3. Criminal profilers 4. Torture 5. Starvation 6. Serial murder investigation 7. Serial murders 8. Teenage girl murder victims 9. Loss (Psychology) 10. Washington, D.C. 11. Thrillers and suspense

LC 2018004438

Focusing on her research after the death of her fiance, an FBI neuroscientist investigates the torturous murder of a senator's daughter before discovering that her dangerously obsessed killer has abducted a second victim.

Cooper, James Fenimore, 1789-1851

The **last** of the Mohicans : a narrative of 1757 / James Fenimore Cooper ; illustrated by N.C. Wyeth. Scribner's, 1986, c1826. x, 372 p. Leatherstocking tales

ISBN 0684187116

1. 18th century 2. Indians of North America -- East (United States) 3. Interracial friendship 4. Frontier and pioneer life 5. Mohegan Indians 6. United States -- History -- French and Indian War, 1754-1763 7. New York (State) -- History -- French and Indian War, 1754-1763 8. Adventure stories 9. Historical fiction 10. War stories 11. Classics

Originally published in 1826.

The classic tale of a disillusioned man who exiles himself from a society whose values he abhors. Despite this exile, he agrees to take two sisters through hostile Indian country with the help of a Mohican scout.

Cooper, Tom

The **marauders** / Tom Cooper. Crown Publishing, 2015. 304 p.

ISBN 9780804140560

1. Treasure hunters 2. Drug use 3. Small towns 4. Obsession 5. Drug traffic 6. Crime 7. Oil spills 8. Shrimpers (Persons) 9. Seafood industry and trade 10. Misadventures 11. BP Deepwater Horizon Explosion and Oil Spill, 2010 12. Environmental disasters 13. Working class 14. Louisiana 15. Crime fiction 16. Noir fiction 17. Southern fiction

What does a pill-addicted, one-armed treasure hunter have in common with violent, marijuana-growing identical twin brothers? They all haunt the moonlit swamps of tiny Jeannette, Louisiana, situated near Gulf Coast waters devastated by the massive BP oil spill. Add to this toxic mix are a shifty BP rep trying to get folks to take low-ball settlements, two inept ex-con newcomers, and a troubled widower and his 17-year-old son, who blames his dad for his mom's death during Hurricane Katrina. This gritty, funny, evocative debut novel will please fans of Elmore Leonard and Donald E. Westlake. -- Description by Dawn Towery.

"With withering contempt for BP, Cooper offers a believable portrait of a bayou town and a cast of deeply engaging characters wrestling inchoately with the likely extinction of the only life they know. There is real substance and humanity in this fine debut novel." Booklist.

Coover, Robert

Going for a beer : selected short fictions / Robert Coover ; introduction by T. C. Boyle. W. W. Norton & Company, 2018. 336 p.

ISBN 9780393608465

1. Anthologies 2. Short stories 3. Experimental fiction

LC 2017051773

A collection of the best short fictions from the grandmaster of postmodernism.

Coover, Robert

Huck out west / Robert Coover. W. W. Norton & Company, 2017 308 p.

ISBN 9780393608441

1. 1870s 2. 1860s 3. Male friendship 4. Misadventures 5. Voyages and travels 6. Pony Express 7. Teenage boys 8. Young men 9. United States Civil War, 1861-1865 10. Scouting (Reconnaissance) 11. Separated friends, relatives, etc 12. Husband and wife 13. Lakota Indians 14. Gold rush 15. The West (United States) -- History -- 19th century 16. Adventure stories

LC 2016027492

This title is meant to be a sequel to: Mark Twain's The adventures of Huckleberry Finn.

In the author's interpretation of what happened after Mark Twain's Huckleberry Finn, Huck joins the Pony Express, scouts for both sides in the Civil War, joins a bandit gang, finds an ill-fated pal in a Lakota tribe and finds himself in the Black Hills just ahead of the 1876 Gold Rush, in a book that sees the return of Tom Sawyer, Becky Thatcher and Jim.

Coover, Robert

Noir / Robert Coover. Overlook Press, 2010. 224 p.

ISBN 9781590202944

1. Detectives 2. Widows 3. City life 4. Murderers 5. Murder investigation 6. Violence 7. Crime 8. Black humor

LC 2009040215

A mysterious young widow hires Philip M. Noir to find her husband's killer--if he was killed. She suddenly is killed and her body disappears. At once wry, absurd, and desolate--most people will think what's happening is pretty funny.

"With its flashbacks and glittering allusions, Noir is an exuberant, edgy laugh in the dark. . . . If you're looking for a Sam Spade, Mr. Noir is not your sleuth. He's an empty trench coat, which makes the ending so delicious. If you're a Coover groover, you'll love how the writer gooses this classic subgenre. Noir is an obsidian gem." Dallas Morning News.

Coover, Robert

The **origin** of the Brunists : a novel / Robert Coover. Grove Press , 2000, c1966. 441 p.

ISBN 0802137431

1. Cults 2. Small towns 3. Poverty 4. Coal mine accidents 5. Prophets 6. Religion 7. Doomsayers 8. Pennsylvania 9. Literary fiction

Originally published: New York : G.P. Putnam, 1966.

The lone survivor of a catastrophic mine explosion announces that the end of the world is at hand and begins a new cult that, sweeping the mining towns, gathers believers in anticipation of the Coming of the End of the World.

Coover, Robert

Pinocchio in Venice / Robert Coover. Linden Press/Simon and Schuster, 1991. 330 p.

ISBN 9780671644710

1. College teachers 2. Senior men 3. Puppets 4. Venice, Italy 5.

Farcical fiction 6. Adaptations, retellings, and spin-offs

LC 90045706

A very old professor returns to Venice to finish work on his final book, but as he searches for the proper ending, he slowly begins to turn back into wood.

"The ribaldry and the fun are a lot more strenuous and obsessive than self-denial ever was. But then, that is Coover's specialism--the joke on the joker, that the world without soul, far from being easy, is absurdly hard." Times Literary Supplement.

Coplin, Amanda

* The **orchardist** / Amanda Coplin. Harper, 2012. 448 p.

ISBN 9780062188502

1. Fruit growers 2. Orchards 3. Pregnant teenagers 4. Sisters 5. Families 6. Runaways 7. Courage 8. Men and nature 9. Foster fathers 10. Compassion 11. Pacific Northwest 12. Historical fiction 13. Literary fiction 14. Pacific Northwest fiction

LC 2012005466

First published: London : Weidenfeld & Nicolson, 2012.

At the turn of the 20th century in a rural stretch of the Pacific Northwest, a gentle solitary orchardist, Talmadge, tends to apples and apricots. Then two feral, pregnant girls and armed gunmen set Talmadge on an irrevocable course not only to save and protect but to reconcile the ghosts of his own troubled past.

Corby, Gary

The **Marathon** conspiracy / Gary Corby. Soho Crime, 2014. 350 p. Athenian mysteries

ISBN 9781616953874

1. Ancient Greece (800 BCE-640 CE) 2. Civilization, Ancient 3. Private investigators 4. Missing children 5. Schools 6. Crimes against children 7. Newlyweds 8. Women priests 9. Diotima (Legendary character) 10. Ancient Greece -- History -- Athenian supremacy, 479-431 BC 11. Athens, Greece 12. Historical mysteries 13. Mysteries

LC 2013033925

Traveling to Athens to marry, investigator Nicolaos helps his bride look into the murder and disappearance of two students from the famous Sanctuary of Artemis in as case that is bizarrely tied to findings about a tyrannical ruler who supposedly died 30 years earlier.

"Corby serves up a bubbly cocktail of clear history, contemporary wit, and heart-stopping action." Booklist.

Corby, Gary

The **Pericles** Commission / Gary Corby. Minotaur Books, 2010. 304 p. Athenian mysteries

ISBN 9780312599027

1. Ancient Greece (800 BCE-640 CE) 2. 5th century 3. Civilization, Ancient 4. Murder investigation 5. Politicians 6. Seduction 7. Conspiracies 8. Private investigators 9. Diotima (Legendary character) 10. Ancient Greece -- History -- Athenian supremacy, 479-431 BC 11. Athens, Greece 12. Historical mysteries 13. Mysteries

LC 2010030462

Patrolling Classical Athens as an agent for the young politician Pericles, Nicolaos searches for an assassin whose murder of a democratic statesman has thrown the city into chaos, a case that his complicated by his infatuation with the virgin priestess Diotima.

Corey, James S. A

Abaddon's gate / James S. A. Corey. Orbit, 2012. 576 p. Expanse

ISBN 9780316129077

1. Life on other planets 2. Space warfare 3. Space flight 4. Revenge

5. Conspiracies 6. Murder 7. Violence 8. Soldiers 9. Secrets 10. Science fiction 11. Space opera

James S.A. Corey is the pseudonym for Daniel Abraham and Ty Franck.

Locus Award for Best Science Fiction Novel, 2014.

A latest entry in the acclaimed series that includes Leviathan Wakes follows the discovery of a massive alien gate in Uranus's orbit that is examined by Jim Holden and the crew of the Rocinante, who are placed in mortal danger by a complex human plot.

Corey, James S. A

Babylon's ashes / James S. A. Corey. Orbit, 2016. 608 p. Expanse

ISBN 9780316334747

1. Space colonies 2. Life on other planets 3. Space warfare 4. Space flight 5. Black market 6. Space exploration 7. Planets -- Colonization 8. Violence 9. Soldiers 10. Alien artifacts 11. Secrets 12. Science fiction 13. Space opera

James S.A. Corey is the pseudonym for Daniel Abraham and Ty Franck.

Summoned by the remnants of old political powers for a desperate mission to reach Medina Station at the heart of the gate network, James Holden and the crew of the Rocinante are challenged by alliance vulnerabilities, an alien mystery and a band of desperate vigilantes.

Corey, James S. A

Caliban's war / James S. A. Corey. Orbit, 2012. 672 p. Expanse

ISBN 9780316129060

1. Life on other planets 2. Space warfare 3. Space flight 4. Missing girls 5. Conspiracies 6. Murder 7. Violence 8. Soldiers 9. Secrets 10. Science fiction 11. Space opera

LC 2011031646

RUSA Reading List, 2013.

An alien's attack on the outer-planet territory of Ganymede triggers instability throughout the solar system, prompting James Holden and the crew of the Rocinante to engage in peacekeeping efforts and search for a missing child.

Corey, James S. A

Cibola burn / James S. A. Corey. Orbit, 2014. 592 p. Expanse

ISBN 9780316217620

1. Space colonies 2. Life on other planets 3. Space warfare 4. Space flight 5. Plague 6. Space exploration 7. Planets -- Colonization 8. Violence 9. Soldiers 10. Secrets 11. Science fiction 12. Space opera

James S.A. Corey is the pseudonym for Daniel Abraham and Ty Franck.

In this follow-up to Abbadon's Gate, the human race -- both Earth-based and "Belter" -- has gained access to a seemingly infinite number of worlds outside of our solar system. As interstellar travel increases exponentially, so do conflicts between inner and outer system populations. At the center of the dispute is newly discovered, lithium-rich planet Ilus, forcing UN representative James Holden and the crew of the Rocinante to try their hands at diplomacy. Fans of sweeping, dramatic space operas that combine deft characterization with detailed world-building will want to get their hands on this 4th book in the Expanse series, which begins with Leviathan Wakes, followed by Caliban's War. -- Description by Gillian Speace.

"Combining an exploration of real human frailties with big sf ideas and exciting thriller action, Corey (pen name for authors Ty Franck and Daniel Abraham) cements the series as must-read space opera." Library Journal.

Corey, James S. A

* **Leviathan** wakes / James S. A. Corey. Orbit, 2011. 592 p. Expanse

ISBN 9780316129084

1. Detectives 2. Space flight 3. Space warfare 4. Missing girls 5. Conspiracies 6. Secrets 7. Space opera 8. Science fiction

Leviathan Wakes inspired the 2015 Syfy series "The Expanse."

James S.A. Corey is the pseudonym for Daniel Abraham and Ty Franck.

Originally published: 2011.

RUSA Reading List, 2012.

When Captain Jim Holden's ice miner stumbles across a derelict, abandoned ship, he uncovers a secret that threatens to throw the entire system into war. Attacked by a stealth ship belonging to the Mars fleet, Holden must find a way to uncover the motives behind the attack, stop a war and find the truth behind a vast conspiracy that threatens the entire human race.

Corey, James S. A

Nemesis games / James S. A. Corey. Orbit, 2015. 608 p. Expanse

ISBN 9780316217583

1. Space colonies 2. Life on other planets 3. Space warfare 4. Space flight 5. Plague 6. Space exploration 7. Planets -- Colonization 8. Violence 9. Soldiers 10. Secrets 11. Science fiction 12. Space opera

James S.A. Corey is the pseudonym for Daniel Abraham and Ty Franck.

As an intergalactic land rush gets into full swing--causing new alliances, grand acts of violence, and a new human order--James Holden and the crew of the Rocinante must struggle to survive and get back to the only home they have left.

Corey, James S. A

Persepolis rising / James S.A. Corey. Orbit, 2017. 549 p. Expanse

ISBN 9780316332835

1. Space colonies 2. Life on other planets 3. Space warfare 4. Space vehicles 5. Enemies 6. Imaginary wars and battles 7. Interplanetary relations 8. Science fiction 9. Space opera

LC 2017042094

As humanity's presence in space expands and new colony worlds struggle to survive, the crew of the aging gunship Rocinante struggles to keep the fragile peace as ancient patterns of war and subjugation return.

"Corey's tense, tightly plotted story is stuffed to the brim with intrigue, action, awesome alien tech, multidimensional characters, and provocative ideas." Publishers Weekly.

Corey, James S. A

Tiamat's wrath / James S.A. Corey. Orbit, 2019, c2018. 608 p. Expanse

ISBN 9780316332873

1. Imaginary empires 2. Life on other planets 3. Space warfare 4. Space vehicles 5. Imaginary wars and battles 6. Interplanetary relations 7. Intrigue 8. Science fiction 9. Space opera

LC 2018054213

Originally published in Great Britain, 2018.

While Elvi Okoye weighs the consequences of uncovering the truth about weapons tied to an ancient genocide, Teresa Duarte navigates secrets and dangerous intrigues to fulfill her father's godlike ambition.

"Part of what is projected to be a nine-book series, this story at once provides a satisfying conclusion and maneuvers the story lines to a propulsive confrontation that will have readers eagerly awaiting the final chapter." Booklist.

Corleone, Douglas

Gone cold / Douglas Corleone. St. Martin's Press, 2015. 320 p. Simon Fisk novels

ISBN 9781250065780

1. Cold cases (Criminal investigation) 2. Missing persons investigation 3. Murder suspects 4. Missing children 5. Kidnapping 6. Private investigators 7. Former marshals 8. Missing children 9. Police 10. Rescues 11. United States marshals 12. Crimes against children 13. Fathers of kidnapping victims 14. Thrillers and suspense

Renewing his effort to solve the case of his young daughter's abduction, former U.S. marshal Simon Fisk journeys to Dublin to investigate a murder suspect who bears a striking family resemblance.

Corleone, Douglas

Good as gone / Douglas Corleone. Minotaur Books, 2013. 304 p. Simon Fisk novels

ISBN 9781250017208

1. Private investigators 2. Former marshals 3. Missing children 4. Police 5. Rescues 6. Kidnapping 7. Child custody 8. United States marshals 9. Crimes against children 10. Fathers of kidnapping victims 11. Paris, France 12. Thrillers and suspense

LC 2013009828

Finds a former U.S. Marshal haunted by the unsolved disappearance of his daughter reluctantly investigating a terrifying international child abduction case.

Corleone, Douglas

Payoff / Douglas Corleone. Minotaur Books, 2014. 304 p. Simon Fisk novels

ISBN 9781250040732

1. Missing children 2. Kidnapping 3. Private investigators 4. Former marshals 5. Police 6. Rescues 7. Kidnapping 8. Child custody 9. United States marshals 10. Crimes against children 11. Fathers of kidnapping victims 12. Thrillers and suspense

LC 2014007862

First published in the United States of America 2014 by St Martin's Press.

"When movie studio mogul Edgar Trenton's teenage daughter Olivia is kidnapped during a violent home invasion in Calabasas, California, former U.S. Marshal Simon Fisk is called upon to ensure a smooth ransom exchange. But once it becomes clear that the kidnappers never intended to return Olivia to her parents, Simon must follow a lethal trail that will lead him from the powdery white sand beaches of the Cayman Islands through the wild jungles of Costa Rica, and into some of the darkest and deadliest cities of South America"--Amazon.com.

Corman, Avery

Prized possessions / Avery Corman. Simon & Schuster, 1991. 320 p.

ISBN 0671692984

1. Daughters 2. Rape victims 3. Family relationships 4. Upper class 5. Life change events 6. Coping in women 7. New York City 8. Psychological fiction 9. Domestic fiction

LC 90022666

This story of a young woman's rape and its effect on her family takes place in the world of Manhattan's upper middle class, tracing Elizabeth Mason's recovery, her parent's pain and guilt, and the family's gradual transformation.

"With Liz's story, Corman takes a tense, disturbing look at the nature of consent and raises critical questions about negative ways in which society still views female sexuality." Publishers Weekly.

Cornell, Paul

London falling / Paul Cornell. Tor, 2013. 352 p. London falling novels

ISBN 9780765330277

1. Anne Boleyn,, Queen, consort of Henry VIII, King of England, 1507-1536 2. West Ham United (Soccer team) 3. Detectives 4. Supernatural 5. Murder investigation 6. Occult crime 7. Organized crime 8. Witches 9. Child sacrifice 10. Kidnapping 11. Rape 12. Undercover operations 13. Crime bosses 14. Good and evil 15. London, England 16. Urban fantasy 17. Police procedurals

LC 2012043356

"A Tom Doherty Associates book."

Originally published: 2012.

While investigating the mysterious death of a mobster, four police officers come in contact with a strange artifact that grants them the supernatural ability to see the true otherworldly evils that haunt London's streets.

Cornwell, Bernard

1356 / Bernard Cornwell. HarperCollins, 2013, c2012. 464 p.

ISBN 9780061969676

1. Medieval period (476-1492) 2. Plantagenet period (1154-1485) 3. 14th century 4. Relics 5. Hundred Years' War, 1339-1453 6. Battles 7. Military strategy 8. Archers 9. British in France 10. Great Britain -- History -- Edward III, 1327-1377 11. France -- History -- 14th century 12. Historical fiction 13. War stories

Maps on endpages.

First published: London: HarperCollins, 2012.

Bringing to life the violence, action and heroism of the battlefield, this brilliant recreation of the Battle of the Poitiers in 1356 follows a severely outnumbered English army as they, through the ingenious planning of Edward the Black Prince, defeated the French and captured the Poiters and French King John II.

Cornwell, Bernard

The archer's tale / Bernard Cornwell. HarperCollins, 2001. 374 p. Grail Quest (Bernard Cornwell)

ISBN 0066210844

1. Medieval period (476-1492) 2. Plantagenet period (1154-1485) 3. 14th century 4. Grail 5. Hundred Years' War, 1339-1453 6. Knights and knighthood -- France 7. Archers 8. British in France 9. Great Britain -- History -- Edward III, 1327-1377 10. France -- History -- 14th century 11. Historical fiction 12. War stories

LC 2001024333

Originally published in Great Britain under the title: Harlequin.

After surviving a vicious attack on his village in 1343 A.D., archer Thomas of Hookton joins the army of King Edward III as he prepares to launch an invasion into France, but his search for vengeance takes him on an epic quest for the Holy Grail.

"Authentically detailed and appropriately gruesome, the medieval battle scenes fairly crackle with tension; however, what sets Cornwell's work apart from most run-of-the-mill military adventures are his meticulously developed story lines and his razor-sharp characterizations." Booklist.

Cornwell, Bernard

Enemy of God : a novel of Arthur / Bernard Cornwell. St. Martin's Press, 1997, c1996. 396 p. Warlord chronicles

ISBN 0312155239

1. Arthur,, King 2. Knights and knighthood 3. Political corruption 4. Betrayal 5. Rulers 6. Wizards 7. Queen Guinevere (Legendary character) 8. Lancelot (Legendary character) 9. Galahad (Legendary

character) 10. Men/women relations 11. Imaginary wars and battles 12. Great Britain -- History -- Anglo-Saxon period, 449-1066 13. Arthurian fantasy 14. Historical fantasy

LC 97-12884

While fighting the Saxons and trying to unite the Christians and the Druids, Arthur succeeds in gaining the throne for King Mordred and establishes the Round Table before Guinevere and Lancelot betray him.

"This complex and superbly wrought narrative easily eclipses the more sanitized and tepid versions of Arthur's exploits." Booklist.

Cornwell, Bernard

Excalibur : a novel of Arthur / Bernard Cornwell. St. Martin's Press, 1998, c1997. 435 p. Warlord chronicles

ISBN 0312185758

1. Arthur,, King 2. Knights and knighthood 3. Political corruption 4. Rulers 5. Wizards 6. Queen Guinevere (Legendary character) 7. Lancelot (Legendary character) 8. Merlin (Legendary character) 9. Men/women relations 10. Heirs and heiresses 11. Imaginary wars and battles 12. Great Britain -- History -- Anglo-Saxon period, 449-1066 13. Arthurian fantasy 14. Historical fantasy

LC 9810247

Illustrated with endpaper map.

Originally published: London: Michael Joseph, 1997.

Describes King Arthur's final battle with Mordred, who has summoned the power of the gods to help his evil cause.

"The action is gripping and skillfully paced, cadenced by passages in which the characters reveal themselves in conversation and thought, convincingly evoking the spirit of the time. Ways of ancient ritual, battle and daily life are laid out in surprising detail." Publishers Weekly.

Cornwell, Bernard

The last kingdom : a novel / Bernard Cornwell. HarperCollins, 2005. 352 p. Saxon stories (Bernard Cornwell)

ISBN 0060530510

1. Alfred,, King of England, 849-899 2. Medieval period (476-1492) 3. Anglo-Saxon period (449-1066) 4. 9th century 5. Vikings 6. Soldiers 7. Warriors 8. Uncles 9. Kidnapping 10. Religion 11. Betrayal 12. Murder 13. Inheritance and succession 14. Great Britain -- History -- Alfred, 871-899 15. Northumbria (Kingdom) -- History -- 9th century 16. Historical fiction

LC 2004054236

Captured and raised by Danes in the ninth century, dispossessed nobleman Uhtred witnesses the unexpected defeat of his adoptive Viking clan by Alfred of Wessex and longs to recover his father's land.

Cornwell, Bernard

Sword of kings / Bernard Cornwell. HarperCollins, 2019. 336 p. Saxon stories (Bernard Cornwell)

ISBN 9780062563217

1. Anglo-Saxon period (449-1066) 2. Medieval period (476-1492) 3. 10th century 4. Warriors 5. Saxons 6. Vikings 7. Duty 8. Oaths 9. Inheritance and succession 10. Political intrigue 11. Power (Social sciences) 12. Battles 13. Enemies 14. Great Britain -- History -- 10th century 15. Northumbria (Kingdom) -- History 16. Historical fiction

A latest entry in the series that inspired, The Last Kingdom, continues the epic conquests and challenges of Uhtred of Bebbanburg as they shaped a fledgling Britain.

Cornwell, Bernard

War of the wolf : a novel / Bernard Cornwell. Harper, 2018 333 p. Saxon stories (Bernard Cornwell)

ISBN 9780062563170

1. Anglo-Saxon period (449-1066) 2. Medieval period (476-1492) 3.

10th century 4. Warriors 5. Saxons 6. Vikings 7. Duty 8. Devotedness 9. Betrayal 10. Enemies 11. Inheritance and succession 12. Power (Social sciences) 13. Great Britain -- History -- 10th century 14. Northumbria (Kingdom) -- History 15. Historical fiction

Uhtred of Bebbanburg has regained his family's fortress, but must now defend it against two enemies, one from Wessex, where a dynastic struggle is going on, and the other, a Norseman named Skoll who wants to be the King of Northumbria.

"Once again, Cornwell has placed his irascible and cunning hero in the midst of personal and political conflict and provided another exciting story." Library Journal.

Cornwell, Bernard

The winter king : a novel of Arthur / Bernard Cornwell. St. Martin's Press, 1996, c1995. 431 p. Warlord chronicles

ISBN 9780312144470

1. Arthur,, King 2. Knights and knighthood 3. Political corruption 4. Rulers 5. Wizards 6. Queen Guinevere (Legendary character) 7. Lancelot (Legendary character) 8. Galahad (Legendary character) 9. Men/women relations 10. Heirs and heiresses 11. Imaginary wars and battles 12. Great Britain -- History -- Anglo-Saxon period, 449-1066 13. Arthurian fantasy 14. Historical fantasy

Originally published: London : Michael Joseph, 1995.

In Dark Age Britain, a land from which Arthur has been banished and Merlin has disappeared, a child-king sits unprotected on the throne, and it is up to Arthur, a courageous and honorable man, to preserve the lonely embers of civilization in a barbaric world.

"Cornwell's Arthur is fierce, dedicated and complex, a man with many problems, most of his own making. His impulsive decisions sometimes have tragic ramifications... The secondary characters are equally unexpected, and are ribboned with the magic and superstition of the times." Publishers Weekly.

Cornwell, Patricia Daniels

Chaos / Patricia Daniels Cornwell. William Morrow, 2016. 400 p. Kay Scarpetta mysteries

ISBN 9780062436689

1. Women forensic pathologists 2. Lightning strike victims 3. Threat (Psychology) 4. Murder 5. Coroners 6. Harassment 7. Women coroners 8. Forensic medicine 9. Anonymous letters 10. Murder investigation 11. Women physicians 12. Cambridge, Massachusetts 13. Mysteries

Suspicious of a bizarre death by lightning strike, Cambridge forensics examiner Kay Scarpetta identifies links between the case and a series of poetry emails being sent to her by an anonymous cyber-stalker who has gained access to Kay's personal information.

Cornwell, Patricia Daniels

Postmortem / Patricia Daniels Cornwell. C. Scribner's Sons, 1990. 293 p. Kay Scarpetta mysteries

ISBN 0684191415

1. Serial murders 2. Women forensic pathologists 3. Violence against women 4. Women coroners 5. Forensic medicine 6. Serial murder investigation 7. Women murder victims 8. Richmond, Virginia 9. Psychological suspense 10. Mysteries

LC 89010177

"A mystery introducing Dr. Kay Scarpetta."

Macavity Award for Best First Mystery Novel, 1991.

Edgar Allan Poe Award for Best First Mystery Novel, 1991.

John Creasey Memorial Award (Best First Crime Novel), 1990.

Anthony Award for Best First Novel, 1991.

Medical examiner Kay Scarpetta is introduced in this story of a psychopath who is brutally murdering women. Scarpetta must find out why--before she becomes the next victim.

"This mystery about a serial killer features Dr. Kay Scarpetta, Chief Medical Examiner for the Commonwealth of Virginia. . . . From the moment that the strangler makes his fourth killing (one of two that figure prominently in the plot), the tension is up. No less than the police, Dr. Scarpetta is baffled by the absence of the usual sick motivational pattern; but she can read the physical evidence, and she has the brains and the gizmos--computers, fingerprint-matching processor, DNA-testing equipment, F.B.I. profiling systems--to give the madman chase." New York Times Book Review.

Corry, Jane

* The **dead** ex / Jane Corry. Pamela Dorman Books/Viking, 2019 352 p.
    ISBN 9780525561194
    1. Missing men 2. Former husbands 3. Divorced women 4. Police 5. Missing persons investigation 6. Innocence (Law) 7. Mothers and daughters 8. Foster children 9. Drug dealers 10. Memory 11. Men/women relations 12. Great Britain 13. Psychological suspense
    LC 2018041545
    "A Pamela Dorman Book/Viking."
    A man's disappearance throws the lives of four women into chaos, including his ex-wife, who struggles to prove her innocence in spite of an unreliable memory.

Corry, Jane

My husband's wife / Jane Corry. Pamela Dorman Books, 2017. 352 p.
    ISBN 9780735220959
    1. Women lawyers 2. Husband and wife 3. Consequences 4. Neighbors 5. Nine-year-old girls 6. Murderers 7. Deception 8. Secrets 9. London, England 10. Psychological suspense
    Resolving to leave her secrets behind when she gets married, a young lawyer is strangely drawn to a convicted killer during her first murder case in ways that shape her psychologically charged relationship with a young neighbor years later.

Cortazar, Julio

Hopscotch / Julio Cortazar ; translated from the Spanish by Gregory Rabassa. Pantheon Books, 1966, c1963. 564 p.
    1. Mistresses 2. Bohemianism 3. Interpersonal relations 4. Philosophy 5. Missing women 6. Men/women relations 7. Buenos Aires, Argentina 8. Paris, France 9. Psychological suspense 10. Translations -- Spanish to English
    LC 66010409
    Translation from the Spanish of: Rayuela.
    Originally published: Buenos Aires : Editorial Sudamerican, 1963.
    When La Maga, his mistress, disappears, Horacio Oliveira, an Argentinian writer living in Paris, decides to return home to Buenos Aires.

Cosse, Laurence

A **novel** bookstore / Laurence Cosse ; translated by Alison Anderson. Europa Editions, 2010. 424 p.
    ISBN 9781933372822
    1. Bookstores 2. Books and reading 3. Publishers and publishing 4. Critics 5. Mainstream fiction 6. Translations -- French to English
    A mysterious death, unusual car accident, and anonymous threats have one thing in common-- the victims are all members of the Good Novel bookstore's secret selection committee. Set in Paris, this tale combines mystery, romance, and French theology and literature.

"The book begins with descriptions of the committee members' menacings, provoking a reader's quick interest and sympathy. Then follows the booksellers' lengthy interview with a sympathetic police inspector, in which the history of their individual lives and mutual enterprise is told. After that, the rest of the plot unfolds. Several mysteries are plumbed, if not necessarily solved, in this most engaging and winning novel." San Francisco Chronicle.

Cossette, Connilyn

* **Shelter** of the most high / Connilyn Cossette. Bethany House, 2018. 352 p. Cities of refuge
    ISBN 9780764219870
    1. Bible. Old Testament 2. Strangers 3. Pagans 4. Jews 5. Faith 6. Options, alternatives, choices 7. Secrets 8. Interpersonal attraction 9. Men/women relations 10. Christian historical romances 11. Bible novels
    LC 2018019432
    Christy Award for Historical Category, 2019.
    Captured by raiders in 1388 B.C., Sofea narrowly escapes slavery. Bargaining her way to a city of refuge in Israel, she finds herself in more danger. Can she find safety in this city of strangers, accept their God as hers, and be satisfied with His justice instead of her own?

Costello, Mark, 1936-

Big if / Mark Costello. W. W. Norton & Co., 2002. 315 p.
    ISBN 0393051161
    1. United States. Secret Service Officials and employees 2. Primaries 3. Vice-presidents -- United States 4. Presidential candidates -- Protection 5. Assassination 6. Assassins 7. Brothers and sisters 8. Computer software developers 9. Computer software 10. Computer games 11. Computer game designers 12. Women bodyguards 13. Women real estate agents 14. New Hampshire 15. Political fiction 16. Humorous stories
    LC 2002000512
    National Book Award for Fiction finalist, 2002
    In the wake of her father's death and the vice president's campaign for the presidency, Secret Service agent Vi Asplund returns home to her computer genius brother, who is poised to make a fortune on a nihilistic video game.

"The novel ends not with a bang but a shiver, in a masterfully orchestrated scene that is vividly cinematic. But true to his materials and vision--and to life--Costello slyly defuses the emotional catharsis in a manner that would be anathema to the feel-good demands of a major Hollywood production." New York Times Book Review.

Coster, Naima

Halsey Street / Naima Coster. Little A, 2018. 336 p.
    ISBN 9781503941175
    1. Mother-deserted children 2. Mother and adult daughter 3. Women artists 4. Sick fathers 5. Homecomings 6. Neighborhoods 7. Social change 8. Belonging 9. Landlords 10. Loss (Psychology) 11. Family relationships 12. Brooklyn, New York City 13. Dominican Republic 14. Literary fiction 15. Family sagas
    Kirkus Prize for Fiction finalist, 2018.
    A modern-day story of family, loss, and renewal, Halsey Street captures the deeply human need to belong--not only to a place but to one another.

"Coster is a masterful observer of family dynamics: her characters, to a one, are wonderfully complex and consistently surprising. Absorbing and alive, the kind of novel that swallows you whole." Kirkus.

Cotter, Bill, 1964-

Fever chart / Bill Cotter. McSweeney's Books, 2009. 305 p.

ISBN 9781934781418

1. Homeless men -- New Orleans, Louisiana 2. Mental illness 3. Misadventures 4. Psychoses 5. New Orleans, Louisiana 6. Psychological fiction

"Having spent most of his life medicated, electroshocked, and institutionalized, Jerome Coe finds himself homeless on the coldest night of the century--and so, with nowhere else to go, he accepts a ride out of New England from an old love's ex-girlfriend. It doesn't quite work out, but he makes it to New Orleans, and a new life--complete with a bandaged hand, world-champion grilled-cheese sandwiches, and only the occasional psychotic break. Things get better, and then, of course, they get worse."--Publisher's website.

"Cotter gives only the briefest of nods to plot, but Fever Chart is not about the destination so much as the reckless, driving-with-your-knees journey, and Jerome Coe is an antihero for the ages." Texas Monthly.

Cotterill, Colin

The **coroner's** lunch / Colin Cotterill. Soho Press, 2004. 272 p. Dr. Paiboun novels

ISBN 1569473765

1. 1970s 2. Murder investigation 3. Coroners 4. Senior men 5. Men psychics 6. Ghosts 7. Physicians 8. Communists 9. Communism -- Laos 10. Murder 11. Laos -- History -- 1975- 12. Mysteries

LC 2004048191

Sequel: Thirty-three teeth.

Laos, 1972. The Communist Pathet Lao has taken over. Most of the educated class has fled, but 72-year-old Dr. Siri Paiboun, a Paris-trained doctor, remains and is appointed state coroner. When three bodies are recovered from a reservoir, Dr. Siri establishes that the cause of death was not drowning -- they seem to have been electrocuted. And then there is the inexplicable death of a Party bigwig's wife at a banquet. Dr. Siri doesn't think her death was from natural causes. In the course of his investigations, he travels to his birthplace, where he makes a discovery.

"Cotterill's engaging whodunit [is] set in Laos a year after the 1975 Communist takeover." Publishers Weekly.

Cotterill, Colin

Disco for the departed / Colin Cotterill. Soho Press, 2006. 247 p. Dr. Paiboun novels

ISBN 1569474281

1. 1970s 2. Senior men 3. Coroners 4. Murder investigation 5. Supernatural 6. Mysticism 7. Murder 8. Rites and ceremonies 9. Paranormal phenomena 10. Laos -- History -- 1975- 11. Mysteries

LC 2005055462

Coroner Siri Paiboun must identify a corpse found near the mansion of the new Laotian president, an investigation which includes communication with the dead, sacrificial rituals, a marriage proposal, and strange disco music that only the doctor can hear.

Cotterill, Colin

* **Don't** eat me / Colin Cotterill. Soho Crime, 2018. 304 p. Dr. Paiboun novels

ISBN 9781616959401

1. 1980s 2. Seniors 3. Coroners 4. Dead 5. Filmmaking 6. Friendship 7. Detectives 8. Corruption 9. Black market 10. Laos 11. Mysteries

LC 2017055447

Between getting into a tangle with a corrupt local judge, and discovering a disturbing black-market business, Dr. Siri and his friend Inspector Phosy have their hands full.

"The eccentric Siri, who's possessed by spirits (including those of a dog, his dead mother, and a transvestite fortune-teller), continues to stand out as a unique and endearing series sleuth." Publishers Weekly.

Cotterill, Colin

Grandad, there's a head on the beach : a Jimm Juree mystery / Colin Cotterill. Minotaur Books, 2012. 384 p. Jimm Juree mysteries

ISBN 9780312564544

1. Women journalists 2. Murder investigation 3. Dismemberment 4. Murder 5. Women amateur detectives 6. Thailand 7. Mysteries

LC 2012005482

Reluctantly abandoning her crime-reporting job to accompany her family to her mother's newly acquired "holiday camp" on Thailand's Gulf of Siam, Jimm Juree investigates a morbid local mystery in the hopes of revamping her career.

Cotterill, Colin

* **Killed** at the whim of a hat / Colin Cotterill. St. Martin's Press, 2011. 320 p. Jimm Juree mysteries

ISBN 9780312564537

1. Murder investigation 2. Women journalists 3. Murder suspects 4. Murder 5. Hippies 6. Buddhist monks 7. Investigative journalists 8. Eccentrics and eccentricities 9. Women amateur detectives 10. Thailand 11. Mysteries

LC 2011008722

"First published in Great Britain in 2011 by Quercus"--T.p. verso.

Forced to relocate to rural Thailand with her eccentric family, crime reporter Jimm Juree fears that her career is over until the bodies of two hippies are discovered in a local farmer's field and a Buddhist abbot is murdered, a case that implicates a monk and a nun.

"Cotterill combines plenty of humor with fascinating and unusual characters, a solid mystery, and the relatively unfamiliar setting of southern Thailand to launch what may be the best new international mystery series since the No. 1 Ladies' Detective Agency." Booklist.

Cotterill, Colin

The **second** biggest nothing / Colin Cotterill. Soho Crime, 2019. 264 p. Dr. Paiboun novels

ISBN 9781641290616

1. 1970s 2. Coroners 3. Museums 4. Death threats 5. Investigations 6. Prisoners of war 7. Laos 8. Mysteries

LC 2018057751

Receiving a sinister threat against everyone he loves, Laotian coroner Dr. Siri searches for clues in three incidents from his past, including an encounter with an old friend, a disruptive visit to a Saigon museum and a Vietnam prisoner-of-war negotiation.

Cotterill, Colin

Slash and burn : a Dr. Siri Mystery set in Laos / Colin Cotterill. Soho Crime, 2011. 300 p. Dr. Paiboun novels

ISBN 9781616951160

1. 1970s 2. Murder investigation 3. Missing in action 4. Missing persons investigation 5. Excavation 6. Helicopters -- Accidents 7. Americans in Laos 8. Murder 9. Airmen 10. Coroners 11. Seniors 12. Laos 13. Mysteries

LC 2011030330

Things have been hectic for Dr. Siri, so he decides to go on a therapeutic vacation with his wife and friends. Unfortunately, trouble follows as the doctor is blackmailed into helping an American MIA team searching for a pilot downed ten years earlier. Sifting through debris, navigating acres of unexploded munitions, and trying to discover who the killer is in their midst make things interesting for Dr. Siri and the morgue team.

Coughlin, Jack, 1966-

In the crosshairs : a sniper novel / Gunnery Sgt. Jack Coughlin, USMC (Ret.), with Donald A. Davis. St. Martin's Press, 2017. 304 p. Sniper thrillers (Jack Coughlin)
ISBN 9781250103536
1. CIA 2. Drug lords 3. Snipers 4. Bombings 5. Widows 6. Revenge 7. Traitors 8. CIA agents 9. Military intelligence 10. International intrigue 11. Afghanistan 12. United States 13. Thrillers and suspense
LC 2017013454
CIA field operative Kyle Swanson must find a former top-level Russian sniper who was working for the United States, but appears to have gone rogue, killing a marine in the latest addition to the series following Long Shot.

Coughlin, Jack, 1966-

Long shot : a sniper novel / Gunnery Sgt. Jack Coughlin USMC (Ret.) with Donald A. Davis St. Martin's Press, 2016. 304 p. Sniper thrillers (Jack Coughlin)
ISBN 9781250072955
1. Defectors 2. Double agents 3. Military intelligence 4. Traitors 5. Snipers 6. Deception 7. CIA agents 8. International intrigue 9. Terrorism -- Prevention 10. Special operations (Military science) 11. Russia -- Foreign relations -- United States 12. United States -- Foreign relations -- Russia 13. Thrillers and suspense
LC 2016003177
A special contractor with the CIA interviews a defector who happens to be a top Russian intelligence agent and finds he is full of amazing secrets.

Coulter, Catherine

The **devil's** triangle / Catherine Coulter and J.T. Ellison. Gallery Books, 2017. 352 p. Brit in the FBI
ISBN 9781501150326
1. Great Britain. Metropolitan Police Office. Criminal Investigation Department 2. FBI 3. Undercover operations 4. Weather 5. Terrorism 6. Terrorists 7. British in the United States 8. FBI agents 9. Police 10. New York City 11. Thrillers and suspense
LC 2016031234
Entering their new roles as heads of the Covert Eyes team, Nicholas Drummond and Michaela Caine are in a race against time when a dangerous thief known as the Fox resurfaces asking them for help.

Coulter, Catherine

The **end** game / Catherine Coulter, J.T. Ellison. Penguin, 2015. 464 p. Brit in the FBI
ISBN 9780399173806
1. Great Britain. Metropolitan Police Office. Criminal Investigation Department 2. FBI 3. Undercover operations 4. Terrorism 5. Terrorists 6. British in the United States 7. FBI agents 8. Police 9. New York City 10. Thrillers and suspense
Investigating a ecoterrorist group suspected in a series of bombings, FBI agent Nicholas Drummond and his partner, Mike Caine, work with an undercover counter-terrorism agent to stop an assassination plot against the president.

Coulter, Catherine

The **final** cut / Catherine Coulter ; with J. T. Ellison. G. P. Putnam's Sons, 2013 400 p. Brit in the FBI
ISBN 9780399164736
1. Great Britain. Metropolitan Police Office. Criminal Investigation Department 2. FBI 3. Murder investigation 4. Jewel thieves 5. Jewelry theft 6. British in the United States 7. FBI agents 8. Police 9. New York City 10. Thrillers and suspense
LC 2013024511
Chief inspector Nicholas Drummond of Scotland Yard investigates after the centerpiece of an exhibit of crown jewels is stolen from the Metropolitan Museum of Art and his colleague is murdered.

Coulter, Catherine

Labyrinth / Catherine Coulter. Gallery Books, 2019. 512 p. FBI suspense thriller series
ISBN 9781501193651
1. Power (Social sciences) 2. FBI agents 3. Traffic accidents 4. Deception 5. Missing men 6. Women kidnapping victims 7. Murder 8. Washington, D.C. 9. Virginia 10. Thrillers and suspense
LC 2019006760
While Sherlock searches for the missing CIA analyst involved in her recent car crash, Griffin is targeted by a sheriff whose son has been implicated the murders of three girls.

Coulter, Catherine

The **last** second / Catherine Coulter and J.T. Ellison. Gallery Books, 2019. 448 p. Brit in the FBI
ISBN 9781501138225
1. FBI agents 2. Nuclear weapons 3. Treasure hunters 4. International intrigue 5. Space vehicles 6. Immortalism 7. British in the United States 8. New York City 9. Thrillers and suspense
LC 2018049650
When an eccentric treasure hunter finances a private space agency and augments its first satellite with a nuclear device, special agents Drummond and Caine race to prevent a corrupt scientist's apocalyptic plot.

Coulter, Catherine

The **lost** key / Catherine Coulter, J.T. Ellison. G. P. Putnam's Sons, 2014. 448 p. Brit in the FBI
ISBN 9780399164767
1. Great Britain. Metropolitan Police Office. Criminal Investigation Department 2. FBI 3. Murder investigation 4. Treasure troves 5. Treasure hunters 6. British in the United States 7. FBI agents 8. Police 9. New York City 10. Thrillers and suspense
Investigating the stabbing of a rare book dealer who had been secretly looking for a missing World War I U-boat full of treasure, Nicholas Drummond and his partner, Mike Caine, try to track down the victim's missing children.

Coulter, Catherine

Paradox / Catherine Coulter. Gallery Books, 2018. 434 p. FBI suspense thriller series
ISBN 9781501138126
1. FBI Officials and employees 2. FBI agents 3. Psychopaths 4. Bones 5. Murder victims 6. Revenge 7. Murderers 8. Maryland 9. Thrillers and suspense
LC 2018007876
When divers discover the bones of multiple murder victims during a search of Lake Massey, agents Sherlock and Savich make a connection between the bones and an escaped psychopath who attempted to kidnap five-year-old Sean Savich.

Coulter, Catherine

The **sixth** day / Catherine Coulter and J.T. Ellison. Simon & Schuster, 2018 448 p. Brit in the FBI

ISBN 9781501138171

1. FBI 2. Voynich manuscript 3. FBI agents 4. Assassination 5. International intrigue 6. Betrayal 7. Terrorism 8. Cryptography 9. Blood -- Diseases 10. British in the United States 11. Police 12. New York City 13. Thrillers and suspense

When several major political figures who are linked to sophisticated drone assassinations die under mysterious circumstances, the Covert Eyes team follows leads to a wealthy cybersecurity genius and descendant of Vlad the Impaler who is desperate to unlock the secret of curing his severely ill twin brother's blood disorder.

Coupland, Douglas

Eleanor Rigby : a novel / Douglas Coupland. Bloomsbury, 2004. 256 p.

ISBN 9781582345239

1. 1990s 2. Loneliness 3. Loneliness in women 4. Single women 5. Middle-aged women 6. Overweight women 7. Birthmothers 8. Caregivers 9. Hospital patients 10. People with multiple sclerosis 11. Adoptees 12. Sales personnel 13. Mother and adult son 14. Birthparent/adoptee relations 15. Visions 16. Self-fulfillment 17. Hale-Bopp comet 18. Life change events 19. Vancouver, British Columbia 20. Canada 21. Italy 22. Psychological fiction

LC 2004046437

Liz Dunn has little to keep her going until a strange young man named Jeremy arrives in her life, upsetting her quiet routine and triggering events that take Liz around the world, into danger, and maybe, for the first time, in reach of happiness.

"Liz Dunn is fat, lonely and has no friends. . . . The only exciting incident ever to brighten Liz's life was a class trip to Rome when she was 16, during which she attended a party where she drank so much she can't remember what happened. Nine months after she returned home, she gave birth to a son, an event hidden from her family because of her natural rotundity. Liz gave the child up for adoption and then launched into a life of perpetual loneliness (hence the title's nod to the lonely lady of Beatles fame). All this changes when her now 20-year-old son, Jeremy, shows up. He's a great kid, but his story is tragic-he bounced around foster homes until he could take care of himself, he has multiple sclerosis and his body is rapidly deteriorating. Coupland . . . avoids the pitfalls of weepy melodrama with sarcastic humor, inspired treatment of the weirdness of everyday life and dark mystical interludes." Publishers Weekly.

Coupland, Douglas

Microserfs / Douglas Coupland. HarperCollins, 1995. 371 p.

ISBN 9780060391485

1. Microsoft Corporation 2. 1990s 3. Computer programmers 4. Eccentrics and eccentricities 5. Technology 6. Young men 7. Office workers 8. Misfits (Persons) 9. Independence (Personal quality) 10. New businesses 11. Humorous stories

LC 95011472

They are Microserfs--six code-crunching computer whizzes who spend upward of sixteen hours a day "coding" and eating "flat" foods (food which, like Kraft singles, can be passed underneath closed doors) as they fearfully scan company e-mail to learn whether the great Bill is going to "flame" one of them. But now there's a chance to become innovators instead of cogs in the gargantuan Microsoft machine. The intrepid Microserfs are striking out on their own?living together in a shared digital flophouse as they desperately try to cultivate well-rounded lives and find love amid the dislocated, subhuman whir and buzz of their computer-driven world.

Couto, Mia, 1955-

Rain : and other stories / Mia Couto ; translated by Eric M. B. Becker. Biblioasis, 2019. 168 p.

ISBN 9781771962667

1. Civil war 2. Colonialism 3. Postwar life 4. Loss (Psychology) 5. Hope 6. Mozambique 7. Africa 8. Short stories 9. Literary fiction 10. Translations -- Portuguese to English

Published in the aftermath of Mozambique's bloody civil war, Mia Couto's third collection seeks out the places violence could not reach, the places where, the author writes, "every man is the same: pretending he's here, dreaming of going away, and plotting his return." Shifting masterfully between forms?creation tale to meditation, playful comedy to magical twist?these stories grapple with questions of what's been lost and what can be reclaimed, what future exists for a country that broke the yoke of colonialism only to descend into internecine war, what is Mozambican and what is Mozambique.

Couto, Mia, 1955-

* Sleepwalking land / Mia Couto ; translated from the Portuguese by David Brookshaw. Serpent's Tail, 2006, c1992. 256 p.

ISBN 185242897X

1. 1970s 2. 1980s 3. Senior men 4. Boys 5. Refugees 6. Civil war 7. Children and war 8. Africans 9. Insurgency 10. Warriors 11. Soldiers 12. Men/women relations 13. Quests 14. Storytelling 15. Companionship 16. Survival 17. Mozambique -- History -- 1975-1992 18. Mozambique -- Politics and government -- 1975-1992 19. Mozambique -- Race relations 20. Translations -- Portuguese to English 21. War stories 22. Magical realism 23. Literary fiction

Originally published: Lisboa : Caminho, 1992.

"Many great novels have shown a world torn to shreds by the brutality of war. To do so, their authors ground their texts in the details of destruction and decay. But Couto's novel stands apart: it shows the world that war creates, a dreamscape of uncertainty where characters and readers alike marvel not at the abnormal becoming normal but at the way we come to accept the impossible as reality." New York Times Book Review.

Cowell, Stephanie

Claude & Camille : a novel of Monet / Stephanie Cowell. Crown Publishers, 2010. 352 p.

ISBN 9780307463210

1. Monet, Claude, 1840-1926 2. Monet, Camille, 1847-1879 3. Painters -- France 4. Artists' spouses -- France 5. Impressionist artists 6. Painters' spouses -- France -- Biography 7. Giverny, France 8. Biographical fiction

LC 2009023383

A vividly rendered portrait of both the rise of Impressionism and of Monet, the artist at the center of the movement. It is, above all, a love story of the highest romantic order.

Coyle, Matt

Yesterday's echo / Matt Coyle. Oceanview Publishing, 2013. 297 p. Rick Cahill crime novels

ISBN 9781608090761

1. Murder suspects 2. Former police 3. Secrets 4. Widowers 5. Women television journalists 6. Chases 7. Police corruption 8. Detectives 9. Murder 10. California 11. La Jolla, California 12. Mysteries 13. Hardboiled fiction

Anthony Award for Best First Novel, 2014.

Still under suspicion for his wife's death eight years earlier, Rick Cahill finds new love with Melody Malana, but when she is accused of murder, Rick's attempts to help her go wrong, and he finds himself the target of a manhunt.

Coyne, John

The **caddie** who played with hickory / John Coyne. Thomas Dunne Books, 2008. ix, 321 p.

ISBN 9780312372446

1. Hagen, Walter, 1892-1969 2. Golfers 3. Golf 4. Revenge in men 5. Caddies 6. Country clubs 7. Illinois 8. Biographical fiction 9. Historical fiction

LC 2008003997

When a legendary golfer returns to Midlothian Country Club in the summer of 1946 to play a ceremonial round with the hickory clubs he used when he won his first U.S. Open, his arrival is anticipated by two caddies who have colorful stories of their own.

Crace, Jim

The **gift** of stones / Jim Crace. C. Scribner's Sons, 1989, c1988. 169 p.

ISBN 9780684190709

1. Prehistoric humans 2. Stone age 3. Change (Psychology) 4. Storytellers 5. Art, Prehistoric 6. Allegories 7. Literary fiction

LC 88031587

A community of stoneworkers in the era before the advent of bronze find their lives and their peace disrupted by the return of an adventurous storyteller

"As the fabulist tale unwinds, Crace looks into the role of the artist in society-here, a storyteller-considering both the impact and limits of imagination in guiding us toward new horizons. A marvelous literary effort." Library Journal.

Crace, Jim,

Harvest / Jim Crace. Nan A. Talese/Doubleday, 2013. 240 p.

ISBN 9780385520775

1. Medieval period (476-1492) 2. Xenophobia 3. Villages 4. Malicious accusation 5. Arson 6. Crime 7. Strangers 8. Punishment 9. Cartographers 10. Criminal investigation 11. Hysteria (Social psychology) 12. England -- History -- Medieval period, 1066-1485 13. Historical fiction 14. Psychological fiction 15. Literary fiction

LC 2012026208

International IMPAC Dublin Literary Award, 2015.
James Tait Black Memorial Prize for Fiction, 2013.
Shortlisted for the Man Booker Prize, 2013.
Shortlisted for the Walter Scott Prize for Historical Fiction, 2014

A stable fire in a remote English village leads to disputes between newcomers who are wrongly accused and long-term residents who refuse to believe one of their own could be responsible, a situation that is further exacerbated by the observations and meticulous note-taking of another outsider.

Crace, Jim,

Quarantine / Jim Crace. Farrar, Straus and Giroux, 1997. 242 p.

ISBN 0374239622

1. Jesus Christ 2. Fasting -- Religious aspects 3. Pilgrims and pilgrimages 4. Expectation (Psychology) 5. Wilderness survival 6. Husband and wife 7. Violence in men 8. Bible novels 9. Historical fiction 10. Literary fiction

LC 9761489

Whitbread Book Award for Novel, 1997.
Shortlisted for the Booker-McConnell Prize, 1997.

Shortlisted for the International IMPAC Dublin Literary Award, 1999

Retells the story of Jesus Christ's forty-day sojourn in the wilderness and its impact on a small group of individuals

"Crace's prose is startlingly specific about ancient life and Judea's harsh, terrible beauty. Unlike many authors of biblical fiction, he blends his research smoothly into his narrative and adds a leavening pinch of humor." Time.

Craddock, Curtis

An **alchemy** of masques and mirrors / Curtis Craddock. Tor, 2017. 384 p. Risen kingdoms

ISBN 9780765389596

1. Civil war 2. Princesses 3. Imaginary empires 4. Magic 5. Mathematics 6. Arranged marriage 7. Social acceptance 8. Steampunk 9. Fantasy fiction

In a retrofuturistic world of skyships and sorcerers, Isabelle des Zephyrs prepares to marry a man she's never met -- one whose two previous fiancées were assassinated. Determined not to meet the same fate, Isabelle must rely on her wits as well as the aid of her swashbuckling guardian, musketeer Jean-Claude. -- Description by Gillian Speace

Craddock, Curtis

A **labyrinth** of scions and sorcery / Curtis Craddock. Tor, 2019. 416 p. Risen kingdoms

ISBN 9780765389626

1. Coups d'etat 2. Imaginary empires 3. Courts and courtiers 4. Magic 5. Nobility 6. Princesses 7. Serial murderers 8. Murder investigation 9. Malicious accusation 10. Steampunk 11. Fantasy fiction

LC 2018044549

"A Tom Doherty Associates Book."

Isabelle des Zephyrs is unfairly convicted of breaking the treaty she helped write and has her political rank and status taken away. Now bereft, she nevertheless finds herself drawn into mystery when her faithful musketeer Jean-Claude uncovers a series of gruesome murders by someone calling themselves the Harvest King.

"Readers who already enjoyed the Romanticism-inspired worldbuilding of the first in Craddock's Risen Kingdoms trilogy will be pleased to discover even more nuances here. The types of magic are especially fleshed out and, with them, competing political factions. A fun, complicated tale, filled with adventure and intrigue." Booklist.

Crafts, Hannah

The **bondwoman's** narrative / Hannah Crafts ; edited by Henry Louis Gates. Warner Books, 2002. 338 p.

ISBN 0446530085

1. Crafts, Hannah 2. Women slaves 3. Fugitive women slaves 4. African American women 5. Plantations -- North Carolina 6. United States -- Social life and customs -- 19th century 7. Autobiographical fiction 8. African American fiction

LC 2001098325

A novel written in the 1850s by a runaway slave follows a young slave from a North Carolina plantation as she flees to the North and, after being pursued by slave hunters and forced to serve a difficult new mistress, finally obtains freedom in New Jersey.

Craig, Charmaine

Miss Burma / Charmaine Craig. Grove Press, 2017, c2016. 368 p.

ISBN 9780802126450

1. 20th century 2. Interethnic marriage 3. Interethnic conflict 4. Minorities 5. Civil war 6. Political persecution 7. Husband and wife 8. Nationalism 9. Betrayal 10. Identity (Psychology) 11. Daughters

12. Jewish men 13. Karen (Southeast Asian people) 14. Family relationships 15. Burma -- History -- 20th century 16. Political fiction 17. Literary fiction 18. Historical fiction

LC 2016047415

Longlisted for the National Book Award for Fiction, 2017.

Longlisted for The Women's Prize for Fiction, 2018.

In 1939, Benny, an Anglo-Indian pugilist from Rangoon's Jewish quarter, falls in love with Khin, a Karen woman. Their daughter, Louisa, grows up to be a beauty queen and an unlikely symbol of unity in a divided nation. Based on author Charmaine Craig's own family history, this sweeping saga brings to life a tumultuous half-century in the history of Burma (Myanmar) that includes British colonial rule, World War II and Japanese occupation, independence, and military dictatorship. -- Description by Gillian Speace

Craig, Philip R., 1933-2007

A **shoot** on Martha's Vineyard : a Martha's Vineyard mystery / Philip R. Craig. Scribner, 1998. 285 p. Martha's Vineyard mysteries

ISBN 9780684834542

1. Pedophiles 2. Biologists 3. Film locations 4. Murder investigation 5. Former police 6. Island life 7. Martha's Vineyard, Massachusetts 8. Mysteries

LC 9751141

Former policeman J.W. Jackson, now a fisherman in Martha's Vineyard, has a fight with a state environmental officer over the closure of a beach during a film shoot. When the officer is murdered, Jackson is a suspect and must clear his name.

"When J.W. Jackson's long-time nemesis arrives in town and is murdered, J.W. can avoid suspicion only by finding the murderer. A handsome Hollywood movie scout, meanwhile, takes a shine to Jackson's new wife. A lively and entertaining addition to the series." Library Journal.

Craig, Philip R., 1933-2007

Third strike : a Brady Coyne-J.W. Jackson mystery / Philip R. Craig and William G. Tapply. Scribner, 2007. 323 p. Brady Coyne and J. W. Jackson mysteries

ISBN 9781416532569

1. Strikes -- Transport workers 2. Ferryboats 3. Bombs 4. Frameups 5. Criminal investigation 6. Smuggling 7. Lawyers 8. Former police 9. Island life 10. Martha's Vineyard, Massachusetts 11. Mysteries

Features Brady Coyne from the Brady Coyne mysteries and Jeff Jackson from the Martha's Vineyard mysteries.

When a union striker is killed in an engine room explosion and accused of setting the bomb that ended his life, J.W. Jackson is entreated by the victim's widow to prove the man's innocence.

"Tapply's Boston lawyer, Brady Coyne, responds to an anguished call for help from an old client living on Martha's Vineyard, where the late Philip Craig's ex-cop, J.W. Jackson, is being urged by his wife to investigate the death of a striking ferry boat worker. . . . The two friends pursue their cases separately and together as tensions caused by the ferry strike mount and a murder raises the stakes. This marks the highly enjoyable and poignant end to a short, sweet series." Publishers Weekly.

Craig, Philip R., 1933-2007

A **vineyard** killing : a Martha's Vineyard mystery / Philip R. Craig. Scribner, 2003. 229 p. Martha's Vineyard mysteries

ISBN 9780743205245

1. Real estate developers 2. Fencing 3. Loyalty 4. Murder investigation 5. Former police 6. Island life 7. Martha's Vineyard, Massachusetts 8. Mysteries

LC 2002042878

When a visitor to Vineyard Haven survives a murder attempt, sometime private investigator J.W. Jackson looks into the deeds of a real estate developer who is buying deeds and evicting home owners.

"This installment begins with a bang: an unknown assailant shoots someone outside the delicatessen where series private investigator J. W. Jackson is eating with his wife. Jackson is soon embroiled in a murder case involving grabby real estate developers and recalcitrant islanders. Off-season atmosphere and the usual high-caliber sleuthing." Library Journal.

Crais, Robert

Chasing darkness / Robert Crais. Simon & Schuster, 2008. 256 p. Elvis Cole/Joe Pike novels

ISBN 9780743281645

1. Murder 2. Cold cases (Criminal investigation) 3. Police cover-ups 4. Private investigators 5. Police 6. Vietnam veterans 7. Detectives 8. Suicide 9. Murder investigation 10. Guilt in men 11. Los Angeles, California 12. Mysteries 13. Hardboiled fiction

LC 2008010709

Having cleared a man of a murder charge three years earlier, Elvis Cole and his sideick, Joe Pike, find themselves on trial when the former defendant is found dead holding photographs of the victim he had been accused of killing.

Crais, Robert

A **dangerous** man / Robert Crais. G.P. Putnam's Sons, 2019. 336 p. Elvis Cole/Joe Pike novels

ISBN 9780525535683

1. Kidnapping victims 2. Private investigators 3. Missing persons investigation 4. Murder 5. Whistle blowers 6. Murder investigation 7. Witnesses -- Protection 8. Los Angeles, California 9. Mysteries 10. Hardboiled fiction

Rescuing a bank teller from an abduction attempt, Joe Pike tackles the most perilous case of his career when the would-be kidnappers are found murdered and the bank teller goes missing.

Crais, Robert

Demolition angel : a novel. Doubleday, 2000. 386 p.

ISBN 0385495846

1. Policewomen 2. Bombings 3. Terrorists 4. Bomb squads 5. Murder 6. Women detectives 7. Bombing investigation 8. Bombers (Persons) 9. Los Angeles, California 10. Thrillers and suspense 11. Police procedurals

LC 00029054

Carol Starkey, a Los Angeles bomb squad detective who suffered permanent scarring and watched her lover/partner die in a prior detonation, embarks on a dangerous investigation into explosions rocking the city that are designed specifically to kill bomb technicians.

"The book features one of the most complex heroines to grace a thriller since Clarice Starling locked eyes with Hannibal Lecter, a deliciously spooky villain in the person of a mad bomber known as Mr. Red, and an aggressively involving plot." Publishers Weekly.

Crais, Robert

The **first** rule / Robert Crais. G. P. Putnam's Sons, 2010. 320 p. Elvis Cole/Joe Pike novels

ISBN 9780399156137

1. Home invasions 2. Drug traffic 3. Deception 4. Revenge 5. Criminals 6. Former police 7. Vietnam veterans 8. Former Marines 9. Crimes against married people 10. Private Investigators 11. Los Angeles, California 12. Mysteries 13. Hardboiled fiction

LC 2009036928

Elvis Cole's taciturn partner, Joe Pike, investigates an attack on former associate Frank Meyer, a one-time mercenary whose family has been murdered by a professional hit crew and who police suspect has been keeping a dangerous secret.

"Righteous vengeance, a reckless pace, a stratospheric body count and just enough surprises to keep you turning the pages. The pleasures may be primitive, but they're genuine." Kirkus.

Crais, Robert

Suspect / Robert Crais. G. P. Putnam's Sons, 2013. 320 p.
ISBN 9780399161483
1. Post-traumatic stress disorder 2. Police 3. Police dogs 4. Human/animal relationships 5. Murder investigation 6. Psychic trauma 7. Los Angeles, California 8. Thrillers and suspense

Struggling to reclaim his career after the devastating murder of his partner eight months earlier, LAPD cop Scott James is teamed with a traumatized military canine named Maggie who assists Scott in an effort to track down his late partner's killer.

Cramer, W. Dale

Levi's will : a novel / W. Dale Cramer. Bethany House, 2005. 394 p.
ISBN 0764229958
1. 1940s 2. Amish 3. Former Amish 4. Married men 5. Fathers 6. Amish families 7. Families 8. Father and adult son 9. Fathers and sons 10. Family relationships 11. Generation gap 12. Inheritance and succession 13. Soldiers 14. New identities 15. Reconciliation 16. Ohio 17. Florida 18. Europe 19. Christian fiction 20. Family sagas
LC 2005004602
Christy Award for Contemporary (Stand Alone) Category, 2006.

"A family saga of pain and reconciliation set behind the closed doors of an Amish community. Spanning three generations, the story follows the life of Will McGruder, who having fled as a young man, seeks to heal the past by bringing his new family to meet his Amish relatives"--Provided by publisher.

Crandall, Susan

Whistling past the graveyard / Susan Crandall. Gallery Books, 2013. 320 p.
ISBN 9781476707723
1. 1960s 2. Runaway girls 3. Race relations -- Mississippi 4. African American women 5. Interracial friendship 6. Civil Rights Movement -- Mississippi 7. Voyages and travels 8. Mississippi -- History -- 20th century 9. Coming-of-age stories 10. Southern fiction
LC 2012045961
Fleeing her strict grandmother's home in 1963 Mississippi, 9-year-old Starla Claudelle becomes an unlikely companion to an African-American woman at whose side she learns harsh lessons about period segregation and family.

Crane, Stephen, 1871-1900

* **Maggie** : a girl of the streets / Stephen Crane. Prometheus Books, 1995, c1893. 90 p.
ISBN 1573920371
1. Gilded Age (1865-1898) 2. City life 3. Poor girls 4. Families 5. Alcoholic mothers 6. Prostitutes 7. Conflict in families 8. Unhappiness in women 9. Manipulation by women 10. Naturalism 11. Dysfunctional families 12. Slums 13. New York City 14. Bowery, New York City 15. Psychological fiction
LC 959642
The harrowing story of a young girl living in the slums of New York City.

Crane, Stephen, 1871-1900

* The **red** badge of courage : an episode of the American Civil War / Stephen Crane, with an introduction by Shelby Foote. Modern Library, 1993, c1895. li, 246 p.
ISBN 0679602968
1. American Civil War era (1861-1865) 2. Courage in men 3. Union soldiers 4. Civil war 5. Cowardice in men 6. Shame in men 7. Second chances 8. Chancellorsville, Battle of, 1863 9. Naturalism 10. United States Civil War, 1861-1865 11. Virginia -- History -- Civil War, 1861-1865 12. United States -- History -- Civil War, 1861-1865 13. War stories 14. Historical fiction 15. Classics
LC 92027135
Originally published: New York : D. Appleton and company, 1895.

During his service in the Civil War, a young Union soldier matures to manhood and finds peace of mind as he comes to grips with his conflicting emotions about war.

Crawford, Isis

A **catered** Christmas cookie exchange / Isis Crawford. Kensington, 2013. 304 p. Mystery with recipes
ISBN 9780758274892
1. Contests 2. Television programs 3. Murder investigation 4. Octogenarian women 5. Women amateur detectives 6. Caterers and catering 7. Murder investigation 8. Women caterers 9. New York (State) 10. Cozy mysteries 11. Culinary mysteries 12. Gentle reads Includes recipes.

When Bernie and Libby are tasked with judging a highly competitive Christmas-cookie-baking contest, things get too hot in the kitchen when one of the contestants ends up dead.

Creech, Sarah

The **whole** way home / Sarah Creech. William Morrow & Co., 2017. 368 p.
ISBN 9780062409294
1. Country musicians 2. Former lovers 3. Secrets 4. Women musicians 5. Singers 6. Scandals 7. Country music 8. First loves 9. Nashville, Tennessee 10. Mainstream fiction

A radiant talent on the brink of making it big in Nashville must confront her small-town past and an old love she's never forgotten in this engaging novel--a soulful ballad filled with romance, heartbreak, secrets, and scandal from the author of Season of the Dragonflies.

Crews, Harry, 1935-2012

A **feast** of snakes : a novel / Harry Crews. Scribner, 1998, c1976. 177 p.
ISBN 0684842483
1. Discontent in men 2. Snakes 3. Rattlesnakes 4. Festivals 5. Small towns 6. Georgia 7. Black humor 8. Southern Gothic 9. Literary fiction 10. Southern fiction
LC 97031155
"The novel is set in the backwoods hamlet of Mystic, Georgia, where the annual festival begins with the crowning of the high-school Rattlesnake Queen , continues with a pit-bull championship fight, and ends with a Rattlesnake Roundup. The festival this year is a total nightmare: a black girl with a razor emasculates Sheriff Buddy Matlow, Big Joe Mackey kicks his losing dog to death, and Joe Lon Mackey aged twenty-two, practically illiterate, miserably married, with two screaming babies, his years of glory as an all-around athlete . . . behind him goes out of control with a twelve-gauge shotgun." The New Yorker.

Crichton, Michael, 1942-2008

Next : a novel / Michael Crichton. HarperCollins, 2006. 431 p.

ISBN 0060872985

1. Genetic engineering 2. Mutation (Biology) 3. Clones and cloning 4. Scientists 5. Venture capitalists 6. Lawyers 7. Talking animals 8. Parrots 9. Apes 10. Human/animal relationships 11. Genetics 12. Biotechnology 13. Heredity 14. Greed 15. Ethics 16. Bio-thrillers

LC 2006046905

In a near-future world where biotechnology and genetic research has become big business, the discovery of several transgenic animals leads to a legal and ethical battle over the rights to genes that can be used for commercial purposes.

"Despite its seemingly controversial subject matter, 'Next' is not one of Mr. Crichton's polarizing books . . . . Its' emphasis is on excitement, and on the strange moral wilderness in which geneticists and biotech profiteers suddenly find themselves." New York Times.

Crichton, Michael, 1942-2008

Micro / Michael Crichton and Richard Preston. HarperCollins, 2011. 448 p.

ISBN 9780060873028

1. Graduate students 2. Biotechnology 3. Rain forests 4. Robots 5. Microbiologists 6. Nanotechnology 7. Wilderness survival 8. Business -- Corrupt practices 9. Hawaii 10. Thrillers and suspense

The acclaimed late author of Jurassic Park and the award-winning author of The Hot Zone present the story of a group of graduate students who accept work with a mysterious biotech company in Hawaii only to be abandoned in a treacherous wilderness when they discover their employer's dark agenda.

Crichton, Michael, 1942-2008

Pirate latitudes / Michael Crichton. HarperCollins, 2009. 320 p.

ISBN 9780061929373

1. 17th century 2. Pirates 3. Treasure hunting 4. Raids (Military science) 5. Violence 6. Gold 7. Islands 8. Caribbean area 9. Adventure stories 10. Thrillers and suspense

English Captain Charles Hunter and his crew of ruffians sail from colonial Jamaica to infiltrate a Spanish-controlled port, commandeering the galleon El Trinidad and its fortune in gold after a bloody battle.

"Pirate fans will love the book for its flashy characters and historical authenticity. Crime fans will enjoy the caper-novel structure and the way the author keeps them on their toes." Booklist.

Crichton, Michael, 1942-2008

Prey : a novel / Michael Crichton. HarperCollins, 2002. 367 p.

ISBN 0066214122

1. Nanotechnology 2. Evolution 3. Artificial life 4. Technology and civilization 5. High technology industry and trade 6. Computer software 7. Computer programs 8. Military intelligence 9. Women executives 10. Molecular biologists 11. Stay-at-home fathers 12. Deserts 13. Nevada 14. California 15. Techno-thrillers

LC 2002032338

Deep in the remote Nevada desert, eight people are trapped inside of the Xymos Corporation by a rapidly evolving swarm of predatory molecules that have massed together to form a powerful and intelligent organism that is targeting its creators.

"Despite its absurd moments, 'Prey' is irresistibly suspenseful. You're entertained on one level and you learn something on another, even if the two levels do ultimately diverge." New York Times Book Review.

Criswell, Millie

What to do about Annie? / Millie Criswell. Ivy Books, 2001. 316 p. Baltimore novels (Millie Criswell)

ISBN 0804119511

1. Little Italy, Baltimore, Maryland 2. Contemporary romances 3. Romantic comedies

LC 2001116593

When Annie encounters Joe, the man who broke her heart years earlier when he became a priest, she decides it is time to get over him and move on, but Joe has other ideas as he prepares to leave the priesthood and pursue his beloved Annie.

Croft, Pippa

* The **second** time I saw you / Pippa Croft. Penguin U.K., 2016 360 p. Oxford Blue

ISBN 9781405917049

1. College students 2. Americans in England 3. Aristocracy 4. Young women 5. Studying abroad 6. Universities and colleges 7. Options, alternatives, choices 8. Sexual attraction 9. Men/women relations 10. England 11. New adult fiction

It's the beginning of a new term at Wyckham College, Oxford, and a fresh start for Lauren Cusack. Her fingers were badly burnt when a whirlwind romance with gorgeous English aristocrat, Alexander Hunt, became too hot to handle - and now she's determined to keep her distance.

Crombie, Deborah

A **bitter** feast / Deborah Crombie. William Morrow & Co, 2019 384 p. Duncan Kincaid and Gemma James mysteries

ISBN 9780062271662

1. Scotland Yard. 2. Husband-and-wife detectives 3. Criminal investigation 4. Family estates 5. Rich families 6. Villages 7. Flashbacks 8. Traffic accident victims 9. Murder 10. Secrets 11. England 12. Mysteries 13. Police procedurals

Invited to spend a weekend at a tranquil Cotswolds village, husband-and-wife Scotland Yard detectives Kincaid and James are drawn into a dangerous web of secrets involving an up-and-coming star chef and a series of mysterious deaths.

Crombie, Deborah

Kissed a sad goodbye / Deborah Crombie. Bantam Books, 1999. 322 p. Duncan Kincaid and Gemma James mysteries

ISBN 055310943X

1. Scotland Yard 2. Police 3. Murder investigation 4. Family businesses 5. Detectives 6. Women tea industry and trade executives 7. Businesspeople 8. Fiances 9. Crimes against women 10. Guilt in men 11. Tea industry and trade 12. London, England 13. Mysteries 14. Police procedurals

LC 9850186

Detective Kincaid of Scotland Yard investigates the murder of a promiscuous woman whose tea warehouse in the dockland of London was coveted by a builder. Sex crime or business crime?

"The murder of a beautiful businesswoman in London's Isle of Dogs neighborhood calls both local police and Scotland Yard into play. The Yard's Duncan Kincaid and Gemma James . . . create a psychological profile of the victim and thoroughly investigate the thriving family tea concern." Library Journal.

Crombie, Deborah

Mourn not your dead / Deborah Crombie. Scribner, 1996. 281 p. Duncan Kincaid and Gemma James mysteries

ISBN 0684801310

1. Scotland Yard 2. Detectives 3. Police murders 4. Murder

investigation 5. Villages 6. Police 7. Murder 8. London, England 9. England 10. Mysteries 11. Police procedurals

LC 9526166

In England, the romantic police pair of Duncan Kincaid and Gemma James investigate the murder of their commander, Superintendent Gilbert, an unloved man, even by his wife.

"Ms. Crombie keeps this series on its toes with her smooth procedural techniques and engagingly eccentric characters." New York Times Book Review.

Crombie, Deborah

Water like a stone : a novel / Deborah Crombie. William Morrow, 2007. viii, 407 p. Duncan Kincaid and Gemma James mysteries

ISBN 0060525274

1. Scotland Yard. 2. Police 3. Child murder victims 4. Family visits 5. Brothers and sisters 6. Crimes against children 7. Children -- Death 8. Drowning 9. Murder 10. Christmas Eve 11. Christmas 12. Marital conflict 13. Men/women relations 14. Policewomen 15. Cheshire, England 16. Mysteries 17. Police procedurals

LC 2006046841

Sequel to: In a dark house.

In the aftermath of a teenager's drowning in a Cheshire countryside canal, Scotland Yard detectives Duncan Kincaid and Gemma James investigate strange connections between the victim and two past murder cases.

"As in books by Elizabeth George and P. D. James, the intriguing personal relationships and family dynamics drive this well-crafted, impressive mystery-drama." Booklist.

Crompton, Richard, 1973-

Hell's gate : a novel / Richard Crompton. Sarah Crichton Books/Farrar, Straus and Giroux, 2015. 256 p. Detective Mollel mysteries

ISBN 9780374280581

1. Masai (African people) 2. Murder investigation 3. Detectives 4. Police corruption 5. Extortion 6. Organized crime 7. Bribery 8. Conspiracies 9. Kenya 10. Nairobi, Kenya 11. Mysteries

LC 2014030528

A former Maasai warrior who now works as a detective uncovers a murder plot, as well as extortion and bribery outside a national park.

"A classic lone-wolf detective story with enough plot twists to keep readers guessing until the end, this novel will appeal to those looking for both a psychological and an action thriller." Library Journal.

Crompton, Richard, 1973-

Hour of the red god / Richard Crompton. Sarah Crichton Books, 2013. 272 p. Detective Mollel mysteries

ISBN 9780374171995

1. Masai (African people) 2. Crimes against prostitutes 3. Political corruption 4. Conspiracies 5. Murder investigation 6. Detectives 7. Kenya 8. Nairobi, Kenya 9. Mysteries

LC 2012034612

Originally published as an e-book titled, The Honey Guide

Detective Mollel, a former Maasai warrior in Nairobi, investigates the brutal murder of a prostitute and suspects the killing is part of a far more extensive plot associated with the turbulent elections of 2007.

"[Crompton's] debut novel combines a sinuous plot, a wonderfully complex and tragic protagonist, and a remarkable portrait of a city that is simultaneously exotic yet familiar." Booklist.

Cronin, A. J. (Archibald Joseph), 1896-1981

* Citadel / A.J. Cronin Little, 1937. 401 p.

1. Physicians 2. Ambition in men 3. Husband and wife 4. Wales 5. London, England 6. Mainstream fiction

A sincere, conscientious young doctor faces the realization that he can achieve great material success only at the cost of his self-image.

Cronin, A. J. (Archibald Joseph), 1896-1981

The **keys** of the kingdom / A.J. Cronin. Little, 1941. 344 p.

ISBN 0316161845

1. Christian missions -- China 2. Priests -- China 3. China -- History 4. Christian fiction

LC 83-83064

Sent to China, a Scottish priest struggles to create and maintain a mission where famine, disease, and civil war prevail.

Cronin, Justin

The **city** of mirrors / Justin Cronin. Random House, 2016. 704 p. Passage trilogy

ISBN 9780345505002

1. Vampires 2. Revenge 3. Good and evil 4. Viruses 5. Survival 6. Immortality 7. Violence 8. Human experimentation in medicine 9. End of the world 10. Horror 11. Apocalyptic fiction

"The third and final installment in the Passage trilogy. With The Twelve destroyed, many wonder if the threat to humankind also has vanished. But then a terrifying threat shudders the gates of the colony...and Amy--the girl who must save the world, Peter, Alicia, and Michael must at last confront their destinies"--, Provided by publisher.

"Not only does this title bring the series to a thrilling and satisfying conclusion, but it also exhibits Cronin's moving exploration of love as both a destructive force and an elemental need, elevating this work among its dystopian peers." Library Journal.

Cronin, Justin

* The passage / Justin Cronin. Ballantine Books, 2010. 640 p. Passage trilogy

ISBN 9780345504968

1. Vampires 2. Viruses 3. Survival 4. Immortality 5. Good and evil 6. Violence 7. Human experimentation in medicine 8. End of the world 9. California 10. Horror 11. Apocalyptic fiction

First published: 2010.

The latest test subject in a covert government experiment, abandoned six-year-old Amy is rescued by an FBI agent who hides them in the Oregon hills, from which Amy emerges a century later to save the human race from a terrifying virus.

"The Passage owes a substantial debt to both King's 1978 epic and Cormac McCarthy's 2007 Pulitzer winner, and he is not immune to some of the hoarier tropes of Armageddon fiction (mystical children, cryptic-wisdom-spouting old folks, impossibly arduous vision quests). But his bogeymen, the vampiric, blood-hungry beasts known as virals, are magnificently unnerving, and his power to compel readers to the next page seldom flags." Entertainment Weekly.

Cronin, Justin

The **twelve** / Justin Cronin. Ballantine, 2012. 640 p. Passage trilogy

ISBN 9780345504982

1. Vampires 2. Viruses 3. Survival 4. Immortality 5. Good and evil 6. Violence 7. Human experimentation in medicine 8. End of the world 9. Horror 10. Apocalyptic fiction

Goodreads Choice Award, 2012.

Survivors of a government-induced apocalypse endure their violent and disease-stricken world while protecting their loved ones; while a century into the future, members of a transformed society determinedly search for the original twelve virals.

Crosbie, Lynn, 1963-

Where did you sleep last night? / Lynn Crosbie. House of Anansi, 2015. 381 p.

ISBN 1770899316

1. Cobain, Kurt, 1967-1994 2. Rock musicians 3. Teenage girls 4. Drug addicts 5. Couples 6. Marital conflict 7. Fame 8. Washington (State) 9. Mainstream fiction

When Evelyn Gray, a lonely sixteen-year old from Carnation, Washington, overdoses, she wakes up in the hospital with her idol, Kurt Cobain, convalescing in the bed beside her, with no memory of his former life. Once united, they quickly become addicted to drugs and each other. They run off together and become infamous musicians. But as their celebrity grows, so does their jealousy and an incident of sexual violence explodes shockingly into murder.

Cross, Amanda, 1926-2003

The **collected** stories / Amanda Cross. Ballantine Books, 1997. 192 p.

ISBN 9780345408174

1. Women detectives 2. United States 3. Mysteries 4. Short stories
LC 97-15301

Ten literary mystery stories starring Kate Fansler, academic sleuth.

"Kate Fansler, a university professor normally involved with things academic, also dabbles in solving mysteries. In these short stories, she deals with cases ranging from missing persons to murder. Cross presents a complex jumble of seemingly enigmatic clues that Kate proceeds to study and resolve into a simple answer based on logic and deduction. The author camouflages the clues, facts, and answers by placing them in total view during the entire story." School Library Journal.

Cross, Neil

Luther. The calling / Neil Cross. Simon & Schuster, 2012, c2011. 362 p.

ISBN 9781451673098

1. Detectives 2. Police 3. Murder 4. Murder investigation 5. Obsession 6. Gifted men 7. London, England 8. Mysteries 9. Police procedurals 10. TV tie-ins

Originally published: London : Simon & Schuster UK, 2011.

Ngaio Marsh Award for Best Crime Novel, 2012.

DCI John Luther takes us into his past and his mind. It is the story of the serial killer case that tore his personal and professional relationships apart and propelled him over the precipice beyond fury, beyond vengeance, all the way to the other side of the law.

Cross-Smith, Leesa, 1978-

Whiskey & ribbons / Leesa Cross-Smith. Hub City Press, 2018. 272 p.

ISBN 9781938235382

1. African American families 2. Police 3. African American widows 4. Murder victims 5. Assaults on police 6. Adoptees 7. Grief 8. Coping 9. Loss (Psychology) 10. African American police 11. Spouses of pregnant women 12. Parenthood 13. Blizzards 14. African American fiction 15. Domestic fiction

Leesa Cross-Smith's anticipated novel following a contemporary African American family caught in the wake of a tragic police shooting. Set in contemporary Louisville, the death of a police officer is a requiem for marriage, friendship and family.

Crouch, Blake

Dark matter : a novel / Blake Crouch. Crown Publishers, 2016. 336 p.

ISBN 9781101904220

1. College teachers 2. Parallel universes 3. Kidnapping victims 4. Life change events 5. Scientists 6. Reality 7. Married men 8. Families 9. Chicago, Illinois 10. Science fiction
LC 2015040107

A mind-bending, relentlessly paced science-fiction thriller, in which an ordinary man is kidnapped, knocked unconscious--and awakens in a world inexplicably different from the reality he thought he knew.

"Suspenseful, frightening, and sometimes poignant--provided the reader has a generously willing suspension of disbelief." Kirkus.

Crouch, Blake

Recursion / Blake Crouch Crown, 2019. 336 p.

ISBN 9781524759780

1. 21st century 2. Memories 3. Deception 4. High technology 5. Neuroscientists 6. False memory syndrome 7. Memory 8. Couples 9. Loss (Psychology) 10. Near future 11. Time travel 12. Reality 13. Science fiction

Goodreads Choice Award, 2019

Assigned to the case of a suicide victim who claimed her son's existence had been erased, investigator Barry Sutton follows leads to the outbreak of a memory-altering disease and the technological innovations of a controversial neuroscientist.

"This latest technological thriller from Crouch (Dark Matter) is completely engrossing and should have wide appeal. Highly recommended, especially for readers who enjoy suspenseful, fast-moving, well-crafted, science-based sf." Library Journal.

Crowell, Jenn, 1978-

* **Etched** on me : a novel / Jenn Crowell. Washington Square Press, 2013. 320 p.

ISBN 9781476739069

1. Child custody 2. Mothers and daughters 3. Adult child sexual abuse victims 4. Psychic trauma 5. Self-harm 6. Mental illness 7. Unplanned pregnancy 8. Cutting (Self-harm) 9. Psychiatric hospitals 10. London, England 11. Coming-of-age stories 12. Mainstream fiction
LC 2013014712

A coming-of-age story about a young woman who overcomes a troubled adolescence, only to lose custody of her daughter when her mental health history is used against her.

Crowley, John, 1942-

Lord Byron's novel : the evening land / John Crowley. William Morrow, 2005. 480 p.

ISBN 0060556587

1. Byron, George Gordon Byron,, Baron, 1788-1824 2. Lovelace, Ada King,, Countess of, 1815-1852 3. Regency period (1811-1820) 4. Codes (Communication) 5. Fiction writing 6. Fathers and daughters 7. Manuscripts -- Collectors and collecting 8. Women mathematicians 9. Literary historians 10. Poets 11. Authors 12. Fathers -- Death 13. Nobility 14. Great Britain -- History -- Regency, 1811-1820 15. Novels-within-novels 16. Epistolary novels 17. Gothic fiction 18. Psychological fiction
LC 2004063575

"Crowley's real achievement in Lord Byron's Novel is not a convincing imitation of Byron--not even Byron, who was pudgy and pale and walked with a limp, could always pull that off. More persuasive by far is the suffocating world of encryption and code, coincidence and conspiracy, paranoia and parapsychology that Crowley summons from his

19th-century documents and 21st-century decoders." New York Times Book Review.

Crownover, Jay

Honor / Jay Crownover. William Morrow Paperbacks, 2016 400 p. The Breaking Point

ISBN 9780062435569

1. Criminals 2. Stripteasers 3. Sex clubs 4. Inner city 5. Assassins 6. Business partnership 7. Sexual attraction 8. Men/women relations 9. Denver, Colorado 10. New adult fiction 11. Romantic suspense 12. Contemporary romances 13. Erotic romances

LC 2016017339

With money as no object, a good man who has seen things no one should have and done things no one should talk about will stop at nothing to find the woman he believes to be his equal, dancer Keelyn Foster, who has disappeared, and claim her as his.

Crucet, Jennine Capo

Make your home among strangers / Jennine Capo Crucet. St. Martin's Press, 2015. 352 p.

ISBN 9781250059666

1. Young women 2. College students 3. Immigrants 4. Family relationships 5. Divorce 6. Social classes 7. Cuban-Americans 8. Miami, Florida 9. Mainstream fiction 10. Coming-of-age stories

Upsetting her family by attending an elite college far from home, Cuban-American Lizet struggles with identity issues and her father's abandonment before meeting a young boy whose mother's death enmeshes Lizet's family in Florida's heated immigration debates.

"An emblematic story of both immigrant America and the coming-of-age struggle, told by an a PEN/O. Henry and Iowa Short Fiction award winner." Library Journal.

Crumley, James, 1939-2008

Bordersnakes / James Crumley. Mysterious Press, 1996. 320 p. Mino Minodragovitch Mysteries

ISBN 0892965738

1. Revenge 2. Violence 3. Gunshot victims 4. Automobile travel 5. Victims of crimes 6. Alcoholics 7. Inheritance and succession 8. Drug use 9. Vietnam veterans 10. Korean War veterans 11. Bankers 12. Drug lords 13. Private investigators 14. Mexican-American Border Region 15. West Texas 16. Hardboiled fiction

LC 9634405

Detective C.W. Sughrue joins forces with Detective Milo Milodragovitch to search for two would-be assassins and a thief, in a journey that takes them across the American Southwest and into Mexico

Crumley, James, 1939-2008

The **final** country / James Crumley. Mysterious Press, 2001. 310 p. Milo Milodragovitch mysteries

ISBN 0892966661

1. Violence 2. Alcoholics 3. Drug use 4. Private investigators 5. Missing persons 6. African American fugitives 7. Cross-country automobile trips 8. Victims of crimes 9. Political corruption 10. Korean War veterans 11. Mexico 12. Texas 13. Mysteries 14. Hardboiled fiction

LC 2001030640

Silver Dagger Award for Fiction, 2002.

On the lookout for a local man's vanished wife, Milo has a drink with an African-American ex-con that ends in the ex-con blowing out the brains of the local cocaine merchant. Milo need to track the ex-con down to save him from the hands of the Texas police but in the process becomes embroiled in his own set of difficulties.

"Plot twists and details seem loose and easy, yet every thread is sewn tight as a hardball. This is a brilliant achievement, with Crumley returned to his full powers, seeming to say with each assured sentence, Yeah, I'm an old dog, but I still wag the baddest bone." Publishers Weekly.

Crumley, James, 1939-2008

The **last** good kiss : a novel / James Crumley. Random House, 1978. 259 p. C. W. Sughrue mysteries

ISBN 0394419464

1. Missing persons 2. Alcoholics 3. Murder investigation 4. Prostitutes 5. Criminal investigation 6. Vietnam veterans 7. Topless bars 8. Amateur detectives 9. Haight-Ashbury District, San Francisco, California 10. San Francisco, California 11. Montana 12. Mysteries 13. Hardboiled fiction

LC 77090286

C.W. Sughrue, a Montana private eye, is hired to track down a failing author and winds up searching for Betty Sue Flowers, a woman missing for ten years in Haight-Ashbury.

Crumley, James, 1939-2008

* The **wrong** case / James Crumley. Random House, 1975. 272 p. Milo Milodragovitch mysteries

ISBN 9780394496184

1. Private investigators 2. Alcoholics 3. Missing persons investigation 4. Murder investigation 5. Brothers and sisters 6. Cynicism 7. Small towns 8. Korean War veterans 9. Pacific Northwest 10. Mysteries 11. Hardboiled fiction

LC 85-8882

In the small Northwest town of Meriwether, onetime prosperous private investigator Milo is lured from his reveries of lost opportunities into love, dope-dealing, and murder by one Helen Duffy who asks him to find her lost brother

"This is an exceptionally good example of the genre. Properly deferring to hallowed conventions, Crumley writes about damaged people seen through a haze of jaded romanticism, but he asserts his own tone of voice . . . . Crumley is a vivid writer. He makes Milo much more vulnerable, more involved in this sordid case than Hammett or Chandler would have done." Newsweek.

Crummey, Michael, 1965-

Galore / Michael Crummey. Doubleday Canada, 2009. 336 p.

ISBN 9780385663144

1. Fishing villages 2. Whales 3. Family relationships 4. Small town life 5. Interpersonal relations 6. Storytelling 7. Newfoundland and Labrador 8. Canada 9. Family sagas 10. Historical fiction

Canadian Authors Association Literary Awards, MOSAID Technologies Inc. Award for Fiction, 2010.

Shortlisted for the International IMPAC Dublin Literary Award, 2011

Governor General's Literary Awards, English-language Fiction finalist

Narrates the stories of six generation of two families who live in the small town of Deep Paradise set in Newfoundland, describing their loves and hates combined with elements of folklore and tales of witches, and ghosts.

"Crummey has created an unforgettable place of the imagination. Paradise Deep belongs on the same literary map as Faulkner's Yoknapatawpha and Garcia Marquez's Macondo." Boston Globe.

Crummey, Michael, 1965-

The **innocents** / Michael Crummey. Doubleday, 2019.
304 p.

ISBN 9780385545426

1. 19th century 2. Orphans 3. Survival 4. Loyalty 5. Forgiveness
6. Social isolation 7. Brothers and sisters 8. Islands 9. Shipwrecks
10. Newfoundland and Labrador 11. Literary fiction 12. Historical
fiction

LC 2018059408

ALA Notable Book, 2020.
Rogers Writers' Trust Fiction Prize finalist, 2019.
Shortlisted for the Scotiabank Giller Prize, 2019.

Two orphans forage for survival on an isolated Newfoundland cove
during years marked by storms and ravaging illness, before the mystery
of their nature tests the limits of their bond.

Crummey, Michael, 1965-

Sweetland / Michael Crummey Liveright Publishing,
2015, c2014 322 p.

ISBN 9780871407900

1. Misfits (Persons) 2. Eminent domain 3. Home (Concept) 4.
Eccentrics and eccentricities 5. Rural families 6. Newfoundland and
Labrador 7. Literary fiction 8. Domestic fiction

First published: Canada: Doubleday Canada, 2014.

Originally published in Canada in 2014 (Toronto : Doubleday Canada, 2014)

Newfoundland and Labrador Book Award for Fiction, 2016.

Governor General's Literary Awards, English-language
Fiction finalist

Sweetland is a story about one man's struggles against the forces of
nature on a remote island just off Newfoundland.

"The small cast of accompanying characters is well and wittily delineated, and Crummey's characteristic switching between past and present
is done craftily." Booklist.

Cruz, Angie

Dominicana : a novel / Angie Cruz. Flatiron Books, 2019.
336 p.

ISBN 9781250205933

1. 1960s 2. Arranged marriage 3. Teenage girls 4. Immigration and
emigration 5. Young women -- Relations with older men 6. Families
7. Duty 8. Abusive men 9. Brothers-in-law 10. Growing up 11.
Determination in teenage girls 12. Self-discovery in teenage girls 13.
Identity (Psychology) 14. New York City 15. Dominican Republic
16. Historical fiction 17. Coming-of-age stories

LC 2019012554

ALA Notable Book, 2020.

The author draws on her mother's story in a tale set in a turbulent
1960s Dominican Republic, where a young teen agrees to marry a man
twice her age to help her family's immigration to America.

Cullin, Mitch, 1968-

Undersurface / Mitch Cullin. Permanent Press, 2002. 166
p.

ISBN 1579620779

1. Undercover operations 2. Police murders 3. Married men 4.
Witnesses 5. Gay men 6. Homeless men 7. Ethics 8. Psychological
fiction

LC 2001036621

Based roughly on real events, this fictional account follows its
oblique protagonist as he moves through the loitering subculture found
within public toilets and pornographic arcades, and, in the process, finds
himself losing everything he values, including his own grip on reality.

"An account of a Tucson teacher's descent into the lurid, furtive
world of illicit gay sex, which lands him in the wrong place at the wrong
time when a murder is committed. John Connor is the ordinary, sensitive
narrator whose descent begins when he finds himself frequenting adult
video stores after his sex life with his wife sours. . . . As a crime narrative
based on a true story, the book is a chilling if somewhat dated tale of a
misstep morphing into free fall; as a literary character study, Connor's
attempt to come to terms with his situation is both haunting and compelling." Publishers Weekly.

Cumming, Charles, 1971-

A **colder** war / Charles Cumming. St. Martin's Press,
2014. 400 p. Thomas Kell novels

ISBN 9781250020611

1. M I 6 2. 1970s 3. Sabotage 4. Moles (Spies) 5. Former spies --
Great Britain 6. Spies 7. Espionage 8. Former spies 9. Assassination
10. Intelligence service 11. International relations 12. Turkey 13.
Middle East 14. Spy fiction 15. Thrillers and suspense

LC 2014010053

Sequel to: A Foreign Country.

Disgraced MI6 agent Thomas Kell is assigned to investigate the murders of an Iranian defector, an investigative journalist, and an Iranian nuclear scientist who had been recently recruited by Western intelligence,
a case that is further complicated by a senior agent's suspicious death.

Cumming, Charles, 1971-

A **divided** spy / Charles Cumming. St. Martin's Press,
2017. 368 p. Thomas Kell novels

ISBN 9781250021045

1. M I 6 2. Former spies 3. Espionage 4. Revenge 5. Terrorism 6.
Loss (Psychology) 7. Spies 8. Intelligence service 9. Voyages and
travels 10. Options, alternatives, choices 11. Spy fiction 12. Thrillers
and suspense

LC 2016037568

"Thomas Kell thought he was done with spying. A former MI6 officer, he devoted his life to the Service, but it has left him with nothing but
grief and a simmering anger against the Kremlin. Then Kell is offered
an unexpected chance at revenge. Taking the law into his own hands, he
embarks on a mission to recruit a top Russian spy who is in possession
of a terrifying secret. As Kell tracks his man from Moscow to London,
he finds himself in a high stakes game of cat and mouse in which it
becomes increasingly difficult to know who is playing whom. As the
mission reaches boiling point, the threat of a catastrophic terrorist attack
looms over Britain. Kell is faced with an impossible choice. Loyalty to
MI6--or to his own conscience?"--, Provided by publisher.

"Cumming not only tells a moving human story here, he also constructs an airtight espionage plot full of unanticipated twists and leading
up to a perfectly orchestrated finale." Booklist.

Cumming, Charles, 1971-

A **foreign** country / Charles Cumming. St. Martin's Press,
2012. 368 p. Thomas Kell novels

ISBN 9780312591335

1. M I 6 2. 1970s 3. Former spies -- Great Britain 4. Conspiracies
5. Kidnapping investigation 6. Political corruption 7. Women
kidnapping victims 8. France 9. Tunisia 10. Spy fiction 11. Thrillers
and suspense

LC 2012010921

Sequel: A Colder War.

Ian Fleming Steel Dagger Award, 2012.

When a newly appointed first female Chief of MI6 disappears weeks
after two possibly related cases, disgraced former MI6 officer Thomas

Kell is offered a chance to redeem his career by conducting a discreet operation that uncovers a shocking conspiracy.

Cumming, Charles, 1971-

The **Moroccan** girl / Charles Cumming. St. Martin's Press, 2019, c2018. 358 p.

ISBN 9781250129956

1. Authors 2. Intelligence service -- Great Britain 3. Revolutionaries 4. International intrigue 5. Espionage 6. Terrorism 7. Left-wing extremists 8. Betrayal 9. Options, alternatives, choices 10. Morocco 11. Spy fiction

Originally published as "The man between": London : HarperCollins Publishers, 2018.

A simple assignment for MI6 during a literary festival lands a successful novelist on the trail of a revolutionary leader who is being targeted by the world's competing intelligence services.

"Carradine is about to find out the hard way that real-life espionage bears little resemblance to his page-turning depictions. Cumming channels the dreamy romance of classic spy movies (think Casablanca, Notorious, The Thirty-Nine Steps) and juxtaposes it with a modern, relentlessly intense and staccato delivery." BookPage.

Cumming, Charles, 1971-

* The **Trinity** Six / Charles Cummin. St. Martin's Press, 2011. 368 p.

ISBN 9780312675295

1. Spies -- Russia 2. Intelligence service 3. Traitors 4. Espionage 5. Murder 6. Cold War 7. England 8. Cambridge, England 9. Spy fiction

LC 2010040197

The identity of a secret member of a modern espionage ring becomes a matter of survival to a Russian history academic who, in the wake of several suspicious deaths, is entangled in a plot involving MI-6 and the highest levels of Russian government.

"Taut, atmospheric and immersive--an instant classic." Kirkus.

Cumyn, Alan, 1960-

Losing it / Alan Cumyn. St. Martin's Press, 2003. 365 p.

ISBN 9780312306915

1. Teacher-student relationships 2. Fetishism (Sexuality) 3. College students 4. Husband and wife 5. Women poets 6. Mother and adult daughter 7. People with Alzheimer's disease 8. Middle class families 9. Ottawa, Ontario 10. Psychological fiction 11. Erotic fiction

LC 2002031882

Middle-aged English professor Bob Sterling finds his marriage and career on the brink of ruin after he takes a trip with a young poetry student who brings him face-to-face with a previously unexplored sexual fetish.

"The nuanced persuasive characterization propels the story forward and provides depth and texture. . . . A bonus is that Cumyn spices up this essentially sad story with some horrifyingly funny scenes." Booklist.

Cunningham, Michael, 1952-

By nightfall / Michael Cunningham. Farrar, Straus and Giroux, 2010. 256 p.

ISBN 9780374299088

1. Married people 2. City dwellers 3. Art museums 4. Brothers 5. Art and culture 6. Crushes (Interpersonal relations) 7. New York City 8. SoHo, New York City 9. Literary fiction

LC 2010012614

Peter and Rebecca Harris have settled into a comfortable mid-life--with their careers as an art dealer and editor, respectively, blossoming and their daughter in college--until Rebecca's brother with a history of drug problems shows up and makes Peter question his life.

"Cunningham is a cool observer of the New York art scene, and he has fun with the contrasts between the makers of art, toiling away in obscurity, and the buyers cocooned in expensive suburbs. His descriptions of the objects themselves are also worth the price of the book. . . . [This] is a good book, even a challenging one. But for a story about the power of passion to upend lives, it lacks juiciness and messiness. Cunningham's prose is so exact and so careful that it actually takes away from the story, putting an arid, intellectual distance between Peter and the reader. The result: Instead of a novel overflowing with flesh and sweat, rage and craziness, Cunningham has given us a well-considered treatise." Cleveland Plain Dealer.

Cunningham, Michael, 1952-

Flesh and blood / Michael Cunningham. Farrar, Straus, and Giroux, 1995. 465 p.

ISBN 0374181136

1. Family secrets 2. Dysfunctional families 3. Identity (Psychology) 4. Family violence 5. Fathers 6. Family relationships 7. Family sagas 8. Literary fiction

LC 94024628

Lambda Literary Award for Gay Men's Fiction, 1995.

Follows the Stassos family through four generations of ambition, love, violence, and change, focusing on the turbulent lives of the Stassos children

Cunningham, Michael, 1952-

* The **hours** / Michael Cunningham. Farrar, Straus, Giroux, 1998. 229 p.

ISBN 0374172897

1. Woolf, Virginia, 1882-1941 2. Women authors, English -- 20th century 3. Joy and sorrow in women 4. Identity (Psychology) 5. Women with mental illnesses 6. Mothers and sons 7. Mother-deserted children 8. Women with depression 9. Women -- Identity 10. Mothers 11. Lesbian editors 12. AIDS caregivers 13. People with AIDS 14. Pregnant women -- California 15. Literary fiction 16. Parallel narratives

LC 9834188

Pulitzer Prize for Fiction, 1999.

PEN-Faulkner Award, 1999.

Stonewall Book Award for the Barbara Gittings Literature Award, 1999.

ALA Notable Book, 2000.

Shortlisted for the International IMPAC Dublin Literary Award, 2000

National Book Critics Circle Award for Fiction finalist, 1998

The spirit of Virginia Woolf permeates the lives of several American readers as evidenced in this trio of tales about the author Woolf, a New Yorker planning a party to honour a writer, and a young mother reading Woolf's Mrs. Dalloway.

"After a brief prologue, the stories alternate in an intricate sequence, rather like a rhyme scheme. . . . The whole book does sound a little fussy in description, an exercise in echoes, but it doesn't read that way." New York Times Book Review.

Cunningham, Michael, 1952-

The **snow** queen : a novel / Michael Cunningham. Farrar, Straus and Giroux, 2014. 240 p.

ISBN 9780374266325

1. Brothers 2. Spirituality 3. Drug addiction 4. People with cancer 5. Conversion 6. New York City 7. Literary fiction 8. Psychological

fiction

LC 2013038712

First published in Great Britain by Fourth Estate in 2014.

A heartbroken man turns to religion after seeing a vision in the sky above Central Park, while his musician brother takes drugs he thinks will help him compose a ballad for his seriously ill wife.

"In concise yet descriptive language, Cunningham weaves the secret of transcendence through the mundane occurrences of everyday life." Library Journal.

Cunningham, Michael, 1952-

Specimen days / Michael Cunningham. Farrar, Straus, and Giroux, 2005. 320 p.

ISBN 0374299625

1. Whitman, Walt, 1819-1892 Influence 2. 19th century 3. 21st century 4. 22nd century 5. Poets 6. City life 7. Identity (Psychology) 8. Boys 9. Young women 10. Senior men 11. Terrorists 12. Refugees 13. Human/alien encounters 14. Industrial revolution 15. Machinery 16. Technology and civilization 17. Bombings 18. New York City 19. Literary fiction

LC 2005040518

3 linked stories.

Prophetic poet Walt Whitman presides over each interlinked episode in a visionary novel set in the city of New York, featuring the same group of characters--a young boy, an older man, and a young woman.

"As much as Cunningham's novel is haunted by the ghost of Whitman's prophecies, it is profoundly informed by the events of September 11, 2001. . . . Cunningham's brilliantly imagined dystopian future represents the final betrayal of Walt Whitman's joyously democratic America." The New Leader.

Curran, Kitty

My lady's choosing : an interactive romance novel / Kitty Curran, Larissa Zageris. Quirk Books, 2018. 351 p.

ISBN 9781683690139

1. Regency period (1811-1820) 2. Mate selection 3. Independence in women 4. Live-in companions 5. Aunt and niece 6. Sexual attraction 7. Men/women relations 8. Women/women relations 9. Regency romances 10. Historical romances 11. Plot-your-own stories

The romance novel that lets you pick your path, follow your heart, and find happily ever after. And in every path you pick, beguiling illustrations bring all the lust and love to life. --Amazon.

Currie, Ron, 1975-

Everything matters! / Ron Currie, Jr. Viking, 2009. 320 p.

ISBN 9780670020928

1. Prophecies (Occultism) 2. Adult children of dysfunctional families 3. Purpose in life 4. Self-fulfillment 5. End of the world 6. Comet collisions 7. Options, alternatives, choices 8. Men/women relations 9. Dysfunctional families 10. Apocalyptic fiction

LC 2008046686

Junior Thibodeau, who was encoded at birth with a prophecy about the world ending in thirty-six years, grapples with the question of whether or not anything he does matters.

"Junior Thibodeau of Waterville, ME--the fourth-smartest person in human history--is born with the certain knowledge that an asteroid will destroy Earth in 36 years. In that case, what is the point of living? In this radical reimagining of Frank Capra's It's a Wonderful Life, Junior tells his own story, while in alternating chapters his wildly dysfunctional family and friends provide commentary." Library Journal.

Currie, Ron, 1975-

* **Flimsy** little plastic miracles : a true story / Ron Currie, Jr. Viking, 2013. 352 p.

ISBN 9780670025343

1. Staged deaths 2. Fame 3. Authors 4. Men/women relations 5. Missing persons 6. Grief in men 7. Fathers -- Death 8. Deception 9. Fires 10. Islands 11. Metafiction 12. Satirical fiction

LC 2012028931

Mourning the death of his father and pining for an elusive woman he has loved since childhood, a writer who has lost his latest book in a fire fakes his own death and exiles himself to a small Caribbean island, where unexpected fame reveals the price of his deception.

Cush, Jean Love

Endangered / Jean Love Cush. Amistad Press, 2014 320 p.

ISBN 9780062316233

1. Trials (Murder) 2. Racism 3. African Americans 4. Murder suspects 5. Mothers and sons 6. Teenage boys 7. Race relations 8. injustice 9. Single mothers 10. Philadelphia, Pennsylvania 11. Mainstream fiction

When her 15-year-old son Malik is accused of murder, Janae, who cannot pay for his defense, reluctantly agrees to let a white human rights attorney represent him, and as she battles to save her son, his trial sparks a national firestorm of debate over race, prison and politics.

Cusk, Rachel, 1967-

* **Kudos** / Rachel Cusk. Farrar, Straus and Giroux, 2018. 224 p. Outline

ISBN 9780374279868

1. Freedom 2. Women authors 3. Identity (Psychology) 4. Art 5. Authors 6. Married women 7. Writers' retreats 8. Publishers and publishing 9. Brexit, 2016-2020 10. Europe 11. Psychological fiction 12. Literary fiction

LC 2018002527

A literary visit to a Europe in transition finds a material-seeking writer deeply identifying with the people she meets before evaluating difficult questions about acclaim, justice and the ultimate value of suffering.

"Brilliantly aware without being indulgent or preachy, this novel has the intense beauty of form that has marked Cusks trilogy from the beginning, and the final installment does not disappoint." Booklist.

Cusk, Rachel, 1967-

* **Outline** : a novel / Rachel Cusk. Farrar, Straus and Giroux, 2015, c2014. 256 p. Outline

ISBN 9780374228347

1. English language teachers 2. Self-disclosure 3. Self-deception 4. Truth 5. Conversation 6. Self-perception 7. Identity (Psychology) 8. Creative writing teachers 9. Observation (Psychology) 10. Teacher-student communication 11. Athens, Greece 12. Psychological fiction 13. Literary fiction

LC 2014016969

Originally published: London : Faber and Faber, 2014.

Shortlisted for The Baileys Women's Prize for Fiction, 2015

Shortlisted for the Giller Prize, 2015

Governor General's Literary Awards, English-language Fiction finalist

Captures 10 conversations involving the narrator, a novelist teaching a course in creative writing during one oppressively hot summer in Athens.

"And as the profile of her main character grows more defined in relief, so does Cusk's underlying message about love, loss, and feminine identity in the modern world, evident not only in her story but also in its delivery." Booklist.

Cusk, Rachel, 1967-

Transit / Rachel Cusk. Farrar, Straus and Giroux, 2017, c2016. 260 p. Outline

ISBN 9780374278625

1. English language teachers 2. Mothers and sons 3. Self-discovery in women 4. Self-perception 5. Transformations, Personal 6. Identity (Psychology) 7. London, England 8. Psychological fiction 9. Literary fiction

LC 2016025619

Sequel to: Outline.

Originally published: London : Jonathan Cape, 2016.

Shortlisted for the Giller Prize, 2017.

Moving to London with her two young sons in the wake of a family collapse, a writer endures personal, moral, artistic and practical transitions while confronting difficult questions about her vulnerability and power.

"Brilliantly written and structured, which is nothing new from this superlatively gifted writer, but with a chastened empathy for human weakness that was absent from her last two novels. Its return is most welcome." Kirkus.

Cusset, Catherine, 1963-

Life of David Hockney : a novel / Catherine Cusset ; translated by Teresa Fagan. Other Press, 2019, c2017. 192 p.

ISBN 9781590519837

1. Hockney, David, 1937- 2. Artists -- Great Britain 3. Gay men 4. Painters 5. Success (Concept) 6. Belonging 7. Eccentrics and eccentricities 8. Gay painters 9. Men/men relations 10. England 11. United States 12. Biographical fiction 13. LGBTQIA fiction 14. Translations -- French to English

LC 2018045824

Originally published: Paris : Gallimard, 2017

A compelling hybrid of novel and biography, Life of David Hockney offers an insightful overview of a painter whose art is as accessible as it is compelling, and whose passion to create has never been deterred by heartbreak or illness or loss.

Cussler, Clive, 1931-2020

Blue gold : a novel from the Numa files / By Clive Cussler, with Paul Kemprecos. Pocket Books, 2000. 378 p. NUMA files

ISBN 067178546X

1. National Underwater and Marine Agency 2. Desalting of water 3. Women scientists 4. Missing persons 5. Water-supply 6. Terrorism 7. Eco-terrorists 8. Billionaires -- California 9. South America 10. Venezuela 11. Adventure stories 12. Thrillers and suspense

LC 00057480

With the world running short of drinkable water, Kurt Austin and his NUMA team races against time to hunt down the missing scientist who has invented a process for turning salt water into fresh water.

Cussler, Clive, 1931-2020

Celtic empire / Clive Cussler, Dirk Cussler. G.P. Putnam's Sons, 2019 416 p. Dirk Pitt adventures

ISBN 9780735218994

1. National Underwater and Marine Agency 2. International intrigue 3. Diseases 4. Tombs 5. Archaeology 6. Murder 7. Secrets 8. Thrillers and suspense 9. Adventure stories

LC 2018056946

The murders of a U.N. science team in El Salvador, a deadly collision in the Detroit waterways and an attack on the Nile are linked to the ancient story of a fugitive Egyptian princess.

Cussler, Clive, 1931-2020

* The **chase** / Clive Cussler. G.P. Putnam's Sons, 2007. 416 p. Isaac Bell thrillers

ISBN 9780399154386

1. 1910s 2. Bank robberies 3. Detectives 4. Crime 5. Stealing 6. California -- History -- 1850-1950 7. Historical thrillers 8. Adventure stories

LC 2007017291

In 1906 detective Isaac Bell goes after the Butcher Bandit who has committed a string of bank robberies and murders in the western states of America and becomes the hunted.

"Cussler clearly had a lot of fun writing this. The details of early 20th-century America and the novel's thrill-a-minute pace will add another best seller to his resume." Library Journal.

Cussler, Clive, 1931-2020

The **cutthroat** / Clive Cussler and Justin Scott. G.P. Putnam's Sons, 2017. 393 p. Isaac Bell thrillers

ISBN 9780399575600

1. 1900s (Decade) 2. Detectives 3. Missing women 4. Serial murder investigation 5. Women murder victims 6. Murder investigation 7. Serial murders 8. New York City 9. Adventure stories 10. Historical thrillers

LC 2017002791

Hired to find a young woman who ran away from home to become an actress in 1911, Chief Investigator Isaac Bell begins a manhunt that is complicated by the acts of a serial killer whose victims resemble the missing girl.

Cussler, Clive, 1931-2020

* **Final** option / Clive Cussler and Boyd Morrison. G. P. Putnam's Sons, 2019. 390 p. Oregon files

ISBN 9780525541813

1. Mercenaries 2. Intelligence service 3. Secrecy 4. Enemies 5. Technology 6. Weapons 7. Thrillers and suspense 8. Adventure stories

LC 2019037432

Juan Cabrillo and his team of expert operatives return in this latest entry in Clive Cussler's Oregon Files series. Aboard the Oregon, one of the most advanced spy ships ever built, they face new challenges and nemeses as they undertake another dangerous mission.

Cussler, Clive, 1931-2020

Ghost ship / Clive Cussler and Graham Brown. G. P. Putnam's Sons, 2014. 440 p. NUMA files

ISBN 9780399167317

1. National Underwater and Marine Agency 2. Scientists 3. Human trafficking 4. Amnesia 5. International intrigue 6. Human trafficking victims 7. Thrillers and suspense 8. Adventure stories

LC 2014008875

Waking with conflicted memories after an injury sustained while trying to rescue passengers from a sinking yacht, Kurt Austin searches for answers from a state-sponsored cybercrime ring that takes him from Monaco to North Korea.

Cussler, Clive, 1931-2020

* **Golden** Buddha / Clive Cussler and Craig Dirgo. Berkley Books, 2003. 420 p. Oregon files

ISBN 0425191729

1. 1950s 2. 2000s (Decade) 3. Businesspeople 4. Special operations (Military science) 5. International relations 6. Oil wells 7. Dalai lamas 8. Art thefts 9. Intelligence officers 10. CIA agents 11. Ship captains 12. Spy ships 13. Mercenaries 14. Statues 15. Tibet 16. Cuba 17. Spy fiction 18. Sea stories 19. Adventure stories 20. Thrillers and suspense

LC 2003052217

Captain Cabrillo and his intelligence agents plan to strike a deal with the Russians and Chinese to exchange a golden Buddha containing records of oil reserves for Tibet's freedom, but his enemies will do anything to stop him.

Cussler, Clive, 1931-2020

* The **Gray** Ghost / Clive Cussler and Robin Burcell. G. P. Putnam's Sons, 2018. 388 p. Fargo adventures

ISBN 9780735218734

1. Antique and classic cars 2. Greed 3. Malicious accusation 4. Automobile thieves 5. Private investigators 6. Criminal investigation 7. Adventure stories 8. Thrillers and suspense

LC 2018012901

The grandson of a man who was wrongly accused of stealing a recovered Rolls-Royce prototype a century earlier hires husband-and-wife team Sam and Remi Fargo to solve the mystery and clear his grandfather's name, a case that is complicated by dangerous enemies and the rare vehicle's repeat disappearance.

Cussler, Clive, 1931-2020

Havana storm / Clive Cussler and Dirk Cussler. G. P. Putnam's Sons, 2014. 452 p. Dirk Pitt adventures

ISBN 9780399172922

1. National Underwater and Marine Agency 2. Treasure hunting 3. International intrigue 4. Underwater warfare 5. Cuba 6. Thrillers and suspense 7. Adventure stories

LC 2015001483

Investigating a toxic outbreak in the Caribbean Sea that is threatening the United States, Dirk Pitt is embroiled in a post-Castro power struggle for control of Cuba; while his children, Dirk Jr. and Summer, embark on a high-stakes treasure hunt.

Cussler, Clive, 1931-2020

The **Mediterranean** caper / Clive Cussler. Pyramid Books, 1973. 220 p. Dirk Pitt adventures

ISBN 9780515031799

1. Air bases -- Greece 2. Conspiracies -- Greece 3. Drug smuggling -- Greece 4. Nazi fugitives -- Greece 5. Sabotage -- Greece 6. War criminals -- German 7. Germans in Greece 8. Greece 9. Adventure stories

LC 9553364

Originally published in Great Britain as: May day!

A Luftwaffe ace, a Nazi war criminal, a beautiful and untrustworthy brunette, and a deadly billion-dollar cargo are the objects of a desperate search.

Cussler, Clive, 1931-2020

Nighthawk : a novel from the NUMA Files / Clive Cussler and Graham Brown. G.P. Putnam's Sons, 2017. 464 p. NUMA files

ISBN 9780399184017

1. National Underwater and Marine Agency 2. Weapons 3. Threat (Psychology) 4. International intrigue 5. Thrillers and suspense 6. Adventure stories

LC 2016043196

When the most advanced aircraft ever designed vanishes over the South Pacific, Kurt Austin and Joe Zavala are drawn into a deadly race to recover the fallen technology, which carries a secret payload of exotic matter capable of triggering an Armageddon-level catastrophe.

Cussler, Clive, 1931-2020

Odessa Sea / Clive Cussler and Dirk Cussler. G. P. Putnam's Sons, 2016. 464 p. Dirk Pitt adventures

ISBN 9780399575518

1. National Underwater and Marine Agency 2. Nuclear weapons 3. Smugglers 4. International intrigue 5. War -- Prevention 6. Ships 7. Secrets 8. Women oceanographers 9. Marine engineers 10. Voyages and travels 11. Thrillers and suspense 12. Adventure stories

Dirk Pitt and his NUMA team race to prevent a global war linked to the 1917 effort to preserve the Romanov Empire, the loss of a Cold War bomber's deadly cargo, mysterious Black Sea deaths and modern-day nuclear-materials smugglers.

Cussler, Clive, 1931-2020

* The **oracle** / Clive Cussler and Robin Burcell. G. P. Putnam's Sons, 2019 399 p. Fargo adventures

ISBN 9780525539612

1. Treasure hunters 2. Hostage taking 3. Criminals 4. Treasure troves 5. Schools 6. Curses 7. Scrolls 8. North Africa 9. Nigeria 10. Adventure stories 11. Thrillers and suspense

LC 2019020942

Searching for a cache of cursed scrolls from sixth-century northern Africa, treasure hunters Sam and Remi Fargo confront rival crime bands that have taken students hostage to steal supply shipments from a charity-funded Nigerian school.

Cussler, Clive, 1931-2020

Pacific vortex! / Clive Cussler. Bantam Books, 1983, c1982. 270 p. Dirk Pitt adventures

ISBN 9780553276329

1. International intrigue 2. Nuclear submarines 3. Underwater rescue operations 4. Heroes and heroines 5. Thrillers and suspense 6. Adventure stories 7. Sea stories

LC 85000832

The author recommends reading the Dirk Pitt adventures in the order they were written. According to his website, "Pacific Vortex" was written first but published much later. Please see the author's website for more information.

When a top secret American nuclear submarine mysteriously disappears from the depths of the ocean, Dirk Pitt is ordered to locate and salvage the submarine.

Cussler, Clive, 1931-2020

The **Pharaoh's** secret / Clive Cussler and Graham Brown. G. P. Putnam's Sons, 2015. 422 p. NUMA files

ISBN 9780399174117

1. National Underwater and Marine Agency 2. Weapons 3. Threat (Psychology) 4. International intrigue 5. Thrillers and suspense 6.

Adventure stories

When a power broker's scheme to build a new Egyptian empire requires his manipulation of a Saharan aquifer, Kurt and Joe race to learn the truth about an underworld plant extract at his disposal that may have the power to restore life to the dead.

Cussler, Clive, 1931-2020

* The **rising** sea : a novel from the NUMA files / Clive Cussler and Graham Brown. G. P. Putnam's Sons, 2018. 416 p. NUMA files

ISBN 9780735215535

1. National Underwater and Marine Agency 2. International intrigue 3. High technology 4. Power (Social sciences) 5. Sea level 6. Weapons 7. Pacific Ocean 8. Thrillers and suspense 9. Adventure stories

LC 2017033074

Investigating an alarming rise in the world's sea levels, Kurt, Joe and the rest of the NUMA scientific team uncover a diabolical plot to upset the Pacific balance of power by triggering natural disasters to displace billions of people.

Cussler, Clive, 1931-2020

The **Romanov** ransom / Clive Cussler and Robin Burcell. G. P. Putnam's Sons, 2017. 388 p. Fargo adventures

ISBN 9780399575549

1. Kidnapping 2. Missing persons investigation 3. Treasure hunters 4. Treasure troves 5. Adventure stories 6. Thrillers and suspense

LC 2017021532

Husband-and-wife team Sam and Remi Fargo investigate a kidnapping that may be linked to the Nazi-stolen Romanov ransom, a case that is complicated by the heinous acts of a guerrilla faction that would establish the Fourth Reich.

Cussler, Clive, 1931-2020

Sacred stone / Clive Cussler and Craig Dirgo. Berkley Books, 2004. 404 p. Oregon files

ISBN 0425198480

1. Ship captains 2. Businesspeople 3. Spies 4. Mercenaries 5. Terrorists 6. Muslims 7. Terrorism -- Prevention 8. Prejudice 9. Relics 10. Meteorites 11. Radioactivity 12. Atomic bomb 13. Special operations (Military science) 14. International intrigue 15. Private security services 16. Spy ships 17. Fundamentalism 18. Islam 19. Greenland 20. Spy fiction 21. Sea stories 22. Adventure stories 23. Thrillers and suspense

LC 2004050206

Juan Cabrillo and his fellows on the Oregon are charged with protecting a deadly radioactive stone. Beset by two militant terrorist factions, Juan and his mates must act quickly to prevent WWIII.

Cussler, Clive, 1931-2020

* **Sea** of greed : a novel from the NUMA files / Clive Cussler and Graham Brown. G. P. Putnam's Sons, 2018 416 p. NUMA files

ISBN 9780735219021

1. National Underwater and Marine Agency 2. Offshore oil 3. International intrigue 4. Oil industry and trade 5. Billionaires 6. Submarines 7. Military missions 8. Alternative energy development 9. Genetically engineered organisms 10. Mediterranean Sea 11. Gulf of Mexico 12. Thrillers and suspense 13. Adventure stories

LC 2018037962

The world's oil supply is vanishing, the stock market is plummeting and the NUMA team must solve a baffling historical mystery in order to save the future.

Cussler, Clive, 1931-2020

Serpent : a novel from the NUMA Files / Clive Cussler with Paul Kemprecos. Pocket Books, 1999. 474 p. NUMA files

ISBN 0671026682

1. National Underwater and Marine Agency 2. Andrea Doria (Steamship) 3. Assassins 4. Underwater archaeology -- North Atlantic Ocean 5. Shipwrecks -- North Atlantic Ocean 6. Archaeological expeditions 7. Women underwater archaeologists 8. Thrillers and suspense 9. Adventure stories

Kurt Austin, leader of a National Underwater and Marine Agency exploration team, and a marine archaeologist embark on a deadly mission to uncover a priceless pre-Columbian antiquity.

Cussler, Clive, 1931-2020

Shadow tyrants / Clive Cussler and Boyd Morrison. G. P. Putnams Sons, 2018. 387 p. Oregon files

ISBN 9780735219069

1. Mercenaries 2. Intelligence service 3. Secrecy 4. Enemies 5. Technology 6. Weapons 7. Thrillers and suspense 8. Adventure stories

When the descendants of a legendary band of imperial secret-keepers threaten humanity, Juan Cabrillo and his team aboard the Oregon race to protect the world from a plot to eliminate all technology.

"Readers probably won't lie awake worrying whether all this could really happen. Fast-moving, implausible fun." Kirkus.

Cussler, Clive, 1931-2020

* The **Titanic** secret / Clive Cussler and Jack Du Brul. G.P. Putnam's Sons, 2019. 390 p. Isaac Bell thrillers

ISBN 9780735217263

1. Titanic (Steamship) 2. 1910s 3. Detectives 4. Private investigators 5. International intrigue 6. Coal mines and mining 7. Coal mine accidents 8. Submersibles 9. Submarines 10. Shipwrecks 11. New York City 12. Colorado 13. Adventure stories 14. Historical thrillers 15. Parallel narratives

LC 2019028820

Investigating a mine tragedy in 1911 Colorado that killed nine people, Isaac Bell discovers a larger puzzle involving an international power scheme aimed at seizing control of a rare element.

Cussler, Clive, 1931-2020

Typhoon fury / Clive Cussler and Boyd Morrison. G. P. Putnam's Sons, 2017. 436 p. Oregon files

ISBN 9780399575570

1. Intelligence service 2. Mercenaries 3. Ocean travel 4. Painting 5. Drug industry and trade 6. Thrillers and suspense 7. Adventure stories

LC 2017012116

Juan Cabrillo and the crew of the Oregon sail into a perfect storm of danger to try to stop a new world war, in a thrilling suspense novel from the #1 New York Times-bestselling grand master of adventure.

Cussler, Clive, 1931-2020

The **wrecker** / Clive Cussler and Justin Scott. G.P. Putnam's Sons, 2009. 480 p. Isaac Bell thrillers

ISBN 9780399155994

1. 1900s (Decade) 2. Sabotage 3. Railroad accidents 4. Railroads 5.

Detectives 6. Murderers 7. Murder investigation 8. The West (United States) -- History -- 20th century 9. Adventure stories 10. Historical thrillers

LC 2009017216

Investigating a series of attacks on the Southern Pacific Railroad's Cascades express lines, Detective Bell learns of the existence of an elusive saboteur who recruits and murders his own accomplices while engineering schemes of maximum havoc.

Czerneda, Julie, 1955-

A **turn** of light / Julie E. Czerneda. Penguin Group USA, 2013. 854 p. Night's edge

ISBN 9780756407070

1. Sunrise and sunset 2. Interdimensional travel 3. Transformations (Magic) 4. Frontier and pioneer life 5. Protectiveness in men 6. Desire in women 7. Young women 8. Good and evil 9. Dragons 10. Magic 11. Fantasy fiction

Sequel: A play of shadow.

Prix Aurora: Best Novel, 2014.

A debut fantasy novel set in an isolated refugee community where the magic and mortal worlds intersect and where young Jenn Nalynn, an unknowing member of both worlds, accidentally transforms her dragon protector into a man before encountering hostile strangers.

D

D'Agostino, Kris, 1978-

The **antiques** / Kris D'Agostino. Scribner, 2017. 320 p.

ISBN 9781501138973

1. Dysfunctional families 2. Hurricanes 3. Last days 4. People with cancer 5. Wills 6. Antiques 7. Brothers and sisters 8. Homecomings 9. Floods 10. Memories 11. Family relationships 12. New York (State) 13. Domestic fiction

Gathering at the deathbed of their antiques-store-owner father, three adult siblings and his wife reinforce the store against a record-breaking hurricane and become consumed by past memories, present-day dilemmas and the realities of managing a death as floodwaters overtake the town.

"DAgostino balances scathing and humorous commentary on the foibles of family with keen insight into his characters who, despite their myriad flaws, deserve a satisfactory ending to the worst week ever." Publishers Weekly.

D'Eramo, Luce, 1925-2001

Deviation / Luce D'Eramo ; translated from the Italian by Anne Milano Appel. Farrar, Straus and Giroux, 2018. 368 p.

ISBN 9780374138455

1. World War II 2. Women -- Italy 3. Fascists 4. Holocaust (1933-1945) 5. Teenage girls 6. Concentration camps 7. Violence 8. Fear 9. Atrocities 10. Life change events 11. Autobiographical fiction 12. Historical fiction 13. Translations -- Italian to English

LC 2018000169

Originally published: Milan : Mondadori, 1979.

A devoted fascist changes her mind and her life after witnessing the horrors of the Holocaust.

D'Erasmo, Stacey

The **sky** below / Stacey D'Erasmo. Houghton Mifflin, 2009. 288 p.

ISBN 9780618439256

1. Life change events 2. Gay men -- Manhattan, New York City

3. Men -- Mortality 4. Change (Psychology) 5. Homosexuality 6. Manhattan, New York City 7. Mexico 8. Psychological fiction

LC 2008025673

Working as an obituary writer at a failing newspaper in lower Manhattan in the wake of 9/11, thirty-seven-year-old Gabriel Callahan has a halfhearted approach to life, until a brush with his own mortality sends him to Mexico on a quest to put himself back together and transform his life.

"This novel tells the story of a misanthropic obituary writer for a dying New York newspaper, who views his life through a series of memory boxes modelled on the assemblage art of Joseph Cornell. I assiduously collected interesting junk, filling my pockets with pebbles and wire and old nails: the stuff of transformation, he says. He narrates the drudgery of the daily grind and scrutinizes his dysfunctional, fatherless childhood, during which he rebelled against his mother by dealing drugs and engaging in sex with men for money. Now nearing forty and spiritually broken, he is given a diagnosis of cancer and travels to a commune in Mexico, where he reluctantly receives the help of a clairvoyant eight-year-old girl. Although the book strays into portentous magic realism, its lyrical prose and telling detail create a powerful atmosphere." The New Yorker.

D'Souza, Tony

The **Konkans** / Tony D'Souza. Harcourt, 2008. 308 p.

ISBN 9780151015191

1. 1970s 2. Kokna (Indic people) 3. East Indians in the United States 4. Culture conflict 5. Identity (Psychology) 6. Identity (Religion) 7. Families 8. Husband and wife 9. Fathers and sons 10. Extramarital affairs 11. Brothers 12. India 13. Domestic fiction

LC 2007015303

Francisco D'Sai, the son of a Konkan father, Lawrence, and an American mother, Denise, grows up surrounded by the colorful tales of India and Konkan history, stories that feed his imagination and give him a profound sense of his heritage and its meaning in his life.

"This is more than an ethnographic study--D'Souza stays character-focused throughout the novel, gently mixing irony and fatalism with a warm affection for humans and the stupid things they do." Washington City Paper.

D'Souza, Tony

Whiteman / Tony D'Souza. Harcourt, 2006. 279 p.

ISBN 9780151011452

1. Americans in West Africa 2. International relief -- Africa 3. Political violence -- Africa 4. Race relations -- Africa 5. Muslims 6. AIDS (Disease) -- Study and teaching 7. Friendship 8. Cote d'Ivoire 9. West Africa 10. Psychological fiction

LC 2005025459

Refusing to leave his violence-charged post in an African Muslim village after his funding is cut off, maverick American relief worker Jack Diaz, at the side of his village guardian, Mamadou, gains insights into the region's hunting, farming, culture, and struggles with AIDS.

"One significant virtue of D'Souza's storytelling rests in his ability to present Jack's experiences of African life with a vividness that reveals the continent's allure without sentimentalizing its exoticism. . . . Much of the drama that unfolds in the 12 loosely chronological parts of Whiteman (each a story that could stand on its own) rests in the gentle progression that ferries Jack away from a form of blindness to a new kind of sight." New York Times Book Review.

Dahl, Arne, 1963-

Bad Blood / Arne Dahl ; translated from the Swedish by Rachel Willson-Broyles. Pantheon Books, 2013, c1998. 352 p. Intercrime

ISBN 9780375425363

1. 1990s 2. Police 3. Serial murder investigation 4. Serial murders 5. Torture 6. Americans in Sweden 7. Stockholm, Sweden 8. Sweden 9. Mysteries 10. Police procedurals 11. Translations -- Swedish to English 12. Scandinavian crime fiction

LC 2012046772

Translated from the Swedish of: Ont Blod (1998).

Originally published as Ont blod in 1998 by Bra Brocker AB, Stockholm.

First published with the title 'Ont blod' by Bra Bocker in 1998.

TV tie-in.

Detective Paul Hjelm and his team receive an urgent call from the FBI. A murderer whose methods bear a frightening resemblance to a serial killer they believed long dead is on his way to Sweden. If they are to capture the killer, the team must collaborate with their colleagues in the FBI on a desperate hunt that will take them from rainswept city streets to deserted Kentucky farmhouses, and will push them to the limits of their endurance.

Dahl, Arne, 1963-

Misterioso : a crime novel / Arne Dahl ; translated from the Swedish by Tiina Nunally. Pantheon Books, 2011, c1999. 352 p. Intercrime

ISBN 9780375425356

1. 1990s 2. Police 3. Serial murders 4. Serial murder investigation 5. Crimes against rich people 6. Murder investigation 7. Mafia -- Russia 8. Secret societies 9. Stockholm, Sweden 10. Sweden 11. Mysteries 12. Police procedurals 13. Translations -- Swedish to English 14. Scandinavian crime fiction

LC 2010032837

Also known as: The blinded man.

Detective Paul Hjelm is unexpectedly placed into an elite team of officers and sent on a mission to track down a killer who has been systematically targeting business leaders, a case that pits them against the Russian Mafia, Sweden's secret wealthy societies and the country's persistent xenophobia.

"[The author] sets a full plate for himself in the first of a series about Hjelm and his colleagues. He describes a once comfortable country fragmented by racial malaise; East European Mafias; a financial collapse brought on by greedy, reckless bankers and government deregulation; postindustrial capitalism; and a gnawing fear that Sweden has lost its way." Booklist.

Dahl, Julia, 1977-

Conviction / Julia Dahl. Minotaur Books, 2017. 312 p. Rebekah Roberts novels

ISBN 9781250083692

1. Cold cases (Criminal investigation) 2. Innocence (Law) 3. Women journalists 4. Women amateur detectives 5. Jews 6. Tabloid newspapers 7. Hasidism 8. Police 9. Murder 10. Murder investigation 11. Secrets 12. New York City 13. Mysteries

Investigating when a Jewish man convicted 22 years earlier for the brutal murders of a Crown Heights black family writes to her, pleading his innocence, journalist Rebekah Roberts is challenged to infiltrate Brooklyn's insular Hasidic community, where she is targeted by a determined killer.

"Dahl excels at revealing the inner workings of enigmatic subcultures while maintaining peak suspense." Publishers Weekly.

Dahl, Kjell Ola, 1958-

The **courier** / Kjell Ola Dahl ; translated from the Norwegian by Don Bartlett. Orenda Books, 2019. 276 p.

ISBN 9781912374434

1. 1940s 2. 2010s 3. World War II -- Underground movements 4. Guerrillas 5. Jewish women 6. Former lovers 7. Absence and presumption of death 8. Oslo, Norway 9. Norway -- History -- German occupation, 1940-1945 10. Historical mysteries 11. Mysteries 12. Translations -- Norwegian to English

"Dahl deftly binds the story's alternating time periods, creating depth and mixing gut-churning tension with haunting tragedy." Booklist.

Dahl, Roald

Collected stories / Roald Dahl ; edited and introduced by Jeremy Treglown. Alfred A. Knopf, 2006. xxxvii, 850 p.

ISBN 9780307264909

1. Short stories

LC 2006046523

Originally published: The collected short stories of Roald Dahl. London : Michael Joseph, c1991. With new introduction.

A definitive compilation of short fiction for adults from the author of Charlie and the Chocolate Factory and other children's classics blends the macabre with humor and the grotesque.

"With the inventive power of a Thomas Edison and the imagination of a Lewis Carroll . . . Roald Dahl is a wizard of comedy and the grotesque, an artist with a marvelously topsy-turvy sense of the ridiculous in life." Cleveland Plain Dealer.

Dahlie, Michael

The **best** of youth : a novel / Michael Dahlie. W.W. Norton & Co., 2013. 288 p.

ISBN 9780393081855

1. Authors, American 2. Young men 3. Ghostwriters 4. Publishers and publishing 5. Drifters 6. Inheritance and succession 7. Men with depression 8. Brooklyn, New York City 9. Coming-of-age stories 10. Mainstream fiction

LC 2012029249

After inheriting a large sum of money, Henry Lang moves to Brooklyn to live like a 20-something hipster and pursue his dream of a publishing career but instead finds himself in increasingly disturbing situations.

Daisley, Stephen, 1955-

Coming rain / Stephen Daisley. Text Publishing, 2015. 320 p.

ISBN 9781922182029

1. 1950s 2. Agricultural laborers 3. Rural life -- Australia 4. Sheep shearing 5. Male friendship 6. Sheep ranches 7. Grief in men 8. Widowers 9. Ranchers 10. Droughts 11. Dingo 12. Australia 13. Historical fiction

Ockham New Zealand Book Awards, Fiction, 2016.

"They returned to the main part of the shed and it was Lew's turn to sharpen his cutters. The woolshed now bright and well lit. Painter walked to his stand and connected the handpiece to the down-rod. He drizzled oil over the comb and the cutter, adjusted the tension and pulled the rope to engage the running gear."

Dallas, Sandra

The **last** midwife / Sandra Dallas. St. Martin's Press, 2015. 352 p.

ISBN 9781250074461

1. American Westward Expansion (1803-1899) 2. 1880s 3. Midwives 4. Infanticide 5. Trust 6. Secrets 7. Communities 8. Innocence (Law)

9. Murder investigation 10. Malicious accusation 11. Frontier and pioneer life 12. Colorado -- Social life and customs -- 19th century 13. Historical fiction 14. Gentle reads

LC 2015017976

Spur Awards, Best Western Traditional Novel, 2016.

Wrongly accused when a baby is found dead, a 19th-century Colorado midwife who has witnessed the secrets of countless families considers in the face of her own secrets whether or not it is worth it to prove her innocence.

Dallas, Sandra

The **Persian** Pickle Club / Sandra Dallas. St. Martin's Press, 1995. 196 p.

ISBN 9780312135867

1. 1930s 2. Women's organizations 3. Quilting 4. Small town life -- Kansas 5. Women 6. Quiltmakers 7. Historical fiction 8. Gentle reads

LC 95031032

In 1930s Harveyvile, Kansas, Rita Ritter, a recent arrival, is invited to join the Persian Pickle Club, but her interest in journalism brings her dangerously close to a secret the club has sworn to keep.

"This is a simple but endearing story that depicts small-town eccentricities with affection and adds dazzle with some latebreaking surprises. Dallas hits all the right notes, combining an authentic look at the social fabric of Depression-era life with a homespun suspense story." Publishers Weekly.

Dallas, Sandra

Tallgrass / Sandra Dallas. St. Martin's Press, 2007. 320 p.
ISBN 0312360193

1. Second World War era (1939-1945) 2. 1940s 3. Japanese Americans -- Forced removal and incarceration, 1942-1945 4. Missing persons 5. Farmers 6. Teenagers 7. Soldiers 8. Concentration camps 9. Murder 10. Secrets 11. Interpersonal conflict 12. Suspicion 13. World War II 14. Colorado 15. The West (United States) 16. Historical fiction 17. Gentle reads

LC 2006051271

Spur Award for Best Western Novel (Short Novel), 2008.

Her life turned upside-down when a Japanese internment camp is opened in their small Colorado town, Rennie witnesses the way her community places suspicion on the newcomers when a young girl is murdered.

"Rennie Stroud looks back to 1942, when she was 13, to tell a powerful coming-of-age story. That year, the U.S. government opened a Japanese internment camp outside Ellis, CO, less than a mile from where Rennie and her family farmed sugar beets. Rennie observes the prejudice of some of the townspeople as well as her parents' strong moral code and their entanglement in the emotions of the time. Her father, Loyal, not only shows open support for the Japanese, whom he views as Americans, but offers to hire them to work on the farm. When a young girl is murdered, suspicion naturally turns to the camp, and the town is divided by fear. Dallas's strong, provocative novel is a moving examination of prejudice and fear that addresses issues of community discord, abuse, and rape." Library Journal.

Dallas, Sandra

Westering women : a novel / Sandra Dallas. St. Martin's Press, 2020. 304 p.

ISBN 9781250239662

1. 1850s 2. American Westward Expansion (1803-1899) 3. Wagon trains 4. Overland journeys to the Pacific 5. Abused women 6. Escapes 7. Mothers and daughters 8. Secrets 9. Female friendship 10. Clergy 11. Frontier and pioneer life 12. The West (United States)

-- History -- 19th century 13. Historical fiction

LC 2019034031

Joining other mail-order brides on a dangerous wagon journey to the gold mines of 1852 Chicago, a seamstress with painful secrets discovers strengths she did not know she possessed among a growing sisterhood of fellow women pioneers.

"Readers will enjoy this modern take on the journey West that's rife with girl power." Publishers Weekly.

Dalton, Trent

Boy swallows universe / Trent Dalton Harper, 2019, c2018. 452 p.

ISBN 9780062898104

1. 1980s 2. Drug traffic 3. Brothers 4. Growing up 5. Boys who are mute 6. Drug dealers 7. Crime 8. Violence 9. Addiction 10. Criminal justice system 11. Brisbane, Queensland 12. Australia 13. Literary fiction 14. Coming-of-age stories 15. Autobiographical fiction

Originally published in Australia: Fourth Estate, 2018.

Australian Book Industry Awards, Book of the Year, 2019.

Australian Book Industry Awards, Literary Fiction Book of the Year, 2019.

Australian Book Industry Awards, Newcomer of the Year, 2019.

Librarians' Choice (Australia), 2018.

Shortlisted for the Russell Prize for Humour Writing (Australia), 2018.

Exiled in a drug-oppressed refugee suburb in 1980s Australia, a 12-year-old boy dreams of a career in journalism while fending off the local criminal element to protect his imprisoned mother.

"A captivating and quirky life story that leads the reader on an intense and rewarding journey; highly recommended." Library Journal.

Daly, Paula

* **Clear** my name / Paula Daly. Atlantic Monthly Press, 2019. 304 p.

ISBN 9780802147837

1. Women prisoners 2. Innocence (Law) 3. Investigations 4. Mentoring 5. Charities 6. Witnesses 7. Trials (Murder) 8. Judicial error 9. Murder investigation 10. Great Britain 11. Thrillers and suspense

A jaded investigator from a UK charity that helps exonerate wrongly convicted people teams up with a naive trainee to follow leads related to a witness who could clear an innocent woman's name.

Daly, Paula

Open your eyes / Paula Daly. Grove Press, 2018. 339 p.
ISBN 9780802128454

1. Authors 2. Victims of violent crimes 3. Married people and secrets 4. Secrets 5. Enemies 6. Married people 7. Interracial marriage 8. Stay at home mothers 9. Suspense story writing 10. Liverpool, England 11. England 12. Thrillers and suspense

LC 2018028233

When her husband, a bestselling crime writer, is brutally attacked in the driveway of their home, Jane Campbell must face the problems in her life--and secrets that have been kept from her--as she attempts to discover who would commit such a crime.

"This is an evenly paced thriller; Daly delivers just enough clues and twists, a little bit at a time, to keep the reader guessing. It's easy to relate to Jane; her general passiveness leads to few character surprises, but she firmly gains and keeps our sympathy, unlike many more unreliable narrators who pepper domestic suspense novels these days. After the shocking beginning, Jane's dogged pursuit of the truth keeps the novel grounded. A satisfyingly original thriller." Kirkus.

Dane, Lauren

The **best** kind of trouble / Lauren Dane. HQN Books, 2014. 384 p. Hurley boys
ISBN 9780373779345
1. Librarians 2. Rock musicians 3. Small towns 4. Former lovers 5. Family relationships 6. Sexual attraction 7. Men/women relations 8. Oregon 9. Contemporary romances
When Paddy Hurley returns to the small town of Hood River after years of the rock 'n' roll lifestyle, librarian Natalie Clayton, a former party girl who had a hot two-week affair with him years earlier, finds her control slipping as he tempts her into picking up where they left off.

Dane, Lauren

Broken open / Lauren Dane. HQN Books, 2014. 378 p. Hurley boys
ISBN 9780373779352
1. Small towns 2. Sexual attraction 3. Second chances 4. Lust 5. Musicians 6. Ranchers 7. Interracial romance 8. African American women 9. Recovering addicts 10. Men/women relations 11. Oregon 12. Contemporary romances
"Dane continues to evolve, and this strong, widely appealing, and memorable story will gain new readers while satisfying fans." Booklist

Dangerous women / George R.R. Martin and Gardner Dozois, ed. Tor Books, 2013. 736 p. Song of ice and fire prequel stories
ISBN 9780765332066
1. Women warriors 2. Women 3. Independence in women 4. Courage in women 5. Superheroines 6. Women rulers 7. Femmes fatales 8. Short stories 9. Anthologies
LC 2013018473
Dangerous Women also released in 3 separate volumes by Tor, 2014.
'The Princess and the Queen' is a prequel story to George R. R. Martin's series 'A Song of Ice and Fire.'
A collection of 21 short stories by best-selling authors celebrates women heroines and villains.

Daniel, Ray, 1962-

Hacked : a Tucker mystery / Ray Daniel. Midnight Ink, 2017. 360 p. Tucker mysteries
ISBN 9780738751108
1. Hackers 2. Widowers 3. Serial murder investigation 4. Cyberbullying 5. Cousins 6. Revenge 7. Chat rooms 8. Threat (Psychology) 9. Frameups 10. Computer programmers 11. Boston, Massachusetts 12. Cyber-thrillers 13. Thrillers and suspense
LC 2016047687
Aloysius Tucker vows vengeance when a hacker terrorizes his ten-year-old cousin, Maria. Promising Maria that he?ll unmask the hacker and get an apology, Tucker goes online to get justice. But the resulting flame war turns deadly when the hacker is murdered.

Daniel, Susanna

Stiltsville : a novel / Susanna Daniel. Harper, 2010. 310 p.
ISBN 9780061963070
1. Marriage 2. Husband and wife 3. Family relationships 4. Families 5. Loss (Psychology) 6. Intimacy (Psychology) 7. Friendship 8. Mothers and daughters 9. Florida 10. Mainstream fiction
Miami,1969. Frances is captivated by the community of houses built on pilings in the middle of Biscayne Bay. On the dock of one stilt house, she meets Dennis, and turns away from her predictable life. Stiltsville becomes their island oasis-- until suddenly it's gone, and Francis is forced to figure out how to make her family work on dry land.

"This is a love story but not one that should be mistaken for a romance. This lyrically written work, which follows the ebb and flow of a long marriage, is just intimate enough to draw the reader close. It isn't until well into the novel that you realize just how much you've come to care about author Susana Daniel's narrator and her story." Denver Post..

Danielewski, Mark Z.

* The **familiar.** Mark Z. Danielewski. Pantheon Books, 2017. 880 p. Familiar novels
ISBN 9780375715006
1. Girls and cats 2. Human nature 3. Videos 4. Human/animal communication 5. Options, alternatives, choices 6. Human/animal relationships 7. Familiars (Spirits) 8. Consequences 9. Supernatural 10. Families 11. Cats 12. Girls 13. Experimental fiction 14. Literary fiction
"The author is innovating wildly not only with text but also with narrative flow, structure, and multiplicity of meaning. Loose, imagistic words are followed by tightly layered prose and pictures; this varied density creates a deeply nuanced reading experience that works." Library Journal.

Danielewski, Mark Z.

* **House** of leaves : a novel / Mark Z. Danielewski. Pantheon Books, 2000. xxiii, 709 p.
ISBN 9780375420528
1. Photojournalists 2. Manuscripts 3. Houses 4. Families 5. Tattoo artists 6. Documentary films 7. Supernatural 8. Paranormal phenomena 9. Transformations, Personal 10. Mental illness 11. Haunted houses 12. Experimental fiction 13. Horror 14. Literary fiction
LC 99036024
A family relocates to a small house on Ash Tree Lane and discovers that the inside of their new home seems to be without boundaries.
"This work is a kaleidoscopically layered and deconstructed H. P. Lovecraft-style horror story. It hums and resonates with wonder, dread, and insight." Booklist.

Danielewski, Mark Z.

Only revolutions / Mark Z. Danielewski. Pantheon Books, 2006. 360 p.
ISBN 9780375421761
1. Sixteen-year old boys 2. Sixteen-year-old girls 3. Teenagers 4. Love 5. Automobile travel 6. Boy/girl relations 7. Voyages and travels 8. Time travel 9. Freedom 10. Experimental fiction
LC 2006040996
National Book Award for Fiction finalist, 2006
Moving back and forth between the two main characters, Hailey and Sam, a kaleidoscopic novel follows two wayward teenagers who never grow up as they crash New Orleans parties, barrel up the Mississippi, crash through the Badlands, and more, from the Civil War to the Iraq War and beyond.
"This novel consists of the dual free-verse narratives of 16-year-old Hailey and Sam, which are meant to be read in tandem... This creative paean to the velocity of young lovers and the vibrancy of American culture is sure to wow the experimental-fiction camp." Booklist.

Danielewski, Mark Z.

The **familiar.** Mark Z. Danielewski. Pantheon Books, 2015 880 p. Familiar novels
ISBN 9780375714948
1. Girls 2. Familiars (Spirits) 3. Cats 4. Supernatural 5. Human/animal relationships 6. Human/animal communication 7. Options,

alternatives, choices 8. Experimental fiction 9. Literary fiction

LC 2014028320

"Strangely, it works, though not without studied effort on the reader's part. And as for all the loose ends? No worries--there are 26 volumes to come in which to tie them up." Kirkus.

Daniels, Natalie

Too close / Natalie Daniels. Harper, 2019. 312 p.

ISBN 9780062917485

1. Women with amnesia 2. Women forensic psychiatrists 3. Psychiatric hospitals 4. Female friendship 5. Life change events 6. Traffic accidents 7. Psychiatrist and patient 8. Crime 9. Secrets 10. England 11. Psychological suspense

A veteran forensic psychiatrist assigned to the case of a wife and mother who committed an unforgiveable crime finds her professional and personal limits tested as she begins to feel sympathy for her.

"Each chapter, alternatively narrated by Connie or Emma, reveals each woman's darkest secrets and perceived sins. Daniels presents an unflinching, visceral look into the nature of love, fidelity, and betrayal." Publishers Weekly.

Danler, Stephanie

Sweetbitter / Stephanie Danler. Alfred A. Knopf, 2016. 356 p.

ISBN 9781101875940

1. Self-fulfillment in women 2. City life 3. Waitresses 4. Restaurants 5. Young women 6. Lovers 7. Bartenders 8. Friendship 9. Men/women relations 10. Manhattan, New York City 11. New York City 12. Coming-of-age stories

LC 2015037137

A year in the life of a beguiling young woman in the wild world of a famous downtown New York restaurant follows her burning effort to become someone of importance through a backwaiter job that enables her indulgences in culinary and intellectual interests.

"Throughout, Danler evokes Tess's voice--intimate, confiding, wonderstruck, depressed--with deft skill." Publishers Weekly.

Danticat, Edwidge, 1969-

Claire of the sea light / Edwidge Danticat. Alfred A. Knopf, 2013. 238 p.

ISBN 9780307271792

1. Crimes against girls 2. Missing children 3. Community life 4. Secrets 5. Coastal towns 6. Loss (Psychology) 7. Fathers and daughters 8. Interpersonal relations 9. Communities -- Haiti 10. Options, alternatives, choices 11. Humans -- Effect of environment on 12. Haiti 13. Literary fiction 14. Psychological fiction

LC 2012043876

ALA Notable Book, 2014

Andrew Carnegie Medal for Excellence in Fiction finalist, 2014.

When a vibrant 7-year-old disappears from her Haitian community at the same time her father agonizingly decides to give her up so that she can have a better life, an ensuing search reveals the painful stories of neighbors whose lives the child touched.

"In interlocking stories moving back and forth in time, Danticat weaves a beautifully rendered portrait of longing in the small fishing town of Ville Rose in Haiti." Booklist.

Danticat, Edwidge, 1969-

The **dew** breaker / Edwidge Danticat. Knopf, 2004. 244 p.

ISBN 9781400041145

1. Torturers 2. Redemption 3. Haitian Americans 4. Remorse 5. Barbers 6. Daughters 7. Immigrants 8. Neighbors 9. Landlord and tenant 10. Torture victims 11. Torture 12. Violence 13. Hope 14.

Compromise 15. Secrets 16. Memories 17. Haiti 18. Brooklyn, New York City 19. Psychological fiction

LC 2003060788

National Book Critics Circle Award for Fiction finalist, 2004

A scarred Brooklyn resident remembers his past life as a Haitian torturer in the 1960s, a period during which he waged personal and political battles before moving to New York, where his past continued to haunt him throughout his marriage and parenthood.

"Beautifully written fiction about the real-life horror that is Haiti. Seamlessly blending the personal and political, it deals with what happens to a country and its people when mothers and fathers disappear for their political transgressions." USA Today.

Danticat, Edwidge, 1969-

* Everything inside : stories / Edwidge Danticat. Alfred A. Knopf, 2019. ix, 223 p.

ISBN 9780525521273

1. Interpersonal relations 2. Human nature 3. Friendship 4. Divorce 5. Miami, Florida 6. Haiti 7. Caribbean Area 8. Port-au-Prince, Haiti 9. Short stories 10. Literary fiction

LC 2018047646

ALA Notable Book, 2020.

National Book Critics Circle Award for Fiction, 2019.

A single-volume collection of short stories by the National Book Critics Circle Award-winning author is set in such locales as Miami, Port-au-Prince and the Caribbean and poignantly explores the forces that unite and divide.

Danticat, Edwidge, 1969-

The **farming** of bones : a novel / Edwidge Danticat. Soho Press, 1998. 312 p.

ISBN 9781569471265

1. 1930s 2. Massacres -- Dominican Republic 3. Sugar workers -- Haiti 4. Haitians in the Dominican Republic 5. Women -- Haiti 6. Dominican-Haitian Conflict, 1937 7. Genocide 8. Dominican Republic 9. Historical fiction

LC 98003655

ALA Notable Book, 1999.

In 1937, on the Dominican side of the Haiti border, Amabelle, an orphaned maid to an army colonel's wife, falls in love with Sebastien, an itinerant sugarcane cutter, but their relationship is threatened by the violent persecution of the Haitians.

"It's a testament to Danticat's skill that Amabelle's musical, sorrowing voice never falters, even during her stark descriptions of the bloodbath." The New Yorker.

Danticat, Edwidge, 1969-

Krik? Krak! / Edwidge Danticat. Soho Press, 1995. 224 p.

ISBN 9781569470251

1. Dictatorship 2. Haitian Americans -- Social life and customs 3. Haiti -- Social life and customs 4. Short stories

LC 9441999

"Nine ... stories about life under Haiti's dictatorships."

National Book Award for Fiction finalist, 1995

In a land where vicious dictators crush dreams and lives on a whim, Haitian people have only faith and hope to sustain them. Perhaps it is the faith that a tiny, leaky boat packed with refugees will successfulyly navigate the ocean and reach Florida. Or perhaps it is the macabre hope that a daughter will find her mother's body in a mass grave, so she can wrap it in a homemade patchwork quilt.

"The author touches upon life both in Haiti and in New York's Haitian community, though we spend most of our time in Port-au-Prince and the country town of Ville Rose. The best of these stories humanize, particularize, give poignancy to the lives of people we may have come to think of as faceless emblems of misery, poverty and brutality." New York Times Book Review.

Daoud, Kamel

The **Meursault** investigation / Kamel Daoud ; translated by John Cullen. Other Press, 2015, c2013. 160 p.

ISBN 9781590517512

1. Brothers -- Death 2. Identity (Psychology) 3. Postcolonialism 4. Mothers and sons 5. Loneliness in men 6. Bars (Drinking establishments) 7. Flashbacks 8. Algeria 9. Psychological fiction 10. Political fiction 11. Adaptations, retellings, and spin-offs 12. Literary fiction 13. Translations -- French to English

LC 2015010736

"Originally published in French as Meursault, contre-enquete by Editions Barzakh in Algeria in 2013, and by Actes Sud in France in 2014"--Title page verso.

Originally published: 2013.

Harun, the brother of "the Arab" killed by Meursault in Albert Camus' "The Stranger," details the events that led to his brother's murder on an Algerian beach.

"An eye-opening, humbling read, splendid whether or not you know and love the original." Library Journal.

Dare, Abi

The **girl** with the louding voice / Abi Dare. Dutton, 2020. 336 p.

ISBN 9781524746025

1. Education 2. Teenage girls 3. Women's rights 4. Forced marriage 5. Sexual violence 6. Children's rights 7. Runaway girls 8. Indentured servants 9. Right to education 10. Independence in teenage girls 11. Nigeria 12. Coming-of-age stories 13. Literary fiction

LC 2019029365

Adunni, a 14-year-old Nigerian girl who longs for an education, must find a way for her voice to be heard loud and clear in a world where she and other girls like her are taught to believe, through words and deeds, that they are nothing.

"Dare's arresting prose provides a window into the lives of Nigerians of all socioeconomic levels and shows readers the beauty and humor that may be found even in the midst of harrowing experiences." Booklist.

Dare, Tessa

* The **duchess** deal / Tessa Dare. Avon Books, 2017 370 p. Girl meets duke

ISBN 9780062697202

1. Regency period (1811-1820) 2. Dukes and duchesses 3. Mate selection 4. Interclass romance 5. Jilted men 6. Heirs and heiresses 7. Seamstresses 8. Veterans 9. Interpersonal attraction 10. Men/women relations 11. England -- Social life and customs -- 19th century 12. Regency romances 13. Historical romances

When seamstress Emma Gladstone approaches the formidable Duke of Ashbury with the bill for his ex-fianc?e's wedding dress, she receives a marriage proposal instead. Believing that his battle-scarred face may deter potential brides, Ashbury offers Emma a house and financial independence if she's willing to live with him until she conceives the heir he desperately needs. But what if Emma wants a real marriage? Witty banter and comedic situations add levity to an emotionally intense Beauty and the Beast story. -- Description by Gillian Speace

"RITA Award-winning Dare once again works her own irresistible brand of magic by taking a cast of richly nuanced characters (including an emotionally and physically scarred hero and the feisty heroine who refuses to give up on him), a deliciously clever plot that manages to be both superbly sexy as well as thoroughly romantic, and a generous

measure of addictively tart wit, and then she spins the whole thing into pure literary gold." Booklist.

Dare, Tessa

Do you want to start a scandal / Tessa Dare. Avon Books, 2016 384 p. Castles ever after

ISBN 9780062349040

1. Regency period (1811-1820) 2. Marquis and marchionesses 3. Scandals 4. Women marriage resisters 5. Rumor 6. Reputation 7. Investigations 8. Balls (Parties) 9. Aristocracy 10. Country homes 11. Intelligence officers 12. Secret identity 13. England -- Social life and customs -- 19th century 14. Great Britain 15. Regency romances 16. Historical romances

In order to avoid a forced marriage to Piers Brandon, Charlotte Highwood must uncover the identities of the two lovers involved in a scandalous library tryst the night of the Parkhurst ball, proving that she wasn't involved.

"The irresistibly provocative, classy love scenes set the bar high for other historical romance novels." Publishers Weekly.

Dare, Tessa

* The **governess** game / Tessa Dare. Avon Books, 2018. 352 p. Girl meets duke

ISBN 9780062851673

1. Regency period (1811-1820) 2. Dukes and duchesses 3. Governesses 4. Womanizers 5. Aristocracy 6. Guardian and ward 7. Mate selection 8. Interclass romance 9. Interpersonal attraction 10. Men/women relations 11. England -- Social life and customs -- 19th century 12. Regency romances 13. Historical romances

When the governess he has hired to turn a pair of wild orphans into proper young ladies tries to reform him, self-respecting libertine Chase Reynaud decides to teach her a lesson in pleasure.

Dare, Tessa

* A **night** to surrender / Tessa Dare. Avon Books, 2011. 389 p. Spindle Cove

ISBN 9780062049834

1. Regency period (1811-1820) 2. Earls and countesses 3. Soldiers 4. Coastal towns 5. Men/women relations 6. Interpersonal attraction 7. Independence in women 8. Single women 9. England -- History -- 19th century 10. Regency romances 11. Historical romances

RITA Award for Best Regency Historical Romance, 2012.

While in the town of Spindle Cove, a haven for ladies with delicate constitutions, to gather a militia, the new Earl of Rycliff meets his match in Susanna Finch, a woman who is determined to save her personal utopia from the invasion of his makeshift army.

Dare, Tessa

* **Romancing** the duke / Tessa Dare. Avon Books, 2014. 370 p. Castles ever after

ISBN 9780062240194

1. Regency period (1811-1820) 2. Single women 3. Poor women 4. Inheritance and succession 5. Romantic love 6. Castles 7. Dukes and duchesses 8. England -- Social life and customs -- 19th century 9. Historical romances 10. Regency romances

RITA Award for Best Historical Romance (Short), 2015.

Although Isolde Ophelia Goodnight's father made a fortune as the author of the bestselling series of novels that immortalized her as "Little Izzy Goodnight," he died without a penny to his name, leaving Izzy destitute and homeless. An inheritance from her godfather in the form of Gostley Castle proves a welcome surprise, even if a more appropriate name for the crumbling ruin is "ghostly" or "ghastly." Its current occupant, Lord Ransome Vane, the blind, brooding Duke of Rothbury, is considerably less charming...and unwilling to surrender his claim to the castle. However, as Izzy lays siege to his solitary existence, he may end up surrendering his heart. -- Description by Gillian Speace.

"Humor, whimsy, and joy overflow as a most unlikely pair find their happy ending in this fairy tale-come-to-life." Library Journal.

Dare, Tessa

* **Say** yes to the marquess / Tessa Dare. Avon Books, 2014. 374 p. Castles ever after

ISBN 9780062240200

1. Regency period (1811-1820) 2. Castles 3. Engaged persons 4. Love triangles 5. Womanizers 6. Boxers (Sports) 7. Inheritance and succession 8. Marquis and marchionesses 9. England -- Social life and customs -- 19th century 10. Historical romances 11. Regency romances

Determined that his brother marry Miss Clio Whitmore, hardened fighter Rafe Brandon decides to plan the wedding himself but has a change of heart when he falls hopelessly in love with the bride-to-be.

"With the latest sterling addition to her Castles Ever After series, RITA awardwinning Dare (Romancing the Duke, 2014) continues to charm and captivate readers with her droll sense of humor, clever plotting, and engaging characters. This flawlessly written Regency historical is guaranteed to hit the sweet spot for most romance readers." Booklist.

Dare, Tessa

* The **wallflower** wager / Tessa Dare. Avon Books, 2019. 384 p. Girl meets duke

ISBN 9780062952561

1. Dukes and duchesses 2. Womanizers 3. Single women 4. Aristocracy 5. Rich men 6. Neighbors 7. Animal rescue 8. Interpersonal attraction 9. Men/women relations 10. England -- Social life and customs -- 19th century 11. Regency romances 12. Historical romances

They call him the Duke of Ruin... To an undaunted wallflower, he's just the beast next door.

Dare, Tessa

A **week** to be wicked / Tessa Dare. Avon Books, 2012. 375 p. Spindle Cove

ISBN 9780062049872

1. Regency period (1811-1820) 2. 19th century 3. Young women 4. Voyages and travels 5. Protectiveness in men 6. Women scientists 7. Deception 8. Men/women relations 9. Interpersonal attraction 10. England -- History -- 19th century 11. Regency romances 12. Historical romances

During one week, unlikely partners Minerva Highwood, one of Spindle Cove's confirmed spinsters, and Lord Payne must fake an elopement, convince family and friends they are "in love", outrun armed robbers and travel 400 miles without killing each other--or falling in love for real.

Dare, Tessa

When a Scot ties the knot / Tessa Dare. Avon, 2015. 384 p. Castles ever after

ISBN 9780062349026

1. Regency period (1811-1820) 2. Soldiers 3. Heirs and heiresses 4. Extortion 5. Love letters 6. Secrets 7. Shyness in women 8. Castles 9. Inheritance and succession 10. Scotland 11. Regency romances 12. Historical romances

RUSA Reading List Short List, 2016.

To escape the social obligations of the London season, painfully shy Madeline "Maddy" Gracechurch invents a fianc?: Captain Logan MacKenzie, a dashing soldier with whom she carries on a lengthy fictional correspondence until -- no longer in need of the ruse -- she kills him off. Imagine Maddy's surprise when the real-life Logan MacKenzie arrives at Lannair Castle, where she lives, insisting that they wed immediately. Has Maddy's dream lover become her worst nightmare? Find out in this 3rd book in the Castles Ever After series. -- Description by Gillian Speace.

"Dare's latest begins with a fairy-tale twist of fate, then leads readers on a mesmerizing and intense emotional journey that explores love in many forms and the powerful pull of dreams. A brilliant, enchanting, and soul-satisfying romance." Kirkus.

Dark, Alice Elliott

Think of England : a novel / Alice Elliott Dark. Simon & Schuster, 2002. 271 p.

ISBN 068486522X

1. Single mothers 2. Life change events 3. Children of separated parents 4. Mothers and daughters 5. Psychological fiction

LC 2002017554

"Everything in this spare, eccentrically paced book is a pleasure to read, from the exposition of nine-year-old Jane MacLeod's home life in Pennsylvania to a family reunion, thirty-six years later. . . . It's almost impossible to write about the kind of subtle, inward sorrows and tensions that animate this story, and the author manages the challenge handsomely." The New Yorker.

Darnielle, John

Universal harvester / John Darnielle. Farrar, Straus and Giroux, 2017. 214 p.

ISBN 9780374282103

1. 1990s 2. Young men 3. Video stores 4. Small town life 5. Loss (Psychology) 6. Small towns 7. Recluses 8. Videos 9. Cults 10. Grief 11. Iowa 12. Rural noir 13. Literary fiction

LC 2016025809

Working for a 1990s small-community video rental store under threat by a major chain competitor, Jeremy is reluctantly drawn into a mystery involving chilling footage of criminal activity that has been recorded onto the store's VHS tapes.

"Darnielle's contemporary ghost story may confound with its elusiveness (who is the mysterious I narrator?), but its impact will stick with readers." Library Journal.

Darnielle, John

Wolf in white van : a novel / John Darnielle. Farrar, Straus and Giroux, 2014. 207 p.

ISBN 9780374292089

1. Role playing games 2. Social isolation 3. Men with disfigurements 4. Alienation in men 5. Survival 6. Suicidal behavior 7. High school students 8. California 9. Psychological fiction

LC 2014015427

Creating fantastical mail-order role-playing games from his apartment where he endures a life of solitude after a disfiguring injury, Sean is blamed for a disaster involving two high school student clients, an event that compels him to reevaluate his own past.

"Sean Phillips was an unremarkable, moody teenager until tragedy left him with a horrific injury, changing his life forever. Who or what drove him to his fate? Can anyone be blamed? Is there a lesson to be learned? These questions are explored but never fully answered in Darnielle's first full-length novel...As senseless as a car accident, and as hard to look away from, the inconclusiveness of this journey will either captivate or madden readers." Booklist.

LIST OF FICTIONAL WORKS

Darznik, Jasmin, 1973-

Song of a captive bird : a novel / Jasmin Darznik. Ballantine Books, 2018. 401 p.

ISBN 9780399182310

1. Farrukhzad, Furugh 2. 20th century 3. Poets 4. Women's role 5. Women poets 6. Sexism 7. Feminists 8. Women filmmakers 9. Independence in women 10. Iran -- History -- 20th century 11. Biographical fiction 12. Historical fiction

Reimagines the life of rebel poet Forugh Farrokzhad, a passionate young writer in search of freedom and independence from the restrictions imposed on women in mid-twentieth-century Iran.

Dastgir, Rosie

A **small** fortune / Rosie Dastgir. Riverhead Books, 2012. 384 p.

ISBN 9781594488108

1. Pakistanis in Great Britain 2. Life change events 3. Divorce settlements 4. Conflict in families 5. Promises 6. Patriarchs 7. Family relationships 8. London, England 9. Mainstream fiction

LC 2011050598

Resolving to give away a divorce settlement to his most deserving relative, devout Muslim Harris, the presumed head of a large extended family in England and Pakistan, rashly bequeaths his fortune to a prosperous cousin, complicating a difficult web of familial debt and obligation.

"Dastgir's smartly written first novel entertains even as it captures the essence of the changing immigrant community and the slow urban decline of contemporary England." Library Journal.

Dau, Stephen

The **book** of Jonas / Stephen Dau. Blue Rider Press, 2012. 256 p.

ISBN 9780399158452

1. Life change events 2. Soldiers 3. Orphans 4. Teenage boys 5. Moving to a new country 6. Middle East 7. United States 8. Psychological fiction

When his family is killed during an errant U.S. military operation in the Middle East, 15-year-old Jonas is sent to live with a foster family in America and struggles to adapt before revealing the heroics of a missing soldier who saved his life, a story that reveals a shocking secret to the soldier's grieving mother.

Daugherty, Christi

A **beautiful** corpse / Christi Daugherty. Minotaur Books, 2019. 368 p. Harper McClain novels

ISBN 9781250148872

1. Women journalists 2. Women murder victims 3. Newspapers 4. Adult children of murder victims 5. Murder investigation 6. Stalkers 7. Detectives 8. City life 9. Sexual attraction 10. Men/women relations 11. Savannah, Georgia 12. Thrillers and suspense

LC 2018046205

When a 24-year-old bartender is found murdered, crime reporter Harper McClain investigates three men, including the victim's former-criminal boyfriend, her stalker boss and her acrimonious ex, the son of the district attorney.

Daugherty, Christi

The **echo** killing / Christi Daugherty. Minotaur Books, 2018. 320 p. Harper McClain novels

ISBN 9781250148841

1. Women journalists 2. Cold cases (Criminal investigation) 3. Families of murder victims 4. Murder investigation 5. Serial murder investigation 6. Savannah, Georgia 7. Thrillers and suspense

LC 2017044453

When a murder echoing a fifteen-year-old cold case rocks the Southern town of Savannah, crime reporter Harper McClain risks everything to find the identity of this calculated killer.

Daugherty, Christi

Revolver road : a Harper McClain mystery / Christi Daugherty. Minotaur Books, 2020. 336 p. Harper McClain novels

ISBN 9781250235886

1. Women journalists 2. Threat (Psychology) 3. Missing men 4. Murder victims 5. Murderers 6. Murder investigation 7. Adult children of murder victims 8. Islands 9. Hiding 10. Secrets 11. Determination in women 12. Sexual attraction 13. Men/women relations 14. Georgia 15. Thrillers and suspense

LC 2019039542

Crime reporter Harper McClain is back on the beat when a troubled musician vanishes.

"Daugherty has created a complex, likable heroine whom readers will root for, fully fleshed-out secondary characters, and a compelling plot." Library Journal.

Daughters, Amy Weinland

* **You** cannot mess this up : a true story that never happened / Amy Weinland Daughters. She Writes Bress, 2019. 272 p.

ISBN 9781631525834

1. 1970s 2. 2010s 3. Stay-at-home mothers 4. Time travel (Past) 5. Childhood 6. Family relationships 7. Memories 8. Attempted rape 9. Houston, Texas 10. Dayton, Ohio 11. Autobiographical fiction 12. Mainstream fiction

Forty-six-year-old Amy Daughters flies home to Houston for Thanksgiving -- and is mysteriously hurled back through time to 1978, where she's forced to visit her childhood home, including her ten-year old self, for thirty-six hours.

Davidson, Andrew, 1969-

The **gargoyle** / Andrew Davidson. Doubleday, 2008. 468 p.

ISBN 9780385524940

1. Burns and scalds 2. Men/women relations 3. Traffic accident victims 4. Hospital wards 5. Reincarnation 6. Stone carvers 7. Redemption 8. Love stories 9. Psychological fiction

LC 2007037258

Sunburst Award for Excellence in Canadian Literature of the Fantastic, 2009.

Awakening in a burn ward after being horribly burned over much of his body after a terrible car accident, the cynical narrator is visited by a beautiful and enigmatic sculptress of gargoyles who tells him that they had once been lovers in medieval Germany and spins a tale of deathless love.

Davidson, Andy, 1978-

The **boatman's** daughter : a novel / Andy Davidson. MCD, 2020. 416 p.

ISBN 9780374538552

1. Smuggling 2. Corruption 3. Supernatural 4. Swamps 5. Clergy 6. Witches 7. Drug traffic 8. Mutism 9. Human sacrifice 10. Women criminals 11. Police corruption 12. Black magic 13. Good and evil 14. Arkansas 15. Literary fiction 16. Horror 17. Southern Gothic

LC 2019025806

A swampy literary horror novel about a young woman facing down drug dealers, a crooked cop, and a mad preacher on the banks of an Arkansas river.

"A stunning supernatural Southern gothic." Kirkus.

Davidson, Diane Mott

Killer pancake / Diane Mott Davidson. Bantam Books, 1995. 301 p. Goldy Bear mysteries

ISBN 0553095889

1. Caterers and catering 2. Murder investigation 3. Women caterers 4. Women amateur detectives 5. Women cooks 6. Divorced women 7. Gourmets 8. Colorado 9. Culinary mysteries 10. Gentle reads 11. Cozy mysteries

LC 95010852

"A culinary mystery."

Includes ten recipes.

Caterer and amateur sleuth Goldy B. Schulz gets caught between a ruthless cosmetic company and a violent animal rights group.

"The author includes recipes as she brings events to a proper boil in this latest lively and satisfying outing for Goldy, who not only solves the mystery but also finds, much to her delight, that coffee can save your life." Publishers Weekly.

Davidson, Diane Mott

The **last** suppers / Diane Mott Davidson. Bantam Books, 1994. 283 p. Goldy Bear mysteries

ISBN 0553095870

1. Caterers and catering 2. Murder investigation 3. Missing men 4. Weddings 5. Women caterers 6. Women amateur detectives 7. Women cooks 8. Cooking, American 9. Divorced women 10. Gourmets 11. Culinary mysteries 12. Gentle reads 13. Cozy mysteries

LC 94018886

Includes 10 recipes.

When her wedding is called off last minute after the priest is murdered, Goldy fears that her homicide detective fiance, Tom, who was the first to arrive at the murder scene and who disappeared before anyone else got there, may be responsible.

"An appealing mixture of food and crime." Library Journal.

Davies, Carys

West / Carys Davies. Scribner, 2018. 149 p.

ISBN 9781501179341

1. American Westward Expansion (1803-1899) 2. Widowers 3. Quests 4. Frontier and pioneer life 5. Farms 6. Fossils 7. Fathers and daughters 8. Girls 9. Shawnee Indians 10. Life change events 11. The West (United States) -- History -- 19th century 12. Pennsylvania -- History -- 19th century 13. Historical fiction 14. Literary fiction

Prompted by reports of giant animal bones found in Kentucky, a 19th century Pennsylvania mule breeder leaves his daughters behind on his small, failing farm and sets out with an American Indian guide into the harsh and strange Western landscape.

Davies, Peter Ho, 1966-

The **fortunes** / Peter Ho Davies. Houghton Mifflin Harcourt, 2016. 272 p.

ISBN 9780544263703

1. Chinese Americans 2. Immigrants 3. Identity (Psychology) 4. Assimilation (Sociology) 5. Culture conflict 6. Chinese in the United States 7. Families 8. Yellowface 9. United States -- History -- 19th century 10. United States -- History -- 20th century 11. China 12. Literary fiction

LC 2016005161

Asian Pacific American Award for Literature: Adult Fiction Honor Book, 2017.

Four interlinked stories examine the Chinese-American experience from the 19th century to the present. "Gold" follows a mixed-race im-

migrant from the Pearl River Delta who becomes the valet of a railroad baron. "Silver" introduces 1930s Hollywood actress Anna May Wong, whose career ambitions are thwarted by institutional racism. "Jade," set against the backdrop of 1980s Detroit's struggling auto industry, recounts a hate crime, while the contemporary "Pearl" describes a biracial writer's adoption of a child from China. Like The Welsh Girl, author Peter Ho Davies' debut novel, The Fortunes sensitively explores issues of identity and belonging. -- Description by Gillian Speace.

"Davies' nuanced contemplation of how America has affected the Chinese (and vice versa) forces the reader to confront what is both singular and similar about all cross-cultural transactions." Kirkus.

Davies, Robertson, 1913-1995

The **cunning** man : a novel / Robertson Davies Viking, 1994. 469 p.

ISBN 9780670859115

1. Physicians 2. Priests -- Death 3. Reminiscing in old age 4. Alternative medicine 5. Memories 6. Canada 7. Toronto, Ontario 8. Psychological fiction 9. Literary fiction

LC 94031874

Following a mysterious death at the High Altar on Good Friday, holistic doctor Jonathan Hullah takes a critical look at his past and the individuals who shaped his life, and reevaluates his personal philosophies.

"Robertson entertains with an old-fashioned fictional mixture that he seems to have invented anew: keen social observations delivered with wit, intelligence and free-floating philosophical curiosity." Time.

Davies, Robertson, 1913-1995

Fifth business / Robertson Davies. Viking, 1970. 308 p. Deptford trilogy

ISBN 0670312134

1. Magicians 2. Psychoanalysis 3. Guilt 4. History teachers 5. Fathers and sons 6. Psychoanalyst and patient 7. Canadians in Switzerland 8. World War I veterans 9. Christian saints 10. Single men 11. Psychological fiction 12. Literary fiction

LC 70128346

A retiring Canadian history professor reveals the true nature of his eerie, mystical influence on those around him.

Davies, Robertson, 1913-1995

Murther and walking spirits / Robertson Davies. Viking Press, 1991. 357 p.

ISBN 9780670841899

1. Film festivals 2. Life after death 3. Murder victims 4. Extramarital affairs 5. Death 6. Self-discovery in men 7. Guilt in men 8. Ghosts 9. Canada 10. Family sagas 11. Literary fiction

LC 91029844

Murdered by his wife's lover, Gil must spend his afterlife seated next to his murderer at a film festival, where he views the exploits of his ancestors from the Revolutionary era to his parents' time.

"The films convey more than sight and sound, making our hero eerily privy to his relatives' thoughts and feelings. Davies has great fun with this device, giving full rein to his sense of drama, love of gritty, historical detail, and delight in satire." Booklist.

Davies, Robertson, 1913-1995

* The **rebel** angels / Robertson Davies. Penguin, 1983, c1981. 326 p. Cornish trilogy (Robertson Davies)

ISBN 9780140062717

1. Universities and colleges 2. Love triangles 3. Women graduate students 4. Men/women relations 5. Manuscripts -- Collectors and collecting -- Canada 6. College teachers 7. Romanies 8. Family relationships 9. Husband and wife 10. Canada 11. Psychological

fiction 12. Literary fiction

LC 81051907

Sequel: What's bred in the bone.

Two professors--one a goodhearted priest, the other a dabbler in the darker arts--becomes involved with graduate student Maria Theotoki, who knows the gospel of the angels who betrayed heaven's secrets.

Davies, Valentine, 1905-1961

Miracle on 34th Street / Valentine Davies Harcourt Brace Jovanovich, 1991, c1947. 144 p.

ISBN 9780156604550

1. New York City 2. Christmas stories

LC 91-76211

"Nice blend of fantasy, fun and humor with the universal and wholesome appeal of the Christmas spirit." Library Journal.

Davis, Amanda, 1971-

Wonder when you'll miss me / Amanda Davis. William Morrow, 2003. 259 p.

ISBN 0688167810

1. Runaway teenagers 2. Teenage girls 3. Teenagers 4. Sixteen-year-old girls 5. Sixteen-year-olds 6. High school students 7. Rape victims 8. Weight loss 9. Revenge 10. Circus 11. Southern States 12. Coming-of-age stories

LC 2002024118

Losing a considerable amount of weight in her attempt to commit suicide, sixteen-year-old Faith Duckle returns to the school where she had been tormented, haunted by painful memories and working to exact retribution from those who hurt her.

"Davis's writing is at its finest when the protagonist is struggling through the constant trials with her distant mother, her ineffectual teachers, and her one true friend's suicide. . . . The author succeeds in making this character unique, with flaws that teens will relate to. Readers will root for Faith, and the heartwarming conclusion will leave them satisfied." School Library Journal.

Davis, Fiona, 1966-

The **Chelsea** girls / Fiona Davis. Dutton, 2019. 368 p.

ISBN 9781524744588

1. Chelsea Hotel 2. 20th century 3. McCarthyism 4. Entertainment industry and trade 5. Female friendship 6. Women screenwriters 7. Actors and actresses 8. Malicious accusation 9. City life 10. Creativity 11. New York City -- Social life and customs -- 20th century 12. Historical fiction

A 20-year friendship between a playwright and an actress with Broadway ambitions is tested by the impact of McCarthy-era witch hunts among the creative residents of New York City's Chelsea Hotel.

Davis, Fiona, 1966-

The **masterpiece** / Fiona Davis. E.P. Dutton, 2018. 368 p.

ISBN 9781524742959

1. New York City. Grand Central Terminal. 2. 1920s 3. 1970s 4. Women artists 5. Independence in women 6. Art schools 7. Art 8. Sexism 9. Divorced women 10. Cancer survivors 11. Railroad stations 12. City life 13. New York City 14. Historical fiction

A recently divorced information-booth worker stumbles on an abandoned art school within a crumbling Grand Central Terminal before learning the story of a talented woman artist who went missing 50 years earlier.

Davis, Kathryn, 1946-

Duplex / Kathryn Davis. Graywolf Press, 2013. 195 p.

ISBN 9781555976538

1. Time travel 2. Couples 3. Wizards 4. Interdimensional travel 5. Life change events 6. Suburban life 7. Supernatural 8. Families 9. Robots 10. Time 11. Love 12. Science fiction 13. Science fantasy 14. Literary fiction

In the duplex, a magical doorway to the past and future, human and robot and space and time, Mary and Eddie, existing in an eternal present, are meant for each other, but discover that love is no guarantee when the past and future fold into each other after the arrival of a sorcerer.

Davis, Lindsey

A **body** in the bathhouse / Lindsey Davis. Mysterious Press, 2002, c2001. 354 p. Marcus Didius Falco mysteries

ISBN 9780892967711

1. Roman Britain (55 BCE-449 CE) 2. 1st century 3. Romans in Great Britain 4. Families 5. Building 6. Palaces 7. Contractors 8. Murder investigation 9. Private investigators 10. Great Britain -- History -- Roman period, 55 BC-449 AD 11. Rome -- History -- Vespasian, 69-79 12. Rome -- History -- Empire, 30 BC-476 AD 13. Historical mysteries 14. Mysteries

LC 2002023071

Ancient Roman investigator Marcus Didius Falco finds trouble on the site of a new palace being built by the king of the Atrebtes tribe in distant Britain.

"In this Marcus Didius Falco adventure various circumstancesincluding a dead body under his father's new bathhouse, a sister in danger from a spurned love interest, and a request from the emperor for help in auditing a British building projectconverge to send Falco, his family, and his frightened sister to the damp and uncivilized frontier. . . . Davis delivers her usual entertaining family dynamics and historically accurate details." Booklist.

Davis, Lindsey

The **ides** of April : a Flavia Albia mystery / Lindsey Davis. Minotaur Books, 2013. 341 p. Flavia Albia mysteries

ISBN 9781250023698

1. Roman Empire (27 BCE-476 CE) 2. 1st century 3. Women private investigators 4. Murder investigation 5. Private investigators 6. Murder 7. Murder suspects 8. Suspicion 9. Rome -- History -- Vespasian, 69-79 10. Rome -- History -- Empire, 30 BC-476 AD 11. Historical mysteries 12. Mysteries

Flavia Albia, the adopted daughter of Falco, works as a private informer in Rome during the reign of Domitian and is hired to investigate a fatal accident that turns sinister when her client dies under suspicious circumstances that place Flavia Albia's reputation at stake.

Davis, Lindsey

One virgin too many / Lindsey Davis. Mysterious Press, 2000, c1999. 304 p. Marcus Didius Falco mysteries

ISBN 9780892967162

1. Roman Empire (27 BCE-476 CE) 2. 1st century 3. Cults 4. Monasticism and religious orders -- Rome 5. Geese 6. Murder 7. Murder investigation -- Rome 8. Private investigators 9. Rome -- History -- Vespasian, 69-79 10. Rome -- History -- Empire, 30 BC-476 AD 11. Historical mysteries 12. Mysteries

LC 00031053

Marcus Didius Falco, the cynical, hard-boiled investigator from the rough end of Rome, is back from a difficult mission in North Africa. As a result of his hard work, Emperor Vespasian awards Falco with the title of Procurator of Poultry for the Senate and People of Rome, or keeper of the city's sacred geese. Not much of a salary, of course, but the title does give him a better standing with his in-laws. Now, all Falco wants is to spend time relaxing at home with his family. But there is no rest for Falco as he finds himself drawn into the world of the Roman religious cults...and the murder of a member of the Sacred Brotherhoods. And then there's the disappearance of the most likely new candidate for the Order of Vestal Virgins. Falco soon uncovers a sinister cover-up-and is too deeply involved to back away from the truth.

"For sharply etched characters, wry humor, and a powerfully evoked Rome, this historical can't be beaten." Library Journal.

Davis, Lydia, 1947-

* The **collected** stories of Lydia Davis / Lydia Davis. Farrar, Straus and Giroux, 2009. xi, 733 p.

ISBN 9780374270605

1. Short stories

LC 2009025451

Includes index.

A single-volume compilation of the National Book Award finalist's short stories.

"This volume presents a body of work probably unique in American writing, in its combination of lucidity, aphoristic brevity, formal originality, sly comedy, metaphysical bleakness, philosophical pressure, and human wisdom. I suspect that The Collected Stories of Lydia Davis will in time be seen as one of the great, strange American literary contributions, distinct and crookedly personal, like the work of Flannery O'Connor, or Donald Barthelme, or J. F. Powers." The New Yorker.

Davys, Tim

Amberville / Tim Davys. HarperCollins, 2009. 352 p. Mollisan Town quartet

ISBN 9780061625121

1. Stuffed animals (Toys) 2. Missing persons 3. Organized crime 4. Good and evil 5. Escapes 6. Toys 7. Disappeared persons 8. Crime bosses 9. Mysteries 10. Hardboiled fiction 11. Translations -- Swedish to English

A fantastical noir tale populated by animal characters finds Eric Bear, a successful advertising executive, confronting his checkered past when notorious crime boss Nicholas Dove threatens Eric's wife, Emma Rabbit, unless Eric and his former teammates prevent an attack on Dove's life.

Dazieri, Sandrone, 1964-

Kill the angel / Sandrone Dazieri. Simon & Schuster, 2018 384 p. Caselli and Torre novels

ISBN 9781501174650

1. Women detectives 2. Private investigators 3. Murder investigation 4. Trains 5. Captives 6. Terrorism 7. Mass murder 8. Biological weapons 9. Rome, Italy 10. Italy 11. Thrillers and suspense 12. Translations -- Italian to English

LC 2017051621

Translated from the Italian Antony Shugaar.

Originally published in Italy in 2016 by Mondadori as L'Angelo.

A follow-up to Kill the Father finds investigators Colomba Caselli and Dante Torre examining clues on a high-speed train found with a carriage full of murder victims, an act committed by a murderously damaged killer who has staged the scene to look like a terrorist attack.

Dazieri, Sandrone, 1964-

Kill the father / Sandrone Dazieri ; translated from the Italian by Antony Shugaar. Scribner, 2017, c2014. 512 p. Caselli and Torre novels

ISBN 9781501130731

1. Missing children 2. Kidnapping 3. Murder investigation 4.

Kidnappers 5. Women detectives 6. Psychic trauma 7. Fugitives 8. Government conspiracies 9. Terrorism 10. Revenge 11. People with post-traumatic stress disorder 12. Rome, Italy 13. Italy 14. Thrillers and suspense 15. Translations -- Italian to English

LC 2016015605

Originally published: Segrate, Italy : Mondadori, 2014.

When a woman is beheaded in a park outside Rome and her six-year-old son goes missing, two of Italy's top analytical minds are assigned to the case: Deputy Captain Colomba Caselli, a fierce warrior-like detective, and Dante Torre, a man who spent his childhood trapped inside a concrete silo, fed through the gloved hand of a masked kidnapper who called himself "the Father". And now evidence suggests that the Father is coming back.

Dazieri, Sandrone, 1964-

Kill the king / Sandrone Dazieri. Scribner, 2020, c2018. 384 p. Caselli and Torre novels

ISBN 9781501174728

1. Women detectives 2. Coworkers 3. Missing men 4. Teenage boys 5. Boys with autism 6. Murder 7. Bombings 8. Psychic trauma 9. Frameups 10. Murder investigation 11. Rome, Italy 12. Italy 13. Thrillers and suspense 14. Translations -- Italian to English

Series complete in three volumes.

Originally published: Milan : Mondadori, 2018.

Reeling from a deadly bombing in Venice and her investigative partner Dante's disappearance, Detective Colomba Caselli retreats to the rural countryside outside Rome to nurse her wounds. When an apparently autistic teenager appears in her yard, covered in blood, he leads her to a brutal crime scene where nothing is what it seems. As Colomba gets pulled into the investigation and the body count spirals upward, she is implicated in the violence.

De Bernieres, Louis

Birds without wings / Louis de Bernieres Knopf, 2004. xi, 553 p.

ISBN 9781400043415

1. Ataturk, Kemal, 1881-1938 2. Villages -- Turkey 3. Religious fanaticism 4. Interfaith romance 5. Communities 6. Muslims 7. Christians 8. Soldiers 9. Extramarital affairs 10. Men/women relations 11. Love triangles 12. Islam -- Relations -- Christianity 13. Christianity -- Relations -- Islam 14. Fathers and sons 15. World War I -- Turkey 16. Nationalism -- Turkey 17. Forced relocations 18. Coastal towns -- Turkey 19. Gallipoli Campaign, Turkey, 1915 20. Turkey -- History -- 20th century 21. Gallipoli Peninsula, Turkey 22. Historical fiction 23. War stories 24. Literary fiction

LC 2004014529

Map on lining papers.

ALA Notable Book, 2005.

In a small town in Anatolia in the finals days of the Ottoman Empire, the lives of its inhabitants--Armenians, Christians, and Muslims--peacefully intertwine, until Mustafa Kemal, a powerful military leader, conscripts the young men of the village to battle the invading Western European forces during the Great War, and religious fanaticism and nationalism destroy the peace.

"This epic about the tragedy of borders is likely to cross all borders, moving readers everywhere as it describes the harrowing cost of remaking faraway places in the image of our dreams." Christian Science Monitor.

De Giovanni, Maurizio, 1958-

The **bastards** of Pizzofalcone / Maurizio De Giovanni ; translated from Italian by Antony Shugaar. Europa Editions, 2016, c2013. 288 p. Giuseppe Lojacono mysteries

ISBN 9781609453145

1. Detectives 2. Police 3. Murder investigation 4. Murder 5. Police corruption 6. Police internal affairs investigation 7. Naples, Italy 8. Italy 9. Police procedurals 10. Mysteries 11. Translations -- Italian to English

After every officer of the investigative branch of the Pizzofalcone police precinct of Naples is suspended for corruption, a new team of officers is assembled from around the city and thrown into a high profile murder case led by Inspector Lojacono.

De Giovanni, Maurizio, 1958-

The **crocodile** / Maurizio de Giovanni ; translated from Italian by Antony Shugaar. Europa Editions, 2013, c2012. 278 p. Giuseppe Lojacono mysteries

ISBN 9781609451196

1. Malicious accusation 2. Detectives 3. Women lawyers 4. Marital conflict 5. Serial murders 6. Revenge 7. Loneliness in men 8. Interpersonal relations 9. Naples, Italy 10. Italy 11. Police procedurals 12. Hardboiled fiction 13. Translations -- Italian to English

Originally published: Milano : Mondadori, 2012.

Given a second chance and a shot at clearing his name, Inspector Giuseppe Lojacono, who has been accused of leaking sensitive information to the mob, arrives in Naples, at the behest of a beautiful magistrate, to catch a serial killer called "The Crocodile."

De Kretser, Michelle

* The **life** to come / Michelle de Kretser. Catapult, 2018, c2017. 344 p.

ISBN 9781936787821

1. Interpersonal relations 2. Coping 3. Self-fulfillment 4. Loneliness 5. Interpersonal attraction 6. Loss (Psychology) 7. Authors 8. Extramarital affairs 9. Married men 10. Success (Concept) 11. Literary fiction

Originally published: Sydney : Allen & Unwin, 2017.

Librarians' Choice (Australia), 2017.

Miles Franklin Award, 2018.

Shortlisted for the Stella Prize, 2018.

Connected stories set in Australia, France and Sri Lanka follow a writer longing for success, a woman seeing a married man and a man with commitment issues stemming from a childhood tragedy.

De Leon, Aya

Side chick nation / Aya De Leon. Dafina Books, 2019. 352 p. Justice hustlers

ISBN 9781496715791

1. Female gang leaders 2. Women thieves 3. West Indian Americans 4. Cheating (Interpersonal relations) 5. Rich men 6. Fugitives 7. Journalists 8. Hurricane Maria, 2017 9. Organized crime 10. Betrayal 11. Ambition 12. African American women 13. Hispanic American women 14. Miami, Florida 15. New York City 16. Puerto Rico 17. Caribbean Area 18. Urban fiction 19. African American fiction

Fed up with her married Miami boyfriend, savvy Dulce has no problem stealing his drug-dealer stash and fleeing to her family in the Caribbean. But when she gets bored in rural Santo Domingo, she escapes on a sugar daddy adventure to Puerto Rico. Meanwhile, New York-based mastermind thief Marisol already has her hands full fleecing a ruthless CEO who's stealing her family's land in Puerto Rico, while trying to get her relatives out alive after the hurricane. An extra member in her crew could be game-changing, but she's wary of Dulce's unpredictability and reputation for drama.

De Robertis, Carolina

Cantoras / Carolina De Robertis. Alfred A. Knopf, 2019. 320 p.

ISBN 9780525521693

1. 20th century 2. 21st century 3. Lesbians 4. Independence in women 5. Violence against gay men and lesbians 6. Homophobia 7. Communities 8. Secrets 9. Female friendship 10. Dictatorship 11. Violence against women 12. Women -- Psychology 13. Identity (Psychology) 14. Families 15. Women/women relations 16. Uruguay 17. Political fiction 18. LGBTQIA fiction 19. Literary fiction

Stonewall Book Award for the Barbara Gittings Literature Award, 2020.

Kirkus Prize for Fiction finalist, 2019.

Enduring the rampant violence against women and the LGBTQ community in the decades of the Uruguayan dictatorship, five women heartbreakingly unite as lovers, friends and family.

De Robertis, Carolina

* **Perla** / Carolina De Robertis. Alfred A. Knopf, 2012. 235 p.

ISBN 9780307599599

1. Family secrets 2. Fathers and daughters 3. Teenage girls -- Identity 4. Military service 5. Dictatorship 6. Argentina -- History -- Dirty War, 1976-1983 7. Buenos Aires, Argentina 8. Coming-of-age stories 9. Psychological fiction

A coming-of-age tale set in post-dictatorship Buenos Aires finds privileged Correa safeguarding the interests of her family by hiding her beloved father's military past from others until an uninvited visitor forces her to confront the unease she has suppressed her entire life.

De Robertis, Carolina

The **gods** of tango / Carolina De Robertis. Alfred A. Knopf, 2015. 367 p.

ISBN 9781101874493

1. Gender identity 2. Violinists 3. Lesbians 4. Tango music 5. Male impersonators 6. Secret identity 7. Buenos Aires, Argentina 8. Coming-of-age stories 9. LGBTQIA fiction

Stonewall Book Award for the Barbara Gittings Literature Award, 2016.

As soon as Italian immigrant Leda Mazzoni steps off the boat in Argentina in 1913, she learns that she's a widow: her husband has been killed during a political protest. Since returning home isn't an option, Leda dons his clothes and takes his name. Playing the violin on the streets of Buenos Aires, "Dante" earns a living as a busker until a local bandleader recruits the young musician for his troupe. What follows is a lush and lyrical coming-of-age story, set against the vivid backdrop of a city obsessed with the seductive rhythms of the tango. -- Description by Gillian Speace.

"The novel is a plea to embrace 'the bright jagged thing you really are,' and in its hero's more contemplative, interior moments, De Robertis captures the enormity of that struggle." Kirkus.

De la Motte, Anders, 1971-

MemoRandom : a thriller / Anders De La Motte ; translated by Neil Smith. Pocket Books, 2015. 448 p. MemoRandom

ISBN 9781476788067

1. Men with amnesia 2. Intelligence service 3. Competition 4. Police 5. Traffic accident victims 6. Intelligence officers 7. Organized crime 8. Informers 9. Amnesia 10. Ambition 11. Trust 12. Stockholm,

Sweden 13. Scandinavian crime fiction 14. Thrillers and suspense 15. Translations -- Swedish to English

Originally published: Stockholm : Forum 2014.

After suffering a stroke and a violent car crash, a handler at the Intelligence Unit of the Stockholm Police Force loses all memory of an important informant, putting the entire operation at risk.

De la Motte, Anders, 1971-

Ultimatum : a thriller / Anders de la Motte. Atria, 2017. 368 p. MemoRandom

ISBN 9781476788098

1. Informers 2. Intelligence service 3. Intelligence officers 4. Organized crime 5. Secrets 6. Betrayal 7. Trust 8. Stockholm, Sweden 9. Scandinavian crime fiction 10. Thrillers and suspense 11. Translations -- Swedish to English

In a sequel to the thriller MemoRandom, David Sarac of the Stockholm Police Force's Intelligence Unit, recovering from gunshot wounds after a violent encounter with the enigmatic high-level informant Janus, is slipped an anonymous note by his nurse that contains clues to the person responsible for betraying him during the Janus shoot-out.

De la Roche, Mazo, 1879-1961

Jalna / Mazo de la Roche. Little, Brown, 1955, c1927. 347p. Whiteoaks of Jalna

1. Centenarians 2. Grandmother and grandson 3. Intergenerational relations 4. Mansions 5. Love triangles 6. Family relationships 7. Ontario 8. Family sagas

Sequel to Whiteoak brothers.

Sequel: Whiteoaks of Jalna.

First published in 1927.

The sequel to The Whiteoak Brothers includes representatives of each generation up to 99-year-old Gran.

De los Santos, Marisa, 1966-

The **precious** one / Marisa De los Santos. William Morrow & Co., 2015. 359 p.

ISBN 9780061670893

1. Sisters 2. Fathers and daughters 3. Manipulation (Social sciences) 4. People who have had heart attacks 5. Father-separated families 6. Family relationships 7. Sibling rivalry 8. Family secrets 9. Domestic fiction

A tale told in alternating voices traces the collaborative efforts of an estranged millionaire father and the daughter he abandoned 17 years earlier to reconcile and write his memoir.

DeBoard, Paula Treick

The **fragile** world / Paula Treick DeBoard. Harlequin MIRA, 2014. 432 p.

ISBN 9780778316763

1. Families 2. Children -- Death 3. Loss (Psychology) 4. Healing 5. Grief 6. Revenge 7. Obsession 8. Life-change events 9. Domestic fiction

The sudden death of their college-age son in a car crash sends the Kaufmans reeling and leads the father, Curtis, to pack up his life?and his anxious teenage daughter, Olivia--and set out to seek revenge.

DeCarlo, Melissa

The **art** of crash landing : a novel / Melissa DeCarlo. Harper, 2015. 405 p.

ISBN 9780062390547

1. Mothers and daughters 2. Family secrets 3. Forgiveness 4. Family relationships 5. Pregnant women 6. Inheritance and succession 7.

Life change events 8. Small town life -- Oklahoma 9. Self-discovery in women 10. Oklahoma 11. Domestic fiction

LC 2015010374

Chasing a possible inheritance from her grandmother, Mattie Wallace, homeless and pregnant, travels to her mother's hometown in Oklahoma, where she tries to reconcile the town's memory of her mother with the broken alcoholic she became and stop her own downward spiral.

"DeCarlo bursts on the scene with a fascinating, mysterious novel. The pacing is excellent and the prose fluid as the story unfolds in a combination of flashbacks and present-day scenes. This debut is thick with secrets; it will cause readers to question everyone and everything. The author does an outstanding job combining suspense with heartache, adding a dash of romance and, at the end, hope." Library Journal.

DeLillo, Don

Falling man : a novel / Don DeLillo. Scribner, 2007. 246 p.

ISBN 9781416546023

1. September 11 Terrorist Attacks, 2001 2. Terrorism -- Psychological aspects 3. Separated couples 4. Escapes 5. Victims of terrorism 6. Reconciliation in marriage 7. Family relationships 8. Terrorists -- Arab countries 9. Terrorists -- Psychology 10. Manhattan, New York City 11. New York City 12. Psychological fiction 13. Literary fiction

LC 2006052306

Escaping from the World Trade Center during the September 11 attacks, Keith makes his way to the uptown apartment where his ex-wife and young son are living and considers how the day's events have irrevocably changed his perception of the world.

"Scenes are laid out like cards face up in some mysterious game of solitaire, except that each card, each sequence, seems to carry some larger import. It's not clear even at the novel's end what its finishing up might mean. On one narrative level, the game is already over the characters are living in an unknown afterworld. But on another level DeLillo inserts several time-jumps into the pre-Sept. 11 past we see his terrorist preparing himself. . . . Though the setup feels stylized, it is also riveting." Los Angeles Times Book Review.

DeLillo, Don

Libra / Don DeLillo. Viking, 1988. 456 p.

ISBN 9780670823178

1. Oswald, Lee Harvey, 1939-1963 2. Kennedy, John F (John Fitzgerald), 1917-1963 Assassination 3. 1960s 4. Presidents -- United States -- Assassination 5. Assassination 6. Assassins -- Texas 7. Defectors -- United States 8. Former CIA agents 9. CIA agents 10. Immigrants, Cuban 11. Conspiracies 12. Defection 13. United States -- History -- 1961-1969 14. Dallas, Texas -- History 15. Biographical fiction 16. Literary fiction

LC 87040649

National Book Award for Fiction finalist, 1988

National Book Critics Circle Award for Fiction finalist, 1988

The scheme of two disgruntled CIA agents to stage an unsuccessful attempt on the life of President Kennedy and link it to Cuba backfires when the erratic Lee Harvey Oswald goes too far.

"This novel provokes the reader with its clever use of history, its dramatic pacing and its immaculate and detailed construction." Publishers Weekly.

DeLillo, Don

The **names** / Don DeLillo. A. A. Knopf, 1982. 339 p.

ISBN 9780394528144

1. Americans in Greece 2. Cults 3. Murder 4. Language and languages 5. Political risk insurance 6. Working abroad 7. Separated men (Marital relations) 8. Expatriates 9. Alienation in men 10.

Literary fiction

LC   82048012

In an expatriate's world of turmoil and danger, American risk analyst James Axton learns of a ritual-murder cult in the Aegean and follows the trail to its secret meanings in the ancient city of Lahore

"Nearly every page testifies to DeLillo's exceptional gifts as a writer." The New Republic.

DeLillo, Don

* **Underworld** / Don DeLillo. Scribner, 1997. 827 p.
ISBN 0684842696
1. 1950s 2. Baseball -- History -- 20th century 3. Cold War 4. African Americans 5. African American teenage boys 6. Professional baseball teams 7. Baseball fans 8. Former lovers 9. Senior nuns 10. New York City 11. United States -- Popular culture -- History -- 20th century 12. Literary fiction

LC 97-13825

Prologue also published separately in 2001 under the title Pafko at the wall.

Earlier version of prologue published in Harper's magazine (October 1992).

National Book Award for Fiction finalist, 1997

National Book Critics Circle Award for Fiction finalist, 1997

Pulitzer Prize for Fiction finalist, 1998.

Shortlisted for the International IMPAC Dublin Literary Award, 1999

A work combining fiction and history in a collaboration that encompasses fifty years gives readers a glimpse into the realities upon which America's modern culture is based and explores the complex relationship between "waste analyst" Nick Shay and artist Klara Sax.

"The dialogue is a rockingly comic attack on our mental excreta: the distortions and sound bites of the television age. DeLillo was absent from his fiction before, an unbodied intelligence, but here is an undertow of personal pain he has never touched. This is his most demanding novel and yet his most transparent, giving the reader the privileged intimacy that comes from seeing a writer whole." New York Times Book Review.

DeLillo, Don

* **White** noise / Don DeLillo. Viking, 1985. 326 p.
ISBN 9780670803736
1. Industrial accidents 2. Universities and colleges 3. College teachers 4. Poisonous gases 5. Husband and wife 6. Eccentrics and eccentricities 7. Middle West 8. Literary fiction 9. Black humor 10. Satirical fiction

LC   84040375

National Book Award for Fiction, 1985.

National Book Critics Circle Award for Fiction finalist, 1985

A Midwestern family navigates the rocky passages of family life while a lethal cloud resulting from an industrial accident hovers over them.

"This is a stunning performance from one of our finest and most intelligent novelists. DeLillo's reach is broad and deep, combining acute observation of the textures of American life and analytic rigor." The New Republic.

DeLillo, Don

Zero K : a novel / Don DeLillo. Scribner, 2016. 288 p.
ISBN 9781501135392
1. Cryonics 2. Scientists 3. Fathers and sons 4. Death 5. Billionaires 6. Stepmothers 7. Human nature 8. Family relationships 9. Science -- Social aspects 10. People with terminal illnesses -- Family relationships 11. Kyrgyzstan 12. Social science fiction

LC 2015040210

"Jeffrey Lockhart's father, Ross, is a George Soros-like billionaire now in his sixties, with a younger wife, Artis, whose health is failing. Ross is the primary investor in a deeply remote and secret compound where death is controlled and bodies are preserved until a future moment when medicine and technology can reawaken them. Jeffrey joins Ross and Artis at the compound to say "an uncertain farewell" to her as she surrenders her body."

"DeLillo's rich language and rhythmic prose draw readers deep into a rumination on both the inescapability and alluring possibilities of the eternal return." Library Journal.

DeLuca, Jen

* **Well** met / Jen DeLuca Berkley Jove, 2019. 328 p.
ISBN 9781984805386
1. Teachers 2. Renaissance fairs 3. Women volunteers 4. Actors and actresses 5. Role playing 6. Flirtation 7. Moving to a new city 8. Interpersonal attraction 9. Men/women relations 10. Small towns 11. Maryland 12. Romantic comedies 13. Contemporary romances

LC 2019001004

While in the small town of Willow Creek, Maryland, to help her sister, Emily is roped into volunteering for the local Renaissance Faire with her teenaged niece where she, after meeting an irritating, yet handsome, schoolteacher, finally finds a place to call home.

"DeLuca turns in an intelligent, sexy, and charming debut romance sure to resonate with Renaissance Faire enthusiasts and those looking for an upbeat, lighter read." Library Journal.

DeMille, Nelson

* The **Cuban** affair : a novel / Nelson DeMille. Simon & Schuster, 2017. 416 p.
ISBN 9781501101724
1. Treasure hunting 2. Veterans 3. Fishing boat captains 4. Ocean travel 5. Fishing 6. Fishing boats 7. Treasure troves 8. Cubans 9. Cuban Americans 10. Cuba 11. Mainstream fiction

LC 2017017727

When his shaky finances compel him to accept a lucrative job for a 10-day fishing tournament to Cuba, Army combat veteran-turned-charter boat captain Mac learns that one of his clients is seeking to claim millions hidden by her grandfather, who was forced to flee Castro's revolution years earlier.

DeMille, Nelson

* The **deserter** : a novel / Nelson DeMille and Alex DeMille. Simon & Schuster, 2019. 448 p.
ISBN 9781501101755
1. Assassins 2. Missing persons 3. Military police 4. Veterans 5. Special forces 6. Criminal investigation 7. Men/women relations 8. Sexual attraction 9. Deserters 10. Thrillers and suspense

LC 2019013504

A year after a trained assassin with classified Army intelligence disappears under suspicious circumstances, an Army investigator's efforts to capture the man alive are complicated by his partner's inexperience and suspected role as a CIA spy.

DeMille, Nelson

Wild fire / Nelson DeMille. Warner Books, 2006. 519 p.
John Corey novels
ISBN 9780446579674
1. 2000s (Decade) 2. Nuclear terrorism 3. Government investigators 4. Husband-and-wife detectives 5. Detectives 6. Women FBI agents 7. Husband and wife 8. Terrorism -- Prevention 9. Secrets 10. Conspiracies 11. Former police 12. Detectives 13. Terrorism 14. Revenge 15. Murder 16. Adirondack Mountains, New York 17.

Thrillers and suspense

LC 2006020982

While investigating the death of a member of the Federal Anti-Terrorist Task Force, Detective John Corey and his wife, FBI Agent Kate Mayfield, stumble into the middle of a terrifying nuclear conspiracy that leads them to the inner circle of the Custer Hill Club, a luxurious Adirondack hunting lodge whose members include America's most powerful leaders.

"As usual, DeMille appears to have done a ton of research; what sets his thrillers apart from those of some of his competitors is the way he seamlessly incorporates real technology and real government organizations into his stories." Booklist.

DePoy, Phillip

Sidewalk saint / Phillip Depoy. Severn House, 2019. 192 p. Foggy Moskowitz novels

ISBN 9780727889577

1. 1970s 2. Amateur detectives 3. Missing children 4. Social workers 5. Children of criminals 6. Florida 7. Mysteries

Foggy Moscowitz knows he's having a bad night when he wakes to find a gun pressed to his face. Nelson Roan has busted out of his prison cell and broken into Foggy's house, demanding Foggy finds his eleven-year-old daughter, Etta. But as Foggy searches for Etta, it seems her father is not the only person who wants her found...

DeSilva, Bruce

Providence rag / Bruce DeSilva. Forge Books, 2014. 351 p. Liam Mulligan mysteries

ISBN 9780765374295

1. Teenage serial murderers 2. Investigative journalists 3. Parole 4. Investigative journalism -- Moral and ethical aspects 5. Murder investigation 6. Political corruption 7. Journalistic ethics 8. Serial murderers 9. Frameups 10. Murder 11. Providence, Rhode Island 12. Rhode Island 13. Mysteries

LC 2013025786

A tale inspired by a true story finds Mulligan, his friend Mason, and the newspaper they work for confronting an ethical dilemma involving a juvenile serial murderer's parole and corrupt police activities.

"[T]here is real suspense here. And Mulligan's character, played off the vicissitudes of his job, is skillfully layered and engaging." Booklist.

DeSilva, Bruce

Rogue Island / Bruce DeSilva. Forge, 2010. 302 p. Liam Mulligan mysteries

ISBN 9780765327260

1. Investigative journalists 2. Arson 3. Neighborhoods 4. Murder 5. Police 6. Arsonists 7. Criminals 8. Providence, Rhode Island 9. Rhode Island 10. Mysteries

Edgar Allan Poe Award for Best First Novel by an American Author, 2011.

Macavity Award for Best First Mystery Novel, 2011.

When journalist Liam Mulligan realizes that someone is systematically burning down his childhood neighborhood in Providence, Rhode Island, he ignores his bosses and his budding relationship to figure out the firebug's identity.

DeSilva, Bruce

A **scourge** of vipers / Bruce DeSilva. Forge, 2015. 368 p. Liam Mulligan mysteries

ISBN 9780765374318

1. Gambling 2. Investigative journalists 3. Sports betting -- Corrupt practices 4. Murder 5. Corruption 6. Governors 7. Organized crime 8. Political corruption 9. Murder investigation 10. State governments

-- Finance 11. Crime bosses 12. Providence, Rhode Island 13. Rhode Island 14. Mysteries

Investigating an upsurge in organized crime when Rhode Island's colorful governor proposes the legalization of sports gambling, rogue journalist Liam Mulligan is targeted by shadowy forces when he unearths suspicious clues in the death of a powerful senator.

"DeSilva is spot-on, as only a journalist with a 40-year newspaper career behind him can be, when it comes to corruption. His dialogue, however, has everyone, including the former nun, sounding as if theyve just completed a 'Talk like a Martin Scorsese thug' course." Booklist.

DeWoskin, Rachel

Big girl small : a novel / Rachel DeWoskin. Farrar, Straus and Giroux, 2011. 294 p.

ISBN 9780374112578

1. Teenage girls -- Sexuality 2. Date rape 3. Humiliation 4. Little people 5. High school students 6. Scandals 7. Popularity 8. Social acceptance 9. Coming-of-age stories

LC 2010033106

Sixteen-year-old Judy Lohden finds her three feet nine inches tall, incredibly talented self in the middle of a scandal, with the national media on her trail and the students at Darcy Academy, a local performing arts high school, involved in the mayhem.

"Bright and sardonic Judy Lohden, a 16-year-old dwarf freshly enrolled in Ann Arbor's Darcy Arts Academy, falls victim to the worst Steven King Carrie prank in the history of dating at the hands of popular boy Jeff Legassic, who becomes an object of desire as soon as he and Judy meet cute the first week of school. The book opens with Judy hiding out in a seedy motel; throughout the novel, she slowly unveils her secret and reveals her two visions of herselfthat of a pretty teenage girl with an hourglass figure who happens to be three feet nine inches tall, and that of a sideshow attraction. It's a rare author who is willing to subject her protagonist to the extreme ranges of degradation and redemption to which DeWoskin subjects Judy; thankfully, she manages it beautifully." Publishers Weekly.

Dean, Anna

Bellfield Hall / Anna Dean. Minotaur Books, 2010, c2008 304 p. Dido Kent mysteries

ISBN 9780312562946

1. Georgian era (1714-1837) 2. Engaged persons 3. Missing men 4. Upper class 5. Missing persons investigation 6. Women murder victims 7. Murder investigation 8. Single women 9. Women detectives 10. Great Britain -- History -- George III, 1760-1820 11. England -- Social life and customs -- 19th century 12. Historical mysteries 13. Gentle reads 14. Cozy mysteries

LC 2009041130

Sequel: A gentleman of fortune, or, the suspicions of Miss Dido Kent. Originally published: A moment of silence. London : Allison & Busby, 2008.

Visiting Bellfield Hall to comfort her niece, who has been seemingly abandoned by her wealthy fiancé, Miss Dido Kent investigates the possibly related death of a young woman, a situation that is complicated by surprising secrets and an unexpected romance for Dido.

Dean, Anna

A **place** of confinement : the investigations of Miss Dido Kent / Anna Dean. Minotaur Books, 2013. 414 p. Dido Kent mysteries

ISBN 9781250029676

1. Georgian era (1714-1837) 2. 19th century 3. Missing persons investigation 4. Women amateur detectives 5. Haunted places 6. Missing persons 7. Upper class 8. Hypochondriacs 9. Aunts 10.

Amateur detectives 11. Heirs and heiresses 12. Great Britain -- History -- George III, 1760-1820 13. England -- Social life and customs -- 19th century 14. Historical mysteries 15. Cozy mysteries 16. Gentle reads

LC 2013011842

Sequel to: A woman of consequence: the investigations of Miss Dido Kent.

Thwarting her sister-in-law's efforts to marry her off to a decidedly unwanted suitor, the sharp-witted Miss Dido Kent is sent to live with a wealthy hypochondriac aunt and investigates the disappearance of a visiting heiress amid false accusations, dark secrets and a crying ghost.

Dean, Anna

A **woman** of consequence : the investigations of Miss Dido Kent / Anna Dean. Minotaur Books, 2012. 336 p. Dido Kent mysteries

ISBN 9780312626846

1. Georgian era (1714-1837) 2. Single women 3. Abbeys 4. Haunted places 5. Murder investigation 6. Upper class 7. Great Britain -- History -- George III, 1760-1820 8. England -- Social life and customs -- 19th century 9. Historical mysteries 10. Gentle reads 11. Cozy mysteries

Sequel to: A gentleman of fortune, or, the suspicions of Miss Dido Kent.

Refusing to believe that Penelope Lambe suffered a dangerous fall at an abbey ruin because of a ghost sighting, Miss Dido Kent uncovers a human skeleton at the scene and investigates clues linking the remains to Miss Lambe's accident.

Dean, Debra, 1957-

The **madonnas** of Leningrad : a novel / Debra Dean. William Morrow, 2006. 231 p.

ISBN 9780060825300

1. Hermitage Museum, St. Petersburg, Russia 2. 1940s 3. Russian Americans 4. Reminiscing in old age 5. People with Alzheimer's disease 6. Russian American women 7. Senior women 8. World War II 9. Weddings 10. Art treasures in war 11. Museums 12. St Petersburg, Russia -- Siege, 1941-1944 13. Soviet Union 14. Seattle, Washington 15. Psychological fiction 16. Historical fiction 17. War stories 18. Pacific Northwest fiction

LC 2005050233

ALA Notable Book, 2007.

In a novel that moves back and forth between the Soviet Union during World War II and modern-day America, Marina, an elderly Russian woman, recalls vivid images of her youth during the height of the siege of Leningrad.

"Like her adoring museum audiences 60 years earlier, readers will absorb Marina's glorious, lush accounts of classical beauties as she traces them in her mind. Dean eloquently depicts the ravages of Alzheimer's disease and convincingly describes the inner world of the afflicted." Library Journal.

Dean, Louise

The **idea** of love / Louise Dean. Houghton Mifflin Harcourt, 2009. 320 p.

ISBN 9780151013852

1. Drug industry and trade 2. Married people -- Psychology 3. Americans in France 4. Middle-aged men 5. Extramarital affairs 6. Parent and child 7. Depression 8. British in France 9. Provence, France 10. Psychological fiction

LC 2008050150

A pair of expatriate couples find their new home in Provence challenged by pharmaceutical salesman Richard's womanizing and promotion of antidepressants in Africa, where idealistic Rachel hopes to adopt a second child.

Dean, Margaret Lazarus, 1972-

The **time** it takes to fall / Margaret Lazarus Dean. Simon & Schuster, 2007. 305 p.

ISBN 9780743297226

1. United States. National Aeronautics and Space Administration 2. Twelve-year-old girls -- Florida 3. Girls -- Career aspirations 4. Families -- Florida 5. Unemployed persons -- Family relationships 6. Marital conflict 7. Mother-deserted families 8. Coping in men 9. Growing up 10. Boy/girl relations 11. Challenger (Space shuttle) Accident, January 28, 1986 12. Florida 13. Coming-of-age stories

LC 2006052213

Dreaming of a future in space travel while growing up in 1980s Cape Canaveral, young Dolores Gray struggles with the harsh realities of her increasingly unstable home life and is shocked by the devastating 1986 explosion of the space shuttle Challenger.

"A gripping judgment of American culture with a harrowing depiction in the epilogue of the last few minutes in the lives of the Challenger's seven astronauts." Library Journal.

Dean, Michael, 1949-

I, Hogarth / Michael Dean. Overlook Duckworth, 2013, c2012. 261 p.

ISBN 9781468303421

1. Hogarth, William, 1697-1764 2. Artists -- History 3. Dysfunctional families 4. Apprenticeship 5. Lust in men 6. Rogues 7. Sexuality 8. Sex in art 9. Engravers 10. Seduction 11. Social classes 12. Art and society 13. Great Britain -- Social life and customs -- 17th century 14. Biographical fiction 15. Historical fiction

A tale inspired by the life of the 18th-century London artist famed for such works as "Gin Lane" and "The Rake's Progress" imagines his youth in a debtor's prison, struggles to establish the Copyright Act on behalf of artists and childless marriage to Jane Thornhill.

Dean, Pamela, 1953-

Tam Lin / Pamela Dean Tom Doherty Associates, 1991. 468 p. Fairy tales: a series of fantasy novels retelling classic tales

ISBN 0312851375

1. 1970s 2. Universities and colleges -- Middle West 3. Women college students 4. Roommates 5. College teachers 6. Men/women relations 7. Love triangles 8. Ghosts 9. Suicide 10. Magic 11. Women rulers 12. Fairies 13. Ballads, Scottish 14. Fairy tales 15. Middle West 16. Minneapolis, Minnesota 17. Adaptations, retellings, and spin-offs 18. Contemporary fantasy 19. Fantasy fiction

LC 90049033

An original novel based on the classic fairy tale.

Includes text of the Scottish ballad.

This Scottish-based tale for adults offers a pregnant heroine who must rescue the man who seduced her in the woods from his captor, the Fairie Queen.

Deane, Seamus, 1940-

* **Reading** in the dark / Seamus Deane. A. A. Knopf, 1997, c1996. 245 p.

ISBN 9780394574400

1. 1940s 2. 1950s 3. Boys 4. Family secrets 5. Betrayal 6. Murder 7. Family relationships 8. Growing up 9. Loss (Psychology) 10. Resistance to government 11. Northern Ireland 12. Coming-of-age stories 13. Literary fiction

LC 96-49635

Originally published: London: Jonathan Cape, 1996.

ALA Notable Book, 1998.

Guardian First Book Award, 1996.

Shortlisted for the Booker-McConnell Prize, 1996.

A young boy describes growing up amid the violence and tragedy of Northern Ireland during the 1940s and 1950s, detailing the deadly, unspoken betrayal born out of political enmity that shapes the lives of himself and his family.

"A Catholic boy growing up hard by the border between Donegal and Derry is fascinated by the local ghost stories and neighborhood lore, and this fascination leads him to secrets at the heart of a family feud. His search for the truth runs through a labyrinth of Irish detours and delights: elaborate catechisms, mad poets, mute idiots, drunken hyperbole, death-bed revelations, and a clever reprisal involving an unwitting bishop." The New Yorker.

Deaver, Jeffery

* The **coffin** dancer / Jeffery Deaver. Simon & Schuster, 1998. 358 p. Lincoln Rhyme mysteries

ISBN 0684852853

1. New York City. Police Department 2. Serial murderers 3. Violence 4. Forensic scientists 5. People with quadriplegia 6. Serial murder investigation 7. Jealousy 8. Love triangles 9. Women detectives 10. Police 11. New York City 12. Mysteries

LC 98-13537

Detective Lincoln Rhyme and his protege have 48 hours to keep three federal witnesses alive, as they frantically search for an elusive murderer.

"Quadriplegic forensic specialist Lincoln Rhyme is called in to track down a contract killer, known as the Coffin Dancer, who has been hired to eliminate three witnesses in the upcoming federal trial of Philip Hansen. The trial is set to begin just 48 hours from the novel's (literally) explosive beginning. Rhyme and his beautiful assistant, detective Amelia Sachs, have just that much time to ID the Dancer and keep him from murdering the remaining witnesses. . . . The pace, energized by Deaver's precise attention, never flags." Publishers Weekly.

Deaver, Jeffery

Edge : a novel / Jeffery Deaver. Simon & Schuster, 2010 397 p.

ISBN 9781439156353

1. Detectives 2. Criminals 3. Kidnapping 4. Torture 5. Revenge 6. Washington, D.C. 7. Thrillers and suspense

Targeted by a ruthless hired criminal seeking to extract information for a mysterious employer, Washington, D.C. police detective Ryan Kessler places the safety of his family in the hands of a federal protection officer who takes incrementally extreme measures to outmaneuver his adversary.

Deaver, Jeffery

The **empty** chair / Jeffrey Deaver. Simon & Schuster, 2000. 411 p. Lincoln Rhyme mysteries

ISBN 0684855631

1. Environmental crimes 2. Innocence (Law) 3. Kidnapping victims 4. Forensic pathologists 5. People with quadriplegia 6. Women detectives 7. Bounty hunters 8. North Carolina 9. New York City 10. Mysteries

LC 00024220

Detective Lincoln Rhyme is in North Carolina for an experimental surgery when he is asked by local authorities to search for two young women who have been abducted.

"Deaver is the master of the plot twist, and readers will only drive themselves crazy trying to outguess him. Better just to enjoy the ride. A magnificent thriller." Booklist.

Deaver, Jeffery

Garden of beasts : a novel of Berlin 1936 / Jeffery Deaver. Simon & Schuster, 2004. 416 p.

ISBN 0743222016

1. Olympic Games (11th :, 1936 :, Berlin, Germany) 2. 1930s 3. Assassins 4. Nazis 5. Criminals 6. Assassins 7. German Americans 8. Americans in Germany 9. Impostors 10. Police -- Berlin, Germany 11. International intrigue 12. Deals 13. Berlin, Germany -- History -- 1918-1945 14. Germany -- History -- 1933-1945 15. Historical mysteries 16. Mysteries

LC 2004045206

Ian Fleming Steel Dagger Award, 2004.

Reputed for his vow to take only morally righteous assignments in 1936 New York City, a German-American hit man is forced by the government to pose as an Olympic contender and kill a member of Hitler's regime.

"Top Nazis, including Hitler, Himmler and Gring, make colorful cameos, but it's the smart, shaded-gray characterizations of the principals that anchor the exciting plot." Publishers Weekly.

Deaver, Jeffery

* The **never** game / Jeffery Deaver. G.P. Putnam's Sons, 2019. 400 p. Colter Shaw novels

ISBN 9780525535942

1. Trackers 2. Video games 3. Missing persons investigation 4. Video games industry and trade 5. Business -- Corrupt practices 6. Serial murder investigation 7. Serial murderers 8. Missing women 9. Silicon Valley, California 10. Cyber-thrillers 11. Thrillers and suspense

LC 2019003019

Searching for a missing woman in Silicon Valley, an expert tracker is pitted against dark elements in the billion-dollar gaming industry and a serial killer who stages scenes from his favorite game.

"Fans of twisty suspense that pushes the envelope of plausibility without inviting disbelief will be enthralled." Publishers Weekly.

Deaver, Jeffery

The **October** list / Jeffery Deaver. Grand Central Publishing, 2013. 208 p.

ISBN 9781455576647

1. Kidnapping 2. Ransom 3. Secrets 4. Venture capitalists 5. Personal assistants 6. Thrillers and suspense

LC 2013018524

After Gabriela McKenzie's daughter is kidnapped, her abductors demand two things: $400,000 in cash and a document known only as the October List.

Deaver, Jeffery

The **stone** monkey : a Lincoln Rhyme novel / Jeffery Deaver. Simon & Schuster, 2002. 424 p. Lincoln Rhyme mysteries

ISBN 0743221990

1. New York City. Police Department 2. Human smuggling 3. Undocumented immigrants 4. Serial murderers 5. Sabotage 6. Attempted murder 7. People with quadriplegia 8. Serial murder investigation 9. Women detectives 10. Forensic scientists 11. Police 12. Chinatown, New York City 13. New York City 14. Mysteries

Recruited to help the FBI and the INS perform the nearly impossible, Lincoln Rhyme and his partner, Amelia Sachs, manage to track down a cargo ship headed for New York City carrying two dozen illegal Chinese immigrants, as well as the notorious human smuggler and killer known as "the Ghost." But when the Ghost's capture goes disastrously wrong, Lincoln and Amelia find themselves in a horrifying race against time.

"The methodical, technical way in which the detectives conduct their search stands in stark contrast to the Ghost's paranoid, frenetic manner; thankfully, Rhyme's and Sachs' characters, first introduced in The Bone Collector (1996), are more well developed here than they were in earlier outings. The series' mass popularity, however, is certain to continue with or without improved characterization." Booklist.

Deb, Siddhartha, 1970-
The **point** of return : a novel / Siddhartha Deb. Ecco, 2003. 304 p.
ISBN 9780060501518
1. 1970s 2. 1980s 3. Young men 4. Teenage boys 5. Children of veterinarians 6. Veterinarians 7. Civil service workers 8. Public officials 9. Retirees 10. People who have had strokes 11. Fathers and sons 12. Bengali (South Asian people) in India 13. Alienation in men 14. Alienation (Social psychology) 15. Belonging 16. Generation gap 17. Memories 18. Ethics 19. Integrity 20. Honesty 21. Personal conduct 22. Fathers -- Death 23. Violence 24. Political corruption 25. Interethnic conflict 26. Culture conflict 27. Small town life 28. Villages 29. Rural families 30. Families 31. Family relationships 32. Postcolonialism 33. Ethnic groups 34. India -- History -- 20th century 35. India -- History -- 1947-1971 36. India -- Politics and government -- 1947-1971 37. India -- Politics and government -- 20th century 38. Northeast India -- Social conditions 39. Northeast India -- Interethnic relations 40. Assam, India (State) 41. Family sagas
LC 2002035300
A tale told in reverse chronological order is set against the political violence of the 1970s and 1980s in northeast India, during which the willful, curious Babu and his father, a doctor and enigmatic product of British colonial rule and Nehruvian nationalism, find themselves strangers living in the same home.

"To allow Dr. Dam to evolve through most of the book in a self-generated fog of benevolence and to shatter it in the last pages is a brillant stroke. . . . Storytelling of the kind Deb lavishes, for most of his book, on Dr. Dam is rare and precious and uplifting." New York Times Book Review.

Dee, Jonathan, 1962-
The **locals** : a novel / Jonathan Dee. Random House, 2017. 383 p.
ISBN 9780812993226
1. Small towns 2. Contractors 3. Billionaires 4. Working class families 5. Local government 6. Politicians 7. Class conflict 8. Inequality 9. Real estate investment 10. Global Financial Crisis, 2008-2009 11. Berkshire Hills, Massachusetts 12. New England 13. Mainstream fiction 14. Domestic fiction
LC 2016055310
A rural, working-class town in New England elects as its mayor a New York hedge fund millionaire who slowly transforms the community in his image, triggering unexpected changes in the life of a financially strapped contractor and his extended family.

"An absorbing panorama of small-town life and a study of democracy in miniature, with both the people and their polity facing real and particular contemporary pressures." Kirkus.

Dee, Jonathan, 1962-
The **privileges** : a novel / Jonathan Dee. Random House, 2010. 258 p.
ISBN 9781400068678
1. Rich people 2. Families 3. Success (Concept) 4. Husband and wife

5. Ambition in men 6. Impatience 7. Upper class 8. Manhattan, New York City 9. New York City 10. Mainstream fiction
LC 2009012900
Pulitzer Prize for Fiction finalist, 2011.
Becoming wealthier and more socially connected throughout their marriage, Adam and Cynthia Morey also find themselves increasingly subject to the temptations of excess and risky behavior while their children struggle with their own privilege-based challenges.

"The tale of a family scaling the heights of finance in New York City, a family born, nursed and prep-schooled on the fiscally rich milk of the hedge fund. The novel begins with the wedding of Cynthia and Adam-two glossy, self-absorbed 22-year-olds. . . . [They] go on to live the life of insider-trading zillionaires, obtaining the Manhattan penthouse, the villa in Anguilla, the halfhearted charitable trust. But where a lesser novelist might rely on sarcasm and satire, Dee opts for old-fashioned complexity. The wedding scene, a 32-page masterpiece, begins with a panoramic perspective that dips into the brains of all involved, from the wedding planner to her stoned son to Cynthia's jealous mother. His characters are stories in and of themselves, particularly Cynthia, a sexy savant who calls people skanks and pays off her estranged father's girlfriend to leave his deathbed. Yet Dee approaches her--and all his characters--with understanding." Time Out New York.

Dee, Jonathan, 1962-
A **thousand** pardons : a novel / Jonathan Dee. Random House, 2012. 256 p.
ISBN 9780812993219
1. Public relations 2. Divorced women 3. Business -- Corrupt practices 4. Businesspeople 5. Men/women relations 6. Political corruption 7. Family problems 8. Apologizing 9. Film actors and actresses 10. Dysfunctional families 11. Satirical fiction 12. Mainstream fiction
LC 2012018513
Forced back into the working world after her corporate lawyer husband's spectacular downfall, Helen discovers a talent for public relations and is tempted away from her dysfunctional family by her childhood crush, now a movie star who needs her professional assistance.

Dees, Cindy
Beyond the limit / Cindy Dees. Sourcebooks Casabkabca, 2019. 352 p. Valkyrie Ops
ISBN 9781492679097
1. Navy SEALs 2. Women soldiers 3. Determination in women 4. Women and the military 5. Military training camps 6. Men/women relations 7. Sexual attraction 8. Women and war 9. Terrorists 10. Romantic suspense
Navy SEAL Griffin Caldwell is not happy with his team's top-secret mission, training the first female SEALs. Griffin's determined to prove that that his trainee Sherri Tate - a former beauty queen no less - doesn't have what it takes to join the world's most elite warrior's club. Until he sees what she's capable of, and even this hard-nosed SEAL has to admit she's tough as nails. What he won't admit to is the attraction sizzling between them.

Defoe, Daniel, 1661?-1731
* **Moll** Flanders / Daniel Defoe ; with an introduction by John Mullan. Knopf, 1991. xxxiii, 338 p.
ISBN 9780679405481
1. Prostitutes -- Great Britain 2. Great Britain -- Social life and customs -- 17th century 3. Picaresque fiction 4. Classics
Original ed. published in 1722 under title: The fortunes and misfortunes of the famous Moll Flanders.

Moll is born in Newgate prison to a petty thief and is soon left at the mercy of whoever will take her in. From this unfavorable beginning, the lusty, resourceful Moll loves and bargains her way from rags to riches, from prostitution in the streets of London to prosperity on a Virginia plantation. Along the way, she offers a charmingly candid view of her life and times.

Defoe, Daniel, 1661?-1731

* **Robinson** Crusoe / Daniel Defoe. TOR, 1996. 340 p.
ISBN 0812557360
1. Survival (after airplane accidents, shipwrecks, etc) 2. Shipwrecks 3. Solitude 4. Castaways 5. Adventure stories 6. Survival stories 7. Classics

Originally published in 1719.

In 1659, after becoming the sole survivor of a shipwreck, Englishman Robinson Crusoe lives on a deserted island for more than twenty-eight years.

Deighton, Len, 1929-

Berlin game / Len Deighton. Knopf, 1984, c1983. 345 p. Bernard Samson novels
ISBN 0394534077
1. KGB 2. Moles (Spies) 3. Intelligence service -- Great Britain 4. Secret service -- Great Britain 5. International intrigue 6. Cold War 7. Informers 8. Defectors 9. Husband and wife 10. Moles (Spies) 11. Escapes 12. Rescues 13. Traitors 14. Defection 15. Berlin, Germany 16. London, England 17. Spy fiction

LC 83048104

Sequel: Mexico set.

Originally published: [London] : Hutchinson, 1983.

East is East and West is West - and they meet in Berlin. He was the best source the Department ever had, but now he desperately wanted to come over the Wall. 'Brahms Four' was certain a high-ranking mole was set to betray him. There was only one Englishman he trusted any more: someone from the old days. So they decided to put Bernard Samson back into the field after five sedentary years of flying a desk. The field is Berlin. The game is as baffling, treacherous and lethal as ever.

"This novel is a decent entertainment that rattles swiftly along to its payoff. Two things especially recommend ita devious contrivance of plot that has probably never been used before in an espionage novel; and the city of Berlin, mecca to spies and spy novelists. The second is the greater asset. Although the book is elaborately plotted, its best moments derive from the setting and from the force of this particular setting upon behavior and psychology." New York Times Book Review.

Deighton, Len, 1929-

London match / Len Deighton. A. A. Knopf, 1985. 407 p. Bernard Samson novels
ISBN 9780394549378
1. KGB 2. Intelligence service -- Great Britain 3. Defectors 4. Suspicion 5. Spies 6. Moles (Spies) 7. Traitors 8. International intrigue 9. Cold War 10. Defection 11. England 12. Spy fiction

LC 85040454

Sequel to: Mexico set.

British agent Bernard Samson discovers compelling evidence that there is yet another traitor at the highest level of British intelligence and finds himself in direct confrontation with this British KGB agent

"The strength of (this novel) is not in its plot but its characterization. . . . Mr. Deighton portrays each character of his large cast fully and sympathetically. However, the best character is the city of Berlin. It is a living presence, and in some of the descriptions one can almost hear the stones breathing." New York Times Book Review.

Dekker, Ted, 1962-

Black : the birth of evil / Ted Dekker. WestBow Press, 2004. 408 p. Books of history chronicles. Circle trilogy
ISBN 0849917905
1. Generals 2. Insomniacs 3. Men's dreams 4. Authors 5. Parallel universes 6. Virus diseases 7. Vaccines 8. Shooting 9. Chases 10. Reality 11. Dreams 12. Biological terrorism 13. Men/women relations 14. Faith (Christianity) 15. Options, alternatives, choices 16. Denver, Colorado 17. Christian fantasy 18. Christian suspense 19. Gateway fantasy

LC 2003020542

Series inferred from bk. 2 and bk. 3, spine.

"A trilogy - book one"--Spine.

Thomas Hunter narrowly survives a shooting attempt only to awaken in an alternate universe of green forests, a world to which he subsequently travels every time he goes to sleep.

Dekker, Ted, 1962-

The **girl** behind the red rope / Ted Dekker and Rachelle Dekker. Revell, 2019. 336 p.
ISBN 9780800736538
1. Cults 2. Questioning 3. Good and evil 4. Belief and doubt 5. Religious communities 6. End of the world 7. Angels 8. Strangers 9. Tennessee 10. Christian suspense

LC 2018057275

Grace lives in the hills of Tennessee in a religious community with strict rules meant to keep everyone safe, but her brother's questions and the appearance of outsiders for the first time in decades force her to rethink her truth.

"In this mind-bending inspirational thriller, father-daughter writing team Ted Dekker and Rachelle Dekker triumph in their faultlessly structured and deconstructed world of religious extremism." Booklist.

Dekker, Ted, 1962-

Red : the heroic rescue / Ted Dekker. WestBow Press, 2004. 381 p. Books of history chronicles. Circle trilogy
ISBN 0849917913
1. Generals 2. Biological terrorism 3. Virus diseases 4. Authors 5. Insomniacs 6. Men's dreams 7. Parallel universes 8. Vaccines 9. Shooting 10. Chases 11. Reality 12. Dreams 13. Men/women relations 14. Options, alternatives, choices 15. Faith (Christianity) 16. Christian suspense 17. Christian fantasy 18. Gateway fantasy

LC 2004004529

Thomas Hunter finds himself in a desperate quest to rescue two worlds from collapse. In one world, he's a battle-scarred general commanding an army of primitive warriors. In the other, he's racing to out wit sadistic terrorists intent on creating global chaos through an unstoppable virus.

Dekker, Ted, 1962-

White : the great pursuit / Ted Dekker. WestBow Press, 2004. xv, 370 p. Books of history chronicles. Circle trilogy
ISBN 0849917921
1. Authors 2. Chases 3. Virus diseases 4. Generals 5. Insomniacs 6. Men's dreams 7. Parallel universes 8. Vaccines 9. Shooting 10. Reality 11. Dreams 12. Biological terrorism 13. Men/women relations 14. Faith (Christianity) 15. Options, alternatives, choices 16. Christian fantasy 17. Christian suspense 18. Gateway fantasy

LC 2004010579

Time is running out in two realities. In one world, a lethal virus threatens to destroy all life as scientists and governments scramble to find an antidote. In the other, a forbidden love could forever destroy the ragtag resistance known as The Circle. Thomas can bridge both worlds, but he is quickly realizing that he may not be able to save either.

Dektar, Molly

The **Ash** family / Molly Dektar. Simon & Schuster, 2019. 352 p.

ISBN 9781501144868

1. Environmentalists 2. Communes 3. Counterculture 4. Cult leaders 5. Young women 6. Cult behavior 7. Farm life 8. Mountain life 9. Social groups 10. Great Smoky Mountains (NC and Tenn) 11. North Carolina 12. Literary fiction

Drawn by a mysterious stranger to a remote farming community that lives off the fertile mountain lands, a North Carolina teen is seduced by their high ideals before new friends begin to disappear.

Del Amo, Jean-Baptiste

* Animalia / Jean-Baptiste Del Amo ; translated by Frank Wynne. Grove Press, 2019, c2016. 410 p.

ISBN 9780802147578

1. 20th century 2. Farm life 3. Pigs 4. Rural families 5. Animal welfare 6. Pig farming 7. Animal culture 8. Farms 9. Rural life 10. Social change 11. Violence 12. Poverty 13. Pork industry and trade 14. France -- History -- 20th century 15. Translations -- French to English

Originally published: Paris : Gallimard, 2016.

Enduring a hardscrabble childhood on her family's farm in southwest France, a woman becomes the matriarch of a large industrial pig farm, where the casual brutality inflicted on animals reflects the horrors of the 20th century's wars and diseases.

Del Vecchio, John M., 1948-

The **13th** valley : a novel / John Del Vecchio. Bantam Books, 1982. 606 p.

ISBN 0553050222

1. Vietnam War, 1961-1975 2. War stories

LC 81070920

Includes end-paper maps.

"The novel is almost documentary in style and conveys to an extraordinary degree the very 'feel' of ground combat in I Corps. . . . Two elements in this well-written novel are especially praiseworthy: the depiction of the explosive relations between white and black GIs, and the moral corruption by war of a decent, sensitive young man. . . . Despite the presence of too much historical exposition, this is one of the finest novels to come out of the Vietnam War." Publishers Weekly.

Delaney, J. P.

Believe me : a novel / JP Delaney. Ballantine Books, 2018 334 p.

ISBN 9781101966310

1. Baudelaire, Charles, 1821-1867 2. Actors and actresses 3. British in the United States 4. Undercover operations 5. Women murder victims 6. College teachers 7. Poems 8. Men/women relations 9. New York City 10. Psychological suspense

LC 2018009618

An out-of-work British actress plays both sides of a murder investigation while working as a decoy for unfaithful husbands for a New York City divorce firm.

Delaney, J. P.

The **girl** before : a novel / JP Delaney. Ballantine Books, 2017. 336 p.

ISBN 9780425285046

1. Landlord and tenant 2. Control (Psychology) 3. Obsession 4. Architects 5. Widowers 6. Rules 7. Surveillance 8. Personal conduct 9. Young women 10. Loss (Psychology) 11. London, England 12. England 13. Psychological suspense 14. Parallel narratives

Seizing a unique opportunity to rent a one-of-a-kind house, a damaged young woman falls in love with the enigmatic architect who designed the residence, unaware that she is following in the footsteps of a doomed former tenant.

"This haunting Big Brotheresque novel will consume psychological thriller enthusiasts and keep them thinking long after the final page." Library Journal.

Delaney, J. P.

The **perfect** wife : a novel / JP Delaney. Ballantine Books, 2019 432 p.

ISBN 9781524796747

1. Androids 2. Deception 3. Accident victims 4. Married women 5. Married people and secrets 6. Manipulation by men 7. Marriage 8. Robotics 9. Psychological suspense 10. Science fiction

LC 2019007619

A woman miraculously restored to health by the innovations of her tech icon husband struggles with fragmented memories of a past that differs from her husband's accounts.

Delany, Samuel R.

Aye, and Gomorrah : stories / Samuel R. Delany. Vintage Books, 2003. 383 p.

ISBN 0375706712

1. Life on other planets 2. Aliens 3. Far future 4. Short stories 5. Science fiction 6. Fantasy fiction 7. African American fiction 8. Afrofuturism and Afrofantasy

LC 2002035854

Rev. ed. of Driftglass, with 4 new stories added.

An expanded edition of the classic anthology, this collection of science fiction and fantasy tales includes the Nebula and Hugo Award-winning "Time Considered as a Helix of Semi-Precious Stones."

Delany, Samuel R.

Dhalgren / Samuel R. Delany. Vintage Books, 2001, c1975. xiii, 801 p.

ISBN 0375706682

1. Post-apocalypse 2. Survival (after disaster) 3. Extinct cities -- United States 4. Adventurers -- United States 5. Identity (Psychology) 6. Bisexuality 7. Anarchism 8. Poets 9. Faith 10. Self 11. United States 12. Literary fiction 13. Apocalyptic fiction 14. African American fiction 15. Science fiction 16. Afrofuturism and Afrofantasy

LC 00067412

Originally published in the United States by Bantam Books in 1975- -T.p. verso.

Journeying to the central United States city of Bellona, where all have fled save madmen and criminals, a poet and adventurer known only as the Kid wonders at the strange portents that appear in the city's cloud-covered sky.

Delany, Samuel R.

Stars in my pocket like grains of sand / Samuel R. Delaney. Bantam Books, 1984. 368 p.

ISBN 9780553050530

1. Gender role 2. Science fiction 3. Afrofuturism and Afrofantasy 4. African American fiction

LC 84041580

Set against exotic landscapes and strange cultures, this saga concerns a great information war involving every world inhabited by humanity and two people whose relationship shakes civilization to its core.

"Reading this novel is like learning another language, only to realize how much it teaches you about your own, and how relative it makes your cultural assumptions." Publishers Weekly.

Delinsky, Barbara

Lake news : a novel / Barbara Delinsky. Simon & Schuster, 1999. 380 p.

ISBN 0684864320

1. Women singers -- New Hampshire 2. Journalists 3. Rumor 4. Malicious accusation 5. Journalism 6. Small town life -- New Hampshire 7. Journalists -- New Hampshire 8. Men/women relations 9. New Hampshire 10. Psychological fiction

Author's An Accidental Woman, 2002 shares the fictional Lake Henry setting.

After being unjustly accused by a reporter of having had an affair with a newly-appointed Cardinal, famous singer Lily Blake returns to her home town to recover and escape further attention from the press. There she forms an unlikely alliance with a big-city reporter whose career ended disastrously, sending him to the same town to edit the local newspaper.

"The author plots this satisfying, gentle romance with the sure hand of an expert, scattering shady pasts and dark secrets among some of her characters, while giving others destructive family patterns and difficult family dynamics to contend with." Publishers Weekly.

Dell, Kari Lynn

Fearless in Texas / Kari Lynn Dell. Sourcebooks Inc, 2018. 416 p. Texas rodeo

ISBN 9781492658115

1. Bar owners 2. Secrets 3. Interpersonal attraction 4. Men/women relations 5. Texas 6. Western romances 7. Contemporary romances

Refusing to make the same mistakes twice, Melanie Brookman, while trying to rebuild her life, helps smooth-talking rodeo man Wyatt Darrington save his failing bar, and as they work closely together, an undeniable attraction grows between them, forcing Melanie to make a difficult decision.

Dell, Kari Lynn

Mistletoe in Texas / Kari Lynn Dell. Sourcebooks Inc., 2018 448 p. Texas rodeo

ISBN 9781492658146

1. Bullfighters 2. Rodeos 3. Interpersonal attraction 4. Men/women relations 5. Wounds and injuries 6. Redemption 7. Lovers' reunions 8. Texas 9. Western romances 10. Contemporary romances

"Some superfluous plot points draw out the story a little longer than necessary, but the characters and world are so well crafted that readers won't mind the extra pages. Dell continues to be a standout in western romance." Booklist

Dell, Kari Lynn

* Reckless in Texas / Kari Lynn Dell. Sourcebooks Casablanca, 2016. 411 p. Texas rodeo

ISBN 9781492631941

1. Single mothers 2. Bullfighters 3. Rodeos 4. Interpersonal attraction 5. Men/women relations 6. Texas 7. Western romances 8. Contemporary romances

When single mom Violet Jacobs hires a hotshot rodeo bullfighter to take her family's rodeo production company into the big time, she discovers a man who is not afraid to let his guard down around her--and a man who is determined to create a life of his own--with her.

Demirtas, Selahattin, 1973-

Dawn : stories / Selahattin Demirtas ; translated by Amy Spangler and Kate Ferguson. SJP for Hogarth, 2019, c2017. 176 p.

ISBN 9780525576938

1. War and society 2. Distress (Psychology) 3. Women and war 4. Persistence 5. Turkey 6. Middle East 7. Syria 8. Aleppo, Syria 9. Political fiction 10. Short stories 11. Translations -- Turkish to English

LC 2018038558

Originally published in Turkish under title: Seher.
Originally published: Kızılay, Ankara : Dipnot Yayınları, 2017.

An extraordinary short-story collection from the imprisoned pro-Kurdish human-rights lawyer, activist and politician offers a powerful portrait of Turkey and the Middle East that shares insights into the violence, cultural beliefs and humanity shaping the region today.

Dennis-Benn, Nicole

Here comes the sun / Nicole Y. Dennis-Benn. Liveright, 2016. 349 p.

ISBN 9781631491764

1. 1990s 2. Island life 3. Prostitutes 4. Lesbians 5. Sisters 6. Self-fulfillment in women 7. Race relations 8. Social classes 9. Poverty 10. Consequences 11. Hotels 12. Communities 13. Family relationships 14. Women/women relations 15. Jamaica 16. Political fiction 17. LGBTQIA fiction 18. Coming-of-age stories

Lambda Literary Award for Lesbian Fiction, 2017

Working as a prostitute near the pristine beaches and turquoise seas of Jamaica to pay for a younger sister's education, Margot hopes that a new hotel that is reshaping her home will grant her financial independence and allow her to pursue a forbidden affair with another woman.

"Haunting and superbly crafted, this is a magical book from a writer of immense talent and intelligence." Kirkus.

Dennis-Benn, Nicole

* Patsy : a novel / Nicole Dennis-Benn. Liveright Publishing, 2019 400 p.

ISBN 9781631495632

1. Undocumented immigrants 2. Jamaican Americans 3. Unrequited love 4. Lesbians 5. Consequences 6. Childhood friends 7. Family relationships 8. Children with depression 9. Mothers and daughters 10. Women/women relations 11. Mother-deserted children 12. New York City 13. Jamaica 14. Brooklyn, New York City 15. Literary fiction 16. Psychological fiction

LC 2018055787

Receiving her long-coveted visa to America, Patsy leaves behind her family in Jamaica, only to discover that life as an undocumented immigrant is not what her best friend had described.

Deon, Natashia

Grace / Natashia Deon. Counterpoint, 2015. 404 p.
ISBN 9781619027206

1. 19th century 2. Slavery 3. Mothers and daughters 4. Violence against women 5. African American women -- Psychology 6. Women murder victims 7. Motherhood 8. Sexual violence 9. Slaves 10. Freed slaves 11. Flashbacks 12. Ghosts 13. Southern States -- History -- 19th century 14. Family sagas 15. Literary fiction 16. Historical fiction 17. Parallel narratives

BCALA Literary Award for First Novelist, 2017.

The dual stories of a mother, a runaway plantation slave and the child she never knew are woven through the historic events of the mid-19th century, including the Civil War and the Emancipation Proclamation.

"Den stays in control of her complex material, from its clever parallel structure to the women's psychological reactions to relentless tension." Booklist.

Depestre, Rene

Hadriana in all my dreams / Rene Depestre ; introduction by Edwidge Danticat. Akashic Books, 2017. 160 p.
ISBN 9781617755330

1. 1930s 2. Voodoo 3. Zombies 4. Race relations 5. Weddings 6. Creole women 7. Men/women relations 8. Haiti 9. Magical realism 10. Literary fiction 11. Translations -- French to English

Originally published in 1988 as Hadriana dans tous mes reves by Gallimard.

"Legendary Haitian author Depestre combines magic, fantasy, eroticism, and delirious humor to explore universal questions of race and sexuality."--Provided by the publisher.

"Depestre presents a rich and nuanced exploration of large and significant themes expertly couched in one fantastical, expertly translated tale." Booklist.

Dermansky, Marcy, 1969-

Very nice / Marcy Dermansky. Alfred A Knopf, 2019. 304 p.
ISBN 9780525655633

1. Creative writing 2. Rich people 3. Mothers and daughters 4. Love triangles 5. College teachers 6. Teacher-student relationships 7. Divorced women 8. Authors 9. Pakistanis in the United States 10. Lesbians 11. Housesitting 12. Sexuality 13. Black humor

A darkly humorous tale of privilege, race and bad behavior find a wealthy Connecticut divorcé and her college-age daughter becoming unlikely rivals in a romantic triangle involving the latter's creative writing professor.

Desai, Anita, 1937-

* **Clear** light of day / Anita Desai. Harper and Row, 1980. 183 p.
ISBN 9780060109844

1. Women 2. Middle class 3. Sisters 4. Delhi 5. India -- Social life and customs 6. India 7. Literary fiction

LC 80007603

Shortlisted for the Booker-McConnell Prize, 1980.

Explores the traumatic history of India after the departure of the British in a story of an estranged Hindu family in Old Delhi and their complex relationships.

"This work does what only the best novels can do: it totally submerges us. It takes us so deeply into another world that we almost fear we won't be able to climb out again." New York Times Book Review.

Desai, Anita, 1937-

* **Fire** on the mountain / Anita Desai. Harper & Row, 1977. 145 p.
ISBN 9780060110666

1. Great-grandmothers 2. Women 3. Mothers and daughters 4. India 5. Literary fiction

LC 77003788

Nanda Kaul, a woman remote in her self-imposed solitude among the Simla hills of India, her strange and silent great-granddaughter, and the broken old woman who is her only friend are touched in varying ways by the violence of living

"This is a delicate wisp of a story that nevertheless possesses great tensile strength." Booklist.

Desai, Kiran, 1971-

The **inheritance** of loss / Kiran Desai. Atlantic Monthly Press, 2006. 336 p.
ISBN 0871139294

1. 1980s 2. Grandfather and granddaughter 3. Insurgency 4. Interethnic relations 5. Nationalism 6. Modernization (Social sciences) 7. Class conflict 8. Hope 9. Judges -- Retirement 10. East Indians in the United States 11. Teenage romance 12. Social change 13. India -- Social life and customs -- 20th century 14. New York City -- Social life and customs -- 20th century 15. Himalaya Mountains region 16. Political fiction 17. Literary fiction

LC 2005052416

ALA Notable Book, 2007.
Booker Prize, 2006.
National Book Critics Circle Award for Fiction, 2006.
Shortlisted for The Orange Prize for Fiction, 2007

In a crumbling house in the remote northeastern Himalayas, an embittered, elderly judge finds his peaceful retirement turned upside down by the arrival of his orphaned granddaughter, Sai.

"This novel is set in the nineteen-eighties in the northeast corner of India, where the borders of several Himalayan states--Bhutan and Sikkim, Nepal and Tibet--meet. At the head of the novels teeming cast is Jemubhai Patel, a Cambridge-educated judge who has retired from serving a country he finds too messy for justice. He lives in an isolated house with his cook, his orphaned seventeen-year-old granddaughter, and a red setter, whose company Jemubhai prefers to that of human beings. The tranquillity of his existence is contrasted with the life of the cook's son, working in grimy Manhattan restaurants, and with his granddaughter's affair with a Nepali tutor involved in an insurgency that irrevocably alters Jemubhai's life. Briskly paced and sumptuously written, the novel ponders questions of nationhood, modernity, and class, in ways both moving and revelatory." The New Yorker.

Deutermann, Peter T., 1941-

The **Iceman** / P.T. Deutermann. St. Martin's Press, 2018. 304 p.
ISBN 9781250181374

1. Second World War era (1939-1945) 2. World War II -- Naval operations 3. Risk 4. Submarines 5. Armed Forces -- Officers 6. Sailors 7. Memories 8. Pacific Area 9. Historical thrillers

LC 2018003988

A decorated submarine commander haunted by a violent youth unsettles his crew with the incrementally risky measures he takes to sink Japanese ships in the western Pacific during World War II.

"Deutermann packs authentic information on submarine tactics and naval warfare in between the taut underwater action. Fans of old-school submarine novels like Run Silent, Run Deep will be rewarded." Publishers Weekly.

Deutermann, Peter T., 1941-

The **nugget** : a novel / P. T. Deutermann. St Martins Press, 2019. 320 p.

ISBN 9781250205889

1. Second World War era (1939-1945) 2. World War II 3. Fighter pilots 4. Prisoners of war 5. Search and rescue operations 6. Friends' death 7. Revenge 8. Determination in men 9. Pearl Harbor, Attack on, 1941 10. Historical thrillers

LC 2019021340

Compelled by the Pearl Harbor attack to serve in some of World War II's most dangerous air battles, a young naval aviator leads a mission to rescue prisoners from a secluded POW camp.

"Deutermann knows how to reveal navy life to even the casual reader. ... [R]eaders who enjoy WWII stories, especially those involving the air war, will be entranced by Steele's story, which is told in a gripping first-person narrative that extends from the Battle of Midway to a mission in which Steele is charged with rescuing POWs from a Japanese internment camp and, finally, to his appearance in an American military court." Booklist.

Deutermann, Peter T., 1941-

Pacific glory : a novel / Peter T. Deutermann. St. Martin's Press, 2011. 336 p.

ISBN 9780312599447

1. Second World War era (1939-1945) 2. Love triangles 3. Pilots 4. Nurses 5. Widows 6. Soldiers 7. World War II 8. Alcoholic men 9. Savo Island, Battle of, 1942 10. Midway, Battle of, 1942 11. Historical fiction 12. War stories

W. Y. Boyd Literary Award, 2012.

Their military careers forever transformed by the attack on Pearl Harbor, Navy nurse Glory grieves for the loss of her husband while ship officer Marsh battles his way toward Leyte Gulf and fighter pilot Mick struggles with the drinking problem for which he was grounded.

Dev, Sonali

* A **Bollywood** affair / Sonali Dev. Kensington Books, 2014. viii, 288 p.

ISBN 9781617730139

1. Arranged marriage 2. East Indians in the United States 3. Film producers and directors 4. Film industry and trade 5. Villages 6. Divorce 7. Men/women relations 8. Interpersonal attraction 9. Michigan 10. India 11. Multicultural romances 12. Contemporary romances

LC 2015296688

RUSA Reading List, 2015.

Coming to America on a scholarship, Mili Rathod, who has been bound by marriage since she was four years old to a man she has never met, is drawn into the world of her husband's playboy filmmaker brother who has been sent across the world to keep an eye on her.

"Dev's heartfelt debut novel is rich in scenes and images illuminating Indian culture, leaving readers with a greater understanding and appreciation of Indian traditions while beautifully capturing the struggle between familial duty and self-discovery." Booklist.

Dev, Sonali

The **Bollywood** bride / Sonali Dev. Kensington, 2015. 352 p.

ISBN 9781617730153

1. Actors and actresses 2. First loves 3. East Indian Americans 4. Second chances 5. Lovers' reunions 6. Family secrets 7. Mental illness 8. Film industry and trade 9. Men/women relations 10. Interpersonal attraction 11. Chicago, Illinois 12. India 13. Multicultural romances 14. Contemporary romances

Traveling home to Chicago to attend a family wedding and ride out a scandal, Bollywood star Ria Parkar reunites with Vikram Jathar, whose heart she broke to pursue her career.

Dev, Sonali

A **distant** heart / Sonali Dev. Kensington Books, 2017. 302 p.

ISBN 9781496705761

1. Interclass romance 2. Sick persons 3. Social isolation 4. Romantic love 5. Social classes 6. Men/women relations 7. Interpersonal attraction 8. Mumbai, India -- Social life and customs 9. India 10. Contemporary romances 11. Multicultural romances

Stricken with a rare illness, Indian woman of privilege Kimaya grows up isolated in an ivory tower, until she builds a relationship with window washer Rahul Savant, whom she inspires to join the police force; but when Rahul uncovers a gang-run organ ring at the same time Kimaya gets a chance at a life-changing heart transplant, their world gets turned upside down.

"Thrilling action sequences and a complex, weighty romance propel this smart, sensitive story. A natural wordsmith, Dev dives into the psyches of disparate characters with voice-driven prose that includes both chilling insights and quirky humor. She also paints a vivid picture of modern Mumbai, from Kimis pristine mansion to Rahuls overcrowded chawl (tenement), and the many personalities who inhabit it. Subplots and characters overlap in Dev's novels, so even though this is a stand-alone, encourage patrons to read her earlier novels for an even-more-enriching experience. This poignant, sensual, and exciting tale captures a range of emotions and conflicts." Booklist.

Dev, Sonali

* **Pride,** prejudice, and other flavors : a novel / Sonali Dev. William Morrow Paperbacks, 2019. 368 p. The Rajes

ISBN 9780062839053

1. East Indian Americans 2. Immigrant families 3. Interracial dating 4. Classism 5. Racism 6. Prejudice 7. Women neurosurgeons 8. Cooks 9. Multiracial men 10. Overachievers 11. Royal houses 12. Home (Concept) 13. Brothers and sisters 14. San Francisco, California 15. Contemporary romances 16. Multicultural romances 17. Adaptations, retellings, and spin-offs

LC 2019009606

A neurosurgeon from a politically ambitious immigrant family clashes with a talented dessert chef who would prove he is more than his pedigree.

"A workaholic, socially inept Indian-American brain surgeon is caught off guard by her attraction to a Rwandan/Anglo-Indian chef in this rewrite of Pride and Prejudice." Kirkus.

Deveraux, Jude

Someone to love / Jude Deveraux. Atria Books, 2007. 320 p. Montgomery and Taggert clans series

ISBN 9780743437165

1. Grief in men 2. Fiances -- Death 3. Men/women relations 4. Haunted houses 5. Women war correspondents 6. Loss (Psychology) 7. Suicide 8. Ghosts 9. Supernatural 10. Paranormal phenomena 11. England -- History 12. Margate, England 13. Contemporary romances

LC 2006101700

Still grieving three years after his fiancee's mysterious suicide, Jace Montgomery discovers a clue about her death that leads him to purchase an English fortress, where he encounters a headstrong ghost who died under similar circumstances.

"Deveraux never raises the pitch very high, and harmonizes the whole satisfactorily." Publishers Weekly.

Deveraux, Jude

A **willing** murder / Jude Deveraux. Mira Books, 2018. 384 p. Medlar mysteries

ISBN 9780778369295

1. Senior women 2. Aunt and niece 3. Amateur detectives 4. Boarders 5. Renovation (Architecture) 6. Dead 7. Women authors 8. Hometowns 9. Investigations 10. Secrets 11. Small town life 12. Florida 13. Mysteries

The discovery of two bodies in a quiet Florida community exposes old secrets and deadly grudges, prompting a group of improbable friends to try to uncover the truth.

Devon, Cat

Sleeping with the entity / Cat Devon. St. Martin's Press, 2013. 336 p. Entity novels

ISBN 9780312591465

1. Vampires 2. Women bakers 3. Paranormal phenomena 4. Cupcakes 5. Neighborhoods 6. Interpersonal attraction 7. Men/women relations 8. Chicago, Illinois 9. Paranormal romances

When prospective cupcake-shop owner Daniella Delaney threatens to breathe new life into vampire Nick St. George's intentionally barren district of Chicago, the tension between them just may turn into a deep burning passion.

Dexter, Colin

The **daughters** of Cain / Colin Dexter. Crown Publishers, 1995. 295 p. Inspector Morse mysteries

ISBN 9780517700679

1. College teachers 2. Household employees 3. Murder investigation 4. Prostitutes 5. Police 6. Oxford, England 7. England 8. Mysteries 9. Police procedurals

Chief Inspector Morse and Detective Sergeant Lewis probe the baffling murder of Dr. Felix McClure, late of Wolsey College, Oxford, and follow a trail that leads to Edward Brooks, who himself disappears following a museum theft.

"Mr. Dexter is a superb technician who torments the reader with logistical details that contradict every previously established point in his puzzle. Red herrings are a specialty. But the canny author also strews the path with literary quotations to think on, polysyllabic words to look up and characters whose lives are so complicated they turn into richly distracting mini-dramas." New York Times Book Review.

Dexter, Colin

The **remorseful** day / Colin Dexter. Crown Publishers, 1999. 363 p. Inspector Morse mysteries

ISBN 0609606220

1. Cold cases (Criminal investigation) 2. Women murder victims 3. Murder investigation 4. Murder -- Cotswold, England 5. Police 6. Lower Swinstead, England 7. Oxford, England 8. England 9. Mysteries 10. Police procedurals

The final Inspector Morse novel.

An unsolved murder case yields new clues that could implicate Inspector Morse even as he seeks to solve the case

"This finale to a grand series presents a moving elegy to one of mystery fiction's most celebrated and popular characters. . . . Dexter has fashioned another brilliantly intricate puzzle, one of his finest, with the valedictory tone of the narrative lending a particularly rich texture to the tale. Morse leaves us on the highest possible note, perfectly pitched." Publishers Weekly.

Dexter, Colin

The **way** through the woods / Colin Dexter. Crown, 1993, c1992. 296 p. Inspector Morse mysteries

ISBN 9780517594445

1. Missing persons 2. Vacations 3. Newspapers 4. Missing persons investigation 5. Police 6. Oxford, England 7. England 8. Mysteries 9. Police procedurals

LC 92040762

Originally published: London : Macmillan, 1992.

Gold Dagger Award for Best Crime Novel of the Year, 1992.

When a young woman mysteriously vanishes in North Oxford, Chief Inspector Morse unsuccessfully sets out to prove that it is a case of murder, until the arrival of an anonymous letter containing a cryptic poem provides a bizarre clue.

"To say that the investigation is tricky is only to hint at the technical density of the plot, which, once all the tantalizing enigmas have been packed up, hinges on the most basic human frailties. Dazzling." New York Times Book Review.

Dexter, Pete, 1943-

* **Deadwood** / Pete Dexter. Random House, 1986. 365 p.

ISBN 9780394536699

1. Hickok, Wild Bill, 1837-1876 2. Calamity Jane, 1852-1903 3. 19th century 4. Cowboys 5. Gunfighters 6. Prostitutes 7. Fate and fatalism 8. The West (United States) -- History -- 19th century 9. Deadwood, South Dakota -- History -- 19th century 10. Westerns

LC 85019635

This book was released as a movie entitled Wild Bill.

When Wild Bill Hickok takes a wagon train of prostitutes through Deadwood, a pimp hires someone to kill him.

"This novel is unpredictable, hyperbolic and, page after page, uproarious; a joshing book written in high spirits and a raw appreciation for the past." New York Times Book Review.

Dexter, Pete, 1943-

Paris Trout / Pete Dexter Random House, 1988. 306 p.

ISBN 9780394563701

1. 1940s 2. Murder 3. Racism 4. Married people 5. Race relations 6. Psychopaths 7. Mental illness 8. Bribery 9. Small towns 10. Georgia -- Race relations 11. Historical fiction 12. Literary fiction

LC 87043314

National Book Award for Fiction, 1988.

National Book Critics Circle Award for Fiction finalist, 1988

In Cotton Point, Georgia, the murder of a Black girl by a white man, Paris Trout, becomes the catalyst in a tale of obsession, racism, and murder that centers on Trout, an intimidating, unremorseful bully who warps the attitudes of everyone he touches.

"Mr. Dexter has created a character whose racism is a blunt, unregenerate fact, as primitive and willful as an earthquake or a rainstorm--and just as sealed off from argument, examination or questions of mercy. What the town's polite society takes care to disguise in Sunday-go-to-meeting euphemisms, Paris sets in defiant, ugly relief; he makes it easy for them to believe they are innocent of racism." New York Times Book Review.

Dexter, Pete, 1943-

Spooner / Pete Dexter. Grand Central Pub., 2009. 480 p.

ISBN 9780446540728

1. Fathers and sons 2. Stepfathers 3. Bad luck 4. Twins 5. Grief 6. Journalists 7. Mischief 8. Philadelphia, Pennsylvania 9. Washington (State) 10. Psychological fiction 11. Pacific Northwest fiction

LC 2009006087

ALA Notable Book, 2010.

Losing his father shortly after birth, Warren Spooner endures a troubled childhood and even more troubled young adulthood that is marked by his dishonorably discharged stepfather, whose inexhaustible patience is tested by the difficult Warren.

"The title character is one Warren Spooner, a kid dogged by the fact that his mother's favorite child, Spooner's twin brother, died at birth. Spooner's dad dies soon afterward. Into the family's life arrives Ottosson, [a] disgraced young naval officer turned schoolteacher. He is a man of great virtues: smart, tough, capable and wreathed in infinite patience. He will need the latter quality in spades to deal with his troubled stepson. . . . Despite the autobiographical elements in Spooner, the book lacks a narrative arc that permits a complete picture of the protagonist's life. This is not cited as a fault. It is a function of how this picaresque novel serves as a work of memory, real or imagined." Denver Post.

Diachenko, Serhii, 1945-

Vita nostra / Sergiy Dyachenko and Maryna Shyrshova-Dyachenko ; translated from the Russian by Julia Meitov Hersey. HarperCollins, 2018, c2007. 416 p.

ISBN 9780062694591

1. Magic 2. Schools 3. Teenage girls 4. Coercion 5. Obedience 6. Control (Psychology) 7. Sixteen-year-old girls 8. Transformations (Magic) 9. Coming-of-age stories 10. Fantasy fiction 11. Translations -- Russian to English

Originally published in Ukraine, 2007.

A young girl falls under the spell of a strange, sinister man who asks her to perform odd tasks before convincing her to enroll in a strange and magical school called The Institute of Special Technologies.

Diamant, Anita

The **Boston** girl : a novel / Anita Diamant. Scribner, 2015. 256 p.

ISBN 9781439199350

1. 20th century 2. Jewish women 3. Reminiscing in old age 4. Children of immigrants 5. Gender role 6. Female friendship 7. Feminism 8. Octogenarians 9. Men/women relations 10. Family relationships 11. Boston, Massachusetts 12. Historical fiction

LC 2014019284

Amelia Bloomer List, 2016

Recounting the story of her life to her granddaughter, octogenarian Addie describes how she was raised in early-twentieth-century America by Jewish immigrant parents in a teeming multicultural neighborhood.

Diamant, Anita

* The **red** tent / Anita Diamant. St.Martin's Press, 1997. 321 p.

ISBN 0312169787

1. Dinah, (Biblical figure) 2. Bible. Genesis 3. Women in the Bible 4. Matriarchy 5. Gender role 6. Mothers and daughters 7. Betrayal 8. Families 9. Men/women relations 10. Courage in women 11. Bible novels 12. Historical fiction

LC 9716825

Book Sense Book of the Year Adult Fiction, 2001.

The story of Dinah, a tragic character from the Bible whose great love, a prince, is killed by her brother, leaving her alone and pregnant. The novel traces her life from childhood to death, in the process examining sexual and religious practices of the day, and what it meant to be a woman.

"Diamant's fiction debut links the passions of the early Israelites to the ongoing traditions of modern Jews, while the red tent of her title (where women retreat for menstruation, childbirth and illness) becomes a resonant symbol of womanly strength, love and wisdom. Despite a few unprofitable digressions, Diamant succeeds admirably in depicting the lives of women in the age that engendered our civilization and our most enduring values." Publishers Weekly.

Diamond, De'nesha

Boss divas / De'nesha Diamond. Dafina, 2014. 320 p. Divas (De'nesha Diamond)

ISBN 9780758292513

1. Secrets 2. African American women 3. Female gangs 4. Inner city 5. Street life 6. Gangs 7. Competition 8. Revenge 9. Drug dealers 10. Memphis, Tennessee 11. Urban fiction 12. African American fiction

The most lethal ride-or-die women in Memphis now run their gangs and the streets. But the aftermath of an all-out war means merciless new enemies, time-bomb secrets... and one chance to take it all.... Vice Lord chief Lucifer goes after the upstart Crippettes gang one by one--but locking down her power will put everything she lives to protect at risk. Ta'Shara straps on her training wheels to prove she can ride with the best of the Flowers--but does this good-girl-gone-bad really have what it takes to survive? And as Queen G LeShelle viciously body-drops to keep her bloody secrets buried, her husband Python may be the one person that can put her in check. Now these boss divas will go head-to-head for complete domination--because in the end only one can rule.

Diamond, De'nesha

Gangsta divas / De'nesha Diamond. Dafina, 2012. 320 p. Divas (De'nesha Diamond)

ISBN 9780758247599

1. Revenge 2. African American women 3. Female gangs 4. Inner city 5. Street life 6. Gangs 7. Competition 8. Drug dealers 9. Memphis, Tennessee 10. Urban fiction 11. African American fiction

The deadliest ride-or-die chicks in Memphis have a new rival. Meet the Cripettes. They're the realest of the real--raging war with both the Queen Gs and the Flowers. But when all's said and done, only one gang can reign supreme. Cover.

Diamond, De'nesha

King divas / De'nesha Diamond. Kensington Books., 2015. 320 p. Divas (De'nesha Diamond)

ISBN 9780758292551

1. Secrets 2. African American women 3. Female gangs 4. Inner city 5. Street life 6. Gangs 7. Competition 8. Revenge 9. Drug dealers 10. Memphis, Tennessee 11. Urban fiction 12. African American fiction

Street Lit Book Award Medal: Adult Fiction, 2016.

While Python resolves to negotiate a peace meeting with his brother in the aftermath of their aunt's brutal murder, Ta'Shara barely saves Lucifer's life from a rival gang and worries that Lucifer's injuries will cause her to lose her child.

Diamond, De'nesha

Street divas / De'nesha Diamond. Dafina, 2011. 343 p. Divas (De'nesha Diamond)

ISBN 9780758247575

1. Revenge 2. African American women 3. Female gangs 4. Inner city 5. Street life 6. Competition 7. Drug dealers 8. Memphis, Tennessee 9. Urban fiction 10. African American fiction

Sisters LaShelle and Ta'Shara fall out over Ta'Shara's involvement with Profit, a gangster who runs with the Vice Lords, as Python remains the main hustler the Memphis, Tennessee girls truly want to be with.

Diamond, Elizabeth

An **accidental** light / Elizabeth Diamond. Other Press, 2009. 288 p.

ISBN 9781590513019

1. Life change events 2. Police 3. Daughters -- Death 4. Tragedy 5. Grief in families 6. Redemption 7. Forgiveness 8. Ghosts 9. London (England) 10. Mainstream fiction

LC 2008019397

On a quiet road just outside London, in the blue half-light of dusk, a car accident changes the lives of two families. Jack Philips is a happily married policeman with two small daughters, but the accident forces him to reassess everything he loves - and to confront long-buried secrets. For Lisa Jenkins, the devastation seems almost unbearable.

Diaz, Hernan, 1973-

* **In** the distance / Hernan Diaz. Coffee House Press, 2017. 256 p.

ISBN 9781566894883

1. 19th century 2. American Westward Expansion (1803-1899) 3. Immigrants 4. Frontier and pioneer life 5. Outlaws 6. Swedes in the United States 7. Desert survival 8. Brothers 9. Teenage boys and horses 10. Interpersonal relations 11. Voyages and travels 12. The West (United States) 13. Adventure stories 14. Westerns

LC 2017000413

William Saroyan International Prize for Writing, Fiction category, 2018.

Pen/Faulkner Award Finalist, 2018.

Pulitzer Prize for Fiction finalist, 2018.

After a young Swedish boy finds himself alone in California, he travels east to find his brother, having a series of adventures and encountering naturalists, criminals, religious fanatics, Indians, and lawmen along the way.

"Stitched through with humor, this often-unpredictable novel will keep readers running along with every step of Hakans odd escapades." Booklist.

Diaz, Junot, 1968-

The **brief** wondrous life of Oscar Wao / Junot Diaz. Riverhead Books, 2007. 336 p.

ISBN 9781594489587

1. Misfits (Persons) 2. Family curses 3. Eccentrics and eccentricities 4. Loss (Psychology) 5. Persistence 6. Family relationships 7. Social acceptance 8. Interpersonal relations 9. Men/women relations 10. Ghettoes, Hispanic American 11. Dominican Americans 12. Hispanic Americans 13. New Jersey 14. Literary fiction

LC 2007017251

Hurston/Wright Legacy Award: Fiction, 2008.

Massachusetts Book Awards, Fiction Award, 2008.

National Book Critics Circle Award for Fiction, 2007.

Pulitzer Prize for Fiction, 2008.

Shortlisted for the International IMPAC Dublin Literary Award, 2009

Living with an old-world mother and rebellious sister, an urban New Jersey misfit dreams of becoming the next J. R. R. Tolkien and believes that a long-standing family curse is thwarting his efforts to find love and happiness.

"In this novel Diaz presents a slice of the vast history of Santo Domingo and the intricate past and present of a doomed family. . . . Diaz weaves the stories of Lola, his troubled but supportive sister, and Belicia, his hardened mother, along with various other family members, to portray a colorful and complex portrait of mad love, old-world superstition, and the continual strivings of a diaspora." Christian Science Monitor.

Diaz, Junot, 1968-

* **This** is how you lose her / Junot Diaz. Riverhead Books, 2012. 240 p.

ISBN 9781594487361

1. Social behavior 2. Loss (Psychology) 3. Intimacy (Psychology) 4. Love 5. Companionship 6. Social isolation 7. Human behavior 8. Family relationships 9. Interpersonal relations 10. United States -- Social life and customs -- 21st century 11. Literary fiction 12. Short stories

ALA Notable Book, 2013

Andrew Carnegie Medal for Excellence in Fiction finalist, 2013.

National Book Award for Fiction finalist, 2012

A collection of stories that explores the heartbreak and radiance of love as it is shaped by passion, betrayal and the echoes of intimacy.

Dibdin, Michael

Ratking / Michael Dibdin. Bantam Books, 1989. 266 p. Aurelio Zen mysteries

ISBN 9780553053371

1. Kidnapping 2. Political corruption 3. Families 4. Detectives 5. Police 6. Italy 7. Perugia, Italy 8. Police procedurals 9. Mysteries

LC 88047832

The TV miniseries Zen is based on the books Vendetta, Cabal, and Ratking.

Gold Dagger Award for Best Crime Novel of the Year, 1988.

Police Commissioner Aurelio Zen of Rome becomes involved in a kidnapping case that quickly plummets into a case of murder and leads Zen into dangerous and shocking territory in the ancient city.

Dick, Philip K.

* **Do** androids dream of electric sheep? / Philip K. Dick. Ballantine Books, 1996, c1968. 244 p.

ISBN 0345404475

1. Androids 2. Bounty hunters 3. Post-apocalypse 4. Dystopias 5. Detectives 6. Near future 7. Los Angeles, California 8. Cyberpunk 9. Science fiction

LC 9696117

"In a future where technological sophistication has made the ersatz virtually indistinguishable from the real, the hero is a bounty hunter who must track down and eliminate androids passing for human. . . . A key novel in Dick's canon." Anatomy of Wonder, 5th edition.

Dick, Philip K.

* **The man** in the high castle / Philip K. Dick. Vintage Books, 1992, c1962. 259 p.

ISBN 9780679740674

1. 1960s 2. World War II 3. Spies 4. International intrigue 5. Religion 6. Meaning (Psychology) 7. Alternative histories 8. Science fiction

LC 91050895 //r92

First published: New York: Putnam, 1962.

Hugo Award for Best Novel, 1963.

After the defeat of the Allies during World War II, the United States is divided up and ruled by the Axis powers.

"An alternate history in which Germany and Japan won World War II and partitioned the U.S. except for the Rocky Mountain States, which were left in a kind of political limbo. Faction-ridden Nazism oppressively rules the eastern U.S. In the west, the Japanese overlords are reconciling Oriental and American cultural values. . . . This is Dick's most important early book." Anatomy of Wonder, 5th edition.

Dick, Philip K.

The **minority** report / Philip K. Dick. Pantheon Books, 2002, c1956. 103 p.

ISBN 9780375421877

1. Crime prevention 2. Precognition 3. Police 4. New York City 5. Science fiction

LC 2002072313

Originally published as: The little black box.

Commissioner John Anderton's clever use of the Precrime System, which uses "precogs," people with the ability to see into the future, to identify criminals before they can do any harm, is confronted with a serious glitch when his precogs identify Anderton himself as the next criminal and he must race against time to save himself.

"Police Commissioner John Anderton finds himself at the mercy of his own crime-prevention system when the prescient precogs he's hired to stop crime before it starts peg him as a soon-to-be murderer." Publishers Weekly.

Dickens, Charles, 1812-1870

* **Bleak** House / Charles Dickens ; with the original illustrations by Phiz. Knopf, 1991. xlix, 891 p.

ISBN 9780679405689

1. 19th century 2. Judicial system -- Great Britain 3. Orphans 4. Social classes 5. Lawyers 6. Detectives 7. England -- Social life and customs -- 19th century 8. England -- Social conditions -- 19th century 9. Satirical fiction 10. Classics

Originally published in 1853.

The English equity court of the nineteenth century is satirized in Dicken's tale about the suit of Jarndyce vs. Jarndyce.

Dickens, Charles, 1812-1870

* A **Christmas** carol / Charles Dickens ; with illustrations by Arthur Rackham. A.A. Knopf, 1994. 155 p.

ISBN 9780679436393

1. Grouches 2. Miserliness 3. Transformations, Personal 4. Ghosts 5. Christmas 6. Greed in men 7. London, England -- Social life and customs -- 19th century 8. Christmas stories 9. Classics

Through the intervention of four ghosts, Ebenezer Scrooge is shown the spirit of Christmas.

Dickens, Charles, 1812-1870

* **David** Copperfield / Charles Dickens. Dover Publications, 2004, c1850. 719 p.

ISBN 0486436659

1. 19th century 2. Child labor 3. Orphans 4. Poor boys -- Employment 5. Young men 6. Stepfathers 7. London, England -- History -- 19th century 8. England -- History -- 19th century 9. Coming-of-age stories 10. Classics

LC 43018839

First published: 1850.

Originally published under title: The personal history of David Copperfield. London : Bradbury and Evans, 1850.

The story of an abandoned waif who discovers life and love in an indifferent world, this classic tale of childhood is populated with a cast of eccentrics, innocents, and villains who number among the author's greatest creation.

Dickens, Charles, 1812-1870

Dombey and Son / Charles Dickens ; edited, with an introduction and notes by Andrew Sanders. Penguin Classics, 2002, c1848. 1040 p.

ISBN 9780140435467

1. 19th century 2. Family businesses 3. Fathers and daughters 4. Family relationships 5. Loss (Psychology) 6. Grief in men 7. Fathers and sons 8. Family problems 9. Businesspeople 10. London, England -- Social life and customs -- 19th century 11. England -- Social life and customs -- 19th century 12. Classics 13. Literary fiction

LC 81016959

Includes introduction, explanatory notes, and period illustrations. "Complete and unabridged".

This edition published 1995 by Wordsworth Editions, illustrations, introduction and notes added 2002.

Originally published 1848 by Bradbury and Evans.

In this carefully crafted novel, Dickens reveals the complexity of London society in the enterprising 1840s as he takes the listener into the business firm and home of one of its most representative patriarchs, Paul Dombey. A sensitive family drama unfolds between this stern father, his two children and aloof wife in which time and fateful events bring a slow, inexorable pressure to bear upon the hearts of all. In Paul Dombey we witness the force of social and personal arrogance wrestling with his own stubborn, but not unredeemable, heart.

Dickens, Charles, 1812-1870

* **Great** expectations / Charles Dickens ; illustrated by F.W. Pailthrope with an introduction by Michael Slater. Knopf, 1992, c1861. xxxiv, 469 p.

ISBN 0679405798

1. 19th century 2. Orphans 3. Revenge 4. Classism 5. Victoriana 6. Poor children 7. Young men 8. Men/women relations 9. Former convicts 10. Benefactors 11. Senior women 12. London, England -- History -- 19th century 13. London, England -- Social conditions -- 19th century 14. London, England -- Social life and customs -- 19th century 15. Coming-of-age stories 16. Literary fiction 17. Classics

LC 9153219

Originally published: Philadelphia : T. B. Peterson & brothers, 1861.

The orphan, Pip, and the convict, Magwitch, the beautiful Estella, and her guardian, the embittered and vengeful Miss Havisham, the ambitious lawyer, Mr. Jaggers -- all have a part to play in the mystery.

Dickens, Charles, 1812-1870

Little Dorrit / Charles Dickens. Knopf, 1992, c1855. xxxvii, 836 p.

ISBN 0679417257

1. Children of prisoners 2. Prisons 3. Debtor and creditor 4. Poverty 5. Young women 6. Inheritance and succession 7. Fathers and daughters 8. Civil service workers 9. England -- Social life and customs -- 19th century 10. London, England -- History -- 19th century 11. England -- Social conditions -- 19th century 12. England -- History -- 19th century 13. Satirical fiction 14. Classics

LC 92052919

Originally published: London : Bradbury & Evans, 1855.

Little Dorrit grows up in Marshalsea prison, where her father is confined for his debts, and she helps to feed the family with her needlework until her father receives an inheritance when she is in her teens, and more problems ensue.

Dickens, Charles, 1812-1870

Martin Chuzzlewit / Charles Dickens ; with forty illustrations by "Phiz" ; introduced by William Boyd. A.A. Knopf, 1994, c1844. xlvii, 851 p.

ISBN 067943884X

1. Grandfathers 2. British in the United States 3. Greed 4. Selfishness 5. Men/women relations 6. Young men 7. Voyages and travels 8. United States -- Description and travel 9. England 10. Satirical fiction 11. Adventure stories 12. Coming-of-age stories 13. Classics

LC 95136833

Originally published The life and adventures of Martin Chuzzlewit: New York, 1844.

. Martin Chuzzlewit's wealthy grandfather forces him to emigrate to America after the selfish Martin falls in love with the wrong girl; upon his return, Martin seems to prove his worth.

Dickens, Charles, 1812-1870

* **Nicholas** Nickleby / Charles Dickens ; with an introduction by John Carey A.A. Knopf, 1993. 843 p.

ISBN 0679423079

1. 19th century 2. Orphans 3. Uncle and nephew 4. Money lenders 5. Boys' boarding schools 6. Cruelty in men 7. Child abuse 8. Eccentrics and eccentricities 9. England -- Social conditions -- 19th century 10. England -- Social life and customs -- 19th century 11. Coming-of-age stories 12. Classics 13. Picaresque fiction

LC 93001856 //r94

After Nicholas Nickleby's father dies bankrupt, Nicholas becomes the unhappy ward of his uncle, a moneylender, and survives many adventures before finding happiness.

Dickens, Charles, 1812-1870

The **old** curiosity shop / Charles Dickens. Alfred A. Knopf, 1995, c1848. 624 p.

ISBN 0679443738

1. 19th century 2. Grandparent and child 3. Gambling 4. Antique dealers 5. Voyages and travels 6. Gamblers 7. Girl orphans 8. Grandfathers 9. England -- Social life and customs -- 19th century 10. Domestic fiction 11. Classics

LC 95075208

Originally published: London : Chapman and Hall, 1848.

"Complete and unabridged".

Introduction, illustrations and notes (c)2001.

After Little Nell's grandfather loses his money gambling, and they roam the country as beggars, even more tragedy ensues.

Dickens, Charles, 1812-1870

Oliver Twist, or The parish boy's progress / Charles Dickens ; with 24 illustrations by George Cruikshank ; introduced by Michael Slater. Knopf, 1992, c1829. xlvi, 427 p.

ISBN 0679417249

1. 19th century 2. Orphans 3. Thieves -- 19th century 4. Pickpockets 5. Criminals 6. Murder 7. Kidnapping victims 8. Poor people 9. Boy thieves -- 19th century 10. Children and adults -- 19th century 11. Victoriana 12. London, England -- Social life and customs -- 19th century 13. Coming-of-age stories 14. Classics

Originally published Oliver Twist: Philadelphia : Lea & Blanchard, 1829.

Originally published Oliver Twist; or, The parish boy's progress: Philadelphia : Carey, Lea and Blanchard, 1837.

Released as a movie entitled Oliver Twist.

Born in a workhouse, Oliver Twist, an orphan, walks to London where he gets involved with Fagin and his gang of young thieves.

Dickens, Charles, 1812-1870

Our mutual friend / Charles Dickens ; with an introduction by Andrew Sanders. A.A. Knopf, 1994, c1864. xliii, 832 p.

ISBN 0679420282

1. 19th century 2. Inheritance and succession 3. Murder 4. Businesspeople 5. City life 6. Social classes -- 19th century 7. Poor families 8. Deception 9. London, England -- Social conditions -- 19th century 10. London, England -- Social life and customs -- 19th century 11. Love stories 12. Satirical fiction 13. Classics

LC 93081033

Originally published: New York : J. Bradburn, 1864-65.

John Harmon will inherit a fortune if he marries a girl whose personality has been affected by her wealth, and friends and events conspire to prove her true worth.

Dickens, Charles, 1812-1870

The **Pickwick** papers / Charles Dickens ; with forty-three illustrations by Seymour and 'Phiz' ; introduced by Peter Washington. Alfred A. Knopf, 1998, c1837. lxii, 813 p.

ISBN 0375405488

1. 19th century 2. Misadventures 3. Voyages and travels 4. Men's organizations 5. Male friendship 6. England -- Social life and customs -- 19th century 7. England -- Social conditions -- 19th century 8. Classics 9. Picaresque fiction 10. Satirical fiction

The posthumous papers of The Pickwick Club were first published in monthly parts between 1936-7 and as a single volume in 1837.

Four members of a nineteenth-century London social club journey to places outside the city and become involved in romantic adventures and a few legal scrapes.

Dickens, Charles, 1812-1870

* A **tale** of two cities / Charles Dickens ; with an introduction by Simon Schama and sixteen illustrations by Phiz. Knopf , 1993, c1859. xxviii, 413 p.

ISBN 0679420738

1. Revolutionary France (1789-1799) 2. Georgian era (1714-1837) 3. 18th century 4. French in England 5. Fathers and daughters 6. Classism 7. Executions and executioners 8. Look-alikes 9. Self-sacrifice 10. French Revolution, 1789-1799 11. France -- History -- Revolution, 1789-1799 12. Paris, France -- History -- 1789-1799 13. London, England -- History -- 18th century 14. Classics 15. Historical fiction

First published in the United Kingdom in 1859 by Chapman & Hall.

When the starving French masses rise to overthrow a corrupt and decadent government, both the guilty and innocent become victims of their frenzied anger.

Dickey, Eric Jerome

Bad men and wicked women / Eric Jerome Dickey. E.P. Dutton, 2018. 400 p. Ken Swift novels

ISBN 9781524742195

1. Father and adult daughter 2. Enforcers (Criminals) 3. Extortion 4. Pregnant women 5. Divorced men 6. Revenge 7. Crime 8. Lust 9. African Americans 10. City life 11. Men/women relations 12. Los Angeles, California 13. Drama lit 14. African American fiction

When his pregnant and bitter daughter blackmails him for $50,000, Los Angeles enforcer Ken Swift embarks on a clash of wills that is complicated by a contract that spirals out of control, revealing the vengeful nature of a dangerous adversary.

Dickey, Eric Jerome

Before we were wicked / Eric Jerome Dickey. Dutton, 2019. 368 p. Ken Swift novels

ISBN 9781524744038

1. Unplanned pregnancy 2. College students 3. Enforcers (Criminals) 4. Men/women relations 5. Sexual attraction 6. Lust 7. Postpartum depression 8. Options, alternatives, choices 9. African American fiction 10. Drama lit

Ken Swift from Bad Men and Wicked Women falls obsessively in love with a Harvard-bound beauty before a one-night stand culminates in an unplanned pregnancy that is further complicated by their disparate backgrounds.

Dickey, Eric Jerome

The **blackbirds** / Eric Jerome Dickey. Dutton, 2016 384 p.

ISBN 9781101984109

1. Female friendship 2. African American women 3. Sexuality 4. Secrets 5. Lovers 6. Sexual attraction 7. African American men/women relations 8. Drama lit 9. African American fiction

LC 2015045477

Four women, best friends who are closer than sisters, find their friendship tested as they struggle with their own personal demons, drama, and desires.

Dickey, Eric Jerome

The **business** of lovers / Eric Jerome Dickey. E.P. Dutton, 2020. 400 p.

ISBN 9781524745202

1. Brothers 2. African American families 3. Life change events 4. Sexuality 5. Lust 6. Decision-making 7. City life 8. Family relationships 9. Men/women relations 10. Los Angeles, California 11. African American fiction 12. Erotic fiction

While a father struggles to reconnect with his estranged son and spiteful ex, his bodyguard brother is invited by three women escorts to consider a job as a male prostitute.

Dickey, Eric Jerome

Finding Gideon / Eric Jerome Dickey. Dutton, 2017 448 p.

ISBN 9781101985496

1. African American men 2. Former lovers 3. Assassins 4. Revenge 5. Enemies 6. Death threats 7. Mercenaries 8. Women assassins 9. Protectiveness in men 10. Buenos Aires, Argentina 11. Thrillers and suspense 12. Drama lit 13. African American fiction

LC 2016055134

Calling in support from the beautiful Hawks when his latest job takes an unprecedented toll, jet-setting contract killer Gideon launches a plan to take down his nemesis, Midnight, who has assembled a team of mercenaries targeting Gideon's loved ones.

"Prolific best-seller Dickey returns to his Gideon thriller series after a long hiatus, following Resurrecting Midnight (2009) with a fifth installment. ... Dickey steadily generates a taut, deadly atmosphere throughout the book, and readers will not be able to predict who will be the last man standing. Given Dickey's popularity, collections may want to stock the entire series." Booklist.

Dickinson, Peter, 1927-

The **yellow** room conspiracy / Peter Dickinson. Mysterious Press, 1994. 261 p.

ISBN 9780892965564

1. Scandals 2. Murder 3. Reminiscing in old age 4. Mansions 5. Arson 6. Suspicion 7. Men/women relations 8. Extramarital affairs 9. England 10. Mysteries

LC 94001980

Two lifelong lovers sort through their shared history of secrets and suspicions, dating back to World War II, to find the truth behind a fatal weekend that became a public scandal.

Dicks, Matthew

* **Memoirs** of an imaginary friend / Matthew Dicks. St. Martin's Press, 2012. 314 p.

ISBN 9781250006219

1. Imaginary playmates 2. Boys with autism 3. Kidnapping 4. Bullying and bullies 5. Friendship 6. Psychological fiction 7. Coming-of-age stories

A tale imparted from the perspective of long-time imaginary friend, Budo, traces his awareness of his advancing age and constant thoughts of the inevitable day when 8-year-old Max, an autistic boy, will stop believing in him, a progression that is complicated by a teasing bully and Max's abduction by an overly-possessive therapist.

Dicks, Matthew

The **perfect** comeback of Caroline Jacobs : a novel / Matthew Dicks. St. Martin's Press, 2015. 216 p.

ISBN 9781250006301

1. Mothers and daughters 2. Former friends 3. Self-fulfillment in women 4. Betrayal 5. Homecomings 6. Childhood friends 7. Automobile travel 8. Secrets 9. Mainstream fiction

LC 2015017808

A suddenly enlightened former pushover uses her newfound assertiveness to return home to tell off her childhood friend who betrayed her in public 25 years before.

"Heartwarming and often darkly humorous, this road trip for vengeance fairly cries out for filming." Kirkus.

Dicks, Matthew

Unexpectedly, Milo / Matthew Dicks. Broadway Books, 2010. 272 p.

ISBN 9780307592309

1. Missing persons 2. Obsessive-compulsive disorder in men 3. Men nurses 4. Eccentrics and eccentricities 5. Secrets 6. Marital conflict 7. Separation (Marital relations) 8. Guilt in women 9. Humorous stories

Stumbling on a video confession detailing a decade-old missing-persons cold case, the neurotic Milo embarks on a madcap journey to solve the mystery, which enables unexpected personal revelations.

Didion, Joan

A **book** of common prayer / Joan Didion. Vintage International, 1995, c1977. 272 p.

ISBN 9780679754862

1. Women and politics 2. Revolutions 3. People with cancer 4. Missing persons 5. Murder 6. Violence 7. Women with terminal illnesses 8. Mother and adult daughter 9. California 10. El Salvador 11. Latin America -- Politics and government 12. Literary fiction 13. Political fiction

Originally published : Simon, 1977.

National Book Critics Circle Award for Fiction finalist, 1977

The disappearance of her politically active daughter, forces Charlotte to abandon her apathetic, comfortable existence and become involved in the dangerous politics of a South American nation.

"Didion's exposition of situations and details adroitly conceals their significanceuntil much later their meaning flares before our eyes. This is a remarkably good novel." Newsweek.

Didion, Joan

* **Play** it as it lays : a novel / Joan Didion. Farrar, Straus, and Giroux, 2005, c1970. 213 p.

ISBN 9780374529949

1. 1960s 2. Film industry and trade -- Hollywood, California 3. Alienation in women 4. Men/women relations 5. Divorced women 6. Abortion 7. Sexuality 8. Drug use 9. Women -- Alcohol use 10. Regret in women 11. California 12. Psychological fiction 13. Literary fiction

Originally published in 1970.

"Using a phrenetic millieu of drugs, pills, sexual aberrancy, Didion elliptically etches the self-destructive life of Maria Wyeth. Didion with authorial legerdemain skillfully controls the suspense as Maria dangerously exists: she cannot relate and adjust. Her father has told her life was a crap game and to play it as it lays, not the hard way. But Maria plays it the hardest way, trying to anesthetize herself against pain (almost everyone, anything) and pleasure (Kate, her neurally damaged child), and trying to lose herself in the dead-end life around her." Choice.

Diehl, Heidi,

Lifelines / Heidi Diehl. Houghton Mifflin Harcourt, 2019. 304 p.

ISBN 9781328483720

1. 1970s 2. 2000s (Decade) 3. Artists 4. Funerals 5. Former husbands 6. Mothers and daughters 7. Family relationships 8. Husband and wife 9. Mothers-in-law 10. Conceptual art 11. Women artists 12. Remarriage 13. Oregon 14. Germany 15. Eugene, Oregon 16. Dusseldorf, Germany 17. Domestic fiction 18. Mainstream fiction

LC 2018036017

An American artist returns to the German city where she fell in love and had a child decades earlier to confront her past at her former mother-in-law's funeral.

Diffenbaugh, Vanessa

The **language** of flowers : a novel / Vanessa Diffenbaugh. Ballantine Books, 2011. 336 p.

ISBN 9780345525543

1. Young women -- San Francisco, California 2. Foster care 3. Forgiveness 4. Flower language 5. Interpersonal relations 6. Men/women relations 7. Orphans 8. Coping 9. Happiness in women 10. Florists 11. San Francisco, California 12. Psychological fiction

Previously published: 2011.

First published in the USA: 2011.

RUSA Reading List, 2012.

"The story of a woman whose gift for flowers helps her change the lives of others even as she struggles to overcome her own past"--, Provided by publisher.

"An unusual, overextended romance, fairy tale in parts but with a sprinkling of grit." Kirkus.

Dillard, Annie

The **Maytrees** : a novel / Annie Dillard. HarperCollins, 2007. 224 p.

ISBN 0061239534

1. Poets 2. Husband and wife 3. Caretakers 4. World War II veterans 5. Marriage 6. Separation (Marital relations) 7. Family relationships 8. Provincetown, Massachusetts 9. Massachusetts 10. Domestic fiction

LC 2006052599

"A portion of this work has previously appeared, in different form, in Harper's magazine"--T.p. verso.

Sharing a simple life with his wife and young son in the post-war artist community of his childhood, free-thinking poet Toby Maytree is aided with child-care responsibilities by close friend Deary, who years later comes between Toby and his wife.

"The good news is that in The Maytrees, despite the big words and the name-dropping . . . there is also good old straight narrative and prose that is often, yes, breathtakingly illuminative." New York Times Book Review.

Dimberg, Kelsey Rae

Girl in the rearview mirror / Kelsey Rae Dimberg. Harper-Collins, 2019 352 p.

ISBN 9780062867926

1. Intrigue 2. Young women 3. Politicians' families 4. Nannies 5. Scandals 6. Politicians 7. Deception 8. Rich families 9. Museum directors 10. Power (Social sciences) 11. Phoenix, Arizona 12. Arizona 13. Political thrillers 14. Thrillers and suspense

Accepting what she believes will be a dream job from a prominent political family, a young nanny is dazzled by her employers' glamorous life before a mysterious stranger draws her into a menacing web of secrets.

Dimechkie, Karim

Lifted by the great nothing / Karim Dimechkie. Bloomsbury USA, 2015. 288 p.

ISBN 9781632860583

1. Fathers and sons 2. Mother separated children 3. Identity (Psychology) 4. Lebanese Americans 5. Family secrets 6. Immigrants 7. Lebanon -- History -- Civil War, 1975-1990 8. Coming-of-age stories 9. Political fiction

LC 2014033821

A Lebanese-American comes of age under a loving roof--and a devastating lie.

Dimitri, Francesco, 1981-

The **book** of hidden things / Francesco Dimitri. Titan Books, 2018. 400 p.

ISBN 9781785657078

1. Hometowns 2. Male friendship 3. Missing men 4. Secrets 5. Manuscripts 6. Mafia 7. Home (Concept) 8. Rumor 9. Investigations 10. Violence in men 11. Small town life 12. Men/women relations 13. Italy 14. Literary fiction

When Art, the charismatic leader of their group, mysteriously disappears amidst bizarre and unbelievable rumors, three friends, while searching for the truth, discover a document that he left behind that promises to reveal dark secrets and wonders beyond anything previously known.

Dimon, HelenKay

* **Her** other secret / HelenKay Dimon. Avon Books, 2019. 384 pags Whitaker Island

ISBN 9780062892782

1. Second chances 2. New identities 3. Repairers 4. Loss (Psychology) 5. Escape (Psychology) 6. Sexual attraction 7. Men/women relations 8. Secrets 9. Murder 10. Murderers 11. Washington (State) 12. Romantic suspense 13. Contemporary romances

Is it the perfect escape--or a private trap for two lovers?

Dimon, HelenKay

Mercy / HelenKay Dimon. Berkley, 2014. 336 p. Holton Woods

ISBN 9780425270738

1. Former lovers 2. CIA agents 3. Businesspeople 4. Lust 5. Investigations 6. Betrayal 7. Sexual attraction 8. Men/women

relations 9. Washington, D.C. 10. Erotic romances 11. Contemporary romances

"Dimon 's latest is perfect for readers who appreciate intense intrigue and very erotic romance with overtones of questionable consent." Publishers Weekly.

Dinesen, Isak, 1885-1962

Seven Gothic tales / Isak Dinesen. Vintage, 1991, c1934. 420 p. ; 20 cm.

ISBN 0679736417

1. 19th century 2. Europe -- 19th century 3. Gothic fiction 4. Short stories 5. Translations -- Danish to English

LC 91050030

Includes biographical note.

Originally published: New York : H. Smith and R. Haas, 1934.

Seven short fantasies set in the nineteenth century explore the psychological dimensions of familiar landscapes and human experiences

Dinesen, Isak, 1885-1962

Winter's tales / Isak Dinesen. Vintage Books, 1993, c1942. 313 p.

ISBN 0679743340

1. Short stories 2. Translations -- Danish to English

LC 92050615

Originally published: New York : Random House, 1942.

Tells the stories of a struggling author, Danish country life, a brave Frenchwoman, a young sailor, a young married couple, a dreamer, and a wealthy child

Disher, Garry, 1949-

Under the cold bright lights / Garry Disher. Soho Crime, 2019, c2017. 299 p.

ISBN 9781641290579

1. Murder 2. Cold cases (Criminal investigation) 3. Former police 4. Divorced men 5. Boarding houses 6. Coroners 7. Clues 8. Retirees 9. Australia 10. Australian 11. Mysteries

LC 2018059657

Originally published: Melbourne, Vic. : The Text Publishing Company, 2017.

Librarians' Choice (Australia), 2017.

A cold case investigator looks into a possible murder that the coroner pegged as a suicide and a doctor who killed three women and left no evidence.

"Disher, the prolific Australian great, best known for the Inspector Challis series (Signal Loss, 2017), offers a stand-alone about a veteran detective faced with thorny moral choices. ... As always, Disher writes with clear eyes and a sure hand." Booklist.

Divakaruni, Chitra Banerjee, 1956-

* Oleander girl : a novel / Chitra Banerjee Divakaruni. Free Press, 2013. 304 p.

ISBN 9781451695656

1. Engaged persons 2. Family secrets 3. Fathers and daughters 4. East Indians in the United States 5. Young women 6. Grandparents 7. Multiracial persons 8. Birthparents -- Identification 9. India 10. Kolkata, India 11. United States 12. Coming-of-age stories 13. Mainstream fiction

LC 2012025671

Enjoying a sheltered childhood with adoring grandparents but troubled by the silence surrounding her parents' deaths, 17-year-old Korobi is prompted by a love note among her mother's possessions and a fiance's shattering revelation to travel from India to post-September 11 America in search of her true identity.

"Divakaruni... introduces a cast of characters who defy their stereotypes... [and] has crafted a beautiful, complex story in which caste, class, religion, and race are significant factors informing people's world views." Library Journal.

Dixon, Stephen, 1936-

* Interstate : a novel / Stephen Dixon. H. Holt, 1995. 374 p.

ISBN 9780805026542

1. Drive-by shootings 2. Child murder victims 3. Daughters -- Death 4. Fathers and daughters 5. Roads 6. Mainstream fiction

LC 94040174

National Book Award for Fiction finalist, 1995

A father mentally replays, in eight variations, the shooting of his daughters on an interstate highway.

"Italo Calvino and Alain Robbe-Grillet have also written novels that begin again and again, revising themselves, but the subjects of these novels are only themselves. Neither of them has brought off anything like the broken eloquence of Nathan's voice, which is as distinct and original and American as Mark Twain's, if otherwise very different. . . . Neither Italo Calvino nor Alain Robbe-Grillet ever brought off anything so cruelly audacious (although they tried) or so upsetting as 'Interstate' or even attempted the muted beauty of the novel's last few pages, as Nathan performs the ordinary rituals of fatherhood, haunted by everything that has gone before." New York Times Book Review.

Djavadi, Negar, 1969-

Disoriental / Négar Djavadi ; translated from the French by Tina Kover. Europa Editions, 2018, c2016. 338 p.

ISBN 9781609454517

1. Memories 2. Women immigrants 3. Intergenerational relations 4. Immigrants -- Identity 5. Families -- History 6. Political violence 7. Fertility clinics 8. Dissenters 9. Ancestors 10. Iran -- History 11. Paris, France 12. Family sagas 13. Literary fiction 14. Translations -- French to English

Originally published by Liana Levi in 2016.

Lambda Literary Award for Bisexual Fiction, 2019.

25-year-old Iranian expat Kimia Sadr, facing the future she has built for herself after leaving her family behind, is inundated by her own memories and the stories of her ancestors in the waiting room of a Parisian fertility clinic.

"The novel convincingly and powerfully explores the enormous weight of ones family and culture on individual identity, especially the exile's." Publishers Weekly.

Doan, Amy Mason

The **summer** list / Amy Mason Doan. Graydon House, 2018. 384 p.

ISBN 9781525804250

1. Teenage girls 2. Female friendship 3. Betrayal 4. Best friends 5. Memories 6. Mothers and daughters 7. Adopted girls 8. Scavenger hunts 9. Summer 10. Lakes 11. Reunions 12. Family secrets 13. Childhood friends 14. Women's lives and relationships

Returning home after being away for 17 years, Laura is reunited with her former best friend, Casey, and as they embark on one last scavenger hunt, a devastating secret threatens to tear them apart once again.

Dobyns, Stephen, 1941-

Saratoga payback / Stephen Dobyns. Blue Rider Press, 2017. 352 p. Charlie Bradshaw mysteries

ISBN 9780399576577

1. Former private investigators 2. Former police 3. Retirement 4. Horse thefts 5. Murder investigation 6. Private investigators 7.

Saratoga Springs, New York 8. New York (State) 9. Mysteries

LC 2016041987

Torn between helping and breaking the law when a local trouble-maker is found dead on the sidewalk near his home, erstwhile detective Charlie Bradshaw becomes entangled in a mission to rescue an old acquaintance's stolen horse.

Doctorow, Cory

Radicalized / Cory Doctorow. Tor, 2019. 304 p.

ISBN 9781250228581

1. Corporate power 2. Corporate greed 3. Social classes 4. Hacking 5. Hackers 6. Women hackers 7. Inequality 8. Hierarchy (Social sciences) 9. Social structure 10. Rich people 11. Social marginality 12. Science fiction 13. Dystopian fiction 14. Social science fiction 15. Short stories

Four urgent Sci-fi novellas of America's present and future that are connected by social, technological and economic visions of today and what our nation could be in the near, near future.

Doctorow, Cory

Rapture of the nerds / Cory Doctorow and Charles Stross. Tor, 2012. 349 p.

ISBN 9780765329103

1. 21st century 2. Potters 3. Jury 4. Conspiracies 5. Near future 6. Interplanetary relations 7. Posthumanism 8. Cyberpunk 9. Science fiction 10. Humorous stories

LC 2012019450

"A Tom Doherty Associates book."

At the end of the 21st century, humans who have abandoned Earth to join densethinker clades are carelessly circulating technologies which can change entire cultures and spiritual systems. Huw Jones, a technophobe, is chosen to serve on the tech jury that evaluates new inventions before they are released.

Doctorow, Cory

Walkaway / Cory Doctorow. Tor Books, 2017. 379 p.

ISBN 9780765392763

1. Social classes 2. Inequality 3. Hierarchy (Social sciences) 4. Social structure 5. Identity (Psychology) 6. Kidnapping 7. Rich people 8. Social marginality 9. Survival 10. Canada 11. Science fiction 12. Techno-thrillers

Abandoning formal society to pursue a minimalist counterculture life in a near-future world wrecked by climate change, a disenchanted senior and his heiress paramour inspire a host of followers who become obsessed with cheating death in ways that turn the world upside down.

"Doctorow sticks the landing with a multigenerational saga that extends this tale of the 'first days of a better nation' to a thrilling and unexpected finale. A truly visionary techno-thriller that not only depicts how we might live tomorrow, but asks why we don't already." Kirkus.

Doctorow, E. L., 1931-2015

All the time in the world : new and selected stories / E. L. Doctorow. Random House, 2011. x, 277 p.

ISBN 9781400069637

1. Literary fiction 2. Short stories

A collection of short works includes the stories of a couple who become estranged after a mysterious man claims he grew up in their house, and a Russian bus boy who is entangled with an organized crime ring.

"In the preface to his new book, [Doctorow] reiterates a position he has advocated many times: You write to find out what you're writing. . . . . The surprises in this book come at you as slaps on the back of the head. Even while the plots make the surprises seem inevitable the moment you see them, you have to imagine Doctorow's own shock and relief that the

story has come so far from its premise. You can only imagine it, though, because the writer and his agenda are nowhere to be found. At the emotional heights of this book, you communicate less with Doctorow than with the presiding god of the world of the story. Doctorow is only the medium. The effect is egoless, frank, spontaneous and altogether wonderful." San Francisco Chronicle.

Doctorow, E. L., 1931-2015

Andrew's brain / E. L. Doctorow. Random House, 2014. 200 p.

ISBN 9781400068814

1. Memory 2. Identity (Psychology) 3. Scientists 4. Cognitive science 5. Brain 6. Conversation 7. Loss (Psychology) 8. Consequences 9. Interpersonal relations 10. Psychological fiction 11. Literary fiction

A psychological tale recounts the experiences of Andrew, who confesses to an unknown recipient the memory- and truth-challenging events, loves, and tragedies that have led him to a mysterious act.

Doctorow, E. L., 1931-2015

* **Billy** Bathgate : a novel / E.L. Doctorow. Random House, 1989. 323 p.

ISBN 0394525299

1. Schultz, Dutch, 1900?-1935 2. 1930s 3. Gangsters 4. Organized crime 5. Crime 6. Fifteen-year-old boys 7. Revenge 8. New York City 9. Historical fiction 10. Coming-of-age stories 11. Literary fiction 12. Crime fiction

LC 88042820

National Book Critics Circle Award for Fiction, 1989.

PEN/Faulkner Award, 1990.

National Book Award for Fiction finalist, 1989

Pulitzer Prize for Fiction finalist, 1990.

Young Billy Bathgate witnesses atrocities of the crime world in his introduction to a brutal and unsparing life that takes him through the heart of the city and the rural underworld in Depression-era America.

"Doctorow brings a nice sense of moral ambiguity and creates characters who develop or deteriorate at an appropriate pace. His fecund run-on sentences are a pleasure to read. It all adds up to that rarity: a formal literary work that's also hugely entertaining." Newsweek.

Doctorow, E. L., 1931-2015

* The **book** of Daniel : a novel / E. L. Doctorow. Plume, 1996, c1971. 303 p.

ISBN 9780452275669

1. Rosenberg, Ethel, 1915-1953 2. Rosenberg, Julius, 1918-1953 3. 1950s 4. Spies 5. Parent and child 6. Trials (Espionage) 7. Hypocrisy 8. Jewish Americans 9. Radicals 10. Communists 11. Family relationships 12. United States -- Social life and customs -- 20th century 13. Psychological fiction 14. Literary fiction

Book made into a movie called Daniel.

In 1967, Daniel, the son of two convicted spies executed by their own country, ponders his life, his sister's radicalism, his appreciation for his wife and son, and the hypocrisy of the moralistic ideals upon which this country was based.

Doctorow, E. L., 1931-2015

Doctorow : collected stories / E.L. Doctorow. Random House, 2016. 321 p.

ISBN 9780399588358

1. Literary fiction 2. Short stories

LC 2016006619

"While many of these stories appear in 2011's All the Time in the World: New and Selected Stories , this new volume was compiled by the author just before his death, and it includes revised and updated versions of all of his best stories , which makes it an essential acquisition for many libraries." Library Journal

Doctorow, E. L., 1931-2015

Homer and Langley : a novel / E.L. Doctorow. Random House, 2009. 208 p.

ISBN 9781400064946

1. Collyer, Homer Lusk, 1881-1947 2. Collyer, Langley, 1885-1947 3. Brothers 4. Recluses 5. Compulsive behavior in men 6. Eccentrics and eccentricities 7. Men who are blind 8. Interpersonal relations 9. Family relationships 10. New York City -- History -- 20th century 11. Biographical fiction 12. Literary fiction

LC 2009006959

A tale inspired by a true story finds the blind Homer Collyer closeted within a once-grand Fifth Avenue mansion with his damaged brother and remembering a life marked by colorful characters, political events, and technological achievements.

"Toward the end of E.L. Doctorow's novel Homer & Langley, narrator Homer Collyer, the real-life Manhattanite notorious for his and his brother Langley's reclusive lifestyle and hoarding of sundry objects, frets about their legacy: For what could be more terrible than being turned into a mythic joke? How could we cope, once dead and gone, with no one available to reclaim our history? In attempting to recover the Collyer brothers' history from those who would reduce their existence to eccentricities, Doctorow probes the inner workings of the brothers' minds and extends their lives well beyond 1947, when the real Collyers died." San Antonio Express-News.,Cunningly panoramic. . . . Doctorow has packed this tale with episodes of existential wonder that capture the brothers in all their fascinating wackiness. Elle

Doctorow, E. L., 1931-2015

The **march** : a novel / E.L. Doctorow. Random House, 2005. 363 p.

ISBN 9780375506710

1. Sherman, William Tecumseh, 1820-1891 2. Confederate States of America. Army. 3. American Civil War era (1861-1865) 4. 1860s 5. Sherman's March to the Sea 6. Confederate soldiers 7. Pillage 8. Freed slaves 9. Slaveholders 10. Refugees 11. Sherman's March through the Carolinas 12. Marching 13. War casualties 14. Civil war 15. United States Civil War, 1861-1865 16. Georgia -- History -- Civil War, 1861-1865 17. South Carolina -- History -- Civil War, 1861-1865 18. Historical fiction 19. War stories 20. Literary fiction

LC 2005046452

Michael Shaara Prize for Excellence in Civil War Fiction, 2006
National Book Critics Circle Award for Fiction, 2005.
PEN-Faulkner Award, 2006.
Pulitzer Prize for Fiction finalist, 2006
National Book Award for Fiction finalist, 2005

Chronicles Union General William Tecumseh Sherman's devastating march through Georgia and the Carolinas during the final years of the Civil War and the profound impact it had on the marchers, those in their path, and the outcome of the war.

"The march in question is that of General William Tecumseh Sherman and his Union soldiers as they slash and burn their way through Georgia and the Carolinas, and the march to freedom as liberated slaves fall in step with the liberating army. But it is also, given the poetic depth of Doctorow's vision, the great march of time and of humanity in all its cruelty and glory. As Doctorow dramatizes the fury, conviction, and chaos of the Civil War, he portrays historical figures, as he is wont to do, most electrifyingly Sherman himself. But he focuses most on brilliantly imagined characters who embody the epic conflicts of that cataclysmic era, including Pearl, the smart and courageous daughter of a slave and slave owner; an excessively clinical military surgeon; the valiant daugh-

ter of a Southern judge; a freed slave who becomes a war photographer; and Arly, a scheming Rebel soldier who provides shrewdly comic relief. Doctorow writes with blazing clarity about the brutal romance of war and its gruesome realities, with lyrical splendor about nature, and with wry wisdom and nimble satire about human folly." Booklist.

Doctorow, E. L., 1931-2015

* Ragtime / E.L. Doctorow. Random House, 1975. 270 p.

ISBN 9780394469010

1. 1900s (Decade) 2. Racism -- United States -- History -- 20th century 3. Violence 4. Families -- New Rochelle, New York 5. Family relationships 6. Jewish American families 7. Immigrants 8. African Americans 9. Sexuality 10. Poverty 11. New Rochelle, New York 12. United States -- Social life and customs -- 20th century 13. New York (State) -- Race relations -- History -- 20th century 14. Historical fiction 15. Literary fiction 16. Modern classics

LC 75009613

National Book Critics Circle Award for Fiction, 1975.

In America at the beginning of this century three families become entwined with Henry Ford, Emma Goldman, Harry Houdini, Theodore Dreiser, Sigmund Freud, and Emiliano Zapata.

Doctorow, E. L., 1931-2015

World's Fair / E.L. Doctorow. Random House, 1985. 288 p.

ISBN 0394525280

1. New York World's Fair, (1939-1940) 2. 1930s 3. Depressions -- 1929-1941 4. Jewish American boys 5. Family relationships 6. Nine-year-old boys 7. Growing up 8. Essay contests 9. Bronx, New York City -- History -- 20th century 10. New York City -- History -- 1898-1951 11. Literary fiction 12. Historical fiction

LC 85010728

National Book Award for Fiction, 1986.

Edgar, nine, and his family have difficult times, but Edgar wins tickets for them to attend the New York World's Fair of 1939.

Dodd, Christina

Because I'm watching / Christina Dodd. St. Martin's Press, 2016. 336 p. Virtue Falls

ISBN 9781250130648

1. Veterans 2. Women authors 3. Conspiracies 4. Manipulation (Social sciences) 5. Suicide 6. Depression 7. Eccentrics and eccentricities 8. Romantic suspense

Struggling to build the courage to commit suicide to escape the horrors of his past, veteran Jacob finds his life turned upside-down by a local eccentric who drives her car through the front of his house and who hides her own traumas.

"The tautly written novels plot proves that Dodd knows exactly how to keep readers nerves jangling; at the same time, her irresistibly dry wit helps lighten some of the darker twists and turns. Scary, sexy, and smartly written, Dodd is at the top of her game." Booklist.

Dodd, Christina

Dead girl running / Christina Dodd. Harlequin Books, 2018 384 p. Cape Charade

ISBN 9781335017437

1. Abused women 2. Murder investigation 3. Runaway wives, husbands, etc 4. Resorts 5. Amnesia 6. Mutilation 7. Murderers 8. Women murder victims 9. Washington (State) 10. Pacific Northwest 11. Thrillers and suspense

Surviving a gunshot wound to the head and struggling to remember an entire year of her life, Kellan Adams finds herself on the run from a husband she hopes is dead and takes a job at a Pacific Coast resort, where she is embroiled in a murder investigation that makes her question both her past and her sanity.

Dodd, Christina

Obsession Falls / Christina Dodd. St Martin's Press, 2015. 384 p. Virtue Falls

ISBN 9781250028471

1. Women witnesses 2. Fugitives 3. Secret identity 4. Frameups 5. Hiding 6. Conspiracies 7. Idaho 8. Washington (State) 9. Romantic suspense

Sacrificing herself to protect a young boy from a death threat, Taylor subsequently endures a ruined life in the wilderness before seeking the help of an unlikely ally to defeat a man who would prevent her from reclaiming her life.

Dodd, Christina

Strangers she knows / Christina Dodd. HQN Books, 2019. 335 p. Cape Charade

ISBN 9781335016614

1. Islands 2. Serial murderers 3. Protectiveness in women 4. Obsession 5. Families 6. California 7. Thrillers and suspense

Living on an obscure technology-free island off California to escape a murderer who hunts her and her new family, Kellen Adams must face off against him one last time when he somehow finds them.

"With a fascinating island setting that includes a spooky old mansion, a secondary storyline involving World War II, and an antagonist who could give Villanelle from Killing Eve a pointer or two, this is Dodd at her brilliant best." Booklist.

Dodd, Christina

Virtue Falls / Christina Dodd. St. Martin's Press, 2014. 448 p. Virtue Falls

ISBN 9781250028419

1. Reunions 2. Murder witnesses 3. False imprisonment 4. Secrets 5. FBI agents 6. Coastal towns 7. Former husbands 8. Women geologists 9. Murder investigation 10. Father and adult daughter 11. Washington (State) 12. Thrillers and suspense

LC 2014016827

Growing up believing that her father was responsible for murdering her mother twenty years earlier, Elizabeth returns to her hometown in search of answers and discovers evidence of her father's innocence and the ongoing agenda of the real killer.

Dodd, Christina

What doesn't kill her / Christina Dodd. HQN, 2019. 384 p. Cape Charade

ISBN 9781335005786

1. Women with amnesia 2. Chases 3. Wilderness survival 4. Mothers and daughters 5. Memories 6. Life change events 7. Protectiveness in women 8. Secrets 9. Enemies 10. Revenge 11. Washington (State) 12. Pacific Northwest 13. Thrillers and suspense

Kellen Adams suffers from a yearlong gap in her memory. A bullet to the brain will cause that. But she's discovering the truth, and what she learns changes her life, her confidence and her very self. She finds herself in the wilderness, on the run, unprepared, her enemies unknown?and she is carrying a priceless burden she must protect at all costs. The consequences of failure would break her.

Dodd, Christina

The **woman** who couldn't scream / Christina Dodd. St Martins Pr., 2017. 352 p. Virtue Falls

ISBN 9781250028488

1. Trophy wives 2. Former lovers 3. Revenge in women 4. Violence against women 5. Sheriffs 6. Stalking 7. Serial murders 8. Stalkers 9. Romantic suspense

Following her wealthy husband's death, Merida reinvents herself and vows revenge on those responsible for a traumatic accident years earlier that cost her the ability to speak and left her bound to her elderly partner's obsessions.

"Dodd's (Because I'm Watching, 2017, etc.) new title delivers complex storytelling, a rollicking pace, and surprising twists and turns, plus sly humor, a touch of the supernatural, and a full cast of interesting and diverse characters." Kirkus.

Doerr, Anthony, 1973-

* **All** the light we cannot see : a novel / Anthony Doerr. Scribner, 2014. 448 p.

ISBN 9781476746586

1. Second World War era (1939-1945) 2. People who are blind 3. War and society 4. World War II 5. Personal conduct 6. Coastal towns 7. Germans in France 8. Fathers and daughters 9. Orphans 10. Men/women relations 11. Family relationships 12. France -- History -- German occupation, 1940-1945 13. Germany -- History -- 1933-1945 14. Historical fiction 15. Literary fiction

LC 2013034107

ALA Notable Book, 2015.

Andrew Carnegie Medal for Excellence in Fiction, 2015.

Australian Book Industry Awards, International Book of the Year, 2015.

Goodreads Choice Award, 2014.

Pulitzer Prize for Fiction, 2015.

National Book Award for Fiction finalist, 2014

A blind French girl on the run from the German occupation and a German orphan-turned-Resistance tracker struggle with their respective beliefs after meeting on the Brittany coast.

"Doerr captures the sights and sounds of wartime and focuses, refreshingly, on the innate goodness of his major characters." Kirkus.

Doerr, Harriet, 1910-2002

* **Stones** for Ibarra / Harriet Doerr. Viking Press, 1984. 214 p.

ISBN 9780670192038

1. Americans in Mexico 2. Husband and wife 3. Married people 4. Copper mines and mining -- Mexico 5. Villages -- Mexico 6. Mexico 7. Domestic fiction

LC 83047861

National Book Critics Circle Award for Fiction finalist, 1984

Richard and Sara Everton move to Ibarra, Mexico to reopen Richard's grandfather's copper mine and learn that Richard is dying of leukemia.

Doetsch, Richard

Half-past dawn / Richard Doetsch. Atria Books, 2011. 356 p.

ISBN 9781439183977

1. Men with amnesia 2. Missing persons 3. District attorneys 4. Conspiracies 5. Thrillers and suspense

Waking up with suspicious injuries and no memory of the previous night, attorney Harper Keller is horrified to discover that he has been reported murdered and that his wife is missing.

Doig, Ivan

The **bartender's** tale / Ivan Doig. Riverhead Books, 2012. 387 p.

ISBN 9781594487354

1. 1960s 2. Fathers and sons -- Montana 3. Bars -- Montana 4. Life change events 5. Former lovers -- Montana 6. Twelve-year-olds 7. Small town life -- Montana 8. Paternity 9. Montana 10. Coming-of-age stories 11. Historical fiction 12. Modern Westerns 13. Gentle reads

LC 2012017498

Running a venerable bar in 1960 Montana while raising his 12-year-old son, single father Tom Harry finds his world upended by the arrival of a woman from his past and her beatnik daughter, who claims Tom as her father and upends the town with her passionate and pretentious modern views.

Doig, Ivan

Dancing at the Rascal Fair / Ivan Doig. Atheneum, 1987. 405 p. Montana trilogy (Ivan Doig)

ISBN 9780689117640

1. Frontier and pioneer life 2. Ranch life -- Montana 3. Scots in Montana 4. Male friendship 5. Families -- Montana 6. Immigrants 7. Unrequited love 8. Betrayal 9. Montana -- History -- 19th century 10. Montana -- History -- 20th century 11. Historical fiction 12. Pacific Northwest fiction 13. Gentle reads

LC 87018672

A tale of a fateful contest of the heart between Scottish immigrants Anna Ramsay and Angus McCaskill, walled apart by their obligations as they and their stormy kith and kin vie to tame the brutal, beautiful Two Medicine county in Rocky Mountains at the turn of the century.

"If the thorny individualism of Rob and Angus results in lives that are never easy, they are rich in incident and growth, beautifully described in Doig's strong, savory prose. America's frontier history comes vividly to life in this absorbing saga filled with memorable characters." Publishers Weekly.

Doig, Ivan

* **Last** bus to wisdom : a novel / Ivan Doig. Riverhead Books, 2015. 320 p.

ISBN 9781594632020

1. 1950s 2. Bus travel 3. Orphans 4. Uncles 5. Travelers 6. Eleven-year-old boys 7. Boys 8. Coming-of-age stories 9. Historical fiction 10. Gentle reads

LC 2015014721

Rejected by his domineering great aunt during the summer of 1951, imaginative eleven-year-old Donal travels back to his ailing grandmother's home accompanied by his German great uncle while experiencing haphazard adventures along the way.

"Doig's superb storytelling does not disappoint. The dialog is snappy, funny, and true to the charming characters. With the author's passing in April, this is the last journey into familiar Doig territory we've come to admire." Library Journal.

Doig, Ivan

Mountain time : a novel / Ivan Doig. Scribner, 1999. 316 p.

ISBN 068483295X

1. People with leukemia 2. Loss (Psychology) 3. Fathers and sons 4. Senior men -- Family relationships 5. Fathers -- Death 6. Inheritance and succession 7. Familial love 8. Forgiveness 9. Sisters 10. Middle-aged men 11. Divorced persons 12. Men/women relations 13. Family feuds 14. Montana 15. Seattle, Washington 16. Domestic fiction 17. Pacific Northwest fiction 18. Gentle reads

LC 99014324

In a novel set in Seattle, Montana, and Alaska but centering around a single family, one man strives to uncover his father's darkest secrets so he can learn to love himself.

"A worthy addition to Doig's impressive saga of the twentieth-century West." Booklist.

Doig, Ivan

Ride with me, Mariah Montana / Ivan Doig. Atheneum, 1990. 324 p. Montana trilogy (Ivan Doig)

ISBN 9780689120190

1. 1980s 2. Father and adult daughter 3. Voyages and travels 4. Recreational vehicles 5. Widowers 6. Men/women relations 7. Women photojournalists 8. Journalists 9. Montana -- Description and travel 10. Pacific Northwest fiction 11. Gentle reads

LC 90035834

Jick takes his daughter Mariah on a tour of Montana as the state leaves its pioneer past for an unknown future.

Doig, Ivan

The **whistling** season / Ivan Doig. Harcourt, 2006. 352 p. Morrie Morgan novels (Ivan Doig)

ISBN 0151012377

1. 1900s (Decade) 2. Frontier and pioneer life 3. Household employees 4. Brothers and sisters 5. Men/women relations 6. Fathers and sons 7. Teachers 8. Schools 9. Widowers -- Montana 10. Housekeepers 11. Montana 12. The West (United States) 13. Historical fiction 14. Coming-of-age stories 15. Pacific Northwest fiction 16. Gentle reads

LC 2005025457

ALA Notable Book, 2007.

Hired as a housekeeper to work on the early 1900s Montana homestead of widower Oliver Milliron, the irreverent Rose and her brother, Morris, endeavor to educate the widower's sons while witnessing local efforts on a massive irrigation project.

"Set in the early 1900s, this novel is a nostalgic, bittersweet story about a widower, his three sons, and the year these boys spend in a one-room country schoolhouse. The novel begins with the father, Oliver, hiring a widowed housekeeper named Rose from Minneapolis (her advertisement reads Can't Cook but Doesn't Bite). She arrives with her unconventional brother, Morrie, in tow. Morrie is something of a scholar, and he soon finds himself pressed into service as a replacement teacher. During the course of the novel, these intriguing and unpredictable characters come together in surprising and uplifting ways. This is an affectionate, heartwarming tale that also celebrates a vanished way of life and laments its passing." Library Journal.

Doiron, Paul

Almost midnight / Paul Doiron. Minotaur Books, 2019. 320 p. Mike Bowditch novels

ISBN 9781250102416

1. Game wardens 2. Prisoners 3. Conspiracies 4. Prisons 5. Wolves 6. Friendship 7. Law enforcement 8. Maine 9. Mysteries

LC 2019005587

When his best friend is released from prison under suspicious circumstances, warden investigator Mike Bowditch races to protect his friend's family only to uncover a violent criminal conspiracy.

Doiron, Paul

Bad Little Falls : a novel / Paul Doiron. Minotaur Books, 2012. 320 p. Mike Bowditch novels

ISBN 9780312558482

1. Game wardens 2. Murder investigation -- Maine 3. Wilderness areas -- Maine 4. Drug dealers 5. Blizzards -- Maine 6. Murder -- Maine 7. Maine 8. Thrillers and suspense

LC 2012007787

Summoned to a rustic cabin during a blizzard, Maine game warden Mike Bowdich embarks on a dangerous investigation involving a notorious drug dealer, a beautiful woman with a dark past and her troubled young son.

Doiron, Paul

The **poacher's** son / Paul Doiron. Minotaur Books, 2010. 336 p. Mike Bowditch novels

ISBN 9780312558468

1. Game wardens 2. Poachers 3. Fathers and sons 4. Fugitives 5. Murder suspects 6. Alcoholics 7. Wilderness areas -- Maine 8. Maine 9. Thrillers and suspense

LC 2009041136

Desperate and alone, game warden Mike Bowditch strikes up an uneasy alliance with a retired warden pilot, and together the two men journey deep into the Maine wilderness in search of a runaway fugitive--Mike's father. But the only way for Mike to save his father is to find the real killer--which could mean putting everyone he loves in the line of fire.

"Along with nostalgic laments about the old-growth woods and modest settlements that have already fallen to civilization, Doiron provides wonderful scenes of present-day bear-tracking and man-hunting through the kind of terrain that attracts hikers, hunters and the odd paranoid militia freak like the one causing so much trouble in this story." New York Times Book Review.

Doiron, Paul

The **precipice** / Paul Doiron. Minotaur Books, 2015. 320 p. Mike Bowditch novels

ISBN 9781250063694

1. Game wardens 2. Wilderness areas -- Maine 3. Hikers 4. Murder investigation 5. Murder 6. Maine 7. Thrillers and suspense

When a pair of lovers are declared the victims of a coyote attack on a remote stretch of the Appalachian Trail, Mike Bowditch clashes with his biologist girlfriend, who believes that the victims were murdered.

"Bowditch is an uncomplicated good guy who might even be considered boring except for the lively conversations on topics as diverse as atheism, sexuality, and animal rights. This unexpected thoughtfulness makes his character appealing enough for readers to cheer him on." Library Journal.

Doiron, Paul

Stay hidden / Paul Doiron. Minotaur Books, 2018. 320 p. Mike Bowditch novels

ISBN 9781250102386

1. Game wardens 2. Women murder victims 3. Islands 4. Communities 5. Sisters 6. Women authors 7. Secrets 8. Maine 9. Mysteries

LC 2018004439

When a woman is killed in an apparent hunting accident on an island off the coast of Maine, newly promoted Warden Investigator Mike Bowditch discovers that the victim, a controversial author writing about a local recluse, died of other causes.

"The plot is complex, and the action intense, made all the more so by forbidding terrain. The characters are well developed and clearly defined despite the dense fog that surrounds them, literally and figuratively." Booklist.

Dolan, Harry

Bad things happen / Harry Dolan. Amy Einhorn Books, 2009. 352 p. David Loogan mysteries

ISBN 9780399155635

1. Periodical editors 2. Murder investigation 3. Extramarital affairs 4. Women detectives -- Michigan 5. Single mothers 6. Murder suspects 7. Ann Arbor, Michigan 8. Mysteries

LC 2008054628

The man who calls himself David Loogan is leading a quiet, anonymous life in the college town of Ann Arbor, Michigan. He's hoping to escape a violent past he would rather forget. But his solitude is broken when he finds himself drawn into a friendship with Tom Kristoll, publisher of the mystery magazine Gray Streets--and into an affair with Laura, Tom's sleek blond wife. When Tom offers him a job as an editor, Loogan sees no harm in accepting. What he doesn't realize is that the stories in Gray Streets tend to follow a simple formula: Plans go wrong. Bad things happen. People die.--From publisher's description.

"Although the plot is fairly outlandish, the narrative comes with startling developments and nicely tricky reversals. There's also something appealingly offbeat about the wry, dry tone of its academic humor, which has much to do with the self-important authors who figure in the hectic plot." New York Times Book Review.

Dolan, Harry

Very bad men / Harry Dolan. Amy Einhorn Books, 2011. 412 p. David Loogan mysteries

ISBN 9780399157493

1. Periodical editors 2. Manuscripts 3. Confession (Law) 4. Criminal Investigation 5. Murder investigation 6. Ann Arbor, Michigan 7. Mysteries

Living a quiet life with Detective Elizabeth Waishkey and her daughter, mystery magazine editor David Loogan receives a sinister manuscript that begins with a murder confession and names individuals who are being stalked and killed for their involvement in a notorious robbery years earlier.

"Anthony Lark's mission is simple: to kill three of the men involved in a fatally botched bank robbery 17 years ago. He's already dispatched two of his targets--an impressive feat, considering that one of them, Terry Dawtrey, is serving 30 years in Kinross Prison--when he identifies them both and announces his third, nurse practitioner Sutton Bell, in an anonymous letter to Loogan . . . , who promptly shares it with his ladylove, police detective Elizabeth Waishkey. The timely intervention of aspiring tabloid reporter Lucy Navarro saves Bell from Lark's initial attempt and gives Dolan a chance to fill in some back story. . . . Dolan mixes his pitches with an ace's judgment, steadily complicating Lark's quest while keeping the psychology of his characters considerably more plausible than in Loogan's equally baroque debut. The rare crime novel with something for everyone who reads crime fiction." Kirkus.

Dolan-Leach, Caite

We went to the woods : a novel / Caite Dolan-Leach. Random House, 2019 352 p.

ISBN 9780399588884

1. Communes 2. Farm life 3. Idealism 4. Social isolation 5. Twenties (Age) 6. Farms 7. Rural life 8. Secrets 9. Sexuality 10. Interpersonal relations 11. New York (State) 12. Literary fiction

Convinced that society is on the brink of collapse, five disillusioned twenty-somethings create a self-sustaining socialist commune, before their utopian vision is marred by desire, suspicion and betrayal.

"Equal parts slow-burning thriller and intelligent analysis of the pros and cons of intentional communities, the novel will appeal to those who would rather read about such endeavors from a safe distance than be immersed in their messy reality." Kirkus.

Donati, Sara, 1956-

Where the light enters / Sara Donati. Berkley, 2019. xi, 652 p. Gilded hour novels

ISBN 9780425271827

1. Gilded Age (1865-1898) 2. Women physicians 3. Violence against women 4. Multiracial women 5. Abortion 6. Serial murderers 7. Women -- Social conditions 8. Public health 9. Violence in men 10. Serial murder investigation 11. Loss (Psychology) 12. Families 13. Family relationships 14. New York (State) -- History -- 19th century 15. Historical fiction

LC 2019008855

A black obstetrician returns to Manhattan in 1884 to move in with her best friend and fellow physician after the tragic loss of her family.

"As she brings the sights, sounds, smells, and social mores of 1884 New York into sharp focus, Donati creates a timely tale of the past that illuminates the ongoing struggle for women's reproductive rights and sheds light on the passionate, centuries-long fight over abortion." Booklist.

Donoghue, Emma, 1969-

Akin / Emma Donoghue. Little Brown & Co, 2019. 304 p.

ISBN 9780316491990

1. 21st century 2. Retirees 3. Widowers 4. French Americans 5. Guardian and ward 6. Coastal towns 7. World War II 8. Family and war 9. Family secrets 10. Senior men 11. Preteen boys 12. Loss (Psychology) 13. Technology 14. Family relationships 15. Nice, France 16. France 17. Literary fiction

A retired New York professor's life is thrown into chaos when he takes a young great-nephew to the French Riviera in hopes of uncovering his own mother's wartime secrets.

Donoghue, Emma, 1969-

* **Frog** music / Emma Donoghue. Little, Brown & Co., 2014. 405 p.

ISBN 9780316324687

1. Gilded Age (1865-1898) 2. 1870s 3. Murder investigation 4. Mothers 5. Amateur detectives 6. Friendship 7. Identity (Psychology) 8. Prostitutes 9. Mother-separated children 10. Abandonment (Psychology) 11. San Francisco, California -- History -- 19th century 12. The West (United States) -- History -- 19th century 13. Historical mysteries 14. Literary fiction

Burlesque dancer Blanche Beunon tries to discover who murdered her friend Jenny, who was shot through a window in a railroad saloon in 1876 San Francisco, amidst a record-breaking heat wave and smallpox epidemic.

"[A]n engrossing and suspenseful tale about moral growth, unlikely friendship, and breaking free from the past." Booklist.

Donoghue, Emma, 1969-

* **Room** : a novel / Emma Donoghue. Little, Brown and Co., 2010. ix, 321 p.

ISBN 9780316098335

1. Antisocial personality disorders 2. Captives 3. Boys 4. Mother and child 5. Captivity 6. Psychological fiction 7. Literary fiction

LC 2010006983

This book was made into film under the same name in 2015, directed by Lenny Abrahamson, and starring Brie Larson, Joan Allen, William H. Macy and Jacob Tremblay.

ALA Notable Book, 2011.

CBA Libris Award for Fiction Book of the Year, 2011.

Evergreen Award (Ontario), 2011.

Goodreads Choice Award, 2010.

Kentucky Bluegrass Award for Grades 9-12, 2012.

Rogers Writers' Trust Fiction Prize, 2010.

Shortlisted for the Man Booker Prize, 2010.

Shortlisted for The Orange Prize for Fiction, 2011

Governor General's Literary Awards, English-language Fiction finalist

A 5-year-old narrates a riveting story about his life growing up in a single room where his mother aims to protect him from the man who has held her prisoner for seven years since she was a teenager.

"Though the story's chilling circumstances reflect the horrors endured by tabloid-famous abductees, Donoghue avoids all sensationalism. Instead, she gracefully distills what it means to be a mother and what it's like for a child whose entire world measures just 11 x 11." Entertainment Weekly.

Donoghue, Emma, 1969-

Slammerkin / Emma Donoghue. Harcourt, 2001, c2000. 336 p.

ISBN 9780151006724

1. Saunders, Mary, died 1764 2. Georgian era (1714-1837) 3. 18th century 4. Teenage prostitutes 5. Women murderers 6. Young women 7. Clothing 8. Great Britain -- History -- George III, 1760-1820 9. London, England -- History -- 18th century 10. Monmouth, Wales 11. Biographical fiction 12. Historical fiction 13. Literary fiction

LC 00049867

Originally published: London : Virago, 2000.

Born to poverty in eighteenth-century London, Mary Saunders' love of fine clothes and a dream of a better life take her from the world of prostitution to life as a household seamstress in Monmouth to a search for true freedom.

"In her storytelling, the author shrewdly alternates the point of view, a technique that, rather than feeling gratuitous and shticky as it so often does these days, works to put Mary in a delicious pickle, since the satisfaction of her deepest desires, and the revelation of her secret career, could crush those for whom sheand wecome to feel real affection." New York Times Book Review.

Donoghue, Emma, 1969-

* The **wonder** / Emma Donoghue. Little, Brown and Company, 2016. 291 p.

ISBN 9780316393874

1. 1850s 2. Belief and doubt 3. Faith (Christianity) 4. Villages 5. Fasting 6. Miracles 7. Nurses 8. Murder 9. Ireland -- History -- 19th century 10. Historical fiction 11. Literary fiction

Shortlisted for the Giller Prize, 2016

Hired to care for a small Irish village girl said to have miraculously survived on nothing but "manna from heaven" for months, a journalist and nurse veteran of Florence Nightingale's Crimean campaign quickly finds herself fighting to save the child's life.

"Donoghue's most recent offering is as startlingly rewarding as her celebrated novel Room. Heart-hammering suspense builds as Lib monitors Anna's quickening pulse, making this book's bracing conclusion one of the most satisfying in recent fiction." Library Journal.

Donohue, Keith

The **stolen** child / Keith Donohue. Nan A. Talese, Double-day, 2006. 336 p.

ISBN 0385516169

1. Boy kidnapping victims 2. Goblins 3. Identity (Psychology) 4. Changelings 5. Doppelgangers 6. Pianists 7. Kidnapping victims 8. Young men -- Identity 9. Kidnapping 10. Impostors 11. Secret identity 12. Magic 13. Coping 14. Loss (Psychology) 15. Belonging 16. Alienation (Social psychology) 17. New England 18. Contemporary fantasy

LC 2005053828

Stolen from his family by changelings, Henry Day is given the name "Aniday" by the ageless and magical beings, who replace him with another child who takes his place with his parents, a young boy who possesses an extraordinary gift of music.

"On the surface, Donohue may seem to have written a clever debut novel about fairies. But the real triumph of the book is that, while our backs were turned, he has performed a switch and delivered a luminous and thrilling novel about our humanity." Washington Post Book World.

Dorris, Michael

Cloud chamber : a novel / Michael Dorris. Scribner, 1997. 316 p.

ISBN 0684815672

1. Irish Americans 2. Interracial families 3. Family relationships 4. Men with amnesia 5. Women -- Identity 6. African-Native American girls 7. Kentucky 8. Pacific Northwest 9. Family sagas

LC 96042544

Sequel to: A yellow raft in blue water.

From late nineteenth century Ireland to present-day America, the diverse members of a family--men, women, and children--speak out in their own voices about their emotions, passions, determination, memories, and the persistence of the love that binds them together.

"Though not unflawed--a few voices sound confusingly similar and a few characters are more types than people--this is a compellingly readable and emotionally satisfying novel, full of secrets and surprises." Booklist.

Dorris, Michael

* A **yellow** raft in blue water / Michael Dorris Warner Books, 1988, c1987. 372 p.

ISBN 9780446387873

1. Native American women 2. Indian reservations 3. Family relationships 4. Fifteen-year-old girls 5. Family secrets 6. Resentfulness 7. Families 8. Interpersonal relations 9. African-Native American girls 10. Montana 11. Pacific Northwest 12. Family sagas

Sequel: Cloud chamber.

Moving backward in time, Dorris's critically acclaimed debut novel is a lyrical saga of three generations of Native American women beset by hardship and torn by angry secrets.

"The bitter rifts and inevitable bonds between generations are highlighted as a teenaged daughter, mother, and grand matriarch of an American Indian family tell their life stories. Humorous and poignant, with unique characters." School Library Journal.

Dos Passos, John, 1896-1970

* **1919** / John Dos Passos. Houghton Mifflin, 2000, c1932. xv, 380 p. U.S.A. series

ISBN 0618056823

1. Edison, Thomas A (Thomas Alva), 1847-1931 2. Carnegie, Andrew, 1835-1919 3. First World War era (1914-1918) 4. Sailors -- United States 5. Manners and customs 6. Jewish Americans 7.

Poets, American 8. Social problems -- United States 9. World War I -- Influence and results 10. World War I 11. Children of clergy 12. Women -- Texas 13. United States -- History -- 1913-1921 14. United States -- History -- 1900-1945 15. New York City -- History -- 1900-1945 16. United States -- History -- 20th century 17. New York City -- History -- 20th century 18. Literary fiction 19. Modern classics

LC 00027609

Originally published: New York : Harcourt, Brace and Company, 1932.

"A Mariner book."

"1919' is literally what so many books are erroneously called, 'a slice of life.' With infinite skill that slicing is done by the author, and the raw surface which meets the reader's eye is the actual living, breathing record of a period in its most intense manifestation." Chicago Daily Tribune.

Dos Passos, John, 1896-1970

* The **42nd** parallel / John Dos Passos ; illustrated by Reginald Marsh ; with an introduction by Alfred Kazin. Signet Classics, 1969. 414 p. U.S.A. series

ISBN 0451524578

1. United States -- History -- 1913-1921 2. Literary fiction 3. Modern classics

The narrator presents life in the United States through a variety of methods, incidents, and characters.

Dos Passos, John, 1896-1970

Manhattan transfer / John Dos Passos. Houghton Mifflin Co., 2000, c1925. 342 p.

ISBN 9780618381869

1. 1920s 2. City life 3. Alienation (Social psychology) 4. Social change 5. Fate and fatalism 6. Modernization (Social sciences) 7. Capitalism -- Moral and ethical aspects 8. Immigrants 9. Rich people 10. Poor people 11. New York City 12. Psychological fiction 13. Experimental fiction 14. Literary fiction

LC 2003272269

Originally published: New York : Harper & Brothers, 1925.

Vignettes in the lives of numerous characters create a picture of life in New York City during the early twenties.

Dostoyevsky, Fyodor, 1821-1881

The **best** short stories of Dostoevsky / Fyodor Dostoyevsky ; translated with an introduction by David Magarshack. Modern Library, 1992, c1955. 348 p.

ISBN 9780679600206

1. Russia -- History -- 19th century 2. Classics 3. Psychological fiction 4. Short stories 5. Translations -- Russian to English

LC 55010655

7 short stories.

Offers a collection of the Russian author's shorter fiction that features both his best known works and less familiar writing, including early sketches that reveal the development of his style and his understanding of psychology.

Dostoyevsky, Fyodor, 1821-1881

* The **brothers** Karamazov / Fyodor Dostoevsky ; translated from the Russian by Richard Pevear and Larissa Volokhonsky ; introduced by Malcolm V. Jones. Knopf, 1992. xxxiii, 796 p.

ISBN 9780679410034

1. Romanov Dynasty (1613-1917) 2. Brothers 3. Parricide

4. Peasantry 5. Fathers and sons 6. Sibling rivalry 7. Guilt -- Psychological aspects 8. Personal conduct 9. Religion 10. Fathers -- Death 11. Russia -- History -- 19th century 12. Classics 13. Psychological fiction 14. Translations -- Russian to English

Driven by intense, uncontrollable emotions of rage and revenge, the four Karamazov brothers all become involved in the brutal murder of their despicable father.

Dostoyevsky, Fyodor, 1821-1881

* **Crime** and punishment / Fyodor Dostoyevsky ; translated by Constance Garnett. Dover Publications, 2001. xii, 430 p.

ISBN 0486415872

1. 19th century 2. Murderers -- Psychology 3. Conscience 4. Guilt in men 5. Criminals 6. Murder 7. Crime 8. Poverty 9. Russia 10. St Petersburg, Russia 11. Psychological fiction 12. Translations -- Russian to English 13. Classics

Originally published: London : Heinemann, 1914.

Believing he can commit the perfect crime, Roderick Raskolnikov robs and murders an elderly pawnbroker. He eventually finds himself engaged in a battle of wits with inspector Porfiry, a policeman who is determined to wring a confession from the once confident Raskolnikov, a killer whose conscience is slowly beginning to destroy him.

Dostoyevsky, Fyodor, 1821-1881

Notes from underground / Fyodor Dostoevsky ; translated from the Russian by Richard Pevear and Larissa Volkhonsky [sic] ; with an introduction by Richard Pevear. Alfred A. Knopf, 2004, c1864. xxxi, 126 p.

ISBN 1400041910

1. Romanov Dynasty (1613-1917) 2. Suffering in men 3. Social isolation 4. Humiliation 5. Middle-aged men 6. Individuality 7. Misfits (Persons) 8. Loners 9. Russia -- History -- 1801-1917 10. Psychological fiction 11. Black humor 12. Translations -- Russian to English 13. Classics

LC 2003059216

First published in 1864.

Written in 1864, this classic novel recounts the apology and confession of a minor nineteenth-century official, an account of the man's separation from society, and his descent "underground."

Douglas, Lloyd C. (Lloyd Cassel), 1877-1951

Magnificent obsession / Lloyd C. Douglas. Houghton Mifflin, 1929. 330 p. Dr. Hudson series

1. Neurosurgeons 2. Near-death experience 3. Redemption 4. Christian life 5. Philanthropists 6. Faith (Christianity) 7. Life change events 8. Obsession 9. Self-sacrifice 10. Diaries 11. Detroit, Michigan -- History -- 20th century 12. Michigan -- History -- 20th century 13. Psychological fiction 14. Christian fiction

A local hero, Dr Wayne Phillips, dies because the equipment that could save him is being used to help Bob Merrick, a spoiled rich man who has wrecked his speed boat. Dr Phillips gave selflessly and in secret to many people and causes, which Merrick now takes up too. However his efforts end in failure and also alienate Dr Phillips' widow, Helen, with whom he is besotted.

Dovlatov, Sergei, 1941-1990

Pushkin Hills / Sergei Dovlatov. Counterpoint Press, 2014. 160 p.

ISBN 9781619022454

1. Authors, Russian 2. Alcoholic men 3. Divorced men 4. Tour guides (Persons) 5. Literary fiction 6. Satirical fiction 7. Translations

-- Russian to English

LC 2013028859

An unsuccessful writer and an inveterate alcoholic, Boris Alikhanov has recently divorced his wife Tatyana, and he is running out of money. The prospect of a summer job as a tour guide at the Pushkin Hills Preserve offers him hope of regaining some balance in life as his wife makes plans to emigrate to the West with their daughter Masha, but during Alikhanov's stay in the rural estate of Mikhaylovskoye, his life continues to unravel.

Dow, David R.

Confessions of an innocent man / David R. Dow. Dutton, 2019. 304 p.

ISBN 9781524743888

1. Death row prisoners 2. Judicial error 3. Criminal justice system 4. Innocence (Law) 5. Women murder victims 6. Mexican Americans 7. Revenge 8. Prisons 9. Death row 10. Women billionaires 11. Justice 12. Prisoners 13. DNA fingerprinting 14. Criminal evidence 15. Houston, Texas 16. Texas 17. Legal thrillers 18. Thrillers and suspense

When an Austin billionaire is murdered, her husband, Rafael Zhettah, the son of poor Mexican immigrants, is sent to death row, only to have DNA evidence vindicate him six years later, spurring him to take revenge on the people that ruined his life.

Dowlatabadi, Mahmoud

The **colonel** / Mahmoud Dowlatabadi ; translated from the Persian by Tom Patterdale. Melville House, 2012. v, 247 p.

ISBN 9781612191324

1. Father and child 2. Political corruption 3. Soldiers 4. Ayatollahs 5. Islam and state 6. Torture 7. Daughters -- Death 8. Guilt in men 9. Iran -- History -- Islamic revolution, 1979-1997 10. Political fiction 11. Psychological fiction 12. Translations -- Persian to English

In a small Iranian town on a dark rain-soaked night, the Colonel paces back and forth waiting for the inevitable knock on the door. The secret police take him to the tortured body of his youngest daughter, for the Islamic revolution is devouring its own children. This shocking diatribe leaves no taboo unbroken.

Downie, Ruth, 1955-

Caveat emptor : a novel of the Roman Empire / Ruth Downie. Bloomsbury USA, 2010. 338 p. Ruso mysteries

ISBN 9781596916081

1. Roman Britain (55 BCE-449 CE) 2. 2nd century 3. Physicians -- Rome 4. Missing persons 5. Romans 6. Military physicians 7. Treasure troves 8. Revenue agents 9. Conspiracies 10. Great Britain -- History -- Roman period, 55 BC-449 AD 11. Historical mysteries 12. Mysteries

LC 2010034525

In the far reaches of the Roman Empire, there are three certainties in life for Doctor Gaius Petreius Ruso: death, taxes, and angry barbarians. The hero finds himself trapped at the heart of an increasingly treacherous conspiracy involving theft, forgery, buried treasure, and the legacy of Boudica, the rebel queen.

"Serial physician (medicus) and de facto detective Gaius Petreius Ruso is assigned to investigate the suspicious disappearance of both tax collector Julius Asper and money owed to the coffers of Emperor Hadrian. Ruso traces a path between the Roman command center in Londinium and the northern metropolis (Verulamium) whence Asper and his brother (also missing) have presumably fled. When it appears both fugitives were murdered, Asper's pregnant common-law wife begins hurling accusations. Ruso's former servant and present wife Tilla does what she usually does, helping out, investigating on her own and attracting the threatening attentions of assorted suspects. . . . As always, Downie displays a virtuoso's command of pertinent period detail." Kirkus.

Downie, Ruth, 1955-
Medicus : a novel of the Roman Empire / Ruth Downie. Bloomsbury, 2007, c2006. 386 p. Ruso mysteries
ISBN 9781596912311
1. Roman Britain (55 BCE-449 CE) 2. 2nd century 3. Murder investigation 4. Prostitutes -- Great Britain 5. Military physicians 6. Slaves -- Emancipation 7. Romans 8. Divorced men 9. Military medicine 10. Women murder victims 11. Rome -- History -- Empire, 30 BC-476 AD 12. Great Britain -- History -- Roman period, 55 BC-449 AD 13. Historical mysteries 14. Mysteries
LC 2006013179
Originally published in the UK as Medicus and the Disappearing Dancing Girls, London: Michael Joseph, 2006.
A down-on-his-luck Roman army doctor, Gaius Petreius Ruso decides to seek his fortune in one of the far outposts of the Roman Empire, journeying to Britannia, where he rescues an injured slave girl, Tilla, from her abusive owner.

Downie, Ruth, 1955-
Semper Fidelis : a novel of the Roman Empire / Ruth Downie. Bloomsbury, 2013. 330 p. Ruso mysteries
ISBN 9781608197095
1. Roman Britain (55 BCE-449 CE) 2. Physicians 3. Rulers 4. Roman emperors 5. Crimes against soldiers 6. Romans 7. Military physicians 8. Murder investigation 9. Murder suspects 10. Great Britain -- History -- Roman period, 55 BC-449 AD 11. Historical mysteries 12. Mysteries
Resuming his medical duties in the Twentieth legion in Roman-occupied Britain, Gaius Petreius Ruso investigates an outbreak of mysterious injuries and deaths among the native recruits to Britannia's imperial army and discovers possible links to the revered Centurion Geminus and the long-awaited Emperor Hadrian, findings that place his wife in jeopardy.

Downie, Ruth, 1955-
Tabula rasa : a crime novel of the Roman Empire / Ruth Downie. Bloomsbury USA, 2014. 352 p. Ruso mysteries
ISBN 9781608197088
1. Roman Britain (55 BCE-449 CE) 2. Physicians 3. Hadrian's Wall 4. Missing persons 5. Romans 6. Culture conflict 7. Rulers 8. Roman emperors 9. Military physicians 10. Military occupation 11. Missing persons investigation 12. Great Britain -- History -- Roman period, 55 BC-449 AD 13. Historical mysteries 14. Mysteries
The medicus Ruso and his wife Tilla are back in the borderlands of Britannia, this time helping to tend the builders of Hadrian's Great Wall. Having been forced to move off their land, the Britons are distinctly on edge and are still smarting from the failure of a recent rebellion that claimed many lives.
"Downie writes with quiet authority and surprising depth, offering an engaging depiction of an obscure slice of history." Kirkus.

Downie, Ruth, 1955-
Terra incognita : a novel of the Roman Empire / Ruth Downie. Bloomsbury, 2008. 400 p. Ruso mysteries
ISBN 9781596912328
1. Roman Britain (55 BCE-449 CE) 2. 2nd century 3. Murder investigation 4. Military physicians 5. Romans 6. Divorced men 7. Military medicine 8. Murder 9. Rome -- History -- Hadrian, 117-138 10. Rome -- History -- Empire, 30 BC-476 AD 11. Great Britain -- History -- Roman period, 55 BC-449 AD 12. Historical mysteries

13. Mysteries
LC 2007044474
"Published in the United Kingdom with the title Ruso and the Demented Doctor by Penguin Books Ltd. in 2008"--T.p. verso.
Army doctor Gaius Petrius Ruso journeys to early second-century Britannia in the hope of securing a quieter life, only to encounter local turbulence, a circumstance that is complicated by the vengeful plans of his slave, Tilla.
"Saving this novel from a certain gritty grimness often found in mysteries is Downie's wry and witty humor." Library Journal.

Downing, David, 1946-
Diary of a dead man on leave / David Downing. Soho Press, 2019. 312 p.
ISBN 9781616958435
1. Second World War era (1939-1945) 2. World War II 3. Spies -- Russia 4. Soldiers 5. Espionage 6. Undercover operations 7. Diary writing 8. Father figures 9. Women boarding house owners 10. Boys 11. Children and war 12. World War II -- Children 13. Communists 14. Communism -- Germany 15. Germany 16. Spy fiction 17. Historical thrillers 18. Diary novels
LC 2018046837
Stumbling across the hidden diary of a boarder who had been a father figure to him half a century earlier, Walter discovers the man's life-risking undercover work as an anti-Nazi Moscow spy.
"This is a quiet, largely introspective spy novel, very different in mood from Downing's adventure-fueled Jack McColl novels, but it packs an equal if not greater emotional wallop." Booklist.

Downing, Samantha
He started it / Samantha Downing. Berkley, 2020. 384 p.
ISBN 9780451491756
1. Inheritance and succession 2. Brothers and sisters 3. Family secrets 4. Automobile travel 5. Funerals 6. Murderers 7. Greed 8. Family relationships 9. Thrillers and suspense
LC 2019050012
In the latest thrillingly savage stand-alone from the twisted mind behind mega hit My Lovely Wife comes the story of a family--not unlike your own--just with a few more violent tendencies thrown in....
"With our need to know ramped up through a series of teasers offering more to come, this tale is virtually impossible to put down." Booklist.

Downing, Samantha
My lovely wife / Samantha Downing. Berkley, 2019. 384 p.
ISBN 9780451491725
1. Husband and wife 2. Murderers 3. Marriage burn out 4. Married people -- Psychology 5. Married people and secrets 6. Boredom 7. Suburban life 8. Copycat murderers 9. Serial murderers 10. Psychological suspense
A seemingly typical suburban husband discloses the secret ways that his wife of 15 years and he keep their marriage alive and chase away domestic boredom by orchestrating creative ways to get away with murder.

Doyle, Arthur Conan,, Sir, 1859-1930
* The **complete** Sherlock Holmes / Sir Arthur Conan Doyle ; with a preface by Christopher Morley. Doubleday, 1930. 1323 p. Sherlock Holmes mysteries
ISBN 9780385006897
1. 19th century 2. Criminal investigation 3. Amateur detectives 4. Private investigators 5. Murder investigation 6. Eccentrics and eccentricities 7. London, England -- Social life and customs -- 19th

century 8. Short stories 9. Mysteries 10. Classics

LC 30023546

Here, collected in one volume, are all four full-length novels and 56 short stories chronicling the colorful adventures of Sherlock Holmes--every word Sir Arthur Conan Doyle ever wrote about Baker Street's most famous resident.

Doyle, Brian, 1956 November 6-

* The **plover** : a novel / Brian Doyle. Thomas Dunne Books, 2014. 311 p.

ISBN 9781250034779

1. Ship captains 2. Self-discovery 3. Voyages and travels 4. Ocean travel 5. Interpersonal relations 6. Misadventures 7. Oregon 8. Sea stories 9. Pacific Northwest fiction

LC 2013032101

Voyaging into the Pacific to escape his troubled life in Oregon, Declan O'Donnell bonds with his crewmates and learns of their own respective quests for self, exchanges that lead to a shared celebration of life's unexpected paths.

"Doyle ... has written a novel in the adventurous style of Jack London and Robert Louis Stevenson but with a gentle mocking of their valorization of the individual as absolute. Readers will enjoy this bracing and euphoric ode to the vastness of the ocean and the unexpectedness of life." Library Journal.

Doyle, Rob

Threshold / Rob Doyle. Bloomsbury, 2020. 316 p.

ISBN 9781635574142

1. Voyages and travels 2. Travelers 3. Authors 4. Writing 5. Creativity in men 6. Art 7. Drug use 8. Spirituality 9. Sexuality 10. Literary fiction 11. Epistolary novels

An uninhibited portrait of the artist as a perpetual drifter and truthseeker--a funny, profound, compulsive read that's like traveling with your wildest and most philosophical friend.

"Doyle's musings are always intriguing and often enlightening, offering a glimpse of the anxious yet pleasing rationale of a mind struggling to live in a rational world." Publishers Weekly.

Doyle, Roddy, 1958-

The **guts** / Roddy Doyle. Viking Press, 2014, c2013. 327 p. Barrytown novels

ISBN 9780670016433

1. Musicians 2. Middle-aged men 3. Fathers and sons 4. Middle age 5. People with cancer 6. Dublin, Ireland 7. Ireland 8. Humorous stories

Sequel to: The van.

Originally published: London: Jonathan Cape, 2013.

A follow-up to The Commitments finds a middle-aged Jimmy battling cancer and reconnecting with his musical past by tracking down the resurrected albums of old bands, practicing the trumpet, reuniting with his long-lost brother and rediscovering the joys of fatherhood.

Doyle, Roddy, 1958-

* **Paddy** Clarke, ha-ha-ha / Roddy Doyle. Viking, 1993. 282 p.

ISBN 9780670853458

1. 1960s 2. Working class families 3. Childhood 4. Catholic boys 5. Growing up 6. Family relationships 7. Ten-year-old boys 8. Father-deserted families 9. Dublin, Ireland 10. Literary fiction 11. Coming-of-age stories

LC 93216955

Booker Prize, 1993.

Paddy Clarke, a ten-year-old boy who longs to be a missionary, experiences life's joys and setbacks--specifically his parent's fights--as he grows up in the north of Liffey, Ireland, in the late 1960s.

"Doyle's triumph in this novel is to replenish our sense of how children think and speak and explain the adult world to themselves." London Review of Books.

Doyle, Roddy, 1958-

* **Smile** / Roddy Doyle. Viking, 2017. 214 p.

ISBN 9780735224445

1. Christian Brothers 2. Memory 3. Psychic trauma 4. Men -- Psychology 5. Marital conflict 6. Former friends 7. Memories 8. Reunions 9. Schools 10. Ireland 11. Psychological fiction

Approached by a man he does not remember who claims they attended secondary school together, a man on his own for the first time in years reluctantly reflects on unhappy memories from the past, including those of a brutal teacher who left him traumatized and struggling to hold fast to his sanity.

"Doyle's ability to convey so much meaning through rapid-fire dialog in the Irish vernacular is unsurpassed. His commentary about the Catholic Church, sexuality, and repression is searing." Library Journal.

Doyle, Roddy, 1958-

A **star** called Henry / Roddy Doyle. Viking, 1999. 343 p. The last roundup (Roddy Doyle)

ISBN 9780670887576

1. Irish Republican Army 2. Easter Rising, 1916 3. Rebels -- Ireland -- History -- 20th century 4. Irish resistance and revolts 5. Dublin, Ireland 6. Ireland -- History -- 20th century 7. Picaresque fiction 8. Historical fiction

LC 99-25310

ALA Notable Book, 2000.

Offers a portrait of an adventuresome Irishman named Henry Smart, an IRA assassin and 1916 Easter Rebellion fighter, from his Dublin birth to his adulthood, when he becomes the father of a young rebel.

"In Doyle's hands, the grand patriotic narrative is tempered with a sharp sense of humanity and human frailty." Times Literary Supplement.

Drabble, Margaret, 1939-

A **day** in the life of a smiling woman : complete short stories / Margaret Drabble ; edited by Jose Francisco Fernandez. Houghton Mifflin Harcourt, 2011. 208 p.

ISBN 9780547550404

1. Female friendship 2. Interpersonal relations 3. Short stories

LC 2010049798

A single-volume compilation of the 2008 Dame of the British Empire's previously uncollected short works offers insight into her use of irony, female friendships and personal passions and is complemented by an introduction that places her works in a context of her life and novels.

"The discursive spaciousness of Margaret Drabble's voice and vision lends itself to the long form, as her 17 splendid novels demonstrate. This may help to explain why her complete short stories make up so slender a volume. Drabble, it seems, just didn't have enough time to write short stories (with apologies to Mark Twain). Of those collected here, 14 in all, the earliest dates from the 1950s, the most recent from the 1990s. Some are reed slim, but many glimmer with the irony, lyricism, moral vision and (despite their page counts) amplitude we associate with Drabble's novels. They reflect back to us the last half of the 20th century, albeit in Drabble's often 19th-century voice." New York Times Book Review.

LIST OF FICTIONAL WORKS

Doyle, Roddy, 1958-

* The **woman** who walked into doors / Roddy Doyle. Viking, 1996. 226 p. Paula Spencer novels

ISBN 9780670867752

1. Working class women 2. Middle-aged women 3. Alcoholic women 4. Abused women 5. Ireland 6. Psychological fiction

LC 95-418650

Sequel: Paula Spencer.

ALA Notable Book, 1997.

Relates the story of Paula Spencer, a woman approaching forty and struggling with alcoholism and a violent marriage.

"Doyle is a very, very good writer. 'The Woman Who Walked Into Doors' honors not the female experience in the abstract, but the experience of this one woman, Paula Spencer; it examines it with tenderness, but with fearless clearsightedness. And it's funny in places too. Paula Spencer is neither a victim nor a flawless Madonna; she inhabits the complexity of her mind and history; she acts to buy a better future for her children." New York Times Book Review.

Drabble, Margaret, 1939-

* The **dark** flood rises / Margaret Drabble. Farrar, Straus and Giroux, 2017, c2016. 336 p.

ISBN 9780374134952

1. Aging 2. Caregivers 3. Senior women 4. May/December romance 5. Men/women relations 6. Family relationships 7. Men/men relations 8. Septuagenarians 9. Mortality 10. Seniors 11. England 12. Canary Islands 13. Literary fiction 14. Psychological fiction

LC 2016025620

Originally published in 2016 by Canongate Books.

Driven to live life to its fullest while she still can, a housing expert for the elderly balances her challenging career with the cares of her loved ones, in a tale that juxtaposes her interconnected social circle in England against her contacts in an idyllic expat community in the Canary Islands.

"For women of a certain age, it is a pure pleasure to grow older alongside Drabble... For all others, there's plenty of joy to be had in this thoughtful meditation on aging and mortality." Library Journal.

Drabble, Margaret, 1939-

The **pure** gold baby / Margaret Drabble. Houghton Mifflin Harcourt, 2013. 291 p.

ISBN 9780544158900

1. Mothers of children with disabilities 2. Women anthropologists 3. Children with disabilities 4. Female friendship 5. Motherhood 6. Fate and fatalism 7. Single mothers 8. Change 9. Aging 10. London, England 11. Literary fiction 12. Psychological fiction

LC 2013021736

Her promising career in 1960s London interrupted by an affair with a married professor that renders her a single mother, anthropology student Jessica Speight faces wrenching questions about responsibility, potential and compassion when her sunny child reveals unique needs.

Drabble, Margaret, 1939-

The **sea** lady / Margaret Drabble. Harcourt, 2007. 352 p.
ISBN 0151012636

1. Reunions 2. Social acceptance 3. Memories 4. Marine biologists 5. Women scholars and academics 6. Feminists 7. Children -- Friendship 8. Autobiographical memory 9. Men/women relations 10. Secrets 11. Celebrities 12. England -- Social life and customs -- 1945- 13. Psychological fiction 14. Literary fiction

LC 2006023778

Traveling separately to Ornemouth, England, a town by the North Sea where they had spent a summer together as children, Humphrey

Clark and Ailsa Kelman reassess the course of their individual lives and decisions over the past thirty years of separation.

"The author has a keen sense of the past and the ways in which intellectual fashions evolve. She is pitiless--and very funny--about the flimsiness of Ailsa's various posturings. Where Humphrey craves knowledge, Ailsa craves exposure. Their love affair mirrors the age they are living through. . . . Drabble writes beautifully about the passing of time and the sad, incomplete experience of human love." New Statesman.

Drabble, Margaret, 1939-

The **witch** of Exmoor / Margaret Drabble. Harcourt Brace, 1996. 281 p.

ISBN 0151003637

1. Families 2. Eccentric women 3. Women authors 4. Grandmothers 5. Misfits (Persons) 6. Mother and child 7. Missing persons 8. Conflict in families 9. Family relationships 10. Dysfunctional families 11. Inheritance and succession 12. England 13. Satirical fiction 14. Psychological fiction

LC 97-10952

Frieda, the peculiar matriarch of the Palmer family, makes her family wonder what escapade she will think of next and whether her foreign grandson will inherit all her money or if the sinister atmosphere of Exmoor has caused her to lose her mind

"Can politics ever amount to more than the conspiracies we hatch against our parents and the spells we cast on our children? The humbling surprise of Drabble's novel is not that it refuses to resolve this question but that we gradually lose our lofty perspective and begin to have an emotional stake in the answer." The New Yorker.

Drake, Laura, 1954-

The **sweet** spot / Laura Drake. Forever, 2013. 384 p. Sweet on a cowboy novels

ISBN 9781455521951

1. Divorced couples 2. Lovers' reunions 3. Cowboys 4. Second chances 5. Children -- Death 6. Bereavement 7. Second chances 8. Loss (Psychology) 9. Bull riding 10. Ranch life 11. Men/women relations 12. Texas 13. Contemporary romances 14. Western romances

RITA Award for Best First Book, 2014.

Everything changed the day their son died. Driven apart by guilt and grief, Charla Rae and JB go their separate ways... but a cowboy's love doesn't die easily. A chance encounter a year later, JB wants nothing more than to be the man that Charla needs but can she see beyond her broken heart? Can this cowboy get her to love again?

Draper, Sharon M. (Sharon Mills)

* **Forged** by fire / Sharon M. Draper. Atheneum Books for Young Readers, 1997. 151 p. Hazelwood High trilogy

ISBN 068980699X

1. Mother-separated boys 2. African American stepbrothers and stepsisters 3. Incest victims 4. African American teenage boys 5. Sexually abused children 6. African American stepfathers 7. Children of African American drug abusers 8. Fires 9. Great-aunt and child 10. Cincinnati, Ohio 11. Realistic fiction 12. African American fiction 13. Books for reluctant readers

LC 962763

Companion volume to: Tears of a tiger.

Coretta Scott King Award, Author Category, 1998.

Young Hoosier Book Award, Middle Books, 2001.

After surviving a fire, Gerald experiences separation from his mother, the loss of his great aunt, and life with his stepsister's abusive father.

Draven, Grace

Phoenix unbound / Grace Draven. Ace, 2018. 384 p.
Fallen empire
ISBN 9780451489753
1. Imaginary empires 2. Human sacrifice 3. Magic 4. Executions and executioners 5. Interpersonal attraction 6. Men/women relations 7. Good and evil 8. Deception 9. Slavery 10. Fantasy romances
LC 2018018971
A woman with power over fire and illusion and an enslaved son of a chieftain battle a corrupt empire.

Drayson, Nicholas

A **guide** to the birds of East Africa / Nicholas Drayson. Houghton Mifflin Co., 2008. 201 p.
ISBN 9780547152585
1. Ornithologists 2. Bird watching 3. Love triangles 4. Wildlife watching 5. Wildlife refuges -- Kenya 6. Widowers 7. Crushes (Interpersonal relations) 8. Bets 9. Kenya 10. Mainstream fiction
LC 2008017183
ACT Book of the Year, 2009.
Working up the nerve to invite Rose Mbikwa to the Nairobi Hunt Club Ball, Mr. Malik, a reserved, honorable widower, is suddenly confronted by the return of his school nemesis, the flashy Harry Kahn, who also sets his sights on Rose.
"With captivating character sketches and glimpses into Kenyan life and politics, Drayson meets the inevitable comparisons to Alexander McCall Smith without breaking a sweat." Publishers Weekly.

Dreiser, Theodore, 1871-1945

* An **American** tragedy / Theodore Dreiser ; with a new introduction by Richard Lingeman. Signet Classic, 2000, c1925. xv, 859 p.
ISBN 9780451527707
1. Ambition in men 2. Success (Concept) 3. Poor children 4. Murder 5. Men/women relations 6. Murderers 7. Literary fiction 8. Classics
The movie called A place in the sun was inspired by the book.
Originally published: New York : Boni & Liveright, 1925.
The author's classic vision of the dark side of American life looks at the failings of the American dream, in the story of the rise and fall of Clyde Griffiths, who sacrifices everything in his desperate quest for success.

Dreiser, Theodore, 1871-1945

* **Sister** Carrie / Theodore Dreiser. Penguin, 1994, c1900. 499 p.
ISBN 9780140188288
1. 19th century 2. Mistresses 3. Success (Concept) 4. Actors and actresses 5. Moving to a new city 6. Extramarital affairs 7. Men/women relations 8. Survival 9. Coming-of-age stories 10. Classics
LC 78183140
Title of later film version: Carrie (1952).
Originally published: New York : Doubleday, Page & Co., 1900.
Young Caroline Meeber leaves home for the first time and experiences work, love, and the pleasures and responsibilities of independence in late-nineteenth-century Chicago and New York.

Drndic, Dasa, 1946-2018

* **Trieste** / Dasa Drndic ; translated from the Croatian by Ellen Elias-Bursac. Houghton Mifflin Harcourt, 2014, c2007. 359 p.
ISBN 9780547725147
1. Women Holocaust survivors 2. Mother and adult son 3. World War II 4. Jewish women 5. Senior women 6. Reminiscing in old age 7. Nuremberg war crime trials, 1946-1949 8. Italy 9. Trieste, Italy 10. Literary fiction 11. Translations -- Croatian to English
Originally published: Zagreb : Fraktura, 2007.
An old Italian woman seeks a reunion with her son, fathered by an SS officer and taken away by German authorities 62 years ago while she remembers and discusses the atrocities committed in Northern Italy during World War II.
"Trieste's originality lies not just in its structure and forceful, unflinching imagery . . . but also in how it brings the lingering effects of the Nazis' merciless racial policies forward into the present." Booklist.

Druon, Maurice, 1918-2009

The **iron** king / Maurice Druon ; translated from the French by Humphrey Hare. Scribner's, 1956. 269 p. Accursed kings
ISBN 0712608761
1. Philip IV,, King of France, 1268-1314 2. Molay, Jacques de, ca 1243-1314 3. Knights Templar (Masonic order) 4. Medieval period (476-1492) 5. 14th century 6. Curses 7. Feudalism -- France 8. Rulers 9. France -- Rulers 10. France -- History -- Philip IV, 1285-1314 11. France -- History -- Capetians, 987-1328 12. France -- History -- 14th century 13. Historical fiction 14. Biographical fiction
LC 56010197
First published in Great Britain by Rupert Hart-Davis 1956.
Originally published in France in 1955, this sweeping 1st volume in a seven-book saga about the Hundred Years' War finally makes its English-language debut. Set in the year 1314, the story takes place during the reign of despotic French King Philip the Fair and focuses on disenfranchised Lord Robert of Artois, whose attempts to reclaim his birthright ignite a conflict that will engulf all of France and destroy a dynasty. Steeped in sex, violence, and political intrigue, this book will captivate readers of sprawling, dramatic, and intricately plotted historical fiction. - Description by Gillian Speace.

Drury, Tom

The **driftless** area / Tom Drury. Atlantic Monthly Press, 2006. 215 p.
ISBN 9780871139436
1. Young men 2. Bartenders 3. Optimism 4. Thieves 5. Criminals 6. Senior men 7. Men/women relations 8. Revenge 9. Ice-skating 10. Curiosities and wonders 11. Stealing 12. Accidents 13. Paranormal phenomena 14. Secrets 15. Cross-country automobile trips 16. Hitchhiking 17. Small towns 18. Eccentrics and eccentricities 19. Middle West 20. Iowa 21. Coming-of-age stories
LC 2006040787
A young bartender with a knack for finding trouble wherever he goes, Pierre Hunter falls in love with the mysterious Stella Rosmarin, becoming the central figure in a revenge drama that he must unravel, and finding himself in sudden possession of a stolen bundle of money, in a novel set in an eccentric small town in the American Midwest.
"Deadpan wit, cosmic melancholy, characters both ethereal and down and dirty, predicaments a Beckett character would accept as inevitable, and a porous divide between the living and the dead add up to a delectably unnerving outlaw fairy tale." Booklist.

Drury, Tom

Pacific / Tom Drury. Atlantic Monthly Press, 2012. 352 p.
ISBN 9780802119995
1. Mothers and sons 2. Second chances 3. Rich people 4. Actors and actresses 5. Private investigators 6. Swindlers and swindling 7. Teenagers 8. City life 9. Small town life 10. Drug use 11. Los Angeles, California 12. Iowa 13. Southern California 14. Middle

West 15. Coming-of-age stories
LC bl2012006262
A story alternating between Iowa and Los Angeles follows Joan Gower, a mother who deserted her family but wants a second chance with her son, Micah, who moves with her to L.A. and has trouble adjusting to its fast and furious life of excess.

Du Maurier, Daphne, 1907-1989
Frenchman's creek / Daphne Du Maurier. Sourcebooks Landmark, 2009, c1941. 283 p.
ISBN 9781402217104
1. Restoration England (1660-1688) 2. Stuart period (1603-1714) 3. Pirates 4. Nobility -- History -- 17th century 5. Men/women relations 6. Cornwall, England -- History -- 17th century 7. Great Britain -- History -- Charles II, 1660-1685 8. Great Britain -- History -- Restoration, 1660-1688 9. Historical fiction
Originally published: London : V. Gollancz, 1941.
During the reign of Charles II, a rebellious noblewoman abandons her Cornwall estate to sail with her pirate lover.
"The lovely Lady St. Columb fled by coach from the boredom of London society, and an unloved husband to their wild and unused Cornish coast estate. There she discovered an aristocratic French pirate who secreted his ship and crew in the hidden creek and as a game preyed gaily upon the dull Cornish gentry. [The book describes] the love between the two and the thrilling adventure they shared." Booklist.

Du Maurier, Daphne, 1907-1989
Jamaica Inn / Daphne duMaurier. Avon Books, 1971, c1936. 302 p.
ISBN 9780380000722
1. Smuggling 2. Murder 3. Secrets 4. Wreckers (Plunderers of ships) 5. Shipwrecks 6. Aunt and niece 7. Men/women relations 8. Cornwall, England -- History -- 19th century 9. Historical romances 10. Romantic suspense
Originally published: London: Gollancz, 1936.
Originally published in the U.S.: Garden City, N.Y. : Doubleday, Doran & Co., 1936.
After her mother dies, Mary Yellan goes to live with her aunt and uncle at the mysterious Jamaica Inn where she is terrified by the ruthless lawbreakers that frequent the roadhouse.

Du Maurier, Daphne, 1907-1989
* **Rebecca** / Daphne Du Maurier Avon Books, 1997, c1938. 410 p.
ISBN 9780380730407
1. Remarriage 2. Family estates 3. Rich people -- Cornwall, England 4. Widowers 5. Household employees 6. Secrets 7. Men/women relations 8. Obsession 9. Housekeepers 10. Cornwall, England 11. Gothic fiction 12. Psychological suspense 13. Modern classics
Sequel: Mrs. de Winter, by Susan Hill.
Originally published: London : V. Gollancz, 1938.
A classic novel of romantic suspense finds the second Mrs. Maxim de Winter entering the home of her mysterious and enigmatic new husband and learning the story of the house's first mistress, to whom the sinister housekeeper is unnaturally devoted.

DuPree, Kia
Shattered / Kia DuPree. Grand Central Pub., 2012. 384 p.
ISBN 9780446547772
1. African American women 2. Street life 3. Sexual violence 4. Foster children 5. Prostitution 6. Drug use 7. Rape 8. Sexually abused women 9. Family violence 10. Inner city teenagers 11. African Americans 12. Washington, D.C. 13. Urban fiction 14.

African American fiction
LC 2011052226
Sequel to: Damaged.
Running away after being put into foster care, Kiki and her friend are lured into a life of captivity by a pedophile until a neighbor helps them escape.

Dubus, Andre, 1959-
Dirty love / Andre Dubus III. W. W. Norton & Company, 2013. 320 p.
ISBN 9780393064650
1. Desire 2. Extramarital affairs 3. Small towns 4. Life change events 5. Sexuality 6. Need (Psychology) 7. Shame 8. Men/women relations 9. Massachusetts 10. Psychological fiction 11. Short stories
LC 2013017214
A collection of short stories examines the lives of suburbanites seeking solace and gratification in food, sex, work, and love.

Due, Tananarive, 1966-
Ghost summer : stories / Tananarive Due ; introduction by Nalo Hopkinson. Prime Books, 2015 256 p.
ISBN 9781607014539
1. Fantasy fiction 2. Science fiction 3. Short stories 4. Afrofuturism and Afrofantasy 5. African American fiction
In this collection of 15 short stories and a novella, award-winning author Tananarive Due portrays human depravity in the guise of monstrous creatures. With a liberal dollop of ghosts (including the story titled "Summer"), occasional zombies ("Patient Zero" and "Danger World"), werewolves ("Afternoon"), and glimpses into the future, Due expertly reveals what lies under the surface. With an introduction by Nalo Hopkinson and an afterword by Steven Barnes, Ghost Summer offers a terrifying sampler of gourmet treats. -- Description by Katherine Bradley Johnson.

Duenas, Maria, 1964-
The **time** in between : a novel / Maria Duenas ; translated by Daniel Hahn. Atria, 2011. 624 p.
ISBN 9781451616880
1. 1930s 2. Seamstresses 3. Spaniards in Morocco 4. World War II 5. Espionage 6. Courage in women 7. Jilted women 8. Spain -- History -- Civil War, 1936-1939 9. Morocco -- History -- 20th century 10. Historical fiction
"The Time In Between follows the story of a seamstress who becomes the most sought-after couturiere during the Spanish Civil War and World War II"--, Provided by publisher.

Duffy, Brendan
House of echoes : a novel / Brendan Duffy. Ballantine Books, 2015. 384 p.
ISBN 9780804178112
1. Houses 2. Local history 3. Moving, Household 4. Life change events 5. Small town life 6. Forests 7. Secrets 8. Family relationships 9. New York State 10. Gothic fiction
LC 2014024343
Frustrating career setbacks and a heartbreaking diagnosis challenge the lives of Ben and Caroline, who after starting over in a nostalgic new hometown encounter disconcerting secrets that threaten their survival.
"Debut author Duffy has delivered a fluid, suspenseful yet subtle thriller, with touches of humor, evocative writing, and characters that are both familiar and uniquely fascinating. A wonderfully tense and heart-wrenching debut." Kirkus.

Dufresne, John

Deep in the shade of paradise / John Dufresne. Norton, 2002. 364 p.

ISBN 9780393020205

1. Plantation life 2. Weddings 3. Conjoined twins 4. Priests 5. Love triangles 6. Boy prodigies 7. Bayous 8. Families 9. Brides 10. Bridegrooms 11. Men/women relations 12. Small town life 13. Family secrets 14. People with Alzheimer's disease 15. Women songwriters 16. Eleven-year-old boys 17. Plantation houses 18. Extramarital affairs 19. Eccentrics and eccentricities 20. Louisiana 21. Mainstream fiction 22. Southern fiction

LC 2001044487

As family and friends arrive at Paradiso, the Loudermilk family ancestral home in the swamp country of Shiver-de-Freeze, Louisiana, for the marriage of Grisham Loudermilk and Arlane Thevenot, all kinds of romantic entanglements arise to complicate the wedding.

"The people in this small town are surprisingly endearing, despite their quirks. Numerous asides sprinkled throughout the novel make for a clever and memorable narrative style." Booklist.

Dufresne, John

Requiem, Mass. : a novel / John Dufresne. W. W. Norton & Co., 2008. 316 p.

ISBN 9780393057904

1. Dysfunctional families 2. Extramarital affairs 3. Family relationships 4. Memories 5. Autobiography 6. Massachusetts 7. Mainstream fiction

LC 2008001343

Struggling with his mother's latest delusions, his father's fantasy-born absence, and his sister's social withdrawal, young Johnny becomes increasingly obsessed with saving his family.

"Dufresne's characters are poignant, their frailties both pitiful and hilarious in this novel of the strong push and pull of family entanglements." Booklist.

Dugoni, Robert

The **conviction** / Robert Dugoni. Touchstone, 2012. 384 p. David Sloane thrillers

ISBN 9781451606720

1. Widowers 2. Fathers and sons 3. Juvenile corrections 4. Judicial corruption 5. Lawyers 6. Rescues 7. Seattle, Washington 8. Washington (State) 9. Thrillers and suspense 10. Legal thrillers

Bringing his teenage son on a camping trip with an old friend and his friend's son, lawyer David Sloane embarks on a legal rescue mission when the boys are caught vandalizing a general store and sentenced to six months in a detention camp with ties to a corrupt judge.

Dugoni, Robert

The **eighth** sister : a thriller / Robert Dugoni. Thomas & Mercer, 2019. 478 p.

ISBN 9781503903036

1. Espionage 2. CIA agents 3. International intrigue 4. Intelligence service 5. Assassins 6. Spies 7. Sixties (Age) 8. Married men 9. United States -- Foreign relations -- Russia 10. Russia -- Foreign relations -- United States 11. Spy fiction 12. Thrillers and suspense

A pulse-pounding thriller of espionage, spy games, and treachery by the New York Times bestselling author of the Tracy Crosswhite Series.

Dugoni, Robert

* The **extraordinary** life of Sam Hell / Robert Dugoni. Lake Union Press, 2018. 448 p.

ISBN 9781503949003

1. Growing up 2. Misfits (Persons) 3. Small town life 4. Small towns 5. Albinos and albinism 6. Physicians 7. Hometowns 8. Self-discovery 9. Secrets 10. Regret 11. Coming-of-age stories

Born with ocular albinism, small-town eye doctor Sam Hill, who was called "Devil Boy" in his youth, must finally face a past tragedy that caused him to turn his back on his friends, his hometown and the life he'd always known--a journey that makes him realize what truly matters.

Dugoni, Robert

Murder one / Robert Dugoni. Simon & Schuster, 2011. 384 p. David Sloane thrillers

ISBN 9781451606690

1. Murder investigation 2. Drug traffic 3. Widowers 4. Wrongful death 5. Drugs -- Overdose 6. Lawyers 7. Attorney and client 8. Corporate lawyers 9. Seattle, Washington 10. Washington (State) 11. Thrillers and suspense 12. Legal thrillers

A year after the murder of his wife, attorney David Sloane reconnects with former adversary Barclay Reid, who upon losing her daughter to a drug overdose has launched a campaign against Russian drug trafficking, only to be accused of murdering a dealer.

"While many will anticipate the ending twist, Dugoni conveys the legalese in digestible form." Publishers Weekly.

Dugoni, Robert

My sister's grave / Robert Dugoni. Thomas & Mercer, 2014. 416 p. Tracy Crosswhite novels

ISBN 9781477825570

1. Women detectives 2. Missing women 3. Cold cases (Criminal investigation) 4. Murderers 5. Sisters 6. Lawyers 7. Dead 8. Frameups 9. Seattle, Washington 10. Washington (State) 11. Mysteries 12. Police procedurals

Twenty years after Seattle homicide detective Tracy Crosswhite's sister, Sarah, was murdered, Tracy sees a chance to find the real killer when Sarah's remains are discovered near their hometown in the northern Cascade mountains of Washington State.

Dumas, Alexandre, 1824-1895

* **Camille** / Alexandre Dumas, fils; introduction by Edmund Gosse. The Modern Library, 1925 270 p.

ISBN 9780451529206

1. 19th century 2. Prostitutes 3. Lovers 4. Counts and countesses 5. Courtesans 6. Nobility 7. Mistresses 8. Paris, France -- Social life and customs -- 19th century 9. Classics 10. Love stories 11. Translations -- French to English

LC 26008619

Camille, a fashionable Paris courtesan, escapes to the country with her poor lover Armand Duval, from a Count who wants her as his mistress, but she later leaves Duval to placate his family.

Dumas, Alexandre, 1802-1870

* The **count** of Monte Cristo / Alexandre Dumas. Modern Library, 1996, c1845. xiv, 1462 p.

ISBN 9780679601999

1. Chateau d'If (France) 2. 19th century 3. Escapes 4. Prisoners -- France 5. Revenge 6. Sailors 7. Treason 8. Malicious accusation 9. France -- History -- Restoration, 1814-1830 10. Adventure stories 11. Translations -- French to English 12. Classics

LC 96-3397

First published in 1845.

Movie entitled Forever mine is inspired by this book.

Television series entitled Revenge is inspired by this book.

The Count of Monte Cristo is the story of Edmond Dantes, who is imprisoned in the island fortress of the Chateau d'If on a false political charge; after escaping, he finds the fabulous treasure of Monte Cristo and sets upon the course of revenge against his old enemies.

Dumas, Alexandre, 1802-1870

* The **man** in the iron mask / Alexandre Dumas ; translated by Joachim Neugroschel ; introduction by Francine du Plessix Gray. Penguin Books, 2003, c1848. xxv, 470 p. Three musketeers series

ISBN 9780140439243

1. Man in the Iron mask 2. 17th century 3. Rulers 4. Prisoners -- France 5. Musketeers 6. Twin brothers 7. Political corruption 8. Conspiracies 9. Rescues 10. France -- Rulers 11. Historical fiction 12. Swashbuckling tales 13. Adventure stories 14. Translations -- French to English 15. Classics

First published in 1848.

Translated from the French.

Deep inside the dreaded Bastille, a twenty-three-year-old prisoner called merely "Philippe" has languished for eight long, dark years. He does not know his real name or what crime he is supposed to have committed. But Aramis, one of the original Three Musketeers, has bribed his way into the cell to reveal the shocking secret that has kept Philippe locked away from the world. That carefully concealed truth could topple Louis XIV, king of France, which is exactly what Aramis is plotting to do! A daring jailbreak, a brilliant masquerade, and a terrifying fight for the throne may make Aramis betray his sacred vow, "All for one, and one for all!"

Dumas, Alexandre, 1802-1870

* The **three** musketeers / Alexandre Dumas ; translated from the French with an introduction by Richard Pevear. Viking, 2006. xxiii, 704 p.

ISBN 9780670037797

1. Louis XIII,, King of France, 1601-1643 2. Richelieu, Armand Jean du Plessis, Cardinal, duc de, 1585-1642 3. Musketeers 4. Soldiers -- France 5. Male friendship 6. Revenge 7. Swordplay 8. Swordfighters 9. Courts and courtiers 10. France -- History -- Bourbons, 1589-1790 11. Swashbuckling tales 12. Adventure stories 13. Historical fiction 14. Translations -- French to English 15. Classics

A major new translation depicts the epic adventures of musketeer-hopeful d'Artagnan and his swordsmen companions in a faithful rendition that endeavors to preserve the original author's wit, romance, and rollicking pace.

"Richard Pevear's brisk, agile new translation succeeds, I think, because it does justice to the pure nuttiness of Dumas's writing: the nonindustrial, nonformulaic, downright peculiar qualities that make a work of popular fiction memorable." New York Times Book Review.

Dumas, Alexandre, 1802-1870

Twenty years after / Alexandre Dumas. Oxford University Press, 2009, c1845. xxv, 845 p. Three musketeers series

ISBN 9780199537266

1. 17th century 2. Musketeers 3. Swordplay 4. Political corruption 5. Soldiers -- France 6. France -- History -- 17th century 7. Paris, France -- History -- 17th century 8. Swashbuckling tales 9. Adventure stories 10. Historical fiction 11. Translations -- French to English 12. Classics

Sequel to: The three musketeers.

Two decades have passed since the musketeers triumphed over Cardinal Richelieu and Milady. Time has weakened their resolve, and dispersed their loyalties. But treasons and strategems still cry out for justice: civil war endangers the throne of France, while in England Cromwell threatens to send Charles I to the scaffold. But their greatest test is a titanic struggle with the son of Milady, who wears the face of Evil.

Dunant, Sarah

The **birth** of Venus : a novel / Sarah Dunant. Random House, 2004. 400 p.

ISBN 1400060737

1. Savonarola, Girolamo, 1452-1498 2. 15th century 3. Women painters 4. Married women 5. Men/women relations 6. Teenage girls 7. Painters 8. Arranged marriage 9. Love 10. Dilemmas 11. Options, alternatives, choices 12. Family relationships 13. Political science 14. Religion 15. Florence, Italy -- History -- 1421-1737 16. Historical fiction

LC 2003046932

Turning fifteen in Renaissance Florence, Alessandra Cecchi becomes intoxicated with the works of a young painter whom her father has brought to the city to decorate the family's Florentine palazzo.

"Part feverish thriller, part historical romance, the story of the outspoken heroine's sentimental education--a curriculum including every conceivable transgression--sometimes comes off as a heady blend of Browning's My Last Duchess and Anas Nin. But Dunant's skill lies in combining these elements with a finely textured and pertinent depiction of a cultured citizenry in the grip of rampant fundamentalism." The New Yorker.

Dunant, Sarah

Blood and beauty : a novel / Sarah Dunant. Random House, 2013. 506 p.

ISBN 9781400069293

1. Borgia, Lucrezia, 1480-1519 2. Borgia family 3. Renaissance (1300-1600) 4. 16th century 5. Political corruption 6. Nobility -- Italy 7. Church and state 8. Brothers and sisters 9. Ambition 10. European Renaissance 11. Power (Social sciences) 12. Italy -- History -- 1492-1559 13. Biographical fiction 14. Historical fiction

LC 2012042215

A tale inspired by the lives of Borgia siblings Lucretia and Cesare traces the family's rise in the aftermath of Rodrigo Borgia's rise to the papacy, during which war, a terrifying sexual plague, and the family's notorious reputation forge an intimate bond between brother and sister.

"An impressively confident, capable sweep through the corrupt politics and serpentine relationships of a legendary family." Kirkus.

Dunant, Sarah

In the company of the courtesan : a novel / Sarah Dunant. Random House, 2006. 400 p.

ISBN 1400063817

1. Renaissance (1300-1600) 2. 16th century 3. Courtesans 4. Little people 5. Courts and courtiers 6. Women who are blind 7. Lovers 8. Women -- Italy -- Social conditions -- 16th century 9. Men/women relations 10. Friendship 11. Interpersonal relations 12. European Renaissance -- Italy 13. Venice, Italy -- History -- 1508-1797 14. Venice, Italy -- Social life and customs -- 16th century 15. Rome, Italy -- History -- 1420-1798 16. Rome, Italy -- Social life and customs -- 16th century 17. Italy -- Courts and courtiers 18. Italy -- History -- 1492-1559 19. Italy -- Social life and customs -- 16th century 20. Historical fiction

LC 2005051649

In 1527, when the city of Rome is sacked and burned by an invading army, the famed courtesan Fiammetta Bianchini and her dwarf companion, Bucino Teodoldi, escape to the wealthy and powerful city of Venice in order to rebuild their business.

"This historical novel follows the fortunes of a beautiful, flame-haired courtesan, Fiammetta Bianchini, who, after escaping from the 1527 pillage of Rome, sets up shop in Venice. The novel, narrated by Fiammetta's servant, a dwarf, chronicles the pair's horrific scrapes and their dizzying triumphs, which include Fiammetta's becoming Titian's model for his Venus of Urbino. Along the way, Dunant presents a lively and detailed acccount of the glimmering palaces and murky alleys of Renaissance Venice, and examines the way the city's clerics and prostitutes alike are bound by its peculiar dynamic of opulence and restraint." The New Yorker.

Dunant, Sarah

Sacred hearts : a novel / Sarah Dunant. Random House, 2009. 432 p.

> ISBN 9781400063826
>
> 1. 16th century 2. Nuns -- Italy 3. Imprisonment 4. Convents -- Italy 5. Interpersonal conflict 6. Women -- Italy -- Social conditions -- 16th century 7. Betrayal 8. Teenage girls 9. Resistance (Psychology) in teenage girls 10. Anger 11. Forbidden love 12. Italy -- History 13. Ferrara, Italy 14. Historical fiction
>
> LC 2009002246
>
> Originally published: 2009.
>
> Shortlisted for the Walter Scott Prize for Historical Fiction, 2010

1570 in the Italian city of Ferrara. Sixteen-year-old Serafina is ripped by her family from an illicit love affair and forced into the convent of Santa Caterina, renowned for its superb music. Serafina's one weapon is her glorious voice, but she refuses to sing. Madonna Chiara, an abbess as fluent in politics as she is in prayer, finds her new charge has unleased a power play rebellion, ecstasies and hysterias within the convent. However, watching over Serafina is Zuana, the sister in charge of the infirmary, who understands and might even challenge her incarceration.

Duncan, Glen, 1965-

By blood we live / Glen Duncan. Alfred A. Knopf, 2014. 357 p. The last werewolf trilogy

> ISBN 9780307595102
>
> 1. Werewolves 2. Vampires 3. Animal behavior 4. Supernatural 5. London, England 6. Literary fiction 7. Horror

A conclusion to the best-selling saga finds Talulla settling down with her werewolf family only to be tormented by a fanatical cult and nagging thoughts about ancient vampire Remshi, who believes he knows Talulla from another time.

"[T]here are plenty of battles, blood, and sexy escapades; but the real treats continues to be Duncan's beautifully twisted way with language and the profound thesis he poses about humanity." Booklist.

Duncan, Glen, 1965-

The **last** werewolf / Glen Duncan. Alfred A. Knopf, 2011. 293 p. The last werewolf trilogy

> ISBN 9780307595089
>
> 1. Werewolves 2. Self-destructive behavior in men 3. Animal behavior 4. Human behavior 5. Love 6. London, England 7. Horror 8. Literary fiction
>
> Sequel: Talulla Rising.

Rendered the last of his kind after a colleague's death, two-hundred-year-old werewolf Jake struggles with depression and contemplates suicide until powerful forces that have personal agendas and the power to keep him alive take over his life.

"A yarn about a Kant-quoting lycanthrope on the run from monster hunters bent on rendering his species extinct. ʃr Take that, True Blood

fans! Duncan creates a world that is completely imagined, if occasionally implausible." Entertainment Weekly.

Duncan, Glen, 1965-

Talulla rising / Glen Duncan. Alfred A. Knopf, 2012. 368 p. The last werewolf trilogy

> ISBN 9780307595096
>
> 1. Werewolves 2. Single mothers 3. Mother and child 4. Protectiveness in women 5. Animal behavior 6. Supernatural 7. London, England 8. Literary fiction 9. Horror
>
> Sequel to: The Last Werewolf.

After losing her werewolf lover Jake and giving birth to a son, Talullah confronts a psychotic new WOCOP leader, an unlikely human lover, blood-drinking religious fanatics, a pack of London werewolves, and the world's oldest living vampire.

Dundas, Chad

The **blaze** / Chad Dundas. G. P. Putnam's Sons, 2020. 374 p.

> ISBN 9780399176098
>
> 1. Veterans 2. Amnesia 3. Psychic trauma 4. Women journalists 5. Murder investigation 6. Childhood friends 7. Arson 8. Homecomings 9. Brain injury 10. Montana 11. Thrillers and suspense

One man knows the connection between two extraordinary acts of arson, 15 years apart, in his Montana hometown?if only he could remember it.

"Dundas's insightful look at a former soldier's attempts to reenter civilian life elevates this poignant, action-packed story. The plot soars with each believable twist and realistic characters worth rooting for." Publishers Weekly.

Dunmore, Evie

* **Bringing** down the duke / Evie Dunmore. Berkley Jove, 2019. 368 p. League of extraordinary women novels

> ISBN 9781984805683
>
> 1. Victorian era (1837-1901) 2. Suffragist movement 3. Dukes and duchesses 4. Universities and colleges 5. Gender role 6. Rich men 7. Poor women 8. Determination in women 9. Independence in women 10. Women college students 11. Men/women relations 12. Interpersonal attraction 13. Oxford, England 14. England 15. Victorian romances 16. Historical romances
>
> LC 2018060569

Recruiting men of influence to champion the rising women's suffrage movement of 1879 England, a daring Oxford rebel targets a cold and calculating duke before their unexpected romance threatens to upend the British social order.

Dunmore, Helen, 1952-2017

Exposure / Helen Dunmore. Atlantic Monthly Press, 2016. 391 p.

> ISBN 9780802124937
>
> 1. 1960s 2. Cold War 3. Espionage 4. Secrets 5. Spies 6. England 7. Spy fiction 8. Historical thrillers

A missing top-secret file poses a terrible dilemma for colleagues Giles Holloway and Simon Callington at the height of the Cold War in London, where Simon's wife, Lily, resolves to protect their family, only to be devastatingly exposed.

"Dunmore deftly creates a noir atmosphere, revealing layers of complexity in personal relationships darkened by non-battlefield conflict and blending psychological observations reminiscent of Henry James with le Carre-esque betrayals." Publishers Weekly.

Dunmore, Helen, 1952-2017

The **lie** / Helen Dunmore. Atlantic Monthly Press, 2014. 294 p.

ISBN 9780802122544

1. Between the Wars (1918-1939) 2. 1920s 3. Veterans 4. Memories 5. World War I 6. Villages 7. Loss (Psychology) 8. Coping 9. Grief in men 10. Dishonesty 11. Postwar life 12. England -- History -- 20th century 13. France -- History -- 20th century 14. Historical fiction

First published: London: Hutchinson, 2014.

Shortlisted for the Walter Scott Prize for Historical Fiction, 2015

Returning to the small Cornish town where he was born after surviving World War I, Daniel is haunted by memories of his closest friend and his first love before suffering the unforeseen consequences of a lie.

"From the first page, Dunmore shares Daniel's inner life, building an increasing sense of dread while exposing the tragedy of great promise thwarted by forces beyond Daniel's control. Dunmore's crystalline prose is almost too good; the pain she describes is often unbearable to read, yet the emotional power resonates, and Daniel is impossible to forget." Kirkus.

Dunn, Kate

The **Dragonfly** / Kate Dunn. Aurora Metro, 2017. 320 p.

ISBN 9781911501039

1. Fathers and sons 2. Grandfather and granddaughter 3. Dysfunctional families 4. Widowers 5. Nine-year-old girls 6. Boats 7. Fishing 8. Murder suspects 9. Interpersonal relations 10. Secrets 11. Mainstream fiction

When Colin discovers his son is being held on a murder charge in France, he trails his boat, The Dragonfly, across the channel to help. There he meets his granddaughter for the first time, and they embark on a journey through the French canals, where they land big fish and uncover burning secrets. But can Colin get his son off the hook?

Dunn, Katherine, 1945-2016

* **Geek** love / Katherine Dunn. A. A. Knopf, 1989. 347 p.

ISBN 9780394569024

1. Little people 2. Birth defects 3. People with disabilities 4. Carnivals 5. Sideshows 6. Sideshow performers 7. Black humor 8. Transgressive fiction 9. Picaresque fiction

LC 88045776

National Book Award for Fiction finalist, 1989

Aloysious and Lillian Binewski, proprietors of a traveling carnival, attempt to reduce overhead by breeding their own freak show, with tragic results.

"This raw, shocking view of the human condition, a glimpse of the tormented people who live on the fringe, makes readers confront the dark, mad elements in every society. . . . A brilliant, suspenseful, heartbreaking tour de force." Publishers Weekly.

Dunn, Mark, 1956-

Ella Minnow Pea : a progressively lipogrammatic epistolary fable / Mark Dunn. MacAdam/Cage Pub., 2001. 205 p.

ISBN 9780967370163

1. Communes 2. Islands 3. Lipograms 4. South Carolina 5. Epistolary novels

LC 2001042585

Recounts what happens when the citizens of an island must rely on all their ingenuity to communicate in an increasingly limited language when the goverment progressively bans letters from the alphabet.

Dunne, Dominick

* **People** like us : a novel / Dominick Dunne. Crown Publishers, 1988. 403 p.

ISBN 0345430549

1. 1980s 2. Rich people 3. Upper class 4. Divorced men 5. Journalists 6. Scandals 7. Nouveaux riches 8. Gossiping and gossips 9. Manhattan, New York City 10. New York City -- Social life and customs 11. Satirical fiction

LC 88000353

Sequel: Too much money.

Gus Bailey, the confidant of New York society, observes the social repercussions of socialite Justine Altemus's engagement to TV anchorman Bernie Slatkin and inadvertently precipitates a social explosion.

"Engaging us in his characters' concerns and then pulling multiple story strands into a tight knot, Dominick Dunne demonstrates with wit and accuracy the delicate, merciless distinction between 'people like that' and 'people like us'." New York Times Book Review.

Dunne, Dominick

Too much money / Dominick Dunne. Crown Publishers, 2009. 275 p.

ISBN 9780609603871

1. Rich people 2. Upper class 3. Journalists 4. Authors 5. Senior men 6. Socialites 7. Gossiping and gossips 8. Libel and slander 9. Murder 10. Manhattan, New York City 11. New York City -- Social life and customs 12. Satirical fiction

Sequel to: People like us.

Writer Gus Bailey witnesses the disappearance of the old-money society that once occupied him and investigates the murder of one of the world's wealthiest men, an effort that is sabotaged by the man's calculating wife and schemers within Gus's own set.

"The novel opens with an Easter luncheon in a vast Park Avenue apartment that ironically marks the decline of its owner, a well-bred old guard woman named Lil Altemus. Gus Bailey, Dunne's alter ego, is in attendance. He's a journalist who works for a high-society magazine and is about to write a novel about widowed Perla Zacharias, one of the wealthiest women in the world, who, because of dubious origins, has been held down from New York society's highest ranks. Zacharias is not happy with the news about the novel and takes appropriate measures to block it. . . . Dunne shows a little more affection for his subjects than Capote, but not that much. Too little sympathy and you have acid satire. Too much and you have a sentimental portrait. Dunne does it just about right. After you finish his portrayal of the very rich, you may somehow be satisfied with the knowledge of just how poorly they live." San Francisco Chronicle.

Dunne, John Gregory, 1932-2003

The **red,** white, and blue : a novel / John Gregory Dunne. Simon and Schuster, 1987. 475 p.

1. Rich families 2. San Francisco, California

LC 86026025

"An insightfully provocative slice of Americana." Booklist.

Dunnett, Dorothy

Niccolo rising / Dorothy Dunnett. Random House, 1999, c1986. viii, 470 p. House of Niccolo

ISBN 9780375704772

1. Renaissance (1300-1600) 2. 15th century 3. Widows 4. Heirs and heiresses 5. Apprentices 6. Mercenaries 7. Upper class 8. Political corruption 9. Nobility 10. Europe -- History -- 15th century 11. Family sagas 12. Historical fiction 13. Adventure stories

LC 86045306

Includes endpaper maps.

Originally published: London : Michael Joseph, 1986.

Sent to Italy by his guardian Marian, the widowed owner of a Bruges trading house, Claes, a reckless boy and seeming simpleton, develops into a sophisticated adventurer known as Niccolo, in a colorful novel of late fifteenth-century Europe.

Dunning, John, 1942-

Booked to die : a mystery introducing Cliff Janeway / John Dunning. Maxwell Macmillan International, 1992. xiv, 321 p. Cliff Janeway mysteries

ISBN 0684193833

1. Former police 2. Murder investigation 3. Booksellers 4. Antiquarian booksellers 5. Police 6. Rare books 7. Book collectors 8. Amateur detectives 9. Colorado 10. Denver, Colorado 11. Mysteries

LC 91026889

"This is a soundly plotted, evenly executed whodunit in the classic mode." New York Times Book Review.

Dunning, John, 1942-

The **bookman's** wake : a mystery with Cliff Janeway / John Dunning. Scribner, 1995. 351 p. Cliff Janeway mysteries

ISBN 0684800039

1. Criminal investigation 2. Booksellers 3. Stealing 4. Missing persons 5. Former police 6. Antiquarian booksellers 7. Rare books 8. Book collectors 9. Amateur detectives 10. Seattle, Washington 11. Colorado 12. Denver, Colorado 13. Mysteries

LC 94034328

Surprised by a visit from a difficult-to-manage former cop from his old precinct, bookstore owner Cliff Janeway is unable to resist Slater's invitation to help recover a stolen edition of a rare and valuable book

"The author can't resist writing lengthy, luxurious passages about the craftsmanship of the great print men. Strictly speaking, these eloquent lectures on the art of the printer and the beauty of the book get in the way of the action; but that shouldn't bother anyone who loves booksand their covers." New York Times Book Review.

Dupont, Eric, 1970-

The **American** fiancee : a novel / Eric Dupont ; translated from the French by Peter McCambridge. HarperCollins, 2020, c2012. 608 p.

ISBN 9780062947451

1. 20th century 2. Families 3. War 4. Love 5. Womanizers 6. Generations 7. Fate and fatalism 8. Quebec (Province) 9. Literary fiction 10. Family sagas 11. Translations -- French to English

LC 2019030730

Originally published: Montreal : Marchand de feuilles , 2012.

Follows three generations of the Lamontagnes family as they travel the world experiencing passion, jealousy, revenge and death, from the family patriarch, Louis, who served in World War II to his ladies' man grandson, Gabriel.

"While the intensity of Dupont's prose can be maddening, the sweet, sour, and salty world he creates is thoroughly addictive." Kirkus.

Durham, David Anthony, 1969-

* **Gabriel's** story / David Anthony Durham. Doubleday, 2001. 291 p.

ISBN 9780385498142

1. African American families -- Kansas 2. African American cowboys -- The West (United States) 3. Pioneer men 4. Young men 5. Homesteaders 6. Homesteading 7. Kansas 8. Westerns 9. Coming-of-age stories 10. African American fiction

LC 00025291

BCALA Literary Award for First Novelist, 2002.

Hurston/Wright Legacy Award: Debut Fiction, 2002.

Reluctantly moving with his mother and younger brother from the urban East to join his stepfather, a Kansas homesteader, Gabriel hates their primitive, harsh new life and runs away to seek adventure as a cowboy, in a coming-of-age story of a young black man in the American West of the 1870s.

"The moral gravity of Durham's narrative is offset by his attentiveness to the primacy of nature in the Western landscape." The New Yorker.

Durrell, Lawrence

* **Balthazar** / Lawrence Durrell. Penguin Books, 1991, c1958. 250 p. Alexandria quartet

ISBN 9780140153217

1. 1940s 2. Extramarital affairs 3. Married women 4. Men/women relations 5. Friendship 6. Illegal arms transfers 7. Alexandria, Egypt -- History -- 1900-1945 8. Literary fiction 9. Modern classics

Originally published: London : Faber & Faber, 1958.

Presents a reading of the novel concerning love and murder in the streets, brothels, and drawing-rooms of Alexandria, Egypt.

"Once again [Durrell] writes of Justine, Melissa, Clea, Nessim, Pursewarden, Scobie, Pombalbut from a fresh point of view. The new insights are provided by the psychiatrist, Balthazar, who convinces the narrator that the first volume of the story was almost wholly inaccurate. . . . So this second volume is a correction and an expansion of the first." New York Times Book Review.

Durrell, Lawrence

* **Clea** / Lawrence Durrell. Penguin Books, 1991, c1960. 287 p. Alexandria quartet

ISBN 9780140153224

1. 1940s 2. Women artists 3. War and society 4. Authors 5. Men/women relations 6. Alexandria, Egypt -- History -- 1900-1945 7. Literary fiction 8. Modern classics

Originally published: London : Faber & Faber, 1960.

After the war Irish emigre Darley becomes involved with Clea, a bisexual artist

Durrell, Lawrence

* **Justine** / Lawrence Durrell. Penguin Books, 1991, c1957. 253 p. Alexandria quartet

ISBN 9780140153194

1. Between the Wars (1918-1939) 2. Extramarital affairs 3. Authors 4. Jewish women 5. Married women 6. Copts 7. Mistresses 8. City life 9. Men/women relations 10. Alexandria, Egypt 11. Egypt -- History -- 1900-1945 12. Literary fiction 13. Modern classics

Originally published: London : Faber & Faber, 1957.

Justine is the first volume of the author's Alexandria quartet, four interlinked novels set in Alexandria, Egypt just before the Second World War.

"Set in Alexandria the story concerns the amorous adventures of a penniless young man, a prostitute who lives with him, the rich and beautiful Justine with whom he has an affair, and Justine's husband." Publishers Weekly.

Durrell, Lawrence

* **Mountolive** / Lawrence Durrell. Penguin Books, 1991, c1958. 320 p. Alexandria quartet

ISBN 9780140153200

1. 1940s 2. Young men -- Relations with older women 3. Diplomats 4. War and society 5. Men/women relations 6. Alexandria, Egypt -- History -- 1900-1945 7. Literary fiction 8. Modern classics

Originally published: London : Faber & Faber, 1958.

A new view of the complex relationship between the members of a romantic quadrangle in Alexandria, Egypt is offered through the eyes of British diplomat

Durrow, Heidi W., 1969-

* The **girl** who fell from the sky : a novel / Heidi W. Durrow. Algonquin Books of Chapel Hill, 2010. 264 p.

ISBN 9781565126800

1. Multiracial children 2. Identity (Psychology) 3. Intergenerational relations 4. Children of suicide victims 5. Abandoned girls 6. Witnesses 7. Survival 8. Psychological fiction 9. Coming-of-age stories 10. Literary fiction

LC 2009027572

Bellwether Prize for Fiction, 2008.

After a family tragedy orphans her, Rachel, the daughter of a Danish mother and a black G.I., moves into her grandmother's mostly black community in the 1980s, where she must swallow her grief and confront her identity as a biracial woman in a world that wants to see her as either black or white.

"Set in the 1980s and focusing luminously on one unusually sympathetic girl overcoming apocalyptic tragedy and navigating her way through nascent sexuality and racial tensions, Durrow's novel transcends topicality." Christian Science Monitor.

Durst, Sarah Beth

The **queen** of blood / Sarah Beth Durst. Harper Voyager, 2016. 353 p. Queens of Renthia

ISBN 9780062413345

1. Women students 2. Warriors 3. Quests 4. Women rulers 5. Spirits 6. Imaginary kingdoms 7. Political intrigue 8. Magic 9. Epic fantasy

LC 2015044319

Daleina, a young student, joins forces with a disgraced warrior, Ven, to embark on an epic and treacherous quest to save their realm from the spirits that want to rid it of all human life.

"In addition to a solid cast of characters and great political intrigue, Durst delivers some fascinating worldbuilding, and the spirits are malevolent, cunning, wild, and mysterious antagonists." Publishers Weekly.

Dybek, Nick

The **Verdun** affair : a novel / Nick Dybek. Scribner, 2018 320 p.

ISBN 9781501191763

1. Between the Wars (1918-1939) 2. 1950s 3. Postwar life 4. War casualties 5. People with amnesia 6. Widows 7. Missing in action 8. Loss (Psychology) 9. Men/women relations 10. World War I -- Influence 11. World War II -- Influence 12. France 13. Verdun, France 14. Italy 15. Historical fiction 16. Parallel narratives

LC 2017061760

A sweeping novel, set in Europe in the aftermath of World War I and Los Angeles in the 1950s follows a lonely young man, a beautiful widow and the amnesiac soldier whose puzzling case binds them together even as it tears them apart.

Dybek, Stuart, 1942-

I sailed with Magellan / Stuart Dybek. Farrar, Straus and Giroux, 2003. 307 p.

ISBN 9780374174071

1. 1950s 2. 1960s 3. Polish American boys 4. Polish American men 5. Polish Americans 6. Polish American families 7. Neighborhoods 8. Growing up 9. Uncle and nephew 10. Men/women relations 11. Love 12. Loss (Psychology) 13. Memories 14. South Side, Chicago, Illinois 15. Chicago, Illinois -- Social life and customs -- 20th century 16. Short stories

LC 2003049052

Eleven interlocking short stories.

ALA Notable Book, 2005.

A collection of eleven short works is set in the urban areas of Chicago's South Side, where imaginative protagonist Perry Katzek encounters such events as a boy's musical performances on behalf of a drinking uncle, and a thug's distraction by multiple ex-girlfriends.

"The episodes that intersect and surround young Perry Katzek's upbringing in the Polish-Mexican ghetto of Chicago's South Side are simultaneously daring and compassionate, intimate in detail and mythic in scale. Dybek has the rare ability to dart back and forth in time and slide around recklessly in space while carrying the reader effortlessly with him." Washington Post Book World.

Dyer, Geoff

Jeff in Venice, death in Varanasi / Geoff Dyer. Pantheon Books, 2009. 296 p.

ISBN 9780307377371

1. Journalists 2. British in India 3. Desire in men 4. Forties (Age) 5. Men/women relations 6. Romantic love 7. Americans in Italy 8. Self-perception 9. Self-fulfillment 10. Venice, Italy 11. India 12. Literary fiction

LC 2008023759

Jeff Atman is a British journalist on assignment in Venice who feels disillusioned with his hedonistic way of living, while a narrator in the Indian holy city of Varanasi practices detachment and meditates on art and spiritual matters.

"This novel is zany and deceptively light, even as Atman explores the meaning of life and enlightenment. Does it matter whether the unnamed hero of the second part is Jeff or Geoff? Or whether the stories in Venice and Varanasi are the same story? You can read this novel as if you're munching a burger or savoring a ribeye." St. Louis Post-Dispatch.

Dykes, Amanda

Whose waves these are / Amanda Dykes. Bethany House, 2019. 361 p.

ISBN 9780764234132

1. War memorials 2. Loss (Psychology) 3. Women anthropologists 4. Great-uncles 5. Letter carriers 6. Anxiety in women 7. People in comas 8. Family secrets 9. Family relationships 10. Maine 11. Christian fiction

LC 2018048925

In the wake of WWII, a grieving fisherman submits a poem to a local newspaper asking readers to send rocks in honor of loved ones to create something life-giving--but the building halts when tragedy strikes. Decades later, Annie returns to the coastal Maine town, where stone ruins spark her curiosity and her search for answers faces a battle against time.

E

Earley, Tony, 1961-

Jim the boy : a novel / Tony Earley. Little, Brown, 2000. 227 p.

ISBN 9780316199643

1. Depression era (1929-1941) 2. Ten-year-old boys -- North Carolina 3. Boys -- North Carolina 4. Small town life -- North Carolina 5. Families -- North Carolina 6. Father-separated boys -- North Carolina 7. Depressions -- 1929-1941 -- North Carolina 8. Uncles -- North Carolina 9. Children of single parents -- North Carolina 10. North Carolina 11. Historical fiction 12. Coming-of-age

stories 13. Southern fiction

LC 9942901

Sequel: The blue star.

Describes the life of a young boy in a small southern town in the early twentieth century as he begins to explore the confusing adult world that surrounds him and begins to take his own first steps toward maturity.

"The genius of a novel like this is Earley's trust in the purity of his style and the plainness of his story. Perhaps all things done very well look simple." Christian Science Monitor.

Earley, Tony, 1961-

Mr. Tall : a novella and stories / Tony Earley. Little, Brown & Co., 2014. 242 p.

ISBN 9780316246125

1. Small towns 2. Couples 3. Interpersonal relations 4. Southern states 5. Short stories 6. Literary fiction

A collection of short stories and one novella features tales about a widow being visited by Bigfoot and an elderly woman plagued by Jesse James' ghost.

Eason, K. (Kathryn F.)

How Rory Thorne destroyed the multiverse / K. Eason. DAW Books, 2019. 408 p. Thorne chronicles

ISBN 9780756415297

1. Princesses 2. Royal pretenders 3. Magic 4. Inheritance and succession 5. Space stations 6. Engaged persons 7. Betrayal 8. Truth 9. Deception 10. Insurgency 11. Alliances 12. Space opera 13. Science fiction

Rory Thorne is a princess with thirteen fairy blessings, the most important of which is to see through flattery and platitudes. As the eldest daughter, she always imagined she?d inherit her father's throne and govern the interplanetary Thorne Consortium. Then her father is assassinated, her mother gives birth to a son, and Rory is betrothed to the prince of a distant world. When Rory arrives in her new home, she uncovers a treacherous plot to unseat her newly betrothed and usurp his throne. An unscrupulous minister has conspired to name himself Regent to the minor (and somewhat foolish) prince. With only her wits and a small team of allies, Rory must outmaneuver the Regent and rescue the prince.

Ebershoff, David

The **19th** wife : a novel / David Ebershoff. Random House, 2008. 514 p.

ISBN 9781400063970

1. Young, Ann Eliza, b 1844 2. 19th century 3. 21st century 4. Mormons 5. Polygamy 6. Fundamentalists 7. Gay men 8. Families 9. Murder 10. Murder investigation 11. Utah 12. Parallel narratives 13. Historical fiction

LC 2008000074

The complex history of polygamy in the Mormon Church intertwines the story of Ann Eliza Young, the nineteenth and final wife of Brigham Young, who in 1875 leaves her husband and embarks on crusade to end polygamy, and a modern-day murder mystery in which a polygamous man has been found dead and one of his wives is accused of the crime.

"This novel tells two parallel stories of polygamy. The first recounts Brigham Young's expulsion of one of his wives, Ann Eliza, from the Mormon Church; the second is a modern-day murder mystery set in a polygamous compound in Utah. Unfolding through an impressive variety of narrative forms--Wikipedia entries, academic research papers, newspaper opinion pieces--the stories include fascinating historical details. . . . Ebershoff demonstrates abundant virtuosity, as he convincingly inhabits the voices of both a nineteenth-century Mormon wife and a contemporary gay youth excommunicated from the church, while also

managing to say something about the mysterious power of faith." The New Yorker.

Ebershoff, David

The **Danish** girl : a novel / David Ebershoff. Viking, 2000. 270 p.

ISBN 9780670888085

1. Elbe, Lili, died 1931 2. Painters 3. Trans women 4. Transitioning (Gender identity) 5. Love 6. Married men -- Sexuality 7. Marriage 8. Gender role 9. Identity (Psychology) 10. Men/women relations 11. Biographical fiction 12. Psychological fiction 13. Historical fiction

LC 99034890

Lambda Literary Award for Transgender/Bisexual, 2000.

Set in decadent 1920s Copenhagen, this tender tale of love and marriage in the midst of fundamental crisis introduces a man who discovers he's a woman and the woman who will do anything for him.

"Ebershoff's poignant and visionary conclusion is a fitting one for what is, above all, and despite its sensationalist trimmings, a profound and beautifully realized love story." Publishers Weekly.

Echenoz, Jean

Lightning : a novel / Jean Echenoz ; translated from the French by Linda Coverdale. The New Press, 2011, c2010. 142 p.

ISBN 9781595586490

1. Tesla, Nikola, 1856-1943 2. Inventors 3. Electrical engineers 4. Electrical engineering 5. Obsessive-compulsive disorder 6. Competition 7. Phobias 8. Pigeons 9. Eccentrics and eccentricities 10. Biographical fiction 11. Literary fiction

LC 2011001157

Originally published in France as Des eclairs by Les Editions de Minuit, Paris, 2010.

Inspired by the life of Nikola Tesla, the author tells the story of Gregor, a young engineer from Eastern Europe, who travels to America to work alongside Thomas Edison, with whom he later holds a long-lasting rivalry.

"This is a fictional portrait of Nikola Tesla (here depicted as Gregor), a talented immigrant who begins life in the U.S. as an underpaid troubleshooter for Thomas Edison but whose exceptional gifts eventually make him Edison's formidable rival. But readers see much more than the extensively chronicled Edison-Tesla rivalry. Probing deep into Tesla's tangled psyche, Echenoz illuminates unexpected tensions. . . . Coverdale's nuanced translation of Echenoz's highly successful French original permits English-speaking readers to contemplate the human mystery that persists long after the scientific puzzles have been solved." Booklist.

Echlin, Kim

The **disappeared** / Kim Echlin. Black Cat, 2009. 235 p.

ISBN 9780802170668

1. 1970s 2. Young women 3. Rock musicians 4. Refugees, Cambodian -- Canada 5. Cambodian Canadians 6. First loves 7. Interethnic romance 8. Memory 9. Loss (Psychology) 10. Disappeared persons -- Cambodia 11. Genocide -- Cambodia 12. Cambodian genocide, 1975-1979 13. Cambodia -- History -- 20th century 14. Phnom Penh, Cambodia 15. Montreal, Quebec 16. Literary fiction 17. Coming-of-age stories

Also published: Toronto : Hamish Hamilton/Penguin Canada, 2009.

Shortlisted for the Giller Prize, 2009

Traces one woman's three-decades-long journey from the peaceful streets of Montreal to the war-torn villages of Cambodia, as a brief affair turns into a grand passion of loss and remembrance, set against one of the most brutal genocides of our time.

"There is something of Marguerite Duras in these pages, something of the lust between the young Western girl and the Asian man that drove novels like The Lover and The North China Lover. But while Duras focuses mostly on desire, Echlin focuses on absolute love--physical desire coupled with the need to know everything about the beloved, to follow him even to the grave and beyond. . . . [An] exquisite novel." New York Times Book Review.

Eco, Umberto

Baudolino / Umberto Eco; translated from the Italian by William Weaver. Harcourt, 2002. 528 p.

ISBN 0151006903

1. Medieval period (476-1492) 2. 12th century 3. Storytelling 4. Dishonesty 5. Courts and courtiers 6. Adopted children 7. Crusades -- Fourth, 1202-1204 8. Europe -- History -- 476-1492 9. Historical fiction 10. Literary fiction 11. Translations -- Italian to English

LC 2002002345

Born a simple peasant in northern Italy, Baudolino narrates the story of his life, from his adoption by Emperor Frederick Barbarossa and his education in Paris to his arrival in Constantinople during the turmoil of the Fourth Crusade.

"In this whimsical yet deadly earnest tale, Eco puts forth the question that perpetually beguiles him and with which he beguiles the rest of us: If a teller of tales tells us he's telling the truth, how can we know for sure what really happened?." The New Yorker.

Eco, Umberto

* **Foucault's** pendulum / Umberto Eco ; translated from the Italian by William Weaver. Harcourt Brace Jovanovich, 1989. 641 p.

ISBN 9780151327652

1. Conspiracy theories 2. Secret societies 3. Missing persons 4. Literary fiction 5. Translations -- Italian to English

LC 89032212

A wily group of editors devises a mock formula for tapping the mystical powers of the universe, only to set off a series of mysterious disappearances.

"This book is not meant to be easy. . . . [But] great are the rewards for those who actually manage to read it. For while it is not a novel in the strict sense of the word, it is a truly formidable gathering of information delivered playfully by a master manipulating his own inventionin effect, a long, erudite joke." New York Times Book Review.

Eco, Umberto

The **island** of the day before / Umberto Eco ; translated from the Italian by William Weaver. Harcourt Brace & Co., 1995. 515 p.

ISBN 0151001510

1. Jesuits 2. 17th century 3. Shipwrecks 4. Flashbacks 5. Paradoxes 6. Missing persons 7. Europe -- History -- 17th century 8. Literary fiction 9. Translations -- Italian to English

LC 95007594

Translation of L'isola del giorno prima.

A panoramic historical novel set in the seventeenth century follows a young aristocrat who goes to sea to find love and an old Jesuit with a boundless scientific knowledge

"Umberto Eco's narrative surface is sensually alluring, cool and glittery, but for all its lucidity and charm, there is always something else going on. . . . This novel is really a book about telling, reminding us that the only clarity we are capable of reaching is the story we tell to compel time and the universe to take on meaning." New York Times Book Review.

Eco, Umberto

The **mysterious** flame of Queen Loana : an illustrated novel / Umberto Eco ; translated from the Italian by Geoffrey Brock. Harcourt, 2004. 480 p.

ISBN 0151011400

1. People with amnesia 2. Memory 3. Memories 4. Antiquarian booksellers 5. Amnesia 6. Identity (Psychology) 7. Family estates 8. Attics 9. Souvenirs (Keepsakes) 10. First loves 11. Italy 12. Milan, Italy 13. Psychological fiction 14. Literary fiction 15. Translations -- Italian to English

LC 2004029105

Having suffered a complete loss of memory regarding every aspect of his identity, Yambo withdraws to a family home outside of Milan, where he sorts through boxes of old records and experiences memories in the form of a graphic novel.

"Those who don't enjoy the occasional ramble through Bartlett's Quotations may quickly lose patience with Queen Loana, but bookworms will get an added kick out of puzzling out the dozens of literary allusions." Christian Science Monitor.

Eco, Umberto

* The **name** of the rose / Umberto Eco ; translated from the Italian by William Weaver. Harcourt Brace, 1994. 536 p.

ISBN 0156001314

1. Franciscans Italy 2. Benedictines Italy. 3. Medieval period (476-1492) 4. 14th century 5. Librarians 6. Monastic libraries -- Italy 7. Murder 8. Monks 9. European Renaissance -- Italy 10. Abbeys -- Italy -- History 11. Libraries -- Italy 12. Monasticism and religious orders for men 13. Secrets 14. Italy -- History -- 14th century 15. Medieval mysteries 16. Historical mysteries 17. Literary fiction 18. Translations -- Italian to English 19. Modern classics

LC 94013818

"A Helen and Kurt Wolff book".

This translation originally published: London;: Secker & Warburg, 1983. Originally published in Italy in 1980 under the title Il nome della rose.

In 1327, finding his sensitive mission at an Italian abbey further complicated by seven bizarre deaths, Brother William of Baskerville turns detective.

"This novel is an antidetective-story detective story; as a semiotic murder mystery it is superbly entertaining; it is also an extraordinary work of novelistic art." Harper's..

Eco, Umberto

Numero zero / Umberto Eco ; translated from the Italian by Richard Dixon. Houghton Mifflin Harcourt, 2015. 191 p.

ISBN 9780544635081

1. 1990s 2. Journalism 3. Corruption 4. Newspapers 5. Journalists 6. Ghostwriters 7. Paranoia 8. Editors 9. Gossiping and gossips 10. Extortion 11. Conspiracies 12. Murder 13. Men/women relations 14. Italy -- History -- 20th century 15. Political fiction 16. Satirical fiction 17. Literary fiction 18. Translations -- Italian to English

Originally published in Italian: Milan : Bompiani, 2015.

Follows the employees of a mudslinging newspaper in 1992 as they try to identify a dead body that appears in a back alley in Milan.

"Eco combines his delight in suspense with astute political satire in this brainy, funny, neatly lacerating thriller." Booklist.

Edgarian, Carol

Three stages of amazement : a novel / Carol Edgarian. Scribner, 2011. 304 p.

ISBN 9781439198308

1. Marital conflict 2. Money 3. Moving, Household 4. Family relationships 5. Uncles 6. Marriage 7. Married people 8. Domestic fiction

LC 2010044448

In San Francisco during the first year of Barack Obama's presidency, Lena Rusch and her husband Charlie Pepper must deal with a stillborn child, an economic crash, a ruthless business rival and the attentions of an old lover.

"Edgarian's characters fully inhabit this all-too-familiar world of marital squabbles, wounded pride and unpaid bills. Her depiction of the frustrations and joys of motherhood is hilariously on target, when its not tragic. Her characters are caught in the rhythms of trying, failing and trying again--patterns that superbly mimic those of everyday life." BookPage.

Edgerton, Clyde, 1944-

* **Walking** across Egypt : a novel / Clyde Edgerton. Algonquin Books of Chapel Hill, 1987. 216 p.

ISBN 9780912697512

1. Juvenile delinquents (Boys) 2. Intergenerational relations 3. Widows -- North Carolina 4. Senior women -- North Carolina 5. Septuagenarians 6. Teenage boys 7. Small town life 8. Teenage orphans 9. Friendship 10. North Carolina 11. Southern States 12. Southern fiction 13. Gentle reads

LC 86020645

Sequel : Killer diller.

Mattie Rigsbee, seventy-eight and set in her ways, decides to help out Wesley Benfield, a troubled adolescent just out of reform school for car theft.

"This novel is warm, innocent, and has a charming central character." Booklist.

Edghill, India

Queenmaker : a novel of King David's Queen / India Edghill. St. Martin's Press, 2002. 376 p.

ISBN 0312289189

1. Michal, (Biblical figure) 2. David,, King of Israel 3. Bible. Old Testament History of Biblical events 4. Women in the Bible 5. Women rulers 6. Political intrigue 7. Rulers 8. Bible novels

LC 2001048603

Sequel: Wisdom's daughter.

A retelling of the biblical story of King David and Queen Michal follows Michal, who lived and reigned in David's court for more than forty years, as she speaks about her hopes and fears while war, betrayal, death, and prophecy rage through the Promised Land.

"With its excellent writing, dynamic characters, and galloping pace, Edghill's work is highly recommended for all historical fiction collections." Library Journal.

Edugyan, Esi

Half-blood blues / Esi Edugyan. Picador, 2012, c2011. 321 p.

ISBN 9781250012708

1. 1940s 2. 1990s 3. Multiracial men 4. Jazz musicians 5. Race (Social sciences) 6. Secrets 7. Betrayal 8. Nazism -- Germany 9. Berlin, Germany 10. Paris, France 11. Germany -- Social conditions -- 20th century 12. Literary fiction 13. Historical fiction

Originally published: London: Serpent's Tail : 2011.

ALA Notable Book, 2013

BC Book Prizes, Ethel Wilson Fiction Prize, 2012

Hurston/Wright Legacy Award: Fiction, 2013.

Scotiabank Giller Prize, 2011.

Governor General's Literary Awards, English-language Fiction finalist

Rogers Writers' Trust Fiction Prize finalist, 2011.

Shortlisted for the Man Booker Prize, 2011.

Shortlisted for The Orange Prize for Fiction, 2012

Shortlisted for the Walter Scott Prize for Historical Fiction, 2012.

Sid, the only one to witness his bandmate's disappearance at the hands of the Gestapo, breaks his silence on the incident over fifty years later when the men are reunited at a documentary premiere.

Edugyan, Esi

* **Washington** Black : a novel / Esi Edugyan. Alfred A. Knopf, 2018. 333 p.

ISBN 9780525521426

1. 1830s 2. 19th century 3. Slaves 4. Betrayal 5. Fugitives 6. Science 7. Airships 8. Self-discovery 9. Interracial friendship 10. Malicious accusation 11. Barbados 12. Historical fiction

LC 2017058436

ALA Notable Book, 2019.

Scotiabank Giller Prize, 2018.

Andrew Carnegie Medal for Excellence in Fiction finalist, 2019.

Shortlisted for the Man Booker Prize, 2018.

Unexpectedly chosen to be a family manservant, an 11-year-old Barbados sugar-plantation slave is initiated into a world of technology and dignity before a devastating betrayal propels him throughout the world in search of his true self.

Edvardsson, M. T.

A **nearly** normal family / M. T. Edvardsson ; translated by Rachel Willson-Broyles. Celadon Books, 2019, c2018. 400 p.

ISBN 9781250204431

1. Teenage murder suspects 2. Family relationships 3. Trials (Murder) 4. Teenage girls -- Psychology 5. Seventeen-year-old girls 6. Parent and teenager 7. Defense attorneys 8. Parent and child 9. Clergy 10. Ethics 11. Sweden 12. Legal thrillers 13. Psychological suspense 14. Thrillers and suspense 15. Scandinavian crime fiction 16. Translations -- Swedish to English

Originally published by Bokf?rlaget Forum, 2018.

A legal thriller told in three acts follows the trial of a 17-year-old girl from an upstanding family who has been implicated in the murder of a shady businessman, testing the limits of her father's faith and mother's ethics.

Edwards, Kim, 1958-

The **memory** keeper's daughter / Kim Edwards. Viking, 2005. 401 p.

ISBN 9780670034161

1. Children with Down syndrome 2. Fraternal twins 3. Family secrets 4. Abandoned children 5. Married people 6. Mothers 7. Fathers 8. Twins 9. Physicians 10. Nurses 11. Parent and child 12. Mother and child 13. Separation (Psychology) 14. Child custody 15. Down syndrome 16. Deception 17. Dishonesty 18. Loss (Psychology) 19. Grief in families 20. Lexington, Kentucky 21. Pittsburgh, Pennsylvania 22. Psychological fiction 23. Mainstream fiction 24. Domestic fiction

LC 2005042257

British Book Award for Popular Fiction, 2008.

In a tale spanning twenty-five years, a doctor delivers his newborn twins during a snowstorm and, rashly deciding to protect his wife from their baby daughter's affliction with Down Syndrome, turns her over to a nurse, who secretly raises the child.

Edwards, Rachel

Darling / Rachel Edwards. Fourth Estate, 2018. 352 p.
ISBN 9780008281113
1. Teenage girls 2. Resentfulness 3. Stepmothers 4. Stepdaughters 5. Racism in teenagers 6. Racism 7. Race relations 8. Brexit, 2016-2020 9. England 10. Psychological suspense

Lola doesn't particularly want a new stepmother. Especially not one who has come out of nowhere and only been with her dad for three months. And she's not racist or anything but since when did her dad fancy black women anyway? Darling didn't particularly want a new stepdaughter. Especially not one as spiteful and spoilt as Lola. She does want Lola's dad though. And he wants her, so that's that: Darling and Lola will just have to get used to each other. Unless Lola can find a way to get rid of Darling.

Edwards, Yvvette

The **mother** / Yvvette Edwards. Amistad Press, 2016. 192 p.
ISBN 9780062440778
1. Mothers 2. Grief in women 3. Trials (Murder) 4. Mothers of murder victims 5. Criminal evidence 6. Loss (Psychology) 7. Marital conflict 8. Teenagers 9. Secrets 10. Psychological fiction

A mother copes with the death of her murdered teen after learning disturbing truths about the killer's dysfunctional family.

Edwardson, Ake, 1953-

Sail of stone / Ake Edwardson ; translated from the Swedish by Rachel Willson-Broyles. Simon & Schuster, 2012. 409 p. Erik Winter mysteries
ISBN 9781451608502
1. Missing persons investigation 2. Murder investigation 3. World War II veterans 4. Smuggling 5. Women detectives 6. Family violence 7. Detectives 8. Murder investigation 9. Scotland 10. Sweden 11. Mysteries 12. Police procedurals 13. Scandinavian crime fiction 14. Translations -- Swedish to English
LC 2011028497

Originally published in Swedish as Segel av sten.

While Chief Inspector Erik Winter of the Gothenburg police investigates the disappearance of a man who may have gone to Scotland to search for his World War II victim father, African-Swedish detective Aneta Djanali is threatened during her search for an abused woman who has been leaving mysterious phone calls.

Egan, Greg, 1961-

Perihelion summer / Greg Egan. St Martins Pr, 2019 208 p.
ISBN 9781250313782
1. Disasters 2. Black holes (Astronomy) 3. Global environmental change 4. Science -- Public opinion 5. Climate change 6. Aquaculture 7. Scientists 8. Sea level 9. Survival 10. Australia 11. Earth 12. Solar system 13. Hard science fiction 14. Apocalyptic fiction 15. Science fiction

Taraxippus is coming: a black hole one tenth the mass of the sun is about to enter the solar system. By the time it leaves, the conditions of life across the globe will be changed forever.

Egan, Greg, 1961-

* **Phoresis** / Greg Egan. Subterranean Press, 2018. 168 p.
ISBN 9781596068667
1. Planets 2. Women 3. Aliens (Humanoid) 4. Space colonies 5. Intergenerational relations 6. Risk 7. Survival 8. Hard science fiction

Welcome to Tvibura and Tviburi, the richly imagined twin planets that stand at the center of Greg Egan's extraordinary new novella.

Egan, Greg, 1961-

Schild's ladder / Greg Egan. EOS, 2002. 342 p.
ISBN 9780061050930
1. Far future 2. Scientists 3. Space flight 4. Vacuum 5. Research 6. Refugees 7. Mathematics 8. Posthumanism 9. Space and time 10. Quantum theory 11. Life on other planets 12. Space 13. Hard science fiction 14. Science fiction
LC 2001055583

Twenty-thousand years in the future, a dangerous experiment in quantum physics creates an expanding vacuum in space that threatens to wipe out all humanity.

"Egan writes rather forbidding novels, always grounded in real science and imbued with serious scientific speculations. This is his most uncompromising book to date." Booklist.

Egan, Jennifer

The **keep** / Jennifer Egan. Alfred A. Knopf, 2006. 239 p.
ISBN 9781400043927
1. Castles 2. Revenge 3. Prisoners 4. Cousins 5. Thirties (Age) 6. Rich men 7. Luddites 8. Drug abuse 9. Technology 10. Nobility 11. Creative writing 12. Practical jokes 13. Eastern Europe 14. Thrillers and suspense 15. Gothic fiction 16. Novels-within-novels
LC 2006011573

Two decades after taking part in a childhood prank whose devastating repercussions changed their lives forever, two cousins are reunited to work on the renovation of a medieval castle in Eastern Europe, a remote, eerie site profoundly influenced by its bloody past, where the two are cut off from the outside world and doomed to reenact the horrific event from their past.

"This novel makes us think hard about one of the murkiest mysteries of all: the mystery of perception, that uncertain border where reality and imagination meet. . . . In a novel full of unexpected shifts and interruptions, it's amazing how deftly Egan builds a logic for her characters." Los Angeles Times.

Egan, Jennifer,

* **Manhattan** Beach : a novel / Jennifer Egan. Scribner, 2017. 352 p.
ISBN 9781476716732
1. Second World War era (1939-1945) 2. World War II -- United States 3. Young women 4. Corruption 5. Deals 6. Divers 7. Daughters 8. Missing men 9. Girls with disabilities 10. Depressions -- 1929-1941 11. Navy-yards and naval stations 12. New York City -- History -- 20th century 13. Historical fiction 14. Literary fiction
LC 2017029043

Map on endpapers.

Andrew Carnegie Medal for Excellence in Fiction, 2018.
Longlisted for the National Book Award for Fiction, 2017.
Longlisted for The Women's Prize for Fiction, 2018.
Shortlisted for the Walter Scott Prize for Historical Fiction, 2018

Years after she is placed in the hands of a stranger vital to her family's survival, Anna takes a job at the Brooklyn Naval Yard during the war while meeting with the man who helped them and learning important truths about her father's disappearance.

"Realistically detailed, poetically charged, and utterly satisfying: apparently there's nothing Egan can't do." Kirkus.

Egan, Jennifer
 * A **visit** from the Goon Squad / Jennifer Egan. Alfred A. Knopf, 2010. 273 p.
 ISBN 9780307592835
 1. Punk rock musicians 2. Music industry and trade 3. Change 4. Sound recording executives and producers 5. Senior men 6. Young women 7. Secrets 8. Kleptomania 9. Psychological fiction 10. Literary fiction
           LC 2009046496
 ALA Notable Book, 2011.
 National Book Critics Circle Award for Fiction, 2010.
 Pulitzer Prize for Fiction, 2011.
 Shortlisted for the International IMPAC Dublin Literary Award, 2012
 Working side-by-side for a record label, former punk rocker Bennie Salazar and the passionate Sasha hide illicit secrets from one another while interacting with a motley assortment of equally troubled people from 1970s San Francisco to the post-war future.
 "This novel is centered, nominally, on the aging owner of an independent record label and his comely, kleptomania-prone assistant. But it is in fact a frequently dazzling piece of layer-cake meta-fiction, told via a sprawling constellation of characters and linked vignettes that spill from the late'70s Bay Area punk scene to the African plains, the dissolute slums of Naples, and the flush New York suburbs of the '90s boom. Egan's expert flaying of human foibles has the compulsive allure of poking at a sore tooth: excruciating but exhilarating, too." Entertainment Weekly.

Eggers, Dave
 The **circle** / Dave Eggers. Knopf, 2013. 504 p.
 ISBN 9780385351393
 1. Near future 2. Technology 3. Surveillance 4. Internet industry and trade 5. Social media 6. Memory 7. Privacy 8. Satirical fiction
           LC 2013032894
 Adapted into a film by the same title in 2016.
 Hired to work for the Circle, the world's most powerful Internet company, Mae Holland begins to questions her luck as life beyond her job grows distant, a strange encounter with a colleague leaves her shaken, and her role at the Circle becomes increasingly public.

Eggers, Dave
 A **hologram** for the king : a novel / Dave Eggers. McSweeney's Books, 2012. 312 p.
 ISBN 9781936365746
 1. Americans in Saudi Arabia 2. Businesspeople 3. Recession (Economics) 4. Household finances 5. Interracial friendship 6. Families 7. Saudi Arabia 8. Social science fiction 9. Science fiction
 Adapted into a film in 2016 under the same title.
 ALA Notable Book, 2013
 National Book Award for Fiction finalist, 2012
 In a Saudi Arabian city, far from weary, recession-scarred America, a struggling businessman attempts to avoid foreclosure, pay his daughter's college tuition, and finally do something great.

Eggers, Dave
 How we are hungry : stories / Dave Eggers. Vintage, 2005. 240 p.
 ISBN 1400095565
 1. Friendship 2. Family relationships 3. Interpersonal relations 4. Men/women relations 5. Social acceptance 6. Self-acceptance 7.

Self-discovery 8. Psychological fiction 9. Short stories
           LC 2005042321
 A debut collection of short stories presents a compelling cast of characters who struggle with inconvenient revelations, from the deserts of Egypt to the side of Interstate 5.

Eggers, Dave
 What is the what : the autobiography of Valentino Achak Deng / Dave Eggers. McSweeney's, 2006. 386 p.
 ISBN 1932416641
 1. Deng, Valentino Achak 2. Father-separated boys 3. Civil war 4. Survival 5. Refugees, Sudanese 6. Poverty 7. Voyages and travels 8. Loss (Psychology) 9. Belonging 10. Globalization (Economics) 11. Sudan -- History -- Civil War, 1955-1972 12. Biographical fiction
 National Book Critics Circle Award for Fiction finalist, 2006
 A biographical novel traces the story of Valentino Achak Deng, who as a boy was separated from his family when his village in southern Sudan was attacked, and became one of the estimated 17,000 "lost boys of Sudan" before relocating from a Kenyan refugeecamp to Atlanta in 2001.
 "Eggers has made the outlines of the tragedy in East Africa--so vague to so many Americans--not only sharp and clear but indelible. An eloquent testimony to the power of storytelling, What Is the What is an extraordinary work of witness, and of art." New York Times Book Review.

Ehirim, Nnamdi
 Prince of monkeys / Nnamdi Ehirim. Counterpoint, 2019. 304 p.
 ISBN 9781640091672
 1. Young men 2. Friendship 3. Social mobility 4. Political persecution 5. Corruption 6. Identity (Psychology) 7. Options, alternatives, choices 8. Lagos, Nigeria 9. Nigeria 10. Coming-of-age stories 11. Literary fiction
           LC 2018044345
 Growing up in middle-class Lagos, Nigeria during the late 1980s and early 1990s, Ihechi forms a band of close friends discovering Lagos together as teenagers with differing opinions of everything from film to football, Fela Kuti to spirituality, sex to politics. They remain close-knit until tragedy unfolds during an anti-government riot. Nnamdi Ehirim's debut novel, Prince of Monkeys, is a lyrical, meditative observation of Nigerian life, religion, and politics at the end of the twentieth century.

Eisenberg, Deborah
 The **twilight** of the superheroes / Deborah Eisenberg. Farrar, Straus and Giroux, 2006. 225 p.
 ISBN 9780374299415
 1. Families 2. Friendship 3. Men/women relations 4. New York City -- Social life and customs 5. Short stories 6. Literary fiction
           LC 2005042659
 Six short stories.
 A collection of short works includes the tales of a group of friends whose efforts to acquire a luxurious Manhattan sublet are halted by the September 11 attacks, a teacher's Roman holiday in the wake of her husband's life-threatening illness, and a brother's painful love for his schizophrenic sister.
 "Using her playwright's ear for dialogue and a journalistic eye for the askew detail, Ms. Eisenberg gives us--in just a handful of pages--a visceral sense of these characters' daily routines, the worlds they inhabit and the families they rebel against or allow to define them. . . . Instead of forcing her characters' stories into neat, arbitrary, preordained shapes, she allows them to grow asymmetrical narratives -- narratives that possess all the surprising twists and dismaying turns of real life." New York Times.

Eisler, Barry

All the devils / Barry Eisler. Thomas & Mercer, 2019. 364 p. Livia Lone novels

ISBN 9781542094238

1. Women detectives 2. Serial rapists 3. Missing girls 4. Government investigators 5. Thai Americans 6. Sexual violence victims 7. Violence against women 8. Missing persons investigation 9. Corruption 10. Thrillers and suspense

Ordered against investigating a series of disappearances linked to his daughter's unsolved kidnapping a decade earlier, a Homeland Security agent pleads for help from Seattle detective Livia Lone, who follows leads to a twisted pair of Special Forces veterans.

Eisler, Barry

The **god's** eye view / Barry Eisler. Thomas & Mercer, 2016. 374 p.

ISBN 9781503951518

1. National security 2. Intelligence service 3. Secrecy in government 4. Spies 5. Intrigue 6. Sadists 7. Assassins 8. Men/women relations 9. Attempted assassination 10. Spy fiction 11. Political thrillers 12. Thrillers and suspense

Working as a camera surveillance tech for a zealous security director, Evelyn stumbles on a mysterious program code connected to a string of journalist and whistle-blower deaths before finding herself and her deaf son in the crosshairs of a sadistic bomber and her boss's enforcer.

"The agent sent to monitor her is not quite what the boss thinks, and the personal and cyberfink stories are blended beautifully." Booklist.

Eisler, Barry

The **killer** collective / Barry Eisler. Thomas & Mercer, 2019. 401 p. John Rain novels

ISBN 9781503904262

1. Assassins 2. Elite operatives 3. Women detectives 4. Sex crimes 5. Conspiracies 6. Intelligence service 7. Political corruption 8. Spy fiction 9. Thrillers and suspense

When a joint FBI-Seattle Police investigation into an international child pornography ring gets too close to powerful enemies, sex-crimes detective Livia Lone becomes the target of a hit that is offered to a retired John Rain.

Eisler, Barry

Livia Lone / Barry Eisler. Thomas & Mercer, 2016. 368 p. Livia Lone novels

ISBN 9781503939660

1. Sisters 2. Detectives 3. Human trafficking 4. Police 5. Revenge 6. Thai Americans 7. Women detectives 8. Kidnapping victims 9. Sex crime investigation 10. Sexual violence victims 11. Missing persons investigation 12. Seattle, Washington 13. Thrillers and suspense

RUSA Reading List Short List, 2017

Seattle PD sex-crimes detective, and former human-trafficking victim, Livia Lone must relive the horrors of the past when she gets a fresh lead as to the whereabouts of her little sister, Nason.

Eisler, Barry

The **night** trade / Barry Eisler. Thomas & Mercer, 2018. 320 p. Livia Lone novels

ISBN 9781477820049

1. Women detectives 2. Former Marines 3. Conspiracies 4. Intelligence service 5. Human trafficking 6. Sex crimes 7. Thai Americans 8. Sexual violence victims 9. Americans in Thailand 10. Thailand 11. Thrillers and suspense

When an effort to arrest a trafficking kingpin goes violently wrong, sex-crimes detective Livia Lone forges a partnership with a former Marine sniper who is tracking the same criminal, only to uncover a conspiracy with ties to the highest levels of American intelligence.

El Akkad, Omar, 1982-

* **American** war / Omar El Akkad. Alfred A. Knopf, 2017. 333 p.

ISBN 9780451493583

1. 21st century 2. Civil war 3. Near future 4. Child soldiers 5. Refugee camps 6. Child refugees 7. Atrocities 8. Ideology 9. War 10. United States -- History -- 21st century 11. Louisiana 12. Political fiction 13. War stories 14. Dystopian fiction

LC 2016963038

ALA Notable Book, 2018.

Longlisted for the Andrew Carnegie Medal for Excellence in Fiction, 2018.

Rogers Writers' Trust Fiction Prize finalist, 2017.

Shortlisted for the James Tait Black Memorial Prize for Fiction, 2017

A second American Civil War and devastating plague in the late 21st century forces a family into a camp for displaced people, where a young woman is befriended by a mysterious functionary who would transform her into a living weapon.

"El Akkad has created a brilliantly well-crafted, profoundly shattering saga of one family's suffering in a world of brutal power struggles, terrorism, ignorance, and vengeance." Booklist.

El-Mohtar, Amal

* **This** is how you lose the time war / Amal El-Mohtar, Max Gladstone. Saga Press, 2019. 198 p.

ISBN 9781534431003

1. Space and time 2. Imaginary wars and battles 3. Romantic love 4. Enemies 5. Letter writing 6. Time travel 7. Competition 8. High technology 9. Secrets 10. Science fiction 11. Epistolary novels 12. Love stories 13. Literary fiction

Two time-traveling agents from warring futures, working their way through the past, begin to exchange letters?and soon fall in love.

"The authors pack their narrative full of fanciful ideas and poignant moments, weaving a tapestry stretching across the millennia and through multiple realities that's anchored with raw emotion and a genuine sense of wonder. This short novel warrants multiple readings to fully unlock its complexities." Publishers Weekly.

Elias, Gerald

Danse macabre / Gerald Elias. Minotaur Books, 2010. 304 p. Daniel Jacobus mysteries

ISBN 9780312541897

1. Violin teachers 2. Murder investigation 3. Murder suspects 4. Violin 5. Violinists 6. African American men 7. Malicious accusation 8. Murder 9. Men who are blind 10. Amateur detectives 11. New York City 12. Mysteries

LC 2010021994

When a beloved violinist is brutally murdered and a rival performer sentenced to death for the crime, blind concert master and amateur sleuth Daniel Jacobus reluctantly reopens the investigation at his own peril.

Elias, Gerald

* **Death** and transfiguration : a Daniel Jacobus novel / Gerald Elias. Minotaur Books, 2012. 320 p. Daniel Jacobus mysteries

ISBN 9780312678357

1. Conductors (Music) 2. Suicide investigation 3. Violin teachers 4.

Violinists 5. Musicians 6. harassment 7. Amateur detectives 8. Men who are blind 9. Crimes against musicians 10. New York City 11. Mysteries

LC 2012005488

When an aspiring concertmaster commits suicide after being dismissed by the tyrannical conductor of a world-famous touring orchestra, blind violin teacher Daniel investigates allegations about the conductor's harassment.

Eliot, George, 1819-1880

* **Adam** Bede / George Eliot ; introduction by Joanna Trollope ; notes by Hugh Osborne. Modern Library, 2002, c1859. xvii, 592 p.

ISBN 0375759018

1. Carpenters 2. Love triangles 3. Rural life 4. Clergywomen 5. Rich men 6. Social classes 7. Villages 8. England -- Social life and customs -- 19th century 9. Literary fiction 10. Classics

LC 2001044873

Originally published: 1859.

Arthur's seduction of an innocent, young country girl results in remorse, suffering, and regret.

Eliot, George, 1819-1880

* **Middlemarch** : a study of provincial life / George Eliot ; with a new introduction by Michael Faber. Signet Classic, 2003, c1872. xx, 892 p.

ISBN 9780451529176

1. 1830s 2. Women's role 3. Young women -- Relations with older men 4. Inheritance and succession 5. Physicians 6. Scholars and academics 7. Suffering 8. Medical care reform 9. Rural life 10. Men/women relations 11. England -- Social life and customs -- 19th century 12. Psychological fiction 13. Classics 14. Domestic fiction

LC 200354205

Originally published: 1872.

A sensitive young woman marries a bitter, despotic scholar 30 years her senior, who lives just long enough to blight her spirit. She inherits his fortune, only to learn she will forfeit it if she marries her husband's young cousin, whom she loves. When Dorothea tries to find happiness without Ladislaw, the intricate plots, subplots and character portraits lead to a satisfying conclusion in this masterpiece of 19th-century morals and social issues.

Eliot, George, 1819-1880

* The **mill** on the Floss / George Eliot ; edited with an introduction and notes by A.S. Byatt Penguin, 2003, c1860. 579 p.

ISBN 9780141439624

1. 19th century 2. Women's role 3. Brothers and sisters 4. Family relationships 5. Self-fulfillment in women 6. Growing up 7. Forgiveness 8. Floods 9. Family feuds 10. Psychological fiction 11. Classics

First published in 1860.

Evokes nineteenth-century rural England through the story of Maggie Tulliver, who attempts to adapt to her life until her brother forbids her to see the one person who understands her after she is found in a compromising situation.

Eliot, George, 1819-1880

* **Silas** Marner : the weaver of Raveloe / George Eliot. Knopf, 1993, c1861. xxx, 206 p.

ISBN 9780679420309

1. 19th century 2. Recluses 3. Malicious accusation 4. Abandoned children 5. Rural life 6. Stealing 7. Truthfulness and falsehood 8.

Fathers and daughters 9. Happiness 10. Redemption 11. Weavers 12. Frameups 13. Psychological fiction 14. Domestic fiction 15. Classics

The 1994 film A simple twist of fate is loosely based on Silas Marner.

Originally published: Edinburgh : William Blackwood & Sons, 1861.

Here is a tale straight from the fireside. We are compelled to follow the humble and mysterious figure of the linen weaver Silas Marner, on his journey from solitude and exile to the warmth and joy of family life. His path is a strange one; when he loses his hoard of hard-earned coins all seems to be lost, but in place of the golden guineas come the golden curls of a child and from desolate misery comes triumphant joy.

Elison, Meg

The **book** of Etta / Meg Elison. 47North, 2017. 314 p. Road to Nowhere

ISBN 9781503941823

1. Post-apocalypse 2. Midwives 3. Far future 4. Survival (after epidemics) 5. Dictators 6. Despotism 7. Women's role 8. Gender identity 9. Women's rights 10. Sex discrimination 11. Transgender persons 12. Apocalyptic fiction 13. Social science fiction 14. Science fiction

Etta comes from Nowhere, a village of survivors of the great plague that wiped away the world that was. In the world that is, women are scarce and childbearing is dangerous, yet desperately necessary for humankind's future. Mothers and midwives are sacred, but Etta has a different calling. As a scavenger. Loyal to the village but living on her own terms, Etta roams the desolate territory beyond: salvaging useful relics of the ruined past and braving the threat of brutal slave traders, who are seeking women and girls to sell and subjugate.

"Elison continues to startle her readers with unexpected gender permutations and fascinating relationships worked out in front of a convincingly detailed landscape." Publishers Weekly.

Elison, Meg

The **book** of Flora / Meg Elison. 47North, 2019. 332 p. Road to Nowhere

ISBN 9781542042093

1. Post-apocalypse 2. Far future 3. Gender identity 4. Belief and doubt 5. Survival (after epidemics) 6. Librarians 7. Women's role 8. Women's rights 9. Sex discrimination 10. Transgender persons 11. Imaginary wars and battles 12. Apocalyptic fiction 13. Social science fiction 14. Science fiction

Navigating a blighted landscape, Flora--an outsider everywhere she goes--her friends, and a sullen young slave she adopts as her own child leave their oppressive pasts behind to find their place in a post-apocalyptic world. When the promise of a miraculous hope for humanity's future tears Flora's makeshift family asunder, she must choose: protect the safe haven she's built or risk everything to defy oppression, whatever its provenance.

Elison, Meg

* The **book** of the unnamed midwife / Meg Elison. Sybaratic Press, 2014. 185 p. Road to Nowhere

ISBN 9781495116360

1. Post-apocalypse 2. Midwives 3. Sex discrimination 4. Survival (after epidemics) 5. Male impersonators 6. Voyages and travels 7. Diary writing 8. Death 9. Sexuality 10. Apocalyptic fiction 11. Social science fiction 12. Science fiction

Philip K. Dick Award for Science Fiction, 2015.

"Elison takes readers on an exciting and often excruciating journey, navigating issues of gender and sex in a scorched, disease-ridden world." Booklist.

LIST OF FICTIONAL WORKS

Elkin, Stanley, 1930-1995

The **MacGuffin** / Stanley Elkin. Linden Press, 1991. 283 p.

ISBN 9780671673246

1. Politicians 2. Middle-aged men 3. Humorous stories

LC 90013233

National Book Award for Fiction finalist, 1991

Bobbo Druff, the fifty-eight-year-old commissioner of streets, finds his ordinary life turned upside down by a series of bizarre events and the people in his life--his wife, his son, his new lover, and his chauffeur.

"Here, MacGuffins of adultery, smuggling, and drug abuse merely provide a context for inspired, Joycean wordplay based on cliches, shoptalk, and technical jargon. Language itself is the real topic." Library Journal.

Elkins, Aaron J.

Dying on the vine / Aaron J. Elkins. Berkley, 2012. 294 p. Gideon Oliver mysteries

ISBN 9780425247884

1. Forensic anthropologists 2. Murder investigation 3. Deception 4. Vintners 5. Families 6. Wine and wine making 7. Forensic anthropology 8. Dead -- Identification 9. College teachers 10. Amateur detectives 11. Tuscany, Italy 12. Italy 13. Florence, Italy 14. Mysteries

Italian detective Gideon Oliver investigates what is believed by the local Tuscan authorities to be a murder-suicide when a couples' remains are discovered in a vineyard.

Elkins, Aaron J.

A **long** time coming / Aaron J. Elkins. Thomas & Mercer, 2018. 268 p.

ISBN 9781503902381

1. Art curators 2. Art thefts 3. Nazi plunder 4. Divorced men 5. Forties (Age) 6. Murder 7. Art 8. Amateur detectives 9. Milan, Italy 10. New York City 11. Mysteries

Art curator Val Caruso is not a happy camper. His promotion has just been nixed, his divorce has become final, and he's dug himself into a nice little rut for his fortieth birthday. The uplift? A trip to Milan to help Holocaust survivor Sol Bezzecca recover a pair of cherished sketches by Renoir. They'd once been given to Sol's family by the then-unknown artist, looted by the Italian Fascist militia, and now after decades in hiding have turned up for auction. It's Val's job to get them back. The trip takes a dangerous turn thanks to an intricate web that reaches back to World War II-- and someone among the art thieves and forgers wants Val out of the picture-- permanently.

"Classy work, deserving patience." Booklist.

Elkins, Aaron J.

Unnatural selection / Aaron Elkins. Berkley Prime Crime, 2006. 288 p. Gideon Oliver mysteries

ISBN 0425210057

1. Forensic anthropologists 2. Environmentalists 3. Murder 4. College teachers 5. Anthropologists 6. Husband and wife 7. Americans in Italy 8. Women amateur detectives 9. Forensic anthropology 10. Dead -- Identification 11. Biodiversity 12. Amateur detectives 13. Sicily, Italy 14. Mysteries

LC 2006002173

Heading for the Isles of Scilly, off the Cornwall coast, with his wife, who has been invited to attend a consortium hosted by Russian expatriate Vasily Kozlov, forensics professor Gideon Oliver is delighted to spend the time puttering around local Neolithic sites, until he stumbles upon a much newer bone that could be tied to a brand-new murder.

Elliot, Laura

Guilty / Laura Elliot. Grand Central Publishing, 2019, 400 p.

ISBN 9781538764275

1. Teenage girl murder victims 2. Women investigative journalists 3. Malicious accusation 4. Uncle and niece 5. Murder investigation 6. Violence in mass media 7. Revenge 8. Dublin, Ireland 9. Thrillers and suspense

Originally published: Ickenham, United Kingdom : Bookouture, 2017.

On a warm summer's morning, thirteen-year-old school girl Constance Lawson is reported missing. A few days later, Constance's uncle, Karl Lawson, suddenly finds himself swept up in a media frenzy created by journalist Amanda Bowe implying that he is the prime suspect. Six years later, Karl's life is in ruins. His marriage is over, his family destroyed. But the woman who took everything away from him is thriving. With a successful career, husband and a gorgeous baby boy, Amanda's world is complete. Until the day she receives a phone call and in a heartbeat, she is plunged into every mother's worst nightmare.

Elliott, Lexie,

The **missing** years / Lexie Elliott. Berkley, 2019. 320 p.

ISBN 9780399586958

1. Women television producers and directors 2. Half-sisters 3. Manors 4. Missing persons investigation 5. Missing men 6. Fathers 7. Family secrets 8. Highlands, Scotland 9. Scotland 10. Gothic fiction

LC 2018043170

When Ailsa Calder inherits her childhood home in the craggy peaks of the Scottish Highlands, she must contend with memories of her 27-years-gone father, a half-sister she's hardly known, the fact that neighborhood animals avoid the garden - and the nighttime intruder.

Ellis, Bella

The **vanished** bride / Bella Ellis. Berkley, 2019. 304 p. Bronte sisters mystery

ISBN 9780593099056

1. Bronte, Charlotte, 1816-1855 2. Bronte, Emily, 1818-1848 3. Bronte, Anne, 1820-1849 4. Victorian era (1837-1901) 5. 1840s 6. Women amateur detectives 7. Women authors, English 8. Gender role 9. Missing women 10. Sisters 11. Sexism 12. Missing persons investigation 13. Families 14. Yorkshire, England 15. England -- Social life and customs -- 19th century 16. Historical mysteries

LC 2019015852

In 1845 Yorkshire, a young wife and mother has gone missing from her home, leaving behind two small children and a large pool of blood, and it is up to the Bronte sisters to investigate.

Ellis, Bret Easton

Lunar Park / Bret Easton Ellis. Knopf, 2005. 307 p.

ISBN 9780375412912

1. Ellis, Bret Easton 2. Suburban life 3. Drug abuse 4. Missing boys 5. Fathers and sons 6. Murder 7. Alcoholism 8. Hallucinations and illusions 9. Suspicion 10. Family relationships 11. Autobiographical fiction 12. Psychological fiction 13. Domestic fiction

LC 2005040923

International Horror Guild Award for Best Novel, 2005.

Becoming a best-selling novelist and wealthy celebrity while still in college, only to have his fame disintegrate in a sea of booze, drugs, and vilification, the narrator gets a new chance at life married to the mother of a previously unacknowledged son and living in suburbia, but now his new life unravels in the wake of a series of grotesque murders and the disappearance of young boys.

"The whole book swirls, surreally, pushing the limits of tolerable confusion while sending up laughably familiar horror story shticks. For a while, it looks as if nothing will be resolved. It works precisely because it is a ghost story, replete with eviscerated livestock, freshly dug graves, and messages written in ashand because everything, ultimately, is resolved." New Criterion.

Ellis, Bret Easton

Imperial bedrooms / Bret Easton Ellis. Alfred A. Knopf, 2010. 288 p.

ISBN 9780307266101

1. Middle-aged men 2. Generation X 3. City life -- Los Angeles, California 4. Conspiracies 5. Friendship 6. Personal conduct 7. Los Angeles, California 8. Psychological fiction

LC 2009041690

Sequel to: Less than zero.

With his screenwriting career at its peak, Clay returns to Los Angeles to hire the cast for an upcoming blockbuster. There he comes across his former girlfriend Blair and her philandering husband Trent, whose nightlife and sexual tastes have made him the talk of the town. He also comes into contact with Julian, an old friend turned junkie, and his sinister drug dealer. However, when his life starts spiraling out of control, Clay is forced to face his own past.

"As with Chandler's work, the details of the twists and turns are beside the point particularly since Ellis puckishly reveals at the start which character is going to wind up as a corpse in a Tom Ford suit. But the author uses the thriller framework to infuse nerve-rending unease into this look at Tinseltown mores, a dissection that also comes nicely weighted with both bleak hilarity and firsthand authorial experience." Entertainment Weekly.

Ellis, David, 1967-

In the company of liars / David Ellis. G.P. Putnam's Sons, 2005. 378 p.

ISBN 9780399152474

1. Women authors 2. Women authors 3. Women murder suspects 4. Divorced persons 5. Former husbands 6. Mothers and daughters 7. Lawyers 8. Women FBI agents 9. Terrorists 10. Conspiracies 11. Extortion 12. Political corruption 13. Lobbyists -- Washington, D.C. 14. Terrorism -- Prevention 15. Thrillers and suspense

LC 2004057342

A thriller told in reverse centers on a woman who is undergoing a murder trial that is being overseen by a prosecutor who is strongly pursuing a death penalty and an FBI agent who would force the defendant to betray her family.

Ellis, Helen

American housewife : stories / Helen Ellis. Doubleday, 2016. xi, 188 p.

ISBN 9780385541039

1. Women 2. Married women 3. Femininity 4. Anger in women 5. Revenge 6. Satirical fiction 7. Short stories

LC 2015021779

A collection of stories featuring conventional, if ruthless, housewives features a rigged reality television show, a unique book club initiation ritual, and the fitting room of a legendary lingerie shop.

"With monstrous children and cats, hopeless husbands, and covertly dangerous women, Ellis takes down the entire housewife concept with a sniper's precision. These are delectably revved up, marauding, sometimes macabre tales of ruined marriages, illness, infertility, crass commercialism (literary product placement), desperation, ghosts, even murder, featuring women of shrewd calculation, secret sorrows, and deep sympathy." Booklist.

Ellis, M. Henderson

Keeping bedlam at bay in the Prague Cafe / M. Henderson Ellis. Steerforth Press, 2013. 208 p.

ISBN 9780982578186

1. 1990s 2. Eccentrics and eccentricities 3. City life 4. Capitalism 5. Expatriates 6. Americans in Poland 7. Drug abusers 8. Prostitutes 9. Baristas 10. Prague, Czech Republic 11. Experimental fiction

After a young Chicago barista loses his job at his beloved global coffee chain, he tries to open a franchise of the café in postcommunist Prague, and falls in with an arcade game-obsessed prostitute and a pair of Golem hunters.

Ellison, J. T.

Good girls lie / J. T. Ellison. MIRA, 2019. 464 p.

ISBN 9780778309185

1. Girls' boarding schools 2. Teenage girls 3. Murder 4. Transfer students 5. Prep schools 6. Secret societies 7. Hazing 8. Friendship 9. Dishonesty 10. Secrets 11. Serial murderers 12. British in the United States 13. Rich people 14. United States 15. Virginia 16. Psychological suspense

In a follow-up to Lie to Me and Tear Me Apart, a popular transfer student at an elite prep school races to protect a dangerous secret when a killer sets her up for a string of murders.

Ellison, J. T.

Tear me apart / J. T. Ellison. MIRA Books, 2018. 368 p.

ISBN 9780778308263

1. Teenage girls 2. Daughters 3. Infants switched at birth 4. Skiers 5. Accident victims 6. People with leukemia 7. Deception 8. Family secrets 9. Identity (Psychology) 10. Colorado 11. Psychological suspense

When a life-threatening illness reveals that she is not related to her parents, a competitive skier uncovers the sinister impact of lies and desperation on two families.

Ellison, Jan

A small indiscretion / Jan Ellison. Random House, 2015. 336 p.

ISBN 9780812995442

1. Redemption 2. Married women 3. Married people and secrets 4. Traffic accident victims -- Family relationships 5. Desire in women 6. Consequences 7. Love triangles 8. Photographs 9. Secrets 10. Families 11. Lovers 12. San Francisco, California 13. London, England 14. Literary fiction 15. Psychological fiction

Successful designer and family woman Annie Black journeys to London to piece together the events of a fateful night of indiscretions from her past.

Ellison, Ralph

* Invisible man / Ralph Ellison. Vintage International, 1995, c1952. xxiii, 581 p.

ISBN 9780679732761

1. Race relations 2. African Americans 3. Identity (Psychology) 4. African American men -- Harlem, New York City 5. New York City 6. Harlem, New York City 7. African American fiction 8. Literary fiction 9. Modern classics

Originally published: New York : Random House, 1952.

National Book Award for Fiction, 1953.

An African-American man's search for success and the American dream leads him out of college to Harlem and a growing sense of personal rejection and social invisibility.

Ellison, Ralph

Three days before the shooting . . . / Ralph Ellison ; edited by John Callahan. Modern Library, 2010. 896 p.

ISBN 9780375759536

1. Attempted assassination 2. Race relations 3. Politicians 4. Caretakers 5. African Americans -- Identity 6. African American clergy 7. Racism 8. Orphans 9. Jazz music 10. Literary fiction 11. African American fiction

"Culled from Ellison's drafts, his notes, and those of his wife, Fanny, this book brings together four decades of work, a portion of which was published posthumously as Juneteenth in 1999. The allegorical, lyrical novel is presented in three books in various stages of completion. It centers on the complex relationship between A. Z. Hickman, a blues musician turned preacher, and Bliss, an orphan of undetermined race, whom Hickman raises as a boy preacher. ... He is masterful at evoking the language of common black folks, preachers, press and politicians, and charlatans and flimflammers." Booklist.

Ellmann, Lucy, 1956-

* Ducks, Newburyport / Lucy Ellmann. Biblioasis, 2019. 728 p.

ISBN 9781771963077

1. 21st century 2. Mothers 3. Obsession 4. Popular culture 5. Family relationships 6. Anxiety 7. Resistance (Psychology) in children 8. Protectiveness in women 9. Parents 10. Women-headed families 11. Ohio 12. Literary fiction 13. Experimental fiction

Shortlisted for the Booker Prize, 2019.

Peeling apple after apple for the tartes tatin she bakes for local restaurants, an Ohio mother wonders how to exist in a world of distraction and fake facts, besieged by a tweet-happy president and trigger-happy neighbors, and all of them oblivious to what Dupont has dumped into the rivers and what's happening at the factory farm down the interstate?not to mention what was done to the land's first inhabitants.

Ellory, R. J. (Roger Jon)

The **anniversary** man / R. J. Ellory. Penguin Group USA., 2010 400 p.

ISBN 9781590203279

1. Serial murderers 2. Police 3. Detectives 4. Serial murder investigation 5. Attempted murder 6. Violence 7. New York City 8. Thrillers and suspense

Twenty years ago, John Costello and his girlfriend, Nadia, became victims of the deranged "Hammer of God," a serial killer who went after young courting couples in an attempt to "save their souls." Nadia was killed by the first blow of the hammer. John survived but was physically and psychologically scarred to an extent that few people could comprehend. He withdrew from society and hid in his apartment and emerges now only to work as a crime researcher for a major newspaper.

Ellory, R. J. (Roger Jon)

Bad signs / R. J. Ellory. Overlook Pr, 2016 440 p.

ISBN 9781468311273

1. Orphans 2. Brothers 3. Hostages 4. Free will and determinism 5. Death row prisoners 6. Life change events 7. Hostage-taking 8. Psychopaths 9. Murderers 10. California 11. Texas 12. Thrillers and suspense

LC 2015044766

Originally published: 2011.

Orphaned by an act of senseless violence that took their mother from them, half-brothers Clarence Luckman and Elliott Danziger have been raised in state institutions, unaware of any world outside. But their lives take a sudden turn when they are seized as hostages by a convicted killer en route to death row. Earl Sheridan is a psychopath of the worst kind, but he has the potential to change the boys' lives for ever. As the trio set off on a frenetic escape from the law through California and Texas, the two brothers must come to terms with the ever-growing tide of violence that follows in their wake--something that forces them to make a choice about their lives and their relationship to one another.

Ellory, R. J. (Roger Jon)

Saints of New York : a novel / R. J. Ellory. Overlook Press, 2011. 400 p.

ISBN 9781590204610

1. Detectives 2. Murder investigation 3. Crimes against teenage girls 4. Murder 5. New York City 6. Mysteries

Includes reading group notes.

Investigating the murder of a young heroin dealer's teenage sister, New York detective Frank Parrish uncovers a disturbing pattern of killings while battling painful personal demons about his legendary detective father.

Ellory, R. J. (Roger Jon)

A **simple** act of violence : a thriller / R. J. Ellory. Overlook Press, 2011. 464 p.

ISBN 9781590203187

1. Detectives -- Washington, D.C. 2. Murder investigation -- Washington, D.C. 3. Serial murders -- Washington, D.C. 4. Corruption investigation 5. Murder -- Washington, D.C. 6. Washington, D.C. 7. Mysteries

Theakston Old Peculier Crime Novel of the Year Award, 2010

Veteran D.C. Detective Robert Miller arrives at the house of Catherine Sheridan, the fourth victim of the Ribbon Killer. As the case unfolds, the motive behind the murders of these female victims is somehow linked to much larger political issues.

Ellroy, James, 1948-

American tabloid : a novel / James Ellroy. A.A. Knopf, 1995. 571 p. Underworld U.S.A. trilogy

ISBN 9780679403913

1. Kennedy, John F (John Fitzgerald), 1917-1963 2. CIA 3. 1960s 4. Political corruption 5. Criminals -- United States 6. Labor unions -- United States 7. Organized crime 8. United States -- Politics and government -- 1961-1963 9. Noir fiction 10. Political fiction

LC 94042898

Reprinted in 2019 with "The Cold Six Thousand".

Offers a story of the dark secrets behind Kennedy's election and assassination, the Bay of Pigs, and the roles of the underworld, the CIA, Howard Hughes, Hoover, and three renegade law-enforcement officers.

Ellroy, James, 1948-

Blood's a rover / James Ellroy. Knopf, 2019, 583 p. Underworld U.S.A. trilogy

ISBN 9781101908143

1. Democratic Party. National Convention, Chicago, Illinois, 1968 2. 1960s 3. Organized crime 4. Political corruption 5. Conspiracies 6. Assassination 7. Racism 8. Communism 9. Gangsters 10. United States -- Politics and government -- 1963-1969 11. Noir fiction 12. Political fiction

Originally published in 2009.

Blood's A Rover takes us into the seventies. MLK and RFK are dead. The Democratic National Convention in Chicago has spawned chaos. There's a punk-kid private eye in L.A. He's clashing with a mob goon and an enforcer for J. Edgar Hoover. There's an armored-car heist and a cache of missing emeralds. There's bad voodoo in the Dominican Republic and Haiti. Amidst it all is a revolutionary, Joan Rosen Klein. The kid P.I., the mob goon, and Hoover's enforcer love her unto death.

Blood's A Rover gives us the private nightmare of public policy on an epic scale.

"Ellroy employs a huge cast and hyper-pulp prose to create a convincingly horrific universe run by the F.B.I., the Mob, and a host of other sinister organizations." The New Yorker.

Ellroy, James, 1948-

The **cold** six thousand : a novel / James Ellroy. Knopf, 2001. 669 p. Underworld U.S.A. trilogy

ISBN 9780679403920

1. King, Martin Luther,, Jr, 1929-1968 Assassination 2. Kennedy, John F (John Fitzgerald), 1917-1963 Assassination 3. Hoover, J Edgar, 1895-1972 4. 1960s 5. Political corruption 6. Conspiracies -- United States 7. Assassins 8. Drug smugglers 9. Police 10. Mafia 11. United States -- Politics and government -- 1963-1969 12. Noir fiction 13. Political fiction

Reprinted in 2019 with "American Tabloid".

Politics and conspiracies are interwoven in this story of a young policeman from Las Vegas who becomes intangled with the events and people who shaped the Sixties.

"A look at the dark side of American life during the 1960s, focusing on a Las Vegas police officr, Wayne Tedrow Jr., and his inadvertent role in the cover-up of John F. Kennedy's assassination. The narrative spans a five-year period and traces Tedrow's dealings with the Mafia, the Ku Klux Klan, and various political and cultural icons of that time period." Library Journal.

Ellroy, James, 1948-

* **L.A.** confidential / James Ellroy. Warner Books, 1997, c1990. 496 p. L. A. quartet

ISBN 9780446674249

1. 1950s 2. Police 3. Detectives 4. Police corruption 5. Mass murder 6. Los Angeles, California 7. Crime fiction

Originally published: New York : Mysterious Press, 1990.

Three troubled cops-- Ed Exley, desperately seeking glory; vengeful Bud White, a witness to his mother's murder by his father; and Jack Vincennes, a shakedown artist with a dark secret-- tread a fine line between right and wrong in 1950s Los Angeles.

"The author merges raw-edged period detail with sleazy celluloid lore, producing a dark and dazzling descent into the criminal underworld of the 1950s." Booklist.

Ellroy, James, 1948-

Perfidia / James Ellroy. Random House Inc., 2014. 608 p. Second L. A. quartet

ISBN 9780307956996

1. Second World War era (1939-1945) 2. 1940s 3. Japanese Americans -- Forced removal and incarceration, 1942-1945 4. World War II -- United States 5. Violence against minorities 6. Forced relocations 7. Men/women relations 8. Murder investigation 9. Forensic scientists 10. War and society 11. Police 12. Los Angeles, California -- History -- 20th century 13. Police procedurals 14. Historical mysteries

A debut entry in a second L.A. Quartet follows a post-Pearl Harbor murder of a Japanese family that entangles a brilliant Japanese-American forensic chemist, an adventurous woman, a future police chief and an arch villain.

"Regardless of what Ellroy intends or means, what hes achieved is a disturbing, unforgettable, and inflammatory vision of how the men in charge respond to the threat of war." Booklist.

Ellroy, James, 1948-

This storm : a novel / James Ellroy. Alfred A. Knopf, 2019. 589 p. Second L. A. quartet

ISBN 9780307957009

1. 1940s 2. Second World War era (1939-1945) 3. Police 4. Military intelligence 5. Murder investigation 6. Murder 7. Profiteering 8. War and society 9. Police corruption 10. Forensic scientists 11. Fascism -- United States 12. Japanese Americans -- Forced removal and incarceration, 1942-1945 13. Los Angeles, California -- History -- 20th century 14. Police procedurals 15. Historical mysteries

LC 2018048538

A corrupt vice cop, a crime-lab whiz facing Japanese internment, a fascist police consultant to Army Intelligence and a rogue profiteer investigate a historically relevant murder in 1942 Los Angeles.

"Just when it seems that things couldn't get darker, Ellroy peels back a deeper level of corruption. This obsessive, wholly satisfying probing of 20th-century American history deserves a wide readership." Publishers Weekly.

Emezi, Akwaeke

Freshwater / Akwaeke Emezi. Grove Press, 2017 229 p.

ISBN 9780802127358

1. Emezi, Akwaeke 2. Women with mental illnesses 3. Identity (Psychology) 4. Self 5. Nigerians in the United States 6. Igbo (African people) 7. Gods and goddesses 8. Women -- Psychology 9. Loss (Psychology) 10. Nigeria 11. Virginia 12. Autobiographical fiction 13. Literary fiction

LC 2017028925

Otherwise Award, 2019.

Longlisted for The Women's Prize for Fiction, 2019.

Traces the experiences of a deeply troubled young woman who alarms her devout Nigerian family as she succumbs to multiple personality disorder and begins to display increasingly dark and dangerous traits in accordance with her fractured personalities.

"Emezi's brilliance lies not just in her expert handling of the conflicting voices in Ada's head but in delivering an entirely different perspective on just what it means to go slowly mad. Complex and dark, this novel will simultaneously challenge and reward lovers of literary fiction. A must-read." Booklist.

Emshwiller, Carol

The **secret** city / Carol Emshwiller. Tachyon Publications, 2007. 209 p.

ISBN 1892391449

1. Aliens (Humanoid) 2. Rescues 3. Humans 4. Human/alien encounters 5. Assimilation (Sociology) 6. Labor exploitation 7. Men/women relations 8. Interpersonal attraction 9. Options, alternatives, choices 10. Social science fiction 11. Science fiction

The Secret City, hidden high in a mountain range, harbors a handful of aliens stranded on Earth, waiting for rescue and running out of time. Over years of increasing poverty, an exodus to the human world has become their only chance for survival. The aliens are gradually assimilating, not as a discrete culture, but rather as a source of cheap labor. But the sudden arrival of ill-prepared rescuers will touch off divided loyalties, violent displacement, and star-crossed love. As unlikely human allies are pitted against xenophobic aliens, the stage is set for a final standoff at the Secret City.

"First and foremost, Emshwiller is a poetwith a poet's sensibility, precision, and magic. She revels in the sheer taste and sound of words, she infuses them with an extraordinary vitality and sense of life." Newsday

Enard, Mathias, 1972-

Compass / Mathias Enard ; translated by Charlotte Mandell. New Directions, 2017. 464 p.

ISBN 9780811226622

1. Obsession 2. Voyages and travels 3. Interpersonal relations 4. Musicologists 5. Learning and scholarship 6. Memories 7. Unrequited love 8. Opium 9. Dreams 10. Insomnia 11. Literary fiction 12. Translations -- French to English

LC 2016039665

Shortlisted for the International Dublin Literary Award, 2019.

Franz Ritter, an insomniac musicologist, spends a restless night drifting between dreams and memories, revisiting the important chapters of his life, including his elusive, unrequited love, Sarah, a brilliant French scholar caught in the complex tension between Europe and the Middle East.

Endo, Shusaku, 1923-1996

* **Deep** river / Shusaku Endo ; translated by Van C. Gessel. New Directons, 1994, c1993. 216 p.

ISBN 9780811212892

1. Japanese in India 2. Pilgrims and pilgrimages 3. Ganges River 4. India 5. Translations -- Japanese to English

LC 94038913

Originally published: Tokyo : Kodansha, 1993.

Offers a religious vision combining Christian faith with Buddhist acceptance in the story of a group of Japanese tourists who converge at the Ganges River in India

"This is a beautifully wrought, lyrically suggestive story. . . . If Christianity holds up to us the lonely individual challenged by a God who entered history, Buddhism gives us people who are ready to surrender, finally, a measure of their human and spiritual particularity and who, with acceptance, join their fellow creatures as part of the great tide of humanity. Mr. Endo manages to merge both of these streams of faith, bringing them together in a flow that is, indeed, deep. His work is a soulful gift to a world he keeps rendering as unrelievedly parched." New York Times Book Review.

Endo, Shusaku, 1923-1996

* **Silence** / Shusaku Endo ; translated by William Johnston. Sophia University; in cooperation with the C.E. Tuttle Co., 1969 306 p.

ISBN 0800871863

1. 17th century 2. Christian missionaries 3. Priests 4. Christians 5. Religious persecution 6. Portuguese in Japan 7. Faith (Christianity) 8. Belief and doubt 9. Torture 10. Japan -- History -- 17th century 11. Translations -- Japanese to English 12. Christian historical fiction 13. Christian fiction

LC 68058912

Sustained by dreams of glorious martyrdom, a seventeenth-century Purtuguese missionary in Japan administers to the outlawed Christians until Japanese authorities capture him and force him to watch the torture of his followers, promising to stop if he will renounce Christ.

Engelmann, Karen, 1954-

The **Stockholm** octavo / Karen Engelmann. Ecco, 2012. 432 p.

ISBN 9780061995347

1. 18th century 2. Fortune telling 3. Conspiracies 4. Revolutions 5. Mate selection for men 6. Scandals 7. Magic 8. Stockholm, Sweden 9. Historical fiction 10. Adventure stories

In Stockholm of 1791, self-satisfied bureaucrat Emil Larsson is informed by a fortune teller that in order to find love and connection, he must first find eight individuals who can help him realize this vision--a search that becomes dangerous when he must pull his country back from rebellion and chaos.

Enger, Leif,

Virgil Wander / Leif Enger. Grove Press, 2018. 300 p.

ISBN 9780802128782

1. Film theater managers 2. Survival (after automobile, truck, train accidents, etc) 3. Amnesia 4. Memory 5. Interpersonal communication 6. Missing men 7. Traffic accidents 8. Loss (Psychology) 9. Eccentrics and eccentricities 10. Small towns 11. Minnesota 12. Mainstream fiction 13. Psychological fiction

LC 2018026619

Emerging from an accident with damaged memories and compromised language skills, a movie-house owner from a small Midwestern town pieces together his story against a backdrop of community history, which is shaped by a prodigal son's return.

Enger, Lin

The **high** divide : a novel / Lin Enger. Algonquin Books of Chapel Hill, 2014. 304 p.

ISBN 9781616203757

1. 1880s 2. Father-deserted families 3. Frontier and pioneer life 4. Voyages and travels 5. Families 6. Wilderness areas 7. Indians of North America 8. Redemption 9. Family relationships 10. The West (United States) 11. Westerns 12. Literary fiction

LC 2014014702

Abandoned by her husband and her two sons who went out to search for him, Gretta Pope must follow her family across the rugged badlands of 1880s Montana.

Enger, Lin

Undiscovered country : a novel / Lin Enger. Little, Brown and Co., 2008. 320 p.

ISBN 9780316006941

1. Fathers and sons 2. Suicide 3. Revenge 4. Family secrets 5. Married people 6. Forgiveness 7. Minnesota 8. Domestic fiction

LC 2007030138

While hunting in the cold Minnesota woods, 17-year-old Jesse Matson's life is forever changed when he discovers his father, dead by a self-inflicted gunshot wound. But would easygoing Harold Matson really kill himself? If so, why? And just where was Jesse's uncle Clay--always jealous of Harold, and a bit too friendly with Jesse's mother--that cold afternoon?

"A modern-day Hamlet story set in rural northern Minnesota. Teenage Jesse's father, the mayor of Battlepoint, apparently committed suicide with his own hunting rifle. But Jesse suspects his Uncle Clay, who had more than one motive for murder. Is Jesse's suspicion simply his inability to accept his father's senseless act? Or is Clay really guilty and how complicit is Jesse's mother? If Clay is guilty, what should he do about it? The obvious parallels with Shakespeare's play are even acknowledged by some of the characters, but Enger doesn't let this conceit overwhelm the story. He skillfully draws a portrait of small-town life and all its barely concealed secrets and effectively narrates Jesse's torment." Library Journal.

Englander, Nathan

The **ministry** of Special Cases / Nathan Englander. Alfred A. Knopf, 2007. 352 p.

ISBN 9780375404931

1. Missing persons -- Argentina 2. Missing children 3. Human rights -- Argentina 4. Jews 5. Loss (Psychology) 6. Family relationships 7. Identity (Psychology) 8. Murder 9. Fathers and sons 10. Options,

alternatives, choices 11. Argentina -- History -- 1955-1983 12. Political fiction 13. Literary fiction

LC 2006048731

Sophie Brody Medal, 2008

In the heart of Argentina's Dirty War, Kaddish Poznan struggles with a son who won't accept him; strives for a wife who forever saves him; and spends his nights protecting the good name of a community that denies his existence--and denies a checkered history that only Kaddish holds dear.

"The author bravely wrangles the themes of political liberty and personal loss with the swift style and knowing humor of folklore. In the spirit of the simple ambiguity of its title, The Ministry of Special Cases is carefully contradictory, wise and off-kilter, funny and sad." New York Observer.

Englander, Nathan

* **What** we talk about when we talk about Anne Frank : stories / Nathan Englander. Knopf, 2012. 288 p.

ISBN 9780307958709

1. Jews 2. Mother and child 3. Holocaust (1933-1945) 4. Holocaust survivors 5. Jewish way of life 6. Literary fiction 7. Short stories

LC 2011033756

Pulitzer Prize for Fiction finalist, 2013.

A collection of short stories includes the title story about two marriages in which the Holocaust is played out as a devastating parlor game, and a dark story of vigilante justice undertaken by a troop of geriatric campers.

Enright, Anne, 1962-

Actress : a novel / Anne Enright. W. W. Norton & Co., 2020. 264 p.

ISBN 9781324005629

1. Mothers and daughters 2. Theater actors and actresses 3. Celebrities 4. Children of actors and actresses 5. Fame 6. Sexuality 7. Growing up 8. Aging 9. Familial love 10. Family relationships 11. Family secrets 12. Ireland 13. Family sagas 14. Literary fiction

LC 2019046238

When her Irish-theater-legend mother succumbs to alcohol and instability, Norah draws on her experiences of surviving a crime and growing up in the wings of her mother's career to rediscover herself as a wife, mother and writer.

"Another triumph for Enright: a confluence of lyrical prose, immediacy, warmth, and emotional insight." Kirkus.

Enright, Anne, 1962-

The **forgotten** waltz / Anne Enright. W. W. Norton & Co., 2011. 263 p.

ISBN 9780393072556

1. Memories 2. Extramarital affairs 3. Desire 4. Boredom in women 5. Fathers and daughters 6. Epilepsy 7. Ireland 8. Psychological fiction 9. Literary fiction

Andrew Carnegie Medal for Excellence in Fiction, 2012.

Shortlisted for The Orange Prize for Fiction, 2012

During a peaceful snowfall in a suburb in Dublin, a woman remembers her younger days spent with her lover in various hotel rooms as she awaits the arrival of his 12-year-old daughter.

"The Forgotten Waltz meditates on the way personal responsibility can twist the most well-meaning, loving relationship into a holding tank for accusations and tears. . . . Enright allows her main character the thrill of remembered joys, without letting her slip away from blame." A.V. Club.

Enright, Anne, 1962-

* The **gathering** / Anne Enright. Black Cat, 2007. 260 p.

ISBN 0802170390

1. Middle-aged women 2. Brothers -- Death 3. Catholics -- Ireland 4. Resentfulness 5. Unhappiness in women 6. Discontent in women 7. Frustration in women 8. Anger 9. Family secrets 10. Betrayal 11. Disappointment 12. Dublin, Ireland 13. Ireland 14. Psychological fiction 15. Literary fiction

First published in Great Britain in 2007 by Jonathan Cape.

Man Booker Prize, 2007.

Veronica--once an attention-deprived middle child among 12 siblings, and now an unfulfilled wife and mother--has come to London to claim the body of her beloved yet estranged brother Liam who drowned himself at sea. As the nine surviving members of the Hegarty clan converge in Dublin for Liam's wake, Veronica wants to protect the past-- and the secret of what transpired in her grandmother's house during the winter of 1968.

"You will love this book or loathe it. It doesn't take prisoners, it doesn't simper or seek to be liked. Abrasively honest and toweringly moving, it grabs and shakes you, rabbiting on in a manic monologue, comical, tragic, lost and profound." The Scotsman.

Enright, Anne, 1962-

The **Green** Road : a novel / Anne Enright. W. W. Norton & Co., 2015. 304 p.

ISBN 9780393248210

1. Mothers 2. Home (Concept) 3. Voyages and travels 4. Mother and adult child 5. Growing up 6. Families 7. Family relationships 8. Ireland 9. Family sagas 10. Literary fiction

Shortlisted for the Baileys Women's Prize for Fiction, 2016.

Shortlisted for the International Dublin Literary Award, 2017.

When Christmas day reunites the Madigan children, who all left their mother Rosaleen behind to follow their dreams, under one roof in County Clare, Ireland, they each must confront the terrible weight of family ties and the journey that brought them home.

"Long introductions to the principal characters precede the theatrical format of the reunion, allowing Enright plenty of space to convey her brilliant ear for dialogue, her soft wit, and piercing, poetic sense of life's larger abstractions." Kirkus.

Enright, Anne, 1962-

Yesterday's weather : stories / Anne Enright. Grove Press, 2008. 308 p.

ISBN 9780802118745

1. Change -- Psychological aspects 2. Ireland -- Social conditions -- 21st century 3. Short stories

LC bl2008017676

A collection of short fiction chronicles the lives of ordinary men and women struggling to cope with the bonds of love, family, and community, in an increasingly disconnected, transient, and changing Ireland.

"Enright's subjects are family, children, love, domestic horror. The stories are strong and hard bitten. Something in them is always snagging and catching on grief, large or small. She is a confident writer, letting stories unfold at their own speed. Her best pieces have a fluid shape that feels close to the way we actually think, choose, muse." Washington Post Book World.

Enriquez, Mariana

Things we lost in the fire : stories / Mariana Enriquez. Hogarth, 2017, c2016. 208 p.

ISBN 9780451495112

1. Poverty 2. Violence 3. Human behavior 4. Murder 5. Family violence 6. Argentina 7. Translations -- Spanish to English 8.

Literary fiction 9. Short stories

LC 2016034008

Previously published in Spanish as Las cosas que perdimos en el fuego. First edition. Narrativas hispánicas ; 559. Barcelona : Editorial Anagrama, 2016.

A U.S. release of an anthology of stories by a debut writer from Buenos Aires explores macabre dimensions of life in contemporary Argentina, from women who set themselves on fire to protest domestic violence to a 9-year-old serial killer who acts out in gruesome ways in her classroom.

"A rich and malcontent stew of stories about the everyday terrors that wait around each new corner." Kirkus.

Ephron, Hallie

Careful what you wish for / Hallie Ephron. HarperCollins, 2019 304 p.

ISBN 9780062473653

1. Compulsive hoarding 2. Married women 3. Marital conflict 4. Orderliness 5. House cleaning 6. Personal belongings 7. Murder investigation 8. Boston, Massachusetts 9. Thrillers and suspense 10. Domestic fiction

A professional organizer whose husband is a hoarder distracts her growing relationship troubles by focusing on her new clients, one of which takes her tipsy fantasy about life being more pleasant without spouses a little too far.

Ephron, Hallie

Night night, sleep tight : a novel of suspense / Hallie Ephron. William Morrow & Co., 2015 287 p.

ISBN 9780062117632

1. 1980s 2. Fathers and daughters 3. Fame 4. Memory 5. Fathers -- Death 6. Murder 7. Tragedy 8. Murderers 9. Secrets 10. Friendship 11. Hollywood, California 12. Los Angeles, California 13. Thrillers and suspense

Discovering her bitter father's drowned body in his 1980s Beverly Hills swimming pool, Deirdre reconnects with an old friend who confessed to killing her mother's boyfriend decades earlier.

"As the daughter of screenwriters, Ephron (There Was an Old Woman, 2013) knows the old Hollywood scene and re-creates it vividly in her fourth novel, inspired in part by the 1958 stabbing of Lana Turner's lover. A fast-moving tale, with building suspense and the price of fame at its center." Booklist.

Ephron, Hallie

You'll never know, dear / Hallie Ephron. William Morrow & Co., 2017. 304 p.

ISBN 9780062473615

1. Missing children 2. Mother and adult daughter 3. Dolls 4. Sisters 5. Grief 6. Guilt in women 7. Loss (Psychology) 8. South Carolina 9. Psychological suspense

An addictive novel of psychological suspense from the award-winning author of Night Night, Sleep Tight, about three generations of women haunted by a little girl's disappearance, and the porcelain doll that may hold the key to the truth . . .

Epperson, Tom

Sailor / Tom Epperson. Forge, 2012. 352 p.

ISBN 9780765328922

1. Organized crime 2. Mothers and sons 3. Attempted murder 4. Diamonds 5. Federal Witness Protection Program 6. Sailors 7. Los Angeles, California 8. Thrillers and suspense

LC 2011047593

"A Tom Doherty Associates book."

Turning in her mafia-affiliated husband and fleeing with her son and a cache of stolen diamonds, Gina is vengefully targeted by her father-in-law and meets sailor Gray, whose trustworthiness Gina doubts.

Epstein, Jennifer Cody

* **Wunderland** : a novel / Jennifer Cody Epstein. Crown Publishing, 2019. 371 p.

ISBN 9780525576907

1. Hitler Youth. 2. Nazi Party (Germany) 3. 20th century 4. Mothers and daughters 5. World War II 6. Women and war 7. Persecution by Nazis 8. Kristallnacht, 1938 9. Jews -- Persecutions 10. Betrayal 11. Female friendship 12. Childhood friends 13. Interfaith friendship 14. Family secrets 15. Letter writing 16. Nazism -- Germany 17. German Americans 18. Berlin, Germany 19. Germany -- History -- 1933-1945 20. East Village, New York City 21. New York City 22. Historical fiction 23. Parallel narratives

A German-American woman in 1989 New York City evaluates her relationship with her late mother, whose childhood best friendship was shattered in the wake of a betrayal involving the Hitler Youth movement and a family secret.

"A vividly written and stark chronicle of Nazism and its legacies." Kirkus.

Epstein, Joseph, 1937-

* The **love** song of A. Jerome Minkoff, and other stories / Joseph Epstein. Houghton Mifflin Harcourt, 2010. 260 p.

ISBN 9780618721955

1. Jewish Americans 2. Jewish American men 3. Family relationships 4. Men/women relations 5. Chicago, Illinois 6. Short stories 7. Short stories

LC 2009034898

A collection of short stories features everyday Jewish men in Chicago who confront life-defining moments during complex love affairs, unspoken rivalries, and family triumphs.

"It's a rare and welcome thing to find a collection of short stories that define a place. . . . Epstein delivers one about a neighborhood on the far north of Chicago called West Rogers Park. It is a polyglot area, but Epstein has chosen to write about the Jews who dominate it. . . . If his voice is wry, it is also sympathetic. Life is hard, and he knows it. He invests his collection with a peerless take on a particular slice of Jewish life today. Each story stands strong as a discrete work, but together they become profound." Boston Globe.

Erdrich, Louise

* The **beet** queen : a novel Holt, 1986. 338 p.

ISBN 9780805000580

1. Native American women 2. Loneliness 3. Abandonment (Psychology) 4. Jealousy 5. Mothers and daughters 6. Abandoned children 7. Sexuality 8. Butcher shops 9. Women -- North Dakota 10. Family relationships 11. Miracles (Christianity) 12. North Dakota 13. Literary fiction 14. Coming-of-age stories

LC 86004788

Sequel to: Love Medicine.

Sequel: Tracks.

National Book Critics Circle Award for Fiction finalist, 1986

Orphaned fourteen-year-old Carl and his eleven-year-old sister, Mary, travel to Argus, North Dakota, to live with their mother's sister, in this tale of abandonment, sexual obsession, jealousy, and unstinting love.

Erdrich, Louise

Four souls : a novel / Louise Erdrich. HarperCollins, 2004. 210 p.

ISBN 9780066209753

1. Land tenure 2. Revenge in women 3. Native American women 4. Ojibwa Indians 5. Indian reservations 6. Married people 7. Families 8. Launderers 9. Rich people 10. Identity (Psychology) 11. Deception in women 12. Crimes against Native American women 13. Minneapolis, Minnesota 14. North Dakota 15. Psychological fiction 16. Literary fiction

LC 2003065243

Sequel to: Tracks.

After taking her mother's name, Four Souls, for strength, the strange and compelling Fleur Pillager walks from her Ojibwe reservation to the cities of Minneapolis and Saint Paul. She is seeking restitution from and revenge on the lumber baron who has stripped her tribe's land. But revenge is never simple, and her intentions are complicated by her dangerous compassion for the man who wronged her.

"The shifting of voices and stories, ranging back and forth in time and place, may sound dauntingly complicated; luckily, it doesn't read that way. In fact, the progression of events feels natural and unforced, full of satisfying yet unexpected twists. The book begins with clean, spare prose, but finishe's in gorgeous incantation and poetry." New York Times Book Review.

Erdrich, Louise

Future home of the living god / Louise Erdrich. Harper, 2017 368 p.

ISBN 9780062694058

1. Ojibwa Indians 2. Pregnant women 3. Human evolution 4. Adoption 5. Fugitives 6. Birthparents 7. Post-apocalypse 8. Authoritarianism 9. Humans -- Extinction 10. Minnesota 11. Dystopian fiction 12. Literary fiction 13. Apocalyptic fiction

Longlisted for the Andrew Carnegie Medal for Excellence in Fiction, 2018.

A tale set in a world of reversing evolution and a growing police state follows pregnant twenty-six-year-old Cedar Hawk Songmaker, who investigates her biological family while awaiting the birth of a child who may emerge as a member of a primitive human species.

"A tornadic, suspenseful, profoundly provoking novel of lifes vulnerability and insistence." Booklist.

Erdrich, Louise

* LaRose / Louise Erdrich. HarperCollins, 2016. 256 p.

ISBN 9780062277022

1. Sons 2. Atonement 3. Hunting accidents 4. Grief 5. Families 6. Boys -- Death 7. Sweat lodges 8. Ojibwa Indians 9. Accidental death 10. Native American mysticism 11. Indians of North America -- Rites and ceremonies 12. North Dakota 13. Literary fiction 14. Magical realism 15. Domestic fiction

National Book Critics Circle Award for Fiction, 2016.

Pen/Faulkner Award Finalist, 2017

Horrified when he accidentally kills his best friend's 5-year-old son while hunting, Landreaux Iron gives away his own young son to his friend's family according to ancient tradition, a decision that helps both families reach a tenuous peace that is threatened by a vengeful adversary.

"Electric, nimble, and perceptive, this novel is about 'the phosphorous of grief' but also, more essentially, about the emotions men need, but rarely get, from one another." Kirkus.

Erdrich, Louise

The **last** report on the miracles at Little No Horse / Louise Erdrich. HarperCollins, 2001. 361 p.

ISBN 0060187271

1. Ojibwa Indians -- North Dakota 2. Impostors -- North Dakota 3. Indian reservations 4. Priests -- North Dakota 5. Male impersonators 6. Deception in women 7. North Dakota 8. Literary fiction

LC 00047198

Illustrations on lining papers.

National Book Award for Fiction finalist, 2001

As a priest nears the end of his life, he is asked to prove or disprove the sainthood of a woman he knows well and struggles to guard his own secret identity in the process.

"Even the small incidents in this novel are moments of tremendous power, stripped of sentimentality or pretension. Erdrich has developed a style that can sound as serious as death or ring with the haunting simplicity of ancient legend." Christian Science Monitor.

Erdrich, Louise

* Love medicine : a novel / Louise Erdrich. Harper Perennial, 1993, c1984. 272 p.

ISBN 9780805027983

1. Extended families 2. Indian reservations 3. Family secrets 4. Grandparents 5. Love potions 6. Poverty 7. Secrets 8. Men/women relations 9. Native American women 10. Tradition (Philosophy) 11. North Dakota 12. Literary fiction

LC 84003774

Sequel: The Beet Queen.

National Book Critics Circle Award for Fiction, 1984.

Expanded to include previously unpublished chapters, this collection of interrelated stories of love, betrayal, mystery, and madness concerns men and women bound by blood, legend, tradition, and need.

Erdrich, Louise

The **Master** Butchers Singing Club : a novel / Louise Erdrich. HarperCollins, 2002. 389 p.

ISBN 9780066209777

1. Married people 2. Widows 3. Immigrants 4. Love triangles 5. World War I veterans 6. German Americans 7. Butchers 8. Singers 9. North Dakota 10. The West (United States) 11. Literary fiction 12. Historical fiction 13. Love stories 14. Domestic fiction

LC 2002068501

Returning to his quiet German village home after World War I, trained killer Fidelis Waldvogel, accompanied by his new wife, starts a new life in America and finds his life irrevocably changed by a new relationship.

Erdrich, Louise

* The night watchman / Louise Erdrich. HarperCollins, 2020. 416 p.

ISBN 9780062671189

1. 1950s 2. Guards 3. Factories 4. Ojibwa Indians 5. Uncles 6. Native American men 7. Native American women 8. Blue collar women 9. Exploitation 10. Family violence 11. Night work 12. North Dakota 13. Literary fiction 14. Biographical fiction 15. Historical fiction

A historical novel based on the life of the author's grandfather traces the experiences of a Chippewa Council night watchman in mid-19th-century rural North Dakota who fights Congress to enforce Native American treaty rights.

"National Book Award winner Erdrich once again calls upon her considerable storytelling skills to elucidate the struggles of generations of Native people to retain their cultural identity and their connection to the land." Library Journal.

Erdrich, Louise

The **painted** drum : a novel / Louise Erdrich. HarperCollins, 2005. 277 p.

ISBN 9780060515102

1. Multiracial women 2. Ojibwa Indians -- Antiquities 3. Grief 4. Divorced women 5. Women travelers 6. Mothers and daughters 7. Sisters -- Death 8. Children -- Death 9. Indian reservations 10. Family relationships 11. Drum -- History 12. Antiquities -- Collection and preservation 13. Extramarital affairs 14. Bereavement 15. Villages 16. New England 17. North Dakota 18. The West (United States) 19. Psychological fiction 20. Domestic fiction 21. Literary fiction

LC 2005040227

Discovering a cache of valuable Native American artifacts while appraising a family estate in New Hampshire, Faye Travers investigates the history of a ceremonial drum, which possesses spiritual powers and changes the lives of people who encounter it.

"There is searing pain and loss aplenty in this book, but one of Erdrich's strengths as a writer is the way in which she controls emotion. . . . Readers familiar with her works will recognize characters from the North Dakota native families who populate other of her works. But again, it doesn't really matter. Her themes transcend that terrain." Christian Science Monitor.

Erdrich, Louise

The **plague** of doves / Louise Erdrich. HarperCollins, 2008. 313 p.

ISBN 9780060515126

1. Small town life -- North Dakota 2. Lynching 3. Multiracial women 4. Grandfather and granddaughter 5. Indian reservations 6. Ojibwa Indians 7. Stamp collecting 8. Interethnic marriage 9. Revenge 10. Coping 11. Family relationships 12. North Dakota 13. Domestic fiction 14. Literary fiction

LC 2007033626

ALA Notable Book, 2009.

Pulitzer Prize for Fiction finalist, 2009

Unaware of a violent event that marked the beginning of her mixed ancestry, ambitious young Evelina Harp, a part-Ojibwe, part-white girl prone to falling hopelessly in love, learns disturbing truths from her gifted storyteller grandfather, while a sentimental judge weighs the legacy of a century-old crime as reflected by his own love life.

"This novel is about the unsolved murder of a farm family, but it is also an allegory about blood (and bloody) connections that develop as the descendants of killers and victims continue to live alongside one another near the Ojibwe reservation in North Dakota. As always with Erdrich, the bloodlines are both white and Native American, churned by the passions of characters with wonderful names like Mooshum Milk and Holy Track, whose lives and stories make the question of whodunit seem like an afterthought. Mooshum, one of three Indians falsely accused of the 1911 crime and the only one who survives the lynch mob tells of finding the murdered farm family and the infant who lived. Evelina, his granddaughter, becomes the central narrator of Mooshum's story amidst the intertwining tales of deathless romantic encounters that follow. Evelina and others detail the dramas of her family, including her own budding romantic encounters with the descendant of the murdered family and a nun whose lineage goes back to the lynch mob." New York Daily News.

Erdrich, Louise

The **red** convertible : selected and new stories, 1978-2008 / Louise Erdrich. HarperCollins, 2009. x, 496 p.

ISBN 9780061536076

1. Literary fiction 2. Short stories

LC bl2008029054

A collection of three dozen short works includes six previously unpublished pieces and offers insight into the author's use of plot twists and contrasting psychological landscapes.

"Louise Erdrich is an immensely satisfying storyteller who molds her novels from the clay of her short fiction. . . . This anthology returns 30 of those stories, which eventually became parts of 11 novels, to their original, unentangled forms. The book also includes six other stories, some of which are being published for the first time. Like Faulkner, Erdrich has created a fictional community an Ojibwe reservation in North Dakota from which her work can unfold. Her stories stretch back 100 years or more and venture as far away as New Hampshire, looping elliptically, intersecting through a priest, a place, a hidden parentage. But where her novels develop these relationships, The Red Convertible, in dislodging the stories, creates a new arc between them." Los Angeles Times Book Review.

Erdrich, Louise

* The **round** house : a novel / Louise Erdrich. Harper, 2012. 336 p.

ISBN 9780062065247

1. Ojibwa Indians 2. Life change events 3. Indian reservations 4. Revenge 5. Teenage boys 6. Loss (Psychology) 7. Family relationships 8. Crimes against women 9. Rape victims 10. Native-American women 11. Native-American families 12. North Dakota 13. Literary fiction 14. Coming-of-age stories

LC 2012005381

ALA Notable Book, 2013

National Book Award for Fiction, 2012.

Andrew Carnegie Medal for Excellence in Fiction finalist, 2013.

When his mother, a tribal enrollment specialist living on a reservation in North Dakota, slips into an abyss of depression after being brutally attacked, fourteen-year-old Joe Coutz sets out with his three friends to find the person that destroyed his family.

Erdrich, Louise

* **Shadow** tag : a novel / Louise Erdrich. Harper, 2010. 255 p.

ISBN 9780061536090

1. Husband and wife 2. Family relationships 3. Identity (Psychology) 4. Marriage 5. Artists 6. Self-discovery 7. Jealousy 8. Dysfunctional families 9. Emotional abuse 10. Compulsive behavior 11. Psychological fiction 12. Literary fiction 13. Diary novels

LC 2009033699

After she discovers that her husband has been reading her diary, Irene America turns it into a manipulative farce, while secretly keeping a second diary that includes her true thoughts, through which the reader learns of Irene's shaky marriage, its affect on her children and her struggles with alcohol.

"Erdrich is a muscular and fearless writer, and she explores her characters with both compassion and criticism and through lyrical and visceral prose." BookPage.

Erdrich, Louise

Tracks : a novel / Louise Erdrich. Harper Perennial, 2004, c1988. 226 p.

ISBN 9780060972455

1. Indians of North America -- Relations with European-Americans 2. Widowers 3. Pride and vanity 4. Men/women relations 5. Multiracial women 6. Native American women 7. Indian reservations 8. Ojibwa Indians 9. Tradition (Philosophy) 10. Magic 11. Communities 12. North Dakota 13. Literary fiction

LC 88009321

Sequel to: The Beet Queen.

Sequel: The Bingo Palace.

Set in North Dakota at a time in the past century when Indian tribes were struggling to keep what little remained of their lands, Tracks is a tale of passion and deep unrest. Over the course of ten crucial years, as tribal land and trust between people erode ceaselessly, men and women are pushed to the brink of their endurance--yet their pride and humor prohibit surrender.

"Ms. Erdrich is, as always, the generous kind of storyteller, passing along not only everything her characters know, but the story of the stories as well. Giving life and shape and sense to what's happened, she lets the designs spring clear." New York Times Book Review.

Eriksson, Kjell, 1953-

The **princess** of Burundi / Kjell Eriksson ; translated from the Swedish by Ebba Segerberg. Thomas Dunne Books, 2006, c2002. 288 p. Ann Lindell novels

ISBN 0312327676

1. Murder investigation 2. Women detectives 3. Revenge 4. Policewomen 5. Police 6. New mothers 7. Maternity leave 8. Murder 9. Small town life -- Sweden 10. Sweden 11. Mysteries 12. Psychological suspense 13. Translations -- Swedish to English 14. Scandinavian crime fiction

LC 2005050965

Translation from the Swedish of Prinsessan av Burundi, published in 2002.

When a jogger stumbles upon the mutilated body of the local reformed troublemaker, Inspector Ann Lindell takes time off from maternity leave to uncover the killer and is drawn into a deadly game of cat-and-mouse with a vicious murderer.

"The brilliance of Eriksson's richly detailed crime novel, . . . lies in its psychological and even sociological insights. Eriksson not only reveals a deep, sympathetic understanding for his large cast of characters but also evokes a pervasive sense of despair, reminiscent of Henning Mankell's, in the face of the violent, amoral nature of contemporary society and the challenges it places on the police." Publishers Weekly.

Erpenbeck, Jenny, 1967-

The **book** of words / Jenny Erpenbeck ; translated, with an afterword, by Susan Bernofsky. New Directions, 2007. 93 p. New Directions paperback

ISBN 9780811217064

1. State-sponsored terrorism 2. Political violence 3. Teenage girls 4. Immigrant families 5. Totalitarianism 6. Authoritarianism 7. Awareness 8. Tropics 9. Political fiction 10. Literary fiction 11. Translations -- German to English

"Erpenbeck . . . eschews specific geographical detail, letting the eeriness rise to the universal. Susan Bernofsky's remarkably fluid translation does a seamless job of capturing Erpenbeck's swirl of language as the voice of her narrator trips along like uninterrupted thought.. . . . This is writing so intense you don't even notice the brevity." Guardian (UK).

Erpenbeck, Jenny, 1967-

* **Go,** went, gone : a novel / Jenny Erpenbeck ; translated from the German by Susan Bernofsky. New Directions Books, 2017, c2015. 286 p.

ISBN 9780811225946

1. Refugees -- Europe 2. Retirees 3. Psychic trauma 4. Immigration and emigration 5. Former college teachers 6. Unemployed persons 7. Immigrants 8. Hunger strikes 9. Purpose in life 10. Survival 11. Africans in foreign countries 12. Berlin, Germany 13. Literary fiction 14. Translations -- German to English

LC 2017013730

First published in German as Gehen, ging, gegangen. Munich : Albrecht Knaus Verlag, 2015.

Richard is a widower and a retired classics professor who lives in Berlin, and whose life is routine until the day he spies some African refugees staging a hunger strike. As he visits their shelter, interviews them, and becomes embroiled in their harrowing fates, he finds he has more in common with them than he realizes.

Erpenbeck, Jenny, 1967-

Visitation / Jenny Erpenbeck ; translated from the German by Susan Bernofsky. New Directions Pub., 2010, c2008. 151 p.

ISBN 9780811218351

1. Houses 2. Caretakers 3. Violence 4. Holocaust (1933-1945) 5. Murder victims 6. Nazis 7. Communism 8. Architects 9. Germany -- History 10. Literary fiction 11. Translations -- German to English

LC 2010011144

First published: Frankfurt am Main : Eichborn Verlag, 2008.

By the side of a lake in Brandenburg, a young architect builds the house of his dreams - a summerhouse with wrought-iron balconies, stained-glass windows the color of jewels, and a bedroom with a hidden closet, all set within a beautiful garden. But the land on which he builds has a dark history of violence that began with the drowning of a young woman in the grip of madness and that grows darker still over the course of the century...

"This novel's central character is a place. In a grand house and its grounds, by a lake in Brandenburg, a succession of occupants dislodge each other, borne along by the political calamities of 20th century Europe. The Jewish family who own the property in the 1930s are forced to sell while they wait for visas out of the Third Reich. An architect renovates the house; at the end of the second world war, it's requisitioned by the Russian army; then, under the GDR, the architect has to flee for having done illegal business with the west. The place is reclaimed by returning exiles from Siberia, then resold by estate agents. . . . The one person known to all the owners and occupants and thus the thread that binds the narrative together is the gardener. Periodic updates are given of his activities, describing his routines in detail. . . . No word is ever heard from him, and Erpenbeck allows no access to his mind, but we end up feeling great relief whenever he reappears, and deep sadness as this increasingly frail figure does what he can to forestall his Eden's incremental slide into ruin. Indeed, the amount of emotional engagement Erpenbeck manages to win from us, in a mere 150 pages, is just one proof of her mastery." The Guardian (UK).

Ervin, Keisha

Gunz and roses / Keisha Ervin. Urban Books, 2009. x, 305 p.

ISBN 9781601621566

1. Sexuality 2. Street life 3. African American men/women relations 4. Interpersonal attraction 5. Drug dealers 6. African Americans 7. Women editors 8. Murder 9. Inner city 10. City life 11. St Louis, Missouri 12. African American fiction 13. Drama lit

LC bl2009025102

Fashion editor Gray Rose finds the man of her dreams in St. Louis kingpin Gunz Marciano, but their obsessive love soon turns complicated when she discovers the identity of the new woman in his life.

Ervin, Keisha

Mina's joint / Keisha Ervin. Triple Crown Publications, 2005. vii, 265 p. Mina's joint

ISBN 9780976789451

1. African American women 2. Ambition 3. Love triangles 4. Self-fulfillment in women 5. African American businesspeople 6. Beauty shops 7. Independence in women 8. Former lovers 9. Self-doubt in

women 10. Engagement 11. St Louis, Missouri 12. African American fiction 13. Drama lit

LC 2005936179

Mina, who has her own salon and is engaged to the son of the mayor of St. Louis, finds her perfect life shattered when her childhood sweetheart, Victor, comes back into her life and everything she thought was true turns out to be a lie.

Eskens, Allen, 1963-

The **heavens** may fall / Allen Eskens. Seventh Street Books, 2016. 270 p. Max Rupert novels

ISBN 9781633882058

1. Male friendship 2. Wife-killing 3. Widowers 4. Lawyers 5. Detectives 6. Murder investigation 7. Memories 8. Disagreement 9. Minnesota 10. Mysteries

Two friends take opposite sides of a murder investigation and trial, each convinced that he is right.

"Eskens keeps the reader guessing as the tale takes several unexpected twists before reaching the satisfying denouement." Publishers Weekly.

Eskens, Allen, 1963-

Nothing more dangerous : a novel / Allen Eskens. Mulholland Books, 2019. vii, 293 p.

ISBN 9780316509725

1. 1970s 2. Race relations 3. Male friendship 4. Small town life 5. Racism 6. Missing women 7. African Americans 8. Ozark Mountain region 9. Coming-of-age stories 10. Mysteries

A high school boy growing up in the Ozark hills rethinks his understanding of the world, race and class when he befriends a black family that moves in across the street.

Esquivel, Laura, 1950-

* **Like** water for chocolate : a novel in monthly installments, with recipes, romances, and home remedies / Laura Esquivel ; translated by Carol Christensen and Thomas Christensen. Doubleday, 1992. 245 p.

ISBN 0385420161

1. Cooking, Mexican 2. Responsibility 3. Love triangles 4. Families -- Mexico 5. Women cooks -- Mexico 6. Mothers and daughters -- Mexico 7. Men/women relations 8. Women caregivers 9. Expectation (Psychology) 10. Youngest child 11. Duty 12. Family traditions 13. Sisters 14. Marriage 15. Unrequited love 16. Lovers' reunions 17. Mexico 18. Magical realism 19. Love stories 20. Translations -- Spanish to English 21. Literary fiction

LC 91047188

Recipes precede each chapter.

Includes recipes.

"Previously published as Like water for hot chocolate."

Book Sense Book of the Year Adult Trade, 1994.

Despite the fact that she has fallen in love with a young man, Tita, the youngest of three daughters born to a tyrannical rancher, must obey tradition and remain single and at home to care for her mother

"A poignant, funny story of love, life, and food which proves that all three are entwined and interdependent." Library Journal.

Essbaum, Jill Alexander

Hausfrau : a novel / Jill Alexander Essbaum. Random House, 2015 324 p.

ISBN 9780812997538

1. Married women 2. Extramarital affairs 3. Self-fulfillment in women 4. Americans in Switzerland 5. Marital conflict 6. Change (Psychology) 7. Secrets 8. Deception 9. Sexuality 10. Switzerland

11. Psychological fiction

LC 2014026118

Enduring private misery in spite of a well-appointed life in suburban Zurich with her distant Swiss banker husband and young children, Anna Benz experiments with unfulfilling hobbies before engaging in a series of surprising sexual affairs.

"Isolated and tormented, Anna shares more than her name with that classic adulteress, Anna Karenina, but Essbaum has given a deft, modern facelift to the timeless story of a troubled marriage and tragic love." Booklist.

Estleman, Loren D.

The **adventures** of Johnny Vermillion : a novel / Loren D. Estleman. Forge, 2006. 272 p.

ISBN 9780765309143

1. 1870s 2. Swindlers and swindling 3. Outlaws 4. Tricksters 5. Criminals 6. Bank robbers 7. Detectives 8. Theater companies 9. Bank robberies 10. Competition 11. Gunfights 12. Westerns

LC 2006042532

"A Tom Doherty Associates book."

Republished in 2016 with The Long High Noon.

Heading a theater troupe that journeys throughout the wild western frontier, Johnny Vermillion uses their performances as a clever cover-up for a bank robbery operation that is investigated by a suspicious Pinkerton agent.

"Johnny Vermillion, operator and featured performer of the Prairie Rose Repertory Company, travels the Wild West putting on plays in towns like Lockjaw, Diablo, and Purgatory. But that's just his cover: in fact, he and his small troop are bank robbers. And when a determined Pinkerton agent tips to what Johnny has been up to, an all-out pursuit results, culminating in a wickedly clever trap. Once again, Estleman proves why he is among the best of our contemporary western novelists . . . . Johnny and his merry band of thieves are thoroughly delightful characters, a bunch of good-natured rogues, colorful without being cartoony." Booklist.

Estleman, Loren D.

* **Amos** Walker : the complete story collection / Loren D. Estleman. Tyrus Books, 2010. 637 p. Amos Walker novels

ISBN 9781935562245

1. Private investigators 2. Crime 3. Criminals 4. Detroit, Michigan 5. Michigan 6. Hardboiled fiction 7. Mysteries

Collects every short story featuring Detroit detective Amos Walker, including a brand-new story never before published.

"All the elements that have made Estleman one of the best hardboiled writers of all time--just a notch below Chandler and Hammett--are present in these 32 short stories. Remarkably, he has kept his Detroit-based Amos Walker series (Motor City Blue) fresh after three decades and 20 novels, and any fan of the genre who has yet to encounter the ex-cop turned PI will get a great introduction through this collection. What's most impressive is Estleman's ability to blend sharp-edged language, cynical characters, betrayals, twists, and a memorable narrative voice within the short story format. He also manages to inject dark humor into his work that keeps the violence, corruption, and double-crosses from becoming too grim. . . . Longtime fans will welcome the author's informative introduction." Publishers Weekly.

Estleman, Loren D.

Frames / Loren D. Estleman. Forge, 2008. 272 p. Valentino mysteries

ISBN 9780765315755

1. Greed (Motion picture) 2. Archivists 3. Murder investigation 4. Film -- Preservation 5. Film industry and trade -- History 6. Women

law students 7. Men/women relations 8. Women forensic scientists 9. Hollywood, California 10. California 11. Gentle reads 12. Cozy mysteries

LC 2008004505

"A Tom Doherty Associates book."

Discovering a skeleton in a decrepit movie palace he hopes to restore, UCLA firm archivist Valentino also finds a priceless original director's cut of a long-lost classic film and must solve the mystery of the skeleton before the police claim the film as evidence and doom it to destruction.

"Estleman first introduced Valentino in a series of short stories for Ellery Queen Mystery Magazine and promises that Frames is the first in a series of novels featuring the film detective. As with every Estleman novel, Frames is written in crisp, vivid prose, the characters well-drawn. And the author's meticulous research of movie history adds another layer of richness." San Francisco Chronicle.

Estleman, Loren D.

* **Gas** City / Loren D. Estleman. Forge, 2008. 304 p.

ISBN 9780765319562

1. Mafia 2. Serial murders 3. Police 4. Police chiefs 5. Husband and wife 6. Power (Social sciences) 7. Men/women relations 8. Betrayal 9. Police corruption 10. Serial murders 11. Violence 12. Crime bosses 13. Noir fiction 14. Crime fiction

LC 2007034927

"A Tom Doherty Associates book."

The black heart of a seemingly stable well-run city is pitched into violence and chaos when a serial killer's rampage pits the police chief, a mafia boss and the press against each other.

"The shades of Frank Norris and Upton Sinclair must have been looking over Loren D. Estleman's shoulder when he wrote Gas City. Set in a Midwestern metropolis that grew up around a refinery, his muscular novel initially takes a long view of the cynical bargain struck between civic leaders and organized crime--and only moves in for the kill when a key figure in this devil's dance decides to reform. Like earlier muckraking writers, Estleman is always looking for the tipping point where our frontier values of independent entrepreneurship and community justice tumble into criminality. And his characters never stop asking whether it's possible to go back and get it right." New York Times Book Review.

Estleman, Loren D.

Infernal angels / Loren D. Estleman. Forge, 2011 304 p. Amos Walker novels

ISBN 9780765319555

1. Private investigators 2. Murder investigation 3. Drug smuggling 4. Criminals 5. High definition television 6. Stealing 7. Heroin 8. Drug traffic 9. Detroit, Michigan 10. Michigan 11. Hardboiled fiction 12. Mysteries

Detroit private investigator Amos Walker is hired to recover HDTV converter boxes stolen from a retailer whose shop also does vintage resale business. Before long, the case turns old school: both a suspect and the man who lost the boxes are murdered, and Walker ends up working with both the local police and the feds.

"A novel featuring Detroit PI Amos Walker.... Reuben Crossgrain, proprietor of Past Presence (Everything you require for the Modern Regressive Lifestyle), hires Walker to recover 25 TV converter boxes that allow the owner to watch HDTV on an analog set, although the total value of the loss isn't much more than Walker's standard retainer. The detective hits the pavement to identify the likely recipients of the hot items, and his digging soon attracts the attention of ex-Detroit police detective Mary Ann Thaler, who now works in D.C. on homeland security. As the bodies start to drop, Estleman presents a powerful view of the battered inner city, where federally funded housing ends up der-

elict. Three decades on, Estleman and Walker show no signs of slowing down." Publishers Weekly.

Estleman, Loren D.

* The **master** executioner / Loren D. Estleman. Forge, 2001. 270 p.

ISBN 0312869703

1. 19th century 2. Capital punishment 3. Executions and executioners 4. Civil War veterans 5. Frontier and pioneer life 6. The West (United States) 7. Westerns 8. Psychological fiction

LC 2001023181

Western Heritage Award for Outstanding Western Novel, 2002.

Hangman Oscar Stone is a master executioner, who prides himself on his careful and exacting work, until a sudden moment of realization and devastating truth forces him to come to terms with himself and his profession.

"Estleman has created an unforgettable character in Stone. . . . A dark, compelling journey into a previously unexplored facet of the old West." Booklist.

Estleman, Loren D.

* **Something** borrowed, something black / Loren D. Estleman. Forge, 2002. 236 p. Peter Macklin novels

ISBN 031287863X

1. Assassins 2. Honeymoons 3. Assassins 4. Los Angeles, California 5. San Antonio, Texas 6. Thrillers and suspense

LC 2001054752

"A Tom Doherty Associates book."

Retired hit man Peter Macklin is enjoying his honeymoon with his beautiful new wife Laurie when his past catches up to him, and he is forced to leave to take care of old business that will not wait.

"The story vibrates with letter-perfect details, and the plot, with changing locations and changing points of view, is deftly handled." Publishers Weekly.

Estleman, Loren D.

A **smile** on the face of the tiger / Loren D. Estleman. Mysterious Press, 2000. 295 p. Amos Walker novels

ISBN 0892967064

1. Private investigators 2. Mystery story writing 3. Missing persons 4. Murder investigation 5. Detroit, Michigan 6. Hardboiled fiction 7. Mysteries

LC 00022284

Detroit private detective Amos Walker is hired by scheming book editor Louise Starr to find the missing Eugene Booth, an aging pulp fiction writer from the 1950s, to uncover why he has turned down his first book contract in forty years.

"Detroit gumshoe Amos Walker, a serious drinker-thinker who lives by a tough-guy code that went out of fashion with the Edsel, is sick of hearing that he looks as if he just slouched out of a 1950's (pbk.) novel. But when a publisher hires him to find Eugene Booth, a has-been pulp legend who skipped out on a lucrative contract to reissue his best book, Walker finds himself staring at a streaky mirror image of himself--if he lives so long. . . . Estleman pays handsome homage to Goodis and Woolrich and all the other 'paper tigers' to whom he dedicates this wonderful book." New York Times Book Review.

Eugenides, Jeffrey

Fresh complaint : stories / Jeffrey Eugenides. Farrar, Straus and Giroux, 2017. 285 p.

ISBN 9780374203061

1. Misfits (Persons) 2. Life change events 3. Human nature 4. Embezzlers 5. Travelers 6. Students 7. Self-discovery 8. Short

stories 9. Literary fiction

LC 2017007576

Longlisted for the Andrew Carnegie Medal for Excellence in Fiction, 2018.

A first collection of short stories by the Pulitzer Prize winner includes the tales of a failed poet-turned-embezzeler, a young traveler seeking enlightenment, and a high schooler whose drastic decision upends a British physicist's life.

"Pulitzer Prizewinning Eugenides first story collection . . . is gifted with the strong voices and luminous prose his novels are known for." Booklist.

Eugenides, Jeffrey

* The **marriage** plot / Jeffrey Eugenides. Farrar Straus & Giroux, 2011. 406 p.

ISBN 9780374203054

1. 1980s 2. Compulsive behavior in men 3. Love triangles 4. Men/women relations 5. Semiotics 6. Loners 7. Self-discovery in men 8. Unrequited love 9. Men with bipolar disorder 10. Universities and colleges 11. Literary fiction 12. Psychological fiction

National Book Critics Circle Award for Fiction finalist, 2011

Madeleine Hanna breaks out of her straight-and-narrow mold when she enrolls in a semiotics course and falls in love with charismatic loner Leonard Morten, a time which is complicated by the resurfacing of a man who is obsessed with the idea that Madeleine is his destiny.

Eugenides, Jeffrey

* **Middlesex** / Jeffrey Eugenides. Farrar, Straus, and Giroux, 2002. 544 p.

ISBN 9780374199692

1. People who are intersex 2. Greek Americans 3. Identity (Psychology) 4. City life 5. Suburban life -- Michigan 6. Girls' boarding schools 7. Teenage girls 8. Desire 9. Detroit, Michigan 10. Michigan 11. Coming-of-age stories 12. Literary fiction 13. LGBTQIA fiction

LC 2002019921

Great Lakes Book Awards, Fiction category, 2003.

Pulitzer Prize for Fiction, 2003.

National Book Critics Circle Award for Fiction finalist, 2002

Shortlisted for the International IMPAC Dublin Literary Award, 2004

Shortlisted for the James Tait Black Memorial Prize for Fiction, 2003

Calliope's friendship with a classmate and her sense of identity are compromised by the adolescent discovery that she is a hermaphrodite, a situation with roots in her grandparent's desperate struggle for survival in the 1920s.

"Eugenides pitches a big tent, but one of the delights of 'Middlesex' is how soundly it's constructed, with motifs and characters weaving through the novel's various episodes, pulling it tight." New York Times Book Review.

Eugenides, Jeffrey

* The **virgin** suicides / Jeffrey Eugenides. Farrar Straus Giroux, 1993. 249 p.

ISBN 9780374284381

1. 1970s 2. Suicide 3. Suburban families 4. Teenage boys 5. Teenage girls 6. Sisters 7. Suburban teenagers 8. Boy/girl relations 9. Survivors of suicide victims 10. Detroit, Michigan 11. Michigan 12. Coming-of-age stories 13. Psychological fiction 14. Literary fiction

LC 92033466

ALA Notable Book, 1994.

The narrator and his friends piece together the events that led up to suicides of the Lisbon girls, brainy Therese, fastidious Mary, ascetic Bonnie, libertine Lux, and saintly Cecilia.

"The author's engrossing writing style keeps one reading despite a creepy feeling that one shouldn't be enjoying it so much. A black, glittering novel that won't be to everyone's taste but must be tried by readers looking for something different." Library Journal.

Evanovich, Janet

Look alive twenty-five / Janet Evanovich. G.P. Putnam's Sons, 2018. 311 p. Stephanie Plum mysteries

ISBN 9780399179228

1. UFO abductions 2. Missing persons investigation 3. Women bounty hunters -- Trenton, New Jersey 4. Women bail bond agents 5. Bounty hunters 6. Delicatessens 7. New Jersey 8. Trenton, New Jersey 9. Mysteries 10. Chick lit

LC 2018038157

When three consecutive managers from a famous deli go missing, leaving no clues behind but a single shoe each, latest manager Stephanie Plum navigates Lula's theories about alien abductions to avoid becoming the next victim.

Evanovich, Janet

One for the money / Janet Evanovich. C. Scribner's Sons, 1994. 290 p. Stephanie Plum mysteries

ISBN 9780684196398

1. Women bounty hunters -- Trenton, New Jersey 2. Fugitives -- Trenton, New Jersey 3. Family businesses 4. Police 5. Cousins 6. Women bail bond agents 7. Men/women relations 8. Trenton, New Jersey 9. Mysteries 10. Chick lit

LC 9350733

John Creasey Memorial Award (Best First Crime Novel), 1995.

When Stephanie Plum needs money (she's been laid off, her Miata has been repossessed, her rent is due, etc.), she turns to bounty hunting for quick cash...even though she has no idea what to do and doesn't own a gun. Luckily, her first quarry, an ex-cop accused of murder, turns out to be her first lover, with whom she still shares a powerful chemistry; unluckily, he's better at getting away than she is at catching him. With the help of a mysterious (and hot!) new friend, Ranger, who shows her some tricks of the trade, Stephanie just might turn this new job into a career. -- Description by Dawn Towery.

"A wonderful sense of humor, an eye for detail, and a self-deprecating narrative endow Stephanie Plum with the easy-to-swallow believability that accounts for her appeal as heroine. . . . A witty, well-written, and gutsy debut." Library Journal.

Evanovich, Janet

Turbo twenty-three / Janet Evanovich. Bantam Books, 2016. 288 p. Stephanie Plum mysteries

ISBN 9780345543004

1. Women bounty hunters -- Trenton, New Jersey 2. Women bail bond agents 3. Men/women relations 4. Bounty hunters 5. Love triangles 6. New Jersey 7. Trenton, New Jersey 8. Mysteries 9. Chick lit

Bounty hunter Stephanie Plum receives support from prostitute-turned-bounty hunter Lula, gun-toting Grandma Mazur, on-again-off-again paramour Joe Morelli, and mentor Ranger.

Evanovich, Stephanie

Under the table / Stephanie Evanovich. William Marrow, 2019. 336 p.

ISBN 9780062415929

1. Women caterers 2. Computer programmers 3. Millionaires

4. Separation (Marital relations) 5. Self-discovery 6. Sisters 7. Makeovers (Beauty care) 8. Image consultants 9. Men/women relations 10. Love triangles 11. Self-fulfillment in women 12. Geeks (Computer enthusiasts) 13. New York City 14. Chick lit

The best-selling author of Big Girl Panties presents a modern adaptation of My Fair Lady in the story of a canny young divorcee who makes over her socially awkward millionaire client, with unexpected results.

Evans, Diana, 1971-

Ordinary people : a novel / Diana Evans. Liveright Publishing, 2018. 326 p.

ISBN 9781631494819

1. Husband and wife 2. New mothers 3. Marital conflict 4. Identity (Psychology) 5. Extramarital affairs 6. Identity (Psychology) 7. Self-perception 8. London (England) 9. Mainstream fiction
Shortlisted for The Women's Prize for Fiction, 2019.

In South London and the surrounding suburbs, two couples--longtime friends whose bonds are no longer clearly defined--struggle through a year of marital crisis.

Evans, Harriet, 1974-

A **place** for us / Harriet Evans. Gallery Books, 2015, c2014. 432 p.

ISBN 9781476786780

1. Senior women 2. Family secrets 3. Family reunions 4. Family relationships 5. Coping 6. England 7. Mainstream fiction 8. Domestic fiction
First published in the United Kingdom in 2014 by Headline Review.

Inviting her extended family to a party in celebration of her 80th birthday, Martha Winter prepares to reveal a long-hidden secret that has the potential to destroy everything that her husband and she built together.

Evans, Justin

The **white** devil : a novel / Justin Evans. Harper, 2011. 366 p.

ISBN 9780061728273

1. Byron, George Gordon Byron,, Baron, 1788-1824 2. Harrow School 3. Seventeen-year-old boys 4. Boarding schools 5. Ghosts 6. Teenage boys -- Interpersonal relations 7. Americans in England 8. Mistaken identity 9. Haunted schools 10. Tuberculosis 11. Librarians 12. Murder 13. England 14. Horror 15. Ghost stories 16. Gothic fiction 17. Coming-of-age stories

LC 2010051662

When 17-year-old Andrew Taylor is sent to the 400-year-old Harrow School, a British institution for privileged adolescents, he is soon cast as an outsider and, spurned by nearly all of his peers, becomes immersed in a 200-year-old literary mystery when he finds a friend in the school's poet-in-residence.

Evans, Nicholas, 1950-

* The **horse** whisperer : a novel / Nicholas Evans. Delacorte Press, 1995. 404 p.

ISBN 9780385315234

1. Accidents 2. Horse whisperers 3. Human/animal communication 4. Ranchers 5. Humans and horses 6. Horses 7. Extramarital affairs 8. Women editors 9. Thirteen-year-old girls 10. Montana 11. Mainstream fiction 12. Love stories

LC 95-37603

After her daughter and the girl's horse are injured in a tragic accident, Annie Graves journeys across the continent in search of Tom Booker, the Horse Whisperer, hoping he can use his ancient gift to help both the horse and the maimed girl.

"Evans can give equally clipped but clear descriptions of a prosthetic device or a Montana vista, and the lead characters emerge through carefully constructed, seemingly effortless scenes and dialog, not in histrionics." Library Journal.

Evaristo, Bernardine, 1959-

Blonde roots / Bernardine Evaristo. Riverhead Books, 2009. 288 p.

ISBN 9781594488634

1. Slaves 2. Farmers 3. Kidnapping victims 4. Freedom 5. Slavery 6. Young women 7. Escapes 8. Alternative histories

LC bl2008028928

In an alternate world in which Africans enslaved Europeans, Doris, an Englishwoman, is captured and taken to the New World, where the hardships she endures as a slave are offset by dreams of escape and home.

"The whole story is a riotous, bitter course in the arbitrary nature of our cultural values. Don't be fooled; slavery might have ended 150 years ago, but you've still got time to be enlightened by this bracing novel." Washington Post Book World.

Evaristo, Bernardine, 1959-

* **Girl,** woman, other / Bernardine Evaristo. Grove Press, 2019. 452 p.

ISBN 9780802157706

1. Identity (Psychology) 2. Women -- Social life and customs 3. Black British 4. England 5. Great Britain 6. Literary fiction
12 interconnected short stories.
Originally published in London by Hamish Hamilton, 2019.
ALA Notable Book, 2020.
Man Booker Prize, 2019.

From one of Britain's most celebrated writers of color, a magnificent portrayal of the intersections of identity among an interconnected group of Black British women.

"Anglo-Nigerian writer Evaristo's (Mr. Loverman, 2014) courageous and intersectional novel explores Black British identity and unfolds in a single night, or over the course of 100 years, depending on how readers look at it." Booklist.

Evaristo, Bernardine, 1959-

Mr. Loverman / Bernardine Evaristo. Akashic Books, 2014. 284 p.

ISBN 9781617752896

1. Gay seniors 2. Closeted gay men 3. West Indians in England 4. Families 5. City life 6. Secrets 7. Gay men 8. Gay husbands 9. Coming out (Sexual or gender identity) 10. Men/men relations 11. London, England 12. LGBTQIA fiction 13. Love stories

Barrington Jedidiah Walker is 74 and leads a double life. A flamboyant, wisecracking character with a dapper taste in retro suits and a fondness for Shakespeare, Barrington is a husband, father, grandfather, and also secretly gay, lovers with his childhood friend, Morris. With an abundance of laugh-out-loud humor and wit, Evaristo explodes cultural myths and shows the extent of what can happen when people fear the consequences of being true to themselves.

"In this vibrant novel, Evaristo draws wonderful character portraits of complex individuals as well as the West Indian immigrant culture in Britain." Booklist.

Everett, Percival L.

God's country / Percival Everett Faber and Faber, 1994. 219 p.

ISBN 9780571198320

1. 1870s 2. African American men 3. Women kidnapping victims 4.

Kidnapping 5. Frontier and pioneer life 6. Race relations 7. Racism 8. Trackers 9. The West (United States) -- Race relations -- History -- 19th century 10. Westerns 11. Satirical fiction 12. Literary fiction 13. African American fiction

The unlikely narrator through this tale of misadventures is one Curt Marder: gambler, drinker, cheat, and would-be womanizer. It's 1871, and he's lost his farm, his wife, and his dog to a band of marauding hooligans. With nothing to live on but a desire to recover what is rightfully his, Marder is forced to enlist the help of the best tracker in the West: a black man named Bubba.

Everett, Percival L.

* **Erasure** : a novel / Percival Everett. University Press of New England, 2001. 265 p.

ISBN 9781584650904

1. Identity (Psychology) 2. Fiction writing 3. African American authors 4. African American men 5. Mothers and sons 6. Anonyms and pseudonyms 7. Brothers 8. African American gay men 9. People with Alzheimer's disease 10. Washington, D.C. 11. Satirical fiction 12. Literary fiction 13. Novels-within-novels 14. African American fiction

LC 2001002535

ALA Notable Book, 2002.
Hurston/Wright Legacy Award: Fiction, 2002.

Thelonious "Monk" Ellison's writing career has bottomed out: his latest manuscript has been rejected by seventeen publishers, which stings all the more because his previous novels have been "critically acclaimed." He seethes on the sidelines of the literary establishment as he watches the meteoric success of We's Lives in Da Ghetto, a first novel by a woman who once visited "some relatives in Harlem for a couple of days." In his rage and despair, Monk dashes off a novel meant to be an indictment of Juanita Mae Jenkins's bestseller. He doesn't intend for My Pafology to be published, let alone taken seriously, but it is?under the pseudonym Stagg R. Leigh?and soon it becomes the Next Big Thing.

Everett, Percival L.

I am Not Sidney Poitier / Percival L. Everett. Graywolf Press, 2009. 234 p.

ISBN 9781555975272

1. Race relations 2. African American men -- Identity 3. Identity (Psychology) 4. Class conflict 5. Orphans 6. Look-alikes 7. Murder 8. Rich men 9. Georgia 10. Alabama 11. Satirical fiction 12. Literary fiction 13. African American fiction 14. Southern fiction

Hurston/Wright Legacy Award: Fiction, 2010.

Rendered an orphan at a young age, Not Sidney Poitier bears an uncanny resemblance to the actor who inspired his name, grows up in the home of a less-than-watchful foster father, and struggles to balance his considerable fortune with the inherent disadvantages of his skin color.

"Not only is the novel smart and without a trace of pretentiousness, it shows Everett as a novelist at the height of his narrative and satirical powers." Publishers Weekly.

Everett, Percival L.

Percival Everett by Virgil Russell / Percival L. Everett. Graywolf Press, 2013. 227 p.

ISBN 9781555976347

1. Father and adult son 2. Authors 3. Autobiography 4. Assisted living for seniors 5. Guilt in men 6. Identity (Psychology) 7. Invalids 8. Literary fiction 9. Metafiction 10. African American fiction

A man visits his aging father in a nursing home, where his father writes the novel he imagines his son would write. Or is it the novel that the son imagines his father would imagine, if he were to imagine the kind of novel the son would write?

Everett, Percival L.

* **Everyday** people : the color of life--a short story anthology / [edited by] Jennifer Baker. Atria Paperback, 2018. 320 p.

ISBN 9781501134944

1. Immigrants 2. Loss (Psychology) 3. Self-discovery 4. African Americans 5. Asian Americans 6. Hispanic Americans 7. City life 8. Interpersonal relations 9. Multiculturalism 10. Short stories 11. Literary fiction 12. Anthologies

LC 2017060013

Also includes stories by Mia Alvar, Nana Brew-Hammond, Mitchell S. Jackson, Dennis Norris II, Nelly Rosario, and Hasanthika Sirisena.

A selection of short stories from a variety of award-winning authors highlights the moments that linger in life, from doubts to epiphanies and loss to discovery.

Suder / Percival Everett. Louisiana State University Press, 1999. 171 p.

ISBN 0807123870

1. African American men 2. Women with mental illnesses 3. Family relationships 4. Baseball players 5. Mothers and sons 6. Runaways 7. Elephants 8. Drug dealers 9. Marriage 10. African American families 11. Jazz music 12. Seattle, Washington 13. Psychological fiction 14. Humorous stories 15. African American fiction

Suder, Percival Everett's acclaimed first novel, follows the exploits and ordeals of Craig Suder, a struggling black third baseman for the Seattle Mariners. In the midst of a humiliating career slump and difficulties with his demanding wife and troubled son, Suder packs up his saxophone, phonograph, and Charlie Parker's Ornithology and begins a personal crusade for independence, freedom, and contentment. -- Amazon.

Evison, Jonathan

All about Lulu : a novel / Jonathan Evison. Soft Skull Press, 2008. 340 p.

ISBN 9781593761967

1. Blended families 2. Stepsisters 3. Unrequited love 4. Grief 5. Teenage boys 6. Mothers -- Death 7. Secrets 8. Crushes (Interpersonal relations) 9. Bodybuilders 10. Vegetarians 11. Eccentrics and eccentricities 12. Los Angeles, California 13. United States -- Social life and customs -- 20th century 14. Coming-of-age stories 15. Mainstream fiction

LC 2007046761

Loner William Miller tries to cope after his mother dies of cancer, his bodybuilding father remarries a grief counselor, and he falls in love with his stepsister Lulu.

"Evison provides readers a viciously funny and deeply felt portrayal of a blended family and one man's thwarted longing." Publishers Weekly.

Evison, Jonathan

* **Lawn** boy : a novel / Jonathan Evison. Algonquin Books of Chapel Hill, 2018. 312 p.

ISBN 9781616202620

1. Mexican Americans 2. Working class 3. American Dream 4. Libraries 5. Librarians 6. Self-fulfillment in men 7. Self-improvement 8. Landscape gardening 9. Social classes 10. Inequality 11. Families 12. Interpersonal relations 13. Washington (State) 14. Coming-of-age stories

LC 2017032613

Faced by a life of menial prospects in the years after high school, Mike Munoz, a young Mexican-American, attempts over and over to change his life for the better and achieve the American dream, only to be stymied by social-class distinctions and cultural discrimination.

Evison, Jonathan

The **revised** fundamentals of caregiving : a novel / Jonathan Evison. Algonquin Books of Chapel Hill, 2012. 288 p.

ISBN 9781616200398

1. Caregivers 2. Teenagers with muscular dystrophy 3. Automobile travel 4. Loss (Psychology) 5. People with muscular dystrophy 6. Washington (State) 7. Mainstream fiction 8. Pacific Northwest fiction
LC 2012002956

After losing virtually everything meaningful in his life, Benjamin trains to be a caregiver, but his first client, a fiercely independent teen with muscular dystrophy, gives him more than he bargained for and soon the two embark on a road trip to visit the boy's ailing father.

Evison, Jonathan

This is your life, Harriet Chance! : a novel / Jonathan Evison. Algonquin Books of Chapel Hill, 2015. 296 p.

ISBN 9781616202613

1. Widows 2. Mother and adult daughter 3. Pleasure cruises 4. Senior women 5. Aging 6. Loss (Psychology) 7. Secrets 8. Husband and wife 9. Family relationships 10. Seniors 11. Psychological fiction
LC 2015004221

RUSA Reading List Short List, 2016.

Embarking on an ill-conceived Alaskan cruise, septuagenarian Harriet reunites with her estranged daughter and confronts pivotal events from her life surrounding the true character of the husband who died two years earlier.

"Evison writes humanely and with good humor of his characters, who, like the rest of us, muddle through, too often without giving ourselves much of a break. A lovely, forgiving character study that ' s a pleasure to read." Kirkus.

Evison, Jonathan

West of here : a novel / Jonathan Evison. Algonquin Books of Chapel Hill, 2011. 496 p.

ISBN 9781565129528

1. 1880s 2. 2000s (Decade) 3. Men and nature 4. Small town life -- Washington (State) 5. Eccentrics and eccentricities 6. Dams 7. Consequences 8. Dysfunctional families 9. Clallam Indians 10. Washington (State) -- Social life and customs 11. Literary fiction 12. Parallel narratives 13. Pacific Northwest fiction 14. Literary fiction

The stories of the people who first inhabited the mythical town of Port Bonita in Washington State from 1887-1891, and then who live there in 2005-2006 and must deal with the damage done by their predecessors.

Ewan, Chris, 1976-

Dark tides : a thriller / Chris Ewan. Minotaur Books, 2015. 440 p.

ISBN 9781250074423

1. Halloween 2. Policewomen 3. Murder investigation 4. Practical jokes 5. Police 6. Revenge 7. Isle of Man 8. Thrillers and suspense

When another Halloween brings another death, a young police officer on the Isle of Man suspects they are connected to dark secrets in her own past.

Ewan, Chris, 1976-

Long time lost / Chris Ewan. Minotaur Books, 2017. 464 p.

ISBN 9781250117397

1. Witnesses -- Protection 2. New identities 3. Crime 4. Escapes 5. Murderers 6. Death threats 7. Attempted murder 8. Protectiveness in men 9. Isle of Man 10. Europe 11. Thrillers and suspense
LC 2016044901

Providing a unique, highly illegal service giving new identities to at-risk individuals and relocating them across Europe, Nick, a man who spent years under an assumed name, prevents a murder attempt on a witness in hiding, triggering a chain of events that threatens everyone he protects.

Extence, Gavin, 1982-

The **universe** versus Alex Woods / Gavin Extence. Orbit, 2013. 320 p.

ISBN 9780316246576

1. Misfits (Persons) 2. Teenage boys 3. Intergenerational friendship 4. Books and reading 5. Widowers 6. Curses 7. Bullying and bullies 8. Meteorites 9. Coming-of-age stories 10. Mainstream fiction

Alex Woods was struck by a meteorite when he was ten years old, leaving scars that marked him for an extraordinary life. The son of a fortune teller, bookish, and an easy target for bullies, he hasn't had the most conventional childhood. When he meets curmudgeonly widower Mr. Peterson, he finds an unlikely friend. Someone who teaches him that that you only get one shot at life. That you have to make it count. So when, aged seventeen, Alex is stopped at Dover customs with 113 grams of marijuana, an urn full of ashes on the passenger seat, and an entire nation in uproar, he's fairly sure he's done the right thing."-- Publisher description.

"Most teens think the universe is against them at some point. Seventeen-year-old Alex Woods has plenty of evidence for his case: a tarot-reading witch for a mother, his father a one-night Solstice stand long since forgotten, a chunk of meteorite crashing through the roof and smashing into him, the onset of epileptic seizures, and school bullies eager to target him...A bittersweet, cross-audience charmer, this debut novel will appeal to guys, YA readers, and Vonnegut and coming-of-age fiction fans." Library Journal.

F

Faber, Michel

The **book** of strange new things / Michel Faber. Hogarth Press, 2014. 500 p.

ISBN 9780553418842

1. Clergy 2. Life on other planets 3. Husband and wife 4. Married men 5. Environmental disasters 6. Aliens 7. Letter writing 8. Faith (Christianity) 9. Corporations 10. Literary fiction 11. Science fiction

Called to perform missionary work in a world light years away where the natives are fascinated by the concepts he introduces, man of faith Peter Leigh finds his beliefs tested when he learns of natural disasters that are tearing Earth apart.

Faber, Michel

The **crimson** petal and the white / Michel Faber. Harcourt, 2002. 838 p.

ISBN 9780151006922

1. Victorian era (1837-1901) 2. 19th century 3. Rich men 4. Prostitutes 5. Social status -- Great Britain 6. Young women 7. Married men -- Relations with single women 8. Women with mental illnesses 9. Men/women relations 10. Upper class 11. Prostitution 12. Perfumes industry and trade 13. London, England -- Social life and customs -- 19th century 14. Great Britain -- Social life and customs -- Victoria, 1837-1901 15. England -- Social life and customs -- 19th century 16. Historical fiction
LC 2002024138

Originally published: Edinburgh : Canongate, 2002.

Shortlisted for the James Tait Black Memorial Prize for Fiction, 2003

Yearning to escape her life of prostitution in 1870s London, Sugar finds her fate entangled in the complicated family life of patron William, an egotistical perfume magnate.

"The large themes that interwine the characters with one another-religion, health, sexuality, death, and, reluctantly, love--are juxtaposed against the most minute and intimate details of Victorian life. . . . This massive work is startling and absorbing." Booklist.

Faber, Michel
The **courage** consort : three novellas / Michel Faber. Harcourt, 2004. 240 p.
ISBN 0151010617
1. Vocal ensembles 2. Twin brothers and sisters 3. Archaeologists 4. Singers 5. Castles -- Belgium 6. Twins 7. Children of anthropologists 8. Children of eccentrics 9. Excavations (Archaeology) 10. Sexuality 11. Manuscripts 12. Women's dreams 13. Vocal music 14. Murder 15. Abbeys 16. Belgium 17. Whitby, England 18. Arctic regions 19. Psychological fiction
LC 2004005912
Three novellas include the title story, in which an a cappella ensemble is torn by conflicting artistic temperaments and sexual needs; and "The Fahrenheit Twins," in which abandoned children of anthropologists create a ritual civilization.

Fabry, Chris, 1961-
The **promise** of Jesse Woods / Chris Fabry. Tyndale House Publishers, 2016. 400 p.
ISBN 9781414387772
1. Life change events 2. Family secrets 3. Friendship 4. Reunions 5. Children of clergy 6. Small town life -- West Virginia 7. Teenagers 8. Summer 9. Promises 10. Loss (Psychology) 11. West Virginia 12. Christian fiction 13. Coming-of-age stories
LC 2016005373
Christy Award for Contemporary (Stand Alone) Category, 2017.
Matt Plumley moves to West Virginia and falls in love with an Appalachian girl, Jesse Woods, but she ends their relationship after he joins her in a rescue that causes a death, and years later, Matt returns to find out the truth about that night.

Fabry, Chris, 1961-
War room : prayer is a powerful weapon / Chris Fabry. Tyndale House Pub, 2015 424 p.
ISBN 9781496407290
1. Marital conflict 2. Suburban life 3. Prayer 4. Faith (Christianity) 5. Working mothers 6. Sales personnel 7. Real estate agents 8. Family relationships 9. Dysfunctional families 10. Marriage 11. Domestic fiction 12. Christian fiction 13. Movie tie-ins
LC 2015011970
"Based on the screenplay by Alex Kendrick and Stephen Kendrick."
When real-estate agent Elizabeth Jordan meets elderly widow Clara Williams, a visit to the elder woman's prayer room helps Elizabeth realize that her mounting problems at home are surmountable with the help of God.

Fagan, Jenni
The **Panopticon** : a novel / Jenni Fagan. Hogarth, 2013, c2012. 288 p.
ISBN 9780385347860
1. Juvenile correctional institutions 2. Problem youth 3. Teenage girls 4. Foster care 5. Juvenile delinquents 6. Self-discovery in teenage girls 7. Scotland 8. Coming-of-age stories
LC 2013006072

Shortlisted for the James Tait Black Memorial Prize for Fiction, 2012
Sent to a home for chronic offenders, 15-year-old foster child Anais is unable to remember the events that led to her sentencing and considers her bleak life in the hands of untrustworthy adults before discovering herself within an ad hoc family that helps her take first steps toward friendship and personal strength.

Fairstein, Linda A.
Blood oath / Linda A. Fairstein. Dutton, 2019. 400 p. Alexandra Cooper novels
ISBN 9781524743109
1. Women assistant district attorneys 2. Sex crimes 3. Sexually abused women 4. Detectives 5. Biomedical engineering 6. Women lawyers 7. City life 8. Secrets 9. New York City 10. Thrillers and suspense 11. Legal thrillers
A key witness' revelation about a sexual assault at the hands of a prominent official is complicated by rumors about a colleague's abusive conduct and another associate's violent, mysterious collapse.

Fairstein, Linda A.
Entombed / Linda Fairstein. Scribner, 2005. 416 p. Alexandra Cooper novels
ISBN 0743254880
1. Poe, Edgar Allan, 1809-1849 Homes and haunts 2. Women lawyers 3. Serial rape 4. Murder 5. Women public prosecutors 6. Literary societies 7. Sex crimes 8. New York City 9. Upper East Side, New York City 10. Thrillers and suspense 11. Legal thrillers
LC 2004052189
When a former residence of Edgar Allan Poe is demolished, a human skeleton is found behind the walls. Soon, Cooper is digging into Poe's tormented life, hoping to discover a clue that will break open the case.
"It's a tribute to Fairstein's integrity and her clear, measured prose that the novel never tips into prurience. Her methodical presentation of authentic detail engages reader interest more than narrative flourish or cheap thrills." Publishers Weekly.

Fajardo-Anstine, Kali
* **Sabrina** & Corina : stories / Kali Fajardo-Anstine. One World, 2019. 212 p.
ISBN 9780525511298
1. Hispanic American women 2. Mothers and daughters 3. Social marginality 4. Poverty 5. Racism 6. Family relationships 7. Ethnic identity 8. Denver, Colorado 9. The West (United States) 10. Literary fiction 11. Short stories
LC 2018023965
ALA Notable Book, 2020.
National Book Award for Fiction finalist, 2019.
A debut story collection about female relationships and the deep-rooted truths of our homelands features Latina protagonists of indigenous descent who cautiously navigate the violence and changes in a Denver, Colorado community.

Falcones de Sierra, Ildefonso, 1959-
Cathedral of the sea / Ildefonso Falcones ; translated from the Spanish by Nick Caistor. Dutton, 2008. 612 p.
ISBN 9780525950486
1. Medieval period (476-1492) 2. Inquisition -- Spain 3. Peasant men 4. Brothers 5. Men/women relations 6. Jewish women 7. Prejudice 8. Church and State -- Spain 9. Interfaith romance 10. Love 11. Interpersonal attraction 12. Civilization, Medieval 13. Spain -- History -- 14th century 14. Historical fiction 15. Translations --

Spanish to English

LC 2007046077

Follows the fortunes of the Estanyol family in medieval Barcelona, whose rise from peasantry is marked by their stoneworker son's role in building the Santa Maria del Mar cathedral and his forbidden love for a Jewish woman.

Faletti, Giorgio, 1950-

A **pimp's** notes / Giorgio Faletti ; translated from the Italian by Antony Shugaar. Farrar, Straus and Giroux, 2012. 400 p.

ISBN 9780374231408

1. 1970s 2. Terrorists 3. Kidnapping -- Italy 4. Crimes against politicians 5. Organized crime -- Italy 6. Crime bosses 7. Italy 8. Milan, Italy 9. Noir fiction 10. Crime fiction

LC 2011046064

Set in the seedy underworld of 1970s Milan against a backdrop of politician Aldo Moro's kidnapping by the Red Brigades terrorist group, Bravo, a caterer to the wealthy, has an affair with a mysterious woman only to find himself pursued by the authorities and organized crime bosses.

Fallada, Hans, 1893-1947

Every man dies alone / Hans Fallada ; translated by Michael Hofmann, with an afterword by Geoff Wilkes. Melville House Pub., 2009, c1947. 544 p.

ISBN 9781933633633

1. Hampel, Otto Hermann, 1897-1943 2. Hampel, Elise, 1903-1943 3. World War II 4. Nazism 5. Civil disobedience 6. Resistance to government 7. Grief 8. Husband and wife 9. Germany -- History -- 20th century 10. Biographical fiction 11. Historical fiction 12. Translations -- German to English

LC 2008027489

First published in German as Jeder stirbt fur sich allein. Berlin : Aufbau, 1947.

Also known as Alone in Berlin: London : Penguin Classics, 2009.

Tells the story of a working-class German couple who lose their son to war and begin to a small resistance against Nazi power.

"This is a readable, suspense-driven novel from an author who a) knew what he was doing when it came to writing commercial fiction, and b) had lived through, and so knew intimately, the period he was writing about. This is an extraordinary combination. I hesitate to use a word like serendipity, but cruelly enough, that's exactly what it was. Thus, the characters and what characters they are, the good, the bad and the ugly of the Berlin working class during the war are drawn from life. They are alive." Globe and Mail.

Fallon, Siobhan

* **You** know when the men are gone / Siobhan Fallon. G.P. Putnam's Sons, 2011. 240 p.

ISBN 9780399157202

1. Military spouses 2. Families of military personnel 3. Iraq War, 2003-2011 4. Military life 5. Coping in women 6. Texas 7. Short stories

LC 2010029597

"Amy Einhorn books."

A collection of interconnected stories relate the experiences of Fort Hood military wives who share a poignant vigil during which they raise children while waiting for their husbands to return.

"In this book of eight stories, connected by young families stationed at Fort Hood, Texas, Siobhan Fallon sees military life as an alternate universe. It can be many times better and so much worse than its civilian counterparts. . . . Fallon is a superb writer with a delicate perception of this raw material. Her characters may be invented or based on people she

herself knew as an army wife. In either case, the stories are powerful." Providence Journal.

Farah, Nuruddin, 1945-

Crossbones / Nuruddin Farah. Riverhead Books, 2011. 400 p. Links trilogy

ISBN 9781594488160

1. Americans in Somalia 2. Journalists 3. College teachers 4. Political refugees 5. Somali Americans 6. Warlords 7. Missing persons 8. Insurgency 9. Violence 10. Somalia 11. Mogadishu, Somalia 12. Political fiction 13. Literary fiction

Jeebleh returns to Mogadiscio to discover that it is being rigidly controlled by white-robed oppressors; while Ahl searches for his missing stepson, who he fears has been recruited for a religious insurgency.

"Gripping but utterly humane thriller set in one of the least-understood regions on earth." Kirkus.

Farah, Nuruddin, 1945-

Knots / Nuruddin Farah. Riverhead Books, 2007. 432 p. Links trilogy

ISBN 9781594489242

1. Americans in Somalia 2. Warlords 3. Feminism -- Somalia 4. Muslim women -- Africa 5. Peace activists 6. Peace -- Somalia 7. Women's role 8. Property rights 9. Real estate -- Somalia 10. Self-discovery in women 11. Home (Concept) 12. Veils 13. Mogadishu, Somalia 14. Political fiction 15. Literary fiction

LC 2006023107

Returning to her native home in Somalia after being raised in North America and suffering a failed marriage, self-reliant Cambara struggles to reclaim her family's home from a warlord and finds support from a group of women activists.

"Despite its weaknesses, there is beauty in this story of reclamation and resurrection. When Farah's heroine sheds her veil of conformity, it is as if Somalia itself is emerging from a cocoon of despair." Time Out New York.

Farah, Nuruddin, 1945-

Links / Nuruddin Farah. Riverhead Books, 2004. 352 p. Links trilogy

ISBN 1573222658

1. Americans in Somalia 2. Political refugees 3. Somali Americans 4. Male friendship 5. Mothers -- Death 6. Warlords -- Mogadishu, Somalia 7. Kidnapping 8. Hometowns -- Somalia 9. Violence 10. Somalia 11. Mogadishu, Somalia 12. Political fiction 13. Literary fiction

LC 2003065969

Returning to Mogadishu, Somalia, from New York after a twenty-year exile, Jeebleh finds a troubled and devastated city ruled by clan warlords and patrolled by violent gangs of thugs.

"This novel is both alien and familiar, a haunting exploration of the desire to help and the attendant costs of doing so." Christian Science Monitor.

Farnsworth, Christopher

Flashmob / Christopher Farnsworth. William Morrow & Company, 2017 388 p. John Smith (Christopher Farnsworth)

ISBN 9780062568496

1. Psychic ability 2. Technology 3. Social media 4. Internet 5. Murderers 6. CIA agents 7. Fugitives 8. Corporations 9. Cyber-thrillers

Gifted troubleshooter John Smith, introduced in the acclaimed thriller Killfile, must take down a shadowy figure who has weaponized the internet, using social media to put a price on the heads of his targets.

Farnsworth, Christopher

Killfile / Christopher Farnsworth. William Morrow & Co., 2016. 336 p. John Smith (Christopher Farnsworth)

ISBN 9780062416407

1. Psychic ability 2. Intellectual property 3. Technology 4. CIA agents 5. Fugitives 6. Corporations 7. Cyber-thrillers

A man who can hear other people's thoughts is hired to track a former tech employee who stole some valuable intellectual property.

Farrell, Henry, 1920-2006

* **What** ever happened to Baby Jane? / Henry Farrell. Carroll & Graf, 1991, c1960. 245 p.

ISBN 9780881847253

1. Sisters 2. Former film actors and actresses 3. Sibling rivalry 4. Psychological fiction

Originally published: New York : Rinehart, 1960.

Baby Jane, a former child star of early vaudeville who resented having to grow up in the shadow of her prettier sister, Blanche, is now casting her own sinister shadow over Blanche, an invalid who must rely on Jane for her care.

Farrow, John, 1947-

* The **storm** murders : a thriller / John Farrow. St Martins Pr, 2015 384 p. Emile Cinq-Mars mysteries

ISBN 9781250057686

1. Blizzards 2. Weather 3. Farms 4. Murder 5. Murder investigation 6. Police -- Montreal, Quebec 7. French-Canadians 8. Detectives 9. Quebec (Province) 10. Mysteries

"City of Ice, John Farrow's first book in his acclaimed Emile Cinq-Mars series, which has been hailed by Booklist as "the best series in crime fiction today," has been published in over 17 countries. Now with The Storm Murders, the series continues. On the day after a massive blizzard, two policemen are called to an isolated farm house sitting all by itself in the middle of a pristine snow-blanketed field. Inside the lonely abode are two dead people. But there are no tracks in the snow leading either to the house or away. What happened here? Is this a murder/suicide case? Or will it turn into something much more sinister? John Farrow is the pen name of Trevor Ferguson, a Canadian writer who has been named Canada's best novelist in both Books in Canada and the Toronto Star. This is the first of a trilogy he is writing for us called The Storm Murders trilogy. Each book features Emile Cinq-Mars, the Hercule Poirot of Canada, and extreme weather conditions"--, Provided by publisher.

"Farrow (a pseudonym for Canadian author Trevor Ferguson) brings a literary fiction writer's sensitivity to nuance and feel for landscape to this fine, character-rich thriller with a bang-up finish." Booklist.

Faulkner, Colleen

Finding Georgina / Colleen Faulkner. Kensington, 2018. 304 p.

ISBN 9781496711557

1. Kidnapping 2. Kidnapping victims 3. Mothers and daughters 4. Missing children 5. Motherhood 6. Teenage girls 7. Veterinarians 8. Catholics 9. Jews 10. Interfaith relations 11. New Orleans, Louisiana 12. Mainstream fiction

What happens after you get what you?ve always wanted? In Colleen Faulkner's thought-provoking and emotionally compelling novel, a mother is reunited with the daughter who was abducted as a toddler?only to face unexpected and painful challenges . . .

Faulkner, William, 1897-1962

* **Absalom**, Absalom! / William Faulkner. Vintage Books, 1990, c1936. 313 p.

ISBN 9780679732181

1. Poor people 2. Plantation life 3. Mississippi 4. Literary fiction 5. Family sagas 6. Historical fiction 7. Modern classics 8. Southern Gothic 9. Southern fiction

The story of Thomas Sutpen, an enigmatic stranger who came to Jefferson in the early 1830s to wrest his mansion out of the muddy bottoms of the north Mississippi wilderness. He was a man, Faulkner said, "who wanted sons and the sons destroyed him."

Faulkner, William, 1897-1962

* **As** I lay dying : the corrected text / William Faulkner. Modern Library, 1992. vii, 261 p.

ISBN 9780375504525

1. Death 2. Farm life 3. Dysfunctional families 4. Southern Gothic 5. Southern fiction 6. Literary fiction 7. Psychological fiction 8. Modern classics

LC 00056254

Originally published: 1930.

The members of a Southern family contribute their individual tribulations to this encompassing impression of rural poverty.

Faulkner, William, 1897-1962

* **Go** down, Moses / William Faulkner. Vintage Books, 1990, c1942. 365 p.

ISBN 9780679732174

1. Race relations 2. Plantation life 3. Slavery 4. Nature 5. Mississippi -- Social life and customs 6. Literary fiction 7. Short stories 8. Modern classics 9. Southern Gothic 10. Southern fiction

LC 90050209

"Originally published by Random House, Inc., in 1942"--T.p. verso.

Set in mythical Yoknapatawpha County, seven interrelated stories deal with the complex, changing relationships between Blacks and whites and between man and nature.

Faulkner, William, 1897-1962

The **hamlet** / William Faulkner. Random House, 1940. 366 p. Snopes Family

ISBN 9780394427591

1. Small town life -- Mississippi 2. Obsession 3. Family relationships 4. Sharecroppers 5. Bankers 6. Mississippi -- History 7. Family sagas 8. Literary fiction 9. Modern classics 10. Southern fiction

LC 64007972

Later film version: Long hot summer

Traces the growing power of Flem Snopes, a white-trash farmer, in the Mississippi town of Frenchman's Bend.

Faulkner, William, 1897-1962

Intruder in the dust / William Faulkner. Vintage International, 1991, c1948. 241 p.

ISBN 9780679736516

1. Trials (Murder) 2. African American defendants 3. Racism -- Mississippi 4. Race relations 5. Lynching 6. Murder 7. Mississippi 8. Literary fiction 9. Modern classics 10. Southern fiction

LC 91050014

Originally published in 1948.

Dramatizes the events that surround the murder of a white man in a volatile Southern community.

Faulkner, William, 1897-1962

* **Light** in August / William Faulkner. Modern Library, 2002, c1932. vii, 512 p.

ISBN 067964248X

1. Racism 2. Pregnant women 3. Multiracial men 4. Drifters 5. Misfits (Persons) 6. Ostracism 7. Clergy 8. Mississippi 9. Literary fiction 10. Modern classics 11. Southern Gothic 12. Southern fiction

LC 67012716

Originally published: Harrison Smith and Robert Haas, 1932.

In a novel about hopeless perseverance in the face of mortality, guileless Lena Grove searches for the father of her unborn child, Reverend Hightower is plagued by visions of Confederate horsemen, and drifter Joe Christmas is consumed by his mixed ancestry.

Faulkner, William, 1897-1962

Pylon / William Faulkner. Random House, 1935. 315 p.

1. 1930s 2. Polyamory 3. Stunt flying 4. Stunt pilots 5. Husband and wife 6. Sexuality 7. Drinking 8. Journalists 9. Mardi Gras 10. New Orleans, Louisiana 11. Literary fiction 12. Modern classics 13. Southern fiction

Relates the experiences of four individuals competing in an aviation contest during the Mardi Gras celebration in New Valois.

Faulkner, William, 1897-1962

The **reivers** : a reminiscence / William Faulkner. Random House, 1962. 305 p.

ISBN 0394442296

1. 1900s (Decade) 2. Automobile travel 3. Eleven-year-old boys 4. Boys and men 5. African American men 6. Automobile thefts 7. Thieves 8. Coming-of-age stories 9. Literary fiction 10. Modern classics 11. Southern fiction

LC 62010335

Pulitzer Prize for Fiction, 1963.

Boon Hogganbeck persuades Lucius Priest, 11, to borrow his grandfather's car in 1905, and after they arrive at a bordello, the black Ned McCaslin trades the car for a horse.

Faulkner, William, 1897-1962

Requiem for a nun / William Faulkner. Random House, 1951. 286p.

ISBN 9780394442747

1. Child murders 2. Household employees 3. African American women 4. Rape victims 5. Nurses 6. Confession (Law) 7. Husband and wife 8. Housekeepers 9. Literary fiction 10. Modern classics 11. Southern fiction

LC 51012731

Sequel to: Sanctuary

In order to save a nurse convicted of murder, Temple Stevens decides to confess that she killed her own daughter.

Faulkner, William, 1897-1962

* **Sanctuary** / William Faulkner Vintage, 1993, c1931. 309 p.

ISBN 9780679748144

1. Crimes against women 2. Rape 3. Kidnapping 4. Murder 5. College students 6. Young women 7. Small towns 8. Bootleggers 9. Trials (Murder) 10. Rape victims 11. Mississippi 12. Literary fiction 13. Modern classics 14. Southern fiction 15. Rural noir

Sanctuary was the basis for the films The story of Temple Drake (1933) and Sanctuary (1960).

Sequel: Requiem for a nun.

First published: [London] : Chatto & Windus, 1931.

An assortment of perverse characters act out this dramatic story of the kidnapping of a Mississippi debutante

Faulkner, William, 1897-1962

* The **sound** and the fury / William Faulkner. Random House, 1929. 401 p.

ISBN 0394532414

1. 1920s 2. Men with developmental disabilities 3. Dysfunctional families 4. Incest 5. Suicide 6. African Americans 7. Literary fiction 8. Psychological fiction 9. Modern classics 10. Southern Gothic 11. Southern fiction

Retells the tragic times of the Compson family, including beautiful, rebellious Caddy; manchild Benjy; haunted, neurotic Quentin; Jason, the brutal cynic; and Dilsey, their Black servant.

Faulkner, William, 1897-1962

Uncollected stories of William Faulkner / William Faulkner ; edited by Joseph Blotner. Random House, 1979. 716 p.

ISBN 0394400445

1. Family relationships 2. Small towns 3. Rural life 4. Mississippi -- Social life and customs 5. Short stories 6. Literary fiction 7. Modern classics 8. Southern fiction

LC 78021803

Forty-six stories never before published in any collection include twenty that were incorporated into longer works after magazine publication, eleven that appeared in periodicals, and fifteen never published at all

Faulks, Sebastian

* **Birdsong** / Sebastian Faulks. Random House, 1993. 402 p. French trilogy

ISBN 9780091773731

1. Great Britain. Army Officers France 2. First World War era (1914-1918) 3. World War I 4. Soldiers -- Great Britain -- History -- 20th century 5. Extramarital affairs 6. Trench warfare 7. British in France 8. Men/women relations 9. Love triangles 10. Romantic love 11. Loss (Psychology) 12. Identity (Psychology) 13. France -- History -- German occupation, 1914-1918 14. War stories 15. Historical fiction 16. Literary fiction

LC 9523721

In 1910, Stephen Wraysford, a young Englishman, journeys to France and becomes embroiled in a series of traumatic events, including a clandestine love affair, and is later trapped amid the horrors of the First World War.

"[The author] proves himself a grand storyteller here." Publishers Weekly.

Faulks, Sebastian

Charlotte Gray : a novel / Sebastian Faulks. Random House, 1998. 399 p. French trilogy

ISBN 037550169X

1. Second World War era (1939-1945) 2. 1940s 3. British in France 4. World War II 5. Resistance to military occupation 6. Holocaust (1933-1945) -- France 7. Nazi collaborators -- France 8. Anti-Nazis -- France 9. Men/women relations 10. Missing in action 11. Determination in women 12. France -- History -- German occupation, 1940-1945 13. England 14. Historical fiction 15. War stories 16. Literary fiction

LC 9833658

A young Scottish woman who falls in love with a World War II RAF pilot shortly before his plane is lost over France joins the Resistance movement to find him, only to discover a larger meaning in her new role.

"Faulks has written one of those rare books that is adventurous enough to attract a popular audience while thoughtful enough to sustain the more serious reader." Library Journal.

Faulks, Sebastian

* Jeeves and the wedding bells / Sebastian Faulks. St. Martin's Press, 2013 336 p.
 ISBN 9781250047595
 1. Butlers 2. Misadventures 3. Rich people 4. Men/women relations 5. Weddings 6. Characters and characteristics in literature 7. England 8. Humorous stories 9. Gentle reads
 Originally published: London: Hutchinson, 2013.

When young man about town Bertie Wooster, nursing a broken heart, agrees to help his old friend Peregrine Woody Beeching, whose own romance is failing, hilarity and chaos ensue as Jeeves, the very epitome of the modern manservant, steps in to save Bertie from himself.

Faulks, Sebastian

On Green Dolphin Street : a novel / Sebastian Faulks. Random House, 2001. 351 p.
 ISBN 0375502254
 1. 1960s 2. British in the United States 3. Extramarital affairs 4. Diplomats' spouses 5. Married women 6. Cold War 7. Washington, D.C. 8. New York City 9. Love stories 10. Literary fiction
          LC 2001041753

In 1960, Mary van der Linden, a loyal wife and mother approaching forty, moves with her family from London to Washington, D.C., where she escapes her narrow world for the larger issues of politics and the Cold War with the help of Frank, a New York journalist.

"The outline of this archetypal love story may sound familiar, but everything about Faulks' telling of it is fresh. . . . It is a love story above all, but it is also a New York story, the sights, sounds, and smells of the city perfectly evoked to capture one of those moments when the forces of change collide with the proprieties of the past." Booklist.

Faulks, Sebastian

Paris echo : a novel / Sebastian Faulks. Henry Holt and Company, 2018 272 p.
 ISBN 9781250305657
 1. Women historians 2. Americans in Paris, France 3. Immigrants 4. History 5. Identity (Psychology) 6. Interethnic friendship 7. Women and war 8. World War II -- Paris, France 9. Paris, France -- History -- German occupation, 1940-1944 10. France -- History -- German occupation, 1940-1945 11. Literary fiction 12. Psychological fiction
          LC 2018013873

An American historical researcher in World War II Paris and a Moroccan teen who risked his life to enter France find the realities of the Nazi occupation transforming their ideas about sacrifice and happiness.

Faulks, Sebastian

A **week** in December / Sebastian Faulks. Doubleday, 2010, c2009. 392 p.
 ISBN 9780385532914
 1. Rich people 2. Dinners and dining 3. Banks and banking 4. Reality 5. Greed 6. Self-deception 7. Redemption 8. London, England 9. Literary fiction 10. Psychological fiction
          LC 2009030109
 Originally published: London: Hutchinson, 2009.

A novel set in 2007 London follows seven diverse characters, exploring the complex patterns and crossings of modern urban life and culminating in a climax where each character is forced to confront the true nature of the world they inhabit.

"The events of the novel span seven days close to Christmas, 2007. It's a time when fears of terrorism are, as now, real and the financial markets are on the brink of disaster. Faulks employs a sizable cast, and a fast bicyclist who rides without a light, to reveal a social DNA that reverberates through the present. The characters are introduced on Sunday, Dec. 16, as Sophie Topping begins final preparations for an important dinner party the following Saturday. Her husband, Lance, has recently been elected to Parliament, and this gathering is meant to show party leadership that Lance moves in powerful circles. The guest list is a combination of financial, social, business, journalism and sports figures, culled from Sophie's broad network. From this assemblage, which Faulks will allow the reader to follow over the coming week, several leading characters emerge. . . . This, at its heart, is fiction about folks, and it's darned compelling." Denver Post.

Faust, Christa

Choke hold / Christa Faust. Hard Case Crime, 2011. 256 p.
 ISBN 9780857682857
 1. Former erotic film actors and actresses 2. Murder 3. Sex industry and trade 4. Federal Witness Protection Program 5. Violence 6. Mixed martial arts 7. Revenge 8. Crime fiction 9. Pulp fiction
 Sequel to: Money Shot.

After a shoot-out at the restaurant where she works leaves a former costar dead, Angel Dare begins to protect his son Cody, a mixed martial artist, and they wind up on the run from drug dealers who think that Cody stole drugs from them.

Faust, Christa

Money shot / Christa Faust. Hard Case Crime, 2008. 250 p.
 ISBN 9780843959581
 1. Former erotic film actors and actresses 2. Revenge 3. Sex industry and trade 4. Pornographic film actors and actresses 5. Murder 6. Rape 7. Malicious accusation 8. Former police 9. Fugitives 10. Violence 11. Crime fiction 12. Pulp fiction
 Sequel: Choke Hold.

Angel Dare, a retired porn star and owner of an adult modeling agency, seeks revenge on the people who framed her for murder after locking her in the trunk of a car, battered, raped, and shot.

"Former porn star Angel Dare (nee Gina Moretti), who stopped acting to establish Daring Angels, a firm that manages women in the business, is lured to perform once more by a hot young male star. Instead, she's beaten, raped, shot, and left for dead in the trunk of a car, and that's just the start--all because of money from the international sex trade. With the help of her company's ex-cop security escort, Lalo Malloy, Angel untangles the plot and players, depending finally on nothing but her own resources for the vengeance she craves. A rip-roaring story with nonstop action and an inside look at X-rated movie making, this is clearly not for all readers or collections; but the title (which originated in the porn industry) and cover art are indicators of its contents." Library Journal.

Fay, Juliette

The **shortest** way home / Juliette Fay. Penguin Books, 2013. 368 p.
 ISBN 9780143121916
 1. Brothers and sisters 2. Small town life -- Massachusetts 3. Family relationships 4. Huntington's disease 5. Interpersonal relations 6. Men nurses 7. Friendship 8. Men/women relations 9. Massachusetts 10. Pelham, Massachusetts 11. Mainstream fiction
          LC 2012025149

Sean, burnt out after spending twenty years in the Third World, returns home to Massachusetts and reconnects with his family and a woman from his past, who may just rewrite his future.

Fay, Kim

The **map** of lost memories : a novel / Kim Fay. Ballantine Books, 2012. 336 p.

ISBN 9780345531346

1. 1920s 2. Women adventurers 3. Treasure hunting 4. Quests 5. Scrolls 6. Seattle, Washington 7. Shanghai, China 8. Cambodia 9. Adventure stories 10. Historical fiction

LC 2012004142

Teaming up in 1925 Shanghai to find a priceless set of scrolls believed to contain the lost history of the Khmer empire, Irene Blum and temple-robber Simone Merlin commit a shockingly violent act before discovering unexpected commonalities in their respective pasts.

Faye, Gael, 1982-

* **Small** country : a novel / Gael Faye. Hogarth Press, 2018. 183 p.

ISBN 9781524759872

1. 1990s 2. Boys -- Africa 3. Civil war 4. Childhood innocence (Concept) 5. Genocide 6. Survival 7. Interracial families 8. Brothers and sisters 9. Burundi 10. Rwanda -- History -- Civil War, 1994 11. Africa 12. Coming-of-age stories 13. Literary fiction 14. Translations -- French to English

In Burundi in 1992, ten-year-old Gabriel enjoys carefree days with his friends, but his idyllic existence and his innocence come to a brutal end when Burundi and neighboring Rwanda are hit by civil war and genocide.

Faye, Lyndsay

The **gods** of Gotham / Lyndsay Faye. G. P. Putnam's Sons, 2012 432 p. Gods of Gotham

ISBN 9780399158377

1. 1840s 2. Police 3. Serial murderers 4. Irish Americans -- Discrimination 5. Immigrants, Irish 6. Crimes against children 7. Brothels 8. Social workers 9. Anti-Catholicism 10. People with disfigurements 11. Political corruption 12. New York City 13. Historical mysteries 14. Mysteries

RUSA Reading List, 2013.

Joining the newly formed NYPD in 1845, Timothy reluctantly assumes his duties near the notorious Five Points slum, where in the middle of the night he hears a little girl's claim that dozens of bodies have been buried in a local forest.

Faye, Lyndsay

Jane Steele / Lyndsay Faye. G. P. Putnam's Sons, 2016. 400 p.

ISBN 9780399169496

1. 19th century 2. Murderers 3. Inheritance and succession 4. Governesses 5. Women murderers 6. Orphans 7. Serial murders 8. Undercover operations 9. Mansions 10. Deception 11. London, England -- History -- 19th century 12. England -- History -- 19th century 13. Adaptations, retellings, and spin-offs 14. Gothic fiction

"A reimagining of Jane Eyre as a gutsy, heroic serial killer, from the author whose work The New York Times described as "riveting" and The Wall Street Journal called "thrilling.""--, Provided by publisher.

"Fayes skill at historical mystery was evident in her nineteenth-century New York trilogy, but this slyly satiric stand-alone takes her prowess to new levels. A must for Bronte devotees; wickedly entertaining for all." Booklist.

Faye, Lyndsay

* The **Paragon** Hotel / Lyndsay Faye. G.P. Putnam's Sons, 2019 432 p.

ISBN 9780735210752

1. Ku-Klux Klan 2. 1920s 3. Women fugitives 4. Racism 5. Hotels 6. Gunshot victims 7. Mafia 8. Train rides 9. Porters 10. African Americans 11. African American businesspeople 12. Nightclubs 13. Women singers 14. Segregation 15. Race relations 16. Multiracial children 17. Missing boys 18. New York City 19. Portland, Oregon 20. Historical mysteries

LC 2018012903

Fleeing to 1921 Oregon, Alice takes refuge in the city's only black hotel and helps new friends search for a missing child, hide from KKK violence and navigate painful secrets.

"A riveting multilevel thriller of race, sex, and mob violence that throbs with menace as it hums with wit." Kirkus.

Faye, Lyndsay

Seven for a secret / Lyndsay Faye. G. P. Putnams Sons, 2013. 464 p. Gods of Gotham

ISBN 9780399158384

1. Antebellum America (1820-1861) 2. 1840s 3. Free African Americans 4. Slave trade 5. Missing persons investigation 6. Kidnapping 7. Underground Railroad 8. Police 9. Political corruption 10. New York City 11. Historical mysteries 12. Mysteries

LC 2013008127

A police officer investigates a ring of "blackbirders" who kidnap free people of color in the North and sell them to Southern plantations.

Faye, Lyndsay

The **whole** art of detection : lost mysteries of Sherlock Holmes / Lyndsay Faye. Mysterious Press, 2017. 388 p.

ISBN 9780802125927

1. Victorian era (1837-1901) 2. 1880s 3. Criminal investigation 4. Private investigators 5. Crime 6. London, England -- History -- 19th century 7. England 8. Adaptations, retellings, and spin-offs 9. Short stories 10. Victorian mysteries 11. Historical mysteries

LC 2016037116

In this superb short story collection, Edgar Award-nominated Lyndsay Faye presents a collection of 15 Sherlock Holmes tales, including two new works (such as the clever "The Adventure of the Thames Tunnel") as well as stories that were previously published. Though Sherlock Holmes pastiches abound, not very many place him in his prime on Baker Street as Lyndsay Faye often does here. Read and enjoy, Sherlockians! -- Description by Dawn Towery

"Fans and neophytes alike should cheer Faye's reinvigoration of Conan Doyle's hero and his panoramic world." Kirkus.

Feehan, Christine

Dark illusion / Christine Feehan. Berkley, 2019. 432 p. Dark series

ISBN 9781984803467

1. Women wizards 2. Vampires 3. Interspecies romance 4. Mate selection 5. Good and evil 6. Warriors 7. Families 8. Sexual attraction 9. Men/women relations 10. Carpathian Mountains 11. Paranormal romances

LC 2019003736

Fleeing her controlling family to warn the Carpathians of an imminent threat, mage Julija Brennan resists her explosive connection to centuries-old warrior Isai Florea, who recognizes her as his lifemate.

Feehan, Christine

Shadow rider / Christine Feehan. Jove Books, 2016. 432 p. Shadow riders novels

ISBN 9780515156133

1. Organized crime 2. Psychic ability 3. Secrets 4. Determination in men 5. Rich families 6. Escapes 7. Interpersonal attraction 8. Men/women relations 9. Paranormal phenomena 10. Chicago, Illinois 11. Paranormal romances

Gifted with the ability to manipulate light and dark, shadow rider Stefano Ferraro, the head of a Chicago crime family, meets his match in Francesca Cappello, a mysterious?and dangerously beautiful?woman whose powers rival his own.

Feeney, Alice

* **I** know who you are : a novel / Alice Feeney. Flatiron Books, 2019. 304 p.

ISBN 9781250147349

1. Actors and actresses 2. Married women 3. Stalkers 4. Missing men 5. Secrets 6. Threat (Psychology) 7. Psychological suspense

LC 2018037893

An actress on the brink of fame finds her sense of reality thrown into question by her husband's baffling disappearance at the same time a young runaway lands in mortal danger.

Feeney, Alice

* **Sometimes** I lie / Alice Feeney. Flatiron Books, 2018, c2017. 272 p.

ISBN 9781250144843

1. Coma -- Patients 2. Married women 3. Betrayal 4. Sisters 5. Secrets 6. Memories 7. Consciousness 8. Radio personalities 9. Extramarital affairs 10. London, England 11. Psychological suspense

LC 2017045151

Depicts the harrowing experiences of a coma patient with shut-in syndrome who while unable to move or speak must listen to those around her to figure out what happened and who is responsible for her injuries.

Ferencik, Erica

Into the jungle / Erica Ferencik. Scout Press, 2019. 320 p.

ISBN 9781501168925

1. Jungles 2. Foster teenagers 3. Runaway teenagers 4. Indians of South America 5. Determination (Personal quality) 6. Interpersonal attraction 7. Jungle animals 8. Jungle survival 9. Teenage girls 10. Missionaries 11. Poachers 12. Survival 13. Bolivia 14. Survival stories 15. Thrillers and suspense

LC 2018047677

Taking a job in Bolivia to escape foster care and group homes, Lily apprehensively follows the man she loves into a ruthless, life-threatening jungle region of lawless poachers, bullheaded missionaries and desperate indigenous tribes.

Ferber, Edna, 1887-1968

So big / Edna Ferber ; introduction by Maria K. Mootry. University of Illinois Press, 1995, c1924. xvi, 212 p.

ISBN 0252063767

1. Gamblers 2. Children of gamblers 3. Fathers and daughters 4. Mothers and sons -- Illinois 5. Families 6. Family relationships 7. Women farmers -- Illinois 8. Truck farming -- Illinois 9. Determination in women 10. Independence in women 11. Self-sacrifice in women 12. Farmers 13. Success (Concept) 14. Chicago, Illinois 15. Coming-of-age stories 16. Modern classics 17. Domestic fiction

LC 94024615

Originally published: Garden City, N. Y. : Doubleday, Page & Company, 1924.

Pulitzer Prize for Fiction, 1925.

Fernandez, Macedonio, 1874-1952

* The **museum** of eterna's novel : the first good novel / Macedonio Fernandez ; translated from the Spanish by Margaret Schwartz. Open Letter, 2010. 240 p.

ISBN 9781934824061

1. Writing 2. Books and reading 3. Authors 4. Philosophy 5. Interpersonal relations 6. Literary fiction 7. Translations -- Spanish to English

LC 2009048625

"This novel was initiated in 1925 and worked on until [the author's] death in 1952 and is only now available in English. With its 29 prologues of metaphysical indecision and despair, this book never really begins and thus never has to actually end. Its chapters, framed by letters to the critics and to the WINDOW SHOPPING READER, deliver a cumulative script of adoration and gratitude formed around a woman named Eterna, a character based on the author's great love and benefactor, Consuelo Bosch de Senz Valiente. . . . Fernndez's theme is love in the face of death, and to get to this, he will combine the metaphysics of Schopenhauer with the fatalist frenzy of Poe." Dallas Morning News

Ferrante, Elena

* The **lost** daughter / Elena Ferrante ; translated from the Italian by Ann Goldstein. Europa, 2008. 125 p.

ISBN 9781933372426

1. Mothers and daughters 2. Divorced women 3. Motherhood 4. Parent and child 5. Vacations 6. Italy 7. Domestic fiction 8. Translations -- Italian to English

Original title: La figlia oscura.

The author revisits the story of this book in her children's book, The Beach at Night.

When Leda's daughters leave home to be with their father, she decides to take a trip to a small coastal town in Italy, but soon after she arrives memories from her unsettled past come back to haunt her.

"In this brutally frank novel of maternal ambivalence, the narrator, a forty-seven-year-old divorcée summering alone on the Ionian coast, becomes obsessed with a beautiful young mother who seems ill at ease with her husband's rowdy, slightly menacing Neapolitan clan. When this woman's daughter loses her doll, the older woman commits a small crime that she can't explain even to herself. Although much of the drama takes place in her head, Ferrante's gift for psychological horror renders it immediate and visceral." The New Yorker.

Ferrante, Elena

My brilliant friend / Elena Ferrante ; translated from the Italian by Ann Goldstein. Europa Editions, 2012, c2011. 336 p. Neapolitan novels

ISBN 9781609450786

1. 1950s 2. Growing up 3. Teenage girls -- Friendship 4. Poverty 5. Violence 6. Inner city -- Naples, Italy 7. Ambition in teenage girls 8. Childhood friends 9. Postwar life 10. Italy 11. Naples, Italy 12. Mainstream fiction 13. Translations -- Italian to English

Originally published: Rome : Edizioni, 2011.

Beginning in the 1950s Elena and Lila grow up in Naples, Italy, mirroring two different aspects of their nation.

Ferrante, Elena

*The **story** of a new name / Elena Ferrante ; translated from the Italian by Ann Goldstein. Europa Editions, 2013, c2012. 480 p. Neapolitan novels

ISBN 9781609451349

1. Marriage 2. Unhappiness in women 3. Self-discovery in women 4. Female friendship 5. Childhood friends 6. Creativity in women 7. Women authors 8. Italy 9. Naples, Italy 10. Mainstream fiction 11. Translations -- Italian to English

Translation from the Italian of: Storia del nuovo cognome.

Originally published: Rome : Edizione, 2012.

In this follow-up to My Brilliant Friend, Lila is imprisoned by marriage, while Elena continues her journey of self-discovery, until their friendship, which is at the center of their emotional lives, forces them both to mature into women.

"Ferrante's writing is captivating and insightful. She delves deeply into the character of the girls' friendship, ushering them into womanhood with an honesty that is acutely personal." Booklist.

Ferrante, Elena

* The **story** of the lost child / Elena Ferrante ; translated from the Italian by Ann Goldstein. Europa Editions, 2015, c2014. 464 p. Neapolitan novels

ISBN 9781609452865

1. 1970s 2. 1980s 3. Female friendship 4. Middle-aged women 5. Women authors 6. Independence in women 7. Childhood friends 8. Social change 9. Organized crime 10. Camorra 11. City life 12. Italy 13. Naples, Italy 14. Mainstream fiction 15. Translations -- Italian to English

Translation from the Italian of: Storia della bambina perduta

Originally published: Rome : E/O, 2014.

Follows the continuing story of the friendship between fiery Lina and bookish Elena, now grown with children and successful in their chosen careers, and both again living in Naples, the city of their birth.

"Although the eponymous child is of profound importance here, its the disappearance revealed at the series' onset and to which Ferrante returns, after navigating the 40-plus-year span covered in the story, that will compel readers forward, puzzling over it and anticipating resolution. As Elena ages, struggling to understand her relationship to her books success, she writes--and we read, a level removed--a story about story and its authorship. A friendship so reflective and yet so repellent, so truthfully plumbed, is a rare thing written." Booklist.

Ferrante, Elena

* **Those** who leave and those who stay / Elena Ferrante ; translated from the Italian by Ann Goldstein. Europa Editions, 2014, c2013. 400 p. Neapolitan novels

ISBN 9781609452339

1. Self-fulfillment in women 2. Female friendship 3. Creativity in women 4. Women authors 5. Women employees 6. Self-discovery in women 7. Single mothers 8. Childhood friends 9. Italy 10. Naples, Italy 11. Mainstream fiction 12. Translations -- Italian to English

Translation from the Italian of: Storia di chi fugge e di chi resta.

Originally published: Rome : E/O, 2013.

Continues the story of Lina and Elena as they push against boundaries in 1970s Italy, where Lina has left her husband and is working in a factory while taking care of her son and Elena has graduated college and published a novel.

"Ferrante continues to imbue this growing saga with great magic, treating the girls' years of marriage and motherhood with breathtaking honesty while envisaging the turbulence of political and social unrest in 1970s Italy." Booklist.

Ferraris, Zoe

Finding Nouf / Zoe Ferraris. Houghton Mifflin, 2008. 320 p. Katya Hijazi novels

ISBN 9780618873883

1. Sixteen-year-old girls 2. Gender role 3. Murder investigation 4. Teenage girl murder victims 5. Brothers and sisters 6. Engaged persons 7. Detectives 8. Women -- Saudi Arabia 9. Saudi Arabia 10. Middle East 11. Mysteries

LC 2007038411

Sequel : City of veils.

When sixteen-year-old Nouf goes missing and is found drowned in the desert outside Jeddah, Nayir--a desert guide hired by her prominent family to search for her--feels compelled to find out what really happened.

"Sixteen-year-old Nouf ash-Shrawi, daughter of a wealthy Saudi Arabian family, mysteriously disappears and is eventually found drowned in the desert. . . . Nouf's brother, Othman, asks his friend Nayir Sharqi, a local desert guide, to find out what happened to his sister. Nayir's investigation leads him into unknown territorynotably, the secret realm of women in a segregated Middle Eastern society. In an unusual partnership that challenges his traditional ideas, Nayir works on the case with Othman's fiancée, a laboratory technician in the medical examiner's office. Ferraris's debut novel gives a fascinating peek into the lives and minds of devout Muslim men and women while serving up an engrossing mystery." Library Journal.

Ferraris, Zoe

Kingdom of strangers : a novel / Zoe Ferraris. Little, Brown and Company, 2012. 304 p. Katya Hijazi novels

ISBN 9780316074247

1. Crimes against women -- Saudi Arabia 2. Serial murders -- Saudi Arabia 3. Murder investigation -- Saudi Arabia 4. Missing persons 5. Extramarital affairs 6. Muslims 7. Women detectives -- Saudi Arabia 8. Saudi Arabia 9. Middle East 10. Mysteries

LC 2011046158

Sequel to : City of veils .

Saudi lead inspector Ibrahim Zahrani discovers that a serial killer has been burying women's bodies in Jeddah for more than 10 years at the same time his mistress disappears and seeks assistance from Katya, one of the few women on the force.

Ferris, Joshua

To rise again at a decent hour : a novel / Joshua Ferris. Little, Brown and Company, 2014. 337 p.

ISBN 9780316033978

1. Dentists 2. Compulsive behavior in men 3. Identity (Psychology) 4. False personation 5. Online identity theft 6. Internet 7. Religious fanatics 8. Belief and doubt 9. Interpersonal relations 10. Psychological fiction 11. Literary fiction 12. Satirical fiction

Shortlisted for the Man Booker Prize, 2014.

After noticing his identity has been stolen and used to create various social media accounts, a man with a troubled past, Paul O'Rourke, begins to wonder if his virtual alter ego is actually a better version of himself.

"The protagonist's sharp inner dialogues are laugh-out-loud hilarious, combining New York nihilism with an Ivy League vocabulary." Booklist.

Ferris, Joshua

* The **unnamed** / Joshua Ferris. Little, Brown and Co., 2010. 320 p.

ISBN 9780316034012

1. Compulsive behavior 2. Husband and wife 3. Identity (Psychology) 4. Lawyers 5. Diseases 6. Family relationships 7. Domestic fiction

8. Mainstream fiction

LC 2009010264

Their wealthy lifestyle marred only by a two-time occurrence of a short-lived illness, Tim and Jane Farnsworth are devastated when the illness returns in ways that frighteningly alter Tim's behavior and test Jane's endurance.

"Audacious, risky and powerfully bleak, with the author's unflinching artistry its saving grace." Kirkus.

Fesperman, Dan, 1955-
Safe houses : a novel / Dan Fesperman. Alfred A. Knopf, 2018. 336 p.
ISBN 9780525520191
1. CIA 2. 1970s 3. Intelligence service 4. Conspiracies 5. Cold War 6. Children of murder victims 7. Mothers and daughters 8. Murder investigation 9. Secrets 10. Berlin, Germany 11. West Germany 12. Spy fiction 13. Thrillers and suspense

LC 2017058898

RUSA Reading List, 2019.

A CIA safe house inspector uncovers a nefarious secret at the heart of Agency operations in postwar Berlin, triggering a life on the run, her brutal murder and her daughter's search for answers.

Fforde, Jasper
* **Early** riser : a novel / Jasper Fforde. Viking Press, 2019, c2018. 402 p.
ISBN 9780670025039
1. Winter 2. Civil service workers 3. Sleep 4. Misfits (Persons) 5. Hibernation 6. Dreams 7. Death 8. Nightmares 9. Wales 10. Dystopian fiction

The best-selling author of the Nursery Crimes series imagines the reader as a first-winter employee with the misfit Winter Consuls, who protect the world's hibernating masses until an outbreak of viral nightmares starts triggering mysterious deaths.

"Readers familiar with Fforde's (The Woman Who Died a Lot, 2012) gleefully pun-heavy world building will relish this stand-alone novel, confident that everything will work out in the end for the underdog." Booklist.

Fforde, Jasper
The **Eyre** affair : a novel / Jasper Fforde. Viking, 2002. 374 p. Thursday Next novels
ISBN 9780670030644
1. 1980s 2. Fathers and daughters 3. Censorship 4. Time travel 5. Women detectives 6. Crimean War, 1853-1856 7. Literary historians 8. Characters and characteristics in literature 9. England 10. Wales 11. Fantasy mysteries 12. Metafiction

LC 2001043775

In a world where one can literally get lost in literature, Thursday Next, a Special Operative in literary detection, tries to stop the world's Third Most Wanted criminal from kidnapping characters, including Jane Eyre, from works of literature.

"This rambunctious caper could be taken as a warning about what might happen if society considered literature really important--like, say, energy futures or accounting." The New Yorker.

Fforde, Jasper
Lost in a good book : a Thursday Next novel / Jasper Fforde. Viking, 2003 416 p. Thursday Next novels
ISBN 0670031909
1. 1980s 2. Women detectives -- Great Britain 3. Multinational corporations 4. Time travel 5. Characters and characteristics in literature 6. Literary historians 7. Husband and wife 8. England 9.

Great Britain 10. Fantasy mysteries 11. Metafiction

LC 2002071304

In order to rescue the love of her life from the corrupt multinational Goliath, Thursday seeks out a believed-vanquished enemy from the pages of The Raven and finds unexpected assistance from Great Expectation's Miss Havisham.

"Time flies--and leaps and zigzags--while reading this wickedly funny and clever fantasy. Would-be wordsmiths and mystery fans will find the surreal genre-buster irresistible." Publishers Weekly.

Fforde, Jasper
Shades of grey : a novel / Jasper Fforde. Viking, 2009. 400 p. Chromatacia novels
ISBN 9780670019632
1. Color blindness 2. Dystopias 3. Social classes 4. Technology -- Social aspects 5. Post-apocalypse 6. Color 7. Men/women relations 8. Insurgency 9. Conspiracies 10. England 11. Fantasy fiction 12. Literary fiction

LC 2009030813

Color Control Agency employee and House of Red member Eddie Russet experiences discontent with his limited vision when he meets Gray Nightseer Jane, who suggests that their color-blind world was brought about by a disaster that nobody is allowed to acknowledge.

"The world is wildly but closely imagined, so the result is as internally coherent as it is unlikely. Distinctive wordplay abounds. All the fooling around is built on a good mystery, and Fforde telegraphs no punches. In short, Shades of Grey is everything that Fforde fans love, and distinctly different from what has come before." Denver Post.

Fielding, Helen, 1958-
Bridget Jones's diary : a novel / Helen Fielding. Viking, 1998, c1996. 271 p. Bridget Jones
ISBN 0670880728
1. Single women 2. Dieting for women 3. Dating (Social customs) 4. Female friendship 5. Single people 6. Self-improvement for women 7. Men/women relations 8. Office romance 9. Publishers and publishing 10. Love triangles 11. London, England 12. Chick lit 13. Diary novels

LC 9818687

Sequel: Bridget Jones : the edge of reason.
British Book Award for Book of the Year, 1998.
The daily chronicle of a 30-something single English woman who is convinced her life would be perfect if she could lose weight, stop smoking and develop "Inner Poise."

"Brimming with a deliciously irreverent sense of humor and a keen sense of women's deepest insecurities, Bridget Jones's Diary is a must-read." Booklist.

Fielding, Henry, 1707-1754
* The **history** of Tom Jones, a foundling / Henry Fielding ; edited with explanatory notes by Thomas Keymer and Alice Wakely with an introduction by Thomas Keymer. Penguin Books, 2005, c1749. xlvii, 975 p.
ISBN 9780140436228
1. Elopement 2. Interclass romance 3. Abandoned children 4. Illegitimacy 5. Social classes 6. Misadventures 7. Arranged marriage 8. Voyages and travels 9. Men/women relations 10. England -- Social life and customs -- 18th century 11. Picaresque fiction 12. Satirical fiction 13. Classics

Title of later film version: Tom Jones.
Originally published: London : A. Millar, 1749.
A foundling of mysterious parentage, Tom Jones is brought up by the benevolent and wealthy Squire Allworthy as his own son. Tom falls

in love with the beautiful and unattainable Sophia Western, a neighbor's daughter, whose marriage has already been arranged. When Tom's sexual misadventures around the countryside get him banished, he sets out to make his fortune and find his true identity. Against the vivid background of eighteenth-century London, Tom encounters passion, corruption, danger, and intrigue before finally claiming his fortune, legitimacy, and true love.

Fielding, Joy

All the wrong places : a novel / Joy Fielding. Ballantine Books, 2019 240 p.

ISBN 9780399181559

1. Murderers 2. Online dating 3. Crimes against women 4. Women -- Interpersonal relations 5. Dating (Social customs) 6. Men/women relations 7. Murder investigation 8. Serial murderers 9. Thrillers and suspense

LC 2018051132

Driven to desperation by divorce, boredom, infidelity and loss, four women turn to online dating for companionship, only to find themselves in the crosshairs of a tech-savvy killer.

Fielding, Joy

The **bad** daughter : a novel / Joy Fielding. Ballantine Books, 2018. 368 p.

ISBN 9780399181528

1. Family secrets 2. Home invasions 3. Homecomings 4. Women psychotherapists 5. Blended families 6. Family estates 7. Family relationships 8. Small towns 9. California 10. Thrillers and suspense

LC 2017051448

Estranged from her family because of her difficulties getting along with her stepmother, Robin returns home in the aftermath of a brutal home invasion, hoping to mend fences, only to uncover horrible family secrets that may have led to the attack.

Fields, Hilary

Last Chance Llama Ranch / Hilary Fields. Orbit, 2015. 350 p.

ISBN 9780316277426

1. Women journalists 2. Ranches 3. Cowboys 4. Former athletes 5. Llamas 6. Interpersonal attraction 7. Men/women relations 8. Romantic comedies

"From Olympic skier to llama farmer? Now that is a serious jump. When a close encounter with an eighty-foot spruce steals Merry's dreams of Olympic gold, the former ski champ finds herself falling into a career she never expected -- the life of a travel writer. Picturing glamorous trips to exotic places, Merry is speechless when her boss assigns her to the blog, "Don't Do What I Did," and sends her to, place of all places, a llama ranch. Soon she's eyeball-deep in alpacas, llamas, goats and more. But when Last Chance Llama Ranch starts to grow on her, Merry finds that ranch life, while still just as gross, might be just what she's been missing. You know what they say... When life gives you llamas."--, Provided by publisher.

Finch, Charles (Charles B.)

A **beautiful** blue death / Charles Finch. St. Martin's Minotaur, 2007. 320 p. Charles Lenox chronicles

ISBN 9780312359775

1. Scotland Yard 2. Victorian era (1837-1901) 3. 19th century 4. 1860s 5. Amateur detectives 6. Murder investigation 7. Murder 8. Deception 9. Butlers 10. Police 11. London, England -- Social life and customs -- 19th century 12. England -- Social life and customs -- 19th century 13. Historical mysteries 14. Victorian mysteries 15.

Mysteries

LC 2007011273

When Victorian gentleman Charles Lenox begins to investigate the apparent suicide of a friend's former servant, he suspects murder--but to find the killer, he must untangle a complex web of loyalties and animosities before it's too late.

Finch, Charles (Charles B.)

The **last** passenger / Charles Finch. Minotaur Books, 2020. 304 p. Charles Lenox chronicles

ISBN 9781250312204

1. 1850s 2. 19th century 3. Private investigators 4. Trains 5. Impostors 6. Murder investigation 7. Locomotive engineers 8. England 9. London, England 10. Historical mysteries

LC 2019049215

Finds Victorian detective Charles Lenox defying Scotland Yard and navigating the dual challenges of royal obstinance and class prejudice to investigate the murder of a first-class passenger at Paddington Station.

"Set 10 years before series debut A Beautiful Blue Death (2007), this tightly plotted mystery, winding through the back alleys of Whitechapel to the halls of Parliament itself, is rich in historical detail and quite enjoyable on its own merits but will be of particular interest to fans of the series, as it provides useful backstory to favorite characters." Booklist.

Finch, Charles (Charles B.)

The **September** Society / Charles Finch. St. Martin's Minotaur, 2008. 310 p. Charles Lenox chronicles

ISBN 9780312359782

1. Scotland Yard 2. Lincoln College (University of Oxford) 3. Victorian era (1837-1901) 4. 1860s 5. Amateur detectives 6. Missing persons investigation 7. College students 8. Murder 9. Secret societies 10. Cold cases (Criminal investigation) 11. London, England -- Social life and customs -- 19th century 12. England -- Social life and customs -- 19th century 13. Historical mysteries 14. Victorian mysteries 15. Mysteries

LC 2008003452

Amateur detective and Victorian gentleman Charles Lenox heads for his alma mater at Oxford to investigate the disappearance of a student and encounters a series of bizarre clues, including a card bearing the name The September Society.

"Finch, a superb hand at plotting, gives nothing away, and even the most astute reader will be guessing to the end." Library Journal.

Finch, Charles (Charles B.)

The **vanishing** man / Charles Finch. Minotaur Books, 2019. 320 p. Charles Lenox chronicles

ISBN 9781250311368

1. 1850s 2. 19th century 3. Private investigators 4. Aristocracy 5. Art thefts 6. Scandals 7. Rich families 8. Family secrets 9. Murder 10. Power (Social sciences) 11. Criminal investigation 12. London, England 13. England -- Social life and customs -- 19th century 14. Victorian mysteries 15. Historical mysteries

A second entry in a prequel trilogy to the best-selling series finds the theft of an antique painting sending a young Charles Lenox on a hunt for a criminal mastermind.

Finder, Joseph

Buried secrets / Joseph Finder. St. Martin's Press, 2011. 400 p. Nick Heller novels

ISBN 9780312379148

1. Kidnapping 2. Missing persons 3. Secrets 4. Criminal investigation 5. Greed 6. Billionaires 7. Kidnapping investigation 8. Premature burial 9. Hedge funds 10. Security consultants 11. Corporations

12. Investments 13. Former Special Forces members 14. Boston, Massachusetts 15. Financial thrillers

LC 2011004443

Hoping to set up his own spy operation in his Boston home town, Nick Heller is contacted by a desperate family friend to rescue his kidnapped daughter, whose terrifying incarceration in an underground crypt is being broadcast on the Internet.

"Finder's compulsively readable sequel to Vanished opens fast and never slows down. When 17-year-old Alexa Marcus, the spoiled daughter of Marshall Marcus, a wildly successful money manager, is kidnapped from a Boston club and buried alive in a coffin equipped with an air hose and a video camera (for Internet streaming, of course!), Marshall asks his old intelligence expert friend, Nick Heller, to find her. The search leads into an expanding world of buried secrets, from Marshall's gold-digging trophy wife, Belinda, and his crumbling investment empire to allegations of government funding for covert operations and the Russian mafia. . . . Self-effacing, wry, and ridiculously competent, Heller makes a reasonably engaging protagonist, but this thriller's real star is the suspenseful, expertly paced plot." Publishers Weekly.

Finder, Joseph

The **fixer** / Joseph Finder. Dutton/Penguin Random House, 2015. 416 p.

ISBN 9780525954613

1. Family secrets 2. Fathers and sons 3. Life change events 4. People who have had strokes -- Family relationships 5. Hiding-places (Secret chambers, etc) 6. Houses -- Maintenance and repair 7. Unemployment 8. Journalists 9. Criminals 10. Survival 11. Secrets 12. Murder 13. Massachusetts 14. Financial thrillers

LC 2015006982

Forced to move to the ramshackle home of his youth after a career setback, Rick Hoffman begins a laborious renovation only to make a discovery that threatens his life and challenges everything he thought he knew about his late father.

Finder, Joseph

Guilty minds / Joseph Finder. Penguin, 2016. 400 p. Nick Heller novels

ISBN 9780525954620

1. Security consultants 2. Intrigue 3. Conspiracies 4. Criminal investigation 5. Corruption 6. Judges 7. Former Special Forces members 8. Political thrillers 9. Thrillers and suspense

Summoned to investigate potentially explosive charges of corruption levied by a gossip website against the chief justice of the Supreme Court, private intelligence operative Nick Heller is given 48 hours to prove that the story is baseless.

Finder, Joseph

* **House** on fire : a novel / Joseph Finder. Dutton, 2020, c2019 384 p.

ISBN 9781101985847

1. Veterans 2. Drug industry and trade -- Corrupt practices 3. Opioid epidemic 4. Rich families 5. Whistle blowers 6. Friends' death 7. Private investigators 8. Addiction 9. Intrigue 10. Secrets 11. Thrillers and suspense

LC 2019039182

Originally published in Great Britain by Head of Zeus, 2019.

Eagerly accepting a job investigating whistleblower claims about the manufacturer of an opioid that contributed to an army buddy's death, Nick Heller uncovers dangerous secrets implicating a powerful family.

"This thriller is not only topical but beautifully driven by the intricacies of personal agendas, both obvious and hidden. Easily read as a stand-alone as well as part of the series, this is sure to captivate a new audience and bring them to the Joseph Finder backlist." Library Journal.

Finder, Joseph

* **Judgment** / Joseph Finder. Dutton, 2019. 384 p.

ISBN 9781101985816

1. Women judges 2. Strangers 3. One-night stands (Interpersonal relations) 4. Married women 5. Extramarital affairs 6. Errors 7. Promotions 8. Trials 9. Videos 10. Frameups 11. Conspiracies 12. Boston, Massachusetts 13. Chicago, Illinois 14. Legal thrillers 15. Thrillers and suspense

LC 2018026165

Sharing a one-night stand with a gentle stranger during a moment of weakness, a state superior court judge reencounters the man during a high-profile case and discovers that a conspiracy is threatening her family and federal court prospects.

Finder, Joseph

Suspicion / Joseph Finder. Dutton Adult, 2014. 384 p.

ISBN 9780525954606

1. Drug traffic 2. Single fathers 3. Options, alternatives, choices 4. Drug enforcement agents 5. Undercover operations 6. Father and teenager 7. Teenage girls 8. Deception 9. Rich men 10. Betrayal 11. Boston, Massachusetts 12. Financial thrillers

LC 2013049012

Unable to afford the private school his daughter adores, single father Danny Goodman reluctantly accepts a loan from a wealthy man only to be forced to choose between false drug charges and an undercover DEA assignment targeting his best friend.

Finder, Joseph

The **switch** : a novel / Joseph Finder. Dutton, 2017 384 p.

ISBN 9781101985786

1. United States. Congress. Senate 2. Intelligence service 3. Government cover-ups 4. National security 5. Politicians 6. Security classification (Government documents) 7. Laptop computers 8. Conspiracies 9. Assassins 10. Secrets 11. Errors 12. Boston, Massachusetts 13. Political thrillers 14. Thrillers and suspense

LC 2017006234

Picking up a politician's laptop by mistake, Michael Tanner discovers stolen files before finding himself targeted by an unscrupulous fixer at the same time the owners of the files hatch a deadly plot.

Finder, Joseph

Vanished / Joseph Finder. St. Martin's Press, 2009. 400 p. Nick Heller novels

ISBN 9780312379087

1. Security consultants 2. Missing persons 3. Brothers 4. Corporate culture 5. Former Special Forces members 6. International businesses 7. Secrets 8. Washington, D.C. 9. Financial thrillers

LC 2009013029

After an assault leaves his estranged brother nowhere to be found and his sister-in-law in a coma, security investigator and ex-intelligence agent Nick Heller is forced to seek help even from his despised convict father as Nick contends with one of the most powerful and secretive corporations in the world, an endeavor which may get him and everyone he's trying to protect killed.

"The first title in a new series featuring Nick Heller, a high-powered international investigator and corporate security consultant. Through a brilliant piece of detection, Heller has just tracked down 12 cargo containers packed with Library Journal.

Findley, Timothy

The **piano** man's daughter / Timothy Findley. Crown Publishers, 1995. 461 p.

ISBN 0517703076

1. Women with mental illnesses 2. Mothers and sons 3. Fathers 4. Music 5. Families 6. Ontario 7. Canada 8. Literary fiction 9. Historical fiction 10. Psychological fiction

Shortlisted for the Giller Prize, 1995

After Lily Kilworth dies in a 1939 asylum fire, her illegitimate son tries to piece together her life and, in so doing, creates a history of Canadian life from the 1890s to the 1930s.

"Brilliantly told, powerfully affecting." Booklist.

Fine, Julia

What should be wild / Julia Fine. Harper, 2018. 350 p.

ISBN 9780062684134

1. Family curses 2. Family estates 3. Social isolation 4. Superhuman abilities 5. Forests 6. Teenage girls -- Sexuality 7. Growing up 8. Missing men 9. Ancestors 10. Women 11. Coming-of-age stories 12. Gothic fiction

Born with the power to kill or restore life at a touch, a young woman endures a childhood of objectification and a complete inability to experience physical contact before she ventures into the woods at the edge of her village to remove a curse that has plagued the women in her family for centuries.

Finlay, Mick

The **murder** pit / Mick Finlay. Harlequin MIRA, 2019, c2018 336 p. Arrowood novels (Mick Finlay)

ISBN 9780778369301

1. Victorian era (1837-1901) 2. 1890s 3. Private investigators 4. Missing women 5. Missing persons investigation 6. Working class 7. Poverty 8. Corruption 9. Murder 10. Murder investigation 11. London, England 12. Victorian mysteries 13. Hardboiled fiction 14. Historical mysteries

Receiving less recognition and income than his contemporary, Sherlock Holmes, private detective William Arrowood investigates a simple missing person's case that turns into a complicated murder investigation.

"This is a welcome grittier take on a familiar genre trope." Publishers Weekly.

Finn, A. J.

* The **woman** in the window / A. J. Finn. William Morrow & Co., 2018. 368 p.

ISBN 9780062678416

1. Women recluses 2. Neighbors 3. Surveillance 4. Obsession 5. Agoraphobia 6. Women witnesses 7. Women psychologists 8. Secrets 9. New York City 10. Psychological suspense

Librarians' Choice (Australia), 2017.

An agoraphobic recluse languishes in her New York City home, drinking wine and spying on her neighbors, before witnessing a terrible crime through her window that exposes her secrets and raises questions about her perceptions of reality.

"An astounding debut from a truly talented writer, perfect for fans in search of more like Gone Girl and The Girl on the Train." Booklist.

Fisher, Kerry

The **silent** wife / Kerry Fisher. Forever, 2018. 352 p.

ISBN 9781538714652

1. Blended families 2. Married women 3. Family secrets 4. Brothers 5. Second wives 6. Secrecy 7. Mothers 8. Mothers-in-law 9. Family relationships 10. Women's lives and relationships

A heart-wrenching, emotionally gripping read for fans of Liane Moriarty and Diane Chamberlain.

Fisher, Sharon Lynn

The **absinthe** earl / Sharon Lynn Fisher. Blackstone Publishing, 2019. 288 p.

ISBN 9781982684419

1. Women anthropologists 2. Earls and countesses 3. Interpersonal attraction 4. Absinthe 5. Fairies 6. Historic buildings 7. Winter solstice 8. Secrets 9. Women rulers 10. Men/women relations 11. Ireland 12. Paranormal romances

"Although the quick shifts between Ada and Edward's perspectives are distracting and disruptive, persevering readers will still enjoy Fisher's inventive premise and the heady romance between two independent and well-matched protagonists." Publishers weekly.

Fisher, Tarryn

* The **wives** / Tarryn Fisher. Graydon House, 2019. 320 p.

ISBN 9781525805127

1. Polygamy 2. Married men 3. Partner abuse 4. Married women 5. Nurses 6. Businesspeople 7. False personation 8. Washington (State) 9. Seattle, Washington 10. Psychological suspense

A woman in a voluntarily bigamous marriage befriends one of her husband's other wives by chance, only to discover that the gentle husband she knows may be abusing his other families.

"Fisher smoothly inserts moments of self-doubt, longing, paranoia, and triumph into her unsettling narrative as she draws the reader into Thursday s conflicted and increasingly complicated life." Publishers Weekly.

Fitch, Janet, 1955-

Paint it black : a novel / Janet Fitch. Little, Brown, 2006. 400 p.

ISBN 0316182745

1. 1980s 2. Young women 3. Art students 4. First loves 5. Punk rock music 6. Suicide -- Los Angeles, California 7. Grief in women 8. Death -- Psychological aspects 9. Only child 10. Mothers and sons -- Psychological aspects 11. Los Angeles, California 12. Psychological fiction

LC 2006010211

Following the suicide of her lover, art student Michael Faraday, Josie Tyrell, an art model and teenage runaway, struggles to come to terms with his death and to deal with his mother, Meredith, who holds her responsible for the tragedy.

"Fitch has given us a courageous and interesting young woman who handles the bad cards she has been dealt with grace and resolve. No one, not even Cinderella, knows better than Josie Tyrell that life isn't fairand no one, despite some very long odds, seems more likely to transcend the role of victim and succeed with or without her fairy-tale prince." Washington Post Book World.

Fitch, Janet, 1955-

White oleander : a novel / Janet Fitch. Little, Brown, 1999. 390 p.

ISBN 0316569321

1. Women poets 2. Children of prisoners 3. Identity (Psychology) 4. Women murderers 5. Single mothers 6. Mothers and daughters 7. Foster children 8. Women prisoners 9. California 10. Los Angeles, California 11. Psychological fiction 12. Literary fiction

LC 9850371

At the age of 12, Astrid has her world blown away when her mother is sentenced to life in prison for murdering her lover. Sharpened by harsh foster home environments, Astrid remakes herself as a survivor, and ultimately, an artist.

"This sensitive exploration of the mother daughter terrain . . . offers a convincing look at what Adrienne Rich has called 'this womanly splitting of self,' in a poignant, virtuosic, utterly captivating narrative." Publishers Weekly.

Fitten, Marc, 1974-
Elza's kitchen : a novel / Marc Fitten. Bloomsbury USA, 2012. 224 p.

ISBN 9781608197699

1. Divorced women 2. Self-fulfillment in women 3. Unhappiness in women 4. Women restaurateurs 5. Food columnists 6. Interpersonal conflict 7. Second chances 8. Change (Psychology) 9. Cooks 10. Hungary 11. Mainstream fiction

LC 2011039009

Divorcée and restauranteur Elza falls into a rut, having become irritated serving the same dishes and customers, and devises a challenge for herself that entails wooing an internationally renowned food critic to her humble restaurant.

"Fitten, having lived in Hungary for several years, paints a vivid and charming picture of life in the country. While Elzas story is an easy and engaging read, Fitten also manages to subtly track the progress of a nation and its people--specifically its women (they're the only ones given proper names)--as they pursue a better life." Publishers Weekly.

FitzGerald, Gerry, 1949-
Redemption Mountain : a novel / Gerry FitzGerald. Henry Holt and Co., 2013. 448 p.

ISBN 9780805094893

1. Love triangles 2. Businesspeople 3. Small town life -- West Virginia 4. Homemakers 5. Mineral industry and trade 6. Mothers and sons 7. Mountain life 8. Cultural differences 9. Family farms 10. Men/women relations 11. Resistance to land development 12. West Virginia 13. Love stories

LC 2012034073

Hoping for a chance at meaningful work away from his status-obsessed wife, New York executive Charlie visits West Virginia to oversee a mining project and finds a friendship with Natty, who longs to escape her own unfulfilling existence.

Fitzgerald, F. Scott (Francis Scott), 1896-1940
* The **beautiful** and damned / F. Scott Fitzgerald. Scribner, 1922. 449 p.

ISBN 9781847497390

1. Inheritance and succession 2. Married people 3. Rich people -- United States 4. Socialites 5. Alcoholics 6. Young men 7. Men/women relations 8. New York City 9. Psychological fiction 10. Satirical fiction 11. Modern classics

LC 22004437

Set in the heady Jazz Age of New York, "The beautiful and damned" chronicles the relationship between Anthony Patch, a Harvard-educated aspiring aesthete, and his beautiful trophy wife, Gloria, as they wait to inherit his grandfather's fortune. Anticipating easy millions, they embrace the glittering, hedonistic lifestyle of the pretentious nouveaux riches, but find that they are living a dream that is all too fleeting.

Fitzgerald, F. Scott (Francis Scott), 1896-1940
* The **last** tycoon : an unfinished novel / F. Scott Fitzgerald Scribner, 1958, c1941 163 p., 21 cm.

ISBN 0684153114

1. 1930s 2. Film industry and trade executives 3. Men/women relations 4. American dream 5. Workaholism 6. Failure (Psychology)

7. Film industry and trade -- Hollywood, California 8. Hollywood, California 9. Love stories 10. Modern classics

LC 58014792

The Last Tycoon inspired the film The Last Tycoon in 1976.

Features Life & Times - a fascinating insight into the author, their work and the time of publication - and glossary of classic literature.

Original ed. published in 1941 by Scribner, New York.

In this tragic tale, unfinished at the time of his death, F. Scott Fitzgerald exposes the corruption, sex and towering ambition at the dark heart of 1930s Hollywood.

Fitzgerald, F. Scott (Francis Scott), 1896-1940
Novels and stories, 1920-1922 / F. Scott Fitzgerald. Library of America, 2000. 1082 p.

ISBN 9781883011840

1. Princeton University 2. 1920s 3. College students -- New Jersey 4. Rich people -- United States 5. Manners and customs 6. New Jersey 7. United States -- Social life and customs -- 1919-1933 8. Short stories 9. Modern classics

LC 00024287

A compilation of the novelist's work, including This Side of Paradise, The Beautiful and Damned and his short stories reflects American society during the 1920s and portrays the aristocratic class of the era.

Fitzgerald, F. Scott (Francis Scott), 1896-1940
* The **short** stories of F. Scott Fitzgerald : a new collection / edited and with a preface by Matthew J. Bruccoli. Scribner, 1989. xix, 775 p.

ISBN 9780684191607

1. Manners and customs 2. United States -- Social life and customs -- 20th century 3. Short stories 4. Modern classics

LC 89006351

43 short stories.

Gathers more than forty Fitzgerald stories and provides brief background information on each piece.

Fitzgerald, F. Scott (Francis Scott), 1896-1940
Six tales of the jazz age and other stories / F. Scott Fitzgerald. Scribner, 1960. 192 p.

ISBN 9780684717623

1. 1920s 2. Manners and customs 3. United States -- Social life and customs -- 20th century 4. Short stories 5. Modern classics

LC 60006410

Faced with exposure, a young woman, who has been leading conflicting lives separately and secretly, begins to plan her own death.

Fitzgerald, F. Scott (Francis Scott), 1896-1940
* **This** side of paradise / F. Scott Fitzgerald. Scribner, 1970, c1920. 282 p.

ISBN 9780684101644

1. Princeton University 2. Debutantes 3. Interclass romance 4. Social status 5. Young men 6. Classism 7. Rich people -- New Jersey 8. World War I veterans 9. College students -- New Jersey 10. Rejection (Psychology) in men 11. Coming-of-age stories 12. Literary fiction 13. Modern classics

A young man searches for himself in the American upper-class society of the pre- and post-World War I era.

Fitzgerald, Penelope

The **blue** flower / Penelope Fitzgerald. Houghton Mifflin, 1997, c1995 225 p.

ISBN 0395859972

1. Novalis, 1772-1801 2. College students 3. Courtship 4. Poets 5. Girls and men 6. Romantic love 7. Obsession 8. Teenage girls 9. Family relationships 10. Men/women relations 11. Germany -- History -- 1740-1806 12. Historical fiction 13. Literary fiction

LC 9652911

"A Mariner original."

Illustrated with black-and-white photos.

Originally published: London : Flamingo, 1995.

National Book Critics Circle Award for Fiction, 1997.

Presents a fictionalized account of the relationship between the eighteenth-century German poet known as Novalis and his true love, Sophie

Fitzgerald, Penelope

The **means** of escape : stories / Penelope Fitzgerald. Houghton Mifflin, 2000. 117 p.

ISBN 9780618079940

1. Social classes 2. Interpersonal relations 3. Short stories 4. Literary fiction

LC 0038914

A collection of stories skips across the globe from England to New Zealand between the seventeenth century and the modern day, exploring the shifting fortunes of class and wealth.

"Strange, whimsical, sometimes gothic or bizarre, these tales demonstrate Fitzgerald's cool and civilized wit and the merciless eye she casts on worldly pretensions." Publishers Weekly.

Fitzpatrick, Lydia, 1982-

Lights all night long : a novel / Lydia Fitzpatrick. Penguin Press, 2019. 352 p.

ISBN 9780525558736

1. Exchange students 2. Brothers 3. Culture shock 4. Russians in the United States 5. Murder suspects 6. Addiction 7. Friendship 8. Investigations 9. Teenagers 10. Secrets 11. Guilt 12. Louisiana 13. Russia 14. Coming-of-age stories

LC 2018034986

With the help of his American host family's daughter, Sadie, who has secrets of her own, Russian exchange student Ilya embarks on a mission to prove his brother Vladimir's innocence in the murders of three girls back in Russia.

Flagg, Fannie

* **Fried** green tomatoes at the Whistle Stop Cafe / Fannie Flagg. Random House, 1987. 403 p.

ISBN 039456152X

1. 1930s 2. 1980s 3. Reminiscing in old age 4. Female friendship 5. Self-discovery in women 6. Women -- Alabama 7. Lesbians 8. Race relations 9. Restaurants -- Alabama 10. Men/women relations 11. Murder 12. Abusive men 13. Violence in men 14. Family secrets 15. Senior women 16. Loneliness in women 17. Alabama 18. Humorous stories 19. Women's lives and relationships 20. Parallel narratives 21. Southern fiction

LC 87012813

Includes recipes.

Book made into movie called Fried green tomatoes.

Mrs. Threadgoode's tale of two high-spirited women of the 1930s, Idgie and Ruth, helps Evelyn, a 1980s woman in a sad slump of middle age, to begin to rejuvenate her own life.

"This novel is set in a rural hamlet outside of Birmingham, Alabama. Bulletins from a gossipy town newsletter produced in the 1940s by Dot Weems are interspersed with the recollections of Mrs. Cleo (Vinnie) Throughgoode uttered (40 years later) in a nursing home to a depressed, menopausal visitor, Evelyn Couch (whose life is rejuvenated by these Sunday afternoon chats). Flagg also supplies basic narrative passages illuminating the news shared by Dot and Vinnie. The pace of the novel is as swift as the life of the small town is slowat least it seems slow until Vinnie drops hints of a murder and of riotous pranks played upon the local minister. The story is carefully plotted, with the moods and people of pre- and post-World War II Alabama splendidly evoked." Booklist.

Flagg, Fannie

Standing in the rainbow : a novel / Fannie Flagg. Random House, 2002. 464 p.

ISBN 0679426159

1. 1940s 2. Women radio broadcasters 3. Pharmacists 4. Gospel singers 5. Mothers and sons 6. People who are blind 7. Musicians 8. Sales personnel 9. Boys' fantasies 10. Family relationships 11. Small town life -- Missouri 12. Missouri 13. Humorous stories 14. Southern fiction 15. Gentle reads

LC 2002021977

Sequel to: Welcome to the world, Baby Girl!.

As the story begins, it is 1945, the war is over, the American economy is booming, and there is no better place in the world than Elmwood Springs, Missouri. Ten-year-old Bobby Smith's father is the town pharmacist and his mother is a local radio personality. Over the next several decades, the plot expands to include numerous beguiling characters who interact with the Smith family--among them, the Oatman Family Southern Gospel Singers.

"Beneath the sentImentality, there's a real celebration of life here, an affirmation that success and happiness are the results of simple kindness gratituder and courage." Christian Science Monitor.

Flanagan, Richard, 1961-

Gould's book of fish : a novel in twelve fish / Richard Flanagan. Grove Press, 2001. 404 p.

ISBN 9780802117113

1. Gould, William Buelow, 1803-1853 2. Colonial Australia (1788-1901) 3. Marine animals in art 4. Prisoners -- Australia 5. Penal colonies -- Australia 6. Fishes in art 7. Prisoners -- Australia 8. Painters -- Australia 9. Prisoners' art 10. Australia -- History -- 19th century 11. Australia -- Social conditions -- 19th century 12. Historical fiction 13. Literary fiction

LC 2001055747

Originally published: Sydney, N.S.W.: Picador, 2001.

Australian Literature Society Gold Medal, 2002.

Shortlisted for the Miles Franklin Literary Award, 2002

In the early nineteenth century, forger and thief William Buelow Gould lands in prison in Australia, where the prison doctor utilizes his painting talents to create an illustrated taxonomy of the country's exotic sea creatures.

"This remarkable novel is a meditation on colonialism--indeed, on history itself--couched in the story of an English guttersnipe." The New Yorker.

Flanagan, Richard, 1961-

* The **narrow** road to the deep north / Richard Flanagan. Knopf, 2014, c2013. 467 p.

ISBN 9780385352857

1. Burma-Siam Railroad. 2. 1940s 3. Lovers 4. Forced labor 5. World War II -- Prisoners and prisons, Japanese 6. Violence 7. Guilt in men 8. Prisoners of war, Australian 9. Loss (Psychology) 10. Men/women relations 11. Survival (in concentration camps, prisons, etc) 12. Survivor guilt 13. Thailand -- History -- 20th century 14.

Australia -- History -- 20th century 15. Australian 16. Literary fiction 17. Love stories 18. Historical fiction

Originally published: North Sydney, N.S.W.: Knopf, 2013.

ALA Notable Book, 2015.

Man Booker Prize, 2014.

Tasmania Book Prizes, Margaret Scott Prize, 2015.

Prime Minister's Literary Awards: Fiction, 2014.

Queensland Literary Awards, Fiction Book Award, 2014.

Western Australian Premier's Book Awards, Fiction category, 2014.

Western Australian Premier's Book Awards, Premier's Prize, 2014.

Shortlisted for the Miles Franklin Literary Award, 2014

Shortlisted for the International Dublin Literary Award, 2015

Haunted by the death of his wife while attending brutally sick and injured soldiers at a World War II Japanese POW camp, surgeon Dorrigo Evans receives a letter that irrevocably shapes the subsequent decades of his life in Australia.

"A supple meditation on memory, trauma, and empathy that is also a sublime war novel." Publishers Weekly.

Flanagan, Richard, 1961-

The **unknown** terrorist / Richard Flanagan. Grove, 2007, c2006. 336 p.

ISBN 9780802118516

1. Terrorism 2. Hysteria (Social psychology) 3. Stripteasers 4. Mass media -- Social aspects 5. Malicious accusation 6. Young women -- Sydney, New South Wales 7. Women fugitives 8. Television journalists 9. Terrorists 10. Broadcast journalists 11. Sydney, New South Wales 12. Australia 13. Political fiction

Originally published: Sydney : Picador, 2006.

What would you do if you turned on the television and saw you were the most wanted terrorist in the country? After spending a night with an attractive stranger, Gina Davies becomes a prime suspect in an attempted terrorist attack. When police find three unexploded bombs at a stadium, Gina goes on the run and witnesses every truth of her life turned into a betrayal. A devastating picture of a world where the cease-less drumbeat of terror alerts, news breaks, and fear of the unknown push one woman ever closer to breaking point.

"A page-turning thriller worthy of John le Carre, with a plot so cred-ible a reader might feel it's nonfiction, except for a few too many coin-cidences. But even those can't dampen the chilling effect of the story, written in a fresh, exhilarating prose style in which the author makes each sentence a small work of art." Seattle Times.

Flanagan, Thomas, 1923-2002

The **tenants** of time E. P. Dutton, 1988. 824p. Irish trilogy
ISBN 0525246061

1. 19th century 2. Irish War of Independence, 1919-1921 3. Men -- Ireland 4. Nationalism -- Ireland 5. Irish resistance and revolts 6. Ireland -- History -- 19th century 7. Historical fiction 8. Literary fiction

LC 87013632

"This novel is enormously long and unfalteringly rich in its delinea-tion of the sometimes thorny connection between the public associations and private needs and loyalties of people who live energetically, and even recklessly, through times of political turbulence." Commonwealth.

Flanagan, Thomas, 1923-2002

The **year** of the French : a novel / Thomas Flanagan. New York Review Books, 2004, c1979. xi, 516 p. Irish trilogy
ISBN 9781590171080

1. Catholic Church Ireland History 18th century 2. 18th century 3. Soldiers -- France -- History -- 18th century 4. Revolutions 5. Insurgency 6. Military occupation 7. Protestantism -- Ireland

-- History -- 18th century 8. Soldiers -- Ireland -- History -- 18th century 9. Ireland -- History -- Rebellion of 1798 10. Ireland -- History -- French invasion, 1798 11. Historical fiction 12. Literary fiction

Originally published: New York : Holt, Rinehart, and Winston, 1979.

National Book Critics Circle Award for Fiction, 1979.

"The author writes well, taking care to approximate . . . the spoken and written language of the time. The result is, I'm convinced, not only a serious book, free of the irony and satire that informs so many of the more literary historical fictions written today, but a distinguished one as well." Newsweek.

Flanery, Patrick, 1975-

Absolution : a novel / Patrick Flanery. Riverhead Books, 2012. 388 p.

ISBN 9781594488177

1. Women authors 2. Apartheid 3. Forgiveness 4. Biographers 5. Truth 6. Reconciliation 7. Anti-apartheid activists 8. Missing persons 9. Mothers and daughters 10. Loyalty 11. Betrayal 12. South Africa 13. Cape Town, South Africa 14. Literary fiction

Shortlisted for the International IMPAC Dublin Literary Award, 2014

In modern-day South Africa, Clare Walde tells the story of her sister's death and disappearance of her daughter during apartheid 20 years earlier.

Flaubert, Gustave, 1821-1880

* **Madame** Bovary : patterns of provincial life / Gustave Flaubert ; translated from the French by Francis Steegmuller. Alfred A. Knopf, 1993, c1857. xxxviii, 330 p.

ISBN 9780679420316

1. Married women -- France 2. Physicians' spouses -- France 3. Boredom in women 4. Extramarital affairs 5. Married people -- France 6. Husband and wife 7. Marriage 8. Middle class women 9. Women's role 10. Expectation (Psychology) 11. France 12. Domestic fiction 13. Translations -- French to English 14. Classics

Originally published in book form: Paris : Michel Levy Freres, 1857.

The classic tale of a woman who craves passion and intima-cy, but finds only greed, betrayal, and heartbreak, as she stumbles towards suicide.

Flaubert, Gustave, 1821-1880

Madame Bovary : provincial ways / Gustave Flaubert ; a new translation by Lydia Davis Viking Press, 2010. 342 p.

ISBN 9780670022076

1. Married women -- France 2. Physicians' spouses -- France 3. Boredom in women 4. Extramarital affairs 5. Married people -- France 6. Husband and wife 7. Marriage 8. Middle class women 9. Women's role 10. Expectation (Psychology) 11. France 12. Domestic fiction 13. Translations -- French to English 14. Classics

A new translation of Flaubert's classic tale, in which the title char-acter turns to spending and a series of affairs to combat the boredom of married life and, heartbroken and crippled by debts, takes drastic action that results in tragedy.

"The power of Madame Bovary stems from Flaubert's determina-tion to render each object of his scrutiny exactly as it looks, or sounds or smells or feels or tastes. . . . Given the pressure Flaubert applied to each sentence, there is no greater test of a translator's art than Madame Bovary. Faithful to the style of the original, but not to the point of slav-ishness, Davis's effort is transparent the reader never senses her pres-ence. For Madame Bovary, hers is the level of mastery required." New York Times Book Review.

Flaubert, Gustave, 1821-1880

* **Sentimental** education / Gustave Flaubert ; translated with an introduction by Robert Baldick. Penguin Books, 1964, c1869 429 p.

ISBN 0140441417

1. Flaubert, Gustave, 1821-1880 Criticism and interpretation 2. 19th century 3. Disillusionment in men 4. Alienation in men 5. Idealism 6. Young men 7. Married women 8. France -- History -- February Revolution, 1848 9. Paris, France -- Social life and customs -- 19th century 10. Translations -- French to English 11. Classics

Originally published in French as L'education sentimentale: 1869.

Fleischmann, Raymond

How quickly she disappears / Raymond Fleischmann. Berkley, 2020. 320 p.

ISBN 9781984805171

1. 1940s 2. Second World War era (1939-1945) 3. Twin sisters 4. Missing women 5. Violent crimes 6. Crimes against women 7. Strangers 8. German Americans 9. Murderers 10. Prisoners 11. Secrets 12. Married women 13. Small towns 14. Manipulation (Social sciences) 15. Alaska 16. Historical thrillers

LC 2019019798

A woman whose twin disappeared 30 years earlier is approached in her small Alaskan town by a dangerous man claiming to know what happened to her sister, but requesting from her three specific gifts in exchange for the information.

"As the narrative toggles between the present of 1941-42 and the past, shortly before Jacqueline disappeared, Elizabeth is forced to make dreadful choices, leading to a pulse-pounding climax. Fleischmann proves to be an author to watch on the literary-thriller scene." Booklist.

Fleming, Ian, 1908-1964

* **Casino** royale : a James Bond novel / Ian Fleming. Penguin Books, 2002. 181 p. James Bond series

ISBN 014200202X

1. Secret service -- Great Britain 2. Spies -- Great Britain 3. Gambling -- France 4. International intrigue 5. Spies -- Russia 6. Intelligence service -- Great Britain 7. British in France 8. Casinos -- France 9. Baccarat 10. Assassins 11. Bond, James (Fictional character) 12. France 13. Spy fiction 14. Adventure stories

LC 2002024602

In his first mission, James Bond (Agent 007) must neutralize a Russian agent known as "Le Chiffre" by ruining him at the baccarat table, thus forcing his "retirement." However, a beautiful female agent leads him to disaster--and an unexpected savior.

Fleming, Ian, 1908-1964

Doctor No / Ian Fleming. Macmillan, 1958. 256 p. James Bond series

ISBN 9789997512338

1. Spies -- Great Britain 2. Missing persons 3. Sadists 4. Murder 5. Intelligence service -- Great Britain 6. Guano 7. Bond, James (Fictional character) 8. Secret service -- Great Britain 9. British in Jamaica 10. International intrigue 11. Jamaica 12. Spy fiction 13. Adventure stories

Hidden on a tropical island paradise is the evil empire of Dr. No. Dr. No's obsession is power. His only gifts are strictly pain-shaped. He will be a worthy adversary for James Bond.

Fleming, Ian, 1908-1964

From Russia with love / Ian Fleming. J. Cape, 1972. 253 p. James Bond series

ISBN 9789997407191

1. Spies -- Great Britain 2. Betrayal 3. Encoding machines 4. Intelligence officers 5. Bond, James (Fictional character) 6. Intelligence service -- Great Britain 7. British in Europe 8. International intrigue 9. Women -- Soviet Union 10. Women spies -- Soviet Union 11. Men/women relations 12. Europe 13. Istanbul, Turkey 14. Soviet Union 15. Spy fiction 16. Adventure stories

First published: [London]: Jonathan Cape, 1957.

The light nudge at his ankle wakes Bond. He doesn't move. His senses come to life like an animal's. What has woken him? The spectral eye of the nightlight casts its deep velvet sheen over the little room. No sound comes from the upper bunk. By the window, Captain Nash sits in his place, his book open on his lap, a flicker of moonlight from the edge of the blind showing white on the double page.

Fleming, Ian, 1908-1964

* **Goldfinger** / Ian Fleming. Charter Books, 1987, c1959. 262 p. James Bond series

ISBN 9780441298068

1. Gold thefts 2. Robbery 3. Spies -- Great Britain 4. Women murder victims 5. Bond, James (Fictional character) 6. International intrigue 7. Canasta (Game) 8. Intelligence service -- Great Britain 9. Secret service -- Great Britain 10. Gold smuggling 11. Kentucky 12. Spy fiction 13. Adventure stories

Originally published: London : Cape, 1959.

"A friendly game of two-handed canasta that turns out thoroughly crooked. And a beautiful golden girl who ends up thoroughly dead ... In Bond's first encounter with the world's cleverest, cruellest criminal, useful lessons are learned. Soon the game will change and the stakes will rise ... to fifteen billion dollars' worth of US government bullion. But 007 knows that Auric Goldfinger's rules remain brutally simple - Heads I win, tails you die."

Fleming, Ian, 1908-1964

The **man** with the golden gun / Ian Fleming. New American Library, 1965. 235 p. James Bond series

ISBN 9780859974400

1. Spies -- Great Britain 2. Assassins 3. Undercover operations 4. Assassins 5. Secret service -- Great Britain 6. Bond, James (Fictional character) 7. Intelligence service -- Great Britain 8. International intrigue 9. Jamaica 10. Spy fiction 11. Adventure stories

Pitted against the sophisticated and deadly villain Scaramanga and his arch rival Hi Fat, Bond is assigned to recover a small piece of equipment which can be utilized to harness the sun's energy.

Fleming, Ian, 1908-1964

On Her Majesty's secret service / Ian Fleming. New American Library, 1963. 190 p. James Bond series

ISBN 9780451154323

1. Spies -- Great Britain 2. Mafia 3. Undercover operations 4. Conspiracies 5. Chases 6. Men/women relations 7. International intrigue 8. Bond, James (Fictional character) 9. Intelligence service -- Great Britain 10. Spy fiction 11. Adventure stories

In this tale, Secret Agent James Bond finds himself once again against the SPECTRE archfiend, Blofeld, and his plot to destroy the world. Bond also finds himself falling for Tracy, the daughter of Marc-Ange Draco, head of the Corsican mafia.

Fleming, Ian, 1908-1964

You only live twice / Ian Fleming. J. Cape, 1964. 255 p.
James Bond series
ISBN 9780685116319
1. Codes (Communication) 2. Assassination 3. Recluses 4. Spies -- Great Britain 5. Intelligence service -- Great Britain 6. Grief in men 7. Men with depression 8. Bond, James (Fictional character) 9. International intrigue 10. Japan 11. Spy fiction 12. Adventure stories
After the death of his wife, Bond leaves for Japan to accomplish an impossible mission far removed from his usual duties.
"Bond, near-prostrate from his bride's death, is given a Japanese assignment to snap him out of his torpor. . . . [The story] involves Bond's making up as a Japanese and venturing into the den of a foreign 'death collector,' a madman who has set up a poisonous garden complete with noxious plants, volcanic geysers, snakes, and, in a lake, piranha fish. Very grisly and chilling. The ending is an epitome of horror." Publishers Weekly.

Flight or fright / edited by Stephen King and Bev Vincent. Cemetery Dance Pubns, 2018 304 p.
ISBN 9781587676796
1. Flight 2. Air travel 3. Airplanes 4. Fear of flying 5. Flights 6. Horror 7. Short stories 8. Anthologies
Best-selling author Stephen King presents an anthology about all the things that can go horribly wrong during air travel, with story contributions from Richard Matheson, Ray Bradbury, Roald Dahl, Dan Simmons and King himself.
"This entertaining anthology of horror, mystery, and literary tales about aircraft (most reprinted) will have the reader thinking twice about flying." Publishers Weekly.

Flint, Emma

* **Little** deaths : a novel / Emma Flint. Hachette Books, 2017. 304 p.
ISBN 9780316272476
1. 1960s 2. Single mothers 3. Child murder victims 4. Public opinion 5. Malicious accusation 6. Journalists 7. Detectives 8. Mothers of murder victims 9. Working-class 10. Bad mother (Concept) 11. Casual sex 12. Cocktail servers 13. Women prisoners 14. New York City -- Social life and customs -- 20th century 15. Queens, New York City 16. Literary fiction 17. Psychological suspense
LC 2016037331
Librarians' Choice (Australia), 2017
Longlisted for The Baileys Women's Prize for Fiction, 2017.
A tale set in 1960s New York and inspired by true events follows the investigation of a cocktail waitress whose two young children have been brutally murdered and a rookie tabloid reporter who would uncover the truth.
"This accomplished debut novel will intrigue fans of both true crime and noir fiction. Flint, a technical writer in London, is a welcome addition to the world of literary crime fiction." Library Journal.

Flores, Fernando A., 1982-

Tears of the trufflepig / Fernando A. Flores. Farrar, Straus and Giroux, MCD x FSG Originals, 2019. 336 p.
ISBN 9780374538330
1. Mexican Americans 2. Widowers 3. Criminals 4. Cartels 5. Conspiracies 6. Smuggling 7. Grief in men 8. Extinct animals 9. Imaginary creatures 10. Near future 11. Mexican-American Border Region 12. Texas 13. Mexico 14. Magical realism
LC 2018044001
"A surreal debut novel set on the Texas-Mexico border, blending magical realism, sci-fi, and political parable to tell the story of an everyday man's tumble into a bizarre and sinister criminal underworld"--, Provided by publisher.

Florio, Gwen, 1955-

Silent hearts / Gwen Florio. Atria Books, 2018. 336 p.
ISBN 9781501181924
1. 2000s (Decade) 2. Women interpreters 3. Americans in Afghanistan 4. Female friendship 5. Humanitarian assistance 6. Cultural differences 7. Non-governmental organizations 8. Arranged marriage 9. Husband and wife 10. War 11. Military occupation 12. Kabul, Afghanistan 13. Afghanistan 14. Literary fiction 15. Political fiction
LC 2017057630
An American aid worker and her local interpreter forge an unexpected friendship in spite of disparate life experiences and the increasing violence that surrounds them in 2001 Kabul. By the author of the Lola Wicks series.

Flournoy, Angela

The **Turner** house / Angela Flournoy. Houghton Mifflin Harcourt, 2015. 320 p.
ISBN 9780544303164
1. African American families 2. Intergenerational relations 3. Houses 4. Families 5. Change 6. Sick mothers 7. Loss (Psychology) 8. African Americans 9. Parent and adult child 10. Recession (Economics) 11. Options, alternatives, choices 12. Detroit, Michigan 13. Domestic fiction 14. African American fiction
LC 2014034423
BCALA Literary Award for First Novelist, 2016.
Finalist for the Hurston/Wright Legacy Awards for Fiction, 2016
National Book Award for Fiction finalist, 2015
Learning after a half-century of family life that their house on Detroit's East Side is worth only a fraction of its mortgage, the members of the Turner family gather to reckon with their pasts and decide the house's fate.
"Flounoy's debut is a lively, thoroughly engaging family saga with a cast of fully realized characters. . . . [She] evokes the intricacies of domestic situations and sibling relationships, depicting how each of the Turners lives has been shaped by the social history of their generation." Publishers Weekly.

Flynn, Gillian, 1971-

Dark places / Gillian Flynn. Shaye Areheart Books, 2009. 368 p.
ISBN 9780307341563
1. Children of murder victims 2. Teenage murderers 3. Brothers and sisters 4. Crimes against family 5. Secret societies 6. Witnesses 7. Survival 8. Deception 9. Satanism 10. Missouri 11. Kansas City, Missouri 12. Psychological suspense
LC 2008040244
Libby Day was seven when her mother and two sisters were murdered in "The Satan Sacrifice of Kinnakee, Kansas". She escaped and survived to later testify that her 15-year-old brother Ben was the killer. Twenty-five years later she is contacted by "The Kill Club" and pumped for information they hope to use to free Ben. Libby hatches a plan to profit from her tragic past but ends up being chased by a killer.
"Flynn's well-paced story deftly shows the fallibility of memory and the lies a child tells herself to get through a trauma." The New Yorker.

Flynn, Gillian, 1971-

* **Gone** girl : a novel / Gillian Flynn. Crown, 2012. 416 p.
ISBN 9780307588364
1. Murder suspects 2. Missing women 3. Marital conflict 4. Husband

and wife 5. Married people 6. Crimes against women 7. Deception 8. Secrets 9. Psychological suspense

LC 2011041525

Goodreads Choice Award, 2012.

RUSA Reading List, 2013.

When beautiful Amy Dunne disappears from her Missouri home, it looks as if her husband Nick is to blame. But though he protests his innocence, it's clear that he's not being entirely truthful. Gone Girl is not only the story of a disappearance, but a truly frightening glimpse of a souring marriage. -- Description by Shauna Griffin.

Flynn, Gillian, 1971-

* **Sharp** objects : a novel / Gillian Flynn. Shaye Areheart Books, 2006. 272 p.

ISBN 9780307341549

1. Self-harm 2. Women journalists 3. Girl murder victims 4. Murder investigation 5. Women journalists 6. Mother and adult daughter 7. Half-sisters 8. Self-destructive behavior 9. Cutting (Self-harm) 10. Men/women relations 11. Poisoning 12. Deception 13. Drug abuse 14. Sexuality 15. Secrets 16. Missouri 17. Psychological suspense

LC 2005035046

Ian Fleming Steel Dagger Award, 2007.

New Blood Dagger Award, 2007.

Returning to her hometown after a long absence to investigate the murders of two girls, reporter Camille Preaker is reunited with her neurotic mother and enigmatic half-sister as she works to uncover the truth about the killings.

"The author offers up a literary thriller that's a doozy. . . and she does it with wit and grit, a sort of Hitchcock visits Stephen King, with plenty of the former's offstage and often only implied violence, and the latter's sense of pacing and facility with dialogue. . . . This is not a comfortable novel of touchy-feely family fun. Rather, it is a tough tale told with remarkable clarity and dexterity." Denver Post.

Flynn, Michael (Michael F.)

Eifelheim / Michael Flynn. Tor Books, 2006. 320 p.

ISBN 0765300966

1. 14th century 2. Historians 3. Women physicists 4. Research 5. Villages -- Germany 6. Space vehicles 7. Aliens (Insectoid) 8. Priests 9. Human/alien encounters 10. Converts to Christianity 11. Plague -- Germany -- History -- 14th century 12. Consequences 13. Extinct cities -- Germany 14. Germany -- History -- 1273-1517 15. Earth -- Invasions 16. Alternative histories 17. Hard science fiction 18. Science fiction

LC 2006005468

"A Tom Doherty Associates book."

Tom, a contemporary historian and his physicist girlfriend Sharon become interested in a one small town in Germany that disappeared in 1349 and was never resettled. Father Deitrich the priest of the village is the first contact between humanity and an alien race from a distant star when their interstellar ship crashes in the nearby forest in 1348, the year the Black Death spread across Europe.

"Tom, a young historian, obsesses about Eifelheim, a German village that mysteriously disappeared from all maps in 1349. His lover Sharon, a theoretical physicist, occupies herself with testing the limits of conventional theories of time and space. Their interests merge when they discover the remarkable story of Father Dietrich, Eifelheim's parish priest during the Black Death and a believer in travelers from the stars. With a sure grasp of both speculative science and medieval history, Flynn . . . compellingly weaves past and present together in a dialog of faith and science." Library Journal.

Flynn, Michael (Michael F.)

The **January** dancer / Michael Flynn. Tor, 2008. 352 p. January dancer

ISBN 9780765318176

1. Antiquities, Prehistoric 2. Space flight 3. Collectors and collecting 4. Life on other planets 5. Life after death 6. Men/women relations 7. Competition 8. Science fiction 9. Space opera

LC 2008029772

"A Tom Doherty Associates book."

Follows the adventures of Captain Amos January and a host of rivals struggling to obtain an ancient pre-human artifact of great power that incites murderous actions in those who seek it.

"The characters zip through so many worlds that it's hard to keep track of them, but Flynn includes enough clever references to the long-abandoned Earth to keep the journey amusing. . . . The balladic framework can be heavy-handed at times, but it adds a mythical quality to what could have been run-of-the-mill space fantasy." Washington Post Book World.

Flyte, Magnus

City of dark magic : a novel / Magnus Flyte. Penguin Books, 2012. 368 p. City of dark magic

ISBN 9780143122685

1. Music students 2. Magic 3. Mentors 4. Murder 5. Murder investigation 6. Paranormal phenomena 7. Men/women relations 8. Prague, Czech Republic 9. Thrillers and suspense 10. Urban fantasy

LC 2012028676

A music student working in Prague cataloging Beethoven's manuscripts discovers clues that her deceased mentor may not have committed suicide and becomes involved with a time-travel drug, a 400-year-old dwarf, a handsome Prince and a powerful U.S. senator.

Flyte, Magnus

City of lost dreams : a novel / Magnus Flyte. Penguin Books, 2013. 368 p. City of dark magic

ISBN 9780143123279

1. Music students 2. Magic 3. Mentors 4. Enemies 5. Paranormal phenomena 6. Men/women relations 7. Prague, Czech Republic 8. Thrillers and suspense 9. Urban fantasy

LC 2013031311

Maps on inside cover.

A sequel to City of Dark Magic finds Sara and Nicolas's search for an alchemical cure for a gravely ill friend threatened by an old enemy and a bloodthirsty horseman, while Prince Max tries to explain the strange reappearance of a saint while outmaneuvering a scheming historian.

"Sensual, witty and sometimes laugh-out-loud funny, set forth in sparkling prose and inhabited by characters well-worth getting to know." Kirkus.

Foer, Jonathan Safran, 1977-

Everything is illuminated : a novel / Jonathan Safran Foer. Houghton Mifflin Co., 2002. 276 p.

ISBN 0618173870

1. Grandfather and child 2. Holocaust (1933-1945) 3. Translators 4. World War II 5. Guilt in men 6. Jewish Americans in Ukraine 7. Ukraine -- History -- German occupation, 1941-1944 8. Novels-within-novels 9. Epistolary novels 10. Magical realism 11. Literary fiction

LC 2001051610

Guardian First Book Award, 2002.

National Jewish Book Award for Fiction, 2001.

William Saroyan International Prize for Writing, Fiction category, 2003.

Hilarious, energetic, and profoundly touching, a debut novel follows a young writer as he travels to the farmlands of eastern Europe, where he embarks on a quest to find Augustine, the woman who saved his grandfather from the Nazis, and, guided by his young Ukrainian translator, he discovers an unexpected past that will resonate far into the future.

"Foer deftly handles the intricate story-within-a-story plot, and the layers of suspense build as the shtetl hurtles toward the devastation of the 20th century while Alex and Jonathan and Grandfather close in on the object of their search. An impressive, original debut." Publishers Weekly.

Foer, Jonathan Safran, 1977-

Extremely loud and incredibly close / Jonathan Safran Foer. Houghton Mifflin, 2005. 368 p.

ISBN 9780618329700

1. 21st century 2. Fathers -- Death 3. Loss (Psychology) 4. Quests 5. Locks and keys 6. Boys 7. Nine-year-old boys 8. Gifted children 9. Senior men 10. Men who are mute 11. Survival 12. Memories 13. September 11 Terrorist Attacks, 2001 14. New York City 15. Dresden, Germany -- Bombing, 1945 -- Influence 16. Hiroshima, Japan -- Atomic bombing, 1945 -- Influence 17. Mainstream fiction 18. Psychological fiction 19. Illustrated books

LC 2004065131

ALA Notable Book, 2006.

Shortlisted for the International IMPAC Dublin Literary Award, 2007

Oskar Schell, the nine-year-old son of a man killed in the World Trade Center attacks, searches the five boroughs of New York City for a lock that fits a black key his father left behind.

"The author's depiction of Oskar's reaction to phone messages left by his father as he awaited rescue in the burning World Trade Center, his description of Oskar's grandfather's love affair . . . and his experiences during the bombing of Dresden--these passages underscore Mr. Foer's ability to evoke, with enormous compassion and psychological acuity, his characters' emotional experiences, and to show how these private moments intersect with the great public events of history." New York Times.

Foer, Jonathan Safran, 1977-

Here I am : a novel / Jonathan Safran Foer. Farrar, Straus and Giroux, 2016. 512 p.

ISBN 9780374280024

1. Dysfunctional families 2. Jewish families 3. Family relationships 4. Jewish Americans 5. Self-discovery in men 6. Parent and child 7. Washington, D.C. 8. Israel 9. Domestic fiction

LC 2016007096

A tale told over four tumultuous weeks in present-day Washington, D.C traces the fracturing of a family in crisis when the three sons of Jacob and Julia confront the paradoxes between the lives they think they want and the lives they are actually living.

"That he can provide such a redemptive denouement, at once poignant, inspirational, and compassionate, is the mark of a thrillingly gifted writer." Publishers Weekly.

Foley, Lucy

The **hunting** party / Lucy Foley. William Morrow Co., 2019. 327 p.

ISBN 9780062868909

1. Country homes 2. Blizzards 3. Flashbacks 4. Thirties (Age) 5. Winter 6. Friendship 7. Murder 8. Secrets 9. New Year's Eve 10. Men/women relations 11. Childhood friends 12. Highlands, Scotland 13. Scotland 14. Psychological suspense

A group of thirty-something Oxford friends celebrate New Year's Eve in the Scottish Highlands as a historic blizzard hits, trapping and isolating them, only to discover one of them is a murderer.

Follett, Ken

A **column** of fire / Ken Follett. Viking, 2017. 1024 p. Pillars of the Earth

ISBN 9780525954972

1. Elizabethan era (1558-1603) 2. Tudor period (1485-1603) 3. Renaissance (1300-1600) 4. Church and state -- Great Britain 5. Men/women relations 6. Interpersonal attraction 7. Ambition 8. Humanism (14th-16th centuries) 9. European Renaissance 10. Revenge 11. Cathedrals -- Great Britain 12. Monks 13. Peasantry 14. Peasant women 15. Knights and knighthood 16. Nuns 17. Great Britain -- History -- Elizabeth I, 1558-1603 18. Historical fiction

LC 2017025384

The relationship between a man in service to Elizabeth I and a woman on the opposing side of England's religious divide is challenged by violent ideological power shifts, torn loyalties, and the queen's circle of spies.

"Follett's sprawling novel is a fine mix of heart-pounding drama and erudite historicism." Publishers Weekly.

Follett, Ken

Edge of eternity / Ken Follett. Dutton, 2014. 1120 p. Century trilogy

ISBN 9780525953098

1. 20th century 2. World politics 3. Social change 4. Civil Rights Movement 5. Vietnam War, 1961-1975 6. Assassination 7. Espionage 8. Cold War 9. War 10. Families 11. Interpersonal relations 12. Historical fiction 13. Family sagas 14. Epic fiction

Continues the experiences of five intertwined international families as they confront the social, political, and economic turmoil of the second half of the twentieth century.

"This mesmerizing final installment is an exhaustive but rewarding reading experience dense in thematic heft, yet flowing with spicy, expertly paced melodrama, character-rich exploits, familial histrionics, and international intrigue." Publishers Weekly.

Follett, Ken

Eye of the needle / Ken Follett. Dark Alley, 2005, c1978. 339, 14 p.

ISBN 006074815X

1. M I 6 2. Second World War era (1939-1945) 3. 1940s 4. Spies -- Germany 5. Intelligence service -- Great Britain 6. World War II 7. Germans in Great Britain 8. Married women 9. Islands 10. Ethics 11. Men/women relations 12. Extramarital affairs 13. Betrayal 14. Secrets 15. Spies -- Great Britain 16. Submarines, German 17. Double agents 18. Secret service 19. Scotland 20. Spy fiction 21. Historical thrillers

LC 2004061876

Published in England as: Storm Island.

Originally published: London : Futura, 1978.

Edgar Allan Poe Award for Best Mystery Novel, 1979.

One enemy spy knows the secret of the Allies' greatest deception, a brilliant aristocrat and ruthless assassin -- code name: "The Needle" -- who holds the key to the ultimate Nazi victory. Only one person stands in his way: a lonely Englishwoman on an isolated island, who is coming to love the killer who has mysteriously entered her life. Ken Follett's unsurpassed and unforgettable masterwork of suspense, intrigue, and dangerous machinations of the human heart.

"An absolutely terrific thriller, so pulse-pounding, so ingenious in its plotting, and so frighteningly realistic that you simply cannot stop reading, this World War II espionage tale is right up there with the best of them." Publishers Weekly.

Follett, Ken

Fall of giants / Ken Follett. Dutton, 2010. xiv, 985 p. Century trilogy

ISBN 9780525951650

1. First World War era (1914-1918) 2. 20th century 3. World War I 4. World politics 5. Suffrage 6. War -- History -- 20th century 7. Families 8. Postwar life 9. Historical fiction 10. Family sagas 11. Epic fiction

LC 2010009279

Sequel: Winter of the World.

Col. map on endpapers.

Goodreads Choice Award, 2010.

Follows the fates of five interrelated families--American, German, Russian, English, and Welsh--as they move through the dramas of the First World War, the Russian Revolution, and the struggle for women's suffrage.

"Follett entwines fiction and factual events well. Creating characters of numerous, actual historical figures is a big risk. How do you write about Trotsky without being facile? Follett successfully assails the dilemma from a couple of angles, most importantly by knowing a lot about the period but not making the reader aware of how arduously he is working." Chicago Sun-Times.

Follett, Ken

Hornet flight / Ken Follett. Dutton, 2002. 420 p.

ISBN 9780525946892

1. Second World War era (1939-1945) 2. 1940s 3. Spies 4. Military intelligence -- History -- World War II 5. World War II -- Radar 6. Radar -- History 7. Nazis 8. Military intelligence officers 9. Biplanes 10. Teenagers and war 11. Teenagers -- Denmark 12. Denmark -- History -- German occupation, 1940-1945 13. Great Britain -- History -- 20th century 14. War stories 15. Spy fiction 16. Thrillers and suspense

In June 1944, with the war not going well for the British, the lives of three people on both sides of the English Channel intertwine as one of them makes a discovery that could change the course of the war.

"Tale of amateur spies pursued by Nazi collaborators in occupied Denmark in 1941. Harald Olufsen is an 18-year-old physics student who stumbles into espionage when he accidentally discovers a secret German radar installation on the island where he lives. . . . Follett starts out fast and keeps up the pace, revealing how ordinary people who want to do the right thing are undone by their own enthusiasm and inexperience. He also paints a vivid and convincing picture of life in occupied Denmark, of easy collaboration with the Nazis and of the insidious, creeping persecution of the Jews." Publishers Weekly.

Follett, Ken

Jackdaws / Ken Follett. Dutton, 2001. 384 p.

ISBN 0525946284

1. Great Britain Special operations executive 2. Second World War era (1939-1945) 3. 1940s 4. Women spies -- Great Britain 5. Military intelligence 6. World War II 7. Secret service 8. Telephones 9. Spies -- Great Britain 10. French Resistance (World War II) 11. World War II -- Women's participation 12. Women -- France 13. France -- History -- German occupation, 1940-1945 14. War stories 15. Spy fiction 16. Historical thrillers

LC 2001037087

On the eve of World War II, Special Operations agent, Felicity 'Flick' Clairet is sent undercover to destroy the German lines of communica-tion. An all woman team dubbed the Jackdaws is hastily trained to aid her in this very difficult mission.

"This thriller is about a mission to take out a German telephone exchange near Reims in the last few hours before D-Day. ... All of this may sound like cliched melodrama, but when Follett starts the clock and slips the narrative gearshift into synchromesh, one's literary misgivings are abandoned in the wake of the plot's forward thrust." Booklist.

Follett, Ken

The **pillars** of the earth / Ken Follett W. Morrow, 1989. 973 p. Pillars of the Earth

ISBN 9780688046590

1. Medieval period (476-1492) 2. Norman period (1066-1154) 3. 12th century 4. Church and state -- Great Britain 5. Revenge -- Great Britain 6. Betrayal 7. Cathedrals -- Great Britain 8. Stone building 9. Stonemasons 10. Monks 11. Natural disasters 12. Building 13. Great Britain -- History -- Stephen, 1135-1154 14. Historical fiction

LC 89009405

Sequel: World without end (2007).

Set in twelfth-century England, this epic of kings and peasants juxta-poses the building of a magnificent church with the violence and treach-ery that often characterized the Middle Ages.

"Follett has skillfully crafted an extraordinary epic buttressed by a succession of suspenseful subplots. A towering triumph of romance, ri-valry, and spectacle from a major talent." Booklist.

Follett, Ken

* Whiteout / Ken Follett. Dutton, 2004. 400 p.

ISBN 0525948430

1. Biological terrorism 2. Competition 3. Betrayal 4. Drug industry and trade 5. Animal rights advocates 6. Security consultants 7. Hazardous materials 8. Former policewomen 9. Viruses 10. Vaccines 11. Television journalists 12. Biological research 13. Lost articles 14. Greed 15. Jealousy 16. Dishonesty 17. Redemption 18. Stealing 19. Christmas 20. Scotland 21. Thrillers and suspense

LC 2004010373

First published: Macmillan, 2004.

A missing canister containing a deadly virus forms the center of a storm that traps Stanley Oxenford, director of a medical research firm, and a violent trio of thugs in a remote house during a Christmas Eve blizzard.

Follett, Ken

Winter of the world / Ken Follett. Dutton, 2012. 1008 p. Century trilogy

ISBN 9780525952923

1. 20th century 2. Atomic bomb 3. World War II 4. War 5. Families 6. Nazism 7. Communism 8. World politics 9. Social change 10. Interpersonal relations 11. Spain -- History -- Civil War, 1936-1939 12. Historical fiction 13. Family sagas 14. Epic fiction

LC 2012004653

Sequel to: Fall of Giants.

Maps on lining papers.

Originally published: London : Macmillan, 2012.

A follow-up to Fall of Giants continues the stories of five interre-lated families from different world regions who struggle with social, political and economic turmoil in the years leading up to World War II, during which Carla considers a dangerous act against the Nazis, brothers Woody and Chuck pursue separate paths to key world events and Lloyd takes a stand against Communism.

Follett, Ken

World without end / Ken Follett. Dutton, 2007. 992 p. Pillars of the Earth

ISBN 0525950079

1. Plantagenet period (1154-1485) 2. 14th century 3. Medieval period (476-1492) 4. Church and state -- Great Britain 5. Greed 6. Ambition 7. Humanism (14th-16th centuries) 8. European Renaissance 9. Revenge 10. Black Death 11. Plague 12. Cathedrals -- Great Britain 13. Monks 14. Peasantry 15. Peasant women 16. Knights and knighthood 17. Nuns 18. Civilization, Medieval 19. Great Britain -- History -- 14th century 20. Great Britain -- History -- Edward III, 1327-1377 21. Great Britain -- History -- Medieval period, 1066-1485 22. Historical fiction

Sequel to The pillars of the Earth (1989)

Sequel to: The pillars of the earth.

First published: London : Macmillan, 2007.

"A war that lasts a hundred years. A plague that ravages a continent. A rivalry that could destroy everything. On the day after Halloween, in the year 1327, four children slip away from the cathedral city of Kingsbridge. In the forest they see two men killed. As adults, their lives become braided together by desire, determination, avarice and retribution. They will see prosperity and famine, plague and war. Yet they will always live under the shadow of the unexplained killing on that fateful childhood day." - back cover.

"Populated with an immense cast of truly remarkable characters-the rich and powerful, the weak and downtrodden, clergy, guildsmen and nobility-this novel explores the lives and fortunes of the ancestors of the original inhabitants of Kingsbridge." Library Journal.

Forbes, Curdella

* A **tall** history of sugar / Curdella Forbes. Akashic Books, 2019. 372 p.

ISBN 9781617757518

1. 20th century 2. Artists 3. Adopted children 4. Misfits (Persons) 5. Childhood friends 6. Political activists 7. Men/women relations 8. Searching 9. Race relations 10. Postcolonialism 11. Child-separated fathers 12. Jamaica 13. England 14. Magical realism 15. Love stories 16. Literary fiction

Tells the story of Moshe Fisher, a man who was "born without skin," so that no one is able to tell what race he belongs to; and Arrienne Christie, his quixotic soul mate who makes it her duty in life to protect Moshe from the social and emotional consequences of his strange appearance.

Force, Marie

Deceived by desire / Marie Force. Zebra Books, 2019. 320 p. Gilded novels

ISBN 9781420147872

1. Regency period (1811-1820) 2. Industrialists 3. Housekeepers 4. Rich men 5. Dukes and duchesses 6. Vacations 7. Vacation homes 8. Class consciousness 9. Protectiveness in men 10. Secrets 11. Women murder suspects 12. Interpersonal attraction 13. Men/women relations 14. Newport, Rhode Island 15. Regency romances 16. Historical romances

From New York Times bestselling author Marie Force comes a glittering tale of star-crossed romance set amid the lavish mansions and decadent lifestyles of early 20th century Newport, Rhode Island. But even in an age of great fortune, the heart has its own idea of true riches . . .

Force, Marie

Five years gone / Marie Force. Zebra Books, 2018. 325 p.

ISBN 9781420149036

1. Love triangles 2. Soldiers 3. Lovers 4. Options, alternatives, choices 5. Loss (Psychology) 6. Sexual attraction 7. Men/women relations 8. New York City 9. Contemporary romances

The most brazen terrorist attack in history. A country bent on revenge. A love affair cut short. A heart that never truly heals.

Ford, Ford Madox, 1873-1939

* The **good** soldier : a tale of passion / Ford Madox Ford. Knopf, 1991, c1915. 220 p.

ISBN 0679406654

1. Americans in Germany 2. Extramarital affairs 3. Friendship 4. British in Germany 5. Leisure class 6. Suicide 7. Secrecy 8. Married people and secrets 9. Bad Nauheim, Germany 10. Germany 11. Literary fiction 12. Psychological fiction 13. Classics

LC 91052977

Four wealthy and socially prominent individuals are forced to see each other realistically

Ford, Ford Madox, 1873-1939

Parade's end / Ford Madox Ford ; with an introduction by Robie Macauley Knopf, 1966, c1950. xxii, 836 p. Parade's end

ISBN 0679417281

1. First World War era (1914-1918) 2. Social change 3. Married people 4. World War I -- Great Britain 5. Marriage 6. Suffragists 7. War neuroses 8. Social order 9. Mental illness 10. Men -- Psychology 11. Extramarital affairs 12. Europe -- History -- 1871-1918 13. Great Britain -- History -- 20th century 14. War stories 15. Psychological fiction 16. Historical fiction 17. Modern classics

Adapted into a television series of the same name (2012).

Reprinted in 2019 with a new introduction by Julian Barnes.

The four Tietjens novels depicting the breakdown of the English Tory world are presented under one title.

Ford, Jamie

Songs of Willow Frost : a novel / Jamie Ford. Ballantine Books, 2013. 256 p.

ISBN 9780345522023

1. 1930s 2. 1920s 3. Orphans 4. Chinese American boys 5. Mother and child 6. Actors and actresses 7. Films 8. Orphanages 9. Friendship 10. Families 11. Seattle, Washington 12. Historical fiction 13. Parallel narratives 14. Pacific Northwest fiction

LC 2013011007

Confined to Seattle's Sacred Heart Orphanage during the Great Depression, Chinese-American boy William Eng becomes convinced that a certain movie actress is actually the mother he has not seen since he was 7 years old, a belief that compels a determined search for answers.

Ford, Jeffrey, 1955-

The **empire** of ice cream / Jeffrey Ford ; with an introduction by Jonathan Carroll. Golden Gryphon Press, 2006. 300 p.

ISBN 1930846398

1. Supernatural 2. Fantasy fiction 3. Short stories

LC 2005024035

"Giants and unidentifiable alien creatures, fairy tales, the intertwining of wonder and terror, and fantastic views of both the strange and the ordinary all appear in this marvelous collection, with Ford's comments on his inspiration and motivations appended to each story. Ford is nothing if not versatile, as this collection confirms to great effect." Booklist.

Ford, Jeffrey, 1955-

The **shadow** year : a novel / Jeffrey Ford. William Morrow, 2008. 304 p.

ISBN 9780061231520

1. 1960s 2. Teenage boys 3. Cities and towns 4. Murder 5. Kidnapping 6. Alcoholism 7. Brothers and sisters 8. Mysteries 9. Domestic fiction

LC 2007037319

Shirley Jackson Awards, Novel, 2008.

World Fantasy Award, 2009.

In the wake of a classmate's disappearance, a sixth grader and his older brother observe strange events in 1960s Long Island, including the appearance of a man in a large white car and the deteriorating mental state of the school librarian.

"A masterly literary adventure that is at once a hypnotically compelling mystery and a stunningly evocative portrait of small-town adolescence." Pittsburgh Press.

Ford, Richard, 1944-

Canada / Richard Ford. Ecco Press, 2012. 432 p.

ISBN 9780061692048

1. Fifteen-year old boys 2. Children of prisoners 3. Coping in teenage boys 4. Violence in men 5. Self-fulfillment in teenage boys 6. Saskatchewan 7. Psychological fiction 8. Literary fiction

ALA Notable Book, 2013

Andrew Carnegie Medal for Excellence in Fiction, 2013.

After his parents are arrested and imprisoned for robbing a bank, 15-year-old Dell Parsons is taken in by Arthur Remlinger who, unbeknownst to Dell, is hiding a dark and violent nature that interferes with Dell's quest to find grace and peace on the prairie of Saskatchewan.

Ford, Richard, 1944-

* **Independence** Day / Richard Ford. A.A. Knopf, 1995. 451 p. Frank Bascombe novels

ISBN 0679492658

1. 1980s 2. Fathers and sons 3. Divorced men 4. Real estate agents 5. Teenage boys 6. Families 7. Men/women relations 8. Fourth of July 9. New Jersey 10. Psychological fiction 11. Literary fiction

LC 95003126

Sequel to: The sportswriter.

Sequel: The lay of the land.

PEN-Faulkner Award, 1996.

Pulitzer Prize for Fiction, 1996.

National Book Critics Circle Award for Fiction finalist, 1995

Real estate agent Frank Bascombe moves into his newly married ex-wife's old home, and is looking forward to the upcoming Fourth of July weekend, but somehow nothing turns out the way he expects

"One is constantly struck by the rich, dense mixture of Ford's narrative. No one writes better--and with more inventive brio--about the bland wasteland of US suburbia; that shopping-malled, subdivisioned terrain that has rapidly become the true defining landscape of late 20th-century America." New Statesman.

Ford, Richard, 1944-

The **lay** of the land / Richard Ford. Alfred A. Knopf, 2006. 496 p. Frank Bascombe novels

ISBN 0679454683

1. 2000s (Decade) 2. Remarriage 3. Mortality 4. Aging 5. Men/women relations 6. Fathers and sons 7. Men with prostate cancer 8. Marital conflict 9. Real estate agents 10. Married men 11. Presidents -- United States -- Election 12. Thanksgiving Day 13. Fifties (Age) 14. New Jersey 15. Psychological fiction 16. Literary fiction

LC 2006025570

Sequel to: Independence Day.

National Book Critics Circle Award for Fiction finalist, 2006

In the fall of 2000, with the results of the presidential election still hanging in the balance, Frank Bascombe confronts the perils of Thanksgiving as he contends with health, marital, and family issues and works as a realtor at the Jersey shore.

"This is as as vibrant a book as any that Richard Ford has written. It bristles with energy, with a natural assurance on the part of its writer. . . . And what a slice of life at the turn of the century and millennium this novel is. There is so much trenchant criticism of what is wrong with American society: the economic royalism, the greed, the lack of common decency and civility in so many walks of life, and above all perspective. . . . As people today read Theodore Dreiser for his acute portraits of industrialized America in its gilded age and Sinclair Lewis for his insights into his nation's struggles to come to terms with 20th-century changes in its social structures, one day readers will turn to Richard Ford to discover just what the United States was like on the homefront during his particular fin de siecle." Christian Science Monitor.

Ford, Richard, 1944-

Let me be Frank with you / Richard Ford. Ecco Press, 2014. 240 p. Frank Bascombe novels

ISBN 9780061692062

1. Hurricanes 2. Sixties (Age) 3. Mortality 4. Aging 5. Voyages and travels 6. Divorced men 7. Interpersonal relations 8. Hurricane Sandy, 2012 9. New Jersey 10. Psychological fiction 11. Literary fiction

Pulitzer Prize for Fiction finalist, 2015.

In the aftermath of Hurricane Sandy, Frank Bascombe travels to the site of his former home on the shore, visits his ex-wife, who is suffering with Parkinson's, and meets a dying former friend.

"In each neatly linked tale, Frank ruminates misanthropically, wittily, and wisely about love, family, friendship, race, politics, and the mystery of the self." Booklist.

Ford, Richard, 1944-

A **multitude** of sins : stories / Richard Ford. Alfred A. Knopf :, 2001. 286 p.

ISBN 0375412123

1. Men/women relations 2. Intimacy (Psychology) 3. Interpersonal relations 4. Failure (Psychology) 5. Love 6. Extramarital affairs 7. Montreal, Quebec 8. Grand Canyon 9. Psychological fiction 10. Short stories

LC 2001038402

"Originally published in Great Britain by The Harvill Press, London"--T.p. verso.

A collection of short stories that explores the theme of love and intimacy looks inside the relationships between men and women--both in and out of marriage--and the sense of right and wrong.

"Tracing the blueprint of human interaction in this latest collection . . . Ford signals the master text of lust standing behind the multitude of small sins he so tersely and poignantly chronicles. To err is human, and, in Ford's worldview, little is so human as the act of cheating on a wife or husband." Publishers Weekly.

Forester, C. S. (Cecil Scott), 1899-1966

Admiral Hornblower in the West Indies / C.S. Forester. Little, Brown, 1989, c1958. 329 p. Horatio Hornblower saga

ISBN 9781405936958

1. Great Britain. Royal Navy Officers 2. Sailing ships 3. Ship captains 4. British in the West Indies 5. Great Britain -- History, Naval -- 19th century 6. Adventure stories 7. Sea stories 8. Historical fiction

LC 58007862

Horatio Hornblower faces a new Bonapartist uprising in the West Indies while trying to stamp out slave trade and piracy.

Forester, C. S. (Cecil Scott), 1899-1966

The **African** Queen / C.S. Forester. Little, Brown, 1984, c1935. 307 p.

ISBN 9780316289108

1. First World War era (1914-1918) 2. World War I -- Africa 3. Women Christian missionaries 4. River boat pilots 5. British in Africa 6. Men/women relations 7. River travel 8. Africa 9. Adventure stories 10. Historical fiction

Originally published: 1935.

The African Queen tells the story of Rose Sayer, a respectable missionary who is in Africa with her brother the Reverend Samuel Sayer, and Charles Alnutt the hard-bitten and disreputable skipper of the African Queen. Upon the death of her brother the pair become the unlikeliest of allies as marooned in German Central Africa during the First World War, they fight their ramshacle old launch, laden with explosives, downriver to strike a blow for England.

Forester, C. S. (Cecil Scott), 1899-1966

Beat to quarters / C.S. Forester. Little, Brown, 1985, c1937. 324 p. Horatio Hornblower saga

ISBN 9780316289320

1. Great Britain. Royal Navy Officers 2. Spain. Navy History 19th century 3. 19th century 4. Sailing ships 5. Naval battles 6. Napoleonic Wars, 1800-1815 -- Naval operations, British 7. Great Britain -- History, Naval -- 19th century 8. Adventure stories 9. Sea stories 10. Historical fiction

LC 85-11609

Plot elements of Horatio Hornblower saga titles Beat to quarters, Ship of the line, and Flying colours were used in the 1951 movie "Captain Horatio Hornblower."

Originally published as The happy return: London : Michael Joseph, 1937.

Hornblower sails the South American waters and comes face to face with a mad revolutionary in a novel that ripples with risk and gripping adventure. Through his escapades Forester's hero remains resourceful and courageous.

"There is plenty of action. But there is also an unusual character study." New York Times Book Review.

Forester, C. S. (Cecil Scott), 1899-1966

Commodore Hornblower / C.S. Forester. Little, Brown, 1989, c1945 320 p. Horatio Hornblower saga

ISBN 9780316289382

1. Great Britain. Royal Navy Officers 2. 19th century 3. Napoleonic Wars, 1800-1815 4. Military campaigns 5. Sailing ships 6. Ship captains 7. Naval battles 8. Naval history 9. Spain 10. Great Britain -- History, Naval -- 19th century 11. Historical fiction 12. Adventure stories 13. Sea stories 14. War stories

Originally published as The Commodore: London : Michael Joseph, 1945.

Commodore Hornblower's new mission is a delicate one because he must maintain good diplomatic relations with Russia and Sweden at all costs and, at the same time, keep Napoleon's forces out of the Baltic.

"It is a spirited piece of work, and full of interesting detail where matters naval, military, and diplomatic in that year of decision are concerned." Times Literary Supplement.

Forester, C. S. (Cecil Scott), 1899-1966

Flying colours / C.S. Forester. Little, Brown, 1986, c1938. 294 p. Horatio Hornblower saga

ISBN 9780316289399

1. Great Britain. Royal Navy Officers 2. 19th century 3. Napoleonic Wars, 1800-1815 -- Naval operations, British 4. Sailing ships 5. Naval battles 6. Prisoners of war, British 7. Great Britain -- History, Naval -- 19th century 8. Adventure stories 9. Historical fiction 10. Sea stories 11. War stories

Plot elements of Horatio Hornblower saga titles Beat to quarters, Ship of the line, and Flying colours were used in the 1951 movie "Captain Horatio Hornblower."

Originally published: London : Michael Joseph, 1938.

James Tait Black Memorial Prize for Fiction, 1938.

Hornblower becomes a national hero when he escapes a French firing squad. But the Terror of the Mediterranean becomes Europe's most wanted man, forced to fight alone for England - and liberty.

Forester, C. S. (Cecil Scott), 1899-1966

Hornblower and the Atropos / C.S. Forester. Little, Brown, 1985, c1953. 325 p. Horatio Hornblower saga

ISBN 9780316289290

1. 19th century 2. Salvage 3. Naval battles 4. Napoleonic Wars, 1800-1815 -- Naval operations, British 5. Sailing ships 6. Ship captains 7. Great Britain -- History, Naval -- 19th century 8. Adventure stories 9. Sea stories 10. Historical fiction

Originally published: London : Michael Joseph, 1953.

Captain Horatio Hornblower takes his 22-gun sloop into the Mediterranean, where he and his crew search for sunken treasure, harass Napoleon's fleet, and face off against a Spanish frigate.

Forester, C. S. (Cecil Scott), 1899-1966

Hornblower and the Hotspur / C.S. Forester. Little, Brown, 1998, c1962. 344 p. Horatio Hornblower saga

ISBN 9780316290463

1. Great Britain. Royal Navy History Napoleonic Wars, 1800-1815 2. 19th century 3. Naval battles 4. Napoleonic Wars, 1800-1815 -- Naval operations, British 5. Sailing ships 6. Ship captains 7. Great Britain -- History, Naval -- 19th century 8. Adventure stories 9. Sea stories 10. Historical fiction

LC 62013907

Originally published: London : Michael Joseph, 1962.

In the midst of his wedding reception, Hornblower receives orders to report the next day to his command in the Channel Fleet and help protect England against Napoleon's threatened invasion.

Forester, C. S. (Cecil Scott), 1899-1966

Lieutenant Hornblower / C.S. Forester. Little, Brown, 1998, c1952. 306 p. Horatio Hornblower saga

ISBN 9780316290630

1. Great Britain. Royal Navy Officers 2. 19th century 3. Sailing ships 4. Napoleonic Wars, 1800-1815 -- Naval operations, British 5. Naval battles 6. Resourcefulness in young men 7. Courage in young men 8. Great Britain -- History, Naval -- 19th century 9. Adventure stories 10. Sea stories 11. Historical fiction

LC 52005530

Originally published: London : Michael Joseph, 1952.

His cool judgement under fire shows that young Hornblower is maturing as he repeatedly defeats the Spanish warships.

"The author interprets the navy, certainly in its Napoleonic period, with the help of a character that represents the navy at its best and action that is grandly exciting without being melodramatic; helped, too, by a sense of order and a mastery of technique that puts his work on a high plane of artistry." Christian Science Monitor.

Forester, C. S. (Cecil Scott), 1899-1966

Lord Hornblower / C.S. Forester. Little, Brown, 1989, c1946. 322 p. Horatio Hornblower saga

ISBN 9780316289436

1. Great Britain. Royal Navy Officers 2. 19th century 3. Sailing ships 4. Napoleonic Wars, 1800-1815 -- Naval operations, British 5. Naval battles 6. Ship captains 7. Great Britain -- History, Naval -- 19th century 8. Bordeaux, France 9. Adventure stories 10. Sea stories 11. Historical fiction

Originally published: London : Michael Joseph, 1946.

The Admiral's face was grim as he gave Commodore Hornblower his orders. The situation was critical: mutiny was an infection that could spread through the fleet like the plague and, furthermore, the crew were threatening to go over to the French.

Forester, C. S. (Cecil Scott), 1899-1966

Mr. Midshipman Hornblower / C.S. Forester. Little, Brown, 1984, c1950. 310 p. Horatio Hornblower saga

ISBN 9780316289122

1. Great Britain. Royal Navy 2. Sailing ships 3. Napoleonic Wars, 1800-1815 -- Naval operations, British 4. Naval battles 5. Ship captains 6. Great Britain -- History, Naval -- 19th century 7. Adventure stories 8. Sea stories 9. Historical fiction

Originally published: London : Michael Joseph, 1950.

Horatio Hornblower rises to lieutenant after serving as a midshipman

Forester, C. S. (Cecil Scott), 1899-1966

Ship of the line / C.S. Forester. Little, Brown, 1985, c1938. 323 p. Horatio Hornblower saga

ISBN 9780316289368

1. Great Britain. Royal Navy Officers 2. 19th century 3. Napoleonic Wars, 1800-1815 -- Naval operations, British 4. Sailing ships 5. Naval battles 6. Great Britain -- History, Naval -- 19th century 7. Adventure stories 8. Sea stories 9. Historical fiction

LC 85-12856

Plot elements of Horatio Hornblower saga titles Beat to quarters, Ship of the line, and Flying colours were used in the 1951 movie "Captain Horatio Hornblower."

Originally published: London : Michael Joseph, 1938.

James Tait Black Memorial Prize for Fiction, 1938.

Her Majesty's ship Sutherland is a humdrum ship of the line. But in command none other than the heroic Captain Hornblower and, with his crew from the Lydia, looks set to take on commando raids, hurricanes at sea and Napoleons's gun batteries.

Forman, Gayle

Leave me : a novel / Gayle Forman. Algonquin Books of Chapel Hill, 2016. 352 p.

ISBN 9781616206178

1. Working mothers 2. Self-fulfillment in women 3. Workaholics 4. Married women 5. People who have had heart attacks 6. Mother deserted families 7. Adoption 8. Identity (Psychology) 9. Friendship 10. Secrets 11. Family relationships 12. Women's lives and relationships

LC 2016006430

A harried working mom, who is so busy that she fails to recognize the signs of a heart attack, leaves the family that resents helping her recover and gradually confronts the painful secrets she has been ignoring.

"With humor and pathos, Forman depicts Maribeths complicated situation and her thoroughly satisfying arc, leaving readers feel-

ing as though theyve really accompanied Maribeth on her journey." Publishers Weekly.

Forna, Aminatta

Happiness / Aminatta Forna. Atlantic Monthly Press, 2018. 312 p.

ISBN 9780802127556

1. Interpersonal relations 2. Loss (Psychology) 3. Self-fulfillment 4. Missing children 5. Psychiatrists 6. Scientists 7. Friendship 8. Foxes 9. Happiness 10. London, England 11. Literary fiction

LC 2017043798

Shortlisted for the RSL Ondaatje Prize, 2019.

An American scientist and a Ghanaian psychologist become unlikely partners and friends during a search for a missing child that challenges their perspectives on their careers and happiness.

Forna, Aminatta

The **hired** man / Aminatta Forna. Grove Press, 2013. 304 p.

ISBN 9780802121912

1. War and civilization 2. Houses -- Conservation and restoration 3. Collective memory 4. Mosaics 5. Revenge 6. Small town life 7. British in Croatia 8. Croatia 9. Literary fiction

LC 2013375768

Originally published: 2013.

Originally published: London : Bloomsbury, 2013.

Gost is surrounded by mountains and fields of wild flowers. The summer sun burns. The Croatian winter brings freezing winds. Beyond the boundaries of the town an old house which has lain empty for years is showing signs of life. One of the windows, glass darkened with dirt, today stands open, and the lively chatter of English voices carries across the fallow fields. Laura and her teenage children have arrived. A short distance away lies the hut of Duro Kolak who lives alone with his two hunting dogs. As he helps Laura with repairs to the old house, they uncover a mosaic beneath the ruined plaster and, in the rising heat of summer, painstakingly restore it. But Gost is not all it seems; conflicts long past still suppurate beneath the scars.

"A low-key but sophisticated portrait of history--and evil--at a local level." Kirkus.

Forna, Aminatta

The **memory** of love / Aminatta Forna. Atlantic Monthly, 2011, c2010. 464 p.

ISBN 9780802119650

1. War -- Psychological aspects 2. Men/women relations 3. Hospitals 4. Surgeons 5. Psychiatrists 6. British in West Africa 7. Reminiscing in old age 8. Sierra Leone -- History -- Civil War, 1991-2002 9. Literary fiction

First published in Great Britain, 2010.

Shortlisted for the International IMPAC Dublin Literary Award, 2012

Shortlisted for The Orange Prize for Fiction, 2011

While a gifted young surgeon is haunted by memories of the civil war that has decimated his Sierra Leone home, a patient relates disturbing stories about the post-colonial years and a well-intentioned British psychiatrist draws all of them into the path of an enigmatic woman.

Forster, E. M. (Edward Morgan), 1879-1970

* Howards End / E.M. Forster ; introduction and notes by David Lodge. Penguin Books, 2000, c1910. xxx, 302 p.

ISBN 9780141182131

1. Rich people -- Relations with poor people 2. Social classes 3. Family estates 4. Classism 5. Women 6. Young women 7. Middle

class 8. Poor people 9. England -- Social life and customs -- 1910-1936 10. Literary fiction 11. Domestic fiction 12. Modern classics
Originally published: London : Edward Arnold, 1910.

Howards End, an English country house, passes to the moneyed, the cultured, and then to the lower class.

Forster, E. M. (Edward Morgan), 1879-1970

Maurice : a novel / E.M. Forster. Norton, 1971. 256 p.
1. Gay men 2. Loneliness in men 3. Coming out (Sexual or gender identity) 4. Homosexuality 5. Men/men relations 6. Literary fiction 7. Modern classics 8. LGBTQIA fiction
LC   76170181

While a student at Cambridge, Maurice Hall discovers that he is sexually attracted to men rather than women.

"This posthumous novel ... would have been sensational had it been published when written in 1913. Appearing in the 1970's, it is not sensational, but it is an interesting novel--well written as all of E. M. Forster's works are. . . . It is filled with keen insight and sympathetic character analysis, valuable for an understanding of the author and his works." Choice.

Forster, E. M. (Edward Morgan), 1879-1970

* A **passage** to India / E.M. Forster. Harcourt Brace Jovanovich, 1984, c1924. 322 p.
ISBN 9780156711425
1. British Raj (1858-1947) 2. British in India 3. Imperialism, British 4. Trials (Rape) 5. Physicians 6. Psychological fiction 7. Literary fiction 8. Modern classics
LC   8422375

Originally published: London : E. Arnold & Co., 1924.
James Tait Black Memorial Prize for Fiction, 1924.

Two women come to Chandrapore, India, and their lack of understanding of the culture causes one of them to make an unjust accusation.

Forster, E. M. (Edward Morgan), 1879-1970

* A **room** with a view / E.M. Forster. Knopf, 1968, c1908. 318 p.
ISBN 9781444736281
1. British in Italy 2. Young women 3. Middle class 4. Upper class 5. Classism 6. England -- Social life and customs -- 1910-1936 7. Literary fiction 8. Modern classics 9. Love stories
Originally published: 1908.

Lucy Honeychurch falls in love while on a visit to Florence and must choose between fulfilling her social role or following her heart.

Forsyth, Frederick, 1938-

The **fox** / Frederick Forsyth. G. P. Putnam's Sons, 2018. xiii, 286 p.
ISBN 9780525538424
1. Hackers 2. International intrigue 3. Espionage 4. Political intrigue 5. Spies 6. Teenage boys 7. Cyberterrorism 8. Computer crimes 9. Politicians 10. Secrets 11. Cyber-thrillers 12. Thrillers and suspense
When America's intelligence agencies are breached by a teen hacker, a British MI6 leader endeavors to use the boy's talents to safeguard both nations from unseen enemies.

Forsyth, Frederick, 1938-

The **kill** list / Frederick Forsyth. G. P. Putnam's Sons, 2013. 352 p.
ISBN 9780399165276
1. Undercover operations 2. Fathers -- Death 3. Assassins 4. Government missions 5. Fundamentalism 6. Terrorism -- Prevention

7. Islam 8. Thrillers and suspense 9. Spy fiction
LC 2013015342

A counter-terrorist unit hunts down the Preacher, a terrorist who radicalizes young muslims into carrying out assassinations.

Fortier, Anne, 1971-

Juliet : a novel / Anne Fortier. Ballantine Books, 2010. 448 p.
ISBN 9780345516107
1. 14th century 2. Family secrets 3. Voyages and travels 4. Family feuds 5. Americans in Italy 6. Inheritance and succession 7. Counts and countesses 8. Quests 9. Treasure hunting 10. Men/women relations 11. Siena, Italy 12. Love stories 13. Parallel narratives
LC 2010002093

After she visits Italy per the instructions of her late aunt's will, Juliet Jacobs is thrust into a centuries-old feud, uncovering the story of her ancestor, Giulietta, whose love for a man named Romeo proved ill-fated, and finding herself under threat after the past and present begin to resemble one another.

"Fortier navigates around false clues and twists, resulting in a dense, heavily plotted love story that reads like a Da Vinci Code for the smart modern woman." Publishers Weekly.

Fortier, Anne, 1971-

The **lost** sisterhood / Anne Fortier. Ballantine Books, 2014. 528 p.
ISBN 9780345536228
1. Excavations (Archaeology) 2. Women college teachers 3. Women warriors 4. Women priests 5. Kidnapping 6. Philology 7. Grandmother and granddaughter 8. Men/women relations 9. Adventure stories 10. Parallel narratives

While a band of ancient-world Amazon priestesses in training embark on a brave quest to rescue their kidnapped companions, a modern-day scholar is led by an enigmatic Middle Easterner on a dangerous search for an Amazonian treasure in the Sahara.

Fossum, Karin, 1954-

Bad intentions / Karin Fossum ; translated from the Norwegian by Charlotte Barslund. Houghton Mifflin Harcourt, 2011, c2008. 224 p. Inspector Sejer novels
ISBN 9780547483344
1. Police 2. Detectives 3. Suicide investigation 4. Murder investigation 5. Drowning victims 6. Men with mental illnesses 7. Drug addicts 8. Men -- Interpersonal relations 9. Secrets 10. Widowers 11. Norway 12. Scandinavian crime fiction 13. Psychological suspense 14. Mysteries 15. Translations -- Norwegian to English
Sequel to: The water's edge.
Sequel: The caller.
Original English translation published: London : Harvill Secker, 2010.
Originally published in Norway in 2008.

Konrad Sejer must face down his memories and fears as he struggles to determine why the corpses of troubled young men keep surfacing in local lakes. As Sejer begins to feel his age weigh on him, he wonders if he has the strength to pursue the elusive explanations for human evil.

Fossum, Karin, 1954-

Eva's eye / Karin Fossum ; translated from the Norwegian by James Anderson. Houghton Mifflin Harcourt, 2013, c1995. 336 p. Inspector Sejer novels
ISBN 9780547738758
1. Police 2. Murder investigation 3. Secrets 4. Violence against

prostitutes 5. Widowers 6. Detectives 7. Norway 8. Scandinavian crime fiction 9. Psychological suspense 10. Mysteries 11. Translations -- Norwegian to English

Sequel: Don't look back.

Translated from the Norwegian.

Published as In the darkness: London : Harvill Secker, 2012.

Originally published under the title, Evas Oye which translates to Eva's Eye in 1995 (Oslo : J.W. Cappelen, 1995).

Investigating the murder of a man who had been missing for months, Inspector Sejer and his team discover that his death is linked to the murder of a prostitute and to Eva, a struggling artist who holds the key to solving both murders.

Foster, Alan Dean, 1946-

Relic / Alan Dean Foster. Del Rey, 2018. 304 p.

ISBN 9781101967638

1. Humans 2. Quests 3. Aliens 4. Loneliness in men 5. Epidemics 6. Extinction (Biology) 7. Experiments 8. Space 9. Science fiction

LC 2018009535

A lone surviving human of a destructive engineered virus is rendered a research subject by his alien rescuers, who outmaneuver his reluctance by offering to help him find the mythical planet Earth.

Foster, Lori, 1958-

Run the risk / Lori Foster. HQN, 2012. 384 p. Love undercover

ISBN 9780373776955

1. Detectives 2. Undercover operations 3. Women murder witnesses 4. Hiding 5. Trust in women 6. Cold cases (Criminal investigation) 7. Sexual attraction 8. Men/women relations 9. Romantic suspense

Going deep undercover as a construction worker to find Pepper Yates, a potential link to his best friend's unsolved murder, Detective Logan Riske must convince the elusive beauty to trust him before she becomes the next target of a relentless killer.

Foster, Lori, 1958-

Sisters of summer's end / Lori Foster. Harlequin Books, 2019 304 p. Love at the resort

ISBN 9781335007681

1. Single mothers 2. Businesspeople 3. Female friendship 4. Men/women relations 5. Family relationships 6. Lifestyle change 7. Beaches 8. Resorts 9. Contemporary romances

Abandoning her stressful life to take a job at a lakeside resort, a single mom reconsiders romance at the urging of a new friend, a dedicated businesswoman who also starts wondering what she might be missing.

Foster, Lori, 1958-

Under pressure / Lori Foster. HQN Books, 2017 384 p. Body Armor novels

ISBN 9780373789931

1. Bodyguards 2. Women witnesses 3. Threat (Psychology) 4. Protectiveness in men 5. Women teachers 6. Martial artists 7. Private security services 8. Conspiracies 9. Sexual attraction 10. Men/women relations 11. Cincinnati, Ohio 12. Romantic suspense

Librarians' Choice (Australia), 2017

When Body Armor security guard Leese Phelps is hired to protect Catalina Nicholson, he is immediately drawn to her, which is a dangerous complication, especially since it could be the very man who hired Leese who's threatening her.

"Romantic thriller veteran Foster has been honing her skill for a long time, and it's clear she's at the top of her game here." Kirkus.

Founds, Kathleen

When mystical creatures attack! / Kathleen Founds. University of Iowa Press, 2014. 206 p.

ISBN 9781609382834

1. High school teachers 2. Teacher-student relationships 3. Nervous breakdown 4. Women with mental illnesses 5. Texas 6. Short stories 7. Surrealist fiction

Set against a South Texas landscape where cicadas hum and the air smells of taco stands and jasmine flowers, these stories range from laugh-out-loud funny to achingly poignant. This surreal, exuberant collection mines the dark recesses of the soul while illuminating the human heart.

"Each story adds a layer of feeling, understanding and history to the characters as they slide back and forth through time and relationships. They handle, gracefully, the whiplash switch between depression and hilarity, between the ghost of a suicidal mother and a love-struck boy promising to invent a time machine. A surreal, dark and very funny collection that has the emotional punch of a novel." Kirkus.

Fountain, Ben

* Billy Lynn's long halftime walk / Ben Fountain. Ecco Press, 2012. 307 p.

ISBN 9780060885595

1. Soldiers 2. Young men -- Personal conduct 3. Iraq War, 2003-2011 4. Self-discovery in men 5. Patriotism 6. Veterans 7. War and society 8. Football and war 9. Heroes and heroines 10. Dallas, Texas 11. Texas 12. Satirical fiction 13. Literary fiction

Billy Lynn's Long Halftime Walk inspired the 2016 movie of the same name, directed by Ang Lee and starring Kristen Stewart, Garrett Hedlund, and Vin Diesel.

ALA Notable Book, 2013

National Book Critics Circle Award for Fiction, 2012.

National Book Award for Fiction finalist, 2012

Asked to be part of the Dallas Cowboys' halftime show on Thanksgiving, Specialist Billy Lynn, one of the eight surviving men of Bravo Squad, finds his life forever changed by this event that will help him understand difficult truths about himself.

Fowler, Christopher

Bryant & May : hall of mirrors : Christopher Fowler. Bantam, 2018. 432 p. Bryant and May mysteries

ISBN 9781101887097

1. 1960s 2. Eccentrics and eccentricities 3. Whistle blowers 4. Bodyguards 5. Detectives 6. Country homes 7. Deception 8. Social isolation 9. Murder 10. Murder investigation 11. England 12. Mysteries

LC 2018023627

An early Peculiar Crimes Unit case from 1969 London finds a younger Bryant and May struggling to protect a playboy star witness and solve a murder mystery at an old-fashioned manor house estate.

"The inspired idea of revisiting the youth of his aged sleuths in swinging England is matched by Fowler's customary gusto in sweating the details. More fully fleshed-out suspects, clues, red herrings, twists, and honest mystery and detection than in the last three whodunits you read." Kirkus.

Fowler, Christopher

Bryant & May : the lonely hour / Christopher Fowler. Bantam, 2019. 448 p. Bryant and May mysteries

ISBN 9780525485827

1. Detectives 2. Octogenarians 3. Serial murders 4. Serial murder investigation 5. Night 6. Parks 7. Arson 8. Kidnapping 9. Extortion 10. Loneliness 11. Occultism 12. Eccentrics and eccentricities 13.

England 14. London, England 15. Mysteries

LC 2019034750

Tangled in a cat-and-mouse hunt with a killer who has been performing ritual murders at 4 A.M., Bryant and May explore technological and academic leads that are bizarrely connected by arson, kidnapping and blackmail.

"Perfect for fans of police procedurals with nontraditional, especially older, detectives." Library Journal.

Fowler, Christopher

Bryant & May : strange tide / Christopher Fowler. Random House, 2016. 448 p. Bryant and May mysteries

ISBN 9781101887035

1. Detectives 2. Drowning victims 3. Police 4. Refugees 5. Occultism 6. Octogenarians 7. Criminal evidence 8. Murder investigation 9. Swindlers and swindling 10. London, England 11. Mysteries

When a woman is found drowned in the Thames after being roped to a pillar at low tide, the Peculiar Crimes Unit is baffled to discover only the victim's footprints leading to the spot where she was killed.

"Fowler once again perfectly balances farce and deduction." Publishers Weekly.

Fowler, Earlene

* The **road** to Cardinal Valley / Earlene Fowler. Berkley, 2012 304 p. Ruby McGavin novels

ISBN 9780425252840

1. Alcoholic men 2. Families 3. Family secrets 4. Widows 5. Brothers and sisters 6. Second chances 7. Homecomings 8. Separated friends, relatives, etc 9. Alcoholism -- Intervention 10. Cowboys 11. Traffic accidents 12. Forgiveness 13. Hope 14. Ranches -- California 15. Domestic fiction

Hoping to help her deceased husband's alcoholic brother, Nash, make a fresh start, Ruby McGavin returns to Cardinal, California, where she must confront her estranged mother and a terrible secret.

Fowler, Karen Joy

The **Jane** Austen book club / Karen Joy Fowler. G. P. Putnam's Sons, 2004. 256 p.

ISBN 0399151613

1. Austen, Jane, 1775-1817 Appreciation 2. 21st century 3. Book clubs 4. Friendship 5. Books and reading 6. Fiction -- Appreciation 7. California 8. Humorous stories 9. Women's lives and relationships

LC 2003047244

"A Marian Wood book."

Originally published: 2004.

Six Californians join to discuss Jane Austen's novels. Over the six months they meet, marriages are tested, affairs begin, unsuitable arrangements become suitable, and love happens.

"This novel is essentially a character study of six people who meet regularly over several months to discuss six of Austen's works. Jocelyn, in her 50s and never married, is the originator of the club, a control freak who handpicked all the members; Sylvia, her good friend, is in a funk because her husband of 32 years has just left her for another woman; Sylvia's daughter, Allegra, is an attractive 30-year-old lesbian who recently broke up with her lover; Prudie is a twentysomething high school French teacher; the much-married Bernadette, 67, is now single; and Grigg, in his 40s, would love to get married." Library Journal.

Fowler, Karen Joy

Sarah Canary / Karen Joy Fowler. H. Holt, 1991. 390 p.

ISBN 9780805017533

1. 1870s 2. 19th century 3. Suffragists -- Washington (State) 4. Chinese American men -- Washington (State) 5. Frontier and pioneer life -- Pacific Northwest 6. Voyages and travels 7. Misadventures 8. Perception 9. Racism 10. Sexism 11. Washington (State) 12. The West (United States) -- Race relations -- History -- 19th century 13. Pacific Northwest fiction 14. Science fiction

LC 91009746

First published in 1991.

When a hideous woman appears without warning in Washington territory, Chin Ah Kin--certain that she is an immortal sent to enchant him--decides to return her to her white world, and their journey together becomes a magnet for a cast of eccentric characters

"This novel is similar in scope to E. L. Doctorow's 'Ragtime,' and yet Ms. Fowler's book is as much a dreamscape as a panorama. Each of her 19 chapters has a contemporaneous and often cryptic epigraph from Emily Dickinson's poetry that, amazingly, seems to dictate the narrative that follows." New York Times Book Review.

Fowler, Karen Joy

* **We** are all completely beside ourselves / Karen Joy Fowler. Marian Wood, 2013 320 p.

ISBN 9780399162091

1. Sisters 2. Bonding (Human/animal) 3. Humans and chimpanzees 4. Familial love 5. Animal rights 6. Chimpanzees 7. Loss (Psychology) 8. Family relationships 9. Identity (Psychology) 10. Animal experimentation 11. Human/animal relationships 12. Human experimentation in psychology 13. Literary fiction

PEN-Faulkner Award, 2014.

Shortlisted for the Man Booker Prize, 2014.

Coming of age in middle America, 18-year-old Rosemary evaluates how her entire youth was defined by the presence and forced removal of an endearing chimpanzee who was secretly regarded as a family member and who Rosemary loved as a sister.

"A fantastic novel: technically and intellectually complex, while emotionally gripping." Kirkus.

Fowler, Therese

*A **good** neighborhood / Therese Anne Fowler. St. Martin's Press, 2020. 288 p.

ISBN 9781250237279

1. Racism 2. Suburbs 3. Teenage romance 4. Ecology 5. Multiracial boys 6. Teenage girls 7. Interracial romance 8. Television celebrities 9. Trees 10. Property 11. North Carolina 12. Literary fiction 13. Domestic fiction

LC 2019035018

The single mother of a mixed-race college student and a thriving business owner with a troubled daughter clash over a historic oak tree on their property line and the blossoming romance between their children.

"This page-turner delivers a thoughtful exploration of prejudice, preconceived notions, and what it means to be innocent in the age of an opportunistic media." Publishers Weekly.

Fowler, Therese

A **well-behaved** woman : a novel of the Vanderbilts / Therese Anne Fowler. St. Martin's Press, 2018. 352 p.

ISBN 9781250095473

1. Belmont, Alva, 1853-1933 2. Vanderbilt family 3. Gilded Age (1865-1898) 4. Rich women 5. Ambition in women 6. Women's role 7. Suffragist movement 8. Socialites 9. Wealth 10. Poverty 11. Balls (Parties) 12. Mansions 13. Divorce 14. Scandals 15. New York City 16. New York (State) 17. United States -- Social life and customs -- 1865-1918 18. Historical fiction 19. Biographical fiction

LC 2018019687

RUSA Reading List Short List, 2019.

Marrying into the newly rich but socially scorned Vanderbilt clan, a formerly impoverished Alva navigates society snubs and dark undercurrents in the lives of her in-laws and friends while testing the limits of her ambitious rule-breaking.

"Though the novels lavish sweep and gorgeous details evoke a vanished world, Fowler's exploration of the way powerful women are simultaneously devalued and rewarded resonates powerfully." Publishers Weekly.

Fowler, Therese

* **Z** : a novel of Zelda Fitzgerald / Therese Anne Fowler. St. Martin's Press, 2013. 352 p.

ISBN 9781250028655

1. Fitzgerald, Zelda, 1900-1948 2. Fitzgerald, F Scott (Francis Scott), 1896-1940 3. 1920s 4. Alcoholism 5. Authors' spouses 6. Marital conflict 7. Socialites 8. Women with mental illnesses 9. Interpersonal conflict 10. Authors, American -- 20th century 11. United States -- History -- 1919-1933 12. Biographical fiction 13. Historical fiction

A tale inspired by the marriage of F. Scott and Zelda Fitzgerald follows their union in defiance of her father's opposition and her scandalous transformation into a Jazz Age celebrity in the literary party scenes of New York, Paris, and the French Riviera.

Fowles, John, 1926-2005

* The **French** lieutenant's woman / John Fowles. Back Bay Books, 1998, c1969. 467 p.

ISBN 9780316291163

1. Victorian era (1837-1901) 2. 1860s 3. 19th century 4. Love triangles 5. Scientists 6. Women 7. Men/women relations 8. Interpersonal attraction 9. England -- Social life and customs -- 19th century 10. Great Britain -- History -- Victoria, 1837-1901 11. Historical fiction 12. Literary fiction 13. Love stories 14. Modern classics 15. Metafiction

Originally published: Boston : Little, Brown, 1969.

Charles Smithson, a conventional young scientist, breaks his proper Victorian engagement upon becoming involved with the devastating Sarah Woodruff, whom the townspeople have linked with scandal and forbidden pleasures.

Fowles, John, 1926-2005

* The **magus** / John Fowles. Little Brown, 1966, c1965. 582 p.

ISBN 9780316290975

1. Manipulation (Social sciences) 2. Hallucinations and illusions 3. Sexuality 4. Islands -- Greece 5. Freedom 6. Millionaires 7. Greece 8. Islands of the Aegean 9. Psychological fiction 10. Literary fiction 11. Modern classics 12. Metafiction

LC 65021357

Nicholas Urfe, a young Englishman, accepts a teaching position on a remote Greek island, where an eccentric millionaire manipulates him with hallucinations, riddles, and psychological tests.

"With the narrative skill and literary sleight of hand . . . Fowles again provides hours of engrossing entertainment for an audience susceptible to a massive blend of sensuous realism, suspenseful romanticism, hypertheatrical mystification, psychic intervention, and a gallery of unusual or exotic characters in the vivid setting of the golden, craggy, threatening beauty of an isolated Greek island." Booklist.

Fox, Candice

Crimson Lake / Candice Fox. Forge, 2018, c2017. 304 p. Crimson Lake

ISBN 9780765398482

1. Former police 2. Private investigators 3. Missing persons investigation 4. Missing persons 5. Innocence (Law) 6. Pariahs 7. Authors 8. Australia 9. Thrillers and suspense

Originally published: North Sydney, N.S.W. : Bantam Australia, 2017.

RUSA Reading List Short List, 2019.

Wrongly accused of the abduction of a thirteen-year-old girl, Sydney detective Ted Conkaffey is forced to hide in the crocodile-infested wetlands of Crimson Lake, where he agrees to help convicted killer Amanda Pharrell in a case involving dangerous secrets.

Fox, Candice

Gone by midnight / Candice Fox. Forge, 2020, c2019. 352 p. Crimson Lake

ISBN 9781250317582

1. Missing children 2. Crimes against children 3. Kidnapping 4. Kidnapping victims 5. Missing persons investigation 6. Private investigators 7. Mothers 8. Mothers and sons 9. Women murderers 10. Australia 11. Mysteries 12. Thrillers and suspense

Originally published by Bantam Australia, c2019.

Librarians' Choice (Australia), 2018

When her son goes missing from a hotel room of kids while their parents dine downstairs, Sara teams up with a disgraced cop and a convicted killer to investigate the region's worst suspects.

"Fox ramps up the suspense, leading to a climactic scene in a crocodile-infested swamp. Compelling plot aside, it's the humanity of both Conkaffey and the appealingly eccentric Pharrell that lifts this well above the standard suspense thriller." Booklist.

Fox, Candice

Redemption point / Candice Fox. a Tom Doherty Associates Book, 2019, c2018. 400 p. Crimson Lake

ISBN 9780765398512

1. Kidnapping 2. Missing persons investigation 3. Former police 4. Revenge 5. Innocence (Law) 6. Pariahs 7. Fathers 8. Private investigators 9. Murder investigation 10. Australia 11. Thrillers and suspense

"A Forge Book."

Originally published: North Sydney, NSW : Bantam Australia, c2018.

When the father of a kidnapped girl launches a plan to kill those he holds responsible, Ted Conkaffey races to identify the real abductor; while private detective Amanda Pharrel and Pip Sweeney conduct the latter's first homicide investigation.

Fox, Lauren

Days of awe : a novel / Lauren Fox. Alfred A. Knopf, 2015. 272 p.

ISBN 9780307268129

1. Female friendship 2. Mothers and daughters 3. Marital conflict 4. Husband and wife 5. Separated women (Marital relations) 6. Loss (Psychology) 7. Mother and teenager 8. Motherhood 9. Grief in women 10. Domestic fiction

LC 2015013533

RUSA Reading List Short List, 2016.

Enduring a year marked by her husband's abandonment, her daughter's rebelliousness, and her best friend's shattering death, Isabel gains new insights into her friend's difficulties while considering a new relationship prospect.

Frame, Janet
* **Between** my father and the king : new and uncollected stories / Janet Frame. Counterpoint, 2013. 252 p.
ISBN 9781619021693
1. Literary fiction 2. Short stories
Originally published by Penguin Group (NZ), 2012 as Gorse is not people.
Presents a collection of short stories by the New Zealand author dealing with themes of memory, family, and loss.

Frame, Janet
Prizes : selected short stories / Janet Frame. Counterpoint, 2009. 294 p.
ISBN 9781582435152
1. Short stories 2. Literary fiction
LC 2009032954
"This new anthology spans her lifetime and includes the best of four published collections, plus five previously unpublished stories. Often melancholy but containing wonderful detail, imagery, and emotion, her works cover a wide range of topics like childhood, madness, relationships, identity, and more." Library Journal.

Frame, Ronald, 1953-
Havisham / Ronald Frame. Picador, 2013, c2012. 357 p.
ISBN 9781250037275
1. Rich women 2. Family businesses 3. Upper class 4. Breweries 5. Obsession 6. Jilted women 7. Social classes 8. Obsession in women 9. Women -- Psychology 10. Fathers and daughters 11. Great Britain -- Social life and customs -- 19th century 12. Adaptations, retellings, and spin-offs 13. Historical fiction 14. Literary fiction
Originally published: London : Faber and Faber, 2012.
Catherine Havisham was born into privilege. Handsome, imperious, she is the daughter of a wealthy brewer, and lives in luxury in Satis House. But she is never far from the smell of hops and the arresting letters on the brewhouse wall - Havisham. A reminder of all she owes to the family name and the family business.

Frampton, Megan
The **duke's** guide to correct behavior / Megan Frampton. Avon Books, 2014. 384 p. Dukes behaving badly
ISBN 9780062352200
1. 1840s 2. 19th century 3. Dukes and duchesses 4. Nobility 5. Governesses 6. Men/women relations 7. Interpersonal attraction 8. Secrets 9. Historical romances
All of London knows the Duke of Rutherford has position and wealth. They also whisper that he's dissolute, devilish, and determinedly unwed. So why, everyone is asking, has he hired a governess?
"Framptons romance has charm to spare, and readers will find it impossible to resist her flawless characterization, fanciful plotting, and deliciously fizzy wit." Booklist.

Frampton, Megan
Put up your duke / Megan Frampton. Avon Books, 2015. 384 p. Dukes behaving badly
ISBN 9780062352224
1. Victorian era (1837-1901) 2. Dukes and duchesses 3. Arranged marriage 4. Seduction 5. Inheritance and succession 6. Nobility 7. Husband and wife 8. Boxers (Sports) 9. Sexual attraction 10. Men/women relations 11. London, England -- Social life and customs -- 19th century 12. England -- Social life and customs -- 19th century 13. Great Britain -- History -- Victoria, 1837-1901 14. Victorian romances 15. Historical romances

"Rich in subtle characterization, deftly seasoned with plenty of piquant wit, and spiced with just the right amount of sexy passion, the second tale in the Dukes Behaving Badly series (following The Dukes Guide to Correct Behavior, 2014) is a romantic tour de force. With this splendidly satisfying love story, Frampton proves that she is one of the rising new stars in the historical romance genre." Booklist.

Francis, David, 1958-
Wedding Bush Road : a novel / David Francis. Counterpoint Press, 2016. 300 p.
ISBN 9781619027879
1. Rural life 2. Homecomings 3. Family relationships 4. Families 5. Lawyers 6. Family problems 7. Extramarital affairs 8. Parent and adult child 9. Interpersonal relations 10. Australia 11. South Australia 12. Domestic fiction
LC 2016020224
A young lawyer in Los Angeles returns to his family's farm in rural Australia, where he is plunged into a complex struggle involving his father's mistress, an unstable half-sibling and his mother's failing health.
"Domestic drama with an offbeat, rural flavor." Kirkus.

Francis, Dick
Smokescreen / Dick Francis. Harper & Row, 1972. 213 p.
ISBN 0060113340
1. Actors and actresses 2. Horse racing 3. Attempted murder 4. Gold mines and mining -- South Africa 5. Steeplechasing 6. Jockeys 7. Men/women relations 8. South Africa 9. Kruger National Park, South Africa 10. Thrillers and suspense
LC 72009095
Edward Lincoln, a movie star who plays daring detectives on the silver screen, travels to South Africa to find out who is tampering with his grandmother's race horses. Edward discovers that he is the target and not the horses.
"Even given Francis's high standards [this novel is] an elegant construction, in which we see the parts and their potentialities, and are as much excited to discover how he put them together as what happens when he does. . . . A symphony tumultuous with thrills." Times Literary Supplement.

Francis, Felix
Crisis / Felix Francis. G. P. Putnams Sons, : 384 p. Dick Francis novels
ISBN 9780525536765
1. Horse racing 2. Race horses 3. Arson 4. Fires 5. Stables 6. Murder 7. Murder investigation 8. Arson investigation 9. Amateur detectives 10. Rich families 11. Thrillers and suspense
LC 2018953955
Investigating a stable fire that has killed a Derby favorite, London crisis manager Harrison Foster discovers a human victim and is reluctantly thrust into the dysfunctional rivalries of a racing dynasty.

Francis, Felix
Guilty not guilty / Felix Francis. G. P. Putnams Sons, 2019. 384 p. Dick Francis novels
ISBN 9780525536796
1. Horse racing 2. Married women -- Death 3. Murder suspects 4. Murder investigation 5. Amateur detectives 6. Race horses 7. Murder 8. Greed 9. Jealousy 10. Thrillers and suspense
A volunteer horseracing steward finds his life upended by sensational media allegations about the violent death of his beloved wife and his dangerous efforts to clear his name by capturing the true killer.

Francis, Felix

Pulse / Felix Francis. G.P. Putnam's Sons, 2017. 384 p.
Dick Francis novels

ISBN 9780399574733

1. Horse racing 2. Physicians 3. Attempted murder 4. Murder 5. Jockeys 6. Murder investigation 7. Corruption investigation 8. Thrillers and suspense

LC 2017022753

When a smartly dressed man dies in the hospital after being found unconscious at a local racetrack, doctor Chris Reynolds, a specialist struggling with mental health challenges, searches for the victim's identity and clues about what happened only to be targeted by a ruthless killer.

Francis, Patry

The **orphans** of Race Point : a novel / Patry Francis. Harper, 2014. 336 p.

ISBN 9780062281302

1. Murder 2. Priests 3. First loves 4. Malicious accusation 5. Orphans 6. Betrayal 7. Families 8. Psychic trauma 9. Redemption 10. Memories 11. Provincetown, Massachusetts 12. Literary fiction

LC 2013031980

When priest Gus Silva, the man she has never stopped loving, is charged with murder, Hallie Costa, who has known Gus since childhood, must not only free him from prison, but from the curse of his past.

Franck, Julia

Blindness of the heart / Julia Franck ; translated from the German by Anthea Bell. Grove Press, 2010. 416 p.

ISBN 9780802119674

1. Abandoned children 2. World War II 3. Jewish women 4. Multiracial persons 5. War -- Moral and ethical aspects 6. Germany -- History -- 20th century 7. Historical fiction 8. War stories 9. Literary fiction 10. Translations -- German to English

A family story spanning two world wars and several generations in a German family centers on Helene, a woman who must make the most of a tumultuous time, in a book that reveals the scope of German citizens' denial--or "blindness of the heart"--as a survival mechanism during World War II.

"There are no easy answers or pat resolutions in this dark novel, just a compelling narrative and solid writing." Library Journal.

Frank, Dorothea Benton, 1951-2019

Folly Beach : a Lowcountry tale / Dorothea Benton Frank. William Morrow, 2011. 336 p. Lowcountry tales (Dorothea Benton Frank)

ISBN 9780061961274

1. Family relationships 2. Widows 3. Self-discovery in women 4. Homecomings 5. Identity (Psychology) 6. Loss (Psychology) 7. Debt 8. South Carolina 9. Folly Beach, South Carolina 10. Domestic fiction 11. Southern fiction 12. Gentle reads

Returning to Folly Beach, her childhood home, newly widowed Cate Cooper, whose late husband's financial exploits have left her homeless and broke, discovers that it is possible to go home again and discover the person she was meant to become.

"The recently widowed protagonist's journey to rediscovering joy and love will thrill readers, especially with the addition of a suavely integrated story-within-a-story involving a one-woman play about the lovers who wrote Porgy and Bess. There's a certain authenticity to the lives Frank tells that will resonate with many women. Frank's telling of this tale will help readers celebrate love and sexuality after 60." Publishers Weekly.

Frank, Dorothea Benton, 1951-2019

Queen bee / Dorothea Benton Frank. William Morrow & Co., 2019. 384 p. Lowcountry tales (Dorothea Benton Frank)

ISBN 9780062861214

1. Island life 2. Beekeepers 3. Women -- Interpersonal relations 4. Mother and adult daughter 5. Men/women relations 6. Single fathers 7. Sibling rivalry 8. Domestic fiction 9. Women's lives and relationships 10. Southern fiction 11. Gentle reads

A Sullivan's Island beekeeper navigates her demanding hypochondriac mother and flamboyant rival sister while immersing herself in the lives of two young neighbor boys and their widowed father.

Frankel, Laurie

Goodbye for now : a novel / Laurie Frankel. Doubleday, 2012. 288 p.

ISBN 9780385536189

1. Computer programmers 2. Small business 3. Loss (Psychology) 4. Online dating 5. Social networks 6. Soul mates 7. Satirical fiction 8. Mainstream fiction

LC 2011051266

First published in Great Britain in 2012.

Creating an algorithm to improve his Internet dating employer's match success rate only to be fired for being too effective, Sam Elliot, who used his innovation to meet the love of his life, develops a computer program that creates compelling human simulations that allow people to say final goodbyes to lost loved ones.

Frankel, Laurie

This is how it always is / Laurie Frankel. Flatiron Books, 2017. 327 p.

ISBN 9781250088550

1. Transgender children 2. Family secrets 3. Identity (Psychology) 4. Social acceptance 5. Families 6. Familial love 7. Loyalty 8. Domestic fiction

LC 2016037633

A family reshapes their ideas about family, love and loyalty when youngest son Claude reveals increasingly determined preferences for girls' clothing and accessories and refuses to stay silent.

"This is a wonderfully contradictory storyheartwarming and generous, yet written with a wry sensibility." Publishers Weekly.

Franklin, Ariana

Mistress of the art of death / Ariana Franklin. G. P. Putnam's Sons, 2007. 384 p. Adelia Aguilar series

ISBN 0399154140

1. Henry II,, King of England, 1133-1189 2. Medieval period (476-1492) 3. Plantagenet period (1154-1485) 4. 12th century 5. Women physicians 6. Child murder victims 7. Serial murder investigation 8. Jews 9. Rulers 10. Serial murderers 11. Revenue agents 12. Serial murders 13. Malicious accusation 14. Prejudice 15. Witchcraft 16. Cambridge, England 17. England -- History -- Medieval period, 1066-1485 18. Historical mysteries 19. Mysteries

LC 2006024710

Ellis Peters Historical Dagger Award, 2007.
RUSA Reading List, 2008.
Sue Feder Historical Mystery Award, 2008.

Sent to medieval Cambridge in order to exonerate Jewish prisoners with financial ties to King Henry II, University of Salerno medical examiner Adelia struggles to avoid being accused of witchcraft and discovers that the killer may be a former crusader.

"This novel will surely please mystery fans as well as lovers of historical fiction." Library Journal.

Franklin, Ariana

The **serpent's** tale / Ariana Franklin. G. P. Putnam's Sons, 2008. 371 p. Adelia Aguilar series

ISBN 9780399154645

1. Henry II,, King of England, 1133-1189 2. Eleanor,, of Aquitaine, Queen, consort of Henry II, King of England, 1122?-1204 3. Medieval period (476-1492) 4. Plantagenet period (1154-1485) 5. 12th century 6. Women physicians 7. Murder 8. Mistresses 9. Men/women relations 10. Interpersonal relations 11. Murder suspects 12. Rulers 13. Poisoning 14. Women forensic pathologists 15. Great Britain -- History -- Henry II, 1154-1189 16. Historical mysteries 17. Mysteries

LC 2007038585

Also published as: "The Death Maze"

Ordered by Henry II to establish the possible role of Eleanor of Aquitaine in the poisoning death of Henry's mistress, a reluctant Adelia Aguilar joins forces with her infant daughter's father, the Bishop of St. Albans, during the investigation.

"This excellent adventure delivers high drama and lively scholarship from its heroine's feminist perspective." New York Times Book Review.

Franklin, Ariana

The **siege** winter / Ariana Franklin, Samantha Norman. William Morrow & Co., 2015. 352 p.

ISBN 9780062282569

1. Matilda,, Empress, consort of Henry V, Holy Roman Emperor, 1102-1167 2. Stephen,, King of England, 1097?-1154 3. Medieval period (476-1492) 4. Norman period (1066-1154) 5. Apprentices 6. War and society 7. Political intrigue 8. Rulers 9. Kidnapping victims 10. Disguises 11. Archers 12. Young women 13. Apprenticeship 14. Peasantry 15. Monks 16. Siege warfare 17. Great Britain -- History -- Stephen, 1135-1154 18. Historical fiction

A traumatized apprentice archer, disguised as a boy, and the young chatelaine of a strategically important fortress risk their lives to support the Empress Matilda's campaign for the throne of mid-12th-century England.

"The cheeky wit and precise descriptions that were Franklins hallmarks are as sharp as ever, and the major characters are delightfully human. The book also has a genuine feel for medieval life and times. This unique collaboration is a worthy conclusion to one remarkable career and a promising beginning to another." Booklist.

Franklin, Miles, 1879-1954

* **My** brilliant career / Miles Franklin. St. Martin's Press, 1980, c1901. 232 p.

ISBN 9780312555993

1. Franklin, Miles, 1879-1954 2. 19th century 3. Teenage nonconformists 4. Independence in teenage girls 5. Women marriage resisters 6. Teenagers -- Career aspirations 7. Teenage girls -- Australia 8. Independence in young women 9. Women employees -- Australia -- History 10. Women -- Social conditions -- 19th century 11. Australia -- Social life and customs -- 19th century 12. Autobiographical fiction 13. Teenagers' writings

LC 80052658

Sequel: My career goes bung.

Originally published: Edinburgh : William Blackwood & Sons, 1901.

This captivating Australian novel transcends time and genre in the classic tale of an extraordinarily ambitious young woman who passionately evades marriage to pursue her envisioned brilliant career

Franklin, Tom

Crooked letter, crooked letter : a novel / Tom Franklin. William Morrow, 2010. 288 p.

ISBN 9780060594664

1. Male friendship 2. Small town life -- Mississippi 3. Missing girls 4. Reconciliation in men 5. Childhood friends 6. Mississippi 7. Psychological suspense 8. Southern Gothic 9. Southern fiction

LC 2010005423

ALA Notable Book, 2011.

Gold Dagger Award for Best Crime Novel of the Year, 2011.

African-American Constable Silas Jones must confront his white former friend Larry Ott, who has lived under suspicion for twenty years since a girl disappeared while on a date with him, after another girl disappears and Larry is blamed once again.

"Franklin writes with quiet economy. There are no great flights of dialogue or rambling description; everything is sharply focused to achieve its purpose. The resulting novel winds through its path as crookedly as the letters of its title, and arrives at a nicely achieved ending. It's an ending that isn't without complication but, given what precedes it, a conclusion that is fitting and right." Denver Post.

Frantz, Laura

The **lacemaker** / Laura Frantz. Revell, 2018. 416 p.

ISBN 9780800726638

1. Revolutionary America (1775-1783) 2. Revolutionaries 3. Jilted women 4. Protectiveness in men 5. Malicious accusation 6. Loyalty 7. Interpersonal attraction 8. Men/women relations 9. Williamsburg, Virginia 10. United States -- History -- Revolution, 1775-1783 11. Christian historical romances 12. Historical romances

LC 2017031367

Christy Award for Historical Romance Category, 2018.

On the eve of her wedding, Lady Elisabeth Lawson's world is shattered, as surely as the fine glass windows of her colonial Williamsburg home. In a town seething with Patriots ready for rebellion, her protection comes from an unlikely source--now if she could only protect her heart.

Franzen, Jonathan

* The **corrections** / Jonathan Franzen. Farrar, Straus and Giroux, 2001. 576 p.

ISBN 0374129983

1. People with Parkinson's disease 2. Parent and adult child 3. Dysfunctional families 4. Family relationships 5. Married women 6. Middle West 7. Philadelphia, Pennsylvania 8. Vilna, Lithuania 9. New York City 10. Literary fiction 11. Psychological fiction

LC 2001033478

ALA Notable Book, 2002.

James Tait Black Memorial Prize for Fiction, 2002.

National Book Award for Fiction, 2001.

National Book Critics Circle Award for Fiction finalist, 2001

Pulitzer Prize for Fiction finalist, 2002

Shortlisted for the International IMPAC Dublin Literary Award, 2003

Enid Lambert begins to worry about her husband when he begins to withdraw and lose himself in negativity and depression as he faces Parkinson's disease.

"The novel has the absorbing treacheries of married life, the comic squalors of cruise-shop travel and the shenanigans of global capitalism. It also has language that builds in powerful, rolling strides. And it has characters, the separately unraveling Lamberts, who get very deeply under your skin." Time.

Franzen, Jonathan

* Freedom / Jonathan Franzen. Farrar, Straus and Giroux, 2010. 576 p.

ISBN 9780374158460

1. Husband and wife 2. Love triangles 3. Dysfunctional families 4. Family relationships 5. Neighbors 6. Interpersonal relations 7. Sexuality 8. Self-fulfillment 9. Self-discovery 10. St Paul, Minnesota 11. Literary fiction

LC 2010010273

ALA Notable Book, 2011.

National Book Critics Circle Award for Fiction finalist, 2010

The idyllic lives of civic-minded environmentalists Patty and Walter Berglund come into question when their son moves in with aggressive Republican neighbors, green lawyer Walter takes a job in the coal industry, and go-getter Patty becomes increasingly unstable and enraged.

"Franzen performs a kind of literary MRI on the marriage, micro-slicing its many nuances. He innately grasps how desires can shift in an instant, and how getting what we want can lead to disappointment or self-doubt. And he remains a keen observer of modern culture. . . . Freedom isn't flawless: Patty's journal reads more like Franzen than his character, and he gets sidetracked by quirky tangents. But this is a deep dive into a fascinating family that feels very real, and fully grounded in our time." Entertainment Weekly.

Franzen, Jonathan

Purity / Jonathan Franzen. Farrar, Straus and Giroux, 2015. 563 p.

ISBN 9780374239213

1. Identity (Psychology) 2. Internet 3. Whistle blowing 4. Young women 5. Interpersonal relations 6. Men/women relations 7. Secrets 8. Birthfathers 9. Literary fiction 10. Psychological fiction

Struggling with identity issues and student loans as the daughter of a mother who hides a mysterious past, Pip takes an internship with an illicit activist group and falls for its charismatic fugitive leader.

"... Franzen is burrowing deep into each person's questionable sense of his or her own goodness and suggests that the moral rot can metastasize to the levels of corporations and government. And yet the novel's prose never bogs down into lectures, and its various back stories are as forceful as the main tale of Purity's fate. Franzen is much-mocked for his primacy in the literary landscape (something he himself mocks when Charles grouses about a plague of literary Jonathans). But here, he's admirably determined to think big and write well about our darkest emotional corners. An expansive, brainy, yet inviting novel that leaves few foibles unexplored." Kirkus.

Frayn, Michael

Headlong : a novel / Michael Frayn. Metropolitan Books, 1999. 342 p.

ISBN 0805062858

1. Art investigators 2. Husband and wife 3. Painting -- Private collections 4. Philosophers 5. Women art historians 6. England 7. Humorous stories

Shortlisted for the Booker-McConnell Prize, 1999.

When a frustrated philosopher uncovers what he believes is a lost painting by Bruegel in a boorish neighbor's basement, he embarks on a quest to separate the work from its owner

"Martin Clay seems to have all he might reasonably wish for: a new career as an art historian, a loving wife, an adorable baby daughter, and a summer cottage in the English countryside, where he is supposed to be completing his book on fifteenth-century Netherlandish art. Instead, he stumbles upon an unsigned Brueghel (at least, he's almost positive it's a Brueghel) stashed in a fireplace of his neighbor's crumbling estate. Overwhelmed by high-minded professional curiosity and base greed, Martin resolves to acquire it by whatever means necessary. What follows is part detective story, part art-history lesson, part cautionary tale, and entirely funny." The New Yorker.

Frayn, Michael

Spies : a novel / Michael Frayn. Metropolitan Books, 2002. 261 p.

ISBN 0805070583

1. Boys -- Friendship 2. Friendship 3. World War II -- Children 4. Secrets 5. Women spies -- Germany 6. London, England 7. Thrillers and suspense

LC 2001039840

Whitbread Book Award for Novel, 2002.

When a long-forgotten scent forces Stephen Wheatley to confront his past, he starts to remember a troubling childhood summer in wartime London where an imaginative child's game of playing spies wreaked havoc upon innocent lives.

"A compelling story about secrecy and betrayal. . . . What is truly remarkable about this novel, though, is the way Frayn perfectly captures the dynamics of childhood friendships." Booklist.

Frazier, Charles, 1950-

* Cold Mountain / Charles Frazier. Atlantic Monthly Press, 1997. 356 p.

ISBN 0871136791

1. American Civil War era (1861-1865) 2. 1860s 3. Confederate soldiers 4. Deserters 5. Farm life 6. Lovers' reunions 7. Soldiers 8. Mountain life 9. Voyages and travels 10. Women farmers 11. Civil war 12. United States Civil War, 1861-1865 13. North Carolina -- History -- Civil War, 1861-1865 14. Historical fiction 15. Literary fiction 16. Southern fiction

LC 97275

Illustrated with endpaper map.

ALA Notable Book, 1998.

Book Sense Book of the Year Adult Trade, 1998.

National Book Award for Fiction, 1997.

Sir Walter Raleigh Award for Fiction, 1997.

National Book Critics Circle Award for Fiction finalist, 1997

After Inman escapes from a war hospital in 1864 and starts walking to Cold Mountain, Ada struggles to save her mountain farm with the help of Ruby, an illiterate but efficient farmer.

"This novel's landscape is finely drawn, full of dark beauty and presentiment, and so are its characters. They give voice to a classical, peculiarly American feeling of nostalgia--the pain of returning home." The New Yorker.

Frazier, Charles, 1950-

Nightwoods : a novel / Charles Frazier. Random House, 2011. 272 p.

ISBN 9781400067091

1. 1960s 2. Children who are mute 3. Aunts 4. Orphans 5. Rural women 6. Solitude 7. Sisters -- Death 8. Murder 9. Loss (Psychology) 10. Small towns -- North Carolina 11. Twins 12. Twin brothers and sisters 13. Wife-killing 14. Greed in men 15. North Carolina -- History -- 20th century 16. Appalachian Region 17. Rural noir 18. Literary fiction 19. Southern fiction

LC 2011014629

Sir Walter Raleigh Award for Fiction, 2012.

Named the guardian of her murdered sister's troubled twins, Luce struggles to build a family with the children before being targeted by the twins' father--her sister's killer--who believes that the children are in possession of a stolen cache of money.

"Not surprisingly, things get messy, but Nightwoods is no typical thriller. It hits hard because you come to care so much about the characters, all of them drawn with that precise enchanted prose. By the book's climactic scenes in the shadowy mountain forest that gives Nightwoods its title, the unhurried, poetic suspense is both difficult to bear and impossible to shake." Entertainment Weekly.

Frazier, Charles, 1950-

Thirteen moons : a novel / Charles Frazier. Random House, 2006 422 p.
ISBN 9780375509322
1. 19th century 2. Interracial romance 3. Indians of North America 4. Cherokee Indians 5. Courage in men 6. Loss (Psychology) 7. Fate and fatalism 8. Voyages and travels 9. Twelve-year-old boys 10. Men/women relations 11. Love 12. Interethnic relations 13. Coming-of-age stories 14. Historical fiction 15. Southern fiction
From the age of twelve, when he is sent alone into the wilderness to run an Indian trading post, Will's life becomes intertwined with the destiny of the Cherokee Indians, as he falls in love with a girl named Claire, and builds a friendship with a chief named Bear.
"The author uses his sense of time and place and his lyrical, pointillist prose to give the reader an aching appreciation of the Indians' plight. ... [He] recounts Will's melancholy adventures with plenty of narrative brio, giving the reader a succession of suspensefuland in some cases touchingset pieces." New York Times.

Frazier, Charles, 1950-

Varina / Charles Frazier. Ecco, 2018. 288 p.
ISBN 9780062405982
1. Davis, Varina, 1826-1906 2. American Civil War era (1861-1865) 3. Civil War 4. Married women 5. Politicians' spouses 6. War 7. Social conflict 8. Women fugitives 9. Women -- History 10. Men/women relations 11. United States -- History -- Civil War, 1861-1865 12. Confederate States of America 13. Mississippi 14. Biographical fiction 15. Historical fiction

LC bl2018002826
Forced by limited prospects to marry much-older widower Jefferson Davis, teenaged Varina Howell finds her expectations as the wife of a Mississippi landowner upended by his appointment as the leader of the Confederacy, a situation that renders her and her children fugitives in a divided and increasingly hostile nation.

Frear, Caz

Stone cold heart / Caz Frear. HarperCollins, 2019. 368 p. Cat Kinsella
ISBN 9780062849885
1. Women detectives 2. Women murder victims 3. Murder investigation 4. Marital conflict 5. Dishonesty 6. Boyfriends 7. Dysfunctional families 8. Secrets 9. London, England 10. England 11. Great Britain 12. Police procedurals 13. Thrillers and suspense
When a coffee-shop owner is implicated in the death of a young Australian woman, DC Cat Kinsella of the London Metropolitan Police investigates the chief suspect's hostile wife to discern which of them is telling the truth.

Frear, Caz

Sweet little lies / Caz Frear. Harper, 2018, c2017. 480 p. Cat Kinsella
ISBN 9780062823199
1. 1990s 2. Fathers and daughters 3. Women detectives 4. Missing persons 5. Murder investigation 6. Trust 7. Family relationships 8. Deception 9. London, England 10. England 11. Great Britain 12. Police procedurals 13. Thrillers and suspense

Originally published: London : Zaffre, 2017.
A London policewoman from a troubled family is forced to investigate dark secrets in her estranged father's past to solve the murder of a young housewife and the disappearance of a teen girl years earlier.

Fredericks, Mariah

* Death of a new American : a mystery / Mariah Fredericks. Minotaur Books, 2019. 304 p. Jane Prescott novels
ISBN 9781250152992
1. 1910s 2. Upper class 3. Household employees 4. Women amateur detectives 5. Weddings 6. Mafia 7. Rich families 8. Women murder victims 9. Murder investigation 10. Long Island, New York 11. Historical mysteries

LC 2018049423
A follow-up to A Death of No Importance finds ladies' maid Jane Prescott accompanying her employers to a family wedding in Long Island that is threatened by a nanny's murder, mafia threats against their host and dark secrets.
"Fredericks has a sharp eye for the complexities of human nature and how even good people are capable of committing terrible deeds to protect the ones they love. This is a touching portrait of early-20th-century New York in all its glory and ugliness." Publishers Weekly.

Freed, David, 1954-

Hot start : a Cordell Logan mystery / David Freed. The Permanent Press, 2016 312 p. Cordell Logan mysteries
ISBN 9781579624330
1. Big game hunters 2. Animal rights advocates 3. Malicious accusation 4. Murder suspects 5. Buddhists 6. Intelligence officers 7. Buddhism 8. Murder 9. California 10. Mysteries

LC 2016017186
A notorious, international big game hunter and his beautiful, former flight attendant wife are gunned down at long range late one sweltering summer night while swimming naked on their seaside estate in opulent Rancho Bonita, California. Police investigators are convinced that the killer is a strident, outspoken animal rights activist with both military experience and a criminal record. The evidence against him would appear overwhelming--until rumors begin to surface that others may have had their own reasons for committing murder. The last thing flight instructor, aspiring Buddhist, and ex-government assassin Cordell Logan wants to do is become involved in the investigation. He and the accused, however, have mutual friends.

Freedman, Benedict

Mrs. Mike : the story of Katherine Mary Flannigan / Benedict and Nancy Freedman. Berkley Books, 2002, c1947. 313 p. Mrs. Mike series
ISBN 9780425183236
1. Flannigan, Katherine Mary 2. Royal Canadian Mounted Police Northwest, Canadian 3. Frontier and pioneer life -- Northwest, Canadian 4. Irish American women 5. Police 6. Men/women relations 7. Canada 8. Historical fiction 9. Biographical fiction
Sequel: The Search for Joyful.
Originally published: New York : Coward-McCann, 1947.
Mrs. Mike is the love story of Katherine Mary O'Fallon, a young Irish girl from Boston, and Sergeant Mike Flannigan of the Canadian Mounted Police, who is a priest, doctor and magistrate to all in the great Canadian wilderness area under his supervision.

Freeman, Anna

The **fair** fight : a novel / Anna Freeman. Riverhead Books, 2015, c2014. 480 p.

ISBN 9781594633294

1. Georgian era (1714-1837) 2. Boxing 3. Social classes 4. Poor women 5. Women boxers 6. Gambling 7. Scars 8. Brothers and sisters 9. Self-fulfillment 10. Gay men 11. England -- Social life and customs -- 18th century 12. Bristol, England 13. Historical fiction

LC 2014019046

Originally published: London: Weidenfeld & Nicolson, 2014.

Born in a Bristol whorehouse, scrappy Ruth stumbles into a career as a pugilist after a brawl with her half-sister attracts a betting audience. As Ruth enters the gritty, brutal world of professional prize-fighters, she encounters aspiring boxer Charlotte Sinclair, for whom the ring serves as an escape from her abusive marriage and a place where her smallpox scars do not attract notice; and gambler George Bowden, who hopes that backing the right fighter will make him a wealthy man. Bouncing between brothel and boxing ring, this debut skillfully depicts the seamy underbelly of Georgian England. -- Description by Gillian Speace.

"Freeman doesnt shy away from the grim realities of sexism, homophobia, and illness that afflict the lives of her characters, and readers will appreciate her blunt look at the English caste system. Freeman is at her best in moments when the characters transcend their societal roles and break free of expectations." Booklist.

Freeman, Brian, 1963-

Goodbye to the dead / Brian Freeman. Quercus, 2016, c2015. 448 p. Jonathan Stride novels

ISBN 9781623659110

1. Widowers 2. Murder witnesses 3. Innocence (Law) 4. Women murder suspects 5. Human trafficking 6. Detectives 7. Women detectives 8. Lovers 9. Men/women relations 10. Minnesota 11. Duluth, Minnesota 12. Thrillers and suspense

First published in Great Britain in 2015 by Quercus.

When fellow detective Serena witnesses a brutal murder with ties to a case from the last year of his wife's life, detective Stride investigates human-trafficking activity in the Duluth port and struggles with the possibility that he may have sent an innocent woman to prison.

"Freeman skillfully weaves together diverse story lines, from the old murder to a sex-slavery operation, with twists that build suspense, in this fine, character-driven addition to a strong series." Booklist.

Freeman, Brian, 1963-

Marathon / Brian Freeman. Quercus, 2017. 408 p. Jonathan Stride novels

ISBN 9781681442419

1. Bombings 2. Terrorism 3. Criminal investigation 4. Marathons 5. Fugitives 6. Minnesota 7. Duluth, Minnesota 8. Thrillers and suspense

When a bombing at the Duluth Marathon kills and injures numerous victims, detective Jonathan Stride teams up with Serena Dial, Maggie Bei and their FBI contacts to track down a suspicious man with a backpack in the wake of media misinformation. By the award-winning author of Immoral.

Freeman, Brian, 1963-

The **night** bird / Brian Freeman. Thomas & Mercer, 2017. 350 p. Frost Easton novels

ISBN 9781503943568

1. Memory 2. Psychoses 3. Serial murders 4. Serial murder investigation 5. Mental illness -- Treatment 6. Experimental medicine 7. Murder investigation 8. Psychiatrists 9. Detectives 10. Murder 11. San Francisco, California 12. Thrillers and suspense

Homicide detective Frost Easton doesn't like coincidences, so when a series of bizarre deaths rock San Francisco?during which seemingly random women suffer violent psychotic breaks?Frost looks for a connection that leads him to controversial psychiatrist Francesca Stein.

Freeman, Brian, 1963-

Thief River Falls / Brian Freeman. Thomas and Mercer, 2020. 314 p.

ISBN 9781542093361

1. Women authors 2. Child witnesses 3. Runaways 4. Protectiveness in women 5. Runaway boys 6. Police cover-ups 7. Murder 8. Memories 9. Rural life 10. Minnesota 11. Psychological suspense

A best-selling writer living in seclusion after losing her family to a series of tragedies risks her life to protect a child who is being targeted by both killers and police who would cover up the murder he witnessed.

"Readers will admire the skillful way Freeman plays tricks with thriller conventions." Publishers Weekly.

Freeman, Castle, 1944-

All **that** I have : a novel / Castle Freeman Jr. Steerforth Press, 2009. 176 p.

ISBN 9781586421519

1. Small-town life 2. Sheriffs 3. Middle-aged men 4. Criminals 5. Personal conduct 6. Ethics 7. Misbehavior 8. Robbery 9. Vermont 10. Psychological fiction

LC 2008043223

Sheriff Lucian Wing deals with unexpected crises in his quiet Vermont jurisdiction, including the theft of a safe from Russian mobsters by a local bad boy, a deputy who wants Lucian's job, and marital problems.

"Sheriff Lucian Wing, the narrator of Freeman's wonderfully wry fourth novel, is a laconic, old-fashioned lawman who discovers an outpost of nefarious Russians in his sleepy Vermont county. Wing's Fargoesque delivery is hysterical, but what makes this spare tale a standout is Freeman's keen ear for dialogue and his affection for the quietly complex characters of small-town life. " People.

Freeman, Dianne

A **lady's** guide to etiquette and murder / Dianne Freeman. Kensington Books, 2018 304 p. Countess of Harleigh mysteries

ISBN 9781496716873

1. Victorian era (1837-1901) 2. Counts and countesses 3. Independence in women 4. Women amateur detectives 5. Americans in Great Britain 6. Murder investigation 7. Rich women 8. Aristocracy 9. Debutantes 10. Widows 11. London, England 12. Victorian mysteries 13. Historical mysteries

Agatha Award for Best First Novel, 2018.

A wealthy young widow encounters the pleasures?and scandalous pitfalls--of a London social season.

Frei, Max

The **stranger's** magic / Max Frei ; translated by Polly Gannon and Astamur Moore. Overlook Press, 2012. 464 p. Labyrinths of Echo

ISBN 9781590204795

1. Twenties (Age) 2. Parallel universes 3. Slackers 4. Magic 5. Crime 6. Dreams 7. Misfits (Persons) 8. Supernatural mysteries 9. Translations -- Russian to English

More adventures of Max, a hopeless smoker, glutton, and loafer, who discovers a parallel world where magic is commonplace and he fits right in.

French, Albert

Billy / Albert French. Viking, 1993. 214 p.

ISBN 0670850136

1. 1930s 2. Racism 3. African American boys 4. Ten-year-old boys 5. Murder 6. Mothers and sons 7. Capital punishment 8. Racism in capital punishment 9. Segregation 10. Small towns 11. Small town life 12. Mississippi 13. Historical fiction 14. African American fiction

LC 93014676

An anonymous observer narrates the tale of spirited ten-year-old Billy Lee, a Black boy who is convicted and executed for the murder of a white girl in Banes, Mississippi, in the 1930s.

French, Jonathan (Jonathan P.)

* The **Grey** Bastards / Jonathan French. Crown Publishing, 2018. 424 p. Lot Lands

ISBN 9780525572442

1. Half-human hybrids 2. Quests 3. Orcs 4. Goblins 5. Secrets 6. Black magic 7. Wizards 8. Exiles 9. Sword and sorcery 10. Apocalyptic fiction 11. Horror

Jackal, a proud member of a group of half-orcs tasked with protecting human civilization from their full-blooded brethren, discovers a dark secret that threatens to dissolve the tenuous peace between species.

French, Jonathan (Jonathan P.)

The **true** Bastards / Jonathan French. Crown Publishers, 2019. 583 p. Lot lands

ISBN 9780525572473

1. Half-human hybrids 2. Women warriors 3. Alliances 4. Orcs 5. Wanderers and wandering 6. Exiles 7. Humans 8. Gangs 9. Famines 10. Enemies 11. Leadership in women 12. Sick persons 13. Sword and sorcery 14. Apocalyptic fiction

Sequel to: The Grey Bastards.

Fetching--the female leader of her own hoof, a loyal group of orcs sworn to her--fights off famine, desertions, other orcs and humans who are plotting against her.

French, Marilyn, 1929-2009

* The **women's** room / Marilyn French. Summit Books, 1977. 471 p.

ISBN 067140010X

1. 1970s 2. Women graduate students 3. Sexism 4. Self-awareness in women 5. Middle-aged women 6. Feminists 7. Sexism in universities and colleges 8. Protests, demonstrations, vigils, etc 9. Suburban life 10. Loss (Psychology) 11. Men/women relations 12. Literary fiction

LC 77024918

A portrait of Mira Ward, erstwhile suburban doctor's wife and mother of two and latter-day Harvard graduate student, depicts a 1950s world of men and women in bondage to one another and the 1970s world of liberation and radical reassessment.

"[The author's] dialogue, her characterizations, her knowledge of the changing relationships, sexual and otherwise, between men and women in a complex world of shifting values, are all extraordinary." Publishers Weekly.

French, Nicci

* **Blue** Monday / Nicci French. Pamela Dorman Books/ Viking, 2012, c2011. 400 p. Frieda Klein novels

ISBN 9780670023363

1. Missing children 2. Psychotherapists 3. Psychotherapist and patient 4. Captives 5. Missing persons investigation 6. Police 7. Detectives 8. Abandoned children 9. Suspicion 10. London, England

11. Psychological suspense

Originally published in UK in 2011 (London: Michael Joseph)

Frieda Klein is a brilliant psychotherapist who finds herself hunting down a kidnapper. When five-year-old Matthew Farraday goes missing, all of London is in an uproar--including Frieda, who recalls a patient haunted by dreams of snatching a child matching Matthew's description. To find the child before it's too late, Frieda must journey to a very dangerous place--the mind of a psychopath.

"With its smart plot, crisp prose, and a stunning final twist, this is psychological suspense at its best. Absolutely riveting." Booklist.

French, Nicci

Dark Saturday / Nicci French. William Morrow & Co., 2017. 390 p. Frieda Klein novels

ISBN 9780062676665

1. Murder suspects 2. Women psychotherapists 3. Cold cases (Criminal investigation) 4. Murder investigation 5. Murderers 6. Suspicion 7. Guilt (Law) 8. Great Britain 9. Psychological suspense

Reluctantly agreeing to assess a woman who was incarcerated in a secure psychiatric hospital a decade earlier for murder, psychotherapist Frieda Klein begins to suspect that the girl is innocent, only to find herself targeted by someone who would keep the truth hidden.

French, Nicci

* The **day** of the dead : a novel / Nicci French. William Morrow, 2018. 304 p. Frieda Klein novels

ISBN 9780062846082

1. Murder suspects 2. Women psychotherapists 3. Psychopaths 4. Stalking 5. Murder investigation 6. Murderers 7. Suspicion 8. Obsession 9. Criminology 10. Stalkers 11. Great Britain 12. Psychological suspense

LC 2017061678

Series complete in 8 volumes.

Finds psychologist Frieda Klein driven into hiding by obsessed psychopath Dean Reeve, while criminology student Lola Hayes places herself at risk to follow in Frieda's footsteps.

French, Nicci

Friday on my mind : a Frieda Klein mystery / Nicci French. Penguin Books, 2016. 352 p. Frieda Klein novels

ISBN 9780143127222

1. Women psychotherapists 2. Murder suspects 3. Fugitives 4. Suspicion 5. Former boyfriends 6. Police 7. Stalkers 8. Murder investigation 9. Malicious accusation 10. Stalking 11. Suffolk, England 12. Psychological suspense

LC 2016013489

Maps on end papers.

When the body of her ex-boyfriend turns up in the Thames, London psychotherapist Frieda Klein becomes the prime suspect in the murder investigation and goes on the run to save herself and find the real killer, who she believes is a man who has never stopped haunting her, but who the police think has been dead for years.

French, Nicci

* The **lying** room / Nicci French. William Morrow & Co, 2019. 304 p.

ISBN 9780062676726

1. Married women 2. Extramarital affairs 3. Deception 4. Murder victims 5. Murderers 6. Detectives 7. Crime scenes 8. England 9. Psychological suspense

In this thrilling standalone from the internationally bestselling author of the Frieda Klein series, a married woman's affair with her boss spirals into a dangerous game of chess with the police when she discovers he's been murdered and she clears the crime scene of all evidence.

French, Nicci

* Sunday silence / Nicci French. William Morrow & Co., 2018, c2017. 403 p. Frieda Klein novels

   ISBN 9780062819840

   1. Murder suspects 2. Women psychotherapists 3. Stalking 4. Psychopaths 5. Murder investigation 6. Murderers 7. Suspicion 8. Guilt (Law) 9. Stalkers 10. Great Britain 11. Psychological suspense

Maps on endpapers.

Originally published: London : Penguin, 2017 as Sunday morning coming down.

Declared a person of interest when a body is discovered beneath the floorboards of her own home, London psychologist Frieda Klein realizes that a copycat killer of the chief suspect is responsible before she finds herself in a deadly game of tug-of-war between two obsessive murderers.

French, Nicci

Thursday's children / Nicci French. Michael Joseph, 2014. 420 p. Frieda Klein novels

   ISBN 9780718156992

   1. Women psychotherapists 2. Rape investigation 3. Hometowns 4. Murder 5. Police 6. Reunions 7. Memories 8. Former friends 9. Teenage girl murder victims 10. Women psychotherapists 11. Crimes against teenage girls 12. Murder investigation 13. Suffolk, England 14. Psychological suspense

When psychotherapist Frieda Klein left the sleepy Suffolk coastal town in which she grew up she never intended to return. Left behind were friends, family, lives and loves but alongside them, painful memories; a past she wouldn't allow to destroy her.

"A skillfully woven plot and deftly drawn characters complement the central mystery, which engages and satisfies while developing the series arc." Publishers Weekly.

French, Nicci

Tuesday's gone / Nicci French. Pamela Dorman Books/Viking, 2013, c2012. 384 p. Frieda Klein novels

   ISBN 9780670025671

   1. Swindlers and swindling 2. Women psychotherapists 3. Fraud 4. Detectives 5. False personation 6. Family relationships 7. Murder investigation 8. Police 9. London, England 10. Psychological suspense 11. Thrillers and suspense

           LC 2012040052

First published: Michael Joseph, 2012.

Psychotherapist Frieda Klein is called upon by DCI Karlsson to help solve a grisly murder in which the prime suspect is afflicted with a strange mental disorder. As the pair dig into the dead man's past, they find plenty of motive for murder, but questions remain about whether the real killer is still on the loose.

French, Nicci

Waiting for Wednesday : a Frieda Klein mystery / Nicci French. Pamela Dorman Books/Viking, 2014, c2013. 384 p. Frieda Klein novels

   ISBN 9780670015771

   1. Murder investigation 2. Innocence (Law) 3. Women psychotherapists 4. Sabotage 5. Secrets 6. Robbery 7. Police 8. London, England 9. Psychological suspense

Originally published: London : Michael Joseph, 2013.

While consulting on the murder of housewife, who was hiding a shocking secret, brilliant psychotherapist Frieda Klein is brought closer to a serial killer who has long escaped detection and wonders if she

is solving both cases or if she just the victim of her own paranoid, fragile mind.

"French's darkly ambitious tale piles on the complications until you beg for mercy. Hard-core fans of detective work as a vehicle for revealing the depths of the human soul will find it irresistible." Kirkus.

French, Tana

* Broken harbor / Tana French. Viking, 2012. 464 p. Dublin Murder Squad novels

   ISBN 9780670023653

   1. Police 2. Murder investigation 3. Memories 4. Families of murder victims 5. Dublin, Ireland 6. Psychological suspense 7. Police procedurals

           LC 2011042397

In the aftermath of a brutal attack that left a woman in intensive care and her husband and young children dead, brash cop Scorcher Kennedy and his rookie partner, Richie, struggle with perplexing clues and Scorcher's haunting memories of a shattering incident from his childhood.

French, Tana

Faithful place : a novel / Tana French. Viking, 2010. 464 p. Dublin Murder Squad novels

   ISBN 9780670021871

   1. Police 2. Missing persons 3. First loves 4. Family relationships 5. Dysfunctional families 6. Undercover operations 7. Missing persons investigation 8. Dublin, Ireland 9. Psychological suspense 10. Police procedurals

           LC 2010003212

Frank Mackey appeared in The Likeness.

Sequel to: The Likeness.

Detective Frank Mackey finds himself straight back in the dark tangle of relationships he left behind twenty-two years ago when the suitcase belonging to his first love, Rosie Daly, shows up behind a fireplace in a derelict house on Faithful Place.

"The first thing that Ms. French does so well in Faithful Place is to inhabit fully a scrappy, shrewd, privately heartbroken middle-aged man. The second is to capture the Mackey family's long-brewing resentments in a way that's utterly realistic on many levels. Sibling rivalries, class conflicts, old grudges, adolescent flirtations and memories of childhood violence are all deftly embedded in this novel, as is the richly idiomatic Dublinese." New York Times.

French, Tana

In the woods / Tana French. Viking, 2007. 464 p. Dublin Murder Squad novels

   ISBN 9780670038602

   1. Coworkers 2. Girl murder victims 3. Detectives 4. Cold cases (Criminal investigation) 5. Murder investigation 6. Crimes against children 7. Police 8. Dublin, Ireland 9. Police procedurals 10. Psychological suspense

           LC 2006033498

Adapted into the television series Dublin Murders, Fall 2019.

Anthony Award for Best First Novel, 2008.

Edgar Allan Poe Award for Best First Novel by an American Author, 2008.

Macavity Award for Best First Mystery Novel, 2008.

Twenty years after witnessing the violent disappearances of two companions from their small Dublin suburb, detective Rob Ryan investigates a chillingly similar murder that takes place in the same wooded area, a case that forces him to piece together his traumatic memories.

"French sets a vivid scene for her complex characters, who seem entirely capable of doing the unexpected. Drawn by the grim nature of her plot and the lyrical ferocity of her writing, even smart people who should know better will be able to lose themselves in these dark woods." New York Times Book Review.

French, Tana

The **likeness** / Tana French. Viking, 2008. 448 p. Dublin Murder Squad novels

ISBN 9780670018864

1. Graduate students 2. Undercover operations 3. Women murder victims 4. Women detectives 5. Murder investigation 6. Detectives 7. Deception 8. Couples 9. Coworkers 10. Secrets 11. Police procedurals 12. Psychological suspense

LC 2008003940

Cassie Maddox appeared in In the Woods.

Sequel to: In the woods.

Sequel: Faithful Place.

Adapted into the television series Dublin Murders, Fall 2019.

This novel finds Detective Cassie Maddox still scarred by her last case. When her boyfriend calls her to a chilling murder scene, Cassie is forced to face her inner demons. A young woman has been found stabbed to death outside Dublin, and the victim looks just like Cassie.

"Cassie Maddox, the partner of the self-destructing detective who narrated In the Woods, is drawn into a ménage à cinque of college students living a seeming charmed existence in an Irish country house. One of the five, a girl who is Cassie's doppelgänger and has been living under an alias Cassie once used as an undercover narcotics agent, turns up murdered in a ruined cottage. Cassie is given the unlikely task of pretending to be a woman who was pretending to be a woman whom Cassie once pretended to be. As you might expect, The Likeness wrestles with matters of identity and intimacy as its heroine comes to prefer this triply false life to her real one. The hypnotic prose and eerie atmosphere conspire to make this ostensible mystery novel much, much more than it appears to be." Salon.com.

French, Tana

* The **secret** place / Tana French. Viking, 2014. 464 p. Dublin Murder Squad novels

ISBN 9780670026326

1. Girl boarding school students 2. Boarding schools 3. Cliques 4. Teenage girls 5. Police 6. Murder investigation 7. Secrets 8. Dublin, Ireland 9. Psychological suspense 10. Police procedurals

LC 2014004500

Investigating a photograph of a boy whose murder was never solved, aspiring Murder Squad member Stephen Moran partners with detective Antoinette Conway to search for answers in the cliques and rivalries at a Dublin boarding school.

"Beyond the murder mystery, which leaves the reader in suspense throughout, the novel explores the mysteries of friendship, loyalty and betrayal, not only among adolescents, but within the police force as well. Everyone is this meticulously crafted novel might be playing--or being played by--everyone else." Kirkus.

French, Tana

* The **witch** elm : a novel / Tana French. Viking, 2018. 509 p.

ISBN 9780735224629

1. Family secrets 2. Life change events 3. Assault and battery 4. Uncles 5. Secrets 6. Family estates 7. Identity (Psychology) 8. Traumatic brain injury 9. Ireland 10. Thrillers and suspense

LC 2018022167

Published in the UK as The Wych Elm, 2018.

Left for dead by burglars while partying with friends, a happy-go-lucky charmer takes refuge at his dilapidated ancestral home before a grisly discovery reveals an unsuspected family history.

Freudenberger, Nell

The **dissident** / Nell Freudenberger. ECCO, 2006. 448 p.

ISBN 0060758716

1. Performance artists 2. Psychiatrists 3. Teenagers 4. Host families of foreign students 5. Dysfunctional families 6. Chinese in California 7. Exhibitions 8. Families 9. Family relationships 10. Moving to a new country 11. Extramarital affairs 12. Interpersonal relations 13. Men/women relations 14. Xenophobia 15. Secrets 16. Social isolation 17. Solitude 18. Obsession in men 19. Art 20. Identity (Psychology) 21. Culture conflict 22. Los Angeles, California 23. China 24. Mainstream fiction

LC 2006042617

Accepting an artist residency from a wealthy Beverly Hills family, a famous performance artist and political activist becomes increasingly entangled in the lives of his hosts and reveals the artistic subculture that shaped his Beijing past.

"Freudenberger demonstrates great talent for capturing the subtleties of cross-cultural and intergenerational relationships, as the dissident's struggles with his past and with his art intersect with Cece's unravelling." The New Yorker.

Freudenberger, Nell

* **Lost** and wanted : a novel / Nell Freudenberger. Alfred A Knopf, 2019. 336 p.

ISBN 9780385352680

1. Ghosts 2. Female friendship 3. Grief 4. Women scientists 5. College teachers 6. Loss (Psychology) 7. Memories 8. Mothers 9. Literary fiction 10. Psychological fiction

Receiving an unsettling phone call from her late college roommate, a rationally minded MIT professor reflects on their once-close friendship, her friend's tragic death and her own rediscovered feelings for a fellow scientist.

"Narrator Helen, a theoretical physicist who graduated from Harvard and is now an MIT professor of repute, must ponder her place among those in her orbit when she begins, inexplicably, receiving text and email messages from her recently deceased best friend's telephone." Library Journal.

Freudenberger, Nell

* The **newlyweds** / Nell Freudenberger. Knopf, 2012. 304 p.

ISBN 9780307268846

1. Muslim women 2. Interethnic marriage 3. Arranged marriage 4. Newlyweds 5. Interethnic romance 6. Mail order brides 7. Women immigrants 8. Families 9. Interpersonal relations 10. Secrets 11. Betrayal 12. Marriage 13. Rochester, New York 14. New York (State) 15. India 16. Literary fiction

LC 2011044116

Leaving her Bangladesh home to marry a New Yorker who wooed her online, Amina finds the marriage challenged by secrets and her struggles to find a place for herself in America.

Fridlund, Emily

* **History** of wolves : a novel / Emily Fridlund. Atlantic Monthly Press, 2017. 288 p.

ISBN 9780802125873

1. Teenage girls 2. Belonging 3. Options, alternatives, choices 4. Fourteen-year-old girls 5. Social acceptance 6. Consequences 7. Secrecy 8. Christian Scientists 9. Minnesota 10. Psychological

fiction 11. Literary fiction 12. Coming-of-age stories

LC 2016027800

Longlisted for the Andrew Carnegie Medal for Excellence in Fiction, 2018.

Shortlisted for the International Dublin Literary Award, 2019.

Shortlisted for the Man Booker Prize, 2017.

Living with her parents in a nearly abandoned counterculture commune, 14-year-old Linda finds her perspectives and desires changed by the scandal-marked arrest of a teacher and the secrets of a new neighbor family as she wrestles with the consequences of actions and failures in the name of love.

"The novel has a tinge of fairy tale, wavering on the blur between good and evil, thought and action. But the sharp consequences for its characters make it singe and singa literary tour de force." Kirkus.

Friedland, Elyssa

The **floating** Feldmans / Elyssa Friedland. Berkley Pub Group, 2019 368 p.

ISBN 9780399586897

1. Family vacations 2. Pleasure cruises 3. Dysfunctional families 4. Senior women 5. Grandmothers 6. Birthdays 7. Pleasure cruises 8. Septuagenarian women 9. Family secrets 10. Sibling rivalry 11. Domestic fiction 12. Humorous stories

Organizing a family reunion cruise for her 70th birthday in the hopes of resolving long estrangements, Annette reveals difficult secrets that challenge long-held perceptions about the more troublesome members of her clan.

Friedland, Elyssa

The **intermission** / Elyssa Friedland. Penguin Group USA, 2018 368 p.

ISBN 9780399586866

1. Separation (Marital relations) 2. Married people and secrets 3. Married people 4. Marital conflict 5. Husband and wife 6. New York City 7. Los Angeles, California 8. Domestic fiction

A novel told from the alternating perspectives of a husband and wife who both have something to hide pulls back the curtain on a seemingly-happy marriage, posing the question: how much do we really know?and how much should we want to know?about the people we love the most?

Friedman, Daniel, 1981-

* **Don't** ever get old / Daniel Friedman. Minotaur Books, 2012. 304 p. Buck Schatz mysteries

ISBN 9780312606930

1. Senior men 2. Nazi plunder 3. Former police 4. Former prisoners of war 5. Private investigators 6. Murderers 7. Former Nazis 8. Memphis, Tennessee 9. Mysteries

LC 2012005485

Macavity Award for Best First Mystery Novel, 2013.

Learning that an old adversary may have escaped Germany with a fortune in stolen gold, retired Memphis cop Buck Schatz teams up with his plugged-in, smart-alecky grandson in a vigilante investigation involving a Mississippi loan shark, a 7-foot-tall Hasidic Jewish man and a bloodthirsty maniac.

Friedman, Daniel, 1981-

Riot most uncouth : a Lord Byron mystery / Daniel Friedman. Minotaur Books, 2015. 304 p. Lord Byron mysteries

ISBN 9781250027597

1. Byron, George Gordon Byron,, Baron, 1788-1824 2. Georgian era (1714-1837) 3. Poets, English 4. Amateur detectives 5. College students 6. Murder 7. Murder investigation 8. Impulsiveness in men 9. Overdoing things 10. Egotism in men 11. Drinking 12. Sexuality

13. England -- Social life and customs -- 19th century 14. Cambridge, England 15. Historical mysteries

LC 2015033767

"A Thomas Dunne book."

When a young woman is found murdered in a local boarding house, Trinity College student Lord Byron resolves to prove his genius by solving the case while finding time for his regular pursuits of excessive drinking, seducing women and causing mischief.

"Friedman manages to make one of the most obnoxious leads in recent memory oddly endearing and even sympathetic." Publishers Weekly.

Friedman, Daniel, 1981-

Running out of road / Daniel Friedman. Minotaur Books, 2020. 288 p. Buck Schatz mysteries

ISBN 9781250058485

1. Death row prisoners 2. Senior men 3. Retirees 4. Jewish men 5. Former police 6. Coercion 7. Aging 8. Married men 9. Memphis, Tennessee 10. Mysteries

LC 2019041960

Retired Memphis detective Buck Schatz must confront a new challenge in NPR producer Carlos Watkins, who claims that Buck coerced a confession out of a man slated for execution.

"Should you, will you, and how can you fight the reaper are questions Friedman handles with amazing grace. Screamingly funny and achingly sad." Kirkus.

Frost, Keziah

The **reluctant** fortune-teller / Keziah Frost. Park Row Books, 2018. 320 p.

ISBN 9780778312819

1. Senior men 2. Shyness in men 3. Fortune-tellers 4. Senior women 5. Observing things 6. Small towns 7. Chihuahuas (Dogs) 8. Young women 9. Missing women 10. Mainstream fiction

A down-on-his-luck septuagenarian curmudgeon is taken under the wing of a group of fun-loving seniors who use his special skills at observation to remake him as a community fortune teller, a situation that is complicated by the disappearances of two young women.

"As Norbert's readings force his clients to address their depression, secrets, and fear, the whole crew learns about friendship, honesty, and the importance of healing. For extra detail and fun, every chapter begins with a card description that foreshadows coming events. The Reluctant Fortune Teller will charm any reader looking for a sweet, witty, zany read." Booklist.

Fu, Kim

For today I am a boy / Kim Fu. Houghton Mifflin Harcourt, 2014. 256 p.

ISBN 9780544034723

1. 1970s 2. Transgender persons 3. Chinese Canadians 4. Brothers and sisters 5. Fathers and sons 6. Chinese in Canada 7. Gender identity 8. Expectation (Psychology) 9. Canada 10. Coming-of-age stories 11. LGBTQIA fiction

LC 2013027720

Peter, the only boy among four siblings born to Chinese immigrants, is convinced he is a girl and must fight the confines of a small town as well as the expectations of his parents to forge his own path into adulthood.

LIST OF FICTIONAL WORKS

Fuentes, Carlos

The **crystal** frontier : a novel in nine stories / Carlos Fuentes ; translated from the Spanish by Alfred Mac Adam. Farrar, Straus and Giroux, 1997, c1995. 266 p.

ISBN 0374132771

1. Families -- Mexico 2. Mexicans in the United States 3. Entrepreneurs -- Mexico 4. Maquiladoras -- Mexico 5. Cooks -- Mexico 6. Middle class -- Mexico 7. Mexico 8. Rio Grande 9. Mexican-American Border Region -- Social conditions 10. Short stories 11. Translations -- Spanish to English

LC 9711230

Translation of La frontera de cristal: una novela en neuve cuentos (1995).

"Leonardo Barroso is an unscrupulous Mexican oligarch whose fortress of a villa is only a short drive from the 'crystal frontier' of the title, and each one of the nine stories comprising this work explores the life of someone touched by him." Library Journal.

Fuentes, Carlos

The **death** of Artemio Cruz / Carlos Fuentes ; translated from the Spanish by Alfred MacAdam. Farrar, Straus and Giroux, 2009, c1952 307 p.

ISBN 9780374531805

1. Death 2. Businesspeople 3. Memories 4. Rich men 5. Men/women relations 6. Senior men 7. Mexico 8. Historical fiction 9. Translations -- Spanish to English

Originally published: Mexico : Fondo de cultura economica, 1952

As the novel opens, Artemio Cruz, the all-powerful newspaper magnate and land baron, lies confined to his bed and, in dreamlike flashes, recalls the pivotal episodes of his life.

Fuentes, Carlos

Destiny and desire : a novel / Carlos Fuentes ; translated by Edith Grossman. Random House, 2011, c2008. 416 p.

ISBN 9781400068807

1. Beheading 2. Friendship 3. Revenge 4. Orphans 5. Mexico 6. Magical realism 7. Literary fiction 8. Translations -- Spanish to English

LC 2010015078

Originally published in Spanish as La voluntad y la fortuna by Alfaguara, Mexico City, in 2008.

The severed head of Josue Nadal, floating in the Pacific Ocean off the shore of Mexico, remembers his life, friends, enemies, and lovers, and his involvement in the drug trade and the corruption frequently encountered in his country.

"A towering work. No character enters its pages lightly, and escape for each carries a price. Fuentes's language is rich, evoking character, place and, perhaps most memorably, the human decisions that propel society. It is a novel of wheels turning within wheels and of convoluted but ultimately meaningful connections." Denver Post.

Fuentes, Carlos

The **eagle's** throne : a novel / Carlos Fuentes ; translated by Kristina Cordero. Random House, 2006, c2003. 384 p.

ISBN 1400062470

1. Presidents -- Mexico 2. Oil industry and trade 3. Armed Forces -- Foreign countries 4. Revenge 5. Communication technology 6. Political corruption 7. Betrayal 8. Near future 9. Mexico -- Foreign relations -- United States 10. United States -- Foreign relations -- Mexico 11. Letters 12. Political fiction 13. Satirical fiction 14. Translations -- Spanish to English

LC 2006040806

Originally published: Mexico, D.F. : Alfaguara, 2003.

"While Fuentes is concerned, as always, about the destiny of his native country, his story focuses more on down-and-dirty political means than serious political ends, leaving us to draw our own conclusions about what sort of good can possibly come of his characters' byzantine strategies and counterstrategies:their opportunistic alliances, their calculated secret-keeping and secret-leaking, their posturing, their watchful waiting, their sly brutalities. What results is the most wickedly entertaining novel of Fuentes's career." New York Times Book Review.

Fuentes, Carlos

* The **old** gringo / Carlos Fuentes ; translated by Margaret Sayers Peden. Farrar Straus Giroux, 1985. 199 p.

ISBN 0374225788

1. Bierce, Ambrose, 1842-1914? 2. Mexican Revolution (1910-1920) 3. Americans in Mexico 4. Soldiers 5. Revolutionaries 6. Authors 7. Revolutions 8. Mexico -- Foreign relations -- United States 9. United States -- Foreign relations -- Mexico 10. Mexico -- History -- 1910-1946 11. Biographical fiction 12. Translations -- Spanish to English

LC 85016266

Originally published in Spanish as El Gringo viejo: Mexico : Fondo de cultura economica, 1985.

"We have in this novel a fastidious American governess stranded in Pancho Villa's revolution, where she attracts the erotic interest of an intellectual fellow countryman and a nature-boy Mexican general. On this inanely trite foundation Mr. Fuentes has erected a narrative of brilliant complexity and sophistication, describing brisk military action and philosophically contrasting national character, or social tradition, or styles of revolt, or regional strengths, weaknesses, and prejudices." The Atlantic.

Fuentes, Carlos

The **years** with Laura Diaz / Carlos Fuentes ; translated from the Spanish by Alfred Mac Adam. Farrar, Straus and Giroux, 2000, c1998. 518 p.

ISBN 0374293414

1. Kahlo, Frida 2. Rivera, Diego, 1886-1957 3. Mexican Revolution (1910-1920) 4. Women artists 5. Mexican Americans 6. Political science 7. Women 8. Mexico -- Politics and government -- 20th century 9. Mexico -- History -- Revolution, 1910-1920 10. Mexico -- History -- 20th century 11. Veracruz, Mexico 12. Mexico -- Social conditions -- 20th century 13. Political fiction 14. Literary fiction 15. Translations -- Spanish to English

LC 00037648

Originally published in Spanish as Anos con Laura Diaz: Madrid : Santillana, 1999.

Shortlisted for the International IMPAC Dublin Literary Award, 2002

The life and fate of Laura Díaz becomes entwined in the history, culture, and politics of Mexico, in a novel that chronicles her life from 1905 to 1978 as she becomes a politically active artist, wife, mother, and lover.

"Fuentes's emotional commitment to his subject shows in the lucidity of the book's underlying intellectual dialoguesthe opposition of communism and fascism, the corrosion of individual identities by historical processes--which Fuentes is able to animate with a learned lyricism that should make this volume one of his most admired and memorable." Publishers Weekly.

Fuller, Claire

* **Bitter** orange / Claire Fuller. Tin House Books, 2018. 320 p.

ISBN 9781947793156

1. 1960s 2. 1980s 3. Manors 4. Neighbors 5. Voyeurism 6. Friendship 7. Deception 8. England 9. Domestic fiction 10. Gothic fiction 11. Parallel narratives

LC 2018024161

An architect spending the summer of 1969 in a dilapidated English country mansion discovers a peephole that allows her to observe the increasingly sinister private lives of her hedonist neighbors.

"Desmond Elliott Prize-winning Fuller's stunning third novel (after Swimming Lessons) is a masterpiece that takes us to the dark places of human emotions." Library Journal.

Fuller, Claire

Our endless numbered days : a novel / Claire Fuller. Tin House Books, 2015. 386 p.

ISBN 9781941040171

1. Fathers and daughters 2. Wilderness survival 3. Survivalists 4. Parental kidnapping 5. Family secrets 6. Homecomings 7. Mental illness 8. Psychic trauma 9. Mother-separated girls 10. Family relationships 11. Wilderness areas 12. England 13. Germany 14. Coming-of-age stories 15. Literary fiction

LC 2014037937

Peggy is eight when her survivalist father tells her that the world has been destroyed and takes her to live in a remote cabin, but years later, her search for the owner of a pair of found boots unwittingly leads her back to civilization.

Fuller, Jack

Abbeville / Jack Fuller. Unbridled Books, 2008. 257 p.

ISBN 9781932961478

1. Grandparent and child 2. Business failures -- Illinois 3. Families -- History 4. Grandfathers 5. Failure (Psychology) 6. Banks and banking -- Corrupt practices 7. Stock market crash, October 1929 8. Generations -- United States 9. Family relationships 10. Illinois 11. Family sagas

LC 2008000989

"There is a framing story involving Karl's grandson that isn't particularly well integrated into the rest of the plot, and many of the characters, particularly Karl and Cristina, don't really come to life until the book 's concluding chapters. But the book has some true things to say about very American ideas of manhood and success and the relationships among fathers, sons, brothers, grandfathers, and grandsons." Library Journal.

Fuqua, Jonathon Scott

* **Gone** and back again / Jonathon Scott Fuqua. Soft Skull Press, 2007. 176 p.

ISBN 9781933368771

1. 1970s 2. Children with depression 3. Divorce 4. Sixth-graders 5. Eleven-year-old boys 6. Coping in children 7. Blended families 8. People with mental illnesses -- Family relationships 9. Misfits (Persons) 10. Children of divorced parents 11. Family problems 12. Identity (Psychology) 13. Addiction 14. Self-hate (Psychology) 15. Self-esteem in boys 16. Self-discovery in boys 17. Virginia 18. Florida 19. Coming-of-age stories 20. Psychological fiction

LC 2007028305

Caley tries to survive as he deals with his parents' divorce, moving from place to place, insomnia, and an eventual descent into depression.

Furnivall, Kate

The **red** scarf / Kate Furnivall. Berkley Books, 2008. 480 p.

ISBN 9780425221648

1. 1930s 2. Women prisoners 3. Love triangles 4. Freedom 5. Interpersonal attraction 6. Men/women relations 7. Missing persons 8. Friendship 9. Forced labor 10. Escapes 11. Soviet Union -- History 12. Siberia -- History -- 20th century 13. Historical thrillers

LC 2007040037

Once, Russia was a place split between breathtaking wealth and desperate poverty. Now, as the country conforms under Stalin's violent rule, a young woman becomes a fugitive, and a storied hero turns into a living, breathing man.

"Sophia Morozova's relationship with fragile Anna Fedorina begins through a small act of kindness at a 1930s Siberian labor camp. As the two inmates struggle daily to survive, they increasingly rely on each other for hope and comfort; when Anna falls ill, Sophia escapes, intending to find Anna's lifelong love, Vasily, and rescue Anna. Beautiful and charismatic, Sophia quickly becomes a force to reckon with in the town of Tivil, where she hopes to find Vasily, and her connections with powerful gypsy Rafik, the handsome factory director Mikhail Pashin and the stern but unreadable Aleksei Fomenko become satisfying sources of danger and desire. Furnivall . . . paints a stark picture of rampant scarcity, grim regimentation and blaring propaganda in pre-WWII Soviet Russia." Publishers Weekly.

Furst, Alan

Blood of victory : a novel / Alan Furst. Random House, 2002. 288 p. Night soldiers

ISBN 0375505741

1. Second World War era (1939-1945) 2. 1940s 3. Journalists 4. Oil industry and trade 5. Spies 6. Resistance to government 7. Government investigators 8. World War II 9. Resistance to military occupation 10. Secret service 11. Refugees 12. Russians in France 13. Russians in Romania 14. Romania 15. Historical thrillers 16. War stories 17. Spy fiction

LC 2002021312

In 1940, Russian emigre journalist I.A. Serebin is recruited by the British secret service to take part in a desperate operation to prevent Hitler's conquest of Europe by stopping the export of Romanian oil to Germany.

"As usual, Furst adheres strictly to the rules of the genre: the protagonist, a Russian expatriate writer, is seduced into service both by the prospect of heroism and by a mysterious Frenchwoman, and embarks on a globetrotting, spy-versus-spy adventure. But his debts to convention work in his favor. Densely atmospheric and genuinely romatic, the novel is most reminiscent of the Hollywood films of the forties, when moral choices were rendered not in black-and-white but in smoky shades of gray." The New Yorker.

Furst, Alan

Dark voyage : a novel / Alan Furst. Random House, 2004. 272 p. Night soldiers

ISBN 1400060184

1. 1940s 2. Ship captains 3. Merchant sailors 4. Refugees 5. Dutch in Sweden 6. Shipping 7. Freighters 8. Deception 9. World War II 10. Secret service 11. Sweden 12. War stories 13. Spy fiction 14. Sea stories 15. Historical thrillers

LC 2004046674

"The author lulls us into the atmosphere, allows us to imbibe his descriptions and then, in the last 50 pages, turns the screws. The denouement of Dark Voyage is both breathless and utterly relaxed, not so pellmell that Furst can't stop to be amused at the ironies of shifting alliances. If he ever breaks a sweat, it doesn't show." New York Times Book Review.

Furst, Alan

The **foreign** correspondent : a novel / Alan Furst. Random House, 2006. 288 p. Night soldiers

ISBN 1400060192

1. Ovra (Organization : Italy) 2. Gestapo. 3. 1930s 4. Nazis 5. Secrets 6. Attempted murder 7. Expatriates -- Paris, France 8. Murder 9. Underground newspapers -- Paris, France 10. Insurgency 11. Journalists -- Paris, France 12. Multiracial men 13. Political crimes and offenses 14. Spies -- Great Britain 15. Italians in France 16. Fascism -- Europe -- History -- 20th century 17. Europe -- History -- 1918-1945 18. Historical thrillers 19. Spy fiction

LC 2006040417

In 1939 Paris, the murder of an Italian political émigré by OVRA, Mussolini's secret police, brings new danger to his successor, Carlo Weisz, who finds himself the target of OVRA, MI6, Stalin's NKVD, and Hitler's Gestapo.

"In an interview in 2002, Furst said that he had difficulty understanding why none of his bestselling novels had yet been filmed. With no apparent preciousness about what might be lost in a transfer to the screen, he added, These really are movies. In a sense, this is true. He has the ability to invent plots that work all on their own, which is, as Somerset Maugham once pointed out, a very rare gift indeed." The Atlantic.

Furst, Alan

* A **hero** of France / Alan Furst. Random House, 2016. 256 p. Night soldiers

ISBN 9780812996494

1. 1940s 2. Second World War era (1939-1945) 3. French Resistance (World War II) 4. Nazis 5. Resistance to government 6. National liberation movements 7. Fascism -- Europe -- History -- 20th century 8. France -- History -- German occupation, 1940-1945 9. Spy fiction 10. War stories 11. Historical thrillers

A tale set in World War II occupied Paris follows the experiences of French Resistance network members from diverse walks of life who engage in clandestine actions to regain the country's freedom.

Furst, Alan

* **Mission** to Paris / Alan Furst. Random House, 2012. 272 p. Night soldiers

ISBN 9781400069484

1. 1930s 2. Film actors and actresses 3. Films -- Production and direction 4. Nazis 5. Fascism -- Europe -- History -- 20th century 6. Spies 7. France -- History -- 20th century 8. Spy fiction 9. War stories 10. Historical thrillers

Arriving in Paris on the eve of the Munich Appeasement in 1938, Hollywood star Frederic Stahl is unwittingly entangled in the region's shifting political currents when he discovers that his latest film is linked to the destinies of fascists, German Nazis and Hollywood publicists.

Furst, Alan

Spies of the Balkans : a novel / Alan Furst. Random House, 2010. 256 p. Night soldiers

ISBN 9781400066032

1. 1940s 2. Police 3. World War II 4. Resistance to military occupation 5. Nazis 6. Spies 7. War 8. Refugees, Jewish 9. Men/women relations 10. Secrets 11. Conspiracies 12. Greece -- History -- 1917-1944 13. Balkan Peninsula 14. Thessalonike, Greece 15. Historical thrillers 16. Spy fiction

LC 2010007755

As war approaches northern Greece, the spies begin to circle--from the Turkish legation to the German secret service. In the ancient port of Salonika, Costa Zannis, a senior police official, head of an office that handles special "political" cases, risks everything to secure an escape route for those hunted by the Gestapo.

"Furst is not in the least imitative--he has own style, and intricate sense of detail--but in his hands the mastery of the traditional spy novel has firmly passed to the other side of the Atlantic, and all I can say is that Eric Ambler and Graham Greene would have read his books with pleasure, and that somebody like Orson Welles (think of him playing Harry Lime in The Third Man) or Otto Preminger could have made a marvelous movie out of Spies of the Balkans. A pity that it probably won't happen--somehow, Furst seems to write in black and white, not Technicolor, just as Greene did--but in the meantime, this is a book, written for adults, to sit down and read in one gulp if you can." Daily Beast.

Furst, Alan

The **spies** of Warsaw / Alan Furst. Random House, 2008. 256 p. Night soldiers

ISBN 9781400066025

1. 1930s 2. Double agents 3. Soldiers 4. Spies -- France 5. Spies -- Germany 6. Engineers 7. Women lawyers 8. Aristocracy 9. Men/women relations 10. Interpersonal attraction 11. Secrets 12. Conspiracies 13. World War II 14. Warsaw, Poland -- History 15. Poland -- History -- 1918-1945 16. Historical thrillers 17. Spy fiction

In 1937 Warsaw, on the eve of World War II, intelligence operatives on both sides of the forthcoming struggle wage their own espionage battle in a world of betrayal, intrigue, and abduction.

"Rather than Eric Ambler thrillers or Graham Greene entertainments, the comparisons Mr. Furst's novels most often draw, they might more accurately be seen as extended series of Talk of the Town pieces. There's the same soupçon of irony, the expert deployment of detail and, above all, a thick helping of knowingness--only with military secrets, machine pistols and Gestapo agents instead of celebrity quirks or outerborough oddities." New York Observer.

Furst, Alan

* **Under** occupation : a novel / Alan Furst. Random House, 2019. 224 p.

ISBN 9780399592300

1. Second World War era (1939-1945) 2. Authors 3. French Resistance (World War II) 4. Spies 5. World War II 6. World War II -- Prisoners and prisons, German 7. Forced labor 8. Prisoners of war, Polish 9. Nazis 10. Fiction writing 11. France -- History -- German occupation, 1940-1945 12. Paris, France -- History -- German occupation, 1940-1944 13. Spy fiction 14. War stories 15. Historical thrillers

LC 2019010340

A historical novel based on the true stories of Polish prisoners in Nazi Germany finds a young member of the French resistance in occupied Paris navigating increasingly dangerous assignments and the machinations of an enigmatic spy.

G

Gabaldon, Diana

* A **breath** of snow and ashes / Diana Gabaldon. Delacorte Press, 2005. 992 p. Outlander novels

ISBN 0385324162

1. Revolutionary America (1775-1783) 2. 1770s 3. 18th century 4. Fate and fatalism 5. Dilemmas 6. Loyalty 7. Options, alternatives, choices 8. Scots in America 9. Husband and wife 10. Families 11.

Love 12. Men/women relations 13. Rape 14. Women physicians 15. Revolutions -- United States 16. American Revolution, 1775-1783 17. North Carolina -- History -- Revolution, 1775-1783 18. United States -- History -- Revolution, 1775-1783 19. Time travel romances 20. Historical fiction

LC 2005051948

In 1772, on the eve of the American Revolution, Jamie Fraser is asked by the governor to help protect the colonies for King and Crown, but, thanks to his time-traveling twentieth-century wife, Claire, Jamie is aware of the ultimate result of the rebellion.

"This vivid and haunting novel, therefore, brings an aching sadness, but it is balanced with sheer joy, revelation, and solace. The large scope of the novel allows Gabaldon to do what she does best, paint in exquisite detail the lives of her characters." Booklist.

Gabaldon, Diana

* An **echo** in the bone / Diana Gabaldon. Delacorte Press, 2009. 992 p. Outlander novels

ISBN 9780385342452

1. Revolutionary America (1775-1783) 2. 1770s 3. 18th century 4. Protectiveness in women 5. Ocean travel 6. Scots in America 7. Dilemmas 8. Love 9. Men/women relations 10. War 11. Husband and wife 12. Families 13. Women physicians 14. Time travel (Past) 15. Revolutions -- United States 16. American Revolution, 1775-1783 17. North Carolina -- History -- Revolution, 1775-1783 18. United States -- History -- Revolution, 1775-1783 19. Time travel romances 20. Historical fiction

Goodreads Choice Award, 2009.

While Jacobite Jamie Fraser reluctantly participates in the American rebellion with a foreknowledge of the fledgling country's victory, his time-traveling wife, Claire, worries about the ultimate price of the war while struggling to safeguard her family.

Gabaldon, Diana

* **Dragonfly** in amber / Diana Gabaldon. Delacorte Press, 1992. 743 p. Outlander novels

ISBN 9780385302319

1. Charles Edward,, Prince, grandson of James II, King of England, 1720-1788 2. Jacobite Rebellions (1689-1746) 3. 18th century 4. Mothers and daughters 5. Time travel (Past) 6. Jacobites 7. Dueling 8. Prisoners 9. Culloden, Battle of, 1746 10. Political intrigue 11. Nurses 12. Love 13. Husband and wife 14. Men/women relations 15. Rape 16. Scotland -- History -- 18th century 17. France -- History -- 18th century 18. Time travel romances 19. Historical fiction

LC 92004904

Twenty years after her voyage to Scotland, Claire Randall, now a doctor, returns to Scotland with her daughter to locate the stone that sent her on her magical journey years before.

Gabaldon, Diana

* **Drums** of autumn / Diana Gabaldon. Delacorte Press, 1997. 880 p. Outlander novels

ISBN 9780385311403

1. Colonial America (1600-1775) 2. 18th century 3. 20th century 4. Quests 5. Time travel (Past) 6. Mothers and daughters 7. Scots in America 8. Husband and wife 9. Love 10. Men/women relations 11. Families 12. Rape 13. Women physicians 14. Indians of North America 15. Charleston, South Carolina -- History -- Colonial period, 1600-1775 16. Time travel romances 17. Historical fiction

LC 9614035

Twice, Claire has used an ancient stone circle to travel back to the 18th century. The first time she found love with a Scottish warrior but had to return to the 1940s to save their unborn child. The second time,

twenty years later, she reunited with her lost love but had to leave behind the daughter that he would never see. Now Brianna, from her 1960s vantage point, has found a disturbing obituary and will risk everything in an attempt to change history.

Gabaldon, Diana

* The **fiery** cross / Diana Gabaldon. Delacorte Press, 2001. ix, 979 p. Outlander novels

ISBN 0385315279

1. Colonial America (1600-1775) 2. 1770s 3. 18th century 4. Militias and irregular armies 5. Insurgency 6. Mothers and daughters 7. Scots in America 8. Love 9. Men/women relations 10. Husband and wife 11. Women physicians 12. North Carolina -- History -- Colonial period, 1600-1775 13. Time travel romances 14. Historical fiction

LC 2001047063

In 1771, Scotsman James Fraser and his wife Claire Randall, a time-traveler from the twentieth century, have emigrated to the Royal County of North Carolina. Dissidents are stirring throughout the colonies. Claire forewarns James of the impendng war and the dangers it may bring them. Will her knowledge of America's tumultuous revolution be enough to guide them through a dangerously uncertain future?

Gabaldon, Diana

* **Outlander** / Diana Gabaldon. Delacorte Press, 1991. 627 p. Outlander novels

ISBN 0385302304

1. Jacobite Rebellions (1689-1746) 2. 18th century 3. Time travel (Past) 4. Nurses 5. Jacobites 6. Love 7. Clans 8. Men/women relations 9. Husband and wife 10. Prisons 11. Escapes 12. Rape 13. Scotland -- History -- 18th century 14. Time travel romances 15. Historical fiction

LC 90019122

First published in Great Britain by Century in 1991 as Cross stitch. RITA Award for Best Romance of 1991.

Hurtled back through time more than two hundred years to Scotland in 1743, Claire Randall finds herself caught in the midst of an unfamiliar world torn apart by violence, pestilence, and revolution and haunted by her growing feelings for James Fraser, a young soldier.

Gabaldon, Diana

* **Voyager** / Diana Gabaldon. Delacorte Press, 1994. viii, 870 p. Outlander novels

ISBN 9780385302326

1. 18th century 2. Voyages and travels 3. Shipwrecks -- Atlantic Coast (United States) 4. Women physicians 5. Culloden, Battle of, 1746 6. Time travel (Past) 7. Love 8. Men/women relations 9. Husband and wife 10. Jacobites 11. Slaves 12. Scotland -- History -- 18th century 13. West Indies -- History -- 18th century 14. Historical fiction 15. Time travel romances

LC 93021907

Time-travelling Claire Randall returns to her own time, pregnant and weary, and resumes her life, but her memories of her eighteenth-century Scottish lover Jamie Fraser will not die, leading her to a desperate decision to return to him.

Gabaldon, Diana

Written in my own heart's blood / Diana Gabaldon. Delacorte Press, 2014. 832 p. Outlander novels

ISBN 9780385344432

1. Revolutionary America (1775-1783) 2. 1770s 3. 18th century 4. Protectiveness in women 5. Family secrets 6. Scots in America 7. Dilemmas 8. Love 9. Men/women relations 10. War 11. Husband and wife 12. Families 13. Women physicians 14. Time travel (Past)

15. Revolutions -- United States 16. American Revolution, 1775-1783 17. United States -- History -- Revolution, 1775-1783 18. Historical fiction

Goodreads Choice Award, 2014.

After being presumed dead, Jamie Fraser returns to find that his best friend has married his wife, his illegitimate son has discovered who his father is, and his nephew has decided to marry a Quaker.

Gabel, Aja,

The **ensemble** : a novel / Aja Gabel. Riverhead Books, 2018. 352 p.

ISBN 9780735214767

1. 1990s 2. Musicians 3. Stringed instruments 4. Ambition 5. String quartets (Groups) 6. Friendship 7. Art 8. Secrets 9. Interpersonal relations 10. San Francisco, California 11. Coming-of-age stories

LC 2017004103

Forging a familial bond over their shared artistic talents and secrets, four young people navigate a cutthroat world and their complex relationships with each other, as ambition, passion and love reinforce and divide them throughout the course of their lives.

Gaddis, William, 1922-1998

Agape agape / William Gaddis ; foreword by Matthew Gaddis ; afterword by Joseph Tabbi. Viking, 2002. 128 p.

ISBN 0670031313

1. Men with terminal illnesses 2. Fathers and daughters 3. Technology -- Social aspects 4. Inheritance and succession 5. Player-piano 6. Psychological fiction 7. Literary fiction

LC 2002020676

A dying man lies in bed thinking about how he will write a book and grumbling about the pending fall of civilization.

"Gaddis has compressed 50 years of research on the social history of the player piano into a novel narrated by a dying elderly man who is as concerned with his own physical collapse as he is with his piano-based literary project.... As usual, Gaddis's avant-garde style requires patience and staying power from readers, who must parse long, elliptical sentences that wander from idea to idea while barely advancing the narrative. But his thoughts and ruminations remain fascinating and challenging." Publishers Weekly

Gaddis, William, 1922-1998

A **frolic** of his own : a novel / William Gaddis. Poseidon Press, 1994. 586 p.

ISBN 0671669842

1. College teachers 2. Copyright 3. Dramatists, American -- 20th century 4. Lawyers 5. Greed 6. Satirical fiction 7. Literary fiction

LC 9326098

National Book Award for Fiction, 1994.

National Book Critics Circle Award for Fiction finalist, 1994

A satirically jaundiced view of modern law and justice chronicles the fortunes of Oscar Crease, a middle-aged college instructor and playwright, as he sues a Hollywood producer for pirating a play.

"The medium is exceptionally dense. The mere effort of sorting out the voices, of tracking them, can be exhausting. . . . In any case, I hope the reader will persevere. 'A Frolic of His Own' is an exceptionally rich, even important novel." New York Times Book Review.

Gaddis, William, 1922-1998

* **J** R : a novel / William Gaddis. Penguin Books, 1993, c1975. 725 p.

ISBN 9780140187076

1. Free enterprise 2. Capitalists and financiers 3. Eleven-year-old boys 4. Wealth 5. Satirical fiction 6. Literary fiction

Originally published: New York : A.A. Knopf, 1975.

National Book Award for Fiction, 1976.

"Conversations are the timber from which Gaddis ' imposing structure is constructed; from the continuous flow of dialog the outrageous story is realized. A unique process of character exposition; to follow it is like shooting rapids in a raft: adventuresome but not easy and finishing is rewarded with a sense of accomplishment." Booklist.

Gaddis, William, 1922-1998

* The **recognitions** / William Gaddis ; with an introduction by William H. Gass. Penguin Books, 1993. 956 p.

ISBN 0140187081

1. Art forgeries 2. Painters 3. Painting, Flemish -- Forgeries 4. Paranoia 5. Literary fiction 6. Modern classics

LC 85556

Originally published by Harcourt Brace in 1955.

Obsessed with seventeenth-century Flemish masterpieces, Wyatt Gwyon forges original artwork amazingly faithful to the spirit and techniques of the time.

Gage, Eleni N.

The **ladies** of Managua : a novel / Eleni N. Gage. St. Martin's Press, 2015. 352 p.

ISBN 9781250058645

1. 20th century 2. Mothers and daughters 3. Generation gap 4. Women artists 5. Gender role 6. Revolutionaries 7. Women -- Psychology 8. Couples 9. Funerals 10. Loss (Psychology) 11. Family secrets 12. Family relationships 13. Men/women relations 14. Nicaragua 15. Family sagas

LC 2015007273

A grandmother, mother and daughter from a Nicaraguan family reunite during a beloved patriarch's funeral and confront painful secrets and losses in order to repair their severed bonds to their country and each other.

Gaige, Amity, 1972-

Schroder / Amity Gaige. Twelve, 2013. 288 p.

ISBN 9781455512133

1. Fathers and daughters 2. Child custody 3. Identity (Psychology) 4. Immigrants 5. Family relationships 6. Parental kidnapping 7. Voyages and travels 8. Secrets 9. Alienation (Social psychology) 10. Divorced men 11. Loss (Psychology) 12. Eccentrics and eccentricities 13. Psychological fiction

LC 2012013882

Ensconced in a correctional facility at the height of a custody battle with his estranged wife, Eric, a first-generation East German immigrant who changed his name as a youth, surveys his life to consider the disparity between his original and assumed identities.

Gaige, Amity, 1972-

Sea wife / Amity Gaige. Alfred A Knopf, 2020. 288 p.

ISBN 9780525656494

1. Seafaring life 2. Sailboats 3. Marital conflict 4. Life change events 5. Husband and wife 6. Families 7. Women with depression 8. Ocean travel 9. Diary writing 10. Conservatives 11. Psychological fiction

A young family escapes suburbia for a year-long sailing trip that upends all of their lives.

"This surprising novel is stunning and deep." Booklist.

Gailey, Sarah

Magic for liars / Sarah Gailey. Tor Books, 2019. 320 p.

ISBN 9781250174611

1. Women private investigators 2. Women wizards 3. Twin sisters 4.

Schools 5. Teachers 6. Secrets 7. Murder 8. Murder investigation 9. Magic 10. Wizards 11. Family relationships 12. California 13. Urban fantasy 14. Mysteries

A private investigator and talented liar embarks on a search for a killer at a California private academy for mages where her estranged, magically gifted twin hides in plain sight.

"There's something for almost all readers here: family drama, romance, high-school gossip, fantasy-world building. Above all, Gailey shows us that humans are humans, even when they are magic, and they are still flawed, damaged, and oh so interesting." Booklist.

Gaiman, Neil

* **American** gods : a novel / Neil Gaiman. W. Morrow, 2001. 465 p.

ISBN 9781117970486

1. Gods and goddesses 2. National characteristics, American 3. Spiritual warfare 4. Former convicts 5. Bodyguards 6. Widowers 7. Death 8. Contemporary fantasy 9. Mythological fiction

LC 2001030407

Adapted into a television series on the Starz network in 2017.

Annotated edition released: New York :

Bram Stoker Award for Best Novel, 2001.

Hugo Award for Best Novel, 2002.

Locus Award for Fantasy Novel, 2002.

Nebula Award for Best Novel, 2002.

Days before his release from prison, Shadow learns that his wife has been killed in an accident. On the plane ride back home for the funeral, he meets Mr. Wednesday, who offers Shadow a job. Shadow accepts but soon discovers that Mr. Wednesday is far more dangerous than he could ever have imagined.

"A noirish sci-fi road trip novel in which the melting pot of the United States extends not merely to mortals but to a motley assortment of disgruntled gods and deities." New York Times Book Review.

Gaiman, Neil

* **Anansi** boys : a novel / Neil Gaiman. William Morrow, 2005. 368 p.

ISBN 006051518X

1. Tricksters 2. Gods and goddesses, African 3. Magic 4. Anansi (Legendary character) 5. Fathers and sons 6. Fathers -- Death 7. Brothers 8. Engaged persons 9. Enemies 10. Love triangles 11. Storytelling 12. Stealing 13. England 14. Florida 15. Mythological fiction 16. Fantasy fiction

LC 2005047176

Locus Award for Fantasy Novel, 2006.

Mythopoeic Award for Adult Literature, 2006.

His past marked by his father's embarrassing taunts and untimely death, Fat Charlie meets the brother he never knew and is introduced to new and exciting ways to spend his time.

"A fun book with a little of everything:horror, mystery, magic, comedy, song, romance, ghosts, scary birds, ancient grudges, and trademark British wit." Library Journal.

Gaiman, Neil

Fragile things : short fictions and wonders / Neil Gaiman. William Morrow, 2006. 400 p.

ISBN 0060515228

1. Horror 2. Fantasy fiction 3. Short stories 4. Anthologies 5. Poetry

LC 2006048135

Collects approximately twenty previously published pieces of short fiction - stories, verse, and an American Gods novella - plus one new piece written especially for this volume -- Author's website.

Locus Award for Best Collection, 2007.

A collection of more than twenty-five short fictional works follows a theme of the intersections between life and death, perception and reality, and darkness and light

"Gaiman follows no overarching theme, but that is what makes these stories charming, at times creepy, and good fun. They read like dreams and meditations, with a stream-of-consciousness quality to their presentation. Gaiman also explains some of the inspiration behind the stories to help put them in perspective." Library Journal.

Gaiman, Neil

* **Good** omens : the nice and accurate prophecies of Agnes Nutter, witch / Neil Gaiman and Terry Pratchett. William Morrow, 2006, 384 p.

ISBN 9780060853969

1. End of the world 2. Demons 3. Angels 4. Fantasy fiction 5. Humorous stories

LC 2006-41944

Originally published: New York : Workman Pub., 1990.

The world is going to end next Saturday, but there are a few problems--the Antichrist has been misplaced, the Four Horseman of the Apocalypse ride motorcycles, and the representatives from heaven and hell decide that they like the human race.

"The end of the world is nigh! At least according to the prophecies of Agnes Nutter, a witch whose predictions are usually accurate but seldom heeded. Eleven years before the deadly Last Saturday Night, the ancient rivals of good and evil personified by the angelic Aziraphale (otherwise living as a London book dealer) and the demonic devil and former serpent Crowley clash in substituting the Antichrist during the birth of a baby. But the babies are switched as an unexpected third child enters the picture. The confusion picks up pace as witch hunters Sgt. Shadwell and Newton Pulsifer pursue modern Nutter follower Anathema Device. Along the way, countless puns, humorous footnotes, and satirical illusions enliven the story." School Library Journal.

Gaiman, Neil

* **Norse** mythology / Neil Gaiman. W.W. Norton & Co., 2017. 256 p.

ISBN 9780393609097

1. Gods and goddesses, Norse 2. Heroes and heroines, Norse 3. Mythology, Norse 4. End of the world 5. Mythical creatures 6. Odin (Norse deity) 7. Thor (Norse deity) 8. Loki (Norse deity) 9. Balder (Norse deity) 10. Creation (Norse religion) 11. Valkyries (Norse mythology) 12. Mythological fiction 13. Mythology, folklore, and legends

Presents a rendering of the major Norse pantheon that traces the genesis of the legendary nine worlds and the exploits of its characters, illuminating the characters and natures of iconic figures Odin, Thor, and Loki.

"Just the thing for the literate fantasy lover and the student of comparative religion and mythology alike." Kirkus.

Gaiman, Neil

* **The** **ocean** at the end of the lane / Neil Gaiman. HarperCollins, 2013. 192 p.

ISBN 9780062255655

1. Good and evil 2. Memories 3. Farms 4. Funerals 5. Senior women 6. Children 7. England 8. Sussex, England 9. Fantasy fiction 10. Contemporary fantasy

British Book Award for Book of the Year, 2013.

Goodreads Choice Award, 2013.

Locus Award for Fantasy Novel, 2014.

Returning to his childhood home in the English countryside for a funeral, the unnamed middle-aged narrator of this haunting, lyrical fable finds himself drawn to an ordinary-looking farmhouse that's anything but. As long-buried memories surface, he recalls events that occurred at Hempstock Farm when he was seven. When the malevolent Ursula Monkton insinuates herself into the fabric of his close-knit family, the farm's inhabitants, especially 11-year-old Lettie, offer their friendship and later their protection to the lonely, abused boy. However, their aid comes at a price, requiring a sacrifice he's unprepared to make. - Description by Gillian Speace.

Gaiman, Neil
Stardust / Neil Gaiman ; illustrated by Charles Vess. Spike/ Avon Books, 1999. 238 p.

ISBN 0380977281

1. Victorian era (1837-1901) 2. Quests 3. Fairies 4. Magic 5. Walls 6. Gems 7. Precious stones 8. Topaz 9. Meteorites 10. Magic rocks 11. Wisdom 12. Transformations (Magic) 13. Witches 14. Historical fantasy 15. Gateway fantasy

LC 988773

Includes reading group questions.
Mythopoeic Award for Adult Literature, 1999.

Living in a Victorian countryside town overshadowed by an imposing stone barrier, Tristran is compelled to retrieve a fallen star for the woman he loves and crosses to the wondrous other side of the barrier, where he encounters dangerous rivals for the star.

Gaiman, Neil
Trigger warning : short fictions and disturbances / Neil Gaiman. HarperCollins, 2015 400 p.

ISBN 9780062330260

1. Ghosts 2. Death 3. Months 4. Magic 5. Characters and characteristics in literature 6. Fantasy fiction 7. Horror 8. Short stories 9. Anthologies

Locus Award for Best Collection, 2016.

A latest collection of short fiction by the #1 best-selling author of Fragile Things includes previously published stories, verses and a 50th anniversary Doctor Who tale, as well as an original short story. Reading-group guide available.

"Full of all manner of witches and monsters and things that creep in the night, this collection will thoroughly satisfy faithful fans and win new onesif there's anyone out there left unconverted." Kirkus.

Gaines, Ernest J., 1933-2019
* The **autobiography** of Miss Jane Pittman / Ernest J. Gaines. Bantam Books, 1996, c1971. x, 245 p.

ISBN 0553263579

1. 19th century 2. 20th century 3. African American women 4. Race relations 5. Leadership in women 6. Women slaves -- Louisiana 7. African Americans -- Civil rights -- History 8. Christian African American women 9. Centenarians 10. Slavery -- Louisiana 11. Racism 12. Reconstruction (United States history) 13. Segregation 14. Civil Rights Movement 15. Communities 16. Louisiana 17. Historical fiction 18. Family sagas 19. African American fiction 20. Southern fiction

LC 96208552

Originally published: New York : Dial Press, 1971.

Presents the story of the long life of Miss Jane Pittman, who began her life as a slave in the South and who marched for her civil rights in the 20th century at the age of 110.

Gaines, Ernest J., 1933-2019
* A **gathering** of old men / Ernest J. Gaines. Knopf, 1983. 213 p.

ISBN 9780394514680

1. 1970s 2. Race relations 3. Revenge 4. Rural African Americans 5. African American men -- Louisiana 6. Senior men 7. African American senior men 8. Cajuns -- Louisiana 9. Murder -- Louisiana 10. Plantations -- Louisiana 11. Louisiana -- Race relations 12. Literary fiction 13. African American fiction 14. Southern fiction

LC 83049000

When Sheriff Mapes is summoned to a sugarcane plantation to find a dead Cajun farmer, he knows who committed the crime. Mapes finds himself powerless, however, when nearly 20 elderly black men confess to the murder. Can justice be served, or will the dead man's brutish father pass judgment his way?

Gainza, Maria, 1975-
The **optic** nerve / Maria Gainza ; translated from the Spanish by Thomas Bunstead. Catapult, 2019, c2014. 208 p.

ISBN 9781948226165

1. Women 2. Art 3. Observing things 4. Art museums 5. Obsession 6. Interpersonal relations 7. Context effects (Psychology) 8. Art 9. Artists 10. Women art historians 11. Social classes 12. Domestic fiction 13. Buenos Aires, Argentina 14. Buenos Aires (Argentina) 15. Psychological fiction 16. Literary fiction 17. Translations -- Spanish to English

Originally published: Buenos Aires : Mansalva, 2014.

"With playfulness and startling psychological acuity, Gainza explores the spaces between others, art, and the self, and how what one sees and knows form the ineffable hodgepodge of the human soul." Publishers Weekly.

Gaitskill, Mary, 1954-
Don't cry : stories / Mary Gaitskill. Pantheon Books, 2009. 240 p.

ISBN 9780375424199

1. Life change events 2. Personal conduct 3. Sex crimes 4. One-night stands (Interpersonal relations) 5. Interpersonal relations 6. Veterans 7. Former prostitutes 8. Adoption 9. United States -- Social life and customs -- 20th century 10. United States -- Social life and customs -- 21st century 11. Literary fiction 12. Psychological fiction 13. Short stories

LC 2008025231

A collection of stories unfolding against the backdrop of American life over the last thirty years includes "College Town 1980," "The Little Boy," and "Mirrorball," in which a young man steals a girl's soul during a one-night stand.

"There is always a moment in a Mary Gaitskill story when you wince. And then you shrug. The wince means, Wow, that's a pretty creepy aspect of human nature to point out, while the shrug is a way of acknowledging, But it's true. Life's really like that, isn't it? The Gaitskill two-step that wince-and-shrug maneuver her work inspires is what elevates her above other fiction writers who, though talented, are content to give us surfaces. Gaitskill never stops at surfaces. She's too adventurous for that, too reckless." Newsday.

Gaitskill, Mary, 1954-
The **mare** : a novel / Mary Gaitskill. Pantheon Books, 2015. 400 p.

ISBN 9780307379740

1. Girls and horses 2. Interethnic relations 3. Life change events 4. Hispanic American girls 5. Horses 6. Rich people -- Relations with poor people 7. Women artists 8. Married people 9. Academics 10.

Communities 11. Brooklyn, New York City 12. New York (State) 13. Coming-of-age stories

LC 2015007973

Longlisted for The Baileys Women's Prize for Fiction, 2017.

Taken in by a near-alcoholic artist and a jaded academic, a young Dominican girl in Brooklyn's Fresh Air Fund program explores the contrasts between her inner-city life and her hosts' privileged world and finds her realities powerfully shaped by her relationship with a horse.

"Gaitskill explores the complexities of love (mares, meres) to bring us a novel that gallops along like a bracing bareback ride on a powerful thoroughbred." Kirkus.

Gaitskill, Mary, 1954-

Veronica / Mary Gaitskill. Pantheon Books, 2005. 240 p. ISBN 0375421459

1. 1980s 2. Female friendship 3. Memories 4. Young women 5. Fashion models 6. Middle-aged women 7. Household employees 8. Sick women 9. Women with AIDS 10. People with AIDS 11. Friends' death 12. Eccentric women 13. Women proofreaders 14. Feminine beauty (Aesthetics) 15. Love 16. Intergenerational friendship 17. Death 18. Grief 19. Housekeepers 20. Manhattan, New York City 21. New York City 22. Paris, France 23. Literary fiction 24. Psychological fiction 25. Short stories

LC 2005043143

"With a new introduction by the author" -- Cover.

Originally published: USA : Pantheon Books, 2005.

ALA Notable Book, 2006.

National Book Critics Circle Award for Fiction finalist, 2005

National Book Award for Fiction finalist, 2005

As a teenager on the streets of San Francisco, Alison is discovered by a photographer and swept into the world of fashion modelling in Paris and Rome. When her career crashes and a love affair ends disastrously, she moves to New York City to build a new life. There she meets Veronica -- an older wisecracking eccentric with her own ideas about style, a proofreader who comes to work with a personal "office kit" and a plaque that reads "Still Anal After All These Years." Improbably, the two women become friends. Their friendship will survive not only Alison's reentry into the seductive nocturnal realm of fashion, but also Veronica's terrible descent into the then-uncharted realm of AIDS. The memory of their friendship will continue to haunt Alison years later, when she, too, is aging and ill and is questioning the meaning of what she experienced and who she became during that time.

"The author's fierce, night-blooming new novel is about a close friendship between two women. But it should not be confused with anything cozy. Imagine a buddy story from the mind of William S. Burroughs, illustrated with images by Robert Mapplethorpe or David Cronenberg, and you get some idea of the tenderness to be found here. . . .Ms.Gaitskill writes so radiantly about violent self-loathing that the very incongruousness of her language has shocking power." New York Times.

Gala, Marcial, 1963-

* The **Black** Cathedral / Marcial Gala ; translated from the Spanish by Anna Kushner. Farrar, Straus and Giroux, 2020, c2012. 192 p.

ISBN 9780374118013

1. Cathedrals 2. Religious fanatics 3. Neighborhoods 4. Race relations 5. Neighbors 6. Building 7. Violent crimes 8. Families 9. Poverty 10. Cuba 11. Literary fiction 12. Translations -- Spanish to English

LC 2019037907

Originally published in Spanish in 2012 by Letras Cubanas, Cuba, as La catedral de los negros.

After the Stuart family moves to Cienfuegos, Cuba, Arturo Stuart?a charismatic, visionary preacher?discovers soon after arriving that God has given him a mission: to build a temple that surpasses any before seen in Cuba, and to make of Cienfuegos a new Jerusalem.

"Gala's raw, compelling, and highly readable novel lays bare a Cuba that, just like everywhere else, has not found an answer to human desperation, envy, or evil." Booklist

Galbraith, Robert

Career of evil / Robert Galbraith. Mulholland Books, 2015. 464 p. Cormoran Strike novels

ISBN 9780316349932

1. Private investigators 2. Enemies 3. Secrets 4. Murder 5. Murder investigation 6. Revenge 7. Cruelty 8. Men/women relations 9. Missing persons investigation 10. Interpersonal relations 11. Mysteries

J. K. Rowling writing under the name Robert Galbraith

When a mysterious package is delivered to Robin Ellacott, she is horrified to discover that it contains a woman's severed leg, and Cormoran Strike must look to his past to determine who is behind the horrid parcel.

"The real appeal here . . . is Robin and Strikes relationship. A contemporary thriller with characters whose emotional journey is just as page-turningly gratifying as the most high-stakes manhunt." Booklist.

Galbraith, Robert

The **cuckoo's** calling / Robert Galbraith. Mulholland Books, 2013. 464 p. Cormoran Strike novels

ISBN 9780316206846

1. Private investigators 2. Fashion models 3. Suicide investigation 4. Celebrities 5. Rich people 6. Multiracial women 7. Brothers and sisters 8. Afghan War, 2001- 9. Veterans 10. Mysteries

J. K. Rowling writing under the name Robert Galbraith

Private investigator Cormoran Strike has a day he'll not soon forget. The 35-year-old, who lost a leg in Afghanistan, spends the night in his bare-bones London office after a relationship-ending fight with his girlfriend. That morning, he sports a cut on his face (she threw an ashtray) as he rushes out the door, barreling into a new temp secretary he can't afford, almost sending her down a staircase. The forgiving temp, Robin, quickly proves useful when they get a case: a famous young model supposedly jumped from the top of her penthouse apartment, but her brother believes she was murdered. Entering the realm of the mega-rich, Strike and Robin question celebrities and fashionistas, trying to uncover the truth in a beautifully written book that was pseudonymously written by none other than J.K. Rowling. - Description by Dawn Towery.

Galbraith, Robert

Lethal white / Robert Galbraith. Mulholland Books, 2018. 656 p. Cormoran Strike novels

ISBN 9780316422734

1. Private investigators 2. Cold cases (Criminal investigation) 3. Secrets 4. Murder 5. Murder investigation 6. Politicians 7. Manors 8. Men/women relations 9. Missing persons investigation 10. Interpersonal relations 11. Mysteries

LC bl2018157218

Originally published: London: Sphere, 2018.

When a troubled young man asks him to investigate a crime he thinks he saw as a child, Cormoran Strike sets off on a twisting trail that leads from London's backstreets, into a secretive inner sanctum within Parliament, and to a country manor house.

Galbraith, Robert

The **silkworm** / Robert Galbraith. Mulholland Books, 2014. 464 p. Cormoran Strike novels

ISBN 9780316206877

1. Private investigators 2. Authors -- Death 3. Secrets 4. Murder 5. Murder investigation 6. Writing 7. Missing persons investigation 8. Veterans 9. Interpersonal relations 10. Mysteries

J. K. Rowling writing under the name Robert Galbriath

Cormoran Strike investigates the disappearance of a novelist who, in his most recent book, unflatteringly portrayed people from his life.

"In her Galbraith persona, author J.K. Rowling has created memorable characters who develop and grow throughout the course of the novel. The mystery itself is clever, and the frequent darts aimed at the publishing world are entertaining." Library Journal.

Galchen, Rivka

American **innovations** : stories / Rivka Galchen. Farrar, Straus and Giroux, 2014. 176 p.

ISBN 9780374280475

1. Short stories 2. Literary fiction

LC 2013039912

Reimagines the themes of canonical short stories from the perspectives of female characters and includes the tales of a young woman whose furniture walks out on her and a property transaction that illuminates painful family dynamics.

"Galchen's stories feel remarkably believable, despite their suggestion of alternate worlds and lives." Kirkus.

Galen, Shana

Third son's a charm / Shana Galen. Sourcebooks Inc, 2017 384 p. Survivors (Shana Galen)

ISBN 9781492657033

1. Regency period (1811-1820) 2. Veterans 3. Kidnapping 4. Dukes and duchesses 5. Napoleonic Wars veterans 6. Napoleonic Wars, 1800-1815 7. Men/women relations 8. Men with dyslexia 9. Bodyguards 10. Intrigue 11. England -- Social life and customs -- 19th century 12. Regency romances 13. Historical romances

Taking a job watching the Duke of Ridington's stubbornly independent daughter, former soldier Ewan Mostyn, who is trying desperately trying to settle back into peaceful Society, is drawn into a world of subterfuge and betrayal as he tries to save Lady Lorraine from kidnappers--and from herself.

Galen, Shana

When you give a duke a diamond / Shana Galen. Sourcebooks Casablanca, 2012. 352 p. Jewels of the Ton

ISBN 9781402269738

1. Regency period (1811-1820) 2. Nobility 3. Scandals 4. Prostitutes 5. Gossiping and gossips 6. Men/women relations 7. London, England -- History -- 19th century 8. Regency romances 9. Historical romances

Juliette, a famous courtesan who is falsely linked to the straightlaced William, the Duke of Pelham, must turn to him for help when she witnesses the murder of his fiancée and the killer targets her.

Gallagher, Stephen

The **bedlam** detective : a novel / Stephen Gallagher. Crown Publishers, 2012. 256 p. Sebastian Becker mysteries

ISBN 9780307406644

1. Edwardian era (1901-1914) 2. 1910s 3. Detectives 4. Murder investigation 5. Monsters 6. Rich people 7. Eccentrics and eccentricities 8. People with mental illnesses 9. Crimes against girls 10. England -- History -- 20th century 11. Supernatural mysteries

LC 2011018605

Investigating a wealthy landowner whose sanity has come into question, Sebastian Becker stumbles on a murder case involving two young girls, a traumatized suffragette and monsters who hide in plain sight.

Gallagher, Stephen

The **kingdom** of bones : a novel / Stephen Gallagher. Shaye Areheart Books, 2007. 368 p. Sebastian Becker mysteries

ISBN 9780307382801

1. Victorian era (1837-1901) 2. 19th century 3. Detectives 4. Serial murderers 5. Vampires 6. Sadism 7. Theater 8. Actors and actresses 9. Malicious accusation 10. Secrets 11. Men/women relations 12. Supernatural mysteries

LC 2007013288

Escaping from custody after being arrested for the serial killings of pauper children, former boxing champion Tom Sayers, desperate to prove himself innocent and to reveal the true murderer, searches for the dark truth and ancient evil behind the murders.

"Vividly set in England and America during the booming industrial era of the late 19th and early 20th centuries, this stylish thriller conjures a perfect demon to symbolize the age and its appetites, an entity that inhabits characters eager to barter their souls for fame and fortune." New York Times Book Review.

Galloway, Gregory

As **simple** as snow / Gregory Galloway. G. P. Putnam's Sons, 2005. 308 p.

ISBN 0399152318

1. High school students 2. Teenage boys 3. Teenage girls 4. Teenagers 5. Teenage boy/girl relations 6. Missing persons 7. Missing persons investigation 8. Goth culture (Subculture) 9. Psychological fiction 10. Coming-of-age stories

LC 2004044500

In awe of high school girl Anna Cayne and her penchant for affectionate magic tricks and riddles, a man is baffled by her mysterious disappearance just before Valentine's Day and retraces the time they spent together for clues to her fate.

Galsworthy, John, 1867-1933

* The **Forsyte** saga / John Galsworthy. Scribner, 2002, c1922. 878 p. Forsyte saga

ISBN 9780743245029

1. Victorian era (1837-1901) 2. Middle class families 3. Lawyers 4. Husband and wife 5. Women -- Social conditions -- 19th century 6. Personal property 7. Ownership 8. Possessiveness 9. Unrequited love 10. Family relationships 11. Social classes 12. Obsession in men 13. Extramarital affairs 14. Men/women relations 15. London, England -- Social life and customs -- 19th century 16. Great Britain -- Social life and customs -- Victoria, 1837-1901 17. England -- Social life and customs -- 19th century 18. Family sagas 19. Modern classics

Collects the original trilogy: The man of property, In chancery and To let, as well as the related short stories "The Indian Summer of a Forsyte" and "Awakening."

First published together: London : Penguin Books, 1978.

Originally collected: New York : C. Scribner's, 1922.

The saga begins with Soames Forsyte, a successful solicitor who buys land at Robin Hill on which to build a house for his wife Irene and future family. Eventually, the Forsyte family begins to disintegrate when Timothy Forsyte, the last of the old generation, dies at the age of 100.

Gamboa, Santiago, 1965-

Necropolis / Santiago Gamboa ; translated from the Spanish by Howard Curtis. Europa Editions, 2012. 500 p.

ISBN 9781609450731

1. Professional conferences 2. Drinking 3. Sexuality 4. Lust 5. Former convicts 6. Pornographic film actors and actresses 7. Murder 8. Israel 9. Literary fiction 10. Surrealist fiction 11. Translations -- Spanish to English

An author attends a conference featuring a series of extraordinary life stories, where the story of formerly troubled evangelical pastor José Maturana captures his imagination and causes him to seek answers when Maturana is later found dead.

Gander, Forrest, 1956-

As **a** friend / Forrest Gander. New Directions Pub., 2008. 192 p.

ISBN 9780811217453

1. Eccentrics and eccentricities 2. Friendship 3. Betrayal 4. Interpersonal attraction 5. Men/women relations 6. Loyalty 7. Adopted boys 8. Betrayal 9. Admiration in men 10. Male friendship 11. Men/women relations 12. Suicide 13. Guilt in women 14. Mainstream fiction

LC 2008023125

"The story is a small one, with no ambitions to be the Great American Novel or to chronicle our time. It sets itself the task of seeing up close the lines of one man's very particular life, and how those lines are walked and read, stumbled over and misread, by those nearby." New York Times Book Review.

Ganek, Danielle

* The **summer** we read Gatsby : a novel / Danielle Ganek. Viking, 2010. 304 p.

ISBN 9780670021789

1. Sisters 2. Rich people -- Hamptons, New York 3. Inheritance and succession 4. Aunts 5. Cottages 6. Artists 7. Men/women relations 8. Hamptons, New York -- Social life and customs 9. Humorous stories

LC 2009049273

Forced to set aside their differences when they jointly inherit a run-down cottage in the Hamptons, practical-minded Cassie and her dreamer half-sister Peck struggle to decide what to do with the house, which comes with a resident artist plagued by bad luck.

Ganshert, Katie

Life after / Katie Ganshert. WaterBrook Press, 2017. 352 p.

ISBN 9781601429025

1. Accident victims 2. Widowers 3. Life change events 4. Survival -- Psychological aspects 5. Guilt 6. Survivor guilt 7. Men/women relations 8. Faith (Christianity) 9. Bombing victims 10. Coping 11. Survival (after automobile, truck, train accidents, etc) 12. Chicago, Illinois 13. Christian fiction 14. Women's lives and relationships

LC 2016053315

Christy Award for Contemporary (Stand Alone) Category, 2018.

A bomb goes off on a Chicago train, killing 22 people. Autumn Manning survives, but a year later still can't remember what happened, and can't seem to move on either. Wondering why God let her live when so many lost their lives, she's drawn to the victims' families and records them sharing memories of their loved ones. Autumn connects with one family in particular, a husband and kids who lost their wife and mother -- but secrets from the past complicate matters for everyone. Addressing grief and guilt, this poignant, thought-provoking book is unputdownable. -- Description by Dawn Towery

Ganshert, Katie

* **No** one ever asked : a novel / Katie Ganshert. WaterBrook, 2018 368 p.

ISBN 9781601429049

1. P. T. A. 2. Schools 3. Prejudice 4. Class conflict 5. Income distribution 6. Christian women 7. School districts 8. Race relations 9. Social conflict 10. Teachers 11. Parents 12. Missouri 13. Christian fiction

LC 2017048918

Christy Award for Contemporary (Stand Alone) Category, 2019.

The absorbtion of an impoverished school district by the affluent community of Crystal Ridge brings three women together as tensions rise, leading to an unforeseen event that impacts them all.

"Ganshert's (Life After) emotionally charged and powerful novel will have readers examining their own personal biases. Recommended for book groups looking for a story with loads of discussion potential." Library Journal.

Gao, Xingjian

Soul mountain / Gao Xingjian ; translated from the Chinese by Mabel Lee. HarperCollins, 2000. xi, 510 p.

ISBN 0066210828

1. Semantics (Philosophy) 2. Revolutions -- China 3. Villages -- China 4. Wanderers and wandering 5. Spiritual journeys 6. People with cancer 7. Self-discovery 8. Dissenters 9. Culture 10. Exiles 11. China 12. Literary fiction 13. Allegories 14. Translations -- Chinese to English 15. Second person narratives

Threatened with time on a prison farm for defying his country's laws of cultural conformity, artist/writer Gao Xingjian embarked on an epic search for his inner self and for his freedom. The author's journey through southern China's ancient mountains and forests inspired this story.

"It is not easy to say what the novel is aboutand it is lacking in plot, descriptions and character developmentand yet the marvel is that somehow it is still both engaging and elegant." New York Times Book Review

Gappah, Petina, 1971-

* **Out** of darkness, shining light / Petina Gappah. Scribner, 2019. 320 p.

ISBN 9781982110338

1. Livingstone, David, 1813-1873 2. 19th century 3. Colonialism 4. Voyages and travels 5. Slavery 6. Colonized peoples 7. Exploration 8. Explorers 9. Dead 10. Research 11. Determination (Personal quality) 12. Life change events 13. Africa -- History -- 19th century 14. Historical fiction

A sharp-tongued cook and a rigidly pious freed slave confront complicated race dynamics to join the followers of the late Dr. Livingstone on a 19th -century voyage from Africa to the doctor's home in England.

Garcia Marquez, Gabriel, 1928-2014

* The **autumn** of the patriarch / Gabriel Garcia Marquez ; translated from the Spanish by Gregory Rabassa. Harper & Row, 1976. 269 p.

ISBN 9780060114190

1. Dictators -- South America 2. Senior men 3. Death 4. Patriarchs 5. Despotism 6. Cruelty in men 7. South America 8. Magical realism 9. Translations -- Spanish to English 10. Literary fiction 11. Modern classics

LC 75030349

The discovery of a South American dictator's rotting corpse in the deserted tangle of his crumbling palace prompts a search through his past and a colorful chronicle of his progression from popular, beloved, unafraid ruler to isolated, frightened despot.

Garcia Marquez, Gabriel, 1928-2014
  Chronicle of a death foretold / Gabriel Garcia Marquez ; translated from the Spanish by Gregory Rabassa. Knopf, 1983, c1982. 120 p.
  ISBN 9780394530741
  1. Murder 2. Brothers and sisters 3. Villages -- Colombia 4. Passivity (Psychology) 5. Apathy 6. Violence in men 7. Weddings 8. Chastity 9. Colombia 10. Translations -- Spanish to English 11. Literary fiction 12. Modern classics 13. Magical realism
  LC 82048884
  The Nobel laureate weaves a story of a fantastic wedding, the return of the bride to her parents, her brothers' resolve to murder her corruptor, and the townspeoples' refusal to depart from routine.
  "This investigation of an ancient murder takes on the quality of a hallucinatory exploration, a deep groping search into the gathering darkness of human intentions for a truth that continually slithers away." The New York Review of Books.

Garcia Marquez, Gabriel, 1928-2014
  Collected novellas / Gabriel Garcia Marquez. Harpercollins, 1999, c1990. 281 p.
  ISBN 9780060932664
  1. Magical realism 2. Translations -- Spanish to English 3. Literary fiction 4. Modern classics
  Three novellas deal with such themes as life in Colombia and the effects of violence

Garcia Marquez, Gabriel, 1928-2014
  The **general** in his labyrinth / Gabriel Garcia Marquez ; translated from the Spanish by Edith Grossman. A. A. Knopf, 1990. 285 p.
  ISBN 9780394582580
  1. Bolivar, Simon, 1783-1830 2. 19th century 3. Politicians 4. Death -- Psychological aspects 5. Men with terminal illnesses 6. Assassination 7. Unhappiness in men 8. Political corruption 9. Insomnia 10. Tuberculosis 11. South America -- History -- 19th century 12. Literary fiction 13. Modern classics 14. Biographical fiction 15. Translations -- Spanish to English 16. Magical realism
  LC 90052957
  In his last days, Simon Bolivar, the Liberator of South America, is prematurely aged, but though he has announced his exile, he hopes to be restored to power.
  "Seldom has there been a more fitting match between author and subject. Mr. Garcia Marquez wades into his flamboyant, often improbable and ultimately tragic material with enormous gusto, heaping detail upon sensuous detail, alternating grace with horror." New York Times Book Review.

Garcia Marquez, Gabriel, 1928-2014
  In evil hour / Gabriel Garcia Marquez ; translated from the Spanish by Gregory Rabassa. Harper & Row, 1978. 183 p.
  ISBN 9780060114145
  1. Mayors 2. Gossiping and gossips 3. Villages 4. Good and evil 5. Paranoia 6. Political corruption 7. Translations -- Spanish to English 8. Literary fiction 9. Modern classics
  The acclaimed Colombian writer's earlier novel about the slanders, defamations, infidelities, and torrential rains that afflict a small town and the sacrifice of a boy that brings torment and chaos to an end.

"The reader is carried along effortlessly in the current of this gifted storyteller's prose. Both heroes and villains elicit sympathy because their basic human foibles, while true to local circumstances, can be recognized by people of any culture." Library Journal.

Garcia Marquez, Gabriel, 1928-2014
  Leaf storm, and other stories / Gabriel Garcia Marquez ; translated from the Spanish by Gregory Rabassa. Harper & Row, 1972. 146 p.
  ISBN 9780060127794
  1. Magical realism 2. Short stories 3. Translations -- Spanish to English 4. Literary fiction 5. Modern classics
  LC 76138784
  "As with Emerson, Poe, Hawthorne, every sentence breaks the silence of a vast emptiness, the famous New World 'solitude' that is the unconscious despair of his characters but the sign of Márquez's genius." The New York Times Book Review.

Garcia Marquez, Gabriel, 1928-2014
  * **Love** in the time of cholera / Gabriel Garcia Marquez ; translated from the Spanish by Edith Grossman. A. A. Knopf, 1988. 348 p.
  ISBN 0394561619
  1. Romantic love 2. Unrequited love 3. Love triangles 4. Courtship 5. Men/women relations 6. Latin America 7. Love stories 8. Translations -- Spanish to English 9. Literary fiction 10. Modern classics 11. Magical realism
  LC 87040484
  Translation of: El amor en los tiempos del colera.
  This English translation first published in the United States by Alfred A. Knopf, 1988.
  Florentino Ariza has never forgotten his first love. He has waited nearly a lifetime in silence since his beloved Fermina married another man. But now her husband is dead. Finally Florentino has another chance to declare his eternal passion and win her back. Will love that has survived half a century remain unrequited?

Garcia Marquez, Gabriel, 1928-2014
  Memories of my melancholy whores / Gabriel Garcia Marquez ; translated by Edith Grossman. Knopf, 2005. 128 p.
  ISBN 140004460X
  1. 1950s 2. Senior men -- Sexuality 3. Teenage prostitutes 4. Reminiscing in old age 5. Aging 6. Nonagenarians 7. Journalists 8. Fourteen-year-old girls 9. Teenage girls -- Relations with older men 10. Sexual ethics 11. Sexuality 12. Lust 13. Love 14. Memories 15. Self-discovery in men 16. Colombia 17. Translations -- Spanish to English 18. Literary fiction 19. Modern classics 20. Magical realism
  LC 2005043591
  Having decided to celebrate his ninetieth birthday by spending the night with a young virgin, an old man falls deeply in love for the first time in his life when he spots the girl at a local brothel.

Garcia Marquez, Gabriel, 1928-2014
  * **One** hundred years of solitude / Gabriel Garcia Marquez ; translated from the Spanish by Gregory Rabassa. Harper & Row, 1970. 422 p.
  ISBN 0072434236
  1. Families 2. Villages 3. Ghosts 4. Murder 5. Good and evil 6. Patriarchs 7. Insurgency 8. Solitude 9. Unrequited love 10. Latin America 11. Magical realism 12. Literary fiction 13. Family sagas 14. Translations -- Spanish to English 15. Modern classics
  LC 74083632

The evolution and eventual decadence of a small South American town is mirrored in the family history of the Buendias.

Garcia Marquez, Gabriel, 1928-2014

* **Strange** pilgrims : twelve stories / Gabriel Garcia Marquez ; translated from the Spanish by Edith Grossman. A. A. Knopf, 1993. 188 p.

ISBN 0679425667

1. Latin Americans in Europe 2. Expatriates 3. Loss (Psychology) 4. Disorientation 5. Fear 6. Magical realism 7. Short stories 8. Literary fiction 9. Translations -- Spanish to English 10. Modern classics
LC 93012257

12 stories "written over the last eighteen years."

Twelve stories recount the peculiar experiences of Latin Americans visiting or residing in Europe

"Exile and loss are the principal subjects of these 12 stories . . . which capture with lyrical precision the emotions of disorientation and fear, coupled with a sense of new possibility, experienced by Latin Americans in Europe." Publishers Weekly.

Garcia, Cristina, 1958-

The **Aguero** sisters / Cristina Garcia. A. A. Knopf, 1997. 299 p.

ISBN 9780679450900

1. Businesspeople -- Florida 2. Cuban American women 3. Families -- Cuba 4. Family secrets -- Cuba 5. Fathers and daughters -- Cuba 6. Husband and wife -- Cuba 7. Naturalists -- Cuba 8. Sisters -- Cuba 9. Sisters -- Florida 10. Wife-killing -- Cuba 11. Women -- Cuba 12. Women electricians -- Cuba 13. Cuba 14. Florida 15. Family sagas
LC 9652204

ALA Notable Book, 1998.

Explores the complexities of Cuban-American family life in the story of two middle-aged Cuban sisters--one living in Havana, one in New York City--who have been estranged for more than thirty years.

"Unmoored by the reverberating effects of the revolution, Garcia's characters search for stability and meaning in a world where fatalism is their only belief. They all endure 'the fidelity of certain, unshakable pain,' but sudden insights illuminate their different routes to salvation." Publishers Weekly.

Garcia, Cristina, 1958-

Dreaming in Cuban / Cristina Garcia. A. A. Knopf, 1992. 245 p.

ISBN 0345381432

1. Cuban American women 2. Cubans 3. Home (Concept) 4. Voodoo 5. Black magic 6. Revolutionaries -- Cuba 7. Mothers and daughters 8. Women 9. Cuba -- Civilization 10. Brooklyn, New York City 11. Havana, Cuba 12. Women's lives and relationships
LC 91020755

Spanish translation published 1993 under title: Sonar en Cubano.

National Book Award for Fiction finalist, 1992

A vivid and funny first novel about three generations of a Cuban family divided by conflicting loyalties over the Cuban revolution, set in the world of Havana in the 1970s and '80s and in an emigre neighborhood of Brooklyn. It is a story of immense charmabout women and politics, women and witchcraft, women and their men.

"While taking very seriously those ideas that have truly riven so many families in recent years, leaving many obsessed with the politics of Cuba, Ms. Garcia also portrays the costliness of such an obsession and the fading of the light between mothers and daughters, between lovers, as communication fails." New York Times Book Review.

Garcia, Cristina, 1958-

King of Cuba : a novel / Cristina Garcia. Scribner, 2013. 256 p.

ISBN 9781476710242

1. Dictators -- Cuba 2. Cubans in the United States 3. Senior men 4. Revolutions 5. Revenge 6. Dictatorship 7. State-sponsored terrorism 8. Assassination 9. Havana, Cuba 10. Miami, Florida 11. Political fiction
LC 2012037553

A tale told from the alternating viewpoints of an aging Castro-like dictator and a Miami exile obsessed with avenging himself against the dictator for personal betrayals traces the impact of a six-decade revolution on their lives and a homeland that has paid the price of constant violence.

Garcia, Cristina, 1958-

The **Lady** Matador's hotel : a novel / Cristina Garcia. Scribner, 2010 224 p.

ISBN 9781439181744

1. Hotels 2. Unhappiness 3. Political science 4. Revenge 5. Desire 6. Human nature 7. Interpersonal relations 8. Political violence 9. Latin America 10. Political fiction

A novel about the intertwining lives of the denizens of a hotel in an unnamed Latin American country in the midst of political turmoil.

"Garca has created a half-magical world in which blood runs close to the surface and flesh is transitory, opening the door to the big questions of existence: Who am I, and what is my purpose in life? The answers she offers such as they are come with a sly wit and strong visual style that explodes with color and life." Miami Herald.

Garcia-Roza, L. A. (Luiz Alfredo)

Alone in the crowd : an Inspector Espinosa mystery / Luiz Alfredo Garcia-Roza ; translated from the Portuguese by Benjamin Moser. Henry Holt and Co., 2009, c2007. 240 p. Inspector Espinosa mysteries

ISBN 9780805079593

1. Fatal traffic accidents 2. Criminal psychology 3. Loners 4. Detectives 5. Murder 6. Stalkers 7. Bank tellers 8. Senior women 9. Murder suspects 10. Murder investigation 11. Stalking 12. Rio de Janeiro, Brazil 13. Mysteries 14. Hardboiled fiction 15. Translations -- Portuguese to English
LC 2008050135

Originally published as Na Multidao: Sao Paulo : Companhia das Letras, 2007.

After leaving the precinct in Copacabana without speaking to the chief, Dona Laureta is killed when she is hit by a bus two hours later, leading veteran police chief inspector Espinosa to investigate the strange accident and the woman's personal connection to a new suspect involved in an old murder.

Garcia-Roza, L. A. (Luiz Alfredo)

December heat / Luiz Alfredo Garcia-Rosa ; translated from the Portuguese by Benjamin Moser. H. Holt, 2003. 288p. Inspector Espinosa mysteries

ISBN 0805068902

1. Police 2. Detectives -- Rio de Janeiro, Brazil 3. Former police 4. Prostitutes 5. Crimes against prostitutes 6. Murder 7. Rio de Janeiro, Brazil 8. Mysteries 9. Hardboiled fiction 10. Translations -- Portuguese to English
LC 2002038825

Inspector Espinosa agrees to take on the case of an old friend and retired police officer, who awoke one morning to find his prostitute girlfriend murdered, his wallet and keys missing, and no memory of the previous night's occurrences.

"An exciting procedural, infused with exotic ambience, sympathetic detectives, and a little romance." Library Journal.

Gardam, Jane

The **flight** of the maidens / Jane Gardam. Carroll & Graf, 2001, c2000. 278 p.

ISBN 0786708794

1. 1940s 2. Young women 3. Life change events 4. Yorkshire, England 5. England -- Social life and customs -- 20th century 6. Coming-of-age stories

Originally published: London : Chatto & Windus, 2000.

Follows three unforgettable Yorkshire women--independent Hetty Fallowes, rebellious Una Vane, and Jewish refugee Liselotte Klein--as they prepare for their departure for university in Cambridge and London in 1946.

"Gardam has thrown out the usual too-sensitive-for-you boilerplate of the coming-of-age novel, for which we can be thankful. Luckily, the generational conflict that remains is usually all the better for her wry indirection." New York Times Book Review.

Gardam, Jane

God on the rocks / Jane Gardam. Europa Editions, 2010, c1978. 195 p.

ISBN 9781933372761

1. 1930s 2. Children of rich people 3. Conflict in families 4. Child neglect 5. Gifted girls 6. Family relationships 7. Curiosity in girls 8. Family secrets 9. Regret 10. Fundamentalists 11. England -- History -- 20th century 12. Coming-of-age stories

Originally published: London : H. Hamilton, 1978.

Shortlisted for the Booker-McConnell Prize, 1978.

To escape her religious father and bitter mother, Margaret Marsh roams the meadows and beaches of coastal England, where she meets childhood friends of her mother that expose her to a side of her mother Margaret has never known.

"This novel dexterously exposes the misapprehensions wrought by class, sex, love, and religion among the members of two families in a seaside town in the north of England during the interwar years. Gardam has been compared to Anita Brookner, but her view, though equally dark, is far less dreary. Few can present tragedy with such humor." The Atlantic.

Gardam, Jane

Last friends / Jane Gardam. Europa Editions, 2013 304 p. Old Filth trilogy

ISBN 9781609450939

1. Reminiscing in old age 2. Lawyers 3. Social classes 4. Trials 5. Competition 6. Love triangles 7. Poor people 8. Marriage 9. Men/women relations 10. England 11. Psychological fiction 12. Literary fiction

Originally published: London: Little, Brown, 2013.

The marriage of Edward Feathers and Betty as seen through the eyes of Edwards friend and Betty's lover Terry Veneering.

Gardam, Jane

The **man** in the wooden hat / Jane Gardam. Europa Editions, 2009. 240 p. Old Filth trilogy

ISBN 9781933372891

1. Husband and wife 2. Childlessness 3. Married women 4. Lawyers 5. Marriage 6. Love triangles 7. Loyalty 8. Hong Kong 9. England 10. Psychological fiction 11. Literary fiction

Originally published: London: Chatto & Windus, 2009.

Tells the story of the fifty-year marriage of barrister Filth and his wife Betty, which is filled with secrets and hidden desires.

"In this understated novel, Gardam returns to the successful barrister and judge Sir Edward Feathers, the protagonist of her deliciously acerbic Old Filth. The complementary tale, told largely from the point of view of Feathers's wife, Betty, a fellow Raj orphan, begins as the two make a prudent marriage not for love, in Hong Kong after the Second World War. The story briskly follows their fifty-year union from adulterous beginnings and unhappy childlessness to a companionable old age in England, after the handover of Hong Kong." The New Yorker.

Gardam, Jane

Old Filth / Jane Gardam. Europa, 2006. 289 p. Old Filth trilogy

ISBN 9781933372136

1. Lawyers 2. Reminiscing in old age 3. Personal conduct 4. Boy orphans 5. Seniors 6. Married women -- Death 7. Redemption 8. Colonialism 9. Social isolation 10. London, England -- History -- 20th century 11. Great Britain -- Colonies 12. Hong Kong 13. Psychological fiction 14. Literary fiction

Shortlisted for The Orange Prize for Fiction, 2005

"FILTH is a lawyer with a practice in the Far East. A few remember that his nickname stands for Failed In London Try Hong Kong. But Old Filth is not as pompous as people imagine, and his past contains many secrets and dark hiding places"--Publisher.

"Gardam's prose is so economical that no moment she describes is either gratuitous or wasted." The New Yorker.

Gardam, Jane

The **people** on Privilege Hill and other stories / Jane Gardam. Europa Editions, 2008, c2007. 196 p.

ISBN 9781933372525

1. Manners and customs 2. England -- Social life and customs 3. Short stories

Originally published: London : Chatto & Windus, 2007.

"The 14 stories in Gardam's marvelously titled new collection, The People on Privilege Hill, focus to a large extent on members of her generation (she was born July 11, 1928, soon to turn 80) or that of her parents. These generally feisty individuals recall sometimes troubling events from their prime while they cope with the affronts of aging in a changing world. Not all the stories are winners, but even the slightest offer the pleasures of Gardam's brisk, sharp sensibility. The title story brings back the splendid character Filth from her last novel. He's approaching 90, a widower who's retired to Dorset and misses the warm tropical rains of the Orient, where he practiced law for many years." Christian Science Monitor.

Gardiner, Meg

The **dark** corners of the night / Meg Gardiner. Blackstone Pub, 2020. 352 p. Unsub novels

ISBN 9781982627515

1. Women FBI agents 2. Criminal profilers 3. Psychic trauma 4. Family-killing 5. FBI agents 6. Secrets 7. Child witnesses 8. Serial murderers 9. Serial murder investigation 10. Los Angeles, California 11. Thrillers and suspense

Hunting a serial killer who has been murdering parents in front of their children, FBI behavioral analyst Caitlin Hendrix discovers that the killer holds a devastating secret from Caitlin's own past.

"Gardiner has mastered the art of the serial-killer saga without an ounce of fat." Kirkus.

Gardiner, Meg

The **Dirty** Secrets Club / Meg Gardiner. Dutton, 2008. 304 p. Jo Beckett series

ISBN 9780525950660

1. Women forensic psychiatrists 2. Suicide 3. Secrets 4. Forensic sciences 5. Women psychiatrists 6. Murder 7. Murder investigation 8. San Francisco, California 9. California 10. Pacific Coast (United States) 11. Mysteries

LC 2007046757

In the wake of an ongoing string of high-profile murder-suicides in San Francisco, forensic psychiatrist Jo Beckett is hired by the SFPD to perform investigative autopsies and discovers a harrowing commonality among the suicide victims.

"As Beckett gets in touch with her inner Rambo, Ericksen's acid-tinged delivery suddenly works just fine." Publishers Weekly.

Gardiner, Meg

Into the black nowhere / Meg Gardiner. Dutton, 2018 384 p. Unsub novels

ISBN 9781101985557

1. Women FBI agents 2. Criminal profilers 3. Women murder victims 4. Serial murderers 5. Serial murder investigation 6. FBI agents 7. Saturday 8. Murder suspects 9. Texas 10. Thrillers and suspense

LC 2017045253

An FBI profiler is forced to navigate the twisted mind of a charismatic, ruthless serial killer responsible for the murders of a series of women in southern Texas, in a thriller inspired by the case of Ted Bundy.

Gardiner, Meg

Phantom instinct / Meg Gardiner. Dutton, 2014. 368 p.

ISBN 9780525954316

1. Lovers -- Death 2. Former police 3. Investigations 4. Murderers 5. People with brain injuries 6. Dogs 7. Murder 8. Men/women relations 9. Los Angeles, California 10. California 11. Thrillers and suspense

LC 2013048812

Struggling to rebuild after a club shooting, bartender Harper Flynn searches for the escaped gunman with the help of L.A. Deputy Sheriff Aiden Garrison, whose injuries in the same incident left him with a rare type of perception blindness.

Gardiner, Meg

Unsub : a novel / Meg Gardiner. Dutton, 2017 384 p. Unsub novels

ISBN 9781101985526

1. Serial murderers 2. Women detectives 3. Serial murder investigation 4. Obsession 5. Revenge in women 6. Fathers and daughters 7. Determination in women 8. Cold cases (Criminal investigation) 9. San Francisco Bay Area 10. Northern California 11. California 12. Thrillers and suspense

LC 2016041608

A psychological thriller inspired by the unsolved case of the Zodiac Killer follows the efforts of a young detective who resolves to apprehend the serial murderer who destroyed her family and terrorized a city 20 years earlier.

Gardner, Lisa

Alone / Lisa Gardner. Bantam Books, 2005. 336 p. Detective D. D. Warren novels

ISBN 0553802534

1. Snipers 2. Police -- Massachusetts 3. Girl kidnapping victims 4. State police -- Massachusetts 5. Former convicts 6. Psychopaths

7. Widows 8. Police shootings 9. Serial murders 10. Revenge 11. Burial 12. Manipulation by women 13. Sexuality and power (Social sciences) 14. Police -- Special Weapons and Tactics units 15. Boston, Massachusetts 16. Thrillers and suspense 17. Psychological suspense

LC 2004057577

When Bobby Dodge, a sniper with the Massachusetts State Police SWAT team, saves a woman and her young son from her armed husband, he finds himself investigating the shooting of a man who had accused his wife of poisoning their son.

"The protagonist of this thriller is Massachusetts police sniper Bobby Dodge. He meets his match in Catherine Gagnon, who as a girl was snatched, raped and nearly murdered. Now she's the wife of erratic, rich Jimmy Gagnon and mother of perpetually ill four-year-old Nathan. When Bobby kills Jimmy during a hostage situation at the Gagnons, he does it to save Catherine and Nathan. But was it a righteous shoot, or did Catherine engineer the killing? Judge James Gagnon and his wife, Maryanne, think Bobby murdered their son out of lust for Catherine. As other people start dying, very messily, and the DA and cops come down hard on Bobby, Gardner keeps the tension high and the pace fast." Publishers Weekly.

Gardner, Lisa

Fear nothing : a Detective D. D. Warren Novel / Lisa Gardner. Penguin, 2014. 400 p. Detective D. D. Warren novels

ISBN 9780525953081

1. Murder investigation 2. Women detectives 3. Vigilantes 4. Memory 5. Deception 6. Police -- Massachusetts 7. State police -- Massachusetts 8. Boston, Massachusetts 9. Thrillers and suspense

Seriously injured after stumbling into a crime scene she cannot remember, Boston Detective D. D. Warren learns about a second murder with the same characteristics only to discover that she is being personally targeted by the killer.

Gardner, Lisa

Find her / Lisa Gardner. Dutton, 2016. 402 p. Detective D. D. Warren novels

ISBN 9780525954576

1. Missing persons investigation 2. Vigilantes 3. Murder investigation 4. Women detectives 5. Rape victims 6. Kidnapping 7. Deception 8. Police -- Massachusetts 9. State police -- Massachusetts 10. Boston, Massachusetts 11. Thrillers and suspense

LC 2015038503

Requesting the assistance of a survivor of an extended abduction experience who has become obsessed with the cases of girls who never made it home, Boston detective D. D. Warren becomes suspicious of the woman's agenda upon discovering her relationships with other victims.

"A gritty, complicated heroine like Flora Dane deserves a better plot than this needlessly complicated story." Kirkus.

Gardner, Lisa

* Look for me : a novel / Lisa Gardner. Dutton, 2018 400 p. Detective D. D. Warren novels

ISBN 9781524742058

1. Family-killing 2. Missing teenage girls 3. Women vigilantes 4. Women detectives 5. Foster care 6. Child abuse 7. Murder investigation 8. Missing persons investigation 9. Boston, Massachusetts 10. Thrillers and suspense

LC 2017042389

Librarians' Choice (Australia), 2018.

Detective D. D. Warren teams up with Flora Dane from Find Her in an investigation involving the sinister disappearance of a 16-year-old girl whose family has been brutally murdered.

Gardner, Lisa

Love you more : a Detective D.D. Warren novel / Lisa Gardner. Bantam Books, 2011. 368 p. Detective D. D. Warren novels

ISBN 9780553807257

1. Murder investigation 2. Women detectives 3. Abused women 4. Family secrets 5. Missing girls 6. Family violence 7. Mothers 8. Missing persons investigation 9. Police -- Massachusetts 10. State police -- Massachusetts 11. Boston, Massachusetts 12. Thrillers and suspense

Brian Darby lies dead on the kitchen floor. His wife, state police trooper Tessa Leoni, claims to have shot him in self-defense, and bears the bruises to back up her tale. For veteran detective D. D. Warren, it should be an open-and-shut case. But where is their six-year-old daughter? As the homicide investigation ratchets into a frantic statewide search for a missing child, D. D. Warren must partner with former lover Bobby Dodge to break the case.

"Gardner sprinkles plenty of clues and inventive twists to keep readers off-kilter as the suspense builds to a realistic, jaw-dropping finale." Publishers Weekly.

Gardner, Lisa

The **neighbor** / Lisa Gardner. Bantam Books, 2009. 373 p. Detective D. D. Warren novels

ISBN 9780553807233

1. Missing persons 2. Murder investigation 3. Mother-separated families 4. Husband and wife 5. Young women 6. Family secrets 7. Murder suspects 8. Boston, Massachusetts 9. Thrillers and suspense

Thriller Award for Best Novel, 2010.

A young mother, blond and pretty, disappears without a trace from her South Boston home, leaving behind her four-year-old daughter as the only witness and her handsome, secretive husband as the prime suspect.

Gardner, Lisa

* **Never** tell : a novel / Lisa Gardner. Dutton, 2019. 416 p. Detective D. D. Warren novels

ISBN 9781524742089

1. Women vigilantes 2. Women detectives 3. Women murder suspects 4. Secrets 5. Murder 6. Murder investigation 7. Guilt 8. Boston, Massachusetts 9. Thrillers and suspense

LC 2018042977

While D. D. Warren investigates a pregnant woman's suspicious role in the murders of her father and husband, Flora draws on her own haunted past to identify an unsettling link to one of the victims.

Gardner, Lisa

* **When** you see me : a novel / Lisa Gardner. Dutton, 2020. 400 p.

ISBN 9781524745004

1. Women FBI agents 2. Women detectives 3. Serial murderers 4. Cold cases (Criminal investigation) 5. Secrets 6. Clues 7. Small towns 8. Georgia 9. Thrillers and suspense

LC 2019041316

FBI Special Agent Kimberly Quincy and Sergeant Detective DD Warren join forces with Flora Dane and true-crime savant Keith Edgar to investigate the secrets of a deceased serial killer.

"A frightening climax provides an appropriate wrap-up to the Ness saga and the story of evil flourishing in a small mountain town. This is top-notch suspense by a best-selling master of the genre." Booklist.

Garey, Juliann

Too bright to hear too loud to see / Juliann Garey. Soho Press, 2012. 224 p.

ISBN 9781616951290

1. 1980s 2. Film industry and trade executives -- Hollywood, California 3. Bipolar disorder 4. Self-discovery in men 5. Fathers and daughters 6. Marriage 7. Executives 8. Voyages and travels 9. Self-discovery in men 10. Mental illness 11. Father-deserted children 12. Electric shock therapy 13. Dysfunctional families 14. Mainstream fiction 15. Psychological fiction

LC 2012026028

ALA Notable Book, 2014

In a look at mental illness that weaves together three timelines, Greyson Todd leaves his successful Hollywood career and wife and young daughter to travel the world, giving free reign to the bipolar disorder he has been forced to keep hidden for almost twenty years.

Garner, Helen, 1942-

The **spare** room / Helen Garner. Text Publishing Co., 2008. 195 p.

ISBN 9781921351396

1. Women with cancer 2. Death -- Psychological aspects 3. Female friendship 4. Women with terminal illnesses 5. Women caregivers 6. Cancer -- Alternative treatment 7. Melbourne, Victoria 8. Literary fiction

Queensland Premier's Literary Awards, Fiction Book Award, 2008.

Barbara Jefferis Award, 2009.

Offering a room to an old friend who is undergoing treatment for cancer, Helen finds her advice disregarded in the face of her friend's faith in alternative medicine, a situation that turns both of their lives upside-down.

"Humour is not just an occasional relief in The Spare Room, it's actually the lifeblood of the book. The old cliche that you've got to laugh in the face of tragedy is given new meaning by Garner. For all the sickness and suffering and thankless service involved in the story, it's only an acute sense of the absurdity of the situation that keeps the heroine . . . sane. Garner's dealings with terminal illness are truly refreshing. Instead of focusing on the sufferer, Nicola, she delves inwards, exploring the impact on the carer. And she dares to express the unspeakable thoughts we often think when confronted by another's illness." PopMatters.

Garrett, Kellye, 1978-

* **Hollywood** homicide / Kellye Garrett. Midnight Ink, 2017 312 p. Detective by day novels

ISBN 9780738752617

1. Women amateur detectives 2. Women witnesses 3. Poor women 4. Actors and actresses 5. Murder investigation 6. Hit-and-run accidents 7. Female friendship 8. Crime 9. City life 10. African Americans 11. Hollywood, California 12. California 13. Mysteries 14. African American fiction

LC 2017007797

Agatha Award for Best First Novel, 2017.

Anthony Award for Best First Novel, 2018.

After witnessing a deadly hit-and-run, broke actress Dayna investigates and pursues the reward money in an effort to help her parents keep their house, but she soon finds herself wanting justice for the victim even more.

Garriott, Leah

Promised / Leah Garriott. Shadow Mountain, 2020. 368 p.

1. Regency period (1811-1820) 2. Young women 3. Nobility 4. Arranged marriage 5. Breaking up (Interpersonal relations) 6. Mate

selection 7. Womanizers 8. Secrets 9. Interpersonal attraction 10. Men/women relations 11. England -- Social life and customs -- 19th century 12. Regency romances 13. Historical romances

LC 2019019684

After the heartbreak and humiliation of a broken engagement, Margaret Brinton is determined to never allow her heart to be hurt again. But will her resolve hold when her father arranges for her to marry Lord Williams, a man who had once publically snubbed her, but who might be more than he appears?

"Garriott's impressive debut distinguishes itself with its expertly evoked Regency setting, a cast of realistically flawed yet eminently relatable characters, and a sweetly satisfying love story." Booklist.

Garwood, Julie

The **bride** / Julie Garwood. Pocket Books, 1989. 358 p. MacAlister family

ISBN 0671737791

1. Medieval period (476-1492) 2. Widowers 3. Arranged marriage 4. Men/women relations 5. Nobility 6. Sexuality 7. Suspicion 8. Remarriage 9. England -- History -- 12th century 10. Medieval romances 11. Highland romances 12. Historical romances

Garwood, Julie

Wired / Julie Garwood. Berkley, 2017. 336 p. Buchanan novels (Julie Garwood)

ISBN 9780525954460

1. FBI 2. Technology 3. Protectiveness in men 4. Computer programmers 5. Brothers and sisters 6. Men/women relations 7. Interpersonal attraction 8. Attempted murder 9. Boston, Massachusetts 10. Romantic suspense

"Allison Trent doesn't look like a hacker. In fact, when she's not in college working on her degree, she models on the side. But behind her gorgeous face is a brilliant mind for computers and her real love is writing--and hacking--code. Her dream is to write a new security program that could revolutionize the tech industry. Hotshot FBI agent Liam Scott has a problem: a leak deep within his own department. He needs the skills of a top-notch hacker to work on a highly sensitive project: to secretly break into the FBI servers and find out who the traitor is. But he can't use one of his own. He finds the perfect candidate in Allison. Only, there's one problem--she wants nothing to do with his job and turns him down flat. What Liam doesn't know is that Allison is hiding secrets that she doesn't want the FBI to uncover. But Liam will do nearly anything to persuade her to join his team, even break a few rules if that's what it takes. A temptation that could put his job--and both of their futures--on the line." Provided by publisher.

"Engaging and easily relatable characters and a compelling plot that seems to have been ripped from todays headlines." Booklist.

Gash, Jonathan,

The **rich** and the profane / Jonathan Gash. Viking, 1999, c1998. 344 p. Lovejoy mysteries

ISBN 9780670883462

1. Antique dealers 2. Amateur detectives 3. East Anglia, England 4. England 5. Mysteries

LC 98-38951

Originally published: London : Macmillan, 1998.

In Britain, antique dealer Lovejoy organizes a break-in to assess the worth of a priory's antiques after fears are expressed that the prior will sell them to pay gambling debts. The operation has unforeseen results.

"With this dervish of comic activity and a romp that ends in a circus-like venue, Gash is in top form." Publishers Weekly.

Gaskell, Elizabeth Cleghorn, 1810-1865

* **Cranford** / Elizabeth Gaskell ; edited with an introduction by Elizabeth Porges Watson. Oxford University Press, 1972, c1906. xix, 200 p.

ISBN 9780192553515

1. Rural life -- 19th century 2. Women 3. Sisters -- 19th century 4. England -- Social life and customs -- 19th century 5. Literary fiction 6. Classics

Originally serialized in Household Words, 1851-1853.

Adapted into three separate British television series.

A comic portrait of early Victorian life in a country town which describes with poignant wit the uneventful lives of its lady-like inhabitants, offering an ironic commentary on the separate spheres and diverse experiences of men and women.

Gaskell, Elizabeth Cleghorn, 1810-1865

* **North** and South / Elizabeth Gaskell ; edited by Angus Easson ; with an introduction by Sally Shuttleworth. Oxford University Press, 1996, c1855. xlii, 452 p.

ISBN 9780192831941

1. Factories 2. Young women 3. Class conflict 4. Manners and customs 5. Factory owners 6. Industrialization 7. Industrialists 8. Former clergymen 9. Strikes 10. Interclass friendship 11. Family relationships 12. Men/women relations 13. England 14. Literary fiction 15. Love stories 16. Classics

Originally serialized in Household Words, 1854-1855.

Moving from the industrial riots of discontented millworkers through to the unsought passions of a middle-class woman, and from religious crises of conscience to the ethics of naval mutiny, the novel poses fundamental questions about the nature of social authority and obedience. Through the story of Margaret Hale, the middle-class southerner who moves to the northern industrial town of Milton, Gaskell skilfully explores issues of class and gender in the conflict between Margaret's ready sympathy with the workers and her growing attraction to the charismatic mill owner, John Thornton.

Gaspar de Alba, Alicia, 1958-

Desert blood : the Juarez murders / Alicia Gaspar de Alba. Arte Publico Press, 2005. 352 p.

ISBN 1558854460

1. Women amateur detectives 2. Women college teachers 3. Lesbians 4. Americans in Mexico 5. Serial murders -- Mexico 6. Crimes against pregnant women 7. Crimes against young women 8. Lesbian couples 9. Adoption 10. Hometowns 11. Women/women relations 12. Maquiladoras -- Mexico 13. Mexican-American Border Region 14. El Paso, Texas 15. Ciudad Juarez, Mexico 16. Mexico 17. Mysteries 18. LGBTQIA fiction

LC 2004055417

Lambda Literary Award for Lesbian Mystery, 2005.

Ivon Villa, a women's studies professor who travels to Mexico to arrange for an adoption of a baby for herself and her female lover, discovers the pregnant mother has been murdered, an apparent victim of a serial killer, and vows to find the person responsible for the killings.

Gass, William H., 1924-2017

Middle C / William H. Gass. Alfred A. Knopf, 2013. 352 p.

ISBN 9780307701633

1. Deception 2. Human nature 3. College teachers 4. False personation 5. Mediocrity 6. Music teachers 7. Jewish Americans 8. Crimes against humanity 9. World War II -- Jews -- Rescue 10. Middle West 11. Historical fiction 12. Black humor

"A Borzoi book."

Investigates the multifaceted nature of human identity and follows the experiences of Joseph, who flees Austria in 1938 and pretends to be Jewish before disappearing from London under mysterious circumstances.

Gavin, Rick

Beluga / Rick Gavin. St Martins Press, 2012. 304 p. Nick Reid novels

ISBN 9781250015228

1. Criminals 2. Money laundering 3. Swindlers and swindling 4. Death threats 5. Assassins 6. Rural life 7. Delta Region, Mississippi 8. Humorous stories 9. Noir fiction 10. Crime fiction

Launching a money laundering and lending operation after outwitting a meth dealer, Nick Reid and his partner, Desmond, reluctantly participate in a former in-law's scheme involving a trailer full of stolen tires, which pits them against a ninja schoolgirl assassin and a pair of Delta gangsters.

Gay, Roxane

* **Ayiti** / Roxane Gay. Grove Press, 2018, c2011. 320 p.

ISBN 9780802128263

1. African diaspora 2. Immigrants 3. Interpersonal relations 4. Ethnic identity 5. Culture conflict 6. Haitians in the United States 7. Assimilation (Sociology) 8. Haiti 9. United States 10. Literary fiction 11. African American fiction 12. Short stories

Originally published: New York : Artistically declined press, 2011.

Released for the first time to mainstream readers, a debut story collection by the award-winning author of An Untamed State is a poignant exploration of the Haitian diaspora experience and is complemented by several new stories.

Gay, Roxane

* **Difficult** women / Roxane Gay. Grove Press, 2017. 272 p.

ISBN 9780802125392

1. Independence in women 2. Women -- Psychology 3. Women -- Interpersonal relations 4. Short stories 5. Literary fiction

BCALA Literary Award for Fiction, 2018.

Telling the stories of strong, imperfect, fully realized women, award-winning author Roxane Gay offers diverse protagonists and settings and unusual, often troubling situations in which women are haunted by pain and loss. In "The Mark of Cain," a woman pretends not to know that her abusive husband and his gentler identical twin have switched places; women participate in fight clubs in another story, while a priest refuses to feel bad about an affair in a third. With complex characters and straightforward writing, this is a memorable collection. -- Description by Shauna Griffin

"Whether focusing on assault survivors, single mothers, or women who drown their guilt in wine and bad boyfriends, Gay's fantastic collection is challenging, quirky, and memorable." Publishers Weekly.

Gay, Roxane

* An **untamed** state / Roxane Gay. Black Cat, 2014. 368 p.

ISBN 9780802122513

1. Kidnapping 2. Ransom 3. Women kidnapping victims 4. Rape 5. Mental illness 6. Psychic trauma 7. Rich women 8. Haiti 9. Literary fiction

A novel about a woman kidnapped for ransom, her captivity as her father refuses to pay and her husband fights for her release over thirteen days, and her struggle to come to terms with the ordeal in its aftermath.

"Among the strongest achievements of this novel is that Mireille's story feels complete and whole while emphasizing its essential brokenness. A cutting and resonant debut." Kirkus.

Gaylin, Alison

Never look back / Alison Gaylin. William Morrow & Co., 2019. 384 p.

ISBN 9780062884350

1. Teenage murderers 2. Podcasts 3. Amateur detectives 4. Families of murder victims 5. Murder investigation 6. Family secrets 7. Mother and adult daughter 8. Threat (Psychology) 9. Home invasions 10. Psychological suspense

More than four decades after a 1976 killing spree by two teens, a young podcaster blames his troubled upbringing on the murders before receiving a terrifying message that one of the killers may still be alive.

"A mind-bending mystery, an insightful exploration of parent-child relationships, and a cautionary tale about bitterness and blame." Kirkus.

Gaynor, Hazel

The **lighthouse** keeper's daughter / Hazel Gaynor. Harper-Collins, 2018 384 p.

ISBN 9780062869302

1. 1930s 2. 1830s 3. Hurricanes 4. Lighthouses 5. Teenage girls 6. Search and rescue operations 7. Lighthouse keepers 8. Teenage pregnancy 9. Shipwrecks 10. Portraits 11. Storms 12. Northumberland, England 13. Newport, Rhode Island 14. Historical fiction 15. Parallel narratives

Pregnant and disgraced, a 1938 Irish teen is sent to stay with a lighthouse keeper relative, where she discovers an unfinished portrait and delves into the story of a woman who lived there a hundred years prior.

Gaynor, Hazel

* **Meet** me in Monaco : a novel / Hazel Gaynor and Heather Webb. William Morrow, 2019. 384 p.

ISBN 9780062913548

1. Grace,, Princess of Monaco, 1929-1982 2. 1950s 3. Film actors and actresses 4. Friendship 5. Second chances 6. Paparazzi 7. Perfumes industry and trade 8. Divorced fathers 9. Interpersonal attraction 10. Men/women relations 11. Royal weddings 12. Film festivals 13. Monaco 14. France 15. Historical fiction 16. Love stories

LC 2018059053

A struggling perfumer who has forged an unlikely friendship with Grace Kelly against a backdrop of the latter's high-profile wedding considers what she is prepared to sacrifice when she falls in love with a British press photographer.

Geagley, Brad, 1950-

Year of the hyenas / Brad Geagley. Simon & Schuster, 2005. 304 p. Semerket mysteries

ISBN 074325080X

1. Ramses III,, King of Egypt 2. Ancient Egypt (3100 BCE-640 CE) 3. Semerket 4. Government investigators 5. Detectives 6. Alcoholics 7. Alcoholic men 8. Divorced men 9. Murder investigation 10. Women priests 11. Conspiracies 12. Former wives 13. Grave robbing -- Egypt 14. Thebes (Egypt : Extinct city) 15. Nile River 16. Egypt -- Rulers 17. Ancient Egypt -- History -- To 332 BC 18. Egypt -- Politics and government 19. Historical mysteries 20. Mysteries

LC 2004058979

Sequel: Day of the False King.

A mystery inspired by ancient transcripts documenting the "Harem Conspiracy of Ramses III" finds investigations clerk Semerket exploring clues to the murder of a Theban princess and discovering a threat on the life of Pharaoh Ramses III.

Gear, Kathleen O'Neal

People of the masks / Kathleen O'Neal Gear and W. Michael Gear. Forge, 1998. 416 p. First North Americans

ISBN 0312858574

1. Iroquois Indians -- Canada -- History 2. Curses 3. Kidnapping 4. Indians of North America 5. Prehistoric humans 6. Prophets 7. Iroquois Indians -- New York (State) -- History 8. Iroquois Indians -- Social life and customs 9. Historical fiction

LC 98-8695

With the help of a young village girl named Wren, Rumbler, the foretold "Manitou Child," escapes from Jumping Badger, the ruthless war leader who murdered his mother, destroyed his home, and kidnapped him in an attempt to seize control of the child of power.

Gear, Kathleen O'Neal

People of the mist / Kathleen O'Neal Gear and W. Michael Gear. Forge, 1997. 432 p. First North Americans

ISBN 031285854X

1. 14th century 2. Algonquian Indians -- Chesapeake Bay Region -- History -- 14th century 3. Women murder victims -- Chesapeake Bay Region 4. Algonquian Indians -- Social life and customs -- 14th century 5. Shamans 6. Chesapeake Bay Region -- History 7. Historical fiction

LC 9704682

"Set during the period archaeologists call Late Woodland II ... around 1300 A.D."

A bitter old recluse, feared as a terrible sorcerer, retreats to an island in the middle of the Chesapeake Bay where only the bravest venture to his lair, until a frightened young man arrives bearing news of a terrible murder that will sunder the great chieftainships.

"Simple prose brightened by atmospheric detail sweeps this fluid, suspenseful mix of anthropological research and character-driven mystery to a solid, satisfying resolution." Publishers Weekly.

Gelman, Laurie

Class mom : a novel / Laurie Gelman. Henry Holt & Company, 2017. 290 p. Class Mom

ISBN 9781250124692

1. P. T. A. 2. Middle-aged women 3. Kindergarten 4. Parenting 5. Mothers 6. Competition 7. Interpersonal relations 8. Personal conduct 9. Middle-aged mothers 10. Mothers and sons 11. Email correspondence 12. Elementary schools 13. Kansas City, Missouri 14. Missouri 15. Domestic fiction 16. Women's lives and relationships

LC 2016052495

Frowned upon by conservative fellow PTA members for her past as a single parent, Jen reluctantly agrees to become class mom during her youngest child's kindergarten year, a role that is challenged by parent drama, hypersensitive allergies and a former flame.

"Gelman pens an uproariously funny first novel with a relatable protagonist. Moms will clamor for this story, trying to hold back tears of laughter as Jen establishes her voice and place as the class mom." Library Journal.

Gelman, Laurie

You've been volunteered : a class mom novel / Laurie Gelman. Henry Holt & Co., 2019. 304 p. Class Mom

ISBN 9781250301857

1. P. T. A. 2. Middle-aged women 3. Third graders 4. Parenting 5. Mothers and sons 6. Mother and adult daughter 7. Children of aging parents 8. Married women 9. Interpersonal relations 10. Personal conduct 11. Middle-aged mothers 12. Email correspondence 13. Elementary schools 14. Missouri 15. Kansas City, Missouri 16.

Mainstream fiction 17. Women's lives and relationships

LC 2018050182

A follow-up to Class Mom finds Jen Dixon agreeing to school-parent her son's third-grade class only to find herself overwhelmed by her husband's late hours, her daughters' early adulthood and the needs of her aging parents.

"The tone and pacing are excellent, and new characters, who come with their own issues and snark, are delightful." Library Journal.

Geni, Abby

* The **lightkeepers** : a novel / Abby Geni. Counterpoint, 2016. 375 p.

ISBN 9781619026001

1. Women photographers 2. Social isolation 3. Wildlife refuges 4. Interpersonal relations 5. Islands 6. Wildlife 7. Scientists 8. Assault and battery 9. Murder 10. Mysteries

LC 2015037125

Traveling to a dangerous archipelago off the coast of California for a one-year residency, photographer Miranda is assaulted by a local who is later found dead, an event that leaves Miranda speculating about the region's wild beauty and the natures of her companions.

"As the plot turns violent and suspenseful, and the mesmerizingly vivid descriptions reach shivery crescendos of shocking revelations, Geni dramatically meshe's the grand, menacing power of the ruthless wild with the mysteries and aberrations of the equally untamed human psyche." Booklist.

Geni, Abby

The **wildlands** : a novel / Abby Geni. Counterpoint, 2018. 288 p.

ISBN 9781619022348

1. Orphans 2. Domestic terrorism 3. Animal rights advocates 4. Brothers and sisters 5. Animal rights 6. Survival (after tornadoes) 7. Child kidnapping victims 8. Violence in men 9. Life change events 10. Oklahoma 11. Literary fiction

LC 2018008262

Losing her home and parents to a tornado, a young girl becomes her radical older brother's unwitting accomplice as he declares war on humanity and engages in acts of increasing violence.

Genova, Lisa

Every note played / Lisa Genova. Gallery Books, 2018. 307 p.

ISBN 9781476717807

1. Pianists 2. Reconciliation 3. Amyotrophic lateral sclerosis -- Patients 4. Nervous system -- Degeneration 5. Degeneration (Pathology) 6. Men/women relations 7. Family relationships 8. Former wives 9. Caregivers 10. Mainstream fiction

Librarians' Choice (Australia), 2018.

A once-celebrated concert pianist who is gradually succumbing to ALS is forced to accept help from the estranged wife he pushed away, a situation that forces the couple to reconcile their past before time runs out.

Genova, Lisa

Inside the O'Briens : a novel / Lisa Genova. Gallery Books, 2015. 320 p.

ISBN 9781476717777

1. People with terminal illnesses -- Family relationships 2. Life change events 3. Parent and adult child 4. People with Huntington's disease 5. Children of people with terminal illnesses 6. Police 7. Coping 8. Families 9. Medical genetics 10. Huntington's disease 11.

Massachusetts 12. Domestic fiction

LC 2014034832

When a beloved Irish Catholic police officer is diagnosed with Huntington's Disease, his grown children witness their father's demise and consider whether they want to be tested to see if they have inherited the condition.

Genova, Lisa

Left neglected : a novel / Lisa Genova. Gallery Books, 2011. 320 p.

ISBN 9781439164631

1. Life change events 2. Self-fulfillment in women 3. Women with brain injuries 4. Caretakers 5. Convalescence 6. Forgiveness 7. Husband and wife 8. Family relationships 9. Massachusetts 10. Mainstream fiction 11. Mainstream fiction

LC 2010025568

Presents the story of a woman in her thirties who suffers a traumatic brain injury in a car accident that leaves her unable to perceive left-side information, a disability that prompts her struggle to recover and heal an estrangement.

"Some readers will likely find a few of the plot elements a bit too neat. . . . Despite these contrivances, Left Neglected is a novel worth reading for the way it informs a little-known medical condition, as well as the engaging story of a character who transcends what could have been a tragedy to find a fresh appreciation for life." Boston Globe.

Gentry, Amy,

Last woman standing / Amy Gentry. Houghton Mifflin Harcourt, 2019 288 p.

ISBN 9780544962538

1. Betrayal 2. Revenge in women 3. Sexual harassment 4. Computer programmers 5. Sexism in employment 6. Men/women relations 7. Comedians 8. Thrillers and suspense

LC 2018017517

Prompted by sexual harassment and assaults to exact revenge, an aspiring comedienne and her tough computer-programmer friend engage in an escalating series of betrayals that trigger unexpected consequences.

George, Elizabeth, 1949-

A **banquet** of consequences / Elizabeth George. Viking, 2015 736 p. Thomas Lynley mysteries

ISBN 9780525954330

1. Scotland Yard. 2. Criminal investigation 3. Detectives 4. Police 5. London, England 6. England 7. Mysteries 8. Police procedurals

"As Inspector Thomas Lynley investigates the London angle of an ever more darkly disturbing case, his partner, Barbara Havers, is looking behind the peaceful façade of country life to discover a twisted world of desire, deceit, and murder. The suicide of William Goldacre is devastating to those left behind. But what was the cause of his tragedy and how far might the consequences reach? Is there a link between the young man's leap from a Dorset cliff and a horrific poisoning in Cambridge? After various career-threatening issues with her department, Barbara Havers is desperate to redeem herself. So when a past encounter with a bestselling feminist writer and her pushy personal assistant gives her a connection to the Cambridge murder, Barbara begs Thomas Lynley to let her pursue the crime" --, provided by publisher.

"This nineteenth Lynley novel is a sterling addition to George's acclaimed character-centered series: even the most minor characters are full-bodied...." Booklist.

George, Elizabeth, 1949-

Believing the lie / Elizabeth George. Dutton, 2012 624 p. Thomas Lynley mysteries

ISBN 9780525952589

1. Scotland Yard. 2. Undercover operations 3. Murder investigation 4. Family secrets 5. Drowning 6. Recovering drug abusers 7. Rich families 8. Deception 9. Murder suspects 10. Police 11. London, England 12. England 13. Mysteries 14. Police procedurals

In this novel Inspector Thomas Lynley is mystified when he's sent undercover to investigate the death of Ian Cresswell at the request of the man's uncle, the wealthy and influential Bernard Fairclough. The death has been ruled an accidental drowning, and nothing on the surface indicates otherwise. But when Lynley enlists the help of his friends Simon and Deborah St. James, the trio's digging soon reveals that the Fairclough clan is awash in secrets, lies, and motives. Deborah's investigation of the prime suspect, Bernard's prodigal son Nicholas, a recovering drug addict, leads her to Nicholas' wife, a woman with whom she feels a kinship, a woman as fiercely protective as she is beautiful. Lynley and Simon delve for information from the rest of the family, including the victim's bitter ex-wife and the man he left her for, and Bernard himself. As the investigation escalates, the Fairclough family's veneer cracks, with deception and self-delusion threatening to destroy everyone from the Fairclough patriarch to Tim, the troubled son Ian left behind.

George, Elizabeth, 1949-

Careless in red / Elizabeth George. HarperCollins, 2008. 640 p. Thomas Lynley mysteries

ISBN 9780061160875

1. Scotland Yard. 2. Murder investigation 3. Murder suspects 4. Police 5. Women detectives 6. Loss (Psychology) 7. Grief in men 8. Earls and countesses 9. Cornwall, England 10. England 11. Mysteries 12. Police procedurals

LC 2007044629

Scotland Yard's Thomas Lynley discovers the body of a young man who appears to have fallen to his death. The closest town, better known for its tourists and its surfing than its intrigue, seems an unlikely place for murder. However, it soon becomes apparent that a clever killer is indeed at work, and this time Lynley is not a detective but a witness and possibly a suspect.

"As with George's other books, the reader is soon plunged into a vast back story of relationships and psychologically complex characters. It's a level of literary sophistication readers have come to expect from George." Seattle Times.

George, Elizabeth, 1949-

* **Just** one evil act / Elizabeth George. Dutton, 2013. 736 p. Thomas Lynley mysteries

ISBN 9780525952961

1. Scotland Yard. 2. Child kidnapping victims 3. Kidnapping investigation 4. British in Italy 5. Policewomen 6. Parents' rights 7. Child custody 8. Police 9. London, England 10. England 11. Italy 12. Mysteries 13. Police procedurals

Supporting a friend who has lost custody of his young daughter, Barbara and her partner, Inspector Thomas Lynley, are further shocked when the girl's mother reports that the child has been kidnapped from an Italian marketplace as part of a complex plot that risks Barbara's career.

George, Elizabeth, 1949-

The **punishment** she deserves / Elizabeth George. Viking, 2018. 692 p. Thomas Lynley mysteries

ISBN 9780525954347

1. Police 2. Women detectives 3. Suicide investigation 4. Politicians 5. Murder investigation 6. London, England 7. England 8. Mysteries

9. Police procedurals

Inspector Thomas Lynley of Scotland Yard and the pugnacious but loyal detective sergeant Barbara Havers tackle one of the most sinister murder cases they have ever encountered.

George, Elizabeth, 1949-

This body of death : an Inspector Lynley novel / Elizabeth George. HarperCollins, 2010. 692 p. Thomas Lynley mysteries

ISBN 9780061160882

1. Scotland Yard. 2. Murder investigation 3. Crimes against women 4. Police 5. Women detectives 6. Murder suspects 7. Public relations 8. Murder 9. London, England 10. England 11. Mysteries 12. Police procedurals

LC 2009035547

After a woman is found dead in an isolated cemetery, Inspector Thomas Lynley and his former partner, Barbara Havers, find that the roots of the crime trace to a long-ago act of violence that has poisoned subsequent generations.

"As always, [George's] story is credible and commanding, and her characters--particularly Lynley and Havers--continue to evolve while remaining the reader's old and dear friends. George's perceptive characterizations find a worthy complement in her descriptive powers, which evoke a strong sense of place. . . . A book for neither the faint of heart nor the short of patience, This Body of Death is a rich, unsettling work, one whose darkness is lightened by Lynley's steady emergence from grief." Richmond Times-Dispatch.

George, Elizabeth, 1949-

What came before he shot her / Elizabeth George. HarperCollins, 2006. 560 p. Thomas Lynley mysteries

ISBN 0060545623

1. Boy murderers 2. Drug traffic 3. Revenge 4. Dysfunctional families 5. Protectiveness in children 6. Multiracial children 7. Family problems 8. Poverty 9. Murder 10. Classism 11. London, England 12. England 13. Mysteries 14. Police procedurals

LC 2006043520

Novel tells of the events prior to the murder of Thomas Lynley's wife. Thomas Lynley and Barbara Havers do not appear in this book.

"In North Kensington three orphaned mixed-race children are bounced from one home to another. The middle child Joel takes care of the youngest, Toby, who isn't quite right. When a local gang threatens Toby, Joel makes a pact with the devil that ends in the murder of Thomas Lynley's wife."--From source other than the Library of Congress

"This is crime writing at its finest, with an almost painfully sharp view of the world and evil." Rocky Mountain News.

George, Margaret, 1943-

The confessions of young Nero / Margaret George. Berkley Books, 2017. 528 p. Nero novels

ISBN 9780451473387

1. Nero,, Emperor of Rome, 37-68 2. Roman Empire (27 BCE-476 CE) 3. Rulers 4. Inheritance and succession 5. Political intrigue 6. Mothers and sons 7. Ambition in women 8. Manipulation (Social sciences) 9. Civilization, Ancient 10. Rome -- History -- Nero, 54-68 11. Historical fiction 12. Biographical fiction

LC 2016024945

RUSA Reading List Short List, 2018.

Lucius Domitius Ahenobarbus was born to rule. At least, that's what his mother Agrippina (a woman with a penchant for poisoning her husbands) believes. An intelligent, sensitive boy who loves music and chariot races, Lucius can only be an improvement over his uncle, Caligula. Even as he benefits from Agrippina's scheming, Lucius strives to break free of his family's influence; by age 16, he's Emperor Nero. However, he quickly discovers that staying in power requires a certain amount of ruthlessness. This is an unusual coming-of-age story that imagines the life of a notorious ruler. -- Description by Gillian Speace

"Highly acclaimed for the detail and personality she gives to epic subjects, George's heavily researched novel flows dynamically among multiple points of view." Library Journal.

George, Margaret, 1943-

Elizabeth I : a novel / Margaret George. Viking, 2011. 688 p.

ISBN 9780670022533

1. Elizabeth I,, Queen of England, 1533-1603 2. Elizabethan era (1558-1603) 3. 16th century 4. Tudor period (1485-1603) 5. Women rulers -- Great Britain 6. Courts and courtiers 7. Cousins 8. Men/women relations 9. Great Britain -- History -- Elizabeth I, 1558-1603 10. Historical fiction 11. Biographical fiction

LC 2010035382

Growing up at the side of her cousin, Elizabeth I, Lettice Knollys struggles to regain power and position for her family while competing against the queen for the love of Robert Dudley, a rivalry that is set against a backdrop of the flourishing Elizabethan age.

"Set in the final 20 years of Elizabeth's reign, George's novel is the portrait of an aging powerful woman, one who struggles at times with her waning sexual allure even as she refuses to let its loss diminish her power. . . . This historical novel has considerable strengths, from impressive detail and a wonderfully evocative setting to dialogue that feels appropriately old without ever veering into hokeyness. George brings the queen's two major foreign-policy challenges--conflict with Spain and with Ireland--to life in a way that feels both immediate and relevant. But these achievements are at times outweighed both by the inclusion of (seemingly) everything that happened in England during the time period covered, and by the jarring choice to divide the story between two first-person narrators: Elizabeth herself, and her cousin, Lettice Knollys, who was wife to one of Elizabeth's favorite courtiers and mother to another. The two narrators slow the pace down a problem in such a lengthy tome and the stories don't intersect enough for a reader to gain traction. . . . Nevertheless, the contrast between the two narrative voices successfully illustrates two very different modes of female power: the Virgin Queen vs. the seductive noblewoman." Boston Globe.

George, Margaret, 1943-

Helen of Troy / Margaret George. Viking, 2005. 624 p.

ISBN 0670037788

1. Helen of Troy (Greek mythology) 2. Trojan War 3. Self-sacrifice 4. Love triangles 5. War 6. Battles 7. Fate and fatalism 8. Greeks in Turkey 9. Consequences 10. Men/women relations 11. Beauty 12. Mythology, Greek 13. Folklore, Greek 14. Mycenae (Extinct city) 15. Troy (Extinct city) 16. Biographical fiction 17. Historical fiction

LC 2005058473

Married at a tender age to the Spartan king Menelaus, the beautiful Helen bears him a daughter and anticipates a passionless marriage before falling in love with the Trojan prince Paris, with whom she flees to Troy with devastating consequences.

"George's characters are precisely crafted, and the lovely Helen, clear-eyed and intelligent, is a sympathetic narrator. Despite the novel's length, the pages practically turn themselves. An absorbing retelling of the classic Trojan War myth, and a sobering look at the utter futility of trying to change one's fate." Booklist.

George, Margaret, 1943-

The **splendor** before the dark : a novel of the Emperor Nero / Margaret George. Berkley, 2018. 528 p. Nero novels

ISBN 9780399584619

1. Nero,, Emperor of Rome, 37-68 2. Roman Empire (27 BCE-476 CE) 3. Roman emperors 4. Political intrigue 5. Power (Social sciences) 6. Fire 7. Betrayal 8. Rulers 9. Civilization, Ancient 10. Rome -- History -- Nero, 54-68 11. Historical fiction 12. Biographical fiction

LC 2017060014

When a fire engulfs ancient Rome, Nero Augustus is targeted with suspicion about his complicity, forcing him to navigate a web of false friends and spies to save the empire, in a follow-up to The Confessions of a Young Nero.

George, Nina, 1973-

The **book** of dreams / Nina George. Crown Publishing, 2019. 352 p.

ISBN 9780525572534

1. Fathers and sons 2. People in comas 3. Former lovers 4. Hospitals 5. Romantic love 6. Purpose in life 7. Loss (Psychology) 8. Teenage boys 9. Genius 10. Synesthesia 11. Memories 12. Interpersonal relations 13. London, England 14. Mainstream fiction 15. Translations -- German to English

Rendered comatose after an act of heroism, a man revisits memories of his British youth, while his ex forges an unexpected, profound friendship with the teenage son he has never known.

George, Nina, 1973-

The **little** Paris bookshop / Nina George ; translated by Simon Pare. Crown, 2015, c2013. 320 p.

ISBN 9780553418774

1. Booksellers 2. Books 3. Lost love 4. Voyages and travels 5. Rivers 6. Self-fulfillment in men 7. Interpersonal relations 8. Paris, France 9. France 10. Mainstream fiction 11. Translations -- German to English

Originally published in Germany as Das Lavendelzimmer by Knaur Verlag in 2013.

""A book is both doctor and medicine. It makes diagnoses and provides therapy. Bringing the right novels together with the appropriate people is the way I sell books."

"Through its well-drawn characters, this novel carefully explores these relationships between lovers, friends, and family, and the painful sacrifices made selflessly for them." Booklist.

Gerritsen, Tess

The **apprentice** : a novel / Tess Gerritsen. Ballantine Books, 2002. 344 p. Jane Rizzoli and Maura Isles series

ISBN 0345447859

1. Serial murders 2. Imitation 3. Escaped convicts 4. Police 5. Policewomen 6. Women detectives 7. Serial murderers 8. Serial rape 9. Serial rapists 10. Women kidnapping victims 11. FBI agents 12. Revenge 13. Men/women relations 14. Attempted murder 15. Boston, Massachusetts 16. Medical thrillers

Sequel to: The surgeon.

Sequel: The sinner.

It's a boiling summer in Boston. Adding to the city's woes is a series of shocking crimes that end in abduction and death. The pattern suggest "the Surgeon," serial killer Warren Hoyt. But Hoyt is behind bars, so this time it's a copycat killer. Detective Jane Rizzoli is on the case, determined to finally end Hoyt's influence.

"Boston detective Jane Rizzoli is called to a crime scene out of her jurisdiction. The victim is a wealthy doctor, found with his throat slashed, sitting on the floor of his living room in his pajamas, with a teacup in his lap. His wife is missing, but her nightgown is found folded neatly on a chair in the bedroom. There are unmistakable similarities to the work of serial killer Warren Hoyt, nicknamed 'the Surgeon,' but he is in prison, which leads Rizzoli to suspect a copcat killer." Library Journal.

Gerritsen, Tess

The **bone** garden / Tess Gerritsen. Ballantine Books, 2007. 368 p.

ISBN 0345497600

1. 19th century 2. 1830s 3. 21st century 4. Serial murders 5. Forensic sciences 6. Women detectives 7. Divorced women 8. Murder 9. Murder investigation 10. Women murder victims 11. Women medical scientists 12. Women forensic pathologists 13. Women forensic scientists 14. Medical students 15. Boston, Massachusetts 16. Thrillers and suspense

The discovery of the skeleton of a woman murdered nearly two centuries earlier sends Boston medical examiner Maura Isles on the trail of a long-dead serial killer who terrorized Boston with crimes in which Norris Marshall, a Harvard Medical School student and reluctant resurrectionist, had become the prime suspect and enlisted the help of classmate Oliver Wendell Holmes to find and stop the murderer.

Gerritsen, Tess

I know a secret / Tess Gerritsen. Ballantine, 2017. 336 p. Jane Rizzoli and Maura Isles series

ISBN 9780345543882

1. Serial murder investigation 2. Women detectives 3. Horror films 4. Filmmakers 5. Fans 6. Serial murderers 7. Police 8. Medical thrillers

Jane Rizzoli and Maura Isles--the crime-solving duo who inspired the smash hit TNT series--return to investigate the gruesome staged murder of a horror film producer in this edge-of-your-seat thriller.

Gerritsen, Tess

Playing with fire / Tess Gerritsen. Ballantine Books, 2015. 288 p.

ISBN 9781101884348

1. Change (Psychology) 2. Violence 3. Music 4. Women violinists 5. Mothers and daughters 6. Sheet music 7. Secrets 8. Family secrets 9. Thrillers and suspense

Discovering an old and strikingly unusual musical composition that causes her to black out and has a violently transformative effect on her daughter, Julia Ansdell travels to Venice to find the man behind the music and uncovers a dark secret dating back to the Holocaust.

"Gerritsens narrative weaves back and forth between Julia's time and that of musical prodigy Lorenzo Todesco, who faces the growing anti-Semitism in WWII Italy. These story lines arch, intertwine, and combust in a riveting finale." Booklist.

Gerritsen, Tess

* The **shape** of night : a novel / Tess Gerritsen. Ballantine Books, 2019. 268 p.

ISBN 9781984820952

1. Haunted houses 2. Ghosts 3. Single women 4. Guilt 5. Seduction 6. Social isolation 7. Coastal towns 8. Small town life 9. Women murder victims 10. Moving to a new state 11. Secrets 12. Men/women relations 13. Maine 14. Gothic fiction

LC 2019013895

Moving to a coastal community in Maine, a woman trying to outrun her past is confronted by a string of murders and the ghost of a sea captain who is haunting her isolated home.

Gerritsen, Tess

The **surgeon** / Tess Gerritsen. Ballantine Books, 2001. 359 p. Jane Rizzoli and Maura Isles series
ISBN 0345447832

1. Serial murders 2. Mutilation 3. Rape victims 4. Women heart surgeons 5. Stalkers 6. Police 7. Policewomen 8. Women detectives 9. Women -- Death 10. Serial murder investigation 11. Men/women relations 12. Serial rapists 13. Stalking 14. Boston, Massachusetts 15. Medical thrillers

LC 2001035901

Sequel: The apprentice.
RITA Award for Best Romantic-Suspense Gothic, 2002.

A female heart surgeon, terrorized by a serial killer in Boston using the same MO as a killer who attacked her during her internship years in Savannah, works with a detective to solve the crime while trying to stay alive.

"A fascinating story with a gripping plot and believably human characters." Booklist.

Gertler, Stephanie

* **Drifting** / Stephanie Gertler. Dutton, 2003. 258 p.
ISBN 0525947353

1. Women psychologists 2. Married women 3. Husband and wife 4. Separation (Psychology) 5. Mothers and daughters 6. Maternal deprivation 7. College freshmen 8. Hotel managers 9. Girls who are blind 10. Seven-year-old girls 11. Seven-year-olds 12. Fathers and daughters 13. Single fathers 14. Parental kidnapping 15. Love 16. Loss (Psychology) 17. Connecticut 18. Psychological fiction 19. Domestic fiction

LC 2002155035

Haunted by the mother who abandoned her in babyhood, Connecticut innkeeper Claire finds herself bonding with a blind seven-year-old girl and struggling to help the child, whose father harbors a darker nature.

Gessen, Keith

All the sad young literary men / Keith Gessen. Viking, 2008. 256 p.
ISBN 9780670018550

1. Young men 2. Authors 3. Men/women relations 4. Love 5. Growing up 6. Coming-of-age stories 7. Domestic fiction

LC 2007021009

A portrait of young adulthood at the opening of the twenty-first century, charting the lives of Sam, Mark and Keith during their college years.

"Gessen's humor is persistently Seinfeldian, avoiding the excesses of savage comedy or satire, or anything like raging spiritual despair, for All the Sad Young Literary Men is a post-postmodernist work of fiction in which spiritual impotence is the great subtextual theme, even as sexual promiscuity is the norm." The New York Review of Books.

Gessen, Keith

A **terrible** country / Keith Gessen. Penguin Group USA, 2018. 352 p.
ISBN 9780735221314

1. 2000s (Decade) 2. Grandmother and grandson 3. Seniors -- Care 4. Capitalism 5. Communism 6. Senior women 7. Culture conflict 8. Political activists 9. Russian Americans 10. Family relationships 11. Intergenerational relations 12. Moscow, Russia 13. Russia 14. Satirical fiction 15. Literary fiction

After Andrei Kaplan returns to Moscow to care for his ailing grandmother, he becomes entangled with a group of leftists and he is forced to come to terms with the Russian society he was born into and the American one he has enjoyed since he was a kid.

"With a realistic approach that nods to William Dean Howells and Tolstoy in equal measure, and like the fiction of his n+1 cohorts Chad Harbach and Benjamin Kunkel, Gessen presents a measured, socially engaged novel that is moving, often funny, and deeply thought-provoking." Booklist.

Gestern, Helene, 1971-

The **people** in the photo / Helene Gestern ; translated from the French by Emily Boyce and Ros Schwartz. Gallic Books, 2014, c2011. 240 p.
ISBN 9781908313546

1. Birthparents 2. Family secrets 3. Women archivists 4. Biologists 5. Photographs 6. Adopted girls 7. Letter writing 8. Families -- History 9. Family relationships 10. Interpersonal relations 11. Paris, France 12. Literary fiction 13. Translations -- French to English

First published in France as Eux sur la photo by Editions Arlea, c2011.

A photograph taken in 1971 sets two people on the path to uncovering the truth about their parents.

Ghaffari, Rabeah

* **To** keep the sun alive / Rabeah Ghaffari. Catapult, 2019. 176 p.
ISBN 9781948226097

1. 1970s 2. Extended families 3. Social change 4. Revolutions 5. Orchards 6. Family estates 7. Religious fanaticism 8. Family relationships 9. Life change events 10. Iran -- History -- Islamic revolution, 1979-1997 11. Political fiction 12. Family sagas

A cinematic novel about an Iranian family and their fruit orchard, caught up in the Revolution of 1979.

Ghosh, Amitav, 1956-

Flood of fire / Amitav Ghosh. Farrar, Straus & Giroux, 2015. 528 p. Ibis trilogy
ISBN 9780374174248

1. 19th century 2. 1830s 3. Voyages and travels 4. Opium industry and trade 5. Sailors 6. Schooners 7. Seafaring life 8. Travelers 9. Caste 10. China 11. India -- History -- 19th century 12. Historical fiction 13. Literary fiction

First published in Great Britain in 2015 by John Murray (Publishers).

A conclusion to the internationally best-selling series that began with Sea of Poppies and River of Smoke follows an East India Company soldier's 1839 journey to Hong Kong to end a costly embargo on the eve of the Opium Wars.

"Forbidden and betrayed love are the primary forces here, enacted with bawdy comedy and outright melodrama amid family concerns, secret deals, brutality, military battles, and the horrors of the drug trade. This feverishly detailed, vividly panoramic, tumultuous, funny, and heartbreaking tale offers a vigorous conclusion to Ghosh's astutely complex and profoundly resonant geopolitical saga." Booklist.

Ghosh, Amitav, 1956-

The **glass** palace / Amitav Ghosh. Random House, 2000. 512 p.
ISBN 0375501487

1. 1880s 2. 20th century 3. Courts and courtiers 4. Exiles 5. Colonialism 6. Political intrigue 7. Friendship 8. Men/women relations 9. Family relationships 10. Burma -- History 11. India -- History 12. Historical fiction 13. Literary fiction 14. Family sagas

LC 00041477

Unable to forget the girl he befriended during the British invasion of 1885 when soldiers forced the royal family of Burma into exile, Rajkumar is lifted on the tides of political and social chaos to create an empire in the Burmese teak forests.

"Ghosh renders the polite imprisonment of the Burmese royal family in India and the lush, dangerous atmosphere of teak camps in the Burmese forest with fine detail--a perfect balance for the broad stroke of romance and serendipity that drive the story forward." The New Yorker.

Ghosh, Amitav, 1956-

* **Gun** Island / Amitav Ghosh. Farrar Straus & Giroux, 2019. 288 p.

ISBN 9780374167394

1. Storytelling 2. Climate change 3. East Indian Americans 4. Voyages and travels 5. Antiquarian booksellers 6. Family history 7. Characters and characteristics in mythology 8. Bengali Americans 9. Self-discovery 10. Literary fiction

A rare books dealer unexpectedly embarks on a journey of discovery through nations and cultures where the people he meets impart insights into the Bengali legends of his childhood.

Ghosh, Amitav, 1956-

The **hungry** tide / Amitav Ghosh. Houghton Mifflin, 2005. 352 p.

ISBN 0618329978

1. Dolphins 2. Women marine biologists 3. Wildlife conservation 4. Americans in Sundarbans (Bangladesh and India) 5. Fishers 6. Guides (Persons) 7. Interpreters 8. Revolutionaries 9. Diaries 10. Sundarbans (Bangladesh and India) -- History 11. India 12. Psychological fiction 13. Literary fiction

LC 2004060942

ALA Notable Book, 2006.

Off the eastern coast of Inda lies an extraordinary cluster of islands known as the Sundarbans. It is a raw but a beautiful sea--a place of man-eating tigers, river dolphins, huge crocodiles and devistating tides that sweep across the terrain without remorse. In this exotic land, marine biologist Piya, fisherman Fokir and translator Kanai meet. As they travel deep into the remote archipelago, they experience a territory at risk not only from natural disaster, but also from human foolishness and volatile politics.

Ghosh, Amitav, 1956-

River of smoke / Amitav Ghosh. Farrar, Straus & Giroux, 2011. 528 p. Ibis trilogy

ISBN 9780374174231

1. 19th century 2. 1830s 3. Voyages and travels 4. Opium industry and trade 5. Sailors 6. Schooners 7. Cyclones 8. Seafaring life 9. Botanists 10. Travelers 11. Caste 12. China 13. Mauritius 14. India -- History -- 19th century 15. Historical fiction 16. Literary fiction

Amid a cyclone in the Bay of Bengal, three vessels, and the diverse occupants within, converge on Canton's Fanqui-Town, or Foreign Enclave, which is a powder keg awaiting a spark to ignite the Opium Wars.

"Ghosh's fascination with the multicultural ferment of Canton inspires thrilling descriptions of everything from local cuisine to the geopolitics of the opium wars. And his delight in language, especially the inventiveness of pidgin, further vitalizes his canny and dazzling tale, which, for all its historical exactitude, subtly reflects the hypocrisy and horrors of today's drug trafficking." Booklist.

Ghosh, Amitav, 1956-

Sea of poppies / Amitav Ghosh. Farrar, Straus and Giroux, 2008. 528 p. Ibis trilogy

ISBN 9780374174224

1. 1830s 2. Schooners 3. Opium industry and trade 4. Sailors 5. Voyages and travels 6. Travelers 7. Caste 8. India -- History -- 19th century 9. Historical fiction 10. Literary fiction

LC 2008030854

First published, 2008.

Shortlisted for the Man Booker Prize, 2008.

Preparing to fight China's nineteenth-century Opium Wars, a motley assortment of sailors and passengers establish family-like ties that eventually span continents, races, and generations.

"An adventure story set in nineteenth-century Calcutta against the backdrop of the Opium Wars. On the Ibis, a ship engaged in transporting opium across the Bay of Bengal, varied life stories converge. A fallen raja, a half-Chinese convict, a plucky American sailor, a widowed opium farmer, a transgendered religious visionary are all united by the smoky paradise of the opium seed. Ghosh writes with impeccable control, and with a vivid and sometimes surprising imagination." The New Yorker.

Gibb, Camilla

Sweetness in the belly / Camilla Gibb. Penguin Press, 2006. 432 p.

ISBN 159420084X

1. Muslim women 2. Muslims 3. Muslims -- Ethiopia 4. Immigrants 5. British in Ethiopia 6. Women 7. Race awareness 8. Islam 9. Loss (Psychology) 10. Harer, Ethiopia 11. London, England 12. Africa 13. Psychological fiction 14. Political fiction

LC 2005053451

Trillium Book Award, 2005.

Shortlisted for the Giller Prize, 2005

"Utterly convincing and authentic . . . a novel that will take you to a place so far from yourself that you may wonder, from time to time, whether you are ever coming back." San Francisco Chronicle.

Gibbons, Kaye, 1960-

Charms for the easy life / Kaye Gibbons. HarperCollins, 2005, c1993. 254 p.

ISBN 9780060760250

1. Grandmother and granddaughter 2. Independence in women 3. Mother and adult daughter 4. Midwives 5. Homeopathy 6. Women -- North Carolina 7. Women healers 8. Depressions -- 1929-1941 9. World War II 10. Family relationships 11. Men/women relations 12. North Carolina 13. Family sagas 14. Southern fiction 15. Gentle reads

LC 92040690

A tale of three generations of North Carolina women that has charmed readers from coast to coast. Their men may come and go-- but for Margaret, Sophia and Charlie Kate, the hopes, hurts, large losses and small victories are the stuff that bind family together.

"A touching picture of female bonding and solidarity. Related with the simple, tart economy of a folktale, the narrative brims with wisdom and superstition, with Southern manners and insights into human nature." Publishers Weekly.

Gibbons, Kaye, 1960-

* **Ellen** Foster : a novel / Kaye Gibbons. Algonquin Books of Chapel Hill, 1987. 146 p. Ellen Foster duology

ISBN 9781565122055

1. Foster children 2. Child abuse victims 3. Identity (Psychology) 4. Runaways 5. Eleven-year-old girls 6. Children of alcoholics 7. Southern States 8. North Carolina 9. Coming-of-age stories 10. Domestic fiction 11. Southern fiction

LC 86022136

Sequel: The life all around me by Ellen Foster.

Having suffered abuse and misfortune for much of her life, a young child searches for a better life and finally gets a break in the home of a loving woman with several foster children.

"What might have been grim, melodramatic material in the hands of a less talented author is instead filled with lively humor, . . . compassion and intimacy. This short novel focuses on Ellen's strengths rather than her victimization, presenting a memorable heroine who rescues herself." New York Times Book Review.

Gibbons, Kaye, 1960-

The **life** all around me by Ellen Foster / Kaye Gibbons. Harcourt, 2006. 224 p. Ellen Foster duology

ISBN 0151012040

1. Gifted teenagers 2. Independence (Personal quality) 3. Self-fulfillment in teenage girls 4. Teenage girls 5. Fifteen-year-old girls 6. Orphans 7. Foster children 8. Foster mothers 9. Best friends 10. Neighbors 11. Foster home care 12. Poetry writing 13. Independence in teenage girls 14. Small town life -- North Carolina 15. North Carolina 16. Domestic fiction 17. Coming-of-age stories 18. Southern fiction

LC 2005014552

Sequel to: Ellen Foster.

Now fifteen, Ellen Foster is settled into a permanent home with a new mother. Strengthened by adversity and blessed with enough intelligence to design a salvation for herself, she still feels ill at ease in the world. While she holds fast to the shreds of her childhood, humoring her best friend Stuart who is determined to marry her. She protects her old neighbor, slow-witted Starletta and sells her poetry for money to pay her way to a camp for gifted students.

"This book lacks the strong story arc of its predecessor, which may make some readers impatient. But Ellen is still a remarkable creation, and her narrative voice, while it has matured and grown more sophisticated, remains compelling and unique." Booklist.

Gibson, Claire

Beyond the point : a novel / Claire Gibson. HarperCollins Publishers, 2019. 528 p.

ISBN 9780062853745

1. United States Military Academy 2. Women soldiers 3. Female friendship 4. September 11 Terrorist Attacks, 2001 5. Women's role 6. Sexism 7. Ambition in women 8. Self-doubt 9. Interpersonal relations 10. Coping 11. United States -- Armed Forces -- Women 12. Mainstream fiction 13. Women's lives and relationships

In this powerful debut novel set at the U.S. Military Academy at West Point, three women-a nationally-ranked point guard, the granddaughter of an Army general, and a rebellious Homecoming Queen-are brought together in an enthralling story of friendship, heartbreak, and resilience.

Gibson, William, 1948-

* **Agency** / William Gibson. Berkley, 2020. 496 p. Peripheral

ISBN 9781101986936

1. 21st century 2. 22nd century 3. Artificial intelligence 4. Space and time 5. End of the world 6. High technology 7. Consequences 8. Parallel narratives 9. Cyberpunk

LC 2019023019

Sequel to: The Peripheral.

Originally published in Great Britain, 2019.

Verity Jane is hired to test a digital assistant that is accessed through a pair of ordinary glasses for a San Francisco start-up. One hundred years in the future and a different timeline, Wilf Netherton works amid survivors of the slow and steady apocalypse known as the jackpot. His employer can look into alternate pasts and nudge their ultimate directions. Verity has become his boss's current project, which will lead to their own version of the jackpot.

"Gibson blurs the line between real and speculative technology in a fast-paced thriller that will affirm to readers that it was well worth the wait." Booklist.

Gibson, William, 1948-

* **Neuromancer** / William Gibson ; with an afterword by Jack Womack. Ace Books, 2000, c1984. 276 p. Sprawl trilogy

ISBN 9780441007462

1. Hackers 2. Cyberspace 3. Betrayal 4. Computers 5. Near future 6. Dystopias 7. Second chances 8. Cyberpunk 9. Science fiction

Sequel: Count Zero.

Contains an exerpt from "Count zero".

Originally published: New York : Ace Books, 1984.

Nebula Award for Best Novel, 1984.

Phillip K. Dick Award for Science Fiction, 1984.

Hugo Award for Best Novel, 1985.

The Matrix unfolds like neon origami beneath clusters and constellations of data. Constructs, AIs, live here. Somewhere, concealed by ice, Neuromancer is evolving. As entropy goes into reverse, Molly's surgical implants broadcast trouble from the ferro-concrete geodesic of the Sprawl. Maelcum, Rastafarian in space, is her best hope of rescue. But she and Case, computer cowboy, are busy stealing data from the almighty Megacorps. If the Megacorps do not get them both, perhaps Case will fall prey to the cheap treachery of Linda Lee, someone as lost as himself.

"An adventure story much enlivened by elaborate technical jargon and sleazy, streetwise characters: the pioneering cyberpunk novel and arguably the most influential SF novel of the 1980s." Anatomy of Wonder, 5th edition.

Gibson, William, 1948-

Pattern recognition / William Gibson. G.P. Putnam's Sons, 2003. 368 p. Blue Ant trilogy

ISBN 0399149864

1. 21st century 2. Marketing research 3. Pattern perception 4. Hackers 5. Fathers and daughters 6. Grief 7. Paranoia 8. Mafia -- Russia 9. Phobias 10. London, England 11. Tokyo, Japan 12. Bournemouth, England 13. Moscow, Russia 14. Cyberpunk 15. Science fiction mysteries 16. Science fiction

LC 2002067955

Hired to investigate a mysterious video collection that has been appearing on the Internet, market research consultant Cayce Pollard realizes that there is more to the assignment when her computer is hacked.

"Cayce Pollard is a brand consultant whose father disappeared on September 11th. She becomes fascinated by mysterious scraps of film footage--seemingly random scenes, luminously shot--that are disseminated on the Web and have spawned cults of viewers. Gibson wisely avoids addressing the import of 9/11 head on, but he somehow establishes a powerful correlative for it in Cayce's strange quest--through the Tokyo red-light district and the Moscow underworld--to find the anonymous filmmaker. In Gibson's eerie vision of our time, the future has come crashing upon us, fragmentary and undecipherable." The New Yorker.

Gibson, William, 1948-

The **peripheral** / William Gibson. Putnam's Sons, 2014. 400 p. Peripheral

ISBN 9780399158445

1. Dystopias 2. Brothers and sisters 3. Computer software -- Testing 4. Murder 5. Intrigue 6. Veterans 7. Far future 8. Deception 9. Drug traffic 10. Time travel 11. Video games 12. Brain implants 13. Former Marines 14. Cyberpunk 15. Science fiction 16. Parallel narratives

LC 2014028558

Whenever she can, gamer Flynne Fisher tries to help her brother Burton, a disabled veteran. So when Burton asks her to beta-test a virtual reality game as part of his lucrative but illegal part-time job, Flynne agrees to sub in. During her shift, Flynne witnesses a murder and soon realizes that she's not playing a game, she's seeing the future. But how? Cutting-edge technology and crossed time lines create an intricately plotted and thought-provoking science fiction story that slowly builds suspense through parallel, yet intersecting, narratives. -- Description by Gillian Speace.

"All of Gibson's characters are intensely real, and Flynne is a clever, compelling, stereotype-defying, unhesitating protagonist who makes this novel a standout." Publishers Weekly.

Gide, Andre, 1869-1951

* The **immoralist** / Andre Gide ; translated from the French by Richard Howard. Knopf, 1970, c1958. 171 p.

ISBN 0394605004

1. Gay men -- Relations with women 2. Gay men -- Sexuality 3. Married men 4. Gay men's wives 5. Unhappiness in men 6. Self-discovery in men 7. Moving to a new city 8. Sexuality 9. Lust 10. Interpersonal conflict 11. Homosexuality 12. Pederasty 13. Translations -- French to English 14. Modern classics 15. Literary fiction

LC 70098648

Michel, a young Frenchman living in an Algerian village nearly succumbs to a fatal illness and, after recovering, rebels against his former standards of morality.

Gideon, Melanie, 1963-

Wife 22 / Melanie Gideon. Ballantine, 2012 480 p.

ISBN 9780345527950

1. Marital conflict 2. Husband and wife 3. Boredom in women 4. Self-discovery in women 5. Family relationships 6. Purpose in life 7. Women's lives and relationships

Baring her soul in an anonymous survey for a marital happiness study, Alice catalogues her stale marriage, unsatisfying job and unfavorable prospects and begins to question virtually every aspect of her life.

Gifford, Barry, 1946-

The **stars** above Veracruz / Barry Gifford. Thunder's Mouth Press, 2006. 256 p.

ISBN 1560258071

1. 1960s 2. 1980s 3. Prostitutes 4. Murder 5. Violence in men 6. Storytelling 7. Sexuality 8. Suicide 9. Men/women relations 10. Unrequited love 11. Voyages and travels 12. South America 13. New Zealand 14. Los Angeles, California 15. Noir fiction 16. Short stories 17. Crime fiction

"While the stories take place in cities from Berlin to Havana to San Francisco and involve characters as disparate as a prizefighter, a schoolboy, and a one-legged ex-Legionnaire, each concerns the naked bravery of characters stepping into maturity. Gifford's great talent is capturing defining moments with the casual grace of anecdote. Each of these 16 stunning tales makes the anecdotal monumental." San Francisco Magazine.

Gifford, Barry, 1946-

Wyoming / Barry Gifford. Seven Stories Press, 2004, c2000. 94 p.

ISBN 1583226362

1. 1950s 2. Mothers and sons 3. Runaway wives, husbands, etc 4. Nine-year-old boys 5. Boys 6. Father-separated boys 7. Sick fathers 8. Family relationships 9. Husband and wife 10. Automobile travel 11. Separation (Psychology) 12. Loss (Psychology) 13. Divorce 14. Dishonesty 15. Middle West 16. Southern States 17. Psychological

fiction

LC 2004007762

Originally published: New York : Arcade Pub., 2000.

"This is a tender and understated story. . . . That Gifford forges these characters almost entirely out of dialogue makes their affecting humanity doubly impressive; by the novel's end, Roy and his mother are likely to live as vividly in the reader's mind as their unseen Wyoming lives in theirs." New York Times Book Review.

Gilb, Dagoberto, 1950-

The **Flowers** : a novel / Dagoberto Gilb. Grove, 2008. 250 p.

ISBN 9780802118592

1. Apartment house life 2. Mexican American teenage boys 3. Mothers and sons 4. Prejudice 5. Blended families 6. Stepfathers 7. Fifteen-year-old boys 8. Teenage boys 9. Mexican Americans 10. Hispanic American teenage boys 11. Hispanic Americans 12. Interracial marriage 13. Interpersonal relations 14. City life 15. Coming-of-age stories 16. Domestic fiction

Sonny Bravo is a tender, unusually smart fifteen-year-old who is living with his vivacious mother in a large city where intense prejudice is not just white against black, but also brown. When his mother, Silvia, suddenly marries an Okie building contractor named Cloyd Longpre, they are uprooted to a small apartment building, Los Flores. As Sonny sweeps its sidewalks, he meets his neighbors and becomes ensnared in their lives.

"A tightly woven narrative about a boy coming of age in a community bubbling with racial tension. It's beautifully rendered in part because Mr. Gilb nails the voice of 15-year-old narrator Sonny Bravo with pinpoint accuracy." Dallas Morning News.

Gilbert, David, 1967-

& sons : a novel / David Gilbert. Random House, 2013. 496 p.

ISBN 9780812993967

1. Dysfunctional families 2. Authors, American 3. Fathers and sons 4. Family relationships 5. Rich people 6. Family secrets 7. Recluses 8. Senior men 9. Eccentric men 10. Book industry and trade 11. New York City 12. Upper East Side, New York City 13. Literary fiction

LC 2012031308

A novel about a famous reclusive writer and his three sons finds their bond tested by the weight of long-held secrets and a cumbersome legacy shaped by boarding school, Hollywood and the elite circles of the publishing world.

Gilbert, Elizabeth, 1969-

* **City** of girls / Elizabeth Gilbert. Riverhead Books, 2019. 432 p.

ISBN 9781594634734

1. 1940s 2. Theater companies 3. Memories 4. Female friendship 5. Reminiscing in old age 6. Scandals 7. Aunt and niece 8. Rich people 9. Sexuality 10. Social classes 11. Race relations 12. City life 13. Men/women relations 14. New York City 15. Historical fiction

Eighty-nine-year-old Vivian recounts her life after being kicked out of Vassar College, living in Manhattan with her Aunt Peg and the personal mistake that resulted in a professional scandal.

"Tart-voiced Vivian and her adventures in 20th-century Manhattan will please readers who enjoyed Kathleen Rooney's Lillian Boxfish Takes a Walk." Library Journal.

Gilbert, Elizabeth, 1969-

* The **signature** of all things : a novel / Elizabeth Gilbert. Viking, 2013. 512 p.

ISBN 9780670024858

1. 18th century 2. Painters 3. Women botanists 4. Men/women relations 5. Women -- Spiritual life 6. Interpersonal attraction 7. Enlightenment (European intellectual movement) 8. Industrial revolution 9. Philadelphia, Pennsylvania -- History -- 18th century 10. Family sagas 11. Epic fiction 12. Historical fiction

LC 2013017045

A multi-generational saga of the Whittaker family, whose progenitor makes a fortune in the quinine trade before his daughter, a gifted botanist, researches the mysteries of evolution while falling in love with an utopian artist against a backdrop of the Age of Enlightenment and the Industrial Revolution.

Gilchrist, Ellen, 1935-

* **Collected** stories / Ellen Gilchrist. Little, Brown, 2000. 563 p.

ISBN 0316299480

1. Women 2. Human nature 3. Southern States -- Social life and customs 4. Short stories

34 short stories.

Presents a collection of stories selected by the author from her fifteen previous collections of short fiction.

"Gilchrist is an important voice in contemporary Southern fiction, and this book belongs in every library." Library Journal.

Gillham, David R.

City of women / David R. Gillham. Amy Einhorn Books, 2012. 400 p.

ISBN 9780399157769

1. Second World War era (1939-1945) 2. 1940s 3. Military spouses 4. Married women 5. Nazis 6. World War II 7. Secrets -- Germany 8. Former lovers 9. Berlin, Germany -- History -- 1918-1945 10. Germany -- History -- 1918-1945 11. Historical fiction

LC 2012011002

Hiding her clandestine activities behind the persona of a model Nazi soldier's wife at the height of World War II, Sigrid Schroeder dreams of her former Jewish lover and risks everything to hide a mother and two young children who she believes might be her lover's family.

Gilman, Carolyn Ives

Dark orbit / Carolyn Ives Gilman. St. Martin's Press, 2015. 304 p.

ISBN 9780765336293

1. Women scientists 2. Aliens (Non-humanoid) 3. Aliens 4. Exiles 5. Prophets 6. Space exploration 7. Life on other planets 8. Human/alien encounters 9. Dark matter (Astronomy) 10. Space 11. Science fiction

Recruited to monitor an unstable scientist who is investigating a habitable new planet, exoethnologist Sara Callicot navigates the culture of the planet's extrasensory indigenous race while her charge battles delusions to warn their crewmates of an impending danger.

"Blending mystery, philosophy, and science gracefully in a twisty plot, Gilman (Ison of the Isles) has written a challenging but ultimately satisfying space adventure that explores how the most basic preconceptions can distort our outlook. It's a winner for any sf fan, of special appeal to those with interests in epistemology, ethics, or physics." Library Journal.

Gilman, Charlotte Perkins, 1860-1935

Herland / Charlotte Perkins Gilman ; with an introduction by Ann J. Lane. Pantheon Books, 1979, c1915. xxiv, 147 p.

ISBN 9780394736655

1. 1910s 2. Utopias 3. Sexism 4. Prejudice 5. Explorers 6. Culture conflict 7. Parthenogenesis 8. Men/women relations 9. Gender role 10. Women's role 11. Social science fiction 12. Science fiction

LC 78020418

Jacket subtitle: A lost feminist utopian novel.

Originally published: 1915.

On the eve of World War I, an all-female society is discovered somewhere in the distant reaches of the earth by three male explorers who are now forced to re-examine their assumptions about women's roles in society.--Publisher's description.

Gilman, Dorothy, 1923-2012

Kaleidoscope / Dorothy Gilman. Ballantine Books, 2002. 244 p. Madame Karitska mysteries

ISBN 0345448200

1. Clairvoyance 2. Psychometry 3. Murder 4. Counts and countesses 5. Women amateur detectives 6. Psychics 7. Women psychics 8. Police 9. Detectives 10. Violinists 11. Cults 12. Madame Karitska 13. Maine 14. Mysteries

Madame Karitska, blessed with the gift of clairvoyance, joins forces with Detective Lieutenant Pruden when she is confronted by several objects, filled with violence, greed, passion, and obsession, that hold the key to many mysteries.

"This [is a] well-written episodic adventure." Library Journal.

Gilman, Felix

The **half-made** world / Felix Gilman. Tor, 2010. 480 p. Half-made world novels

ISBN 9780765325525

1. Magic 2. Dystopias 3. Industries 4. Machinery 5. Terrorism 6. Hope 7. Psychologists 8. Supernatural 9. Reality 10. Demonic possession 11. Imaginary wars and battles 12. Weird Westerns 13. Steampunk 14. Historical fantasy

LC 2010032564

"A Tom Doherty Associates book."

A steampunk reimagining of the American West follows the efforts of a spiritually protected doctor to analyze two rival factions that are oppressing the world's people, a study that leads to her discovery of a broken general from a mythological resistance force.

"Sick of predictable books that fill your subgenre bingo card with the same subgenre elements over and over? .... Felix Gilman has blended elements from alternate history, Steampunk, Westerns, and epic fantasy to create something truly original." io9.

Gilman, Laura Anne

* The **cold** eye / Laura Anne Gilman. Saga Press, 2017. 400 p. Devil's West

ISBN 9781481429719

1. American Westward Expansion (1803-1899) 2. Frontier and pioneer life 3. Devil 4. Voyages and travels 5. Young women 6. Power (Social sciences) 7. Mentors 8. Magic 9. Supernatural 10. The West (United States) -- History -- 19th century 11. Weird Westerns 12. Historical fantasy

LC 2016029456

While serving as the Left Hand of the Devil, Isobel has her power tested as she tries to figure out the cause of a growing and mysterious danger throughout the Territory, in a sequel to Silver on the Road.

Gilman, Laura Anne

Flesh and fire / Laura Anne Gilman. Pocket Books, 2009. 384 p. Vineart war trilogy

ISBN 9781439101414

1. Wizards 2. Wine and wine making 3. Magic potions 4. Power (Social sciences) 5. Vineyards 6. Good and evil 7. Boy slaves 8. Apprentices 9. Fantasy fiction 10. Coming-of-age stories

LC 2009012786

Jerzy--a young slave who has just begun an apprenticeship to become a Vineart, a mage who can create spell-making wines--must work with his master to stop a plot to complete the work of the dreaded Sin-Washer and rid the world of the last few Vinearts.

Gilman, Laura Anne

Hard magic / Laura Anne Gilman. Luna, 2010. 352 p. Paranormal scene investigations

ISBN 9780373803132

1. Murder investigation 2. Magic 3. Spells (Magic) 4. Detectives 5. Bisexual women 6. Paranormal phenomenon investigation 7. Urban fantasy 8. Mysteries

Bonnie Torres and four other paranormal investigators are hired to prove that the deaths of two Talents were murder, not suicide, while dealing with a vast array of high-profile people who want to shut them down.

"Spinning off a minor character from the Retrievers books (Staying Dead, etc.), Gilman launches an entertaining new series set in her Cosa Nostradamus world of magic-using Talented humans. Following up on a mysterious job lead, college grad Bonita Torres joins the Private Unaffiliated Paranormal Investigations (PUPI), a freelance CSI-style unit for Talent-related crimes. The puppies refine and practice spells until they get their first big case: an apparent double suicide. As they follow the evidence, trail and interrogate suspects, and defend themselves against attacks, the investigators develop comfortable and engaging team dynamics and create the field of forensic magic. Gilman's deft plotting and first-class characters complement her agile blend of science and spell craft." Publishers Weekly.

Gilman, Laura Anne

Silver on the road / Laura Anne Gilman. Saga Press, 2015. 400 p. Devil's West

ISBN 9781481429689

1. American Westward Expansion (1803-1899) 2. Young women 3. Devil 4. Manipulation (Social sciences) 5. Deals 6. Faustian bargains 7. Voyages and travels 8. The West (United States) -- History -- 19th century 9. Weird Westerns 10. Historical fantasy

Taking a job in the untamed American West serving a being of immense power who makes deals with people and gives them exactly what they deserve, Izzy receives training in the manipulations of human desire and travels throughout the territory to spread magical chaos.

"Refreshingly, her vision of the American West includes respectful portrayals of Native Americans. Isobel's coming-of-age story is very accessible to teens, and There's plenty for adventure-minded adults to enjoy as well." Publishers Weekly.

Gilman, Susan Jane

* **Donna** has left the building / Susan Jane Gilman. Grand Central Publishing, 2019. 384 p.

ISBN 9781538762417

1. Automobile travel 2. Decision-making 3. Recovering alcoholics 4. Transformations, Personal 5. Married women 6. Mothers 7. Extramarital affairs 8. Former rock musicians 9. Punk rock music 10. Life change events 11. Friendship 12. Mainstream fiction

LC 2018048056

Leaving behind her family and her suburban home when her world implodes, forty-five-year-old Donna Koczynski sets off on a road trip to rebuild her life.

Gilman, Susan Jane

The **ice** cream queen of Orchard Street : a novel / Susan Jane Gilman. Grand Central Publishing, 2014. 512 p.

ISBN 9780446578936

1. 20th century 2. Immigrants 3. Entrepreneurs 4. People with disabilities 5. Abandoned girls 6. Street vendors 7. Identity (Psychology) 8. Fame 9. Celebrities 10. Women entrepreneurs 11. Ice cream trucks 12. Jews, Russian 13. Men/women relations 14. United States 15. Mainstream fiction

LC 2013030543

Russian immigrant Malka arrives in 1913 Manhattan, where she struggles to survive and learns trade secrets from an Italian ices peddler before setting off across America in an ice cream truck with a handsome, illiterate radical to seek their fortunes.

"With its vivid depictions of old New York City tenement life and its tale of the American ice cream business set against the backdrop of the major events of the 20th century, this rags-to-riches saga will appeal greatly to readers of American historical novels." Library Journal.

Gilmore, Jennifer

The **mothers** / Jennifer Gilmore. Scribner, 2013. 352 p.

ISBN 9781451697254

1. Adoption 2. Motherhood 3. Despair 4. Marital conflict 5. Childlessness 6. Adoptive parents 7. Infertility 8. Cancer survivors 9. Waiting 10. New York City 11. Brooklyn, New York City 12. Mainstream fiction

Applying for an open adoption after several unsuccessful years of trying to conceive, Jesse and Ramon are disheartened by the bureaucratic labyrinth of red tape, training sessions and approvals they endure as well as their being targeted by con artists, a situation that challenges their views about culture, class and changing family dynamics.

Gingrich, Newt

Gettysburg : a novel of the Civil War / Newt Gingrich and William Forstchen. St. Martin's Press, 2003. 480 p. Gettysburg trilogy

ISBN 031230935X

1. 1860s 2. Gettysburg, Battle of, 1863 3. Military strategy 4. Battles 5. Civil war 6. United States Civil War, 1861-1865 7. Pennsylvania -- History -- Civil War, 1861-1865 8. United States -- History -- Civil War, 1861-1865 9. Gettysburg, Pennsylvania 10. Alternative histories

LC 2003041381

"On July 1, 1863, the Army of Virginia, under the command of Gen. Robert E. Lee, and the Army of the Potomac, under Gen. George G. Meade, clashed in deadly combat near Gettysburg, PA. Of course, Union forces won, but Gingrich and Forstchen imagine a different outcome in which Confederate forces do a surprise march around Union lines to flank and cut off the Union troops from their supply and information routes. In the course of their narrative, the authors depict the gallantry and heroism of Lee, Longstreet, Chamberlain, Hancock, Hunt, and many other officers and enlisted men on both sides of the conflict." Library Journal.

Gingrich, Newt

Grant comes east : a novel of the Civil War / Newt Gingrich and William R. Forstchen. Thomas Dunne Books/St. Martin's Press, 2004. 400 p. Gettysburg trilogy

ISBN 0312309376

1. Grant, Ulysses S, 1822-1885 2. Lee, Robert E (Robert Edward), 1807-1870 3. 1860s 4. Generals 5. Military strategy 6. Battles 7. Command of troops 8. Civil war 9. United States Civil War, 1861-1865 10. United States -- History -- Civil War, 1861-1865 11. Alternative histories

LC 2004043894

A fictionalized account of an alternate American Civil War recounts events following the capture of Vicksburg by General Ulysses S. Grant and traces the northern army's journey to Gettysburg.

Ginzburg, Natalia, 1916-1991

A **family** lexicon / Natalia Ginzburg ; translated by Jenny McPhee ; afterword by Peg Boyers. New York Review of Books, 2017. 224 p. New York Review Books classics

ISBN 9781590178386

1. Ginzburg, Natalia, 1916-1991 2. Authors 3. Families 4. Intimacy (Psychology) 5. Family relationships 6. Friendship 7. World War II 8. Fascism -- Italy 9. Intellectual life 10. Italy 11. Autobiographical fiction 12. Domestic fiction 13. Family sagas 14. Literary fiction 15. Translations -- Italian to English

LC 2016026803

Originally published: Turin : Einaudi, 1963.

Re-creates with extraordinary objectivity the small world of a family enduring some of the most difficult years of the twentieth century, the period from the rise of Mussolini through World War II and its immediate aftermath.

Giordano, Mario, 1963-

Auntie Poldi and the Vineyards of Etna / Mario Giordano ; translated by John Brownjohn. Houghton Mifflin Harcourt, 2019, c2016. 352 p. Auntie Poldi novels

ISBN 9781328919021

1. Women amateur detectives 2. Senior women 3. Vineyards 4. Nephews 5. Murder investigation 6. Mafia 7. Sicily, Italy 8. Italy 9. Mysteries 10. Translations -- German to English

Published in the UK by Bitter Lemon Press as Auntie Poldi and the fruits of the Lord, 2018.

Originally published by Bastei, 2016.

A follow-up to Auntie Poldi and the Sicilian Lions finds Prosecco-loving Auntie Poldi defending her community when a dog is poisoned and a respected handyman goes missing amid a rise in local Mafia activities.

"Readers will look forward to the further adventures of the irrepressible Auntie Poldi." Publishers Weekly.

Giordano, Paolo, 1982-

The **human** body / Paolo Giordano ; translation from the Italian by Anne Milano Appel. Pamela Dorman Books/Viking, 2014. 336 p.

ISBN 9780670015641

1. Afghan War, 2001- 2. Soldiers -- Italy 3. War -- Psychological aspects 4. Young men 5. Military missions 6. Military life 7. Conflict (Psychology) 8. Adulthood 9. Human body 10. Italians in Afghanistan 11. War stories 12. Literary fiction 13. Psychological fiction 14. Translations -- Italian to English

LC 2014006927

A platoon in one of the world's most dangerous war zones--the Forward Operating Base in the Gulistan district of Afghanistan--endure deadly engagements and psychological trauma before a mission gone wrong changes everything.

"[A] memorable entry in the literature of the Afghan war, the characters crisply drawn and the writing full of telling details." Booklist.

Giordano, Paolo, 1982-

Like family / Paolo Giordano ; translated from the Italian by Anne Milano Appel. Pamela Dorman Books/Viking, 2015, c2014. 160 p.

ISBN 9780525428763

1. Housekeepers 2. People with terminal illnesses 3. Families 4. Widows 5. Scientists 6. People with cancer 7. Marriage 8. Interpersonal relations 9. Family relationships 10. Literary fiction 11. Translations -- Italian to English

Translation from the Italian of: Nero e l'argento.

Originally published: Torino : Einaudi, 2014.

The delicate fabric of a young family unravels when a beloved maid who has become the glue in their household falls ill and reveals poignant incidents from her past, including a tragically short marriage. By the best-selling author ofThe Solitude of Prime Numbers.

"And at his best, Giordano muses gorgeously on our inability to blend our life essences; even love leaves us lonely. A lovely remembrance played in a minor key." Kirkus.

Giordano, Paolo, 1982-

* The **solitude** of prime numbers : a novel / Paolo Giordano ; translated from the Italian by Shaun Whiteside. Pamela Dorman Books/Viking, 2010, c2008. 288 p.

ISBN 9780670021482

1. Life change events -- Psychological aspects 2. Solitude 3. Loss (Psychology) 4. Anorexia nervosa 5. Anger in women 6. Self-destructive behavior in teenagers 7. Shame 8. Coping 9. Guilt 10. Grief 11. Social acceptance 12. Self-acceptance 13. Men/women relations 14. Italy 15. Psychological fiction 16. Love stories 17. Literary fiction 18. Translations -- Italian to English

LC 2009041165

Originally published: Milano : Mondadori, 2008.

Misfits Alice and Mattia bond as teens over shared experiences of suffering before mathematically gifted Mattia accepts a research position that takes him far away, a situation that restores their isolation before they meet by chance years later.

"This is a book about communication: in lacking a facility for self-expression, our stunted protagonists exist almost solely, and safely, in their own minds. Despite its heavy subject matter, it reads easily, due in part to the almost seamless translation. A quietly explosive ending completes the novel in just the fashion it was started, as an intimate psychological portrait of two prime numbers--together alone and alone together." Booklist.

Gladstone, Max

* **Empress** of forever / Max Gladstone. Tor, 2019. 480 p.

ISBN 9780765395818

1. Women computer scientists 2. Time travel (Future) 3. Dystopias 4. Women rulers 5. Artificial intelligence 6. Monks 7. Insurgency 8. Imaginary wars and battles 9. Alliances 10. Space opera 11. Science fiction

LC 2018054087

"A Tom Doherty Associates Book."

After being thrown into a dark future ruled by the powerful Empress, radical billionaire tech genius Vivian Liao assembles a group of unlikely allies to aid in her attempt to break free of the Empress's stranglehold and save the galaxy.

Glass, Jenna

The **women's** war / Jenna Glass. Del Rey, 2019. 560 p. Women's war

ISBN 9781984817204

1. Spells (Magic) 2. Reproductive rights 3. Women rulers 4. Women exiles 5. Magic 6. Revolutions 7. Men/women relations 8. Widows 9. Patriarchy 10. Social change 11. Empowerment (Social sciences) 12. Political intrigue 13. Imaginary kingdoms 14. Epic fantasy

LC 2018015835

When a world-altering spell gives women the ability to control their own fertility, a disinherited princess and a powerless queen trigger changes in their patriarchal kingdoms before a caravan of exiles stumbles on a new source of women's magic.

"Glass's substantial debut stands out as both social commentary on contemporary issues of bodily autonomy, gender, and social power and as feminist retribution fantasy, made manifest through an appealing epic fantasy setting and grounded in a carefully designed magic system." Publishers Weekly.

Glass, Julia, 1956-

* **Three** Junes / Julia Glass. Pantheon Books, 2002. 368 p.

ISBN 0375421440

1. Family relationships 2. Loss (Psychology) 3. Fathers and sons 4. Familial love 5. Scots in the United States 6. Gay men 7. Summer 8. Death 9. Betrayal 10. Life change events 11. Scots in Long Island, New York 12. Long Island, New York 13. Scotland 14. Psychological fiction 15. Literary fiction

LC 2001055448

National Book Award for Fiction, 2002.

Reveals the interconnected lives, loves, and relationships of different generations of the McLeod family over the course of three crucial summers.

"Free of gimmickry, Three Junes brilliantly rescues, then refurbishes, the traditional plot-driven novel." New York Times Book Review.

Glass, Julia, 1956-

The **whole** world over / Julia Glass. Pantheon Books, 2006. 528 p.

ISBN 0375422749

1. Women cooks 2. Marital conflict 3. Women bakers 4. Husband and wife 5. Psychiatrists 6. Mothers and sons 7. Family secrets 8. Women with disfigurements 9. Gay men 10. Governors 11. Fate and fatalism 12. September 11 Terrorist Attacks, 2001 13. Manhattan, New York City 14. New Mexico 15. Maine 16. Psychological fiction 17. Domestic fiction 18. Literary fiction

LC 2005054043

Fenno McLeod found in this book was first mentioned in the author's debut novel, Three Junes.

Hired as the personal chef to the governor of New Mexico, Greenie Duquette leaves behind her Greenwich Village pastry business and her husband to head west with her four-year-old son, prompting a period of upheaval and reflection for herself.

"Glass is too capable to need recipes and four-legged friends to make her fiction a pleasure. It's a tribute to this unassuming but conspicuously talented novelist that even with far too many of them, The Whole World Over so often manages to sing." New York Times Book Review.

Glass, Julia, 1956-

The **widower's** tale / Julia Glass. Pantheon Books, 2010. 448 p.

ISBN 9780307377920

1. Senior men 2. Family relationships 3. Father and adult child 4. Widowers 5. Former librarians 6. Sisters 7. Preschools 8. Eco-terrorism 9. Literary fiction

Enjoying an active but lonely rural life, 70-year-old Percy haplessly allows a progressive preschool to move into his barn and transform his quiet home into a lively, youthful community that compels him to reexamine the choices he made in the decades after his wife's death.

"Percy Darling, 70, is the titular widower, a rigid man still sorely missing his long-deceased wife. He holds the center of Glass' [novel], . . . set in a bucolic town outside of Boston. Orbiting around Percy are two grown daughters: one a divorced flibbertigibbet and the other a renowned oncologist who is as stern with her family as she is open and available to her patients. Add to the mix a wayward Harvard grandson, a Guatemalan gardener, a gay preschool teacher, and a salt-of-the-earth artist who reminds Percy that he is still very much alive. It's a large, endearing cast, bursting with emotional and social issues, and Glass slips effortlessly between their individual and enmeshed dramas." Entertainment Weekly.

Gleason, Colleen

Murder at the capitol / C. M. Gleason. Kensington Books, 2020. 304 p. Lincoln's White House mysteries

ISBN 9781496723987

1. Lincoln, Abraham, 1809-1865 2. White House, Washington, D.C. 3. American Civil War era (1861-1865) 4. 1860s 5. Presidents -- United States 6. Espionage 7. Private investigators 8. Murder 9. Murder investigation 10. War and society 11. Military strategy 12. Washington, D.C. 13. United States -- Politics and government -- 19th century 14. Historical mysteries

In July 1861, just months after the Battle of Fort Sumter plunges the young nation into civil war, President Lincoln's top priority is to unite the country, while Adam Quinn finds himself on the trail of a murderer . . .

"Gleason follows Murder in the Oval Library with a riveting historical mystery set on the eve of the first major battle of the Civil War. Fans of descriptive historical mysteries will appreciate the mix of real people and intriguing fictional characters." Library Journal.

Gloss, Molly

The **hearts** of horses / Molly Gloss. Houghton Mifflin Co., 2007. 304 p.

ISBN 9780618799909

1. 1910s 2. Young women 3. Horse trainers 4. Farmers 5. Horses 6. Farms 7. Farm life -- Oregon 8. Tomboys 9. Oregon 10. Historical fiction 11. Pacific Northwest fiction 12. Gentle reads

LC 2007008521

Martha Lessen, a female horse whisperer, is trying to make a go of it in a man's world. It was thought that the only way to break a horse was to buck the wild out of it, and broken ribs and tough falls just went with the job. But over several long, hard winter months, many of the townsfolk in this remote county of eastern Oregon witness Martha's way of talking in low, sweet tones to horses believed beyond repair---and getting miraculous, almost immediate results---and she thereby earns a place of respect in the community.

"Gloss bases her novel on historical accounts of cowgirls in the American West. With obvious appeal for horse lovers, it has a homespun quality, and varies in action between a gentle canter and energetic gallop." Library Journal.

Glynn, Alan, 1960-

Paradime / Alan Glynn. Faber & Faber, 2016. 304 p.

ISBN 9780571316229

1. Debt 2. Unemployment 3. Doppelgangers 4. Secret identity 5. Rich men 6. Capitalists and financiers 7. Obsession in men 8. Conspiracies 9. Stealing 10. New York City 11. Thrillers and suspense

"Until Danny and Teddy have their one face-to-face encounter, the story maintains a deliciously creepy atmosphere, with dark humor as Danny manages to sneak into Teddy's life. The plot keeps moving with plenty of effective surprises, and the final chapters successfully navigate to an even darker tone. So the not-quite-resolved ending seems perfectly appropriate, even if you have to read it over to make sense of it." Kirkus.

Glynn, Alan, 1960-

Receptor / Alan Glynn. St Martins Pr, 2019 288 p. Limitless novels

ISBN 9781250061805

1. 1950s 2. 2010s 3. Mind control 4. Power (Social sciences) 5. Experimental drugs 6. Addiction 7. Elitism 8. Pharmaceutical research -- Corrupt practices 9. Techno-thrillers

LC 2018036692

Originally published as "Under the Night" by Faber & Faber, 2018.

From the author of Limitless comes Receptor, an irresistible thriller that reveals the origins of MDT-48 and the consequences of unlocking the human mind.

Goddard, Robert

Beyond recall : a novel / Robert Goddard. Henry Holt, 1998, c1997. 310 p.

ISBN 9780805051100

1. Cold cases (Criminal investigation) 2. Innocence (Law) 3. Secrets 4. Men 5. Greed in men 6. Revenge 7. Inheritance and succession 8. Deception 9. Suicidal behavior 10. Cornwall, England 11. England 12. Thrillers and suspense

LC 97-28895

Originally published: London: Bantam, 1997.

The suicide of the black sheep of the family at a wedding party in Cornwall, England, drives Chris Napier into his clan's dark past, where he discloses more than one skeleton, including child abuse and old-fashioned revenge.

"There's an elegant arc to Goddard's fluid style, which gracefully orchestrates the story over its broad time span and through the ambiguous testimony of its complex characters." New York Times Book Review.

Goddard, Robert

* Into the blue / Robert Goddard. Poseidon Press, 1990. 415 p. Harry Barnett series

ISBN 0671704826

1. Frameups 2. British in Greece 3. Missing persons investigation 4. Betrayal 5. Extortion 6. Deception 7. Detectives 8. Redemption 9. Failure (Psychology) 10. Greece 11. England 12. Psychological suspense 13. Thrillers and suspense

LC 90042481

A disgraced caretaker on the island of Rhodes is suspected in the murder of a woman, and his quest to clear his name leads him to his native England, where he investigates the victim's past and regains his self-esteem.

"During this quest, Harry's courage is tested as well as his judgment of people--all of whom turn out to be totally and depressingly human. An everyman's hero, against all mental and emotional odds, Harry finds Heather and renewed self-respect. A very satisfying novel in every way." Booklist.

Goddard, Robert

* Long time coming : a novel / Robert Goddard. Bantam Books Trade Paperbacks, 2010. 432 p.

ISBN 9780385343619

1. Former convicts 2. Art forgeries 3. World War II 4. Diamond industry and trade 5. War crimes -- History -- World War II 6. Uncle and niece 7. Secrets 8. England 9. Mysteries

LC 2009044547

Edgar Allan Poe Award for Best Paperback Original, 2011.

Astonished to learn that the uncle he believed was killed in the Blitz has been in prison for nearly four decades, Stephen Swan finds himself in the middle of a conspiracy involving forged Picassos and the disinherited family an Antwerp diamond dealer.

Goddard, Robert

Never go back / Robert Goddard. Bantam Dell, 2007. 336 p. Harry Barnett series

ISBN 9780385340632

1. Great Britain. Royal Air Force Veterans 2. Suspicion 3. Senior men 4. Human experimentation in medicine 5. Murder 6. Secrets 7. Conspiracies 8. Murder suspects 9. Castles -- Scotland 10. Reunions -- Scotland 11. Murder investigation 12. Scotland 13. Psychological suspense 14. Thrillers and suspense

LC 2007006336

"Goddard's latest offering marks the return of unlikely hero Harry Barnett, star of Into the Blue (1990) and Out of the Sun (1997). It's a crackling good read, with clipped prose, complex characters, and a smart, sinuous plot." Booklist.

Godden, Rumer, 1907-1998

Battle of the Villa Fiorita Viking, 1963. 312 p.

1. Italy 2. Literary fiction

First published: Great Britain: Macmillan & Co. Ltd, 1963.

"Godden's characters live and linger in the mind, and the very feel of golden Italy counterpoints the sharp battle in which both sides so tragically lose." Library Journal.

Godden, Rumer, 1907-1998

The **greengage** summer : a novel Viking, 1958. 218p.

ISBN 9781447211013

1. British in France 2. France 3. Literary fiction 4. Classics

LC 58007066

Originally published: London: Macmillan, 1958.

"Some will quarrel with the betrayals at the end; all readers will appreciate the deft handling of budding adolescence; nobody can read the story and remain emotionally untouched. And yet, for this reader- a long time admirer of Rumer Godden in her many phases- this stems back to the mood and tension of Breakfast with the Nikolides (1942) rather than the gentler quality of her most popular book , An Episode of Sparrows." Kirkus.

Godden, Rumer, 1907-1998

Pippa passes : a novel / Rumer Godden. W. Morrow, 1994. 171 p.

ISBN 0688133975

1. Seventeen-year-old girls 2. Teenage ballet dancers 3. British in Italy 4. Literary fiction

LC 94018336

A young English ballet dancer, Pippa Fane, journeys to Venice with a touring company and discovers love, evil, and the vast complexities of the adult world

"In less able hands, these highly romantic goings-on would seem contrived, but Godden's graceful storytelling keeps readers enthralled, with gorgeous Venice and the nitty-gritty of the dance troupe's routine providing a convincing backdrop for her winsome ingenue." Publishers Weekly.

Godwin, Gail

Flora : a novel / Gail Godwin. Bloomsbury, 2013. 288 p.
ISBN 9781620401200
1. 1940s 2. Loss (Psychology) 3. Family secrets 4. Girls 5. Guardian and ward 6. World War II 7. Aunt and niece 8. Grandmother and granddaughter 9. Grief in girls 10. Women authors 11. Haunted houses 12. Poliomyelitis 13. North Carolina 14. Historical fiction 15. Coming-of-age stories 16. Literary fiction 17. Southern fiction
LC 2012036741
Isolated in a decaying family home while her father performs secret work at the end of World War II, 10-year-old Helen, grieving the losses of her mother and grandmother, bonds with her sensitive young aunt while desperately clinging to the ghosts and stories of her childhood.

Godwin, Gail

* Grief cottage : a novel / Gail Godwin. Bloomsbury USA, 2017. 324 p.
ISBN 9781632867056
1. Cottages 2. Recluses 3. Eleven-year-old boys 4. Ghosts 5. Island life 6. Hurricanes 7. Local history 8. Aunt and nephew 9. Loss (Psychology) 10. South Carolina 11. Southern Gothic 12. Literary fiction 13. Coming-of-age stories
LC 2016036527
Moving in with his reclusive artist aunt after his mother's death, 11-year-old Marcus learns the story of a local cottage from which a family disappeared during a hurricane half a century earlier, a tragedy that compels him to explore the cottage, where he meets a ghost with a mysterious agenda.

"The book moves between the fantastical and the everyday with ease; Marcus is just as likely to shop for his elderly neighbors as to whisper encouragement to loggerhead hatchlings or offer friendship to the restless spirits of the island. But nothing and no one on the island can break free of the forces that build and destroy, that give life and bring death. As time pushes him forward, Marcus must decide how to grieve: to raze his identity completely or memorialize his tragedies. His choice and its consequences will echo with readers, and Godwins forceful prose captivates with the quiet, renewing power of a persistent tide." Publishers Weekly.

Godwin, Gail

* Unfinished desires / Gail Godwin. Random House, 2009. 416 p.
ISBN 9780345483201
1. Competition in girls 2. Nuns 3. Scandals 4. Girls' schools 5. Friendship 6. Loyalty 7. Betrayal 8. Redemption 9. Small town life -- North Carolina 10. North Carolina 11. Literary fiction 12. Southern fiction
Working title was originally: The Red Nun: A Tale of Unfinished Desires.
Sparking enthusiasm for a play about the founding of their North Carolina mountains Catholic girls' school, a charismatic ninth grader and her recently orphaned best friend set in motion a series of events that have decades-long ramifications.

"Told from multiple points of view, Unfinished Desires puts the author's twin talents--storytelling and characterization--on dazzling display. Godwin brings each of the girls and women fully alive and tells her well-conceived and well-executed story in a leisurely but suspenseful fashion." Richmond Times-Dispatch.

Goenawan, Clarissa, 1988-

The **perfect** world of Miwako Sumida / Clarissa Goenawan. Soho Press, 2020. 278 p.
ISBN 9781641291194
1. College students 2. Suicide victims 3. Friends' death 4. Villages 5. Friendship 6. Clues 7. Secrets 8. Shame 9. Families 10. Japan 11. Psychological fiction
LC 2019036361
A Japanese university student investigates the mysterious suicide of a classmate in a remote mountainside village, discovering secrets that may lead to his own unraveling.

"Goenawan's luminous prose captures the deep emotions of her characters as they grapple with questions about family history, gender, and sexuality. The tug of Miwako's strange, troubled spirit will wrench readers from the beginning." Publishers Weekly.

Goenawan, Clarissa, 1988-

Rainbirds / Clarissa Goenawan. Soho Press, 2018. 336 p.
ISBN 9781616958558
1. Brothers and sisters 2. Sisters -- Death 3. Murder 4. Murder investigation 5. Teachers 6. Rich men 7. Politicians 8. Japan 9. Literary fiction 10. Psychological fiction
LC 2017055165
After his sister, Keiko, is mysteriously murdered in a desolate, small town far from Tokyo, Ren finds himself stepping into her shoes, accepting her teaching position and a job reading to the catatonic wife of a wealthy politician while investigating what really happened.

Gogol, Nikolai Vasilievich, 1809-1852

The **collected** tales of Nikolai Gogol / Nikolai Vasilevich Gogol ; translated and annotated by Richard Pevear and Larissa Volokhonsky. Pantheon Books, 1998. xxii, 435 p.
ISBN 9780679430230
1. Russia 2. St Petersburg, Russia 3. Short stories 4. Anthologies 5. Translations -- Russian to English 6. Classics
LC 97037228
A new translation offers thirteen satirical and fantastic stories of downtrodden characters who are set upon by the powers that be.

Gogol, Nikolai Vasilievich, 1809-1852

Dead souls / Nikolai Gogol ; translated from the Russian, and with a foreword, by Bernard Guilbert Guerney. Modern Library, 1997, c1842. 674 p.
ISBN 0679602658
1. Romanov Dynasty (1613-1917) 2. Swindlers and swindling 3. Social classes 4. Serfdom 5. Gossiping and gossips 6. Political corruption 7. Landowners 8. Deception 9. Greed 10. Russia -- History -- 19th century 11. Translations -- Russian to English 12. Classics
LC 9629784
Originally published: 1842.

Gohlke, Cathy

Promise me this / Cathy Gohlke. Tyndale House Publishers, 2012. 416 p.
ISBN 9781414353074
1. Titanic (Steamship) 2. First World War era (1914-1918) 3. Promises 4. Long-distance romance 5. Interpersonal attraction 6. Last words 7. Brothers and sisters 8. Men/women relations 9. Loss (Psychology) 10. World War I 11. Christian historical romances
LC 2011034977

Michael, a Titanic survivor living in New Jersey, develops a friendly correspondence with Annie, an Englishwoman whose brother died in the disaster, that evolves into love, but their budding relationship is threatened by the onset of World War I.

Goldberg, Lee, 1962-

* **Fake** truth / Lee Goldberg. Thomas & Mercer, 2020. 298 p. Ian Ludlow novels

ISBN 9781542014694

1. Authors 2. Dissenters 3. Actors and actresses 4. Women CIA agents 5. Fake news 6. Xenophobia 7. International intrigue 8. United States -- Relations -- Russia 9. Spy fiction 10. Thrillers and suspense

When author Ian Ludlow helps a Chinese movie star defect to the United States, he accidentally winds up becoming the hero in a real-life espionage thriller in the latest addition to the series following Killer Thriller.

"Who says preventing global destruction can t be funny? Goldberg continues to inject a welcome dose of levity into the thriller genre." Publishers Weekly.

Goldberg, Myla

Feast your eyes / Myla Goldberg. Scribner, 2019. 326 p.

ISBN 9781501197840

1. 20th century 2. Women photographers 3. Mothers and daughters 4. Creativity in women 5. Obscenity (Law) 6. Photographs 7. Memories 8. Women artists 9. Ambition in women 10. Single mothers 11. Motherhood 12. Literary fiction

Andrew Carnegie Medal for Excellence in Fiction finalist, 2020.

National Book Critics Circle Award for Fiction finalist, 2019

The life of a controversial mid-20th-century photographer is chronicled through her daughter's memories, interviews with her intimates and excerpts from journals and letters documenting her quest for artistic legitimacy in the face of public notoriety.

"This is a novel of infinite depth, of caring authenticity both intimate and societal, of mothers and daughters, art and pain, and transcendent love." Booklist.

Goldberg, Tod

* **Gangsterland** : a novel / Tod Goldberg. Counterpoint, 2014. 464 p.

ISBN 9781619023444

1. Gangsters 2. Assassins 3. Deception 4. Crime 5. Rabbis 6. Judaism 7. Plastic surgery 8. Murder 9. Drug use 10. FBI agents 11. Crime bosses 12. Organized crime 13. Chicago, Illinois 14. Las Vegas, Nevada 15. Crime fiction

LC 2014014920

After his botched assassination attempt leaves three FBI agents dead, hit man Sal Cupertine agrees to the Chicago Mafia's insane plan to save his skin--several reconstructive surgeries and a new identity as "Rabbi David Cohen" of Las Vegas--but just as he is settling into his new life, he learns of the mafia's intentions to use the synagogue cemetery in a crime scheme.

"Clever plotting, a colorful cast of characters and priceless situations make this comedic crime novel an instant classic." Kirkus.

Goldbloom, Goldie, 1964-

On division / Goldie Goldbloom. Farrar, Straus and Giroux, 2019. 240 p.

ISBN 9780374175313

1. Jewish families 2. Pregnant women 3. Middle-aged women -- Sexuality 4. Extended families 5. Hasidism 6. Communities 7. Shame 8. Secrets 9. Self-discovery in women 10. Faith (Judaism)

11. Family relationships 12. Brooklyn, New York City 13. New York City 14. Literary fiction 15. Religious fiction

LC 2018060811

Anticipating the birth of her first great-grandchild, a 57-year-old Chasidic woman in Williamsburg, Brooklyn feels exposed and ashamed by a late-in-life pregnancy that slowly separates her from her community.

Golden, Arthur, 1957-

* **Memoirs** of a geisha : a novel / Arthur Golden. A. A. Knopf, 1997. 434 p.

ISBN 0375400117

1. 1930s 2. 1940s 3. Geishas 4. Artisans 5. Competition in women 6. Women entertainers 7. Sisters -- Kyoto, Japan 8. Prostitution -- Kyoto, Japan 9. Female friendship 10. Jealousy in women 11. First loves 12. Men/women relations 13. Kyoto, Japan -- History -- 20th century 14. Kyoto, Japan -- Social life and customs 15. Historical fiction

LC 9774747

Originally published: London : Chatto & Windus, 1997.

Also published: Toronto : Vintage Canada, 1999.

The "memoirs" of one of Japan's most celebrated geishas describes how, in 1929, as a little girl, she is sold into slavery; her efforts to learn the arts of the geisha; the impact of World War II; and her struggle to reinvent herself to win the man she loves.

"Rarely has a world so closed and foreign been evoked with such natural assurance, from the aesthetics of the Kyoto geisha's art--to the fetishized sexuality of Gion in the thirties and forties, at once delicate and crude, repressed and flagrant." The New Yorker.

Golden, Christopher

Ararat / Christopher Golden. St. Martin's Press, 2017. 305 p. Ben Walker novels

ISBN 9781250117052

1. Survival (after disaster) 2. Archaeological expeditions 3. Archaeologists 4. Mountains 5. Caves 6. Tombs 7. Noah's ark 8. Blizzards 9. Explorers 10. Wilderness survival 11. Good and evil 12. Mount Ararat 13. Turkey 14. Horror

Bram Stoker Award for Best Novel, 2017.

RUSA Reading List Short List, 2018.

After an avalanche uncovers an ancient boat (maybe Noah's Ark) on Turkey's Mt. Ararat, an archaeological team finds human-like remains inside a coffin -- and the skeleton has horns! Then the explorers are trapped by a blizzard, and terrifying things happen. Is the evil coming from a supernatural power? -- Description by Katherine Bradley Johnson

Golden, Christopher

The **pandora** room : a novel / Christopher Golden. St. Martin's Press, 2019. 320 p. Ben Walker novels

ISBN 9781250192103

1. International intrigue 2. Extinct cities 3. Archaeologists 4. Plague 5. Militants 6. Supernatural 7. Characters and characteristics in mythology 8. Horror

LC 2018041160

When what appears to be the original Pandora's box of mythological fame is discovered in an ancient city, neighboring countries fight for ownership before chaos-minded jihadi forces unleash a terrible plague.

"Golden provides a detailed setting and excellent character development. Where this novel shines is in the horror. The tension and fear are eerily realistic, while the supernatural monsters are unique and utterly terrifying." Booklist.

Goldin, Megan

The **escape** room / Megan Goldin. St. Martin's Press, 2019, c2018. 368 p.

ISBN 9781250219657

1. Resentfulness 2. Murderers 3. Secrets 4. Feuds 5. Office politics 6. Survival 7. Deception 8. Investment bankers 9. Elevators 10. Finance 11. Claustrophobia 12. Escapes 13. Wall Street, New York City 14. Thrillers and suspense

Originally published: North Sydney, Australia : Penguin Random House Australia, 2018.

Ordered to participate in a corporate team-building exercise that requires them to escape from a locked elevator, four ruthless Wall Street high-flyers struggle to put aside rivalries shaped by workplace intimidation, deception, and sexual harassment.

Golding, Melanie

Little darlings / Melanie Golding. Crooked Lane Books, 2019. 304 p.

ISBN 9781683319979

1. New mothers 2. Changelings 3. Motherhood 4. Imaginary creatures 5. Twins 6. Change (Psychology) 7. Infant kidnapping victims 8. Women detectives 9. Criminal investigation 10. England 11. Psychological suspense

Discounted by everyone when after the traumatizing birth of her twins she is threatened by a mysterious being, an exhausted mother risks the unthinkable when she becomes convinced that her infants have been replaced by changelings.

Golding, William, 1911-1993

Close quarters / William Golding. Farrar, Straus, Giroux, 1987. 281 p. Sea trilogy

ISBN 0374125104

1. 1810s 2. Ocean travel 3. Shipwrecks 4. Young men 5. Nobility 6. Classism 7. Sailors 8. Misadventures 9. Incompetence 10. Voyages and travels 11. Men/women relations 12. Self-discovery in men 13. Napoleonic Wars, 1800-1815 14. Atlantic Ocean 15. Indian Ocean 16. Historical fiction 17. Sea stories 18. Literary fiction

LC 87005351

In the sequel to Rites of Passage, an old ship transporting cargo and passengers from England to Australia in the 19th century disintegrates after a sailor's error.

"This second volume of the trilogy begun with Rites of passage is a tale of the tragic misadventures befalling an 18th century fighting ship now converted to transporting cargo and passengers on the treacherous voyage from England to Australia. The novel is cast as a journal written by Edmund FitzHenry Talbot, a well-meaning, somewhat uncertain, slightly pompous officer and gentleman enroute to Sydney and a career in His Majesty's service. As a result of a green sailor's blunder, the ship's masts shatter, and it founders. Golding's principal achievement is the vivid, detailed depiction of a disintegrating vessel in the tropical seas, its progressive decay, and the wretchedness and despair of its passengers." Publishers Weekly.

Golding, William, 1911-1993

* **Darkness** visible / William Golding. Farrar Straus Giroux, 2007, c1979. 259 p.

ISBN 0374530513

1. People with disfigurements 2. Mental illness 3. Religious fanaticism 4. Loneliness 5. Burn victims 6. Burns and scalds 7. Human nature 8. Kidnapping 9. Medicine 10. Great Britain 11. Literary fiction 12. Psychological fiction

Originally published: London : Faber and Faber, 1979.

James Tait Black Memorial Prize for Fiction, 1979.

Wartime firestorms in London mutilate a child, Matty, whose physical appearance keeps others from forming relationships with him.

"A child hideously maimed in the bombing of London during World War II grows up to inspire the messianic fantasies of the people with whom he comes in contact. In Golding's dark world the horrors of the physically deformed are mirrored in--but are no match for--the spiritual monsters who inhabit the novel's strange vision of contemporary life. A powerful contemplation of the evil at the root of human behavior." Booklist.

Golding, William, 1911-1993

Fire down below / William Golding. Farrar, Straus, Giroux, 1989. 5], 313 p. Sea trilogy

ISBN 0374253811

1. 1810s 2. Ocean travel 3. Sailors 4. Young men 5. Nobility 6. Classism 7. Immigrants 8. Incompetence 9. Voyages and travels 10. Storms 11. Self-discovery in men 12. Australia -- History -- 19th century 13. Indian Ocean 14. Historical fiction 15. Sea stories

LC 88018079

Edmund Talbot learns about survival in a terrible storm off the Cape of Good Hope, in the sequel to Close Quarters.

"Golding is translucent and economical. In his writing, allegorical motifs are revealed fleetingly in the everyday and in the ordinary. He is at once a complex and highly readable novelist." The Economist.

Golding, William, 1911-1993

The **inheritors** / William Golding. Harcourt, Brace & World, 1962, c1955. 233 p.

ISBN 0156443791

1. Prehistoric humans 2. Cave dwellers 3. Stone age 4. Prehistoric women 5. Survival 6. Human evolution 7. Kinship-based society 8. Culture conflict 9. Cannibalism 10. Hunters 11. Hunting 12. Good and evil 13. Jealousy 14. Envy 15. Goddess worship 16. Historical fiction 17. Literary fiction

LC 62016724

Reprint. Originally published in London : Faber and Faber, 1955.

A happy group of mild-mannered Neanderthals cannot survive when the more technologically advanced beings, homo sapiens, arrive at their campsite.

Golding, William, 1911-1993

* **Lord** of the flies : a novel / William Golding. Coward-McCann, 1955, c1954 243 p.

ISBN 0884116956

1. Survival (after airplane accidents, shipwrecks, etc) 2. Human nature 3. Child castaways 4. Teenage boys 5. Boys 6. Civilization, Western 7. Good and evil 8. Islands 9. Wilderness survival 10. Regression (Psychology) 11. Psychological fiction 12. Literary fiction 13. Modern classics

LC 55010081

First published: 1954.

"William Golding centenary"--Cover.

Originally published: 1954.

Reprint. Originally published in London : Faber and Faber, 1954.

The classic study of human nature which depicts the degeneration of a group of schoolboys marooned on a desert island.

Golding, William, 1911-1993

Rites of passage / William Golding. Farrar, Straus, Giroux, 1980. 278 p. Sea trilogy

ISBN 0374250863

1. 1810s 2. Ocean travel 3. Clergy 4. Immigrants 5. Nobility 6. Young men 7. Sailors 8. Classism 9. Voyages and travels 10. Faith 11. Death

12. Homosexuality 13. Personal conduct 14. Self-discovery in men 15. Napoleonic Wars, 1800-1815 16. Atlantic Ocean 17. England -- History -- 19th century 18. Historical fiction 19. Sea stories 20. Literary fiction

LC 80016809

Booker Prize, 1980.

Edmund Talbot recounts his voyage from England to the Antipodes, and the humiliating confrontation between the stern Captain Anderson and the nervous parson, James Colley, which leads to the latter's death.

"In a sense the novel seems highly artificial, not only in its careful, detailed recreation of the period, but also in the elaborate system of correspondences and parallels--some clear, some obscure--which underpins the narration. Yet at the same time it is an extremely lively, enjoyable piece of work. Readers who know only the early Golding will be surprised by its humor." Times Literary Supplement.

Goldman, Matt, 1962-

The **shallows** / Matt Goldman. Forge, 2019. 320 p. Nils Shapiro novels

ISBN 9781250191311

1. Private investigators 2. Divorced men 3. Murder suspects 4. Law firms 5. Suspicion 6. Murder victims 7. Murder investigation 8. Minnesota 9. Hardboiled fiction 10. Mysteries

Sequel to: Broken ice.

Investigating the brutal murder of a Minnesota lawyer, private investigator Nils Shapiro and his partners are unexpectedly overwhelmed by an influx of complicated cases, additional murders and an unknown adversary that would keep the truth hidden.

"Fans of classic hard-boiled crime novels of the 1930s and 1940s will appreciate Nils's intelligence and likable coworkers, who star in a novel that is timely, not old-fashioned, and featuring a riveting story." Library Journal.

Goldman, William, 1931-2018

* The **princess** bride : S. Morgenstern's classic tale of true love and high adventure : abridged by [i.e. written by] William Goldman. Harcourt Brace Jovanovich, 1973. 308 p.

ISBN 0151730857

1. Princesses 2. Swordfighters 3. Kidnapping 4. Imaginary kingdoms 5. Agricultural laborers 6. Rescues 7. Princes 8. Giants 9. Fantasy fiction 10. Humorous stories 11. Metafiction 12. Classics

LC 73006812

Originally published: New York : Harcourt Brace Jovanovich, c1973.

A classic swashbuckling romance retells the tale of a drunken swordsman and a gentle giant who come to the aid of Westley, a handsome farm boy, and Buttercup, a princess in dire need of rescue from the evil schemers surrounding her.

Goldstein, Rebecca, 1950-

36 arguments for the existence of God : a work of fiction / Rebecca Newberger Goldstein. Pantheon Books, 2010. 416 p.

ISBN 9780307378187

1. Faith and reason 2. Psychology teachers 3. Men -- Religious life 4. Men/women relations 5. Love triangles 6. Belief and doubt 7. Religion and culture 8. Religion 9. Philosophy 10. Academics 11. Humorous stories 12. Literary fiction

LC 2009017022

Elevated to celebrity by his best-selling book, psychology professor Cass Seltzer finds his relationship with a fellow theorist challenged by a former girlfriend's invitation to join her biochemistry experiment in immortality, an effort that is further complicated by his ongoing quest to understand religion.

"This is without a doubt the funniest work of existential philosophy you'll read.... Thoughtful, witty, and -- really entertaining, 36 Arguments is part campus comedy, part romantic farce, part philosophical treatise." Christian Science Monitor.

Goldstone, Lawrence, 1947-

Assassin of shadows / Lawrence Goldstone. Pegasus Books, 2019. 352 p.

ISBN 9781643131306

1. McKinley, William, 1843-1901 Assassination 2. Czolgosz, Leon F, 1873?-1901 3. United States. Secret Service 4. 1900s (Decade) 5. Assassins 6. Presidents -- United States -- Assassination 7. Anarchists 8. Assassination -- United States 9. Conspiracy theories 10. Secret service 11. Assassination investigation 12. Historical thrillers

The latest historical thriller by New York Times Notable mystery author Lawrence Goldstone plunges readers into the dramatic events surrounding the assassination of President William McKinley.

Gonzales, Laurence, 1947-

Lucy : a novel / Laurence Gonzales. Alfred A Knopf, 2010. 320 p.

ISBN 9780307272607

1. Genetic engineering 2. Human experimentation in medicine 3. Biotechnology 4. Primatologists 5. Secrets 6. Chicago, Illinois 7. Congo (Brazzaville) 8. Techno-thrillers

LC 2010003898

"This is a Borzoi book."

The result of experimental breeding between a human and ape, 14-year-old Lucy is rescued from the Congo jungle where she has lived exclusively among apes and experiences stunning revelations about herself when she is relocated to a Chicago suburb.

"Splicing DNA has been a science-fiction plot device as far back as the 19th century, when H.G. Wells was mixing the test tubes. But the results were always horrific crimes against nature. Here, the mutant hybrid couldn't be lovelier or more charming it's the people who behave like monsters.... [The author has] Crichton's gift for page-turning storytelling, but also a vivid, literary-grade prose style, and a knack for getting inside his characters' heads." Entertainment Weekly.

Goodis, David, 1917-1967

Nightfall / David Goodis. Vintage Books, 1991, c1947. 139 p.

ISBN 0679734740

1. Fugitives 2. Gangsters 3. Police 4. Chases 5. Lost articles 6. Men/women relations 7. Helplessness (Psychology) 8. Identity (Psychology) 9. Despair in men 10. Crime fiction

LC 90050592

"Nightfall's real story is about Vanning's despair about how to behave rationally when he knows he's being watched and the detective's self-questioning about whether a man can ever act with integrity without falling under suspicion. It's a relatively big theme for a noir, but Goodis keeps the story earthbound, rooting it in cynical observations designed to keep the mood of paranoia going." Washington City Paper.

Goodman, Allegra

The **cookbook** collector : a novel / Allegra Goodman. Dial Press, 2010. 352 p.

ISBN 9780385340854

1. Self-fulfillment in women 2. Rare books 3. Trust 4. Greed 5. Men/women relations 6. Women executives 7. Sisters 8. Women booksellers 9. California 10. Cambridge, Massachusetts 11. Mainstream fiction

LC 2009047594

While executive Emily questions her choices about her career and a long-distance relationship with a successful man, her environmental activist sister, Jessamine, struggles with her own doubts about her beliefs and love affair.

"As the story opens in 1999, twentysomething sisters Emily and Jessamine Bach are a study in contrasts: One's a driven tech executive in Silicon Valley; the other, an impoverished Berkeley grad student/bookstore employee with a penchant for sprout sandwiches and seductive tree huggers. A revolving constellation of characters-- Emily's goldenboy fiance and instant-millionaire colleagues, Jess' brusque, ponytailed boss, George-- are made fully flesh and blood by Goodman; sometimes more so, even, than her protagonists. She especially excels at capturing the precipitous rush of the then-nascent tech boom, with its breakneck innovations and backroom intrigues, while simultaneously recounting Jess' increasing absorption into the ornate and distinctly analog world of high-end bibliophilia. Even as Cookbook strikes a rare bum note with a late, left-field revelation, Goodman delivers a novel of impressive elan and real emotional resonance." Entertainment Weekly.

Goodman, Carol

The **night** villa : a novel / Carol Goodman. Ballantine Books, 2008. 432 p.

ISBN 9780345479600

1. Pythagoras 2. College teachers 3. Excavations (Archaeology) 4. Cults 5. Women classicists 6. Herculaneum (Extinct city) 7. Italy 8. Mysteries 9. Psychological suspense

LC 2008008519

Narrowly escaping with her life after a gunman storms the University of Texas campus, classics professor Sophie Chase joins an expedition to recover ancient papyrus manuscripts buried in the eruption of Mt. Vesuvius and uncovers the gripping story of an ancient Roman slave girl, while a secret and powerful cabal will stop at nothing to gain control of the scrolls.

"The pleasure of a Carol Goodman novel is in her enviable command of the classical canon--and the deft way she [writes] a book that's light enough for a weekend on the beach but literary enough for a weekend in the Hamptons." Chicago Tribune.

Goodman, Carol

The **sea** of lost girls / Carol Goodman. William Morrow, 2020. 336 p.

ISBN 9780062979636

1. Women teachers 2. Married people 3. Sons 4. Boarding schools 5. Murder 6. Teenage girl murder victims 7. Murder suspects 8. Murder investigation 9. Secrets 10. Police 11. Beaches 12. Coastal towns 13. United States 14. Maine 15. Psychological suspense

A teacher with a secret past endures attacks on her family when her son is implicated in the death of his girlfriend just before she discovers her husband's involvement.

"Readers will have a hard time putting this one down thanks to Goodman͏rs storytelling powers." Publishers Weekly.

Goodman, Jo, 1953-

In want of a wife / Jo Goodman. Berkley, 2014. 384 p.

ISBN 9780425264171

1. 1890s 2. Frontier and pioneer life 3. Mail-order brides 4. Ranches 5. Determination in women 6. Interpersonal attraction 7. Men/women relations 8. Husband and wife 9. Misunderstanding 10. Secrets 11. Wyoming 12. Western romances 13. Historical romances

Responding to an ad for a mail-order bride needed in Bitter Springs, Wyoming, Jane Middlebourne arrives on the Morning Star ranch where she must prove to her new husband that she is the perfect woman to stand by his side.

Goodman, Jo

A **touch** of forever / Jo Goodman. Jove, 2019. 402 p. Cowboys of Colorado

ISBN 9780440000648

1. Independence in women 2. Young widows 3. Railroad workers 4. Frontier and pioneer life 5. Railroad engineers 6. Secrets 7. Interpersonal attraction 8. Men/women relations 9. Colorado 10. The West (United States) 11. Western romances 12. Historical romances

Lily Salt has sworn off men. After finally gaining her independence, the last thing she needs is another man telling her what to do. But the handsome railroad engineer from New York isn't at all what she expected. He's kind, gentle...and tempting enough to make her wonder what a second chance at love might be worth.

"Crisp descriptions, insightful character development, and four savvy kids bring depth to this romantic historical charmer that is pure gold. " Library Journal.

Goodwin, Bobi Gentry

Revelation / Bobi Gentry Goodwin. She Writes Press, 2019. 256 p.

ISBN 9781631526060

1. Family secrets 2. Addiction 3. Social workers 4. Family problems 5. Faith (Christianity) 6. African American families 7. Family relationships 8. San Francisco, California 9. African American fiction 10. Mainstream fiction

When Angela walked into her social work office for the first time, she vowed her work with traumatized families would be meaningful. But when one family intrudes into her personal life, all bets are off. Discovering her father's picture alongside an overdosed client is just the beginning as her life and family unravels as she searches to uncover the truth.

"Wonderfully realistic dialogue and relatably fallible characters mark Goodwin's debut for readers who appreciate Vanessa Davis Griggs and Kimberla Lawson Roby." Booklist.

Goodwin, Daisy

The **American** heiress / Daisy Goodwin. St. Martin's Press, 2011, c2010. 480 p.

ISBN 9780312658656

1. Gilded Age (1865-1898) 2. 1890s 3. Heirs and heiresses 4. Aristocracy 5. Americans in England 6. Dukes and duchesses 7. Cultural differences 8. Husband and wife 9. Country homes 10. Great Britain -- Social life and customs -- Victoria, 1837-1901 11. England -- Social life and customs -- 19th century 12. Historical fiction

Originally published as My Last Duchess, London : Headline Review, 2010.

Presents the story of vivacious Cora Cash, whose early twentieth-century marriage to England's most eligible duke is overshadowed by his secretive nature and the traps and betrayals of London's social scene.

"A shrewd, spirited historical romance with flavors of Edith Wharton, Daphne du Maurier, Jane Austen, Upstairs, Downstairs and a dash of People magazine that charts a bumpy marriage of New World money and Old World tradition." Kirkus.

Goonan, Kathleen Ann

In war times / Kathleen Ann Goonan. Tor, 2007. 400 p.

ISBN 9780765313553

1. 1940s 2. World War II 3. Saxophonists 4. Time travel (Future) 5. Technology 6. Jazz music 7. Jazz musicians 8. Soldiers 9. Brothers -- Death 10. Technology and civilization 11. Women physicists 12. Men/women relations 13. Alternative histories 14. Science fiction

LC 2007005165

Sequel: This Shared Dream.

"A Tom Doherty Associates Book."

John W. Campbell Memorial Award for Best Science Fiction Novel, 2008.

RUSA Reading List, 2008.

In an alternate-universe depiction of World War II, Sam enlists in the military after his brother is killed at Pearl Harbor and receives plans for a mysterious device from one of his instructors that he spends the war constructing, with unexpected and bizarre results.

"Goonan weaves a remarkable tale of quantum physics, human nature and jazz." SF Signal

Goonan, Kathleen Ann

This shared dream / Kathleen Ann Goonan. Tor, 2011. 368 p.

ISBN 9780765313546

1. Kennedy, John F (John Fitzgerald), 1917-1963 Assassination 2. Brothers and sisters 3. Abandoned children 4. Memories 5. Parallel universes 6. Family secrets 7. Alternative histories 8. Science fiction

LC 2011013444

"A Tom Doherty Associates book."

Sequel to: In War Times.

Struggling with memories of an alternate existence in which their mother prevented JFK's assassination and enabled several other societal improvements, the three adult Dance siblings work through inconsistencies in history to discover the truth about the parents who seemingly abandoned them.

Gordimer, Nadine

The **conservationist** / Nadine Gordimer. Penguin, 1978, c1974. 267 p.

ISBN 9780140047165

1. 1970s 2. Industrialists 3. Farms -- South Africa 4. Injustice 5. Conservation of natural resources 6. Superiority and inferiority (Psychology) 7. Self-preservation 8. European Africans 9. Suffering 10. Middle-aged men 11. Apartheid 12. South Africa 13. Literary fiction

Originally published: London : Cape, 1974.

Booker Prize, 1974.

Mehring, a wealthy, dominating South African industrialist moves to preserve his way of life, his power, and his possessions in the face of massive injustice and suffering, changing times, and death.

"The author probes the way of life that exists in South Africa today, and some aspects of the tensions that exist among English and Afrikaaners, Blacks, coloreds, Indian shopkeepers. . . . Mehring is rich, white, bored. His farm is a weekend pleasure place to which he once brought the mistress whose flirtations with left wing causes have now exiled her forever. His teenage son won't even come home for the holidays and wants out of all that South Africa stands for. Mehring is kind enough to his blacks, keeps them in their place, avoids his Boer neighbors with whom he has nothing in common. A loner, living for himself, deliberately isolated from any unpleasantness that might intrude, only gradually does he begin to perceive that there are forces at work in nature, in the closeness between the blacks and the land by which some day his way of life will be forever changed." Publishers Weekly.

Gordimer, Nadine

Get a life / Nadine Gordimer. Farrar, Straus and Giroux, 2005. 208 p.

ISBN 0374161704

1. Ecologists 2. People with cancer -- Family relationships 3. Mortality 4. Quarantine 5. Parent and adult child 6. Husband and wife 7. Cancer -- Treatment 8. Change (Psychology) 9. Extramarital

affairs 10. Archaeological expeditions -- Mexico 11. South Africa 12. Mexico 13. Literary fiction 14. Psychological fiction 15. Domestic fiction

LC 2005007199

Paul Bannerman, an ecologist living in South Africa, begins to re-examine his life after he is diagnosed with thyroid cancer and begins radiation treatments--an isolating experience that forces him to confront his relationships with family and friends.

"Gordimer confronts the reader with questions of conservation, social welfare, and emotional ecosystems. The austere Gordimer's mastery of her craft means she never needs to point at herself, thus highlighting the difference between art and performance." Harper's

Gordimer, Nadine

* **July's** people / Nadine Gordimer. Viking, 1981. 160 p.

ISBN 0140061401

1. Household employees 2. Insurgency -- South Africa 3. Families -- South Africa 4. Race relations 5. Villages -- South Africa 6. Apartheid 7. Housekeepers 8. South Africa -- Race relations 9. Literary fiction

LC 80024877

When South Africa is riven by war and the Smales, a white couple, take refuge in the village of their former servant July, their relationships are completely transformed

Gordimer, Nadine

Life times : stories, 1952-2007 / Nadine Gordimer. Farrar, Straus and Giroux, 2010. 560 p.

ISBN 9780374270537

1. Politics and culture -- South Africa 2. Sexuality 3. Race (Social sciences) 4. South Africa 5. Short stories

LC 2010023403

A collection of short fictional works offers insight into the author's use of rich language to convey themes ranging from politics and sexuality to race and family life, in a volume that includes such pieces as "Friday's Footprint" and "Something Out There."

"Gordimer has been writing for more than 60 years now, but her concerns have been constant: race, justice, the South African land. ... Four of the stories are new, an added pleasure for admirers of Gordimer's work. A welcome collection by a master of English prose--lucid and precisely written, if often bringing news only of disappointment, fear and loss." Kirkus.

Gordimer, Nadine

* **My** son's story / Nadine Gordimer. Farrar Straus Giroux, 1990. 277 p.

ISBN 0374217513

1. Human rights activists 2. Fathers and sons -- South Africa 3. Interracial romance 4. Interracial families 5. Extramarital affairs 6. South Africa 7. South Africa -- Race relations 8. Literary fiction

LC 9083232

Will, an adolescent black South African, finds his already unsettled relationship with his father further confused by his father's political activism and his affair with a young white woman.

"This is a thoughtful, poised, quietly poignant novel that not only recognizes the value and cost of political commitment, but also takes account of recent developments in South Africa and Eastern Europe in a way that Gordimer's previous work did not." Christian Science Monitor.

LIST OF FICTIONAL WORKS

Gordimer, Nadine

No time like the present : a novel / Nadine Gordimer. Farrar, Straus and Giroux, 2012. 421 p.

ISBN 9780374222642

1. Interracial marriage 2. Race relations 3. Suburban life 4. Postapartheid era 5. Collective memory 6. College teachers 7. Political corruption 8. Extramarital affairs 9. Fathers and daughters 10. Women lawyers 11. South Africa -- History -- 1989- 12. South Africa -- Social life and customs 13. Literary fiction 14. Psychological fiction

LC bl2012005508

"Gordimer trains her keen eye on Steve and Jabulile, an interracial couple living in a newly, tentatively, free South Africa. They have a daughter, Sindiswa; they move to the suburbs; Steve becomes a lecturer at a university; Jabulile trains to become a lawyer; there is another child, a boy this time. There is nothing so extraordinary about their lives, and yet, in telling their story and the stories of their friends and families, Gordimer manages to capture the tortured, fragmented essence of a nation struggling to define itself post-apartheid."--Publisher's website.

Gordimer, Nadine

None to accompany me / Nadine Gordimer. Farrar, Straus and Giroux, 1994. 324 p.

ISBN 0374222975

1. Women lawyers 2. Men/women relations 3. Marriage 4. Political violence 5. Family problems 6. South Africa -- Race relations 7. Literary fiction

LC 94-7553

Set in South Africa during the last days of the white regime, the heroine Vera Stark, a white lawyer, works to restore land taken from blacks by the government.

"A novel that raises more questions than it answers, 'None to Accompany Me' is an unflinching and perceptive exploration of people living on the brink of changes--political and personal--with little but their own sense of self-reliance to guide them." Christian Science Monitor.

Gordimer, Nadine

The **pickup** / Nadine Gordimer. Farrar, Straus and Giroux, 2001. 270 p.

ISBN 0374232105

1. Undocumented immigrants 2. Interethnic relations 3. Women 4. Men/women relations 5. Immigrants, Arab 6. Husband and wife 7. Children of rich people 8. Post-apartheid era 9. Arab countries 10. Literary fiction

LC 2001023041

ALA Notable Book, 2002.

Julie is from an affluent white family and is always searching for new ideas and adventures. When her car breaks down in a South African city she is immediately drawn to Abdu the mechanic who comes to her aid. He has left his home and family in the north to find work in the new South Africa. As their relationship develops into passionate love, they must both confront the prejudices of their past and the uncertainties of the future.

"Gordimer writes so tenderly and so searchingly about Julie's gradual transcendence of her western self that she manages to hold sceptism at bay." Women's Review of Books.

Gordon, Jaimy, 1944-

* **Lord** of misrule : a novel / Jaimy Gordon. McPherson & Co., 2010. 296 p.

ISBN 9780929701837

1. 1970s 2. Horse trainers 3. Race horses 4. Deception 5. Horse racing 6. Race tracks 7. Horse racing industry and trade 8. West

Virginia 9. Literary fiction

National Book Award for Fiction, 2010.

Set in 1970s West Virginia, this National Book Award winner examines the bottom rung of the sport of kings. In the ruthless and often violent world of cheap horse racing, trainers and jockeys, grooms and hotwalkers, loan sharks and touts all struggle to take an edge, or prove their luck, or just survive. -- Description by Dawn Towery.

"Gordon clearly loves the subculture of grifters and ne'er-do-wells whose lives center on a venue that obviously has never and will never bring them success. Her lowlifes have names like Two-Tie, Medicine Ed, Kidstuff and Deucey, and they're capable of speaking a kind of racetrack patois occasionally reminiscent of Damon Runyon characters. . . . Exceptional writing and idiosyncratic characters make this an engaging read." Kirkus.

Gordon, Mary, 1949-

The **liar's** wife : four novellas / Mary Gordon. Pantheon, 2014. 304 p.

ISBN 9780307377432

1. Americans in foreign countries 2. Life change events 3. Europeans in the United States 4. Interpersonal relations 5. Literary fiction

LC 2013043926

Four novellas about relationships at home and abroad are set in different historical periods and explore the experiences of such protagonists as an American grad student who escapes to Italy after a compromising love affair.

Gorman, Edward

Bad moon rising : a Sam McCain mystery / Ed Gorman. Pegasus Books, 2011. 256 p. Sam McCain mysteries

ISBN 9781605982601

1. 1960s 2. Hippies 3. Murder investigation 4. Innocence (Law) 5. Communes 6. Vietnam veterans 7. Prejudice 8. Small towns 9. Teenage murder victims 10. Lawyers -- Iowa 11. Iowa -- Social life and customs -- 20th century 12. Mysteries

Caught in the middle of a dispute over a hippie commune that has moved into Black River Falls, lawyer and private investigator Sam McCain doubts claims that a troubled commune member is responsible for a local murder.

"One of my favorite parts about the McCain series is Gorman's cultural insight. The McCain books are some of the best-written portrayals of the complexities of small-town America, like Winesburg, Ohio with a noir twist. This isn't a nostalgic view of the good old days. Gorman's 1950s and 1960s are as politically diverse and socially complex as today. Even though it is a small town, the crimes are anything but quaint. Gorman reveals the dark undercurrents, seething anger, and boiled-up oppression of mid-century Middle America." Pulp Serenade.

Gorman, Edward

Riders on the storm : a Sam McCain mystery / Ed Gorman. Pegasus Books, 2014. 252 p. Sam McCain mysteries

ISBN 9781605986258

1. 1970s 2. Vietnam veterans 3. Violence against radicals 4. Murder investigation 5. Male friendship 6. Peace activists 7. Small towns 8. Prejudice 9. Veterans 10. Lawyers 11. Iowa -- Social life and customs -- 20th century 12. Mysteries

Returning to his hometown after recovering from his Vietnam War injuries, lawyer Sam McCain investigates a charge against a veteran friend who has been accused of murdering a peace protestor.

"This is an extended, nuanced fictional biography with an occasional mystery thrown in. Great reading." Booklist.

Goss, Theodora

The **sinister** mystery of the mesmerizing girl / Theodora Goss. Saga Press, 2019. 416 p. Extraordinary adventures of the Athena Club

ISBN 9781534427877

1. Victorian era (1837-1901) 2. Characters and characteristics in literature 3. Secret societies 4. Conspiracies 5. Kidnapping victims 6. Enemies 7. Human experimentation in medicine 8. Women -- Social conditions 9. Female friendship 10. London, England -- Social life and customs -- Victoria, 1837-1901 11. Great Britain -- History -- Victoria, 1837-1901 12. Historical fantasy 13. Adaptations, retellings, and spin-offs

Mary Jekyll and the Athena Club race to save Alice?and foil a plot to unseat the Queen--in the conclusion to the trilogy that began with the Nebula Award finalist and Locus Award winner The Strange Case of the Alchemist's Daughter.

Goss, Theodora

The **strange** case of the alchemist's daughter / Theodora Goss. Saga Press, 2017 352 p. Extraordinary adventures of the Athena Club

ISBN 9781481466509

1. Victorian era (1837-1901) 2. Characters and characteristics in literature 3. Secret societies 4. Alchemists 5. Fugitives 6. Monsters 7. Serial murderers 8. Female friendship 9. Fathers and daughters 10. Human experimentation in medicine 11. London, England -- Social life and customs -- Victoria, 1837-1901 12. Great Britain -- History -- Victoria, 1837-1901 13. Historical fantasy 14. Adaptations, retellings, and spin-offs

Locus Award for First Novel, 2018.

Alone and penniless, Mary Jekyll hunts for her father's killer, a former friend named Edward Hyde, along with help from Sherlock Holmes and Dr. Watson resulting in the discovery of a secret society of immoral and power-crazed scientists.

Gottlieb, Eli, 1956-

Best boy : a novel / Eli Gottlieb. Liveright Publishing Corporation, 2015 248 p.

ISBN 9781631490477

1. People with autism 2. Roommates 3. Escapes 4. People with disabilities 5. Housing 6. Autism 7. Homecomings 8. Life change events 9. Middle aged men 10. Psychological fiction

LC 2014048573

A middle-aged autistic resident of a therapeutic community where he was sent as a young child rebels against changes in his environment by attempting to return to a family home and younger sibling he only partially remembers.

"Gottlieb merits praise for both the endearing eloquence of Todd's voice and a deeply sympathetic parable that speaks to a time when rising autism rates and long-lived elders force many to weigh tough options." Kirkus.

Goudge, Elizabeth, 1900-1984

Green Dolphin Street / Elizabeth Goudge. Hodder & Stoughton, 1974, c1944. 503 p.

1. 1830s 2. Sisters 3. Love triangles 4. British in New Zealand 5. Immigrants 6. Nuns 7. Spiritual journeys 8. Maori (New Zealand people) 9. Lumber industry and trade 10. Channel Islands 11. New Zealand 12. Love stories 13. Historical fiction 14. Gentle reads

After William emigrates to New Zealand, he writes the father of the woman he loves for her hand in marriage, but he mistakenly puts her sister's name in the letter instead, and the sister comes to New Zealand.

Gowar, Imogen Hermes

The **mermaid** and Mrs. Hancock / Imogen Hermes Gowar. HarperCollins, 2018. 488 p.

ISBN 9780062859952

1. Georgian era (1714-1837) 2. Courtesans 3. Mermaids 4. Captives 5. Unhappiness in women 6. Merchants 7. Gender role 8. Marriage 9. City life 10. Sexual attraction 11. Men/women relations 12. England -- Social life and customs -- 18th century 13. London, England 14. Historical fantasy 15. Literary fiction

Shortlisted for The Women's Prize for Fiction, 2018.

When one of his trading vessels returns to 18th-century London with the remarkable body of a mermaid, Jonah gains entry into high society and falls in love with a highly accomplished courtesan, with unexpected consequences.

Gowdy, Barbara

Helpless : a novel / Barbara Gowdy. Metropolitan Books, 2007. 320 p.

ISBN 0805082883

1. Kidnapping victims 2. Obsession in men 3. Stalkers 4. Nine-year-old girls 5. Single mothers 6. Beauty 7. Power failures 8. Kidnapping 9. Ransom 10. Loyalty 11. Stalking 12. Thrillers and suspense

LC 2006047348

Trillium Book Award, 2007.

Governor General's Literary Awards, English-language Fiction finalist

"There is a clean urgency to Gowdy's tale. We are helpless before her sure and beguiling hand because ultimatelyand breathlesslywe are drawn in." Vancouver Sun.

Graedon, Alena

The **word** exchange : a novel / Alena Graedon. Doubleday, 2014. 304 p.

ISBN 9780385537650

1. Dystopias 2. Language and technology 3. Missing persons 4. English language 5. Technology -- Social aspects 6. Communication technology 7. Young women 8. Digital communications 9. Fathers and daughters 10. Dictionaries 11. Near future 12. North America 13. Literary fiction 14. Dystopian fiction 15. Science fiction

LC 2013033165

In a world where the "death of print" has become a near reality, Anana Johnson, an employee at the North American Dictionary of the English Language (NADEL), searches for her missing father and stumbles upon the spiritual home of the written world and a pandemic "word flu."

"A wildly ambitious, darkly intellectual and inventive thriller about the intersection of language, technology and meaning." Kirkus.

Grafton, Sue, 1940-2017

"A" is for alibi / Sue Grafton. Holt, Rinehart, and Winston, 1982. 274 p. Kinsey Millhone mysteries

ISBN 0805013342

1. Women private investigators 2. Frameups 3. Murder investigation 4. Widows 5. Murder 6. Murderers 7. Santa Teresa (Calif : Imaginary place) 8. California 9. Mysteries

LC 81007128

After serving time for the murder of her husband, Nikki Fife is out on parole and wants private investigator Kinsey Millhone to find the real killer.

"Kinsey Millhone is a cut above the usual woman private eye who flounces through fiction. Millhone is neither a sex bomb nor a detached cerebrum, but a believable, straightforward character." Booklist.

Grafton, Sue, 1940-2017

X / Sue Grafton. G. P. Putnam's Sons, 2015. 400 p. Kinsey Millhone mysteries

ISBN 9780399163845

1. 1980s 2. Serial murderers 3. Psychopaths 4. Women private investigators 5. Murder investigation 6. California 7. Mysteries

A serial killer who leaves no trace of his crimes challenges Kinsey Milhone's skills to solve the case before she becomes his next victim.

"Grafton's endless resourcefulness in varying her pitches in this landmark series (W Is for Wasted, 2013, etc.), graced by her trademark self-deprecating humor, is one of the seven wonders of the genre." Kirkus.

Grafton, Sue, 1940-2017

Y is for yesterday / Sue Grafton. Marian Wood, 2017. 483 p. Kinsey Millhone mysteries

ISBN 9780399163852

1. 1980s 2. Rapists 3. Extortion 4. Criminals 5. Psychopaths 6. Women private investigators 7. Murder investigation 8. California 9. Mysteries

Series complete in 25 volumes.

Kinsey Millhone monitors the release from prison of a sociopath who is determined to exact revenge on a fellow perpetrator who went missing after they sexually assaulted a fourteen-year-old classmate.

"The series may be coming to a close, but Grafton (W Is for Wasted) constructs an intricate plot following two time lines with at least a dozen characters in play while rarely slowing the pace. Kinseys fans may have to take notes to keep up with her as she untangles a web of lies and cover stories to solve the current blackmail case as well as the older murder." Library Journal.

Graley, Lisa

The **current** that carries : stories / Lisa Graley. The University of Georgia Press, 2016., 176 p.

ISBN 9780820349879

1. Rural life 2. Loss (Psychology) 3. Interpersonal relations 4. Appalachian region 5. Short stories 6. Literary fiction 7. Southern fiction

LC 2015047529

This collection bristles and hums with the rugged resilience one encounters in southern and Appalachian fiction, where ghosts of loved ones and livestock alike haunt an underworld of lonely trails.

"Eight stories that give voice to incommunicable aspects of love and loss." Kirkus.

Grames, Juliet

The **seven** or eight deaths of Stella Fortuna / Juliet Grames. Ecco Press, 2019. 445 p.

ISBN 9780062862822

1. Teenage girls 2. Sisters 3. Protectiveness in teenagers 4. Immigration and emigration 5. Italian-American women 6. Abusive men 7. Father-separated families 8. Curses 9. Near-death experience 10. Gender role 11. Independence in women 12. Italy 13. Connecticut 14. Historical fiction 15. Domestic fiction 16. Coming-of-age stories

Believed cursed in her rugged Italian village, a tough, intelligent teen protects her younger sister during World War II, enduring challenges that transform her views about survival and independence.

"With her story of an ordinary woman who is anything but, Grames explores not just the immigrant experience but the stages of a womans life. This is a sharp and richly satisfying novel." Publishers Weekly.

Gran, Sara

Claire DeWitt and the city of the dead / Sara Gran. Houghton Mifflin Harcourt, 2011. 288 p. Claire DeWitt mysteries

ISBN 9780547428499

1. Women private investigators 2. Missing persons investigation 3. Drug use 4. Murder investigation 5. Public prosecutors 6. Gang members 7. Hurricane Katrina, 2005 -- Social aspects 8. Women's dreams 9. Women psychics 10. Brooklyn, New York City 11. New Orleans, Louisiana 12. Hardboiled fiction 13. Mysteries

LC 2010021449

Macavity Award for Best Mystery Novel, 2012.

Augmenting her brilliant deductive skills with dream analysis, marijuana, and the written work of a mysterious French detective, private investigator Claire DeWitt reluctantly returns to post-Katrina New Orleans to solve the disappearance of an unpopular prosecutor.

"The novel is is difficult to categorize, offering a strangely appealing mix of the mystical and the hardboiled. The book is beautifully written in a tight, quirky style that distinguishes Gran as one of the more original writers working today." Miami Herald.

Gran, Sara

* The **infinite** blacktop : a novel / Sara Gran. Atria Books, 2018. 304 p. Claire DeWitt mysteries

ISBN 9781501165719

1. Women private investigators 2. Hit-and-run accidents 3. Cold cases (Criminal investigation) 4. Missing persons investigation 5. Murder investigation 6. Female friendship 7. Survival (after automobile, truck, train accidents, etc) 8. Artists 9. Purpose in life 10. Existentialism 11. Identity (Psychology) 12. Hardboiled fiction 13. Mysteries

LC 2018026234

Acclaimed detective Claire DeWitt navigates three cases from different turning points in her life, including the disappearance of a childhood friend, the cold-case double murder that shaped her PI license, and a near-fatal attack by a homicidal driver.

Grant, Helen, 1964-

The **glass** demon / Helen Grant. Bantam Dell, 2011. 320 p.

ISBN 9780385344203

1. Fathers and daughters 2. Relics 3. Demons 4. Supernatural 5. Teenage girls 6. Stained glass 7. Dysfunctional families 8. Stained glass windows 9. Emotional problems 10. Families 11. Horror stories 12. Mystery and detective stories 13. Germany 14. Germany 15. Horror

When seventeen-year-old Lin and her family move to an ancient German castle for a year while her medievalist father searches for the famed Allerheiligen glass--lost stained glass windows that are said to be haunted by a terrifying demon--she becomes involved in a horrific murder mystery.

"With its fascinating information on medieval folklore, unique setting, and increasingly claustrophobic sense of terror, this is an exhilarating page-turner that offers a cerebral blend of horror and mystery." Booklist.

Grant, Helen, 1964-

The **vanishing** of Katharina Linden / Helen Grant. Delacorte, 2010. 304 p.

ISBN 9780385344173

1. Villages -- Germany 2. Missing persons 3. Secrets 4. Ten-year-old girls 5. Bullying and bullies 6. Teasing 7. Misfits (Persons) 8. Senior men 9. Intergenerational friendship 10. Germany 11. Mysteries 12. Coming-of-age stories

Reviled in her German village home where her only friends are a fellow outcast and an elderly storyteller, eleven-year-old Pia investigates the disappearances of three local girls whom she believes are tied to unsolved missing persons cases from decades earlier.

"Set in the small German town of Bad Mnstereifel during a cold, dreary winter when little girls seem to be disappearing left and right, this dark story gains immeasurably from Grant's choice of narrator: Pia Kolvenbach, who is socially ostracized (shunned as the Potentially Explosive Schoolgirl) after her grandmother dies in a bizarre accident. Feeling even more isolated when her English mother and German father begin quarreling, Pia finds companionship with StinkStefan, the most unpopular boy in the class, and Herr Schiller, a kindly old gent who spins terrifying but oddly comforting horror stories. Although thin on plot, the novel has nice atmosphere and takes a tender view of lonely children trying to make sense of a grown-up world." New York Times Book Review.

Grant, Linda, 1951-
We had it so good / Linda Grant. Simon & Schuster, 2011. 272 p.

ISBN 9781451617405

1. 1960s 2. Baby boom generation 3. Middle class 4. Idealism 5. Friendship 6. Fathers and sons 7. Parent and child 8. England 9. Literary fiction

American Rhodes scholar Stephen Newman remains in England to avoid the Vietnam War. He marries an Englishwoman, and together they raise their family, experiencing all the cultural and personal touchstones of the Baby Boomer generation.

Grant, Mira
Blackout / Mira Grant. Orbit, 2012. 560 p. Newsflesh

ISBN 9780316081078

1. Conspiracies 2. Viruses 3. Zombies 4. Near future 5. Dystopias 6. Political corruption 7. Apocalyptic fiction 8. Horror

In 2041, Georgia Mason, held hostage by a team of CDC researchers, must find her way back to Shaun Mason, who is dealing with his own problems, such as zombie bears, mad scientists and rogue government agencies, before things get worse in her post-zombie, post-resurrection America.

Grant, Mira
Deadline / Mira Grant. Orbit, 2011. 560 p. Newsflesh

ISBN 9780316081061

1. Conspiracies 2. Viruses 3. Zombies 4. Near future 5. Dystopias 6. Blogs 7. Journalists 8. Political corruption 9. Apocalyptic fiction 10. Horror

When a CDC researcher, after faking her own death, arrives on his doorstep with a ravenous pack of zombies in tow, Shaun Mason, the head of a news organization, is plunged into the biggest story of his life.

Grant, Mira
Feed / Mira Grant. Grand Central Pub., 2010. 560 p. Newsflesh

ISBN 9780316081054

1. Conspiracies 2. Viruses 3. Zombies 4. Near future 5. Mind control 6. Dystopias 7. Blogs 8. Journalists 9. Political corruption 10. Campaigning 11. Apocalyptic fiction 12. Horror

Goodreads Choice Award, 2010.

In the year 2014, a new virus emerges, taking over bodies and minds with one, unstoppable command, FEED, and, now, 20 years later, two reporters will stop at nothing to expose the dark conspiracy behind the infected.

"Shunning misogynistic horror tropes in favor of genuine drama and pure creepiness, McGuire has crafted a masterpiece of suspense with engaging, appealing characters who conduct a soul-shredding examination of what's true and what's reported." Publishers Weekly.

Grant, Mira
Feedback / Mira Grant. Orbit, 2016. 512 p. Newsflesh

ISBN 9780316379342

1. Viruses 2. Zombies 3. Journalists 4. Dystopias 5. Near future 6. Mind control 7. Conspiracies 8. Campaigning 9. Political culture 10. Political corruption 11. Apocalyptic fiction 12. Horror

LC 2016013017

Story overlaps the timeline of Feed (2010).

Twenty years after the Rising--the start of an infection that caused people to have a single uncontrollable impulse to feed--a team of scrappy underdog reporters relentlessly pursue dangerous truths on the presidential campaign trail.

"This mashup of medical and media ethics, politics and the living undead, is a whip-smart thriller overflowing with sharp ideas and social commentary." Kirkus.

Grant, Mira
Into the drowning deep / Mira Grant. Orbit, 2017. 512 p. Into the drowning deep

ISBN 9780316379403

1. Shipwrecks 2. Vanished ships 3. Sea monsters 4. Ocean travel 5. Scientists 6. Mermaids 7. Sisters 8. Mariana Trench 9. Contemporary fantasy 10. Horror

LC 2017020686

This novel is a sequel to the author's 2015 novella Rolling in the deep.

Victoria Stewart and her crew sail to the Mariana Trench in the hopes of discovering the fate of the Atargatis, which, along with its crew, including Victoria's sister, was lost at sea during the crew's attempt to film a mockumentary on ancient sea creatures of legend.

Grant, Mira
Parasite / Mira Grant. Little, Brown, 2013. 608 p. Parasitology

ISBN 9780316218955

1. Parasites 2. Near future 3. Genetic engineering 4. Amnesia 5. Immunity 6. Tapeworms 7. Corporations 8. Biotechnology 9. Consciousness 10. Bio-thrillers 11. Science fiction

In the future, a genetically engineered tapeworm protects most of the human populace from illness, boosts everyone's immune system and even secretes designer drugs, but now the organisms have begun to change and want out of human bodies they occupy--at all costs.

Grass, Gunter, 1927-2015
The **box** : tales from the darkroom / Gunter Grass ; translated from the German by Krishna Winston. Houghton Mifflin Harcourt, 2010. 208 p.

ISBN 9780547245034

1. Photography 2. Childhood 3. Growing up 4. Father and child 5. Memories 6. Families 7. Literary fiction

LC 2010008479

Grass writes in the voices of his eight children as they record memories of their childhoods and of their father.

Grass, Gunter, 1927-2015

The **call** of the toad / Gunter Grass ; translated from the German by Ralph Manheim Harcourt Brace Jovanovich, 1992. 248 p.

1. Middle-aged persons 2. Cemeteries 3. Germany 4. Translations -- German to English

LC 92020233

"This book is a skillful balancing act that juggles some very timely questions about the conflict between calls for ethnic self-determination and calls for international unity and cooperation." Christian Science Monitor.

Grass, Gunter, 1927-2015

Cat and mouse / Gunter Grass ; translated from the German by Ralph Manheim Harcourt, 1963. 189p.

1. Humorous stories 2. Translations -- German to English

LC 63013499

To compensate for his unusually large Adam's apple - source of both comfort and stress - 14-year-old Mahlke turns himself into an athlete and ace driver. Soon he is known to the nation as "The Great Mahlke" but remains a target to his enemies. He is different, and doomed.

Grass, Gunter, 1927-2015

Crabwalk / Gunter Grass ; translated from the German by Krishna Winston. Harcourt, 2002. 240 p.

ISBN 0151007640

1. Shipwrecks 2. Journalists 3. Fathers and sons 4. Guilt 5. Memories 6. Survival (after airplane accidents, shipwrecks, etc) 7. Submarines, Soviet 8. Ships 9. World War II -- Post-war aspects 10. Refugees, German 11. Mothers and sons 12. Grandmother and grandson 13. Postwar life 14. Literary fiction 15. Translations -- German to English

LC 2002013205

Presents a fictional exploration of the worst maritime disaster in history, the 1945 sinking of a German cruise ship packed with refugees by a Soviet sub--a disaster that killed nine thousand people.

"A writer who refuses to avert his eyes from unpleasant truths, Grassremains an eloquent explorer of his country's troubled 20th-century history." Publishers Weekly.

Grass, Gunter, 1927-2015

Dog years / Gunter Grass ; translated from the German by Ralph Manheim Harcourt, 1965. 570 p.

1. Epistolary novels 2. Translations -- German to English

LC 65014715

Eddi Amsel, a half-Jewish scarecrow maker, forms a friendship with Walter Matern that deteriorates as the Nazis rise in power.

Grass, Gunter, 1927-2015

The **flounder** / Gunter Grass ; translated from the German by Ralph Manheim Harcourt, 1978. 547p.

1. Immortality 2. Women -- History 3. Sexism 4. Cooks 5. Fishes 6. Fishers 7. Literary fiction 8. Translations -- German to English

LC 78053891

"It is perhaps best to take this fantasy . . . as a celebration of life in all its gross particularity, with Grass still telling the German people to beware of the abstractions that have too often made them flounder in a nordic mist." Times Literary Supplement.

Grass, Gunter, 1927-2015

* The **tin** drum / Gunter Grass ; a new translation by Breon Mitchell. Houghton Mifflin Harcourt, 2009, c1959. 591 p.

ISBN 9780151014163

1. World War II 2. Nazism 3. Little people 4. Drum 5. Germany -- History -- 20th century 6. Historical fiction 7. Picaresque fiction 8. Modern classics 9. Translations -- German to English

LC 2009013272

Originally published in Germany under the title: Die blechtrommel (1959).

Originally translated by Ralph Manheim: London : Secker & Warburg, 1962.

On his third birthday, Oskar decides to stop growing. Haunted by the deaths of his parents and wielding his tin drum, Oskar recounts the events of his extraordinary life; from the long nightmare of the Nazi era to his anarchic adventures in post-war Germany.

Grass, Gunter, 1927-2015

Too far afield / Gunter Grass ; translated from the German by Krishna Winston. Harcourt, 2000. 658 p.

ISBN 0151002304

1. Senior men -- Berlin, Germany 2. German reunification 3. Berlin, Germany -- History -- 20th century 4. East Germany 5. Political fiction 6. Translations -- German to English

LC 00029586

Follows two old German men--one a former Eastern diplomat, the other a Prussian spy who has served many masters--as they make their way in modern Germany.

"The narrative's focus is German reunification, in particular, the fate of the German Democratic Republic after the Wall came down in 1989. At the center of the novel are two characters, locked in a sort of political marriage: Theo Wuttke, a former East German cultural figure and long-winded raconteur, and Ludwig Hoffstaller, a professional spy who served for years as Wuttke's shadow. They are both about to turn 70 in this new Germany and are now both employees of the agency responsible for privatizing state-held companies." Booklist.

Gratton, Tessa

The **queens** of Innis Lear / Tessa Gratton. Tom Doherty Associates Book, 2018. 544 p. Queens of Innis Lear

ISBN 9780765392466

1. Princesses 2. Rulers -- Succession 3. Inheritance and succession 4. Magic 5. Prophecy 6. Leadership 7. Competition 8. Imaginary kingdoms 9. Imaginary wars and battles 10. Epic fantasy 11. Adaptations, retellings, and spin-offs

LC 2017039670

A fantasy inspired by Shakespeare's "King Lear" depicts a once-bountiful isle decimated by a prophecy-obsessed king's erratic decisions, where three rival princesses prepare for a war that will determine their realm's leadership and survival.

Grau, Shirley Ann

The **keepers** of the house / Shirley Ann Grau. Knopf, 1964. 309 p.

ISBN 9780394431826

1. Interracial marriage 2. Interracial families 3. Small town life 4. Politicians 5. Race relations 6. Family secrets 7. Southern States 8. Literary fiction 9. Southern fiction

LC 64012306

Pulitzer Prize for Fiction, 1965.

Abigail is the last keeper of the house, the last to know the Howland family's secrets. Now in the name of all her brothers and sisters, she must take her bitter revenge on the small-minded Southern town that shames them.

Graves, Robert, 1895-1985

Claudius the god and his wife Messalina : the troublesome reign of Tiberius Claudius Caesar, Emperor of the Romans (born B.C. 10, died A.D. 54), as described by himself : Robert Graves. Vintage, 1989, c1934. viii, 533 p.

ISBN 0679725733

1. Claudius I,, Emperor of Rome, 10 BC-54 AD 2. Roman Empire (27 BCE-476 CE) 3. Roman emperors 4. Rome -- History -- Empire, 30 BC-284 AD 5. Historical fiction

Sequel to: I, Claudius.

Originally published: London : Arthur Barker, 1934.

James Tait Black Memorial Prize for Fiction, 1934.

Depicts the turbulent life of a Roman emperor, reconstructing the decadence of the Roman world

"A vivid picture of profligate Rome during the years in which Claudius conquered Britain and instituted many reforms at home. A story complete in itself, though a continuation of 'I, Claudius.' " Booklist.

Graves, Robert, 1895-1985

* I, Claudius : from the autobiography of Tiberius Claudius, born 10 B.C., murdered and deified A.D. 54 / Robert Graves. Vintage Books, 1989, c1934. x, 468 p.

ISBN 067972477X

1. Claudius I,, Emperor of Rome, 10 BC-54 AD 2. Augustus, Emperor of Rome, 63 BC-14 AD 3. Tiberius, Emperor of Rome, 42 BC-37 AD 4. Caligula, Emperor of Rome, 12-41 5. Roman Empire (27 BCE-476 CE) 6. Roman emperors 7. Rome -- History -- Empire, 30 BC-284 AD 8. Biographical fiction 9. Historical fiction 10. Modern classics

Sequel: Claudius the god and his wife Messalina.

Originally published: London : Arthur Barker, 1934.

James Tait Black Memorial Prize for Fiction, 1934.

Claudius, born weak and with a stutter, was shamed and dismissed by his family as an idiot. This allowed him to live under the public radar and avoid his family's scandals and murders to become the emperor of Rome in 41 A.D.

Gray, Anissa,

The **care** and feeding of ravenously hungry girls / Anissa Gray. Berkley Books, 2019. 294 p.

ISBN 9781984802439

1. 2010s 2. Aunt and niece 3. Mothers and daughters 4. African American families 5. Sisters 6. Women prisoners 7. Family secrets 8. Small town life 9. Communities 10. Michigan 11. Literary fiction 12. Domestic fiction 13. African American fiction

LC 2018018552

When their formidably strong-willed eldest sister is arrested, abruptly transitioning their family from respectability to disgrace, two younger sisters confront complicated dynamics in their family and identities to uncover what really happened.

Gray, Erick S.

Love & a gangsta : a novel / Erick S. Gray. Augustus Pub., 2009. 261 p. Crave all, lose all novels

ISBN 9780979281648

1. Drug traffic 2. Ambition in men 3. Criminals 4. Gangsters 5. Men/women relations 6. Violence 7. Street life 8. Inner city 9. African Americans 10. New York City 11. Queens, New York City 12. Urban fiction 13. African American fiction

LC bl2010011393

Sequel to: Crave all, lose all. New York :

Soul completes a four-year stint in prison but rejects America's request for him to live honestly, returning to the Queens drug scene and severely testing the strength of their relationship.

Gray, Juliana, 1972-

A **duke** never yields / Juliana Gray. Berkley Sensation, 2013. viii, 312 p. Affairs by moonlight

ISBN 9780425251188

1. Single women 2. Dukes and duchesses 3. Vow of chastity 4. Curses 5. Single men 6. Womanizers 7. Seduction 8. Men/women relations 9. British in Italy 10. Tuscany, Italy 11. Italy -- Social life and customs -- 19th century 12. Historical romances

Miss Abigail Harewood, who is determined to reject stifling convention and take a lover, sets her sights on the Duke of Wallingford, who is dissatisfied with his life of debauchery and has resolved to remain chaste for a year.

Gray, Juliana, 1972-

How to tame your duke / Juliana Gray. Berkley Sensation, 2013. 320 p. Princess in hiding

ISBN 9780425265666

1. Victorian era (1837-1901) 2. Princesses 3. Secret identity 4. Dukes and duchesses 5. Governesses 6. Interpersonal attraction 7. Men with disfigurements 8. Men/women relations 9. England -- Social life and customs -- 19th century 10. Great Britain -- History -- Victoria, 1837-1901 11. Historical romances 12. Victorian romances

No longer safe in her beloved homeland, the tiny principality of Holstein-Schweinwald-Huhnhof, scholarly Princess Emilie makes the most of her enforced exile by disguising herself as a man and accepting a position as tutor to the teenage son of the Duke of Ashland. The Duke, a disfigured former soldier whose wife abandoned him and their child years ago, is intrigued by his new employee once he discovers her secret. Shades of Jane Eyre and Beauty and the Beast enhance this lyrical, emotionally intense romance, set in Victorian England. - Description by Gillian Speace.

Gray, Juliana, 1972-

A **lady** never lies / Juliana Gray. Berkley Sensation, 2012. viii, 311 p. Affairs by moonlight

ISBN 9780425250921

1. Widows 2. Inventors 3. Sexual attraction 4. Eccentrics and eccentricities 5. Scandals 6. Aristocracy 7. British in Italy 8. Automobiles -- Design and construction 9. Automobile racing 10. Castles 11. Bets 12. Men/women relations 13. Tuscany, Italy 14. Italy -- Social life and customs -- 19th century 15. Historical romances

Although Lady Alexandra Morely has a reputation as a beautiful and wealthy widow, only the first part is true. Her "fortune" consists of her late husband's title and 20,000 shares in the near-defunct Manchester Machine Company. Plotting her return to London society, Alexandra leases modest digs in Castel Sant'Agata in Tuscany, where she meets brilliant inventor Phineas "Finn" Burke, who is developing an unusual horseless carriage. Finn's success may her company, but can their companionship outlast this scandalous start? Captivating leads with chemistry and witty banter will charm readers. -- Description by Gillian Speace.

Greaves, C. Joseph

Hard twisted : a novel / C. Joseph Greaves. Bloomsbury, 2012. 304 p.

ISBN 9781608198559

1. Depression era (1929-1941) 2. 1930s 3. Serial murders 4.

Psychopaths 5. Teenage girls -- Relations with older men 6. Former convicts 7. Swindlers and swindling 8. Drifters 9. Depressions -- 1929-1941 10. Texas -- History -- 20th century 11. Historical fiction 12. Psychological suspense 13. Crime fiction 14. Rural noir

LC 2011051902

A tale based on a true story finds the 13-year-old daughter of a homeless man lured by a charismatic drifter to Depression-era Texas, where she is forced to participate in a year-long crime spree that culminates in the notorious Greenville "skeleton murder" trial of 1935.

Greaves, Chuck

* **Hush** money : a mystery / Chuck Greaves. Minotaur Books, 2012. 304 p. Jack MacTaggart mysteries

ISBN 9781250005236

1. Insurance fraud 2. Show jumping 3. Horses 4. Lawyers 5. Fraud investigation 6. Murder investigation 7. Mysteries

LC 2012004489

Investigating a socialite's insurance claim for a champion show horse's sudden death, elite Pasadena law firm newcomer Jack MacTaggart uncovers links to an old blackmail scheme before he is falsely accused of murder.

Grebe, Camilla

After she's gone : a novel / Camilla Grebe ; translated from the Swedish by Elizabeth Clark Wessel. Ballantine Books, 2019, c2017. 304 p. Psychological profiler novels (Camilla Grebe)

ISBN 9780425284407

1. Criminal profilers 2. Cross-dressers 3. Women with amnesia 4. Secrets 5. Cold cases (Criminal investigation) 6. Murder investigation 7. Murder victims 8. Diary writing 9. Teenage boys 10. Sweden 11. Scandinavian crime fiction 12. Translations -- Swedish to English

LC 2018050773

Sequel to: The Ice Beneath Her

"Originally published in Swedish in Sweden by Wahlstrom & Widstrand, a division of the Bonnier Group, Stockholm, Sweden, in 2017."

Finds an amnesia-stricken psychological profiler struggling to figure out what happened, while a teen with a difficult secret considers exposing himself to save the profiler's life.

"Grebe delivers an unflinching, heart-wrenching message about the plight of refugees in this scorching thriller." Publishers Weekly.

Grebe, Camilla

The **ice** beneath her : a novel / Camilla Grebe ; translated from the Swedish by Elizabeth Clark Wessel. Ballantine Books, 2016, 368 p. Psychological profiler novels (Camilla Grebe)

ISBN 9780425284322

1. Missing persons 2. Murder investigation 3. Criminal profilers 4. Dementia 5. Murder suspects 6. Thrillers and suspense 7. Scandinavian crime fiction 8. Translations -- Swedish to English

LC 2016013298

Originally published: Stockholm : Wahlstrom & Widstrand, 2015.

Investigating a grisly murder in a business tycoon's Stockholm residence, detective Peter Lindgren and psychological profiler Hanne Lagerlind-Schon navigate complications in their own relationship while tracking down the businessman, who may have been having an affair with the victim.

"A tour de force that lifts its author to the front rank among the increasingly crowded field of Nordic noir." Kirkus.

Grecian, Alex

The **saint** of wolves and butchers / Alex Grecian. G.P. Putnam's Sons, 2018. 388 p.

ISBN 9780399176111

1. Nazis 2. Nazi hunters 3. War criminals 4. Nazism 5. Deception 6. Big churches 7. False personation 8. Tracking and trailing 9. African American policewomen 10. Kansas 11. Thrillers and suspense

LC 2017012118

Also published in Great Britain under the title The Wolf.

An enigmatic hunter and his highly skilled dog track a Nazi concentration-camp administrator who has been hiding in the United States, a case that is complicated by the man's secret ongoing work and his band of fanatical followers.

Greeley, Molly

The **clergyman's** wife / Molly Greeley. William Morrow & Co., 2019. 304 p.

ISBN 9780062942913

1. Regency period (1811-1820) 2. Married women 3. Romantic love 4. Spouses of clergy 5. Options, alternatives, choices 6. Interclass friendship 7. Social classes 8. Men/women relations 9. England -- Social life and customs -- 19th century 10. Great Britain -- History -- Regency, 1811-1820 11. Historical fiction 12. Adaptations, retellings, and spin-offs

"A Pride & Prejudice novel" -- cover.

When she makes the acquaintance of Mr. Travis, the tenant of her vicar husband's condescending patroness, Charlotte, for the first time in her life, feels appreciated, heard and seen and must question the role of love and passion in her life.

"With tight prose and expert characterization (and, sadly, a finale true to those times), Greeley easily draws readers into the world she's created while largely staying true to Pride and Prejudice's original plot." Publishers Weekly.

Green, George Dawes

Ravens / George Dawes Green. Grand Central Pub., 2009. 350 p.

ISBN 9780446538961

1. Hostages 2. Lottery winners 3. Greed 4. Social isolation 5. Death threats 6. Money-making projects 7. Georgia 8. Psychological suspense

Stopping at a convenience store to fix a leaky tire, Shaw McBride and Romeo Zderko learn that a winning lottery ticket was purchased from the same location and devise a plot to steal half of the prize money.

"The stark good and evil imagery of Christianity stands in contrast to the ever-shifting quicksand of moral dilemmas, and what comes through in Ravens, despite the coincidences needed to spur along the narrative, is how the naked need for money, power and love strips away the prospect of a cathartic journey to redemption, turning hope inside out and back upon itself." Los Angeles Times Book Review.

Green, Hank,

An **absolutely** remarkable thing : a novel / Hank Green. Penguin Group USA, 2018 320 p.

ISBN 9781524743444

1. Fame 2. Social media 3. Young women 4. Self-discovery 5. Robots 6. Bisexual women 7. Life change events 8. New York City 9. Science fiction 10. Coming-of-age stories

LC 2018010156

The first to document the appearance of the Carls, giant robot-like statues popping up around the world, April May finds herself at the center of an intense international media spotlight that puts her relationships, identity and safety at risk.

"At once funny, exciting, and a tad terrifying, this exploration of aliens and social-media culture is bound to have wide appeal to readers interested in either theme." Booklist.

Green, Jocelyn

The **mark** of the king / Jocelyn Green. Bethany House, 2017. 400 p.

ISBN 9780764219061

1. 1720s 2. Colonial America (1600-1775) 3. Midwives 4. Exiles 5. Voyages and travels 6. Colonists 7. New France 8. Christian historical fiction

LC 2016034521

Christy Award for Historical Category, 2017.

After being unjustly imprisoned for the death of her client, midwife Julianne Chevalier trades her life sentence for exile to the French colony of Louisiana in 1720. She marries a fellow convict in order to sail, but when tragedy strikes--and a mystery unfolds--Julianne must find her own way in this dangerous new land while bearing the brand of a criminal.

Green, Norman, 1954-

The **angel** of Montague Street : a novel / Norman Green. HarperCollins, 2003. 293 p.

ISBN 0060188197

1. 1970s 2. Vietnam veterans 3. Brothers 4. Missing persons 5. Missing persons investigation 6. Revenge 7. Gangsters 8. Gangs 9. Family secrets 10. Men/women relations 11. Italian American families 12. Organized crime 13. Brooklyn, New York City 14. Crime fiction 15. Noir fiction

LC 2002032885

Wishing to leave his troubled past in Brooklyn behind, Silvano Iurata's brother suddenly disappears, making it necessary for him to return to his childhood home to solve the mystery.

"Silvano Iurata should never be in Brooklyn in the first place. It's 1973, the city is broke and mean, and he's ben bumming around since he got out of Vietnam, avoiding his Mafia-employed family and keeping clear of his loco cousin, Domenic, who wants to settle and old family quarrel by killing him with his bare hands. But Iurata is on some private redemptive mission, and he figures that if he can find out what happened to his sweet, mildly retarded brother, last seen in Brooklyn Heights, he might be able to give up the dead and rejoin the living. . . . Green writes about mobster families with a knowledge that is unnerving in its intimacy." New York Times Book Review.

Greenberg, Joanne, 1932-

I never promised you a rose garden : a novel / Hannah Green Holt, Rinehart and Winston, 1964. 300 p.

ISBN 9780030437250

1. Greenberg, Joanne, 1932- 2. Teenage girls with mental illnesses 3. Psychotherapist and patient 4. Teenage girls -- Psychology 5. Teenagers with schizophrenia 6. Psychiatric hospital patients 7. Mental illness -- Treatment 8. Jewish teenage girls 9. Imagination in teenage girls 10. Autobiographical fiction 11. Psychological fiction

LC 64011018

Chronicles the three-year battle of a mentally ill, but perceptive, teenage girl against a world of her own creation, emphasizing her relationship with the doctor who gave her the ammunition of self-understanding with which to destroy that world of fantasy.

"The hospital world and Deborah's fantasy world are strikingly portrayed, as is the girl's violent struggle between sickness and health, a struggle given added poignancy by youth, wit, and courage." Library Journal.

Greene, Amy, 1975-

Bloodroot : a novel / Amy Greene. Alfred A. Knopf, 2010. 304 p.

ISBN 9780307269867

1. Rural families 2. Mountain life 3. Women psychics 4. Men/women relations 5. Women's role 6. Violence in men 7. Poverty 8. Forgiveness 9. Families 10. Appalachian Region 11. Tennessee 12. Literary fiction 13. Southern fiction

LC 2009019483

Myra Lamb of Bloodroot Mountain has troubling "haint" blue eyes and a grandma whose touch charms people and animals alike. When their neighbor John Odom tries to tame Myra, he meets a with shocking, violent disaster.

"As a first novel, Bloodroot has its awkward moments, and some segments that work less well than others. . . . When Bloodroot works, however, its power is awesome, peeling away layers of the human experience like an onion until it reaches a message of redemption. Greene proves herself a newcomer to watch." Wilmington Star News

Greene, Amy, 1975-

* **Long** Man / Amy Greene. Alfred A Knopf, 2014. 272 p.

ISBN 9780307593436

1. 1930s 2. Rivers 3. Missing children 4. Farms 5. Small town life 6. Dams 7. Storms 8. Family relationships 9. Interpersonal relations 10. Tennessee 11. Historical fiction 12. Literary fiction 13. Southern fiction

Refusing to evacuate the East Tennessee hometown that is being flooded by a newly constructed dam, Annie Clyde Dodson battles with a husband who would start over elsewhere only to begin a frantic search when their toddler goes missing.

"A smart and moody historical novel that evokes the best widescreen Southern literature." Kirkus.

Greene, Graham, 1904-1991

* **Brighton** Rock / Graham Greene ; introduction by J.M. Coetzee. Penguin Books :, 2004, c1938. xvi, 270 p.

ISBN 0142437972

1. Psychopaths 2. Murder 3. Gangsters 4. Journalists 5. Teenage murderers 6. Street life 7. Catholic women 8. Growing up 9. Men/women relations 10. Betrayal 11. Secrets 12. Teenage boy/girl relations 13. England 14. Brighton, England 15. Psychological suspense 16. Literary fiction 17. Crime fiction 18. Modern classics

LC 2004275123

"Graham Greene Centennial, 1904-2004"--Cover.

Originally published: New York : The Viking press, 1938.

Originally published in Great Britain: William Heinemann, 1938.

Originally published: 1938.

Set in Brighton among the criminal rabble, the story depicts the tragic career of a 17 year-old boy named Pinkie whose primary ambition is to lead a gang to rival that of the wealthy and established Calleoni.

Greene, Graham, 1904-1991

The **captain** and the enemy / Graham Greene. Penguin, 2005. 154 p.

ISBN 9780143039297

1. Foster fathers 2. Gun smugglers 3. Abandoned boys 4. Father-separated boys 5. Impostors 6. England 7. Psychological fiction 8. Literary fiction

"Vintage Greene"--Cover.

Originally published: London: Reinhardt, 1988.

Originally published: New York: Viking, 1988.

This evocative novel centers on the life of Victor Baxter, a young boy growing up amid odd and touching circumstances, and on his relationships with various unusual and enigmatic people.

"The author wastes not a word in distilling the fictional preoccupations of a lifetime, omitting descriptive padding and elaborate transitions. But stripped down, the narrative runs fast and true across that bleak and poignant emotional landscape that is uniquely, immortally his." Time.

Greene, Graham, 1904-1991

Collected stories : including May we borrow your husband? A sense of reality, Twenty-one stories / Graham Greene. Viking Press, 1973, c1972. xii, 561 p.

ISBN 0670229113

1. Violence 2. Vandalism 3. Gay men 4. Honeymoons 5. Men/women relations 6. Great Britain -- Social life and customs -- 20th century 7. Short stories 8. Literary fiction

LC 73002334

Forty stories by the popular British novelist show his mastery of narrative, suspense, and atmosphere.

Greene, Graham, 1904-1991

* The **end** of the affair / Graham Greene. Penguin, 2004, c1951. 192 p.

ISBN 0142437980

1. Love triangles 2. Extramarital affairs 3. Loss (Psychology) 4. Former lovers 5. Authors, English 6. Faith 7. Male friendship 8. Men with terminal illnesses 9. World War II 10. London, England 11. Psychological fiction 12. Love stories 13. Literary fiction 14. Modern classics

LC 51013559

Originally published : London : Heinemann, 1951.

The love affair between Maurice Bendix and Sarah, flourishing in the turbulent times of the London Blitz, ends when she suddenly and without explanation breaks it off. After a chance meeting rekindles his love and jealousy two years later, Bendix hires a private detective to follow Sarah, and slowly his love for her turns into an obsession.

Greene, Graham, 1904-1991

* The **heart** of the matter / Graham Greene. Penguin Books, 1999, c1948. 242 p.

ISBN 9780140283327

1. British in West Africa 2. Extramarital affairs 3. Personal conduct 4. Catholic men 5. Police -- West Africa 6. Married men 7. Widows 8. Young women -- Relations with older men 9. West Africa 10. Love stories 11. Psychological fiction 12. Literary fiction 13. Modern classics

LC 48007530

Originally published: London : Heinemann, 1948.

James Tait Black Memorial Prize for Fiction, 1948.

Scobie, a police officer serving in a war-time West African state, is distrusted, being scrupulously honest and immune to bribery. But then he falls in love, and in doing so he is forced to betray everything he believes in, with drastic and tragic consequences.

Greene, Graham, 1904-1991

The **honorary** consul / Graham Greene. Simon and Schuster, 1973. 315 p.

ISBN 9780671215699

1. Hostage taking -- Argentina 2. Diplomats 3. International intrigue 4. Physicians 5. Political science 6. Betrayal 7. Extramarital affairs 8. Brothels 9. Ethics 10. Personal conduct 11. Argentina 12. Paraguay

13. Thrillers and suspense 14. Literary fiction 15. Modern classics

LC 73005254

Book made into a movie called Beyond the limit.

Although Paraguayan revolutionaries make the mistake of kidnapping the British Consul instead of the American Ambassador, they continue to threaten violence.

Greene, Graham, 1904-1991

* The **human** factor / Graham Greene. Knopf, 1992, c1978. 338 p.

ISBN 9780679409922

1. Spies -- Great Britain 2. Double agents 3. Interracial marriage 4. Defectors 5. Intelligence service -- Great Britain 6. Betrayal 7. Cold War 8. International intrigue 9. Fear 10. Apartheid 11. Police 12. Families 13. Loneliness in men 14. South Africans in England 15. Defection 16. Spy fiction 17. Literary fiction

Originally published: London : The Bodley Head, 1978.

The senior officers of Britain's secret service move to plug a leak by eliminating a junior colleague, unmindful of a veteran intelligence processor whose decency, courage, and capacity for love threaten all security.

Greene, Graham, 1904-1991

The **last** word and other stories / Graham Greene. Penguin Books, 1999, c1990. vii, 149 p.

ISBN 0141181575

1. Spies 2. Human nature 3. Senior men 4. People with amnesia 5. Christianity 6. Great Britain -- Social life and customs -- 20th century 7. Short stories 8. Literary fiction

LC 99200035

"Collection of stories dating from 1923-89, of which only four have appeared before in book form and none of which are included in Collected short stories, published in 1972"--Pref.

"This modest volume gathers uncollected stories from the entire range of Greene's career. The earliest dates from 1923 (!) and the latest from 1989." Library Journal.

Greene, Graham, 1904-1991

Our man in Havana / Graham Greene ; introduction by Christopher Hitchens. Penguin, 2007, c1958. 247 p.

ISBN 9780142438008

1. Single fathers 2. Intelligence service -- Great Britain 3. Spies -- Great Britain 4. Fathers and daughters 5. British in Cuba 6. Divorced men 7. Vacuum cleaner sales personnel 8. Classism 9. International intrigue 10. Seventeen-year-old girls 11. Supplementary employment 12. Dishonesty 13. Havana, Cuba 14. Satirical fiction 15. Spy fiction

"This edition first published by Collector's Library 2015"--Title page verso.

Originally published: New York : Viking Press, 1958.

Follows the plight of Wormold, a former vacuum cleaner salesman, who becomes a slave to the expensive whims of his thirteen-year-old daughter, Milly, and takes on a job for MI6 as Secret Agent 5920015 to pay for them.

Greene, Graham, 1904-1991

The **power** and the glory / Graham Greene. Viking Press, 1990, c1940. xviii, 295 p.

ISBN 9780670835362

1. Catholic Church Clergy. 2. 1930s 3. Religious persecution -- Mexico 4. Priests -- Mexico 5. Faith (Christianity) 6. Faith in men 7. Alcoholic priests 8. Personal conduct 9. Catholics 10. Mexico -- History -- 20th century 11. Literary fiction 12. Modern classics

Movies inspired by this book are: The fugitive and The power and the glory.

Originally published: London : W. Heinemann, 1940.

The time is 1938 and the place is one of Mexico's southern states. They are undergoing a religious purge, arresting every Catholic priest they can find, charging them with treason and then killing them in a firing squad. Those that aren't caught get married or go into hiding. One such priest has tried to escape through the jungles, villages, and plantations. A policeman is after him and shooting a hostage in each village until someone turns in the priest.

Greene, Graham, 1904-1991

* The **.quiet** American / Graham Greene ; text and criticism edited by John Clark Pratt. Penguin Books, 1996, c1955. 515 p.

ISBN 014024350X

1. 1950s 2. Love triangles 3. Americans in Vietnam 4. War correspondents -- Great Britain 5. British in Vietnam 6. Husband and wife 7. Extramarital affairs 8. Disillusionment in men 9. Communism 10. Drug traffic 11. Ethics 12. Fanaticism 13. Idealism 14. Vietnam 15. Indochina -- History -- War for national liberation, 1946-1954 16. Political fiction 17. War stories 18. Psychological fiction 19. Literary fiction 20. Historical fiction 21. Modern classics

LC 95023183

Originally published in 1955.

This novel is a study of New World hope and innocence set in an Old World of violence. The scene is Saigon in the violent years when the French were desperately trying to hold their footing in the Far East. The principal characters are a skeptical British journalist, his attractive Vietnamese mistress, and an eager young American sent out by Washington on a mysterious mission.

"Mr. Greene has always been a master of suspense, and the particular excellence of 'The Quiet American' lies in the way in which he builds up the situation finally to explode the moral problem which for him lies at the heart of the matter." Times Literary Supplement.

Greene, Graham, 1904-1991

The **tenth** man / Graham Greene. Simon and Schuster, 1985. 157 p.

ISBN 9780671507947

1. 1940s 2. Rich men -- France 3. World War II -- Prisoners and prisons, German 4. Cowardice in men 5. Shame in men 6. Good and evil 7. Lawyers 8. France -- History -- German occupation, 1940-1945 9. Psychological fiction 10. Literary fiction

LC 84029830

This recently recovered novel, written in 1944, focuses on Jean-Louis Charlot, who returns to his home after a four-year absence knowing that strangers live there and that one moment of panic has cost him the right to call it his own.

"A fatal series of events follows, entwining narrative excitement with broader questions of identity, fate, and morality. As always with Greene, the basic plot is heightened by the novelist's compelling view of the human condition." Library Journal.

Greenfeld, Karl Taro, 1964-

True / Karl Taro Greenfeld. Amazon Pub, 2018 225 p.

ISBN 9781542046831

1. Soccer 2. Teenage girls 3. Soccer players 4. Brothers and sisters of children with autism 5. Family and death 6. Family problems 7. Mothers -- Death 8. Ambition in girls 9. Los Angeles, California 10. Coming-of-age stories

After her mother passes away, True, who only feels free from anxiety when she's playing soccer, must balance caring for her autistic sister

and grieving father with realizing her dream of being the greatest soccer player of her generation.

Greengrass, Jessie, 1982-

Sight : a novel / Jessie Greengrass. Hogarth, 2018 198 p.

ISBN 9780525574606

1. Motherhood 2. Mother and child 3. Identity (Psychology) 4. Loss (Psychology) 5. Grief 6. Mothers -- Death 7. Literary fiction

LC 2017060526

Shortlisted for the James Tait Black Memorial Prize for Fiction, 2018

Shortlisted for The Women's Prize for Fiction, 2018.

A first novel by an award-winning writer draws on the history of psychoanalysis and the origins of modern surgery to explore the complexities and poignant birth-and-death cycles of being a child, choosing to become a parent and letting go.

Greenidge, Kaitlyn

We love you, Charlie Freeman : a novel / Kaitlyn Greenidge. Algonquin Books of Chapel Hill, 2016. 368 p.

ISBN 9781616204679

1. Families 2. Sign language 3. Human-animal relationships 4. Chimpanzees 5. African American families 6. Human-animal communication 7. Teenage girls 8. Race relations 9. Massachusetts 10. Coming-of-age stories 11. Literary fiction 12. African American fiction

LC 2015031336

An African-American, sign-language-fluent family is hired by a private research institute?with a shocking, secret past?to teach sign language to a chimpanzee who will live as part of their household.

"A vivid and poignant coming-of-age story that is also an important exploration of family, race, and history." Kirkus.

Greenwell, Garth

Cleanness / Garth Greenwell. Farrar, Straus and Giroux, 2020. 208 p.

ISBN 9780374124588

1. Gay men -- Sexuality 2. Teachers 3. Americans in Eastern Europe 4. Intimacy (Psychology) 5. Sexual attraction 6. Sex customs 7. Desire in men 8. Memories 9. Options, alternatives, choices 10. Men/men relations 11. Bulgaria 12. LGBTQIA fiction 13. Psychological fiction 14. Literary fiction

LC 2019028457

Sequel to: What belongs to you.

In a follow-up to What Belongs to You, set in Sofia, Bulgaria?a landlocked city in Southern Europe?an American teacher grapples with the intimate encounters that have marked his years abroad as he prepares to leave the place he's come to call home.

"Greenwell's writing on language, desire, and sex in all their complex choreography vibrates with intensity, reading like brainwaves and heartbeats as much as words." Booklist.

Greenwell, Garth

What belongs to you : a novel / Garth Greenwell. Farrar, Straus and Giroux, 2015. 208 p. What belongs to you

ISBN 9780374288228

1. Men/men relations 2. Obsession 3. Gay men 4. Self-destructive behavior 5. Americans in Bulgaria 6. Intimacy (Psychology) 7. Sex workers 8. Obsession in men 9. Sexual attraction 10. Desire in men 11. Memories 12. Bulgaria 13. LGBTQIA fiction 14. Psychological fiction 15. Literary fiction

LC 2015003932

"Part one of 'What Belongs to You' was originally published in a very different form as a novella, 'Mitko', in June 2011 by the Miami University Press"--Title page verso.

Sequel: Cleanness.

Shortlisted for the James Tait Black Memorial Prize for Fiction, 2016

Pen/Faulkner Award Finalist, 2017

Drawn by hunger, loneliness, and risk, an American teacher embarks on a sexual relationship with a young hustler and discovers that desire has far-reaching consequences when he is forced to grapple with his own fraught history and that of the lover with whom he is obsessed.

"The book breaks up the adult protagonists story with a long middle section devoted to exploring the professors difficult childhood, as well as his first love, and it is here that the mans struggles--sexual and emotional--come alive." Publishers Weekly.

Greenwood, Kerry

Death by water / Kerry Greenwood. Poisoned Pen Press, 2008, c2005. 259 p. Phryne Fisher mysteries

ISBN 9781590582398

1. 1920s 2. Women amateur detectives 3. Pleasure cruises 4. Jewelry theft 5. Jewel thieves 6. Melbourne, Victoria 7. Australia 8. Historical mysteries 9. Mysteries

LC 2008923264

Sequel to: Queen of the flowers.

Sequel: Murder in the dark.

Originally published: Crows Nest, N.S.W. : Allen & Unwin, 2005.

With a series of jewelry thefts targeting the first-class passengers on P&O ocean liners, the powers-that-be ask Phryne Fisher to mingle with the upper classes to solve a case of theft on the S.S. Hinemoa, during a luxury cruise to New Zealand.

"While memories of the Titanic linger among the ships passengers, readers are treated to descriptions of sumptuous meals and snippets of Maori lore, along with a tantalizing mystery. Those who long to revel in a glamorous if imperfect past will be satisfied." Publishers Weekly.

Greenwood, Kerry

Out of the Black Land / Kerry Greenwood. Poisoned Pen Press, 2013. 250 p.

ISBN 9781464200380

1. Nefertiti,, Queen of Egypt, 14th cent BC 2. Akhenaten,, King of Egypt 3. Ancient Egypt (3100 BCE-640 CE) 4. Political intrigue 5. Women priests 6. Rulers 7. Scribes 8. Ancient Egypt -- Civilization -- To 332 BC 9. Historical mysteries

Appointed by a dream-plagued young pharaoh to the unwanted position of Great Royal Scribe, peasant boy Ptah-hotep finds himself surrounded by envious rivals; while the beautiful Nefertiti participates in a shocking scheme to bear children to an impotent king; and zealous monotheist Akhnaten plots to suppress the worship of all other gods in the Black Land.

Greenwood, Kerry

Unnatural habits / Kerry Greenwood. Poisoned Pen Press, 2013, c2012. 250 p. Phryne Fisher mysteries

ISBN 9781464201233

1. 1920s 2. Missing persons 3. Teenage pregnancy 4. Women journalists 5. Women amateur detectives 6. Human trafficking 7. Human trafficking victims 8. Child trafficking 9. Child trafficking victims 10. Australia 11. Historical mysteries 12. Mysteries

Sequel to: Dead man's chest.

Sequel: Murder and Mendelssohn.

Originally published: 2012.

In 1929 Melbourne, Australia, three unmarried pregnant girls working at a convent laundry go missing weeks before they are due to give birth -- and then an ambitious reporter, Polly Kettle, who was investigating the girls' whereabouts, disappears, too. It's a good thing for them all that brave, intelligent Honourable Miss Phryne Fisher, who'd just met Polly, decides to sort it all out. Phryne, who's wealthy, glamorous, and a good shot, uses her skills and connections to solve a case that is dark at its core. Unnatural Habits is part of a fun, vibrant flapper-era series, which inspired the Australian TV program Miss Fisher's Murder Mysteries. - Description by Dawn Towery.

Greenwood, T. (Tammy),

Rust & stardust / T. Greenwood. St. Martin's Press, 2018. 336 p.

ISBN 9781250164193

1. Horner, Sally 2. 1940s 3. Girl kidnapping victims 4. Former convicts 5. Child abusers 6. Eleven-year-old girls 7. Deception 8. Child abuse 9. Sex crimes 10. Consequences 11. Historical fiction

LC 2018001891

Traces the story of the 11-year-old kidnapping victim whose 1948 abduction inspired Nabokov's *Lolita*, recreating in chilling detail Sally Horner's exploitation and assault by predatory former inmate Frank LaSalle.

Greer, Andrew Sean

The **impossible** lives of Greta Wells / Andrew Sean Greer. Ecco, 2013. 304 p.

ISBN 9780062213785

1. Electric shock therapy 2. Time travel (Past) 3. Loss (Psychology) 4. Parallel universes 5. Identity (Psychology) 6. Reincarnation 7. Family relationships 8. Men/women relations 9. Options, alternatives, choices 10. San Francisco, California 11. Psychological suspense 12. Literary fiction

"After the death of her beloved twin brother, Felix, and the breakup with her longtime lover, Nathan, Greta Wells embarks on a radical psychiatric treatment to alleviate her suffocating depression. But the treatment has unexpected effects, and Greta finds herself transported to the lives she might have had if she'd been born in different eras."--from publisher's description.

"Philosophically intriguing as well as gorgeously imagined and executed, this novel will catch fire with the same audience that propelled Audrey Niffeneggers The Time Travelers Wife (2003) to the top of the best-seller list." Booklist.

Greer, Andrew Sean

* **Less** / Andrew Sean Greer. Lee Boudreaux Books/Little, Brown and Company, 2017. 263 p.

ISBN 9780316316125

1. Americans in foreign countries 2. Middle-aged men 3. Gay men 4. Birthdays 5. Authors 6. Former boyfriends 7. Voyages and travels 8. Memories 9. Men/women relations 10. LGBTQIA fiction 11. Romantic comedies 12. Literary fiction

ALA Notable Book, 2018.

Australian Book Industry Awards, International Book of the Year, 2019.

Librarians' Choice (Australia), 2018.

Pulitzer Prize for Fiction, 2018.

Longlisted for the Andrew Carnegie Medal for Excellence in Fiction, 2018.

Receiving an invitation to his ex-boyfriend's wedding, Arthur, a failed novelist on the eve of his 50th birthday, embarks on an international journey that finds him falling in love, risking his life, reinventing himself and making connections with the past.

Greer, Robert O.

* First of state / Robert Greer. North Atlantic Books, 2010. 400 p. C. J. Floyd mysteries

ISBN 9781556439155

1. 1970s 2. African American men 3. Murder investigation 4. Stealing 5. Automobile license plates 6. Vietnam veterans 7. Post-traumatic stress disorder 8. African American bail bond agents 9. Bounty hunters 10. Depression 11. Denver, Colorado 12. Mysteries 13. African American fiction

LC 2010020235

It is 1972 and CJ returns from Vietnam with PTSD, but quickly befriends a fellow vet and collector of western memorabilia; however, the friend and a mysterious Chinese man are soon found murdered, prompting CJ to take on the first case of his life.

"This prequel to Greer's always thoughtful and multilayered Floyd series reveals the pain behind the protagonist's curmudgeonly, emotionally guarded personality and his reluctance to employ violence. CJ Floyd is one of crime fiction's hidden gems, and this is a satisfying entry in a rewarding, underappreciated series." Booklist.

Gregory, Daryl

Afterparty / Daryl Gregory. Tor Books, 2014. 320 p.

ISBN 9780765336927

1. Mental illness 2. Drug control 3. Near future 4. Lesbians 5. Prisons 6. Drug industry and trade 7. Religious awakening 8. Drug addiction 9. Drug abuse 10. Visions 11. Medical thrillers 12. Science fiction

LC 2013025194

When a girl who was addicted to a drug she helped develop dies in a detention facility, Lyda Rose, a scientist and patient at the same facility, receives help from an imaginary, drug-induced doctor to make things right while finding the other survivors of her development team.

"This taut, brisk, gripping narrative, dazzlingly intercut with flashbacks and sidebars, oozes warmth and wit. A hugely entertaining, surprising and perhaps prophetic package." Kirkus.

Gregory, Daryl

The **devil's** alphabet / Daryl Gregory. Ballantine Books, 2009. 384 p.

ISBN 9780345501172

1. Small town life -- Tennessee 2. Mutants 3. Secrets 4. Syndromes 5. Human evolution 6. Murder 7. Retroviruses 8. Tennessee 9. Mysteries 10. Horror

Returning to his small hometown in the aftermath of a neighbor's suicide, Paxton Martin remembers how the community was radically transformed by a mysterious retrovirus that mutated many of its survivors, a seemingly short-lived incident that he discovers has caused additional changes.

"Small-town peace and quiet are turned upside-down when Transcription Divergence Syndrome (TDS) kills a third of the inhabitants of Switchcreek, Tennessee, and transforms most of the rest into mutants: argos (gray-skinned giants), betas (seal-like people whose women get pregnant spontaneously), and charlies (the morbidly obese whose males leak a narcotic called the vintage). One of the few unaffected is 14-year-old Paxton Martin. After losing his mother and watching his father (a charlie) hideously changed by the disease, Paxton leaves for Chicago. Fifteen years later, following news of a friend's death, he returns, forced to revisit the horror of his previous life and to solve a murder. The larger question, of what eventually might become of these evolutionary exiles as they move into second and third generations, seems to move us back into Theodore Sturgeon territory, and it's fortunately a territory that Gregory has mastered well. The novel's quiet ending, in a snowbound South Dakota winter, is haunting." Locus Magazine.

Gregory, Daryl

We are all completely fine / Daryl Gregory. Tachyon Publications, 2014. 192 p.

ISBN 9781616961718

1. Supernatural 2. Good and evil 3. Victims 4. Survival 5. Psychotherapists 6. Support groups 7. Paranormal phenomena 8. Interpersonal relations 9. Horror

A group of outcasts with questionable states of mental health--including Stan, who was partially eaten by cannibals, and Greta, who may be a mass-murdering arsonist--are sought by a psychotherapist to uncover internal and external monsters.

"Blending the stark realism of pain and isolation with the liberating force of the fantastic, Gregory (Afterparty) makes it easy to believe that the world is an illusion, behind which lurks an alternative truthdark, degenerate, and sublime." Publishers Weekly.

Gregory, Philippa

The **Boleyn** inheritance / Philippa Gregory. Touchstone, 2006. 416 p. Tudor novels (Philippa Gregory)

ISBN 0743272501

1. Boleyn, Jane,, Viscountess Rochford, d 1542 2. Henry VIII,, King of England, 1491-1547 3. Anne,, of Cleves, Queen, consort of Henry VIII, King of England, 1515-1557 4. Catherine Howard,, Queen, consort of Henry VIII, King of England, d 1542 5. Boleyn family 6. Tudor period (1485-1603) 7. 16th century 8. Marriages of royalty and nobility -- Great Britain 9. Courts and courtiers 10. Ladies-in-waiting 11. Nobility 12. Ambition 13. Jealousy in women 14. Men/women relations 15. Husband and wife 16. Divorce -- History 17. Great Britain -- History -- Henry VIII, 1509-1547 18. Biographical fiction 19. Historical fiction

An only survivor of the ambitious Boleyn family, lady-in-waiting Jane Boleyn testifies against Henry VIII's latest queen, Anne of Cleves, and conspires to place her young cousin, Katherine Howard, on the throne.

"Rich in intrigue and irony, this is a tale where readers will already know who was divorced, beheaded or survived, but will savor Gregory's sharp staging of how and why." Publishers Weekly.

Gregory, Philippa

The **constant** princess / Philippa Gregory. Simon & Schuster, 2005. 400 p. Tudor novels (Philippa Gregory)

ISBN 074327248X

1. Catharine,, of Aragon, Queen, consort of Henry VIII, King of England, 1485-1536 2. Arthur,, Prince of Wales, 1486-1502 3. Henry VIII,, King of England, 1491-1547 4. Henry VII,, King of England, 1457-1509 5. Ferdinand V,, King of Spain, 1452-1516 6. Isabella I,, Queen of Spain, 1451-1504 7. Tudor period (1485-1603) 8. 16th century 9. Renaissance (1300-1600) 10. Marriages of royalty and nobility -- Great Britain 11. Catholic women 12. Determination in women 13. Widows 14. Brothers 15. Spaniards in England 16. Courts and courtiers 17. Married men -- Death 18. Nobility 19. Extramarital affairs 20. Love triangles 21. Men/women relations 22. Husband and wife 23. Arranged marriage 24. Faith in women 25. Great Britain -- History -- Henry VII, 1485-1509 26. Great Britain -- History -- Henry VIII, 1509-1547 27. Spain -- History -- 15th century 28. Spain -- History -- Arab period, 711-1492 29. Biographical fiction 30. Historical fiction

LC 2005052303

"A Touchstone book."

"I am Catalina, Princess of Spain, daughter of the two greatest monarchs the world has ever known ... and I will be Queen of England." Thus, bestselling author Philippa Gregory introduces one of her most unforgettable heroines: Katherine of Aragon. Daughter of Queen Isabella and King Ferdinand of Spain, Katherine has been fated her whole life to marry Prince Arthur of England. When they meet and are married, the match becomes as passionate as it is politically expedient.

Gregory, Philippa

The **kingmaker's** daughter / Philippa Gregory. Simon & Schuster, 2012. 432 p. Cousins' war

ISBN 9781451626070

1. Edward IV,, King of England, 1442-1483 2. Neville, Richard,, Earl of Warwick, 1428-1471 3. Medieval period (476-1492) 4. Plantagenet period (1154-1485) 5. Conspiracies -- Great Britain 6. Ambition in men 7. Fathers and daughters -- Great Britain 8. Power (Social sciences) 9. Royal houses 10. Marriage 11. War -- History 12. Ambition 13. Great Britain -- History -- Edward IV, 1461-1483 14. Historical fiction 15. Biographical fiction

Presents a tale inspired by the daughters of "Kingmaker" Richard, 15th-century Earl of Warwick, who uses his daughters as political pawns before their strategic marriages place them on opposing sides in a royal war that will cost them everyone they love.

Gregory, Philippa

The **lady** of the rivers / Philippa Gregory. Simon & Schuster, 2011. 448 p. Cousins' war

ISBN 9781416563709

1. Henry VI,, King of England, 1421-1471 2. Joan of Arc,, Saint, 1412-1431 3. Ambition 4. Greed 5. Women psychics 6. Wars of the Roses, 1455-1485 7. Loyalty 8. Power (Social sciences) 9. Royal houses 10. Marriage 11. Widows 12. Independence in women 13. Inheritance and succession 14. Great Britain -- History -- Henry VI, 1422-1461 15. Great Britain -- History -- Wars of the Roses, 1455-1485 16. Historical fiction 17. Biographical fiction

The duchess--kin to half the crowned heads of Europe and mother of England's White Queen--walks a perilous path through the battle lines of the tumultuous War of the Roses.

Gregory, Philippa

The **last** Tudor / Philippa Gregory. Simon & Schuster, 2017 432 p. Cousins' war

ISBN 9781476758763

1. Grey, Jane,, Lady, 1537-1554 2. Mary I,, Queen of England, 1516-1558 3. Hertford, Katherine Seymour,, Countess of, 1540-1568 4. Tudor period (1485-1603) 5. 16th century 6. Inheritance and succession 7. Religious persecution 8. Women rulers 9. Executions and executioners 10. Courts and courtiers 11. Political corruption 12. Politicians 13. Nobility 14. Power (Social sciences) 15. Royal houses 16. Great Britain -- History -- Mary I, 1553-1558 17. England -- History -- 16th century 18. Great Britain -- History -- Tudors, 1485-1603 19. Historical fiction 20. Biographical fiction

Reimagines the lives of Lady Jane Grey and her two sisters, who respectively endure imprisonment, a secret marriage and marginalization under the suspicious eyes of Tudor queens Mary and Elizabeth.

Gregory, Philippa

The **other** Boleyn girl : a novel / Philippa Gregory. Scribner Paperback Fiction, 2002, c2001. 664 p. Tudor novels (Philippa Gregory)

ISBN 9780743227445

1. Boleyn, Mary, 1508-1543 2. Anne Boleyn,, Queen, consort of Henry VIII, King of England, 1507-1536 3. Henry VIII,, King of England, 1491-1547 4. Catharine,, of Aragon, Queen, consort of Henry VIII, King of England, 1485-1536 5. Boleyn family 6. Tudor period (1485-1603) 7. Mistresses 8. Nobility 9. Sibling rivalry 10. Ambition 11. Brothers and sisters 12. Sisters 13. Marriages of royalty and nobility -- Great Britain 14. Courts and courtiers 15. Extramarital affairs 16. Great Britain -- History -- Henry VIII, 1509-1547 17. Biographical fiction 18. Historical fiction

LC 2001057646

The daughters of a ruthlessly ambitious family, Mary and Anne Boleyn are sent to the court of Henry VIII to attract the attention of the king, who first takes Mary as his mistress, in which role she bears him an illegitimate son, and then Anne as his wife.

"This is as much a tale of love and lust as it is a saga about an ambitious family who used their kin as negotiable assets. . . . Absorbing tale of a Renaissance family determined to climb as high as they can, whatever the cost." Kirkus.

Gregory, Philippa

The **red** queen : a novel / Philippa Gregory. Simon & Schuster, 2010. 382 p. Cousins' war

ISBN 9781416563723

1. Beaufort, Margaret,, Countess of Richmond and Derby, 1443-1509 2. Henry VII,, King of England, 1457-1509 3. Medieval period (476-1492) 4. Plantagenet period (1154-1485) 5. Ambition 6. Power (Social sciences) 7. Conspiracies 8. Widows 9. Deception 10. Wars of the Roses, 1455-1485 11. Inheritance and succession 12. Revenge 13. Royal houses 14. Marriage 15. Success (Concept) 16. Great Britain -- History -- Edward IV, 1461-1483 17. Great Britain -- History -- House of York, 1461-1485 18. Great Britain -- History -- Richard III, 1483-1485 19. Great Britain -- History -- Wars of the Roses, 1455-1485 20. Historical fiction 21. Biographical fiction

Determined to see her son Henry on the throne of England, pious Margaret Beaufort arranges politically advantageous marriages, sends her son out of the country for his safety and lays secret plans for a battle between the houses of York and Lancaster.

Gregory, Philippa

The **taming** of the queen / Philippa Gregory. Touchstone, 2015. 432 p.

ISBN 9781476758794

1. Catharine Parr,, Queen, consort of Henry VIII, King of England, 1512-1548 2. Henry VIII,, King of England, 1491-1547 3. Tudor period (1485-1603) 4. 16th century 5. Women rulers 6. Forced marriage 7. Royal houses 8. Widows 9. Independence in women 10. Murderers 11. Great Britain -- History -- Henry VIII, 1509-1547 12. Biographical fiction 13. Historical fiction

LC 2015018375

Reimagines the story of Henry VIII's sixth wife, Kateryn Parr, who after being forced to marry the king, struggles against dangerous adversaries to observe her own faith and promote religious reforms.

"Tracing Kateryn's path to intellectual independence requires more religious discussion than some readers will prefer, but Gregory's portrait of the complex, aging king and his sensual, scholarly bride will satisfy Tudor enthusiasts." Publishers Weekly.

Gregory, Philippa

* **Tidelands** / Philippa Gregory. Atria Books, 2019. 480 p. Fairmile novels

ISBN 9781501187155

1. Stuart period (1603-1714) 2. English Civil War, 1642-1649 3. Women healers 4. Independence in women 5. Midwives 6. Priests 7. Father-deserted families 8. Superstition 9. Social classes 10. Power (Social sciences) 11. Puritans 12. Men/women relations 13. Family relationships 14. Great Britain -- History -- Civil War, 1642-1649 15. England -- Social life and customs -- 17th century 16. Historical fiction 17. Family sagas

LC 2019005706

During England's 17th century civil war, Alinor, a woman without a husband and skilled with herbs, helps a young man on the run and unwittingly brings disaster into the heart of her life.

Gregory, Philippa

The **white** princess / Philippa Gregory. Simon & Schuster, 2013. 400 p. Cousins' war

ISBN 9781451626094

1. Elizabeth,, Queen, consort of Henry VII, King of England, 1465-1503 2. Medieval period (476-1492) 3. Plantagenet period (1154-1485) 4. Arranged marriage 5. Lovers 6. Rulers 7. Ambition 8. Loyalty 9. Power (Social sciences) 10. Royal houses 11. Marriage 12. War -- History 13. Great Britain -- History -- Edward IV, 1461-1483 14. Historical fiction 15. Biographical fiction

Passionately in love with Richard III in spite of her arranged marriage to pretender to the throne Henry Tudor, Princess Elizabeth of York is forced to marry the man who murdered her lover and create a royal family.

Grenville, Kate, 1950-

The **idea** of perfection / Kate Grenville. Viking, 2002, c1999. 401 p.

ISBN 9780670030804

1. Small town life -- New South Wales 2. Men/women relations 3. Wilderness areas 4. Middle-aged women 5. Women museum curators 6. Divorced men 7. Engineers 8. Middle-aged men 9. New South Wales 10. Australia 11. Literary fiction

LC 200158133

Originally published: Sydney : Picador, 1999.

Orange Prize for Fiction, 2001.

The story of an unlikely romance in the Australian bush between Douglas Cheesman, a shy and awkward engineer, and Harley Savage, a plain, large-boned woman who works as a museum curator.

"Grenville does her characters the honor of taking their pain seriously and is gracious enough to allow them their hard-earned pleasure. Her ability to move between these elements gives her novel a beautiful balance." New York Times Book Review.

Grenville, Kate, 1950-

The **lieutenant** / Kate Grenville. Atlantic Monthly Press, 2009, c2008. 307 p.

ISBN 9780802119162

1. Colonial Australia (1788-1901) 2. Astronomers 3. Aboriginal Australians -- Relations with whites -- 18th century 4. British in Australia 5. Misfits (Persons) 6. Colonialism 7. Interracial communication 8. Astronomical observatories 9. Indigenous peoples -- Relations with missionaries, traders, etc 10. Indigenous peoples' rights 11. Friendship 12. Australia -- History -- 1788-1851 13. Historical fiction

Previously published: 2008.

Originally published: Melbourne, Vic. : Text Pub., 2008.

In 1787 Lieutenant Thomas Rooke, officer and astronomer, sets sail from Portsmouth with the First Fleet and its cargo of convicts destined for New South Wales. As the newcomers struggle to establish a settlement, Rooke comes to know the aboriginal people and forges a remarkable connection with one child which will change his life in ways he never imagined. Based on real events.

"Grenvilles thematic relentlessness can be stultifying, but the honest beauty of her story wins out." The New Yorker.

Grenville, Kate, 1950-

Sarah Thornhill / Kate Grenville. Grove Press, 2011. 307 p.

ISBN 9780802120243

1. Colonial Australia (1788-1901) 2. Young women 3. Family secrets 4. Families -- History 5. Multiracial persons 6. Postcolonialism 7. Sealing 8. Men/women relations 9. Australia -- Race relations 10. New Zealand -- History -- 19th century 11. Australia -- History -- 19th century 12. Hawkesbury River (New South Wales) 13. New South Wales 14. Historical fiction 15. Love stories

Sequel to: The secret river

Originally published: Melbourne, Vic. : Text Publishing, 2011.

Australian Book Industry Awards, General Fiction Book of the Year, 2012.

Sarah is the youngest child of William Thornhill, an uneducated ex-convict from London who has built his fortune on the blood of Aboriginal people. With a fine stone house and plenty of money, Thornhill has re-invented himself. As he tells his daughter, he "never looks back," and Sarah grows up learning not to ask about the past. Instead her eyes are on handsome Jack Langland, whom she's loved since she was a child. Their romance seems destined, but the ugly secret in Sarah's family is poised to ambush them both.

Grenville, Kate, 1950-

The **secret** river / Kate Grenville. Canongate U.S., 2006. 352 p.

ISBN 9781841957975

1. Colonial Australia (1788-1901) 2. Exiles -- Great Britain 3. Criminals 4. Prisoners 5. Penal colonies -- Australia 6. Serfdom 7. Indigenous peoples -- Relations with missionaries, traders, etc 8. Indigenous peoples -- Land rights 9. Indigenous peoples' rights 10. Colonized peoples 11. Squatter settlements 12. Land tenure 13. Ethics 14. Remorse 15. New South Wales -- History -- 19th century 16. Australia -- History -- 19th century 17. Historical fiction 18. Literary fiction

ALA Notable Book, 2007.

Australian Book Industry Awards, Literary Fiction Book of the Year, 2006.

Nielsen BookData Australian Booksellers' Choice Award, 2006.

Shortlisted for the Man Booker Prize, 2006.

Shortlisted for the Miles Franklin Literary Award, 2006

Moving between the slums of nineteenth-century London and the convict colonies of Australia, a compelling historical novel chronicles the lives and fortunes of the early pioneers of New South Wales, in a volume based on the author's own family history.

"[A]n unflinching exploration of modern Australia's origins. Like the settlers, we instinctively turn away from the ugly truths behind every cleared riverbank and every posted fence. But Grenville's psychological acuity, and the sheer gorgeousness of her descriptions of the territory being fought over, pulls us ever deeper into a time when one community's opportunity spelled another's doom." The New Yorker.

Grey, Zane, 1872-1939

* **Riders** of the purple sage / Zane Grey. Penguin Books, 1990. 280 p.

ISBN 0140184406

1. Texas Rangers 2. Outlaws -- Texas 3. Women ranchers 4. Gunfighters 5. Mormon women 6. Polygamy 7. Utah 8. Westerns

LC 89-29702

Collected with The Rainbow Trail and Desert Gold in an omnibus entitled Western Colors by Forge, 2014.

Released in one volume with The Rainbow Trail in 2015 by Tor Books. ISBN 9780765382399.

First published 1912 by Harper & Brothers.

Refusing to marry the grim, brutal Elder Tull, Jane Withersteen is dismayed when her Utah ranch and hired hands are targeted in retaliation, and the mysterious gunfighter Lassiter offers Jane protection and a chance at love.

"Well handled melodramatic story of hairbreadth escapes from Mormon vengeance in southwestern Utah in 1871." Booklist.

Grey, Zane, 1872-1939

West of the Pecos / Zane Grey. Grosset, 1937. 314 p.

1. Westerns

Colonel Terrill is brutally murdered, and Pecos Smith rides to rescue his daughter from the desperados.

Grey, Zane, 1872-1939

Woman of the frontier : a western story / Zane Grey. Five Star, 1998. 320 p.

ISBN 0786211563

1. Frontier and pioneer life 2. Abandoned girls 3. Apache Indians 4. Families 5. Homesteaders 6. Husband and wife 7. Multiracial boys 8. Parent and child 9. Rape victims 10. Arizona (Territory) 11. Westerns

LC 9822717

Details the harsh realities of frontier life in the story of a former Army scout and his wife, settling in central Arizona, where they deal with oppressive loneliness, the wife's rape, and their twenty-year struggle to achieve prosperity

"This tale, written in 1934, was rejected by magazines because of its vivid portrayal of the hardships of pioneer life, including the rape of Grey's heroine by a renegade Apache. A heavily edited version called 30,000 on the Hoof was finally published in 1940, a year after the author's death. This version, completely restored by Grey's son, Loren, recounts the trials and tribulations of Arizona rancher Logan Huett, his heroic wife, Lucinda, their three sons, and a girl named Barbara, who is abandoned by wagon-train travelers and raised by the Huetts." Booklist.

Griffin, Anne, 1969-

When all is said : a novel / Anne Griffin. Thomas Dunne Books, 2019. 352 p.

ISBN 9781250200587

1. Senior men 2. Life change events 3. Reminiscing in old age 4. Options, alternatives, choices 5. Loss (Psychology) 6. Parent and child 7. Octogenarians 8. Memories 9. Families 10. Secrets 11. Toasts 12. Ireland 13. Psychological fiction 14. Domestic fiction

LC 2018041302

An 84-year-old loner, sitting at a grand hotel bar in Ireland, toasts the five people who have meant the most to him while recalling unspoken losses and joys, a tragic secret and a fierce love.

"Newcomer Griffin's storytelling, while economical, is rich and evocative, and her deft pacing maintains suspense across several narrative arcs spanning multiple time lines...Highly recommended; this unforgettable first novel introduces Griffin as a writer to watch." Library Journal.

Griffin, Kate, 1986-

The **glass** god / Kate Griffin. Little, Brown, 2013. 544 p. Magicals Anonymous

ISBN 9780316187275

1. Women shamans 2. Missing persons investigation 3. Misfits (Persons) 4. Good and evil 5. Supernatural 6. Magic 7. Support groups 8. Vampires 9. Druids and druidism 10. Banshees 11. Goblins 12. Trolls 13. London, England 14. Urban fantasy

"Sharon Li: apprentice shaman and community support officer for the magically inclined. It wasn't the career Sharon had in mind, but she's getting used to running Magicals Anonymous and learning how to Be One with the City. When the Midnight Mayor goes missing, leaving only a suspiciously innocent-looking umbrella behind him, Sharon finds herself promoted. Her first task: find the Midnight Mayor. The only clues she has are a city dryad's cryptic warning and several pairs of abandoned shoes"--, Back cover.

Griffin, Kate, 1986-

Stray souls / Kate Griffin. Orbit, 2012. 457 p. Magicals Anonymous

ISBN 9780316187268

1. Women shamans 2. Soul 3. Misfits (Persons) 4. Good and evil 5. Supernatural 6. Magic 7. Support groups 8. Vampires 9. Druids and druidism 10. Banshees 11. Goblins 12. Trolls 13. London, England 14. Urban fantasy

After discovering she is a shaman, Sharon Li starts a magical beings support group and soon learns that she and her fellow support group attendees must stop someone from stealing London's soul.

Griffith, Nicola

Hild : a novel / Nicola Griffith. Farrar, Straus and Giroux, 2013. 560 p.

ISBN 9780374280871

1. Hilda,, of Whitby, Saint, 614-680 2. Anglo-Saxon period (449-1066) 3. 7th century 4. Medieval period (476-1492) 5. Women saints 6. Civilization, Medieval 7. Bisexual women 8. Christian saints 9. Christian women 10. Leadership in women 11. Women and nature 12. England 13. Great Britain -- History -- Anglo-Saxon period, 449-1066 14. Historical fiction 15. Biographical fiction

LC 2013022510

Daughter of a poisoned prince and a crafty noblewoman, quiet, bright-minded Hild arrives at the court of King Edwin of Northumbria, where the six-year-old takes on the role of seer/consiglieri for a monarch troubled by shifting allegiances and Roman emissaries attempting to spread their new religion.

Griffiths, Elly

The **crossing** places / Elly Griffiths. Houghton Mifflin Harcourt, 2009. 304 p. Ruth Galloway mysteries

ISBN 9780547229898

1. Missing girls 2. Bogs 3. Women archaeologists 4. Detectives 5. Criminal investigation 6. Men/women relations 7. Amateur detectives 8. Women amateur detectives 9. Norfolk, England 10. Mysteries

LC 2009007006

"First published in Great Britain in 2009 by Quercus."

Edgar Allan Poe Awards: Mary Higgins Clark Award, 2011.

When a child's bones are found near an ancient henge in the wild saltmarshes of Norfolk's north coast, Ruth Galloway, a university lecturer in forensic archaeology, is asked to date them by DCI Harry Nelson who thinks they may be the bones of a child called Lucy who has been missing for ten years.

Griffiths, Elly

The **dark** angel / Elly Griffiths. Houghton Mifflin Harcourt, 2018., 336 p. Ruth Galloway mysteries

ISBN 9780544750326

1. Women archaeologists 2. Murder 3. Forensic sciences 4. Murder investigation 5. Archaeology 6. Archaeological sites 7. Detectives 8. Amateur detectives 9. Women amateur detectives 10. Italy 11.

Mysteries

LC 2017057874

Asked by archaeologist Angelo Morelli for help in identifying bones found in the tiny hilltop town of Fontana Liri in Italy, Ruth Galloway soon realizes that there is darkness lurking in this seemingly picturesque town when she discovers a link between the bones and a modern-day murder.

"A sure bet for fans of strong-minded women and wry humor in the tradition of Rhys Bowen and M. C. Beaton." Booklist.

Griffiths, Elly

A **dying** fall : a Ruth Galloway mystery / Elly Griffiths. Houghton Mifflin Harcourt, 2013, c2012. 240 p. Ruth Galloway mysteries

ISBN 9780547798165

1. Arthur,, King 2. Women archaeologists 3. Forensic sciences 4. Murder investigation 5. Universities and colleges 6. Skeleton 7. Right-wing extremists 8. Arson 9. New mothers 10. Infants 11. Detectives 12. Amateur detectives 13. Women amateur detectives 14. Lancashire, England 15. England 16. Norfolk, England 17. Mysteries

Originally published: London : Quercus, 2012.

An old friend's death sends Ruth to Lancaster to investigate an important archaeological discovery, but what she finds is a mystery that may have gotten her friend murdered.

Griffiths, Elly

* The **house** at sea's end : a Ruth Galloway mystery / Elly Griffiths. McClelland & Stewart, 2011. 356 p. Ruth Galloway mysteries

ISBN 9780771036002

1. Forensic sciences 2. New mothers 3. Skeleton 4. Women archaeologists 5. Detectives 6. Norfolk, England 7. Mysteries

"Solid characterization, believable forensic science, great atmosphere, and a mystery that stretches back decades all make this another winner from the talented Griffiths." Booklist.

Griffiths, Elly

The **Janus** stone / Elly Griffiths. Houghton Mifflin Harcourt, 2011. 336 p. Ruth Galloway mysteries

ISBN 9780547237442

1. Child murder victims 2. Criminal investigation 3. Pregnant women 4. Women archaeologists 5. Detectives 6. Amateur detectives 7. Women amateur detectives 8. Norfolk, England 9. Mysteries

LC 2010005740

Ruth Galloway is called in to investigate when builders, demolishing a large old house in Norwich to make way for a housing development, uncover the bones of a child beneath a doorway -- minus the skull. Is it some ritual sacrifice or just plain straightforward murder? DCI Harry Nelson would like to find out -- and fast. It turns out the house was once a children's home. Nelson traces the Catholic priest who used to run the home. Father Hennessey tells him that two children did go missing from the home forty years before -- a boy and a girl. They were never found. When carbon dating proves that the child's bones predate the home and relate to a time when the house was privately owned, Ruth is drawn ever more deeply into the case. But as spring turns into summer it becomes clear that someone is trying very hard to put her off the scent by frightening her half to death ...

Griffiths, Elly

The **stone** circle / Elly Griffiths. Houghton Mifflin Harcourt, 2019. 368 p. Ruth Galloway mysteries

ISBN 9781328974648

1. Women archaeologists 2. Forensic sciences 3. Murder investigation 4. Archaeological sites 5. Cold cases (Criminal investigation) 6. Stone circles 7. Skeleton 8. Letters 9. Death Threats 10. Detectives 11. Women amateur detectives 12. England 13. Great Britain 14. Police procedurals

LC 2019001733

The past returns in ominous ways when both Ruth Galloway and DCI Nelson begin receiving threatening letters from the man responsible for their partnership, Ruth's believed-dead former mentor.

"This superb series (The Dark Angel, 2018, etc.) never disappoints. Its' patented combination of mysterious circumstances, police procedure, and agonizing relationship problems will keep you reading, and feeling, all night." Kirkus.

Griffiths, Elly,

The **stranger** diaries / Elly Griffiths. Houghton Mifflin Harcourt, 2019, c2018 352 p.

ISBN 9781328577856

1. Literature teachers 2. Murder investigation 3. Women amateur detectives 4. Women 5. Authors, English 6. Small towns 7. Suspicion 8. Teachers 9. Police 10. England 11. West Sussex, England 12. Gothic fiction 13. Mysteries

LC 2018035768

Originally published: London : Quercus, 2018.

A high-school English teacher chronicles her suspicions about the murder of a colleague before discovering a sinister message in her own diary.

"Alternating among the voices of Clare, Georgia, and Det. Sgt. Harbinder Kaur, who investigates the killings, Griffiths weaves a tale replete with ghosts, the occult, forbidden desire, and murder." Publishers Weekly.

Grimes, Linda

In a fix / Linda Grimes. Tor, 2012. 320 p. Ciel Halligan novels

ISBN 9780765331809

1. Shapeshifters 2. Kidnapping 3. Rescues 4. Businesspeople 5. Vikings 6. Impersonation 7. Men/women relations 8. Matchmaking 9. Shapeshifting 10. Urban fantasy

LC 2012019453

"A Tom Doherty Associates Book."

When her current client's fiancé is kidnapped by neo-Vikings, Ciel finds herself caught between two men who play havoc with her emotions.

Grimes, Linda

Quick fix / Linda Grimes. Tor Books, 2013. 368 p. Ciel Halligan novels

ISBN 9780765331816

1. Shapeshifters 2. Impersonation 3. Genetic research 4. Zoo employees 5. Shapeshifting 6. Orangutan 7. Scientists 8. Genetics -- Experiments 9. Men/women relations 10. Urban fantasy

LC 2013017712

Aura adaptor Ciel Halligan escapes from the National Zoo with a new baby orangutan after her little sister, Molly, takes on the form of the animal and can't change herself back.

Grimes, Martha

The **Old** Wine Shades : a Richard Jury mystery / Martha Grimes. Viking, 2006. 432 p. Richard Jury mysteries

ISBN 0670034797

1. Scotland Yard. 2. Police 3. Murder 4. Missing persons investigation 5. Physicists 6. Dogs 7. Bars 8. Murder investigation 9. Missing women 10. Missing children 11. Missing boys 12. London, England 13. England 14. Mysteries

Richard Jury considers the authenticity of a fantastical tale, told by a stranger and fellow patron at the Old Wine Shades pub in London, about a string theory scientist's wife, son, and dog, who disappeared without a trace nine months earlier.

"The scheme Jury [the Scotlant Yard detective] ultimately detects is ingeniously clever and sufficiently consistent with the personalities Grimes has created to overcome disbelief." Publishers Weekly.

Grimes, Martha

The **winds** of change : a Richard Jury mystery / Martha Grimes. Viking, 2004. 432 p. Richard Jury mysteries

ISBN 0670033278

1. Scotland Yard 2. Police 3. Child murder investigation 4. Pedophiles 5. Child sexual abuse 6. Crimes against girls 7. England 8. Mysteries
LC 2004052636

Declan Scott stood inside the room looking at Jury as if he were one more disappointment in a long list of them. Police, private investigators- all had failed to find the child Flora. Brian Macalvie of the Devon and Cornwell police takes this failure especially hard.

"This Richard Jury mystery involves the murder of an anonymous five-year-old girl, shot in the back. . . . When he learns that the child was found near a house frequented by pedophiles, he's convinced there's a link. His suspicions grow stronger when the man supposedly behind the operation turns out to be the father of a child who mysteriously disappeared three years before from a country estate." Booklist.

Grindle, Lucretia W.

Villa Triste / Lucretia Grindle. Grand Central Pub, 2013, c2010. 400 p.

ISBN 9781455505371

1. World War II 2. Resistance to military occupation 3. Murder investigation 4. Betrayal 5. Crimes against seniors 6. Revenge 7. Fascists 8. Sisters 9. Women 10. Righteous Gentiles in the Holocaust 11. Police 12. Florence, Italy 13. Italy -- History -- German occupation, 1943-1945 14. Historical mysteries 15. Parallel narratives

Originally published in 2010 (London: Macmillan,c2010.)

One of Florence's most senior policemen, agrees to oversee a murder investigation, after it emerges the victim was once a Partisan hero over sixty years ago.

Grippando, James, 1958-

Black horizon / James Grippando. Harper,An Imprint of HarperCollinsPublishers, 2014. 384 p. Jack Swyteck novels

ISBN 9780062109880

1. Explosions 2. International intrigue 3. Widows 4. Honeymoons 5. Offshore oil well drilling rigs 6. Oil spills 7. Men/women relations 8. Florida Keys 9. Miami, Florida 10. Legal thrillers 11. Thrillers and suspense
LC 2013020660

"Three summers after the biggest man-made environmental disaster in history, millions of gallons of oil are again spewing from a hole in the ocean floor. But this rig explosion was in Cuban waters, just 50 miles away from Florida, and the situation is complex. The consortium doing the work is state-owned Venezuelan, Chinese and Russian, controlled by a mineral lease from the Cuban government. And the Cubans not only refuse assistance from the U.S., they also vow to fire on "hostile" American vessels that enter Cuban waters. Enter Jack Swyteck, who's honeymooning with his new wife Andie in the lower Keys. As an ominous black slick appears in the water, CIA agent Andie is called back to an undercover assignment. So Jack heads to Key West to see his buddy Theo Knight. There Jack is transformed from bystander to player in the unfolding oil catastrophe when he takes on a client whose husband was on the rig that blew up. She wants Jack to file a wrongful death in U.S. court. Takingon this unimaginably complicated case pitches Jack into a dangerous world, only to find that his case and Andie's assignment may be lethally connected Provided by publisher.

Grippando, James, 1958-

* The **girl** in the glass box / James Grippando. Harper, 2019. 352 p. Jack Swyteck novels

ISBN 9780062657831

1. Undocumented immigrants 2. Lawyers 3. Deportation 4. Legal assistance to poor people 5. Women immigrants 6. Enemies 7. Violence against women 8. Secrets 9. Miami, Florida 10. Florida 11. Legal thrillers 12. Thrillers and suspense
LC 2018022312

Miami attorney Jack Swyteck lands in the heart of the contentious immigration debate when he takes on the heart-wrenching case of an undocumented immigrant who fled to America to protect her daughter and save herself, in this timely and pulse-pounding thriller that explores the stories behind the headlines.

Grippando, James, 1958-

Lying with strangers / James Grippando. Harper Collins Publishers, 2007. 400 p.

ISBN 006113838X

1. Stalking victims 2. Trust 3. Manipulation by men 4. Women stalking victims 5. Rescues 6. Women physicians 7. Harassment 8. Obsession in men 9. Ambition in women 10. Determination in women 11. Stalkers 12. Stalking 13. Boston, Massachusetts 14. Psychological suspense
LC 2006050956

Peyton Shields finds her life irrevocably changed by an attack that she barely survives, an event that causes her to realize that she can trust no one when everyone close to her denies her story that the attack was deliberate.

"Grippando excels at the ordinary-person-in-extraordinary-circum- stances story, and this one uses the premise expertly, building enough suspense to keep readers looking in dark corners and over their shoul- ders." Booklist.

Grippando, James, 1958-

Money to burn : a novel of suspense / James Grippando. Harper, 2010. 368 p.

ISBN 9780061556302

1. Capitalists and financiers 2. Stealing 3. Frameups 4. Missing persons 5. Business intelligence 6. Married women -- Death 7. Hacking 8. Greed 9. Murder 10. Deception 11. Innocence (Law) 12. Financial thrillers
LC 2009024828

Michael Centella is a rising star at Wall Street investment bank Sax- ton Silvers. Everything is going according to plan until the love of his life, Ivy Layton, vanishes on their honeymoon in the Bahamas. Seven years later, Michael's got undercover FBI agents afoot, spyware on his computer, and mysterious e-mails from a "JBU." Embroiled in corporate espionage, he's desperate to clear his name. He doesn't want to believe it, but the signs point to his first wife, Ivy. Could she be back from the dead to destroy him?

"Grippando keeps the energy level high in Money To Burn while also showing the behind-the-scenes machinations of money schemes. A surprise twist is not only believable but also seamlessly woven into the plot." South Florida Sun-Sentinel.

Grisham, John

The **client** / John Grisham. Doubleday, 1993. 421 p.
ISBN 038542471X
1. Trials (Murder) -- New Orleans, Louisiana 2. Mafia -- New Orleans, Louisiana 3. Witnesses 4. Secrets 5. Eleven-year-old boys -- New Orleans, Louisiana 6. Women lawyers -- New Orleans, Louisiana 7. Suicide -- New Orleans, Louisiana 8. New Orleans, Louisiana 9. Thrillers and suspense 10. Legal thrillers
LC 92039079
Colorado Blue Spruce YA Book Award, 1995.

Present at the suicide of a New Orleans defense attorney, a young boy hires a lawyer to protect himself, sharing with her the dead attorney's shocking last words and hiding from her some dangerous information.

"This thriller is unique in its theme and in its suspense mixed with humor. A sure all-night read." School Library Journal.

Grisham, John

* The **firm** / John Grisham. Doubleday, 1991. 421 p.
ISBN 0385416342
1. FBI 2. Mafia 3. FBI informants 4. Law firms 5. Lawyers 6. Corruption investigation 7. Organized crime 8. Government investigators 9. Tennessee 10. Memphis, Tennessee 11. Thrillers and suspense 12. Legal thrillers
LC 90003945
Mitch McDeere, a Harvard Law graduate, becomes suspicious of his Memphis tax firm when mysterious deaths, obsessive office security, and the Chicago mob figure into its operations.

"The aphorism between a rock and a hard place aptly describes the dilemma of a young attorney pressed by the FBI to reveal crime-related secrets of his firm, while also hounded by his employers to simply take his huge salary and zip his lip. No aphorism, though, can convey the suspense, wit, and polished writing of this laser-sharp candidate for the best recent updating of the David and Goliath story." Library Journal.

Grisham, John

Ford County : stories / John Grisham. Doubleday, 2009. 272 p.
ISBN 9780385532457
1. Small town life 2. Mississippi 3. Short stories 4. Mainstream fiction
The author returns to Ford County, Mississippi--the setting of his popular first novel, "A Time to Kill"--in a surprising collection of stories.

"In Ford County, John Grisham's first collection of stories, we meet a weird and endearing group of misfits with one thing in common: each has lived in Clanton, the seat of fictional Ford County, Mississippi. . . . Grisham's prose is smooth and controlled as he deftly moves between narrators and storylines, and his skilled storytelling makes even the wackier scenes believable. One of Ford County's greatest assets is its abundant but understated humor." BookPage.

Grisham, John

* The **guardians** / John Grisham. Doubleday, 2019. 368 p.
ISBN 9780385544184
1. Lawyers 2. African American prisoners 3. Innocence (Law) 4. Frameups 5. Murder 6. Judicial error 7. Legal services 8. Post-conviction remedies 9. Murder investigation 10. Legal thrillers

Guardian handles only a few innocence cases at a time, and Cullen Post is its only investigator. He travels the South fighting wrongful convictions and taking cases no one else will touch. With Quincy Miller, though, he gets far more than he bargained for. Powerful, ruthless people murdered Keith Russo, and they do not want Quincy exonerated. They killed one lawyer twenty-two years ago, and they will kill another one without a second thought.

"Grisham's readers are legion, and they will be prepped for his latest, which finds the perennial chart-topper in great form." Booklist.

Grisham, John

The **last** juror / John Grisham. Doubleday :, 2004. 355 p.
ISBN 0385510438
1. 1970s 2. Former convicts 3. Murderers 4. Jurors -- Mississippi 5. Newspaper publishers and publishing -- Mississippi 6. Rape 7. Murder 8. Lawyers 9. Trials (Murder) 10. Newspaper publishers and publishing 11. Revenge 12. Jury 13. Mississippi 14. Thrillers and suspense

LC 2004043818

The future of a bankrupt paper looked grim until a young mother was brutally raped and murdered by a member of the notorious Padgitt family. Willie Traynor reported all the gruesome details, and his newspaper began to prosper. Nine years after Danny Padgitt was convicted, he managed to get himself paroled. He returned to Ford County and the retribution began.

Grisham, John

* The **pelican** brief / John Grisham. Doubleday, 1992. 371 p.
ISBN 9780385421980
1. United States Supreme Court Justices Assassination 2. Assassination 3. Government cover-ups -- United States 4. Witnesses 5. Crimes against judges 6. Women law students 7. Journalists 8. Washington, D.C. 9. Louisiana 10. Legal thrillers 11. Thrillers and suspense

LC 91033235

Two members of the Supreme Court are assassinated by a professional killer on the same night. A law student thinks that she has figured it out, and must protect herself and her theory.

"Mr. Grisham has written a genuine page-turner. He has an ear for dialogue and is a skillful craftsman. Like a composer, he brings all his themes together at the crucial moment for a gripping, and logical, finale." New York Times Book Review.

Grisham, John

A **time** to kill / John Grisham. Doubleday, 1993, c1989. 415 p.
ISBN 9780385470810
1. Revenge 2. Trials (Murder) -- Mississippi 3. Race relations 4. African American defendants -- Mississippi 5. Defense attorneys -- Mississippi 6. Mississippi -- Race relations 7. Mississippi 8. Legal thrillers

LC 89005760

Sequel to: Sycamore row (2013).

Criminal lawyer Jake Brigance faces the fight of his life when he is asked to defend Carl Hailey, who, in a rage of anger, shot and killed the men on trial for the rape of his daughter.

Grodstein, Lauren

* A **friend** of the family : a novel / Lauren Grodstein. Algonquin Books of Chapel Hill, 2009. 304 p.

ISBN 9781565129160

1. Interns (Medicine) 2. Suburban life -- New Jersey 3. Middle class families 4. Fathers and sons 5. Young men -- Relations with older women 6. Family relationships 7. Men/women relations 8. New Jersey 9. Psychological fiction 10. Literary fiction

LC 2009024476

After his best friend's daughter, Laura, sets her sights on his son, Alec, Pete Dizinoff sees his plans for a perfect son not just unraveling but being destroyed completely and sets out to derail the romance.

"The novel is spot-on in its depiction of affection and jealousy among longtime friends; boozy suburban bashes; unrequited love; and adjusting to middle age. . . . [It] beautifully captures the ever-striving angst of parents who will take any step to ensure their children's lives are easier or better." USA Today.

Grodstein, Lauren

Our short history / Lauren Grodstein. Algonquin Books of Chapel Hill, 2017. 352 p.

ISBN 9781616206222

1. Mothers and sons 2. Mortality 3. Parenthood 4. Six-year-old boys 5. Mothers with terminal illnesses 6. Children and death 7. Child-separated fathers 8. New York City 9. Washington (State) 10. Domestic fiction 11. Literary fiction

Karen Neulander has always been fiercely protective of her son, Jacob, now six. She's had to be: when Jacob's father, Dave, found out Karen was pregnant and made it clear that fatherhood wasn?t in his plans, Karen walked out of the relationship. But now Jake is asking to meet his dad, and with good reason: Karen is dying. Lauren Grodstein has created an unforgettable story about parenthood, sacrifice, and life itself.

"Grodstein's...heartbreaking, character-driven story is told in the remarkable, believable voice of a courageous, sympathetic character." Library Journal.

Groen, Hendrik

On the bright side : the new secret diary of Hendrik Groen, 85 years old / Hendrik Groen ; translated from the Dutch by Hester Velmans. Grand Central Pub, 2019 384 p. Secret diary of Hendrik Groen

ISBN 9781538746639

1. Seniors 2. Senior men 3. Retirement communities 4. Clubs 5. Aging 6. Mischief 7. Friendship 8. Octogenarians 9. Nursing homes 10. Amsterdam, Netherlands 11. Netherlands 12. Humorous stories 13. Diary novels 14. Translations -- Dutch to English

Finds octogenarian curmudgeon Hendrik emerging from a year of mourning to help the Old-But-Not-Dead Club save their homes from demolition plans.

Groff, Lauren

* **Arcadia :** a novel / Lauren Groff. Hyperion, 2012. 291 p.

ISBN 9781401340872

1. 1960s 2. Communes 3. Hippies 4. Introspection 5. Growing up 6. Epidemics 7. Perfection 8. Homecomings 9. New York (State) 10. Literary fiction 11. Coming-of-age stories

LC 2011009956

In a haunting story of the American dream, Bit, born in a back-to-nature commune in 1970s New York State, must come to grips with the outside world when the commune eventually fails.

Groff, Lauren

Delicate edible birds and other stories / Lauren Groff. Hyperion, 2009. 320 p.

ISBN 9781401340865

1. Short stories

LC 2008044002

Short stories.

Presents a volume of nine stories that reflects the use of different styles and structures, including a recreation of the tale of Abelard and Heloise during the 1918 New York flu epidemic, and the experiences of a group of war correspondents in France.

"An innovative and beautifully written collection that covers a wide swath of humanity, from east coast resort towns, to the early 20th century flu epidemic, to WWII Europe. . . . Even in the less successful stories, Groff's prose is lovely, and when she nails a storylike the title story about journalists fleeing Nazi-occupied Paristhe results are sublime." Publishers Weekly.

Groff, Lauren

* **Fates** and furies / Lauren Groff. Riverhead Books, 2015. 390 p.

ISBN 9781594634475

1. Marriage 2. Husband and wife 3. Married people and secrets 4. Love 5. Families 6. Secrets 7. Creativity 8. Dramatists 9. Maine 10. Literary fiction 11. Domestic fiction

LC 2015013565

National Book Award for Fiction finalist, 2015
National Book Critics Circle Award for Fiction finalist, 2015
Kirkus Prize for Fiction finalist, 2015.

Marrying in a glamorous whirlwind amid predictions of future greatness, Lotto and Mathilde are shaped throughout a subsequent shared decade by complications, secrets and powerful creative drives.

"The first half of the novel, entitled 'Fates,' gives lanky lothario Lottos perspective on the marriage. He sees nothing but Mathilde's goodness ('the best person I know') and her unerring belief in his talent, and, after some years of struggling as an actor, Lotto finds great success as a playwright, which brings the couple both fame and wealth. The second half of the novel, 'Furies,' turns the lens on Mathilde and will upend readers' expectations, for she is possessed of a cold calculation that will surprise and even dismay." Booklist.

Groff, Lauren

* **Florida** / Lauren Groff. Riverhead Books, 2018. 272 p.

ISBN 9781594634512

1. Florida 2. Short stories 3. Literary fiction

LC 2017042916

National Book Award for Fiction finalist, 2018
Kirkus Prize for Fiction finalist, 2018.

A collection of stories spanning centuries of time in mercurial Florida examines the decisions and connections behind life-changing events in characters ranging from two abandoned sisters to a conflicted family woman.

"The flora and fauna of the Sunshine State vine and prowl through Groffs second short story collection and first book since the smash-hit novel Fates and Furies (2015). With sympathy for her characters and a keen sensitivity to the natural world, Groff gets readers wondering who or what will triumph or succumb." Booklist.

Groom, Winston, 1944-

El Paso : a novel / Winston Groom. Liveright Publishing, 2016. 477 p.

ISBN 9781631492242

1. Villa, Pancho, 1878-1923 2. Mexican Revolution (1910-1920)

3. 1910s 4. Kidnapping 5. Outlaws 6. Capitalists and financiers 7. Frontier and pioneer life 8. Railroads 9. Ranches 10. Texas -- History -- 20th century 11. Mexico -- History -- 20th century 12. Southwest (United States) -- History -- 20th century 13. Westerns

LC 2016021007

After feared outlaw and revolutionary Pancho Villa kidnaps his grandchildren, railroad tycoon John Shaughnessy, known as the Colonel, ventures to El Paso with his adopted son and a band of hired cowboys on a rescue mission.

"An engaging epic that could be headed for the best-seller lists and then the big screen." Booklist.

Groot, Tracy, 1964-

Flame of resistance / Tracy Groot. Tyndale House, 2012. 416 p.

ISBN 9781414359472

1. 1940s 2. Spies -- United States 3. Undercover operations 4. Prostitutes 5. Fighter pilots 6. French Resistance (World War II) 7. Helpfulness in women 8. World War II 9. Resistance to military occupation 10. Americans in France 11. Spies -- France 12. Normandy 13. War stories 14. Christian historical fiction

LC 2011052924

Christy Award for Historical Category, 2013.

Years of Nazi occupation have stolen much from Brigitte Durand, but that changes the day American fighter pilot Tom Jaeger is shot down over occupied France and is picked up by the Resistance, giving her hope for a new future.

"This is a superior, page-turning entry." Publishers Weekly.

Groot, Tracy, 1964-

The **sentinels** of Andersonville / Tracy Groot. Tyndale House, 2014. 400 p.

ISBN 9781414359489

1. Andersonville Prison 2. 1860s 3. Prisoners of war 4. Compassion 5. Redemption 6. Civil war 7. Prisons 8. Confederate soldiers 9. Small towns 10. Consequences 11. Interpersonal relations 12. United States -- Civil War, 1861-1865 13. Confederate States of America 14. Christian historical fiction

LC 2013031516

Christy Award for Historical Category, 2015.

Three young Confederates and an entire town come face-to-face with Andersonville Prison's atrocities and learn the cost of compassion, when withheld and when given.

"Groot unflinchingly examines the consequences of becoming a good Samaritan in this richly detailed, engrossing historical fiction." Kirkus.

Gross, Andrew, 1952-

Button man / Andrew Gross. Minotaur Books, 2018. 371 p.

ISBN 9781250179982

1. 1930s 2. Between the Wars (1918-1939) 3. Jewish families 4. Organized crime 5. Immigrant families 6. Betrayal 7. Brothers 8. Corruption 9. Gangsters 10. Clothing industry and trade 11. New York City -- Social life and customs -- 20th century 12. Historical fiction

LC 2018013607

A disadvantaged but once happy immigrant family is brought together and torn apart by the birth of organized crime in 1930s New York City.

"Alternately frightful and fascinating, the story viscerally describes the era, exposing the motives and fears that drive each character and play out on the streets. Neil Kleid's graphic novel Brownsville? (2006) also vividly portrays many of the same criminals, along with District

Attorney Thomas Dewey, who fought them in court. Readers might also like the fast-paced Quinn mystery series by Michael Mayo for another perspective on the same period." Booklist.

Gross, Andrew, 1952-

Eyes wide open : a novel / Andrew Gross. HarperCollins, 2011. 352 p.

ISBN 9780061655968

1. Nephews 2. Cults 3. Surgeons 4. Murder 5. Murder investigation 6. Suicide victims 7. California 8. Thrillers and suspense
Published in UK/Australia/NZ as Killing Hour.

When disaster strikes his older brother Charlie, who once fell under the sway of a deeply disturbed cult-like figure, Jay Erlich is drawn back into his brother's past of secrets, terror, and lies.

"The issues of what family truly means, the struggles of mental illness that affect both the victims and those surrounding them, and the bad decisions of the past that come back with a vengeance are all displayed like an open wound.... Gross has written his best book to date." Denver Post.

Gross, Andrew, 1952-

The **one** man / Andrew Gross. Minotaur Books, 2016. 384 p.

ISBN 9781250079503

1. Auschwitz (Concentration camp) 2. Second World War era (1939-1945) 3. Physicists 4. Intelligence service 5. Holocaust (1933-1945) 6. Concentration camp inmates 7. Undercover operations 8. Knowledge 9. Nazis 10. Jewish men 11. World War II 12. Interpersonal relations 13. Poland -- History -- 20th century 14. United States -- History -- 20th century 15. Historical thrillers

LC 2016007570

RUSA Reading List Short List, 2017.

When a World War II physics professor with information vital to Allied forces is sent to a Nazi concentration camp, intelligence officer Nathan Blum is sent undercover to infiltrate Auschwitz and bring the professor to safety.

"Alternating between scenes of American hope-against-hope optimism and Nazi brutality, Blums deadly odyssey into and out of this 20th-century hell drives toward a compelling celebration of the human will to survive, remember, and overcome." Publishers Weekly.

Gross, Andrew, 1952-

Reckless : a novel / Andrew Gross. William Morrow, 2010. 352 p. Ty Hauck novels

ISBN 9780061655951

1. Murder investigation 2. Business -- Corrupt practices 3. Conspiracies 4. Corruption investigation 5. Detectives 6. Floor traders (Finance) 7. Greenwich, Connecticut 8. Financial thrillers

LC 2009044799

Ty Hauck is shattered when a close friend from his past is brutally murdered by vicious home intruders, and risks everything he loves to avenge her death. But it leads to a sinister conspiracy involving the sudden bank transfers of millions in cash and a dangerous plot to unleash global panic.

Grossman, David

Be my knife / David Grossman. Farrar, Straus and Giroux, 2002. 320 p.

ISBN 0374299773

1. Middle-aged men 2. Middle-aged women 3. Antiquarian booksellers 4. Rare books -- Collectors and collecting 5. Extramarital affairs 6. Intimacy (Psychology) 7. Literary fiction 8. Translations --

LIST OF FICTIONAL WORKS

Hebrew to English

LC 2001033645

When Yair, an awkward, neurotic seller of rare books, encounters a gorgeous stranger named Miriam at a class reunion, he begins writing her letters, which ignites a powerful love affair of words between these two people who are dissatisfied with their lives.

"When a thirty-three-year-old man named Yair catches a glimpse of Miriam at a class reunion, he senses a bond with her that goes beyond sexual attraction; because he is a practiced philanderer who is in search of something extraordinary, he implores her to enter a ruthlessly honest correspondence with him, on the understanding that they will never meet. . . . Most of the book is devoted to Yair's letters, and so we don't get to hear Miriam's responses until near the end. But it is Grossman's achievement that we understand from the start that Yair's vision of Miriam (and thus ours) is almost painfully incomplete." The New Yorker.

Grossman, David

Falling out of time / David Grossman ; translated by Jessica Cohen. Alfred A. Knopf, 2014, c2011 208 p.

ISBN 9780385350136

1. Bereavement 2. Death 3. Parent and child 4. Grief 5. Tragedy 6. Literary fiction 7. Translations -- Hebrew to English

LC 2013017532

Originally published in Hebrew as Nofel mi-huts la-zeman.

Announcing that he must embark on a journey in search of his dead son, a man walks in ever-widening circles around his town and beyond, picking up similarly bereaved companions with whom he explores questions about the potential for overcoming death and reconnecting with lost loved ones.

"Grossman's lyrical approach to the silent suffering of mourning is both a literary study in processing grief and a reminder that healing often comes through the action of putting into words the pain we thought was unspeakable." Library Journal.

Grossman, David

*A **horse** walks into a bar / David Grossman ; translated from the Hebrew by Jessica Cohen. Alfred A. Knopf, 2016, c2011. 208 p.

ISBN 9780451493972

1. Comedians 2. Autobiography 3. Stand-up comedy 4. Jokes 5. Judges 6. Storytelling 7. Psychic trauma 8. Loss (Psychology) 9. Men -- Psychology 10. Adult child abuse victims 11. Children of Holocaust victims 12. Israel 13. Psychological fiction 14. Literary fiction 15. Translations -- Hebrew to English

LC 2016014688

Previously published as Sus ehad nikhnas le-bar in 2011.

Man Booker International Prize, 2017.

National Jewish Book Award, 2017.

An Israeli comedian a bit past his prime conveys with semi-questionable humor anecdotes from his violence-stricken youth during a night of standup, while a judge in the audience wrestles with his own part in the comedian's losses.

"In this latest from award-winning Israeli author Grossman, a stand-up comedy routine quickly turns into a harrowing and soul-searching experience for both audience and performer. ... Dov's emotions are thoroughly spent as this oral memoir reaches its climax, a defining moment in his life told with such power and resonance that the audience is shocked and becomes totally submissive to this significant performance." Library Journal.

Grossman, David

* **To** the end of the land / David Grossman ; translated from the Hebrew by Jessica Cohen. Alfred A. Knopf, 2010. 592 p.

ISBN 9780307592972

1. Coping in women 2. Family relationships 3. War and society 4. Men/women relations 5. Hiking 6. Mothers and sons 7. Motherhood 8. Memories 9. Israel 10. Translations -- Hebrew to English 11. Literary fiction 12. Psychological fiction

LC 2010003915

"This is a Borzoi book."

Translation from the Hebrew of: Ishah borahat mi-besorah.

National Jewish Book Award for Fiction, 2010.

National Book Critics Circle Award for Fiction finalist, 2010

Fleeing to Galilee in despair when her son voluntarily rejoins the Israeli army, Ora drags along estranged family friend Avram, a tortured former POW to whom she relates her experiences of motherhood against a backdrop of constant war and fear.

"Grossman weaves the essences of private life into the tapestry of history with deliberate and delicate skill; he has created a panorama of breathtaking emotional force, a masterpiece of pacing, of dedicated storytelling, with characters whose lives are etched with extraordinary, vivid detail. While his novel has the vast sweep of pure tragedy, it is also at times playful, and utterly engrossing." New York Times Book Review.

Grossman, Lev

The **magician** king : a novel / Lev Grossman. Viking, 2011. 400 p. Magician novels (Lev Grossman)

ISBN 9780670022311

1. Magic 2. Wizards 3. Rulers 4. Voyages and travels 5. Young men 6. College graduates 7. Good and evil 8. Schools 9. Imaginary wars and battles 10. Massachusetts 11. Contemporary fantasy 12. Gateway fantasy

LC 2011019733

Sequel to: The magicians.

After Quentin and his old friend Julia leave Fillory on a magical sailing ship, they end up back in Quentin's home in Chesterton, Massachusetts, and only Julia's dark magic can get them back to the realm they have grown to love.

"Quentin Coldwater, the wizard who traveled to a mythical land to be its king in the first book, has gotten past most of his misery and settled into bored complacency, wondering whether hanging out in a castle and getting drunk is really all there is to rulership. Isn't he meant for great things? Shouldn't he be carrying out some giant quest? In the book's opening chapter, the quest he's already on unravels disappointingly, so he decides to embark to the farthest edge of the land he rules, a speck of an island in the middle of the sea, and he winds up on an even stranger journey. The Magicians was terrific, but loose, with a plot that moved from incident tox incident with only the barest connecting material. The Magician King, which is better in almost every way, feels as if it might be even looser in the early going, with plenty of opportunities to worry whether Grossman can pull his narrative together. But once he reaches his devastating climax, neatly knitting together story threads readers won't have even realized were major plot points, the novel reaches a level of poignancy the first could only hope to attain." A. V. Club.

Grossman, Lev

The **magician's** land : a novel / Lev Grossman. Viking, 2014. 416 p. Magician novels (Lev Grossman)

ISBN 9780670015672

1. Magic 2. Wizards 3. Rulers 4. Voyages and travels 5. Young men 6. College graduates 7. Good and evil 8. Schools 9. Imaginary wars and battles 10. Massachusetts 11. Contemporary fantasy

"Quentin Coldwater has been cast out of Fillory, the secret magical land of his childhood dreams. With nothing left to lose he returns to where his story began, the Brakebills Preparatory College of Magic. But he can't hide from his past, and it's not long before it comes looking for him. Along with Plum, a brilliant young undergraduate with a dark secret of her own, Quentin sets out on a crooked path through a magical demimonde of gray magic and desperate characters. But all roads lead back to Fillory, and his new life takes him to old haunts, like Antarctica, and to buried secrets and old friends he thought were lost forever. He uncovers the key to a sorcery masterwork, a spell that could create magical utopia, a new Fillory--but casting it will set in motion a chain of events that will bring Earth and Fillory crashing together. To save them he will have to risk sacrificing everything"--, Provided by publisher.

"This novel serves as an elegantly written third act to Quentin's bildungsroman, in which he at last learns responsibility and to not simply put childish things aside but understand them--and himself--anew." Publishers Weekly.

Grossman, Lev

The **magicians** : a novel / Lev Grossman. Viking, 2009. 402 p. Magician novels (Lev Grossman)

ISBN 9780670020553

1. Teenage wizards 2. Magic -- Study and teaching 3. Young men 4. Good and evil 5. Schools 6. Imaginary wars and battles 7. New York (State) 8. Contemporary fantasy

LC bl2009000464

Sequel: The magician king.

Harboring secret preoccupations with a magical land he read about in a childhood fantasy series, Quentin Coldwater is unexpectedly admitted into an exclusive college of magic and rigorously educated in modern sorcery.

"Quentin Coldwater is a geeky high-school senior in Brooklyn who is convinced that happiness and the life he should be living are elsewhere--for example, in the series of nineteen-thirties British adventure novels that he was obsessed with as a child. When Quentin stumbles on a portal that takes him to a college for magicians in upstate New York, he learns that the world depicted in these novels, known as Fillory, is real, and he is forced to square his youthful ideas with the realities that exist there, too: boredom, regret, shame, and despair. Quentin's journey becomes an unexpectedly moving coming-of-age story in which he learns that magical worlds are much like the real one." The New Yorker.

Grossman, Paul

Children of wrath / Paul Grossman. St. Martin's Press, 2012 320 p. Willi Kraus novels

ISBN 9780312601911

1. 1920s 2. Crimes against children 3. Serial murderers 4. Serial murder investigation 5. Jews, German 6. Detectives 7. Police -- Germany 8. Antisemitism 9. Murder 10. Germany -- History -- 1918-1933 11. Berlin, Germany 12. Historical mysteries 13. Mysteries

Detective Willi Kraus investigates the 1929 discovery of a burlap sack filled with children's bones and enclosed with a biblical phrase, a grisly finding with links to the dark side of Germany's capital.

Gruber, Michael, 1940-

The **book** of air and shadows / Michael Gruber. William Morrow, 2007. 480 p.

ISBN 0060874465

1. Shakespeare, William, 1564-1616 2. Lost books 3. Antiquities 4. Booksellers 5. Books 6. Rare books 7. Men/women relations 8. Secrets 9. England 10. New York City 11. Thrillers and suspense

LC 2006046767

Desperately typing out the details of a case that puts him at the center of a deadly conspiracy, intellectual property lawyer Jake Mishkin recounts how a bookstore fire led to the discovery of the whereabouts of one of the most valuable historical items in the world.

"Few thrillers will surpass [this book] when it comes to energetic writing, compellingly flawed characters, literary scholarship and mathematical conundrums." USA Today.

Gruber, Michael, 1940-

The **forgery** of Venus : a novel / Michael Gruber. William Morrow, 2008. 336 p.

ISBN 9780060874483

1. Art forgeries 2. Delusions 3. Extortion 4. Painters 5. Art dealers 6. Art forgers 7. Advertising 8. Time travel (Past) 9. Men's fantasies 10. Hallucinations and illusions 11. Deception 12. Thrillers and suspense

LC 2008002363

Although Chaz Wilmot's father is a famed illustrator, and Chaz has far surpassed his father in talent. Desperately in need of money, Chaz accepts a job restoring an antique fresco in a European castle. But when he gets there, he finds that there is so little to restore, it will really be more of a forgery--one that Chaz can pull off perfectly.

"Gruber writes passionately and knowledgeably about art and its historyand he writes brilliantly about the shadowy lines that blur reality and unreality. Fans of intelligent, literate thrillers will be well rewarded." Publishers Weekly.

Gruber, Michael, 1940-

Night of the jaguar : a novel / Michael Gruber. Morrow, 2006. 384 p. Jimmy Paz series

ISBN 0060577681

1. Police -- Miami, Florida 2. Supernatural 3. Shamanism 4. Shamans 5. Gods and goddesses 6. Jaguar 7. Murder 8. Cuban American men 9. Businesspeople 10. Cuban Americans 11. Serial murders 12. Miami, Florida 13. Thrillers and suspense

LC 2005040011

Miami detective Jimmy Paz risks everything to save his daughter and stop a series of murders involving the gruesome killings of affluent Cuban-American businessmen, crimes that could be tied to the murder in Colombia of an American priest.

"Hotly spiced with hit men and guns, demon gods and piranhas, this one offers more social satire than its predecessors, mostly at the expense of do-gooder environmentalists." Publishers Weekly.

Gruber, Michael, 1940-

The **return** : a novel / Michael Gruber. Henry Holt and Co., 2013. 320 p.

ISBN 9780805091298

1. Revenge 2. Violence in men 3. Ethics 4. Editors 5. Justice 6. Voyages and travels 7. Vietnam veterans 8. Widowers 9. Drug cartels 10. Mexico 11. New York, City 12. Thrillers and suspense

LC 2012045307

When a shattering piece of news awakens his buried desire for vengeance, Richard Marder, with nothing left to lose, sets out to punish the people whose actions, years earlier, changed his life and, with an old army buddy by his side, encounters a colorful cast of dangerous characters along the way.

Gruber, Michael, 1940-

Valley of bones : a novel / Michael Gruber. William Morrow, 2005. 448 p. Jimmy Paz series

ISBN 0060577665

1. Police -- Miami, Florida 2. Supernatural 3. Women psychiatric

hospital patients 4. Cuban American men 5. Catholic women 6. Nuns 7. Women murder suspects 8. Women psychologists 9. Rookie police 10. Monasticism and religious orders for women 11. Confession 12. Memories 13. Notebooks 14. Murder investigation 15. Belief and doubt 16. Miami, Florida 17. Africa 18. Thrillers and suspense

LC 2004045756

Sequel to: Tropic of night.

Investigating the murder of an oil tycoon, detective Jimmy Paz interviews an unlikely suspect in pious young Emmylou Dideroff, whose claim about her ability to commune with saints places her sanity in question.

"The author is at least as eager to fathom the violent and the unknown as he is to exploit these things. Some books simply relish the darker sides of human nature. Mr. Gruber summons them with troubled inquisitiveness, with both brio and regret." New York Times.

Gruen, Sara

The **ape** house / Sara Gruen. Spiegel & Grau, 2010. 320 p. ISBN 9780385523219

1. Bonobos 2. Apes 3. Human/animal relationships 4. Human/animal communication 5. American Sign Language 6. Primatologists 7. Journalists 8. Animal welfare 9. Animal rights advocates 10. Humans and apes 11. Reality television programs 12. Animal stealing 13. Literary fiction

LC 2010008928

Also published: Toronto : Bond Street Books, 2010.

A group of apes are kidnapped from a language laboratory and subsequently cast on a reality television show that calls into question scientific assumptions about common DNA that is shared by apes and people.

"This novel portrays a group of six bonobo apes housed in the fictional Great Ape Language Lab in Kansas City and the humans who either come to love them or seek to profit from their surprisingly advanced communication skills. Led by Bonzi, the matriarch and undisputed leader, the bonobo group includes Sam, the charismatic oldest male, Jelani, an adolescent showoff, and Makena, Jelani's biggest fan, who is pregnant and due any day. Isabel Duncan is a research scientist overseeing the bonobos and their unique ability to communicate via lexigrams on their computers, supplemented by American Sign Language. . . . Gruen enlivens this charming story of their emotional bonding with multiple villlains--including Isabel's fiancé, the head of the Great Ape Language Lab, who she discovers has a history of animal cruelty and a desire to profit from the bonobos under his control. There's also a purveyor of porn who sees the bonobos as the perfect stars for his new reality TV show, enticing viewers with their healthy sex lives 24 hours a day. Ape House turns into a romp, but Gruen never loses the thread of the enviable bond Isabel has nurtured with her ape friends." BookPage.

Gruen, Sara

* **Water** for elephants : a novel / Sara Gruen. Algonquin Books, 2006. 352 p. ISBN 1565124995

1. Circus performers 2. Reminiscing in old age 3. Depressions -- 1929-1941 4. Human/animal relationships 5. Parents -- Death 6. Veterinarians 7. Love triangles 8. Women circus performers 9. Circus animals 10. Elephants 11. Human/animal communication 12. Circus 13. Literary fiction

LC 2005052700

Book Sense Book of the Year Adult Fiction, 2007.

Great Lakes Book Awards, Fiction category, 2007.

Ninety-something-year-old Jacob Jankowski remembers his time in the circus as a young man during the Great Depression, and his friendship with Marlena, the star of the equestrian act, and Rosie, the elephant, who gave them hope.

"Life is good for Jacob Jankowski. He's about to graduate from veterinary school and about to bed the girl of his dreams. Then his parents are killed in a car crash, leaving him in the middle of the Great Depression with no home, no family, and no career. Almost by accident, Jacob joins the circus. There he falls in love with the beautiful performer Marlena, who is married to the circus' psychotic animal trainer. He also meets the other love of his life, Rosie the elephant. This lushly romantic novel travels back and forth in time between Jacob's present day in a nursing home and his adventures in the surprisingly harsh world of 1930s circuses. The ending of both stories is a little too cheerful to be believed, but just like a circus, the magic of the story and the writing convince you to suspend your disbelief. The book is partially based on real circus stories and illustrated with historical circus photographs." Booklist.

Grunberg, Arnon,

Tirza / Arnon Grunberg ; translated from the Dutch by Sam Garrett. Open Letter, 2013, c2006. 452 p.

ISBN 9781934824696

1. Compulsive behavior in men 2. Suspicion 3. Middle-aged men 4. Fathers and daughters 5. Marital conflict 6. Family secrets 7. Parties 8. Terrorism 9. Deserts 10. Searching 11. Racism 12. Amsterdam, Netherlands 13. Namibia 14. Africa 15. Psychological suspense 16. Translations -- Dutch to English

LC 2012044299

Originally published: Amsterdam : Nijgh & Van Ditmar, 2006.

With its meandering pace, sometimes-grotesque characters, and unflinching look at some unsavory personality traits, this story is for the reader of the hard-to-like yet quite-well-written novel." Booklist.

Grushin, Olga, 1971-

The **line** / Olga Grushin. G.P. Putnam's Sons, 2010. 336 p. ISBN 9780399156168

1. Hope 2. Rumor 3. Friendship 4. Interpersonal relations 5. Music 6. Composers 7. Exiles 8. Power (Social sciences) 9. Concerts 10. Moscow, Russia -- Social life and customs 11. Literary fiction

LC 2009042733

When rumors about an exiled composer's return to Moscow for a farewell symphony spark power abuses among officials and bureaucrats, a disparate gaggle of strangers evolves into a community of friends bonded by long-buried memories and unexpected acts of kindness.

"In the world of The Line, no desire, no matter how trifling, is met without a herculean struggle, and Anna's stymied attempts to present her family with something as simple as a date cake sometimes devolve into farce. But for the most part, Grushin expertly maintains a dreamlike tone to sell the novel's more preposterous (albeit historically grounded) elements, and characters who initially appear one-dimensional become intensely empathetic by the novel's end, as they bristle or cave under a society that grinds down the exceptional to make way for the pedestrian." A. V. Club

Guhrke, Laura Lee

Governess gone rogue / Laura Lee Guhrke. Avon Books, 2019 352 p. Dear Lady Truelove

ISBN 9780062890689

1. Victorian era (1837-1901) 2. Tutors 3. Deception 4. Male impersonators 5. Seduction 6. Aristocracy 7. Governesses 8. Advice columnists 9. Earls and countesses 10. Interpersonal attraction 11. Men/women relations 12. England 13. Great Britain 14. Victorian romances 15. Historical romances

Disguising herself as a man to score her dream job--being the tutor for the Earl of Kenyon's wild young sons-- Miss Amanda Leighton, when her deception is exposed, vows to teach the Earl some lessons in love, seduction and second chances.

Guhrke, Laura Lee

How to lose a duke in ten days / Laura Lee Guhrke. Avon Books, 2014. 384 p. An American heiress in London

ISBN 9780062118196

1. Heirs and heiresses 2. Dukes and duchesses 3. Husband and wife 4. Separated couples 5. Homecomings 6. Reconciliation in marriage 7. Interpersonal attraction 8. Americans in England 9. Men/women relations 10. England -- Social life and customs -- 19th century 11. London, England -- Social life and customs -- 19th century 12. Historical romances

"A spirited yet emotionally fragile heroine and a resourceful hero find love in this flawlessly written, lushly sensual tale that balances sexual abuse issues with flashes of humor and treats readers to a beautifully depicted and tender courtship." Library Journal.

Guhrke, Laura Lee

The **truth** about love and dukes / Laura Lee Guhrke. Avon Books, 2017 369 p. Dear Lady Truelove

ISBN 9780062469854

1. Victorian era (1837-1901) 2. Dukes and duchesses 3. Advice columnists 4. Newspaper publishers and publishing 5. Women columnists 6. Scandals 7. Nobility 8. Interclass romance 9. Interpersonal attraction 10. Men/women relations 11. England 12. Great Britain 13. Victorian romances 14. Historical romances

When his mother elopes after receiving advice from columnist Lady Truelove, causing a huge scandal, Henry, Duke of Torquil, is determined to expose the author's true identity before she can ruin any more lives, but his plan backfires when he, instead, embarks on an affair with the beauty.

Guhrke, Laura Lee

When the marquess met his match / Laura Lee Guhrke. Avon, 2013. 384 p. An American heiress in London

ISBN 9780062118172

1. Matchmakers 2. Womanizers 3. Heirs and heiresses 4. Marquis and marchionesses 5. Nobility 6. Aristocracy 7. Americans in England 8. Widows 9. Mate selection 10. England -- Social life and customs -- 19th century 11. London, England -- Social life and customs -- 19th century 12. Historical romances

Nicholas, Marquess of Trubridge, wants to marry a rich American heiress--until he meets the beautiful matchmaker, Lady Belinda Featherstone.

"Graced with an abundance of memorable characters and rich in lush sensuality." Booklist.

Guillory, Jasmine

The **proposal** / Jasmine Guillory. Jove/Berkley, 2018. 336 p. Wedding dates

ISBN 9780399587689

1. Interracial romance 2. Dating (Social customs) 3. Social media 4. Physicians 5. Women authors 6. Friendship 7. Lovers 8. City life 9. Sexual attraction 10. Men/women relations 11. Los Angeles, California 12. California 13. Multicultural romances 14. Contemporary romances 15. African American fiction

LC 2018022593

After a handsome doctor helps Nikole escape a ridiculous, public proposal, she starts having a series of hookups with him, but when things begin to get out of hand, one of them has to put the brakes on things.

Guillory, Jasmine

Royal holiday / Jasmine Guillory. Berkley, 2019. 304 p. Wedding dates

ISBN 9781984802217

1. Christmas 2. Middle-aged couples 3. Dating (Social customs) 4. Personal assistants 5. Women fashion designers 6. Royal houses 7. Vacations 8. Americans in Great Britain 9. African American women 10. Sexual attraction 11. Men/women relations 12. England 13. Holiday romances 14. Multicultural romances 15. Contemporary romances 16. African American fiction

LC 2019024644

A spontaneous holiday vacation turns into an unforgettable romance.

Guillory, Jasmine

* The **wedding** date / Jasmine Guillory. Berkley, 2018. 304 p. Wedding dates

ISBN 9780399587665

1. Women politicians 2. Physicians 3. Interracial romance 4. Long-distance romance 5. African American women 6. Weddings 7. Sexual attraction 8. Men/women relations 9. California 10. Multicultural romances 11. Contemporary romances 12. African American fiction

LC 2017034041

RUSA Reading List Short List, 2019.

Stranded together in an elevator during a power outage, Drew and Alexa agree to pose as a couple at an ex's wedding and discover afterwards that they are unable to forget each other.

"This incredibly delicious meet-cute brings two people together who would not have met otherwise, and though it could have become predictable, Guillory keeps this contemporary romance fresh with well-drawn multicultural characters navigating the perils of long-distance relationships." Booklist.

Guillory, Jasmine,

The **wedding** party / Jasmine Guillory. Jove, 2019. 320 p. Wedding dates

ISBN 9781984802194

1. Wedding planning 2. Interpersonal conflict 3. One-night stands (Interpersonal relations) 4. Aversion 5. Friendship 6. Weddings 7. Men/women relations 8. African American men 9. Interpersonal attraction 10. California 11. Multicultural romances 12. Contemporary romances 13. African American fiction

LC 2018057817

Maddie and Theo have two things in common: Alexa is their best friend, and they hate each other. After an "oops, we made a mistake" night together, neither one can stop thinking about the other. With Alexa's wedding rapidly approaching, Maddie and Theo both share bridal party responsibilities that require more interaction than they're comfortable with.

Guinn, Matthew

The **scribe** : a novel / Matthew Guinn. W. W. Norton & Company, 2015 304 p.

ISBN 9780393239294

1. Gilded Age (1865-1898) 2. 1880s 3. Serial murder investigation 4. Crimes against African Americans 5. Police 6. Racism 7. Mutilation 8. Detectives 9. Upper class 10. Serial murderers 11. Crimes against rich people 12. Atlanta, Georgia -- Social life and customs -- 19th century 13. Historical mysteries

LC 2015013780

Investigating a series of murders targeting post-Civil War Atlanta's wealthiest black entrepreneurs, a disgraced former detective partners with the city's first African-American officer in a case marked by fierce racial, political, and personal tensions.

"This is an absorbing historical mystery filled with evocative period detail, a brooding atmosphere of corruption and pervasive evil, and compelling characters who could be developed further." Booklist.

Gunaratne, Guy, 1984-

In our mad and furious city / Guy Gunaratne. MCD x FSG Originals, 2018. 288 p.

ISBN 9780374175771

1. City life 2. Immigrants 3. Public housing 4. Riots 5. Inner city 6. Young men 7. Anger 8. Inequality 9. Extremism 10. Families 11. London, England 12. Literary fiction 13. Political fiction

LC 2018039534

Longlisted for the Man Booker Prize, 2018.

While Selvon, Ardan, and Yusuf organize their lives around soccer, girls, and grime, Caroline and Nelson struggle to overcome pasts that haunt them. Each voice is uniquely insightful, impassioned, and unforgettable, and when stitched together, they trace a brutal and vibrant tapestry of today's London. In a forty-eight-hour surge of extremism and violence, their lives are inexorably drawn together in the lead-up to an explosive, tragic climax.

Gundar-Goshen, Ayelet, 1982-

Waking lions / Ayelet Gundar-Goshen ; translated from the Hebrew by Sondra Silverston. Little, Brown and Company, 2017, c2016. 352 p.

ISBN 9780316395434

1. Hit-and-run accidents 2. Hit-and-run drivers 3. Extortion 4. Refugees 5. Surgeons 6. Reputation 7. Married men 8. Families 9. Widows 10. Israel 11. Psychological suspense

Originally published in Hebrew as "Leha'ir arajot" in 2014.

After neurosurgeon Eitan Green hits and kills an African migrant while driving on a deserted road late at night, the victim's wife tracks him down and confronts him the next day, and her price for silence shatters his safe existence.

"As characters reveal previously hidden facets, Gundar-Goshens mesmerizing novel, her first to be published in English, moves continually into unexpected territory." Booklist.

Gunday, Hakan, 1976-

The **few** / Hakan Gunday, translated by Alexander Dawe. Arcade Publishing, 2018, c2015 335 p.

ISBN 9781628727098

1. Human trafficking 2. Eleven-year-olds 3. Immigrants, Turkish 4. Adult child abuse victims 5. Authors 6. Fame 7. Betrayal 8. Orphans 9. London, England 10. Turkey 11. Literary fiction 12. Coming-of-age stories 13. Translations -- Turkish to English

Originally published:Istanbul : Dogan Kitap, 2015

Sold by her mother as a wife to a conservative tribesman, Derda, after five years of abuse in London, escapes only to find herself preyed upon by Turkish immigrants in London's underworld; while, in Turkey, an unstable writer targets two authors whom he believes stole his fame.

Gunesekera, Romesh

* **Suncatcher** : a novel / Romesh Gunesekera. The New Press, 2020, c2019. 312 p.

ISBN 9781620975596

1. 1960s 2. Teenage boys 3. Friendship 4. Families 5. Entitlement attitudes 6. Class consciousness 7. Growing up 8. Sri Lanka 9. Historical fiction 10. Literary fiction 11. Coming-of-age stories

LC 2019051382

Originally published: London : Bloomsbury Publishing, 2019.

Set in post-independence Sri Lanka, a coming-of-age novel follows young Kairo as he discovers a world of privilege through his new friend, Jay, a budding naturalist and a born rebel, and embarks on a journey of devastating consequences.

"A lyrical and evocative portrait of a Sri Lankan boyhood friendship and the life lessons that came." Kirkus.

Gunn, James E., 1923-

Transcendental / James Gunn. Tor Books, 2013. 320 p. Transcendental novels

ISBN 9780765335012

1. Far future 2. Pilgrims and pilgrimages 3. Faith 4. Space flight 5. Veterans 6. Assassins 7. Prophets 8. Belief and doubt 9. Storytelling 10. Betrayal 11. Aliens 12. Artificial intelligence 13. Space opera 14. Hard science fiction 15. Science fiction

LC 2013023856

"A Tom Doherty Associates Book."

As it travels to its destination at the end of the galaxy, where a Prophet offers guidance in achieving Transcendence, dilapidated spaceship Geoffrey plays host to a motley crew of pilgrims who pass the time by telling their stories. In addition to Aldebaran "flower child" 4107 (a sentient plant), heavy-world tripod Tordor, "weasel-faced" alien Xi, and captive-born human Asha, there's also mercenary Riley, a war veteran hired by anonymous but powerful employers to identify the Prophet and kill him. Fans of Dan Simmons' Hyperion, which also draws inspiration from The Canterbury Tales to present multiple narratives from diverse perspectives, should enjoy this richly detailed, thought-provoking novel. - Description by Gillian Speace.

Gurganus, Allan, 1947-

* **Local** souls : novellas / Allan Gurganus. Liveright Publishing Corporation, 2013. 352 p.

ISBN 9780871403797

1. Interpersonal relations 2. Small town life 3. North Carolina 4. Southern States 5. Short stories

LC 2013016662

Returning to his mythological Falls, North Carolina home of Widow, the author presents three novellas set in today's South, a place revolutionized around freer sexuality, looser family ties and superior telecommunications.

Gurganus, Allan, 1947-

Oldest living Confederate widow tells all A. A. Knopf, 1989. 718 p.

ISBN 0394545370

1. Antietam, Battle of, Md, 1862 2. Husband and wife 3. Widows 4. Nonagenarians 5. Senior women 6. Senior women -- Friendship 7. Men/women relations 8. Partner abuse 9. Civil war 10. United States Civil War, 1861-1865 11. Southern States -- History 12. Historical fiction 13. Southern fiction

LC 88045870

Sir Walter Raleigh Award for Fiction, 1990.

"In a way, 'Oldest Living Confederate Widow Tells All' is as much about language and myth-making as it is about love and war. Whether one feels that it succeeds depends on how much leeway one is willing to give to this indomitable 'veteran of the veteran,' as Lucy describes herself." New York Times Book Review.

Gurganus, Allan, 1947-

The **practical** heart : four novellas / Allan Gurganus. Knopf, 2001. 322 p.

ISBN 0679437630

1. Women immigrants 2. Houses -- Remodeling 3. Fathers 4. Villages 5. United States -- Social life and customs -- 20th century

FICTION CORE COLLECTION
TWENTIETH EDITION

6. Short stories

LC 2001032665

Lambda Literary Award for Gay Men's Fiction, 2001.
Sir Walter Raleigh Award for Fiction, 2002.
A collection of four novellas includes "He's One, Too," about a pillar of the community whose attraction to boys turns him into a pariah, and "Saint Monster," a love story that celebrates one boy's feelings for his father.

Gurganus, Allan, 1947-
White people : stories and novellas / Allan Gurganus. Vintage Books, 2000, c1990. 252 p.
ISBN 9780375704277
1. European Americans 2. Short stories
Originally published: New York : Knopf, 1990.
A collection of eleven comic short stories by the author of The Oldest Living Confederate Widow Tells All features tales of love and money among American WASPs.

Guskin, Sharon
The **forgetting** time / Sharon Guskin. Flatiron Books, 2016. 304 p.
ISBN 9781250076427
1. Single mothers 2. Mothers and sons 3. Memory 4. Men with terminal illnesses 5. Missing persons 6. Regret 7. Grief 8. Reincarnation 9. Literary fiction
While a mother's life abruptly stops after receiving an emergency phone call from her son's preschool, a driven former Ivy League professor confronts the realities of his terminal diagnosis and helps a woman whose child has been missing for years.

Gustine, Amy, 1970-
You should pity us instead : stories / Amy Gustine. Sarabande Books, 2016. 256 p.
ISBN 9781941411193
1. Interpersonal relations 2. Family relationships 3. Literary fiction 4. Short stories
LC 2015017017
Debut story collection explores love in its many guises -- family, romance, friendship -- through the lens of religion, international conflict, and complicated relationships.
"Gustine's language is uniformly remarkable for its clarity and forthrightness." Publishers Weekly.

Guterson, David
Ed King : a novel / David Guterson. Alfred A. Knopf, 2011. 320 p.
ISBN 9780307271068
1. Young men -- Relations with older women 2. Orphans 3. Rich men 4. Free will and determinism 5. Fate and fatalism 6. Millionaires 7. Technology -- Social aspects 8. Literary fiction 9. Satirical fiction 10. Adaptations, retellings, and spin-offs
LC 2011010255
"This is a Borzoi book."
Left on a doorstep after his illegal au pair mother exacts a brutal revenge on his father, Edward is raised by an adoring family and grows up to become a famous billionaire Internet tycoon who hurtles toward a fate that he is powerless to control.
"Guterson's narrative voice by turns savage and sad, amused and outraged becomes a kind of Greek chorus of one. From the self-reverential blather of Seattle liberals to the gaming industry's nihilistic love of violence to the winner-take-all world of software and search engines, Guterson skewers it all.... He interweaves the story with enough myth-

ological references to keep even the most ardent classicist entertained." Seattle Times.

Guterson, David
The **other** / David Guterson. Alfred A. Knopf, 2008. 272 p.
ISBN 9780307263155
1. Male friendship 2. Recluses 3. Men and nature 4. Class conflict 5. Secrets 6. Friendship 7. Irish American men 8. Men -- Decision-making 9. Washington (State) 10. Psychological fiction 11. Literary fiction 12. Pacific Northwest fiction
LC 2007041098
A deeply engrossing story about friendship, youth, and idealism from the bestselling author of Snow falling on cedars. When John William Barry and Neil Countryman met in 1972, the 16-year-old boys find they share a youthful idealism and a love of the outdoors. But after high school, their paths diverge. John William eventually drops out of society, and only Neil knows his whereabouts. He remains loyal to his oath of secrecy, until years later, when a shocking truth is revealed.

Guterson, David
Our Lady of the Forest / David Guterson. Alfred A. Knopf, 2003. 336 p.
ISBN 0375412115
1. Mary,, Blessed Virgin, Saint Apparitions and miracles 2. Catholic Church 3. Manipulation (Social sciences) 4. Homeless teenagers 5. Visions 6. Teenage abuse victims 7. Runaway teenagers 8. Teenage girls 9. Lumber workers 10. Clergy 11. Migrant agricultural laborers 12. Mushroom industry and trade 13. Small town economic development 14. Washington (State) 15. Psychological fiction 16. Literary fiction 17. Pacific Northwest fiction
LC 2002043322
Sixteen-year-old runaway and unlikely spiritual candidate Ann Holmes, surviving by living in a tent and working as a mushroom picker, experiences a vision of the Virgin Mary in the foggy woods of a Washington November afternoon.
"When Ann Holmes starts having visions of the Virgin Mary, the bedraggled teen runaway becomes the last hope for the inhabitants of a dank, economically depressed logging town and the hordes of miracle-seekers who descend on it. In this panoramic, psychologically dense novel, she also becomes a symbol of the intimate intertwining of the sacred and the profane in American life." Publishers Weekly.

Guterson, David
* **Snow** falling on cedars / David Guterson. Harcourt Brace, 1994. x, 345 p.
ISBN 0151001006
1. 1950s 2. Japanese Americans 3. Trials (Murder) 4. Racism 5. Journalists 6. People who have had amputations 7. World War II veterans 8. Interracial romance 9. Washington (State) 10. Literary fiction 11. Psychological suspense 12. Pacific Northwest fiction
LC 94007535
Originally published: 1995.
Book Sense Book of the Year Adult Trade, 1994.
PEN-Faulkner Award, 1995.
Presents a tense courtroom drama, a poignant love story, and a haunting reflection on the delicate balance between the mind and heart.

Guthrie, A. B. (Alfred Bertram), 1901-1991
* The **big** sky / A.B. Guthrie, Jr. Houghton Mifflin, 2002, c1947. 386 p. Western saga (A.B. Guthrie, Jr.)
ISBN 9780618154630
1. American Westward Expansion (1803-1899) 2. 19th century 3.

Frontier and pioneer life 4. Adventurers 5. Indians of North America -- Relations with missionaries, traders, etc 6. Mountain men 7. Piegan Indians 8. Siksika Indians 9. Mandan Indians 10. The West (United States) 11. Oregon Trail 12. Missouri River 13. Westerns Sequel: The way west.

Includes map.

Relates the adventures of Boone Caudill, a mountain man in the American West of the mid-nineteenth century.

Guttridge, Peter

The **thing** itself / Peter Guttridge. Severn House, 2012. 213 p. Brighton novels

ISBN 9780727880819

1. Former police chiefs 2. Cold cases (Criminal investigation) 3. Murder investigation 4. Women detectives 5. Women investigative journalists 6. Conspiracies 7. Police -- Brighton, England 8. Gangsters 9. Crime -- Brighton, England 10. Procedure (Law) 11. Brighton, England 12. England -- History -- 20th century 13. Mysteries

LC bl2012021985

Ex-Chief Constable Bob Watts investigates what really happened in the unsolved Brighton Trunk Murder of 1934; Sarah Gilchrist probes the Milldean Massacre; and Jimmy Tingley tails the Balkan gangsters who wreaked havoc in Brighton.

Gyasi, Yaa

* **Homegoing** : a novel / Yaa Gyasi. Alfred A. Knopf, 2016. 304 p.

ISBN 9781101947135

1. 18th century 2. 19th century 3. 20th century 4. Half-sisters 5. Race relations 6. Separated friends, relatives, etc 7. Slavery 8. Ancestors 9. African Americans 10. Racism 11. Families 12. Family history 13. Africa -- History -- 18th century 14. Ghana -- History 15. United States -- History -- 19th century 16. Historical fiction 17. Family sagas 18. African American fiction

LC 2015039411

ALA Notable Book, 2017.

Hemingway Foundation/PEN Award, 2017.

RUSA Reading List Short List, 2017

Two half-sisters, unknown to each other, are born into different villages in 18th-century Ghana and experience profoundly different lives and legacies throughout subsequent generations marked by wealth, slavery, war, coal mining, the Great Migration and the realities of 20th-century Harlem.

"Gyasi's characters are vividly drawn, sympathetic yet not simplistically heroic. It's wrenching to leave them behind, but readers will be quickly enthralled by the next generation's story." Library Journal.

H

Hackwith, A. J.

The **library** of the unwritten / A.J. Hackwith. Ace Books, 2019. 336 p. Hell's library novels

ISBN 9781984806376

1. Librarians 2. Magical books 3. Angels 4. Hell 5. Demons 6. Muses (Persons) 7. Power (Social sciences) 8. Magic 9. Books 10. Books -- Conservation and restoration 11. Chases 12. Adventure stories 13. Fantasy fiction

LC 2019012345

Assigned to watch the restless characters of books left unfinished by their authors, a head librarian of Hell's neutral Unwritten Wing tracks an escaped Hero before an angel attack reveals the existence of a powerful literary weapon.

Haddam, Jane, 1951-

Cheating at solitaire : a Gregor Demarkian novel / Jane Haddam. St. Martin's Minotaur, 2008. 391 p. Gregor Demarkian mysteries

ISBN 0312343086

1. Celebrities 2. Paparazzi 3. Actors and actresses 4. Armenian American men 5. Former FBI agents 6. Private investigators 7. Massachusetts 8. Philadelphia, Pennsylvania 9. Mysteries

LC 2007049770

Former FBI agent Gregor Demarkian, fleeing from his own wedding preparations, is hired to review a case--one that he finds has little evidence and twisted by an out-of-control media--in what may be the most compelling case of his entire career.

"Moving slowly through the landscape of her story, Haddam turns the island and its ambiance into a vividly visual experience for readers. Brilliantly introspective, intellectual ruminations and multiple narrators--who fully convey the craziness of the paparazzi and the cutthroat attitudes of those with power--intersperse with Haddam's own unique and frequently unexpected conclusions." Library Journal.

Haddam, Jane, 1951-

Hardscrabble road / Jane Haddam. St. Martin's Minotaur, 2006. 320 p. Gregor Demarkian mysteries

ISBN 0312353731

1. Radio talk show hosts and guests 2. Right-wing extremists 3. Prescription drug abuse 4. Homeless men 5. Nuns 6. Drug abuse treatment centers and clinics 7. Poisoning 8. Murder 9. Armenian American men 10. Former FBI agents 11. Private investigators 12. Philadelphia, Pennsylvania 13. Mysteries

LC 2005054793

Retired FBI agent Gregor Demarkian probes the circumstances surrounding the death of a former client, following a maze of clues that could be tied to the arrest of a local Philadelphia right-wing radio talk-show host for illegal drugs.

"Those new to Haddam will snap up her earlier work based on this captivating literate mystery, which shows how well a classic fair play whodunit can work in a contemporary setting." Publishers Weekly.

Haddam, Jane, 1951-

True believers / Jane Haddam. St. Martin's Minotaur, 2001. 328 p. Gregor Demarkian mysteries

ISBN 0312209290

1. Suicide 2. Widowers 3. Poisoning 4. Armenian American men 5. Former FBI agents 6. Private investigators 7. Philadelphia, Pennsylvania 8. Mysteries

LC 00051794

Gregor Demarkian is asked to investigate after a woman's body turns up in Philadelphia's St. Anselm's church, her husband, a local parishioner, commits suicide, and it is discovered that the woman was the victim of arsenic poisoning.

"Haddam's large cast pulses with petty jealousies, vanities and fears as they confront the mysteries of life and religion. This is an engrossingly complex mystery that should win further acclaim for its prolific and talented author." Publishers Weekly.

Haddon, Mark, 1962-

* The **curious** incident of the dog in the night-time : a novel / Mark Haddon. Doubleday, 2003. 256 p.

ISBN 9780385512107

1. Fifteen-year-old boys 2. Autism 3. Savant syndrome 4. Dogs --

Death 5. Neighbors 6. Social phobia 7. Family secrets 8. England 9. Mysteries 10. Psychological fiction

LC 2002031355

ALA Notable Book, 2004.

British Book Award for Children's Book of the Year, 2004.

British Book Award for Literary Fiction, 2004.

Garden State Teen Book Award (New Jersey), Fiction (Grades 9-12), 2006.

Whitbread Book Award for Novel, 2003.

Whitbread Book of the Year Award, 2003.

Shortlisted for the James Tait Black Memorial Prize for Fiction, 2003

Despite his overwhelming fear of interacting with people, Christopher, a mathematically-gifted, autistic fifteen-year-old boy, decides to investigate the murder of a neighbor's dog and uncovers secret information about his mother.

"Unable to feel emotions himself, his story evokes emotions in readers: heartache and frustration for his well-meaning but clueless parents and deep empathy for the wonderfully honest, funny, and lovable protagonist. Readers will never view the behavior of an autistic person again without more compassion and understanding." School Library Journal.

Hadley, Tessa

Bad dreams and other stories / Tessa Hadley. HarperCollins, 2017. 288 p.

ISBN 9780062476661

1. Human nature 2. Family relationships 3. Interpersonal relations 4. Families 5. Life 6. Short stories 7. Literary fiction

A collection of stories by the award-winning author of The Past explores a theme of the exceptional nature of seemingly mundane things, depicting such characters as sisters who quarrel over an inheritance and new baby, a child who explores her home in the middle of the night and a housekeeper who uncovers an elderly charge's secrets.

"Achingly lovely, though never sentimental, Hadley's collection renders common lives with exquisite grace." Kirkus.

Hadley, Tessa

Clever girl / Tessa Hadley. HarperCollins, 2014, c2013. 272 p.

ISBN 9780062270399

1. Middle-aged women 2. Memory 3. Single mothers 4. Teenage mothers 5. Growing up 6. Gifted girls 7. Family relationships 8. Men/women relations 9. England 10. Literary fiction

Originally published: London: Jonathan Cape, 2013.

Captures the beauty, innocence, and irony of ordinary life in a story that follows a woman named Stella from her childhood growing up with a single mother in a Bristol bedsit in the 1960s to middle age.

Hadley, Tessa

The **past** / Tessa Hadley. HarperCollins, 2016. 320 p.

ISBN 9780062270412

1. Adult children of dysfunctional families 2. Brothers and sisters 3. Family secrets 4. Intergenerational relations 5. Family relationships 6. Abandoned children 7. Marital conflict 8. Married people 9. House selling 10. Cottages 11. Families 12. Domestic fiction

Hawthornden Prize, 2016.

Over five novels and two collections of stories Tessa Hadley has earned a reputation as a fiction writer of remarkable gifts, and been compared with Elizabeth Bowen and Alice Munro. In her new novel three sisters and a brother meet up in their grandparents' old house for three long, hot summer weeks. The house is full of memories of their childhood and their past - their mother took them there when she left their father - but now they may have to sell it. And under the idyllic surface,

there are tensions. Roland has come with his new wife and his sisters don't like her. Kasim, the twenty-year-old son of Alice's ex-boyfriend, makes plans to seduce Molly, Roland's teenage daughter. Fran's children uncover an ugly secret in a ruined cottage in the woods. Passion erupts where it's least expected, blasting the quiet self-possession of Harriet, the oldest sister. A way of life - bourgeois, literate, ritualised - winds down to its inevitable end. With uncanny precision and extraordinary sympathy, Tessa Hadley charts the squalls of lust and envy disrupting this ill-assorted house party, as well as the consolations of memory and affection, the beauty of the natural world, the shifting of history under the social surface. From the first page the reader is absorbed and enthralled, watching a superb craftsman at work --, Source other than Library of Congress.

"Hadley is the patron saint of ordinary lives; her trademark empathy and sharp insight are out in force here." Kirkus.

Hagberg, David

Abyss / David Hagberg. Tor, 2011. 496 p. Kirk McGarvey adventures

ISBN 9780765324108

1. Women scientists 2. Terrorism -- Prevention 3. Business -- Corrupt practices 4. Environmental degradation 5. Intelligence service 6. Former CIA agents 7. Florida 8. Hutchinson Island (Fla) 9. Thrillers and suspense 10. Spy fiction

LC 2011007891

"A Tom Doherty Associates book."

When an NOAA scientist has a breakthrough that could enable a sustainable energy source and prevent dangerous weather systems, legendary former CIA director Kirk McGarvey begins a frantic cat-and-mouse chase with a contract killer who would trigger an unprecedented nuclear disaster.

"This is a timely and frightening novel. Readers will be left thinking, This could really happen." Kirkus.

Hage, Rawi

Beirut Hellfire Society : a novel / Rawi Hage. W. W. Norton & Company, 2019., 288 p.

ISBN 9781324002918

1. 1970s 2. Undertakers 3. Existentialism 4. Death 5. Misfits (Persons) 6. Burial 7. Cremation 8. Rites and ceremonies 9. Funerals 10. Religion 11. Grief 12. Secret societies 13. War 14. Loss (Psychology) 15. Fathers and sons 16. Beirut, Lebanon -- History -- 20th century 17. Lebanon -- History -- Civil War, 1975-1990 18. Literary fiction

Previously published in Toronto : Alfred A. Knopf Canada, 2018.

It's 1978 in Beirut, Lebanon. When his father dies, Pavlov is approached by a member of the mysterious Beirut Hellfire Society, and agrees to take up his father's work for the Society, arranging burial or cremation for those have been denied last rites.

Hage, Rawi

De Niro's game / Rawi Hage. Steerforth Press, 2007, c2006. 277 p.

ISBN 9781581952230

1. 1980s 2. Civil war 3. Militias and irregular armies 4. War and society 5. Young men 6. Best friends 7. War and civilization 8. Childhood 9. Crime 10. Violence 11. War -- Psychological aspects 12. Escapes 13. Separated friends, relatives, etc 14. Exiles 15. Beirut, Lebanon -- History -- 20th century 16. Lebanon -- History -- Civil War, 1975-1990 17. France 18. Political fiction 19. War stories 20. Literary fiction

Originally published: Canada: House of Anansi, 2006.

International IMPAC Dublin Literary Award, 2008.

Quebec Writers' Federation Literary Awards, Hugh MacLennan Prize for Fiction, 2006.

Quebec Writers' Federation Literary Awards, McAuslan First Book Prize, 2006.

Governor General's Literary Awards, English-language Fiction finalist

Shortlisted for the Giller Prize, 2006

Follows the lives and choices of two best friends, Bassam and George, caught in Lebanon's civil war. Both men are desparate to escape Beirut but choose different paths to accomplish their goals.

"This is a grim, flat book. Hage's flatness gives it the right tone of bruised emotion, disconnectedness, and violence; it's what makes this such an effective debut." Quill & Quire.

Haig, Francesca

The **fire** sermon : a novel / Francesca Haig. Gallery Books, 2015. 320 p. Fire sermon

ISBN 9781476767185

1. Dystopias 2. Post-apocalypse 3. Twins 4. Perfection 5. Power (Social sciences) 6. Equality 7. Dystopian fiction 8. Science fiction

LC 2014031292

In a world turned primitive following a nuclear fire, every person is born with a twin and of each pair, one is an Alpha, perfect in every way, and the other is an Omega, burdened with a deformity that makes them ostracized; and psychic Cass, a rare Omega, dares to envision a world of equality.

"Haig's experience as a poet shows in her writing, which is clear, forceful and laced with bright threads of beauty. [A] well-built world [with] vivid characters and [a] suspenseful plot." Kirkus.

Haig, Matt, 1975-

The **humans** : a novel / Matt Haig. Simon & Schuster, 2013. 256 p.

ISBN 9781476727912

1. Aliens 2. Mathematicians 3. Immortality 4. Disguises 5. Human/alien encounters 6. Social science fiction 7. Science fiction

LC 2013003203

Regarding humans unfavorably upon arriving on Earth, a reluctant extraterrestrial assumes the identity of a Cambridge mathematician before realizing that there is more to the human race than he suspected and embarking on a darkly comic effort to save humanity from itself.

Haigh, Jennifer, 1968-

Baker Towers : a novel / Jennifer Haigh. William Morrow, 2005. 352 p.

ISBN 0060509414

1. Coal mining towns 2. Working class families 3. Small town life 4. Ambition 5. Single mothers 6. Widows 7. Families 8. Italian American women 9. Children of widows 10. Children of single parents 11. Brothers and sisters 12. Coal mines and mining 13. Small towns 14. Hometowns 15. Communities 16. World War II -- Pennsylvania -- Post-war aspects 17. Postwar life 18. Pennsylvania 19. Historical fiction 20. Family sagas

LC 2004049073

L. L. Winship/PEN New England Award for Fiction, 2006.

The decade following World War II becomes one of tragedy, excitement, and unexpected change for the five Novak children and the residents of their western Pennsylvania community of company houses, church festivals, union squabbles, and firemen's parades.

"This novel is set in Bakerton, a mining town in post-World World II Pennsylvania. Haigh's focus is the Novak family, particularly the five children being raised by their Italian mother after their Polish father drops dead. All five make attempts to escape Bakerton at one point or another; some are successful, others are not. George, a veteran of WW II, neglects his Bakerton fiancee and marries a cold socialite. Dorothy goes to the nation's capital to work, but a nervous breakdown brings her home. Brilliant, cold Joyce thinks her future lies with the military, but she is sorely disappointed. Sandy is the golden son who escapes to dubious success. And Lucy is the youngest, who finds herself in college despite the nagging feeling that she never wanted to leave home in the first place. Haigh creates a real sense of a community and brings her mining town to life through a large cast of minor characters who pass in and out of the Novaks' lives." Booklist.

Haigh, Jennifer, 1968-

Mrs. Kimble : a novel / Jennifer Haigh. Morrow, 2003. 400 p.

ISBN 0060509392

1. Men/women relations 2. Strength and weakness 3. Quarreling 4. Married men 5. Married women 6. Marriage 7. Engagement 8. Engaged persons 9. Babysitters 10. Loneliness 11. College dropouts 12. Manipulation by men 13. Vulnerability in women 14. Women with depression 15. Alcoholic women 16. Abandoned wives 17. Father-deserted children 18. Swindlers and swindling 19. Single mothers 20. Birthmarks 21. Breast cancer 22. Women cancer survivors 23. Real estate agents 24. Former clergymen 25. Bigamy 26. Literary fiction

LC 2002070304

Hemingway Foundation/PEN Award, 2004.

Follows twenty-five years in the life of a charismatic opportunist as seen through the eyes of his three wives.

"Original and compelling." Library Journal.

Hair, David, 1965-

Mage's blood / David Hair. Jo Flectcher Books, 2013. 686 p. Moontide quartet

ISBN 9781623650148

1. Wizards 2. Twelve-year-olds 3. Imaginary wars and battles 4. Tides 5. Magic 6. Bridges 7. Good and evil 8. Social conflict 9. Mercenaries 10. Imaginary empires 11. Heroes and heroines 12. Epic fantasy

When a third 12-year cycle causes the tides to sink so that an underwater realm is rendered accessible to above-ground trade, the people of the East, under the rule of power-hungry Magi who would conquer the Moontide world, trigger a cataclysmic battle that falls on the shoulders of three ordinary individuals.

Hair, David, 1965-

Scarlet tides / David Hair. Jo Fletcher Books, 2014, c2013. 684 p. Moontide quartet

ISBN 9781623658298

1. Imaginary empires 2. Imaginary wars and battles 3. Heroes and heroines 4. Wizards 5. Warriors 6. Magic 7. Bridges 8. Power (Social sciences) 9. Epic fantasy

A key magical artifact still eludes capture by Emperor Constant and is also being sought by a failed mage, a gypsy and a poor, lowly merchant girl, who vow to restore peace to Urte.

"The second volume in Hairs Moontide Quartet (after Mages Blood) is mostly dizzying movement, plunging headfirst into a convoluted series of plots, unraveling alliances, and tightening nooses... Some parts of the plot that feel slower or less tense are only the eye of the storm, and will keep Hair's fans satisfied while the storm builds." Publishers Weekly.

Haldane, Sean

* The **devil's** making / Sean Haldane. Minotaur Books, 2015, c2013. 367 p.

ISBN 9781250069405

1. 1860s 2. Police -- Victoria, British Columbia 3. Frontier and pioneer life 4. Race relations 5. Colonists 6. British in Canada 7. Murder investigation 8. Victoria, British Columbia 9. British Columbia 10. Great Britain -- Colonies -- Social conditions 11. Historical mysteries

Arthur Ellis Award for Best Novel, 2014.

In 1869 Victoria, British Columbia, policeman Chad Hobbes, recently arrived from England, must solve the murder of an American alienist, whose methods included phrenology, Mesmerism and sexual-mystical magnetation, and discovers that everyone who knew him seems to have something to hide.

"A good match for readers who relish suspense drawn out at a leisurely pace, lavish details of Pacific Northwest Coast Indian life, and the particular edginess of unreliable narrators." Booklist.

Haldeman, Joe W.

* The **forever** war / Joe Haldeman. EOS, 2003, c1974. 277 p. Forever series (Joe W. Haldeman)

ISBN 9780345324894

1. Space warfare 2. Space flight 3. Aging 4. Aliens 5. War -- Moral and ethical aspects 6. Relativity (Physics) 7. Time 8. Far future 9. Imaginary wars and battles 10. Military science fiction 11. Hard science fiction 12. Science fiction

Originally published: New York : St Martin's Press, 1974.

Hugo Award for Best Novel, 1976.

Locus Award for Best Science Fiction Novel, 1976.

Nebula Award for Best Novel, 1975.

Drafted into the ranks of Earth's interstellar warriors, private William Mandella finds his fight against the Taurans secondary to the side-effects of faster-than-light space travel, which affects the rate at which he ages.

Hale, Benjamin

The **evolution** of Bruno Littlemore / Benjamin Hale. Twelve, 2011. 592 p.

ISBN 9780446571579

1. Chimpanzees 2. Animal intelligence 3. Human/animal relationships 4. Human/animal communication 5. Alienation (Social psychology) 6. Bestiality 7. Behavior evolution 8. Chicago, Illinois 9. Satirical fiction 10. Literary fiction

LC 2010012098

Bruno Littlemore, the world's first chimpanzee with the ability to speak, tells the story of primatologist Lydia Littlemore's efforts to educate him; his untimely outbursts, which ultimately cost Lydia her job; and the unforgettable road trip that follows.

"Bruno, the novel's singular protagonist, is a 25-year-old chimp born at a zoo and raised by researchers who taught him to read, write, and speak. The trappings of humanity, unfortunately, have come with unexpected wants and desires, and Bruno ends up falling in love with one of his handlers. Deeply. Making your main character a talking ape and one who engages in a romantic liaison with a human being, no less is ambitious, to say the least. But from the first page, it is clear that Bruno is more than mere literary gimmickry; he is fascinating and fully formed. You learn as much by what he withholds as by what he provides, and he withholds a lot . . . . Where the novel should be offensive, it is often tender, and where it should be risible, it is genuinely funny." Entertainment Weekly.

Hale, Shannon

Austenland : a novel / Shannon Hale. Bloomsbury, 2007. 197 p. Austenland novels

ISBN 1596912855

1. Single women 2. Idealism in women 3. Gardeners 4. Thirties (Age) 5. Romantic love 6. Vacations 7. Resorts 8. Role playing 9. Interpersonal attraction 10. Men/women relations 11. Self-discovery in women 12. England 13. New York City 14. Chick lit

LC 2006034165

Because her obsession with Jane Austen's Mr. Darcy, as played by Colin Firth in the BBC adaptation of "Pride and Prejudice," is ruining her love life, Jane Hayes is delighted when she gets the chance to take a trip to an English resort catering to Austen-crazed women.

"The author's charming first book for adults is chick lit with soul. Though there's a laugh on nearly every page. Hale, like Austen, is adept at subtly skewering the ridiculous--there's also the more serious story of a woman learning the difference between fantasy and reality, and discovering that real life can be better than your dreams." BookPage.

Halfon, Eduardo

Mourning / Eduardo Halfon ; translated by Lisa Dillman & Daniel Hahn. Bellevue Literary Press, 2018. 192 p. Polish boxer novels

ISBN 9781942658443

1. Family history 2. Family secrets 3. Identity (Philosophical concept) 4. Jews 5. Immigrant families 6. Holocaust survivors 7. Violence -- Psychological aspects 8. Loss (Psychology) 9. Voyages and travels 10. Literary fiction 11. Translations -- Spanish to English

LC 2017059202

Originally published in Spanish in 2017 as Duelo by Libros del Asteroide.

Edward Lewis Wallant Award, 2018.

Kirkus Prize for Fiction finalist, 2018.

A mysterious family tragedy inspires a journey across the globe, into the past, and through the tangled memories of childhood.

Hall, Adam

The **quiller** memorandum / Adam Hall. Forge, 2004, c1965. 220 p. Quiller adventures

ISBN 076530967X

1. Spies -- Great Britain 2. Nazis -- West Germany 3. Intelligence officers 4. British in Germany 5. Berlin, Germany 6. Great Britain 7. Spy fiction 8. Adventure stories

LC 2003069455

"A Tom Doherty Associates book."

Also known as: The Berlin memorandum.

Edgar Allan Poe Award for Best Mystery Novel, 1966.

Set in West Berlin fifteen years after the end of World War II, a British agent takes on a neo-Nazi underground organization and its war-criminal leader.

Hall, Alexis

For real / Alexis Hall. Riptide Publishing, 2015 470 p. Spires novels

ISBN 9781626492806

1. Gay men 2. Men/men relations 3. Sexual dominance and submission 4. Middle-aged men -- Relations with younger men 5. Leather lifestyle (Sexuality) 6. Sadomasochism 7. Homosexuality 8. LGBTQIA romances 9. Contemporary romances 10. LGBTQIA fiction

RITA Award for Best Erotic Romance, 2016.

"In this charming May-December romance, Hall delights the reader with endless reversals of expectations...Hall blends pleasure and pain, both erotic and emotional, to create an engrossing romance with sharpness hidden in the sweetly traditional power-exchange relationship. The characters are charmingly flawed, with enough chemistry to see them through some serious ups and downs. Many classic images of dominance and submission are beautifully upended even as more traditional romance manages to bloom. Full of poetry and honesty, Laurie and Toby's journey together makes each victory feel earned." Publishers Weekly.

Hall, James W. (James Wilson), 1947-

Buzz cut / James W. Hall. Bantam Books, 1996. 374 p. Thorn novels
ISBN 0385312342
1. Cruise ships -- Florida 2. Murderers -- Florida 3. Missing women 4. Robbery 5. Pleasure cruises 6. Florida 7. Thrillers and suspense
LC 96-50425
Armed with electric fingertips, a terrorist plans to turn a cruise ship into a floating bomb. The reclusive Thorn, a ship employee, must work against the clock to sabotage the plan.
"Butler Jack's love of words comes to him naturally, from an author who uses language with great delicacy, even when his characters are sticking knives into one another." New York Times Book Review.

Hall, James W. (James Wilson), 1947-

Red sky at night / James W. Hall. Delacorte Press, 1997. 326 p. Thorn novels
ISBN 0385316380
1. Men with disabilities 2. Medical researchers 3. Marine animals in medicine 4. Dolphins 5. Murder 6. Pain treatment centers 7. Paralysis 8. Vietnam veterans 9. Key Largo, Florida 10. Thrillers and suspense
LC 96045621
Thorn checks into a pain clinic run by a childhood friend and uncovers a series of horrifying experiments being performed on handicapped Army veterans, placing his own life in danger
"Popular fiction at its absolute best." Booklist.

Hall, Louisa, 1982-

Speak / Louisa Hall. HarperCollins, 2015 352 p.
ISBN 9780062391193
1. Artificial intelligence 2. Robots 3. Technology and civilization 4. Communication 5. Science fiction 6. Social science fiction 7. Epistolary novels
Exploring the creation of artificial intelligence and illuminating the very human need for communication, connection and understanding, a thought-provoking novel is told from the perspectives of five very different people from different times and places.
"Hall subtly weaves a thread through a temporally diverse cast of narrators. Like all good robot novels, Speak raises questions about what it means to be human as well as the meaning of giving voice to memory." Booklist.

Hall, Parnell

Lights! Camera! Puzzles! / Parnell Hall ; ; with puzzles from ... Will Shortz. Pegasus Crime, 2019 263 p. Puzzle lady mysteries
ISBN 9781643130590
1. Crossword puzzles 2. Crossword puzzle makers 3. Women amateur detectives 4. Filmmaking 5. Biographical films 6. Former husbands 7. Murder investigation 8. New York City 9. Hobby mysteries 10. Cozy mysteries
Sequel to: The purloined puzzle.

When her ex's sensational tell-all about their lives is optioned for a movie, Puzzle Lady Cora Felton reluctantly accepts a producer role's in the much-despised production before a body is found on set, staged with a crossword puzzle clue.

Hall, Tarquin

The **case** of the deadly butter chicken : a Vish Puri mystery / Tarquin Hall. McClelland & Stewart, 2012. 288 p. Vish Puri mysteries
ISBN 9780771038297
1. Detectives 2. Murder investigation 3. Secrets 4. Poisoning 5. Cricket (Sports) 6. Sports betting 7. Gambling 8. Private investigators 9. Pakistan 10. India 11. Mysteries
Previously published Great Britain : Hutchinson, 2012.
Mustachioed sleuth Vish Puri tackles his greatest fears in a case involving the poisoning death of the elderly father of a leading Pakistani cricketer, whose demise is linked to the Indian and Pakistani mafias and the violent 1947 partition of India.

Hall, Tarquin

The **case** of the love commandos : from the files of Vish Puri, India's most private investigator / Tarquin Hall. Simon & Schuster, 2013. 310 p. Vish Puri mysteries
ISBN 9781451613261
1. Private investigators 2. Social classes 3. Missing persons 4. Romantic love 5. Families 6. Missing persons investigation 7. Pakistan 8. India 9. Mysteries
LC 2013009100
Includes recipes and glossary p.297-310.
Coming to the rescue of Ram and Tulsi, only to have Ram disappear, India's Love Commandos, a real-life group of volunteers dedicated to helping mixed-caste couples, asks Vish Puri, India's Most Private Investigator, to help them reunite the star-crossed lovers.

Hallberg, Garth Risk

* **City** on fire / Garth Risk Hallberg. Alfred A. Knopf, 2015. 944 p.
ISBN 9780385353779
1. 1970s 2. Interpersonal relations 3. Punk culture 4. Detectives 5. Betrayal 6. Power failures 7. Shooting 8. Heirs and heiresses 9. Friendship 10. Husband and wife 11. Teenagers 12. New York City 13. Literary fiction
LC 2014041963
A tale set against a backdrop of the infamous 1977 blackout follows the experiences of two New York heirs, their paramours, two punk-loving teens, an obsessive reporter and a detective who would learn what any of them have to do with a Central Park shooting.
"Graceful in execution, hugely entertaining, and most concerned with the longing for connection, a theme that reaches full realization during the blackout of 1977, this epic tale is both a compelling mystery and a literary tour de force." Booklist.

Halliday, Lisa

* **Asymmetry** / Lisa Halliday. Simon & Schuster, 2018. 275 p.
ISBN 9781501166761
1. Art 2. Writing 3. Inequality 4. Interpersonal relations 5. Men/women relations 6. Literary fiction
Explores the imbalances that drive dramatic human relations, tracing the overlapping stories of a young American editor's relationship with a famous older writer during the early years of the Iraq War, and an Iraqi-American man who is detained by immigration officers in Heathrow.

Hallinan, Timothy

Crashed / Timothy Hallinan. Soho Crime, 2012, c2010. 356 p. Junior Bender mysteries

ISBN 9781616952747

1. Organized crime 2. Sabotage 3. Pornographic films 4. Thieves 5. Extortion 6. Private investigators 7. Pornographic film actors and actresses 8. Former child actors and actresses 9. Drug addicts 10. Single fathers 11. Crime bosses 12. Interpersonal conflict 13. Attempted murder 14. Los Angeles, California 15. Mysteries

Master thief Junior Bender is blackmailed by a powerful crime boss into finding out who is causing all the problems on the set of his pornographic film, which features a destitute and strung-out former child star.

Hallinan, Timothy

* Fields where they lay / Timothy Hallinan. Soho Crime, 2016. 384 p. Junior Bender mysteries

ISBN 9781616957469

1. Thieves 2. Christmas 3. Shopping malls 4. Gangsters 5. Shoplifting 6. Murder 7. Organized crime 8. Hollywood, California 9. Mysteries

"It's the week before Christmas in Tinsel Town, and the Edgerton Mall isn't exactly full of holiday cheer, despite its two Santas. The mall is a fossil of an industry in decline; many of its stores are closed, and to make matters worse, there is a rampant shoplifting problem. Enter burglar Junior Bender, the unwilling fixer for LA's various underworld bosses. The murderous Russian gangster who owns the mall hires Junior to look into the shoplifting problem for him. But Junior's surveillance operation doesn't go well: within two days, two people are dead. It's obvious that shoplifting is the least of the mall's problems. Meanwhile, Junior must confront his own deep-seated melancholy at the very notion of Christmas--both present and past"--, Provided by publisher.

"A plum pudding stuffed with cynical disillusionment, organized and disorganized crime, two Santas, a seasonal miracle, and an ending that earns every bit of its uplift." Kirkus.

Hallinan, Timothy

Fools' river / Timothy Hallinan. Soho Crime, 2017. 360 p. Poke Rafferty Bangkok thrillers

ISBN 9781616957506

1. Travel writers 2. Amateur detectives 3. Kidnapping victims 4. Missing persons investigation 5. Thieves 6. Expatriates 7. City life 8. Bangkok, Thailand 9. Thailand 10. Thrillers and suspense

LC 2017011761

When his daughter's friend begs for help tracking down his father, Bangkok writer Poke Rafferty discovers that the missing man has been abducted by a pair of killers who kidnap people and drain their accounts before murdering them, a finding that triggers a desperate race against time.

Hambly, Barbara

Lady of perdition / Barbara Hambly. Severn House, 2020, c2019. 246 p. Benjamin January mysteries

ISBN 9780727889096

1. Antebellum America (1820-1861) 2. Freed slaves 3. Amateur detectives 4. African American men 5. Musicians 6. Violence against women 7. Murder investigation 8. Women murder suspects 9. Political intrigue 10. Slavery 11. Texas -- History -- 19th century 12. Historical mysteries

First published in 2019.

Risking his freedom in New Orleans to help a loved one in the Republic of Texas in 1840, Benjamin January navigates land disputes and racism to locate a kidnapped girl while proving the innocence of a murdered landowner's widow.

"It's a stark and occasionally brutal story, and Hambly tells it superbly, in prose that is vivid and empathetic." Booklist.

Hamer, Kate

The **girl** in the red coat / Kate Hamer. Melville House, 2016, c2015. 378 p.

ISBN 9781612195001

1. Missing girls 2. Single mothers 3. Eight-year-old girls 4. Captives 5. Captivity 6. Mother-separated girls 7. Men with mental illnesses 8. Religion 9. Kidnapping 10. England 11. Great Britain 12. Psychological suspense

Originally published: London : Faber and Faber, 2015.

When her daughter Carmel disappears during an outdoor festival, Beth, despite being told by authorities she may be gone for good, embarks on a mission to find her.

"Telling the story in two remarkable voices, with Beth's chapters unfurling in past tense and Carmel's in present tense, the author weaves a page-turning narrative. The trajectories of the novel's two leads--through despair, hope, and redemption--are believable and nuanced, resulting in a morally complex, haunting read." Publishers Weekly.

Hamid, Mohsin, 1971-

* Exit west : a novel / Mohsin Hamid. Riverhead Books, 2017. 240 p.

ISBN 9780735212176

1. Couples 2. Refugees 3. Political violence 4. Civil war 5. Culture conflict 6. Guerrilla warfare 7. Fundamentalism 8. Voyages and travels 9. Religious persecution 10. Immigration and emigration 11. Literary fiction 12. Love stories 13. War stories 14. Political fiction

LC 2016036296

ALA Notable Book, 2018.

Kirkus Prize for Fiction finalist, 2017.

Shortlisted for the Man Booker Prize, 2017.

Longlisted for the Andrew Carnegie Medal for Excellence in Fiction, 2018.

National Book Critics Circle Award for Fiction finalist, 2017

Shortlisted for the International Dublin Literary Award, 2019.

Presents the story of two young lovers whose furtive affair is shaped by local unrest on the eve of a civil war that erupts in a cataclysmic bombing attack, forcing them to abandon their previous home and lives.

"Hamid's storytelling is stripped down, and the books sweeping allegory is timely and resonant." Publishers Weekly.

Hamill, Pete, 1935-

Forever / Pete Hamill. Little, Brown and Co., 2003. 624 p.

ISBN 0316341118

1. Revenge 2. Orphans 3. Immortality 4. Peasant men 5. Earls and countesses 6. Irish in the United States 7. Magic swords 8. Mythology, Celtic 9. Ireland 10. Manhattan, New York City 11. Urban fantasy

LC 2002114241

Moving from Ireland to New York City in 1741, Cormac O'Connor witnesses the city's transformation into a thriving metropolis while he explores the mysteries of time, loss, and love.

"In 1740, an Irish Jew named Cormac O'Connor heads to New York in pursuit of the man who killed his father and gets tangled up in a rebellion against the English. Through a series of events involving an African slave with shamanistic powers, he is granted eternal life, provided that he never leaves Manhattan. There follows a tour of the city's history through Cormac's eyes: the political corruption and the poverty, but also the majestic growth of the metropolis through its culture, its buildings, and its people." The New Yorker.

LIST OF FICTIONAL WORKS

Hamill, Pete, 1935-

Tabloid city : a novel / Pete Hamill. Little, Brown and Co., 2011. 288 p. Sam Briscoe novels

ISBN 9780316020756

1. Newspaper editors 2. Women murder victims 3. Terrorism 4. Murder investigation 5. Extremists 6. Socialites 7. Journalists 8. Manhattan, New York City 9. New York City 10. Crime fiction

LC 2010026166

When a wealthy socialite and her secretary are found murdered in a stately West Village townhouse, a flurry of seemingly unrelated people spring into action. A reporter chases the story while a tabloid executive holds the presses, a ruined financer attempts to leave the country, a war veteran plots revenge, and a terrorist plans an attack.

"Just as the last ever edition of the New York World is getting put to bed, veteran editor Sam Briscoe stops the presses for a sensational murder: socialite Cynthia Harding and her personal secretary are found stabbed to death in Harding's Manhattan town house. The story unfolds in time-stamped, you-are-there bursts that follow a large cast, including several journalists; Cynthia's adopted daughter; a disgraced Madoff-like financier; a media blogger; the murdered secretary's husband, a police officer assigned to a counterterrorism task force, as well as their son, a convert to radical Islam; and best of all by the weary and worldly Briscoe himself. Hamill is at his best in the Briscoe portions, rich in print anecdotes and mournful for a passing age." Publishers Weekly.

Hamill, Shaun

A **cosmology** of monsters / Shaun Hamill. Pantheon Books, 2019. 336 p.

ISBN 9781524747671

1. Monsters 2. Family problems 3. Obsession 4. Supernatural 5. Sexuality 6. Haunted houses 7. Family history 8. Loss (Psychology) 9. Family relationships 10. Texas 11. Horror 12. Coming-of-age stories

Shielded by his mother and sisters from his father's obsessive construction of a haunted house attraction, young Noah considers an ultimate sacrifice when he chooses to acknowledge a monster that his family members have tried to ignore.

Hamilton, Jane, 1957 July 13-

A **map** of the world / Jane Hamilton. Doubleday, 1994. 389 p.

ISBN 0385473109

1. Guilt in women 2. Drowning 3. Women prisoners 4. Scapegoats (Persons) 5. Mothers 6. Dairy farmers 7. School nurses 8. Families 9. Separated friends, relatives, etc 10. Friendship 11. Wisconsin 12. Middle West 13. Mainstream fiction

LC 94-42531

On a dairy farm in the midwest, Alice is watching her neighbor's daughter when she drowns in the pond. This marks the beginning of a series of events that turns Alice into a scapegoat and brings about her family's downfall.

"This is not an easy or light read; indeed, it takes on some of the toughest issues of modern life. But the writer's skill in describing a community and a way of life, as well as her insight into the hearts of her characters, render this story difficult to forget." Christian Science Monitor.

Hamilton, Peter F.

The **dreaming** void / Peter F. Hamilton. Del Rey/Ballantine Books, 2008. 640 p. Void trilogy

ISBN 9780345496539

1. 34th century 2. Telepathy 3. Religious fanatics 4. Life on other planets 5. Visions 6. Space vehicles 7. Scientists 8. Police 9. Genetic engineering 10. Power (Social sciences) 11. Space opera 12. Science fiction

LC 2007029244

Originally published: London : Macmillan, 2007.

At the center of the galaxy is the Dreaming Void, an artificial black hole that may hold paradise within its walls. When a human named Inigo begins dreaming of what lies within the Void, the word spreads, triggering a religious pilgrimage into the Void and possibly a catastrophic expansion that threatens the peace of the Commonwealth Universe.

"There is a generous cast of characters and a handful of storylines involved here and it takes the overall story a while to get going. But once it does, it feels like putting on a comfortable jacket; space opera is what Hamilton does and he does it well." SF Signal

Hamilton, Peter F.

Great North Road / Peter F. Hamilton. Del Rey/Ballantine Books, 2012. 976 p.

ISBN 9780345526663

1. 22nd century 2. Serial murder investigation 3. Clones and cloning 4. Rich families 5. Human/alien encounters 6. Life on other planets 7. Energy resources 8. Corporations 9. Scientific expeditions 10. Aliens 11. Detectives 12. Secrets 13. Men/women relations 14. Science fiction mysteries 15. Science fiction

LC 2012033593

In 2143 Newcastle, a naked corpse is dredged from the River Tyne. Although there's no physical evidence, police detective Sidney Hurst must discover the identity of both the murderer and the victim, who seems to be one of the hundreds of clones comprising the North family. Their wealthy and powerful dynasty began with three brothers who pioneered technology allowing humans access to other star systems -- and the off-world production of Earth's primary fuel source, bioil. In this deadly web of money, politics, and family secrets, Hurst has just one lead: a decades-old crime with striking similarities to his present-day case. - Description by Gillian Speace.

Hamilton, Peter F.

Pandora's star / Peter F. Hamilton. Del Rey, 2004. 768 p. Commonwealth saga

ISBN 0345461622

1. 24th century 2. Wormholes (Astrophysics) 3. Aliens (Non-humanoid) 4. Space exploration 5. Humans 6. Space flight 7. Science fiction 8. Space opera

LC 2003068753

Sequel: Judas unchained.

Originally published: London: Macmillan, 2004.

The year is 2380. The Intersolar Commonwealth, a sphere of stars some four hundred light-years in diameter, contains more than six hundred worlds, interconnected by a web of transport "tunnels" known as wormholes. At the farthest edge of the Commonwealth, astronomer Dudley Bose observes the impossible: Over one thousand light-years away, a star ... vanishes. It does not go supernova. It does not collapse into a black hole. It simply disappears. Since the location is too distant to reach by wormhole, a faster-than-light starship, the Second Chance, is dispatched to learn what has occurred and whether it represents a threat.

"By the 24th century, the vast human Commonwealth has spread from Earth via artificial wormholes. Various benign or seemingly indifferent alien races have been encountered during exploration of new planets, but an astronomer sparks curiosity by announcing that a pair of stars is enclosed by a mysterious energy barrier. Unfortunately, a space expedition discovers that the shield was created to imprison an insatiably greedy mass mind that sees any other race as a mortal threat. When the barrier somehow is lowered, the alien immediately attacks the largely unprepared Commonwealth, while humans begin wondering if yet another inhuman power has manipulated events that unleashed this threat. The author deftly juggles many characters in multiple plot lines." Publishers Weekly.

Hamilton, Steve, 1961-

* The **lock** artist / Steve Hamilton. Minotaur Books, 2010. 304 p.

ISBN 9780312380427

1. Safecrackers 2. Men who are mute 3. Psychic trauma in men 4. Former convicts 5. Criminals 6. Safecracking 7. Secrets 8. Lock picking 9. Crime fiction

LC 2009034523

Edgar Allan Poe Award for Best Novel, 2011.

Ian Fleming Steel Dagger Award, 2011.

Traumatized at the age of eight and pushed into a life of crime by reason of his unforgiveable talent--lock picking--Michael sees his chance to escape, and with one desperate gamble risks everything to come back home to the only person he ever loved, and to unlock the secret that has kept him silent for so long.

Hamilton, Steve, 1961-

* The **second** life of Nick Mason : a novel / Steve Hamilton. Putnam Pub. Group, 2016 304 p. Nick Mason novels

ISBN 9780399574320

1. Organized crime 2. Former convicts 3. Thieves 4. Manipulation (Social sciences) 5. Control (Psychology) 6. Second chances 7. Detectives 8. Families 9. Crime 10. Deals 11. Chicago, Illinois 12. Crime fiction

LC 2015022076

Reprieved from a long prison term in exchange for committing increasingly dangerous crimes on behalf of a criminal kingpin, Nick Mason is relentlessly haunted by the detective who initially placed him behind bars.

Hammad, Isabella

* The **Parisian,** or, Al-Barisi : a novel / Isabella Hammad. Grove Press, 2019. ix, 566 p.

ISBN 9780802129437

1. 1910s 2. First World War era (1914-1918) 3. Ottoman Empire (1299-1922) 4. Palestinians -- Identity 5. Immigrants, Arab 6. Social conflict 7. Lost love 8. Colonialism 9. Social change 10. Arab nationalism 11. Medical students 12. Arranged marriage 13. World War I -- France 14. National liberation movements 15. Paris, France -- History 16. Palestine -- History 17. Middle East -- History 18. Literary fiction 19. Historical fiction

LC 2018058113

Studying medicine and falling in love in 1914 France, the son of a wealthy Palestinian textile merchant finds his loyalties tested by conflicts between the British government and the independence-minded nationalists of his community.

"Richly textured prose drives the novels spellbinding themes of the ebb and flow of cultural connections and people who struggle with love, familial responsibilities, and personal identity." Publishers Weekly.

Hammett, Dashiell, 1894-1961

The **glass** key / Dashiell Hammett. Vintage Books, 1989, c1931. 214 p.

ISBN 0679722629

1. Frameups 2. Politicians 3. Heirs and heiresses 4. Male friendship 5. Gamblers 6. Organized crime 7. Amateur detectives 8. Political corruption 9. Men/women relations 10. Interpersonal attraction 11. Lust 12. Murder 13. Hardboiled fiction 14. Mysteries

LC 88040517

Originally published by A. A. Knopf in 1931.

This classic work of detective fiction combines an airtight plot, authentically venal characters, and writing of telegraphic crispness. -- Amazon

Hammett, Dashiell, 1894-1961

* The **Maltese** falcon / Dashiell Hammett. Vintage Books, 1992, c1957. 217 p.

ISBN 0679722645

1. 1920s 2. Femmes fatales 3. Private investigators 4. Business partners 5. Widows 6. Police 7. Soviets in the United States 8. Murder suspects 9. Deception 10. Dishonesty 11. Betrayal 12. Gems 13. Decoys 14. Murder 15. Murder investigation 16. Extramarital affairs 17. San Francisco, California -- History -- 20th century 18. Hardboiled fiction 19. Mysteries 20. Modern classics

LC 85672450

Sam Spade's partner is murdered while working on a case, and it is Spade's responsibility to find the killer. In his search, Spade runs mortal risks as he comes closer to the answer.

Hammett, Dashiell, 1894-1961

* The **thin** man / Dashiell Hammett. Vintage Books, 1992, c1934. 201 p.

ISBN 9780679722632

1. Husband-and-wife detectives 2. Married people 3. Missing persons 4. Private investigators 5. New York City 6. Noir fiction

LC 9150920

Originally published: New York : Knopf ; London : Barker, 1934.

Nick Charles searches for a wealthy inventor who is the prime suspect in a New York City murder case

Hampton, Brenda (Brenda M.)

Stalker / Brenda Hampton. Urban Books, 2017. 288 p.

ISBN 9781622867974

1. Divorced women 2. Stalkers 3. Threat (Psychology) 4. Men/women relations 5. Interpersonal attraction 6. African-American women 7. Stalking 8. Drama lit 9. Thrillers and suspense 10. African American fiction

After a brutal divorce, Abigal Wilson vowed to never love again, but when Brent Carson crosses her path, she simply can't resist his good-guy persona that exemplifies perfection, but then he gives her the bad news.

Han, Kang, 1970-

* **Human** acts : a novel / Han Kang ; translated from the Korean and introduced by Deborah Smith. Hogarth, 2016, c2014. 218 p.

ISBN 9781101906729

1. 20th century 2. 21st century 3. Protests, demonstrations, vigils, etc 4. Political violence 5. Consequences 6. Life change events 7. Dissenters 8. Murder 9. Teenage boys -- Death 10. Loss (Psychology) 11. Grief 12. Student movements 13. Interpersonal relations 14. South Korea -- Politics and government 15. Political fiction 16. Literary fiction 17. Translations -- Korean to English

Originally published as: Sonyon i onda = The boy is coming : Changbi Publishers, 2014.

ALA Notable Book, 2018.

Longlisted for the Andrew Carnegie Medal for Excellence in Fiction, 2018.

Shortlisted for the International Dublin Literary Award, 2018.

Follows the aftermath of a young boy's shocking death during a violent student uprising as told from the perspectives of the event's victims and their loved ones.

"A fiercely written, deeply upsetting, and beautifully human novel." Kirkus.

Han, Kang, 1970-

The **white** book / Han Kang ; translated from the Korean by Deborah Smith. Hogarth, 2019, c2016. 157 p.

ISBN 9780525573067

1. Han, Kang, 1970- Family 2. White (Color) 3. Infant death 4. Grief 5. Loss (Psychology) 6. Death 7. Sisters 8. Mourning customs 9. Autobiographical fiction 10. Literary fiction

Originally published in Korean: Seoul: Munhak Dongne, 2016.

"This translation originally published in Great Britain by Portobello Books, London in 2017. This edition published by arrangement with Portobello Books."--Title page verso.

Shortlisted for the Man Booker International Prize, 2018.

An exploration of personal grief, conveyed through the prism of the color white, finds a nameless writer grappling with a haunting family tragedy involving the infancy death of her older sister.

"Though thin on conventional narrative, the novel resonates as a prayer for the departed, and only gains power upon rereading." Publishers Weekly.

Hand, Elizabeth

Available dark : a thriller / Elizabeth Hand. Minotaur Books, 2012. 256 p. Cass Neary novels

ISBN 9780312585945

1. Women photographers 2. Violence 3. Serial murders 4. Photographs 5. Death 6. Fashion photographers 7. Human sacrifice 8. Former lovers 9. Finland 10. Iceland 11. Thrillers and suspense 12. Scandinavian crime fiction

LC 2011032833

Sequel to: Generation loss

Fleeing for her life after she is shown photographs of ritual killings during a mysterious job in Helsinki, Cass Neary encounters a former lover and exiled musician in Iceland only to be inundated by a series of unsolved murders.

Hand, Elizabeth

* **Curious** toys / Elizabeth Hand. Mulholland Books, 2019. 336 p.

ISBN 9780316485883

1. Darger, Henry, 1892-1973 2. 1910s 3. Male impersonators 4. Violence in men 5. City life 6. Misfits (Persons) 7. Amusement parks 8. Drug dealers 9. Amateur detectives 10. Murderers 11. Teenage girls 12. Artists 13. Summer 14. Murder investigation 15. Chicago, Illinois 16. Historical mysteries

Joining a gang near the famous Riverview amusement park in 1915 Chicago, the daughter of a fortune teller teams up with a reclusive artist to track down a serial killer responsible for a child's disappearance.

Hand, Elizabeth

* **Generation** loss : a novel / Elizabeth Hand. Small Beer Press, 2007. 320 p. Cass Neary novels

ISBN 1931520216

1. Women photographers 2. Secrets 3. Redemption 4. Self-destructive behavior in women 5. Islands 6. Interviews 7. Death 8. Artists 9. Communes 10. New York City 11. Maine 12. Thrillers and suspense

LC 2006102024

Sequel: Available dark

Shirley Jackson Awards, Novel, 2007.

Cass, a photographer who made a name for herself in the seventies, now finds herself adrift when someone sends her on a mercy gig where she stumbles across an old mystery that is still claiming victims.

"This is a crossover novel, difficult to classify, uncomfortable, spiky. Hand is one of those writers who has challenged the restrictions of genre writing. Here, she both fights with and against the conventions of the thriller genre to get at an evil deeper than its mere perpetrator. . . . So although Generation Loss moves like a thriller, it detonates with greater resound. It's a dark and beautiful novel that should not be read by anyone under the age of 30." Washington Post Book World.

Hand, Elizabeth

Hard light / Elizabeth Hand. Minotaur Books, 2016. 336 p. Cass Neary novels

ISBN 9781250030382

1. Women photographers 2. Violence 3. Smuggling 4. Photographs 5. Death 6. Murder 7. Threat (Psychology) 8. Former lovers 9. London, England 10. Thrillers and suspense

As the story opens Cass arrives in London where she's arranged to meet her long-lost lover, Quinn O'Boyle. When Quinn fails to show at their rendezvous point, Cass meets the eccentric couple Mallo and Morven Dunfries. When Mallo catches Cass rifling his medicine cabinet in search of drugs, he threatens to turn her in to the authorities, then puts her to work as a runner for his illegal goods.

Hand, Elizabeth

Mortal love : a novel / Elizabeth Hand. William Morrow, 2004. 384 p.

ISBN 0061051705

1. 19th century 2. 2000s (Decade) 3. Obsession in men 4. Desire 5. Artists 6. Unrequited love 7. Creation (Literary, artistic, etc) 8. Authors 9. Muses (Persons) 10. Americans in England 11. People with mental illnesses 12. Psychiatrists 13. Despair 14. Sexuality 15. Psychiatric hospitals 16. Supernatural 17. London, England 18. New York City 19. Historical fantasy 20. Mythological fiction

LC 2003062398

In a tale that explores the link between creativity and madness, artist Radborne Comstock interacts with a captivating woman who both inspires him and becomes an object of obsession.

"What lies behind the complex, even violent process that we call artistic inspiration? That is the final mystery evoked in Elizabeth Hand's ambitious and richly imagined novel. By tracing the turbulence and reverberations of that process back to its source, Mortal Love offers its readers the satisfactions of a detective thriller. Here, however, the mystery goes deeper than murder. Nothing, Hand convinces us, is quite as mysterious as art." Washington Post Book World.

Handke, Peter

* **Don** Juan : his own version / Peter Handke ; translated from the German by Krishna Winston. Farrar, Straus and Giroux, 2010. 112 p.

ISBN 9780374142315

1. Cooks -- France 2. Don Juan (Legendary character) 3. Seduction 4. Innkeepers 5. France 6. Literary fiction

LC 2009029526

"In this quick and airy fantasia, the quintessential womanizer becomes instead a sad and mostly passive man, possessing a certain magnetism but emphatically not a seducer, who feels pursued by time itself. Handke's multilayered structure has a sympathetic narrator relaying Don Juan's account of travel through contemporary Europe, the Middle East, and North Africa. ... The novel's action is obscured behind screens of philosophically tinted analysis touching on the nature of relationships, storytelling, and time. And yet the story itself is suffused with the freshness of the French countryside in which it largely takes place." The New Yorker.

Hannah, Kristin,

The **great** alone / Kristin Hannah. St. Martin's Press, 2018. 464 p.

ISBN 9780312577230

1. 1970s 2. Vietnam veterans 3. Wilderness survival 4. Moving, Household 5. Post-traumatic stress disorder 6. Communities 7. Thirteen-year-old girls 8. Violence in men 9. Friendship 10. Families 11. Alaska 12. Domestic fiction

LC 2017036271

Goodreads Choice Award, 2018

When her volatile, former POW father impulsively moves the family to mid-1970s Alaska to live off the land, young Leni and her mother are forced to confront the dangers of their lack of preparedness in the wake of a dangerous winter season.

"[The novel is] a heart-tugger written in borderline young adult style, combining terrible troubles with notes of overripe romance . . . [The book] is packed with rapturous descriptions of Alaskan scenery, which are the most reliably alluring part of it. . . .Characters are good or bad in 'The Great Alone,' happy or miserable." New York Times.

Hannah, Kristin

Home front / Kristin Hannah. St. Martin's Press, 2012. 400 p.

ISBN 9780312577209

1. Married people 2. Husband and wife 3. Marital conflict 4. Defense attorneys 5. Helicopter pilots 6. Families of military personnel 7. Women pilots 8. Post-traumatic stress disorder 9. Iraq War, 2003-2011 10. War -- Psychological aspects 11. United States -- National Guard 12. Washington (State) 13. Domestic fiction 14. Women's lives and relationships

LC 2011033805

Struggling with a marital estrangement that is further complicated when one of them is deployed, military couple Michael and Joleen Zarkades are forced to confront their problems while protecting the security of their family.

Hannah, Kristin

The **nightingale** / Kristin Hannah. St. Martin's Press, 2015. 384 p.

ISBN 9780312577223

1. Second World War era (1939-1945) 2. Sisters 3. War and society 4. World War II 5. Rescues 6. Resistance to military occupation 7. Families of military personnel 8. French Resistance (World War II) 9. Loss (Psychology) 10. Secrets 11. Reminiscing in old age 12. Family relationships 13. Men/women relations 14. France 15. Historical fiction

LC 2014033303

RUSA Reading List Short List, 2016.

Reunited when the elder's husband is sent to fight in World War II, French sisters Vianne and Isabelle find their bond as well as their respective beliefs tested by a world that changes in horrific ways.

Hannah, Sophie, 1971-

The **cradle** in the grave / Sophie Hannah. Penguin Books, 2011, c2010. 464 p. Simon Waterhouse and Charlie Zailer novels

ISBN 9780143119944

1. Serial murderers 2. Women television producers and directors 3. Sudden infant death syndrome 4. Police 5. Crimes against mothers 6. London, England 7. Thrillers and suspense 8. Psychological suspense 9. Police procedurals

LC 2011014075

Originally published under the title A room swept white (London: Hodder, 2010).

A television producer finds herself at the heart of a mystery after receiving an anonymous card in the mail that matches one found in the pocket of a murder victim who had been featured in a documentary about crib-death.

"The novel concludes in a fashion that manages to be both surprising and, in retrospect, somewhat inevitable, which is further testament to Hannah's storytelling prowess. The author has certainly chosen to work with a lot of ingredients here, and yet the subtlety with which she does so makes for a hearty literary meal-one in which each part feels as if it's essential. If good books are those that entertain while simultaneously provoking thought, then this one certainly qualifies." Hartford Examiner.

Hannah, Sophie, 1971-

Keep her safe / Sophie Hannah. HarperCollins, 2017. 384 p.

ISBN 9780062388322

1. Frameups 2. Witnesses 3. Teenage girl murder victims 4. Staged deaths 5. Deception 6. Resorts 7. Thrillers and suspense

A British woman's relaxing holiday at a sunny Arizona resort transforms into a dark, obsessive quest for the truth when she becomes convinced that another guest is the woman who disappeared in a sensational headline case years earlier.

Hannah, Sophie, 1971-

* The **mystery** of three quarters : the new Hercule Poirot mystery / Sophie Hannah. William Morrow, 2018. 320 p. New Hercule Poirot mysteries

ISBN 9780062792341

1. Between the Wars (1918-1939) 2. 1920s 3. Private investigators 4. Murder suspects 5. Malicious accusation 6. Murder victims 7. Murder investigation 8. Strangers 9. Historical mysteries

LC 2018019740

At head of title: Agatha Christie.

"Agatha Christie" -- Cover.

Accused by strangers of trying to set them up for murder, Hercule Poirot teams up with Scotland Yard policeman Edward Catchpool to investigate the drowning death of an elderly man.

"In her third Poirot mystery, Hannah, authorized to continue the series by Agatha Christie's estate, once again nails the style and substance of her beloved predecessor, producing another treat for Christie fans." Booklist.

Hannah, Sophie, 1971-

* **Perfect** little children / Sophie Hannah. William Morrow, 2020. 416 p.

ISBN 9780062978202

1. Former friends 2. Mothers 3. Children 4. Aging 5. Snooping 6. Stalking 7. Women amateur detectives 8. Secrets 9. England 10. Cambridge, England 11. United States 12. Florida 13. Psychological suspense

Spying on a former best friend she has not seen in years, Beth is alarmed when she discovers that the woman's children do not appear to have aged.

"A tightly wound tale of love gone awry." Booklist.

LIST OF FICTIONAL WORKS

Hannah, Sophie, 1971-

The **wrong** mother / Sophie Hannah. Penguin Books, 2009, c2008. 432 p. Simon Waterhouse and Charlie Zailer novels

ISBN 9780143116301

1. Married women 2. Extramarital affairs 3. Secret identity 4. Murder 5. Deception 6. Police 7. England 8. Psychological suspense 9. Police procedurals

LC 2009027521

Originally published as The point of rescue: London : Hodder, 2008.

A year after a brief vacation affair, Sally Thorning hears her one-time lover's name on the news and is shocked to hear that the man's wife and daughter have died, a situation that quickly escalates to the point that Sally's own family is placed in danger.

"Shockingly (and refreshingly) blunt riffs about the violent emotions of motherhood and the familial yearnings of men, along with chilling and darkly funny revelations about lust and loyalty, make this novel one of the season's most absorbing reads." O magazine.

Hannaham, James

* **Delicious** foods / James Hannaham. Little Brown & Co., 2015. 371 p.

ISBN 9780316284943

1. Widows 2. Drug addiction 3. Captivity 4. Mother separated boys 5. Farms 6. Captives 7. Drugs 8. Mothers and sons 9. Survival 10. Psychological fiction 11. Literary fiction 12. African American fiction

ALA Notable Book, 2016.

Hurston/Wright Legacy Award: Fiction, 2016.

PEN-Faulkner Award, 2016.

A young widow with an addiction is lured away to a remote farm by a shady company called Delicious Foods, where she is held captive and forced into hard labor while she struggles to become reunited with her young son.

"If the plot sounds like tough going, Hannahams masterpiece is anything but. The writing makes it 'great,' and the themes of pain, forgiveness, exploitation, and self-creation make it American." Booklist.

Hansen, Ron, 1947-

* The **assassination** of Jesse James by the coward Robert Ford / Ron Hansen. A. A. Knopf, 1983. 304 p.

ISBN 9780394516479

1. Ford, Robert, 1862-1892 2. James, Jesse, 1847-1882 3. Outlaws 4. Enemies 5. Obsession in men 6. Biographical fiction 7. Westerns

LC 83047851

Jesse James was a fabled outlaw, a charismatic, spiritual, larger-than-life bad man whose bloody exploits captured the imagination and admiration of a nation hungry for antiheroes. Robert Ford was a young upstart torn between dedicated worship and murderous jealousy, the "dirty little coward" who coveted Jesse's legend. The story of their interweaving paths-- and twin destinies that would collide in a rain of blood and betrayal.

"Hansen's Jesse is in no way romanticized; his interest derives from the complexity of his psychopathology. The Jesse that emerges here is prematurely decrepit; he'll murder when he doesn't need to, but he reads his Bible and talks about God's peace. Canny, intuitive, he seems to welcome the disciple who will betray him, even gives him the pistol for the job. . . . The novel works not despite our knowledge of what will happen, but because of it a sense of fatality hangs over every scene." Newsweek.

Hansen, Ron, 1947-

Mariette in ecstasy / Ron Hansen. HarperPerennial, 1991. 179 p.

ISBN 9780060182144

1. Teenage nuns 2. Stigmatization 3. Christian church controversies 4. Nuns 5. Teenage girls -- New York (State) 6. Ecstasy (Christianity) 7. Convents 8. New York (State) 9. Historical fiction 10. Psychological fiction

When miraculous wounds appear on a seventeen-year-old postulant in an upstate New York convent who claims to have been seduced by God, a religious controversy ensues.

"The novel pulls its taut plot-thread smartly along from start to finish, weaving flash-forward patches of dialogue from the investigation of Mariette's case into the unfolding action of her entry into the life of the convent. The finale is a stunner." New York Times Book Review.

Hansen, Ron, 1947-

A **wild** surge of guilty passion : a novel / Ron Hansen. Scribner, 2011 272 p.

ISBN 9781451617559

1. Snyder, Ruth, died 1928 2. Gray, Henry Judd, 1892-1928 3. 1920s 4. Husband-killing 5. Extramarital affairs 6. Marital conflict 7. Unhappiness in women 8. Traveling sales personnel 9. Violence 10. Sexual attraction 11. Homemakers 12. Women murderers 13. Trials (Murder) 14. Queens, New York City 15. Historical fiction 16. Crime fiction

A tale based on a true story from 1920s Manhattan follows the affair between voluptuous Ruth Snyder and undergarment salesman Judd Gray, whose plot to kill Ruth's husband triggers an explosive police investigation.

"This is a gripping, entertaining novel. You can feel Hansen's fascination with this story and his delight at the wealth of material; the memoirs written by both murderers, the news and court reports, the testimony of lesser characters, the secondary material that flowed for years following the trial and execution of Ruth and Gray. The restraint is evident in his measured tone this is fiction but the author still relies on the factual material the times, dates, places." Los Angeles Times.

Hanson, Hart

The **driver** / Hart Hanson. E.P. Dutton, 2017. 327 p.

ISBN 9781101986363

1. Veterans 2. Murder suspects 3. Intuition 4. Chauffeurs 5. Special forces 6. Ghosts 7. Women detectives 8. Men/women relations 9. Interpersonal attraction 10. Innocence (Law) 11. Attempted murder 12. Murder investigation 13. Los Angeles, California 14. Mysteries 15. Hardboiled fiction

A debut thriller by the award-winning creator of Bones traces the experiences of an Army special forces sergeant turned limo driver who, after hearing a ghost's warning of imminent danger, finds himself implicated in a murder, a situation that is further complicated by his crush on the case's lead detective.

Harding, Paul, 1967-

Tinkers / Paul Harding. Bellevue Literary Press, 2009. 192 p.

ISBN 9781934137123

1. Fathers and sons 2. Reminiscing in old age 3. People with dementia 4. Grandfathers 5. Seniors -- Identity 6. Epilepsy 7. Coping 8. Deathbed hallucinations 9. Clocks and watches -- Repairing and adjusting 10. Senior men -- Family relationships 11. Identity (Psychology) in old age 12. New England 13. Psychological fiction 14. Literary fiction

LC 2008039887

ALA Notable Book, 2010.

Pulitzer Prize for Fiction, 2010.

On his deathbed, surrounded by his family, George Washington Crosby's thoughts drift back to his childhood and the father who abandoned him when he was twelve.

"In Harding's skillful evocation, Crosby's life, seen from its final moments, becomes a mosaic of memories." The New Yorker.

Hardy, Thomas, 1840-1928

* **Far** from the madding crowd / Thomas Hardy. Vintage Books, 2015, c1874. 434 p.

ISBN 9780345804006

1. Victorian era (1837-1901) 2. Rural life 3. Courtship 4. Classism 5. Men/women relations 6. Shepherds 7. Mate selection for women 8. England -- Social life and customs -- 19th century 9. Classics 10. Psychological fiction 11. Love stories

Originally published serially in 1874 in "Cornhill Magazine."

After an unfortunate marriage to Sergeant Troy and an affair with Farmer Boldwood, Bathsheba Everdene finally becomes the wife of the man who has always loved her.

Hardy, Thomas, 1840-1928

* **Jude** the obscure / Thomas Hardy. Bantam Books, 1996. 444 p.

ISBN 0553211919

1. Cousins 2. Extramarital affairs 3. Stonemasons 4. Great-aunts 5. Husband and wife 6. Marriage 7. Men/women relations 8. Teacher-student relationships 9. Working class men 10. England -- Social life and customs -- 19th century 11. England -- Social conditions -- 19th century 12. Wessex, England 13. Love stories 14. Classics

This book was released as a movie entitled Jude.

First published in the United Kingdom in 1895 by Osgood, McIlvaine, & Co.

The story of the tragic relationship between Jude Fawley, a village stonemason who is thwarted in his aspirations to the ministry, and Sue Bridehead, a free-thinking cousin who is shunned by society for her social and sexual rebellion.

Hardy, Thomas, 1840-1928

* The **return** of the native / Thomas Hardy. Bantam, 1991, c1878 512 p.

ISBN 9780553212693

1. Moors and heaths 2. Lovers 3. Rural life 4. Women 5. England -- Social life and customs -- 19th century 6. Love stories 7. Psychological fiction 8. Classics

First published in 1878.

A young beauty who feels trapped living in the country with her grandfather plots her escape with a dashing suitor. But her plans are shaken when a handsome local man returns from Paris, hoping to make her his bride. Torn by her passion for two men, and a dream she will never abandon, Eustacia Vye learns that fate holds all the answers.

Hardy, Thomas, 1840-1928

* **Tess** of the d'Urbervilles : a pure woman faithfully presented / Thomas Hardy. Oxford University Press, 2005, c1891. 1, 443 p.

ISBN 9780192840691

1. Young women -- Relations with older men 2. Rape victims 3. Unplanned pregnancy 4. Guilt in women 5. England -- Social life and customs -- 19th century 6. Wessex, England 7. Psychological fiction 8. Classics

The movie "Trishna" is loosely based on this book.

Originally serialized in The Graphic, 1891.

Originally published in 1891. This revised edition first published in 1912.

Tess Durbeyfield is driven by family poverty to claim kinship with the wealthy D'Urbervilles, and meeting her "cousin" Alec proves to be her downfall. When Angel Clare offers her love and salvation, she must choose whether to reveal her past or remain silent in the hope of a peaceful future.

Harkaway, Nick, 1972-

Angelmaker / Nick Harkaway. Alfred A. Knopf, 2012. 477 p.

ISBN 9780307595959

1. Women spies 2. International intrigue 3. End of the world 4. Clocks and watches -- Repairing and adjusting 5. Children of gangsters 6. Fathers and sons 7. Senior women 8. Dictators 9. Weapons of mass destruction 10. Good and evil 11. London, England 12. Spy fiction 13. Science fiction mysteries 14. Science fiction

LC 2011028261

Avoiding the lifestyle of his late gangster father by working as a clock repairman, Joe Spork fixes an unusual device that turns out to be a former secret agent's doomsday machine and incurs the wrath of the government and a diabolical South Asian dictator.

Harkaway, Nick, 1972-

Gnomon : a novel / Nick Harkaway. Alfred A. Knopf, 2018. 560 p.

ISBN 9781524732080

1. Dystopias 2. Dissenters 3. Government investigators 4. Subversive activities 5. Murder investigation 6. Attitude change 7. Surveillance 8. Near future 9. Conformity 10. Authors 11. Dystopian fiction 12. Literary fiction 13. Science fiction

LC 2017039289

A tale set in a near-future, high-tech surveillance state follows the suspicious death of a dissident in custody and finds state inspector Mielikki Neith immersing herself in the victim's world, where she encounters a panorama of characters and innovations that transform her perspectives.

Harkaway, Nick, 1972-

The **gone-away** world / Nick Harkaway. Alfred A. Knopf, 2008. 512 p.

ISBN 9780307268860

1. End of the world 2. Power (Social sciences) 3. Friendship 4. Conspiracies 5. Greed 6. Dystopias 7. Post-apocalypse 8. Imaginary wars and battles 9. Apocalyptic fiction 10. Science fiction 11. Humorous stories

LC 2008008701

With a fire burning along the Jorgmund Pipe, a vital protection from the bandits and monsters left in the wake of the Go-Away War, Gonzo Lubitsch and his colleagues at the Haulage and HazMat Emergency Civil Freebooting Company are hired to put it out.

"This novel is set in a dystopian future where humanity huddles in the shadow of the Jorgmund Pipe. The ragtag bunch of heroes are sent to put out a fire on the Pipe, a mission both dangerous and imperative, since the Pipe, like a vast futuristic Glade room-freshener, releases the only substance that keeps the psychic stinks and foul odours of this post-apocalyptic world at bay. On the way there, the unnamed narrator reminisces about his upbringing, college days, military service, the Go Away Bombs that created their surreal present, and above all his friend Gonzo, to whom he's always felt closer than a brother. Somehow their story brings in ninjas, first loves, pirate-kings, mime-artists, human monsters and, well, monster monsters. . . . The revelation of Gonzo's relationship to his nameless best friend (and the ways in which Harkaway keeps on teasing around us not knowing his name is one of the novel's joys) is both unexpected and obvious. The Gone-Away World is brakes-off fiction." The Scotsman.

Harkaway, Nick, 1972-
Tigerman / Nick Harkaway. Alfred A. Knopf, 2014. 384 p.
ISBN 9780385352413
1. Veterans 2. Vigilantes 3. Comic book fans 4. Islands 5. Pollution 6. Criminals 7. Corruption 8. Gifted boys 9. British in Asia 10. Boys and men 11. International crime 12. Protectiveness in men 13. Environmental degradation 14. Asia 15. Superhero stories 16. Apocalyptic fiction
ALA Notable Book, 2015.
Assigned to a ceremonial post in Mancreu, British consul and Afghanistan war veteran Lester Ferris is compelled to disregard widespread underworld activities while bonding with a comic-addicted youth who during a violent uprising desperately relies on him for help.
"Harkaway has created an immensely likable hero who rises to the occasion in amusing and spectacularly improbable fashion." Publishers Weekly.

Harkness, Deborah E., 1965-
The **book** of life / Deborah Harkness. Viking, 2014. 560 p. All souls trilogy
ISBN 9780670025596
1. Women scholars and academics 2. Witches 3. Vampires 4. Alchemy 5. Manuscripts 6. Men/women relations 7. Interpersonal attraction 8. Magic 9. Libraries 10. Contemporary fantasy
Goodreads Choice Award, 2014.
Historian and witch Diana Bishop and her vampire scientist husband Matthew Clairmont return from a trip to the past still searching for the elusive alchemy tome Ashmole 782 in the final installment of the bestselling trilogy following Shadow of Night.
"There is no shortage of action in this sprawling sequel, and nearly every chapter brings a wrinkle to the tale. The storytelling is lively and energetic, and Diana remains an appealing heroine even as her life becomes ever more extraordinary." Publishers Weekly.

Harkness, Deborah E., 1965-
A **discovery** of witches : a novel / Deborah Harkness. Viking, 2011. 579 p. All souls trilogy
ISBN 9780670022410
1. Women scholars and academics 2. Witches 3. Manuscripts 4. Vampires 5. Alchemy 6. Men/women relations 7. Interpersonal attraction 8. Magic 9. Libraries 10. Contemporary fantasy
LC 2010030425
Discovering a magical manuscript in Oxford's library, scholar Diana Bishop, a descendant of witches who has rejected her heritage, inadvertently unleashes a fantastical underworld of daemons, witches and vampires whose activities center around an enchanted treasure.
"A riveting tale full of romance and danger that will have you on the edge of your seat, yet its chief strength lies in the wonderfully rich and ingenious mythology underlying the story. Entwining strands of science and history, Harkness creates a fresh explanation for how such creatures could arise that is so credible, you'll have to keep reminding yourself this is fiction." BookPage.

Harkness, Deborah E., 1965-
Shadow of night / Deborah Harkness. Viking, 2012. 592 p. All souls trilogy
ISBN 9780670023486
1. 16th century 2. Women scholars and academics 3. Witches 4.

Vampires 5. Alchemy 6. Time travel (Past) 7. Manuscripts 8. Men/women relations 9. Interpersonal attraction 10. Magic 11. Libraries 12. Historical fantasy
LC 2012005843
Goodreads Choice Award, 2012.
A follow-up to A Discovery of Witches finds Oxford scholar and reluctant witch Diana and vampire geneticist Matthew Clairmont in Elizabethan London, where Diana seeks a magical tutor and Matthew confronts elements from his past at the same time the mystery of Ashmole 782 deepens.

Harkness, Deborah E., 1965-
Time's convert / Deborah Harkness. Viking, 2018 436 p. All souls universe
ISBN 9780399564512
1. Revolutionary America (1775-1783) 2. Surgeons 3. Vampires 4. American Revolution, 1775-1783 5. Men -- Personal conduct 6. Transformations (Magic) 7. Consequences 8. Ethics 9. Paris, France 10. London, England 11. United States -- History -- Revolution, 1775-1783 12. Historical fantasy
A Revolutionary War-era doctor seizes a chance to become a vampire, only to find the ancient traditions governing his new life clashing with the deeply held beliefs of his former one.

Harman, Patricia, 1943-
The **midwife** of Hope River : a novel / Patricia Harman. HarperCollins, 2012. 320 p. Hope River novels
ISBN 9780062198891
1. Depression era (1929-1941) 2. 1930s 3. Midwives 4. Poverty 5. Home birth 6. Depressions -- 1929-1941 7. Secrets 8. Women and nature 9. Midwifery 10. Motherhood 11. Childbirth 12. West Virginia -- History -- 20th century 13. Appalachian Region -- Social life and customs 14. Historical fiction
LC 2012010944
Midwife Patience Murphy has a gift: a talent for escorting mothers through the challenges of bringing children into the world. Working in the hardscrabblle conditions of Appalachia during the Depression, Patience takes the jobs that no one else wants, helping those most in need.

Harmel, Kristin
The **room** on Rue Amelie / Kristin Harmel. Gallery Books, 2018. 368 p.
ISBN 9781501171406
1. Second World War era (1939-1945) 2. World War II -- France 3. Military occupation 4. Survival 5. War 6. Soldiers 7. Courage 8. Newlyweds 9. Jewish girls 10. British in France 11. Americans in France 12. Resistance to military occupation 13. Paris, France -- History -- German occupation, 1940-1944 14. War stories 15. Historical fiction
LC 2017047966
An American newlywed whose romantic dreams are shattered by the realities of war, an 11-year-old Jewish girl witnessing the horrors of mass deportations and a British Royal Air Force soldier who wonders if he is making a difference are brought together by fate and loss in Nazi-occupied Paris, where together they find the courage to survive.

Harper, Jane (Jane Elizabeth)
* The **dry** / Jane Harper. Flatiron Books, 2017, c2016. 320 p. Aaron Falk novels
ISBN 9781250105608
1. Alibi 2. Deception 3. Revenge 4. Government investigators 5. Droughts 6. Best friends 7. Small towns 8. Murder 9. Murder suspects 10. Secrets 11. Australia 12. Mysteries

Originally published: Australia : Macmillan, 2016.

RUSA Reading List Short List, 2018.

Receiving a sinister anonymous note after his best friend's suspicious death, federal agent Aaron Falk is forced to confront the fallout of a twenty-year-old false alibi against a backdrop of the worst drought Melbourne has seen in a century.

"From the ominous opening paragraphs, all the more chilling for their matter-of-factness, Harper, a journalist who writes for Melbournes Herald Sun, spins a suspenseful tale of sound and fury as riveting as it is horrific." Publishers Weekly.

Harper, Jane (Jane Elizabeth)

The **lost** man / Jane Harper. Flatiron Books, 2019, c2018 340 p.

ISBN 9781250105684

1. Cattle ranches 2. Rural life 3. Family problems 4. Brothers 5. Ranches 6. Cattle ranchers 7. Ranchers 8. Death 9. Grief in men 10. Families 11. Gravestones, mausoleums, etc 12. Small towns 13. Secrets 14. Queensland 15. Australia 16. Mysteries

Originally published: Pan Macmillan Australia, 2018.

Davitt Awards, Readers' Choice, 2019.

Ned Kelly Award for Best Novel, 2019.

Thriller Award for Best Paperback Original, 2019.

Meeting at the remote fence line separating their cattle ranches on an isolated belt of the Australian outback, two brothers navigate the haunting realities of the isolation that ended their third brother's life.

"The mystery of Cam's death is at the dark heart of an unfolding family drama that will leave readers reeling, and the final reveal is a heartbreaker. A twisty slow burner by an author at the top of her game." Kirkus.

Harper, Karen (Karen S.)

The **poyson** garden : an Elizabethan mystery / Karen Harper. Delacorte Press, 1999. 310 p. Elizabeth I mysteries

ISBN 0385332831

1. Elizabeth I,, Queen of England, 1533-1603 2. Elizabethan era (1558-1603) 3. 16th century 4. Tudor period (1485-1603) 5. Poisoning 6. Women rulers 7. Half-sisters 8. Princesses 9. Women detectives 10. Historical mysteries 11. Mysteries

LC 98-36420

Released from the Tower of London by an insurrection against Queen Mary, her half sister, the twenty-five-year-old Princess Elizabeth immediately puts herself back into harm's way by investigating a multiple poisoning

"Elizabeth's active role may strain credulity a bit, but this one is great fun all the same." Booklist.

Harrington, Anna

An **inconvenient** duke / Anna Harrington. Sourcebooks Casablanca, 2020. 352 p. Lords of the Armory

ISBN 9781728200088

1. Regency period (1811-1820) 2. Dukes and duchesses 3. Veterans 4. Young women 5. Sisters -- Death 6. Best friends 7. Grief 8. Murder investigation 9. Women's shelters 10. Men/women relations 11. Interpersonal attraction 12. Protectiveness in men 13. Independence in women 14. England -- Social life and customs -- 19th century 15. Great Britain -- History -- Regency, 1811-1820 16. Historical romances 17. Regency romances

Marcus Braddock, former general and newly appointed Duke of Hampton, is back from war. Now, not only is he surrounded by the utterly unbearable ton, he's mourning the death of his beloved sister, Elise. Marcus believes his sister's death wasn't an accident, and he's determined to learn the truth - starting with Danielle Williams, his sister's beautiful best friend.

"Action, suspense, seduction, and two determined lovers fighting for what is right provide a host of reasons to read well into the night. Danielle is an extremely compelling heroine who is willing to forgo her own prospects to correct wrongdoing. When combined with Marcus's conviction and refusal to abandon those he cares about, they make a perfect pair to kick off Hampton's (How I Married a Marquess) latest Regency series." Library Journal.

Harris, C. S.

Good time coming / C. S. Harris. Severn House Pub., 2016. 309 p.

ISBN 9780727886491

1. American Civil War era (1861-1865) 2. Families 3. Civil War 4. Women and war 5. Confederate soldiers 6. Oppression (Psychology) 7. Civilians in war 8. Ostracism 9. Soldiers 10. Trust 11. Rape 12. Louisiana -- History -- Civil War, 1861-1865 13. Mississippi -- History -- Civil War, 1861-1865 14. Historical fiction 15. War stories

"A novel of the American Civil War" -- cover.

As the Civil War comes ever closer to her vulnerable village of St. Francisville in Louisiana, young Amrie St. Pierre is forced to grow up quickly when she encounters a Union captain named Gabriel who threatens to destroy all she holds dear.

"Harris offers an evocative, intimate, disturbing, mesmerizing tale of the American Civil War, seen through the eyes of a 12-year-old girl, Amrie St. Pierre. ... When two Federals attack Amries home, she defends it with all her might, but the results are as terrifying as they are shocking. This story of love, loss, and growing up under some of the most difficult circumstances imaginable is beautifully written, superbly researched, emotionally engaging, and gripping from first page to last. A must for old-school fans of historical fiction." Booklist.

Harris, E. Lynn

Basketball Jones : a novel / E. Lynn Harris. Doubleday, 2009. 256 p.

ISBN 9780767926270

1. African American gay men 2. Professional basketball players 3. Extortion 4. Homosexuality 5. Identity (Psychology) 6. Image -- Social aspects 7. Gay men -- Social life and customs 8. African American men -- Sexuality 9. Betrayal 10. Men/men relations 11. United States 12. LGBTQIA fiction 13. African American fiction 14. Drama lit 15. Mainstream fiction

Aldridge James "AJ" Richardson's comfortable life with his longtime lover, famed NBA star Dray Jones, is threatened by the need to hide their relationship to maintain Dray's public image and by Dray's marriage to Judi, a beautiful and ambitious woman.

Harris, E. Lynn

* **I** say a little prayer : a novel / E. Lynn Harris. Doubleday, 2006. 256 p.

ISBN 0385512724

1. Bisexual African American men 2. African American singers 3. African American churches 4. African Americans 5. African American gay men 6. Bisexuals -- Religious life 7. Gay men -- Religious life 8. Singing 9. Lovers 10. Revivals 11. Fundamentalism 12. Homophobia 13. Prejudice 14. Social acceptance 15. Scandals 16. Sexuality 17. Men/men relations 18. Identity (Psychology) 19. Georgia 20. Atlanta, Georgia 21. LGBTQIA fiction 22. African American fiction 23. Mainstream fiction

LC 2005055452

Chauncey Greer, the bisexual owner of a thriving card company in Atlanta, is inspired to pursue his old dream of a musical career, a career that had ended in scandal thanks to a teenage love affair with his fellow bandmate in a popular boy band.

Harris, E. Lynn

Invisible life : a novel / E. Lynn Harris Anchor Books, 1994, copyright 1991. 268 p. Invisible life trilogy

ISBN 0385469683

1. African American men -- Sexuality 2. Bisexual African American men 3. Sexuality 4. Identity (Psychology) 5. Love triangles 6. African American lawyers 7. Homosexuality 8. African American fiction 9. LGBTQIA fiction 10. Mainstream fiction

LC 93008731

A young man graduating from college discovers his bisexuality and spends the next eight years alternately trying to face and deny the truth of his passions.

Harris, E. Lynn

Not a day goes by : a novel / E. Lynn Harris. Doubleday, 2000. 271 p.

ISBN 0385498241

1. Separation (Psychology) 2. Bisexual African American men 3. African American men/women relations 4. African American actors and actresses 5. African-American sports agents 6. Former football players 7. Bisexuality 8. Weddings 9. Secrets 10. Romantic comedies 11. Drama lit 12. African American fiction 13. Mainstream fiction

LC 00038368

John "Basil" Henderson and Yancey Harrington Braxton believe that they have found the perfect mate in each other. A lavish wedding is planned but just before the nuptials, fate and a little comeuppance from the past threaten the happy couple's future.

"When John 'Basil' Henderson, ex-football player and sports agent on the rise, falls in love with haughty, ambitious Broadway star Yancey Harrington Braxton, it seems like a perfect match. But on the couple's wedding day, which opens the book, the extravagant nuptials are suddenly canceled. The narrative retraces the couple's rocky courtship. . . . Determined to marry, have children, and keep his homosexual proclivities a secret, Basil doesn't realize that Yancey has a few secrets of her own." Publishers Weekly.

Harris, Joanne, 1964-

* Chocolat : a novel / Joanne Harris. Viking, 1999. 242 p. Chocolat novels (Joanne Harris)

ISBN 0670881791

1. Single mothers 2. Mothers and daughters 3. Chocolate 4. Small town life -- France 5. Villages -- France 6. Priests 7. Churches 8. Lent 9. France -- Social life and customs 10. Literary fiction

LC 9821771

Sequel: The girl with no shadow (which has also been published as: The Lollipop Shoes).

Originally published: London: Doubleday, 1999.

When an exotic stranger, Vianne Rocher, arrives in the French village of Lansquenet and opens a chocolate boutique directly opposite the church, Father Reynaud identifies her as a serious danger to his flock - especially as it is the beginning of Lent, the traditional season of self-denial. War is declared as the priest denounces the newcomer's wares as the ultimate sin.

"Harris' writing conveys a multitude of images and captures the self-absorption of small town life in France." Booklist.

Harris, Oliver, 1978-

A **shadow** intelligence / Oliver Harris. Houghton Mifflin Harcourt, 2020. 359 p.

ISBN 9780358206651

1. M I 6 2. Spies 3. Missing women 4. Intelligence service 5. Psychological warfare 6. Data encryption (Computer science) 7. Geopolitics 8. International intrigue 9. Espionage 10. Lovers 11. Surveillance 12. Kazakhstan 13. Spy fiction 14. Thrillers and suspense

LC 2019041570

A modern but classically styled spy novel in the spirit of John Le Carré and Chris Pavone, A Shadow Intelligence follows a mercurial MI6 agent, Elliot Kane, as he goes off script to find his lover, who went missing while embroiled in a dangerous scheme in Kazakhstan.

"An absorbing, superbly written novel likely to stand as one of the best spy novels of the year." Kirkus.

Harris, Robert, 1957-

Archangel : a novel / Robert Harris. Random House, 1999, c1998. 373 p.

ISBN 9780679428886

1. Stalin, Joseph, 1879-1953 Influence 2. Spies 3. Americans in Moscow, Russia 4. Sovietologists -- United States 5. Stalinism -- Russia 6. Soviet Union 7. Russia 8. Russia -- Politics and government -- 1991- 9. Archangel, Russia 10. Thrillers and suspense

LC 9833655

Originally published: London : Hutchinson, 1998.

While in Moscow, historian Fluke Kelso is approached by someone claiming to have been present when Stalin died, but a simple check into the old man's story turns into a murderous chase into the dark forests of northern Russia near the White Sea port of Archangel.

"The sinewy plot never slackens, but what makes the book memorable are the vividly observed backgrounds. . . . No less authentic are the fragmented but undead relics of the old Soviet system." The National Review.

Harris, Robert, 1957-

* Enigma / Robert Harris. Random House, 1995. 320 p.

ISBN 0679428879

1. Enigma machine 2. World War II 3. Cryptographers 4. Secret service 5. Cryptography 6. Mathematicians 7. England 8. War stories 9. Spy fiction 10. Historical thrillers

LC 95-47628

A fictional account of the desperate efforts to break the Nazi's Enigma code takes place in a British railway town, a struggle that becomes complicated by the pivotal disappearance of a beautiful cryptographer

"As one expects from a thriller-writer, Harris ensures the tension builds inexorably as the plot unfolds. Unlike some, however, he creates characters that linger in the mind, and he never bores his readers with gratuitous technical detail." The New Scientist.

Harris, Robert, 1957-

* Fatherland / Robert Harris. Random House, 1992. 338 p.

ISBN 0679412735

1. Hitler, Adolf, 1889-1945 2. Nazism 3. Nazis 4. Conspiracies -- Germany 5. Police 6. Holocaust (1933-1945) 7. Government cover-ups -- Germany 8. Totalitarianism -- Germany 9. Germany 10. Mysteries 11. Alternative histories

LC 91051026

Illustrated with maps and endpaper drawings.

"Fatherland' is a bleak book. But what concerns the author is the indestructibility of the human spirit, as exemplified by Xavier March. If

Hitler's Germany is hell, at least a few angels are floating around." New York Times Book Review.

Harris, Robert, 1957-

The **ghost** : a novel / Robert Harris. Simon & Schuster, 2007. 352 p.

ISBN 9781416551812

1. Ghostwriters 2. Political corruption 3. Deception 4. Spies 5. Former prime ministers 6. War on Terrorism, 2001-2009 7. Secrets 8. Writing 9. London, England 10. England 11. Northeastern States 12. Thrillers and suspense

LC 2007029670

Thriller Award for Best Novel, 2008.

Having served as Great Britain's longest-enduring prime minister, Adam Lang accepts a large cash advance to write a tell-all memoir of his life and controversial political career, an effort for which he hires a ghostwriter who uncovers dangerous secrets about the former leader's term.

"From the first paragraph, Harris' novel tugs the reader on through a thriller blessedly short on shoot'emup and long on character nuance, dead-on media satire and the damned-either-way consequences of wielding power in the murky wake of 9/11." Pittsburgh Post-Gazette.

Harris, Robert, 1957-

An **officer** and a spy / Robert Harris. Random House, 2014, c2013. 304 p.

ISBN 9780385349581

1. Dreyfus, Alfred, 1859-1935 2. Belle Epoque (1871-1914) 3. 19th century 4. 1890s 5. Dreyfus Affair, 1894-1906 6. Antisemitism 7. Spies 8. Exiles 9. Espionage 10. Traitors 11. Scandals 12. France 13. Historical thrillers

First published: London: Hutchinson, 2013.

British Book Award for Popular Fiction, 2013.

Ian Fleming Steel Dagger Award, 2014.

Walter Scott Prize for Historical Fiction, 2014.

Paris, 1895: Captain Alfred Dreyfus, a Jewish army officer, is convicted of treason, stripped of his rank, and sentenced to a lifetime of hard labor on Devil's Island, French Guiana. Ordered to investigate the case on behalf of the military's new counter-espionage force, Colonel Georges Picquart uncovers evidence of anti-Semitism as well as a conspiracy that reaches the highest levels of the government. Inspired by the events of the Dreyfus Affair, a real-life political scandal that engulfed Europe in the late 19th century, this gripping tale brings history to life. -- Description by Gillian Speace.

"Harris combats the predictability that can haunt fictional accounts of well-known events by teasing out the tale through Picquart's training in espionage and investigation, his unsanctioned detecting, and the complex intrigues he navigates to secure a reexamination of Dreyfus' case." Booklist.

Harris, Robert, 1957-

Pompeii : a novel / Robert Harris. Random House, 2003. 288 p.

ISBN 0679428895

1. Pliny, the Elder, 23-79 2. 1st century 3. Civilization, Ancient 4. Aqueducts 5. Coastal towns 6. Engineers 7. Civil engineers 8. Rich people 9. Volcanoes 10. Italy -- Antiquities 11. Pompeii (Extinct city) 12. Vesuvius -- Eruption -- 79 13. Rome, Italy 14. Historical fiction

LC 2003058446

When the aqueduct that brings fresh water to thousands of people around the bay of Naples fails, Roman engineer Marius Primus heads to the slopes of Mount Vesuvius to investigate, only to come face to face with an impending catastrophe.

"Lively writing, convincing but economical period details and plenty of intrigue keep the pace quick." Publishers Weekly.

Harris, Robert, 1957-

* The **second** sleep : a novel / Robert Harris. Knopf, 2019. 464 p.

ISBN 9780525656692

1. Civilization, Medieval 2. Priests 3. Heretics 4. Young men 5. Funerals 6. Antiquities 7. Communities 8. Faith 9. Far future 10. Villages 11. Post-apocalypse 12. England 13. Apocalyptic fiction 14. Mysteries

LC 2019012429

Arriving in a remote mid-15th-century Exmoor village, a young priest discovers his late predecessor's possibly fatal obsession with the ancient coins, glass and human bones strewn throughout the region.

Harris, Sarah J., 1971-

The **color** of Bee Larkham's murder : a novel / Sarah J. Harris. Touchstone, 2018, c2018. 448 p.

ISBN 9781501187896

1. Synesthesia 2. Perception 3. Missing persons 4. Senses and sensation 5. Clues 6. Teenage boys 7. Face perception 8. People with autism 9. Amateur detectives 10. Murder investigation 11. Missing persons investigation 12. London, England 13. England 14. Literary fiction 15. Mysteries 16. First-person narratives

Originally published: London : Harper Collins, 2018.

Librarians' Choice (Australia), 2018.

A boy with synesthesia--a condition that causes him to see colors when he hears sounds--tries to uncover what happened to his beautiful neighbor, and if he was ultimately responsible.

Harris, Thomas, 1940-

Hannibal / Thomas Harris Delacorte, 1999. 486 p. Hannibal Lecter novels

ISBN 038529929X

1. FBI Officials and employees, Women 2. Violence against women 3. Women murder victims 4. Psychiatrists with mental illnesses 5. Serial murderers 6. Men with mental illnesses 7. Psychopaths 8. Villains 9. Women FBI agents 10. Fugitives 11. Escaped convicts 12. Italy 13. Psychological suspense 14. Horror

A showdown between two psychopathic killers with a beautiful FBI agent caught in the middle. From his respirator, Mason Verger orders the capture of Hannibal Lecter, the man who put him there, and the bait is Clarice Starling with whom Lecter crossed swords in The Silence of the Lambs.

"Where Silence haunted and tantalized, Hannibal grosses out and gratifies. Yet there's still a basso ostinato of serious questions, and the answers are darker than in Silence." The Nation.

Harris, Thomas, 1940-

Red dragon / Thomas Harris. G. P. Putnam's Sons, 1981. 348 p. Hannibal Lecter novels

ISBN 9780399124426

1. FBI Officials and employees 2. Serial murderers 3. Adult child abuse victims 4. Psychopaths 5. People with disabilities 6. Cleft palate 7. Serial murders 8. Former FBI agents 9. Forensic scientists 10. Tabloid newspapers 11. Journalists 12. Government investigators 13. Psychological suspense 14. Horror

LC 81008674

Will Graham's unusual, fearful ability to project himself into the minds of psychopaths puts him on the trail of Francis Dolorhyde, whose bizarre and bloody murders of two suburban families have been triggered by his viewing of a William Blake watercolor.

Harris, Thomas, 1940-

Hannibal rising / Thomas Harris. Delacorte, 2006. 336 p. Hannibal Lecter novels

ISBN 0385339410

1. Child abuse victims 2. Uncle and nephew 3. Revenge 4. Childhood 5. Sisters -- Death 6. Orphans 7. Nazis 8. Villains 9. Violence 10. World War II 11. France 12. Coming-of-age stories 13. Psychological suspense 14. Horror

This novel is a prequel to: Red Dragon.

The villainous Hannibal Lecter--from Red Dragon and Silence of the Lambs--returns in a chilling new novel that describes the cannibalistic serial killer's early life in Eastern Europe, from the ages of six to twenty, following the loss of his entire family during World War II.

"There are images of morbid beauty here. . . . Harris' handling of the wartime violence is also impressive, as swift and vicious as the blitz-krieg itself." Los Angeles Times.

Harris, Thomas, 1940-

* The **silence** of the lambs / Thomas Harris St. Martin's Press, 1988. 338 p. Hannibal Lecter novels

ISBN 0312022824

1. FBI Officials and employees 2. Women FBI agents 3. Violence against women 4. Psychopaths 5. Women murder victims 6. Psychiatrists 7. Serial murderers 8. Serial murders 9. Men with mental illnesses 10. Psychological suspense 11. Horror

LC 88018203

Bram Stoker Award for Best Novel, 1988.

Anthony Award for Best Novel, 1989.

FBI trainee Clarise Starling is assigned to interview a brilliant, imprisoned psychopathic killer, Dr. Hannibal Lecter. She needs him to bring in a psychotic serial killer.

"Harris places his clues with precision, and his characterizations . . . are superbly developed and richly complex." Booklist.

Harrison, Cora

Beyond absolution : a mystery set in 1920s Ireland / Cora Harrison. Severn House, 2017. 249 p. Reverend Mother mysteries

ISBN 9780727887139

1. 1920s 2. Nuns 3. Women amateur detectives 4. Clergy 5. Murder investigation 6. Antiques 7. Robbery 8. Murder victims 9. Cork, Ireland 10. Ireland -- History -- 20th century 11. Historical mysteries

LC bl2017031596

Reverend Mother Aquinas aids in the investigation of the murder of a beloved priest, which may be linked to a string of antique thefts.

Harrison, Jim, 1937-2016

* The **great** leader / Jim Harrison. Grove Press, 2011. 288 p. Detective Sunderson novels

ISBN 9780802119704

1. Religious fanatics 2. Cults 3. Sex offenders 4. Pedophiles 5. Former sheriffs 6. Retirement 7. Alcoholics 8. Leadership in men 9. Michigan 10. Arizona 11. Black humor 12. Noir fiction 13. Literary fiction

Retired Detective Sunderson must get past his troubles with alcohol if he and an unlikely 16-year-old sidekick are ever going to expose an elusive cult leader called The Great Leader.

"Some of the funniest and profoundest bits in The Great Leader are the detective's alcohol-soaked musings just before he passes out. The novel serves up Sunderson's old-school field notes, which range from serious case observations to stream-of-consciousness ramblings. This is all the better, for it is fun to hear police quote Marx to each other in the field, where the outlaw and his pursuer find they have things in common, and where religion and sex intersect under the canopy of trees in the Upper Peninsula." Cleveland Plain Dealer.

Harrison, M. John (Michael John), 1945-

Light / M. John Harrison. Gollancz, 2002. 336 p.

ISBN 0553382950

1. 1990s 2. 25th century 3. Physicists 4. Quantum computers 5. Serial murderers 6. Options, alternatives, choices 7. Aliens 8. Men's fantasies 9. Violence in men 10. Virtual reality 11. Psychoses 12. Hallucinations and illusions 13. Mind control 14. Space vehicles 15. Space flight 16. Space opera 17. Science fiction

Companion to: Nova Swing.

James Tiptree, Jr. Award, 2002.

The stories of three people--modern-day Michael Kearney, a serial killer; Seria Mau Genlicher, a spaceship pilot; and Ed Chainese, a down-and-out drifter--are linked by the mysteries of the Kefahuchi Tract.

Harrison, M. John (Michael John), 1945-

Nova swing / M. John Harrison. Victor Gollancz, 2006. 304 p.

ISBN 0575070277

1. Young women 2. Police 3. Detectives 4. Aliens 5. Tourism 6. Physics 7. Men/women relations 8. Space and time 9. Space flight 10. Interstellar relations 11. Interplanetary relations 12. Obsession in men 13. Human/alien encounters 14. Consciousness transfer 15. Personal conduct 16. Planets 17. Cities and towns 18. Cyberpunk 19. Science fiction

Companion to: Light.

Arthur C. Clarke Award, 2007.

Philip K. Dick Award for Science Fiction, 2007.

Years after Ed Chianese's trip into the Kefahuchi Tract, the Tract begins to expand and change, with pieces falling to Earth and transforming the landscape with strange artifacts and organisms that threaten surrounding areas.

Harrison, Mette Ivie, 1970-

The **bishop's** wife / Mette Ivie Harrison. Soho Crime, 2014. 352 p. Linda Wallheim mysteries

ISBN 9781616954765

1. Mormon Church 2. Mormons 3. Married women 4. Missing persons 5. Families 6. Faith 7. Secrets 8. Utah 9. Mysteries 10. Mormon fiction

In the predominantly Mormon city of Draper, Utah, some seemingly perfect families have deadly secrets. Inspired by an actual crime and written by a practicing Mormon, The Bishop's Wife is both a fascinating look at the lives of modern Mormons as well as a grim and cunningly twisted mystery. Linda Wallheim is the mother of five grown boys and the wife of a Mormon bishop. As bishop, Kurt Wallheim is the ward's designated spiritual father, and that makes Linda the ward's unofficial mother, and her days are filled with comfort visits, community service, and informal counseling. But Linda is increasingly troubled by the church's patriarchal structure and secrecy, especially as a disturbing situation takes shape in the ward. One cold winter morning, a neighbor, Jared Helm, appears on the Wallheims' doorstep with his 5-year-old daughter, claiming that his wife, Carrie, disappeared in the middle of the night, leaving behind everything she owns. The circumstances surrounding Carrie's disappearance become more suspicious the more Linda learns about them, and she becomes convinced that Jared has murdered his wife and painted himself as an abandoned husband. Kurt asks Linda not to get involved in the unfolding family saga, but she has become obsessed with Carrie's fate, and with the well-being of her vulnerable young daughter. She cannot let the matter rest until she finds out the truth. Is she wrong to go against her husband, the bishop, when her inner convictions are so strong Provided by publisher.

"This decidedly adult tale adds twists aplenty to an insider's look at a religion replete with its own mysteries." Kirkus.

Harrison, Nicola, 1979-

Montauk / Nicola Harrison. St. Martin's Press, 2019. 400 p.

ISBN 9781250200112

1. 1930s 2. Self-fulfillment in women 3. Married women 4. Social classes 5. Islands 6. Resorts 7. Underclass 8. Interclass romance 9. Interpersonal attraction 10. Montauk, New York 11. Long Island, New York 12. Historical fiction

LC 2018055447

Distancing herself from her unfaithful spouse and her fellow society wives at seaside Montauk Manor, Bea Bordeaux is drawn by the village's natural beauty and community spirit before falling for a man who is nothing like her husband.

Harrison, Rachel, 1989-

The **return** / Rachel Harrison. Berkley, 2020. 368 p.

ISBN 9780593098660

1. Missing women 2. Female friendship 3. Women with amnesia 4. Change (Psychology) 5. Reunions 6. Hotels 7. Secrets 8. Storms 9. Catskill Mountains Region, New York 10. Gothic fiction 11. Horror

LC 2019027223

When their friend returns ill and haggard from a two-year absence with no memory of what happened, a circle of women, trapped inside a hotel by bad weather, become targeted by malevolent otherworldly phenomena.

"This girls' trip has teeth. A stylish and well-crafted horror debut." Kirkus.

Harrison, Thea

Dragon bound / Thea Harrison. Berkley Sensation, 2011. 336 p. Elder races

ISBN 9780425241509

1. Stealing 2. Dragons 3. Sexual attraction 4. Thieves 5. Extortion 6. Supernatural 7. Goblins 8. Seduction 9. Misunderstanding 10. Paranormal romances

RITA Award for Best Paranormal Romance, 2012.

When she is blackmailed into stealing a coin from the hoard of a dragon, Pia Giovanni, half human and half wyr, goes up against Dragos Cuelebre, who, after catching her in the act, spares her life, but claims her as his own.

Harrod-Eagles, Cynthia,

Game over : a Bill Slider mystery / Cynthia Harrod-Eagles. Severn House, 2008. 234 p. Inspector Bill Slider mysteries

ISBN 9780727866158

1. Murder investigation 2. Death threats 3. Detectives 4. Marriage 5. Journalists 6. Police 7. Crimes against journalists 8. Spouses of pregnant women 9. London, England 10. Mysteries 11. Police procedurals

Sequel to: Dear departed.

When ex-BBC correspondent Ed Stonax is found dead, the last thing Detective Inspector Slider needs to complicate his life is the reappearance of an old enemy issuing death threats. Trevor Bates, aka The Needle, is on the loose and trying to kill him, and with a high-profile murder to solve, Slider must try to find a spare moment to marry Joanna before their baby is born and stay alive long enough to do it.

"The various plot lines neatly intersect at the highest levels of government by the end of this appealing English whodunit." Publishers Weekly.

Harrod-Eagles, Cynthia

Headlong / Cynthia Harrod-Eagles. Severn House, 2018. 256 p. Inspector Bill Slider mysteries

ISBN 9780727888365

1. Murder 2. Literary agents 3. Murder investigation 4. Detectives 5. Secrets 6. Scandals 7. Former wives 8. Former lovers 9. Murder suspects 10. Men/women relations 11. Mutilation 12. Police 13. London, England 14. Mysteries 15. Police procedurals

Bill Slider and his team investigate the death of a prominent literary agent.

Harrod-Eagles, Cynthia

Old bones / Cynthia Harrod-Eagles. Severn House, 2017. 256 p. Inspector Bill Slider mysteries

ISBN 9780727886651

1. Bones 2. Cold cases (Criminal investigation) 3. Missing teenage girls 4. Detectives 5. Murder investigation 6. London, England 7. England 8. Police procedurals

A couple discover human remains buried in the garden of their new house: could this be the resting place of 14-year-old Amanda Knight, who disappeared from the same garden two decades before? With a murder twenty years in the past, this is the coldest of cold cases. Most of the suspects are now dead too, and all passion is long spent. Or is it?

"Another sterling entry in a truly outstanding series." Booklist.

Hart, Carolyn G.

Death walked in : a death on demand mystery / Carolyn Hart. William Morrow, 2008. 304 p. Death on Demand mysteries

ISBN 9780060724054

1. Murder suspects 2. Coin collecting 3. Booksellers 4. Women amateur detectives -- South Carolina 5. Detectives 6. Mystery bookstore owners -- South Carolina 7. South Carolina 8. Gentle reads 9. Cozy mysteries

LC 2007043589

A fortune in gold coins stolen from a house filled with visiting family members lies at the root of this Max and Annie Darling mystery.

"This tight, Agatha Christie-style puzzler will keep readers guessing to the end." Publishers Weekly.

Hart, Carolyn G.

Ghost gone wild / Carolyn Hart. Berkley Hardcover, 2013. 320 p. Bailey Ruth mysteries

ISBN 9780425260753

1. Ghosts 2. Rescues 3. Women amateur detectives 4. Death 5. Murder investigation 6. Crime 7. Supernatural 8. Oklahoma 9. Mysteries 10. Supernatural mysteries

LC 2013025898

When well-meaning ghost Bailey Ruth Raeburn returns to Earth and saves Nick Magruder from being shot, she loses her ability to disappear and is trapped unless she can discover who wants Nick dead.

Hart, Carolyn G.

Letter from home / Carolyn Hart. Berkley Prime Crime, 2003. 272 p.

ISBN 0425191796

1. 1940s 2. Small town life -- Oklahoma 3. Crimes against women 4. Women journalists 5. Teenage girls 6. Teenage girl journalists 7. Memories 8. Murder 9. Loss (Psychology) 10. World War II -- Women 11. Oklahoma 12. Letters 13. Historical mysteries 14. Mysteries

LC 2003051953

Agatha Award for Best Novel, 2004.

Working at the local newspaper during the summer of 1944, Gretchen Gilman investigates the mysterious death of Faye Tatum, found dead in her own living room, supposedly murdered by her husband, a World War II veteran.

"Set in a small-town America that lives only in memory, this artfully narrated whodunit observes the residents of an unnamed Oklahoma hamlet over the hot and dusty summer of 1944 as they ration their food, count their war dead and turn on their neighbors." New York Times Book Review.

Hart, Carolyn G.

Murder walks the plank : a death on demand mystery / Carolyn Hart. William Morrow & Co., 2004. 298 p. Death on Demand mysteries

ISBN 0060004746

1. Cruise ships 2. Murder 3. Secrets 4. Mystery bookstore owners 5. Women booksellers 6. Booksellers 7. Women amateur detectives 8. Mystery story writers 9. Murder parties 10. Pleasure cruises 11. South Carolina 12. Gentle reads 13. Cozy mysteries

LC 2003051095

Pleased with the success of her murder-mystery cruise, Annie Darling and her husband, Max, are suddenly on the hunt for a killer when one of the cruise participants falls overboard, the first in a series of suspicious deaths.

"This novel can only reinforce Hart's high standing among the cozy mystery cognoscenti." Publishers Weekly.

Hart, Carolyn G.

Resort to murder : a Henrie O mystery / Carolyn Hart. William Morrow, 2001. 294 p. Henrie O mysteries

ISBN 0380977737

1. Fathers and daughters 2. Weddings 3. Murder investigation 4. Murder suspects 5. Women mystery story writers 6. Widows 7. Women amateur detectives 8. Resorts -- Bermuda Islands 9. Senior women 10. Women journalists 11. Bermuda Islands 12. Gentle reads 13. Cozy mysteries

LC 00059446

When Henrie O accompanies her grandchildren to Bermuda for the remarriage of their father to a wealthy widow, she begins an investigation into a mysterious ghost and two murders as she finds herself becoming the sole protector of her family.

"Recovering from pneumonia, Henrie O isn't sure she feels up to the task of dealing with the emotional maelstrom stewing around the Bermuda wedding of her son-in-law, Lloyd Drake, and beautiful Connor Bailey, a wealthy widow. . . . The hotel where the party has gathered witnessed tragedy the year before, when Roddy Worrell, the manager's husband, plunged to his death from a tower. According to rumor, Roddy had been infatuated with Connor, who spurned his advances. When a ghost is sighted at the tower, word spreads that Roddy has come back to haunt Connor. The subsequent death of a hotel employee who knew more than he should about the apparition puts Henrie O on the murder scent once again." Publishers Weekly.

Hart, Carolyn G.

White elephant dead : a death on demand mystery / Carolyn Hart. Avon Twilight, 1999. 277 p. Death on Demand mysteries

ISBN 0380975300

1. Booksellers 2. Extortion -- South Carolina 3. Murder suspects 4. Murder investigation 5. Socialites 6. Husband-and-wife detectives 7. Women booksellers 8. Women amateur detectives 9. Mystery bookstore owners -- South Carolina 10. South Carolina 11. Gentle

reads 12. Cozy mysteries

LC 99020833

Annie and Max Darling work to clear their friend of the murder of a woman who had been blackmailing several members of their community.

"This Death on Demand mystery, delivers charming characters, . . . a tantalizing mystery, and plenty of appealing descriptions of coastal landscapes." Booklist.

Hart, Carolyn G.

Yankee Doodle dead : a death on demand mystery / Carolyn G. Hart. Avon Twilight, 1998. 273 p. Death on Demand mysteries

ISBN 0380975297

1. Booksellers 2. Festivals 3. Murder investigation 4. Murder suspects 5. Island life -- South Carolina 6. Husband-and-wife detectives -- South Carolina 7. Women booksellers 8. Women amateur detectives 9. Mystery bookstore owners -- South Carolina 10. Fourth of July 11. Library trustees -- South Carolina 12. Retired military personnel -- South Carolina 13. Resorts -- South Carolina 14. South Carolina 15. Gentle reads 16. Cozy mysteries 17. Holiday mysteries

LC 9813565

A Fourth of July festival finds Annie and Max Darling watching not only fireworks but murder as well. A newcomer to town, a retired Brigadier General is murdered. As Annie has witnessed the murder, she feels an obligation to find the real murderer, and not the person the police have just arrested.

Hart, Elsa

City of ink : a mystery / Elsa Hart. Minotaur Books, 2018. 352 p. Li Du novels

ISBN 9781250142795

1. 1700s (Decade) 2. Former librarians 3. Mentors 4. Intrigue 5. Homecomings 6. Memories 7. Murder 8. Murder investigation 9. Secrets 10. City life 11. China -- History -- 18th century 12. Historical mysteries

LC 2018004086

Forced to return home to unravel the mystery surrounding his mentor's execution, Li Du confronts painful memories while investigating a double murder, the secrets of several Beijing residents and threats against his safety.

Hart, Erin, 1958-

The **book** of Killowen / Erin Hart. Scribner, 2013. 302 p. Nora Gavin and Cormac Maguire series

ISBN 9781451634846

1. Cold cases (Criminal investigation) 2. Women pathologists 3. Murder investigation 4. Television personalities 5. Archaeologists 6. Conspiracies 7. Secrets 8. Ireland 9. Mysteries

LC 2012028465

Returning to the bogs after a year away from the field, archaeologist Cormac Maguire and pathologist Nora Gavin investigate a ninth-century corpse found in the trunk of a car along with the body of a provocative television philosopher, a case that is tied to an ancient volume of philosophical heresy.

Hart, Erin, 1958-

Haunted ground : a crime novel / Erin Hart. Scribner, 2003. 328 p. Nora Gavin and Cormac Maguire series

ISBN 9780743235051

1. Bogs 2. Family estates 3. Women pathologists 4. Landowners 5. Archaeologists 6. Americans in Ireland 7. Families of missing persons 8. Missing women 9. Bog bodies 10. Men/women relations

11. Ireland 12. Mysteries

LC 2002030679

The Irish landscape holds secrets past and present as archaeologist Cormac Maguire and pathologist Nora Gavin encounter a mystery when a decapitated woman is found in the bogs who may be related to a recent mother/child disappearance.

Hart, Erin, 1958-
Lake of sorrows / Erin Hart. Scribner, 2004. 352 p. Nora Gavin and Cormac Maguire series
ISBN 0743247965
1. Celts -- Material culture 2. Human sacrifice 3. Excavations (Archaeology) 4. Women pathologists 5. Archaeologists 6. Serial murders 7. Forensic scientists 8. Bog bodies 9. Men/women relations 10. Bogs 11. Ireland 12. Mysteries

LC 2004052234

Pathologist Nora Gavin investigates two bodies discovered at the site of an Irish midland industrial site--one ancient, the other recent--and teams up with archaeologist Cormac Maguire, with whom she has fallen in love, for an unexpectedly dangerous case.

Hart, John, 1965-
Down river / John Hart. Thomas Dunne Books/St. Martin's Minotaur, 2007. 352 p.
ISBN 0312359314
1. Small town life -- North Carolina 2. Murder suspects 3. Family secrets 4. Forgiveness 5. Families 6. Fathers and sons 7. Murderers 8. Abandonment (Psychology) 9. Rejection (Psychology) 10. Greed 11. Interpersonal conflict 12. North Carolina 13. Mysteries 14. Southern fiction

LC 2007021540

Edgar Allan Poe Award for Best Novel, 2008.

Five years after fleeing to New York in the wake of a murder acquittal, Adam Harston returns to North Carolina, only to find himself trapped in the middle of a new case of murder as the people around him begin to die and he becomes the prime suspect in the crimes.

"This work is reminiscent of Raymond Chandler's novels, hard-boiled and rich with evocative metaphors." Library Journal.

Hart, John, 1965-
Iron house / John Hart. Thomas Dunne Books/St. Martin's Press, 2011. 352 p.
ISBN 9780312380342
1. Organized crime 2. Second chances 3. Revenge 4. Secrets 5. Brothers 6. Orphans 7. Murder 8. Former assassins 9. Men/women relations 10. North Carolina 11. New York City 12. Thrillers and suspense 13. Crime fiction

LC 2011006909

At the Iron Mountain Home for Boys, there was nothing but time. Time to burn and time to kill, time for two young orphans to learn that life isn't won without a fight. Julian survives only because his older brother, Michael, is fearless and fiercely protective. When tensions boil over and a boy is brutally killed, there is only one sacrifice left for Michael to make: He flees the orphanage and takes the blame with him. For two decades, Michael has been an enforcer in New York's world of organized crime, a prince of the streets so widely feared he rarely has to kill anymore. But the life he's fought to build unravels when he meets Elena, a beautiful innocent who teaches him the meaning and power of love. He wants a fresh start with her, the chance to start a family like the one he and Julian never had. But someone else is holding the strings. And escape is not that easy... The mob boss who gave Michael his blessing to begin anew is dying, and his son is intent on making Michael pay for his betrayal. Determined to protect the ones he loves, Michael spirits

Elena- who knows nothing of his past crimes, or the peril he's laid at her door- back to North Carolina, to the place he was born and the brother he lost so long ago. There, he will encounter a whole new level of danger, a thicket of deceit and violence that leads inexorably to the one place he's been running from his whole life: Iron House.--From book jacket.

"Hart deftly interweaves a complex family history story with Stevan's intense, bloody quest for vengeance." Publishers Weekly.

Hart, John, 1965-
The **king** of lies / John Hart. St. Martin's Press, 2006. 320 p.
ISBN 031234161X
1. Murder suspects 2. Fathers and sons 3. Lawyers 4. Defense attorneys 5. Families of murder victims 6. Married men 7. Families 8. Fathers -- Death 9. North Carolina 10. Legal thrillers 11. Psychological suspense

LC 2005049774

When Work Pickens finds his father murdered, the investigation pushes a repressed family history to the surface and he sees his own carefully constructed façade begin to crack. Work's troubled sister, her combative girlfriend, his gold digging socialite wife, and an unrequited lifelong love join a cast of small town characters that create no shortage of drama in this extraordinary, fast-paced suspense novel.

"More than anything else--more than a terrific whodunit, an unsentimental, clear-eyed story of love and forgiveness, and a gripping family saga: The King of Lies is a masterful piece of writing." Raleigh News & Observer

Hart, John, 1965-
The **last** child / John Hart. Minotaur Books, 2009. 373 p.
ISBN 9780312359324
1. Missing children 2. Twins 3. Small town life -- North Carolina 4. Detectives 5. Dysfunctional families 6. Brothers and sisters 7. North Carolina 8. Psychological suspense

LC 2008045678

"A Thomas Dunne book for Minotaur Books" --T.p. verso.
Ian Fleming Steel Dagger Award, 2009.
Edgar Allan Poe Award for Best Novel, 2010.

After his twin sister Alyssa disappears, thirteen year-old Johnny Merrimon is determined to find her. When a second girl disappears from his rural North Carolina town, Johnny makes a discovery that sends shock waves through the community in this multi-layered tale of broken families and deadly secrets.

"The author has produced a novel that is elegant, haunting, and memorable. His characters are given an emotional depth that genre characters seldom have, and the graceful, evocative prose lifts his stories right out of their genre and into the realm of capital-L literature. A must-read for every variety of fiction reader." Booklist.

Hart, John, 1965-
Redemption road / John Hart. Thomas Dunne Books, 2016. 432 p.
ISBN 9780312380366
1. Murder 2. Revenge 3. Women detectives 4. Former convicts 5. Boys 6. Ethics 7. Secrets 8. Betrayal 9. Thrillers and suspense

"Over 2 million copies of his books in print. The first and only author to win back-to-back Edgars for Best Novel. Every book a New York Times bestseller. Now after five years, John Hart is back with a stunning literary thriller. Imagine: A boy with a gun waits for the man who killed his mother. A troubled detective confronts her past in the aftermath of a brutal shooting. After thirteen years in prison, a good cop walks free. But for how long? And deep in the forest, on the altar of an abandoned church, the unthinkable has just happened... This is a town on the brink. This is a road with no mercy. Since his debut bestseller, The King of Lies, reviewers across the country have heaped praise on John Hart, comparing his writing to that of Pat Conroy, Cormac Mc-Carthy and Scott Turow. With each novel Hart has climbed higher on the New York Times Bestseller list, with his last two books - The Last Child and Iron House - landing squarely in the top ten. His masterful writing and assured evocation of place have won readers around the world and earned history's only consecutive Edgar Awards for Best Novel. After five years, John Hart returns with Redemption Road, his most powerful story yet"--, Provided by publisher.

"Hart plays brilliantly on the tradition of the southern gothic, but his grasp of character gives this novel--and all his works--the extra dimension that extends his audience well beyond adrenaline junkies." Booklist.

Hart, Josephine
Damage : a novel / Josephine Hart. Virago, 2011, c1991. 195 p.
ISBN 9781844087181
1. Fathers and sons 2. Love triangles 3. Extramarital affairs 4. Obsession in men 5. Politicians 6. Lust 7. England 8. Psychological suspense

LC 90053393

This book was released as a movie entitled Fatale.
Originally published: London: Chatto & Windus, 1991.
The narrator's erotic obsession with a woman who wields a dominant sexual and psychological power over him draws him into a headlong plunge toward tragedy for his family and his own self-destruction.

Hart, Rob
The **warehouse** : a novel / Rob Hart. Crown Publishing, 2019 358 p.
ISBN 9781984823793
1. Near future 2. Corporations 3. Undercover operations 4. Dystopias 5. Online shopping 6. Business intelligence 7. Corporate culture 8. Business -- Corrupt practices 9. High technology 10. Men/women relations 11. Dystopian fiction 12. Thrillers and suspense
Set in a near-future America wracked by violence, unemployment and climate change, two employees of a world-saving global giant discover their employers' true agenda.

"Part video game, part Sinclair Lewis, part Michael Crichton; it adds up to a terrific puzzle." Kirkus.

Harte, Bret, 1836-1902
* The **best** short stories of Bret Harte / edited, and with an introduction, by Robert N. Linscott. Modern Library, 1947. x, 517 p.
ISBN 9780394602509
1. 1860s 2. Frontier and pioneer life 3. Gold rush 4. California -- History -- 19th century 5. The West (United States) -- History -- 19th century 6. Westerns 7. Short stories

LC 47030278

Twenty-five stories of the Western frontier

Haruf, Kent
Benediction / Kent Haruf. Alfred A. Knopf, 2013. 272 p.
ISBN 9780307959881
1. Family relationships 2. Men with terminal illnesses -- Family relationships 3. People with cancer 4. Bereavement in families 5. Death 6. Loss (Psychology) 7. Alienation in families 8. Father and adult son 9. Colorado 10. Psychological fiction

LC 2012028744

"This is a Borzoi book."

Shortlisted for the James Tait Black Memorial Prize for Fiction, 2013

A terminally ill cancer patient is attended throughout his final days by his wife and daughter while the trio contemplates their relationships with an estranged son, a situation that stirs up painful memories for a new next-door neighbor who has recently lost her mother.

Haruf, Kent
Eventide / Kent Haruf. Alfred A. Knopf, 2004. 320 p.
ISBN 0375411585
1. Ranchers 2. Single men 3. Brothers 4. Boys 5. Single mothers 6. People with disabilities 7. Neighbors 8. Communities 9. Small town life 10. Winter 11. Colorado 12. Psychological fiction 13. Domestic fiction

LC 2003060480

Sequel to: Plainsong.
A novel of small-town life in the high plains region around Holt, Colorado, follows the challenges, emotional upheaval, tragedies, and intertwined destinies of the local inhabitants as they cope with the changes they encounter.

"This novel takes up where the author's Plainsong left off, in the windy high-plains country in and around the tiny town of Holt, Colorado. ... It's rare that such slow, deliberate prose is this highly charged, but Haruf's writing draws power from his sense of characterits limitations and its possibilities--and how it propels action." The New Yorker.

Haruf, Kent
* **Our** souls at night / Kent Haruf. Alfred A. Knopf, 2015 176 p.
ISBN 9781101875896
1. Widowers 2. Small town life 3. Loneliness 4. Friendship 5. Memories 6. Men/women relations 7. Neighbors 8. Grandmother and child 9. Second chances 10. Colorado 11. Literary fiction 12. Love stories
Addie Moore and Louis Waters, a widow and widower each living alone, forge a loving bond over their shared loneliness, provoking local gossip and the disapproval of their grown children in ways that are further complicated by an extended visit by a sad young grandchild.

"Haruf, who died in 2014, returns to the landscape and daily life of Holt County, Colo. where his previous novels (Plainsong, Eventide, The Tie That Binds) have also been set, this time with a stunning sense of all that's passed and the precious importance of the days that remain." Publishers Weekly.

Haruf, Kent
* **Plainsong** / Kent Haruf. A. A. Knopf, 1999. 301 p.
ISBN 0375406182
1. Small town life 2. High school teachers 3. Ranchers 4. Single men 5. Pregnant teenagers 6. Brothers 7. Nine-year-old boys 8. Ten-year-old boys 9. Fathers and sons 10. Homeless teenagers 11. Colorado 12. Domestic fiction 13. Psychological fiction 14. Literary fiction

LC 9915606

Sequel: Eventide.
National Book Award for Fiction finalist, 1999
An unlikely extended family is formed when a high school teacher helps a pregnant student make a home with two elderly bachelor ranchers.

"From simple strands of language and cuttings of talk, from the look of the high Colorado plains east of Denver almost to the place where Nebraska and Kansas meet, Haruf has made a novel so foursquare, so delicate and lovely, that it has the power to exalt the reader." New York Times Book Review.

Harvey, John, 1938-

Cold in hand / John Harvey. William Heinemann, 2008. 405 p. Charlie Resnick mysteries

ISBN 9780434016945

1. Police -- Nottingham, England 2. Human trafficking 3. Teenage murder victims 4. Murder investigation -- Nottingham, England 5. Private investigators 6. Police corruption 7. Human trafficking victims 8. Child trafficking 9. Child trafficking victims 10. Nottingham, England 11. England 12. Police procedurals

LC 2008396522

"Resnick is now living with a much younger DI, Lynn Kellog, and their relationship is one of the best aspects of this fine crime novel, subtly described and convincing. . . . Cold in Hand reveals modern England in all its most depressing messiness while engaging the reader with characters whose warmth and humanity give real pleasure. There is no melodrama here; all the actions and motives that are eventually revealed are rooted in reality; and yet at the heart of the novel is an event so shocking in the context that it could rival anything in the most lurid thriller." Times Literary Supplement.

Harvey, John, 1938-

* Darkness, darkness / John Harvey. Pegasus Books, 2014. 352 p. Charlie Resnick mysteries

ISBN 9781605986166

1. 1980s 2. 21st century 3. Dead 4. Strikes 5. Miners 6. Police 7. Missing women 8. Murder investigation 9. Retirement 10. Nottingham, England 11. England 12. Police procedurals 13. Parallel narratives

LC bl2014031493

"Resnick's last case"--cover.

In 1984, young police inspector Charlie Resnick ran an intelligence gathering team during the British Miners' Strike, a terrible time of civil unrest that pitted close friends and family members against each other; back then, a vocal young supporter of the strike, Jenny Hardwick, went missing. Now her body's been discovered, and though he's retired, Charlie teams up with DS Catherine Njoroge, who has problems of her own, to dig into the past and solve the case. -- Description by Dawn Towery.

"Harvey's first Resnick novel, 1989's Lonely Hearts, is one of the London Times List of 100 Best Crime Novels of the last century and there has been no diminishment in quality in the 11 books since. This is Resnick's final case, and every reader of contemporary mystery fiction should be acquainted with this outstanding series and its jazz-loving protagonist whose stories limn the changing world around him. Increasingly, Charlie is an observer more than an actor, but he remains an unforgettable creation." Library Journal.

Harvey, John, 1938

A **darker** shade of blue : stories / John Harvey. Pegasus Books, 2012. 368 p.

ISBN 9781605982847

1. Detectives 2. Criminal investigation 3. Former police 4. Private investigators 5. England 6. Short stories 7. Mysteries

This collection of short stories from a master of British crime fiction feature tales of ex-cops, private eyes and investigators who wade through broken families, revenge, prostitution, drugs and corruption in their search for justice.

Harvey, John, 1938-

Far cry / John Harvey. William Heinemann, 2009. 500 p.

ISBN 9780434016921

1. Missing persons 2. Parents of missing children 3. Parents of murder victims 4. Missing persons investigation 5. Cold cases (Criminal investigation) 6. Police 7. Detectives 8. Cambridgeshire,

England 9. England 10. Mysteries

First published: William Heinemann, 2009.

Ruth and Simon Graham's rare romantic break is shattered by devastating news: their daughter, Heather, on holiday in Cornwall with a friend's family, has disappeared. The loss is more than they - or their marriage - can bear. But time does heal, and slowly Ruth builds a new life for herself, a new husband, Andrew, even a second daughter, Beatrice. The chances that history should repeat itself are next-to-impossible - that is until, years later, a desperate phone call launches D.I. Will Grayson and his partner, D.S. Helen Walker, into an investigation which will test their professional and emotional resources to the very limit. Yet as Grayson becomes increasingly obsessed with a recently-released child abuser and Helen is drawn deeper into a destructive love affair with a married colleague, there is a real danger that their most testing investigation yet will slip fatefully through their hands.

"The architecture of Harvey's storytelling begs to be admired, with its multiple narratives, shifting time lines and elaborate plot details. But it's his handling of difficult characters and provocative themes that gives the book weight. All the adults in this story love children, some selflessly and others in ways that make your skin crawl, and they all react differently when the children they love are taken away from them. Harvey's touch is so subtle, his style so seductive, that he distracts us from the fact that Ruth isn't the only person whose choices are determined, or tragically derailed, by love for a child even if it's someone else's child." New York Times Book Review.

Harvey, John, 1938-

Gone to ground / John Harvey. Harcourt, 2007. 400 p.

ISBN 9780151013630

1. Police -- Nottingham, England 2. Murder -- Nottingham, England 3. Violence against gay men and lesbians 4. Detectives 5. Marital conflict 6. Women detectives 7. Criminal investigation 8. Gay men 9. Film actors and actresses 10. Women journalists 11. Hate crimes 12. Family secrets 13. Cambridge, England 14. Nottingham, England 15. England 16. Mysteries

LC 2006037390

"An Otto Penzler Book."

Originally published: London: Heinemann, 2007.

Investigating the murder of Stephen Bryan, a gay Cambridge academic, detective Will Grayson and his partner, Helen Walker, discover that the killing could be tied to a book Bryan had been writing about the mysterious death of fifties film star Stella Lombard.

"The author, best known for his now-complete Charlie Resnick series, follows Cambridge police detectives Will Grayson and Helen Walker as they investigate the disfiguring murder of gay film professor Stephen Bryan. Initially focused on Bryan's love life, they soon sense secrets around a book he was writing on '50s movie queen Stella Leonard. Flashbacks from the star's last film add a noir chill to the tale. Bryan's sister, a journalist, uses her position to look into things on her own, with potentially dangerous results as Leonard's family grows fiercely protective. Harvey keeps the devastating secret at the center of the tale well hidden until the end." Rocky Mountain News.

Harvey, Michael T.

Brighton / Michael Harvey. Ecco, 2016. 304 p.

ISBN 9780062442970

1. Male friendship 2. Investigative journalists 3. Murder suspects 4. Organized crime 5. Murder 6. Violence 7. Women lawyers 8. Secrets 9. Irish Americans 10. Childhood friends 11. Boston, Massachusetts 12. Thrillers and suspense 13. Crime fiction

Before he became a Pulitzer Prize-winning journalist, Kevin Pearce grew up in gritty Brighton, MA, where he committed a horrible act of violence -- one that he got away with. Nearly three decades on, having avoided Brighton ever since, he's returned to a neighborhood embroiled in a series of murders that could bring to light his own bloody past. Told from multiple points of view, this is an intense and descriptive novel. -- Description by Shauna Griffin.

"Sharp as the blades used to gut the guilty and innocent alike, Harvey's fierce stand-alone is a blood-soaked tribute to finding your past and living with the consequences." Kirkus.

Harvey, Michael T.

The **Chicago** way / Michael Harvey. Knopf, 2007. 320 p. Michael Kelly mysteries

ISBN 9780307266866

1. Private investigators 2. Cold cases (Criminal investigation) 3. Police cover-ups 4. Police 5. Deception 6. Murder 7. Murder investigation 8. Chicago, Illinois 9. Hardboiled fiction 10. Mysteries

LC 2007007796

Sequel: The Fifth Floor

"This is a Borzoi book."

A former Chicago cop and tough, street-smart private detective, Michael Kelly is hired by his former partner, John Gibbons, to solve an eight-year-old rape and battery case, a crime that is complicated by Gibbons's own murder.

"Harvey's tightly plotted evocation of the Chicago underworld is set in the present but brings to mind the voices of Chandler and Hammett." New York Magazine.

Harvey, Michael T.

The **fifth** floor / Michael Harvey. Alfred A. Knopf, 2008. 288 p. Michael Kelly mysteries

ISBN 9780307266873

1. Political corruption 2. Cold cases (Criminal investigation) 3. Private investigators 4. Frameups 5. Police 6. Abusive men 7. Murder 8. Secrets 9. Violence in men 10. Murder 11. Great Fire, Chicago, Ill, 1871 12. Chicago, Illinois 13. Hardboiled fiction 14. Mysteries

LC 2008001484

Sequel to: The Chicago way

Hired by a former lover to follow her abusive husband, private detective Michael Kelly follows the subject to an old house on Chicago's North Side, where he stumbles upon a body and a possible answer to the mystery about who actually started the Great Chicago Fire of 1871, in the atmospheric sequel to The Chicago Way.

"This Michael Kelly thriller has the ex-Chicago cop taking on what he thinks is a simple domestic violence case. But when he tails Johnny Woods, a fixer for the city's powerful mayor, to what turns out to be a grisly murder scene, Kelly realizes he's stumbled onto a scandal that began with the great Chicago Fire of 1871. Digging deeper, Kelly unearths what was once considered an urban legend: two of Chicago's most eminent families conspiring to eradicate Irish immigrants by burning down the city's slums. As more bodies pile up and he becomes romantically involved with a judge with secrets of her own, Kelly vows to expose the conspiracy, even if that means putting himself on the wrong side of the city's most powerful men. Harvey's plot twists in all the right places, and his noir-inspired dialogue crackles without sounding showy. Marlowe and Spade would readily welcome Michael Kelly into their fold." Publishers Weekly.

Harvey, Michael T.

The **governor's** wife / Michael Harvey. Alfred A. Knopf, 2015. 256 p. Michael Kelly mysteries

ISBN 9780307958648

1. Private investigators 2. Political corruption 3. Ambition 4. Missing persons investigation 5. Secrets 6. Married women 7. Chicago,

Illinois 8. Hardboiled fiction 9. Mysteries

LC 2014014535

Receiving a lucrative anonymous offer to track down an escaped criminal, private investigator Michael Kelly unwinds the past of the fugitive's wife, who harbors deeply complicated and dangerous reasons for standing by her husband.

"Harvey makes political corruption personal: this isn't a story of anonymous millions being shuffled between various offshore accounts. The consequence of every decision in Kelly's gritty world bleeds." Kirkus.

Harvey, Michael T.

Pulse / Michael Harvey. HarperCollins, 2018 304 p.

ISBN 9780062443038

1. 1970s 2. Psychic ability 3. Murder investigation 4. College football players 5. Police 6. Visions 7. Brothers 8. Boy psychics 9. Boston, Massachusetts 10. Mysteries 11. Police procedurals 12. Supernatural mysteries

Investigating the murder of a Harvard football star, a pair of veteran detectives are stunned when the victim's teen-runaway brother arrives at the scene, claiming to have metaphysical knowledge of the crime before it occurred.

Harvey, Michael T.

We all fall down / Michael Harvey. Alfred A. Knopf, 2011. 320 p. Michael Kelly mysteries

ISBN 9780307272515

1. Private investigators 2. Biological terrorism 3. Terrorism -- Prevention 4. Gangs 5. Former police 6. Chicago, Illinois 7. Hardboiled fiction 8. Mysteries

LC 2011004681

When Chicago is targeted by a brutal biological attack that threatens millions of lives, Michael Kelly begins a desperate search through the tangled underworld of the city's West Side gangs, where he confronts the covert practices of dark science in one of the nation's premiere laboratories.

"A gripping crime novel with a frightening message about very plausible biological warfare." Booklist.

Hashemzadeh Bonde, Golnaz, 1983-

What we owe / Golnaz Hashemzadeh Bonde ; translated from the Swedish by Elizabeth Clark Wessel. Mariner Books/ Houghton Mifflin Harcourt, 2018., 200 p.

ISBN 9781328995087

1. Women -- Iran 2. Mothers and daughters 3. Women with cancer 4. Pregnant women 5. Immigrants 6. Revolutions 7. Family relationships 8. Anger in women 9. Memories 10. Men/women relations 11. Iran -- History -- Islamic revolution, 1979-1997 12. Sweden 13. Domestic fiction 14. Literary fiction 15. Translations -- Swedish to English

LC 2017058741

Originally published: Stockholm : Wahlstrom & Widstrand, 2017.

Standing on the precipice of her own death, 50-year-old Nahid, who has never had the ability or opportunity to live life to the fullest, is filled with both new fury and long dormant rage when she learns that her daughter Aram is pregnant with her first child.

"Hashemzadeh Bonde, unafraid of ugliness and seemingly unconcerned with likability, has produced a startling meditation on death, national identity, and motherhood. Always arresting, never sentimental; gut-wrenching, though not without hope." Kirkus.

Haslett, Adam

* **Imagine** me gone : a novel / Adam Haslett. Little, Brown and Company, 2016. 368 p.

ISBN 9780316261357

1. Depression 2. Married people 3. Family and mental illness 4. Coping 5. Fathers 6. Familial love 7. Mental illness 8. Faith 9. Parent and child 10. Families 11. Psychological fiction 12. Literary fiction
LC 2015028890

Kirkus Prize for Fiction finalist, 2016.

National Book Critics Circle Award for Fiction finalist, 2016.

Pulitzer Prize for Fiction finalist, 2017.

Electing to marry the fianc? who is hospitalized for depression, a woman commits to decades of love and faith involving their brilliant musical eldest son, their responsible daughter and a tightly controlled younger son who helps her care for her increasingly troubled husband.

"This touching chronicle of love and pain traces half a century in a family of five from the parents' engagement in 1963 through a father's and son's psychological torments and a final crisis." Kirkus.

Haslett, Adam

Union Atlantic / Adam Haslett. Nan A. Talese/Doubleday, 2010. 304 p.

ISBN 9780385524476

1. Social classes 2. Banks and banking 3. Personal conduct 4. Interpersonal relations 5. Bankers 6. Senior women 7. High school students 8. Mental illness 9. Bank failures 10. Land claims 11. House construction 12. Betrayal 13. Massachusetts 14. Literary fiction

Lambda Literary Award for Gay Men's Fiction, 2010.

Banker Doug Fanning begins building a massive mansion on land formerly owned by retired teacher Charlotte Graves' grandfather. The land was once donated to the local town, and now Charlotte is trying to stop Doug's construction efforts by any means necessary.

"A novel about Doug Fanning, a handsome, renegade Boston securities trader whose imprudent bets on the Japanese markets threaten to cause systemic bank failure. . . . Unfolding in the fictional town of Finden, Massachusetts, the novel's central narrative pits Doug in an oblique battle of wills with his neighbor Charlotte Graves, a former history teacher and dismayed old-school liberal who resents the size and style of his massive new house. While the two ostensibly wrangle over property rights, the real stakes of their disagreement is not taste but ideologyor perhaps better, pathology. . . . Set during the run-up to the invasion of Iraq, Union Atlantic is like a pressure-compacted version of a Tom Wolfe zeitgeist doorstop, complete with a diffuse cast of characters (bankers, pot-smoking teenagers, a conflicted corporate whistle-blower, the president of the Federal Reserve Bank of New York) and myriad cultural obsessions: about the corporatization of war, the joyless hedonism of American society and the soullessness of suburban life." Time Out New York.

Hassib, Rajia

A **pure** heart : a novel / Rajia Hassib. Viking, 2019. 320 p.

ISBN 9780525560050

1. Sisters 2. Muslim women 3. Egyptian-Americans 4. Women -- Egypt 5. Women archaeologists 6. Egyptologists 7. Sisters -- Death 8. Suicide bombings 9. Arab Spring, 2010- 10. Secrets 11. Husband and wife 12. Sibling rivalry 13. Identity (Psychology) 14. Self-perception 15. Cairo, Egypt 16. New York City 17. Literary fiction
LC 2018060355

Follows the divergent fates of two Egyptian sisters--Rose, married to an American journalist and living in New York City, and Gameela, a devout Muslim who remained in Cairo--when Rose returns to Egypt after Gameela is killed in a suicide bombing.

"...A multifaceted look at the complicated legacies of identity, religion, and politics in Egypt after the Arab Spring emerges. Even the story of the suicide bomber is given careful consideration in this enlightening, heartrending novel." Booklist.

Hatcher, Robin Lee

Cross my heart / Robin Lee Hatcher. Thomas Nelson, 2019 320 p. Legacy of faith novels

ISBN 9780785219309

1. Horse farms 2. Recovering alcoholics 3. Trust 4. Faith (Christianity) 5. Men/women relations 6. Interpersonal attraction 7. Brothers 8. Opioid abuse 9. Forgiveness 10. Redemption 11. Great-great-grandfathers 12. Small towns 13. Idaho 14. Christian romances
LC 2018059440

Ashley and Ben have a lot in common and a possible love connection, but Ben is a recovering alcoholic and after dealing with her drug addicted brother, Ashley refuses to enter a relationship where addiction is present.

Hatcher, Robin Lee

Who I am with you / Robin Lee Hatcher. Thomas Nelson, 2018. 320 p. Legacy of faith novels

ISBN 9780785219262

1. Pregnant women 2. Widows 3. Politicians 4. Scandals 5. Loss (Psychology) 6. Great-grandfathers 7. Secrets 8. Faith (Christianity) 9. Small towns 10. Idaho 11. Christian romances
LC 2018031310

A pregnant woman embittered by the deaths of her husband and daughter finds healing and renewal in her great-grandfather's Bible before opening her heart to a disgraced businessman who would withdraw from the world.

Hauck, Rachel, 1960-

How to catch a prince / Rachel Hauck. Zondervan, 2015, c2014. 320 p. Royal wedding novels

ISBN 9780310315544

1. Friends' death 2. Former lovers 3. Married people 4. Men/women relations 5. Heirs and heiresses 6. Princes 7. Women journalists 8. Secrets 9. Life change events 10. Florida 11. Christian romances
LC 2014033423

Corina Del Rey's life as a journalist in Melbourne, Florida, is complicated when professional rugby player and prince Stephen of Brighton Kingdom re-enters her life.

"Hauck has written a sensitive, emotion-filled story about the effects of war on a relationship. Her characters are flawed and realistic. This engaging, faith-based book is part of the Royal Wedding Series." Booklist.

Hauck, Rachel, 1960-

Once upon a prince / Rachel Hauck. Zondervan, 2013. 320 p. Royal wedding novels

ISBN 9780310315476

1. God (Christianity) -- Will 2. Faith (Christianity) 3. Royal weddings 4. Princes 5. Life change events 6. Royal houses 7. Duty 8. Women -- Southern States 9. Islands 10. Men/women relations 11. St Simon's Island, Georgia 12. Georgia 13. Christian romances
LC 2013001023

When a jilted girlfriend meets a reluctant crown prince, they discover the power of God's love to heal hearts and change a nation.

Hauck, Rachel, 1960-

The **wedding** chapel / Rachel Hauck. Zondervan, 2015 352 p.

ISBN 9780310341529

1. Retirees 2. Women photographers 3. Husband and wife 4. Advertising executives 5. Marital conflict 6. Homecomings 7. Weddings 8. Family secrets 9. Men/women relations 10. New York City 11. Tennessee 12. Christian romances

LC 2015023680

Christy Award for Contemporary Romance Category, 2016.

When photographer Taylor Branson elopes with top ad man Jack Forester and then returns to her home town in Tennessee, her doubts about her relationship are put into perspective by a retired football coach who has been holding onto a dream since 1949.

Hawkins, Paula

* The **girl** on the train : a novel / Paula Hawkins. Riverhead Books, 2015. 336 p.

ISBN 9781594633669

1. Divorced women 2. Secrets 3. Murder witnesses 4. Crime 5. Murder victims 6. Murder 7. Alcoholic women 8. Railroad travel 9. Commuters 10. Strangers 11. London, England 12. Psychological suspense

LC 2014027001

Adapted into a film in 2016 under the same title.

Obsessively watching a breakfasting couple every day to escape the pain of her losses, Rachel witnesses a shocking event that inextricably entangles her in the lives of strangers.

"The novel is alternately narrated by three equally unlikable women, and Hawkins very deliberately doles out tantalizing information, but what really gives this novel its compulsive readability is the way she so expertly mines female archetypes: the jealous ex-wife, the smug mistress, the emotionally damaged femme fatale." Booklist.

Hawkins, Scott

* The **library** at Mount Char / Scott Hawkins. Crown Publishers, 2015 400 p.

ISBN 9780553418606

1. Orphans 2. Libraries 3. Imprisonment 4. Gods and goddesses 5. Secrets 6. Magic 7. Fantasy fiction

Carolyn and a dozen other children being raised by "Father," a cruel man with mysterious powers, begin to think he might be God, so when he dies, they square off against each other to determine who will inherit his library, which they believe holds the power to all Creation.

"Hawkins's cunning plotting is backed up by crisp dialogue, a sensation of constant dread, and a solid, subtly weird setting." Publishers Weekly.

Hawley, Noah

Before the fall / Noah Hawley. Grand Central Pub., 2016. 384 p.

ISBN 9781455561780

1. Airplane accidents 2. Accident victims 3. Rich people 4. Four-year-old boys 5. Business -- Corrupt practices 6. Recovering alcoholics 7. Private airplanes 8. Millionaires 9. Painters 10. Survival 11. Secrets 12. Artists 13. Massachusetts 14. Thrillers and suspense

Edgar Allan Poe Award for Best Novel, 2017.

Thriller Award for Best Novel, 2017.

The stories of ten wealthy victims of a plane crash intertwine with those of a down-on-his-luck painter and a four-year-old boy, the tragedy's only survivors, as odd coincidences surrounding the crash point to a possible conspiracy.

"This is a gritty tale of a man overwhelmed by unwelcome notoriety, with a stunning, thoroughly satisfying conclusion." Publishers Weekly.

Hawley, Noah

The **good** father / Noah Hawley. Doubleday, 2012. 320 p.

ISBN 9780385535533

1. Parents of children with mental illnesses 2. Children of divorced parents 3. Father and adult son 4. Physicians 5. Assassination 6. Guilt in men 7. Self-discovery in men 8. Psychological suspense

LC 2011017657

Establishing a specialty in diagnosing otherwise abandoned patients with conflicting symptoms, Chief of Rheumatology Paul Allen is placed in the impossible position of having to unlock the mind of his 20-year-old son, who has attempted to assassinate a presidential candidate.

Hawthorne, Nathaniel, 1804-1864

* The **house** of the seven gables / Nathaniel Hawthorne. Modern Library, 2001, c1851. xix, 312 p.

ISBN 9780375756870

1. Curses 2. Families 3. Haunted houses 4. Revenge 5. Greed in men 6. Witch hunting 7. Malicious accusation 8. Salem, Massachusetts 9. New England 10. Family sagas 11. Gothic fiction 12. Classics

First published 1851.

Book inspired a 1940 film of the same name but differs dramatically from the plot of the novel.

The sins of the Pyncheon father are visited upon his children over a period of several generations, until such time as one of his descendants unites with a member of the family he has wronged. Love conquers hate, and new blood washes away the original crime. This intriguing and insightful novel truly deserves its significant place in the canon of American literature.

Hawthorne, Nathaniel, 1804-1864

* The **scarlet** letter : a romance / Nathaniel Hawthorne ; with an introduction by Alfred Kazin. Knopf, 1992, xxvii, 273 p.

ISBN 0679417311

1. Colonial America (1600-1775) 2. Married women 3. Puritans 4. Revenge 5. Husband and wife 6. Pariahs 7. Clergy 8. Physicians 9. Extramarital affairs 10. Love triangles 11. Atonement 12. Sin 13. Secrets 14. Ostracism 15. Villages 16. Massachusetts -- History -- Colonial period, 1600-1775 17. Historical fiction 18. Classics

LC 92052902

First published in 1850.

Originally published: Boston: J.R. Osgood and company, 1878.

In early colonial Massachusetts, a young woman endures the consequences of her sin of adultery and spends the rest of her life in atonement.

Hay, Elizabeth, 1951-

Late nights on air / Elizabeth Hay. McClelland & Stewart, 2007. 376 p.

ISBN 9780771038112

1. 1970s 2. Radio newscasters and commentators 3. Fuel industry and trade 4. Land claims 5. Women radio newscasters and commentators 6. Radio stations 7. Interpersonal relations 8. Shyness in women 9. Coping 10. Emotions 11. Summer 12. Yellowknife, Northwest Territories 13. Northwest Territories 14. Canada 15. Literary fiction

CBA Libris Award for Fiction Book of the Year, 2008.

Ottawa Book Award for English Fiction, 2008.

Scotiabank Giller Prize, 2007.

Accepting a position at a northern Canadian radio station in 1975, Dido Paris disarms a hard-bitten broadcaster with her beauty and vocal talents before controversy surrounding a proposed gas pipeline triggers call-in-listener debates on the air.

"The plot of this novel is a faint signal, a series of short moments, sometimes funny, sometimes poignant, often flecked with intimations of tragedy. Hay's writing is so alluring and her lost souls so endearing that you'll lean in to catch the story's delicate developments as these characters shuffle along through quiet desperation and yearning." Washington Post Book World.

Hayder, Mo

Birdman / Mo Hayder. Doubleday, 1999. 327 p. Detective Inspector Jack Caffery mysteries

ISBN 9780385496940

1. Violence against women 2. Mutilation 3. Serial murders 4. Coping 5. Pedophiles 6. Suspicion 7. Surgeons 8. Serial murder investigation 9. Men/women relations 10. Detectives 11. Serial murderers 12. Drug dealers 13. Police 14. London, England 15. Greenwich, England 16. England 17. Police procedurals 18. Mysteries

Detective Inspector Jack Caffery must confront the demons of his own past while searching for the psychopathic killer responsible for the brutal murders and mutilations of five young women, all of whom had worked at a strip club near a local medical school

Hayder, Mo

Gone / Mo Hayder. Atlantic Monthly Press, 2011, c2010 416 p. Detective Inspector Jack Caffery mysteries

ISBN 9780802119643

1. Carjacking 2. Kidnapping 3. Missing girls 4. Eleven-year-old girls 5. Detectives 6. Police 7. England 8. Bristol, England 9. Police procedurals 10. Mysteries

Originally published: London : Bantam, 2010.

Edgar Allan Poe Award for Best Novel, 2012.

Investigating a serial carjacker whose actual targets are young children in back seats, Jack Caffery teams up once again with police diver Sergeant Flea Marley, whose life is endangered by a discovery in an abandoned, half-submerged tunnel.

"A crime novel featuring Detective Inspector Jack Caffery of Bristol's Major Crime Investigation Unit and Sgt. Flea Marley, who heads up the Underwater Search Unit. This artfully constructed procedural opens with a car-jacking that becomes a kidnapping after the thief drives off with a little girl in the back seat. The narrative takes its first chilling turn when Caffery's team detects a pattern of other accidental kidnappings, indicating that the carjacker was stalking little girls all along. More shocks are in store, but for once the visceral thrills don't come at the expense of character. By giving her villain the intelligence to inflict as much emotional as physical pain, Hayder makes him less of a monster and more of a terror." New York Times Book Review.

Hayder, Mo

Hanging hill / Mo Hayder. Grove/Atlantic, 2012. 432 p.

ISBN 9780802120069

1. Murder investigation 2. Pornography 3. Teenage girls 4. Policewomen 5. Sisters 6. Crimes against women 7. Divorced women 8. Fashion models 9. Secrets 10. Bath, England 11. England 12. Thrillers and suspense

After a popular Bath teen's murder, police detective Zoe Benedict looks beyond the usual motives to solve the crime; while her divorced sister, Sally, takes a housekeeping job for a wealthy entrepreneur who behaves in increasingly suspicious ways.

Hayder, Mo

Poppet / Mo Hayder. Grove/Atlantic, 2013. 400 p. Detective Inspector Jack Caffery mysteries

ISBN 9780802121073

1. Detectives 2. Escapes 3. Psychiatric hospitals 4. Self-harm 5. Psychiatric hospital patients 6. Fugitives 7. Cutting (Self-harm) 8. Police 9. England 10. Bristol, England 11. Mysteries 12. Police procedurals

"The new Jack Caffery thriller"--Cover.

When a dangerous mental patient named Isaac, who is linked to a series of unexplained episodes of self-harm among the ward's patients, is released in error, Detective Jack Caffery must track him down before he kills again.

Hayder, Mo

Ritual / Mo Hayder. Atlantic Monthly Press, 2008. 416 p. Detective Inspector Jack Caffery mysteries

ISBN 9780871139924

1. Witchcraft 2. Torture 3. Detectives 4. Missing persons investigation 5. Violence 6. Women divers 7. Drug abuse 8. Police 9. Bristol, England 10. England 11. Mysteries 12. Police procedurals
LC bl2008017802

Originally published: London : Bantam, 2008.

Police diver Flea Marley's discovery of a human hand underwater, as well as evidence that it had been recently amputated while the victim was alive, sends Flea and Detective Inspector Jack Caffery on a search for a young man who recently vanished.

"Hayder vividly evokes torture and drug abuse, but the violence is never gratuitous. Readers looking for visceral thrills need look no further than this gritty English series." Publishers Weekly.

Hayder, Mo

Skin / Mo Hayder. Grove Press, 2010. 288 p. Detective Inspector Jack Caffery mysteries

ISBN 9780802119308

1. Mutilation 2. Suicide 3. Missing persons investigation 4. Detectives 5. Murder investigation 6. Police 7. Witchcraft 8. Missing persons 9. Serial murderers 10. England 11. Bristol, England 12. Mysteries 13. Police procedurals

Detective Jack Caffery and police driver Flea Marley follow a trail of apparent suicides to Elf's Grotto, a nearly bottomless network of flooded quarries, where someone--or something--lurks, ready to disappear into darkness or slip into houses unseen.

Hayder, Mo

The **treatment** / Mo Hayder. Doubleday, 2002, c2001. 357 p. Detective Inspector Jack Caffery mysteries

ISBN 0385496958

1. Child kidnapping victims 2. Murder 3. Detectives 4. Pedophilia 5. Coping 6. Brothers -- Death 7. Missing persons 8. Violence against children 9. Police 10. Greenwich, England 11. England 12. Mysteries 13. Police procedurals

A Detective Jack Caffery thriller in which Jack is called in to investigate the mysterious disappearance of a south London couple's young son.

Haydon, Elizabeth

Destiny : child of the sky / Elizabeth Haydon. Tor, 2001 555 p. Symphony of Ages

ISBN 0312867506

1. Women adventurers 2. Demons 3. Rulers 4. Dragons 5. Good and evil 6. Magic 7. Music 8. Epic fantasy

LIST OF FICTIONAL WORKS

Sequel to Prophecy: child of earth.

Three great heroes--Rhapsody the Singer, Achmed the assassin-king, and Grunthor the giant Sergeant-Major--continue their struggle against their elusive enemy as they face the final battle for the future of the world.

Haydon, Elizabeth

The **Merchant** Emperor / Elizabeth Haydon. Tor Books, 2014. 384 p. Symphony of Ages

ISBN 9780765305664

1. Women rulers 2. Motherhood 3. Demons 4. Intrigue 5. Imaginary wars and battles 6. Weapons 7. Magic 8. Dragons 9. Epic fantasy

While Ashe, Gwydion Navarne, and Lord Marshal Anborn prepare to combat the forces of throne-seeking Talquist, the Merchant Emperor of Sorbold forges an alliance with two demons and Rhapsody goes into hiding to protect her infant son.

"For those familiar with the history of Rhapsody and Ashe, two of the main characters from previous books, this volume will provide additional depth to their personalities as they are forced to make difficult decisions to save not only themselves and those they love but also perhaps the world they live in... followers of the series will be delighted with it." Booklist.

Haydon, Elizabeth

Prophecy : child of earth / Elizabeth Haydon Tor, 2000. 448 p. Symphony of Ages

ISBN 0312867514

1. Good and evil 2. Giants 3. Assassins 4. Women adventurers 5. Demons 6. Quests 7. Men/women relations 8. Magic 9. Music 10. Epic fantasy

LC 00026836

Sequel to: Rhapsody.

The Prophecy of the Three--Rhapsody, a talented singer; Achmed, an assassin with unearthly powers; and the giant Grunthor--must find their elusive enemy before his darkness consumes them all.

"The skysinger Rhapsody and her two FirBolg companions seek to carve out a place for themselves in a new world even as their lives move inexorably toward the fulfillment of an ancient prophecy. As momentous events take shape around the three heroes, other forces work hard to undermine their hope and bring the powers of evil closer to victory. . . . Haydon's epic saga of the endless battle between light and darkness resounds with the richness of ancient myths reworked into new forms." Library Journal.

Hayes, Terry

I am Pilgrim / Terry Hayes. Atria Books, 2014. 608 p.

ISBN 9781439177723

1. Genius 2. Terrorists 3. Antiterrorists 4. Former spies 5. Crime prevention 6. Forensic sciences 7. Mass murder 8. Detectives 9. Extremism 10. Murder 11. Middle East 12. Turkey 13. New York City 14. Spy fiction 15. Thrillers and suspense

First published: London: Bantam Press, 2013.

British Book Award for Crime Thriller of the Year, 2014.

Suspense Fiction. This explosive thriller starts with the perfect murder -- the victim has had her teeth removed, her identifiable features have been destroyed by acid, and the scene has been liberally sprayed with DNA-destroying disinfectant. But more alarmingly, a jihadist is building a biological weapon he's planning on letting loose in the U.S. The connection between the two is Pilgrim, a retired CIA operative, who's called in to stop the terrorist -- and whose textbook on criminal investigations may have been the blueprint for the murder. -- Description by Shauna Griffin.

"[T]he race against time to save the world has been done before but seldom this well. . . . [A] taut and muscular thriller." Library Journal.

Haynes, Dana

Crashers / Dana Haynes. Minotaur Books, 2010. 352 p. Crashers

ISBN 9780312599881

1. National Transportation Safety Board. 2. Airplane accident investigation 3. Government investigators 4. Spies 5. Forensic sciences 6. Terrorism 7. Portland, Oregon 8. Thrillers and suspense 9. Pacific Northwest fiction

LC 2009046155

When a passenger plane, a Vermeer One Eleven, slams into the ground outside Portland, Oregon, a team--the "crashers"-- is quickly assembled to investigate the cause. Usually the team has months to determine the cause of a crash. But this time it's different. This time, the plane was brought down deliberately, without leaving a trace, and this was only a trial run.

Haywood, Gar Anthony

Cemetery Road / Gar Anthony Haywood. Severn House, 2010. 224 p.

ISBN 9780727868510

1. Murder investigation 2. Drug dealers 3. Revenge 4. Repairers 5. Friendship 6. Grief 7. Murder 8. Secrets 9. Criminals 10. Crime 11. Los Angeles, California 12. Mysteries 13. African American fiction

When Errol "Handy" White returns to his native Los Angeles to attend the funeral of his old friend R. J. Burrow, who has been brutally murdered, a terrible secret threatens to reveal itself.

Haywood, Sarah

The **cactus** / Sarah Haywood. Park Row, 2018. 368 p.

ISBN 9780778318996

1. Mothers -- Death 2. Loss (Psychology) 3. Pregnant women 4. Self-discovery in women 5. Coping 6. Middle-aged women 7. Forties (Age) 8. Women's lives and relationships

Susan has a hard time adjusting when her mother dies and she discovers she's about to become a mother herself.

Hazzard, Shirley, 1931-2016

* The **great** fire / Shirley Hazzard. Farrar, Straus and Giroux, 2003. 352 p.

ISBN 9780374166441

1. 1940s 2. Soldiers 3. World War II veterans 4. Girls 5. Children with terminal illnesses 6. Brothers and sisters 7. Family relationships 8. Love 9. Self-discovery in girls 10. War crimes 11. World War II -- Influence 12. World War II -- Post-war aspects 13. Reconstruction (1939-1951) 14. Postwar life 15. England 16. Japan 17. Hong Kong 18. Japan -- History -- Allied occupation, 1945-1952 19. Literary fiction

LC 2003049189

Miles Franklin Award, 2004.

National Book Award for Fiction, 2003.

Shortlisted for the International IMPAC Dublin Literary Award, 2005

Shortlisted for The Orange Prize for Fiction, 2004

In war-torn Asia and stricken Europe, men and women, still young but veterans of harsh experience, must reinvent their lives and expectations, and learn, from their past, to dream again. Some will fulfill their destinies, others will falter. At the center of the story, a brave and brilliant soldier finds that survival and worldly achievement are not enough. His counterpart, a young girl living in occupied Japan and tending her dying brother, falls in love, and in the process discovers herself.

"The time is 1947-48, and the place is, primarily, East Asia. . . . Our hero, and indeed he fills the requirements to be called one, is Aldred Leith, who is English and part of the occupation forces in Japan; his particular military task is damage survey. He has an interesting past, including, most recently, a two-year walk across civil-war-torn China to write a book. In the present. . .he meets the teenage daughter and younger son of a local Australian commander. And, as Helen is growing headlong into womanhood, this novel of war's aftermath becomes a story of love--or more to the point, of the restoration of the capacity for love once global and personal trauma have been shed." Booklist.

Hazzard, Shirley, 1931-2016

* The **transit** of Venus / Shirley Hazzard. Viking Press, 1980. 337 p.

ISBN 9780670724260

1. Sisters 2. Men/women relations 3. Romantic love 4. Australians in foreign countries 5. Literary fiction

LC 79021754

First published in the United States by Viking 1980 and in Great Britain by Macmillan & Co 1980.

National Book Critics Circle Award for Fiction, 1980.

National Book Award for Fiction finalist, 1981

"This is an exceedingly ambitious novel; a stunning and at times bewildering galaxy of ideas. From a literary and intellectual standpoint it is a challenge. . . . Miss Hazzard's greatest achievement in this novel is the suspense she creates from unfinished relationships. Instead of spinning off in different directions through space, these characters collide once again, drawn together by an ineluctable magnetism." Christian Science Monitor.

Heacox, Kim

Jimmy Bluefeather : a novel / Kim Heacox. Alaska Northwest Books, 2015. 256 p.

ISBN 9781941821688

1. Grandfather and grandson 2. Spiritual journeys 3. Indians of North America 4. Canoes 5. Villages 6. Communities 7. Corporations 8. Wilderness areas 9. Alaska 10. Literary fiction 11. Adventure stories

LC 2015007906

National Outdoor Book Award for Outdoor Literature, 2015.

Canoe carver Keb Wisting and his grandson James, who is despondent after a logging injury derails the future he envisioned, embark on a great canoe journey into the wild Alaska.

"Heacox does a superb job of transcending his characters unique geography to create a heartwarming, all-American story. Jinkaat, Alaska, can stand beside Twain's Missouri and Anderson's Winesburg, Ohio." Booklist.

Headley, Maria Dahvana, 1977-

The **mere** wife / Maria Dahvana Headley. Farrar, Straus and Giroux, 2018. 308 p.

ISBN 9780374208431

1. Mothers and sons 2. Gated communities 3. Misfits (Persons) 4. Women veterans 5. Stay-at-home mothers 6. Motherhood 7. Suburban life 8. Interpersonal conflict 9. Literary fiction 10. Adaptations, retellings, and spin-offs

LC 2017058628

A modern retelling of Beowulf recasts classic themes from the perspectives of the attackers and finds a suburban housewife and a battle-hardened veteran navigating dark realities to protect the sons they love.

Healey, Emma, 1985-

* **Elizabeth** is missing / Emma Healey. HarperCollins, 2014. 303 p.

ISBN 9780062309662

1. Female friendship 2. Memory disorders 3. People with dementia 4. Missing persons 5. Memory 6. Senior women 7. Compulsive behavior 8. Dementia 9. Sisters 10. Interpersonal relations 11. England 12. Psychological suspense

Costa First Novel Award, 2014.

When Maud, an aging grandmother who is slowly losing her memory, is convinced that her best friend Elizabeth is missing and in terrible danger, she becomes obsessed with saving her beloved friend despite the fact that no one believes her.

"Part mystery, part meditation on memory, part Dickensian revelation of how apparent charity may hurt its recipients, this is altogether brilliant." Booklist.

Heath, Lorraine

Falling into bed with a duke / Lorraine Heath. Avon Books, 2015. 384 p. Hellions of Havisham

ISBN 9780062391018

1. Victorian era (1837-1901) 2. Dukes and duchesses 3. Heirs and heiresses 4. Lovers 5. Secret identity 6. Mate selection 7. Courtship 8. Photography of the nude 9. Sexual attraction 10. Men/women relations 11. England -- Social life and customs -- 19th century 12. Great Britain -- History -- Victoria, 1837-1901 13. Victorian romances 14. Historical romances

Choosing spinsterhood over fortune-hungry suitors, Miss Minerva Dodger decides to enjoy one night of pleasure at the Nightingale Club where she is drawn into an intimate affair with the Duke of Ashebury, who, once he discovers her true identity, sets out to win her heart.

Heathcock, Alan

Volt : stories / Alan Heathcock. Graywolf Press, 2011. 208 p.

ISBN 9781555975777

1. Small towns 2. Grief in men 3. Women sheriffs 4. Fatal traffic accidents 5. Murder 6. Short stories 7. Rural noir 8. Literary fiction

A debut collection by a National Magazine Award winner features stark tales set in brutal landscapes, depicting such protagonists as a grief-stricken farmer who takes to walking after running over his son and a female sheriff who covers up a murder in a flood-stricken town.

"Heathcock displays a real talent for describing a character in a telling phrase and shows a deep appreciation of the petty and serious violence of daily life. Recommend Volt to fans of Cormac McCarthy, Larry Brown, and Tom Franklin." Booklist.

Heger, Amanda

Crazy cupid love / Amanda Heger. Sourcebooks Casablanca, 2019. 352 p. Let's get mythical

ISBN 9781492672753

1. Enchantment 2. Family businesses 3. Matchmaking 4. Mentors 5. Characters and characteristics in mythology 6. Gods and goddesses, Greek 7. Love spells 8. Sexual attraction 9. Men/women relations 10. California 11. Romantic comedies 12. Paranormal romances

In a magical rom-com, the descendants of Greek mythology must learn to live and love in a mundane world where Aphrodite's blessing can sure feel like a real pain in the quiver.

Heggen, Thomas, 1919-1949

Mister Roberts / Thomas Heggen ; illustrated by Samuel Hanks Bryant. Houghton Mifflin, 1946. 221 p..

ISBN 1557507236

1. United States. Navy Officers 2. 1940s 3. World War II -- Naval operations -- Pacific Ocean 4. World War II -- Naval operations, American 5. Seafaring life 6. Pacific Ocean 7. War stories 8. Sea stories 9. Historical fiction

LC 46025229

The popular First Lieutenant of a cargo ship leads the otherwise idle crew in a fight against boredom and the captain.

"The leisurely narrative is told in a very few incidents, all centering about an admirable young lieutenant miserably defeated in his desire to get into fighting. A quiet, credible story of the corroding effects of apathy and boredom on men who, in battle, might have been heroes." The New Yorker.

Hegi, Ursula

Children and fire : a novel / Ursula Hegi. Simon & Schuster, 2011. 272 p.

ISBN 9781451608298

1. 1930s 2. Family secrets 3. Nazism 4. Women teachers 5. Fear in women 6. School children 7. Nazis 8. Villages 9. Influence (Psychology) 10. Germany -- History -- 1933-1945 11. Historical fiction

Protecting her beloved students from the devastating world outside of their 1934 Berlin classroom, Thekla Jansen sacrifices some of her personal freedoms to retain her teaching position until activities within Hitler's early regime test her moral courage.

"A thoughtful, sidelong approach to the worst moment in Germany's history that invites us to understand how decent people come to collaborate with evil." Kirkus.

Hegi, Ursula

Stones from the river / Ursula Hegi. Poseidon Press, 1994. 507 p.

ISBN 0671780751

1. 20th century 2. Small town life 3. Librarians 4. Secrets 5. Women librarians 6. World War II 7. Misfits (Persons) 8. Sexual violence 9. Revenge 10. Hate 11. Little people 12. Small towns 13. West Germany 14. Literary fiction

LC 93033533

A dwarf becomes the librarian of a small German town. The work makes her privy to many of the town's secrets and she uses them to set people against each other. It's her way of paying them back for the taunts and humiliations.

"The author imbues her novel with a strong spirit of place. When Trudi wrestles with despair, she goes to the nearby Rhine for help. It never fails her. . . . Americans still tend to view Germany with horror or (sometimes gleeful) condescension. This moving, elegiac novel commands our compassion and respect for the wisdom and courage to be found in unlikely places, in unlikely times." New York Times Book Review.

Hegi, Ursula

The **vision** of Emma Blau / Ursual Hegi. Simon & Schuster, 2000. 432 p.

ISBN 0684829975

1. Family relationships 2. Young women 3. Deception 4. Runaways 5. Ambition in men 6. Restaurateurs 7. Widowers 8. Single fathers 9. Men/women relations 10. Married people 11. German Americans 12. World War II 13. Immigrants 14. Women 15. New Hampshire 16. Family sagas 17. Literary fiction

LC 99056392

A novel of immigration and love follows a German man who flees to the U.S. at the start of the century and makes a life for himself, spawning four generations of descendants

"Hegi has created a milieu full of sexual energy--the book is often erotic--and has captured both the tension and love endemic to all tight-knit families. Compelling and absorbing, this old-fashioned saga is rife with passion, tragedy, and redemption." Library Journal.

Heinlein, Robert A. (Robert Anson), 1907-1988

The **moon** is a harsh mistress / Robert A. Heinlein. T. Doherty, 1997. 382 p.

ISBN 0312863551

1. Artificial intelligence 2. Space warfare 3. Revolutions -- Moon 4. Computers 5. Supercomputers 6. Far future 7. Dystopias 8. Moon 9. Hard science fiction 10. Dystopian fiction 11. Social science fiction 12. Science fiction

LC 9553750

Hugo Award for Best Novel, 1967.

The moon, 2075. Working to produce wheat for earth, lunar residents live like sharecroppers, kept prisoners of the mother planet by a tight web of control. A small group of dissidents are planning a revolution that will change this relationship forever.

Heinlein, Robert A. (Robert Anson), 1907-1988

* **Starship** troopers / Robert A. Heinlein. G. P. Putnam's Sons, 1959. 309 p.

1. Aliens (Non-humanoid) 2. Space warfare 3. Human/alien encounters 4. Life on other planets 5. Violence 6. Dystopias 7. Military policy -- Philosophy 8. Imaginary wars and battles 9. Science fiction

LC 59012950

"A much abridged version ... was published in Fantasy and science fiction magazine under the title 'Starship soldier.' "

Originally published: New York: Putnam, 1959; Great Britain: New English Library, 1960.

Hugo Award for Best Novel, 1960.

With Earth embroiled in a vast interplanetary war with the "Bugs," a young recruit in the Federal Reserves relates his experiences training in boot camp and as a junior officer in the Terran Mobile Infantry.

Heinlein, Robert A. (Robert Anson), 1907-1988

* **Stranger** in a strange land / Robert A. Heinlein. G. P. Putnam's Sons, 1961. 408 p.

ISBN 9780399107726

1. Messiahs 2. Sexual freedom 3. Religion 4. Rich men 5. Men psychics 6. Cult leaders 7. Martians 8. Sexuality 9. Civilization, Western 10. Religion and culture 11. Cults 12. Innocence (Personal quality) 13. Mars (Planet) -- Exploration 14. Social science fiction 15. Science fiction

LC 61011702

Hugo Award for Best Novel, 1962.

A nonhuman visitor brings into doubt the values and self-evident truths of Western society.

Heller, Joseph

* **Catch-22** / Joseph Heller. Simon & Schuster Paperbacks, 2004, c1961. 463 p.

ISBN 0684833395

1. United States. Air Force 2. 1940s 3. Soldiers -- United States 4. World War II 5. Survival 6. Military missions 7. Mental illness 8. Airmen 9. War 10. Italy 11. Satirical fiction 12. Black humor 13. War

stories 14. Modern classics

LC 2004558446

Sequel: Closing time.

Originally published: New York: Simon & Schuster, 1961.

Presents the contemporary classic depicting the struggles of a United States airman attempting to survive the lunacy and depravity of a World War II airbase

Heller, Joseph

Good as Gold / Joseph Heller. Simon and Schuster, 1979. 447 p.

ISBN 0671229230

1. 1970s 2. Jewish men 3. Middle-aged men 4. Midlife crisis in men 5. Jewish American families 6. Fathers and sons 7. Jewish Americans 8. Husband and wife 9. Family relationships 10. Ambition in men 11. United States -- Politics and government -- 20th century 12. Domestic fiction 13. Satirical fiction 14. Political fiction

LC 78023894

Dr. Bruce Gold, a forty-eight-year-old Jewish professor of English, faces the possibilities of being appointed to a high State Department position and being disowned by his family.

Heller, Peter, 1959-

Celine : a novel / Peter Heller. Alfred A. Knopf, 2017. 352 p.

ISBN 9780451493897

1. Missing persons investigation 2. Women private investigators 3. Senior women 4. Cold cases (Criminal investigation) 5. Families of missing persons 6. Husband and wife 7. Photographers 8. Bear attacks 9. Socialites 10. Secrets 11. Artists 12. Yellowstone National Park 13. Wyoming 14. Colorado 15. New York City 16. Mysteries

LC 2016026943

Establishing an excellent record as a missing-persons tracker who specializes in reuniting families to make amends for a loss in her own past, Celine searches for a presumed-dead photographer in Yellowstone, only to be targeted by a shadowy figure who would keep the case unsolved.

"Heller (The Painter) blends suspense with beautiful descriptive writing of both nature and civilization to create a winner." Library Journal.

Heller, Peter, 1959-

* The **dog** stars : a novel / Peter Heller. Alfred A. Knopf, 2012. 272 p.

ISBN 9780307959942

1. Pilots 2. End of the world 3. Survival 4. Risk 5. Epidemics 6. Apocalyptic fiction

LC 2011050429

"This is a Borzoi book."

ALA Notable Book, 2013

Surviving a pandemic disease that has killed everyone he knows, a pilot establishes a shelter in an abandoned airport hangar before hearing a random radio transmission that compels him to risk his life to seek out other survivors.

Heller, Peter, 1959-

* The **painter** : a novel / Peter Heller. Alfred A. Knopf, 2014. 363 p.

ISBN 9780385352093

1. Artists 2. Violence in men 3. Former convicts 4. Abstract expressionism 5. Life change events 6. Murder 7. Psychological fiction

LC 2013045522

Struggling with dark impulses after serving time for attempted murder, a successful artist gives in to his obsessions to kill an abusive troublemaker before fleeing authorities and the man's vengeful clan.

"[E]mbraces themes of personal loss and growth, drama and suspense, while also including plenty for those who enjoy art or nature fiction." Library Journal.

Heller, Peter, 1959-

The **river** : a novel / Peter Heller. Alfred A. Knopf, 2019. 253 p.

ISBN 9780525521877

1. Canoeing 2. Male friendship 3. Wilderness survival 4. Survival 5. Friendship 6. Young men 7. Forest fires 8. Abusive men 9. Abused women 10. Men and nature 11. Interpersonal conflict 12. Canada 13. Survival stories 14. Psychological fiction

Two college students on a wilderness canoe trip find their survival skills and longtime best friendship tested by a wildfire, white-water hazards and two mysterious strangers.

"An exhilarating tale delivered with the pace of a thriller and the wisdom of a grizzled nature guide." Kirkus.

Heller, Zoe

What was she thinking? : notes on a scandal / Zoe Heller. Henry Holt, 2003. 256 p.

ISBN 0805073337

1. 1990s 2. Women teachers 3. Senior women 4. Middle-aged women 5. Female friendship 6. Teacher-student relationships 7. Fifteen-year-old boys -- Relations with older women 8. Extramarital affairs 9. Sex scandals 10. Loneliness 11. Obsession in women 12. Love 13. Envy 14. London, England 15. Psychological fiction 16. Satirical fiction

LC 2002038809

Book made into a movie called Notes on a scandal.

Shortlisted for the Man Booker Prize, 2003.

Schoolteacher Barbara Covett has known none but the most solitary of lifestyles until new teacher Sheba Hart joins St. George's. Starting by sharing lunches, then family events, the new art teacher draws Barbara into a touching confidence. Sheba has begun a passionate affair with an underage male student. When the details come to light and Sheba falls prey to the inevitable media circus, Barbara decides to write an account in her friend's defense, revealing not only Sheba's secrets but her own.

"Barbara Covett, a sixtyish history teacher, is the kind of unmarried-woman-with-cat whose female friends sooner or later decide she is 'too intense.' Thus when a beautiful new pottery teacher, Sheba Hart. . .chooses Barbara as a confidante, she is deeply, even rather sinisterly, gratified. Sheba's secret is explosive: married with two kids, she is having an affair with a fifteen-year-old student. . . . Equally adroit at satire and at psychological suspense, Heller charts the course of a predatory friendship and demonstrates the lengths to which some people go for human company." The New Yorker.

Helprin, Mark

In sunlight and in shadow / Mark Helprin. Houghton Mifflin Harcourt, 2012. 752 p.

ISBN 9780547819235

1. 1940s 2. Veterans 3. Love triangles 4. Heirs and heiresses 5. Courtship 6. Engagement 7. Actors and actresses 8. Jews 9. Crime 10. Corruption 11. New York City 12. Love stories 13. Historical fiction 14. Literary fiction

LC 2012016242

Returning home after serving in World War II to run his family business in New York, paratrooper Harry Copeland falls in love with young singer and heiress Catherine Thomas Hale, who risks everything to break off her engagement to another man.

Helprin, Mark

Paris in the present tense / Mark Helprin. Overlook Press, 2017. 394 p.

ISBN 9781468314762

1. Holocaust survivors 2. Personal conduct 3. Widowers 4. Cellists 5. Seniors 6. Loss (Psychology) 7. Life change events 8. Jewish men 9. Sick children 10. City life 11. Family relationships 12. Interpersonal attraction 13. Men/women relations 14. Paris, France 15. France 16. Literary fiction

When faced with a series of challenges to his principles, livelihood and home, Jules-- 74-year-old maitre at Paris-Sorbonne, cellist, widow, veteran of the war in Algeria and child of the Holocaust--must confront his complex past and find a way forward.

Helprin, Mark

* **Winter's** tale / Mark Helprin. Harcourt, 2005. 748 p.

ISBN 0156031191

1. Gilded Age (1865-1898) 2. Love 3. Death 4. Mortality 5. Irish Americans 6. Thieves 7. Orphans 8. Sick women 9. Heirs and heiresses 10. Men/women relations 11. Reincarnation 12. Supernatural 13. Human nature 14. Personal conduct 15. Ambition 16. Dreams 17. Upper West Side, New York City 18. New York City 19. Magical realism 20. Literary fiction

LC 2006272912

Originally published: San Diego : Harcourt Brace Jovanovich, 1983.

When master mechanic Peter Lake attempts to rob a mansion on the Upper West Side, he is caught by young Beverly Penn, the terminally ill daughter of the house, and their subsequent love sends Peter on a desperate personal journey

Hemingway, Ernest, 1899-1961

* A **farewell** to arms / Ernest Hemingway. Scribner, 1995, c1929. 332 p.

ISBN 9780684801469

1. Americans in Italy 2. World War I -- Italy 3. Ambulance drivers -- History -- World War I 4. British women in Italy 5. Nurses -- History -- World War I 6. War -- Relief of sick and wounded 7. Men/women relations 8. Italy -- History -- 1914-1922 9. War stories 10. Love stories 11. Historical fiction 12. Modern classics 13. Literary fiction

First published: [New York] : Charles Scribner's Sons, 1929.

An American's love for an English nurse during the First World War ends in tragedy.

Hemingway, Ernest, 1899-1961

For whom the bell tolls / Ernest Hemingway. Scribner, 1995, c1940. 471 p.

ISBN 9780684803357

1. Americans in Spain 2. Disillusionment in men 3. Soldiers 4. Guerrillas 5. Anti-fascism 6. Guerrilla warfare 7. Civil War 8. Death -- Psychological aspects 9. War -- Psychological aspects 10. Spain -- History -- Civil War, 1936-1939 11. War stories 12. Historical fiction 13. Modern classics 14. Literary fiction

LC 95-15746

The story of an American fighting in the Spanish Civil War, his loyalty and courage and his eventual disillusionment with love and defeat.

Hemingway, Ernest, 1899-1961

The **Nick** Adams stories / Ernest Hemingway ; preface by Philip Young. Scribner, 1972. 268 p.

ISBN 9780684124858

1. Young men 2. Coming-of-age stories 3. Short stories 4. Modern classics 5. Literary fiction

LC 77159759

Eight of these stories never before published.

Events in the life of Hemingway's memorable character are presented chronologically in this arrangement of the stories.

"The volume presents Nick as a child in the northern woods, as adolescent, as soldier, veteran, writer, husband and parent. The last Nick Adams story appeared in 1933, and what surprises here, in these . . . [stories] of varying length, quality and intent, is their freshness and immediacy." Publishers Weekly.

Hemingway, Ernest, 1899-1961

* The **old** man and the sea / Ernest Hemingway ; illustrations by C.F. Tunnicliffe and Raymond Sheppard. Scribner, 1996, 93 p.

ISBN 9780684830490

1. Fishers -- Cuba 2. Marlin fishing -- Cuba 3. Courage in men 4. Senior men -- Cuba 5. Male friendship 6. Cuba 7. Coming-of-age stories 8. Allegories 9. Modern classics 10. Literary fiction

LC 96011419

First published: London : Jonathan Cape, 1952.

"Vintage Hemingway".

Originally published: New York : Scribner, 1952.

Pulitzer Prize for Fiction, 1953.

Santiago is a Cuban fisherman who encounters a giant marlin in the Gulf Stream and the battle for his catch becomes one of survival against a band of marauding sharks.

Hemingway, Ernest, 1899-1961

The **short** stories / Ernest Hemingway. Scribner Classics, 1997. 457 p.

ISBN 9780684837864

1. Manners and customs 2. Short stories

Forty-nine stories reflect much of the intensity of Hemingway's own life and environment.

Hemingway, Ernest, 1899-1961

The **snows** of Kilimanjaro and other stories / Ernest Hemingway. Scribner, 1995, c1961. 143 p.

ISBN 9780684862217

1. Safaris -- Africa 2. Death -- Psychological aspects 3. Kilimanjaro 4. Short stories 5. Adventure stories 6. Modern classics 7. Literary fiction

Contains ten of Hemingway's classic stories including "The snows of Kilimanjaro," "A day's wait," "Fathers and sons," "The killers," and "The short happy life of Francis Macomber"

Hemingway, Ernest, 1899-1961

* The **sun** also rises / Ernest Hemingway. Scribner, 1995, c1954. 251 p.

ISBN 9780684800714

1. 1920s 2. Expatriates -- Spain 3. Americans in Europe 4. Disillusionment 5. Bullfights -- Spain 6. Alienation (Social psychology) 7. Femmes fatales 8. World War I veterans 9. Drinking 10. Men/women relations 11. Europe -- Social life and customs -- 20th century 12. Modern classics 13. Literary fiction

LC 95-130282

The story of a group of Americans and English on a sojourn from Paris to Paloma, evokes in poignant detail, life among the expatriates on Paris's Left Bank, during the 1920s and conveys in brutally realistic descriptions the power and danger of bullfighting in Spain.

Hemingway, Ernest, 1899-1961

To have and have not / Ernest Hemingway. Scribner, 1999, c1937. 174 p.

ISBN 9780684859231

1. 1930s 2. Smuggling -- Cuba 3. Fishing boat captains -- Florida Keys 4. Married people 5. Americans in Cuba 6. Havana, Cuba 7. Key West, Florida 8. Modern classics 9. Literary fiction

Titles of later film versions: To have and have not (1944), The breaking point (1950), and The gun runners (1958).

In an attempt to keep his family above water, Harry Morgan runs contraband rum shipments between Cuba and Key West during the 1930s, in a humorous tale that also follows an unlikely love affair.

Hemmings, Kaui Hart

The **possibilities** : a novel / Kaui Hart Hemmings. Simon & Schuster, 2014. 288 p.

ISBN 9781476725796

1. Sons -- Death 2. Bereavement 3. Families 4. Life change events 5. Grief 6. Mothers and sons 7. Parenthood 8. Pregnant women 9. Secrets 10. Coping 11. Breckenridge, Colorado 12. Colorado 13. Mainstream fiction

LC 2013027385

A grieving mother struggles to overcome her son's death, when a strange girl enters her life with a secret that changes them both forever.

"Hemmings writes a piercing, empathetic story about parenthood and unfathomable heartbreak and manages to bring humor and hope to her characters. Emotionally complex and relatable to all." Kirkus.

Hempel, Amy

Sing to it : new stories / Amy Hempel. Scribner, 2019. 149 p.

ISBN 9781982109110

1. Interpersonal relations 2. Family relationships 3. Options, alternatives, choices 4. Short stories 5. Literary fiction

LC 2018045523

Finely tuned and brilliantly written, a heartbreaking new collection of 15 stories introduces characters, lonely and adrift, searching for connection.

Henderson, Smith (Joshua Smith)

Fourth of July Creek / Smith Henderson. Ecco Press, 2014. 512 p.

ISBN 9780062286444

1. 1980s 2. Social workers 3. Survivalists 4. Wilderness areas 5. Missing persons 6. Eleven-year-old boys 7. FBI agents 8. Extremists 9. Family relationships 10. Montana 11. Literary fiction

New Blood Dagger Award, 2015.

Shortlisted for the James Tait Black Memorial Prize for Fiction, 2014

Set in the mountains, valleys and close-knit communities of rural Montana in the early 1980s, this novel is about a young social worker called Pete, who struggles to hold together the lives of the most dysfunctional inhabitants of the town of Tenmile, as his own life begins to fall apart.

Henderson, Susan, 1967-

The **flicker** of old dreams / Susan Henderson. Perennial, 2018. 320 p.

ISBN 9780062834072

1. Funeral homes 2. Misfits (Persons) 3. Change (Psychology) 4. Undertakers 5. Small town life 6. Friendship 7. Communities 8. Loss (Psychology) 9. Montana 10. Modern Westerns

Spur Awards, Best Western Contemporary Novel, 2019.

WILLA Literary Awards: Contemporary Fiction, 2019.

Finding fulfillment in her job as an embalmer in her father's small town mortuary, outsider Mary bonds with a villainized local who was blamed for a fatal accident twenty years earlier, a friendship that compels her to consider what might happen if she were to leave their fading community.

Hendricks, Greer

An **anonymous** girl / Greer Hendricks and Sarah Pekkanen. St. Martin's Press, 2019, c2018. 352 p.

ISBN 9781250133731

1. Makeup artists 2. Psychology teachers 3. Psychology -- Experiments 4. Ethics 5. Obsession 6. Human behavior 7. Control (Psychology) 8. Women -- Psychology 9. Manipulation (Social sciences) 10. New York City 11. Manhattan, New York City 12. Psychological suspense 13. Second person narratives

LC 2018029126

Originally published: PanMacmillan, 2018.

Participating in a psychological study under the mysterious Dr. Shields, Jessica endures intense, invasive sessions and oppressive behavioral restrictions before she begins to lose her grasp on reality.

"The movement here from small tests to bigger ones masterfully escalates the suspense. The juxtaposed points of view, with reactions of each protagonist to the other, keep the reader guessing until the end." Booklist.

Hendrix, Grady

My best friend's exorcism / Grady Hendrix. Quirk Books, 2016. 336 p.

ISBN 9781594748622

1. 1980s 2. Female friendship 3. Demonic possession 4. Exorcism 5. Exorcists 6. Best friends 7. Suburban life 8. Interclass friendship 9. High school students 10. Rejection (Psychology) 11. Teenagers -- Friendship 12. Charleston, South Carolina 13. South Carolina 14. Horror

RUSA Reading List Short List, 2017

The year: 1988. The place: Charleston, South Carolina. Abby and Gretchen have been BFFs since fifth grade, but now that they're in high school, Gretchen seems different. After a series of bizarre events, Abby realizes that Gretchen has a demon living inside her -- and it's up to Abby to rescue her friend. Author Grady Hendrix hits a home run with his spectacular, gripping exorcism scene. Don't miss this terrifying tale, filled with spot-on 1980s popular culture references and framed at the beginning and end with yearbook-style layouts. -- Description by Katherine Bradley Johnson.

Henry, O., 1862-1910

* The **complete** works of O. Henry / O. Henry ; foreword by Harry Hansen. Doubleday, 1960, c1953. 1692p.

ISBN 0385009615

1. Short stories 2. Christmas stories 3. Anthologies

LC 60051825

"286 stories and poems."

Includes "The gift of the Magi."

Entertaining collection of two hundred eighty-six stories and poems generally about simple people in various situations with surprise endings.

Henry, Patti Callahan

* Becoming Mrs. Lewis : the improbable love story of Joy Davidman and C. S. Lewis / Patti Callahan. Thomas Nelson, 2018. 432 p.

ISBN 9780785224501

1. Davidman, Joy, 1915-1960 2. Lewis, C S (Clive Staples), 1898-1963 3. Authors 4. Faith (Christianity) 5. Literature 6. Divorced women 7. College teachers 8. Love 9. Thought and thinking 10. Marriage 11. Americans in England 12. Independence in women 13. Loss (Psychology) 14. Historical fiction 15. Love stories 16. Biographical fiction

Christy Award for Book of the Year, 2019.

Christy Award for Historical Romance Category, 2019.

Fictionalizes the romance between beloved author C.S. Lewis and his wife Joy Davidman, as she begins writing letters to Lewis searching for spiritual answers and eventually finds love.

Hensher, Philip

King of the badgers / Philip Hensher. Faber and Faber, 2011. 436 p.

ISBN 9780865478633

1. Missing girls 2. Privacy 3. Missing persons investigation 4. Social classes 5. Interpersonal relations 6. Coastal towns 7. Mass media 8. Gay men 9. Surveillance 10. Neighborhood watch programs 11. England 12. Literary fiction

LC 2011024407

When a child goes missing in the English community of Hanmouth, the ensuing investigation and blurred views about privacy reveal deep economic divisions while exposing the personal secrets of everyday individuals.

"A rich and ambitious novel, which manages both to offer a convincing picture of different levels of English society today and to explore the shifting certainties of individual lives. It is certainly easier to read than to summarise, and this is as it should be." The Scotsman.

Hensher, Philip

Scenes from early life : a novel / Philip Hensher. Faber and Faber, 2013, c2012. 312 p.

ISBN 9780865477612

1. Mahmood, Zaved, 1970- 2. Families -- History 3. Culture conflict 4. Social conflict 5. Bangladeshi families 6. Genocide 7. Bangladesh -- History -- Revolution, 1971 8. Bangladesh -- Social conditions 9. Biographical fiction 10. Literary fiction

Originally published: London: Fourth Estate, 2012.

RSL Ondaatje Prize, 2013.

Traces the experiences of young Zaved's upper-middle-class Bengali family, whose strong bond is made more resilient in the face of brutal violence as Bangladesh fights for independence.

Henson, Pene

Into the blue / Pene Henson. Interlude Press, 2016. 236 p.

ISBN 9781941530849

1. Surfers 2. Professional athletes 3. Roommates 4. Best friends 5. Misunderstanding 6. Men/men relations 7. Gay men 8. Demisexuals 9. Bisexuals 10. Asexuals 11. Hawaii 12. LGBTQIA romances 13. Contemporary romances 14. New adult fiction

Lambda Literary Award for Gay Romance, 2017

"Readers eager for more diversity in romance will appreciate the nuanced portrayals of the leads (one gay, one demisexual) and the women they live with (one bisexual, one asexual) but may wish that Tai's

Samoan heritage and its meaning for him had been explored, rather than just repeatedly referred to in passing." Publishers Weekly.

Hepworth, Sally

The **secrets** of midwives / Sally Hepworth. St. Martin's Press, 2015. 352 p.

ISBN 9781250051899

1. Midwives 2. Pregnant women 3. Family secrets 4. Mothers and daughters 5. Granddaughters 6. Midwifery 7. Storms 8. Family relationships 9. New England 10. Women's lives and relationships

LC 2014033628

Determined to hide the identity of her baby's father from others, a third-generation midwife is separated from and bound to her mother and grandmother by a similar secret from the past.

"Hepworth makes some interesting, though not always successful, choices in her narratives (chapters alternate among Neva, Grace and Floss), painting an irksome portrait of Grace and a rather opaque picture of Neva, whose secret is kept from the reader until the finale. Fans of Call the Midwife will enjoy the vignettes of childbirth and the multigenerational female saga." Kirkus.

Herbert, Frank

* Dune / Frank Herbert. G. P. Putnam's Sons, 1984, c1965. 517 p. Dune novels. Main series

ISBN 0399128964

1. Revolutions 2. Psychic ability 3. Rulers 4. Dukes and duchesses 5. Sabotage 6. Betrayal 7. Genetic engineering 8. Space flight 9. Aliens (Humanoid) 10. Life on other planets 11. Space opera 12. Coming-of-age stories 13. Science fiction

LC 83016030

A deluxe (hbk.) edition was published in 2019 by Ace Books.

Includes map.

Originally published: Philadelphia : Chilton Books, 1965.

Hugo Award for Best Novel, 1966.

Nebula Award for Best Novel, 1965.

Set on the desert planet Arrakis, this is the story of the boy Paul Atreides, who would become the mysterious man known as Muad'Dib, avenge the traitorous plot against his noble family, and bring to fruition humankind's most ancient and unattainable dream.

Herlihy, James Leo, 1927-1993

Midnight cowboy : a novel / James Leo Herlihy. Simon and Schuster, 1960. 253 p.

1. 1960s 2. Male prostitutes 3. Male friendship 4. Loneliness 5. Men -- Sexuality 6. Swindlers and swindling 7. American dream 8. New York City 9. Psychological fiction

Inarticulate man, after twenty-seven years of dependency upon his grandmother, decides to sell what he considers his dashing cowboy charms in New York.

Hersey, John, 1914-1993

* A bell for Adano / John Hersey. Vintage Books, 1988, c1944. 269 p.

ISBN 0394756959

1. Soldiers -- United States 2. World War II -- Italy 3. Americans in Italy 4. Small towns 5. Italian Americans 6. Compassion 7. Sicily, Italy -- History 8. War stories 9. Historical fiction 10. Literary fiction

LC 8745943

Originally published: New York : A.A. Knopf, 1944.

Pulitzer Prize for Fiction, 1945.

An American major attempts to rebuild ravaged Italian town during the World War II occupation.

Hertmans, Stefan

* The **convert** : a novel / Stefan Hertmans ; translated from the Dutch by David McKay. Pantheon Books, 2019, c2016. 304 p.

ISBN 9781524747084

1. Hertmans, Stefan 2. 11th century 3. Young women 4. Jewish men 5. Jews -- Persecutions 6. Conversion to Judaism 7. Voyages and travels 8. Religious persecution 9. Crusades -- First, 1096-1099 10. Jewish children 11. Men/women relations 12. Authors, Dutch 13. France 14. Egypt 15. Cairo, Egypt 16. Historical fiction 17. Translations -- Dutch to English

LC 2019025351

Originally published: Amsterdam : De Bezige Bij, 2016.

English translations originally published London : Harvill Secker, 2019.

Abandoning her privileged life after falling in love with a Jewish man, a Medieval Christian noblewoman embarks on a dangerous journey to southern France, where their brief happiness is upended by the vicious anti-Semitism of the First Crusade.

"The horrors of anti-Semitism and the unintended consequences of the First Crusade are pitilessly portrayed, resulting in a story that is tragic and harrowing, yet beautifully told, with an ambience that is fully realized for both the eleventh century and our own." Booklist.

Hess, Joan

Maggody and the moonbeams : an Arly Hanks mystery / Joan Hess. Simon & Schuster, 2001. 240 p. Arly Hanks mysteries

ISBN 0743202295

1. Camps 2. Communes 3. Murder investigation 4. Police -- Arkansas 5. Police chiefs -- Arkansas 6. Small town life -- Arkansas 7. Women detectives -- Arkansas 8. Women sheriffs -- Arkansas 9. Women police chiefs -- Arkansas 10. Maggody, Arkansas 11. Arkansas 12. Ozark Mountain region 13. Mysteries

LC 2001020208

Spending a miserable week at camp with ten teenagers, the Mayor's stern wife, the high school shop teacher, and preacher Brother Verber, police chief Arly Hanks must attempt to catch a killer after one of the teens discovers the corpse of a woman.

Hesse, Hermann, 1877-1962

The **fairy** tales of Hermann Hesse / Hermann Hesse ; translated and with an introduction by Jack Zipes ; woodcut illustrations by David Frampton. Bantam Books, 1995. xxxi, 266 p.

ISBN 0553377760

1. Belonging 2. Normality (Psychology) 3. Individuality 4. Social acceptance 5. Allegories 6. Anthologies 7. Translations -- German to English

LC 94049166

Translation from the German of: Marchen.

A collection of twenty-two fairy tales by the Nobel Prize winning novelist, most translated into English for the first time, show the influence of German Romanticism, psychoanalysis, and Eastern religion on his development as an author

"Quirky and evocative, Hesse's fairy tales stand alone, but also amplify the ideas and utopian longings of such counterculture avatars as Siddhartha and Steppenwolf." Publishers Weekly.

Hesse, Hermann, 1877-1962

Narcissus and Goldmund / Hermann Hesse ; translated from the German by Ursule Molinaro. Random House, 1992. 320 p.

ISBN 9780553275865

1. Medieval period (476-1492) 2. Monasticism and religious orders for men 3. Civilization, Medieval 4. Meaning (Psychology) 5. Young men 6. Artists 7. Opposites 8. Monks -- Germany 9. Germany -- Church history -- 843-1517 10. Coming-of-age stories 11. Historical fiction 12. Literary fiction 13. Psychological fiction 14. Translations -- German to English

Narcissus, an ascetic instructor at a cloister school, has devoted himself solely to scholarly and spiritual pursuits. One of his students is the sensual, restless Goldmund, who is immediately drawn to his teacher's fierce intellect and sense of discipline. When Narcissus persuades the young student that he is not meant for a life of self-denial, Goldmund sets off in pursuit of aesthetic and physical pleasures, a path that leads him to a final, unexpected reunion with Narcissus.

Hesse, Hermann, 1877-1962

* **Siddhartha** : a new translation / Hermann Hesse ; translated from the German by Sherab Chodzin Kohn ; with an introduction by Paul W. Morris. Shambhala, 2002, c1922. xxiii, 159 p.

ISBN 1570629706

1. Gautama Buddha 2. Spiritual life -- Buddhism 3. Self-fulfillment 4. Enlightenment (Buddhism) 5. Buddhism 6. Courtesans 7. Sexuality 8. Asceticism 9. Gambling 10. Rivers 11. Meaning (Psychology) 12. Brahmins 13. India 14. Psychological fiction 15. Translations -- English to German 16. Modern classics

LC 2002073423

Translated from the German.

Originally published: Berlin : S. Fischer, 1922.

Blends elements of psychoanalysis and Asian religions to probe an Indian aristocrat's efforts to renounce sensual and material pleasures and discover spiritual truths.

Hesse, Hermann, 1877-1962

* **Steppenwolf** / Hermann Hesse ; introduction by Joseph Mileck. H. Holt, 1990, c1963. vi, 218 p.

ISBN 9780805012477

1. 1920s 2. Alienation in men 3. Men with mental illnesses 4. Self-discovery in men 5. Middle-aged men 6. Intellectuals 7. Germany -- Social conditions -- 1918-1933 8. Psychological fiction 9. Literary fiction 10. Translations -- German to English 11. Modern classics

Harry Haller is a sad and lonely figure, a reclusive intellectual for whom life holds no joy. He struggles to reconcile the wild primeval wolf and the rational man within himself without surrendering to the bourgeois values he despises. His life changes dramatically when he meets a woman who is his opposite, the carefree and elusive Hermine. With its blend of Eastern mysticism and Western culture, Hesse's best-known and most autobiographical work, originally published in English in 1929, Steppenwolf continues to speak to our souls and marks it as a classic of modern literature.

Hewson, David, 1953-

The **garden** of evil / David Hewson. Delacorte Press, 2008. 416 p. Nic Costa mysteries

ISBN 9780385339575

1. Art 2. Murder investigation 3. Violence against prostitutes 4. Murder 5. Detectives 6. Police 7. Rome, Italy 8. Italy 9. Mysteries

LC 2007045762

RUSA Reading List, 2009.

The discovery of two corpses next to an unknown Caravaggio masterpiece in an art studio in Rome sends Detective Nic Costa on a quest to uncover the truth about a modern-day crime and a centuries-old secret concealed in the painting.

"A thought-provoking blend of art history and mystery, The Garden of Evil is . . . a treat for readers who like their entertainment literate." Richmond Times-Dispatch

Hewson, David, 1953-

A **season** for the dead / David Hewson. Delacorte Press, 2004. 386 p. Nic Costa mysteries

ISBN 0385337221

1. Catholic Church 2. Women college teachers 3. Former lovers 4. Religious corruption 5. Religious fanatics 6. Serial murders 7. Painting 8. Martyrs 9. Detectives 10. Police 11. Vatican 12. Rome, Italy 13. Vatican City 14. Mysteries

LC 2003062522

The first installment in a new crime series features detective Nic Costa on the trail of a serial killer who stalks and kills victims according to a heavenly play book--Catholic martyrs--leaving behind a trail of clues that read like bloody chapters from Lives of the Saints.

"Outsized, eccentric characters, a complex story and an abundance of historical detail make this engrossing book more than just another cookie-cutter, religious-nut serial killer thriller." Publishers Weekly.

Heyer, Georgette, 1902-1974

Black sheep / Georgette Heyer. Sourcebooks, 2008, c1966. 279 p.

ISBN 9781402210785

1. Regency period (1811-1820) 2. Aunts 3. Single women 4. Mate selection 5. Black sheep 6. Fortune hunters 7. Bath, England -- Social life and customs -- 19th century 8. Regency romances 9. Historical romances

LC 2007050205

Originally published: London : Bodley Head, 1966.

"A lovely young spinster is both charmed and infuriated by the wealthy, unconventional black sheep uncle of the fortune hunter on whom her young niece has her heart set. This character-driven novel . . . is considered one of Heyer's best." Library Journal.

Heyer, Georgette, 1902-1974

The **grand** Sophy / Georgette Heyer. Sourcebooks Casablanca, 2009, c1950. 372 p.

ISBN 9781402218941

1. Regency period (1811-1820) 2. Independence in women 3. Cousins 4. Engagement 5. Helpfulness in women 6. Men/women relations 7. Single women 8. Interpersonal relations 9. Family relationships 10. London, England -- Social life and customs -- 19th century 11. England -- Social life and customs -- 19th century 12. Great Britain -- History -- Regency, 1811-1820 13. Regency romances 14. Historical romances 15. Gentle reads

When Lady Ombersley agrees to take in her young niece, no one expects Sophy, who sweeps in and immediately takes the ton by storm. Sophy discovers that her aunt's family is in desperate need of her talent for setting everything right: Cecila is in love with a poet, Charles has tyrannical tendencies that are being aggravated by his grim fiancee, her uncle is of no use at all, and the younger children are in desperate need of some fun and freedom. By the time she's done, Sophy has commandeered Charles's horses, his household, and finally, his heart.

Heyer, Georgette, 1902-1974

These **old** shades / Georgette Heyer. Sourcebooks Casablanca, 2009, c1926. 378 p.

ISBN 9781402219474

1. Georgian era (1714-1837) 2. 1770s 3. Dukes and duchesses 4. Mistaken identity 5. Men/women relations 6. Guardian and ward 7. Nobility 8. Revenge 9. Paris, France -- Social life and customs -- 18th century 10. Georgian romances 11. Historical romances

Sequel: The Devil's Cub.

First published 1926.

Set in the Georgian period, about 20 years before the Regency, "These Old Shades" features two of Heyer's most memorable characters: Justin Alastair, the Duke of Avon, and Leonie, whom he rescues from a life of ignominy and comes to love and marry.

Hiaasen, Carl

Bad monkey / Carl Hiaasen. Alfred A. Knopf, 2013. 368 p. Andrew Yancy novels

ISBN 9780307272591

1. Real estate development 2. Police 3. Murder investigation 4. Widows 5. Florida 6. Crime fiction 7. Humorous stories

LC 2013005863

Anticipating his retirement from the Key West Police, Andrew Yancy tackles a murder case involving a human arm in his freezer, an investigation that pits him against a twitchy widow, a clueless real estate developer and a voodoo witch with a string of hapless lovers.

Hiaasen, Carl

Basket case / Carl Hiaasen. Alfred A. Knopf, 2002. 317 p.

ISBN 0375411070

1. Obituary writers 2. Investigative journalists 3. Newspaper publishers and publishing 4. Rock musicians -- Death 5. Women newspaper editors 6. Florida 7. Mysteries 8. Humorous stories

LC 2001038317

Once a hotshot investigative reporter, middle-aged Jack Tagger now bangs out obituaries for a South Florida daily. When Jimmy Stoma, the infamous front man of Jimmy and the Slut Puppies, dies in a diving "accident, " Jack uses clues from the singer's own music to unravel the mystery and resurrect his career in the process.

"Hiaasen skewers both corporate media operations and the world of pop stardom." New York Times Book Review.

Hiaasen, Carl

Lucky you : a novel / Carl Hiaasen. A. A. Knopf, 1997. 353 p.

ISBN 9780679454441

1. Women lottery winners 2. Stolen property recovery 3. Newspapers 4. Journalists 5. Militia movement 6. Lottery winners 7. Men/women relations 8. Florida 9. Humorous stories

LC 9736885

A romantic comedy featuring two people recovering a stolen $14-million lottery ticket. It belongs to JoLayne Lucks, a black veterinary assistant in Florida and was stolen by white supremacists. With the help of reporter Tom Krome, JoLayne goes after the thieves and love blooms.

"Hiaasen writes witty dialogue that crackles, and his characters are eccentrically colorful." New York Times Book Review.

Hiaasen, Carl

Nature girl / Carl Hiaasen. Alfred A. Knopf, 2006. 320 p.

ISBN 0307262995

1. Mistresses 2. Real estate agents 3. Tour guides (Persons) 4. Mothers and sons 5. Twelve-year-old boys 6. Stalkers 7. Former

husbands 8. Bipolar disorder 9. Telemarketing 10. Wildlife refuges -- Florida 11. Dead 12. Men/women relations 13. Stalking 14. Florida 15. Everglades, Florida 16. Humorous stories 17. Mysteries

LC 2006049360

Honey Santana, the bipolar, self-proclaimed "queen of lost causes," has plans to give Boyd Shreave and his mistress a lesson in civility, unaware that she is being followed by her obsessed ex-employer and her one-time drug runner ex-husband.

"As usual, Hiaasen throws his colorful characters into an increasingly frenetic mix, and the fun lies in watching how, or if, they'll manage to extricate themselves. One reason Nature Girl works so well is the fact that much of the action is confined to a single island, allowing the characters to intermingle and weave in and out of view." San Francisco Chronicle.icle

Hiaasen, Carl

Skin tight / Carl Hiaasen. Ballantine, 1990, c1989. 373 p.
ISBN 9780449219416

1. Retirees 2. Attempted murder 3. Plastic surgery 4. Criminals 5. Political corruption 6. Florida 7. Black humor 8. Thrillers and suspense

A man with a gun foolishly enters retired PI Mike Stranahan's house with bad intentions and ends up fatally gored by a taxidermied blue marlin. Now, the laid-back Stranahan needs to figure out who wants him dead and why. As he tries to sort out the mystery, more wild and crazy things happen. -- Description by Dawn Towery.

Hiaasen, Carl

Skinny dip : a novel / Carl Hiaasen. Alfred A. Knopf, 2004. 368 p.
ISBN 0375411089

1. Former police 2. Married women 3. Marine scientists 4. Marine biologists 5. Married people 6. Attempted murder 7. Agribusiness 8. Hazardous wastes 9. Water -- Pollution 10. Absence and presumption of death 11. Revenge 12. Revenge in women 13. Men/women relations 14. Everglades, Florida 15. Florida 16. Thrillers and suspense 17. Satirical fiction

LC 2004044106

Story includes the character Mick Stranahan, who first appeared in Skin tight.

Doctoring water samples to help his corrupt agribusiness employer continue illegal dumping in the Everglades, biologist Chaz Perrone attempts to murder his wife, who has figured out his scam and who survives to plot her husband's downfall.

"The squirm-inducing mayhem that follows in this sometimes side-splitting novel almost makes you feel sorry for Chaz. It has rarely been this much fun to read about the act of revenge. All of the trademark characters and Florida locales are used to maximum effect." Library Journal.

Hiaasen, Carl

Star Island / Carl Hiaasen. Alfred A. Knopf, 2010. 337 p.
ISBN 9780307272584

1. Celebrities 2. Mistaken identity 3. Kidnapping 4. Pop musicians 5. Second chances 6. Women impostors 7. Paparazzi 8. Alcoholic women 9. Kidnapping victims 10. Women singers 11. Rescues 12. Fame 13. Florida 14. Mysteries 15. Humorous stories

Ann DeLuisa, body double for drug-addled pop star Cherry Pye, is kidnapped by an obsessed paparazzo, and Cherry's entourage must rescue her while keeping her existence a secret from Cherry's public--and from Cherry herself.

"Trying to follow the plot, which involves a supporting cast of crooked politicians and predatory developers, is a little like walking a puppy. But the outlandish events soar on the exuberance of Hiaasen's

manic style, a canny blend of lunatic farce and savage satire." New York Times Book Review.

Hiaasen, Carl

Strip tease : a novel / Carl Hiaasen. A. A. Knopf, 1993. 353 p.
ISBN 9780679419815

1. United States. Congress. House 2. Politicians -- Florida 3. Stripteasers -- Florida 4. Extortion -- Florida 5. Sugar industry and trade 6. Sugar industry and trade -- Corrupt practices 7. Strip club competition -- Florida 8. Florida 9. Humorous stories

LC 93012358

A Florida congressman falls for a gorgeous stripper who's also a damsel in distress. In pursuit of this woman, the congressman ripples through the strip club, sugar cane fields in South Florida, and some powerful political careers.

"In among Hiaasen's freaks and obsessives, his corrupters and corrupted, his brain-dead and his frenetically active, the author has dropped a real honest-to-God human being, an appealing young woman named Erin Grant. Her presence, her history and goals, make the cartoon nastiness around her less cartoony and more nasty than in previous Hiaasen novels." New York Times Book Review.

Hibbert, Talia

* Get a life, Chloe Brown / Talia Hibbert. Avon Books, 2019. 384 p. The Brown sisters
ISBN 9780062941206

1. People with chronic illnesses 2. Repairers 3. Lists 4. Geeks (Computer enthusiasts) 5. Artists 6. Rich families 7. Interracial romance 8. Interpersonal relations 9. Men/women relations 10. England 11. Contemporary romances 12. Multicultural romances 13. Romantic comedies

Emerging from a life-threatening illness, a fiercely organized but unfulfilled computer geek recruits a mysterious artist to help her establish meaning in her life, before finding herself engaged in reckless but thrilling activities.

Hibbert, Talia

A **girl** like her / Talia Hibbert. Nixon House, 2018. 296 p. Ravenswood
ISBN 9781916404304

1. Single women 2. Veterans 3. Neighbors 4. Villages 5. Ostracism 6. Gossiping and gossips 7. Secrets 8. Sexual attraction 9. Men/women relations 10. England 11. Contemporary romances 12. Multicultural romances

After years of military service, Evan Miller wants a quiet life. The small town of Ravenswood seems perfect--until he stumbles upon a vicious web of lies with his new neighbour at its centre. Ruth Kabbah is rude, awkward, and--according to everyone in town--bad news. ... The more Evan's isolated, eccentric neighbour pushes him away, the more he wants her. Her--and all her secrets. --, Provided by publisher.

Hicks, Robert, 1951-

The **widow** of the South / Robert Hicks. Warner Books, 2005. 409 p.
ISBN 0446500127

1. McGavock, Caroline E Winder, 1829-1905 2. McGavock Confederate Cemetery (Franklin, Tenn.) 3. Carnton Mansion (Franklin, Tenn.) 4. American Civil War era (1861-1865) 5. 1860s 6. Franklin, Battle of, 1864 7. Plantation owners' spouses 8. Women caregivers 9. Cemetery managers 10. Plantation owners 11. Confederate soldiers 12. Plantation life 13. Plantations 14. Women and war 15. Battles 16. Military hospitals 17. Grief 18. Civil war 19.

United States Civil War, 1861-1865 20. Williamson County (Tenn) 21. Tennessee -- History -- Civil War, 1861-1865 22. United States -- History -- Civil War, 1861-1865 23. Biographical fiction 24. War stories 25. Historical fiction 26. Southern fiction

LC 2005010568

A story based on the true experiences of a Civil War heroine finds Carrie McGavock witnessing the bloodshed of the Battle of Franklin, falling in love with a wounded man, and dedicating her home as a burial site for fallen soldiers.

Higashino, Keigo, 1958-
* The **devotion** of suspect X / Keigo Higashino ; translated from the Japanese by Alexander O. Smith. St. Martin's Minotaur, 2011. 304 p. Detective Galileo mysteries
ISBN 9780312375065
1. Mathematics teachers 2. Abused women 3. Murder 4. Former husbands 5. Murder suspects 6. Physicists 7. Divorced women 8. Detectives 9. Japan 10. Mysteries 11. Psychological suspense

LC 2010039022

RUSA Reading List, 2012.

Ishigami is a lonely Japanese math teacher infatuated with his next-door neighbor Yasuko, a lovely woman who has killed her deadbeat ex-husband to protect her daughter. Not only does Ishigami help her dispose of the body, he also devises a clever cover story for her when the police begin to investigate. But problems build as the involvement of an old colleague threatens to destabilize both Ishigami's ability to counter every police move and his plans for himself and Yasuko, who begins to break down -- and pull away. -- Description by Shauna Griffin.

Higashino, Keigo, 1958-
Malice / Keigo Higashino ; translated by Alexander O. Smith. Minotaur Books, 2014, c2001. 276 p. Kyoichiro Kaga mysteries
ISBN 9781250035608
1. 1990s 2. Detectives 3. Authors, Japanese 4. Police 5. Enemies 6. Strangling 7. Childhood friends 8. Murder suspects 9. Murder investigation 10. Japan -- Social life and customs -- 20th century 11. Mysteries 12. Translations -- Japanese to English

LC 2014019885

Malice was originally published fourth in the Kyoichiro Kaga mystery series, but is the first to have been translated into English.
This translation originally published: London: Little, Brown, 2014. Originally published in Japanese as Akui by Kodansha.
Originally published: Tokyo : Kodansha, 2001.

When a best-selling Japanese novelist is found murdered the night before he was scheduled to move to another country, police detective Kyochiro Kaga uncovers a deadly game involving the victim's best friend and rival.

"Each time you're convinced Higashino's wrung every possible twist out of his golden-age setup, he comes up with a new one. If you still miss the days of The Murder of Roger Ackroyd, you can't do better than this fleet, inventive retro puzzler." Kirkus.

Higashino, Keigo, 1958-
The **miracles** of the Namiya General Store / Keigo Higashino ; translated from the Japanese by Sam Bett. Yen ON, 2019. 314 p.
ISBN 9781975382575
1. Shopkeepers 2. Retail stores 3. Thieves 4. Juvenile delinquents 5. Letter writing 6. Counseling 7. Time travel 8. Space and time 9. Japan 10. Magical realism 11. Translations -- Japanese to English

LC 2019023608

When three delinquents hole up in an abandoned general store after their most recent robbery, to their great surprise, a letter drops through the mail slot in the store's shutter. This seemingly simple request for advice sets the trio on a journey of discovery as, over the course of a single night, they step into the role of the kindhearted former shopkeeper who devoted his waning years to offering thoughtful counsel to his correspondents.

"More than a time travel mystery, the story is a rather earnest tale of human decision-making, and the author is adept at drawing an emotional response from readers. Inventive and always surprising, this book is easy to get drawn into and difficult to put down. An endearing tale about a magical correspondence." Kirkus.

Higashino, Keigo, 1958-
Newcomer / Keigo Higashino. Minotaur Books, 2018. 320 p. Kyoichiro Kaga mysteries
ISBN 9781250067869
1. 1990s 2. Murder suspects 3. Detectives 4. Police 5. Secrets 6. Strangling 7. Divorced women 8. Murder investigation 9. Interpersonal relations 10. Japan -- Social life and customs -- 20th century 11. Tokyo, Japan 12. Mysteries 13. Translations -- Japanese to English

Newcomer is the second Kyoichiro Kaga mystery published in English by Minotaur Books. It was originally published in Japanese as Shinzanmono in 2009, the seventh book in the Police Detective Kaga series.

Newly transferred to a precinct in the Nihonbashi area of Tokyo, Detective Kyochiro Kaga, while investigating the puzzling murder of a woman, soon discovers that nearly all the people living and working in the business district of Nihonbashi are suspects.

Higgins, C. A. (Caitlin A.)
Lightless / C.A. Higgins. Del Rey, 2015. 304 p. Lightless
ISBN 9780553394429
1. Women engineers 2. Terrorists 3. Space travelers 4. Space vehicles 5. Terrorists 6. Sabotage 7. Prisoners 8. Space opera 9. Hard science fiction 10. Science fiction

LC 2014037514

A female engineer, Althea, fights for her life when her small spacecraft is invaded by two mysterious terrorists on a dark mission, one of whom is a revolutionary harboring deep secrets.

"A suspenseful, emotional story that asks plenty of big questions about identity and freedom." Kirkus.

Higgins, George V., 1939-1999
The **friends** of Eddie Coyle / George Higgins. Knopf, 1972. 183 p.
ISBN 0394473272
1. Criminals -- United States 2. Swindlers and swindling 3. Informers 4. Assassins 5. Illegal arms transfers 6. Massachusetts 7. Boston, Massachusetts 8. Thrillers and suspense

LC 71163134

A crime classic about gunrunner Eddie Coyle and his dangerous relations with bank robber Jimmy Scalisi, a cop named Foley, and Dillon, a bartending hitman, features a new introduction by Elmore Leonard.

Higgins, Jack, 1929-
Bad company / Jack Higgins. G. P. Putnam's Sons, 2003. 304 p. Sean Dillon thrillers
ISBN 0399149708
1. Hitler, Adolf, 1889-1945 Diaries 2. Intelligence officers 3. Presidents 4. Secrets 5. World politics 6. Government conspiracies 7. International intrigue 8. Secret service 9. Spies -- Great Britain

10. World War II 11. Spy fiction 12. Political thrillers 13. Thrillers and suspense

LC 2003041365

Near the end of World War II, Hitler gave his personal diary to an aid for safekeeping. Containing minutes from a secret meeting between emissaries of Hitler and Roosevelt, it outlined plans to join forces against the Soviet Union. Ironically, the American representative was a direct relative of Jake Cazalet, the current U.S. president. Now this diary has become a powerful weapon.

"As the war is drawing to a close in 1945, Hitler gives his diary to an aide for safekeeping. The diary contains an account of a meeting between representatives of Hitler and President Roosevelt at which they discussed ways to negotiate a peace treaty and then to attack Russia. The aide, Max von Berger, is now (in 2003) a billionaire industrialist and a silent partner with an international crime family. Seeking revenge for a killing, Berger vows to reveal the diary's secret that would destroy the current U.S. president. It's up to an American and a British agent to get the diary before it falls into the hands of the president's enemies." Booklist.

Higgins, Jack, 1929-

Confessional / Jack Higgins. Stein and Day, 1985. 278p. Liam Devlin thrillers

ISBN 0812830253

1. John Paul II,, Pope, 1920-2005 2. Irish Republican Army 3. KGB 4. Undercover operations 5. Assassins 6. Spies 7. Impostors 8. Intelligence service 9. Canterbury Cathedral 10. Ukraine 11. Thrillers and suspense 12. War stories 13. Spy fiction

LC 84040777

"This novel is tense. It is riveting. It is what a thriller should be. If Mr. Higgins's prose is dull and his understanding of humanity shallow, it may only be because good prose and a deeper understanding would inhibit the race to the plot's final twist." New York Times Book Review.

Higgins, Jack, 1929-

Day of reckoning / Jack Higgins. G. P. Putnam's Sons, 2000. 295 p. Sean Dillon thrillers

ISBN 0399145850

1. Organized crime 2. Revenge in men 3. Spies -- Great Britain 4. Women investigative journalists 5. Women murder victims 6. Murder 7. Husband and wife 8. Former FBI agents 9. Mafia 10. Secret service 11. Undercover operations 12. Gambling and crime 13. Shipwrecks 14. Robbery 15. Weapons 16. Elite operatives 17. Brooklyn, New York City 18. Thrillers and suspense 19. Spy fiction 20. Political thrillers

LC 9934847

When his wife is killed, a former FBI agent seeks vengeance by destroying the killer's illegal holdings from the United States to the Middle East.

"The journalist wife of Sean Dillon's old comrade Blake Johnson is killed in Brooklyn on orders of her latest object of investigation, Jack Fox, heir apparent to the powerful Solazzo crime family. The law can't touch Fox, but Blake and Dillon can and will. Aided by Dillon's black-ops boss Brigadier Charles Ferguson, and his crew, plus a father/son team of British gangsters, Blake and Dillon strike again and again at Fox's wallet: shutting down his London gambling den; sinking a boat laden with his gold; destroying a cache of his weapons in Ireland; foiling his plans for a major robbery in London. . . . The action is sleek and intensely absorbing." Publishers Weekly.

Higgins, Jack, 1929-

The **eagle** has flown / Jack Higgins. Simon and Schuster, 1991. 335 p. Liam Devlin thrillers

1. Churchill, Winston, 1874-1965 2. Irish Republican Army 3. Tower of London (London, England) 4. 1940s 5. Search and rescue operations 6. Betrayal 7. World War II 8. Secret service 9. Hostage taking 10. Parachute troops 11. Undercover operations 12. Norfolk, England 13. War stories 14. Historical thrillers

LC 91004368

IRA assassin Liam Devlin returns to Britain in an attempt to effect the escape of German soldier Kurt Steiner from the Tower of London and return with him to Berlin.

"Mr. Higgins is an expert storyteller, and he goes about 'The Eagle Has Flown' with typical gusto. Everything is carefully arranged, little pieces fitting into other little pieces to form an action-packed mosaic." New York Times Book Review.

Higgins, Jack, 1929-

The **eagle** has landed / Jack Higgins. Holt, Rinehart and Winston, 1975. 352 p. Liam Devlin thrillers

ISBN 9780030137464

1. Churchill, Winston, 1874-1965 2. Irish Republican Army 3. 1940s 4. Undercover operations 5. Hostage taking 6. World War II 7. Secret service 8. Parachute troops 9. Norfolk, England 10. War stories 11. Historical thrillers

LC 74015475

Combines fact and speculation in a fictionalized reconstruction of the events leading up to and including the November 1943 mission of a small force of German paratroopers landed in Britain to capture Prime Minister Winston Churchill

"There are elements of heroism, duplicity, and heavy irony, plus considerable bloodshed, in this action-oriented yarn." Christian Science Monitor.

Higgins, Jack, 1929-

Edge of danger / Jack Higgins. G. P. Putnam's Sons, 2001. 273 p. Sean Dillon thrillers

ISBN 0399147012

1. Presidents -- United States -- Attempted assassination 2. Attempted assassination 3. Revenge 4. International intrigue 5. Rich families 6. Mothers -- Death 7. Assassins 8. Honor in men 9. Arabs in Great Britain 10. Assassins 11. Terrorists -- Ireland 12. Secret service 13. Spies -- Great Britain 14. Undercover operations 15. Elite operatives 16. Middle East 17. Scotland 18. England 19. Thrillers and suspense 20. Spy fiction 21. Political thrillers

LC 00040268

The Rashid family, half British, half Arab, is directing its rage against the United States, whose president they hold responsible for a series of attacks against their power and honor. From opposite ends of the world, hints are picked up by Blake Johnson, head of the clandestine White House operation known as the Basement, and his Irish colleague, Sean Dillon, but hints to what and by whom?

"Pitting returning antihero Sean Dillon, once of the IRA, now with British intelligence, against an aristocratic English-Arab family bent on vengeance that threatens world order, the story whips along. From London to the Middle East, from Ireland to the White House, it swirls with intrigue and snaps with violence." Publishers Weekly.

Higgins, Jack, 1929-

Eye of the storm / Jack Higgins. G. P. Putnam's Sons, 1992. 320 p. Sean Dillon thrillers

ISBN 9780399137587

1. Major, John, 1943- Attempted assassination 2. Irish Republican Army 3. International intrigue 4. Undercover operations 5. Secret service 6. Spies -- Great Britain 7. Assassins 8. Persian Gulf War, 1991 9. Terrorists -- Ireland 10. Terrorism 11. London, England 12. Thrillers and suspense 13. Spy fiction 14. Political thrillers 15. War stories

LC   91046736

Also published under the title: Midnight man.

Elusive master terrorist Sean Dillon reemerges during the Gulf War when Saddam Hussein hires him to assassinate Margaret Thatcher, and only Martin Brosnan can stop him.

"Early in 1991, while the Gulf war is in full bloom, operatives of Saddam Hussein hire legendary terrorist Sean Dillon to take the war to the enemy. A master of disguise and subterfuge, Dillon began his career with the IRA, earning the enmity of Liam Devlin--the unforgettable antihero of The Eagle Has Landed, who makes a featured appearance here--and of Martin Brosnan, an American Special Forces hero and IRA member turned college professor. After Dillon's attempt to assassinate former Prime Minster Margaret Thatcher during a visit to France fails, he decides to go after her successor John Major. . . . Although readers can be sure that Dillon's scheme will be foiled, fun remains in the how and why." Publishers Weekly.

Higgins, Jack, 1929-

Flight of eagles / Jack Higgins. G. P. Putnam's Sons, 1998. 328 p. Dougal Munro and Jack Carter thrillers

ISBN 0399143769

1. Eisenhower, Dwight D (Dwight David), 1890-1969 Attempted assassination 2. Great Britain. Royal Air Force 3. Germany. Air Force 4. World War II 5. International intrigue 6. Dishonesty 7. Twin brothers 8. Americans in Great Britain 9. Pilots 10. Barons and baronesses 11. Loyalty 12. War stories 13. Historical thrillers

LC 9737582

Separated as boys, now military pilots on opposing sides in World War II, two brothers are brought together again by a massive intrigue that forces them to question their deepest loyalties, as the war's outcome hangs in the balance.

Higgins, Jack, 1929-

Luciano's luck / Jack Higgins. Stein and Day, 1981. 238 p.

1. Luciano, Lucky, 1897-1962 2. 1940s 3. World War II 4. Undercover operations 5. Mafia 6. Nuns 7. Special forces 8. Spies 9. Former convicts 10. Strategic alliances (Military) 11. Sicily, Italy 12. War stories 13. Historical thrillers

LC   81040330

In 1943, a British intelligence operative, two American Rangers, one extraordinary woman, and American Lucky Luciano parachute into Nazi-occupied Sicily. Their dangerous mission: to persuade the Don to rally the people of Sicily to run the Axis forces off the Island and pave the way for the Allied invasion of Italy.

"[A] fast-paced, action-crammed plot, suspenseful to the last page. The fictionalized Luciano is sympathetically portrayed, and although the romanticizing of the Mafia figures jars a little, the historical premises are acceptably plausible." Library Journal.

Higgins, Jack, 1929-

Midnight runner / Jack Higgins. Putnam's, 2002. 289 p. Sean Dillon thrillers

ISBN 0399148337

1. United States. Congress. Senate 2. Terrorism -- Prevention 3. Intelligence officers 4. Oil industry and trade 5. Brothers -- Death 6. Women terrorists 7. Daughters -- Death 8. Poisoning 9. Drug use 10. Revenge 11. Secret service 12. Spies -- Great Britain 13. Undercover operations 14. Elite operatives 15. Middle East 16. England 17. Scotland 18. Thrillers and suspense 19. Spy fiction 20. Political thrillers

LC 2001048124

After British agent Sean Dillon and his associates kill the three Rasid brothers--Kate Rashid takes control and vows revenge. She plans to kill Dillon and plots an interruption of the world's oil supply.

Higgins, Jack, 1929-

Night of the fox / Jack Higgins. Simon and Schuster, 1986. 316 p. Dougal Munro and Jack Carter thrillers

1. 1940s 2. Search and rescue operations 3. Undercover operations 4. Impostors 5. Germans in France 6. Soldiers -- United States 7. Hiding-places (Secret chambers, etc) 8. World War II 9. Resistance to military occupation 10. Secret service 11. Women spies 12. French Resistance (World War II) 13. Normandy Invasion, June 6, 1944 14. Military campaigns 15. France -- History -- German occupation, 1940-1945 16. War stories 17. Spy fiction 18. Historical thrillers

LC   86029662

"Higgins combines powerful narrative with documentary detail in an exceptional tale that relies upon the interweaving histories of the various characters." Library Journal.

Higgins, Jack, 1929-

Rough justice / Jack Higgins. G.P. Putnam's Sons, 2008. 288 p. Sean Dillon thrillers

ISBN 9780399155130

1. Spies 2. Organized crime 3. Terrorists 4. Terrorism 5. Revenge 6. Assassins 7. Intelligence officers 8. International intrigue 9. Fundamentalists 10. Muslims 11. Islam 12. Kosovo (Republic) 13. Moscow, Russia 14. Thrillers and suspense 15. Spy fiction 16. Political thrillers

LC 2008008905

Sent to Kosovo on a mission, agent Blake Johnson joins forces with British operative Harry Miller to stop a Russian officer in the act of torching a mosque, a lethal action that will have profound repercussions for both agents.

"The action moves swiftly amid a variety of foreign locales, including Moscow, London and Beirut, to a climax that will leave readers asking themselves, evidence to the contrary, whether the great game is really over." Publishers Weekly.

Higgins, Jack, 1929-

Touch the devil / Jack Higgins. Stein and Day, 1982. 251 p. Liam Devlin thrillers

ISBN 9780007283316

1. Irish Republican Army 2. Kidnapping 3. International intrigue 4. Spies 5. Terrorism 6. Secret service 7. Undercover operations 8. Ireland -- Politics and government -- 20th century 9. War stories 10. Spy fiction 11. Thrillers and suspense

LC   82040080

Retired agent Liam Devlin is forced to undertake a deadly mission that involves British and Soviet intelligence, hired killer Martin Brosnan, and combat photographer Anne-Marie Audin.

Higgins, Jack, 1929-

The **White** House connection / Jack Higgins. G. P. Putnam's Sons, 1999. 323 p. Sean Dillon thrillers

ISBN 0399144897

1. International intrigue 2. Women assassins 3. Spies -- Great Britain 4. Women sexagenarians 5. Revenge 6. Secret societies 7. Terrorists -- Ireland 8. Mothers and sons 9. Sons -- Death 10. Married men -- Death 11. Secret service 12. Undercover operations 13. Elite operatives 14. New York City 15. Washington, D.C. 16. London, England 17. Ireland 18. Thrillers and suspense 19. Spy fiction 20. Political thrillers

LC 9842577

As a mysterious female assassin stalks members of a splinter group known as the Sons of Erin, Sean Dillon, the former IRA terrorist, is called in to stop her before her actions can derail the Irish peace process.

"When it comes to thrillers, Jack Higgins wrote the book. In fact, he wrote lots of them, and this is one of the best." Booklist.

Higgins, Kristan

* The **best** man / Kristan Higgins. HQN, 2012. 432 p. Blue Heron romances

ISBN 9780373777921

1. Homecomings 2. Jilted women 3. Police chiefs 4. Interpersonal attraction 5. Wineries 6. Family businesses 7. Men/women relations 8. New York (State) 9. Contemporary romances

Finally ready to return to the Blue Heron Winery, her family's vineyard, and face her past, Faith Holland is drawn to Levi Cooper, the local police chief and best friend of her former fianc?, but has a hard time forgetting his role in ruining her wedding years ago.

Higgins, Kristan

* **Life** and other inconveniences / Kristan Higgins. Berkley, 2019. 448 p.

ISBN 9780451489425

1. Grandmother and adult child 2. Single mothers 3. Reconciliation 4. Terminal illness 5. Family relationships 6. Clothing industry and trade 7. Fashion 8. Abandonment (Psychology) 9. Grief 10. Forgiveness 11. Women's lives and relationships

A blue-blood grandmother and her black-sheep granddaughter discover they are truly two sides of the same coin.

Higgins, Kristan

Now that you mention it / Kristan Higgins. HQN Books, 2017 406 p.

ISBN 9781335915276

1. Homecomings 2. Family problems 3. Near-death experience 4. Hometowns 5. Reconciliation 6. Small town life 7. Life change events 8. Women physicians 9. Family relationships 10. Dysfunctional families 11. Maine 12. Boston, Massachusetts 13. Women's lives and relationships

RITA Award, 2018.

Returning to her hometown in the hopes of reconciling with her estranged family, a woman who recently survived a brush with death makes discoveries with the potential to heal the rift or permanently separate her from her surviving relatives.

Higgins, Kristan

The **perfect** match / Kristan Higgins. HQN, 2012. 448 p. Blue Heron romances

ISBN 9780373778195

1. Jilted women 2. Small towns 3. Betrayal 4. British in the United States 5. College teachers 6. Immigrants 7. Stepsons 8. Jealousy 9.

Wineries 10. Family businesses 11. Former friends 12. Interpersonal attraction 13. Men/women relations 14. New York (State) 15. Contemporary romances

After Honor Holland agrees to a marriage of convenience to help British professor Tom Barlow stay in the country, she begins to wonder if there isn't something more between them.

"Higgins once again blends sweet romance, quirky humor, and realistic emotion in a story that will keep readers entranced." Booklist.

Highsmith, Patricia, 1921-1995

The **Highsmith** reader : selected novels and short stories / Patricia Highsmith ; edited with an introduction by Joan Schenkar. W. W. Norton & Co., 2011. xvi, 644 p.

ISBN 9780393080131

1. Short stories 2. Psychological suspense

LC 2010034589

Features key works in the psychological thriller genre from the author of "The Talented Mr. Ripley," including "Strangers on a Train," which was made into a legendary Alfred Hitchcock film, and "The Price of Salt."

Hijuelos, Oscar

Beautiful Maria of my soul / Oscar Hijuelos. HarperCollins, 2010. 352 p.

ISBN 9781401323349

1. 1950s 2. First loves 3. Cuban American women 4. Cubans in the United States 5. Reminiscing in old age 6. Men/women relations 7. Commitment (Psychology) 8. Interpersonal conflict 9. Musicians 10. Cuban Americans 11. New York City 12. Literary fiction

Companion to The Mambo Kings Play Songs of Love

In a part sequel and part retelling of "The Mambo Kings Play Songs of Love," the inspiration for the Mambo King's biggest hit, Maria, now 60 years old, reminisces about her days and nights in Havana, offering a completely different perspective on the Mambo Kings' story.

"The rare sequel that can be enjoyed independently of the original work or as a complement to it. . . . There's a simmering backdrop of revolution in the middle of the book that provides the story with historical heft. And, in the novel's bold ending, Hijuelos seamlessly welds fact and fiction, with the author himself making an appearance to discuss his books with the characters that inhabit them." Cleveland Plain Dealer.

Hijuelos, Oscar

* The **mambo** kings play songs of love : a novel / Oscar Hijuelos. Farrar, Straus, Giroux, 1989. 407 p.

ISBN 0374201250

1. 1950s 2. Cubans in the United States 3. Reminiscing in old age 4. Men/women relations 5. First loves 6. Commitment (Psychology) 7. Gender role 8. Interpersonal conflict 9. Cuban Americans 10. Musicians 11. Fame 12. Brothers 13. New York City 14. Literary fiction

LC 89001248

Pulitzer Prize for Fiction, 1990.

National Book Critics Circle Award for Fiction finalist, 1989

National Book Award for Fiction finalist, 1989

"The novel alternates crisp narrative with opulent musings--the language of everyday and the language of longing. When Mr. Hijuelos falters, as from time to time he does, it's through an excess of self-consciousness: he strives too hard for all-encompassing description or grows distant and dutiful in an effort to get period details just right." New York Times Book Review.

Hijuelos, Oscar

Twain & Stanley enter paradise / Oscar Hijuelos. Grand Central Pub, 2015. 592 p.

ISBN 9781455561490

1. Twain, Mark, 1835-1910 2. Stanley, Henry M (Henry Morton), 1841-1904 3. 19th century 4. Male friendship 5. Voyages and travels 6. Journalists 7. Intellectual life 8. Women artists 9. Authors 10. Explorers 11. Married people 12. Writing 13. United States -- History -- 19th century 14. Cuba -- History -- 19th century 15. Historical fiction 16. Biographical fiction 17. Diary novels 18. Epistolary novels

Chronicles the sojourn of journalist-explorer Henry Stanley; his wife, the painter Dorothy Tennant; and Mark Twain, Stanley's longtime friend, as they head for Cuba in search of Stanley's father.

Hilderbrand, Elin

The **perfect** couple / Elin Hilderbrand. Little Brown & Co, 2018. 471 p.

ISBN 9780316375269

1. Weddings 2. Rich families 3. Couples 4. Vacation homes 5. Summer 6. Murder suspects 7. Women murder victims 8. Murder investigation 9. Police chiefs 10. Family secrets 11. Family relationships 12. Men/women relations 13. Massachusetts 14. Nantucket, Massachusetts 15. Women's lives and relationships 16. Mysteries

When a bride-to-be is found dead in the harbor, Chief of Police Ed Kapenash searches for the killer within her own wedding party.

Hilderbrand, Elin

* **Summer** of '69 / Elin Hilderbrand. Little Brown & Co, 2019 432 p.

ISBN 9780316420013

1. 1960s 2. Family secrets 3. Brothers and sisters 4. Vietnam War, 1961-1975 5. Families 6. Social change 7. Civil rights workers 8. Younger brothers and sisters 9. Grandmother and granddaughter 10. Nantucket, Massachusetts 11. Massachusetts 12. Historical fiction

A pregnant eldest sibling, a middle-sister civil rights activist, an infantry soldier brother deployed to Vietnam and a lonely 13-year-old youngest child find their lives upended by troubling family secrets.

Hilderbrand, Elin

* **What** happens in paradise / Elin Hilderbrand. Little Brown & Co, 2019. 272 p. Paradise (Elin Hilderbrand)

ISBN 9780316435574

1. Widows 2. Adult children 3. Secrets 4. Truth 5. Coping in women 6. Mothers and sons 7. Married men -- Death 8. Betrayal 9. Island life 10. Family relationships 11. Interpersonal attraction 12. Men/women relations 13. West Indies 14. Virgin Islands of the United States 15. Women's lives and relationships

A follow-up to *Winter in Paradise* finds Irene and her sons returning to St. John to investigate her late husband's secret double life before uncovering surprising truths about their own realities and futures.

Hilderbrand, Elin

* **Winter** in paradise : a novel / Elin Hilderbrand. Little Brown & Co., 2018 viii, 310 p. Paradise (Elin Hilderbrand)

ISBN 9780316435512

1. Married people and secrets 2. Extramarital affairs 3. Coping in women 4. Secrets 5. Betrayal 6. Island life 7. Family problems 8. Married men -- Death 9. West Indies 10. Virgin Islands of the United States 11. Women's lives and relationships

A suburban wife confronts the loss of everything at the same time her husband is found dead on the beaches of St. John, where he harbored a secret second family.

"As usual, Hilderbrand's characters are as familiar as old friends, and her smooth prose is as tender and welcoming...Readers will be happy to lose themselves in paradise while getting to know these irresistible new characters." Publishers Weekly Annex.

Hill Gumbao, Toni

The **good** suicides : a thriller / Antonio Hill ; translation by Laura McGloughlin. Crown Publishers, 2014. 338 p. Inspector Hector Salgado mysteries

ISBN 9780770435905

1. Suicide victims 2. Suicide investigation 3. Business -- Corrupt practices 4. Cold cases (Criminal investigation) 5. Detectives 6. Spain 7. Barcelona, Spain 8. Mysteries 9. Translations -- Spanish to English

LC 2013019691

"Originally published in Spanish as Los Buenos Suicidas in June 2012 by Random House Mondadori."

"This translation originally published, in slightly different form, in Great Britain by Doubleday, an imprint of Transworld Publishers, a division of Random House, Inc., London, in 2013."

A follow-up to The Summer of Dead Toys finds Inspector Salgado infiltrating the icy personal lives of a group of young executives who committed suicide after returning from a team-building retreat and receiving grisly e-mail photos.

"The characters are intriguingly complex and the author skillfully pulls the rug out with a flourish at the end." Library Journal.

Hill Gumbao, Toni

The **summer** of dead toys / Antonio Hill. Doubleday, 2012, c2011. 320 p. Inspector Hector Salgado mysteries

ISBN 9780857520821

1. Falls (Accidents) 2. Human trafficking 3. Elite (Social sciences) 4. Corruption 5. Witnesses 6. Police 7. Argentines 8. Sexual slavery 9. Police misconduct 10. Murder investigation 11. Detectives 12. Human trafficking victims 13. Child trafficking 14. Child trafficking victims 15. Spain 16. Barcelona, Spain 17. Mysteries 18. Translations -- Spanish to English

Translated from the Spanish by Laura McGlouglin.

Translation of El verano de los juguetes muertos, originally published Barcelona : Debolsillo, 2011.

Inspector Hector Salgado is sent to investigate the death of a high society Barcelona teenager and manages to uncover some dangerous secrets from among the city's most powerful families.

Hill, Edwin J., 1970-

Little comfort / Edwin Hill. Kensington Books, 2018. 343 p. Hester Thursby novels

ISBN 9781496715906

1. Librarians 2. Women private investigators 3. Swindlers and swindling 4. Missing men 5. Rich people 6. Male friendship 7. Secrets 8. Boston, Massachusetts 9. Mysteries

Harvard librarian Hester Thursby must track down charismatic--and deadly--con man Sam Blaine before he bilks another widow out of her life savings.

Hill, Joe

The **Fireman** : a novel / Joe Hill. William Morrow, 2016. 608 p.

ISBN 9780062200631

1. Spontaneous combustion 2. End of the world 3. Plague 4. Fires 5.

Spores 6. Nurses 7. Secrets 8. Survival 9. Epidemics 10. Pregnant women 11. New Hampshire 12. Apocalyptic fiction 13. Horror

LC 2015042212

Goodreads Choice Award, 2016

Locus Award for Dark Fantasy-Horror Novel, 2017.

RUSA Reading List Short List, 2017

When a bizarre virulent plague breaks out in the world's major cities, causing victims to spontaneously combust, a dedicated nurse resolves to survive until her baby is born and receives protection from a mysterious infected man who uses his fire symptoms to help others.

"This is a long book, but with a curiously ominous tone set from the very first line, a brisk pace throughout, and dozens of detailed action scenes, readers will be hard-pressed to stop turning the pages." Booklist.

Hill, Joe

* **Full** throttle : stories / Joe Hill. William Morrow, 2019. 480 p.

ISBN 9780062200679

1. Horror 2. Short stories

LC 2019014759

Dissects timeless human struggles in thirteen relentless tales of supernatural suspense.

Hill, Joe

Heart-shaped box / Joe Hill. William Morrow, 2007. 384 p.

ISBN 0061147931

1. Ghosts 2. Rock musicians 3. Supernatural 4. Secrets 5. Men/women relations 6. Life after death 7. Paranormal phenomena 8. Apparitions 9. Interpersonal relations 10. Ghost stories 11. Horror

LC 2006046548

"With a new introduction by the author" -- Back cover.

Bram Stoker Award for Best First Novel, 2007.

Locus Award for First Novel, 2008.

Thriller Award for Best First Novel, 2008.

RUSA Reading List, 2008.

A collector of obscure and macabre artifacts, unscrupulous metal band musician Judas Coyne is unable to resist purchasing a ghost over the Internet, which turns out to be the vengeful spirit of his late girlfriend's stepfather.

"The author has created a wild, mesmerizing, perversely witty tale of horror. In a book much too smart to sound like the work of a neophyte, he builds character invitingly and plants an otherworldly surprise around every corner." New York Times.

Hill, Joe

* **Horns** / Joe Hill. William Morrow & Co, 2010. 384 p.

ISBN 9780061147951

1. Lovers -- Death 2. Transformations (Magic) 3. Revenge 4. Grief in men 5. Devil 6. Monsters 7. Murder victims 8. Magic 9. Rich men 10. Telepathy 11. New Hampshire 12. Horror

After his childhood sweetheart is brutally killed and suspicion falls on him, Ig Parrish goes on a drinking binge and wakes up with horns on his head, hate in his heart, and an incredible new power which he uses in the name of vengeance.

"The strange thing about Horns is that its opening scenes aren't all that strange. Its author, Joe Hill, is able to make Ig's problem seem like the most natural thing in the world. Mr. Hill writes with such palpable enthusiasm that he has no trouble hooking readers. . . . [He] is able to combine intrigue, editorializing, impassioned romance and even fiery theological debate in one well-told story." New York Times.

Hill, Joe

* **NOS4A2** / Joe Hill. William Morrow & Co., 2013. 384 p.

ISBN 9780062200570

1. Secret places 2. Boy kidnapping victims 3. Transformations, Magic 4. Monsters 5. Christmas 6. Kidnapping 7. Supernatural 8. Good and evil 9. Mothers and sons 10. Courage in women 11. Horror

When Charles Talent Manx, an unstoppable monster who transforms children into his own terrifying likeness, kidnaps her son, Victoria McQueen, the only person to ever escape his unmitigated evil, must engage in a life-and-death battle of wills to get her son back.

Hill, Joe

Strange weather : four short novels / Joe Hill. William Morrow & Co., 2017. 432 p.

ISBN 9780062663115

1. Supernatural 2. Paranormal phenomena 3. Horror 4. Short stories

Bram Stoker Award for Best Fiction Collection, 2017.

Librarians' Choice (Australia), 2017.

"Hill is back with a collection of four short novels that each showcases his talent for mining modern lives for fear." Booklist.

Hill, Lawrence, 1957-

Someone knows my name : a novel / Lawrence Hill. W.W. Norton & Co., 2007. 384 p.

ISBN 9780393065787

1. Revolutionary America (1775-1783) 2. 18th century 3. Child kidnapping victims 4. Slavery 5. African American loyalists (United States history) 6. Black Canadian women 7. Girl slaves 8. Women freed slaves 9. Voyages and travels 10. Anti-slavery movements -- Great Britain 11. American Revolution, 1775-1783 12. Nova Scotia 13. United States -- History -- Revolution, 1775-1783 14. Canada 15. Sierra Leone 16. Historical fiction 17. Literary fiction

Originally published as The Book of Negroes in Canada (Toronto : HarperCollins, 2007).

Evergreen Award (Ontario), 2008.

Rogers Writers' Trust Fiction Prize, 2007.

Kidnapped at the age of 11 by British slavers, Aminata survives the Middle Passage and is reunited in South Carolina with Chekura, a boy from a village near hers. Her story gets entwined with his, and with those of her owners: nasty indigo producer Robinson Appleby and, later, Jewish duty inspector Solomon Lindo. During her long life of struggle, she does what she can to free herself and others from slavery, including learning to read and teaching others to, and befriending anyone who can help her, black or white.

"What makes this novel extraordinary is Hill's ability to transcend the facts--to make something magical out of them. Despite the unpalatable subject matter, he compels our attention and manages to delight. His Aminata is a heroic figure, a little larger than life, residing within and outside of history. You can never forget this character. She embeds herself in your heart." Toronto Star.

Hill, Nathan, 1975-

The **nix** : a novel / Nathan Hill. Knopf, 2016. 512 p.

ISBN 9781101946619

1. 1960s 2. 2010s 3. Family secrets 4. Mothers and sons 5. Self-fulfillment 6. Women criminals 7. Loss (Psychology) 8. Elections 9. Popular culture 10. Psychological fiction 11. Domestic fiction

LC 2015046704

ALA Notable Book, 2017.

Astonished to see the mother who abandoned him in childhood throwing rocks at a presidential candidate, a bored college professor struggles to reconcile the radical media depictions of his mother with his small-town memories and decides to draw her out by penning a tell-all biography.

"As more subplots build, including the mesmerizing tale of young Samuel's relationships with twins fearless Bishop and violin prodigy Bethany, Hill takes aim at hypocrisy, greed, misogyny, addiction, and vengeance with edgy humor and deep empathy." Booklist.

Hill, Reginald

The **stranger** house / Reginald Hill. Harper Collins, 2005. 480 p.

ISBN 0060820810

1. Searching 2. Small town life 3. Ancestors 4. Women graduate students 5. Strangers 6. Australians in England 7. Spaniards in England 8. Difference (Psychology) 9. Historians 10. Deception 11. Secrets 12. Supernatural 13. Villages 14. Cumbria, England 15. England 16. Psychological suspense

LC 2005040274

Things move slowly in the village of Illthwaite, but that's about to change with the arrival of two strangers intent on digging up bits of the past the locals would rather keep buried.

"Twentysomething Aussie math whiz Samantha Flood has fiery red hair and a fierce determination to learn the truth about her paternal grandmother, an orphan shipped from her native England to Australia under suspicious circumstances. Sober Spaniard Miguel Madero, who experiences ghostly visions and painful sensations in his feet and hands, has abandoned pursuit of the priesthood to engage in research about English Catholics during the Reformation. The paths of Samantha and Miguel (known to all as Mig) cross in the tiny English village of Illthwaite, home to the Stranger House, an inn that has hosted weary travelers for more than 500 years. Samantha and Mig, an unlikely duo, are drawn to one another as each discovers secrets simmering beneath the surface of Illthwaite's deceptively serene facade." Booklist.

Hill, Reginald

The **woodcutter** : a novel / Reginald Hill. Harper, 2011, 528 p.

ISBN 9780062060747

1. Innocence (Law) 2. Betrayal 3. Family secrets 4. Revenge 5. Former convicts 6. Entrepreneurs 7. Men who are mute 8. Psychiatrists 9. Lumber workers 10. Truth 11. Recovered memory 12. Homecomings 13. Cumbria, England 14. England 15. Psychological suspense 16. Thrillers and suspense

LC 2010053608

Originally published: London: HarperCollins, 2010.

"Near the end, a character refers to the fate of the dreadful, drab English. There's nothing drab about this dark and compelling novel, although some of its characters are dreadful human beings." Kirkus.

Hill, Ruth Beebe

Hanta Yo / Ruth Beebe Hill. Doubleday, 1979. 834 p.
ISBN 0385135548

1. 18th century 2. 19th century 3. Dakota Indians 4. Dakota men 5. Male friendship 6. Indians of North America 7. Family sagas 8. Historical fiction

LC 77016922

Western Heritage Award for Outstanding Western Novel, 1980.

"The practice of using the multi-generational family story to reflect changing times and/or historical events is almost a genre unto itself. This is such a novel. . . . The historical accuracy, linguistic acrobatics, and ethnological acuity do not limit the book's appeal. A superb style transcends the few minor flaws, and despite the scholarly impression given by the introduction, chronology notes, and glossaries, this book is first and foremost a well-written story." Library Journal.

Hill, Susan, 1942-

The **pure** in heart : a Simon Serrailler crime novel / Susan Hill. Overlook Press, 2007, c2005. 370 p. Simon Serrailler crime novels

ISBN 9781585679287

1. Kidnapping investigation 2. Stalking 3. Police 4. Detectives 5. Nine-year-old boys 6. Kidnapping 7. Kidnapping victims 8. Interpersonal relations 9. Coping in men 10. Sisters -- Death 11. Bereavement 12. Stalkers 13. England 14. Mysteries 15. Police procedurals

Originally published: London : Chatto & Windus, 2005.

Detective Chief Inspector Simon Serrailler investigates the kidnapping of a young boy, a case that is influenced by a critically ill disabled woman and an ex-con who is struggling to stay honest.

"A nine-year-old boy is kidnapped in broad daylight while waiting for his school ride outside his home in the British cathedral town of Lafferton, and the case falls squarely in the lap of Detective Chief Inspector Serrailler. It's a copper's worst nightmarebroken and grieving parents, intense media interest, and extreme pressure from the top police brass to solve the case yesterday. But there are few leads and no apparent motive, and as the days go by and the child isn't found, hope drains away. Although the case hits Simon and his team exceptionally hard, he has other problems to deal with. . . . This is realistic, gritty, and gut-wrenching crime fiction, but it's also a poignant and thoughtful character study." Booklist.

Hill, Susan, 1942-

The **risk** of darkness / Susan Hill. Overlook Press, 2009, c2006. 374 p. Simon Serrailler crime novels

ISBN 9781585679270

1. Widowers 2. Grief in men 3. Criminal investigation 4. Detectives 5. Police 6. Women priests 7. Loss (Psychology) 8. Families 9. Social isolation 10. Obsessive-compulsive disorder 11. England 12. Mysteries 13. Police procedurals

Originally published: London : Chatto & Windus, 2006.

Simon Serailler takes on the case of an obsessive widower engaging in increasingly violent acts, a case that is further complicated by Serailler's troubled feelings for the Cathedral's newest recruit, a red-haired woman Anglican priest.

Hill, Susan, 1942-

The **shadows** in the street : a Simon Serrailler mystery / Susan Hill. Overlook, 2010. 372 p. Simon Serrailler crime novels

ISBN 9781590204085

1. Missing women 2. Murder investigation 3. Women murder victims 4. Missing persons investigation 5. Crimes against prostitutes 6. Police 7. Detectives 8. Vacations 9. England 10. Scotland 11. Mysteries 12. Psychological suspense 13. Police procedurals

Simultaneously published in the UK: London : Chatto & Windus, 2010.

Simon Serrailler has just wrapped up a particularly exhausting and difficult case and is on sabbatical on a far-flung Scottish island when he is called back to Lafferton by the Chief Constable. Two local prostitutes have been found strangled. When the wife of the St. Michael's Cathedral Dean goes missing and then another respectable woman is taken on her way to work, the townspeople grow angry and afraid. Serrailler is in the greatest danger of his life.

Hill, Susan, 1942-

The **various** haunts of men : a Simon Serrailler crime novel / Susan Hill. Overlook Press, 2007, c2004. vii, 437 p. Simon Serrailler crime novels

ISBN 9781585678761

1. Police 2. Missing persons 3. Murder investigation 4. Policewomen 5. Detectives 6. Small towns 7. Husband and wife 8. Men/women relations 9. Widows 10. Murder 11. England 12. Mysteries 13. Police procedurals

LC 2006051546

Originally published: London : Chatto & Windus, 2004.

A lonely woman of fifty-three vanishes in a fog and a twenty-two year old never returns from an early morning walk. Experienced policemen know that missing persons either turn up or go missing on purpose. But fresh young D.S. Freya Graffham won't drop it- until she discovers what links the people who dissapear on The Hill.

"Lafferton, an idyllic village just far enough from the madness of London, is a paragon of tranquility and peace, with a lovely cathedral and a stand of ancient stones on the Hill. But then a woman goes missing from there, and then another, and another. Young policewoman Freya Graffham is assigned to investigate the suspected serial killings. Recently transferred from London, she is young, bright, inquisitive, dedicated, and smitten with Detective Chief Inspector Simon Serrailler. . . . As their relationship and the investigation unfold, the killer is revealed in a series of eerie first-person passages. . . . Readers will be instantly drawn to her likable characters and beautiful landscape and will be carried along by the plot, right up to the shocking final twist." Library Journal.

Hillerman, Tony

The **shape** shifter / Tony Hillerman. HarperCollins, 2006. 288 p. Joe Leaphorn and Jim Chee mysteries

ISBN 0060563451

1. Native American men 2. Former police 3. Criminal investigation 4. Murder investigation 5. Navajo Indians 6. Tribal police 7. Fugitives 8. Missing persons 9. Husband and wife 10. Stealing 11. Secrets 12. Cold cases (Criminal investigation) 13. New Mexico 14. Mysteries 15. Police procedurals

LC 2005052602

Spur Award for Best Western Novel (Short Novel), 2007.

Retired Police Lieutenant Joe Leaphorn returns to put together the clues from his last unsolved case--a mystery involving the disappearance of a priceless Navajo rug--without the help of Jim Chee and Bernie Manuelito, who are on their honeymoon.

"Only Hillerman could so masterfully connect such disparate elements as an ancient cursed weaving, two stolen buckets of pion sap and the Vietnam War. The conclusion is sure to startle longtime fans of this acclaimed mystery series." Publishers Weekly.

Hillerman, Tony

The **sinister** pig / Tony Hillerman. HarperCollins, 2003. 304 p. Joe Leaphorn and Jim Chee mysteries

ISBN 006019443X

1. Smuggling 2. Native American men 3. Former police 4. Detectives 5. Tribal police 6. Criminal investigation 7. Murder investigation 8. Navajo Indians 9. New Mexico 10. Mysteries 11. Police procedurals

LC 2003042316

Discovering a link between the woman he loves and a political murder and a twisted conspiracy, Navajo tribal police Sergeant Chee joins a map-wielding Joe Leaphorn on the heels of a fleeing Washington power broker.

"With his usual up-front approach to issues concerning Native Americans such as endlessly overlapping jurisdictions, Hillerman delivers a masterful tale that both entertains and educates." Publishers Weekly.

Hillerman, Tony

The **wailing** wind / Tony Hillerman. HarperCollins, 2002. 224 p. Joe Leaphorn and Jim Chee mysteries

ISBN 0060194448

1. Navajo shamans 2. Murder suspects 3. Police -- New Mexico 4. Tribal police 5. Gold mines and mining 6. Native American men 7. Former police 8. Detectives 9. Criminal investigation 10. Murder investigation 11. Navajo Indians 12. New Mexico 13. Mysteries 14. Police procedurals

LC 2001051734

The mishandling of a murder scene places Navajo Tribal Police sergeant Jim Chee on the bad side of the FBI and brings ex-lieutenant Joe Leaphorn out of retirement into an old crime he hoped to forget involving an obsessive love and memories of a missing woman.

"Hillerman is never better than when he is circling a puzzle from various angles, playing with the perceptions of his detectives as well as the reader's." New York Times Book Review.

Hilton, James, 1900-1954

* **Good-bye,** Mr. Chips / James Hilton. Little, Brown, and Co., 2004, c1934. 132 p.

ISBN 9780316010139

1. Boarding schools 2. Boys' schools 3. Teachers 4. England -- Social life and customs -- 19th century 5. England -- Social life and customs -- 20th century 6. Classics

Depicts the life of Mr. Chipping, a gentle English schoolmaster known familiarly to the schoolboys at Brookfield as Mr. Chips.

Hilton, James, 1900-1954

* **Lost** horizon : a novel / James Hilton. Perennial, 2004, c1933. 241 p.

ISBN 9780060594527

1. Utopias 2. Survival (after airplane accidents, shipwrecks, etc) 3. Himalaya Mountains region 4. Adventure stories 5. Classics

Originally published: New York : W. Morrow & Co., 1933.

Following a plane crash in the Himalayan mountains, a lost group of Englishmen and Americans stumble upon the dream-like, utopian world of Shangri-La, where life is eternal and civilization refined.

Hilton, James, 1900-1954

Random harvest / James Hilton. Carroll and Graf, 1985, c1969. 326 p.

ISBN 0818841250

1. Men with amnesia 2. Politicians -- 20th century 3. World War I veterans 4. England 5. Love stories

Charles Rainier, a prosperous Briton, loses his memory as a result of shellshock in the First World War.

Hilton, L. S., 1974-

Maestra / L.S. Hilton. Penguin Group USA, 2016. 320 p. Maestra novels

ISBN 9780399184260

1. Femmes fatales 2. Women swindlers 3. Art industry and trade 4. Murder 5. Sexuality 6. Art forgeries 7. Social classes 8. Revenge in women 9. Swindlers and swindling 10. Art galleries, Commercial 11. Personal assistants 12. London, England 13. Crime fiction 14. Erotic fiction

Maestra is the beginning of a razor-sharp trilogy that introduces the darkly irresistible Judith Rashleigh, a femme fatale for the ages whose vulnerability and ruthlessness will keep you guessing until the last page.

"With the book already optioned for a movie, interest will be high for this scandalous, thrilling tour through Europe and the art world." Library Journal.

Himes, Chester B., 1909-1984

Cotton comes to Harlem / Chester Himes Vintage Books, 1965. 159 p. Coffin Ed Johnson and Grave Digger Jones mysteries

ISBN 9780394759999

1. 1950s 2. African American men 3. Murder investigation 4. Murder 5. Swindlers and swindling 6. Detectives 7. Racism 8. Race relations 9. Street life 10. Crime 11. Criminals 12. Drug addicts 13. New York City 14. Harlem, New York City 15. Mysteries 16. African American fiction 17. Hardboiled fiction 18. Urban fiction

First published in France in 1964 under title: Retour en Afrique.

Set in Harlem's underside in the 1950s, a fast-paced tale of mystery and intrigue unfolds as Coffin Ed Johnson and Grave Digger Jones work to halt the theft of thousands of dollars marked for the Back-to-Africa movement.

Hoang, Helen

* The **bride** test / Helen Hoang. Jove, 2019. 300 p.
ISBN 9780451490827

1. Romantic love 2. People with autism 3. Arranged marriage 4. Multiracial women 5. Vietnamese Americans 6. Single mothers 7. Rich men 8. Cultural differences 9. Class conflict 10. Vietnamese in the United States 11. Secrets 12. Families 13. Interpersonal attraction 14. Men/women relations 15. California 16. Multicultural romances 17. Contemporary romances

LC 2018053953

Believing he cannot experience big emotions--like love, or grief, Khai Diep avoids relationships, until his mother travels to Vietnam and returns with Esme Tran.

Hoang, Helen,

* The **kiss** quotient / Helen Hoang. Berkley/Jove, 2018. 336 p.

ISBN 9780451490803

1. People with Asperger's syndrome 2. Dating (Social customs) 3. Women mathematicians 4. Escort services (Prostitution) 5. Autism 6. Single women 7. Interpersonal attraction 8. Asperger's syndrome 9. Men/women relations 10. Contemporary romances 11. Erotic romances

LC 2017061141

Goodreads Choice Award, 2018
Librarians' Choice (Australia), 2018.
RUSA Reading List Short List, 2019.

A 30-year-old math whiz with Asperger's tries to make her love life as rich as her career by hiring an escort to help her with her lack of knowledge and experience in the dating department.

"A compulsively readable erotic romance that is equal parts sugar and spice. Highly recommended." Library Journal.

Hobbs, Allison

Stealing candy / Allison Hobbs. Strebor Books, 2010. 353 p. Saleema Sparks thrillers

ISBN 9781593092801

1. Prostitutes 2. Human trafficking 3. Missing teenage girls 4. Kidnapping 5. Nonprofit organizations 6. Street life 7. Murder 8. Pimps 9. Teenage prostitution 10. Human trafficking victims 11. Child trafficking 12. Child trafficking victims 13. Philadelphia, Pennsylvania 14. Urban erotica 15. Thrillers and suspense 16.

African American fiction 17. Drama lit

LC 2010925102

Teenagers Gianna, Brielle, and Portia suffer under a pimp who forced them into prostitution, until a nonprofit worker who offers a safe haven to troubled teens risks her life to find Portia, one of her members, when she goes missing.

Hockensmith, Steve

Holmes on the range / Steve Hockensmith. St. Martin's Minotaur, 2006. 320 p. Holmes on the range mysteries

ISBN 0312347804

1. Doyle, Arthur Conan,, Sir, 1859-1930 Appreciation 2. 1890s 3. Murder 4. Cowboys 5. Amateur detectives 6. Brothers 7. Ranch life 8. Ranching 9. Ranches 10. Cattle ranches 11. Crimes against cowboys 12. Montana -- History -- 19th century 13. Historical mysteries 14. Westerns

LC 2005050406

In 1893, inspired by their hero, master sleuth Sherlock Holmes, two cowboys, Big Red and Old Red Amlingmeyer, put their detecting skills to use to uncover the truth about the murder of a ranch hand on their Montana cattle ranch.

"This is a great reworking of the Holmes conceit, and one suspects Hockensmith will have a steady readership as long as the Amlingmeyers are on the case." Booklist.

Hockensmith, Steve

On the wrong track / Steve Hockensmith. St. Martin's Press, 2007 304 p. Holmes on the range mysteries

ISBN 0312347812

1. Doyle, Arthur Conan,, Sir, 1859-1930 Appreciation 2. 1890s 3. Cowboys 4. Train robberies 5. Murder investigation 6. Amateur detectives 7. Trains 8. Murder 9. Brothers 10. Ranch life 11. Ranching 12. Ranches 13. Cattle ranches 14. Montana -- History -- 19th century 15. Historical mysteries 16. Westerns

Hired to guard the Pacific Express during a trip to San Francisco, crime-solving cowboy sleuths Gustav "Old Red" Amlingmeyer and his brother, "Big Red," deal with a scheming gang of outlaws and a killer hiding among the train's passengers.

"As a lively Holmes takeoff, as an inventive melding of mystery and western genres, and as a new source of damn good reading, this series demands attention." Booklist.

Hodder, Mark, 1962-

The **strange** affair of Spring Heeled Jack / Mark Hodder. Pyr, 2010. 384 p. Burton & Swinburne

ISBN 9781616142407

1. Burton, Richard F, 1821-1890 2. Swinburne, Algernon Charles, 1837-1909 3. Victoria,, Queen of Great Britain, 1819-1901 Assassination attempts 4. 19th century 5. Attempted assassination 6. Time travel 7. Werewolves 8. Robots 9. End of the world 10. Criminal investigation 11. Spring-heeled Jack (Legendary character) 12. Great Britain -- Social conditions -- 19th century 13. Science fantasy 14. Steampunk 15. Science fiction mysteries

LC 2010020632

Philip K. Dick Award for Science Fiction, 2010.

When the supposedly mythical Spring Heeled Jack begins terrorizing 1861 London, it's up to adventurer Sir Richard Francis Burton to track down the monster. Accompanied by his louche and libidinous sidekick, poet Algernon Swinburne, Burton tracks the beast and attempts to thwart a werewolf invasion by enlisting the help of everyone who was anyone in 19th-century Britain, except Queen Victoria (sorry, she was assassinated). -- Description by Gillian Speace.

Hodgen, Christie, 1974-

Elegies for the brokenhearted : a novel / Christie Hodgen. W. W. Norton & Co., 2010. 271 p.

ISBN 9780393061406

1. Young women -- Identity 2. Dysfunctional families 3. Belonging 4. Disappointment 5. Redemption 6. Abandonment (Psychology) 7. Women's lives and relationships

LC 2010011149

Mary Murphy searches for identity and purpose as she tells the story of her erratic childhood, her runaway sister, and the histories of people with whom she's crossed paths.

"Despite its gritty realities, Elegies for the Brokenhearted ultimately has an almost mythic grandeur, in part because the story is propelled by associative rather than linear logic, in part because the action, played out largely in places that are entirely familiar but hardly ever named, acquires a strange universality, and in part because Hodgen's interest lies in questions of blood and parentage of the ties that bind us together or drive us apart." New York Times Book Review.

Hodges, Cheris F.

Rumor has it / Cheris Hodges. Dafina, 2015 368 p. Rumor novels (Cheris F. Hodges)

ISBN 9781617733796

1. Revenge 2. Cheating (Interpersonal relations) 3. Engaged persons 4. Best friends 5. Women lawyers 6. African American men/women relations 7. Competition 8. Interpersonal attraction 9. Men/women relations 10. North Carolina 11. Contemporary romances 12. Multicultural romances 13. African American fiction

RUSA Reading List Short List, 2016.

Public relations professional Liza Palmer is proud to work for North Carolina senatorial candidate Robert Montgomery, who also happens to be her best friend Chante's fianc? -- until she catches him in flagrante delicto with a woman who's not his bride-to-be. Armed with enough information to destroy his political career, Liza approaches Robert's opponent, Jackson Franklin. But Jackson refuses to play dirty, at least when it comes to elections. The bedroom, however, is a whole other story. As their relationship heats up, Liza and Jackson must learn to balance their personal lives and professional ambitions, and without compromising their integrity. -- Description by Gillian Speace.

Hodgkinson, Amanda

22 Britannia Road : a novel / Amanda Hodgkinson. Pamela Dorman Books/Viking, 2011. 336 p.

ISBN 9780670022632

1. Husband and wife 2. War -- Psychological aspects 3. Polish people in England 4. Parent and child 5. Secrecy 6. World War II -- Poland 7. England 8. Psychological fiction 9. Historical fiction

LC 2010045353

Originally published: London: Fig Tree, 2011.

Leaving Poland for England at the end of World War II, Silvana is accompanied by 8-year-old, near-feral Aurek, with whom she shares traumatic wartime memories that set them apart from her husband, who has remade himself as an Englishman to forget the past.

"Hodgkinson enters boldly into well-trodden, sensitive territory and distinguishe's herself with freshness and empathy." Kirkus.

Hodgson, Antonia

* The **last** confession of Thomas Hawkins / Antonia Hodgson. Houghton Mifflin Harcourt, 2016, 388 p. Tom Hawkins novels

ISBN 9780544639683

1. 1720s 2. Innocence (Law) 3. Murder suspects 4. Murder 5. Mistresses 6. Rulers 7. Political intrigue 8. Prisoners 9. Interpersonal relations 10. London, England -- History -- 18th century 11. Historical mysteries

LC 2015028196

Sequel to: The Devil in the Marshalsea.

"First published in Great Britain in 2015 by Hodder & Stoughton"--Title page verso.

An early 18th-century gentleman with a penchant for trouble, facing hanging for a crime he did not commit, endeavors to secure his freedom while reflecting on the careless choices that led to his condemnation, including placing trust in a calculating royal.

"Hodgson maintains pitch-perfect suspense, craftily constructs a fairly clued whodunit, and convincingly evokes the period." Publishers Weekly.

Hoeg, Peter, 1957-

Borderliners / Peter Hoeg ; translated by Barbara Haveland. Farrar, Straus and Giroux, 1994, c1993. 277 p.

ISBN 9780374115548

1. Orphans 2. Misfits (Persons) 3. Private schools 4. Experimental psychology 5. Special education 6. Resistance (Psychology) in children 7. Child abuse victims 8. Copenhagen, Denmark 9. Denmark 10. Psychological fiction 11. Translations -- Danish to English

LC 9418892

Originally published: Copenhagen : Rosinante, 1993.

A novel that challenges ideas of education and childhood relates the tale of a boy who grows up in institutions and becomes drawn to outsiders at an elite private school.

"The author avoids simple storytelling, preferring instead to explore the nature of time. 'What is time?' are the book's opening words, and later Mr. Hoeg actually provides brief historical passages on the development of theories of time. In a related device, the novel employs a dreamy, associative narrative, moving back and forth through the years, including flash-forwards to the adult Peter's family life. . . . 'Borderliners' is written from the heart, and its portrait of the embittered survivor Peter is moving." New York Times Book Review.

Hoeg, Peter, 1957-

The **history** of Danish dreams / Peter Hoeg ; translated by Barbara Haveland. Farrar, Straus and Giroux, 1995. 356 p.

ISBN 9780374171384

1. Social change 2. Families -- History 3. Eccentrics and eccentricities 4. Social classes 5. Family relationships 6. Intergenerational relations 7. Denmark -- History 8. Family sagas 9. Magical realism 10. Translations -- Danish to English 11. Literary fiction

LC 95018355

Originally published: Charlottenlund : Rosinante, 1988.

"If Dreams is regarded not as a novel, but as a marvelous trunkful of loosely related funny bits, . . . it is a great success." Time.

Hoeg, Peter, 1957-

The **quiet** girl / Peter Hoeg ; translated by Nadia Christensen. Farrar, Straus, and Giroux, 2007. 424 p.

ISBN 9780374263690

1. Clowns 2. Child psychics 3. Extrasensory perception 4. Gamblers 5. Tax evasion 6. Nuns 7. Identity (Psychology) 8. Secrets 9. Faustian bargains 10. Denmark 11. Thrillers and suspense 12. Translations -- Danish to English 13. Scandinavian crime fiction

LC 2007008187

Originally published: Copenhagen: Rosinante, 2006, as Den Stille Pige.

Originally published in English: London: Harvill Secker, 2007.

A mysterious order of nuns promises Kaspar Krone, a circus clown with a gambling debt and wanted for tax evasion, a reprieve from the authorities in exchange for his help in safeguarding children with mystical abilities--talents that he also shares.

"In the end, The Quiet Girl seems like two different novels—one a philosophical treatise, the other an adrenaline-laced thriller—that don't easily meet on common ground. It is a story wrapped in enigmas that build to a screeching pitch and leave you dizzy and stunned. But it's the melancholy wit of Hoeg's writing that keeps you engaged, and hoping Kasper finally does comes to terms with his place in the world." Chicago Sun-Times.

Hoeg, Peter, 1957-

* **Smilla's** sense of snow / Peter Hoeg ; translated from the Danish by Tiina Nunnally. Farrar Straus and Giroux, 1993, c1992. 453 p.

ISBN 9780374266448

1. Conspiracies 2. Women detectives 3. Murder investigation 4. Inuit women 5. Inuit children 6. Copenhagen, Denmark 7. Greenland 8. Crime fiction 9. Translations -- Danish to English 10. Scandinavian crime fiction

LC 93017742

Winner of the Glass Key Award in 1993.

Originally published: Copenhagen : Rosinante, 1992.

Silver Dagger Award for Fiction, 1994.

When her six-year-old neighbor falls to his death, and no one is willing to suspect foul play, Smilla Qaavigaaq Jasperson finds her own investigation taking her into the files of a Danish company

"Selfishness, menace and systematic corruption form the fabric of this mysterious novel. Relationships are all based on suspicion, and love has to be 'like a military operation.'. . . Peter Hoeg has a remarkable feeling for sinister surprises." Times Literary Supplement.

Hoffman, Alice

Blackbird house / Alice Hoffman. Doubleday, 2004. 240 p.

ISBN 0385507615

1. Home (Concept) 2. Place (Philosophy) 3. Farmhouses 4. Houses 5. Home ownership 6. Massachusetts 7. Cape Cod, Massachusetts 8. Historical fiction 9. Short stories 10. Literary fiction

LC 2004007958

Presents a series of interlinking stories that capture the lives and fortunes of the various occupants of an old Massachusetts house over the course of two centuries.

"The relationship of the characters to their surroundings is seen as a kind of magical bond, expressed in language that is both eerie and beautiful. The house of the title is one in which, from story to story, we glimpse various families over the course of two centuries. . . . Hoffman lets Blackbird House stand as an emblem for the transforming power of any long-established home, while reveling in the haunting quality of her own distinctive literary style." New York Times Book Review.

Hoffman, Alice

The **dovekeepers** / Alice Hoffman. Scribner, 2011. 504 p.

ISBN 9781451617474

1. Women 2. Identity (Psychology) 3. Mass suicide 4. Tragedy 5. Grief 6. Men/women relations 7. Masada (Fortress), Israel -- Siege, 72-73 8. Historical fiction 9. Literary fiction

A tale inspired by the tragic first-century massacre of hundreds of Jewish people at Masada presents the stories of a hated daughter, a baker's wife, a girl disguised as a warrior, and a medicine woman who keep doves and secrets while Roman soldiers draw near.

"Hoffman put years of research into The Dovekeepers, and at times the story slows from a scholar's desire to dwell on details of custom or ritual. But for those ... who'll follow the novelist anywhere, that pacing becomes its own powerful incantation." Entertainment Weekly.

Hoffman, Alice

The **ice** queen : a novel / Alice Hoffman. Little, Brown and Co., 2005. 224 p.

ISBN 0316058599

1. Loss (Psychology) 2. Wishing and wishes 3. Self-acceptance in women 4. Secrets 5. Women librarians 6. Lightning strike victims 7. Lightning 8. Life change events 9. Near-death experience 10. Fear 11. Small town life 12. Psychological fiction 13. Literary fiction

LC 2004026610

After a small town librarian survives a lightning strike, she seeks out a fellow survivor in a quest for meaning, only to begin an obsessive love affair between two opposites joined by a single common thread.

"As Hoffman's spellbinding and wonderfully insightful tale unfurls, she pays charming tribute to librarians, revels in metaphors of hot and cold, and poetically explores the meaning of trust, the chemistry of healing, and the reach of love." Booklist.

Hoffman, Alice

Illumination night / Alice Hoffman. G. P. Putnam's Sons, 1987. 224 p.

ISBN 9780399132827

1. Interpersonal relations 2. Unrequited love 3. Agoraphobia in women 4. Short boys 5. Men/women relations 6. Family relationships 7. Martha's Vineyard, Massachusetts 8. Literary fiction

LC 86030472

"Hoffman probes the mythic connotations of the situation as she supplies convincing portraits of the man and woman and of the young girl who is determined to come between them. . . . All of this is delineated with both depth and clarity in a novel that encapsulates and transforms the characters' experiences into broader symbols of yearning and passion." Booklist.

Hoffman, Alice

Local girls / Alice Hoffman. G. P. Putnam's Sons, 1999. 197 p.

ISBN 0399145079

1. Dysfunctional families 2. Family relationships 3. Girls and women 4. Teenage girls -- Identity 5. Women -- Identity 6. Female friendship 7. Families 8. Suburbs 9. Long Island, New York 10. Domestic fiction 11. Literary fiction

LC 98-50632

An anthology of interconnected short stories captures the lives and destinies of the Samuelsons, a family struggling with tragedy and divorce, in a series of portraits that chronicle Gretel Samuelson's journey through betrayal, grief, conflicting loyalties, friendship, and loss

"A collection of interlinked stories about a Jewish Long Island family locked in a downward spiral after the parents' divorce. Most of the stories are told from the viewpoint of Gretel Samuelson as she moves from high-school years to young adulthood. . . . Hoffman doesn't sentimentalize her characters' lives: the tragedies they suffer are ordinary, after all. She has a light touch and a poet's knack for making diffuse elements fall into place with seeming effortlessness." Publishers Weekly.

Hoffman, Alice

The **marriage** of opposites : a novel based on the life of Rachel Pizzarro / Alice Hoffman. Simon & Schuster, 2015. 369 p.

ISBN 9781451693591

1. Pissarro, Camille, 1830-1903 2. Pissarro, Rachel, 1795-1889 3. 19th century 4. Gender role 5. Scandals 6. Ambition in girls 7. Refugees, Jewish 8. Widows 9. Impressionist artists 10. Family estates 11. Arranged marriage 12. Remarriage 13. West Indies 14. France 15. Magical realism 16. Historical fiction 17. Love stories 18. Literary fiction 19. Biographical fiction

LC 2014047743

Dreaming of an exotic life in Paris while coming of age in a St. Thomas refugee community, young Rachel is forced to marry a widower before falling scandalously in love and becoming the mother of Impressionist master Camille Pissarro.

"As witty as she is lyrical, she writes ricocheting dialogue. This rhapsodic blend of keenly observed historical elements and vibrantly fabulistic invention generates an entrancing saga of sacrifice, forbidden loves, betrayals, and family tragedies endured in a world fractured by religion, class, and race and redeemed by art and by love. Hoffman is at her resplendent best in this trenchant and revelatory tale of a heroic woman and her world-altering artist son. ... Given the resounding success of her previous two novels, Hoffman's latest, with zealous publisher support, will lure her fans and readers curious about the lives of artists." Booklist.

Hoffman, Alice

The **Museum** of Extraordinary Things : a novel / Alice Hoffman. Scribner, 2014. 384 p.

ISBN 9781451693560

1. 1900s (Decade) 2. Freak shows 3. Fires 4. Young women 5. Photographers 6. Missing women 7. Immigrants, Jewish 8. Freaks (Entertainers) 9. Men/women relations 10. Fathers and daughters 11. Russians in the United States 12. Coney Island, New York City 13. New York City -- History -- 20th century 14. New York (State) -- History -- 20th century 15. Historical fiction 16. Parallel narratives

LC 2013036572

The daughter of a Coney Island boardwalk curiosities museum's front man pursues an impassioned love affair with a Russian immigrant photographer who after fleeing his Lower East Side Orthodox community has captured poignant images of the infamous Triangle Shirtwaist Factory fire.

Hoffman, Alice

Practical magic / Alice Hoffman. G. P. Putnam's Sons, 1995. 244 p. Practical magic novels

ISBN 0399140557

1. Sisters 2. Witches 3. Spells (Magic) 4. Aunts 5. Witchcraft 6. Abused women 7. Protectiveness 8. Ostracism 9. Love spells 10. New England 11. Magical realism 12. Literary fiction

LC 94047013

The story of two sisters, Gillian and Sally Owens, brought up by their elderly guardian aunts in a small New England town. The aunts possess magic that they in turn hand down to their nieces.

"The tale of the Owenses' struggle is charmingly told, and a good deal of fun. Dark comedy and a light touch carry the story along to a truly Gothic climax." New York Times Book Review.

Hoffman, Alice

The **probable** future / Alice Hoffman. Doubleday, 2003. 320 p.

ISBN 0385507607

1. Mothers and daughters 2. Women psychics 3. Supernatural 4. Death 5. Love 6. Dreams 7. Betrayal 8. Murder suspects 9. New England 10. Massachusetts 11. Magical realism 12. Literary fiction 13. Domestic fiction

LC 2003040960

Struggling to cope with her unwanted ability to see the future, Stella must confront her legacy when her father is jailed, wrongly accused of homicide, and Stella joins forces with her grandmother and mother to uncover the truth.

"Filled with vivid (if sometimes sketchy) characters and cinematic descriptions of New England landscapes, this book will be a hit wherever Hoffman is in demand." Library Journal.

Hoffman, Alice

The **red** garden / Alice Hoffman. Shaye Areheart Books, 2010. 256 p.

ISBN 9780307393876

1. Small towns 2. Small town life 3. Place (Philosophy) 4. Massachusetts 5. Literary fiction 6. Short stories

LC 2010006246

Traces the multi-generational story of wintry Blackwell town through the experiences of such characters as a wounded Civil War soldier who is saved by a passionate neighbor and a woman who meets a fiercely human historical figure.

"[A] collection of 14 stories set in Blackwell, Mass., a fictional village deep in the woods of the Berkshires. Beginning with Blackwell's founding in 1786 by a handful of inept, unprepared settlers, these stories span more than 200 years. Each one, complete in itself, offers a time-stamped snapshot of the lives of Blackwell's inhabitants--the temporal equivalent of a holograph. If this book has a plot, it is not the usual kind. Instead, against a background of far-off historical events Hoffman sets the ongoing life of one small town and its episodic interaction with the natural world that surrounds it." Boston Globe.

Hoffman, Alice

The **river** king / Alice Hoffman. G. P. Putnam's Sons, 2000. 324 p.

ISBN 0399145990

1. Superstition 2. Private schools 3. Small town life 4. Murder 5. Prep school students 6. Teenage boys 7. Teenage girls 8. Death 9. Massachusetts 10. Magical realism 11. Literary fiction

LC 00023870

A town divided by class lines is thrown into turmoil by a mysterious death, which begins to unravel the lives of a fifteen-year-old girl, a young boy, and a woman running from her own destiny.

"It can be hard to find an example of good old-fashioned storytelling these days, but storytelling, refreshingly, is Alice Hoffman's strength." New York Times Book Review.

Hoffman, Alice

The **rules** of magic : a novel / Alice Hoffman. Simon & Schuster, 2017. 367 p. Practical magic novels

ISBN 9781501137471

1. 1950s 2. Sisters 3. Witches 4. Spells (Magic) 5. Witchcraft 6. Brothers and sisters 7. Love spells 8. New England 9. New York City 10. Magical realism 11. Literary fiction

LC 2016054138

Librarians' Choice (Australia), 2017

A prequel to Practical Magic traces the story of the children of Susanna Owens, who, in spite of their mother's fierce edicts against witchcraft, develop powerful abilities while struggling to escape the family curse that leads to tragedy if they fall in love.

"The spellbinding story, focusing on the strength of family bonds through joy and sorrow, will appeal to a broad range of readers." Publishers Weekly.

Hoffman, Alice

Skylight confessions : a novel / Alice Hoffman. Little, Brown and Co., 2007. 272 p.

ISBN 0316058785

1. Magic 2. Life change events 3. Fate and fatalism 4. Opposites 5. Architects 6. Married people 7. Husband and wife 8. Brothers and sisters 9. Self-destructive behavior 10. Ambition 11. Dysfunctional families 12. Identity (Psychology) 13. New England 14. Psychological fiction 15. Magical realism 16. Literary fiction

LC 2006001391

The marriage of Arlyn Singer and John Moody, opposites who are drawn to each other despite a mutual lack of understanding, has a profound and lasting impact on them, their children, and their grandchildren.

"This novel, about the magic of love and the perils of fate, may be the saddest book [Hoffman's] ever written, but it is also one of her very best. . . . [Arlie's] ephemeral self is what fuels the taleshe is a fairy-tale creature, to be sure, and yet she is also obviously a flesh-and-blood woman with deep and compelling desires." Baltimore Sun.

Hoffman, Alice

The **story** sisters : a novel / Alice Hoffman. Shaye Areheart Books, 2009. 256 p.

ISBN 9780307393869

1. Adult child sexual abuse victims 2. Sisters 3. Dysfunctional families 4. Coping in women 5. Mothers and daughters 6. Loss (Psychology) 7. Imagination in women 8. Honesty 9. Familial love 10. Fate and fatalism 11. United States 12. Paris, France 13. Coming-of-age stories 14. Magical realism 15. Literary fiction

LC 2008051054

A family drama and coming of age story follows the lives of three sisters who create a magical world on their street to escape a tragedy that has changed them forever.

"The sisters' struggle to grow and thrive in the real world will keep you riveted to the pages of this heartbreaking novel about the powers and limits of love. Redbook,The Story sisters, Elv, Meg, and Claire, are dark-haired beauties clustered in the attic of their old Long Island house, while their lonely mother broods below. Their all-female household, a sly variation on Little Women, is under a grim fairy-tale spell, and not even sojourns with their fairy-godmother-like grandmother in Paris can protect them. . . . Meg is practical, while Elv and Claire share a tragic secret, and Elv channels her anguish into elaborate, demon-haunted tales of an imaginary parallel world until she discovers more effective means of self-punishment." Booklist.

Hoffman, Alice

The **third** angel : a novel / Alice Hoffman. Shaye Areheart Books, 2008. 288 p.

ISBN 9780307393852

1. 1990s 2. 1960s 3. 1950s 4. Independence in women 5. Love triangles 6. Women 7. Girls 8. Ghosts 9. Interpersonal attraction 10. Helpfulness in women 11. Men/women relations 12. Unhappiness in women 13. London, England 14. England 15. Psychological fiction 16. Women's romantic fiction

LC 2007028071

Follows the lives of three women in love with the wrong men--Madeleine Heller, attracted to her sister's fiance; Frieda Lewis, the muse to an ill-fated rock star; and Bryn Evans, engaged to be married but secretly obsessed with her ex-husband.

"This is the tale of three women, all terribly in love with the wrong men. The novel is . . . constructed in three sections, narrated in three different time periods. The women in each section stay on the seventh floor of the haunted Lion Park Hotel in London. The first woman, Maddy Heller, stays at the Lion Park in 1999 for her sister's wedding. Her story is compelling in that she is secretly and tragically in love with her sister's fiance. In 1966, the second woman, Frieda Lewis, falls in love with a guest at the hotel: an American rock star and drug addict who happens to be engaged to someone else. And in 1952, the third woman, Bryn Evans, betrays her fiance at the Lion Park, to disastrous results. At the very end of the novel, Hoffman reveals the tragedy of the Lion Park ghost, the suspenseful event that connects all the women in powerful and mystical ways." Rocky Mountain News.

Hoffman, Alice

Turtle moon / Alice Hoffman. G. P. Putnam's Sons, 1992. 255 p.

ISBN 0399137203

1. Single-parent families 2. Missing children 3. Murder 4. Men/women relations 5. Sea turtles 6. Mothers and sons 7. Divorced persons 8. Murder suspects 9. Florida 10. Magical realism 11. Literary fiction

LC 91037222

ALA Notable Book, 1993.

Determined to begin life anew in Verity, Florida, with her son, Keith, transplanted New Yorker Lucy Rosen finds everything she ever hoped for and everything she ever feared in her new community

"Hoffman handles romance, suspense, and the healing properties of love and understanding with aplomb and a dash of magic." Booklist.

Hoffman, Alice

* The **world** that we knew / Alice Hoffman. Simon & Schuster, 2019. 384 p.

ISBN 9781501137570

1. Second World War era (1939-1945) 2. Golem 3. Protectiveness 4. Holocaust (1933-1945) 5. Jewish girls 6. Persecution by Nazis 7. French Resistance (World War II) 8. Loss (Psychology) 9. Love 10. Courage in women 11. Determination (Personal quality) 12. Faith (Judaism) 13. Men/women relations 14. Berlin, Germany -- History -- 20th century 15. France -- History -- 20th century 16. Magical realism 17. Literary fiction 18. Historical fiction

Sent away to 1941 Paris when Berlin becomes too dangerous for Jewish families, a young girl bonds with her protective mystical golem; while her friend, a rabbi's daughter, rises to become a defender of their people.

Hogan, Chuck

Devils in exile : a crime novel / Chuck Hogan. Scribner, 2010. 312 p.

ISBN 9781416558866

1. Drug traffic 2. Veterans 3. Organized crime 4. Drug enforcement agents 5. Criminals 6. Love triangles 7. Boston, Massachusetts 8. Thrillers and suspense

Neal returns to Boston from his tour in Iraq only to discover that the country he vowed to protect has little use for him now. Royce, a fellow vet, offers him a much-needed job-- using his military skills to intercept major drug deals, taking the dirty money while destroying the product. It's almost too good to be true...

"This is a compelling portrait of a good man who makes bad choices and in the end must battle his way out of a destructive and deadly life." Publishers Weekly.

Holbert, Bruce

Whiskey / Bruce Holbert. MCD/Farrar, Straus and Giroux, 2018. 255 p.

ISBN 9780374289188

1. 1990s 2. Family relationships 3. Brothers 4. Dysfunctional families 5. Religious fanaticism 6. Runaways 7. Alcoholism 8. Failure (Psychology) 9. Indians of North America 10. Divorce 11. Washington (State) 12. The West (United States) 13. Literary fiction
LC 2017040456

Two self-destructive, but fiercely loyal adult brothers find themselves entwined in domestic troubles, alcoholic benders, their parents? ongoing tangles with the law and religious fanaticism and must work together after one of their daughters runs off with a zealot.

Holdstock, Pauline, 1948-

Here I am! / Pauline Holdstock. Biblioasis, 2019 292 p.

ISBN 9781771963091

1. Boys 2. Mothers -- Death 3. Stowaways 4. Ocean travel 5. Intergenerational relations 6. Fathers and sons 7. Teachers 8. Families 9. England 10. France 11. Literary fiction

"A John Metcalf book."

After Frankie's mother dies, he can't seem to get anyone to listen to him. So the six-year-old comes up with a plan: go to France, find a police station, and ask the officers to ring his father.

"A wide range of readers from late adolescence on will find this compelling story of one youngster's adventure full of psychological depth and rich characterization." Library Journal.

Holland, Cecelia, 1943-

Jerusalem / Cecelia Holland. Forge, 1996. 318 p.

ISBN 0312859562

1. 12th century 2. Crusades 3. Power (Social sciences) 4. Knights and knighthood 5. People with leprosy -- Jerusalem 6. Crusaders (Middle Ages) 7. Battles 8. Jerusalem, Israel -- History -- Latin Kingdom, 1099-1244 9. Jerusalem, Israel -- Rulers 10. Historical fiction 11. Movie tie-ins 12. Franchise books
LC 9538814

A recreation of the Crusader Kingdom of Jerusalem captures the religious passions and political intrigues of the Holy Land in A.D. 1187, as seen through the eyes of Rannulf Fitzwilliam, a Knight Templar who loves the princess Sibylla.

"The narrative structure may be simple, but Holland's masterful layering of subplots, historical detail and multiple perspectives makes for a great read." Publishers Weekly.

Holland, Travis

The **archivist's** story / Travis Holland. Dial Press, 2007. 256 p.

ISBN 038533995X

1. Babel, I (Isaak), 1894-1941 Manuscripts 2. Communist Party of the Soviet Union Purges 3. KGB Moscow operations. 4. 1930s 5. Authors, Jewish -- Soviet Union 6. Dissenters -- Soviet Union 7. Political prisoners -- Soviet Union 8. Prisoners -- Soviet Union 9. Archivists 10. Information policy -- Soviet Union 11. State-sponsored terrorism -- Soviet Union 12. Manuscripts, Russian 13. Manuscript smuggling -- Soviet Union 14. Soviet Union -- History -- 1925-1953 15. Soviet Union -- Politics and government -- 1936-1953 16. Historical fiction
LC 2006031932

Shortlisted for the International IMPAC Dublin Literary Award, 2009

In 1939 Moscow, Pavel Dubrov, a reluctant young archivist, is sent into the infamous Lubyanka prison to authenticate an unsigned story confiscated from one of the political prisoners, Isaac Babel, and is given the task of destroying the great writer's final works.

"There is a quiet authenticity about Holland's writing that draws you in, and soon you will find yourself sitting on the edge of your seat, silently cheering for his characters." Library Journal.

Hollinghurst, Alan

* The **Sparsholt** affair / Alan Hollinghurst. Alfred A. Knopf, 2018, c2017. 417 p.

ISBN 9781101874561

1. 20th century 2. Social change 3. Social classes 4. Sexuality 5. Gay men 6. Aging 7. Great Britain -- Social life and customs -- 20th century 8. Literary fiction 9. LGBTQIA fiction
LC 2017032901

Originally published: London : Picador, 2017.

A World War II-era Oxford engineering student who hides secret ambitions to join the Royal Air Force and the lonely son of a celebrated novelist forge a fateful bond that reverberates throughout seven decades of shared family life and friendship.

Hollinghurst, Alan

The **stranger's** child : a novel / Alan Hollinghurst. Alfred A. Knopf, 2011. 464 p.

ISBN 9780307272768

1. 1910s 2. Love triangles 3. Family secrets 4. Homosexuality 5. Biographers 6. Poets 7. Family estates 8. Great Britain -- Social life and customs -- 20th century 9. Literary fiction 10. Family sagas
LC 2011010256

Also published: Toronto : Vintage Canada, 2012, c2011.

National Book Critics Circle Award for Fiction finalist, 2011

Shortlisted for the Walter Scott Prize for Historical Fiction, 2012

Embraced by the family of his Cambridge schoolmate, Cecil Valance writes an inspiring poem in an autograph album that becomes a staple of every English classroom after he is killed during World War I.

"Hollinghurst divides the novel into five novella-length sections set in 1913, 1926, 1967, 1980 and 2008. In each of them, he demonstrates his knack for conjuring the moments between events, the seeming down time in which the ramifications of turning points in life sort themselves out. His immersion in each period is fluid and free of false notes, collectively fusing into a single symphonic epic." Seattle Times.

Hollingshead, Greg, 1947-

Bedlam : a novel / Greg Hollingshead. Thomas Dunne Books, 2006, c2004. 320 p.

ISBN 0312354746

1. Bethlem Royal Hospital (London, England) 2. Georgian era (1714-1837) 3. 1790s 4. 18th century 5. Men with mental illnesses 6. Pharmacists 7. Husband and wife 8. Physician and patient 9. Psychiatric hospitals 10. Psychiatric research 11. Mental illness -- Causes 12. Mental illness -- Treatment -- History 13. Delusions 14. London, England -- History -- 18th century 15. Historical fiction
LC 2006044416

Originally published: Toronto : HarperCollins, 2004.

"Bedlam has no end of gorgeous writing. Ostentatious language is always a danger when using narrators from the distant past, but Hollingshead's descriptions stand tastefully back from such overexuberance." New York Times Book Review.

LIST OF FICTIONAL WORKS

Hollis, Lee

Poppy Harmon investigates / Lee Hollis. Kensington Books, 2018 282 p. Desert Flowers mysteries

ISBN 9781496713889

1. Women amateur detectives 2. Retirement communities 3. Women retirees 4. Widows 5. Jewelry theft 6. Senior women 7. Murder investigation 8. California 9. Palm Springs, California 10. Cozy mysteries 11. Gentle reads

Poppy Harmon and her friends find that life after retirement can be much busies--and deadlier--than any of them ever anticipated.

Holmes, J. M. (Jeff M.)

How are you going to save yourself / J. M. Holmes. Little Brown & Co, 2018. 248 p.

ISBN 9780316514880

1. African American men 2. Working class 3. Male friendship 4. Multiracial men 5. Social classes 6. Racism 7. Identity (Psychology) 8. Growing up 9. Ambition 10. Families 11. Men/women relations 12. Rhode Island 13. Literary fiction 14. Coming-of-age stories 15. African American fiction

Four friends come of age in a Rhode Island postindustrial enclave and struggle to liberate themselves from the limitations imposed on African Americans while navigating the dynamics of sex, drugs, class and family.

Holmes, Linda

* Evvie Drake starts over : a novel / Linda Holmes. Ballantine Books, 2019. 304 p.

ISBN 9780525619246

1. Widows 2. Young women 3. Baseball players 4. Coastal towns 5. Pitchers (Baseball) 6. Men/women relations 7. Maine 8. Contemporary romances 9. Chick lit

LC 2018051134

Young widow Evvie Drake and major league pitcher Dean Tenney, who has lost his game and needs a chance to reset his life, form an unlikely relationship when Dean moves into an apartment at the back of Evvie's house.

"The charm of Holmes novel comes not only from a genuine friendship turned sweet romance between Evvie and Dean but also from watching amiable Evvie stumble through the process of finding herself. A warm and funny book that will captivate fans of Abbi Waxman and Taylor Jenkins Reid." Booklist.

Holmes, Shannon

Bad girlz : a novel / Shannon Holmes. Atria Books, 2003. 208 p. Bad girlz novels

ISBN 074348620X

1. African American women 2. Women -- Philadelphia, Pennsylvania 3. African American women -- Philadelphia, Pennsylvania 4. Young women 5. Stripteasers 6. Sex industry and trade 7. Drug use 8. Survival 9. Murder 10. Street life -- Philadelphia, Pennsylvania 11. City life -- Philadelphia, Pennsylvania 12. Street life 13. Pennsylvania 14. Philadelphia, Pennsylvania 15. Thrillers and suspense 16. Urban fiction 17. African American fiction

LC 2003062767

Sequel: Bad girlz 4 life.

Taken under the wing of Kat, a veteran stripper, Tender and Goldie must turn to the streets and strip clubs as a way to survive difficult times.

Holmes, Shannon

* B-more careful : a novel / Shannon Holmes. Meow Meow Productions, 2001 281 p.

ISBN 0967224918

1. African American young women 2. African American families 3. African Americans 4. Inner city 5. Street life 6. City life 7. Drug dealers 8. Drug abuse and crime 9. Prostitution 10. Men/women relations 11. Dysfunctional families 12. Revenge 13. Mothers and daughters 14. Family and addiction 15. Family problems 16. Baltimore, Maryland 17. Maryland 18. Urban fiction 19. African American fiction

LC 2002113967

Street Lit Book Award Medal: Adult Fiction, 2002

Fatherless and with an addict mother, Netta, the leader of the Pussy Pound, relies on her body and her wiles to survive the harsh streets of Baltimore, but finds there is more to life after her heartbroken lover Black swears revenge on her.

Holsinger, Bruce W.

The **gifted** school : a novel / Bruce Holsinger. Riverhead Books, 2019. 304 p.

ISBN 9780525534969

1. Schools 2. Social conflict 3. Parents -- Psychology 4. Competition 5. Class conflict 6. Resentfulness 7. Race relations 8. Parent and child 9. Colorado 10. Mainstream fiction 11. Domestic fiction

LC 2018057642

The students and parents of a tight-knit community find their bonds nearly destroyed by competitiveness when an exclusive school for gifted children opens nearby, in a story told from both adult and child perspectives.

Holt, Anne, 1958-

Odd numbers : a Hanne Wilhelmsen novel / Anne Holt ; translated from the Norwegian by Anne Bruce. Scribner, 2017, c2015. 326 p. Hanne Wilhelmsen novels

ISBN 9781451634730

1. Bombings 2. Terrorism investigation 3. Terrorism -- Prevention 4. Mass murder 5. Fathers and sons 6. Former policewomen 7. Murder investigation 8. Lesbians 9. Oslo, Norway 10. Norway 11. Mysteries 12. Scandinavian crime fiction 13. Translations -- Norwegian to English

LC 2016056265

Originally published in 2015 by Vigmostad & Bjørke as Offline.

A devastating bombing attack in the Islamic Cooperation Council's offices in Oslo brings special adviser Hanne Wilhelmsen out of her secluded home to investigate rumors of an imminent second attack and assist a long-lost friend's efforts to reach out to his troubled son.

Holt, Victoria, 1906-1993

The **black** opal / Victoria Holt. Fawcett Crest, 1994, c1993. 373 p.

ISBN 9780449222713

1. Abandoned children 2. Family secrets 3. Murder 4. Scandals 5. Illegitimacy 6. Trials (Murder) 7. Men/women relations 8. Cold cases (Criminal investigation) 9. England 10. Romantic suspense

Originally published: New York : Doubleday, 1993.

Returning to England many years after a murder had taken away her adoptive family, Carmel March searches her memory for the truth behind her past and wonders about the role played by her childhood friend, Lucian.

Holthe, Tess Uriza

When the elephants dance : a novel / Tess Uriza Holthe. Crown, 2002. xi, 368 p.

ISBN 0609609521

1. World War II -- Philippines 2. Brothers and sisters 3. Families 4. Philippines -- History -- Japanese occupation, 1942-1945 5. Historical fiction

In the final weeks of the Japanese occupation of the Philippines during World War II, three different Filipino narrators recount the experiences of a people desperately struggling in the midst of the horrors of war.

"Full of weird, fantastic twists and folkloric wisdom, the stories become both a touchstone to and a respite from the horrific events unfolding outside." New York Times Book Review

Hood, Ann, 1956-

The **obituary** writer / Ann Hood. W. W. Norton & Company, 2013. 320 p.

ISBN 9780393081428

1. 1960s 2. 1910s 3. Homemakers 4. Women journalists 5. Loss (Psychology) 6. Regret 7. Marital conflict 8. Obituary writers 9. Extramarital affairs 10. United States -- Social life and customs 11. Historical fiction 12. Mainstream fiction 13. Parallel narratives

LC 2012040074

An obituary writer searching for her missing lover at the turn of the 20th century is linked to a woman considering leaving her loveless marriage in 1963 in this literary mystery from the best-selling author of The Red Thread.

Hooper, Emma

Etta and Otto and Russell and James : a novel / Emma Hooper. Simon & Schuster, 2015. 320 p.

ISBN 9781476755670

1. Walking 2. Memories 3. Octogenarians 4. Voyages and travels 5. Senior couples 6. Self-fulfillment 7. Love triangles 8. Veterans 9. Farmers 10. Coyotes 11. Desire 12. Canada 13. Literary fiction

Embarking on a more than 3,000-kilometer walking journey from rural Canada to the East coast so that she can see the ocean for the first time in her life, an octogenarian woman has experiences that blur her perspectives between illusion, memory and reality.

"Hooper has written an irresistibly enchanting debut novel that explores mysteries of love old and new, the loyalty of animals and dependency of humans, the horrors of war and perils of loneliness, and the tenacity of time and fragility of memory." Booklist

Hooper, Kay

Stealing shadows / Kay Hooper. Bantam Books, 2000. 356 p. Bishop special crimes unit

ISBN 0553575538

1. Women psychics 2. FBI agents 3. Serial murder investigation 4. Women sheriffs 5. Sisters 6. Small town life 7. Men/women relations 8. Paranormal phenomena 9. North Carolina 10. Romantic suspense 11. Thrillers and suspense

Cassie Neill has a powerful but troubling gift. She can see inside the minds of murderers as they are planning their crimes. Tormented by her ability, she takes refuge in a secluded North Carolina town. But there's no escaping her visions, and soon she senses the fury and perverse exhilaration of a madman on the loose. The sheriff refuses to take Cassie seriously, until a body surfaces just where she predicts. Suddenly Cassie isn't just a psychic -- she's also a suspect.

"The first in a . . . thrill-ogy of suspense novels, this is a serial killer tale charged with deeply felt dread and romance that will steal readers' hearts. Cassie Neill has inherited a psychic gift from her mother that is a mixed blessing at best because it enables her to enter the minds of serial rapists and killers. From her aunt, she inherits a house tucked away in a corner of quiet little Ryan's Bluff, North Carolina, where she takes refuge, hoping to distance herself from the grueling work she's done for the Los Angeles Police Department. But, just as there's no rest for the weary, there's no rest for the wicked either, and visions of a deranged man's plans to kill prompt Cassie to visit Ben Ryan, the small town's prosecuting attorney. Skeptical but interested, Ben finds himself drawn toward the oddly bewitching Cassie, just as she is pulled ever further into the psychotic soul of evil." Booklist.

Hoover, Colleen

All your perfects / Colleen Hoover. Atria Books, 2018. 308 p.

ISBN 9781501193323

1. Husband and wife 2. Marital conflict 3. Infertility 4. Communication 5. Promises 6. Life change events 7. Marriage 8. Secrets 9. Men/women relations 10. New adult fiction 11. Contemporary romances

A damaged couple in a troubled marriage grapple with the memories and mistakes they've made and secrets they've kept as they try to repair their love.

Hoover, Colleen

It ends with us / Colleen Hoover. Atria Books, 2016. 320 p.

ISBN 9781501110368

1. Adult children of dysfunctional families 2. Women florists 3. Surgeons 4. Family violence 5. Former boyfriends 6. Abusive men 7. Abused women 8. Commitment (Psychology) 9. Trust in women 10. Love triangles 11. Men/women relations 12. Boston, Massachusetts 13. New adult fiction 14. Contemporary romances 15. Mainstream fiction

Goodreads Choice Award, 2016

"The newest, highly anticipated novel from beloved #1 New York Times bestselling author, Colleen Hoover. Sometimes it is the one who loves you who hurts you the most. Lily hasn't always had it easy, but that's never stopped her from working hard for the life she wants. She's come a long way from the small town in Maine where she grew up--she graduated from college, moved to Boston, and started her own business. So when she feels a spark with a gorgeous neurosurgeon named Ryle Kincaid, everything in Lily's life suddenly seems almost too good to be true. Ryle is assertive, stubborn, maybe even a little arrogant. He's also sensitive, brilliant, and has a total soft spot for Lily. And the way he looks in scrubs certainly doesn't hurt. Lily can't get him out of her head. But Ryle's complete aversion to relationships is disturbing. Even as Lily finds herself becoming the exception to his "no dating" rule, she can't help but wonder what made him that way in the first place. As questions about her new relationship overwhelm her, so do thoughts of Atlas Corrigan--her first love and a link to the past she left behind. He was her kindred spirit, her protector. When Atlas suddenly reappears, everything Lily has built with Ryle is threatened. With this bold and deeply personal novel, Colleen Hoover delivers a heart-wrenching story that breaks exciting new ground for her as a writer. Combining a captivating romance with a cast of all-too-human characters, It Ends With Us is an unforgettable tale of love that comes at the ultimate price"--, Provided by publisher.

Hoover, Michelle

The **quickening** / Michelle Hoover. Other Press, 2010. 224 p.

ISBN 9781590513460

1. 1900s (Decade) 2. Neighbors 3. Farm life -- Upper Midwest 4. Female friendship -- Middle West 5. Secrets 6. Families -- Upper

Midwest 7. Upper Midwest 8. Historical fiction

LC 2010005199

With the coming of the Great Depression to the upper Midwest, two farmer's wives are pitted against one another, exposing the dark secrets they hide and triggering a series of events that will unravel their friendship--and their families.

"In Hoover's debut, the quiet struggle between two Midwestern farm women has the stark simplicity of a Biblical parable. ... If Hoover's symbolism, like the characters' heavy-handed surnames, is at times too overt, the book's lament for a lost way of life . . . has a mournful beauty." The New Yorker.

Hope, Anthony, 1863-1933

The **prisoner** of Zenda : being the history of three months in the life of an English gentlemen / Anthony Hope. Buccaneer Books, 1976, c1894. 182 p.

ISBN 9780141033747

1. Look-alikes 2. Rulers 3. Adventure stories 4. Historical fiction

LC 81071632

First published 1894.

Originally published: 1894.

English gentleman, Rupert Rassendyll, arrives in the kingdom of Ruritania on the eve of King Rudolf's coronation. That night the king is abducted and held prisoner in a castle in the small town of Zenda. Rupert, who bears an uncanny resemblance to Rudolf, is persuaded to impersonate the King in order to stop the king's brother, Prince Michael, from seizing the throne. Rupert is determined to rescue the King but can he defeat the dastardly villain, Rupert of Hentzau?

Horan, Nancy

Loving Frank : a novel / Nancy Horan. Ballantine Books, 2007. 384 p.

ISBN 0345494997

1. Borthwick, Mamah Bouton, 1869-1914 2. Wright, Frank Lloyd, 1867-1959 3. Architects 4. Women intellectuals 5. Extramarital affairs 6. Scandals 7. Married women 8. Married men 9. Feminists 10. Independence in women 11. Women's role -- United States -- History -- 20th century 12. Men/women relations 13. Women murder victims 14. Illinois -- History -- 20th century 15. Wisconsin -- History -- 20th century 16. Europe -- Social life and customs -- 20th century 17. Biographical fiction 18. Historical fiction 19. Love stories

James Fenimore Cooper Prize, 2009

Fact and fiction blend in a historical novel that chronicles the relationship between seminal architect Frank Lloyd Wright and Mamah Cheney, from their meeting, when they were each married to another, to the clandestine affair that shocked Chicago society.

"In 1904, Frank Lloyd Wright started work on a house for an Oak Park couple, Edwin and Mamah Cheney, and, before long, he and Mamah had begun a scandalous affair. In her first novel, Horan, viewing the relationship from Mamahs perspective, does well to avoid serving up a bodice-ripper for the smart set. If anything, she cleaves too faithfully to the sources, occasionally giving her story the feel of a dissertation masquerading as a novel. But she succeeds in conveying the emotional center of her protagonist, whom she paints as a proto-feminist, an educated woman fettered by the role of bourgeois matriarch. Horan best evokes Mamahs troubled personality by means of delicately rendered reflections on the power of the natural world, from which her lover drew inspiration." The New Yorker.

Horlock, Mary

The **book** of lies : a novel / Mary Horlock. Harper Perennial, 2011. 304 p.

ISBN 9780062065094

1. Life change events 2. Family secrets 3. Truthfulness and falsehood 4. Teenagers -- Friendship 5. Teenage girls 6. Friendship 7. Murder 8. Confession (Law) 9. Betrayal 10. Memories 11. Germans in Guernsey (Channel Islands) 12. Guernsey (Channel Islands) 13. Channel Islands -- History -- German occupation, 1940-1945 14. Historical fiction 15. Diary novels

LC 2010046608

When Nicolette, the popular new girl at her all-girls high school on the tiny island of Guernsey, takes her under her wing, Cat, an overweight bookworm, enters a world of parties and shoplifting until a perceived betrayal tears them apart, resulting in a scandal that mirrors her uncle's hidden story of the island's Nazi occupation in WWII.

"The narrative shifts may initially disorient readers, but their subtle, skillfully built connections underscore Horlock's themes of the powerful, shadowy reach of history and the slippery nature of truth . . . while Cat's indelible, darkly funny voice offers unsparing insights into the adolescent jungle." Booklist.

Horn, Dara, 1977-

All other nights : a novel / Dara Horn. W. W. Norton, 2009. 384 p.

ISBN 9780393064926

1. American Civil War era (1861-1865) 2. 1860s 3. Jewish Americans 4. Life change events 5. Ethics 6. Assassination 7. Spies 8. Union soldiers 9. Civil war 10. Men/women relations 11. United States Civil War, 1861-1865 12. United States -- History -- Civil War, 1861-1865 13. Spy fiction 14. Historical thrillers

LC 2008053412

Jacob Rappaport, a Jewish soldier in the Union army, struggles with difficult moral questions when he is ordered to murder his own uncle, who has been plotting an assassination attempt against President Lincoln.

"The author both unearths a fascinating, relatively unexplored aspect of American historythe role of Jewish Americans in the Civil Warand delivers a novel rich in human emotion and ambiguity. A triumph." Booklist.

Horn, Dara, 1977-

Eternal life : a novel / Dara Horn. W. W. Norton & Co., 2018. 236 p.

ISBN 9780393608533

1. Faustian bargains 2. Jewish women 3. Immortality 4. Death 5. Families 6. First loves 7. Reincarnation 8. Senior women 9. Mother and adult son 10. New York City 11. Jerusalem, Israel -- History -- To 70 AD 12. Literary fiction

LC 2017044684

Ever since she made a deal to save her son's life in Roman-occupied Jerusalem, Rachel has been doomed to live eternally|having hundreds of children and being stalked by an obsessed man|but as her descendants develop new technologies for immortality, she realizes that, for them to live fully, she must die.

"Horn constructs a deeply satisfying novel, rich not only in history and the great philosophical conundrums of living and dying but also in humor and passion." Booklist.

Horn, Dara, 1977-

The **world** to come : a novel / Dara Horn. W.W. Norton & Co., 2006. 320 p.

ISBN 0393051072

1. Chagall, Marc, 1887-1985 Appreciation 2. Art -- Provenance 3.

Jewish families 4. Twins 5. Fugitives 6. Painters 7. Brothers and sisters 8. Jewish American men 9. Parents -- Death 10. Art thefts 11. Painting 12. Museum thefts 13. Museum employees 14. Orphanages 15. Vietnam War, 1961-1975 16. Families 17. Loss (Psychology) 18. New York City 19. Soviet Union 20. Vietnam 21. Literary fiction

LC 2005014586

National Jewish Book Award for Fiction, 2006.

Having stolen a million-dollar Marc Chagall masterpiece, thirty-year-old quiz-show writer Benjamin Ziskind and his twin sister work to evade the police and evaluate the eighty-year-old link between their family and the famous painting.

"There is much to be said for this novel. Dara Horn is skillful with words. She is serious about writing Jewish literature, and she knows her Jewish sources and treats them sensitively. Good at describing people and places, she is also good at dialogue. And she has the ability to construct a complex story from a large number of components and to build an utterly coherent whole out of them. The World to Come is architecturally complicated, but as architecture it works beautifully." Commentary.

Horowitz, Anthony, 1955-

The **House** of Silk : a Sherlock Holmes novel / Anthony Horowitz. Mulholland Books, 2011. 320 p. Sherlock Holmes novels (Anthony Horowitz)

ISBN 9780316196994

1. 1890s 2. Detectives 3. Organized crime 4. Train robberies 5. Conspiracies 6. Murder 7. Clues 8. London, England -- History -- 19th century 9. Boston, Massachusetts -- History -- 19th century 10. Adaptations, retellings, and spin-offs 11. Historical mysteries

LC 2011030839

It is 1890. A year after Holmes's death, Watson--now in a retirement home--narrates a tale of Sherlockian detection that could tear apart the very fabric of society. The story opens with a train robbery in Boston, and moves to the innocuous setting of Wimbledon.

Horowitz, Anthony, 1955-

* **Magpie** murders / Anthony Horowitz. Harper, 2017, c2016. 368 p.

ISBN 9780062645227

1. 1950s 2. Detectives 3. Editors 4. Holocaust survivors 5. Accidental death 6. Murder investigation 7. Housekeepers 8. Murder suspects 9. Books and reading 10. England -- Social life and customs -- 20th century 11. Mysteries 12. Metafiction

LC 2016045021

Originally published: London : Orion, 2016.

Macavity Award for Best Mystery Novel, 2018.

RUSA Reading List Short List, 2018.

"From New York Times bestselling author Anthony Horowitz comes Magpie Murders, a brilliant and strikingly original reimagining of the classic whodunit (à la Agatha Christie) with a contemporary mystery wrapped around it"--, Provided by publisher.

"Fans who still mourn the passing of Agatha Christie, the model who's evoked here in dozens of telltale details, will welcome this wildly inventive homage /update/commentary as the most fiendishly clever puzzle--make that two puzzles--of the year." Kirkus.

Horowitz, Anthony, 1955-

Moriarty / Anthony Horowitz. Harper, 2014. 288 p. Sherlock Holmes novels (Anthony Horowitz)

ISBN 9780062377180

1. 1890s 2. Detectives 3. Organized crime 4. Enemies 5. Villains 6. Murder 7. Clues 8. London, England -- History -- 19th century 9. Boston, Massachusetts -- History -- 19th century 10. Adaptations, retellings, and spin-offs 11. Historical mysteries

Pinkerton agent Frederick Chase arrives in London to help Scotland Yard Inspector Athelney Jones track down the sinister figure determined to be Moriarty's successor.

"Horowitz's mystery bona fides are impeccable: not only did his previous Sherlock Holmes novel, The House of Silk, sell over 450,000 copies worldwide in more than 35 countries, but he created both Midsomer Murders and the BAFTA-winning Foyle's War. Here he reimagines what happened after the presumably lethal scuffle between Holmes and Moriarty at the Reichenbach Falls." Library Journal.

Horowitz, Anthony, 1955-

* The **sentence** is death / Anthony Horowitz. HarperCollins, 2019. 464 p. Daniel Hawthorne novels

ISBN 9780062676832

1. Detectives 2. Authors 3. Mystery story writers 4. Secrets 5. Deception 6. Former police 7. Murder 8. Murder investigation 9. England 10. Mysteries 11. Metafiction

Also published as Another word for death: HarperCollins Canada, 2019.

Detective Daniel Hawthorne and his literary sidekick risk their lives to expose dangerous secrets while investigating the murder of a celebrity divorce lawyer and teetotaler who was bludgeoned to death with an expensive bottle of wine.

"Horowitz plays fair with the reader all the way to the surprise reveal of the killers identity. Fans of traditional puzzle mysteries will be enthralled." Publishers Weekly.

Horowitz, Anthony, 1955-

* The **word** is murder / Anthony Horowitz. Harper, 2018, c2017. 400 p. Daniel Hawthorne novels

ISBN 9780062676788

1. Detectives 2. Authors 3. Mystery story writers 4. Secrets 5. Deception 6. Former police 7. Murder 8. Murder investigation 9. England 10. Mysteries 11. Metafiction

Originally published: London : Cornerstone, 2017.

When a wealthy woman is found murdered after planning her own funeral service, disgraced police detective Daniel Hawthorne and his sidekick, author Anthony Horowitz, investigate.

"Deduction and wit are well-balanced, and fans of Peter Lovesey and other modern channelers of the spirit of the golden age of detection will clamor for more." Publishers Weekly.

Horrocks, Caitlin, 1980-

The **vexations** / Caitlin Horrocks. Little Brown & Co., 2019. 451 p.

ISBN 9780316316910

1. Satie, Erik, 1866-1925 2. Belle Epoque (1871-1914) 3. Obsession 4. Composers 5. Brothers and sisters 6. Genius 7. Loyalty 8. Orphans 9. Loss (Psychology) 10. Family relationships 11. Art -- Psychological aspects 12. Paris, France -- Social life and customs -- 19th century 13. Biographical fiction 14. Historical fiction

Devoted to her talented composer brother after becoming orphaned in childhood, Louise is forced to confront the realities of her brother's obsessions in the wake of a devastating loss.

"Finely written and deeply empathetic, a powerful portrait of artistic commitment and emotional frustration." Kirkus.

Hosking, Jay

Three years with the rat : a novel / Jay Hosking. Thomas Dunne Books, 2017. 271 p.

ISBN 9781250116307

1. Brothers and sisters 2. Graduate students 3. Missing persons 4. Missing persons investigation 5. Rats 6. Physics 7. Space and time

8. Parallel universes 9. Eccentrics and eccentricities 10. Time 11. Toronto, Ontario 12. Science fiction

Originally published: Toronto, Ontario : Hamish Hamilton, 2016.

Alarmed by his sister's raging meltdowns that point to a serious mental illness, a young man embarks on a quest for answers when his sister goes missing, an effort that is complicated by her seemingly devoted boyfriend's suspicious knowledge.

"A potent, sophisticated combination of science-fiction novel and psychological thriller." Kirkus.

Hosseini, Khaled

* The **kite** runner / Khaled Hosseini. Riverhead Books, 2003. 368 p.

ISBN 1573222453

1. Boys -- Friendship -- Afghanistan 2. Afghan War, 2001- 3. Social classes -- Afghanistan 4. Rich boys -- Afghanistan 5. Household employees 6. Betrayal 7. Bullying and bullies -- Afghanistan 8. Gang rape -- Afghanistan 9. Male rape victims -- Afghanistan 10. Male rape -- Afghanistan 11. Housekeepers 12. Afghanistan 13. Kabul, Afghanistan 14. Literary fiction 15. Coming-of-age stories

LC 2003043106

ALA Notable Book, 2004.

Afghanistan, 1975: Twelve-year-old Amir is desperate to win the local kite-fighting tournament and his loyal friend Hassan promises to help him. But neither of the boys can foresee what will happen to Hassan that afternoon, an event that is to shatter their lives. After the Russians invade and the family is forced to flee to America, Amir realises that one day he must return to Afghanistan under Taliban rule to find the one thing that his new world cannot grant him: redemption.

"Khaled Hosseini gives us a vivid and engaging story that reminds us how long his people have been struggling to triumph over the forces of violence." New York Times Book Review.

Hosseini, Khaled

* **Sea** prayer / Khaled Hosseini. Riverhead Books, 2018. 48 p.

ISBN 9780525539094

1. Refugees, Syrian 2. Fathers and sons 3. Child refugees 4. Children and war 5. Family and war 6. Syria -- History -- Civil War, 2011- 7. War stories 8. Illustrated books 9. Epistolary novels

LC 2018022980

Presents an evocatively illustrated tribute to the tragic human realities of today's refugee crisis in the form of a father's letter to his young son on the eve of a dangerous journey.

Houellebecq, Michel

The **map** and the territory / Michel Houellebecq ; translated from the French by Gavin Bowd. Knopf, 2012, c2010. 272 p.

ISBN 9780307701558

1. Painters 2. Fathers 3. Mortality 4. Artists 5. Russians in France 6. Police 7. Men -- Identity 8. Criminal investigation 9. France 10. Literary fiction 11. Translations -- French to English

Originally published with the title La Carte et le Territoire in France by Flammarion, 2010.

Shortlisted for the International IMPAC Dublin Literary Award, 2013

Traces the experiences of artist Jed Martin, who rises to international success as a portrait photographer before helping to solve a heinous crime that has lasting repercussions for his loved ones.

Houellebecq, Michel

Submission / Michel Houellebecq ; Translated from the French by Lorin Stein. Farrar Straus & Giroux, 2015. 256 p.

ISBN 9780374271572

1. Near future 2. Elections 3. College teachers 4. Muslims 5. Social change 6. Personal conduct 7. Middle-aged men 8. Intellectual life 9. Political science 10. France 11. Literary fiction 12. Satirical fiction 13. Translations -- French to English

Translation from the French of: Soumission.

Originally published: Paris : Flammarion, 2015.

In a near-future France, François, a middle-aged academic, is watching his life slowly dwindle to nothing. His sex drive is diminished, his parents are dead, and his lifelong obsession--the ideas and works of the novelist Joris-Karl Huysmans--has led him nowhere. In a late-capitalist society where consumerism has become the new religion, François is spiritually barren, but seeking to fill the vacuum of his existence. And he is not alone. As the 2022 Presidential election approaches, two candidates emerge as favorites: Marine Le Pen of the Front National, and Muhammed Ben Abbes of the nascent Muslim Fraternity. Forming a controversial alliance with the mainstream parties, Ben Abbes sweeps to power, and overnight the country is transformed. Islamic law comes into force: women are veiled, polygamy is encouraged and, for François, life is set on a new course.

"Submission is well crafted, but the pornographic sex scenes are as tired as their rationale. Houellebecq's faltering is Francois' failure writ large: the inability to believe there might be any meaning in or meaningful differences between diverse points of view or ways of life." Booklist.

House, Silas, 1971-

A **parchment** of leaves : a novel / Silas House. Algonquin Books of Chapel Hill, 2002. 288 p.

ISBN 9781565123670

1. 1910s 2. Cherokee women 3. Irish American men 4. Interracial marriage 5. Mountain life 6. Homesickness 7. Family relationships 8. Marriage 9. Childbirth 10. Interpersonal relations 11. Brothers-in-law 12. Sawmill workers 13. Violence 14. Kentucky 15. Historical fiction 16. Domestic fiction 17. Southern fiction

LC 2002066570

In 1917, a Cherokee woman who leaves her community to marry a white man finds herself isolated and discriminated against as she tries to settle in to her new life.

"This is a moving love story set against a stunningly beautiful background, and House seems to capture it all -- the deep emotion, the love of land, the customs of mountain people -- quietly eloquent prose." Booklist.

Howard, Ravi

Driving the king : a novel / Ravi Howard. Harper, 2015. 336 p.

ISBN 9780060529611

1. Cole, Nat "King,", 1919-1965 2. 1950s 3. Racism 4. Chauffeurs 5. African Americans -- Social conditions -- To 1964 6. Racism in the judicial system 7. Violence against minorities 8. African American singers 9. Male friendship 10. Prejudice 11. Injustice 12. Loyalty 13. United States -- Race relations 14. Montgomery, Alabama -- Race relations 15. Los Angeles, California -- Race relations 16. Biographical fiction 17. Historical fiction 18. African American fiction

LC 2014015054

Explores race and class in 1950s America, witnessed through the experiences of Nat King Cole and his driver, Nat Weary.

"Alternating between the cities and Wearys past and present, Howard explores race relations in the pre-civil rights era and the strong ties forged between two extraordinary men." Booklist.

Howarth, Paul, 1978-

Only killers and thieves : a novel / Paul Howarth. Harper, 2018. 319 p.

ISBN 9780062690968

1. 1880s 2. Frontier and pioneer life 3. Wilderness areas -- Australia 4. Atrocities 5. Aboriginal Australians 6. Racism 7. Murder 8. Brothers 9. Anger in teenage boys 10. Justice 11. Revenge 12. Australia 13. Historical fiction 14. Coming-of-age stories

It is 1885, and a crippling drought threatens to ruin the McBride family. Their land is parched, their cattle starving. When the rain finally comes, it is a miracle that renews their hope for survival. But returning home from an afternoon swimming at a remote waterhole filled by the downpour, fourteen-year-old Tommy and sixteen-year-old Billy meet with a shocking tragedy.

Howatch, Susan

Cashelmara / Susan Howatch. Simon and Schuster, 1974. 702 p.

ISBN 9780671217365

1. British in Ireland 2. Families -- Ireland 3. Ireland 4. Ireland -- History -- 19th century 5. Family sagas 6. Historical fiction

LC 73022333

Some printings issued by Fawcett Crest.

The dynastic history of three generations of an English/Irish family and the great house that obsesses them.

"Divided into six sections, each narrated by a different character, this novel charts the lives of three generations of the Anglo-Irish de Salis family between 1859 and 1891. They move between London homes, a Warwickshire estate, New York and Bostonwhere two Lords de Salis find their wives--but end always at the great white house on their Irish estate, Cashelmara. In the background are the simmering troubles between starving Irish tenants and callous English landlords." Christian Science Monitor.

Howatch, Susan

The **heartbreaker** : a novel / Susan Howatch. Knopf, 2004. 496 p. St. Benet's trilogy

ISBN 9781400041473

1. Widows 2. Faith healing 3. Deception 4. Faith healers 5. Redemption 6. Male prostitutes 7. Women psychics 8. Closeted gay men 9. Church fund raising 10. Men/women relations 11. Forgiveness 12. London, England 13. Christian fiction 14. Psychological fiction

LC 2003062493

Sequel to: The High Flyer.

Gavin Blake, desperate to escape his world of prostitution, violence, and pornography, seeks refuge at St. Benet's, a church in the heart of London, where he becomes involved with Carta Graham, a church fundraiser struggling with her own demons.

"Plot improbabilities and long sections of spiritual musing are redeemed by Howatch's strongly drawn characters: if Carta can come across as brittle and prudish, Gavin's self-absorbed cant is continually entertaining." Publishers Weekly.

Howland, Bette

Calm sea and prosperous voyage / Bette Howland. A Public Space, 2019. 230 p.

ISBN 9780998267500

1. Women 2. Family relationships 3. Interpersonal relations 4. Autobiographical fiction 5. Short stories

With the publication of Bette Howland's CALM SEA AND PROSPEROUS VOYAGE, A Public Space Books restores to the literary canon an extraordinarily gifted writer, who was recognized as a major talent, with Guggenheim and MacArthur "genius" fellowships, before all but disappearing from public view for decades. With direct and powerful use of language in the tradition of Lucia Berlin, Kathleen Collins, and Grace Paley, Bette Howland chronicles the tensions of her generation.

Howrey, Meg

The **wanderers** / Meg Howrey. G. P. Putnam's Sons, 2017. 400 p.

ISBN 9780399574634

1. Astronauts 2. Family relationships 3. Introspection 4. Space flight to Mars 5. Ambition 6. Social isolation 7. Engineers 8. Utah 9. Literary fiction 10. Psychological fiction

"Station Eleven meets The Martian in this brilliantly inventive novel about three astronauts training for the first-ever mission to Mars, an experience that will push the boundary between real and unreal, test their relationships, and leave each of them--and their families--changed forever. In an age of space exploration, we search to find ourselves. In four years Prime Space will put the first humans on Mars. Helen Kane, Yoshi Tanaka, and Sergei Kuznetsov must prove they're the crew for the job by spending seventeen months in the most realistic simulation ever created. Retired from NASA, Helen had not trained for irrelevance. It is nobody's fault that the best of her exists in space, but her daughter can't help placing blame. The MarsNOW mission is Helen's last chance to return to the only place she's ever truly felt at home. For Yoshi, it's an opportunity to prove himself worthy of the wife he has loved absolutely, if not quite rightly. Sergei is willing to spend seventeen months in a tin can if it means travelling to Mars. He will at least be tested past the point of exhaustion, and this is the example he will set for his sons. As the days turn into months the line between what is real and unreal becomes blurred, and the astronauts learn that the complications of inner space are no less fraught than those of outer space. The Wanderers gets at the desire behind all exploration: the longing for discovery and the great search to understand the human heart"--. Provided by publisher.

"Although the contours of a space drama may seem familiar to a 21st-century readership, Howrey, through the poetry of her writing and the richness of her characters, makes it all seem new. A lyrical and subtle space opera." Kirkus.

Hoyt, Elizabeth, 1970-

Wicked intentions / Elizabeth Hoyt. Grand Central Pub., 2010. 392 p. Maiden Lane romances

ISBN 9780446558945

1. Georgian era (1714-1837) 2. Nobility 3. Desire 4. Deals 5. Nobility 6. Slums 7. Secrets 8. Widows 9. Men/women relations 10. Murder investigation 11. Orphanages 12. Interpersonal attraction 13. London, England -- History -- 18th century 14. Georgian romances 15. Historical romances

Lord Caire, who needs help searching for a killer in London's most notorious slum, turns to Temperance Dews, a young widow who knows the area well, and agrees to help launch her in high society if she will assist him.

"With a dash of sharp wit; a rare literary flair for creating complex, compelling characters; and lively writing that packs a powerful emotional punch, Hoyt delivers the first sensually charged, danger-infused installment in a new Georgian-set series." Booklist.

Huang, S. L.
Zero sum game / S. L. Huang. Tor, 2018. 336 p. Cas Russell novels
ISBN 9781250180254
1. Mathematics 2. Telepathy 3. Mercenaries 4. Corporations 5. Conspiracies 6. Mind control 7. Science fiction
LC 2018023931
"A Tom Doherty Associates Book."
Cas Russell wields her math skills like a superpower, using vector calculus to dodge bullets and beat up armed men, but is very surprised to find someone with a power more dangerous than her own, the ability to control minds.

Hubbard, Ladee
The **talented** Ribkins / Ladee Hubbard. Melville House, 2017. 300 p.
ISBN 9781612196367
1. African American families 2. Superhuman abilities 3. Family relationships 4. Civil Rights Movement 5. Race relations 6. Social classes 7. Maps 8. Senior men 9. Uncle and niece 10. Identity (Psychology) 11. Debt 12. Burglary 13. Florida 14. Magical realism 15. Literary fiction
LC 2017018187
Tells the story of Johnny Ribkins, a 72-year-old African-American antiques dealer and patriarch of a gifted family, the members of which sometimes stumble in their efforts to succeed in life.
"Hubbard's voice mixes wry humor and superhero pop culture while addressing issues that continue to challenge our country's African American community." Library Journal.

Hughes, Langston, 1902-1967
Not without laughter / Langston Hughes ; with a new introduction by Maya Angelou ; foreword by Arna Bontemps. Scribner Paperback Fiction, 1995, c1930. 299 p.
ISBN 9780020209850
1. Growing up -- Kansas 2. African American boys -- Kansas 3. Small town life -- Kansas 4. Kansas 5. African American fiction 6. Coming-of-age stories 7. Modern classics 8. Literary fiction
Originally published: New York : Knopf, 1930.
Depicts a Black family's attempts to deal with life in a small Kansas town
"A sympathetic portrayal, unmarred by bitterness or sentimentality, of a people to whom life, no matter how hard, was not without laughter." Booklist.

Hughes, Langston, 1902-1967
* **Short** stories / Langston Hughes ; edited by Akiba Sullivan Harper ; with an introduction by Arnold Rampersad. Hill and Wang, 1996. 299 p.
ISBN 9780809016037
1. African Americans -- Social life and customs 2. Race relations 3. Social classes 4. Men/women relations 5. Survival 6. Poverty 7. Racism 8. New York City -- Social life and customs 9. Harlem, New York City -- Social life and customs 10. United States -- Race relations 11. Short stories 12. Autobiographical fiction 13. African American fiction
LC 95-19554
47 short stories.
Offers a collection of stories written between 1919 and 1963 that follow Hughes' literary development and the growth of his personal and political concerns.

"[T]hese pieces vary in theme... If you crave good reading don't pass up this gem." Library Journal.

Hughes, Langston, 1902-1967
Simple speaks his mind / Langston Hughes. Simon and Schuster, 1950. 231 p.
1. 1940s 2. Race relations 3. African Americans 4. Conversation 5. Civil rights 6. City life 7. New York City 8. Harlem, New York City 9. Humorous stories 10. African American fiction
"Simple is completely frank in his opinions about white people; he dislikes them intensely. The race problem is never absent, but the flow of the book is light-hearted and easy." New York Times Book Review.

Hugo, Victor, 1802-1885
* The **hunchback** of Notre Dame / Victor Hugo ; revised translation and notes by Catherine Liu ; introduction by Elizabeth McCracken. Modern Library, 2002, c1831. xxviii, 483 p.
ISBN 9780679642572
1. Notre Dame Cathedral, Paris 2. Catholic Church. 3. People with disfigurements 4. Romani women 5. Love 6. Frameups 7. Jealousy in men 8. Romanticism -- France 9. People with kyphosis 10. Paris, France -- History -- To 1515 11. France -- History -- Louis XI, 1461-1483 12. Historical fiction 13. Translations -- French to English 14. Classics
Television mini-series of the same title as the book were based on The Hunchback of Notre-Dame in 1966 and 1977, and a television movie in 1982.
First published in French as Notre Dame de Paris in 1831.
Originally published: Paris : Gosselin, 1831.
The archdeacon of Notre Dame, Claude Frollo, falls in lust with Esmerelda, a gypsy dancer who is much admired in Paris and convinces Quasimodo, the hunchbacked bell-ringer of Notre Dame, to kidnap her. Esmerelda is rescued by the Captain of the Royal Archers and falls mistakenly in love with his bravery when he is in reality, something of a rogue and a braggart.

Hugo, Victor, 1802-1885
* **Les** miserables / Victor Hugo ; translated from the French by Charles E. Wilbour ; with an introduction by Peter Washington. Knopf, 1997, c1862. xxxvii, 1432 p.
ISBN 9780375403170
1. French Revolution, 1789-1799 2. Fate and fatalism 3. Revolutions 4. State-sponsored terrorism 5. Revolutionaries 6. Rich men 7. Fathers 8. Prisoners -- France 9. France -- Social conditions -- 19th century 10. France -- History -- Revolution, 1789-1799 11. Literary fiction 12. Classics 13. Translations -- French to English
Originally published: Paris : J. Hetzel, 1862.
Story of Valjean, the ex-convict who rises against all odds from galley slave to mayor, and the fanatical police inspector who dedicates his life to recapturing Valjean.

Hulme, Keri
* The **bone** people : a novel / Keri Hulme. Louisiana State University Press, 1985, c1983. 450 p.
ISBN 0807112844
1. Maori (New Zealand people) 2. Love triangles 3. Multiracial women 4. Interpersonal relations 5. Foster child abuse 6. Culture conflict 7. Ethnic identity 8. Race relations 9. Foster fathers 10. Redemption 11. New Zealand 12. Literary fiction 13. Magical realism
LC 85012937
Originally published: Wellington : Spiral, 1983.

New Zealand Book Award for Fiction, 1984.

Booker Prize, 1985.

A novel of the charged relationships between European and Polynesian descendents in New Zealand explores the fluctuating bonds connecting three South Sea natives as they struggle to endure.

"This novel is unforgettably rich and pungent. . . . Set on the harsh South Island beaches of New Zealand, bound in Maori myth and entwined with Christian symbols, Miss Hulme's provocative novel summons power with words, as in a conjurer's spell." New York Times Book Review.

Hulse, S. M.

* Black River / S. M. Hulse. Houghton Mifflin Harcourt, 2015. 256 p.

ISBN 9780544309876

1. Widowers 2. Correctional personnel 3. Confrontation (Interpersonal relations) 4. Prison riots 5. Redemption 6. Hostage taking 7. Parolees 8. Prisoners 9. Blended families 10. Conversion to Christianity 11. Loss (Psychology) 12. Montana 13. Psychological fiction 14. Literary fiction

LC 2014027025

ALA Notable Book, 2016.

Meditative and Montana-set, this debut is a modern American Western that tells the story of former prison guard Wes Carver, tortured 20 years ago by an inmate who's now up for parole, claiming to have found religion. Though Wes moved away, he's back in Black River (with his wife's ashes) to speak against the parole hearing. He's also got some work to do in repairing his damaged relationship with his stepson. Awash in bluegrass music, this is a wrenching story of a broken man trying to find his way back. -- Description by Shauna Griffin.

"Hulse clearly loves Montana, and her own experience playing the fiddle and knowledge of horses shine through the novel. She maintains suspense and manages to avoid the cliches of redemption stories." Booklist.

Hulse, S. M.

Eden mine / S.M. Hulse. Farrar, Straus and Giroux, 2020. 256 p.

ISBN 9780374146474

1. People with disabilities 2. Brothers and sisters 3. Bombing 4. Domestic terrorism 5. Sheriffs 6. Eminent domain 7. Terrorists 8. Women artists 9. Painting 10. Interpersonal relations 11. Faith 12. Redemption 13. Montana 14. Literary fiction 15. Westerns

LC 2019036405

After the state seizes through eminent domain the home near Den Mine that Jo and her brother, Samuel, inherited, she is packing up her things when a tragedy rocks the town - and the lives of those she loves.

"Especially fine is her rendering of a person of faith struggling with doubt and the nature of evil. Fans of Annie Proulx may appreciate the novel's pensive mood and the exploration of a place where people have few options and little hope." Booklist.

Humphreys, Helen, 1961-

Afterimage : a novel / Helen Humphreys. Metropolitan Books, 2001, c2000. 240 p.

ISBN 0805066667

1. Victorian era (1837-1901) 2. Women photographers 3. Photographers' models 4. Household employees 5. Love triangles 6. Housekeepers 7. England 8. Great Britain -- History -- Victoria, 1837-1901 9. Historical fiction

LC 00046907

Originally published: Toronto : HarperCollins, 2000.

Rogers Writers' Trust Fiction Prize, 2000.

When Annie Phelan goes to work for the Dashells, she enters a world her strict upbringing did not prepare her for, where she is asked to be the Muse for Isabel's portraits and a member of Eldon's imaginary Arctic expeditions.

"Inspired by the work of Julia Margaret Cameron, this urgent, well-made novel charts the boundaries where light becomes shadow, and the known can suddenly appear awful and astonishing." The New Yorker.

Humphreys, Josephine

Nowhere else on earth / Josephine Humphreys. Viking, 2000. 341 p.

ISBN 0670891762

1. American Civil War era (1861-1865) 2. Lumbee Indians 3. Teenage girls 4. Native American women 5. Civil war 6. Multiracial persons 7. United States Civil War, 1861-1865 8. Robeson County, North Carolina 9. North Carolina -- History -- Civil War, 1861-1865 10. Historical fiction

LC 00036666

A North Carolina town struggles to preserve its sanity in 1864 as the Civil War approaches to shatter the peace, while sixteen-year-old Rhoda Strong falls in love with outlaw Henry Berry Lowrie.

"In 1864, Rhoda Strong is a teenager of mixed ancestry in Scuffletown, an Indian settlement on the Lumbee River, in North Carolina. As the town's inhabitants find themselves caught between marauding Union soldiers and Confederates attempting to conscript their children for labor, Rhoda falls in love with a local outlaw who is fighting to protect the community. Humphreys has always been a master of telling a larger story through a deceptively intimate narrative, and Rhoda's tale, with its clear, distinct voice, is no exception." The New Yorker.

Humphreys, Sara Taney

Trouble walks in / Sara Humphreys. Sourcebooks Casablanca, 2016. 309 p. McGuire brothers

ISBN 9781402293702

1. Police 2. Women real estate agents 3. Threat (Psychology) 4. Protectiveness in men 5. Police dogs 6. Sexual attraction 7. Men/women relations 8. Police dogs 9. New York City 10. Contemporary romances

When an old friend moves into his jurisdiction, K-9 cop Ronan McGuire will do anything to get Maddy Morgan's attention, and when his work places her life in danger, his resolve is tested beyond anything he's experienced before.

Hunt, Andrew E., 1968-

City of saints : a mystery / Andrew Hunt. Minotaur Books, 2012. 320 p. Art Oveson novels

ISBN 9781250015792

1. 1930s 2. Socialites 3. Political corruption 4. Murder investigation 5. Police 6. Mormons 7. Physicians' spouses 8. Children of murder victims 9. Cold cases (Criminal investigation) 10. Salt Lake City, Utah 11. Utah 12. Historical mysteries 13. Mysteries

LC 2012030078

"A Thomas Dunne Book."

A historical mystery set in 1930s Salt Lake City finds a rookie investigator and Mormon family man partnering with a foul-mouthed, vice-ridden former strikebreaker to solve the murder of a beautiful socialite that is complicated by a sheriff's reelection campaign, a corrupt doctor and a scandalous affair.

Hunt, Laird

The **evening** road / Laird Hunt. Little, Brown and Company, 2017. 278 p.

ISBN 9780316391283

1. 1920s 2. Race relations 3. Small towns 4. African American women 5. Lynching 6. Married women 7. Interracial couples 8. Sexism 9. Racism 10. Coping 11. Small town life 12. Indiana 13. Historical fiction

In the summer of 1920 in small-town Indiana, two extraordinary women--beautiful Ottie Lee Henshaw and Calla Destry, a young black woman--cross paths and they soon move through an America plagued by fear and hatred, determined to flee the secrets they have left behind.

"Though the novels meandering odysseys sometimes feel frustrating, Hunts striking prose and visionary imagery capture Americas community bonds, violent prejudices, falling darkness, and searing light." Publishers Weekly.

Hunt, Laird

Neverhome / Laird Hunt. Little Brown & Co, 2014. 224 p.

ISBN 9780316370134

1. American Civil War era (1861-1865) 2. 1860s 3. Married women 4. Disguises 5. Gender role 6. Union soldiers 7. Women soldiers 8. Civil war 9. Deception 10. United States Civil War, 1861-1865 11. United States -- History -- Civil War, 1861-1865 12. Historical fiction

"I was to go and he was to stay," says Constance Thompson, recounting her decision to disguise herself as a man, leave her husband behind to tend their Indiana farm, and enlist in the Union Army as "Ash Thompson." Though Ash may be physically stronger than her spouse and more suited to military life, she finds the battlefield carnage tough to stomach. And that's before she's wounded in combat, captured by bounty hunters, imprisoned, and worse. Spare and compelling, Neverhome offers a different perspective on the American Civil War. -- Description by Gillian Speace.

"Historical fiction fans will not be disappointed by this wonderful story of Ash's struggles with her identity and of her personal ties to the war. An amazing book." Library Journal.

Hunt, Samantha

The **dark** dark : stories / Samantha Hunt. Farrar, Straus & Giroux, 2017. 256 p.

ISBN 9780374282134

1. Paranormal phenomena 2. Magic 3. Loneliness 4. Lust 5. Anxiety 6. Men/women relations 7. Literary fiction 8. Magical realism

LC 2016050909

Pen/Faulkner Award Finalist, 2018

A first collection of stories by the award-winning author of The Invention of Everything Else imagines lives that are disrupted by otherworldly manifestations, from a woman who inadvertently cheats on her husband when she turns into a deer by night, to an FBI agent who falls in love with a robot built for a suicide mission.

"This excellent, inventive collection . . . is rife with observant asides, sly humor, and surprises." Publishers Weekly.

Hunt, Samantha

The **invention** of everything else / Samantha Hunt. Houghton Mifflin Co., 2007. 272 p.

ISBN 9780618801121

1. Tesla, Nikola, 1856-1943 2. 1940s 3. Hotel workers 4. Interpersonal attraction 5. Love 6. Electrical engineers 7. Inventors 8. New York City 9. Biographical fiction 10. Historical fiction

LC 2007009416

Shortlisted for The Orange Prize for Fiction, 2009

Eccentric inventor, Nikola Tesla, and a young hotel chambermaid, Louisa, who is obsessed with radio dramas and the secret lives of the hotel guests have an unlikely friendship. Louisa first catches sight of the hotel's most famous resident on New Year's Day, 1943, and is determined to befriend the strange man.

"Set in New York City in 1943, the book focuses on Nikola Tesla, the underappreciated Serbian inventor. . . . Hunt's story unfolds over the last week of Tesla's life: He is 86 years old, destitute, and maybe a little crazy. He is also, of course, a genius. Tesla is an ideal person to bring back to life through fiction; technically, he's famous, but he's also largely unfamiliar. Because his actual story is so incredible (he was pals with Mark Twain, he fell in love with a bird, he tried to invent a death ray), it's tricky to separate the pieces of Hunt's account that are drawn from fact from those that she's invented. Tesla is well balanced by the entirely fictional character of Louisa, a sensible, inquisitive young chambermaid who works at the hotel and befriends the inventor after he catches her snooping through his things. A classic sort of heroine, she treats the fading man like an oracle as she juggles her own daily dramas." Village Voice.

Hunt, Samantha

* **Mr.** Splitfoot / Samantha Hunt. Houghton Mifflin Harcourt, 2016. 320 p.

ISBN 9780544526709

1. Teenage orphans 2. Swindlers and swindling 3. Aunt and niece 4. Voyages and travels 5. Women mediums 6. Supernatural 7. Pregnant women 8. Cults 9. Women who are mute 10. New York (State) 11. Gothic fiction 12. Parallel narratives

A contemporary gothic from an author in the company of Kelly Link and Aimee Bender, Mr. Splitfoot tracks two women?Ruth (a scam-artist foster kid), and, decades later, Cora (her pregnant niece)?as they march, each in her own time, toward a mysterious reckoning.

"Hunt's use of a split narrative to measuredly disclose snippets of Ruth's past and Cora's present in alternating, interconnected chapters builds suspense while keeping readers guessing about what crazy turn might happen next. Hints of what's in store for readers include a cult of Etherists, a noseless man, a pile of lost money, and a scar-like pattern of meteorite landings." Publishers Weekly.

Hunter, Evan, 1926-2005

The **blackboard** jungle : a novel / Evan Hunter. Bentley, 1971, c1954. 309p.

1. 1950s 2. High school teachers -- Inner city 3. Inner city schools 4. Violence in schools 5. Violence in teenage boys 6. Juvenile delinquency 7. Husband and wife 8. Pregnant women 9. Interracial friendship 10. Intergenerational friendship 11. Families 12. Public schools 13. Gangs 14. Inner city teenage boys 15. Fear in teenage boys 16. Gang rape 17. Frustration 18. Apathy 19. Stealing 20. Vandalism 21. Psychological fiction

LC 73183139

Rick Dadier encounters insolence and violence as a new teacher at a New York City vocational school as he tries to reach a group of violent, rebellious New York City teenagers, in a fiftieth anniversary edition of the classic novel.

Hunter, Evan, 1926-2005

The **moment** she was gone : a novel / Evan Hunter. Simon & Schuster, 2002. 288 p.

ISBN 9780743237482

1. Brothers and sisters 2. Missing persons 3. People with schizophrenia 4. Twins 5. New York City 6. Psychological suspense

LC 2002070532

When Andrew Gulliver's mother tells him that his erratic twin sister, Annie, has disappeared again, he makes a desperate effort to find her and to figure out whether Annie does, indeed, have schizophrenia.

"Hunter is a masterfully adept storyteller and a very shrewd observer of human behavior. . . . Powerful reading." Booklist.

Hunter, Jillian

Forbidden to love the duke / Jillian Hunter. Onyx Books, 2015. 352 p. Fenwick Sisters affairs

ISBN 9780451470133

1. Regency period (1811-1820) 2. Dukes and duchesses 3. Single fathers 4. Governesses 5. Fathers -- Death 6. Debtor and creditor 7. Interpersonal attraction 8. Men/women relations 9. Nobility 10. Historical romances 11. Regency romances

Her family desperately in need of income, Lady Ivy Fenwick takes work as governess to James the Duke of Ellsworth's wards, and when another suitor moves in on Ivy, James must decide whether to surrender Ivy or fight for the woman he has come to love.

Hunter, Madeline

The **conquest** of Lady Cassandra / Madeline Hunter. Jove, 2013. 325 p. Fairbourne quartet

ISBN 9780515151114

1. Georgian era (1714-1837) 2. 1790s 3. Auctions 4. Young women 5. Jewelry 6. Nobility 7. Sexual attraction 8. Men/women relations 9. Debtor and creditor 10. Scandals 11. Misunderstanding 12. Independence in women 13. Women marriage resisters 14. Dysfunctional families 15. Family secrets 16. London, England -- History -- 18th century 17. Great Britain -- History -- George III, 1760-1820 18. England 19. Historical romances 20. Georgian romances

The impoverished and scandalous Lady Cassandra Vernham tries to get Viscount Ambury to pay her the considerable sum of money that he owes her, but Ambury, who blames her for the death of his friend, is reluctant to help her.

Hunter, Madeline

The **surrender** of Miss Fairbourne / Madeline Hunter. Jove, 2012. 352 p. Fairbourne quartet

ISBN 9780515150469

1. Georgian era (1714-1837) 2. 1790s 3. Auctions 4. Business partners 5. Independence in women 6. Sexual attraction 7. Men/women relations 8. Secrets 9. London, England -- History -- 18th century 10. Great Britain -- History -- George III, 1760-1820 11. England 12. Historical romances 13. Georgian romances

As reluctant business partners, Emma Fairbourne's defiance and Darius Alfreton's demands make it difficult to manage one of London's most eminent auction houses. But their passionate personalities find common ground in an unforgettable affair, until the devastating truth behind their partnership comes to light.

Hunter, Stephen, 1946-

The **47th** samurai / Stephen Hunter. Simon & Schuster, 2007. 480 p. Bob Lee Swagger novels

ISBN 9780743238090

1. Greed 2. Murder investigation 3. Revenge 4. Vietnam veterans 5. Voyages and travels 6. Swords 7. Samurai 8. Murder 9. Tokyo, Japan 10. Japan 11. Thrillers and suspense

LC 2007006627

With a high opinion of loyalty as well as a need to bring about justice -- by any means necessary -- Bob Lee Swagger is a former Marine whose skills are frequently required as he rights wrongs and clears conspiracies. The 47th Samurai takes him to Japan to return a samurai sword to the son of the rightful owner. After he does so, someone slaughters the entire family in order to get the historic sword. Vowing to avenge their murders and retrieve the sword, Bob Lee is drawn into the world of the samurai. -- Description by Shauna Griffin.

"Although heavy on both the explanations of Japanese customs and the sordid world of incredibly savage Japanese criminals, this work is compelling, exciting, and satisfying, a dark adventure that will appeal to thriller fans." Library Journal.

Hunter, Stephen, 1946-

Black light / Stephen Hunter. Doubleday, 1996. 463 p. Bob Lee Swagger novels

ISBN 9780385480420

1. Cold cases (Criminal investigation) 2. Escaped convicts 3. Conspiracies 4. Snipers 5. Fathers -- Death 6. Vietnam veterans 7. Thrillers and suspense

LC 9543079

Forty years after his state trooper father was gunned down by two robbers, Bob Swagger returns to Blue Eye, Arkansas, to find out what really happened and discovers unanswered questions about the shootout and dark secrets that someone will do anything to keep hidden

"Mr. Hunter, who is a powerful and disturbing writer, tells this unholy story in a heroic style that gives mythic sweep to the generational waves of violence that seem to have had no beginning and threaten to have no end." New York Times Book Review.

Hunter, Stephen, 1946-

Dead zero / Stephen Hunter. Simon & Schuster, 2010. 384 p. Bob Lee Swagger novels

ISBN 9781439138656

1. Vietnam veterans 2. Conspiracies 3. Snipers 4. Former Marines 5. International intrigue 6. Afghanistan -- Boundaries 7. Pakistan -- Boundaries 8. Thrillers and suspense

Finds the Marine Corps Master Sniper Bob Lee Swagger traveling to the remote deserts and caves of Afghanistan to track down a renegade Marine who is using extreme measures to complete a mission.

Hunter, Stephen, 1946-

Dirty white boys : a novel / Stephen Hunter. Random House, 1994. 436 p.

ISBN 9780679437512

1. Escaped convicts 2. Chases 3. Violence in men 4. Murderers 5. Escapes 6. State police 7. Oklahoma 8. Texas 9. Thrillers and suspense

LC 9415359

After killing a black inmate, sadistic Lamar Pye flees Oklahoma's McAlester State Pen and embarks on a bloody flight across the Southwest. He's accompanied by his retarded giant of a cousin Odell (who lives for Lamar) and artist-turned-felon Richard Peed (who was allowed to live by Lamar, who likes his crude artwork), and is pursued by Trooper Bud Pewtie (who blames himself for the death of his partner at the hands of this murderous group). Their next face-off can have only one survivor. -- Description by Shauna Griffin.

"The blood-soaked packaging of Mr. Hunter's big, mythic theme is thrilling, in the manner of the ancient storytellers, with battles fierce enough for a war and characters crazy enough to fight them to the death. There is no place to run for cover from this author's proseno glades of pretty writing to cool his vision of a land of lost children, forgotten values and total desolation." New York Times Book Review.

LIST OF FICTIONAL WORKS

Hunter, Stephen, 1946-

Game of snipers : a Bob Lee Swagger novel / Stephen Hunter. G. P. Putnam's'S Son, 2019 400 p. Bob Lee Swagger novels

ISBN 9780399574573

1. Mossad 2. FBI 3. Snipers 4. Extremists 5. Tracking and trailing 6. Guns 7. Assassins 8. Retirement 9. Ammunition 10. Law enforcement 11. Military intelligence 12. Assassination -- Prevention 13. Middle East 14. Idaho 15. Thrillers and suspense

LC 2018044740

Obsessively tracking a sniper with skills that match his own, Bob Lee Swagger teams up with the Mossad, the FBI and local law enforcement to identify the killer's next target.

Hunter, Stephen, 1946-

Havana : an Earl Swagger novel / Stephen Hunter. Simon & Schuster, 2003. 480 p. Earl Swagger novels

ISBN 0743238087

1. Castro, Fidel, 1926-2016 2. CIA. 3. KGB 4. 1950s 5. Americans in Cuba 6. Detectives 7. Organized crime 8. Assassins 9. Revolutionaries 10. World War II veterans 11. Casinos 12. Violence 13. Ethics 14. Cuba -- History -- 1933-1959 15. Thrillers and suspense

LC 2003054461

Sent by the CIA to 1950s Cuba to eliminate young revolutionary Fidel Castro, ex-Marine hero Earl Swagger finds himself confronting outdated ideals about honor and duty as the world around him erupts into early Cold War violence.

"Havana's story line bobs and weaves like a prizefighter, taking the reader in many directions, from barely exciting scenes to intense ones." USA Today.

Hunter, Stephen, 1946-

Hot springs : a novel / Stephen Hunter. Simon & Schuster, 2000. 478 p. Earl Swagger novels

ISBN 068486360X

1. 1940s 2. Violence 3. Gangsters 4. World War II veterans 5. Detectives 6. Coal mining towns 7. World War II veterans 8. Crime bosses 9. Public prosecutors 10. Hot Springs, Arkansas 11. Arkansas 12. Thrillers and suspense

LC 9988530

While many people come to Hot Springs, Arkansas to take the cure in the mineral-rich 142 degree water that bubbles from the earth. In the summer of 1946, the main source of income for the town are the brothels and casinos, run by English-born gangster Owney Maddox, who represents the New York syndicate.

"Once upon a time, hard-boiled implied more than a style; Hunter shows us what the real thing was all about." Booklist.

Hunter, Stephen, 1946-

I, sniper : a Bob Lee Swagger novel / Stephen Hunter. Simon & Schuster, 2010. 400 p. Bob Lee Swagger novels

ISBN 9781416565154

1. Vietnam veterans 2. Peace activists 3. Radicals 4. Murder 5. Murder investigation 6. Conspiracies 7. Snipers 8. Former Marines 9. Tennessee 10. Thrillers and suspense

LC 2009019792

Special Agent Nick Memphis enlists the help of retired Marine sniper Bob Lee Swagger to unravel a sophisticated conspiracy involving the deaths of four famed '60s radicals--a conspiracy that would require the highest level of warcraft by the most superb special operations professionals.

"As with all of Hunter's Swagger novels, there is much more than meets the eye, with cover-ups and nasty villains galore. Swagger is a loner, a paladin, and a violent and politically incorrect corrector of injustice, a cousin to Lee Child's Jack Reacher." Library Journal.

Hunter, Stephen, 1946-

Pale horse coming : a novel / Stephen Hunter. Simon & Schuster, 2001. 491 p. Earl Swagger novels

ISBN 0684863618

1. 1950s 2. Detectives 3. Prisons 4. African American prisoners 5. Conspiracies 6. Racism 7. World War II veterans 8. Missing persons 9. Mississippi -- History -- 20th century 10. Thrillers and suspense

LC 2001047386

In 1951, the disappearance of Sam Vincent, who was investigating a prison for violent African American convicts in Thebes, Mississippi, draws Earl Swagger into a confrontation with a town guarded by a private army of brutal, Klan-type thugs and rednecks.

"In this sequel to Hot Springs, Hunter continues the story of Arkansas state cop Earl Swagger. ʃr The character of Earl Swagger, equal parts gristle and determination, remains compelling, both as archetype and as complex human being." Booklist.

Hunter, Stephen, 1946-

Soft target : a thriller / Stephen Hunter. Simon & Schuster, 2011. 384 p. Ray Cruz novels

ISBN 9781439138700

1. Snipers 2. Terrorism -- Prevention 3. Hostages 4. Former Marines 5. Minneapolis, Minnesota 6. Thrillers and suspense

Ray Cruz first appeared in Stephen Hunter's Dead zero.

Black Friday. America's largest shopping mall, suburban Minneapolis. 3:00 pm. Twelve gunmen open fire in the mall corridors, and take more than a thousand hostage. Cruz, a retired Marine sniper, is taken captive along with his fiancée and her family. He has a plan-- now all he needs is a gun...

Hunter, Stephen, 1946-

Time to hunt : a novel / Stephen Hunter. Doubleday, 1998. 467 p. Bob Lee Swagger novels

ISBN 0385480431

1. CIA 2. Conspiracies 3. Murder 4. Vietnam veterans 5. Snipers 6. Moles (Spies) 7. Assassins 8. Idaho 9. Washington, D.C. 10. Thrillers and suspense

LC 9746985

Vietnam War hero and master sniper Bob Lee Swagger must call on his deadly talents to protect his family from an old foe

"Swagger is a near-mythic character without peer in mystery fiction. He was born to soldier but longs to stop. As we revel in his adventures and triumphs, we also experience his pain." Booklist.

Hunting, Helena

* Handle with care / Helena Hunting. St Martins Pr, 2019. 320 p.

ISBN 9781250183996

1. Chief executive officers 2. Women public relations consultants 3. Families 4. Family businesses 5. Fathers -- Death 6. Brothers 7. Scandals 8. Family secrets 9. Sexual attraction 10. Men/women relations 11. Contemporary romances

He wants to lose control... She's trying to hold it together.

Hurley, Andrew Michael, 1975-

Devil's Day / Andrew Michael Hurley. Houghton Mifflin Harcourt, 2018, c2017. 295 p.

ISBN 9781328489883

1. Newlyweds 2. Superstition 3. Grandfathers -- Death 4. Devil 5. Sheep 6. Farmers 7. Shepherds 8. Rites and ceremonies 9. England 10. Lancashire, England 11. Horror 12. Gothic fiction

LC 2018000259

Originally published: London : John Murray, 2017.

John Pentecost returns to his family farm each autumn to gather the sheep down from the moors, but this year his grandfather has died, and with him the village's protection from the Devil.

"[T]his beautifully told gothic story of love, obligation, and legacy blends genres superbly. Hurley is considered one of the leading figures in what is called the British folk-horror revival." Booklist.

Hurley, Kameron

* The **light** brigade / Kameron Hurley. SAGA Press, 2019. 356 p.

ISBN 9781481447966

1. Women soldiers 2. Teleportation 3. Imaginary wars and battles 4. War 5. Time travel 6. Space and time 7. Soldiers 8. Martians 9. Transportation 10. Corporations 11. Corporate greed 12. Corporate power 13. Mars (Planet) 14. Mars (Planet) -- Colonization 15. Military science fiction 16. Science fiction

To fight a war on Mars, soldiers are broken down into particles of light, but those who survive are experiencing an alarming type of combat madness.

"...this book is both a gripping story of future warfare and an incisive antiwar fable. Readers will savor this striking novels ambitious structure and critique of rapacious, militarized capitalism." Publishers Weekly.

Hurley, Kameron

The **stars** are legion / Kameron Hurley. Simon & Schuster, 2017. 400 p.

ISBN 9781481447935

1. Imaginary wars and battles 2. Royal houses 3. Armistices 4. Sisters 5. Intrigue 6. Revenge 7. Rescues 8. Space vehicles 9. Mothers and daughters 10. Marriage -- Political aspects 11. Manipulation (Social sciences) 12. Space 13. Space opera 14. Science fiction

Amnesiac Zan is a prisoner, although her family?insists that it's for her own good. They also claim that she represents their best hope for saving the Legion, their dying civilization of "world-ships." Yet Zan can't shake the feeling she's been here before, and that her family isn't really her family. Flawed characters and inventive world-building make this novel a good bet for fans of Iain M. Banks' Culture novels. -- Description by Gillian Speace

Hurston, Zora Neale

Hitting a straight lick with a crooked stick : stories from the Harlem Renaissance / Zora Neale Hurston. Amistad Press, 2020. 192 p.

ISBN 9780062915795

1. African Americans 2. Race relations 3. Social classes 4. Prejudice 5. Racism 6. Sexism 7. Short stories 8. Literary fiction 9. African American fiction

Featuring eight lesser-known stories, a collection of Harlem Renaissance tales by the revered folklorist and author of Their Eyes Were Watching God explores subjects ranging from class and migration to racism and sexism.

"With biting wit, Hurston gets to the heart of the human condition, including racism, sexism, and classism, through the circuitous path of her characters, that is, the straight lick with a crooked stick." Booklist.

Hurston, Zora Neale

* **Their** eyes were watching God / Zora Neale Hurston ; with a foreword by Edwidge Danticat. Harper Collins, 2000, c1937. xxii, 231 p.

ISBN 9780060199494

1. 1930s 2. Independence in African American women 3. Scandals 4. Self-fulfillment in African American women 5. African American women 6. Women murder suspects 7. African American men/women relations 8. African American women -- Friendship 9. African American women -- Spiritual life 10. Marriage 11. African American women -- Identity 12. Husband and wife 13. Florida 14. Modern classics 15. Literary fiction 16. Psychological fiction 17. Love stories 18. African American fiction 19. Southern fiction

LC 00058186

Originally published: Philadelphia : J.B. Lippincott Co., 1937.

When Janie Starks returns home, she seeks identity and independence as the small southern black community buzzes with gossip about the outcome of her affair with a younger man.

Hurwitz, Gregg Andrew

The **crime** writer / Gregg Hurwitz. Viking, 2007. 320 p.

ISBN 9780670063215

1. Authors 2. Murder -- Los Angeles, California 3. Good and evil 4. Former fiancées 5. Murder investigation -- Los Angeles, California 6. Crime writing 7. Authors 8. Amateur detectives 9. Los Angeles, California 10. California 11. Mysteries

LC 2006052822

Drew Danner, a crime novelist with a house off L.A.'s storied Mulholland Drive, awakens in a hospital bed with a scar on his head and no memory of being found convulsing over his ex-fiancée's body the previous night. He was discovered holding a knife, her blood beneath his nails. He himself doesn't know whether he's guilty or innocent. To reconstruct the story, the writer must now become the protagonist, searching the corridors of his life and the city he loves. Soon Drew closes in on clues he may or may not have left for himself, and as another young woman is similarly murdered he has to ask difficult questions--not of others but of himself.

"Successful crime-novelist Drew Danner has gained true tabloid fame-as the murderer of his ex-fiancée. Found by the police in the midst of a brain-tumor-induced grand mal seizure, with her blood covering his hands and his fingerprints on the murder weapon, Danner seems to be the only person in L.A. who isn't sure he is a killer. Emergency surgery after his arrest removes the tumor, and a temporary insanity defense frees him, but his comfortable life is shattered. He can't live without knowing if he killed a woman he once loved. His only choice is to become a character in a story he hasn't written. Danner's anguish is compellingly described, and the plot has more twists and turns than Mulholland Drive." Booklist.

Hurwitz, Gregg Andrew

Hellbent : an orphan X novel / Gregg Hurwitz. Minotaur Books, 2018. 416 p. Evan Smoak thrillers

ISBN 9781250119179

1. Assassins 2. Intelligence service 3. Secrecy in government 4. Former assassins 5. Assassination 6. Fugitives 7. Captives 8. Justice 9. Thrillers and suspense

LC 2017036261

When the man who raised and trained him warns him that secret government forces are trying to eliminate all surviving members of the

Orphan Program, Evan Smoak is challenged to track down and protect his teacher's last protégé from a brutal new Program leader.

"This is a great novel, perhaps the darkest in the series so far. ... The story moves as fast as a bullet train, and we've never seen Evan Smoak as emotionally exposed as he is here. Do not miss this one." Booklist.

Hurwitz, Gregg Andrew
* **Into** the fire / Gregg Hurwitz. Minotaur Books, 2020. 400 p. Evan Smoak thrillers
ISBN 9781250120458
1. Former assassins 2. Money laundering 3. Protectiveness in men 4. Murder victims 5. Murder 6. Crime bosses 7. Organized crime 8. Secrets 9. Men/women relations 10. Thrillers and suspense
LC 2019035900

Helping a murder victim's cousin who is being violently pursued for a mysterious key, Nowhere Man Evan Smoak eliminates a series of dangerous threats before discovering that he is being personally targeted.

"Another exceptional installment in the Orphan X series, full of action, excitement, and adventure. A must-read for thriller fans." Library Journal.

Hurwitz, Gregg Andrew
The **Nowhere** Man / Gregg Hurwitz. Minotaur Books, 2017. 352 p. Evan Smoak thrillers
ISBN 9781250067852
1. Assassins 2. Kidnapping 3. Intelligence service 4. Secrecy in government 5. Former assassins 6. Assassination 7. Fugitives 8. Captives 9. Justice 10. Thrillers and suspense
In this sequel to Orphan X, former assassin Evan Smoak (now a freelance vigilante delivering justice) is being pursued by his ex-colleagues from the Orphan Program. They taught him everything he knows about killing, escaping, and disappearing, and they consider him a huge threat to their shadowy organization. Kidnapped and held hostage as his enemies get closer, the story really picks up when his captors realize that though they've trapped him, they're also trapped?with?him. Moving at a blistering pace, this white-hot read combines the moves of Jack Reacher, the skills of Jason Bourne, and the brains and money of Tony Stark.? -- Description by Shauna Griffin

"Thriller fans craving action and violence will enjoy this one." Kirkus.

Hurwitz, Gregg Andrew
Orphan X / Gregg Hurwitz. Minotaur Books, 2016. 352 p. Evan Smoak thrillers
ISBN 9781250067845
1. Secrecy in government 2. Former assassins 3. Vigilantes 4. Assassins 5. Intelligence service 6. Assassination 7. Fugitives 8. Justice 9. Thrillers and suspense
RUSA Reading List, 2017.
Evan Smoak, the Nowhere Man a protector of the truly desperate and deserving, finds himself a target of someone with similar training and knowledge of his Orphan X identity.

"Hurwitz, known for this kind of adrenaline-producing fiction . . . adds enough humanity to the action to make this a standout, and readers should get in at the start." Booklist.

Hurwitz, Gregg Andrew
* **Out** of the dark : the return of Orphan X / Gregg Hurwitz. Minotaur Books, 2019. 400 p. Evan Smoak thrillers
ISBN 9781250120427
1. Assassins 2. Former assassins 3. Presidents -- United States -- Assassination plots 4. Secrecy in government 5. Assassination 6.

Fugitives 7. Justice 8. Thrillers and suspense
LC 2018029794

Evan Smoak, a.k.a., the Nowhere Man, is pitted against one of his own for the future of the country when a murderous President Bennett activates the Orphan program's first recruit.

Hurwitz, Gregg Andrew
The **survivor** / Gregg Hurwitz. St. Martin's Press, 2012, c2011. 416 p.
ISBN 9780312625511
1. Veterans 2. Bank robbers -- Los Angeles, California 3. Coercion 4. Kidnapping 5. Men 6. Death threats 7. Protectiveness in men 8. Suicidal behavior 9. Los Angeles, California 10. Psychological suspense
LC 2012013914

Attempting suicide only to foil a bank robbery and receive a blackmail note from a robbers, Nate, a traumatized former soldier with ALS, is kidnapped by a Russian mobster who threatens Nate's family to force him to complete the robbery.

Hurwitz, Gregg Andrew
They're watching / Gregg Hurwitz. St. Martin's, 2010, c2009. 368 p.
ISBN 9780312534905
1. Electronic surveillance 2. Stalking 3. Films -- Production and direction 4. Marital conflict 5. Married people 6. Husband and wife 7. Screenwriters 8. Privacy 9. Paranoia 10. Film actors and actresses 11. Frameups 12. Stalkers 13. California 14. Thrillers and suspense
LC 2009047039

Originally published in the UK under the title, Or she dies (London: Sphere,2009)/

Struggling with setbacks in his marriage and Hollywood ambitions, Patrick Davis begins receiving mysterious DVDs that reveal that he and his wife are being stalked, a situation that is thrown into further turmoil by a mysterious e-mail offer of assistance.

"This is a very well constructed thriller, full of twists and turns and unexpected revelations. Hurwitz frequently sets us up to expect one thing but delivers something entirely different. He keeps us constantly on our toes, and--this is especially good--he keeps us guessing right until the very last pages about exactly who has targeted Patrick and why. ." Booklist.

Hurwitz, Gregg Andrew
You're next / Gregg Hurwitz. St. Martin's Press, 2011. 416 p.
ISBN 9780312534912
1. Death threats 2. Protectiveness in men 3. Orphans 4. Family secrets 5. Threat (Psychology) 6. Foster care 7. Assassins 8. Married men 9. Husband and wife 10. Fathers and daughters 11. Psychological suspense
LC 2011006869

The Boss Man has an unexpected motive in destroying Mike Wingate, who's worked his way up from the bottom to become a successful home contractor in Lost Hills, California. To protect his family and himself, Mike, who was raised in a foster home, summons his only friend from those days, the formidable Shep, who has grown up to be a career criminal of considerable skill.

"A thriller that grabs readers by the seat of the pants and gives them a Wow, what next! action thrill ride." Kirkus.

Huston, Charlie

Caught stealing / Charlie Huston. Ballantine, 2004. 272 p. Henry Thompson novels

ISBN 034546477X

1. Former baseball players 2. Mafia -- Russia 3. Bartenders 4. Money 5. Cats 6. Neighbors 7. Men and cats 8. Violence 9. Manhattan, New York City 10. Lower East Side, New York City 11. Crime fiction

Henry "Hank" Thompson, who once played California baseball, has moved to the Lower East Side of Manhattan, and works as a bartender. Hank's neighbor Russ has to leave town in a rush and hands over his cat Bud to Hank to take care of. When two Russians in tracksuits beat Hank to a pulp, he starts to get the idea: someone wants something from him.

"[This book] definitely belongs on every Elmore Leonard fan's to-read list. One note of caution: Lovers of mystery-solving felines should place paws over eyes during the hair-raising cat torture scene." Booklist.

Huston, Charlie

Every last drop : a novel / Charlie Huston. Del Rey, 2008. 272 p. Joe Pitt casebook

ISBN 9780345495884

1. Vampires 2. Enemies 3. Violence 4. Crime 5. Private investigators 6. Manhattan, New York City 7. Fantasy mysteries

LC 2008026441

An outcast among his fellow vampires in Manhattan, vampire P.I. Joe Pitt is coerced by Dexter Predo, the minister of the Coalition Clan, into infiltrating Cure, the newest Clan, only to find himself trying to discover where the powerful Coalition gets all their blood.

Huston, Charlie

Half the blood of Brooklyn : a novel / Charlie Huston. Del Rey Ballantine Books, 2008. 240 p. Joe Pitt cas(ebk.)

ISBN 9780345495877

1. People with AIDS 2. Murder 3. Vampires 4. Crime 5. Private investigators 6. Brooklyn, New York City 7. Fantasy mysteries

LC 2007028330

Sent to Brooklyn to investigate the murder of a blood dealer, vampyre detective Joe Pitt comes face to face with the most peculiar Vampyres he has ever encountered, all the while struggling to deal with his ailing girlfriend, Evie, who is rapidly running out of time.

"Huston's formidable writing chops are on full display: his action scenes are unparalleled in crime fiction and his dialogue is so hip and dead-on that Elmore Leonard should be getting nervous." Publishers Weekly.

Huston, Charlie

The **shotgun** rule : a novel / Charlie Huston. Ballantine Books, 2007. 248 p.

ISBN 9780345481351

1. 1980s 2. Teenage boys 3. Drug control 4. Drug dealers 5. Working class teenagers 6. Suburbs 7. Stealing 8. Drug industry and trade 9. Secrets 10. Police misconduct 11. California 12. Coming-of-age stories 13. Thrillers and suspense

LC 2007020511

Seeking revenge for the theft of a bicycle, four teenage friends discover that the missing item is in the hands of the Arroyo brothers, one of whom is just out of prison, and set out to retrieve it, stumbling upon a methamphetamine lab in the process.

"From a sharp pitch, staccato dialogue and volatile action, durable characters and an intricate plot emerge, demonstrating Huston can still deliver the expected thriller goods." Paste.

Huston, Charlie

Skinner / Charlie Huston. Mulholland Books/Little, Brown and Company, 2013. 320 p.

ISBN 9780316133722

1. CIA 2. Intelligence officers 3. Cyberterrorism 4. Terrorists 5. Bodyguards 6. Guerrilla warfare 7. Fear 8. Robotics 9. Mumbai, India 10. Thrillers and suspense 11. Cyber-thrillers

LC 2013001055

A fringe CIA agent unites with a roboticist to help bring down an elaborate cyber-terrorist attack that originated in Mumbai.

Hustvedt, Siri

The **blazing** world / Siri Hustvedt. Simon & Schuster, 2014. 320 p.

ISBN 9781476747231

1. Women artists 2. Gender role 3. Anger in women 4. Scandals 5. Death 6. Deception 7. Widows 8. Art -- Collectors and collecting 9. Art critics 10. Feminism 11. Identity (Psychology) 12. Women with depression 13. Psychological fiction 14. Literary fiction

LC 2013027172

Kirkus Prize for Fiction finalist, 2014.

A provocative tale told through a series of scholarly texts draws on notebooks and conflicting accounts about the life and work of an acclaimed artist who after years of being marginalized conceals her female identity behind three male fronts.

"Hustvedt subtly explores the intricate workings of the brain and the mysteries of the mind as she shrewdly investigates gender differences, parodies art criticism, and contrasts diabolical ambition and the soul-scouring inquiries of expressive art." Booklist.

Huxley, Aldous, 1894-1963

* **Brave** new world / Aldous Huxley. Perennial Classics, 1998, c1932. xvii, 270 p.

ISBN 0060929871

1. 26th century 2. Dystopias 3. Far future 4. Totalitarianism 5. Passivity (Psychology) 6. Genetic engineering 7. Collectivism 8. Dystopian fiction 9. Science fiction 10. Modern classics

LC 98008385

Originally published: Garden City, N.Y. : Doubleday, Doran & company, inc., 1932.

Cloning, feel-good drugs, anti-aging programs, and total social control through politics, programming and media--has Aldous Huxley accurately predicted our future? With a storyteller's genius, he weaves these ethical controversies in a compelling narrative that dawns in the year 632 A.F. (After Ford, the deity). When Lenina and Bernard visit a savage reservation, we experience how Utopia can destroy humanity.

Huyler, Frank, 1964-

The **laws** of invisible things / Frank Huyler. H. Holt, 2004. 320 p.

ISBN 9780805073300

1. Physicians 2. Physician and patient 3. Sick persons 4. Diseases 5. Communicable diseases 6. Guilt 7. North Carolina 8. Medical thrillers

LC 2003051116

A young doctor's struggle to understand what appears to be a deadly new virus takes him on a journey into the hinterland between religion and science, leading him to question his beliefs and search for new modes of thinking.

"Although the story elements are melodramatic, the intimate tone of Huyler's elegiac voice invites us to rise above our disgust and think again about the things we think we know." New York Times Book Review.

Hynes, James

Kings of infinite space / James Hynes. St. Martin's Press, 2004. 341 p.

ISBN 031245645X

1. Temporary employees 2. Office workers 3. Divorced men 4. Technical writing 5. Government contractors 6. Loss (Psychology) 7. Supernatural 8. Cat ghosts 9. Work 10. Office romance 11. Men/women relations 12. Faustian bargains 13. Texas 14. Black humor 15. Thrillers and suspense 16. Satirical fiction

LC 2003058563

Contains characters from "Queen of the jungle," a short story found in author's Publish and perish collection.

"This is social satire that slides smoothly and surreally into horror, and if it loses a little of its emotional heft in the process, you don't really miss it. The glee with which Hynes choreographs an in-office zombie-vs.-stapler fight scene is compensation enough." Time.

Hynes, James

Next : a novel / James Hynes. Little, Brown and Co., 2010. 320 p.

ISBN 9780316051927

1. Middle-aged men -- Psychology 2. Self-discovery in men 3. Life change events 4. Second chances 5. Midlife crisis 6. Job hunting 7. Terrorism 8. Men/women relations 9. Austin, Texas 10. Satirical fiction 11. Literary fiction

LC 2009008490

ALA Notable Book, 2011.

Flying to a secret job interview in Texas in the wake of an unsatisfying relationship and career, Kevin Quinn falls for a fellow passenger and obsessively worries about terrorist threats in Europe while spending an ensuing eight hours hoping for personal reinvention.

I

Ibrahim, Abubakar Adam

Season of crimson blossoms / Abubakar Adam Ibrahim Cassava Republic Press, 2016 313 p.

ISBN 9781911115007

1. Widows 2. Drug dealers 3. May-December romance 4. Loyalty 5. Propriety 6. Public opinion 7. Interclass romance 8. Family relationships 9. Men/women relations 10. Nigeria -- Social conditions 11. Love stories 12. Literary fiction

LC 2016387320

"Parresiq koos"

An affair between 55-year-old widow Binta Zubairu and 25-year-old weed dealer Reza was bound to provoke condemnation in conservative Northern Nigeria. Brought together in unusual circumstances, Binta and Reza faced a need they could only satisfy in each other.

Ide, Joe

* **Hi** five : an IQ novel / Joe Ide. Mulholland Books, 2020. 341 p. IQ novels

ISBN 9780316509534

1. African Americans 2. Private investigators 3. Dissociative identity disorder 4. Women witnesses 5. Women murder suspects 6. Organized crime 7. Murder investigation 8. Clues 9. City life 10. Men/women relations 11. Los Angeles, California 12. Mysteries

Finds genius private investigator Isaiah Quintabe's efforts to build a quiet life with Grace challenged by unexpected new threats.

"Ide goes dark with the skill of a noir master, leaving Isaiah in a very bad place and the reader gasping for breath. A stunning change of pace from one of crime fiction's new stars." Booklist.

Iggulden, Conn

The **abbot's** tale / Conn Iggulden. Pegasus Books, 2018. 480 p.

ISBN 9781681777306

1. Alfred,, King of England, 849-899 2. Medieval period (476-1492) 3. Anglo-Saxon period (449-1066) 4. 9th century 5. Rulers 6. Clergy 7. Ambition in men 8. Political intrigue 9. Battles 10. Imperialism 11. Manipulation (Social sciences) 12. Great Britain -- History -- Alfred, 871-899 13. Historical fiction

At the side of Alfred the Great in 973, priest Dunstan of Glastonbury helps guide England into a unified country.

Ignatius, David, 1950-

Body of lies : a novel / David Ignatius. W. W. Norton & Co., 2007. 320 p.

ISBN 9780393065039

1. CIA 2. Intelligence service -- United States 3. International intrigue 4. Terrorists 5. Terrorism 6. Deception 7. Soldiers 8. Spies 9. Antiterrorists 10. Europe 11. Middle East 12. Spy fiction

LC 2006102362

Emerging from a tour of duty in Iraq with a badly injured leg, CIA soldier Roger Ferris takes on a mission to infiltrate the network of a master terrorist and bases his plan on a British intelligence operation from World War II.

"Unlike most of the folks writing fiction about the CIA these days, [Ignatius] understands the gestalt of the place and the internal and external pressure under which the agency's denizens operate." Washington Times.

Ignatius, David, 1950-

A **firing** offense / David Ignatius. Random House, 1997. 333 p.

ISBN 9780679448600

1. CIA 2. Journalists 3. Spy fiction

LC 96-29518

Journalist Eric Truell risks his career and his life when his source at the CIA, a maverick CIA agent, leaks word about a private trade war between France, China, and the U.S., a competition in which his own newspaper may be playing an unwitting role.

"Thanks to great writing and an all-too-human protagonist, the preaching is kept to a minimum, but the sermon--about good journalism and bad, truth and lies--is there in bold letters." Publishers Weekly.

Ignatius, David, 1950-

The **increment** : a novel / David Ignatius. W. W. Norton & Co., 2009. 400 p.

ISBN 9780393065046

1. CIA 2. Nuclear weapons -- Iran 3. Nuclear physicists -- Iran 4. Intelligence officers -- United States 5. Spies 6. Codes (Communication) 7. Escapes 8. Intelligence officers 9. Tehran, Iran 10. Spy fiction

LC 2008053857

When a Tehrani scientist sends encrypted messages to the CIA about Iran's secret nuclear program, Harry Pappas commences communication with him, positive that his information is legitimate. As the agency looks into pretexts for attacking Iran, the scientist grows certain that his life is in danger. Therefore, Pappas enlists the help of British operatives, the Increment, who possess licenses to kill. As the ordeal grows in complexity, Pappas may have to betray his country to find a resolution.

"The author immerses readers in a totally believable universe. Jargon, geography and detail all ring true as his meticulously crafted, tightly woven tale moves from Washington to London and Iran. The plot grabs everything in its path like a snowball rolling down a hill." Kirkus.

Ignatius, David, 1950-

The **sun** king : a novel / David Ignatius. Random House, 1999. 305 p.

ISBN 9780679448617

1. Publishers and publishing 2. Women journalists 3. Billionaires 4. Men/women relations 5. Washington, D.C. 6. Political thrillers
LC 99013490

Charismatic billionaire Sandy Galvin comes to the nation's capital and proceeds to turn it upside down by purchasing the city's most powerful newspaper to challenge the power brokers of Washington, D.C., until he encounters his former Harvard flame, Candace Ridgway, a beautiful journalist known as the "Mistress of Fact"

"A thoroughly involving narrative with a sharp, satiric edge, Ignatius's contemporary take on the tragic confluence of love, power and ambition is a sophisticated look at the media mystique and the movers and shakers in our nation's capitol. His stylish, fluent prose, anchored with fine atmospheric detail, gives the story texture and momentum." Publishers Weekly.

Iles, Greg

Black cross / Greg Iles. Dutton, 1995. 516 p.

ISBN 9780525938293

1. 1940s 2. Concentration camps 3. Assassins 4. Physicians 5. World War II 6. Secret service 7. Holocaust (1933-1945) 8. Nazis 9. Chemical warfare 10. Germany -- History -- 20th century 11. Thrillers and suspense
LC 94034642

An American doctor and a Jewish soldier embark on a perilous mission into Nazi Germany to ensure a D-Day victory for Allied forces by uncovering a doomsday weapon and committing a soul-destroying act of devastation.

"This novel tells the story of a physician from Georgia and a German Jew who manage to forestall Hitler's use of poison nerve gas during World War II by destroying a secret laboratory hidden in a Nazi death camp. The rash plan for infiltrating the camp and destroying the laboratory has been developed by the Allies and led by Winston Churchill and will require nerves of steel, physical and emotional stamina, unparalleled bravery, and incredible luck. If it works, millions of lives will be saved. But there is a horrible price to pay for the larger victoryhundreds of Jewish prisoners interred in the camp may also die. From the very first page, Iles takes his readers on an emotional roller-coaster ride, juxtaposing tension-filled action scenes, horrifying depictions of savage cruelty, and heart-stopping descriptions of sacrifice and bravery." Booklist.

Iles, Greg

* The **bone** tree : a novel / Greg Iles. William Morrow, 2015 816 p. Penn Cage novels

ISBN 9780062311115

1. Ku-Klux Klan 2. Malicious accusation 3. Police corruption 4. Father and adult son 5. Race relations 6. Justice 7. Duty 8. Mississippi 9. Natchez, Mississippi 10. Thrillers and suspense 11. Legal thrillers
LC 2014042113

A follow-up to Natchez Burning finds Southern lawyer Penn Cage desperately struggling to protect his father from false charges and corrupt officers by confronting the puppet master behind the Double Eagles terrorist group.

"In a scenario swarming with FBI agents . . . villains, reporters, and a red herring or two, Iles allows Cage and Masters plenty of room to

operate--and so they do, with all the missteps of ordinary people, unlike the supercops and superagents of so many other procedurals." Kirkus.

Iles, Greg

Cemetery road : a novel / Greg Iles. William Morrow, 2019. 752 p.

ISBN 9780062824615

1. Investigative journalists 2. Secret societies 3. Small town life 4. Amateur detectives 5. Rich people 6. Friendship 7. Betrayal 8. Secrets 9. Corruption 10. Murder 11. Murder investigation 12. Mississippi 13. Mysteries

His father's terminal illness, his family's struggling newspaper, and a politically charged murder trial force a Washington journalist to return to his small Mississippi hometown.

"Iles once again delivers a sweeping tale of family dysfunction, sexually charged secrets, and the power of wealth, with an overlay of violence and Southern sensibility. Despite the novels length, it all goes by in a flash." Publishers Weekly.

Iles, Greg

The **devil's** punchbowl / Greg Iles. Simon & Schuster, 2009. 480 p. Penn Cage novels

ISBN 9780743292511

1. Mayors 2. Murder 3. Gambling and crime 4. Racism 5. Violent crimes 6. Betrayal 7. Violence 8. Mississippi 9. Natchez, Mississippi 10. Legal thrillers 11. Thrillers and suspense

A deep river pit in Natchez, Mississippi, reputed to be the hiding spot for Jean Lafitte's hidden treasure and a dumping ground for numerous murder victims, becomes the site of a dangerous showdown for Penn Cage.

"Penn Cage, a former prosecuting attorney-turned-novelist, is now mayor of Natchez, MS, his hometown. But all is not well, for the promises he made as a candidate seem all but impossible to achieve as a working mayor. When one of his childhood friends is murdered a day after contacting him with information concerning dog fighting, prostitution, drugs, and money laundering presided over by the manager of a Natchez gambling casino, Cage takes on an investigation that makes him the target of organized crime, endangers the lives of his family and closest friends, and draws the wrath of the Justice Department and Homeland Security. . . . Provides a thrill a minute." Library Journal.

Iles, Greg

The **footprints** of God / Greg Iles. Scribner, 2003. 459 p.

ISBN 9780743234696

1. United States. National Security Agency. 2. Artificial intelligence 3. Scientists 4. Murder 5. Fugitives 6. Assassins 7. Technological innovations 8. Information technology 9. Medical ethics 10. Women psychiatrists 11. Dreams 12. Nightmares 13. Chess 14. North Carolina 15. Techno-thrillers 16. Thrillers and suspense
LC 2003045733

Resisting those who would use a revolutionary new technology for unethical purposes, doctor David Tennant and psychiatrist Rachel Weiss run for their lives from ruthless NSA agents and turn to David's unusual dreams for guidance.

"Readers interested in the exploration of religious themes without the usual New Age blather or window-dressed dogma will snap up this novel of cutting-edge science." Publishers Weekly.

Iles, Greg

* **Mississippi** blood : a novel / Greg Iles. William Morrow, 2017. 694 p. Penn Cage novels

ISBN 9780062311153

1. Ku-Klux Klan 2. Hate groups 3. Murder suspects 4. Father and

adult son 5. African American authors 6. Murder investigation 7. White supremacists 8. Police corruption 9. Trials (Murder) 10. Hate crimes 11. Racism 12. Mississippi -- Race relations 13. Natchez, Mississippi 14. Thrillers and suspense 15. Legal thrillers

LC 2016043631

Grief-stricken and with his world collapsing around him, Penn Cage is shut out of trial preparations by his once-revered Southern doctor father, who is about to be tried for murder in the wake of revelations about a mixed-race child and KKK associations.

"Iles wraps up his massively ambitious Natchez Burning trilogy with a book that is (in keeping with its predecessors) compelling, dark, surprising, and morally ambiguous." Booklist.

Iles, Greg

Mortal fear / Greg Iles. Dutton, 1997. 564 p.

ISBN 9780525937920

1. FBI 2. Sex crimes 3. Serial murders 4. Innocence (Law) 5. Virtual sex 6. Internet pornography 7. Impostors 8. Internet 9. Thrillers and suspense

When the woman with whom he has been having an online affair is murdered by a serial killer specializing in female clients of EROS, an exclusive, erotic online service, Harper Cole devises a plan to impersonate his dead lover online, hoping to lead the killer out into the open.

"Despite the artifice of the characters operating it, the technology involved in their ingenious computer chase which gives new meaning to the term 'network' is fascinating." New York Times Book Review.

Iles, Greg

* **Natchez** burning : a novel / Greg Iles. William Morrow, 2014. 656 p. Penn Cage novels

ISBN 9780062311078

1. Ku-Klux Klan 2. Father and adult son 3. Malicious accusation 4. Cold cases (Criminal investigation) 5. Race relations 6. Justice 7. Duty 8. Mississippi 9. Natchez, Mississippi 10. Thrillers and suspense 11. Legal thrillers

LC 2013031971

Penn Cage must investigate when his father, a beloved family doctor and pillar of the community, is accused of murdering Viola Turner, the beautiful nurse with whom he worked in the dark days of the early 1960s.

"Much more than a thriller. . . . This superlative novel's main strength comes from the lead's struggle to balance family and honor." Publishers Weekly.

Iles, Greg

Third degree : a novel / Greg Iles. Scribner, 2007. 528 p.

ISBN 9780743292504

1. Pregnant women 2. Extramarital affairs 3. Anger in men 4. Married people 5. Physicians 6. Marital conflict 7. Tax evasion investigation 8. Hostage taking 9. Love triangles 10. Secrets 11. Threat (Psychology) 12. Thrillers and suspense

A tale spanning a traumatic single day follows Liz Pike, who awakens in her small-town home to discover her husband frantically preparing for what he claims is an IRS audit. She soon realizes, however, that he has discovered the truth about her affair with another man.

Iles, Greg

Turning angel / Greg Iles. Scribner, 2005. 501 p. Penn Cage novels

ISBN 9780743234719

1. Crimes against teenage girls 2. Physicians 3. Murder investigation 4. Lawyers 5. Attorney and client 6. Murder suspects 7. Widowers 8. Best friends 9. Teenage girls -- Relations with older men 10. Teenage drug users 11. Trials (Murder) 12. Private schools 13. Murder 14.

Sexuality 15. Mississippi 16. Natchez, Mississippi 17. Legal thrillers 18. Thrillers and suspense

LC 2005054469

When the body of Kate Townsend turns up near the Mississippi River and his close friend, physician Drew Elliott, admits to a love affair with the murdered girl, attorney Penn Cage once again tangles with the dark side of his hometown of Natchez, Mississippi, to investigate the secret world of an elite nearby high school, teenage sex, drugs, and violence.

"All this is lurid in the extreme and, in Iles's hands, entirely gripping, but there is more to Turning Angel than sex and scandal. Iles offers an insider's heartfelt picture of a Southern town that is dying because of lousy schools, a failing economy and racial tensionsand, again, there is no reason to think Natchez is unique. Iles populates this town with characters who are all too real and makes clear that its privileged young people no longer live isolated lives. . . . This is a powerful piece of popular fiction." Washington Post Book World.

Inbinder, Gary

The **hanged** man : a mystery in fin-de-siecle Paris / Gary Inbinder. Pegasus Crime, 2016 236 p. Inspector Lefebvre novels

ISBN 9781681771649

1. Belle Epoque (1871-1914) 2. 1880s 3. Vacations 4. Seaside resorts 5. Spies 6. Suicide 7. Trust in men 8. Detectives 9. Murder investigation 10. Historical mysteries

A seaside holiday for Inspector Lefebvre and his wife is disrupted by a suspicious suicide that forces the inspector to team up with his former partner, Inspector Rousseau, in a shadowy underworld of international intrigue, espionage and terrorism.

"Will the Inspector risk Delphine's life along with his own to save half of Paris from being blown to bits? A case every bit as baffling as the hero's debut. Here's hoping for another entry in this atmospheric series." Kirkus.

Irvin, Kelly

Tell her no lies / Kelly Irvin. Thomas Nelson, 2018 352 p.

ISBN 9780785223115

1. Women journalists 2. Uncles -- Death 3. Malicious accusation 4. Family relationships 5. Lawyers 6. Family secrets 7. Faith (Christianity) 8. Trust 9. San Antonio, Texas 10. Texas 11. Christian romantic suspense

LC 2018028548

"Nina Fischer carries a camera wherever she goes--so she can view life through a filter. Safely. After her mother abandoned her to the streets, Nina has kept people at a distance, including her uncle, who adopted Nina and her sister. Wealthy and proud, he is a good man, a fair judge, and someone many in San Antonio admire. But when he is murdered, and the detective assigned to the case accuses Nina of the crime, she knows she must act. She's determinedto use her journalism background to find the real killer. The two men in her life want to help, but can she trust them? She's known Rick since they were children, but now he's an attorney whose political aspirations seem more important than Nina's tragic loss. And then there's Aaron, a news videographer; using their friendship could break the biggest story of his career. Following the evidence leads Nina on a journey of discovery into her father's shocking masquerade as a law-abiding, family-loving Christian. Unlocking these secrets could prove fatal, but it's the only way Nina will ever be able to trust love again."--, Provided by publisher.

Irving, John, 1942-

Avenue of mysteries : a novel / John Irving. Simon & Schuster, 2015. 460 p.

ISBN 9781451664164

1. Fate and fatalism 2. Memory 3. Dreams 4. Aging 5. Voyages and travels 6. Space and time 7. Philippines 8. Mexico 9. Literary fiction 10. Psychological fiction

LC 2015005193

Embarking on a trip to the Philippines, senior-aged Juan Diego reflects on dreams and memories of his childhood in Mexico before his past and present intersect in unexpected ways.

"Irving works his familiar themes--Catholicism, sex, death--with a light and assured touch, and though the dream-narrative construct is a little shelf-worn, it serves the story well. Though not as irresistible as early works such as The World According to Garp and The Hotel New Hampshire, a welcome return to form." Kirkus.

Irving, John, 1942-

* The **Cider** House rules : a novel / John Irving. W. Morrow, 1985. 560 p.

ISBN 9780688030360

1. Orphans -- Maine 2. Orphanages -- Maine 3. Physician drug abusers 4. Obstetricians -- Maine 5. Rural life -- Maine 6. Abortion 7. Ether (Anesthetic) 8. Intergenerational relations 9. Maine 10. Literary fiction 11. Modern classics

LC 84027195

Set in rural Maine in the first half of the 20th century, it tells the story of Dr. Wilbur Larch--saint and obstetrician, founder and director of the orphanage in the town of St. Cloud's, ether addict and abortionist. It is also the story of Dr. Larch's favorite orphan, Homer Wells, who is never adopted.

"The Cider House Rules is filled with people to love and to feel for. . . . The characters in John Irving's novel break all the rules, and yet they remain noble and free-spirited. Victims of tragedy, violence, and injustice, their lives seem more interesting and full of thought-provoking dilemmas than the lives of many real people." Houston Post.

Irving, John, 1942-

In one person : a novel / John Irving. Simon & Schuster, 2012. 424 p.

ISBN 9781451664126

1. Authors, American 2. Bisexuality 3. AIDS and sexuality 4. Secrecy 5. Bisexual men 6. Identity (Psychology) 7. Vermont 8. New England 9. Psychological fiction

LC 2011039707

Lambda Literary Award for Bisexual Literature

A tale inspired by the U.S. AIDS epidemic in the 1980s follows the experiences of individuals--including the bisexual narrator, Billy--who are torn by devastating losses and whose perspectives on tolerance and love are shaped by awareness of what might have been.

Irving, John, 1942-

* A **prayer** for Owen Meany : a novel / John Irving. W. Morrow, 1989. 543 p.

ISBN 9780688077082

1. 1950s 2. Misfits (Persons) 3. Messiahs 4. Christians -- New Hampshire 5. Tallness and shortness 6. Male friendship 7. Precognition 8. New Hampshire 9. Psychological fiction 10. Modern classics

LC 88013839

A prayer for Owen Meany was the inspiration for the movie Simon Birch.

ALA Notable Book, 1990.

Owen Meany hits a foul ball while playing baseball in the summer of 1953 that kills his best friend's mother, an accident that Owen is sure is the result of divine intervention.

"Despite its theological proppings, A Prayer for Owen Meany is a fable of political predestination. As usual, Irving delivers a boisterous cast, a spirited story line and a quality of prose that is frequently underestimated even by his admirers. On the other hand, the novel invites trespass by symbol hunters. . . . To get lost in critical rummage would be to miss the point. Irving's litany of error and folly may strike some as too righteous; but it is effective." Time.

Irving, John, 1942-

* The **world** according to Garp : a novel / John Irving. Modern Library, 1998, c1978. xvi, 688 p.

ISBN 9780679603061

1. Authors, American -- 20th century 2. Feminism 3. Eccentrics and eccentricities 4. Mothers and sons 5. Children of single parents 6. Coming-of-age stories 7. Modern classics

40th anniversary edition published by EP Dutton, 2018.

National Book Critics Circle Award for Fiction finalist, 1978

T. S. Garp, a man with high ambitions for an artistic career and with obsessive devotion to his wife and children, and Jenny Fields, his famous feminist mother, find their lives surrounded by an assortment of people including teachers, whores, and radicals.

"This is a long family novel, spanning four generations and two continents, crammed with incidents, characters, feelings and craft. The components of black comedy and melodrama, pathos and tragedy, mesh effortlessly in a tale that can also be read as a commentary on art and the imagination." Time.

Irwin, Stephen M.

The **broken** ones : a novel / Stephen M. Irwin. Doubleday, 2012. 368 p.

ISBN 9780385534659

1. Detectives 2. Life after death 3. Serial murder investigation 4. Police corruption 5. Ghosts 6. Crimes against young women 7. Supernatural mysteries

When everyone in the world finds themselves suddenly accompanied by a personal ghost that only the haunted can see, the situation throws society into chaos and creates complications for homicide detective Oscar Mariani.

Irwin, Stephen M.

The **dead** path : a novel / Stephen M. Irwin. Doubleday, 2010. 400 p.

ISBN 9780385533430

1. Widowers 2. Psychics 3. Missing children 4. Ghosts 5. Soul 6. Guilt 7. Violence 8. Murder 9. Australia 10. Horror

LC 2009053661

RUSA Reading List, 2011.

After the death of his wife, Nicholas Close becomes haunted, literally, by ghosts. Torn by guilt and fearing for his sanity, he returns home to Tallong, Australia, and becomes entangled in a disturbing series of disappearances and murders--both as a suspect and as the next victim of the malignant evil lurking in the heart of the woods.

"Irwin writes in a lyrical style that expresses both the poignancy of Nicholas's distressing supernatural experiences and the mood of horror those experiences conjure." Publishers Weekly.

LIST OF FICTIONAL WORKS

Isaac, Kara

Then there was you / Kara Isaac. Bellbird Press, 2017. 344 p.

ISBN 9780473396534

1. Musicians 2. Americans in foreign countries 3. Big churches 4. Contemporary Christian music 5. Church management 6. Faith (Christianity) 7. Christian church music 8. Interpersonal attraction 9. Men/women relations 10. Sydney, New South Wales 11. Christian romances 12. Romantic comedies

RITA Award, 2018.

Paige McAllister leaves her life in Chicago to move to Sydney, Australia where she becomes a logistics planner for one of Australia's biggest churches. Her boss's son, Josh Tyler, fronts a top-selling worship band. When Josh and Paige are thrown together to organize his band's next tour, the sparks fly.

Isaacs, Susan, 1943-

After all these years / Susan Isaacs. Harper Collins, 1993. 343 p.

ISBN 9780060167684

1. Teachers 2. Millionaires 3. Married men -- Death 4. Executives' spouses 5. Women fugitives 6. Widows 7. Women amateur detectives 8. Extramarital affairs 9. Innocence (Law) 10. Long Island, New York 11. New York (State) 12. Mysteries

LC 92056200

Soon after her wealthy husband of twenty-five years leaves her for a younger woman, Rosie Meyers finds herself the prime suspect in his murder and goes underground as a fugitive in Manhattan to find the killer.

"Isaacs has a field day lampooning upper-class mores . . . but also weaves into this thoroughly diverting caper unexpected moments of genuine tenderness and sly social commentary." Publishers Weekly.

Isaacs, Susan, 1943-

As **husbands** go : a novel / Susan Isaacs. Simon & Schuster, 2010. 352 p.

ISBN 9781416573012

1. Rich people 2. Families of murder victims 3. Murder investigation 4. Grief in women 5. Widows 6. Triplets 7. Grandmothers 8. Murder 9. Marriage 10. Plastic surgeons 11. Prostitutes 12. Jewish women 13. Suburban life 14. Bereavement -- Psychological aspects 15. Long Island, New York 16. Mysteries

Married to a handsome and successful plastic surgeon, Susie B. Anthony Rabinowitz Gersten thought she had the perfect life. But when her husband is found murdered in a sleazy apartment with a cheap call girl, Susie is left scratching her head. Pegged as a suspect and ridiculed by her husband's family, she turns to her tough-as-nails Grandma Ethel for help.

"The mystery is barely there, but Isaacs' fans will enjoy another sharp-tongued romp through the New York privileged classes and their foibles." Kirkus.

Isherwood, Christopher, 1904-1986

* The **Berlin** stories : The last of Mr. Norris, Goodbye to Berlin / Christopher Isherwood. James Laughlin, 1946, c1945. 191, 207 p.

ISBN 9780811218047

1. Isherwood, Christopher, 1904-1986 2. 1930s 3. City life -- Berlin, Germany 4. British in Germany 5. Gay men -- Berlin, Germany 6. Berlin, Germany 7. Literary fiction 8. Historical fiction 9. Autobiographical fiction 10. Modern classics

LC 46002158

Two previously published novels reissued here together under a new collective title.

"A New directions book".

Ishiguro, Kazuo, 1954-

An **artist** of the floating world / Kazuo Ishiguro. Faber and Faber, 1986. 206 p.

ISBN 0571136087

1. World War II -- Art and the war 2. Fathers and daughters 3. Artists 4. Senior men 5. Responsibility 6. Imperialism, Japanese -- History -- 20th century 7. Japan -- History -- Allied occupation, 1945-1952 8. Historical fiction 9. Literary fiction 10. Psychological fiction

LC 86214424

Whitbread Book Award for Novel, 1986.

Whitbread Book of the Year, 1986.

Shortlisted for the Booker-McConnell Prize, 1986.

This is the story of an artist as an aging man, struggling through the wreckage of Japan's World War II experience. Ishiguro's first novel.

"The tensions stay tight. And this is what makes Mr. Ishiguro not only a good writer but also a wonderful novelist." New York Times Book Review.

Ishiguro, Kazuo, 1954-

The **buried** giant : a novel / Kazuo Ishiguro. Alfred A. Knopf, 2015. 304 p.

ISBN 9780307271037

1. Anglo-Saxon period (449-1066) 2. Quests 3. Memory 4. Husband and wife 5. Loss (Psychology) 6. Characters and characteristics in literature 7. Warriors 8. Meaning (Psychology) 9. Sons 10. People with amnesia 11. Magic 12. War -- Psychological aspects 13. Great Britain -- History -- Anglo-Saxon period, 449-1066 14. Arthurian fantasy 15. Historical fantasy 16. Literary fiction

LC 2014028378

"This is a Borzoi book."

As the wars that have ravaged Britain fade into the past, Axl and Beatrice, a couple of elderly Britons, set out on a journey to find the son they have not seen in years, and are joined in their travels by a Saxon warrior, his orphaned charge, and a knight.

"Ishiguro's story is a deceptively simple one, for enfolded within its elemental structure are many profound truths, including its beautiful and memorable portrait of a long-term marriage and its subtle commentary on the eternity of war, all conveyed in the authors mesmerizing prose." Booklist.

Ishiguro, Kazuo, 1954-

* **Never** let me go / Kazuo Ishiguro. Alfred A. Knopf, 2005. 304 p.

ISBN 1400043395

1. 1970s 2. 1990s 3. Clones and cloning 4. Organ donors 5. Ethics 6. Women 7. Young women 8. Friendship 9. Donation of organs, tissues, etc 10. Private schools 11. Secrets 12. Memories 13. England 14. Literary fiction 15. Science fiction

LC 2004048966

ALA Notable Book, 2006.

Shortlisted for the Man Booker Prize, 2005.

Shortlisted for the James Tait Black Memorial Prize for Fiction, 2005

National Book Critics Circle Award for Fiction finalist, 2005

A reunion with two childhood friends--Ruth and Tommy--draws Kath and her companions on a nostalgic odyssey into the supposedly idyllic years of their lives at Hailsham, an isolated private school in the serene English countryside, and a dramatic confrontation with the truth about their childhoods and about their lives in the present.

"Ishiguro serves up the saddest, most persuasive science fiction you'll read. Set in England, late 1990s, the novel posits a technological breakthrough whose effect is to condemn the children of Hailsham to a fate that was, until this novel, unthinkable. Ishiguro's imagining of the children's misshapen little world is profoundly thoughtful, and their hesitant progression into knowledge of their plight is an extreme and heartbreaking version of the exodus of all children from the innocence in which the benevolent but fraudulent adult world conspires to place them." The Atlantic.

Ishiguro, Kazuo, 1954-

* The **remains** of the day / Kazuo Ishiguro. A. A. Knopf, 1989. 245 p.

ISBN 9780394573434

1. Butlers 2. Social classes 3. Men -- Psychology 4. Loyalty 5. Country homes 6. Household employees 7. Discontent 8. Self-deception 9. Nazi collaborators 10. Housekeepers 11. England 12. Psychological fiction 13. Literary fiction

LC 89080445

Originally published: 1989.

"Originally published in Great Britain by Faber and Faber Limited, London"--T.p. verso.

Booker Prize, 1989.

ALA Notable Book, 1990.

Stevens, an aging butler dedicated to the dignity of his profession, takes to the road to convince Ms. Bent -- a now-married former housekeeper -- to resume her duties at Darlington Hall. As Stevens journeys, he reflects on their prior acquaintance; his memories reveal Stevens? deeply personal desires, and how he has rewritten events to maintain his ideal image of service and discretion. -- Description by Kimberly S. Burton.

Ishiguro, Kazuo, 1954-

The **unconsoled** / Kazuo Ishiguro. A. A. Knopf, 1995. 535 p.

ISBN 9780679404255

1. Pianists -- Europe 2. Celebrities -- Europe 3. Memory 4. Interpersonal relations 5. Expectation (Psychology) 6. Creativity 7. Europe 8. Surrealist fiction 9. Literary fiction

LC 9515829

ALA Notable Book, 1996.

Arriving in an European city with significant gaps in his memory, Ryder, a renowned pianist, is overwhelmed by an onslaught of strangers who seem to know him and of whom he has vague, dreamlike recollections.

"In this novel, prominent concert pianist Ryder is at odds with his surroundings. Ryder arrives in an unidentified European city at a bit of a loss. Everyone he meets seems to assume that he knows more than he knows, that he is well acquainted with the city and its obscure cultural crisis. A young woman he kindly consents to advise seems to have been an old lover and her son quite possibly his own; he vaguely recalls past conversations. The world he has entered is a surreal, Alice-in-Wonderland place where a door in a cafe can lead back to a hotel miles away. The result is at once dreamy, disorienting, and absolutely compelling; Ishiguro's paragraphs, though Proust-like, are completely lucid and quite addictive to read." Library Journal.

Ishiguro, Kazuo, 1954-

When we were orphans / Kazuo Ishiguro. A. A. Knopf, 2000. 335 p.

ISBN 9780375410543

1. 1930s 2. Detectives -- Shanghai, China 3. British in China 4. Orphans -- China 5. Parent-separated boys 6. Cold cases (Criminal investigation) 7. Parents -- Death 8. Missing persons -- Shanghai, China 9. Shanghai, China -- Social life and customs -- 20th century 10. Mysteries 11. Literary fiction 12. Psychological fiction

LC 00026120

Shortlisted for the Booker-McConnell Prize, 2000.

Christopher Banks, an English boy born in early-20th-century Shanghai, is orphaned at age nine when both his mother and father disappear under suspicious circumstances. He grows up to become a renowned detective, and more than 20 years later, returns to Shanghai to solve the mystery of the disappearances.

"For all its ellipses and evasions, When We Were Orphans, will linger in the mind as an often fascinating, imaginative work of surpassing intelligence and taste." Times Literary Supplement.

It occurs to me that I am America : new stories and art / edited by Jonathan Santlofer. Touchstone Books, 2018. xix, 374 p.

ISBN 9781501179600

1. Democracy 2. Freedom 3. Compassion 4. Justice 5. United States 6. Short stories 7. Anthologies

Published to coincide with the one-year anniversary of the Trump inauguration and the Women's March, a provocative anthology of original short stories by 30 best-selling and award-winning writers--including Alice Walker, Alice Hoffman and Lee Child--considers the fundamental ideals of a free, just and compassionate democracy as expressed through fiction and graphic artwork.

"Marking the first anniversary of Trump's inauguration, this resounding gathering of major literary and artistic talent will inspire avid interest." Booklist.

Itani, Frances, 1942-

Deafening / Frances Itani. Atlantic Monthly Press, 2003. 378 p. Deafening novels (Frances Itani)

ISBN 9780871139023

1. First World War era (1914-1918) 2. Deafness 3. Women who are deaf 4. Veterans' families 5. Love 6. Newlyweds 7. Sign language 8. Canadians in Europe 9. Intimacy (Psychology) 10. Language and languages 11. World War I 12. War -- Relief of sick and wounded 13. Trench warfare 14. Ontario -- History -- 20th century 15. Deseronto, Ontario 16. Canada -- History -- 20th century 17. Historical fiction 18. Love stories 19. Literary fiction

LC 2003045108

Shortlisted for the International IMPAC Dublin Literary Award, 2005

Left profoundly deaf following a bout with scarlet fever, Grania O'Neill grows up at the Ontario School for the Deaf, where she spends her entire time, protected from the hearing world outside and learning sign language and speech, but her life is changed forever when she falls in love with Jim Lloyd, a hearing man, in a debut novel set on the eve of the Great War.

"This novel is not only a beautifully crafted love story but also an exploration of the possibilities of language and the eloquence of silence." Library Journal.

Itani, Frances, 1942-

Tell : a novel / Frances Itani. Atlantic Monthly Press, 2015, c2014. 321 p. Deafening novels (Frances Itani)

ISBN 9780802123367

1. 1910s 2. World War I veterans 3. Marital conflict 4. Husband and wife 5. Aunt and niece 6. Post-traumatic stress disorder 7. Alienation (Social psychology) 8. Love 9. Loss (Psychology) 10. Secrets 11. Ontario -- History -- 20th century 12. Deseronto, Ontario 13. Historical fiction 14. Literary fiction 15. Love stories

Originally published: Toronto : HarperCollins, 2014.

Shortlisted for the Giller Prize, 2014

LIST OF FICTIONAL WORKS

Two sisters who created their own secret language to compensate for one's deafness have grown up and are now facing problems with their respective husbands who have returned home from the war, in a follow-up to Deafening.

"The slow-moving novel circulates among Kenan and Tress, Maggie and Am; an exceptionally awkward ending is summarized in a letter. Though attentive to period detail, Itani seems more constricted than liberated by the past in her sixth novel." Kirkus.

Ivey, Eowyn

The **snow** child : a novel / Eowyn Ivey. Little, Brown and Co., 2012. 389 p.

ISBN 9780316175678

1. 1920s 2. Frontier and pioneer life -- Alaska 3. Transformations (Magic) 4. Childlessness 5. Adopted children 6. Husband and wife 7. Alaska -- History -- 1867-1959 8. Magical realism 9. Literary fiction
LC 2011024937

Pulitzer Prize for Fiction finalist, 2013.

A childless couple working a farm in the brutal landscape of 1920 Alaska discover a little girl living in the wilderness, with a red fox as a companion, and begin to love the strange, almost-supernatural child as their own.

Ivey, Eowyn

* **To** the bright edge of the world / Eowyn Ivey. Little, Brown and Company, 2016. 417 p.

ISBN 9780316242851

1. 1880s 2. Explorers 3. Attitude change 4. Army spouses 5. Eyak Indians 6. Polar expeditions 7. Native American women 8. Indians of North America 9. Alaska 10. Historical fiction 11. Epistolary novels
ALA Notable Book, 2017.
RUSA Reading List Short List, 2017.

Leaving his wife, Sophie, behind in the Vancouver barracks, U.S. Army Colonel Allen Forrester embarks on an expedition to map the interior of the newly acquired Alaska Territory. As Forrester and his crew venture into the wilderness, encountering danger, hardship, and astounding natural beauty, free-spirited Sophie chafes against the restrictions placed upon military spouses, recording her experiences in her diary. With its sympathetic characters and lyrical depictions of the 19th-century American frontier, this historical epistolary novel may appeal to fans of Diane Smith's Letters from Yellowstone and Pictures from an Expedition. -- Description by Gillian Speace.

"In this splendid adventure novel, Ivey captures Alaskas beauty and brutality, not just preserving history, but keeping it alive." Publishers Weekly.

Iweala, Uzodinma

* **Speak** no evil / Uzodinma Iweala. Harper, 2018. 214 p.
ISBN 9780061284922

1. Gay teenagers 2. Homophobia 3. Nigerian Americans 4. Immigrants 5. Interethnic friendship 6. Parent and child 7. Belonging 8. Cultural differences 9. Teenage girls 10. Coming out (Sexual or gender identity) 11. Family relationships 12. Washington, D.C. 13. Nigeria 14. Literary fiction 15. LGBTQIA fiction

An Ivy League-bound star athlete from a prestigious private school in Washington, D.C., and his best friend, the daughter of prominent government insiders, struggle with brutal responses to the young man's sexual orientation before finding themselves speeding toward a violent and senseless future.

J

JaQuavis

The **dopefiend** / JaQuavis Coleman. Urban Books, 2010. 230 p. Dopeman's trilogy

ISBN 9781601622662

1. African American women 2. Drug addicts 3. Street life 4. Revenge 5. African American drug abusers 6. Urban fiction 7. African American fiction
LC bl2010010260

Hazel Brown is alone in the world, and the only thing she has to her name is a strong addiction to heroin.

JaQuavis

The **dopeman's** wife / JaQuavis Coleman. Urban Books, 2009. 230 p. Dopeman's trilogy

ISBN 9781601621597

1. African American women 2. Drug dealers 3. African American men/women relations 4. Street life 5. Abused women 6. Jealousy in men 7. Escapes 8. Secrets 9. Murder 10. African Americans 11. Flint, Michigan 12. Baltimore, Maryland 13. Urban fiction 14. African American fiction

JaQuavis

* The **streets** have no king / JaQuavis Coleman. Griffin, 2017. 320 p.

ISBN 9781250081278

1. Drug lords 2. College teachers 3. Mentors 4. Drug traffic 5. Drug dealers 6. Consequences 7. Betrayal 8. Urban fiction 9. African American fiction

While teaching a college class, drug mogul Kane takes on a student, heroin dealer Basil, as a protege and they build a drug trafficking business, but when Basil meets Kane's daughter, lines are crossed and the business union becomes a deadly rivalry.

Jackson, Brenda (Brenda Streater)

Forged in desire / Brenda Jackson. HQN, 2017. 384 p. The Protectors (Brenda Jackson)

ISBN 9780373790005

1. Bodyguards 2. Heirs and heiresses 3. Women jurors 4. Threat (Psychology) 5. Protectiveness in men 6. Security consultants 7. Interpersonal attraction 8. African Americans 9. Men/women relations 10. Romantic suspense 11. Multicultural romances 12. African American fiction

Jury duty isn't usually this exciting: soon after Margo Connelly and her fellow jurors deliver a guilty verdict, people involved in the trial start dying. Once the judge, the court clerk, and the bailiff are gunned down in cold blood outside the courthouse, it becomes clear that Margo needs protection, too. Tasked with protecting Margo from a crime boss' hired killer, bodyguard Lamar "Striker" Jennings must stay by her side, day and night. Naturally, Margo and Lamar get to know each other very, very well. But Lamar has reservations about a relationship: not only is Margo his mentor's niece, but Lamar fears that his law-breaking past may change her mind about him.? -- Description by Gillian Speace

"Jackson's deft plotting and effective red herrings keep the suspense high as her multidimensional characters command the readers attention." Publishers Weekly.

Jackson, Charles, 1903-1968

The **lost** weekend / Charles Jackson. R. Bentley, 1979, c1944. 244 p.

ISBN 9780837604305

1. Middle-aged men 2. Alcoholics 3. Alcoholism 4. Depression 5. Family relationships 6. Hallucinations and illusions 7. Self-destructive behavior 8. Psychological fiction

LC 78026163

Originally published: New York :

This frank examination, written before the disease of alcoholism was understood, offers no solution, no moral, just an unblinking look into the life and mind of an addict." Publishers Weekly.

Jackson, Joshilyn

The **almost** sisters / Joshilyn Jackson. William Morrow, 2017. 352 p.

ISBN 9780062105714

1. Unplanned pregnancy 2. Family secrets 3. Stepsisters 4. One-night stands (Interpersonal relations) 5. People with dementia -- Care 6. Intergenerational relations 7. Family relationships 8. Comic book writers 9. Multiracial children 10. Race relations 11. Grandmothers 12. Alabama 13. Southern States 14. Women's lives and relationships 15. Domestic fiction 16. Southern fiction

LC 2016056529

RUSA Reading List, 2018.

"With empathy, grace, humor, and piercing insight, the author of Gods in Alabama pens a powerful, emotionally resonant novel of the South that confronts the truth about privilege, family, and the distinctions between perception and reality---the stories we tell ourselves about our origins and who we really are. Superheroes have always been Leia Birch Briggs' weakness. One tequila-soaked night at a comics convention, the usually level-headed graphic novelist is swept off her barstool by a handsome and anonymous Batman. It turns out the caped crusader has left her with more than just a nice, fuzzy memory. She's having a baby boy--an unexpected but not unhappy development in the thirty-eight year-old's life. But before Leia can break the news of her impending single-motherhood (including the fact that her baby is biracial) to her conventional, Southern family, her step-sister Rachel's marriage implodes. Worse, she learns her beloved ninety-year-old grandmother, Birchie, is losing her mind, and she's been hiding her dementia with the help of Wattie, her best friend since girlhood. Leia returns to Alabama to put her grandmother's affairs in order, clean out the big Victorian that has been in the Birch family for generations, and tell her family that she's pregnant. Yet just when Leia thinks she's got it all under control, she learns that illness is not the only thing Birchie's been hiding. Tucked in the attic is a dangerous secret with roots that reach all the way back to the Civil War. Its exposure threatens the family's freedom and future, and it will change everything about how Leia sees herself and her sister, her son and his missing father, and the world she thinks she knows"--, Provided by publisher.

"Jackson (The Opposite of Everyone, 2016, etc.) has written another spirited page-turner set in a new South still haunted by the ghosts of the old." Kirkus.

Jackson, Joshilyn

Never have I ever / Joshilyn Jackson. William Morrow, 2019 352 p.

ISBN 9780062855312

1. Secrets 2. Betrayal 3. Book clubs 4. Diving 5. Families 6. Extortion 7. Deception 8. Suburban women 9. Women -- Psychology 10. Southern States 11. Thrillers and suspense 12. Southern fiction

When her loved ones are put in danger by a blackmailer who threatens to expose dangerous secrets, a devoted family woman struggles to keep the upper hand in an escalating war of betrayal.

Jackson, Naomi A.

The **star** side of Bird Hill / Naomi Jackson. Penguin Press, 2015. 298 p.

ISBN 9781594205958

1. 1980s 2. Sisters 3. Family relationships 4. West Indian Americans 5. West Indian American families 6. Grandmother and granddaughter 7. Children of immigrants 8. Fathers and daughters 9. Sixteen-year-old girls 10. Ten-year-old girls 11. Home (Concept) 12. Barbados 13. Brooklyn, New York City 14. Domestic fiction 15. Literary fiction

Suddenly sent from their home in Brooklyn to Bird Hill in Barbados after their mother can no longer care for them, sisters Phaedra and Dionne spend the summer of 1989 living with their grandmother Hyacinth, a midwife and practitioner of the local spiritual practice of obeah.

"A charming, laid-back bildungsroman and an uplifting story about the importance of a stable, loving home and the embrace of ones culture." Booklist.

Jackson, Shirley, 1916-1965

* The **haunting** of Hill House / Shirley Jackson. Penguin, 1984, c1959. 246 p.

ISBN 9780140071085

1. Haunted houses 2. Loners 3. Paranormal phenomenon investigation 4. Poltergeists 5. Ghosts 6. Single women 7. Interpersonal relations 8. Horror 9. Gothic fiction

Later editions published as: The Haunting.

Book made into a movie called The haunting.

Originally published: New York : Viking, 1959.

An 80-year-old mansion harboring dark secrets comes to menacing life in this classic spine-tingling tale from Shirley Jackson. Anthropologist and ghost hunter Dr. John Montague invites three strangers to stay in haunted Hill House for the summer. One of the guests is 32-year-old Eleanor, for whom three months in a haunted house is preferable to caring for her invalid mother. Soon, Eleanor begins to see and hear things that the other guests cannot. Is it all in her imagination, or is she the only one who can perceive the evil that lurks in Hill House? -- Description by Dawn Towery.

Jackson, Shirley, 1916-1965

* The **lottery** : and other stories / Shirley Jackson. Farrar, Straus, Giroux, 1982, c1949. 306 p.

ISBN 9780141191430

1. Manners and customs 2. Villages 3. Stoning 4. Small town life 5. Lotteries 6. Murder 7. Horror 8. Classics 9. Short stories

Original title: The lottery, or, The adventures of James Harris.

A collection of stories including "The Lottery."

Jackson, Shirley, 1916-1965

We have always lived in the castle / Shirley Jackson. Penguin Books, 1984, c1962. 214 p.

ISBN 9780140071078

1. Family estates 2. Eccentric families 3. Poisoning 4. Social isolation 5. Superstition 6. Sisters 7. Arsenic poisoning 8. Family relationships 9. Horror 10. Gothic fiction

A deliciously unsettling novel about a perverse, isolated, and possibly murderous family and the dramatic struggle that ensues when an unexpected visitor interrupts their unusual way of life.

Jacobs, Nova

The **last** equation of Isaac Severy : a novel in clues / Nova Jacobs. Touchstone, 2018. 352 p.

ISBN 9781501175121

1. Women booksellers 2. Mathematicians 3. Secret societies 4. Grandfathers -- Death 5. Clues 6. Books 7. Adoptees 8. Murder 9. Free will and determinism 10. Investigations 11. Families 12. Family secrets 13. Los Angeles, California 14. Seattle, Washington 15. Mysteries 16. Literary fiction

LC 2017032828

Receiving a cryptic letter from her famous mathematician grandfather just before his suicide, adopted granddaughter Hazel, the owner of a struggling bookstore in Seattle, is charged with tracking down and protecting a dangerous equation before dangerous enemies can exploit it.

Jacobson, Howard

The **Finkler** question / Howard Jacobson. Bloomsbury, 2010. 307 p.

ISBN 9781408808870

1. Men -- Psychology 2. Identity (Psychology) 3. Belonging 4. Jewish men 5. Jewish way of life 6. Friendship 7. Obsession in men 8. Jews -- Identity 9. London, England 10. Literary fiction 11. Psychological fiction

Man Booker Prize, 2010.

Julian Treslove, a radio producer, and Samuel Finkler, a Jewish philosopher, have been friends since childhood and, as they enter middle age, they reminisce over their struggles with self-identity, anti-Semitism, women, love, and the past.

"Not everyone will love The Finkler Question. Hilarious and romantic at the start, it becomes more and more discomfiting as it progresses, especially in its chilling depiction of modern anti-Semitism. If the reader yearns . . . for Jewish happiness, Jacobson truly one of our funniest writers is more than willing to provide it. It's just that happiness isn't the whole story." Globe and Mail (Toronto)

Jacobson, Howard

The **mighty** walzer : a novel / Howard Jacobson. St. Martins Press, 2011. 400 p.

ISBN 9781608196852

1. 1950s 2. Table tennis players 3. Shyness in men 4. Men/women relations 5. Manchester, England 6. Coming-of-age stories 7. Historical fiction

In 1950s Manchester, England, Oliver Walzer, a shy Jewish boy, comes of age in a household dominated by women and finds that he has a natural talent for ping-pong, but things do not go as smoothly for him when it comes to women and sex.

Jaeggy, Fleur

I am the brother of XX / Fleur Jaeggy ; translated by Gini Alhadeff. New Directions, 2017, c2014. 128 p.

ISBN 9780811225984

1. Interpersonal relations 2. Short stories 3. Literary fiction 4. Translations -- Italian to English

LC 2017000508

Translated from the Italian Sono il fratello di XX.

Originally published by Adelphi, 2014.

"As concentrated as bullets, new stories by the inimitable Fleur Jaeggy."--Publisher's description.

"In prismatic translation from the Italian, these tiny tales sparkle with wit and worldly wisdom." Kirkus.

Jakeman, Jane

In the kingdom of mists / Jane Jakeman. Berkley Prime Crime, 2004. 355 p.

ISBN 0425195120

1. Monet, Claude, 1840-1926 2. Monet, Camille, 1847-1879 3. Savoy Hotel, London, England 4. 1900s (Decade) 5. French in England 6. Detectives 7. Mutilation 8. Murder investigation 9. Murder suspects 10. Upper class 11. Soldiers -- Great Britain 12. Impressionism (Art) 13. Painting 14. Serial murders 15. Nostalgia 16. Memories 17. Classism 18. Sexism 19. Prejudice 20. Boer War, 1899-1902 21. Painters 22. London, England 23. Thames River 24. Historical mysteries 25. Mysteries

LC 2003062800

Beautifully illustrated in colour with twelve paintings by Monet.

When the bodies of two young women are pulled from the Thames, prompting fears that Jack the Ripper has returned, London investigators are unaware of the horror that lurks above the suite inhabited by renowned French painter Claude Monet.

"The novel tells a dramatic story about crime and perception, art and reality through the eyes of the famous painter, the policeman and a young diplomat. Multilayered and voiced, this is a fascinating attempt to add an extra dimension to this historical crime novel." Guardian (UK).

Jakes, John, 1932-

Love and war / John Jakes. Harcourt Brace Jovanovich, 1984. 1019 p. North and South trilogy

ISBN 9780151544967

1. American Civil War era (1861-1865) 2. 1860s 3. Family relationships 4. Abolitionists 5. War 6. Slavery 7. Revenge 8. Civil war 9. United States Civil War, 1861-1865 10. Confederate States of America 11. United States -- History -- Civil War, 1861-1865 12. War stories 13. Family sagas 14. Historical fiction

LC 84012895

"This sequel to North and South carries forward the entwined sagas of the Hazards of Pennsylvania, industrialists, and the Mains of South Carolina, plantation owners. . . . The story moves from action on the battlefield to the corridors of Washington to the shipyards of Liverpool. It encompasses deeds heroic and dastardly; passions licit and illicit; spying, assassination plotting and cynical profiteering; and the trying out of new military interventions." Publishers Weekly.

Jakes, John, 1932-

* **North** and South / John Jakes. Harcourt Brace Jovanovich, 1982. 740 p. North and South trilogy

ISBN 9780151669981

1. 1940s 2. Family relationships 3. Abolitionists 4. Slavery 5. Revenge 6. Confederate States of America 7. West Point, New York 8. United States -- History -- 19th century 9. War stories 10. Family sagas 11. Historical fiction

LC 81047898

Chronicles two great American dynasties over three generations. Though brought together in a friendship that neither jealousy nor violence could shatter, the Hazards and the Mains are torn apart by the storm of event that has divided the nation.

Jakes, John, 1932-

On secret service : a novel / John Jakes. Dutton, 2000. 464 p.

ISBN 052594544X

1. American Civil War era (1861-1865) 2. 1860s 3. Intelligence service 4. Secret service -- United States -- History -- Civil War, 1861-1865 5. Spies 6. Men/women relations 7. Slavery 8. Socialites 9. Spies -- Confederate States of America 10. Actors and actresses

11. Civil war 12. United States Civil War, 1861-1865 13. United States -- History -- Civil War, 1861-1865 -- Secret Service 14. Washington, D.C. 15. War stories 16. Historical fiction

LC 99047951

Retraces the early years of the "Secret Service," from the Pinkertons to the assassination of Lincoln, following four main characters--a spy, a rebel, an actress, and an officer

"Numerous historical figures are represented accurately and plausibly, and lesser-known events like the horrific Draft Riots in New York are vividly portrayed." Library Journal.

Jakes, John, 1932-

Savannah, or, A gift for Mr. Lincoln / John Jakes. Dutton, 2004. 304 p.

ISBN 0525948031

1. Sherman, William Tecumseh, 1820-1891 2. American Civil War era (1861-1865) 3. 1860s 4. Women plantation owners -- Savannah, Georgia 5. Sherman's March to the Sea 6. Determination in women 7. Twelve-year-old girls 8. Widows 9. Generals 10. Mothers and daughters 11. Courage 12. Determination in girls 13. Men/women relations 14. Christmas 15. Civil war 16. United States Civil War, 1861-1865 17. United States -- History -- Civil War, 1861-1865 18. Georgia -- History -- Civil War, 1861-1865 19. Savannah, Georgia 20. Historical fiction 21. War stories

LC 2004049417

Sherman's army marches from Atlanta to the sea, with Savannah in its path. The Lester ladies--attractive widowed Sara and her feisty twelve-year-old daughter Hattie--struggle to save the family rice plantation. Hattie and the general find themselves on a collision course that will astonish both of them when Sherman offers the city to Lincoln as "a Christmas gift."

"This historical novel recounts the taking of Savannah by Gen. William Tecumseh Sherman's Union Army during Christmas 1864. Fundamentally, it is the story of Sara Lester and her precocious 12-year-old daughter, Hattie, who has an aversion to General Sherman until she finds herself in need of his help. The novel includes a rich cast of characters who, as Union forces move north, are ultimately left to their own devices. The narrative offers adventure, romance, humor, and crime along with the trials of an American city living under what is, to its citizens, occupation by a foreign army." Library Journal.

Jalaluddin, Uzma

* Ayesha **at** last / Uzma Jalaluddin. Berkley, 2019, c2018. 368 p.

ISBN 9781984802798

1. Muslim families 2. Expectation (Psychology) 3. Women poets 4. Women teachers 5. Independence in women 6. Arranged marriage 7. Communities 8. Cousins 9. Islamic values 10. Family relationships 11. Interpersonal attraction 12. Men/women relations 13. Toronto, Ontario 14. Canada 15. Chick lit 16. Romantic comedies 17. Adaptations, retellings, and spin-offs

LC 2018058488

A modern Muslim adaptation of Pride and Prejudice finds a reluctant teacher who would avoid an arranged marriage setting aside her literary ambitions before falling in love with her perpetually single cousin's infuriatingly conservative fiance.

James, Eloisa

Desperate duchesses / Eloisa James. Avon Books, 2007. 384 p. Desperate duchesses series

ISBN 9780060781934

1. Georgian era (1714-1837) 2. 18th century 3. Aristocracy -- History -- 18th century 4. Men/women relations 5. Chess players 6. Mate

selection for women 7. Love triangles 8. Seduction 9. Dukes and duchesses 10. Mate selection for men 11. Interpersonal attraction 12. Marriage 13. Interpersonal conflict 14. England -- Social life and customs -- 18th century 15. Great Britain -- History -- George II, 1727-1760 16. Georgian romances 17. Historical romances

When Lady Roberta St. Giles, a marquess's sheltered only daughter, gambles on love with notorious scoundrel Damon Reeve, the Earl of Gryffyn, she plays a high-stakes game of seduction and passion where the winner takes all.

"James's (Pleasure for Pleasure) Georgian romp is the sparkling debut of a new series that promises to be remarkable." Library Journal.

James, Eloisa

Four nights with the duke / Eloisa James. Avon Books, 2015 384 p. Desperate duchesses by the numbers

ISBN 9780062223913

1. Georgian era (1714-1837) 2. 1800s (Decade) 3. Dukes and duchesses 4. Husband and wife 5. Marital conflict 6. Forced marriage 7. Women authors 8. Revenge 9. Extortion 10. Interpersonal attraction 11. Men/women relations 12. Marriage 13. England -- Social life and customs -- 19th century 14. Great Britain -- History -- George III, 1760-1820 15. Georgian romances 16. Historical romances

Takes place in 1800.

When Mia Carrington is forced to beg Evander Brody, Duke of Pindar, whom she once swore she would never marry, to enter into a marriage of convenience with her, he sets some conditions of his own before agreeing to her offer.

"With peeks at Thorn and India from Lady X, as well as other secondary characters and storylines that enhance and add texture to an already complex plot, James gives readers a welcome opportunity to revisit a popular community and flexes her powerful romantic storytelling muscles, somehow getting even stronger. Historical romance at its smart, poignant best." Kirkus.

James, Eloisa

Kiss me, Annabel / Eloisa James. Avon Books, 2005. 400 p. Essex sisters series

ISBN 0060732105

1. Regency period (1811-1820) 2. Earls and countesses 3. Mate selection for women 4. Sisters 5. Orphans 6. Nobility 7. Men/women relations 8. Engaged persons 9. Kissing 10. Games 11. England -- Social life and customs -- 19th century 12. London, England -- Social life and customs -- 19th century 13. Scotland -- Social life and customs -- 19th century 14. Regency romances 15. Historical romances

Sequel to Much ado about you.

Heading for London to acquire a wealthy husband, Annabel Essex finds her plans taking a detour when she encounters the seductive but impoverished Earl of Ardmore, a Scottish nobleman.

James, Eloisa

* **Seven** minutes in heaven / Eloisa James. Avon Books, 2017. 384 p. Desperate duchesses by the numbers

ISBN 9780062660121

1. Georgian era (1714-1837) 2. 1800s (Decade) 3. Widows 4. Inventors 5. Abduction 6. Guardian and ward 7. Governesses 8. Illegitimacy 9. Misunderstanding 10. Aristocracy 11. Dukes and duchesses 12. Mate selection 13. Interpersonal attraction 14. Men/women relations 15. England -- Social life and customs -- 19th century 16. Great Britain -- History -- George III, 1760-1820 17. Historical romances 18. Georgian romances

Story takes place in 1801.

Eugenia Snowe's professional reputation depends on supplying the upper classes with England's finest governesses. So when one of her placements proves unsuitable, she takes a personal interest in rectifying the situation. Edward "Ward" Reeve is desperate to find someone who can handle his rambunctious younger half-siblings, whose behavior threatens his status as their guardian. A witty and heartfelt tale of opposites attracting. -- Description by Gillian Speace

"Another bright, delightful read from a queen of historical romance." Kirkus.

James, Eloisa

* Three weeks with Lady X / Eloisa James. Avon Books, 2014. 384 p. Desperate duchesses by the numbers

ISBN 9780062223890

1. Georgian era (1714-1837) 2. Rich men 3. Women mentors 4. Nobility 5. Aristocracy 6. Social status 7. Illegitimacy 8. Mate selection 9. Interpersonal attraction 10. Men/women relations 11. London, England -- Social life and customs -- 18th century 12. Great Britain -- History -- George III, 1760-1820 13. England -- Social life and customs -- 18th century 14. Georgian romances 15. Historical romances

Having sworn off marriage to start her own business, Lady Xenobia India St. Clair has made quite the name for herself as society's most in-demand interior designer. Hired by Tobias "Thorn" Dautry, illegitimate son of the Duke of Villiers, to refurbish his newly acquired country house, India finds herself drawn to Thorn, who's equally enchanted by "Lady X." However, since Thorn has employed India for the express purpose of designing a comfortable home for his future bride, their steadily escalating flirtation proves problematic. Readers who enjoy this installment of the Desperate Duchesses series will want to read more about Thorn's childhood in A Duke of Her Own. -- Description by Gillian Speace.

"Emotionally rewarding and elegantly written, with textured characters and a captivating plot." Kirkus.

James, Eloisa

Too Wilde to wed / Eloisa James. Avon Books, 2018. 384 p. Wildes of Lindow Castle

ISBN 9780062692467

1. Georgian era (1714-1837) 2. Adventurers 3. Aristocracy 4. Mate selection 5. Independence in women 6. Fame 7. Nobility 8. Families 9. Sexual attraction 10. Men/women relations 11. England -- Social life and customs -- 19th century 12. Great Britain -- History -- 1714-1837 13. Georgian romances 14. Historical romances

Returning home from war only to discover that the ton has labeled him "too wild to wed," Lord Roland Northbridge Wilde is determined to prove them wrong as he sets out to win the heart of Miss Diana Belgrave, the woman who jilted him two years earlier.

"RITA award-winner James again elevates historical romance to sublime new heights through the lithe elegance of her writing, her exceptional gift for creating richly nuanced characters, and her ability to flawlessly marry potent sensuality with a deliciously dry sense of humor." Booklist.

James, Eloisa

* The ugly duchess / Eloisa James. Avon Books, 2012. 384 p. Happily ever afters (Eloisa James)

ISBN 9780062021731

1. Regency period (1811-1820) 2. Dukes and duchesses 3. Separated couples 4. Married people and secrets 5. Romantic love 6. Feminine beauty (Aesthetics) 7. Pirates 8. Men/women relations 9. London, England -- Social life and customs -- 19th century 10. England -- Social life and customs -- 19th century 11. Regency romances 12.

Historical romances

When she discovers that her husband James married her only for her dowry, Theodora Saxby, known by the town as The Ugly Duchess, is devastated until James launches a campaign to prove that he really loves her.

James, Eloisa

When Beauty tamed the Beast / Eloisa James. Avon Books, 2011. 384 p. Happily ever afters (Eloisa James)

ISBN 9780062021274

1. Men/women relations 2. Scandals 3. Mate selection for women 4. Beauty 5. Earls and countesses 6. Physicians 7. Wales -- Social life and customs -- 19th century 8. England -- Social life and customs -- 19th century 9. Historical romances

An unparalleled beauty, Miss Linnet Berry Thynne gives herself two weeks to make her fiance, the Earl of Marchant, who is rumored to be immune to the charms of any woman, fall in love with her, but the tables turn when she loses her own heart to a man who may never love her in return.

James, Eloisa

Wilde in love / Eloisa James. Avon Books, 2017. 384 p. Wildes of Lindow Castle

ISBN 9780062697288

1. Georgian era (1714-1837) 2. Adventurers 3. Celebrities 4. Aristocracy 5. Mate selection 6. Independence in women 7. Castles 8. Fame 9. Nobility 10. Families 11. Sexual attraction 12. Men/women relations 13. England -- Social life and customs -- 19th century 14. Great Britain -- History -- 1714-1837 15. Georgian romances 16. Historical romances

Includes a note about bogs, Egyptian ducks, and melodramatic plays.

After returning home from dangerous adventures, the notoriously rakish Lord Alaric Wilde, son of the Duke of Lindow, finds himself drawn to the very private, but very witty, Miss Willa Ffynche.

James, Henry, 1843-1916

Complete stories, 1864-1874 / Henry James. Library of America, 1999. 972 p.

ISBN 9781883011703

1. Americans in Europe Fiction 2. Manners and customs 3. United States -- Social life and customs -- 19th century 4. Europe -- Social life and customs -- 19th century 5. Short stories 6. Anthologies

LC 98053919

The complete stories of Henry James spans the creative life of the writer and includes his first twenty-four published stories, including thirteen never collected by him.

James, Henry, 1843-1916

Complete stories, 1874-1884 / Henry James. Library of America, 1999. 941 p.

ISBN 1883011639

1. 19th century 2. Americans in Europe 3. Europe -- Social life and customs -- 19th century 4. Short stories 5. Psychological fiction 6. Classics

LC 9819252

"Second volume in The Library of America's complete, five-volume edition."

James, Henry, 1843-1916

Complete stories, 1884-1891 Library of America, 1999. 904 p.

ISBN 1883011647

1. 19th century 2. Americans in Europe 3. Europe -- Social life and customs -- 19th century 4. Short stories 5. Psychological fiction 6. Classics

LC 9819250

"Third volume in the Library of America's complete, five-volume edition."

James, Henry, 1843-1916

Complete stories, 1892-1898 / Henry James. Library of America, 1996. 948 p.

ISBN 1883011094

1. 19th century 2. Americans in Europe 3. Europe -- Social life and customs -- 19th century 4. Short stories 5. Psychological fiction 6. Classics

Twenty-one stories include "The Turn of the Screw," and "The Figure in the Carpet."

James, Henry, 1843-1916

Complete stories, 1898-1910 / Henry James. Library of America, 1996. 946 p.

ISBN 1883011108

1. Americans in Europe 2. Europe -- Social life and customs 3. Short stories 4. Psychological fiction 5. Classics

LC 95-23462

Gathers thirty-one stories, including "The Great Good Place," "The Jolly Corner," and "The Beast in the Jungle."

James, Henry, 1843-1916

Daisy Miller / Henry James. Dover Publications, 1995. 59 p.

ISBN 0486287734

1. Americans in Europe 2. Scandals 3. Voyages and travels 4. Young women -- Europe 5. Rich women 6. Personal conduct 7. Expatriates 8. Men/women relations 9. Social acceptance 10. Sexuality 11. Feminism 12. Classism 13. Prejudice 14. Europe 15. Psychological fiction 16. Classics

LC 95021203

"An unabridged republication of the work originally published in The Cornhill magazine, 1878"--T.p. verso.

Daisy Miller, a young American girl, flirts and partakes of young life to its fullest while visiting Europe. Daisy meets the more subtle and self-aware Winterbourne and their romance ends in misfortune.

James, Henry, 1843-1916

The **golden** bowl / Henry James. A.A. Knopf, 1992, c1904. 596 p.

ISBN 0679417338

1. Father and adult daughter 2. Extramarital affairs 3. Marriage 4. Deception 5. Psychological fiction 6. Classics

LC 92052927

Originally published 1904.

The close relationship between American millionaire Adam Venuer and his daughter Maggie threatens their respective marriages.

James, Henry, 1843-1916

The **portrait** of a lady / Henry James. Alfred A. Knopf, 1991, c1881. 626 p.

ISBN 9780679405627

1. Heirs and heiresses 2. Americans in England 3. Marriage 4. Manors 5. Young women 6. Men/women relations 7. Women's role 8. Mate selection for women 9. Betrayal 10. Independence in women 11. Family relationships 12. Inheritance and succession 13. Disillusionment 14. Love triangles 15. Fathers and daughters 16. Married women 17. Italy 18. Psychological fiction 19. Coming-of-age stories 20. Classics

LC 91052999

First published: 1881.

When Isabel Archer, a beautiful, spirited American, is brought to Europe by her wealthy Aunt Touchett, it is expected that she will soon marry. But Isabel, resolved to determine her own fate, does not hesitate to turn down two eligible suitors. She then finds herself irresistibly drawn to Gilbert Osmond, who, beneath his veneer of charm and cultivation, is cruelty itself.

James, Henry, 1843-1916

* The **turn** of the screw / Henry James. Dover Publications, 1991. 87 p.

ISBN 0486266842

1. Ghosts 2. Governesses 3. Orphans 4. Men/women relations 5. Supernatural 6. Paranormal phenomena 7. Deception 8. Children 9. Mental illness 10. Good and evil 11. England 12. Ghost stories 13. Gothic fiction 14. Psychological fiction 15. Classics

LC 90-20572

New introduction and notes (c)2000.

The story unfolds with the arrival of a new governess at a remote country estate, who has been hired by the uncle of two young orphans to take complete charge of the children's lives and upbringing. Her first peaceful weeks are disturbed by the apparition of the ghosts of two evil servants who once served in the house.

James, Henry, 1843-1916

The **wings** of the dove / Henry James. Modern Library, 1993, c1907. 711 p.

ISBN 0679600671

1. Americans in Europe 2. Heirs and heiresses 3. Manipulation (Social sciences) 4. Terminal illness 5. Upper class 6. Love triangles 7. People with terminal illnesses 8. Young women 9. Fortune hunters 10. London (England) 11. Venice (Italy) 12. Psychological fiction 13. Classics

LC 93015338

Beautiful Kate Croy may have been left penniless by her relatives, but her bold, ambitious nature ensures she will not succumb meekly to a life of poverty. If the financial circumstances of Merton Densher, the man she is passionately in love with, are not sufficient to secure her future, perhaps her cunning will. Her scheming is flawed, though, for it fails to take into account the inconstancies of the human heart.

James, Julie, 1974-

Something about you / Julie James. Berkley Sensation, 2010. x, 323 p. FBI/US Attorney novels

ISBN 9780425233382

1. FBI Officials and employees 2. Women lawyers 3. FBI agents 4. Murder witnesses 5. Murder 6. Murder investigation 7. Betrayal 8. Forgiveness 9. Public prosecutors 10. Interpersonal attraction 11. Men/women relations 12. Chicago, Illinois 13. Contemporary romances

Sequel: A lot like love.

Becoming involved in a murder investigation, which brings her face-to-face with FBI Special Agent Jack Pallas, who still blames her for almost ruining his career three years earlier, Assistant U.S. Attorney Cameron Lynde tries to deny the attraction between them by focusing on the case at hand.

"Delivers an addictively readable combination of sharp humor, sizzlingly sexy romance, and a generous measure of nail-biting suspense." Chicago Tribune.

James, Lorelei

I want you back / Lorelei James. Berkley, 2019. 320 p. Need you series

ISBN 9780451492746

1. Former girlfriends 2. Former hockey players 3. Single mothers 4. Coparenting 5. Life change events 6. Trust 7. Hockey 8. Sexual attraction 9. Men/women relations 10. Minneapolis, Minnesota 11. Sports romances 12. Contemporary romances

When former NHL star Jaxson Lund returns home, he is determined to prove to Lucy, his ex-girlfriend and mother of his daughter, that he is ready to be a father and the man she has always wanted.

James, Marlon, 1970-

* Black leopard, red wolf / Marlon James. Riverhead Books, 2019. 720 p. Dark star trilogy (Marlon James)

ISBN 9780735220171

1. Missing boys 2. Quests 3. Shapeshifters 4. Private investigators 5. Imaginary creatures 6. Mercenaries 7. Missing persons investigation 8. Afrofuturism and Afrofantasy 9. Epic fantasy 10. Literary fiction

LC 2018035102

National Book Award for Fiction finalist, 2019.

Hired to find a mysterious boy who disappeared three years before, Tracker joins a search party that is quickly targeted deadly creatures.

James, Marlon, 1970-

The **book** of night women / Marlon James. Riverhead Books, 2009. 432 p.

ISBN 9781594488573

1. 18th century 2. Slaves 3. Secrets 4. Supernatural 5. Plantations 6. Violence 7. Conspiracies 8. Psychic ability 9. Identity (Psychology) 10. Growing up 11. Jamaica 12. Historical fiction

LC 2008046309

National Book Critics Circle Award for Fiction finalist, 2009

Feared from birth for her vivid green eyes, which her fellow slaves believe to be evidence of her dark powers, young slave Lilith is both revered and avoided throughout her childhood and becomes a key in the success of a long-planned slave revolt.

"This novel is both beautifully written and devastating. While the gruesome history of slavery in the Americas is a story we may dare to think we already know, every page of The Book of Night Women reminds us that we don't know nearly enough. . . . While his cast includes sadistic plantation owners and vicious overseers, house Negroes and field slaves, James deftly avoids the cliched melodrama such characters all too often inspire." New York Times Book Review.

James, Marlon, 1970-

* A brief history of seven killings : a novel / Marlon James. Riverhead Books, 2014. 704 p.

ISBN 9781594486005

1. Marley, Bob Assassination attempts 2. 20th century 3. Reggae musicians 4. Drug traffic 5. Assassins 6. Attempted murder 7. Political corruption 8. Rastafarians 9. Journalists 10. Violence 11. Jamaica -- History -- 20th century 12. New York City -- History -- 20th century 13. Historical fiction 14. Literary fiction

LC 2014018475

Man Booker Prize, 2015.

Shortlisted for the International Dublin Literary Award, 2016

National Book Critics Circle Award for Fiction finalist, 2014

A tale inspired by the 1976 attempted assassination of Bob Marley spans decades and continents to explore the experiences of journalists, drug dealers, killers and ghosts against a backdrop of period social and political turmoil.

"This is a breakthrough novel not only for the author but also for Caribbean and world literature. The Kingston milieu (and its extensions, including New York) is made horrifyingly believable; the patois is rhythmic, slangy, and often quite funny." Booklist.

James, P. D.

The **black** tower / P.D. James. Scribner, 1975. 271 p. Adam Dalgliesh mysteries

ISBN 9780684142630

1. Scotland Yard 2. Police 3. Murder investigation 4. Priests 5. Detectives 6. Mortality 7. Dorset, England 8. Mysteries 9. Police procedurals

Silver Dagger Award for Fiction, 1975.

Responding to an old friend's call, Commander Adam Dalgliesh travels to Toynton Grange, a convalescence home in Dorset, where he finds his friend dead and, himself weakened by a recent illness, encounters multiple murder and malicious intrigue.

James, P. D.

A **certain** justice / P.D. James. Random House, 1997. 364 p. Adam Dalgliesh mysteries

ISBN 0375401091

1. Scotland Yard 2. Murder investigation 3. Police 4. Women lawyers 5. Lawyers 6. Courts 7. London, England 8. Mysteries 9. Police procedurals

When noted criminal lawyer Venetia Aldridge turns up murdered after defending young Garry Ashe for the brutal killing of his mother, Commander Adam Dalgliesh and his team struggle to unravel the case, which involves him in a series of deadly crimes linked to the complexities of the legal system

"In obedience to the classic crime-writing genre, James finally offers up the guilty party, resolving a complicated plot with impeccable logic. But there the symmetry ends, for the moral and emotional questions she asks do not admit of such neatness." New York Times Book Review.

James, P. D.

Death in holy orders / P. D. James. Knopf, 2001. 415 p. Adam Dalgliesh mysteries

ISBN 9780375412554

1. Scotland Yard 2. Police -- East Anglia, England 3. Theological seminaries -- East Anglia, England 4. Murder investigation 5. Secrets 6. East Anglia, England 7. Mysteries 8. Police procedurals

The body of a student at a theological college on the East Anglian coast is found on the shore, suffocated by a fall of sand. Dalgliesh is called upon to reexamine the verdict of accidental death which the student's father would not accept. When another visitor to the college dies, Dalgliesh realizes that this is the most horrific case of his career.

"It's a pleasure to read James at the top of her form, as she often is here." The New Yorker.

James, P. D.

* **Death** of an expert witness / P. D. James. Scribner, 1977. 322 p. Adam Dalgliesh mysteries

ISBN 9780684152677

1. Scotland Yard 2. Police 3. Forensic scientists 4. Murder investigation 5. Crime laboratories 6. Mysteries 7. Police procedurals

LC 77021530

A community of forensic scientists are taken by surprise when a member of their own team is found in a bloody pool on the laboratory floor. Dalgliesh faces too many suspects as he tries to discover who might have wanted to kill the universally hated Edward Lorrimer.

"Basically James is a novelist who happens to put her character into mystery stories. She is just as much interested in people and their relationships as she is in the conventions of the genre. And being the perceptive and sensitive writer she is, she constructs books that can be read on several levels." New York Times Book Review.

James, P. D.

Devices and desires / P.D. James. Knopf, 1990, c1989. 433 p. Adam Dalgliesh mysteries

ISBN 9780394580708

1. Scotland Yard 2. Police 3. Serial murder investigation 4. Nuclear power plants 5. Serial murderers -- Great Britain 6. Norfolk, England 7. Mysteries 8. Police procedurals

LC 89045305

Scotland Yard's Adam Dalgliesh leaves London to vacation in Norfolk and becomes enmeshed in the hunt for the perpetrator of a series of murders of young women, which continues even after the murderer's capture

"As always with P. D. James, the whodunit element is the lagniappe, so interesting are her characters, so absorbing her depiction of time and place, so rich the texture of the tale she tells." New York Times Book Review.

James, P. D.

Innocent blood / P.D. James. Scribner, 1980. 311 p.

ISBN 9780684165912

1. 1970s 2. Adoptees -- Identity 3. Adult children of murderers 4. Birthparent/adoptee relations 5. Women adoptees 6. Eighteen-year-old women 7. Birthmothers 8. Women prisoners 9. Fathers of murder victims 10. Mothers and daughters 11. Self-discovery in women 12. Revenge 13. Murder 14. England 15. Psychological suspense 16. Thrillers and suspense

LC 79028699

Adopted at age eight, Philippa Palfrey learns that she is the daughter of a rapist and a murderess who is soon to be paroled from a life sentence for killing a child whose father seeks revenge.

James, P. D.

The **lighthouse** / P.D. James. Knopf, 2005. 320 p. Adam Dalgliesh mysteries

ISBN 9780307262912

1. Scotland Yard 2. Seaside resorts 3. Police 4. Murder investigation 5. Policewomen 6. Resorts 7. Authors -- Death 8. Murder suspects 9. Murder 10. Men/women relations 11. Islands 12. Mysteries 13. Police procedurals

LC 2005051039

Commander Adam Dalgliesh and his team are called in to solve a sensitive high profile case on Combe island off the Cornish coast of England at a time when Dalgliesh is dealing with his uncertain future with Emma Lavenham, Kate Miskin struggles with her own personal turmoil, and Sergeant Francis Benton-Smith must cope with resentment over a female superior.

"This novel is too rooted in genre conventions to count originality as its strong suit. But it has deviousness to burn, and it also offers other enticements. It's the kind of book that boasts a wryly humorous Scrabble scene, not to mention a Scrabble-lover's vocabulary." New York Times Book Review.

James, P. D.

Original sin / P.D. James. A. A. Knopf, 1995, c1994. 416 p. Adam Dalgliesh mysteries

ISBN 9780679438892

1. Scotland Yard 2. Police 3. Murder investigation 4. Publishers and publishing 5. Revenge 6. Thames River 7. London, England 8. England 9. Mysteries 10. Police procedurals

LC 9426094

As Commander Adam Dalgliesh and his team probe the bizarre death of publishing magnate Gerard Etienne, a ruthless man with many enemies, they uncover a complex web of dark secrets and revenge and a desperate killer prepared to strike again

"A mystery featuring Commander Adam Dalgliesh of Scotland Yard. Innocent House, a nineteenth-century pile on the Thames that accommodates the Peverell Press, presides over this novel of revenge. After Gerard Etienne, the new chairman of the press, announces his plan to sell the house, he ends up dead, with the head of a toy snake stuffed in his mouth. In this elaborate novel, the author . . . does what she does best: shows that guilt and blame have no single address." The New Yorker.

James, P. D.

The **private** patient / P.D. James. Alfred A. Knopf, 2008. 368 p. Adam Dalgliesh mysteries

ISBN 9780307270771

1. Scotland Yard. 2. Women journalists 3. Murder investigation 4. Plastic surgery 5. Police 6. Policewomen 7. Plastic surgeons 8. Crimes against women journalists 9. Dorset, England 10. Mysteries 11. Police procedurals

LC 2008027137

"This is a Borzoi book"--T.p. verso.

When investigative journalist Rhoda Gradwyn turns up dead after seeing renowned plastic surgeon George Chandler-Powell for a routine surgical procedure, Commander Adam Dalgliesh is called in to investigate.

"The book begins by introducing investigative journalist Rhoda Gradwyn, whose face is marked by a disfiguring scar. She chooses prominent plastic surgeon George Chandler-Powell to remove it at his private clinic in Cheverell Manor. . . . It's a place where the comfortably situated can have their cosmetic work done in privacy and not everyone welcomes the arrival of a professional snoop. The evening after her surgery, Gradwyn is murdered. Dalgleish and his team are called in to solve the mystery, then have to deal with a second murder. . . . The investigation disrupts lives and disturbs secrets far beyond the little group at the manor. James is in excellent form in Patient. She engages the brain as she entertains with apt descriptions and wry asides, and sets the reader to thinking beyond the obvious." St. Louis Post-Dispatch.

James, P. D.

The **skull** beneath the skin / P.D. James. Scribner, 1982. 416 p. Cordelia Gray mysteries

ISBN 9780684177731

1. Women private investigators 2. Murder investigation 3. Anonymous letters 4. Actors and actresses 5. Islands 6. England 7. Mysteries

LC 82005981

Hired as a bodyguard to faded actress Clarissa Lisle, the recent recipient of numerous death threats, Cordelia Gray accompanies the actress to an island castle, whose owner collects funeral paraphernalia.

"Fading actress Clarissa Lisle has been receiving frightening notes and is terrified of failing in her comeback performance, a revival of 'The Duchess of Malfi', held on a small private island off Dorset. Her husband hires detective Cordelia Gray to stop the notes. Once on the island, Cordelia discovers that nearly everyone there has a good reason to hate Clarissa, who is soon found gruesomely battered to death. The isolated group of suspects, hidden clues, and macabre atmosphere of an island castle complete with skulls and underground passageways make a pleasant traditional mystery. But James is never superficial, and her in-depth characterizations and excellent writing reveal complex relationships, motives, and human frailties." Library Journal.

James, P. D.

A **taste** for death / P.D. James. Knopf, 1986. 459 p. Adam Dalgliesh mysteries
ISBN 9780394555836
1. Scotland Yard 2. Police 3. Murder investigation 4. Social classes 5. Hoboes 6. Aristocracy 7. London, England 8. Mysteries 9. Police procedurals
LC 86045273
Macavity Award for Best Mystery Novel, 1987.
Silver Dagger Award for Fiction, 1986.
Commander Adam Dalgliesh investigates the throat-slash murders, in a London Church, of Sir Paul Berowne, former Minister of State, and a tramp named Harry Mack, murders that lead Dalgliesh onto surprising English pathways

"This book is about murder and the way murder changes everything. . . . It is also about the human condition in London today, enlarged by a sense of the British past that stretches back like a rich and barely dwindling perspective." New York Times Book Review.

James, P. D.

* An **unsuitable** job for a woman / P.D. James. Scribner, 2001, c1972. 250 p. Cordelia Gray mysteries
ISBN 9780743219556
1. University of Cambridge Students 2. Women private investigators 3. College students -- Cambridge, England 4. Murder investigation 5. Suicide 6. Cambridge, England 7. Mysteries
LC 200118202
Left alone by her partner's suicide, Cordelia Gray struggles to manage the private detective agency they once shared.

Jance, Judith A.

Birds of prey : a novel of suspense / J.A. Jance William Morrow, 2001 384 p. J. P. Beaumont mysteries
ISBN 038097407X
1. Pleasure cruises -- Gulf of Alaska 2. Murder investigation -- Gulf of Alaska 3. Religious fanaticism 4. Former detectives 5. Police -- Seattle, Washington 6. Detectives -- Seattle, Washington 7. Physicians 8. Grandmothers 9. Seniors 10. Mysteries 11. Pacific Northwest fiction
LC 00059445
Retired from the Seattle P.D. after twenty years, Jonas Piedmont Beaumont agrees to chaperon his newlywed grandmother on her honeymoon cruise to Alaska. But Beau's brief idyll is abruptly shaken when a security videotape shows a passenger taking a fatal fall overboard.

"Retired Seattle cop J. P. Beaumont accompanies his newlywed, eightysomething grandmother and her crusty hubby, Lars Jenssen, on an Alaskan cruise to act as a chaperone of sorts. The jaded protagonist is inadvertently forced to masquerade as an FBI agent when Dr. Harrison Featherman's shrill blonde wife Margaret is tossed overboard, and the crime is captured on ship security cameras." Library Journal.

Jance, Judith A.

Queen of the night / J. A. Jance. William Morrow, 2010. 368 p. Walker family
ISBN 9780061239243
1. Tohono O'Odham Indians -- Arizona 2. Cold cases (Criminal investigation) 3. Legends 4. Grandmother and grandson 5. Cactus 6. Arizona 7. Mysteries
LC 2009038976
Three separate families find their relationships threatened by murders committed fifty years apart as they uncover evidence about the crimes and are faced with self-sacrifice and unspeakable evils.

Jance, Judith A.

Skeleton Canyon : a Joanna Brady mystery / J. A. Jance. Avon Books, 1997. 373 p. Joanna Brady mysteries
ISBN 9780380973958
1. Women sheriffs 2. Murder investigation 3. Interracial romance 4. Widows 5. Cochise County, Arizona 6. Bisbee, Arizona 7. Arizona 8. Mysteries
LC 97-3217
The sheriff of Cochise County, Arizona, widow Joanna Brady becomes caught up in a deadly family tragedy initiated by a pair of star-crossed lovers, while trying to prove herself in the male-dominated world of law enforcement and struggling to cope with echoes of Tombstone's infamous Clanton gang.

"When high-school valedictorian Bree O'Brien is found dead in the southeastern Arizona mountains, suspicion falls on her boyfriend, Ignacio Ybarra, who refuses to explain his fresh cuts and bruises. But the case isn't that simple, as Coshise County Sheriff Joanna Brady learns. . . . Jance's regional knowledge runs deep, whether she writes about troubled Anglo-Hispanic relations along the border or the surprising power of Arizona thunderstorms." Publishers Weekly.

Jarvis, Stephen, 1958-

* **Death** and Mr. Pickwick : a novel / Stephen Jarvis. Farrar, Straus and Giroux, 2015. 802 p.
ISBN 9780374139667
1. Seymour, Robert, 1798-1836 2. Dickens, Charles, 1812-1870 3. Publishers and publishing 4. Caricaturists 5. Authors, English -- 19th century 6. Characters and characteristics in literature 7. Popular culture 8. Creation (Literary, artistic, etc) 9. Popularity 10. Fame 11. Great Britain -- Popular culture -- History -- 19th century 12. Biographical fiction 13. Historical fiction 14. Literary fiction
LC 2015002954
Illustrations on end papers.
Originally published: Great Britain : Jonathan Cape, 2015.
A novel based on the life of the artist Robert Seymour--the caricaturist behind The Pickwick Papers, and the extraordinary events surrounding the birth of Charles Dickens' first novel--departs from the accepted origin of Pickwick put forward by Dickens and his publisher, Edward Chapman; and it does so for good reason:the accepted origin is a lie.

"Readers don't have to buy Jarvis' argument to appreciate his teeming chronicle. Packed with interesting characters and tall tales, and ranging in setting from sporting clubs (read drinking clubs) to the theater to a factory floor to a debtors prison, this is fiction writ large." Booklist.

Jaswal, Balli Kaur

Erotic stories for Punjabi widows / Balli Kaur Jaswal. William Morrow & Co., 2017. 304 p.

ISBN 9780062645128

1. Multiculturalism 2. Creativity 3. Books and reading 4. Communities 5. Female friendship 6. Friendship 7. Panjabis (South Asian people) 8. Identity (Psychology) 9. Culture conflict 10. Panjabis (South Asian people) 11. Sikhs 12. Sexuality 13. London, England 14. England 15. Literary fiction

A lively, sexy, and thought-provoking East-meets-West story about community, friendship, and women's lives at all ages?a spicy and alluring mix of Together Tea and Calendar Girls.

"Jaswal's charming debut features an engaging protagonist who longs to break free from her more traditional mothers expectations and who is still smarting from her fathers death, but its the portrayal of the women in Nikkis' class that is the highlight: these women are considered invisible, but through their writing they can be seen and their desires and dreams can be acknowledged." Publishers Weekly

Jeffries, Sabrina

The **art** of sinning / Sabrina Jeffries. Pocket Books, 2015. 416 p. Sinful suitors

ISBN 9781476786063

1. Georgian era (1714-1837) 2. Americans in England 3. Painters 4. Artists' models 5. Heirs and heiresses 6. Aristocracy 7. Missing women 8. Artists 9. Brothels 10. Scandals 11. Sexual attraction 12. Men/women relations 13. Historical romances 14. Regency romances

Refusing to return home and take over his father's business, American artist Jeremy Keane, in search of a model for the provocative masterpiece he's driven to create, finally finds his muse in Lady Yvette Barlow, who agrees to be his subject in exchange for his help in solving a family mystery.

Jeffries, Sabrina

Project Duchess / Sabrina Jeffries. Zebra Books, 2019. 352 p. Duke dynasty

ISBN 9781420148558

1. 19th century 2. Dukes and duchesses 3. Nobility 4. Debutantes 5. Funerals 6. Arrogance in men 7. Vulnerability 8. Family relationships 9. Independence in women 10. Sexual attraction 11. Men/women relations 12. England 13. Great Britain 14. Historical romances

Being prepared for her debut by the Duke of Greycourt at the behest of his mother, Beatrice Wolf, as she gets to know the man beneath the arrogant facade, must decide where her loyalties lie--with her family or with him--when her family's secrets come to light.

Jeffries, Sabrina

'**Twas** the night after Christmas / Sabrina Jeffries. Gallery Books, 2012. 384 p. Hellions of Halstead Hall

ISBN 9781451642469

1. Regency period (1811-1820) 2. Nobility 3. Mothers and sons 4. Reconciliation 5. Widows 6. Live-in companions 7. Womanizers 8. Men/women relations 9. Sexual attraction 10. Regency romances 11. Christmas stories 12. Historical romances

LC 2012015020

This book bridges two of the author's series: The Hellions of Halstead Hall and The Duke's Men.

Summoned to visit the seriously ill mother from whom he has been estranged most of his life, Pierce Waverly, the Earl of Devonmont, learns that Camilla, his mother's beautiful companion, has tricked him to orchestrate a holiday reconciliation that progresses with conciliatory steps on both sides at the same time Pierce finds himself falling for Camilla.

Jeffries, Sabrina

What the duke desires / Sabrina Jeffries. Pocket Books, 2013. 386 p. The Duke's men

ISBN 9781451693461

1. Dukes and duchesses 2. British in France 3. Kidnapping 4. Missing men 5. Private investigators 6. Pretending 7. Sexual attraction 8. Men/women relations 9. Interclass romance 10. England -- Social life and customs -- 19th century 11. Paris, France -- Social life and customs -- 19th century 12. Historical romances

Maximilian Cale, the Duke of Lyons, and Lisette Bonnaud, pose as husband and wife to seek out their respective siblings in Regency Paris, a ruse that proves to seduce the two into each others arms.

Jemc, Jac, 1983-

* The **grip** of it / Jac Jemc. Farrar, Strauss and Giroux, 2017. 272 p.

ISBN 9780374536916

1. Suspicion 2. Paranoia 3. Psychoses 4. Married people 5. Homeowners 6. Lifestyle change 7. Home (Concept) 8. Small town life 9. Gambling 10. Spirit possession 11. Psychological suspense 12. Horror

LC 2016041347

Julie and James settle into a house in a small town outside the city where they met. As they settle into their home and their marriage, the house and its surrounding terrain become the locus of increasingly strange happenings. Together the couple embark on a panicked search for the source of their mutual torment, a journey that mires them in the history of their peculiar neighbors and the mysterious residents who lived in the house before them.

"Shivery and smart. A book that brings the legacy of Henry James into the modern world with great effect." Kirkus.

Jemisin, N. K.

* The **fifth** season / N. K. Jemisin. Orbit, 2015. 498 p. Broken Earth novels

ISBN 9780316229296

1. End of the world 2. Mothers 3. Superhuman abilities 4. Imaginary empires 5. Murder 6. Betrayal 7. Secrets 8. Searching 9. Prejudice 10. Discrimination 11. Social science fiction 12. Afrofuturism and Afrofantasy 13. Apocalyptic fiction 14. African American fiction

Hugo Award for Best Novel, 2016.

RUSA Reading List Short List, 2016.

When her husband murders their son and abducts their daughter, grief-stricken and vengeful Essun pursues him across The Stillness, a vast and dynamic super-continent on the brink of catastrophe that will usher in a "fifth season," a time of uncertainty and hardship. But Essun is as formidable as the land she traverses -- she's an orogene, which means that she can shape the contours of the land. Although she's spent much of her life hiding from those who would kill her on account of her race, Essun is about to prove how dangerous a woman on a mission can be. Set in a richly detailed, fully realized world inhabited by numerous well-drawn and complex cultures, The Fifth Season launches the Broken Earth series. -- Description by Gillian Speace.

"Jemisin's graceful prose and gritty setting provide the perfect backdrop for this fascinating tale of determined characters fighting to save a doomed world." Publishers Weekly.

Jemisin, N. K.

How long 'til black future month? / N. K. Jemisin. Orbit, 2018. 400 p.

ISBN 9780316491341

1. Magic 2. African Americans 3. Short stories 4. Afrofuturism and Afrofantasy 5. Science fiction 6. Fantasy fiction 7. African American

fiction

LC 2018034027

Locus Award for Best Collection, 2019.

Offers a collection of the author's short fiction, including "The City Born Great," where a young street kid fights to give birth to an old metropolis's soul.

"In this career-spanning collection, Jemisin ("The Broken Earth" trilogy) delivers 22 thrilling stories of black strength in the face of worldly and otherworldly adversity. ... This robust collection is a worthy introduction to three-time Hugo Award winner Jemisin's powerful work for curious newcomers and is sure to delight the author's many fans." Library Journal.

Jemisin, N. K.

The **hundred** thousand kingdoms / N.K. Jemisin. Orbit, 2010. 432 p. Inheritance trilogy (N. K. Jemisin)

ISBN 9780316043915

1. Gods and goddesses 2. Heirs and heiresses 3. Family secrets 4. Imaginary kingdoms 5. Slaves 6. Rulers 7. Epic fantasy 8. Afrofuturism and Afrofantasy 9. African American fiction

LC 2009002075

Republished in a single volume with the titles: The broken kingdoms ; The kingdom of gods ; and The awakened kingdom: New York : Orbit, 2014.

Locus Award for First Novel, 2011.

After Yeine Darr is summoned to the majestic city of Sky and named an heiress to the king of the Hundred Thousand Kingdoms, she is thrust into a vicious power struggle with cousins she never knew she had, drawing ever closer to the secrets of her mother's death and her family's bloody history.

"Debut author Jemisin creates a mesmerizingly exotic world where fallen gods serve as slaves to the ruling class and murder and ambition go hand in hand." Library Journal.

Jemisin, N. K.

The **killing** moon / N.K. Jemisin. Orbit, 2012. 448 p. Dreamblood duology

ISBN 9780316187282

1. Political corruption 2. Dreams 3. Conspiracies 4. Deserts 5. Priests 6. Gods and goddesses 7. Magic 8. Murder 9. Protectiveness in men 10. Faith 11. Secrecy in government 12. Afrofuturism and Afrofantasy 13. Middle Eastern-influenced fantasy 14. Fantasy fiction 15. African American fiction

LC 2011028110

Sequel: The shadowed sun.

Republished with The shadowed sun as The dreamblood duology: Little, Brown, 2016.

In a city where Gatherers harvest the magic of the sleeping mind and use it to judge the corrupt, Ehiru, the most famous of the city's Gatherers, learns that he must protect the woman he was sent to kill or watch the city be devoured by forbidden magic.

Jemisin, N. K.

* The **obelisk** gate / N. K. Jemisin. Orbit, 2016. 433 p. Broken Earth novels

ISBN 9780316229265

1. End of the world 2. Mothers 3. Superhuman abilities 4. Imaginary empires 5. Murder 6. Betrayal 7. Secrets 8. Searching 9. Prejudice 10. Discrimination 11. Social science fiction 12. Afrofuturism and Afrofantasy 13. Apocalyptic fiction 14. African American fiction

Hugo Award for Best Novel, 2017.

In this sequel to the Hugo Award-winning novel, The Fifth Season, the world known as Stillness is on the verge of collapse. Essun, who can harness geological forces to physically reshape her surroundings, may be able to prevent the apocalype. However, Essun's priority is searching for her lost daughter, Nassun, who travels with her father -- Essun's ex-husband who murdered their son and attempted to kill Essun for possessing an orogene's abilities. Complex characters, detailed world-building, and thought-provoking meditations on identity and human nature make this book a must-read. -- Description by Gillian Speace.

"The Stillness and those who dwell there are vividly drawn, and the threats they face are both timely and tangible. Once again Jemisin immerses readers in a complex and intricate world of warring powers, tangled morals, and twisting motivations." Publishers Weekly.

Jemisin, N. K.

* The **stone** sky / N. K. Jemisin. Orbit, 2017. 445 p. Broken Earth novels

ISBN 9780316229241

1. End of the world 2. Mothers 3. Superhuman abilities 4. Imaginary empires 5. Murder 6. Betrayal 7. Secrets 8. Searching 9. Prejudice 10. Discrimination 11. Social science fiction 12. Afrofuturism and Afrofantasy 13. Apocalyptic fiction 14. African American fiction

Hugo Award for Best Novel, 2018.

Locus Award for Fantasy Novel, 2018.

Nebula Award for Best Novel, 2017.

In this concluding volume of N.K. Jemisin's acclaimed Broken Earth trilogy, orogene Essun and her daughter Nassun find themselves on opposite sides of an ideological battle for the future of the Stillness. Like its predecessors, this novel boasts a vivid apocalyptic setting and thoughtful explorations of the nature of personhood and the ways in which systems of oppression operate. Due to the complexity of the story, newcomers will want to start with the first of the series, The Fifth Season. -- Description by Gillian Speace

"Vivid characters, a tautly constructed plot, and outstanding world-building meld into an impressive and timely story of abused, grieving survivors fighting to fix themselves and save the remnants of their shattered home." Publishers Weekly.

Jen, Gish

* The **resisters** / Gish Jen. Knopf, 2020. 320 p.

ISBN 9780525657217

1. Near future 2. Families 3. Social classes 4. Totalitarianism 5. Artificial intelligence 6. Surveillance 7. Baseball 8. Girl baseball players 9. Olympic games 10. Multiracial girls 11. African Americans 12. Asian Americans 13. Racism 14. Class conflict 15. Survival (after floods) 16. Resistance to government 17. United States 18. Dystopian fiction 19. Science fiction 20. Mainstream fiction

Enduring life on the margins in a near-future world ruthlessly divided between the employed and unemployed, a once-professional couple give birth to an athletically gifted child, whose attention by the government compels her mother to challenge society's foundations.

"While some of Jen's fans might miss the overt humor of her previous work, her intelligence and control shine through in a chilling portrait of the casual acceptance of totalitarianism." Publishers Weekly.

Jen, Gish

World and town : a novel / Gish Jen. Alfred A. Knopf, 2010. 386 p.

ISBN 9780307272195

1. Widows 2. Identity (Psychology) 3. Cambodian Americans 4. Former lovers 5. Social acceptance 6. Grief 7. Chinese American women 8. Coping 9. Violence 10. Interpersonal relations 11. Families 12. Refugees 13. City life 14. Literary fiction

LC 2010007057

Massachusetts Book Awards, Fiction Award, 2011.

Two years after burying her husband and best friend, 68-year-old Hattie Kong moves to a small New England town where she is joined by a Cambodian family and reunited with an ex-lover before tackling challenges in the form of fundamentalist Christians and struggling family farms.

"Gish sets this novel in an idyllic New England town, the kind of place we like to carelessly fetishize as the real America. At the center is 68-year-old Hattie Kong, a descendant of Confucius who's still reeling from the back-to-back deaths of her husband and her best friend. Her life, flattened by grief, is shaken up when a former lover moves to town and a family of Cambodian immigrants takes up in the trailer down the hill. Everybody in these pages, it seems, is in desperate need of a fresh start and a sense of belonging. It's into this mix that Jen gracefully introduces some of the great issues of our time: how the shock of 9/11 reverberated from city to town; how lost souls can cling meanly to fundamentalism; how it feels when a chain store bulldozes into a mom-and-pop community, or a family farm finally collapses." Entertainment Weekly.

Jenkins, Beverly, 1951-

Breathless / Beverly Jenkins. Avon Books, 2017 384 p. Old West series

ISBN 9780062389022

1. 1880s 2. Women hotel managers 3. Drifters 4. Cowboys 5. Former friends 6. Independence in women 7. Frontier and pioneer life 8. Interpersonal attraction 9. Men/women relations 10. African Americans 11. Arizona (Territory) 12. The West (United States) -- History -- 19th century 13. Western romances 14. Historical romances 15. Multicultural romances 16. African American fiction

Portia Carmichael's mother was a prostitute who abandoned Portia and her sister when they were children. Fortunately, her aunt and uncle (Forbidden's Eddy Carmichael and Rhine Fontaine) stepped in; thanks to them, Portia is now an Oberlin graduate who manages the finest hotel in the Arizona Territory. Due to her experiences, Portia has no desire to marry. But the return of an old family friend, Kent Randolph, soon has her rethinking her stance on romance -- despite his youthful reputation as a lady's man. As Kent patiently woos Portia, he must prove to her that he's matured into the kind of man she could marry. -- Description by Gillian Speace

"Her writing is both sexy and smart, and her characters come to life as real people the reader will want to know better. A thrilling and enjoyable read." Kirkus.

Jenkins, Beverly, 1951-

* **Forbidden** / Beverly Jenkins. Avon Books, 2016 384 p. Old West series

ISBN 9780062389008

1. 1870s 2. Women cooks 3. Multiracial men 4. Passing (Identity) 5. Secret identity 6. Civil War veterans 7. Politicians 8. Rich men 9. Rescues 10. African Americans 11. Social conflict 12. Interpersonal attraction 13. Men/women relations 14. Frontier and pioneer life 15. Nevada 16. The West (United States) -- History -- 19th century 17. Western romances 18. Historical romances 19. Multicultural romances 20. African American fiction

RUSA Reading List, 2017.

The son of a slave and a plantation owner, Union Army veteran?Rhine Fontaine moves to Virginia City, Nevada, where his light skin and green eyes enable him to pass for white.Convinced that passing is his best bet for helping the local black community, Rhine questions his choice after meeting cook and aspiring restaurant owner Eddy Carmichael. Eddy insists that she's bound for California as soon as she can save enough money; Rhine wants her stay, but convincing her would mean sacrificing the life he's built for himself. Fans of Beverly Jenkins' African-Ameri-

can historical romances will recognize Rhine from his supporting role in Through the Storm. -- Description by Gillian Speace.

"The characters are strong and appealing in this excellent western historical romance, with its fascinating background and modern implications." Booklist.

Jenkins, Beverly, 1951-

Rebel / Beverly Jenkins. Avon Books, 2019. 373 p. Women who dare

ISBN 9780062861689

1. 1860s 2. Postwar life 3. Determination in women 4. Architects 5. Protectiveness in men 6. Ambition in women 7. African Americans 8. Racism 9. Freed slaves 10. Revenge 11. Families 12. New Orleans, Louisiana -- History -- 19th century 13. Multicultural romances 14. Historical romances 15. African American fiction

After the Civil War, Captain Drake LeVeq, an architect from an old New Orleans family, is drawn into an irresistible intrigue when he encounters a rebellious young woman who is on a mission to help the newly emancipated community survive and flourish.

"So often, stories drawn from the African-American past deal largely with struggle, and Jenkins does not shy away from depictions of injustice and violence. But she also gives us characters who are able to thrive and love and find their ways to happy endings. A satisfying start to a new historical series from one of romance's finest writers." Kirkus.

Jenkins, Beverly, 1951-

Tempest / Beverly Jenkins. Avon Books, 2018. 373 p. Old West series

ISBN 9780062389046

1. American Westward Expansion (1803-1899) 2. Mail order brides 3. Widowers 4. African Americans 5. Single fathers 6. Fathers and daughters 7. Families 8. Men/women relations 9. Interpersonal attraction 10. Wyoming -- History -- 19th century 11. The West (United States) -- History -- 19th century 12. United States -- History -- 19th century 13. Historical romances 14. Western romances 15. Multicultural romances 16. African American fiction

RUSA Reading List Short List, 2019.

When Regan Carmichael, his mail-order bride, arrives, widower Dr. Colton Lee, who is in need of someone to care for his daughter, gets the unexpected in the form of this independent beauty who makes him believe in second chances.

Jenkins, Victoria, 1945-

An **unattended** death / Victoria Jenkins. The Permanent Press, 2012. 264 p. Irene Chavez novels

ISBN 9781579622848

1. Women detectives 2. Murder investigation 3. Crimes against rich people 4. Widows 5. Prejudice 6. Secrets 7. Small towns 8. Women psychiatrists 9. Mother and teenager 10. Single mothers 11. Puget Sound 12. Washington (State) 13. Police procedurals 14. Mysteries

LC 2012016405

Police detective Irene Chavez, newly returned to a small town in Puget Sound with her fourteen-year-old-son, finds herself in the middle of a mystery as she investigates what appears to be a sailing accident when the body of a young psychiastrist, Anne Paris, is found on the grounds of the victim's family's summer home.

Jenoff, Pam

* The **ambassador's** daughter / Pam Jenoff. Harlequin MIRA, 2013. 331 p.

ISBN 9780778315094

1. Paris Peace Conference, 1919-1920. 2. Young women 3. City life -- France 4. Interpersonal attraction 5. Engaged persons 6.

Ambassadors 7. New experiences 8. Soldiers -- Germany 9. Fathers and daughters 10. Female friendship 11. Men/women relations 12. Postwar reconstruction 13. Paris, France -- History -- 20th century 14. Historical fiction

Includes Discussion Guide Questions.

Republished in 2019 by Park Row.

Bored and torn between duty and the desire to be free, Margot strikes up unlikely alliances that make her question everything she thought she knew about where her true loyalties should lie.

Jenoff, Pam

The **lost** girls of Paris / Pam Jenoff. Park Row, 2019. 377 p.

ISBN 9780778308614

1. 1940s 2. Postwar life 3. Women spies 4. Women and war 5. World War II 6. Photographs 7. Determination in women 8. Courage in women 9. Widows 10. Historical fiction

After discovering an abandoned, photograph-filled suitcase in Grand Central Station in 1946 a young widow sets out to discover who the people in the pictures are.

Jensen, Nancy, 1961-

The **sisters** : a novel / Nancy Jensen. St. Martin's Press, 2011. 304 p.

ISBN 9780312542702

1. Sisters 2. Family secrets 3. Separated friends, relatives, etc 4. Separation (Psychology) 5. Family relationships 6. Misunderstanding 7. Familial love 8. Betrayal 9. Mothers and daughters 10. Child sexual abuse 11. Kentucky 12. Indiana 13. Historical fiction

LC 2011025854

Growing up in hardscrabble Kentucky in the 1920s, with their mother dead and their stepfather an ever-present threat, Bertie Fischer and her older sister Mabel have no one but each other--with perhaps a sweetheart for Bertie waiting in the wings. But on the day that Bertie receives her eighth-grade diploma, good intentions go terribly wrong. A choice made in desperate haste sets off a chain of misunderstandings that will divide the sisters and reverberate through three generations of women.

Jerkins, Grant

The **ninth** step / Grant Jerkins. Berkley Prime Crime, 2012. 304 p.

ISBN 9780425255988

1. Fatal traffic accidents 2. Hit-and-run accidents 3. Guilt in women 4. Drunk drivers 5. Secrets 6. Women veterinarians 7. Mathematics teachers 8. Alcoholic women 9. Psychological suspense

LC 2012014770

Working a 12-step recovery program after being involved in a hit and run accident, Helen works up the courage to meet the husband of the woman she killed, but becomes involved with him after lying about her identity.

Jewell, Lisa

The **family** upstairs / Lisa Jewell. Atria Books, 2019. 320 p.

ISBN 9781501190100

1. Orphans 2. Birthparents 3. Inheritance and succession 4. Young women 5. Mansions 6. Family secrets 7. Abandoned houses 8. Women musicians 9. Identity (Psychology) 10. London, England 11. Great Britain 12. Thrillers and suspense

Discovering the identity of her birth parents and her inheritance of a valuable mansion, 25-year-old Libby makes horrifying discoveries about the massacre and disappearances of her biological family.

Jewell, Lisa

I found you : a novel / Lisa Jewell. Atria Books, 2017. 320 p.

ISBN 9781501154591

1. Coastal towns 2. Amnesia 3. Strangers 4. Missing persons 5. Memories 6. Husband and wife 7. Single mothers 8. Brothers and sisters 9. Yorkshire, England 10. England 11. Psychological suspense 12. Gothic fiction 13. Parallel narratives

LC 2016023147

First published in Great Britain by Century in 2016.

A lonely single mom who offers shelter to an amnesiac man and a young bride who is told that her missing husband never existed struggle to make sense of their transforming worlds and connection to a sister and brother whose lives where shattered by secrets more than two decades earlier.

Jewell, Lisa

The **making** of us / Lisa Jewell. Century, 2011. 400 p.

ISBN 9781846055744

1. Half-brothers and sisters 2. Artificial insemination 3. Families 4. Identity (Psychology) 5. Fathers 6. Sperm donors 7. Men with terminal illnesses 8. London, England 9. England 10. Mainstream fiction

Originally published: London: Century, 2011.

In a hospice in Bury St Edmunds, a man called Daniel is slowly fading away. His friend Maggie sits with him every day; she holds his hand and she listens to the story of his life, to his regrets and to his secrets. And then he tells her about the children he has never met and never will. He talks of them wistfully. His legacy, he calls them. Lydia, Dean and Robyn don't know each other. Yet. And they are all facing difficult changes. Lydia is still wearing the scars from her traumatic childhood and although she is wealthy and successful, her life is lonely and disjointed. Dean is a young man, burdened with unexpected responsibility, whose life is going nowhere. And Robyn wants to be a doctor, just like her father, a man she's never met. Three people leading three very different lives. All lost. All looking for something. But when they slowly find their way into each other's lives, everything starts to change.

Jewell, Lisa

Then she was gone : a novel / Lisa Jewell. Atria Books, 2018. 359 p.

ISBN 9781501154645

1. Single fathers 2. Divorced women 3. Parents of missing children 4. Cold cases (Criminal investigation) 5. Men/women relations 6. Life change events 7. Loss (Psychology) 8. Missing teenagers 9. Suspicion 10. London, England 11. Psychological suspense

LC 2017032784

Struggling to put her life back together a decade after her beloved teen daughter's disappearance, a divorced woman bonds with a charming single father whose young child eerily resembles the woman's own lost daughter and who compels a wrenching search for answers.

Jewell, Lisa

Watching you / Lisa Jewell. Pocket Books, 2018. 324 p.

ISBN 9781501190070

1. Headmasters 2. Obsession 3. Neighborhoods 4. Secrets 5. Murder 6. Neighbors 7. Middle-aged men 8. Interpersonal relations 9. England 10. Thrillers and suspense

When a murder occurs in Melville Heights, one of the nicest neighborhoods in Bristol, England, dangerous obsessions come to light involving the headmaster at a local school, in this place where everyone has a secret.

"Expert misdirection keeps the reader guessing, and the rug-pulled-out-from-beneath-your-feet conclusioncoupled with one final, bone-chilling revelationis stunning." Booklist.

Jewett, Sarah Orne, 1849-1909

The **country** of the pointed firs and other stories / Sarah Orne Jewett. Modern Library, 1995. 296 p.

ISBN 0679601732

1. 1890s 2. Rural life -- Maine 3. Small town life -- Maine 4. Women authors 5. Senior women 6. Female friendship 7. Neighbors 8. Community life 9. New England -- Social life and customs -- 19th century 10. Maine 11. Short stories 12. Classics

LC 95002831

A wandering writer, who boards at an herbalist's house in Maine, finds herself becoming more and more involved in the lives of the villagers.

Jhabvala, Ruth Prawer, 1927-2013

At the end of the century : the stories of Ruth Prawer Jhabvala. / Ruth Prawer Jhabvala ; introduction by Anita Desai. Counterpoint, 2019. 448 p.

ISBN 9781640091375

1. Human nature 2. Europeans in India 3. Men/women relations 4. Social classes 5. India 6. Short stories 7. Literary fiction

LC 2018041024

In this vivid collection of stories, pathos, despair, sensuality and liberation are explored with sensitivity, wit and affection.

Jhabvala, Ruth Prawer, 1927-2013

* **Heat** and dust / Ruth Prawer Jhabvala. Harper & Row, 1976, c1975. 181 p.

ISBN 9780060121976

1. Extramarital affairs 2. Women nonconformists 3. Sex scandals 4. Race relations 5. Interracial sex 6. British in India 7. British women in India 8. India -- Race relations 9. India -- Rulers 10. Literary fiction 11. Parallel narratives

LC 72025088

Originally published: London : J. Murray, 1975.
Booker Prize, 1975.

In a narrative intermingling past and present, a young English woman journeys to India to reconstruct the behavior of her grandfather's first wife, Olivia, who left husband and friends in 1923 out of love for an Indian prince.

Jhabvala, Ruth Prawer, 1927-2013

My nine lives : chapters of a possible past / , Ruth Prawer Jhabvala ; illustrations by C.S.H. Jhabvala. Shoemaker & Hoard, 2004. 277 p.

ISBN 1593760280

1. Cultural differences 2. Women 3. Family relationships 4. Parents 5. Parent and child 6. Married men 7. Husband and wife 8. Married women 9. Love triangles 10. Spiritual journeys 11. Hollywood, California 12. Literary fiction

Nine vignettes offer a view of lives lived in between the cultures of London, Delhi, Hollywood, and New York--all creatively linked to portray a rich life filled with an international cast of characters.

"Jhabvala name-drops Chekhov, and this is no pretension given the grace of her spiraling plots, the depth of her psychology, the elegance of her humor, the subtly of her eroticism, and her masterfully concise descriptions of imperiled households, eccentric personalities, sexual enthrallment, unexpected alliances, and transcendent love." Booklist.

Jiang, Rong, 1946-

Wolf totem : a novel / Jiang Rong ; translated from the Chinese by Howard Goldblatt. Penguin Press, 2008. ix, 526 p.

ISBN 9781594201561

1. 1960s 2. Nomads 3. Human/animal relationships 4. Religion and culture 5. Wolves 6. Shepherds 7. Chinese in Mongolia 8. Mongolia -- History -- 20th century 9. Political fiction 10. Literary fiction 11. Translations -- Chinese to English

LC 2007037554

Man Asian Literary Prize, 2007.

In the 1960s on the eve of the Cultural Revolution, Beijing intellectual Chen Zhen undertakes a spiritual journey into the world of the nomadic Mongols, a dying culture that honors the endangered Mongolian wolf and follows a philosophy about maintaining a balance with nature.

"The novel's literary claims are shaky; and Jiang Rong's apparent wish to transform China's national character through a benign conservationism is compromised by his boy-scoutish arguments for toughness. Yet few books about today's China can match Wolf Totem as a guide to the troubled self-images of so many of its people as they stumble, grappling with some inconvenient truths of their own, into modernity." New York Times Book Review.

Jiles, Paulette, 1943-

The **color** of lightning : a novel / Paulette Jiles. William Morrow, 2009. 349 p.

ISBN 9780061690440

1. American Westward Expansion (1803-1899) 2. Freed slaves -- Texas 3. Kidnapping -- Texas 4. Battles 5. Kiowa Indians -- Wars 6. Comanche Indians -- Wars 7. Freedom 8. African American men 9. Texas -- History -- 19th century 10. Historical fiction

LC 2008046339

Sequel: News of the World.

In post-Civil War Texas, ex-slave Britt Johnson, returning from a trip, discovers his family members murdered and kidnapped as a result of an Indian raid, and sets out to rescue his loved ones and seek revenge.

"Based on the true story of an African American who was legendary for his ability to bargain with Native Americans for the return of captives, the novel also tells the fictional tale of a well-meaning, but naive young Quaker from Philadelphia, Samuel Hammond, who is sent to run a regional Bureau of Indian Affairs. The contrast between Johnson, a pragmatic man of action, and Hammond, an idealist who struggles with the ambiguities of reality, echoes the history of a period when government programs and westward expansion collided, ruinously, with Native cultures. Jiles' spare and melancholy prose is the perfect language for this tale in which survival necessitates brutality." Seattle Times.

Jiles, Paulette, 1943-

* **News** of the world : a novel / Paulette Jiles. William Morrow, 2016. 213 p.

ISBN 9780062409201

1. American Westward Expansion (1803-1899) 2. 1870s 3. Voyages and travels 4. Widowers 5. Families 6. Friendship 7. Orphans 8. Kidnapping victims 9. Kiowa Indians 10. Options, alternatives, choices 11. Texas -- History -- 19th century 12. San Antonio, Texas -- History -- 19th century 13. United States -- History -- 19th century 14. Historical fiction

LC 2015041173

Sequel to: The Color of Lightning.
RUSA Reading List Short List, 2017.

A live news reader traveling the antebellum south is offered $50 to bring an orphan girl, who was kidnapped and raised by Kiowa raiders, back to her family in San Antonio.

Jimenez, Abby

The **friend** zone / Abby Jimenez. Forever, 2019. 367 p.
ISBN 9781538715604

1. Women business owners 2. Fire fighters 3. Friendship 4. Weddings 5. Secrets 6. Infertility 7. Uterine fibroids 8. Interpersonal attraction 9. Men/women relations 10. Contemporary romances 11. Romantic comedies

Kristen Peterson doesn't do drama, will fight to the death for her friends, and has no room in her life for guys who just don't get her. She's also keeping a big secret: facing a medically necessary procedure that will make it impossible for her to have children.

"Biting wit and laugh-out-loud moments take priority, but the novel remains subtle in its sentimentality and sneaks up on the reader with unanticipated depth." Publishers Weekly.

Jimenez, Simon, 1989-

* The **vanished** birds / Simon Jimenez. Del Rey, 2020 400 p.

ISBN 9780593128985

1. Space flight 2. Space and time 3. Decision-making 4. Boys who are mute 5. Music 6. Loss (Psychology) 7. Options, alternatives, choices 8. Corporations 9. Life on other planets 10. Love 11. Interpersonal relations 12. Space 13. Space opera 14. Science fiction
LC 2019034925

An out-of-time space traveler who only aged months while decades passed back home navigates the loss of everyone she knew before finding new purpose caring for a mysterious broken child who communicates through a wooden flute.

"This powerful, suspenseful story asks us to consider what we'd sacrifice for progress--or for the ones we love. The best of what science fiction can be: a thought-provoking, heart-rending story about the choices that define our lives." Kirkus.

Jin, Ha, 1956-

* The **boat** rocker : a novel / Ha Jin. Pantheon Books, 2016. 256 p.

ISBN 9780307911629

1. 2000s (Decade) 2. Journalists 3. Chinese in the United States 4. Personal conduct 5. Asian Americans 6. Communism -- China 7. Investigative journalism 8. Ethics 9. Expatriates 10. Former wives 11. Women authors 12. New York City -- Social life and customs -- 21st century 13. Political fiction 14. Black humor 15. Literary fiction
LC 2016007449

Rendered famous for his explosive anti-Communist expose, a fiercely principled Chinese expatriate reporter endures an excruciating assignment investigating his own ex-wife, an unscrupulous novelist who has become a pawn of the Chinese government.

"Ha Jin's prose is always pleasurable to read." Publishers Weekly.

Jin, Ha, 1956-

The **crazed** / Ha Jin. Pantheon Books, 2002. 352 p.
ISBN 0375421815

1. 1980s 2. Communism 3. Loss (Psychology) 4. Teacher-student relationships 5. Grief 6. People who have had strokes 7. Graduate students 8. College teachers 9. Caretakers 10. Memories 11. Breaking up (Interpersonal relations) 12. Tiananmen Square Massacre, Beijing, China, June 3-4, 1989 13. China -- History -- 20th century 14. Psychological fiction 15. Political fiction 16. Literary fiction
LC 2002022427

Assigned to care for his fiancée's father, Professor Yang, after he suffers a stroke, Jian Wan is disturbed when the professor begins to rave against his family and colleagues, and takes great risks to uncover the truth.

"Writing with a searing restraint born of long-brewing grief over the Chinese government's surreal savageness, Ha Jin depicts a warped society in which everyone is driven mad by viciousness and injustice. But Ha Jin's dramatic indictment does not preclude love, or the ancient power of story to memorialize, awaken compassion, and shore up hope." Booklist.

Jin, Ha, 1956-

A **free** life / Ha Jin. Pantheon Books, 2007. 624 p.
ISBN 9780375424656

1. Assimilation (Sociology) 2. Disillusionment 3. Poetry writing 4. Poets 5. Chinese in the United States 6. Immigrants 7. Communism 8. Tiananmen Square Massacre, Beijing, China, June 3-4, 1989 9. Social change 10. Men/women relations 11. Interpersonal relations 12. Detachment (Psychology) 13. Literary fiction
LC 2007006177

In the wake of the Tiananmen Square massacre, Nan Wu, who had studied in the U.S. in the mid-1980s, leaves China with his wife and son to seek the freedom of the West, embarking on a migration that takes them through the heart of contemporary America.

"At each location Jin creates a rich community of characters writers, artists, political dissidents, waiters, shopkeepers, even the Dalai Lama makes an appearance that give this quiet story of modest triumph a universal dimension." Seattle Times.

Jin, Ha, 1956-

A **good** fall : stories / Ha Jin. Pantheon Books, 2009. 256 p.

ISBN 9780307378682

1. Chinese in the United States 2. Americanization 3. Identity (Psychology) 4. Immigrants 5. Queens, New York City 6. Short stories 7. Literary fiction

LC 2009008638

An anthology presents detailed pieces illuminating the experiences of Chinese immigrants in America, from a lonely composer who takes comfort in a parakeet's song to a group of children who want to change their names.

"Its an uneven collection in the best sense of the word, combining superfluous vignettes with moments of stark insight into an amalgamation that itself resembles a melting pot. . . . A few missteps dont spoil a collection of sublime moments, not the least of which occurs in the title story, its plot capturing the entire arc of the immigrant experience." Denver Post.

Jin, Ha, 1956-

* A **map** of betrayal : a novel / Ha Jin. Pantheon, 2014. 320 p.

ISBN 9780307911605

1. Former CIA agents 2. Diary writing 3. Chinese American women 4. Loyalty 5. Parents -- Death 6. Moles (Spies) 7. Espionage 8. Family secrets 9. Family relationships 10. China -- Foreign relations -- United States 11. United States -- Foreign relations -- China 12. Literary fiction 13. Spy fiction 14. Parallel narratives

LC 2014008892

"From the award-winning author of Waiting: a spare, haunting tale of espionage and conflicted loyalties that spans half a century in the entwined histories of two countries--China and the United States--and two families as it explores the complicated terrain of love and honor. When Lilian Shang, born and raised in America, discovers her father's diary after the death of her parents, she is shocked by the secrets it contains. She knew that her father, Gary, convicted decades ago of being a mole in the CIA, was the most important Chinese spy ever caught. But his diary--an astonishing chronicle of his journey from 1949 Shanghai to Okinawa to Langley, Virginia--reveals the pain and longing that his double life entailed. The trail leads Lilian to China, to her father's long-abandoned other family, whose existence she and her Irish American mother never suspected. As Lilian begins to fathom her father's dilemma--torn between loyalty to his motherland and the love he came to feel for his adopted country--she sees how his sense of duty distorted his life. But as she starts to understand that Gary, too, had been betrayed, she finds that it is up to her to prevent his tragedy from damaging yet another generation of her family"--, Provided by publisher.

"A sharply ironic, stealthily devastating tale of the tragic cost of 'blind' patriotism, told by a master of clarifying fiction, that unites the personal and the geopolitical." Booklist.

Jin, Ha, 1956-

Nanjing requiem : a novel / Ha Jin. Pantheon Books, 2011. 320 p.

ISBN 9780307379764

1. 1930s 2. Women missionaries 3. Americans in China 4. Sino-Japanese Conflict, 1937-1945 5. Nanking Massacre, Nanjing, Jiangsu Sheng, China, 1937 6. Self-fulfillment in women 7. Genocide 8. China -- History -- 20th century 9. Historical fiction 10. War stories 11. Literary fiction

LC 2010047608

During the 1937 attack on Nanjing, American missionary and women's college dean Minnie Vautrin decides to remain at her school during a violent Japanese attack that renders the school a refugee center for ten thousand women and children.

"Jin paints a convincing, harrowing portrait of heroism in the face of brutality." Publishers Weekly.

Jin, Ha, 1956-

* **Waiting** / Ha Jin. Pantheon Books, 1999. 308 p.

ISBN 0375406530

1. Love triangles 2. Men/women relations 3. Waiting 4. Physicians 5. Arranged marriage 6. Military life 7. Divorce 8. Duty 9. China -- Social life and customs -- 1949-1976 10. Literary fiction

LC 9921334

ALA Notable Book, 2000.
National Book Award for Fiction, 1999.
PEN/Faulkner Award, 2000.
Pulitzer Prize for Fiction finalist, 2000.

An ambitious and dedicated Chinese doctor, Lin Kong finds himself torn between two very different women--the educated and dynamic nurse with whom he has fallen in love and the traditional, meek, and humble woman to whom his family married him when they were both very young

"This novel provides a dual education: a crash course in Chinese society during and since the Cultural Revolution, and more leisurely but nonetheless compelling exploration of the less exotic terrain that is the human heart." New York Times Book Review.

Jin, Ha, 1956-

War trash / Ha Jin. Pantheon Books, 2004. 368 p.

ISBN 0375422765

1. Prisoners of war, Chinese 2. Survival (in concentration camps, prisons, etc) 3. Korean War, 1950-1953 -- Prisoners and prisons 4. Chinese in Korea 5. Separated friends, relatives, etc 6. Communists -- China 7. Loneliness in men 8. Anti-Communist movements 9. South Korea -- History -- 20th century 10. War stories 11. Historical fiction 12. Literary fiction

LC 2004043428

PEN-Faulkner Award, 2005.
Pulitzer Prize for Fiction finalist, 2005.

Captured by enemy forces, Yu Yuan, a Chinese army officer serving in Korea in 1951, takes on the role of interpreter due to his proficiency in English, a role that places him in a conflict between his fellow prisoners and their captors.

"Written in the modest, uninflected prose of a soldier's letter home, Ha Jin's story, a mixture of authentic historical detail and realistic invention, is a powerful work of the imagination whose psychic territory is not the hunger and humiliation of the prison camp but the haunted past that was the old, lost China and the mysterious future that is in the process of becoming Mao Zedong's chimerical new China." Washington Post.

Jin, Meng

Little gods / Meng Jin. Custom House, 2020. 279 p.

ISBN 9780062935953

1. Chinese American women 2. Mothers and daughters 3. Ambition in women 4. Love triangles 5. Mothers -- Death 6. Women physicists 7. Memories 8. Loss (Psychology) 9. Identity (Psychology) 10. Secrets 11. China 12. Literary fiction

Explores the complex web of grief, memory, time, physics, history and selfhood in the immigrant experience, and the complicated bond between daughters and mothers.

"Artfully composed and emotionally searing, Jin's debut about lost girls, bottomless ambition, and the myriad ways family members can hurt and betray one another is gripping from beginning to end." Publishers Weekly.

Jin, Yong, 1924-2018

A **hero** born : a novel / Jin Yong ; translated from the Chinese by Anna Holmwood. St. Martin's Press, 2019, c2018. 394 p. Legends of the condor heroes

ISBN 9781250220608

1. Genghis Khan, 1162-1227 2. Heroes and heroines 3. Kung fu 4. Warriors 5. Martial arts 6. Political intrigue 7. Ambition in men 8. Fathers -- Death 9. Fate and fatalism 10. China 11. Translations -- Chinese to English 12. Historical fantasy 13. Epic Fantasy

LC 2019016755

A U.S. release of an epic Chinese classic is set in the years between the Song Empire and the rise of Genghis Khan and traces the story of a murdered patriot's son who fulfills his destiny in a divided China.

"Filled to the brim with characters and action, this translation will allow English-speaking readers to finally enjoy a classic of the wuxia fantasy genre, and hopefully whet their appetites for more." Booklist.

Jio, Sarah

The **last** camellia : a novel / Sarah Jio. Plume, 2013. 320 p.

ISBN 9780452298392

1. 2000s (Decade) 2. 1940s 3. Women botanists 4. Rare and endangered plants 5. Manors 6. Secrets 7. Extortion 8. Camellias 9. Smuggling 10. Americans in England 11. Women amateur detectives 12. England -- History -- 20th century 13. Historical mysteries 14. Parallel narratives 15. Mysteries

LC 2012049474

When garden designer Addison takes up residence at an old English manor, she stumbles upon a mystery dating back to World War II that involves the enchanting camellia orchard and an old gardener's notebook, which conceals a series of horrible crimes.

John, Elnathan

Born on a Tuesday / Elnathan John. Black Cat, 2016. 256 p.

ISBN 9780802124821

1. Muslims 2. Growing up 3. Political violence 4. Students 5. Street

life 6. Apprentices 7. Islam 8. Mosques 9. Men/women relations 10. Nigeria 11. Coming-of-age stories 12. Political fiction 13. Literary fiction

Hired by the Small Party to stir up trouble during an election, a Muslim street boy in northwestern Nigeria is forced to run for his life and finds shelter in a mosque before becoming an apprentice to a sheikh as the world around him erupts into political and religious turbulence.

"Nigerian author John's story is an absorbing and sometimes disquieting look inside the contemporary Muslim world." Booklist.

Johnson, Adam, 1967-

Fortune smiles : stories / Adam Johnson. Random House, 2015 304 p.

ISBN 9780812997477

1. Literary fiction 2. Short stories

ALA Notable Book, 2016.

National Book Award for Fiction, 2015.

This short story collection by Pulitzer Prize-winning author Adam Johnson features only six items, but they're full-fledged doozies that demand careful reading. Despite differences in plot and setting (like Silicon Valley and North Korea), what they all have in common is realistic characters enduring tragic events and challenges. Taken together, they give the impression that these stories could very well be about real people (one, "Interesting Facts," has some similarities to Johnson's own life). -- Description by Shauna Griffin.

"Often funny, even when they're wrenchingly sad, the stories provide one of the truest satisfactions of reading: the opportunity to sink into worlds we otherwise would know little or nothing about, ones we might even cross the street to avoid." Publishers Weekly.

Johnson, Adam, 1967-

* The **orphan** master's son : a novel / Adam Johnson. Random House, 2011. 512 p.

ISBN 9780812992793

1. Orphanages 2. Spies 3. Kidnapping 4. Torture 5. Dictatorship 6. Political corruption 7. Violence 8. Political violence 9. North Korea 10. Political fiction 11. Literary fiction

LC 2011013410

ALA Notable Book, 2013

Pulitzer Prize for Fiction, 2013.

National Book Critics Circle Award for Fiction finalist, 2012

The son of a singer mother whose career forcibly separated her from her family and an influential father who runs an orphan work camp, Pak Jun Do rises to prominence using instinctive talents and eventually becomes a professional kidnapper and romantic rival to Kim Jong Il.

Johnson, Angela, 1961-

The **first** part last / Angela Johnson. Simon & Schuster Books for Young Readers, 2003. 144 p. Heaven trilogy

ISBN 0689849222

1. Teenage fathers 2. African American teenage boys 3. Father and child 4. Sixteen-year-old boys 5. Teenage parents 6. Infants 7. Parental love 8. Single teenage fathers 9. Teenagers in comas 10. Parenthood 11. African Americans 12. New York City 13. Coming-of-age stories 14. Realistic fiction 15. African American fiction 16. Books for reluctant readers

LC 2002036512

Coretta Scott King Award, Author Category, 2004.

Georgia Peach Book Award for Teen Readers, 2005.

Michael L. Printz Award, 2004.

When his girlfriend Nia announces that she is pregnant, sixteen-year-old Bobby, a typical urban New York City teenager, must cast aside his life of partying to visit obstetricians and social workers, who try to convince them to give their baby up for adoption, until tragedy strikes.

"Brief, poetic, and absolutely riveting." School Library Journal.

Johnson, Caleb (Caleb Rick)

Treeborne / Caleb Johnson. Picador, 2018. 308 p.

ISBN 9781250169082

1. Women -- Southern States 2. Small towns 3. Change 4. Orchards 5. Home (Concept) 6. Local history 7. Memories 8. Alabama 9. Southern states -- Social life and customs 10. Southern fiction 11. Family sagas

LC 2017060104

Anticipating the end of her small Alabama community, an orchard keeper seeks to preserve its story by imparting the experiences of the ancestors who endured hardships and loss against a backdrop of regional history.

Johnson, Charles Richard, 1948-

* **Middle** Passage / Charles Johnson. Atheneum, 1990. 209 p.

ISBN 0689119682

1. 19th century 2. Slave ships -- Atlantic Ocean 3. Mutiny 4. Freed slaves -- New Orleans, Louisiana 5. Middle passage (Atlantic slave trade) 6. Slave trade 7. Cannibalism 8. Sea stories 9. Adventure stories 10. Diary novels 11. Literary fiction 12. African American fiction

LC 90032713

National Book Award for Fiction, 1990.

National Book Critics Circle Award for Fiction finalist, 1990

In 1830, seeking to escape an unwanted marriage, Rutherford Calhoun, a newly freed slave, becomes a stowaway aboard "The Republic," unaware that the ship is a slave clipper bound for West Africa

"Johnson's exciting sea narrative provides an unusual historical look at the horrifying Middle Passage experience. . . . Like Moby-Dick's Ahab, the captain of the Republic is on his own special quest (in this case, the capture of the African trickster god). . . . Above all, the book is valuable in offering a rare perspective of the shocking experience of the slave trade and the consequences of that event for American blacks." Choice.

Johnson, Craig, 1961-

Another man's moccasins / Craig Johnson. Viking, 2008. 290 p. Walt Longmire mysteries

ISBN 9780670018611

1. Vietnam veterans 2. Human trafficking 3. Vietnamese in the United States 4. Indians of North America 5. Small town life -- Wyoming 6. Sheriffs 7. Human trafficking victims 8. Wyoming 9. Absaroka Range (Mont and Wyo) 10. The West (United States) 11. Mysteries 12. Modern Westerns

Spur Award for Best Western Novel (Short Novel), 2009.

Unsettled by similarities between a recent murder case and his first investigation as a Marine in Vietnam, Sheriff Walt Longmire wonders about a strangely familiar photograph found in the recent victim's purse.

Johnson, Craig, 1961-

Dark horse : a Walt Longmire mystery / Craig Johnson. Viking, 2009. 336 p. Walt Longmire mysteries

ISBN 9780670020874

1. Suspicion 2. Murder suspects 3. Violence against men 4. Murder investigation 5. Revenge 6. Helpfulness in men 7. Small town life -- Wyoming 8. Sheriffs 9. Wyoming 10. Absaroka Range (Mont and Wyo) 11. The West (United States) 12. Mysteries 13. Modern

Westerns

LC 2008054093

When Walt Longmire meets a woman jailed for her husband's death, he travels outside his usual haunts to discover the truth behind this unusual murder case.

"Johnson's deft, twisty storytelling immediately grips the reader. His latest has a heart as big as a Wyoming sky." Library Journal.

Johnson, Craig, 1961-

Death without company / Craig Johnson. Viking, 2006. 271 p. Walt Longmire mysteries

ISBN 0670034673

1. Abusive men 2. Cheyenne Indians 3. Violence in men 4. Murder 5. Murder investigation 6. Small town life -- Wyoming 7. Sheriffs 8. Wyoming 9. Absaroka Range (Mont and Wyo) 10. The West (United States) 11. Mysteries 12. Modern Westerns

When a resident at the Durant Home for Assisted Living is found poisoned, Sheriff Longmire finds her death proving as dramatic as her life, which was marked by connections to the coal-bed methane industry and an abusive husband.

"Johnson combines a vivid sense of the dailiness of life--and the way human relationships take root in that dailiness--with a sure--handed touch for jolting both his characters and his readers out of their comfort zones and deep into harm's way." Booklist.

Johnson, Craig, 1961-

Hell is empty : a Walt Longmire mystery / Craig Johnson. Viking, 2011. 320 p. Walt Longmire mysteries

ISBN 9780670022779

1. Confession (Law) 2. Child murder victims 3. Native American mysticism 4. Justice 5. FBI agents 6. Murderers 7. Escapes 8. Escaped convicts 9. Small town life -- Wyoming 10. Sheriffs 11. Wyoming 12. Absaroka Range (Mont and Wyo) 13. The West (United States) 14. Mysteries 15. Modern Westerns

LC 2010048021

Transporting a confessed murderer only to learn that the man's crime falls under his jurisdiction and that the killer has escaped, Sheriff Walt Longmire taps insights from Indian mysticism and Dante's "Inferno" in a manhunt through the icy Cloud Peak Wilderness Area.

Johnson, Craig, 1961-

Land of wolves / Craig Johnson. Viking Press, 2019 336 p. Walt Longmire mysteries

ISBN 9780525522508

1. Sheriffs 2. Suicide investigation 3. Wolves 4. Shepherds 5. Vietnam veterans 6. Basque Americans 7. Law enforcement 8. Wyoming 9. Modern Westerns 10. Mysteries 11. TV tie-ins 12. Franchise books

LC 2019014874

Investigating the suspicious suicide of a Wyoming shepherd, sheriff Walt Longmire uncovers disturbing connections to a violent family before the case is further complicated by the appearance of a giant wolf.

Johnson, Craig, 1961-

Spirit of steamboat : a Walt Longmire story / Craig Johnson. Viking, 2013. 112 p. Walt Longmire mysteries

ISBN 9780670015788

1. Sheriffs 2. Reunions 3. Christmas 4. World War II veterans 5. Accident victims 6. Young women 7. Memories 8. Secrets 9. Mysteries 10. Modern Westerns

LC 2013017053

A holiday entry in the best-selling series finds Sheriff Walt Longmire making the acquaintance of a scarred young woman who raises questions about his predecessor while imparting the story of a tragic car accident during a blizzard that marked Walt's first year as sheriff.

Johnson, D. E. (Dan E.)

Detroit shuffle / D.E. Johnson. Minotaur Books, 2013. 336 p. Will Anderson novels

ISBN 9781250006769

1. Attempted murder 2. Detectives -- Detroit, Michigan 3. Suffragists 4. Protectiveness in men 5. Conspiracies 6. Cousins 7. Murder suspects 8. Detroit, Michigan 9. Historical mysteries 10. Mysteries

LC 2013013935

Thwarting an attempt on Elizabeth Hume's life only to be accused of having a hallucination, Will Anderson resolves to prove his sanity against a backdrop of key suffrage legislation that is further complicated by a suspicious death and Detective Riordan's secretive behavior.

Johnson, Daisy, 1990-

Everything under / Daisy Johnson. Graywolf Press, 2018. 264 p.

ISBN 9781555978266

1. Mother-separated girls 2. Mothers and daughters 3. Lexicographers 4. Canals 5. Houseboats 6. Imaginary creatures 7. People with dementia 8. Transgender children 9. Family relationships 10. Secrets 11. Identity (Psychology) 12. Gender fluid 13. Consequences 14. Oxfordshire, England 15. Great Britain 16. Literary fiction 17. Horror

Shortlisted for the Man Booker Prize, 2018.

An eerie, watery reimagining of the Oedipus myth set on the canals of Oxford, from the author of Fen. In this electrifying reinterpretation of a classical myth, Daisy Johnson explores questions of fate and free will, gender fluidity, and fractured family relationships.

"Johnson's harrowing, singular first novel (following the story collection Fen) retells the myth of Oedipus Rex, putting a modern spin on a familiar tale." Publishers Weekly.

Johnson, Denis, 1949-2017

The **largesse** of the sea maiden : stories / Denis Johnson. Random House, 2018. 208 p.

ISBN 9780812988635

1. Purpose in life 2. Mortality 3. Aging 4. Short stories 5. Literary fiction

LC 2017027298

National Book Critics Circle Award for Fiction finalist, 2018

A posthumous story collection by the National Book Award-winning author contemplates subjects ranging from old age and mortality to the unexpected ways the mysteries of the universe manifest, depicting haunted characters who would atone for the past, remember departed loved ones or come to terms with lifelong obsessions.

"The second story collection from the late Johnson (Jesus' Son) is a masterpiece of deep humanity and astonishing prose." Publishers Weekly.

Johnson, Denis, 1949-2017

Nobody move : a novel / Denis Johnson. Farrar, Straus and Giroux, 2009. 208 p.

ISBN 9780374222901

1. Gamblers 2. Money 3. Organized crime 4. Good luck 5. Escapes 6. Alcoholic women 7. Swindlers and swindling 8. Money-making projects 9. Violence 10. Noir fiction 11. Crime fiction

LC 2008043420

In Bakersfield, California, an assortment of unscrupulous characters engages in a cat-and-mouse game over a multimillion-dollar claim.

LIST OF FICTIONAL WORKS

Johnson, Denis, 1949-2017

* **Train** dreams / Denis Johnson. Farrar, Straus and Giroux, 2011. 128 p.

ISBN 9780374281144

1. Railroad workers 2. Widowers 3. Grief in men 4. Solitude 5. Ghosts 6. Curses 7. The West (United States) -- History -- 1848-1950 8. Idaho 9. Magical realism 10. Historical fiction 11. Literary fiction 12. Pacific Northwest fiction

LC 2011007505

Pulitzer Prize for Fiction finalist, 2012.

Presents the story of early twentieth-century day laborer Robert Grainer, who endures the harrowing loss of his family while struggling for survival in the American West against a backdrop of radical historical changes.

"The story concerns the life of Robert Grainier, a fictional orphan shipped by train in 1893 into the woods of the Idaho panhandle. He grows up, works on logging gangs, falls in love, and loses his wife and baby daughter to a particularly pernicious wildfire. What Johnson builds from the ashe's of Grainier's life is a tender, lonesome and riveting story, an American epic writ small, in which Grainier drives a horse cart, flies in a biplane, takes part in occasionally hilarious exchanges and goes maybe 42 percent crazy. It's a love story, a hermit's story and a refashioning of age-old wolf-based folklore like Little Red Cap. It's also a small masterpiece. You look up from the thing dazed, slightly changed." New York Times Book Review.

Johnson, Denis, 1949-2017

Tree of smoke / Denis Johnson. Farrar, Straus and Giroux, 2007. 672 p.

ISBN 9780374279127

1. 1970s 2. 1960s 3. Intelligence officers 4. Vietnam War, 1961-1975 5. Loneliness 6. Brothers 7. Undercover operations 8. Interpersonal relations 9. Spies 10. Vietnam 11. War stories 12. Psychological fiction 13. Literary fiction

LC 2007006562

National Book Award for Fiction, 2007.

Pulitzer Prize for Fiction finalist, 2008

The lives of Skip Sands, a spy-in-training engaged in psychological operations against the Vietcong, and brothers Bill and James Houston, young men who drift out of the Arizona desert into a war, intertwine in a novel of America during the Vietnam War.

"Mr. Johnson not only succeeds in conjuring the anomalous, hallucinatory aura of the Vietnam War as authoritatively as Stephen Wright or Francis Ford Coppola, but he also shows its fallout on his characters with harrowing emotional precision. He has written a flawed but deeply resonant novel that is bound to become one of the classic works of literature produced by that tragic and uncannily familiar war." New York Times.

Johnson, Keith Lee

* **Little** black girl lost / Keith Lee Johnson. Urban Books, 2005. 324 p. Little black girl lost

ISBN 0974702552

1. 1950s 2. Prostitution 3. Race relations 4. African American women 5. Girl slaves 6. Mothers and daughters 7. Fifteen-year-old girls 8. African American teenage girls 9. Inequality 10. Men/women relations 11. New Orleans, Louisiana 12. Urban fiction 13. Thrillers and suspense

In 1950s New Orleans, beautiful fifteen-year-old Johnnie Wise is sold to a corrupt white insurance man named Earl Shamus, while being pursued by a crime boss who will stop at nothing to possess her, against a backdrop of murder, greed, jealousy, and lust.

Johnson, Keith Lee

Little black girl lost 2 / Keith Lee Johnson. Urban, 2006. 372 p. Little black girl lost

ISBN 9781893196391

1. 1950s 2. Prostitution 3. Race relations 4. Rich families 5. Betrayal 6. Extramarital affairs 7. Organized crime 8. Inequality 9. Murder 10. African American teenage girls 11. Men/women relations 12. New Orleans, Louisiana 13. Thrillers and suspense 14. Urban fiction

LC oc2007041833

In this sequel to Little Black Girl Lost, Johnnie Wise, haunted by the murder of her mother's killer and the subsequent riots, is unable to stop thinking about ruthless crime boss Napolean Bentley even though she loves Lucas Matthews, the current man in her life.

Johnson, Kij

* The **dream-quest** of Vellitt Boe / Kij Johnson. Tor.com, 2016. 169 p.

ISBN 9780765391414

1. Women college teachers 2. Quests 3. Dreams 4. Gods and goddesses 5. Women students 6. Imaginary creatures 7. Universities and colleges 8. Secrets 9. Fantasy fiction

Professor Vellitt Boe teaches at the prestigious Ulthar Women's College. When one of her most gifted students elopes with a dreamer from the waking world, Vellitt must retrieve her. But the journey sends her on a quest across the Dreamlands and into her own mysterious past, where some secrets were never meant to surface.

"Superb worldbuilding and gorgeous prose will hold readers rapt." Publishers Weekly.

Johnson, Lindsey Lee

The **most** dangerous place on earth : a novel / Lindsey Lee Johnson. Random House, 2016. 272 p.

ISBN 9780812997279

1. High school students 2. High school teachers 3. Upper class 4. Suburban life 5. Teenagers 6. Overachievers 7. Self-destructive behavior 8. Risk-taking (Psychology) 9. Cyberbullying 10. High schools 11. San Francisco Bay Area 12. California 13. Psychological fiction 14. Literary fiction

LC 2015035537

Arriving as a replacement teacher in a privileged Bay Area school, Molly becomes intrigued with the hidden lives and challenging ambitions of her students, who are struggling with a tragedy from their middle-school years.

"Readers may find themselves so swept up in this enthralling novel that they finish it in a single sitting." Publishers Weekly.

Johnson, Liz, 1981-

A **sparkle** of silver / Liz Johnson. Revell, 2018 368 p. Georgia coast novels

ISBN 9780800729622

1. Mansions 2. Treasure hunting 3. Private security services 4. Grandmothers 5. Family secrets 6. Islands 7. Interpersonal attraction 8. Men/women relations 9. Georgia 10. Christian romances

LC 2018014357

A young woman and an unlikely partner race to capture her grandmother's fading memories and find the fortune they both desperately need . . . before treasure hunters claim it for themselves.

"The romance between Millie and Ben is on a constant simmer, creating a breathtaking dynamic that will satisfy romantic suspense fans. Johnson's followers will be lining up for this new series." Library Journal.

Johnson, Mat

Pym : a novel / Mat Johnson. Spiegel & Grau, 2011. 272 p.

ISBN 9780812981582

1. Poe, Edgar Allan, 1809-1849 Narrative of Arthur Gordon Pym of Nantucket 2. Race relations 3. Monsters 4. African American college teachers 5. African Americans 6. Voyages and travels 7. Arctic regions -- Exploration 8. Satirical fiction 9. Fantasy fiction

LC 2010029331

A comic reimagining of America's racial history by a Hurston-Wright Legacy Award-winning writer follows a book collector's enslavement by giant Antarctic ice creatures after he learns that Edgar Allan Poe's unfinished novel is actually a true story.

"Relentlessly entertaining. . . . It's no easy task to balance social satire against life-threatening adventure, the allegory against the gory, but Johnson's hand is steady and his ability to play against Poe's text masterly." New York Times Book Review.

Johnson, Melonie

Smitten by the Brit / Melonie Johnson. St Martins Press, 2019. 320 p. Sometimes in love

ISBN 9781250193056

1. Women college teachers 2. Dukes and duchesses 3. Americans in Great Britain 4. Nobility 5. Betrayal 6. Weddings 7. Best man (Weddings) 8. Families 9. Sexual attraction 10. Men/women relations 11. England 12. Chicago, Illinois 13. Contemporary romances
Definitely, maybe...or love, actually?

Johnson, R. M. (Rodney Marcus)

No one in the world : a novel / R.M. Johnson and E. Lynn Harris. Simon & Schuster, 2011. 320 p.

ISBN 9781439178096

1. Secrets 2. Closeted gay men 3. African Americans 4. District attorneys 5. Criminals 6. Inheritance and succession 7. Family businesses 8. Deception 9. Debt 10. Twin brothers 11. Thrillers and suspense 12. African American fiction

LC 2010043440

Follows the experiences of a gay social climber and his career criminal brother, who reunite thirty years after being separated as children.

Johnson, Susan, 1939-

Blaze / Susan Johnson. Bantam Books, 1992, c1986. 486 p. Braddock-Black Absarokee series

ISBN 9780553299571

1. Crow Indians 2. Native American men 3. Interracial romance 4. Heirs and heiresses 5. Interpersonal attraction 6. Men/women relations 7. Boston, Massachusetts -- History -- 19th century 8. Historical romances 9. Erotic romances
Originally published: New York : Berkley Books, 1986.

In her attempts to persuade Jon Hazard Black, the Harvard-educated son of an Absarokee chief, to sell his land claim to her father, Boston heiress Blaze Braddock unwittingly captures Black's heart with her fiery spirit.

Johnson, Tara, 1978-

Engraved on the heart / Tara Johnson. Tyndale House Pub, 2018 400 p.

ISBN 9781496428318

1. American Civil War era (1861-1865) 2. Debutantes 3. Physicians 4. Underground Railroad 5. Abolitionists 6. Women with epilepsy 7. Family secrets 8. Men/women relations 9. Faith (Christianity) 10. United States Civil War, 1861-1865 11. Savannah, Georgia 12. Pennsylvania 13. Christian historical fiction

LC 2017043706

Reluctant debutante Keziah Montgomery lives beneath the weighty expectations of her staunch Confederate family, forced to keep her epilepsy secret for fear of a scandal. As the tensions of the Civil War arrive on their doorstep in Savannah, Keziah sees little cause for balls and courting. Despite her discomfort, she cannot imagine an escape from her familial confines--until her old schoolmate Micah shows her a life-changing truth that sets her feet on a new path . . . as a conductor in the Underground Railroad.

Johnston, Tim, 1962-

The **current** : a novel / Tim Johnston. Algonquin Books of Chapel Hill, 2019. 352 p.

ISBN 9781616206772

1. College students 2. Traffic accidents 3. Cold cases (Criminal investigation) 4. Accident investigation 5. Murder investigation 6. Life change events 7. Loss (Psychology) 8. Small towns 9. Sheriffs 10. Minnesota 11. Thrillers and suspense

LC 2018020534

Surviving the accident that killed her friend, a young woman delves into the case of another victim from a decade earlier to identify a killer among her neighbors.

"An apt title that functions as a beautiful metaphor for all the secrets and emotions roiling beneath the surface of every human life." Kirkus.

Johnston, Wayne

The **colony** of unrequited dreams / Wayne Johnston. Doubleday, 1999, c1998. 562 p. Newfoundland novels (Wayne Johnston)

ISBN 9780385495424

1. Smallwood, Joseph R, 1900-1991 2. 20th century 3. Labor organizers 4. Women columnists 5. Men/women relations 6. Newfoundland and Labrador -- History -- 20th century 7. Historical fiction 8. Biographical fiction 9. Literary fiction

LC 9919144

Sequel: The custodian of paradise.
Originally published: Toronto, Ont. : Knopf Canada, 1998.
ALA Notable Book, 2000.
Canadian Authors Association Literary Awards, MOSAID Technologies Inc. Award for Fiction, 1999.
Thomas Head Raddall Atlantic Fiction Prize, 1999.
Governor General's Literary Awards, English-language Fiction finalist, 1998.
Shortlisted for the Giller Prize, 1998

Joe Smallwood, an impoverished boy intent on making a name for himself, and Sheilagh Fielding, a journalist who pens his rise to power, confront their own frailties, secrets, and mutual love, in a novel of twentieth-century Newfoundland

"The very human story of Smallwood and Fielding and its historical counterpoint may both appear inauspicious, even contrived, at first, but as the book proceeds they and their pairing gather momentum to achieve a mesmerizing inevitability." New York Times Book Review.

Joinson, Suzanne

A **lady** cyclist's guide to Kashgar / Suzanne Joinson. Bloomsbury, 2012. 370 p.

ISBN 9781608198115

1. 1920s 2. Women missionaries 3. Voyages and travels 4. Friendship 5. Interpersonal relations 6. Sisters 7. Women travelers 8. Women -- Social conditions -- 20th century 9. Kashi, China 10. London, England -- Social life and customs -- 20th century 11. Historical

fiction 12. Adventure stories

LC 2011046720

In 1923, devout Eva English and her not-so-religious sister Lizzie embark on a journey to be missionaries in the ancient Silk Road city of Kashgar.

Joinson, Suzanne

The **photographer's** wife / Suzanne Joinson. Bloomsbury, 2016. 338 p.

ISBN 9781620408308

1. Between the Wars (1918-1939) 2. 1920s 3. 1930s 4. Parks 5. Political intrigue 6. British in Palestine 7. Married women 8. Pilots 9. Photographers 10. Architects 11. Secrets 12. Espionage 13. Fathers and daughters 14. Husband and wife 15. Interpersonal attraction 16. Men/women relations 17. Palestine -- History -- 1917-1948 18. Jerusalem, Israel -- History 19. Great Britain -- History -- 20th century 20. Historical fiction

Years after photographer William Harrington participates in a 1920s project to redesign Jerusalem with British parks against a backdrop of growing nationalist unrest, his revelations about long-buried secrets transform the life of his former employer's daughter.

"Atmospheric, romantic, yet refreshingly acerbicJoinson's timely portrayal of the difficult relationships between different cultures is rivaled by her heartbreaking delineation of the fragile relationships between individuals." Kirkus.

Jonasson, Jonas, 1961-

The **accidental** further adventures of the hundred-year-old man / Jonas Jonasson ; translated from the Swedish by Rachel Willson-Broyles. William Morrow & Co., 2019, c2018. 368 p. 100 year old man novels

ISBN 9780062846136

1. Senior men 2. Voyages and travels 3. Chases 4. Centenarians 5. Escapes 6. Smuggling 7. Misadventures 8. Seniors 9. Aging 10. Picaresque fiction 11. Humorous stories 12. Translations -- Swedish to English

Originally published by Piratforlaget, 2018.

When a hot air balloon ride ends with a sea landing and an unexpected rescue from a North Korean ship, one hundred-year-old Allan Karlsson and his sidekick Julius find themselves in the middle of a diplomatic crisis of epic proportions.

Jónasson, Ragnar, 1976-

The **island** / Ragnar Jonasson. Minotaur Books, 2019, 352 p. Inspector Hulda Hermannsdottir

ISBN 9781250193377

1. Hunting lodges 2. Islands 3. Women detectives 4. Wilderness areas 5. Reunions 6. Women murder victims 7. Falls (Accidents) 8. Murder investigation 9. Vacations 10. Iceland 11. Scandinavian crime fiction 12. Translations -- Icelandic to English

Prequel to The darkness.

Originally published: Reykjavik : Verold, 2016.

Autumn of 1987 takes a young couple on a romantic trip in the Westfjords holiday?a trip that gets an unexpected ending and has catastrophic consequences. Ten years later a small group of friends go for a weekend to an old hunting lodge in Ellidaey. A place completely cut off from the outside world, to reconnect. But one of them isn't going to make it out alive. And Detective Inspector Hulda Hermannsdottir is determined to find the truth in the darkness.

Jones, Darynda

A **bad** day for sunshine / Darynda Jones. St. Martin's Press, 2020. 352 p. Sunshine Vicram

ISBN 9781250149442

1. Women sheriffs 2. FBI agents 3. Missing girls 4. Kidnapping 5. Small towns 6. Men/women relations 7. Former lovers 8. New Mexico 9. Police procedurals

LC 2019048698

Challenged to prove herself when her New Mexico community becomes the center of a nationwide manhunt, police chief Sunshine Vicram is seduced by an alluring FBI agent and a sultry U.S. Marshal who test her feelings for a childhood crush.

"Compelling characters and a sexy, angst-filled bunch of mysteries add up to a winning series debut." Kirkus.

Jones, Darynda

Second grave on the left / Darynda Jones. St. Martin's Press, 2011. viii, 307 p. Charley Davidson novels

ISBN 9780312360818

1. Women psychics 2. Dreams 3. Ghosts 4. Devil 5. Paranormal phenomena 6. Demons 7. Women mediums 8. Men/women relations 9. Women amateur detectives 10. Urban fantasy 11. Fantasy mysteries

Awakened in the middle of the night by a friend who has been texted by a missing woman, Charley discovers clues linking the disappearance to the murder of a woman two weeks earlier, a situation that is complicated by the handsome son of Satan's efforts to protect Charley from demons.

"The fiery relationship between Charley and Reyes will satisfy paranormal romance fans, but it's the distinctive characters, dead and alive, and the almost constant laughs that will leave readers eager for the next installment." Publishers Weekly.

Jones, Diana Wynne

A **sudden** wild magic / Diana Wynne Jones. W. Morrow, 1992. 412 p.

ISBN 9780688118822

1. Witches 2. Space warfare 3. Men/women relations 4. Magic 5. Science fantasy

LC 92010860

An adventurous group of good witches embarks on a perilous mission to save the earth from attack by an evil predator bent on stealing the planet's ideas, innovations, and technologies.

"Jones's sly sense of humor and her accurate, affectionate depiction of relations between women and men give an extra kick to this effervescent tale." Publishers Weekly.

Jones, Douglas C. (Douglas Clyde), 1924-1998

* The **court-martial** of George Armstrong Custer / Douglas C. Jones. Scribner, 1976. 291 p.

ISBN 0684147386

1. Custer, George A (George Armstrong), 1839-1876 2. 19th century 3. Courts-martial and courts of inquiry 4. Little Big Horn, Battle of the, 1876 5. Indians of North America 6. Westerns

LC 76012606

Spur Award for Best Western Novel (Short Novel), 1977.

An alternative historical novel considers the life of George Armstrong Custer if he had lived beyond his 7th Cavalry battles and places him on trial, where he is called upon to explain what really happened at Little Bighorn.

"Slowly building the cases for the prosecution and defense, Jones does well by mixing the drama of courtroom proceedings with the color of a controversial incident." Booklist.

Jones, Edward P.

The **known** world / Edward P. Jones. Amistad, 2003. 400 p.

ISBN 9780060557546

1. Antebellum America (1820-1861) 2. African American plantation owners 3. African American slaveholders 4. Freed slaves 5. African Americans 6. Slaves 7. Fugitive slaves 8. Men with disfigurements 9. Women with disabilities 10. Sheriffs 11. Husband and wife 12. Plantation life 13. Slavery 14. Virginia -- Social conditions -- 19th century 15. Historical fiction 16. Literary fiction 17. African American fiction

LC 2003040389

ALA Notable Book, 2004.

BCALA Literary Award for First Novelist, 2004.

International IMPAC Dublin Literary Award, 2005.

National Book Critics Circle Award for Fiction, 2003.

Pulitzer Prize for Fiction, 2004.

National Book Award for Fiction finalist, 2003

Jones's ambitious novel, which ranges between the past and future and back again to the present, weaves together the lives of freed and enslaved blacks, whites, and Indians -- and allows readers a deeper understanding of the enduring multidimensional world created by the institution of slavery.

"There are few certified villains in the novel, white or black, because slavery poisons moral judgements at the root. . . . The freshness of this story lies in its very incongruity and strangeness." New York Times Book Review.

Jones, J. Sydney

The **silence** / J. Sydney Jones. Severn House, 2011. 229 p. Viennese mysteries (J. Sydney Jones)

ISBN 9780727880840

1. Gross, Hans, 1847-1915 2. Wittgenstein, Karl, 1847-1913 3. Belle Epoque (1871-1914) 4. 1900s (Decade) 5. Criminologists 6. Suicide investigation 7. Suicide 8. Journalists 9. Corruption 10. Lawyers 11. Political corruption 12. City council members 13. Missing persons investigation 14. Vienna, Austria -- History -- 20th century 15. Historical mysteries 16. Mysteries

In 1900 Vienna, lawyer Karl Werthen finds himself investigating a puzzling suicide, the disappearance of a wealthy heir, and the murder of a journalist.

Jones, James, 1921-1977

* **From** here to eternity / James Jones. Delta, 1998, c1951. 850 p.

ISBN 9780385333641

1. World War II 2. War 3. Soldiers 4. War stories 5. Literary fiction 6. Modern classics

Originally published: New York : Scribner, 1951.

National Book Award for Fiction, 1952.

Two young soldiers and the women they love are caught up in the events preceding the bombing of Pearl Harbor

"Mr. Jones has grappled with a variety of materials and handles some of them less successfully than others. There is a good deal of weak stuff in the two love affairs and the characterizations of the women, and the sorties into the field of general ideas are unimpressive. The book as a whole, however, is a spectacular achievement; it has tremendous vitality and driving power and graphic authenticity." The Atlantic.

Jones, James, 1921-1977

* The **thin** red line / James Jones. The Dial Press, 1998, c1962. 510 p.

ISBN 9780385324083

1. 1940s 2. Soldiers 3. Guadalcanal, Battle of, 1942-1943 4. Military campaigns 5. World War II 6. War stories 7. Historical fiction

LC 62012099

Originally published: New York: Scribner, 1962.

C-for-Charlie, an Army rifle company, struggles against death, depression, and cowardice during the invasion of Guadalcanal.

Jones, Sandie

The **other** woman / Sandie Jones. Minotaur Books, 2018. 294 p.

ISBN 9781250191984

1. Mother and adult son 2. Possessiveness 3. Manipulation by women 4. Couples 5. Widows 6. Mothers-in-law 7. Men/women relations 8. London, England 9. Psychological suspense

LC 2018011480

A blissful romance between Adam and Emily is challenged by Adam's manipulative mother, who resorts to dire measures to keep all other women out of her son's life.

Jones, Sadie

The **outcast** / Sadie Jones. Harper Collins, 2008. 352 p.

ISBN 0061374032

1. 1950s 2. 1950s 3. Postwar life 4. Homecomings 5. Fathers and sons 6. Family relationships 7. Secrets 8. Neighbors 9. Middle class families 10. Drowning 11. Mother-separated families 12. Grief 13. Guilt 14. Alcoholism 15. Social isolation 16. England 17. Historical fiction

Originally published: Great Britain : Chatto & Windus, 2007.

Costa First Novel Award, 2008.

Shortlisted for The Orange Prize for Fiction, 2008

Neglected by his father and stepmother in the years after his mother's death, seventeen-year-old Lewis Aldridge commits an act of violence that lands him in prison and returns two years later to a community that no longer welcomes him.

"An explosive drama, fuelled by the repression of 1950s Britain. Troubled 19-year-old Lewis Aldridge has never recovered from the death of his mother. After a stint in prison, he heads home and attempts to convince his father of his worth. But his good intentions crumble in the face of his father's disapproval, and Lewis reveals the horrifying realities that lie under the seemingly sedate rural community. Devastatingly good." Marie Claire.

Jones, Sadie

Small wars : a novel / Sadie Jones. Harper, 2010, c2009. 376 p.

ISBN 9780061929885

1. 1950s 2. Military spouses 3. War -- Psychological aspects 4. Marital conflict 5. Atrocities 6. Soldiers -- Great Britain 7. British in Cyprus 8. Colonialism 9. Cyprus -- History -- 20th century 10. Historical fiction 11. War stories

First published: London : Chatto & Windus, 2009.

After career soldier Hal Treherne is transferred to the British colony of Cyprus, his wife, Clara, and two daughters follow, but Clara becomes fearful of her increasingly distant husband and the atrocities that take him further from her.

"Jones is excellent at evoking fraught moments in both halves of the Trehernes' lives." Christian Science Monitor.

LIST OF FICTIONAL WORKS

Jones, Sadie

The **uninvited** guests / Sadie Jones. Harper, 2012. 262 p.
ISBN 9780062116505

1. Edwardian era (1901-1914) 2. 1910s 3. Eccentric families 4. Supernatural 5. Houseguests 6. Manors 7. Railroad accidents 8. Ghosts 9. England -- Social life and customs -- 20th century 10. Historical fiction 11. Satirical fiction

Originally published: London: Chatto & Windus, 2012.

One late spring evening in 1912, in the kitchens at Sterne, preparations begin for an elegant supper party in honour of Emerald Torrington's twentieth birthday.

Jones, Sherry, 1961-

Four sisters, all queens / Sherry Jones. Gallery Books, 2012. 434 p.
ISBN 9781451633245

1. Marguerite,, Queen, consort of Louis IX, King of France, 1221-1295 2. Eleanor,, of Provence, Queen, consort of Henry III, King of England, 1223 or 1224-1291 3. Beatrice,, of Provence, Queen of Sicily, consort of Charles I, King of Naples, 1234-1267 4. Sancha,, of Provence, Queen, consort of Richard, King of the Romans, 1225-1261 5. 13th century 6. Sisters -- Europe 7. Courts and courtiers 8. Women rulers -- Europe 9. Europe -- History -- 476-1492 10. Biographical fiction 11. Historical fiction

LC 2011044484

Advised by their mother to place their family first in all things, medieval royal sisters Marguerite, Eleanor, Sanchia and Beatrice become influential queens who further their kingdoms' respective agendas and advance family power until the death of their father tears them apart.

Jones, Stephen Graham, 1972-

Mongrels : a novel / Stephen Graham Jones. HarperCollins, 2016 240 p.
ISBN 9780062412690

1. Werewolves 2. Preteen boys 3. Wanderers and wandering 4. Identity (Psychology) 5. Aunts and uncles 6. Self-discovery 7. Shapeshifting 8. Growing up 9. Families 10. Drifters 11. Southern States 12. Horror 13. Coming-of-age stories

LC 2015041168

Enduring a hardscrabble, marginalized existence with his impoverished family outside of a society that does not understand or want him, a young boy travels in the night to escape legal harassment while his family watches diligently to see if he will display the same differences that have shaped their unusual lives.

Jones, Tanen

The **better** liar : a novel / Tanen Jones. Ballantine Books, 2020. 306 p.
ISBN 9781984821225

1. Sisters 2. Impersonation 3. Wills 4. Swindlers and swindling 5. Fathers -- Death 6. Mothers and daughters 7. Deception 8. Secrets 9. Psychological suspense

LC 2019034777

Desperate to safeguard a much-needed inheritance that is dependent on the legacy of a long-estranged runaway sibling, Leslie orchestrates a reckless bargain with an imposter who hides her own dangerous secrets.

"A stunning twist ending will leave readers waiting to see what Jones will give them next." Booklist.

Jones, Tayari

* An **American** marriage : a novel / Tayari Jones. Algonquin Books of Chapel Hill, 2018. 308 p.
ISBN 9781616201340

1. Marriage 2. African American families 3. False imprisonment 4. Husband and wife 5. Life change events 6. Extramarital affairs 7. Racism 8. African Americans 9. Letter writing 10. Loss (Psychology) 11. Consequences 12. Men/women relations 13. Atlanta, Georgia 14. Louisiana 15. Literary fiction 16. Southern fiction 17. Domestic fiction 18. African American fiction

LC 2017030582

ALA Notable Book, 2019.
Women's Prize for Fiction, 2019.
BCALA Literary Award for Fiction, 2019.

When her new husband is arrested and imprisoned for a crime she knows he did not commit, a rising artist takes comfort in a longtime friendship, only to encounter unexpected challenges in resuming her life when her husband's sentence is suddenly overturned.

"Jones crafts an affecting tale that explores marriage, family, regret, and other feelings made all the more resonant by her well-drawn characters and their intricate conflicts of heart and mind." Booklist.

Jones, Tayari

Silver sparrow : a novel / Tayari Jones. Algonquin Books of Chapel Hill, 2011. 352 p.
ISBN 9781565129900

1. 1980s 2. African American families 3. Polygamy 4. Family secrets 5. African American teenage girls 6. Betrayal 7. Half-sisters 8. Mothers and daughters 9. Fathers and daughters 10. Teenage boy/girl relations 11. Atlanta, Georgia 12. Literary fiction 13. Coming-of-age stories 14. Literary fiction 15. African American fiction 16. Southern fiction

LC 2010048098

BCALA Literary Award for Fiction, 2012.

In 1980s Atlanta, James Witherspoon is living a double life. He has two families, a public one and a secret one. When the daughters from each family become friends, James' secrets are revealed and lives are changed forever.

"A tense, layered and evocative tale. . . . Jones explores the rivalry and connection of siblings, the meaning of beauty, the perils of young womanhood, the complexities of romantic relationships and the contemporary African-American experience." Minneapolis Star Tribune.

Jong, Erica

* **Fear** of flying : a novel / Erica Jong. Holt, Rinehart and Winston, 1973. 340 p.
ISBN 9780030107313

1. Women poets 2. Marital conflict 3. Self-fulfillment in women 4. Extramarital affairs 5. Men/women relations 6. Independence in women 7. Jewish American women 8. Sexuality 9. Erotic fiction 10. Psychological fiction

LC 73003697

Sequel: How to save your own life.

Records the erotic fantasies and outrageous adventures of Isadora Wing who travels constantly in spite of her phobia of flight.

"At times, Jong gets caught in cliches about women, men, sex, and Jewish mothers, all [of] which she could do without. However, when she takes herself more seriously, the language is penetrating, paying tribute to her worth as a poet." Library Journal.

Jordan, Hillary, 1963-

Mudbound : a novel / Hillary Jordan. Algonquin Books Of Chapel Hill, 2008. 328 p.

ISBN 9781565125698

1. 1940s 2. Racism 3. Farm life -- Mississippi 4. African American veterans 5. World War II veterans 6. Prejudice 7. Race relations -- Mississippi 8. Mississippi 9. Historical fiction 10. Southern fiction
LC 2007044471

Bellwether Prize for Fiction, 2006.

In 1946, Laura McAllan tries to adjust after moving with her husband and two children to an isolated cotton farm in the Mississipi Delta.

"With authentic, earthy prose . . . Jordan picks at the scabs of racial inequality that will perhaps never fully heal and brings just enough heartbreak to this intimate, universal tale, just enough suspense, to leave us contemplating how the lives and motives of these vivid characters might have been different." San Antonio Express-News.

Jordan, Hillary, 1963-

When she woke : a novel / Hillary Jordan. Algonquin Books of Chapel Hill, 2011. 352 p.

ISBN 9781565126299

1. Women former convicts 2. Stigmatization 3. Self-discovery in women 4. Abortion -- Political aspects 5. Dystopias 6. Church and state 7. Texas 8. Political fiction 9. Literary fiction

Amelia Bloomer List, 2012

In the middle of the 21st century, a young woman in Texas awakens to a nightmarish new life: her skin has been genetically altered, turned bright red as punishment for the crime of having an abortion. Stigmatized and in a hostile and frightening world, Hannah Payne must make a perilous journey northward to safety.

"Jordan manages to open up powerful feminist and political themes without becoming overly preachyand the parallels with Hawthorne are fun to trace." Kirkus.

Joseph, Fabiola

Niya : rainbow dreams / Fabiola Joseph. Urban Books, 2016. 288 p.

ISBN 9781622867851

1. Lesbian teenagers 2. Friendship 3. Love triangles 4. Self-discovery 5. Coping 6. Musicians 7. Women/women relations 8. Urban fiction 9. LGBTQIA fiction 10. African American fiction

Do you know who you are? Are you comfortable in your skin? Outed by her best friend in front of the whole neighborhood, Niya is trying to come to terms with being a lesbian. When she falls for her straight neighbor, Jamilla, there is no more denying who she really is. Niya will do whatever it takes to prove her love, even if it means taking a life. What will happen when family issues, fame, the struggle for love, and reality set in? How will Niya deal with a Hip-Hop career as she tries to repair her broken heart and family issues?

Joshi, Alka

The **henna** artist / Alka Joshi. Mira Books, 2020. 368 p.

ISBN 9780778309451

1. 1950s 2. Women artists 3. Runaway wives, husbands, etc 4. Abusive men 5. Young women 6. Arranged marriage 7. Henna 8. Mehndi (Body painting) 9. Upper class 10. Secrets 11. Families 12. Self-discovery in women 13. India 14. Historical fiction

A talented henna artist for wealthy confidantes finds her efforts to control her own destiny in 1950s Jaipur threatened by the abusive husband she fled as a teenage girl.

"Joshi has constructed a bewitching glimpse into the not-so-distant past with a tough heroine well worth cheering on." Booklist.

Joss, Morag

Among the missing : a novel / Morag Joss. Delacorte Press, 2011. 272 p.

ISBN 9780385342742

1. Love triangles 2. New identities 3. Missing persons 4. Secrets 5. Pregnant women 6. Immigrants 7. Former convicts 8. Loss (Psychology) 9. Identity (Psychology) 10. Former convicts 11. Scotland 12. Psychological suspense
LC 2010052989

When a bridge collapses in Scotland, dozens of people plunge into the freezing water below. Only an amateur video and the bridge's security camera record the tragedy. A woman whose car was among those on the bridge is assumed to be among the dead. However, she sold the car and house before and begins life anew with a clean slate and a new name: Annabel. Now living with Silva, an illegal immigrant whose husband and child has disappeared, Annabel befriends Ron, a boatman who has his own secrets.

"[Joss] builds the relationships among her sad trio slowly, through excruciatingly subtle modulations of tone. But the ending fully justifies every intimation of imminent doom." Kirkus.

Joss, Morag

Half broken things / Morag Joss. Delacorte Press, 2005 303 p.

ISBN 0385339402

1. Misfits (Persons) 2. Loners 3. Housesitting 4. Discontent 5. Women housesitters 6. Senior women 7. Pregnant teenagers 8. Criminals 9. Manors 10. Country homes 11. Nontraditional families 12. Love triangles 13. Loss (Psychology) 14. England 15. Psychological suspense 16. Literary fiction

Silver Dagger Award for Fiction, 2003.

Follows the lives of three strangers--an aging housesitter, a struggling con man, and a young pregnant woman--who seek refuge at Walden Manor, a remote country estate, as they attempt to rebuild their individual lives.

Joss, Morag

The **night** following / Morag Joss. Delacorte Press, 2008. 354 p.

ISBN 9780385341189

1. Hit-and-run drivers 2. Deception 3. Guilt in women 4. Married people and secrets 5. Married women 6. Physicians' spouses 7. Extramarital affairs 8. Hit-and-run accidents 9. Accidental death 10. Manslaughter 11. Secrets -- Psychological aspects 12. Obsession in women 13. England 14. Wiltshire, England 15. Psychological suspense 16. Literary fiction

Moments after discovering that her husband has been having an affair, a woman driving along a winding country lane strikes and kills a woman on a bicycle and then drives away, in a psychological portrait of the repercussions of deception.

"In The Night Following, a bleak, exquisitely written novel, Morag Joss braids together three stories of shattering loneliness that intersect in surprising, haunting ways." Entertainment Weekly.

Joyce, Graham, 1954-

The **limits** of enchantment : a novel / Graham Joyce. Atria Books, 2005. 272 p.

ISBN 9780743463447

1. 1960s 2. Witches 3. Women herbalists 4. Herbalists 5. Midwives 6. Teenage girls 7. Adopted teenage girls 8. Children of sick persons 9. Young women 10. Herbal medicine 11. Manners and customs 12. Hippies 13. Communes 14. Beat culture 15. Social marginality 16. Prejudice 17. Social change 18. Change (Psychology) 19. Life

change events 20. Secrets 21. Rural life 22. Villages 23. Family businesses 24. Midlands, England 25. England -- Social life and customs -- 20th century 26. Domestic fiction 27. Contemporary fantasy 28. Coming-of-age stories

LC 2004056683

Growing up in the 1960s under the tutelage of unconventional mid-wife Mammy, Fern Cullen finds the people of their small English village rallying against them when a patient dies, forcing Fern to turn to former adversaries for support.

"Generally the prose is economical, hurrying along a plot which engages as a whole, despite the weight of Fern's introspection." Times Literary Supplement.

Joyce, Graham, 1954-

Some kind of fairy tale : a novel / Graham Joyce. Doubleday, 2012. 352 p.

ISBN 9780385535786

1. Missing persons 2. Memory 3. Fairy tales 4. Absence and presumption of death 5. Forests 6. Small towns 7. England 8. Urban fantasy

LC 2012001946

Returning to her English family home on Christmas 20 years after her inexplicable disappearance, young Tara Martin, who seems to have not aged a day, imparts a fantastical tale that her brother, Peter, is unable to believe.

Joyce, James, 1882-1941

* **Dubliners** / James Joyce. A. A. Knopf, 1991. 287 p.
ISBN 9780679405740

1. Dublin, Ireland -- Social life and customs -- 20th century 2. Ireland -- Social life and customs -- 20th century 3. Short stories 4. Modern classics 5. Literary fiction

LC 91053001

Dubliners first published 1914.

Originally published: London : Grant Richards, 1914.

In this collection of masterful stories, steeped in realism, James Joyce creates an exacting portrait of his native city, showing how it reflects the general decline of Irish culture and civilization.

Joyce, James, 1882-1941

* **Finnegans** wake / James Joyce. Penguin Books, 1999, c1939. 628 p.

ISBN 9780141181264

1. Senior men -- Ireland 2. Dreams 3. Men's dreams 4. Men -- Psychology 5. Dublin, Ireland -- Social conditions -- 20th century 6. Ireland -- Social conditions -- 20th century 7. Psychological fiction 8. Experimental fiction 9. Modern classics 10. Literary fiction

'Riverrun past Eve and Adam's, from swerve of shore to bend of bay, brings us by a commodius vicus of recirculation back to Howth Castle and Environs ..." So starts Finnegans wake, the greatest challenge in twentieth-century literature. Who is Humphrey Chimpden Earwicker? And what did he get up to in Phoenix Park? And what did Anna Livia Plurabelle have to say about it? In the rich night time language of dreams here is history, anecdote, myth, folk tale -- and above all, a wondrous sense of humour coloured by a clear sense of humanity.

Joyce, James, 1882-1941

* A **portrait** of the artist as a young man / James Joyce. Knopf, 1991, c1916. xli, 318 p.

ISBN 9780679405757

1. Joyce, James, 1882-1941 2. Catholic Church Ireland Social aspects 3. Young men 4. Artists 5. Families 6. Catholics 7. Self-fulfillment in men 8. Ireland -- Social conditions -- 20th century 9.

Dublin, Ireland -- History -- 20th century 10. Coming-of-age stories 11. Autobiographical fiction 12. Modern classics 13. Literary fiction

Originally serialized in The Egoist, 1914-1915 and collected in book form in 1916.

This edition first published: United States : Vintage International, 1993.

Stephen Dedalus, a sensitive and creative youth, rebels against his family, his education, and his country by committing himself to the artist's life.

Joyce, James, 1882-1941

* **Ulysses** / James Joyce. Modern Library, 1992, c1922. 783 p.

ISBN 9780679600114

1. Men -- Personal conduct 2. Married people 3. City life -- Dublin, Ireland 4. Alienation (Social psychology) 5. Dublin, Ireland -- Social conditions -- 20th century 6. Ireland -- Social conditions -- 20th century 7. Psychological fiction 8. Modern classics 9. Literary fiction

Originally published: Paris : Shakespeare & Company, 1922.

A day in the life of Leopold Bloom, whose odyssey through the streets of turn-of-the-century Dublin leads him through trials that parallel those of Ulysses on his epic journey home.

July, Miranda, 1974-

No one belongs here more than you : stories / Miranda July. Scribner, 2007. 224 p.

ISBN 9780743299398

1. Love 2. Social acceptance 3. Interpersonal relations 4. Reality 5. Short stories

LC 2006051156

Collected here are 16 pieces of short fiction written with July's signature wit. Both touching and dangerous, July's stories continually surprise and will be a treat for anyone who loves daring fiction.

"July writes about desire to be understood, to be part of another person. . . . The engine that drives these stories is July's voice the book is full of wistful, wonderful observations about the limits of connection, about the hopes and disappointments of intimacy." Los Angeles Times.

Jungstedt, Mari, 1962-

The **inner** circle / Mari Jungstedt ; translated from the Swedish by Tiina Nunnally. St. Martin's Minotaur, 2008, c2005. 280 p. Detective Anders Knutas mysteries

ISBN 9780312363789

1. Detectives -- Sweden 2. Occult crime 3. Murder 4. Murder investigation 5. Occult crime victims 6. Men/women relations 7. Archaeology 8. Archaeological sites 9. Gotland, Sweden 10. Police procedurals 11. Mysteries 12. Scandinavian crime fiction 13. Translations -- Swedish to English

LC 2008024761

Originally published: Stockholm : Bonnier, 2005.

Working on an archaeological dig to uncover an ancient Viking fortification on the Swedish island of Gotland, a group of students becomes caught up in a web of horror when a young woman turns up dead, naked, and hanging from a tree, the victim of a ritual killing, as Inspector Knutas races against time to find the link between the victim and other local violence.

Just, Ward

Rodin's debutante / Ward Just. Houghton Mifflin Harcourt, 2011. 263 p.

ISBN 9780547504193

1. Sculptors -- United States 2. Boarding schools 3. Sex crimes 4. Friendship 5. Sculpture 6. Growth (Psychology) 7. Chicago, Illinois

-- History -- 20th century 8. Coming-of-age stories 9. Historical fiction

Sculptor Lee Goodell reflects on his time at a Chicago boys' school, as well as on the sexual assault of a childhood friend, who has no memory of the attack on her.

"Rodin's Debutante is a surprising story, never going where you expect it to, and Just's spare prose packs a solid emotional punch." Entertainment Weekly.

Just, Ward

* An **unfinished** season / Ward Just. Houghton Mifflin, 2004. 251 p.

ISBN 9780618036691

1. 1950s 2. Young men 3. Teenage boys 4. Nineteen-year-old men 5. Parent and child 6. Printing industry and trade 7. Labor unions 8. Strikes 9. Social classes 10. Newspaper publishers and publishing 11. Loss (Psychology) 12. Family problems 13. Teenage boy/girl relations 14. Secrets 15. Memories 16. Illinois 17. Chicago, Illinois 18. Coming-of-age stories 19. Domestic fiction 20. Historical fiction

LC 2004042722

Great Lakes Book Awards, Fiction category, 2005.
Pulitzer Prize for Fiction finalist, 2005.

Class struggle and family tensions explode in this novel of life in a Chicago suburb in the 1950s, as a teenager watches his father's psyche crumble in the wake of union problems and marital difficulties.

"Even if the setting of Just's . . . novel is the Midwest instead of Washington, Saigon or Paris, the territory is familiar: it's the world of memory tinged with regret. It's the early 1950s, the dawn of the cold war and the Red scare. . . This is vintage Just: elegant writing that captures the wounded spirit of the times." Newsweek

K

K'wan

* **Animal** /   K'wan. Cash Money Content, 2012. 407 p. Animal novels (K'wan)

ISBN 9781936399253

1. Street life 2. Revenge 3. Fugitives 4. Attempted murder 5. Secrets 6. African Americans 7. New York City 8. Harlem, New York City 9. Urban fiction 10. African American fiction

LC bl2012025014

Street Lit Book Award Medal: Adult Fiction, 2013
Street Lit Book Award Medal: Emerging Classic, 2013

When Animal returns to Harlem and learns of the attempt on his soul mate's life, he wages a personal war against those responsible, only to discover the frightening truth in the process.

K'wan

Animal II : the omen / K'Wan. Cashmoney, 2013. 336 p. Animal novels (K'wan)

ISBN 9781936399291

1. Street life 2. Revenge 3. Father and adult son 4. Cooperation 5. Enemies 6. Secrets 7. Inner city 8. African Americans 9. New York City 10. Harlem, New York City 11. Urban fiction 12. African American fiction

When Animal returns to Harlem, he is captured by Shai Clark and sentenced to death by the crime boss, only to discover that the executioner is actually his missing father, and the two band together to defeat a common enemy.

K'wan

The **Diamond** empire / K'wan. St Martin's Griffin, 2017. 260 p. Diamonds and Pearl

ISBN 9781250102638

1. Drug lords 2. Business competition 3. African Americans 4. Street life 5. Drug traffic 6. Organized crime 7. Men/women relations 8. Power (Social sciences) 9. New York City 10. New Orleans, Louisiana 11. Urban fiction 12. African American fiction

When his crew is usurped by an ambitious rival, an exiled Diamond carefully plans his comeback only to be outmaneuvered by an unexpected enemy from the past; while a grieving Pearl finds herself pushed into the very life her father worked to prevent.

K'wan

* **Diamonds** and Pearl / K'wan. St Martin's Griffin, 2016. 320 p. Diamonds and Pearl

ISBN 9781250102614

1. Street life 2. Criminals 3. African Americans 4. Murder 5. Survival 6. Robbery 7. Drug lords 8. Drug traffic 9. Drug dealers 10. Children of criminals 11. Men/women relations 12. New York City 13. New Orleans, Louisiana 14. Urban fiction

LC 2016021589

"They say that good girls like bad boys, and this was especially true for Pearl Stone. A child born of privilege to a drug baron and reputed killer known in the streets as Big Stone. Although the flashy, fast-paced nature of the streets calls to Pearl, she's been brought up to look but not touch. But when a young hustler named Diamonds crawls up from the swamps of Louisiana and sets up shop in New York City, everything Pearl was taught flies out the window."--Provided by publisher.

K'wan

The **fix** / K'wan. Urban Books, 2014. 288 p. Fix novels

ISBN 9781601625854

1. Street life 2. Drug use 3. Life change events 4. Addiction 5. African Americans 6. Lifestyle change 7. Drug addicts 8. Sexuality 9. Men/women relations 10. Harlem, New York City 11. New York City 12. Urban fiction

LC bl2014000550

Persia reunites with her old Harlem friends, a situation that becomes dangerous when she starts dating a drug dealer who brings her into his world of sex, money, and drugs.

K'wan

Gangsta /   K'wan. Urban Books, 2013, c2003. 263 p. Gangsta novels

ISBN 9781601625762

1. Crips (Gang) 2. Gang members 3. African American men 4. Friendship 5. African American authors 6. African Americans 7. African American gangs 8. Gangs 9. Violence in gangs 10. Street life 11. Moving to a new state 12. Ambition in men 13. California 14. New York City 15. Urban fiction 16. African American fiction

Sequel: Gutter.
Originally published: Columbus, Ohio : Triple Crown, 2003.

Crip assassin Lou-Loc, who wants to be a writer, and his sociopath counterpart Gutter, who has dreams of being a kingpin, leave Los Angeles for New York, each with his dream in tow.

K'wan

Gutter / K'wan. St. Martin's Griffin, 2008. 416 p. Gangsta novels

ISBN 9780312360092

1. Crips (Gang) 2. Bloods (Gang) 3. Gang members 4. African

American men 5. Violence in men 6. Street life 7. Best friends 8. Revenge 9. Pregnant women 10. Competition 11. Hate in men 12. Organized crime 13. African American gangs 14. Gangs 15. Harlem, New York City 16. Urban fiction 17. African American fiction

LC 2008021526

Sequel to: Gangsta

After Lou-loc's brutal murder, his best friend, Gutter, vows to seek revenge on the entire Blood faction in New York City in retaliation, despite the pleas of his pregnant girlfriend, Sharell, unaware that a vicious adversary named Major Blood has plans to shut down the Harlem Crips and eliminate Gutter and all those who matter to him.

K'wan

Hoodlum / K'wan. St. Martin's Griffin, 2005. 336 p. ISBN 0312333080

1. African American young men 2. Street life 3. Organized crime 4. Young men 5. African American brothers 6. Brothers 7. Adult children of gangsters 8. African American men 9. College dropouts 10. African American basketball players 11. Fathers -- Death 12. African Americans 13. African American families 14. Families of murder victims 15. Adult children of murder victims 16. Families 17. Murder 18. Revenge 19. Business competition 20. Ghettoes, African American -- Harlem, New York City 21. Organized crime and heroin traffic 22. Loyalty 23. Street life 24. Harlem, New York City 25. Urban fiction 26. African American fiction

Later published as The good son. Write 2 Eat Concepts, 2017.

Street Lit Book Award Medal: Adult Fiction, 2006

After waging a war on the streets that lasts nearly three years, Shai feels that he can finally try to legitimize his family's business, but when enemies old and new come out of the woodwork, it becomes clear that the previous battle was just a warm-up.

K'wan

Lawless / K'wan. Urban Books, 2019. 266 p. ISBN 9781601621245

1. Murder investigation 2. African American women 3. Married people and secrets 4. Marketing consultants 5. African Americans 6. Lawyers 7. Murder 8. Secrets 9. Atlanta, Georgia 10. New Orleans, Louisiana 11. Urban fiction 12. African American fiction

Atlanta marketing mogul Bernadette "Bernie" Hunt falls for and marries high-powered lawyer Keith Davis, but when she and Keith must go to his native New Orleans to solve a murder mystery, she begins to learn about his dark past.

K'wan

Revelations / K'wan. Cashmoney, 2014. 336 p. Animal novels (K'wan)

ISBN 9781936399932

1. Street life 2. Protectiveness in men 3. Single mothers 4. Former lovers 5. Enemies 6. Secrets 7. Inner city 8. African Americans 9. New York City 10. Harlem, New York City 11. Urban fiction 12. African American fiction

Forced to return to street life by the shocking revelation that he has fathered a child, Animal embarks on a deadly mission to stop a powerful drug dealer, who would kill Animal's daughter and the girl's mother.

K'wan

Section 8 : a hood rat novel / K'wan. St. Martin's Griffin, 2009. 368 p. Hood rat novels

ISBN 9780312536961

1. Street life 2. Public housing 3. African American single mothers 4. Prisoners 5. Criminals 6. Drug traffic 7. Women swindlers 8. Rap music industry and trade 9. Men/women relations 10. Father-

separated families 11. Brooklyn, New York City 12. New York City 13. Urban fiction 14. African American fiction

LC 2009012530

Includes characters from Hood rat and Still Hood.

With two kids, her boyfriend Duhan in prison, and no back up plan, Tionna moves back to her old rough-and-tumble neighborhood, where she is reunited with her friends Gucci, Boots, and Tracy and must again live by her wits to maintain the lifestyle she has become accustomed to.

K'wan

Street dreams / K'wan. St. Martin's Griffin, 2004. 310 p. ISBN 0312333064

1. African American young men 2. Ghettoes, African American -- Harlem, New York City 3. Ambition in men 4. African American men 5. Young men 6. African American former convicts 7. Former convicts 8. African American teenagers 9. African American young women 10. Sexually abused teenagers 11. Soul mates 12. African American men/women relations 13. Street life 14. Ambition 15. Ambition in women 16. Drug traffic 17. Harlem, New York City 18. Coming-of-age stories 19. Urban fiction 20. African American fiction

LC 2004046805

Two young people--Darius, a.k.a. Rio, the hustler son of an alcoholic singer who did prison time for a friend, and his soulmate, Trinity, the daughter of an abusive father--find solace in their love from the troubled realities of their lives, all the while dreaming of an escape from the mean streets of ghetto Harlem.

K'wan

Welfare wifeys : a hood rat novel / K'wan. St. Martin's Griffin, 2010. 320 p. Hood rat novels

ISBN 9780312536978

1. Street life 2. Rap musicians 3. Hip-hop culture 4. City life 5. Betrayal 6. Revenge 7. Sexuality 8. Murderers 9. Rap music 10. African Americans 11. Harlem, New York City 12. New York City 13. Urban fiction 14. African American fiction

LC 2010030122

Includes characters from Hood rat, Still hood, and Section 8.

After he finds fame and fortune as a recording artist in Texas, Animal returns home to his girlfriend, Gucci, bringing with him a hidden agenda that will have life-altering consequences, while Malika meets the man of her dreams, who happens to be married, and bad-blooded Jada Butler meets her match.

Kadare, Ismail

Agamemnon's daughter : a novella and stories / Ismail Kadare ; translated from the French of Tedi Papavrami and Jusuf Vrioni by David Bellos. Arcade, 2006. 240 p.

ISBN 9781559707886

1. Dictatorship 2. Political corruption 3. Communism 4. Political culture -- History -- 20th century 5. Men/women relations 6. Stalinism 7. May Day 8. Former lovers 9. Self-sacrifice 10. Albania -- History -- 1944-1990 11. Literary fiction 12. Political fiction 13. Translations -- French to English

LC 2006018639

Sequel to: The Successor.

The first work, Agamemnon's Daughter, is a tale of a disappointed lover's odyssey through a single day and his gradual realization of how the utter cruelty of dictatorship can express itself even in matters of the heart. The second work, The Blinding Order is a parable about the uses of terror set in the Ottoman Empire, and the third story, The Great Wall is a chilling duet between a Chinese official and a soldier in the invading army of the great Central Asian conqueror of the 14th century, Tamerlane.

"This miscellany contains the title novella, finished in 1985 and published here in English for the first time, and two stories. The novella, a companion to Kadare's The Successor, follows one day in the life of a young, unnamed journalist about to attend a celebratory May Day parade. . . . His half-girl, half-woman lover, Suzana, whose father's political star is on the rise, has just left the journalist in a sort of political sacrifice (the journalist is practically engaged to someone else and it looks bad). Through a wry and compelling set of ruminations on the grandstand, the journalist finds that a government that would deny young love denies humanity, and seeks the isolation of every citizen-which in turn pits neighbor against neighbor in a fever of paranoid denunciation. That simple but powerful insight also lies behind the two shorter, more allegorical works in the collection, The Blinding Order and The Great Wall, which were completed in 1984 and 1993 respectively." Publishers Weekly.

Kadare, Ismail

The **general** of the dead army / Ismail Kadare ; translated from the French of Jusuf Vrioni by Derek Coltman. Arcade Pub., 2008. 264 p.

ISBN 9781559707909

1. Death 2. War -- Moral and ethical aspects 3. Despair 4. Generals -- Italy 5. Veterans -- Identity 6. Search and rescue operations 7. Exhumation 8. Duty 9. Guilt in men 10. Loss (Psychology) 11. Albania -- History -- 20th century 12. Literary fiction 13. War stories 14. Political fiction 15. Historical fiction 16. Translations -- French to English

Translation from the French of Le general de l'armee morte which was translated from the Albanian Gjenerali i ushterise se vdekur.

Originally published in English: London : W. H. Allen, 1971.

An Italian general accompanies a priest on his mission to Albania to retrieve the remains of soldiers who had fallen 20 years previously in World War II.

"The book's protagonist is an Italian army officer who has come to Albania to recover the bodies of soldiers who died twenty years earlier in World War II. The General and his team carry crudely drawn maps and directions to burial sites supplied by aging war veterans. At first, the General fantasizes about returning home in triumph with his army of dead soldiers, but his optimism quickly fades. Rain and cold weather make recovery difficult, and the sullen Albanians continue to treat the Italians as invaders. . . . Before long, the General is haunted by terrifying dreams and hallucinations. He starts to see living people as skeletal remains and, fatally, begins to feel sympathy for the Albanians. This gloomy but powerful antiwar novel provides an excellent introduction to Albania's best-known author." Library Journal.

Kadare, Ismail

The **successor** : a novel / Ismail Kadare ; translated from the French of Tedi Papavrami by David Bellos. Arcade Pub., 2005. 207 p.

ISBN 9781559707732

1. Murder investigation 2. Politicians -- Death 3. Power (Social sciences) 4. Intelligence officers 5. Father and child 6. Family relationships 7. Suicide investigation 8. Political science 9. Albania -- Politics and government 10. Political fiction 11. Literary fiction 12. Translations -- French to English

LC 2005010311

Translation from the French, which was translated from the Albanian Pasardhesi.

Sequel: Agamemnon's daughter.

A fictionalized political tale based on true-life events and the author's conversations with the victim's son follows the events surrounding the death of Mehmet Shehu, a hand-picked successor to hated ailing Albanian dictator Enver Hoxha who succumbs to an unlikely suicide and sparks a government maelstrom.

"Drawing on real events--Mehmet Shehu was poised to succeed Albanian dictator Enver Hoxha in 1981 when he mysteriously died--Kadare successfully builds suspense by portraying multiple suspects with the motivation to commit murder; all believe they are guilty of the crime in some small or large way." Library Journal.

Kadare, Ismail

* The **three-arched** bridge / Ismail Kadare ; translated from the Albanian by John Hodgson. Arcade Publishing, 1997. 184 p.

ISBN 1559703687

1. 14th century 2. Bridges -- Design and construction 3. Monks -- Albania -- 14th century 4. Villages -- Albania -- 14th century 5. Prophecies (Occultism) 6. Men with mental illnesses 7. Dissenters 8. Balkan Peninsula -- History -- To 1501 9. Allegories 10. Literary fiction 11. Translations -- Albanian to English

When engineers build a bridge in Albania, a monk records its construction and the people's belief that a body buried in it gave the bridge a soul.

"In this matter-of-fact parable, a fourteenth-century Albanian monk attempts to 'record the lie we saw and the truth we did not see' about the building of a stone bridge that is a threatening wonder to the local people. The lie is the myths and legends exploited by the foreign builders to destroy their competitors; the truth is the mercenary nature of their crime. Kadare manages to appeal to a sense of outrage and hunger for evidence even as he suggests the outlines of today's Balkans." The New Yorker.

Kadrey, Richard

The **grand** dark / Richard Kadrey. HarperCollins, 2019 400 p.

ISBN 9780062672490

1. Ambition 2. Postwar life 3. Class conflict 4. Power (Social sciences) 5. Bicycle messengers 6. Political intrigue 7. Social conflict 8. Conspiracies 9. Hedonism 10. Addiction 11. Science fantasy 12. Science fiction 13. Steampunk

The Great War is over. The city of Lower Proszawa celebrates the peace with a decadence and carefree spirit as intense as the war's horrifying despair. Unlike others who live strictly for fun, Largo is an addict with ambitions. Dreams can be a dangerous thing in a city whose mood is turning dark and inward. Others have a vision of life very different from Largo's, and they will use any methods to secure control. The threat of new war always looms.

Kafka, Franz, 1883-1924

The **castle** : a new translation, based on the restored text / Franz Kafka ; translated and with a preface by Mark Harman. Schocken Books, 1998. xxiii, 328 p.

ISBN 0805241183

1. Castles 2. Alienation in men 3. Meaning (Psychology) 4. Authority (Psychology) 5. Futility (Psychology) 6. Bureaucracy 7. Allegories 8. Literary fiction 9. Translations -- German to English 10. Modern classics 11. Dystopian fiction

LC 97018117

Originally published in German as: Das schloss.

The story of K., the unwanted Land Surveyor who is never admitted to the Castle nor accepted in the village, and yet cannot go home, seems to depict like a dream from the deepest recesses of consciousness, an inexplicable truth about the nature of existence.

Kafka, Franz, 1883-1924
* **Collected** stories / Franz Kafka ; edited and introduced by Gabriel Josipovici. Knopf, 1993. lv, 503 p.
  ISBN 9780679423034
  1. Identity (Psychology) 2. Purpose in life 3. Belonging 4. Short stories 5. Parables 6. Anthologies
  LC 93001858
Collects Kafka's short stories and parables, each reflecting his concern for modern man's search for identity, place, and purpose.

Kafka, Franz, 1883-1924
* The **metamorphosis** / Franz Kafka ; translated and edited by Stanley Corngold. Bantam Books, 1986, c1915. xxii, 201 p.
  ISBN 9780553213690
  1. Loneliness in men 2. Transformations (Magic) 3. Insects 4. Coping 5. Rejection (Psychology) 6. Conflict in families 7. Allegories 8. Modern classics 9. Literary fiction 10. Translations -- German to English
  Originally published: Leipzig : Kurt Wolff Verlag, 1915.
A seemingly typical man wakes up one morning to discover that he has been transformed into a gigantic insect, and must deal with the depression over his new physical alteration, as well as the rejection of his family.

Kafka, Franz, 1883-1924
* The **trial** / Franz Kafka ; translated from the German by Willa and Edwin Muir ; revised, with additional notes, by Professor E.M. Butler. Knopf, 1992, c1925. xxxiii, 299 p.
  ISBN 9780679409946
  1. Trials 2. Bureaucracy 3. Totalitarianism 4. Alienation (Social psychology) 5. Guilt 6. Fairness 7. Existentialism 8. Responsibility 9. Bank employees 10. Allegories 11. Literary fiction 12. Surrealist fiction 13. Translations -- German to English 14. Modern classics
  LC BL 99729791
Narrates the experiences and reactions of a respectable bank functionary after his abrupt arrest on an undisclosed charge

Kamal, Sheena
  It all falls down / Sheena Kamal. William Morrow & Co., 2018. 384 p. Nora Watts novels
  ISBN 9780062565778
  1. Fathers and daughters 2. Family and suicide 3. Drug traffic 4. First Nations (Canada) 5. Private investigators 6. Family secrets 7. Identity (Psychology) 8. City life 9. British Columbia 10. Detroit, Michigan 11. Canada 12. Thrillers and suspense
To find the truth about her father's life and violent death, Nora Watts, focused on the mysterious events of her father's past and the clues they provide to her own fractured identity, is led to a private investigator whose latest is case is somehow connected to her.

Kamali, Marjan
* The **stationery** shop / Marjan Kamali. Gallery Books, 2019. 312 p.
  ISBN 9781982107482
  1. 1950s 2. 2010s 3. Teenage romance 4. Political violence 5. Fate and fatalism 6. Engagement 7. Jilted women 8. Secrets 9. Men/women relations 10. Loss (Psychology) 11. Reconciliation 12. Bookstores 13. Letter writing 14. Coups d'etat 15. Tehran, Iran 16. Iran -- History -- Coup d'etat, 1953 17. Boston, Massachusetts 18.

Historical fiction
  LC 2018052061
A young couple who meet and fall in love at a neighborhood stationery shop in 1953 Tehran are separated by a violent coup d'etat on the eve of their marriage and reunite by chance after more than half a century.
"The unfurling stories in Kamali's sophomore novel (after Together Tea) will stun readers as the aromas of Persian cooking wafting throughout convince us that love can last a lifetime. For those who enjoy getting caught up in romance while discovering unfamiliar history of another country." Library Journal.

Kaminsky, Stuart M.
  Dancing in the dark / Stuart M. Kaminsky. Mysterious Press, 1996. 228 p. Toby Peters mysteries
  ISBN 9780892965281
  1. Astaire, Fred, 1899-1987 2. 1940s 3. Murder investigation 4. Gangsters 5. Women murder victims 6. Dancing 7. Film actors and actresses 8. Private investigators 9. World War II 10. Hollywood, California 11. Historical mysteries 12. Hardboiled fiction 13. Mysteries
  LC 95013095
Includes appearance by Fred Astaire.
In 1940s Hollywood, PI Toby Peters is hired by Fred Astaire to serve as a dancing partner for a gangster's moll learning to dance. A strenuous assignment as Peters is no dancer, but before you know it the moll is killed and Peters is once again in his element.
"The author effortlessly choreographs Hollywood history, colorful cast and dirty doings." Publishers Weekly.

Kaminsky, Stuart M.
  A **fatal** glass of beer / Stuart M. Kaminsky. Mysterious Press, 1997. 246 p. Toby Peters mysteries
  ISBN 9780892966301
  1. Fields, W C, 1879-1946 2. 1940s 3. Impostors 4. Swindlers and swindling 5. Stealing 6. Film comedians 7. Murder investigation 8. Film actors and actresses 9. Private investigators 10. World War II 11. Hollywood, California 12. Historical mysteries 13. Hardboiled fiction 14. Mysteries
  LC 96-49494
The Hollywood detective, Toby Peters, is hired by the 1940s comedian, W.C. Fields, to help catch a swindler. The swindler has found a way to gain access to Fields' bank accounts in various parts of the country and is emptying them one by one.
"The author balances one-liners from Fields with headlines about the war effort in this amiable adventure that delivers a nicely twisted plot with fully dimensioned characters, including the usually caricatured misanthropic comedian." Publishers Weekly.

Kaminsky, Stuart M.
  Murder on the Trans-Siberian Express / Stuart M. Kaminsky. Mysterious Press, 2001. 277 p. Inspector Porfiry Rostnikov mysteries
  ISBN 9780892967476
  1. Police -- Moscow, Russia 2. Murder investigation 3. Kidnapping 4. Railroad travel 5. Murder 6. Father and child 7. Women with mental illnesses 8. Skinheads 9. Jews, Russian 10. Detectives 11. People who have had amputations 12. Siberia 13. Moscow, Russia 14. Mysteries 15. Hardboiled fiction
  LC 2001026218
Chief Inspector Rostnikov heads for Vladivostok aboard the Trans-Siberian Express to find an extortionist who may possess information that could bring down the Russian government.

"The action reaches back to Siberia in 1894, when one man in a band of starving, disease-ridden convicts, sentenced to work on constructing the great rail line from Moscow to Vladivostok, buries his treasure: a leather pouch containing a tiny gold box with a letter inside. More than a century later, Inspector Porfiry of the Moscow Police is sent on the 6,000-mile rail line to find this box. Porfiry leaves behind two other investigations: the kidnapping of a skinhead rock star and a series of murders in the Moscow Metro. How Kaminsky weaves these tangled plot lines into a taut suspense fabric, while providing fascinating, sad-funny commentary on his characters and the tensions inherent in the new Russian social order, is a matter of wonder." Booklist.

Kaminsky, Stuart M.

To catch a spy : a Toby Peters mystery / Stuart M. Kaminsky. Carroll & Graf Publishers, 2002. 230 p. Toby Peters mysteries

ISBN 0786710233

1. Grant, Cary, 1904-1986 2. 1940s 3. Murder investigation 4. Nazis 5. Spies -- Great Britain 6. Film actors and actresses 7. Private investigators 8. World War II 9. Hollywood, California 10. Historical mysteries 11. Hardboiled fiction 12. Mysteries

LC 2002067254

"An Otto Penzler book."

While trying to deliver a package for film superstar Cary Grant, private detective Toby Peters stumbles upon a corpse and joins forces with the movie star to follow a trail of clues that leads them to a gang of Nazi sympathizers.

Kaminsky, Stuart M.

Tomorrow is another day / Stuart M. Kaminsky. Mysterious Press, 1995. 201 p. Toby Peters mysteries

ISBN 9780892965274

1. Gable, Clark, 1901-1960 2. Gone With the Wind (Motion picture) 3. 1940s 4. Murder investigation 5. Murder witnesses 6. Film actors and actresses 7. Private investigators 8. World War II 9. Hollywood, California 10. Historical mysteries 11. Hardboiled fiction 12. Mysteries

LC 94018987

It is 1943 and PI Toby Peters is hired by Clark Gable, the movie star, to catch a killer. The man is bumping off actors who were in the film, Gone with the Wind. He has sent a note saying Gable's turn will come. Peters suspects the killer is eliminating people who may have witnessed a murder disguised as an accident during the burning of Atlanta, a scene in the film.

"Nostalgic readers with a yen for the good old days--when men were men and movies were movies--will find Kaminsky's story entertaining, clever, eminently readable, and chock-full of snippets from Hollywood's Golden Age." Booklist.

Kandasamy, Meena

When I hit you, or, A portrait of the writer as a young wife / Meena Kandasamy. Europa Editions, 2020, c2017. 210 p.

ISBN 9781609455996

1. Abused women 2. Married women 3. Women authors 4. Partner abuse 5. Courage in women 6. Manipulation by men 7. Control (Psychology) 8. Gender role 9. Violence in men 10. Coastal towns 11. Social isolation 12. India -- Social conditions 13. Literary fiction 14. Autobiographical fiction

Originally published: London : Atlantic Books, 2017.

Shortlisted for The Women's Prize for Fiction, 2018.

Set in modern India, the unnamed narrator falls in love with a university professor and agrees to be his wife. Based on the author's own experience of marriage, soon the newly-wed experiences extreme violence at her husband's hands and finds herself socially isolated. ... Yet hope keeps her alive. Writing becomes her salvation, a supreme act of defiance.

"Kandasamy (The Gypsy Goddess, 2014, etc.) divides her time between Chennai and London, and the novel was shortlisted for the Women's Prize for Fiction and the Jhalak Prize and longlisted for the Dylan Thomas Prize." Kirkus.

Kane, Ben

* Spartacus : the gladiator / Ben Kane. St. Martin's Press, 2012. 466 p.

ISBN 9781250001160

1. Spartacus, d 71 BC 2. Roman Empire (27 BCE-476 CE) 3. Gladiators 4. Soldiers 5. Jealousy in men 6. Women priests 7. Escapes 8. Battles 9. Rome -- History -- Vespasian, 69-79 10. Historical fiction 11. War stories

Sequel: Spartacus: the rebellion.

Returning to his village after escaping the Roman army, Spartacus is betrayed by his jealous king and forced into life as a gladiator before executing a daring overthrow and assuming leadership over an army of escaped slaves.

Kane, Jessica Francis, 1971-

Rules for visiting / Jessica Francis Kane. Penguin Books, 2019. 304 p.

ISBN 9780525559221

1. Women gardeners 2. Middle age 3. Loners 4. Female friendship 5. Vacations 6. Visiting 7. Houseguests 8. Voyages and travels 9. Eccentrics and eccentricities 10. Literary fiction

At forty, May Attaway is more at home with plants than people. Over the years, she's turned inward, finding pleasure in language, her work as a gardener, and keeping her neighbors at arm's length while keenly observing them. But when she is unexpectedly granted some leave from her job, May is inspired to reconnect with four once close friends. She knows they will never have a proper reunion, so she goes, one-by-one, to each of them. A student of the classics, May considers her journey a female Odyssey.

Kanon, Joseph

Los Alamos : a novel / Joseph Kanon. Broadway Books, 1997. 403 p.

ISBN 0553062247

1. Manhattan Project (U.S.) 2. 1940s 3. Military intelligence officers 4. Atomic bomb 5. Espionage 6. Extramarital affairs 7. Physicists 8. Gay men 9. Men/women relations 10. Murder investigation -- Los Alamos, New Mexico 11. World War II -- Los Alamos, New Mexico 12. Los Alamos, New Mexico 13. Spy fiction 14. Romantic suspense

LC 96-44055

Edgar Allan Poe Award for Best First Mystery Novel, 1998.

A thriller set in Los Alamos, New Mexico, during the final years of World War II follows a murder investigation that leads into the top-secret heart of the Manhattan Project

Kantaria, Annabel

I know you : a novel of suspense / Annabel Kantaria. Crooked Lane Books, 2019, c2018. 384 p.

ISBN 9781643851105

1. Stalkers 2. Friendship 3. Social media 4. Moving, Household 5. Moving to a new country 6. Loneliness 7. Pregnancy 8. Secrets 9. England 10. Psychological suspense

Originally published: London : HQ, 2018.

A twisted domestic thriller in the vein of B. A. Paris and Shari Lapena that asks: How well do you know your friends?

Kantor, MacKinlay, 1904-1977

* **Andersonville** / MacKinlay Kantor. Plume, 1993, c1955. 766 p.

ISBN 0452269563

1. Andersonville, Georgia Military Prison 2. American Civil War era (1861-1865) 3. Prisoners of war, Confederate 4. Prisons -- Confederate States of America 5. Civil war 6. United States Civil War, 1861-1865 7. United States -- History -- Civil War, 1861-1865 -- Prisoners and prisons 8. Historical fiction 9. War stories 10. Literary fiction

LC 9235802

Originally published: New York : New American Library, 1955.

Pulitzer Prize for Fiction, 1956.

In 1864, thirty-three thousand Yankee prisoners of war suffer the horrors of imprisonment at the Confederate prison of Andersonville.

Kantra, Virginia

* **Meg** and Jo / Virginia Kantra. Berkley, 2019. 400 p.

ISBN 9780593100349

1. Sisters 2. Mothers and daughters 3. Family relationships 4. Young women 5. Ambition in women 6. Men/women relations 7. North Carolina 8. Mainstream fiction 9. Domestic fiction 10. Adaptations, retellings, and spin-offs

LC 2019022562

When their mother falls ill, the March sisters--reliable Meg, independent Jo, stylish Amy and shy Beth, --return home to North Carolina for the holidays where they'll rediscover what really matters.

"Kantra blends just enough of Alcott's story of four close-knit sisters and their myriad tribulations with clever and timely new elements (unexpected pregnancies, the girls' father as a military chaplain, parents separating), a mix that will satisfy Alcott fans as well as entice Kantra's existing fans." Publishers Weekly.

Karlsson, Jonas, 1971-

The **room** : a novel / Jonas Karlsson ; translated from the Swedish by Neil Smith. Hogarth, 2015. 176 p.

ISBN 9780804139984

1. Office workers 2. Conformity 3. Coworkers 4. Office environment 5. Rooms 6. Civil service workers 7. Secrets 8. Surrealist fiction 9. Literary fiction 10. Translations -- Swedish to English

LC 2014014601

Translation from the Swedish of: Rummet.

Originally published: 2009.

Surrounded by intolerable coworkers in his open-plan office, Björn is thrilled to discover a small, secret room where he can work with exceptional efficiency, but his bizarre behavior outside the room may drive his colleagues to a point of no return.

"Part psychological drama documenting a disturbed man's possible descent into madness and part satirical take on corporate culture and the alienated workers it produces, Karlsson succeeds admirably in creating the perfect combination of funny, surreal, and disturbing." Booklist.

Karnezis, Panos, 1967-

The **maze** / Panos Karnezis. Farrar, Straus and Giroux, 2004. 224 p.

ISBN 0374204802

1. 1920s 2. Journalists 3. Soldiers 4. Widowers 5. Deserters 6. Priests 7. Prostitutes 8. Greeks in Turkey 9. Small town life -- Turkey 10. Villages -- Turkey 11. Robbery 12. Desert survival 13. Despair 14. Executions and executioners 15. Memories 16. Deserts 17. Greco-Turkish War, 1921-1922 18. Turkey 19. Historical fiction 20. War stories

LC 2003060261

In retreat from a failed 1922 invasion of Turkey, Greek soldiers stumble across a quiet town where an odd cast of characters seems to be living untouched by the war.

"As with many an imperial expedition, the soldiers seem to be lost without honor; they massacre civilians on their fool's errand undertaken for worthless ends. Karnezis dramatizes their plight with remorseless clarity and dry humor." New York Times Book Review.

Karon, Jan, 1937-

At home in Mitford / Jan Karon. Lion Publishing, 1994. 446 p. Mitford years

ISBN 0745926290

1. Episcopal Church Clergy 2. Small town life -- North Carolina 3. Clergy 4. Christianity 5. Neighbors 6. Loneliness in men 7. Men/women relations 8. Small towns -- North Carolina 9. North Carolina 10. Christian fiction 11. Gentle reads

Longing for change in the face of burnout, Episcopal rector Father Tim finds his lonely bachelor existence enriched by a stray dog, a lonely boy, and a pretty neighbor.

Karon, Jan, 1937-

In this mountain / Jan Karon. Viking, 2002. 368 p. Mitford years

ISBN 0670031046

1. Episcopal Church Clergy 2. Small town life -- North Carolina 3. Clergy 4. Christianity 5. Neighbors 6. Episcopalians 7. North Carolina 8. Christian fiction 9. Gentle reads

LC 2002016877

Though Father Tim dislikes change, he dislikes retirement even more. When he decides to take on a difficult ministry, he begins to think he likes change -- until an unexpected event propels him on a journey that shakes his faith, his marriage, and the whole town of Mitford.

"Homespun dialogue, fresh and lively descriptions, laugh-out-loud moments and poignant scenes mark the heartfelt book, which is a happy reunion form Mitford devotees." Publishers Weekly.

Karon, Jan, 1937-

A **new** song / Jan Karon. Viking, 1999. 400 p. Mitford years

ISBN 0670878103

1. Episcopal Church Clergy 2. Small town life -- North Carolina 3. Islands -- North Carolina 4. Clergy 5. Christianity 6. Neighbors 7. Christian fiction 8. Gentle reads

LC 9855141

Christy Award for Contemporary/General Category, 2000.

Gold Medallion Book Award, 2000.

Recently retired, Episcopal priest Father Tim and his wife, Cynthia, discover new challenges and adventures when Tim agrees to serve as interim minister of a small church on Whitecap Island.

Karon, Jan, 1937-

Out to Canaan / Jan Karon. Viking, 1997. 342 p. Mitford years

ISBN 067087485X

1. Episcopal Church Clergy 2. Small town life -- North Carolina 3. Clergy 4. Christianity 5. Neighbors 6. Real estate development -- North Carolina 7. Mayors -- North Carolina 8. Elections -- North Carolina 9. North Carolina 10. Christian fiction 11. Gentle reads

LC 975867

In the small town of Mitford, Father Tim and his wife Cynthia ponder their retirement plans and try to raise their young charge, Dooley, while a brash mayoral candidate is calling for development and "progress."

"Racing from one good deed to another, Father Timothy takes in stray sick folk, finds an abandoned child, and helps his favorite baker write a winning jingle. A mayoral race pitting the long-time mayor Esther Cunningham against the possibly corrupt Mack Stroupe makes for some colorful sparring. Father Timothy applies his own unique, time-honored method of intuition, prayer, or dietary indulgence to a multitude of problems big and small. His late-in-life marriage to Cynthia continues to be a blessing readers will feel privileged to share." Library Journal.

Karunatilaka, Shehan

The **legend** of Pradeep Mathew : a novel / Shehan Karunatilaka. Graywolf Press, 2011. 397 p.

ISBN 9781555976118

1. Mathew, Pradeep Sivanathan, 1965- 2. Sportswriters 3. Alcoholic men 4. Former professional athletes 5. Cricket (Sports) 6. Cricket players 7. Friendship 8. Misadventures 9. Fans (Persons) 10. Sri Lanka 11. Literary fiction

Originally published: London : Jonathan Cape, 2011.

Succumbing to poor health after years of drinking, aging sportswriter W. G. Karunasena and his friend embark on a madcap search for a legendary cricket bowler during which they encounter a mysterious six-fingered coach, a Tamil Tiger warlord and startling truths.

Kasasian, M. R. C. (Martin R. C.)

Dark dawn over Steep House / M.R.C. Kasasian. Pegasus Books, 2017 473 p. Gower Street detectives

ISBN 9781681775647

1. Victorian era (1837-1901) 2. Murder investigation 3. Private investigators 4. Women amateur detectives 5. Gangsters 6. Rape victims 7. Murder victims 8. Guardian and ward 9. Nobility -- Germany 10. Crimes against women 11. London, England 12. England -- History -- 19th century 13. Victorian mysteries 14. Historical mysteries

Detective Sidney Grice and his ward, March Middleton, must solve a mystery that involves a Prussian Count, two damsels in distress, a Chinese man from Wales, a gangster looking for love and the shadowy ruin of a once-loved family home, Steep House.

Kasischke, Laura, 1961-

The **raising** : a novel / Laura Kasischke. Perennial, 2011. 464 p.

ISBN 9780062004789

1. Secrets 2. Revenge 3. Campus life 4. Fatal traffic accidents 5. Sororities 6. Witnesses 7. Obsession 8. Missing women 9. Middle West 10. Coming-of-age stories 11. Psychological suspense

LC 2010021605

Released in the UK as Sweet things.

The accident was tragic, yes. Bloody and horrific and claiming the life of a beautiful young sorority girl. Nicole was a straight-A student from a small town. Sweet-tempered, all-American, a former Girl Scout, and a virgin. But it was an accident. And that was last year. It's fall again, a new semester, a fresh start.

"Kasischke excels at depicting the psychology of the young and the traumatized even as she delivers a scathing indictment of the siege mentality of college administrators. In this literary page-turner, reminiscent of Donna Tartt's Secret History (1992), the talented author inlays her academic novel with a touch of the supernatural and a deep sense of foreboding." Booklist.

Kate, Jessica

A **girl's** guide to the Outback : a novel / Jessica Kate. Thomas Nelson, 2020. 358 p.

ISBN 9780785229612

1. Clergy 2. Church work 3. Women entrepreneurs 4. Dairy farms 5. Farm life 6. Deals 7. Family businesses 8. Interpersonal attraction 9. Men/women relations 10. Australia 11. United States 12. Virginia 13. Christian romances 14. Contemporary romances

LC 2019032265

How far will a girl go to win back a guy she can?t stand?

"Kate (Love and Other Mistakes) brings the outback to life in this stand-alone Christian romance that features two people struggling to figure out what they want." Library Journal.

Kate, Jessica

Love and other mistakes / Jessica Kate. Thomas Nelson, 2019. 344 p.

ISBN 9780785229582

1. Nannies 2. Single fathers 3. Former fiances 4. Children of clergy 5. Men with cancer 6. Sick fathers 7. Faith (Christianity) 8. Christian families 9. Forgiveness 10. Communities 11. Life change events 12. Interpersonal attraction 13. Men/women relations 14. Virginia 15. Christian romances

LC 2019000983

When Jeremy Walters, the fiance who left her weeks before their marriage seven years ago, comes back to town, Natalie Groves, who has just lost her job, reluctantly agrees to work as the nanny for his infant daughter.

Katsu, Alma

The **deep** / Alma Katsu. G.P. Putnam's Sons, 2020. 420 p.

ISBN 9780525537908

1. Titanic (Steamship) 2. Britannic (Ship) 3. 1910s 4. Ocean travel 5. Ocean liners 6. Paranormal phenomena 7. Nurses 8. Shipwreck survivors 9. Memories 10. Secrets 11. Loss (Psychology) 12. Supernatural 13. Historical horror

Surviving the sinking of the Titanic, Annie takes a job as a nurse on the Britannic before encountering a fellow survivor who forces her to reckon with past demons.

"A riveting, seductively menacing tale of love, loss, and betrayal set amid the glamour of the Titanic, filled with seances, sea witches, and second chances." Library Journal.

Katsu, Alma

The **hunger** : a novel / Alma Katsu. G. P. Putnam's Sons, 2018 400 p.

ISBN 9780735212510

1. American Westward Expansion (1803-1899) 2. 1840s 3. Donner Party 4. Wagon trains 5. Good and evil 6. Cannibalism 7. Supernatural 8. Violence 9. Murder 10. Malicious accusation 11. Wilderness survival 12. Interpersonal relations 13. The West (United States) -- History -- 19th century 14. Horror 15. Historical horror 16. Weird Westerns

LC 2017019689

Western Heritage Award for Outstanding Western Novel, 2019.

A supernatural reimagining of the Donner Party story follows a group of wagon-train pioneers who navigate sanity-testing misfortunes, including the mysterious death of a little boy and a series of disappearances that cause a beautiful member of the group to be accused of witchcraft.

LIST OF FICTIONAL WORKS

Katzenbach, John

Just cause / John Katzenbach. G. P. Putnam's Sons, 1992. 431p.

ISBN 0399136266

1. Journalists 2. African-American death row prisoners 3. Serial murders 4. Innocence (Law) 5. Violence 6. Serial murderers 7. Miami, Florida 8. Mysteries 9. Psychological suspense

LC 91015135

When Florida newpaperman Matthew Cowart receives a note from an inmate on death row, he tries to ignore its plea, but Cowart becomes convinced of the prisoner's innocence and his investigative articles contribute to the pardon of a monster

"Despite some extraneous subplots, the story generally proceeds at a breakneck pace, enhanced by ear-perfect dialogue and complex characterization." Publishers Weekly.

Katzenbach, John

The **analyst** / John Katzenbach. Ballantine Books, 2002. 424 p.

ISBN 0345426266

1. Psychoanalysts 2. Death threats -- Manhattan, New York City 3. Stalkers 4. Stalking 5. Serial murderers 6. Violence 7. Manhattan, New York City 8. Psychological suspense

LC 2001043841

Dr. Frederick Starks, a New York psychoanalyst on the brink of a much-needed vacation, is plunged into a deadly game of revenge where a mysterious tormentor waits in the darkness to destroy him.

"The author has potently chronicled a long journey of revenge and redemption. Some of his psychological plot points . . . are a stretch, but the novel's fine sense of pacing, sudden switchbacks and chilling characterizations far overshadow its minor faults." Publishers Weekly.

Katzenbach, John

What comes next / John Katzenbach. Mysterious Press, 2012. 320 p.

ISBN 9780802126115

1. Women kidnapping victims 2. Internet 3. Torture 4. Missing persons investigation 5. Sadism 6. Kidnappers 7. Psychological suspense

After the police falter in their investigation, a retired college professor vows to track down a young woman he witnessed being snatched off the street, kidnapped by a sadistic couple who put their victim's slow torture up for public display on the Internet.

Kaufman, Bel

Up the down staircase / Bel Kaufman Prentice Hall, 1965, c1964. 340p.

1. Teaching -- Philosophy 2. High school teachers 3. High schools 4. New York City 5. Mainstream fiction

LC 64024258

Chronicles the goings-on in a large metropolitan high school, detailing the experiences of an idealistic first-year teacher who is plagued by difficulties arising from an overwhelming bureaucracy, inadequate facilities, and some unforgettable students.

Kaufman, Sue, 1926-1977

Diary of a mad housewife / Sue Kaufman. Thunder's Mouth Press : 2005, c1967. 311 p.

ISBN 1560256877

1. 1960s 2. Homemakers 3. Identity (Psychology) 4. Gender role 5. Women -- Identity 6. Husband and wife 7. Mothers and daughters 8. Snobs and snobbishness 9. Social mobility 10. Extramarital affairs 11. Marital conflict 12. Self-awareness in women 13. New York City 14. Manhattan, New York City 15. Diary novels

Originally published: New York : Random House, c1967.

First published in 1967, this novel of life in New York is written in the form of a diary of a disenchanted housewife who offers a frank, unsparing portrait of her terrors and passions.

Kaufmann, Nicholas, 1969-

Dying is my business / Nicholas Kaufmann. St Martin's Griffin, 2013. 369 p.

ISBN 9781250036100

1. Thieves 2. Immortalism 3. Magic boxes 4. Good and evil 5. Men with amnesia 6. Gangsters 7. Supernatural 8. Brooklyn, New York City 9. Urban fantasy

Sequel: Die and stay dead.

Trent, who can cheat death, but loses all memory of his past identity each time he does so, must steal an antique box for his mysterious boss, a mission that reveals a secret world of magic and monsters that threatens to destroy New York City.

Kava, Alex

Hotwire : a Maggie O'Dell novel / Alex Kava. Doubleday, 2011. 291 p. Maggie O'Dell novels

ISBN 9780385532013

1. Criminal profilers 2. Serial murder investigation 3. Crimes against teenagers 4. Crimes against children 5. Biological warfare 6. Conspiracies 7. Women FBI agents 8. Thrillers and suspense

LC 2010052991

Investigating the bizarre deaths of three hard-partying teens, Special Agent Maggie O'Dell sifts through conflicting accounts only to discover that surviving partygoers are being targeted and systematically killed, a case that is complicated by a bizarre illness that is sweeping through a Virginia elementary school.

"A sizzling plot, achingly real characters, and government officials working their backsides off to save their backsides, all strike as lethally as lightning." Publishers Weekly.

Kawabata, Yasunari, 1899-1972

The **sound** of the mountain / Yasunari Kawabata ; translated from the Japanese by Edward M. Seidensticker. Vintage, 1996, c1954. 276 p.

ISBN 9780679762645

1. Senior men 2. Emotions 3. Anxiety 4. Memory 5. Mountains 6. Loneliness 7. Alienation (Social psychology) 8. Family relationships 9. Japan 10. Historical fiction 11. Literary fiction 12. Translations -- Japanese to English

LC 77098666

Focuses on the anxieties, desires, and emotions of a sensitive old Japanese man.

"The language is delicate, allusive, intensely Japanese; and, since plot and character development count for little, the style is all-important. We are fortunate that it should have been a writer with Mr. Seidensticker's gifts who ventured to convey [Kawabata's] rarefied novels into English." New York Times Book Review.

Kawakami, Mieko, 1976-

Ms. Ice Sandwich / Mieko Kawakami ; translated by Louise Heal Kawai. Pushkin Press, 2018. 160 p.

ISBN 9781782273301

1. Women merchants 2. Strangers 3. Crushes in boys 4. Friendship 5. Portraits 6. Drawing 7. First loves 8. Literary fiction 9. Coming-of-age stories 10. Translations -- Japanese to English

Obsessed with a woman who sells sandwiches, a young boy, who endlessly draws her portrait, finds his hopes dashed when a friend hears about his hesitant adoration, which changes everything.

Kay, Guy Gavriel

* A **brightness** long ago / Guy Gavriel Kay. Berkley, 2019. 422 p.

ISBN 9780451472984

1. Courts and courtiers 2. Women assassins 3. Social classes 4. Counts and countesses 5. Rebels 6. Fate and fatalism 7. War 8. Warlords 9. Mercenaries 10. Epic fantasy

LC 2018039450

A brilliant servant under a despotic count and a would-be assassin who has forfeited a life of comfort join an extraordinary group of companions when a rivalry between two mercenary commanders threatens the world balance.

"Fans of Kay's previous work will find his usual elements in play: strong historical research and worldbuilding, a vast cast of characters, world-changing events, and prose that sometimes gets carried away with itself. An epic tale filled with characters compelling enough to bear the weight of the high stakes." Kirkus.

Kay, Guy Gavriel

* **Children** of earth and sky / Guy Gavriel Kay. New American Library, 2016. 560 p.

ISBN 9780451472960

1. Voyages and travels 2. Interpersonal relations 3. Imaginary wars and battles 4. Revenge 5. Intrigue 6. Artists 7. Rulers 8. Spies 9. Fantasy fiction 10. Historical fantasy 11. Middle Eastern-influenced fantasy

LC 2015047832

RUSA Reading List Short List, 2017

A khalif from the Ottoman Empire sends an enormous army to attack the fortress that separates the Western World from the Turkish lands.

"This intricately plotted literary novel will appeal to Kays many fans as well as readers who enjoy character-driven historical fiction with just a touch of fantasy." Booklist.

Kay, Guy Gavriel

The **last** light of the sun / Guy Gavriel Kay. ROC, 2004. 512 p.

ISBN 0451459652

1. 9th century 2. 10th century 3. Vikings 4. Princes 5. Magic 6. Fate and fatalism 7. Northmen and Northwomen 8. Anglo-Saxons 9. Celts 10. Rulers 11. Northern Europe 12. Historical fantasy 13. Epic fantasy 14. Celtic fantasy

LC 2003019316

The fates of three powerful civilizations--the Erlings of Vinmark, the Anglcyn kindom, and the Cyngael--clash in a fantasy based on the legends of the ancient Celts, Anglo-Saxons, and Norse.

"Kay's novel is an ambitious entertainment that transcends the historical record, offering cogent observations on fathers and sons, on the power of grief, on faith, courage, loyalty and the inevitability of change." Quill & Quire.

Kay, Guy Gavriel

* **River** of stars / Guy Gavriel Kay. Roc, 2013. 639 p. Under heaven

ISBN 9780451464972

1. 9th century 2. Power (Social sciences) 3. Women's role 4. Life change events 5. Political intrigue 6. War 7. Gender role 8. Imaginary wars and battles 9. China -- History -- Sung dynasty, 960-1279 10. Historical fantasy 11. Epic fantasy 12. Asian-influenced fantasy

Sequel to: Under heaven.

Four-hundred years after the events of Under Heaven, the region ruled by the Tang Dynasty in China is still populated with prideful emperors, soldiers, robbers and people fighting to find their place in the world.

"An elegant, imaginative inhabitation of Song-dynasty China of 1,000 years ago." Kirkus.

Kay, Guy Gavriel

The **summer** tree / Guy Gavriel Kay. Roc, 2001, c1984. 383 p. Fionavar tapestry

ISBN 9780451458223

1. Parallel universes 2. Imaginary wars and battles 3. Magic 4. College students 5. Good and evil 6. Wizards 7. Dwarves (Fantasy characters) 8. Elves 9. Princes 10. Gods and goddesses 11. Fate and fatalism 12. Epic fantasy 13. Gateway fantasy

LC 0045803

Originally published: New York : Arbor House, 1984.

Five young professionals and students are dramatically precipitated out of their lives in this world into the realm of Fionavar, the true world, of which our own is only shadow. Led by Silvercloak, the wizard, the five are caught up in the opening forays of a devastating war as the renegade god, Rakoth Maugrim, breaks free from his thousand-year imprisonment. In a world gripped by the timeless war between the forces of Light and Dark, a rich tapestry is woven as the five are confronted by wood and water spirits, dwarves, supernatural animals and the titanic magics of the gods, against which the strengths of humans seem weak and small.

Kay, Guy Gavriel

Tigana / Guy Gavrial Kay. Penguin Books, 1990. 673 p.

ISBN 9780451450289

1. Magic 2. Wizards 3. Psychological warfare 4. Singers 5. Guilt 6. Revenge 7. Good and evil 8. Rulers 9. Imaginary kingdoms 10. Epic fantasy

LC 90034423

Includes end-paper maps.

Prix Aurora: Best Novel, 1991.

Allesan, son of the king of Tigana, and other survivors of the forgotten world band together to plot the demise of Brandin of Ygrath.

"Memorable characters and cultures add depth to a gracefully plotted story." Library Journal.

Kay, Guy Gavriel

Under heaven / Guy Gavriel Kay. Roc, 2010. 573 p. Under heaven

ISBN 9780451463302

1. Tang dynasty (618-907) 2. 8th century 3. Honor 4. Power (Social sciences) 5. Horses 6. Life change events 7. Voyages and travels 8. Fathers and sons 9. Gifts 10. Funerals 11. Imaginary wars and battles 12. China -- History -- Tang dynasty, 618-907 13. Historical fantasy 14. Epic fantasy 15. Asian-influenced fantasy

LC 2010004833

Sequel: River of stars

RUSA Reading List, 2011.

Sunburst Award for Excellence in Canadian Literature of the Fantastic, 2011.

To honor the memory of his father, who was a general in the Tang Dynasty of 8th-century China, Tai spends the two years of official mourning in isolation and in service, which elicits an honor he hasn't sought and which changes his life forever.

"Virtually everything a reader could want in a book: a thrilling adventure, a love story, a coming-of-age tale, a military chronicle, a court-intrigue drama, a tragedy and on and on. It is a sumptuous feast of story-telling." Globe and Mail (Toronto)

Kay, Guy Gavriel

* **Ysabel** : a novel / Guy Gavriel Kay. Roc, 2007. 421 p.
ISBN 9780451461292

1. Spirit possession 2. Celts -- History 3. Love triangles 4. Spirits 5. Teenage boys 6. Fathers and sons -- France 7. Americans in France 8. Cathedrals -- France 9. Romans in Provence 10. Romans -- Provence, France 11. Celtic magic (Occultism) 12. Supernatural 13. Imaginary wars and battles 14. Aix-en-Provence, France 15. Contemporary fantasy

LC 2006028326

World Fantasy Award, 2008.

While his famed photographer father works to record Saint-Saveur Cathedral of Aix-en-Provence, Ned Marriner wanders the halls and rooms of the ancient structure, uncovering some of the many secrets of the monument and discovering that it is not as empty as it appears.

"The author's historical detail, evocative writing and fascinating characters--both ancient and modern--will enthrall mainstream as well as fantasy readers." Publishers Weekly.

Kazantzakis, Nikos, 1883-1957

The **last** temptation of Christ / Nikos Kazantzakis ; translated from the Greek by P.A. Bien. Simon and Schuster, 1960. 506 p.
ISBN 9780671407100

1. Jesus Christ 2. Historical fiction 3. Translations -- Greek to English
LC 60010985

Jesus lives and works in Nazareth where, as any man might, he asserts his beliefs.

Kazantzakis, Nikos, 1883-1957

Zorba the Greek / Nikos Kazantzakis ; translated by Carl Wildman Simon and Schuster, 1952. 311 p.

1. Senior men -- Crete 2. Enthusiasm in senior men -- Crete 3. Male friendship 4. Mines and mineral resources 5. Optimism 6. Failure (Psychology) 7. Grief 8. Men/women relations 9. Crete 10. Psychological fiction 11. Modern classics 12. Translations -- Greek to English

Zorba, an irrepressible, earthy hedonist, sweeps his young disciple along as he wines, dines, and loves his way through a life dedicated to fulfilling his copious appetites.

Kazinski, A. J.

The **last** good man : a novel / A.J. Kazinski ; translated from the Danish by Tiina Nunnally. Scribner, 2012 384 p.
ISBN 9781451640755

1. Detectives 2. Murder investigation 3. Good and evil 4. Religious adherents 5. Women scientists 6. Metaphysics 7. Pattern perception 8. Mythology, Judaic 9. Denmark 10. Mythological fiction 11. Thrillers and suspense

A. J. Kazinski is the pseudonym of Anders Ronnow Klarlund and Jacob Weinreich.

According to Jewish legend, there are 36 righteous people on Earth at any given time. Without them, humanity would perish. But the 36 do not know they are the chosen ones, and many are dying.

Keane, Mary Beth

Fever / Mary B. Keane. Simon & Schuster, 2013. 352 p.
ISBN 9781451693416

1. Typhoid Mary, 1869-1938 2. 1900s (Decade) 3. Cooks 4. Typhoid fever 5. Communicable diseases 6. Ostracism 7. Quarantine 8. Sick women 9. Women cooks 10. Consequences 11. Separated couples 12. New York City -- History -- 20th century 13. Biographical fiction 14. Historical fiction

In 1883, Irish immigrant Mary Mallon arrives in New York to pursue her dream of becoming a cook. Success seems within reach when she's hired by a wealthy Manhattan family, but quickly recedes when her employers fall violently ill. She flees, but the pattern repeats itself and the death toll rises until the New York Department of Health catches up to her. As an asymptomatic carrier of salmonella typhi, the strain of bacteria responsible for typhoid fever, Mary appears healthy but is capable of infecting others. Dubbed "Typhoid Mary," the city's notorious patient zero is placed under quarantine and spends the rest of her life alternately campaigning for her freedom and, despite the danger to all involved, attempting to return to the work she loves. - Description by Gillian Speace.

Kearsley, Susanna, 1966-

A **desperate** fortune / Susanna Kearsley. Sourcebooks, 2015. 448 p.
ISBN 9781492602026

1. 18th century 2. 21st century 3. Self-discovery in women 4. Jacobites 5. Diaries 6. Trust 7. Women 8. Betrayal 9. Loyalty 10. France -- History -- 18th century 11. Paris, France 12. Historical fiction 13. Romantic suspense 14. Parallel narratives
RUSA Reading List Short List, 2016.

Hired to crack the cipher in the journal of Jacobite exile Mary Dundas, amateur codebreaker Sara Thomas encounters complications that require her to let go of everything she thought she knew about loyalty, love, and herself.

Kearsley, Susanna, 1966-

The **firebird** / Susanna Kearsley. Sourcebooks, 2013. 544 p.
ISBN 9781402276637

1. 1710s 2. Jacobite Rebellions (1689-1746) 3. Psychics 4. Visions 5. Young women 6. Bird carving 7. Jacobites 8. Courage 9. Redemption 10. Scotland -- History -- 1689-1745 11. Russia -- History -- 18th century 12. Love stories 13. Historical fiction 14. Parallel narratives
Companion book to: The winter sea.
Originally published: London : Allison & Busby, 2013.
RITA Award for Best Paranormal Romance, 2014.

A modern day woman with psychic abilities helps uncover the provenance of a small wooden carving, tracing it all the way back to eighteenth century Scotland and Russia.

Keating, H. R. F. (Henry Reymond Fitzwalter), 1926-2011

The **soft** detective St. Martin's, 1998. 268 p.
ISBN 0312193351

1. Nobel Prize winners 2. Detectives 3. East Indians in England 4. Fathers and sons 5. London, England 6. Mysteries
LC 98-8817

When Detective Chief Inspector Phil Benholme investigates the baffling murder of Nobel Prize-winning Professor Unwala, he is disturbed to discover that his own teenage son could be the prime suspect in the crime

"Keating's latest is a gripping examination of one of a police officer's worst nightmaresa portrait of a man faced with the choice between defending his son and helping to prove he's a killer." Booklist.

Keesey, Anna, 1962-

* **Little** century : a novel / Anna Keesey. Farrar, Straus and Giroux, 2012. 304 p.

ISBN 9780374192044

1. Eighteen-year-old women 2. Range wars 3. Loyalty 4. Homesteading -- Oregon 5. Orphans 6. Rangelands 7. Frontier and pioneer life -- Oregon 8. Cousins -- Oregon 9. Oregon 10. Westerns

LC 2011046308

After she moves near the lawless frontier town of Century, Oregon, to become a homesteader, eighteen-year-old Esther Chambers finds herself in a full-out range war that tests her loyalty to her cousin, rancher Ferris Pickett.

Kehlmann, Daniel, 1975-

Tyll / Daniel Kehlmann ; translated from the German by Ross Benjamin. Pantheon Books, 2020, c2017. 336 p.

ISBN 9781524747466

1. 17th century 2. Postwar life 3. Tricksters 4. Adventurers 5. Adventure 6. Voyages and travels 7. Entertainers 8. Characters and characteristics in fairy tales 9. Interpersonal relations 10. Europe -- History -- 17th century 11. Literary fiction 12. Picaresque fiction 13. Historical fiction 14. Magical realism 15. Translations -- German to English 16. Adaptations, retellings, and spin-offs

Originally published in Germany, c2017.

A vagabond and trickster from the 17th century embarks on a journey of discovery as he travels through history.

"Located somewhere between German romanticism and modernism, superstition and science, history and high fantasy, this is a rapturous and adventuresome novel of ideas that, like Tyll's roaming sideshow, must be experienced to be believed." Publishers Weekly.

Keilson, Hans, 1909-2011

Life goes on / Hans Keilson ; translated from the German by Damion Searls. Farrar, Straus and Giroux, 2012, c1933. 288 p.

ISBN 9780374191955

1. Keilson, Hans, 1909-2011 2. War and society 3. Jewish men 4. Depressions -- 1929-1941 5. Nationalism 6. Men with depression 7. Fathers and sons 8. Political corruption 9. World War I veterans 10. Businesspeople 11. Germany -- History -- 1918-1933 12. Autobiographical fiction 13. Historical fiction 14. Translations -- German to English

LC 2012012326

Originally published in Germany: S. Fischer Verlag, 1933.

Originally published as Leben geht weiter: Berlin : S. Fischer, 1933.

Life Goes On paints a dark portrait of Germany between the world wars. It tells the story of Max Seldersen - a Jewish store owner modeled on the author's father, a textile merchant and decorated World War I veteran - along with his wife, Else, and son, Albrecht, and the troubles they encounter as the German economy collapses and politics turn rancid. Banned by the Nazis in 1934, it has finally been reissued and translated.

Keller, Julia

* **Bone** on bone / Julia Keller. Minotaur Books, 2018. 304 p. Bell Elkins mysteries

ISBN 9781250190925

1. Former lawyers 2. Former convicts 3. Drug addiction 4. People with paraplegia 5. Former sheriffs 6. Murder 7. Murder investigation 8. Despair 9. Drug addicts 10. Small town life 11. West Virginia 12. Mysteries 13. Southern fiction

LC 2018023688

An investigation involving the suspicious deaths of a drug addict's parents is complicated by former deputy Jake Oakes' struggles to adjust to his physical challenges and Bell's grief over the loss of her sister.

"This haunting, thought-provoking story proves Keller is one of a kind. Readers of Julia Spencer-Fleming's mysteries of communities torn apart by crime may also want to try." Library Journal.

Keller, Julia

* **Fast** falls the night / Julia Keller. Minotaur Books, 2017. vii, 286 p. Bell Elkins mysteries

ISBN 9781250089618

1. Women lawyers 2. Drugs -- Overdose 3. Drug traffic 4. Drug dealers 5. Addiction 6. Small towns 7. Murder 8. Murder investigation 9. Mountain life 10. Secrets 11. Family relationships 12. West Virginia 13. Mysteries 14. Southern fiction

LC 2017008618

In a 24-hour period, Raythune County, West Virginia faces a record number of overdose victims thanks to heroin laced with elephant tranquilizer. Sheriff's deputy Jake Oakes, other cops, and EMTs try to save who they can, but not everyone lives, and opinions vary among locals if an addict's death matters. Investigating the source of the tainted drug in her Appalachian hometown, prosecutor Bell Elkins learns more about her past and new secrets from her ex-convict sister in this beautifully written, gritty 6th in the Bell Elkins series. -- Description by Dawn Towery.

"Keller's prose is so pure that her exploration of the desperate scourge of drugs and poverty and her forecast of a grim future for her heroine are a joy to read." Kirkus.

Keller, Julia

* **A killing** in the hills / Julia Keller. Minotaur Books, 2012. 416 p. Bell Elkins mysteries

ISBN 9781250003485

1. Teenage girls 2. Murder witnesses 3. Small town life -- West Virginia 4. Mothers and daughters 5. Crimes against seniors 6. Murder 7. Drug traffic 8. Women lawyers 9. West Virginia 10. Mysteries 11. Southern fiction

LC 2012016583

First published in the United Kingdom in 2012 by Headline Publishing Group.

Prosecuting attorney Bell Elkins and her estranged teenage daughter, Carla, try to protect their town and each other in the aftermath of a shocking triple murder committed by an unknown shooter whose identity is gradually realized by Carla.

Keller, Julia

Last ragged breath / Julia Keller. Minotaur Books, 2015. 384 p. Bell Elkins mysteries

ISBN 9781250044747

1. Recluses 2. Murder suspects 3. Real estate developers 4. Secrets 5. Small town life 6. Women lawyers 7. Public prosecutors 8. Inheritance and succession 9. Murder investigation 10. Floods 11. West Virginia 12. Mysteries 13. Southern fiction

LC 2015017000

RUSA Reading List Short List, 2016.

A tale inspired by a true event in West Virginia history finds prosecuting attorney Bell Elkins struggling to discover the truth when a survivor of the 1972 Buffalo Creek disaster is implicated in the murder of a development company president.

"With bits of her backstory still being revealed, Elkins is certainly among the best-drawn characters in crime fiction today." Booklist.

LIST OF FICTIONAL WORKS

Kellerman, Faye

The **forgotten** / Faye Kellerman. William Morrow, 2001. 374 p. Peter Decker and Rina Lazarus mysteries
ISBN 0688156142
1. Antisemitism 2. Orthodox Jews 3. Criminal investigation 4. Synagogue vandalism 5. Husband-and-wife detectives 6. Detectives 7. Police 8. Los Angeles, California 9. Mysteries

Having submitted for counseling a troubled wealthy teen who desecrated a synagogue, Rina Lazarus discovers there is more to the case when the boy and his therapists are murdered.

"The depiction of how teens and parents push and pull at one another's emotions is dead on." Booklist.

Kellerman, Faye

Jupiter's bones / Faye Kellerman. W. Morrow, 1999. 375 p. Peter Decker and Rina Lazarus mysteries
ISBN 0688156126
1. Cults 2. Orthodox Jews 3. Criminal investigation 4. Detectives 5. Police 6. Husband-and-wife detectives 7. Parent and child 8. Los Angeles, California 9. Mysteries

Ten years after prominent astrophysicist Dr. Emil Euler Ganz disappeared and became Father Jupiter, the founder of a pseudoscientific cult, he is found dead with a fifth of vodka and a vial of pills by his bedside. As LAPD Lieutenant Peter Decker begins to investigate the death, the cult turns violent and erupts into mayhem that threatens not only the lives of its naive adult members but also scores of helpless children.

"Kellerman has pulled together elements of suspense, violence, humor, pathos, and love and wrapped them into a potent plot certain to captivate genre fans." Booklist.

Kellerman, Faye

Milk and honey : a novel / Faye Kellerman. W. Morrow, 1990. 384p. Peter Decker and Rina Lazarus mysteries
ISBN 9780688086039
1. Murder 2. Orthodox Jews 3. Office romance 4. Police 5. Detectives 6. Widows 7. Jewish American women 8. Murder investigation 9. Beekeepers 10. Divorced men 11. Los Angeles, California 12. Mysteries

LC 89039592
One dark night, LAPD sergeant Peter Decker finds a blood-spattered two-year-old--all alone in the woods, with no one to claim her.

Kellerman, Faye

Prayers for the dead / Faye Kellerman. W. Morrow, 1996. 406 p. Peter Decker and Rina Lazarus mysteries
ISBN 0688143679
1. Medical research fraud 2. Orthodox Jews 3. Murder investigation 4. Husband-and-wife detectives 5. Murder suspects 6. Criminal investigation 7. Detectives 8. Police 9. Los Angeles, California 10. Mysteries

LC 967494
When celebrated heart surgeon Dr. Azor Sparks is brutally murdered, the suspects include the doctor's six children, a jealous colleague, and a gang of biker buddies, and it is up to Lieutenant Peter Decker to sort out the truth

"This mystery begins with the brutal murder and mutilation of renowned heart surgeon, researcher and fundamentalist Christian Azor Sparks. LAPD Lieutenant Decker gets the call. He also gets an abundance of suspects. . . . Religion and morality are integral to Kellerman's mysteries--built on the bedrock of the Deckers' orthodox Judaism. Here she deftly casts her net around the commanding victim, whose shadow lay equally over family and colleagues, and his son, the theologian Fa-

ther Abram, whose past connection with Rina may force Decker off the case." Publishers Weekly.

Kellerman, Faye

Serpent's tooth / Faye Kellerman. W. Morrow, 1997. 400 p. Peter Decker and Rina Lazarus mysteries
ISBN 0688143687
1. Mass murder 2. Criminal investigation 3. Orthodox Jews 4. Husband-and-wife detectives 5. Detectives 6. Police 7. Malicious accusation 8. Los Angeles, California 9. Mysteries

LC 97-10685
In the aftermath of a horrific mass murder at a trendy L.A. restaurant, Lieutenant Peter Decker, with the support of Rina Lazarus, risks his career and his reputation to investigate the alleged mad triggerman, ex-bartender and would-be actor Harlan Manz

"The scope of the investigation is broad and the moralizing is kept to a minimum, giving Decker a rare chance to do some solid police work." New York Times Book Review.

Kellerman, Jesse

The **genius** / Jesse Kellerman. G.P. Putnam's Sons, 2008. 374 p.
ISBN 9780399154591
1. Former police 2. Assistant district attorneys 3. Women assistant district attorneys 4. Fathers and daughters 5. Murder victims 6. Recluses 7. Cold cases (Criminal investigation) 8. Painting 9. Art museums 10. Drawing -- Psychological aspects 11. New York City 12. Mysteries 13. Psychological fiction

When a retired cop recognizes the faces of murdered children in an art gallery exhibit, he and his assistant DA daughter Susan begin a search to find the artist of the portraits--and possibly crack open a forty-year murder case.

"When Manhattan art dealer Ethan Muller is shown a dingy rent-controlled apartment bursting with fabulous work, he jumps on it, soon mounting a show even though the artist, Victor Cracke, has vanished. Who was Cracke, and why do some of the faces in his drawings look like young boys murdered years ago, the crimes unsolved? Prodded by a retired cop, Ethan begins to investigate first unwillingly, then compulsively and it becomes clear that Cracke's story is intertwined with that of Ethan's own family. Despite some cumbersome flashbacks, Jesse Kellerman's The Genius boasts a masterful plot and dead-on pacing." Entertainment Weekly.

Kellerman, Jonathan

Bones : an Alex Delaware novel / Jonathan Kellerman. Ballantine Books, 2008. 368 p. Alex Delaware novels
ISBN 9780345495136
1. Crimes against women 2. Marshes 3. Psychologists 4. Telephone calls 5. Murder 6. Murder investigation 7. Prostitutes 8. Private investigators 9. Detectives 10. California 11. Mysteries 12. Psychological suspense

LC bl2008020492
When an anonymous tip leads to the skeletal remains of victims whose right hands have been removed and a box containing six human hands, LAPD detective Milo Sturgis calls in Alex Delaware, whose investigation takes them to a reclusive tycoon's mansion.

"Kellerman's strength is that he can set up an intriguing situation and keep things moving at a breakneck pace. He can also, when he wants to, write well. He's good at short, vivid descriptions. . . . I don't think the plot of Bones will withstand scrutiny, but most readers probably won't care. The story sweeps them along, offering plenty of snappy dialogue and cheap thrills, plus a fair amount of suspense that is relieved by the final unveiling of the killer." Washington Post Book World.

Kellerman, Jonathan

The **clinic** / Jonathan Kellerman. Bantam Books, 1997, c1996. 370 p. Alex Delaware novels

ISBN 0553089226

1. Women authors 2. Human body parts industry and trade 3. Obsession in men 4. Psychologists 5. Detectives 6. Revenge 7. California 8. Mysteries 9. Psychological suspense

LC 9624626

Originally published: London : Little, Brown, 1996.

After an unsuccessful three-month investigation into the murder of psychology professor Hope Devane, author of a controversial anti-male best-seller, homicide detective Milo Sturgis calls in psychologist Alex Delaware to help uncover a motive for the cold-blooded stalking and killing

"The author has crafted another masterly, darkly psychological tale, drawing upon timely issues ranging from abortion to organ harvesting." Library Journal.

Kellerman, Jonathan

Devil's waltz / Jonathan Kellerman. Bantam Books, 1993. 416p. Alex Delaware novels

ISBN 9780553092059

1. Child abuse victims 2. Greed in men 3. Hospital administrators 4. Psychologists 5. Detectives 6. Physicians -- California 7. Sick children 8. Children's hospitals -- California 9. California 10. Mysteries 11. Psychological suspense

LC 92018089

Called in as a consultant for a possible child-abuse case, child psychologist Alex Delaware begins to suspect that the hospital has come under the sway of Chuck Jones, the financial whiz administrator who seems overly interested in profits

"Despite Mr. Kellerman's over-elaborate approach, he maintains the harrowing suspense of a medical mystery too horrid to be anything but real." New York Times Book Review.

Kellerman, Jonathan

Gone / Jonathan Kellerman. Ballantine Books, 2006. 384 p. Alex Delaware novels

ISBN 0345452615

1. Art students 2. Hoaxes 3. Psychologists 4. Psychologists 5. Police 6. Kidnapping 7. Murder 8. Murder investigation 9. Detectives 10. California 11. Mysteries 12. Psychological suspense

Psychologist Alex Delaware and L.A.P.D. detective Milo Sturgis investigate the bizarre case of two students whose claims of abduction are revealed to be a hoax, a case that takes an odd turn when one student is found murdered and the other vanishes.

"While the murderer's identity may not be that surprising, the author's ability to convey the unrelenting sadness of his characters' lives and his deep psychological insights will satisfy those looking for more than mere thrills." Publishers Weekly.

Kellerman, Jonathan

Monster / Jonathan Kellerman. Random House, 1999. 396 p. Alex Delaware novels

ISBN 067945960X

1. Precognition 2. Men with mental illnesses 3. Women psychologists 4. Serial murders 5. Serial murder investigation 6. Psychologists 7. Detectives 8. California 9. Mysteries 10. Psychological suspense

Dr. Alex Delaware and his friend and partner Detective Sturgis must penetrate the mind of a psychotic prisoner in order to stop a series of brutal slayings.

Kellerman, Jonathan

Private eyes / Jonathan Kellerman. Bantam Books, 1992. 475 p. Alex Delaware novels

1. Fear in women 2. Women college students 3. Protectiveness 4. Heirs and heiresses 5. Actors and actresses 6. Mothers and daughters 7. Former convicts 8. Psychologists 9. Detectives 10. California 11. Mysteries 12. Psychological suspense

LC 91017314

Twenty years after an assailant permanently scarred and crippled her actress mother, Gina, Melissa Dickinson is convinced that the attacker, now out of prison and back in L.A., will return to finish the job and enlists the aid of Dr. Alex Delaware to help protect her and her mother.

"Kellerman deftly handles the strings of his plot." Publishers Weekly.

Kellerman, Jonathan

Self-defense / Jonathan Kellerman. Bantam Books, 1995. 390 p. Alex Delaware novels

ISBN 055308920X

1. Recovered memory 2. Nightmares 3. Psychologists 4. Women's dreams 5. Interpersonal relations 6. Deception 7. Detectives 8. California 9. Mysteries 10. Psychological suspense

LC 94026175

Dr. Alex Delaware doesn't see many private patients anymore, but the young woman called Lucy is an exception. So is her dream. Lucy Lowell is referred to Alex by Los Angeles police detective Milo Sturgis. A juror at the agonizing trial of a serial killer, Lucy survived the trauma only to be tormented by a recurring nightmare: a young child in the forest at night, watching a strange and furtive act. Now Lucy's dream is starting to disrupt her waking life, and Alex is concerned ...

"Psychologist Alex Delaware is treating 25-year-old Lucy Lowell for a recurring nightmare that she has been having ever since serving on the hanging jury that convicted a serial killer. . . . When Lucy's terrifying dream is complicated by incidents of sleepwalking, bed-wetting, narcolepsy and a possible suicide attempt, Alex suspects a repressed childhood memory. After putting his patient through hypnotic regression, he is convinced that she witnessed a murder and he sets out to prove it. . . . An exciting story that is loaded with tension and packed with titillating insights into abnormal psychology." New York Times Book Review.

Kellerman, Jonathan

Therapy / Jonathan Kellerman. Ballantine, 2004. 400 p. Alex Delaware novels

ISBN 0345452593

1. Women psychotherapists 2. Psychotherapy patients 3. Confidential communications 4. Psychologists 5. Police 6. Women psychologists 7. Psychotherapist and patient 8. Murder investigation 9. Serial murders 10. Secrets 11. Men/women relations 12. Detectives 13. California 14. Mysteries 15. Psychological suspense

The brutal killings of a young couple--the troubled Gavin Quick and an unidentified female victim--draws LAPD Detective Milo Sturgis and psychologist Alex Delaware into a search for a cold-blooded killer.

"The author manages to take the story of a lovers' lane double murder near Mulholland Drive to the point where it involves human rights atrocities in Rwanda. Along the way Mr. Kellerman packs in the descriptive detail that is one of his hallmarks and one of the incidental attractions in his fiction." New York Times.

Kellerman, Jonathan

Time bomb / Jonathan Kellerman. Bantam Books, 1990. 468 p. Alex Delaware novels

1. Antisemitism 2. Women with mental illnesses 3. Psychologists 4. Racism 5. Snipers 6. Men with mental illnesses 7. School shootings 8. Psychological autopsy 9. Detectives 10. Mass shootings

11. California 12. Los Angeles, California 13. Mysteries 14. Psychological suspense

LC 90000349

When psychologist, Alex Delaware, is called in to conduct a psychological autopsy on a playground sniper in order to clear the name of the sniper's family, he soon becomes the target for an obsessive hatred.

Kelly, Cathy

Secrets of a happy marriage / Cathy Kelly. Grand Central Publishing, 2018, c2016. 464 p.

ISBN 9781538728796

1. Newlyweds 2. Husband and wife 3. Stepdaughters 4. Dysfunctional families 5. Resentfulness 6. Birthdays 7. Celebrations 8. Family relationships 9. Remarriage 10. Blended families 11. Ireland 12. Women's lives and relationships

Originally published as an e-book in the U.K. by Orion, 2017.

While planning her new husband's big birthday celebration, Bess, finds her May-December romance going into a tailspin as she quickly realizes that joining his family isn't going to be as easy as she thought.

Kelly, Erin, 1976-

* The **burning** air : a novel / Erin Kelly. Pamela Dorman Books, 2013. 336 p.

ISBN 9780670026722

1. Family secrets 2. Revenge 3. Rich families 4. Country homes 5. Bereavement in families 6. Mothers -- Death 7. England 8. Psychological suspense

LC 2012029302

Old wounds and long-buried family secrets come crashing down on the seemingly untouchable MacBride clan not long after matriarch Lydia MacBride dies. Connecting everything is a mysterious confession in Lydia's extensive diaries and an outsider bent on exacting terrible revenge on the MacBrides. -- Description by Shauna Griffin.

Kelly, Erin, 1976-

Broadchurch : a novel / Erin Kelly, Chris Chibnall. Minotaur Books., 2014. 433 p.

ISBN 9781250055507

1. Women detectives 2. Child murder victims 3. Small town life 4. Murder 5. Secrets 6. Suspicion 7. Detectives 8. Murder investigation 9. News media -- Social aspects 10. England 11. Dorset, England 12. Police procedurals 13. Mysteries 14. TV tie-ins

A novelization of the hit television show follows detectives Alec Hardy and Ellie Miller as they search for a young boy's killer among numerous suspects and a brewing media storm.

"Kelly's novelization of the eponymous British TV series . . . works as both a classic puzzle and an unnerving portrait of a little English town wracked by a young boy's murder." Kirkus.

Kelly, Erin, 1976-

The **poison** tree / Erin Kelly. Hodder & Stoughton, 2010. 340 p.

ISBN 9781444701036

1. 1990s 2. Women college students 3. Brothers and sisters 4. Love triangles 5. Orphans 6. Secrets 7. Bohemianism 8. Flashbacks 9. London, England 10. Psychological suspense

Originally published: London : Hodder & Stoughton, 2010.

Just out of university, Karen Clarke finally gets a taste of the excitement that's been sorely lacking from her life as a conscientious student: she comes to live in a crumbling London mansion with the free-spirited Biba, her brother Rex, and a bunch of others whose lives seem to revolve around sex, drugs, and irresponsibility. Before long, Karen becomes aware of the sad and tangled history that underlies their bohemian

lifestyle, but by then it's too late to disentangle herself. -- Description by Shauna Griffin.

"Veteran mystery fans looking for nail-biting thrills will find plenty that is fresh and surprising about The Poison Tree, and Kelly's masterful plotting and intricately crafted story make the comparisons to Tana French and Donna Tartt well-deserved." BookPage.

Kelly, Jim, 1957-

The **fire** baby / Jim Kelly. St. Martin's Minotaur, 2004. 352 p. Philip Dryden novels

ISBN 0312321457

1. Journalists 2. Amateur detectives 3. Women with terminal illnesses 4. People with cancer 5. People in comas -- Family relationships 6. Husband and wife 7. Serial murders 8. Last words 9. Secrets 10. Family secrets 11. Airplane accidents 12. Communication 13. The Fens, England 14. Cambridgeshire, England 15. Mysteries

LC 2004048691

Laura, who is slowly emerging from a coma, overhears a confession that could solve the murder case currently being investigated by her journalist husband, Philip, and struggles to tell him what she has learned in order to keep him out of danger.

Kelly, Jim, 1957-

The **moon** tunnel / Jim Kelly. St. Martin's Minotaur, 2005. 336 p. Philip Dryden novels

ISBN 031234922X

1. Journalists 2. People in comas -- Family relationships 3. Husband and wife 4. Excavations (Archaeology) 5. Treasure hunting 6. Tunnels 7. Dead 8. Cold cases (Criminal investigation) 9. Prisoners of war, British 10. World War II -- Prisoners and prisons, British 11. The Fens, England 12. Cambridgeshire, England 13. England 14. Mysteries

LC 2005049449

At the scene of an archaeological dig searching for buried Anglo-Saxon treasure on the site of a former POW camp, journalist Philip Dryden is stunned when excavators uncover the skeletal remains of a much more recent corpse.

Kelly, Julia, 1986-

The **light** over London / Julia Kelly. Gallery Books, 2019. 288 p.

ISBN 9781501196416

1. Second World War era (1939-1945) 2. Antique dealers 3. Women and war 4. World War II 5. Men/women relations 6. Antiaircraft guns 7. Diaries 8. Secrets 9. Cornwall, England -- History 10. London, England -- History -- Bombardment, 1940-1941 11. Parallel narratives 12. Historical fiction

LC 2018010178

Unable to confront the challenges in her own life, Cara Hargraves immerses herself in work for her antiques-dealer boss, uncovering relics from the life of World War II British "Gunner Girl" Louise Keene and her complicated relationship with a man named Paul.

Kelly, Martha Hall

Lilac girls / Martha Hall Kelly. Ballantine Books, 2016. 496 p.

ISBN 9781101883075

1. Ravensbruck (Concentration camp) 2. Second World War era (1939-1945) 3. World War II 4. Women 5. Secrets 6. Nazis 7. Teenage girls 8. Couriers 9. Women physicians 10. Concentration camps 11. Second chances 12. Freedom 13. Paris, France -- History -- German occupation, 1940-1944 14. Germany -- History -- 1933-1945 15. Historical fiction

"On a September day in Manhattan in 1939, twenty-something Caroline Ferriday is consumed by her efforts to secure the perfect boutonniere for an important French diplomat and resisting the romantic advances of a married actor. Meanwhile across the Atlantic, Kasia Kuzmerick, a Polish Catholic teenager, is nervously anticipating the changes that are sure to come since Germany has declared war on Poland. As tensions rise abroad - and in her personal life - Caroline's interest in aiding the war effort in France grows and she eventually comes to hear about the dire situation at the Ravensbruck all-female concentration camp. At the same time, Kasia's carefree youth is quickly slipping away, only to be replaced by a fervor for the Polish resistance movement. Through Ravensbruck - and the horrific atrocities taking place there told in part by an infamous German surgeon, Herta Oberheuser - the two women's lives will converge in unprecedented ways and a novel of redemption and hope emerges that is breathtaking in scope and depth"--, Provided by publisher.

Kelly, Martha Hall

Lost roses : a novel / Martha Hall Kelly. Ballantine Books, 2019. 448 p.

ISBN 9781524796372

1. First World War era (1914-1918) 2. Russian Revolution and Civil War (1917-1921) 3. Female friendship 4. Voyages and travels 5. Revolutions -- Russia 6. Friendship 7. Life change events 8. Women travelers 9. Russia -- History -- 20th century 10. United States -- History -- 20th century 11. Historical fiction

Originally published: North Sydney, NSW : Michael Joseph, 2019.

Based on true events, a tale set a generation before Lilac Girls traces the stories of three women, including Caroline Ferriday's mother, a Romanov cousin and a fortune-teller's daughter, against a backdrop of the Russian revolution and World War I.

Kelly, Stephen

The **wages** of desire : a World War II mystery / Stephen Kelly. Pegasus Books, 2016. 314 p. Inspector Lamb novels

ISBN 9781681771496

1. 1940s 2. Second World War era (1939-1945) 3. Detectives 4. Villages 5. World War II 6. Cold cases (Criminal investigation) 7. Conscientious objectors 8. World War I veterans 9. Murder investigation 10. Abandoned wives 11. Murder 12. England -- Social life and customs -- 20th century 13. Historical mysteries

Detective Chief Inspector Thomas Lamb risks his life to uncover links between a series of killings from the past and present in a Hampshire village brimming with dark secrets.

Kelman, James, 1946-

How late it was, how late / James Kelman. W. W. Norton, 1995, c1994. 373 p.

ISBN 9780393038170

1. Working class men 2. Men who are blind 3. Former convicts 4. Missing persons 5. Glasgow, Scotland 6. Literary fiction

Booker Prize, 1994.

Sammy, an ex-convict living in Glasgow, gets into a fight with some soldiers, only to regain consciousness in a jail cell and be questioned by the police about his girlfriend's disappearance.

"The novel is a tour de force, both in its convincingly claustrophobic rendering of what it's like to be newly sightless and in its rhythmic prose." Newsweek.

Kelton, Elmer

Badger boy / Elmer Kelton. Tom Doherty Associates, 2001. 286 p. Texas Rangers (Elmer Kelton)

ISBN 9780312873196

1. Texas Rangers 2. American Civil War era (1861-1865) 3. 1860s 4. Racism 5. Indians of North America 6. Boy orphans 7. Comanche Indians 8. Farmers 9. Lost love 10. Self-evaluation 11. Law enforcement 12. Civil war 13. United States Civil War, 1861-1865 14. United States -- History -- Civil War, 1861-1865 15. Texas 16. Historical fiction

LC 00048457

After his company of Texas rangers is disbanded, David "Rusty" Shannon returns home to his land on the Red River, where he encounters a young white boy known as Badger Boy who had been taken from his murdered parents by a Comanche warrior.

Kelton, Elmer

Hard ride / Elmer Kelton. Forge, 2018. 411 p.

ISBN 9781250161284

1. Ranchers 2. Outlaws 3. Rodeos 4. Justice 5. Gunfights 6. Cattle drives 7. Men/women relations 8. Frontier and pioneer life 9. The West (United States) 10. Short stories 11. Westerns

LC 2018044737

Collects stories originally published in the 1950s.

"A Tom Doherty Associates Book."

Imbued with an adventurous spirit, Hard Ride is filled with many heartfelt glimpses into the authentic experience of the American West. These stories encompass an enormous array of scenes from the early days of the Wild West into the twentieth century.

Kelton, Elmer

Texas vendetta / Elmer Kelton. Forge, 2004. 301 p. Texas Rangers (Elmer Kelton)

ISBN 0765305720

1. Texas Rangers 2. 1870s 3. Family feuds 4. Murder 5. Prisoners 6. Revenge 7. Trials (Murder) 8. Law enforcement 9. Escapes 10. Bank robbers 11. Former convicts 12. Texas 13. Westerns

LC 2003017352

Andy, a young Texas Ranger, joins forces with Farley, a Confederate soldier turned ranger, to deliver a prisoner to stand trial for murder, but the two lawmen soon find themselves in the middle of two warring families.

"Within the exciting context of a western adventure, [Kelton] explores paternal relationships-good and bad-and the crippling consequences of hanging on too tightly to a painful past." Booklist.

Kelton, Elmer

* The **way** of the coyote / Elmer Kelton. Forge, 2001. 283 p. Texas Rangers (Elmer Kelton)

ISBN 0312873182

1. Texas Rangers History 2. 1860s 3. Kidnapping 4. Loyalty 5. Political corruption 6. Comanche Indians 7. Boy orphans 8. Adopted boys 9. Former Texas Rangers 10. Indians of North America 11. Racism 12. Ranchers 13. Freed slaves 14. Texas 15. Westerns

LC 2001040482

Spur Award for Best Western Novel (Short Novel), 2002.

Former Comanche captive Rusty Shannon tries to resume a normal life after the end of the Civil War, but instead finds himself confronted by racial tension, murderous outlaws, brutal Comanche bands, and his nemesis--the deadly Oldham brothers.

"Kelton covers a wide swath of history with aplomb, illuminating a little-known period in Western history. California is still Mexican, Indians are a real threat and outlaws rule the land in this rough-riding adventure tale." Publishers Weekly.

Kemelman, Harry

Monday the rabbi took off G. P. Putnam's Sons, 1972. 316 p. Rabbi David Small mysteries

ISBN 9780449210017

1. Americans in Israel 2. Criminal investigation 3. Murder 4. Murder investigation 5. Rabbis 6. Amateur detectives 7. Israel 8. Barnard's Crossing, Massachusetts 9. Mysteries

LC 75175264

Equipped with the ability to see the third side of every question, Rabbi David Small, determined to have a peaceful day at the park, unexpectedly finds himself in the middle of an international incident.

Kemelman, Harry

One fine day the rabbi bought a cross / Harry Kemelman W. Morrow, 1987. 234 p. Rabbi David Small mysteries

ISBN 9780688056315

1. Illegal arms transfers 2. Criminal investigation 3. Murder 4. Murder investigation 5. Vacations 6. Rabbis 7. Amateur detectives 8. Jerusalem, Israel 9. Barnard's Crossing, Massachusetts 10. Mysteries

LC 86023571

As a favor, the rabbi looks in on Jordan Goodman, son of the local grocer. Jordan has adopted the beliefs of a fundamentalist Jewish group, and before long, he is the only suspect in a local murder.

Kemelman, Harry

Thursday the Rabbi walked out / Harry Kemelman. Morrow, 1978. 250 p. Rabbi David Small mysteries

ISBN 9780688033620

1. Criminal investigation 2. Antisemites 3. Murder 4. Murder investigation 5. Rabbis 6. Amateur detectives 7. Barnard's Crossing, Massachusetts 8. Mysteries

LC 78008466

When several members of his congregation become suspects in the murder of a cantankerous curmudgeon who has offended the Jewish community, Rabbi Small is forced to match wits with the killer.

Keneally, Thomas

* The **daughters** of Mars / Tom Keneally. Atria Books, 2013, c2012. 544 p.

ISBN 9781476734613

1. First World War era (1914-1918) 2. Military nurses 3. Sisters 4. World War I 5. Military campaigns 6. Battle casualties 7. Nurses -- Australia 8. Soldiers -- Australia 9. War -- Psychological aspects 10. Gallipoli Campaign, Turkey, 1915 11. Gallipoli, Turkey 12. France -- History -- 20th century 13. Egypt -- History -- 20th century 14. Historical fiction 15. War stories 16. Literary fiction

Includes author's note.

Originally published: North Sydney, N.S.W. : Vintage Books, 2012.

Colin Roderick Award (Australia), 2012.

Shortlisted for the Walter Scott Prize for Historical Fiction, 2013

Joining the war effort as nurses in 1915, two spirited Australian sisters, carrying a guilty secret, become the friends they never were at home and find themselves courageous in the face of extreme danger as they serve alongside remarkable women during the first World War.

"Keneally must have done copious research, but historical details and information about wartime medical treatment are presented organically, without the weight of historical retrospection... Highly recommended." Library Journal.

Keneally, Thomas

* **Schindler's** list / Thomas Keneally. Simon and Schuster, 1994, c1982. 398 p.

ISBN 9780671516888

1. Schindler, Oskar, 1908-1974 2. Holocaust (1933-1945) -- Poland 3. Righteous Gentiles in the Holocaust -- Germany 4. Ghettoes, Jewish -- Krakow, Poland 5. Holocaust survivors -- Poland 6. World War II -- Jews -- Rescue -- Poland 7. Poland -- History -- Occupation, 1939-1945 8. Germany -- Social conditions -- 1933-1945 9. Historical fiction 10. Biographical fiction 11. Literary fiction

Simultaneously published in 1982: New York : Simon and Schuster, as Schindler's list; and, London : Hodder and Stoughton, as Schindler's ark.

Booker Prize, 1982.

A wealthy German-Catholic industrialist and Nazi Party member named Oskar Schindler builds a factory near a concentration camp to save the lives of over 1,300 Jews.

Keneally, Thomas

Shame and the captives : a novel / Thomas Keneally. Atria Books, 2015, c2013. 400 p.

ISBN 9781476734644

1. Escapes 2. Prisoners of war, Japanese 3. Prisoners of war, Australian 4. World War II 5. Prisoners' spouses 6. Suicidal behavior 7. Culture conflict 8. Consequences 9. Young women 10. Anarchists 11. Shame 12. Australia -- History -- 20th century 13. New South Wales -- History -- 20th century 14. Literary fiction 15. Historical fiction 16. War stories

LC 2014034535

Originally published: North Sydney, NSW : Random House Australia, 2013.

A tale inspired by true events follows the experiences of a World War II prisoner's wife who befriends an Italian anarchist in the hopes of alleviating her husband's suffering, only to be swept up in a violent prison break.

"Keneally explores multiple and multifaceted themes of courage, loyalty, empathy, and cultural dissonance." Booklist.

Keneally, Thomas

Woman of the inner sea / Thomas Keneally. Nan A. Talese/ Doubleday, 1993, c1992. 277 p.

ISBN 9780385467957

1. Runaway wives, husbands, etc -- Australia 2. Small town life -- Australia 3. Wilderness areas -- Australia 4. Women -- Australia 5. Grief in women 6. Australia 7. Psychological fiction

LC 92028554

Originally published: Sydney : Hodder & Stoughton, 1992.

Distraught after a family crisis, Kate Gaffney-Kozinski disappears into the Australian outback, where she assumes a new identity and works as a barmaid, while her wealthy husband's enforcer tries to track her down.

"This novel succeeds on many fronts. It is a picaresque and often hilarious adventure story, recounting one woman's unforgettable if improbable travels. It is a series of love stories, as Kate meets the man who is appropriate for her at each stage of her life, and it is a mystery story as well. But the novel is also very much an exploration of ethics." New York Times Book Review.

Kennedy, Douglas, 1955-

The **big** picture / Douglas Kennedy. Hyperion, 1997. 374 p.

ISBN 078686298X

1. Lawyers 2. Photographers 3. Women authors 4. New identities

5. Deception 6. Husband and wife 7. Midlife crisis 8. Boredom 9. Extramarital affairs 10. Redemption 11. Murder 12. Father-separated children 13. New York City 14. Connecticut 15. Montana 16. Psychological suspense

LC 96044446

Years after giving up his dreams of becoming a photographer for law, Ben Bradford finds his perfect life falling apart when his wife begins having an affair with a neighbor, a professional photographer, and Ben is suddenly faced with a dangerous choice

"The book is more than just a compelling read: it also has poignant and moving things to say about lost opportunities and wasted lives in America, the cynical quality of sudden fame, the awfulness of willed seperation from deeply loved children." Publishers Weekly.

Kennedy, Douglas, 1955-

The **moment** / Douglas Kennedy. Pocket Books, 2011. 448 p.

ISBN 9781439180792

1. Cold War 2. Men/women relations 3. Memories 4. Travel writers 5. Betrayal 6. Espionage 7. Men -- Psychology 8. West Berlin, Germany 9. Psychological suspense 10. Literary fiction

Enduring a very private midlife while contemplating the end of a long marriage, Thomas is unsettled by the arrival of a package from Berlin and remembers an intense love affair with a police state refugee who was haunted by the city's division and the Cold War.

"A newly divorced American novelist living alone in Maine, Thomas Nesbitt reflects on a distant relationship he's never quite recovered from. As he looks back on his life in Germany, he must confront his unforgotten passion for Petra Dussmann, the betrayal that ended their relationship and the sorrowful regret that has haunted him since. Thomas' story begins as the launch of his writing career leads him to Cold War Berlin, where everyone is filled with suspicion and uncertainty. He finds himself living in a flat with an emotionally erratic, yet talented painter from Ireland and secures a job that not only pays his rent, but also introduces him to a beautiful translator named Petra. Their relationship quickly evolves into something serious, only to be challenged by her unbearable situation with the German police. In a moment of distrust and forgotten loyalty, the two lovers part ways, leaving Thomas' life forever altered by his missed opportunity with Petra." Yakima Herald.

"Despite his rambling pace, Kennedy's evocative prose makes the eventual spellbinding finish worth the trip." Kirkus.

Kennedy, Randy

Presidio / Randy Kennedy. Simon & Schuster, 2018. 304 p.

ISBN 9781501153860

1. 1970s 2. Drifters 3. Automobile thefts 4. Girl kidnapping victims 5. Stolen money 6. Thieves 7. Brothers 8. Kidnappers 9. Mennonites 10. Automobile travel 11. Diary writing 12. Families 13. Texas 14. Texas Panhandle 15. Crime fiction 16. Modern Westerns

Two brothers in the 1970s Texas panhandle steal a car to search for one's wife who ran off with their tiny amount of money and accidentally kidnap a Mennonite girl who was asleep in the backseat.

Kennedy, William, 1928-

Chango's beads and two-tone shoes / William Kennedy. Viking, 2011. 304 p. Albany cycle

ISBN 9780670022977

1. 1950s 2. 1960s 3. Journalists 4. Race relations 5. Political corruption 6. Men/women relations 7. Americans in Cuba 8. Irish Americans 9. Cuba -- History -- 1933-1959 10. Albany, New York 11. Literary fiction 12. Historical fiction

LC 2011019764

His life radically changed by an encounter with Ernest Hemingway in Cuba, journalist Daniel Quinn embarks on a turbulent journey marked by such historical events as the Albany race riots, the rise of Fidel Castro, and the assassination of Robert Kennedy.

Kennedy, William, 1928-

* **Ironweed** : a novel / William Kennedy. Viking Press, 1983. 227 p. Albany cycle

ISBN 0670401765

1. 1930s 2. Alcoholic men 3. Gravediggers 4. Former baseball players 5. Murderers 6. Runaway wives, husbands, etc 7. Fathers and sons 8. Families -- Albany, New York 9. Murder 10. Homecomings 11. Albany, New York 12. Noir fiction 13. Historical fiction 14. Literary fiction

LC 82040370

National Book Critics Circle Award for Fiction, 1983.
Pulitzer Prize for Fiction, 1984.

"With this tale of skid-row life in the Depression, Kennedy adds another chapter to his Albany cycle." Booklist.

Kenney, John, 1962-

Talk to me / John Kenney. Penguin Group, 2019 320 p.

ISBN 9780735214378

1. Reputation 2. Life change events 3. Television newscasters and commentators 4. Families 5. Discontent 6. Self-fulfillment 7. Television news 8. Family relationships 9. Men -- Family relationships 10. Family problems 11. New York City 12. Mainstream fiction 13. Domestic fiction

Losing his job and reputation in the wake of an ill-timed live tirade, a disgraced television anchor finds himself reconnecting with his family and the man he used to be.

Kenney, John, 1962-

Truth in advertising / John Kenney. Simon & Schuster, 2013. 320 p.

ISBN 9781451675542

1. Advertising executives 2. Middle-aged men 3. Breaking up (Interpersonal relations) 4. Father and adult son 5. Self-discovery in men 6. New York City 7. Mainstream fiction

LC 2012009173

"A Touchstone book."
Thurber Prize for American Humor, 2014.

Struggling with encroaching middle age and a broken engagement, advertising agent Finbar Dolan is forced to cancel his Christmas plans to tackle a last-minute work assignment only to learn that his estranged and abusive father has taken ill and that his siblings are unwilling to help, a situation that forces Fin to re-evaluate his choices.

Kent, Christobel

The **loving** husband / Christobel Kent. Farrar, Straus and Giroux, 2017, c2016. 416 p.

ISBN 9780374194123

1. Malicious accusation 2. Husband-killing 3. Widows 4. Police 5. Farms 6. Secrets 7. Small towns 8. Social isolation 9. Murder suspects 10. Murder investigation 11. Married people and secrets 12. England 13. Psychological suspense

LC 2016025969

"Sarah Crichton Books."

Wrongly targeted for her husband's shattering murder, Fran struggles with isolation and paranoia while their claustrophobic community is increasingly unraveled by dark secrets.

"There is something about Fran's complexity that sets this one apart and makes for a truly chilling, absorbing read." Kirkus.

LIST OF FICTIONAL WORKS

Kent, Hannah, 1985-

* **Burial** rites : a novel / Hannah Kent. Little, Brown and Company, 2013. 256 p.

ISBN 9780316243919

1. Magnusdottir, Agnes 2. 1820s 3. Women murderers 4. Capital punishment 5. Rural families -- Iceland 6. Malicious accusation 7. Attitude change 8. Perception 9. Farm life 10. Priests 11. Iceland -- History -- 19th century 12. Biographical fiction 13. Historical fiction

LC 2013014305

Australian Book Industry Awards, Literary Fiction Book of the Year, 2014.

Davitt Awards, Debut Crime, 2014.

Davitt Awards, Readers' Choice, 2014.

Nielsen BookData Australian Booksellers? Choice Award, 2014.

Shortlisted for the Stella Prize, 2014.

Shortlisted for the International Dublin Literary Award, 2015

Shortlisted for The Baileys Women's Prize for Fiction, 2014

Set against Iceland's stark landscape, Hannah Kent brings to vivid life the story of Agnes, who, charged with the brutal murder of her former master, is sent to an isolated farm to await execution. Horrified at the prospect of housing a convicted murderer, the family at first avoids Agnes. Only Tóti, a priest Agnes has mysteriously chosen to be her spiritual guardian, seeks to understand her. But as Agnes's death looms, the farmer's wife and their daughters learn there is another side to the sensational story they've heard. . . . BURIAL RITES evokes a dramatic existence in a distant time and place --, provided by publisher.

Kent, Kathleen, 1953-

The **burn** / Kathleen Kent. Mulholland Books, 2020. 352 p. Detective Betty

ISBN 9780316450584

1. Drug cartels 2. Women detectives 3. Narcotics investigation 4. Women/women relations 5. Organized crime 6. Culture conflict 7. Post-traumatic stress disorder 8. Drug traffic 9. Lesbians 10. Stalkers 11. Police 12. Cults 13. Stalking 14. Dallas, Texas 15. Police procedurals 16. LGBTQIA fiction

A Dallas detective struggles to adjust at work and home after a run-in with an apocalyptic cult while trying to track down crooked cops and the cult leader who had taken her hostage.

"Betty's struggles with PTSD and challenges to her identity as a cop spark compelling character evolution as she lowers walls to bond with a pair of old souls she meets on the streets. A gripping, powerfully human procedural." Booklist.

Kent, Kathleen, 1953-

The **dime** / Kathleen Kent. Mulholland Books, 2017. 352 p. Detective Betty

ISBN 9780316311038

1. Drug cartels 2. Women detectives 3. Narcotics investigation 4. Women/women relations 5. Organized crime 6. Culture conflict 7. Drug traffic 8. Lesbians 9. Stalkers 10. Police 11. Cults 12. Stalking 13. Dallas, Texas 14. Police procedurals 15. LGBTQIA fiction

RUSA Reading List, 2018.

Betty Rhyzyk, Brooklyn's toughest female police detective, relocates to rough-and-tumble Dallas, Texas, where she must contend with a group of unruly subordinates, a persistent stalker, a formidable criminal organization, and her girlfriend's unsupportive family.

"A worthy addition to the ranks of strong female detectives." Booklist.

Kent, Kathleen, 1953-

The **heretic's** daughter : a novel / Kathleen Kent. Little, Brown, 2008. 352 p.

ISBN 9780316024488

1. 17th century 2. Courage in girls 3. Witchcraft -- Salem, Massachusetts 4. Trials (Witchcraft) -- Salem, Massachusetts -- History 5. Mothers and daughters 6. Loss (Psychology) 7. Mothers -- Death 8. Coping in girls 9. Imprisonment 10. Superstition 11. Smallpox 12. Salem, Massachusetts -- History -- Colonial period, 1626-1775 13. Historical fiction

LC 2008001887

Prequel: The wolves of Andover.

David J. Langum, Sr. Prize in American Historical Fiction, 2008

A witchcraft accusation in their Salem, Massachusetts, home further complicates the challenging relationship between Martha Carrier and her equally willful daughter, Sarah, who are forced to stand together against the escalating hysteria and superstition of the trials that are threatening Martha's life.

Kent, Kathleen, 1953-

The **outcasts** : a novel / Kathleen Kent. Little, Brown and Company, 2013. 320 p.

ISBN 9780316206129

1. Frontier and pioneer life 2. Outlaws 3. Lovers 4. Treasure hunting 5. Brothels 6. Second chances 7. Police 8. Gunfighters 9. Determination (Personal quality) 10. Travelers 11. Men/women relations 12. The West (United States) -- History -- 19th century 13. Gulf Coast (United States) -- History -- 19th century 14. Westerns

LC 2013017705

RUSA Reading List, 2014.

"It's the 19th century on the Gulf Coast, a time of opportunity and lawlessness. After escaping the Texas brothel where she'd been a virtual prisoner, Lucinda Carter heads for Middle Bayou to meet her lover, who has a plan to make them both rich, chasing rumors of a pirate's buried treasure. Meanwhile Nate Cannon, a young Texas policeman with a pure heart and a strong sense of justice, is on the hunt for a ruthless killer named McGill who has claimed the lives of men, women, and even children across the frontier. Who--if anyone--will survive when their paths finally cross? As Lucinda and Nate's stories converge, guns are drawn, debts are paid, and Kathleen Kent delivers an unforgettable portrait of a woman who will stop at nothing to make a new life for herself"--, Provided by publisher.

Kenyon, Sherrilyn, 1965-

Dark bites : a short story collection / Sherrilyn Kenyon. St. Martin's Press, 2014 448 p. Dark-Hunter novels

ISBN 9780312376864

1. Good and evil 2. Supernatural 3. Paranormal romances 4. Short stories

LC 2013038823

The complete collection of short stories written for the Dark-Hunter series includes "Phantom Lover" and "Love Bytes" as well as a new, previously unreleased title and tales that have only been published exclusively on the author's website.

Kepler, Lars

The **hypnotist** : a novel / Lars Kepler ; translated from the Swedish by Miranda Dawson. Vintage Crime/Black Lizard, 2018, c2009. 528 p. Detective Inspector Joona Linna mysteries

ISBN 9780525433125

1. Boy murder witnesses 2. Murder victims 3. Hypnotists 4. Murderers -- Identification 5. Children of murder victims 6. Murder

investigation -- Sweden 7. Detectives 8. Police 9. Sweden 10. Mysteries 11. Scandinavian crime fiction 12. Translations -- Swedish to English

LC 2010044603

Originally published in Sweden with the title Hypnotisoren by Albert Bonniers Forlag, 2009.

Swedish Detective Inspector Joona Linna investigates the murders of three family members whose killing was witnessed by a fourth intended victim, a traumatized child whose shock Linna hopes to penetrate through hypnotism.

"Linna and Bark make a great crime-solving pair precisely because they puzzle each other so thoroughly; says Bark, for instance, 'The patient always speaks the truth under hypnosis. But it's only a matter of what he himself perceives as the truth'. To which Linna responds, 'What is it you're trying to say?' Indeed. What Bark is trying to say is that there are monsters hiding everywhere beneath the reasonable and rational, and Kepler's book makes for a satisfying and scary testimonial." Kirkus.

Kepler, Lars

The **rabbit** hunter : a novel / Lars Kepler ; translated from the Swedish by Neil Smith. Alfred A Knopf, 2020, c2016. 412 page Detective Inspector Joona Linna mysteries

ISBN 9781524732288

1. Prisoners 2. Serial murder investigation 3. Violence 4. Murder investigation 5. Detectives 6. Secrets 7. Sweden 8. Scandinavian crime fiction 9. Mysteries 10. Translations -- Swedish to English

Summoned from prison by the Swedish prime minister to help investigate the murder of a high-ranking political official, detective Joona Linna teams up with security police detective Saga Bauer to uncover the complex scheme of a vengeful killer.

"Fast-paced and fluent, with all the authors' trademark stratagems. Sure to be a hit, though best read by those with strong stomachs." Kirkus.

Kepler, Lars

The **sandman** / Lars Kepler ; translated from the Swedish by Neil Smith. Alfred A. Knopf, 2018. 443 p. Detective Inspector Joona Linna mysteries

ISBN 9781524732240

1. Cold cases (Criminal investigation) 2. Serial murders 3. Detectives 4. Police 5. Psychiatric hospital patients 6. Serial murder investigation 7. Sweden 8. Stockholm, Sweden 9. Translations -- Swedish to English 10. Mysteries 11. Scandinavian crime fiction

Originally published in 2012 by Albert Bonniers Forlag, Sweden, as Sandmannen.

"During a cold winter night in Stockholm a man is found walking alongside a railway bridge, suffering from hypothermia and legionella. After he's rushed to the hospital, it's discovered that, according to a death certificate, the man has been dead for over seven years. He is believed to be a victim of notorious serial killer Jurek Walter, who was arrested years ago by Detective Inspector Joona Linna and sentenced to a life of total isolation in forensic psychiatric care. As Joona Linna investigates where the "dead man" has been all these years, some unexpected evidence leads to the reopening of a cold case"--www.amazon.ca.

Kepler, Lars

Stalker / Lars Kepler ; translated from the Swedish by Neil Smith. Alfred A Knopf, 2019, c2014. 528 p. Detective Inspector Joona Linna mysteries

ISBN 9781524732264

1. Serial murders 2. Psychiatric hospital patients 3. Women murder victims 4. Hypnotists 5. Serial murder investigation 6. Detectives 7. Sweden 8. Stockholm, Sweden 9. Scandinavian crime fiction 10. Translations -- Swedish to English

Previously published in English by McClelland & Stewart, c2016. Originally published: Stockholm : A Bonnier, c2014.

When the police receive video clips of women who later fall victim to violent murders, criminal psychiatrist and hypnotist needs the help of Detective Joona Linna, who has been missing for over a year and is presumed dead.

Kerangal, Maylis de,

The **cook** / Maylis de Kerangal ; translated from the French by Sam Taylor. Farrar, Straus and Giroux, 2019, c2016. 112 p.

ISBN 9780374120900

1. Cooks 2. Cooking, French 3. Men and success 4. Men 5. Cooking 6. Friendship 7. Self-fulfillment 8. Personal conduct 9. Life change events 10. Interpersonal relations 11. Interpersonal attraction 12. France 13. Coming-of-age stories 14. Literary fiction 15. Psychological fiction 16. Translations -- French to English

LC 2018044068

Originally published by Raconter la Vie, 2016.

A follow-up to The Heart follows the coming-of-age of a self-taught chef who endures setbacks in his career, relationships and mental stability before rediscovering his passions, a journey witnessed by a nameless narrator who might be in love with him.

Kerangal, Maylis de

The **heart** : a novel / Maylis de Kerangal ; translated by Sam Taylor ; British edition translated by Jessica Moore. Farrar, Straus and Giroux, 2016, c2014. 256 p.

ISBN 9780374240905

1. Transplantation of organs, tissues, etc 2. Organ donors 3. Traffic accidents 4. Grief 5. Loss (Psychology) 6. Heart -- Transplantation 7. Second chances 8. France 9. Literary fiction 10. Psychological fiction 11. Translations -- French to English

LC 2015023340

"Originally published in French in 2014 by Verticales, an imprint of Editions Gallimard, France, as Reparer les vivants" -- Verso title page.

Also translated by Jessica Moore under the title Mend the living, 2016

"The Heart" takes place over the twenty-four hours surrounding a fatal accident and a resulting heart transplant as life is taken from a young man and given to a woman close to death. In gorgeous, ruminative prose it examines the deepest feelings of everyone involved--grieving parents, hardworking doctors and nurses--as they navigate decisions of life and death.

"It's clear de Kerangal has done extensive research, and the novel contains a wealth of medical knowledge. But her prose is more than just technical; the writing is uncommonly beautiful and never lacking humanity." Publishers Weekly.

Kerley, Jack

* The **death** collectors / Jack Kerley. Dutton, 2005. 336 p. Carson Ryder and Harry Nautilus mysteries

ISBN 0525948775

1. Psychopaths 2. Serial murder investigation 3. Collectors and collecting 4. Police -- Mobile, Alabama 5. Brothers 6. Women television journalists 7. Serial murderers 8. Artists 9. Painters 10. Conspiracies 11. Serial murders 12. Art -- Collectors and collecting 13. Death in art 14. Alabama 15. Mobile, Alabama 16. Mysteries

LC 2004028816

Thirty years after a renowned artist and serial killer is shot dead in the courtroom on the day of his sentencing, homicide detectives Carson Ryder and Harry Nautilus investigate a murder scene that resembles the work of the long-dead killer.

Kerouac, Jack, 1922-1969

The **dharma** bums / Jack Kerouac. Penguin Books, 1990, c1958. xxviii, 187 p.

ISBN 9780140042528

1. Kerouac, Jack, 1922-1969 2. Young men 3. Zen Buddhism 4. Counterculture 5. Hedonism 6. Dharma (Buddhism) 7. Beat culture 8. Self-discovery in men 9. Truth -- Religious aspects -- Buddhism 10. Sierra Nevada Mountains 11. San Francisco, California 12. Literary fiction 13. Autobiographical fiction 14. Modern classics
Sequel: Desolation Angels.

Originally published: New York : Viking Press, 1958.

During the 1950s the search for Buddhist truths takes two young Bohemians through a series of bizarre experiences in California

"This novel deals with Zen Buddhism. It's about two young men who are seeking to find themselves through meditation, voluntary poverty, separation from society, and intimate contact with nature, especially the Western mountains. . . . Sometimes Kerouac seems a little foolish, often he is extreme, but he is genuine, he is alive, and he is native." Library Journal.

Kerouac, Jack, 1922-1969

* **On** the road / Jack Kerouac. Penguin Books, 1976, c1957. 310 p.

ISBN 9780140042597

1. Kerouac, Jack, 1922-1969 2. 1950s 3. Travelers -- United States 4. Counterculture 5. Friendship 6. Hitchhiking 7. Companionship 8. Automobile travel 9. Voyages and travels 10. Beat culture 11. Men/women relations 12. Self-fulfillment in men 13. Autobiographical fiction 14. Modern classics 15. Literary fiction

Originally published: New York : Viking Press, 1957.

On the Road is a thinly fictionalized autobiography, filled with a cast made of Kerouac's real life friends, lover, and fellow travelers. Narrated by Sal Paradise, one of Kerouac's alter-egos, On the Road is a cross-country bohemian odyssey that not only influenced writing in the years since its 1957 publication but penetrated into the deepest level of American thought and culture.

"The biggest immediate difference between the first draft and the finished product . . . is that while we know On the Road as a novel--the great novel of the Beat Generation--the scroll is essentially nonfiction, a memoir that uses real names and is far less self-consciously literary. It is a dazzling piece of writing for all of its rough edges, and, stripped of affectations that in the novel can sometimes verge on bathos, as well as of gratuitous punctuation supplied by editors more devoted to rules than to music, it seems much more immediate and even contemporary. The scroll clarifies the book's connection to the past--to Mark Twain and tramp narratives and Woody Guthrie and cowboy sagas--and underlines the features it shares with its nearest contemporaneous cultural relative, Robert Frank's great photographic road book The Americans." New York Times Book Review.

Kerouac, Jack, 1922-1969

* **Road** novels 1957-1960 / Jack Kerouac ; edited by Douglas Brinkley. Library of America, 2007 864 p.

ISBN 9781598530124

1. 1950s 2. Counterculture 3. Beat culture 4. Beat generation 5. Wanderers and wandering 6. Literary fiction 7. Autobiographical fiction 8. Modern classics

LC 2007924522

A collector's edition of five works by the late Beat Generation classic writer.

"Kerouac's work marked the articulation of a new voice far more interesting for what the author had to say and the way in which he said it

than for the technical breakthroughs that it was heralded--and scorned--for at the time." San Francisco Chronicle.

Kerr, Laurel

Wild on my mind / Laurel Kerr. Sourcebooks Casablanca, 2018. 384 p. Where the wild hearts are

ISBN 9781492670858

1. Zoos 2. Single fathers 3. Helpfulness in women 4. Animals 5. Animal rescue 6. Bullying and bullies 7. Matchmaking 8. Badgers 9. Sexual attraction 10. Men/women relations 11. Contemporary romances

Love runs wild at the Sagebrush Flats Zoo, where a motley crew of big-hearted animals helps the most unlikely couples find love.

Kerr, Philip

Field gray / Philip Kerr. G. P. Putnam's Sons, 2011. 448 p. Bernhard Gunther mysteries

ISBN 9780399157417

1. 1950s 2. 1930s 3. International intrigue 4. Murder 5. Suspicion 6. World War II 7. Private investigators 8. Germans 9. Hardboiled fiction 10. Historical mysteries 11. Mysteries

LC 2010045006

In a historical suspense novel, chain-smoking, hard-drinking Bernie Gunther moves from riot-torn Berlin in 1931 to Adenauer's Germany in 1954--with a stop at a Russian prisoner-of-war camp along the way.

Kerr, Philip

* **Greeks** bearing gifts : a Bernie Gunther novel / Philip Kerr. G.P. Putnam's Sons, 2018 511 p. Bernhard Gunther mysteries

ISBN 9780399177064

1. 1950s 2. Second World War era (1939-1945) 3. Nazi plunder 4. Former detectives 5. Insurance companies 6. Murderers 7. Postwar life 8. Murder investigation 9. International intrigue 10. Germany 11. Historical mysteries 12. Hardboiled fiction

LC 2017037137

"A Marian Wood book."

Working undercover in 1956 Munich, Bernie Gunther investigates a murder with ties to Nazi plunder that prompts his collaboration with a lieutenant who has been looking for an opportunity to bring a killer to justice.

Kerr, Philip

Hitler's peace : a novel of the Second World War / Philip Kerr. G.P. Putnam's Sons, 2005. 464 p.

ISBN 0399152695

1. Hitler, Adolf, 1889-1945 2. Roosevelt, Franklin D (Franklin Delano), 1882-1945 3. Stalin, Joseph, 1879-1953 4. Churchill, Winston, 1874-1965 5. Himmler, Heinrich, 1900-1945 6. United States. Office of Strategic Services 7. Teheran Conference, (1943) 8. 1940s 9. Spies 10. Politicians 11. World politics -- 20th century 12. Political science 13. Negotiation 14. Deception 15. Betrayal 16. Ethics 17. World War II -- Peace 18. Alternative histories 19. Spy fiction 20. Thrillers and suspense

LC 2004043170

Realizing in the aftermath of Stalingrad that Germany will not win the war, Adolph Hitler considers the demands of FDR, Stalin, and Churchill, while OSS operative Willard Mayer, serving as FDR's envoy, finds his beliefs in the period's stylish philosophies put to the test.

Kerr, Philip

* The **lady** from Zagreb : a Bernie Gunther Novel / Philip Kerr. G. P. Putnam's Sons, 2015. 421 p. Bernhard Gunther mysteries

ISBN 9780399167645

1. 1940s 2. Actors and actresses 3. Propaganda 4. Atrocities 5. Mass burials 6. Murder 7. Nazis 8. Prague, Czech Republic -- History -- 20th century 9. Hardboiled fiction 10. Historical mysteries 11. Mysteries

Former Berlin homicide bull Bernie Gunther and a rising star in Germany's most prominent film company become pawns in the ambitious agendas of Hitler's dangerous Propaganda Minister.

"Kerr unspools a whopping good historical thriller here, brilliantly evoking not only wartime Berlin, but also Switzerland and Croatia, as well as portraying the German cinema in a time of peril. And, of course, there is the ever-fascinating Bernie, neither as tough nor as cynical as he pretends to be." Booklist.

Kerr, Philip

A **man** without breath / Philip Kerr. Marian Wood Books, 2013. 448 p. Bernhard Gunther mysteries

ISBN 9780399160790

1. 1940s 2. Private investigators 3. Atrocities 4. Mass burials 5. Murder 6. Nazis 7. Prague, Czech Republic -- History -- 20th century 8. Hardboiled fiction 9. Historical mysteries 10. Mysteries

Working in the Wehrmacht's War Crime Bureau of 1943 at the behest of an old friend, sardonic Berlin cop Bernie Gunther struggles to find proof of Russian responsibility for a mass shooting of Polish army officers in the hopes of destabilizing the Western Alliance.

Kerr, Philip

March violets / Philip Kerr. Viking, 1989. 245 p. Bernhard Gunther mysteries

ISBN 9780670824311

1. 1930s 2. Murder investigation 3. Nazis 4. Missing persons investigation 5. Robbery investigation 6. Stolen property recovery 7. Extramarital affairs 8. Private investigators 9. Criminal evidence 10. Undercover operations 11. Political corruption 12. Germans 13. Nazism 14. Former police 15. Berlin, Germany -- History -- 1918-1945 16. Germany -- History -- 1918-1945 17. Hardboiled fiction 18. Historical mysteries 19. Mysteries

"Berlin...1936."

First published by Viking 1989, published in Penguin Books 1990, reissued in this edition 2015.

The first book of the Berlin noir trilogy, March violets introduces readers to Bernie Gunther, an ex-policeman who thought he'd seen everything on the streets of 1930s Berlin--until he turned freelance and each case he tackled sucked him further into the grisly excesses of Nazi subculture. Hard-hitting, fast-paced, and richly detailed, March violets is noir writing at its blackest and best.

"The first volume in Kerrs Bernhard Gunther series, starring a classic Chandler-Hammett PI in Germany in 1936, captures a moment ideal for detective fiction: a country in the wake of a gloriously decadent era, the Weimar Republic, confronted by a new regime of unimagined repression." Booklist.

Kerr, Philip

* **Metropolis** : a Bernie Gunther novel / Philip Kerr. G.P. Putnam's Sons, 2019 400 p. Bernhard Gunther mysteries

ISBN 9780735218895

1. 1920s 2. Between the Wars (1918-1939) 3. Police 4. Young men 5. Serial murder investigation 6. Murder investigation 7. World War I veterans 8. Crimes against prostitutes 9. Germany -- History -- 1918-1933 10. Berlin, Germany 11. Historical mysteries 12. Hardboiled fiction

LC 2018046712

A Bernie Gunther origin story is set during his first weeks on Berlin's Murder Squad and finds a twentysomething Bernie investigating a particularly violent wave of murders targeting the city's vulnerable prostitutes and homeless veterans.

"The banter is priceless. Going against the grainas usual--by writing an origin novel as his swan song, Kerr leaves his fans happy." Kirkus.

Kerr, Philip

***Prussian** blue / Philip Kerr. Marian Wood Books/Putnam, 2017. 544 p. Bernhard Gunther mysteries

ISBN 9780399177057

1. Gestapo 2. 1950s 3. Second World War era (1939-1945) 4. Former detectives 5. Coercion 6. Assassination 7. Nazi fugitives 8. Murder investigation 9. Spies 10. Double agents 11. International intrigue 12. Postwar life 13. French Riviera 14. France 15. Germany 16. Hardboiled fiction 17. Historical mysteries

LC 2016046341

"A Marian Wood book."

Longlisted for the Walter Scott Prize for Historical Fiction, 2018

When his cover is blown, Bernie Gunther plays a game of cat-and-mouse with an old enemy before escaping to Berlin seeking help from a group of former allies.

"As always, Kerr lets Bernie have fun with genre conventions without losing sight of the horror behind the tough talk. At the top of everyones WWII mystery list." Booklist.

Kerstan, Lynn

The **golden** leopard / Lynn Kerstan. NAL, 2002 384 p. Big cat trilogy

ISBN 0451410572

1. Regency period (1811-1820) 2. England -- Social life and customs -- 19th century 3. Regency romances 4. Historical romances

After a heart-wrenching romantic betrayal, Lady Jessica Carville abandons love to become a dealer of rare antiquities for Christie's auction house in London, but her new job takes a bizarre turn when Lord Hugo Duran, the man she had once loved, makes her a tempting offer to find a missing priceless artifact.

Kerstan, Lynn

Heart of the tiger / Lynn Kerstan. New American Library, 2003 384 p. Big cat trilogy

ISBN 9780451410856

1. Regency period (1811-1820) 2. Women 3. Women murder suspects 4. Poor people 5. Sick fathers 6. Brothers 7. Nobility 8. Dukes and duchesses 9. Revenge 10. Murder 11. Honor 12. Redemption 13. Determination (Personal quality) 14. London, England 15. England -- Social life and customs -- 19th century 16. Historical romances 17. Romantic suspense 18. Regency romances

Unable to trust men after being victimized by the Duke of Tallant, Mira Holcombe, a stunning beauty, embarks on a mission of vengeance against the Duke, but her plans are thwarted by his younger brother, Michael Keynes, who vows to gain her trust and free her heart from her dark past.

Kesey, Ken

* **One** flew over the cuckoo's nest / Ken Kesey. Viking, 2002, c1962. xxiv, 281 p.

ISBN 9780670030583

1. Psychiatric hospitals 2. Psychiatric hospital care 3. People with

mental illnesses -- Care and treatment 4. Mental illness -- Treatment 5. Psychiatric hospital patients 6. Native American men 7. Nurses 8. Oregon 9. Satirical fiction 10. Modern classics 11. Literary fiction 12. Pacific Northwest fiction

LC 200146923

Originally published: Viking, 1962.

McMurphy, a criminal who feigns insanity, is admitted to a mental hospital where he challenges the autocratic authority of the head nurse.

Kesey, Ken

Sometimes a great notion : a novel / Ken Kesey. Penguin Books, 1988, c1964. 628 p.

ISBN 9780140045291

1. Strikebreakers 2. Lumber workers -- Oregon 3. Strikes 4. Small town life 5. Lumber industry and trade 6. Brothers -- Oregon 7. Oregon 8. Pacific Northwest fiction 9. Modern classics 10. Literary fiction

LC 87029184

Originally published: New York : Viking Press, 1964.

The aggressive scion of an Oregon lumber empire struggles against the conformity of townspeople. -- Multnomah County Library, Portland, Oregon.

Khadivi, Laleh

* **A good** country : a novel / Laleh Khadivi. Bloomsbury, 2017. 239 p. Khourdi trilogy

ISBN 9781632865847

1. Iranian Americans 2. Friendship 3. Radicalism 4. Jihad 5. Growing up 6. Teenagers 7. Terrorism 8. Arab American teenagers 9. Terrorists 10. Muslims 11. Coming-of-age stories 12. Literary fiction

LC 2016050042

Alireeza Courdee, son of Iranian immigrants, changes from a typical American teenager to a political radical, making his way to Syria with two of his friends, and is soon faced with the harsh reality of his choice.

"The story unfolds deftly, beautifully capturing the psychology of an American teen who goes down the path of radicalization; readers will understand what would motivate a sheltered, shortsighted young person to run away to join extremists." School Library Journal.

Khadra, Yasmina

The **swallows** of Kabul : a novel / Yasmina Khadra ; translated from the French by John Cullen. Nan A. Talese/Doubleday, 2004. 208 p..

ISBN 0385510012

1. Taliban 2. Prison guards 3. Women prisoners -- Afghanistan 4. State-sponsored terrorism -- Afghanistan 5. Married people 6. Life change events 7. Violence 8. Death 9. Extramarital affairs 10. Fundamentalists 11. Islam 12. Muslims 13. Afghanistan -- Social conditions 14. Kabul, Afghanistan 15. Literary fiction 16. Translations -- French to English

LC 2003050769

ALA Notable Book, 2005.

Shortlisted for the International IMPAC Dublin Literary Award, 2006

Their lives as a diplomat and lawyer frozen by the ascendancy of the Taliban, Moshen and Zunaira find their situation becoming a nightmare when Zunaira is arrested and condemned to death.

"The author is intimately familiar with the consequences that war and religious extremism have on people's daily lives, and in this book he gives the reader a tactile sense of what life under the Taliban might have been like." New York Times.

Khalfah, Khlid, 1964-

Death is hard work : a novel / Khaled Khalifa ; translated from the Arabic by Leri Price. Farrar, Straus and Giroux, 2019. 192 p.

ISBN 9780374135737

1. Civil war 2. Brothers and sisters 3. Fathers -- Death 4. Father and child 5. Cemeteries 6. Voyages and travels 7. War and society 8. Personal conduct 9. Family relationships 10. Syria -- History -- Civil War, 2011- 11. Literary fiction 12. War stories 13. Translations -- Arabic to English

LC 2018033289

National Book Award for Translated Literature finalist, 2019.

Draws on first-person experiences in the story of three siblings who set aside their differences and risk their lives during the Syrian civil war to honor their late father's final wishes.

"Flawlessly translated and exquisitely written, this novel from the winner of the Naguib Mahfouz Prize is a genuine tour de force as well as a thoughtful and provocative examination of what it means to be alive." Library Journal.

Khan, Ausma Zehanat

Among the ruins / Ausma Zehanat Khan. Minotaur Books, 2017. 336 p. Rachel Getty and Esa Khattak novels

ISBN 9781250096739

1. Political prisoners 2. Muslim men 3. Detectives 4. Missing persons investigation 5. Women murder victims 6. Political surveillance 7. Murder investigation 8. Canadians 9. Iran 10. Toronto, Ontario 11. Canada 12. Police procedurals

Investigating the murder of a filmmaker in Iran at a notorious prison, detectives Esa Khattak and Rachel Getty become embroiled in the country's tumultuous politics and a conspiracy linked to the Shah and the decades-old murders of famous dissidents.

"Khan uses an involving mystery in a vividly portrayed setting to illustrate unspeakable violations undertaken by governments in religious and political chaos. In Khan's hands, mysteries carry powerful messages." Booklist.

Khan, Ausma Zehanat

The **unquiet** dead / Ausma Zehanat Khan. Minotaur Books, 2015. 336 p. Rachel Getty and Esa Khattak novels

ISBN 9781250055118

1. War criminals 2. Deception 3. Muslim men 4. Detectives 5. Murder investigation 6. Consequences 7. War crimes 8. Murder victims 9. Secret identity 10. Secrets 11. Toronto, Ontario 12. Canada 13. Police procedurals

LC 2014032396

Arthur Ellis Award for Best First Novel, 2016.

Detective Esa Khattack and his partner, Detective Rachel Getty, investigate the death of a local man who may have been a Bosnian war criminal with ties to the Srebrenica massacre of 1995.

"Khan's stunning debut is a poignant, elegantly written mystery laced with complex characters who force readers to join them in dealing with ugly truths." Kirkus.

Khan, Vaseem, 1973-

The **perplexing** theft of the jewel in the crown / Vaseem Khan. Redhook Books, 2016. 362 p. Baby Ganesh Agency investigations

ISBN 9780316386845

1. Former police 2. Jewelry theft 3. Elephants 4. Diamonds 5. Crown jewels 6. Retirees 7. Investigations 8. India 9. Mumbai, India 10. Mysteries

Shamus Award for Best P.I. Paperback Original, 2017.

When the priceless Koh-i-noor diamond is stolen from an exhibition of the British Crown Jewels in Mumbai, Inspector Chopra and his elephant are left with the task of discovering the perpetrators of the seemingly impossible heist.

"The second in the Baby Ganesh Agency series, following last year's The Unexpected Inheritance of Inspector Chopra, is every bit as captivating as its predecessor. The reason has much to do with Khan's ability to craft such quirky, three-dimensional characters and the fact that he places them in such believable difficulties amid the rich stew of Mumbai." Booklist.

Khoury, Raymond

Empire of lies / Raymond Khoury. Forge, 2019. 448 p.

ISBN 9781250210968

1. Time travel 2. History 3. Civilization 4. Caliphate 5. Culture 6. War 7. International intrigue 8. Intelligence service 9. Sultans 10. Imaginary empires 11. Physicians 12. Women lawyers 13. Espionage 14. Terrorism 15. Islam 16. Paris, France 17. Europe 18. Science fiction 19. Alternative histories

Published in the U.K. under the title The Ottoman secret, Michael Joseph, 2019.

Paris, 2017: Ottoman flags have been flying over the great city for three hundred years, ever since its fall--along with all of Europe -- to the empire's all-conquering army. Notre Dame has been renamed the Fatih Mosque. Public spaces are segregated by gender. And Kamal Arslan Agha, a feted officer in the sultan's secret police, is starting to question his orders.

Kibler, Julie

Home for erring and outcast girls / Julie Kibler. Random House Inc, 2019 336 p.

ISBN 9780451499332

1. 1900s (Decade) 2. Female friendship 3. Women's shelters 4. Women -- Social conditions 5. Librarians 6. Friendship 7. Local history 8. Single mothers 9. Maternity homes 10. Texas -- History -- 20th century 11. Historical fiction 12. Parallel narratives

Inspired by historical events, a follow-up to the best-selling Calling Me Home follows the deep friendship between two women at an early 20th-century rehabilitation home for cast-out single mothers, and the reclusive librarian who discovers their story a century later.

Kidd, Jess

* **Things** in jars / Jess Kidd. Simon & Schuster, 2020. 384 p.

ISBN 9781982121280

1. Victorian era (1837-1901) 2. Aristocracy 3. Supernatural 4. Eccentrics and eccentricities 5. Anatomy 6. Detectives 7. Women detectives 8. Kidnapping 9. Missing children 10. Missing persons investigation 11. Curiosities and wonders 12. London, England -- History -- 19th century 13. Historical fantasy

Previously published in Great Britain, 2019.

Woman detective Bridie Devine investigates the kidnapping of a nobleman's illegitimate daughter, whose reputed supernatural powers have captured the attention of sinister collectors in the underworld's curiosities trade.

"With so much detail and so many clever, Dickensian characters, readers might petition Kidd to give Bridie her own series. Creepy, violent, and propulsive; a standout gothic mystery." Kirkus.

Kidd, Sue Monk

* The **book** of longings / Sue Monk Kidd. Viking, 2020. 384 p.

ISBN 9780525429760

1. Jesus Christ 2. Ethics 3. Marriage 4. Ambition in women 5. Women authors 6. Writing 7. Civilization, Ancient 8. Escapes 9. Secrets 10. Historical fiction

LC 2019049624

A first-century intellectual fights the limitations imposed on women before an encounter with an 18-year-old Jesus leads to their marriage, his dangerous public ministry and her flight to safety in Alexandria.

"Kidd is a library favorite, and the bold subject of this novel will increase buzz tenfold." Booklist.

Kidd, Sue Monk

* The **invention** of wings : a novel / Sue Monk Kidd. Viking, 2014. 384 p.

ISBN 9780670024780

1. Grimke, Sarah Moore, 1792-1873 2. Antebellum America (1820-1861) 3. 19th century 4. Anti-slavery movements 5. Feminists 6. Women's rights 7. Women abolitionists 8. Slavery 9. South Carolina -- History -- 19th century 10. Charleston, South Carolina -- History -- 19th century 11. Historical fiction 12. Biographical fiction 13. Southern fiction

LC 2013028185

Traces more than three decades in the lives of a wealthy Charleston debutante who longs to break free from the strictures of her household and pursue a meaningful life; and the urban slave, Handful, who is placed in her charge as a child before finding courage and a sense of self.

Kidd, Sue Monk

The **secret** life of bees / Sue Monk Kidd. Viking, 2002. xii, 301 p.

ISBN 9780670894604

1. 1960s 2. African American women -- South Carolina 3. Interracial friendship 4. Teenage girls -- South Carolina 5. Sisters -- South Carolina 6. Beekeepers -- South Carolina 7. African-American women beekeepers -- South Carolina 8. Small town life -- South Carolina 9. Fourteen-year-old girls -- South Carolina 10. Fathers and daughters -- South Carolina 11. Racism -- South Carolina 12. South Carolina -- Race relations 13. Coming-of-age stories 14. Mainstream fiction 15. Southern fiction

LC 2001026310

Book Sense Book of the Year Paperback, 2004.

After her "stand-in mother," a bold black woman named Rosaleen, insults the three biggest racists in town, Lily Owens joins Rosaleen on a journey to Tiburon, South Carolina, where they are taken in by three black, bee-keeping sisters.

Kiefer, Christian, 1971-

The **infinite** tides : a novel / Christian Kiefer. Bloomsbury USA, 2012. 320 p.

ISBN 9781608198108

1. Astronauts 2. Grief in men 3. Friendship 4. Loss (Psychology) 5. Immigrants 6. Ukrainians in the United States 7. Suburban life 8. Self-discovery in men 9. Midlife crisis in men 10. Coping 11. Mainstream fiction

LC 2011045534

Achieving the goal of a lifetime when he arrives aboard the International Space Station, astronaut and math genius Keith Corcoran is shattered to receive news that his wife has left him and that his 16-year-old daughter has died in a car accident, a situation from which he gradually recovers at the side of an unlikely friend.

LIST OF FICTIONAL WORKS

Kienzle, William X.

The **rosary** murders / William X. Kienzle. Andrews and McMeel, 1989, c1979. 257 p. Father Koesler mysteries

ISBN 9780836261011

1. Serial murders 2. Priests 3. Serial murder investigation 4. Clergy 5. Young men 6. Consequences 7. Amateur detectives 8. Murder investigation 9. Crimes against clergy 10. Options, alternatives, choices 11. Detroit, Michigan 12. Mysteries

LC 78031833

The investigators on the Detroit homicide team headed by Lieutenant Walter Koznicki are unable to solve a string of senseless murders in the city's Catholic community until Father Koesler breaks the madman murderer's code

Kiernan, Caitlin R.

The **drowning** girl : a memoir / Caitlin R. Kiernan. Roc, 2012. 352 p.

ISBN 9780451464163

1. People with schizophrenia 2. Self-fulfillment in women 3. Identity (Psychology) 4. Visions 5. Schizophrenia 6. Dreams 7. Reality 8. Providence, Rhode Island 9. Contemporary fantasy 10. Gothic fiction 11. Psychological fiction

LC 2011044675

Bram Stoker Award for Best Novel, 2012
James Tiptree, Jr. Award, 2012.

Imp, a struggling schizophrenic, fights to determine whether or not the strange mythological creatures she meets are due to her condition or are from something else entirely.

Kiernan, Caitlin R.

The **very** best of Caitlin R. Kiernan / Caitlin R. Kiernan ; introduction by Richard Kadrey. Tachyon Publications, 2019. xi, 424 p.

ISBN 9781616963026

1. Horror 2. Fantasy fiction 3. Anthologies 4. Short stories

Caitlin R. Kiernan is one of dark fantasy and horror's most acclaimed and influential short fiction writers. Her powerful, unexpected stories shatter morality, gender, and sexuality.

"This versatile retrospective offers something for nearly every fan of the strange and macabre, and cements Kiernan's legacy as the reigning queen of dark fantasy." Kirkus.

Kilalea, Katharine

Ok, Mr. Field : a novel / Katharine Kilalea. Tim Duggan Books, 2018. 218 p.

ISBN 9780525573630

1. Pianists 2. Wounds and injuries 3. Architecture 4. Houses 5. Men with mental illnesses 6. Married men 7. Retirees 8. Cape Town, South Africa 9. Literary fiction

LC 2018003397

Retiring to a Cape Town beachhouse inspired by Le Corbusier's Villa Savoye, an injured concert pianist begins to experience the psychological consequences of the house's unusual design.

Kim, Angie, 1969-

Miracle Creek / Angie Kim. Sarah Crichton Books/Farrar, Straus and Giroux, 2019. 352 p.

ISBN 9780374156022

1. Secrets 2. Trials (Murder) 3. Human experimentation in medicine 4. Rural life 5. Small towns 6. Boys with autism 7. Korean Americans 8. Immigrants, Korean 9. Hyperbaric oxygenation 10. Mothers of children with autism 11. Virginia 12. Legal stories

LC 2018037096

A dramatic murder trial in the aftermath of an experimental medical treatment and a fatal explosion upends a rural Virginia community where personal secrets and private ambitions complicate efforts to uncover what happened.

"Intricate plotting and courtroom theatrics, combined with moving insight into parenting special needs children and the psychology of immigrants, make this book both a learning experience and a page-turner." Kirkus.

Kim, Crystal Hana, 1987-

If you leave me / Crystal Hana Kim. William Morrow & Co., 2018. 417 p.

ISBN 9780062645173

1. 1950s 2. 1960s 3. Love triangles 4. War and society 5. Korean War, 1950-1953 6. Refugees 7. Life change events 8. Cousins 9. Marriage 10. Families 11. Consequences 12. Men/women relations 13. Korea 14. Family sagas 15. Historical fiction

Forced into the life of a refugee when the North Korean army invades her home, 16-year-old Haemi is forced to choose between love and security in ways that resonate throughout generations of her family.

Kim, Eugenia (Eugenia SunHee)

The **kinship** of secrets / Eugenia Kim. Houghton Mifflin Harcourt, 2018. 292 p.

ISBN 9781328987822

1. 20th century 2. Separated sisters 3. Immigrant families 4. Koreans in the United States 5. Sisters 6. Life change events 7. Korean War, 1950-1953 8. Assimilation (Sociology) 9. Cultural differences 10. Family relationships 11. United States 12. South Korea 13. Family sagas 14. Historical fiction

LC 2017061490

The story of two sisters separated by the Korean War follows Miran, who grows up living with her parents in a prosperous American suburb, and her sister Inja who struggles with life in war-torn Korea and ties to a family she doesn't remember.

"How she copes with the cultural change, and how the sisters gradually forge the bond they had only dreamed about, make up the remainder of Kim's heartfelt story, one which will greatly appeal to readers who enjoy the multicultural novels of Lisa See and Amy Tan, stories that enlighten as well as entertain." Booklist.

Kim, Young-ha, 1968-

Diary of a murderer : and other stories / Young-ha Kim ; translated by Krys Lee. Mariner Books, 2019. 224 p.

ISBN 9781328545428

1. Murder 2. Sexuality 3. Writing 4. Short stories 5. Literary fiction 6. Translations -- Korean to English

LC 2018042555

An electric collection that captivates and provokes in equal measure, exploring what it means to be on the edge--between life and death, good and evil."--Provided by publisher.

Kimani, Peter, 1971-

Dance of the Jakaranda / Peter Kimani. Akashic Books, 2017. 342 p.

ISBN 9781617754968

1. 1900s (Decade) 2. 1960s 3. Railroads 4. Social change 5. Intergenerational communication 6. Interethnic relations 7. Racism 8. Colonialism -- Africa 9. Singers 10. Railroad construction workers 11. Hotels 12. British in Africa 13. East Indians in Africa 14. Kenya -- History -- 1895-1963 15. Historical fiction 16. Literary fiction

Set in the shadow of Kenya's independence from Great Britain, Kimani reimagines the rise and fall of colonialism in Africa, and the special circumstances that brought black, brown, and white men together to lay the railroad that heralded the birth of the nation.

"Kimani's complex novel will leave readers questioning the meanings of citizenship and belonging during an era of significant social upheaval in Kenya's history." Booklist.

Kimmel, Fran, 1955-

No good asking : a novel / Fran Kimmel. ECW Press, 2018. 300 p.

ISBN 9781770414389

1. Former police 2. Family relationships 3. Family problems 4. Women with depression 5. Moving to a new state 6. Neighbors 7. Girls 8. Child abuse victims 9. Kindness 10. Christmas 11. Resilience (Personal quality) 12. Dysfunctional families 13. Abused children 14. Domestic fiction 15. Canada 16. Canada 17. Domestic fiction

"Kimmel's novel has only a few characters, but they all possess presence and depth and experience honest changes. The strong sense of place serves as an additional relationship for the characters to negotiate." Library Journal.

Kincaid, Jamaica

* Annie John / Jamaica Kincaid. Farrar, Straus, Giroux, 1985. 148 p.

ISBN 0374105219

1. Teenage girls 2. Family relationships 3. Self-discovery in teenage girls 4. West Indians 5. Girl rebels 6. Girls -- Antigua and Barbuda 7. Mothers and daughters 8. Family problems 9. Families 10. Love-hate relationships 11. Betrayal 12. Dishonesty 13. Social structure 14. Islands 15. Island life 16. Antigua and Barbuda 17. Antigua and Barbuda -- Social conditions 18. Coming-of-age stories 19. Domestic fiction 20. Literary fiction

LC 84028630

"Episodes from the young life of Annie John, aged 10 to 17, as she grows up on the Caribbean island of Antigua. This is a magical coming-of-age tale, ripe with the special ambience of its tropical setting and sustained by Annie's far from naive awareness of the world around her. Death, illness, and poverty intrude on the narrator's perceptive sensibility from time to time, but even these experiences instruct her and expand her understanding of life and its shifting reality. . . . A poetic and intensely moving work." Booklist.

Kincaid, Jamaica

The **autobiography** of my mother / Jamaica Kincaid. Farrar Straus Giroux, 1996. 228 p.

ISBN 0374107319

1. Island life 2. Multiracial persons 3. Power (Social sciences) 4. Women -- Dominica 5. West-Indian women 6. Imperialism 7. Postcolonialism 8. Social classes 9. Infertility 10. Dominica 11. Literary fiction

LC 9424580

Shortlisted for the International IMPAC Dublin Literary Award, 1998

National Book Critics Circle Award for Fiction finalist, 1996

"In Kincaid's poised and crystalline prose, precise and serene as a knife drawn through water, she now gives us this starkly memorable 'self-portrait' of a calm, thoughtful, utterly alienated woman who has learned to lead a life devoid of love, but not devoid of dignity." Christian Science Monitor.

Kincaid, Jamaica

* Lucy / Jamaica Kincaid. Farrar, Straus, Giroux, 2002, 176 p.

ISBN 9780374527358

1. Young women 2. Au pairs 3. Culture shock 4. West Indian women 5. Women immigrants 6. Rich people 7. Mothers and daughters 8. Postcolonialism 9. Alienation (Social psychology) 10. Sexuality 11. Literary fiction 12. Coming-of-age stories

Lucy, a nineteen-year-old girl from the West Indies, comes to North America to work as an au pair and observes the unhealthy realities of the seemingly happy family that employs her.

"The great motifs of Western literature, like goodness and evil, innocence and experience, resonate in Kincaid's novel in a completely updated and unselfconscious way. In other hands, this story of a West Indian au pair would just be sociology. In Kincaid's recasting, it is both art and argument." Christian Science Monitor.

Kincaid, Jamaica

See now then / Jamaica Kincaid. Farrar, Straus and Giroux, 2013. 176 p.

ISBN 9780374180560

1. Marriage 2. Family relationships 3. Anger in women 4. Archetype (Psychology) 5. Romantic love 6. Betrayal 7. Loss (Psychology) 8. Marital conflict 9. Literary fiction

LC 2012029932

A mother and father and their two children, living in a small village in New England, move, in their own minds, between the present, the past and the future.

Kinder, Chuck

Honeymooners : a cautionary tale / Chuck Kinder. Farrar, Straus and Giroux, 2001. 357 p.

ISBN 0374172587

1. 1970s 2. Male friendship -- California 3. Married people -- California 4. Partying 5. Authors, American -- California 6. Extramarital affairs 7. Drug use 8. California 9. Literary fiction

LC 00063616

Chronicles the misadventures of promising writers Ralph Crawford and Jim Stark and their wives, in a story of friendship, betrayal, and the ups and downs of the writer's life.

"Both wives emerge as major characters, reflecting the humor and anguish of living with men who, despite their successes, seem headed for rock bottom. Kinder's speedy, wry prose transports the reader to a time when drug use and personal freedom were unquestioned." Library Journal.

King, Camryn

Stiletto justice / Camryn King. Dafina Books, 2016 320 p.

ISBN 9781496702166

1. Judicial error 2. Married women 3. African American women 4. Prisoners 5. Revenge 6. Justice 7. Power (Social sciences) 8. Lawyers 9. Politicians 10. Thrillers and suspense

LC bl2016033017

Includes a reading group guide.

After Kim, Jayda, and Harley's husbands are incarcerated by former prosecutor Hammond Grey, the three women plan the ultimate, lethal payback.

King, Deja

Bitch / Deja King. Triple Crown Publications, 2004. 196 p. Precious Cummings novels

ISBN 097623498X

1. African American women 2. Revenge 3. Deception 4. Sexuality 5. Betrayal 6. Murder 7. Street life 8. African American fiction 9. Drama lit

Street Lit Book Award Medal: Adult Fiction, 2005

Precious Cummings came from nothing but was determined to have it all. Using her most deadly weapons - undeniable beauty, body and street savvy brains, Precious sets out to change the cards that she'd been dealt. After meeting Nico Carter, a man who can help her achieve her goals, virtually overnight she is on her way. Precious quickly transforms from Project Chick to Hood Queen and is determined to hold on to her position even if it means crossing the man who made it possible. Set on revenge, Precious gambles it all in her quest to gain everything.

King, Laurie R.

The **beekeeper's** apprentice : or, on the segregation of the Queen / Laurie R. King. St. Martin's Press, 1994. 347 p. Mary Russell and Sherlock Holmes mysteries

ISBN 9780312104238

1. 1910s 2. Mentors 3. Detectives 4. Women detectives 5. Young women 6. Kidnappers 7. World War I 8. England -- History -- 20th century 9. Historical mysteries 10. Adaptations, retellings, and spin-offs 11. Mysteries

LC 93043522

This title takes place in Spring of 1914.

When Mary Russell meets famous detective Sherlock Holmes, she discovers that he is also a beekeeper. Soon she finds herself on the trail of kidnappers and discovers a plot to kill both Holmes and herself.

King, Laurie R.

* The **game** : a Mary Russell novel / Laurie R. King. Bantam Books, 2004. 369 p. Mary Russell and Sherlock Holmes mysteries

ISBN 9780553801941

1. 1920s 2. Husband-and-wife detectives 3. Spies 4. Missing persons investigation 5. Jewish women 6. Detectives 7. Brothers-in-law 8. Intelligence officers 9. Missing persons 10. British in India 11. Ocean travel 12. Passenger ships 13. Social classes 14. Cultural differences 15. India 16. Historical mysteries 17. Adaptations, retellings, and spin-offs 18. Mysteries

LC 2003055684

This title takes place in January 1924.

Traveling incognito, Mary Russell and her famed spouse, Sherlock Holmes, head for India to search for a missing spy, the famous orphan who inspired Rudyard Kipling's Kim, and find themselves caught up in a dangerous, high-level game of intrigue and political machinations.

"Whatever this grueling land journey lacks in urgency, it repays in scenes of vibrant local color, described by Russell in the droll tongue of a woman with the wit to realize that, while she may be dirty and tired and in constant danger, she is having the time of her life." New York Times Book Review.

King, Laurie R.

Keeping watch : a novel / Laurie R. King. Bantam Books, 2003. 352 p.

ISBN 0553801910

1. Rescues 2. Vigilantes 3. Child abuse victims 4. Vietnam veterans 5. Redemption 6. Crimes against children 7. Child abuse 8. Child custody 9. Kidnapping 10. Thrillers and suspense

LC 2002034266

Vietnam veteran Allen Carmichael has lived on the fringe of society since the war, rescuing abused children from hostile environments and placing them with foster families. Now in California, he comes to the aid of 12-year-old Jamie, who is being tormented by his entrepreneur father. Allen abducts Jamie from his home and takes him to a waiting family in Montana. But as Allen continues investigating the boy's tragic background, he realizes that everyone involved may be in danger.

"At its simplest, this is the story of a man who helps rescue women and/or children from dangerously abusive men. King's lengthy, brilliantly executed backstory of Allen Carmichael's experiences in Vietnam, his disastrously unhappy return home and his eventual discovery of his 'calling' showcase some of her finest writing." Publishers Weekly.

King, Lily

* **Euphoria** / Lily King. Atlantic Monthly Press, 2014. 368 p.

ISBN 9780802122551

1. 1930s 2. Love triangles 3. Anthropologists 4. Kinship-based society 5. Matriarchy 6. Husband and wife 7. Life change events 8. Interpersonal relations 9. Papua New Guinea 10. Historical fiction

Kirkus Prize for Fiction, 2014.

National Book Critics Circle Award for Fiction finalist, 2014

Frustrated by his research efforts and depressed over the death of his brothers, Andre Banson runs into two fellow anthropologists, a married couple, in 1930s New Guinea and begins a tumultuous relationship with them.

"King does not shy from showing the uncomfortable relationship among all three anthropologists and those they study. . . . A small gem, disturbing and haunting." Kirkus.

King, Lily

Father of the rain / Lily King. Atlantic Monthly Press, 2010. 384 p.

ISBN 9780802119490

1. Fathers and daughters 2. Familial love 3. Self-discovery in women 4. Alcoholic fathers 5. Family relationships 6. Dysfunctional families 7. Interracial romance 8. Women -- Identity 9. Boston, Massachusetts 10. Psychological fiction 11. Literary fiction

"Gardiner Amory is a New England WASP who is beginning to feel the cracks in his empire. Nixon is about to be impeached, his wife is leaving him, and his worldview is rapidly becoming outdated. His daughter, Daley, has spent the first eleven years of herlife carefully negotiating her parents' conflicting worlds: the liberal, socially committed realm of her mother and the conservative, decadent, liquor-soaked life of her father. As she grows into adulthood, Daley rejects the narrow world that nourished her father's fears and prejudices, and embarks on her own separate life, until he hits rock bottom"--Dust jacket flap.

"There's something so raw and affecting about Daley's love for her damaged father that the book will linger in your mind long after you've finished it." Entertainment Weekly.

King, Lily

Writers & lovers : a novel / Lily King. Grove Press, 2020. 320 p.

ISBN 9780802148537

1. 1990s 2. Grief 3. Women authors 4. Love triangles 5. Moving to a new city 6. Waitresses 7. Extramarital affairs 8. Mothers -- Death 9. Debt 10. Men/women relations 11. Massachusetts 12. Literary fiction 13. Coming-of-age stories 14. Love stories

LC 2019045257

Blindsided by her mother's sudden death, and wrecked by a recent love affair, Casey Peabody has arrived in Massachusetts in the summer of 1997 without a plan. When she falls for two very different men at the same time, her world fractures even more. Casey's fight to fulfill her creative ambitions and balance the conflicting demands of art and life is challenged in ways that push her to the brink.

"Read this for insights about writing, about losing one's mother, about dealing with a cranky sous-chef and a difficult four-top." Kirkus. Reviews

King, Ross, 1962-

Domino / Ross King. Walker & Company, 2002. 435 p.
ISBN 0802733786
1. 18th century 2. Upper class 3. Disguises 4. Mistresses 5. Castrati 6. Singers 7. Artists 8. Physiognomists 9. Europe -- History -- 18th century 10. London, England -- History -- 18th century 11. London, England -- Social life and customs -- 18th century 12. Milan, Italy -- History -- 18th century 13. Historical thrillers 14. Picaresque fiction
LC 2002029620

From the garret room of poor artist George Cautley to the busy streets of 1770s London to the glittering drawing rooms of the elite, this historical novel brings to life the turbulent and exciting world of eighteenth-century England.

"Replete with mystery and suspense and immersed in vivid historical details, this work is also a sharp, philosophical musing on the disguises of the world and the search for the truth that lies beneath." Library Journal.

King, Stephen, 1947-

11/22/1963 Scribner, 2011. 960 p.
ISBN 9781451627282
1. Kennedy, John F (John Fitzgerald), 1917-1963 Assassination 2. 1950s 3. Time travel (Past) 4. High school teachers 5. Men/women relations 6. Rescues 7. Life change events 8. Consequences 9. Nuclear warfare 10. Dallas, Texas 11. Maine 12. Alternative histories 13. Thrillers and suspense
Goodreads Choice Award, 2011.
Thriller Award for Best Novel, 2012.

Receiving a horrific essay from a GED student with a traumatic past, high-school English teacher Jake Epping is enlisted by a friend to travel back in time to prevent the assassination of John F. Kennedy, a mission for which he must befriend troubled loner Lee Harvey Oswald.

"Though his scenarios aren't always plausible in strictest terms, King's imagination, as always, yields a most satisfying yarn." Kirkus.

King, Stephen, 1947-

* Carrie / Stephen King. Doubleday, 1974. 199 p.
ISBN 9780812419726
1. Psychokinesis 2. Bullying and bullies 3. Teenage psychics 4. High school students 5. Teenage girls 6. High schools 7. Family relationships 8. Supernatural 9. Small town life 10. Maine 11. Horror
LC 73009037

A repressed teenager uses her telekinetic powers to avenge the cruel jokes of her classmates.

"A terrifying treat for both horror and parapsychology fans." School Library Journal.

King, Stephen, 1947-

Cujo / Stephen King. Viking Press, 1981. 319 p.
ISBN 0670451932
1. Dogs 2. Rabies in animals 3. Animal attacks 4. Alcoholic men 5. Families 6. Marital conflict 7. Villages -- Maine 8. Maine 9. Horror
LC 81050265

A family's two-hundred-pound Saint Bernard is transformed by rabies and the insidious guidance of demonic forces into a terrifying monster.

King, Stephen, 1947-

Doctor Sleep : a novel / Stephen King. Scribner, 2013. 544 p.
ISBN 9781476727653
1. Good and evil 2. Psychics 3. Supernatural 4. Psychic ability 5. Telepathy 6. Family relationships 7. Violence in men 8. Torture 9. Immortalism 10. Seniors 11. New Hampshire 12. Horror
LC 2013000431
Sequel to: The shining (1977).
Adapted into a film entitled "Doctor Sleep" in 2019.
Bram Stoker Award for Best Novel, 2013.
Goodreads Choice Award, 2013.

After decades as an itinerant alcoholic, middle-aged Dan Torrance uses his remnant powers to assist the dying before coming to the aid of a twelve-year-old girl being tortured by a tribe of murderous paranormals.

King, Stephen, 1947-

Dolores Claiborne / Stephen King. Viking, 1993. 305 p.
ISBN 9780670844524
1. Husband-killing 2. Incest 3. Household employees 4. Family violence 5. Women murderers 6. Marital conflict 7. Housekeepers 8. Maine 9. Psychological suspense
LC 92015467

Forced by overwhelming evidence to confess her life of crime, Dolores Claiborne, a foul-tempered New Englander, describes how her disintegrating marriage years before caused her heart to turn murderous.

"What drives Dolores Claiborne is a powerful characterization of the title figure, a cranky old Maine islander who takes no guff from life or death. . . . King's mimicry is startlingly good." Time.

King, Stephen, 1947-

Elevation / Stephen King. Scribner, 2018. 144 p.
ISBN 9781982102319
1. Prejudice 2. Body weight 3. Weightlessness 4. Divorced men 5. Diseases 6. Social justice 7. Neighbors 8. Supernatural 9. Lesbians 10. Small town life 11. Maine 12. Contemporary fantasy
Goodreads Choice Award, 2018

The latest from legendary master storyteller Stephen King, a riveting, extraordinarily eerie, and moving story about a man whose mysterious affliction brings a small town together?a timely, upbeat tale about finding common ground despite deep-rooted differences.

King, Stephen, 1947-

End of watch : a novel / Stephen King. Scribner, 2016. 496 p. Bill Hodges novels
ISBN 9781501129742
1. Psychic ability 2. People with brain injuries 3. Private investigators 4. Psychopaths 5. Suicide 6. Murder 7. Former police 8. Mass murderers 9. Murder investigation 10. Middle West 11. Thrillers and suspense
LC 2015039639
Goodreads Choice Award, 2016

A conclusion to the trilogy finds mental patient Brady Hartsfield manifesting powers to commit deadly acts without leaving his hospital room, while retired detective Bill Hodges and his partner investigate a suicide with ties to the Mercedes Massacre.

"King's mystery experiment has been page-flipping fun from the start, and no ones going to want to miss seeing how it all pans out." Booklist.

King, Stephen, 1947-

Finders keepers / Stephen King. Simon & Schuster, 2015 448 p. Bill Hodges novels

ISBN 9781501100079

1. Books and reading 2. Obsession 3. Authors 4. Recluses 5. Fans (Persons) 6. Psychopaths 7. Middle West 8. Thrillers and suspense

After Morris Bellamy discovers that not(ebk.)s and money belonging to his favorite author were taken by Pete Saubers, only Bill Hodges, Holly Gibney, and Jerome Robinson can rescue the Saubers family from the deranged and vengeful criminal.

"This being a King novel, the narrative hums and roars along like a high-performance vehicle, even though there are times when its readers may find themselves several tics ahead of the book's plot developments. But such qualms are overcome by the plainspoken, deceptively simple King style, which has once again fashioned a rip-snorting entertainment; one that also works as a sneaky-smart satire of literary criticism and how even the most attentive readers can often miss the whole point behind making up characters and situations. Reading a King novel as engrossing as this is a little like backing in a car with parking assist: after a while, you just take your hands off the wheel and the pages practically turn themselves." Kirkus.

King, Stephen, 1947-

Firestarter / Stephen King. Viking Press, 1980. 428 p.

ISBN 9780670315413

1. Psychic ability 2. Psychokinesis 3. Fires 4. Supernatural 5. Seven-year-old girls 6. Voyages and travels 7. Political corruption 8. Secrecy in government 9. Human experimentation in medicine 10. Horror

LC 80014793

Andy and Vicky McGee's eight-year-old daughter, Charlie, has the ability to set things on fire and a secret government agency is determined to make use of Charlie's horrifyingly destructive gift.

"This is your advanced post-Watergate cynical American thriller with some eerie parapsychological twists, and it's been done so distinctively well that we'd better talk about genius rather than genre." Quill & Quire.

King, Stephen, 1947-

The **girl** who loved Tom Gordon / Stephen King. Scribner, 1999. 224 p.

ISBN 0684867621

1. Lost girls -- Appalachian Trail 2. Professional baseball players -- Boston, Massachusetts 3. Wilderness survival 4. Children of divorced parents -- Maine 5. Girl hikers -- Appalachian Trail 6. Self-reliance in girls 7. Pitchers (Baseball) 8. Imagination in girls 9. Bears -- Appalachian Trail 10. Appalachian Trail 11. Maine 12. New Hampshire 13. Thrillers and suspense

LC 9913109

When a 9-year-old girl becomes lost on a hike on the Appalachian Trail, she relies on her courage and faith, as she imagines her hero, baseball pitcher Tom Gordon, is with her.

"Nine-year-old Trisha McFarland is hopelessly lost in the woods. Out for a morning hike with her bickering mother and brother, she runs off to relieve herself and discovers she can't find her way back to the path. . . . Trisha wanders for a week in the mosquito-infested forest with nothing but her wits, her Walkman and the pitching prowess of her hero, the dreamy Red Sox reliever Tom Gordon, to guide her. As Trisha fights to stay alive, King demonstrates his empathy for the inner lives of children and an outdoorsman's knowledge of the edible wild flora of Maine." New York Times Book Review.

King, Stephen, 1947-

The **Institute** / Stephen King. Scribner, 2019. 576 p.

ISBN 9781982110567

1. Children 2. Superhuman abilities 3. Captivity 4. Torture 5. Manipulation (Social sciences) 6. Psychokinesis 7. Telepathy 8. Child abuse 9. Kidnapping 10. Imprisonment 11. Captives 12. Good and evil 13. Thrillers and suspense 14. Horror

Goodreads Choice Award, 2019

Published to coincide with the release of *It: Chapter Two*, a supernatural thriller finds an abducted youth imprisoned in an inescapable institute, where teens with psychic abilities are subjected to torturous manipulation.

King, Stephen, 1947-

It / Stephen King. Viking, 1986. 1138 p.

ISBN 9780670813025

1. Children 2. Murder 3. Clowns 4. Sewers 5. Fear in children 6. Crimes against children 7. Supernatural 8. Good and evil 9. Homecomings 10. Friendship 11. Violence 12. Small town life -- Maine 13. Maine 14. Horror

LC 85041062

Colorado Blue Spruce YA Book Award, 1994.

They were seven teenagers when they first stumbled upon the horror. Now they were grown-up men and women who had gone out into the big world to gain success and happiness. But none of them could withstand the force that drew them back to Derry, Maine to face the nightmare without an end, and the evil without a name.

"Six adults, living separately in a blessed fog of forgetfulness, are summoned back to their hometown to complete the destruction of a horrific, shape-changing entity who breakfasts on the city's children. This same group first encountered the menace more than a quarter century before, as schoolchildren in the 1950s. Their quest breeds some riveting chase scenes as adults and children alike flee from an assortment of menacing humans and slavering monsters--most of which are manifestations of an evil so vile its true nature can never be known. King's considerable talent for grounding this supernatural stuff in the minutiae of everyday life is evident." Booklist.

King, Stephen, 1947-

* **Misery** / Stephen King. Viking, 1987. 310 p.

ISBN 0670813648

1. Obsession in women 2. Captives 3. Fans (Persons) 4. Horror story authors 5. Captivity 6. Nurses 7. Torture 8. Fear in men 9. Manipulation by women 10. Psychological suspense 11. Horror

LC 86040504

Bram Stoker Award for Best Novel, 1987.

Rescued from a car crash by a psychotic woman claiming to be a fan, novelist Paul Sheldon becomes a captive invalid in her secluded Colorado farmhouse.

"Even if 'Misery' is less terrifying than his usual work--no demons, no witchcraft, no nether-world horrors--it creates strengths out of its realities. Its excitements are more subtle. And, as such, it is an intriguing work." New York Times Book Review.

King, Stephen, 1947-

Mr. Mercedes : a novel / Stephen King. Scribner, 2014. 496 p. Bill Hodges novels

ISBN 9781476754451

1. Mass murder 2. Former police 3. Psychopaths 4. Retirees 5. Mass murderers 6. Death threats 7. Mercedes automobile 8. Letter writing 9. Middle West 10. Thrillers and suspense

LC 2013046172

Edgar Allan Poe Award for Best Novel, 2015.

Goodreads Choice Award, 2014.

"In a mega-stakes, high-suspense race against time, three of the most unlikely and winning heroes Stephen King has ever created try to stop a lone killer from blowing up thousands. In the frigid pre-dawn hours, in a distressed Midwestern city, hundreds of desperate unemployed folks are lined up for a spot at a job fair. Without warning, a lone driver plows through the crowd in a stolen Mercedes, running over the innocent, backing up, and charging again. Eight people are killed; fifteen are wounded. The killer escapes. In another part of town, months later, a retired cop named Bill Hodges is still haunted by the unsolved crime. When he gets a crazed letter from someone who self-identifies as the "perk" and threatens an even more diabolical attack, Hodges wakes up from his depressed and vacant retirement, hell-bent on preventing another tragedy. Brady Hartfield lives with his alcoholic mother in the house where he was born. He loved the feel of death under the wheels of the Mercedes, and he wants that rush again. Only Bill Hodges, with a couple of highly unlikely allies, can apprehend the killer before he strikes again. And they have no time to lose, because Brady's next mission, if it succeeds, will kill or maim thousands. Mr. Mercedes is a war between good and evil, from the master of suspense whose insight into the mind of this obsessed, insane killer is chilling and unforgettable"--, Provided by publisher.

"This exists outside of the usual Kingverse (Pennywise the Clown is referred to as fictive); add that to the atypical present-tense prose, and this feels pretty darn fresh. Big, smashing climax, too." Booklist.

King, Stephen, 1947-

Night shift / Stephen King. Doubleday, 1978. xxii, 336 p.
ISBN 9780385129916

1. Supernatural 2. Paranormal phenomena 3. Horror

LC 77075146

Boogeyman, Children of the corn, The lawnmower man, and Mangler, and Graveyard shift were each released as a movie under the same title as the short story. The 1985 film Cat's eye was inspired by The ledge, and Quitters, Inc.

More than twenty-five stories of horror and nightmarish fantasy transform everyday situations into experiences of compelling terror in the worlds of the living, the dying, and the nonliving.

King, Stephen, 1947-

Pet sematary / Stephen King. Doubleday, 1983. 373 p.
ISBN 9780385182447

1. Undead 2. Pets 3. Cemeteries -- Maine 4. Loss (Psychology) 5. Supernatural 6. Small town life -- Maine 7. Maine 8. Horror

LC 82045360

Republished in 2019 by Gallery Books.
Colorado Blue Spruce YA Book Award, 1991.

When the Creed family's beloved cat, Winston Churchill, dies, Dr. Louis Creed -- on the instructions of his elderly neighbor -- buries the animal not in the "Pet Sematary" where local children inter their deceased pets, but rather in the haunted Indian burial ground behind it. The next day, a changed Churchill comes back, a little smellier and more vicious than before. What will happen when a person dies and is buried in the same area? -- Description by Dawn Towery.

King, Stephen, 1947-

Salem's lot / Stephen King. Doubleday, 1975. 439 p.
ISBN 9780385007511

1. Vampires 2. Small towns -- Maine 3. Authors -- Maine 4. Good and evil 5. Supernatural 6. Maine 7. New England 8. Horror

When a writer returns to his small Maine hometown, he discovers that the peaceful hamlet is being overrun by vampires and sets out to curb this ancient evil before it can spread.

King, Stephen, 1947-

* The **shining** / Stephen King. Doubleday, 1977. 447 p.
ISBN 9780385121675

1. Haunted hotels 2. Caretakers 3. Supernatural 4. Boy psychics 5. Telepathy 6. Resorts 7. Winter 8. Alcoholics 9. Family relationships 10. Violence in men 11. Colorado 12. Horror

LC 76024212

Sequel: Doctor Sleep (2013).

Jack Torrance sees his stint as winter caretaker of a Colorado hotel as a way back from failure, his wife sees it as a chance to preserve their family, and their five-year-old son sees the evil waiting just for them.

"In a fast-paced and gory denouement, the terror comes to a violent end. King is a masterful technician of suspense whose readers as well as characters are the victims of his relentless heightening of horror." Library Journal.

King, Stephen, 1947-

Sleeping beauties : a novel / Stephen King and Owen King. Scribner, 2017. 720 p.
ISBN 9781501163401

1. Epidemics 2. Near future 3. Small towns 4. Poverty 5. Violence 6. Supernatural 7. Sleep disorders 8. Women prisoners 9. Prisons for women 10. Women -- Diseases 11. Violence against women 12. Appalachian region 13. Horror 14. Apocalyptic fiction 15. Social science fiction

LC 2017002473

Goodreads Choice Award, 2017

In a near-future where women succumb to a sleeping disease and men revert to their primal natures, one mysteriously immune woman struggles to survive in an Appalachian town where she is treated as both a demon and a lab specimen.

King, Stephen, 1947-

* The **stand** / Stephen King. Doubleday, 1990, c1978. xix, 1153 p.
ISBN 9780385199575

1. Plague 2. Epidemics 3. Survival (after epidemics) -- United States 4. Influenza -- United States 5. Good and evil 6. Supernatural 7. Post-apocalypse 8. Horror 9. Apocalyptic fiction

LC 89027548

A monumentally devastating plague leaves only a few survivors in a desert world who move toward the ultimate confrontation of good and evil, in the expanded original version of King's novel.

Kingsbury, Karen

When we were young / Karen Kingsbury. Howard Books, 2018. 352 p. Baxter family series. Standalone novels
ISBN 9781501170010

1. Instagram (Electronic resource) 2. Social media 3. Husband and wife 4. Second chances 5. Marital conflict 6. Christian life 7. Obsession 8. LIfe change events 9. Faith (Christianity) 10. Christian fiction 11. Gentle reads

LC 2018015676

While reality show lovebirds Noah and Emily prepare to announce a wrenching separation, Kari prays for a miracle to resolve a crisis in her own marriage that is granted in astonishing ways for both couples.

Kingsolver, Barbara

* The **bean** trees : a novel / Barbara Kingsolver. Harper & Row, 1988. 232 p.
ISBN 0060158638

1. Abandoned children 2. Single mothers 3. Friendship 4. Female

friendship 5. Cherokee girls 6. Cherokee Indians -- Oklahoma 7. Automobile travel 8. Motherhood 9. Tucson, Arizona 10. Women's lives and relationships 11. Mainstream fiction

LC 87045633

Sequel: Pigs in heaven.

Taylor Greer hits the road wanting only to get as far away from Kentucky as possible, ending up in Arizona with a 3-year-old Cherokee girl she has inherited from a woman in a bar.

"This book gives readers something that's increasingly hard to find today--a character to believe in and laugh with and admire." Christian Science Monitor.

Kingsolver, Barbara
* **Flight** behavior / Barbara Kingsolver. HarperCollins, 2012. 400 p.

ISBN 9780062124265

1. Global warming 2. Small towns 3. Women farmers 4. Mothers 5. Poverty 6. Social isolation 7. African American scientists 8. Married people 9. Curiosities and wonders 10. Farmers 11. Butterflies 12. Rural families 13. Ecology 14. Tennessee 15. Appalachian Region, Southern 16. Literary fiction

Shortlisted for The Women's Prize for Fiction, 2013

Tired of living on a failing farm and suffering oppressive poverty, bored housewife Dellarobia Turnbow, on the way to meet a potential lover, is detoured by a miraculous event on the Appalachian mountainside that ignites a media and religious firestorm that changes her life forever.

Kingsolver, Barbara
Pigs in heaven / Barbara Kingsolver. Harper Collins, 1993. 343 p.

ISBN 0060168013

1. Single mothers 2. Runaways 3. Self-acceptance in women 4. Cherokee girls 5. Cherokee Indians -- Oklahoma 6. Adoptive mothers 7. Native American women lawyers -- Oklahoma 8. Six-year-old girls 9. Women's lives and relationships 10. Mainstream fiction

LC 92054739

Sequel to: The bean trees.

Western Heritage Award for Outstanding Western Novel, 1994.

When a six-year-old child named Turtle is the sole witness to a freak accident at the Hoover Dam, she and her adoptive mother Taylor have a moment of celebrity that will change their lives forever. Turtle is claimed by Annawake Fourkiller, a Cherokee activist, to have been wrongly taken from the Cherokee nation. Fear of losing Turtle sends Taylor fleeing across the country with her mother Alice, pursued by Annawake. In the course of their journey, the three find love and wisdom in surprising places.

"Possessed of an extravagantly gifted narrative voice, [Kingsolver] blends a fierce and abiding moral vision with benevolent, concise humor." New York Times Book Review.

Kingsolver, Barbara
* The **Poisonwood** Bible : a novel / Barbara Kingsolver. HarperFlamingo, 1998. 546 p.

ISBN 9780060175405

1. Christian missionaries 2. Americans in Africa 3. Culture conflict 4. Christian families 5. Americans in Congo (Democratic Republic) 6. Religious fanatics 7. Baptists 8. Emotionally abusive men 9. Colonialism 10. Congo (Democratic Republic) 11. Historical fiction 12. Literary fiction

LC 9819901

Book Sense Book of the Year Adult Fiction, 2000.

Pulitzer Prize for Fiction finalist, 1999.

Shortlisted for The Orange Prize for Fiction, 1999

The family of a fierce evangelical Baptist missionary--Nathan Price, his wife, and his four daughters--begins to unravel after they embark on a 1959 mission to the Belgian Congo, where they find their lives forever transformed over the course of three decades by the political and social upheaval of Africa.

"Buttressing her suspenseful chronicle with authentic background detail, Kingsolver's narrative is at once a compelling family saga and an astute look at Western imperialism in Africa." Publishers Weekly.

Kingsolver, Barbara
* **Unsheltered** / Barbara Kingsolver. Harper, 2018. 464 p.

ISBN 9780062684561

1. Treat, Mary, 1830-1923 2. 21st century 3. 19th century 4. Home (Concept) 5. Utopias 6. Social change 7. Houses -- History 8. Ethics 9. Courage 10. Scientists 11. Belief and doubt 12. Interpersonal relations 13. Family relationships 14. New Jersey 15. Literary fiction 16. Political fiction 17. Parallel narratives

Traces the experiences of a woman whose efforts to protect her family from sudden unemployment are shaped by the story of an ostracized 19th-century science teacher.

Kinsale, Laura
Lessons in French / Laura Kinsale. Sourcebooks, 2010. 458 p.

ISBN 9781402237010

1. Regency period (1811-1820) 2. 19th century 3. Jilted women 4. Forgery 5. Men/women relations 6. Lost love 7. England -- Social life and customs -- 19th century 8. Great Britain -- History -- Regency, 1811-1820 9. Historical romances 10. Regency romances

Callie realizes that she still has feelings for childhood sweetheart Trevelyan when he returns from France to care for his mother with a fortune and a secret scandalous past.

Kipling, Rudyard, 1865-1936
* **Collected** stories / Rudyard Kipling ; selected and introduced by Robert Gottlieb. A.A. Knopf, 1994. xxxvii, 911 p.

ISBN 9780679435921

1. Manners and customs 2. Short stories

LC 94005854

A selection of stories from across the author's entire career.

Kirk, David, 1985-
* **Sword** of honor / David Kirk. Doubleday, 2015. 416 p.

ISBN 9780385536653

1. 17th century 2. Samurai 3. Fugitives 4. Honor 5. Swordfighters 6. Attempted murder 7. Warriors 8. Battles 9. Japan -- History -- 17th century 10. Historical fiction

LC 2015002270

Sequel to : Child of vengeance.

Great samurai Musashi Miyamoto travels to Kyoto for a reckoning after a price is put on his head and falls in love with a blind witch.

"Kirk doesn't shrink from the violence these warriors mete out to each other and even finds both poetic and excruciatingly exact ways to describe the many duels that take place." Kirkus.

Kirkpatrick, Jane, 1946-
One more river to cross / Jane Kirkpatrick. Revell, 2019. 368 p.

ISBN 9780800727024

1. American Westward Expansion (1803-1899) 2. 1840s 3. Overland journeys to the Pacific 4. Wagon trains 5. Winter storms 6. Disaster

victims 7. Survival 8. Frontier and pioneer life 9. Communities 10. Pioneers 11. Decision-making 12. Faith (Christianity) 13. Sierra Nevada Mountains 14. The West (United States) -- History -- 19th century 15. Christian historical fiction

LC 2019006997

Based on true events, this compelling survival story by award-winning novelist Jane Kirkpatrick is full of grit and endurance. Beset by storms, bad timing, and desperate decisions, 8 women, 17 children, and one man must outlast winter in the middle of the Sierra Nevada Mountains in 1844.

"Sibling disagreements, marital stress, faith-based doubts, and fear all bear witness to the gumption, solidarity, and effort vital to the pioneering experience. Kirkpatrick is a commanding innovator of the historical genre with her depth of research and lifelike characters." Booklist.

Kirkpatrick, Jane, 1946-

This road we traveled / Jane Kirkpatrick. Revell, 2016. 352 p.

ISBN 9780800722333

1. 1840s 2. American Westward Expansion (1803-1899) 3. Faith (Christianity) 4. Frontier and pioneer life 5. Family relationships 6. Christian life 7. Men/women relations 8. Oregon Trail 9. Oregon Territory -- History -- 19th century 10. Christian historical fiction 11. Pacific Northwest fiction

Though her son thinks she's too feeble to make the rough Oregon Trail journey, 66-year-old widow Tabitha "Tabby" Moffat Brown disagrees. Hiring her own wagon and heading out from Missouri with her elderly brother-in-law, Tabby joins other family members making the trek, including her reluctant daughter and her forward-thinking granddaughter. Facing life-threatening danger and other obstacles, Tabby and the others try to keep their faith. Based on the life of the real Tabby (who's known as the "mother of Oregon" and was a founder of Pacific University), This Road We Traveled is a thoroughly researched, engaging tale. -- Description by Dawn Towery.

"This is more than one woman's story of courage and faith; it is the story of a family that journeys, grows, and heals together. Kirkpatrick's vivid, rich prose will keep readers in awe and on the edges of their seats." Publishers Weekly.

Kirshenbaum, Binnie

Rabbits for food / Binnie Kirshenbaum. Soho Press, 2019 371 p.

ISBN 9781641290531

1. Women authors 2. Women with depression 3. Nervous breakdown 4. Women with mental illnesses 5. Psychiatric hospitals 6. Women psychiatric hospital patients 7. Forties (Age) 8. Married women 9. Interpersonal relations 10. New York City 11. Literary fiction

LC 2018059655

"Master of razor-edged literary humor Binnie Kirshenbaum returns with her first novel in a decade, a devastating, laugh-out-loud funny story of a writer's slide into depression and institutionalization. It's New Year's Eve, the holiday of forced fellowship, mandatory fun, and paper hats. While dining out with her husband and their friends, Kirshenbaum's protagonist--an acerbic, mordantly witty, and clinically depressed writer--fully unravels. Her breakdown lands her in the psych ward of a prestigious New York hospital where she refuses all modes of recommended treatment. Instead, she passes the time chronicling the lives of her fellow "lunatics" and writing a novel about how she got to this place. Her story is a hilarious and harrowing deep dive into the disordered mind of a woman who sees the world all too clearly. Propelled by stand-up comic timing and rife with pinpoint insights, Kirshenbaum examines what it means to be unloved and loved, to succeed and fail,

to be at once impervious and raw. Rabbits for Food shows how art can lead us out of--or into--the depths of disconsolate loneliness and piercing grief. A bravura literary performance from one of our most witty and indispensable writers." Provided by publisher.

Kitt, Sandra

Celluloid memories / Sandra Kitt. Kimani, 2007 320 p.

ISBN 9780373830152

1. Men/women relations 2. Father and adult daughter 3. Loss (Psychology) 4. African American women 5. Actors and actresses 6. Lawyers 7. Female friendship 8. Interpersonal attraction 9. Los Angeles, California 10. Contemporary romances 11. African American fiction 12. Multicultural romances

When Savannah Shelton discovers an old Hollywood secret among her late father's possessions that would make a great screenplay, she is determined to take L.A. by storm, until a fender bender introduces her to a charming attorney who makes her rethink her hasty decision.

Kittredge, William

The **willow** field / William Kittredge. Knopf, 2006. 352 p.

ISBN 1400040973

1. 1930s 2. 1940s 3. 1950s 4. Fathers and sons 5. Fifteen-year-old boys 6. Rodeo performers 7. Fathers and daughters 8. Pregnant women 9. Adopted girls 10. Marines -- United States -- History -- World War II 11. Casinos 12. Ranch life -- Nevada 13. Voyages and travels 14. Marriage 15. Growing up 16. Men/women relations 17. Teenage boy/girl relations 18. Reno, Nevada 19. Calgary, Alberta 20. Montana 21. The West (United States) -- Social life and customs -- 20th century 22. Coming-of-age stories 23. Pacific Northwest fiction 24. Modern Westerns

LC 2006045157

"This multigenerational saga begins with a stunning set piecea classic horse drive, more than 200 head, from Nevada to Calgary. Rossie, a veteran ranch hand but still barely 20, signs on for the drive as a way of breaking ties with a girl and winds up forging even stronger ties with another girl, Eliza Stevenson, the unmarried but pregnant daughter of a rancher in Montana's Bitterroot Mountains. 'We could be it, entirely it,' Eliza says shortly after she meets Rossie, and as we watch their lives unfold, from the Depression through World War II and on into the 1960s, we realize that this strong-willed woman was both right and wrong. . . . Rossie and Eliza are entirely it, but--fiery individuals both--they are also in perpetual conflict, cherishing their union just as they struggle not to be consumed by the other. This transcendent love story is at the heart of Kittredge's novel, but it is set against not one but two imposing landscapes: Bitterroot and the Nevada desert, both of which demand their own allegiance from the characters' minds and hearts." Booklist.

Klassen, Julie, 1964-

The **painter's** daughter / Julie Klassen. Bethany House, 2015 400 p.

ISBN 9780764216022

1. Regency period (1811-1820) 2. Love triangles 3. Young women 4. Women artists 5. Pregnancy 6. Brothers 7. Soldiers 8. Family estates 9. Birthfathers 10. Husband and wife 11. England -- History -- 19th century 12. Christian historical romances

LC 2015024522

In 1815, a painter's daughter on the north Devon coast agrees to marry a stranger to avoid scandal, but her choice is complicated by the return of a former lover and a growing affection for the husband she barely knows.

LIST OF FICTIONAL WORKS

Klaussmann, Liza

Tigers in red weather : a novel / Liza Klaussmann. Little, Brown and Co., 2012. 336 p.

ISBN 9780316211338

1. 1960s 2. Cousins 3. Family secrets 4. Murder -- Martha's Vineyard, Massachusetts 5. Martha's Vineyard, Massachusetts 6. United States -- Social life and customs -- 20th century 7. Thrillers and suspense
LC 2011050204

Old secrets are revealed and lives become unraveled when the children of a well-heeled New England family discover the body of a murder victim near Tiger House, their estate on Martha's Vinyard.

Klein, Matthew, 1968-

Con ed / Matthew Klein. Warner Books, 2007. 304 p.

ISBN 0446579556

1. Swindlers and swindling 2. Mafia 3. Fathers and sons 4. Middle-aged men 5. Billionaires 6. Married women 7. Rich women 8. Former convicts 9. Debt 10. Crime fiction 11. Thrillers and suspense
LC 2006018438

After spending five years in prison, con man Kip Largo is approached by the wife of billionaire Ed Napier for help in stealing her husband's money, a job that Kip turns down, until his son gets in trouble with the Russian mafia.

Klein, Rachel, 1953-

The **moth** diaries : a novel / Rachel Klein. Counterpoint, 2002. 249 p.

ISBN 1582432058

1. 1960s 2. Sixteen-year-old girls 3. Girls' boarding schools 4. Teenage girls 5. Diary novels 6. Psychological suspense 7. Historical fiction
LC 2001007226

"The unnamed narrator of Klein's first novel is a studious, thoughtful 16-year-old at an elite boarding school in the late '60s. Her closest friend is her sweet, friendly roommate, Lucy, who navigates the school's social system with ease. The arrival of quiet, mysterious Ernessa upsets the balance between the friends when Ernessa befriends and seemingly takes Lucy away from the narrator. . . . Thanks to reading LeFanu's vampire story 'Carmilla' and other tales, and to Ernessa's odd behavior and Lucy's mysterious wasting illness, the narrator begins to suspect that Ernessa is a vampire. . . . The diary format of Klein's story gives it immediacy, and a menacing atmosphere permeates it." Booklist.

Kleypas, Lisa

Christmas Eve at Friday Harbor / Lisa Kleypas. St. Martin's Press, 2010. 211 p. Friday Harbor novels

ISBN 9780312605865

1. Family secrets 2. Guardian and ward 3. Grief 4. Death 5. Widows 6. Brothers and sisters 7. Christmas 8. Interpersonal attraction 9. Washington (State) 10. San Juan Islands 11. Contemporary romances 12. Holiday romances
LC 2010035779

After a radio DJ in the close-knit community of Friday Harbor reads a heartwrenching letter to Santa written by widower Zachary Nolan's daughter, Zachary's family and friends get caught up in a holiday matchmaking frenzy.

Kleypas, Lisa

* **Cold-hearted** rake / Lisa Kleypas. Avon Books, 2015. 384 p. The Ravenels

ISBN 9780062371812

1. Victorian era (1837-1901) 2. Earls and countesses 3. Widows

4. Inheritance and succession 5. Family estates 6. Womanizers 7. Transformations, Personal 8. Responsibility 9. Sexual attraction 10. Men/women relations 11. England -- Social life and customs -- 19th century 12. Great Britain -- History -- Victoria, 1837-1901 13. Victorian romances 14. Historical romances

When the death of his cousin, an earl, lands him with responsibility for an estate riddled with debt and the late earl's three sisters, Devon Ravenel finds himself drawn to his cousin's widow and committed to restoring the estate.

"Kleypas begins a new historical romance series with two damaged characters who might find happiness if they can ever learn to trust themselves and one another. Intricately and elegantly crafted, intensely romantic, and with secondary characters and an epilogue that will leave readers anxiously awaiting more." Kirkus.

Kleypas, Lisa

Devil in spring / Lisa Kleypas. Avon Books, 2017. 370 p. The Ravenels

ISBN 9780062371874

1. Victorian era (1837-1901) 2. Scandals 3. Women marriage resisters 4. Womanizers 5. Nobility 6. Mate selection 7. Sexual attraction 8. Men/women relations 9. England -- Social life and customs -- 19th century 10. Great Britain -- History -- Victoria, 1837-1901 11. Victorian romances 12. Historical romances

Preferring a career to participating in the London season, strong-willed debutante Lady Pandora Ravenel unexpectedly meets her match in notorious rake Lord St. Vincent, who talks her into a marriage of convenience as part of his plan to win her heart.

"Her signature formula, the suave and sexy hero falling for a frumpy wallflower, still produces a captivating read. Fans will appreciate cameos by some of the author's most beloved characters, and the world of Victorian England is drawn with Kleypas' usual sharp wit and well-researched political nuances. A funny and charming story that will delight readers from the first page to the last." Kirkus.

Kleypas, Lisa

Marrying Winterborne / Lisa Kleypas. Avon Books, 2016. 384 p. The Ravenels

ISBN 9780062371867

1. Victorian era (1837-1901) 2. Nobility 3. Rich men 4. Family secrets 5. Interclass romance 6. Businesspeople 7. Retail industry and trade 8. Sexual attraction 9. Men/women relations 10. England -- Social life and customs -- 19th century 11. Great Britain -- History -- Victoria, 1837-1901 12. Victorian romances 13. Historical romances

Achieving wealth and success through his savage ambitions, tycoon Rhys Winterborne resolves to marry shy, aristocratic Lady Helen Ravenel, who in spite of her gentle upbringing responds to Rhys's seductions with her own unexpected passions.

Kleypas, Lisa

* **Secrets** of a summer night / Lisa Kleypas. Avon, 2004 384 p. Wallflower series

ISBN 0060091290

1. Victorian era (1837-1901) 2. 1840s 3. Young women -- Friendship 4. Women 5. American women in England 6. Mate selection 7. Men/women relations 8. Financial crises 9. Social acceptance 10. Social classes 11. Great Britain -- History -- Victoria, 1837-1901 12. England -- Social life and customs -- 18th century 13. Victorian romances 14. Historical romances

Desperate to save her family from ruin, Annabelle Peyton plans to use her beauty and wit to marry a wealthy aristocrat, but her plans are undermined by the intriguing Simon Hunt, who offers seduction but not marriage.

"By turns amusing, sensual and sober, but always compelling, this is a first-rate offering from a truly talented storyteller." Publishers Weekly.

Kline, Christina Baker, 1964-

Orphan train : a novel / Christina Baker Kline. William Morrow, 2012. 288 p.

ISBN 9780061950728

1. Friendship 2. Second chances 3. Families 4. Orphans 5. Young women 6. Orphan trains 7. Penobscot Indians 8. Community service (Punishment) 9. Senior women 10. Maine 11. Literary fiction 12. Parallel narratives

LC 2012027409

Close to aging out of the foster care system, Molly Ayer takes a position helping an elderly woman named Vivian and discovers that they are more alike than different as she helps Vivian solve a mystery from her past.

Knausgaard, Karl Ove, 1968-

* **My** struggle. Karl Ove Knausgaard ; translated from the Norwegian by Don Bartlett and Martin Aitken. Archipelago Books, 2018, c2011. 1156 p. My struggle

ISBN 9780914671992

1. Authors 2. Memory 3. Existentialism 4. Anxiety 5. Identity (Psychology) 6. Group identity 7. Language and languages 8. Consequences 9. Women with depression 10. Interpersonal relations 11. Fame 12. Norway 13. Autobiographical fiction 14. Literary fiction 15. Metafiction 16. Translations -- Norwegian to English

Published in the UK by Harvill Secker as The end : my struggle 6, 2018.

In the final volume of My Struggle, Karl Ove Knausgaard examines with ruthless, unsparing rigour his life, his ambitions and frailties, his uncertainties and doubts, and his relationships with friends and exes, his wife and children, his mother and father.

"A fittingly bulky end to a radical feat of oversharing." Kirkus.

Kneale, Matthew, 1960-

English passengers / Matthew Kneale. Nan A. Talese/Doubleday, 2000. 446 p.

ISBN 9780385497435

1. Aboriginal Tasmanians 2. Ship captains 3. Voyages and travels -- 19th century 4. Smuggling -- Australia 5. Tasmania -- History -- 1803-1900 6. Historical fiction 7. Literary fiction

LC 99016402

ALA Notable Book, 2001.

Whitbread Book Award for Novel, 2000.

Whitbread Book of the Year Award, 2000.

Shortlisted for the Booker-McConnell Prize, 2000.

Shortlisted for the Miles Franklin Literary Award, 2001

While two Englishmen head for Tasmania on a confiscated pirate ship in search of the Garden of Eden, the British continue their violent "civilization" of the natives in this "paradise."

Kneale, Matthew, 1960-

When we were Romans : a novel / Matthew Kneale. Nan A. Talese, 2008. 240 p.

ISBN 9780385524339

1. Dysfunctional families 2. Father-deserted families 3. Stalking 4. Moving to a new country 5. Homecomings 6. Nine-year-old boys 7. Families 8. British in Italy 9. Interpersonal relations 10. Self-reliance in women 11. Stalkers 12. Rome, Italy 13. Domestic fiction

LC 2007045523

"We, the adult readers of When We Were Romans, learn to peer through the screen of Lawrence's limited point of view to see what's re-ally going on even as our narrator begins to guess at what lies behind his mother's version of events and even to catch a glimpse of the mysteries of his own heart. In life as well as in books, there are some truths that it's much better to sneak up on." Salon.com.

Knight, Deidre

Butterfly tattoo / Deidre Knight. Samhain Publishing, 2010. 296 p.

ISBN 9781605045443

1. Bisexual men 2. Interpersonal attraction 3. Grief 4. Bisexuality 5. Men/women relations 6. Gay men -- Relations with women 7. Stepdaughters 8. Interpersonal relations 9. Men/men relations 10. LGBTQIA romances 11. Contemporary romances 12. LGBTQIA fiction

Michael Warner struggles to put his life back together after a car crash that left his lover dead and his daughter scarred, but begins to find comfort with Rebecca, a former celebrity with insecurities and scars of her own.

"Making a compelling case for bisexuals who recognize no gender boundaries when it comes to true love, Knight's engrossing romance includes another keen twist regarding families." Publishers Weekly.

Knight, Renee

* **The** **secretary** : a novel / Renee Knight. Harper, 2019. 292 p.

ISBN 9780062362353

1. Personal assistants 2. Loyalty 3. Rich women 4. Secrets 5. Celebrities 6. Social classes 7. London, England 8. England 9. Psychological suspense

Serving 20 years as the Personal Assistant to the celebrated Mina Appleton, and amassing many, many secrets, Christine Butcher, discovering that years of loyalty and discretion come with a high price, shows everyone why they should never underestimate a steadfast woman.

"A cinematic page-turner steeped in atmosphere and just awaiting its adaptation to miniseries." Kirkus.

Knopf, Chris

* **Dead** anyway / Chris Knopf. The Permanent Press, 2012. 248 p. Arthur Cathcart novels

ISBN 97815796228312

1. Staged deaths 2. Organized crime 3. Life change events 4. Hiding 5. Secrets 6. Revenge 7. Assassins 8. New identities 9. Loss (Psychology) 10. Attempted murder 11. Connecticut 12. Stamford, Connecticut 13. Mysteries

LC 2012016404

Sequel: Cries of the Lost.

After surviving being shot by a gunman who killed his wife, Arthur Cathcart has his sister--a doctor--declare him dead so that he can assume a new identity and track down his wife's killer.

Knopf, Chris

The **last** refuge / Chris Knopf. Permanent Press, 2005. 292 p. Sam Acquillo mysteries

ISBN 157962118X

1. Murder 2. Executors and administrators 3. Crimes against women 4. Crimes against seniors 5. Carpenters 6. Amateur detectives 7. Neighbors 8. Social isolation 9. Life change events 10. Southampton, New York 11. Hamptons, New York 12. Mysteries 13. Hardboiled fiction

LC 2004065314

Sam Acquillo is at the end of the line. A middle-aged corporate dropout living in a ramshackle cottage in Southampton's North Sea, Sam has abandoned friends, family, and a big-time career to sit on his porch, drink vodka, and stare at the Little Peconic Bay. But then the old lady next door ends up floating dead in her bathtub, and it seems that Sam is the only one who wonders why. Despite himself, burned out, busted up, and cynical, the ex-engineer, ex-professional boxer, ex-loving father and husband finds himself uncovering secrets no one could have imagined, least of all Sam himself.

"While [Sam's] low-key investigation is only minimally suspenseful, the characters he chats up are such original oddballs and their conversation so bracing that you want to kick off your shoes and spend some time on the porch with them, just taking in the view and enjoying the talk." New York Times Book Review.

Knopf, Chris,

You're dead / Chris Knopf. Permanent Press, 2018 288 p.
ISBN 9781579625665
1. Frameups 2. Psychologists 3. Aerospace industry and trade 4. Murder 5. Murder suspects 6. People with autism 7. Personality assessment 8. Business -- Corrupt practices 9. Connecticut 10. New Haven, Connecticut 11. Mysteries

LC 2018039060

"Knopf plays fair as he matches well-developed characters with a crafty whodunit plot, one whose resolution few readers will anticipate." Publishers Weekly.

Knott, Robert, 1954-

Robert B. Parker's Buckskin / Robert Knott. G.P. Putnam's Sons, 2019 304 p. Virgil Cole and Everett Hitch
ISBN 9780735218277
1. Serial murderers 2. United States marshals 3. Mines and mineral resources 4. Blizzards 5. Gunfighters 6. Gunfights 7. Murder investigation 8. The West (United States) -- History -- 19th century 9. Westerns

LC 2019001337

A campaign for sheriff in Appaloosa is thrown into turmoil by a nearby gold strike and a dangerous snowstorm, pitting marshals Virgil Cole and Everett Hitch against rival mining factions and a vicious serial killer.

Knowles, John, 1926-2001

* A **separate** peace / John Knowles. Scribner Classics, 1996, 204 p.
ISBN 0684833662
1. Second World War era (1939-1945) 2. 1940s 3. Teenage boys -- New Hampshire 4. Betrayal 5. Friendship 6. Prep school students 7. Prep schools -- New Hampshire 8. Sixteen-year-old boys -- New Hampshire 9. Death 10. Boys 11. World War II 12. New Hampshire 13. Coming-of-age stories 14. Modern classics 15. Literary fiction

LC 96025844

Originally published: London : Secker & Warburg, 1959.

A conflict of loyalties between Gene and his fearless friend, Phineas, leads to tragedy.

Knox, Tyler

Kockroach / Tyler Knox. William Morrow, 2007. 368 p.
ISBN 0061143332
1. 1950s 2. Cockroaches 3. Metamorphosis 4. Transformations (Magic) 5. Interpersonal relations 6. Male friendship 7. Organized crime 8. Ethics 9. Violence 10. Greed 11. New York City 12. Noir fiction 13. Magical realism

LC 2006048138

When a 1950s cockroach awakens only to discover that he has been transformed into a human being, he awkwardly learns human skills while wondering how his primitive insect desires and amorality will mesh with the values of people.

"Literary fiction is not often this wildly funny. . . . Knox shifts voices and perspective, from hard-boiled to modern-hip, dropping allusions to people as varied as Richard Nixon and the Ramones. You can tell when an author is having a good time, and Knox has a ball." Seattle Times.

Ko, Lisa

* The **leavers** / Lisa Ko. Algonquin Books of Chapel Hill, 2017. 352 p.
ISBN 9781616206888
1. Undocumented immigrants 2. Mothers and sons 3. Abandonment (Psychology) 4. Parent-separated boys 5. Assimilation (Sociology) 6. Cultural differences 7. Children of immigrants 8. Immigrants, Chinese 9. Adoptive families 10. Family relationships 11. New York City 12. China 13. Coming-of-age stories 14. Literary fiction
Asian Pacific American Award for Literature: Adult Fiction, 2018.
Bellwether Prize for Fiction, 2016.
National Book Award for Fiction finalist, 2017

"One morning, Deming Guo's mother, an undocumented Chinese immigrant named Polly, goes to her job at the nail salon and never comes home. With his mother gone, eleven-year-old Deming is left with no one to care for him. He is eventually adopted by two white college professors who move him from the Bronx to a small town upstate. Set in New York and China, the Leavers is the story of how one boy comes into his own when everything he's loved has been taken away--and how a mother learns to live with the mistakes of her past"--, Provided by publisher.

"Kos stunning tale of love and loyalty -- to family, to country -- is a fresh and moving look at the immigrant experience in America, and is as timely as ever." Publishers Weekly.

Koch, Herman, 1953-

The **dinner** / Herman Koch ; translated from the Dutch by Sam Garrett. Text Publishing, 2013, c2009. 304 p.
ISBN 9780770437855
1. Middle class families 2. Life change events 3. Parent and child 4. Teenage boys -- Personal conduct 5. Candidates for public office 6. Personal conduct 7. Protectiveness 8. Responsibility 9. Liberalism 10. Families 11. Netherlands 12. Satirical fiction 13. Psychological suspense 14. Translations -- Dutch to English
Adapted into a film by the same name in 2017.
Originally published: Amsterdam : Anthos, 2009.
ALA Notable Book, 2014

Over the course of a meal at a fashionable Amsterdam restaurant, two couples move from small talk during the appetizer to weightier issues. While discussing their sons -- who have done something terrible -- we learn more about what ties the families together, and what seems to be a skewering of upper-class values turns into something far more serious. -- Description by Shauna Griffin.

"In a single setting, Koch successfully deploys multiple narratives of a single event to effectively show that our construction of history, and constant attempts at overdetermining the future, is problematic. A shocking, humorous, and entertaining novel." Library Journal.

Koen, Karleen

Before Versailles : a novel of Louis XIV / Karleen Koen. Crown, 2011. 480 p.
ISBN 9780307716576
1. Louis XIV,, King of France, 1638-1715 2. 1660s 3. 17th century 4. Rulers 5. Love triangles 6. Extramarital affairs 7. Independence in women 8. Scandals 9. Upper class 10. Conspiracies 11. Power (Social sciences) 12. France -- History -- Louis XIV, 1643-1715 13.

Biographical fiction 14. Historical fiction

LC 2010035562

Assuming the responsibilities of governing France after the death of his prime minister, Louis XIV embarks on a love affair with his sister-in-law, Henriette, triggering a scandal that is complicated by a finance minister's growing power and a mysterious boy with an iron mask.

Koen, Karleen

Through a glass darkly / Karleen Koen. Random House, 1986. 743 p. Barbara Devane novels

ISBN 1402200447

1. 18th century 2. Innocence (Psychology) 3. Upper class 4. Politics and culture 5. Nobility 6. Dowries 7. Extramarital affairs 8. Arranged marriage 9. Secrets 10. Independence in women 11. Gay men 12. Former lovers 13. Young women 14. France -- Social life and customs -- 18th century 15. England -- Social life and customs -- 18th century 16. Coming-of-age stories 17. Historical fiction

LC 86000422

Sequel to: Dark angels.

Sequel: Now face to face.

Barbara Alderly's marriage to Roger Montgeoffrey--twenty-seven years her senior--seems a dream come true, until his plans for building a magnificent estate with the proceeds of her dowry turn the marriage into a nightmare.

"Expertly paced, the novel blends quaint historical romance with a sharp-edged, contemporary psychodramatic style. Its characters are memorable and full-bodied, maturing through a series of rapidly escalating tragedies that bring the sweetly naive heroine into full womanhood and force her to make a decision that will forever change her life. A sophisticated, atmospheric work." Booklist.

Koenig, Minerva

Nine days : a mystery / Minerva Koenig. Minotaur Books, 2014. 304 p. Julie Kalas novels

ISBN 9781250051943

1. Widows 2. Murder investigation 3. Small towns 4. Secrets 5. Determination in women 6. Witnesses -- Protection 7. Illegal arms transfers 8. Police chiefs 9. Amateur detectives 10. Criminals 11. Murder suspects 12. Bars (Drinking establishments) 13. Texas 14. Mysteries

LC 2014016747

Long-time home-renovator--and career criminal--Julia Kalas must enter the witness protection program after the Aryan Brotherhood makes her a widow; and, relocating to the tiny town of Azula, Texas, must soon contend with a murder at the bar where she has started working.

"Small-town Texas is vividly brought to life in this atmospheric and entertaining debut that also introduces a memorable and unusual protagonist. It's bound to delight fans of Tricia Fields, Lori G. Armstrong, or James Lee Burke's Hackberry Holland books." Library Journal.

Koepp, David

Cold storage : a novel / David Koepp. Ecco, 2019. 256 p.

ISBN 9780062916433

1. Epidemics 2. Biological terrorism 3. Government investigators 4. Mutation (Biology) 5. Predation (Biology) 6. Bio-thrillers 7. Thrillers and suspense

LC 2018057661

When Pentagon bioterror operative Roberto Diaz was sent to investigate a suspected biochemical attack, he found something far worse: a highly mutative organism capable of extinction-level destruction. He contained it and buried it in cold storage deep beneath a little-used military repository.

Koestler, Arthur, 1905-1983

Darkness at noon / Arthur Koestler ; translated by Daphne Hardy. Macmillan, 1987, c1940. 267 p.

ISBN 0025652109

1. 1930s 2. Political prisoners 3. Revolutionaries 4. Moscow, Russia, Trials, 1936-1937 5. Stalinism 6. Trials 7. Revolutions 8. Confession (Law) 9. Questioning 10. Trials (Political crimes and offenses) -- Soviet Union 11. Totalitarianism -- Soviet Union 12. Totalitarianism 13. Soviet Union -- History -- 1925-1953 14. Historical fiction 15. Political fiction 16. Translations -- Hungarian to English 17. Modern classics 18. Dystopian fiction

Originally published: London : J. Cape, 1940.

An aging revolutionary is imprisoned by his own political party and forced to confess to crimes he never committed. Where once he saw promise for humanity, he now sees only darkness.

Kohnstamm, Thomas B.

Lake City / Thomas Kohnstamm. Counterpoint, 2019 256 p.

ISBN 9781640091429

1. 2000s (Decade) 2. Gentrification of cities 3. Ambition in men 4. Class conflict 5. Underclass 6. Birthmothers 7. Adoptive parents 8. Personal conduct 9. September 11 Terrorist Attacks, 2001 10. Seattle, Washington 11. Humorous stories

The setting is Seattle's Lake City neighborhood during the 2001 holiday season. In the wake of the 9/11 tragedy and at the peak of Seattle's first wave of tech-boom gentrification-a wave that never quite made it to his neighborhood-Lane Bueche schemes how to win back his wife (and her trust fund). In his childhood bedroom in his mother's decrepit old house, the idealistic but self-serving striver Lane licks his wounds and hatches a plot.

Kolpan, Gerald

Magic words : the tale of a Jewish boy-interpreter, the frontier's most estimable magician, a murderous harlot, and America's greatest Indian chief / Gerald Kolpan. W. W. Norton & Co., 2012. 384 p.

ISBN 9781605983691

1. 1860s 2. Immigrants, Jewish 3. Interpreters 4. Magicians 5. Ponca Indians 6. Men/women relations 7. Nebraska -- History -- 19th century 8. Westerns

A young Jewish immigrant to the New World, Julius Meyer is captured by the Ponca Indian tribe, where he becomes interpreter for Standing Bear and falls in love with the chief's daughter, Prairie Flower, only to see his idyllic life begin to unravel after his magician cousin begins an affair with a murderous prostitute.

Konar, Affinity

* Mischling : a novel / Affinity Konar. Little, Brown and Company, 2016. 344 p.

ISBN 9780316308106

1. Mengele, Josef, 1911-1979 2. Auschwitz (Concentration camp) 3. Second World War era (1939-1945) 4. Twin sisters 5. Human experimentation in medicine 6. Holocaust, 1933-1945 7. Concentration camp survivors 8. Persecution by Nazis 9. Jews -- Persecutions 10. Atrocities 11. Twins 12. Missing persons 13. Searching 14. Poland -- History -- 20th century 15. Historical fiction 16. Literary fiction

Arriving at Auschwitz in 1944, twin sisters Pearl and Stasha Zagorski take refuge in each other when they become part of the experimental population of twins known as Mengele's Zoo, where they experience horrors unknown to other inmates.

"Konar makes every sentence count; its to her credit that the girls never come across as simply victims: they're flawed, memorable characters trying to stay alive. This is a brutally beautiful novel." Publishers Weekly.

Koontz, Dean R. (Dean Ray), 1945-

The **darkest** evening of the year / Dean Koontz. Bantam, 2007 416 p.

ISBN 0739327429

1. Psychopaths 2. Golden retrievers 3. Stalking 4. Women and dogs 5. Dogs 6. Stalkers 7. Children with Down syndrome 8. Lovers 9. Revenge 10. Secrets 11. Animal welfare 12. Animal liberation 13. Human/animal relationships 14. Thrillers and suspense

Amy Redwing risks her own well-being to come to the aid of Nickie, a very special golden retriever, unaware that she has drawn the attentions of an unknown and ruthless enemy whose attacks escalate with stunning ferocity.

"Amy Redwing, the survivor of a horrifying marriage, establishes Golden Heart to rescue golden retrievers. . . . A supernatural chain of events ensues after Amy and her architect boyfriend, Brian McCarthy, rescue Nickie during a violent intervention in a family dispute. Soon the pair are on a mission that leads to a transformative confrontation with a number of ugly character: Gunther Schloss, a frustrated aspiring novelist turned killer-for-hire; Moonglow, a psychobitch in the Mommie Dearest league; and Moonglow's lover, Harrow, a self-obsessed sicko. This is the perfect book for thriller addicts who know the darkest hour is just before dawn and for canine lovers who remember dog spelled backwards is god." Publishers Weekly.

Koontz, Dean R. (Dean Ray), 1945-

The **husband** / Dean Koontz. Bantam Books, 2006. 416 p.

ISBN 0553804790

1. Psychopaths 2. Kidnapping 3. Women kidnapping victims 4. Husband and wife 5. Gardeners 6. Ransom 7. Murder 8. Murderers 9. Murder witnesses 10. Dysfunctional families 11. Betrayal 12. Child pornography 13. Detectives 14. Police 15. Southern California 16. Thrillers and suspense

LC 2006042696

When Mitchell Rafferty receives a phone call that his wife has been kidnapped and there is a two million dollar ransom, his extraordinary commitment to his wife will take him on a seventy-two-hour journey of sacrifice and redemption.

"Koontz focuses relentlessly on Mitch and, in chapters scattered judiciously throughout the latter 230 pages, Holly. Not for him the flirtation with evil thinking that an Elmore Leonard does so well or the temptation to sympathize with evildoers that an Alfred Hitchcock offers. And yet Koontz is no less an artist for his championing of the good and his determination to have readers identify with it, as this hair-raising thriller attests." Booklist.

Koontz, Dean R. (Dean Ray), 1945-

Innocence : a novel / Dean Koontz. Bantam Books, 2013. 352 p.

ISBN 9780553808032

1. Social isolation 2. Misfits (Persons) 3. Good and evil 4. Murder 5. Solitude 6. Secrets 7. Mysticism 8. Former Marines 9. People with disfigurements 10. Interpersonal attraction 11. Thrillers and suspense

LC 2013014516

Foraging for supplies by night in a beautiful but hostile urban world where strangers would kill him on sight, Addison endures a solitary existence before meeting a quicksilver girl engaged in a dangerous duel of wits with a malicious, well-placed enemy.

"The narrative is intense, with an old-fashioned ominousness and artistically crafted descriptions. . . . Koontz's allegory on morality and love (agape rather than sensual) probes the idea that evil is woven through humankind." Kirkus.

Koontz, Dean R. (Dean Ray), 1945-

Intensity : a novel / Dean Koontz. Ballantine Books, 1996, c1995. 436 p.

ISBN 9780345384362

1. Psychopaths 2. Women murder witnesses 3. Mass murder 4. Adult child abuse victims 5. Stalking 6. Stalkers 7. California 8. Napa Valley, California 9. Thrillers and suspense

LC 9517120

The sole survivor of a homicidal sociopath's latest killing spree, Chyna Shepherd unwittingly discovers the identity of the murderer's intended next victim and confronts her own troubled past and overwhelming fear to protect herself and the life of a complete stranger from the ultimate evil

"The velocity of the plot is the book's true pleasure; the story does not move so much as rocket up the portentously gloomy highway with the reader in violent pursuit." New York Times Book Review.

Koontz, Dean R. (Dean Ray), 1945-

Velocity / Dean Koontz. Bantam Books, 2005. 352 p.

ISBN 0553804154

1. Serial murderers 2. Psychopaths 3. Anonymous letters 4. Good and evil 5. Bartenders 6. Police 7. People in comas 8. Dilemmas 9. Options, alternatives, choices 10. Threat (Psychology) 11. Death threats 12. Serial murders 13. Thrillers and suspense

A series of communications from a deranged killer in which he is offered a number of devastating choices and deadlines draws Bill Wile into a confrontation with pure evil.

"Graphic, fast-paced action, well-developed characters and relentless, nail-biting scenes show Koontz at the top of his game." Publishers Weekly.

Koryta, Michael

The **Cypress** House / Michael Koryta. Little, Brown and Co., 2011. 400 p.

ISBN 9780316053723

1. Depression era (1929-1941) 2. Depressions -- 1929-1941 3. Political corruption 4. Precognition 5. Boarding houses 6. Railroad travel 7. Hurricanes 8. Gulf Coast, Florida 9. Historical thrillers

LC 2010011405

When Arlen Wagner, who can see impending death in people's eyes, warns fellow rail passengers that the train is going to crash, only Paul Brickhill heeds his warning, but the two end up stranded at The Cypress House, an isolated Gulf Coast boarding house.

"Though Koryta's evocation of the Depression could be stronger, the novel builds to a richly satisfying climax in which Arlen is guided by the spirit of his father and voices of the recently departed. A commanding performance in the field of supernatural noir." Kirkus.

Koryta, Michael

* **How** it happened / Michael Koryta. Little, Brown, 2018. 400 p.

ISBN 9780316293938

1. False confessions (Law) 2. Murder suspects 3. FBI agents 4. Murder investigation 5. Drug abusers 6. Evidence (Law) 7. Maine 8. Mysteries

After a troubled teen, no stranger to the law, admits to her involvement in a brutal murder, Rob Barrett, an FBI investigator and interrogator stakes his reputation on her confession only to have the information she provided prove false.

Koryta, Michael

If she wakes / Michael Koryta. Little Brown & Co, 2019 416 p.

ISBN 9780316294003

1. Attempted murder 2. Accident investigation 3. Insurance investigators 4. Locked-in syndrome 5. College students 6. Murder for hire 7. Stunt driving 8. Assassins 9. Paralysis 10. Thrillers and suspense

An insurance investigator finds herself on the run from a mysterious young hit man while examining the case of a young college student who has been rendered a locked-in syndrome patient by a suspicious accident.

Koryta, Michael

* The **prophet** / Michael Koryta. Little Brown & Co., 2012. 432 p.

ISBN 9780316122610

1. Families of murder victims 2. Small towns 3. Brothers 4. Murder 5. Bail bond agents 6. High school football coaches 7. Murder suspects 8. Murder investigation 9. Thrillers and suspense

Two brothers, estranged since their sister's abduction and murder when they were teens, are forced into a reunion through a new killing in their small Midwestern town.

Koryta, Michael

The **ridge** / Michael Koryta. Little, Brown and Co., 2011. 448 p.

ISBN 9780316053662

1. Murder 2. Good and evil 3. Supernatural 4. Lighthouses 5. Sheriffs 6. Animal sanctuaries 7. Ghosts 8. Kentucky 9. Horror 10. Ghost stories

LC 2011011377

RUSA Reading List, 2012.

From the lighthouse he built on top of a ridge in an eastern Kentucky forest, Wyatt French makes two rambling phone calls about murder and suicide. When Chief Deputy Kevin Kimble and journalist Roy Darmus find him dead in the lighthouse and discover old photographs and maps with names written on them, they realize Wyatt has been collecting information that relates to mysterious and deadly local events that date back decades. As more disturbing events occur, Kimble and Darmus find they are confronting an old, old evil. -- Description by Dawn Towery.

"Koryta . . . matches an original and complex plot line with prose full of understated menace." Publishers Weekly.

Koryta, Michael

So cold the river / Michael Koryta. Little, Brown and Co., 2010. 528 p.

ISBN 9780316053631

1. Documentary films 2. Hallucinations and illusions 3. Supernatural 4. Film producers and directors 5. Resort towns 6. Senior men 7. Rich men 8. Mineral waters 9. Good and evil 10. Hotels 11. Indiana 12. Horror

LC 2009032414

After he is hired by Alyssa Bradford to research the life of her 95-year-old billionaire father-in-law, Eric Shaw visits the man's hometown, where he discovers a restored hotel that has a checkered past--and a newly reawakened evil bent on revenge.

"Koryta spins a spellbinding tale of an unholy lust for power that reaches from beyond the grave and suspends disbelief through the believable interactions of fully developed characters. A cataclysmic finale

will put readers in mind of some of the best recent works of supernatural horror, among which this book ranks." Publishers Weekly.

Koryta, Michael

Those who wish me dead / Michael Koryta. Little Brown & Co, 2014. 400 p.

ISBN 9780316122559

1. Wilderness areas 2. Murder witnesses 3. Wilderness survival 4. Murderers 5. Teenage boys 6. Wildfires 7. Mountains 8. Protectiveness 9. Montana 10. Thrillers and suspense

Pennsylvania Young Reader's Choice Awards, Young Adult, 2016.

"When 13-year-old Jace Wilson witnesses a brutal murder, he's plunged into a new life, issued a false identity and hidden in a wilderness skills program for troubled teens. The plan is to get Jace off the grid while police find the two killers. The result is the start of a nightmare. The killers, known as the Blackwell Brothers, are slaughtering anyone who gets in their way in a methodical quest to reach him. Now all that remains between them and the boy are Ethan and Allison Serbin, who run the wilderness survival program; Hannah Faber, who occupies a lonely fire lookout tower; and endless miles of desolate Montana mountains. The clock is ticking, the mountains are burning, and those who wish Jace Wilson dead are no longer far behind." --, from publisher's web site.

"Koryta . . . has upped his game with this stand-alone's seamless blend of western-wilderness thriller and mainstream crime fiction, with a prickly dab of horror." Booklist.

Koryta, Michael

Tonight I said goodbye / Michael Koryta. Thomas Dunne Books, 2004. 304 p. Lincoln Perry mysteries

ISBN 0312332459

1. Former police 2. Real estate developers 3. Russian American criminals 4. Crimes against police 5. Mafia 6. Rich people 7. Missing persons 8. Sons -- Death 9. Former police 10. Private investigators 11. Murder investigation 12. Cleveland, Ohio 13. Myrtle Beach, South Carolina 14. Mysteries

LC 2004046781

When an alleged suicide victim's wife and six-year-old daughter go missing, private investigator Lincoln Perry and his partner, Joe Pritchard, pursue a theory that the man was actually murdered.

"The hardboiled cliche works beautifully here as these two men find themselves chasing Russian Mafiya, a real estate mogul, and an ex-Marine while dodging bullets, cops, and the FBI. The Cleveland setting is a nice change from the usual East Coast/West Coast locales." Library Journal.

Kosinski, Jerzy, 1933-1991

* **Being** there / Jerzy Kosinski Harcourt Brace Jovanovich, 1971, c1970. 142 p.

ISBN 9780151117000

1. Television -- Social aspects 2. United States -- Social conditions 3. Psychological fiction

LC 70147229

Tells the tale of Chauncey "Chance" Gardiner, who appears out of nowhere to become the heir to the empire of a Wall Street tycoon, a presidential policy adviser, and a media mogul.

Kosinski, Jerzy, 1933-1991

The **devil** tree / Jerzy Kosinski Harcourt Brace Jovanovich, 1973. 208 p.

ISBN 0802139655

1. Rich people -- United States 2. Self-fulfillment 3. Mainstream fiction

LC 72088804

Unable to cope with his huge inheritance, Jonathan Whalen searches for an escape in the drug culture.

Kosinski, Jerzy, 1933-1991

* The **painted** bird / Jerzy Kosinski. Grove Press, 1995, c1965. xxvi, 234 p.

ISBN 9780802134226

1. Kosinski, Jerzy, 1933-1991 2. Holocaust (1933-1945) 3. Jews, Eastern European 4. World War II -- Poland 5. Abandoned children -- Eastern Europe 6. Poland -- History -- Occupation, 1939-1945 7. Autobiographical fiction

Originally published: Boston : Houghton Mifflin, 1965.

When the war separates a youth from his parents, he begins a terrible odyssey of suffering as he wanders from village to village.

Kosmatka, Ted, 1973-

The **games** / Ted Kosmatka. Del Rey, 2012. 368 p.

ISBN 9780345526618

1. Geneticists 2. Genetic engineering 3. Gladiators 4. DNA 5. Olympic games 6. Women biologists 7. Monsters 8. Science fiction 9. Bio-thrillers

Set in a future world where genetically engineered monsters represent competing nations during the Games, a cutting-edge gladiator designed by U.S. Games Committee head Dr. Silas Williams demonstrates signs of hyper-intelligence and violent tendencies that threaten more than athletic opponents.

Kostova, Elizabeth

* The **historian** : a novel / Elizabeth Kostova. Little, Brown and Co., 2005. 656 p.

ISBN 0316011770

1. 1970s 2. Historians 3. Vampires 4. Books 5. Widowers 6. Teenage girls 7. Missing persons 8. Fathers and daughters 9. Americans in Europe 10. Inheritance and succession 11. Amsterdam, Netherlands 12. Netherlands 13. Horror 14. Gothic fiction 15. Literary fiction

LC 2004022563

Book Sense Book of the Year Adult Fiction, 2006.

Discovering a medieval book and a cache of letters, a motherless American girl becomes the latest in a series of historians, including her late father, who investigate the possible surviving legacy of Vlad the Impaler.

"Kostova's vampire is no campy Lugosi knockoff but a blend of the cunning, powerful count who debuts in Bram Stoker's 1897 classic novel and the actual Dracula, Vlad the Impaler, a 15th-century Romanian prince who was both a nationalist hero and a sadistic torturer. Blending history and myth, Kostova has fashioned a version so fresh that when a stake is finally driven through a heart, it inspires the tragic shock of something happening for the very first time." Newsweek.

Kostova, Elizabeth

The **shadow** land : a novel / Elizabeth Kostova. Ballantine Books, 2017. 528 p.

ISBN 9780345527868

1. Americans in foreign countries 2. Post-communism 3. Political corruption 4. Dissenters 5. Women teachers 6. Political activists 7. Poets 8. Taxicab drivers 9. Social change 10. Violinists 11. Communist countries 12. Political persecution 13. Family secrets 14. Bulgaria -- History 15. Eastern Europe 16. Literary fiction 17. Psychological fiction 18. Parallel narratives

LC 2016036489

Librarians' Choice (Australia), 2017

Accidentally taking a parcel from a family with whom she shared a cab, a young American tourist in Bulgaria is horrified to discover that the parcel contains an urn of ashes and embarks on an effort to return it to its family, making astonishing discoveries along the way.

"A compelling and complex mystery, strong storytelling, and lyrical writing combine for an engrossing read set in the former Soviet-bloc nation of Bulgaria." Publishers Weekly.

Kotzwinkle, William

The **bear** went over the mountain / William Kotzwinkle. Doubleday, 1996. 306 p.

ISBN 0385484283

1. Bears 2. Publishers and publishing 3. Best sellers (Books) 4. Authors 5. College teachers 6. Impersonators 7. Manuscripts 8. New York City 9. Maine 10. Satirical fiction

LC 962296

A black bear finds a manuscript in the woods of Maine and becomes a literary sensation from coast to coast, as money-hungry executives shape his image into the next Hemingway.

"This genuine parable for our time is as full of truth as it is of humor." The Nation.

Kowal, Mary Robinette, 1969-

The **calculating** stars : a lady astronaut novel / Mary Robinette Kowal. Tor.com, 2018. 431 p. Lady astronaut novels

ISBN 9780765378385

1. 1950s 2. Women astronauts 3. Women's role 4. Disasters 5. Women pilots 6. Meteors 7. Space exploration 8. Space colonies 9. Climate change 10. Jewish women 11. Racism 12. Sexism 13. Globalization 14. Survival (after disaster) 15. Alternative histories 16. Science fiction 17. Social science fiction

Follows the e-novella "The lady astronaut of Mars" (2014).

Hugo Award for Best Novel, 2019.

Locus Award for Best Science Fiction Novel, 2019.

Nebula Award for Best Novel, 2018.

RUSA Reading List, 2019.

Sidewise Awards for Alternate History, 2018.

On a cold spring night in 1952, a meteorite falls to earth and destroys much of the eastern seaboard of the United States, including Washington D.C. The Meteor, as it is popularly known, decimates the U.S. government and paves the way for a climate cataclysm that will eventually render the earth inhospitable to humanity. This looming threat calls for a radically accelerated timeline in the earth's efforts to colonize space, and allows a much larger share of humanity to take part in the process.

Kowal, Mary Robinette, 1969-

The **fated** sky : a lady astronaut novel / Mary Robinette Kowal. Tor.com, 2018. 320 p. Lady astronaut novels

ISBN 9780765398949

1. 1960s 2. Civil Rights Movement 3. Women astronauts 4. Space exploration 5. Space colonies 6. Jewish women 7. Racism 8. Sexism 9. Gender role 10. Alternative histories 11. Social science fiction 12. Science fiction

Continuing the grand sweep of alternate history begun in The Calculating Stars, The Fated Sky looks forward to 1961, when mankind is well-established on the moon and looking forward to its next step: journeying to, and eventually colonizing, Mars.

Kracht, Christian, 1966-

Imperium : a fiction of the South Seas / Christian Kracht ; translated from the German by Daniel Bowles. Farrar, Straus and Giroux, 2015, c2012. 160 p.

ISBN 9780374175245

1. Engelhardt, August, 1877-1919 2. 20th century 3. Islands 4. Nonconformists 5. Nudists 6. Radicals 7. Vegetarians 8. Coconut 9.

Islands of the Pacific 10. Literary fiction 11. Translations -- German to English

LC 2014039370

Translation from the German of: Imperium.

Originally published: 2012.

A satirical indictment of extremism follows the exploits of a radical vegetarian and nudist from Nuremberg who voyages to 1902's Bismarck Archipelago to establish a colony based on the worship of the sun and coconuts.

"Comparable to the adventure stories of Robert Louis Stevenson, Jack London, and Daniel Defoe, albeit with a definite philosophical inclination, this amusing, fantastical tale features fabulous language, delightfully concocted descriptions, and an excellent translation by Bowles." Library Journal.

Krall, Hanna

Chasing the king of hearts / Hanna Krall ; translated from the Polish by Philip Boehm ; afterword by Mariusz Szczygiel. The Feminist Press at CUNY, 2017, c2006. 192 p.

ISBN 9781558619449

1. Regensberg, Izold 2. Auschwitz (Concentration camp) 3. Second World War era (1939-1945) 4. Ghettoes, Jewish -- Warsaw, Poland 5. Holocaust (1933-1945) 6. Resilience in women 7. Holocaust survivors 8. Suffering 9. Escapes 10. Disguises 11. Jewish families -- Warsaw, Poland 12. Poland 13. Historical fiction 14. Love stories

LC 2016034906

Based on a true story.

Previously published in Polish as Krol kier znow na wylocie. Warszawa : "wiat Ksiki", 2006.

When her husband is arrested in Nazi-occupied Poland, Izolda endures seemingly unending brutality to ensure his safety.

"A quirky but exceptional story of infinite love and life-sustaining commitment." Kirkus.

Kramer, Larry

Search for my heart / Larry Kramer. Farrar Straus & Giroux, 2015. 880 p. American people

ISBN 9780374104399

1. AIDS (Disease) 2. Gay men 3. Homosexuality 4. People with AIDS 5. Conspiracies 6. McCarthyism 7. Homophobia 8. Gay culture 9. Political persecution 10. Sexuality 11. Eugenics 12. United States -- History 13. Satirical fiction 14. LGBTQIA fiction 15. Transgressive fiction 16. Historical fiction

Presents a satirical history of homosexuality in America that imagines the alternate motivations behind key events.

"There is nary a dog in these pages that is not supremely shaggy, never a missed opportunity to offend someone. Kramer ranges among voices, eras and styles, the dominant ones being steely anger shading into Pynchon-esque goofiness but always with serious intent. Breathtakingly well-written. And how could one not keep reading, no matter how endless, a book with a line such as 'You don't just drop a penis like Tibby's into the narrative and let it go'?" Kirkus.

Krauss, Nicole

Forest Dark / Nicole Krauss. HarperCollins, 2017 288 p.

ISBN 9780062430991

1. Life change events 2. Self-discovery 3. Identity (Psychology) 4. Retirees 5. Jews 6. Divorced men 7. Clergy 8. Senior men 9. Filmmakers 10. Women authors 11. Writers' block 12. Transformations, Personal 13. Americans in Israel 14. Tel Aviv, Israel 15. Israel 16. Literary fiction

Jules Epstein, a man whose drive, avidity, and outsized personality have, for sixty-eight years, been a force to be reckoned with, is undergoing a metamorphosis. In the wake of his parents' deaths, his divorce from his wife of more than thirty years, and his retirement from the New York legal firm where he was a partner, he's felt an irresistible need to give away his possessions, alarming his children and perplexing the executor of his estate. With the last of his wealth, he travels to Israel, with a nebulous plan to do something to honor his parents. In Tel Aviv, he is sidetracked by a charismatic American rabbi planning a reunion for the descendants of King David who insists that Epstein is part of that storied dynastic line.

"Krauss's elegant, provocative, and mesmerizing novel is her best yet. Rich in profound insights and emotional resonance, it follows two characters on their paths to self-realization." Publishers Weekly.

Krauss, Nicole

Great house : a novel / Nicole Krauss. W. W. Norton & Co., 2010 352 p.

ISBN 9780393079982

1. Loss (Psychology) 2. Memories 3. Desks 4. Secrets 5. Recluses 6. Joy and sorrow 7. Grief 8. Lost love 9. Coping 10. Literary fiction

National Book Award for Fiction finalist, 2010.

Shortlisted for The Orange Prize for Fiction, 2011.

A young novelist inherited the desk from a poet taken by Pinochet's police. Then the desk is stolen from her by the poet's supposed daughter. In its drawers, another man discovers a long-kept secret about his wife. And a Jerusalem antiques dealer uses the desk in his family's study, which was devastated by the Nazis in 1944.

"For most of the novel, it's unclear what the desk represents or whether the book's far-flung characters will ever meet. But Krauss has a unique way of assembling novelsbaroque, complex, and with a stunning tidiness that isn't clear until the very last page. All the parts do fit together in the end. The shape they form is a ghostly Great House, and its walls are ideas that leave the reader reverberating." The Atlantic.

Krauss, Nicole

The **history** of love / Nicole Krauss. Norton, 2005. 248 p.

ISBN 0393060349

1. Senior authors 2. Books and reading 3. Loss (Psychology) 4. Immigrants, Polish 5. Teenage girls 6. Widows 7. Holocaust survivors 8. Loneliness 9. Romantic love 10. Lost love 11. New York City 12. Poland 13. Novels-within-novels 14. Psychological fiction 15. Literary fiction

LC 2005000936

Edward Lewis Wallant Award, 2005.

William Saroyan International Prize for Writing, Fiction category, 2008.

Shortlisted for The Orange Prize for Fiction, 2006

Sixty years after a book's publication, its author remembers his lost love and missing son, while a teenage girl named for one of the book's characters seeks her namesake, as well as a cure for her widowed mother's loneliness.

"Beyond the vigorous whiplash that keeps Ms. Krauss's [book] moving (and keeps its reader off-balance until a stunning finale), this novel is tightly packed with ingenious asides. They range from parodying various publications' characteristic obituaries of a very famous writer, a man who was best known for a single, ecstatic five-page paragraph (Ms. Krauss perfectly mimics the syntax of both The Times and The New Republic) to skewering the kind of editor whom all writers dread." New York Times.

Krentz, Jayne Ann

Copper Beach / Jayne Ann Krentz. G. P. Putnam's Sons, 2012. 352 p. Dark legacy

ISBN 9780399157875

1. Rare books 2. Paranormal phenomena 3. Women psychics 4. Collectors and collecting 5. Books and reading 6. Extortion 7. Men/women relations 8. Interpersonal attraction 9. Washington (State) 10. Paranormal romances 11. Romantic suspense 12. Pacific Northwest fiction

A rare book. An ancient code. Abby's psychic talents have made her an expert in books of the paranormal-- and now an old alchemical text know as The Key has reappeared on the black market. Convinced that she needs an investigator who can also be a body guard, she hires Sam. Passion flares immediately between them, yet neither entirely trust the other. Both have their own agendas...

Krentz, Jayne Ann

River road / Jayne Ann Krentz. G. P. Putnam's Sons, 2014. 336 p.

ISBN 9780399165122

1. Women private investigators 2. Traffic accidents 3. Missing persons 4. Men/women relations 5. Murder investigation 6. Bereavement 7. Small town life 8. California 9. Mysteries 10. Romantic suspense

LC 2013036136

Returning thirteen years after an embarrassing incident from her teens to the hometown of her beloved late aunt, forensic genealogist Lucy Sheridan makes shocking discoveries about her aunt's death, the disappearance of a cold-blooded local, and an attractive former cop.

"An irresistible mix of scintillating humor, stunning suspense, and sexy romance." Booklist.

Krentz, Jayne Ann

Running hot / Jayne Ann Krentz. G.P. Putnam's Sons, 2008. 352 p. Arcane society novels

ISBN 9780399155215

1. Former police 2. Librarians 3. Men/women relations 4. Murder 5. Psychic ability 6. Murder investigation 7. Maui, Hawaii 8. Romantic suspense

LC 2008028340

Reluctantly paired for a murder investigation by the paranormal Arcane Society, former cop Luther Malone and aura-reading librarian Grace Renquist find their mutual disgust dissolving into a powerful attraction, during a case that is further complicated by operatives for a ruthless underground psychic group.

"This arresting tale combines witty humor with clever plotting to weave an exceptionally memorable romance." Library Journal.

Krentz, Jayne Ann

Secret sisters / Jayne Ann Krentz. Berkley Books, 2015. 368 p.

ISBN 9780399174483

1. Trust 2. Secrets 3. Female friendship 4. Crimes against girls 5. Hotels 6. Revenge 7. Murderers 8. Security consultants 9. Men/women relations 10. Romantic suspense

LC 2015016234

Reuniting at the hotel where one of them was brutally attacked as a child decades earlier, Madeline and Daphne are forced to confront painful memories and truths in order to solve the mysterious death of Madeline's father.

"Krentz scores another winner with complex characters and seamless plotting." Publishers Weekly.

Krentz, Jayne Ann

When all the girls have gone / Jayne Ann Krentz. Berkley Books, 2016 304 p. Cutler, Sutter & Salinas

ISBN 9780399174490

1. Stepsisters 2. Missing women 3. Investment clubs 4. Private investigators 5. Conspiracies 6. Threat (Psychology) 7. Secrets 8. Jilted women 9. Divorced men 10. Seattle, Washington 11. Romantic suspense

"Jayne Ann Krentz, the New York Times bestselling author of Secret Sisters, delivers a thrilling novel of the deceptions we hide behind, the passions we surrender to, and the lengths we'll go to for the truth... When Charlotte Sawyer is unable to contact her step-sister, Jocelyn, to tell her that one her closest friends was found dead, she discovers that Jocelyn has vanished. Beautiful, brilliant--and reckless--Jocelyn has gone off the grid before, but never like this. In a desperate effort to find her, Charlotte joins forces with Max Cutler, a struggling PI who recently moved to Seattle after his previous career as a criminal profiler went down in flames--literally. Burned out, divorced and almost broke, Max needs the job. After surviving a near-fatal attack, Charlotte and Max turn to Jocelyn's closest friends, women in a Seattle-based online investment club, for answers. But what they find is chilling...When her uneasy alliance with Max turns into a full-blown affair, Charlotte has no choice but to trust him with her life. For the shadows of Jocelyn's past are threatening to consume her--and anyone else who gets in their way..."--, Provided by publisher.

"Krentz returns with an intricately plotted romantic suspense novel that satisfies on every level, includes some clever twists with the senior community, and may open the door for a sequel. A terrific read by a stellar author." Kirkus.

Krentz, Jayne Ann

White lies / Jayne Ann Krentz. G. P. Putnam's Sons, 2007. 384 p. Arcane Society novels

ISBN 9780399153730

1. Women psychics 2. Half-sisters 3. Men/women relations 4. Murder 5. Family secrets 6. Family businesses 7. Financial planners 8. Deception 9. Secrets 10. Conspiracies 11. Secret societies 12. Arcane Society (Imaginary organization) 13. Thirties (Age) 14. California 15. Arizona 16. Romantic suspense 17. Paranormal romances

LC 2006044829

Fearing that her psychic abilities have damaged her chances of having a healthy relationship, Clare Lancaster travels to California to assist her father's business and meets financial consultant Jake Salter, with whom she shares an unlikely chemistry.

Kress, Nancy

After the fall, before the fall, during the fall / Nancy Kress. Tachyon Publications, 2012. 189 p.

ISBN 9781616960650

1. Time travel (Future) 2. Post-apocalypse 3. Aliens 4. Disasters 5. Teenage boys 6. Women mathematicians 7. Kidnapping investigation 8. Apocalyptic fiction 9. Science fiction

An FBI analyst in the year 2013 formulates a plan that involves sending children into the future to 2035 to save the dying survivors of an alien attack who are trapped in an enclosure on Earth's remains.

Kress, Nancy

Beggars in Spain / Nancy Kress. William Morrow, 1993. 438 p. Beggars trilogy

ISBN 9780380718771

1. 21st century 2. Perfectionism in children 3. Genetic engineering 4. Prejudice 5. Millionaires 6. Envy 7. Ostracism 8. Women lawyers

9. Pariahs 10. Posthumanism 11. Hard science fiction 12. Science fiction

LC 92025070

The product of an experiment in genetic manipulation, superintelligent Leisha Camden is forced to live a life apart from most "ordinary" people and seeks the companionship of other superhumans.

"This book is an intellectual roller-coaster ride, supplying no simple conclusions about right and wrong, and racing along with its brisk prose, stimulating ideas, and a variety of challenging characters." School Library Journal.

Kress, Nancy
If tomorrow comes / Nancy Kress. Tor, 2018. 288 p. Yesterday's kin

ISBN 9780765390325

1. United Nations 2. Aliens 3. Scientists 4. Epidemics 5. Human/alien encounters 6. Disasters -- Prevention 7. Life on other planets 8. High technology 9. Space flight 10. Plague 11. Hard science fiction 12. Science fiction

Ten years after the Aliens left Earth, humanity succeeds in building a ship, Friendship, to follow them home to Kindred. Aboard are a crew of scientists, diplomats, and a squad of Rangers to protect them. But when the Friendship arrives, they find nothing they expected. No interplanetary culture, no industrial base?and no cure for the spore disease.

Kress, Nancy
Tomorrow's kin / Nancy Kress. Tor, 2017. 349 p. Yesterday's kin

ISBN 9780765390295

1. United Nations 2. Aliens 3. Scientists 4. Xenophobia 5. Human/alien encounters 6. Disasters -- Prevention 7. Conflict in families 8. High technology 9. Social conflict 10. Isolationism 11. Geneticists 12. New York City 13. Hard science fiction 14. Science fiction

Tomorrow's Kin is an expansion of the author's 2014 novella Yesterday's Kin.

Follows the arrival of alien embassies who meet with the United Nations amid human fear and speculation before obscure scientist Dr. Marianne Jenner is secretly invited to visit the aliens and prevent an imminent disaster.

Kristen Omarsdottir, 1962-
Children in Reindeer Woods / Kristin Omarsdottir ; translated from the Icelandic by Lytton Smith. Open Letter, 2012, c2004. 198 p.

ISBN 9781934824351

1. Soldiers 2. Violence in men 3. Eleven-year-old girls 4. War 5. Orphans 6. Murder 7. Farmers 8. Life on other planets 9. Lifestyle change 10. Girls 11. Literary fiction 12. Translations -- Icelandic to English

LC 2011043995

Originally published as Her: Iceland : Salka, 2004.

When paratroopers invade Children in Reindeer Woods, a "temporary home for children," and kill everyone except eleven-year-old Billie before turning on one another, the last soldier decides to adopt the peaceful lifestyle of a farmer with young Billie.

Krivak, Andrew
The **bear** / Andrew Krivak. Bellevue Literary Press, 2020. 221 p.

ISBN 9781942658702

1. Post-apocalypse 2. Wilderness survival 3. Fathers and daughters 4. Human/animal relationships 5. Voyages and travels 6. Bears 7. Solitude 8. Fathers -- Death 9. Anonymous persons 10. Burial 11.

Storytelling 12. Mountains 13. Apocalyptic fiction 14. Coming-of-age stories

LC 2018061687

Living close to the land in an Eden-like post-civilization world, a girl learns the secrets of hunting and star navigation before finding herself in an unknown landscape, where a bear imparts powerful natural-world lessons.

"Poignant but not tragic, this end-of-civilization story shows that there's no loneliness in this world when we are one with nature." Library Journal.

Krivak, Andrew
* The **signal** flame : a novel / Andrew Krivak. Scribner, 2017. 288 p. Sojourn novels (Andrew Krivak)

ISBN 9781501126376

1. 20th century 2. Small towns 3. Grief 4. Families 5. Soldiers 6. Veterans 7. War and society 8. Loss (Psychology) 9. World War I 10. World War II 11. Vietnam War, 1961-1975 12. Mountain life 13. Widows 14. Family relationships 15. Pennsylvania 16. Family sagas 17. Historical fiction

The stunning second novel from National Book Award finalist Andrew Krivak--a heartbreaking, captivating story about a family awaiting the return of their youngest son from the Vietnam War. In a small town in Pennsylvania's Endless Mountains Hannah and her son Bo mourn the loss of the family patriarch, Jozef Vinich. They were three generations under one roof. Three generations, but only one branch of a scraggy tree; they are a war-haunted family in a war-torn century. Having survived the trenches of World War I as an Austro-Hungarian conscript, Vinich journeyed to America and built a life for his family. His daughter married the Hungarian-born Bexhet Konar, who enlisted to fight with the Americans in the Second World War but brought disgrace on the family when he was imprisoned for desertion. He returned home to Pennsylvania a hollow man, only to be killed in a hunting accident on the family's land. Finally, in 1971, Hannah's prodigal younger son, Sam, was reported MIA in Vietnam. And so there is only Bo, a quiet man full of conviction, a proud work ethic, and a firstborn's sense of duty. He is left to grieve but also to hope for reunion, to create a new life, to embrace the land and work its soil through the seasons. The Signal Flame is a stirring novel about generations of men and women and the events that define them, brothers who take different paths, the old European values yielding to new world ways, and the convalescence of memory and war. Beginning shortly after Easter in 1972 and ending on Christmas Eve this ambitious novel beautifully evokes ordinary time, a period of living and working while waiting and watching and expecting. The Signal Flame is gorgeously written, honoring the cycles of earth and body, humming with blood and passion, and it confirms Andrew Krivak as a writer of extraordinary vision and power. Provided by publisher.

"This family saga is quiet at its core, but its Krivak's gorgeous prose and deep grasp of the relationship between longing and loss that make the book such a stunner." Publishers Weekly.

Krivak, Andrew
The **sojourn** / Andrew Krivak. Bellevue Literary Press, 2011. 192 p. Sojourn novels (Andrew Krivak)

1. First World War era (1914-1918) 2. World War I 3. Soldiers -- Austria 4. Trench warfare 5. Growing up 6. Sharpshooters 7. Austria 8. Historical fiction

LC 2010053027

National Book Award for Fiction finalist, 2011

Uprooted from a nineteenth century mining town in Colorado by a shocking family tragedy, young Jozef Vinich returns with his father to an impoverished shepherd's life in rural Austria-Hungary. When war comes, Jozef is sent as a sharpshooter to the southern front, where he must survive the killing trenches, a perilous trek across the frozen Italian Alps, and capture by a victorious enemy.

"Krivak dexterously exposes the stark, brutal realities of trench warfare, the horror of a POW camp, and the months of violent bloodshed that stole the boys' innocence. Once home from war, the author's depiction of Jozef's arduous return to life, love, and family is charged with emotion and longing." Publishers Weekly.

Kroese, Robert

The **last** iota / Robert Kroese. Thomas Dunne Books, 2017. 302 p. Erasmus Keane novels

ISBN 9781250088468

1. 21st century 2. Private investigators 3. Lost articles 4. Near future 5. Eccentrics and eccentricities 6. Film industry and trade executives 7. Missing women 8. Women murder victims 9. Money 10. Conspiracies 11. City life 12. Los Angeles, California 13. Science fiction mysteries

LC 2017001074

Hired by a movie mogul to find rare coins lost somewhere in the Disincorporated Zone of LA, eccentric private investigator Erasmus Keane struggles to unravel the mystery while his partner, Blake, is framed for murder, which plunges them both into a conspiracy that reaches the highest levels of government.

Krueger, Paul, 1989-

Steel crow saga / Paul Krueger. Del Rey, 2019. 516 p.

ISBN 9780593128220

1. Princes 2. Imaginary empires 3. Magic 4. Women soldiers 5. Thieves 6. Princesses 7. Secret identity 8. Fantasy fiction 9. Asian-influenced fantasy

LC 2019014522

A band of rogues and royals that should be enemies join forces for a common purpose: to defeat an unstoppable killer who defies the laws of magic in a battle that forges bonds of friendship and love that will change their lives and the world.

"With a well-realized world and strong characters, many of whom are queer, Krueger's novel will feel as fast-paced and exciting as its animated influences and leave the reader longing for more." Booklist.

Krueger, William Kent

Ordinary grace : a novel / William Kent Krueger. Atria Books, 2013. 320 p.

ISBN 9781451645828

1. 1960s 2. Family secrets 3. Murder 4. Grief 5. Extramarital affairs 6. Betrayal 7. Methodism 8. Redemption 9. Teenage boys 10. Coming-of-age stories 11. Psychological fiction 12. Mysteries

LC 2012034884

Anthony Award for Best Novel, 2014.

Edgar Allan Poe Award for Best Novel, 2014.

Macavity Award for Best Mystery Novel, 2014.

Looking back at a tragic event that occurred during his 13th year, a man explores how a complicated web of secrets, adultery and betrayal shattered his Methodist family and their small 1961 Minnesota community.

Krueger, William Kent

This tender land : a novel / William Kent Krueger. Atria Books, 2019. 464 p.

ISBN 9781476749297

1. Depression era (1929-1941) 2. 1930s 3. Orphans 4. Voyages and travels 5. Native American children 6. Separated friends, relatives, etc 7. Schools 8. Child abuse 9. Indians of North America 10. River travel 11. Belonging 12. Home (Concept) 13. Good and evil 14.

Minnesota 15. Historical fiction 16. Adventure stories 17. Coming-of-age stories

LC 2019015067

Fleeing the Depression-era school for Native American children who have been taken from their parents, four orphans share a summer marked by struggling farmers, faith healers and lost souls.

Krueger, William Kent

Vermilion drift / William Kent Krueger. Simon & Schuster, 2010. 336 p. Cork O'connor mysteries

ISBN 9781439153840

1. Private investigators 2. Secrets 3. Murder 4. Cold cases (Criminal investigation) 5. Nightmares 6. Security consultants 7. Former sheriffs 8. Former police 9. Multiracial men 10. Small town life 11. Ojibwa Indians 12. Indians of North America 13. Minnesota 14. Mysteries

Assigned to protect security at a mine where protestors are trying to prevent the storage of nuclear waste, Cork O'Connor discovers the bodies of five long-missing people and a recently murdered sixth victim who was killed with Cork's own gun.

Kuang, R. F. (Rebecca F.)

* The **dragon** republic / R. F. Kuang. Harper Voyager, 2019. 560 p. Poppy war

ISBN 9780062662637

1. 20th century 2. Shamans 3. Opium addiction 4. Gods and goddesses 5. Rulers 6. Betrayal 7. Revenge 8. War -- Psychological aspects 9. Imaginary wars and battles 10. Women warriors 11. Assassination plots 12. Martial arts 13. Social classes 14. Racism 15. Military occupation 16. Atrocities 17. Asian-influenced fantasy 18. Historical fantasy 19. Military fantasy

A sequel to The Poppy War finds shaman-warrior Rin haunted by personal demons including the choice she made to save her people, an atrocity that compels a precarious alliance to defeat the Empress.

Kuang, R. F. (Rebecca F.)

The **poppy** war / R.F. Kuang. Harper Voyager, 2018. 530 p. Poppy war

ISBN 9780062662569

1. 20th century 2. Orphans 3. Apprentices 4. Shamans 5. Gods and goddesses 6. Martial arts 7. Social classes 8. Weapons 9. Military education 10. Racism 11. Military occupation 12. Revenge 13. War 14. Atrocities 15. Asian-influenced fantasy 16. Historical fantasy 17. Military fantasy

RUSA Reading List Short List, 2019.

An epic historical military fantasy, inspired by the violent history of China's 20th century, follows the efforts of an unexpected, dark-skinned war orphan to obtain an education at Nikan's most elite military school in spite of prejudice and the challenges of her lethal shaman skills, which raise her awareness about the existence of gods and the imminence of war.

Kubica, Mary

* The **other** Mrs. / Mary Kubica. Park Row, 2020. 384 p.

ISBN 9780778369110

1. Inheritance and succession 2. Coastal towns 3. Neighbors 4. Secrets 5. Moving to a new city 6. Suicide 7. Sisters -- Death 8. Murder victims 9. Murder suspects 10. Suspicion 11. Orphans 12. Child custody 13. Families 14. Extramarital affairs 15. Married people 16. Maine 17. Psychological suspense

Unnerved by her husband's inheritance of a decrepit coastal property and the presence of a disturbed relative, community newcomer Sadie uncovers harrowing facts about her family's possible role in a neighbor's murder.

"What is satisfying and most effective is the oppressive sense of unease that permeates this intense psychological suspense drama. For fans of A.J. Finn and Gillian Flynn." Library Journal.

Kubica, Mary

Pretty baby / Mary Kubica. MIRA Books, 2015 380 p.
ISBN 9780778317708

1. Married women 2. Teenage mothers 3. Homeless persons 4. Strangers 5. Dishonesty 6. Secrets 7. Infants 8. Kindness in women 9. Middle-class families 10. Chicago, Illinois 11. Psychological suspense

The charitable Heidi Wood horrifies her husband and daughter by inviting an apparently homeless teenager and her infant to take refuge in their home, a situation that quickly devolves as details from the girl's past begin to surface.

"Kubica's debut novel, The Good Girl (2014), also employed multiple points of view and timelines, but Kubica serves up a much more cohesive tale this time aroundthe story is almost hypnotic and anything but predictable. The writing is compelling, but Kubica's strong point is being able to juggle a complicated plot and holding the reader's interest without dropping any of the balls she has in the air. This book will give insomniacs a compelling reason to sit up all night." Kirkus.

Kundera, Milan

* Immortality / Milan Kundera ; translated from the Czech by Peter Kussi. Grove Weidenfeld, 1991. 345 p.
ISBN 9780802111111

1. Love 2. Sexuality 3. Immortality 4. Identity (Psychology) 5. Men/women relations 6. Philosophy 7. Literary fiction 8. Translations -- Czech to English
LC 90028628

Through the actions of three characters--Agnes, her husband, and her sister--and others in contemporary France and Weimar Germany, the author reflects on the image of the individual, the Western cult of sentiment, and the meaning of love.

"Immortality swings easily, almost imperceptibly, from narrative to rumination and back again, Time.

Kundera, Milan

* The unbearable lightness of being / Milan Kundera ; translated from the Czech by Michael Henry Heim. Harper & Row, 1984. 314 p.
ISBN 9780060152581

1. 1960s 2. Men/women relations 3. Totalitarianism -- Czechoslovakia 4. Sexuality 5. Jealousy 6. Czechoslovakia -- History -- Soviet invasion, 1968 7. Literary fiction 8. Translations -- Czech to English
LC 83048363

After the 1968 Soviet invasion of Czechoslovakia, a married surgeon, Tomas, becomes a window washer while trying to reconcile himself to decisions that he and his wife must make about their relationship.

Kunzru, Hari, 1969-

* Gods without men / Hari Kunzru. Alfred A. Knopf, 2012. 352 p.
ISBN 9780307957115

1. 2000s (Decade) 2. Children with autism 3. Missing children 4. Human/alien encounters 5. Vacations 6. Former cult members 7. Refugees, Iraqi 8. Eccentrics and eccentricities 9. Deserts 10. Interracial marriage 11. Husband and wife 12. Marital conflict 13. Former rock musicians 14. Mojave Desert 15. Literary fiction

Publicly shattered when their autistic son disappears during a family vacation to the California desert, Jaz and Lisa Matharu organize searches from a remote town near the Pinnacles rock formation and bond with a sequence of eccentric locals including a debauched British rock star, a former extraterrestrial cult member and a teenage Iraqi refugee.

Kunzru, Hari, 1969-

The **impressionist** / Hari Kunzru. Dutton, 2002. 383 p.
ISBN 052594642X

1. East Indians 2. Impostors 3. Multiracial persons 4. Illegitimacy 5. Identity (Psychology) 6. Passing (Identity) 7. East Indians in England 8. Deception 9. Race relations 10. England 11. India 12. Psychological fiction 13. Historical fiction 14. Coming-of-age stories 15. Literary fiction
LC 2001047137

Betty Trask Award, 2002.
Somerset Maugham Award, 2003.

At the age of fifteen, Pran Nath Razdan is thrown out onto the streets when the truth of his parentage is revealed, forcing him to reinvent himself over and over to survive as he journeys from Victorian India to Edwardian London.

"This novel includes a multitude of richly imagined characters. A bold, unfashionably omniscient voice narrates the story as it tackles such subjects as race, class, colonialism, and the roots of personal identity." The New Leader.

Kunzru, Hari, 1969-

My revolutions / Hari Kunzru. Dutton, 2008. 304 p.
ISBN 9780525949329

1. 1970s 2. Radicalism 3. Terrorists 4. Impostors 5. Middle-aged men 6. Former lovers 7. Idealism 8. Protests, demonstrations, vigils, etc 9. Identity (Psychology) 10. England 11. Psychological fiction 12. Literary fiction
LC 2007039459

Having briefly worked as a terrorist to protest the Vietnam War, Chris Carver hides his past from his suburban family and friends before a ghost from his past forces him to flee, a circumstance during which he remembers his isolated youth and violent relationships with two fellow radicals.

"This novel is, as Virginia Woolf said of George Eliot's Middlemarch, a book for grownup people (although that shouldn't imply it is at all ponderous or worthy) and it is very much a book about the process of growing up. My Revolutions is impassioned, intelligent and profoundly serious literature." Sydney Morning Herald.

Kunzru, Hari, 1969-

White tears / Hari Kunzru. Alfred A. Knopf, 2017. 288 p.
ISBN 9780451493699

1. Hoaxes 2. Blues music 3. Cultural appropriation 4. Racism 5. Rich families 6. Record collecting 7. Institutional racism 8. Murder investigation 9. Informal sector (Economics) 10. African American blues musicians 11. Sound recording executives and producers 12. Mississippi -- Race relations 13. New York City 14. Literary fiction 15. Coming-of-age stories
LC 2016011904

"This is a Borzoi book."
Kirkus Prize for Fiction finalist, 2017.
Longlisted for the Andrew Carnegie Medal for Excellence in Fiction, 2018.
Shortlisted for the James Tait Black Memorial Prize for Fiction, 2017

Two ambitious young musicians, one shy, the other a glamorous heir, are drawn into the dark underworld of blues-record collecting while navigating the ghosts of a repressive past and the fallout of a scam involving one's claim that a viral video of an unknown singer is long-lost recording of a famous blues musician.

"Record collecting turns dangerous in a smart, time-bending tale about cultural appropriation." Kirkus.

Kurland, Lynn

Star of the morning / Lynn Kurland. Berkley Sensation, 2006. 336 p. Nine kingdoms

ISBN 0425212122

1. Women warriors 2. Magic 3. Men/women relations 4. Wizards 5. Nobility 6. Rulers 7. Strangers 8. Quests 9. Magic swords 10. Fantasy romances

LC 2006025855

As the dark forces and evil magic of the black mage threaten to engulf the kingdom of Neroche, the fate of the Nine Kingdoms lies in the hands of the woman destined to wield one of two magical swords in the possession of the king of Neroche.

Kushner, Rachel

The **Mars** room / Rachel Kushner. Scribner, 2018, c2018. 338 p.

ISBN 9781476756554

1. 2000s (Decade) 2. Single mothers 3. Women prisoners 4. Prisons 5. Women murderers 6. Prison sentences 7. Stalking 8. Stripteasers 9. Drug abusers 10. Judicial system 11. Life imprisonment 12. Mothers and sons 13. San Francisco, California 14. California 15. Literary fiction

LC 2017061764

ALA Notable Book, 2019.

National Book Critics Circle Award for Fiction finalist, 2018

Shortlisted for the Man Booker Prize, 2018.

A woman begins serving two life sentences at Stanville Women's Correctional Facility deep in 2003 California's Central Valley, reflecting on the San Francisco of her youth and her relationship with her young son while navigating the harsh realities of a bare-essentials life of casual violence at the hands of the guards and her fellow inmates.

"This is a gorgeously eviscerating novel of incarceration writ large, of people trapped in the wrong body, the wrong family, poverty, addiction, and prejudice. The very land is chained and exploited. Rooted in deeply inquisitive thinking and executed with artistry and edgy wit, Kushner's dramatic and disquieting novel investigates with verve and compassion societal strictures and how very difficult it is to understand each other and to be truly free." Booklist.

Kutsukake, Lynne

* The **translation** of love : a novel / Lynne Kutsukake. Doubleday, 2016. 318 p.

ISBN 9780385540674

1. 1940s 2. Deportation 3. Japanese Canadians 4. Letter writing 5. Culture conflict 6. Female friendship 7. Military occupation 8. Translating and interpreting 9. Political letter-writing 10. Separated sisters 11. Sisters 12. Tokyo, Japan -- History -- 20th century 13. Japan -- History -- 20th century 14. Historical fiction

Canada-Japan Literary Awards, 2016

Deported back to post-war Japan with her father after their release from a Canadian internment camp, thirteen-year-old Aya Shimamura struggles at school, where she is bullied for being foreign, before one of her tormentors asks for Aya's help in finding her missing sister.

"A vivid delight chronicling a fascinating--and little-discussed--chapter in world history." Kirkus.

Kuznetsov, Anatolii Petrovich, 1929-1979

Babi Yar : a document in the form of a novel / A. Anatoli (Kuznetsov). Translated by David Floyd. Farrar, Straus and Giroux, 1970. 477 p.

ISBN 0374107610

1. 1940s 2. Babi Yar Massacre, 1941 3. Atrocities 4. Soviet Union -- History -- German occupation, 1941-1944 5. Historical fiction 6. Translations -- Russian to English

LC 70125154

The author documents the German massacre from 1941 to 1943 of two million people, including 50,000 Jews, outside Kiev.

Kwan, Kevin

China rich girlfriend / Kevin Kwan. Knopf Doubleday, 2015 400 p. Rich novels (Kevin Kwan)

ISBN 9780385539081

1. Heirs and heiresses 2. Weddings 3. Birthfathers 4. Father-separated families 5. Rich people 6. Men/women relations 7. Engaged persons 8. China 9. Mainstream fiction

Sequel to Crazy rich Asians.

Feeling incomplete because her unknown birth father cannot walk her down the aisle, Rachel Chu, on the brink of marrying one of Asia's richest bachelors, is brought into the elite circles of Shanghai by a shocking revelation.

"Lovers of clothes, cuisine, and cars will find themselves at home in Kwan's second smart and snarky send-up of the Chinese jet set." Booklist.

Kwan, Kevin

Crazy rich Asians / Kevin Kwan. Doubleday, 2013. 416 p. Rich novels (Kevin Kwan)

ISBN 9780385536974

1. Engaged persons 2. Americans in Singapore 3. Rich families 4. Social conflict 5. Chinese American women 6. Singapore 7. Mainstream fiction

LC 2012032395

Envisioning a summer vacation in the humble Singapore home of a boy she hopes to marry, Chinese American Rachel Chu is unexpectedly introduced to a rich and scheming clan that strongly opposes their son's relationship with an American girl.

Kwan, Kevin

Rich people problems / Kevin Kwan. Doubleday, 2017. 384 p. Rich novels (Kevin Kwan)

ISBN 9780385542234

1. Rich people 2. Inheritance and succession 3. Families 4. Divorced persons 5. Family relationships 6. Men/women relations 7. Singapore 8. Manila, Philippines 9. Mainstream fiction

Rushing to the deathbed of his grandmother, Nicholas Young encounters a massive clan eager to claim a share of the family fortune, win the hearts of loved ones, destroy each other's reputations and outmaneuver professional rivals.

"The fairy tale/soap opera/lux-a-thon that began with Crazy Rich Asians (2013) and China Rich Girlfriend (2015) comes to a fittingly majestic and hilarious end in Kwan's third novel." Kirkus.

Kwok, Jean

Searching for Sylvie Lee / Jean Kwok. William Morrow & Co., 2019. 304 p.

ISBN 9780062834300

1. Missing persons 2. Sisters 3. Children of immigrants 4. Family secrets 5. Immigrants, Chinese 6. Belonging 7. Identity (Psychology)

8. Chinese in the United States 9. Cultural differences 10. Racism 11. Families 12. New York City 13. Netherlands 14. Literary fiction

A poignant and suspenseful drama that untangles the complicated ties binding three women--two sisters and their mother--in one Chinese immigrant family and explores what happens when the eldest daughter disappears, and a series of family secrets emerge, from the New York Times bestselling author of Girl in Translation.

L

L'Amour, Louis, 1908-1988

*Bendigo Shafter / Louis L'Amour. Bantam, 1983, c1979. 323 p.

ISBN 9780553264463

1. Frontier and pioneer life -- The West (United States) 2. Brothers -- The West (United States) 3. Eighteen-year-old men 4. Widows 5. The West (United States) -- History -- 19th century 6. Wyoming -- History -- 19th century 7. Westerns

Bendigo Shafter and his followers build a town in the heart of Wyoming Indian country, where the crack-shot leader falls in love with two women: the dignified Widow Macken and the beautiful Ninon.

L'Amour, Louis, 1908-1988

The **Californios** / Louis L'Amour. Bantam Books, 1996, c1974. 188 p.

ISBN 9780553253221

1. Widows 2. Ranches -- California 3. Gold prospecting 4. Native American mystics 5. Brothers 6. California -- History -- To 1846 7. The West (United States) -- History -- 19th century 8. Westerns

The Mulkerin Brothers, in a desperate attempt to settle the debt on their ranch, follow an Indian mystic to California in search of gold, with a gang of greedy gunfighters riding hard on their heels.

"An expert blend of the fascinating settling of California in the 1840's; strong, self-reliant characters . . . and a plot of evil doings but triumphant good. The theme of mysticism and the legends of The Old Ones is what lifts this book above the typical western. Intriguing even for those who aren't westerns fans." Library Journal.

L'Amour, Louis, 1908-1988

End of the drive / Louis L'Amour. Bantam Books, 1997. 257 p. The Sacketts

ISBN 9780553578980

1. Frontier and pioneer life -- The West (United States) 2. The West (United States) -- History -- 19th century 3. Westerns

Comprised of seven unforgettable, never-before-published tales, together with one complete novella.

"The courting of Griselda" is part of L'Amour's Sacketts series. This story takes place between The Daybreakers and Lando.

L'Amour, Louis, 1908-1988

The **last** of the breed / Louis L'Amour. Bantam Books, 1986. 358 p.

ISBN 9780553051629

1. Test pilots 2. Native American men 3. Airplane accidents 4. Military secrets 5. Wilderness survival -- Siberia 6. Native American prisoners -- Soviet Union 7. Escapes 8. Siberia 9. Adventure stories

LC 86003622

Includes end-paper maps.

When his experimental aircraft is forced down over the Bering Sea by Russians, U.S. Air Force Major Joseph "Joe Mack" Makatozi must seek his safety in the uncharted wilds of Siberia, pursued by Colonel Zamatev of the GRU and by a Yakut tracker

"Joe Mack is a classic American hero, thrown back into the wilderness and forced to rely on his wits and his ancestral skills to survive the deadly cold and elude his Soviet pursuers, including his nemesis, a Siberian tracker. L'Amour brings the same colorful realism to this sweeping adventure that has made his Westerns so beloved." Publishers Weekly.

L'Amour, Louis, 1908-1988

May there be a road / Louis L'Amour. Bantam Books, 2001. 276 p.

ISBN 0553802135

1. Americans in Mexico 2. Boxers (Sports) 3. Detectives 4. Escapes -- Tibet 5. Pioneer men 6. Freighters -- Brazil 7. Gamblers 8. Orphans 9. Ship captains -- Brazil 10. Small town life 11. World War II 12. Brazil 13. Mexico 14. Tibet 15. Adventure stories 16. Short stories 17. Westerns

LC 2001018127

Ten short adventure stories range from the intrigue of South America during World War II to tales of the American frontier, in a collection of works that appeared in short story magazines during the 1950s and were never before published in book format.

L'Amour, Louis, 1908-1988

To the far blue mountains / Louis L'Amour. Bantam Books, 1977, c1976. 287 p. The Sacketts

ISBN 9780553027570

1. Colonial America (1600-1775) 2. 17th century 3. Frontier and pioneer life -- Virginia 4. British in the United States 5. Fugitives 6. Virginia -- History -- Colonial period, 1600-1775 7. Blue Ridge Mountains 8. Great Britain -- History -- Elizabeth I, 1558-1603 9. Westerns 10. Family sagas

LC 75029190

Wanted by the law, Barnabas Sackett leaves England to seek his fortune in the New World and heads west with his wife Abigail and a few friends to begin a new life in the wilderness.

"This tale is much more leisurely and nonviolent than the usual L'Amour story, but it has its share of suspense and gives us a different kind of look at colonial America." Publishers Weekly.

L'Engle, Madeleine

Certain women / Madeleine L'Engle. Farrar, Straus and Giroux, 1992. 351 p.

ISBN 9780374120252

1. David,, King of Israel 2. Fathers and daughters 3. Men with terminal illnesses 4. Actors and actresses 5. Death 6. Families 7. Divorce 8. Family storytelling 9. Family sagas 10. Bible novels 11. Parallel narratives

LC 91034048

As David Wheaton's enormous family gathers around his deathbed, Emma Wheaton, his actress daughter, compares her father's life with a play about the Old Testament King David written by her estranged husband.

"L'Engle describes complex truths very simply. . . . Because she also details the emotional cost of discovering and accepting such concepts, many readers will find these observations memorable but never simplistic." Library Journal.

LaPlante, Alice, 1958-

A **circle** of wives / Alice LaPlante. Atlantic Monthly Press, 2014. 375 p.

ISBN 9780802122346

1. Women detectives 2. Married women 3. Bigamy 4. Secrets 5.

Plastic surgeons 6. Murder 7. Murder investigation 8. Palo Alto, California 9. Mysteries

Small-town detective Samantha Adams investigates the murder of a well-known and well-liked plastic surgeon who turns out to have been a closeted polygamist when his three wives show up at his funeral.

"The narration alternates from chapter to chapter and from woman to woman. An investigation of a crime becomes an exploration of the choices these women made and the resulting impact." Library Journal.

LaPlante, Alice, 1958-

Turn of mind / Alice Laplante. Atlantic Monthly Press, 2011. 320 p.

ISBN 9780802119773

1. Friends' death 2. Memory disorders 3. People with Alzheimer's disease 4. Murder 5. Dementia 6. People with dementia 7. Alzheimer's disease 8. Women murder victims 9. Women with memory disorders 10. Murder investigation 11. Senior women 12. Aging 13. Seniors 14. Memory 15. Mysteries 16. Psychological suspense

Implicated in the murder of her best friend, Jennifer White, a brilliant retired surgeon with dementia, struggles with fractured memories of their complex relationship and wonders if she actually committed the crime.

"LaPlante has a gift for rhythm, crafting rat-a-tat passages that are their own pleasures." Entertainment Weekly.

LaValle, Victor D., 1972-

The **changeling** : a novel / Victor LaValle. Spiegel & Grau, 2017 431 p.

ISBN 9780812995947

1. Antiquarian booksellers 2. New parents 3. Fatherhood 4. Infanticide 5. Parenthood 6. Family violence 7. Husband and wife 8. Life change events 9. African Americans 10. Children of single parents 11. New York City 12. Queens, New York City 13. Contemporary fantasy 14. Literary fiction 15. Horror

LC 2016049361

Locus Award for Dark Fantasy-Horror Novel, 2018.

World Fantasy Award, 2018.

Resolving to commit to marriage and parenthood unlike the father who abandoned him, Apollo Kagwa, who suffers from bizarre dreams, is shocked when his wife commits an act of astounding violence before disappearing, compelling Apollo's odyssey through a world he barely understands.

"The Changeling is an example of how good urban horror fantasy can be, a layered story that joins themes important to modern readers with the mystery and wonder of the darker side of fantasy. LaValle's story is reminiscent of Clive Barker's Imajica (1991) and the way China Mieville marries the fantastical with the contemporary." Booklist.

LaValle, Victor D., 1972-

The **devil** in silver : a novel / Victor LaValle. Spiegel & Grau, 2012. 288 p.

ISBN 9781400069866

1. Psychiatric hospital patients 2. Psychiatric hospitals 3. Monsters 4. False imprisonment 5. People with schizophrenia 6. People with bipolar disorder 7. Obsessive-compulsive disorder in men 8. New York City 9. Queens, New York City 10. Horror 11. Psychological suspense 12. African American fiction

LC 2011034970

Landing in a budget-strapped mental institution after being accused of a crime he does not remember, Pepper is assaulted by a monstrous creature that has been attacking patients but that the hospital staff does not believe exists.

Läckberg, Camilla, 1974-

The **hidden** child / Camilla Läckberg ; translated from the Swedish by Steven T. Murray. HarperCollins, 2011. 400 p. Patrik Hedstrom mysteries

ISBN 9780007419470

1. Family secrets 2. Nazis 3. Murder 4. Women authors 5. New mothers 6. Diary writing 7. Police 8. Families 9. Suspicion 10. Detectives 11. Small towns 12. Sweden 13. Fjällbacka, Sweden 14. Police procedurals 15. Scandinavian crime fiction 16. Mysteries 17. Translations -- Swedish to English

Translated from the Swedish.

First published in Swedish as Tyskungen.

Living in her childhood home in the village of Fj?llbacka, Sweden, it's only natural that crime writer Erica Falck would come across old family possessions. But she never expected to find a Nazi medal wrapped in blood-stained baby clothing among her late mother's belongings. Nor did she expect the historian to whom she showed the medal -- a friend of her mother during World War II -- to be murdered weeks after she talked to him. Though her police detective husband Patrik is on paternity leave caring for their one-year-old daughter while Erica works, he becomes involved in the official murder case, and together the new parents search for answers among Erica's mother's wartime diaries. -- Description by Dawn Towery.

"Though the flashbacks to the 1940s can be distracting, this secondary plot is just as intriguing as the main story line. Though dealing with the serious subjects of extremist groups and prisoners of war, the novel has its humorous moments." Library Journal.

Läckberg, Camilla, 1974-

The **ice** princess / Camilla Läckberg ; translated from the Swedish by Steven T. Murray. Free Press, 2011, c2008. 393 p. Patrik Hedstrom mysteries

ISBN 9781605980928

1. Women murder victims 2. Women authors 3. Obsessive-compulsive disorder 4. Police 5. Detectives 6. Murder 7. Winter 8. Secrets 9. Small towns 10. Sweden 11. Fjallbacka, Sweden 12. Police procedurals 13. Scandinavian crime fiction 14. Mysteries 15. Translations -- Swedish to English

Translated from the Swedish.

Originally published in English: London : HarperCollins, 2009.

After she returns to her hometown to learn that her friend, Alex, was found in an ice-cold bath with her wrists slashed, biographer Erica Falck researches her friend's past in hopes of writing a book and joins forces with Detective Patrik Hedstrom, who has his own suspicions about the case.

Läckberg, Camilla, 1974-

The **lost** boy / Camilla Läckberg ; translated from the Swedish by Tiina Nunnally HarperCollins, 2013, c2009 497 p. Patrik Hedstrom mysteries

ISBN 9780007473212

1. Businesspeople 2. Lovers 3. Secrets 4. Murder 5. Detectives 6. Sweden 7. Scandinavian crime fiction 8. Mysteries 9. Translations -- Swedish to English

First published in Swedish as Fyrvaktaren in 2009.

"Läckberg weaves fine lines through this multilayered thriller, connecting a ghostly historic backstory, tragic portrayals of domestic violence, shady business dealings, and series regulars various personal dramas." Booklist.

Läckberg, Camilla, 1974-

The **preacher** / Camilla Läckberg ; translated from the Swedish by Steven T. Murray. Free Press, 2011, c2009. 422 p. Patrik Hedstrom mysteries

ISBN 9781605981734

1. Women murder victims 2. Missing girls 3. Murder 4. Police 5. Detectives 6. Religious fanaticism 7. Secrets 8. Small towns 9. Sweden 10. Fjällbacka, Sweden 11. Police procedurals 12. Scandinavian crime fiction 13. Mysteries 14. Translations -- Swedish to English

LC 2011023707

Translated from the Swedish.

Originally published in English: London : HarperCollins, 2009.

In a sequel to Ice Princess, the discovery of two murder victims who were killed 20 years earlier is complicated by the body of a third, recent victim at the same location, a case that compels detective Patrik Hedstrom to focus his investigation on a feuding clan of misfits, religious fanatics and criminals.

"This mystery featuring detective Patrik Hedstrom is again set in the small Swedish village of Fjällbacka. The story opens with the discovery of the skeletons of two women who disappeared more than 20 years ago, along with a fresh victim killed in a similar manner. In researching the decades-old murders, the police are led to the dysfunctional family of a religious fanatic, Ephraim Hult, who was known as a preacher and healer. Hedstrom must find the key to connect the old crimes with the new. In addition, Patrik's girlfriend, Erica, is about to give birth, and he must come to terms with his feelings about becoming a father. Erica, in turn, is deeply troubled by her sister's increasingly serious marriage problems. Läckberg's many-layered story features plot twists and turns galore." Library Journal.

Läckberg, Camilla, 1974-

The **stonecutter** / Camilla Läckberg ; translated from the Swedish by Steven T. Murray. Pegasus Books, 2011, c2010. 480 p. Patrik Hedstrom mysteries

ISBN 9781605983301

1. Girl drowning victims 2. Murder 3. Family feuds 4. Girl murder victims 5. Police 6. Detectives 7. Secrets 8. Child pornography 9. Small towns 10. Sweden 11. Fjällbacka, Sweden 12. Police procedurals 13. Scandinavian crime fiction 14. Mysteries 15. Translations -- Swedish to English

Translated from the Swedish.

This translation originally published: London : HarperCollins, 2010.

First published in Swedish as Stenhuggaren.

Originally published in English: London : HarperCollins, 2010.

When a young girl's body is pulled out of the harbor in the small Swedish resort town of Fjällbacka, Det. Patrik Hedstrom becomes the lead investigator as he struggles with lazy and inept colleagues and an even remoter-than-usual boss. It's his grim task to discover who could be behind the murder of the child both he and his partner Erica knew well.

"A perfectly plotted and paced mystery bolstered by strong, realistic characters." Booklist.

Lackey, Mercedes

The **fairy** godmother / Mercedes Lackey. Luna, 2004. 417 p. Five hundred kingdoms

ISBN 9780373802029

1. Courtship 2. Fairy godmothers 3. Twenties (Age) 4. Stepmothers 5. Stepsisters 6. Debtor and creditor 7. Women apprentices 8. Magic 9. Young women 10. Wizards 11. Princes 12. Quests 13. Anger 14. Marriage 15. Imaginary kingdoms 16. Fantasy romances

LC BL2003016748

In the mystical realm of the Five Hundred Kingdoms, the newest Fairy Godmother tries to help three impossible princes find the women of their dreams, while fending off an evil sorcerer who is determined to destroy her kingdom.

"A spirited, resourceful, though somewhat impulsive heroine, a prince who needs to learn a lesson in manners, humility, and compassion, and a host of magical creatures--including some delightful house elves and besotted unicorns--result in a lively, humorous fantasy romance." Library Journal.

Lafferty, Mur

Ghost train to New Orleans / Mur Lafferty. Orbit, 2014. 342 p. Shambling Guides

ISBN 9780316221146

1. City dwellers 2. Vampires 3. Women editors 4. Incubi 5. Publishers and publishing 6. Supernatural 7. Young women 8. Social conflict 9. Men/women relations 10. Cities and towns 11. Gods and goddesses 12. New Orleans, Louisiana 13. Urban fantasy

LC 2013030554

Sequel to: The Shambling Guide to New York City

In this exciting sequel to the Shambling Guide to New York City, Zoë Norris, who writes travel guides for the undead, arrives in the Big Easy where she, trying to save her boyfriend from zombism, deals with jealous supernatural colleagues and a dangerous new threat.

"Funny, smart, and original, this outing, with its appealing characters and unusual take on urban fantasy tropes, is a delightful addition to the series." Library Journal.

Lafferty, Mur

The **shambling** guide to New York City / Mur Lafferty. Orbit, 2013. 358 p. Shambling Guides

ISBN 9780316221177

1. City dwellers 2. Vampires 3. Women editors 4. Incubi 5. Publishers and publishing 6. Supernatural 7. Young women 8. Social conflict 9. Men/women relations 10. Cities and towns 11. Gods and goddesses 12. New York City 13. Urban fantasy

LC 2012032172

Sequel: Ghost train to New Orleans.

Fleeing North Carolina after a career-derailing lapse in judgment, travel writer Zoë Norris returns to her native New York City in an attempt to make a fresh start. She talks her way into a job with Underground Publishing, a vampire-owned press whose city-themed guidebooks cater to the "coterie" (members of this highly secretive supernatural community take offense at the term "monster"). However, as the only human on staff, Zoë must quickly learn to navigate a society whose citizens would sooner eat her than employ her. - Description by Gillian Speace.

"This is a funny, thoughtfully conceived, and thoroughly entertaining romp that will be a sure bet for urban-fantasy readers--and might even surprise people who don't think they'd enjoy a paranormal novel". " Booklist.

Lafferty, Mur

Six wakes / Mur Lafferty. Little Brown & Co, 2017 352 p.

ISBN 9780316389686

1. 25th century 2. Clones and cloning 3. Space vehicles 4. Murder victims 5. Murder investigation 6. Military missions 7. Space flight 8. Astronauts 9. Murderers 10. Secrets 11. Science fiction mysteries 12. Science fiction

Awakening in a cloning vat, streaked with blood and possessing no memory of how she died, new clone Maria Arena discovers the clones of six former starship crew members and must identify their murderers before the killer strikes again.

"Lafferty delivers a tense nail-biter of a story fueled by memorable characters and thoughtful worldbuilding. This space-based locked-room murder mystery explores complex technological and moral issues . . ." Publishers Weekly.

Lagercrantz, David

The **girl** in the spider's web : a Lisbeth Salander novel / David Lagercrantz ; translated from the Swedish by George Goulding. Knopf, 2015. 400 p. Millennium novels (Stieg Larsson)

ISBN 9780385354288

1. Political intrigue 2. Hackers 3. Investigative journalists 4. Violence against women 5. Sweden 6. Scandinavian crime fiction 7. Mysteries 8. Translations -- Swedish to English

Originally published in Sweden as Det som inte dodar oss by Norstedts, Sweden, in 2015. First published in Great Britain in 2015 by MacLehose Press.

After receiving a call from a trusted source claiming to have vital information to the United States, journalist Mikael Blomkvist turns to hacker Lisbeth for help.

"A very fine thriller, true to the characters and the world Larsson created but also taking the ongoing story in some new and exciting directions." Booklist.

Lagercrantz, David

The **girl** who lived twice : a Lisbeth Salander novel / David Lagercrantz. Knopf, 2019. 416 p. Millennium novels (Stieg Larsson)

ISBN 9780451494344

1. Political intrigue 2. Hackers 3. Investigative journalists 4. Organized crime 5. Violence against women 6. Sweden 7. Scandinavian crime fiction 8. Mysteries 9. Translations -- Swedish to English

"Continuing Stieg Larsson's Millenium series" -- cover.

The best-selling author of The Girl in the Spider's Web presents a latest entry in the internationally acclaimed series starring punk hacker heroine, Lisbeth Salander.

Lagercrantz, David

The **girl** who takes an eye for an eye / David Lagercrantz. Knopf, 2017. 416 p. Millennium novels (Stieg Larsson)

ISBN 9780451494320

1. Political intrigue 2. Hackers 3. Investigative journalists 4. Organized crime 5. Violence against women 6. Sweden 7. Scandinavian crime fiction 8. Mysteries 9. Translations -- Swedish to English

"Continuing Stieg Larsson's Millenium series" -- cover.

"Originally published in Sweden as Mannen som sökte sin skugga by Norstedts, Stockholm, in 2017."--Title page verso.

Accepting help from Mikael Blomkvist to uncover the truth about her traumatic childhood, Lisbeth Salander navigates obstacles in the form of an anti-Muslim gang, her mafia-connected twin, and the conductors of a pseudoscientific experiment.

"Once again, Lagercrantz succeeds in carefully staying true to the framework created by the late Stieg Larsson in his original trilogy, and fans can continue to follow their favorite hacker heroine from obscurity to notoriety to unsought fame and unwanted attention." Booklist.

Lahiri, Jhumpa

* The **lowland** : a novel / Jhumpa Lahiri. Alfred A. Knopf, 2013. 339 p.

ISBN 9780307265746

1. Brothers 2. Love triangles 3. Loss (Psychology) 4. Insurgency 5. Widows 6. Naxalite Movement 7. Guilt 8. Husband and wife 9. Parenthood 10. India 11. Psychological fiction 12. Literary fiction 13. Family sagas

LC 2012043878

National Book Award for Fiction finalist, 2013.

Shortlisted for The Baileys Women's Prize for Fiction, 2014

Shortlisted for the Man Booker Prize, 2013.

Brothers Subhash and Udayan Mitra pursue vastly different lives--Udayan in rebellion-torn Calcutta, Subhash in a quiet corner of America--until a shattering tragedy compels Subhash to return to India, where he endeavors to heal family wounds.

Lahiri, Jhumpa

The **namesake** / Jhumpa Lahiri Houghton Mifflin, 2003. 304 p.

ISBN 0395927218

1. 20th century 2. East Indian Americans -- Social life and customs 3. Culture conflict 4. Immigrant families 5. College students 6. Young men 7. East Indian-American immigrants 8. Children of immigrants 9. Names, Personal 10. Identity (Psychology) 11. Assimilation (Sociology) 12. Alienation (Social psychology) 13. Family relationships 14. Cultural differences 15. Men/women relations 16. Arranged marriage 17. Electrical engineers 18. Massachusetts 19. Cambridge, Massachusetts 20. New Haven, Connecticut 21. New York City 22. Literary fiction

LC 2003041718

First published in Great Britain by Flamingo, 2003.

A portrait of the immigrant experience follows the Ganguli family from their traditional life in India through their arrival in Massachusetts in the late 1960s and their difficult melding into an American way of life.

"Its incorrigible mildness and its ungilded lilies aside, Lahiri's novel is unfailingly lovely in its treatment of Gogol's relationship with his father. This is the classic American parent-child bond." New York Times Book Review.

Lai, Larissa,

The **tiger** flu / Larissa Lai. Arsenal Pulp Press., 2018. 296 p.

ISBN 9781551527314

1. 22nd century 2. Survival 3. Epidemics 4. Women exiles 5. Quests 6. Villages 7. Near future 8. Organ donors 9. Mutation (Biology) 10. Women physicians 11. Regeneration (Biology) 12. Women/women relations 13. Apocalyptic fiction 14. Science fiction

Lambda Literary Award for Lesbian Fiction, 2019.

After her lover dies of the tiger flu brought into their village, Kirilow, a doctor, travels to the city to find a new "starfish", a person capable of regrowing organs.

Lake, Jay

Endurance / Jay Lake. Tor, 2011. 320 p. Green Universe

ISBN 9780765326768

1. Assassins 2. Gods and goddesses 3. Survival 4. Heroes and heroines 5. Former prostitutes 6. Lesbians 7. Bisexuality 8. Magic 9. Enemies 10. LGBTQIA fiction 11. Fantasy fiction

LC 2011021613

Sequel to: Green.

Sequel: Kalimpura.

Courtesan and trained assassin Green returns to Copper Downs where she must defend the gods from the Godslayers, magicians dedicated to the destruction of all deities, by tracking them down and removing the threat.

"Lake deftly weaves complicated, stubborn characters into a plot that reaches the grandest and most personal scales without ever straining credulity." Publishers Weekly.

Lake, Jay

Green / Jay Lake. Tor, 2009. 368 p. Green Universe
ISBN 9780765321855
1. Strangers 2. Assassins 3. Heroes and heroines 4. Poor families 5. Girls 6. Magic 7. Gods and goddesses 8. Lesbians 9. Bisexuality 10. Enemies 11. Survival 12. LGBTQIA fiction 13. Fantasy fiction
LC 2008050608
"A Tom Doherty Associates book."

In a world of political power and magic, and of Gods and mortals, a courtesan and trained assassin who calls herself "Green" finds intrigue and adventure, and many enemies, in the Undying Duke's city of Copper Downs.

Laker, Rosalind

To dance with kings : a novel of Versailles / Rosalind Laker. Doubleday, 1988. 564 p.
1. Chateau de Versailles (Versailles, France) 2. 17th century 3. 18th century 4. Women -- France 5. Women -- Family relationships 6. Mistresses 7. Nobility 8. Huguenots 9. Fans 10. Courts and courtiers -- France 11. Versailles, France -- History 12. France -- History -- Louis XIV, 1643-1715 13. France -- History -- Louis XV, 1715-1774 14. France -- History -- Louis XVI, 1774-1793 15. France -- History -- Revolution, 1789-1799 16. Historical fiction 17. Family sagas
LC 88003698

Lalami, Laila, 1968-

* The **Moor's** account : a novel / Laila Lalami. Pantheon Books, 2014. 323 p.
ISBN 9780307911667
1. Narvaez, Panfilo de, -1528 2. Nunez Cabeza de Vaca, Alvar, active 16th century 3. Voyages and travels 4. Survival 5. Slaves 6. Slavery 7. Explorers 8. Indians of North America 9. First contact (Anthropology) 10. Escapes 11. North America -- Exploration 12. Morocco 13. Historical fiction 14. Political fiction
LC 2013045255
Hurston/Wright Legacy Award: Fiction, 2015.
Pulitzer Prize for Fiction finalist, 2015.

A tale inspired by the experiences of the New World's first explorer of African descent describes how Moroccan slave Estebanico barely survives his early 16th-century expedition's encounters with storms, disease and hostile natives while traveling to the Gulf Coast and beyond.

"Estebanicos' account alternates between this disastrous mission and his past as a merchant, with the two threads combining to create a deeply layered, complex portrait of all-too-familiar characters in an unfamiliar world. The result is a totally engrossing and captivating novel that reconsiders the overlooked roles of Africans in New World exploration." Booklist.

Lalami, Laila, 1968-

The **other** Americans : a novel / Laila Lalami. Pantheon Books, 2019. 320 p.
ISBN 9781524747145
1. Immigrant families 2. Family relationships 3. Hit-and-run accidents 4. Accident investigation 5. Immigration and emigration 6. Undocumented immigrants 7. Race relations 8. Fathers -- Death 9. Grief 10. Widows 11. Mothers and sons 12. Life change events 13. Mojave Desert 14. California 15. Mysteries 16. Literary Fiction
Kirkus Prize for Fiction finalist, 2019.
National Book Award for Fiction finalist, 2019.

The suspicious death of a Moroccan immigrant impacts the lives of a diverse cast of characters, including his jazz-composer daughter, an undocumented witness and an Iraqi War veteran. By the award-winning author of The Moor's Account.

"Though structured like a murder mystery, the novel delves into much deeper themes." Library Journal.

Lalli, Sonya

The **matchmaker's** list / Sonya Lalli. Berkley Books, 2019. 329 p.
ISBN 9780451490940
1. Immigrant families 2. Matchmaking 3. Grandmother and granddaughter 4. East Indians in Canada 5. Culture conflict 6. Women -- Identity 7. Matchmakers 8. Communities 9. Expectation (Psychology) 10. Family relationships 11. Men/women relations 12. Toronto, Ontario 13. Canada 14. Romantic comedies 15. Multicultural romances
Navigating a series of disastrous dates, Raina Anand attempts to balance her Indian-immigrant community's expectations with her personal idea of modern romance.

"Lalli's sharp-eyed tale of cross-cultural dating, family heartbreak, the strictures of culture, and the exuberance of love is both universal and timeless." Publishers Weekly.

Lam, Vincent

The **headmaster's** wager : a novel / Vincent Lam. Hogarth, 2012. 426 p.
ISBN 9780307986467
1. School principals 2. Fathers and sons 3. Gambling 4. Men/women relations 5. Vietnam War, 1961-1975 6. Political corruption 7. Vietnam -- History -- 1945-1975 8. Historical fiction
ALA Notable Book, 2013
Governor General's Literary Awards, English-language Fiction finalist
Enjoying his position as the headmaster of Saigon's best English school while indulging in a gambling and womanizing lifestyle, Percival Chen becomes aware of the local violence when his son lands in trouble with the authorities.

Lamb, Alex

Roboteer / Alex Lamb. Gollancz/Orion Publishing Group, 2017. 448 p. Roboteer novels
ISBN 9781473206090
1. Genetically engineered men 2. Space colonies 3. Far future 4. Espionage 5. Human/alien encounters 6. Space vehicles 7. Genetic engineering 8. Survival 9. Robotics 10. Robots 11. Religion 12. Space warfare 13. Hard science fiction
Colonization of the stars has turned out to be anything but easy; civilization on Earth has collapsed, while small human settlements on barely habitable planets have developed ways of life heavily dependent on robotics and genetic engineering. Will is a man bred to interface with the robots that his home-world Galatea needs to survive, and is sent on a mission to discover the secret of a new weapon. What he discovers will transform his understanding of both science and civilization forever... but at a cost.

"Lamb's excellent first novel is an exciting and fast-paced, fresh take on space warfare and the future of humankind." Booklist.

Lambdin, Dewey

Hostile shores : an Alan Lewrie naval adventure / Dewey Lambdin. St Martins Press, 2013. 368 p. Alan Lewrie naval adventures

ISBN 9780312595722

1. Great Britain. Royal Navy History 18th century 2. Great Britain. Royal Navy Officers 3. 19th century 4. Ship captains 5. Naval battles -- History -- 18th century 6. Sailors -- Great Britain -- History -- 18th century 7. Men/women relations 8. Privateers 9. Traitors 10. Great Britain -- History, Naval -- 18th century 11. France -- History, Naval -- 18th century 12. Sea stories 13. Adventure stories 14. Historical fiction

Participating in the 1805 Battle of Cape Town after the death of Admiral Nelson, Captain Lewrie voyages to South America to assist Britain's campaigns on the Spanish colonies only to confront a formidable adversary that places his career and life at risk.

Lambdin, Dewey

King's captain : an Alan Lewrie naval adventure / Dewey Lambdin. Thomas Dunne Books, 2000. 358 p. Alan Lewrie naval adventures

ISBN 0312268858

1. Great Britain. Royal Navy History 18th century 2. Great Britain. Royal Navy Officers 3. 1790s 4. Seafaring life 5. Womanizers 6. Mutiny 7. Industrial revolution 8. Naval battles 9. Men/women relations 10. Cape Saint Vincent, Portugal, Battle of, 1797 11. Sailors -- Great Britain -- History -- 18th century 12. Great Britain -- History, Naval -- 18th century 13. Adventure stories 14. Sea stories 15. Historical fiction

LC 00031764

Promoted to frigate captain after proving himself in the Battle of Cape St. Vincent, Alan Lewrie confronts a mutiny that rages through the British fleet and the reappearance of an old enemy.

"A rip-roaring sea yarn brimming with riveting action and lusty diversions." Booklist.

Lamberson, Gregory, 1964-

The **frenzy** way / Gregory Lamberson. Medallion, 2010 340 p. Frenzy cycle

ISBN 9781605421070

1. Serial murder investigation 2. Werewolves 3. Police 4. Material culture 5. Supernatural 6. Secret societies 7. Serial murders 8. New York City 9. Mysteries 10. Horror

Detective Anthony Mace, recently promoted to captain of New York City's homicide unit, investigates a series of murders that may have been committed by a werewolf.

Lambert, Charles, 1953-

The **children's** home : a novel / Charles Lambert. Scribner, 2016. 224 p.

ISBN 9781501117398

1. Recluses 2. People with disfigurements 3. Abandoned children 4. Household employees 5. Good and evil 6. Physicians 7. Mansions 8. Factories 9. Secrets 10. England 11. Allegories 12. Horror

LC 2015027042

Disfigured from a terrible childhood incident, wealthy Morgan Fletcher lives alone in his country house, avoiding mirrors and other people except for his housekeeper and the local doctor. Since he's so antisocial, it's surprising that he welcomes two abandoned children into his home. When more children arrive and their behavior becomes increasingly strange, Morgan and the doctor wonder if the kids have a dark purpose. Author Charles Lambert escalates the level of dread as he gradually reveals Morgan's full story in this thought-provoking novel. -- Description by Katherine Bradley Johnson.

"Despite the strangeness of the novel's world, the story retains its subtlety, and though it is profoundly symbolic--and not always easy to decode--it remains compulsively readable." Kirkus.

Lanagan, Margo, 1960-

The **brides** of Rollrock Island / Margo Lanagan. Alfred A. Knopf, 2012. 305 p.

ISBN 9780375869198

1. Selkies 2. Witches 3. Enchantment 4. Shapeshifters 5. Magic 6. Islands 7. Fantasy fiction

Orginally published as: Sea hearts. Crows Nest, N.S.W. : Allen & Unwin, 2012.

Aurealis Awards, Best Fantasy Novel, 2012.

Aurealis Awards, Best Young Adult Novel, 2012.

Barbara Jefferis Award, 2014.

Children's Book of the Year Award for Older Readers (Children's Book Council of Australia), 2013.

Children's Book Council of Australia: Notable Australian Children's Book

Ditmar Award, 2013.

Western Australian Premier's Book Awards, Young Adult category, 2012.

Shortlisted for the Stella Prize, 2013.

Lured by the witch Misskaella, who possesses secrets for luring beautiful sea-wives from their underwater homes and transforming them out of their sealskins, a fisherman on remote Rollrock Island becomes the witch's victim when he falls desperately in love with the woman he has captured.

Lancaster, Jen, 1967-

Here I go again / Jen Lancaster. New American Library, 2012. 320 p.

ISBN 9780451236722

1. Second chances 2. Time travel 3. Transformations, Personal 4. Personal conduct 5. Bullying and bullies 6. Self-discovery in women 7. Suburban life 8. Popularity 9. Karma 10. Cliques 11. High school students 12. Options, alternatives, choices 13. Life change events 14. Parallel universes 15. Chicago, Illinois 16. Chick lit

LC 2012021417

Longing for the high-school days when she was popular and feared, 37-year-old Lyssy Ryder moves back into her parents' home after being dumped by her husband and losing her job, a situation that compels her to start her own business and try to change the mean person she was as a teenager.

Lanchester, John

Fragrant Harbor / John Lanchester. G.P. Putnam's Sons, 2002. 342 p.

ISBN 0399148663

1. 1930s 2. British in Hong Kong 3. Young men -- Hong Kong 4. Ships 5. Nuns 6. Businesspeople 7. Voyages and travels 8. Emotions 9. Bets 10. Undercover operations 11. World War II 12. Language and languages 13. Hong Kong 14. Historical fiction 15. Literary fiction

LC 2001057876

"A Marian Wood book."

Shortlisted for the James Tait Black Memorial Prize for Fiction, 2002

In the 1930s, a young Englishmn named Tom Stewart heads to Hong Kong in search of adventure.

"This is not an enormous novel, but it feels like one--it is bursting with ideas. Lanchester takes on almost every major theme and succeeds with most of them: race, class, love, war, the fall of rulers and the rise of the ruled." New York Times Book Review.

Landay, William

Defending Jacob : a novel / William Landay. Delacorte Books, 2012. 432 p.

ISBN 9780385344227

1. Child murders 2. Murder investigation 3. Marital conflict 4. Suburban life 5. Murder suspects 6. Loyalty 7. Families 8. Conflict in families 9. Family secrets 10. Guilt in men 11. Betrayal 12. Public prosecutors 13. Massachusetts 14. Legal thrillers 15. Psychological suspense

LC 2011011623

Includes reading group notes.

Andy Barber has been an assistant district attorney in his suburban Massachusetts county for more than twenty years. He is respected in his community, tenacious in the courtroom, and happy at home with his wife, Laurie, and son, Jacob. But when a shocking crime shatters their New England town, Andy is blindsided by what happens next. His fourteen-year-old son is charged with the murder of a fellow student.

Landis, Jill Marie

Heartbreak hotel / Jill Marie Landis. Ballantine Books, 2004. 352 p. Twilight Cove trilogy

ISBN 0345453301

1. Secret identity 2. Guilt in men 3. Second chances 4. Single mothers 5. Widows 6. Women hotel managers 7. Hotel managers 8. Authors 9. Resilience in women 10. Hotels 11. Debt 12. California 13. Contemporary romances 14. Romantic suspense

LC 2004063654

Stunned by her husband's sudden death, Tracy Potter retreats with her son and stepdaughter to Heartbreak Hotel, planning to reopen the abandoned inn, but the arrival of her first guest, Wade MacAllister, transforms her life.

Landon, Sydney

Wishing for us / Sydney Landon. Berkley Sensation, 2016. 260 p. Danvers novels

ISBN 9780399583209

1. Single fathers 2. Executives 3. Single women 4. Fiances -- Death 5. Interpersonal attraction 6. Men/women relations 7. Contemporary romances

When, after a wild Vegas bachelorette party, Lydia Cross wakes up next to corporate hotshot Jacob Hay -- as his wife -- she is shocked, especially when Jacob doesn't seem inclined to end their hasty merger, but instead wants to give her everything she's been missing in her life.

Landvik, Lorna, 1954-

Chronicles of a radical hag : with recipes / Lorna Landvik. University of Minnesota Press, 2019. 320 p.

ISBN 9781517905996

1. Columnists 2. Newspapers 3. Small town life 4. Secrets 5. Journalists 6. Teenage boys 7. People in comas 8. Mothers and sons 9. Parent and teenager 10. Community newspapers 11. Intergenerational relations 12. Minnesota 13. Humorous stories 14. Mainstream fiction 15. Gentle reads

When beloved columnist Haze Evans falls into a coma, Susan Mc-Grath, filling the void with Haze's past columns, stumbles upon secrets that have been locked in the files for decades.

Lange, Richard, 1961-

Angel baby : a novel / Richard Lange. Mulholland Books/ Little, Brown and Company, 2013. 288 p.

ISBN 9780316219822

1. Drug lords 2. Motherhood 3. Daughters 4. Drug dealers 5. Corruption 6. Human smuggling 7. Violent crimes 8. Murder 9. Family relationships 10. Men/women relations 11. Tijuana, Mexico 12. Mexico 13. California 14. Noir fiction 15. Crime fiction

LC 2012037350

After escaping her violent, drug cartel-running husband with only the clothes she was wearing, a gun and money from their safe, Luz risks her life again years later to return for the daughter she left behind.

Langton, Jane

The **deserter** : murder at Gettysburg / Jane Langton. Thomas Dunne Books, 2003. 322 p. Homer Kelly mysteries

ISBN 0312301863

1. Murder investigation 2. Civil war 3. Deserters 4. College teachers 5. Amateur detectives 6. Husband and wife 7. Gettysburg, Battle of, 1863 8. Murder 9. United States Civil War, 1861-1865 10. Gettysburg, Pennsylvania 11. Concord, Massachusetts 12. United States -- History -- Civil War, 1861-1865 13. Mysteries

LC 2002191961

As Homer and Mary Kelly research the life of Mary's ancestor Seth Morgan, the story of Seth's life and disappearance during the battle of Gettysburg unfolds.

Langton, Jane

Murder at Monticello : a Homer Kelly mystery / Jane Langton ; illustrations by the author. Viking, 2001. 256 p. Homer Kelly mysteries

ISBN 0670894621

1. Jefferson, Thomas, 1743-1826 Homes and haunts 2. Monticello (Va.) History 3. Serial murderers 4. Crimes against young women 5. Presidents 6. Fourth of July 7. College teachers 8. Amateur detectives 9. Charlottesville, Virginia 10. Mysteries

LC 00043369

A murder on the ground of Jefferson's mansion at Monticello leads history buff Homer Kelly on a search for Tom Dean, a young man seen trespassing on the property, who has become the prime suspect in the killings of several local women.

"Like the previous Kelly novels, this one features a smart mystery, delightful characters, and vastly entertaining dialogue." Booklist.

Langton, Jane

The **thief** of Venice : a Homer Kelly mystery / Jane Langton ; illustrations by the author. Viking, 1999. 247 p. Homer Kelly mysteries

ISBN 0670882100

1. Treasure troves 2. Missing persons 3. Secrets 4. Murder 5. College teachers 6. Amateur detectives 7. Christian relics -- Venice, Italy 8. Americans in Italy 9. Book collectors 10. Venice, Italy 11. Italy 12. Cambridge, Massachusetts 13. Mysteries

LC 9954894

Illustrated with black-and-white drawings, and a reproduction.

Homer Kelly's and his wife Mary's trip to Venice turns into a life-and-death adventure when some holy relics begin to vanish.

"With a master hand, Langton develops the various subplots into a sophisticated, elegantly constructed thriller." Publishers Weekly.

Lansdale, Joe R., 1951-

* The **bottoms** / Joe R. Lansdale. Mysterious Press, 2000. 328 p.

ISBN 0892967048

1. 1930s 2. Serial murders 3. Depressions -- 1929-1941 4. Serial murderers 5. Eleven-year-old boys 6. Nine-year-old girls 7. Brothers and sisters 8. East Texas -- Race relations 9. Texas 10. Mysteries 11. Coming-of-age stories 12. Southern fiction

LC 00032886

Edgar Allan Poe Award for Best Mystery Novel, 2001.

When young Harry Crane stumbles upon a mutilated body in the local river bottoms, the region becomes trapped in a nightmare of fear and racial tension, as a vicious serial killer stalks the town.

"An emotionally charged tale very reminiscent of To Kill a Mockingbird. Effectively combining mystery and family history, it offers a vivid, multifaceted glimpse back to a simpler, but not necessarily better, time." Booklist.

Lansdale, Joe R., 1951-

The **complete** Drive-in : three novels of anarchy, aliens, & the popcorn king / Joe R. Lansdale. Underland Press, 2010. 376 p., 12 unnumbered p. of plates

ISBN 9780980226041

1. Human-alien encounters 2. Drive-in theaters 3. Texas 4. Horror 5. Science fiction

"The festivities get started with The Drive-In, the story of Jack and his friends Bob, Willard, and Randy, and the trip they take to the All Night Horror Show at the Orbit, a drive-in movie theater with six screens full of murder, mayhem, and madness. One special Friday, a comet comes out of the sky, grins at the crowd, and takes the rest of the outside world away. Without an exit, the Orbit's audience turns into a small country of starving psychotics, and whoever's running the show keeps throwing in plot twists to keep life interesting. Twists like the Popcorn King, a crazed despot made of twisted flesh, lightning, and concession-stand treats. Lansdale followed the original novel with The Drive-In: Not Just One Of Them Sequels and The Drive-In: The Bus Tour. In both, things continue to go downhill. It's no surprise that Lansdale's story loses some steam by the end. Given how much power he's able to wring out of the premise's stark simplicity, the real wonder is that the sequels work as well as they do." A. V. Club.

Lansdale, Joe R., 1951-

Devil red / Joe R. Lansdale. Knopf, 2011. 288 p. Hap Collins and Leonard Pine novels

ISBN 9780307270986

1. Cults 2. Cold cases (Criminal investigation) 3. Serial murders 4. Inheritance and succession 5. Vampires 6. Assassins 7. Texas 8. Mysteries

LC 2010047476

Investigating a cold-case double murder to earn extra cash, amateur detectives Hap and Leonard discover that one of the victims was a member of a vampire cult and that many similar killings have taken place.

"Nobody's better at smacking us with the look, feel, and smell of derring-do. Along the way, there is the usual camaraderie, banter, and sex." Library Journal.

Lansdale, Joe R., 1951-

Edge of dark water / Joe R. Lansdale. Mulholland Books/ Little, Brown and Co., 2012. 288 p.

ISBN 9780316188432

1. Depression era (1929-1941) 2. 1930s 3. Female friendship 4. Friends' death 5. Small towns 6. Murder victims 7. Murder investigation 8. Loss (Psychology) 9. Mothers -- Death 10. Rural families 11. Secrets 12. Racism 13. Depressions -- 1929-1941 14. Historical fiction

LC 2011030557

Trying to escape her worthless life leads to unexpected and disastrous consequences when Sue Ellen steals money and a raft and embarks on a journey to dig up her best friend's body, burn it, and sprinkle the ashes in Hollywood.

Lansdale, Joe R., 1951-

A **fine** dark line / Joe R. Lansdale. Mysterious Press, 2003. 304 p.

ISBN 0892967293

1. 1950s 2. Race relations 3. Drive-in theaters 4. Desire 5. Lovers 6. Religion 7. Power (Social sciences) 8. Child abuse victims 9. Violence in men 10. Thirteen-year-old boys 11. Alcoholic men 12. African-American women cooks 13. Stalkers 14. Tribal police 15. Senior men 16. Stalking 17. Former police 18. Texas 19. Coming-of-age stories 20. Historical mysteries 21. Southern fiction

LC 2002071387

Young Stanley Mitchell, Jr., enters the underworld of his 1958 East Texas home when he discovers a cache of love letters by a murdered girl and experiences his first encounters with blues music, racism, and lost dreams.

Lansdale, Joe R., 1951-

* **Honky** tonk samurai / Joe R. Lansdale. Mulholland Books, 2016. 352 p. Hap Collins and Leonard Pine novels

ISBN 9780316329408

1. Cold cases (Criminal investigation) 2. Missing persons investigation 3. Prostitutes 4. Extortion 5. Interracial friendship 6. African American gay men 7. Texas 8. Mysteries

Blackmailed into accepting a missing-persons cold case, rebel Hap and gay veteran Leonard search for their client's long-missing granddaughter, who they discover was involved in a prostitution ring.

"This shambolic, action-packed novel will ensnare new readers and satisfy devoted fans alike." Publishers Weekly.

Lansdale, Joe R., 1951-

* **Paradise** sky / Joe R. Lansdale. Mullholland Books, 2015. 416 p.

ISBN 9780316329378

1. Love, Nat, 1854-1921 2. Hickok, Wild Bill, 1837-1876 3. African American cowboys 4. Frontier and pioneer life -- United States 5. African Americans -- Social conditions -- 19th century 6. Misunderstanding 7. Race relations 8. Gunfighters 9. Revenge 10. Survival 11. Mentors 12. Racism 13. Texas -- History -- 19th century 14. South Dakota -- History -- 19th century 15. The West (United States -- Social life and customs -- 19th century 16. Westerns 17. Biographical fiction

Spur Awards, Best Western Historical Novel, 2016.

RUSA Reading List Short List, 2016.

On the run after an infamous landowner murders his father, Willie becomes an expert marksman before turning Buffalo Soldier, befriending Wild Bill Hickok and earning the nickname "Deadwood Dick."

"Loosely based on the true story of African American cowboy Nat Love (1854-1921), this fast-paced Western with its multicultural cast of characters is a winner." Library Journal.

Lansdale, Joe R., 1951-

* Sunset and sawdust / Joe R. Lansdale. Alfred A. Knopf, 2004. 320 p.

ISBN 0375414533

1. Depression era (1929-1941) 2. Women sheriffs 3. Pregnant women 4. Depressions -- 1929-1941 -- Texas 5. Murder investigation 6. Policewomen 7. Widows 8. Race relations 9. Land tenure 10. East Texas 11. Historical mysteries 12. Mysteries

LC 2003060478

Sunset Jones has just killed her husband. Never mind that he was raping her. Pete Jones was constable of a small sawmill settlement called Camp Rapture, where no woman refuses her husband. So everyone is angrily surprised when, thanks to the amazing understanding of her mother-in-law -- who owns three-quarters of the mill -- Sunset becomes the new constable and begins to investigate the murders of a woman and unborn baby in which her late husband might be implicated. Yet, no one is more surprised than Sunset when the murders lead her -- through a labyrinth of greed, corruption, and unspeakable malice -- not only to the conclusion of the case, but to a well of inner strength she never knew she had.

"The mystery is only mildly engrossing here; the great pleasure of Lansdale's work lies in his pitch-perfect vernacular prose.... The book opens with a cyclone, ends with a plague of grasshoppers and in between there's insanity, extreme violence, sex, grotesques aplenty and an excellent dog. What's not to like?" Publishers Weekly.

Lansdale, Joe R., 1951-

The **thicket** / Joe R. Lansdale. Mulholland Books, 2013. 288 p.

ISBN 9780316188456

1. 1930s 2. Orphans 3. Kidnapping 4. Outlaws 5. Brothers and sisters 6. Bounty hunters 7. Rescues 8. Race relations 9. East Texas 10. Adventure stories 11. Historical mysteries

LC 2013016949

Recently orphaned, Jack Parker witnesses his grandfather's murder and his sister's kidnapping by bank robbers while traveling to his uncle's farm in East Texas and vows revenge.

Lansdale, Joe R., 1951-

Vanilla Ride / Joe R. Lansdale. Alfred A. Knopf, 2009. 256 p. Hap Collins and Leonard Pine novels

ISBN 9780307270979

1. African American gay men 2. Drug dealers 3. Mafia 4. Interracial friendship 5. African American men 6. Texas 7. Mysteries 8. Humorous stories

LC 2009008821

"This is a Borzoi book."

Best friends and freelance troublemakers Hap Collins and Leonard Pine assist an old friend in rescuing his daughter from an abusive drug dealer, and wind up enraging the Dixie Mafia.

"Lansdale's storytelling skills are as sharp as ever." Publishers Weekly.

Larison, John

Whiskey when we're dry / John Larison. Viking Press, 2018. 400 p.

ISBN 9780735220447

1. American Westward Expansion (1803-1899) 2. Women sharpshooters 3. Male impersonators 4. Outlaws 5. Orphans 6. Teenage girls 7. Identity (Psychology) 8. Frontier and pioneer life 9. Brothers and sisters 10. Voyages and travels 11. Determination in women 12. The West (United States) -- History -- 19th century 13. Westerns 14. Coming-of-age stories 15. Literary fiction

Facing starvation and worse when she is orphaned on her family's 1885 homestead, a 17-year-old sharpshooter cuts off her hair and disguises herself as a boy to journey across the mountains in search of her outlaw brother.

Larkwood, A. K.

The **unspoken** name / A. K. Larkwood. Tor, 2020. 448 p. Serpent Gates

ISBN 9781250238900

1. Wizards 2. Women bodyguards 3. Interdimensional travel 4. Women warriors 5. Gods and goddesses 6. Human sacrifice 7. Treasure troves 8. Betrayal 9. Orcs 10. Fantasy fiction

LC 2019042768

Destined to become a sacrifice on behalf of her superstitious people, Csorwe accepts a powerful mage's alternate offer to become his bodyguard and spy to help him reclaim his power in the land from where he was exiled.

"Larkwood's intricately woven plot is jam-packed with intrigue and excitement. Lyrical, immersive prose masterfully conveys complex worldbuilding. Epic fantasy fans are sure to be impressed by this expertly crafted adventure." Publishers Weekly.

Larsen, Nella

Passing / Nella Larsen. Modern Library, 2002, c1929. 215 p.

ISBN 0375758135

1. 1920s 2. African American women -- Identity 3. Identity (Psychology) 4. Race relations 5. Middle class women 6. Married women 7. Passing (Identity) 8. Prejudice 9. Change (Psychology) 10. Jealousy 11. Husband and wife 12. Interracial marriage 13. Secrets 14. Risk-taking in women 15. Loneliness in women 16. Love triangles 17. Harlem, New York City 18. New York City 19. Chicago, Illinois 20. United States -- Social conditions -- 1918-1932 21. Psychological fiction 22. Literary fiction 23. Modern classics

LC 29009990

Originally published: New York : A.A. Knopf, 1929.

First published in 1929, Passing is a remarkable exploration of the shifting racial and sexual boundaries in America. Larsen, a premier writer of the Harlem Renaissance, captures the rewards and dangers faced by two negro women who pass for white in a deeply segregated world.

"This is a shrewdly conceived and finely executed novella that raises questions not only of racial identity in a realistically rendered middle and upper-middle-class Negro society (in Harlem and Chicago, 1927) but of the murderous rage one woman might feel for another who has passed beyond her." The New York Review of Books.

Larsen, Reif

The **selected** works of T. S. Spivet / Reif Larsen. Penguin Press, 2009. 352 p.

ISBN 9781594202179

1. Gifted boys 2. Ranch life 3. Voyages and travels 4. Mothers and sons 5. Grief in families 6. Brothers 7. Fathers and sons 8. Loss (Psychology) 9. Cartography 10. Guilt 11. Railroad travel 12. Montana 13. Coming-of-age stories 14. Picaresque fiction 15. Illustrated books

LC 2009006277

Book made into a movie in 2013 called The Young and Prodigious T.S. Spivet, directed by Jean-Pierre Jeunet and starring Helena Bonham Carter.

Shortlisted for the James Tait Black Memorial Prize for Fiction, 2009

When twelve-year-old cartography genius T.S. Spivet receives a prestigious award, he leaves his quiet ranch home in Montana for Washington, D.C., and he learns more about himself and the world around him on his journey.

"Only at the end does Larsen lose control of the already outlandish plot, but that's to be forgiven. His debut is oddly affecting, and T.S. Spivet is a character to root for." Dallas Morning News.

Larsen, Reif

I am Radar : a novel / Reif Larsen. Penguin Press, 2015. 656 p.

ISBN 9781594206160

1. Protest art 2. Secret societies 3. Human skin color 4. Puppetry 5. Young men 6. Radio waves 7. Ethnic identity 8. Performance art 9. Parent and child 10. Identity (Psychology) 11. War -- History -- 20th century 12. New Jersey -- Social life and customs -- 20th century 13. Norway 14. Literary fiction

Born inexplicably to white parents, black youth Radar falls in with a secretive group of scientific puppeteers who stage experimental art in the world's war zones, where he is forced to confront the true nature of his identity.

"If Larsen's story makes demands of its readers, it also offers plenty of rewards. Imaginative, original, nicely surreal--and hyperpigmentarily so." Kirkus.

Larsson, Asa, 1966-

Until thy wrath be past / Asa Larsson ; translated from the Swedish by Laurie Thompson. SilverOak, 2011, c2009. 416 p. Rebecka Martinsson mysteries

ISBN 9781402787164

1. Women lawyers 2. Murder investigation 3. Women murder victims 4. Women detectives 5. Missing men 6. Women's dreams 7. Police 8. Secrets 9. Nazi collaborators 10. Murder 11. Sweden 12. Kiruna, Sweden 13. Mysteries 14. Translations -- Swedish to English 15. Scandinavian crime fiction

Originally published: Stockholm : Bonnier, 2009.

It is the first thaw of spring and the body of a young woman surfaces in the River Thorne in the far north of Sweden. Rebecka Martinsson is working as a prosecutor in nearby Karuna. Her sleep has been disturbed by haunting visions of a shadowy, accusing figure. Could the body belong to the ghost in her dreams?

"The novel shows that Larsson is ready to confront unpalatable truths. Among the current batch of Nordic writers, the new Larsson is one to be followed with the most minute attention." The Independent (UK).

Larsson, Stieg, 1954-2004

* The **girl** who kicked the hornet's nest / Stieg Larsson ; translated from the Swedish by Reg Keeland. Alfred A. Knopf, 2010, c2007. 512 p. Millennium novels (Stieg Larsson)

ISBN 9780307269997

1. Political corruption -- Sweden 2. Revenge 3. Gunshot wounds 4. Murder investigation 5. Conspiracies 6. Violence against women 7. Hackers 8. Investigative journalists 9. Sweden 10. Mysteries 11. Translations -- Swedish to English 12. Scandinavian crime fiction

LC 2010006361

Sequel to: The girl who played with fire.

Originally published in Sweden as Luftslottet Som Sprangdes in 2007.

Originally published in Sweden as Luftslottet som sprangdes by Norstedts, Stockholm, in 2007.

Goodreads Choice Award, 2010.

Lisbeth Salander is in the intensive care unit of a provincial Swedish city hospital, fighting for her life in more ways than one: when she's well enough, she'll stand trial for a triple murder. While journalist Mi-

kael Blomkvist helps to prove her innocence, Lisbeth plots her revenge against the man who tried to kill her, and the government institutions that very nearly destroyed her life.

Larsson, Stieg, 1954-2004

The **girl** who played with fire / Stieg Larsson ; translated from the Swedish by Reg Keeland. Alfred A. Knopf, 2009, c2006. 512 p. Millennium novels (Stieg Larsson)

ISBN 9780307269980

1. Sexual slavery 2. Murder 3. Police misconduct 4. Murder investigation 5. Sex industry and trade 6. Violence against women 7. Hackers 8. Investigative journalists 9. Sweden 10. Mysteries 11. Translations -- Swedish to English 12. Scandinavian crime fiction

Translation from the Swedish of: Flickan som lekte med elden.

Originally published in Sweden as Flickan Som Lekte Med Elden by Norstedts in 2006.

Originally published: Stockholm : Norstedts, 2006.

Goodreads Choice Award, 2009.

On the eve of the publication of a sex-trafficking expos?, two reporters responsible for the magazine story are murdered, and the fingerprints on the murder weapon belong to Lisbeth Salander, a genius hacker, prompting the magazine's publisher, Mikael Blomkvist, to launch his own investigation to vindicate Lisbeth, just as she becomes the prey of a murderous hunt.

"For all the complications of the melodramatic story, which advances at a brisk, violently cinematic clip in Reg Keeland's translation, it's clear where Larsson's strongest interests liein his heroine and the ill-concealed attitudes she brings out in men." New York Times Book Review.

Larsson, Stieg, 1954-2004

The **girl** with the dragon tattoo / Stieg Larsson ; translated from the Swedish by Reg Keeland. Alfred A. Knopf, 2008, c2005. 480 p. Millennium novels (Stieg Larsson)

ISBN 9780307269751

1. Murder investigation 2. Missing persons 3. Violence against women 4. Cold cases (Criminal investigation) 5. Investigative journalists 6. Hackers 7. Fathers and daughters 8. Sweden 9. Scandinavian crime fiction 10. Mysteries 11. Translations -- Swedish to English

LC 2008017771

Originally published as: Man som hatar kvinnor. Stockholm : Norstedt, 2005.

Originally published under the title Man som hatar kvinnor: Stockholm : Norstedt, 2005.

Anthony Award for Best First Novel, 2009.

British Book Award for Crime Thriller of the Year, 2009.

Macavity Award for Best First Mystery Novel, 2009.

Journalist Mikael Blomkvist and hacker Lisbeth Salander investigate the disappearance of Harriet Vanger, which took place forty years ago.

"First title in the author's Millennium trilogy. Convicted of libeling a prominent businessman and awaiting imprisonment, financial journalist Mikael Blomkvist agrees to industrialist Henrik Vanger's request to investigate the 40-year-old disappearance of Vanger's 16-year-old niece, Harriet. In return, Vanger will help Blomkvist dig up dirt on the corrupt businessman. Assisting in Blomkvist's investigation is 24-year-old Lisbeth Salander, a brilliant but enigmatic computer hacker." Library Journal.

Lasdun, James

Afternoon of a faun : a novel / James Lasdun. W. W. Norton & Co., 2019. 160 p.

ISBN 9781324001942

1. 2010s 2. Rape 3. Truth 4. Journalists 5. Loyalty 6. Secrets 7.

Suspicion 8. Expatriates 9. Consequences 10. Rape suspects 11. British in New York City 12. New York City 13. Literary fiction 14. Psychological fiction

LC 2018057124

When his expat journalist friend is accused of sexual assault in a former girlfriend's memoir, a man finds himself caught between loyalty and an urgent desire to uncover the truth.

Lasdun, James

The **fall** guy : a novel / James Lasdun. W. W. Norton & Co., 2016. 245 p.

ISBN 9780393292329

1. Rich people 2. Obsession 3. Revenge 4. Bankers 5. Secrets 6. Cousins 7. Betrayal 8. Guilt 9. New York (State) 10. Psychological suspense

LC 2016018259

couple and their troubled cousin are caught in a deadly web of secrets, obsession and revenge during a scalding, psychologically complex summer spent in their idyllic mountaintop home.

"An undercurrent of menace and threat finally erupts, and Lasdun presents the inexorable turnings of fate in a subtle and disconcerting way." Publishers Weekly.

Lashner, William

A **killer's** kiss / William Lashner. William Morrow, 2007. 336 p. Victor Carl novels

ISBN 9780061143465

1. Former lovers 2. Murder suspects 3. Deception 4. Murder 5. Betrayal 6. WIdows 7. Greed 8. Innocence (Law) 9. Lawyers 10. Defense attorneys 11. Love triangles 12. Murder 13. Murder investigation 14. Philadelphia, Pennsylvania 15. Thrillers and suspense 16. Legal thrillers

LC 2007061202

Unable to resist a reconciliation with his former fiancee Julia, second-rate lawyer Victor learns that Julia's wealthy husband has been murdered, a crime in which Victor finds himself targeted as the prime suspect when the police begin questioning him.

"Chandler and Hammett fans looking for a fix will be well rewarded." Publishers Weekly.

Lasser, Scott

Say nice things about Detroit / Scott Lasser. W.W. Norton & Co., 2012. 288 p.

ISBN 9780393082999

1. Life change events 2. Homecomings 3. Murder investigation -- Detroit, Michigan 4. Second chances 5. Family relationships 6. Detroit, Michigan -- Economic conditions -- 21st century 7. Detroit, Michigan -- Social conditions 8. Detroit, Michigan -- Race relations 9. Literary fiction 10. Psychological fiction

LC 2012006784

After losing his son and divorcing his wife, a Detroit native returns home after 25 years and becomes involved with the sister of his murdered high school girlfriend as he tries to put back the pieces of his life.

Lathen, Emma

Brewing up a storm / Emma Lathen. St. Martin's Press, 1996. 248 p. John Putnam Thatcher mysteries

ISBN 0312145543

1. Breweries 2. Bankers 3. Nonalcoholic beer 4. Murder 5. Amateur detectives 6. Corporate intrigue 7. Murder investigation 8. Grassroots movement 9. Teenagers -- Alcohol use 10. Fast food restaurants, chains, etc 11. Wall Street, New York City 12. New York City 13. Cozy mysteries 14. Gentle reads

LC 96-22116

When the leader of No-Beer Buying Youngsters (NOBBY) is murdered during a protest, it is up to John Putnam Thatcher to discover whether it was a brewery owner, a politician, or one of her own supporters who was responsible for the killing

Lathen, Emma

East is east / Emma Lathen. Simon & Schuster, 1991. 255 p. John Putnam Thatcher mysteries

ISBN 9780671737078

1. Bankers 2. Corporate mergers 3. Business competition 4. Murder 5. Business travel 6. Amateur detectives 7. Financial intrigue 8. Corporate intrigue 9. Murder investigation 10. Business -- Corrupt practices 11. Japan 12. Wall Street, New York City 13. Cozy mysteries 14. Gentle reads

LC 91032789

In Japan to head off a possible takeover, Sloan Guaranty Trust's executive vice president, John Putnam Thatcher, finds himself caught up in a tea ceremony that involves unscrupulous business practices, murder, and mystery

"Ms. Lathen has a wonderful knack for turning the driest, most complicated corporate maneuvers into high drama, and occasionally burlesque." New York Times Book Review.

Lathen, Emma

Something in the air / Emma Lathen. Pocket Books, 1989, c1988. 255 p. John Putnam Thatcher mysteries

ISBN 9780671683566

1. Airlines 2. Stock market 3. Bankers 4. Pilots 5. Murder 6. Financial intrigue 7. Amateur detectives 8. Corporate intrigue 9. Murder investigation 10. Chief executive officers 11. Boston, Massachusetts 12. Wall Street, New York City 13. Cozy mysteries 14. Gentle reads

LC 88004491

Originally published: New York : Simon & Schuster, 1988.

Wall Street banker/detective John Putnam Thatcher encounters intrigue along with a loan request from Sparrow Flyways, an airline whose expansion plans are not to be deterred, even by opposition from its shareholders.

Latin@ rising : an anthology of Latin@ science fiction and fantasy / edited by Matthew David Goodwin ; introduction by Frederick Luis Aldama. Wings Press, 2016. 272 p.

ISBN 9781609405243

1. Latin Americans 2. Hispanic Americans 3. Science fiction 4. Fantasy fiction 5. Short stories 6. Anthologies

LC 2016027239

The first anthology of science fiction and fantasy written by Latinos/as living in the United States. The book gives an overview to the field of Latino/a speculative fiction, showing the great variety of stories being told by Latino/a writers.

"Sloughing off the worn veil of magical realism, Goodwins anthology amplifies a new generation of Latin' speculative fiction voices." Booklist.

Latour, Jose, 1940-

The **Havana** World Series / Jose Latour. Grove Press, 2003. 320 p.

ISBN 0802117546

1. Lansky, Meyer, 1902-1983 2. World Series (Baseball) 3. 1950s 4. Mafia 5. Criminals 6. Organized crime 7. Organized crime and gambling 8. Casinos -- Cuba 9. Sports betting 10. Gambling 11. Robbery 12. Cuba -- History -- 1933-1959 13. Havana, Cuba 14.

Historical thrillers

LC 2003060716

At the height of the World Series in 1958, the gambling empire of Meyer Lansky enjoys unprecedented profits much to the chagrin of rival mafia boss Joe Bonanno, who plots to hijack Lansky's winnings with deadly consequences.

"The author tells the story of a gang of Cuban crooks, funded by New York Mob boss Joe Bonanno, who sets out to rob Meyer Lansky's Capri casino on the last day of the 1958 World Series (when the coffers are overflowing). The portraits of Lansky, Bonnano, and the other gangsters are full-bodied, but it's the fictional blue-collar crooks, led by mastermind Ox Contreras, who give the novel its appeal and afford the best view of Cuban life. Although the documentary style occasionally seems flat, it contrasts nicely with the richness of detail and quirkiness of character." Booklist.

Laukkanen, Owen

Criminal enterprise / Owen Laukkanen. G. P. Putnam's Sons, 2013. 384 p. Kirk Stevens and Carla Windermere novels
ISBN 9780399157905
1. Government investigators 2. Bank robberies 3. FBI agents 4. Police 5. Robbery investigation 6. Secrets 7. Employees -- Dismissal 8. Accountants 9. Minnesota 10. Thrillers and suspense

LC 2012028673

When a secretly unemployed man begins robbing banks in a desperate struggle to hold onto his once-successful life, FBI Special Agent Carla Windermere and Minnesota state investigator Kirk Stevens approach the case from respective angles and reconnect when the robber develops a taste for violence.

Laukkanen, Owen

Deception Cove / Owen Laukkanen. Mulholland Books, 2019 372 p. Neah Bay novels
ISBN 9780316448703
1. Widows 2. Police corruption 3. Afghan War veterans 4. Sheriffs 5. Rescues 6. Extortion 7. Dognapping 8. Service dogs 9. Women veterans 10. People with post-traumatic stress disorder 11. Thrillers and suspense

A recently widowed marine suffering PTSD from her time in Afghanistan has her service dog kidnapped by a corrupt deputy sheriff who wants to blackmail her into delivering goods allegedly stolen by her husband before his death.

Laukkanen, Owen

Gale force / Owen Laukkanen. G. P. Putnam's Sons, 2018. 384 p.
ISBN 9780735212633
1. Women ship captains 2. Organized crime 3. Ocean travel 4. Deep-sea sounding 5. Salvage 6. Ships 7. Rescues 8. Leadership 9. Alaska 10. Thrillers and suspense

LC 2017020483

Playing it safe in spite of significantly reduced profits after witnessing her father's death in a freak maritime accident and assuming his rank as captain of an Alaskan salvage boat, McKenna and her crew take a last-chance job helping an imperiled freighter only to discover that it contains valuable cargo that is being targeted by powerful enemies.

Laukkanen, Owen

The **professionals** / Owen Laukkanen. G. P. Putnam's Sons, 2012. 372 p. Kirk Stevens and Carla Windermere novels
ISBN 9780399157899
1. Kidnappers 2. Crimes against rich people 3. Organized crime 4. College graduates 5. Unemployed persons 6. Kidnapping 7. Ransom 8. Police 9. FBI agents 10. Kidnapping investigation 11. Violence 12. Michigan 13. Thrillers and suspense

When a joke about making illicit money in the poor economy escalates to a kidnapping scheme, four friends enjoy the proceeds of a low-risk operation until they abduct the wrong target and capture the attentions of state investigator Kirk Stevens, hotshot FBI agent Carla Windermere and a vengeful organized-crime ring.

"Author Laukkanen deftly cuts back and forth among the kidnappers, the thugs and the authorities hot on their trails, engendering reader empathy for members of each group--no easy feat!" BookPage.

Laukkanen, Owen

The **watcher** in the wall : a Stevens and Windermere novel / Owen Laukkanen. G. P. Putnam's Sons, 2016 368 p. Kirk Stevens and Carla Windermere novels
ISBN 9780399174544
1. Government investigators 2. FBI agents 3. Suicide investigation 4. Suicide 5. Internet predators 6. Crimes against teenagers 7. Thrillers and suspense

LC 2015026298

Kirk Stevens and Carla Windermere of the joint FBI-BCA violent crime task force investigate a teen suicide chat group presided over by a psychopath who seems to be spurring the others on.

Laureano, C. E. (Carla E.)

* The **Saturday** Night Supper Club / Carla Laureano. Tyndale House Pub, 2018 416 p. Saturday Night Supper Club novels
ISBN 9781496428271
1. Women cooks 2. Ambition in women 3. Journalists 4. Reputation 5. Dinners and dining 6. Critics 7. Helpfulness in men 8. Interpersonal attraction 9. Men/women relations 10. Denver, Colorado 11. Christian romances

LC 2017049829

RITA Award, 2019.

After an essay he writes results in chef Rachel Bishop's firing, a repentent Alex Kanin partners with Rachel to host an exclusive pop-up dinner party that they hope will restore her career.

Lauren, Christina

Dating you / Hating you / Gallery Books, 2017 320 p.
ISBN 9781501165818
1. Talent agents 2. Coworkers 3. Workaholics 4. Competition 5. Love-hate relationships 6. Sabotage 7. Sexual attraction 8. Men/women relations 9. Hollywood, California 10. Contemporary romances 11. Romantic comedies

First published in the US in 2017 by Gallery Books, an imprint of Simon & Schuster, Inc.

Sparks fly when Hollywood agents Carter and Evie meet at a party (dressed as Harry Potter and Hermione Granger, respectively). Then their agencies merge, turning them into bitter rivals as they compete for the same job. Fans of witty workplace-set romantic comedies such as Sally Thorne's The Hating Game should enjoy this stand-alone novel, which presents both sides of the story in alternating chapters. -- Description by Gillian Speace

Lauren, Christina,

Roomies / Christina Lauren. Gallery Books, 2017. 358 p.
ISBN 9781501165832
1. Irish in the United States 2. Musicians 3. Women authors 4. Visas 5. Immigrants 6. City life 7. Couples 8. Men/women relations 9. Interpersonal attraction 10. New York City 11. Contemporary

romances

LC 2017036788

When a struggling musician on the brink of stardom reveals he is in the country illegally, besotted Holland Bakker enters a marriage of convenience that becomes more real than either anticipated.

Lauren, Christina

Sweet filthy boy / Christina Lauren. Gallery Books, 2014 352 p. Wild seasons

ISBN 9781476751801

1. Young women 2. One-night stands (Interpersonal relations) 3. Lawyers 4. Women college graduates 5. Sexual attraction 6. Men/women relations 7. Twenties (Age) 8. Self-discovery 9. Americans in France 10. Paris, France 11. Erotic romances 12. New adult fiction 13. Contemporary romances

After a one night stand, Mia Holland makes an impulsive decision to follow her fling to France for the summer where she gets caught up in erotic masquerades that leave her reconsidering her plan to attend business school in the fall.

"This roller-coaster ride of a novel has humorous, punchy female characters who share a strong bond that doesn't seem to fall on tired tropes." Library Journal.

Laurens, Stephanie

By winter's light / Stephanie Laurens. Mira, 2014. 352 p. Cynsters: Next generation

ISBN 9780778317470

1. Victorian era (1837-1901) 2. 1830s 3. Tutors 4. Widows 5. Christmas 6. Trust 7. Family relationships 8. Interpersonal attraction 9. Men/women relations 10. Scotland -- Social life and customs -- 19th century 11. Historical romances 12. Holiday romances 13. Victorian romances

It's frosty December and six Cynster families come together at snowbound Casphairn Manor with members of their households to celebrate the season in true Cynster fashion-and where Cynsters gather, love is never far behind. The festive occasion brings together Daniel Crosbie, tutor to Lucifer Cynster's sons, and Claire Meadows, widow and governess to Gabriel Cynster's daughter. Daniel and Claire have met before and the embers of an unexpected passion smolder between them. However, Claire, once bitten, twice shy, believes a second marriage is not in her stars. Yet Daniel is determined. He's seen the kind of love the Cynsters share, and Claire is the lady with whom he dreams of sharing his life. Assisted by a bevy of Cynsters-innate matchmakers every one-Daniel strives to persuade Claire that trusting him with her hand and her heart is her right path to happiness. Claire is increasingly drawn to Daniel and despite her misgivings, their relationship deepens. But then catastrophe strikes, and by winter's light, she learns that love-true love-is worth any risk, any price.

Laurens, Stephanie

* **Devil's** bride / Stephanie Laurens. Avon Books, 1998. 388 p. Cynster novels

ISBN 038079456X

1. Regency period (1811-1820) 2. Governesses 3. Men/women relations 4. Cousins -- Death 5. Murder 6. Women adventurers 7. Independence in women 8. Women's dreams 9. Rescues 10. Dukes and duchesses 11. England -- History -- 19th century 12. Regency romances 13. Romantic suspense 14. Historical romances

LC 97-94313

When Devil Cynster and Honoria Wetherby are caught in a comprising position, he offers her marriage, but the spirited Honoria is not about to conform to conventions and decides that solving a mystery and seeing the world is more to her liking, despite her passionate longing for Devil.

Laurens, Stephanie

The **pursuits** of Lord Kit Cavanaugh / Stephanie Laurens. Harlequin Books, 2019 330 p. Cavanaughs (Stephanie Laurens)

ISBN 9780778369899

1. Victorian era (1837-1901) 2. 19th century 3. Schools 4. Nobility 5. Sabotage 6. Yachts 7. Business competition 8. Men/women relations 9. Interpersonal attraction 10. Independence in women 11. Determination (Personal quality) 12. England 13. Victorian romances 14. Historical romances

Kit Cavanugh and Sylvia Buckleberry fight to secure her school and to expose the blackguard trying to sabotage his yacht business; yet an even more dastardly villain lurks, one who threatens the future both discover they now hold dear.

"Laurens' subtle nods to forgiveness, community-building, and second chances lend extra character and warmth to a winning love story." Kirkus.

Laurens, Stephanie

A **rake's** vow / Stephanie Laurens. Avon Books, 1998. 374 p. Cynster novels

ISBN 0380794578

1. Regency period (1811-1820) 2. Single women 3. Men/women relations 4. Thieves 5. Godmothers 6. Loyalty 7. Protectiveness in men 8. Families 9. Sexuality 10. Independence in women 11. Brothers and sisters 12. Teenage boys 13. Spirits 14. Marriage 15. England -- History -- 19th century 16. Regency romances 17. Historical romances

LC 98-92766

Accustomed to organizing her own affairs and those of her teenage brother, lovely Patience Debbington finds her life turned upside down by the dashing Vane Cynster, an arrogant rake with an antipathy toward matrimony.

Lavery, Daniel M.

* The **merry** spinster : Tales of everyday horror / Daniel Lavery. Henry Holt & Co., 2018. 190 p.

ISBN 9781250113429

1. Fairy tales 2. Feminism 3. Women in folklore and mythology 4. Women in literature 5. Storytelling 6. Gender role 7. Fantasy fiction 8. Horror 9. Adaptations, retellings, and spin-offs 10. Short stories

Adapted from the author's "Children Stories Made Horrific" series, a collection of darkly whimsical stories based on classic fairy tales updates familiar favorites with elements of psychological horror, emotional clarity and feminist mischief.

"[Lavery] infuses [his] stories with unsettling surrealism, sharp social commentary, a mordant sense of humor, and little in the way of true love. [Lavery] successfully pinpoints a kernel of real horror in each of the stories [he] recasts, and although [his] smart, weird writing might not be for everyone, it will bewitch macabre, literary-minded readers." Booklist.

Lawler, Liz

Don't wake up / Liz Lawler. Harper Paperbacks, 2019, c2017 368 p.

ISBN 9780062886224

1. Rape victims 2. Violence against women 3. Skepticism 4. Women physicians 5. Memory 6. Hospitals 7. Life change events 8. England 9. Psychological suspense

Originally published: London : Twenty7 Books, 2017.

Dr. Alex Taylor awakens after an assault with no physical proof of the attack and must try to convince everyone of what really happened.

Lawrence, D. H. (David Herbert), 1885-1930
  * **Lady** Chatterley's lover / D.H. Lawrence ; with an afterword by Harry T. Moore. Penguin, 1962, c1928 299 p.
  ISBN 0451524985
  1. Extramarital affairs 2. Interclass romance 3. Married women 4. Sexual ethics 5. Sexuality 6. Gamekeepers 7. England -- Social life and customs -- 20th century 8. Literary fiction 9. Erotic fiction 10. Modern classics
  Bold, passionate, and erotic, this classic tale of love and discovery pits the paralyzed and callous Clifford Chatterley against his indecisive wife and her persuasive lover.

Lawrence, D. H. (David Herbert), 1885-1930
  The **rainbow** / D. H. Lawrence ; Introduction by Jeffrey Meyers Bantam Books, 1991, c1915. 460 p.
  ISBN 0553213903
  1. Young women -- Sexuality 2. Self-fulfillment 3. Personal conduct 4. Marriage 5. Brothers and sisters 6. Sexuality 7. Families 8. Family relationships 9. Widows 10. Manners and customs 11. Husband and wife 12. Industrial Revolution 13. Men/women relations 14. England -- Social life and customs -- 20th century 15. Modern classics 16. Literary fiction 17. Family sagas
  Set in the rural midlands of England, this story revolves around three generations of the Brangwen family over a period of more than sixty years, setting them against the emergence of modern England. When Tom Brangwen marries a Polish widow and adopts her daughter as his own, he is unprepared for the conflict and passion that erupt.

Lawrence, D. H. (David Herbert), 1885-1930
  * **Sons** and lovers / D.H. Lawrence. Penguin Classics, 2010, c1913. 420 p.
  ISBN 9780141195445
  1. Mothers and sons 2. Young men 3. Family relationships 4. Marriage 5. Sexuality 6. Grief in men 7. Growing up 8. Working class families 9. Coal miners 10. Men/women relations 11. Interpersonal attraction 12. England -- Social life and customs -- 20th century 13. Nottingham, England 14. Literary fiction 15. Coming-of-age stories 16. Modern classics
  LC 13021105
  Under the shadow of his parents' unsatisfactory marriage and the profound influence of his mother, Paul Morel faces a painful struggle to emancipate himself. His spiritual friendship with Miriam Lievers and a passionate sexual awakening with Clara Dawes together with the anguish caused by his mother's death, brings Paul Morel to manhood.

Lawrence, D. H. (David Herbert), 1885-1930
  * **Women** in love / D.H. Lawrence ; edited by David Farmer, Lindeth Vasey, and John Worthen ; introduction by Melvyn Bragg Cambridge University Press, 1988, c1920. 448 p.
  ISBN 9780521235655
  1. 1900s (Decade) 2. Women -- Sexuality 3. Men/women relations 4. Ideas (Philosophy) 5. Sisters 6. Sexuality 7. Couples 8. Social classes 9. Industrialization 10. Industrial Revolution 11. England -- Social life and customs -- 20th century 12. Love stories 13. Literary fiction 14. Modern classics
  LC 85031367
  The 2nd volume of the author's trilogy, the 1st of which in The rainbow, and the 3rd, Aaron's rod.
  Originally published: London : Thomas Seltzer, 1920.
  Women in Love follows the passionate relationships of two sisters, Gudrun and Ursula Brangwen, with their respective lovers, the ominous Gerald Crich and the charismatic but fragile Rupert Birkin. Beginning in a narrow-minded English colliery town and culminating amidst the ice and snow of the Alps, the abortive alliance between the two men and the couples' affairs are played out against the derangements of industrialism and the need to find new ways of living and better ways of dying.

Lawrence, David, 1942-
  The **dead** sit round in a ring / David Lawrence. Thomas Dunne Books, 2004. 448 p. Stella Mooney mysteries
  ISBN 0312327102
  1. Policewomen 2. Police 3. Mafia 4. Prostitutes 5. Serbs in England 6. Murder investigation 7. Suicide 8. Nightmares 9. Men/women relations 10. London, England 11. Mysteries
  LC 2004041878
  Published in 2005 in (pbk.) as: Circle of the dead.
  "This mystery offers a perspective on London that is darker and grittier than in conventional treatments. But the writing is the thing. Whether he's describing a bizarre death scene . . . or observing a group of streetwalkers plying their night trade . . . Lawrence, a published poet, writes with a delicacy and restraint rare in the genre." New York Times Book Review.

Lawrence, Margaret (Margaret K.)
  Hearts and bones / Margaret Lawrence Avon Books, 1996. 307 p. Hannah Trevor novels
  ISBN 0380973510
  1. 1780s 2. Independence in women 3. Single mothers 4. Murder 5. Rape victims 6. Children with disabilities 7. Midwives 8. Revolutions -- United States -- Post-war aspects 9. Former lovers 10. Men/women relations 11. Postwar life 12. United States -- Politics and government -- 18th century 13. Maine -- History -- 18th century 14. Historical mysteries
  LC 962394
  A midwife in a small Maine town, Hannah Trevor discovers the body of a young wife and mother, along with a note naming Hannah's secret past lover and the father of her illegitimate daughter as her murderers.
  "Through a combination of diary entries, trial records, autopsy reports, and engrossing narrative, Lawrence reveals the story of a witness and a participant in a brutal war crime and their decade-long silence." Booklist.

Lawson, Mary, 1946-
  Crow Lake / Mary Lawson. Dial Press, 2002 288 p.
  ISBN 038533611X
  1. Women zoologists 2. Brothers and sisters 3. Rural families -- Canada 4. Farm life -- Canada 5. Orphans 6. Dysfunctional families 7. Ontario 8. Psychological fiction
  LC 2001053779
  Books in Canada First Novel Award, 2002.
  Evergreen Award (Ontario), 2005.
  "Lawson achieves a breathless anticipatory quality in her surprisingly adept first novel, in which a child tells the story, but tells it very well indeed." Booklist.

Lawton, John, 1949-
  Hammer to fall / John Lawton. Atlantic Monthly Press, 2020. 352 p. Joe Wilderness novels
  ISBN 9780802148124
  1. M I 6 2. 1960s 3. Espionage 4. Intelligence service 5. International intrigue 6. Smuggling 7. KGB agents 8. Former lovers 9. Atomic bomb 10. Mines and mineral resources 11. London, England 12. Finland 13. Prague, Czech Republic 14. Thrillers and suspense 15. Spy fiction
  LC 2019045235

Posted in disgrace to remote northern Finland under the guise of a cultural exchange representative, 1960s MI6 spy Joe Wilderness earns money on the side as a vodka smuggler before uncovering a mining operation with possible atomic ties.

"Lawton does a brilliant job of incorporating backstory here, deepening our understanding of and feelings for rule-breaking Joe, who cares more for people than governments, while delivering a jaw-dropping finale that will leave readers palpitating for more." Booklist.

Lawton, John, 1949-
Then we take Berlin / John Lawton. Grove/Atlantic, 2013. 400 p. Joe Wilderness novels

ISBN 9780802121967

1. 1960s 2. Private investigators 3. Swindlers and swindling 4. Former spies 5. Smuggling 6. Royal Air Force veterans 7. Espionage 8. Men/women relations 9. Berlin, Germany 10. Historical fiction 11. Crime fiction

In 1963, freelance P.I. Joe Wilderness, a former MI6 agent and black market con-artist, agrees to one last Berlin scam, which involves smuggling people and brings the old gang back together once again.

Layne, Lauren,
Passion on Park Avenue / Lauren Layne. Gallery Books, 2019. 288 p. Central Park pact

ISBN 9781501191572

1. Women executives 2. Rich men 3. Interpersonal attraction 4. Elite (Social sciences) 5. Misfits (Persons) 6. New neighbors 7. Social classes 8. People with dementia 9. Housekeepers 10. Upper class 11. Revenge 12. Upper East Side, New York City 13. New York City 14. Contemporary romances

LC 2018045881

Naomi Powell, the strong-willed CEO of one of the biggest jewelry empires in the country, fights to find her place in Manhattan's upper class while engaging in a battle of wits with her new neighbor?and former childhood tormentor--Oliver Cunningham.

Layton, Edith
To wed a stranger / Edith Layton. Avon, 2003. 384 p. C' series

ISBN 0060502177

1. Regency period (1811-1820) 2. Viscounts and viscountesses 3. Husband and wife 4. Nobility 5. Sick women 6. Men/women relations 7. Arranged marriage 8. Influenza 9. Feminine beauty (Aesthetics) 10. London, England -- Social life and customs -- 19th century 11. England -- History -- 19th century 12. London, England -- History -- 19th century 13. Regency romances 14. Historical romances

Lazarin, Danielle
* **Back** talk : stories / Danielle Lazarin. Penguin Books, 2018 256 p.

ISBN 9780143131472

1. Loss (Psychology) 2. Grief 3. Coping 4. Interpersonal relations 5. Marriage 6. Mothers 7. Literary fiction 8. Short stories

LC 2017013074

A collection of stories from an award-winning, emerging author includes tales about a nearly-divorced woman who befriends the neighbor trying to buy her apartment and a teenage girl who experiences first love while still grieving her mother's death.

"With poignant imagery and a fresh voice, Lazarin portrays these women honestly and relatably. Her exceptional craftsmanship speaks to the heart, as she paints these tales with empathy and a compassion that extends to all humankind." Booklist.

Le Carre, John, 1931-
Agent running in the field / John Le Carre. Viking Press, 2019. 272 p.

ISBN 9781984878878

1. 2010s 2. Political intrigue 3. Spies 4. Intelligence service 5. Middle-aged persons 6. Young men 7. Disillusionment 8. Anger 9. Brexit, 2016-2020 10. Husband and wife 11. Badminton (Game) 12. Young women 13. London, England 14. Spy fiction

London 2018. In a desperate attempt to resist the new political turbulence swirling around him, Nat makes connections that will take him down a very dangerous path.

Le Carre, John, 1931-
The **constant** gardener : a novel / John Le Carre. Scribner, 2001. 492 p.

ISBN 0743215052

1. International businesses -- Corrupt practices -- Kenya 2. Diplomats 3. Pharmaceutical research -- Corrupt practices 4. Conspiracies 5. Business -- Corrupt practices -- Kenya 6. Murder -- Kenya 7. Greed 8. Grief in men 9. Loss (Psychology) 10. Kenya 11. Political thrillers 12. Thrillers and suspense

LC 00053340

Also published: Toronto : Penguin Group Canada, 2010, c2001.

When the young and beautiful wife of a much older embassy worker and amateur gardener is found murdered near northern Kenya's Lake Turkana, his personal pursuit of the killers not only sets him up as their next target, but as a suspect among his embassy colleagues.

"Globalization in its uglier aspects . . . has replaced the Cold War as the moral backdrop in Le Carre's work. His Cold War novels did not spare the conscience even of citizens on the 'right' side, confronting them with crimes committed in their names, and the globalization novels do not spare the stockholder." The Atlantic.

Le Carre, John, 1931-
* A **delicate** truth / John Le Carre. Viking, 2013. 432 p.

ISBN 9780670014897

1. Terrorism -- Prevention 2. Government cover-ups 3. Arms dealers 4. Political corruption 5. Conspiracies 6. Diplomats 7. Spies -- Great Britain 8. Intelligence service 9. Spy fiction

Three years after the launch of a delicate counter-terrorist operation organized to capture a high-value jihadist arms buyer, a disgraced Special Forces solider delivers a message that raises questions about the operation's success and a possible cover-up, a situation that forces the soldier to choose between his conscience and his duty.

Le Carre, John, 1931-
* The **honourable** schoolboy / John le Carre. Knopf, 1977. 533 p. George Smiley novels

ISBN 9780394416458

1. 1970s 2. Spies -- Great Britain 3. Intelligence service -- Great Britain 4. Cold War 5. Spies -- Soviet Union 6. Intelligence service -- Soviet Union 7. Spy fiction

LC 77075001

Gold Dagger Award for Best Crime Novel of the Year, 1977.

James Tait Black Memorial Prize for Fiction, 1977.

George Smiley, of England's Secret Service, goes onto the attack, manipulating old Asian hand Jerry Westerby through the Far East and a tangle of money, defection, passion, loyalty, and love that tests severely Westerby's hitherto unfaltering allegiances.

"This is superbly well-organized, combining a grandiose sweep with an intricate pattern. It has hard-edged reality instead of fuzzy near-fantasy, a host of sharply etched characters instead of a few eccentric caricatures, and a style which, subtle and flexible . . . never obtrudes, yet never goes unnoticed." Times Literary Supplement.

Le Carre, John, 1931-
A **most** wanted man : a novel / John Le Carre. Scribner, 2008. 323 p.
ISBN 9781416594888
1. Intelligence officers 2. War on Terrorism, 2001-2009 3. Spies 4. Terrorism 5. Muslims 6. Intelligence service 7. Germany 8. Thrillers and suspense 9. Spy fiction
LC 2008030704
Smuggled into Hamburg, Issa, a young Russian man carrying a large amount of cash and claiming to be a devout Muslim, forms an unlikely alliance with Annabel, an idealistic young German civil rights lawyer, and Tommy Brue, a sixty-year-old scion of a failing British bank, as they become victims of rival intelligence operations in the War on Terror.

"Le Carre's dialogue has snap, rhythm and wit, particularly in those passages where intelligence chiefs maneuver to gain an edge on each other. Too, his immaculate timing helps him fold in different plot lines without smudging narrative pace and tone. Ever the spymaster, he also differentiates the challenges faced by spies today from those of their Cold War counterparts." St. Louis Post-Dispatch.

Le Carre, John, 1931-
* **Our** kind of traitor : a novel / John Le Carre. Viking, 2010. 305 p.
ISBN 9780670022243
1. Mafia 2. Spies 3. Money laundering 4. Defectors 5. Vacations 6. Women lawyers 7. Banks and banking -- Corrupt practices 8. College teachers 9. Betrayal 10. Defection 11. Antigua and Barbuda 12. Spy fiction 13. Thrillers and suspense
LC 2010019513
Vacationing at a posh tennis resort in Antigua, Perry and Gail are recruited by big-time Russian money launderer Dima to help him defect, an arrangement for which Dima promises to expose financial corruption but renders the hapless couple pawns in a deadly international scheme.

"Le Carre seems positively re-invigorated in a retro sort of way. The story carries on with an extra spring in the step that harkens back, both in the manner of plotting and the style, to Le Carre's earliest and still greatest novels. That's due in large part to how he engages with current events: the teetering economy, Britain (and Europe's) austerity-oriented response, and the rise of state surveillance even as the events of September 11 grow more distant." Daily Beast

Le Carre, John, 1931-
Smiley's people / John le Carre. Knopf, 1980, c1979. 374 p. George Smiley novels
ISBN 9780394508436
1. Spies -- Great Britain 2. Intelligence service -- Great Britain 3. International intrigue 4. Spies -- Soviet Union 5. Intelligence service -- Soviet Union 6. Spy fiction
LC 79002299
"This novel is a complete winner, exciting, well-paced, and convincing. . . . There is a lot of the Le Carre gloom, but now it seems almost elegiac and touching. Absolutely not to be missed." Library Journal.

Le Carre, John, 1931-
The **spy** who came in from the cold / John Le Carre. Coward, McCann & Geoghegan, 1978, c1963. 256 p. George Smiley novels
ISBN 0698109163
1. Spies -- Great Britain 2. Intelligence service -- Great Britain 3. Double agents 4. Cold War 5. Intelligence officers 6. International intrigue 7. Murder 8. Secrets 9. Communism 10. Berlin, Germany 11. Spy fiction
LC 78001799
Originally published: London : Victor Gollancz, 1963.
First published: London : Victor Gollancz, 1963.
Edgar Allan Poe Award for Best Mystery Novel, 1965.
Gold Dagger Award for Best Crime Novel of the Year, 1963.
Somerset Maugham Award, 1964.
Secret agent Leamas is on a mission in East Berlin, but he has doubts about the organization he serves.

"The story of Alec Leamas, 50-year-old professional secret agent who has grown stale in espionage, who longs to come in from the cold and how he undertakes one last assignment before that hoped-for retirement. Over the years Leamas has grown unsure where his workday carapace ends and his real self begins. . . . Recalled from Berlin after the death of his last East German contact at the Wall, Leamas lets himself be seduced into a pretended defection-thereby providing the East Germans with data from which they can deduce that the head of their own spy apparatus is a double agent." New York Times Book Review.

Le Carre, John, 1931-
The **tailor** of Panama / John le Carre. Alfred A. Knopf, 1996. 331 p.
ISBN 0679454462
1. 1980s 2. Conspiracies 3. Spies -- Great Britain 4. Secret identity 5. British in Panama 6. Tailors -- Panama 7. Intelligence service -- Great Britain 8. Jewish men 9. Men/women relations 10. Soldiers 11. Ghosts 12. Greed 13. Jealousy 14. Dishonesty 15. Political corruption 16. Americans in Panama 17. Panama 18. Spy fiction
LC 96034802
First published by Hodder & Stoughton 996.
Seldom has the hidden eye of British Intelligence selected such an unlikely champion as Harry Pendel, a British tailor living in Panama City.

"Le Carre reveals in the contortions of British diplomats, aghast at the arriviste spy masters whom they pretend to accept, all the while struggling to extricate themselves from absurd but inevitable catastrophe. Readers who wonder whether Graham Greene was not here 40 years ago are right, and Mr Le Carre acknowledges his debt to 'Our Man in Havana'. This tale, told with wit and ingenuity, is a splendid homage from one master of political thrillers to another." The Economist.

Le Carre, John, 1931-
* **Tinker,** tailor, soldier, spy / John Le Carre. Knopf, 1974. 355 p. George Smiley novels
ISBN 9780241323410
1. Spies -- Great Britain 2. Spies -- Soviet Union 3. Intelligence service -- Great Britain 4. Husband and wife 5. Extramarital affairs 6. Intelligence service -- Soviet Union 7. Spy fiction
LC 74005084
Originally published: London: Hodder & Stoughton, 1974.
George Smiley, who is a troubled man of infinite compassion, is also a single-mindedly ruthless adversary as a spy. The scene which he enters is a Cold War landscape of moles and lamplighters, scalp-hunters and pavement artists, where men are turned, burned or bought for stock. Smiley's mission is to catch a Moscow Centre mole burrowed thirty years deep into the Circus itself.

"Smiley instinctively realises from the outset who the traitor is but refuses to confront the embarrassing truth. A perceptive reader will sense the secret too, but one goes on reading entranced not so much by the ramifications of the plot, beautifully engineered though it is, as by concern for the characters, a rare thing in thrillers." New Statesman.

Le Guin, Ursula K., 1929-2018

The **beginning** place / Ursula K. LeGuin Tor, 2005, c1980. 230 p.

ISBN 9780765346254

1. Quests 2. Magic 3. Growing up 4. Happiness 5. Love 6. Good and evil 7. Men/women relations 8. Coming-of-age stories 9. Fantasy fiction

Two young people who cross over from everyday reality and meet in the magical village of Tembreadbrezi volunteer to take on and destroy the unknown malevolent force that is threatening the village with destruction.

Le Guin, Ursula K., 1929-2018

The **birthday** of the world : and other stories / Ursula K. Le Guin. HarperCollins, 2002. 362 p.

ISBN 9780066212531

1. Life on other planets 2. Aliens (Humanoid) 3. Human/alien encounters 4. Gender role 5. Women's role 6. Short stories 7. Social science fiction 8. Science fiction

LC 2001039508

A collection of stories that are filled with love, lust, sex, marriage, gender, and other annoying problems that people must deal with no matter where they reside in the universe.

"Le Guin appears to have the most fun with her investigations of sex and gender . . . but the costs of revolution, religious bliss, and technology are also provicatively explored, and one returns to the current headlines with a fresh awareness of the exotic providional nature of human arrangements." The New Yorker.

Le Guin, Ursula K., 1929-2018

* The **dispossessed** : an ambiguous utopia / Ursula K. Le Guin. Harper & Row, 1974. 341 p. Hainish series

ISBN 0060125632

1. Dystopias 2. Utopias 3. Far future 4. Life on other planets 5. Anarchists 6. Revolutions 7. Rebels 8. Physicists 9. Voyages and travels 10. Political corruption 11. Gender role 12. Women's role 13. Dystopian fiction 14. Social science fiction 15. Science fiction

LC 73018667

Hugo Award for Best Novel, 1975.
Locus Award for Best Science Fiction Novel, 1975.
Nebula Award for Best Novel, 1974.

A physicist from isolated Anarres travels to the mother planet, Urras, in hopes of dissolving the hatred that exists between them.

Le Guin, Ursula K., 1929-2018

Four ways to forgiveness / Ursula Le Guin. HarperPrism, 1995. 228 p. Hainish series

ISBN 0061052345

1. Slave resistance and revolts 2. Sexism 3. Far future 4. Life on other planets 5. Slaves 6. Slavery 7. Women slaves 8. Space colonies 9. Women's resistance and revolts 10. Social science fiction 11. Science fiction

LC 95011459

4 novellas.
Locus Award for Best Collection, 1996.

Four interconnected novellas are set on the twin planets Werel and Yeowe and follow the stories of such characters as the disgraced revolutionary Abberkam, the callow "space brat" Solly, and the androgynous artist Batikam.

"Four interrelated novellas deal with the Hainish culture on the twin planets of Werel and Yeowe and examine the relationship between love, freedom and forgiveness." Publishers Weekly.

Le Guin, Ursula K., 1929-2018

The **lathe** of heaven / Ursula K. Le Guin Scribner, 1971. 184 p.

ISBN 0684125293

1. Near future 2. Dreams 3. Psychiatrist and patient 4. Psychic ability 5. Portland, Oregon 6. Oregon 7. Pacific Northwest fiction 8. Science fiction

LC 77162760

"First published in Amazing stories magazine."
Locus Award for Best Science Fiction Novel, 1972.

George Orr discovers that his dreams possess the remarkable ability to change the world, and when he falls into the hands of a power-mad psychiatrist, he counters by dreaming up a perfect world that can overcome his nightmares.

Le Guin, Ursula K., 1929-2018

* The **left** hand of darkness / Ursula Le Guin. Ace Books, 1969. 286 p. Hainish series

ISBN 0441007317

1. Far future 2. Androgyny (Psychology) 3. Life on other planets 4. Culture conflict 5. Ethnologists 6. Voyages and travels 7. Aliens (Humanoid) 8. Human/alien encounters 9. Gender role 10. Women's role 11. Social science fiction 12. Science fiction

Hugo Award for Best Novel, 1970.
James Tiptree, Jr. Award, 1995.
Nebula Award for Best Novel, 1969.

While on a mission to the planet Gethen, earthling Genly Ai is sent by leaders of the nation of Orgoreyn to a concentration camp from which the exiled prime minister of the nation of Karhide tries to rescue him.

Le Guin, Ursula K., 1929-2018

Orsinian tales / Ursula K. LeGuin Harpercollins, 2004, c1976. 179 p.

ISBN 9780060763435

1. Freedom 2. State-sponsored terrorism 3. Political persecution 4. Eastern Europe 5. Short stories 6. Historical fiction

LC 76005545

Originally published: New York : Harper, 1976.

The universal need for human freedom and love and the horrors of government oppression are recurring themes in this collection of eleven haunting pieces of short fiction, all set in the imaginary Eastern European country of Orsinia.

"This is a cycle of interrelated short stories. Set in a vaguely Middle-European country, Le Guin's tales deal with love, freedom, and tyranny in a society which over a series of historical periods appears to be perpetually in the last stages preceding cataclysm." Booklist.

Le Guin, Ursula K., 1929-2018

The **other** wind / Ursula K. Le Guin. Harcourt, 2001. 256 p. Earthsea series

ISBN 0151006849

1. Dragons 2. Wizards 3. Magic 4. Rulers 5. Widowers 6. Earthsea 7. Dreams 8. Grief in men 9. Loss (Psychology) 10. Death 11. High fantasy 12. Fantasy fiction

LC 2001024632

World Fantasy Award, 2002.

Haunted by dreams of the dead who seek to invade Earthsea through him, the sorcerer Alder enlists the aid of Ged, a former Archmage, who advises him to find the holiest place in the world, which holds the key to preserving Earthsea.

Le Guin, Ursula K., 1929-2018

The **telling** / Ursula Le Guin Harcourt, 2000 272 p. Hainish series

ISBN 0151005672

1. Life on other planets 2. Aliens (Humanoid) 3. Far future 4. Social science fiction 5. Science fiction

LC 00029574

Locus Award for Best Science Fiction Novel, 2001.

On a world in which ancient beliefs and customs are banned, Sutty journeys deep into the countryside and discovers the Telling, the old faith of the Akans, a banned religion that teaches her about the meaning of her own existence.

"This parable of the modern world's headlong rush toward monocultural sterility exemplifies the author's elegant simplicity and keen insight." Library Journal.

Lea, Caroline

The **glass** woman / Caroline Lea. HarperCollins, 2019, c2019. 400 p.

ISBN 9780062935106

1. 17th century 2. Second wives 3. Superstition 4. Winter 5. Secrets 6. Rumor 7. Villages 8. Paganism 9. Married women 10. Husband and wife 11. Married people and secrets 12. Iceland -- History -- 17th century 13. Historical fiction 14. Gothic fiction

Originally published in the UK February, 2019.

A young bride in gothic 17th-century Iceland navigates ancient superstitions, disturbing secrets and her husband's enigmatic nature amid rumors about his first wife's mysterious death.

Leavitt, David, 1961-

* The **two** Hotel Francforts : a novel / David Leavitt. Bloomsbury, 2013. 257 p.

ISBN 9781596910423

1. 1940s 2. Life change events 3. Expatriates 4. Marital conflict 5. Extramarital affairs 6. Gay men 7. Homosexuality 8. Jewish women 9. Bohemianism 10. Interpersonal relations 11. Lisbon, Portugal 12. Portugal 13. Historical fiction 14. LGBTQIA fiction

LC 2013015952

As Europe prepares for war during the summer of 1940, two couples--expatriate Americans fleeing Paris and wealthy bohemians beset by the social and sexual anxieties of their class--arrive in Portugal where their lives become inexplicably entwined in unimaginable--and dangerous--ways.

"Leavitt's clever, engaging tale of marriage's hidden shadows, lies, and half-truths demonstrates that husbands and wives are only as happy as they've already decided to allow themselves to be." Publishers Weekly.

Lebrecht, Norman, 1948-

The **song** of names / Norman Lebrecht. Anchor Books, 2019, c2002. 311 p.

ISBN 9781400034895

1. 20th century 2. Refugees 3. Jews 4. Boys -- Friendship 5. Self-discovery 6. Violinists 7. Children and war 8. War -- Psychological aspects 9. City life 10. London, England 11. Literary fiction 12. Historical fiction

Originally published: London : Headline Review, 2002.

Whitbread Book Award for First Novel, 2002.

Martin is growing up as an only child in wartime London until Dovidl, a refugee violinist from Warsaw, comes to stay. His arrival brings merriment and love, mischief and menace. Blood-brothers, they roam the ruined city, finding tragedy and triumph, sex and crime, until Dovidl disappears.

"Lebrecht's story delves into the horrors of the Holocaust and the Blitz, as well as the quiet communities of Hasidic Judaism that developed in Britain after the flight of so many refugees. What emerges is a vivid and outstanding story that sings about artistry, genius, music, love, envy, friendship, and revenge." Booklist.

Leckie, Ann

* **Ancillary** justice / Ann Leckie. Orbit, 2013. 432 p. Imperial Radch

ISBN 9780316246620

1. Aliens 2. Space flight 3. Revenge 4. Immortalism 5. Rulers 6. Imperialism 7. Weapons 8. Quests 9. Space opera 10. Science fiction

LC 2012051135

Arthur C. Clarke Award, 2014.

BSFA Award for Best Novel, 2013.

Hugo Award for Best Novel, 2014.

Locus Award for First Novel, 2014.

Nebula Award for Best Novel, 2013.

One Esk -- an electronic artificial intelligence -- once commanded an entire starship, the formidable Justice of Tore. Now confined to a mortal body cobbled together from interchangeable human parts as the entity called "Breq," the AI must survive as a multisegmented, ancillary humanoid being in a galactic empire ruled by an oppressive government -- without disobeying the law that forbids AIs from harming their creators. - Description by Gillian Speace.

"Using the format of sf military adventure blended with hints of space opera, Leckie explores the expanded meaning of human nature and the uneasy balance between individuality and membership in a group identity." Library Journal.

Leckie, Ann

* **Ancillary** sword / Ann Leckie. Orbit, 2014. 432 p. Imperial Radch

ISBN 9780316246651

1. Aliens 2. Space flight 3. Revenge 4. Immortalism 5. Rulers 6. Imperialism 7. Weapons 8. Quests 9. Space opera 10. Science fiction

LC 2014018730

BSFA Award for Best Novel, 2014.

Locus Award for Best Science Fiction Novel, 2015.

Fleet Captain Breq Mianaai has acquired both a human body and command of a starship. Not the worst fate in the universe for a several-thousand-year-old AI component (or "ancillary") separated from her former vessel's hive mind. Sent to the planet Athoek as an envoy of the many-bodied Lord of the Radch, Breq must prevent a civil war that threatens the stability of the Radchaai Empire while engaging in a more personal quest for answers about the past. -- Description by Gillian Speace.

"Breq's struggle for meaningful justice in a society designed to favor the strong is as engaging as ever." Publishers Weekly.

Leckie, Ann

* **Ancillary** mercy / Ann Leckie. Orbit, 2015. 432 p. Imperial Radch

ISBN 9780316246682

1. Aliens 2. Space flight 3. Revenge 4. Immortalism 5. Rulers 6. Imperialism 7. Weapons 8. Quests 9. Space opera 10. Science fiction

LC 2015020915

Locus Award for Best Science Fiction Novel, 2016.

Housed in a composite human body not her own, Fleet Captain Breq is the last remaining "ancillary" fragment of a fallen starship's AI, as well as the commander of her own vessel. With civil war raging throughout the rapidly fracturing Radchaai Empire, Breq and her crew devise a plan to defend Atheok Station from ancient nemesis Anaander Mianaai,

Lord of the Radch. Action-packed heroics unfold side-by-side with reflections on identity and personhood in this dramatic conclusion of the Imperial Radch trilogy, which begins with Ancillary Justice and Ancillary Sword. -- Description by Gillian Space.

"Leckie creates a grand backdrop to tell an intimate, cerebral story about identity and empowerment. She devotes as much attention to the characters' personal relationships and their mental and emotional difficulties as she does to the wider conflict." Kirkus.

Leckie, Ann

Provenance / Ann Leckie. Orbit, 2017. 432 p.
ISBN 9780316388672
1. Ambition in women 2. Political intrigue 3. Material culture 4. Thieves 5. Prisoners 6. Power (Social sciences) 7. Rescues 8. Families 9. Foster parents 10. Space opera 11. Science fiction
LC 2017018846

Ingray Aughskold has never been her mother's favorite child; that distinction belongs to her brother, who will almost certainly be named heir. But will a scheme to shame one of her family's political rivals win Ingray enough plaudits to change her fate? Although set in the universe of the author's Imperial Radch trilogy, Provenance stands on its own. -- Description by Gillian Space

"Leckie again uses large-scale worldbuilding to tell a deeply personal story--in this case, to explore what binds children to their families. As always, she impels the reader to consider the power language, and specifically names, has to shape perception and reality." Kirkus.

Leckie, Ann

* The **Raven** tower / Ann Leckie. Orbit, 2019. 432 p.
ISBN 9780316388696
1. Imaginary kingdoms 2. Gods and goddesses 3. Rulers 4. Warriors 5. Secrets 6. Political intrigue 7. Power (Social sciences) 8. Faith 9. Magic 10. Revenge 11. Epic fantasy 12. Second person narratives
LC 2018040311

The kingdom of Iraden, under the protection of a god known as the Raven, faces unrest and challenges from invaders when a usurper takes over the throne and discovers that the Raven's power is weakening.

"Sharp, many layered, and, as always for Leckie, deeply intelligent." Kirkus.

Ledgard, J. M.

Submergence : a novel / J. M. Ledgard. Coffee House Press, 2013. 208 p.
ISBN 9781566893190
1. Hostages 2. Oceans 3. Torture 4. Culture conflict 5. Espionage 6. Memory 7. Lovers 8. Violence 9. Undercover operations 10. Women marine biologists 11. Men/women relations 12. Fundamentalists 13. Islam 14. Muslims 15. Somalia 16. Literary fiction
LC 2012036524

Originally published: London : Jonathan Cape, 2011.

James More, held captive by jihadists, and Danielle Flinders, diving in a submersible to the ocean floor, each remember the love they shared and the Christmas they spent together the year before.

Lee, Chang-rae

A **gesture** life / Chang-rae Lee. Riverhead Books, 1999. 356 p.
ISBN 1573221465
1. Japanese Americans 2. Comfort women 3. Memories 4. Soldiers -- Japan 5. Koreans in Japan 6. Fathers and daughters 7. World War II -- Japan 8. Suburban life -- New York (State) 9. New York (State) 10. Japan -- History -- 1926-1945 11. Literary fiction
ALA Notable Book, 2000.

"This is a wise, humane, fully rounded story, deeply but unsentimentally moving, and permeated with insights about the nature of human relationships." Publishers Weekly.

Lee, Chang-rae

* **On** such a full sea / Chang-rae Lee. Riverhead Books, 2014. 336 p.
ISBN 9781594486104
1. Social classes 2. Dystopias 3. Quests 4. Post-apocalypse 5. Missing persons 6. Crime 7. Chinese American women 8. Regression (Civilization) 9. Forced labor 10. Men/women relations 11. United States 12. Dystopian fiction 13. Literary fiction
LC 2013036600

ALA Notable Book, 2015.
Andrew Carnegie Medal for Excellence in Fiction finalist, 2015.
National Book Critics Circle Award for Fiction finalist, 2014

In a class-divided future America where urban neighborhoods function as labor colonies for elite charter villages, Fan, a female fish-tank diver, embarks on what becomes a legendary quest to find the man she loves in a region overcome by anarchic forces.

"A harrowing and fully imagined vision of dystopian America. . . . Welcome and surprising proof that there's plenty of life in end-of-the-world storytelling." Kirkus.

Lee, Chang-rae

* The **surrendered** / Chang-rae Lee. Riverhead Books, 2010. 480 p.
ISBN 9781594489761
1. Orphans -- Korea 2. Soldiers 3. Women missionaries 4. Secrets 5. Korean War, 1950-1953 6. Korea 7. Epic fiction 8. Literary fiction
LC 2009030887

ALA Notable Book, 2011.
Pulitzer Prize for Fiction finalist, 2011.

At the end of the Korean War, the lives of orphan June Han and American soldier Hector Brennan collide. Thirty years later, they meet again and are forced to come to terms with the secrets of their devastating past.

"In its ineffably quiet way, there really is something Tolstoyan in this searching fiction's determination to understand the characters specifically as members of families and products of other people's influences. The characterizations of Hector and Sylvie are astonishingly rich and complex, and the risk taken in depicting the adult June as the woman readers will hope she would not become is triumphantly vindicated." Kirkus.

Lee, Don, 1959-

Country of origin : a novel / Don Lee. W.W. Norton & Co., 2004. 352 p.
ISBN 0393058123
1. 1980s 2. Police -- Tokyo, Japan 3. Diplomats 4. Anthropology students 5. Women graduate students 6. Multiracial women 7. Multiracial persons 8. Identity (Psychology) 9. Ethnic identity 10. Crimes against young women 11. Sex-oriented businesses 12. Americans in Japan 13. Missing persons 14. Missing persons investigation 15. Alienation (Social psychology) 16. Belonging 17. Racism 18. Conformity 19. Tokyo, Japan 20. Mysteries
LC 2004004722

Edgar Allan Poe Award for Best First Mystery Novel, 2005.

When a young American woman goes missing in 1980 Tokyo's sexual underworld, a young U.S. Embassy official considers his prospects for finding her and enlists the help of a neurotic and unpopular Japanese police officer.

"Issues of race, class, and national identity drive this clear-eyed story of closure, redemption, and carving out a place in the world." Booklist.

Lee, Fonda

Jade City / Fonda Lee. Orbit, 2017. 498 p. Green Bone saga

ISBN 9780316440868

1. Jade 2. Organized crime 3. Power (social sciences) 4. Imaginary wars and battles 5. Cities and towns 6. Political intrigue 7. Black market 8. Martial arts 9. Drug traffic 10. Gangs 11. Magic 12. Epic fantasy 13. Asian-influenced fantasy

Prix Aurora: Best Novel, 2018.

World Fantasy Award, 2018.

In this action-packed series opener, Green Bone warriors use the magic-enhancing powers of jade to protect their island nation of Kekon and its capital, Janloon. But times are changing, as rival syndicates headed by the feuding Ayt and Kaul families go to extreme lengths to consolidate their power and gain control of the city. Detailed world-building and exciting martial-arts battles enhance this gritty crime drama, which takes place in an East Asia-inspired fantasy world. -- Description by Gillian Speace

Lee, Fonda

Jade war / Fonda Lee. Orbit, 2019. 512 p. Green Bone saga

ISBN 9780316440929

1. Jade 2. Power (Social sciences) 3. Imaginary wars and battles 4. International relations 5. Brothers and sisters 6. Organized crime 7. Political intrigue 8. Martial arts 9. Alliances 10. Magic 11. Epic fantasy 12. Asian-influenced fantasy

LC 2019000760

In a sequel to *Jade City*, the Kaul siblings forge new and dangerous alliances to fight political rivals and mercenary kingpins for control over the capital city and its supply of magical jade.

Lee, Harper

* **Go** set a watchman / Harper Lee. HarperCollins, 2015. 288 p. To kill a mockingbird

ISBN 9780062409850

1. 1950s 2. Homecomings 3. Independence in women 4. Fathers and daughters 5. Race relations 6. Racism 7. Small town life 8. Social change 9. Hometowns 10. Men/women relations 11. Alabama 12. Southern States 13. Literary fiction 14. Southern fiction

Twenty years after the trial of Tom Robinson, Scout returns home to Maycomb to visit her father and struggles with personal and political issues as her small Alabama town adjusts to the turbulent events beginning to transform the United States in the mid-1950s.

Lee, Harper

* **To** kill a mockingbird / Harper Lee. Lippincott, 1960. 296 p. To kill a mockingbird

ISBN 0397001517

1. Racism 2. Single-parent families 3. Fathers and daughters 4. Race relations 5. Trials (Rape) 6. Girls 7. African Americans 8. Lawyers 9. Family relationships 10. Southern States 11. Alabama 12. Coming-of-age stories 13. Modern classics 14. Literary fiction 15. Southern fiction

LC 60007847

Pulitzer Prize for Fiction, 1961.

Scout Finch, daughter of the town lawyer, likes to spend her summers building treehouses, swimming, and catching lightning bugs with her big brother Jem. But one summer, when a black man is accused of raping a white woman, Scout's carefree days come to an end. In the county courtroom, she will join her father in a desperate battle against ignorance and prejudice.

Lee, Min Jin

Pachinko / Min Jin Lee. Grand Central Publishing, 2017. 496 p.

ISBN 9781455563937

1. 20th century 2. 1910s 3. Families 4. Unplanned pregnancy 5. Intergenerational relations 6. Identity (Psychology) 7. Immigrant families 8. Koreans in Japan 9. Home (Concept) 10. Prejudice 11. Korea -- History -- Japanese occupation, 1910-1945 12. Japan -- Social life and customs -- 20th century 13. Family sagas 14. Historical fiction

LC 2016023353

ALA Notable Book, 2018.

National Book Award for Fiction finalist, 2017

RUSA Reading List Short List, 2018.

In early 1900s Korea, prized daughter Sunja finds herself pregnant and alone, bringing shame on her family until a young tubercular minister offers to marry her and move with her to Japan, in the saga of one family bound together as their faith and identity are called into question.

"Those who enjoy historical fiction with strong characterizations will not be disappointed as they ride along on the emotional journeys offered in the author's latest page-turner." Library Journal.

Lee, Ji-min

* The **starlet** and the spy / Ji-min Lee ; translated from the Korean by Chi-Young Kim. HarperCollins, 2019 256 p.

ISBN 9780062930262

1. Monroe, Marilyn, 1926-1962 2. 1950s 3. Postwar life 4. Interpreters 5. Actors and actresses 6. Friendship 7. Women and war 8. War and society 9. Love triangles 10. Regret in women 11. Korean War, 1950-1953 12. South Korea 13. Seoul, Korea 14. Historical fiction 15. Translations -- Korean to English

Published in the UK as Marilyn and Me, 2019.

A Korean war survivor is assigned as translator for Marilyn Monroe during a 1954 USO tour to a Korea still struggling to return to normalcy and develops a deep kinship with the star.

Lee, Patrick, 1976-

Dark site / Patrick Lee. Minotaur Books, 2019. 391 p. Sam Dryden novels

ISBN 9781250030795

1. Former Special Forces members 2. Military secrets 3. Kidnappers 4. Secrets 5. Memories 6. Government conspiracies 7. Retired military personnel 8. California 9. Iowa 10. Techno-thrillers 11. Thrillers and suspense

LC 2018055980

Escaping an attempted abduction, former Special Forces operative Sam Dryden narrowly rescues another potential target, an unfamiliar woman in possession of a heavily redacted file about a secret military site where they both lived as children.

Lee, Patrick, 1976-

Runner / Patrick Lee. Minotaur Books, 2014. vii, 328 p. Sam Dryden novels

ISBN 9781250030733

1. Retired military personnel 2. Escapes 3. Amnesia 4. Special forces 5. Girls 6. Prisoners 7. Conspiracies 8. Secrecy in government 9. Human experimentation in psychology 10. Girl psychics 11. California 12. Southern California 13. Thrillers and suspense 14. Techno-thrillers

LC 2013032586

In this series debut starring retired special forces soldier Sam Dryden, our hero is out for a run (at 3am) when he encounters a young girl being chased by a group of men who are armed to the teeth. Of course he helps her, putting himself in immediate danger. The girl -- who can remember only her first name and the last two months of her life -- appears to have been imprisoned for most of her 11 years, and has a skill that makes her extremely dangerous to a lot of powerful people. -- Description by Shauna Griffin.

"Tension mounts right from the start in this nonstop action-packed narrative and seldom flags, as Lee . . . continually blurs the lines between the good guys and the bad guys." Library Journal.

Lee, Patrick, 1976-

Signal / Patrick Lee. Minotaur Books, 2015. 320 p. Sam Dryden novels

ISBN 9781250030788

1. Escapes 2. Kidnapping victims 3. Special forces 4. Girls 5. Rescues 6. Conspiracies 7. Secrecy in government 8. Retired military personnel 9. Business -- Corrupt practices 10. California 11. Southern California 12. Thrillers and suspense 13. Techno-thrillers

Former Special Forces operative Sam Dryden is back on the run in this sequel to successful series opener?Runner. Here, the rescue of four kidnapped girls leads to the discovery that a murderous cabal known only as the Group has stolen cutting-edge technology that will allow them to influence the future (it's complicated, but there's just enough scientific explanation to make it plausible). With plenty of action, plus continued references to world-changing technologies, the Sam Dryden novels offer an exhilarating ride. -- Description by Shauna Griffin.

"A credible hero and a plot filled with nonstop cinematic action will leave thriller fans eager for the next installment." Publishers Weekly.

Lee, Yoon Ha, 1979-

Ninefox gambit / Yoon Ha Lee. Solaris, 2016. 384 p. Machineries of empire

ISBN 9781781084496

1. Imaginary empires 2. Women soldiers 3. Space warfare 4. Trust 5. Traitors 6. Alliances 7. Life after death 8. Political intrigue 9. Command of troops 10. Power (Social sciences) 11. Imaginary wars and battles 12. Space 13. Military science fiction 14. Space opera 15. Science fiction

Locus Award for First Novel, 2017.

Given the opportunity to redeem herself for past crimes, Captain Kel Cheris is tasked with retaking the Fortress of Scattered Needles, a star fortress under the control of heretics, a mission that requires her to partner with an untrustworthy ally.

Lee, Yoon Ha, 1979-

Raven stratagem / Yoon Ha Lee. Solaris, 2017. 400 p. Machineries of empire

ISBN 9781781085370

1. Imaginary empires 2. Power (Social sciences) 3. Space warfare 4. Political intrigue 5. Military strategy 6. Deception 7. Enemies 8. Space 9. Military science fiction 10. Space opera 11. Science fiction

When Kel Cheris, a young captain, summons the ghost of a long-dead General Shuos Jedao to stop a rebellion, the general possesses her and takes over General Khiruev's fleet.

"This follow up to the Nebula- and Hugo-nominated Ninefox Gambit combines exciting space opera action with dazzling, imaginative worldbuilding." Library Journal.

Lee, Yoon Ha, 1979-

Revenant gun / Yoon Ha Lee. Solaris, 2018. 400 p. Machineries of empire

ISBN 9781781086070

1. Imaginary empires 2. Imaginary wars and battles 3. Power (Social sciences) 4. Space warfare 5. Political intrigue 6. Life after death 7. Rulers 8. War crimes 9. Memories 10. Soldiers 11. Space 12. Military science fiction 13. Space opera 14. Science fiction

Shuos Jedao wakes up thinking he is a seventeen-year-old cadet, but his body is that of an older man. The soldiers he commands hate him thanks to a massacre he can't remember committing. Even worse, he is being hunted by an enemy who knows more about Jedao and his crimes than he does himself...

Lefteri, Christy, 1980-

The **beekeeper** of Aleppo : a novel / Christy Lefteri. Ballantine Books, 2019. 317 p.

ISBN 9781984821218

1. Beekeepers 2. Refugees 3. Voyages and travels 4. Blindness 5. Women who are blind 6. Husband and wife 7. Loss (Psychology) 8. Syria 9. Great Britain 10. Mainstream fiction

A beekeeper and his artist wife have their lives upended and must flee after war destroys their home in Aleppo, Syria, and they set off on a dangerous journey through Turkey and Greece, towards an uncertain future in England.

"Lefteri perceptively and powerfully documents the horrors of the Syrian civil war and the suffering of innocent civilians. Readers will find this deeply affecting for both its psychological intensity and emotional acuity." Publishers Weekly.

Lehane, Dennis

The **given** day / Dennis Lehane. William Morrow, 2008. 704 p. Coughlin novels

ISBN 9780688163181

1. 1910s 2. Strikes 3. Race relations 4. Civil rights 5. Police 6. Social classes 7. Labor unions 8. Boston, Massachusetts -- History -- 20th century 9. Historical fiction

Sequel: Live by Night.

An epic tale set at the end of World War I follows the experiences of a family whose lives mirror the political unrest of an America caught between its well-patterned past and an unpredictable future.

"Lehane laces his narrative with melodrama--two brothers in love with the same woman, who harbors a secret past; a viciously racist cop out to destroy Luther and frame the burgeoning N.A.A.C.P.and a subplot, involving Babe Ruth, feels stale and unnecessary. But he brings vividly to life the struggles that the working classes faced in pursuit of decent working conditions and a fair wage." The New Yorker.

Lehane, Dennis

* **Live** by night / Dennis Lehane. William Morrow & Co., 2012. 401 p. Coughlin novels

ISBN 9780060004873

1. 1920s 2. Prohibition 3. Gangsters 4. Betrayal 5. Violence 6. Bootleggers 7. Fathers and sons 8. Organized crime 9. Men/women relations 10. Crime bosses 11. Black market 12. Young men -- Psychology 13. United States -- History -- 1919-1933 14. Historical fiction 15. Crime fiction

Sequel to: The Given Day.

Edgar Allan Poe Award for Best Novel, 2013.

In 1926, during the Prohibition, Joe Coughlin defies his strict law-and-order upbringing by climbing a ladder of organized crime that takes him from Boston to Cuba where he encounters a dangerous cast of characters who are all fighting for their piece of the American dream.

Lehane, Dennis

* **Mystic** river / Dennis Lehane. William Morrow, 2001. 401 p.

ISBN 9780688163167

1. Adult child sexual abuse victims 2. Men -- Psychology 3. Blue

collar families 4. Working class neighborhoods 5. Murder 6. Murder investigation 7. Detectives 8. Children -- Friendship 9. Sex crimes 10. Life change events 11. Secrets 12. Grief in men 13. Revenge 14. Urban violence 15. Childhood friends 16. Boston, Massachusetts 17. Back Bay, Boston, Massachusetts 18. Massachusetts 19. Noir fiction 20. Thrillers and suspense 21. Psychological fiction

Anthony Award for Best Novel, 2002

Massachusetts Book Awards, Fiction Award, 2002.

Sean Devine must confront the world of violence and pain he tried to forget when his childhood friend's daughter is murdered, and the investigation brings him face-to-face with a vigilante killer and a man with a dangerous secret.

"Lehane spares nothing in his wrenching descriptions of how a crime in the neighborhood kills the neighborhood, taking it down house by house, family by family." New York Times Book Review.

Lehane, Dennis

Prayers for rain : a novel / Dennis Lehane. W. Morrow, 1999. 337 p. Patrick Kenzie and Angela Gennaro novels

ISBN 9780688153335

1. Private investigators 2. Psychopaths 3. Urban violence 4. Mind control 5. Family secrets 6. Psychotherapy malpractice 7. Antisocial personality disorders 8. Accidental death investigation 9. Suicide 10. Boston, Massachusetts 11. Dorchester, Boston, Massachusetts 12. Back Bay, Boston, Massachusetts 13. Hardboiled fiction 14. Mysteries

LC 9922048

When a former client jumps from the twenty-sixth floor, private investigator Patrick Kenzie digs into her past to uncover the psychopath responsible for her self-destruction.

"Lehane's love of Boston, its neighborhoods, and its people shines through in his hard-edged prose." Library Journal.

Lehane, Dennis

Sacred / Dennis Lehane. W. Morrow, 1997. 320 p. Patrick Kenzie and Angela Gennaro novels

ISBN 9780688143817

1. Billionaires 2. Missing persons investigation 3. Fathers and daughters 4. Private investigators 5. Cults 6. Missing women 7. Widowers 8. Heroin smuggling 9. Cults and crime 10. Grief counseling programs 11. Boston, Massachusetts 12. Florida 13. Hardboiled fiction 14. Mysteries

LC 96-53115

When dying billionaire Trevor Stone hires two private detectives, Patrick Kenzie and Angela Gennaro, to find his missing daughter, the trail takes the two experienced detectives down a road of half-truths and corruption that leads them from Boston to Florida's Gulf Coast and back again

Lehane, Dennis

Shutter Island / Dennis Lehane. Morrow, 2003. ix, 325 p.

ISBN 9780688163174

1. 1950s 2. Psychiatric hospitals 3. United States marshals 4. Escaped convicts 5. Criminals with mental illnesses 6. Islands -- Massachusetts 7. Hurricanes 8. Delusions 9. Mind control 10. Conspiracies 11. Psychiatric hospital patients 12. Brainwashing 13. Drug testing 14. Eugenics 15. Massachusetts -- Social life and customs -- 20th century 16. Psychological suspense

U.S. Marshal Teddy Daniels and his partner, Chuck Aule, come to Shutter Island's Ashcliffe Hospital in search of an escaped mental patient, but uncover true wickedness as Ashcliffe's mysterious patient treatments propel them to the brink of insanity.

"The atmosphere is properly dark and moody, and so long as Teddy and Chuck stick to the manhunt and their investigation of Ashecliffe's creepy medical staff, they play their roles with muscle and grace." New York Times Book Review.

Lehane, Dennis

Since we fell / Dennis Lehane. Ecco Press, 2017. 400 p.

ISBN 9780062129383

1. Married women 2. Agoraphobia in women 3. Psychic trauma 4. Deception 5. Betrayal 6. Former journalists 7. Businesspeople 8. Remarried persons 9. Life change events 10. Murder 11. Men/women relations 12. Boston, Massachusetts 13. Thrillers and suspense 14. Literary fiction

Retreating from the world in the aftermath of a traumatizing reporting assignment, Rachel finds happiness with a raffish businessman before witnessing activities surrounding a conspiracy that tests the limits of her fragile psyche.

"He produces one of crime fiction's most exciting and well-orchestrated finales--rife with dramatic tension and buttressed by rich psychological interplay between the characters." Booklist.

Lehane, Dennis

* **World** gone by : a novel / Dennis Lehane. William Morrow, 2015. 416 p. Coughlin novels :

ISBN 9780060004903

1. Second World War era (1939-1945) 2. Organized crime 3. Spies 4. Criminals 5. Single fathers 6. Fathers and sons 7. Secrets 8. Family relationships 9. Crime bosses 10. Tampa, Florida 11. Cuba -- History -- 20th century 12. Historical thrillers 13. Crime fiction

LC 2014027026

Working as a consigliere to the Bartolo crime family, traveling between Tampa and Cuba, former crime kingpin Joe Coughlin, who has everything--money, power, anonymity and a beautiful mistress, is forced to pay for his lifetime of sin when the dark truth of his past emerges.

"A multilayered, morally ambiguous novel of family, blood and betrayal." Kirkus.

Leigh, Eva

Forever your earl / Eva Leigh. Avon Books, 2015. 384 p. Wicked quills of London

ISBN 9780062358622

1. Regency period (1811-1820) 2. Gossip columnists 3. Earls and countesses 4. Gossiping and gossips 5. Womanizers 6. Deception 7. Disguises 8. Sexual attraction 9. Men/women relations 10. London, England -- Social life and customs -- 19th century 11. England -- Social life and customs -- 19th century 12. Great Britain -- History -- Regency, 1811-1820 13. Regency romances 14. Historical romances

Gossip writer Eleanor Hawke is invited to indulge in the illicit pursuits of Daniel Balfour, the notorious Earl of Ashford, but when Daniel falls for Eleanor, she discovers that the earl's true scandal may involve herself.

"Leigh (the pseudonym of best-selling romance author Zoe Archer) launches the Wicked Quills of London series on a high note with this fabulously fun Regency-set historical that superbly showcases the authors flair for mixing sharp wit and sexy romance." Booklist.

Leigh, Eva

Scandal takes the stage / Eva Leigh. Avon Books, 2015. 370 p. Wicked quills of London

ISBN 9780062358646

1. Regency period (1811-1820) 2. Women dramatists 3. Viscounts and viscountesses 4. Writer's block 5. Country homes 6. Nobility 7. Theater 8. Interclass romance 9. Sexual attraction 10. Men/

women relations 11. London, England -- Social life and customs -- 19th century 12. England -- Social life and customs -- 19th century 13. Great Britain -- History -- Regency, 1811-1820 14. Regency romances 15. Historical romances

When writer's block threatens the delivery of her new play, playwright Maggie Delamere accepts the offer of the theater-loving Viscount Marwood to write at his country estate, where passion sparks between them.

"This lighthearted romp is full of rambunctious characters, witty repartee, and believable emotional development." Publishers Weekly.

Leigh, Eva

Temptations of a wallflower / Eva Leigh. Avon Books, 2016. 384 p. Wicked quills of London

ISBN 9780062358660

1. Regency period (1811-1820) 2. Clergymen 3. Women erotica writers 4. Husband and wife 5. Newlyweds 6. Secret identity 7. Secrets 8. Nobility 9. Sexual attraction 10. Men/women relations 11. London, England -- Social life and customs -- 19th century 12. England -- Social life and customs -- 19th century 13. Great Britain -- History -- Regency, 1811-1820 14. Regency romances 15. Historical romances

Lady Sarah Frampton has a scandalous secret: she is A Lady of Dubious Quality, the pseudonymous author of bestselling erotica. Country vicar Jeremy Cleland has no idea that the demure wallflower he's falling in love with is the woman whose identity he's been ordered to publicly expose by his father, the Earl of Hutton, as part of the elder man's crusade against immorality. -- Description by Gillian Speace.

"Leigh's latest is a thoughtful and sensuous romance." Publishers Weekly.

Leimbach, Marti, 1963-

The **man** from Saigon : a novel / Marti Leimbach. Nan A. Talese/Doubleday, 2010. 352 p.

ISBN 9780385529860

1. 1960s 2. Prisoners of war, American 3. Vietnam War, 1961-1975 4. Women war correspondents 5. Photojournalists 6. Secrets 7. Americans in Vietnam 8. Women prisoners of war 9. Vietnam 10. Historical fiction

LC 2009030332

One of the first women correspondents on assignment in 1967 Saigon, Susan Gifford teams up with a Vietnamese photographer eager to break into American media and is captured by Vietcong soldiers in the treacherous jungle.

"Sent by a women's magazine to find human-interest stories in 1967 Saigon, journalist Susan Gifford forms a fateful alliance with Son, a Vietnamese photographer. Traveling with U.S. troops, Gifford and Son survive an ambush only to be captured by the Vietcong. What follows is harrowing, as Leimbach vividly recreates the chemical strafing of the countryside, the misery of the refugee camps and the suffocating humidity of the jungle. This impressive novel finds a new way of illuminating the horrors of an old war." People.

Leine, Kim, 1961-

The **prophets** of Eternal Fjord / Kim Leine ; translated from the Danish by Martin Aitken. Liveright Publishing, 2015, c2012. 608 p.

ISBN 9780871406712

1. 18th century 2. Missionaries 3. Inuit 4. Culture conflict 5. Colonies 6. Colonialism 7. Self-doubt 8. Clergy 9. Sects 10. Communities 11. Greenland -- History -- 18th century 12. Historical fiction 13. Literary fiction 14. Translations -- Danish to English

LC 2015013260

Translation from the Danish of: Profeterne i Evighedsfjorden.

Originally published: Copenhagen : Gyldendal, 2012.

ALA Notable Book, 2016.

Shortlisted for the International Dublin Literary Award, 2017

A saga of a Greenlandic community torn by the forces of colonialism follows the experiences of a misguided late-18th-century priest whose faith is tested during his tragic efforts to convert the Inuit.

"Epic in sweep and noteworthy for its large cast of skillfully drawn characters, this is a lush, brave book about idealism and faith." Library Journal.

Leithauser, Brad, 1953-

The **art** student's war / Brad Leithauser. Alfred A. Knopf, 2009. 512 p.

ISBN 9780307271112

1. Second World War era (1939-1945) 2. 1940s 3. World War II 4. Women artists 5. Family and war 6. Soldiers 7. Portrait artists 8. Ambition in women 9. Eighteen-year-old women 10. Convalescence 11. Family relationships 12. World War II home front 13. Detroit, Michigan -- History -- 20th century 14. Coming-of-age stories 15. Historical fiction

LC 2009019468

Heading to her home in Detroit during World War II, passionate art student Bianca Paradise accepts a job drawing portraits of wounded soldiers and experiences a spectrum of emotions that compromise her balance.

"This novel is, at its core, a traditional American wartime love story. As such, it is timely and engrossing." Boston Globe.

Leithauser, Brad, 1953-

* The **promise** of elsewhere / Brad Leithauser. Alfred a Knopf, 2019 336 p.

ISBN 9780525655039

1. Travelers 2. Midlife crisis 3. Voyages and travels 4. Americans in foreign countries 5. Men with bipolar disorder 6. Retinal degeneration 7. Men -- Psychology 8. College teachers 9. Architecture 10. Glaciers 11. Aging 12. Rome, Italy 13. London, England 14. Greenland 15. Denmark 16. Michigan 17. Humorous stories

In the face of devastating existential crisis stemming from a collapsing marriage and a health scare, a Midwestern professor decides to tour the world's most beautiful architectural sites and becomes sidetracked with a jilted bride in Rome.

Lelchuk, Saul

Save me from dangerous men : a novel / Saul Lelchuk. Flatiron Books, 2019. 320 p. Nikki Griffin novels

ISBN 9781250170248

1. Women private investigators 2. Women vigilantes 3. Bookstores 4. Books and reading 5. Violence against women 6. Crimes against women 7. Business intelligence 8. Corporate intrigue 9. Secret identity 10. Abusive men 11. San Francisco Bay Area 12. California 13. Northern California 14. Thrillers and suspense

LC 2018046994

Operating a private investigator business from an office above her bookstore, bibliophile and part-time vigilante Nikki Griffin becomes the target of dangerous adversaries when she breaks cover to save a woman's life.

"A credible plot and solid prose are pluses, but the books real appeal stems from its powerful, distinctive protagonist." Publishers Weekly.

Lelic, Simon

The **child** who : a novel / Simon Lelic. Penguin Books, 2012. 303 p.

ISBN 9780143120919

1. Juvenile delinquents 2. Crimes against children 3. Lawyers 4. Trials (Murder) 5. Anger 6. Small town life 7. England, Southern 8. Legal thrillers 9. Thrillers and suspense

LC 2011045210

When provincial attorney Leo Curtice handles a case involving a child murdering another child, he finds himself pitted against an enraged community and fearing for his family's safety.

Lem, Stanislaw

Eden / Stanislaw Lem ; translated from the Polish by Marc E. Heine. Harcourt Brace Jovanovich, 1989. 262 p.

ISBN 9780151275809

1. Misunderstanding 2. Human/alien encounters 3. Space vehicle accidents 4. Survival (after spacecraft accidents) 5. Life on other planets 6. Comprehension 7. Communication 8. Consequences 9. Cruelty 10. Translations -- Polish to English 11. Hard science fiction 12. Science fiction

LC 89001963

Six men crash-land on a planet in another solar system and, in an attempt to communicate with its inhabitants, they encounter violence and human cruelty.

"No one writes sf more intellectually challenging or of greater literary distinction than Lem." Booklist.

Lem, Stanislaw

Fiasco / Stanislaw Lem ; translated from the Polish by Michael Kandel. Harcourt Brace Jovanovich, 1987. 322 p.

ISBN 9780151306404

1. Scientific expeditions 2. Human/alien encounters 3. Aliens (Non-humanoid) 4. Life on other planets 5. Interstellar relations 6. Misunderstanding 7. Communication 8. Human nature 9. Expeditions 10. Scientists 11. Disasters 12. Translations -- Polish to English 13. Hard science fiction 14. Science fiction

LC 86031816

When a crew of earthmen--among them a space pilot, a military leader, a scientist, and a priest--reach the planet Quinta, the travelers descend into the very depths of the human condition.

"The crew's dense, challenging discussions--of physics, philosophy, military tactics, morality, cybernetics, psychology, game theory, etc.-- are punctuated by bursts of action whose initial release only serves to increase the tension, as new data disproves old theses and one fiasco follows another. Brilliant and demanding, this is one of Lem's best novels, putting the reader through an intellectual and emotional wringer." Publishers Weekly.

Lem, Stanislaw

His master's voice / Stanislaw Lem ; translated from the Polish by Michael Kandel. Harcourt Brace Jovanovich, 1983. 199 p.

ISBN 9780156403009

1. Scientists 2. Interstellar communication 3. Cosmic background radiation 4. Aliens 5. Cold war 6. Near future 7. Incompetence 8. Secrecy in government 9. Codes (Communication) 10. Human/alien encounters 11. Diary novels 12. Translations -- Polish to English 13. Hard science fiction 14. Science fiction

LC 82015765

A secret team of scientists study a pulsating stream of radiation from outer space and attempt to determine if it is a message from another world.

"A stream of 'signals' from outer space is the subject of various attempted decodings and an excuse for all kinds of wild hypotheses about who might have sent the message and why, in which are reflected various human hopes and fears. Good satire." Anatomy of Wonder, 4th edition.

Lem, Stanislaw

* **Solaris** / Stanislaw Lem ; afterword by Darko Suvin ; translated from the French by Joanna Kilmartin and Steve Cox. Walker, 1970. 204 p.

ISBN 9780802755261

1. Scientists 2. Consciousness 3. Aliens (Non-humanoid) 4. Oceans 5. Memories 6. Space flight 7. Psychologists 8. Space colonies 9. Communication 10. Life on other planets 11. Human/alien encounters 12. Hard science fiction 13. Literary fiction 14. Science fiction 15. Translations -- Polish to English

LC 75123267

Upon landing at an interplanetary station, Kris Kelvin discovers that an advanced power has taken over.

Lemaitre, Pierre, 1951-

Inhuman resources / Pierre Lemaitre ; translated from the French by Sam Gordon. MacLehose Press, 2018. 384 p.

ISBN 9781635060812

1. Fifties (Age) 2. Role playing 3. Unemployment 4. Employment interviewing 5. Life change events 6. Violence in men 7. Crime 8. Crime fiction 9. Translations -- French to English

When Alain Delambre lost his job four years ago, he lost everything, and now he's breaking all the rules for one last shot at the life he thinks he deserves.

"A high-quality experience for readers with a taste for real pessimism." Booklist.

Lemaitre, Pierre, 1951-

* **Irene** : the Commandant Camille Verhoeven trilogy / Pierre Lemaitre ; translated by Frank Wynne. MacLehose Press, 2014, c2006. 416 p. Commandant Camille Verhoeven trilogy

ISBN 9781623658007

1. Violence against women 2. Married men 3. Serial murder investigation 4. Detectives 5. Pregnant women 6. Journalists 7. Serial murders 8. Short people 9. Men/women relations 10. Paris, France 11. Police procedurals 12. Hardboiled fiction 13. Translations -- French to English

First published as Travail soigne, Jean-Claude Lattes, 2006.

Draws on five contemporary and classic literary murder scenes in a prequel to "Alex" that finds Camille Verhoeven linking a brutal double murder to a cold case before his pregnant wife is abducted by the killer.

"Verhoeven is a one-of-a-kind detective, and Lemaitre does an excellent job surrounding him with characters who demand their share of the limelight." Booklist.

Lennon, J. Robert, 1970-

Castle / J. Robert Lennon. Graywolf Press, 2009. 224 p.

ISBN 9781555975227

1. Homecomings 2. Violence 3. Guilt 4. Farms 5. Renovation (Architecture) 6. Secrets 7. Small town life 8. Memories 9. New York (State) 10. Psychological suspense

Purchasing hundreds of acres of farmland near his childhood home in upstate New York, Eric Loesch embarks on a renovation project that is halted when he discovers a section of land in the middle of his woods that he does not own, a finding with links to an eighteenth-century Native American massacre, a luminous white deer, and community paranoia.

"Like two other powerful novels of recent years--James Lasdun's Horned Man and Peter Cameron's Andorra--Castle is told by an egomaniacal, unlikable man with a precarious grasp on reality, especially his own. . . . Castle tells a terrific story, dire and confusing and convincing." New York Times Book Review.

Lennon, J. Robert, 1970-

Familiar / J. Robert Lennon. Graywolf, 2012. 208 p.
ISBN 9781555976255
1. Parallel universes 2. Children -- Death 3. Grief in women 4. Self-discovery in women 5. Brothers 6. Mother and adult son 7. Psychological suspense

After she returns from visiting her son Silas' grave, Elisa Brown finds her life completely changed--she is more voluptuous, her marriage is stronger and Silas is still alive while his brother is disturbingly changed--and she must embark on a journey of self-discovery if she is ever going to find out whether this is all is a result of a psychotic break, an alternate reality or something else.

Lent, Jeffrey

Lost nation / Jeffrey Lent. Atlantic Monthly Press, 2002. 370 p.
ISBN 0871138433
1. Men -- New Hampshire 2. Social marginality 3. Wilderness areas 4. Teenage girls 5. England 6. New Hampshire 7. Historical fiction
LC 2001056495

Seeking to make a fresh start and establish himself as a trader, Blood heads for Indian Stream, a wild, ungoverned territory in northern New Hampshire, but his arrival triggers an escalating series of clashes and violence.

"In 1838, a man called Blood opens a tavern and one-girl brothel in an ungoverned area on the New HampshireCanada border. His prostitute, Sally, is a teenager he won in a game of cards. While the territory is already home to a number of society's escapees, Blood's presence introduces a new volatility. Blood and Sally's relationship grows in unpredictable ways, the law threatens to descend, and Blood's secret past returns in a surprising manner. . . . The author has tremendous literary gifts: a fine ear for speech, a keen eye for period detail, the ability to craft a well-turned phrase and create rich interior lives for his characters." Booklist.

Lent, Jeffrey

A **slant** of light : a novel / Jeffrey Lent. Bloomsbury USA, 2015. 357 p.
ISBN 9781620404966
1. American Civil War era (1861-1865) 2. Redemption 3. Civil war veterans 4. Murder 5. Power (Social sciences) 6. Authority 7. United States Civil War, 1861-1865 8. United States -- History -- Civil War, 1861-1865 9. Historical fiction 10. Literary fiction
LC 2014021632

At the close of the Civil War, veteran Malcolm Hopeton, returning home to western New York State, commits a horrific crime that leaves the people around him struggling to make sense of his actions, including a judge who bows to the wisdom of a more human truth within the vision of a nation on the cusp of the modern era.

"There's an overabundance of detail on farming, but many sentences demand rereading for their sheer beauty, and each love story--some tragic, others newly born--has a poignant emotional charge. Lent offers eloquent insight into what makes his characters tick, yet enough unknowns remain to keep the novel unpredictable through the final pages." Booklist.

Leon, Donna

About face / Donna Leon. Atlantic Monthly, 2009. 272 p. Guido Brunetti mysteries
ISBN 9780802118967
1. Police -- Venice, Italy 2. Pollution 3. Crime 4. Murder investigation 5. Corruption investigation 6. Solid waste disposal 7. Garbage collection -- Corrupt practices 8. Venice, Italy 9. Italy 10. Mysteries 11. Police procedurals

Environmental concerns become significant in Brunetti's work when an investigator from the Carabiniere, looking into the illegal hauling of garbage, asks for a favor. But the investigator is not the only one with a special request. His father-in-law needs help and a mysterious woman comes into the picture. Brunetti soon finds himself in the middle of an investigation into murder and corruption more dangerous than anything he's seen before.

"It would be easy to punch holes in a contrived subplot, thick with symbolism, about a beautiful young woman whose face was ruined by cosmetic surgery. But who would want to, when Leon is being so generous with the humanizing details that make this series special? There are long walks in Brunetti's warm company and lively talks with his clever wife and even more engaging father-inlaw. . . . As detective work goes, it's a tiny masterpiece of analysis." New York Times Book Review.

Leon, Donna

Beastly things : a Commissario Guido Brunetti mystery / Donna Leon. Atlantic Monthly Press, 2012. 288 p. Guido Brunetti mysteries
ISBN 9780802120236
1. Police -- Venice, Italy 2. Murder investigation 3. Men with disfigurements 4. Animal rights 5. Venice, Italy 6. Italy 7. Mysteries 8. Police procedurals

Commissario Brunetti investigates the death of an animal lover whose decomposed body was found in a Venice canal.

Leon, Donna

* **Blood** from a stone / Donna Leon. Atlantic Monthly Press, 2005. 288 p. Guido Brunetti mysteries
ISBN 9780871138873
1. Police -- Venice, Italy 2. Murder investigation 3. Political corruption 4. Immigrants 5. Undocumented workers 6. Africans in Italy 7. Crimes against street vendors 8. Assassination 9. Police misconduct 10. Secrets 11. Racism 12. Diamonds 13. Undocumented immigrants 14. Venice, Italy 15. Italy 16. Mysteries 17. Police procedurals
LC 2005040961

Commissario Guido Brunetti plunges into the Venetian underworld of illegal African immigrants as he investigates the killing of a street vendor.

Leon, Donna

Drawing conclusions : a Commissario Guido Brunetti mystery / Donna Leon. Grove/Atlantic, 2011. 256 p. Guido Brunetti mysteries
ISBN 9780802119797
1. Widows 2. Heart attack 3. Old age homes 4. Murder investigation 5. Police -- Venice, Italy 6. Venice, Italy 7. Italy 8. Mysteries 9. Police procedurals

When Anna Maria Giusti returns from holiday to find her elderly neighbour Constanza Altavilla dead, with blood on the floor near her head, she immediately alerts the police. Commissario Brunetti is called to the scene and it seems the woman has suffered a fatal heart attack.

Patta, the Vice-Questore, is eager to dismiss the case as a death from natural causes.

"This installment epitomizes what we treasure most about this series: a feeling for the life of a sublimely beautiful city and a sensitivity to the forces that are reshaping it. Not to mention the pleasure of being in Brunetti's company when this shrewd but scrupulously honest man is having a crisis of ethics at the flower market or trying to pry information from a hostile nun." New York Times Book Review.

Leon, Donna

Falling in love : a Commissario Guido Brunetti mystery / Donna Leon. Atlantic Monthly Press, 2015. 264 p. Guido Brunetti mysteries

ISBN 9780802123534

1. Police -- Venice, Italy 2. Stalking 3. Opera singers 4. Obsession 5. Fans 6. Stalkers 7. Venice, Italy 8. Italy 9. Mysteries 10. Police procedurals

Attending a performance by a opera star he saved in Death at La Fenice, Brunetti learns that the singer is being stalked by an obsessed fan who subsequently attacks a fellow performer.

"This is a dark novel with an ironic title that resonates on multiple levels. In particular, it explores the nature of loveand hatein a manner that will haunt readers well after they have finished the book. Another provocative addition to a fine series, certain to appeal to aficionados of profound literary mysteries such as Louise Penny's How the Light Gets In." Library Journal.

Leon, Donna

The **girl** of his dreams : a Commissario Guido Brunetti mystery / Donna Leon. Atlantic Monthly, 2008. 272 p. Guido Brunetti mysteries

ISBN 9780871139801

1. Police -- Venice, Italy 2. Murder investigation 3. Police corruption 4. Romani girls -- Death 5. Priests 6. Suspicion 7. Undercover operations 8. Murder 9. Trust 10. Venice, Italy 11. Italy 12. Mysteries 13. Police procedurals

One cold and rainy morning, the body of a gypsy girl is found floating in a canal. Brunetti suspects she fell off a nearby roof while fleeing an apartment she had robbed--but something about the case continues to haunt him.

"Political reality prevails over justice, and a child's death goes unpunished despite the best efforts of Commissario Guido Brunetti in Leon's . . . Venetian mystery. When 11-year-old Ariana Rocich drowns in a canal and goes unidentified for days, she begins to haunt Brunetti's dreams. But Ariana is a Rom, or gypsy, found with stolen jewelry items secreted in and on her person, a discovery that makes Brunetti's investigation particularly sensitive in the face of new departmental directives regarding multicultural issues. The book opens with the funeral of Brunetti's mother before segueing into a subplot about a religious charlatan; so religion, as well as politics, becomes a topic around the family table for Brunetti, wife Paola, daughter Chiara, and son Raffi." Library Journal.

Leon, Donna

The **golden** egg / Donna Leon. Atlantic Monthly Press, 2013. 256 p. Guido Brunetti mysteries

ISBN 9780802121011

1. Police -- Venice, Italy 2. Murder investigation 3. Extortion 4. Scandals 5. Men with developmental disabilities 6. Venice, Italy 7. Italy 8. Mysteries 9. Police procedurals

Maps on cover linings and endpapers.

Commissario Guido Brunetti investigates the death of a man who never existed on paper.

Leon, Donna

A **question** of belief : a Commissario Guido Brunetti mystery / Donna Leon. Atlantic Monthly, 2010. 288 p. Guido Brunetti mysteries

ISBN 9780802119421

1. Political corruption 2. Police -- Venice, Italy 3. Murder investigation 4. Justice 5. Violence 6. Venice, Italy 7. Italy 8. Mysteries 9. Police procedurals

Under the stifling summer sun, Venice is flooded with tourism. Commissario Guido Brunetti is planning the perfect mountain vacation where he can catch up on his reading. However, before he can go, an old friend has him look into a court corruption case. As he probes deeper, Commissario Brunetti quickly becomes embroiled in a shocking murder case that is linked to his own investigation.

Leon, Donna

Trace elements / Donna Leon. Atlantic Monthly Press, 2020. 320 p. Guido Brunetti mysteries

ISBN 9780802148674

1. Detectives 2. Last words 3. Public health 4. Murder investigation 5. Criminal investigation 6. Crime 7. Italy 8. Venice, Italy 9. Police procedurals

A woman's cryptic dying words in a Venetian hospice lead Guido Brunetti to uncover a threat to the entire region in Donna Leon's haunting twenty-ninth Brunetti novel.

"As usual, Leon adroitly portrays the complex questions of what constitutes justice and the sad consequences that can result from its pursuit." Publishers Weekly.

Leon, Donna

Uniform justice / Donna Leon. Atlantic Monthly Press, 2003. 280 p. Guido Brunetti mysteries

ISBN 0871139030

1. Police -- Venice, Italy 2. Military cadets 3. Political corruption 4. Detectives 5. Suicide -- Venice, Italy 6. Parent and child -- Venice, Italy 7. Military academies -- Venice, Italy 8. Secrets -- Venice, Italy 9. Scandals -- Venice, Italy 10. Police misconduct 11. Politicians -- Venice, Italy 12. Husband and wife -- Venice, Italy 13. Venice, Italy 14. Italy 15. Mysteries 16. Police procedurals

LC 2003044326

Commissario Guido Brunetti is called in to investigate when a young cadet at an elite military academy is found hanged, a presumed suicide.

"As a thinking man, Brunetti reads Cicero for moral direction, looks to his wife for doses of cynical realism and humbly consults his secretary, the terrifyingly efficient Signorina Elettra, on practical matters. But it is as a man of sensibility that this endearing detective most engages us." New York Times Book Review.

Leon, Donna

Unto us a son is given / Donna Leon. Atlantic Monthly Press, 2019. 320 p. Guido Brunetti mysteries

ISBN 9780802129116

1. Murder investigation 2. Family relationships 3. Detectives 4. Inheritance and succession 5. Criminal investigation 6. Adoption policy 7. Suspicion 8. Prejudice 9. Gay men 10. Italy 11. Venice, Italy 12. Police procedurals

LC 2018058492

When an elderly family friend is urged to bequeath his fortune to a specific heir before suddenly dropping dead, Commissario Guido Brunetti untangles a disturbing mystery from the victim's past.

"Far more than whodunit, the real subject of this novel (and Leons work in general) is what we all do to one another." Booklist.

Leon, Sarah, 1995-

Wanderer / Sarah Leon ; translated from the French by John Cullen. Other Press, 2019, c2016. 201 p.

ISBN 9781590519257

1. Students 2. Reunions 3. Composers 4. Classical music 5. Child prodigies 6. Pianists 7. Interpersonal relations 8. Men/men relations 9. Betrayal 10. Literary fiction 11. Coming-of-age stories 12. Translations -- French to English

Originally published by H?lo'se d'Ormesson, 2016.

Inspired by Schubert's recurring theme and German Romanticism, explores the stifled, complicated feelings between a music teacher living in seclusion and his prodigy former student after years of silence.

"Leon's staggering debut uses musical structure and allusion to explore friendship and secrecy between two gifted young men...Leon's innovative blending of events across time and her delicate emotional precision make for a bewitching, immersive experience." Publishers Weekly

Leonard, Elmore, 1925-2013

* Be cool : everyone is looking for the next big hit / Elmore Leonard. Delacorte Press, 1999. 292 p.

ISBN 9780385333917

1. Film producers and directors -- Hollywood, California 2. Record industry and trade -- Hollywood, California 3. Film industry and trade -- Hollywood, California 4. Cool (Personal quality) 5. Entertainment industry and trade -- Hollywood, California 6. Hollywood, California 7. Caper novels 8. Crime fiction

LC 989836601

Sequel to: Get Shorty.

Chili Palmer is ready to move into the recording industry, but his next big singing star may have ties to the mob.

"Aside from the wit, the fun and the colorful figures that populate Elmore Leonard's novels, the real magic of his work is in the language. . . . This is Elmore Leonard at his best, the sweeping synaptic prose effortlessly echoing the argot of the gutter." New York Times Book Review.

Leonard, Elmore, 1925-2013

Charlie Martz and other stories : the unpublished stories / Elmore Leonard. William Morrow, 2015. 300 p.

ISBN 9780062364920

1. Crime 2. Outlaws 3. Law enforcement 4. Gangsters 5. United States marshals 6. New Mexico 7. Detroit, Michigan 8. Westerns 9. Thrillers and suspense 10. Short stories

LC 2015008625

An anthology of 15 stories by the award-winning author include 11 previously unpublished tales and selections from the early years of his career.

"[T]his posthumous collection showcases the early writing of the author of westerns and crime stories, revealing his particular genius in embryonic, pulpish form." Publishers Weekly.

Leonard, Elmore, 1925-2013

* The **complete** Western stories of Elmore Leonard. William Morrow, 2004. 544 p.

ISBN 0060724250

1. United States. Army. Cavalry. 2. 19th century 3. Indians of North America -- Southwest (United States) 4. Frontier and pioneer life 5. Apache Indians 6. Arizona 7. Southwest (United States) 8. The West (United States) 9. Westerns 10. Short stories

LC 2004055969

Seven of the titles were later published as: Trail of the Apache and other stories.

A collection of short fiction features pieces written over the course of five decades and includes the author's first short story, "The Trail of the Apache."

Leonard, Elmore, 1925-2013

Freaky deaky / Elmore Leonard. Warner Books, 1989, c1988. 341 p.

ISBN 9780446350396

1. Police 2. Radicals 3. Bombs 4. Extortion 5. Detroit, Michigan 6. Mysteries

Originally published: New York : Arbor House, 1988.

"Leonard excels here with his trademark menace and his deadpan, throwaway humor. His superlative ear for the vernacular makes all the characters spring to life; Woody, 'always in low with his dims on,' is a brilliant creation." Publishers Weekly.

Leonard, Elmore, 1925-2013

* Get Shorty / Elmore Leonard. HarperTorch, 2002, c1990. 359 p.

ISBN 9780385301411

1. Money lenders -- Hollywood, California 2. Horror film producers and directors -- Hollywood, California 3. Film industry and trade -- Corrupt practices -- Hollywood, California 4. Gamblers -- Hollywood, California 5. Hollywood, California 6. Caper novels 7. Crime fiction

Sequel: Be cool.

Originally published: New York : Delacorte Press, 1990.

Chili Palmer, a Miami loanshark, and Harry Zimm, a film producer in debt, become reluctant partners as they become embroiled in the seductive but deadly Hollywood scene.

"Leonard's strongest books make you stand up and sit down a lot during their tight moments, but 'Get Shorty,' despite its occasional white-knuckle passages, belongs to that vast vinegary canon known as the Hollywood novel. . . . Best of all is the portrait Leonard gives us of a seven-million-dollar-a-picture star named Michael Weir." The New Yorker.

Leonard, Elmore, 1925-2013

Glitz / Elmore Leonard. Arbor House, 1985. 251 p.

ISBN 9780877956327

1. Former convicts 2. Revenge 3. Police -- Miami, Florida 4. Atlantic City, New Jersey 5. Miami, Florida 6. Mysteries

LC 84016794

When Miami Beach detective Vincent Mora's quirky girl friend turns up dead, only seven days after taking a hostess job in Atlantic City, Mora investigates the circumstances and comes up against La Cosa Nostra

"There is a steady flow of intrigue and action set just outside the law in a world both dirty and glamorous. Several characters develop into complex personalities, but Mora is never quite clear." Library Journal.

Leonard, Elmore, 1925-2013

The **Hot** Kid / Elmore Leonard. William Morrow, 2005. 304 p.

ISBN 0060724226

1. Depression era (1929-1941) 2. 1930s 3. United States deputy marshals 4. Fame 5. Criminals 6. Gangsters 7. Former convicts 8. Bank robbers 9. Children of millionaires 10. Police -- Oklahoma 11. Journalists 12. Enemies 13. Oil executives 14. Millionaires 15. Mistresses 16. Fathers and sons 17. Extortion 18. Kidnapping 19. Depressions -- 1929-1941 20. Oklahoma 21. Westerns

LC 2004063578

Having made his name by killing notorious bank robber Emmet Long, Deputy U.S. Marshal Carl Webster embarks on a dangerous

LIST OF FICTIONAL WORKS

search for Jack Belmont, the son of an oil millionaire who dreams of becoming Public Enemy Number One.

"Where so much of Leonard's recent fiction has a sharp, almost hyperrealistic quality, The Hot Kid is noirish and even a little pulpy at times, in the fashion of 30's movies and detective magazines. . . . Tony Antonelli isn't a portrait of the artist as young man, exactly, but rather a fond wink at the tradition of potboilers and genre writing that gave rise to Leonard himself and from which, for all his success, he has never cut himself off." New York Times Book Review.

Leonard, Elmore, 1925-2013
* Killshot / Elmore Leonard. Warner Books, 1990, c1989. 321 p.
   ISBN 9781557100412
   1. Witnesses 2. Federal Witness Protection Program 3. Men criminals 4. Terrorism 5. Assassins 6. Crime fiction
   Originally published: New York : Arbor House, 1989.
   Innocent witnesses to a mob-related murder, Carmen and Wayne Colson discover that the Witness Protection Program is not exactly a safe haven when they learn that the killers are on the loose and that the authorities are not protecting them from harm.

Leonard, Elmore, 1925-2013
LaBrava / Elmore Leonard. Arbor House, 1983. 283 p.
   ISBN 9780877955276
   1. United States. Secret Service. 2. Photographers 3. Film actors and actresses 4. Men/women relations 5. South Miami Beach, Florida 6. Thrillers and suspense
                                                LC 83072676
   Edgar Allan Poe Award for Best Mystery Novel, 1984.
   Joe LaBrava, a photographer and former Secret Service agent, observes a murder and becomes involved in an unusual confidence scheme in South Miami Beach
   "What makes the author's work memorable is his uncompromisingly direct prose, his affectionately crafted yet very real characters, and, of course, the fact that Leonard knows that providing entertainment is the novelist's first commandment. Nobody brings the illogic of crime and criminals to life better." Christian Science Monitor.

Leonard, Elmore, 1925-2013
Mr. Paradise / Elmore Leonard. Morrow, 2004. 256 p.
   ISBN 0060083956
   1. Prostitutes 2. Women murder witnesses 3. Assassins 4. Detectives -- Detroit, Michigan 5. Fashion models 6. Young women 7. Roommates 8. Young women -- Relations with older men 9. Police -- Detroit, Michigan 10. Senior men 11. Octogenarians 12. Retirees 13. Football fans 14. Former lawyers 15. Assassins 16. Secret identity 17. Detroit, Michigan 18. Mysteries
   When party games involving a beautiful escort, her model roommate, lawyer Tony Paradiso, and his aide Montez Taylor go murderously wrong, Detroit detective Frank Delsa finds himself with a double homicide on his hands.
   "Leonard addresses those who think they hear the same music he does, but who are open to questioning the familiar, to listening carefully and seeing when something has a different emphasis. . . . Mr. Paradise is about deception. People deceive through false identity (appropriating, dissembling), just as they, themselves, have been deceived whether by the implied promise of collapsed dot-coms or by positive, false assumptions about family." New York Times Book Review.

Leonard, Elmore, 1925-2013
Pagan babies / Elmore Leonard. Delacorte Press, 2000. 263 p.
   ISBN 0385333927
   1. Americans in Rwanda 2. Swindlers and swindling 3. Criminals 4. Priests 5. Women stand-up comedians 6. Detroit, Michigan 7. Rwanda 8. Crime fiction
                                                LC 00029506
   Father Terry Dunn returns to Detroit from a stint in Rwanda, and begins a search for the perfect money-raising scam.
   "This is one of Mr. Leonard's funniest books, with a typically colourful cast of oddballs. The dialogue, too, is snappy. . . . Mr. Leonard steers the reader effortlessly through a maze of plots and counterplots, then brings the whole thing in with a bravura flourish and stops on a dime." The Economist.

Leonard, Elmore, 1925-2013
* Raylan / Elmore Leonard. William Morrow, 2012. 263 p. Raylan Givens thrillers
   ISBN 9780062119469
   1. United States marshals 2. Drug dealers 3. Human body parts industry and trade 4. Criminal investigation 5. Brothers 6. Kentucky 7. Harlan County, Kentucky 8. Crime fiction
                                                LC 2011024392
   After discovering his quarry naked in the bathtub, doped up and missing his kidneys, Federal Marshall Raylan Givens becomes involved, both literally and figuratively, in a case involving the harvesting of organs for sale on the black market where this time the bad guys are girls.

Leonard, Elmore, 1925-2013
Rum punch / Elmore Leonard. Delacorte, 1992. 297 p.
   ISBN 9780385301435
   1. Gun smugglers 2. Bail bond agents 3. Betrayal 4. Flight attendants 5. Thrillers and suspense
                                                LC 91038738
   When the feds arrest her for running machine guns for gun dealer Ordell Robbie, former flight attendant Jackie Burke must decide whether to keep quiet about her boss or spill the beans and face his wrath
   "Mr. Leonard never tells you; he shows you. The story is all action, a scam within a scam. . . . His style is the absence of style, stripped of fancy baggage . . . the absence, as far as it's possible, of an authorial ego." New York Times Book Review.

Leonard, Elmore, 1925-2013
Tishomingo blues : a novel / Elmore Leonard. Morrow, 2002. 308 p.
   ISBN 9780060008727
   1. Murder witnesses 2. Divers 3. Daredevils (Stunt performers) 4. Crime 5. Casinos 6. Mafia 7. Civil war 8. United States Civil War, 1861-1865 9. Southern States 10. United States -- History -- Civil War, 1861-1865 -- Campaigns -- Reenactment 11. Crime fiction
                                                LC 2001044405
   Warned by the local Dixie underworld to keep silent after witnessing a murder, daredevil diver Dennis Lenahan is recruited by Detroit gangster Robert Taylor for a showdown that takes place during a Civil War reenactment.

Leonard, Elmore, 1925-2013
When the women come out to dance : stories / Elmore Leonard. William Morrow, 2002. 228 p.
   ISBN 9780060083977
   1. Law enforcement 2. Criminals 3. Men/women relations 4. Short

stories 5. Crime fiction 6. Westerns 7. Anthologies

LC 2002026426

A collection of stories includes two novella-length works featuring surprising plot twists.

"Reading the clipped, unfailingly accurate dialogue that comes out of the mouths of Leonard's characters can make you feel as if you're in the presence of a writer who is both ventriloquist and psychic. It's not just that Leonard captures the cadences and elisions of each character's speech, it's that he has an uncanny sense of knowing what each will say next." New York Times Book Review.

Lepionka, Kristen

The **last** place you look / Kristen Lepionka. Minotaur Books, 2017. 320 p. Roxane Weary novels

ISBN 9781250120519

1. Judicial error 2. Death row prisoners 3. Missing teenage girls 4. Missing persons investigation 5. Women private investigators 6. Private investigators 7. Bisexual women 8. Race relations 9. Ohio 10. Mysteries

Shamus Award for Best First P.I. Novel, 2018.

Nine months after her cop father died on duty, PI Roxane Weary is still a mess. Even so, she agrees to help the desperate sister of a man on death row. The woman thinks she's seen her black brother's white girlfriend, who could clear his name... but if it's really her, where's she been for the last 15 years, gone since the day her parents were murdered? Roxane finds solace in whiskey and sex, but also finds purpose in her search, even as she gets harassed by cops and links the missing girl to one of her late father's cases. This accomplished debut set in Columbus, Ohio has a hardboiled feel, great dialogue, complex characters, and a tough female detective. -- Description by Dawn Towery

"Introducing a fascinating protagonist who combats her emotional demons with the aid of sugar, booze, and sex, this suspenseful, original, and confident debut will please fans of the hard-boiled PI genre." Library Journal.

Lerner, Ben, 1979-

Leaving the Atocha Station : a novel / Ben Lerner. Coffee House Press, 2011. 186 p.

ISBN 9781566892742

1. Poets 2. Americans in Spain 3. Self-discovery in men 4. Art and literature 5. Scholarships and fellowships 6. Identity (Psychology) 7. Spain 8. Madrid, Spain 9. Coming-of-age stories

LC 2011024105

Shortlisted for the James Tait Black Memorial Prize for Fiction, 2012

"The main character of Lerner's novel is an unhappy young poet named Adam Gordon, who's been awarded a prestigious fellowship to study in Spain. Adam sets himself up in a bare-bones apartment in Madrid, studies Spanish, and spends his days at cafes and museums, battling his isolation and anxiety. The novel has a beguiling mixture of lightness and weight. There are wonderful sentences and jokes on almost every page. Lerner is attempting to capture something that most conventional novels, with their cumbersome caravans of plot and scene and conflict, fail to do: the drift of thought, the unmomentous passage of undramatic life." The New Yorker.

Lerner, Ben, 1979-

* The **Topeka** school / Ben Lerner. Farrar Straus & Giroux, 2019. 272 p.

ISBN 9780374277789

1. 1990s 2. Middle-class families 3. Violence -- Psychological aspects 4. High school students 5. Debates and debating 6. Identity (Psychology) 7. Psychologists 8. Teenagers with mental illnesses

9. Marital conflict 10. Consequences 11. Family relationships 12. Kansas 13. Middle West 14. Literary fiction

ALA Notable Book, 2020.

National Book Critics Circle Award for Fiction finalist, 2019

A family drama set in the American Midwest at the turn of the century: a tale of adolescence, transgression, and the conditions that have given rise to the trolls and tyrants of the new right.

Leroy, Margaret

Postcards from Berlin a novel / Margaret Leroy. Little, Brown, 2003. 304 p.

ISBN 0316738131

1. Married women 2. Mothers and daughters 3. Sick children 4. Secrets 5. Suspicion 6. Marriage 7. Postcards 8. Adult children of alcoholics 9. Munchausen syndrome by proxy 10. London, England 11. Domestic fiction 12. Psychological suspense

LC 2003040069

When disturbing postcards begin to arrive in the mail, Catriona Lydgate finds her happy family life succumbing to her secret past, a situation that is complicated when she is accused of deliberately trying to make her daughter ill.

"The resolution of Leroy's novel has a fairy-tale aspect, but fairy tales can nevertheless be very absorbing. Despite the occasional straining of her plot, Leroy succeeded in making me care about these characters; even at my most incredulous." New York Times Book Review.

Les Becquets, Diane

Breaking wild / Diane Les Becquets. Berkley Books, 2016. 309 p.

ISBN 9780425283783

1. Missing persons 2. Wilderness areas 3. Search and rescue operations 4. Secrets 5. Bow hunters 6. Park rangers 7. Missing women 8. Wilderness survival 9. Colorado 10. Thrillers and suspense 11. Parallel narratives

LC 2015015383

Searching for a mysterious mother of two who has gone missing during an outdoors adventure in a remote area, ranger Pru Hathaway makes unexpected discoveries about the woman, who she believes is still alive in spite of dangerous weather conditions.

"The reimagining of a romantic West through the experiences of two strong women both challenges the dominant stereotype of 'cowboy country' and simultaneously offers the comment that gender has no place when it comes to matters of survival." Kirkus.

Lescroart, John T.

The **first** law / John Lescroart. Dutton, 2003. 384 p. Dismas Hardy novels

ISBN 0525947051

1. Police misconduct 2. Murder investigation 3. Innocence (Law) 4. Police 5. Lawyers 6. Defense attorneys 7. Detectives 8. Former police 9. Mysteries 10. Legal thrillers

Lieutenant Abe Glitsky becomes involved in the investigation of a murdered family friend when the prime suspect's lawyer turns to him for help, a request that places both of their careers in jeopardy.

Lescroart, John T.

Guilt / John Lescroart. Delacorte Press, 1997. 462 p.

ISBN 0385316550

1. Catholic Church 2. Guilt 3. Trials (Murder) 4. Ethics 5. Married men 6. Extramarital affairs 7. Marital conflict 8. Murder suspects 9. Catholic men 10. Religious corruption 11. Lawyers 12. San Francisco, California 13. Legal thrillers 14. Thrillers and suspense

LC 96-43756

A standalone novel starring attorneys Wes Farrell and Mark Dooher and homicide detective Abe Glitsky set in the same San Francisco milieu as the Dismas Hardy novels.

When Mark Dooher becomes a suspect in his wife's murder, all the San Francisco attorney--who gets what he wants, including a beautiful mistress and the power of the Church behind him--has to fear is the truth

Lescroart, John T.

The **hearing** / John Lescroart. Dutton, 2001. 451 p. Dismas Hardy novels

ISBN 052594575X

1. Political corruption 2. Murder 3. Secrets 4. Defense attorneys 5. Police 6. Lawyers 7. Murder suspects 8. Heroin addicts 9. Former police 10. Detectives 11. San Francisco, California 12. Mysteries 13. Legal thrillers

LC 00034119

Dismas Hardy encounters political corruption and conspiracy when he takes on San Francisco's embattled, ambitious D.A. by defending a homeless heroin addict on trial for the murder of a homicide lieutenant's daughter.

Lescroart, John T.

Nothing but the truth / John Lescroart. Delacorte Press, 1999. 435 p. Dismas Hardy novels

ISBN 0385333536

1. Murder 2. Former police 3. Secrets 4. Deception 5. Grand jury 6. Marital conflict 7. Women witnesses 8. Lawyers' spouses 9. Murder suspects 10. Defense attorneys 11. San Francisco, California 12. Mysteries 13. Legal thrillers

LC 99032584

San Francisco defense attorney Dismas Hardy finds himself caught up in a high-stakes murder case when his wife, Frannie, is jailed for refusing to reveal the secret of a man accused of killing his wife, a friend whose children attend the same school as Hardy's own.

Lescroart, John T.

The **oath** / John Lescroart. Dutton, 2002. 408 p. Dismas Hardy novels

ISBN 0525945768

1. Medical care -- Corrupt practices 2. Murder 3. Medical ethics 4. Hospital patients -- Mortality 5. Hospitals 6. Murder investigation 7. Lawyers 8. Defense attorneys 9. Health maintenance organizations 10. Trials (Murder) 11. Medical malpractice 12. Detectives 13. Former police 14. San Francisco, California 15. Mysteries 16. Legal thrillers

LC 2001047055

When the head of San Francisco's largest HMO dies in his own hospital, everyone is startled to learn that it was not as a result of a random hit-and-run accident--instead it was an overdose of potassium. Dismas Hardy is defending the prime suspect, attending physician Erick Kensing. Hardy soon discovers that all is not well with the HMO--that too many patients have been dying, many of them victims of murder. And it looks like it is the hospital that is killing them.

"The author wisely steers clear of taking cheap shots at the HMO industry, yet manages to direct a sharp beam into some of its darker crevices." Publishers Weekly.

Lessing, Doris May, 1919-2013

* The **fifth** child / Doris Lessing. A. A. Knopf, 1988. 133 p.

ISBN 9780394571058

1. Violence in boys 2. Family problems 3. Misfits (Persons) 4. Mothers and sons 5. Large families 6. Family relationships 7. Children with disabilities 8. Birth defects 9. Brothers and sisters 10. Rejection (Psychology) 11. Betrayal 12. Cruelty 13. Exploitation 14. Gangs 15. London, England 16. Psychological fiction 17. Literary fiction

LC 88002680

Sequel: Ben, in the world.

A self-satisfied couple intent on raising a happy family is shocked by the birth of an abnormal and brutal fifth child.

"Acting as a social moralist, Lessing exposes the division between the warm and comfortable domestic scene and the harsh reality of the outside world, piercing the boundary between the two as human desires clash with a more brutal vision of existence. A psychologically probing and emotionally powerful performance." Booklist.

Lessing, Doris May, 1919-2013

The **four-gated** city : a novel / Doris Lessing. Harper Perennial, 1995, c1969. 668 p. Children of violence series

ISBN 0060976675

1. Identity (Psychology) 2. Women with mental illnesses 3. Women -- Identity 4. Men/women relations 5. London, England 6. Psychological fiction 7. Literary fiction

LC 95031487

After moving to London, Martha Quest finds herself being drawn toward a Bohemian way of life.

Lessing, Doris May, 1919-2013

* The **golden** notebook / Doris Lessing ; with an introduction by the author. Harper Perennial, 1994. xxix, 623 p.

ISBN 0060975903

1. Women authors 2. Communism 3. Feminists 4. Identity (Psychology) 5. Women authors 6. Mothers and daughters 7. Writer's block 8. Sexuality 9. Nervous breakdown 10. Women with depression 11. Men/women relations 12. Motherhood 13. Selfishness 14. Women with mental illnesses 15. London, England 16. Psychological fiction 17. Literary fiction 18. Diary novels 19. Modern classics

LC 93044125

The experiences of two women provide the framework for an intense literary study of liberated womanhood.

Lessing, Doris May, 1919-2013

The **good** terrorist / Doris Lessing. A. A. Knopf, 1985. 375 p.

ISBN 9780394543390

1. 20th century 2. Communes 3. Women terrorists 4. Women radicals 5. Communism 6. Terrorism 7. Gay men 8. Middle-aged women 9. Politics and culture 10. Homeless women 11. Parent and adult child 12. Squatters 13. Revolutionaries 14. Anger in women 15. Behavior and culture 16. London, England 17. Psychological fiction 18. Literary fiction 19. Political fiction

LC 85040214

Shortlisted for the Booker-McConnell Prize, 1985.

In her mid-thirties, intelligent, resourceful, and sensitive, Alice Mellings is the organizer, the mother-figure of a vagabond radical group, some of whose members become active terrorists, confronting the group with dissension, real danger, and the necessity of making crucial decisions.

"Unsparingly, fiercely, often satirically, Lessing is writing a narrative about death: the death of the heart when ideology tyrannizes over just, kindly human relations, abstractions over common sense." Ms.

Lessing, Doris May, 1919-2013

The **grass** is singing / Doris Lessing. Perennial Classics, 2000. 245p.

ISBN 0060953462

1. Love triangles 2. Sexual attraction 3. Interracial romance 4. European Africans 5. Young women 6. Self-confidence in teenage girls 7. Independence in teenage girls 8. Women with depression 9. Married women 10. Husband and wife 11. Marriage 12. Frustration 13. Farm life -- Africa 14. Household employees 15. Fate and fatalism 16. Housekeepers 17. South Africa -- Race relations 18. Psychological fiction 19. Literary fiction

LC 99035316

"This novel, besides being very well-written, is an extremely mature psychological study. It is full of those terrifying touches of truth, seldom mentioned but instantly recognized. By any standards, this book shows remarkable powers and imagination." New Statesman.

Lessing, Doris May, 1919-2013

Landlocked / Doris Lessing. Harper Perennial, 1995. 347 p. Children of violence series

ISBN 0060976659

1. British in South Africa 2. Marital conflict 3. Extramarital affairs 4. Race relations 5. Women -- Zimbabwe 6. Communism 7. Disillusionment 8. Social movements 9. Revolutionaries 10. Unhappiness 11. World War II 12. Zimbabwe 13. Literary fiction 14. Psychological fiction 15. Domestic fiction

LC 95031489

When Martha Quest's second marriage begins to fall apart, she fights her growing disillusionment by engaging in a love affair that proves to be only temporarily successful.

Lessing, Doris May, 1919-2013

Love, again : a novel / Doris Lessing. Harper Collins, 1995. 352 p.

ISBN 0060176873

1. Love triangles 2. May-December romance 3. Senior women -- Psychology 4. Women dramatists 5. Widows -- Sexuality 6. Jealousy in women 7. Senior women -- Sexuality 8. Actors and actresses 9. Theater -- Production and direction 10. Intergenerational relations 11. Men/women relations 12. Desire 13. Self-discovery in women 14. London, England 15. Psychological fiction 16. Literary fiction

A story of love and desire in an older woman finds sixty-five-year-old Sarah Durham in relationships with two younger men and follows her struggles with the feelings of her youth.

"Although the book is long and rambling, asking much of a reader's patience and willingness to spend so much time inside Sarah's head, Lessing, wields a formidable analytic intelligence that makes this work provocative and often astonishingly beautiful." Publishers Weekly.

Lessing, Doris May, 1919-2013

Martha Quest / Doris Lessing. Harper Perennial, 1995. 333 p. Children of violence series

ISBN 0060976667

1. 1930s 2. British in South Africa 3. Growing up -- Africa 4. Race relations 5. Young women 6. Women -- Zimbabwe 7. Farm life -- Africa 8. Sexuality 9. Teenage girls 10. Self-discovery in teenage girls 11. Racism 12. Southern Africa 13. Zimbabwe 14. Psychological fiction 15. Coming-of-age stories 16. Literary fiction

LC 95033106

Martha Quest, a passionate and intelligent young British woman growing up on a farm in Africa, rebels against her snobbish parents as she determines to live her life to the fullest.

Lessing, Doris May, 1919-2013

A **proper** marriage / Doris Lessing. Plume, 1991?, c1964. 345 p. Children of violence series

ISBN 0452265770

1. 1930s 2. Extramarital affairs 3. Married women 4. British in South Africa 5. Marital conflict 6. Marriage 7. Women -- Zimbabwe 8. Unhappiness 9. Options, alternatives, choices 10. Family violence 11. Misunderstanding 12. Failure (Psychology) 13. Frustration 14. Africa 15. Psychological fiction 16. Literary fiction 17. Domestic fiction

LC 90022046

Feeling trapped and alienated by her husband, Martha Quest must choose between the security of marriage and the sacrifices of independence.

Lessing, Doris May, 1919-2013

A **ripple** from the storm / Doris Lessing. Harper Perennial, 1995. 334 p. Children of violence series

ISBN 0060976640

1. 1940s 2. Feminists 3. World War II 4. Racism 5. British in Africa 6. British in Central Africa 7. Women -- Political activity 8. Communists -- Central Africa 9. Central Africa -- Race relations 10. Great Britain -- Colonies -- Central Africa 11. Psychological fiction 12. Literary fiction

LC 95031488

Martha Quest enters into a curious and uncertain second marriage and becomes active in Communist politics in racially intolerant British Africa.

Lessing, Doris May, 1919-2013

The **sweetest** dream / Doris Lessing. HarperCollins, 2002. 478 p.

ISBN 0066213347

1. 1960s 2. Extended families 3. Self-sacrifice in women 4. Widows 5. Runaway wives, husbands, etc 6. Daughters-in-law 7. Divorced women 8. Women journalists 9. Grandmothers 10. Courage in women 11. Compassion in women 12. AIDS (Disease) 13. Communism 14. Aging 15. London, England 16. Africa 17. Family sagas 18. Psychological fiction 19. Literary fiction

As Frances Lennox and her two sons try to make the best of their situation living with her conservative mother-in-law, her ex-husband dumps his second wife's problem child at her feet, in a novel that recreates the tumultuous political landscape of the 1960s.

Lethem, Jonathan

Chronic city / Jonathan Lethem. Doubleday, 2009. 480 p.

ISBN 9780385518635

1. Women astronauts 2. Socialites 3. Social criticism 4. Celebrities 5. Critics 6. Male friendship 7. Engaged persons 8. Drug use 9. Rumor 10. Truth 11. Manhattan, New York City 12. Literary fiction

Exchanging love letters with a fiancée who is trapped on the Space Station, Chase Insteadman apathetically attends social engagements before pop critic Perkus Tooth introduces him to a side of Manhattan that causes Chase to question everything he believes.

Lethem, Jonathan

Dissident gardens / Jonathan Lethem. Doubleday, 2013. 468 p.

ISBN 9780385534932

1. Dysfunctional families 2. Jewish women 3. Communism 4. Mothers and daughters 5. Interracial romance 6. Extramarital affairs 7. Self-discovery 8. Popular culture 9. New York City -- Social life

and customs 10. Family sagas 11. Literary fiction 12. Political fiction 13. Satirical fiction

A multigenerational saga focuses on two extraordinary women, including Rose, a tyrannical Communist who terrorizes her neighborhood with her absolute beliefs, and her daughter Miriam, who embraces the counterculture of Greenwich Village.

"The cast makes for a heady, swirly mix of fascinating, lonely people. Lethem's writing, as always, packs a witty punch." Publishers Weekly.

Lethem, Jonathan

The **feral** detective / Jonathan Lethem. Ecco Press, 2018. 272 p.

ISBN 9780062859068

1. 21st century 2. Subcultures 3. Deserts 4. Misfits (Persons) 5. Missing teenage girls 6. Private investigators 7. Women amateur detectives 8. Political science 9. Options, alternatives, choices 10. Men/women relations 11. California 12. Mysteries 13. Literary fiction

Convincing an enigmatic loner to help her search for a friend's missing daughter, Phoebe traverses the outskirts of California's stunning Inland Empire, where she discovers her companion's complicated relationship with warring tribes of outcasts.

"Nearly two decades after his last mystery, Motherless Brooklyn (1999), Lethem gives us another, a funny but rage-fueled stunner about a New Yorker tracking her mentors missing daughter on the West Coast." Booklist.

Lethem, Jonathan

Motherless Brooklyn / Jonathan Lethem. Doubleday, 1999. 311 p.

ISBN 9780788751837

1. Tourette syndrome 2. Private investigators 3. Murder investigation 4. Orphans 5. Brooklyn, New York City 6. Hardboiled fiction 7. Literary fiction

Adapted into a film entitled "Motherless Brooklyn" in 2019.

ALA Notable Book, 2000.

Gold Dagger Award for Best Crime Novel of the Year, 2000.

National Book Critics Circle Award for Fiction, 1999.

A walk on the wild side of Brooklyn's criminal underclass with a hero known as "The Human Freakshow," a would-be detective also answering to the name of Lionel Essrog. Essrog is a victim of Tourette's Syndrome; hapless and veering out of control, he fights himself and his disease.

"The short and shady life of Frank Minna ends in murder, shocking the four young men employed by his dysfunctional Brooklyn detective agency/limo service. The 'Minna Men' have centered their lives around Frank. . . . Tourette's-afflicted Lionel has found security as a Minna Man and is shattered by Frank's death. Lionel determines to become a genuine sleuth and find the killer. The ensuing plot twists are marked by clever wordplay, fast-paced dialog, and nonstop irony." Library Journal.

Letts, Elizabeth

Finding Dorothy : a novel / Elizabeth Letts. Ballantine Books, 2019 351 p.

ISBN 9780525622109

1. Baum, Maud Gage 2. Baum, L Frank (Lyman Frank), 1856-1919 Wizard of Oz 3. Garland, Judy 4. 1930s 5. 1870s 6. Widows 7. Ambition in women 8. Women singers 9. Film actors and actresses 10. Protectiveness in women 11. Flashbacks 12. Film industry and trade 13. Independence in women 14. Biographical fiction 15. Historical fiction

LC 2018039473

Reimagines the story behind the creation of The Wonderful Wizard of Oz from the perspective of L. Frank Baum's intrepid wife, whose hardscrabble life on the Dakota prairie inspires her husband's masterpiece and her advocacy of an exploited Judy Garland.

"This well-researched novelization weaves various moments that shaped Maud and Frank's life together and led to his writing The Wonderful Wizard of Oz and her desire to fight for a young actress she just met." Library Journal.

Levack, Simon

Demon of the air : an Aztec mystery / Simon Levack. Thomas Dunne Books/St. Martin's Minotaur, 2005. 320 p. Aztec mysteries

ISBN 0312348347

1. Montezuma II,, Emperor of Mexico, ca 1480-1520 2. 16th century 3. Indians of Mexico 4. Aztecs 5. Former priests 6. Slaves 7. Rulers 8. Shapeshifters 9. Divination 10. Prophecies 11. Human sacrifice 12. Suicide 13. Rumor 14. Dreams 15. Secrets 16. Death threats 17. Tenochtitlan (Extinct city) 18. Mexico -- History -- 16th century 19. Historical mysteries 20. Mysteries

LC 2005043976

Sequel: Shadow of the lords.

In 1517, plagued by enigmatic visions and disturbing dreams, Aztec emperor Montezuma is also faced with a strange prophecy uttered by a would-be sacrificial victim, who escapes the knife with his own suicide.

Leveen, Lois, 1968-

The **secrets** of Mary Bowser / Lois Leveen. William Morrow & Co., 2012. 496 p.

ISBN 9780062107909

1. Bowser, Mary Elizabeth, ca 1840- 2. 19th century 3. Slavery 4. Freed slaves 5. Women spies 6. Women slaves 7. Freedom 8. African Americans 9. Racism 10. Race relations 11. Family secrets 12. Virginia -- History -- 1775-1865 13. Historical fiction

A slave to one of the wealthiest families in Richmond, Virginia, Mary Bowser, sent to Philadelphia to be educated, secretly joins the abolition movement to bring fugitive slaves to freedom - a cause that leads her to deceive even those who are closest to her as she engages in a deadly game of espionage to end slavery.

"Deftly balancing history, romance and adventure, Leveen honors the life and historical importance of a brave, resourceful woman." Kirkus.

Levi, Primo

If not now, when? / Primo Levi ; translated from the Italian by William Weaver ; introduction by Irving Howe. Summit Books, 1985. 349 p.

ISBN 0671493361

1. World War II 2. Resistance to military occupation 3. Jewish resistance and revolts 4. Guerrillas 5. Europe 6. Literary fiction 7. War stories 8. Historical fiction 9. Translations -- Italian to English

LC 85002526

From 1943 to 1945, a band of Jewish partisans engages in guerilla warfare against the Germans in eastern Europe.

Levien, David

City of the sun : a novel / David Levien. Doubleday, 2007. 320 p. Frank Behr novels

ISBN 9780385523660

1. Private investigators 2. Missing boys 3. Parents of missing children 4. Human trafficking 5. Loss (Psychology) 6. Former police 7. Teenage boys 8. Human trafficking victims 9. Child trafficking

10. Child trafficking victims 11. Indianapolis, Indiana 12. Mexico 13. Thrillers and suspense

LC 2007028002

Fourteen months after their young son Jamie vanishes while delivering newspapers in his suburban Indianapolis neighborhood, Paul and Carol Gabriel hire private detective Frank Behr to uncover the truth about their son's fate.

"While it deals with the practical mechanics of how a private detective tracks down a boy who has been missing for more than a year, this relentless novel is really about how parents suffer the loss of a child. As such, the story conveys a piercing sense of honesty, even when the investigation itself seems implausibly free of complications." New York Times Book Review.

Levin, Ira

* The **boys** from Brazil : a novel / Ira Levin. Random House, 1976. 312 p.

ISBN 9780394402673

1. Hitler, Adolf, 1889-1945 2. Mengele, Josef, 1911-1979 3. Racism 4. Conspiracies 5. Clones and cloning 6. Nazis -- Brazil 7. Antisemitism 8. Thrillers and suspense

Six former SS men, dispatched from Brazil by the notorious former commandant of Auschwitz to kill ninety-four men, become the targets of aging, increasingly shortsighted Nazi-hunter Yakov Liebermann.

Levin, Ira

A **kiss** before dying / Ira Levin. Simon and Schuster, 1953. 244 p.

ISBN 0786711647

1. Psychopaths 2. Antisocial personality disorders 3. Deception 4. Twin sisters 5. Ambition in men 6. Greed in men 7. Charisma 8. Murder 9. Murder investigation 10. Noir fiction 11. Thrillers and suspense

LC 53002041

Edgar Allan Poe Award for Best First Mystery Novel, 1954.

A charming young man who will stop at nothing, including murder, to get to where he wants to go, must deal with Dorothy, his pregnant girlfriend, and the solution involves some desperate measures.

Levin, Ira

* **Rosemary's** baby : a novel / Ira Levin. Penguin, 1997, c1967. 319 p.

ISBN 9780451194008

1. Husband and wife 2. Rape 3. Antichrist 4. Apartment houses 5. Unplanned pregnancy 6. Faustian bargains 7. Satanism 8. Spirit possession 9. Manhattan, New York City 10. Horror

Sequel: Son of Rosemary.

Originally published: New York : Random House, 1967.

Witchcraft and terror await Rosemary and Guy Woodhouse when they move into the ominous Bramford apartment building

Levin, Ira

The **Stepford** wives : a novel / Ira Levin. Random House, 1972. 145 p.

ISBN 0394481992

1. Suburban life 2. Gender role 3. Men's organizations 4. Homemakers 5. Robots 6. Deception 7. Secrets 8. Horror

LC 72002481

"There is a broad current of humor beneath the horrific surface of this little ambush of Women's Lib, life and the pursuit of happiness." New York Times Book Review.

Levine, David D., 1961-

* **Arabella** of Mars / David D. Levine. Tor, 2016. 320 p. Adventures of Arabella Ashby

ISBN 9780765382818

1. 18th century 2. Space flight 3. Young women 4. Male impersonators 5. Space vehicles 6. Frontier and pioneer life 7. Mars (Planet) 8. Science fiction 9. Alternative histories 10. Steampunk 11. Swashbuckling tales

Nebula Awards: Andre Norton Award for YA Science Fiction and Fantasy, 2016.

Arabella Ashby loves her life on the British colony of Mars. Her parents, however, despair of Arabella's refusal to act like a proper English lady and sends her to Oxfordshire, where she must endure an endless succession of social events for the purpose of finding a husband. But when Arabella receives word that her brother, still on Mars, is in danger, she disguises herself as a boy and joins the crew of the?Diana, a Mars Trading Company vessel. But will she arrive in time to save him? With its Steampunk-infused Regency-era setting and swashbuckling adventure among the stars,?Arabella of Mars'should appeal to fans of Jules Verne and Edgar Rice Burroughs. -- Description by Gillian Speace.

"The alternate-world science is novel, the plot thrilling, and the romance appropriately chaste, but with her wits, resourcefulness, and courage, Arabella cuts a dashing figure as the heroine of this story." Booklist.

Levine, James, 1963-

Bingo's run / James A. Levine. Spiegel & Grau, 2014. 304 p.

ISBN 9781400068838

1. Orphans 2. Drug smuggling 3. Swindlers and swindling 4. Drug couriers 5. Poverty 6. Murder witnesses 7. Corruption 8. Slums 9. Short boys 10. Fifteen-year-old boys 11. Artists 12. Characters and characteristics in mythology 13. Nairobi, Kenya 14. Kenya 15. Literary fiction

A mythology-infused tale set against the backdrop of Kenya's poverty-stricken slums and luxury resorts follows the experiences of a charismatic young drug runner who makes deliveries to a reclusive artist before his witness of murder leads to his adoption by a woman who tests his sense of morality.

"As Bingo asserts many times throughout Levine's second novel (after The Blue Notebook), I am the greatest runner in Kibera, Nairobi, and probably the world.... Bingo is a fascinating and inimitably likable character. Levine, a Mayo clinic professor of medicine and well-known child advocate, excels at telling his adventurous, comic, and realistically gritty story with humor but not with pathos, successfully addressing the harsh and sometimes tragic story of a child at risk." Library Journal.

Levitt, Paul M.

Come with me to Babylon / Paul M. Levitt. University of New Mexico Press, 2008. 240 p.

ISBN 9780826341785

1. Jews, Russian 2. Jews 3. Families 4. Assimilation (Sociology) 5. Love triangles 6. Betrayal 7. Family secrets 8. Culture conflict 9. Poverty 10. Hope 11. Farms 12. Factories 13. Disappointment 14. Immigrants 15. New York City 16. New Jersey 17. Domestic fiction 18. Historical fiction

LC 2007039410

In 1910 the Cohen family, in search of the Golden Medina, undertakes a dangerous journey from Russia to the United States, where the new world, exposes family secrets, cultural conflicts, the corruption of the American Dream, and love's divides.

"This historical novel follows the Cohen family from their village in Russia to the United States, led by strong-willed Esther Cohen. Under the auspices of the Baron de Hirsch Fund, an agency focused on emigration, the Cohens are supposed to become farmers in rural New Jersey. But the bucolic occupation doesn't interest her husband, the gently raised Meyer Cohen. . . . All too soon, the Cohens have become a tenement family. Daughter Fanny is disabled in the Triangle Shirtwaist Co. fire, which killed more than 100 garment workers in a locked building. Son Ben begins dating a whore and running errands for a strikebreaking criminal. . . . Levitt hooks and plays his readers well. One influential character never appears directly: Jacob, Meyer and Esther's estranged son. The story of how he left the family, and how it grieves both parents, is a subtle but unmistakable undercurrent to Babylon." Rocky Mountain News.

Levy, Andrea, 1956-2019

* The **long** song / Andrea Levy. Farrar, Straus and Giroux, 2010. 320 p.

ISBN 9780374192174

1. Slavery -- Jamaica 2. Master and servant 3. Women slaves 4. Race relations 5. Plantation life 6. Love triangles 7. Freedom 8. Freed slaves 9. Slave resistance and revolts 10. Interracial romance 11. Sugar plantations -- Jamaica 12. Jamaica -- History -- 19th century 13. Historical fiction

LC 2009043181

"A Frances Coady book."

Contains reading group questions.

Walter Scott Prize for Historical Fiction, 2011.

Shortlisted for the Man Booker Prize, 2010.

You do not know me yet but I am the narrator of this work. My son Thomas, who is publishing this book, tells me it is customary at this place in a novel to give the reader a little taste of the story that is held within these pages. As your storyteller, I am to convey that this tale is set in Jamaica during the last turbulent years of slavery and the early years of freedom that followed.

"For all its power to disturb, this is a beautifully written and cleverly constructed novel that projects convincing personal relationships on to the feral backdrop of the Jamaican plantations." Times (London).

Levy, Andrea, 1956-2019

Small island / Andrea Levy. Review, 2004. 448 p.

ISBN 0755307496

1. 1940s 2. Racism 3. Prejudice 4. Race relations 5. Interracial friendship 6. Husband and wife 7. Jamaicans in Great Britain 8. Landlord and tenant 9. World War II veterans 10. Immigration and emigration 11. World War II -- Post-war aspects 12. Adaptability (Psychology) 13. Postwar life 14. England -- Social conditions -- 20th century 15. England -- Race relations 16. England -- Immigration and emigration 17. Historical fiction 18. Literary fiction

Orange Prize for Fiction, 2004.

Whitbread Book Award for Novel, 2004.

Whitbread Book of the Year Award, 2004.

National Book Critics Circle Award for Fiction finalist, 2005

Returning to England after the war Gilbert Joseph is treated very differently now that he is no longer in an RAF uniform. Joined by his wife Hortense, he rekindles a friendship with Queenie who takes in Jamaican lodgers. Can their dreams of a better life in England overcome the prejudice they face?.

"The narrative voice jumps between the characters, a technique that embeds familiar cultural observations in closely observed and surprising lives. If the plot sometimes verges on the operatic, Levy's writing deftly illuminates the complex and contradictory motives behind each character's behavior." The New Yorker.

Levy, Deborah

Hot milk : a novel / Deborah Levy. Bloomsbury USA, 2016. 217 p.

ISBN 9781620406694

1. Parent and adult child 2. Mothers and daughters 3. Self-fulfillment in women 4. Uncertainty 5. Purpose in life 6. Anthropologists 7. Family relationships 8. Spain 9. Literary fiction

LC 2016001369

Shortlisted for the Man Booker Prize, 2016

Driven to cure her mother's inexplicable illness, a young anthropologist seeks the advice of a famous but controversial consultant on the arid coast of southern Spain, where the transient desert environment shapes her own desires.

"Levy has crafted a great character in Sofia, and witnessing a pivotal point in her life is a pleasure." Publishers Weekly.

Levy, Deborah

Swimming home : a novel / Deborah Levy ; with an introduction by Tom McCarthy. Bloomsbury USA, 2012, c2011. 157 p.

ISBN 9781620401699

1. 1990s 2. Middle class families 3. Family vacations 4. Strangers 5. Interpersonal relations 6. Poets 7. Husband and wife 8. Women -- Psychology 9. Home (Concept) 10. Women war correspondents 11. Depression 12. Control (Psychology) 13. Nice, France 14. French Riviera 15. Psychological fiction 16. Literary fiction

LC 2011535684

Originally published: High Wycombe, England : And Other Stories, c2011.

Shortlisted for the Man Booker Prize, 2012.

A mysterious woman who suffers from mental illness suddenly appears at a vacation villa where two families are staying and her interactions with them reveal secret details about their past and tensions within their relationships with each other.

Lewis, Beverly, 1949-

The **brethren** / Beverly Lewis. Bethany House, 2006. 352 p. Annie's people

ISBN 0764202316

1. Children of clergy 2. Family secrets 3. Amish families 4. Women artists 5. Amish -- Social life and customs 6. Family relationships 7. Art appreciation 8. Faith (Christianity) 9. Men/women relations 10. Christian life 11. Pennsylvania 12. Christian fiction 13. Domestic fiction

LC 2006019314

Sequel to: The Englisher.

Christy Award for Contemporary (Series, Sequels, and Novellas) Category, 2007.

Annie Zook, the Amish preacher's daughter, is caught between two worlds. Living with shunned friend Esther, Annie longs to return to her forbidden art and the idyllic days spent with Englisher Ben Martin, before her father ordered her never to see him again. Stunned when family secrets come to light, Ben determines to solve the mystery of his past. Will his future include Annie--or will the Brethren always stand between them?

Lewis, Beverly, 1949-

The **ebb** tide / Beverly Lewis. Baker Pub Group, 2017. 352 p.

ISBN 9780764219092

1. Amish 2. Amish women 3. Nannies 4. College students 5. Men/women relations 6. Interpersonal attraction 7. Mate selection 8. Cape

May, New Jersey 9. Christian romances

LC 2016041992

Spending the summer working as a nanny in Cape May, young Amish woman Sallie meets a marine biology student and makes discoveries about herself and the world outside her community that compel her to question her commitments to the home she has always loved.

Lewis, Beverly, 1949-

The **missing** / Beverly Lewis. Bethany House, 2009. 332 p. Seasons of grace (Beverly Lewis)

ISBN 9780764207242

1. Amish 2. People with terminal illnesses 3. Mothers and daughters 4. Female friendship 5. Missing women 6. Family secrets 7. Family relationships 8. Redemption 9. Pennsylvania 10. Christian fiction

Longing to find her missing mother and uncover the secrets that led to her leaving three weeks earlier, 21-year-old Grace Byler strikes up a fast friendship with Heather Lang, an "Englisher" contemplating her own grave medical prognosis, and the two young women travel together in hopes of finding Grace's mother and bringing her home.

Lewis, Beverly, 1949-

The **preacher's** daughter / Beverly Lewis. Bethany House, 2005. 349 p. Annie's people

ISBN 0764201050

1. 1890s 2. Amish women 3. Children of clergy 4. Women artists 5. Pen pals 6. Women art teachers 7. Amish -- Social life and customs 8. Amish families 9. Family relationships 10. Friendship 11. Faith (Christianity) 12. Men/women relations 13. Christian life 14. Pennsylvania 15. Christian historical fiction 16. Domestic fiction 17. Coming-of-age stories

LC 2005018581

Collected in 2014 with The Englisher and The Brethren under the title Annie's People.

Annie Zook's greatest passion is drawing, but it's forbidden by her father, an Old Order Amish preacher in Paradise, Pennsylvania. She must even sacrifice marriage and happiness with the love of her life, Rudy Esh, in order to secretly practice her art. But when longtime pen pal, fellow artist and "Englisher" Louisa Stratford visits seeking solace after a broken engagement, Annie must come to terms with her unhappiness and decide whether to stay with her Plain community or pursue her dream.

Lewis, C. S. (Clive Staples), 1898-1963

Till we have faces : a myth retold / C.S. Lewis ; drawings by Fritz Eichenberg. Harcourt Brace & Co., 1984, c1956. 313 p.

ISBN 9780156904360

1. Love 2. Identity (Psychology) 3. Princesses 4. Psyche (Greek deity) 5. Cupid (Roman deity) 6. Mythological fiction 7. Fantasy fiction

Originally published in 1956.

This reinterpretation of the tale of Cupid and Psyche, combines elements of barbarism and fantasy with an understanding of human nature and psychology.

Lewis, Kristyn Kusek

Half of what you hear / Kristyn Kusek Lewis. HarperCollins, 2018 400 p.

ISBN 9780062673350

1. Secrets 2. Small town life 3. Women -- Interpersonal relations 4. Inns 5. Families 6. Scandals 7. Female friendship 8. Family businesses 9. Family relationships 10. Virginia 11. Women's lives and relationships

A novel about a woman moving to a small community and uncovering the many secrets that hide behind closed doors.

Lewis, M. G (Matthew Gregory), 1775-1818

* The **monk** : a romance / Matthew Lewis. Penguin, 2012. xii, 424 p.

ISBN 9780141199467

1. Monks 2. Temptation (Christianity) 3. Satanism 4. Good and evil 5. Lust 6. Sin 7. Sexuality 8. Madrid, Spain 9. Gothic fiction 10. Classics 11. Horror

First published: 1796.

The respected monk Ambrosio, the Abbot of a Capuchin monastery in Madrid, is overwhelmed with desire for a young girl; once having abandoned his monastic vows he begins a terrible descent into immorality and violence. His appalling fall from grace embraces blasphemy, black magic, torture, rape, and murder, and places his very soul in jeopardy.

Lewis, Sinclair, 1885-1951

* **Babbitt** / Sinclair Lewis. Harcourt, 1950, c1922. 401 p.

ISBN 0140189025

1. 1920s 2. Hypocrisy 3. Real estate agents 4. Conformity 5. Middle class men 6. Satirical fiction 7. Modern classics

Originally published in 1922.

On the surface, everything is all right with Babbitt's world of the solid, successful businessman. But in reality, George F. Babbit is a lonely, middle-aged man. He doesn't understand his family, has an unsuccessful attempt at an affair, and is almost financially ruined when he dares to voice sympathy for some striking workers. Babbitt finds his only safety lies deep in the fold of those who play it safe. He is a man who has added a new word to our language: a "Babbitt," meaning someone who conforms unthinkingly, a sheep.

Lewis, Sinclair, 1885-1951

Dodsworth / Sinclair Lewis. Harcourt, 1929. 377 p.

ISBN 9789997412379

1. Middle-aged men 2. Executives -- United States 3. Climacteric, Male 4. Automobile industry and trade -- United States 5. Rich men -- United States 6. Husband and wife 7. Marriage -- United States 8. Americans in Europe 9. Europe -- Social life and customs -- 1918-1945 10. United States -- Social life and customs -- 1918-1945 11. Domestic fiction 12. Satirical fiction

Touring Europe with his beautiful but spoiled wife Fran, millionaire Sam Dodsworth, known as the American Captain of Industry, witnesses the clash of American and English cultures at the same time his marriage falls apart.

Lewis, Sinclair, 1885-1951

* **Elmer** Gantry / Sinclair Lewis. New American Library, 1980, c1927. 430 p.

ISBN 9780451522511

1. Ambition 2. Hypocrisy 3. Revivals 4. Itinerant preachers 5. Evangelists -- United States 6. Men/women relations 7. Modern classics 8. Satirical fiction

Originally published: New York : Harcourt, Brace and Co., 1927.

A vulgar and licentious college football captain becomes a messenger of God as a suave evangelist preacher, in this classic story that is universally recognized as a landmark in American literature.

Lewis, Sinclair, 1885-1951

It can't happen here / Sinclair Lewis, with an introduction by Jay Richard Kennedy New American Library, 1963. 331 p.
ISBN 9780451216588

1. 1930s 2. State-sponsored terrorism 3. Newspaper editors 4. Extremism -- United States 5. Totalitarianism -- United States 6. Dictators -- United States 7. Imperialism, American 8. United States -- Politics and government 9. Fascism -- United States 10. United States -- Foreign relations -- Mexico 11. Mexico -- Foreign relations -- United States 12. Minnesota 13. Political fiction

It is 1936. America has just elected Berzelius Windrip to the presidency-and his fascist policies turn the U.S. into a totalitarian state.

"In an enigmatic election year, Sinclair Lewis's 1935 political satire It Can't Happen Here holds unexpectedly fresh warnings." Chronicle of Higher Education

Lewis, Sinclair, 1885-1951

* **Main** street : the story of Carol Kennicott / Sinclair Lewis ; with an introduction and notes by Martin Bucco. Penguin Books, 1995, c1920. 415 p.
ISBN 0140189017

1. 1920s 2. Physicians' spouses 3. Small town life 4. Hypocrisy 5. Gossiping and gossips 6. Greed 7. Friendship 8. Minnesota 9. Satirical fiction 10. Modern classics
LC 95016373 //r96

Originally published: New York : Harcourt, Brace, 1920.

Raised in free-thinking St. Paul, Carol Milford is slightly disheartened when she marries Dr. Will Kennicott, moves to a rural town, and reverts to a life of domesticity. Although her husband is not to blame for her unhappiness, Carol quickly becomes disillusioned and begins to contemplate leaving the good doctor.

Lewis, Ted, 1940-1982

* **GBH** / Ted Lewis. Soho Crime, 2015, c1980. 323 p.
ISBN 9781616955502

1. 1970s 2. Criminals 3. Paranoia 4. Pornography 5. Power (Social sciences) 6. Violence 7. Sex industry and trade 8. Intrigue 9. Coastal towns 10. Organized crime 11. London, England 12. England 13. Noir fiction 14. Parallel narratives 15. Crime fiction
LC 2014033183

Originally published: London : Sphere, 1980

In 1970s London, George Fowler is a producer and distributor of illegal pornography, but he becomes increasingly suspicious that his company is being undermined and as he retreats to his hideout in a coastal town, his paranoia threatens to overwhelm him.

"Though he narrates his own story, Fowlers lack of self-awareness makes this book about a bad man a great one." Booklist.

Li, Yiyun, 1972-

The **vagrants** : a novel / Yiyun Li. Random House, 2009. 337 p.
ISBN 9781400063130

1. Chinese Cultural Revolution (1966-1976) 2. 1970s 3. Communism 4. Executions and executioners 5. Human body parts industry and trade 6. Violence 7. Friendship 8. China -- Politics and government -- 20th century 9. China -- Social conditions -- 20th century 10. China -- History -- 20th century 11. Historical fiction
LC 2008023467

ALA Notable Book, 2010.

Shortlisted for the International IMPAC Dublin Literary Award, 2011

In 1979 Muddy River, a provincial Chinese city, the Gu family struggles to deal with the imminent loss of their daughter, Gu Shan, about to be executed as a counterrevolutionary, while their neighbors deal with the realities of life in China.

"Li offers both a bleak view of a historical moment when people were the most dangerous animals in the world and a meditation on the act of martyrdom, which is presented both as a duty and as a luxury that few could afford." The New Yorker.

Liardet, Frances

We must be brave / Frances Liardet. G.P. Putnam's Sons, 2019. 464 p.
ISBN 9780735218864

1. 20th century 2. Childlessness 3. Married women 4. Lost children 5. Loss (Psychology) 6. Villages 7. Friendship 8. Small town life 9. England -- History -- 20th century 10. Historical fiction
LC 2018041587

Caring for a lost child during the chaotic 1940 evacuation of her once-quiet Southampton village, a woman who never believed she wanted children finds herself unexpectedly at a loss when the child is taken away.

Lightman, Alan P., 1948-

The **diagnosis** / Alan Lightman. Pantheon Books, 2000. 369 p.
ISBN 0679436154

1. Identity (Psychology) 2. Amnesia 3. Technology -- Social aspects 4. Executives 5. Men with amnesia 6. People with amnesia 7. Businesspeople 8. Psychiatry 9. Boston, Massachusetts 10. Psychological fiction
LC 00024543

National Book Award for Fiction finalist, 2000

Businessman Bill Chalmers descends into a nightmare as he pursues a diagnosis for his strange illness, which involves a bizarre memory loss and a strange numbness that gradually affects his entire body.

"A work of vivid sensuousness, sparkling intelligence, and poignant beauty, Lightman's gripping tale contrasts the needs of the body and spirit with the acquisitiveness of the mind and ponders the potential lethality of ideologies, be they cultural or technological." Booklist.

Lightman, Alan P., 1948-

* **Einstein's** dreams / Alan Lightman. Pantheon Books, 1993. 179 p.
ISBN 0679416463

1. Einstein, Albert, 1879-1955 2. Dreams 3. Time 4. General relativity (Physics) 5. Physicists 6. Physics 7. Literary fiction
LC 92050465

A fictional recreation of Einstein's discovery of the nature of time follows the young Albert through 1905 Bern, Switzerland, as he sorts through the dreams that have persisted in his mind for several months

"Lightman starts out with commonplaces, neurological conditions or abstractions of our personal experience of time. Then, with one or two exceptions, he embodies the concept in brilliant, folkloric tales with extraordinary assurance." New Statesman.

Lim, Eugene

Dear cyborgs / Eugene Lim. Farrar, Straus and Giroux, 2017. 163 p.
ISBN 9780374537111

1. Superheroes 2. Korean American boys 3. Storytelling 4. Friendship 5. Villains 6. Detectives 7. Near future 8. Creation (literary, artistic, etc) 9. Purpose in life 10. Capitalism -- Social aspects 11. Protest movements 12. Alienation (Social psychology) 13. Science fiction 14. Experimental fiction 15. Metafiction 16. Parallel narratives
LC 2016045039

Interweaves the story of two Asian American outcast boys bonding over their mutual appreciation of comic books, with a team of superheroes on their coffee breaks who discuss their ennui, artistic malaise and complain about the pragmatic demands of modern capitalism.

A colorful meditation on friendship and creation nested within a fictional universe.

Lim, Roselle

Natalie Tan's book of luck and fortune / Roselle Lim. Berkley, 2019. 304 p.

ISBN 9781984803252

1. Women cooks 2. Chinese Americans 3. Families 4. Cooking, Chinese 5. Women -- Family relationships 6. Homecomings 7. Chinatown, San Francisco, California 8. San Francisco, California 9. Mainstream fiction 10. Women's lives and relationships

LC 2018041137

Inheriting her grandmother's restaurant in a crumbling San Francisco Chinatown neighborhood, Natalie Tan is advised by the local seer to prepare three recipes from her grandmother's cookbook to help their struggling community.

"Readers will fall in love with Natalie, her multifaceted supporting cast, and the sights, sounds, and smells of San Francisco. This big-hearted and deeply-felt story stirs together mourning, nostalgia, and the freedom of new possibilities." Booklist.

Limon, Martin, 1948-

Mr. Kill / Martin Limon. Soho Crime, 2011. 368 p. George Sueno and Ernie Bascom mysteries

ISBN 9781569479346

1. United States. Army Criminal Investigation Command 2. 1970s 3. Murder investigation 4. Violence against women 5. Detectives 6. Soldiers 7. Alliances 8. Rape investigation 9. Americans in Korea 10. Korea 11. South Korea 12. Seoul, Korea 13. Mysteries 14. Political fiction

LC 2011024936

When a brutal rape escalates tensions between locals and American soldiers stationed in early 1970s South Korea, Army investigators George Sueño and Ernie Bascom team up with a legendary Korean detective in a desperate search that is hampered by military apologists who deny that Americans were involved.

Limon, Martin, 1948-

The **line** / Martin Limon. Soho Press, 2018. 336 p. George Sueno and Ernie Bascom mysteries

ISBN 9781616959661

1. United States. Army Criminal Investigation Command 2. 1970s 3. Murder investigation 4. Racism 5. Racism in the military 6. Innocence (Law) 7. Scapegoats (Persons) 8. Military police 9. Americans in Korea 10. Missing persons investigation 11. Missing persons 12. Intelligence service 13. Mexican Americans 14. Korean Demilitarized Zone 15. Korea 16. South Korea 17. Mysteries 18. Political fiction

LC 2018016742

After discovering a body on the Korean Demilitarized Zone in the 1970s, Sueño and Bascom try to find the perpetrator despite little cooperation between the two countries' governments.

"Limn has never been better at incorporating a logical mystery plot into the politics of his chosen time and place." Publishers Weekly.

Lin, Jeannie

The **dragon** and the pearl / Jeannie Lin. Harlequin Books, 2011 288 p. Tang Dynasty

ISBN 9780373296620

1. Tang dynasty (618-907) 2. Assassins 3. Political corruption 4. Nobility 5. Courts and courtiers 6. Rulers 7. Mistresses 8. Warriors 9. Rescues 10. Courtesans 11. Women rulers 12. Men/women relations 13. Interpersonal attraction 14. Protectiveness in men 15. China -- History -- T'ang dynasty, 618-907 16. Historical romances 17. Category romances

Former Emperor's consort Ling Suyin is renowned for her beauty. She lives quietly alone until the most ruthless warlord in the region steals her away, intent on uncovering her mystery without falling under her spell.

Lin, Jeannie

The **lotus** palace / Jeannie Lin. HQN, 2013. 384 p. Lotus Palace

ISBN 9780373777730

1. Tang dynasty (618-907) 2. Medieval period (476-1492) 3. Nobility 4. Murder investigation 5. Civilization, Medieval 6. Interclass romance 7. Deception 8. Mate selection 9. China -- History -- T'ang dynasty, 618-907 10. Historical romances

Even without her disfiguring birthmark, maidservant Yue-ying knows she could never attract the attention of Lord Bai Huang -- not when he could have her mistress, Mingyu, the Lotus Palace's most desirable courtesan and one of the Four Beauties of the Pingkang li, the famed entertainment district of capital city Chang'an. However, as Yue-ying discovers when they're thrown together during a murder investigation, Bai is more than the charming wastrel he seems at first. Can their mutual attraction overcome their different stations in life? Set in during China's 9th-century Tang Dynasty, The Lotus Palace delivers romance loaded with lavish, atmospheric historical details. - Description by Gillian Speace.

"Lin once again effortlessly evokes the colorful, intriguing world of Tang dynasty China in her latest dazzlingly different romance, and the books mystery-rich plot and exotic historical setting also make The Lotus Palace an excellent read-alike suggestion for fans of Laura Joh Rowland's mysteries." Booklist.

Linden, Rachel

Ascension of larks / Rachel Linden. Thomas Nelson, 2017. 336 p.

ISBN 9780718095734

1. Family secrets 2. Self-discovery in women 3. Women photographers 4. Loss (Psychology) 5. Widows 6. First loves 7. Second chances 8. Options, alternatives, choices 9. Grief 10. Women's lives and relationships

LC 2017004213

Risking her career to care for the widow and young children of the only man she's ever loved, globetrotting photographer Magdalena Henry finds joy after tragedy and embraces the beauty of an unexpected life.

Linden, Rachel

The **enlightenment** of bees / Rachel Linden. Thomas Nelson, 2019. 336 p.

ISBN 9780785221401

1. Humanitarian assistance 2. Self-fulfillment in women 3. Breaking up (Interpersonal relations) 4. Volunteers 5. Food relief 6. Faith (Christianity) 7. Life change events 8. International relief 9. Men/women relations 10. Transformations, Personal 11. Young women -- Psychology 12. Hungary 13. Mumbai, India 14. Seattle, Washington

15. Christian fiction

LC 2019002201

Rachel Linden's newest story speaks to the universal struggle of what it means to live a meaningful life where the passions we have meet the needs of the world.

Lindsay, Jeffry P.

Just watch me / Jeffry P. Lindsay. E.P. Dutton, 2019. 320 p. Riley Wolfe novels

ISBN 9781524743949

1. Thieves 2. Jewelry theft 3. Ambition 4. Parkour 5. Diamonds 6. Personal conduct 7. Criminals 8. Art forgers 9. FBI agents 10. Mothers and sons 11. Caper novels

Targeting a crown jewel collection that is protected by airtight security, a Robin Hood-type master thief finds his efforts complicated by an equally skilled nemesis cop and an expert forger with dubious loyalties.

Link, Charlotte

The **other** child / Charlotte Link. Pegasus Books, 2013, c2010. 416 p.

ISBN 9781605984308

1. Women detectives 2. Engagement 3. Rural life 4. Coastal towns 5. Orphans 6. Murder investigation 7. Murder 8. Deception 9. World War II 10. Evacuation of civilians 11. Secrets 12. Interpersonal relations 13. Yorkshire, England 14. London, England 15. Mysteries 16. Parallel narratives 17. Translations -- German to English

Originally published in English: 2012. First published in Germany as Das andere Kind. 2009.

Originally published: Wolfenbuttel : Bundesakademie fur Kulturelle Bildung, 2010.

Investigating two murders that occurred months apart in the quiet seaside town of Scarborough, detective Valerie Almond seeks a connection between the two victims and instead discovers a link to the evacuation of children to Scarborough during World War II.

Link, Charlotte

The **watcher** : a novel of crime / Charlotte Link ; translated from the German by Stefan Tobler. Pegasus Books, 2014, c2012. 400 p.

ISBN 9781605985596

1. Murder suspects 2. Men 3. Nosiness 4. Murder 5. Snooping 6. Neighbors 7. Sisters-in-law 8. Former detectives 9. Apartment dwellers 10. Murder investigation 11. London, England 12. Psychological suspense 13. Translations -- German to English

Der beobachter originally published: Munich : Blanvalet Verlag, 2012.

After two of his high-rise neighbors are murdered in their apartments, a would-be good Samaritan with a fondness for spying on the other residents, Samson Segal, comes under intense suspicion as the possible killer.

"In Link's skilled hands, seemingly disparate story lines come together in a nail-biting climax. This is the second novel (following The Other Child, 2013) by a best-selling author in her native Germany to be released in the U.S. Fans of Tana French's twisty crime novels will devour this suspenseful read." Booklist.

Link, Kelly

Magic for beginners / Kelly Link. Small Beer Press, 2005. 272 p.

ISBN 1931520151

1. Haunted houses 2. Convenience stores 3. Teenagers 4. Zombies 5. Clerks (Retail industry and trade) 6. Short stories 7. Contemporary

fantasy 8. Fantasy fiction

LC 2005005394

9 short stories.

Locus Award for Best Collection, 2006.

A follow-up collection to Stranger Things Happen celebrates the intersection between the worlds of reality and the supernatural, in an anthology that features such topics as a haunted convenience store and a weekly apocalyptic poker party.

"Link's second collection has a McSweeney's-like tendency to digress, but does so without irony. Whether describing witches filled with ants that carry pieces of time, or an orange-juice-colored corduroy couch that looks as if it has just escaped from a maximum security prison for criminally insane furniture, these stories examine American middle and lower-middle-class life from unexpected angles that mix fairy tale, science fiction, and zaniness. . . . Reading Link, one has a sense that sometimes a person needs to wander off for a better perspective, and sometimes a person simply needs to wander off." The New Yorker.

Lipman, Elinor

The **dearly** departed, Elinor Lipman. Random House, 2001. 256 p.

ISBN 0679463127

1. Self-discovery 2. Brothers and sisters 3. Funerals 4. Mothers -- Death 5. Family secrets 6. Women golfers 7. New Hampshire 8. Mainstream fiction

LC 00067368

The untimely death of her single mother, Margaret Batten, brings Sunny back to small-town King George, New Hampshire, the scene of her unhappy adolescence, where she discovers old family secrets and a possible half-brother she never knew she had.

Lipman, Elinor

The **family** man / Elinor Lipman. Houghton Mifflin Harcourt, 2009. 320 p.

ISBN 9780618644667

1. Gay lawyers 2. Stepdaughters 3. Fathers and daughters 4. Gay men -- Relations with women 5. Former wives 6. Secrets 7. Family reunions 8. Family relationships 9. Upper West Side, New York City 10. Mainstream fiction 11. Domestic fiction

LC 2008046222

A successful but lonely man reconnects with a long-lost stepdaughter and her newly widowed mother and finds his life turned upside down.

"Hilarious, literate and unnervingly accurate in its observations of the quirks of human nature, The Family Man proclaims that whatever bizarre sort of family you have, you're better off with it than without." PopMatters.

Lipman, Elinor

Good riddance / Elinor Lipman. Houghton Mifflin Harcourt, 2019. 290 p.

ISBN 9780544808256

1. School yearbooks 2. Neighbors 3. Family secrets 4. Mothers -- Death 5. Class reunions 6. Father and adult daughter 7. Documentary filmmakers 8. Interpersonal relations 9. Men/women relations 10. New York City 11. New Hampshire 12. Romantic comedies

LC 2018006362

Discarding her late mother's cherished and heavily annotated high school yearbook, Daphne is entangled in a series of absurdities when the yearbook is discovered by a busybody documentary filmmaker.

Lipman, Elinor

The **inn** at Lake Devine : a novel / Elinor Lipman Random House, 1998. 253 p.

ISBN 0679456937

1. Hotels -- Vermont 2. Antisemitism -- Vermont 3. Interfaith romance -- Vermont 4. Jewish American women -- Vermont 5. Revenge -- Vermont 6. Women cooks 7. Hotel owners 8. Vermont 9. Mainstream fiction

LC 971307

When her mother receives a notice about a Vermont inn that caters especially to non-Jewish guests, Natalie Marx becomes obsessed with the once-restricted, family-owned resort and wangles an invitation to join a friend on a vacation there

"Skillfully interweaving the bittersweet narrative with threads of both tragedy and comedy, Lipman displays a healthy amount of empathy and affection for her flawed and slightly eccentric cast of characters." Booklist.

Lipman, Elinor

The **pursuit** of Alice Thrift : a novel / Elinor Lipman. Random House, 2003. 269 p.

ISBN 9780679463139

1. Courtship 2. Swindlers and swindling 3. Self-discovery 4. Self-fulfillment 5. Women physicians 6. Women interns (Medicine) 7. Nurses 8. Interpersonal relations 9. Men/women relations 10. Boston, Massachusetts 11. Mainstream fiction

LC 2002031864

Workaholic wallflower Alice Thrift, a socially inept surgical intern at a Boston hospital, is pursued romantically by Ray Russo, a social-climbing, somewhat shady purveyor of carnival fudge, until her roommate, nurse Leo Frawley, and neighbor, Dr. Sylvie Schwartz, decide to take on the task of guiding Alice through the social complexities of life.

"The eponymous Alice is a sleep-deprived surgical intern at a Boston hospital. A graduate of MIT and Harvard and a congenital workaholic, she's also devoid of social skills, a sense of humor or elementary tact. Though miserably unequipped with self-esteem, Alice is an intelligent, well-brought-up offspring of upper-middle-class parents. Why, then, does she fall prey to the romantic blandishments of Ray Russo, a vulgar loudmouth and con artist whoit turns outlies every time he opens his mouth? That Lipman can make this story plausible, and tell it with humor, pschological insight and rising suspense, is a triumph." Publishers Weekly.

Lippman, Laura, 1959-

* **After** I'm gone / Laura Lippman. William Morrow, 2014. 334 p.

ISBN 9780062083395

1. Missing men 2. Coping 3. Family relationships 4. Cold cases (Criminal investigation) 5. Women murder victims 6. Married women 7. Mistresses 8. Criminals 9. Secrets 10. Baltimore, Maryland 11. Psychological suspense

LC 2013018550

Anthony Award for Best Novel, 2015.

Working a twenty-six-year-old cold case involving the murder of a convicted felon's mistress, retired Baltimore detective Roberto Sanchez discovers a web of bitterness, jealousy, and greed involving five women which spans five decades.

"Lippman incisively explores marriage, Jewish family life, class distinctions, and the power and liability of physical beauty, thus creating an involving and elegant novel of the psychological ravages of crime." Booklist.

Lippman, Laura, 1959-

* **And** when she was good / Laura Lippman. William Morrow, 2012. 384 p.

ISBN 9780061706875

1. Madams (Prostitution) 2. Crimes against prostitutes 3. Death threats 4. Murderers 5. Former lovers 6. Betrayal 7. Thrillers and suspense

Suburban madam Heloise, with no one left to trust, decides to get out of the game when another suburban madam is brutally murdered, forcing her to stay one step ahead of a killer--and the father of her child--who is just as lethal behind bars as he was on the outside.

Lippman, Laura, 1959-

Hardly knew her : stories / Laura Lippman ; with an introduction by George Pelecanos. William Morrow & Co, 2008. ix, 292 p.

ISBN 9780061584992

1. Murder 2. Women detectives 3. Women murder suspects 4. Crime 5. Women 6. Noir fiction 7. Short stories

Collection of 17 short stories and the novella Scratch a woman.

"Lippman clearly agrees with Kipling that the female of the species is deadlier than the male. Women's victims here include a female friend, boyfriends (both current and ex), a husband, and one-night stands and strangers; their murders are all the more chilling. The novella Scratch A Woman, featuring a single suburban Maryland soccer mom who works as a prostitute, and one of several stories featuring Tess [Monaghan] are the only entries not published previously. But those that have been published are scattered in a variety of anthologies over the last seven years, including Baltimore Noir. Here are nearly all of the short stories Lippman has ever written in one volume; read them fast, like a glutton, or slowly to savor each one. Either way, this is a treasure." Library Journal.

Lippman, Laura, 1959-

* **Hush** hush / Laura Lippman. HarperCollins, 2015. 384 p. Tess Monaghan mysteries

ISBN 9780062083425

1. Infanticide 2. Child-separated mothers 3. Parent and child 4. Mental illness 5. Child custody 6. Murder investigation 7. Women private investigators 8. Men/women relations 9. Baltimore, Maryland 10. Mysteries

Hush blends mystery with an unflinching look at new parenthood. Beautiful, upper-crust Melisandre Dawes purposefully left her baby in a hot car ten years ago; scandalously found not guilty of murder by reason of insanity, she fled the country. Now D back in Baltimore, Dawes has hired a down-and-out documentary filmmaker to tell her story and hopes to mend matters with her 15- and 17-year-old daughters. PI Tess Monaghan, worn out from caring for her strong-willed three-year-old daughter, must discover who's sending Dawes threatening notes and track down a killer in this excellent series installment. -- Description by Dawn Towery.

"With an intriguing cast of characters, stinging dialogue, hilarious moments, and a superbly convoluted and suspenseful plot, Lippman has created an incisive and provocative tale about parents good and evil." Booklist.

Lippman, Laura, 1959-

I'd know you anywhere / Laura Lippman. William Morrow, 2010. 384 p.

ISBN 9780061706554

1. Serial rapists 2. Death row 3. Women crime victims 4. Capital punishment 5. Fear in women 6. Guilt in women 7. Memories 8. Virginia 9. Psychological suspense

Eliza Benedict's peaceful suburban life is shattered after she is contacted by Walter Bowman, the man who kidnapped and held her hostage as a teen in 1985, and who now claims to want forgiveness while on death row.

"I'd Know You Anywhere is a crime story, but it's not a whodunit. Rather, it's an exquisitely sensitive story about the psychological impact of crime on its victims. It's a story about shame, about anger, about survivor's guilt." Ft. Worth Star-Telegram

Lippman, Laura, 1959-

* Lady in the lake : a novel / Laura Lippman. William Morrow, 2019. 384 p.

ISBN 9780062390011

1. 1960s 2. Journalists 3. Race relations 4. Murder investigation 5. Ghosts 6. Racism 7. Sexism 8. Jewish women 9. Drowning victims 10. Ambition in women 11. Women amateur detectives 12. Crimes against African Americans 13. Baltimore, Maryland -- Race relations -- 20th century 14. Historical thrillers

LC 2018058807

A divorced reporter in racially torn 1966 Baltimore triggers unanticipated consequences for vulnerable community members while investigating the murder of an African-American party girl.

Lippman, Laura, 1959-

The **most** dangerous thing / Laura Lippman. William Morrow & Co., 2011 384 p.

ISBN 9780061706516

1. Best friends 2. Secrets 3. Deception 4. Guilt 5. Children -- Interpersonal relations 6. Fatal traffic accidents 7. Childhood friends 8. Psychological suspense 9. Thrillers and suspense

Once the best of friends until a terrible secret tore them apart, a group of friends are suddenly brought back together under tragic circumstances and wonder if their long-ago lie is the reason for their troubles today and if someone is out to destroy them.

"No one explores the delicate interplay between children and the adults they grow into better than Lippman." Kirkus.

Lippman, Laura, 1959-

No good deeds / Laura Lippman. William Morrow, 2006. 352 p. Tess Monaghan mysteries

ISBN 0060570725

1. Homeless teenagers 2. Murder investigation 3. Witnesses 4. Detectives 5. Women private investigators 6. Public prosecutors 7. Murder 8. Men/women relations 9. Government attorneys 10. Fifteen-year-old boys 11. FBI agents 12. Baltimore, Maryland 13. Mysteries

LC 2005058358

Anthony Award for Best Novel, 2007.

For Tess Monaghan, the unsolved murder of a young federal prosecutor is nothing more than a theoretical problem, one of several cases to be deconstructed in her new gig as a consultant to the local newspaper. But then her boyfriend brings home a street kid who doesn't even realize he holds an important key to the man's death. Tess agrees to protect the boy's identity no matter what, especially when one of his friends is killed in an apparent case of mistaken identity. But with federal agents determined to learn the boy's name at any cost, Tess finds out just how far even official authorities will go to get what they want. Soon she's facing felony charges--and her boyfriend has gone into hiding with his protégé, so Tess can't deliver the kid to investigators even if she wants to.--From publisher description.

"Lippman has pulled off the near-impossible: writing a conventional procedural that still feels fresh. It's impossible not to like the complex, all-too-real Monaghan, a strong, wry detective prone to derailing my own gravy train." Washington Post Book World.

Lippman, Laura, 1959-

* Sunburn / Laura Lippman. William Morrow & Co, 2018. 292 p.

ISBN 9780062389923

1. 1990s 2. Strangers 3. Lovers 4. Femmes fatales 5. Wanderers and wandering 6. Married women 7. Secrets 8. Murder 9. Revenge 10. Redheads 11. Summer 12. Sexual attraction 13. Men/women relations 14. Delaware 15. Noir fiction

Librarians' Choice (Australia), 2018.

A pair of travelers, one of whom may be playing a dangerous psychological game with the other, embark on a steamy summertime affair that is thrown into chaos by dark secrets and a suspicious death, in a story inspired by the classics of James M. Cain.

Lippman, Laura, 1959-

What the dead know / Laura Lippman. William Morrow, 2007. 376 p.

ISBN 9780061128851

1. Police -- Baltimore, Maryland 2. Cold cases (Criminal investigation) 3. Kidnapping 4. Detectives -- Baltimore, Maryland 5. Girl kidnapping victims 6. Gravestones, mausoleums, etc 7. Missing persons 8. Secrets 9. Murder investigation 10. Murder 11. Baltimore, Maryland 12. Maryland 13. Mysteries

LC 2006052495

Anthony Award for Best Novel, 2008.
Macavity Award for Best Mystery Novel, 2008.

Interviewing a distressed and disoriented woman who has fled the scene of an accident, Baltimore County police department detective Kevin Infante is amazed when she claims to be the younger of a pair of sisters who were abducted thirty years earlier, a statement that she seems completely unable to prove.

"As artful as she is at interweaving disarming scenes of two spirited girls on the day they vanished with painful moments in the lives of their parents--maintaining all the while a thread of continuity in the current-day police investigation--Lippman pulls off something more ambitious than a high-wire act of technical virtuosity. With great thought and compassion, she uses her fractured narrative style to delve into the ways in which every serious crime tears to shreds the lives of its victims." New York Times Book Review.

Lippman, Laura, 1959-

Wilde Lake / Laura Lippman. William Morrow & Co., 2016. 352 p.

ISBN 9780062083456

1. Trials (Murder) 2. District attorneys 3. Cold cases (Criminal investigation) 4. Women district attorneys 5. Brothers and sisters 6. Assault and battery 7. Investigations 8. Memories 9. Childhood 10. Drifters 11. Maryland 12. Psychological suspense

Luisa "Lu" Brant is the newly elected-- and first female-- state's attorney of Howard County, Maryland, a job in which her widower father famously served. Fiercely intelligent and ambitious, she sees an opportunity to make her name by trying a mentally disturbed drifter accused of beating a woman to death in her home. It's not the kind of case that makes headlines, but peaceful Howard County doesn't see many homicides. As Lu prepares for the trial, the case dredges up painful memories, reminding her small, but tight-knit, family of the night when her brother, AJ, saved his best friend at the cost of another man's life. Only eighteen, AJ was cleared by a grand jury. Now, Lu wonders if the events of 1980 happened as she remembers them. What details might have been withheld from her when she was a child?

"As shocking secrets are revealed, the reader realizes that nothing and no one can be taken at face value in Lippman's brainy, witty, socially conscious, and all-consuming inquiry into human nature and our slowly evolving sense of justice and equality." Booklist.

Lipsyte, Sam, 1968-

* The **ask** / Sam Lipsyte. Farrar, Straus and Giroux, 2010. 304 p.

ISBN 9780374298913

1. Marriage 2. Failure (Psychology) 3. Family relationships 4. Artists 5. Classism 6. Expectation (Psychology) 7. Universities and colleges -- Administration 8. Benefactors 9. Arts fund raising 10. Satirical fiction

LC 2009029508

After he loses his job as a development officer at a university, family man Milo Burke is given a chance to regain his position, but only if he can reel in a potential donor, one who has requested his involvement and turns out to be his sinister college classmate.

"The Ask's narrative heft comes from the reappearance of a wealthy friend from Milo's college days and the tragicomic scenarios that follow the plight of socialist daycare workers and legless Iraq-war vets among them. But the gift is Sam Lipsyte's writing: a chewy, corrosive, and syntactically dazzling prose style that doesn't so much run across the page as pick it up and throttle it. You may want to throttle Milo yourself frequently, but you won't stop reading." Entertainment Weekly.

Lispector, Clarice

The **besieged** city / Clarice Lispector ; translated from the Portuguese by Johnny Lorenz ; edited by Benjamin Moser. New Directions, 2019, c1949. 208 p.

ISBN 9780811226714

1. Change 2. Growing up 3. Observing things 4. Young women 5. Married women 6. Interpersonal relations 7. Small town life 8. Economic development 9. Men/women relations 10. Families 11. Gender role 12. Sick persons 13. Literary fiction 14. Translations -- Portuguese to English

LC 2018046582

Originally published: Rio de Janeiro : Janeiro, A Noite, 1949.

Unlike any of her other novels, this story from a noted Brazilian writer is about simply seeing the eternal world as it follows a heroine free of the burden of thought as she marries a rich man, travels the globe and lives happily ever after.

Liss, David, 1966-

A **spectacle** of corruption / David Liss. Random House, 2004. 384 p. Benjamin Weaver novels

ISBN 0375508554

1. Georgian era (1714-1837) 2. 18th century 3. Conspiracies 4. False imprisonment 5. Jewish men 6. Amateur detectives 7. Former boxers 8. Jews, English 9. Fugitives 10. Judicial error 11. Escapes 12. Frameups 13. Political science 14. Elections 15. Social classes 16. Secret identity 17. London, England -- History -- 18th century 18. London, England -- Social life and customs -- 18th century 19. Historical mysteries 20. Mysteries

LC 2003054806

Realizing at the moment of his conviction for a crime he did not commit that someone is determined to see him dead and another to set him free, Benjamin Weaver works to expose a conspiracy with links to the coming election.

"Weaver turns out to be the hard-outside, soft-inside private investigator of the noir thrillers inserted into 1720s London: Philip Marlowe done up in a wig and buckles." Washington Post Book World.

Littell, Robert, 1935-

The **company** : a novel of the CIA / Robert Littell. Overlook Press, 2002. 894 p.

ISBN 9781585671977

1. CIA 2. International relations 3. Intelligence officers 4. Cold War 5. International intrigue 6. CIA agents 7. Spy fiction

LC 2001051383

A novel of Cold War espionage traces the struggles of two generations of CIA operatives fighting Communism and battling one another in the complex world of international intrigue.

"There is plenty here to amuse anyone with even a network news interest in current events--and a gold mine for true conspiracy theorists." New York Times Book Review.

Littell, Robert, 1935-

The **Mayakovsky** tapes : a novel / Robert Littell. Thomas Dunne Books, 2016. 243 p.

ISBN 9781250100566

1. Mayakovsky, Vladimir, 1893-1930 2. Creativity in men 3. Poets 4. Memories 5. Former lovers 6. Suicide victims 7. Revolutionaries 8. Idealism 9. Futurism (Literary movement) -- Soviet Union 10. Censorship 11. Consequences 12. Conversation 13. Sexuality 14. Men/women relations 15. Soviet Union -- Politics and government 16. Historical fiction 17. Biographical fiction

LC 2016010551

A tale inspired by the life of 20th-century Russian poet Vladimir Mayakovsky is told from the perspectives of four women who loved him and share with each other memories of pivotal moments in his life, from his early years as a Futurist leader, to his work as a Revolution propagandist, to the censorship battles that turned him against the State.

"...Littell uses four sophisticated women who had relationships with the poet to illuminate his life and character. ... Separately and together they paint a vivid picture of a gifted poet, a tireless womanizer, and a man beset by wild mood swings. The ladies' narration is both raunchy and often hilarious. It also illuminates a tumultuous period of Russian history." Booklist.

Littell, Robert, 1935-

The **Stalin** epigram / Robert Littell. Simon & Schuster, 2009. 384 p.

ISBN 9781416598640

1. Mandelshtam, Osip Emilievich, 1891-1938 2. 1930s 3. Poets 4. Censorship 5. Political corruption 6. Exiles 7. Soviet Union 8. Historical fiction

LC 2008052277

A tale inspired by the life of twentieth-century Russian poet Osip Mandelstam recounts his criticism of the Stalin regime, the verbal distribution of his famous "Stalin Epigram" that led to his arrest, and his exile and death in a Siberian transit camp.

"This is a timeless story of courage and truth confronting the madness of absolute power. It's a brilliant work, always readable, sometimes funny and often heartbreaking. There are many books about Stalin's terror, but there cannot be many that bring its truths more vividly, painfully to life." Washington Post Book World.

Littell, Robert, 1935-

Vicious circle : a novel of complicity / Robert Littell. Overlook Hardcover, 2006. 304 p.

ISBN 1585678554

1. Women presidents 2. Palestinian men 3. Palestinians 4. Muslims 5. Jews 6. Israelis 7. Terrorists 8. Rabbis 9. Hostages 10. Israeli-Palestinian relations 11. Interfaith relations 12. Interpersonal relations 13. Terrorism 14. Peace 15. Fundamentalism 16. Hostage

taking 17. Hostage negotiations 18. Revenge 19. Friendship 20. Fundamentalists 21. Middle East 22. Political thrillers 23. Thrillers and suspense

The global community, led by a visionary U.S. president, brokers a major compromise between Israel and the Palestinian authority in order to snuff out the violent flashpoint of global terrorism. It seems to work until a well known fundamentalist rabbi is taken hostage by a legendary Palestinian terrorist.

"This novel takes place in the volatile Holy Land of the near future. When the Arab leader of a terrorist faction kidnaps a rabbi who heads an ultraconservative settlers' group, Israeli security services go on red alert. In adding a smart-alecky American reporter to the mix, Littell . . . ratchets up the action to a heart-bursting sprint that stops only for big gulps of violence and torture. What makes this book unforgettable is the extraordinary relationship between kidnapper and victim. Extremists both, they joust with vehement hatred yet are strangely drawn together. Littell's acute portrayal of their inflamed psychological states illuminates an understanding that goes far beyond the day's headlines." Library Journal.

Little, Terra

Where there's smoke / Terra Little. Q-Boro Books, 2009. 288 p. Where there's smoke novels

ISBN 9781933967783

1. Drug dealers 2. Cocaine addicts 3. Fathers and sons 4. Single mothers 5. Drug addicts 6. Men/women relations 7. African Americans -- Drug use 8. City life 9. Inner city 10. Street life 11. Urban fiction 12. African American fiction

Sequel: Where there's smoke 2.

Trying to put his past as a drug dealer behind him, Alec, formerly known as Smoke, runs into one of his old clients, who, now a successful businesswoman, claims that he is the father of her troubled teenaged son who is heading down the wrong path.

Littlejohn, Emily

Inherit the bones / Emily Littlejohn. Minotaur, 2016. 336 p. Detective Gemma Monroe novels

ISBN 9781250089397

1. Small towns 2. Women detectives 3. Pregnant women 4. Secret identity 5. Circus 6. Clowns 7. Family secrets 8. Mayors 9. Politicians 10. Murder investigation 11. Detectives 12. Colorado 13. Mysteries

While investigating a traveling circus, detective Gemma Monroe discovers that a murdered clown is actually the mayor's missing son and must trace back a chain of events that began nearly 40 years ago.

Littlejohn, Emily

Lost Lake : a detective Gemma Monroe mystery / Emily Littlejohn. Minotaur Books, 2018. 304 p. Detective Gemma Monroe novels

ISBN 9781250178305

1. Women detectives 2. Missing women 3. Lakes 4. Friendship 5. Museum curators 6. Missing persons investigation 7. Murder 8. Secrets 9. Small towns 10. Colorado 11. Mysteries

LC 2018025709

Detective Gemma Monroe must figure out who is lying to her after three friends make a missing person's report about the fourth member of their camping party.

"The mysteries involved, one of which hints at the supernatural, are satisfying and wrapped up in a way that readers won't see coming." Booklist.

Liu, Cixin

Ball lightning / Cixin Liu ; translated by Joel Martinsen. Tor, 2018. 352 p.

ISBN 9780765394071

1. Scientific discoveries 2. Parents -- Death 3. Weapons 4. Physicists 5. Soldiers 6. Ethics 7. Secrecy 8. Life change events 9. China 10. Science fiction 11. Translations -- Chinese to English

After witnessing his parents' bizarre death by ball lightning, Chin uncovers a new frontier in particle physics that pits him against a weapons-obsessed army major and an unscrupulous physicist.

Liu, Cixin

* **Death's** end / Cixin Liu ; translated from the Chinese by Ken Liu. Tor, 2016, 604 p. Remembrance of Earth's past

ISBN 9780765377104

1. Aliens 2. Scientists 3. Human nature 4. Life on other planets 5. Space flight 6. Peace 7. China 8. Hard science fiction 9. Science fiction 10. Translations -- Chinese to English

First published in Chinese in 2010 by Chongqing Publishing Group. Locus Award for Best Science Fiction Novel, 2017.

Half a century after the Doomsday Battle, twenty-first-century aerospace engineer Cheng Xin awakens from hibernation, bringing with her knowledge of a long-forgotten program that threatens the peaceful coexistence of humans and Trisolarans.

"The time scale is an obstacle to emotional engagement, but there are emotionally moving moments that ground the intriguing speculations about science and human nature." Publishers Weekly.

Liu, Cixin

* The **dark** forest / Cixin Liu ; translated from the Chinese by Joel Martinsen. Tor Books, 2015 480 p. Remembrance of Earth's past

ISBN 9780765377081

1. Aliens 2. Human nature 3. Research 4. Physicists 5. Life on other planets 6. Scientists 7. China 8. Hard science fiction 9. Science fiction 10. Translations -- Chinese to English

A continuation of a near-future trilogy follows humanity's desperate plan to outmaneuver alien invaders by placing all defensive strategies in the hands of four men, including an anonymous astrologer who is baffled by his new status.

"The book's large cast of characters form a latticework of precisely placed focal points around which the story weaves and connects to wonderful moments of revelation." Booklist.

Liu, Cixin

* The **three-body** problem / Cixin Liu ; translated by Ken Liu. Tor Books, 2014, c2007. 336 p. Remembrance of Earth's past

ISBN 9780765377067

1. Chinese Cultural Revolution (1966-1976) 2. Aliens 3. Revolutions -- China 4. Physics 5. Loss (Psychology) 6. Human nature 7. Research 8. Physicists 9. Life on other planets 10. Scientists 11. China 12. Hard science fiction 13. Science fiction 14. Translations -- Chinese to English

Originally published: 2007.

Hugo Award for Best Novel, 2015.

Set against the backdrop of China's Cultural Revolution, a secret military project's signal is received by an alien civilization on the brink of destruction, which plans to invade Earth; meanwhile, on Earth, different camps start forming, planning to either welcome the superior beings and help them take over a world seen as corrupt, or to fight against the invasion.

"The narrative will grab readers' attention with its passionate and fascinating critique of early Communist China, augmented by translator Liu's lean but informative footnotes for the likely uninformed English readers. But the high-minded premise is really just a vessel for a collection of surreal and hauntingly beautiful scenes that will hook you deep and drag you relentlessly across every page." Booklist.

Liu, Ken, 1976-

The **grace** of kings / Ken Liu. Saga Press, 2015 800 p. ; Dandelion dynasty

ISBN 9781481424271

1. Rebels 2. Insurgency 3. Friendship 4. Imaginary wars and battles 5. Gods and goddesses 6. Interpersonal conflict 7. Imaginary empires 8. Attitude change 9. Class conflict 10. Coups d'etat 11. Ideology 12. Epic fantasy 13. Asian-influenced fantasy

LC 2014019957

Locus Award for First Novel, 2016.

Warrior Mata Zyndu, scion of his once-powerful Clan, believes that it is his destiny to rule. His best friend, wily bandit Kuni Garu, just wants to get rich and have a grand time doing so. Although they bond during the rebellion against the empire, their different goals and philosophies will ultimately make them bitter adversaries. Author Ken Liu has won Hugo, Nebula, Locus, and World Fantasy awards for his short fiction and his translations (most notably of Cixin Liu's The Three-Body Problem). This 1st book in the Dandelion Dynasty series, which vividly evokes the politics and culture of China's Han dynasty, marks his novel-writing debut. -- Description by Gillian Speace.

Liu, Ken, 1976-

Invisible planets : contemporary Chinese science fiction in translation / Ken Liu. Tor, 2016. 383 p.

ISBN 9780765384195

1. Social problems 2. Dystopias 3. Technology -- Social aspects 4. Totalitarianism 5. Science fiction 6. Science fiction 7. Social science fiction 8. Translations -- Chinese to English 9. Anthologies 10. Essays

"A phenomenal anthology of short speculative fiction." Kirkus.

Liu, Ken, 1976-

The **wall** of storms / Ken Liu. Simon & Schuster, 2016. 600 p. Dandelion dynasty

ISBN 9781481424301

1. Rulers 2. Imaginary empires 3. Imaginary wars and battles 4. Aggression (International relations) 5. Adult children of politicians 6. International relations 7. Political leadership 8. Military strategy 9. Armies 10. Epic fantasy 11. Asian-influenced fantasy

A sequel to Grace of Kings finds newly declared Emperor Kuni Garu struggling to meet the demands of his people and vision before an unexpected invading force compels him to dispatch his grown children to defend the shores of Dara.

"This tale of divided loyalties, deadly ambition, and 'silkpunk' technology delivers enough excitement and sense of wonder to enchant any fan of epic fantasy." Publishers Weekly.

Lively, Penelope, 1933-

How it all began : a novel / Penelope Lively. Viking, 2012, c2011. 229 p.

ISBN 9780670023448

1. Mugging 2. Family relationships 3. Interpersonal relations 4. Retired teachers 5. Mugging victims 6. Senior women 7. Secrets 8. Extramarital affairs 9. Uncle and niece 10. Mothers and daughters 11. London, England 12. Mainstream fiction

"First published in Great Britain by Fig Tree, an imprint of Penguin Books Ltd 2011." -- Title page verso.

The mugging of a retired schoolteacher on a London street has unexpected repercussions for her friends and neighbors when it inadvertently reveals an illicit love affair, leads to a business partnership, and helps an immigrant to reinvent his life.

Lively, Penelope, 1933-

* **Moon** tiger / Penelope Lively. Grove Press, 1987. 208 p.

ISBN 9780802110275

1. Women historians 2. Senior women authors 3. Women with terminal illnesses 4. Psychological fiction 5. Literary fiction

LC 87023798

Originally published: London : Deutsch, 1987.

Booker Prize, 1987.

Claudia Hampton, writer of best-selling popular history books, lies in a London hospital bed and looks back on her own life, including an unforgettable love affair.

Livesey, Margot

Criminals : a novel / Margot Livesey. Knopf, 1996, c1995. 271 p.

ISBN 0679444874

1. Abandoned children 2. Women with mental illnesses 3. Bankers 4. Voyages and travels 5. Brothers and sisters 6. Family relationships 7. Secrets 8. Birthfathers 9. London, England 10. Scotland 11. Great Britain 12. Novels-within-novels 13. Psychological suspense

LC 9531512

The discovery of a baby girl abandoned in a bus station restroom becomes the catalyst for linking five distinct lives in a web of responsibility, affection, and filial, maternal, and romantic love

"The reader becomes enmeshed in the complex windings of Ms. Livesey's plot, a web of criminal circumstance and moral consequence that conveys the awful randomness of life even as it offers the abiding pleasures of artfully constructed fiction." New York Times Book Review.

Livesey, Margot

The **missing** world : a novel / Margot Livesey. Knopf, 2000. 325 p.

ISBN 037540581X

1. People with amnesia 2. Accident victims 3. African American men 4. Couples 5. Men with depression 6. Amnesia 7. Convalescence 8. Memory 9. Memories 10. Secrets 11. Men/women relations 12. Control (Psychology) 13. Dominance (Psychology) 14. Deception in men 15. London, England 16. Thrillers and suspense

LC 99035785

Troubled by his betrayal of the woman he professes to love, Jonathan takes advantage of an unexpected opportunity to rewrite his relationship with Hazel, a woman robbed by an accident of her memories of the last three years, while two other misfits, also tormented by troubling memories, are drawn into his orbit.

"Adroitly paced, meticulously plotted and increasingly suspenseful, the novel transcends its genre as psychological thriller." Publishers Weekly.

The **living** dead / edited by John Joseph Adams. Night Shade Books, 2008. 487 p.

ISBN 9781597801430

1. Zombies 2. Dead 3. Fear 4. Horror 5. Short stories 6. Anthologies

"These stories range from the truly disgusting (Poppy Z. Brite's Calcutta: Lord of Nerves) to the nearly wistful (Followed by Will McIntosh) and even one with no supernatural elements at all (Joe Hill's Bobby Conroy Comes Back from the Dead). Included are pieces by big names in horror like Stephen King and Clive Barker but also contributions by less obvious suspects like Harlan Ellison, Sherman Alexie, and George R.R. Martin. The final treat is John Langan's How the Day Runs Down, a nasty little play best described as Our Town with zombies. Highly recommended for all horror fiction collections." Library Journal.

Llewellyn, Richard

* How green was my valley / Richard Llewellyn. Scribner, 1997, c1939. 495 p.

ISBN 9780684825557

1. 1880s 2. 1890s 3. Coal miners' families 4. Families -- Wales 5. Boys 6. Young men 7. Coal miners -- Wales 8. Family relationships 9. Wales -- Social life and customs 10. Great Britain -- Social conditions -- Victoria, 1837-1901 11. Coming-of-age stories 12. Family sagas 13. Historical fiction

Sequel: Up into the singing mountain.

Originally published: London : M. Joseph, 1939.

The youngest son of a Welsh coal-mining family recalls the tender and tragic experiences of his youth at the turn of the century with his courageous and loving parents and brothers and sisters.

"A remarkably beautiful novel of Wales. And although it follows stirringly in the romantic traditions, there is the resonance of a profound and noble realism in its evocation, its intensity and reach of truth." New York Times Book Review.

Lloyd, Catherine, 1963-

Death comes to the nursery / Catherine Lloyd. Kensington Books, 2020. 304 p. Kurland St. Mary mysteries

ISBN 9781496723222

1. Regency period (1811-1820) 2. Pregnant women 3. Husband and wife 4. Amateur detectives 5. Household employees 6. Deception 7. Murder 8. Murder investigation 9. Actors and actresses 10. Great Britain -- History -- Regency, 1811-1820 11. Historical mysteries

When their new nursery maid from London is found dead, Lady Lucy, who is expecting another child, and Major Sir Robert Kurland suspect foul play and set out to find the truth, which leads them to the London theater world?and into great danger.

"A charming Regency mystery/romance with plenty of local color and unexpected twists and turns." Kirkus.

Llywelyn, Morgan

1916 / Morgan Llywelyn. Forge, 1998. 447 p. Irish independence series

ISBN 031286101X

1. Pearse, Padraic Henry, 1879-1916 2. Irish Republican Brotherhood 3. Easter Rising, 1916 4. Revolutionaries -- Dublin, Ireland 5. Brothers and sisters 6. Irish resistance and revolts 7. Irish American women 8. Students -- Dublin, Ireland 9. Ireland -- History -- Easter Rising, 1916 10. Dublin, Ireland -- History -- 20th century 11. New York City -- History -- 1898-1951 12. Historical fiction

LC 97-29838

A fictional portrait of Ireland's Easter Rising of 1916 follows the events and personalities of the rebellion as chronicled by some of its passionate participants, including poet-rebels Patrick Pearse, Thomas MacDonagh, and Joseph Plunkett.

"Battle scenes are both accurate and compelling. The betrayals, slaughters and passions of the day are all splendidly depicted as Llywelyn delivers a blow-by-blow account of the rebellion and its immediate aftermath. The novel's abundant footnotes should satisfy history buffs; its easy, gripping style will enthrall casual readers." Publishers Weekly.

Llywelyn, Morgan

1921 / Morgan Llywelyn. Forge, 2001. 445 p. Irish independence series

ISBN 0312867549

1. Pearse, Padraic Henry, 1879-1916 2. Collins, Michael, 1890-1922 3. 1920s 4. Irish Civil War, 1922-1923 5. Journalists -- Ireland 6. Civil war 7. British in Ireland -- History -- 20th century 8. Ireland -- History -- 1910-1921 9. Ireland -- History -- Civil War, 1922-1923 10. Ireland -- Politics and government -- 20th century 11. Historical fiction

LC 00049021

Jacket subtitle: A book of the Irish century.

A novel of the Irish Civil War follows the division of a nation and the passion it inspired in an Irish journalist and the Englishwoman he loves.

"The lucid narrative and the compelling subject matter will enthrall both Irish history buffs and fans of sweeping historical fiction." Booklist.

Llywelyn, Morgan

1949 : a novel of the Irish Free State / , Morgan Llywelyn. Forge, 2003. 414 p. Irish independence series

ISBN 0312867530

1. 1940s 2. Revolutionaries -- Ireland 3. Rebels -- Ireland -- History -- 20th century 4. Women revolutionaries -- Ireland 5. British in Ireland -- History -- 20th century 6. Anglo-Irish relations -- History -- 20th century 7. Catholics -- Ireland 8. Single mothers -- Ireland 9. Women radio broadcasters -- Ireland 10. Pilots -- Great Britain 11. Civil service workers -- Ireland 12. Men/women relations 13. Politicians -- Ireland 14. Ireland -- History -- 1922-1949 15. Ireland -- History -- Civil War, 1922-1923 16. Ireland -- Politics and government -- 20th century 17. Historical fiction 18. Domestic fiction 19. Coming-of-age stories

LC 2002032525

"A Tom Doherty Associates Book."

Continuing the chronicle of the Irish fight for independence, idealistic Ursula rebels against the repressive Catholic state when she bears a child out of wedlock and runs her family farm in a neutral part of the country.

Llywelyn, Morgan

After Rome : a novel of Celtic Britain / Morgan Llywelyn. Forge, 2013. 336 p.

ISBN 9780765331236

1. 5th century 2. Cousins 3. Political intrigue 4. Ambition 5. Power (Social sciences) 6. Men/women relations 7. Great Britain -- History -- 5th century 8. Historical fiction

LC 2012027562

Remaining on the virtually abandoned island of Britannia after centuries of Roman rule, two cousins pursue very different efforts to unite disparate tribes and factions throughout the land, including throne-seeking Dinas and reluctant leader Cadogan.

Locascio, Lisa

Open me : a novel / Lisa Locascio. Grove Press, 2018. 288 p.

ISBN 9780802128072

1. Teenage girls -- Sexuality 2. Studying abroad 3. Change (Psychology) 4. Self-discovery 5. Political science 6. Lovers 7. Desire 8. Rural life 9. Refugees 10. Women -- Body 11. Americans in Europe 12. Sexual attraction 13. Men/women relations 14. Denmark 15. Coming-of-age stories 16. Literary fiction

LC 2017044112

Redirected to Copenhagen by a logistical mix-up, a college student studying abroad falls for her guide and embarks on an erotically charged transformative journey of self-discovery that is overshadowed by her lover's dark temperament.

Lock, Norman, 1950-

American meteor / Norman Lock. Bellevue Literary Press, 2015. 208 p. American novels (Norman Lock)

ISBN 9781934137949

1. American Westward Expansion (1803-1899) 2. 1870s 3. 1860s 4. Wanderers and wandering 5. Transcontinental railroad (United States) 6. Assassins 7. Orphans 8. Soldiers 9. Teenage boys 10. Buglers 11. Photographs 12. Little Big Horn, Battle of the, 1876 13. The West (United States) 14. Historical fiction 15. Literary fiction

A scrappy Brooklyn orphan-turned-assassin comes of age, befriends Walt Whitman, apprentices under William Henry Jackson and stalks General George Custer as railroad construction advances the nation's Manifest Destiny goals.

Lock, Norman, 1950-

A **fugitive** in Walden Woods / Norman Lock. Bellevue Literary Press, 2017. 238 p. American novels (Norman Lock)

ISBN 9781942658221

1. Thoreau, Henry David, 1817-1862 2. Emerson, Ralph Waldo, 1803-1882 3. Hawthorne, Nathaniel, 1804-1864 4. 19th century 5. Fugitive slaves 6. Inequality 7. Interclass friendship 8. Freedom 9. Slavery 10. Underground Railroad 11. Transcendentalists (New England) 12. Racism 13. Social classes 14. Idealism 15. Walden Woods, Massachusetts 16. Massachusetts 17. Historical fiction 18. Biographical fiction

After escaping slavery in Virginia, Samuel Long travels the Underground Railroad to Walden Pond where he meets Henry David Thoreau, Ralph Waldo Emerson, Nathaniel Hawthorne and a host of other transcendentalists and abolitionists and experiences his coming-of-age while his hosts receive a lesson in human dignity.

Locke, Attica

Bluebird, bluebird / Attica Locke. Mulholland Books, 2017. 336 p. Highway 59

ISBN 9780316363297

1. Texas Rangers. 2. African American men 3. Detectives 4. Race relations 5. Murder investigation 6. Small towns 7. Identity (Psychology) 8. Hate crimes 9. Racism 10. Texas 11. Mysteries 12. African American fiction

Anthony Award for Best Novel, 2018.

Edgar Allan Poe Award for Best Novel, 2018.

Ian Fleming Steel Dagger Award, 2018.

In a rural East Texas town of fewer than 200 people, the body of an African American lawyer from Chicago is found in a bayou, followed several days later by that of a local white woman. What's going on? African American Texas Ranger Darren Mathews hopes to find out, which means talking to relatives of the deceased, including the woman's white supremacist husband -- and Mathews soon discovers things are more complex than they seem. With fully realized characters and a timely look at race relations in the U.S., this book by award-winning novelist Attica Locke (who's also written and produced for TV's Empire) is the 1st in her Highway 59 series. -- Description by Dawn Towery

"Locke . . . deserves a career breakthrough for this deftly plotted whodunit whose writing pulses throughout with a raw, blues-inflected lyricism." Kirkus.

Locke, Attica

The **cutting** season / Attica Locke. Harper, 2012. 384 p.

ISBN 9780061802058

1. Migrant workers 2. Families -- History 3. Plantations -- Louisiana 4. Farms 5. Murder 6. Secrets 7. Slavery 8. Civil war 9. Plantation life 10. Family secrets 11. Murder investigation 12. Louisiana 13. Southern States 14. Mysteries

When the dead body of a young woman is found on the grounds of Belle Vie, the estate's manager, Caren Gray, launches her own investigation into Belle Vie's history, which leads her to a centuries old mystery involving the plantation's slave quarters--and her own past.

Locke, Attica

* Heaven, my home / Attica Locke. Mulholland Books, 2019. 304 p. Highway 59

ISBN 9780316363402

1. Texas Rangers. 2. African American men 3. Detectives 4. Missing boys 5. Missing persons investigation 6. Race relations 7. Small towns 8. White supremacists 9. Racism 10. Marital conflict 11. Secrets 12. Texas 13. Southern States -- Race relations 14. Mysteries 15. African American fiction

In this follow-up to <I>Bluebird, Bluebird</I>, Texas Ranger Darren Matthews must battle centuries-old suspicions and prejudices, as well as threats that have been reignited in the current political climate, to find a missing boy and save himself.

Locke, Thomas, 1952-

Emissary / Thomas Locke. Revell, 2015. 304 p. Legends of the realm

ISBN 9780800723859

1. Young men 2. Fate and fatalism 3. Quests 4. Magic 5. Outlaws 6. Linguists 7. Christian fantasy

LC 2014029802

With magic largely outlawed, and its legitimate practitioners tightly controlled, a young man begins to find that the astonishing powers he has discovered in himself may be the key to facing a growing menace from beyond the badlands.

"Locke (a pseudonym for Christy-winning inspirational thriller author Davis Bunn) launches the Legends of the Realm fantasy series with this competent story that owes more to the Lord of the Rings trilogy than the Bible . . . Even if fans of Bunns international thrillers dont follow him over to the fantasy realm, readers of inspirational fantasy will enjoy his foray into a new genre." Publishers Weekly.

Locke, Thomas, 1952-

Enclave / Thomas Locke. Revell, 2018 278 p.

ISBN 9780800735470

1. Traders 2. Faith 3. Quests 4. Dystopias 5. Superhuman abilities 6. Heroes and heroines 7. Political intrigue 8. Secrets 9. Gold mines and mining 10. Government cover-ups 11. Christian science fiction 12. Dystopian fiction

LC 2018020850

Fifty years after the collapse of the United States, Caleb attempts to institute a dangerous plan to secure his enclave's future. But if his secret is exposed, he won't live to see another dawn.

Lockridge, Ross Franklin, 1914-1948

Raintree County / Ross Lockridge Jr. Chicago Review Press, 2007, c1948. 1066 p.

ISBN 9781556527104

1. Rural life 2. Civil war 3. United States Civil War, 1861-1865 4. United States -- History -- Civil War, 1861-1865 5. Indiana 6.

Modern classics

LC 48000245
Originally published: Boston, Mass. : Houghton Mifflin, 1948.

Throughout a single day in 1892, John Shawnessy recalls the great moments of his life: from the love affairs of his youth in Indiana, to the battles of the Civil War, to the politics of the Gilded Age, to his homecoming as schoolteacher, husband, and father. Shawnessy is the epitome of the place and period in which he lives, a rural land of spring-like women, shady gamblers, wandering vagabonds, and soapbox orators. Yet here on the banks of the Shawmucky River, which weaves its primitive course through Raintree County, Indiana, he also feels and obeys ancient rhythms.

Lodato, Victor

Edgar and Lucy : a novel / Victor Lodato. St. Martin's Press, 2017. 533 p.

ISBN 9781250096982

1. Mothers and sons 2. Boy kidnapping victims 3. Survivors of suicide victims 4. Kidnappers 5. Grief in boys 6. Family and suicide 7. Life change events 8. Eight-year-old boys 9. Dysfunctional families 10. Kidnapping investigation 11. Parenting by grandparents 12. New Jersey 13. Literary fiction 14. Domestic fiction

A grieving little boy who had been cared for by his late grandmother during his mother's dysfunctional episodes becomes an at-risk youth in the New Jersey Pine Barrens home of an unsettlingly attentive adult who harbors dubious intentions.

"Lodato's remarkable novel traces a family's spiritual journey toward healing in moving, magical prose." Booklist.

Lodato, Victor

Mathilda Savitch / Victor Lodato. Farrar, Straus and Giroux, 2009. 304 p.

ISBN 9780374204006

1. Grief in families 2. Worry in girls 3. Alcoholic mothers 4. Loss (Psychology) 5. Compassion in teenagers 6. Teenage girls 7. Sisters -- Death 8. Family secrets 9. Dysfunctional families 10. Murder investigation 11. Thirteen-year-old girls 12. Psychological fiction 13. Literary fiction

LC 2009004719

Mathilda investigates her older sister's shattering death and learns perplexing truths when she accesses her sister's computer journals and reads about a secret underworld life.

"A novel about a preteen whose older sister has died, pushed off a train platform. Logging in to her sister's e-mail, Mathilda eventually adopts her sister's life, contacting her old boyfriends and trying to retrace the footsteps of her last days. . . . Trying to provoke her parents, Mathilda dresses up in her dead sister's birthday dress. Numb, in search of deeper numbness, her mother downs the vodka, and crawls on the kitchen floor, howling, in search of another bottle. Mathilda's original observations carry these incidents--blending imagination, intelligence and kookily beautiful imagery. . . . For the most part, this is a delight and a devil of a book, a tale that fills you with despair and pleasureoften at the same time." Time Out New York.

Lodge, David, 1935-

Paradise news : a novel / David Lodge. Viking, 1992, c1991. 293 p.

ISBN 0670842281

1. Families 2. Middle-aged men 3. Voyages and travels 4. British in Hawaii 5. Fathers and sons 6. Caretakers 7. Men/women relations 8. Hawaii 9. Humorous stories

LC 91032128
Originally published: London : Secker & Warburg, 1991.

"Mr. Lodge is a serious author who bravely uses coincidence and contrivance to tie up loose ends. And just under the surface of the spirited and often comic adventures of his travelers he runs an undercurrent of understanding about their longings for the perfection of paradise. This comes to us in graceful and disciplined prose that offers vivid glimpses of what lies beyond the tourist hotels of Wakiki: the natural and imperfect world." New York Times Book Review.

Loh, Vyvyane

Breaking the tongue , by Vyvyane Loh. W.W. Norton & Co., 2004. 448 p.

ISBN 0393057925

1. Second World War era (1939-1945) 2. Young men 3. Expatriates 4. Spies 5. Chinese in Singapore 6. Ethnic identity 7. Identity (Psychology) 8. Family relationships 9. Language and languages 10. Racism 11. Social classes 12. Extramarital affairs 13. Betrayal 14. Torture 15. World War II -- Singapore 16. Singapore -- History -- Japanese occupation, 1942-1945 17. Historical fiction 18. Domestic fiction 19. War stories 20. Coming-of-age stories

LC 2003015870

Shortlisted for the International IMPAC Dublin Literary Award, 2006

As the Japanese prepare to invade Singapore, an Anglophile Chinese family struggles to survive and preserve its dignity in the face of shifting loyalties of spies, expatriates, and nationalists.

"The author explores such concepts as loyalty to one's family and country, the place of language in culture, and the roles of race, racism and ethnicity in how we perceive ourselves and others. In doing so, she has skillfully touched on questions at the very heart of politics, culture and global relations today." Washington Post Book World.

Lohmann, Jennifer

Winning Ruby Heart / Jennifer Lohmann. Harlequin Books, 2014. 384 p.

ISBN 9780373608690

1. Women athletes 2. Journalists 3. Scandals 4. Olympic athletes 5. Olympic medal winners 6. Doping in sports 7. Running 8. People with paraplegia 9. Women runners 10. Redemption 11. Former college football players 12. Interpersonal attraction 13. Men/women relations 14. Sports romances 15. Contemporary romances 16. Category romances

Exposing world-class athlete Ruby Heart's cheating scandal five years ago made reporter Micah Blackwell's career. Falling in love with her now could end it. Yet watching her determination to return to the top, he can't resist the woman she has become.

"Librarian and author Lohmann, a Romance Writers of America Librarian of the Year, has written a remarkable story of a heroine who refuses to let her past mistakes define her future. Lohmanns realistically flawed characters and emotionally compelling plot will resonate with readers." Booklist.

Loigman, Lynda Cohen

The **two-family** house / Lynda Cohen Loigman. St. Martin's Press, 2016. viii, 290 p.

ISBN 9781250076922

1. 1940s 2. Girls -- Friendship 3. Apartment dwellers 4. Interpersonal conflict 5. Family relationships 6. Shared housing 7. Jewish families 8. City dwellers 9. Growing up 10. Friendship 11. Secrets 12. Brooklyn, New York City 13. New York City -- Social life and customs -- 20th century 14. Historical fiction 15. Domestic fiction

Two women, sisters by marriage who share a two-family brownstone in Brooklyn in the 1950s, form a strong bond when they each give birth minutes apart on the same night, but as the years pass, a deeply buried family secret causes their friendship to unravel.

"In her first novel, Loigman uses complex characters to deconstruct the anatomy of family relationships and expose deep-rooted emotions, delivering a moving story of love, loss, and sacrifice." Booklist.

Loigman, Lynda Cohen

The **wartime** sisters : a novel / Lynda Cohen Loigman. St. Martin's Press, 2019. 304 p.

ISBN 9781250140708

1. Second World War era (1939-1945) 2. Sisters 3. Family and war 4. World War II -- Women 5. Family relationships 6. Women and success 7. Ambition in women 8. Conflict in families 9. Brooklyn, New York City 10. Massachusetts 11. New York City 12. Historical fiction

LC 2018029127

Reunited after an estrangement at the beginning of World War II, two Brooklyn sisters, one an officer's wife, the other a widow and factory laborer, are shattered by the revelations of a mysterious figure from the past.

Lombardo, Claire, 1988-

The **most** fun we ever had : a novel / Claire Lombardo. Doubleday, 2019. 544 p.

ISBN 9780385544252

1. Married people 2. Sisters 3. Family relationships 4. Daughters 5. Sibling rivalry 6. Parenthood 7. Family secrets 8. Self-doubt 9. Individuality 10. Classism 11. Options, alternatives, choices 12. Adoption reunions 13. Men/women relations 14. Chicago, Illinois 15. Illinois 16. Family sagas 17. Literary fiction

LC 2018036701

The four adult daughters of two Chicago parents who have been madly in love for decades recklessly ignite old rivalries, until a long-buried secret threatens to shatter the lives they built.

"The result is an affectionate, sharp, and eminently readable exploration of the challenges of love in its many forms." Booklist.

London, Jack, 1876-1916

* The **call** of the wild / Jack London ; illustrations by Philippe Munch. Viking, 1996. 126 p.

ISBN 9780670869183

1. Sled dogs -- Alaska 2. Wolves -- Alaska 3. Prospectors 4. Men and dogs 5. Dogs 6. Klondike gold fields 7. Alaska 8. Adventure stories 9. Classics

LC 95-61728

The Call of the Wild has inspired three films, released in 1923, 1935, and 1972.

"An unabridged republication of the story originally published in book form by the Macmillan Co., New York, in 1903"--T.p. verso.

The adventures of an unusual dog, part St. Bernard, part Scotch Shepherd, that was kidnapped and shipped off to Alaska to work on the Klondike Gold Rush. Buck the dog quickly learns how to survive in the wild and also learns the call of the wolf.

London, Jack, 1876-1916

Martin Eden / Jack London. Penguin Books, 1993, c1909. 482 p.

ISBN 9780140187724

1. London, Jack, 1876-1916 2. Sailors 3. Working class men 4. Social status 5. Interclass romance 6. Individualism in men 7. Disillusionment in men 8. Classism 9. Working class 10. Authors, American 11. Men/women relations 12. Autobiographical fiction 13. Classics

Originally serialized in Pacific Monthly, September 1908-September 1909. Published in book format: New York, Macmillan, 1909.

Recounts the story of Martin Eden, a young seaman struggling to obtain social and intellectual recognition as a writer

London, Jack, 1876-1916

The **sea-wolf** / Jack London Macmillan, 1969, c1904. 366 p.

1. Ship captains 2. Sealing 3. Rescues 4. Sea stories 5. Adventure stories

First published 1904.

At the center of this exciting sea adventure, lies the battle between Humphrey Van Weyden and Wolf Larsen - the battle to determine who is the fittest to survive ; a battle for life, love and one man's soul.

London, Jack, 1876-1916

* **White** Fang / Jack London. Scholastic, 2001, c1906. 252 p.

ISBN 9780439236195

1. Wild animals as pets 2. Men and dogs 3. Gold rush -- Klondike River Valley, Yukon Territory 4. Human/animal relationships 5. Mixed-breed dogs 6. Dogfighting 7. Animal welfare 8. Yukon Territory 9. Klondike River Valley, Yukon Territory 10. Northwest, Canadian 11. Adventure stories 12. Classics

Originally serialized in The Outing Magazine, May-October 1906.

The adventures in the northern wilderness of a dog who is part wolf and how he comes to make his peace with man.

"White Fang is about a dog, a cross-breed, sold to Beauty Smith. This owner tortures the dog to increase his ferocity and value as a fighter. A new owner Weedon Scott, brings the dog to California, and, by kind treatment, domesticates him. White Fang later sacrifices his life to save Scott. Thesaurus of Book Digests.

London, Joan, 1948-

The **golden** age / Joan London. Europa Editions, 2016, c2014. 221 p.

ISBN 9781609453329

1. 1950s 2. People with poliomyelitis 3. Hospital patients 4. Refugees, Hungarian 5. Boy/girl relations 6. Poetry writing 7. Romantic love 8. Convalescence 9. Perth, Western Australia 10. Australia 11. Historical fiction 12. Love stories

Originally published: North Sydney, N.S.W. : Vintage Australia, 2014.

Nita B. Kibble Literary Award, 2015.

Queensland Literary Awards, Fiction Book Award, 2015.

Prime Minister's Literary Awards: Fiction, 2015.

Western Australian Premier's Book Awards, Fiction category, 2016.

Shortlisted for the Stella Prize, 2015

Shortlisted for the Miles Franklin Literary Award, 2015

Escaping the perils of World War II to the safety of Australia, 13-year-old Jewish Hungarian Frank is diagnosed with polio and sent to a sprawling children's hospital, where he falls in love with incandescent fellow patient Elsa while their families back home struggle to adjust to life in a new culture.

"Like Sister Penny, London sees past peoples exteriors to their complex and desirous interiors, and she generously offers those people to us in all their fullness. The novel was a recipient of multiple awards in Londons native Australia, and deservedly so: it is pretty much perfect." Publishers Weekly.

London, Julia

The **charmer** in chaps / Julia London. Berkley Pub Group, 2019. 336 p. Princes of Texas

ISBN 9780451492357

1. Rich men 2. Self-discovery 3. Homecomings 4. Womanizers 5. Men with dyslexia 6. Secrets 7. Small towns 8. Sexual attraction 9. Men/women relations 10. Texas 11. Western romances 12. Contemporary romances

A Texas prince meets his match...

London, Julia

The **trouble** with honor / Julia London. HQN, 2014. 384 p. Cabot Sisters

ISBN 9780373778454

1. Regency period (1811-1820) 2. Inheritance and succession 3. Reputation 4. Dukes and duchesses 5. Illegitimate children of royalty 6. Stepbrothers and stepsisters 7. Swindlers and swindling 8. Interpersonal conflict 9. Seduction 10. Scandals 11. Regency romances 12. Historical romances

When her stepbrother's fiance threatens to steal away her inheritance, Honor Cabot conspires with the illegitimate son of a duke to ruin the woman's reputation, but working in close quarters with such a rogue has its dangers ... and its pleasures.

London, Julia

Wild wicked Scot / Julia London. HQN Books, 2016 352 p. Highland grooms

ISBN 9780373789665

1. Jacobite Rebellions (1689-1746) 2. Stuart period (1603-1714) 3. Political intrigue 4. Seduction 5. Espionage 6. Aristocracy 7. English in Scotland 8. Secrets 9. Pretending 10. Highlands, Scotland -- History -- 18th century 11. Scotland -- Social life and customs -- 18th century 12. Highland romances 13. Historical romances

Forced to return to her husband, whom she fled three years earlier, English beauty Margot Armstrong must outmaneuver Arran McKenzie in games of espionage and seduction as their respective countriesÆ fragile unity threatens to unravel.

"This absorbing and passionate romance bodes well for future Highland Grooms titles." Booklist.

London, Julia

The **year** of living scandalously / Julia London. Pocket Books, 2010. 423 p. Secrets of Hadley Green

ISBN 9781439175453

1. Georgian era (1714-1837) 2. Arranged marriage 3. Identity theft 4. Jewelry theft 5. Criminal investigation 6. Cousins 7. Secrets 8. Nobility 9. Men/women relations 10. West Sussex, England 11. England 12. Great Britain -- History -- George III, 1760-1820 13. Georgian romances 14. Historical romances

LC bl2010028104

Keira Hannigan assumes her cousin's identity to avoid an arranged marriage, but when the Earl of Donnelly comes to visit, she must convince him to guard her secret and help her solve a mystery involving missing jewels and murder.

London, Stefanie

The **Aussie** next door / Stefanie London. Entangled Amara, 2019. 350 p.

ISBN 9781640636682

1. Americans in Australia 2. Neighbors 3. Single women 4. Former foster children 5. Options, alternatives, choices 6. Coastal towns 7. Small towns 8. Australia 9. Contemporary romances

To stay in the tiny seaside town of Margaret River, Australia, Angie Donovan, who has finally found a place to call home -- and whose 6-month visa is about to run out, asks her neighbor for help in finding a man whom she can marry.

Long, Jeff

The **reckoning,** Jeff Long. Atria Books, 2004. 275 p.

ISBN 0743463005

1. Vietnam War, 1961-1975 -- Missing in action 2. Missing in action -- Cambodia 3. Americans in Cambodia 4. Women photographers 5. Women photojournalists 6. Archaeologists 7. Archaeological sites -- Cambodia 8. Civilization, Ancient 9. Jungles -- Cambodia 10. Cambodia 11. Thrillers and suspense

LC 2004043657

Assigned to cover an army search for a thirty-years-missing military plane and its pilot in the former killing fields of Cambodia, photojournalist Molly is warned by a local overseer to avoid ghostly wanderers who appear to move within the pictures Molly takes.

"A journey into the dark past-and present-of Cambodia's former killing fields. Molly Drake, a would-be photojournalist, accompanies a U.S. Army-led search for the bones of a pilot shot down during the war. She meets Duncan O'Brian, an archeologist at a local dig, and John Kleat, who has come back to the country repeatedly, seeking his brother's remains. When bones unexpectedly turn up, Molly photographs them, breaking her agreement with the army not to take pictures of bodies. The captain in charge dismisses her along with O'Brian and Kleat, and the trio make their way to an ancient, fog-enshrouded Angkor-like city where they have evidence an army patrol went missing years ago. . . . Long's considerable knowledge of Cambodian folklore and history is put to good use as he superbly depicts the war-scarred country, its people and its beautiful, hazardous landscape." Publishers Weekly.

Long, Julie Anne

Angel in a devil's arms / Julie Anne Long. Avon Books, 2019. 352 p. Palace of rogues

ISBN 9780062867490

1. Regency period (1811-1820) 2. Nobility 3. Inheritance and succession 4. Revenge 5. Rumor 6. Courtship 7. Sexual attraction 8. Men/women relations 9. London, England 10. England -- Social life and customs -- 19th century 11. Regency romances 12. Historical romances

Sweeping into London with vengeance on his mind, Lucien Durand, seeking to reclaim his true birthright, finds himself brought to his knees by the beautiful Angelique Breedlove and the dangerous passion they share.

"With a sizzling romance, an intriguing revenge plot, and a cast of quirky Palace guests, this next installment of Long's luscious new series is smart and deliciously sensual." Library Journal.

Long, Julie Anne

Dirty dancing at Devil's Leap / Julie Anne Long. Avon Books, 2017. 369 p. Hellcat Canyon

ISBN 9780062672889

1. Former lovers 2. Mansions 3. Rich people 4. Caretakers 5. Competition 6. Sexual attraction 7. Men/women relations 8. Sierra Nevada Mountains 9. Contemporary romances

When Avalon Harwood buys the old Coltrane mansion at auction, she discovers that the property's caretaker is Mac Coltrane, Avalon's first crush, who is desperate to return the Coltranes to their former fortune and glory.

Long, Julie Anne

Hot in Hellcat Canyon / Julie Anne Long. Avon Books, 2016 384 p. Hellcat Canyon

ISBN 9780062397614

1. Actors and actresses 2. Waitresses 3. Small towns 4. Rural women 5. Widows 6. Abused women 7. Sexual attraction 8. Men/women relations 9. California 10. Sierra Nevada Mountains 11. Western romances 12. Contemporary romances

John Tennessee "J.T." McCord's 15 minutes of fame ended years ago along with his hit TV show. These days, he'll take any job, anywhere -- which is how he ends up stranded in Hellcat Canyon, California, when his car breaks down en route to a location shoot. Britt Langley, a waitress at the Misty Cat Cavern, can't take her eyes off the man. However, a disastrous past relationship has made Britt reluctant to pursue anything more than a fling, while J.T. has his own demons to overcome.?Best known for her Pennyroyal Green Regencies, author Julie Anne Long switches gears with this contemporary series opener, which offers small-town charm and a quirky supporting cast.?-- Description by Gillian Speace.

"This laugh-out-loud treat is warmly emotional and richly satisfying." Publishers Weekly.

Long, Julie Anne

* **Lady** Derring takes a lover / Julie Anne Long. Avon Books, 2019. 384 p. Palace of rogues

ISBN 9780062867469

1. Regency period (1811-1820) 2. Widows 3. Boarding houses 4. Ship captains 5. Counts and countesses 6. Debt 7. Smuggling 8. Independence in women 9. Duty 10. Sexual attraction 11. Men/women relations 12. London, England 13. England -- Social life and customs -- 19th century 14. Regency romances 15. Historical romances

On the hunt for a notorious smuggler, Captain Tristan Hardy is led to the Rogue's Palace, a London boarding house, and sets out to seduce its beautiful blue-blooded proprietress, the Countess of Derring, to get the answers he seeks.

Long, Julie Anne

The **legend** of Lyon Redmond / Julie Anne Long. Avon, 2015. 384 p. Pennyroyal Green

ISBN 9780062334855

1. Regency period (1811-1820) 2. First loves 3. Family feuds 4. Lovers' reunions 5. Mate selection 6. Ultimatums 7. Abandoned women 8. Soul mates 9. Prophecies 10. Curses 11. Rich families 12. Sexual attraction 13. Men/women relations 14. Sussex, England 15. England -- Social life and customs -- 19th century 16. Regency romances 17. Historical romances

As Olivia Eversea's wedding to another man approaches, Lyon Redmond decides it's time for a reckoning with the woman he loves, and they must decide whether their love is a curse that will tear their families apart or something legendary.

Long, Julie Anne

Wild at Whiskey Creek / Julie Anne Long. Avon Books, 2016 370 p. Hellcat Canyon

ISBN 9780062397638

1. Women singers 2. Sheriffs 3. Small towns 4. Sexual attraction 5. Men/women relations 6. California 7. Sierra Nevada Mountains 8. Western romances 9. Contemporary romances

RUSA Reading List Short List, 2018.

When a betrayal threatens aspiring musician Glory Greenleaf's big break, her former lover--and the man who put her brother in jail--Sheriff Eli Barlow, will risk everything to make it right ... because the best way to love the girl from Whiskey Creek might mean setting her free forever. "A splendid, delectable romance." Kirkus.

Longworth, M. L. (Mary Lou), 1963-

Death at the Chateau Bremont / M.L. Longworth. Penguin Books, 2011. 288 p. Verlaque and Bonnet mysteries

ISBN 9780143119524

1. Judges 2. Murder investigation 3. Mafia 4. Women law teachers 5. Crimes against brothers 6. Brothers 7. Organized crime 8. Former lovers 9. Murder suspects 10. Aix-en-Provence, France 11. Southern France 12. Mysteries

LC 2011007573

"A Penguin mystery."

Antoine Verlaque, the handsome chief magistrate of Aix and his sometimes love interest, law professor Marine Bonnet, investigate the death of a local French nobleman who fell from the family chîeau in charming and historic Aix-en-Provence.

Longworth, M. L. (Mary Lou), 1963-

Murder in the Rue Dumas / M.L. Longworth. Penguin Books, 2012. 288 p. Verlaque and Bonnet mysteries

ISBN 9780143121541

1. College students 2. College teachers 3. Universities and colleges 4. Judges 5. Murder investigation 6. Women law teachers 7. Murder suspects 8. Aix-en-Provence, France 9. Southern France 10. Mysteries

LC 2012023725

Judge Antoine Verlaque and his law professor girlfriend, Marine Bonnet, investigate the murder of the university's director of theology in this new mystery from the author of Death at the Chateau Bremont.

Longworth, M. L. (Mary Lou), 1963-

Murder on the Ile Sordou : a Verlaque and Bonnet Provencal mystery / M.L. Longworth. Penguin Books, 2014. 303 p. Verlaque and Bonnet mysteries

ISBN 9780143125549

1. Husband and wife 2. Vacations 3. Hotels 4. Storms 5. Wine and wine making 6. Murder 7. Murder investigation 8. Men/women relations 9. France 10. Mysteries

LC 2014010451

"A Penguin mystery."

While vacationing at the opulent Locanda Sordou hotel, Judge Antoine Verlaque and his girlfriend, law professor Marine Bonnet, investigate a murder and find things going from bad to worse when a violent storm cuts off all communication with the mainland, trapping them with a killer.

"Longworth once again immerses readers in French culture with this whodunit, which will delight Francophiles and fans of Donna Leon and Andrea Camilleri. The setting will also appeal to readers who enjoy trapped-on-the-island mysteries in the tradition of Agatha Christie's And Then There Were None." Library Journal.

Lopez Barrio, Cristina, 1970-

The **house** of the impossible loves / Cristina Lopez Barrio ; translated from the Spanish by Lisa Carter. Houghton Mifflin Harcourt, 2013. 319 p.

ISBN 9780547661193

1. Curses 2. Mothers and daughters 3. Father-deserted children 4. Hope 5. Jilted women 6. Fate and fatalism 7. Brothels 8. Intergenerational relations 9. Free will and determinism 10. Women -- Family relationships 11. Spain -- History -- 20th century 12.

France -- History -- 20th century 13. Magical realism 14. Literary fiction 15. Family sagas 16. Translations -- Spanish to English

Cursed to suffer tragic love affairs and give birth to equally cursed daughters, a family of women in 20th-century Spain and France and their colorful inner circle watch over a youngest daughter's passionate affair with a landowner who leaves her pregnant and determined to make redemptive changes.

Lopez, Julian, 1965-

A **beautiful** young woman : a novel / Julian Lopez ; translated from the Spanish by Samuel Rutter. Melville House, 2017, c2013. 160 p.

ISBN 9781612196817

1. 1970s 2. Children of disappeared persons 3. Mothers and sons 4. Political violence 5. Dissenters 6. Abduction 7. Loss (Psychology) 8. Dictatorship 9. Memories 10. Family relationships 11. Argentina -- History -- 20th century 12. Political fiction 13. Literary fiction 14. Translations -- Spanish to English

LC 2017026694

Set in the midst of Argentina's military dictatorship, a poignant and evocative debut novel about family, political violence, and the consequences of dissidence.

Lordan, Beth

But come ye back , Beth Lordan Morrow, 2004. 278 p.

ISBN 0060530367

1. 1990s 2. Americans in Ireland 3. Irish in the United States 4. Married people 5. Husband and wife 6. Parent and child 7. Retirees -- Ireland 8. Men/women relations 9. Extramarital affairs 10. Ireland 11. Galway, Ireland 12. Psychological fiction 13. Domestic fiction

LC 2003056217

A collection of interconnected short stories chronicles more than thirty years in the lives and marriage of Lyle Sullivan and his Irish-born wife, Mary Curtin, as they fall in love and make a life together with their two sons.

Loren, Roni

* The **one** for you / Roni Loren. Sourcebooks Casablanca, 2019. 352 p. Ones who got away

ISBN 9781492693192

1. Single women 2. Best friends 3. School shootings 4. Life change events 5. Psychic trauma 6. Second chances 7. Secrets 8. Interpersonal attraction 9. Men/women relations 10. Contemporary romances

Still haunted by a school shooting on prom night years earlier, Kincaid Breslin runs into an old classmate with whom she embarks on a romantic relationship until she discovers the truth about that night - and his involvement in it.

"Loren nimbly addresses heavy topics, emphasizing emotional resilience and recovery." Publishers Weekly.

Loren, Roni

The **one** you can't forget / Roni Loren. Sourcebooks, 2018. 352 p. Ones who got away

ISBN 9781492651437

1. Women lawyers 2. Divorced men 3. Secrets 4. Mugging 5. Men/women relations 6. Interpersonal attraction 7. Contemporary romances

"Loren's second title in a series that revolves around survivors of a high school shooting (The Ones Who Got Away, 2018) maintains the complexity and emotional intensity that earned the first book huge acclaim but never loses its way as a sexy, captivating romance." Kirkus.

Loren, Roni

The **one** you fight for / Roni Loren. Sourcebooks Casablanca, 2019. 352 p. Ones who got away

ISBN 9781492651468

1. Women college teachers 2. Athletic trainers 3. New identities 4. Interracial romance 5. Brothers and sisters 6. School shootings 7. Violence -- Psychological aspects 8. Loss (Psychology) 9. Guilt 10. Loneliness 11. Forgiveness 12. Secrets 13. Romantic love 14. Sexual attraction 15. Men/women relations 16. Austin, Texas 17. Multicultural romances 18. Contemporary romances

When Taryn, whose younger sister was killed in a school shooting, and Shaw, whose brother was one of the shooters, meet years later, they find themselves falling in love despite their positions on opposite sides of the tragedy.

"Loren delivers another stunning and moving addition to her series about survivors of a school shooting. She realistically and vividly depicts guilt and loneliness while also showcasing the power and importance of love and friendship." Booklist.

Lorret, Vivienne

How to forget a duke / Vivienne Lorret. Avon Books, 2018. 384 p. Misadventures in matchmaking

ISBN 9780062685483

1. 19th century 2. Regency period (1811-1820) 3. Dukes and duchesses 4. Amnesia 5. Women with amnesia 6. Matchmakers 7. Family secrets 8. Mate selection 9. Men/women relations 10. Interpersonal attraction 11. Regency romances 12. Historical romances

Washing up ashore at the Duke of Rydstrom's crumbling cliffside estate with no memory of who she is or what brought her there, matchmaker Miss Jacinda Bourne tries to regain her memory with the help of this handsome, enigmatic man whose amorous attentions hide a dark secret.

Lostetter, Marina J.

Noumenon / Marina J. Lostetter. Harper Voyager, 2017. 496 p. Noumenon

ISBN 9780062497840

1. Space vehicles 2. Clones and cloning 3. Space exploration 4. Space flight 5. Interpersonal relations 6. Survival -- Space 7. Science fiction 8. Hard science fiction

With nods to Arthur C. Clarke's Rama series and the real science of Neal Stephenson's Seveneves, a touch of Hugh Howey's Wool, and echoes of Octavia Butler's voice, a powerful tale of space travel, adventure, discovery, and humanity that unfolds through a series of generational vignettes.

Louis, Edouard

The **end** of Eddy : a novel / Edouard Louis ; translated from the French by Michael Lucey. Farrar, Straus and Giroux, 2017. 192 p.

ISBN 9780374266653

1. Young men 2. Working class families 3. Self-acceptance in gay men 4. Working poor people 5. Gay teenagers 6. Rural families 7. Homophobia 8. Gay men 9. Villages 10. France 11. LGBTQIA fiction 12. Autobiographical fiction 13. Coming-of-age stories 14. Literary fiction 15. Translations -- French to English

LC 2016041340

First published in French as En finir avec Eddy Bellegueule (Paris : Editions du Seuil, 2014).

Traces how a young gay man in a violent French factory village navigates his orientation and intellectually precocious nature while enduring pressure to become a strong man in accordance with local beliefs.

"In this excellent autobiographical novel, a middle school boy struggles to forge an identity in a French industrial town hostile in every way to his homosexuality." Publishers Weekly.

Lourey, Jess, 1970-
* **January** thaw : a murder-by-month mystery / Jess Lourey. Midnight Ink, 2014. 288 p. Murder by month mysteries
ISBN 9780738738758
1. Women amateur detectives 2. Murder investigation 3. Small town life -- Minnesota 4. Women librarians 5. Women journalists 6. Eccentrics and eccentricities 7. Dead 8. January 9. Men/women relations 10. Minnesota 11. Mysteries
LC 2013027483
In her new home in small town Minnesota, private-detective-in-training Mira James must investigate a 150-year cold case, as well as a present-day spate of drug-trafficking.

Lourey, Jess, 1970-
Unspeakable things / Jessica Lourey. Thomas & Mercer, 2020. 299 p.
ISBN 9781542008785
1. 1980s 2. Family secrets 3. Preteen girls 4. Child sexual abuse 5. Missing boys 6. Small towns 7. Rural life 8. Change (Psychology) 9. Families 10. Girl amateur detectives 11. Minnesota 12. Thrillers and suspense
Inspired by a terrifying true story from the author's hometown, a heart-pounding novel of suspense about a small Minnesota community where nothing is as quiet--or as safe--as it seems.
"Lourey may be known for comic capers (March of Crime), but this tense novel combines the best of a coming-of-age story with suspense, and an unforgettable young narrator." Library Journal.

Lourie, Richard, 1940-
A **hatred** for tulips / Richard Lourie. Thomas Dunne Books, 2007. 192 p.
ISBN 9780312349332
1. Frank, Anne, 1929-1945 2. 1940s 3. Betrayal 4. World War II 5. Jews -- Persecutions 6. Informers 7. Boys 8. Family relationships 9. Options, alternatives, choices 10. Fathers and sons 11. Secrets 12. Antisemitism 13. Marital conflict 14. Tragedy 15. Historical fiction
LC 2006048862
In modern-day Amsterdam, an elderly man named Joop describes his desperate efforts to feed his starving family during the Nazi occupation of World War II and reveals how his struggle to provide for them set in motion a horrifying chain of events.

Lovecraft, H. P. (Howard Phillips), 1890-1937
* **Tales** / H.P. Lovecraft. Library of America : 2005. 850 p.
ISBN 1931082723
1. Short stories 2. Horror
LC 2004048979
"If you spend enough time in Lovecraft's lonely landscapes, fear really does develop: not the fear that you will come across unearthly creatures, but the fear that you will come across little else. And what first seems horridly overdone accumulates a creepy minimalism. Taken as a whole, Lovecraft's work exhibits a hopeless isolation not unlike that of Samuel Beckett: lonely man after lonely man, wandering aimlessly through a shadowy city or holing up in rural emptiness, pursuing unspeakable secrets or being pursued by secret unspeakables, all to little avail and to no comfort. There is something funny about this--in small doses. But by the end of this collection, one does not hear giggling so much as the echoes of those giggles as they vanish into the ether lonely, desperate and, yes, very, very scary." New York Times Book Review.

Lovesey, Peter
Beau death / Peter Lovesey. Soho Crime, 2017. 416 p. Peter Diamond mysteries
ISBN 9781616959050
1. Nash, Richard, 1674-1761 2. Dead 3. Detectives 4. Building sites 5. Cold cases (Criminal investigation) 6. Murder investigation 7. Local history 8. England 9. Bath, England 10. Police procedurals 11. Mysteries
When human remains in 18th-century clothing are discovered on a demolition site, Chief Inspector Peter Diamond eagerly embarks on a mission to prove that a scandal-marked fashion icon from Bath may have had quite a different end than the one popularly believed.

Lovesey, Peter
Bertie and the seven bodies / Peter Lovesey Mysterious Press, 1990. 196 p. Prince of Wales mysteries
ISBN 9780892963997
1. Edward VII, King of Great Britain, 1841-1910 2. 19th century 3. Murder 4. Country homes 5. Actors and actresses 6. Murder investigation 7. Victoriana 8. Mysteries
LC 89012405
Republished with the other Prince of Wales mysteries by Soho Crime in 2019.
In 1890 twelve guests gather at Desborough Hall for a week's shooting party hosted by the beautiful Lady Amelia Hammond. Months of planning have left nothing to chance, for the main guests are the Prince and Princess of Wales...
"Narrated by Bertie himself, the voice here is perfectly accurate; Lovesey gives his main character just the right tone of sophistication, charm, anti-intellectualism, and savoir faire, mixed in with ennui. A wonderfully put together puzzle." Booklist.

Lovesey, Peter
* **Diamond** dust / Peter Lovesey. Soho Press, 2002. 343 p. Peter Diamond mysteries
ISBN 9781569472910
1. Police -- Bath, England 2. Widowers 3. Gunshot victims 4. Murder investigation 5. Birthdays 6. Bath, England 7. England 8. London, England 9. Mysteries 10. Police procedurals
LC 2002017567
When his beloved wife becomes the latest victim in a string of police-spouse killings, Detective Superintendent Peter Diamond becomes determined to track down the murderer despite his superior's order to leave the case to someone else.
"In a bold display of virtuosity, Lovesey takes his hero to emotional places he's never been before while constructing a plot of infernal ingenuity." New York Times Book Review.

Lovesey, Peter
Diamond solitaire / Peter Lovesey. Mysterious Press, 1993, c1992. 345 p. Peter Diamond mysteries
ISBN 9780892965359
1. Abandoned children 2. Children with autism 3. Guards 4. Former police 5. Sumo wrestlers 6. England 7. London, England 8. Mysteries 9. Police procedurals
LC 92050660
When an autistic Japanese child is mysteriously abducted in London, ex-police detective Peter Diamond begins a desperate search that takes him from the sumo wrestling world of Japan to New York's high finance district
"Peter Diamond is plagued by bad karma. Formerly detective superintendent of police in Bath, he's sunk to being a security guard at Harrod's, until a small Asian child is found in the area of the store Peter

patrols. Out of a job once again (security breaches are no laughing matter at terrorist-obsessed Harrod's), Diamond becomes intrigued by the Asian child, who is autistic and who remains unclaimed despite massive publicity. What starts out as a kindly effort to restore the child to her parents turns into an international adventure as Diamond travels from London to New York to Japan and confronts millionaire sumo wrestlers, unethical drug researchers, and corrupt businessmen." Booklist.

Lovesey, Peter

The **house** sitter / Peter Lovesey. Soho Press, 2003. 304 p. Peter Diamond mysteries

ISBN 1569473269

1. Police 2. Widowers 3. Serial murder investigation 4. Policewomen 5. Criminal profilers -- Death 6. Murder investigation 7. Serial murders 8. Bereavement in men 9. Grief in men 10. Bath, England 11. Sussex, England 12. Bognor Regis, England 13. London, England 14. Mysteries 15. Police procedurals

LC 2002042626

First published: London: Little, Brown, 2003.

Macavity Award for Best Mystery Novel, 2004.

"The identity of the killer, when finally revealed, is genuinely startling, and not because of authorial obfuscation. The writing is as smooth as polished steel." Publishers Weekly.

Lovesey, Peter

The **last** detective / Peter Lovesey. Doubleday, 1991. 331 p. Peter Diamond mysteries

ISBN 0385421141

1. Murder investigation 2. Murder suspects 3. Police 4. Forensic sciences 5. Bath, England 6. England 7. London, England 8. Mysteries 9. Police procedurals

LC 91011859

"A Perfect crime book."

Anthony Award for Best Novel, 1992.

Challenged by departmental red tape and a dearth of clues, British detective Peter Diamond must solve the murder of a down-on-her-luck soap opera actress, who was found floating face down in a reservoir.

"An intricate, many-tiered examination of police work, especially modern forensic technology, complete with computers and genetic fingerprinting. Everything meshe's perfectly in this airtight tale." Booklist.

Lovesey, Peter

Skeleton Hill / Peter Lovesey. Soho Press, 2009. 336 p. Peter Diamond mysteries

ISBN 9781569475980

1. Cold cases (Criminal investigation) 2. Forensic anthropology 3. Vigilantes 4. Skeleton 5. Women murder victims 6. Murder 7. Murder investigation 8. Police -- Bath, England 9. Bath, England 10. England 11. London, England 12. Mysteries 13. Police procedurals

LC 2009011128

On Lansdown Hill, near Bath, England, a battle between Roundheads and Cavaliers that took place over 350 years ago is annually reenacted. Two of the reenactors discover a skeleton that is female, headless, and only about twenty years old. One of them, a professor who played a Cavalier, is later found murdered.

"Another of Lovesey's convoluted plots, layered with historical lore and teeming with comic characters up to their necks in no good. Diamond is a classic--better catch him while you can." New York Times Book Review.

Lovesey, Peter

The **tooth** tattoo / Peter Lovesey. Soho Press, 2013. 348 p. Peter Diamond mysteries

ISBN 9781616952303

1. Crimes against women 2. Violinists 3. Classical music industry and trade 4. Detectives 5. Murder investigation 6. Serial murderers 7. Police 8. Bath, England 9. London, England 10. Mysteries 11. Police procedurals

LC 2012043412

Investigating the murder of a young woman whose only identifying mark is a tattoo on one of her teeth, British criminal investigator Peter Diamond teams up with violinist Mel Farran, who is being scouted by a mysterious and elite classical quartet that reveals frightening truths about fandom and the cutthroat world of professional music.

Lovesey, Peter

Upon a dark night / Peter Lovesey. Mysterious Press, 1998, c1997. 374 p. Peter Diamond mysteries

ISBN 0892966696

1. Homeless women 2. Suicide 3. Women with amnesia 4. Former police 5. Police -- Bath, England 6. Farmers 7. Young women 8. Bath, England 9. London, England 10. Mysteries 11. Police procedurals

LC 9748922

Ebullient homicide detective Peter Diamond takes on a case in Bath, England, involving a mysterious female amnesiac who is somehow tied to two alleged suicides.

"A triumph of plotting from this master of the classic puzzle form." New York Times Book Review.

Lovesey, Peter

The **vault** / Peter Lovesey. Soho Press, 2000, c1999. 331 p. Peter Diamond mysteries

ISBN 1569472084

1. Murder investigation 2. Monsters 3. Authors 4. Police -- Bath, England 5. Former police -- Bath, England 6. Bath, England 7. London, England 8. Mysteries 9. Police procedurals

LC 00041010

"A wealth of good things fills this novel: Lovesey's deft plotting, his hilarious send-ups of the Brits through the perspective of the American professor, and his intriguing allusions to the architecture and literary history of Bath." Booklist.

Lovesey, Peter

Waxwork / Peter Lovesey. Pantheon Books, 1978. 239 p. Sergeant Cribb mysteries

ISBN 0394500660

1. Scotland Yard. 2. Victorian era (1837-1901) 3. 1880s 4. Extortion 5. Confession (Law) 6. Police 7. Detectives 8. Murder 9. Murder investigation 10. False confessions (Law) 11. London, England -- History -- 19th century 12. England -- History -- 19th century 13. Historical mysteries 14. Victorian mysteries 15. Mysteries

Originally published: London : Macmillan, 1978.

Silver Dagger Award for Fiction, 1978.

Sergeant Cribb of Scotland Yard investigates Miriam Cromer's confession to the murder of her husband with potassium cyanide.

Lovestam, Sara, 1980-

The **truth** behind the lie : a novel / Sara Lovestam ; translated from the Swedish by Laura A. Wildeburg. Minotaur Books, 2019, c2015. 336 p.

ISBN 9781250300072

1. Missing children 2. Mothers 3. Private investigators 4.

Undocumented immigrants 5. Immigrants, Iranian 6. Fear 7. Guilt 8. Mysteries 9. Scandinavian crime fiction 10. Translations -- Swedish to English

LC 2019009082

Originally published: Stockhom : Pocketforlaget, 2015.

After her young daughter disappears, a desperate mother turns to an undocumented Iranian refugee moonlighting as a private investigator, an expert at living and working off the grid, to help her locate her little girl before it's too late.

Lovett, Charles C.

The **bookman's** tale : a novel of obsession / Charlie Lovett. Viking, 2013. 368 p.

ISBN 9780670026470

1. Shakespeare, William, 1564-1616 Authorship 2. 16th century 3. 1990s 4. Booksellers 5. Widowers 6. Searching 7. Americans in England 8. Books 9. Obsession 10. Murder 11. Portraits 12. Forgery 13. Grief in men 14. Men/women relations 15. Mysteries 16. Love stories 17. Parallel narratives

LC 2013001559

Relocating to the English countryside after the death of his wife, antiquarian book enthusiast Peter Byerly discovers an 18th-century study of Shakespeare forgeries that contains a Victorian portrait strongly resembling his late wife, a finding that sparks an obsessive search through the bard's historical period.

Lovett, Charles C.

The **lost** book of the Grail : or a visitor's guide to Barchester Cathedral / Charlie Lovett. Viking, 2017. 320 p.

ISBN 9780399562518

1. Grail 2. Obsession 3. College teachers 4. Libraries 5. Searching 6. Cathedrals 7. Books and reading 8. Americans in England 9. England 10. Mysteries

An obsessive bibliophile and Holy Grail fanatic combs through centuries of history to uncover a long-lost secret about the medieval Barchester Cathedral library at the side of a young American charged with digitizing the library's manuscripts.

"A solidly built, innocently bookish diversion with a distinct Masterpiece Theater flavor." Kirkus.

Lowe, Kathryn A.

The **furies** / Katie Lowe. St. Martin's Press, 2019. 352 p.
ISBN 9781250297891

1. 1990s 2. Witchcraft 3. Revenge 4. Boarding schools 5. Murder 6. Friendship 7. Female friendship 8. Teenage girls 9. Obsession 10. Magic (Occultism) 11. Student secret societies 12. Secret societies 13. Drug use 14. Rape 15. England 16. Thrillers and suspense 17. Coming-of-age stories

LC 2019016759

In 1990s England, at an elite boarding school connected to seventeenth-century witch trials, troubled sixteen-year-old Violet is drawn into a circle of friends dabbling in witchcraft to avenge wrongs done to them.

Lowell, Elizabeth, 1944-

Pearl Cove / Elizabeth Lowell. Avon Books, 1999. 376 p. Donovan Family
ISBN 0380974045

1. Pearl industry and trade 2. Jewelry theft 3. Men/women relations 4. Black pearls 5. Widows -- Australia 6. Australia 7. Romantic suspense

LC 99-21639

Confronted by her late husband's suspicious death, the prospect of bankruptcy, and the disappearance of a priceless black pearl necklace called the "Black Trinity," young widow Hannah McGarry reluctantly turns for help to the seductive Archer Donovan, the silent partner in her husband's pearl farm enterprise

"This is a riveting mix of suspense and romance." Booklist.

Lowenthal, Michael

Charity girl / Michael Lowenthal. Houghton Mifflin, 2007. 336 p.

ISBN 0618546294

1. First World War era (1914-1918) 2. Sexually transmitted diseases -- Government policy 3. Quarantine 4. World War I 5. Young women 6. Prisons 7. Soldiers -- United States -- History -- World War I 8. Men/women relations 9. One-night stands (Interpersonal relations) 10. Women prisoners 11. Friendship 12. United States -- History -- 1913-1921 13. Historical fiction

LC 2005037775

During World War I, after an impulsive night with an infected soldier, Frieda Mintz, a seventeen-year-old Jewish girl, is sent to a makeshift detention center for medical treatment with other "charity girls" in similar circumstances.

"Lowenthal's narrative style is perfect for a heroine who suffers but remains a survivor, striking just the right mix of dark and light, worldly and innocent. Providing Frieda with flickers of humor and joy, he guarantees her our sympathy." New York Times Book Review.

Lowry, Malcolm, 1909-1957

* **Under** the volcano / Malcolm Lowry. Reynal & Hitchcock, 1947. 375 p.

ISBN 9780060153670

1. 1930s 2. Regret 3. Alcoholics 4. British in Mexico 5. Consuls 6. All Souls' Day 7. Interpersonal relations 8. Love triangles 9. Redemption 10. Loss (Psychology) 11. Former wives 12. Desire 13. Reconciliation in marriage 14. Mexico 15. Modern classics 16. Literary fiction

LC 65011640

Geoffrey Firmin, a former British consul, struggles to surmount the forces which threaten to destroy him.

Ludlum, Robert, 1927-2001

The **Bourne** identity / Robert Ludlum. R. Marek Publishers, 1980. 535 p. Jason Bourne series

ISBN 0399900705

1. Amnesia 2. Assassins 3. International intrigue 4. Spies 5. Thrillers and suspense

LC 79023638

A shooting victim, suffering from amnesia, finds himself with a Swiss bank account in the name of Jason Bourne, a professional assassin being manipulated by a top-secret American government organization to kill his arch rival, the dreaded Carlos.

Ludlum, Robert, 1927-2001

The **Bourne** supremacy / Robert Ludlum. Random House, 1986. 597 p. Jason Bourne series

ISBN 9780394543963

1. Impostors 2. International intrigue 3. Assassins 4. China 5. Thrillers and suspense

LC 85018318

Super-diplomat Raymond Havilland sets up the kidnapping of Jason Bourne's wife, in order to draw Bourne out of retirement and into a Taiwanese plot to seize Hong Kong and incite China against the West.

LIST OF FICTIONAL WORKS

Ludlum, Robert, 1927-2001

The **Bourne** ultimatum / Robert Ludlum. Random House, 1990. 611 p. Jason Bourne series

ISBN 9780394584089

1. Carlos, 1949- 2. International intrigue 3. Assassins 4. Spies 5. Thrillers and suspense

LC 89043201

Professor David Webb must once again become his alter ego, assassin Jason Bourne, as he approaches a final confrontation with his arch-nemesis, terrorist Carlos the Jackal

Ludlum, Robert, 1927-2001

The **Prometheus** deception / Robert Ludlum. St. Martin's Press, 2000. 509 p.

ISBN 031225346X

1. Intelligence officers 2. Conspiracies 3. International intrigue 4. Counterintelligence 5. CIA agents 6. Former CIA agents 7. Thrillers and suspense 8. Spy fiction

LC 00062585

For fifteen years Nicholas Bryson was a top deep-cover operative for the Directorate, a clandestine branch of U.S. intelligence. Bryson retired and has been a college professor. Now, five years later, the CIA has contacted Bryson to tell him that his former employer was in fact using him against his own country's interests. The CIA wants Bryson's knowledge and expertise to help shut down the Directorate for good.

"The pace is fast, the action plentiful, and the story confusing enough to keep us turning the pages." Booklist.

Ludlum, Robert, 1927-2001

The **Sigma** protocol St. Martin's Press, 2001 528 p.

ISBN 0312276885

1. United States. Department of Justice 2. CIA 3. Government investigators 4. Serial murders 5. International intrigue 6. Investment bankers 7. Americans in Switzerland 8. Senior men 9. Deception 10. Aging -- Prevention 11. Former Nazis 12. Switzerland 13. Thrillers and suspense

While on vacation in Switzerland, financier Ben Hartman encounters a childhood friend. Suddenly, the friend tries to shoot him, and ends up killing himself and everyone except Ben. At the same time, DOJ field agent Anna Navarro has commenced an investigation on a suspicius series of worldwide killings of elderly men, linked only by an old OSS code named Sigma.

Ludwig, Benjamin, 1974-

Ginny Moon / Benjamin Ludwig. Park Row, 2017. 368 p.

ISBN 9780778330165

1. Girls with autism 2. Foster children 3. Birthmothers 4. Autism 5. Adoption 6. Teenage girls 7. Abusive women 8. Foster daughters 9. Obsession in girls 10. Girls with developmental disabilities 11. Mainstream fiction

Librarians' Choice (Australia), 2017

Despite being placed in the ideal foster home, autistic 14-year-old girl Ginny Moon is intent on running back to her abusive, drug-addict birth mother, Gloria.

"Ludwig's excellent debut is both a unique coming-of-age tale and a powerful affirmation of the fragility and strength of families." Publishers Weekly.

Luesse, Valerie Fraser,

Missing Isaac / Valerie Fraser Luesse. Baker Pub Group, 2018 341 p.

ISBN 9780800728786

1. 1960s 2. Missing persons investigation 3. Race relations 4. African Americans 5. Small towns 6. Searching 7. Friendship 8. Men/women relations 9. Prejudice 10. Racism 11. Alabama -- Social life and customs 12. Christian historical fiction

LC 2017032966

Christy Award for First Novel Category, 2018.

When Pete McLean's close friend Isaac, who is African American, goes missing in 1960s Alabama, Pete's efforts to find him lead him into parts of their small town he has never seen before, and to a girl who will change his life.

Luiselli, Valeria, 1983-

* **Lost** children archive : a novel / Valeria Luiselli. Alfred A. Knopf, 2019. 416 p.

ISBN 9780525520610

1. Cross-country automobile trips 2. Child immigrants 3. Apache Indians 4. Undocumented immigrants 5. Marital conflict 6. Lost children 7. Missing children 8. Families 9. United States -- Immigration and emigration 10. United States -- History -- 21st century 11. Literary fiction

LC 2018018390

ALA Notable Book, 2020.

Andrew Carnegie Medal for Excellence in Fiction, 2020.

National Book Critics Circle Award for Fiction finalist, 2019

Kirkus Prize for Fiction finalist, 2019.

Longlisted for the Booker Prize, 2019.

Longlisted for The Women's Prize for Fiction, 2019.

A novel about a family of four, on the cusp of fracture, who take a trip across America--a story told through varying points of view, and including archival documents and photographs.

"Intense and keenly timely, Luiselli's latest work is perhaps her most politically relevant, and themes of translation and migration resonate, making it one of few novels that fully and powerfully convey the urgency of this unsettling situation." Booklist.

Luiselli, Valeria, 1983-

The **story** of my teeth / Valeria Luiselli ; translation, Christina MacSweeney. Coffee House Press, 2015, c2013. 184 p.

ISBN 9781566894098

1. Auctions 2. Teeth 3. Storytelling 4. Eccentrics and eccentricities 5. Fathers and sons 6. Deception 7. Auctioneers 8. Personal belongings 9. Mexico City 10. Literary fiction 11. Translations -- Spanish to English

LC 2015009759

Translation from the Spanish of: La historia de mis dientes.

Originally published: 2013.

National Book Critics Circle Award for Fiction finalist, 2015

Shortlisted for the International Dublin Literary Award, 2017

Kirkus Prize for Fiction finalist, 2015.

"Bon vivant, world traveler, auctioneer-the story of Highway and his teeth is like Johnny Cash meets Robert Walser in Mexico"--, Provided by publisher.

"Reminiscent of the serialized novels used to entertain and educate Cuban cigar-rollers, Luiselli marvelously redefines the relationship between author and audience." Booklist.

Lukas, Michael David

The **last** watchman of Old Cairo : a novel / Michael David Lukas. Spiegel & Grau, 2018. 288 p.

ISBN 9780399181160

1. Synagogues 2. Ancestors 3. Family secrets 4. Torah scrolls 5. College students 6. Faith 7. Duty 8. Jews 9. Muslims 10. Interfaith families 11. Families 12. Cairo, Egypt 13. California 14. Literary

fiction 15. Family sagas

LC 2017007153

National Jewish Book Award, 2018.

Sophie Brody Medal, 2019.

A Berkeley literature student from a mixed-faith family receives a mysterious package that draws him into a quest to uncover his ancestors' tangled history as watchmen for Old Cairo's storied Ibn Ezra Synagogue.

"Lukas enlivens a fascinating epoch when Jews and Muslims bridged cultural divides for a common cause. Part mystery, part character study, yet historically accurate, this book should appeal to a broad swath of readers." Library Journal.

Lukas, Michael David

The **Oracle** of Stamboul : a novel / Michael David Lukas. Harper, 2011. viii, 294 p.

ISBN 9780062012098

1. Oracles 2. Savant syndrome 3. Epilepsy 4. Prophecies 5. Girls 6. Rulers 7. Turkey 8. Literary fiction

Raised by a carpet merchant father and resentful stepmother after a prophesied birth, Eleonora is recognized as a prodigy before stowing away to Stamboul, where she charms the eccentric Sultan Abdul Amid II and changes the course of history.

"Lukas' book is an appealing blend of magical and historical realism. Its story line is as loosely drawn, and as purposeful, as that flock of hoopoes that accompany the protagonist everywhere she goes. Lukas, too, is a graceful and inventive writer, and reflects his travels across Turkey and his love especially for Istanbul in dozens of polished and elegant passages scattered through the narrative. . . . And while it might seem a novel for young readers, this is a polished literary work that will appeal to a wide readership." Cleveland Plain Dealer.

Luna, Louisa

The **Janes** / Louisa Luna. Doubleday, 2020. 368 p. Alice Vega novels

ISBN 9780385545518

1. Women private investigators 2. Human trafficking 3. Sex crimes 4. Teenage girl murder victims 5. Private investigators 6. Murder investigation 7. San Diego, California 8. Thrillers and suspense

Private investigator Alice Vega and her partner, Cap, search for clues in the murders of two unidentified young women who might be victims of a San Diego sex-trafficking ring.

"In contrast with her debut, Luna this time develops the burgeoning attraction between empathetic Cap and Jack Reacher-esque Vega, resulting in a series duo with legs. Luna's latest entertains while subverting gender stereotypes and confronting the politics of immigration." Kirkus.

Lunde, Maja

The **end** of the ocean : a novel / Maja Lunde ; translated from the Norwegian by Diane Oatley. HarperCollins, 2020. 304 p. Climate novels

ISBN 9780062951366

1. 21st century 2. Climate change 3. Refugees 4. Droughts 5. Sailboats 6. Ocean travel 7. Greed 8. Despair 9. Europe 10. Translations -- Norwegian to English 11. Literary fiction 12. Apocalyptic fiction

LC 2019030722

Explores the threat of a devastating worldwide drought, witnessed through the lives of a father, a daughter and a woman who will risk her life to save the future.

"Two stories on the impact of climate change intersect in this thoughtful and suspenseful novel." Kirkus.

Lundrigan, Nicole

Glass boys : a novel / Nicole Lundrigan. Douglas & McIntyre, 2011. 300 p.

ISBN 9781553657972

1. Abandonment (Psychology) 2. Stepfathers 3. Murder 4. Forgiveness 5. Family problems 6. Men/women relations 7. Single mothers 8. Newfoundland and Labrador 9. Mysteries

When Roy Trench is killed in a drunken prank gone wrong, his brother Lewis blames alcoholic Eli Fagan. Though the courts rule the death an accident, the event causes ongoing hate between the two families of Knife's Point, Newfoundland.

Lupton, Rosamund

Afterwards : a novel / Rosamund Lupton. Crown Publishers, 2012. 386 p.

ISBN 9780307716545

1. Arson investigation 2. Conflict in families 3. Attempted murder 4. Secrets 5. Mothers and daughters 6. Protectiveness in women 7. Burn victims 8. Arson 9. London, England 10. Psychological suspense

LC 2011041524

After a house fire leaves Grace and her daugher, Jenny, in the hospital, Grace must find the true culprit before Jenny's life is once again in danger--and before her mute son is convicted for an arson he didn't commit.,

Lupton, Rosamund

Sister : a novel / Rosamund Lupton. Crown Publishers, 2011. 336 p.

ISBN 9780307716514

1. Grief 2. Sisters -- Death 3. Murder investigation 4. Hallucinogenic drug use 5. Stalkers 6. Suicide 7. Secrets 8. Extramarital affairs 9. Pregnant women 10. Medical research 11. Detectives 12. Compulsive behavior in women 13. Obsession 14. Stalking 15. London, England 16. Epistolary novels 17. Psychological suspense

LC 2010025327

Refusing to believe that her pregnant mercurial artist sister committed suicide, Beatrice begins an obsessive search for the truth and is dismissed by her family and authorities until she closes in on murderous predator.

"Murder mystery? Psychological thriller? Medical-ethical treatise? Yes to all, but so much more, too. Finally, the category doesn?t matter nearly as much as the fact that Lupton's remarkable debut novel is a masterful, superlative-inspiring success that will hook readers (and keep them guessing) from page one." Booklist.

Lurie, Alison

Foreign affairs / Alison Lurie. Random House, 1984. 291 p.

ISBN 039454076X

1. College teachers 2. Americans in London, England 3. Extramarital affairs 4. Middle-aged women -- Relations with younger men 5. Single men 6. London, England 7. England 8. Psychological fiction 9. Literary fiction

LC 84042657

Pulitzer Prize for Fiction, 1985.

National Book Award for Fiction finalist, 1984

National Book Critics Circle Award for Fiction finalist, 1984

Vinnie Miller, a professor of children's literature, and Fred Turner, an assistant professor at the same American university, pursue their separate affairs in London during the same six-month period

LIST OF FICTIONAL WORKS

Lutz, John, 1939-

Burn / John Lutz. H. Holt, 1995. 278 p. Fred Carver mysteries

ISBN 0805034803

1. Stalking 2. Real estate developers 3. Revenge 4. Family secrets 5. Private investigators 6. Detectives 7. Former police 8. People with disabilities 9. Stalkers 10. Florida 11. Mysteries

LC 94032187

Disabled Florida private detective Fred Carver takes on the case of Joel Brandt, a man accused of stalking a woman he claims he has never met and who has become convinced that he is being set up for a kill

"This mystery, in which the motive isn't greed or passion but rather grief and loss, is one of the best in a fine series." Booklist.

Lutz, John, 1939-

Final seconds / John Lutz and David August. Kensington, 1998. 316 p.

ISBN 1575662590

1. Criminal profiling 2. Former FBI agents 3. Bombings 4. Serial murderers 5. Bomb squads 6. Former police 7. New York City 8. Thrillers and suspense

Will Harper, pensioned off by the NYPD Bomb Squad, goes back to work when a letter bomb kills his former partner. Harper hooks up with a former FBI profiler named Alderman and the two try to connect the bombings to seemingly unrelated incidents involving celebrities.

"The most welcome realism in the book comes from the authors' resistance to the far-fetched elements that creep into many thrillers. Their seamless collaboration is notable for the efficiency of the plotting and for the unusual credibility of the story, its characters and the methodical way they do their work." Publishers Weekly.

Lutz, John, 1939-

Lightning / John Lutz. H.Holt, 1996. 296 p. Fred Carver mysteries

ISBN 0805043799

1. Abortion clinic bombings 2. Extramarital affairs 3. Extremists 4. Private investigators 5. Former police 6. Detectives 7. Revenge 8. Florida 9. Mysteries

LC 9543273

Disabled Florida P.I. Fred Carver faces the most painful case of his career when his lover is injured in a bomb blast that kills two abortion clinic workers, and Carver must discover whether the bomb was the work of a religious zealot or a personal vendetta.

"Behind the intransigent and hackneyed rhetoric of both sides, Carver finds venality aplenty as he and Beth attempt to come to terms with their loss. Veteran novelist Lutz ties some nifty twists into his plot, which moves quickly towards a final deadly confrontation." Publishers Weekly.

Lutz, Lisa

Curse of the Spellmans / Lisa Lutz. Simon & Schuster, 2008. 320 p. Spellman files

ISBN 9781416532415

1. Family secrets 2. Family businesses 3. Women private investigators 4. Missing women 5. Sisters 6. Eccentric families 7. Dysfunctional families 8. Familial love 9. Spellman Investigations 10. San Francisco, California 11. Humorous stories 12. Mysteries

LC 2007021152

Sequel to: The Spellman Files (2007)

Izzy struggles to retain her private investigator's license after her fourth arrest., David's marriage to Petra, and Rae's teenage angst.

"Licensed P.I. Isabel Izzy Spellman has been arrested for the fourth time in two months, and no one from her oddball family of fellow investigators will bail her out. Her sister, Rae, has run over Izzy's fianc,

Inspector Henry Stone, during a driving lesson. The senior Spellmans have staged a disappearance, their term for a vacation where no one can reach them. To complicate Izzy's life further, a man with the suspiciously ordinary name of John Brown has moved next door, and she's absolutely positive he's up to no good. . . . Once again, Lutz treats readers to a madcap roller-coaster ride." Library Journal.

Lutz, Lisa

The **last** word : a Spellman novel / Lisa Lutz. Simon & Schuster, 2013. 339 p. Spellman files

ISBN 9781451686661

1. Surveillance 2. Dysfunctional families 3. Women private investigators 4. Secrets 5. Eccentric families 6. Family businesses 7. Family relationships 8. Spellman Investigations 9. San Francisco, California 10. Humorous stories 11. Mysteries

This volume was issued as a (pbk.) in 2014 under the title Spellman six: the next generation.

Targeted by the members of her dysfunctional family for control over Spellman Investigations after staging a retaliatory takeover, Izzy is wrongly accused of embezzling funds from a wealthy Alzheimer's patient.

Lutz, Lisa

The **passenger** : a novel / Lisa Lutz. Simon & Schuster, 2016. ix, 303 p.

ISBN 9781451686630

1. Secrecy 2. Women fugitives 3. False personation 4. Widows 5. Survival 6. Deception 7. Manipulation by men 8. Loneliness in women 9. Men/women relations 10. Psychological suspense

She's left her dead husband -- and within forty-eight hours Tanya Dubois is a fugitive. It's almost impossible to live off the grid today, but Tanya-once-Amelia-now-Debra and Blue, a bartender, have the courage, the ingenuity, and the desperation, to try. Hopscotching from city to city, Debra especially is chased by a very dark secret ... can she outrun her past?

"Lutz develops riveting suspense by slowly revealing the events that first sent Tanya/Amelia on the run, while pouring threats on her gritty heroines increasingly tenuous bids at survival. Binge-worthy fare, especially for those drawn to strong female protagonists." Booklist.

Lutz, Lisa

Revenge of the Spellmans / Lisa Lutz. Simon & Schuster, 2009. 375 p. Spellman files

ISBN 9781416593386

1. Surveillance 2. Family businesses 3. Women private investigators 4. Extortion 5. Psychotherapy 6. Family relationships 7. Dysfunctional families 8. Spellman Investigations 9. San Francisco, California 10. Humorous stories 11. Mysteries

Isabel pursues therapy while trailing her newest client's errant wife, Rae faces skyrocketing expectations in light of her high SAT score, and Henry disrupts the family with a new love interest.

"Those in the market for mayhem and mirth will revel in Lutz's irresistible blend of suspense, irony, and wit." Booklist.

Lutz, Lisa

The **swallows** : a novel / Lisa Lutz. Ballantine Books, 2019. 416 p.

ISBN 9781984818232

1. 2000s (Decade) 2. Private schools 3. Misogyny 4. Entitlement attitudes 5. Creative writing teachers 6. Boarding school students 7. Student secret societies 8. Sexism 9. Sexual harassment victims 10. Social conflict 11. Revenge 12. Secrets 13. Teachers 14. Patriarchy

15. New England 16. Black humor 17. Thrillers and suspense

LC 2019011519

When a creative writing assignment leads to unsettling allegations about her school's indifference to sexual assault, a new teacher organizes a group of marginalized girls in an escalating gender war.

Lutz, Lisa

The **Spellman** files : a novel / Lisa Lutz. Simon & Schuster, 2007. 368 p. Spellman files

ISBN 1416532390

1. Missing persons 2. Women private investigators 3. Cold cases (Criminal investigation) 4. Sisters 5. Familial love 6. Eccentric families 7. Dysfunctional families 8. Spellman Investigations 9. San Francisco, California 10. Humorous stories 11. Mysteries

LC 2006049161

Sequel: Curse of the Spellmans (2008).

Isabel "Izzy" Spellman, a San Francisco private eye with a checkered past, has been working for her family's firm, Spellman Investigations, since age 12. Now 28, Izzy thinks she wants out of the family business, but elects to take on a cold case while dealing with her 14-year-old sister Rae, a nightmarish Nancy Drew, and parents who have no qualms about bugging their children's bedrooms. When Rae suddenly disappears, Izzy and her family must learn some serious lessons in order to find her.

Lyndon, Robert

Hawk quest / Robert Lyndon. Redhook, 2013, c2012. 658 p.

ISBN 9780316219563

1. Medieval period (476-1492) 2. 11th century 3. Quests 4. Warriors 5. Ransom 6. Hawks 7. Battles 8. Voyages and travels 9. Civilization, Medieval 10. Interpersonal relations 11. Men/women relations 12. Historical fiction 13. Adventure stories

LC bl2013013664

"Originally published in Great Britain in 2012 by Sphere"--T.p. verso.

Following the conquest of 1072, English soldier Vallon encounters Viking warlords, Arctic seas, and other obstacles in his quest to capture four rare hawks in order to secure the release of a Norman knight who has been captured by Turks.

Lyon, Annabel, 1971-

The **sweet** girl / Annabel Lyon. Alfred A. Knopf, 2013, c2012. 235 p.

ISBN 9780307962553

1. Aristotle 2. Alexander,, the Great, 356-323 BC 3. Ancient Greece (800 BCE-640 CE) 4. Philosophers -- Ancient Greece 5. Curiosity in teenage girls 6. Thought and thinking 7. Intelligence 8. Logic 9. Teenage girls 10. Fathers and daughters 11. Macedonia, Greece 12. Ancient Greece -- History -- Macedonian expansion, 359-323 BC 13. Historical fiction 14. Literary fiction

Although this is a follow-up to Lyon's The golden mean, it can be read as a stand-alone.

Originally published : Toronto: Random House Canada, 2012.

Resisting the social mores imposed on women in fourth century B.C., Pythias, the daughter of Aristotle, is forced to flee Athens with her family after the death of Alexander the Great and discovers a hostile world of superstition that forces her to test the boundaries of her father's logical methods and her own sharp wits.

Lyons, Jenn, 1970-

The **name** of all things / Jenn Lyons. Tor Books, 2019. 587 p. Chorus of dragons

ISBN 9781250175533

1. Nobility 2. Dragons 3. Prophecies 4. Fugitives 5. Wizards 6. Insurgency 7. Gods and goddesses 8. Demons 9. Magic 10. Magic rocks 11. Adventure 12. Power (Social sciences) 13. Manipulation (Social sciences) 14. Blizzards 15. Epic fantasy

A sequel to *The Ruin of Kings* finds a fugitive Kihrin navigating a secret rebellion and a formidable dragon to help a mysterious Joratese woman prevent the wizard Relos Var from obtaining an artifact of extraordinary power.

Lyons, Jenn, 1970-

The **ruin** of kings / Jenn Lyons. Tor, 2019. 560 p. Chorus of dragons

ISBN 9781250175489

1. Prisoners 2. Political intrigue 3. Power (Social sciences) 4. Nobility 5. Family secrets 6. Conspiracies 7. Quests 8. Imaginary creatures 9. Magic 10. Adventure 11. Epic fantasy

LC 2018045774

"A Tom Doherty Associates book."

Raised on storybook tales of royal adventure, Kihrin discovers his identity as the illegitimate son of a treasonous prince and is rendered a pawn in the royal family's power schemes before embracing his anti-hero destiny.

"Although a cast of well-developed characters and an impressively intricate storyline power this novel, it's Lyons' audacious worldbuilding that makes for such an unforgettable read." Kirkus.

M

Ma, Jian, 1953-

Beijing coma / Ma Jian, Flora Drew. Farrar, Straus and Giroux, 2008. 592 p.

ISBN 9780374110178

1. 1980s 2. Political activists 3. Social change 4. Change (Psychology) 5. People in comas 6. Freedom 7. Medical students 8. Disillusionment 9. Communism 10. Tiananmen Square Massacre, Beijing, China, June 3-4, 1989 11. Prodemocracy movement (China) 12. China -- History -- 20th century 13. Historical fiction 14. Translations -- Chinese to English

LC 2008925628

First published in Great Britain by Chatto & Windus, 2008.

Dai Wei lies in his bedroom, a prisoner in his body, after he was shot in the head at the Tiananmen Square protest ten years earlier and left in a coma. As his mother tends to him, and his friends bring news of their lives in an almost unrecognisable China, Dai Wei escapes into his memories.

"A valuable work. Ma's writing can be lively, and his use of dialogue that embraces everyday chitchat gives the book a sense of reality. The idealism of youth is ably captured. Indeed, the students' frequently lofty and at times naive emotions are touching." The New Leader.

Ma, Jian, 1953-

China dream / Ma Jian ; translated from the Chinese by Flora Drew. Counterpoint, 2019. 176 p.

ISBN 9781640092402

1. Politicians 2. Totalitarianism 3. Dreams 4. Social change 5. Mistresses 6. Rich people 7. Deception 8. Memories 9. Consequences

10. China -- Social conditions 11. Political fiction 12. Satirical fiction
LC 2018057990

"First published in the United Kingdom by Chatto & Windus in 2018."

One of the year's most anticipated novels in translation, written by an acclaimed Chinese author whose entire body of work has been banned by his home country, and published in the thirtieth-anniversary year of the Tiananmen Square Massacre.

Ma, Jian, 1953-

Stick out your tongue / Ma Jian ; translated from the Chinese by Flora Drew. Farrar, Straus and Giroux, 2006. 104 p.
ISBN 9780374269883

1. Voyages and travels 2. Authors, Chinese 3. Burial 4. Rites and ceremonies 5. Funerals 6. Tragedy 7. Child sexual abuse 8. Family violence 9. Voyages and travels 10. Tibet 11. China 12. Short stories 13. Translations -- Chinese to English
LC 2006004282

Traveling to Tibet after the failing of his marriage, a Chinese writer witnesses the sky burial of a woman who died in childbirth, shares a tent with a nomad who is seeking forgiveness for incest, and hears the story of a young woman incarnate lama who died during a Buddhist initiation rite.

"In an afterword, the author notes that his work is controversial among both Tibetans and Chinese. Given their dark and explicitly disturbing nature, these stories will not be appreciated by all readers. But those who have read Xinran's Sky Burial will recognize the irony of hardship placed upon the human spirit set against the striking beauty offered by the Tibetan landscape." Library Journal.

Ma, Ling, 1983-

Severance / Ling Ma. Farrar, Straus and Giroux, 2018 291 p.
ISBN 9780374261597

1. 2010s 2. Children of immigrants 3. Survival (after epidemics) 4. End of the world 5. Chinese Americans 6. Capitalism 7. Habit 8. Young women 9. Epidemics 10. Bloggers 11. Boredom 12. New York City 13. Apocalyptic fiction 14. Satirical fiction
LC 2017038340

Kirkus Prize for Fiction, 2018.

A survivor of an apocalyptic plague maintains a blog about a decimated Manhattan before joining a motley group of survivors to search for a place to rebuild, a goal that is complicated by an unscrupulous group leader.

Maalouf, Amin

Balthasar's odyssey : a novel / Amin Maalouf ; translated from the French by Barbara Bray. Arcade Pub. : 2002. 400 p.
ISBN 155970666X

1. 17th century 2. Quests 3. Rare books 4. Voyages and travels 5. Exiles 6. Merchants 7. Europe -- History -- 17th century 8. Historical fiction 9. Picaresque fiction 10. Translations -- French to English
LC 2002074630

Translated from the French title, Periple de Baldassare.

Shortlisted for the International IMPAC Dublin Literary Award, 2004

In 1665, with prophecies and portents fortelling the forthcoming Apocalypse, Balthasar, an antiquarian merchant and sage, embarks on a perilous quest to find a rare book that could hold the key to the world's salvation.

Maalouf, Amin

Leo Africanus / Amin Maalouf ; translated by Peter Sluglett W. W. Norton, 1989, c1986. 360 p.
ISBN 1561310220

1. Leo Africanus, 1485?-1554? 2. Renaissance (1300-1600) 3. 16th century 4. Geographers -- History -- 16th century 5. Arabs 6. European Renaissance 7. Mediterranean region -- History -- 16th century 8. Travelers 9. Biographical fiction 10. Historical fiction 11. Translations -- French to English
LC 88018027

"This historical novel recreates the era when the Moors were expelled from Spain, and much of North Africa and southern Europe was in turmoil. Hassan al-Wazzan was just a child the year Columbus sailed to the New World. . . . The gradual exile of Hassan's family from Spain is developed through recollections of his proud, erring father, his badly treated mother and her diplomat brother. As a merchant and emissary, Hassan travels from Fez to Cairo to Mecca and--by misadventure--to Rome and the Vatican, where he is later renamed Leo Africanus." Publishers Weekly.

Maaren, Kari, 1975-

* **Weave** a circle round / Kari Maaren Tor, 2017. 336 p.
ISBN 9780765386281

1. Misfits (Persons) 2. Time travel (Past) 3. High school students 4. Chaos 5. Neighbors 6. Immortalism 7. Teenage girls 8. Gifted children 9. Order (Philosophy) 10. Brothers and sisters 11. People who are deaf 12. Gateway fantasy 13. Fantasy fiction

When she runs afoul of her eccentric new neighbors, teen Freddy is sent traveling through time where she encounters numerous versions of her neighbors, Josiah and Cuerva, and she realizes that she might be the third in their group of immortals.

"This is an ambitious, intricate, joyful coming-of-age tale, with memorable characters and a powerful sense of wonder." Publishers Weekly.

Mabanckou, Alain, 1966-

* **Black** Moses / Alain Mabanckou ; translated from the French by Helen Stevenson. The New Press, 2017, c2015. 199 p.
ISBN 9781620972939

1. Boy orphans 2. Self-discovery 3. Survival 4. Escapes 5. Gangs 6. Orphanages 7. Port cities 8. Crime 9. Thieves 10. Corruption 11. Political persecution 12. Teenagers with mental illnesses 13. Congo (Brazzaville) 14. Literary fiction 15. Political fiction 16. Satirical fiction 17. Coming-of-age stories 18. Translations -- French to English

Originally published: Paris : Editions Seuil, 2015.

Hurston/Wright Legacy Award: Fiction, 2018.

Three orphans in 1970s Africa escape their orphanage to the busy port town of Pointe-Noire where they form a gang of petty thieves and become part of the underworld.

"A small book with a big narrative voice, this wacky new novel by Mabanckou follows the existential misfortunes of an orphan whose kilometrically extended name means Thanks be to God, the black Moses is born on the earth of our ancestors.... This mythic, beguiling novel is a journey to discover what is hard-wired in us and what we make up about ourselves." Publishers Weekly.

MacAlister, Katie

The **truth** about Leo / Katie MacAlister. Sourcebooks, 2014. 352 p. Nobles
ISBN 9781402294457

1. Regency period (1811-1820) 2. Princesses 3. Spies 4. Attempted murder 5. Marriage 6. Men/women relations 7. Wealth 8. Voyages

and travels 9. England -- History -- 19th century 10. Denmark -- History -- 19th century 11. Regency romances 12. Historical romances

When she finds Leopold Ernst George Mortimer, defender of the Crown and spy in the service of the King--who, left for dead, has lost his memory--Marie Sophie, impoverished Danish royalty, convinces him that they are husband and wife in an attempt to leave the country and avoid an arranged marriage.

MacBride, Stuart

Blind eye / Stuart MacBride. Minotaur Books, 2009. 528 p. Logan McRae mysteries

ISBN 9780312382643

1. Assault and battery 2. Immigrants 3. Organized crime 4. Violence 5. Gangs 6. Witnesses 7. Pedophiles 8. Crime bosses 9. Police -- Scotland 10. Scotland 11. Aberdeen, Scotland 12. Mysteries 13. Police procedurals

LC 2009021058

It's summer in the Granite City and Aberdeen's growing Polish community is under attack from a serial offender. Detective Sergeant Logan McRae is assigned to the investigation, but with the victims too scared to talk, it's going nowhere fast. When the next victim is bookie, Logan finds himself caught up in a world of drug wars, prostitution rings and gun-running, courtesy of Aberdeen's oldest and most vicious crime lord.

MacBride, Stuart

Close to the bone / Stuart MacBride. HarperCollins, 2013. 438 p. Logan McRae mysteries

ISBN 9780007344260

1. Detectives -- Scotland 2. Police -- Scotland 3. Serial murder investigation 4. Serial murderers 5. Witchcraft 6. Gangs 7. Missing persons 8. Racism 9. Immigrants 10. Scotland 11. Aberdeen, Scotland 12. Mysteries 13. Police procedurals

Detective Inspector Logan McRae is finally getting back on his feet after the events of the last few years. Putting things behind him. Getting better. But it was never going to last. A body turns up on the outskirts of Aberdeen: burned from the neck up, hands chained behind the back. More murders follow all-- gruesome, and with only one obvious connection. The similarities between the real-life killings and the plot of a bestselling novel about witchcraft seem more than coincidental, but the more Logan digs the more dangerous and blurred the line between fact and fiction becomes. It's a small step from police officer to victim. And somebody's got to take it, or everyone will die.

MacBride, Stuart

* Cold granite / Stuart MacBride. St. Martin's Minotaur, 2005. 464 p. Logan McRae mysteries

ISBN 031233995X

1. Police 2. Child murders 3. Serial murders 4. Detectives 5. Crimes against children 6. Serial murder investigation 7. Aberdeen, Scotland 8. Scotland 9. Mysteries 10. Police procedurals

LC 2005042780

Returning to duty after recovering from being stabbed by a murder suspect, Detective Sergeant Logan McRae becomes involved in the ritualistic murder of a three-year-old boy, whose body is found months after being reported missing.

MacBride, Stuart

Dying light / Stuart MacBride. St. Martin's Minotaur, 2006. 448 p. Logan McRae mysteries

ISBN 9780312339975

1. Crimes against prostitutes 2. Police 3. Arson 4. Detectives 5. Murder 6. Violence against women 7. Organized crime 8. Murder investigation 9. Arson investigation 10. Men/women relations 11. Serial murderers 12. Aberdeen, Scotland 13. Mysteries 14. Police procedurals

LC 2006043700

Detective Sergeant Logan MacRae has been bumped to the "Screw-up Squad," a team made up of the most worthless or inexperienced members of the homicide department, and Logan will do anything to prove he doesn't belong there. Including working overtime on two baffling cases: the murder by arson of six people, and the beating to death of a prostitute down by the docks, not a high priority compared to the fire. At least not until another prostitute ends up dead. Although both cases seem simple on the surface--turns out the fire's victims are part of a drug dealer's inner circle, and what fate is to be expected for working girls in Aberdeen's red-light district?--in Stuart MacBride's hands, what's going on in this rainy Scottish city is bound to be much more complicated than it appears.--From publisher description.

MacBride, Stuart

Flesh house / Stuart MacBride. St. Martin's Minotaur, 2008. 467 p. Logan McRae mysteries

ISBN 9780312382636

1. Detectives 2. Cannibalism 3. Violence 4. Police 5. Detectives 6. Serial murders 7. Serial murder investigation 8. Former convicts 9. Breaking up (Interpersonal relations) 10. Stress 11. Aberdeen, Scotland 12. Scotland 13. Mysteries 14. Police procedurals

LC 2008023605

When body parts are discovered in a container at the Aberdeen harbor, police suspect the involvement of Kenneth Wiseman, a vicious killer acquitted on a technicality, sending detective Logan McRae on a feverish quest through two decades of secrets to find a killer.

MacBride, Stuart

Shatter the bones / Stuart MacBride. HarperCollins, 2011. 438 p. Logan McRae mysteries

ISBN 9780007344222

1. Kidnapping investigation 2. Detectives -- Scotland 3. Police -- Scotland 4. Kidnapping 5. Ransom 6. Scotland 7. Aberdeen, Scotland 8. Mysteries 9. Police procedurals

Originally published: London : Harper, 2011.

Alison and Jenny McGregor-- Aberdeen's own mother-daughter singing sensation-- are through to the semi-finals of TV smash-hit Britain's Next Big Star. But their reality-TV dream turns into a real-life nightmare when a ransom demand appears in all the papers, on TV, and the internet, telling the nation to dig deep if they want to keep them alive. Time is running out --and DS Logan McRae and his colleagues have nothing to go on ...

MacDonald, Andrew (Andrew David)

* When we were Vikings / Andrew David MacDonald. Gallery Books, 2020. 336 p.

ISBN 9781982126766

1. Vikings 2. Brothers and sisters 3. Fetal alcohol syndrome 4. Obsession 5. Twenties (Age) 6. Guardian and ward 7. Protectiveness in women 8. Communities 9. Families 10. Men/women relations 11. Coming-of-age stories

When 21-year-old Viking enthusiast Zelda finds out that her older brother, Gert, has resorted to some questionable--and dangerous--methods to make enough money to keep them afloat, Zelda decides to launch her own quest.

"MacDonald avoids oversentimentality and a too-neat resolution, instead depicting Zelda's desire to shape her own life and be the hero of her own legend with frankness and humor." Publishers Weekly.

MacDonald, John D. (John Dann), 1916-1986

Cinnamon skin : the twentieth adventure of Travis McGee / John D. MacDonald. Harper & Row, 1982. 275 p. Travis McGee novels

ISBN 0060149906

1. Terrorists 2. Bombings 3. Private investigators 4. Murder 5. Chases 6. Nieces -- Death 7. Serial murderers 8. Male friendship 9. Attempted murder 10. Murder investigation 11. Men/women relations 12. Fort Lauderdale, Florida 13. Rio Grande Valley 14. Texas 15. Mexico 16. Mysteries

LC 81048159

Travis McGee investigates the explosion of a cruise boat in the Florida Keys, supposedly the work of a Chilean underground organization.

"Travis McGee and his friend Meyer search for Meyer's niece's new husband, who has killed his wife and faked his own death in an explosion. The search is plodding and long, but MacDonald makes it interesting through the diverse and lively characters involved. The showdown, on Mexico's Yucatn Peninsula, is a bit slow but colorful and original." Library Journal.

MacDonald, John D. (John Dann), 1916-1986

The **green** ripper / John D. MacDonald. Lippincott, 1979. 221 p. Travis McGee novels

ISBN 0891907793

1. Cults 2. Terrorists 3. Private investigators 4. Murder 5. Chases 6. Revenge 7. Impostors 8. Fanaticism 9. Secret identity 10. Murder investigation 11. Men/women relations 12. Undercover operations 13. Women murder victims 14. Fort Lauderdale, Florida 15. California 16. Mysteries

LC 79012063

Beautiful girls always grace the Florida beaches, strolling, sailing, relaxing at the many parties on Travis McGee's houseboat, The Busted Flush. McGee was too smart--and had been around too long--for many of them to touch his heart. Now, however, there was Gretel. She had discovered the key to McGee--to all of him--and now he had something to hope for. Then, terribly, unexpectedly, she was dead. From a mysterious illness, or so they said. But McGee knew the truth, that Gretel had been murdered. And now he was out for blood...

"MacDonald is unsurpassed at showing the American brand of loneliness. He catches foibles in a phrase and gives us many-sided, wounded but courageous, characters." Booklist.

MacDonald, John D. (John Dann), 1916-1986

* The **lonely** silver rain / John D. MacDonald. A.A. Knopf, 1985. 231 p. Travis McGee novels

ISBN 0394538994

1. 1970s 2. Middle-aged men 3. Cocaine smuggling 4. Private investigators 5. Yachts 6. Murder 7. Revenge 8. Family reunions 9. Organized crime 10. Trusts and trustees 11. Murder investigation 12. Father and adult daughter 13. Fort Lauderdale, Florida 14. Miami, Florida 15. Mysteries

LC 84023373

Someone is trying to kill Travis McGee, someone linked to southern Florida's drug traffickers--either Miami's old-time underworld or the new generation of Latino drug barons--and in order to save his own life, McGee must detonate a drug war.

MacDonald, John D. (John Dann), 1916-1986

The **long** lavender look / John D. MacDonald. Lippincott, 1972, c1970. 264 p. Travis McGee novels

ISBN 0397007396

1. Police misconduct 2. Private investigators 3. Malicious accusation 4. Murder 5. Secrets 6. Violence 7. Rescues 8. Revenge 9. Murder suspects 10. Traffic accidents 11. Male friendship 12. Murder investigation 13. Men/women relations 14. Assault and battery 15. Police brutality 16. Fort Lauderdale, Florida 17. Everglades, Florida 18. Mysteries

LC 78037010

Featuring an introduction by best-selling author, Carl Hiaasen, another colorful adventure sends freewheeling detective Travis McGee on the trail of millions and murder in a deadly Florida town.

MacDonald, John D. (John Dann), 1916-1986

A **purple** place for dying / John D. MacDonald. Lippincott, 1976, c1964. 204 p. Travis McGee novels

ISBN 0449224384

1. 1960s 2. Snipers 3. Deserts 4. Private investigators 5. Murder 6. Married women 7. Marital conflict 8. Trusts and trustees 9. Murder investigation 10. Extramarital affairs 11. Love triangles 12. Fort Lauderdale, Florida 13. Nevada 14. Mysteries

LC 76004096

While on vacation in the Southwest, Travis McGee reluctantly agrees to help Mona Yeoman retrieve her estate from a wayward husband, only to become an eyewitness to her sudden death.

"Travis McGee is pondering whether to take on the beautiful Mona Yeoman as a client when someone decides for him by shooting her in the back and hiding the body. Mona's husband soon dies of poison, and the killers might have been in the clear if they had not tried to add McGee (and one of those lovely women he always attracts) to their list. The usual literate and fast-paced stuff expected from MacDonald." Booklist.

MacDonald, John D. (John Dann), 1916-1986

The **scarlet** ruse / John D. MacDonald. Lippincott & Crowell, 1980, c1973. 262 p. Travis McGee novels

ISBN 0690018878

1. 1970s 2. Stamp thefts 3. Private investigators 4. Counterfeits and counterfeiting 5. Murderers 6. Senior men 7. Stamp collecting 8. Organized crime 9. Criminal investigation 10. Men/women relations 11. Fort Lauderdale, Florida 12. Mysteries

LC 79024843

Travis McGee agrees to investigate a case involving a rare-stamps swindle and finds himself confronting death, deception, a tantalizing affair, and an ambush aboard a houseboat aground at No Name Island.

MacDonald, John D. (John Dann), 1916-1986

The **turquoise** lament / John D. MacDonald. Lippincott, 1973. 287 p. Travis McGee novels

ISBN 0397009879

1. Private investigators 2. Attempted murder 3. Wife-killing 4. Suspicion 5. Fear in women 6. Treasure hunting 7. Husband and wife 8. Women with mental illnesses 9. Men/women relations 10. Fort Lauderdale, Florida 11. Hawaii 12. Mysteries

LC 73014806

Believing either that her husband is out to kill her or that she is insane, Pidge Brindle contacts a friend of her late father for help.

"One of the best McGee adventures." Publishers Weekly.

MacDonald, Philip

The **list** of Adrian Messenger / Philip MacDonald. Vintage Books, 1983, c1959. 224 p. Anthony Gethryn mysteries

ISBN 0394717120

1. Scotland Yard 2. Murder investigation 3. Detectives 4. Lists 5. Airplane accidents 6. Murder suspects 7. Amateur detectives 8. England 9. Mysteries

LC 83005806

"An Anthony Gethryn mystery"--Cover.

Reprint. Originally published: 1st ed. Garden City, N.Y. : Published for the Crime Club by Doubleday, 1959.

"If some readers find Mr. MacDonald's style a bit stiff and old-fashioned, they will also find that he provides such other old-fashioned elements as honest clues, characters who stick in the mind from page to page, an original idea, and, in Anthony Gethryn, a detective who inspires utter confidence." The New Yorker.

MacGregor, Janna

The **bride** who got lucky / Janna MacGregor. St Martin's Paperbacks, 2017. 352 p. Cavensham heiresses

ISBN 9781250116147

1. Regency period (1811-1820) 2. Nobility 3. Women's rights 4. Interpersonal attraction 5. Murder investigation 6. Men/women relations 7. Forgiveness 8. Forced marriage 9. Abusive men 10. London, England 11. England 12. Great Britain 13. Regency romances 14. Historical romances

After her best friend is murdered by her abusive husband, Lady Emma Cavensham, a women's rights activist, searches for evidence to put him behind bars and ends up in a compromising position that forces her into a marriage of convenience to a wife-averse earl.

MacInnes, Helen, 1907-1985

Prelude to terror / Helen MacInnes. Titan Books, 2013, c1978. 432 p.

ISBN 9781781163368

1. Art -- Collectors and collecting 2. Terrorism 3. Thrillers and suspense

LC 78053888

Originally published: New York : Harcourt Brace Jovanovich, 1978.

Flying to Vienna to purchase at auction a painting whose present owner is a Hungarian planning defection, art consultant Colin Grant finds himself the key piece in a conspiracy of fraud, kidnapping, murder, and wholesale international terror

MacInnes, Helen, 1907-1985

Ride a pale horse / Helen MacInnes. Titan Books, 2013, c1984. 429 p.

ISBN 9781781163382

1. International intrigue 2. Thrillers and suspense

LC 84009037

First published: London, Collins, 1984.

Weaves a web of suspense and intrigue, as Washington journalist Karen Cornell, assigned to cover an international peace convention in Prague, becomes caught up in an adventure of political assassination and murder

"The device of dual protagonists moves the plot along smartly, and the demonstration of the insidious uses of disinformation could hardly be more timely." Booklist.

MacInnes, Helen, 1907-1985

The **Venetian** affair / Helen MacInnes. Titan Books, 2012, c1963. 483 p.

ISBN 9781781163306

1. CIA 2. NATO 3. International intrigue 4. Venice, Italy 5. Spy fiction

LC 63017774

Originally published: New York : Harcourt, Brace & World, 1963.

While on assignment in Paris and Venice, an American journalist works desperately to expose Communist espionage activities... Fenner burned Rosenfeld's message, reminding himself wryly that he was be-

having in the very best tradition. This was a game not too difficult to learn, he thought. A game? A game in deadly earnest.

MacKenzie, Sally

Bedding Lord Ned / Sally Mackenzie. Zebra Books, 2012. 352 p. Duchess of Love

ISBN 9781420123210

1. Regency period (1811-1820) 2. Widowers 3. Single women 4. Aristocracy 5. Interpersonal attraction 6. Men/women relations 7. Sexuality 8. Greed 9. Jealousy 10. Matchmaking 11. London, England -- History -- 19th century 12. England -- Social life and customs -- 19th century 13. Great Britain -- History -- Regency, 1811-1820 14. Regency romances 15. Historical romances

Miss Ellie Bowman, who is determined to find a husband, attends a ball thrown by the Duchess of Greycliffe, where she only has eyes for the duchess's dashing son Ned, who long ago captured her heart and roused her desire.

MacLaughlin, Nina

Wake, siren : Ovid resung / Nina MacLaughlin. FSG/Farrar, Straus and Giroux, 2019. x, 342 p.

ISBN 9780374538583

1. Ovid, 43 BC-17 or 18 AD Metamorphoses 2. Metamorphosis -- Mythology 3. Mythology, Classical 4. Heroes and heroines 5. Women -- Mythology 6. Short stories 7. Adaptations, retellings, and spin-offs

The women of Ovid's Metamorphoses claim their stories and challenge the power of myth.

MacLaverty, Bernard

Midwinter break / Bernard MacLaverty. W. W. Norton & Company, 2017. 243 p.

ISBN 9780393609622

1. Catholic Church 2. Senior couples 3. Vacations 4. Marital conflict 5. Faith (Christianity) 6. Belief and doubt 7. Cynicism 8. Devotedness 9. Marriage 10. Memories 11. Alcoholic men 12. Irish in Europe 13. Amsterdam, Netherlands 14. Domestic fiction 15. Literary fiction

LC 2017015733

Shortlisted for the International Dublin Literary Award, 2019.

A retired couple struggling with his dogmatic forgetfulness and her religious faith attempt to repair their marriage during a vacation in Amsterdam, where they confront painful memories of a troubled time in their native Ireland.

MacLean, Sarah

* **Brazen** and the Beast / Sarah MacLean. Avon Books, 2019. 400 p. Bareknuckle bastards

ISBN 9780062912978

1. Single women 2. Independence in women 3. Swindlers and swindling 4. Brothers 5. Secrets 6. Deals 7. Business competition 8. Men/women relations 9. Interpersonal attraction 10. England -- Social life and customs -- 19th century 11. Historical romances

Henrietta Sedley, who wants to take over her father's shipping company but is passed over in favor of her roguish brother, indulges in a night of passion with a king of smugglers known as Beast, only to find their fates linked.

MacLean, Sarah

Never judge a lady by her cover / Sarah MacLean. Avon Books, 2014. 376 p. Rules of scoundrels

ISBN 9780062068514

1. Regency period (1811-1820) 2. Casinos 3. Secret identity 4. Nobility 5. Single mothers 6. Scandals 7. Newspaper publishers and publishing 8. Secrets 9. Interpersonal attraction 10. Treason 11. Reputation 12. Men/women relations 13. England -- Social life and customs -- 19th century 14. London, England -- Social life and customs -- 19th century 15. Regency romances 16. Historical romances

Lady Georgiana's secret identity as Chase, the founder of London's worst gaming hell, is threatened by Duncan West, who is intrigued by the mysterious beauty and determines to uncover all of her dark secrets.

"Brilliant, seductive, and intensely engaging, this addictive story pairs powerful, driven protagonists with a seemingly unsolvable dilemma in an ingenious, wonderfully satisfying conclusion to MacLean's remarkable quartet." Library Journal.

MacLean, Sarah

No good duke goes unpunished / Sarah MacLean. Avon Books, 2013. 384 p. Rules of scoundrels

ISBN 9780062068545

1. Regency period (1811-1820) 2. Dukes and duchesses 3. Murder suspects 4. Scandals 5. Casinos 6. Missing women 7. Redemption 8. Men/women relations 9. England -- Social life and customs -- 19th century 10. London, England -- Social life and customs -- 19th century 11. Regency romances 12. Historical romances

RITA Award for Best Historical Romance, 2014.

When her brother gets deep in debt to Temple, a disgraced duke who now owns an exclusive casino, Mara Lowe agrees to come forward and clear Temple, who has been accused of her murder, if he will forgive what her brother owes him.

"MacLean once again creates compelling and complex characters and sets them on a path toward love and reconciliation that begins with seemingly impossible odds and ends with exquisite fulfillment." Kirkus.

MacLean, Sarah

One good earl deserves a lover / Sarah MacLean. Avon, 2013. 384 p. Rules of scoundrels

ISBN 9780062068538

1. Regency period (1811-1820) 2. Engagement 3. Aristocracy 4. Social science research 5. Sex customs 6. Desire 7. Eccentric women 8. Sexual attraction 9. Womanizers 10. Earls and countesses 11. Men/women relations 12. England -- Social life and customs -- 19th century 13. London, England -- Social life and customs -- 19th century 14. Regency romances 15. Historical romances

Pippa -- formally known as Lady Philippa Marbury -- is a brainy bluestocking who'd rather devote her energies to scientific inquiry than to maintaining her position in society. Betrothed to a kind but dim-witted earl, Pippa realizes that she has no idea what to expect on her wedding night. After receiving numerous evasive answers from her female relations, Pippa takes matters into her own hands and approaches her brother-in-law's business partner, Cross, the notorious owner of an exclusive gaming hell. Shocked but intrigued by Pippa's boldness, Cross (ever the gambler) makes an unusual wager with her, certain that he'll prevail and simultaneously prevent her ruin. But even if Cross wins the bet, he may lose his heart to Pippa. - Description by Gillian Speace.

MacLean, Sarah

A **rogue** by any other name / Sarah MacLean. Avon Books, 2012. 384 p. Rules of scoundrels

ISBN 9780062068521

1. Regency period (1811-1820) 2. 1830s 3. 1820s 4. Gambling 5. Nobility 6. Inheritance and succession 7. Revenge 8. Letter writing 9. Men/women relations 10. Interpersonal attraction 11. England -- Social life and customs -- 19th century 12. London, England -- Social life and customs -- 19th century 13. Regency romances 14. Historical romances

RITA Award for Best Historical Romance, 2013.

Michael Lawler, Marquess of Bourne, loses his fortune on a bad bet and opens London's most notorious gaming hell, The Fallen Angel, in hopes of buying back his family estate, Falconwell. But Bourne can regain it even more quickly by marrying his childhood friend, Lady Penelope Marbury, the daughter of Falconwell's current owner (who sweetened Penelope's dowry with the estate to offset her reputation as "difficult"). Strong-willed Penelope soon proves to be Bourne's biggest gamble yet. -- Description by Gillian Speace.

MacLean, Sarah

The **rogue** not taken / Sarah MacLean. Avon Books, 2015. 432 p. Scandal & scoundrel

ISBN 9780062379412

1. Regency period (1811-1820) 2. Marquis and marchionesses 3. Pariahs 4. Womanizers 5. Scandals 6. Reputation 7. Stowaways 8. Misadventures 9. Nobility 10. Interpersonal attraction 11. Men/women relations 12. England -- Social life and customs -- 19th century 13. Great Britain -- History -- Regency, 1811-1820 14. Regency romances 15. Historical romances

After stowing away in the Marquess of Eversley's carriage to escape London and scandal, Lady Sophie Talbot must convince the Marquess that she is not trying to trick him into marriage as they try to resist their mutual attraction.

"Readers will be intoxicated by the emotional connection between the lovers, which makes their banter that much more amusing and their eventual physical passion that much more satisfying. Sophie's delightful family will leave readers eager for future installments in the series." Publishers Weekly.

MacLean, Sarah

* **Wicked** and the wallflower / Sarah MacLean. Avon Books, 2018. 360 p. Bareknuckle bastards

ISBN 9780062842640

1. Single women 2. Swindlers and swindling 3. Dishonesty 4. Dukes and duchesses 5. Mate selection 6. Deals 7. Revenge 8. Seduction 9. Manipulation (Social sciences) 10. Men/women relations 11. Interpersonal attraction 12. England -- History -- 19th century 13. Historical romances

Finding the perfect way to exact a revenge years in the making, Devil, bastard son of a duke and king of London's dark streets, offers to help Lady Felicity Faircloth land a suitable husband by transforming her into an irresistible temptress who will destroy his enemy.

MacNeal, Susan Elia

The **king's** justice / Susan Elia MacNeal. Bantam Books, 2020. 352 p. Maggie Hope mysteries

ISBN 9780399593840

1. Second World War era (1939-1945) 2. World War II home front 3. Intelligence service 4. Conscientious objectors 5. Serial murders 6. Serial murder investigation 7. Cryptography 8. Prisoners 9. Couples 10. City life 11. England -- History -- 20th century 12. Historical

mysteries

LC 2019038115

Secret agent and spy Maggie Hope, traumatized by her past and living dangerously, gets entangled in another crime when a stolen violin is linked to a serial killer terrorizing London during World War II.

"Irresistibly readable and brilliantly crafted, this is a story both historical mystery and fiction fans will adore." Library Journal.

Macdonald, Malcolm, 1932-

Tamsin Harte St. Martin's Press, 2000. 345 p.

ISBN 0312206283

1. 1900s (Decade) 2. Young women 3. Social classes 4. Boarding houses 5. Cornwall, England -- Social life and customs -- 20th century 6. England -- History -- 1900-1945 7. England -- Social life and customs -- 20th century 8. Historical fiction 9. Love stories

LC 99088104

Reduced to keeping a boarding house with her mother after the death of her father, Tamsin sees an opportunity to return to a life of ease if she can meet and win the affections of rich and eligible Victor Thorne

Macdonald, Malcolm, 1932-

The **Trevarton** inheritance / Malcolm Macdonald St. Martin's Press, 1995. 395 p.

ISBN 0312147481

1. Grandmother and child 2. Granddaughters 3. Orphans 4. Brothers and sisters 5. Cornwall, England -- Social life and customs -- 19th century 6. England -- Social life and customs -- 19th century 7. Historical fiction

LC 96-20035

After Chrissy Moore, her older sister, and her three younger brothers are orphaned, Chrissy works to find a way to keep the family fed and together, but some secret force is working to split them apart

Macdonald, Ross, 1915-1983

* The **underground** man / Ross Macdonald. Vintage Crime/Black Lizard, 1996, c1971. 273 p. Lew Archer novels

ISBN 0679768084

1. Fires 2. Missing persons investigation 3. Missing children 4. Private investigators 5. Secrets 6. Murder 7. Southern California 8. California 9. Mysteries

As a mysterious fire rages through the hills above a privileged town in Southern California, Lew Archer tracks a missing child who may be the pawn in a marital struggle or the victim of a bizarre kidnapping. What he uncovers amid the ashes is murder ? and a trail of motives as combustible as gasoline.

Macdonald, Ross, 1915-1983

* The **drowning** pool / Ross Macdonald. Vintage Crime/ Black Lizard, 1996, c1950. 244 p. Lew Archer novels

ISBN 0679768068

1. Private investigators 2. Mysteries

Originally published: New York : Knopf, 1950.

When a millionaire matriarch is found floating face down in the family pool, the prime suspects are her good-for-nothing son and his seductive teenage daughter. In The Drowning Pool, Lew Archer takes this case in the Los Angeles suburbs and encounters a moral wasteland of corporate greed and family hatred--and sufficient motive for a dozen murders.

Macdonald, Ross, 1915-1983

* The **far** side of the dollar / Ross Macdonald. Knopf, 1965 247 p. Lew Archer novels

ISBN 0679768653

1. Private investigators 2. Mysteries

LC 65010103

Gold Dagger Award for Best Crime Novel of the Year, 1965.

To reach the Barcelona Hotel you took Sunset and the coast highway. Once starlets and Navy boys had rubbed shoulders with tycoons and hustlers there, but for Lew Archer the old, closed-up palace held the key to a missing teenager and a hot murder. Archer knew that twenty years ago a handful of dreamers and losers had come together in the barcelona. The only question now was what kind of deal had gone down there, and why a mixed-up rich kid and a beautiful blonde were the first to pay the price ...

Macdonald, Ross, 1915-1983

* The **Galton** case / Ross Macdonald. Warner Books, 1990, c1959. 198 p. Lew Archer novels

ISBN 0679768645

1. Private investigators 2. California 3. Mysteries

Almost twenty years have passed since Anthony Galton disappeared, along with a suspiciously streetwise bride and several thousand dollars of his family's fortune. Now Anthony's aging and very rich mother wants him back and has hired Lew Archer to find him. What turns up is a headless skeleton, a boy who claims to be Galton's son, and a con game whose stakes are so high that someone is still willing to kill for them.

Macdonald, Ross, 1915-1983

The **goodbye** look, Ross Macdonald. Vintage Books, 2000, c1969. 243 p. Lew Archer novels

ISBN 0375708650

1. Private investigators 2. Rich people 3. California 4. Mysteries

LC 78308610

Ross Macdonald is the pseudonym of Kenneth Millar.

Originally published: New York : Alfred A. Knopf, 1969.

In searching for a gun used to commit two murders fifteen years apart, Lew Archer is introduced to California hobos and the nouveau riche in his attempt to solve the murder of another private eye.

Macdonald, Ross, 1915-1983

Sleeping beauty / Ross Macdonald. Vintage Books, 2000, c1973. 271 p. Lew Archer novels

ISBN 0375708669

1. Private investigators 2. Rich people 3. Missing persons -- California 4. Extortion -- California 5. Murder -- California 6. California 7. Mysteries

LC 72011037

Originally published: New York : Alfred A. Knopf, 1973.

Private detective Lew Archer challenges the power and ruthlessness of a wealthy oil dynasty responsible for a spill on the Southern California coast and linked to a missing girl, a six-figure ransom, and murder.

Machado, Carmen Maria

Her body and other parties : stories / Carmen Maria Machado. Graywolf Press, 2017 245 p.

ISBN 9781555977887

1. Women 2. Sexuality 3. Short stories 4. Literary fiction 5. Horror

Lambda Literary Award for Lesbian Fiction, 2018

Shirley Jackson Awards, Single-Author Collection, 2017.

Kirkus Prize for Fiction finalist, 2017.

National Book Award for Fiction finalist, 2017

Contains short stories about the realities of women's lives and the violence visited upon their bodies.

"Machado creates eerie, inventive worlds shimmering with supernatural swerves in this engrossing debut collection. Her stories make strikingly feminist moves by combining elements of horror and speculative fiction with womens everyday crises." Publishers Weekly.

Machart, Bruce

The **wake** of forgiveness / Bruce Machart. Houghton Mifflin Harcourt, 2010. 320 p.

ISBN 9780151014439

1. 1900s (Decade) 2. Feuds 3. Redemption 4. Horse racing 5. Dysfunctional families 6. Fathers and sons 7. Horse breeders 8. Landowners 9. Widowers 10. Forgiveness 11. Texas 12. Historical fiction 13. Literary fiction

LC 2009047459

Texas, 1910. Karel rides in the ultimate high-stakes race against a powerful Spanish patriarch and his alluring daughters. Hanging in the balance are his father's fortune, his brother's futures, and his own fate. Fourteen years later, with the stake of the race still driven hard between him and his brothers, Karel is finally forced to dress the wounds of his past and to salvage the tattered fabric of his family.

"[A] tragic family saga in the Faulknerian tradition of sins long simmering and revenge gone wrong. Set in a mythical South Texas town, full of dark deeds and troubled townsfolk, it details a somber world marked by flashes of romance. ... Both eloquent and fast-paced, the novel only bogs down in extremely detailed action scenes." Dallas Morning News.

Mackall, Dandi Daley

With love, wherever you are / Dandi Daley Mackall. Tyndale House Publishers, 2017. 480 p.

ISBN 9781496421227

1. Daley, Helen Eberhart 2. Daley, Frank 3. Second World War era (1939-1945) 4. World War II 5. Physicians 6. Nurses 7. Newlyweds 8. Separated couples 9. War casualties 10. War -- Relief of sick and wounded 11. Military hospitals 12. Mail 13. Europe 14. Love stories 15. Christian historical fiction 16. Biographical fiction

LC 2016040796

Everyone knows that war romances never last . . . After a whirlwind romance and wedding, Helen Eberhart Daley, an army nurse, and Lieutenant Frank Daley, M.D., are sent to the front lines of Europe with only letters to connect them for months at a time. Surrounded by danger and desperately wounded patients, they soon find that only the war seems real--and their marriage more and more like a distant dream.

"The no-holds-barred depictions of war, in-depth characterizations, and suspense make Mackall's historical novel an excellent choice for libraries of all types." Booklist.

Mackintosh, Clare

After the end / Clare Mackintosh. G.P. Putnam's Sons, 2019. 400 p.

ISBN 9780451490568

1. Husband and wife 2. Sick children 3. Decision-making 4. Parenthood 5. Options, alternatives, choices 6. Brain -- Tumors 7. Women physicians 8. Families 9. England 10. Mainstream fiction

LC 2019003453

Disagreeing for the first time when their son falls ill and they receive conflicting doctor recommendations, a devoted couple finds a unique way for both of their preferences to become possible.

Mackintosh, Clare

I let you go : a novel / Clare Mackintosh. Berkley, 2016. 369 p.

ISBN 9781101987490

1. Grief in women 2. Hit-and-run accidents 3. Loss (Psychology) 4. Detectives 5. Hit-and-run drivers 6. Murder investigation 7. Fatal traffic accidents 8. Coping in women 9. Secrets 10. Traffic accidents 11. Wales 12. Psychological suspense

Theakston Old Peculier Crime Novel of the Year Award, 2016

Devastated by a hit-and-run accident that has ended the life of her young son, Jenna moves to the remote Welsh coast to search for healing while two dedicated policemen try to get to the bottom of the case.

"Mackintosh's excellent writing features both memorable characters and a compelling portrayal of the eccentricities of small-town life in a close-knit community. But the author's real skill is in the way she incorporates jaw-dropping, yet plausible, plot twists into the already complex storyline." Kirkus.

Mackintosh, Clare

I see you / Clare Mackintosh. Berkley, 2017. 372 p.

ISBN 9781101988299

1. Stalkers 2. Surveillance 3. Crimes against women 4. Classified advertising 5. Police surveillance 6. Fear in women 7. Young women 8. Near future 9. Obsession 10. Paranoia 11. Stalking 12. London, England 13. Psychological suspense

LC 2016032022

Spotting her own picture in a classified ad referencing a mysterious website, Zoe discovers that other women who have appeared in the ad have become the victims of increasingly violent crimes.

"The author's meticulous detail to investigative accuracy and talent in weaving a thrilling tale set her work apart from others in the field." Kirkus.

Macmillan, Gilly

The **nanny** / Gilly Macmillan. William Morrow & Co, 2019. 384 p.

ISBN 9780062875556

1. Nannies 2. Aristocracy 3. Dead -- Identification 4. Rich families 5. Mother and adult daughter 6. Family estates 7. Detectives 8. Family secrets 9. Deception 10. Memories 11. Married men -- Death 12. Moving, Household 13. England 14. California 15. Psychological suspense

Leaving her home after the mysterious disappearance of her beloved nanny, an embittered woman is forced to return decades later when the discovery of human remains forces her to question everything she thought she knew.

Macmillan, Gilly

The **perfect** girl / Gilly Macmillan. William Morrow & Co., 2016. 448 p.

ISBN 9780062567482

1. Gifted teenagers 2. Teenage musicians 3. Mothers -- Death 4. Teenage girls 5. Former convicts 6. Truth 7. Murder 8. Secrets 9. Psychological suspense

Fighting to start over after serving time for her role in a fatal accident, teen musical prodigy Zoe is horrified when her mother is found dead after a career-launching recital, in a high-suspense tale told over the course of 24 hours.

Macneal, Elizabeth, 1988-

The **doll** factory / Elizabeth Macneal. Emily Bestler Books/ Atria, 2019. 362 p.

ISBN 9781982106768

1. Victorian era (1837-1901) 2. Artists' models 3. Painters 4. Women's role 5. City life 6. Poor people 7. Curiosities and wonders 8. Obsession 9. Historical fiction

In 1850s London beautiful young aspiring artist Iris is asked to model for Pre-Raphaelite artist Louis Frost, whose dark obsession may destroy her world forever.

Macomber, Debbie

If not for you : a novel / Debbie Macomber. Ballantine Books, 2017 400 p.

ISBN 9780553391961

1. Life change events 2. Music teachers 3. Mechanics 4. Self-fulfillment 5. Moving to a new city 6. Men/women relations 7. Parent and adult child 8. Interpersonal attraction 9. Traffic accident victims 10. Portland, Oregon 11. Chicago, Illinois 12. Contemporary romances

LC 2016042032

Moving away from her oppressive parents in hopes of taking charge of her own life, Beth takes a job as a school music teacher and initially resists her attraction to a tattooed mechanic who is the epitome of everything her conservative parents fear.

"A likable supporting cast ... keep the action moving and the plot intriguing in a well-crafted story that includes several romantic relationships and is rich with unresolved interpersonal issues. Wholesome and thoughtful." Library Journal.

Maguire, Gregory

After Alice / Gregory Maguire. HarperCollins, 2015. 273 p.

ISBN 9780060548957

1. Girls 2. Lost girls 3. Friendship 4. Reason 5. Reality 6. Magic 7. Historical fantasy 8. Adaptations, retellings, and spin-offs

A tale inspired by Lewis Carroll's beloved classic follows the experiences of Alice's friend, Ada, who, upon tumbling down the same rabbit hole, embarks on an odyssey to find and reclaim her friend from a surreal world.

"... Maguire firmly sets Wonderland in time and place and weaves an intricate web of symbolism and allegory, asking readers to consider issues of humanity that are as timeless as the original tale itself. The novel is full of the magic, wonder, and fresh twists that his fans have come to expect, and Maguire- and Wonderland-lovers alike will enjoy this fantastic return." Booklist.

Maguire, Gregory

Hiddensee : a tale of the once and future Nutcracker / Gregory Maguire. William Morrow, 2017. xi, 287 p.

ISBN 9780062684387

1. 19th century 2. Toymakers 3. Nutcrackers 4. Resurrection 5. Godfathers 6. Girls 7. Princes 8. Christmas 9. Enchantment 10. Pan (Greek deity) 11. Germany -- History -- 19th century 12. Historical fantasy 13. Adaptations, retellings, and spin-offs

Hiddensee: An island of white sandy beaches, salt marshes, steep cliffs, and pine forests north of Berlin in the Baltic Sea. Godfather Drosselmeier, a one-eyed toy maker, presents a Nutcracker to Klara, his goddaughter. Klara is a young girl in distress on a dark winter evening... and everyone, however lonely or marginalized, has something precious to share.

"A splendid revisitation of folklore that takes us to and from familiar cultural touchstones into realms to make Freud blanch." Kirkus.

Maguire, Gregory

Son of a witch : a novel / Gregory Maguire. Harper Collins, 2005. 352 p. Wicked years

ISBN 0060548932

1. Witches 2. Good and evil 3. Wickedness 4. Young men 5. Teenage boys 6. People in comas 7. Sick men 8. Sick persons 9. Sons of witches 10. Mothers -- Death 11. Childhood 12. Growing up 13. Adaptations, retellings, and spin-offs 14. Fantasy fiction

LC 2005046232

Sequel to: Wicked.

The sequel to Wicked returns to the land of Oz to tell the story of Liir, an adolescent boy last seen hiding in the shadows of the castle after Dorothy did in Elphaba, the Wicked Witch of the West. Bruised, comatose, and left for dead in a gully, Liir is shattered in spirit as well as in form. But he is tended at the Cloister of Saint Glinda by the silent novice called Candle, who wills him back to life with her musical gifts. What dark force left Liir in this condition? Is he really Elphaba's son? He has her broom and her cape, but what of her powers? Can he find his supposed half-sister, Nor, last seen in the forbidding prison, Southstairs? Can he fulfill the last wishes of a dying princess? In an Oz that, since the Wizard's departure, is under new and dangerous management, can Liir keep his head down long enough to grow up?

"This sequel to the adult fairy tale Wicked (1995) . . . begins ten years after the destruction of Elphaba, a.k.a. the Wicked Witch of the West. In Maguire's dark version of the Land of Oz, there's not much to ring the bells for in the Emerald City, despite the tyrannical Wizard's departure. Corruption is rife, political factions compete for power, and radicals proclaim Elphaba lives! Elsewhere, a horribly injured young man called Liir wakes in the religious House of Saint Glinda to many puzzles. . . . Above all, was Elphaba his mother? These and other questions drive a tale that adroitly mixes drama, humor, and political satire into a well-knit examination of good and evil-and leaves several doors open for future journeys over the rainbow into this cleverly constructed dystopia." Library Journal.

Maguire, Gregory

Wicked : the life and times of the wicked witch of the West : Gregory Maguire ; illustrations by Douglas Smith. ReganBooks, 1995. 406 p. Wicked years

ISBN 0060391448

1. Witches 2. Wickedness 3. Social acceptance 4. Good and evil 5. Adaptations, retellings, and spin-offs 6. Fantasy fiction

LC 95000669

Sequel: Son of a witch.

Includes endpaper maps.

Set in an Oz where a morose Wizard battles suicidal thoughts, the story of the green-skinned Elphaba, otherwise known as the Wicked Witch of the West, profiles her as an animal rights activist striving to avenge her dear sister's death.

"Born with green skin and huge teeth, like a dragon, the free-spirited Elphaba grows up to be an anti-totalitarian agitator, an animal-rights activist, a nun, then a nurse who tends the dyingand, ultimately, the headstrong Wicked Witch of the West in the land of Oz. Maguire's strange and imaginative postmodernist fable uses L. Frank Baum's Wonderful Wizard of Oz as a springboard to create a tense realm inhabited by humans, talking animals (a rhino librarian, a goat physician), Munchkinlanders, dwarves and various tribes." Publishers Weekly.

Mahfuz, Najib, 1911-2006

* **Palace** walk / Naguib Mahfouz ; translated from the Arabic by William M. Hutchins with Olive E. Kenny Doubleday, 1990, c1989. 498 p. Cairo trilogy

ISBN 0385264666

1. Muslim families -- Cairo, Egypt 2. Cairo, Egypt 3. Translations -- Arabic to English 4. Political fiction 5. Family sagas 6. Historical fiction

LC 89023348

Originally published in Arabic in 1956.

ALA Notable Book, 1991.

"This is the first volume in the author's trilogy dealing with three generations of a Cairo family in the first half of the twentieth century. The emotional and physical struggles of these middle-class people are depicted with a great deal of sympathy and honesty, from the torments of adolescent love through the banked passions of an established marriage. The novel begins with a series of domestic scenes featuring the five children of a merchant and his wife; later, the setting shifts to Cairo nightclubs, coffee shops, and stores as Mahfouz re-creates the everyday existence of his characters in almost Dickensian detail." Booklist.

Mahfuz, Najib, 1911-2006

Sugar Street / Naguib Mahfouz ; translated from the Arabic by William Maynard Hutchins and Angele Botros Samaan. Anchor Books, 2011, c1992. 331 p. Cairo trilogy

ISBN 9780307947123

1. Muslim families -- Cairo, Egypt 2. Muslim families 3. Egypt -- History -- 1919- 4. Cairo, Egypt 5. Family sagas 6. Literary fiction 7. Translations -- Arabic to English

LC 91012938

Series complete in 3 volumes.

Originally published in Arabic in 1957.

"The ordinary nature of Mr. Mahfouz's world, with its willingness to confront the complexities of human intentions, makes it an extraordinary exception in a marketplace of manufactured ideas and is, for that, all the more admirable." New York Times Book Review.

Mahmoud, Lena

* **Amreekiya** : a novel / Lena Mahmoud. The University Press of Kentucky, 2018. 178 p.

ISBN 9780813176376

1. Palestinian American women 2. Newlyweds 3. Marriage 4. Miscarriage 5. Women's role 6. Reconciliation 7. Arab Americans 8. Independence in women 9. California 10. Domestic fiction 11. Literary fiction

LC 2018027377

After her mother is killed and her father disappears, Isra Shadi, whose parents were Palestinian and white, lives with her aunt and uncle, but when she is encouraged to leave and marry, she chooses a love from her past, as she is caught between two cultures and struggles for identity.

Mailer, Norman

Ancient evenings / Norman Mailer. Little, Brown, 1983. 709 p.

ISBN 9780316544108

1. Ancient Egypt (3100 BCE-640 CE) 2. Reincarnation 3. Power (Social sciences) 4. Rulers 5. Courts and courtiers 6. Incest 7. Sexuality 8. Mothers and sons 9. Ancient Egypt -- History -- To 332 BC 10. Historical fiction

LC 82022839

Menenhetet I rises from peasant stock to become a harem overlord between the reigns of Ramses II and Ramses IX of Egypt.

Mailer, Norman

The **castle** in the forest : a novel / Norman Mailer. Random House, 2007. 496 p.

ISBN 0394536495

1. Hitler, Adolf, 1889-1945 Childhood and youth 2. Hitler family 3. Nazi Party (Germany) 4. S. S. Officers 5. Growing up 6. Dysfunctional families 7. Demons 8. Childhood 9. Fathers and sons 10. Mothers and sons 11. Brothers and sisters 12. Family relationships 13. Teenage boys -- Decision-making 14. Options, alternatives, choices 15. Personal conduct 16. Self-esteem in boys 17. Devil 18. Incest 19. Historical fiction 20. Biographical fiction

LC 2006049389

Explores the early life of Adolf Hitler through the eyes of a mysterious SS man in possession of some extraordinary secrets. Offers revealing portraits of Hitler's parents and siblings.

Mailer, Norman

* The **executioner's** song / Norman Mailer. Little, Brown, 1979. 1056 p.

ISBN 9780316544177

1. Gilmore, Gary Mark, 1941-1977 2. Murderers 3. Capital punishment 4. Violence in men 5. Men/women relations 6. Utah 7. Biographical fiction 8. Psychological fiction 9. Literary fiction

LC 79017193

Pulitzer Prize for Fiction, 1980.

National Book Award for Fiction finalist, 1980

National Book Critics Circle Award for Fiction finalist, 1979

Reconstructs the crime and fate of Gary Gilmore, the convicted murderer who sought his own execution in Utah, based on taped interviews with relatives, friends, lawyers, and law-enforcement officials.

Mailer, Norman

* The **naked** and the dead / Norman Mailer. H. Holt, 1998, c1948. xiii, 721 p.

ISBN 9780805060188

1. Second World War era (1939-1945) 2. World War II 3. Soldiers 4. Self-awareness 5. Self-perception 6. War 7. Battles 8. Authority 9. Interpersonal conflict 10. Islands of the Pacific 11. War stories 12. Modern classics 13. Literary fiction

The Naked and the Dead inspired the film The Naked and the Dead in 1958.

Portrays the contrasting personalities and nostalgic reminiscences of a group of World War II American soldiers engaged in a combat operation against the Japanese

Majmudar, Amit

Partitions : a novel / Amit Majmudar. Metropolitan Books, 2011. 224 p.

ISBN 9780805093957

1. 1940s 2. Political refugees 3. Violence 4. Hindus 5. Mother-separated children 6. Fathers and daughters 7. Physicians 8. Life after death 9. India -- History -- Partition, 1947 10. Pakistan -- History -- 20th century 11. Historical fiction 12. Political fiction

LC 2010045159

A story inspired by the 1947 partition of India finds twin Hindu boys Shankar and Keshav searching for their mother on a refugee-crowded train station, while a young Sikh girl flees the father who would poison her to protect her from infidels, and an elderly Muslim doctor rediscovers new roles as a healer.

Majors, Inman

Love's winning plays / Inman Majors. W. W. Norton & Co., 2012. 256 p.

ISBN 9780393062809

1. Football coaches 2. College sports -- Corrupt practices 3. College football 4. Men/women relations 5. Integrity in men 6. Mainstream fiction

LC 2012020171

Raymond Love, a young, inexperienced coach for a Southeastern Conference football team, falls for the athletic director's daughter and joins her book club to impress her while on a motivational tour of small towns with the team's head coach.

Majors, Inman

Penelope Lemon : game on! / Inman Majors. Louisiana State University Press, 2018. 264 p.

ISBN 9780807169513

1. Divorced women 2. Online dating 3. Misfits (Persons) 4. Single mothers 5. Waitresses 6. Homecomings 7. Parent and child 8. Photographs 9. Internet 10. Small town life 11. Virginia 12. Mainstream fiction 13. Humorous stories

Audacious and laugh-out-loud funny, Inman Majors's new novel holds up a fun-house mirror to the relatable challenges of being a single parent in the digital age. All those who live by the beat of their own drum gain a coconspirator, an accomplice, and a champion in the unstoppable Penelope Lemon.

Makine, Andrei, 1957-

Dreams of my Russian summers / Andrei Makine ; translated from the French by Geoffrey Strachan. Arcade Publishing, 1997, c1995. 241 p.

ISBN 1559703830

1. Grandmother and child 2. French in Russia 3. Reminiscing in old age 4. Storytelling 5. Misfits (Persons) 6. Travelers 7. Russia 8. Autobiographical fiction 9. Translations -- French to English

LC 97-2720

Originally published in France as Le testament francais: Paris : Mercure de France, 1995.

National Book Critics Circle Award for Fiction finalist, 1997

"At first, the narrator's lyrical and poetic memoir is so Proustian that it seems almost a pastiche, but insidiously it brings home the surreal and heartbreaking wonder of this woman's life." The New Yorker.

Makine, Andrei, 1957-

The **life** of an unknown man / Andrei Makine ; translated by Geoffrey Strachan. Sceptre, 2010, c2009. vi, 250 p.

ISBN 9780340998786

1. Authors, Russian 2. Communism 3. Reminiscing in old age 4. Senior men 5. Exiles 6. Survival 7. St Petersburg, Russia 8. Translations -- French to English 9. Literary fiction

Translated from the French.

Originally published in 2009 as La vie d'un homme inconnu by Editions, Paris.

Originally published as La vie d'un homme inconnu: Cergy : A vue d'oeil, 2009.

Jilted by his girlfriend and disillusioned by modern France, the writer Shutov revisits St Petersburg after twenty years in exile, hoping to reconnect with his roots and the woman he loved in his youth. But she, and the brash new Russia that greets him, are not what he was expecting at all. Then he encounters Volsky, a fellow relic of the Communist era who relates his story: of surviving the Siege of Leningrad, the march on Berlin and Stalin's purges, and of a transcendent love affair. It is a tale of extraordinary endurance and courage, yet the old man considers himself unexceptional. Fortunate, too, for he and the woman he loved knew great happiness. To Shutov, his story comes as a revelation, and an inspiration. In this powerful and moving novel, Andre Makine explores what truly matters in life through the prism of Russia's past and present. Drawing on his own experience of growing up in the Soviet Union, he poses an unsettling question: for all its horrors, was life under Communism richer than it is now? In the story of just another unknown, unsung hero lies an answer.

Makine, Andrei, 1957-

Music of a life : a novel / Andrei Makine ; translated from the French by Geoffrey Strachan. Arcade Pub., 2002, c1997. 109 p.

ISBN 9781559706377

1. Pianists 2. Stalinism 3. Secret identity 4. Men/women relations 5. Soldiers 6. State-sponsored terrorism 7. Soviet Union -- History -- 20th century 8. Historical fiction 9. Translations -- French to English

LC 2002025854

Translation of: Musique d'une vie: Paris : Seuil, 1997.

Pursuing a musical career despite the persecution of his performer parents during Stalin's late 1930s reign of terror, young Alexi Berg is forced to flee into a violent world when his parents are arrested.

"Stalin's atrocities are made visceral in this wisp of a book." The New Yorker.

Makine, Andrei, 1957-

The **woman** who waited : a novel / Andrei Makine ; translated from the French by Geoffrey Strachan. Arcade Publishing, 2006, c2003. 192 p.

ISBN 1559707747

1. 1970s 2. Grief in women 3. Folklorists 4. Crushes in men 5. Young men 6. Middle-aged women 7. Men/women relations 8. Love 9. Middle-aged widows 10. Romantic love 11. Soviet Union 12. Love stories 13. Translations -- French to English

LC 2005010314

Originally published in French as La femme qui attendait: Paris : Seuil, 2003.

Shortlisted for the International IMPAC Dublin Literary Award, 2008

"The Woman Who Waited quite deliberately avoids breaking your heart. It just comes very, very close. Vera is perceived only through the eyes of the narrator, but she is clearly more than just the woman who waits: only a fool would fail to understand that she's also the kind of woman worth waiting for, and far kinder and wiser than any romantic fiction." Washington Post Book World.

Makkai, Rebecca

The **borrower** : a novel / Rebecca Makkai. Viking, 2011. 336 p.

ISBN 9780670022816

1. Librarians 2. Boys 3. Books and reading 4. Automobile travel 5. Intergenerational friendship 6. Mothers and sons 7. Mainstream fiction

LC 2010052432

Lucy Hull is an accidental children's librarian who routinely gives her favorite patron, 10-year-old Ian, books that do not conform to the rigid rules his overbearing, fundamentalist mother has set for him. When Ian's parents force him to attend behavior-modification classes that will "cure" his burgeoning homosexuality, Ian determines to run away -- and Lucy decides to go with him. Though this set-up may leave you feeling incredulous, it's actually the start of a warm, moving, and frequently funny book full of literary references and paeans to the power of reading. -- Description by Shauna Griffin.

"A crime farce about a hapless librarian-cum-accidental librarian-cum-accidental kidnapper. Lucy Hull is a 26-year-old whose rebellion against her wealthy Russian mafia parents has taken the form of her accepting a children's librarian job in smalltown Missouri. After an unnecessarily long-winded first act, the novel picks up when Lucy discovers her favorite library regular, 10-year-old Ian Drake, hiding out in the stacks one morning after having run away from his evangelical Christian parents, who censor his book choices and are pre-emptively sending him to SSAD (Same-Sex Attraction Disorder) rehab, and Lucy soon aids and abets his escape. The tale of their subsequent jaunt across several state lines dodging cops, a persistent suitor of Lucy's, and a suspicious black-haired pursuer is fast-paced, suspenseful, and thoroughly enjoyable." Publishers Weekly.

Makkai, Rebecca

* The **great** believers / Rebecca Makkai. Viking, 2018 421 p.

ISBN 9780735223523

1. 1980s 2. 2010s 3. AIDS (Disease) 4. Homophobia 5. Epidemics 6. Mothers and daughters 7. Brothers and sisters 8. Loss (Psychology) 9. Cuban Americans 10. People with AIDS 11. Art museums 12. Chicago, Illinois 13. Paris, France 14. LGBTQIA fiction 15. Literary fiction 16. Parallel narratives

ALA Notable Book, 2019.

Andrew Carnegie Medal for Excellence in Fiction, 2019.

Stonewall Book Award for the Barbara Gittings Literature Award, 2019.

Pulitzer Prize for Fiction finalist, 2019.

A novel set in 1980s Chicago and contemporary Paris follows the director of a Chicago art gallery and a woman looking for her estranged daughter in Paris who both struggle to come to terms with the ways AIDS has affected their lives.

"As her intimately portrayed characters wrestle with painful pasts and fight to love one another and find joy in the present in spite of what is to come, Makkai carefully reconstructs 1980s Chicago, WWI-era and present-day Paris, and scenes of the early days of the AIDS epidemic. A tribute to the enduring forces of love and art, over everything." Booklist.

Makkai, Rebecca

The **hundred-year** house / Rebecca Makkai. Viking, 2014. 336 p.

ISBN 9780525426684

1. 20th century 2. Eccentrics and eccentricities 3. Archives 4. Poets 5. Married men 6. Academics 7. Family secrets 8. Artists' colonies 9. Historic buildings 10. Men/women relations 11. Family relationships 12. Literary fiction 13. Parallel narratives

LC 2013047855

First published: [London] : William Heinemann, 2014.

"A dazzlingly original new novel from the acclaimed author of The Borrower. Now, Makkai returns with an ingenious novel set on an historic estate that once housed an arts colony. Doug, the husband of the estate's heir, desperately needs the colony files to get his stalled academic career back on track. But what he discovers when he finally gets his hands on them is more than he bargained for. Doug may never learn the house's secrets, but the reader will, as Makkai leads us on a thrilling journey into the past of this eccentric family"--, Provided by publisher.

"The book is exceptionally well constructed, with engaging characters busy reinventing themselves throughout, and delightful twists that surprise and satisfy." Publishers Weekly.

Makumbi, Jennifer Nansubuga

Kintu / Jennifer Nansubuga Makumbi ; introduction by Aaron Bady. Transit Books, 2017, c2014. 400 p.

ISBN 9781945492013

1. Family curses 2. Clans 3. Heredity 4. Families 5. National characteristics 6. Culture 7. Family relationships 8. Uganda 9. Family sagas 10. Literary fiction 11. Afrofuturism and Afrofantasy

Originally published: Nairobi : Kwani Trust, 2014.

Though Kintu opens with the death of a man in 2004, this sweeping, literary family saga immediately jumps to 1750, when ambitious Kintu Kidda inadvertently kills his adopted son; the boy's father curses Kintu Kidda, a legacy that generations of his family cannot escape. First published in Kenya in 2014, this debut weaves the history of Uganda into the lives of the members of the Kintu clan. -- Description by Shauna Griffin

"Makumbi's debut novel is a sprawling family chronicle that explores Ugandas national identity through a brilliant interlacing of history, politics, and myth." Publishers Weekly.

Malamud, Bernard, 1914-1986

The **assistant** / Bernard Malamud. Farrar, Straus and Giroux, 2003, xi, 246 p.

ISBN 9780374504847

1. Italian American men 2. Interfaith romance -- Brooklyn, New York City 3. Immigrants 4. Family businesses 5. Families 6. Tragedy 7. Robbery 8. Jewish Americans -- Brooklyn, New York City 9. Jewish American women -- Brooklyn, New York City 10. Brooklyn, New York City 11. Modern classics 12. Literary fiction

LC 57007397

Originally published: New York: Farrar, Straus and Giroux, 1957.

National Jewish Book Award for Fiction, 1958.

A struggling neighborhood Jewish grocer takes on a helper who falls in love with his daughter and steals from his store.

Malamud, Bernard, 1914-1986

* The **complete** stories / Bernard Malamud ; edited and introduced by Robert Giroux. Farrar, Straus and Giroux, 1997. xv, 634 p.

ISBN 0374126399

1. Jews 2. Short stories

LC 9712394

55 short stories.

Brings together all of the late author's short fiction from the past four decades--fifty-three stories in all--ranging from his early work, taken from the National Book Award-winning "The Magic Barrel," to his latest

"Whether, stark, comic or fanciful, Malamud's stories give us immigrant Jews and their descendants pondering moral questions and experiencing moments of magical intervention while enduring life's ridiculous situations. Yet the stories transcend their ethnic settings and achieve a universal resonance." Publishers Weekly.

Malamud, Bernard, 1914-1986

* The **fixer** / Bernard Malamud. Farrar, Straus and Giroux, 2004, c1966. xi, 335 p.

ISBN 9780374529383

1. Antisemitism -- Eastern Europe 2. Self-discovery 3. Malicious accusation 4. Loneliness in men 5. Jews, Eastern European 6. Race relations 7. Russia 8. Literary fiction

Originally published: New York :

National Book Award for Fiction, 1967.

Pulitzer Prize for Fiction, 1967.

A Jew in Tsarist Russia is accused of murdering a Catholic boy and suffers from mistreatment in prison.

Malamud, Bernard, 1914-1986

The **natural** / Bernard Malamud. Farrar, Straus and Giroux, 2003, c1952. 231 p.

ISBN 9780374502003

1. Pitchers (Baseball) 2. Baseball 3. Professional baseball players 4. Purpose in life 5. Magic 6. Gunshot victims 7. Redemption 8. Literary fiction

LC 2003104942

Originally published: New York: Harcourt, Brace, 1952.

This sports novel follows the career of baseball player Roy Hobbs, a natural with a bat whose dreams of playing in the big leagues are deferred by a youthful indiscretion, but who finally becomes a hero.

Malerman, Josh

Bird box : a novel / Josh Malerman. Ecco Pr., 2014. 272 p.

ISBN 9780062259653

1. Survival 2. Monsters 3. Sensory deprivation 4. Hysteria (Social psychology) 5. Mother and child 6. End of the world 7. Mental illness 8. Dystopias 9. Blindness 10. Violence 11. Suicide 12. Horror 13. Apocalyptic fiction

In Bird Box, brilliantly imaginative debut author Josh Malerman captures an apocalyptic near-future world, where a mother and her two small children must make their way down a river, blindfolded. One wrong choice and they will die. And something is following them -- but is it man, animal, or monster? Within these tracks, Malerman, a professional musician, discusses his love of horror and invokes an ethereal and atmospheric experience in an homage to Orson Welles à la War of the Worlds.

"The author uses understatement and allusion to create a lean, spellbinding thriller." Publishers Weekly.

Malerman, Josh

Unbury Carol / Josh Malerman. Del Rey, 2018. 362 p.

ISBN 9780399180163

1. American Westward Expansion (1803-1899) 2. 19th century 3. Coma 4. Rich women 5. Premature burial 6. Murder 7. Outlaws 8. Rescues 9. Assassins 10. Wife-killing 11. Former lovers 12. Married women 13. Death (Personification) 14. The West (United States) -- History -- 19th century 15. Horror 16. Weird Westerns

A woman prone to secret temporary comas that make her appear to be dead receives protection from a redemption-seeking former lover who would save her from being buried alive by her fortune-hunting husband.

Malik, Tania

Three bargains : a novel / Tania Malik. W.W. Norton & company, 2014. 400 p.

ISBN 9780393063400

1. Fathers and sons 2. Social classes 3. Life change events 4. Poverty 5. Children of criminals 6. Faustian bargains 7. Redemption 8. Murder 9. Mentors 10. Forbidden love 11. Consequences 12. India 13. Thrillers and suspense

LC 2014011419

After his drunk, abusive father commits a horrible crime, a 12-year-old boy in a factory town in India has his life altered forever when his quick mind and focused determination catches the attention of his father's wealthy employer.

"Malik's first outing is an absorbing bildungsroman, a lovely and multifaceted tribute to the enduring bonds of family, blood or otherwise." Booklist.

Mallery, Susan

Best of my love / Susan Mallery. HQN, 2016. 384 p. Fools Gold series (Susan Mallery)

ISBN 9780373789191

1. Women bakers 2. Single men 3. Small towns 4. Friendship 5. Trust in women 6. Transformations, Personal 7. Small town life 8. Interpersonal attraction 9. Men/women relations 10. California 11. Contemporary romances

A heartbroken baker and a charming but womanizing tour guide embark on an experiment to prove their respective gender's quality and trustworthiness while regaining self-respect, only to become the subject of gossip in their small hometown.

Mallery, Susan

California girls / Susan Mallery. MIRA, 2019. 461 p.

ISBN 9780778368960

1. Sisters 2. Mother and adult daughter 3. Breaking-up (Interpersonal relations) 4. Jilted women 5. Marital conflict 6. Surrogate motherhood 7. Life change events 8. California 9. Women's lives and relationships

Three sisters wrestling with difficulties in their personal and professional lives tackle secrets and old wounds while helping their mother relocate from the family home to a condo.

"Mallery fans and newcomers alike will adore this tale about the bonds of sisterhood and friendship tested by lifes ups and downs." Publishers Weekly.

Mallery, Susan

The **summer** of Sunshine and Margot / Susan Mallery. HQN Books, 2019. 356 p.

ISBN 9781335659972

1. Twin sisters 2. Self-fulfillment in women 3. Determination in women 4. Summer 5. Family relationships 6. Interpersonal attraction 7. Men/women relations 8. Women's romantic fiction

Descended from a long line of women with disastrous luck in love, twin sisters Margot and Sunshine transform their controversial relationships with a client's son and an employer into unexpected sources of happiness.

"Mallery's approach to the alternating stories of the sisters and their attraction to their powerful employers makes for an enjoyable diversion, perfect for a summer read." Booklist.

Malliet, G. M., 1951-

A **demon** summer : a Max Tudor mystery / G.M. Malliet. Minotaur Books, 2014. 304 p. Max Tudor mysteries

ISBN 9781250021410

1. Clergy 2. Amateur detectives 3. Dinners and dining 4. Vicars 5. Poisons 6. Attempted murder 7. Former spies 8. Villages 9. England 10. Cozy mysteries 11. Gentle reads

LC 2014019884

Investigating what appears to be an attempt on the life of the reviled earl of Lislelivet, former MI5 agent turned vicar Max Tudor interrupts wedding plans and concludes that the event was accidental before a body is discovered in the cloister well.

"The fourth fun entry (after Pagan Spring) in this charming English cozy series is delightful in tone. Think Agatha Christie meets Ian Fleming." Library Journal.

Malliet, G. M., 1951-

A **fatal** winter : a Max Tudor novel / G. M. Malliet. Minotaur Books, 2012. 384 p. Max Tudor mysteries

ISBN 9780312647971

1. Vicars 2. Murder investigation 3. Villages 4. Women murder victims 5. Murder 6. Former spies -- Great Britain 7. Clergy 8. England 9. Cozy mysteries 10. Gentle reads

An investigation into two deaths at Chedrow Castle by former MI5 agent and Anglican priest Max Tudor is complicated by his growing attraction to Awena Owen and the arrival of a raucous group of greedy relatives.

Malliet, G. M., 1951-

Pagan spring : a mystery / G.M. Malliet. Minotaur Books, 2013. 304 p. Max Tudor mysteries

ISBN 9781250021403

1. Clergy 2. Amateur detectives 3. Dinners and dining 4. Vicars 5. Murder 6. Murder investigation 7. Former spies 8. Villages 9. England 10. Cozy mysteries 11. Gentle reads

LC 2013016676

"A Thomas Dunne book for Minotaur Books."

To restore peace in the quaint village of Nether Monkslip, Vicar Max Tudor must unravel the clues, which are linked to long-ago crimes, after one of the village's residents is murdered.

Malliet, G. M., 1951-

Wicked autumn : a Max Tudor novel / G. M. Malliet. Minotaur Books, 2011. 256 p. Max Tudor mysteries

ISBN 9780312646974

1. Vicars 2. Murder investigation 3. Villages 4. Women murder victims 5. Murder 6. Former spies -- Great Britain 7. Clergy 8. England 9. Cozy mysteries 10. Gentle reads

LC 2011019523

His tranquility as the established vicar of a New Age village shattered by the murdered of an unpopular woman, former MI5 agent Max Tudor struggles with past demons while trying to identify a killer in his peaceful community.

"Malliet has mastered the delights of the cozy mystery so completely that she seems to be channeling Agatha Christie, albeit with a hero who adds sex appeal to the mix. She also includes snippets of ironic humor that contribute a little spice to the village charm, making the story even more delicious. Religion, espionage, tea, and crumpets: a winning menu." Booklist.

Mallinson, Allan

A **close** run thing: a novel of Wellington's army of 1815 / Allan Mallinson. Bantam Books, 1999. viii, 306 p. Matthew Hervey novels

ISBN 0553111140

1. Wellington, Arthur Wellesley,, Duke of, 1769-1852 2. Great Britain. Army. Cavalry Officers 3. Napoleonic Wars, 1800-1815 4. Soldiers 5. Waterloo, Battle of, 1815 6. Secrets 7. Military life 8. Great Britain -- History, Military -- 19th century 9. War stories 10. Historical fiction

LC 9852512

Illustrated with a map of the Battle of Waterloo.

Sequel: The Nizam's daughters.

British cavalry soldier Cornet Matthew Hervey and his regiment, the 6th Light Dragoons, journey to Belgium in mid-June, 1815, at the crossroads of Quatre Bras near the small village of Waterloo.

"An exciting historical adventure steeped in authentic military detail." Booklist.

Mallon, Thomas, 1951-

Bandbox / Thomas Mallon. Pantheon Books, 2004. 305 p.

ISBN 9780375421167

1. 1920s 2. Periodical editors 3. Journalists 4. Photographers 5. Actors and actresses 6. Business competition 7. Periodicals 8. Periodical publishers and publishing 9. Organized crime 10. Kidnapping 11. New York City 12. Manhattan, New York City 13. California 14. Historical fiction 15. Humorous stories

LC 2003054861

In Jazz Age New York, Jehoshaphat "Joe" Harris and his offbeat employees battle a sabotaged fiction contest, the NYPD vice squad, the kidnapping of a subscriber, and a gorgeous but murderous film actress cover girl as they struggle to outwit a new competitor to save their popular magazine, Bandbox.

"Mallon, in his other books, has gravitated toward previous eras out of an affinity for something like reticence. Bandbox, then, is a real departure: antic, stylized, and up-tempo. The dialogue has a Kaufman-and-Hart crackle, and the story boasts more lotharios, floozies, mobsters, and wised-up dames than an MGM double feature." The New Yorker.

Mallon, Thomas, 1951-

Fellow travelers / Thomas Mallon. Pantheon Books, 2007. 368 p.

ISBN 0375423486

1. 1950s 2. Politicians 3. College graduates -- Employment 4. Young men 5. Closeted gay men 6. Gay men 7. Young men -- Relations with older men 8. McCarthyism 9. Paranoia in politics and government 10. Young women -- Relations with older men 11. Extramarital affairs 12. Personal conduct 13. Power (Social sciences) 14. Betrayal 15. Political persecution 16. Washington, D.C. -- Social life and customs 17. United States -- Politics and government -- 1953-1961 18. Historical fiction

LC 2006024586

Timothy Laughlin arrives in Washington, D.C. to join the early 1950s crusade against Communism, only to fall for Hawkins Fuller, a State Department official, and struggle to reconcile his political convictions, his love for Fuller, and his faith.

Mallon, Thomas, 1951-

Finale : a novel / Thomas Mallon. Pantheon Books, 2015. 464 p.

ISBN 9780307907929

1. Reagan, Ronald 2. 1980s 3. Presidents -- United States 4. Cold War 5. Politicians 6. Political science 7. United States -- History -- 20th century 8. Iceland 9. Political fiction

LC 2014044333

An analysis of the Reagan Administration shares insights into the 40th President's character and decisions while evaluating key historical events and the influences of such figures as Margaret Thatcher, Jimmy Carter and Richard Nixon.

"Despite all the scene-jumping, the transitions are seamless; There's a whirlwind of activity and abundant snappy dialogue." Booklist.

Mallon, Thomas, 1951-

Landfall : a novel / Thomas Mallon. Pantheon Books, 2019. 480 p.

ISBN 9781101871058

1. Bush, George W (George Walker), 1946- 2. 2000s (Decade) 3. Presidents -- United States 4. Iraq War, 2003-2011 5. Hurricane Katrina, 2005 6. Politicians 7. Women politicians 8. Political science 9. Lovers 10. Life change events 11. United States -- History -- 21st century 12. Political fiction

The award-winning author of Watergate reimagines the turbulent second term and political relationships of a mercurial President George W. Bush from the perspectives of two West Texans with disparate ideological views.

Mallon, Thomas, 1951-

Watergate : a novel / Thomas Mallon. Pantheon Books, 2012. 448 p.

ISBN 9780307378729

1. 1970s 2. Watergate Scandal 3. Journalists 4. Presidents 5. Politicians 6. Washington, D.C. 7. Political fiction 8. Historical fiction

LC 2011017393

Thomas Mallon conveys the drama and high comedy of the Nixon presidency through the urgent perspectives of seven characters we only thought we knew before now. Praised for his "splendid evocation of Washington," Mallon achieves a scope and historical intimacy which surpasses even that attained in his previous novels and turns a "third-rate burglary" into tumultuous, first-rate entertainment.

Malone, Minx

* Bad blood / M. Malone. CrushStar Romance, 2018. 224 p. Left at the altar

ISBN 9781938789670

1. Jilted women 2. Sexual attraction 3. Men/women relations 4. Contemporary romances
RITA Award, 2019.

She's his best friend and business partner's sister. Plus she's engaged to another man. But when she's left at the altar, he steps in to help her out. But will he be able to stop there?

Malouf, David, 1934-

Ransom / David Malouf. Pantheon Books, 2010, c2009. 224 p.

ISBN 9780307378774

1. Ancient Greece (800 BCE-640 CE) 2. Achilles (Greek mythology) 3. Priam (Greek mythology) 4. Grief in men 5. Loss (Psychology) 6. War -- Psychological aspects 7. Warriors 8. Rulers 9. Revenge 10. Sieges 11. Troy (Extinct city) 12. Ancient Greece -- History -- To 146 BC 13. Historical fiction 14. Epic fiction 15. Literary fiction
Originally published: North Sydney, N.S.W. : Knopf, 2009.
Australian Literature Society Gold Medal, 2010.
Shortlisted for the International IMPAC Dublin Literary Award, 2011

A tale of suffering, sorrow, and redemption, "Ransom" is a retelling of one of the most famous stories in all of literature--Achilles's slaughter and desecration of Hector, and Priam's attempt to ransom his son's body in Homer's "The Iliad."

"A retelling of Achilles' desecration of Hector's corpse and his capitulation to Priam's appeal for proper rites and burial for the Trojan hero. Malouf's prose is triumphantly sure, and his characterizations of the subtle and complex bonds between Priam and Achilles, gods and mortals, wives and husbands, parents and children, nobles and commoners, and beasts and men resonate with authority." Library Journal.

Malouf, David, 1934-

Remembering Babylon / David Malouf. Vintage Books, 1994, c1993. 200 p.

ISBN 9780679749516

1. Colonial Australia (1788-1901) 2. Frontier and pioneer life -- Queensland 3. Difference (Psychology) 4. Strangers 5. Racism 6. Aboriginal Australians -- Queensland 7. Queensland -- History -- 19th century 8. Australia -- History -- 19th century 9. Historical fiction 10. Literary fiction

LC 93007888

Originally published: London : Chatto & Windus, 1993.
ALA Notable Book, 1994.
International IMPAC Dublin Literary Award, 1996.
Shortlisted for the Booker-McConnell Prize, 1993.
Shortlisted for the Miles Franklin Literary Award, 1994
Thirteen-year-old Gemmy Fairley is cast ashore in northern Australia and adopted by Australian aborigines during the mid-1840s

"The book is more reflective than polemic. Without excusing the actions of the townsfolk, . . . Malouf shows how difficult original thought is for members of a community that perceives itself as surrounded by danger. The book is a joy to read: richly layered, complex, and dense." Christian Science Monitor.

Malpas, Jodi Ellen

Leave me breathless / Jodi Ellen Malpas. Forever, 2019. 390 p.

ISBN 9781538745212

1. Secret identity 2. Bodyguards 3. Women artists 4. Cabins 5. Handicraft shops 6. Small towns 7. Men/women relations 8. England 9. Romantic suspense

LC 2019017664

Taking a respite in his secluded cabin after an exhausting job, bodyguard Ryan unexpectedly falls for the owner of a local arts and crafts store before uncovering dangerous secrets that risk both their lives.

"Readers will enjoy the multilayered main and supporting characters ... sizzling erotic scenes, and a taut plot loaded with plenty of twists and turns. Malpas will charm her current fans and win new ones with this strong romantic thriller, perfect for those who love a good alpha male and a damsel in distress who doesn?t wait for someone else to rescue her." Publishers Weekly.

Malraux, Andre, 1901-1976

Man's hope / Andre Malraux ; translated by Stuart Gilbert and Alastair Macdonald. Modern Library, 1983, c1938. 511 p.

ISBN 0394604784

1. Revolutionaries 2. Soldiers 3. Revolutions 4. War 5. Spain -- Politics and government 6. Spain -- History -- Civil War, 1936-1939 7. War stories 8. Political fiction 9. Translations -- French to English 10. Modern classics

LC 83042699

Also known as: Days of hope.
Reprint. Originally published: New York : Random House, 1938.
"Vividly realistic as it is, the book is remarkably free from the senseless dwelling upon physical injuries which often weakens the effect of war novels. M. Malraux has concentrated upon the essential rather than the incidental horrors of war, of civil war in particular." Manchester Guardian.

Mamet, David

Chicago : a novel / David Mamet. Custom House, 2018. 332 p.

ISBN 9780062797193

1. 1920s 2. Between the Wars (1918-1939) 3. Mafia 4. Women murder victims 5. Revenge 6. World War I veterans 7. Journalists 8. Organized crime 9. City life 10. Chicago, Illinois 11. Crime fiction 12. Historical fiction

LC 2017044007

A novel set against the backdrop of the 1920s Chicago mob scene follows the experiences of a World War I veteran who seeks vigilante justice against the man responsible for killing the woman he loved.

The **mammoth** book of steampunk : 30 extraordinary tales / edited by Sean Wallace. Constable and Robinson ; 2012. vii, 498 p.

ISBN 9780762444687

1. Scientists 2. Women's role 3. Social classes 4. Technology 5. Steampunk 6. Science fiction 7. Short stories

LC bl2012012763

Presents a collection of thirty short stories which explores alternate worlds from the past in which women and social classes are oppressed and anachronistic technology is used to bring about a better future.

Manchette, Jean-Patrick, 1942-1995

Fatale / J.P. Manchette ; introduction by Jean Echenoz ; translated by Donald Nicholson-Smith. New York Review Books, 2011. 112 p.

ISBN 9781590173817

1. Women assassins 2. Revenge in women 3. Anarchism 4. Men/women relations 5. Crime fiction 6. Noir fiction 7. Translations -- French to English

LC 2010034848

Aimée, an assassin, goes into a coastal town and manipulates the town's wealthy citizens into hiring her to kill the weakest link, but when she develops sympathy for the target, she decides to retaliate against her clients instead.

"Told in tight behaviorist language and laced with deadly black humor, this compact neo-noir follows Joubert as she steps much too far into her self-made career toward a showdown worthy of any action film." Publishers Weekly.

Mandanipour, Shahriar

* **Moon** brow / Shahriar Mandanipour ; translated from the Farsi by Khalili Sara. Restless Books, 2018. 452 p.

ISBN 9781632061287

1. War 2. Angels 3. Soldiers 4. People with post-traumatic stress disorder 5. People who have had amputations 6. Iran-Iraq War, 1980-1988 7. Psychiatric hospitals 8. Brothers and sisters 9. Obsession 10. Memories 11. Lost love 12. Iran 13. Tehran, Iran 14. War stories 15. Literary fiction 16. Magical realism 17. Translations -- Persian to English

A novel steeped in Persian folklore and contemporary Middle Eastern history tells the story of playboy Amir whose whole life changes when his left arm is severed during the Iran-Iraq War and he begins to be haunted by the vision of a mysterious woman.

Mandel, Emily St. John, 1979-

* The **glass** hotel : a novel / Emily St. John Mandel. Alfred A. Knopf, 2020. 320 p.

ISBN 9780525521143

1. Bartenders 2. Missing women 3. Ponzi schemes 4. Hotel owners 5. Greed 6. Guilt 7. Art 8. Shipping industry and trade 9. Ships 10. Wilderness areas 11. City life 12. Brothers and sisters 13. New York City 14. Vancouver, British Columbia 15. Literary fiction 16. Magical realism

LC 2019023840

A tale of crisis and survival in the hidden landscapes of homeless campgrounds, luxury hotels, private clubs and federal prisons, where a massive Ponzi scheme is tied to a woman's disappearance at sea.

"With superb writing and an intricately connected plot that ticks along like clockwork, Mandel offers an unnerving critique of the twinned modern plagues of income inequality and cynical opportunism." Library Journal.

Mandel, Emily St. John, 1979-

* The **singer's** gun : a novel / Emily St. John Mandel. Unbridled Books, 2010 287 p.

ISBN 9781936071647

1. Forgery 2. Former criminals 3. Criminal investigation 4. Conflict in families 5. Extramarital affairs 6. Swindlers and swindling 7. Cousins 8. Deception 9. Secrets 10. Noir fiction

Anton's newly constructed life as a newlywed and manager is in jeopardy after his cousin Aria threatens to expose his criminal past if he does not do one more heist for her.

"This is a gripping story, full of moral ambiguities, where deception and betrayal become the norm, and where the expression, a riddle wrapped in a mystery, inside an enigma, is lifted to new heights." St. Louis Post-Dispatch.

Mandel, Emily St. John, 1979-

* **Station** Eleven / Emily St. John Mandel. Alfred A. Knopf, 2014. 272 p.

ISBN 9780385353304

1. Epidemics 2. End of the world 3. Post-apocalypse 4. Actors and actresses 5. Fame 6. Death 7. Viruses 8. Civilization 9. H1N1 influenza 10. Traveling theater 11. Survival (after epidemics) 12. Family relationships 13. Interpersonal relations 14. Toronto, Ontario 15. Canada 16. Apocalyptic fiction 17. Literary fiction 18. Science fiction

ALA Notable Book, 2015.

Arthur C. Clarke Award, 2015.

Toronto Book Awards, 2015.

National Book Award for Fiction finalist, 2014

One snowy night a famous actor slumps over and dies onstage during a production of King Lear. Hours later, the world as we know it begins to dissolve. Moving back and forth in time--from the actor's early days as a film star to twenty years in the future, when a theater troupe known as the Traveling Symphony roams the wasteland of what remains--this elegiac novel charts the strange twists of fate that connect five people: the actor, the man who tried to save him, the actor's first wife, his oldest friend, and a young actress with the Traveling Symphony, caught in the crosshairs of a dangerous self-proclaimed prophet.

"In this unforgettable, haunting, and almost hallucinatory portrait of life at the edge, those who remain struggle to retain their basic humanity and make connections with the vanished world through art, memory, and remnants of popular culture." Library Journal.

Manfredi, Valerio

A **winter's** night / Valerio Massimo Manfredi ; translated from the Italian by Christine Feddersen Manfredi. Europa Editions, 2012, c2011. 384 p.

ISBN 9781609450762

1. Rural life 2. Family relationships 3. Change 4. Farmers 5. Homeless persons 6. Sharecroppers 7. Charity 8. Poverty 9. Storytelling 10. War 11. Italy -- History -- 1914-1945 12. Literary fiction 13. Family sagas 14. Translations -- Italian to English

Translation from the Italian of: Otel Bruni (2011).

The Brunis, a farming family from the Italian Paduan plain, offer refuge to a host of people during the course of the two World Wars, the difficult times before and after the conflicts, and the rise of fascism.

Mangan, Christine (Christine Rose)

Tangerine : a novel / Christine Mangan. Ecco Press, 2018. 309 p.

ISBN 9780062686664

1. 1950s 2. Female friendship 3. Obsession 4. Expatriates 5.

Married women 6. Fear in women 7. Deception 8. Flashbacks 9. Manipulation by women 10. Morocco 11. Psychological suspense 12. Historical fiction

LC 2017013661

Arriving in Tangier with her new husband only to encounter the estranged best friend she has not seen in more than a year, Alice allows her friend to introduce her to the rhythms and culture of Morocco, only to be quickly stifled by the woman's controlling nature, a situation that turns sinister when her husband goes missing.

Manicka, Rani

The **rice** mother / Rani Manicka. Viking, 2003. 448 p.
ISBN 0670031925
1. Fourteen-year-old girls 2. Matriarchs 3. Women -- Malaysia 4. Mothers and daughters 5. Arranged marriage 6. Deception 7. Betrayal 8. Love 9. Loss (Psychology) 10. Prophecies 11. World War II 12. Malaysia 13. Malaya -- History -- Japanese occupation, 1942-1945 14. Family sagas 15. Historical fiction

LC 2002032421

Her idyllic early childhood in Ceylon lost forever when she is traded in marriage to a stranger in Malaysia, Lakshmi struggles to raise a family and survive the Second World War despite her husband's immaturity.

"When 14-year-old Lakshmi marries a widower of 37, she believes that she is leaving her Sri Lankan village for a life of luxury in Malaysia. Instead, she endures hardship and poverty, giving birth to six children in the years before the Japanese invasion of World War II. In this gripping multigenerational saga, the tumultuous history of Malaysia becomes the backdrop for Lakshmi's indomitable spirit. The barbarity of the Japanese, postwar prosperity, the bursting of the Southeast Asian financial bubble, the vice trades of opium, gambling, and sex all take their toll on Lakshmi's children and grandchildren." Library Journal.

Mankell, Henning, 1948-2015

Before the frost : a Linda Wallander mystery / Henning Mankell ; translated by Ebba Segerberg. New Press ; Distributed by W.W. Norton, 2005. 383 p. Linda Wallander mysteries
ISBN 1565848357
1. Police -- Sweden 2. Father and adult daughter 3. Murder investigation -- Sweden 4. Missing persons investigation 5. Policewomen -- Sweden 6. Rookie police 7. Detectives 8. Missing women 9. Best friends 10. Religious fanaticism 11. Extremism 12. Sweden 13. Translations -- Swedish to English 14. Mysteries 15. Scandinavian crime fiction

LC 2004055197

First in series featuring Kurt Wallander's daughter, Linda, although Kurt appears throughout the book.

"Just graduated from the police academy, Linda Wallander returns to Skane to join the police force, and she already shows all the hallmarks of her father--the maverick approach, the flaring temper. Before she even starts work she becomes embroiled in the case of her childhood friend, Anna, who has inexplicably disappeared. As the case that her father is working on dovetails with her own, something far more dangerous than either could have imagined begins to emerge. They soon find themselves forced to confront a group of extremists bent on punishing the world's sinners." Publisher's website.

Mankell, Henning, 1948-2015

The **dogs** of Riga / Henning Mankell ; translated by Laurie Thompson. Vintage Books, 2004, c1992. 336 p. Kurt Wallander mysteries
ISBN 1400031524
1. 1990s 2. Police -- Sweden 3. Murder investigation 4. Political corruption 5. Detectives 6. Swedes in the Soviet Union 7. Crimes against criminals 8. Life rafts 9. Self-doubt in men 10. Soviet Union -- History -- 1985-1991 11. Latvia 12. Sweden 13. Mysteries 14. Translations -- Swedish to English 15. Scandinavian crime fiction

LC 2003068869

"A Kurt Wallander mystery."
Originally published in Stockholm (Ordfront, 1992).

On the Swedish coastline, two bodies, victims of grisly torture and cold execution, are discovered in a life raft; after the victims are traced to Latvia, Major Liepa of the Riga police takes over the investigation. Thinking his work done, Detective Kurt Wallander slips into the routine once more, until he is called suddenly to Riga and plunged into an alien world in which shadows are everywhere, everything is watched, and old regimes will do anything to stay alive.

"Set against the chaotic backdrop of eastern Europe after the fall of the Berlin Wall, Mankell's intense, accomplished mystery, the last in his Kurt Wallander series. . . explores one man's struggle to find truth and justice in a society increasingly bereft of either. Here the provincial Swedish detective takes on a probably fruitless task: investigating the murders of two unidentified men washed up on the Swedish coast in an inflatable dinghy." Publishers Weekly.

Mankell, Henning, 1948-2015

Firewall / Henning Mankell ; translated from the Swedish by Ebba Segerberg. New Press, 2002, c1998 405 p. Kurt Wallander mysteries
ISBN 9781565847675
1. Police -- Sweden 2. Murder investigation 3. Cyberterrorism 4. Hackers 5. Detectives 6. Middle-aged men 7. People with diabetes 8. Financial intrigue 9. Crime 10. Teenage murderers 11. Crimes against taxicab drivers 12. Power failures 13. Small towns -- Sweden 14. Sweden 15. Mysteries 16. Translations -- Swedish to English 17. Scandinavian crime fiction

LC 2002025543

English translation of: Brandvagg.
Originally published in Stockholm (Ordfront, c1998).

Inspector Kurt Wallander begins to suspect that there is a connection between a series of crimes tormenting Sweden--the brutal murder of a taxi driver by two teenage girls, the escape of one of the culprits from police custody, the sudden death of man who drops dead at an ATM, a bizarre power blackout, and a grisly discovery at the malfunctioning power station.

"Although things get pretty tense at the end in Ebba Segerberg's well-paced translation, this a thinking man's thriller bearing the message that no infernal machine is a match for a decent man with a sense of good and evil." New York Times Book Review.

Mankell, Henning, 1948-2015

The **man** from Beijing / Henning Mankell ; translated from the Swedish Laurie Thompson. Alfred A. Knopf, 2010. 365 p.
ISBN 9780307271860
1. Women judges 2. Grandparents -- Death 3. Murder -- Sweden 4. Diaries 5. Murder investigation -- Sweden 6. Sweden 7. Mysteries 8. Translations -- Swedish to English 9. Scandinavian crime fiction
Originally published under title Kinesen : Stockholm : Leopard, 2008.
English translation originally published: London: Harvill Secker, 2010.

In the aftermath of the 2006 massacre of 19 people in a Swedish village, Judge Birgitta Roslin, a granddaughter of two of the victims, discovers the 19th-century diary of a gang leader that reveals the case's eerie connections to the abuse of Chinese slave workers.

"A sweepingly ambitious tale of corruption, injustice and revenge that ranges over three continents and 140 years. . . . Breathtakingly bold

Mankell, Henning, 1948-2015

The **man** who smiled : a Kurt Wallander mystery / Henning Mankell ; translated from the Swedish by Laurie Thompson. New Press ; distributed by W. W. Norton & Co., 2006. 336 p. Kurt Wallander mysteries

ISBN 1565849930

1. Police -- Sweden 2. Murder investigation 3. Accidental death 4. Detectives 5. Murder suspects 6. Lawyers 7. Murder 8. Small towns -- Sweden 9. Coping 10. Sweden 11. Mysteries 12. Translations -- Swedish to English 13. Scandinavian crime fiction

LC 2006021925

Originally published in Sweden in 1994 as Mannen son log.

A disillusioned Inspector Kurt Wallander is thrown back into the fray when he becomes both hunter and hunted. Crestfallen, dejected, and spiraling into an alcohol-fuelled depression after killing a man in the line of duty, Inspector Wallander has made up his mind to quit the police force for good. When an old acquaintance, a solicitor, seeks Wallander's help and later turns up dead, Wallander realizes that he was wrong not to listen.

"When the bleak landscapes of Henning Mankell's Swedish police procedurals start to look like home, it's time to head for the hills. Either that, or confront the grim truths about modern society that give weight to this author's absorbing but disquieting existential mysteries." New York Times Book Review.

Mankell, Henning, 1948-2015

* **One** step behind / Henning Mankell ; translated from the Swedish by Ebba Segerberg. New Press, 2002, c1997. 408 p. Kurt Wallander mysteries

ISBN 9781565846524

1. Police -- Sweden 2. Murder investigation 3. College students 4. Serial murders 5. Detectives 6. Sweden 7. Mysteries 8. Translations -- Swedish to English 9. Scandinavian crime fiction

LC 2001034254

Originally published: Stockholm : Ordfront, 1997.

Chief Inspector Kur Wallander investigates the deaths of three young celebrants after the Midsummer's Eve ritual.

"The sweep and complexity of Mankell's plot are reason enough for tackling this dense book, thoughtfully translated by Ebba Segerberg. But his meditations on surprising subjects like time travel and 'man's relationship to monsters' make him something special." New York Times Book Review.

Mankell, Henning, 1948-2015

* The **return** of the dancing master / Henning Mankell ; translated by Laurie Thompson. New Press, 2004. 391 p.

ISBN 1565848608

1. 1990s 2. 1940s 3. Police -- Sweden 4. Neo-Nazism 5. Murder investigation 6. People with cancer 7. Villages -- Sweden 8. Former police 9. Murder 10. Nazis 11. Neo-Nazis 12. Sweden 13. Translations -- Swedish to English 14. Mysteries 15. Scandinavian crime fiction

English translation of: Danslararens aterkomst.

"With its expansive time frame and meticulous procedural details, the story (as translated by Laurie Thompson) has a density that demands--and rewards--intellectual involvement." New York Times Book Review.

Mankell, Henning, 1948-2015

The **troubled** man / Henning Mankell ; translated by Laurie Thompson. Knopf, 2011, c2009. 384 p. Kurt Wallander mysteries

ISBN 9780307593498

1. Police -- Sweden 2. International intrigue 3. Missing persons 4. Spies 5. Cold War 6. Small towns 7. Middle-aged men 8. Detectives 9. Sweden 10. Translations -- Swedish to English 11. Thrillers and suspense 12. Scandinavian crime fiction

LC 2010049169

Originally published as: Den orolige mannen, by Leopard Förlag, Stockholm, 2009.

When his father-in-law, a retired naval officer, disappears under suspicious circumstances, Kurt Wallander uncovers disturbing evidence of Cold War espionage, a case that forces him to confront dark truths about his own nature.

"Not only does this novel widen the scope of the detective's investigations into the world of international geopolitics and the relationship of Sweden to the United States and Russia, it is a work of genuine heft and substance, a melancholy, elegiac book that is thoughtful and perceptive about memory, regret and the unfathomability of human nature." PopMatters.

Mann, Thomas, 1875-1955

The **black** swan / Thomas Mann ; translated from the German by Willard R. Trask ; introduction by Nina Pelikan Straus. University of Calif.Press, 1976, c1954. 141 p.

ISBN 9780520070097

1. 1920s 2. Obsession in women 3. Middle-aged women 4. Aging 5. Mother and adult daughter 6. Menopause 7. Psychological fiction 8. Literary fiction 9. Translations -- German to English 10. Modern classics

Originally published in German as Die Betrogene.

"In this novelette Mann returns to the compact dimensions and to the subject matter of Death in Venice--the infatuation of an aging person for a young one. The current novella--though it is not nearly as memorable a piece of storytelling as the masterpiece of 1913--is a provocative addition to Mann's writings." The Atlantic.

Mann, Thomas, 1875-1955

* **Buddenbrooks** / Thomas Mann ; translated from the German by John E. Woods. Vintage International, 1994, c1901. 731 p.

ISBN 9780679752608

1. 19th century 2. Middle class 3. Family relationships 4. Small town life 5. Germany -- History -- 19th century 6. Family sagas 7. Psychological fiction 8. Literary fiction 9. Translations -- German to English 10. Modern classics

A new translation of Mann's classic story of four generations of a wealthy bourgeois family in northern Germany captures the triumphs and tragedies, successes and failures, relationships, loves, and ordinary events of middle-class life.

Mann, Thomas, 1875-1955

Death in Venice and seven other stories / Thomas Mann ; translated from the German by H.T. Lowe-Porter. Modern Library, 1992. 461 p.

ISBN 067960040X

1. Homosexuality 2. Obsession in men 3. Authors 4. Senior men 5. Venice, Italy 6. Psychological fiction 7. Literary fiction 8. Short stories 9. Translations -- German to English 10. Modern classics

LC 92-253225

Includes biographical note.

This translation originally published: United States : Bantam, 1988.

Gustav von Aschenbach succumbs to his desires on a vacation trip to Venice.

Mann, Thomas, 1875-1955

Doctor Faustus / Thomas Mann ; translated from the German by John E. Woods. A. A. Knopf, 1997. 534 p.

ISBN 9780375400544

1. Devil 2. Musicians 3. Faustian bargains 4. Soul 5. Composers 6. Personal conduct 7. Literary fiction 8. Modern classics 9. Translations -- German to English

A new translation of one of Thomas Mann's novel, written in 1948, offers a modern rendering of the Faust legend in which Leverkuhn, a musical genius, promises his body and soul to the devil in exchange for twenty-four years of musical triumph.

Mann, Thomas, 1875-1955

* The **Magic** Mountain / Thomas Mann ; translated from the German by John E. Woods. Vintage International, 1996, c1927. 706 p.

ISBN 9780679772873

1. Sanatoriums 2. Civilization, Western -- 20th century 3. World War I 4. Soldiers 5. Science 6. Religion 7. Philosophy 8. Coming-of-age stories 9. Psychological fiction 10. Allegories 11. Literary fiction 12. Translations -- German to English 13. Modern classics

A sanitorium in the Swiss Alps reflects the societal ills of pre-twentieth-century Europe, and a young marine engineer rises from his life of anonymity to become a pivotal character in a story about how a human's environment affects self identity.

Manning, Kate

My notorious life : a novel / Kate Manning. Scribner, 2013. 416 p.

ISBN 9781451698060

1. Gilded Age (1865-1898) 2. Midwives 3. Women's rights 4. Women's role 5. Families 6. Irish Americans 7. Husband and wife 8. Businesspeople 9. Reproductive rights 10. Contraception 11. New York City -- History -- 19th century 12. Historical fiction

LC 2012031031

Amelia Bloomer List, 2015

A tale based on the life of a controversial Victorian New York City midwife features plucky orphan Axie Muldoon, who recounts her apprenticeship and establishment of a thriving practice that is threatened by a censorious zealot.

Manning, Max

The **victim** : a novel / Max Manning. Sourcebooks Landmark, 2019. 336 p.

ISBN 9781492667018

1. Public relations consultants 2. Carjacking 3. Criminals 4. Options, alternatives, choices 5. Life change events 6. Violent crimes 7. Psychopaths 8. Decision-making 9. London, England 10. Psychological suspense

LC 2018052448

"When public relations executive Gem Golding becomes the victim of a carjacking at the hands of a dangerous criminal bent on her destruction, she must make a choice: Does she surrender to her attacker, or does she stand her ground and fight for her life?What follows are the two strands Gem's life can take, and the chain of causes and effects that leads to Gem's survival...or her eventual demise."-- Provided by publisher.

Mantel, Hilary, 1952-

* **Bring** up the bodies : a novel / Hilary Mantel. Henry Holt and Co., 2012. 432 p. Wolf Hall trilogy

ISBN 9780805090031

1. Cromwell, Thomas,, Earl of Essex, 1485?-1540 2. Henry VIII,, King of England, 1491-1547 3. Anne Boleyn,, Queen, consort of Henry VIII, King of England, 1507-1536 4. Jane Seymour,, Queen, consort of Henry VIII, King of England, 1509?-1537 5. Tudor period (1485-1603) 6. Renaissance (1300-1600) 7. 16th century 8. Conspiracies 9. Courts and courtiers -- History -- 16th century 10. Extramarital affairs 11. Treason 12. Ambition in men 13. Political corruption 14. Politicians 15. Great Britain -- History -- Henry VIII, 1509-1547 16. Great Britain -- Politics and government -- 16th century 17. England -- History -- 16th century 18. Great Britain -- History -- Tudors, 1485-1603 19. Historical fiction 20. Literary fiction

LC 2012006335

Sequel to: Wolf Hall.

Costa Book of the Year Award, 2012.

Costa Novel Award, 2012.

Man Booker Prize, 2012.

RUSA Reading List, 2013.

Shortlisted for the Walter Scott Prize for Historical Fiction, 2013

Shortlisted for The Women's Prize for Fiction, 2013

Depicts the downfall of Anne Boleyn at the hands of Henry VIII and Thomas Cromwell as Anne and her powerful family fight back while she is on trial for adultery and treason.

Mantel, Hilary, 1952-

* **Wolf** Hall / Hilary Mantel. Henry Holt & Co, 2009. 672 p. Wolf Hall trilogy

ISBN 9780805080681

1. Cromwell, Thomas,, Earl of Essex, 1485?-1540 2. More, Thomas,, Sir, Saint, 1478-1535 3. Tudor period (1485-1603) 4. 16th century 5. Courts and courtiers -- History -- 16th century 6. Ambition in men 7. Political corruption 8. Politicians 9. Great Britain -- History -- Henry VIII, 1509-1547 10. Great Britain -- Politics and government -- 16th century 11. England -- History -- 16th century 12. Great Britain -- History -- Tudors, 1485-1603 13. Historical fiction 14. Literary fiction

Sequel: Bring Up the Bodies.

Also published: Toronto : HarperCollins, 2011, c2009.

Man Booker Prize, 2009.

National Book Critics Circle Award for Fiction, 2009.

Walter Scott Prize for Historical Fiction, 2010.

Shortlisted for The Orange Prize for Fiction, 2010

Shortlisted for the James Tait Black Memorial Prize for Fiction, 2009

Assuming the power recently lost by the disgraced Cardinal Wolsey, Thomas Cromwell counsels a mercurial Henry VIII on the latter's efforts to marry Anne Boleyn against the wishes of Rome and many of his people, a successful endeavor that comes with a dangerous price.

"Set in 16th-century Tudor England, Wolf Hall thrusts the reader into Henry VIII's seething court, where the players include Anne Boleyn, her sister Mary, Cardinal Wolsey, Thomas More and Jane Seymour. At the book's center: Thomas Cromwell, the ruthless blacksmith's son who rose to power under Henry VIII because of his intelligence, cunning and work ethic. . . . Mantel's novel is less about Henry's sex life and more about power: how to get it, wield it, keep it, particularly if you like the lowborn Cromwell lived in a merciless world ruled by the rich and titled. Cromwell usually is presented as a bully utterly lacking scruples, but Mantel's Cromwell is a sympathetic character modern readers will understand." USA Today.

LIST OF FICTIONAL WORKS

Mapson, Jo-Ann

Bad Girl Creek : a novel / Jo-Ann Mapson. Simon & Schuster, 2001. 381 p. Bad Girl Creek trilogy

ISBN 0743202562

1. Women with disabilities -- California 2. Boarding houses 3. Flower gardening 4. Single women 5. Women gardeners -- California 6. Female friendship -- California 7. Boarders 8. California 9. Women's lives and relationships

LC 2001027006

Four wounded women heal their hearts by opening a flower farm together, where they rediscover the importance of friendship.

"Mapson combines poignancy with the good-natured banter of girlfriends in her tale of women in transition, waiting to be reborn." Publishers Weekly.

March, Emily

Jackson / Emily March. St Martins Press, 2019. 336 p. Eternity Springs: McBrides of Texas

ISBN 9781250314918

1. Young widows 2. Women booksellers 3. Divorced men 4. Songwriters 5. Ranches 6. Resorts 7. Divorced fathers 8. Second chances 9. Texas 10. Contemporary romances

Sometimes it takes a new beginning . . . to reach a happily-ever-after.

March, William, 1893-1954

The **bad** seed : a novel / William March ; with a new introduction by Elaine Showalter. Harper Perennial, 2005, c1954. 256 p.

ISBN 0060795484

1. Mothers and daughters 2. Moving to a new city 3. Drowning victims 4. Eight-year-old girls 5. Schools 6. Child psychology 7. Secrets 8. Murder 9. Child murderers 10. Thrillers and suspense

Originally published: New York : Rinehart, 1954.

A seemingly normal and attractive young girl, Rhoda Penmark uses her strange powers and talent for evil to force others to give her what she wants.

"Rhoda Penmark at 8 years of age had a mind of her own and a will to match. Aged people doted on her splendid manners, but rogues knew her as one of themselves while older children were afraid of her. Christine, her mother suddenly discovers her daughter's horrible tendencies and also finds out that she is the murderess of two people who stood in her way. Christine resolves to check back and finds that she had been adopted and that the mother she had never known had also been a successful killer. Christine tries to stop the pattern in her daughter, but in the process dies herself." Library Journal.

Marcus, Ben, 1967-

The **flame** alphabet / Ben Marcus. Alfred A. Knopf, 2012. 289 p.

ISBN 9780307379375

1. Speech 2. Epidemics 3. Parent and teenager 4. Parent and child 5. Language and languages 6. Intergenerational relations 7. Postapocalypse 8. Teenage girls 9. Family relationships 10. Jewish families 11. Science fiction 12. Experimental fiction

Follows the outbreak of a deadly phenomenon that causes the speech of children to kill their parents, in a tale in which a desperate father is forced to choose between survival and his family.

Margolin, Phillip

Wild justice / Phillip Margolin. Harper Collins, 2000. 362 p. Amanda Jaffe novels

ISBN 0060196246

1. Serial murders 2. Women lawyers 3. Psychopaths 4. Defense attorneys 5. Surgeons 6. Murder suspects 7. Frameups 8. Portland, Oregon 9. Oregon 10. Mysteries 11. Pacific Northwest fiction

LC 00024351

Vice squad detective Bobby Vasquez joins forces with defense attorney Amanda Jaffe on the case of a heinous crime. Surgeon Vince Cardoni is the prime suspect of the murder. But then Cardoni mysteriously disappears. Four years later, a second set of murders has begun. Bobby and Amanda follow a twisting trail of clues and stay out of the path of the psychopath.

Marias, Javier

A **heart** so white / Javier Marias ; translated from the Spanish by Margaret Jull Costa. Harvill Press, 1995. 278 p.

ISBN 186046002X

1. Translators 2. Family secrets 3. Fathers and sons 4. Literary fiction 5. Translations -- Spanish to English

First published in Spain, 1992, with title Corazon tan blanco.

International IMPAC Dublin Literary Award, 1997.

Newly married Juan Ranz digs into his family's troubled past beginning with the suicide of his father's first wife, Juan's aunt, and finds parallels in his relationships marked by miscommunication and the need for human contact.

Marias, Javier

The **infatuations** / Javier Marias ; translated from the Spanish by Margaret Jull Costa. Alfred A. Knopf, 2013, c2011. 352 p.

ISBN 9780307960726

1. Young women 2. Murder 3. Obsession 4. Widows 5. Murderers 6. Men/women relations 7. Truth 8. Deception 9. Spain 10. Madrid, Spain 11. Psychological suspense 12. Literary fiction 13. Translations -- Spanish to English

LC 2013016429

"Originally published in Spain as Los enamoramientos by Alfaguara, Santillana Ediciones Generales, S. L., Madrid, in 2011."

National Book Critics Circle Award for Fiction finalist, 2013

At the Madrid cafe where she stops for breakfast each day before work, Maria Dolz finds herself drawn to a couple who is also there every morning. Though she can hardly explain it, observing what she imagines to be their "unblemished" life lifts her out of the doldrums of her own existence. But what begins as mere observation turns into an increasingly complicated entanglement when the man is fatally stabbed in the street.

Marias, Javier

* **Thus** bad begins : a novel / Javier Marias ; translated by Margaret Jull Costa. Alfred A. Knopf, 2016, c2014. 464 p.

ISBN 9781101946084

1. 1980s 2. Married people 3. Personal assistants 4. Family secrets 5. Rumor 6. Civil war 7. Men/women relations 8. Madrid, Spain 9. Literary fiction 10. Psychological suspense 11. Translations -- Spanish to English

LC 2015049902

First published in Spanish as "Asi empieza lo malo": Madrid : Alfaguara, 2014.

This translation first published by Hamish Hamilton, 2016.

Taking a job under an eccentric film director while completing his university degree in 1980 Madrid, Juan de Vere is asked to investigate unsavory rumors surrounding a family friend and uncovers complications in his employer's marriage and wartime activities.

"Another challenging, boundary-stretching work from Maras, complete with a jaw-dropping last-chapter revelation." Kirkus.

Marias, Javier

Your face tomorrow, vol.1: fever and spear / Javier Marias ; translated from the Spanish by Margaret Jull Costa. New Directions, 2005, c2002. 387 p.

ISBN 0811216128

1. Husband and wife 2. Military intelligence 3. Secret service 4. Military secrets 5. Secret societies 6. Spies 7. Interpreters 8. Madrid, Spain 9. London, England 10. Translations -- Spanish to English 11. Literary fiction

LC 2005000992

Orginally published: Spain : Alfaguara, 2002.

Jaime Deza is a Spaniard who falls in with a secret British intelligence agency that clandestinely examines subjects to determine what they will do in the future.

Marias, Javier

Your face tomorrow, vol.2: dance and dream / Javier Marias ; translated from the Spanish by Margaret Jull Costa. New Directions, 2005, c2002. 387 p.

ISBN 081121656X

1. Husband and wife 2. Military intelligence 3. Secret service 4. Military secrets 5. Secret societies 6. Spies 7. Interpreters 8. Madrid, Spain 9. London, England 10. Translations -- Spanish to English 11. Literary fiction

Orginally published: Spain : Alfaguara, 2002.

Marias, Javier

Your face tomorrow, vol. 3 : poison, shadow, and farewell / Javier Marias ; translated from the Spanish by Margaret Jull Costa. New Directions, 2009, c2004. 546 p.

ISBN 9780811218122

1. Husband and wife 2. Military intelligence 3. Secret service 4. Military secrets 5. Secret societies 6. Spies 7. Interpreters 8. Madrid, Spain 9. London, England 10. Translations -- Spanish to English 11. Literary fiction

Originally published: Spain : Alfaguara, 2004.

A finale to the author's novel in three parts returns MI6 recruit Jaime Deza to Madrid to spy on and protect his own family, a mission that involves psychologically grueling losses.

"Maras has concluded one of the most striking works in recent memory, giving us the cap to a philosophical espionage trilogy that could have been written by Henry James or Marcel Proust. . . . [He] weaves multi-page disquisitions on the Nationalist takeover of Spain, the collapse of the Cold War spy state and 16th century Italian art with moments of revelry involving Ian Fleming, hairnets, armpits, sex and swordplay. With an elegant, nimble translation by Margaret Jull Costa, the trilogy's 1,273 pages move right along." Los Angeles Times Book Review.

Marillier, Juliet

Daughter of the forest / Juliet Marillier. TOR, 2000. 400 p. Sevenwaters fantasies

ISBN 031284879X

1. Young women 2. Witches 3. Fathers and daughters 4. Brothers and sisters 5. Families 6. Magic 7. Paganism 8. British in Ireland 9. Prisoners 10. Swans 11. Escapes 12. Clans -- Ireland 13. Men/

women relations 14. Kidnapping 15. Spells (Magic) 16. Stepmothers 17. Familial love 18. Loss (Psychology) 19. Loyalty 20. Self-sacrifice 21. Good and evil 22. Mythology, Celtic 23. Folklore, Celtic 24. Ireland 25. Fantasy fiction 26. Mythological fiction 27. Celtic fantasy

LC 00025216

To reclaim the lives of her brothers, Sorcha leaves the only safe place she has known and starts on a journey of pain, loss, and terror.

"The author's keen understanding of Celtic paganism and early Irish Christianity adds texture to a rich and vibrant novel that belongs in most fantasy collections." Library Journal.

Mark, David John, 1977-

Cruel mercy / David J. Mark. Penguin Group USA, 2017. 352 p. Aector McAvoy novels

ISBN 9780399185113

1. Police 2. Detectives 3. Scots in the United States 4. Murder investigation 5. People in comas 6. Serial murderers 7. Organized crime 8. Boxers (Sports) 9. Gangsters 10. Catholics 11. New York City 12. Mysteries 13. Police procedurals

A first U.S. case for Detective Sergeant McAvoy finds the British investigator assisting the NYPD in the aftermath of a shooting attack that has killed a promising young boxer and left his legendary coach in a coma.

"Beautifully crafted, filled with flashbacks, horror, angst, and chilling detail, this one is his most complex and best yet." Kirkus.

Mark, David John, 1977-

The dark winter / David Mark. Blue Rider Press, 2012. 320 p. Aector McAvoy novels

ISBN 9780399158643

1. Murder investigation 2. Serial murders 3. Police misconduct 4. Detectives 5. Crimes against teenage girls 6. Survival 7. England 8. Hull, England 9. Mysteries 10. Police procedurals

LC 2012024256

Investigating a series of suspicious deaths and discovering that each victim was the sole survivor of a tragedy, Detective Sergeant Aector McAvoy of the northern England port of Hull struggles to balance the demand of the case with the needs of his beloved family.

Mark, David John, 1977-

Original skin / David Mark. Blue Rider Press, 2013. 448 p. Aector McAvoy novels

ISBN 9780399158650

1. Drug traffic 2. Political corruption 3. Suicide investigation 4. Murder investigation 5. Gangs 6. Politicians 7. Secrets 8. Fetishism (Sexuality) 9. Detectives 10. England 11. Hull, England 12. Mysteries 13. Police procedurals

Suspecting foul play in the alleged suicide of a depressed man in an East Yorkshire neighborhood where a new gang has recently seized control of the local drug trade, Detective Sergeant Aector McAvoy finds the investigation pitting him against elite political figures and other powerful individuals who murderously protect their secrets.

Mark, David John, 1977-

Sorrow bound / David Mark. Blue Rider Press, 2014. 336 p. Aector McAvoy novels

ISBN 9780399168208

1. Detectives 2. Drug traffic 3. Murder investigation 4. Organized crime 5. Serial murders 6. Secrets 7. England 8. Hull, England 9. Mysteries 10. Police procedurals

LC 2013050353

First published in the U.K. in 2014 by Quercus Editions Ltd.

"Detective Sergeant Aector McAvoy returns for another darkly enthralling case in Sorrow Bound, the third installment of David Mark's internationally acclaimed and bestselling series"--, Provided by publisher.

Markandaya, Kamala, 1924-2004

Nectar in a sieve / Kamala Markandaya. Signet Classic, 2002, c1954. xiii, 190 p.

ISBN 9780451528230

1. Factories 2. Poor families 3. Arranged marriage 4. Brides 5. Tanning 6. Poverty 7. Farmers 8. Consequences 9. Leprosy 10. Husband and wife 11. India 12. Domestic fiction 13. Literary fiction 14. Modern classics

LC 200149544

Originally published: New York : J. Day Co., 1954.

Married as a child bride to a tenant farmer she had never met, Rukmani works side by side in the field with her husband to wrest a living from a land ravaged by droughts, monsoons, and insects. With remarkable fortitude and courage, she meets changing times and fights poverty and disaster.

Markley, Stephen

Ohio / Stephen Markley. Simon & Schuster, 2018. 496 p.

ISBN 9781501174476

1. 2010s 2. Homecomings 3. Drug addiction 4. Recession (Economics) 5. Memories 6. Secrets 7. Hometowns 8. Life change events 9. Interpersonal relations 10. Ohio 11. Middle West 12. Literary fiction

LC 2017040397

Four former classmates converge on their recession- and opioid-ravaged hometown on a fateful summer night that finds them pursuing respective goals based on haunting memories from their shared past.

Markovits, Anouk

I am forbidden : a novel / Anouk Markovits. Hogarth, 2012. 256 p.

ISBN 9780307984739

1. Sisters 2. Belief and doubt 3. Faith (Judaism) 4. Family secrets 5. Jews 6. Hasidism 7. Orphans 8. Romania -- History -- 20th century 9. New York City 10. Family sagas 11. Literary fiction

LC 2011041305

Originally published: London: Hogarth, 2012.

Set inside the insular Hasidic sect, the Satmar, two devoted sisters are forced apart when one begins to question their religion's ancient doctrine.

Marks, John, 1963-

Fangland : a novel / John Marks. Penguin Books, 2007. 400 p.

ISBN 159420117X

1. Women television journalists 2. Americans in Eastern Europe 3. American women in Europe 4. Organized crime 5. Vampires 6. Missing women 7. Women with amnesia 8. Email correspondence 9. Television news 10. Romania 11. Transylvania, Romania 12. New York City 13. Diary novels 14. Horror 15. Adaptations, retellings, and spin-offs

LC 2006049809

Traveling to Romania for her popular television news magazine, Evangeline Harker investigates a crime boss named Ion Torgu, only to disappear and awaken several months later in a Transylvanian monastery with no memory of what happened to her.

Marks, Laurie J.

Fire logic/ Laurie J. Marks. Tor, 2002. 335 p. Elemental logic

ISBN 9780312878870

1. Magic 2. Guerrilla warfare 3. Epic fantasy 4. Fantasy fiction

LC 2001058352

"A Tom Doherty Associates book."

An epic tale of war, betrayal, magic, and love follows three unforgettable characters--Emil, a Shaftali Paladin, an officer, and a scholar; Zanja, a diplomat, traveller, prescient, and the last survivor of a slaughtered tribe; and Karis, a metalsmith and giant who is addicted to a fatal drug--as they join forces to save the peaceful country of Shaftal and change the world forever.

Marlantes, Karl

Deep river / Karl Marlantes. Atlantic Monthly Pr, 2019 820 p.

ISBN 9780802125385

1. 1900s (Decade) 2. Logging 3. Immigrants, Finnish 4. Brothers and sisters 5. Labor unions 6. Imperialism, Russian 7. Women social advocates 8. Washington (State) 9. Finland -- History -- 20th century 10. Literary fiction 11. Historical fiction 12. Pacific Northwest literature

In the early 1900s, as the oppression of Russia's imperial rule takes its toll on Finland, the Koski siblings--Ilmari, Matti and the politicized young Aino--flee to the U.S., settling in a logging community in southern Washington.

Marlantes, Karl

* **Matterhorn** : a novel of the Vietnam War / Karl A. Marlantes. Grove/Atlantic, 2010. 592 p.

ISBN 9780802119285

1. 1960s 2. Vietnam War, 1961-1975 3. Soldiers 4. Marines 5. War 6. Jungles 7. Vietnam 8. War stories 9. Historical fiction 10. Literary fiction

James Fenimore Cooper Prize, 2011

W. Y. Boyd Literary Award, 2011.

ALA Notable Book, 2011.

Shortlisted for the International IMPAC Dublin Literary Award, 2012

Lieutenant Waino Mellas and his fellow Marines venture into the mountain jungle of Vietnam as boys and fight their way into manhood, confronting external obstacles as well as racial tension, competing ambitions, and underhanded officers.

"Matterhorn is one of those countless hills in Vietnam that makes young men's lives so cheap. In this case, it's the Marines of Bravo Company and the hardened NVA (North Vietnamese Army) soldiers. The story revolves around a young Marine lieutenant, Waino Mellas, who must quickly learn the difference between officer candidate school and the reality of life in the bush. Lt. Mellas tries to straddle the line between being one of the guys and a platoon commander. This division between the troops and a low-ranking officer like Mellas (who is only a few years older than his men) can become too vague if he is overly friendly. In combat, that can be disastrous. The delicate balance between life and death resonates throughout Matterhorn, as it does in real combat. What is so fresh and fascinating about this novel is Marlantes' depiction of the specific activities and conflicting motivations that take place in a war zone." BookPage.

Marlette, Doug, 1949-

Magic time / Doug Marlette. Farrar, Straus and Giroux, 2006. 496 p.

ISBN 0374200017

1. Ku-Klux Klan Mississippi 2. 1960s 3. 1990s 4. Journalists 5. Fathers and sons 6. Terrorists 7. Judges 8. Family relationships 9. Homecomings 10. Nervous breakdown 11. Men with depression 12. Cold cases (Criminal investigation) 13. Violence against minorities 14. Racism 15. Suspicion 16. Extortion 17. Terrorism 18. Interpersonal relations 19. Murder 20. Trials 21. Justice 22. Memories 23. Bombing 24. Men/women relations 25. Mississippi 26. Legal thrillers 27. Romantic suspense

LC 2005036396

Sir Walter Raleigh Award for Fiction, 2007.

Following a nervous breakdown, New York City newspaper columnist Carter Ransom returns home to Mississippi to confront his formidable father and a traumatic past marked by a twenty-five-year-old unsolved civil rights murder case that shattered his family.

"Magic Time presents a realistic portrait of the collective amnesia of the South and the generational tensions that the civil rights movement stirred up, then and now. It's a real Mississippi story, not merely a faded imitation." Washington Post Book World.

Maron, Margaret

Bootlegger's daughter / Margaret Maron. Mysterious Press, 1992. 261 p. Deborah Knott mysteries

ISBN 0892964456

1. Elections -- North Carolina 2. Small town life -- North Carolina 3. Fathers and daughters -- North Carolina 4. Women lawyers 5. Women judges 6. Murder investigation 7. Women candidates for public office -- North Carolina 8. North Carolina 9. Mysteries 10. Southern fiction

LC 91058021

Agatha Award for Best Novel, 1993.
Anthony Award for Best Novel, 1993.
Edgar Allan Poe Award for Best Mystery Novel, 1993.
Macavity Award for Best Mystery Novel, 1993.

Deborah Knott, an attorney attempting to infiltrate the old boy network of tobacco country by running for district judge, is distracted from the race, and almost eliminated, when she finds new evidence to an old small-town murder

Maron, Margaret

High country fall / Margaret Maron. Mysterious Press, 2004. 320 p. Deborah Knott mysteries

ISBN 0892968087

1. Aunt and niece 2. Engaged persons 3. Women judges 4. Small town life -- North Carolina 5. Summer resorts 6. Mountain life 7. Mountains -- North Carolina 8. Blue Ridge Mountains 9. North Carolina 10. Mysteries 11. Southern fiction

LC 2004001953

Taking an out-of-town assignment to put distance between herself and her hyper-reactive family, recently engaged judge Deborah Knott finds her peaceful break disrupted by a local murder that she becomes determined to solve.

"Deborah's narrative voice, with its engaging tone of amusement at the human foibles she witnesses in her travels, is just the ticket for this dramatic view of the spectacular Blue Ridge Mountains." New York Times Book Review.

Maron, Margaret

Shooting at loons / Margaret Maron. Mysterious Press, 1994. 229 p. Deborah Knott mysteries

ISBN 0892964472

1. Women judges 2. Murder investigation 3. Fishers 4. Small town life -- North Carolina 5. Fishing 6. Lawyers 7. Women amateur detectives 8. North Carolina 9. Mysteries 10. Southern fiction

LC 93047141

In a picturesque North Carolina village, a struggle between commercial fishermen and real-estate developers leads to murder--and Judge Deborah Knott's ex-lover is implicated

"The down-home prose flows well, spiced by Judge Knott's wit, charm, and extended family as well as by references to the local food and drink." Library Journal.

Maron, Margaret

Storm track / Margaret Maron. Mysterious Press, 2000. 260 p. Deborah Knott mysteries

ISBN 0892966564

1. Hurricanes -- North Carolina 2. Murder investigation 3. Women judges -- North Carolina 4. Small town life -- North Carolina 5. African Americans -- North Carolina 6. Women amateur detectives 7. North Carolina -- Race relations 8. Mysteries 9. Southern fiction

LC 99051761

Agatha Award for Best Novel, 2001.

When the embittered wife of a local attorney is found strangled in a motel by her own skimpy undergarments, Judge Deborah Knott searches for clues as a deadly hurricane bears down on the coastal town.

Maron, Margaret

Uncommon clay / Margaret Maron. Warner Books, 2001. 288 p. Deborah Knott mysteries

ISBN 089296720X

1. Potters -- North Carolina 2. Murder investigation 3. Women judges -- North Carolina 4. Small town life -- North Carolina 5. Women amateur detectives 6. North Carolina 7. Mysteries 8. Southern fiction

LC 00066266

In order to catch a killer, Judge Deborah Knott must unravel a local family's tragic, shameful past, but she may not be able to solve the mystery in time to prevent further bloodshed.

"This mystery does more than honor local folk art and the generations of artisans who carry on the regional heritage. It shows us how deeply these homespun crafts are rooted in the collective artistry of individual families--and what a devastating loss it is when these families die out." New York Times Book Review.

Maron, Margaret

Up jumps the Devil / Margaret Maron. Mysterious Press, 1996. 278 p. Deborah Knott mysteries

ISBN 0892965681

1. Former husbands -- North Carolina 2. Murder investigation 3. Real estate development -- North Carolina 4. Women judges -- North Carolina 5. Small town life -- North Carolina 6. Women amateur detectives 7. North Carolina 8. Mysteries 9. Southern fiction

LC 96007715

Agatha Award for Best Novel, 1997.

Colleton County, North Carolina judge Deborah Knott embarks on a Thanksgiving Day investigation into the murder of a man from her father's moonshine-making past.

"The droll characters and their lilting regional humor seem ever more endearing because we sense their days are numbered." New York Times Book Review.

Marra, Anthony

* A **constellation** of vital phenomena : a novel / Anthony Marra. Hogarth, 2013. 400 p.

ISBN 9780770436407

1. 2000s (Decade) 2. Women physicians 3. Civil war -- Chechnya, Russia 4. Eight-year-old girls 5. Hospitals 6. Father-separated children 7. Refugees 8. Russia -- History -- 1991- 9. Chechnya, Russia -- History -- Civil War, 1994- 10. War stories 11. Literary fiction

LC 2012017444

ALA Notable Book, 2014

Set in rural Chechnya during the region's war with Russia. Though events shift in time, the main focus is a five-day period in 2004, when an eight-year-old girl witnesses her father's abduction by Russian soldiers. Swearing to protect the girl, local doctor Akhmed (whose true passion is portraiture), brings her to a crumbling hospital, run by a hardened but dedicated surgeon, for safety. - Description by Shauna Griffin.

Marra, Anthony

The **tsar** of love and techno : stories / Anthony Marra. Hogarth, 2015. 256 p.

ISBN 9780770436438

1. Families 2. War and society 3. Art 4. Self-sacrifice 5. Interpersonal relations 6. Russia 7. Literary fiction 8. Short stories

ALA Notable Book, 2016.

National Book Critics Circle Award for Fiction finalist, 2015

A collection of interwoven tales explores themes of family, sacrifice, war, and the redemptive power of art.

"As in his previous novel, Marra is deft at managing different characters at different points in time, but the book's brilliance and humor are laced with the somber feeling that the country is allergic to evolution: KGB thugs then, drug dealers and Internet scammers now, with a few stray moments of compassion in between. A powerful and melancholy vision of a nation with long memories and relentless turmoil." Kirkus.

Marren, Susannah

A **Palm** Beach wife / Susannah Marren. St. Martin's Griffin, 2019. 294 p.

ISBN 9781250088918

1. Women 2. Betrayal 3. Social status 4. Image 5. Secrets 6. Scandals 7. Socialites 8. Rich people 9. Husband and wife 10. Palm Beach, Florida 11. Women's lives and relationships 12. Glitz and glamour novels

LC 2018046840

In a town of secrets, gossip and rumors, Faith, who has fought hard for her perfect life, keeps a desperate grip on everything she holds so dear until an unexpected betrayal destroys everything.

"The lavish settings and designer name-dropping bring to mind Kevin Kwan's Crazy Rich Asians (2013), and while Marren's crazy rich Americans aren't as frothy or fun, their dramatic ups and downs are plenty entertaining, providing everything readers are looking for in a beach read." Booklist.

Marrs, John

The **passengers** / John Marrs. Berkley, 2019. 336 p.

ISBN 9781984806970

1. Autonomous vehicles 2. Near future 3. Hostages 4. Options alternatives choices 5. Prejudice 6. Mass media 7. Kidnapping victims 8. Hostage-taking 9. Immigrants 10. Abused women 11. Pregnant women 12. Great Britain 13. Techno-thrillers

LC 2019013185

In a near-future society where self-driving cars are the norm, eight people find themselves trapped in cars which have been hacked, with a mysterious voice telling them they are going to die while their fearful reactions are broadcast around the world from hidden cameras.

"One can almost hear the Hollywood music in the background as the action unfolds; the plot twists are truly gripping. ... As with any story centered around the potential catastrophe of trusting AI to run the mundane moments of our lives, there is an uneasy prescience about this techno-thriller's setup. Summer blockbuster entertainment at its best." Kirkus.

Marsh, Ngaio, 1895-1982

Dead water / Ngaio Marsh. St. Martin's Paperbacks, 1999, c1963. 220 p. Roderick Alleyn mysteries

ISBN 9780312969905

1. Scotland Yard. 2. Islands 3. Health resorts 4. Octogenarian women 5. Police 6. Detectives 7. England 8. Mysteries

Fearless and bold, eighty-year-old Emily Pride embarks on a mission to rid the miraculous "Pixie Falls" healing spring of all its tasteless decorum and attractions, but she is met with major opposition, and when a murder occurs, Superintendent Roderick Alleyn arrives to clear the name of his oldest friend.

"Scotland Yard's Superintendent Roderick Alleyn finds himself involved unofficially in magic and faith healing when his former French teacher, now a formidable lady of 80, inherits an island off the coast of Cornwall which has, as its chief claim to fame and source of income, a Pixie Well supposed to cure warts, asthma and other ills. . . . Skillful writing, convincing atmosphere, and sharply etched characterization will please Ngaio Marsh fans, but the plot is less complex than some of her others." Publishers Weekly.

Marsh, Ngaio, 1895-1982

False scent / Ngaio Marsh. St. Martin's Paperbacks, 1999, c1960. 254 p. Roderick Alleyn mysteries

ISBN 9780312968984

1. Scotland Yard. 2. Actors and actresses -- Great Britain 3. Murder investigation 4. Perfumes 5. Police 6. Detectives 7. England 8. Mysteries

The indomitable Inspector Roderick Alleyn is sent to sniff out the case of the beloved "queen of British theater," Mary Bellamy, who has been found murdered in a cloud of perfume--a case reeking with likely suspects.

Marsh, Ngaio, 1895-1982

Grave mistake / Ngaio Marsh. St. Martin's Paperbacks, 2000, c1978. 256 p. Roderick Alleyn mysteries

ISBN 9780312972974

1. Scotland Yard. 2. Rich people 3. Hypochondriacs 4. Murder investigation 5. Police 6. Detectives 7. England 8. Mysteries

The death of wealthy hypochondriac Sybil Foster at fashionable Greengages is looked into by Superintendent Roderick Alleyn and Sybil's friend, Verity Preston, both of whom are puzzled by the absence of motives and suspects.

Marsh, Ngaio, 1895-1982

Last ditch / Ngaio Marsh. St. Martin's Press, 2000, c1977. 277 p. Roderick Alleyn mysteries

ISBN 9780312972868

1. Scotland Yard. 2. Drug smuggling 3. Accidental death 4. Equestrianism 5. Murder investigation 6. Police 7. Detectives 8. England 9. Mysteries

Superintendent Roderick Alleyn of Scotland Yard visits the Channel Islands after a riding accident leads to charges of premeditated murder.

Marsh, Ngaio, 1895-1982

Light thickens / Ngaio Marsh. St. Martin's Paperbacks, 2000, c1982. 232 p. Roderick Alleyn mysteries

ISBN 9780312973148

1. Scotland Yard. 2. Theater 3. Drama 4. Murder investigation 5. Actors and actresses 6. Police 7. Detectives 8. England 9. Mysteries

Peregrine, owner of the Dolphin Theatre, is putting on Macbeth, the play that, superstition says, always brings bad luck. So it is by chance that Chief Superintendent Alleyn is in the audience when the claymore swings and the dummy's head is very real.

Marsh, Ngaio, 1895-1982

When in Rome / Ngaio Marsh. St. Martin's Paperbacks, 1999, c1971. 213 p. Roderick Alleyn mysteries

ISBN 9780312970970

1. Scotland Yard. 2. Tour guides (Persons) 3. Tour groups 4. Murder investigation 5. Police 6. Detectives 7. Rome, Italy 8. England 9. Mysteries

While vacationing in Rome, Inspector Roderick Alleyn comes face to face with murder when one of the members of his tour group is killed and a shady tour guide mysteriously vanishes.

"Set in Italy, much of the action takes place in an ancient church which reproduces three levels of civilization. . . . The mystery centers on a sinister blackmailing tour entrepreneur who gathers together a motley group of people, some innocent, some with good reason to want him out of the way. Drugs, sex orgies, even more delicate scandals are all grist to his mill and when he meets a very nasty demise the field of suspects is wide open. Not the least of the pleasures here is a charming love affair, and the slightly comic opera encounters between English Inspector Roderick Alleyn and the Rome police." Publishers Weekly.

Marshall, Alex

A **crown** for cold silver / Alex Marshall. Orbit, 2015. 512 p. Crimson Empire (Alex Marshall)

ISBN 9780316277983

1. Women warriors 2. Revenge 3. Mercenaries 4. Imaginary wars and battles 5. Grief 6. Enemies 7. Women generals 8. Middle-aged women 9. Imaginary creatures 10. Epic fantasy 11. Military fantasy

"It was all going so nicely, right up until the massacre." Alas, nothing lasts forever, as retired warrior Cobalt Zosia learns when the Queen of the Crimson Empire sends an army to destroy Cobalt's family and village. In response, Cobalt vows vengeance, puts an end to 20 years of self-imposed exile, and rounds up her former colleagues, the Five Villains, to slaughter her foes (not that the gang needs much persuading). Will Cobalt and company prevail? Find out in this compelling, darkly humorous fantasy saga that introduces a strong female heroine and a cast of spirited misfits. -- Description by Gillian Speace.

"This brawny revenge fantasy feels like a Tarantino movie: a hugely entertaining mix of adventure and comedy, punctuated by moments of darkness, with clever dialogue and explosive set pieces." Booklist.

Marshall, Catherine, 1914-1983

* **Christy** / Catherine Marshall. Avon Books, 1968, c1967. 501 p.

ISBN 0380001411

1. 1910s 2. Mountain life 3. Women teachers 4. Christian women 5. Christian teachers 6. Love triangles 7. Young women 8. Appalachian Region 9. Great Smoky Mountains (NC and Tenn) 10. Christian historical romances

LC 67024957

Previously published by McGraw.

A nineteen-year-old woman leaves her home to teach school in Cutter Gap, Tennessee, in 1912.

Marston, Edward

The **bawdy** basket / Edward Marston. St. Martin's Minotaur, 2002. 262 p. Nicholas Bracewell mysteries

ISBN 0312285019

1. Elizabethan era (1558-1603) 2. 16th century 3. Tudor period (1485-1603) 4. Bribery 5. Frameups 6. Judicial corruption 7. Revenge 8. Actors and actresses 9. Stage managers 10. Theater 11. Amateur detectives 12. Great Britain -- History -- Elizabeth I, 1558-1603 13. Historical mysteries 14. Mysteries

When Moll Comfrey, a woman of ill repute, is mixed up in a murder case, Westfield's Men stage manager Nicholas Bracewell seeks to figure out what Moll is hiding before his theater goes out of business.

"An Elizabethan mystery featuring Nicholas Bracewell, stage manager of Lord Westfield's Men. . . . When a young actor's father is tried, convicted, and hung for a brutal murder he claims he did not commit, his sins are unfortunately visited upon his loyal son. Nicholas agrees to investigate the matter in an effort to clear the unlucky man's name and to restore a promising young thespian to the ranks of his beloved theater company." Booklist.

Marston, Edward

The **devil's** apprentice / Edward Marston. St. Martin's Minotaur, 2001. 273 p. Nicholas Bracewell mysteries

ISBN 9780312265748

1. Elizabethan era (1558-1603) 2. 16th century 3. Tudor period (1485-1603) 4. Hotels 5. Unemployed persons 6. Puritans 7. Actors and actresses 8. Stage managers 9. Theater 10. Amateur detectives 11. Great Britain -- History -- Elizabeth I, 1558-1603 12. Historical mysteries 13. Mysteries

LC 2001019259

Out of work and desperate, the Westfield's Men theatrical troupe accepts an invitation to perform at an Essex manor house, despite the stipulation that they take on a troublesome new apprentice, Davy Stratton, but the job takes on a deadly turn when they come face to face with witchcraft and charges of being the devil's apprentices.

"Lively and entertaining: for fans of Elizabethan historicals." Library Journal.

Marston, Edward

The **roaring** boy : a novel / Edward Marston. St. Martin's Press, 1995. 260 p. Nicholas Bracewell mysteries

ISBN 0312131550

1. Elizabethan era (1558-1603) 2. 16th century 3. Tudor period (1485-1603) 4. Mathematicians 5. Murder investigation 6. Riots 7. Actors and actresses 8. Theater 9. Stage managers 10. Amateur detectives 11. Race riots 12. Great Britain -- History -- Elizabeth I, 1558-1603 13. Historical mysteries 14. Mysteries

LC 95008568

An Elizabethan theater mystery finds theater manager Nicholas Bracewell trying to save his company by solving the murder their play--a domestic drama about a sensational murder case--is based on

"Marston's colorful (and convincing) characterizations shine as Nicholas chases the secrets of the murder in order to save the company. The plot, except for one transparently finagled episode, is expertly wrought, with the suspense building steadily to breathtaking climax and some surprises saved for the very end." Publishers Weekly.

Marston, Edward

The **vagabond** clown / Edward Marston. St. Martin's Minotaur, 2003. 292 p. Nicholas Bracewell mysteries

ISBN 0312307896

1. Elizabethan era (1558-1603) 2. 16th century 3. Tudor period (1485-1603) 4. Clowns 5. Stabbing victims 6. Murder investigation

7. Actors and actresses 8. Stage managers 9. Theater 10. Amateur detectives 11. Kent, England 12. Great Britain -- History -- Elizabeth I, 1558-1603 13. Historical mysteries 14. Mysteries

LC 2002191950

When Lord Westerfield's Men are stricken by an unexpected disaster during a packed performance on the Kent countryside, Nicholas Bracewell investigates a clown's prediction about the end of the troupe.

"Lord Westfield's Men, the actors' troupe for which Bracewell works as stage manager, are forced to leave their theater after a violent act of sabotage trashes the place. Worse, someone has killed one of Westfield's friends during the melee. Bracewell struggles to save the troupe and its reputation. An outstanding historical." Library Journal.

Marston, Edward

The **wanton** angel : a novel / Edward Marston. St. Martin's Press, 1999. 279 p. Nicholas Bracewell mysteries

ISBN 0312203918

1. Elizabethan era (1558-1603) 2. 16th century 3. Tudor period (1485-1603) 4. Revenge 5. Landlords 6. Young women -- Relations with older men 7. Actors and actresses 8. Stage managers 9. Theater 10. Amateur detectives 11. Great Britain -- History -- Elizabeth I, 1558-1603 12. Historical mysteries 13. Mysteries

LC 99-22062

Nicholas Bracewell attempts to save Lord Westfield's Men, a theatrical group threatened by the murder of a star actor and by the elusive identity of a mysterious patron

Martel, Yann

Beatrice and Virgil : a novel / Yann Martel. Spiegel & Grau, 2010. 224 p.

ISBN 9781400069262

1. Authors 2. Taxidermists 3. Animals 4. Fate and fatalism 5. City life 6. Writing 7. Literary fiction

LC 2009048995

In a tale exploring the limitations of language in understanding and describing the Holocaust, a novelist and a taxidermist collaborate on a play about a donkey and a howler monkey who have survived a genocide.

"Whimsy takes a deadly serious turn in a novel that will enchant some readers and exasperate others." Kirkus.

Martel, Yann

The **high** mountains of Portugal : a novel / Yann Martel. Spiegel & Grau, 2016. 332 p.

ISBN 9780812997170

1. 1900s (Decade) 2. 1930s 3. 1980s 4. Quests 5. Loss (Psychology) 6. Material culture 7. Grief in men 8. Spiritual life 9. Automobile travel 10. Autopsy 11. Chimpanzees 12. Priests 13. Crosses (Christianity) 14. Faith 15. Family relationships 16. Portugal 17. Literary fiction

LC 2015022883

Saskatchewan Book Awards, Book of the Year Award, 2017.
Saskatchewan Book Awards, Saskatoon Book Award, 2017.

An allegorical novel in three parts is set in the fictional High Mountains of 17th-century Portugal and beyond, where characters explore questions of loss and faith while on a quest, while tackling ghosts and in the contemporary world.

"Nevertheless, this allegorical tale drives home the ephemeral nature of beauty and joy and the thin line we all walk between normalcy and madness, especially in the wake of loss." Booklist.

Martel, Yann

* **Life** of Pi : a novel / Yann Martel. Harcourt, 2001. 319 p.

ISBN 9780151008117

1. Survival (after airplane accidents, shipwrecks, etc) 2. Human/animal relationships 3. Tigers 4. Storytelling 5. Teenage boys 6. Ocean travel 7. Zoo animals 8. Orphans 9. Pacific Ocean 10. Psychological fiction 11. Literary fiction 12. Survival stories

LC 2001039737

Originally published: Toronto : Alfred A. Knopf Canada, 2001.
Asian Pacific American Award for Literature: Adult Fiction, 2004.
Booker Prize, 2002.
Quebec Writers' Federation Literary Awards, Hugh MacLennan Prize for Fiction, 2001.
Governor General's Literary Awards, English-language Fiction finalist

Possessing encyclopedia-like intelligence, unusual zookeeper's son Pi Patel sets sail for America, but when the ship sinks, he escapes on a life boat and is lost at sea with a dwindling number of animals until only he and a hungry Bengal tiger remain.

"An impassioned defense of zoos, a death-defying trans-Pacific sea adventure à la 'Kon-Tiki,' and a hilarious shaggy-dog story starring a four-hundred-and-fifty-pound Bengal tiger named Richard Parker: this audacious novel manages to be all of these. . . . This breezily aphoristic, unapologetically twee saga of man and cat is a convincing hands-on, how-to guide for dealing with what Pi calls, with typically understated brio, 'major lifeboat pests.'" The New Yorker.

Martin, Alexa

Blitzed / Alexa Martin. Jove, 2019. 323 p. Playbook (Alexa Martin)

ISBN 9780451491992

1. Women business owners 2. African American football players 3. Professional football 4. Bars (Drinking establishments) 5. Female friendship 6. Reality television programs 7. Secrets 8. Men/women relations 9. Interpersonal attraction 10. Interracial couples 11. Denver, Colorado 12. Sports romances 13. Multicultural romances 14. Contemporary romances

LC 2019011707

Professional athlete Maxwell Lewis must convince no-nonsense bar owner Brynn Sterling that he is the perfect man for her, but fate conspires against him--especially when ghosts from both their pasts make a sudden reappearance.

"Martin continues her Playbook series, following Fumbled (2019) and scores again with this perfectly blended sporty-spicy/rom-com cocktail that's so good, you could name a drink after it." Booklist.

Martin, Alexa

Fumbled / Alexa Martin. Berkley, 2019. 320 p. Playbook (Alexa Martin)

ISBN 9780451491978

1. Professional football players 2. Multiracial women 3. Single mothers 4. Professional football 5. Men/women relations 6. Interpersonal attraction 7. Interracial couples 8. Teenage pregnancy 9. Denver, Colorado 10. Sports romances 11. Multicultural romances 12. Contemporary romances

LC 2018045172

"A Jove Book."

Successful single mom, Poppy Patterson, crosses paths with her high school sweetheart, now the hard-partying starting wide receiver for the Denver Mustangs and is shocked to find her feelings rushing back to her in the follow-up to Intercepted.

Martin, Charles, 1969-

* **Long** way gone / Charles Martin. Harpercollins Christian Pub, 2016 352 p.

ISBN 9780718084714

1. Musicians 2. Redemption 3. Fathers and sons 4. Men/women relations 5. Conflict in families 6. Homecomings 7. Burn victims 8. Frameups 9. Memories 10. Families 11. Prodigal son (Parable) 12. Colorado 13. Nashville, Tennessee 14. Christian fiction 15. Coming-of-age stories

LC 2016016302

Christy Award for Book of the Year, 2017.

Having lost everything he stole from his father before being framed for a crime and injured in ways that make his music career impossible, Cooper quietly returns home to seek forgiveness and reconciliation by using his gifts to help others.

Martin, Charles, 1969-

Send down the rain / Charles Martin. Thomas Nelson, 2018 352 p.

ISBN 9780718084745

1. Self-sacrifice 2. Forgiveness (Christianity) 3. Loss (Psychology) 4. Married men -- Death 5. Grief 6. Traffic accidents 7. Vietnam veterans 8. Christian life 9. Faith (Christianity) 10. Post traumatic stress disorder 11. Secrets 12. Men/women relations 13. Interpersonal attraction 14. Second chances 15. Christian romances

LC 2017044610

When Allie loses her second husband to a car accident, traumatized Vietnam War veteran Joseph reemerges from her past in time for them both to find comfort with one another, but a secret from the distant past might stand in the way.

Martin, George R. R.

A **clash** of kings / George R.R. Martin. Bantam Books, 1999 761 p. Song of ice and fire

ISBN 0553108034

1. Ambition 2. Political corruption 3. Magic 4. Nobility 5. Dragons 6. Knights and knighthood 7. Good and evil 8. Violence 9. Rulers 10. Winter 11. Brothers 12. Imaginary kingdoms 13. Imaginary wars and battles 14. Epic fantasy

LC 9837954

Sequel to: A Game of Thrones.

Special 20th anniversary illustrated edition was published by Bantam books in 2019 with illustrations by Lauren K. Cannon

Locus Award for Fantasy Novel, 1999.

Five separate factions vie for control of the Seven Kingdoms, while an ancient form of magic, an everlasting winter, and an unearthly army threaten to return.

"The novel is notable particularly for the lived-in quality of its world, created through abundant detail that dramatically increases narrative length even as it aids suspension of disbelief; for the comparatively modest role of magic . . . and for its magnificent action-filled climax." Publishers Weekly.

Martin, George R. R.

A **dance** with dragons / George R. R. Martin. Spectra, 2011. 1008 p. Song of ice and fire

ISBN 9780553801477

1. Ambition 2. Political corruption 3. Nobility 4. Power (Social sciences) 5. Dragons 6. Women rulers 7. Quests 8. Wizards 9. Magic 10. Winter 11. Betrayal 12. Good and evil 13. Soldiers 14. Slavery 15. Violence 16. Alliances 17. Imaginary kingdoms 18. Epic fantasy Goodreads Choice Award, 2011.

Locus Award for Fantasy Novel, 2012.

New threats emerge to endanger the future of the Seven Kingdoms, as Daenerys Targaryen fights off a multitude of enemies, while Jon Snow faces his foes both in the Watch and beyond the great Wall of ice and stone.

"The heart-hammering conclusion hints that the next installment will see a return to the fiery battles and icy terror that earned the series its fanatic following. Even ostensibly disillusioned fans will be caught up in the interweaving stories, especially when Martin drops little hints around long-debated questions such as Jon's parentage." Publishers Weekly.

Martin, George R. R.

A **feast** for crows / George R.R. Martin Spectra, 2004. 1024 p. Song of ice and fire

ISBN 0553801503

1. Ambition 2. Political corruption 3. Magic 4. Nobility 5. Knights and knighthood 6. Good and evil 7. Violence 8. Alliances 9. Soldiers 10. Assassins 11. Rulers 12. Winter 13. Dragons 14. Imaginary kingdoms 15. Epic fantasy

The uneasy peace is threatened by new plots, intrigues, and alliances that once again will plunge the Seven Kingdoms into all-out war for control of the Iron Throne.

"The author introduces plot twists and characters that continue to flesh out one of the genre's most detailed and intriguing worlds. A must-purchase for libraries owning the series, this panoramic fantasy adventure is highly recommended." Library Journal.

Martin, George R. R.

Fire & blood : 300 years before a Game of Thrones (a Targaryen history) / George R. R. Martin ; illustrated by Doug Wheatley. Bantam Dell Pub Group, 2018. 640 p. Song of ice and fire

ISBN 9781524796280

1. Royal houses 2. Dragons 3. Rulers 4. Imaginary wars and battles 5. Imaginary kingdoms 6. Political intrigue 7. Epic fantasy

Also published Nov. 2018 in the UK by HarperCollins as Fire and Blood: a history of the Targaryen kings from Aegon the conqueror to Aegon III as scribed by Archmaester Gyldayn.

The thrilling history of the Targaryens comes to life in this masterly work by the author of A Song of Ice and Fire, the inspiration for HBO's Game of Thrones.

Martin, George R. R.

* A **game** of thrones / George R. R. Martin. Bantam Books, 1996. 694 p. Song of ice and fire

ISBN 0553103547

1. Ambition 2. Political corruption 3. Magic 4. Nobility 5. Knights and knighthood 6. Good and evil 7. Violence 8. Rulers 9. Winter 10. Dragons 11. Imaginary kingdoms 12. Epic fantasy

LC 95-43936

20th anniversary illustrated edition published: New York : Random House, 2016.

Locus Award for Fantasy Novel, 1997.

The aristocratic Stark family faces its ultimate challenge in the onset of a generation-long winter, the poisonous plots of the rival Lannisters, the emergence of the Neverborn demons, and the arrival of barbarian hordes.

"The first volume in A Song of Ice and Fire saga, combines intrigue, action, romance, and mystery in a family saga. The family is the Starks of Winterfell, a society in crisis due to climatic change that has created decades-long seasons, and a society almost without magic but with human perversity abundant and active. Martin reaches a new plateau in terms of narrative technique, action scenes, and integrating . . . his political views into the story." Booklist.

Martin, George R. R.

A **storm** of swords / George R.R. Martin. Bantam Books, 2000. 800 p. Song of ice and fire

ISBN 0553106635

1. Ambition 2. Political corruption 3. Magic 4. Nobility 5. Knights and knighthood 6. Good and evil 7. Violence 8. Rulers 9. Winter 10. Dragons 11. Imaginary kingdoms 12. Imaginary wars and battles 13. Epic fantasy

LC 00060827

Locus Award for Fantasy Novel, 2001.

The Seven Kingdoms are torn by strife as the three surviving contenders for the throne continue their struggle for power, Robb Stark defends his fledgling kingdom from the ravaging Greyjoys, Winterfell lies in ruins and Jon Snow confronts an escalating threat from behind the Wall, and Danerys Stormborn and her dragon allies continue to grow in power.

"The author's ability to interweave dozens of plot lines and to create memorable characters makes this a rousing saga that should appeal to most fans of grand-scale fantasy. Recommended for most libraries, along with its predecessors, A Game of Thrones and A Clash of Kings." Library Journal.

Martin, Kat

Beyond reason / Kat Martin. Zebra Books, 2017. 395 p. Texas trilogy (Kat Martin)

ISBN 9781420143157

1. Organized crime 2. Trucking industry and trade 3. Women business owners 4. Protectiveness in men 5. Family businesses 6. Truck drivers 7. Rich men 8. Coercion 9. Drug traffic 10. Sexual attraction 11. Men/women relations 12. Texas 13. Romantic suspense

Dealing with the death of her grandfather and Drake Trucking's top driver, Carly Drake, faced with bankruptcy, threats and the fear of failure, is forced to ask the last man she wants to owe for help?Lincoln Cain, the multimillionaire owner of a rival company.

Martin, Steve, 1945-

An **object** of beauty / Steve Martin. Grand Central Pub., 2010. 320 p.

ISBN 9780446573641

1. Women art dealers 2. Ambition in women 3. Art museums 4. Art auctions 5. Popular culture 6. City life 7. Personal conduct 8. New York City -- Social life and customs 9. Satirical fiction

LC 2010007885

Lacey Yeager takes New York City's art world by storm, charming men and women, old and young, rich and even richer with her magnetic charisma and liveliness and experiencing the highs and lows of the art world from the late 1990s into the present day.

"Martin has a gift for rendering an esoteric scene accessible, piercing its sillier pretensions while making a case for art's real aesthetic (if not monetary) value. It takes a certain nimbleness to play the dual roles of proxy art-history professor and compelling storyteller without falling off the literary balance beam. Martin, wry, wise, and keenly observant, rarely misses a step." Entertainment Weekly.

Martin, Steve, 1945-

The **pleasure** of my company : a novella / Steve Martin. Hyperion, 2003. 160 p.

ISBN 0786869216

1. Life change events 2. Men with mental illnesses 3. Single mothers 4. Women students 5. Toddlers 6. Former husbands 7. Grandmothers 8. Obsessive-compulsive disorder 9. Neuroses in men 10. Love 11. Child custody 12. Protectiveness 13. Santa Monica, California 14. Humorous stories 15. Mainstream fiction 16. Psychological fiction

LC 2003049954

Daniel, a troubled man who lives alone, detached from the world, passes his time filling out contest applications and counting ceiling tiles, until his attachment to Clarissa and Teddy helps him rediscover the outside world.

"This novella is a delight, embodying a satisfying story arc, a jeweler's eye for detail, intelligent pacing and a clean, sturdy prose style." Publishers Weekly.

Martin, Steve, 1945-

Shopgirl Hyperion, 2000. 130 p.

ISBN 0786866586

1. Department store employees 2. Clerks (Retail industry and trade) 3. Department stores 4. Prescription drug abuse 5. Young women 6. Artists 7. Men/women relations 8. Beverly Hills, California 9. Mainstream fiction 10. Psychological fiction

LC 00038874

Mirabelle is the shopgirl who sells gloves at Neiman Marcus. She meets Ray Porter, a wealthy businessman twice her age. Together they embark on a relationship and try to decipher the language of love.

"There is an impressive gravity about 'Shopgirl.' Its glints of comedy are sharp and dry. . . . The novella has an edge to it, and a deep, unassuageable loneliness." New York Times Book Review.

Martin, Valerie, 1948-

Property / Valerie Martin. Nan A. Talese, 2003. 200 p.

ISBN 038550408X

1. Antebellum America (1820-1861) 2. 1820s 3. 19th century 4. Plantation owners' spouses 5. Love triangles 6. Slave resistance and revolts 7. Plantation life 8. Women slaves 9. Mistresses 10. Slavery 11. Hate in women 12. Louisiana -- Social life and customs -- 19th century 13. Historical fiction 14. Psychological fiction 15. Literary fiction

LC 2002066846

Orange Prize for Fiction, 2003.

The tragedies and emotional repercussions of slavery in the antebellum South are seen through the eyes of slave owner Manon Gaudet, who marries the owner of a sugar plantation, only to see her own slave, Sarah, become her husband's mistress.

"This work presents itself as a novel about the abuse of power within the loveless marriage between an antebellum plantation owner and his wife, their private suffering amplified by the social context of slavery. Bondage and its invitation to brutality are not unexplored terrain, but embedded within what might be mistaken as a morality play is a more subtle and compelling story: a contest of wills between two women, Manon Gaudet and Sarah, the slave she received from her aunt as a wedding gift." New York Times Book Review.

Martin, William, 1950-

Cape Cod / William Martin. Warner Books, 1991. 652 p.

1. Family feuds 2. Landowners 3. Extortion 4. Land claims 5. Rich people 6. Cape Cod, Massachusetts -- History 7. Historical fiction 8. Family sagas

LC 90050534

Illustrated with black-and-white on end-papers.

Includes genealogy charts.

"Martin embraces the entire sweep of American history with unflagging relish for authentic detail and private moments. He creates generation after generation of feisty Hilyards and cruel Bigelows, pitting them against one another in religious and political skirmishes and joining them in risky love. They endure hardships and shipwrecks, scandal and imprisonment, shame and anger, and contribute their bit to the making of America." Booklist.

Martine, Arkady

* A **memory** called empire / Arkady Martine. Tor, 2019. 464 p. Teixcalaan novels

ISBN 9781250186430

1. Ambassadors 2. Poetry writing 3. Imperialism 4. Cultural differences 5. Imaginary empires 6. Political intrigue 7. Memories 8. Murder 9. Interstellar relations 10. Life on other planets 11. Civilization 12. Identity (Psychology) 13. Women diplomats 14. Technology 15. Space opera 16. Science fiction mysteries

LC 2018046933

"A Tom Doherty Associates Book."

After discovering that the previous ambassador in her post may have been murdered, Mahit Dzmare arrives in the capital of the Teixcalaanli Empire determined to find the killer, as she hides a secret which may save her station from the Teixcalaan's desire for expansion.

"Politics and personalities blend with an immersive setting and beautiful prose in a debut that weaves threads of identity, assimilation, technology, and culture to offer an exceedingly well-done sf political thriller." Library Journal.

Martineau, Maxym M.

Kingdom of exiles / Maxym M. Martineau. Sourcebooks Casablanca, 2019. 448 p. Beast Charmer

ISBN 9781492689386

1. Mythical creatures 2. Human/animal communication 3. Women exiles 4. Assassins 5. Human/animal telepathy 6. Quests 7. Curses 8. Men/women relations 9. Fantasy romances

Forced to sell her beloved magical beasts on the black market -- an offense punishable by death -- exiled beast charmer Leena Edenfrell, with a price on her head, makes a devil's bargain with the realm's most talented assassin in exchange for her life.

Martini, Steve, 1946-

Compelling evidence / Steve Martini. G. P. Putnam's Sons, 1992. 379 p. Paul Madriani novels

ISBN 9780399137129

1. Lawyers 2. Extramarital affairs 3. Frameups 4. Revenge 5. Trials (Murder) 6. Criminal evidence 7. Employees -- Dismissal 8. Former lovers 9. Defense attorneys 10. San Diego, California 11. Legal thrillers

LC 91030253

In a riveting courtroom drama, Talia Potter, indicted for the murder of her judge husband, turns to her lover, Paul Madriani--her husband's ex-law partner--to defend her.

"Besides giving us the scoop on ballistics analysis and post-mortem blood distribution, the author answers just about every cynical question you've ever had about the games lawyers play." New York Times Book Review.

Martinson, T. J.

* The **reign** of the Kingfisher : a novel / T. J. Martinson. Flatiron Books, 2019. 320 p.

ISBN 9781250170217

1. Superheroes 2. Hostages 3. Staged deaths 4. Vigilantes 5. Villains 6. Journalists 7. Police 8. Hackers 9. Secrets 10. City life 11. Chicago, Illinois 12. Superhero stories 13. Crime fiction 14. Presumed dead

LC 2018030160

30 years ago a superhero tried to save Chicago. Now the city is again under siege.

Marwood, Alex

The **killer** next door / Alex Marwood. Penguin Books, 2014. 384 p.

ISBN 9780143126690

1. Boarding houses 2. Neighbors 3. Serial murderers 4. Suspicion 5. Criminals 6. Threat (Psychology) 7. Landlord and tenant 8. London, England 9. Psychological suspense

LC 2014012901

Standard print edition originally published: London: Sphere, 2013. Macavity Award for Best Mystery Novel, 2015.

The secretive tenants of a dodgy old building are forced into an uneasy alliance by a terrible accident that reveals one of them to be a killer.

"Marwood, a British journalist writing under a pseudonym, not only creates a cast of memorable characters, but also ratchets up the suspense, leaving readers to dread what might be around the next corner. Many writers shine at characterization or at creating tension; the trick is in successfully combining the two. In this case, readers will care what happens to Collette and the rest of the boarders while simultaneously waiting for the literary axe to fall. Marwood--whose first novel, The Wicked Girls (2013), won an Edgar Award--proves she's got staying power in this addictive tale." Kirkus.

Mason, Bobbie Ann

Patchwork / Bobbie Ann Mason ; introduction by George Saunders. University Press of Kentucky, 2018. 478 p.

ISBN 9780813175454

1. Human nature 2. Interpersonal relations 3. Family relationships 4. Kentucky 5. Tennessee 6. Short stories 7. Literary fiction 8. Domestic fiction

LC 2018011975

Patchwork contains short stories first published in the New Yorker and other leading periodicals; chapters from Mason's acclaimed novels, including In Country, An Atomic Romance, and The Girl in the Blue Beret; and riveting excerpts from Mason's eclectic nonfiction. Some examples of Mason's recent explorations in flash fiction appear here in print for the first time.

Mason, Bobbie Ann

Shiloh and other stories / Bobbie Ann Mason. Modern Library, 2001, c1982. 240 p.

ISBN 9780375758430

1. Rural life -- Kentucky 2. Kentucky 3. Short stories

LC 82047541

Originally published: New York : Harper & Row, 1982.

Hemingway Foundation/PEN Award, 1983.

National Book Critics Circle Award for Fiction finalist, 1982

National Book Award for Fiction finalist, 1983

A collection of stories, mostly about people raised in western Kentucky, that portrays, in carefully observed detail, their struggle to reconcile family traditions and religion with new societal pressures and lifestyles and charts their search for understanding.

"Capturing in vivid detail the emotional frustrations of her characters and the unsettling ambience of her small-town Kentucky settings, Mason portrays the uneasy feelings of people who don't know what they want out of life but who do know that what they have isn't it." Booklist.

Mason, Daniel (Daniel Philippe)

The **piano** tuner / Daniel Mason. Knopf, 2002. 336 p.

ISBN 0375414657

1. Great Britain. Army Officers 2. Piano tuners 3. Colonialism -- Burma 4. British in Burma 5. Quests 6. Diplomats -- Great Britain 7. Diplomacy 8. Burma -- History -- 19th century 9. Historical fiction

Originally published: New York : Alfred A. Knopf, 2002.

In 1886, piano tuner Edgar Drake leaves London for the jungles of Burma, where he has been asked to repair a grand piano belonging to a British army officer who uses the piano and music to help keep the peace among warring local Burmese princes.

"Mason proves himself equally adept at scenes of wry humor and moments of rapture; most remarkable, he has written a profound adventure story with an unexpected climax, as the mild piano tuner finally becomes the hero of his own life." The New Yorker.

Mason, Jamie

The **hidden** things / Jamie Mason. Gallery Books, 2019. 352 p.

ISBN 9781501177316

1. Isabella Stewart Gardner Museum. 2. Art thefts 3. Social media 4. Fourteen-year-old girls 5. Victims of violent crimes 6. Self-defense 7. Assertiveness in teenage girls 8. Stepfathers 9. Painting, Dutch 10. Art dealers 11. Secrets 12. Deception 13. Museum thefts 14. Thrillers and suspense

A hair-raising, atmospheric thriller from the acclaimed author of Three Graves Full is inspired by the real-life unsolved theft of a 17th-century painting.

Mason, Jamie

Three graves full / Jamie Mason. Gallery Books, 2013. 320 p.

ISBN 9781451685039

1. Murderers 2. Coincidence 3. Missing persons 4. Widowers 5. Psychological suspense

LC 2012014974

"There is very little peace for a man with a body buried in his backyard." So begins Three Graves Full, an often poetic (sometimes almost ornate) debut told from many points of view (including a dog's). Readers quickly learn that mild-mannered Jason Getty uncharacteristically killed a person ("even a eunuch can get angry") and buried the body at the back of his property. Now traumatically averse to yard work, he hires a lawn service to tidy just the front and side yards. Stunningly, the lawn guys dig up two bodies -- and neither of them were buried by Jason, whose life is about to get a lot more complicated. - Description by Dawn Towery.

Mason, Richard, 1978-

Who killed Piet Barol? : a novel / Richard Mason. Alfred A. Knopf, 2017, c2016. 367 p.

ISBN 9780385352888

1. First World War era (1914-1918) 2. Swindlers and swindling 3. Forests 4. Colonialism 5. Greed 6. Race relations 7. Sacred space 8. Arrogance in men 9. Husband and wife 10. Furniture industry and trade 11. Consequences 12. Men/women relations 13. South Africa -- Social life and customs -- 20th century 14. Historical fiction 15. Literary fiction

LC 2016008860

"This is a Borzoi book."

Originally published: London : Weidenfeld & Nicolson, 2016.

European adventurer Piet Barol navigates the turbulence and opportunities of South Africa's Cape Colony of 1914 in the face of dwindling funds and a business prospect that puts him in pursuit of wood from a sacred forest of the Xhosa.

"Luminously reminiscent of Chinua Achebe's Things Fall Apart (1958) and recalling the disastrous culture clash of Barbara Kingsolver's Poisonwood Bible (1998)." Booklist.

Mason, Timothy, 1950-

The **Darwin** affair / Tim Mason. Algonquin Books of Chapel Hill, 2019. 336 p.

ISBN 9781616206345

1. Darwin, Charles, 1809-1882 On the origin of species 2. Victorian era (1837-1901) 3. 1860s 4. Attempted assassination 5. Psychopaths 6. Conspiracies 7. Detectives 8. Investigations 9. Intrigue 10. Murder 11. Secrets 12. Fame 13. City life 14. London, England 15. Great Britain -- History -- Victoria, 1837-1901 16. Germany 17. Victorian mysteries 18. Historical mysteries

LC 2018037996

Unsettling connections between an assassination attempt on Queen Victoria and the gruesome murder of a petty thief lead Chief Detective Inspector Charles Field to a shocking conspiracy related to the publication of Darwin's On the Origin of Species.

Massey, Sujata

The **Satapur** moonstone / Sujata Massey. Soho Crime, 2019 384 p. Perveen Mistry novels

ISBN 9781616959098

1. 1920s 2. British Raj (1858-1947) 3. Women lawyers 4. Rulers -- Succession 5. Courts and courtiers 6. Princes 7. Political intrigue 8. Colonialism 9. Murder investigation 10. Manipulation (Social sciences) 11. India 12. Mumbai, India 13. Historical mysteries

LC 2018046843

India's only female lawyer in 1922 helps the royal ladies of Satapur by getting involved in the power plays and ancient vendettas of the palace.

"Edgar finalist Massey's second whodunit featuring Bombay attorney Perveen Mistry is even better than the series' impressive debut...The winning, self-sufficient Perveen should be able to sustain a long series." Publishers Weekly.

Massey, Sujata

* The **widows** of Malabar Hill : a mystery of 1920s Bombay / Sujata Massey. Soho Crime, 2018 400 p. Perveen Mistry novels

ISBN 9781616957780

1. 1920s 2. Wills 3. Women lawyers 4. Murder investigation 5. Purdah 6. Muslim women 7. Women's rights 8. Guardian and ward 9. Inheritance and succession 10. Manipulation (Social sciences) 11. Mumbai, India 12. India 13. Historical mysteries

LC 2017021391

Agatha Award for Best Historical Novel, 2018.

Edgar Allan Poe Awards: Mary Higgins Clark Award, 2019.

Sue Feder Historical Mystery Award, 2019.

RUSA Reading List, 2019.

Introduces Bombay's first female lawyer, Oxford graduate Perveen Mistry, as she investigates a suspicious will on behalf of three Muslim widows living in strict purdah seclusion who become subject to a murderous guardian's schemes for their inheritances.

Mastai, Elan

All **our** wrong todays : a novel / Elan Mastai. Dutton, 2017. 373 p.

ISBN 9781101985137

1. Time travel 2. Reality 3. Errors 4. Life change events 5. Options, alternatives, choices 6. Technology and civilization 7. Utopias 8. Young men 9. Science fiction 10. Literary fiction 11. Psychological fiction

LC 2016013073

Living in an alternate world of flying cars, moon bases and plentiful food, aimless Tom Barren is blindsided by an accident of fate that leads to a time-travel mishap that lands him in our less-than-ideal 2016, where he discovers wonderful unexpected versions of his own life.

"A potent mixture of sincere introspection and a riveting examination of time travel and alternate realities, this highly recommended novel is reminiscent of Jo Walton's My Real Children with the breeziness of Robin Sloan's Mr. Penumbra's 24-Hour Bookstore." Library Journal.

Matar, Hisham, 1970-

Anatomy of a disappearance : a novel / Hisham Matar. Dial Press, 2011. 256 p.

ISBN 9780385340441

1. Fathers and sons 2. Loss (Psychology) 3. Family secrets 4. Stepmothers 5. Missing persons 6. Exiles 7. Fathers and sons 8. Cairo, Egypt 9. Political fiction 10. Literary fiction 11. Coming-of-age stories

Born into exile, 11-year-old Nuri, the son of worldly parents who fled the revolution in their Arab country, is transfixed along with his widowed father by an Arab-English woman who joins their family, a situation that is complicated by Nuri's father's disappearance.

"Part of what makes Anatomy of a Disappearance worth reading is that its ambiguous and slightly cruel ending does not yield easy transcendence. In fact, it entirely recasts the meaning of the title. There are many disappearances that haunt the narrator not least his own. Though politics take a back seat, they shadow its margins, like the unknown men who kidnap Kamal. . . . For Americans attempting to understand the Middle East, this book provides a poignant picture of grief at the hands of political forces much larger than the individual lives they rupture." Cleveland Plain Dealer.

Matar, Hisham, 1970-

In the country of men / Hisham Matar. Dial Press, 2007. 256 p.

ISBN 0385340427

1. 1970s 2. Nine-year-old boys 3. Deception in men 4. Political prisoners 5. Exiles -- Libya 6. Childhood 7. Family relationships 8. Political crimes and offenses 9. Libya -- Politics and government -- 1969- 10. Coming-of-age stories 11. Political fiction

LC 2006050649

RSL Ondaatje Prize, 2007.

Shortlisted for the Man Booker Prize, 2006.

National Book Critics Circle Award for Fiction finalist, 2007

On a hot day in Tripoli in the summer of 1979, nine-year-old Suleiman spots his father, supposedly away on business, across from the market square and wearing dark glasses, the first portent of grave danger in a previously unsuspected world.

"A remarkably perceptive and affecting portrait of a young boy's premature political awakening. . . . [Matar] expertly builds an atmosphere of palpable tension, and though this novel never delves directly into politics, the menacing pall cast by political tyranny looms over the proceedings." Miami Herald.

MatchUp : the battle of the sexes just got thrilling / edited by Lee Child. Simon & Schuster, 2017. 445 p.

ISBN 9781501141591

1. Detectives 2. Private investigators 3. Criminal investigation 4. Thrillers and suspense 5. Short stories 6. Anthologies

LC 2016046513

A follow-up to FaceOff collects stories written by best-selling thriller authors, 11 women and 11 men partnered in male-female literary pairings, in an anthology that includes contributions by such favorites as Sandra Brown, John Sandford and Eric Van Lustbader.

Matheson, Richard, 1926-2013

Hunted past reason / Richard Matheson. Tor, 2002. 335 p.

ISBN 0765302713

1. Wilderness survival 2. Men with mental illnesses 3. Camping 4. Male friendship 5. Envy in men 6. California 7. Psychological suspense 8. Thrillers and suspense

LC 2001050768

"A Tom Doherty Associates book."

A camping trip in northern California exposes long-hidden rivalries and resentments between two old friends with tensions rising as they get farther from civilization, until the hostility erupts into a life or death struggle for survival.

"Two old friends, Bob (a novelist) and Doug (an actor), head off into the woods for a short hiking trip. Bob wants some hands-on experience for a novel he's working on; Doug is an expert in woodsmanship. From the get-go, there is tension between them: Doug seems excessively demanding; Bob reacts a little too sharply to his friend's criticisms of his stamina and abilities. Soon the mood turns dark, transforming the story into a psychological thriller." Booklist.

Matheson, Richard, 1926-2013

* I am legend / Richard Matheson. TOR, 1997, c1954. 317 p.

ISBN 9780312865047

1. 1970s 2. Survival (after epidemics) 3. Vampires 4. Vampire slayers 5. Loners 6. Survival 7. Plague 8. Loneliness in men 9. Resourcefulness 10. End of the world 11. Courage in men 12. Loss (Psychology) 13. Post-apocalypse 14. Horror 15. Apocalyptic fiction 16. Science fiction

Adapted to films entitled: The last man on Earth(1964), The omega man(1971), and I am legend(2007). It was also an inspiration for NIght of the living dead(1968).

Originally published: Garden City, N.Y., : Nelson Doubleday, 1954.

A lone human survivor in a world that is overrun by vampires, Robert Neville leads a desperate life in which he must barricade himself in his home every night and hunt down the starving undead by day.

Mathews, Brendan

The **world** of tomorrow / Brendan Mathews. Little, Brown, 2017. 416 p.

ISBN 9780316382199

1. Between the Wars (1918-1939) 2. 1930s 3. Brothers 4. Thieves 5. Irish in the United States 6. Extortion 7. Assassins 8. Family relationships 9. Musicians 10. Clergy 11. Post-traumatic stress disorder 12. Fugitives 13. New York City -- Social life and customs -- 20th century 14. Historical fiction

Three brothers caught up in a whirlwind week of love, blackmail, and betrayal culminating in an assassination plot, set in prewar New York.

"With the wit of a 30s screwball comedy and the depth of a thoroughly researched historical novel, this one grabs the reader from the beginning to its suspenseful climax." Publishers Weekly.

Mathis, Ayana

The **twelve** tribes of Hattie / Ayana Mathis. Alfred A. Knopf, 2013. 256 p.

ISBN 9780307959423

1. African Americans -- Migrations -- History -- 20th century 2. African American families 3. Family relationships 4. African American women 5. African American gay men 6. Mother and child 7. Race relations 8. Philadelphia, Pennsylvania 9. Historical fiction 10. Family sagas

LC 2012010779

BCALA Literary Award for First Novelist, 2013.

LIST OF FICTIONAL WORKS

Ayana Mathis tells the story of the children of the Great Migration through the trials of one unforgettable family.

Matlwa, Kopano,

Evening primrose / Kopano Matlwa. Quercus, 2018, c2016 160 p.

ISBN 9781635060324

1. Medicine 2. Women physicians 3. Medical care -- Accessibility 4. Immigrants -- Discrimination 5. Apartheid -- Influence 6. Social conflict 7. Xenophobia 8. Prejudice 9. South Africa -- Politics and government -- 1994- 10. Literary fiction 11. Diary novels

LC 2017045361

First published: South Africa : Jacana Media (Pty) Ltd, 2016.

When Masechaba finally achieves her childhood dream of becoming a doctor, her ambition is tested as she faces the stark reality of South Africa's public healthcare system. As she leaves her deeply religious mother and makes friends with the politically-minded Nyasha, Masechaba's eyes are opened to the rising xenophobic tension that carries echoes of apartheid. Battling her inner demons, she must decide if she should take a stand to help her best friend, even it comes at a high personal cost.

Matthews, Jason, 1951-

* The **Kremlin's** candidate / Jason Matthews. Scribner, 2018 434 p. Dominika Egorova and Nathaniel Nash novels

ISBN 9781501140082

1. Putin, Vladimir Vladimirovich, 1952- 2. Kremlin, Moscow 3. Women spies 4. Double agents 5. Spies -- Russia 6. Espionage 7. CIA agents 8. Moles (Spies) 9. Political intrigue 10. International intrigue 11. Men/women relations 12. Interpersonal attraction 13. Russia -- Foreign relations -- United States 14. United States -- Foreign relations -- Russia 15. Spy fiction 16. Thrillers and suspense

Overhearing a Kremlin plot to install a spy in a high intelligence position so that the Russians can identify CIA assets in Moscow, Dominika launches a desperate mole hunt, only to be exposed and arrested before recklessly immersing herself in Kremlin palace intrigues in the hopes of stealing as much information as possible before her time runs out.

Matthews, Jason, 1951-

Palace of treason / Jason Matthews. Scribner, 2015. 448 p. Dominika Egorova and Nathaniel Nash novels

ISBN 9781476793740

1. Intelligence service 2. Double agents 3. Women spies 4. Spies -- Russia 5. CIA agents 6. Undercover operations 7. Men/women relations 8. Moscow, Russia 9. Russia -- Foreign relations -- United States 10. United States -- Foreign relations -- Russia 11. Spy fiction 12. Thrillers and suspense

Sequel to Red Sparrow

RUSA Reading List Short List, 2016.

Navigating brutal enemies in her espionage work for the CIA, a Russian Intelligence agent pursues a life-threatening affair with her CIA handler before she is discovered by a mole.

"Authentic tradecraft, a complex plot that steadily builds tension, and credible heroes and villains on both sides make this a standout. Recipes at the end of each chapter provide some welcome relief from some brutal violence." Publishers Weekly.

Matthews, Jason, 1951-

Red sparrow : a novel / Jason Matthews. Scribner, 2013. 448 p. Dominika Egorova and Nathaniel Nash novels

ISBN 9781476706122

1. Seduction 2. Women spies 3. Spies -- Russia 4. CIA agents 5. Moles (Spies) 6. Interpersonal attraction 7. Men/women relations 8. Ballet dancers 9. Russia -- Foreign relations -- United States

10. United States -- Foreign relations -- Russia 11. Spy fiction 12. Thrillers and suspense

LC 2012031933

Sequel: Palace of treason

Edgar Allan Poe Award for Best First Novel by an American Author, 2014.

RUSA Reading List, 2014.

Thriller Award for Best First Novel, 2014.

Former ballerina Dominika Egorova serves Vladimir Putin's regime by seducing, then spying on, enemies of the state. CIA officer Nate Nash has been reassigned to Helsinki after nearly blowing the cover of a highly valuable Russian mole, and this is where Dominika latches on, determined to learn the mole's identity. But Dominika is more than a pretty lady -- she's smart, and her synesthesia allows her to tell when someone is lying. As they try to outwit and out-spy each other, readers are treated to vivid, authentic details of spycraft. Author Jason Matthews knows his stuff -- he worked for the CIA for more than 30 years -- and there are shades of John le Carr? in his writing. - Description by Shauna Griffin.

Matthiessen, Peter

Bone by bone : a novel / Peter Matthiessen. Random House, 1999. 410 p. Watson trilogy

ISBN 0375501029

1. 19th century 2. Frontier and pioneer life -- Everglades, Florida 3. Violence in men 4. Murder 5. Sugarcane 6. Swamps -- Florida 7. Entrepreneurs 8. Businesspeople 9. Racism 10. Everglades, Florida 11. Florida -- History -- 1865- 12. South Carolina 13. Historical fiction 14. Family sagas

LC 98-46180

James Fenimore Cooper Prize, 2001

Continues the saga of anti-hero E.J. Watson, an entrepreneurial sugar cane farmer in the Everglades, exile in Indian territory, devoted husband, distant father, and allegedly, a cold-blooded killer

Matthiessen, Peter

* **Far** Tortuga : a novel / Peter Matthiessen. Random House, 1975. 408 p.

1. Ships 2. Turtles 3. Survival (after airplane accidents, shipwrecks, etc) 4. Pirates 5. Oceans 6. Marine biology 7. Caribbean Area 8. Sea stories 9. Literary fiction

LC 74020576

"Almost casually, we have been given a full measure of suspense, adventure, and first-rate descriptive writing; and along with and underneath these things, a group of characters who come fully alive with a complexity and even depth that the usual, traditional story of men at sea never gives us." Choice.

Matthiessen, Peter

In paradise : a novel / Peter Matthiessen. Riverhead Books, A member of Penguin Group (USA), 240 p.

ISBN 9781594633171

1. Auschwitz (Concentration camp) 2. Teachers 3. Jewish women 4. Family secrets 5. Good and evil 6. College teachers 7. Spiritual retreats 8. Concentration camp inmates 9. Holocaust (1933-1945) 10. Literary fiction

LC 2013046176

Joining a diverse group of visitors at the site of a former Nazi concentration camp, Polish-American academic Clements Olin performs research while witnessing personal and political tensions erupting among his fellow participants.

"The strongest sections relate to these more concrete missions--passages about Olin's family history, in particular, stand out. But the novel focuses mainly on the abstract: what it feels like to spend days on end at the death campthe frustration, alienation, and otherworldliness of it." Publishers Weekly.

Matthiessen, Peter

Killing Mister Watson / Peter Matthiessen. Random House, 1990. 372 p. Watson trilogy

ISBN 0394554000

1. 1890s 2. 1910s 3. Frontier and pioneer life 4. Violence in men 5. Murder -- Florida 6. Men -- Florida 7. Friendship 8. Murderers 9. Enemies 10. Pioneers -- Florida 11. Florida 12. Everglades, Florida 13. Historical fiction 14. Family sagas

LC 89043424

Includes end-paper maps.

The arrival of Edgar J. Watson, a complex man with a troubling and violent reputation, spells trouble for the inhabitants of the nineteenth-century Everglades, in a recreation of the life and death of a real-life character

"This historical novel traces the growth of the legend of Edgar J. Watson, a famed outlaw in the Florida Everglades of a hundred years ago. Voice Lit Suppl,By the time he was murdered, Watson was one of the most successful sugar-cane farmers between Tampa and Key West. Everyone liked and admired him, but no one trusted him. Proof was always scant but people wound up dead when Watson was around. . . . Matthiessen tells his story through the voice of Watson's family and neighbors in a series of oral histories, diary entries and old newspaper accounts, all of it fiction. By turns droll, rambunctious, foolish and wise, this collective narration mounts into a carefully orchestrated cacophony of contradictory testimony in which suspicion and mistrust are gradually revealed as the base elements of mystery." Newsweek.

Matthiessen, Peter

* Shadow country : a new rendering of the Watson legend / Peter Matthiessen. Modern Library, 2008. xvi, 892 p.

ISBN 9780679640196

1. Watson, Edgar J, 1855-1910 2. 19th century 3. Frontier and pioneer life 4. Murderers 5. Violence in men 6. Neighbors 7. Murder victims 8. Florida -- History -- 19th century 9. Everglades, Florida -- History -- 19th century 10. Historical fiction 11. Family sagas 12. Literary fiction

LC 2007025117

National Book Award for Fiction, 2008.

Inspired by a near-mythic event of the wild Florida frontier at the turn of the twentieth century, Shadow Country reimagines the legend of the inspired Everglades sugar planter and notorious outlaw E. J. Watson, who drives himself relentlessly toward his own violent end at the hands of neighbors who mostly admired him, in a killing that obsessed his favorite son.--From publisher description.

"Matthiessen is meticulous in creating characters, lyrical in describing landscapes, and resolute in dissecting the values and costs that accompanied the development of this nation." Seattle Times.

Maturin, Charles Robert, 1780-1824

* Melmoth the wanderer : a tale / Charles Maturin ; edited with an introduction and notes by Victor Sage. Penguin Books, 2001, c1820. 704 p.

ISBN 9780140447613

1. Immortality 2. Jews, Spanish 3. Wanderers and wandering 4. Uncles 5. Betrayal 6. Portraits 7. Ancestors 8. Temptation 9. Manuscripts 10. Good and evil 11. Faustian bargains 12. Ireland -- History -- 19th century 13. Gothic fiction 14. Classics

First published 1820.

After striking a deal with the Devil, Sebastian Melmoth spends his extended lifetime searching the world for someone to take his place in the Faustian bargain. Written in 1820 by an Anglican priest, this Gothic novel consists of several tales-within-a-tale. Enthusiasts of the brooding melodrama include Balzac, Poe, Dostoyevsky, and Baudelaire.

Maugham, W. Somerset (William Somerset), 1874-1965

Cakes and ale : or, the skeleton in the cupboard / W. Somerset Maugham. Vintage, 2000, c1930. 202 p.

ISBN 9780375725029

1. Independence in women 2. Social classes 3. Authors 4. Biographers 5. Biography 6. Authors' spouses 7. Fame 8. Remarriage 9. Extramarital affairs 10. Sex customs 11. Men/women relations 12. Great Britain -- History -- Victoria, 1837-1901 13. England 14. Psychological fiction 15. Literary fiction 16. Modern classics

The bitter, witty novel about the business of writing and London literary society between the two World Wars focuses on the lives of a famous writer and his two contrasting wives.

Maugham, W. Somerset (William Somerset), 1874-1965

The **moon** and sixpence / W. Somerset Maugham ; introduction by Robert Calder. Penguin Books, 2005, c1919. 216 p.

ISBN 9780143039341

1. Gauguin, Paul, 1848-1903 2. Painters 3. Ambition 4. Middle-aged men 5. Artists 6. British in Tahiti 7. Gifted men 8. Compulsive behavior in men 9. Obsession in men 10. Creativity in men 11. Poverty 12. Men/women relations 13. London, England 14. Paris, France 15. Psychological fiction 16. Modern classics

A British stockbroker abandons his wife and career to pursue a simple life as an artist in Tahiti.

Maugham, W. Somerset (William Somerset), 1874-1965

* Of human bondage / W. Somerset Maugham ; introduction by Gore Vidal. Modern Library, 1999, c1915. xxxix, 611 p.

ISBN 037575315X

1. Artists 2. People with disabilities 3. Unrequited love 4. Orphans 5. Clubfoot men 6. Boys with clubfoot 7. Waitresses 8. Physicians 9. Poor men 10. Men -- Sexuality 11. Men/women relations 12. London, England 13. England 14. Paris, France 15. France 16. Coming-of-age stories 17. Psychological fiction 18. Literary fiction 19. Modern classics

LC 98046169

Originally published: London : W. Heinemann, 1915.

Considered by many to be W. Somerset Maugham's masterpiece, Of Human Bondage traces the travels of Philip Carey to Germany, Paris, and London while exploring his intellectual, emotional, and psychological development and, later, his destructive relationship with a tawdry waitress.

Maugham, W. Somerset (William Somerset), 1874-1965

* The razor's edge / W. Somerset Maugham ; introduction by Anthony Curtis. Penguin Books, 1992, c1944. xxvii, 314 p.

ISBN 9780140185232

1. Spiritual journeys 2. Purpose in life 3. Self-discovery in men 4. Veterans -- Psychology 5. World War I veterans 6. Expatriates 7. Disillusionment in men 8. Discontent in men 9. Men/women relations 10. United States -- History -- 1919-1933 11. Coming-of-age stories 12. Literary fiction 13. Metafiction 14. Modern classics

Originally published: Garden City, N.Y. : Doubleday, Doran & Co., 1944.

In 1918, Larry Darrell returns home from World War I disillusioned with his materialistic society. The quest for inner peace leads Larry to reject his rich fiancee, Isabel, and go searching for truth in the Himalayas.

But, Larry learns that the path to enlightenment is as painful and narrow as treading the sharp edge of a razor.

Maum, Courtney, 1978-

Costalegre / Courtney Maum. Tin House Books, 2019. 240 p.

ISBN 9781947793361

1. Guggenheim, Peggy, 1898-1979 2. Second World War era (1939-1945) 3. Art and war 4. Women and war 5. Mothers and daughters 6. Artists 7. Dadaism 8. Refugees 9. Rich families 10. Heirs and heiresses 11. Teenage girls 12. World War II -- Social aspects 13. Mexico 14. Biographical fiction 15. Historical fiction

LC 2019005789

A historical novel inspired by the relationship between Peggy and Pegeen Guggenheim finds an American heiress offering safe passage to Nazi-threatened artists, while her emotionally unstable daughter chronicles their wartime experiences.

Maupassant, Guy de, 1850-1893

Like death / Guy De Maupassant ; translated by Richard Howard. New York Review Books, 2017 336 p.

ISBN 9781681370323

1. Belle Epoque (1871-1914) 2. 19th century 3. Painters 4. Counts and countesses 5. Love triangles 6. Mothers and daughters 7. Obsession 8. Jealousy 9. Aging 10. Beauty 11. Psychological fiction 12. Classics 13. Translations -- French to English

LC 2016026783

Originally published as Fort comme la mort, Paris : P. Ollendorff, 1900.

Olivier Bertin is at the height of his career as a painter; Anne, the comtesse de Guilleroy, is a youthful forty, the wife of a busy politician. The painter and the comtesse have been lovers for many years. Anne's daughter, Annette, has finished her schooling and is returning to Paris. Everything is as it should be--until the painter and comtesse are each seized by an agonizing suspicion, like death . . .

Maupin, Armistead

Tales of the city / Armistead Maupin. Harper & Row, 1978. 371 p. Tales of the city

ISBN 0060906545

1. 1970s 2. Gay communities 3. Gay culture 4. City life 5. Men/women relations 6. Sex customs 7. Gay men 8. Lesbians 9. Sexuality 10. Trans women 11. San Francisco, California 12. LGBTQIA fiction

"Published in somewhat different form in the San Francisco Chronicle."

Later published with More tales of the city and Further tales of the city as: 28 Barbary Lane.

A naive young secretary, fresh out of Cleveland, tumbles headlong into a brave new world of laundromat Lotharios, pot-growing landladies, cut throat debutantes, and Jockey Shorts dance contests. The saga that ensues is manic, romantic, tawdry, touching, and outrageous.

Mawer, Simon

The **fall** / Simon Mawer. Little, Brown, 2003. 370 p.

ISBN 9780316097802

1. 1940s 2. 1990s 3. Mountaineers 4. Love triangles 5. Secrets 6. Mountaineering 7. Desire 8. Friends' death 9. Competition in men 10. Male friendship 11. Betrayal 12. World War II 13. London, England -- History -- Bombardment, 1940-1945 14. Great Britain -- History -- George VI, 1936-1952 15. Wales 16. Alps 17. Literary fiction 18. Love stories

LC 2002073193

Hearing that a childhood friend has died in a tragic climbing accident, Rob Ross rushes to comfort the man's widow and finds himself reliving moments from his past, which was marked by a love triangle and a journey to the Alps.

"Intricately weaving time and place, from the bombed-out ruins of World War II London to isolated Alpine mountain peaks, Mawer crafts a sinuously devastating tale of foridden love and faithless betrayal. A haunting and mesmerizing novel from an expert storyteller." Booklist.

Mawer, Simon

The **glass** room / Simon Mawer. Other Press, 2009. 403 p.

ISBN 9781590513965

1. Second World War era (1939-1945) 2. Between the Wars (1918-1939) 3. Architecture, Modern -- 20th century -- Social aspects 4. Houses -- Czechoslovakia -- History -- 20th century 5. World War II -- Social aspects -- Czechoslovakia 6. Rich families 7. War -- Influence 8. Jews 9. Czechoslovakia -- Social conditions -- 20th century 10. Historical fiction 11. War stories

First published in London: Little, Brown, 2009.

Shortlisted for the Man Booker Prize, 2009.

Shortlisted for the Walter Scott Prize for Historical Fiction, 2010

Cool. Balanced. Modern. The precisions of science, the wild variance of lust, the catharsis of confession and the fear of failure - these are things that happen in the Glass Room. High on a Czechoslovak hill, the Landauer House shines as a wonder of steel and glass and onyx built specially for newlyweds Viktor and Liesel Landauer, a Jew married to a gentile. But the radiant honesty that the house, with its unique Glass Room, seems to engender quickly tarnishes as the storm clouds of WW2 gather, and eventually the family must flee, accompanied by Viktor's lover and her child. But the house's story is far from over, and as it passes from hand to hand, from Czech to Russian, both the best and the worst of the history of Eastern Europe becomes somehow embodied and perhaps emboldened within the beautiful and austere surfaces and planes so carefully designed, until events become full-circle.

"Mawer has written this novel as though it were a translation, endowing his prose with a patina of Old World formality that sounds all the more romantic. He claims he doesn't know Czech or German, but his characters speak both fluently, and his attention to foreign languages enriches every episode." Washington Post Book World.

Maxwell, Robin, 1948-

The **queen's** bastard : a novel / Robin Maxwell. Scribner Paperback Fiction, 2000, c1999. viii, 436 p. English history novels

ISBN 068485760X

1. Leicester, Robert Dudley,, Earl of, 1532?-1588 2. Elizabeth I,, Queen of England, 1533-1603 3. Elizabethan era (1558-1603) 4. Tudor period (1485-1603) 5. Illegitimate children of royalty 6. Fathers and sons 7. Scandals 8. Secrets 9. Lovers 10. Men/women relations 11. Political corruption 12. Courts and courtiers 13. Adopted boys 14. Secret identity 15. Great Britain -- History -- Elizabeth I, 1558-1603 16. Historical fiction 17. Biographical fiction

LC 00022781

Originally published: New York : Arcade Pub., 1999

Chronicles the adventures of Arthur Dudley, the illegitimate son of Elizabeth I and Robin Dudley, Earl of Leicester--a child presumed dead by his real parents who learns his true identity upon the death of his adoptive father.

"Arthur's first person narration is cleverly juxtaposed with third-person dramatization of significant events in the queen's life. . . . Maxwell's research examines the biographical gaps in, and documented facts about, the queen's life, making this incredible tale plausible, and the author aptly embellishe's her story with rich period details and the epic dramas of the late 16th century." Publishers Weekly.

Maxwell, Robin, 1948-

The **secret** diary of Anne Boleyn : a novel / Robin Maxwell. Scribner Paperback Fiction, 1998, c1997. 281 p. English history novels

ISBN 9780684849690

1. Anne Boleyn,, Queen, consort of Henry VIII, King of England, 1507-1536 2. Henry VIII,, King of England, 1491-1547 Wives 3. Elizabeth I,, Queen of England, 1533-1603 4. Tudor period (1485-1603) 5. 16th century 6. Women rulers -- Great Britain 7. Betrayal 8. Inheritance and succession 9. Marriage 10. Secrets 11. Royal houses 12. Mothers and daughters 13. Courts and courtiers 14. Executions and executioners -- Great Britain -- History 15. Women's role 16. Great Britain -- History -- Henry VIII, 1509-1547 17. England -- History -- 16th century 18. Great Britain -- History -- Tudors, 1485-1603 19. Biographical fiction 20. Historical fiction 21. Diary novels

LC 97053056

Originally published: New York : Arcade Publishing, 1997.

Upon her coronation as Queen, Elizabeth I receives her mother Ann Boleyn's diary and learns of her love for her and her torment at the hands of Henry VIII.

"Painting vicious court intrigue, national and international politics and the role of the Reformation, Maxwell brings not only the two queens but all of bloody Tudor England vividly to life." Publishers Weekly.

Maxwell, Robin, 1948-

The **wild** Irish / Robin Maxwell. William Morrow, 2003. 393 p. English history novels

ISBN 0060091428

1. Elizabeth I,, Queen of England, 1533-1603 2. O'Malley, Grace, 1530?-1603? 3. Essex, Robert Devereux,, Earl of, 1566-1601 4. Elizabethan era (1558-1603) 5. 16th century 6. Tudor period (1485-1603) 7. Rebellions -- Ireland -- 16th century 8. Courts and courtiers 9. Women revolutionaries 10. Women -- Ireland 11. Women pirates -- Ireland 12. Women rulers 13. Mothers and sons 14. Great Britain -- History -- Elizabeth I, 1558-1603 15. Great Britain -- History -- 16th century 16. Great Britain -- Court and courtiers 17. Ireland -- History -- 1558-1603 18. Ireland -- History -- 1172-1603 19. Ireland -- History -- 16th century 20. Biographical fiction 21. Historical fiction

LC 2003042184

Having fought against the English for its oppression of her country, Irish pirate and gunrunner Grace O'Malley goes head-to-head with Queen Elizabeth I when her son is captured, a confrontation that brings her to England and risks her own life.

"When Grace O'Mally, passionate clan chieftain and legendary Irish pirate, visits the court of Elizabeth I to plead for the release of her imprisoned son, the two most extraordinary women of their time find they have much in common. As Grace relates her incredible life and times to Elizabeth, the aging Bess also revisits her own often tragic past. Caught between these two powerful and magnetic females, Elizabeth's favorite courtier and onetime lover, Robert Devereaux, earl of Essex, is inexorably drawn into the tangled web of the Irish rebellion. . . . Superbly crafted, this dynamic tale brings a host of historical characters vividly to life." Booklist.

May, Peter, 1951-

The **blackhouse** / Peter May. SilverOak, 2012. 432 p. Lewis trilogy

ISBN 9781454901273

1. Murder investigation -- Scotland 2. Detectives -- Scotland 3. Murder -- Scotland 4. Sons -- Death 5. Grief in men 6. Islands -- Scotland 7. Marital conflict 8. Scotland 9. Hebrides 10. Mysteries

LC 2012016939

When a grisly murder occurs on a Scottish island, Edinburgh detective Fin Macleod must confront his past if he is ever going to discover if the killing has a connection to another one that took place on the mainland.

Mayer, Mark, 1984-

Aerialists : stories / Mark Mayer. Bloomsbury Publishing, 2019. 290 p.

ISBN 9781635572179

1. Circus 2. Short stories 3. Literary fiction

LC 2018006312

Through nine surreal stories, a carnival caravan of ordinary misfits grapple with finding happiness, including a sad boy who finds a mentor in a tough female bodybuilder and a navy recruit who builds his childhood neighborhood in code.

"Mayer's high-wire debut exposes the weirdness of everyday life. ... Mayer wittily subverts reader expectations with stories told in a realistic manner about characters or situations that all share a slightly surreal bent, resulting in a clever collection." Publishers Weekly.

Mayor, Archer

Red herring : a Joe Gunther novel / Archer Mayor. Minotaur Books, 2010. 320 p. Joe Gunther mysteries

ISBN 9780312381936

1. Police -- Vermont 2. Betrayal 3. Murder investigation 4. Deception 5. Serial murders 6. Serial murder investigation 7. Violence 8. Pedophiles 9. Loyalty 10. Smuggling 11. Murder 12. Brattleboro, Vermont 13. Vermont 14. New England 15. Mysteries 16. Police procedurals

VBI (Vermont Bureau of Investigation) head Joe Gunther and his team are called in to investigate a series of violent deaths that appear unrelated until telltale clues reveal a link among them.

"With cool forensic details for CSI fans, Mayor's heart-racing tale ends in a dramatic finish that will leave readers gasping." Library Journal.

Mayor, Archer

The **sniper's** wife / Archer Mayor. Mysterious Press, 2002. 312 p., 24 cm. Joe Gunther mysteries

ISBN 9780892967674

1. Vietnam veterans 2. Divorced men 3. Revenge 4. Police 5. Murder 6. Murder investigation 7. New York City 8. Mysteries 9. Police procedurals

LC 2002067183

Seeking revenge for the death of his ex-wife, labeled an accidental overdose by the NYPD, Detective Willy Kunkle leaves Vermont for the busy streets of Manhattan, where his investigation uncovers not only rumors of foul play and dark secrets about his own life.

Mayor, Archer

Tag man : a Joe Gunther novel / Archer Mayor. Minotaur Books, 2011. 320 p. Joe Gunther mysteries

ISBN 9780312681944

1. Assassins 2. Murder investigation 3. Frameups 4. Police -- Vermont 5. Thieves 6. Revenge 7. Crimes against rich people 8. Murderers 9. Innocence (Law) 10. Brattleboro, Vermont 11. Vermont 12. New England 13. Mysteries 14. Police procedurals

LC 2011018779

When a nuisance burglar who breaks into the heavily secured homes of wealthy Vermont citizens but steals nothing discovers evidence of a string of murders in one of the homes, Joe Gunther and his team struggle to untangle conflicting pieces of evidence while the burglar flees for his life.

"Vermont's history and geography again serve Mayor well in this deadly and highly entertaining entry." Publishers Weekly.

McAllister, Tom

* **How** to be safe : a novel / Tom McAllister. Liveright Publishing Corporation, 2018 232 p.

ISBN 9781631494130

1. High school teachers 2. School shootings 3. Blame 4. Malicious accusation 5. Employees -- Dismissal 6. Social media 7. Life change events 8. Guns 9. Prejudice 10. Independence in women 11. Small town life 12. Interpersonal relations 13. Mass shootings 14. Pennsylvania 15. Literary fiction 16. Satirical fiction

LC 2017054671

When high school teacher Anna Crawford is suspended just before a shooting at her school, she is horrified to see that she is considered a suspect, and even though she is exonerated, her moment in the public eye draws judgment and scrutiny, as the community lapses into familiar reactions.

McAllister, Tom

The **young** widower's handbook / Tom McAllister. Algonquin Books, 2017. 282 p.

ISBN 9781616204747

1. Widowers 2. Bereavement 3. Voyages and travels 4. Men/women relations 5. Married women -- Death 6. Coping 7. Memories 8. Life change events 9. Literary fiction 10. Second person narratives

LC 2016016078

"Published simultaneously in Canada by Thomas Allen & Son Limited."

For Hunter Cady, meeting Kait was the greatest thing that ever happened to him. Having spent roughly half his twenty-nine years accomplishing very little, he's the luckiest man on earth when it comes to his wife. When she dies quite suddenly, Hunter is crushed. Numb with grief, he stumbles forward the only way he knows how: by running away.

"McAllister writes with heartfelt emotion about the sudden death of a spouse in this remarkable debut novel. ... Hunters poignant realizations about what his wife meant to him, intermingled with his humorous and spot-on views of the people and places he encounters, as well as how he uses social media to grieve, bring him to the fitting conclusion that even beyond the grave, Kait helps him become the man he always wanted to be for her." Publishers Weekly.

McBain, Ed, 1926-2005

Alice in jeopardy / Ed McBain. Simon & Schuster, 2005. 304 p.

ISBN 0743262506

1. Kidnapping 2. Ransom 3. Life insurance 4. Widows 5. Household employees 6. Police 7. FBI agents 8. Elective mutism 9. Grief in women 10. Single mothers 11. Housekeepers 12. Florida 13. Thrillers and suspense

LC 2004052478

When her children are stolen by a kidnapper who demands her late husband's life insurance premiums in exchange for their return, widowed real estate agent Alice Glendenning turns for help to new friend Charlie Hobbs.

"This is a skilled performance from a master of the genre, the pacing and tone just right to keep you tense, curious and amused at each step." Washington Post Book World.

McBain, Ed, 1926-2005

The **big** bad city : a novel of the 87th precinct / Ed McBain. Simon & Schuster, 1999. 271 p. 87th Precinct mysteries

ISBN 0684855127

1. Police 2. Murder investigation 3. Stalkers 4. Thieves 5. Detectives 6. Nuns 7. Drug abusers 8. City life 9. Italian Americans 10. Stalking 11. New York City 12. Mysteries 13. Police procedurals

LC 9840890

Steve Carella and the men of the 87th Precinct investigate the murder of a nun while a burglar graduates to murder and Carella tries to dodge his own murder by a thug.

McBain, Ed, 1926-2005

Fat Ollie's book : a novel of the 87th Precinct / Ed McBain. Simon & Schuster, 2002. 271 p. 87th Precinct mysteries

ISBN 9780743202701

1. Police 2. Publishers and publishing 3. Manuscripts 4. Murder investigation 5. Detectives 6. City life 7. Italian Americans 8. New York City 9. Mysteries 10. Police procedurals

LC 2002075830

After finishing a murder investigation, Fat Ollie Weeks discovers that his car has been broken into and the manuscript for his new crime novel stolen, sending him on a mission of vengeance to catch the culprit.

"In McBain's howlingly funny sendup, the novel is pure drivel; but Ollie loved it, and darned if we don't like him for that." New York Times Book Review.

McBain, Ed, 1926-2005

The **frumious** bandersnatch : a novel of the 87th Precinct / Ed McBain. Simon & Schuster, 2004. 304 p. 87th Precinct mysteries

ISBN 0743250346

1. Music industry and trade 2. Police 3. Kidnapping 4. FBI agents 5. Detectives 6. Women musicians 7. Women singers 8. Music agents 9. Music videos 10. Yachts 11. Ransom 12. Cable television industry and trade 13. News media 14. City life 15. Italian Americans 16. New York City 17. Mysteries 18. Police procedurals

LC 2003057258

The disappearance of singer Tamar Valparaiso, a young woman on the verge of launching a successful career in hip hop music, draws Steve Carella into the middle of a kidnapping case as he searches for the missing woman.

"Tamar Valparaiso, a hot young singer on the verge of superstardom, is set to launch her debut CD and video Bandersnatch when she is kidnapped in the middle of a performance for a record industry party and the press. The whole episode is caught on camera, but the masked abductors flee, leaving behind few clues. Steve Carella and Cotton Hawes of the 87th Precinct are called in and are soon joined by a Joint Task Force and FBI agents. Detective Ollie Weeks, resident racist, homophobe, and misogynist, is also back on the scene, this time romancing a fellow officer. McBain displays his usual mastery of the police procedural along with an astute grasp of the music industry, the news media, and publicity, as well as political ramifications within the force." Library Journal.

McBain, Ed, 1926-2005

Hark! : a novel of the 87th Precinct / Ed McBain. Simon & Schuster, 2004. 304 p. 87th Precinct mysteries

ISBN 0743250354

1. Police 2. Revenge 3. Murder 4. Detectives 5. Criminals 6. Prostitutes 7. City life 8. Italian Americans 9. Letters 10. New York City 11. Mysteries 12. Police procedurals

LC 2004049102

Setting out to avenge himself after being left for dead, the Deaf Man plants a string of clues taken from the plays of Shakespeare, daring the detectives of the 87th Precinct to prevent a seemingly perfect crime.

"Vintage McBain, complete with pitch-perfect dialogue, subplots that thrust various precinct cops into the spotlight, a pace that encourages the reader to forget about dinner or a good night's rest, and a plot that teases and tantalizes from start to finish." Publishers Weekly.

McBain, Ed, 1926-2005

The **last** dance : a novel of the 87th Precinct / Ed McBain. Simon & Schuster, 2000. 269 p. 87th Precinct mysteries

ISBN 0684855135

1. Police 2. Murder investigation 3. Musicals 4. Detectives 5. City life 6. Italian Americans 7. New York City 8. Mysteries 9. Police procedurals

LC 99053534

The hanging death of a nondescript old man in a shabby little apartment in a meager section of the 87th Precinct was nothing much in this city, especially to detectives Carella and Meyer. But everyone has a story, and this old man's story stood to make some people a lot of money.

"An accomplished mix of police procedure, characterization, social commentary and tight plotting that has long distinguished this landmark series." Booklist.

McBain, Ed, 1926-2005

Nocturne / Ed McBain. Warner Books, 1997. 291 p. 87th Precinct mysteries

ISBN 0446518050

1. Police 2. Murder investigation 3. Crimes against prostitutes 4. Pianists 5. Detectives 6. City life 7. Italian Americans 8. New York City 9. Mysteries 10. Police procedurals

LC 9642030

Detectives Carella and Hawes of the 87th Precinct investigate the murder of an elderly woman, once one of the greatest concert pianists of the century, while Fat Ollie Weeks trails three prep school boys and a crack dealer responsible for a vicious attack on a prostitute.

McBride, Eimear

A **girl** is a half-formed thing / Eimear McBride. Galley Beggar Press Limited, 2013. 205 p.

ISBN 9780957185326

1. Brothers and sisters 2. Family violence 3. Sexuality 4. People with brain tumors 5. Catholics 6. Small town life 7. Growing up 8. Family relationships 9. Ireland 10. Psychological fiction 11. Literary fiction 12. Coming-of-age stories

LC 2013414093

Baileys Women's Prize for Fiction, 2014.

A story of a young woman's relationship with her brother, and the long shadow cast by his childhood brain tumor, touching on everything from family violence to sexuality and the personal struggle to remain intact in times of intense trauma.

"In an uncomfortable but always eye-opening tale, McBride investigates the tensions among family, love, sex and religion.Lovers of straightforward storytelling will shirk, but open-minded readers (specifically those not put off by the unusual language structure) will be surprised, moved and awed by this original novel." Kirkus.

McBride, James, 1957-

* **Deacon** King Kong : a novel / James McBride. Riverhead Books, 2020. 384 p.

ISBN 9780735216723

1. 1960s 2. Drug traffic 3. Communities 4. Murder 5. Gangsters 6. Mafia 7. Drug dealers 8. Clergy 9. Public housing 10. Brooklyn, New York City 11. African American fiction 12. Historical fiction 13. Farcical fiction

LC 2019045146

In the aftermath of a 1969 Brooklyn church deacon's public shooting of a local drug dealer, the community's African-American and Latinx witnesses find unexpected support from each other when they are targeted by violent mobsters.

"McBride has a flair for fashioning comedy whose buoyant outrageousness barely conceals both a steely command of big and small narrative elements and a river-deep supply of humane intelligence." Kirkus.

McBride, James, 1957-

The **good** lord bird / James McBride. Riverhead Books, 2013. 432 p.

ISBN 9781594486340

1. Brown, John, 1800-1859 2. Antebellum America (1820-1861) 3. Abolitionists 4. Female impersonators 5. Fugitive slaves -- United States 6. Self-perception in men 7. Children and adults 8. False personation 9. Twelve-year-olds 10. Gender identity 11. Extremists 12. Obsession 13. Harper's Ferry, West Virginia -- History -- John Brown's Raid, 1859 14. Historical fiction 15. Literary fiction 16. African American fiction

LC 2013004014

BCALA Literary Award for Fiction, 2014.
National Book Award for Fiction, 2013.

Mistaken for a girl on account of his curly hair, delicate features, and sackcloth smock, 12-year-old slave Henry Shackleford realizes that his accidental disguise affords him greater safety and decides to remain female. Dubbed "Little Onion" by his liberator, abolitionist John Brown, Henry accompanies the increasingly fanatical Brown on his crusade to end slavery -- a picaresque journey that takes them from Bloody Kansas to Rochester, New York, where they attempt to enlist the support of such notables as Frederick Douglass and Harriet Tubman before embarking on the infamous, ill-fated 1859 raid on Harpers Ferry. - Description by Gillian Speace.

McBride, James, 1957-

* **Five-carat** soul / James McBride. Riverhead Books, 2017. 288 p.

ISBN 9780735216693

1. Interpersonal relations 2. Interpersonal conflict 3. Race relations 4. Material culture 5. Literary fiction 6. Short stories 7. African American fiction

LC 2017007480

Longlisted for the Andrew Carnegie Medal for Excellence in Fiction, 2018.

Presents a collection of insightful and unpredictable stories that explore the ways people learn from the world and the people around them.

"A versatile, illustrious author brings out his first short-fiction buffet for sampling, and the results are provocatively varied in taste and texture; sometimes piquant, other times zesty." Kirkus.

McBride, James, 1957-

Song yet sung / James McBride. Riverhead Books, 2008. 464 p.

ISBN 9781594489723

1. Antebellum America (1820-1861) 2. 19th century 3. Fugitive slaves 4. Slavery 5. Visions 6. African American women 7. Prophetic dreams 8. Supernatural 9. Civil war 10. United States -- History -- 1815-1861 11. Chesapeake Bay 12. Maryland 13. Historical fiction 14. African American fiction

LC 2007035969

A tale set against a backdrop of slave rights conflicts in the nineteenth-century Chesapeake Bay region finds young runaway Liz Spocott inadvertently inspiring a slave breakout from the attic prison of a notorious slave thief.

"McBride borrows liberally from actual historical events and figures to fabricate this engrossing tale, and then emphasizes the implications of past actions by interspersing them with Liz's recurring nightmares of the future. . . . [His] characters evoke an extraordinary time that spawned ghosts that haunt us still." Seattle Times.

McCabe, Erin Lindsay

I shall be near to you : a novel / Erin Lindsay McCabe. Crown, 2014. 320 p.

ISBN 9780804137720

1. American Civil War era (1861-1865) 2. 1860s 3. Union soldiers 4. Husband and wife 5. Male impersonators 6. Civil war 7. Battles 8. War 9. Romantic love 10. Farm life 11. United States Civil War, 1861-1865 12. United States -- History -- Civil War, 1861-1865 13. Historical fiction 14. War stories

LC 2013028670

A tale inspired by true accounts and a real female soldier's letters home follows the extraordinary experiences of a woman who disguises herself as a man in order to fight next to her husband in the American Civil War, an effort that tests the bonds of their relationship and their respective gender perceptions.

"[A] narrative full of authentic dialogue, historical realism, and great feeling. Loosely based on true events, including the letters of the more than 200 women who are known to have served as men in the Civil War." Booklist.

McCaffrey, Anne

* Acorna : the unicorn girl / Anne McCaffrey and Margaret Ball. HarperPrism, 1997. 291 p. Acorna series

ISBN 0061052965

1. Magic 2. Difference (Psychology) 3. Abandoned children 4. Child abuse 5. Alien children (Humanoid) 6. Unicorns 7. Science fiction 8. Science fantasy

LC 9711099

"Found in a survival pod in space by prospectors, the infant Acorna soon exhibits the ability to analyze deficiencies in plants by taste, purify water and air, and heal. Taken to the planet Kezdet to avoid scientists who want to study her, Acorna discovers barbaric child-labor practices and vows to rescue the children. McCaffrey and Ball have created a magical alien in this fantasy/science fiction story." Library Journal.

McCaffrey, Anne

Dragonflight / Anne McCaffrey. Ballantine Books, 1968. 303 p. Dragonriders of Pern

ISBN 9780345276940

1. Women rulers 2. Household employees 3. Dragons 4. Biological invasions 5. Survival 6. Housekeepers 7. Science fiction 8. Science fantasy

The short stories Weyr Search and Dragonrider are incorporated in this book.

At a time when the number of Dragonriders has fallen too low for safety and only one Weyr trains the creatures and their riders, the Red Star approaches Pern, threatening it with disaster.

McCall Smith, Alexander, 1948-

Blue shoes and happiness / Alexander McCall Smith. Pantheon Books, 2006. 240 p. No. 1 Ladies' Detective Agency

ISBN 9780375422720

1. Women thieves 2. Witchcraft 3. Shoes 4. Women private investigators 5. Women administrative assistants 6. No 1 Ladies' Detective Agency (Imaginary organization) 7. Overweight women 8. Weight loss 9. Dieting 10. Women cooks 11. Advice columnists 12. Engaged persons 13. Feminists 14. Botswana 15. Cozy mysteries 16. Gentle reads

LC 2005052122

Precious Ramotswe and her able assistant, Grace Makutsi, launch an investigation into local advice columnist Aunty Emang, who somehow may be linked to trouble at a local medical clinic and the cobra that somehow ended up in Precious's office, while Grace confronts her own troubles with her greedy uncles and her wealthy fianc?, Phuti Radiphuti.

"McCall Smith renders brisk, seamless tales that are both wry and profound. Amidst the mayhem (like the cobra that slithers its way into the detective agency's headquarters) are eloquent descriptions of the serene African country that holds a special place in his heart." Booklist.

McCall Smith, Alexander, 1948-

The **comforts** of a muddy Saturday : an Isabel Dalhousie novel / Alexander McCall Smith. Pantheon Books, 2008. 256 p. Isabel Dalhousie mysteries

ISBN 9780375425134

1. Middle-aged women 2. Physicians 3. Medical malpractice 4. Women editors 5. Americans in Scotland 6. Americans in Great Britain 7. Household employees 8. Men/women relations 9. Interpersonal relations 10. Housekeepers 11. Women amateur detectives 12. Scotland 13. Mysteries 14. Gentle reads

LC 2008018573

Isabel Dalhousie comes to the aid of a renowned, much respected doctor whose reputation is at stake following the death of a patient because of allegations of scientific fraud in respect to a newly marketed drug.

"While the truth isn't straightforward, the motives of the guilty party prove to be both plausible and rational. The strengths of the book . . . lie in its protagonist's determination to treat others without judgmentand in the author's revealing glimpses into the human soul." Publishers Weekly.

McCall Smith, Alexander, 1948-

* The Department of Sensitive Crimes : a Detective Varg novel / Alexander McCall Smith. Pantheon Books, 2019 208 p. Detective Varg novels

ISBN 9781524748210

1. Police 2. Detectives 3. Criminal investigation 4. Eccentrics and eccentricities 5. Sweden 6. Malmo, Sweden 7. Mysteries 8. Humorous stories 9. Gentle reads

LC 2018040221

Tasked with their Swedish Police Department's most unusual cases, lead detective Ulf Varg and his colorful associates investigate a bizarre stabbing, a lost imaginary boyfriend and a haunted spa.

McCall Smith, Alexander, 1948-

The **Double** Comfort Safari Club / Alexander McCall Smith. Pantheon Books, 2010. 224 p. No. 1 Ladies' Detective Agency

ISBN 9780375424502

1. Women private investigators 2. Marriage 3. Murder investigation 4. Overweight women 5. Husband and wife -- Botswana 6. Homecomings 7. No 1 Ladies' Detective Agency (Imaginary organization) 8. Botswana 9. Africa 10. Okavango River Delta Region, Botswana 11. Cozy mysteries 12. Gentle reads

LC 2009049060

Traveling to northern Botswana where they are impressed by the natural beauty of the Okavango Delta, Mma Ramotswe and Mma Makutsi visit a safari lodge where they encounter discontented locals and struggle with untimely wedding issues.

"It's not in the stories themselves, but in the telling of them, that the secret of McCall Smith's appeal lies. His Botswana may indeed be a kindly place, but he has an ability-- a very rare one-- to write with kindness too. This world, he says, is only ours for a short time, and we realise that more and more with age. And when we cry, he'll point out, how odd it is that we rock forward and back, as our mothers comforted us, as if we were trying to comfort ourselves. Such apecus are, of themselves, not original. What is, is the way McCall Smith effortlessly weaves them into stories of fun and laughter and heartfelt love of place and character." The Scotsman.

McCall Smith, Alexander, 1948-

The **forgotten** affairs of youth / Alexander McCall Smith. Pantheon Books, 2011. 272 p. Isabel Dalhousie mysteries

ISBN 9780307379184

1. Birthparents -- Identification 2. Aunt and niece 3. Engagement 4. Household employees 5. Men/women relations 6. Women editors 7. Women philosophers 8. Housekeepers 9. Scotland 10. Edinburgh, Scotland 11. Mysteries 12. Gentle reads

Originally published: London: Little, Brown, 2011.

When a visiting Australian philosopher on sabbatical in Edinburgh asks for Isabel's help to discover the identity of her father, of course Isabel obliges.

McCall Smith, Alexander, 1948-

The **full** cupboard of life / Alexander McCall Smith. Pantheon Books, 2004, c2003. 208 p. No. 1 Ladies' Detective Agency

ISBN 9780375422188

1. Mate selection 2. Courtship 3. Women private investigators 4. Women administrative assistants 5. Secretaries 6. No 1 Ladies' Detective Agency (Imaginary organization) 7. Engagement 8. Men/women relations 9. Marriage 10. Botswana 11. Africa 12. Cozy mysteries 13. Gentle reads

LC 2003062379

Originally published: Edinburgh : Polygon, 2003.

Worrying about her upcoming marriage, Precious Ramotswe is confronted by the challenges of running her No. 1 Ladies' Detective Agency and an investigation into the would-be suitors of a wealthy woman to determine if any are fortune hunters.

McCall Smith, Alexander, 1948-

The **good** husband of Zebra Drive / Alexander McCall Smith. Pantheon Books, 2007. 240 p. No. 1 Ladies' Detective Agency

ISBN 0375422730

1. Resourcefulness in women 2. Women private investigators 3. Husband and wife 4. Women administrative assistants 5. No 1 Ladies' Detective Agency (Imaginary organization) 6. Married men 7. Parent and child 8. Detectives 9. Overweight women 10. Botswana 11. Cozy mysteries 12. Gentle reads

LC 2006039047

Originally published: Edinburgh: Polygon, 2007.

Mma Ramotswe's devoted husband, J. L. B. Matekoni tries his hand at the detective business, catering to a rude client who suspects her husband of infidelity.

"The author's subtlety of touch and humane portrayal of figures at all levels of society will continue to win him new readers even as his deepening of the ties binding the main figures will satisfy those who have followed the lady detectives from their first recorded case." Publishers Weekly.

McCall Smith, Alexander, 1948-

* **In** the company of cheerful ladies / Alexander McCall Smith. Pantheon Books, 2005, c2004. 240 p. No. 1 Ladies' Detective Agency

ISBN 9780375422713

1. Dancing -- Study and teaching 2. Burglary 3. Extramarital affairs 4. Women private investigators 5. Women administrative assistants 6. Automobile mechanics 7. Furniture sales personnel 8. Newlyweds 9. No 1 Ladies' Detective Agency (Imaginary organization) 10. Marriage 11. Men/women relations 12. Botswana 13. Africa 14. Cozy mysteries 15. Gentle reads

LC 2004056827

Originally published: Edinburgh : Polygon, 2004.

Overwhelmed by work at the No. 1 Ladies' Detective Agency, Precious Ramotswe is further challenged by a strange intruder at her home, the appearance in her yard of a mysterious pumpkin, troubles at her husband's motorworks, and a visitor who forces her to confront a painful secret from her past.

McCall Smith, Alexander, 1948-

The **Kalahari** typing school for men / Alexander McCall Smith. Pantheon Books, 2003, c2002. 186 p. No. 1 Ladies' Detective Agency

ISBN 9780375422171

1. Secretaries 2. Sexism 3. Ethics 4. Women private investigators 5. No 1 Ladies' Detective Agency (Imaginary organization) 6. Men/women relations 7. Engaged persons 8. Orphans 9. Personal conduct 10. Botswana 11. Africa 12. Cozy mysteries 13. Gentle reads

LC 2002030709

Originally published: Edinburgh : Polygon, 2002.

Now that the No. 1 Ladies' Detective Agency is firmly established, founder Precious Ramotswe faces new challenges at home and at work--from problems with her adopted son, to an assistant who dreams of opening a Kalahari Typing School for Men, to a sexist rival who is opening a Satisfaction Guaranteed Detective Agency across town.

McCall Smith, Alexander, 1948-

The **Limpopo** Academy of Private Detection / Alexander McCall Smith. Pantheon Books, 2012. 224 p. No. 1 Ladies' Detective Agency

ISBN 9780307378408

1. Newlyweds 2. Schools 3. Authors 4. Women private investigators 5. No 1 Ladies' Detective Agency (Imaginary organization) 6. Botswana 7. Africa 8. Cozy mysteries 9. Gentle reads

Originally published: London: Little, Brown, 2012.

The formidable talents of Precious Ramotswe are put to the test in the face of a mysterious disciplinary problem at her adopted daughter's school, assistant Grace Makutsi's early marital adjustments and the appearance of the No. 1 Ladies' hero detective.

McCall Smith, Alexander, 1948-

The **lost** art of gratitude / Alexander McCall Smith. Pantheon Books, 2009. 272 p. Isabel Dalhousie mysteries

ISBN 9780375425141

1. Investment bankers 2. Fraud 3. Plagiarism 4. Birthday parties 5. Women editors 6. Men/women relations 7. Women philosophers 8. Single mothers 9. Scotland 10. Edinburgh, Scotland 11. Mysteries 12. Gentle reads

LC 2009022618

Encountering high-flying financier Minty Auchterlonie while attending a birthday party, Isabel learns of Minty's complicated monetary troubles and wonders if the ambitious woman is perpetuating a fraud, a situation that is further complicated by a plagiarism battle with Professor Dove and Cat's problematic new man.

"Smith's trademark humor and telling observations about people heighten the appeal." Publishers Weekly.

McCall Smith, Alexander, 1948-

The **No.** 1 Ladies' Detective Agency / Alexander McCall Smith. Anchor Books, 2002, c1998. 226 p. No. 1 Ladies' Detective Agency

ISBN 9781400031344

1. Women private investigators 2. Missing children 3. Shamans 4. Kidnapping 5. Physicians 6. No 1 Ladies' Detective Agency (Imaginary organization) 7. Dissociative identity disorder 8. Mines and mineral resources 9. Miners 10. Botswana 11. Africa 12. Cozy mysteries 13. Gentle reads

Originally published: Edinburgh : Polygon, 1998.

Working in Gaborone, Botswana, Precious Ramotswe investigates several local mysteries, including a search for a missing boy and the case of the clinic doctor with different personalities for different days of the week.

McCall Smith, Alexander, 1948-

The **Saturday** big tent wedding party / Alexander McCall Smith. Pantheon Books, 2011. 256 p. No. 1 Ladies' Detective Agency

ISBN 9780307378392

1. Missing men 2. Weddings 3. Poisoning 4. Cattle 5. Women private investigators 6. No 1 Ladies' Detective Agency (Imaginary organization) 7. Botswana 8. Africa 9. Cozy mysteries 10. Gentle reads

Originally published: London: Little, Brown, 2011.

Hoping to reclaim a van that was featured in a possible prophetic dream, Precious and Grace find themselves helping an apprentice of Phuti Radiphuti, investigating a cattle poisoning and considering Grace's possible marriage to Phuti.

McCammon, Robert R.

Boy's life / Robert R. McCammon. Pocket Books, 1991. 440 p.

ISBN 0671742264

1. Ku-Klux Klan Alabama 2. 1960s 3. Twelve-year-old boys 4. Murder witnesses 5. Family violence 6. Boys -- Alabama 7. Fathers and sons -- Alabama 8. Murder -- Alabama 9. Murderers 10. Drinking 11. Prejudice 12. Small town life -- Alabama 13. Alabama 14. Coming-of-age stories 15. Mysteries

Bram Stoker Award for Best Novel, 1991.

World Fantasy Award, 1992.

The witnesses to a horrific murder, Cory Mackenson and his father investigate and come face to face with the vicious Blaylock clan, a secret society united by racial hatred, and a reptilian creature inhabiting the river

"McCammon is both a precise and lush writer, and thus the trail Cory takes to deciphering the puzzle the dead man represents quickly firms up into a compelling, even haunting yarn of adult demons being faced and fathomed by the young. This look at life's blacker sides is neither cloying nor jejune." Booklist.

McCann, Colum, 1965-

* Apeirogon : a novel / Colum McCann. Random House, 2020. 464 p.

ISBN 9781400069606

1. Arab-Israeli relations 2. Fathers and daughters 3. Grief 4.

Violence 5. Suicide bombings 6. Peace activists 7. Peace-building 8. Palestinians 9. Israelis 10. Political fiction 11. Literary fiction 12. Biographical fiction

LC 2019022848

Two fathers, a Palestinian and an Israeli, navigate the physical and emotional checkpoints of their conflicted world before devastating losses compel them to work together to use their grief as a weapon for peace.

"National Book Award winner McCann (Let the Great World Spin) bases this masterful novel on the lives of two real men working together toward Middle Eastern peace." Publishers Weekly.

McCann, Colum, 1965-

Let the great world spin : a novel / Colum McCann. Random House, 2009. 349 p.

ISBN 9781400063734

1. Petit, Philippe, 1949- 2. 1970s 3. City life 4. Tightrope walking 5. Traffic accidents 6. Priests 7. Prostitutes 8. Rich women 9. Poor women 10. Irish in New York City 11. Grief 12. Courage 13. Redemption 14. Hope 15. New York City 16. Historical fiction 17. Literary fiction

LC 2008046963

ALA Notable Book, 2010.

International IMPAC Dublin Literary Award, 2011.

National Book Award for Fiction, 2009.

In 1974 Manhattan, a radical young Irish monk struggles with personal demons while making his home among Bronx prostitutes, a group of mothers shares grief over their lost Vietnam soldier sons, and a young grandmother attempts to prove her worth.

McCann, Colum, 1965-

* Transatlantic : a novel / Colum McCann. Random House, 2013. 304 p.

ISBN 9781400069590

1. Douglass, Frederick, 1818-1895 2. 1840s 3. 1910s 4. 1990s 5. Transatlantic voyages 6. Politicians 7. Freed slaves 8. Ireland 9. United States 10. Literary fiction 11. Family sagas 12. Historical fiction 13. Psychological fiction 14. Literary fiction 15. Parallel narratives

LC 2012043294

Shortlisted for the International Dublin Literary Award, 2015

Spanning 150 years and two continents, this literary family saga from National Book Award-winning author Colum McCann ties Frederick Douglass' 1845 journey to Ireland with the first trans-Atlantic flight made in 1919 by two British aviators and the work of U.S. Senator George Mitchell on the 1998 Good Friday Agreement. These great men and the events they're connected to are also linked to a servant girl named Lily, who in 1846 leaves Dublin for New York, and her descendants. Transatlantic is a complex meditation on time, memory, freedom, and war. - Description by Shauna Griffin.

McCann, Colum, 1965-

Zoli : a novel / Colum McCann. Random House, 2007. 336 p.

ISBN 9781400063727

1. 1930s 2. Holocaust (1933-1945) 3. Romanies -- Europe 4. Romani girls 5. Escapes 6. Grandfather and granddaughter 7. Independence in Romani girls 8. Women poets 9. Romani women 10. Communism -- Europe 11. Acculturation 12. Betrayal 13. Exiles 14. Self-discovery in women 15. Europe -- History -- 20th century 16. Historical fiction 17. Parallel narratives

LC 2006042922

Originally published: London: Weidenfeld & Nicolson, 2006.

As fascism spreads across 1930s Europe, Zoli Novotna, a young Gypsy poet, and her grandfather seek refuge with a clan of Romani harpists, where her fame as a poet leads to estrangement from her family, exploitation by the ruling Communists, and a flight to the West as she struggles to find where she truly belongs, in a novel loosely based on the life of Romani poet Papsuza.

"Zoli becomes a flash point for her tribe while raising an important question: In a world driven by conformity and (more lately) consumerism, how can the outsider survive? . . . . McCann's story feels like an important reminder of one dimension that has gladly been left behind: the soul-deadening totalitarianism that snuffs out dissent and difference with the force of its bureaucracy." Seattle Times.

McCarry, Charles

The **mulberry** bush / Charles McCarry. Grove, 2015 320 p.

ISBN 9780802124104

1. Revenge 2. Terrorists 3. Betrayal 4. Spies 5. Espionage 6. Men/women relations 7. Spy fiction 8. Thrillers and suspense

First published in the United Kingdom in 2015 by Head of Zeus Ltd.

Falling in love with a famous Argentinean revolutionary's daughter who he hopes will further his ambition to exact revenge against the handlers who ended his father's career years earlier, a maverick spy is caught in a web of deceit with ties to the Cold War.

"McCarry (The Shanghai Factor, 2013) again creates a richly engaging world of spooks, double agents, terrorists, and Company characters and culture, all delivered in prose that is variously concise, discursive, amusing, insightful, and often gorgeous. The Mulberry Bush is outrageously entertaining." Booklist.

McCarry, Charles

Old boys / Charles McCarry. Overlook Press, 2004. 512 p. Paul Christopher novels

ISBN 1585675458

1. Americans in Foreign countries 2. Intelligence officers 3. Former spies 4. Spies -- United States 5. Spies 6. Senior men 7. Retirees 8. Cousins 9. Missing persons 10. International intrigue 11. Terrorism 12. Scrolls 13. Extremism 14. Religious fanaticism 15. Spy fiction 16. Thrillers and suspense

LC 2004048320

Retired agent Horace Christopher enlists the aid of four other retired colleagues to find his cousin, intelligence operative Paul Christopher, who has mysteriously vanished and is presumed dead.

"The nonstop peregrinations of this league of extraordinary spooks take them to a score of exotic locales, pitting them against Chechen thugs, Chinese secret police, Nazi doctors, and a case of acute myocardial fibrillation. McCarry's commitment to this fanciful premise is absolute, and the resulting yarn combines the intrepid exploits of John Buchan, the cagey intrigue of Eric Ambler, and the clipped cadences of Dashiell Hammett. Tremendous fun." Booklist.

McCarthy, Cormac, 1933-

* **All** the pretty horses / Cormac McCarthy. A. A. Knopf, 1992. 301 p. Border trilogy (Cormac McCarthy)

ISBN 9780394574745

1. 1940s 2. Horse training -- Northern Mexico 3. Americans in Mexico 4. Sixteen-year-old boys -- West Texas 5. Boys and horses 6. Horses 7. Loss (Psychology) 8. Teenagers and horses 9. Children of World War II veterans 10. Northern Mexico 11. West Texas 12. Coming-of-age stories 13. Literary fiction 14. Modern Westerns

LC 91058560

ALA Notable Book, 1993.

National Book Award for Fiction, 1992.

National Book Critics Circle Award for Fiction, 1992.

Western Heritage Award for Outstanding Western Novel, 1993.

Cut off from the life of ranching he has come to love by his grandfather's death, John Grady Cole flees to Mexico, where he and his two companions embark on a rugged and cruelly idyllic adventure.

"Though some readers may grow impatient with the wild prairie rhythms of McCarthy's language, others will find his voice completely transporting." Publishers Weekly.

McCarthy, Cormac, 1933-

* **Blood** meridian, or, The evening redness in the West / Cormac McCarthy. Vintage Books, 1992, c1985. 337 p.

ISBN 9780679728757

1. 1850s 2. 19th century 3. Outlaws 4. Massacres 5. Apache Indians 6. Teenage boys 7. Mexico -- History -- 1821-1867 8. Texas -- History -- 1846-1865 9. Mexican-American Border Region 10. Westerns 11. Literary fiction 12. Southern Gothic 13. Southern fiction

LC 91050742

Based on incidents that took place in the southwestern United States and Mexico around 1850, this novel chronicles the crimes of a band of desperados, with a particular focus on one, "the kid," a boy of fourteen.

McCarthy, Cormac, 1933-

Cities of the plain / Cormac McCarthy. A. A. Knopf, 1998. 291 p. Border trilogy (Cormac McCarthy)

ISBN 0679423907

1. 1950s 2. Americans in Mexico 3. Ranches -- New Mexico 4. Cowboys -- New Mexico 5. Male friendship -- New Mexico 6. Nineteen-year-old men -- New Mexico 7. Prostitutes -- Ciudad Juarez, Mexico 8. New Mexico 9. Ciudad Juarez, Mexico 10. Literary fiction

LC 9811583

Sequel to: The crossing.

The conclusion of the Border trilogy describes the friendship of John Grady Cole and Billy Parham, two cowboys working on a New Mexico ranch in the 1950s

McCarthy, Cormac, 1933-

The **crossing** / Cormac McCarthy. A.A. Knopf, 1994. 425 p. Border trilogy (Cormac McCarthy)

ISBN 0394574753

1. 1930s 2. Wolves 3. Americans in Mexico 4. Sixteen-year-old boys -- New Mexico 5. Boys and wolves 6. Brothers -- New Mexico 7. New Mexico 8. Coming-of-age stories 9. Literary fiction

LC 94004281

In the 1930s, Billy and his family come to Hidalgo County, New Mexico, where he becomes obsessed with a wild wolf that lives a precarious existence threatened by the region's ranchers

McCarthy, Cormac, 1933-

No country for old men / Cormac McCarthy. Knopf, 2005. 320 p.

ISBN 0375406778

1. 1980s 2. Heroin traffic 3. Violence 4. Vietnam veterans 5. Sheriffs 6. World War II veterans 7. Drug lords 8. Former Special forces officers 9. Husband and wife 10. Drug traffic 11. Chases 12. Murder 13. Revenge 14. Texas 15. Mexico 16. Literary fiction 17. Crime fiction 18. Modern Westerns

LC 2004064903

ALA Notable Book, 2006.

Shortlisted for the International IMPAC Dublin Literary Award, 2007

Stumbling upon a bloody massacre, a cache of heroin, and more than $2 million in cash during a hunting trip, Llewelyn Moss removes the money, a decision that draws him and his young wife into the middle of a violent confrontation.

"As devised and refined by James M. Cain, Jim Thompson and their gloomy (pbk.) peers, the crime novel aimed its cheap handgun at the heart of America's most prized beliefs about its destiny: that the loot we've scooped up will belong to us forever and that history allows clean getaways. Cormac McCarthy's No Country for Old Men is as bracing a variation on these noir orthodoxies as any fan of the genre could expect." New York Times Book Review.

McCarthy, Cormac, 1933-

* The **road** / Cormac McCarthy. Knopf, 2006. 256 p.

ISBN 9780307265432

1. Fathers and sons 2. Survival (after nuclear warfare) 3. Familial love 4. Hunger 5. Cannibalism 6. Near future 7. Disasters 8. Catastrophism 9. Ethics 10. Personal conduct 11. Post-apocalypse 12. United States 13. Apocalyptic fiction 14. Literary fiction

LC 2006045158

ALA Notable Book, 2007.

James Tait Black Memorial Prize for Fiction, 2006.

Pulitzer Prize for Fiction, 2007.

National Book Critics Circle Award for Fiction finalist, 2006

Apocalypse grips the earth; wildlife has disappeared; and starvation prevails. Amidst this bleak backdrop, a man and his young son slowly make their way toward the coast. Avoiding roves of marauding cannibals and fighting off starvation, they gain hope and stamina in knowing they are some of the remaining few virtuous people.

McCarthy, Rob

A **handful** of ashes / Rob McCarthy. Pegasus Books, 2018, c2017. 384 p. Dr. Harry Kent novels

ISBN 9781681777719

1. Coroners 2. Suicide investigation 3. Whistle blowers 4. Addiction 5. Hospitals 6. Policewomen 7. Former girlfriends 8. London, England 9. Mysteries

Originally published: London : Mulholland Books, 2017.

In the new Dr. Harry Kent thriller, a whistleblowing doctor commits suicide--or so it seems. When it turns out to be murder, Harry digs deeper to uncover the truth, in this perfect mix of detective novel and medical drama.

"Medical student McCarthy has created humane, fallible characters-notably Kent and Noble, who struggle with addictions--as he spins a taut plot thats part police procedural, part medical thriller." Booklist.

McCarthy, Rob

The **hollow** men / Rob McCarthy. Pegasus Books, 2016. 368 p. Dr. Harry Kent novels

ISBN 9781681772493

1. Police 2. Physicians 3. Hostage taking 4. Murder 5. Secrets 6. Veterans 7. Teenage boys 8. Murder investigation 9. Afghan War veterans 10. London, England 11. Mysteries

Police surgeon Harry Kent is determined to help those the world would rather brush aside, in a smart and electrifying new crime series that evokes the often-hidden medical world of the London Metropolitan Police.

"McCarthy provides a fascinating look at the sociology of crime and policing while deftly exploring the motivations of Idris, Kent, and Lahiri." Publishers Weekly.

McCarthy, Tom, 1969 May 22-

Satin Island : a novel / Tom McCarthy. Knopf, 2015. 192 p.

ISBN 9780307593955

1. Mind and reality 2. Anthropologists 3. Obsession 4. Curiosities and wonders 5. Conspiracies 6. Parachutists 7. Corporations 8. Oil spills 9. Shroud of Turin 10. Turin, Italy 11. Literary fiction 12. Psychological fiction

LC 2014023461

Shortlisted for the Man Booker Prize, 2015.

Struck by a realization that the public's access to the truth seems obscured, a corporate ethnographer is tasked with writing an era-summarizing report that is challenged by his obsessions and overwhelming quantities of data.

"The book itself subtly takes the form of his Great Report, with U. often addressing the reader, and is marked by fascinating philosophical tangents that justify the apparent lack of a story." Publishers Weekly.

McClure, James, 1939-2006

The **steam** pig / James McClure. Soho Crime, 2010, c1971 272 p. Kramer and Zondi mysteries

ISBN 9781569476529

1. 1970s 2. Apartheid 3. Murder investigation 4. Detectives 5. Music teachers 6. Murder 7. Race relations 8. Afrikaner men 9. South Africans 10. South Africa -- Social conditions -- 20th century 11. South Africa -- Race relations 12. Police procedurals 13. Mysteries

LC 72000410

Originally published: London : Gollancz, 1971.

Gold Dagger Award for Best Crime Novel of the Year, 1971.

"Mr. McClure is a new writer with a raffish vigor, humor and originality all within the very easy reach of his talent while so-called 'serious' novels could hardly give you a sharper lesson in apartheid." Kirkus.

McCormack, Mike, 1965-

* **Solar** bones / Mike McCormack. Soho Press, 2017, c2016. 224 p.

ISBN 9781616958534

1. Memories 2. Introspection 3. Meaning (Psychology) 4. Ghosts 5. Civilization 6. Civil engineers 7. Purpose in life 8. Rural life 9. Ireland 10. Literary fiction 11. Psychological fiction

LC 2017007611

Originally published: Dublin : Tramp Press,

ALA Notable Book, 2018.

International IMPAC Dublin Literary Award, 2018.

Longlisted for the Man Booker Prize, 2017.

A man's spirit ruminates on his life and all the entwined events and circumstances in the vast systems of time and history that lead him to that exact moment.

"Deserving a readership far larger than Irish-literature devotees, this is a work of bold risks and luminous creativity." Booklist.

McCracken, Elizabeth

* **Bowlaway** : a novel / Elizabeth McCracken. Ecco, 2019. 384 p.

ISBN 9780062862853

1. 20th century 2. Eccentrics and eccentricities 3. Bowling alleys 4. Family lore 5. Family secrets 6. Love 7. Loss (Psychology) 8. Families 9. Friendship 10. Small town life 11. Massachusetts 12. Family sagas 13. Historical fiction

LC 2018025083

An unconventional New England family faces scandal, inheritance battles and questions of paternities as viewed through their three generations of owning and operating a candlepin bowling alley in the town of Salford, Massachusetts.

McCracken, Elizabeth

The **giant's** house : a romance / Elizabeth McCracken. Dial Press, 1996. 259 p.

ISBN 0385314337

1. 1950s 2. Women librarians 3. Loneliness 4. Loss (Psychology) 5. Misfits (Persons) 6. Boys and women 7. May-December romance 8. Gigantism 9. Tall men 10. Small towns 11. Cape Cod, Massachusetts 12. Historical fiction 13. Love stories

LC 9552433

National Book Award for Fiction finalist, 1996

Befriending an adolescent boy who is ostracized for his unusual height, bereft Cape Cod librarian Peggy Cort finds a soulmate in James and comes to love him as he grows into a man of eight feet.

"The reader is mesmerized by this low-key narrative, first lured by Peggy's alternately acerbic and tender voice, then captivated by James's situation and intrigued by his family, later engulfed by pathos as James's body begins to fail and, finally, amazed by a turn of events that ends the novel with a major surprise. McCracken also invests the narrative with humor, sometimes through Peggy's astringent comments and more often through the use of minor characters who add vivid color and their own distinctive voices." Publishers Weekly.

McCrea, Gavin, 1978-

Mrs. Engels / Gavin McCrea. Catapult, 2015. 389 p.

ISBN 9781936787296

1. Engels, Friedrich, 1820-1895 Family 2. Marx, Karl, 1818-1883 Communist manifesto 3. Burns, Lizzie, 1827-1878 4. 1870s 5. Victorian era (1837-1901) 6. Class conflict 7. Independence in women 8. Working class 9. Philosophers 10. Political science -- Philosophy 11. Class struggle 12. Revolutionaries 13. England -- Social life and customs -- 19th century 14. Great Britain -- History -- Victoria, 1837-1901 15. Historical fiction 16. Love stories 17. Literary fiction 18. Biographical fiction

"First published in Australia and the UK by Scribe Publications."--title page verso.

Shortlisted for the Walter Scott Prize for Historical Fiction, 2016

The enigmatic Irish lover of Communist Manifesto co-author Frederick Engels, Lizzie Burns is a poor worker in the Manchester, England, mill that Engels owns. They are drawn together despite their profound difference. When they move to London to be closer to Karl Marx and family, Lizzie must learn to navigate the complex landscapes of Victorian society.

"Moving, finely detailed, rife with full-bodied, humanizing portraits of historical icons, and told in striking prose, this is a novel to be savored." Booklist.

McCrumb, Sharyn, 1948-

* The **ballad** of Frankie Silver / Sharyn McCrumb. Dutton, 1998. 386 p. Ballad novels

ISBN 9780525939696

1. Sheriffs -- Tennessee 2. Death row prisoners -- Tennessee 3. Pioneer women -- North Carolina 4. Abused women 5. Women murderers -- North Carolina 6. Judicial error 7. North Carolina -- History -- 19th century 8. Tennessee 9. Historical mysteries 10. Parallel narratives 11. Southern fiction

LC 9724867

As a convicted killer awaits execution in Tennessee, Sheriff Spencer Arrowood wonders if he arrested the right man years ago. Searching for answers, he discovers shocking parallels with a case more than a century old--the controversial hanging of a 19-year-old North Carolina

woman. Suddenly he finds himself in a frantic struggle to stop history from repeating itself.

"By working in two time frames and alternating the narrative voice, McCrumb threads both stories into a single pattern, a dense and lovely but very dark design that illustrates the social hypocrisy of the legal system as much as the harshness of mountain justice--then and now." New York Times Book Review.

McCrumb, Sharyn, 1948-

The **ballad** of Tom Dooley / Sharyn McCrumb. St. Martins Press, 2011. 336 p. Ballad novels

ISBN 9780312558178

1. Dula, Tom, 1843 or 4-1868 2. Love triangles 3. Murder -- North Carolina 4. Mountain life -- North Carolina 5. Extramarital affairs 6. Innocence (Law) 7. Ballads, American -- History and criticism 8. North Carolina 9. Historical mysteries 10. Southern fiction

A story inspired by a true crime made famous by the Kingston Trio's folk song recording reimagines the events surrounding the murder of North Carolina mountain girl Laura Foster and the hanging of her lover, Tom Dula, in a meticulously researched account that reveals additional information that may prove Dula's innocence.

McCrumb, Sharyn, 1948-

Foggy Mountain breakdown and other stories / Sharyn McCrumb. Ballantine Books, 1997. 326 p.

ISBN 9780345414939

1. Mountain life -- Appalachian Region, Southern 2. Appalachian Region, Southern 3. Thrillers and suspense 4. Short stories

LC 97-18787

24 short stories.

A collection of suspense and mystery stories evokes the southern Appalachian region

"The author has an uncanny knack for picking up the subtle nuances of dialogue, place, and personality that make her characters and settings sparkle with life. She can perfectly mimic the hillbilly twang of an Appalachian healer or the dulcet, pearshaped tones of an upper-class Briton; she can create the excitement of teenagers in lust, mirror the evil that lurks in a serial killer's heart, or convey the quiet desperation of a woman trapped in a miserable marriage. But most of all, McCrumb can make her readers believe what she writes." Booklist.

McCrumb, Sharyn, 1948-

* **If** ever I return, pretty Peggy-O / Sharyn McCrumb. Ballantine Books, 1991, c1990. 263 p. Ballad novels

ISBN 9780345369062

1. Class reunions 2. Small town life 3. Women folk singers 4. Murder investigation 5. Sheriffs -- Appalachian Region 6. Mountain life 7. Appalachian Region 8. Tennessee 9. Mysteries 10. Southern fiction

Originally published: New York : Scribner, 1990.

Macavity Award for Best Mystery Novel, 1991.

Sheriff Spencer Arrowood investigates the threatening messages being sent to Peggy Muryan, a famous folksinger of the 1960s, who has returned to her hometown of Hamelin, Tennessee, in search of peace and quiet.

"The author's strongly individualized characters give serious and intelligent thought to the ghosts raised by the reunionincluding the tangible spector of a murderer." New York Times Book Review.

McCrumb, Sharyn, 1948-

If I'd killed him when I met him / Sharyn McCrumb. Ballantine Books, 1995. 277 p. Elizabeth MacPherson mysteries

ISBN 9780345382290

1. Women forensic anthropologists -- Virginia 2. Husband-killing 3.

Married women 4. Poisoning 5. Cold cases (Criminal investigation) 6. Murder investigation -- Virginia 7. Virginia 8. Mysteries

LC 94023701 //r94

Agatha Award for Best Novel, 1996.

Southern sleuth Elizabeth MacPherson acts as official investigator for her brother's Virginia law firm and tests her skills solving two sensational murders and a third crime unsolved for a century.

"Buoyed by intriguing characters, a wry--sometimes macabre--wit, and lush Virginia atmosphere, McCrumb's mystery spins merrily along on its own momentum, concluding that justice will triumph . . . but in surprising ways." Publishers Weekly.

McCrumb, Sharyn, 1948-

She walks these hills / Sharyn McCrumb. Scribner, 1994. 336 p. Ballad novels

ISBN 9780684195568

1. Ghosts 2. Escaped convicts 3. Historians 4. Sheriffs 5. Graduate students 6. Wilderness survival 7. Appalachian Trail 8. Appalachian Region 9. Historical mysteries 10. Southern fiction

LC 94009458

Agatha Award for Best Novel, 1995.

Anthony Award for Best Novel, 1995.

Macavity Award for Best Mystery Novel, 1995.

A story of mountain journeys, both literal and figurative, weaves together the tales of a restless spirit from the 1700s, a deranged ex-convict searching the hills for a home that no longer exists, and a shocking murder.

"In 1779, Katie Wyler, 18, was captured by the Shawnee in North Carolina. The story of her escape and arduous journey home through hundreds of miles of Appalachian wilderness is the topic of ethno-historian Jeremy Cobb's thesis. . . . As Cobb begins to retrace Katie's return journey, 63-year-old convicted murderer Hiram (Harm) Sorley escapes from a nearby prison. Suffering from Korsakoff's syndrome, he has no recent memory. . . . Hamelin, Tenn. police dispatcher Martha Ayers uses the opportunity to convince the sheriff to assign her as a deputy. . . . Deftly building suspense, McCrumb weaves these colorful elements into her satisfying conclusion." Publishers Weekly.

McCullers, Carson, 1917-1967

* The **heart** is a lonely hunter / Carson McCullers. Houghton Mifflin, 2000, c1940. 359 p.

ISBN 9780618526413

1. 1940s 2. Misfits (Persons) -- Southern States 3. Social isolation 4. Racism -- Southern States 5. Men who are deaf and mute 6. Interpersonal relations 7. Interpersonal communication 8. Loneliness 9. Belonging 10. Southern States -- Race relations 11. Literary fiction 12. Modern classics 13. Southern Gothic 14. Southern fiction

LC 40010298

Originally published: Boston: Houghton Mifflin, 1940.

A quiet, sensitive girl searches for beauty in a small, but damned Southern town.

McCullers, Carson, 1917-1967

The **member** of the wedding / Carson McCullers Houghton Mifflin, 2004, c1946. 163 p.

ISBN 9780618492398

1. Social isolation 2. Twelve-year-old girls 3. Loneliness 4. Belonging 5. Brothers and sisters 6. Tomboys 7. Weddings 8. Cousins 9. Household employees 10. Girls -- Interpersonal relations 11. Loneliness in girls 12. Housekeepers 13. Southern States -- Social life and customs -- 20th century 14. Georgia -- Social life and customs -- 20th century 15. Coming-of-age stories 16. Literary fiction 17. Southern Gothic 18. Southern fiction

LC 46002022

Presents a drama about Frankie, a motherless twelve-year old girl who sees a solution to her unhappiness in the approaching wedding of her elder brother.

McCullers, Carson, 1917-1967

Reflections in a golden eye / Carson McCullers Houghton Mifflin, 2000, c1941. 136 p.

ISBN 9780618084753

1. 1930s 2. Husband and wife 3. Compulsive behavior 4. Love triangles 5. Military life 6. Men -- Sexuality 7. Closeted gay men 8. Extramarital affairs 9. Women with emotional illnesses 10. Southern States -- Social life and customs -- 20th century 11. Literary fiction 12. Southern Gothic 13. Southern fiction

LC 41002706

Transfered to an army base in the American South of the 1930's, Alison Langdon watches her husband, his commanding officer, and the officer's wife get caught up in a web of passion and jealousy.

McCullough, Colleen, 1937-

* The **first** man in Rome / Colleen McCullough. W. Morrow, 1990. 896 p. Masters of Rome

ISBN 9780688093686

1. Marius, Gaius, 157?-86 BC 2. Sulla, Lucius Cornelius, 138-78 BC 3. Roman Republic (509-27 BCE) 4. Politics and culture 5. Political corruption 6. Ambition in men 7. Social classes -- Rome 8. Families 9. Inheritance and succession 10. Rome -- History -- Republic, 265-30 BC 11. Historical fiction

LC 90037080

Sequel: The grass crown.

Includes end-paper maps.

McCullough's epic tale of ancient Rome explores the power struggle between an ambitious military man and a man who lost his fortune to pleasure.

McCullough, Colleen, 1937-

An **indecent** obsession / Colleen McCullough. Harper and Row, 1981. 317 p.

ISBN 0060149205

1. War -- Psychological aspects 2. Duty 3. Jealousy 4. Nurses 5. People with mental illnesses 6. Military hospitals 7. Soldiers 8. Men/women relations 9. Scandals 10. Violence 11. World War II 12. Pacific Area 13. Historical fiction 14. Psychological fiction

LC 81047547

At the end of World War II, decorated sergeant Michael Wilson enters the mental war of a Pacific military hospital, which contains five remaining patients united by their devotion to their nurse, Honour Langtry.

McDermid, Val

The **distant** echo / Val McDermid. St. Martin's Minotaur, 2003. 404 p. Karen Pirie novels

ISBN 0312301995

1. University of St. Andrews Students 2. Cold cases (Criminal investigation) 3. College students -- Scotland 4. Murder suspects 5. Friendship 6. Police -- Scotland 7. Crimes against young women 8. Revenge 9. Murder 10. Murder investigation 11. DNA testing 12. Scotland 13. St Andrews, Scotland 14. Fife, Scotland 15. Mysteries

LC 2003052902

The first novel in the bestselling Karen Pirie seriesThe award-winning Number One bestseller and Queen of crime fiction Val McDermid carves out a stunning psychological thriller.

"Individually, the characters are sensitively drawn. Collectively, they present the inscrutable face of closed-off communities so terrified of change they would kill for peace." New York Times Book Review.

McDermid, Val

How the dead speak : a Tony Hill and Carol Jordan novel / Val McDermid. Atlantic Monthly Press, 2019. 410 p. Tony Hill and Carol Jordan mysteries

ISBN 9780802147615

1. Former policewomen 2. Prisoners 3. Corruption 4. Lawyers 5. Skeleton 6. Detectives 7. Crime 8. Murder 9. Murder investigation 10. Secrets 11. England 12. Mysteries

LC 2019040561

When skeletal remains are found on the site of an orphanage renovation, imprisoned psychological profiler Tony Hill painfully reunites with ex-DCI Carol Jordan to investigate the discovery of a victim who is believed to be behind bars.

"Series fans will be pleased to see Tony and Carol reunite after a long separation... McDermid is writing at the top of her game." Publishers Weekly.

McDermid, Val

A **place** of execution / Val McDermid. St. Martin's Minotaur, 2000, c1999. 403 p.

ISBN 0312266324

1. Police 2. Missing children 3. Small town life 4. Women journalists 5. Murder 6. Crimes against children 7. England 8. Mysteries

LC 00059145

Anthony Award for Best Novel, 2001.
Macavity Award for Best Mystery Novel, 2001.

Police Inspector George Bennet, who investigated the never-solved disappearance of thirteen-year-old Alison Carter from her cloistered village decades ago, finds shattering new evidence, leading writer Catherine Heathcote to investigate further.

"When a 13-year-old English schoolgirl goes missing from her Derbyshire village in the winter of 1963, George Bennett, the police inspector in charge of the case, quickly realizes that the secrets of the child's life and possible death are locked in the collective mind of Scardale, an isolated hamlet of inbred families united by their common surnames and their hostility to strangers. Through Bennett's exhaustive efforts, the likely villain is caught and hanged--or so it seems, until the story reaches 35 years into the future for its chilling resolution." New York Times Book Review.

McDermott, Alice

After this / Alice McDermott. Farrar, Straus and Giroux, 2006. 288 p.

ISBN 0374168091

1. 1960s 2. 1970s 3. Family relationships 4. Middle class families 5. Vietnam War, 1961-1975 6. Parent and child 7. Brothers and sisters 8. Family traditions 9. Life change events 10. Freedom 11. Families 12. United States -- Social life and customs -- 20th century 13. Domestic fiction 14. Literary fiction

LC 2006005598

Pulitzer Prize for Fiction finalist, 2007.

A portrait of an American family during the middle decades of the twentieth century evokes the social, spiritual, and political turmoil of the era as seen through the experiences of a middle-class couple and their children.

"McDermott's easy authority with this material, combined with her clear-eyed sympathy for her characters, results in a moving, old-fashioned story about longing and loss and sorrow." New York Times.

McDermott, Alice

At weddings and wakes / Alice McDermott. Farrar Straus Giroux, 1992. 213 p.

ISBN 0374106746

1. 1960s 2. Brothers and sisters 3. Irish American families 4. Catholic families 5. Family relationships 6. Long Island, New York 7. Domestic fiction 8. Literary fiction

LC 91042070

Pulitzer Prize for Fiction finalist, 1993.

The bittersweet, lovable, human story of an Irish-Catholic family on Long Island as seen through the eyes of two sisters and a brother.

"Set in Brooklyn during the sixties, this novel tells the story of an extended Irish-American family observed primarily through the eyes of the children, son and two daughters. Time. circles backwards and forwards around a variety of family rituals: holiday meals, vacations at the shore, the wedding of a favorite aunt. The poignant middle-aged romance that develops between the aunt, a former nun, and her suitor, a shy mailman, exacerbates already pronounced family tensions. As they listen to oft-repeated stories about poverty, disease, and early deaths, the children are solemn witnesses to the Irish immigrant experience in America." Library Journal.

McDermott, Alice

* Charming Billy / Alice McDermott. Farrar, Straus and Giroux, 1998. 280 p.

ISBN 0374120803

1. Alcoholic men 2. Irish Americans 3. Unrequited love 4. Alcoholics 5. Death 6. Irish American men 7. Irish American families 8. New York City 9. Literary fiction

LC 9777089

ALA Notable Book, 1999.
National Book Award for Fiction, 1998
Shortlisted for the International IMPAC Dublin Literary Award, 2000

When the late Billy Lynch's relatives and friends gather together to keep his memory alive, stories are woven and memories relived detailing his life in the close Irish-American community and the intricate feelings that resurface

"This novel opens at the wake of the debonair Billy Lynch--gifted talker, abandoned suitor, faithful husband, devout Catholic, raging alcoholic. It then ranges back and forth through dozens of family theories and anecdotes to answer the question of what did or didn't make him who he was. At once a love story, a portrait of Irish Catholic Queens, and an ode to an edenic postwar East Hampton, this novel honors the consequences of everyday decisions, both sacred and profane, burnishing them in the retelling to a high shine." The New Yorker.

McDermott, Alice

Child of my heart / Alice McDermott. Farrar Straus Giroux, 2002. 242 p.

ISBN 9780374121235

1. 1960s 2. Working class families 3. Babysitters 4. Beauty 5. Teenage girls 6. Senior men 7. Fifteen-year-old girls 8. Septuagenarians 9. Cousins 10. Painters 11. Young women -- Relations with older men 12. New York (State) 13. Long Island, New York -- Social life and customs -- 20th century 14. Coming-of-age stories 15. Literary fiction

LC 2002069764

A teenage girl, raised on the east end of Long Island among the country estates of the rich, reflects on her understanding of the complexities and contradictions of human nature during a seemingly idyllic summer spent with her eight-year-old cousin Daisy.

"Child of My Heart is a golden and luminous memory retrieved by a narrator who has achieved a cool and slightly ironic distance from one of those summers in the late fifties or early sixties." Commonwealth.

McDermott, Alice

* The **ninth** hour / Alice McDermott. Farrar, Straus and Giroux, 2017. 240 p.

ISBN 9780374280147

1. 20th century 2. Irish Americans 3. Nuns 4. Family and suicide 5. Immigrants 6. Children of suicide victims 7. Catholics 8. City life 9. Helpfulness in women 10. Belief and doubt 11. Consequences 12. Communities 13. Interpersonal relations 14. Brooklyn, New York City 15. New York City 16. Literary fiction 17. Family sagas 18. Historical fiction

LC 2017011508

Kirkus Prize for Fiction finalist, 2017.

Longlisted for the Andrew Carnegie Medal for Excellence in Fiction, 2018.

National Book Critics Circle Award for Fiction finalist, 2017

A portrait of the Irish-American experience is presented through the story of an Irish immigrant's suicide and how it reverberates through innumerable lives in early twentieth-century Catholic Brooklyn.

"National Book Award winner McDermott (Someone) delivers an immense, brilliant novel about the limits of faith, the power of sacrifice, and the cost of forgiveness." Publishers Weekly.

McDermott, Alice

Someone / Alice McDermott. Farrar, Straus and Giroux, 2013. 232 p.

ISBN 9780374281090

1. Irish Americans 2. Brothers and sisters 3. Self-discovery in women 4. Catholic women 5. Growing up 6. Marriage 7. Faith (Christianity) 8. Homosexuality 9. Brooklyn, New York City 10. Literary fiction 11. Psychological fiction

LC 2013014938

Shortlisted for the International Dublin Literary Award, 2015

National Book Critics Circle Award for Fiction finalist, 2013

Chronicles the ordinary life of a woman named Marie, from her childhood to old age, as she experiences the changing world of her Irish-American enclave in Brooklyn, in this novel that speaks of life as it is daily lived.

McDermott, Alice

* **That** night / Alice McDermott. Farrar, Straus, and Giroux, 1987. 183 p.

ISBN 9780385333306

1. 1960s 2. Men/women relations 3. Suburban life 4. Violence 5. Teenagers 6. Long Island, New York 7. Literary fiction

LC 84045765

National Book Award for Fiction finalist, 1987

Pulitzer Prize for Fiction finalist, 1988.

"In spite of its brevity, 'That Night' is a wonderfully unfettered, ample novel, one that celebrates voice, personality and feeling when so much fiction avoids those rewarding characteristics. Ms. McDermott has invested her novel with a strong sense of historical authority, rendering with sure clarity a time and place marked by both a cultural innocence and the premonition of its inevitable loss." New York Times Book Review.

McDevitt, Jack

The **Cassandra** Project / Jack McDevitt and Mike Resnick. Ace Books, 2012. 400 p.

ISBN 9781937008710

1. Project Apollo (U.S.) 2. United States. National Aeronautics and Space Administration 3. Space flight to the moon 4. Entrepreneurs 5. Alien artifacts 6. Near future 7. Conspiracies 8. Publicity agents 9. Rockets (Aviation) 10. Presidents -- United States 11. Science fiction

LC 2012021236

With interest in the space program waning, a public affairs director at NASA reveals a shocking secret about the Apollo 11 mission from fifty years ago.

McDevitt, Jack

The **engines** of God / Jack McDevitt. Ace Books, 1994. 419 p. Priscilla Hutchins series

ISBN 0441000770

1. Terraforming 2. Monuments 3. Women spaceship captains 4. Space flight 5. Aliens (Non-humanoid) 6. Alien artifacts 7. Hard science fiction 8. Science fiction

LC 94007131

An unknown race called the Monument-Makers creates a stunning array of gorgeous statues, scattering them throughout the galaxy and encoding them with strange inscriptions that hold the key to the survival of humankind.

McDevitt, Jack

A **talent** for war / Jack McDevitt. Ace Books, 1989. 310 p. Alex Benedict novels

ISBN 0441795536

1. Aliens (Non-humanoid) 2. Life on other planets 3. Truth 4. Space warfare 5. Space vehicles 6. Heroes and heroines 7. Far future 8. Alien artifacts 9. Science fiction mysteries 10. Science fiction

When he discovers information that suggests a legendary space fighter may have ties to the alien that he destroyed, Alex ventures into the core of the alien galaxy to learn the truth.

Mcdonald, Gregory, 1937-2008

Fletch / Gregory Mcdonald. Bobbs-Merrill, 1974. 197 p. Fletch mysteries

ISBN 0672520206

1. Drug traffic 2. Undercover operations 3. Investigative journalists 4. Journalists -- United States 5. Murder investigation 6. Disguises 7. Journalists 8. California 9. Mysteries

LC 74003884

Republished in omnibus form under the title Fletch Forever, 1978.

Edgar Allan Poe Award for Best First Mystery Novel, 1975.

When a wealthy California industrialist tells apparent beach bum I.M. Fletcher that he wants to be murdered, the undercover journalist investigates the businessman's private life.

McDonald, Ian, 1960-

The **Dervish** House / Ian McDonald. Pyr, 2010. 410 p.

ISBN 9781616142049

1. European Union 2. 21st century 3. Think tanks 4. Terrorism 5. Carbon dioxide emissions -- Control 6. Power (Social sciences) 7. Interpersonal relations 8. Legends 9. Visions in men 10. Social classes 11. Bombings 12. Genies 13. Istanbul, Turkey 14. European Union countries 15. Cyberpunk 16. Science fiction

LC 2010012843

BSFA Award for Best Novel, 2010.

John W. Campbell Memorial Award for Best Science Fiction Novel, 2011.

RUSA Reading List, 2011.

In 2027 Turkey, sectarian violence threatens, the nation wrestles with whether or not it should leave the European Union, and citizens must carry cards that ration their carbon allowance.

"In 2027, Turkey, still teetering precariously between East and West, has become a member of the European Union and an economic juggernaut. In crowded Istanbul, where stressed-out students guzzle nanofueled energy drinks to boost memory and businessmen wear expensive nanotech suits, the residents of an apartment complex attempt to find their way through-or to profit from-this unstable new world. Among them are an audacious stock trader, an antiquarian searching for a centuries-old mummy rumored to possess mystical powers, and a nine-year-old boy whose ill health keeps him isolated, dreaming of the outside world. When a bizarre terrorist attack afflicts its witnesses with fantastic visions, they are all affected in extraordinary ways. Bookmarks,McDonald brilliantly [imagines] what a world of functional, consumer nano would mean for business, culture, faith, play and terrorism; painting a vivid picture of Istanbul as a gem of human society; and delighting with details of the marvels to be found there." Boing Boing

McDonald, Ian, 1960-

New moon / Ian McDonald. Tor, 2016, c2015. 428 p. Luna novels (Ian McDonald)

ISBN 9780765375513

1. Brothers and sisters 2. Mines and mineral resources 3. Greed 4. Heirs and heiresses 5. Competition 6. Business competition 7. Space colonies 8. Corporations 9. Corporate power 10. Corporate intrigue 11. Upper class 12. Survival 13. Near future 14. Moon -- Colonization 15. Science fiction 16. Cyberpunk 17. Financial thrillers

When her corporation, Corta Helio, which controls the Moon's Helium-3 industry, is confronted by the many enemies she made during her meteoric rise, Adriana Corta and her five children must navigate a world of corporate warfare to save the family empire from those who want to destroy it.

McDonald, Ian, 1960-

River of gods / Ian McDonald. Pyr, 2006, c2004. 583 p. ISBN 1591024366

1. 21st century 2. Caste 3. Genetic engineering 4. Technology and civilization 5. Police 6. Gangsters 7. Husband and wife 8. Police spouses 9. Scientists 10. Stand-up comedians 11. Politicians 12. Journalists 13. Mind reading (Magic tricks) 14. Prophets 15. Religion and culture 16. Communication and technology 17. Gods and goddesses, Indic 18. Near future 19. India -- History -- 21st century 20. Science fiction 21. Cyberpunk 22. Mythological fiction

LC 2005035110

August 15, 2047 -- Happy birthday India.

Originally published: New York :

BSFA Award for Best Novel, 2004.

"It's 2047, and the centennial of India's nationhood approaches. Amid the turmoil and vigor of a nation teeming with people and clogged with information, the lives of nine individuals, including a policeman, a journalist, a scientist, a politician, and a standup comic, intersect in an unanticipated union with the fate of their country at stake. . . . [The author] provides a kaleidoscopic, freewheeling encounter with the near future in one of the most exotic--and impoverished--parts of the world. . . . Every library should purchase this multitextured tale of future perils and possibilities in the land of a thousand gods." Library Journal.

McDonald, L. J., 1970-

The battle sylph / L. J. McDonald. Leisure Books, 2010 336 p. Sylph novels

ISBN 9780843963007

1. Kidnapping victims 2. Human sacrifice 3. Shapeshifters 4. Warriors 5. Good and evil 6. Alliances 7. Desire 8. Sexual attraction 9. Paranormal romances

Kidnapped as a sacrifice for a ruthless battle sylph named Heyou, Solie refuses to succumb without a fight and, using her shape-shifing abilities, takes control of this powerful warrior, unleashing a desire that could change the world.

McDonald, Roger, 1941-

Mr. Darwin's shooter / Roger McDonald. Atlantic Monthly Press, 1998. 365 p.

ISBN 9780871137333

1. Covington, Syms, 1813-1861 2. Darwin, Charles, 1809-1882 3. Beagle Expedition, 1831-1836 4. Biological researchers 5. Evolution and religion 6. Evolution -- Research 7. Hunters 8. Physician and patient 9. Sailors 10. Voyages and travels -- 19th century 11. Australia -- History -- 19th century 12. Biographical fiction 13. Historical fiction

LC 9836819

Shortlisted for the Miles Franklin Literary Award, 1999

Chronicles the life of Syms Covington, who becomes Charles Darwin's shooter and collector of specimens, from his early maritime adventures to his later years as he awaits his copy of "The Origin of Species" and ponders his part in altering the way the world thinks.

"Mr. MacDonald is a generous, leisurely author who gives the reader a large cast of quirky characters, much peripheral detail, lively action, and a view of nineteenth-century social patterns. Covington, moreover, is no plaster saint, and the Beagle's long voyage offers opportunities for adventure. One need not be pro or anti either Darwin or Genesis to enjoy this well-written tale." The Atlantic.

McEwan, Ian

* Amsterdam / Ian McEwan. Nan A. Talese/Doubleday, 1999, c1998. 193 p.

ISBN 0385494238

1. Former lovers -- Death 2. Sex scandals 3. Ambition in men 4. Newspaper editors 5. Composers 6. Politicians -- 20th century 7. Euthanasia -- Amsterdam, Netherlands 8. Suicide pacts 9. Male friendship 10. Fame 11. Amsterdam, Netherlands 12. London, England 13. England 14. Satirical fiction 15. Psychological fiction 16. Literary fiction

LC 9841401

Booker Prize, 1998.

Two old friends, Clive Linley and Vernon Halliday, both former lovers of of the late Molly Lane, meet to pay their last respects and make a pact that will have unforeseen consequences

McEwan, Ian

Atonement : a novel / Ian McEwan. Nan A. Talese, Doubleday, 2002. 351 p.

ISBN 0385503954

1. 1930s 2. Sisters 3. Guilt in women 4. Rich families 5. Shame 6. Thirteen-year-old girls 7. Former convicts 8. Rural life 9. Social classes 10. Regret 11. Redemption 12. England -- History -- 20th century 13. Psychological fiction 14. Historical fiction 15. Literary fiction

LC 2001044291

Originally published: London : Jonathan Cape, 2001.

National Book Critics Circle Award for Fiction, 2002.

ALA Notable Book, 2003.

Shortlisted for the Booker-McConnell Prize, 2001.

In 1935 England, thirteen-year-old Briony Tallis witnesses an event involving her sister Cecilia and her childhood friend Robbie Turner, and she becomes the victim of her own imagination, which leads her on a lifelong search for truth and absolution.

"This is a work of astonishing depth and humanity. . . . The upper-class milieu, the sense of place and time, are rendered with an exactitude worthy of Elizabeth Bowen. . . . Mr McEwan has achieved the difficult task of combining literary sophistication with moral gravity." The Economist.

McEwan, Ian

Black dogs / Ian McEwan. Nan A. Talese, Doubleday, 1992. 149 p.

ISBN 9780385425414

1. Husband and wife 2. Parents-in-law 3. Berlin Wall -- Dismantling, 1989 4. Orphans 5. Communism 6. World War II 7. Honeymoons 8. Difference (Psychology) 9. England 10. Psychological fiction 11. Literary fiction

LC 92007418

Shortlisted for the Booker-McConnell Prize, 1992.

Writing a memoir of his parents-in-law, Jeremy describes how June and Bernhard Iremaine met, fell in love, and committed themselves to the Communist party, in a narrative that spans from post-World War II to the present.

"This novel is compassionate without resorting to sentimentality, clever without ever losing its honesty, an undisguised novel of ideas which is also Ian McEwan's most human work." Times Literary Supplement.

McEwan, Ian

* The **child** in time / Ian McEwan. Anchor Books, 1999, c1987. 263 p.

ISBN 9780385497527

1. Kidnapping 2. Missing children 3. Grief in men 4. Loss (Psychology) 5. Guilt 6. Marital conflict 7. Life change events 8. Children's literature authors, English 9. England 10. Psychological fiction 11. Literary fiction

LC 87008603

Originally published: London : Cape, 1987.

Whitbread Book Award for Novel, 1987.

The abduction of his only child destroys Stephen Lewis' marriage and painfully forces him to look back on his own childhood.

"Many of the plot turns in the novel may seem improbable and even fanciful, but the feelings expressed by the characters and their sense of time (running up, running down and running out) are, without exception, genuine. . . . [This is an] astonishing book." Time.

McEwan, Ian

The **children** act : a novel / Ian McEwan. Nan A. Talese/Doubleday, 2014. 240 p.

ISBN 9780385539708

1. Jehovah's Witnesses 2. Middle-aged women 3. Trials 4. People with cancer 5. Women judges 6. Self-fulfillment in women 7. Religion and law 8. Medical care 9. Extramarital affairs 10. Teenage boys 11. Music 12. England 13. Psychological fiction

LC 2014018448

This book was made into the 2017 film of the same name, directed by Richard Eyre and starring Emma Thompson, Stanley Tucci, and Fionn Whitehead.

ALA Notable Book, 2015.

A highly respected London judge hides behind her professional accomplishments her decision to separate from a husband who wants an open marriage, a loss that challenges her beliefs throughout a case involving parents whose faith forbids a life-saving transfusion for their son.

"In a tranquil mix of exacting word choice and easily flowing sentences, McEwan once again observes with depth and wisdom the universal truth in the uncommon situation." Booklist.

McEwan, Ian

Nutshell / Ian McEwan. Nan A. Talese, Doubleday, 2016. 224 p.

ISBN 9780385542074

1. Married women 2. Pregnant women 3. Extramarital affairs 4. Betrayal 5. Fetus 6. Brothers 7. Deception 8. Murder 9. Murderers 10. London, England 11. Literary fiction 12. Adaptations, retellings, and spin-offs

Originally published: London : Jonathan Cape, 2016.

The nine-month-old inhabitant of Trudy's womb bears witness to a murder plot devised by Trudy and Claude, the brother of Trudy's ex-husband.

"Packed with humor and tinged with suspense, this gem resembles a sonnet the narrator recalls hearing his father recite: brief, dense, bitter, suggestive of unrequited and unmanageable longing, surprising, and surprisingly affecting." Publishers Weekly.

McEwan, Ian

* **On** Chesil Beach / Ian McEwan. Nan A. Talese, Doubleday, 2007. 176 p.

ISBN 9780385522403

1. 1960s 2. 20th century 3. Newlyweds 4. Intimacy (Psychology) 5. Musicians 6. Women musicians 7. Men/women relations 8. College students 9. Husband and wife 10. Sexuality 11. First sexual experience 12. Love 13. Anxiety 14. England 15. London, England 16. Love stories 17. Literary fiction

LC 2006100720

First published: London : Jonathan Cape, c2007.

ALA Notable Book, 2008.

British Book Award for Book of the Year, 2008.

Shortlisted for the Man Booker Prize, 2007

On their wedding day, a young couple--Florence, daughter of an Oxford academic and a successful businessman, and Edward, an earnest history student with little experience of women--looks forward to the future while worrying about their upcoming wedding night.

McEwan, Ian

* **Saturday** / Ian McEwan. Nan A. Talese, Doubleday, 2005. 304 p.

ISBN 0385511809

1. 2000s (Decade) 2. Traffic accidents 3. Assault and battery 4. Forgiveness 5. Neurosurgeons 6. Physicians 7. Middle-aged men 8. Criminals 9. Family reunions 10. World politics 11. Iraq War, 2003-2011 -- Protest movements 12. Road rage 13. Huntington's disease 14. England 15. London, England 16. Literary fiction

LC 2004062127

Originally published: London: Jonathan Cape, 2005.

ALA Notable Book, 2006.

James Tait Black Memorial Prize for Fiction, 2005.

A successful, happily married neurosurgeon, Henry Perowne is drawn into a confrontation with Baxter, a small-time thug, following a minor motor vehicle accident on the way to his regular squash game, an encounter that has savage consequences when Baxter, believing that the doctor has humiliated him, visits the Perowne home that evening during a family reunion.

"It's clear that with this volume, Mr. McEwan has not only produced one of the most powerful pieces of post-9/11 fiction yet published, but also fulfilled that very primal mission of the novel: to show how we--a privileged few of us, anyway--livetoday." New York Times Book Review.

McEwan, Ian

Solar : a novel / Ian McEwan. Nan A. Talese/Doubleday, 2010. 287 p.

ISBN 9780385533416

1. Physicists 2. Nobel Prize winners 3. Egotism in men 4. Selfishness in men 5. Intellectual property 6. Middle-aged men 7. Global warming -- Prevention 8. Extramarital affairs 9. Arctic regions 10. New Mexico 11. Satirical fiction 12. Literary fiction

LC 2009046508

Nobel Prize-winning scientist Michael Beard is coasting through his professional life, making no real contribution since he won his award, while his fifth marriage is in danger due to his, and his wife's, infidelities; but he gets a chance at redemption when he is called on to save humanity from environmental disaster.

McEwan, Ian

Sweet tooth : a novel / Ian McEwan. Nan A. Talese/Doubleday, 2012. 304 p.

ISBN 9780385536820

1. M I 5 2. 1970s 3. Women spies 4. Cold War 5. Intelligence officers 6. Authors 7. Reading 8. Gender role -- Political aspects 9. Politics and literature 10. Intellectuals 11. Intellectual life 12. Men/women relations 13. Interpersonal attraction 14. London, England 15. Spy fiction 16. Metafiction 17. Satirical fiction

LC 2012013932

During the Cold War in Britain, Serena Frome is recruited to work as an intelligence agent for MI5 and her first mission involves getting close to Tom Haley, a promising young writer. Despite her best intentions she starts falling for Tom, with potentially dangerous consquences.

McFadden, Bernice L.

Gathering of waters / Bernice L. McFadden. Akashic Books, 2012 250 p.

ISBN 9781617750328

1. Till, Emmett, 1941-1955 2. 1990s 3. Small towns 4. Lovers' reunions 5. Ghosts 6. Former lovers 7. Homecomings 8. Mississippi 9. Magical realism 10. Literary fiction

Tass Hilson, the girlfriend of Emmett Till, leaves the town of Money, Mississippi, after Emmett's murder and relocates to Detroit where she lives out her life for forty years, until something calls her back to Money.

McFadden, Bernice L.

The **Book** of Harlan / Bernice L. McFadden. Akashic, 2016. 400 p.

ISBN 9781617754456

1. Second World War era (1939-1945) 2. African Americans 3. Prisoners of war 4. Nazis 5. Musicians 6. Concentration camps 7. Europe -- History -- 20th century 8. Historical fiction

In WWII, two African American musicians are captured by the Nazis in Paris and imprisoned at the Buchenwald concentration camp.

"Playing with themes of divine justice and the suffering of the righteous, McFadden presents a remarkably crisp portrait of one average man's extraordinary bravery in the face of pure evil." Booklist.

McFarlane, Fiona, 1978-

The **night** guest / Fiona McFarlane. Faber & Faber, 2013. 256 p.

ISBN 9780865477735

1. Widows 2. Memories 3. Social isolation 4. Caregivers 5. Aging 6. Senior women 7. Fear 8. Australia 9. Psychological suspense

LC 2013022511

Barbara Jefferis Award, 2014.

Shortlisted for the Stella Prize, 2014.

Shortlisted for the Miles Franklin Literary Award, 2014

A widow living alone in an isolated beach house allows a bedraggled woman, claiming to be a governmental care worker, into her home and begins hearing strange sounds at night and is suddenly plagued by childhood memories of Fiji.

McFarlane, Mhairi

Don't you forget about me / Mhairi McFarlane. William Morrow, 2019. 432 p.

ISBN 9780062958464

1. First loves 2. Reunions 3. Women -- Interpersonal relations 4. Lost love 5. Coping in women 6. Men/women relations 7. Breaking up (Interpersonal relations) 8. Romantic comedies 9. Contemporary romances 10. Chick lit

Fired and dumped on the same night, Georgina takes a new job before realizing that her boss is her first love, and does not recognize her.

McGahan, Andrew

The **white** earth / Andrew McGahan. Allen & Unwin, 2004. 376 p.

ISBN 1741141478

1. 1990s 2. Landowners -- Australia 3. Boys -- Australia 4. Land tenure 5. Land claims 6. Family secrets 7. Nine-year-old boys -- Australia 8. Children of widows -- Australia 9. Uncles 10. Inheritance and succession 11. Cholesteatoma 12. Father-separated families 13. Mothers and sons 14. Rural families 15. Family farms 16. Queensland 17. Australia 18. Psychological suspense

Age Fiction or Imaginative Writing Award, 2004.

Miles Franklin Award, 2005.

In late 1992, 8 year-old William looked out from the back verandah of his home and saw the mushroom cloud of a nuclear explosion. There was no sound, but William was aware of the smell of burning.... Later, his father dead by fire and his mother plagued by demons of her own, William is cast upon the charity of his embittered uncle.

"Set in Australia's Queensland province, the novel begins with the blaze of 70 acres of wheat, a conflagration that consumes nine-year-old William's father and sends the boy and his mother packing to his great-uncle John McIvor's rotting mansion on the arid plains of what was once a vast sheep ranch. Chapters alternate between William settling into his new existence (action set in the early 1990s), and the story of John's youth on the ranch, where as the son of the ranch manager he nurtured ambitions to one day own the estate. John recruits William's help in organizing a rally for his right-wing group, which opposes the proposed Native Title laws that would return Aboriginal-claimed land to the original inhabitants. The novel's first half is a slow build, the second half, a well-wrought, meditative reflection on Australia's colonialist demons, brings the book's gothic intimations home to roost." Publishers Weekly.

McGarrity, Michael

Everyone dies : a Kevin Kerney novel / Michael McGarrity. Dutton, 2003. 336 p. Kevin Kerney mysteries

ISBN 0525947612

1. Crimes against gay men and lesbians 2. Death threats 3. Animal mutilations 4. Policewomen 5. Pregnant women 6. Serial murders 7.

Police chiefs 8. Police 9. Santa Fe, New Mexico 10. Mysteries

LC 2003009208

When a prominent homosexual lawyer is murdered, Santa Fe police chief Kevin Kerney directs his staff along elusive leads that result in two additional deaths and the discovery of a chilling series of killings.

"Michael McGarrity is one of those low-key pros who keep the genre honest with realistic crime stories and plain-talking cops who know the procedures." New York Times Book Review.

McGhee, Alison, 1960-

The **opposite** of fate / Alison McGhee. Houghton Mifflin Harcourt, 2020. 256 p.

ISBN 9781328518439

1. Rape victims 2. Pregnancy 3. Missing children 4. Options, alternatives, choices 5. Autonomy 6. Reproductive rights 7. People in comas 8. Consent (Law) 9. New York (State) 10. Literary fiction 11. Women's lives and relationships

Rendered comatose and pregnant by a violent attack, a young woman emerges from her long state of unresponsiveness, only to find herself reckoning with the consequences of decisions that were made about her body without her consent.

"Like its comparable titles, The Opposite of Fate is a prime book-group choice." Booklist.

McGown, Jill

Murder at the old vicarage / Jill McGown. St. Martin's Press, 1988. 256 p. Lloyd and Hill mysteries

ISBN 0312026153

1. Small town life 2. Vicars 3. Policewomen 4. Police 5. England 6. Mysteries

LC 88-30603

"First published in Great Britain by Macmillan London Limited, under the title Redemption"--T.p. verso.

Police duo Lloyd--Acting Chief Inspector--and Judy--Detective Sergeant--spend Christmas in a small village where the indiscreet Reverend George Wheeler's wife-molesting son-in-law is discovered murdered

"McGown's complex plot is masterful and her sleuths and their predicament are enthralling." Publishers Weekly.

McGown, Jill

Verdict unsafe / Jill McGown. Fawcett Columbine, 1997. 327 p. Lloyd and Hill mysteries

ISBN 0449910679

1. Serial rape 2. Rape investigation 3. Trials (Rape) 4. Midlands, England 5. England 6. Mysteries

LC 97-4949

Detective Inspector Judy Hill and her boss and lover, Detective Chief Inspector Lloyd, become caught up in desperate efforts to prove that Colin Arthur Drummond is the serial rapist stalking their East Anglia town, while the young predator privately threatens Judy Hill herself

"The pace is methodical and the cast cheerless, but McGown wraps her grim tale in a complex, satisfying solution." Publishers Weekly.

McGregor, Jon, 1976-

Even the dogs : a novel / Jon McGregor. Bloomsbury USA, 2010. 195 p.

ISBN 9781596913486

1. Homeless persons 2. Drugs -- Overdose 3. Redemption 4. Social marginality 5. Loss (Psychology) 6. Deathwatch 7. Despair 8. Psychological fiction 9. Literary fiction

International IMPAC Dublin Literary Award, 2012.

In a series of fractured narratives, the author tells the stories of a group of addicts, all found dead between Christmas and New Year's

Day, in a novel where it becomes clear that these lost souls are treated with more respect in death than they ever were in their short lives.

"The book is narrated by a group of urban ghosts, victims of drug overdoses who look on as someone they know, Robert Radcliffe, is found dead in his shabby apartment. Other friends, family members and acquaintances, most of whom were part of Robert's life, come in and out of focus as they move around the city looking for their next fixes and, along with the police and investigators, respond to Robert's death. As a novel about the consequences of addiction particularly heroin addiction Even the Dogs is harrowing. . . . But McGregor's devotion to craft comes at a significant cost to a reader's emotional engagement with his characters and story. His technique intrudes, becomes showy." New York Times Book Review.

McGregor, Jon, 1976-

The **reservoir** tapes / Jon McGregor. Catapult, 2018. 176 p. Reservoir novels

ISBN 9781936787913

1. Villages 2. Interviewing 3. Missing teenage girls 4. Memories 5. Small town life 6. Communities 7. Secrets 8. England 9. Literary fiction

Returns readers to the territory of the award-winning author's Reservoir 13, tracing the efforts of an interviewer who collects stories throughout a secretive English village to piece together the fate of a missing girl.

"McGregor demonstrates an extraordinary ability to create complex, multidimensional characters in only a few spare sentences. He is also a master of mood, investing his stories with an air of the ominous while proving also to be a superb stylist.." Booklist.

McGuane, Thomas

* **Cloudbursts** : collected and new stories / Thomas McGuane. Knopf, 2018. 512 p.

ISBN 9780385350211

1. Wilderness areas 2. Literary fiction 3. Short stories

LC 2017039288

An abundant collection of 45 short stories by the acclaimed author of Crow Fair depicts protagonists on the fringes of society whose twisted pasts complicate their future prospects, in a volume set in the seedy corners of Key West, the remote shores of the Bahamas and McGuane's hallmark Big Sky country.

"McGuane is a master, choosing his words with a lapidary's precision and setting them in sentences that burn brightly, finishing his stories with epiphanies to treasure." Booklist.

McGuane, Thomas

Crow fair : stories / Thomas McGuane. Alfred A. Knopf, 2015. 272 p.

ISBN 9780385350198

1. Family relationships 2. Friendship 3. Interpersonal relations 4. Montana 5. Mainstream fiction 6. Short stories

LC 2014018360

A collection of stories set in Big Sky country explores the ties of family and friendship and the many challenges and complications of these relationships.

"The conflicts throughout this book are age-old--indeed, the title story evokes 'Oedipus'--but McGuane's clean writing and psychological acuity enliven them all. A slyly cutting batch of tales." Kirkus.

McGuane, Thomas

Gallatin Canyon / Thomas McGuane. Alfred A. Knopf, 2006. 256 p.

ISBN 1400041562

1. Senior men 2. Self-fulfillment in men 3. Interpersonal relations 4. Failure (Psychology) 5. The West (United States) -- Social life and customs 6. Literary fiction 7. Pacific Northwest fiction 8. Short stories

LC 2005044680

"McGuane has become our poet-philosopher of the arm's length, of the prudently aborted intimacy that keeps both isolation and commitment equally at bay." New York Times Book Review.

McGuire, Ian

The **North** water : a novel / Ian McGuire. Henry Holt & Co., 2016. 255 p.

ISBN 9781627795944

1. Victorian era (1837-1901) 2. Whaling 3. Violence in men 4. Physicians 5. Veterans 6. Seafaring life 7. Murderers 8. Ships 9. Arctic regions 10. Sea stories 11. Historical thrillers

LC 2015023830

Longlisted for the Man Booker Prize, 2016

The Volunteer, a nineteenth-century Yorkshire whaling ship, becomes the stage for a confrontation between brutal harpooner Henry Drax and ex-army surgeon Patrick Sumner, the ship's medic, during a violent, ill-fated voyage to the Arctic.

"There is no light, no letup in this gruesome tale, so there is great significance in the rare but moving acts of kindness and camaraderie between these men in peril. An amazing journey." Publishers Weekly.

McGuire, Seanan

* **Beneath** the sugar sky / Seanan McGuire. Tor, 2018 160 p. Wayward children

ISBN 9780765393586

1. Interdimensional travel 2. Boarding schools 3. Prophecies 4. Magic 5. Boarding school students 6. Mothers and daughters 7. Parallel universes 8. Mermaids 9. Self-acceptance 10. Fantasy fiction 11. Gateway fantasy

Beneath the Sugar Sky returns to Eleanor West's Home for Wayward Children. At this magical boarding school, children who have experienced fantasy adventures are reintroduced to the "real" world. Sumi died years before her prophesied daughter Rini could be born. Rini was born anyway, and now she's trying to bring her mother back from a world without magic.

McGuire, Seanan

Chimes at midnight : an October Daye novel / Seanan McGuire. DAW Books, 2013. 357 p. October Daye novels

ISBN 9780756408145

1. Murder investigation 2. Poisoning 3. Fairies 4. Supernatural 5. Magic 6. Half-human hybrids 7. Counts and countesses 8. Women rulers 9. Changelings 10. San Francisco, California 11. Urban fantasy

When she is exiled by the Queen of the Mists, the only way that Toby Daye can escape the sentence is to locate the legendary Library of the Stars, find the rightful heir to the Kingdom of Mists, and overthrow the Queen.

McGuire, Seanan

* **Down** among the sticks and bones / Seanan McGuire. Tor, 2017. 187 p. Wayward children

ISBN 9780765392039

1. Interdimensional travel 2. Boarding schools 3. Twin sisters 4. Magic 5. Teenage girls 6. Parallel universes 7. Fathers and daughters 8. Mothers and daughters 9. Boarding school students 10. Fantasy fiction 11. Gateway fantasy

Sequel to: Every heart a doorway.

Amelia Bloomer List, 2018.

Rainbow List, 2018.

RUSA Reading List, 2018.

Shares the story of Jack and Jill before they tumbled into Eleanor West's Home for Wayward Children, relating their experiences in a childhood world of monsters, mad scientists and fateful choices.

"Beautifully crafted and smartly written, this fairy-tale novella is everything that speculative fiction readers look for: fantastical worlds, diverse characters, and prose that hits home with its emotional truths." Library Journal.

McGuire, Seanan

* **Every** heart a doorway / Seanan McGuire Tor, 2016. 160 p. Wayward children

ISBN 9780765385505

1. Interdimensional travel 2. Boarding schools 3. Magic 4. Murder 5. Teenagers 6. Parallel universes 7. Murder investigation 8. Boarding school students 9. Sexual minority teenagers 10. Fantasy fiction 11. Gateway fantasy

Rainbow List, 2017.

Children have always disappeared from Eleanor West's Home for Wayward Children under the right conditions; slipping through the shadows under a bed or at the back of a wardrobe, tumbling down rabbit holes and into old wells, and emerging somewhere ... else. But magical lands have little need for used-up miracle children. Nancy tumbled once, but now she's back. The things she's experienced ... they change a person. The children under Miss West's care understand all too well. And each of them is seeking a way back to their own fantasy world. But Nancy's arrival marks a change at the Home. There's a darkness just around each corner, and when tragedy strikes, it's up to Nancy and her new-found schoolmates to get to the heart of the matter. No matter the cost.

McGuire, Seanan

* **In** an absent dream / Seanan McGuire. Tor, 2019, c2018. 176 p. Wayward children

ISBN 9780765399298

1. Nonconformists 2. Parallel universes 3. Deals 4. Consequences 5. Interdimensional travel 6. Gender role 7. Goblins 8. Gateway fantasy 9. Fantasy fiction

LC 2018044548

"A Tom Doherty Associates Book."

Traces the origin story of studious Lundy, who discovers a world founded on logic, reason and riddles before making a fateful bargain.

McGuire, Seanan

* **Middlegame** / Seanan McGuire. Tor, 2019 528 p.

ISBN 9781250195524

1. Twins 2. Alchemy 3. Twin brothers and sisters 4. Magic 5. Time travel 6. Mathematics 7. Parallel universes 8. Power (Social sciences) 9. Language and languages 10. Fantasy fiction

In an alternate-reality world under the shadow of a magical government bent on transmuting the fabric of reality, two alchemical twins, one skilled with language and the other with math, become catalysts in their creator's grab for power.

"Shifts and alterations in timelines demand close attention from readers, but McGuire's rigorous plotting pulls everything together by the end. This is a fascinating novel by an author of consummate skill." Publishers Weekly.

McGuire, Seanan

Night and silence / Seanan McGuire. Daw Books, 2018. x, 352 p.   October Daye novels

ISBN 9780756414764

1. Fairies 2. Half-human hybrids 3. Engaged persons 4. Women private investigators 5. Mother and adult daughter 6. Missing persons 7. Missing persons investigation 8. Kidnapping investigation 9. Malicious accusation 10. Alliances 11. Couples 12. San Francisco, California 13. Urban fantasy

When she is accused of kidnapping Gillian, her estranged human daughter, by her ex-boyfriend and his new secretive wife, October "Toby" Daye investigates and must call upon all of her inner strength and allies to discover which Faerie remembered Gillian existed.

McGuire, Seanan

Once broken faith / Seanan McGuire. Daw Books, 2016. 420 p.   October Daye novels

ISBN 9780756408107

1. Half-human hybrids 2. Women private investigators 3. Fairies 4. Assassination 5. Political intrigue 6. Murder investigation 7. San Francisco, California 8. Urban fantasy

When King Anthony Robinson of Angels is murdered during the grand convocation to discuss the elf-shot cure discovery, Toby, to secure her own future and the distribution of the cure, must solve the murder, clear her own name and unmask a killer with his own agenda.

McGuire, Seanan

Rosemary and rue / Seanan McGuire. DAW Books, 2009. 358 p.   October Daye novels

ISBN 9780756405717

1. Supernatural 2. Women detectives 3. Fairies 4. Elves 5. Magic 6. Half-human hybrids 7. Curses 8. Murder investigation 9. Changelings 10. San Francisco, California 11. Urban fantasy

Half-fae Toby retreats to the human world after being rejected by her Faerie family, but finds her anonymity compromised by the murder of an important countess who binds her to investigate, forcing Toby to resume her fae position.

"Like Dreams and Shadows, this dark, gritty, and richly detailed urban fantasy introduces characters who awkwardly straddle the boundary between the mortal and supernatural worlds, presenting an inventive contemporary take on classic fairy tale lore." Library Journal.

McHugh, Laura

Arrowood :   a novel / Laura McHugh. Spiegel & Grau, 2016. 274 p.

ISBN 9780812996395

1. Family secrets 2. Kidnapping 3. Memory 4. Guilt in women 5. Ghosts 6. Homecomings 7. Family estates 8. Twin sisters 9. Missing girls 10. Iowa 11. Psychological suspense 12. Gothic fiction 13. Literary fiction

LC 2015039961

Inheriting the grand historical Mississippi home of her childhood 20 years after her twin sisters were abducted, Arden endeavors to find out what really happened and confronts devastating family secrets.

"Lyrical prose and in-depth character studies examine the reliability of memory, punctuated by believable suspense and aided by a careful look at a small town." Publishers Weekly.

McHugh, Laura

The **wolf** wants in : a novel / Laura McHugh. Spiegel & Grau, 2019. 260 p.

ISBN 9780399590283

1. Small towns 2. Brothers -- Death 3. Murder investigation 4. Sisters 5. Teenage girls 6. Drug dealers 7. Opioid abuse 8. Missing girls 9. Bones 10. Families 11. Family secrets 12. Teenage boy/girl relations 13. Class conflict 14. Kansas 15. Thrillers and suspense

A woman confronts a dark secret about her brother's death while a teen becomes increasingly desperate to escape their opioid-ravaged community.

McHugh, Maureen F.

After **the** apocalypse : stories /   Maureen F. McHugh. Small Beer Press, 2011. 264 p.

ISBN 9781931520294

1. End of the world 2. Natural disasters 3. Survival 4. Science fiction 5. Short stories

Shirley Jackson Awards, Single-Author Collection, 2011.

Nine stories explore the ways people respond in the aftermath of disasters, from a convict exiled to zombie-controlled Cleveland to debt slavery in China, an illness spread by chicken nuggets, and a participant in a failed clinical trial.

McInerney, Lisa

The **glorious** heresies / Lisa McInerney. John Murray, 2015. 384 p. Glorious heresies

ISBN 9781444798852

1. Catholic Church Ireland. 2. Murder 3. Urban problems 4. Misfits (Persons) 5. Criminals 6. Prostitutes 7. Redemption 8. Organized crime 9. Parents of criminals 10. Teenage drug dealers 11. Cork, Ireland 12. Ireland -- Social conditions 13. Literary fiction

Baileys Women's Prize for Fiction, 2016.

This darkly humorous, gritty debut has a lot in common with novels by Irvine Welsh -- foul language, colorful slang, and seedy characters, to start. Though it ostensibly follows the consequences of Maureen Phelan's clubbing of an intruder using a holy relic (she asks her gangster son to conceal the (accidental) death that results), it also addresses the violence, crime, and despair of an Ireland whose economic hopes have been dashed. Five years pass within these pages, as characters young and old alike are forced into bad choices. Give it a go if you're up for something dark, literary, and profane. -- Description by Shauna Griffin.

"This gritty, urban character study will be perfect for readers favoring strong blends of literary and crime fiction, overlaid with striking dark comedy." Booklist.

McInerny, Ralph, 1929-2010

Celt and pepper / Ralph McInerny. St. Martin's Minotaur, 2002. 210 p., 22 cm. Notre Dame mysteries

ISBN 0312291175

1. University of Notre Dame 2. Campus life 3. Murder investigation 4. College teachers 5. Amateur detectives 6. Brothers 7. Poets 8. Murder 9. South Bend, Indiana 10. Mysteries

LC 2002069938

Becoming suspicious after noting inconsistencies at the site of a young colleague's death, Notre Dame professor Roger Knight and his brother, Philip, draw on their academic expertise, as well as campus gossip, to solve the crime.

"Solid plotting from a practiced hand." Library Journal.

McInerny, Ralph, 1929-2010

Irish coffee / Ralph McInerny. St. Martin's Minotaur, 2003. 247 p. Notre Dame mysteries

ISBN 0312309015

1. University of Notre Dame 2. Murder 3. College sports 4. Campus life 5. Amateur detectives 6. Brothers 7. College teachers 8. Engaged persons 9. College basketball 10. Sports 11. South Bend, Indiana 12. Mysteries

LC 2003050620

Investigating the murder of a Notre Dame athletic department faculty member, professor Roger Knight and his P.I. brother Phil, meet a host of suspects at the victim's wake, including two women who both claim they were secretly engaged to him.

"Everybody likes Fred Neville, who works in Notre Dame's sports information office. Everybody but one person-the person who killed him. A different side of unassuming Fred surfaces when two women arrive at his funeral, each claiming Fred as their fiance. Because South Bend, home of Notre Dame, is always deferential to the university, the locals have no objection when the Knight brothers become unofficial consultants on the case. Phillip Knight is a streetwise PI, and his immensely rotund brother, Roger, is an amateur sleuth and a revered professor of Catholic studies. . . . A fine effort by a deservedly respected genre veteran." Booklist.

McInerny, Ralph, 1929-2010

Requiem for a realtor : a Father Dowling mystery / Ralph McInerny. St. Martin's Minotaur, 2004. 263 p. Father Dowling mysteries

ISBN 0312324170

1. Catholic Church Clergy 2. Real estate agents -- Illinois 3. Extramarital affairs 4. Murder investigation -- Illinois 5. Clergymen -- Illinois 6. Amateur detectives 7. Crimes against real estate agents -- Illinois 8. Catholics -- Illinois 9. Murder -- Illinois 10. Police -- Illinois 11. Married people -- Illinois 12. Husband and wife -- Illinois 13. Marital conflict 14. Inheritance and succession 15. Priests 16. Women singers -- Illinois 17. Nightclubs -- Illinois 18. Illinois 19. Mysteries

LC 2004041858

Father Dowling confronts an ethical dilemma when one of his parishioners reveals information in confidence about a troubled marriage, and the parishioner's spouse later becomes the victim of a brutal hit-and-run "accident" that could be murder.

McKay, Ami, 1968-

The **witches** of New York / Ami McKay Perennial, 2017, c2016. 320 p.

ISBN 9780062359926

1. Gilded Age (1865-1898) 2. 1880s 3. Witchcraft 4. Healing 5. Superhuman abilities 6. Witches 7. Healers 8. Mental illness 9. Missing persons 10. Witches' apprentices 11. New York City 12. Historical fiction

Originally published: Toronto : Knopf Canada, 2016.

RUSA Reading List Short List, 2018.

A tale inspired by Manhattan's 19th-century witchcraft revival finds a celebrated teahouse proprietress and a gifted medium teaming up with a dream interpreter in the aftermath of a psychic colleague's disappearance

McKenzie, Elizabeth, 1958-

* The **portable** Veblen / Elizabeth McKenzie. Penguin Press, 2016 304 p.

ISBN 9781594206856

1. United States. Department of Defense 2. Engaged persons 3. Family relationships 4. Dysfunctional families 5. Values 6. Ambition 7. Rich people 8. Neuroscientists 9. Men/women relations 10. Women -- Psychology 11. Palo Alto, California 12. Literary fiction 13. Satirical fiction

Shortlisted for the Baileys Women's Prize for Fiction, 2016.

An aimless amateur translator struggling under the thumb of an oppressive parent and an ambitious medical researcher from a hippie family endure tests to their bond and question their priorities as their wedding approaches.

"McKenzie's idiosyncratic love story scampers along on a wonderfully zig-zaggy path, dashing and darting in delightfully unexpected directions as it progresses toward its satisfying end and scattering tasty literary passages like nuts along the way." Kirkus.

McKevett, G. A.

Murder in her stocking / G. A. McKevett. Kensington Books, 2018. 304 p. Granny Reid mysteries

ISBN 9781496716262

1. 1980s 2. Christmas 3. Gossiping and gossips 4. Women amateur detectives 5. Memories 6. Murder 7. Murder investigation 8. Neighbors 9. Grandchildren 10. Small town life 11. Georgia 12. Cozy mysteries 13. Gentle reads 14. Holiday mysteries

Chronicles McKevett's character Savannah Reid as a 12-year-old child being raised by her amateur sleuth grandmother, Stella Reid.

When the scandalous Prissy Carr is found dead in an alley behind a tavern just before Christmas, Stella "Granny" Reid decides to investigate and what she finds puts the lives of those she loves in danger.

"Readers will look forward to Stella's further adventures." Publishers Weekly.

McKevett, G. A.

Murder in the corn maze / G. A. McKevett. Kensington Books, 2019 304 p. Granny Reid mysteries

ISBN 9781496716293

1. Women amateur detectives 2. Grandchildren 3. Halloween 4. Murder investigation 5. Senior women 6. Small town life 7. Local history 8. Georgia 9. Cozy mysteries 10. Gentle reads

Chronicles McKevett's character Savannah Reid as a 12-year-old child being raised by her amateur sleuth grandmother, Stella Reid.

During Halloween festivities, Granny Reid and her granddaughter make it to the center of a corn maze on Judge Patterson's antebellum mansion where they discover a human skull.

McKillip, Patricia A.

Alphabet of thorn / Patricia A. McKillip. Ace Books, 2004. 320 p.

ISBN 0441011306

1. Teenage girls 2. Magic 3. Fate and fatalism 4. Orphans 5. Translators 6. Women translators 7. Sixteen-year-old girls 8. Women rulers 9. Wizards 10. Witches 11. Love 12. Books 13. Fantasy fiction

LC 2003062912

Working in the royal library as a translator, Nepenthe becomes obsessed with a strange book, given to her by a young mage during the coronation of the new Queen of Raine, and begins to discover her destiny.

"McKillip . . . creates the atmosphere of a fairy tale with her elegantly lyrical prose and attention to nuance. Her characters are at once intimately personal and larger than life." Library Journal.

McKillip, Patricia A.

Ombria in shadow / Patricia A. McKillip. Ace Books, 2002. 298 p.

ISBN 9780441008957

1. Inheritance and succession 2. Women wizards 3. Rulers 4. Good

and evil 5. Imaginary kingdoms 6. Greed 7. Death 8. Authority 9. Magic 10. Fantasy fiction

LC 2001046388

Mythopoeic Award for Adult Literature, 2003.

World Fantasy Award, 2003.

The death of Ombria's prince leads to chaos as light and dark factions compete for control and the fate of the city rests in the hands of untried forces.

McKinlay, Jenn

The **good** ones / Jenn McKinlay. Berkley Pub Group, 2019. 304 p. Happily ever after (Jenn McKinlay)

ISBN 9780451492432

1. Architects 2. Women college teachers 3. Single fathers 4. Renovation (Architecture) 5. Bookstores 6. Women booksellers 7. Fathers and daughters 8. Small town life 9. Interpersonal attraction 10. Men/women relations 11. North Carolina 12. Contemporary romances

Hired by Maisy Kelly to convert her late aunt's Victorian house into a romance bookstore, architect and single father Ryder Copeland finds his plans of leaving this small town behind thwarted by his attraction to this shy, curly haired professor.

McKinney-Whetstone, Diane

Leaving Cecil Street : a novel / Diane McKinney-Whetstone. William Morrow, 2004. 304 p.

ISBN 0688163858

1. 1960s 2. African American community life 3. Teenage pregnancy 4. Abortion 5. African American teenage girls 6. African American musicians 7. African American families 8. Friendship 9. Homeless women 10. African-American homeless women 11. Former prostitutes 12. African American communities 13. Teenage abortion 14. Guilt 15. Pennsylvania 16. Philadelphia, Pennsylvania 17. Historical fiction 18. Domestic fiction 19. African American fiction

LC 2003055845

BCALA Literary Award for Fiction, 2005.

Surrounded by block parties that liven up the summer nights of their 1969 Philadelphia home, Joe and Louise find their marriage falling apart, a situation that is complicated by the tragic illegal abortion of their daughter's best friend.

"Cecil Street is a quiet, tree-lined haven in West Philadelphia, a place where everyone knows everyone else, a place removed from the turmoil and violence of the late 1960s. Yet the residents of Cecil Street have their problems. Joe and Louise's marriage is strained; Johnetta's sexy niece has arrived, ripe for trouble; and teenaged Shay tries to help best friend Neet deal with an unwanted pregnancy. When Neet's abortion goes tragically wrong, everyone on the street must rally around her, while Joe, Louise, and Neet's mother, Alberta, discover how their pasts have now drawn them together. McKinney-Whetstone's portrayal of African American family life is sensitive and compassionate, with characters who love, work, live, and die without veering into soap opera." Library Journal.

McKinty, Adrian

* The **chain** / Adrian McKinty. Mulholland Books, 2019. 357 p.

ISBN 9780316531269

1. Kidnapping 2. Parent and child 3. Mothers of kidnapping victims 4. Death threats 5. Consequences 6. Divorced women 7. Serial kidnappings 8. Mothers -- Psychology 9. Child kidnapping victims 10. Women -- Personal conduct 11. Manipulation (Social sciences) 12. Massachusetts 13. Thrillers and suspense

A parent receives a panicked phone call from a stranger who reveals that both of their children have been kidnapped by someone who demands that they abduct another child to prevent the murders of their own.

McKinty, Adrian.

The **cold,** cold ground : a Detective Sean Duffy novel / Adrian McKinty. Seventh Street Books, 2012. 320 p. Sean Duffy novels

ISBN 9781616147167

1. Irish Republican Army. 2. Ulster Volunteer Force 3. 1980s 4. Serial murderers 5. Social conflict 6. Homophobia 7. Detectives 8. Police 9. Homophobia 10. Catholic men 11. Murder investigation 12. The Troubles, 1968-1998 13. Northern Ireland 14. Police procedurals
Includes an excerpt from 'I hear the sirens in the street'.

"First published: London: Serpent's Tail, an imprint of Profile Books Ltd., 2012"--T.p. verso.

In a 1981 Northern Ireland rife with sectarian violence, Catholic detective Sean Duffy investigates a serial killer who is targeting gay men, a series of murders that just may have political implications as well.

McKinty, Adrian

In the morning I'll be gone : a Detective Sean Duffy novel / Adrian McKinty. Seventh Street Books, 2014. 315 p. Sean Duffy novels

ISBN 9781616148775

1. Irish Republican Army. 2. Ulster Volunteer Force 3. M I 5 4. 1980s 5. Detectives 6. Revenge 7. Police 8. Veterans 9. Catholic men 10. Social conflict 11. Murder investigation 12. Americans in Northern Ireland 13. The Troubles, 1968-1998 14. Belfast, Northern Ireland 15. Northern Ireland 16. Police procedurals

LC 2013037740

Ned Kelly Award for Best Novel, 2014.

Recruited by MI5 to hunt down Dermot McCann, an IRA master bomber who has escaped from Maze Prison, Sean Duffy, a conflicted Catholic cop, must solve another mystery first in order to discover Dermot's whereabouts before Mrs. Thatcher's keynote speech.

"The Troubles' first two novels were exceptionally smart police procedurals, and McKinty applies the same expertise here, contrasting a classic locked-room puzzle with the gritty, violent Belfast backdrop." Booklist.

McLain, Paula

* **Circling** the sun / Paula McLain. Random House, 2015 368 p.

ISBN 9780345534187

1. Markham, Beryl, 1902-1986 Travel Africa 2. 1920s 3. Women pilots 4. Independence in women 5. British in Africa 6. Love triangles 7. Horse breeders 8. Mother-separated families 9. Horse trainers 10. Kenya 11. East Africa 12. Historical fiction 13. Biographical fiction
Map on endpapers.

Raised by her father and the Kipsigis tribe in 1920s Kenya, Beryl endures painful losses before entering a passionate love triangle and discovering her unconventional true calling.

"McLain's . . . latest showcases her immersive command of setting and character, fictionalizing the exploits of real-life aviator and author Beryl Markham in British Kenya in the early 20th century. . . . Markham's true life was incredibly adventurous, and it's easy for readers to identify with this woman who refused to be pigeonholed by her gender." Publishers Weekly.

McLain, Paula,

Love and ruin / Paula McLain. Ballantine Books, 2018. 352 p.

ISBN 9781101967386

1. Gellhorn, Martha, 1908-1998 2. Hemingway, Ernest, 1899-1961 3. 1930s 4. 1940s 5. Women journalists 6. War correspondents 7. Independence in women 8. Authors 9. Husband and wife 10. Fame 11. Men/women relations 12. Spain -- History -- Civil War, 1936-1939 13. Madrid, Spain 14. Cuba 15. Biographical fiction 16. Historical fiction

LC bl2018020577

The author of The Paris Wife returns to her fan-favorite subject, Ernest Hemingway, in a tale set on the eve of World War II that is inspired by his passionate, stormy marriage to a fiercely independent, ambitious young Martha Gellhorn, who would become one of the 20th century's leading war correspondents.

McLain, Paula

The **Paris** wife : a novel / Paula McLain. Ballantine Books, 2011. xii, 320 p.

ISBN 9780345521309

1. Hemingway, Ernest, 1899-1961 2. Mowrer, Hadley Hemingway, 1891-1979 3. 1920s 4. Authors' spouses -- United States 5. Authors, American -- France 6. Husband and wife 7. Americans in France 8. Expatriate authors -- France 9. Paris, France 10. Biographical fiction 11. Historical fiction

LC 2010037878

Originally published: 2011.

Goodreads Choice Award, 2011.

Meeting through mutual friends in Chicago, Hadley is intrigued by brash "beautiful boy" Ernest Hemingway, and after a brief courtship and small wedding, they take off for Paris, where Hadley makes a convincing transformation from an overprotected child to a game and brave young woman who puts up with impoverished living conditions and shattering loneliness to prop up her husband's career.

"McLain's vivid, clear-voiced novel is a conjecture, an act of imaginary autobiography on the part of the author. Yet her biographical and geographical research is so deep, and her empathy for the real Hadley Richardson so forthright (without being intrusively femme partisan), that the account reads as very real indeed. Big things happen: Hadley is there as Hemingway meets Gertrude Stein and Scott Fitzgerald, as he writes The Sun Also Rises, as he falls in love with bullfighting. But a thousand less glamorous, more quotidian things happen too, as Hadley tries to find a way to live her own life (she's a fine pianist) and support her moody husband, and keep up with hard-drinking company, and run a household in a country not her own. By making the ordinary come to life, McLain has written a beautiful portrait of being in Paris in the glittering 1920s as a wife and one's own woman." Entertainment Weekly.

McLaren, Kaya

The **road** to enchantment / Kaya McLaren. St. Martin's Griffin, 2017. 342 p.

ISBN 9781250058225

1. Wineries 2. Women musicians 3. Children of single parents 4. Self-fulfillment in women 5. Loss (Psychology) 6. Second chances 7. Pregnant women 8. Homecomings 9. Self-discovery 10. Ranches 11. New Mexico 12. Women's lives and relationships

When her mother dies, her boyfriend dumps her and she discovers she is pregnant, Willow returns to the Apache reservation she left behind where she must redefine what home means for her and decide if she can make a go of the legacy her mother left behind.

"Despite its relatively somber tone, this touching novel of homecoming will draw apt comparisons to early Barbara Kingsolver." Booklist.

McLarty, Ron

Art in America : a novel / Ron McLarty. Viking, 2006. 336 p.

ISBN 0316729736

1. Authors 2. Historical societies 3. Summer 4. Playwriting 5. Traffic accidents 6. Water rights 7. Property rights 8. Trials 9. Art 10. Conflict resolution 11. Interpersonal conflict 12. Conflict of interests 13. Land tenure 14. Colorado 15. Thrillers and suspense

LC 2005042406

Taking a three-month stint as a playwright-in-residence at Colorado's Creedemore Historical Society, bumbling writer Steven Kearney is commissioned to write a play based on the town's history, but his efforts are complicated by a local land dispute.

McLaughlin, Emma

The **nanny** diaries : a novel / Emma McLaughlin and Nicola Kraus. St. Martin's Press, 2002. 305 p.

ISBN 0312278586

1. Rich people -- Manhattan, New York City 2. Nannies 3. Upper class 4. Four-year-old boys 5. Women college students 6. Manhattan, New York City 7. Park Avenue, New York City 8. New York City 9. Satirical fiction 10. Chick lit

LC 2001048652

Sequel: Nanny returns

A satirical glimpse into Manhattan's upper class follows Nanny, a struggling NYU student who takes a position caring for the son of the rich and glamorous X family, as she learns how to juggle a vast array of tasks so that a Park Avenue wife never has to lift a well-manicured finger.

"This is a diabolically funny New York story. . . . [Nanny] is a vastly entertaining narrator and impromptu social critic. . . . Not surprisingly, The Nanny Diaries fades slightly when the X's are out of sight, despite the boyfriend and family matters that are meant to fill out Nanny's story. The heart of the matter remains perfectly pitched social satire. . . . This book is saved from self-righteousness not only by the authors' cleverness but also by their compassion. For oblivious parents, lonely offspring and overworked, underpaid employees alike, they're out to fix something that's broken." New York Times.

McLaughlin, James A.

Bearskin / James A. McLaughlin. Ecco Press, 2018. 352 p.

ISBN 9780062742797

1. Poachers 2. Drug cartels 3. Forest conservation 4. Wilderness areas 5. Bears 6. Biologists 7. Appalachian Region 8. Virginia 9. Thrillers and suspense

Edgar Allan Poe Award for Best First Novel by an American Author, 2019.

RUSA Reading List Short List, 2019.

Hiding out from the Mexican drug cartels he betrayed in Arizona, Rice More, while protecting a remote forest preserve in Virginian Appalachia, exposes a bear-poaching scheme that reveals his location to the criminals he was running from in the first place.

McLayne, Alyson

Highland promise / Alyson Mclayne. Sourcebooks Casablanca, 2017. 384 p. Sons of Gregor MacLeod

ISBN 9781492654506

1. Scottish Stewart period (1371-1603) 2. Medieval period (476-1492) 3. Warriors 4. Clans 5. Mate selection 6. Rescues 7. Protectiveness in men 8. Foster brothers 9. Sexual attraction 10. Men/women relations 11. Highlands, Scotland 12. Scotland -- History -- 15th century 13. Highland romances 14. Medieval romances 15. Historical romances

Five boys destined to become Highland lairds are fostered together as brothers. Darach, Lachlan, Callum, Gavin and Kerr fight for their clans, for each other, and for their own true loves.

McLean, Felicity

The **Van** Apfel girls are gone / Felicity McLean. Algonquin Books of Chapel Hill, 2019. 297 p.

ISBN 9781616209643

1. 1990s 2. Suburban life 3. Teenage girls 4. Missing persons 5. Suburbs 6. Crimes against girls 7. Family violence 8. Grief 9. Psychic trauma 10. Loss (Psychology) 11. Australia 12. Psychological fiction 13. Literary fiction

Librarians' Choice (Australia), 2019

Follows the efforts of two sisters who return to their suburban hometown to make sense of the unsolved disappearances of three girls from a strict evangelical family.

"This debut, part coming-of-age story and part crime thriller, is both forceful and unnerving." Publishers Weekly.

McMahon, Jennifer

The **invited** : a novel / Jennifer McMahon. Doubleday, 2019. 336 p.

ISBN 9780385541381

1. Ghosts 2. Local history 3. Historic buildings 4. History 5. Couples 6. Rural life 7. Obsession 8. History teachers 9. Houses -- Remodeling 10. Vermont 11. Ghost stories 12. Horror 13. Thrillers and suspense

LC 2018037320

When an inspired effort to build her dream home is overshadowed by discoveries about her rural property's violent past, a former history teacher becomes obsessed with the stories of three generations of local women who died under suspicious circumstances.

"A city couple trades their fast-paced lifestyle for rural Vermont, running headlong into a few ghosts along the way." Kirkus.

McMahon, Jennifer

The **one** I left behind / Jennifer McMahon. William Morrow, 2013. 422 p.

ISBN 9780062122551

1. Serial murderers 2. Missing women 3. Women murder victims 4. Serial murders 5. Mother-separated girls 6. Crimes against women 7. Women with terminal illnesses 8. Secrets 9. Mothers and daughters 10. Mysteries

Thriller Award for Best Paperback Original, 2014.

In the summer of 1985, teenaged Reggie's mother was the victim of a serial killer called Neptune, who left his victims' severed hands on the police department steps. Her body was never found; the killer was never caught. Twenty-five years later, Reggie is a successful architect who has left her hometown. But when she gets a call revealing that her mother has been found alive, Reggie must confront the ghosts of her past-- and find Neptune before he kills again.

McMillan, Terry

* **How** Stella got her groove back / Terry McMillan. Viking, 1996. 368 p.

ISBN 0670869902

1. Interethnic romance 2. Young men -- Relations with older women 3. Divorced mothers 4. African American women -- Friendship 5. African American women investment advisers 6. Dating (Social customs) 7. Middle-aged women 8. Single mothers 9. Forties (Age) 10. Jamaica 11. Women's lives and relationships 12. African American fiction

Presents a humorous novel about a woman who unexpectedly finds love but who just might be losing her mind

"Readers who have been yearning for a Judith Krantz of the black bourgeoisie--albeit one with a dirty mouth and a more ebullient spirit--will be pleased with this fantasy of sexual fulfillment." Publishers Weekly.

McMillan, Terry

* **It's** not all downhill from here : a novel / Terry McMillan. Ballantine Books, 2020. 368 p.

ISBN 9781984823748

1. Senior women 2. Aging 3. Female friendship 4. Loss (Psychology) 5. Women with diabetes 6. Women business owners 7. African American women 8. Grief in women 9. African American families 10. Family relationships 11. Southern California 12. California 13. Women's lives and relationships 14. Mainstream fiction 15. African American fiction

LC 2019038586

Confident that her best days are still ahead, a successful businesswoman relies on close friends and her resourcefulness when an unexpected loss turns her world upside down.

"McMillan's writing is smart and witty, throwing readers right into the action, and her dialogue is coated with humor that breathes life into her characters." Booklist.

McMillan, Terry

* **Waiting** to exhale / Terry McMillan. Viking, 1992. 409 p.

ISBN 0670839809

1. Dating (Social customs) 2. African American women -- Friendship 3. Friendship 4. Self-discovery in women 5. African American men/ women relations 6. Phoenix, Arizona 7. African American fiction 8. Women's lives and relationships

LC 91046564

Sequel: Getting to happy.

Four African-American women console and support one another in a complex friendship that helps each of them face the middle of their lives as single women

"Terry McMillan's heroines are so well drawn that by the end of the novel, the reader is completely at home with the four of them. They observe men--and contemporary America--with bawdy humor, occasional melancholy and great affection. But the novel is about more than four lives; the bonds among the women are so alive and so appealing they almost seem a character in their own right." New York Times Book Review.

McMurtry, Larry

Boone's Lick : a novel / Larry McMurtry. Simon & Schuster, 2000. 287 p.

ISBN 0684868865

1. Hickok, Wild Bill, 1837-1876 2. Family relationships -- The West (United States) 3. Voyages and travels -- 19th century 4. Runaway wives, husbands, etc 5. Shoshoni Indians -- The West (United States) 6. Fifteen-year-old boys -- The West (United States) 7. Priests -- The West (United States) 8. Father-deserted families -- The West (United States) 9. Pioneer women 10. Teenage boys 11. The West (United States) -- History -- 19th century 12. Westerns

LC 00056342

Fifteen-year-old Shay describes his family's arduous journey from Boone's Lick, Missouri, to Fort Kearny in Wyoming, in search of Shay's father.

McMurtry, Larry

Buffalo girls : a novel / Larry McMurtry. Simon and Schuster, 1990. 351 p.

ISBN 9780671685188

1. Calamity Jane, 1852-1903 2. Buffalo Bill's Wild West Show 3. Women sharpshooters 4. Entertainers 5. Mothers and daughters 6. Wild west shows 7. Pioneer women 8. Indians of North America 9. The West (United States) -- History -- 1848-1950 10. Westerns 11. Biographical fiction 12. Literary fiction

LC 90042486

Western Heritage Award for Outstanding Western Novel, 1991.

Living quietly in her friend Dora's Miles City whorehouse, Calamity Jane is plunged back into one final, bittersweet adventure by the arrival of her old friend and rival, Buffalo Bill Cody

McMurtry, Larry

Comanche moon : a novel / Larry McMurtry. Simon & Schuster, 1997. 752 p. Lonesome Dove saga

ISBN 0684807548

1. Texas Rangers 2. Comanche Indians -- Relations with European-Americans 3. Horse stealing -- Texas 4. Frontier and pioneer life -- The West (United States) 5. Male friendship -- Texas 6. Trackers -- Texas 7. Comanche warriors -- Texas 8. Native American resistance and revolts -- Texas 9. Prostitutes -- Texas 10. Texas 11. The West (United States) -- History -- 19th century 12. Westerns 13. Literary fiction 14. Epic fiction

LC 9729609

"The final volume of the Lonesome Dove saga."

First published 1997 by Simon & Schuster, Inc., New York.

Spur Award for Best Novel of the West (Long Novel), 1998.

As Buffalo Hump becomes older, his Comanche children rise to power, but his son Blue Duck breaks away to form a renegade group favoring guns over bows and arrows, in a prequel to *Lonesome Dove*.

McMurtry, Larry

Dead man's walk : a novel / Larry McMurtry. Simon & Schuster, 1995. 477 p. Lonesome Dove saga

ISBN 068480753X

1. Texas Rangers 2. 19th century 3. Frontier and pioneer life -- The West (United States) 4. Young men -- Friendship 5. Cowboys 6. Indians of North America -- Great Plains (United States) 7. Comanche Indians -- Relations with European-Americans 8. Texas 9. The West (United States) -- History -- 19th century 10. Westerns 11. Coming-of-age stories 12. Literary fiction 13. Epic fiction 14. Adventure stories

LC 95-39995

Book inspired the 1996 TV mini series by the same name starring David Arqette and Jonny Lee Miller.

In a prequel to *Lonesome Dove*, Woodrow Call and Gus McCrae are novice Texas Rangers who, while going to Santa Fe to take it from the Mexicans, come of age.

"If Dead Man's Walk were not a prequel, it would be worth only glancing notice. As things are, it is a satisfactory foothill, with the grand old mountain in view. There are no heroics, though there is plenty of calamity. . . . McMurty has a fine time with youthful damnfoolishness, and so does the reader." Time.

McMurtry, Larry

The **evening** star : a novel / Larry McMurtry. Simon & Schuster, 1999, c1992. 637 p. Houston series

ISBN 0684857510

1. Seniors -- Sexuality 2. Grandmother and adult child 3. Aging -- Psychological aspects 4. Senior women 5. Female friendship 6.

Husband and wife 7. Family relationships 8. Texas 9. Black humor 10. Literary fiction

LC 2003265645

Sequel to: Terms of endearment.

Originally published: New York : Simon & Schuster, 1992.

This is the sequel to Terms of endearment, and follows the ongoing trials and tribulations of a woman raising her grandchildren after the death of her daughter.

"The success of a book like this one depends on the tone the author manages to muster up. Mr. McMurtry's is sentimentality laced with comic irony, and it works very well. . . . And if, in the end, Aurora Greenway and her extended and highly dysfunctional family turn out to be more entertaining than genuinely moving, it's reassuring to know they--and the reader--are in the hands of a real pro." New York Times Book Review.

McMurtry, Larry

* **Lonesome** Dove : a novel / Larry McMurtry. Simon and Schuster, 1985. 843 p. Lonesome Dove saga

ISBN 0671504207

1. Texas Rangers 2. 19th century 3. Cowboys 4. Cattle drives 5. Frontier and pioneer life -- The West (United States) 6. Male friendship 7. Comanche Indians -- Relations with European-Americans 8. Horse stealing 9. Texas 10. The West (United States) -- History -- 19th century 11. Westerns 12. Literary fiction 13. Epic fiction

LC 85002192

Sequel: Streets of Laredo.

Pulitzer Prize for Fiction, 1986.

Spur Award for Best Western Novel (Short Novel), 1986.

National Book Critics Circle Award for Fiction finalist, 1985

Set in the late-nineteenth century, this novel chronicles a cattle drive from Texas to Montana, and follows the lives of Gus and Call, the cowboys heading the drive, Gus's woman, Lorena, and Blue Duck, a sinister Indian renegade

McMurtry, Larry

Rhino ranch : a novel / Larry McMurtry. Simon & Schuster, 2009. 208 p. Last picture show

ISBN 9781439156391

1. Senior men 2. Small town life -- Texas 3. Regret 4. Sexagenarians -- Texas 5. Neighbors 6. Rich women 7. Rhinoceros 8. Interpersonal attraction 9. Texas 10. Literary fiction 11. Psychological fiction 12. Modern Westerns

LC 2009019648

Sequel to: When the light goes.

Returning home to Thalia, Texas, to recover from a heart attack, Duane Moore is charmed by K.K. Slater, a billionairess who intends to open a nature reserve for the endangered black rhinoceros, but Homer Carmichael complicates Duane's romantic intentions.

"In Rhino Ranch, McMurtry gets back to what he does best: the dead-on depiction of this small Texas town and its quirky inhabitants who immediately engage the reader in their less than perfect lives." BookPage.

McMurtry, Larry

Sin killer / Larry McMurtry. Simon & Schuster, 2002. 300 p. Berrybender narratives

ISBN 9780743233026

1. Eccentrics and eccentricities 2. Young women 3. Women immigrants 4. Frontier and pioneer life -- The West (United States) -- 19th century 5. British in The West (United States) 6. The West (United States) -- History -- 19th century 7. Missouri Valley 8.

Westerns 9. Coming-of-age stories 10. Family sagas

LC 2002017616

Journeying up the Missouri River in 1830, the wealthy Berrybenders encounter the challenges of the untamed American West and a variety of people, including Native Americans, pioneers, and explorers, before Tasmin Berrybender falls in love with frontiersman and part-time preacher Jim Snow.

McMurtry, Larry

* Streets of Laredo : a novel / Larry McMurtry. Simon & Schuster, 1993. 589 p. Lonesome Dove saga

ISBN 0671792814

1. Texas Rangers 2. Bounty hunters -- The West (United States) 3. Frontier and pioneer life -- The West (United States) 4. Thieves 5. Outlaws 6. Comanche Indians -- Relations with European-Americans 7. Psychopaths -- The West (United States) 8. Texas 9. The West (United States) -- History -- 19th century 10. Westerns 11. Literary fiction 12. Epic fiction

LC 93019279

Sequel to: Lonesome dove.

Captain Call, a bounty hunter hired to catch bandit Joey Garza, assembles a group of unlikely assistants and travels to Crowtown, Texas.

"This sequel to Lonesome Dove takes place 20 years after the death of Gus McCrae. In this novel, Captain Woodrow Call, McCrae's old partner, tracks a young Mexican train robber, Joe Garza, with the help of a railroad accountant named Brookshire, a Texas deputy named Ted Plunkett and Pea Eye Parker, who is trying to build a family life with his wife Lorena and their children. Across the Texas Panhandle and into northern Mexico, Call pursues his prey. As in some great 19th-century saga, the story has more than its share of improbable coincidences, but these seem only mild contrivances to shape a story packed with action, terror, humor and pathos. Laredo is a fitting conclusion to a remarkable feat of reconstruction and sheer storytelling genius." Publishers Weekly.

McMurtry, Larry

* Terms of endearment : a novel : Larry McMurtry. Scribner Paperback Fiction, 1999. 410 p. Houston series

ISBN 0684853906

1. Women with cancer 2. Mothers and daughters 3. Husband and wife 4. Widows 5. Marriage 6. Motherhood 7. Eccentrics and eccentricities 8. Men/women relations 9. People with cancer 10. Family relationships 11. Texas 12. Houston, Texas 13. Literary fiction

LC 00265299

Sequel to: All my friends are going to be strangers.

Sequel: Evening star.

First published: New York : Simon & Schuster, Inc., 1975.

"The acclaimed novel that inspired the Academy Award-winning film" -- Cover.

Aurora Greenway is the kind of woman who makes the whole world orbit around her, including a string of devoted suitors. Widowed and overprotective of her daughter, Aurora adapts at her own pace until life sends two enormous challenges her way. Her daughter Emma marries hastily and subsequently battles with cancer. Terms of Endearment is the story of an unforgettable mother and her feisty daughter and their struggle to find the courage and humour to live through life's hazards - and to love each other as never before.

"Suddenly, just when we are enjoying ourselves the most, McMurtry changes his style, and we are plunged into a moving but agonizing realistic account of daughter Emma's death from cancer at 37 and the way in which her family and old friends react. . . . The shift of pace may throw some readers off stride badly. McMurtry certainly remains, however, one of our most exciting novelists." Publishers Weekly.

McMurtry, Larry

Zeke and Ned : a novel / Larry McMurtry and Diana Ossana. Simon & Schuster, 1997. 478 p.

ISBN 0684811529

1. Proctor, Ezekial, 1831-1907 2. Christie, Ned, 1852-1892 3. 1890s 4. Frontier and pioneer life 5. Indians of North America -- Relations with European-Americans 6. Cherokee Indians 7. Prejudice 8. European Americans -- Relations with Indians 9. Ozark Mountain Region 10. Oklahoma Territory -- History 11. Westerns 12. Biographical fiction

LC 96044906

Map of the Ozark Region on endpapers.

A case of adultery spirals into racial violence in 1870s Oklahoma Territory. The story begins when a white man seeks justice because a halfbreed is sleeping with his wife. There is a shootout, the races take side and blood flows.

"What gives this well-wrought tale its depth is how McMurtry and Ossana convey the era's various moral shades of gray." Publishers Weekly.

McPhee, Martha

Gorgeous lies / Martha McPhee. Harcourt, 2002. 326 p.

ISBN 9780151006137

1. 1970s 2. Parent and adult child 3. Parents with terminal illnesses 4. Father and child 5. Communes 6. Families 7. Blended families 8. Lovers 9. Psychotherapists 10. Attention seeking 11. New Jersey 12. Domestic fiction 13. Psychological fiction

LC 2002007213

Sequel to: Bright angel time.

National Book Award for Fiction finalist, 2002

In a sequel taking place twenty years after the events in Bright Angel Time, the family of dying therapist Anton Furey finds its precarious balance upset by their efforts to make peace with Anton and each other.

"As the novel unfolds, Anton's unlikely past is revealed: his Texas childhood, his early stint in a Jesuit seminary and his grand passion for the communal haven of Chardin. His insatiable need for connection-particularly with women--can be repellant (as when he pursues one of his stepdaughters), but it is his infectious zest for life that drives this invigorating of convoluted novel." Publishers Weekly.

McPherson, Catriona, 1965-

The **child** garden : a novel / Catriona McPherson. Midnight Ink, 2015 336 p.

ISBN 9780738745497

1. Alternative schools 2. Suicide 3. Cold cases (Criminal investigation) 4. Board and care homes 5. Mothers of children with disabilities 6. Divorced women 7. Stalking 8. Former friends 9. Murder 10. Murder investigation 11. Stalkers 12. Scotland 13. Mysteries

LC 2014050106

Gloria, neighbor to a shuttered alternative school, investigates the suicide that closed the school when the dead begin speaking to her and claiming the death was murder.

"Better known for her Dandy Gilver cozies, McPherson has written a terrific stand-alone that is complex, haunting, and magical. Readers who appreciate Kate Atkinson or Audrey Niffeneger for their intricate plotting and character development will be sure to pounce on this stunning title." Library Journal.

McPherson, Catriona, 1965-

Go to my grave / Catriona McPherson. Minotaur Books, 2018. 297 p.

ISBN 9781250070005

1. Bed-and-breakfast 2. Cousins 3. Practical jokes 4. Revenge 5.

Birthday parties 6. Secrets 7. Guilt 8. Coastal towns 9. Scotland 10. Gothic fiction 11. Psychological suspense

LC 2018020148

A group of cousins staying at a refurbished bed and breakfast in Galloway realize they had stayed there decades ago for a birthday party that started with schnapps and ended with a girl walking into the sea to her death.

"Though some secondary characters are indistinct, this realistically written, gripping suspense tale is one readers will want to finish in a single long sitting, especially if they crave country-house mysteries." Booklist.

McPherson, Catriona, 1965-

* **Quiet** neighbors : a novel / Catriona McPherson. Midnight Ink, 2016 336 p.

ISBN 9780738747620

1. Secrets 2. Bookstores 3. Runaways 4. Small town life 5. Separated couples 6. Pregnant women 7. Birthfathers 8. Arson 9. Bereavement 10. Scotland 11. Mysteries

LC 2015044401

It's the oldest bookshop in a town full of bookshops; rambling and disordered, full of treasures if you look hard. Jude found one of the treasures when she visited last summer, the high point of a miserable vacation. Now, in the depths of winter, when she has to run away, Lowell's chaotic bookshop in that backwater of a town is the safe place she runs to.

"McPhersons literary observations are delightful, her quirky collection of characters intriguing, and the unfolding mystery highly satisfying." Publishers Weekly.

McPherson, Catriona, 1965-

Scot & soda / Catriona McPherson. Midnight Ink, 2019 288 p. Last Ditch mysteries

ISBN 9780738754123

1. Scots in the United States 2. Women amateur detectives 3. Cold cases (Criminal investigation) 4. Murder investigation 5. Marriage counseling 6. Amateur detectives 7. Divorced women 8. Motels 9. California 10. Southern California 11. Mysteries

McPherson, Catriona, 1965-

Scot free / Catriona McPherson. Midnight Ink, 2018. 312 p. Last Ditch mysteries

ISBN 9780738753867

1. Marriage counseling 2. Divorced women 3. Murder suspects 4. Innocence (Law) 5. Marital therapy 6. Amateur detectives 7. Murder investigation 8. Scots in the United States 9. Women amateur detectives 10. Fireworks 11. California 12. Southern California 13. Mysteries

A Scottish marriage counselor living in California finds herself divorced, broke, and contemplating returning home as she tries to clear the name of her last remaining client, who is being accused of using fireworks to kill her husband.

McPherson, Catriona, 1965-

* **A step** so grave / Catriona McPherson. Quercus, 2019, c2018. 336 p. Dandy Gilver murder mysteries

ISBN 9781473682351

1. Between the Wars (1918-1939) 2. 1930s 3. Women private investigators 4. Superstition 5. Family estates 6. Engaged persons 7. Women murder victims 8. Murder investigation 9. Families 10. Scotland -- Social life and customs -- 20th century 11. Historical mysteries

Originally published by Hodder & Stoughton, 2018.

Dandy Gilver investigates after discovering Lady Lavinia, the mother of his son's betrothed, murdered in the middle of her famous knot garden.

McPherson, Catriona, 1965-

Strangers at the gate / Catriona McPherson. Minotaur Books, 2019. 304 p.

ISBN 9781250070012

1. Husband and wife 2. Clergywomen 3. Crime scenes 4. Secrets 5. Options, alternatives, choices 6. Murder investigation 7. Cottages 8. Supervisors 9. Murder 10. Lawyers 11. Noise 12. Scotland 13. Psychological suspense

Moving into her boss's gatehouse in the wake of a law partnership, a deacon's wife is alarmed by otherworldly noises on the property before her boss is brutally murdered. By the Anthony Award-winning author of *Quiet Neighbors*.

McQuiston, Casey

* **Red,** white & royal blue : a novel / Casey McQuiston. Wednesday Books, 2019. 352 p.

ISBN 9781250316776

1. Children of presidents 2. Princes 3. Ambition in men 4. International relations 5. Women presidents 6. Royal houses 7. Liberals 8. Gay men 9. Bisexuals 10. Twenties (Age) 11. Hispanic Americans 12. Multiracial persons 13. Friendship 14. Family relationships 15. Washington, D.C. 16. Great Britain 17. Texas 18. Romantic comedies 19. LGBTQIA romances

LC 2018055526

Goodreads Choice Award, 2019

The First Son falls in love with the Prince of Wales after an incident of international proportions forces them to pretend to be best friends.

"The drama, which involves political rivals, possible betrayals, and even a meeting with the queen, is both irresistible and delicious." Publishers Weekly.

McQuiston, Jennifer

The **spinster's** guide to scandalous behavior / Jennifer McQuiston. Avon Books, 2015. 400 p. Seduction diaries

ISBN 9780062335128

1. Victorian era (1837-1901) 2. Women marriage resisters 3. Marquis and marchionesses 4. Diaries 5. Cottages 6. Secrets 7. Nobility 8. Eccentric women 9. Inheritance and succession 10. Interpersonal attraction 11. Men/women relations 12. Cornwall, England 13. London, England 14. England -- Social life and customs -- 19th century 15. Victorian romances 16. Historical romances

When she inherits a run-down cottage along with an old leather guide that reveals how to live the life of a scandalous spinster, fiercely independent Lucy Westmore matches wits with Lord Thomas Branston who will stop at nothing to buy the property out from under her.

Mda, Zakes

The **Madonna** of Excelsior / Zakes Mda. Farrar, Straus and Giroux, 2004. 272 p.

ISBN 0374200084

1. Anti-apartheid Movement South Africa 2. Multiracial women 3. Multiracial persons 4. Mothers 5. Rape victims 6. Artists' models 7. Multiracial children 8. Multiracial girls 9. Mother and child 10. Families 11. Apartheid -- South Africa 12. Post-apartheid era -- South Africa 13. Freedom 14. Reconciliation 15. Racism 16. Interracial sex 17. Identity (Psychology) 18. Group identity 19. South Africa -- Race relations 20. South Africa 21. South Africa -- History -- 20th century 22. Satirical fiction 23. Literary fiction

LC 2003054728

ALA Notable Book, 2005.

A novel takes readers deep into the heart of apartheid in the early 1970s, focusing on a mixed race family that is trying to survive on the closely regulated line between black and white.

"The voice that emerges suggests not just a writer who can seduce us through beautiful language and unfailing humor. We also encounter a writer who has the power to shock and frighten us, to astound and anger and unsettle us. The Madonna of Excelsior suggests, in short, that his is a voice for which one should feel not only affection but admiration." New York Times Book Review.

Mda, Zakes

The **whale** caller / Zakes Mda. Farrar, Straus and Giroux, 2005. 240 p.

ISBN 0374287856

1. Alcoholic women 2. Humans and whales 3. Middle-aged men 4. Tourists 5. Villages 6. Whales 7. Right whales 8. Whale watching 9. Men/women relations 10. Post-apartheid era -- South Africa 11. South Africa 12. Romantic comedies

LC 2005014196

Charts a tender, funny romance between the "Whale Caller" of a small South African coastal village and the town drunk, Saluni.

"Despite the lighthearted and often hilarious antics, this love triangle, like so many others, is tragically unsustainable. Perhaps this is where The Whale Caller defies expectation: If it is a morality play, these are unusually funny, richly developed characters. If it is a quirky, romantic comedy, it's dispensed with a heaping helping of human frailty, tragic behavior and self-destruction. With an offhanded mastery of lyrical language, this gifted storyteller's prose shimmers without extravagance." Washington Post Book World.

Meacham, Leila, 1938-

Dragonfly : a novel / Leila Meacham. Grand Central Publishing, 2019. 576 p.

ISBN 9781538732229

1. Second World War era (1939-1945) 2. Espionage 3. Americans in Europe 4. French Resistance (World War II) 5. Spies 6. Women spies 7. Spies -- United States 8. World War II 9. Nazis 10. Deception 11. Secrets 12. Friendship 13. Paris, France -- History -- German occupation, 1940-1944 14. Historical fiction

LC 2019001971

Teamed together to infiltrate Nazi ranks in occupied Paris, five idealistic American spies from diverse backgrounds begin questioning who they can trust when one of their number is killed.

"Complex, epic, and rich in historical detail an uplifting story of finding friendship behind enemy lines." Kirkus.

Meader, Kate

Playing with fire / Kate Meader. Pocket Books, 2015 384 p. Hot in Chicago novels

ISBN 9781476785929

1. Women fire fighters 2. Mayors 3. Rescues 4. Political campaigns 5. Former foster children 6. Sexual attraction 7. Men/women relations 8. Chicago, Illinois 9. Contemporary romances

"Meader packs the flawless second Hot in Chicago romance (after Flirting with Fire) with superb relationship development and profane but note-perfect dialogue." Publishers Weekly.

Meadows, Rae

* **I** will send rain : a novel / Rae Meadows. Henry Holt and Co., 2016. 256 p.

ISBN 9781627794268

1. Depression era (1929-1941) 2. 1930s 3. Rural families 4. Farm life 5. Droughts 6. Dust Bowl Era, 1931-1939 7. Marital conflict 8. Extramarital affairs 9. Family relationships 10. Men/women relations 11. Oklahoma -- History 12. Historical fiction 13. Domestic fiction

LC 2015046689

In 1934, as the earliest storms of the Dust Bowl descend on the Bell farm in Mulehead, Oklahoma, Annie Bell and her husband and children struggle against hardship as the wheat harvest dries out and people around them pack up to leave.

"When tragedy strikes or hope emerges, it makes sense and comes to fruition organically. This makes for a vibrant, absorbing novel that stays with the reader." Publishers Weekly.

Means, David, 1961-

* **Hystopia** : a novel / David Means. Farrar, Straus & Giroux, 2016. 336 p.

ISBN 9780865479135

1. 1960s 2. Post-traumatic stress disorder 3. Vietnam veterans 4. Memories 5. Vietnam War, 1961-1975 -- Psychological aspects 6. Authors 7. Psychopaths 8. United States -- History -- 20th century 9. Alternative histories 10. Novels-within-novels

LC 2015035421

Longlisted for the Man Booker Prize, 2016

Describes an alternate history where JFK survived and created an enormous federal agency, the Psych Corps, charged with keeping American citizens happy, even if it means erasing their memories, a practice that is particularly handy for returning Vietnam veterans.

"Means' first novel is a compelling portrait of an imagined counter-history that feels entirely real." Kirkus.

Means, David, 1961-

* **Instructions** for a funeral : stories / David Means. Farrar Straus & Giroux, 2019. 176 p.

ISBN 9780374279813

1. Regret 2. Human nature 3. Interpersonal relations 4. Desire 5. Literary fiction 6. Short stories

LC 2018019100

"A collection of harrowing and personal stories by the O. Henry Prize-winning author David Means."

Meek, James, 1962-

The **heart** broke in / James Meek. Farrar, Straus and Giroux, 2012. 416 p.

ISBN 9780374168711

1. Brothers and sisters 2. Scientists 3. Personal conduct 4. Mass media 5. Vaccines 6. Scandals 7. Secrets 8. Revenge 9. Family relationships 10. Men/women relations 11. Literary fiction

LC 2012012377

When Bec Shepherd, a scientist on the verge of finding a vaccine for malaria, refuses to marry her newspaper editor boyfriend, Val Oatman, she doesn't anticipate the consequences that her decision will have for her family. Oatman runs the Moral Foundation, a website that publishes allegations against well-known figures, and it isn't long before they come after her brother, Ritchie, an aging pop star turned reality TV show producer, threatening to reveal the indescretions of his past unless he'll give up some dirt on his sister.

Meek, James, 1962-

The **people's** act of love / James Meek. Canongate, 2006. 400 p.

ISBN 1841957305

1. Russian Revolution and Civil War (1917-1921) 2. 1910s 3. Widows 4. Women photographers 5. Mothers and sons 6. Czechs in

Siberia 7. Revolutionaries 8. Soldiers 9. Christian sects 10. Shamans 11. Murder 12. Betrayal 13. War -- Psychological aspects 14. War and society 15. Civil war 16. Revolutions 17. Soviet Union -- History -- Revolution, 1917-1921 18. Siberia -- History -- Revolution, 1917-1921 19. Psychological fiction 20. Historical fiction

RSL Ondaatje Prize, 2006.

ALA Notable Book, 2007.

In a remote Siberian town torn apart by civil war and inhabited by a small Christian sect, Anna Petrovna, a beautiful photographer, becomes involved in the fate of Samarin, an escapee from Russia's northernmost prison camp.

Mehl, Nancy

Mind games / Nancy Mehl. Bethany House Publishers, 2018. 336 p. Kaely Quinn profiler

ISBN 9780764231841

1. Criminal profilers 2. Women FBI agents 3. Serial murder investigation 4. Children of murderers 5. Serial murderers 6. FBI agents 7. St Louis, Missouri 8. Christian suspense

LC 2018023849

When an anonymous poem predicts a string of murders, ending with her own, FBI behavior analyst Kaely Quinn is paired up with special agent Noah Hunter, who resents his assignment, but this brazen serial killer breaks all the normal patterns, and soon Noah and Kaely are tested to their limits to catch the murderer before anyone else--including Kaely--is killed.

Mehta, Gita

Raj : a novel / Gita Mehta. Ballantine Books, 1991, c1989. 479 p.

ISBN 9780449905661

1. British Raj (1858-1947) 2. Aristocracy 3. Women 4. India -- History -- 20th century 5. Historical fiction

A novel about the changing social and political face of India in the 1920s, as seen through the eyes of Jaya Singh, a princess of the Royal House of Balmer and eventual political ruler of India during its struggle for independence.

"Grounded in details of ancient royal tradition and Hindu ritual, Jaya's story counterpoints a vanished way of life against the complex political realities involved in the passing of the Raj and the birth of the modern nations of India and Pakistan." Publishers Weekly.

Mehta, Rahul

No other world : a novel / Rahul Mehta. Harper, 2017. 286 p.

ISBN 9780062020468

1. 1980s 2. 1990s 3. Identity (Psychology) 4. Gay teenagers 5. Immigrant families 6. Immigrants -- Identity 7. East Indian Americans 8. Transgender persons 9. Life change events 10. Growing up 11. Gay men 12. Families 13. Rural life 14. New York State 15. India 16. LGBTQIA fiction 17. Coming-of-age stories 18. Literary fiction

LC 2016032306

A 1980s Indian-American immigrant family struggles with cultural differences, past secrets, arranged marriage and a gay son's coming-of-age in a homophobic community.

"Buried secrets, suppressed desires, and the hardships of western New York threaten to tear apart an Indian-American immigrant family in Mehtas (Quarantine, 2011) ruminative first novel of identity and loss. ... Mehta uses vivid, memorable imagery to present likable, complex characters whose conflicts are mostly internal, the invisible things we hold in our hearts, as Pooja puts it. The result is a plot that feels muted and ultimately secondary to shimmering descriptions of emotionally resonant moments." Booklist.

Mehta, Rahul

Quarantine : stories / Rahul Mehta. Harper Perennial, 2011. 224 p.

ISBN 9780062020451

1. Gay men 2. East Indian American men 3. Family relationships 4. Homosexuality -- Psychological aspects 5. Men/men relations 6. Short stories 7. LGBTQIA fiction

LC 2010053604

Lambda Literary Award for Gay Men's Debut Fiction, 2012.

In this groundbreaking collection of stories, openly gay Indian men, wrestling with issues of social acceptance and the right to pursue happiness, struggle to maintain relationships with their families as they find themselves estranged from their culture.

Meier, Leslie

Silver anniversary murder / Leslie Meier. Kensington Books, 2018 304 p. Lucy Stone mysteries

ISBN 9781496710338

1. Weddings 2. Small towns 3. Women amateur detectives 4. Divorced women 5. Murder investigation 6. Suicide investigation 7. Maine 8. Cozy mysteries 9. Gentle reads

Devastated to learn that her strong-willed maid of honor has died under suspicious circumstances while finalizing a fourth divorce, Lucy Stone embarks on a determined investigation through New York in pursuit of a desperate killer.

Melamed, Jennie

Gather the daughters / Jennie Melamed. Little, Brown & Co., 2017. 352 p.

ISBN 9780316463652

1. Women's role 2. Dystopias 3. Child sexual abuse 4. Young women 5. Cults 6. Survival (after disaster) 7. Caste 8. Sexism 9. Near future 10. Misogyny 11. Psychic trauma 12. Apocalyptic fiction 13. Dystopian fiction

Starving herself to fend off adulthood in a radical post-apocalypse community where a few chosen men scavenge for detritus and women are little more than breeders, a teen leader investigates a shocking mystery that is contradictory to law before risking her life to organize a girl uprising.

"Melameds haunting and powerful debut blazes a fresh path in the tradition of classic dystopian works." Publishers Weekly.

Meloy, Maile,

Do not become alarmed : a novel / Maile Meloy. Riverhead Books, 2017. 368 p.

ISBN 9780735216525

1. Pleasure cruises 2. Missing children 3. Families 4. Guilt 5. Blame 6. Parents 7. Kidnapping 8. Parenthood 9. Race relations 10. Interpersonal conflict 11. Families of kidnapping victims 12. Central America 13. Psychological fiction

LC 2016051263

A tropical vacation cruise turns nightmarish for two families whose children go missing during a stop in Central America, a crisis that triggers blame, animosity and new priorities as the once-happy parents scramble to recover their children and their lives.

"This writer can apparently do it all--New Yorker stories, children's books, award-winning literary novels, and now, a tautly plotted and culturally savvy emotional thriller. Do not start this book after dinner or you will almost certainly be up all night." Kirkus.

LIST OF FICTIONAL WORKS

Meloy, Maile

Liars and saints : a novel / Maile Meloy. Scribner, 2003. 260 p.

ISBN 0743244354

1. 1940s 2. 1950s 3. 1960s 4. 1970s 5. 1980s 6. 1990s 7. 20th century 8. Catholic families 9. Catholics 10. Catholic women 11. Catholic men 12. Catholic teenage girls 13. Parent and adult child 14. Parent and child 15. Men/women relations 16. Sexuality 17. Marriage 18. Secrets 19. Deception 20. Families 21. Honesty 22. Dishonesty 23. Jealousy 24. Guilt 25. Incest 26. Teenage pregnancy 27. Generation gap 28. California 29. Family sagas

LC 2002030852

Sequel: A Family Daughter.

Shortlisted for The Orange Prize for Fiction, 2005

Set in California, Liars and saints follows four generations of the Catholic Santerre family from World War II to the present, as they navigate a succession of life-altering events -- through the submerged emotion of the fifties, the recklessness and excess of the sixties and seventies, and the reckonings of the eighties and nineties. In a family driven by jealousy and propriety as much as by love, an unspoken tradition of deceit is passed from generation to generation, and fiercely protected secrets gradually drive the Santerres apart. When tragedy shatters their precarious domestic lives, it takes astonishing courage and compassion to bring them back together.

Meltzer, Brad

The **escape** artist / Brad Meltzer. Grand Central Publishing, 2018, c2017. 384 p.

ISBN 9781455559527

1. Conspiracies 2. Government cover-ups 3. Secrecy in government 4. Women artists 5. Women soldiers 6. Women witnesses 7. Undertakers 8. Deception 9. Flashbacks 10. Thrillers and suspense

LC 2017041729

Discovering that a military artist-in-residence who has been officially declared dead by the government is actually alive and on the run, Zig, a worker at Dover Air Force Base, uncovers disturbing facts about the young woman's past before learning that she witnessed something she was not supposed to see.

Meltzer, Brad

The **inner** circle / Brad Meltzer. Grand Central Pub., 2011. ix, 449 p. Culper Ring novels (Brad Meltzer)

ISBN 9780446577892

1. United States. National Archives and Records Administration 2. Archivists 3. Conspiracies 4. Deception 5. Men/women relations 6. Secrets 7. Murder 8. Presidents 9. Washington (DC) 10. Thrillers and suspense 11. Political thrillers

Sequel: The fifth assassin

After an archivist goes against security protocol to show an ex-crush the president's private room at the National Archives, the two stumble upon a dictionary once owned by George Washington, and are soon entangled in a web of conspiracy and murder.

"Meltzer expertly develops the story, throwing in twists and turns at appropriate intervals, and he does an excellent job of putting us in Beecher's corner and making us care about what happens to him." Booklist.

Meltzer, Brad

The **tenth** justice / Brad Meltzer. R. Weisbach Books, 1997. 389 p.

ISBN 0688150896

1. United States. Supreme Court 2. Extortion 3. Betrayal 4. Confidential communications 5. Trust 6. Law clerks 7. Friendship 8. Washington, D.C. 9. Thrillers and suspense 10. Political thrillers 11. Legal thrillers

LC 9644815

When Ben Addison, a new clerk for a Supreme Court justice, makes an error in judgement that leaves him open to blackmail, he turns for help to Lisa, a fellow clerk, and his housemates, who work in the State Department, a senator's office, and a Washington newspaper

"Meltzer moves the story along at a crisp pace, spicing the action and legalese with lively banter and intriguing D.C. arcana." Publishers Weekly.

Meltzer, Brad

The **zero** game / Brad Meltzer. Warner Books, 2004. 496 p.

ISBN 0446530980

1. Political corruption 2. Congressional aides 3. Gambling 4. Capitol pages 5. Teenagers 6. Legislation 7. Assassins 8. Secrets 9. Death threats 10. Washington, D.C. 11. Capitol Hill (Washington, D.C.) 12. Thrillers and suspense 13. Political thrillers 14. Legal thrillers

LC 2003015157

Bored with their jobs as senior staffers to a respected congressman, Matthew Mercer and Harris Sandler become involved in the clandestine Zero Game, but when someone close to them turns up dead, they discover the sinister intent of the "game."

"This thriller is packed with plenty of backroom D.C. ambience and lots of action." Booklist.

Melville, Herman, 1819-1891

* **Billy** Budd, foretopman / Herman Melville ; Illustrated by Robert Quackenbush. F. Watts, 1968, c1924. 126 p.

1. Sailors 2. Good and evil 3. Symbolism in literature 4. Hanging 5. Murder 6. Sea stories 7. Classics

LC 68010284

Book made into a movie called Billy Budd.

A young sailor is sentenced to be hanged for inadvertently striking and killing an officer. He faces death with a blessing for the benevolent captain who is forced to carry out his execution.

Melville, Herman, 1819-1891

The **complete** shorter fiction / Herman Melville ; with an introduction by John Updike. Alfred A. Knopf, 1997. xli, 478 p.

ISBN 0375400680

1. Short stories 2. Classics

LC 98102392

Gathers all of Melville's short stories and novellas, including "Billy Budd, Sailor," "Bartleby, the Scrivener," and "Benito Cereno."

Melville, Herman, 1819-1891

The **confidence-man** : his masquerade / Herman Melville ; edited with an introduction and notes by Stephen Matterson. Penguin Books, 1990, c1857 351 p.

ISBN 0140445471

1. Swindlers and swindling -- Mississippi River 2. Impostors -- Mississippi River 3. River boats -- Mississippi River 4. River travel -- Mississippi River 5. Mississippi River 6. Satirical fiction 7. Classics

LC 91205777

First published 1857.

On April Fool's Day in 1856, a shape-shifting grifter boards a Mississippi riverboat to expose the pretenses, hypocrisies, and self-delusions of his fellow passengers. Melville's comic allegory addresses themes of sincerity, identity, and morality in its challenge to the optimism and materialism of mid-nineteenth-century America. Misunderstood by the author's contemporaries, the novel is praised today for its stunningly modern techniques.

Melville, Herman, 1819-1891

* **Moby-Dick;** or, The whale / Herman Melville Modern Library, 1992 xxxv, 822 p.

ISBN 9780679600107

1. Whaling 2. Humans and whales 3. Moby Dick (Whale) 4. Obsession in men 5. Sea stories 6. Allegories 7. Classics

The classic American novel about the doomed voyage of the Pequod in pursuit of the enigmatic white whale

Melville, Herman, 1819-1891

Omoo : a narrative of adventures in the South Seas / Herman Melville. Penguin Books, 2007, c1847. 374 p.

ISBN 9780143104926

1. Melville, Herman, 1819-1891 2. Islands 3. Whaling ships 4. Whaling 5. Ships 6. Sailors 7. Polynesia 8. Pacific Ocean 9. Adventure stories 10. Autobiographical fiction 11. Classics
Originally published: Harper & Brothers, 1847.

The nineteenth-century American writer provides a fictionalized account of his experiences in the South Pacific.

Mengestu, Dinaw, 1978-

* **All** our names / Dinaw Mengestu. Alfred A. Knopf, 2014. 255 p.

ISBN 9780385349987

1. Revolutionaries 2. Identity (Psychology) 3. Alienation (Social psychology) 4. Women social workers 5. Lovers 6. Friendship 7. Students 8. Memory 9. Africans in the United States 10. Men/women relations 11. Africa 12. United States 13. Political fiction 14. Psychological fiction

LC 2013031632

Kirkus Prize for Fiction finalist, 2014.

Coming of age during an African revolution, a brilliant university student-turned-fighter eventually flees the escalating violence of his country to resettle in America, where he is haunted by his past and the memory of a charismatic leader's devastating sacrifice.

"Mengestu . . . portrays the intersection of cultures experienced by the immigrant with unsettling perception." Publishers Weekly.

Mengestu, Dinaw, 1978-

The **beautiful** things that heaven bears / Dinaw Mengestu. Riverhead Books, 2006. 240 p.

ISBN 1594489408

1. Fathers -- Death 2. Male friendship 3. Refugees -- United States 4. Ethiopians 5. European American women 6. Immigrants -- Washington, D.C. 7. Immigration and emigration 8. Mothers and daughters 9. Multiracial girls 10. Race relations 11. Prejudice 12. Racism 13. Homesickness 14. Loss (Psychology) 15. Friendship 16. Home (Concept) 17. Convenience stores 18. Washington, D.C. 19. Ethiopia -- History -- Revolution, 1974 20. Psychological fiction 21. African American fiction

LC 2006025058

Published in the U.K. under the title Children of the Revolution: London : Jonathan Cape, 2007.

Guardian First Book Award, 2007.

Seventeen years after fleeing the Ethiopian revolution, Sepha Stephanos runs a grocery store in a poor African-American neighborhood in Washington, D.C., where he reflects on his past and the differences between his prospects and the life he imagined.

Mengestu, Dinaw, 1978-

How to read the air / Dinaw Mengestu. Riverhead Books, 2010. 320 p.

ISBN 9781594487705

1. Immigrants 2. Immigration and emigration 3. Children of immigrants 4. Ethiopians -- United States 5. Intergenerational relations 6. Marital conflict 7. Literary fiction 8. Political fiction 9. African American fiction

LC 2010003045

Comprised of the chronicles of two physical journeys -- the original undertaken by two Ethiopian immigrants to the U.S. and retraced, 30 years later, by their emotionally numb son -- this tale of immigration and the consequences of imperfect communication will appeal to readers interested in the psychological toll taken by immigrating to a new country and culture. -- Description by Shauna Griffin.

Mengiste, Maaza

* The **shadow** king : a novel / Maaza Mengiste. W. W. Norton & Company, 2019 448 p.

ISBN 9780393083569

1. 1930s 2. Second World War era (1939-1945) 3. Women and war 4. World War II -- Women 5. Resistance to military occupation 6. False personation 7. Military occupation 8. Household employees 9. Soldiers -- Italy 10. Courage in women 11. Rulers 12. Exiles 13. Ethiopia -- History 14. Historical fiction 15. Literary fiction 16. African American fiction

LC 2019020502

Tending the wounded when her nation is invaded by Mussolini, an orphaned servant in 1935 Ethiopia helps disguise a gentle peasant as their exiled emperor to rally her fellow women in the fight against fascism.

Meno, Joe

The **boy** detective fails / Joe Meno. Akashic Books, 2006. 320 p.

ISBN 1933354100

1. Life change events 2. Sisters -- Death 3. Depression 4. Gifted children 5. Suicide 6. Former detectives 7. Psychiatric hospitals 8. Halfway houses (for alcoholics, drug addicts, runaways, etc) 9. Memories 10. Bereavement 11. Investigations 12. Coping 13. New York City 14. Mysteries

LC 2006923114

"This is postmodern fiction with a head and a heart, addressing such depressing issues as suicide, death, loneliness, failure, anomie, and guilt with compassion, humor, and even whimsy." Library Journal.

Meno, Joe

Marvel and a wonder / Joe Meno. Akashic Books, 2015. 336 p.

ISBN 9781617753930

1. 1990s 2. Grandfather and grandson 3. Horses 4. Farms 5. Korean War veterans 6. Teenage boys 7. Mother-deserted children 8. Drug addicts 9. Thieves 10. Automobile travel 11. Poverty 12. Race relations 13. Small towns 14. Family relationships 15. Literary fiction

In 1995, Jim Falls is trying to raise his teenage grandson on a farm in southern Indiana and after a pair of troubled, meth-dealing brothers steal a horse from the farm, grandfather and grandson travel the landscape in search of the animal.

"Narrating with piercing empathy in the indelible voices of his characters, Meno parallels the frantic search for the racehorse, an embodiment of natures pure glory, with the complicated troubles of a coltish young woman on the run. Evoking William Faulkner and Cormac Mc-

Carthy, Menos suspenseful, mordantly incisive, many-layered tale can also be read as an equine Moby-Dick." Booklist.

Merbeth, K. S.

* **Fortuna** / Kristyn Merbeth. Orbit, 2019. 448 p. Nova vita protocol

ISBN 9780316453998

1. Smugglers 2. Family businesses 3. Space vehicles 4. Massacres 5. Conspiracies 6. Dysfunctional families 7. Brothers and sisters 8. Life on other planets 9. Interplanetary relations 10. Inheritance and succession 11. Alcoholic women 12. Family relationships 13. Space 14. Space opera 15. Science fiction

LC 2019015305

"Merbeth 's world building is fascinating—five human-settled planets, each distinct and littered with alien technology—but her multifaceted characters and their troubled relationships give this action-packed family drama its heart." Booklist.

Merimee, Prosper, 1803-1870

* **Carmen** / Prosper Merimee ; translated and annotated with an introd. by Walter Frank Charles Ade. Barron's Educational Series, 1977. 99 p.

ISBN 9780812004274

1. Romanies 2. Fortune telling 3. Clocks and watches 4. Prisoners 5. Occultism 6. Women thieves 7. Women -- Spain 8. Men/women relations 9. Manipulation by women 10. Spain -- History -- 19th century 11. Translations -- French to English

LC 75022471

Translated from the French.

Merullo, Roland

The **talk-funny** girl : a novel / Roland Merullo. Crown, 2011. 320 p.

ISBN 9780307452924

1. Teenage girl abuse victims 2. Isolationism 3. Self-fulfillment in young women 4. Courage in young women 5. Cult leaders 6. New Hampshire 7. Psychological suspense

LC 2011003328

Raised by parents so intentionally isolated that they speak their own hybrid dialect, abused youth Marjorie witnesses a nearby town's economic ruin and her parents' submission to a sadistic cult leader before she is rescued by another abuse survivor who teaches her stoneworking skills.

Messud, Claire, 1966-

* The **woman** upstairs : a novel / Claire Messud. Alfred A. Knopf, 2013. 272 p.

ISBN 9780307596901

1. Obsession in women 2. Women artists 3. Teacher-student relationships 4. Elementary school teachers 5. Ambition in women 6. Prejudice 7. Lebanese-Americans 8. Jealousy 9. Betrayal 10. Self-fulfillment in women 11. Massachusetts 12. Cambridge, Massachusetts 13. Psychological fiction 14. Literary fiction

LC 2012017806

"This Is A Borzoi book."

ALA Notable Book, 2014

Relegated to the status of schoolteacher and friendly neighbor after abandoning her dreams of becoming an artist, Nora advocates on behalf of a charismatic Lebanese student and is drawn into the child's family until his artist mother's careless ambition leads to a shattering betrayal.

Meuleman, Sarah, 1975-

Find me gone / Sarah Meuleman. HarperCollins, 2018. 304 p.

ISBN 9780062870704

1. 1960s 2. 2010s 3. Missing persons 4. Women journalists 5. Memories 6. Secrets 7. Friendship 8. Fear 9. Belgium 10. New York City 11. Thrillers and suspense

A successful fashion magazine columnist investigates the mysterious disappearances of Agatha Christie, Barbara Follett and Virginia Woolf before endeavoring to figure out what happened to a friend who went missing during their teen years.

Meyer, Deon

Devil's peak : a novel / Deon Meyer ; English translation by K.L. Seegers. Little, Brown, 2008. 410 p. Benny Griessel novels

ISBN 9780316017855

1. Detectives 2. Former mercenaries 3. Sons -- Death 4. Alcoholic men 5. Detectives 6. Prostitutes 7. Vigilantes 8. Missing children 9. Deception 10. Revenge 11. Violence against children 12. Murder investigation 13. Thrillers and suspense 14. Translations -- Afrikaans to English

LC 2007030129

Main character also appears in the author's title Heart of the hunter.

This translation originally published: London: Hodder & Stoughton, 2007.

First published in Afrikaans under the title Infanta by Lupa, 2005.

In the aftermath of a gruesome child abuse case that has caught the attention of the media, Inspector Benny Griessel struggles to maintain his sobriety in order to bring down a vigilante killer who has won the sympathy of the public.

Meyer, Deon

Heart of the hunter : a novel / Deon Meyer ; translated by K.L. Seegers. Little, Brown and Co., 2004. 384 p.

ISBN 0316935492

1. Xhosa (African people) 2. Motorcyclists 3. Former assassins 4. Kidnapping victims 5. Kidnapping 6. Cape Town, South Africa 7. South Africa 8. Zambia 9. Thrillers and suspense

LC 2003025683

Main character also appears in the author's title Devil's Peak.

Asked to deliver a ransom demand to a friend's kidnappers, former goverment agent Thobela Mpayipheli becomes increasingly suspicious when the ransom, a computer disk, is targeted by the government, the police, and more sinister factions in his South African home.

"Despite the complexity of its tightly woven plot-skillfully revealed through newspaper articles and intelligence reports-Meyer's U.S. debut moves at a breathtaking pace that will carry readers away. A sympathetic protagonist and the landscape of South Africa add color to the story." Library Journal.

Meyer, Deon

Icarus / Deon Meyer. Atlantic Monthly Pr, 2015. 352 p. Benny Griessel novels

ISBN 9780802124005

1. Detectives 2. Internet -- Social aspects 3. Murder investigation 4. Extramarital affairs 5. Businesspeople 6. Murder 7. Murder victims 8. South Africa 9. Thrillers and suspense 10. Translations -- Afrikaans to English

Captain Benny Griessel takes on a high profile murder case after a young tech wiz and the founder of an internet service for cheating spouses is discovered dead in Cape Town.

Meyer, Deon

Trackers / Deon Meyer ; translated from Afrikaans by K.L. Seegers. Atlantic Monthly Press, 2011. 488 p.

ISBN 9780802119933

1. Bodyguards 2. Tracking and trailing 3. Revenge in men 4. Murder -- South Africa 5. Trackers 6. Violence -- South Africa 7. Missing persons 8. Rare and endangered animals 9. South Africa 10. Thrillers and suspense 11. Translations -- Afrikaans to English

The character Lemmer from Deon Meyer's Blood Safari is featured in this novel.

Breaking his impartiality rule when he agrees to help smuggle a pair of rare black rhinos out of Zimbabwe to keep them from being poached, freelance bodyguard Lemmer experiences unexpected complications in the form of a fledgling private investigator and a journalist who recently left her abusive family.

Meyer, Nicholas, 1945-

The **adventure** of the peculiar protocols : adapted from the journals of John H. Watson, M.D. / Nicholas Meyer. Minotaur Books, 2019. 238 p.

ISBN 9781250228956

1. 1900s (Decade) 2. Spies 3. Murder 4. Secret societies 5. Conspiracies 6. Antisemitism 7. Hoaxes 8. Women translators 9. Orient Express (Train) 10. France 11. Russia 12. Diary novels 13. Historical mysteries 14. Mysteries

LC 2019029073

Investigating the murder of a Secret Service agent, Sherlock and Watson, accompanied by an enigmatic woman, uncover a plot by a covert group intent on taking over the world.

"Director and author Meyer puts his own stamp on the Holmes and Watson tradition, basing his story on historic events with contemporary relevance, as lies become accepted as truth by means of willful ignorance. Holmes enthusiasts will relish this well-crafted novel." Library Journal.

Meyer, Nicholas, 1945-

The **seven-per-cent** solution : being a reprint from the reminiscences of John H. Watson, M.D. / as edited by Nicholas Meyer Dutton, 1974. 253 p. Memoirs of John Watson

ISBN 9780525200154

1. Freud, Sigmund, 1856-1939 2. Victorian era (1837-1901) 3. 1890s 4. 19th century 5. Drug abuse 6. Suicide investigation 7. Conspiracies 8. Cocaine abuse 9. Addicts 10. Drug abusers -- Rehabilitation 11. Deception 12. Vienna, Austria 13. Adaptations, retellings, and spin-offs 14. Diary novels 15. Historical mysteries 16. Victorian mysteries 17. Mysteries

LC 74004018

Gold Dagger Award for Best Crime Novel of the Year, 1975.

This "rediscovered" Sherlock Holmes adventure recounts the unique collaboration of Holmes and Sigmund Freud in the solution of a mystery on which the lives of millions may depend.

"In a field replete with pastiche Meyer succeeds because of a superior ear for Conan Doyle's style, a gentle sense of fun, and a talent for plot that few of the imitators have possessed." Library Journal.

Meyer, Philipp, 1974-

American rust : a novel / Philipp Meyer. Spiegel & Grau, 2009. 367 p.

ISBN 9780385527514

1. Small town life -- Pennsylvania 2. Parent and adult-child 3. Despair 4. Hope 5. Manslaughter 6. Young men -- Friendship 7. Steel towns -- Pennsylvania 8. Innocence (Law) 9. Trust in men 10.

Pennsylvania 11. California 12. Rural noir 13. Literary fiction

LC 2008022461

Follows the lives of two young men bound by family, responsibility, inertia, and the ties of home to a dying Pennsylvania steel town, who dream of a future beyond that of the abandoned steel mills, deserted houses, factories, and pollution that rules the world they know, in a debut novel about loyalty, friendship, unrest, and redemption.

"The author conjures up this blue-collar Rust Belt town with the same sort of social detail and emotional verisimilitude that Richard Russo has brought to his depictions of upstate New York and Russell Banks has brought to downstate New Hampshire. He writes about his characters' lives in Buell with sympathy and unsentimental clarity." New York Times.

Meyer, Philipp, 1974-

* The **son** : a novel / Philipp Meyer. Ecco Press, 2013. viii, 561 p.

ISBN 9780062120397

1. Frontier and pioneer life 2. Indian captivities 3. Ambition in men 4. Families -- Texas 5. Ranchers 6. Oil industry and trade 7. Texas -- History 8. The West (United States) 9. Family sagas 10. Westerns 11. Epic fiction

Western Heritage Award for Outstanding Western Novel, 2014.
Pulitzer Prize for Fiction finalist, 2014.

An epic of the American West and a multigenerational saga of power, blood, land, and oil that follows the rise of one Texas family, from the Comanche raids of the 1800s to the to the oil booms of the 20th century.

Meyers, Kent

Twisted tree / Kent Meyers. Houghton Mifflin Harcourt, 2009. 304 p.

ISBN 9780151013890

1. Teenage girl murder victims 2. Bereavement 3. Guilt in girls 4. Missing teenage girls 5. Loss (Psychology) 6. Serial murderers 7. Murder 8. Secrets 9. Small town life -- South Dakota 10. South Dakota 11. Psychological suspense

LC 2009013288

The story of a dead girl, Hayley Jo Zimmerman, is told through the stories of those who knew her, including a supermarket clerk who recalls an encounter with a disturbingly thin Hayley Jo, an ex-priest who remembers baptizing the girl, and her best friend Laura, who regrets all the running they did, and how it fed her addiction.

Meyers, Kent

The **work** of wolves / Kent Meyers. Harcourt, 2004. 407 p.

ISBN 9780151010578

1. Horse trainers 2. Ranchers' spouses 3. Men -- Relations with married women 4. Ranchers 5. Loners 6. Lakota Indians 7. Teenage boys 8. Exchange students 9. Horses 10. Animal welfare 11. Love triangles 12. Love 13. Ranch life 14. Men and horses 15. South Dakota 16. Psychological suspense

LC 2003026365

Carson Fielding is well respected for his ability to train horses, but after reluctantly agreeing to work for a wealthy rancher he despises, he finds his loathing supplanted by his growing desire for his employer's wife.

"Meyer's spare dialogue is brilliantly and often comically expressive, and Carson, his taciturn, rational hero, is an original and compelling character. Strong themes of generational responsibility and family history add resonance to this gratifying, very American novel." Publishers Weekly.

Michaels, Anne, 1958-

Fugitive pieces / Anne Michaels. A. A Knopf, 1997. 294 p.

ISBN 067945439X

1. Jews, Polish 2. Holocaust survivors 3. Rescues 4. Traffic accidents 5. Senior men -- Death 6. Jewish men 7. Geologists 8. Poets 9. Islands of the Aegean 10. Toronto, Ontario 11. Psychological fiction 12. Literary fiction

LC 96-36678

Books in Canada First Novel Award, 1996.
Guardian First Book Award, 1997.
Orange Prize for Fiction, 1997.
Toronto Book Awards, 1997.
Trillium Book Award, 1996.
Canadian Jewish Book Award
Shortlisted for the Giller Prize, 1996

A young orphan smuggled out of Poland during World War II, poet Jakob Beer comes to understand the extraordinary power of language to destroy, restore, and witness as he struggles to cope with both grief and the healing of memory.

"Michaels offers a richly imagined portrait of Jakob's slow progress from reticence to poetic eloquence and of the complex blend of memories, feelings, insights, and experiences that makes him the man he becomes. She even tackles the perpetually troubling question of how so many seemingly ordinary, 'civilized' people could have eagerly committed such monstrous crimes against defenseless children and civilians." Christian Science Monitor.

Michaels, Barbara, 1927-2013

Houses of stone / Barbara Michaels. HarperCollins, 2009, c1993. 368 p.

ISBN 9780061582998

1. Women scholars and academics 2. Manuscripts 3. Anonyms and pseudonyms 4. Women authors -- 19th century 5. Gender role 6. Virginia 7. Gothic romances

Originally published: New York : Simon & Schuster, 1993

"Michaels has composed a mystery that is brimming with suspense yet revolves around authorial research rather than money and multiple murders." Booklist.

Michaels, Fern

Deep harbor / Fern Michaels. Kensington Books, 2019 272 p.

ISBN 9781496714510

1. Congressional aides 2. Political corruption 3. Grief in women 4. Women -- Interpersonal relations 5. Self-fulfillment in women 6. Government cover-ups 7. Loss (Psychology) 8. Brothers -- Death 9. Small town life 10. Friendship 11. Orphans 12. New England 13. Washington, D C 14. Women's lives and relationships

Immersing herself in her job as assistant to a congressman after the death of her only family member, Carol Ann "CJ" Jansen uncovers possible evidence of her boss' corrupt activities before his sudden disappearance.

Michels, Elizabeth

The **rebel** heir / Elizabeth Michels. Sourcebooks Casablanca, 2016. 352 p. The Spare Heirs

ISBN 9781492621362

1. Regency period (1811-1820) 2. Swindlers and swindling 3. Heirs and heiresses 4. Secret identity 5. Deception 6. Nobility 7. Revenge 8. Mate selection 9. Secret societies 10. Sexual attraction 11. Men/women relations 12. England -- Social life and customs -- 19th century 13. Regency romances 14. Historical romances

Determined to avenge the wrongs done to his family and take Lady Evangeline Green's father's money, Ash Claughbane, the fourth son from a titled but poor family, teams up with the Spare Heirs Gentleman's Club to trap this headstrong beauty into marriage.

"Michels expertly delivers a heart-wrenching romance that will leave the reader eagerly anticipating future installments." Publishers Weekly.

Michener, James A. (James Albert), 1907-1997

* The **bridges** at Toko-Ri / James A. Michener. Random House, 1953. 146 p.

ISBN 0394417801

1. United States. Navy Aviation 2. 1950s 3. Korean War, 1950-1953 -- Aerial operations, American 4. Fighter pilots -- United States 5. Bridges 6. Sabotage 7. Bombing 8. Air warfare 9. Husband and wife 10. Airplane accidents 11. Self-discovery in men 12. Korea -- Foreign relations -- United States 13. War stories 14. Historical fiction

LC 52007129

A naval task force tries to destroy the bridges at Toko-ri with jet bombers so that supplies will not reach communist front lines during the Korean War.

Michener, James A. (James Albert), 1907-1997

Caribbean / James A. Michener. Random House, 1989. 672 p.

ISBN 0394565614

1. Island life -- Carribbean area 2. Rastafarians 3. Culture conflict 4. Cuban resistance and revolts 5. Pirates 6. Slaves 7. Nationalism 8. Explorers 9. Superstition 10. Voodoo 11. Taino Indians 12. Arawak Indians 13. Caribbean Area -- History 14. Historical fiction

LC 89042785

The maps are on lining papers.

An epic tale of Caribbean history from the 15th century to the present, following the Rastafarians, Cuban revolution, and nationalism.

"A novel about the Caribbean islands from the days when the peace-loving Arawak Indians were overpowered by cannibalistic Caribs, to a ship's tour of today's still lush, but troubled, paradise. Sir Francis Drake, pirate Henry Morgan, Horatio Nelson, Haitian General Toussaint L'Ouverture, Fidel Castro march across the pages, and while the pace is sometimes achingly slow, the dialogue stilted and the characterization skimpy, Michener laces the whole with fiery Caribbean drama." Publishers Weekly.

Michener, James A. (James Albert), 1907-1997

* **Centennial** / James A. Michener. Random House, 1974 909 p.

ISBN 039447970X

1. American Westward Expansion (1803-1899) 2. Indians of North America -- Relations with missionaries, traders, etc 3. Frontier and pioneer life 4. Homesteaders -- The West (United States) 5. Arapaho Indians 6. Paleontology 7. Cowboys 8. Fur traders 9. Human settlements 10. Immigration and emigration 11. Explorers 12. Overland journeys to the Pacific 13. Ranchers 14. Gold miners -- The West (United States) 15. Colorado 16. The West (United States) -- Exploration 17. Westerns

LC 74005164

Includes maps on end papers.

Western Heritage Award for Outstanding Western Novel, 1975.

The story of Centennial, Colorado, begins when the earth formed the area and ends in the 1970s with human disregard for its benefits and beauties, and also tells the history of relations between the white settlers and Native Americans.

Michener, James A. (James Albert), 1907-1997

Chesapeake / James A. Michener. Random House, 1978. 865 p.

ISBN 0394500792

1. Human settlements 2. Indians of North America 3. Racism 4. Immigration and emigration 5. Rich families 6. Plantation life 7. Race relations 8. Slave trade 9. Quaker families 10. Underground Railroad 11. Freed slaves 12. Chesapeake Bay Region 13. Chesapeake Bay 14. Maryland -- History 15. Family sagas 16. Historical fiction

LC 78002892

Includes end-paper maps.

The Eastern shore of Maryland and Virginia evolves from prehistory into the 20th century and influences the lives of Native Americans, African Americans, and Irish immigrants who live there.

"Through the interwoven stories of three families and the Indians, Blacks, and Irish immigrants with whom they interact, Michener chronicles four centuries of life on Maryland's Eastern Shore. . . . Michener elaborates . . . variations on his themes of personal accountability for social change, man's self-expulsion from paradise, and the interrelated ecological network of all things." Library Journal.

Michener, James A. (James Albert), 1907-1997

The **covenant** / James A. Michener. Random House, 1980. 877 p.

ISBN 0394505050

1. Apartheid 2. Colonialism -- South Africa 3. Race relations 4. Afrikaners 5. Racism 6. Culture conflict 7. San (African people) 8. Zulu (African people) 9. Human evolution 10. Human settlements 11. Immigration and emigration 12. Segregation 13. Dutch in South Africa 14. British in South Africa 15. South Africa -- History 16. Zimbabwe (Kingdom) 17. Historical fiction 18. Family sagas

LC 80005315

Includes glossary and genealogical charts.

The Nxumalos, the Van Doorns, and the Saltwoods interact during several hundred years of South African life.

"This novel spans 500 years of South African history. Three families mingle with the outstanding historic figures of their times. They are the Nxumalos, the Van Doorns, and the Saltwoods, representing respectively the African, Afrikaans, and English. . . . Over several hundred years their descendants make contact, and thrive through the contact, only to become adversaries as contact subsequently gives way to conflict. Finally they find themselves irretrievably stuck in the hard concrete of South Africa's racial policies." Christian Science Monitor.

Michener, James A. (James Albert), 1907-1997

Hawaii / James A. Michener. Random House Paperbacks, 2002, c1959. 937 p.

ISBN 0375760377

1. Island life -- Hawaii 2. Hawaiians 3. Immigrants 4. Christian missions -- Hawaii 5. Christian missionaries 6. Polynesians 7. Human settlements 8. Immigration and emigration 9. Interethnic marriage 10. Asian Americans -- Hawaii 11. Nobility 12. Rulers 13. Farm life 14. Sugar plantations -- Hawaii 15. Hawaii -- History 16. Historical fiction

LC 2002021975

Originally published: New York : Random House, 1959.

Includes family trees and end-paper maps.

Hawaii's prehistory and history appears through the eyes of its natives and the missionaries and Asians who came to influence it.

Michener, James A. (James Albert), 1907-1997

Mexico / James A. Michener. Random House, 1992. 625 p.

ISBN 0679416498

1. 1960s 2. Bullfights -- Mexico 3. Journalists -- United States 4. Indians of Mexico 5. Americans in Mexico 6. Bullfighters 7. Multiracial men 8. Men -- Identity 9. Human sacrifice 10. Inquisition 11. Plantations -- Virginia 12. Silver mines and mining 13. Revolutions -- Mexico 14. Mexico -- History 15. Virginia -- History -- 19th century 16. Historical fiction

LC 92050151

Norman Clay, a New York journalist born in Mexico, returns to tell the story of two rival matadors in 1961, but he also includes vast amounts of Mexican history from the past 1,500 years.

"There are splendid and authentic scenes in the plaza de toros that are as dramatic as any written by Ernest Hemingway or Barnaby Conrad, and one chapter, where the bulls' horns are shaved by the father of a torero, is James Michener the storyteller and parabolist at his finest." New York Times Book Review.

Michener, James A. (James Albert), 1907-1997

Space / James A. Michener ; [cartography by Jean Paul Tremblay]. Random House, 1982. 622 p.

ISBN 0394505557

1. United States. National Aeronautics and Space Administration 2. Space programs 3. Astronautics -- United States 4. Space exploration 5. Rocketry -- History 6. Swindlers and swindling 7. Born again Christians 8. Technology and civilization 9. Space flight 10. Space vehicles 11. World War II 12. Korean War, 1950-1953 13. United States -- Social conditions -- 20th century 14. Moon -- Exploration 15. Mars (Planet) -- Exploration 16. Saturn (Planet) -- Exploration 17. Historical fiction

LC 82040127

Maps on lining papers.

During World War II, scientists and politicians become involved in the program that eventually takes humans into space.

Michener, James A. (James Albert), 1907-1997

* **Tales** of the South Pacific / James A. Michener. Macmillan, 1986, c1947. 326 p.

ISBN 0025845403

1. United States Navy Officers 2. Second World War era (1939-1945) 3. World War II 4. Interethnic romance 5. Military bases, American 6. Men/women relations 7. Interethnic relations 8. Island life -- South Pacific Ocean 9. Patriotism 10. Racism 11. Prejudice 12. Pregnant women 13. Love triangles 14. South Pacific Ocean 15. Oceania 16. War stories 17. Historical fiction 18. Literary fiction

LC 86028450

Tales of the South Pacific was the inspiration for the movie "South Pacific."

Pulitzer Prize for Fiction, 1948.

The people and beauty of the South Pacific's coral islands are viewed through the eyes of a young naval lieutenant.

Mieville, China

The **city** & the city / China Mieville. Del Rey/Ballantine Books, 2009. 416 p.

ISBN 9780345497512

1. Murder investigation 2. Parallel universes 3. City life 4. Missing persons 5. Hallucinations and illusions 6. Eastern Europe 7. Hardboiled fiction 8. Fantasy mysteries

LC 2009013775

Arthur C. Clarke Award, 2010.

BSFA Award for Best Novel, 2009.

Hugo Award for Best Novel, 2010.

Locus Award for Fantasy Novel, 2010.

World Fantasy Award, 2010.

Inspector Tyador Borlu must travel to Ul Qoma to search for answers in the murder of a woman found in the city of Beszel.

"A murder mystery set in two cities, Ul Qoma and Beszel, one rich and one poor, where residents have been trained to unsee each other in order to coexist. . . . The story takes the form of a police procedural as the protagonist, Inspector Tyador Borl of the Extreme Crime Squad, tries to crack the murder case. There are no elves or UFOs. Instead, the story focuses on the lengths to which people will go to enforce borders and maintain separate cultural identities. Evoking such writers as Franz Kafka and Mikhail Bulgakov, Mr. Mieville asks readers to make conceptual leaps and not to simply take flights of fancy." The Wall Street Journal.

Mieville, China

Embassytown / China Mieville. Ballantine Books, 2011. 368 p.

ISBN 9780345524492

1. Human/alien encounters 2. Life on other planets 3. Space warfare 4. Far future 5. Genetic engineering 6. Loyalty 7. Social science fiction 8. Science fiction

Originally published: London: Macmillan, 2011.

Locus Award for Best Science Fiction Novel, 2012.

Embassytown: a city of contradictions on the outskirts of the universe. Avice is an immerser, a traveller on the immer, the sea of space and time below the everyday, now returned to her birth planet. Here on Arieka, humans are not the only intelligent life, and Avice has a rare bond with the natives, the enigmatic Hosts - who cannot lie. Only a tiny cadre of unique human Ambassadors can speak Language, and connect the two communities. But an unimaginable new arrival has come to Embassytown. And when this Ambassador speaks, everything changes. Catastrophe looms. Avice knows the only hope is for her to speak directly to the alien Hosts. And that is impossible.

"It's a joy to find this young author coming into his own, and bringing the craft of science fiction out of the backwaters where it's been caught lately between the regressive drag of publishers marketing to a safe readership and the bewildering promises of change and growth offered by postmodernism in all its forms and formlessness. Embassytown is a fully achieved work of art. Only the trash forms of science fiction are undemanding and predictable; the good stuff, like all good fiction, is not for lazy minds. Where the complexity of realistic novels is moral and psychological, in science fiction it's moral and intellectual; individual character is seldom the key. But Mieville's characters are deftly sketched, and his narrator-protagonist, Avice, is a subtler portrait than she seems at first." The Guardian (UK).

Mieville, China

Perdido Street Station / China Mieville. Del Rey, 2001. 710 p. New Crobuzon series

ISBN 0345443020

1. Dystopias 2. Scientists 3. Flight 4. Garuda (Mythical bird) 5. Caterpillars 6. Post-Industrial society 7. Men/women relations 8. Organized crime 9. Women artists 10. Human-alien hybrids 11. Missing women 12. Monsters 13. Identity (Psychology) 14. Science fantasy 15. Steampunk 16. Science fiction

LC 00067474

Illustrated with a map.

Arthur C. Clarke Award, 2001.

In the squalid, gothic city of New Crobuzon, a mysterious half-human, half-bird stranger comes to Isaac, a gifted but eccentric scientist, with a request to help him fly, but Isaac's obsessive experiments and attempts to grant the request unleash a terrifying dark force on the entire city.

"Scientist Isaac Dan der Grimnebulin and his lover, an insectlike creature named Lin, discover the risks of meddling in the affairs of mobsters, renegades, and revolutionaries when they fall afoul of the powers that rule the sprawling city of New Crobuzon. The author . . . delivers a powerful tale about the power of love and the will to survive in a dystopian universe that combines Victorian elements with a fantasy version of cyberpunk." Library Journal.

Milan, Courtney

The **duchess** war / Courtney Milan. CreateSpace, 2012. 268 p. The Brothers Sinister

ISBN 9781481207478

1. Victorian era (1837-1901) 2. 1860s 3. Dukes and duchesses 4. Single women 5. Secrets 6. Nobility 7. Poor women 8. Radicals 9. Populists 10. Interclass romance 11. Shyness in women 12. Men/women relations 13. Interpersonal attraction 14. England -- Social life and customs -- 19th century 15. Great Britain -- History -- Victoria, 1837-1901 16. Victorian romances 17. Historical romances

"Miss Minerva Lane is a quiet, bespectacled wallflower, and she wants to keep it that way. After all, the last time she was the center of attention, it ended badly so badly that she changed her name to escape her scandalous past. Wallflowers may not be the prettiest of blooms, but at least they don?t get trampled. So when a handsome duke comes to town, the last thing she wants is his attention. But that is precisely what she gets. Because Robert Blaisdell, the Duke of Clermont, is not fooled. When Minnie figures out what he's up to, he realizes there is more to her than her spectacles and her quiet ways. And he's determined to lay her every secret bare before she can discover his. But this time, one shy miss may prove to be more than his match."--annotation by Krista Biggs.

Miles, Jonathan

Anatomy **of** a miracle / Jonathan Miles. Hogarth Press, 2018. 355 p.

ISBN 9780553447583

1. 21st century 2. Veterans 3. People with paraplegia 4. Miracles 5. Belief and doubt 6. Religion and science 7. Secrets 8. Identity (Psychology) 9. Interpersonal relations 10. Mississippi 11. Biloxi, Mississippi 12. Satirical fiction

Confined to a wheelchair after a paralyzing injury, an Afghanistan War veteran endures a hardscrabble existence in his sister's ramshackle Mississippi home before spontaneously regaining his ability to walk, an apparent miracle that subjects him to scientific and religious debates and exposes his most private secrets.

Millay, Katja

The **sea** of tranquility / Katja Millay. Atria Books, 2013. 352 p.

ISBN 9781476730943

1. Psychic trauma 2. Loss (Psychology) 3. Girls who are mute 4. Friendship 5. Teenage girls with disabilities 6. High school students 7. Piano 8. Men/women relations 9. New adult fiction 10. Coming-of-age stories

Teenage former piano prodigy Nastya Kashnikov and Josh Bennett, a lonely boy at her school, enter into an intense relationship, with neither unaware of the dark secrets the other's past holds.

"[F]ans of character-driven fiction will find much to admire in this deeply felt novel that is an excellent example of crossover fiction." Library Journal.

Miller, Andrew, 1961-

Oxygen / Andrew Miller. Harcourt, 2001. 323 p.
ISBN 9780151007219

1. Parents with terminal illnesses 2. Mothers and sons 3. Translators 4. Dramatists 5. Actors and actresses 6. Exiles -- Hungary 7. Failure (Psychology) 8. Memories -- Psychological aspects 9. Hungarians in France 10. Paris, France 11. England 12. Psychological fiction 13. Parallel narratives

LC 2001051459

Shortlisted for the Booker-McConnell Prize, 2001.

As Alec Valentine and his brother Larry return to England to care for their ailing mother, Laszlo Lazar, whose play Alec is translating, finds that he cannot stop thinking about past mistakes.

"Written in elegant, resonant prose, this book breathes with compassion and honesty, and with the rare quality called hope." Publishers Weekly.

Miller, Andrew, 1961-

Pure / Andrew Miller. Europa Editions, 2012, c2011. 346 p.
ISBN 9781609450670

1. 18th century 2. Engineers 3. Cemeteries 4. Exhumation 5. Corpse removals 6. Dead 7. Public health 8. Paris, France -- History -- 1715-1789 9. Paris, France -- Social life and customs -- 18th century 10. Historical fiction 11. Literary fiction

Originally published in the UK (London : Sceptre, 2011).
Originally published: London : Sceptre, 2011.
First published: 2011.
Costa Novel Award, 2011.
Costa Book of the Year Award, 2011.
Shortlisted for the Walter Scott Prize for Historical Fiction, 2012
Shortlisted for the International IMPAC Dublin Literary Award, 2013

Engineer Jean-Baptiste Baratte is tasked with emptying an overflowing cemetery in Paris in 1785, work he considers noble until he begins to suspect that the destruction of the cemetery parallels his own fate and the demise of social order.

Miller, Derek B., 1970-

* **American** by day / Derek B. Miller. Houghton Mifflin Harcourt, 2018. 338 p.
ISBN 9781328876652

1. Women detectives 2. Brothers and sisters 3. Missing persons investigation 4. Police 5. Culture shock 6. Murder suspects 7. Norwegians in the United States 8. Adirondack Mountains, New York 9. New York (State) 10. Mysteries 11. Mysteries

LC 2017045332

Police Chief Inspector Sigrid Odegard from Norwegian by Night departs Oslo for the United States to search for her missing brother, a quest that plunges her into the political minefields and backwoods undercurrents of the Adirondacks.

Miller, Derek B., 1970-

* The **girl** in green / Derek B. Miller. Houghton Mifflin Harcourt, 2017. 336 p.
ISBN 9780544706255

1. Life change events 2. War -- Psychological aspects 3. Captives 4. Muslim girls 5. Journalists 6. Veterans 7. Male friendship 8. Americans in the Middle East 9. British in the Middle East 10. Refugees 11. Persian Gulf War, 1991 12. Syria -- History -- Civil War, 2011- 13. Iraq 14. War stories

LC 2016005409

First published: 2016.

A tale set in the aftermath of Desert Storm finds a British journalist who avoids his family and a reckless American private seeking redemption after failing to save the life of a young girl.

"A penetrating, poetic, and unexpectedly disarming book about the ageless conflict in the Middle East by a writer who has made that topic his specialty." Kirkus.

Miller, Derek B., 1970-

Norwegian by night : a novel / Derek B. Miller. Houghton Mifflin Harcourt, 2013, c2012. 292 p.
ISBN 9780547934877

1. Octogenarians 2. Protectiveness in men 3. Children of murder victims 4. Murder 5. Widowers 6. Albanians 7. Grief in men 8. Murder witnesses 9. Interethnic relations 10. Grandfather and granddaughter 11. Norway 12. Oslo, Norway 13. Scandinavian crime fiction 14. Thrillers and suspense

LC 2012018089

Originally published: Brunswick, Vic. : Scribe Publications, 2012.
New Blood Dagger Award, 2013.

After witnessing a murder in Olso, elderly former Marine sniper and watch repairman Sheldon Horowitz flees to safety with the newly orphaned son of the victim and becomes haunted by memories of his own son who died in Vietnam.

Miller, Henry, 1891-1980

* **Tropic** of Capricorn / Henry Miller. Grove Press, 1987, c1938. 348 p.
ISBN 9780802151827

1. Miller, Henry, 1891-1980 2. 1920s 3. Writing 4. Masculinity 5. Bohemianism 6. Sex customs 7. Sexuality 8. Extramarital affairs 9. Men/women relations 10. Brooklyn, New York City 11. New York City 12. Transgressive fiction 13. Modern classics 14. Erotic fiction 15. Autobiographical fiction 16. Literary fiction

Sequel to: Tropic of Cancer.
Originally published: Paris : Obelisk Press, 1938.

Presents Miller's controversial work candidly depicting the life of an American expatriate in Paris, following the narrator from the ethnic neighborhoods of New York City through a series of sexual adventures to Europe in the 1920s.

Miller, Henry, 1891-1980

* **Tropic** of Cancer / Henry Miller. Grove Press, 1980, c1934. 318 p.
ISBN 9780802131782

1. Miller, Henry, 1891-1980 2. 1930s 3. Americans in France 4. Writing 5. Authors 6. Expatriates 7. Americans in Paris, France 8. Bohemianism 9. Sex customs 10. Poor men 11. Sexuality 12. Men/women relations 13. Paris, France 14. France 15. Transgressive fiction 16. Modern classics 17. Erotic fiction 18. Autobiographical fiction 19. Literary fiction

Sequel: Tropic of Capricorn.
Originally published: Paris : Obelisk Press, 1934.

Chronicles the bawdy adventures of a young expatriate writer, his friends, and the characters they meet in Paris in the 1930s.

Miller, Karen E. Quinones

An **angry-ass** black woman / Karen E. Quinones Miller. Gallery Books, 2012. 288 p.
ISBN 9781451607826

1. Miller, Karen E Quinones 2. People in comas 3. African American authors 4. Growing up 5. Poverty 6. Forties (Age) 7. Race relations 8. Ambition in women 9. Family relationships 10. African American families 11. African-American neighborhoods 12. Harlem, New

York City 13. New York City 14. Autobiographical fiction 15. African American fiction

LC 2011047077

Traces the impoverished early years of Ke-Ke, who awakens from a coma in her midlife to confront events that shaped her resolve to leave Harlem, earn an education, and pursue a writing career.

Miller, Kei

* Augustown / Kei Miller. Pantheon Books, 2017. 256 p.
ISBN 9781101871614

1. 20th century 2. Women -- Jamaica 3. Women who are blind 4. Rastafari Movement 5. Poverty 6. Religion 7. Intuition 8. Great aunts 9. Race relations 10. Aunt and nephew 11. Jamaica 12. Literary fiction 13. Historical fiction 14. Parallel narratives

Longlisted for the Andrew Carnegie Medal for Excellence in Fiction, 2018.

Possessing strong intuitive powers in spite of being unable to see, Ma Taffy comforts her stricken great-nephew while recalling a fantastical story with ties to Jamaican history, the birth of the Rastafari and the human drive for a better life.

"Fusing facts with what-could-have-well-been, Augustown is a gorgeously plotted, sharply convincing, achingly urgent novel deserving widespread attention." Booklist.

Miller, Madeline

* Circe / Madeline Miller. Little Brown & Co., 2018 393 p.
ISBN 9780316556347

1. Ancient Aegean civilizations (3000?1000 BCE) 2. Exiles 3. Witches 4. Gods and goddesses, Greek 5. Supernatural 6. Titans (Mythology) 7. Mythology, Greek 8. Odysseus (Greek mythology) 9. Circe (Greek mythology) 10. Ancient Greece 11. Mythological fiction 12. Historical fantasy 13. Literary fiction

Librarians' Choice (Australia), 2018.

Goodreads Choice Award, 2018

RUSA Reading List Short List, 2019.

Longlisted for The Women's Prize for Fiction, 2019.

Shortlisted for The Women's Prize for Fiction, 2019.

Follows the banished witch daughter of Titans as she hones her powers and interacts with famous mythological beings before a conflict with one of the most vengeful Olympians forces her to choose between the worlds of the gods and mortals.

Miller, Madeline

The **song** of Achilles / Madeline Miller. Ecco Press, 2012, c2011. 352 p.
ISBN 9780062060617

1. Ancient Aegean civilizations (3000?1000 BCE) 2. Princes 3. Exiles 4. Young men -- Interpersonal relations 5. Warriors 6. Trojan War 7. Fate and fatalism 8. Patroclus (Greek mythology) 9. Achilles (Greek mythology) 10. Troy (Extinct city) 11. Ancient Greece 12. Historical fiction 13. War stories 14. Literary fiction 15. Adaptations, retellings, and spin-offs

Originally published: London : Bloomsbury, c2011.

Orange Prize for Fiction, 2012.

Rainbow List, 2013.

Patroclus, an awkward young prince, follows Achilles into war, little knowing that the years that follow will test everything they have learned, everything they hold dear. And that, before he is ready, he will be forced to surrender his friend to the hands of Fate. Set during the Trojan War.

"With language both evocative of her predecessors and fresh, and through familiar scenes that explore new territory, this first-time novelist masterfully brings to life an imaginative yet informed vision of ancient Greece featuring divinely human gods and larger-than-life mortals." Publishers Weekly.

Miller, Mary, 1977-

Biloxi : a novel / Mary Miller. Liveright Publishing Corp, 2019. 224 p.
ISBN 9781631492167

1. Divorced men 2. Men and dogs 3. Options, alternatives, choices 4. Sixties (Age) 5. Human/animal relationships 6. Retirees 7. Dogs 8. Pets 9. Unhappiness 10. Dog adoption 11. Inheritance and succession 12. Second chances 13. Biloxi, Mississippi 14. Mississippi 15. Literary fiction 16. Southern fiction

LC 2018056974

Mary Miller seizes the mantle of Southern literature with this wry tale of middle age and the unexpected turns a life can take.

Miller, Rebecca, 1962-

* Jacob's folly : a novel / Rebecca Miller. Farrar, Straus and Giroux, 2013. 352 p.
ISBN 9780374178543

1. 18th century 2. 21st century 3. Reincarnation 4. Judaism 5. Fathers and sons 6. Hospital patients 7. Transformations, Personal 8. Theater 9. Peddlers 10. Fate and fatalism 11. Men/women relations 12. Long Island, New York 13. Literary fiction 14. Historical fiction

LC 2012022882

First published in the USA in 2013 by Farrar, Straus and Giroux, New York.

Includes reading group questions.

Jacob is a Jewish peddler living in eighteenth-century France; Leslie and Deirdre Senzatimore are a settled American couple; and Masha is an alluring young ultra-Orthodox Jew who is gravely ill. In Jacob's Folly, these four individuals will find their fates intertwined and the courses of their lives irrevocably altered when Jacob is reincarnated as a house fly in contemporary Long Island.

Miller, Sue, 1943-

For love / Sue Miller. Harper Collins, 1993. 301 p.
ISBN 9780060179793

1. Adult children of dysfunctional families 2. Traffic accidents 3. Hometowns -- Massachusetts 4. Familial love 5. Romantic love 6. Divorced women 7. Female friendship 8. Brothers and sisters 9. Men/women relations 10. Massachusetts 11. Cambridge, Massachusetts 12. Women's lives and relationships

LC 92054422

Three childhood chums reunite after years of separation and, when tragedy strikes, they must face their pasts

Miller, Sue, 1943-

The **good** mother / Sue Miller. Harper and Row, 1986. 310p.
ISBN 9780060155513

1. Child custody 2. Psychiatrists 3. Parenting 4. Trials (Child custody) 5. Mothers and daughters 6. Divorced women 7. Former husbands 8. Three-year-old girls 9. Mothers 10. Psychological fiction 11. Women's lives and relationships

LC 85045475

"The fulcrum on which the novel's plot pivots is the allegation by Anna's ex-husband that Anna's lover has molested Molly, and the ensuing custody trial. Miller's treatment of this high point of tension in the novel is dramatic, discreet, compassionate. Each development in the legal process increases the tension. The drama heightens, the suspense builds, character is further developed, and the latitude for choice logically narrowed. Like a final judgment, the custody decision breaks over reader and character alike." Christian Science Monitor.

Miller, Sue, 1943-

The **senator's** wife / Sue Miller. Alfred A. Knopf, 2008. 320 p.

ISBN 9780307264206

1. United States. Congress. Senate 2. Dilemmas 3. Adult children of dysfunctional families 4. Politicians' spouses 5. Married people 6. Marriage 7. Men/women relations 8. Extramarital affairs 9. Marital conflict 10. Pregnant women 11. Female friendship 12. Middle class 13. New England 14. Women's lives and relationships

LC 2007014659

"This is a Borzoi book"--T.p. verso.

Two unconventional women, neighbors in adjacent New England townhouses--Meri Fowler, pregnant, newly married, and discovering the gap between reality and expectation, and Delia Naughton, wife of a notoriously unfaithful liberal senator--confront the costs and challenges of love.

"No one captures the domestic landscape with language as lush as Miller's. She is the Martha Stewart of fictional space. From peeling an orange to laying out Christmas dinner to arranging lilies on a table, her prose is almost erotic. Moreover, her writerly gift extends beyond graceful imagery. She describes sexual encounters with graphic intensity and brings to Meri's labor and delivery a verisimilitude that will flatten you." Houston Chronicle.

Miller, Sue, 1943-

While I was gone / Sue Miller. A. A. Knopf, 1999. 265 p.

ISBN 0375401121

1. 1960s 2. Women veterinarians 3. Housemates 4. Runaway wives, husbands, etc 5. Spouses of clergy 6. Husband and wife 7. Clergy 8. Middle-aged women 9. Murder 10. Roommates 11. Massachusetts 12. Cambridge, Massachusetts 13. Massachusetts 14. Psychological fiction

LC 9814211

Having moved on with her life after a friend was brutally murdered, Jo Becker is now married with a grown family, but when an old housemate moves into the neighborhood, Jo rekindles a relationship that takes her back to the past and threatens her future.

"Miller's narrative is a beautifully textured picture of the psychological tug of war between finding integrity as an individual and satisfying the demands of spouse, children and community." Publishers Weekly.

Miller, Walter M., 1923-1996

* A **canticle** for Leibowitz / Walter M. Miller, Jr. Bantam Books, 2007, c1960. 338 p.

ISBN 9780553273816

1. Survival (after nuclear warfare) 2. End of the world 3. Monks 4. Monasticism and religious orders for men -- United States 5. Mutants 6. Religion 7. Civilization 8. Priests 9. Nuclear warfare 10. Imaginary wars and battles 11. Post-apocalypse 12. Utah 13. Apocalyptic fiction 14. Social science fiction 15. Science fiction

LC 85045444

Sequel: Saint Leibowitz and the wild horse woman (1997).

Hugo Award for Best Novel, 1961.

A monk struggles to preserve spiritual life and wisdom in the years following a nuclear holocaust

Millet, Lydia, 1968-

How the dead dream / Lydia Millet. Soft Skull Press, 2008. 256 p.

ISBN 9781593761844

1. Human/animal relationships 2. Extinction (Biology) 3. Identity (Psychology) 4. Real estate developers 5. Mothers and sons 6. Gay fathers 7. Women 8. Loss (Psychology) 9. Rare and endangered animals 10. Men/women relations 11. Death 12. Suicidal behavior 13. Los Angeles, California 14. California 15. Psychological fiction 16. Literary fiction

LC 2007035242

Sequel: Ghost lights.

Real estate developer "T." finds his life thrown into chaos by his suicidal mother, homosexual father, and two deaths, and develops a growing obsession with vanishing species.

"For the reader, T.'s adventures with animals carry more emotional impact than any of the human encounters. They prompt the serious , sometimes convoluted but always moving meditations that are the spine if this strange, lovely novel." Chicago Sun-Times.

Millet, Lydia, 1968-

Ghost lights : a novel / Lydia Millet. W. W. Norton & Co., 2011. 256 p.

ISBN 9780393081718

1. United States. Internal Revenue Service Officials and employees 2. Midlife crisis in men 3. Extramarital affairs 4. Missing persons 5. Alienation in men 6. Women with disabilities 7. Father and adult daughter 8. Family relationships 9. Psychological fiction 10. Literary fiction

LC 2011026502

Sequel to: How the dead dream.

Sequel: Magnificence.

Suspecting his wife, Susan, is cheating on him with a younger coworker, Hal drunkenly volunteers to search for their missing boss who vanished in a tropical jungle in Belize.

Millet, Lydia, 1968-

Magnificence : a novel / Lydia Millet. W.W. Norton & Co., 2012. 256 p.

ISBN 9780393081701

1. Widows 2. Taxidermy 3. Life change events 4. Inheritance and succession 5. Shared housing 6. Mansions 7. Roommates 8. Identity (Psychology) 9. Loss (Psychology) 10. California 11. Pasadena, California 12. Literary fiction 13. Psychological fiction

LC 2012015145

Sequel to: Ghost lights.

National Book Critics Circle Award for Fiction finalist, 2012

After her husband's death, Susan Lindley moves into her late greatuncle's Pasadena mansion and restores his taxidermy collection while being joined in the residence by an equally strange human menagerie.

Millet, Lydia, 1968-

Sweet lamb of heaven : a novel / Lydia Millet. W. W. Norton & Company, 2016 256 p.

ISBN 9780393285543

1. Marital conflict 2. Mother and child 3. Threat (Psychology) 4. Political campaigns 5. Auditory hallucinations 6. Moving to a new state 7. Hotels 8. Paranoia 9. Coastal towns 10. Maine 11. Psychological suspense

LC 2016000554

Fleeing her cold and unfaithful husband, who has just launched his first campaign for political office, Lydia, accompanied by her 6-year-old daughter, races from Alaska to Maine and hides in a dingy motel as her husband's pursuit escalates from threatening to criminal.

"A top-notch tale of domestic paranoia that owes a debt to spooky psychological page-turners like Rosemary's Baby yet is driven by Millet's particular offbeat thinking." Kirkus.

Millhauser, Steven
* **Martin** Dressler : the tale of an American dreamer / Steve Millhauser. Crown Publishers, 1996. 294 p.
ISBN 051770319X
1. Gilded Age (1865-1898) 2. Obsession in men 3. Entrepreneurs 4. Hotel management 5. Brothers and sisters 6. Visions 7. German Americans 8. Hotels 9. Ambition in men 10. New York City 11. Historical fiction 12. Literary fiction
LC 96683
Pulitzer Prize for Fiction, 1997.
National Book Award for Fiction finalist, 1996
Portrays a businessman at the turn of the century, starting out as a clerk in his father's cigar store, and eventually becoming the proprietor of several hotels, looking at the lessons he learns on his rise to fortune, and after his collapse

Min, Anchee, 1957-
Becoming Madame Mao / Anchee Min. Houghton Mifflin, 2000. 340 p.
ISBN 0618004076
1. Chiang, Ch'ing, 1914-1991 2. Chinese Cultural Revolution (1966-1976) 3. Revolutions -- China 4. Ambition in women 5. Revenge 6. Married women 7. Jealousy in women 8. Politicians -- China 9. China -- History -- 20th century 10. China -- History -- Cultural Revolution, 1966-1976 11. Biographical fiction
LC 99058520
A fictional portrait of Jiang Ching follows her life from her youth as the unwanted daughter of a concubine, to her search for fame as an actress in Shanghai, to her marriage to revolutionary Mao Zedong, to her role in the turbulent Communist rule of China

"Min reveals the complexities of love, betrayal, and ambition in this lyrical and thrilling depiction of a once-powerless woman in the jaws of power, giving us an all-too-rare glimpse into the life of a woman within the machine." Ms.

Min, Anchee, 1957-
Empress Orchid / Anchee Min. Hougton Mifflin, 2004. xiii, 336 p.
ISBN 9780618068876
1. Cixi,, Empress dowager of China, 1835-1908 2. Forbidden City, Beijing, China. 3. Young women 4. Concubinage 5. Women rulers 6. Teenage girls 7. Courtesans 8. Rulers 9. Aristocracy 10. Courts and courtiers 11. Sexual slavery 12. Seduction 13. Jealousy 14. Men/women relations 15. Political science 16. China -- History -- Qing dynasty, 1644-1912 17. China -- History -- 19th century 18. China -- History -- 20th century 19. Biographical fiction 20. Historical fiction
LC 2003056891
Sequel: The last empress.
A fictional portrait of the last empress of China follows Orchid, a beautiful teenager from an aristocratic family, who is chosen to become a low-ranking concubine of the emperor and rises to a position of power in the Chinese court.

"The author has done a prodigious amount of on-site research to capture the glorious, hopeless last days of the Ching dynasty. . . . Readers will be enthralled by the gorgeously woven cultural tapestry and the psychologically astute portrait of the empress a talented girl from the provinces who married (way) up." Publishers Weekly.

Mina, Denise
* **Conviction** / Denise Mina. Mulholland Books, 2019. 376 p.
ISBN 9780316528504
1. Podcasts 2. Stay-at-home mothers 3. Intrigue 4. Family-killing 5. Crime 6. Social media 7. Runaway wives, husbands, etc 8. Judicial error 9. Yachts 10. Secrets 11. Murder investigation 12. Automobile travel 13. Life change events 14. Scotland 15. Europe 16. Thrillers and suspense
LC 2019930999
Originally published in Great Britain by Harvill Secker, an imprint of Penguin Random House UK: May 2019.
An upper-class Edinburgh housewife who enjoys listening to the sordid details of true-crime podcasts has her world turned upside down when a new podcast turns out to have connections to her own dark past.

Mina, Denise
The **dead** hour : a novel / Denise Mina. Little, Brown and Co., 2006. 352 p. Paddy Meehan novels
ISBN 0316735949
1. 1980s 2. Women journalists 3. Women lawyers 4. Murder investigation 5. Women political activists 6. Suicide 7. Bribery 8. Crime 9. Social classes 10. Family violence 11. Murder 12. Glasgow, Scotland 13. Scotland 14. Mysteries
LC 2006001610
Responding to a late-night disturbance call only to be reassured by a blonde women that nothing is wrong, Paddy Meehan is horrified to learn the following morning that the woman, a prosecution lawyer from an upper-crust community, has been murdered, a case that Paddy links to the death of a suicide victim.

"Surely Paddy Meehan is the most unlikely, and most realistic, investigator in recent crime fiction. . . . The Dead Hour is some kind of magnificent." The Wall Street Journal.

Mina, Denise
The **end** of the wasp season : a novel / Denise Mina. Little, Brown and Co., 2011. 390 p. Alex Morrow novels
ISBN 9780316069335
1. Policewomen 2. Pregnant women 3. Murder investigation 4. Violence against women 5. Mothers and sons 6. Fathers -- Death 7. Teenage boys 8. Suicide victims 9. Glasgow, Scotland 10. Mysteries 11. Police procedurals
LC 2011018242
"A Reagan Arthur book."
Theakston Old Peculier Crime Novel of the Year Award, 2012
Detective Inspector Alex Morrow uncovers clues in the savage murder of a young woman in a wealthy suburb of Glasgow that may ultimately be linked to the suicide of a notorious millionaire banker a hundred miles away.

"[I]nsightful observation ... makes Mina's novels so extraordinarily rich and unpredictable. There are the usual rewards in following the evidence... But there's greater satisfaction in watching Mina transform[a] seemingly simple cleaning woman into a complex character, possessed of great depths of feeling." New York Times Book Review.

Mina, Denise
Field of blood : a novel / Denise Mina. Little, Brown, 2005. 304 p. Paddy Meehan novels
ISBN 0316735930
1. 1980s 2. Murderers 3. Child murder victims 4. Injustice 5. Women impostors 6. Ethics 7. Engaged persons 8. Women journalists 9. Crimes against children 10. Child murderers 11. Deception 12. Ambition in women 13. Glasgow, Scotland 14. Scotland 15.

Mysteries

LC 2004023408

When her fiancé's cousin is implicated in the sensational murder of a young boy and a rival reporter leaks the story, fledgling Scottish journalist Paddy Meehan is forced to salvage her relationship with her future in-laws by clearing the cousin's name.

Mina, Denise

Gods and beasts : a novel / Denise Mina. Little, Brown and Co., 2013. 304 p. Alex Morrow novels

ISBN 9780316188524

1. Crimes against seniors 2. Bank robberies 3. Political corruption 4. Conspiracies 5. Deception 6. Policewomen 7. Murder investigation 8. Glasgow, Scotland 9. Mysteries 10. Police procedurals

LC 2012022241

First published: 2012.

Theakston Old Peculier Crime Novel of the Year Award, 2013

In the aftermath of an elderly man's murder during a holiday season bank robbery, DS Alex Morrow discovers that the bank's alarm system had been disabled before the robbery and uncovers a sinister political network that places the entire city at risk.

Mina, Denise

The **long** drop / Denise Mina. Little Brown & Co, 2016. 320 p.

ISBN 9780316380577

1. 1950s 2. Family killing 3. Crimes against women 4. Street life 5. Drinking 6. Murderers 7. Trials (Murder) 8. Crime 9. City life 10. Serial murders 11. Guilt 12. Murder victims 13. Criminals 14. Secrets 15. Glasgow, Scotland 16. Psychological suspense 17. Historical fiction

Centered around the "trial of the century" in Glasgow in 1950, the innocence and guilt of those involved is explored, starting with Peter Manuel who has been found guilty of a string of murders, starting with the Watt family, and is waiting to die by hanging.

"A terrific exploration of crime and oppression." Kirkus.

Mina, Denise

The **red** road / Denise Mina. Little Brown & Co, 2014. 304 p. Alex Morrow novels

ISBN 9780316188517

1. Women detectives 2. Arms dealers 3. Money laundering 4. Violence against women 5. Trials 6. Investigations 7. Lawyers 8. Glasgow, Scotland 9. Mysteries 10. Police procedurals

Preparing to testify against a violent arms dealer, police detective Alex Morrow finds her efforts challenged by a privileged Scottish lawyer's money laundering scheme and a vengeful woman prisoner.

"Mina's at the top of her game here, deftly unveiling the sad truths of the past and present to create a gritty must-read for fans of complex, psychological police procedurals." Booklist.

Mina, Denise

Slip of the knife : a novel / Denise Mina. Little, Brown and Co., 2008. 352 p. Paddy Meehan novels

ISBN 9780316015585

1. Irish Republican Army. 2. Murder investigation 3. Crimes against journalists 4. Women journalists 5. Murder 6. Paranoia 7. Expatriates 8. Glasgow, Scotland 9. Scotland 10. Mysteries

LC 2007042881

"First published in Great Britain as The last breath by Bantam Press, Paddy Meehan is no stranger to murder--as a reporter she lives at crime scenes--but nothing has prepared her for this visit from the police. Her former boyfriend and fellow journalist Terry Patterson has been found hooded and shot through the head. Paddy knows she will be of little help--she had not seen Terry in more than six months. So she is bewildered to learn that in his will he has left her his house and several suitcases full of notes. Drawn into a maze of secrets and lies, Paddy begins making connections to Terry's murder that no one else has seen, and soon finds herself trapped in the most important--and dangerous--story of her career.

"Mina excels at this kind of writing, the back-and-forth of competitors and colleagues, the way tension and love bind people uneasily. She's a leisurely writer; although Terry's murder opens the book, the action plays out slowly, and she lets us soak up the abundant ambience and personality." Boston Globe.

Mina, Denise

Still midnight / Denise Mina. Little, Brown and Co., 2010, c2009. 356 p. Alex Morrow novels

ISBN 9780316015639

1. Policewomen 2. Kidnapping investigation 3. Home invasions 4. Kidnapping 5. Mistaken identity 6. Ransom 7. Office politics 8. Glasgow, Scotland 9. Mysteries 10. Police procedurals

LC 2009022061

"A Reagan Arthur book."

First published: 2009.

Also published: Toronto : McArthur, 2009.

When three armed men invade a quiet Glasgow home and demand audience with a person who does not live there, Alex Morrow investigates their apparent mistake, a situation that escalates as violent acts are committed against the hostages.

"Mina's strength has always been her depiction of her characters' inner lives. With a background in health care, law, and criminology, she knows and can show readers the small choices, the subtle moral nuances that make one sibling a cop, another a gangster. In Still Midnight, she concentrates on such character studies, keeping the action the home invasion and kidnapping, their cause and resolution on a smaller scale than in previous works." Boston Globe.

Minato, Kanae, 1973-

Confessions / Kanae Minato ; translated from the Japanese by Stephen Snyder. Mulholland Books, 2014. 288 p.

ISBN 9780316200929

1. Accidental death 2. Middle school students 3. Bullying and bullies 4. Revenge 5. Middle schools 6. Mother and child 7. Single mothers 8. Women teachers 9. Japan 10. Psychological suspense 11. Translations -- Japanese to English

After calling off her engagement in wake of a tragic revelation, Yko Moriguchi had nothing to live for except her only child, four-year-old Manami. Now, following an accident on the grounds of the middle school where she teaches, Yko has given up and tendered her resignation. But first she has one last lecture to deliver. She tells a story that upends everything her students ever thought they knew about two of their peers, and sets in motion a maniacal plot for revenge. Narrated in alternating voices, with twists you'll never see coming, Confessions explores the limits of punishment, despair, and tragic love, culminating in a harrowing confrontation between teacher and student that will place the occupants of an entire school in danger.

"This award-winning debut novel is a creepy and mesmerizing psychological thriller that challenges the conventions of right vs. wrong, good vs. evil, and law vs. justice. There are no happy endings here, but Minato has pieced together an intriguing puzzle that will keep readers glued to their seats." Library Journal.

LIST OF FICTIONAL WORKS

Minh, Drew

Neon empire / Drew Minh. Rare Bird Books, 2019 220 p.
ISBN 9781947856769

1. Dystopias 2. Social media 3. Near future 4. Filmmakers 5. Missing women 6. Resorts 7. Femmes fatales 8. Terrorism 9. Bombings 10. Cyberpunk 11. Science fiction

"Minh creates a nonstop social media frenzy amid a rich cyberpunk landscape in this vivid debut...With shifting points of view and sharply detailed descriptions, Minh sets up a gripping, if uneven, dynamic between the characters, spicing the intrigue with action. Fans of SF thrillers will enjoy this colorful high-tech mystery and its echoes of the present-day hunger for likes, favorites, and going viral." Publishers Weekly.

Minot, Susan

Evening / Susan Minot. A. A. Knopf, 1998. 264 p.
ISBN 0375400370

1. Women sexagenarians 2. Senior women 3. Memory in senior women 4. Women with terminal illnesses 5. Regret in senior women 6. Redemption 7. Boston, Massachusetts 8. Psychological fiction 9. Literary fiction

LC 9815437

Now ailing and surrounded by her children, sixty-five-year-old Ann Grant Lord reminisces about a glorious summer weekend some forty years earlier during which she met and lost the love of her life.

"Ann Lord's life has been shaped by the men who have married her. As she lies on her deathbed, trying to make some sense of that life, a rediscovered balsam pillow evokes a Maine wedding, in 1954, where she fell in love for the first--and perhaps the last--time. This almost crude conceit produces a narrative of considerable ambition and complexity. . . . For heroine and reader alike, death's painful confusions are tempered by the spirited directness of Ann's younger self, as yet unscathed by time and experience." The New Yorker.

Miranda, Megan

The **last** house guest / Megan Miranda. Simon & Schuster, 2019. 352 p.
ISBN 9781501165375

1. Friends' death 2. Social classes 3. Suspicion 4. Rich families 5. Female friendship 6. Suicide 7. Murder investigation 8. Women murder suspects 9. Coastal towns 10. Tourism 11. Secrets 12. Small town life 13. Maine 14. Thrillers and suspense

LC 2018055887

When her longtime best friend is found murdered, a woman combs through her idyllic Maine tourist community to uncover local secrets and clear her name of suspicion.

Mirvis, Tova

The **outside** world / Tova Mirvis. Alfred A. Knopf, 2004. 320 p.
ISBN 1400041619

1. Jewish families 2. Orthodox Jews 3. Newlyweds 4. Parent and child 5. Culture conflict 6. Acculturation 7. Generation gap 8. Orthodox Judaism 9. Fundamentalism 10. Life change events 11. Belief and doubt 12. Faith 13. Communities 14. Brooklyn, New York City 15. New Jersey 16. Domestic fiction 17. Love stories

LC 2003058923

"Beneath the women's wigs and the men's black fedoras, Mirvis finds reservoirs of belief, doubt, ambition, folly, lust and the rest of the human equation." Washington Post Book World.

Mirza, Fatima Farheen, 1991-

A **place** for us / Fatima Farheen Mirza. SJP for Hogarth, 2018. 385 p.
ISBN 9781524763558

1. Weddings 2. Culture conflict 3. Muslim families 4. East Indian Americans 5. Belonging 6. Family relationships 7. Family secrets 8. California 9. Domestic fiction

A family caught between two cultures yields a resonant story of faith, tradition, identity and belonging.

Mishima, Yukio, 1925-1970

* The **decay** of the angel / Yukio Mishima ; translated from the Japanese by Edward G. Seidensticker A. A. Knopf, 1974. 236 p. Sea of fertility
ISBN 0394466136

1. Senior men -- Japan 2. Mentors -- Japan 3. Adopted children -- Japan 4. Japan 5. Psychological fiction 6. Translations -- Japanese to English

LC 73021525

Originally published 1971 as Tenin gosui.

During the last years of his life, Honda adopts an orphaned boy and teaches him about Japanese society and tradition.

Mishima, Yukio, 1925-1970

The **frolic** of the beasts / Yukio Mishima ; translated from the Japanese by Andrew Clare Vintage International, 2018, c1961. 166 p.
ISBN 9780525434153

1. Violence in men 2. Womanizers 3. Extramarital affairs 4. Married people 5. Young men 6. Human behavior 7. Rural life 8. Men/women relations 9. Japan 10. Translations -- Japanese to English
Originally published: 1961.

Translated into English for the first time, a gripping short novel about an affair gone wrong, from the acclaimed Japanese author, Yukio Mishima.

Mishima, Yukio, 1925-1970

Runaway horses / Yukio Mishima ; translated from the Japanese by Michael Gallagher A. A. Knopf, 1973. 421 p. Sea of fertility
ISBN 0394466187

1. Nationalism -- Japan 2. Terrorism -- Japan 3. Fanaticism -- Japan 4. Japan -- Politics and government -- 1912-1945 5. Psychological fiction 6. Translations -- Japanese to English

LC 72011039

Originally published in Japan as Homma (1969).

"Mishima uses the same literary artistry in this novel as in the first but changes the gently romantic tone to one of martial ideology with a weirdly beautiful emphasis on ritual suicide. In the interplay of entanglements between the two novels, each self-contained, the author experiments with the Buddhist doctrine of reincarnation." Booklist.

Mishima, Yukio, 1925-1970

The **sound** of waves / Yukio Mishima ; translated by Meredith Weatherby ; drawings by Yoshinori Kinoshita. Vintage Books, 1994. 182 p.
ISBN 0679752684

1. Fishers 2. Teenage boys -- Japan 3. Fathers and daughters 4. Teenage romance -- Japan 5. Teenage boy/girl relations 6. First loves 7. Love triangles 8. Gossiping and gossips 9. Rumor 10. Classism 11. Rich families 12. Courtship 13. Jealousy in teenage girls 14. Self-control 15. Persistence in teenage boys 16. Inheritance

and succession 17. Heirs and heiresses 18. Patriarchy -- Japan 19. Island life -- Japan 20. Villages -- Japan 21. Japan -- Social life and customs -- 20th century 22. Love stories 23. Translations -- Japanese to English

LC 94019314

A poor fisherman longs to meet the young and beautiful pearl diver who has enthralled his Japanese village.

Mishima, Yukio, 1925-1970

* **Spring** snow / Yukio Mishima ; translated from the Japanese by Michael Gallagher A. A. Knopf, 1972. 389 p. Sea of fertility

ISBN 0394442393

1. Aristocracy -- Japan 2. Upper class -- Japan 3. Japan 4. Psychological fiction 5. Translations -- Japanese to English

LC 74154940

Originally published in Japan as Haru no yuki (1968).

In Tokyo at the beginning of the 20th century, Satoko is betrothed to an imperial prince but immediately starts an affair with the son of a newly elite family.

Mishima, Yukio, 1925-1970

* The **temple** of dawn / Translated from the Japanese by E. Dale Saunders and Cecilia Segawa Seigle A. A. Knopf, 1973. 334 p. Sea of fertility

ISBN 0394466144

1. Senior men -- Japan 2. Reincarnation 3. Voyeurism 4. Psychological fiction 5. Translations -- Japanese to English

LC 73007277

Originally published in Japan as Akatsuki no tera (1970).

In the sequel to Runaway Horses, Honda goes to Bangkok and India in the 1940s to better understand reincarnation.

Mishima, Yukio, 1925-1970

The **temple** of the golden pavilion / translated by Ivan Morris ; drawings by Fumi Komatsu A. A. Knopf, 1959. 262 p.

ISBN 9784805306376

1. Zen Buddhist acolytes 2. Obsession 3. Monasticism and religious orders (Buddhist) 4. Arson -- Kyoto, Japan 5. Nihilism 6. Beauty 7. Buddhist temples -- Kyoto, Japan 8. Zen Buddhism -- Japan 9. Kyoto, Japan 10. Psychological fiction 11. Translations -- Japanese to English

LC 59007222

"Based on an actual incident in 1950, when a Zen Buddhist acolyte burned down a temple which was a national shrine. Like the real arsonist, the fictional Mizoguchi is ugly and a pathological stutterer, and long before his hostility becomes overt, has developed a compulsion to destroy whatever is morally or physically beautiful. As told by the young acolyte, this is a masterly description of the growth of an obsession and an acute interpretation of the deliberate symbolism underlying Mizoguchi's irrational, perverse behavior." Booklist.

Mistry, Rohinton, 1952-

A **fine** balance : a novel / Rohinton Mistry. A. A. Knopf, 1996, c1995. 603 p.

ISBN 0679446087

1. Political corruption 2. Poor people 3. Apartment houses 4. City life 5. Widows 6. Students 7. Tailors 8. Strangers 9. India -- History -- 1947-1971 10. India -- Politics and government -- 1947-1971 11. Literary fiction 12. Political fiction

LC 95-49317

Originally published: New York : Vintage Books, 1995.

ALA Notable Book, 1997.

Giller Prize, 1995.

Shortlisted for the Booker-McConnell Prize, 1996.

Shortlisted for the International IMPAC Dublin Literary Award, 1997

A portrait of India featuring four characters. Two are tailors who are forcibly sterilized, one is a student who emigrates, and the fourth is a widowed seamstress who decides to hang on. A tale of cruelty, political thuggery and despair by an Indian from Toronto, author of *Such a Long Journey*.

"It is impossible not to seethe at the injustices of the police state, and impossible not to take these characters passionately to heart: this is a novel that can stand with the best of Dickens." The New Yorker.

Mitchard, Jacquelyn

The **deep** end of the ocean / Jacquelyn Mitchard. Viking, 1996. 434 p.

ISBN 0670865796

1. Missing children 2. Parents of missing children 3. Class reunions 4. Family relationships 5. Marital conflict 6. Family reunions 7. Coping 8. Kidnapping 9. Loss (Psychology) 10. Guilt in boys 11. Prayer 12. Chicago, Illinois 13. Thrillers and suspense 14. Domestic fiction

LC 95-26234

Sequel: No time to wave goodbye.

Nine years after three-year-old Ben Cappadora's kidnapping, a twelve-year-old boy knocks at the door of the Cappadora house, looking for yardwork.

"One of the most remarkable things about this rich, moving and altogether stunning first novel is Mitchard's assured command of narrative structure and stylistic resources. Her story about a child's kidnapping and its enduring effects upon his parents, siblings, and extended family is a blockbuster read." Publishers Weekly.

Mitchard, Jacquelyn

No time to wave goodbye : a novel / Jacquelyn Mitchard. Random House, 2009. 240 p.

ISBN 9781400067749

1. Missing persons 2. Kidnapping 3. Family relationships 4. Documentary films 5. Coping 6. Families of missing persons 7. Familial love 8. Loyalty 9. Motherhood 10. Chicago, Illinois 11. California 12. Thrillers and suspense

LC 2009012905

Sequel to: The deep end of the ocean.

In a book that revisits the family featured in the author's best-selling The Deep End of the Ocean, the Cappadora family is once again in peril after adult son Vincent's acclaimed film about the families of abductees leads to Beth Cappadora once again leading her family in search of the truth that can save a life.

"Mitchard charts a tormented family dynamic with shocking ease. This action-packed and emotionally rich drama is every bit as satisfying as its predecessor." Publishers Weekly.

Mitchell, David (David Stephen)

Black Swan Green : a novel / David Mitchell. Random House, 2006. 294 p.

ISBN 9781400063796

1. 1980s 2. Thirteen-year-old boys 3. Stutterers 4. Teenage boys -- Psychology 5. Small town life 6. Family problems 7. Bullying and bullies 8. Villages 9. Change (Psychology) 10. England -- Social life and customs -- 20th century 11. Worcestershire, England 12. Literary fiction 13. Coming-of-age stories

LC 2005052914

ALA Notable Book, 2007.

Follows a single year in the life of thirteen-year-old Jason Taylor as he grows up in what is for him the sleepiest village in Worcestershire, England, in 1982.

"The author does not pull any punches when it comes to the casual cruelty that adolescent boys can inflict on one another, but it is this very brutality that underscores the sweetness of which they are also capable. With its British slang and complex twists and turns, this title is not a selection for reluctant readers, but teens who enjoy multifaceted coming-of-age stories will be richly rewarded." School Library Journal.

Mitchell, David (David Stephen)

* The **bone** clocks : a novel / David Mitchell. Random House, 2014. 624 p.

ISBN 9781400065677

1. 20th century 2. 21st century 3. Paranormal phenomena 4. Mystics 5. Time 6. Voyages and travels 7. Imaginary wars and battles 8. Mortality 9. Secrets 10. Synchronicity (Paranormal phenomena) 11. Interpersonal relations 12. Men/women relations 13. Literary fiction 14. Contemporary fantasy

LC 2014008517

ALA Notable Book, 2015.

World Fantasy Award, 2015.

Beginning in 1984 and moving in linear fashion through the years before ending in the 2040s, this complex, layered novel interweaves several different narratives to tell the story of a secret war between those who would steal souls and those who try to stop them. But it's also the story of Holly Sykes, who belongs to neither of these groups but whose life is nevertheless bound up in them. An expansive, globe-trotting book that takes on themes of aging, youth, and death, The Bone Clocks also features characters who have appeared in author David Mitchell's other books and incorporates genres from absolute realism to heady fantasy. -- Description by Shauna Griffin.

"From gritty realism to far-out fantasy, each section has its own charm and surprises." Publishers Weekly.

Mitchell, David (David Stephen)

* **Cloud** atlas : a novel / David Mitchell. Random House, 2004. 509 p.

ISBN 9780375507250

1. Fate and fatalism 2. Reincarnation 3. Musicians 4. People who are blind 5. Colonialism 6. Racism 7. Conspiracies 8. Deception 9. Exploitation 10. Clones and cloning 11. California 12. Great Britain 13. Korea 14. Experimental fiction 15. Literary fiction

LC 2003069314

ALA Notable Book, 2005.

British Book Award for Literary Fiction, 2005.

British Book Award for the Richard & Judy Best Read of the Year, 2005.

Shortlisted for the Man Booker Prize, 2004.

National Book Critics Circle Award for Fiction finalist, 2004

Many characters live out their lives from 1850 to a postapocalyptic Iron Age Hawaii and eventually their disparate lives intertwine.

"The author presents six narratives that evoke an array of genres, from Melvillean high-seas drama to California noir and dystopian fantasy. There is a nave clerk on a nineteenth-century Polynesian voyage; an aspiring composer who insinuates himself into the home of a syphilitic genius; a journalist investigating a nuclear plant; a publisher with a dangerous bestseller on his hands; and a cloned human being created for slave labor. These five stories are bisected and arranged around a sixth, the oral history of a post-apocalyptic island, which forms the heart of the novel. Only after this do the second halves of the stories fall into place, pulling the novels themes into focus: the ease with which one group

enslaves another, and the constant rewriting of the past by those who control the present. Against such forces, Mitchells characters reveal a quiet tenacity." The New Yorker.

Mitchell, David (David Stephen)

Slade House / David Mitchell. Random House, 2015. 224 p.

ISBN 9780812998689

1. Houses 2. Missing persons 3. Imaginary creatures 4. Supernatural 5. Telepathy 6. Twins 7. Misfits (Persons) 8. Architecture 9. England 10. Literary fiction 11. Horror

Follows the narrative of five different people who disappear through a mysterious door in an unassuming alleyway that leads to Slade House, owned by a peculiar brother and sister, and vanish completely from the outside world.

Mitchell, David (David Stephen)

* The **thousand** autumns of Jacob De Zoet : a novel / David Mitchell. Random House, 2010. 496 p.

ISBN 9781400065455

1. 19th century 2. East and West 3. Trading posts 4. Islands 5. Men/women relations 6. Cultural differences 7. Dutch in Japan 8. Japan -- History -- 1787-1868 9. Deshima (Nagasaki-shi, Japan) 10. Historical fiction 11. Literary fiction

LC 2009047296

ALA Notable Book, 2011.

Shortlisted for the Walter Scott Prize for Historical Fiction, 2011

Dispatched to the influential Japanese port of Dejima in 1799, ambitious clerk Jacob de Zoet resolves to earn enough money to deserve his wealthy fiancee, an effort that is challenged by his relationship with the midwife daughter of a Samurai.

"Mitchell's meticulously reconstructed the lost world of Edo-era Japan, and in doing so he's created his most conventional but most emotionally engaging novel yet: it's as if an acrobatic but show-offy performance artist, adept at mimicry, ventriloquism and cerebral literary gymnastics, had decided to do an old-fashioned play and, in the process, proved his chops as an actor." New York Times.

Mitchell, Margaret, 1900-1949

* **Gone** with the wind / Margaret Mitchell. Warner Books, 1993, c1936. 1024 p.

ISBN 9780446365383

1. American Civil War era (1861-1865) 2. Reconstruction (United States history) 3. Love triangles 4. Survival 5. War 6. Women 7. Husband and wife 8. Married people 9. Plantations 10. Civil war 11. United States Civil War, 1861-1865 12. Georgia -- History -- Civil War, 1861-1865 13. United States -- History -- Civil War, 1861-1865 14. Georgia -- Social life and customs -- 19th century 15. War stories 16. Epic fiction 17. Historical fiction 18. Love stories 19. Modern classics 20. Southern fiction

Sequel: Scarlett, by Alexandra Ripley (1991).

Originally published: New York : Scribner, 1936.

Pulitzer Prize for Fiction, 1937.

A spoiled young Southern belle vows to rebuild her family plantation home after the Civil War and is swept off her feet by a man who infuriates her.

Mitford, Nancy, 1904-1973

* The **pursuit** of love ; and, Love in a cold climate / Nancy Mitford. Modern Library, 1994. xiv, 617 p.

ISBN 9780679600909

1. Rural life 2. Mate selection for women 3. Young women 4. Rich families 5. Aristocracy 6. Upper class 7. Snobs and snobbishness

8. National characteristics, English 9. Manners and customs 10. England -- Social life and customs -- 20th century 11. Satirical fiction 12. Modern classics

LC 93043632

The snobbery and false values of the English country nobility are satirized in these two love stories involving the well-established Radlett and Hampton families.

Miyamoto, Teru

Kinshu = Autumn brocade / Teru Miyamoto ; translated from the Japanese by Roger K. Thomas. New Directions Book, 2005. 224 p.

ISBN 0811216330

1. Former wives 2. Former husbands 3. Divorced persons 4. Mothers 5. Mothers of children with disabilities 6. Suicide 7. Remarriage 8. Marriage 9. Marital conflict 10. Extramarital affairs 11. Grief in women 12. Grief 13. Forgiveness 14. Loss (Psychology) 15. Letters 16. Epistolary novels 17. Domestic fiction 18. Psychological fiction 19. Translations -- Japanese to English

LC 2005020111

Original Japanese language edition published : Tokyo : Shinchosha, 1982.

"Though brief, this novel features a distinctly compelling narrative; credit Thomas's effective translation." Library Journal.

Mizushima, Margaret

Burning ridge / Margaret Mizushima. Crooked Lane Books, 2018. 280 p. Timber Creek K-9 novels

ISBN 9781683317784

1. Police dogs 2. Policewomen 3. Women and dogs 4. Veterinarians 5. Single fathers 6. Family secrets 7. Murder 8. Murder investigation 9. Couples 10. Men/women relations 11. Colorado 12. Police procedurals 13. Mysteries

Investigating the discovery of a shallow grave on Colorado's scenic Redstone Ridge, officer Mattie Cobb; her K-9 partner, Robo; and local veterinarian Cole Walker discover additional remains before realizing that the killer is targeting Mattie.

Mizushima, Margaret

* **Killing** trail / Margaret Mizushima. Crooked Lane Books, 2015. 352 p. Timber Creek K-9 novels

ISBN 9781629533810

1. Small town life 2. Girl murder victims 3. Murder investigation 4. Policewomen 5. Police dogs 6. Drug traffic 7. Women and dogs 8. Veterinarians 9. Single fathers 10. Secrets 11. Fathers and daughters 12. Colorado 13. Mysteries 14. Police procedurals

When she is assigned to investigate the murder of a young girl, Timber Creek Officer Mattie Cobb and her partner, K-9 police dog Robo, discovers that her hometown holds many secrets and that the daughter of a local veterinarian and single father holds the key to solving this mystery that could get them all killed.

Mizushima, Margaret

Stalking ground / Margaret Mizushima. Crooked Lane Books, 2016. 320 p. Timber Creek K-9 novels

ISBN 9781629538334

1. Small town life 2. Women murder victims 3. Murder investigation 4. Serial murderers 5. Blizzards 6. Policewomen 7. Police dogs 8. Women and dogs 9. Veterinarians 10. Single fathers 11. Secrets 12. Fathers and daughters 13. Colorado 14. Mysteries 15. Police procedurals

When Deputy Ken Brody's sweetheart goes missing in the mountains outside Timber Creek, Mattie Cobb and her K-9 partner Robo are

called to search. But it's mid-October and a dark snow storm is brewing over the high country. And they're already too late. By the time they find her body, the storm has broken and the snow is coming down hard. While Brody hikes down to bring back the forensics team and veterinarian Cole Walker gathers supplies to protect them from the storm, Mattie and Robo find themselves alone, guarding the gravesite overnight in the dead of the early winter. And that's only the first long, dark night in a series of them, because as their investigation develops, Mattie, Robo, Brody, and Cole find themselves in the middle of the killer's stalking ground--where the hunters have just become the hunted.

"Realistic characters and believable plot twists distinguish Mizushimas brisk sequel to 2015s Killing Trail." Publishers Weekly.

Modesitt, L. E., Jr., 1943-

The **one-eyed** man : a fugue, with winds and accompaniment / L. E. Modesitt, Jr. Tor Books, 2013. 368 p.

ISBN 9780765335449

1. Ecologists 2. Space colonies 3. Nature -- Effect of humans on 4. Ecological disturbances 5. Business consultants 6. Corporate intrigue 7. Whistle blowers 8. Divorced men 9. Longevity 10. Far future 11. Secrets 12. Hard science fiction 13. Science fiction

LC 2013022128

"A Tom Doherty Associates book."

In a far-future world where the human race is colonizing planets that are ecologically compromised, Dr. Paulo Verano is hired to assess the human impact on the planet of Stittara and endures dangerous elements to investigate mysterious airborne organisms.

Moehringer, J. R., 1964-

Sutton / J. R. Moehringer. Hyperion, 2012. 352 p.

ISBN 9781401323141

1. Sutton, Willie 2. Bank robbers 3. Reminiscing in old age 4. Criminals 5. Journalists 6. Men/women relations 7. Brooklyn, New York City 8. Biographical fiction 9. Historical fiction

LC 2011052473

A fictionalized account of Willie Sutton, one of the most notorious criminals in American history, traces his life, his doomed romance with his first love, and his surprise pardon on Christmas Eve in 1969.

Moggach, Deborah

Tulip fever / Deborah Moggach. Delacorte Press ;, 2000, c1999. 281 p.

ISBN 9780385334891

1. 17th century 2. Portrait artists 3. Tulips 4. Artists -- Netherlands -- History -- 17th century 5. Portraits 6. Deception 7. Husband and wife 8. Men/women relations 9. Extramarital affairs 10. Interpersonal attraction 11. Amsterdam, Netherlands -- History -- 17th century 12. Netherlands -- History -- Wars of Independence, 1556-1648 13. Historical fiction

LC 99-042048

Originally published: London : Heinemann, 1999.

In Amsterdam in the 1630s, a young wife escapes her stifling marriage to an older man into the arms of the artist who is hired to paint their portrait. 3

"A novel set in 17th-century Amsterdam. ſr Moggach's book reads like a thriller: it's a novel that ponders what it means to push things too far, and keenly examines what the consequences might be." New York Times Book Review

LIST OF FICTIONAL WORKS

Mohamed, Nadifa, 1981-
* The **orchard** of lost souls : a novel / Nadifa Mohamed. Farrar, Straus & Giroux, 2014, c2013. 336 p.
ISBN 9780374209148
1. 1980s 2. Civil war 3. War and society 4. Women -- Somalia 5. Nine-year-old girls 6. Women soldiers 7. Widows 8. Violence 9. Somalia 10. Political fiction
LC 2013034411
Originally published: London : Simon & Schuster, 2013.
Somerset Maugham Award, 2014.
The fall of Somalia in the late 1980s is witnessed firsthand by three women in the province of Hargeisa, including Deqo, who left a refugee existence for city security; widow Kawsar, who has been brutalized by the police; and Filsan, a young soldier who helps suppress the growing rebellion.
"Mohamed evokes the burgeoning unrest of a city on the brink of chaos with vibrant, evocative language and imagery, crafting a story that will stay with readers long after the final page is turned." Booklist.

Molloy, Aimee
The **perfect** mother : a novel / Aimee Molloy. Harper, 2018. 317 p.
ISBN 9780062696793
1. New mothers 2. Infant kidnapping victims 3. Motherhood 4. Female friendship 5. Secrets 6. Single mothers 7. Summer 8. City life 9. Brooklyn, New York City 10. New York City 11. Psychological suspense
Librarians' Choice (Australia), 2018.
A group of new moms who all gave birth in the month of May gather twice weekly at the park to offer support and companionship before one of the babies is shatteringly abducted, subjecting his traumatized mother to invasive questions and prompting the others to go to increasingly risky lengths to help.

Momaday, N. Scott, 1934-
The **ancient** child : a novel / N. Scott Momaday. Double-day, 1989. 313 p.
ISBN 9780385279727
1. Billy,, the Kid 2. Kiowa women shamans 3. Native American mysticism 4. Middle-aged men -- Relations with younger women 5. Sexuality -- Spiritual aspects 6. Native American painters 7. Nineteen-year-old women 8. Kiowa Indians -- Religion 9. Vision quests 10. Nervous breakdown 11. Men -- Spiritual life 12. Culture conflict 13. Oklahoma 14. Love stories 15. Literary fiction 16. Mythological fiction
LC 89031304
Based on an Indian myth about a boy who turns into a bear, this mystic novel concerns a young artist who confronts his unusual destiny with the aid of the beautiful medicine woman who loves him.

Momaday, N. Scott, 1934-
House made of dawn / N. Scott Momaday. Perennial Classics, 1999, c1968. 198 p.
ISBN 0060931949
1. 1940s 2. 1950s 3. Indian reservations 4. Culture conflict 5. Native American veterans 6. Native American men 7. Indians of North America 8. Literary fiction
Originally published: New York : Harper & Row, 1968.
Pulitzer Prize for Fiction, 1969.
A young American Indian returning from World War II searches for his place on his old reservation and in urban society.

Moniz, Tomas
Big familia / Tomas Moniz. Acre Books, 2019. 192 p.
ISBN 9781946724229
1. Divorced men 2. Bisexual men 3. Commitment (Psychology) 4. Teenage pregnancy 5. Children of divorced parents 6. Gay couples 7. Race relations 8. Gentrification of cities 9. Fathers -- Death 10. Life change events 11. Extended families 12. Men/men relations 13. Psychological fiction
Follows Juan Gutierrez, a self-employed single father, as he navigates a tumultuous year of inescapable change.

Monroe, Mary
Bad blood / Mary Monroe. Dafina Books, 2015 336 p.
ISBN 9780758274762
1. Success (Concept) 2. Rich families 3. Mate selection 4. Perfection 5. Trust 6. Men/women relations 7. Revenge 8. African Americans 9. Betrayal 10. Drama lit 11. African American fiction
When the man of her dreams, Seth Garrett, dumps her because of her far-from-perfect relatives, beautiful and successful Rachel McNeal, done with forgiving and forgetting, sets out to take his world apart piece by piece.

Monroe, Mary Alice,
Beach house reunion / Mary Alice Monroe. Simon & Schuster, 2018 416 p. Isle of Palms novels
ISBN 9781501193293
1. Aunt and niece 2. Vacation homes 3. Self-fulfillment in women 4. Surfing 5. Reunions 6. Female friendship 7. College graduates 8. Intergenerational relations 9. South Carolina 10. Isle of Palms, South Carolina 11. Women's lives and relationships 12. Southern fiction
Cara Rutledge returns to her Southern home on the idyllic Isle of Palms. Everything is comfortingly the same, yet each detail is rife with painful memories. Only through reconnecting with family, friends, and the rhythms of the lowcountry can Cara release the hold of the past and open herself to the possibility of a new love, career, and hope for the future.

Monroe, Mary
* **God** don't like ugly / Mary Monroe. Dafina Books, 2000. 340 p., 23 cm. God don't novels
ISBN 1575666073
1. Overweight girls 2. African American girls 3. Child abuse victims 4. Girls -- Friendship 5. Best friends 6. Single mothers 7. Father-separated families 8. Ohio 9. Coming-of-age stories 10. Drama lit 11. African American fiction 12. Mainstream fiction
LC 2001274884
Sequel: God still don't like ugly.
Frightened and ashamed, budding teenager Annette Goode, a shy, awkward, overweight girl hides the devastating secret that her mother's boarder has been sexually abusing her, until her life is changed forever by the beautiful and worldly Rhoda Nelson.

Monroe, Mary
God still don't like ugly / Mary Monroe. Dafina Books, 2003. 320 p. God don't novels
ISBN 1575669129
1. Fathers and daughters 2. African American men/women relations 3. Self-discovery 4. Overweight African American women 5. African American young women 6. African American women 7. Adult child abuse victims 8. African American fathers and daughters 9. Friendship 10. Love 11. Ohio 12. Miami, Florida 13. Drama lit 14. African American fiction 15. Mainstream fiction
LC 2003103715

Sequel to: God don't like ugly.

Sequel: God don't play.

Annette, who has recently reconciled with the father she never knew, finds solace with her childhood sweetheart after a dark secret from her past destroys her engagement and a troubled friend unexpectedly comes back into her life.

Monsarrat, Nicholas, 1910-1979

The **cruel** sea / Nicholas Monsarrat. Burford Books, 2000, c1951. 509 p.

ISBN 9781580800464

1. Second World War era (1939-1945) 2. Military campaigns 3. World War II 4. Naval battles 5. North Atlantic Ocean 6. Sea stories 7. Adventure stories 8. War stories

Originally published: New York :

Based on the author's own vivid experiences, The Cruel Sea is the nail-biting story of the crew of HMS Compass Rose, a corvette assigned to protect convoys during World War II. Darting back and forth across the icy North Atlantic, Compass Rose played a deadly cat-and-mouse game with packs of German U-boats lying in wait beneath the ocean waves. Packed with tension and vivid descriptions of agonizing U-boat hunts, this tale of the most bitter and chilling campaign of the war tells of ordinary men who had to master their own fears before they could face a brutal menace-one which would strike without warning from the deep.

Montag, Kassandra

After **the** flood : a novel / Kassandra Montag. William Morrow, 2019. 400 p.

ISBN 9780062889362

1. Post-apocalypse 2. Floods 3. Survival (after environmental catastrophe) 4. Mothers and daughters 5. Mothers of kidnapping victims 6. Pirates 7. Grief in women 8. Ocean travel 9. Despair 10. Quests 11. Fishing 12. Violence 13. Apocalyptic fiction 14. Science fiction

LC 2018044621

A tale set in an anarchic near-future America of mountaintop colonies surrounded by rising oceans finds an independent woman trading for supplies and information about the daughter who was stolen from her eight years earlier.

Montclair, Allison

The **right** sort of man / Allison Montclair. Minotaur Books, 2019. 336 p.

ISBN 9781250178367

1. 1940s 2. Postwar life 3. Matchmakers 4. Women amateur detectives 5. Former spies 6. Murder suspects 7. Murder investigation 8. World War II -- Influence 9. Women-owned businesses 10. London, England 11. Historical mysteries

LC 2019004332

Organizing a matchmaking business together in spite of their differences, two women from 1946 London find their promising company endangered when one of their clients is arrested for the murder of another.

"Fans of M. C. Beaton will relish the wit, and followers of Susan Elia MacNeal and Jacqueline Winspear will enjoy the depth and the period detail." Booklist.

Montero, Mayra, 1952-

Dancing to "Almendra" / Mayra Montero ; translated by Edith Grossman. Farrar, Straus and Giroux, 2007, c2005. 2725 p.

ISBN 0374102775

1. 1950s 2. Journalists 3. Twenties (Age) 4. Zoo keepers 5. Women circus performers 6. Murder investigation 7. Organized crime 8.

Murder 9. Family secrets 10. Men/women relations 11. Crime bosses 12. Violence 13. Havana, Cuba 14. Historical mysteries 15. Translations -- Spanish to English

LC 2006012552

Originally published: Guaynabo, Puerto Rico : Alfaguara, 2005.

Cuban journalist Joaquin Porrata believes there is a connection between the assassination of Mafia boss Albert Anastasia and a dead hippopotamus in the Havana zoo, and Joaquin finds himself caught up in a fight for control of the lucrative casino operations in pre-Castro Cuba.

"Montero probes [the] depths of inner ruin with the gelid calm and lucid exactitude that belies her characters' tortured passions and the story's tropical settings . . . [Her] sentences, planed to a soothing smoothness by Spanish translator extraordinaire Edith Grossman, slide up against each other, inexorably building to a truly tragicand truly disturbingending. [Montero is] a worthy peer for the likes of Mario Vargas Llosa." San Francisco Chronicle.icle

Montgomery, Jess

The **widows** / Jess Montgomery. Minotaur Books, 2019. 320 p. Kinship novels

ISBN 9781250184528

1. Jones,, Mother, 1837-1930 2. Collins, Maude, 1893-1972 3. 1920s 4. Widows 5. Women sheriffs 6. Coal miners 7. Prohibition 8. Communities 9. Corruption 10. Murder victims 11. Missing women 12. Secrets 13. Betrayal 14. Ohio 15. Appalachian Region 16. Historical fiction

LC 2018029795

Vowing revenge against her sheriff husband's killers in 1924 Ohio, Lily offers help to a fellow widow and uncovers dangerous evidence revealing her husband's corrupt secret life and the complexities that triggered his death.

"Inspired by the true story of Maude Collins, Ohio's first female sheriff, and prominent labor and community organizer Mary Harris Mother Jones, Montgomery's debut novel features two tough-as-nails, strong-willed women whose empathy leaves a lasting impression. A simultaneous examination of women's rights, coal mining, prohibition, and Appalachian life, make this is a fantastic choice for historical fiction fans." Library Journal.

Montimore, Margarita

Oona out of order / Margarita Montimore. Flatiron Books, 2020. 280 p.

ISBN 9781250236609

1. Time travel 2. New Year's Eve 3. Women 4. Memories 5. Reality 6. Self acceptance in women 7. Families 8. Friendship 9. Bands (Music) 10. Science fiction 11. Love stories

LC 2019036420

Published in the UK as "The rearranged life of Oona Lockhart" by Orion, 2020.

As the countdown to the New Year begins, soon-to-be-19 Oona Lockhart faints and awakens 32 years in the future in her 51-year-old body; and, greeted by a friendly stranger in a beautiful house she's told is her own, Oona learns that with each passing year she will leap to another age at random.

"Read this to get a bit lost, to root for a character with a strong love for herself, and to connect on a deeply human level with the fear of leading an incomplete life." Kirkus.

Moody, David, 1970-

Hater / David Moody. Thomas Dunne Books, 2009, c2006. 288 p. Hater novels

ISBN 9780312384838

1. Murder victims 2. Murderers 3. Violence 4. Survival 5. Chaos 6.

Family relationships 7. Hate 8. Dystopias 9. Regression (Civilization) 10. England 11. Horror 12. Apocalyptic fiction

LC 2008036519

Sequel : Dog blood.

Originally published: Halesowen, England : Infected Books, 2006.

When ordinary people throughout the world suddenly transform into violent killers, one man struggles to retain normalcy and recognize who is trustworthy in a society escalating out of control.

"The novel moves at a deliberate, relentless pace, feeding readers just enough information to keep them perplexed and paranoid, and the depiction of a society being rent at the seams by violence rings true. Moody creates some truly chilling scenes, but there are also flashes of black comedy. At times savagely brutal--the moments of outrageous violence may be considered over-the-top by some readers--but engrossing and effective." Kirkus.

Moody, Rick

Right livelihoods : three novellas / Rick Moody. Little, Brown, 2007. 256 p.

ISBN 0316166340

1. Disasters 2. Drugs 3. Psychotropic drugs 4. Insurance -- Agents 5. Interpersonal relations 6. Racism 7. New York City 8. Literary fiction 9. Anthologies

LC 2006026937

Presents three novellas, including "K&K," about an office manager who receives frightening notes in a suggestion box, and "The Albertine Notes," in which a mind-altering drug dominates life in post-apocalypse New York City.

"The unreliable and eccentric characters that so often populate Moody's novels again effectively remind us of the nation's collective hysteria. His convoluted narrative may challenge the patience of some readers, but those who persist will find it rewarding." Library Journal.

Moor, Jessica

The **keeper** / Jessica Moor. Viking, 2020. 336 p.

ISBN 9780143134527

1. Partner abuse 2. Family violence 3. Women murder victims 4. Women's shelters 5. Police 6. Murder investigation 7. Secret identity 8. England 9. Mysteries 10. Police procedurals

LC 2019055793

A detective looking into the apparent suicide of a woman who lived at a domestic violence shelter discovers evidence that she was not who she appeared to be and sets out to prove it was actually murder.

"Set in rural England, Moor's clever debut presents a movingly sympathetic portrait of the victims of domestic violence." Publishers Weekly.

Moor, Margriet de., 1941-

The **storm** / Margriet de Moor ; translated from the Dutch by Carol Brown Janeway. Alfred A. Knopf, 2010, c2005. 257 p.

ISBN 9780307264947

1. 1950s 2. Floods -- Netherlands 3. Disaster victims -- Netherlands 4. Sisters -- Netherlands 5. Netherlands 6. Historical fiction 7. Psychological fiction

LC 2009037578

Originally published in the Netherlands as De Verdronkene in 2005.

The 1953 hurricane destruction of southwest Netherlands finds Armada inadvertently triggering fateful events when on the morning of the storm she switches places with her identical sister Lidy, inadvertently placing the latter in the path of danger.

"It's hard to resist using the word symphonic to describe this exquisitely composed, piercingly moving story. De Moor continues to scale increasingly impressive heights." Kirkus.

Moore, Alan, 1953-

Jerusalem : a novel / Alan Moore. Liveright Publishing Corporation, 2016 1184 p.

ISBN 9781631491344

1. Space and time 2. Slums 3. Mortality 4. Public housing 5. Eternity 6. Ancestors 7. Working class 8. Aristocracy 9. Brothers and sisters 10. Angels 11. Demons 12. Humans 13. Dead 14. Fate and fatalism 15. England 16. Northamptonshire, England 17. Literary fiction 18. Fantasy fiction

LC 2016014957

A novel employing a kaleidoscope of literary forms and styles provides a rich cast of characters includes the living, the dead, the celestial, and the infernal in an intricately woven tapestry that presents a vision of an absolute and timeless human reality in all of its exquisite, comical and heartbreaking splendor.

"Moore bundles all his ruminations about space, time, life, and death into an immense interconnected narrative that spans all human existence within the streets of his native Northampton, U.K. Reading this sprawling collection of words and ideas isnt an activity; its an experience." Publishers Weekly.

Moore, Alison, 1971-

The **lighthouse** / Alison Moore. Salt Publishing, 2012. 183 p.

ISBN 9781907773174

1. Middle-aged men 2. Memories -- Psychological aspects 3. Abandonment (Psychology) 4. Compulsive behavior in men 5. Neuroses in men 6. Thought and thinking 7. Separated men (Marital relations) 8. Vacations 9. Germany 10. Psychological fiction 11. Literary fiction

Shortlisted for the Man Booker Prize, 2012.

On the outer deck of a North Sea ferry stands Futh, a middle-aged and newly separated man, on his way to Germany for a restorative walking holiday. As he contemplates an earlier trip to Germany and the things he has done in his life, he does not foresee the potentially devastating consequences of things not done.

Moore, Brian, 1921-1999

The **lonely** passion of Judith Hearne / Brian Moore. New York Review of Books, 2010, c1955. 228 p.

ISBN 9781590173497

1. Catholic women 2. Middle-aged women 3. Loneliness in women 4. Single women 5. Belfast, Northern Ireland 6. Northern Ireland 7. Literary fiction

Originally published: New York : Little, Brown, 1955.

Judith Hearne is an unmarried woman of a certain age who has come down in society. She has few skills and is full of the prejudices and pieties of her genteel Belfast upbringing. But Judith has a secret life. And she is just one heartbreak away from revealing it to the world.

Moore, Christopher, 1957-

A **dirty** job : a novel / Christopher Moore. William Morrow, 2006. 400 p.

ISBN 0060590270

1. Fear in men 2. Death (Personification) 3. Life change events 4. Married men 5. Single fathers 6. Hypochondriacs 7. Fathers and daughters 8. Married women -- Death 9. Widowers 10. Death 11. Occupations 12. San Francisco, California 13. Satirical fiction

LC 2005057501

Sequel : Secondhand souls.

Charlie Asher, a neurotic and anxious hypochondriac who hates change, confronts the challenges of being a widower and a single parent when his wife dies of a freak medical condition on the day his new daughter, Sophie, is born.

"Much of the pleasure of Moore's tale resides not only in the ingeniously unpredictable events but also in the prickly vitality of his language. Striking figures of speech . . . and aphorisms grace the text." Washington Post Book World.

Moore, Christopher, 1957-

Noir / Christopher Moore. William Morrow, 2018 339 p.

ISBN 9780062433978

1. Second World War era (1939-1945) 2. 1940s 3. Femmes fatales 4. Bartenders 5. Rescues 6. Secrecy in government 7. UFOs 8. San Francisco, California 9. Satirical fiction 10. Farcical fiction 11. Noir fiction 12. Pulp fiction

A mad-cap noir set on the streets of post-World War II San Francisco follows a smitten barkeep and unofficial fixer-for-hire as he investigates his paramour's disappearance amid a series of weird events involving an unidentified flying object and a mysterious plane crash.

Moore, Christopher, 1957-

Sacre bleu : a comedy of art / Christopher Moore. William Morrow, 2012 416 p.

ISBN 9780061779749

1. Gogh, Vincent van, 1820-1888 2. Toulouse-Lautrec, Henri de, 1864-1901 3. Belle Epoque (1871-1914) 4. 19th century 5. 1890s 6. Suicide investigation 7. Art 8. Painters 9. Blue (Color) 10. Humorous stories 11. Mysteries

Baker-turned-painter Lucien Lessard and bon vivant Henri Toulouse-Lautrec vow to discover the truth behind the untimely death of their friend Vincent van Gogh, which leads them on a surreal odyssey and brothel-crawl deep into the art world of late-nineteenth-century Paris.

Moore, Christopher, 1957-

The **serpent** of Venice : a novel / Christopher Moore. William Morrow, 2014. 326 p. Fool novels

ISBN 9780061779763

1. Assassination plots 2. Fools and jesters 3. British in Italy 4. Lust 5. Greed 6. Deception 7. Politicians 8. Merchants 9. Conspiracies 10. Sea monsters 11. Armed Forces -- Officers 12. Venice, Italy -- History 13. Adaptations, retellings, and spin-offs 14. Humorous stories

Features characters who appeared previously in Fool.

Three prominent Venetians lure Pocket, an envoy from the Queen of Britain, into a dark dungeon, hoping to drug and kill him, but Pocket has more than a few tricks up his sleeve.

"Pocket fumbles his way through a complicated adventure buoyed by Moore's half-cocked Shakespearean dialogue, puerile humor and ceaseless banter. The setting helps the author's cause, lending a rich historical backdrop that includes trade disputes, political intrigue and Shakespearean spectacle." Kirkus.

Moore, Christopher, 1957-

You suck : a love story / Christopher Moore. William Morrow, 2007. 208 p. Vampire love stories (Christopher Moore)

ISBN 0060590297

1. Vampires 2. Necrophilia 3. Misadventures 4. Teenagers 5. Nineteen-year-old men 6. Women vampires 7. Police 8. Dead 9. Men/women relations 10. Interpersonal relations 11. Friendship 12. Women 13. San Francisco, California 14. Romantic comedies

Sequel to: Bloodsucking fiends.

Sequel: Bite me.

Waking up after a fantastic night only to discover that his girlfriend is a vampire and has transformed him into one, Thomas C. Flood adapts

to his new powers while dealing with a dangerous faction of bloodsuckers trying to kill off all other vampires.

Moore, Edward Kelsey

The **Supremes** at Earl's All-You-Can-Eat / Edward Kelsey Moore. Alfred A. Knopf, 2013. 320 p.

ISBN 9780307959928

1. African American women 2. Female friendship 3. Marriage 4. Women psychics 5. Extramarital affairs 6. Family relationships 7. Indiana 8. Women's lives and relationships 9. African American fiction

LC 2012028743

"This is a Borzoi book."

BCALA Literary Award for First Novelist, 2014.

Forging a friendship at the height of the Civil Rights Movement, Odette, Clarice and Barbara Jean meet regularly at the first diner owned by black proprietors in their Indiana city and are watched throughout the years by a big-hearted man who observes their struggles with school, marriage, parenthood and beyond.

Moore, Edward Kelsey

The **Supremes** sing the happy heartache blues : a novel / Edward Kelsey Moore. Henry Holt and Co., 2017. 320 p.

ISBN 9781250107947

1. Seniors 2. Blues musicians 3. African American women 4. Independence in women 5. Interpersonal relations 6. Transgender persons 7. Family relationships 8. Small town life 9. Self-fulfillment 10. Womanizers 11. Childhood friends 12. Indiana 13. Chicago, Illinois 14. Women's lives and relationships 15. Chick lit 16. African American fiction

LC 2016048172

The late-in-life marriage of two infamous natives of an Indiana community attracts the return of a famous guitar bluesman while compelling numerous locals to resolve long-standing disputes, from a philanderer who would prove his faithfulness, to a transgender woman who would live authentically.

Moore, Graham, 1981-

* The **holdout** : a novel / Graham Moore. Random House, 2020. 336 p.

ISBN 9780399591778

1. Race relations 2. African American men 3. Trials (Murder) 4. Jurors 5. Frameups 6. Defense attorneys 7. Missing girls 8. Jury 9. Teacher-student relationships 10. Rich people 11. True-crime television programs 12. Legal thrillers

LC 2019029712

A woman is wrongly implicated in a murder one decade after convincing the members of a deadlocked jury to return a not-guilty verdict.

"The twists are sharp and the flashbacks that uncover what each juror knows are placed for maximum impact in this rollicking legal thriller." Library Journal.

Moore, Graham, 1981-

The **last** days of night : a novel / Graham Moore. Random House, 2016 368 p.

ISBN 9780812988901

1. Edison, Thomas A (Thomas Alva), 1847-1931 2. Westinghouse, George, 1846-1914 3. Gilded Age (1865-1898) 4. Inventors 5. Competition 6. Lawyers 7. Suing (Law) 8. Ambition in men 9. Businesspeople 10. Electric lighting 11. Patents 12. Technology 13. New York City -- History -- 19th century 14. Historical thrillers 15. Legal thrillers

LC 2015050362

RUSA Reading List, 2017.

When electric light innovator Thomas Edison sues his only remaining rival for patent infringement, George Westinghouse hires untested Columbia Law School graduate Paul Ravath for a case fraught with lies, betrayals and deception.

"Moore's extensive research is apparent, and readers are likely to walk away from the book feeling as informed as they are entertained." Publishers Weekly.

Moore, Graham, 1981-

The **Sherlockian** / Graham Moore. Twelve, 2010. 320 p.
ISBN 9780446572590
1. Doyle, Arthur Conan,, Sir, 1859-1930 2. Stoker, Bram, 1847-1912 3. Authors 4. Serial murderers 5. Murder investigation 6. Literary historians 7. Crimes against scholars 8. Secret societies 9. Diary writing 10. London, England 11. Historical mysteries 12. Parallel narratives

LC 2010009554

Literary researcher and Sherlock Holmes enthusiast Harold White is shocked when a scholar who discovered Sir Arthur Conan Doyle's missing diary is murdered, while in 1890s London, Conan Doyle hunts a serial killer to prove his superiority to his famous character.

"Thanks to the sly self-awareness that keeps The Sherlockian smart and agile, its possible to enjoy this books laughable affectations and still be seduced by them. This is a novel by, for and about Holmes-quoting mystery nuts, and it understands what makes them happy." New York Times.

Moore, Jonathan, 1977-

The **night** market / Jonathan Moore. Houghton Mifflin Harcourt, 2018. 272 p. San Francisco novels (Jonathan Moore)
ISBN 9780544671898
1. Detectives 2. Near future 3. Murder investigation 4. Trust 5. Secrets 6. Neighbors 7. FBI agents 8. Conspiracies 9. Men with amnesia 10. San Francisco, California 11. Noir fiction 12. Science fiction 13. Psychological suspense

LC 2017044907

Investigating a crime scene in a luxurious city home where a victim's body has been contaminated by an unknown substance, Inspector Ross Carver is confronted by FBI agents and awakens in his bed under the care of a neighbor who tells him a suspicious story about what happened.

"A sharp and scary near-future thriller that delivers a dark message about society's love affair with technology." Kirkus.

Moore, Kate (Katherine A.)

Sexy Lexy / Kate Moore. Love Spell/Dorchester, 2005 352 p.
ISBN 0505526239
1. Women innkeepers 2. Women hotel managers 3. Innkeepers 4. Hotel managers 5. Women authors 6. Carpenters 7. Hotels 8. New identities 9. Secret identity 10. Celebrities 11. Fame 12. Hiding 13. Self-help techniques 14. Moving to a new city 15. California 16. Contemporary romances

When her self-help book encouraging fitness through sex causes much controversy, Lexy Clark escapes to Drake's Point, California, where she takes a job as an innkeeper and becomes involved with Sam Worth, but her past soon catches up with her, threatening their newfound love.

Moore, Kate (Katherine A.)

To seduce an angel / Kate Moore. Berkley Sensation, 2011. 304 p. Sons of sin (Kate Moore)
ISBN 9780425243695
1. Regency period (1811-1820) 2. Extortion 3. Aristocracy 4. Malicious accusation 5. Dukes and duchesses 6. Women murder suspects 7. Deception 8. Men/women relations 9. Interpersonal attraction 10. Revenge 11. Great Britain -- History -- Regency, 1811-1820 12. Regency romances 13. Historical romances

Forced by the Duke of Wenlocke to spy on Kit, the Marquess of Daventry, Emma Portland, falsely accused of a murder she didn't commit, takes the position of tutor to Kit's young wards and soon finds herself falling in love with the very same man she has been sent to destroy.

Moore, Laura, 1963-

Making waves / Laura Moore. Ballantine Books, 2017. 390 p. Beach Lane novels
ISBN 9780425284827
1. Personal concierges 2. Women surfers 3. Capitalists and financiers 4. Upper class 5. Unplanned pregnancy 6. Sexual attraction 7. Men/women relations 8. Hamptons, New York 9. Contemporary romances

The owner of a highly successful concierge business serving the needs of the Hamptons' wealthy elite, Dakota Hale must navigate the rough waters of society gossip and devastating secrets after one night of passion with sexy mogul Max Carr leads to unexpected consequences that threaten their already fragile relationship.

Moore, Liz, 1983-

* **Long** bright river / Liz Moore. Riverhead Books, 2020. 496 p.
ISBN 9780525540670
1. Policewomen 2. Women drug abusers 3. Sisters 4. Opioid epidemic 5. Addiction 6. Missing women 7. Violence against women 8. Neighborhoods 9. Single mothers 10. Loneliness in women 11. Flashbacks 12. Philadelphia, Pennsylvania 13. Police procedurals

LC 2018051652

A suspense novel that also looks at the anatomy of a Philadelphia family rocked by the opioid crisis and the relationship between two sisters--one, suffering from addiction, who has suddenly gone missing amid a series of mysterious murders; the other a police officer who patrols the neighborhood from which she disappeared: a story about the formidable ties between place, family, and fate.

"In her fourth novel (following The Unseen World), Rome Prize-winning author Moore blends the reality of today's deadly opioid crisis with a complicated family dynamic to create an intense mystery with stunning twists and turns. Impossible to put down, impossible to forget." Library Journal.

Moore, Liz, 1983-

The **unseen** world / Liz Moore. W. W. Norton & Co., 2016. 416 p.
ISBN 9780393241686
1. 1980s 2. Fathers and daughters 3. Identity (Psychology) 4. Computer scientists 5. Alzheimer's disease 6. Girl prodigies 7. Family secrets 8. Family relationships 9. Artificial intelligence 10. Boston, Massachusetts 11. Literary fiction 12. Coming-of-age stories

LC 2016011031

ALA Notable Book, 2017.

Accompanying her eccentric, socially inept father to his 1980s Boston computer science lab every day, Ada, a shy, homeschooled prodigy, is sheltered by a colleague when her father's mental health and reputation deteriorate in ways that compel her to investigate his hidden past.

Moore, Lorrie

A **gate** at the stairs : a novel / Lorrie Moore. Alfred A. Knopf, 2009. 336 p.

ISBN 9780375409288

1. Racism 2. Adoption 3. Nannies 4. College students 5. Rich families 6. Family relationships 7. Young women 8. Literary fiction 9. Coming-of-age stories

LC 2009003091

Shortlisted for The Orange Prize for Fiction, 2010

In the Midwest just after the September 11 attacks, twenty-year-old Tassie Keltjin comes of age amid such challenges as racism, the War on Terror, and cruelty in the name of love, as she leaves her family's farm to attend college and takes a part-time job as a nanny.

"The novel concludes in a tone of wan hope, with Tassie wiser and stronger, though forever sadder. . . . This book is not above all, but in the service of all-funny. Moore is not shy about the bad joke, and never pushes a great one too far. Her humor, always pointed at insight and elaboration, strikes the perfect balance between taste and feeling." Pop-Matters.

Moore, Meg Mitchell

The **islanders** / Meg Mitchell Moore. William Morrow, 2019 416 p.

ISBN 9780062840066

1. Islands 2. Secrets 3. Friendship 4. Writing 5. Divorce 6. Authors 7. Self-fulfillment 8. Single mothers 9. Men/women relations 10. Stay-at-home mothers 11. Women business owners 12. Rhode Island 13. Block Island, Rhode Island 14. Mainstream fiction

A writer struggling with a second book, the divorced owner of a café and an unfulfilled stay-at-home mom share a season of unexpected romance and secrets on scenic Block Island.

Moore, Susanna

The **life** of objects / Susanna Moore. Alfred A. Knopf, 2012. 256 p.

ISBN 9780307268433

1. Between the Wars (1918-1939) 2. 1930s 3. Women lace makers 4. Self-fulfillment in women 5. Aristocracy -- Germany 6. Nazism -- Germany 7. Jews, German 8. Atrocities -- Germany 9. World War II 10. Postwar life 11. Germany -- History -- 1933-1945 12. Historical fiction

LC 2012019890

"This is a Borzoi book."

Drawn by a mysterious countess into the Berlin household of an aristocratic couple, Beatrice, a young Irish Protestant lace maker, is introduced to the highly rarified world of affluence and art collecting on the eve of World War II.

Mootoo, Shani

Moving forward sideways, like a crab : a novel / Shani Mootoo. Akashic Books, 2017, c2014. 312 p.

ISBN 9781617755347

1. Parent and adult child 2. Child-separated mothers 3. Transgender persons 4. Gender identity 5. Family relationships 6. Authors 7. Toronto, Ontario 8. Trinidad and Tobago 9. Literary fiction 10. Psychological fiction

Originally published: Toronto : Doubleday Canada, 2014.

A young man travels to Trinidad to reconnect with a transgender parent, uncovering the complex realities of love and family.

"A finalist for the Lambda Award, Mootoo's character-driven novel is rich in setting and slow in pace, inviting the reader to linger over its closely observed details." Booklist.

Moran, Michelle

Rebel queen : a novel / Michelle Moran. Touchstone, 2015. 352 p.

ISBN 9781476716350

1. Lakshmibai,, Rani of Jhansi, 1828-1858 2. 1850s 3. Women rulers 4. British in India 5. Women bodyguards 6. Rebels 7. Soldiers 8. Women soldiers 9. India -- History -- 19th century 10. India -- History -- British occupation, 1765-1947 11. Biographical fiction 12. Historical fiction

LC 2014026037

Refusing to surrender to the British Empire, Rani Lakshmibai, ruler of India's Jhansi State, defends her realm with not one but two armies -- one comprised entirely of men, the other, all-female. Narrated by Sita, Rani's trusted bodyguard, Rebel Queen vividly depicts the Indian Rebellion of 1857 and introduces readers to a strong, courageous ruler who fought and died for her country. -- Description by Gillian Speace.

"This often deeply moving novel focuses on its characters, allowing history to play out as a backdrop to the personal story of a young woman who would risk everything, including her own life, for her people. Fans of the authors earlier novels will almost certainly greet this one with enthusiasm, but, because its not tied to Moran's earlier books, its perfect for new historical-fiction readers, too." Booklist.

Morante, Elsa, ca. 1912-1985

* **Arturo's** island : a novel / Elsa Morante ; translated by Ann Goldstein. Liveright Publishing Corporation, 2019, c1957. 384 p.

ISBN 9781631493294

1. Between the Wars (1918-1939) 2. Solitude 3. Stepmothers 4. Fathers and sons 5. Growing up 6. Teenage boys 7. Teenage girls 8. Island life 9. Social isolation 10. Italy -- Social life and customs -- 20th century 11. Modern classics 12. Coming-of-age stories 13. Translations -- Italian to English

LC 2018046181

Originally published: 1957.

Imbued with a spectral grace, as if told through an enchanted looking glass, the novel follows the adolescent Arturo through his days on the isolated Neapolitan island of Procida, where--his mother long deceased, his father often absent, and a dog as his sole companion--he roams the countryside and the beaches or reads in his family's lonely, dilapidated mansion. This quiet, meandering existence is upended when his father brings home a beautiful sixteen-year-old bride, Nunziatella.

More deadly than the male : masterpieces from the queens of horror / edited by Graeme Davis. Pegasus Books, 2019 352 p.

ISBN 9781643130118

1. 19th century 2. Ghosts 3. Haunted houses 4. Haunted places 5. Supernatural 6. Short stories 7. Anthologies 8. Horror 9. Ghost stories

A darkly luminous new anthology collecting the most terrifying horror stories by renowned female authors, presenting anew these forgotten classics to the modern reader.

Moreno-Garcia, Silvia

* **Gods** of jade and shadow : a novel / Silvia Moreno-Garcia. Del Rey, 2019. 352 p.

ISBN 9780525620754

1. 1920s 2. Gods and goddesses, Mayan 3. Young women 4. Quests 5. Families 6. Cousins 7. Twins 8. Competition 9. Social change 10. Mexico 11. Mexican-American Border Region 12. Historical

fantasy 13. Mythological fiction 14. Coming-of-age stories

LC 2019007450

A dark fairy tale inspired by folklore is set against the Jazz age in Mexico's underworld, where a young dreamer is sent by the Mayan God of Death on a life-changing journey.

Morgan Jones, Chris, 1971-

The **jackal's** share / Christopher Morgan Jones. The Penguin Press, 2013. 322 p. Ben Webster novels

ISBN 9781594205354

1. Business intelligence 2. Billionaires 3. Terrorism 4. Extortion 5. Ethics 6. Upper class 7. Lawyers 8. Businesspeople 9. Detectives 10. Thrillers and suspense

Sequel to: The silent oligarch

In this sequel to The Silent Oligarch, British investigator Ben Webster still works for the boutique London firm of Ikertu, which specializes in corporate investigation. This time, a billionaire Iranian refugee named Darius Qazai seeks his services to disprove accusations against him false. Webster lands in a grim world of blackmail, offshore money, arms dealing, and terrorism. Fascinating and one-of-a-kind characters like Webster's man in Dubai or Qazai's pallid assistant will leave readers eager for more adventures from this author. - Description by Shauna Griffin.

Morgan Jones, Chris, 1971-

The **silent** oligarch / Christopher Morgan Jones. Penguin Press, 2012 336 p. Ben Webster novels

ISBN 9781594203190

1. Business intelligence 2. Money laundering 3. Political corruption 4. Upper class 5. Lawyers 6. Businesspeople 7. Detectives 8. Friends' death 9. International intrigue 10. Moscow, Russia 11. Thrillers and suspense

Sequel: The jackal's share

Hired to expose the criminal networks of a Russian bureaucrat who has amassed an illicit fortune, London investigator Benjamin Webster uncovers evidence that his target may also be responsible for the murder of a colleague.

Morgan, C. E., 1976-

* The **sport** of kings / C. E. Morgan. Farrar, Straus & Giroux, 2016. 480 p.

ISBN 9780374281083

1. Horse breeding 2. Horse racing 3. Fathers and daughters 4. Thoroughbred horses 5. African American men 6. Families 7. Family secrets 8. Prejudice 9. Racism 10. Former convicts 11. Ambition 12. Kentucky -- History -- 20th century 13. Literary fiction

LC 2015038512

ALA Notable Book, 2017.

Kirkus Prize for Fiction, 2016.

Pulitzer Prize for Fiction finalist, 2017.

Shortlisted for The Baileys Women's Prize for Fiction, 2017.

Shortlisted for the James Tait Black Memorial Prize for Fiction, 2016

The trailblazing patriarch of a proud Kentucky clan, his daughter, and a black ex-prisoner embark on an effort to reclaim the family's near-mythic legacy by breeding champion horses, an endeavor that is challenged by divided ambitions, the farm's ugly past, and a willful thoroughbred filly.

"A dense meditation on the ugliness that undergirds much of the sublime we as humans strive for and admire in life." Library Journal.

Morgan, Jude, 1962-

The **secret** life of William Shakespeare / Jude Morgan. St. Martin's Press, 2014. 464 p.

ISBN 9781250025036

1. Shakespeare, William, 1564-1616 2. Hathaway, Anne, 1556?-1623 3. Elizabethan era (1558-1603) 4. 16th century 5. Tudor period (1485-1603) 6. Authors' spouses 7. Husband and wife 8. Dramatists 9. Great Britain -- History -- Elizabeth I, 1558-1603 10. England -- Social life and customs -- 16th century 11. Biographical fiction 12. Historical fiction 13. Literary fiction

LC 2013045690

A sumptuously detailed imagining of the private world of the master bard chronicles the transformation of an unwilling craftsman and resentful son into a husband, father and genius playwright in Renaissance London.

"Morgan takes liberties with the Bard's words, motivations, and personality while staying true to the spirit of the Shakespeare we all know and love. An entertaining read." Booklist.

Morgan, Richard K., 1965-

Altered carbon / Richard K. Morgan. Del Rey/Ballantine Books, 2003. 375 p. Takeshi Kovacs novels

ISBN 0345457684

1. United Nations. 2. 25th century 3. Soldiers 4. Consciousness transfer 5. Immortalism 6. Space colonies 7. Conspiracies 8. Mercenaries 9. Murder investigation 10. San Francisco, California 11. Cyberpunk 12. Science fiction mysteries 13. Hardboiled fiction 14. Science fiction

LC 2002031165

Sequel: Broken angels.

Philip K. Dick Award for Science Fiction, 2003.

In a twenty-fifth century world in which death is nearly obsolete, former UN envoy Takeshi Kovacs, re-sleeved into a new body after a brutal death, finds himself caught in the middle of a deadly far-reaching conspiracy.

"A seamless marriage of hardcore cyberpunk and hard-boiled detective tale." Times (London).

Morgan, Richard K., 1965-

Broken angels / Richard K. Morgan. Del Rey, 2004. 366 p. Takeshi Kovacs novels

ISBN 0345457714

1. United Nations Armed forces. 2. 25th century 3. Mercenaries 4. Material culture 5. Space colonies 6. Space flight 7. Space vehicles 8. Soldiers 9. Aliens 10. Consciousness transfer 11. Immortalism 12. Private investigators 13. Betrayal 14. Conspiracies 15. Alien artifacts 16. Cyberpunk 17. Science fiction mysteries 18. Science fiction 19. Hardboiled fiction

LC 2003062515

Sequel to: Altered carbon.

Sequel: Woken furies.

Cynical, quick-on-the-trigger Takeshi Kovacs, the ex-U.N. envoy turned private eye, has changed careers, and bodies, once more . . . trading sleuthing for soldiering as a warrior-for-hire, and helping a far-flung planet's government put down a bloody revolution.

"This novel is clearly the work of a gifted, ambitious storyteller. Morgan's prose is clean and direct, his characters almost uniformly hard-edged, his future convincing, well conceived and decked out with an almost limitless array of technological marvels." Washington Post Book World.

Morgan, Richard K., 1965-

Thirteen / Richard K. Morgan. Del Rey/Ballantine Books, 2007. xii, 544 p.

ISBN 9780345485250

1. 22nd century 2. Assassins 3. Genetic engineering 4. Antiheroes and antiheroines 5. Soldiers 6. Science -- Experiments 7. Government research 8. Identity (Psychology) 9. Life on other planets 10. Prejudice 11. Violence 12. Space colonies 13. Space flight 14. Survival (after spacecraft accidents) 15. Murder 16. Science fiction mysteries 17. Cyberpunk 18. Science fiction

LC 2007010617

Originally published under the title Black man: London : Gollancz, 2007.

Arthur C. Clarke Award, 2008.

The subject of a failed government experiment to produce a more deadly military warrior, Carl Marsalis is a hit man who has lost his taste for killing, but when he is arrested in Miami, government officials come up with a plan to use his talents to achieve their own ends.

"For all that Morgan steps outside some of the usual conventions he is still recognisably working in the format and [Thirteen] comes with some of its bad habits. . . . Morgan's approach is problematic but at the same time it is so utterly different to anything else ou there that it is almost impossible not to admire it." Strange Horizons.

Morgan, Robert, 1944-

The **road** from Gap Creek : a novel / Robert Morgan. Algonquin Books of Chapel Hill, 2013. 352 p.

ISBN 9781616201616

1. 1940s 2. Married women 3. Mountain life 4. Family relationships 5. Young women 6. Rural life 7. Appalachian Region 8. Historical fiction 9. Domestic fiction 10. Coming-of-age stories 11. Southern fiction

LC 2013008906

"A Shannon Ravenel Book."

Sequel: Gap Creek.

Sequel to:

Seen through the eyes of the youngest daughter, Annie, the Richards family faces triumph and hardships during the Great Depression and World War II.

Morgan, Sarah, 1948-

The **Christmas** sisters / Sarah Morgan. HQN Books, 2018 410 p.

ISBN 9781335534699

1. Christmas 2. Adopted girls 3. Homecomings 4. Sisters 5. Families 6. Houseguests 7. Interpersonal attraction 8. Men/women relations 9. Scotland 10. Highlands, Scotland 11. Women's lives and relationships 12. Christmas stories

When their mother's flu and ongoing tensions threaten the holiday season they traditionally share in their snowy Scottish highlands home, three adopted sisters work together to host family guests, including three romance-minded suitors.

Morgan, Sarah, 1948-

Miracle on 5th Avenue / Sarah Morgan. HQN Books, 2016. 384 p. From Manhattan with love

ISBN 9780373789344

1. Mystery story writers 2. Widowers 3. Women caterers 4. Optimism in women 5. Christmas 6. Interpersonal attraction 7. Men/women relations 8. Manhattan, New York City 9. New York City 10. Holiday romances 11. Contemporary romances

RITA Award, 2017.

It will take a Christmas miracle for two very different souls to find each other in this perfectly festive fairy tale of New York.

Morgan, Sarah, 1948-

One summer in Paris / Sarah Morgan. Harlequin Books, 2019 384 p.

ISBN 9781335013422

1. Self-discovery in women 2. Vacations 3. Divorce 4. Self-confidence 5. Divorced women 6. Female friendship 7. Eighteen-year-old women 8. Intergenerational friendship 9. Paris, France 10. Women's lives and relationships

Embarking on a solo Paris vacation after being dumped by her husband of 25 years, cautious Grace unexpectedly bonds with a rebellious London teen who helps her forge new understandings of family, love and self-confidence.

Morgenstern, Erin

* The **night** circus : a novel / Erin Morgenstern. Doubleday, 2011. 387 p.

ISBN 9780385534635

1. 19th century 2. Magicians 3. Magicians' apprentices 4. Competition 5. Circus 6. Games 7. Circus performers 8. Magic 9. Good and evil 10. Historical fantasy

LC 2010050546

Locus Award for First Novel, 2012.

RUSA Reading List, 2012.

Waging a fierce competition for which they have trained since childhood, circus magicians Celia and Marco unexpectedly fall in love with each other and share a fantastical romance that manifests in fateful ways.

Morgenstern, Erin

* The **starless** sea / Erin Morgenstern. Doubleday, 2019. 498 p.

ISBN 9780385541213

1. Libraries 2. Secret societies 3. Graduate students 4. Magic 5. Books 6. Quests 7. Storytelling 8. Interpersonal attraction 9. Men/men relations 10. Fantasy fiction

LC 2018053215

Discovering a mysterious book of prisoner tales, a Vermont graduate student recognizes a story from his own life before following clues to a magical underground library that is being targeted for destruction.

Moriarty, Jaclyn

Gravity is the thing / Jaclyn Moriarity. HarperCollins, 2019. 402 p.

ISBN 9780062883735

1. Self-help psychology 2. Loss (Psychology) 3. Missing persons 4. Grief 5. Coping 6. Brothers and sisters 7. Single mothers 8. Restaurants 9. Self-fulfillment 10. Australia 11. Mainstream fiction

Previoulsy published by Macmillan Australia, 2019.

Librarians' Choice (Australia), 2019

Follows a single mother's heartfelt search for more meaningful truths about the universe, her family and herself.

"With an eye as keen for human idiosyncrasies as Miranda July's, and a sense of humor as bright and surprising as Maria Semple's, this is a novel of pure velocity; it sucks the reader into Abi's problems and her joys in equal, brilliant measure. A complex dissection of the self-help industry, as well as a complete and moving portrait of a difficult, delightful woman, Moriarty proves her adult novels can live up to her YA work's reputation." Publishers Weekly.

Moriarty, Liane

Big little lies / Liane Moriarty. Amy Einhorn Books, 2014 416 p.

ISBN 9780399167065

1. Suburban life 2. Murder 3. Parents 4. Schools 5. Family relationships 6. Suburbs 7. Divorce 8. Mainstream fiction

Davitt Awards, Best Adult Novel, 2015.

An annual school Trivia Night ends in a disastrous riot leaving one parent dead in what appears to be a tragic accident, but evidence shows it might have been premeditated.

"Moriarty demonstrates an excellent talent for exposing the dark, seedy side of the otherwise 'perfect' family unit while keeping the characters believable enough to be someone you might know." Library Journal.

Moriarty, Liane

The **husband's** secret / Liane Moriarty. Amy Einhorn Books, 2013. 416 p.

ISBN 9780399159343

1. Husband and wife 2. Life change events 3. Secrets 4. Mothers 5. Schools 6. Letters 7. Families -- Australia 8. Family relationships 9. Men/women relations 10. Interpersonal relations 11. Women -- Interpersonal relations 12. Australia 13. Sydney, New South Wales 14. Mainstream fiction

LC 2013009340

"We all have secrets. But not like this--"--Cover.

Discovering a tattered letter that says she is to open it only in the event of her husband's death, Cecelia, a successful family woman, is unable to resist reading the letter and discovers a secret that shatters her life and the lives of two other women.

"There is real darkness here, but it is offset by the author's natural wit . . . and irrepressible goodwill toward her characters." Kirkus.

Moriarty, Liane

Nine perfect strangers / Liane Moriarty. Flatiron Books, 2018. 432 p.

ISBN 9781250069825

1. Health resorts 2. Strangers 3. Wellness lifestyle 4. Women authors 5. Secrets 6. Coping 7. Transformations, Personal 8. Australia 9. Mainstream fiction

Librarians' Choice (Australia), 2018

Gathering at a remote health resort for a 10-day fitness program, nine strangers and their enigmatic host become subjects of interest to a brokenhearted novelist who develops uncomfortable doubts about the resort's real agenda.

Moriarty, Liane

Truly madly guilty / Liane Moriarty. Flatiron Books, 2016. 416 p.

ISBN 9781250069795

1. Married people 2. Life change events 3. Consequences 4. Barbecues 5. Friendship 6. Families 7. Parenthood 8. Guilt 9. Neighbors 10. Childhood friends 11. Sydney, New South Wales 12. Australia 13. Mainstream fiction

Goodreads Choice Award, 2016

A busy couple formerly on the brink of realizing their dreams reflects on a fortuitous gathering with their best friends and another couple, in a tale that explores the role of guilt in relationships and the power of everyday moments in family life.

"This novel sheds light on the truths that we all fear as parents, spouses, and friends. It's perfect for those long summer days, but readers will have to pace themselves to not devour it in one sitting." Library Journal.

Morrell, David

Murder as a fine art / David Morrell. Mulholland Books, 2013. 288 p. Thomas De Quincey mysteries

ISBN 9780316216791

1. De Quincey, Thomas, 1785-1859 2. 1850s 3. 19th century 4. Fathers and daughters 5. Serial murderers 6. Opium addiction 7. Authors, English 8. Murder suspects 9. Innocence (Law) 10. London, England -- Social life and customs -- 19th century 11. Historical mysteries

LC 2012020034

First published: 2013.

RUSA Reading List, 2014.

Sue Feder Historical Mystery Award, 2014.

Thomas De Quincey, infamous for his memoir Confessions of an English Opium-Eater, is the major suspect in a series of ferocious mass murders identical to ones that terrorized London forty-three years earlier. Desperate to clear his name but crippled by opium addiction, De Quincey is aided by his devoted daughter Emily and a pair of determined Scotland Yard detectives.

Morrell, David

Ruler of the night / David Morrell. Mulholland Books, 2016. 342 p. Thomas De Quincey mysteries

ISBN 9780316307901

1. De Quincey, Thomas, 1785-1859 2. Victorian era (1837-1901) 3. Trains 4. Fathers and daughters 5. Intrigue 6. Power (Social sciences) 7. Nobility 8. Murder 9. Murder investigation 10. Opium addiction 11. Detectives 12. Secrets 13. London, England -- Social life and customs -- 19th century 14. Victorian mysteries 15. Historical mysteries

Sequel to: Inspector of the dead.

Opium addict Thomas De Quincey and his irrepressible daughter Emily investigate the strangling of a lawyer in what is the first murder on an English train, and they uncover a dangerous secret that reaches the highest levels of British society.

Morris, Heather

Cilka's journey / Heather Morris. St Martin's Press, 2019. 343 p.

ISBN 9781250265708

1. Auschwitz (Concentration camp) 2. 20th century 3. Survival (in concentration camps, prisons, etc) 4. Consequences 5. Resilience (Personal quality) 6. Beauty 7. Holocaust survivors 8. Concentration camp inmates 9. Concentration camp survivors 10. Options, alternatives, choices 11. Courage in women 12. Nurses 13. Men/women relations 14. Poland -- History -- 1918-1945 15. Siberia 16. Historical fiction

Follows a Russian woman who is forced by a concentration-camp commandant to become his lover and is subsquently sent to Siberia after being found guilty of collaborating with the enemy.

"Morris weaves a fast-paced story that captures the immediacy of Cilka's duties caring for prisoners while appeasing guards at every step." Publishers Weekly

Morris, Mary McGarry

Songs in ordinary time / Mary McGarry Morris. Viking, 1995. 740 p.

ISBN 067086014X

1. 1960s 2. Divorced women -- Vermont 3. Mother and teenager 4. Swindlers and swindling -- Vermont 5. Neighbors 6. Alcoholic fathers 7. Families -- Vermont 8. Family relationships 9. Small towns -- Vermont 10. Vermont 11. Domestic fiction 12. Historical fiction

LC 94-44071

A novel set in a small town in Vermont in 1960 offers the story of lonely and vulnerable Marie Fermoyle, her three children, and a dangerous con man.

"The novel is frequently perceptive about the bitter pathos bred by the feeling that you've always lived on someone else's leftovers. . . . The novel is also insightful and frightening on the unshakable resilience of family grudges." New York Times Book Review.

Morris, Michael, 1966-

Man in the blue moon / Michael Morris. Tyndale House, 2012. 400 p.

ISBN 9781414368429

1. First World War era (1914-1918) 2. 1910s 3. Single mothers 4. Land claims 5. World War I 6. Trust in women 7. Murder 8. Men/women relations 9. Father-deserted families 10. Faith (Christianity) 11. Apalachicola, Florida 12. Florida 13. Christian historical fiction
LC 2012016147

Single mother Ella Wallace fights to keep a banker from buying the Florida land that has been in her family for generations when a mysterious stranger shows up and convices Ella he can help her, until his past comes to light.

"A magical and mesmerizing page-turner.." Publishers Weekly.

Morris, Willie

Taps : a novel / Willie Morris. Houghton Mifflin, 2001. 340 p.

ISBN 0618098593

1. 1950s 2. Korean War, 1950-1953 3. Teenage boys 4. Musicians 5. Friends' death 6. Trumpeters 7. Mississippi 8. Delta Region, Mississippi 9. Coming-of-age stories 10. Southern fiction
LC 00068250

Sixteen-year-old Swayze Barksdale watches from his Mississippi Delta front lawn as the town's young men go off into the army, and when he is called to unexpected duty himself, his life becomes filled with funerals and the tragic note of the times.

"Over the course of a year, in intervals framed by a dozen graveside ceremonies for men shipped back from Korea to the summer-baked or winter-frozen cemetery outside town, Swayze tells the story of a passing Southern world and his own troubled growing up. . . . Funerals are its talismans and 'Taps' is at it strongest when it describes them." New York Times Book Review.

Morrison, Toni, 1931-2019

* Beloved : a novel / Toni Morrison. Knopf, 1987. 275 p.
ISBN 0394535979

1. 19th century 2. Freed slaves 3. Children -- Death -- Psychological aspects 4. Coping in women 5. African American women 6. Mothers and daughters 7. Fugitive slaves 8. Slavery 9. Ohio -- History -- 19th century 10. Historical fiction 11. Magical realism 12. Literary fiction 13. African American fiction 14. Modern classics 15. Southern Gothic 16. Southern fiction
LC 86026157

Pulitzer Prize for Fiction, 1988.
Robert F. Kennedy Book Award, 1988.
National Book Critics Circle Award for Fiction finalist, 1987
National Book Award for Fiction finalist, 1987

Sethe, an escaped slave living in post-Civil War Ohio with her daughter and mother-in-law, is persistently haunted by the ghost of her dead baby girl.

Morrison, Toni, 1931-2019

* The bluest eye : a novel / Toni Morrison. Holt, Rinehart and Winston, 1970. 164 p.

ISBN 0030850746

1. Social acceptance 2. Self-acceptance in girls 3. Self-esteem in girls 4. African Americans 5. Family problems 6. Incest 7. Eleven-year-old girls 8. African American girls 9. Eye 10. Appearances 11. Ohio 12. Coming-of-age stories 13. African American fiction 14. Literary fiction 15. Modern classics
LC 79117270

Eleven-year-old Pecola Breedlove, an African-American girl in an America whose love for blonde, blue-eyed children can devastate all others, prays for her eyes to turn blue, so that she will be beautiful, people will notice her, and her world will be different.

Morrison, Toni, 1931-2019

* God help the child / Toni Morrison. Knopf, 2015. 192 p.
ISBN 9780307594174

1. Mothers and daughters 2. Child abuse 3. Psychic trauma 4. Color of African Americans 5. Human skin color 6. Coping 7. Love 8. Child murders 9. Psychological fiction 10. Literary fiction 11. African American fiction
BCALA Literary Award for Fiction, 2016.

Traces the impact of childhood trauma on the lives of a beautiful multiracial woman, the man she loves, and an abused white girl who looks to her for help.

"There are some moves here that may seem obvious, but the pieces all fit together seamlessly in a story about beating back the past, confronting the present, and understanding one's worth." Library Journal.

Morrison, Toni, 1931-2019

Home / Toni Morrison. Knopf, 2012. 144 p.
ISBN 9780307594167

1. African American veterans 2. Brothers and sisters 3. Korean War veterans 4. Psychic trauma in men 5. Racism 6. Redemption 7. African Americans 8. Small towns 9. Georgia 10. Psychological fiction 11. Literary fiction 12. African American fiction
LC 2011043441

A Korean War veteran living a shattered life embarks on a quest to save his younger sister.

Morrison, Toni, 1931-2019

Jazz / Toni Morrison. A. A. Knopf, 1992. 229 p.
ISBN 0679411674

1. 1920s 2. Murder 3. Violence in men 4. Extramarital affairs 5. African American men/women relations 6. African American teenage girls 7. Memories 8. Jazz music 9. May-December romance 10. African American families 11. Sexuality 12. Jealousy 13. Door-to-door selling 14. Harlem, New York City 15. New York City 16. Love stories 17. Literary fiction 18. African American fiction 19. Modern classics
LC 91058555

ALA Notable Book, 1993.

In Harlem, 1926, Joe Trace, a door-to-door salesman in his fifties, kills his teenage lover. A profound love story which depicts the sights and sounds of Black urban life during the Jazz Age.

"This novel tells the story of Violet and Joe Trace, married for over 20 years, residents of Harlem in 1926. . . . Violet works as an unlicensed hairdresser, doing ladies hair in their own homes, and Joe sells Cleopatra cosmetics door to door. . . . When the novel opens, Joe has shot his 18-year-old lover, Dorcas, and Violet has disfigured the dead girl's body at her funeral in a fit of rage. Joe, who was not caught, is in mourning, crying all day in his darkened apartment, and Violet has taken on the task of finding out whatever she can about Dorcas. Voice Lit Suppl, As the story unfolds, we come to understand, if not excuse, what happened. The characters themselves cannot excuse their own behavior, which baffles them. Violet is obsessed by the memory of the dead girl whose face she slashed: What was it about her that Joe found so special? She is driven to visit the girl's aunt Alice, who is understandably frightened. . . . Some of the most interesting scenes in the book are the subsequent meetings of these two very different women who come to respect each other, even before they learn to understand each other." Christian Science Monitor.

Morrison, Toni, 1931-2019

Love / Toni Morrison. Knopf, 2003. 208 p.
ISBN 0375409440
1. Community life 2. African American women 3. African American men 4. Hotel owners 5. African American men/women relations 6. Memories 7. Obsession 8. Seduction 9. Crushes (Interpersonal relations) 10. Power (Social sciences) 11. Dominance (Psychology) 12. Seaside resorts 13. Florida 14. Psychological fiction 15. Literary fiction 16. African American fiction

LC 2003052737
ALA Notable Book, 2004.
The epitome of a group of women's ideals about love, fatherhood, and friendship, wealthy hotel owner Bill Cosey finds his life compromised by his troubled past and his feelings about a spellbinding woman named Celestial.

Morrison, Toni, 1931-2019

A **mercy** : a novel / Toni Morrison. Knopf, 2008. 176 p.
ISBN 9780307264237
1. 17th century 2. Slavery 3. Prejudice 4. African American girls 5. Interracial adoption 6. Racism 7. Religious fanaticism 8. Historical fiction 9. Literary fiction 10. African American fiction

LC 2008021067
ALA Notable Book, 2010.
Shortlisted for the James Tait Black Memorial Prize for Fiction, 2008
In exchange for a bad debt, an Anglo-Dutch trader takes on Florens, a young slave girl, who feels abandoned by her slave mother and who searches for love--first from an older servant woman at her master's new home, and then from a handsome free blacksmith, in a novel set in late seventeenth-century America.
"The fate of a slave child abandoned by her mother animates this allusive novel part Faulknerian puzzle, part dream-song about orphaned women who form an eccentric household in late-17th-century America. Morrison's farmers and rum traders, masters and slaves, indentured whites and captive Native Americans live side by side, often in violent conflict, in a lawless, ripe American Eden that is both a haven and a prison--an emerging nation whose identity is rooted equally in Old World superstitions and New World appetites and fears." New York Times Book Review.

Morrison, Toni, 1931-2019

Paradise / Toni Morrison. A. A. Knopf, 1998. 318 p.
ISBN 0679433740
1. 1890s 2. 1970s 3. African American communities 4. Community life 5. African American men/women relations 6. African Americans 7. Women's shelters 8. Oklahoma 9. African American fiction 10. Literary fiction 11. Modern classics
Shortlisted for the International IMPAC Dublin Literary Award, 2000
Shortlisted for The Orange Prize for Fiction, 1999
Tells the story of Ruby, Oklahoma, an all Black town settled by a dozen families in the 1890s when they were turned away from other

communities. But now it's the 1970s and the men of the town blame the women and the women's shelter for the change in their community's character.

Morrison, Toni, 1931-2019

* **Song** of Solomon / Toni Morrison. A. A. Knopf, 1977. 337 p.
ISBN 0394497848
1. African Americans -- Identity 2. Self-discovery in men 3. Self-acceptance in men 4. African American fathers and sons 5. Rich African American families 6. Racism 7. Detroit, Michigan 8. Family sagas 9. Literary fiction 10. African American fiction 11. Modern classics

LC 77000874
National Book Critics Circle Award for Fiction, 1977.
Milkman Dead was born shortly after a neighborhood eccentric hurled himself off a rooftop in a vain attempt at flight. For the rest of his life he, too, will be trying to fly.

Morrison, Toni, 1931-2019

Sula / Toni Morrison ; with a new foreword by the author. Vintage International, 2004, c1974. xvii, 174 p.
ISBN 1400033438
1. African American women 2. Small town life 3. Friendship 4. African American women -- Friendship 5. Female friendship 6. Separated friends, relatives, etc 7. Reunions 8. African American mothers 9. Leaving home 10. Self-acceptance in African-American women 11. Social acceptance 12. Ohio 13. Literary fiction 14. African American fiction 15. Modern classics

LC 2004555327
At the heart of Sula is a bond between two women, a friendship whose intensity first sustains, then injures. Sula and Nel are both black, both smart, and both poor. Through their girlhood years, they share everything. All this changes when Sula gets out of the Bottom, the hilltop neighborhood where there hides a fierce resentment at the invisible line that cannot be overstepped.

Morrison, Toni, 1931-2019

Tar baby / Toni Morrison. A. A. Knopf, 1981. 305 p.
ISBN 9780394423296
1. Community life 2. Caribbean Area 3. African American fiction 4. Literary fiction 5. Modern classics

LC 80022821
On a tropical island paradise, six people interact with each other in all the tender or hateful ways that human beings are capable of. Rich and poor, black and white, young and old, male and female, each has something to teach the others--and each has something to learn.
"Each of the characters in Toni Morrison's Tar Baby comes with a history, quite a complete history that is given to us in a series of stunning performances." The New Republic.

Morrow, James, 1947-

The **last** witchfinder : a novel / James Morrow. William Morrow, 2006. 448 p.
ISBN 0060821795
1. Franklin, Benjamin, 1706-1790 2. Newton, Isaac, 1642-1727 3. Colonial America (1600-1775) 4. Restoration England (1660-1688) 5. Stuart period (1603-1714) 6. Young women 7. Executions and executioners 8. Indian captivities 9. Women authors 10. Witch hunting 11. Trials (Witchcraft) 12. Witchcraft 13. Fathers and daughters 14. Brothers and sisters 15. Families 16. Men/women relations 17. Independence in women 18. Great Britain -- History -- Restoration, 1660-1688 19. Salem, Massachusetts -- History

-- Colonial period, 1626-1775 20. Philadelphia, Pennsylvania -- History -- Colonial period, 1600-1775 21. Historical fiction

LC 2005047177

"Although steeped in period language and scholarship, the narrative never falters. Morrow's panoramic vision of the Enlightenment encompasses the ideology of that turbulent, transformative era, and his wry commentary--related through the sprightly voice of Newton's Principia Mathematica, speaking for itself--lightens the novel's tone without softening its message. This impeccably researched, highly ambitious novel. . . is a triumph of historical fiction." Booklist.

Mortimer, John, 1923-2009

Felix in the underworld / John Mortimer. Viking, 1997. 246 p.

ISBN 0670860794

1. Malicious accusation 2. Murder investigation 3. Life change events 4. Middle-aged men 5. Authors 6. Fugitives 7. Former lovers 8. Child support 9. London, England 10. Mysteries

LC 9716562

Separated after a childless marriage, Felix Morsom becomes obsessed with his publicist, Brenda Bodkin, and their unconsummated passion, but when a paternity suit leads to murder, Felix finds himself the prime suspect in an underworld of crime and poverty

"This novel is actually about the characters of literary and legal London, and we soon realize that the point is not just to allow these people to circulate in the pages of narrative but, more importantly, to turn character into caricature. . . . John Mortimer's writing is fluent, gently humorous, and possesses the comic's virtue, tact." Times Literary Supplement.

Mortimer, John, 1923-2009

Quite honestly / John Mortimer. Viking, 2006. 224 p.

ISBN 0670034835

1. Former convicts -- Rehabilitation 2. Young women 3. Mentoring 4. Children of clergy 5. Social action 6. Women volunteers 7. Organized crime 8. Secrets 9. Criminals 10. Eccentrics and eccentricities 11. Ethics 12. Clergymen 13. Alcoholic women 14. Family relationships 15. Mentoring 16. Mysteries 17. Satirical fiction

LC 2005053157

Wanting to give something back to society in return for her prestigious education and promising career, Lucinda Purefoy joins an organization that befriends released convicts and finds her life turned upsidedown by career burglar Terry Keegan.

"Good intentions pave Lucy Purefoy's way into all kinds of misadventures in this engaging satire. . . . Mortimer clearly enjoys poking fun at middle-class do-gooders-especially Lucy's dad, a bishop so tolerant that he probably puts a pretty please at the end of the Sixth Commandment. The end result is a tad slight, but fine for readers who enjoy light satire with a little larceny on the side." Christian Science Monitor.

Mortimer, John, 1923-2009

Rumpole's return / John Mortimer. Armchair Detective Library, 1992, c1982. 159 p. Rumpole of the Bailey

ISBN 9781562870379

1. Defense attorneys 2. Lawyers 3. Trials 4. Vacations 5. Criminal investigation 6. Grouches 7. Florida 8. Mysteries 9. Legal stories

LC 91029415

Basking in the Florida sunshine during a well-deserved vacation, barrister Horace Rumpole learns of a case that seems tailor-made for his unique investigative skills.

Morton, Brian, 1955-

Florence Gordon / Brian Morton. Houghton Mifflin Harcourt, 2014. 256 p.

ISBN 9780544309869

1. 2000s (Decade) 2. Senior women 3. Women radicals 4. Independence in women 5. Intellectual life 6. Authors 7. Writing 8. Families 9. Family relationships 10. New York City 11. Upper West Side, New York City 12. Literary fiction

LC 2014011676

Kirkus Prize for Fiction finalist, 2014.

"A wise and entertaining novel about a woman who has lived life on her own terms for seventy-five defiant and determined years, only to find herself suddenly thrust to the center of her family's various catastrophes."--, Provided by publisher.

"Morton's characters are sharply drawn, vivid in temperament and behavior, and his prose smartly reveals Florence's strength and dignity." Publishers Weekly.

Morton, Carson

Stealing Mona Lisa : a mystery / Carson Morton. Minotaur Books, 2011. 304 p.

ISBN 9780312621711

1. Leonardo,, da Vinci, 1452-1519 Mona Lisa 2. Swindlers and swindling -- Argentina 3. Art forgeries 4. Art thefts -- Paris, France 5. Police -- Paris, France 6. Paris, France -- History -- 20th century 7. Argentina -- History -- 20th century 8. Historical mysteries 9. Mysteries

LC 2011009099

Entreated by a beautiful new client to steal the Mona Lisa, art forger Eduardo de Valfierno and a sophisticated band of con artists encounter such challenges as a relentless police inspector and a dangerous flood, in a story inspired by the 1911 theft from the Louvre.

Morton, Kate, 1976-

The **distant** hours : a novel / Kate Morton. Atria Books, 2010. 480 p.

ISBN 9781439152782

1. Mothers and daughters 2. Family secrets 3. World War II 4. Evacuation of civilians 5. Castles 6. Twins 7. Senior women 8. Memory 9. Twin sisters 10. England 11. Kent, England 12. Gothic fiction 13. Psychological suspense 14. Parallel narratives

LC 2010033472

Australian Book Industry Awards, General Fiction Book of the Year, 2011.

Edie Burchill and her mother have never been close, but when a long-lost letter arrives one Sunday afternoon with the return address of Milderhurst Castle, Kent, printed on its envelope, Edie begins to suspect that her mother's emotional distance masks an old secret. Evacuated from London as a thirteen-year-old girl, Edie's mother is chosen by the mysterious Juniper Blythe, and taken to live at the grand and glorious Milderhurst Castle, where she discovers the joys of books and fantasy and writing, but also, ultimately, the dangers. Fifty years later, as Edie chases the answers to her mother's riddle, she, too, is drawn to Milderhurst Castle and the eccentric Sisters Blythe. Inside the decaying castle, Edie begins to unravel her mother's past. But there are other secrets hidden in the stones of Milderhurst Castle, and Edie is about to learn more than she expected. The truth of what happened in the distant hours has been waiting a long time for someone to find it.

Morton, Kate, 1976-

The **house** at Riverton : a novel / Kate Morton. Atria Books, 2008, c2006. vi, 473 p.

ISBN 9781416550518

1. 1920s 2. Family estates 3. Sisters 4. Household employees 5. Reminiscing in old age 6. Secrets 7. Country homes 8. Poets 9. Crimes against poets 10. Americans in England 11. Aristocracy -- History -- 20th century 12. Men/women relations 13. Love triangles 14. Suicide 15. Life change events 16. Housekeepers 17. Essex, England 18. Great Britain -- History -- George V, 1910-1936 19. Great Britain -- Social life and customs -- 20th century 20. Historical fiction

"Originally published in Australia in 2006 as The Shifting Fog by Allen & Unwin"--T.p. verso.

Australian Book Industry Awards, General Fiction Book of the Year, 2007.

Living out her final days in a nursing home, ninety-eight-year-old Grace remembers the secrets surrounding the 1924 suicide of a young poet during a glittering society party hosted by Grace's English aristocrat employers, a family that is shattered by war.

"A suspenseful and beautifully atmospheric novel capturing the transitional time from the end of the Edwardian era through World War I into the Roaring Twenties." Library Journal.

Mosby, Steve

You can run / Steve Mosby. Pegasus Books, 2017. 327 p.

ISBN 9781681775586

1. Serial murderers 2. Fugitives 3. Obsession 4. Women murder victims 5. Authors 6. Detectives 7. Deception 8. England 9. Thrillers and suspense

"But where will you hide your past?" -- Cover.

As the manhunt for the Red River Killer intensifies, Detective Inspector Will Turner finds himself fighting to stay involved in the investigation.

Moses, Kate

Wintering : a novel of Sylvia Plath / Kate Moses. St. Martin's Press, 2003. 292 p.

ISBN 031228375X

1. Plath, Sylvia 2. Hughes, Ted, 1930-1998 3. 1960s 4. Poets 5. Compulsive behavior 6. Self-destructive behavior 7. Mother and child 8. Extramarital affairs 9. Mothers and daughters 10. Women with mental illnesses 11. Separated couples 12. Husband and wife 13. Suicide victims 14. London, England 15. Biographical fiction 16. Psychological fiction

LC 2002036753

"Wintering is beautiful and moving. The narrative voice is a distillation of Plath's diaries, letters and poems; with lyrical dexterity and great economy, Moses portrays a demanding, pitiless woman struggling against the stark fact of her husband's infidelity and her own inner demons." New York Times Book Review.

Mosher, Howard Frank

On Kingdom Mountain / Howard Frank Mosher. Houghton Mifflin Co., 2007. 288 p.

ISBN 9780618197231

1. 1930s 2. Women booksellers 3. Stunt pilots 4. Mountains 5. Women landowners 6. Land development 7. Men/women relations 8. Riddles 9. Treasure hunting 10. Vermont 11. Historical fiction

LC 2006023568

In 1930 Vermont, Jane Hubbell Kinneson, the last resident of a remote mountain on the U.S.-Canadian border that is threatened by a proposed new highway, confronts a mysterious pilot searching for a cache of stolen gold who crashes his plane on her mountain.

"Mosher's passionate geographical hyperbole is both justifiable and charming, producing a wonderfully intriguing sense of place." Washington Post Book World.

Moshfegh, Ottessa

* **Death** in her hands : a novel / Ottessa Moshfegh. Penguin Press, 2020. 272 p.

ISBN 9781984879356

1. Widows 2. Senior women 3. Forests 4. Obsession 5. Women amateur detectives 6. Women murder victims 7. Imagination 8. Social isolation 9. Literary fiction 10. Mysteries

LC 2019045121

Discovering a note and grave while walking her dog in the woods, an elderly widow becomes obsessed with learning the victim's story before her grip on reality is shaken by what she uncovers.

"Cleverly unraveling, linguistically brilliant, and limning the limits of reality, this will speak to fans of literary psychological suspense." Booklist.

Moshfegh, Ottessa

Eileen / Ottessa Moshfegh. Penguin Press, 2015. 260 p.

ISBN 9781594206627

1. 1960s 2. Loneliness in women 3. Crime 4. Female friendship 5. Self-hate in women 6. Obsession 7. Twenties (Age) 8. Juvenile jails 9. Adult children of alcoholics 10. Sexuality 11. Reminiscing in old age 12. Massachusetts 13. Psychological fiction 14. Literary fiction

Hemingway Foundation/PEN Award, 2016.

National Book Critics Circle Award for Fiction finalist, 2015

Shortlisted for the Man Booker Prize, 2016

Dreaming of life in the city while caring for her alcoholic father and working in a 1960s boys' prison, a disturbed young woman is manipulated into committing a psychologically charged crime during the holiday season.

"Moshfegh keeps all options on the table while keeping her heroine coherent. A shadowy and superbly told story of how inner turmoil morphs into outer chaos." Kirkus.

Moshfegh, Ottessa

My year of rest and relaxation / Ottessa Moshfegh. Penguin Press, 2018. 288 p.

ISBN 9780525522119

1. 2000s (Decade) 2. Young women 3. Social isolation 4. Alienation (Social psychology) 5. Drugs 6. Orphans 7. Rich people 8. Psychiatrists 9. Loss of consciousness 10. New York City 11. Upper East Side, New York City 12. Literary fiction 13. Psychological fiction

After losing her parents, a young college graduate in New York City spends a year alienating the world under the influence of a crazy combination of drugs.

Mosley, Walter

All I did was shoot my man : a Leonid McGill mystery / Walter Mosley. Riverhead, 2012 336 p. Leonid McGill mysteries

ISBN 9781594488245

1. Redemption 2. Frameups 3. Robbery investigation 4. Conflict in families 5. Father and adult child 6. Husband and wife 7. Husband-killing 8. African American men 9. Private investigators 10. Murder investigation 11. New York City 12. Mysteries 13. African American fiction

When Zella Grisham is accused of both shooting her boyfriend and stealing more than six million dollars from the Rutgers Assurance Corp., Leonid McGill investigates, while his own family life begins to unravel around him.

Mosley, Walter

And sometimes I wonder about you : a Leonid McGill mystery / Walter Mosley. Doubleday, 2015 304 p. Leonid McGill mysteries

ISBN 9780385539180

1. Missing persons investigation 2. Inheritance and succession 3. Husband and wife 4. Extramarital affairs 5. Family relationships 6. African American men 7. Private investigators 8. Murder investigation 9. New York City 10. Mysteries 11. African American fiction

Investigating the murder of a client he initially refused to help, Leonid navigates difficult personal elements in his own life while uncovering dark secrets about the victim's old-money family and its missing heiress.

"While Mosley is best known for his Easy Rawlins novels, set in the post-WWII and later twentieth-century era, this gritty, present-day series deserves serious attention from all fans of mainstream hard-boiled detective fiction." Booklist.

Mosley, Walter

Bad boy Brawly Brown : an Easy Rawlins mystery / Walter Mosley. Little, Brown, and Co., 2002. 320 p. Easy Rawlins mysteries

ISBN 0316073016

1. 1960s 2. Murder investigation 3. Race relations 4. Working class African Americans 5. African American World War II veterans 6. African American men 7. Private investigators 8. Los Angeles, California -- Race relations 9. Watts, Los Angeles, California 10. Historical mysteries 11. African American fiction 12. Mysteries

LC 2002016232

Set in 1964, Easy is on a mission to lure Brawley Brown back to his mother. But not only is Brawley bad, he's big and not so easily swayed, especially since joining the Urban Revolutionary Party, a political group wary of strangers. Add to that a cache of stolen guns, secret government investigators, a payroll heist, several murders, problems with his son, and everybody lying about everything, plus his own crushing guilt over the apparent death of his best friend, and you've got Easy behind the eight ball once again.

"As Easy persists in his investigation, he is dismissed by black radicals and rousted by racist cops. . . . So he can't really be blamed for spending more time than he should in places like Sam's Hambones soul food diner, engaging in invigorating of often aimless conversations with characters who have little to offer on Brawly's whereabouts but lots to say about whatever is on their minds. Aside from their appealing hero, Mosley's crime novels take their vitality from the racy language and boisterous humanity of his characters, so these neighborhood encounters provide their own joy." New York Times Book Review.

Mosley, Walter

Black Betty : an Easy Rawlins mystery / Walter Mosley. W.W. Norton, 1994. 255 p. Easy Rawlins mysteries

ISBN 0393036448

1. 1960s 2. African American men 3. Missing women 4. Race relations 5. Private investigators 6. Los Angeles, California -- Race relations 7. Historical mysteries 8. African American fiction 9. Mysteries

LC 94-6839

On the shady side of LA in 1961, African-American private eye Easy Rawlins can go places a white detective cannot. So when Saul Lynx needs a missing woman found, he hires Easy to do his dirty work.

"Mosley gives us a recognizable moment in American history viewed through the eyes of a single black man. This perspective, rare in crime fiction, vivifies not only the black experience but the larger event as well. Here we feel the hot winds that would eventually ignite the Watts riots not as abstract issues in race relations, but as emotions in the hearts of individuals we have come to know and care about." Booklist.

Mosley, Walter

Blonde faith / Walter Mosley. Little, Brown and Co., 2008. 320 p. Easy Rawlins mysteries

ISBN 9780316734592

1. 1960s 2. African American men 3. Missing persons 4. Detectives -- Los Angeles, California 5. Male friendship 6. Abandoned children 7. Suspicion 8. Missing persons investigation 9. Race relations 10. Private investigators 11. Los Angeles, California 12. Historical mysteries 13. African American fiction 14. Mysteries

LC 2007026018

Fearing his friend, Christmas Black, has met his demise when the ex-Marine's daughter is left on his doorstep, reluctant L.A. detective Easy Rawlins finds the challenges of caring for a child further complicated by another friend's murder accusation.

Mosley, Walter

Charcoal Joe : an Easy Rawlins mystery / Walter Mosley. Doubleday, 2016. 304 p. Easy Rawlins mysteries

ISBN 9780385539203

1. 1960s 2. African American men 3. Hostages 4. Kidnappers 5. Ransom 6. Boxers (Sports) 7. Detectives -- Los Angeles, California 8. Suspicion 9. Murder suspects 10. Race relations 11. Private investigators 12. Los Angeles, California 13. Historical mysteries 14. African American fiction 15. Mysteries

LC 2015044304

Easy Rawlins' plans to marry his girlfriend and start a new detective agency are interrupted by the case of a promising Stanford student who has been charged with the race-related murder of a white man.

Mosley, Walter

Cinnamon kiss / Walter Mosley. Little, Brown, 2005. 320 p. Easy Rawlins mysteries

ISBN 0316073024

1. 1960s 2. African American men 3. Missing persons investigation 4. Detectives -- Los Angeles, California 5. Sick children 6. Sick girls 7. African American fathers and daughters 8. Missing persons 9. Lawyers 10. Private investigators 11. Los Angeles, California 12. San Francisco, California 13. Historical mysteries 14. African American fiction 15. Mysteries

LC 2005005739

Facing unprecedented financial troubles when his daughter requires a medical treatment, Easy Rawlins takes a job tracking down a missing attorney and legal assistant, but the assignment proves more complicated than anticipated.

"As ever, Mosley is able to capture the era--hippies, Watts, communes--in brief strokes that provide a brilliant background to Easy's search for solutions to both a convoluted mystery and complex personal problems." Publishers Weekly.

LIST OF FICTIONAL WORKS

Mosley, Walter

Debbie doesn't do it anymore : a novel / Walter Mosley. Doubleday, 2014. 272 p.

ISBN 9780385526180

1. Redemption 2. Determination in women 3. Pornographic film industry and trade 4. African-American actors and actresses 5. Pornographic film actors and actresses 6. Married men -- Death 7. Extramarital affairs 8. Organized crime 9. Debt 10. Mothers and sons 11. Drama lit 12. African American fiction 13. Mainstream fiction

Resolving to leave the pornography industry after her husband is found electrocuted in a hot tub with another woman, an adult film star endures a reckoning involving her late husband's debts, her estranged family and the child she had to give up.

Mosley, Walter

Devil in a blue dress / Walter Mosley. W. W. Norton, 1990. 219 p. Easy Rawlins mysteries

ISBN 0393028542

1. 1940s 2. African American men 3. Organized crime 4. Working class African Americans 5. African American World War II veterans 6. Missing women 7. Missing persons investigation 8. Gangsters 9. Political corruption 10. Race relations 11. Private investigators 12. Los Angeles, California -- Race relations 13. Watts, Los Angeles, California 14. Historical mysteries 15. African American fiction 16. Mysteries

LC 89025503

First published: New York : Norton; London : Serpent's Tail, 1990.
John Creasey Memorial Award (Best First Crime Novel), 1991.
Shamus Award for Best First P.I. Novel, 1991.

1948, Los Angeles: The mortgage payment's coming due, so Easy Rawlins accepts the assignment of finding Daphne Monet, a blonde torch singer with a penchant for jazz and criminal black consorts. In his search through a sleazy, fearful city, he is lucky to be under the protection of the murderous Mouse who wants a piece of the action.

"Mosley's prose is a little stiff and his plot is far too complicated. But he has a keen eye for period details. . . . And his lowdown humor never deserts him." Newsweek.

Mosley, Walter

Down the river unto the sea / Walter Mosley. Little Brown & Co, 2018 336 p.

ISBN 9780316509640

1. Frameups 2. Police corruption 3. Private investigators 4. Injustice 5. Police brutality 6. Murder investigation 7. Malicious accusation 8. Corruption investigation 9. African American journalists 10. New York City 11. Mysteries 12. African American fiction

Edgar Allan Poe Award for Best Novel, 2019.

Framed by corrupt enemies within the NYPD and forced to serve a decade in prison, private detective Joe King Oliver receives a confession from a woman who helped set him up, a situation that compels him to investigate his own case at the same time he assists a black radical journalist who has been wrongly accused of murdering two corrupt cops.

Mosley, Walter

Fearless Jones : a novel / Walter Mosley. Little, Brown, 2001. 312 p. Fearless Jones novels

ISBN 0316592382

1. 1950s 2. Missing persons investigation 3. Violence 4. Amateur detectives 5. African American booksellers 6. African American men 7. Holocaust survivors -- Los Angeles, California 8. World War II veterans 9. Race relations 10. Los Angeles, California -- Race relations 11. Watts, Los Angeles, California 12. Historical mysteries

13. Hardboiled fiction 14. African American fiction

LC 00053502

Sequel: Fear itself.

Paris Minton's world is turned upside down when a woman named Elana Love walks into his bookstore and asks a few questions. Within the next 24 hous, Paris is beaten up, made love to, shot at, robbed and his bookstore burned to the ground. He's in so much trouble he gets his friend Fearless Jones out of jail because this man knows violence better than any man should.

"This mystery is narrated by Paris Minton, a black man who sells used books in nineteen-fifties L.A. Paris's life is perfecthe reads all day without interruptionuntil a bewitching young woman named Elana Love walks through his door. She's looking for a religious group called the Messenger of the Divine, but the thug who bursts in after her is looking for a bond worth thousands of dollars. Mayhem and seduction ensue, and when Paris's bookstore is burned to the ground, he knows it's time to seek the aid of the incomparable Fearless Jones. The unlikely friendship of these men--Fearless is all fists and testosterone, Paris is a gun-shy truthseeker--is the source of the novel's humor, and propels the reader through the plot's knottier moments." The New Yorker.

Mosley, Walter

Fortunate son : a novel / Walter Mosley. Little, Brown and Co., 2006. 320 p.

ISBN 0316114715

1. Race relations 2. Stepbrothers and stepsisters 3. Trust 4. Rich boys 5. Boys with disabilities 6. African American boys 7. Personal conduct 8. Boys -- Friendship 9. Mother-separated boys 10. Interracial friendship 11. Reunions 12. Social classes 13. Classism 14. Racism 15. Gratitude 16. Resilience in boys 17. Redemption 18. Cooperation 19. Independence in boys 20. Boston, Massachusetts 21. Psychological suspense 22. African American fiction

LC 2005024477

Sharing a close bond in spite of very different backgrounds, Eric, a handsome white man of privilege, and Tommy, an impoverished black youth with poor health, are separated by tragedy and reunited by a common enemy years later.

"The writing is crisp and the plotting impeccable." Library Journal.

Mosley, Walter

Gone fishin' : an Easy Rawlins novel / Walter Mosley. Pocket Books, 1998, c1997. 244 p. Easy Rawlins mysteries

ISBN 9780671010119

1. 1930s 2. African American men 3. Murder 4. Friendship 5. Parricide 6. African American young men 7. Nineteen-year-old men -- Texas 8. Stepfathers -- Texas 9. Fathers and sons -- Texas 10. Voodoo -- Texas 11. Rural African Americans -- Texas 12. Private investigators 13. Fathers -- Death 14. Texas 15. Mysteries 16. Coming-of-age stories 17. African American fiction

Originally published: Baltimore : Black Classic Press, 1997.

Nineteen-year-old Ezekiel "Easy" Rawlins and his companion, Raymond "Mouse" Alexander, embark on a perilous 1939 odyssey that takes them from Houston to a mysterious bayou world of voodoo, sex, revenge, and death.

"This is in some respects, the best of Mosley's novels. . . . It firmly establishes Mosley as a writer whose work transcends the thriller category and qualifies as serious literature." Time.

Mosley, Walter

* **John** Woman / Walter Mosley. Atlantic Monthly Press, 2018. 377 p.

ISBN 9780802128416

1. Multiracial men 2. College teachers 3. Identity (Psychology)

4. Anonyms and pseudonyms 5. Intellectuals 6. Universities and colleges 7. History 8. Memory 9. Power (Social sciences) 10. Literary fiction 11. Psychological fiction 12. African American fiction

LC 2018012867

A young man reinvents himself as a professor to share his late father's wisdom at an unorthodox university, only to encounter fellow intellectuals who have insights into his father's hidden past.

Mosley, Walter

Known to evil / Walter Mosley. Riverhead Books, 2010. 336 p. Leonid McGill mysteries

ISBN 9781594487521

1. African American men 2. Private investigators 3. Political corruption 4. Fifties (Age) 5. Criminals 6. Organized crime 7. Fathers and sons 8. Murder investigation 9. New York City 10. Mysteries 11. African American fiction

LC 2009042643

Sequel to: The long fall.

New York City private investigator Leonid McGill is given few details when he is hired by the city's top power broker to track down twenty-seven year old Tara Lear, a case that leads him to seek the assistance of some old acquaintants.

"This second installment of Walter Mosley's new detective series opens at the dinner table. He gives you a quick look around the room--walnut cabinet, Blue Danube china, old quart pickle jar doing duty as a flower vase--then takes you inside the protagonist's head. That's how a great portion of the story unfolds: through private detective Leonid McGill's inner musings. If you thought Easy Rawlins was a complicated character, spend a little time with McGill as he tries to find a missing woman, avoid police determined to jail him, deal with his imploding marriage, protect his sons from themselves, fend off a move to evict him from his offices and heal from a broken heart administered by an ex-lover." NPR.

Mosley, Walter

The **last** days of Ptolemy Grey / Walter Mosley. Riverhead Books, 2010. 288 p.

ISBN 9781594487729

1. African American seniors 2. Memory 3. Drive-by shootings 4. Aging 5. African American families 6. Loss (Psychology) 7. People with dementia -- Treatment 8. Nonagenarian men 9. Senior men 10. Seniors 11. South Central Los Angeles, California 12. Los Angeles, California 13. Psychological fiction 14. African American fiction

LC 2010012317

Ptolemy Grey is a 91-year-old man, suffering from dementia and living as a recluse in his Los Angeles apartment. Then Robyn Small, a 17-year-old family friend, appears and helps clean up his apartment and straighten out his life. A reinvigorated Ptolemy volunteers for an experimental medical program that restores his mind, and he uses his last days--shortened now by the medical experiment--to delve into the mystery of the recent drive-by shooting death of his great-nephew, Reggie.

"Narrated in an intimate whisper, the story draws us deep into the mind of an old man wandering through the remnants of his memories, searching for the key to an old mystery. ... The tale of an aged superhero who performs valiant deeds with the aid of a devoted young sidekick (pointedly named Robyn) may sound like the charming stuff of myth. But Mosley invests his wish-fulfillment fantasy with deeper meaning and higher purpose." New York Times Book Review.

Mosley, Walter

Little green : an Easy Rawlins mystery / Walter Mosley. Doubleday, 2014. 304 p. Easy Rawlins mysteries

ISBN 9780385535984

1. 1960s 2. African American men 3. Missing persons 4. Detectives -- Los Angeles, California 5. Suspicion 6. Missing persons investigation 7. Race relations 8. Private investigators 9. Los Angeles, California 10. Historical mysteries 11. African American fiction 12. Mysteries

Originally published: London: Weidenfeld & Nicolson, 2013.

Surviving a near-fatal car wreck and cruising the streets of the Sunset Strip during the heyday of the late 1960s, Easy Rawlins investigates the disappearance of a young African-American, a case that is complicated by Rawlins's changing perspectives. By the O. Henry Award-winning author of the Socrates Fortlow series.

Mosley, Walter

Little Scarlet : an Easy Rawlins mystery / Walter Mosley. Little, Brown and Co., 2004. 320 p. Easy Rawlins mysteries

ISBN 0316073032

1. 1960s 2. African American men 3. Murder investigation 4. Detectives -- Los Angeles, California 5. Watts Riot, Los Angeles, California, 1965 6. Riots -- Los Angeles, California 7. Race relations -- California 8. Race riots 9. Private investigators 10. Los Angeles, California 11. Watts, Los Angeles, California -- History 12. Historical mysteries 13. African American fiction 14. Mysteries

LC 2003023002

When a man who fled the 1965 Watts riots is suspected of killing a woman in a nearby apartment building, Easy Rawlins begins a murder investigation and learns that the case has sobering racial origins.

"This is Mosley's best novel to date: the plot is streamlined and the language simple yet strong, allowing the serpentine story line to support Easy's amazingly complex character and hypnotic narration as Mosley plunges us into his world and, by extension, the world of all blacks in white-run America. Fierce, provocative, expertly entertaining, this is genre writing at its finest." Publishers Weekly.

Mosley, Walter

A **little** yellow dog : an Easy Rawlins mystery / Walter Mosley. W. W. Norton, 1996. 300 p. Easy Rawlins mysteries

ISBN 0393039242

1. 1960s 2. African American men 3. Murder investigation 4. African American janitors 5. Murder 6. Heroin traffic 7. Burglary 8. African American murder suspects 9. Race relations 10. Private investigators 11. Los Angeles, California 12. Historical mysteries 13. African American fiction 14. Mysteries

LC 964231

In Los Angeles' inner city during the fifties, Easy Rawlins takes a job as head custodian at a junior high school, where old enemies and murder catch up with him

"Mosley writes in the grand tradition of the American hard-boiled private investigator. His dialog is sharp and his characters vivid the reader can almost feel the mean L.A. streets." Library Journal.

Mosley, Walter

The **long** fall / Walter Mosley. Riverhead Books, 2009. 320 p. Leonid McGill mysteries

ISBN 9781594488580

1. Fifties (Age) 2. Criminals 3. Organized crime 4. Fathers and sons 5. Murder investigation 6. African American men 7. Private investigators 8. New York City 9. Mysteries 10. African American fiction

LC 2008046238

Sequel: Known to evil.

Getting by as an old-school private investigator in spite of Manhattan's increasingly sophisticated culture, Leonid McGill finds his commitment to living a straight-and-narrow life repeatedly tested when he attempts to obtain information for a high-paying client.

"The novel accomplishes most of what an inaugural installment of a mystery series should. The three major plot strands are solidly developed and neatly resolved. McGill's quest for redemption, however, is far from over, but it will be interesting to watch it play out across a number of subsequent volumes. If The Long Fall is overstuffed with incidental characters whose importance may not be obvious until later installments, that's a minor flaw. Having retired Easy Rawlins, Mosley has devised a worthy successor in Leonid McGill." San Francisco Chronicle.

Mosley, Walter

The **man** in my basement : a novel / Walter Mosley. Little, Brown, 2004. 256 p.

ISBN 0316570826

1. Race relations 2. Power (Social sciences) 3. Manipulation (Social sciences) 4. African American men 5. Unemployed persons 6. European American men 7. Rich men 8. African American families -- History 9. Landlord and tenant 10. Identity (Psychology) 11. Atonement 12. Home ownership 13. Debt 14. Drinking 15. Psychological fiction 16. African American fiction

LC 2003056317

To save the home that has belonged to his family for generations, Charles Blakey, a young black man whose life is slowly crumbling around him, agrees to rent out his basement for the summer to a mysterious stranger.

"In this successful and intriguing departure from his usual work, Mr. Mosley creates a substantial subplot about heritage and history. . . . In the end this audacious novel is about facing up to such brutal realities. But it is also about seeking refuge." New York Times.

Mosley, Walter

A **red** death / Walter Mosley W. W. Norton, 1991. 284 p. Easy Rawlins mysteries

ISBN 9780393029987

1. 1950s 2. African American men 3. Undercover operations 4. Missing persons investigation 5. Working class African Americans -- Watts, Los Angeles, California 6. Private investigators 7. Los Angeles, California 8. Watts, Los Angeles, California 9. Historical mysteries 10. African American fiction 11. Mysteries

LC 90023660

During the McCarthy era, Easy Rawlins is caught between a vengeful IRS employee and an FBI agent who wants to use him as an undercover operative.

Mosley, Walter

* The **right** mistake : the further philosophical investigations of Socrates Fortlow / Walter Mosley. Basic Books, 2008. 288 p. Socrates Fortlow novels

ISBN 9780465005253

1. Former convicts 2. Gangs 3. Violence 4. African American men 5. Meetings 6. Friendship 7. Philosophers 8. Social advocates 9. Los Angeles, California 10. Psychological fiction 11. Political fiction 12. African American fiction

LC bl2008020384

After serving nearly three decades in prison for his deadly crimes, Socrates returns to the streets of South Central L.A. to connect with old friends and encourage new ones to join him in his campaign to get to the heart of gang violence.

Mosley, Walter

RL's dream / Walter Mosley. W.W. Norton, 1995. 267 p.

ISBN 0393038025

1. Johnson, Robert, 1911-1938 2. Poor people 3. African American blues musicians 4. City life 5. Former musicians 6. Young women 7. New York City 8. Psychological fiction 9. Political fiction 10. African American fiction

LC 95-8695

BCALA Literary Award for Fiction, 1996.

Recounting his memories to a young white woman who is also a refugee from a painful Southern past, Soupspoon Wise, a dying blues performer, describes a brief encounter with a famous performer that still haunts him

"A mesmerizing and redemptive tale of friendship, love, and forgiveness. . . . [This] is, without doubt, the author's finest achievement to date, a rich literary gumbo with blue-stinged rhythms that make it a joy to read and a book to remember." San Francisco Review of Books.

Mosley, Walter

Rose gold : an Easy Rawlins mystery / Walter Mosley. Doubleday, 2014. 304 p. Easy Rawlins mysteries

ISBN 9780385535977

1. 1960s 2. African American men 3. Hostages 4. Kidnappers 5. Ransom 6. Boxers (Sports) 7. Detectives -- Los Angeles, California 8. Suspicion 9. Missing persons investigation 10. Race relations 11. Private investigators 12. Los Angeles, California 13. Historical mysteries 14. African American fiction 15. Mysteries

Standard print edition originally published: London: Weidenfeld & Nicolson, 2014.

Clipper. LP3767.

When a boxer-turned-revolutionary kidnaps the daughter of a weapons manufacturer and threatens to publicly execute her in exchange for a lucrative ransom, Easy Rawlins is tapped by the LAPD to make a difficult border crossing to navigate an ensuing standoff.

Mosley, Walter

Six Easy pieces : Easy Rawlins stories / Walter Mosley. Atria Books, 2003. 256 p. Easy Rawlins mysteries

ISBN 0743442520

1. 1960s 2. African American men 3. Race relations 4. Friendship 5. Adopted children 6. Insecurity (Psychology) 7. Grief in men 8. Stealing 9. Extortion 10. Murder 11. Working class African Americans 12. African American janitors 13. Private investigators 14. Los Angeles, California 15. Watts, Los Angeles, California 16. Historical mysteries 17. Short stories 18. African American fiction 19. Mysteries

LC BL2002012425

A collection of six interconnected Easy Rawlins short mysteries includes "Smoke," "Crimson Stain," "Silver Lining," "Lavender," "Gator Green," and "Untitled."

"Mosley is as fine as ever, offering compelling commentary on black-white relations in 1964, writing in a style so simple that it deceives us into thinking writing great fiction is as easy as putting one foot in front of the other. It's not, but turning these pages is." Booklist.

Mosley, Walter

Trouble is what I do : a Leonid McGill mystery / Walter Mosley. Mulholland Books, 2020. 176 p. Leonid McGill mysteries

ISBN 9780316491136

1. Private investigators 2. Blues musicians 3. Assassins 4. Family secrets 5. Criminals 6. Genealogy 7. Protectiveness in men 8. Racism 9. African American men 10. City life 11. New York City

12. Hardboiled fiction 13. Mysteries 14. African American fiction

Detective Leonid McGill is forced to confront the ghost of his felonious past when a nonagenarian Mississippi bluesman is targeted by an infamous assassin.

"Spieled in a powerful, streamlined voice, this wrenching American noir will stick with readers long after the final page." Booklist.

Mosley, Walter

When the thrill is gone / Walter Mosley. Riverhead Books, 2011. 368 p. Leonid McGill mysteries

ISBN 9781594487811

1. Billionaires 2. Extramarital affairs 3. Deception 4. Swindlers and swindling 5. Fathers and sons 6. Husband and wife 7. African American men 8. Private investigators 9. Murder investigation 10. New York City 11. Mysteries 12. African American fiction

LC 2010039098

A beautiful young woman walks into PI Leonid McGill's office with a stack of cash. She's an artist, she tells Leonid, who's escaped poverty via marriage to a rich collector. A rich collector with two ex-wives whose deaths are shrouded in mystery. She says she fears for her life, and needs Leonid's help. Will sorting out the woman's crooked tale bring Leonid straight to death's door?

"This installment finds Leonid McGill still unable to shake his underworld connections as a personal favor he['s undertaking a search for the lost friend of a powerful crime boss. But there are other pressing matters to be taken care of: a man who has been like a father to him lies dying in McGill's apartment, McGill's wife is sleeping with a man half her age and if McGill doesn't get a paying job he won't be able to pay the rent on his office. . . . For a healthy retainer, McGill takes the case of a nervous wife who suspects her billionaire husband of having an affair and planning to murder her to avoid a messy divorce. . . . Unlike the flamboyant criminals who swagger through Mosley's Easy Rawlins novels, the characters who catch your eye here are people who are normally invisible: old folks living on the edges of society and young black men with no notion of their history and no hope for a future except what they were told by the TV. The qualities that make McGill fit to be their hero are the same ones that make him the quintessential New Yorker: he sees it all and knows it all and somehow feels responsible for it all." New York Times Book Review.

Mosley, Walter

White butterfly / Walter Mosley. Norton, 1992. 272 p. Easy Rawlins mysteries

ISBN 9780393033663

1. 1950s 2. African American men 3. Murder investigation 4. Serial murders 5. Murder 6. Stripteasers 7. Women murder victims 8. Private investigators 9. Los Angeles, California 10. Historical mysteries 11. African American fiction 12. Mysteries

LC 91044700

Although little concern is raised by the murder of three black women, the LAPD jumps on the case when the killer's next victim turns out to be Cyndi Starr, a white woman.

"Standard stuff, to be sure--the makings of your typical made-for-television movie. But what elevates it is the character. It is not just that Rawlins is such an engaging fellow. He is a man who both ages and evolves." New York Times Book Review.

Moss, Sarah

Ghost wall : a novel / Sarah Moss. Farrar, Straus and Giroux, 2019, c2018. 144 p.

ISBN 9780374161927

1. Historical reenactments 2. Archaeology 3. Working-class families 4. Iron age 5. Abusive men 6. Teenage girls 7. College students 8.

Family violence 9. Racism 10. Rites and ceremonies 11. Violence 12. Social classes 13. Northern England 14. England 15. Literary fiction 16. Coming-of-age stories

LC 2018026605

Originally published by Granta Books, 2018.

Longlisted for The Women's Prize for Fiction, 2019.

Shortlisted for the RSL Ondaatje Prize, 2019.

Spending her father's vacations at an Iron Age reenactment anthropology field site that requires participants to use period tools and knowledge to survive, Silvie begins to envision her own future before a spiritual ritual involving human sacrifice raises disturbing questions.

"Moss' slender novel follows a working-class family of three from Northern England as they take a proverbial trip back in time, joining an archaeology professor and three of his students on a journey to the wilds of the country to live in the fashion of Iron Age Britons." Booklist.

Mott, Jason

The **returned** / Jason Mott. Mira Books., 2013. 400 p.

ISBN 9780778315339

1. Sons 2. Resurrection 3. Small towns 4. Death 5. Anxiety 6. Violence 7. Redemption 8. Interpersonal relations 9. Family relationships 10. Literary fiction 11. African American fiction

Adapted into the ABC television series: Resurrection.

When their son Jacob, who died tragically at his 8th birthday party in 1966, arrives on their doorstep, still 8 years old, Harold and Lucille Hargrave must navigate a strange new reality as chaos erupts around the world as people's loved ones are returned from beyond.

Moyes, Jojo, 1969-

The **girl** you left behind / Jojo Moyes. Pamela Dorman Books/Viking, 2013, c2012. 384 p.

ISBN 9780670026616

1. First World War era (1914-1918) 2. 1910s 3. Loss (Psychology) 4. Family and war 5. Portraits 6. Soldiers 7. Widows 8. Married women 9. Young women 10. World War I 11. France -- History -- 20th century 12. Historical fiction 13. Parallel narratives

First published: 2012.

Originally published: London : Michael Joseph, 2012.

Unwillingly rendered an object of obsession by the Kommandant occupying her small French town in World War I, Sophie risks everything to reunite with her husband a century before a widowed Liv tests her resolve to claim ownership of Sophie's portrait.

Moyes, Jojo, 1969-

* The **giver** of stars : a novel / Jojo Moyes. Pamela Dorman Books/Viking, 2019. 400 p.

ISBN 9780399562488

1. Depression era (1929-1941) 2. 1930s 3. Volunteers 4. Libraries 5. Traveling libraries 6. Women librarians 7. Independence in women 8. Female friendship 9. Equestrians 10. Rural life 11. Literacy 12. Adventure 13. Purpose in life 14. Kentucky 15. Historical fiction

LC 2019030049

Volunteering for Eleanor Roosevelt's new traveling library in small-town Kentucky, an English bride joins a group of independent women whose commitment to their job transforms the community and their relationships.

Moyes, Jojo, 1969-

Me before you : a novel / Jojo Moyes. Pamela Dorman Books, 2012. 384 p. Me before you

ISBN 9780670026609

1. Resentfulness in men 2. Wheelchair users 3. Caregivers 4. Young women 5. Moods and moodiness 6. Suicidal behavior 7. England 8.

Women's lives and relationships 9. Mainstream fiction

LC 2012029301

Sequel: After You.

RUSA Reading List, 2014.

Taking a job as an assistant to extreme sports enthusiast Will, who is wheelchair bound after a motorcycle accident, Louisa struggles with her employer's acerbic moods and learns of his shocking plans before demonstrating to him that life is still worth living.

Moyes, Jojo, 1969-

* The **peacock** emporium / Jojo Moyes. Penguin Books, 2019, c2004. 432 p.

ISBN 9780735222335

1. Mothers and daughters 2. Socialites 3. Women business owners 4. Coffee shops 5. Married women 6. Dysfunctional families 7. Family relationships 8. Friendship 9. Men/women relations 10. Self-fulfillment 11. England 12. Great Britain 13. Women's lives and relationships

LC 2018058360

Originally published: London : Hodder & Stoughton, 2004.

Struggling to find refuge from her late mother's shameful legacy, Suzanna Peacock finds friendship and escape at her coffee bar and shop, the Peacock Emporium.

Mozley, Fiona

* **Elmet** / Fiona Mozley. Algonquin Books, 2017. 320 p.

ISBN 9781616208424

1. Poor people 2. Father and child 3. Social conflict 4. Violence in men 5. Belonging 6. Loyalty 7. Family relationships 8. Property rights 9. Nonconformists 10. Rural life 11. Violence -- Psychological aspects 12. Yorkshire, England 13. England 14. Literary fiction 15. Psychological fiction

Originally published: London : JM Originals, 2017.

Somerset Maugham Award, 2018.

Shortlisted for the Man Booker Prize, 2017.

Longlisted for The Women's Prize for Fiction, 2018.

Cathy and Daniel live with their father, John, in the remote woods of Yorkshire, in a house the three of them built themselves. John is a gentle brute of a man, a former enforcer who fights for money when he has to, but who otherwise just wants to be left alone to raise his children. When a local landowner shows up on their doorstep, their precarious existence is threatened, and a series of actions is set in motion that can only end in violence.

Mueenuddin, Daniyal

In other rooms, other wonders : connected stories / Daniyal Mueenuddin. W.W. Norton, 2009. 224 p.

ISBN 9780393068009

1. Social classes -- Pakistan 2. Pakistan -- Social conditions 3. Short stories 4. Political fiction

LC 2008040632

National Book Award for Fiction finalist, 2009

Pulitzer Prize for Fiction finalist, 2010.

A volume of linked stories describes the intertwined lives of land-owners and their retainers on the Gurmani family farm in Pakistan, in a collection that explores such themes as culture, class power, and desire.

"In eight beautifully crafted, interconnected stories, Mueenuddin explores the cutthroat feudal society in which a rich Lahore landowner is entrenched. . . . An elegant stylist with a light touch, Mueenuddin invites the reader to a richly human, wondrous experience." Publishers Weekly.

Mukherjee, Abir

A **necessary** evil : a novel / Abir Mukherjee. Pegasus Books, 2018, c2017. 374 p. Sam Wyndham novels

ISBN 9781681776712

1. British Raj (1858-1947) 2. 1920s 3. British in India 4. World War I veterans 5. Detectives 6. Police 7. Murder investigation 8. Colonialism 9. Calcutta, India 10. India -- History -- British occupation, 1765-1947 11. Historical mysteries

Sequel to: A Rising Man.

Sequel: Smoke and ashes.

Originally published: London: Harvill Secker, 2017.

A sequel to the award-winning A Rising Man finds Captain Wyndham and Sergeant Banerjee of the 1920 Calcutta Police Force investigating the assassination of a Maharajah's progressive-minded son, a crime that has left the country in the hands of the victim's brother, a feckless playboy.

"Fans of Elizabeth Peter's Amelia Peabody series will enjoy Wyndhams unashamed internal commentary, social blundering, and witty banter with Banerjee and Grant. A richly detailed period gem boasting the British Rajs exotic setting and a gripping whydunit spun around an intriguing cast of archetypal mystery characters." Booklist.

Mukherjee, Abir,

A **rising** man / Abir Mukherjee. Pegasus Books, 2017, c2016. 400 Sam Wyndham novels

ISBN 9781681774169

1. British Raj (1858-1947) 2. 1910s 3. British in India 4. World War I veterans 5. Detectives 6. Police 7. Murder investigation 8. Colonialism 9. Calcutta, India 10. India -- History -- British occupation, 1765-1947 11. Historical mysteries

Sequel: A Necessary Evil.

Originally published: London : Harvill Secker, 2016.

Ellis Peters Historical Dagger Award, 2017.

Newly arrived in 1919 Calcutta, former Scotland Yard detective Sam Wyndham joins the Imperial Police Force and lands a big case: a murdered British official is found with a sinister note in his mouth. Working with likable Sgt. Banerjee and jealous sub-Inspector Digby, Wyndham travels through all levels of Colonial Indian society to find a killer. With atmosphere to spare, this delightful debut should please fans of India-set historical mysteries. -- Description by Dawn Towery

"Mukherjees outstanding debut and series launch combines a cleverly constructed whodunit with an unusual locale--Calcutta in 1919--portrayed with convincing detail." Publishers Weekly.

Mukherjee, Abir

Smoke and ashes : a novel / Abir Mukherjee. Pegasus Books, 2019, c2018. 332 p. Sam Wyndham novels

ISBN 9781643130149

1. British Raj (1858-1947) 2. 1920s 3. Detectives 4. World War I veterans 5. Serial murder investigation 6. Police 7. Colonialism 8. British in India 9. Opium addiction 10. Murder investigation 11. People with post-traumatic stress disorder 12. Calcutta, India 13. India -- History -- British occupation, 1765-1947 14. Historical mysteries

Sequel to: A necessary evil.

Originally published: London : Random House, c2018.

Haunted by his memories of the Great War, Captain Sam Wyndham is battling a serious addiction to opium that he must keep secret from his superiors in the Calcutta police force.

"This series' third installment ... is pivotal for Sam and Surrender-Not's characters and for colonial India; Mukherjee skillfully manipulates that tension as he darkens the atmosphere in this thoughtful narrative. Definitely the series' best entry so far." Booklist.

Mukherjee, Bharati

Miss new India / Bharati Mukherjee. Houghton Mifflin Harcourt, 2011. 336 p.

ISBN 9780618646531

1. Women's role 2. Arranged marriage 3. Self-fulfillment in women 4. Modernization (Social sciences) 5. Betrayal 6. Identity (Psychology) 7. Violence 8. Eccentrics and eccentricities 9. City life 10. Rape 11. Boarding houses 12. Bangalore, India 13. Mainstream fiction

LC 2010025569

Althought her traditional low middle-class family expects her to go through with her arranged marriage, Anjali Bose wants to make more of her life and self. So she moves to India's fastest growing city, where she learns to sound American, starts working at a call centre and makes friends with a group of young and ambitious Indians who, at first, all seem to share her hopes and dreams.

"Mukherjee subtly continues the stories of the sisters from Desirable Daughters (2002) and The Tree Bride (2004) as she introduces Anjali Bose, a smart, rebellious 19-year-old who flees her provincial town after her father's attempt to arrange her marriage goes catastrophically wrong. ... Each character fascinates, and every detail glints with irony and intent, as Mukherjee brilliantly choreographs her compelling protagonist's struggles against betrayal, violence, and corruption in a dazzling plot that cunningly considers forms of tyranny blatant and insidious in a metamorphosing society." Booklist.

Mukherjee, Neel

A **life** apart / Neel Mukherjee. W. W. Norton & Company, 2016, 371 p.

ISBN 9780393352108

1. Alienation (Social psychology) 2. Loneliness 3. Immigrants 4. East Indians 5. Social isolation 6. Mothers and sons 7. Family relationships 8. London, England 9. Political fiction 10. Parallel narratives 11. Metafiction

LC oc2009075719

Originally published in India as Past Continuous in 2008

Arriving in England from Calcutta, 22-year-old Ritwik Ghosh, recently orphaned, settles in London where he, to stave off his loneliness, drops out of official existence into a shadowy hinterland of illegal immigrants.

"Historical and contemporary, lit with flashes of magic and violence, this intriguing novel offers multifaceted portraits of India and England as seen from the perspective of a clever, burdened misfit." Kirkus.

Mukherjee, Neel

* The **lives** of others / Neel Mukherjee. W. W. Norton & Co., 2014. 516 p.

ISBN 9780393247909

1. 1960s 2. Social classes 3. Social conflict 4. Rich families 5. Family relationships 6. Generation gap 7. Conflict in families 8. Paper industry and trade 9. Naxalite movement 10. Rebels 11. Calcutta, India 12. India -- History -- 20th century 13. India -- Social conditions -- 20th century 14. Literary fiction

Shortlisted for the Man Booker Prize, 2014.

Chronicles the vicissitudes of the extended Ghosh family as internal rivalries accompany the implosion of the family business and external social unrest.

"This is an immensely accomplished, steady-handed achievement, Victorian in its solidity, quietly enthralling in its insightful observation of the ties that bind." Kirkus.

Mukherjee, Neel

* A **state** of freedom / Neel Mukherjee. W. W. Norton & Co., 2018. 278 p.

ISBN 9780393292909

1. Interpersonal relations 2. Caste 3. Poverty 4. Poor people 5. Cooks 6. Freedom 7. Homecomings 8. Homelessness 9. Fathers and sons 10. East Indian Americans 11. Oppression (Psychology) 12. East Indians in Great Britain 13. India 14. Literary fiction

Five characters in very different circumstances--from a domestic cook in Mumbai to a vagrant and his dancing bear--find the meanings of dislocation and the desire to get more out of life.

"Mukherjees diverse perspectives and narrative treatments offer an honest, uncompromising look at the realities of his characters circumstances and, most pointedly, their lack of control over them, as well as a compelling exploration of disparity and identity." Booklist.

Mullen, Thomas

Darktown : a novel / Thomas Mullen. 37 Ink/Atria , 2016. 384 p. Darktown novels

ISBN 9781501133862

1. 1940s 2. Police misconduct 3. Racism 4. Murder 5. Race relations 6. African Americans 7. Veterans 8. Justice 9. Atlanta, Georgia 10. Historical mysteries 11. Police procedurals

LC 2015041687

RUSA Reading List, 2017.

Hired resentfully into the Atlanta Police Department of 1948, war veterans Lucious Boggs and Tommy Smith confront deep hostility from their white peers and are significantly limited in their ability to do their jobs before confronting a corrupt officer who complicates their investigation into the murder of a black woman.

"Mullens writing is extremely evocative in bringing the precivil rights South to life." Booklist.

Mullen, Thomas

Lightning men : a novel / Thomas Mullen. 37 INK/Atria Books, 2017. 384 p. Darktown novels

ISBN 9781501138799

1. 1950s 2. Segregation 3. Racism 4. Hate crimes 5. Hate groups 6. Race relations 7. African Americans 8. Veterans 9. Justice 10. Police 11. Atlanta, Georgia 12. Historical mysteries 13. Police procedurals

LC 2017004468

In this highly anticipated follow-up to last year's Darktown, African American police officers Tommy Smith and Lucius Boggs find themselves once again navigating volatile racial tensions in Atlanta. This time, it's 1950, and their attempt to stop the influx of illegal alcohol and drugs is complicated by the involvement of whites, whom they're not allowed to arrest. Meanwhile, neo-Nazis are in town stirring up trouble as black families move into formerly whites-only neighborhoods. Examining the cops' professional and personal lives, Lightning Men provides a well-rounded look at fascinating characters in an explosive setting. -- Description by Dawn Towery

"Mullen effectively uses the police-procedural format to shine a light on the daily indignities and violence blacks suffered in the precivil rights South, while delivering a plot that never lets up on suspense." Booklist.

Müller, Herta, 1953-

The **fox** was ever the hunter : a novel / Herta Müller ; translated from the German by Philip Boehm. Metropolitan Books, 2016, c1992. 237 p.

ISBN 9780805093025

1. 1980s 2. Informers 3. Lovers 4. Totalitarianism 5. Intellectuals 6. Suspicion 7. Spies 8. Interpersonal relations 9. Men/women relations

10. Romania -- History -- 1944-1989 11. Political fiction 12. Literary fiction 13. Translations -- German to English

LC 2015032783

Originally published: Berlin : Rowohlt Verlag, 1992.

Translation from the German of: Fuchs war damals schon der Jager.

An early work by the winner of the Nobel Prize is set during the final months of the Ceausescu totalitarian regime in Romania and traces the experiences of a teacher, a musician, a factory worker and a lover, one of whom is a spy reporting on the others to the secret police.

"Originally published in German in 1992, this early novel by Nobel laureate Müller ... offers a bleak and poetic portrait of Romanian village life in the final days of the Ceaucescu regime, where deprivation is ubiquitous, cruelty is standard, and spying is a survival skill. ... Thickly lyrical and sometimes downright hallucinatory, Müller's prose is disorienting, even bewildering at times, and it has been suggested that this is the author's most demanding novel. But few descriptions of life under totalitarian rule are as beautifully evocative." Booklist.

Müller, Herta, 1953-

The **hunger** angel / Herta Müller ; translated from the German by Philip Boehm. Metropolitan Books, 2012. 256 p.

ISBN 9780805093018

1. 1940s 2. Hunger 3. Forced labor 4. Closeted gay men 5. Homosexuality 6. Totalitarianism 7. Political corruption 8. Soviet Union 9. Political fiction 10. Historical fiction 11. Literary fiction 12. Translations -- German to English

Originally published as 'Atemschaukel' : Munich Carl Hanser Verlag, 2009.

January 1945, the war is not yet over : the Soviets begin the deportation of the German minority from the labor camps in Ukraine. This is the story of seventeen year old Leo Auberge, who went to the camp with the naive unawareness of a boy eager to escape provincial life. The last five years however he experienced daily hunger and cold, extreme fatigue and death.

"Under Müller's influence, the subject matter not only begs a reader's sympathy, but deftly illuminates the complex psychological state of starvation and displacement." Publishers Weekly.

Müller, Marcia

Both ends of the night / Marcia Müller. The Mysterious Press, 1997. 353 p. Sharon McCone mysteries

ISBN 089296622X

1. Women private investigators 2. Murder investigation 3. Missing persons 4. Airplane accidents 5. Women pilots 6. Political corruption 7. Federal Witness Protection Program 8. Business -- Corrupt practices 9. San Francisco, California 10. Minnesota 11. Mysteries 12. Hardboiled fiction

LC 97010129

Flight instructor Matty is murdered after she confides in private eye Sharon McCone that her boyfriend, John Seabrook, is missing, and Sharon's search for the killer leads her to a frozen wilderness

"Sharon McCone sets out to help a friend and former flying instructor find her missing lover, but soon the friend has been murdered, and a missing-persons case has been transformed into a grudge match. With the help of her own lover and fellow flyer Hy Ripinsky, McCone ventures into the depths of the federal witness protection program, finding first the missing lover and then the killer in the wilds of Minnesota. There's plenty of nicely paced action here, and the flying lore provides effective ballast. Best of all, though, there is McCone at work, both as day-to-day professional detective and as aggrieved friend out for justice." Booklist.

Müller, Marcia

The **broken** promise land / Marcia Müller. Mysterious Press, 1996. 388 p. Sharon McCone mysteries

ISBN 0892966211

1. Women private investigators 2. Extortion 3. Country music industry and trade 4. Country musicians 5. Family relationships 6. Fame 7. Ambition 8. Revenge 9. Brothers-in-law 10. California 11. San Francisco, California 12. Mysteries 13. Hardboiled fiction

LC 95052187

When her brother-in-law, a country music superstar, begins receiving blackmail threats from an enemy from his past, Detective Sharon McCone plunges into the ruthless, play-for-keeps world of the country music industry

"Leading Sharon into the rocky psychological terrain of families, Müller gives her meticulously plotted story, with its absorbing picture of the music industry, a commanding emotional authenticity." Publishers Weekly.

Müller, Marcia

Burn out / Marcia Müller. Grand Central Pub., 2008. 320 p. Sharon McCone mysteries

ISBN 9780446581073

1. Women private investigators 2. Murder investigation 3. Family violence 4. Native American women 5. Dysfunctional families 6. Husband-and-wife detectives 7. Security consultants 8. Secret identity 9. Marital conflict 10. San Francisco, California 11. Mysteries 12. Hardboiled fiction

LC 2008004500

A chance encounter with a troubled, highly secretive Native American woman begins to haunt her dreams, and even though she is determined not to investigate anything during her stay--and perhaps not ever again--McCone is drawn into the plight of the young woman and her dysfunctional family. A murder and traces of violence at a deserted resort lead her across the desert and into Nevada, and finally to a remote and isolated ranch, where danger lies closer that she expects and where her future and life itself may hang in the balance.

"By the upbeat ending, McCone has learned that with judicious use of both her investigative and executive skills she can reshape her life." Publishers Weekly.

Müller, Marcia

The **cavalier** in white / Marcia Müller. St. Martin's, 1986. 207 p. Joanna Stark mysteries

ISBN 0312125399

1. Art thefts 2. Murder investigation 3. Secrets 4. Thieves 5. Family relationships 6. Widows 7. Women amateur detectives 8. San Francisco, California 9. Sonoma, California 10. Mysteries

LC 86003663

Sequel: There hangs the knife.

When a Frans Hals painting is stolen, Joanna Stark is asked by her former San Francisco art security firm partner to return from her retreat to investigate the theft which takes her to the scene of a murder and back into the past

"This mystery features a woman detective named Joanna Stark, who is a widow, and ex-security consultant to art galleries and museums, and now lives in the small, wine-country town of Sonoma in northern California. Making a desultory no-go of starting her own art gallery, and feeling bored and restless after the death of her husband, Stark is visited by her ex-partner, who brings news of the theft of a Frans Hals painting, 'The Cavalier in White,' from a San Francisco museum. Stark is lured back into the detecting business and finds that all clues lead to embarrassing and potentially tragic repercussions that will affect people she

Müller, Marcia

City of whispers / Marcia Müller. Grand Central Pub., 2011. 320 p. Sharon McCone mysteries

ISBN 9780446573337

1. Women private investigators 2. Greed 3. Missing persons 4. Half brothers 5. Heirs and heiresses 6. Murder investigation 7. Rich women 8. San Francisco, California 9. Mysteries 10. Hardboiled fiction

LC 2010051674

Private eye Sharon McCone's search for her emotionally disturbed half-brother in San Francisco turns up a dead body with a connection to the unsolved murder of a young heiress.

"Alternating chapters narrated by different characters add to the suspense of the intricate plot, which propels readers through a San Francisco few tourists see from Colma, the city's necropolis, to the exclusive mansions of Sea Cliff and to a harrowing, haunting denouement." Publishers Weekly.

Müller, Marcia

Cyanide Wells / Marcia Müller. Mysterious Press, 2003. 304 p. Soledad County novels

ISBN 0892967811

1. 1980s 2. Malicious accusation 3. Secret identity 4. Runaway wives, husbands, etc 5. Lesbians 6. Adopted girls 7. Multiracial persons 8. Missing women 9. Betrayal 10. Small town life -- California 11. Northern California 12. Mysteries

LC 2002045516

Sequel to: Point Deception.

Sequel: Cape Perdido.

Learning that his wife, who has been missing for fourteen years, is alive and letting people believe he is responsible for her disappearance, Matthew journeys to California to clear his name.

"Matt Lindstrom leaves the life he has rebuilt in British Columbia to search for his ex-wife, Gwen. After she vanished from their California home, innuendo that he had murdered her ruined him, forcing his relocation. He discovers that she's in a Soledad County town called Cyanide Wells, living with a lesbian lover and an adopted child. When he goes there--for revenge? for solace--he discovers she has taken off again, this time with the child. He and Carly McGuire, publisher of the county newspaper and Gwen's partner, perform an uneasy dance as they try to bring her back." Booklist.

Müller, Marcia

The dangerous hour / Marcia Müller. Mysterious Press, 2004. 304 p. Sharon McCone mysteries

ISBN 0892968044

1. Women private investigators 2. Politicians 3. Credit card fraud 4. Malicious accusation 5. Frameups 6. Conspiracies 7. San Francisco, California 8. Mysteries 9. Hardboiled fiction

LC 2003024625

When one of her investigative operatives is arrested for major credit card fraud, Sharon McCone's efforts to prove the woman's innocence are complicated by the discovery of evidence that supports her guilt and points to a larger conspiracy.

"Müller's plotting isn't quite as tidy as usual . . . , but once again she gives us a solid slice of a San Francisco community and a protagonist with character. Fans of the sturdy, ongoing series will be especially pleased with the final scene, which opens the way for a new chapter in McCone's personal life." Booklist.

Müller, Marcia

* Dead midnight / Marcia Müller. Mysterious Press, 2002. 289 p. Sharon McCone mysteries

ISBN 089296765X

1. Women private investigators 2. Business sabotage 3. Suicide 4. E-zines 5. Hazing 6. Survivors of suicide victims 7. Suicide victims 8. Publishers and publishing 9. San Francisco, California 10. Mysteries 11. Hardboiled fiction

LC 2002020097

Sharon McCone takes on a wrongful-death case in which a grieving family is suing a company for the suicide of a young employee, but as her investigation progresses, she discovers that there may have been more to the death than meets the eye.

"This mystery has Sharon McCone gathering evidence for a wrongful-death suit brought by the family of a sensitive young man driven to kill himself by the deplorable working conditions at a trendy online magazine. But events never advance in a straight line in Muller's complicated narratives, and the job that McCone took on because she thought it would help her come to grips with her own brother's suicide turns into a lethal game of industrial sabotage." New York Times Book Review.

Müller, Marcia

The ever-running man / Marcia Müller. Warner Books, 2007. 320 p. Sharon McCone mysteries

ISBN 9780446582421

1. Women private investigators 2. Bombing investigation 3. Corruption investigation 4. Private security services 5. Security consultants 6. Bombings 7. Bombing suspects 8. Husband-and-wife detectives 9. Marital conflict 10. San Francisco, California 11. Mysteries 12. Hardboiled fiction

LC 2006100803

"The history of corruption may jeopardize Sharon McCone's marriage, but uncovering the secrets of a mysterious firm may be the only way she can save her husband's life, and her own"--Provided by publisher.

Müller, Marcia

Point Deception / Marcia Müller. Mysterious Press, 2001. 304 p. Soledad County novels

ISBN 0892966904

1. Serial murders 2. Women murder victims 3. Murder investigation 4. Cold cases (Criminal investigation) 5. Policewomen 6. Journalists 7. Sheriffs 8. Journalists 9. Mass murder 10. Small town life -- California 11. Family violence 12. Northern California 13. Mysteries

LC 00066265

Sequel: Cyanide Wells.

An unidentified woman's body washes up on shore shortly after journalist Guy Newberry arrives in the small seaside community of Signal Port, California. The community has never recovered from the unsolved murder of two young families 13 years ago. Fear and suspicion abound as Newberry pursues the story. Sheriff Rhoda Swift and Newberry form an uneasy alliance as more women are found murdered and they confront the killer.

"This mystery is set on the California coast in fictitious Soledad County. . . . Nobody who lives between Point Deception and Cape Perdido will dwell on what happened 13 years earlier, when eight residents of a nouveau-hippie enclave were slaughtered in remote Cascada Canyon. But as the anniversary of the massacre looms, coinciding with the rape and murder of a stranger, the dour townspeople of Signal Port are acting weird enough to galvanize a sheriff's deputy named Rhoda Swift into a quest for 'closure'. Although Swift gets the most talk-time in this well-hammered tale, her spooky neighbors might have brought more penetrating insights to its disquieting theme of collective guilt." New York Times Book Review.

Müller, Marcia

There's something in a Sunday : a Sharon McCone mystery / Marcia Müller. Mysterious Press, 1989. 213 p. Sharon McCone mysteries

ISBN 0892962704

1. Women private investigators 2. Surveillance 3. Murder investigation 4. Homeless persons 5. Missing men 6. San Francisco, California 7. Mysteries 8. Hardboiled fiction

LC 88022005

Private eye Sharon McCone takes on a routine surveillance as a favor to a friend, and her target's day proceeds normally until he is murdered

"This is a provocative work, infused with compassion and sensitivity, that explores the complexities of human relationships and the plight of the homeless." Publishers Weekly.

Müller, Marcia

Vanishing point / Marcia Müller. Mysterious Press, 2006. 336 p. Sharon McCone mysteries

ISBN 0892968052

1. Women private investigators 2. Missing persons investigation 3. Cold cases (Criminal investigation) 4. Missing women 5. Mothers and daughters 6. Interpersonal relations 7. Compromise 8. Women artists 9. Family secrets 10. Marital conflict 11. Self-doubt 12. San Francisco, California 13. Mysteries 14. Hardboiled fiction

LC 2005034180

"Sharon McCone is hired to investigate the 22-year-old cold-case of a housewife and artist who vanished inexplicably in the central part of California"--Provided by publisher.

"Now married to longtime boyfriend Hy Ripinsky, Sharon McCone . . . runs a thriving detective agency with more work than her staff can handle comfortably. Then Sharon's former assistant asks if she will look into the 20-year-old disappearance of Lauriel Greenwood, an artist who apparently abandoned two young daughters and a husband. A few days after McCone's agency swings into action, one of Lauriel's now-adult daughters goes missing. . . . This novel lulls the reader into viewing self-centered characters as benign until McCone's investigation reveals ugly, long-hidden truths." Library Journal.

Müller, Marcia

A **walk** through the fire / Marcia Müller. Mysterious Press, 1999. 293 p. Sharon McCone mysteries

ISBN 0892966882

1. Sabotage 2. Murder investigation 3. Drug traffic 4. Women private investigators 5. Women documentary filmmakers 6. Family secrets 7. Political corruption 8. Hawaii 9. San Francisco, California 10. Mysteries 11. Hardboiled fiction

LC 98051314

While investigating sabotage on the set of a controversial film in Hawaii, San Francisco sleuth Sharon McCone finds a violent world of long-buried family secrets, drug dealing, political machinations, and murder

Müller, Marcia

Where echoes live / Marcia Müller. Mysterious Press, 1991. 326 p. Sharon McCone mysteries

ISBN 0892964189

1. Women private investigators 2. Missing persons investigation 3. Kidnapping 4. Murder investigation 5. Gold mines and mining 6. Environmentalists 7. Mineral industry and trade 8. San Francisco, California 9. Mysteries 10. Hardboiled fiction

LC 90084898

When Sharon McCone searches for a missing person, she finds herself caught up in a battle between environmentalists and a mining operation seeking to develop Tufa Lake.

"Private eye Sharon McCone is on the ecological beat, as a renovated gold mine that could lead to environment destruction also leads to several deaths. A good mystery as fresh as today's headlines." Booklist.

Müller, Marcia

While other people sleep / Marcia Müller. Mysterious Press, 1998. 344 p. Sharon McCone mysteries

ISBN 0892966505

1. Women private investigators 2. Women impostors 3. Stalkers 4. Women with mental illnesses 5. Identity theft 6. Revenge 7. Gay men 8. Homophobia 9. Stalking 10. San Francisco, California 11. Mysteries 12. Hardboiled fiction

LC 98013394

It's an identity crisis for PI Sharon McCone when she discovers that someone is pretending to be her. To make matters worse, her office manager, Ted Smalley has been acting oddly. McCone gets caught in a game of cat and mouse through the nightlife of San Francisco.

"Müller's straightforward, no-nonsense writing and fully dimensioned characterizations lend credibility and color to her deftly plotted tale." Publishers Weekly.

Müller, Marcia

A **wild** and lonely place / Marcia Müller. Mysterious Press, 1995. 386 p. Sharon McCone mysteries

ISBN 0892965266

1. Women private investigators 2. Terrorism 3. Missing girls 4. Bombers (Persons) 5. Arab American girls 6. San Francisco, California 7. Caribbean Area 8. Mysteries 9. Hardboiled fiction

LC 94048255

Sharon McCone investigates a terrorist bombing at the consulate of an Arab emirate and tries to save the consul general's granddaughter, who has disappeared, leading Sharon on a high-stakes chase that ends up on the deadly streets of San Francisco

"A mellow, engaging and determined Sharon here heads a diverse and intriguing supporting cast." Publishers Weekly.

Müller, Marcia

Wolf in the shadows / Marcia Müller. Mysterious Press, 1993. 356 p. Sharon McCone mysteries

ISBN 0892965258

1. Women private investigators 2. Missing persons 3. Kidnapping 4. Ransom 5. Environmentalists 6. Murder investigation 7. San Francisco, California 8. Mysteries 9. Hardboiled fiction

LC 92050536

Anthony Award for Best Novel, 1994.

Just when All Souls Legal Cooperative hands her a promotion that will tie her to an uninspiring desk job, Sharon McCone's main squeeze, Hy Ripinsky, disappears. An environmentalist, he seemingly consented to deliver a two million dollar ransom demanded by the kidnappers of a biotech biggie. Putting her career crisis on hold, Sharon discovers Hy's abandoned plane, wrecked rental car and the intrigues of a shady international security firm.

Munier, Paula

A **borrowing** of bones / Paula Munier. Minotaur Books, 2018. 336 p. Mercy and Elvis series

ISBN 9781250153036

1. Women veterans 2. Working dogs 3. Rescue dogs 4. Abandoned children 5. Game wardens 6. Murder investigation 7. Explosives 8. Wilderness areas 9. Murder 10. Murder investigation 11. Loss

(Psychology) 12. Men/women relations 13. Vermont 14. Mysteries
LC 2018011483

Introduces a retired MP and her bomb-sniffing dog, who become embroiled in an investigation involving an abandoned baby, a missing mother and a cold-case murder.

Muñoz Molina, Antonio, 1956-

In her absence / Antonio Muñoz Molina ; translated by Esther Allen. Other Press, 2006, c2001. 126 p.

ISBN 9781590512531

1. Civil service workers -- Spain 2. Husband and wife -- Spain 3. Interclass marriage 4. Marriage -- Spain 5. Women and art 6. Boredom in women 7. Marriage burn out 8. Love 9. Men -- Psychology 10. Perception 11. Reality 12. Spain 13. Psychological fiction 14. Translations -- Spanish to English
LC 2006038139

Originally published: Madrid : Alfaguara, 2001.

Alternating between his daytime persona as a dutiful, bureaucratic employee and his nighttime existence as his beautiful wife's impassioned lover, Mario patiently indulges his wife's avant-garde tastes in spite of his own preferences, until a strange and ominous threat begins to weigh on their marriage.

Muñoz Molina, Antonio, 1956-

A **manuscript** of ashes / Antonio Muñoz Molina ; translated from the Spanish by Edith Grossman. Harcourt, 2007. 320 p.

ISBN 9780151014101

1. Murder 2. Murder investigation 3. College students 4. Poets 5. Family relationships 6. Spain -- History -- 1939-1975 7. Historical fiction 8. Psychological fiction 9. Translations -- Spanish to English
LC 2007036557

Seeking refuge from the police during the last days of Franco's rule, Minaya moves into his uncle's country estate and stumbles upon a dark secrets involving an old poet, his uncle, and the death of the woman they both had loved.

Munro, Alice, 1931-

* **Dear** life : stories / Alice Munro. Alfred A. Knopf, 2012. 336 p.

ISBN 9780307596888

1. Interpersonal relations 2. Fate and fatalism 3. Small town life -- Canada 4. Lake Huron region 5. Canada 6. Short stories 7. Literary fiction
LC 2012020455

"This is a Borzoi book."
Trillium Book Award, 2012.

A collection of stories illuminates moments that shape a life, from a dream or a sexual act to simple twists of fate, and is set in the countryside and towns of Lake Huron.

Munro, Alice, 1931-

Family furnishings : selected stories, 1995-2014 / Alice Munro. Alfred A. Knopf, 2014. 620 p.

ISBN 9781101874103

1. Small town life -- Canada 2. Interpersonal relations 3. Canada -- Social life and customs 4. Ontario -- Social life and customs 5. Literary fiction 6. Short stories
LC 2014023046

"This is a Borzoi book"--Title page verso.

These stories illuminate the extraordinary in the lives of men and women, parents and children, friends and lovers as they discover sex,

fall in love, part, quarrel, suffer defeat, set off into the unknown, or find a way to be in the world.

"Certainly few, if any, narrators are less trustworthy than Munro's; among many other things, she is the ascended master of quiet betrayals, withheld information and unforeseeable reversals of fortune... As is true of so many of Munro's tales, taken straight from the pages of quotidian life, its end is heartbreaking, tragic, not a little mysterious--and entirely unexpected. In fact, all that can be expected from these economical, expertly told stories is that they're near peerless, modern literary fiction at its very best." Kirkus.

Munro, Alice, 1931-

Hateship, friendship, courtship, loveship, marriage : stories / Alice Munro. Alfred A. Knopf, 2001. vii, 323 p.

ISBN 9780375413001

1. Men/women relations 2. Women -- Canada 3. Friendship 4. Canada -- Social life and customs 5. Literary fiction 6. Short stories
LC 2001029870

The short story "The bear came over the mountain" was later made into the motion picture "Away from her".

Published by Penguin Canada in 2007 under the title: Away from her.

National Book Critics Circle Award for Fiction finalist, 2001

A collection of short fiction explores the complexities of human relationships and emotions in stories about a housekeeper entering old-maidhood whose life is transformed by a practical joke and a lifelong philanderer who finds the tables turned.

"Opulent in their beauty and gem-bright psychology, the extraordinary stories in [this] collection span the spectrum from romance to tales of manners to deep meditations on love and mortality, and all evince Munro's profound understanding of the power of memories and the stories we tell ourselves." Booklist.

Munro, Alice, 1931-

Lives of girls and women / Alice Munro. Vintage Contemporaries, 2001, c1971. 277 p.

ISBN 0375707492

1. 1940s 2. Small town life -- Ontario 3. Young women 4. Self-discovery in women 5. Women -- Identity 6. Eccentric men 7. Canada 8. Coming-of-age stories 9. Literary fiction
LC 00063412

Originally published: Toronto : McGraw-Hill Ryerson, 1971.

The story of a young woman who journeys from the carelessness of childhood through an uneasy adolescence in search of love and sexual experience.

Munro, Alice, 1931-

Open secrets : stories / Alice Munro. A.A. Knopf, 1994. 293 p.

ISBN 9780679435754

1. Women 2. Small town life 3. Canada -- Social life and customs 4. Literary fiction 5. Short stories
LC 942099

Eight short stories.

ALA Notable Book, 1995.

Governor General's Literary Awards, English-language Fiction finalist

8 short stories that evoke the devastating power of old love suddenly recollected.

"The author peoples these exquisite tales with sad, lonely eccentrics leading lives of quiet self-deception. Her heroines are often troubled souls with the unforgiving task of fitting into the rigorously confining community that spawned them. ... Munro expertly captures the vagaries of history and geography in this satisfying and immensely pleasurable collection." Booklist.

Munro, Alice, 1931-

Runaway : stories / Alice Munro. Knopf, 2004. 352 p. ISBN 140004281X

1. Senior women 2. Women 3. Young women 4. Married women 5. Family relationships 6. Small town life -- Canada 7. British Columbia 8. Canada -- Social life and customs 9. Literary fiction 10. Short stories

LC 2004046539

Three of these short stories (Chance; Soon; and Silence) later published in an omnibus entitled: Julieta (2016) and made into a Spanish film by the same name.

ALA Notable Book, 2005.

Giller Prize, 2004.

Rogers Writers' Trust Fiction Prize, 2004.

Governor General's Literary Awards, English-language Fiction finalist, 2004.

A collection of short fiction captures the lives of women of all ages and circumstances, as they deal with the limits and lies of passion, unfulfilled dreams, motherhood, betrayal, and the bonds of love.

"Munro's spare style belies the psychological depth of the stories, which feature characters running away from someone or something (often representative of the past) or telling a lie by commission or omission (another form of running away)." Library Journal.

Munro, Alice, 1931-

Selected stories / Alice Munro. A. A. Knopf, 1996. 545 p. ISBN 0679446273

1. Women 2. Small town life 3. Men/women relations 4. Parent and child 5. Canada -- Social life and customs 6. Literary fiction 7. Short stories

LC 96004145

A selection of short fiction drawn from the author's seven collections spans almost thirty years of work and includes twenty-eight tales dealing with such themes as love, parents and children, seduction, marriage, sex, murder, dreams, and death

"Little gems from one of Canada's best writers, drawn from seven collections." Library Journal.

Munro, Alice, 1931-

Too much happiness : stories / Alice Munro. Alfred A. Knopf, 2009. 320 p.

ISBN 9780307269768

1. Women mathematicians 2. Interpersonal relations 3. Women -- Canada 4. Small town life -- Canada 5. Canada -- Social life and customs 6. Literary fiction 7. Short stories

LC 2009020010

Also published: Toronto : Douglas Gibson Books, 2009.

Governor General's Literary Awards, English-language Fiction finalist, 2009.

Nine new short works by the National Book Critics Circle-winning author of Love of a Good Woman include the stories of a grieving mother who is aided by a surprising source, a woman's response to a humiliating seduction, and a nineteenth-century Russian emigre's winter journey to the Riviera.

"The collection's 10 stories take on some sensational subjects. In fact, a quick tally yields all the elements of pulp fiction: violence, adultery, extreme cruelty, duplicity, theft, suicide, murder. But while in pulp fiction the emotional climax coincides with the height of external drama, a Munro story works according to a different scheme. Here the nominally momentous event is little more than an anteroom to an echo chamber

filled with subtle and far-reaching thematic reverberations." New York Times Book Review.

Munro, Alice, 1931-

The **view** from Castle Rock : stories / Alice Munro. Knopf, 2006. 368 p.

ISBN 1400042828

1. Families 2. Immigrants 3. Frontier and pioneer life 4. Women -- Canada 5. Small town life -- Canada 6. Men/women relations 7. Canada -- History -- 19th century 8. Literary fiction 9. Short stories

LC 2006045261

Shortlisted for the James Tait Black Memorial Prize for Fiction, 2006

A collection of short stories in which Munro traces the generations of her Laidlaw ancestors.

"This collection differs from Munro's usual examinations of women in rural Canada leaving home to remake their possibilities. She draws instead on family documents, historical records, and what feels like memoir to piece together, in 12 parts, a fictionalized chronicle of how her tough-minded clan got from the Ettrick Valley near Edinburgh, Scotland, to America. The book shows how much can be done in a simple short story but breaks every rule ever taught in a writing seminar, setting up a writing master class along the way." Time.

Murakami, Haruki, 1949-

After dark / Haruki Murakami ; translated from the Japanese by Jay Rubin. Alfred A. Knopf, 2007. 208 p.

ISBN 0307265838

1. Sisters 2. Prostitutes -- China 3. Night 4. Alienation (Social psychology) 5. Supernatural 6. Fashion models 7. Women college students -- Japan 8. Musicians 9. Interpersonal relations 10. Secrets 11. Violence against women 12. Tokyo, Japan 13. Japan 14. Translations -- Japanese to English 15. Literary fiction

LC 2007004828

"Originally published in Japan as Afutadaku by Kodansha, Tokyo, in 2004"--Titile page verso.

"A Borzoi book."

This translation first published in Great Britain by Harvill Secker, 2007.

First published with the title Afutadaku by Kodansha, Tokyo 2004.

Two sisters--Eri, a fashion model sleeping her way to oblivion, and Mari, a young student--form the center of a novel that documents a series of encounters in Tokyo during the witching hours between midnight and dawn.

"The narrative flows like a jazz ballad, excruciatingly slow yet hypnotically entrancing . . . . Each character is unique in his or her form of loneliness, yet each possesses a capacity for momentary empathy that is both sweet and heartbreaking. Murakami's genius, on both large and small canvases, is to create worlds both utterly alien and disconcertingly familiar." Booklist.

Murakami, Haruki, 1949-

After the quake : stories / Haruki Murakami ; translated from the Japanese by Jay Rubin. Alfred A. Knopf, 2002. 181 p.

ISBN 0375413901

1. 1990s 2. Earthquakes 3. Terrorism -- Japan 4. Poisonous gases 5. Men/women relations 6. Japan 7. Surrealist fiction 8. Short stories 9. Translations -- Japanese to English 10. Literary fiction

LC 2001038829

A collection of stories inspired by the January 1995 Kobe earthquake and the poison gas subway attacks two months later takes place between the two disasters and follows the experiences of people who found their normal lives undone by surreal events.

"These six stories, all loosely connected to the disastrous 1995 earthquake in Kobe, are Murakami. . . at his best. The writer, who returned to live in Japan after the Kobe earthquake, measures his country's suffering and finds reassurance in the inevitability that love will surmount tragedy, mustering his casually elegant prose and keen sense of the absurd in the service of healing." Publishers Weekly.

Murakami, Haruki, 1949-

Blind willow, sleeping woman : 24 stories / Haruki Murakami. Knopf, 2006. 352 p.

ISBN 1400044618

1. Human behavior 2. Paranormal phenomena 3. Identity (Psychology) 4. Supernatural 5. Loneliness 6. Growth (Psychology) 7. Short stories 8. Surrealist fiction 9. Translations -- Japanese to English 10. Literary fiction

LC 2005044544

This translation originally published: London: Harvill Secker, 2006. Kiriyama Prize for Fiction, 2007.

ALA Notable Book, 2007.

From the surreal to the mundane, an anthology of short fiction captures a full range of human experience, emotion, and relationship in works that chronicle a chance reunion in Italy, a holiday in Hawaii, and a romantic exile in Greece.

"Murakami's first collection of short stories in more than a decade again demonstrates his fabulous talent for transporting readers and making the world fade away with a few short strokes of his pen. . . . Murakami's characters are as alienated as any in Albert Camus, and as lost as any in J.D. Salinger. . . . What shines in all of [the stories] is Murakami's love for the open-ended mystery at the core of existence and his willingness to give himself up to the flow in order to capture some of the magic in the mundane." Christian Science Monitor.

Murakami, Haruki, 1949-

Colorless Tsukuru Tazaki and his years of pilgrimage / Haruki Murakami ; translated by Philip Gabriel. Alfred A. Knopf, 2014, c2013. 208 p.

ISBN 9780385352109

1. Friendship 2. Self-discovery in men 3. Voyages and travels 4. Identity (Psychology) 5. Sexuality 6. Railroad stations 7. Locomotive engineers 8. Men/women relations 9. Japan 10. Europe 11. Literary fiction 12. Surrealist fiction 13. Translations -- Japanese to English

Translation from the Japanese of: Shikisai o motanai Tazaki Tsukuru to kare no junrei no toshi.

Originally published in Japan: 2013.

Thirty-six-year-old Tsukuru Tazaki meets a woman named Sara who raises questions about a painful incident from his youth in which his closest friends all cut off relations with him without explanation, and inspires him to find out why.

"A a trademark [Murakami] story that blends the commonplace with the nightmarish in a Japan full of hollow men." Kirkus.

Murakami, Haruki, 1949-

* 1Q84 / Haruki Murakami ; translated from the Japanese by Jay Rubin and Philip Gabriel. Alfred A. Knopf, 2011. 928 p.

ISBN 9780307593313

1. 1980s 2. Authors, Japanese -- 20th century 3. Parallel universes 4. Cults -- Tokyo, Japan 5. Self-discovery 6. Secret societies -- Japan 7. Childhood friends 8. Tokyo, Japan 9. Literary fiction 10. Surrealist fiction 11. Translations -- Japanese to English

LC 2011014274

Originally published in three volumes with the title 1Q84 in 2009 and 2010 by Shinchosa Publishing Co Ltd, Tokyo.

Goodreads Choice Award, 2011.

Shortlisted for the International IMPAC Dublin Literary Award, 2013

An ode to George Orwell's "1984" told in alternating male and female voices relates the stories of Aomame, an assassin for a secret organization who discovers that she has been transported to an alternate reality, and Tengo, a mathematics lecturer and novice writer.

"In typical Murakami fashion, the result is deeply weirdand surprisingly convincing." Entertainment Weekly.

Murakami, Haruki, 1949-

* Kafka on the shore / Haruki Murakami ; translated from the Japanese by Philip Gabriel. Knopf, 2005. 448 p.

ISBN 1400043662

1. Runaway teenage boys 2. Eccentrics and eccentricities 3. Cats 4. Senior men 5. Fate and fatalism 6. Psychic trauma in men 7. Murder 8. Riddles 9. Animal mutilations 10. Japan 11. Surrealist fiction 12. Translations -- Japanese to English 13. Parallel narratives 14. Literary fiction

LC 2004048907

ALA Notable Book, 2006.

World Fantasy Award, 2006.

An unlikely alliance forms between Kafka Tamura, a fifteen-year-old runaway, and the aging Nakata, a man who has never recovered from a wartime affliction, as they embark on a surreal odyssey through a strange, fantastical world.

"Like his characters' quests, Murakami's expeditions off the worn path of literature can be both rewarding and terrifying. Finishing Kafka on the Shore is like waking from a great dream. Nothing has changed, but everything about the world looks different." Newsweek.

Murakami, Haruki, 1949-

Killing commendatore : a novel / Haruki Murakami ; translated from the Japanese by Philip Gabriel and Ted Goossen. Alfred A. Knopf, 2018, c2017. 681 p.

ISBN 9780525520047

1. Artists 2. Painting 3. Lovers 4. Secrets 5. Girls 6. Art 7. History 8. Sexuality 9. Magic 10. Japan 11. Literary fiction 12. Surrealist fiction 13. Translations -- Japanese to English

A portrait painter deals with the upcoming divorce from his wife by moving into an old house in rural Japan that used to belong to a famous artist.

Murakami, Haruki, 1949-

Men without women : stories / Haruki Murakami ; translated from the Japanese by Philip Gabriel and Ted Goossen. Alfred A. Knopf, 2017, c2014. 240 p.

ISBN 9780451494627

1. Human behavior 2. Loneliness 3. Men -- Psychology 4. Short stories 5. Surrealist fiction 6. Literary fiction 7. Translations -- Japanese to English

LC 2016037304

Originally published in Japanese as: Onna no inai otokotachi. Tokyo : Bungei Shunju Ltd, 2014.

A major new collection of stories by the internationally acclaimed author of Colorless Tsukuru Tazaki and His Years of Pilgrimage features male protagonists who find themselves alone in a smoky bar, in a baseball game, in the face of Beatles music, in the presence of women and in the wake of a vanishing cat.

LIST OF FICTIONAL WORKS

Murakami, Haruki, 1949-

South of the border, west of the sun / Haruki Murakami ; translated from the Japanese by Philip Gabriel. A. A. Knopf, 1999, c1998. 213 p.

ISBN 0375402519

1. Extramarital affairs 2. First loves 3. Missing persons 4. Bar owners 5. Interpersonal relations 6. Children -- Friendship 7. Women with disabilities 8. Alienation (Social psychology) 9. Japan 10. Psychological fiction 11. Translations -- Japanese to English 12. Literary fiction

LC 9749459

Years after their separation, two Japanese childhood sweethearts are reunited, and happily married Hajime finds himself prepared to risk everything for the chance to be with his now mysterious first love, Shimamoto.

"The narrative unfolds as an introspective ghost story in which Hajime must exorcise his past in the person of the enigmatic Shimamoto before he can affirm the new direction of his life. The ending, at once tender and hopeful, shows Murakami in a more mellow aspect than his work has exhibited before." Publishers Weekly.

Murakami, Haruki, 1949-

* The **wind-up** bird chronicle / Haruki Murakami ; translated from the Japanese by Jay Rubin. A. A. Knopf, 1997. 611 p.

ISBN 9780679446699

1. Runaway wives, husbands, etc 2. Husband and wife 3. Missing women 4. Alienation (Social psychology) 5. Mystics 6. Paralegals 7. Self-discovery in men 8. Wells 9. Japan 10. Surrealist fiction 11. Translations -- Japanese to English 12. Literary fiction

LC 972813

ALA Notable Book, 1998.

Shortlisted for the International IMPAC Dublin Literary Award, 1999.

The saga of a mysteriously disintegrating marriage, suppressed memories of the tragedies of war, and a young man's search for his personal and national identity is set against the turbulent backdrop of twentieth-century Japan.

"Murakami's protagonist is a harmless fellow who merely wants to recover his cat and his wife. The troubles, real and delusional, that he encounters can be seen as extravagant metaphors for every ill from personal isolation to mass murder. The novel is a deliberately confusing, illogical image of a confusing, illogical world. It is not easy reading, but it is never less than absorbing." The Atlantic.

Murakami, Ryu, 1952-

In the miso soup , Ryu Murakami ; translated by Ralph McCarthy. Kodansha International, 2003. 180 p.

ISBN 4770029578

1. Men 2. Americans in Japan 3. Americans in Tokyo, Japan 4. Teenage girls 5. Psychopaths 6. Serial murders 7. Serial murderers 8. Sex tourism 9. Sex industry and trade 10. Murder suspects 11. Culture conflict 12. Tokyo, Japan 13. Japan -- Social life and customs -- 21st century 14. Transgressive fiction 15. Thrillers and suspense 16. Translations -- Japanese to English

English translation of: In za miso supu.

"Through simple yet chilling language, Murakami doesn't condemn his characters. Instead he takes aim at rampant consumerism and the dumbing-down of Japanese and American culture. No one, Murakami seems to say, is completely guilty because we are shaped by the world around us." USA Today.

Murata, Sayaka, 1979-

Convenience store woman / Sayaka Murata ; translated from the Japanese by Ginny Tapley Takemori. Grove Press, 2018, 163 p.

ISBN 9780802128256

1. Misfits (Persons) 2. Convenience stores 3. Men/women relations 4. Social norms 5. Nonconformity 6. Expectation (Psychology) 7. Alienation (Social psychology) 8. Tokyo, Japan 9. Japan 10. Japan -- Social life and customs 11. Literary fiction 12. Psychological fiction 13. Translations -- Japanese to English

LC 2017051049

Originally published in 2016 as Conbini ningen.

A Japanese woman who has been working at a convenience store for 18 years, much to the disappointment of her family, finds friendship with an alienated, cynical and bitter young man who becomes her coworker.

Murdoch, Iris

* An **accidental** man / Iris Murdoch. Viking, 1972, c1971. 442 p.

ISBN 0670102083

1. Vietnam War, 1961-1975 2. Americans in England 3. Draft resisters 4. Rich people 5. England 6. Psychological fiction 7. Literary fiction

LC 79171893

Austin Gibson Grey, an American living in London, blames fate when he is drafted during the Vietnam War.

"The central figure of this novel is one of those accident-prone figures whose . . . misfortune becomes a substitute source of strength. . . . Ever since his brother injured his hand in a childhood incident, the world owes Austin a blank cheque to cover subsequent reverses--which do not fail to arrive. But someone is always sorry for him, always getting him out of trouble even at the price of their own. His self-pity destroys others in accordance with what Miss Murdoch . . . calls 'whatever deep mythological forces control the destinies of men.'" New Statesman.

Murdoch, Iris

The **bell** : a novel / Iris Murdoch. Viking, 1958. 342 p.

ISBN 9780099470489

1. Convents 2. Nuns 3. Gay men 4. Personal conduct 5. Women -- Sexuality 6. Interpersonal relations 7. England 8. Psychological fiction 9. Literary fiction 10. Modern classics

The story of a lay community of mixed-up people encamped outside Imber Abbey, home of an enclosed order of nuns, including Dora Greenfield, an erring wife who returns to her husband, and Michael Meade, who is confronted by his homosexual former lover.

"The setting is an Anglican lay community attached to an abbey on one of the great estates of England. . . . The members of this community and its temporary residents are on the whole an odd, and certainly an oddly assorted, bunch. And their high-minded leader is a homosexual who was once involved in a scandal that ended his plans for entering the church. The story concerns itself with the relationships between various members of this hothouse world, with the arrival of a new bell for the abbey and the simultaneous discovery in the lake of the lost fourteenth-century bell about which there is a sinister legend. The climax is an eruption of scandal and disaster." The Atlantic.

Murdoch, Iris

The **book** and the brotherhood / Iris Murdoch. Penguin, 1988, c1987. 607 p.

ISBN 9780140104707

1. University of Oxford 2. Friendship 3. Murder 4. Guilt 5. Universities and colleges 6. Interpersonal relations 7. England 8.

Literary fiction

LC 87040294

Shortlisted for the Booker-McConnell Prize, 1987.

In a study of obsession, love, betrayal, and friendship, a group of friends gathers at a midsummer ball at Oxford and the actions of one of them--a radical genius named David Crimond--sets off a crisis.

"Despite its excessive length and passages that can seem almost as self-indulgent as the characters they represent, The Book and The Brotherhood demonstrates again and again that Iris Murdoch is among the most gifted descriptive and narrative writers in Englishand certainly one of the most consistently entertaining." New H209Y Rev Books

Murdoch, Iris

A **fairly** honourable defeat / Iris Murdoch. Viking Press, 1970. 436 p.

ISBN 9780099285335

1. 1970s 2. Manipulation by men 3. Former lovers 4. Interpersonal relations 5. Men/women relations 6. Gambling 7. Gay men 8. England 9. London, England 10. Psychological fiction 11. Literary fiction

Originally published: London: Chatto & Windus, 1970.

A ten guinea wager between a woman and her former lover threatens to disrupt the lives of all those close to them.

"As is usual with a Murdoch novel, the action in summary seems preposterous. But given her inventiveness, her Gothic imagination, her gift for melodrama and suspense, she creates a world that becomes an effective vehicle for her moral vision." Choice.

Murdoch, Iris

The **good** apprentice / Iris Murdoch. Viking Press, 1986, c1985. 522 p.

ISBN 9780670809400

1. Psychiatrists 2. Guilt in men 3. Poisoning 4. Murder 5. Stepbrothers and stepsisters 6. Spiritualism 7. Depression 8. Mental illness 9. Men/women relations 10. England 11. Psychological fiction 12. Literary fiction 13. Modern classics

LC 85040635

Originally published: London : Chatto & Windus, 1985.

Shortlisted for the Booker-McConnell Prize, 1985.

Young Edward Baltram's prank of giving his friend Mark Wilsden a drug-infused sandwich and his stepbrother Stuart's decision to forsake a promising academic career for social work bring consternation to their parents and elders.

"The esthetic puzzle is whether the comic story and the spiritual kernel can be held together by Miss Murdoch's archaic stance as an authorial will. And yet no other contemporary British novelist seems to me of her eminence." New York Times Book Review.

Murdoch, Iris

* The **green** knight / Iris Murdoch. Viking Press, 1994, c1993. 472 p.

ISBN 0670852295

1. Self-defense (Law) 2. Brothers 3. Murder 4. Strangers 5. Guilt in men 6. Extortion 7. London, England 8. Literary fiction 9. Modern classics

LC 93030618

When an attempt by the sharp, feral, uncommonly intelligent Lucas to murder his brother, Clement, backfires and Lucas kills a stranger, the stranger reappears with specific demands for reparation.

"That a cold, dark, evil act should open up a gap through which warmth and light can flood into the world is a paradox characteristic of Iris Murdoch's deeply meditated insight into the nature of the good." London Review of Books.

Murdoch, Iris

The **nice** and the good / Iris Murdoch. Penguin, 1978, c1968. 378 p.

ISBN 9780140030341

1. Married people 2. Murder 3. Spies 4. Extortion 5. Men/women relations 6. Psychological fiction 7. Literary fiction

Shortlisted for the Booker-McConnell Prize, 1969.

A novel originally published in 1968, revolving around a happily married couple and telling of a violent death, blackmail, suspected espionage, Black Arts, stress and terror, over which love conquers all.

"The action begins with a violent death in the chambers of Whitehall faintly suggestive of a Le Carr thriller. . . . At times hilariously funny, slightly shivery (intimations of blackmail, suicide, dabblings in black magic) 'The Nice and the Good' is first and foremost a delightful love story. The friends, relatives, hanger-ons, whose lives revolve around the happily married Octavian and Kate Gray are all seeking after love in their own ways. They find it, too, and sometimes in the most amazing places. The characterizations are superb, the mood that of a happy fairy tale crossed with highly sophisticated sexual comedy." Publishers Weekly.

Murdoch, Iris

Nuns and soldiers / Iris Murdoch. Viking Press, 1981, c1980. 505 p.

ISBN 9780670518265

1. Former nuns 2. Former friends 3. Female friendship 4. Widows 5. Men/women relations 6. Artists 7. Mistresses 8. London, England 9. France 10. Literary fiction

LC 80016935

Originally published: London : Chatto & Windus, 1980.

The lives of Gertrude Openshaw and Anne Cavidge become entangled with the lives of an interesting array of people, including Count, a lonely Pole; Manfred North, a wealthy banker; and Tim Reade, a penniless painter.

"The glory of Iris Murdoch at her best--as she almost always is in Nuns and Soldiers--is that she can convey with total respect the awareness, readjusting and hunger, and at the same time 'place' it, with a severe but not savage irony, in a world which hints at quite different forces and priorities." New Statesman.

Murdoch, Iris

* The **philosopher's** pupil / Iris Murdoch. Viking Press, 1982, c1980. 505 p.

ISBN 9780670551866

1. Teacher-student relationships 2. Philosophers 3. Small towns 4. Health resorts 5. Ethics 6. Mothers and sons 7. Family relationships 8. England 9. Literary fiction

LC 82045901

Originally published: London : Chatto & Windus, 1980.

"This collaboration between Murdoch and her imagination is both challenging and irresistible: a combination of gossip and profundity, modern times and ancient edicts." Time.

Murdoch, Iris

The **sea,** the sea / Iris Murdoch. Penguin Books, 2001, c1978. xxvii, 495 p.

ISBN 9780141186160

1. Senior men 2. Obsession in men 3. Recluses 4. Reminiscing in old age 5. Single men 6. Ghosts 7. England 8. Literary fiction 9. Ghost stories 10. Psychological fiction 11. Modern classics

Originally published: London: Chatto & Windus, 1978.

Booker Prize, 1978.

After a brilliant and fulfilling career, Charles Arrowby revels in his perfect refuge, an isolated home by the sea, but soon his complex past makes unbidden visits.

"The narrator of this novel is Charles Arrowby, a former actor and director who has retired from the theater to take up solitary residence in a remote house on a northern coast. His tale begins as a mixture of diary and memoir: alternately he records his first impressions of his new home and reviews his past life as though the better to understand the man he has become. . . . His recollections largely concern a succession of love-affairs with actresses; but before all these, and dwarfing them in its importance to his development, was an unconsummated but passionate childhood relationship with a girl named Hartley, who disappeared abruptly and woundingly from his life before he was twenty and married another man." Times Literary Supplement.

Murphy, Devin

Tiny Americans / Devin Murphy. Harper Perennial, 2019. 336 p.

ISBN 9780062886248

1. 1970s 2. 2010s 3. Father-deserted children 4. Father and adult child 5. Reconciliation 6. Adult children of alcoholics 7. Brothers and sisters 8. Artists -- Psychology 9. Children of artists 10. New York (State) 11. Literary fiction 12. Domestic fiction

Abandoned by the alcoholic father who idealized the natural world without imparting any survival skills to his children, three siblings in 1970s New York embark on difficult adult lives before their father attempts a reconciliation.

Murphy, Sara Flannery

* The **possessions** / Sara Flannery Murphy. HarperCollins, 2017. 320 p.

ISBN 9780062458322

1. Mediums 2. Spiritualism 3. Spirits 4. Grief 5. Loss (Psychology) 6. Widowers 7. Secrets 8. Suspicion 9. Obsession 10. Psychological suspense 11. Contemporary fantasy

"In an unnamed city, Edie works for the Elysian Society, a private service that allows grieving clients to reconnect with lost loved ones. She and her fellow workers, known as "bodies", wear the discarded belongings of the dead and swallow pills called lotuses to summon their spirits--numbing their own minds and losing themselves in the process. Edie has been with the company for five years, an unusual record. Her success is the result of careful detachment: she seeks refuge in the lotuses' anesthetic effects and avoids personal contact with her clients. But when Edie channels Sylvia, the deceased wife of Patrick Braddock, she becomes obsessed with the glamorous couple ..."--, Provided by publisher.

"This poignant tale is a study of grief and obsession told by a person who will do anything to forget while surrounded by those who refuse to move on." Library Journal.

Murphy, Shirley Rousseau

Cat pay the devil : a Joe Grey mystery / Shirley Rousseau Murphy. William Morrow, 2007. 304 p. Joe Grey mysteries

ISBN 0060578106

1. Cat detectives 2. Kidnapping 3. Serial murder investigation 4. Talking cats 5. Humans and cats 6. Cats 7. Coastal towns 8. Shooting 9. Anthropomorphism 10. California 11. Fantasy mysteries 12. Stories told by animals

LC 2006046768

Nestled quietly on the Pacific Coast below San Francisco, Molena Point is a quaint hamlet--not the kind of place an escaped convict would choose for a hideout. But it just happens to be the home of a state's witness who put a thief named Cage Jones behind bars--until he broke out, that is. Wily tomcat Joe Grey senses trouble is on the way, but he never expected a federal officer would be shot or that two locals would be brutally murdered. With danger closing in, the feline detective, his girlfriend Dulcie, and their tattercoat friend Kit--an indomitable trio with special powers that only a few select humans are privy to--must put paws and whiskers together to capture a very nasty criminal before he strikes again.

Murphy, Timothy, 1969-

Correspondents : a novel / Tim Murphy. Grove Press, 2019. 448 p.

ISBN 9780802129376

1. 20th century 2. 21st century 3. Immigration and emigration 4. Iraq War, 2003-2011 5. War -- Psychological aspects 6. Interracial families 7. Multiracial women 8. Ambition in women 9. Women journalists 10. War correspondents 11. War and society 12. Extended families 13. Family relationships 14. Middle East 15. Massachusetts 16. Iraq 17. Family sagas

LC 2018058108

An enthralling and fast-moving epic of two families: one from New England, the other from the Middle East. Correspondents is a wry, haunting portrait of the best and worst sides of America.

Murphy, Yannick

The **call** : a novel / Yannick Murphy. Harper Perennial, 2011. 240 p.

ISBN 9780062023148

1. Veterinarians 2. Hunting accidents 3. Children in comas 4. Families 5. Marriage 6. Coping 7. Parenthood 8. Small town life 9. New England 10. Domestic fiction 11. Literary fiction

LC 2010051661

L. L. Winship/PEN New England Award for Fiction, 2012.

When a hunting accident leaves his son in a coma, the son's veterinarian father tries to find the man responsible while maintaining normalcy for his family until an unexpected visitor asks a favor that will test his resolve and force him to come to terms with what it truly means to be a family.

"An extraneous plot twist at the end tests the family and the reader's suspension of disbelief, and the emotional resonance seems to recede. But throughout, the most delicate and satisfying snippets answer questions like what the house says at night: I'm closing you in, and buttoning you tight, which quietly and brilliantly speaks to both comfort and threat. In the quotidian details of farm life, Murphy demonstrates how crucial it is to focus on the small, real tasks in the face of something too big and too dark to understand." Time Out New York.

Murphy, Yannick

Signed, Mata Hari : a novel / Yannick Murphy. Little, Brown, 2007. 288 p.

ISBN 9780316112642

1. Mata Hari, 1876-1917 2. 19th century 3. 18th century 4. Women spies 5. Intelligence service 6. Secrets 7. Guilt in women 8. Men/women relations 9. World War I -- Secret service 10. Indonesia 11. Southeast Asia 12. France 13. Biographical fiction 14. Spy fiction 15. Historical thrillers 16. Literary fiction

LC 2006102966

A tale inspired by the life of the infamous spy finds a woman awaiting execution in Paris and attempting to save herself by recounting the story of her Netherlands childhood, self-reinvention after ending a loveless marriage, and performances for the crowned heads of Europe.

"Weaving back and forth in time between Mata Hari's prison cell in Paris and her prior life in its many manifestations, the seductive narrative spins an irresistible tale of a woman whose legendary exploits are still a matter of historical debate. Was she or was she not a victim of time and circumstance? Did she really deserve to be executed as a spy? In the end, it doesn't really matter, but what does matter is that Murphy has fashioned a mesmerizing novel that creatively reimagines the life of one of the most notorious, and perhaps overvilified, women of all time." Booklist.

Murr, Naeem

* The **perfect** man : a novel / Naeem Murr. Random House, 2007, c2006. 429 p.

ISBN 0812977017

1. 1950s 2. Abandoned boys 3. Multiracial boys 4. Children -- Friendship 5. East Indians in the United States 6. Secrets 7. Small town life -- Missouri 8. Prejudice 9. Violence 10. Cold cases (Criminal investigation) 11. Missouri 12. Coming-of-age stories

LC 2006043088

Follows the life of Rajiv Travers, the child of an East Indian mother and an English father but who is raised by an American romance novel author in Pisgah, Missouri, in the 1950s, and whose presence unsettles the small community.

"This novel succeeds in recreating an entire world with a full spectrum of human emotions in a small Missouri town, as Faulkner did in the imaginary Yoknapatawpha County in Mississippi." Times Literary Supplement.

Murray, Paul, 1975-

The **mark** and the void / Paul Murray. Farrar, Straus & Giroux, 2015. 459 p.

ISBN 9780865477551

1. Authors 2. Bankers 3. Financial crises 4. Banks and banking 5. Creativity 6. Waitresses 7. Ireland 8. Literary fiction

LC 2015015136

Originally published : London : Hamish Hamilton, 2015.

Stuck at a dull job at the Investment Bank of Torabundo in Ireland, Claude Martingale falls under the influence of Paul, a luckless author looking for his next subject, and finds his life becoming increasingly more exciting, but both Paul and Claude's employer are not what they seem.

"Here, again, the author displays much of the quick wit of his popular previous novel, but this effort also boasts a more modernist slant, with ever-blurring lines between art imitating life and life imitating art for the characters. The result is another page-turner with smarts, an absurdist riff on our economic follies, one that leaves the impression that its all not so far-fetched, after all." Publishers Weekly.

Murray, Paul, 1975-

Skippy dies / Paul Murray. Faber & Faber, 2010. 672 p.

ISBN 9780865479432

1. Teacher-student relationships 2. Boarding schools 3. Teenage boys -- Death 4. Prescription drug abuse 5. Roommates 6. Drug dealers 7. Social acceptance 8. Love triangles 9. Family relationships 10. High school students 11. Private schools 12. Dublin, Ireland 13. Ireland 14. Coming-of-age stories 15. Literary fiction

ALA Notable Book, 2011.

National Book Critics Circle Award for Fiction finalist, 2010

After fourteen-year-old Skippy ends up dead on the floor of a local donut shop, a number of suspects emerge at Skippy's school in Dublin, in a hilarious portrait of the pain, joy, and occasional beauty of adolescence.

"First off, the title of Skippy Dies should come with a spoiler alert, because Skippy does in fact die. And oh, the humanity! He dies like a fish on the floor of Ed's Doughnut House, where he's been locked in a doughnut-eating contest with his tubby, brilliant, but unhinged prep-

school buddy Ruprecht. . . . Essentially, though, the novel's about a fusty old Catholic school trying to cope and connive after the Skippy Doughnut Tragedy, while dealing with the more commonplace tragedy that being an adolescent sucks, as do being middle-aged and being old. Murray's humor and inventiveness never flag. And despite a serious theme what happens to boys and men when they realize the world isn't the sparkly planetarium they had hoped for Skippy Dies leaves you feeling hopeful and hungry for life. Just not for doughnuts." Entertainment Weekly.

Murray, Victoria Christopher

Lust / Victoria Christopher Murray. Touchstone Books, 2017. 368 p. Seven Deadly Sins (Victoria Christopher Murray)

ISBN 9781501134104

1. Engaged persons 2. Love triangles 3. African American women 4. Lust 5. Sexuality 6. Sexual excitement 7. Men/women relations 8. Interpersonal attraction 9. Drama lit 10. African American fiction

A tale inspired by the seven deadly sins follows the experiences of a woman caught between an entertainment mogul with a shady past and his vengeance-seeking childhood friend.

Murray, Victoria Christopher

Stand your ground / Victoria Christopher Murray. Touchstone, 2015. 400 p.

ISBN 9781476792996

1. Trials (Murder) 2. African American women 3. Crimes against African Americans 4. Husband and wife 5. Life change events 6. Mothers 7. Christian fiction 8. Legal stories 9. African American fiction

LC 2015003165

Follows the experiences of a grieving mother who is reluctant to join a public outcry over her son's murder while the mother of the accused keeps wrenching secrets that she knows will affect her entire family.

Musil, Robert, 1880-1942

* The **man** without qualities / [by] Robert Musil ; translated from the German by Eithne Wilkins and Ernst Kaiser. Vintage Books, 1996, c1930. 1774 p.

ISBN 0394510526

1. Men 2. Character 3. Character in men 4. Meaning (Psychology) 5. Fascism 6. Vienna, Austria 7. Austria -- History -- 1867-1918 8. Hungary -- Politics and government 9. Translations -- German to English 10. Psychological fiction 11. Modern classics

LC 80471287

Originally publised: Berlin: Rohwolt, 1930.

A novel in three volumes on the dying culture of pre-World War I Vienna. The man without qualities of the title is Ulrich, a skeptical type who views with an amused eye all attempts by the rulers of the Austro-Hungarian Empire to instill in their subjects the nationalistic fervor of neighboring Germany.

Mychea

He loves me, he loves you not : a novel / Mychea. Good-2Go Pub., 2012. 216 p.

ISBN 9780615525976

1. Sisters 2. Deception 3. Children of criminals 4. Betrayal 5. Orphans 6. Dishonesty 7. Twin sisters 8. African Americans 9. Men/women relations 10. Dating (Social customs) 11. New York City 12. African American fiction 13. Drama lit

It's been years since their parents were murdered. Twin sisters Shia and Leigh are trying to readjust to life, while caring for their baby sister Remi. With the exception of Leigh's angry, dramatic mood swings every now and then, everything seems to be going great. That is until Demetri;

the mysterious stranger enters their midst, and falls right in the path of the newly single Shia. After dating Trent for so long, she is looking for a man to treat her like a queen, and Demetri is heaven sent...until inexplicable things begin to happen.

Myers, Alex

Continental divide / Alex Myers. Uno Press, 2019. 296 p.
ISBN 9781608011698
1. 1990s 2. Moving to a new state 3. Transgender teenagers 4. Ranches 5. Teenage boys 6. Prejudice 7. Ranchers 8. Belonging 9. Homeless teenagers 10. Rejection (Psychology) 11. Self-discovery in teenage boys 12. Transgender teenagers 13. Transphobia 14. Wyoming 15. LGBTQIA fiction 16. Coming-of-age stories 17. Modern Westerns 18. Literary fiction
Newly out as transgender, Ron finds himself adrift: kicked out by his family, jilted by his girlfriend, unable to afford to return to college in the fall. So he heads out to Wyoming for a new start, a chance to prove that--even though he was raised as a girl, even though everyone in Boston thinks of him as transgender--he can live as a man. A real man.
"A moving meditation on fear, masculinity, and the power of coming out." Kirkus. Reviews

Mysliwski, Wieslaw

Stone upon stone / Wieslaw Mysliwski ; translated from the Polish by Bill Johnston. Archipelago Books, 2011. 500 p.
ISBN 9780982624623
1. Villages 2. Occupations 3. Memory 4. Home (Concept) 5. Interpersonal relations 6. Brothers 7. Poland 8. Literary fiction
Originally published in Polish as: Kamien na kamieniu: Warsaw : Panstw. Inst. Wydawn, 1984.
Relates the experiences of Szymek Piietruszka and life in a Polish farming community before and after World War II.

N

NDiaye, Marie

Ladivine / Marie NDiaye ; translated from the French by Jordan Stump. Alfred A. Knopf, 2016, c2013. 273 p.
ISBN 9780385351881
1. Mothers and daughters 2. Deception 3. Race relations 4. Social classes 5. Family secrets 6. Murder 7. Dogs 8. Voyages and travels 9. Family relationships 10. Literary fiction 11. Translations -- French to English
LC 2015016260
"First published in the French language as Ladivine by Editions Gallimard in Paris, 2013"--title page verso.
Shortlisted for the International Dublin Literary Award, 2018.
After a woman, Clarisse, is murdered on a trip to visit her mother in Bordeaux, her daughter tries to uncover what happened to her with the help of a brown dog who appears to have taken in the spirit of the deceased.
"NDiaye reveals only as much reality as she wants to at any given moment, thoughand therein lies her magic. Come for the promise of a big reveal; stay for the beauty of small moments." Kirkus.

NDiaye, Marie

Three strong women : a novel / Marie NDiaye ; translated from the French by John Fletcher. Alfred A. Knopf, 2012. 293 p.
ISBN 9780307594693
1. Senegalese women in France 2. Self-fulfillment in women 3. No (The word) 4. West Africans in France 5. Women -- France 6. Immigrants 7. France 8. Literary fiction 9. Translations -- French to English
LC 2012003533
First published in French as "Trois femmes puissantes". Paris : Editions Gallimard, 2009.
Shortlisted for the International IMPAC Dublin Literary Award, 2014
Follows the intertwined stories of three women who discover the power of saying no, including a French-born lawyer who must save a victim of her tyrannical father, a Dakar teacher whose happiness is thwarted by a depressed boyfriend and a penniless widow who travels to France to escape homelessness.

Naam, Ramez

Nexus / Ramez Naam. Angry Robot, 2012. 460 p. Nexus novels (Ramez Naam)
ISBN 9780857662934
1. Technology -- Social aspects 2. Scientists 3. Near future 4. Drugs 5. Posthumanism 6. Biotechnology -- Social aspects 7. Telepathy 8. Human evolution 9. Graduate students 10. Drug use 11. Nanotechnology 12. Cyber-thrillers 13. Science fiction
Sequel: Crux.
Thanks to the nanotechnology breakthrough that is Nexus, humans can finally link up mind to mind -- for better or for worse. For every person who wants to enhance Nexus, there are others who want to destroy it or exploit it for personal gain. Although graduate student Kade Lane's only motive is scientific progress, his (illegal) efforts to improve the technology bring him to the attention of the U.S. government. Blackmailed into spying on a Chinese researcher suspected of using Nexus to develop a mind-control program, Kade must rely on operative Samantha Cataranes if he's to succeed in his mission and escape with his life. - Description by Gillian Speace.

Nabb, Magdalen, 1947-2007

Some bitter taste / Magdalen Nabb. Soho Press, 2002. 256 p. Marshal Guarnaccia mysteries
ISBN 156947317X
1. Police 2. Murder investigation 3. Immigrants 4. Senior women 5. Murder 6. Refugees 7. Detectives 8. Prostitution 9. Robbery 10. Fear 11. Florence, Italy 12. Italy 13. Mysteries 14. Police procedurals
LC 2002070579
Investigating the murder of an elderly resident of a store-top flat in Florentine, Marshal Guarnaccia finds clues in a group of Jewish refugees, a band of English expatriates, and an heir to an elegant villa.
"The author has Simenon's knack of unlocking the deeper mysteries of ordinary people's pedestrian lives. . . . In Nabb's world, nothing is simple and no life, after all, is ordinary." New York Times Book Review.

Nabokov, Vladimir Vladimirovich, 1899-1977

Ada : or, Ardor: Vladimir Nabokov. McGraw, 1969. 626 p.
1. Incest 2. Brothers and sisters 3. Reminiscing in old age 4. Sexuality 5. Parallel universes 6. Psychologists 7. Literary fiction 8. Modern classics
Set in a 'dreambright' America, at the turn of the century, the novel depicts an incestuous love affair.

Nabokov, Vladimir Vladimirovich, 1899-1977

King, queen, knave : a novel / Vladimir Nabokov ; translated from the Russian by Dmitri Nabokov in collaboration with the author. McGraw-Hill, 1968, c1928. 272 p.

ISBN 9780070457164

1. 1920s 2. Love triangles 3. Extramarital affairs 4. Husband and wife 5. Lovers 6. Uncle and nephew 7. Murder 8. Berlin, Germany 9. Literary fiction 10. Satirical fiction 11. Modern classics 12. Translations -- Russian to English

Originally published as Korol', dama, valet: Berlin : Slovo, 1928.

Berlin in the late twenties provides the setting for this novel about a woman's scheme to murder her husband to live on his money with his nephew.

Nabokov, Vladimir Vladimirovich, 1899-1977

* **Lolita** / Vladimir Nabokov ; with an introduction by Martin Amis. Knopf, 1992, c1955. xxxi, 335 p.

ISBN 0679410430

1. Pedophilia 2. Obsession in men 3. Pedophiles 4. Men -- Sexuality 5. Sexuality 6. Teenage girls -- Sexuality 7. Literary fiction 8. Modern classics

LC 92052931

Originally published: Paris : Olympia Press, 1955.

A novel that studies the moral disintegration of a man whose obsessive desire to possess his step-daughter destroys the lives of those around him.

Nabokov, Vladimir Vladimirovich, 1899-1977

Look at the harlequins! / Vladimir Nabokov Vintage Books, 1990, c1974. 253 p.

ISBN 9780679727286

1. Authors 2. Exiles -- Russia 3. Reminiscing in old age 4. Men with terminal illnesses 5. Literary fiction 6. Modern classics

LC 74010677

Originally published: New York : McGraw-Hill, 1974.

This is a fictional autobiography narrated by Vadim Vadimovich N. (VV), a Russian-American writer with uncanny biographical likenesses to the novel's author, Vladimir (Vladimirovich) Nabokov. 'Look at the harlequins... Play! Invent the world! Invent reality'. This is the childhood advice given by an aunt to Russian born writer Vadim Vadimovich, who emigrates to England, then Paris, then Germany and then the US, and, now dying, reconstructs his past. He remembers Iris his first wife, Annette his long-necked typist and Bel his daughter, as well as his own bizarre numerical nimbus syndrome.

"This is a book to enchant Nabokov fans and irritate everybody else. . . . [It] is part roman a clef, part fantasy, a tale of 'wives and books interlaced monogrammatically.' It is full of erudite allusions, Russian words in various stages of translation and absurd mistranslation, puns, anagrams, acronyms. Also opinions. . . . Comic, polished, international, [Nabokov] offers sophisticated entertainment, a concoction of romantic and literary matters." Christian Science Monitor.

Nabokov, Vladimir Vladimirovich, 1899-1977

Novels and memoirs, 1941-51 / Vladimir Nabokov. Library of America, 1996. 710 p.

ISBN 1883011183

1. Nabokov, Vladimir Vladimirovich, 1899-1977 2. Authors, Russian -- 20th century 3. Russian Americans 4. Refugees, Russian 5. Authors, American -- 20th century 6. Half-brothers 7. Totalitarianism 8. Philosophy teachers 9. Autobiographies and memoirs 10. Anthologies 11. Modern classics 12. Arts and entertainment Writing and publishing 13. Life stories Arts and culture Writing Authors

LC 96-15237

Illustrated with black-and-white photos.

Includes chronology.

The real life of Sebastian Knight -- Bend sinister -- Speak, memory: an autobiography revisited.

Nabokov, Vladimir Vladimirovich, 1899-1977

* **Pale** fire / Vladimir Nabokov. A. A. Knopf, 1992, c1962. 315 p.

ISBN 0679410775

1. Poetry -- History and criticism 2. College teachers 3. Obsession in men 4. Immigrants 5. Criticism 6. Exiles 7. Satirical fiction 8. Literary fiction 9. Modern classics

LC 91053217 //r92

Originally published: New York : G.P. Putnam's Sons, 1962.

Nabokov's parody, half poem and half commentary on the poem, deals with the escapades of the deposed king of Zemala in a New England college town.

Nabokov, Vladimir Vladimirovich, 1899-1977

Pnin / Vladimir Nabokov. R. Bentley, 1982, c1957. 191 p.

ISBN 9780837604657

1. Exiles -- Russia 2. Russian Americans 3. College teachers 4. Immigrants 5. New York (State) 6. Satirical fiction 7. Literary fiction 8. Modern classics

LC 82001208

Originally published: Garden City, N.Y.: Doubleday; London: Heinemann, 1957.

Professor Timofey Pnin, previously of Tsarist Russia, ia now precariously perched at the heart of an American campus. Battling with American life and language, Pnin must face great hazards in this new world: the ruination of his beautiful lumber-room-as-office; the removal of his teeth and the fitting of new ones; the search for a suitable boarding house; and the trials of taking the wrong train to deliver a lecture in a language he has yet to master. Wry, intelligent and moving, Pnin reveals the absurd and affecting side of one man in exile.

"Not a novel, not really a collection of short stories, but rather a series of sketches, all of them dealing with Timofey Pnin, professor of Russian in a small American university. Each one finds Pnin valiantly trying to cope with the daily crises of American societyPnin on the wrong train, Pnin learning to drive, Pnin giving a party, Pnin and the washing machine. They are all gently amusing, affectionate portraits of a Russian expatriate of the old school caught up in the inexplicable complexities of daily life." Library Journal.

Nabokov, Vladimir Vladimirovich, 1899-1977

The **stories** of Vladimir Nabokov / Vladimir Nabokov ; edited by his son and translator, Dmitri Nabokov. Alfred A. Knopf, 1995. 659 p.

ISBN 0679729976

1. Literary fiction 2. Short stories 3. Translations -- Russian to English 4. Modern classics

LC 95023466

65 stories, "including eleven never before translated into English."

A collection of 65 stories about human relations, human nature, and political satire includes 13 first-time English translations.

Nadel, Barbara

The **Ottoman** cage : a novel of Istanbul / Barbara Nadel. Thomas Dunne Books/St. Martins Minotaur, 2005. 312 p. Inspector Ikmen mysteries

ISBN 0312337698

1. Murder investigation 2. Sex workers 3. Police 4. Coroners 5. Husband and wife 6. Father and adult son 7. People with dementia 8. Armenians in Turkey 9. Violent crimes 10. Murder 11. Apartments 12. Istanbul, Turkey 13. Turkey -- Social life and customs -- 20th century 14. Mysteries 15. Police procedurals

LC 2004061875

Originally published as: A chemical prison. London : Headline Book Pub., c2000.

Called in by the Turkish police when a brutal murder takes place in one of Istanbul's upscale neighborhoods, eccentric, brandy-swilling Inspector Cetin Ikmen plunges into the rich cultural and social life of modern-day Istanbul.

Nadzam, Bonnie

Lamb : a novel / Bonnie Nadzam. Other Press, 2011. 275 p.

ISBN 9781590514375

1. Middle-aged men 2. Teenage girls 3. Teenagers and adults 4. Self-fulfillment 5. Divorced men 6. Automobile travel 7. Loneliness in men 8. Friendship 9. Manipulation (Social sciences) 10. Psychological fiction

LC 2011013263

When his marriage dissolves and his father passes away, David Lamb looks for a way to amend the error of his narcissistic ways. He takes an interest in Tommie, an unpopular eleven-year-old girl. However, when he abducts her and the two embark on cross-country road trip, they both have a life-changing experience.

"People can tell about Lamb, a man whose wife has left him and who finds so little control left in his own life he decides to exert some on Tommie, a seventh-grade girl. Tommie's friends put her up to bumming a cigarette off Lamb just after his dad's funeral. Lamb takes it as an opportunity to teach her and her friends a lesson, pretending to kidnap her (in a manner convincing enough that Tommie's not sure if its real). The two strike up what could charitably be called an uneasy friendship, with Lamb convincing himself he's finally doing right by guiding Tommie, and Tommie happy for the attention and the wealthier Lambs gifts. They both make the very bad decision to road trip to the Rockies together, where pretty much everything goes wrong. Nadzam oversaturates every inch of Lamb's pages. The title character's unacknowledged grief for his father and his own misdirected life floods the subtext, and the writing is both beautiful and unabashedly indulgent. . . . But Nadzam earns that excess. As Lamb always sits on the flinty side of combustion, so does the reader." Time. Out Chicago

Nahai, Gina Barkhordar

The **luminous** heart of Jonah S. / Gina B. Nahai. Akashic Books, 2014. 413 p.

ISBN 9781617753213

1. 1950s 2. 21st century 3. Communities 4. Jewish families 5. Inheritance and succession 6. Exiles 7. Crime 8. Greed 9. Revenge 10. Murder 11. Family relationships 12. Jews, Iranian 13. Tehran, Iran 14. Los Angeles, California 15. Family sagas 16. Magical realism 17. Literary fiction

The Soleymans, an Iranian Jewish family, are tormented for decades by Raphael's Son, a crafty and unscrupulous financier who has futilely claimed to be an heir to the family's fortune. Forty years later in contemporary Los Angeles, Raphael's Son has nearly achieved his goal--until he suddenly disappears, presumed by many to have been murdered.

"With touches of magic realism, extraordinary characters, and a spiraling, multigenerational plot involving fraud, a murder mystery, epic suffering, heroic generosity, womens struggle for freedom, and the clash between East and West, Nahais mythic, tragic, often beautiful immigrant family saga illuminates timeless questions of prejudice, trauma, inheritance, loyalty, and love." Booklist.

Naipaul, V. S. (Vidiadhar Surajprasad), 1932-2018

* A **bend** in the river / V.S. Naipaul. Vintage International, 1989, c1979. 278 p.

ISBN 9780679722021

1. East Indians in Africa 2. Disillusionment in men 3. Villages -- Africa 4. Colonialism 5. Extramarital affairs 6. Africa -- Politics and government 7. Sub-Saharan Africa 8. Political fiction 9. Literary fiction 10. Modern classics

First published in Great Britain by Andre Deutsch, 1979.

Shortlisted for the Booker-McConnell Prize, 1979.

In an African country that has suffered revolution and civil war and that is headed by a man of almost insane energy and crudity, one restless, reflective, and isolated villager and his friends uneasily submit to the tide of events.

Naipaul, V. S. (Vidiadhar Surajprasad), 1932-2018

* **Guerrillas** / V. S. Naipaul. Vintage Books, 1990, c1975. 248 p.

ISBN 9780679731740

1. Guerrillas -- West Indies 2. Love triangles 3. Class conflict 4. European Africans 5. British in the West Indies 6. Revolutionaries 7. West Indies 8. Political fiction 9. Literary fiction

LC 90-50147

A former hero of the South African resistance and his English mistress arrrive on a troubled Caribbean island, where their involvement with a young mulatto revolutionary leader leads to violence

"This is a novel without a villain, and there is not a character for whom the reader does not at some point feel deep sympathy and keen understanding, no matter how villainous or futile he may seem." New York Times Book Review.

Naipaul, V. S. (Vidiadhar Surajprasad), 1932-2018

Half a life / V.S. Naipaul. Knopf, 2001. 211 p.

ISBN 9780375407376

1. East Indians in London, England 2. Men/women relations 3. Interracial romance 4. Colonies -- Africa 5. Authors 6. Portugal -- Colonies -- Africa 7. Africa 8. London, England 9. Literary fiction 10. Psychological fiction

LC 2001033730

Sequel: Magic seeds.

The story of Willy Chandran, who moves from India to the immigrant community of post-war London, seeking something that will set him apart. Then his wife leads him to her home, a province of Portuguese Africa, a country whose inhabitants are all living out the last days of colonialism.

"In the book's last moments a narrative that has seemed to meander pulls suddenly tight, giving 'Half a Life' an interest that lies beyond its relation to Naipaul's other work. . . . The very fissures in its structure, its change from voice to voice, transform 'Half a Life' into a meditation on the difficulties of building a coherent self." New York Times Book Review.

Naipaul, V. S. (Vidiadhar Surajprasad), 1932-2018

* A **house** for Mr. Biswas / V.S. Naipaul Knopf, 1995, c1961. xxxi, 564 p.

ISBN 9780679444589

1. East Indians 2. Married men 3. Middle-aged men 4. Identity (Psychology) 5. Home (Concept) 6. Family relationships 7. Trinidad and Tobago 8. Literary fiction 9. Psychological fiction 10. Modern classics

First published in a different edition: London: Andre Deutsch, 1961.

This is the story of Mohun Biswas, an Indo-Trinidadian who continually strives for success and mostly fails, who marries into the Tulsi family only to find himself dominated by it, and who finally sets the goal of owning his own house. Drawing some elements from the life of the author's father, the work is primarily a sharply drawn look at life that uses postcolonial perspectives to view a vanished colonial world.

Naipaul, V. S. (Vidiadhar Surajprasad), 1932-2018

Magic seeds / V.S. Naipaul. Alfred A. Knopf, 2004. 280 p.

ISBN 0375407367

1. 1950s 2. Revolutionaries 3. Underground movements 4. Middle-aged men 5. East Indians in England 6. Brothers and sisters 7. British in India 8. Social reformers 9. Class conflict 10. Imprisonment 11. Identity (Psychology) 12. Idealism 13. Alienation in men 14. Disillusionment in men 15. England 16. India 17. Psychological fiction 18. Political fiction 19. Literary fiction

LC 2004048964

Sequel to: Half a life.

Willie Chandran feels as though the life he lives is not his own. But his listlessness washes away in a flood of encouragement from his radically political sister. Inspired, he joins an underground liberation movement in India. But after years of revolution and incarceration, he grows disillusioned and returns to England, still hoping to find his true self.

"The author has written a calculated polemic.... Naipaul is suggesting that our racial and ethnic fate is sealed; we can never escape who we are, and must learn to live with our unchosen identities whether we like them or not. It's not a consoling vision; neither is it despairing. It simply is." New York Times Book Review.

Naipaul, V. S. (Vidiadhar Surajprasad), 1932-2018

A **way** in the world : a novel / V.S. Naipaul. Knopf, 1994. 380 p.

ISBN 9780394564784

1. Trinidadians in England 2. Imperialism, European -- Caribbean Area 3. Authors, Trinidadian -- 20th century 4. Autobiographical fiction 5. Literary fiction

LC 93044680

Shortlisted for the International IMPAC Dublin Literary Award, 1996

Integrates examples of British and Spanish imperial history in the Caribbean with a study of the postcolonial experience to reveal the baffling complexities of human inheritance and identity.

"In this autobiographical fiction, Naipaul examines feelings of rootlessness, the realities of the colonial experience, the impact of cultural displacement, and our need to belong. He does so through a series of linked historical narratives.... These are tales of lost souls desperate to find a place at the table but who never quite succeed, leaving them doomed to remain on the fringes of history." Library Journal.

Napolitano, Ann

* **Dear** Edward / Ann Napolitano. The Dial Press, 2020. 340 p.

ISBN 9781984854780

1. Airplane accidents 2. Survival (after airplane accidents, shipwrecks, etc) 3. Boys 4. Life change events 5. Loss (Psychology) 6. Grief 7. Coping 8. Pregnant women 9. Soldiers 10. Families 11. Mainstream fiction

LC 2019000400

A 12-year-old lone survivor of a plane crash investigates the stories of his less-fortunate fellow passengers before making a profound discovery about his life purpose in the face of transcendent losses.

"It is a skillful and satisfying examination of not only what it means to survive, but of what it means to truly live." Booklist.

Narayan, R. K., 1906-2001

* **Malgudi** days / R.K. Narayan. Penguin Books, 2006. xx, 264 p.

ISBN 9780143039655

1. India 2. Short stories

LC 81052204

Originally published: New York : Viking Press, 1982.

"This selection distills, magically, Malgudi's vibrancy, its mythological-animistic throb, the large and small corruptions of its citizens--from bureaucrats to back-street people--and the reassuring backdrop of its cyclical rhythms. Distinguished writing; rewarding reading." Booklist.

Narayan, R. K., 1906-2001

Under the banyan tree and other stories / R.K. Narayan. Viking, 1985. 193 p.

ISBN 9780670804528

1. India 2. Short stories

LC 85003234

28 shories.

Includes glossary.

Twenty-eight stories set in the fictional south Indian town of Malgudi, deal with people from all classes and walks of life

"Narayan's clarity, his mastery of technique, his respect for the spectrum of human predicament, his absence of malice and his freedom from a single philosophy that explains everything away put him in the unique position of being able to turn a teeming cultural life into lucid and enjoyable stories." New Statesman.

Nash, Sophia

Between the Duke and the deep blue sea / Sophia Nash. Avon, 2012. 371 p. Royal entourage

ISBN 9780062022325

1. Regency period (1811-1820) 2. 19th century 3. Nobility 4. Revenge 5. Rescues 6. Gambling 7. Dukes and duchesses 8. Country homes 9. Exile (Punishment) 10. Attempted murder 11. Men/women relations 12. Interpersonal attraction 13. England -- Social life and customs -- 19th century 14. Historical romances 15. Regency romances

After her murderous blackguard of a husband tries to kill her, Roxanne Vanderhaven finds an unlikely champion in the notorious Duke of Kress, who, exiled to Cornwall by the Prince Regent himself, is searching for redemption.

Naslund, Brian

Blood of an exile / Brian Naslund. Tor, 2019. 416 p. Dragons of Terra

ISBN 9781250309631

1. Dragons 2. Attempted assassination 3. Punishment 4. Exile (Punishment) 5. Imaginary kingdoms 6. Environmental degradation 7. Women kidnapping victims 8. Rescues 9. Self-discovery in men 10. Fantasy fiction 11. Epic fantasy

LC 2018052929

"A Tom Doherty Associates book."

Sentenced to fight monsters until he dies, an undefeated dragon slayer is offered his freedom in exchange for assassinating a rival king before finding himself an unlikely defender of an innocent child and the lives of every creature in Terra.

Naslund, Sena Jeter

Abundance : a novel of Marie Antoinette / Sena Jeter Naslund. William Morrow, 2006. 560 p.

ISBN 0060825391

1. Marie Antoinette,, Queen of France, 1755-1793 2. Louis XVI,, King of France, 1754-1793 3. Princesses -- Austria 4. Princes -- France 5. Fourteen-year-old girls 6. Women rulers -- France 7. Revolutionaries -- France -- History -- 18th century 8. Guillotine 9. Executions and executioners -- France -- History 10. Growing up 11. Men/women relations 12. Courts and courtiers -- France 13. Motherhood 14. Escapes 15. French Revolution, 1789-1799 16. France -- History -- Revolution, 1789-1799 17. Versailles, France -- History -- 18th century 18. Austria -- History -- 18th century 19. Historical fiction 20. Biographical fiction

LC 2006043817

A fictional tale of the life of Marie Antoinette presents the story of a teenage empress's daughter who is forced to leave her family home to marry the future king of France and who rebels against the formality and rigid protocol of court life

"With vivid detail and exquisite narrative technique, Naslund exemplifies the best of historical fiction, finding the woman beneath the pose, a queen facing history as it rises up against her." Publishers Weekly.

Naslund, Sena Jeter

Ahab's wife, or, the star gazer : a novel / Sena Jeter Naslund ; illustrations by Christopher Wormell. William Morrow, 1999. xix, 668 p.

ISBN 9780688171872

1. 19th century 2. Ship captains' spouses 3. Whalers 4. Marriage, 5. New England -- History -- 19th century 6. Nantucket, Massachusetts 7. Literary fiction 8. Historical fiction

A rich epic, drawn from the classic Moby Dick, chronicles the life of Una Spenser, wife of the immortal Captain Ahab, from her Kentucky childhood, through her adventures disguised as a whaling ship cabin boy, to her various marriages.

"At age 12, Una escapes her religiously obsessed father in rural Kentucky to live with relatives in a lighthouse off New Bedford, Mass. When she is 16, disguised as a boy, she runs off to sea aboard a whaler, which sinks after being rammed by its quarry. Una and two young men who love her are the only survivors of a group set adrift in an open boat, but the dark secret of their cannibalism will leave its mark. Rescued, Una is wed to one of the young men by the captain of the Pequod, handsome, commanding Ahab -- a, who has not as yet met the white whale that will be his destiny. . . . Una's later marriage to Ahab -- a passionateand intellectually satisfying relationship -- the loss of her mother and her newborn son in one night, and her life as a rich woman in Nantucket are further developments in a plot teeming with arresting events and provocative ideas." Publishers Weekly.

Naslund, Sena Jeter

Four spirits : a novel / Sena Jeter Naslund. Morrow, 2003. 544 p.

ISBN 0066212383

1. 1960s 2. Women civil rights workers 3. African Americans -- Civil rights 4. Civil rights movement -- Birmingham, Alabama 5. Interracial friendship 6. Female friendship 7. College students 8. Race relations 9. Young women 10. Civil rights 11. Courage 12. Southern States -- Race relations -- History -- 20th century 13.

Birmingham, Alabama -- Race relations 14. Historical fiction

LC 2003051170

Stella, a white college student, joins the freedom movement in 1960s Alabama, and her new friendships with black women alter her life forever. So does the dangerous conflagration engulfing everyone and everything she has known.

"Naslund has done something unusually fine--she's written a drifting collective portrait of a city in distress. The characters of 'Four Spirits' are deeply entwined, sometimes without knowing it." New York Times Book Review.

Naslund, Sena Jeter

The **fountain** of St. James Court : or, portrait of the artist as an old woman / Sena Jeter Naslund. William Morrow, 2013. 434 p.

ISBN 9780061579325

1. 18th century 2. 21st century 3. Women authors 4. Divorced women 5. Women artists 6. Family relationships 7. Identity (Psychology) 8. France -- History -- Revolution, 1789-1799 9. Psychological fiction 10. Parallel narratives 11. Historical fiction 12. Novels-within-novels

When writer Kathryn Callaghan finishes her novel about painter Elisabeth Vigee-LeBrun, a French Revolution survivor, she has a hard time leaving the eighteenth-century European world she has researched and returning to her own American life of 2012.

Natt och Dag, Niklas, 1979-

The **wolf** and the watchman : a novel / Niklas Natt Och Dag ; translated from the Swedish by Ebba Segerberg. Atria Books, 2019, c2017. 373 p.

ISBN 9781501196775

1. 18th century 2. Veterans 3. Private investigators 4. Murder investigation 5. Police 6. Physicians 7. Prostitutes 8. Social classes 9. Social conflict 10. Stockholm, Sweden 11. Sweden -- History -- 18th century 12. Historical mysteries 13. Translations -- Swedish to English

Originally published as 1793 by Bokf?rlaget Forum, 2017.

When a mutilated corpse is discovered in a local swamp, watchman Mikel Cardell and lawyer Cecil Winge comb the underworld of eighteenth-century Stockholm to unmask a murderer before a young workhouse laborer becomes the next victim.

"Ideal for readers who enjoy crime thrillers, nail-biting suspense, and historical period dramas. While this debut novel's violent imagery may be too much for some, its an exciting addition to the crime thriller genre and will leave readers on the edge of their seats." Library Journal.

Nava, Michael

* **Carved** in bone / Michael Nava. Persigo Press, 2019. 374 p. Henry Rios mysteries

ISBN 9781733609111

1. 1980s 2. Lawyers 3. Public defenders 4. Gay men 5. Mexican American men 6. Criminal investigation 7. Insurance 8. Men/men relations 9. AIDS (Disease) 10. Los Angeles, California 11. Mysteries 12. LGBTQIA fiction 13. Legal stories

Set in San Francisco in 1984, Henry Rios is hired by an insurance company to investigate the apparently accidental death by carbon monoxide poisoning of Bill Ryan in his Castro Street apartment, but Rios becomes convinced Ryan's death was no accident, and that his young lover is implicated.

Nawaz, Saleema, 1979-

Bone and bread / Saleema Nawaz. House Of Anansi Press, 2013. 448 p.

ISBN 1770890092

1. Sisters 2. Orphans 3. Grief 4. Sikhs 5. Teenage girls -- Body image 6. Pregnancy 7. Anorexia nervosa 8. Group identity 9. Memory 10. Montreal, Quebec 11. Coming-of-age stories 12. Mainstream fiction

Quebec Writers' Federation Literary Awards, Hugh MacLennan Prize for Fiction, 2013.

When sisters Beena and Sadhana are orphaned as teenagers and sent to live with their Sikh uncle in Montreal's Hasidic community, their lives take divergent courses as they deal with their grief in different ways.

Naylor, Gloria

Bailey's Cafe / Gloria Naylor. Harcourt Brace Jovanovich, 1992. 229 p.

ISBN 0151104506

1. 1940s 2. Misfits (Persons) 3. Restaurants 4. Diners (Restaurants) 5. Healing 6. African Americans 7. Historical fiction 8. African American fiction

LC 91042089

ALA Notable Book, 1993.

A motley group of misfits takes on a magical aura at Bailey's Cafe as each character describes his or her motivations, desires, obsessions, and idiosyncracies

"The author takes us many keys down, and sometimes back up, in this virtuoso orchestration of survival, suffering, courage and humor, sounding through the stories of these lives." New York Times Book Review.

Naylor, Gloria

Linden Hills / Gloria Naylor. Ticknor and Fields, 1985. 304 p.

ISBN 9780899193571

1. Identity (Psychology) 2. Hypocrisy 3. Social classes 4. Racism 5. African Americans -- Identity 6. Middle class African Americans 7. Mainstream fiction 8. African American fiction 9. Adaptations, retellings, and spin-offs

LC 84016222

Lester Tilson and Willie Mason, a pair of hip, latter-day poets, work their way down through Linden Hills, experiencing firsthand the lust, pain, hypocrisy, and valor of the hell-bound upper- and middle-class residents.

"The author sketches the development of the community of Linden Hills through its founder, Luther Nedeed, and successive generations of Nedeeds, showing in the decline of the family the corrosive effect of ambition, arrogance and the abuse of power. The residents of Linden Hills are similarly subverted by the accommodations, sacrifices and perversions of soul blacks must endure to live in an affluent community, even, as in this case, an all-black one." Publishers Weekly.

Naylor, Gloria

* **Mama** Day / Gloria Naylor. Ticknor & Fields, 1988. 312 p.

ISBN 9780899197166

1. Independence in women 2. Islands -- South Carolina 3. Married people 4. African American senior women 5. African Americans -- South Carolina 6. African American women 7. Great-aunts 8. Vacations 9. Magic 10. South Carolina 11. New York City 12. Literary fiction 13. African American fiction

LC 87018157

Miranda Day, matriarch of an island off the coast of the U.S., fights a mortal combat with dark forces that threaten her great-niece, Cocoa, who has married and gone to the mainland

"When she is not didactically fostering our spiritual instruction, Gloria Naylor serves another worthy purpose beautifully: she invites us to imagine the lives of complex characters at work and play, and gives us a faithfully rendered community in all its seasons." Ms.

Naylor, Gloria

The **men** of Brewster Place / Gloria Naylor. Hyperion, 1998. 173 p.

ISBN 0786864214

1. Public housing 2. Identity (Psychology) 3. Race relations 4. Self-esteem 5. African American men 6. African American community life 7. City life 8. African American fiction 9. Mainstream fiction

LC 9745987

Sequel to The Women of Brewster Place.

Explores the lives and fates of seven men, from Basil Michael, who marries a woman he does not love for the sake of her children, to Eugene Turner, torn between his homosexuality and his beloved wife

"Ben, a neighborhood janitor (and chorus) resurrected from the previous Brewster Place novel, narrates seven tales of neighborhood men and the women who love them. Their travails feature the familiar ills of the inner city, yet Naylor lends these archetypal situations complexity and depth: Basil yearns to be the kind of father he never had but chooses a path that leads to heartbreak; Eugene's restlessness in his marriage and friendship with a transsexual force him to face a difficult fact about himself; Reverend Moreland T. Woods rehearses his political aspirations with maneuvers on his church's board; and C.C. Baker, involved in local drug trafficking, keeps a startling truth from the police." Publishers Weekly.

Naylor, Gloria

The **women** of Brewster Place / Gloria Naylor. Penguin Books, 1983, c1982. 192 p.

ISBN 9780140066906

1. Urban women 2. Public housing 3. Mother and child 4. Poor families 5. Single mothers 6. African American women 7. City life 8. African American fiction 9. Mainstream fiction

Sequel: The Men of Brewster Place.

Brewster Place is a blind alley feeding into a dead end. It is a story of seven fictitious women characerters; they are "hard-edged, soft-centered, brutally demanding, and easily pleased."

"This novel is set, as the title indicates, in Brewster Place, a block-long dead-end street of run-down apartment buildings in a northern city. In an interrelated series of vignettes, Naylor focuses on seven black women, residents of Brewster Place. She is concerned with the distance between their dreams and realities, problems and solutions; these women are of different ages, come from different backgrounds, react differently to their blackness and to men, and have different notions of personal accomplishment, but all are burdened by being both black and female. Naylor is not angry; she writes with conviction and beautiful language, but spares the reader any bitterness. Characters are not puppets but exist and function as well-rounded personalities." Booklist.

Nebula Awards showcase 2017 : the year's best science fiction and fantasy selected by the Science Fiction and Fantasy Writers of America / edited by Julie E. Czerneda. Pyr Books, 2017. 336 p.

ISBN 9781633882713

1. Science fiction 2. Fantasy fiction 3. Short stories 4. Anthologies

"This compilation of Nebula Award-nominated and winning fiction from 2016 is indispensable reading for anyone interested in fantastic fiction. The three short-fiction winners show the breadth of themes and ideas and the sheer creativity of the genres leading writers." Publishers Weekly.

Neel, Janet

To die for : a mystery / Janet Neel. St. Martin's Press, 1999. 240 p. Francesca Wilson and John McLeish mysteries

ISBN 0312205988

1. Scotland Yard 2. Murder investigation 3. Husband-and-wife detectives 4. Married people 5. Women's shelters 6. Women detectives 7. Murder 8. Police spouses 9. Restaurants 10. Extortion 11. London, England 12. Mysteries

LC 9918077

Pressured to sell their two fashionable restaurants, old friends Selina and Judith refuse, but the stakes become a lot higher when Selina is murdered and amateur sleuth Francesca Wilson investigates

"A mystery featuring Chief Superintendent John McLeish and his wife Francesca. The investors in Judith Delves's London cafe, including her co-owner, want to sell, but Judith is obstinately against the transaction. Shortly after her friend and partner, Selina, comes around to her way of thinking, Selina's body is found stuffed into an unused freezer." Publishers Weekly.

Neely, Barbara, 1941-2020

Blanche cleans up / Barbara Neely. Viking, 1998. 258 p. Blanche White mysteries

ISBN 0670876267

1. Scandals 2. Upper class 3. Murder 4. Household employees 5. African American household employees 6. African American women 7. Politicians 8. Rich people 9. Child sexual abuse 10. Slumlords 11. Lead-poisoning in minority children 12. African American clergy 13. Housekeepers 14. Amateur detectives 15. Women amateur detectives 16. Boston, Massachusetts 17. Mysteries 18. African American fiction

LC 9739834

The series continues as the sharp-eyed, middle-aged black maid-cum-busybody is swept up in a scandal involving a Boston politician, a teen pregnancy, and a phony spiritual advisor

"Blanche's caustic comments, streetwise attitude and lusty approach to life cast an illuminating light on both ends of the social spectrum and add sparks to an already sizzling mystery." Publishers Weekly.

Nelscott, Kris

Days of rage / Kris Nelscott. St. Martin's Minotaur, 2006. 352 p. Smokey Dalton novels

ISBN 0312325290

1. 1960s 2. Private investigators 3. African American men 4. Foster sons 5. Businesspeople 6. Criminologists 7. Undertakers 8. Trials (Political crimes and offenses) 9. Protests, demonstrations, vigils, etc 10. Murder 11. Murder investigation 12. Chicago, Illinois 13. Historical mysteries

LC 2005054791

"Set in 1969 during the trial of the Chicago Eight, . . . [this] Smokey Dalton novel . . . interweaves the issue of race with politics, societal questions and personal relationships, like Smokey's on-again, off-again romance with Laura Hathaway, a white businesswoman. Laura asks Smokey to investigate an empty Queen Anne house that had been bought by her dishonest father's company years earlier. The house, separated into apartments, has slowly emptied over the years until there's only one resident, the manager, Mortimer Hanley. Hanley's death leads to Smokey's inspection, which in turn brings a horrific discovery: the basement is bricked up into many rooms, and each room holds dead bodies. Laura and Smokey bring in Wayne LeDoux, a persnickety criminologist, to do forensic work at the house, and Tim Minton, an expert from a local funeral home, joins him. The two men form a special bond, and like the bond between Smokey and his adopted son, make a suspenseful mystery into something much richer." Publishers Weekly.

Nelscott, Kris

Stone cribs / Kris Nelscott. St. Martin's Minotaur, 2003. 323 p. Smokey Dalton novels

ISBN 0312287844

1. 1960s 2. African Americans 3. Private investigators 4. Child witnesses 5. Child murder witnesses 6. Rape victims 7. Interracial couples 8. Gangs 9. Abortion 10. Racism 11. Revenge 12. Witnesses -- Protection 13. Chicago, Illinois -- Race relations 14. Historical mysteries 15. Mysteries

LC 2003050604

Saving the life of the victim of a botched illegal abortion in 1969, Chicago private investigator Smokey Dalton learns that the woman had been raped, a case that is complicated by the subsequent murder of her vengeful husband.

"Nelscott skillfully recreates a troubled 1960s Chicago, complete with sympathetic protagonists who fight its racial inequalities, widespread ignorance, and political ineptness." Library Journal.

Nelson, Christina Suzann

* If we make it home : a novel of faith and survival in the Oregon wilderness / Christina Suzann Nelson. Kregel Publications, 2017. 272 p.

ISBN 9780825444951

1. Women college friends 2. Wilderness survival 3. Hiking 4. Blizzards 5. Mountain survival 6. Faith (Christianity) 7. Christian suspense

After learning that Hope, their friend from college has died, Jenna, Ireland, and Vicky embark on a wilderness adventure in her honor.

Nelson, Christina Suzann

More than we remember / Christina Suzann Nelson. Bethany House, 2020. 352 p.

ISBN 9780764235504

1. Female friendship 2. Life change events 3. Traffic accidents 4. Psychic trauma 5. Death 6. Drug abuse 7. Faith 8. Families 9. Oregon 10. Christian fiction 11. Women's lives and relationships

LC 2019040450

After a life-altering car accident, one night changes everything for three women. As their lives intersect, they can no longer dwell in the memory of who they've been. Can they rise from the wreck of the worst moments of their lives to become who they were meant to be?

"Readers who are looking for faith-based women's fiction will be quickly drawn into this powerful novel that is, by turns, heartbreaking and uplifting." Booklist.

Nemett, Adam

We can save us all : a novel / Adam Nemett. Unnamed Press, 2018. 363 p.

ISBN 9781944700768

1. College students 2. Misfits (Persons) 3. End of the world 4. Cults 5. Superheroes 6. Drug use 7. Climate change 8. Near future 9. Interpersonal relations 10. Princeton, New Jersey 11. Coming-of-age stories 12. Science fiction

LC 2018021901

A group of alienated Princeton students respond to escalating climate change by forming an endtimes cult inspired by superheroes.

"In this first novel, the drug-fueled, phantasmagoric environment of the college elite intersects with the cogent realities of environmental degradation...This is an unlikely but timely contribution to the ongoing #metoo dialog as well as humorous riposte to concerns about society and the environment." Library Journal.

Nemirovsky, Irene, 1903-1942

Fire in the blood / Irene Nemirovsky; translated by Sandra Smith. Alfred A. Knopf, 2007 176 p.

ISBN 9780307267481

1. Between the Wars (1918-1939) 2. 1940s 3. Family secrets 4. Village communities -- France 5. Reminiscing in old age 6. Men/women relations 7. Love 8. Betrayal 9. Ethics 10. Murder 11. Small towns -- France 12. Secrets 13. Regret in senior men 14. Family relationships 15. Mothers and daughters 16. Forced marriage 17. Class conflict 18. World War II 19. France -- History -- German occupation, 1940-1945 20. Historical fiction 21. Translations -- French to English

Although never published prior to 2007, it was written in 1941.

Originally published in France as Chaleur du sang by Denoel, Paris, in 2007. verso.

A recently discovered but never-before-published novel by an author who died in Auschwitz in 1942 captures life in a small French village in the years before the onset of World War II, as Silvio, a middle-aged man enjoying his wine and his solitude, is drawn back into the life of his family and the village by the arrival of a cousin and the revelation of long-hidden secrets.

"In a book fuelled with images of fire and embers, Nmirovsky brilliantly depicts a closed-in, inward-looking community, then gives what happens in it universal resonance by exhibiting not only what people do to each other but what the passing of time does to us all." London Times

Nemirovsky, Irene, 1903-1942

Suite Francaise / Irene Nemirovsky ; translated from the French by Sandra Smith. Alfred A. Knopf, 2006, c2004. 395 p.

ISBN 9781400044733

1. Second World War era (1939-1945) 2. 1940s 3. 20th century 4. World War II -- France 5. Refugees, French 6. Soldiers -- Germany 7. Military occupation 8. Villages -- France 9. Farm life -- France 10. Farmers -- France 11. Priests 12. Hypocrisy 13. Greed 14. Class conflict 15. Human behavior 16. Men/women relations 17. Interpersonal relations 18. France -- History -- German occupation, 1940-1945 19. War stories 20. Literary fiction 21. Translations -- French to English

LC 2006003461

First published: France : Editions Denoel, 2004. First published in Great Britain by Chatto & Windus, 2006.

Originally written in 1941-42; originally published: Paris : Denoel, 2004.

A story of life in France under the Nazi occupation includes two parts--"Storm in June," set amid the chaotic 1940 exodus from Paris, and "Dolce," set in a German-occupied village rife with resentment, resistance, and collaboration.

"Nemirovsky, a young Russian Jewish emigre, became a celebrated novelist in Paris at age 26 in 1929. She wrote eight more novels; then, even though she was certain that she wouldn't survive Germany's occupation of France, she embarked on a . . . work about France's collaboration with the Nazis. She completed two of five planned movements before she was sent to Auschwitz, a heart-wrenching story meticulously documented in a supplemental section. As for Nemirovsky's masterpiece, it begins with the tumultuous Storm in June, in which diverse Parisians frantically evacuate Paris during the June 1940 German invasion. Nemirovsky's gift for combining the panoramic with the intimate, high emotion with stinging wit, is reminiscent of Turgenev, Babel, and Berberova. Acutely sensitive to class differences, and mordantly scornful of hypocrisy, she orchestrates a veritable carnival of cowardice, lies, larceny, and murder as a panicked populace drops all pretense of civilization. The second movement, Dolce, evokes the eye of the storm in the village of Bussy, where German officers are billeted in French homes,

and life and love resume. Suite Francaise is a magnificent novel of the insidious devastation of occupation, and Nemirovsky is brilliant and heroic, summoning up profound empathy for all, including regretful German soldiers." Booklist.

Nesbit, TaraShea

The **wives** of Los Alamos : a novel / TaraShea Nesbit. Bloomsbury USA, 2014. 233 p.

ISBN 9781620405031

1. Second World War era (1939-1945) 2. Married women 3. Female friendship 4. World War II 5. Scientists 6. Secrets 7. Weapons 8. Research 9. Atomic bomb 10. Partying 11. World War II home front 12. Los Alamos, New Mexico 13. New Mexico 14. Historical fiction

LC 2013036239

"The Wives of Los Alamos is a novel that sheds light onto one of the strangest and most monumental research projects in modern history. It's a testament to a remarkable group of women who carved out a life for themselves, in spite of the chaos of the war and the shroud of intense secrecy"--, Provided by publisher.

"Nesbit uses a collective 'we' to narrate her story, allowing her to explore contradictory points of view among the women. . . . [A] well-researched and fast-paced novel." Library Journal.

Nesbo, Jo, 1960-

The **bat** / Jo Nesbo ; translated from the Norwegian by Don Bartlett. Vintage Crime/Black Lizard, 2013, c1997. 369 p. Detective Harry Hole

ISBN 9780345807090

1. Serial murder investigation 2. Serial murderers 3. Voyages and travels 4. Former detectives 5. Former police 6. Sydney, New South Wales 7. Oslo, Norway 8. Norway 9. Mysteries 10. Translations -- Norwegian to English 11. Scandinavian crime fiction

Originally published as: Flaggermusmannen, by Aschehoug : Oslo, 1997.

Follows Harry Hole's efforts to solve the murder of a television celebrity whose demise is linked to a string of serial killings.

"Inspector Harry Hole's 1997 debut finally follows its seven successors into English translation. . . . Fans of Harry's later adventures (The Redeemer, 2013, etc.) will wait with bated breath to see how long it takes him to break every rule in the book." Kirkus.

Nesbo, Jo, 1960-

Blood on snow / Jo Nesbo ; translated from the Norwegian by Neil Smith. Alfred A. Knopf, 2015. 207 p. Blood on snow

ISBN 9780385354196

1. 1970s 2. Assassins 3. Organized crime 4. Extramarital affairs 5. Love triangles 6. Married men 7. Betrayal 8. Oslo, Norway 9. Scandinavian crime fiction 10. Thrillers and suspense 11. Translations -- Norwegian to English

Originally published in Norway by H. Aschehoug & Co., 2015.

Gifted with an unexpected capacity for love, as well as a talent for murder, Olav, a "fixer" who works for Oslo's crime kingpin, discovers that his boss might want him "fixed" due to the fact that he knows too much about his business--and has fallen in love with his wife.

"Nesbo tells this small but razor-sharp story with precision and understated eloquence, even generating suspense despite the inevitability built into the plot: we know there will be blood on snow, but were not quite sure whose and how much." Booklist.

Nesbo, Jo, 1960-

Cockroaches / Jo Nesbo ; translated from the Norwegian by Don Bartlett. Vintage Crime/Black Lizard, 2014, c1998. 367 p. Detective Harry Hole

ISBN 9780345807151

1. Police 2. Norwegians 3. Murder investigation 4. Bangkok, Thailand 5. Mysteries 6. Translations -- Norwegian to English 7. Scandinavian crime fiction

Originally published in Norwegian as Kakerlakkene : Oslo, [Norway]: H. Aschehoug & Co., 1998.

Sent from Oslo to Thailand to keep the murder of a Norwegian ambassador, who was found dead in a Bangkok brothel, quiet, Inspector Harry Hole discovers that this is much more than a random murder as he tries to piece together the story of the ambassador's death.

Nesbo, Jo, 1960-

The **devil's** star / Jo Nesbo ; translated from the Norwegian by Don Bartlett. Harper, 2010, c2003. 452 p. Detective Harry Hole

ISBN 9780061133978

1. 21st century 2. Murder investigation 3. Detectives 4. Serial murderers 5. Police 6. Murder 7. Oslo, Norway 8. Norway 9. Mysteries 10. Translations -- Norwegian to English 11. Scandinavian crime fiction

This translation originally published: [London]: Harvill Secker, 2004.

Originally published as: Marekors, by H. Aschehoug & Co. (W. Nygaard), Oslo, 2003.

Alcoholic detective Harry Hole has two missions: catch a serial killer obsessed with the number five, who cuts a finger off each victim and adorns her with a red pentagram; and expose his crooked partner, Tom Waaler.

"Scandinavian noir is alive and well, and Nesbo is one of its best authors." Library Journal.

Nesbo, Jo, 1960-

Headhunters / Jo Nesbo ; translated from the Norwegian by Don Bartlett. Vintage Crime/Black Lizard, 2011, c2008. 265 p.

ISBN 9780307948687

1. Art thefts 2. Swindlers and swindling 3. Assassins 4. Murder 5. Chases 6. Escapes 7. Executive search services 8. Painting 9. Husband and wife 10. Stealing 11. Norway 12. Thrillers and suspense 13. Caper novels 14. Translations -- Norwegian to English 15. Scandinavian crime fiction 16. Crime fiction

LC 2011030829

Originally published as: Hodejegerne. Oslo : H. ASchehoug & Co., 2008.

This translation originally published: London : Harvill Secker, 2011.

Roger Brown is a headhunter and art thief living beyond his means and when he meets Clas Greve, a corporate candidate who reveals that he owns a priceless Rubens painting, Roger breaks into his apartment, initiating a series of events which puts Roger's life in danger.

"Roger Brown, a British expat comfortably ensconced in Oslo, has developed a reputation as one of the best corporate headhunters in the business, but money problems lead him to use information he gleans from job applicants about valuable art they own. Brown arranges to steal their art works and replace them with clever fakes. When Clas Greve, the former CEO of a major European GPS company, lets slip that he accidentally discovered a long-lost Rubens painting in the apartment he inherited from his aunt, Brown anticipates making his biggest score. Of course, the heist doesn't go smoothly, and the dizzying reversals of for-tune and situations that would be over-the-top in lesser hands make for a delightful roller-coaster ride." Publishers Weekly.

Nesbo, Jo, 1960-

* The **leopard** / Jo Nesbo ; translated from the Norwegian by Don Bartlett. Alfred A. Knopf, 2011, c2009. 528 p. Detective Harry Hole

ISBN 9780307595874

1. Police -- Oslo, Norway 2. Crimes against women 3. Serial murder investigation 4. Opium addiction 5. Serial murders 6. Detectives -- Oslo, Norway 7. Oslo, Norway 8. Norway 9. Hong Kong 10. Mysteries 11. Translations -- Norwegian to English 12. Scandinavian crime fiction

First published in Great Britain : Harvill Secker, 2011.

First published with the title Panserhjerte in Oslo : H. Aschehong, 2009.

In the depths of winter, a killer stalks the city streets. His victims are two young women, both found with twenty-four inexplicable puncture wounds, both drowned in their own blood. The crime scenes offer no clues, the media is reaching fever pitch, and the police are running out of options. There is only one man who can help them, and he doesn't want to be found. Deeply traumatised by an investigation that threatened the lives of those he holds most dear, Inspector Harry Hole has lost himself in the squalor of Hong Kong's opium dens. But with his father seriously ill in hospital, Harry reluctantly agrees to return to Oslo. He has no intention of working on the case, but his instinct takes over when an MP is found brutally murdered in a city park.

Nesbo, Jo, 1960-

Macbeth / Jo Nesbo. Hogarth Press, 2018 446 p. Hogarth Shakespeare

ISBN 9780553419054

1. 1970s 2. Police 3. Drug dealers 4. Police corruption 5. Murder 6. Casinos 7. Ambition 8. Corruption 9. Police chiefs 10. Men/women relations 11. Manipulation (Social sciences) 12. Crime fiction 13. Literary fiction 14. Adaptations, retellings, and spin-offs

A modern retelling of Macbeth is set in a run-down industrial town in the 1970s and follows the efforts of a popular but increasingly corrupt police officer and his calculating casino owner girlfriend to work with a powerful local drug dealer to murder a professional rival and set up his best friend.

Nesbo, Jo, 1960-

Midnight sun / Jo Nesbo ; translated from the Norwegian by Neil Smith. Alfred A. Knopf, 2016. 273 p. Blood on snow

ISBN 9780385354202

1. Assassins 2. Escapes 3. Betrayal 4. Clergy 5. Cabins 6. Atheists 7. Christians 8. Gangsters 9. Murder for hire 10. Attempted murder 11. Men/women relations 12. Norway 13. Scandinavian crime fiction 14. Thrillers and suspense 15. Crime fiction 16. Translations -- Norwegian to English

First published in Norwegian as: Mere blod : Norway : Aschehoug, 2015.

Arriving in a quiet Norway community where locals ask few questions, a former fixer for a cruel international drug king seeks redemption while becoming the kind of man his former boss and he used to target.

Nesbo, Jo, 1960-

Nemesis / Jo Nesbo ; translated from the Norwegian by Don Bartlett. Harper, 2008, c2002. 474 p. Detective Harry Hole

ISBN 9780061655500

1. Bank robberies 2. Murder 3. Detectives 4. Men/women relations 5. Frameups 6. Violence 7. Oslo, Norway 8. Norway 9. Mysteries

10. Translations -- Norwegian to English 11. Scandinavian crime fiction

LC 2008032976

Originally published as: Sorgenfri, by H. Aschehoug & Co. (W. Nygaard), Oslo, 2002.

Oslo Police Detective Harry Hole is assigned to investigate a series of bank robberies of unparalleled savagery while at the same time absolving himself of the murder of his former girlfriend in a criminal investigation led by his longtime adversary Tom Waaler and Waaler's vigilante police force.

Nesbo, Jo, 1960-

* **Phantom** / Jo Nesbø ; translated from the Norwegian by Don Bartlett. Alfred A. Knopf, 2012, c2011. 400 p. Detective Harry Hole

ISBN 9780307960474

1. Former detectives 2. Former police 3. Murder suspects 4. Murder investigation 5. Drug traffic 6. Drugs 7. Justice 8. Oslo, Norway 9. Norway 10. Mysteries 11. Translations -- Norwegian to English 12. Scandinavian crime fiction

LC 2012019892

"This is a Borzoi book."

"First published with the title Gjenferd in 2011 by Aschehoug & Co (W. Nygaard), Oslo"--T.p. verso.

Originally published as: Gjenferd, by Aschehoug : Oslo, 2011.

Former cop Harry Hole returns to Oslo to prove the innocence of a young man. He embarks on a dangerous investigation linked to Oslo's most virulent street drug.

Nesbo, Jo, 1960-

Police / Jo Nesbo ; translated from the Norwegian by Don Bartlett. Alfred A. Knopf, 2013. 435 p. Detective Harry Hole

ISBN 9780307960498

1. Police murders 2. Former detectives 3. Murder investigation 4. Former police 5. Police 6. Justice 7. Cold cases (Criminal investigation) 8. Oslo, Norway 9. Norway 10. Mysteries 11. Translations -- Norwegian to English 12. Scandinavian crime fiction

First published in Norwegian. Oslo : H. Aschehoug & Co., 2013.

Harry Hole seemingly has his hands tied when the police seek his help in finding a killer who his offing Oslo cops whose cases are unsolved.

Nesbo, Jo, 1960-

The **redbreast** / Jo Nesbo; translated from the Norwegian by Don Bartlett. Harper, 2006, c2000. 519 p. Detective Harry Hole

ISBN 9780061133992

1. 1940s 2. 21st century 3. Cold cases (Criminal investigation) 4. Detectives 5. World War II 6. Police 7. Voyages and travels 8. Alcoholic men 9. Alcoholic police 10. Murder 11. Murder investigation 12. Mysteries 13. Translations -- Norwegian to English 14. Scandinavian crime fiction

Originally published as: Rodstrupe, by H. Aschehoug & Co. (W. Nygaard), Oslo, 2000.

1942: Daniel, a soldier legendary among the Norwegians fighting at the Eastern front, is killed. Eighteen months later in a Vienna hospital, a wounded soldier becomes involved with a young nurse. The consequences will ripple forward to the end of the century. 1999: Having caused an embarrassment in the line of duty, Harry Hole is lumbered with monitoring neo-Nazi activity; a fairly mundane assignment, until reports of a rare weapon being fired attract his interest. Meanwhile, an ex-soldier has been found with his throat cut. Pursuing both his assignment and his hunches, Harry embarks on an investigation in which he has much to gain and everything to lose.

"This is a fine novel, ambitious in concept, skillful in execution and grownup in its view of people and events. In important ways it's also a political novel, one concerned with the threat of fascism, in Norway and by implication everywhere. All in all, The Redbreast certainly ranks with the best of current American crime fiction." Washington Post Book World.

Nesbo, Jo, 1960-

* The **redeemer** / Jo Nesbo ; translated from the Norwegian by Don Bartlett. Alfred A. Knopf, 2013, c2005. 464 p. Detective Harry Hole

ISBN 9780307595850

1. Salvation Army. 2. Serial murderers 3. Police -- Oslo, Norway 4. Murder investigation 5. Detectives -- Oslo, Norway 6. Brothers 7. Oslo, Norway 8. Norway 9. Mysteries 10. Translations -- Norwegian to English 11. Scandinavian crime fiction

Translation of Frelseren. Originally published: Oslo : Aschehoug, 2005.

One freezing night in Oslo Christmas shoppers gather to listen to a Salvation Army street concert. An explosion cuts through the music, and a man in uniform falls to the ground, shot in the head at point-blank range. Harry Hole and his team have little to work with: no immediate suspect, no weapon and no motive.

Nesbo, Jo, 1960-

The **snowman** / Jo Nesbo ; translated from the Norwegian by Don Bartlett. Harvill Secker, 2010, c2007. 454 p. Detective Harry Hole

ISBN 9781846553486

1. Police -- Oslo, Norway 2. Crimes against women 3. Serial murder investigation 4. Cold cases (criminal investigation) 5. Serial murders 6. Detectives -- Oslo, Norway 7. Oslo, Norway 8. Norway 9. Mysteries 10. Translations -- Norwegian to English 11. Scandinavian crime fiction

First published with the title Snomannen in 2007 by H. Aschehoug & Co. (W. Nygaard), Oslo.

First published in Norwegian as "Snomannen": Oslo : H. Aschehoug & Co., 2007. This translation first published: London : Harvill Secker, 2010.

Originally published as: Snomannen, by Aschehoug : Oslo, 2007.

Harry Hole investigates the disappearance of a woman whose scarf is found on a mysteriously built snowman, a case that is complicated by subsequent abductions and a menacing letter.

"This mystery featuring Oslo's Inspector Harry Hole is about a psychopath who waits for the year's first snowfall to build menacing snowmen outside the homes of his victims, all married women cheating on their spouses. Nesbo has a horrormeister's flair for transforming natural scenes into ominous situations, so those recurring images of beady-eyed snowmen can ruin a walk in the woods or a stolen hour of sexual pleasure. The atmosphere of guilt and gloom is also a reflection of Harry's moody thoughts about his own troubled relationships, his obsessive work ethic and his unhealthy preoccupation with the nature of evil. . . . Harry is a cool hero, but whenever his musings get a bit sticky it's worth remembering that he's afraid of the dark." New York Times Book Review.

Nesbo, Jo, 1960-

The **son** : a novel / Jo Nesbo ; translated from the Norwegian by Charlotte Barslund. Alfred A. Knopf, 2014. 401 p.

ISBN 9780385351379

1. Prison corruption 2. Heroin addicts 3. Children of suicide victims 4. Truth 5. Criminals 6. Prisoners 7. Conspiracies 8. Fathers -- Death 9. Prison corruption 10. Escaped convicts 11. Police misconduct

12. Oslo, Norway 13. Norway 14. Scandinavian crime fiction 15. Thrillers and suspense 16. Translations -- Norwegian to English

Serving time for crimes he did not commit in exchange for heroin payouts, Sonny Lofthus uses his spiritual charisma to navigate corrupt and violent elements in his life before learning disturbing truths about his police officer father's suicide.

"A terrific thriller but also a tragic, very moving story of intertwined characters swerving desperately to avoid the dead ends in their paths." Booklist.

Nesbo, Jo, 1960-

The **thirst** / Jo Nesbo ; translated from the Norwegian by Neil Smith. New York : 2017. 461 p. Detective Harry Hole

ISBN 9780385352161

1. Former detectives 2. Serial murder investigation 3. Online dating 4. Murder investigation 5. Former police 6. Police 7. Justice 8. Cold cases (Criminal investigation) 9. Oslo, Norway 10. Norway 11. Mysteries 12. Translations -- Norwegian to English 13. Scandinavian crime fiction

First published with the title Torst. Oslo : H. Aschehoug & Co., 2017.

Harry is inextricably drawn back into the Oslo police force. A serial murderer has begun targeting Tinder daters--a murderer whose MO reignites Harry's hunt for a nemesis of his past.

"This 11th entry (after Police) in Nesbo's Scandinoir series features thoroughly developed characters, an intricate plot, and suspenseful twists, all hallmarks of a master storyteller." Library Journal.

Netzer, Lydia

Shine shine shine / Lydia Netzer. St. Martin's Press, 2012. 312 p.

ISBN 9781250007070

1. Social norms 2. Marital conflict 3. Perfectionism in women 4. Belonging 5. Astronauts 6. Married people 7. Family secrets 8. Mothers -- Death 9. Savant syndrome 10. Space flight to the moon 11. Parents of children with autism 12. Virginia 13. Love stories 14. Science fiction

LC 2012007426

When fabricated aspects of their picture-perfect world are embarrassingly exposed by a car accident, Sunny Mann, a woman longing for an ideal life, and Maxon, her savant astronaut husband, struggle through blame and fear before confronting realities about their deep bond.

Neubauer, Erica Ruth

Murder at the Mena House / Erica Ruth Neubauer. Kensington Books, 2020. 304 p. Jane Wunderly novels

ISBN 9781496725851

1. Between the Wars (1918-1939) 2. Young widows 3. Independence in women 4. Americans in Egypt 5. Women murder victims 6. Women murder suspects 7. Malicious accusation 8. Secrets 9. Women amateur detectives 10. Aunt and niece 11. Bankers 12. Intrigue 13. Men/women relations 14. Egypt -- History -- 20th century 15. Cairo, Egypt 16. Historical mysteries

Well-heeled travelers from around the world flock to the Mena House Hotel--an exotic gem in the heart of Cairo where cocktails flow, adventure dispels the aftershocks of World War I and deadly dangers wait in the shadows.

"Stunning revelations, romance, adventure, and intrigue abound in this multilayered, delightfully entertaining whodunit. Neubauer's debut dazzles, with a smart plot, remarkable scenery, and skilled execution." Library Journal.

Neugeboren, Jay

1940 : a novel / Jay Neugeboren. Two Dollar Radio, 2008. 274 p.

ISBN 9780976389569

1. Bloch, Eduard, 1872-1945 2. Physicians -- Austria 3. Middle-aged men -- Relations with younger women 4. Institutionalized persons 5. Jewish men 6. Men/women relations 7. Bronx, New York City 8. Germany -- History -- 1933-1945 9. Biographical fiction 10. Historical fiction

Dr. Eduard Bloch, who emigrated to New York City with Hitler's help, falls for Elisabeth Rohman, a medical illustrator, and becomes involved in a battle with her ex-husband over the fate of their mentally-ill son, who is hiding in his home.

"Neugeboren traverses the Hitlerian tightrope with all the skill and formal daring that have made him one of our most honored writers of literary fiction and masterful nonfiction. This new book is, at once, a beautifully realized work of imagined history, a rich and varied character study and a subtly layered novel of ideas, all wrapped in a propulsively readable story." Los Angeles Times Book Review.

Neuhaus, Nele

The **ice** queen : a novel / Nele Neuhaus ; translated from the German by Steven T. Murray. Minotaur Books, 2015, c2009. 341 p. Oliver von Bodenstein and Pia Kirchhoff novels

ISBN 9780312604264

1. Murder victims 2. Holocaust survivors 3. Deception 4. Seniors 5. Murder investigation 6. Philanthropists 7. Friendship 8. Nazism 9. Revenge 10. Secrets 11. Germany 12. Police procedurals 13. Mysteries 14. Translations -- German to English

LC 2014033879

Originally published as "Tiefe Wunden". Berlin : List Taschenbuch, 2009.

Pia Kirchhoff and Oliver Bodenstein investigate the murder of a Holocaust survivor who may have had ties to Hitler's SS, and after two other similar murders, follow a trail that leads back to World War II and an area of Poland that previously belonged to East Prussia.

Neuhaus, Nele

Snow White must die / Nele Neuhaus ; translated from the German by Steven T. Murray. Minotaur Books, 2013, c2010. 374 p. Oliver von Bodenstein and Pia Kirchhoff novels

ISBN 9780312604257

1. Police 2. Murder investigation 3. Judicial error 4. Detectives 5. Former convicts 6. Innocence (Law) 7. Crimes against teenage girls 8. Crowd violence 9. Revenge 10. Jealousy 11. Missing persons investigation 12. Germany 13. Police procedurals 14. Mysteries 15. Translations -- German to English

LC 2012038365

"First published in Germany under the title Schneewittchen muss sterben by List Taschenbuch, an imprint of Ullstein Buchverlage GmbH, Berlin, 2010"--Title page verso.

Detectives Pia Kirchhoff and Oliver von Bodenstein race against time after connecting the dramatic murder of a woman to the recent release of her son, who served a 10-year sentence related to the disappearances of two teens.

Nevill, Adam L. G.

The **ritual** / Adam Nevill. St. Martin's Griffin, 2012, c2011. 432 p.

ISBN 9780312641849

1. Hiking 2. Wilderness areas 3. Monsters 4. Camping 5. Sweden 6.

Scandinavia 7. Horror

LC 2011036132

Adapted into a film by the same name in 2017.

Originally published: London: Macmillan, 2011.

RUSA Reading List, 2013.

Unexpectedly clashing with his three old University friends while hiking in the Scandinavian wilderness of the Arctic Circle, Luke takes a shortcut that leads the group to an ancient pagan sacrificial site where they are hunted by a bestial predator.

Nevill, Adam L. G.

The **house** of small shadows / Adam Nevill. St. Martin's Press, 2014. 374 p.

ISBN 9781250041272

1. Art appraisers 2. Haunted houses 3. Collectors and collecting 4. Antique dolls 5. Taxidermy 6. Mansions 7. Dioramas 8. Puppets 9. Women psychotherapy patients 10. Dolls -- Collectors and collecting 11. Historic buildings 12. Supernatural 13. Ghosts 14. England 15. Horror 16. Ghost stories

Forced out of London after being bullied out of her corporate job, antiques expert Catherine is hired to catalog a late millionaire's valuable collections, which conceal a dark message and trigger traumatic memories from Catherine's personal life.

"This is largely a haunted-house story, though Nevill's merciless assault upon primordial fears--darkness, disfigurement, and disablement-does not so much recall the slow, seeping insanity of Stephen Kings The Shining (1977) as it does Stanley Kubricks treatment of the novel, single-minded in its determination to terrorize regardless of which rational concerns are dropped by the wayside." Booklist.

Neville, Katherine, 1945-

The **eight** : a novel / Katherine Neville. Ballantine Books, 1988. 550 p.

ISBN 9780345351371

1. 1970s 2. 18th century 3. Nuns -- France 4. Chess 5. Conspiracies 6. Antique chess sets 7. Algeria 8. France -- History -- Revolution, 1789-1799 9. Adventure stories 10. Historical fiction 11. Parallel narratives

LC 87091363

Sequel: The fire

In a story spanning from the court of Catherine the Great to modern times, the brutal course of history is played out as Catherine "Cat" Velis attempts to thwart world disaster

"Neville has great fun rewriting history and making it all ring true." Publishers Weekly.

Neville, Stuart, 1972-

The **ghosts** of Belfast / Stuart Neville. Soho, 2009. 336 p. Jack Lennon investigations

ISBN 9781569476000

1. Assassins 2. Revenge 3. Guilt 4. Ghosts 5. Violence 6. Former convicts 7. Political violence 8. Detectives 9. Belfast, Northern Ireland 10. Northern Ireland -- Politics and government 11. Thrillers and suspense 12. Noir fiction

LC 2009011312

"Published in Great Britain in 2009 by Harvill Secker Random House as The twelve"--T.p. verso.

Fegan has been a "hard man," an IRA killer in northern Ireland. Now that peace has come, he is being haunted day and night by twelve ghosts: a mother and infant, a schoolboy, a butcher, an RUC constable, and seven other of his innocent victims. In order to appease them, he's going to have to kill the men who gave him orders.

"Neville's debut is as unrelenting as Fegan's ghosts, pulling no punches as it describes the brutality of Ireland's troubles and the crime that has followed, as violent men find new outlets for their skills. Sharp prose places readers in this pitiless place and holds them there. Harsh and unrelenting crime fiction, masterfully done." Kirkus.

Ratlines / Stuart Neville. Soho Crime, 2013. 354 p.

ISBN 9781616952044

1. 1960s 2. Murder investigation 3. Political intrigue 4. Former Nazis 5. Ireland -- History -- 20th century 6. Noir fiction 7. Historical thrillers

Investigating the murders of three German nationals, Lieutenant Albert Ryan, Directorate of Intelligence in 1963 Ireland, finds his loyalties tested after being ordered by the Minister of Justice to hide the truth about the victims' Nazi pasts.

New Cthulhu : the recent weird / edited by Paula Guran. Prime Books, 2011. 520 p.

ISBN 9781607012894

1. Horror 2. Short stories 3. Anthologies

"In the early twenty-first century the best supernatural writers no longer imitate Lovecraft, but they are profoundly influenced by the genre and the mythos he created. New Cthulhu: The Recent Weird presents some of the best of this new Lovecraftian fiction--bizarre, subtle, atmospheric, metaphysical, psychological, filled with strange creatures and stranger characters--eldritch, unsettling, evocative, and darkly appealing."--Page 4 of cover.

The **new** space opera / edited by Gardner Dozois and Jonathan Strahan. EOS; Harper Collins, 2007. 517 p.

ISBN 0060846755

1. Space 2. Space opera 3. Short stories 4. Science fiction

Locus Award for Best Anthology, 2008.

Collection of previously unpublished epic science fiction pieces includes contributions by top genre authors as well as up-and-coming writers, including such names as Stephen Baxter, Gregory Benford, and Nancy Kress.

"An exceedingly fine set of stories written specifically for this collection by some of the best sf authors writing today. These 18 tales run the gamut from technologically centered hard science (think exploding comets and artificial intelligence) to character-driven soft science (settling on new worlds). Alien perspectives are balanced by humanistic introspection. Many of the stories mine the genre's favorite nuggets by exploring political and ethical questions from varied and unusual points of view." Library Journal.

New suns : original speculative fiction by people of color / Nisi Shawl, editor ; introduction by LeVar Burton. Solaris Books, 2019. 384 p.

ISBN 9781781085783

1. Monsters 2. Aliens 3. Space flight 4. Tourism 5. Interplanetary relations 6. Science fiction 7. Fantasy fiction 8. Afrofuturism and Afrofantasy 9. Asian-influenced fantasy 10. Horror 11. Short stories

Showcases emerging and seasoned writers of many races telling stories filled with shocking delights, powerful visions of the familiar made strange.

"This books wide range of stories is its greatest strength; though no reader will love them all, every reader will find something worth rereading. This anthology will appeal most to readers of multiple genres who enjoy exploring the worlds various cultures, and is well suited to library collections." Publishers Weekly.

The **new** voices of fantasy / edited by Peter S. Beagle and

Jacob Weisman. Tachyon Publications, 2017. 325 p.
ISBN 9781616962579

1. Imaginary creatures 2. Fantasy fiction 3. Short stories 4. Anthologies

What would you do if a tornado wanted you to be its Valentine? Or if a haunted spacesuit banged on your door? When is the ideal time to turn into a tiger? Would you post a supernatural portal on Craigslist? In these nineteen stories, the enfants terribles of fantasy have arrived.

Newitz, Annalee, 1969-

* **Autonomous** / Annalee Newitz. Tor, 2017. 304 p.
ISBN 9780765392077

1. Far future 2. Smugglers 3. Medicine 4. Scientists 5. Women scientists 6. Pirates 7. Pharmaceutical research 8. Social classes 9. Patents 10. Addiction 11. Drugs -- Overdose 12. Fugitives 13. Robots 14. Hard science fiction 15. Science fiction

Lambda Literary Award for Lesbian/Gay Science Fiction-Fantasy-Horror, 2018.

Big Pharma is watching you.?In a near-future society dominated by multinational corporations, drug pirate Jack Chen reverse-engineers expensive medications and distributes free copies to those who can't afford the real thing. As a result, her activities have attracted the attention of the International Property Coalition, which sends military robot Paladin and Paladin's human partner, Eliasz, to apprehend Jack. With its noir-tinged dystopian setting, suspenseful plot, and themes of bioethics and artificial intelligence, this debut may remind readers of William Gibson's Neuromancer. -- Description by Gillian Speace

"In a phenomenal debut that's sure to garner significant awards attention, Newitz, cofounder of io9, sends three fascinating characters on an action-packed race against time through a strange yet familiar futuristic landscape." Publishers Weekly.

Newitz, Annalee, 1969-

The **future** of another timeline / Annalee Newitz. St Martins Pr, 2019 272 p.
ISBN 9780765392107

1. Time travel 2. Parallel universes 3. Women's rights -- History 4. Feminism 5. Misogyny 6. Geologists 7. Teenage girls 8. Time machines 9. Murder witnesses 10. Riot grrrl movement 11. Abortion -- Law and legislation 12. United States -- Social conditions 13. California -- Social life and customs -- 20th century 14. Social science fiction 15. Alternative histories 16. Science fiction

A geologist desperate to change the past and a teen rebel who has witnessed a history-changing murder are swept up in a secret historical war in a parallel-world America where time travel is possible.

Newman, Janis Cooke

Mary : a novel / Janis Cooke Newman. MacAdam/Cage Pub., 2006. 707 p.
ISBN 9781931561631

1. Lincoln, Mary Todd, 1818-1882 2. American Civil War era (1861-1865) 3. Presidents' spouses -- United States 4. Widows 5. Feminists 6. Women with mental illnesses 7. Women with anorexia 8. Mothers and sons 9. Female friendship 10. Women lawyers 11. Suffragists 12. Psychiatric hospitals 13. Drug abuse 14. Opium addiction 15. Childhood 16. Memories 17. Mental illness 18. Betrayal 19. Sexuality 20. Extramarital affairs 21. Compulsive shopping in women 22. Civil war 23. United States Civil War, 1861-1865 24. Washington, D.C. 25. United States -- History -- 19th century 26. United States -- History -- Civil War, 1861-1865 27. Historical fiction 28. Biographical fiction

LC 2006015591

While residing in Bellevue Place Sanitarium, Mary Todd Lincoln shares her life story, from her childhood in Kentucky to her marriage to Abraham Lincoln and beyond.

"The first-person narrative and liberal use of descriptive details, perfected perhaps by Newman's extensive experience writing nonfiction, enlist the reader's sympathy for the mentally unstable Mrs. Lincoln. At the same time, we can become dismayed at her seeming lack of common sense. ... Mary's hopes, dreams, feelings, and thoughts are conveyed with depth and subtlety." Library Journal.

Newman, Sandra, 1965-

The **country** of Ice Cream Star / Sandra Newman. Ecco, 2015. 581 p.
ISBN 9780062227096

1. Post-apocalypse 2. Teenage girls 3. Epidemics 4. Power (Social sciences) 5. Voyages and travels 6. Brothers and sisters 7. Plague -- Treatment 8. African Americans 9. Adulthood 10. Survival 11. Apocalyptic fiction 12. Literary fiction 13. Science fiction

Enduring a nomadic existence in the aftermath of a disease that kills all humans once they reach the age of 20, 15-year-old Ice Cream Star risks her freedom and life to travel dangerous territory in search of a cure.

"This suspenseful, provocative tale is The Hunger Games meets Lord of the Flies and The Walking Dead, only much, much better... Could this be the next big book to capture readers all across the age spectrum? Don't bet against it." Booklist.

Newman, Sandra, 1965-

* The **heavens** / Sandra Newman. Grove Press, 2019. 272 p.
ISBN 9780802129024

1. 2000s (Decade) 2. 16th century 3. Dreams 4. Consequences 5. Time travel (Past) 6. Fate and fatalism 7. Purpose in life 8. Multiracial persons 9. Couples 10. Mental illness 11. Men/women relations 12. New York City -- Social life and customs -- 21st century 13. England -- Social life and customs -- 16th century 14. Literary fiction

LC 2018028231

A New Yorker named Kate often dreams she is transported to the past--where she lives a second life as Emilia, the mistress of a nobleman in Elizabethan England--but soon, the dream becomes increasingly real and compelling until it threatens to overwhelm her life.

"A complex, unmissable work from a writer who deserves wide acclaim." Kirkus.

Newton, Charlie

Calumet City : a novel / Charlie Newton. Simon & Schuster, 2008. 320 p.
ISBN 9781416533221

1. Family secrets 2. Policewomen 3. Murder investigation 4. Adult child sexual abuse victims 5. Orphans 6. Betrayal 7. Attempted assassination 8. Revenge 9. Murder 10. Police 11. Dead 12. Criminal investigation 13. Chicago, Illinois 14. Illinois 15. Noir fiction 16. Thrillers and suspense

LC 2007016112

Hiding the truth about her abuse-marked orphan childhood, highly decorated Chicago cop Patti Black finds herself implicated in a series of seemingly unrelated crimes, in a tale based on real-life events.

"An atmospheric shocker. . . . Newton certainly has all the hallmarks and above all the classic noir tone urban and nocturnal, stealthy and smoky, grim determination doing its two-step with gallows humor." Chicago Sun Times

Newton, Charlie

Start shooting : a novel / Charlie Newton. Doubleday, 2012. 305 p.

ISBN 9780385534697

1. Gangs 2. Police corruption 3. Cold cases (Criminal investigation) 4. Murder 5. Police 6. Rape victims 7. Murder investigation 8. Actors and actresses 9. Murder suspects 10. Violence 11. Twin sisters 12. Tabloid newspapers 13. Chicago, Illinois 14. Illinois 15. Thrillers and suspense 16. Noir fiction

Twenty-five years after a gruesome murder rocked Chicago, a dying local newspaper runs a serial exposé on new evidence in the old case--a smear campaign that stirs up bad blood for officer Bobby Vargas and his older brother Ruben--a decorated, high-ranking detective.

Ng, Celeste

* **Everything** I never told you : a novel / Celeste Ng. Penguin Press, 2014. 304 p.

ISBN 9781594205712

1. 1970s 2. Daughters -- Death 3. Loss (Psychology) 4. Interracial families 5. Chinese Americans 6. Drowning 7. Grief 8. Misunderstanding 9. Family secrets 10. Expectation (Psychology) 11. Ambition 12. Family relationships 13. Ohio 14. Psychological fiction

LC 2013039961

Asian Pacific American Award for Literature: Adult Fiction, 2015. Massachusetts Book Awards, Fiction Award, 2015.

Explores the fallout of a favorite daughter's shattering death on a Chinese-American family in 1970s Ohio.

"Ng constructs a mesmerizing narrative that shrinks enormous issues of race, prejudice, identity, and gender into the miniaturist dynamics of a single family." Library Journal.

Ng, Celeste,

* **Little** fires everywhere : a novel / Celeste Ng. Penguin Press, 2017. 384 p.

ISBN 9780735224292

1. Landlord and tenant 2. Adoption 3. Interpersonal conflict 4. Consequences 5. Secrets 6. Artists 7. Single mothers 8. Interracial adoption 9. Child custody 10. Cleveland, Ohio 11. Ohio 12. Literary fiction

LC 2016056762

Goodreads Choice Award, 2017

Fighting an ugly custody battle with an artistic tenant who has little regard for the strict rules of their progressive Cleveland suburb, a strait-laced family woman who is seeking to adopt a baby becomes obsessed with exposing the tenant's past, only to trigger devastating consequences for both of their families.

"The characters she creates here are wonderfully appealing, and watching their paths connect . . . is mesmerizing, casting into new light ideas about creativity and consumerism, parenthood and privilege." Kirkus.

Ng, Fae Myenne, 1956-

Bone / Fae Myenne Ng. Hyperion, 1993. 193 p.

ISBN 9781562829445

1. Chinese American families 2. Sisters 3. Guilt 4. Chinatown, San Francisco, California 5. San Francisco, California 6. Family sagas

LC 92006028

Set in San Francisco's Chinatown, a novel of family ties chronicles the Leongs--a Chinese-American family caught between the traditions of their ancestry and the realities of life in America.

Ngugi wa Thiong'o, 1938-

Minutes of glory, and other stories / Ngg wa Thiong'o. The New Press, 2019, c1975. 224 p.

ISBN 9781620974650

1. Colonialism -- Africa 2. Colonized peoples 3. Droughts 4. Human nature 5. Kenya -- History 6. East Africa -- History 7. Literary fiction 8. Short stories

LC 2018052222

"First published in the Heinemann African Writers Series as Secret Lives and Other Stories, 1975. This edition published in the United States by The New Press, New York, 2019."

A collection of short stories by the Kenyan writer covering the period of British colonial rule and resistance in Kenya to the experience of independence and including two stories that have never before been published in the United States--Provided by publisher.

"Thiongo weaves together disparate stories of people attempting to deal with change in their lives, either chosen or forced upon them, showing his understanding of human nature, its frequent resistance to change, and its ability to surprise. This is a masterful collection." Publishers Weekly.

Nguyen, Kevin

* **New** waves / Kevin Nguyen. One World, 2020. 288 p.

ISBN 9781984855237

1. New businesses 2. Racism 3. Asian American men 4. African American women 5. Twenties (Age) 6. High technology 7. Application software 8. Stealing 9. Friends' death 10. Life change events 11. Race relations 12. Secrets 13. Satirical fiction

LC 2019034574

Fed up with discriminating bosses, an Asian-American customer service representative and a talented African-American programmer conspire to steal their employer's user database before an unexpected setback exposes a secret double life.

"Nguyen's stellar debut is a piercing assessment of young adulthood, the tech industry, and racism." Publishers Weekly.

Nguyen, Phan Que Mai, 1973-

* The **mountains** sing : a novel / Nguyn Phan Que Mai. Algonquin Books of Chapel Hill, 2020. 352 p.

ISBN 9781616208189

1. 20th century 2. War -- Psychological aspects 3. Violence -- Psychological aspects 4. Loss (Psychology) 5. Vietnam War, 1961-1975 6. Families 7. Farms 8. Family relationships 9. Vietnam 10. Translations -- Vietnamese to English 11. Family sagas 12. Literary fiction 13. Historical fiction

LC 2019030591

Years after a family is forced by Vietnam's Communist Land Reforms to abandon their farm, a granddaughter comes of age as her loved ones depart for the Ho Chi Minh Trail.

"This brilliant, unsparing love letter to Vietnam will move readers." Publishers Weekly.

Nguyen, Viet Thanh, 1971-

* The **refugees** / Viet Thanh Nguyen. Grove Press, 2017. 192 p.

ISBN 9780802126399

1. Vietnamese Americans 2. Home (Concept) 3. Self-fulfillment 4. Families 5. Human nature 6. Immigrants -- Identity 7. Identity (Psychology) 8. California 9. Literary fiction 10. Short stories

Author Viet Thanh Nguyen's debut novel The Sympathizer won both the Pulitzer Prize and the Carnegie Medal, among other accolades; readers hungry for more will appreciate the eight stories collected here, written before The Sympathizer was published. While the stories, mostly set in the Vietnamese community in California, represent Vietnamese refugee experiences in the US, the topics they explore -- relationships, grief, the desire for fulfillment -- speak to the human experience. Check them out if you're interested in sympathetic characters, cultural dislocation, or the experiences of refugees. -- Description by Shauna Griffin

"Nguyen is the foremost literary interpreter of the Vietnamese experience in America, to be sure. But his stories, excellent from start to finish, transcend ethnic boundaries to speak to human universals." Kirkus.

Nguyen, Viet Thanh, 1971-

* The **sympathizer** / Viet Thanh Nguyen. Grove/Atlantic, 2015 371 p.

ISBN 9780802123459

1. Viet Cong 2. 1970s 3. 20th century 4. Spies 5. Identity (Psychology) 6. Vietnam War, 1961-1975 7. Vietnamese in the United States 8. Double agents 9. Moles (Spies) 10. Communism 11. Refugees 12. Vietnam -- History -- 20th century 13. Historical fiction 14. Literary fiction 15. Psychological fiction

ALA Notable Book, 2016.

Andrew Carnegie Medal for Excellence in Fiction, 2016.

Asian Pacific American Award for Literature: Adult Fiction, 2016.

Edgar Allan Poe Award for Best First Novel by an American Author, 2016.

Pulitzer Prize for Fiction, 2016.

Shortlisted for the International Dublin Literary Award, 2017

Follows a Viet Cong agent as he spies on a South Vietnamese army general and his compatriots as they start a new life on 1975 Los Angeles.

"Nguyen's probing literary art illuminates how Americans failed in their political and military attempt to remake Vietnam--but then succeeded spectacularly in shrouding their failure in Hollywood distortions. Compelling--and profoundly unsettling." Booklist.

Nicholas, Douglas

Something red : a novel / Douglas Nicholas. Atria Books, 2012. 320 p. Something red

ISBN 9781451660074

1. Medieval period (476-1492) 2. Civilization, Medieval 3. Mountains 4. Monsters 5. Winter 6. Women -- Ireland 7. Good and evil 8. Wilderness survival 9. Magic 10. Orphans 11. Women healers 12. Human/animal communication 13. Crows 14. Castles 15. England -- History -- 13th century 16. Historical fantasy

LC 2011044435

Includes glossary of Irish terms.

Leading a troupe of companions across the mountains of 13th-century northwest England to find shelter from the coldest winter in memory, middle-aged Irishwoman Molly gradually realizes that they are being followed by a mysterious evil force that must be faced and defeated if they are to survive.

Nicholas, Douglas

Throne of darkness : a novel / Douglas Nicholas. Emily Bestler Books/Atria, 2015. 352 p. Something red

ISBN 9781476755984

1. Magna Carta 2. Medieval period (476-1492) 3. 13th century 4. Women rulers 5. Wizards 6. Civilization, Medieval 7. Mountains 8. Warriors 9. Women -- Ireland 10. England -- History -- 13th century 11. Historical fantasy

LC 2014036008

It's 1215 in northwest England--the eve of the signing of the Magna Carta--and mystical Irish queen Maeve and her unlikely band of warriors must protect the region from a chilling fate. Word of a threat reaches the Northern barons: King John has plotted to import an African sorcerer and his sinister clan of blacksmiths, whose unearthly powers may spell destruction for the entire kingdom. Along with her lover, Jack, her gifted niece, Nemain, and Nemain's newlywed husband, Hob (whose hidden talents will soon be revealed), Maeve must overcome a supernatural threat unlike any she's seen before.

Nicholas, Douglas

The **wicked** / Douglas Nicholas. Atria Books, 2014. 368 p. Something red

ISBN 9781451660241

1. Medieval period (476-1492) 2. 13th century 3. Women rulers 4. Civilization, Medieval 5. Mountains 6. Warriors 7. Vampires 8. Women -- Ireland 9. Good and evil 10. Magic 11. Orphans 12. Women healers 13. Human/animal communication 14. Crows 15. Castles 16. Shapeshifters 17. England -- History -- 13th century 18. Historical fantasy

In this sequel to Something Red, mystical Irish queen Molly, with her powers of healing, is the only one who can save the people from an evil nobleman and his equally evil wife, while young warrior Hob and his adopted family work together to destroy the dark powers before all is lost.

"The 13th-century traveling troupe of players from Nicholas's debut, Something Red, returns in another meticulously plotted and researched blend of horror and historical fantasy. . . . The players, especially point-of-view character Hob, are nuanced and interesting, but it is the setting and tense action that make this a gripping read." Library Journal.

Nicholls, Owen

Love, unscripted : a novel / Owen Nicholls. Ballantine Books, 2020, c2019. 384 p.

ISBN 9781984826879

1. Film projectionists 2. Dating (Social customs) 3. Breaking up (Interpersonal relations) 4. Depression 5. Memories 6. Romantic love 7. Self-fulfillment 8. Love in films 9. Film theaters 10. Men/women relations 11. England 12. London, England 13. Love stories 14. Mainstream fiction

LC 2019038100

Originally published in Great Britain in 2019 by Headline Review, an imprint of the Headline Publishing Group.

A romantic movie buff and film projectionist is devastated when his four-year relationship with the leading lady of his dreams ends, compelling him to rewrite history to come to terms with what went wrong.

"Their relationship has cinematic highs and believable lows, with fully rounded characters and smart, snappy, romantic comedy-worthy dialogue. Nick's and Ellie's real lives aren't a movie, but as Nicholls tells it, they might have a happily-ever-after anyway. A delightfully sweet, funny, and heartbreaking ode to love stories, both onscreen and off." Kirkus.

Nicholls, David, 1966-

* **Us** : a novel / David Nicholls. Harper, 2014. 400 p.

ISBN 9780062365583

1. Middle-aged men 2. Husband and wife 3. Families 4. Men/women relations 5. Family vacations 6. Marriage 7. Parenthood 8. Life change events 9. England 10. Europe 11. Psychological fiction 12. Domestic fiction

LC 2014015360

"The highly anticipated new novel from David Nicholls, author of the mega-bestselling fiction sensation One Day, which follows one man's efforts to salvage his marriage--and repair his troubled relationship with his teenaged son--during the course of a trip around Europe"--, Provided by publisher.

"This is Nicholls's most ambitious work to date, and his realistically flawed characters are somehow endearing despite the many bruises they inflict upon each other." Publishers Weekly.

Nichols, John Treadwell, 1940-

The **Milagro** Beanfield War / John Nichols ; illustrations by Rini Templeton. Henry Holt & co., 2000, c1974. 629 p. New Mexico trilogy

ISBN 9780805063745

1. Water rights -- New Mexico 2. Real estate development -- New Mexico 3. Resistance to real estate development -- New Mexico 4. Mexican American farmers -- New Mexico 5. Mexican American resistance and revolts -- New Mexico 6. Farmers' resistance and revolts -- New Mexico 7. Villages -- New Mexico 8. Poor people -- New Mexico 9. New Mexico 10. Literary fiction

LC 74004409

Violence erupts in the poor town of Milagro when one poor dirt farmer impulsively taps the main irrigation channel.

"Nichols has written a bawdy, slangy, modern proletarian novel that is--if finally perhaps excessively sentimental--still a consistently entertaining film scenario while at the same time it manages to make funny-serious sense out of a contemporary situation enduring injustice and imminent violence." Choice.

Nichols, Lisa A., 1972-

Vessel : a novel / Lisa A. Nichols. Emily Bestler Books/ Atria Paperback, 2019. 320 p.

ISBN 9781501168772

1. Women astronauts 2. Space accidents 3. Amnesia 4. Reunions 5. Homecomings 6. Family relationships 7. Loss of consciousness 8. Thrillers and suspense 9. Presumed dead

LC 2018039843

After surviving a deadly incident in deep space, astronaut Catherine Wells is believed to be dead, but miraculously returns to earth years later to find the life she left behind drastically changed.

"The scientific component is kept plausible but light in favor of character drama, interpersonal relationships, and the underlying mystery." Publishers Weekly.

Nichols, Peter, 1950-

* The **rocks** / Peter Nichols. Riverhead Books, 2015 432 p.

ISBN 9781594633317

1. Family secrets 2. Coastal towns 3. Former lovers 4. Men/women relations 5. Islands 6. Separated friends, relatives, etc 7. Spain 8. Majorca, Spain 9. Love stories

LC 2014022801

Two honeymooners, Gerald and Lulu, abruptly split in 1948, and despite residing on the same island for more than sixty years, they live separately, never interacting until children from their rivaling families fall in love.

Nicholson, Christopher, 1956-

The **elephant** keeper / Christopher Nicholson. William Morrow, 2009. 352 p.

ISBN 9780061651601

1. 18th century 2. Elephants 3. Human/animal relationships 4. Companionship 5. Stable hands 6. Villages 7. Violence 8. England -- Social life and customs -- 18th century 9. Historical fiction

LC 2009000852

In the middle of the 18th century, a ship docks at Bristol with an extraordinary cargo: two young elephants. Bought by a wealthy landowner, they are taken to his estate in the English countryside. A stable boy,

Tom Page, is given the task of caring for them. The Elephant Keeper is Tom's account of his life with the elephants. As the years pass, and as they journey across England, his relationship with the female elephant deepens in a startling manner. Along the way they meet incredulity, distrust and tragedy, and it is only their understanding of each other that keeps them together. Christopher Nicholson's charming and captivating novel explores notions of sexuality and violence, freedom and captivity, and the nature of story-telling -- but most of all it is the study of a profound and remarkable love between an elephant and a human being.

"Tom Page is the plain-spoken narrator who begins his working life as a stable boy to Mr. John Harrington, sugar merchant of Bristol, and who later finds his vocation as the elephant keeper to Lord Bidborough of Sussex. In 1773, Tom's master, in the cause of science, instructs Tom to write a full description of the elephant in his care. The elephant's story, as related by Tom, is of course his own story. In Nicholson's hands, however, it is also a lively portrait of 18th-century manners and ideas." Boston Globe.

Nicholson, Geoff, 1953-

The **city** under the skin : a novel / Geoff Nicholson. Farrar, Straus and Giroux, 2014. 256 p.

ISBN 9780374169046

1. Cartography 2. Maps 3. Women kidnapping victims 4. Tattooing 5. Collectors and collecting 6. Noir fiction 7. Thrillers and suspense

LC 2013038778

A cartography-obsessed misfit clerk, an answer-seeking woman and a petty criminal father are bound together in the criminal underworld by a group of mysterious tattooed women.

Nicholson, William

Motherland / William Nicholson. Simon & Schuster, 2013. 448 p.

ISBN 9781451687132

1. Second World War era (1939-1945) 2. 1940s 3. Love triangles 4. Consequences 5. World War II 6. Women ambulance drivers 7. Soldiers 8. Married people 9. Friendship 10. Marital conflict 11. Men/women relations 12. England -- History -- 20th century 13. France -- History -- 20th century 14. India -- History -- 20th century 15. Historical fiction 16. Literary fiction

The character Pamela is the mother of Guy Caulder and grandmother of Alice Dickinson from Nicholson's earlier novels The Secret Intensity of Everyday Life and I Could Love You.

Originally published: London : Quercus, 2013.

Presents the story of a World War II love triangle involving a charismatic war hero whose marriage crumbles in the face of painful realities that culminate in tragedy when his ex-wife returns his best friend's long-unrequited love.

"[I]t's the books quieter moments, infused with realistic dialogue and fastidious attention to historical detail, that will make true romantics swoon and should win over a wide mainstream audience." Booklist.

Nickson, Chris

At the dying of the year / Chris Nickson. Creme de la Crime, 2013. 212 p. Richard Nottingham mysteries

ISBN 9781780290423

1. 1730s 2. Police 3. Child murder victims 4. Murder investigation 5. Serial murders 6. Violence 7. Crimes against children 8. England -- History -- 18th century 9. Leeds, England 10. Historical mysteries 11. Mysteries

In 1733, Richard Nottingham hunts a child-killer preying on the street children of Leeds, but he has to go up against the wealthy and powerful of the city to do it, including the new mayor.

LIST OF FICTIONAL WORKS

Nickson, Chris

Cold cruel winter / Chris Nickson. Creme de la Crime, 2011. 224 p. Richard Nottingham mysteries

ISBN 9781780290058

1. 1730s 2. Murder investigation 3. Police 4. Revenge 5. Murder 6. Grief in men 7. Family relationships 8. England -- History -- 18th century 9. Leeds, England 10. Historical mysteries 11. Mysteries

Richard Nottingham, constable of the city of Leeds, goes in search of the killer of Samuel Graves, a wealthy wool merchant who was found with this throat cut and the skin removed from his back.

Nickson, Chris

Come the fear / Chris Nickson. Creme de la Crime, 2012. 214 p. Richard Nottingham mysteries

ISBN 9781780290300

1. 1730s 2. Murder investigation 3. Police 4. Arson 5. Women murder victims 6. Rich men 7. Wool industry and trade 8. Infant death 9. England -- History -- 18th century 10. Leeds, England 11. Historical mysteries 12. Mysteries

LC bl2012039732

Investigating the deaths of a young woman and a baby whose bodies were found in a deliberately set fire, Richard Nottingham conducts a search through the streets of Leeds before discovering a link to a wealthy wool merchant.

Nickson, Chris

The **constant** lovers / Chris Nickson. Creme de la Crime, 2012. 213 p. Richard Nottingham mysteries

ISBN 9781780295183

1. 18th century 2. 1730s 3. Greed 4. Murder investigation 5. Unrequited love 6. Police 7. Ambition 8. Love letter writing 9. Crimes against women 10. Secrets 11. Murder 12. Family relationships 13. England -- History -- 18th century 14. Leeds, England 15. Historical mysteries 16. Mysteries

When an anonymous but obviously well-off young woman is found stabbed in a ruined abbey near Leeds, England, with a love letter in her pocket, Constable Richard Nottingham investigates, but her husband coming forward still leaves questions.

Nickson, Chris

Gods of gold / Chris Nickson. Severn House, 2014. 212 p. Tom Harper novels

ISBN 9780727884282

1. 1890s 2. Victorian era (1837-1901) 3. Detectives 4. Missing girls 5. Police murders 6. Murder investigation 7. Strikes 8. Missing persons investigation 9. Leeds, England -- History -- 19th century 10. England -- History -- 19th century 11. Police procedurals 12. Historical mysteries 13. Victorian mysteries

Believing that an eight-year-old girl is missing, Detective Inspector Tom Harper sets out to find the child, but is drawn into the growing violence surrounding the gas workers strike.

Nickson, Chris

The **hocus** girl / Chris Nickson. Severn House, 2019. 219 p. Simon Westow novels

ISBN 9780727889355

1. 1820s 2. Georgian era (1714-1837) 3. Private investigators 4. Malicious accusation 5. Spies 6. Intrigue 7. Secrets 8. Married men 9. Women private investigators 10. Thieves 11. Murderers 12. Friendship 13. Northern England 14. Leeds, England 15. Great Britain -- History -- George IV, 1820-1830 16. Historical mysteries

When Simon Westow's friend Davey Ashton is arrested for sedition, he is determined to clear his name. But Davey's not the only one who needs Simon's help - another man has been 'hocussed' by a mysterious young woman. Simon and his assistant Jane encounter murder, lies and betrayal as they attempt to save Davey and find the hocus girl.

"Nickson's latest combines multiple twists, vivid descriptions of life in the early nineteenth century, strong characters, and a surprising ending. A perfect read-alike for David Liss' popular series starring another British thief-taker, Benjamin Weaver." Booklist.

Nickson, Chris

On Copper Street / Chris Nickson. Severn House, 2017. 224 p. Tom Harper novels

ISBN 9780727886965

1. Victorian era (1837-1901) 2. 1890s 3. Prisoners 4. Criminals 5. Detectives 6. Dead 7. Police 8. Social advocates 9. People with cancer 10. Crimes against children 11. Suffragists 12. Socialism 13. Murder 14. Murder investigation 15. Leeds, England -- History -- 19th century 16. England -- History -- 19th century 17. Police procedurals 18. Historical mysteries 19. Victorian mysteries

Leeds, 1895. After his release from prison, Henry White is found stabbed to death on Copper Street. In a neighbourhood where people are hostile to the police, DI Tom Harper finds the investigation tricky. Meanwhile, acid is thrown over a young boy in a local bakery. Harper must uncover the motives in these cases to catch the culprits.

Niffenegger, Audrey

The **time** traveler's wife : a novel / Audrey Niffenegger. MacAdam/Cage Pub., 2002. 518 p.

ISBN 9781931561464

1. Time travel 2. Husband and wife 3. Fate and fatalism 4. Marriage 5. Fathers and daughters 6. Married people 7. Eccentrics and eccentricities 8. Loss (Psychology) 9. Men/women relations 10. Chicago, Illinois 11. Michigan 12. Literary fiction

LC 2003010159

British Book Award for Popular Fiction, 2006.

Passionately in love, Clare and Henry vow to hold onto each other and their marriage as they struggle with the effects of Chrono-Displacement Disorder, a condition that casts Henry involuntarily into the world of time travel.

"Niffenegger writes with the unflinching yet detached clarity of a war correspondent standing at the sidelines of an unfolding battle. She possesses a historian's eye for contextual detail. This is no romantic idyll." USA Today.

Nightmares : a new decade of modern horror / Ellen Datlow. Tachyon, 2016. 427 p.

ISBN 9781616962326

1. Good and evil 2. Reality 3. Horror 4. Short stories 5. Anthologies

An acclaimed horror editor presents 24 terrifying tales that remind us that evil is all around us.

"This volume is not only the perfect discovery tool for readers looking for the very best of modern horror, it should also be used as a collection-development tool by library staff." Booklist.

Nin, Anais, 1903-1977

Cities of the interior / Anais Nin ; introduction by Sharon Spencer. Swallow Press/Ohio University Press, 1991, c1974. xx, 588 p.

ISBN 9780804006668

1. Women 2. Self-discovery in women 3. Literary fiction 4. Psychological fiction 5. Anthologies

LC 91014523

Five interconnected Symbolist and modernist novels in which the inner worlds and lives of three women, Lillian, Djuna, and Sabina, and the relationships they influence are meticulously explored and celebrated.

Nissenson, Hugh

The **pilgrim** : a novel / Hugh Nissenson. Sourcebooks Landmark, 2011. 368 p.

ISBN 9781402209246

1. Colonial America (1600-1775) 2. 17th century 3. Pilgrims (New England settlers) 4. Puritans 5. Self-fulfillment 6. Temptation 7. Interpersonal attraction 8. Redemption 9. Plymouth, Massachusetts -- History -- Colonial period, 1600-1775 10. Massachusetts -- History -- Colonial period, 1600-1775 11. Historical fiction

LC 2011017815

Abandoning his faith after the death of his betrothed, Puritan Charles Wentworth, in hopes of being freed of the temptations that torment him, journeys to Plymouth where he finds unexpected love amidst discovery and danger.

"A marvelously intimate look back through time. Charles' fears and desires are made quite believable as he recalls the everyday horrors of the time--and the bits of Scripture that both justified and aggravated them. And while the young protagonist earnestly seeks salvation, his all-too-human failings--such as when he and the pretty Abigail Winslow flirt on the Sabbath--make him as sympathetic as any young striver since Holden Caulfield. The author's return to historical fiction raises human questions with immediacy and flair." Kirkus.

Noble, Kate, 1978-

The **game** and the governess / Kate Noble. Pocket Books, 2014 418 p. Winner takes all

ISBN 9781476749389

1. Regency period (1811-1820) 2. Governesses 3. Bets 4. Earls and countesses 5. Secret identity 6. Impostors 7. Deception 8. Nobility 9. Men/women relations 10. Interpersonal attraction 11. Interclass romance 12. England -- Social life and customs -- 19th century 13. Regency romances 14. Historical romances

To win a wager, the Earl of Ashby, known as "Lucky Ned," trades places with John Turner, his friend and secretary, and finds his luck suddenly abandoning him--until he meets governess Phoebe Baker, a prim-and-proper beauty who seemingly wants nothing to do with him.

"Nobles buoyant sense of wit gracefully propels the plot of her latest Regency-set historical to its immensely entertaining and eminently satisfying conclusion." Booklist.

Noire

Candy licker : an urban erotic tale / Noire. One World/Ballantine Books, 2005. 304 p.

ISBN 0345486471

1. African American women 2. Sexuality 3. Violence in African American men 4. Urban women 5. Women singers 6. African American lawyers 7. African American chief executive officers 8. Rap music industry and trade 9. African American men/women relations 10. Love triangles 11. Drug traffic 12. Antisocial personality disorders 13. Cruelty 14. Death 15. Harlem, New York City 16. Los Angeles, California 17. Urban erotica 18. Thrillers and suspense 19. African American fiction

LC 2005050880

Candy Raye Montana gets more than she had bargained for when she signs up with the House of Homicide, the hottest recording label on the east coast, and its CEO "Hurricane" Jackson, a man as talented as he is cruel, who gives her a painful lesson in the price of success.

Noire

G-Spot : an urban erotic tale / Noire. One World/Strivers Row, 2005. 320 p.

ISBN 0345477219

1. African American teenage girls 2. Brothers and sisters 3. Middle-aged men 4. Manipulation by men 5. Freedom 6. Nineteen-year-old women 7. African American brothers and sisters 8. African American men/women relations 9. African American fathers and sons 10. Love triangles 11. Sexuality 12. Betrayal 13. Murder 14. Gang rape 15. Violence 16. Urban women 17. Drug traffic 18. Nightclubs 19. Strip clubs 20. Los Angeles, California 21. New York City 22. Urban erotica 23. Thrillers and suspense 24. African American fiction

LC 2004052249

"Noire's heady brew of lethal realism and unbridled sexuality should spell 'hot and bothered' for erotic fiction fans." Publishers Weekly

Nordan, Lewis

* **Wolf** whistle : a novel / Lewis Nordan. Algonquin Books of Chapel Hill, 1993. 290 p.

ISBN 9781565120280

1. Till, Emmett, 1941-1955 2. 1950s 3. Small town life -- Mississippi 4. Women elementary school teachers -- Mississippi 5. Racism -- Mississippi -- History -- 20th century 6. Lynching -- Mississippi 7. Trials (Murder) -- Mississippi 8. Mississippi 9. Mississippi -- Race relations 10. Southern Gothic 11. Southern fiction

LC 93001011

ALA Notable Book, 1994.

In 1955, in Arrow-Catcher, Mississippi, fourth-grade teacher Alice Conroy, hoping to teach her children something important, takes her class on field trips to the bedside of a terminally burned classmate, the sewage plant, a funeral parlor, and a murder trial.

"Propelled by Nordan's musical prose, much of this narrative soars above the commonplace into the realm of myth." Publishers Weekly.

Nordhoff, Charles Bernard, 1887-1947

Men against the sea / By Charles Nordhoff and James Norman Hall Back Bay Books, 2003, 251 p. Mutiny on the Bounty

ISBN 9780316738880

1. Bligh, William, 1754-1817 2. Christian, Fletcher, 1764-1793 3. Bounty Mutiny, 1789 4. Sailors 5. Mutiny 6. Voyages and travels 7. Sea stories 8. Historical fiction

LC 34000685

Originally serialized in The Saturday Evening Post, November 18, 1933-December 9, 1933.

Originally published: Boston, Mass. : Little, Brown and Co., 1934.

Unsurpassed as a gripping tale of historical adventure, Men Against the Sea is the epic account of the eighteen loyal men set adrift on the high seas after the mutiny on the Bounty.

Nordhoff, Charles Bernard, 1887-1947

Pitcairn's Island / By Charles Nordhoff and James Norman Hall Back Bay Books, 2003, 333 p. Mutiny on the Bounty

ISBN 9780316738873

1. Christian, Fletcher, 1764-1793 2. Bligh, William, 1754-1817 3. Bounty Mutiny, 1789 4. Sailors 5. Mutiny 6. Voyages and travels 7. Pitcairn Island -- History 8. Sea stories 9. Historical fiction

LC 888520

Originally serialized in The Saturday Evening Post, September 22, 1934-November 3, 1934.

Illustrated with maps of the route of the Bounty and of Pitcairn's Island.

Originally published: Boston, Mass. : Little, Brown and Co., 1934.

LIST OF FICTIONAL WORKS

The fugitive mutineers from the British ship Bounty meet with terror and bloodshed on an uncharted island.

"A blood-curdling story, not for the squeamish reader." Booklist.

Norfolk, Lawrence, 1963-

John Saturnall's feast / Lawrence Norfolk. Grove Press, 2012. 410 p.

ISBN 9780802120519

1. Stuart period (1603-1714) 2. 17th century 3. English Civil War, 1642-1649 4. Cooks 5. Family secrets 6. Cooking, English -- History -- 17th century 7. Manors 8. Civil war 9. Orphans 10. Fasts and feasts 11. Nobility 12. Men/women relations 13. Great Britain -- History -- James I, 1603-1625 14. Great Britain -- History -- Charles I, 1625-1649 15. Great Britain -- History -- Civil War, 1642-1649 16. Historical fiction

Taken in at the kitchens at Buckland Manor after the cruel death of his mother, young John quickly rises from kitchen boy to cook before catching the attention of the daughter of the lord of the manor, who resolves to starve herself until her father calls off her unwanted engagement.

Norman, Howard A.

* The **bird** artist / Howard A. Norman. Farrar Straus & Giroux, 1994. 289 p.

ISBN 9780374113308

1. 1910s 2. Bird artists 3. Small town life 4. Newfoundland and Labrador 5. Historical fiction

LC 9470542

ALA Notable Book, 1995.

National Book Award for Fiction finalist, 1994

A spare, powerful novel set in Newfoundland in 1911 concerns Fabian, who is studying to be a bird painter, and his relationships with a beautiful woman and his difficult parents, as jealousy, guilt, and regret enter his life.

"This work evokes a way of life, a distinctive community and a fatalistic view of human behavior. The novel sings with tension and sparkles with antic humor." Publishers Weekly.

Norman, Howard A.

The **haunting** of L. / Howard Norman. Farrar, Straus, and Giroux, 2002. 326 p.

ISBN 9780374168254

1. 1920s 2. Love triangles 3. Spirit photography 4. Photographers 5. Young men 6. Accidents 7. Manitoba 8. Psychological fiction 9. Historical fiction

LC 2001051120

When Peter Duvett accepts a position as an assistant to the elusive portraitist Vienna Linn, his life is forever changed as he follows him on a macabre trek across Canada photographing grisly accidents for a private collector, a journey that leads to his employer's wife, who introduces him to the dark world of "spirit pictures"--photographs in which the faces of the long-dead mysteriously appear along with other horrifying images.

"This is a mesmerizing melodrama rendered magical thanks to lyrical evocations of fog and storm, sexual bliss and fear, a conflation of atmospheric conditions and states of mind that makes of the human heart a realm as treacherous and exquisite as the Arctic." Booklist.

Norman, Howard A.

The **museum** guard : a novel / Howard Norman. Farrar, Straus & Giroux, 1998. 310 p.

ISBN 9780374216498

1. 1930s 2. Unrequited love 3. Museum guards 4. Jewish women 5.

Halifax, Nova Scotia 6. Nova Scotia 7. Historical fiction

LC 98-8413

Explores the darkening world of Europe in the 1930s through the story of a Jewish woman who comes under the spell of an unusual painting.

"The author fills this enigmatic novel with elements of fable and fairy tale blended with memorable characterizations and subtle narrative probings into the nature of self and the consequences of actions." Library Journal.

Norman, Howard A.

Next life might be kinder / Howard Norman. Houghton Mifflin Harcourt, 2014. 255 p.

ISBN 9780547712123

1. 1970s 2. Widowers 3. Grief in men 4. Hallucinations and illusions 5. Faith 6. Murder 7. Violence 8. Filmmakers 9. Redemption 10. Biographical films 11. Halifax, Nova Scotia 12. Nova Scotia 13. Canada 14. Literary fiction 15. Psychological fiction

LC 2013045635

Selling his life story to a violent filmmaker in the aftermath of his sensual wife's murder, Sam develops a cat-and-mouse relationship with the filmmaker and begins experiencing wrenching hallucinations.

"The book blends macabre elements, including murder, with an absurdity and humor out of Kafka or Pirandello (a film is in fact being made about the murder). It also includes utterly convincing depictions of human love and compassion." Library Journal.

Norman, Howard A.

What is left the daughter / Howard Norman. Houghton Mifflin Harcourt, 2010. 243 p.

ISBN 9780618735433

1. Second World War era (1939-1945) 2. 1940s 3. Life change events 4. World War II -- Canada 5. Love triangles 6. Germans in Canada 7. Murder 8. Family relationships 9. Unrequited love 10. Compulsive behavior 11. Anxiety in men 12. Men/women relations 13. Nova Scotia 14. Canada 15. Historical fiction 16. Literary fiction 17. Epistolary novels

LC 2009044460

In the aftermath of his parents' double suicides for their separate affairs with the same neighbor, Nova Scotia teen Wyatt moves in with his uncle, aunt and beautiful cousin against a backdrop of World War II and experiences additional life-changing events that culminate in his fathering of a child.

"Norman writes with spare elegance and dry humor, and the extraordinary emotional power of his slim new novel is earned with authentic grace." Entertainment Weekly.

Norris, Frank, 1870-1902

* **McTeague** : a story of San Francisco / Frank Norris. Vintage Books, 1990, c1899. 322 p.

ISBN 9780679732730

1. Greed 2. Materialism 3. Wife-killing 4. Husband and wife 5. Miserliness 6. Dentists 7. San Francisco, California 8. Psychological fiction 9. Classics

LC 90050271

"With an introduction by Alfred Kazin."

Basis for the film, Greed (1924).

Originally published: Garden city, New York, Doubleday, McClure, 1899..

Lack of self-awareness and a weakness for alcohol lead to the moral degradation of San Francisco dentist, McTeague

Norris, Frank, 1870-1902

Novels and essays / Frank Norris. Library of America, 1986. 1232 p.

ISBN 0940450402

1. Essays

LC 85023133

Book reviews and articles accompany the stories of an artist's decline, a dentist's greed, and a clash between California ranchers and the railroad monopoly.

North, Alex

The **Whisper** Man / Alex North. Celadon Books, 2019. 368 p.

ISBN 9781250317995

1. Fathers and sons 2. Moving household 3. Serial murderers 4. Detectives 5. Widowers 6. Married women -- Death 7. Grief 8. Single fathers 9. Imaginary playmates 10. Whispering 11. Copycat murderers 12. Missing boys 13. England 14. Thrillers and suspense 15. Police procedurals

Mourning the death of his wife, a father and his young son move to Featherbank for a fresh start but find their new town has a dark past involving a serial killer named "The Whisper Man."

North, Anna

The **life** and death of Sophie Stark / Anna North. Blue Rider Press, 2015 270 p.

ISBN 9780399173394

1. Fame 2. Filmmakers 3. Humiliation 4. Documentary films -- Production and direction 5. College basketball players 6. Betrayal 7. Manipulation by women 8. Lesbians 9. Former husbands 10. Literary fiction

Lambda Literary Award for Bisexual Literature

An unapologetic filmmaker uses the stories of those around her to create movies that bring her both critical acclaim and ire from the people whose secrets she has exposed.

"As taut and artistically ambitious as its title character, North's novel upends the trope of the lone, tortured genius, considering instead the deeply human consequences of one person's uncompromising vision." Booklist.

North, Claire

The **pursuit** of William Abbey / Claire North. Orbit, 2019. 432 p.

ISBN 9780316316842

1. 19th century 2. 20th century 3. Physicians 4. Curses 5. Imperialism 6. Shadows 7. Guilt 8. Violence -- Psychological aspects 9. Lynching 10. Revenge 11. Truth 12. Supernatural 13. Historical fantasy

A hauntingly powerful novel about how the choices we make can stay with us forever, by the award-winning author of The First Fifteen Lives of Harry August and 84K.

The **Norton** book of science fiction : North American science fiction, 1960-1990 / edited by Ursula K. Le Guin and Brian Attebery ; Karen Joy Fowler, consultant. Norton, 1993. 869 p.

ISBN 9780393035469

1. Science fiction 2. Anthologies 3. Short stories

LC 93016130

"A compilation of intelligent and entertaining sf that belongs in virtually every fiction collection." Booklist.

Norton, Andre

The **elvenbane** : an epic high fantasy of the Halfblood chronicles / Andre Norton and Mercedes Lackey T. Doherty Associates, 1991. 390 p. Halfblood chronicles

ISBN 0312851065

1. Elves 2. Half-human hybrids 3. Power (Social sciences) 4. Magic 5. Dragons 6. Rescues 7. Shamans 8. Oppression (Psychology) 9. Imaginary wars and battles 10. Epic fantasy

LC 91021177

Born in the desert to an exiled concubine and raised by dragons, Shana becomes a wizard of extraordinary power and leads a rebellion against the cruel elven empire ruled by her father

Norton, Andre

Elvenblood : an epic high fantasy / Andre Norton and Mercedes Lackey T. Doherty Associates, 1995. 348 p. Halfblood chronicles

ISBN 0312855486

1. Elves 2. Power (Social sciences) 3. Rulers 4. Magic 5. Dragons 6. Imaginary wars and battles 7. Epic fantasy

LC 95005797

Chaos sweeps through the magical realm after an upstart halfblood known as the Elvenbane challenges the cruel Elvenlords' rule.

"The talents of collaborators Norton and Lackey blend seamlessly as they expand the background to their epic fantasy to include an exotic desert culture, which provides a rich contrast to the stifling atmosphere of elven society." Library Journal.

Norton, Andre

Golden trillium / Andre Norton. Bantam Books, 1993. 296 p. Trillium saga

ISBN 9780553095074

1. Princesses 2. Plague 3. Magic 4. Sisters 5. Good and evil 6. Triplets 7. Women warriors 8. Amulets 9. Talismans 10. Swordplay 11. Sword and sorcery 12. Fantasy fiction

LC 92043875

Kadiya, the fiery, sword-wielding princess, returns to the City of the Garden in order to bury the Three-Orbed Sword and learns that a deadly plague is threatening all of Ruwenda.

"The grande dame of sf and fantasy returns to a favorite themethe discovery of an ancient and highly advanced lost civilizationin this heroic adventure." Library Journal.

Norton, Carla

What doesn't kill her / Carla Norton. Minotaur Books, 2015. 313 p. Reeve LeClaire novels

ISBN 9781250032805

1. Women kidnapping victims 2. Psychic trauma 3. Young women 4. Kidnapping 5. Escapes 6. Psychiatric hospital patients 7. Women college students 8. Kidnapping victims 9. Escaped convicts 10. Thrillers and suspense

When a psychopath who held her prisoner for four years escapes from a mental facility and begins a murderous rampage, college student Reeve LeClaire realizes that she is the only person who knows the killer well enough to stop him.

Not one of us : stories of aliens on Earth / edited by Neil Clarke. Night Shade Books, 2018. 576 p.

ISBN 9781597809573

1. Aliens 2. Aliens (Humanoid) 3. Human/alien encounters 4. Human behavior 5. Group identity 6. Earth 7. Science fiction 8. Short stories 9. Anthologies

LIST OF FICTIONAL WORKS

Mankind comes face to face with extraterrestrial life in this short fiction reprint anthology from publisher Neil Clarke.

Novak, Brenda

This heart of mine / Brenda Novak. Mira, 2015. 400 p. Whiskey Creek novels

ISBN 9780778316725

1. Single fathers 2. Women former convicts 3. Former lovers 4. Child-separated mothers 5. Second chances 6. Families 7. Men/women relations 8. Small town life 9. Small towns -- California 10. California 11. Contemporary romances

After serving time for a crime she did not commit, Phoenix Fuller returns to Whiskey Creek where she hopes to get to know her son, but meets resistance in the form of Riley Stinson, her son's father, who doesn't trust her or believe that she can be a good mother.

Novey, Idra

Ways to disappear : a novel / Idra Novey. Little, Brown and Company, 2016. 258 p.

ISBN 9780316298490

1. Authors 2. Missing persons 3. Translators 4. Gambling 5. Money lenders 6. Parent and adult child 7. Brazil 8. Rio de Janeiro, Brazil 9. Literary fiction

When Brazilian novelist Beatriz Yagoda suddenly disappears, her American translator Emma travels to Brazil to solve the mystery while fending off rapacious loan sharks and the washed-up editor who made Yagoda famous.

Novic, Sara, 1987-

Girl at war / Sara Novic. Random House, 2015. 320 p.

ISBN 9780812996340

1. 1990s 2. War -- Psychological aspects 3. Loss (Psychology) 4. Memory 5. Yugoslav War, 1991-1995 6. Secrets 7. Refugees 8. Families 9. Croatia 10. New York City 11. Coming-of-age stories

Longlisted for the Baileys Women's Prize for Fiction, 2016.

When her happy life in 1991 Croatia is shattered by civil war, 10-year-old Ana Juric is embroiled in a world of guerilla warfare and child soldiers before making a daring escape to America, where years later she struggles to hide her past.

"Elegiac, and understandably if unrelievedly so, with a matter-of-factness about death and uprootedness. A promising start." Kirkus.

Novik, Naomi

His majesty's dragon / Naomi Novik. Del Rey Books, 2006. 384 p. Temeraire

ISBN 0345481283

1. Great Britain. Royal Navy Officers 2. 19th century 3. Ship captains 4. Dragons 5. Napoleonic Wars, 1800-1815 6. Military life 7. Military tactics 8. Alliances 9. Human/animal relationships 10. Human/animal communication 11. Imaginary wars and battles 12. England 13. Historical fantasy 14. Military fantasy 15. Fantasy fiction

LC 2005046342

When the HMS Reliant captures a French ship and its priceless cargo, an unhatched dragon egg, Captain Will Laurence is swept into an unexpected kinship with an extraordinary creature and joins the elite Aerial Corps as a master of the dragon Temaraire, in which role he must match wits with the powerful dragon-borne forces of Napoleon Bonaparte.

"A completely authentic tale, brimming with all the detail and richness one looks for in military yarns as well as the impossible wonder of gilded fantasy." Entertainment Weekly.

Novik, Naomi

* Spinning silver / Naomi Novik. Del Rey, 2018. 466 p.

ISBN 9780399180989

1. Debt 2. Money lenders 3. Pride and vanity 4. Elves 5. Magic 6. Jewish women 7. Consequences 8. Boasts and praises 9. Adaptations, retellings, and spin-offs 10. Fantasy fiction

LC 2018005791

Amelia Bloomer List, 2019.
Librarians' Choice (Australia), 2018.
Locus Award for Fantasy Novel, 2019.
Mythopoeic Award for Adult Literature, 2019.

Deciding to collect on the outstanding debts owed her family of moneylenders, a young woman is overheard boasting about being able to turn silver into gold by the creatures who haunt the wood, in a reimagining of the Rumpelstiltskin story.

Novik, Naomi

* Uprooted / Naomi Novik. Del Rey, 2015. 438 p.

ISBN 9780804179034

1. Curses 2. Witches 3. Wizards 4. Magic 5. Quests 6. Revenge 7. Rescues 8. Best friends 9. Good and evil 10. Life change events 11. Imaginary kingdoms 12. Fantasy fiction 13. Coming-of-age stories

Nebula Award for Best Novel, 2015.
Locus Award for Fantasy Novel, 2016.
Mythopoeic Award for Adult Literature, 2016.
RUSA Reading List, 2016.

A tale inspired by the "Beauty and the Beast" story follows the experiences of Agnieszka, who becomes the latest girl chosen to serve an immortal wizard who protects their village from the malevolent forces of a nearby forest.

"Novik's use of language is supremely skillful as she weaves a tale that is both elegantly grand and earthily humble, familiar as a Grimm fairy tale yet fresh, original, and totally irresistible." Publishers Weekly.

Nugent, Andrew

Soul murder / Andrew Nugent. Minotaur Books, 2009. 288 p.

ISBN 9780312536565

1. Police -- Ireland 2. Boarding schools 3. Murder -- Ireland 4. Malicious accusation 5. Murder investigation -- Ireland 6. Ireland 7. Mysteries

LC 2009017707

In the aftermath of a house master's brutal murder at a boys' boarding school, Superintendent Denis Lennon and Sergeant Molly Power struggle to determine if the killing was related to a bungled kidnapping attempt, an act of revenge, or something more sinister.

Nugent, Liz,

Lying in wait : a novel / Liz Nugent. Gallery/Scout Press, 2018, c2016 320 p.

ISBN 9781501167775

1. Murder 2. Family secrets 3. Consequences 4. Judges 5. Families 6. Extortion 7. Mothers and sons 8. Control (Psychology) 9. Ireland 10. Dublin, Ireland 11. Psychological suspense

LC 2017049456

First published by Penguin Ireland, 2016.

The wife of a respected judge and mother to a beloved son finds their home in Dublin thrown into devastating turmoil by her son's discovery of dark family secrets.

Nunez, Elizabeth

Anna in-between / Elizabeth Nunez. Akashic Books, 2009. 347 p.

ISBN 9781933354842

1. People with breast cancer 2. Mother and adult daughter 3. Frustration in women 4. West Indians 5. Caribbean Americans 6. Family relationships 7. Women editors 8. Medical care 9. Women -- Identity 10. Immigrants 11. West Indians 12. Breast -- Cancer -- Patients 13. Caribbean Area 14. New York City 15. Caribbean Area 16. Domestic fiction 17. Mainstream fiction

Sequel: Boundaries.

Anna, the daughter of an upper-class Caribbean family, returns to her island home on vacation to learn that her mother is suffering from breast cancer, and makes every effort to persuade her mother to go to the United States for treatment.

"The title of her latest novel suggests a sitcom, or the upbeat identity lit marketed to teenagers. But Elizabeth Nunez layers Anna In-Between, a psychologically and emotionally astute family portrait, with dark themes like racism, cancer and the bittersweet longing of the immigrant. Foremost, she explores the late innings of a successful marriage, in which husband and wife cling together in the shadow of mortality." New York Times Book Review.

Nunez, Elizabeth

Grace : a novel / Elizabeth Nunez. One World, 2003. 294 p.

ISBN 0345455339

1. Husband and wife 2. College teachers 3. African American women 4. Married people 5. Trinidadians in the United States 6. Women elementary school teachers 7. Four-year-old girls 8. Men/women relations 9. Separation (Marital relations) 10. Race relations 11. Abandonment (Psychology) 12. Self-fulfillment in women 13. Trust 14. Families 15. Love 16. Brooklyn, New York City 17. Domestic fiction 18. Psychological fiction

LC 2002026260

A Harvard-educated literature professor, Trinidad-born Justin Peters finds his professional and personal life unraveling as his wife, Sally, a one-time poet turned teacher, begins to yearn for something more in her life.

"This is a tender, graceful novel of personal amd material struggle that also explores the power of literature and poetry in everyday life." Booklist.

Nunez, Sigrid

* The **friend** / Sigrid Nunez. Riverhead Books, 2018. 212 p.

ISBN 9780735219441

1. Friends' death 2. Grief in animals 3. Human/animal relationships 4. Survivors of suicide victims 5. Loss (Psychology) 6. Female friendship 7. Women and dogs 8. Great Danes 9. Eviction 10. Coping 11. Grief 12. Psychological fiction 13. Literary fiction

LC 2017011191

National Book Award for Fiction, 2018.

Becoming the guardian of her late best friend's enormous Great Dane, a grieving woman is evicted from her no-pets apartment and forges a deep bond with the equally distraught animal in ways that initially disturb her friends.

"This elegant novel explores both rich memories and day-to-day mundanity, reflecting the way that, especially in grief, the past is often more vibrant than the present." Publishers Weekly.

Nunez, Sigrid

The **last** of her kind : a novel / Sigrid Nunez. Farrar, Straus and Giroux, 2006. 384 p.

ISBN 0374183813

1. Interclass friendship 2. Idealism in women 3. Women radicals 4. Women college students 5. Women roommates 6. Children of rich people 7. Working class women 8. Women murderers 9. Women prisoners 10. Radicals 11. The Sixties generation 12. Counterculture 13. Classism 14. Memories 15. New York City 16. Psychological fiction 17. Coming-of-age stories

LC 2005040098

Chronicles the lives of two women who meet as freshmen in 1968 at Columbia University--Georgette George and her idealistic, radical roommate Ann Drayton--from their first encounter, through the fight that ends their friendship, to Ann's arrest for murder in 1976 and Georgette's search for answers to the riddle of Ann's life.

"This portrait of countercultural America in the sixties and seventies opens in 1968, when two girls meet as roommates at Barnard College. Ann is rich and white and wants to be neither, confiding, 'I wish I had been born poor;' Georgette has no illusions about poverty, having just escaped her depressed home town, where whole families drank themselves to disgrace. Georgette finds Ann at once despicable and mesmerizing, and she's stunned--if not entirely surprised--when, years after the end of their friendship, Ann is arrested for killing a cop. In previous works, Nunez has proved herself a master of psychological acuity. Here her ambitions are grander, and the result is a remarkable and disconcerting vision of a troubled time in American history, and of its repercussions for national and individual identity." The New Yorker.

Nunez, Sigrid

Salvation city / Sigrid Nunez. Riverhead Books, 2010. 288 p.

ISBN 9781594487668

1. Epidemics 2. Teenage boys 3. Orphans 4. Forgiveness 5. Salvation 6. End of the world 7. Rapture (Christian eschatology) 8. Fundamentalists 9. Christianity 10. Indiana 11. Psychological suspense 12. Coming-of-age stories

LC 2010001989

Seeking refuge in the home of an evangelical pastor after a flu pandemic decimates the planet's populations, thirteen-year-old orphan Cole witnesses the community's preparations for a prophesied religious cataclysm and struggles with memories of a very different world.

"The great success of Nunez's book is that the end of the world is filtered through Cole's imperfect perspective, so that the collapse of society is no more devastating than first love, and deeply felt conflict rages as a young man tries to find something worth preserving in a place determined to obliterate the past." Publishers Weekly.

Nunn, Malla

A **beautiful** place to die : a novel / Malla Nunn. Atria Books, 2009. 384 p. Detective Emmanuel Cooper mysteries

ISBN 9781416586203

1. 1950s 2. Police -- South Africa 3. Murder investigation 4. Crimes against police 5. Murder 6. Segregation 7. Apartheid 8. Race relations 9. Afrikaners -- South Africa 10. British in South Africa 11. South Africa -- History -- 1909-1961 12. Mysteries

LC 2008025858

Davitt Awards, Best Adult Novel, 2009.

RUSA Reading List, 2010.

A tale based on the author's childhood in 1950s apartheid southern Africa finds English detective Emmanuel Cooper's investigation into an Afrikaans police officer's murder hampered by the Afrikaner Secret Police's campaign to capture black communist radicals.

LIST OF FICTIONAL WORKS

Nunn, Malla

Blessed are the dead : a novel / Malla Nunn. Atria Books, 2012. 384 p. Detective Emmanuel Cooper mysteries
ISBN 9781451616927
1. 1950s 2. Zulu (African people) 3. Murder investigation 4. Police -- South Africa 5. Missing persons 6. Police misconduct 7. Segregation 8. Apartheid 9. Race relations 10. Afrikaners -- South Africa 11. British in South Africa 12. South Africa -- History -- 1909-1961 13. KwaZulu-Natal, South Africa 14. Mysteries
LC 2011044416

Hired to investigate the disappearance of an adolescent girl in the wild foothills of the Drakensberg, Emmanuel Cooper immerses himself in the class-driven life of transplanted English aristocrats and the traditional world of the old Zulu chiefs, who compel him to break silence to uncover buried secrets.

Nunn, Malla

Present darkness : a novel / Malla Nunn. Atria Books, 2014 337 p. Detective Emmanuel Cooper mysteries
ISBN 9781451616965
1. 1950s 2. Apartheid 3. Murder investigation 4. Police -- South Africa 5. Segregation 6. Race relations 7. Multiracial men 8. Christmas 9. Afrikaners -- South Africa 10. British in South Africa 11. South Africa -- History -- 1909-1961 12. KwaZulu-Natal, South Africa 13. Mysteries

Detective Emmanuel Cooper cancels his holiday plans to learn the truth about his best friend's wrongful murder charge by a high-profile white teen, a case that pits him against violent gangs and corrupt government officials.

Nussbaum, Susan

* **Good** kings, bad kings : a novel / Susan Nussbaum. Algonquin Books of Chapel Hill, 2013. 336 p.
ISBN 9781616202637
1. Institutional care -- Employees 2. Teenagers with disabilities 3. Children with developmental disabilities 4. Children with disabilities 5. Wheelchair users 6. Sex crimes 7. Incest victims 8. Mental illness 9. Chicago, Illinois 10. Mainstream fiction
LC 2013001350

Bellwether Prize for Fiction, 2012.

The residents at a facility for disabled young people in Chicago build trust and make friends in an effort to fight against their living conditions and mistreatment in this debut novel from the playwright behind "Mishuganismo."

"Nussbaum charms, outrages, and enlightens readers as she cycles among these and other characters, boldly contrasting the transcendence of love with the harsh realities of a negligent for-profit nursing home." Booklist.

Nykanen, Harri

Nights of awe / Harri Nykanen ; translated from the Finnish by Kristian London. Bitter Lemon Press, 2012. 252 p. Ariel Kafka novels
ISBN 9781904738923
1. Jews 2. Murder investigation 3. Police 4. Detectives 5. Terrorism 6. Finland 7. Mysteries 8. Translations -- Finnish to English 9. Scandinavian crime fiction
LC bl2012008626

First published in Finnish as Ariel by Werner Soderstrom Ltd (WSOY), Helsinki, 2004.

While investigating the murder of two Arabs near Finland's capital, Inspector Ariel Kafka finds two more bodies at an Iraqi-owned garage, leading him to question whether the perpetrators are part of a gang or international terrorists.

O

* The **O.** Henry prize stories 2019 : 100th anniversary edition / edited by Laura Furman. Anchor Books, 2019. 400 p.
ISBN 9780525565536
1. Anthologies 2. Literary fiction 3. Short stories

A centenary celebration edition of the prestigious annual anthology collects 20 top-selected new short stories from the previous year, including pieces by such leading notables as Lynn Freed, Elizabeth Strout and Lara Vapnyar.

O'Brian, Patrick, 1914-2000

Blue at the mizzen / Patrick O'Brian. W. W. Norton, 1999. 261 p. Jack Aubrey and Stephen Maturin novels
ISBN 9780393048445
1. Great Britain. Royal Navy Officers 2. Sailing ships 3. Ship captains 4. Seafaring life 5. Intelligence officers 6. Naval surgeons 7. Male friendship 8. Great Britain -- History, Naval -- 19th century 9. Chile -- History -- War of Independence, 1810-1824 10. Chile -- Foreign relations -- Great Britain 11. Great Britain -- Foreign relations -- Chile 12. Sea stories 13. Historical fiction 14. Adventure stories
LC 9942043

A Royal Navy warship is dispatched to the Pacific to help Chile fight for its independence from Spain.

"There is nothing in this century that rivals Patrick O'Brian's achievement in his chosen genre. His novels embrace with loving clarity the full richness of the 18th-century world." New York Times Book Review.

O'Brian, Patrick, 1914-2000

* The **commodore** / Patrick O'Brian. W.W. Norton, 1995, c1994. 281 p. Jack Aubrey and Stephen Maturin novels
ISBN 9780393037609
1. Great Britain. Royal Navy Officers 2. Napoleonic Wars, 1800-1815 -- Naval operations, British 3. Intelligence officers 4. Slave-trade -- Gulf of Guinea 5. Sailing ships 6. Ship captains 7. Naval surgeons 8. Male friendship 9. Great Britain -- History, Naval -- 19th century 10. Sea stories 11. Historical fiction 12. Adventure stories
LC 95002653

Originally published: London : HarperCollins, 1994.

Captain Jack Aubrey and Dr. Stephen Maturin of the Royal Navy, are sent to the fever-ridden Gulf of Guinea to disrupt the slave trade. But their ultimate destination is Ireland where the French are mounting an invasion, a mission that will test Aubrey's seamanship and Maturin's talents as a secret agent.

"Another novel in O'Brian's series following Captain (now Commodore) Jack Aubrey and his surgeon friend, Stephen Maturin, through the naval side of the Napoleonic Wars. Although O'Brian is ingenious at devising new adventures, it is the richness of his characters which justifies his readers' continuing enthusiasm. The most arresting moments in this installment come not in battle but in dramas of parenthood and marriage far from the sea. O'Brian acknowledges Jane Austen as one of his inspirations, and she need not be ashamed of the affiliation." The New Yorker.

O'Brian, Patrick, 1914-2000

The **golden** ocean / Patrick O'Brian. W. W. Norton, 1994, c1956. 285 p. Jack Aubrey and Stephen Maturin novels

ISBN 9780393036305

1. Anson, George Anson, 1697-1762 2. Trips around the world 3. Sailors -- Great Britain 4. Great Britain -- History, Naval -- 18th century 5. Sea stories 6. Historical fiction 7. Adventure stories

LC 94011966

In the England of 1740, an Irish parson's gentle son signs up as midshipman on Anson's famous expedition to circumnavigate the globe. In the adventures that follow he grows to become a leader of men, rich and famous. Prequel to the Aubrey/Maturin series.

"This novel is based on the exploits of Commodore George Anson, who set out in 1740 with five men-of-war to circle the globe and returned four years later with one ship and a small but very wealthy crew. The expedition is seen through the eyes of Peter Palafox, a young midshipman who blossoms into an able-bodied seaman. . . . As always, the author's erudition and humor are on display. . . . The attention to period speech and detail is uncompromising, and while the cascades of nautical lore can be dizzying, both aficionados and newcomers will be swept up by the richness of Mr. O'Brian's prodigious imagination." New York Times Book Review.

O'Brian, Patrick, 1914-2000

The **hundred** days / Patrick O'Brian. W. W. Norton, 1998. 280 p. Jack Aubrey and Stephen Maturin novels

ISBN 9780393046748

1. Napoleon I,, Emperor of the French, 1769-1821 Elba and the Hundred Days, 1814-1815 2. Great Britain. Royal Navy Officers 3. Napoleonic Wars, 1800-1815 -- Naval operations, British 4. Sailing ships 5. Ship captains 6. Seafaring life 7. Intelligence officers 8. Naval surgeons 9. Male friendship 10. Great Britain -- History, Naval -- 19th century 11. Sea stories 12. Historical fiction 13. Adventure stories

LC 9835866

On the high seas, Captain Jack Aubrey of the Royal Navy and his co-adventurer, Dr. Stephen Maturin, chase a shipment of gold destined for Napoleon. The emperor has escaped from Elba and the gold would enable him to raise more troops.

"Battles there are aplenty, and O'Brian matches Forester in the excitement, detail and bloody realism of his reconstructions. But these naval tales are blended into a larger panorama of Georgian society and politics, science, medicine, botany and the whole conspectus of contemporary Enlightenment knowledge about the natural world." New York Times Book Review.

O'Brian, Patrick, 1914-2000

* **Master** and commander / Patrick O'Brian. W. W. Norton, 1990, c1970. 411 p. Jack Aubrey and Stephen Maturin novels

ISBN 9780393307054

1. Great Britain. Royal Navy Officers 2. Napoleonic Wars, 1800-1815 -- Naval operations 3. Naval tactics 4. Sailing ships 5. Ship captains 6. Seafaring life 7. Male friendship 8. Great Britain -- History, Naval -- 19th century 9. Sea stories 10. Historical fiction 11. Adventure stories

LC 77085111

Originally published : London: Collins, 1970.

First in the series of Jack Aubrey novels. Establishes the friendship between Captain Aubrey, R.N., and Stephen Maturin, ship's surgeon and intelligence agent, against the backdrop of the Napoleonic wars.

O'Brian, Patrick, 1914-2000

The **unknown** shore / Patrick O'Brian. W. W. Norton, 1995, c1959. 313 p.

ISBN 9780393038590

1. Survival (after airplane accidents, shipwrecks, etc) -- South America 2. Shipwrecks -- South America -- History -- 18th century 3. Mutiny 4. Sailors 5. Great Britain -- History, Naval -- 18th century 6. Sea stories 7. Historical fiction 8. Adventure stories

LC 95032887

Originally published: London : Rupert Hart-Davis, 1959.

In the 18th Century, a Royal Navy ship runs aground during a storm while on a mission to harass Spanish vessels off the coast of South America. A mutiny breaks out and the novel follows two young sailors as they battle the elements and fellow sailors to survive.

"Though this novel isn't quite as polished or stylish as the author's later work, it's a most honorable ancestor." Publishers Weekly.

O'Brian, Patrick, 1914-2000

* The **wine-dark** sea / Patrick O'Brian. W. W. Norton, 1993. 261 p. Jack Aubrey and Stephen Maturin novels

ISBN 9780393035582

1. 1810s 2. Privateers 3. Sailing ships 4. Coups d'etat -- South America 5. Escapes 6. Ship captains 7. Intelligence officers 8. Naval surgeons 9. Male friendship 10. Great Britain -- History, Naval -- 19th century 11. South America 12. Sea stories 13. Historical fiction 14. Adventure stories

LC 93001521

Jack Aubrey and Stephen Maturin pursue a prize into the Great Southern Ocean. Maturin gets caught up in a failed coup in South America and flees across the Andes, while Aubrey makes a desperate voyage in an open boat.

"The naval actions are bang-on and bang-upfast, furious and bloodyand the Andean milieu is as vivid as the shipboard scenes." Publishers Weekly.

O'Brian, Patrick, 1914-2000

The **yellow** admiral / Patrick O'Brian. W.W. Norton, 1996. 261 p. Jack Aubrey and Stephen Maturin novels

ISBN 9780393040449

1. Great Britain. Royal Navy Officers 2. 1810s 3. Sailing ships 4. Naval battles 5. Ship captains 6. Slave trade 7. Intelligence officers 8. Naval surgeons 9. Male friendship 10. Great Britain -- History, Naval -- 19th century 11. Sea stories 12. Historical fiction 13. Adventure stories

LC 96-24149

Captain Jack Aubrey finds his naval career threatened by Admiralty politics, a feud with his neighbor, a disintegrating marriage, and the peace of 1814, until Napoleon escapes from Elba.

"As their careers have advanced and their children have grown, Captain Jack Aubrey and Stephen Maturin have battered Napoleon's ships and thwarted his spies, but here, at last, the Emperor is Elba-bound, and our heroes are left high and dry. Aubrey, ashore at half pay and with scant hope of promotion, prays that peace may not last long a sentiment doubtless shared by O'Brian's readers. Still, Elba is not St. Helena, so war will surely return, if only for a short finale." The New Yorker.

O'Brien, Dan, 1947-

The **contract** surgeon / Dan O'Brien. Lyons Press, 1999. 316 p.

ISBN 1558219323

1. Crazy Horse, approximately 1842-1877 2. Dakota Indians -- Wars, 1876 3. Indians of North America -- Wars 4. Indians of North America -- Wars -- 1866-1895 5. Oglala Indians 6. Oglala Indians

-- Wars 7. Physicians -- North Dakota 8. Surgeons -- North Dakota 9. Interracial friendship 10. North Dakota -- History -- 1889-1918 11. Westerns

LC 9935243

Sequel: The Indian agent.

Western Heritage Award for Outstanding Western Novel, 2000.

Dr. Valentine MacGillycuddy, a contract surgeon pulled from a prestigious practice to become a surgeon for the U.S. Army, meets Crazy Horse and the two discover they had met once before and they develop a friendship despite the war surrounding them.

"This novel is based on the true story of the unusual friendship between Crazy Horse and Dr. Valentine McGillicuddy, a civilian surgeon contracted to serve with the army during the Indian wars on the Great Plains. McGillicuddy relates the tale as an old man. . . . He faces his greatest moral test when Crazy Horse is bayoneted in the back by a soldier, and McGillicuddy is pressured by the army to keep the famous warrior alive, because his death would spur on the Indians to renewed battle. . . . This powerful story is a thinking man's western, in which action is secondary to O'Brien's nuanced exploration of character and the tragic dimensions of a morally fraught conflict." Publishers Weekly.

O'Brien, Edna

* The **country** girls trilogy and epilogue / Edna O'Brien. Farrar Straus Giroux, 1986. 531 p. Country girls trilogy

1. Married women 2. Female friendship 3. Marriage 4. Ireland 5. Psychological fiction 6. Modern classics 7. Literary fiction

LC 85032113

"O'Brien's particular appeal is that she can be tender yet merciless, romantic yet grittily sexual. She resides admirably where quality and popular writing intersect." Booklist.

O'Brien, Edna

* **Girl** / Edna O'Brien. Farrar, Straus and Giroux, 2019 208 p.

ISBN 9780374162559

1. Boko Haram 2. Women kidnapping victims 3. Rape victims 4. Escapes 5. Violence against women 6. Girl kidnapping victims 7. Former captives 8. Ostracism 9. Enemies 10. Captivity 11. Nigeria 12. Literary fiction

LC 2019020325

Abducted by Boko Haram, a young woman makes a hair-raising escape from her northeast Nigerian prison before confronting the hostility and bureaucracy of being the mother of a child fathered by enemies.

O'Brien, Edna

House of splendid isolation / Edna O'Brien. Farrar Straus Giroux, 1994. 232 p.

ISBN 0374173095

1. Widows 2. Terrorists 3. Women hostages 4. Men/women relations 5. Loneliness 6. Northern Ireland -- History -- 1969-1994 7. Psychological fiction 8. Literary fiction

LC 93042602

The heart-breaking dilemmas and the noble and bloody history of Ireland come to life in the tale of Josie, a widow living in a solitary house outside an Irish village, whose home becomes the hideout of a IRA terrorist.

"The author manages to sum up a century of Irish sorrow in this taut, lyrical novel, filled with scenes so vividly rendered they seem captured in a flash of lightning. Not the least of O'Brien's accomplishments is her ability to present both sides of the Irish problem in all their complexity without settling heavily on either side." Library Journal.

O'Brien, Edna

In the forest / Edna O'Brien. Houghton Mifflin, 2002. 262 p.

ISBN 0618197303

1. Murder victims 2. Psychopaths 3. Communities 4. Serial murderers 5. Individuality 6. Fear 7. Kidnapping 8. Villages 9. Ireland 10. Psychological fiction 11. Literary fiction

LC 2001051883

Michen O'Kane, who was born with a killer instinct, unleashes his murderous rage along the countryside of western Ireland, drawing innocent victims into the forest of his twisted fantasies.

"A novel about how a community can be collectively paralyzed by fear. The result is a brilliant illumination of human nature." Booklist.

O'Brien, Edna

Time and tide / Edna O'Brien. Plume, 1999, c1992. 325 p.

ISBN 9780452280519

1. Separated friends, relatives, etc 2. Motherhood 3. Mothers and sons 4. Psychological fiction 5. Literary fiction

LC 92003962

Originally published: New York : Farrar Straus Giroux, 1992.

In her rebellion against the tyranny of her husband, Nell leaves her family to search for love and adventure, while her separation from her husband becomes a battle that eventually pulls her two beloved sons away from her

"This novel is O'Brien's harshest yet most beautiful work. She has a touchy, rich theme: the sexuality of the bond between mothers and sons. . . . O'Brien brings together the earthy and the delicately poetic: she has the soul of Molly Bloom and the skills of Virginia Woolf." Newsweek.

O'Brien, Edna

Wild Decembers / Edna O'Brien. Houghton Mifflin, 1999. 257 p.

ISBN 0618045678

1. Brothers and sisters 2. Landowners 3. Farm life 4. Family feuds 5. Loyalty 6. Love 7. Ireland 8. Literary fiction 9. Psychological fiction

LC 99056110

Offers the story of two siblings, brother and sister, and the dangerous newcomer who would try to steal everything they have

"The novel is a dirge that keens and lulls by turns. The entrancing rhythms and refrains, the density and chant-like, drumming fragmentation work on the reader like magic. . . . O'Brien combines this lyricism with a masterly storytelling instinct, so that [the novel] reads at once like an intricate poem and a taut, suspenseful page-turner." Commonwealth.

O'Brien, Tim, 1946-

Going after Cacciato : a novel / Tim O'Brien. Delacorte Press/S. Lawrence, 1978. 338 p.

ISBN 0440029481

1. Vietnam War, 1961-1975 2. Deserters -- United States 3. Soldiers 4. War and society 5. Courage 6. Coping in men 7. Mortality 8. Vietnam 9. War stories 10. Literary fiction 11. Metafiction

LC 77011723

National Book Award for Fiction, 1979.

Cacciato leaves his unit in Vietnam, announcing that he is going to Paris, but the men chasing him see India and Iran as well.

O'Brien, Tim, 1946-

In the Lake of the Woods / Tim O'Brien. Houghton Mifflin, 1994. 306 p.

ISBN 0395488893

1. Vietnam veterans 2. Secrets 3. Missing persons 4. Married people

5. Politicians 6. War crimes -- History -- Vietnam War, 1961-1975
7. Memories -- Psychological aspects 8. Lake of the Woods 9. Minnesota 10. Literary fiction

LC 94005395

First published: 1994.

ALA Notable Book, 1995.

James Fenimore Cooper Prize, 1995

The story tells of the disintegrating marriage of John and Kathy Wade, living in isolated Lake Of The Woods, Minnesota. John is a politician who lost in a landslide after secrets of his past in Vietnam are revealed to the public. One day John wakes up and finds Kathy missing. John is the main suspect, despite the lack of evidence. The book sets about to solve the mystery of Kathy's diappearance and divulge the dark secrets of John's past.

"What O'Brien really offers is a portrait of one man and woman at the most critical juncture of their relationship. It's a dark portrait, taking issue with a stock notion of commercial fiction: that after suffering comes redemption. Maybe not. Maybe there's only oblivion. A beautifully written, haunting novel that evokes lives in deep crisis." Booklist.

O'Brien, Tim, 1946-

* The **things** they carried : a work of fiction / Tim O'Brien. Houghton Mifflin, 1990. 273 p.

ISBN 039551598X

1. Vietnam veterans 2. Death -- Psychological aspects 3. Soldiers -- United States -- Psychology 4. Vietnam War, 1961-1975 -- Casualties 5. Writing 6. Psychological fiction 7. War stories 8. Short stories 9. Literary fiction 10. Metafiction 11. Modern classics

LC 89039871

ALA Notable Book, 1991.

National Book Critics Circle Award for Fiction finalist, 1990.

Pulitzer Prize for Fiction finalist, 1991.

A collection of award-winning and utterly moving stories about the madness of the Vietnam war.

"This book may be self-conscious . . . but through its determination to treat these men with dignity and decency it proves immensely affecting." Newsweek.

O'Brien, Timothy L., 1961-

The **Lincoln** conspiracy : a novel / Timothy L. O'Brien. Ballantine Books, 2012. 368 p.

ISBN 9780345496775

1. Lincoln, Abraham, 1809-1865 Assassination 2. Lincoln, Mary Todd, 1818-1882 3. Presidents -- United States 4. Conspiracies 5. Assassins 6. Actors and actresses 7. Washington (DC) 8. United States -- History -- 19th century 9. Biographical fiction 10. Historical thrillers

LC 2012022133

As the nation mourns the death of President Abraham Lincoln, Detective Temple McFadden discovers two diaries--one belonging to Mary Todd Lincoln, the other penned by John Wilkes Booth--that reveal a shocking conspiracy behind Lincoln's assassination.

O'Connell, Carol, 1947-

Blind sight / Carol O'Connell. G.P. Putnam's Sons, 2016 400 p. Kathleen Mallory mysteries

ISBN 9780399184239

1. Massacres 2. Missing boys 3. Missing persons investigation 4. Murder 5. Detectives 6. Policewomen 7. Women detectives 8. Boys who are blind 9. Murder investigation 10. New York City 11. Mysteries

LC 2016008417

"The nun was dead. Her body lay on the lawn outside Gracie Mansion, the home of New York City's mayor, and it wasn't alone. There were four of them altogether. They'd been killed at different times, in different places, and dumped there. There should have been five--but the boy was missing. Though he was blind, Jonah Quill saw more than most people did. It was his secret, and he was counting on that to save his life. Detective Kathy Mallory was counting on herself to save his life. It took her a while to realize that the missing-person case she was pursuing was so intimately connected to the massacre on the mayor's lawn."--Provided by publisher.

O'Connell, Carol, 1947-

The **chalk** girl / Carol O'Connell. G. P. Putnam's Sons, 2012. 384 p. Kathleen Mallory mysteries

ISBN 9780399157745

1. Murder investigation 2. Cold cases (Criminal investigation) 3. Extortion 4. Rats 5. Murder 6. Policewomen 7. Williams syndrome 8. Girl murder witnesses 9. Women detectives 10. New York City 11. Mysteries

LC 2011027853

"Before Lisbeth Salander, there was Kathy Mallory. The little girl appeared in Central Park: red-haired, blue-eyed, smiling, perfect-except for the blood on her shoulder. It fell from the sky, she said, while she was looking for her uncle, who turned into a tree. Poor child, people thought -- until they found the body in the tree. For Mallory, newly returned to the Special Crimes Unit after three months' lost time, this girl will lead her to a story of extraordinary crimes: murders stretching back fifteen years, blackmail and complicity and a particularcruelty that only someone with Mallory's history could fully recognize."--, Provided by publisher.

O'Connell, Carol, 1947-

Crime school / Carol O'Connell. G.P. Putnam's Sons, 2002. 341 p. Kathleen Mallory mysteries

ISBN 0399149287

1. Prostitutes 2. Adoptive mothers 3. Bureaucracy 4. Policewomen 5. Women detectives 6. New York City 7. Mysteries

LC 2002022860

New York City policewoman Kathy Mallory investigates the murder of a prostitute named Sparrow, a woman who had taken her in many years ago only to betray her, as part of a crime that seems to mimic one that happened two decades earlier.

"O'Connell's crime-scene investigations techniques ring true, her plotting is breathtaking, and her psychology acute. Searing suspense." Booklist.

O'Connell, Carol, 1947-

Dead famous / Carol O'Connell. G. P. Putnam's Sons, 2003. 304 p. Kathleen Mallory mysteries

ISBN 0399150846

1. Radio personalities 2. Women with disfigurements 3. Trials 4. Policewomen 5. Women detectives 6. FBI agents 7. Jury 8. New York City 9. Chicago, Illinois 10. Mysteries

LC 2003043212

Also known as: The jury must die in the U.S.

Night had fallen, and the woman looked down at the crumpled letter, as if, in absolute darkness, she could read the postscript: Only a monster can play this game. In Chicago, an FBI agent is killed in a psychiatrist's waiting room. In New York, the jurors from a controversial trial are murdered one by one. The only connections between the two: a flamboyant shock-jock, whose on-air comments seem to be taking him dangerously close to the edge, and a woman, her body misshapen since childhood, whose job it is to clean up crime scenes- and maybe create them as well. This is a federal case, and Mallory's been told that the FBI wants no part of her. But she knows something nobody else does--and, besides when has she ever cared what anyone else wanted?

O'Connell, Carol, 1947-

Find me / Carol O'Connell. G.P. Putnam's Sons, 2006. 352 p. Kathleen Mallory mysteries

ISBN 0399153950

1. Mutilation 2. United States Highway 66 3. Automobile travel 4. Women detectives 5. Policewomen 6. Serial murder investigation 7. Missing children 8. Families of murder victims 9. New York City 10. Middle West 11. Mysteries

LC 2006046232

Also known as: Shark music in the U.S.

A mutilated body is found lying on the ground in Chicago, a dead hand pointing down Adams Street, also known as Route 66, a road of many names. And now of many deaths. A silent caravan of cars, dozens of them, drives down that road, each passenger bearing a photograph, but none of them the same. They are the parents of missing children, some recently disappeared, some gone a decade or more--all brought together by word that children's grave sites are being discovered along the Mother Road. Kathy Mallory drives with them. The child she seeks, though, is not like the others'. It is herself--the feral child adopted off the streets, her father a blank, her mother dead and full of mysteries. During the next few extraordinary days, Mallory will find herself hunting a killer like none she has ever known, and will undergo a series of revelations not only of stunning intensity--but stunning effect.

"This isn't a brute-force thriller. It's intelligent, honed and taunting." New York Daily News.

O'Connell, Carol, 1947-

It happens in the dark / Carol O'Connell. G. P. Putnam's Sons, 2013. 368 p. Kathleen Mallory mysteries

ISBN 9780399165399

1. Murder investigation 2. Theaters 3. Dramatists 4. Murder 5. Policewomen 6. Women detectives 7. Detectives 8. Drama 9. New York City 10. Mysteries

LC 2013015334

After two patrons at a play are found murdered on successive nights, detective Kathy Mallory investigates the killings along with mysterious backstage chalkboard messages.

O'Connell, Carol, 1947-

Judas child / Carol O'Connell. G. P. Putnam's Sons, 1998. 340 p.

ISBN 0399143807

1. Women forensic psychologists 2. Twin sisters 3. Men with mental illnesses 4. Police 5. Private schools 6. Priests 7. Kidnapping 8. Thrillers and suspense 9. Christmas stories

LC 9746504

The disappearances of two young girls from a local academy bring back terrifying memories for Rouge Kendall, a young policeman whose own twin sister had been murdered in a similar case some fifteen years earlier, and his classmate, forensic psychologist Ali Cray

"O'Connell thoughtfully tackles material that in other hands would be merely sensational. Dark in tone, gripping suspense, and tempered with the hope of redemption, this is highly recommended." Library Journal.

O'Connell, Carol, 1947-

Killing critics / Carol O'Connell. G.P. Putnam's Sons, 1996. 308 p. Kathleen Mallory mysteries

ISBN 0399141685

1. Art critics 2. Dancers 3. Sculpture 4. Policewomen 5. Women detectives 6. New York City 7. Mysteries 8. Black humor

LC 9543894

As NYPD Detective Sergeant Kathleen Mallory probes the death of a hack artist at a gallery opening, she discovers links to a bizarre twelve-year-old double homicide and dismemberment originally investigated by her late adoptive father

"As mesmerizing as the murder case is, it's heartless, soulless Mallory herself--computer genius, street fighter, provocative waif, peerless investigator, manipulative beauty--who's absolutely the star of this brilliant thriller." Booklist.

O'Connell, Carol, 1947-

Mallory's oracle / Carol O'Connell. G.P. Putnam's, 1994. 286 p. Kathleen Mallory mysteries

ISBN 9780399139758

1. Families of murder victims 2. Fortune-tellers 3. Spirit possession 4. Supernatural 5. Policewomen 6. Women detectives 7. Adoptees 8. Fathers and daughters 9. New York City 10. Mysteries

LC 94002234

Adopted off the streets as a child by a policeman's family, NYC policewoman Kathleen Mallory had never shaken the wild nature of her youth, and when her adoptive father is murdered during a series of stabbings, she is driven to find the truth.

"The author's writing is stunning in its luminosity, originality, simplicity, and power. Her plot is ingenious, inventive, and enigmatic, and her characters sparkle with originality and charm." Booklist.

O'Connell, Carol, 1947-

The man who cast two shadows / Carol O'Connell. G.P. Putnam's Sons, 1995. 278 p. Kathleen Mallory mysteries

ISBN 0399140646

1. Mistaken identity 2. Computers 3. Murder witnesses 4. Supernatural 5. Policewomen 6. Women detectives 7. New York City 8. Mysteries

LC 94043797

Also known as: The man who lied to women in the U.K.

NYPD Detective Sergeant Kathleen Mallory is drawn into a baffling world of peril and illusion when she investigates the brutal murder of a young woman, whose body is found wearing a jacket labeled "Kathleen Mallory."

"This mystery features New York cop Kathleen Mallory. Taken off suspension to cover the murder of a woman at first identified as Mallory herself, she pits her uncanny intelligence and formidable computer skills against a compulsive and evasive adversary. Moments of wry humor invade the author's incisive prose, tempering an admirable female protagonist sure to gather a following." Library Journal.

O'Connell, Carol, 1947-

Stone angel / Carol O'Connell. G. P. Putnam's Sons, 1997. 341 p. Kathleen Mallory mysteries

ISBN 0399142347

1. Children of murder victims 2. Stoning 3. Heredity 4. Policewomen 5. Women detectives 6. Small town life 7. Louisiana 8. Mysteries

LC 96-44504

Also known as: Flight of the stone angel in the U.K.

New York police sergeant Kathleen Mallory returns to her Louisiana hometown to find out who was behind her mother's death by stoning seventeen years earlier--a quest that takes her into a dark and murky past that has unexpected and deadly implications

O'Connor, Flannery

* **Collected** works / Flannery C'Connor ; edited by Sally Fitzgerald Library of America; distributed by Viking Press, 1988. 1281 p.

ISBN 9780940450370

1. Letters 2. Essays 3. Short stories 4. Anthologies 5. Southern Gothic 6. Southern fiction

LC 87037829

This collection includes all the short stories, both novels, the essays, and selected letters of one of the most unique and important writers in the southern tradition.

O'Connor, Flannery

The **complete** stories / Flannery O'Connor. Farrar, Straus and Giroux, 1971. xvii, 555 p.

ISBN 9780374127527

1. Southern States -- Social life and customs 2. Short stories 3. Literary fiction 4. Southern Gothic 5. Southern fiction

LC 72171492

National Book Award for Fiction, 1972.

Thirty-one tales depicting the humorous, if near tragic conditions of life in the Deep South during the fifties.

"This collection is arranged in chronological order from the story she wrote for her master's thesis at the University of Iowa to Judgement Day. . . . The stories here include the original openings and other chapters of her two novels Wise Blood and The Violent Bear It Away." New York Times Book Review.

O'Connor, Flannery

* The **violent** bear it away / Flannery O'Connor. Farrar, Straus & Cudahy, 1960. 243 p.

ISBN 9780374505240

1. Redemption 2. Prophets 3. Religious fanaticism 4. Families -- Southern States 5. Children with Down syndrome 6. Uncle and nephew 7. Conflict in families 8. Fate and fatalism 9. Secularism 10. Baptism 11. Male rape victims 12. Southern States 13. Literary fiction 14. Modern classics 15. Southern Gothic 16. Southern fiction

A back country orphan struggles to defy his uncle's prophesy that he will become a Baptist prophet.

O'Connor, Flannery

* **Wise** blood / Flannery O'Connor. Farrar, Straus and Giroux, 1996, c1962. 232 p.

ISBN 9780374505844

1. Veterans 2. Prophets 3. Grace (Theology) 4. Christianity 5. Eccentrics and eccentricities 6. Unhappiness in men 7. Preaching 8. Nihilism 9. Southern States 10. Literary fiction 11. Modern classics 12. Southern Gothic 13. Satirical fiction 14. Southern fiction

The passengers on the train to Taulkinham show mixed reactions when Haze questions their belief in Jesus.

O'Connor, Frank, 1903-1966

Collected stories / Introduction by Richard Ellmann A. A. Knopf, 1981. 701p.

ISBN 0394516028

1. Short stories

LC 81001253

"The author grew up with 'the troubles,' but the Ireland he evokes in these 72 stories . . . is the provincial life of his Cork boyhood." Library Journal.

O'Connor, Joseph, 1963-

Ghost light : a novel / Joseph O'Connor. Farrar, Straus and Giroux, 2011, c2010. 256 p.

ISBN 9780374161873

1. O'Neill, Maire, 1887-1952 2. Synge, J M (John Millington), 1871-1909 3. 1920s 4. 1950s 5. Dramatists, Irish 6. First loves 7. Theater 8. Men/women relations 9. Actors and actresses 10. Dublin, Ireland -- Social life and customs -- 20th century 11. Literary fiction 12. Biographical fiction 13. Love stories

LC 2010022672

"A Francis Coady Book."

Originally published: London : Harvill Secker, 2010.

Shortlisted for the Walter Scott Prize for Historical Fiction, 2011

A collaborative effort between W. B. Yeats and resident playwright John Synge at the 1907 Abbey Theatre gives way to a barrier-breaking affair with teen actress Molly Allgood, who after World War II looks back on her career and great love.

"O'Connor's impressionistic, intense style delivers a mismatched love story and a social landscape dominated by forceful characters such as W.B. Yeats and Synge's formidable mother, but it is Molly's perspective which prevails, the voice of a comical, intuitive, irrepressible life force. An empathetic act of literary homage offering nuggets of emotional intensity." Kirkus.

O'Connor, Joseph, 1963-

Star of the Sea / Joseph O'Connor. Harcourt, 2003. xxiii, 386 p.

ISBN 0151009082

1. Irish Potato Famine (1845-1852) 2. 19th century 3. 1840s 4. Murderers 5. Ships 6. Ocean travel 7. Immigrants 8. Household employees 9. Nobility 10. Irish in the United States 11. Ireland -- Emigration and immigration 12. England 13. Historical mysteries

LC 2003001984

ALA Notable Book, 2004.

In the middle of the Atlantic Ocean during the summer of 1847, a boatload of Irish refugees heading for the promise of America is stalked by a killer in their ranks who seems bent on some kind of revenge.

"The author brillantly weaves together an intriguing plot, a cast of memorable characters, and some stunningly realistic dialog. Universal themes of love, loyalty, vengeance, and violence are explored in the context of a troubled class-ridden society convulsed by the catastropic potato blight." Library Journal.

O'Connor, Robert

Buffalo soldiers / Robert O'Connor. A. A. Knopf, 1993, c1992. 323 p.

ISBN 9780679415084

1. United States. Army Military life 2. United States Army Germany 3. Heroin traffic 4. Drug dealers 5. Military life 6. Soldiers -- Drug use 7. Germany 8. Political fiction 9. Black humor

LC 92054278

Army man Ray Elwood, battalion commander's clerk and troop heroin dealer, struggles to deal with peacetime boredom while stationed in the no-man's-land of Mannheim in the Federal Republic of Germany.

"O'Connor writes bitter, funny prose and creates bureaucratic snafus of the first order. Alternating scenes of Army idiocy and clinically realistic drug addiction are far more compelling than O'Connor's attempt to attribute his hero's bracing nihilism to his tragic past. Toward its end the book falters, as Elwood flirts with maudlin self-pity. But O'Connor misfires now and then only because he aims high." Publishers Weekly.

O'Dell, Claire

A **study** in honor : a novel / Claire O'Dell. Harper Voyager, 2018 293 p. Janet Watson chronicles
ISBN 9780062699305
1. Civil War 2. Veterans 3. Near future 4. Artificial limbs 5. Military surgeons 6. Intelligence service 7. Murder investigation 8. Women/women relations 9. African American women 10. Washington, D.C. 11. Social science fiction 12. Science fiction mysteries 13. Adaptations, retellings, and spin-offs
Lambda Literary Award for Lesbian Mystery, 2019.

Homeless and jobless after being dishonorably discharged during the New Civil War, Dr. Janet Watson returns to Washington, D.C., where she is offered a place to stay by mysterious covert agent Sara Holmes.

O'Dell, Tawni

Back roads / Tawni O'Dell. Viking, 2000. 338 p.
ISBN 9780670894185
1. Dysfunctional families 2. Children of murderers 3. Children of murder victims 4. Brothers and sisters -- Pennsylvania 5. Coal mining towns -- Pennsylvania 6. Pennsylvania 7. Psychological suspense

A teenaged boy, marooned in a Pennsylvania coal town caring for his three younger sisters, develops an obsession with a young mother. Unspoken truths and family secrets lead to a series of staggering surprises.

"Harley's first-person account of the deterioration of his family and his own slow-motion meltdown is harrowing. O'Dell, a native of western Pennsylvania, renders finely detailed characters and settings in a desperate and failed mining town. This is a riveting first novel of violence, incest, murder, and madness." Booklist.

O'Donnell, Lisa, 1972-

* The **death** of bees : a novel / Lisa O'Donnell. Harper, 2013, c2012. 320 p.
ISBN 9780062209849
1. Sisters 2. Neighbors 3. Family secrets 4. Orphans 5. Teenage girls 6. Loneliness 7. Loss (Psychology) 8. Child abuse victims 9. Suspicion 10. Glasgow, Scotland 11. Coming-of-age stories 12. Literary fiction 13. Black humor
LC 2012031882
"This book was originally published in Great Britain in 2012 by William Heinemann, an imprint of the the Random House Group"--Title page verso.

"I'm Marnie. Too young to smoke, too young to drink, too young to fuck, but who would have stopped me?" Hazlehurst housing estate, Glasgow, Christmas Eve 2006. 15-year-old Marnie and her little sister Nelly have just finished burying their parents in the back garden. Only Marnie and Nelly know how they got there.

O'Donohue, Clare

Beyond the pale : a world of spies mystery / Clare O'Donohue. Midnight Ink, 2018. 360 p. World of spies
ISBN 9780738756509
1. Interpol 2. Husband and wife 3. College teachers 4. Undercover operations 5. Manuscripts 6. Murder 7. Married people 8. Spies 9. Ireland 10. Spy fiction
LC 2017051243
"Interpol asks married college professors Hollis and Finn Larsson to procure a priceless rare book manuscript abroad. They are soon left with fifty thousand euros and a possible death threat"-- Provided by publisher.

O'Donohue, Clare

The **lover's** knot : a Someday Quilts mystery / Clare O'Donohue. Plume, 2008. 304 p. Someday Quilts mysteries
ISBN 9780452289796
1. Quilting 2. Murder 3. Friendship 4. Small town life -- New York (State) 5. Women amateur detectives 6. Quiltmakers 7. Quilts 8. Engaged persons 9. Grandmother and granddaughter 10. Love triangles 11. New York (State) 12. Cozy mysteries 13. Gentle reads 14. Hobby mysteries
LC 2008016909
Overjoyed to receive a handmade quilt from her grandmother as an engagement gift until her fiancé calls off the wedding, Nell seeks refuge at her grandmother's home in picturesque Archers Rest, until the body of a local handyman turns up in the quilt shop and Nell is drawn into the investigation--and to the handsome police chief.

O'Donovan, Gerard, 1965-

Dublin dead : a novel / Gerard O'Donovan. Scribner, 2012. 304 p. Mike Mulcahy and Siobhan Fallon mysteries
ISBN 9781451610635
1. Women journalists 2. Missing persons 3. Drug traffic 4. Detectives 5. Police 6. Bureaucracy 7. Dublin, Ireland 8. Mysteries
LC 2011031170
One year after the events in The Priest, DI Mike Mulcahy finds his dream job hinging on a case involving a Dublin gangster's murder; while reporter Siobhan Fallon buries herself in work to forget her trauma and investigates clues surrounding a suspicious suicide story.

O'Donovan, Gerard, 1965-

The **priest** : a novel / Gerard O'Donovan. Scribner, 2011. 304 p. Mike Mulcahy and Siobhan Fallon mysteries
ISBN 9781451610604
1. Detectives 2. Serial murderers 3. Religious fanatics 4. Police 5. Rape 6. Religious adherents 7. Journalists 8. Violence against women 9. Bureaucracy 10. Dublin, Ireland 11. Mysteries
LC 2010033448
Irish police inspector Mike Mulcahy--along with help from Siobhan Fallon, a ambitious young female reporter--must fight roadblocks from his own department and bureaucratic red tape when he investigates a string of sexually charged murders by a serial killer who brands his victims with a crucifix and is only known to authorities as "The Priest."

"Although it's clear early on who the psycho is . . . Mr. O'Donovan builds suspense carefully and cleverly, leading us to a pulse-raising climax at a huge cross in a Dublin park." Pittsburgh Post-Gazette.

O'Farrell, Maggie, 1972-

The **hand** that first held mine : a novel / Maggie O'Farrell. Houghton Mifflin Harcourt, 2010. 341 p.
ISBN 9780547330792
1. Women painters 2. Motherhood 3. Family secrets 4. Men/women relations 5. Parenthood 6. London, England 7. Psychological fiction 8. Love stories
LC 2009042058
Costa Novel Award, 2010.
Fifty years after an unconventional reporter of genteel origins becomes a single mother, present-day London painter Elina navigates the first weeks of motherhood upon surviving a dangerous labor and learns that her life is disconcertingly linked to the woman from the past.

"O'Farrell constantly fiddles with perspective. Her knowing narrator is so intimate with Lexie, Elina, Ted, and Innes that the story seems to spill directly from their conscious and unconscious voices. She flashes back and forward, revealing secrets about pasts and futures unknown to characters." Boston Globe.

O'Farrell, Maggie, 1972-

This must be the place / Maggie O'Farrell. Alfred A. Knopf, 2016. x, 382 p.

ISBN 9780385349420

1. College teachers 2. Americans in Ireland 3. Divorced men 4. Former actors and actresses 5. Voyages and travels 6. Rural life 7. Children 8. Husband and wife 9. People with disabilities 10. Family secrets 11. Family relationships 12. Men/women relations 13. Ireland 14. Literary fiction

LC 2015044361

Recovering from an ugly divorce and custody battle by marrying a sexual icon who would escape her life of fame, Daniel is threatened by a secret from his past in a story told through his voice and the perspectives of those who have influenced his life.

"There is enough possibility and randomness for three books, yet the story never feels overstuffed, and when it ends, the reader is stunned and grateful, relieved that in the face of all that can go (and have gone) wrong, some things have come right." Publishers Weekly.

O'Farrell, Maggie, 1972-

The **vanishing** act of Esme Lennox / Maggie O'Farrell. Harcourt, 2007. 245 p.

ISBN 9780151014118

1. 2000s (Decade) 2. 1930s 3. Family secrets 4. Institutionalized persons 5. Life change events 6. Senior women 7. Reunions 8. Sisters -- Family relationships 9. Aunt and niece 10. Women psychiatric hospital patients 11. Mental health laws 12. Betrayal 13. Scotland 14. Historical fiction 15. Psychological suspense

LC 2007006079

Iris Lockhart is stunned when she receives news that her great-aunt Esme, a previously unknown woman edited out of her family's history, is being released from Cauldstone Hospital, where she has been confined for more than sixty years, and soon discovers that Esme holds the key to long-hidden family secrets that could change her life forever.

"At the heart of this fantastic new novel is a mystery you want to solve until you start to suspect the truth, and then you read on in a panic, horrified that you may be right." Washington Post Book World.

O'Flynn, Catherine

The **news** where you are : a novel / Catherine O'Flynn. Henry Holt and Co., 2010. 252 p.

ISBN 9780805091809

1. Television newscasters and commentators 2. Loss (Psychology) 3. Hit-and-run accidents 4. Midlife crisis 5. Family relationships 6. England 7. Mysteries

LC 2009045217

Hiding the symptoms of a mid-life crisis behind his famously corny television persona, news anchor Frank Allcroft struggles with his predecessor's mysterious hit-and-run death, the demolition of his architect father's buildings and his tenacious relationship with his aging mother.

"This is a funny, moving, acutely observed story about family and loss, getting old and being alone. That it also manages to take in British architecture and urban space and the problems of celebrity culture, while being disarmingly easy to read, is testament to Catherine O'Flynn's comic timing and lightness of touch." Scotland on Sunday.

O'Hagan, Andrew, 1968-

Be near me / Andrew O'Hagan. Houghton Mifflin Harcourt, 2006. 288 p.

ISBN 9780151013036

1. Catholic Church Clergy 2. Problem youth 3. Intergenerational friendship 4. Scandals 5. Priests 6. Self-deception 7. Gay men -- Psychology 8. Small town life -- Scotland 9. Scotland 10.

Psychological fiction

LC 2006030402

Oxford-educated Father David Anderton, the Catholic priest in a small, working-class Scottish parish, triggers the enmity, suspicions, and simmering hatred of a town that resents strangers when he befriends two rebellious teenagers.

"A distinctive voice resonates clearly through the first-person narrative, clerically portentous at times, a shade trite or unabashedly sentimental at others, yet in all its registers convincing. What it tells us is a story compounded from passion and resurrection as opposed to professional failure or spiritual collapse." Times Literary Supplement.

O'Hara, John, 1905-1970

Appointment in Samarra / John O?Hara. Penguin Classics, 2013, c1934. 269 p.

ISBN 9780143107071

1. 1930s 2. Self-destructive behavior 3. Couples 4. Small towns 5. Pennsylvania -- Social life and customs 6. Modern classics 7. Literary fiction

Originally published 1934.

Julian and Caroline English are at the center of the social elite until Julian makes a fateful decision to break with polite society and embarks on a rapid spiral toward self-destruction.

O'Hara, John, 1905-1970

Butterfield 8 : a novel / John O'Hara. Modern Library, 1935. 310 p.

1. 1930s 2. Extramarital affairs 3. Life change events 4. Women 5. City life 6. Social norms 7. Consequences 8. New York City 9. Literary fiction

Caught up in the fast life of 1930s New York City, Gloria Wandrous becomes tragically involved with a married man.

O'Keefe, Megan E., 1985-

* **Velocity** weapon / Megan E. O'Keefe. Orbit, 2019. 533 p. The Protectorate

ISBN 9780316419598

1. Brothers and sisters 2. Space warfare 3. Artificial intelligence 4. Space flight 5. Women soldiers 6. Politicians 7. Space colonies 8. Human/computer interaction 9. Wounds and injuries 10. Survival 11. Space opera 12. Science fiction

LC 2019000293

Sanda and Biran Greeve were siblings destined for greatness. A high-flying sergeant, Sanda has the skills to take down any enemy combatant. Biran is a savvy politician who aims to use his new political position to prevent conflict from escalating to total destruction. However, on a routine maneuver, Sanda loses consciousness when her gunship is blown out of the sky. Instead of finding herself in friendly hands, she awakens 230 years later on a deserted enemy warship controlled by an AI who calls himself Bero. The war is lost. The star system is dead. Ada Prime and its rival Icarion have wiped each other from the universe. Now, separated by time and space, Sanda and Biran must fight to put things right.

"The short chapters and alternating points of view create strong pacing, the character interaction seamlessly moves from fluid battle scenes and sinister scheming to sarcastic and deeply funny dialogue. The inevitable convergence of disparate story lines will leave readers both satisfied by the ending and eagerly awaiting the next installment." Booklist.

O'Keefe, Molly

Crazy thing called love / Molly O'Keefe. Bantam Books, 2013. 357 p. Crooked Creek Ranch

ISBN 9780345533692

1. Divorced couples 2. Former lovers 3. Interpersonal attraction 4. Men/women relations 5. Lover's reunions 6. Women television personalities 7. Professional hockey players 8. Dallas, Texas 9. Contemporary romances

RITA Award for Best Contemporary Single Title, 2014.

Forced to work with sexy hockey superstar Billy Wilkins, who is also her ex-husband, Dallas TV morning show host Madelyn Cornish finds herself skating on thin ice when he asks for one more shot at making things right.

"Gripping storytelling and convincing character-building allow the story to unfold in the present and in the past, offering windows into the psyches of a damaged hero and his restyled first love." Kirkus.

O'Keefe, Molly

Everything I left unsaid : a novel / M. O'Keefe. Bantam, 2015. 366 p.

ISBN 9781101884485

1. Runaway wives, husbands, etc 2. Abused women 3. Strangers 4. Sex games 5. Seduction 6. Hiding 7. Trust 8. Sexual attraction 9. Men/women relations 10. North Carolina 11. Erotic romances 12. Contemporary romances

LC 2015007597

Sequel: The truth about him.

Picking up a wrong number intended for another person, Annie, a woman on the run from a dangerous husband, embarks on a risky sexual adventure with a mysterious stranger who tempts her to trust again.

O'Leary, Beth

The **flatshare** : a novel / Beth O'Leary. Flatiron Books, 2019. 336 p.

ISBN 9781250295637

1. Roommates 2. Shared housing 3. Apartment house life 4. Men/women relations 5. Sexual attraction 6. Friendship 7. Letter writing 8. Men nurses 9. Women editors 10. Emotional abuse 11. Memories 12. Night work 13. London, England 14. England 15. Romantic comedies

LC 2019004158

Entering a flatshare arrangement with a man on an opposite work shift, a heartbroken woman begins exchanging notes with the roommate she has never met and becomes his best friend, and possibly soulmate, through their correspondence.

O'Malley, Thomas, 1967-

Serpents in the cold / Thomas O'Malley and Douglas Graham Purdy. Mulholland Books/Little, Brown and Company, 2015. 387 p. Boston saga

ISBN 9780316323505

1. 1950s 2. World War II veterans 3. Serial murder investigation 4. Winter 5. Murder 6. Serial murderers 7. Political corruption 8. Amateur detectives 9. Violence against women 10. Private security services 11. Recovering drug abusers 12. Boston, Massachusetts -- History -- 20th century 13. Hardboiled fiction 14. Historical mysteries

LC 2014018353

In 1951, lifelong Boston residents Cal O'Brien and Dante Cooper, struggling to find their identities after World War II, take it upon themselves to track down a serial killer that is terrorizing the city and dis-

cover that there are a few well-placed men that do not want them to solve this case.

O'Malley, Thomas, 1967-

We were kings / Thomas O'Malley, Douglas Graham Purdy. Mulholland Books/Little, Brown and Company, 2016. 369 p. Boston saga

ISBN 9780316323536

1. Irish Republican Army. 2. 1950s 3. Private investigators 4. Drug addicts 5. Irish in the United States 6. Widowers 7. World War II veterans 8. Summer 9. Former police 10. Detectives 11. Loss (Psychology) 12. Murder 13. Murder investigation 14. City life 15. Boston, Massachusetts 16. Massachusetts -- History -- 20th century 17. Hardboiled fiction 18. Historical mysteries

In 1950's Boston, the Irish Republican Army is running guns and killing witnesses. Cal and Dante are committed to stopping them.

O'Mara, Tim

Crooked numbers / Tim O'Mara. Minotaur Books, 2013. ix, 306 p. Raymond Donne novels

ISBN 9781250009005

1. Murder investigation 2. Former police 3. Teachers 4. Gangs 5. Violence in gangs 6. New York City 7. Mysteries

When one of Raymond Donne's former students is found stabbed to death under the Williamsburg Bridge, Ray draws on his past as a cop to find the truth in Tim O'Mara's second New York mystery. Raymond Donne's former student Douglas Lee had everything going for him thanks to a scholarship to an exclusive private school in Manhattan, but all of that falls apart when his body is found below the Williamsburg Bridge with a dozen knife wounds in it. That kind of violence would normally get some serious attention from the police and media except when it's accompanied by signs that it could be gang related. When that's the case, the story dies and the police are happy to settle for the straightforward explanation. Dougie's mom isn't having any of that and asks Ray, who had been a cop before an accident cut his career short, to look into it, unofficially. He does what he can, asking questions, doling out information to the press, and filling in some holes in the investigation, but he doesn't get far before one of Dougie's private school friends is killed and another is put in the hospital. What kind of trouble could a couple of sheltered kids get into that would end like that? And what does is have to do with Dougie's death? None of it adds up, but there's no way Ray can just wait around for something to happen. Following on the heels of his acclaimed debut, Tim O'Mara's Crooked Numbers is another outstanding mystery that brings the streets of Brooklyn and Manhattan to life and further solidifies O'Mara's place among the most talented new crime fiction writers working today. Provided by publisher.

O'Nan, Stewart, 1961-

Emily, alone : a novel / Stewart O'Nan. Viking, 2011. 272 p.

ISBN 9780670022359

1. Widows 2. Aging 3. Life change events 4. Family relationships 5. Senior women 6. Independence in women 7. Parent and adult child 8. Pittsburgh, Pennsylvania 9. Psychological fiction

LC 2010035333

Sequel to: Wish you were here.

Newly independent widow Emily Maxwell dreams of visits by grandchildren and mourns changes in her quiet Pittsburgh neighborhood before realizing an inner strength to pursue developing opportunities.

"This novel revisits the Emily Maxwell of Wish You Were Here [2002] as a widow and traces the course of three-quarters of a year near the end--but decidedly not at the end--of her long life. Born in small-town Appalachia to a building inspector and a teacher, Emily achieved the cultured and refined life for which she yearned by marrying into a gracious Pittsburgh family. She appreciates classical music, visits the library regularly, reserves a table at the club for special occasions, pines for the heyday of Masterpiece Theatre and Mystery! (although not the gritty, Helen Mirren era, much as she admires the actress herself). O'Nan cannot write without nuance, and Emily contains the contradictions and failings of a real person. Her second-guessing of, frustration with, and love for her adult children and grandchildren; her observations concerning her comparatively young neighbors; her dependence on and resentment toward her sister-in-law are all a voyeuristic pleasure." The Atlantic.

O'Nan, Stewart, 1961-

Henry, himself / Stewart O'Nan. Penguin Group USA, 2019 352 p.

ISBN 9780735223042

1. 1990s 2. Senior men 3. Septuagenarians 4. Reminiscing in old age 5. Aging 6. Memory 7. Scruples 8. Self-doubt 9. Family relationships 10. Pittsburgh, Pennsylvania 11. Psychological fiction

Prequel to: Wish You Were Here and Emily, Alone.

A 75-year-old retired engineer looks out on 1998 and sees a world he suspects has passed him by, and weighs his life's dreams against his regrets.

O'Nan, Stewart, 1961-

The **names** of the dead / Stewart O'Nan. Doubleday, 1996. 399 p.

ISBN 0385481926

1. Vietnam veterans 2. Stalking 3. Separated men (Marital relations) 4. Vietnam War, 1961-1975 5. Father and adult son 6. Stalkers 7. New York (State) 8. Thrillers and suspense

LC 95-36745

Oklahoma Book Award for Fiction, 1997.

After his wife leaves him, Larry Markham tries to win her back while confronting several other difficult personal problems, a situation that becomes complicated when he is stalked by an assassin

"O'Nan's language is powerfully restrained; his word pictures of the war and its effect on the men who fought there are fresh and vivid. He rightfully refuses to pander to our desire for easy answers and happy endings." Booklist.

O'Nan, Stewart, 1961-

The **night** country / Stewart O'Nan. Picador, 2004, c2003. 229 p.

ISBN 9780312424077

1. Life change events 2. Traffic accident victims 3. Halloween 4. Ghosts -- Connecticut 5. Teenagers with brain injuries 6. City life 7. Teenagers 8. Connecticut 9. Thrillers and suspense

LC bl2005001507

Originally published as The darkness on the edge of town: New York : Farrar, Straus and Giroux, 2003.

A tragic car accident that kills three teens while leaving one hospitalized with brain damage and another suffering with guilt yields more pain one year later when the spirits of the three dead kids return to torment the survivors.

"O'Nan is wonderful at describing teenage ritual, the simultaneous desire for the comforting familiarity of friends and the lust for speed and novelty and excitement that will lift teenagers out of the confines of their suburban town, the routine of school, out of their own restless bodies." New York Times Book Review.

O'Nan, Stewart, 1961-

The **odds** : a love story / Stewart O'Nan. Viking, 2012. 179 p.

ISBN 9780670023165

1. Husband and wife 2. Debt 3. Second chances 4. Casinos 5. Honeymoons 6. Married people 7. Middle-aged couples 8. Faith 9. Forgiveness 10. Marital conflict 11. Niagara Falls 12. Literary fiction

"A middle aged couple goes all in for love at a Niagara Falls casino."--, Provided by publisher.

O'Nan, Stewart, 1961-

Snow angels / Stewart O'Nan. Doubleday, 1994. 305 p.
ISBN 0385475748

1. Memories 2. Small town life -- Pennsylvania 3. Fifteen-year-old boys -- Pennsylvania 4. Children of divorced parents -- Pennsylvania 5. Pennsylvania 6. Psychological fiction

LC 9412037

ALA Notable Book, 1996.

A small-town tragedy with strong characterization. A grown man recounts two interwoven events which occurred when he was a boy, the break up of his family and the murder of his baby sitter. By the author of In the Walled City.

"The author weaves together these seemingly disparate small-town tragedies--one narrated in the first person, the other in the third--with consummate skill, seamlessly shifting the focus among characters he wishesto make the reader care about." Library Journal.

O'Neill, Heather

* The **Lonely** Hearts Hotel : a novel / Heather O'Neill. Riverhead Books, 2017. 416 p.

ISBN 9780735213739

1. Depression era (1929-1941) 2. First loves 3. Soul mates 4. Child prodigies 5. Separated couples 6. Organized crime 7. Lovers' reunions 8. Orphans 9. Pianists 10. Montreal, Quebec 11. Love stories 12. Historical fiction

LC 2016036295

Quebec Writers' Federation Literary Awards, Hugh MacLennan Prize for Fiction, 2017.

Longlisted for The Baileys Women's Prize for Fiction, 2017.

Two orphaned soul mates in Montreal--one a piano prodigy, the other a dancing savant--dream up a plan for the most extraordinary circus show the world has ever seen against a backdrop of the Great Depression.

"O'Neill's prose is crisp and strange, arresting in its frankness; much like the novel itself, her writing is both gleefully playful and devastatingly sad. Big and lush and extremely satisfying; a rare treat." Kirkus.

O'Neill, Jamie

At **swim,** two boys : a novel / Jamie O'Neill. Scribner, 2002, c1997. 572 p.

ISBN 0743222946

1. 1910s 2. Easter Rising, 1916 3. Male friendship 4. Swimming 5. Teenage boys 6. Gay teenagers 7. Rebels 8. Family relationships 9. Teenage boy/boy relations 10. Ireland -- History -- Easter Rising, 1916 11. Dublin, Ireland 12. LGBTQIA fiction 13. Literary fiction 14. Historical fiction

LC 2001057694

Lambda Literary Award for Gay Men's Fiction, 2002.

In a story set against the backdrop of Dublin in 1915, two boys who meet at the local swimming hole plan to swim to an island in Dublin Bay the following Easter, but their plans coincide with the Easter uprising--a historic rebellion that changes their lives.

"In this novel the cause of Ireland and the cause of gay people fuse with a complete lack of apology or embarrassment. . . . O'Neill is not, however, being patly outrageous; the closeness and exactness of his vision prove that." New York Times Book Review.

O'Neill, Joseph, 1964-
Netherland / Joseph O'Neill. Pantheon Books, 2008. 256 p.

ISBN 9780307377043
1. Marital conflict 2. Cricket (Sports) 3. September 11 Terrorist Attacks, 2001 -- Influence 4. Financial planners 5. Husband and wife 6. Dutch in the United States 7. Trinidadians in the United States 8. West Indian Americans 9. Immigrants 10. Entrepreneurs 11. Hotels 12. Gambling 13. Loneliness in men 14. Single-parent families 15. Self-discovery in men 16. New York City 17. Psychological fiction
LC 2007033711
First published: 2008.
Includes reading group notes.
PEN-Faulkner Award, 2009.
Shortlisted for the International IMPAC Dublin Literary Award, 2010

Abandoned amid the offbeat inhabitants of the Chelsea Hotel when his English wife and son return to London following September 11th, Hans, a banker originally from the Netherlands, struggles to find himself in his adopted country.

"This novel is narrated by a Dutch financier whose privileged Manhattan existence is upended by the events of Sept. 11, 2001. When his wife departs for London with their small son, he stays behind, finding camaraderie in the unexpectedly buoyant world of immigrant cricket players, most of them West Indians and South Asians, including an entrepreneur with Gatsby-size aspirations." New York Times Book Review.

Oakley, Colleen
You were there too / Colleen Oakley. Berkley, 2020. 352 p.

ISBN 9781984806468
1. Married women 2. Strangers 3. Love triangles 4. Dreams 5. Women artists 6. Men/women relations 7. Husband and wife 8. Commitment (Psychology) 9. Fate and fatalism 10. Marriage 11. Infertility 12. Small towns 13. Pennsylvania 14. Love stories 15. Women's lives and relationships 16. Mainstream fiction
LC 2019017291
When she and her husband move to a small town in Pennsylvania, Mia Graydon encounters the stranger she has been dreaming about for years--who, it turns out, has been dreaming of her, too--and together, determined to understand, they search for answers.

"Fans of relationship fiction that explores women's inner lives and choices by Jennifer Weiner or Amy Hatvany will be unable to put this book down." Booklist.

Oates, Joyce Carol, 1938-
The accursed / Joyce Carol Oates Ecco Press, 2013 688 p.

ISBN 9780062231703
1. Wilson, Woodrow, 1856-1924 2. Cleveland, Grover, 1837-1908 3. Sinclair, Upton, 1878-1968 4. 20th century 5. 1900s (Decade) 6. Supernatural 7. Upper class 8. Curses 9. Temptation 10. Weddings 11. Clergy 12. British Americans 13. Missing persons 14. Visions 15. Violence 16. New Jersey 17. Princeton, New Jersey 18. Gothic fiction 19. Literary fiction

While Woodrow Wilson is president of Princeton University at the turn of the 20th century, a strange European prince, possibly the Devil himself, befuddles members of Princeton's social elite. Several disturbing events occur before the prince runs away with a bride who is the granddaughter of a prominent clergyman. Princeton seems to be cursed,

and the question is, can the curse be broken by the end of this surreal historical novel? - Description by Katherine Bradley Johnson.

Oates, Joyce Carol, 1938-
* Because it is bitter, and because it is my heart / Joyce Carol Oates. Dutton, 1990. 405 p.

ISBN 0525248609
1. 1950s 2. Interracial romance 3. Murder 4. Racism 5. Families 6. African Americans 7. Social classes 8. Family problems 9. New York (State) -- Race relations 10. Psychological fiction 11. Literary fiction
LC 89025965
National Book Award for Fiction finalist, 1990
Iris Courtney, a young white woman living in upstate New York in the decade prior to the Civil rights movement, begins a clandestine relationship with Jinx Fairchild, a black man who had defended her in a fatal street fight with a white man

"At its best, the novel awakens the reader to something like the unexpected new comprehensions of the universe that Iris experiences." The New York Review of Books.

Oates, Joyce Carol, 1938-
Blonde : a novel / Joyce Carol Oates. Ecco Press, 2000. 738 p.

ISBN 0060196076
1. Monroe, Marilyn, 1926-1962 2. Film actors and actresses 3. Adult child abuse victims 4. Men/women relations 5. Sexuality 6. Mothers and daughters 7. Dysfunctional families 8. Marital conflict 9. Compulsive behavior in women 10. Expectation (Psychology) 11. Identity (Psychology) 12. Drug use 13. Social acceptance 14. Self-esteem in women 15. Hollywood, California 16. Biographical fiction 17. Literary fiction
National Book Award for Fiction finalist, 2000.
Pulitzer Prize for Fiction finalist, 2001.
A fictional recreation of the life of Marilyn Monroe recounts the tale of her rise to stardom, as seen from Marilyn's perspective.

"Joyce Carol Oates takes the boldest path to comprehending 'the riddle, the curse of Monroe' by proceeding directly and frankly to fiction. Her novel 'Blonde' is fat, messy and fierce. It's part Gothic, part kaleidoscopic novel of ideas, part lurid celebrity potboiler, and it is seldom less than engrossing." New York Times Book Review.

Oates, Joyce Carol, 1938-
A book of American martyrs / Joyce Carol Oates. Ecco, 2017. 768 p.

ISBN 9780062643049
1. Small towns 2. Fundamentalists 3. Violence against abortion clinics 4. Grief 5. Murder 6. Murderers 7. Evangelicalism 8. Abortion providers 9. Families of murder victims 10. Abortion provider shootings 11. Abortion -- Religious aspects -- Christianity 12. Ohio 13. Psychological fiction 14. Crime fiction
LC bl2016053525
Traces the intricately linked lives of a grieving family and an ardent Evangelical patriarch who has assassinated a small-town abortion doctor in the name of God.

Oates, Joyce Carol, 1938-
Broke heart blues : a novel / Joyce Carol Oates. Dutton, 1999. 369 p.

ISBN 0525944516
1. 1960s 2. Teenage murderers 3. Dysfunctional families 4. Celebrities 5. Small towns 6. Family problems 7. Class reunions 8. Fame 9. New York (State) 10. Psychological fiction 11. Literary

fiction

LC 98-51570

John Reddy Heart, a handsome young heartthrob, becomes the obsession of a small town in New York State during a sensational trial after a man is murdered in his mother's house.

"Oates dramatizes how wanting and memory compete. It's about how lonely, unhappy people mythologize their adolescence. . . . This is not a bashful or subtle book. It doesn't woo you so much as run you down." New York Times Book Review.

Oates, Joyce Carol, 1938-

Carthage / Joyce Carol Oates. HarperCollins, 2014 482 p.
ISBN 9780062208125

1. Missing persons 2. Small town life 3. Veterans 4. Iraq War veterans 5. Missing persons investigation 6. Family relationships 7. New York (State) 8. Adirondack Mountains, New York 9. Mysteries

When a young girl disappears near a community in the Adirondacks, the people of the town of Carthage must face the fact that an Iraq War veteran is the prime suspect.

"Once again, Oatess gift for exposing the frailty--and selfishness--of humans is on display." Publishers Weekly.

Oates, Joyce Carol, 1938-

The **doll-master** : and other tales of terror / Joyce Carol Oates. The Mysterious Press, 2016. 317 p.
ISBN 9780802124883

1. Suspicion 2. Obsession 3. Life change events 4. Psychology 5. Horror 6. Short stories

Collects six stories.

Bram Stoker Award for Best Fiction Collection, 2016.

A collection of six psychologically daring stories by the National Book Award-winning author of them includes the tale of a boy's obsession with a doll in the aftermath of a cousin's leukemia-related death and a teen's confrontation with an intruder while housesitting for her teacher.

"This devils half-dozen of dread and suspense is a must read." Publishers Weekly.

Oates, Joyce Carol, 1938-

* **Evil** eye : four novellas of love gone wrong / Joyce Carol Oates. The Mysterious Press, 2013. vii, 216 p.
ISBN 9780802120472

1. Secrets 2. Lovers 3. Husband and wife 4. Entitlement attitudes 5. Revenge 6. Vulnerability in women 7. Men/women relations 8. Family relationships 9. Gothic fiction 10. Short stories

Featuring four stories of love gone horribly wrong, this collection includes "The Flatbed," in which Cecelia, in order to enjoy the pleasures of intimacy with the love of her life, is forced to come face-to-face with the vile man who stole her innocence when she was just a child.

Oates, Joyce Carol, 1938-

* The **falls** : a novel / Joyce Carol Oates. Ecco, 2004. xiv, 481 p.
ISBN 0060722282

1. 20th century 2. Widows 3. Survivors of suicide victims 4. Community life 5. Lawyers 6. Husband and wife 7. Family and suicide 8. Family problems 9. Men/women relations 10. Waterfalls 11. Insecurity (Psychology) 12. Landfills 13. Love Canal Chemical Waste Landfill, Niagara Falls, New York 14. Suing (Law) 15. New York (State) 16. Niagara Falls 17. Psychological fiction 18. Domestic fiction 19. Literary fiction

LC 2004043310

Follows the interconnected and secretive lives of parents and their children when they are challenged by circumstances outside their

family, in a tale set against a backdrop of Niagara Falls in the mid-twentieth century.

"The broad canvas, frank carnality and family melodrama of 'The Falls' may not signal literary sublimity, but they do propel Ms. Oates into the mainstream. This novel could easily be mistaken for the work of a more visceral, less august storyteller. And if she strains to incorporate chemical waste into an otherwise intimate and high-strung narrative, the mixture is as effective as it is forced." New York Times.

Oates, Joyce Carol, 1938-

Foxfire : confessions of a girl gang / Joyce Carol Oates. Dutton, 1993. 328 p.
ISBN 9780525936329

1. 1950s 2. Female gangs 3. Revenge 4. Murder 5. Sexually abused teenagers 6. Courage in teenage girls 7. Teenage girls -- Friendship 8. New York (State) 9. Psychological fiction 10. Literary fiction

LC 92043858

Five teenage girls from upstate New York in the 1950s form a blood sisterhood to protect one another against the world and its oppressors, until their leader's disastrous act of revenge puts all their lives in turmoil.

Oates, Joyce Carol, 1938-

A **garden** of earthly delights / Joyce Carol Oates. Modern Libary, 2003. ix, 404 p.
ISBN 0812968344

1. 1930s 2. Children of migrant workers 3. Fathers and daughters 4. Poor women 5. Independence in women 6. Women's role 7. Mothers and sons 8. Depressions -- 1929-1941 9. Psychological fiction 10. Domestic fiction 11. Literary fiction

LC 2002038012

This complete revision of Oates' book by the same title (originally published in 1967) includes a new afterword.

The daughter of a migrant worker finds her life in the deprived and ugly transient world shaped by her father, lover, husband, and son.

"The book has much to say of society's indifference to the plight of the disadvantaged, and of the shallowness of a way of life based entirely on getting and spending." Library Journal.

Oates, Joyce Carol, 1938-

The **gravedigger's** daughter : a novel / Joyce Carol Oates. Ecco, 2007. 592 p.
ISBN 9780061236822

1. 1960s 2. Gravediggers 3. Children of immigrants 4. Mothers and sons 5. Jewish American families 6. Husband and wife 7. Separated women (Marital relations) 8. Serial murderers 9. Family problems 10. Identity (Psychology) 11. Family violence 12. Mistaken identity 13. Men/women relations 14. Self-discovery in women 15. Resilience (Personal quality) 16. New York (State) 17. Psychological fiction 18. Literary fiction

LC 2006048546

National Book Critics Circle Award for Fiction finalist, 2007

The daughter of a German high school teacher who was forced to work as a gravedigger after immigrating to upstate New York, Rebecca begins a life-changing pilgrimage throughout America in the wake of a prejudice-motivated tragedy.

"This is neither a depressing story nor an uplifting one. Oates succeeds here, as she often does, in making such judgments feel simple-minded. What it all seems is true and therefore moving and somewhat terrible, but in an exhilarating way. Every aspect of the ungainly plot feels right, including its ungainliness." Washington Post Book World.

Oates, Joyce Carol, 1938-

* **I** lock my door upon myself / Joyce Carol Oates. Ecco Press, 1990. 98 p.

ISBN 9780880012607

1. 1900s (Decade) 2. Interracial romance 3. Small town life 4. Married women 5. African American men 6. Farm life 7. Racism 8. Dowsers 9. Grandmothers 10. New York (State) -- Race relations 11. Psychological fiction 12. Historical fiction 13. Literary fiction

LC 90031878

A fictional biography of Edith Margaret Freilicht offers a complex portrait of the willful, eccentric, and enigmatic "Calla"--an elusive woman who views her world as through a dream--and her relationship with Tyrell Thompson, an itinerant black farm worker.

"Is this all a parable of the artist's position as an observer and interpreter of society? Is it an illustration of how a writer constructs a coherent story out of disjointed events? Either way, it provokes thought." The Atlantic.

Oates, Joyce Carol, 1938-

Jack of spades : a tale of suspense / Joyce Carol Oates. The Mysterious Press, 2015. 224 p.

ISBN 9780802123947

1. Secrets 2. Authors 3. Anonyms and pseudonyms 4. Characters and characteristics in literature 5. Plagiarism 6. Reputation 7. Psychological suspense

Enjoying his successful career and devoted family, a best-selling writer secretly authors a masochist-themed series that threatens his respectable community standing and becomes subject to a plagiarism lawsuit.

"As this tour de force reveals, Oates is a master of bleak literary fiction and its (sometimes) poor relation, crime/noir fiction. Examining and delineating insanity, obsession, paranoia, alcoholism, manipulation, and murder, not to mention book collecting and writer's block, this tale of suspense makes for another high-caliber Oatesian outing, displaying flair, noir sophistication, and King-like flourishes." Library Journal.

Oates, Joyce Carol, 1938-

Little bird of heaven : a novel / Joyce Carol Oates. Ecco, 2009. 442 p.

ISBN 9780061829833

1. Loss (Psychology) 2. Murder suspects 3. Suspicion 4. Small towns 5. Young women -- Death 6. Compulsive behavior 7. Obsession 8. Family problems 9. Family relationships 10. Identity (Psychology) 11. Fathers and sons 12. Guilt 13. Fathers and daughters 14. Erotic love 15. New York (State) 16. Psychological fiction 17. Literary fiction

Shortlisted for the International IMPAC Dublin Literary Award, 2011

After Zoe Kruller is murdered, the Sparta, New York, police target her estranged husband Delray Kruller and her lover Eddy Diehl, leading the Krullers' son Aaron and Eddy Diehl's daughter Krista to become obsessed with one another, each believing the other's father is guilty.

"The narrators of this novel, set in upstate New York, are an angry young man whose mother is murdered and a shy, introspective young woman whose father is a suspect. But the character who leaps most off the page is the victim, Zoe Kruller. . . . She abandons her son, Aaron, and her husband, Delray. She has an affair with Eddy Diehl, whose daughter Krista finds life in their small town of Sparta almost impossible to bear. And singing with her band, the Black River Breakdown, she wears spangly outfits, enchants the townspeople and belts out the song that gives the novel its title. . . . Krista and Aaron meet as teenagers. He's a gruff, rough, half-Indian guy with tattoos and little use for school. She is a blond waif, trying to tough it out on the basketball court to win the affection of her daddy and the respect of her peers. But it is her

longing for Aaron that rules her life, particularly after Zoe Kruller is found murdered. Her death seals their connection forever, even though they rarely speak and, when they are together, the conditions are as far from romantic as you can get. . . . Oates deftly merges the personalities of Zoe, Eddy, Krista and Aaron into what is essentially a mystery." St. Louis Post-Dispatch.

Oates, Joyce Carol, 1938-

Marya : a life / Joyce Carol Oates. E. P. Dutton, 1986. 310 p.

ISBN 9780525243748

1. Women -- Identity 2. Self-fulfillment in women 3. Self-discovery in women 4. Identity (Psychology) 5. Women college teachers 6. Family problems 7. Psychological fiction 8. Literary fiction

LC 85016283

Limns an emotionally incisive, hauntingly resonant portrait of a modern woman in search of self-understanding and fulfillment.

"Marya's development and her innermost fears and insecurities are revealed in a very personal, almost autobiographical manner. A major work by an important writer." Library Journal.

Oates, Joyce Carol, 1938-

Middle age : a romance / Joyce Carol Oates. Ecco, 2001. 464 p.

ISBN 0066209463

1. Sudden death 2. Middle-age 3. Rich people -- New York (State) 4. Men/women relations 5. Extramarital affairs 6. Identity (Psychology) 7. Loss (Psychology) 8. New York (State) 9. Psychological fiction 10. Literary fiction

LC 2001023062 d

The death of sculptor Adam Berendt finds his survivors--mostly middle-aged folks living in an upscale community on the Hudson--grieving and unexpectedly influenced by their charismatic friend's untimely demise.

"So often dark and malicious, Oates is oddly lighthearted in this gawky but mordant novel about people caught in that awkward transitional stage between youth and old age." Christian Science Monitor.

Oates, Joyce Carol, 1938-

* **My** life as a rat / Joyce Carol Oates. HarperCollins, 2019. 304 p.

ISBN 9780062899835

1. Dysfunctional families 2. Murder witnesses 3. Racism 4. Family secrets 5. Regret 6. Loyalty 7. Options, alternatives, choices 8. Purpose in life 9. Identity (Psychology) 10. Murder 11. Psychological fiction 12. Literary fiction

Exiled from her family and church since the age of 12 for testifying honestly about a racist murder, a young woman reflects on the wrenching choice she was forced to make between her family and the truth.

Oates, Joyce Carol, 1938-

Pursuit / Joyce Carol Oates. Mysterious Press, 2019. 144 p.

ISBN 9780802147912

1. Newlyweds 2. Nightmares 3. Husband and wife 4. Accidents 5. Secrets 6. Psychic trauma 7. Memories 8. Child abuse 9. Psychological suspense

As a child, Abby had the same recurring nightmare night after night, in which she wandered through a field ridden with human skulls and bones. Now an adult, Abby thinks she's outgrown her demons, until, the evening before her wedding, the terrible dream returns and forces her to confront the dark secrets from her past she has kept from her new husband, Willem. The following day--less than 24 hours after exchanging vows--Abby steps out into traffic. As his wife lies in her hospital bed, sleeping in fits and starts, Willem tries to determine whether this was an absentminded accident or a premeditated plunge, and he quickly discovers a mysterious set of clues about what his wife might be hiding.

Oates, Joyce Carol, 1938-
* **Them** / Joyce Carol Oates. Modern Library, 2006, c1969. xxxiv, 546 p.
ISBN 9780345484406
1. 1960s 2. Dysfunctional families 3. Young women 4. Race relations 5. Working class families 6. Poor women 7. Poor people 8. Violence 9. Rape 10. Detroit, Michigan 11. Michigan 12. Psychological fiction 13. Literary fiction
Originally published: New York : Vanguard Press, 1969.
National Book Award for Fiction, 1970.
From the 1930s through the race riots of 1967, the members of the Wendall family, living in inner-city Detroit, struggle to understand the obscure forces constantly tearing at their lives and happiness. Winner of the National Book Award.

Oates, Joyce Carol, 1938-
* **We** were the Mulvaneys / Joyce Carol Oates. Dutton, 1996. viii, 454 p.
ISBN 0525942238
1. 20th century 2. Rural life 3. Date rape 4. Family problems 5. Family relationships 6. New York (State) 7. Psychological fiction 8. Literary fiction
LC 9617267
Judd Mulvaney, now age 30, and the youngest of the four Mulvaney children, looks back through his memories to tell the secrets that eventually ripped apart the fabric of his storybook family.
"Oates has written an uncharacteristically cathartic book with a provocatively happy ending. . . . Oates eloquently employs daily details, cataloguing Corinne's antiques, mapping Patrick's Ithaca jogging route, calculating the number of paint gallons required to spruce up High Point Farm. She is a vivid storyteller, and the occupations, names and places are rich in allusive imagery. . . . Oates is fascinated by the markings of kinship. Particularly impressive is her shaping of siblings' passions, allegiances and resentments." The Nation.

Oates, Joyce Carol, 1938-
Wild nights! : stories about the last days of Poe, Dickinson, Twain, James, and Hemingway / Joyce Carol Oates. Ecco Press, 2008. 238 p.
ISBN 9780061434792
1. Poe, Edgar Allan, 1809-1849 2. Dickinson, Emily, 1830-1886 3. Twain, Mark, 1835-1910 4. James, Henry, 1843-1916 5. Hemingway, Ernest, 1899-1961 6. Last days 7. Thought and thinking 8. Life change events 9. Death 10. Biographical fiction 11. Short stories 12. Literary fiction
Reimagines the final days of five major American writers, in a collection of short works written in the subtly nuanced language style of each.
"The classic authors who appear as fictionalized characters in Wild Nights! aren't the ones most of us met in Intro to American Literature. Edgar Allan Poe copulating with a one-eyed amphibian? Mark Twain pursuing pubescent girls? Henry James clubbing a cat to death? Joyce Carol Oates may cause a few elderly professors to keel over, but the rest of us can take perverse delight in her five surreal tales. In each, Oates imagines the final days of a famous author, drawing from biographical fact but freely embroidering with Gothic excess." Buffalo News

Obioma, Chigozie, 1986-
* The **fishermen** : a novel / Chigozie Obioma. Little, Brown & Co., 2015 297 p.
ISBN 9780316338370
1. 1990s 2. Brothers 3. Life change events 4. Tragedy 5. Prophecies 6. Family relationships 7. Small town life 8. Fishing 9. Fate and fatalism 10. Death 11. Nigeria 12. Literary fiction 13. Political fiction
Shortlisted for the Man Booker Prize, 2015.
In a Nigerian town in the mid 1990s, four brothers encounter a madman whose mystic prophecy of violence threatens the core of their close-knit family.
"Obioma excels at juxtaposing sharp observation, rich images of the natural world, and motifs from biblical and tribal lore; his novel succeeds as a convincing modern narrative and as a majestic reimagining of timeless folklore." Publishers Weekly.

Obioma, Chigozie, 1986-
* An **orchestra** of minorities / Chigozie Obioma. Little Brown & Co, 2019. 400 p.
ISBN 9780316412391
1. Farmers 2. Determination in men 3. Fate and fatalism 4. Free will and determinism 5. Interclass romance 6. Deception 7. Voyages and travels 8. Spirits 9. Poor men 10. Loss (Psychology) 11. Romantic love 12. Men/women relations 13. Nigeria 14. Cyprus 15. Literary fiction 16. Adaptations, retellings, and spin-offs
Shortlisted for the Booker Prize, 2019.
In a contemporary twist of Homer's *The Odyssey*, a guardian spirit recounts the tragic story of a Nigerian poultry farmer who sacrifices everything for the wealthy woman he loves.
"Influences like Homer's Odyssey, Shakespeare's Othello, and The Divine Comedy inform Obioma's examination of the Igbo tribe's cosmology of destiny vs. the Christian tenet of free will." Library Journal.

Obregon, Nicolas
Blue light Yokohama / Nicolas Obregon. Minotaur Books, 2017. 352 p. Inspector Iwata novels
ISBN 9781250110480
1. Family-killing 2. Signs and symbols 3. Workaholics 4. Detectives 5. Nightmares 6. Serial murders 7. Serial murder investigation 8. City life 9. Tokyo, Japan 10. Japan 11. Police procedurals
Newly reinstated Tokyo Homicide Division Police Inspector Iwata works with reluctant colleagues to investigate the brutal murder of an entire family and other deaths that are identified as the work of the same killer.
"Obregon's full-bodied prose is by turns gritty and poetic, and it's consistently energetic. Given the terrific chemistry between the two lead detectives, here's hoping this debut novel kicks off a new series." Kirkus.

Obreht, Tea
* **Inland** : a novel / Tea Obreht. Random House, 2019. 384 p.
ISBN 9780812992861
1. American Westward Expansion (1803-1899) 2. Pioneer women 3. Outlaws 4. Droughts 5. Loss (Psychology) 6. Sons 7. Ghosts 8. Camels 9. Newspapers 10. Arizona (Territory) 11. Southwest (United States) 12. Literary fiction 13. Historical fiction
LC 2018050729
An unexpected relationship between a frontierswoman riding out the Arizona Territory drought of 1893 and a former outlaw, who has the ability to see ghosts, inspires an epic journey across the West.

LIST OF FICTIONAL WORKS

Obreht, Tea

The **tiger's** wife : a novel / Tea Obreht. Dial Press, 2011. 352 p.

ISBN 9780385343831

1. Women physicians 2. Orphanages 3. Grandparent and child 4. Family secrets 5. Balkan Peninsula 6. Literary fiction 7. Parallel narratives

ALA Notable Book, 2012.

Orange Prize for Fiction, 2011.

National Book Award for Fiction finalist, 2011

Struggling to understand why her beloved grandfather left his family to die alone in a field hospital far from home, a young doctor in a war-torn Balkan country takes over her grandfather's search for a mythical ageless vagabond while referring to a worn copy of Rudyard Kipling's "The Jungle Book."

"Every word, every scene, every thought is blazingly alive in this many-faceted, spellbinding, and rending novel of death, succor, and remembrance." Booklist.

Ocampo, Silvina

Forgotten journey / Silvina Ocampo ; translated from the Spanish by Suzanne Jill Levine and Katie Lateef-Jan. City Lights Books, 2019, c1998. 120 p.

ISBN 9780872867727

1. Working class 2. Death 3. Women 4. Clothing 5. Short stories 6. Surrealist fiction 7. Translations -- Spanish to English

LC 2019027249

Originally published: Buenos Aires : Emece Editores , 1998.

Delicately crafted, intensely visual, deeply personal stories explore the nature of memory, family ties, and the difficult imbalances of love.

Ocampo, Silvina

The **promise** / Silvina Ocampo ; translated from the Spanish by Suzanne Jill Levine and Jessica Powell. City Lights Books, 2019, c2011. 144 p.

ISBN 9780872867710

1. Ship passengers 2. Memories 3. Women authors 4. Accident victims 5. Missing women 6. Self-perception in women 7. Surrealist fiction 8. Metafiction 9. Translations -- Spanish to English

LC 2019027247

Originally published : Lumen Press , 2011.

A dying woman's attempt to recount the story of her life reveals the fragility of memory and the illusion of identity.

Odell, Jonathan, 1951-

The **healing** : a novel / Jonathan Odell. Nan A. Talese/ Doubleday, 2012. 352 p.

ISBN 9780385534673

1. Plantations -- Mississippi 2. Women healers 3. Slavery 4. Healing 5. Loss (Psychology) 6. Grief in women 7. Children -- Death 8. Women slaves 9. Slaveholders 10. Midwives 11. Opium addiction 12. African American senior women 13. Mississippi 14. Historical fiction 15. Psychological fiction

LC 2011005998

Concerned about his wife's extensive grief over the loss of their daughter and worrying about a mysterious illness that is afflicting his slaves, Master Satterfield purchases a slavewoman known as a healer only to be further unsettled by her troubling predictions and possible inauthenticity.

Oe, Kenzaburo, 1935-

The **changeling** / Kenzaburo Oe ; translated from the Japanese by Deborah Boliver Boehm. Grove, 2010. 336 p.

ISBN 9780802119360

1. Brothers-in-law 2. Suicide 3. Loss (Psychology) 4. Male friendship 5. Grief in men 6. Authors 7. Ghosts 8. Memories 9. Self-discovery in men 10. Literary fiction 11. Translations -- Japanese to English

After he rekindles a decades-lost friendship with his brother-in-law, Goro Hanawa, and receives a series of tapes on which Goro has recorded his reflections on their friendship, writer Kogito Choko hears his friend commit suicide on one of the recordings, prompting him to travel to Berlin to confront ghosts from his own past, and that of his friend.

Oe, Kenzaburo, 1935-

* **Death** by water / Kenzaburo Oe ; translated from the Japanese by Deborah Boliver Boehm. Grove Press, 2015, c2009. 424 p.

ISBN 9780802124012

1. Senior men 2. Authors 3. Loss (Psychology) 4. Writer's block 5. Fathers -- Death 6. Drowning 7. Investigations 8. Family secrets 9. Theater companies 10. Japan 11. Literary fiction 12. Translations -- Japanese to English

Translation from the Japanese of: Suishi.

Originally published: Tokyo : Kodansha, 2009.

The recurring and literary alter ego of the Nobel Prize-winning author, Kogito Choko, searches for a red suitcase that may hold documents related to the details of his father's death during World War II.

"This novel, teeming with crises and disclosures, proceeds almost exclusively via conversation made up of intricate, literarily and dramaturgically knowledgeable, politically progressive, long speeches. And it is enchanting." Booklist.

Oe, Kenzaburo, 1935-

Nip the buds, shoot the kids / Kenzaburo Oe ; translated and introduced by Paul St. John Mackintosh and Maki Sugiyama. Marion Boyars, 1995. 189 p.

ISBN 0714529974

1. Juvenile delinquents -- Japan 2. Mountain life -- Japan 3. Plague -- Japan 4. Teenage boys -- Japan 5. Japan 6. Translations -- Japanese to English

LC 94040897

A group of deliquent boys are abandoned in a remote village during the Korean war and manage to survive by stealing food and hunting, only to face the possibility of death when the villagers return.

Oe, Kenzaburo, 1935-

* A **quiet** life / Kenzaburo Oe ; translated from the Japanese by Kunioki Yanagishita and William Wetherall. Grove Press, 1996. 240 p.

ISBN 0802115977

1. Families -- Japan 2. Young women -- Japan 3. Savant syndrome 4. Men with developmental disabilities 5. Young men 6. Children of authors 7. People with developmental disabilities -- Family relationships 8. Composers -- Japan 9. Brothers and sisters -- Japan 10. Japan 11. Literary fiction 12. Translations -- Japanese to English

LC 9625795

Originally published in Japan Shizuka-na seikatsu by Kodansha.

At the age of twenty, Ma-chen, a young woman, is forced to redefine her family and her life when she finds herself the head of the household due to her father's acceptance of a visiting professorship at an American university.

"A famous Japanese writer whose first name begins with K takes off with his wife for a year to become writer in residence at 'one of the several campuses of the University of Carolina,' leaving their almost equally famous son, an idiot savant who is a remarkable composer, in the care of their daughter, Ma-chan. It is Ma-chan, a conscientious young woman acutely aware of the responsibility that devolves on her during her parents' absence, who tells the story related in Kenzaburo Oe's novel 'A Quiet Life,' and the translators, Kunioki Yanagishita and William Wetherall, admirably succeed in conveying a certian archness of style that infuses the work with Ma-chan's personality." New York Times Book Review.

Oe, Kenzaburo, 1935-

Somersault : a novel / Kenzaburo Oe ; translated from the Japanese by Philip Gabriel. Grove Press, 2003. 570 p.

ISBN 0802117384

1. New religious movements 2. Religion 3. Spirituality 4. Faith 5. Charisma 6. Radicals 7. Kidnapping 8. Kidnapping victims 9. Cults 10. Cult leaders 11. Literary fiction 12. Translations -- Japanese to English

LC 2002029746

Ten years after recanting their teachings and abandoning their zealous and violent congregation, two men known only as the Patron and Guide of Humankind seek to overcome a radical faction while leading peaceful followers toward a new future.

"Through the believers' motivations for joining the cult, Oe explores the struggle of contemporary Japanese to situate themselves between a traditional culture and the bullet-train pace of the boom years." The New Yorker.

Offill, Jenny, 1968-

Dept. of speculation / Jenny Offill. Knopf, 2014. 176 p.

ISBN 9780385350815

1. Marriage 2. Families 3. Marital conflict 4. Interpersonal relations 5. College teachers 6. Authors 7. Musicians 8. Extramarital affairs 9. Literary fiction

LC 2013019367

Shortlisted for the International Dublin Literary Award, 2016

The unnamed narrator of this novel writes in short vignettes, starting with odd facts, memories of boys she loved, and recollections from her travels. But as a whole the book itself is a moving portrait of a marriage and a relationship, from early days filled with possibilities to recent difficulties and fears. Wide-ranging and speculative, this novel focuses on the role of a wife and mother. -- Description by Shauna Griffin.

"The 46 short chapters are told mostly in brief fragments and fly through the life of the nameless heroine. Her mind wanders from everyday tasks and struggles, the beginnings of her marriage, the highs and lows with her husband, the joys of having a daughter." Publishers Weekly.

Offill, Jenny, 1968-

* **Weather** / Jenny Offill. Alfred A. Knopf, 2020. 224 p.

ISBN 9780385351102

1. Social obligations 2. Anxiety in women 3. Families 4. Librarians 5. Marital conflict 6. Worry 7. End of the world 8. Everyday life 9. Podcasts 10. Parenting 11. Addicts 12. New York City 13. Literary fiction

LC 2019032408

Hired by her famous podcaster mentor to answer letters from increasingly polarized fans, a librarian who has acquired her education from a lifetime spent reading struggles between the limits of her knowledge and growing crises in the outside world.

"The tension between mundane daily concerns and looming apocalypse, the weather of our days both real and metaphorical, is perfectly captured in Offill's brief, elegant paragraphs, filled with insight and humor." Kirkus.

Offutt, Chris, 1958-

Country dark / Chris Offutt. Grove Press, 2018. 231 p.

ISBN 9780802127792

1. 20th century 2. Life change events 3. Bootleggers 4. Veterans 5. Parents of children with disabilities 6. Social workers 7. Imprisonment 8. Corruption 9. Murder 10. Kentucky 11. Southern Gothic 12. Historical fiction 13. Literary fiction

LC 2017051048

In rural Kentucky in the years after the Korean War, Tucker, a young veteran and bootlegger, is pushed into a life-altering act of violence by threats against his family.

Ogawa, Yoko, 1962-

The **housekeeper** and the professor / Yoko Ogawa ; translated from the Japanese by Stephen Snyder. Picador, 2009. 192 p.

ISBN 9780312427801

1. Men with brain injuries 2. Short-term memory 3. Household employees 4. College teachers 5. Mothers and sons 6. Mathematics 7. Men/women relations 8. Families 9. Housekeepers 10. Psychological fiction 11. Translations -- Japanese to English

LC 2006041568

A strange relationship blossoms between a brilliant math professor suffering from short-term memory problems following a traumatic head injury and the young housekeeper, the mother of a ten-year-old son, hired to care for him, in an enchanting novel that explores what it means to live in the present and to be part of a family, albeit an unusual one.

"A mysterious, suspenseful, and radiant fable. . . . The smart and resourceful housekeeper, the single mother of a baseball-crazy 10-year-old boy the Professor adores, falls under the spell of the beautiful mathematical phenomena the Professor elucidates, as will the reader, and the three create an indivisible formula for love." Booklist.

Ogawa, Yoko, 1962-

* The **memory** police : a novel / Yoko Ogawa ; translated from the Japanese by Stephen Snyder. Pantheon Books, 2019, c1994. 288 p.

ISBN 9781101870600

1. Memory 2. Authors 3. Lost articles 4. Missing persons 5. Loss (Psychology) 6. Power (Social sciences) 7. Authoritarianism 8. Dystopias 9. Islands 10. Memories 11. Police 12. Hiding-places (Secret chambers, etc) 13. Writing 14. Dystopian fiction 15. Translations -- Japanese to English

LC 2018057224

Originally published: Toyko : Kodansha, 1994.

National Book Award for Translated Literature finalist, 2019.

An Orwellian novel about the terrors of state surveillance finds a young novelist hiding her editor from mysterious authorities who would erase all memories of people who once existed.

Ogilvie, Elisabeth, 1917-2006

When the music stopped / Elisabeth Ogilvie. McGraw-Hill, 1989. 326 p.

ISBN 0070477922

1. Sisters -- Maine 2. Women authors -- Maine 3. Maine 4. Thrillers and suspense

LC 88028636

Eden, a writer, realizes that while she was finishing her third book unexpected events were developing in the town of Job's Harbor.

"Author Eden Winters, finds herself in the midst of local scandal and terrifying deaths. Set in a small town along the Maine coast, the plot turns on the return to town of two aging sisters who had left on the wings of scandal decades earlier. While there are plenty of people with reason to despise the returning ladies--who audaciously take up residence in the area's most elegant house--there are just as many people, such as Eden and her family, who are delighted to see them. When the women are found brutally murdered, suspects abound, including a stranger who alternately captures Eden's suspicions and heart. Well-crafted fiction that holds the reader's attention and avoids contrivance." Booklist.

Ohlsson, Kristina, 1979-

The **disappeared** : a novel / Kristina Ohlsson ; translated from the Swedish by Marlaine Delargy. Emily Bestler Books/ Atria, 2014. 406 p. Fredrika Bergman mysteries

ISBN 9781476734002

1. Murder investigation 2. Women detectives 3. Murder suspects 4. Police 5. Innocence (Law) 6. Authors 7. Widowers 8. Snuff films 9. Loss (Psychology) 10. Extramarital affairs 11. Sweden 12. Mysteries 13. Translations -- Swedish to English 14. Police procedurals 15. Scandinavian crime fiction

"Originally published in 2011 in Sweden as Änglavakter"--Title page verso.

Follows Fredrika Bergman's investigation into a missing student's murder, a case that is further complicated by additional killings and clues that lead to Fredrika's lover.

"This is a complicated yet fast-moving story, and the detectives all find themselves with personal connections to the case. Ohlsson excels at creating multilayered stories with substantive characters." Booklist.

Ohlsson, Kristina, 1979-

Hostage : a novel / Kristina Ohlsson ; translated from the Swedish by Marlaine Delargy. Emily Bestler Books/Atria Books, 2015, c2012. 387 p. Fredrika Bergman mysteries

ISBN 9781476734033

1. Terrorism -- Prevention 2. National security 3. Airplanes 4. International relations 5. Hijacking of aircraft 6. Terrorists 7. Former police 8. Sweden 9. Scandinavian crime fiction 10. Police procedurals 11. Translations -- Swedish to English

Originally published: Stockholm : Piratforlaget, 2012.

When a bomb threat is found on a New York-bound Boeing 747 from Stockholm, the demands directed at both the Swedish and U.S. governments, investigative analyst Fredrika Bergman must race against time to unravel a complex hijacking plot to save the plane and its passengers.

Ohlsson, Kristina, 1979-

Silenced : a novel / Kristina Ohlsson. Emily Bestler Books/ Atria, 2013, c2010. 344 p. Fredrika Bergman mysteries

ISBN 9781439198902

1. Murder investigation 2. Women detectives 3. Pregnant women 4. Hit-and-run victims 5. Vicars 6. Revenge 7. Police 8. Police misconduct 9. Rape 10. Immigrants 11. Extramarital affairs 12. Sweden 13. Mysteries 14. Translations -- Swedish to English 15. Police procedurals 16. Scandinavian crime fiction

Originally published as Tusenskonor: Stockholm : Pocketforlaget, 2010.

Finds Fredricka Bergman and her colleagues uncovering sinister connections between three seemingly unrelated cases including an assault that occurred 15 years earlier, a hit-and-run killing and the suspicious double suicide of a clergyman and his wife.

Ohlsson, Kristina, 1979-

Unwanted : a novel / Kristina Ohlsson ; translated from the Swedish by Sarah Death. Emily Bestler Books/Atria, 2012, c2009. 357 p. Fredrika Bergman mysteries

ISBN 9781439198896

1. Missing children 2. Murder investigation 3. Kidnapping 4. First impressions 5. Serial murderers 6. Revenge 7. Police 8. Crimes against children 9. Women detectives 10. Sweden 11. Translations -- Swedish to English 12. Mysteries 13. Police procedurals 14. Scandinavian crime fiction

LC 2011031787

Originally published as Askungar: Stockholm : Pocketforlaget, 2009.

Inspector Fredericka Bergman investigates the kidnapping and murder of a child who had been separated from her mother on a crowded train on a rainy Swedish summer day, a case that points to the work of a brilliant and ruthless killer.

Okorafor, Nnedi

* **Binti** / Nnedi Okorafor. Tom Doherty Asociates, 2015. 106 p. Binti

ISBN 9780765385253

1. Young women 2. Space warfare 3. Conflict resolution 4. Aliens 5. Space flight 6. Culture conflict 7. Himba (African people) 8. Interplanetary relations 9. Human/alien encounters 10. Universities and colleges 11. Space opera 12. Science fiction 13. African American fiction 14. Afrofuturism and Afrofantasy

Trilogy published together in one volume, 2019.

Her name is Binti, and she is the first of the Himba people ever to be offered a place at Oomza University, the finest institution of higher learning in the galaxy. But to accept the offer will mean giving up her place in her family to travel between the stars among strangers who do not share her ways or respect her customs. The world she seeks to enter has long warred with the Meduse, an alien race that has become the stuff of nightmares.

Okorafor, Nnedi

Binti : home / Nnedi Okorafor. Tom Doherty Asociates, 2015. 106 p. Binti

ISBN 9780765393111

1. Young women 2. Diplomacy 3. Aliens 4. Xenophobia 5. Space warfare 6. Homecomings 7. Culture conflict 8. Identity (Psychology) 9. Himba (African people) 10. Interplanetary relations 11. Human/alien encounters 12. Space opera 13. Science fiction 14. African American fiction 15. Afrofuturism and Afrofantasy

Trilogy published together in one volume, 2019.

It's been a year since Binti and Okwu enrolled at Oomza University. A year since Binti was declared a hero for uniting two warring planets. A year since she found friendship in the unlikeliest of places. And now she must return home to her people, with her friend Okwu by her side, to face her family and face her elders. But Okwu will be the first of his race to set foot on Earth in over a hundred years, and the first ever to come in peace. After generations of conflict can human and Meduse ever learn to truly live in harmony?

Okorafor, Nnedi

Binti : the night masquerade / Nnedi Okorafor. Tor Books, 2018 208 p. Binti

ISBN 9780765393135

1. Young women 2. Diplomacy 3. Aliens 4. Xenophobia 5. Homecomings 6. Culture conflict 7. Identity (Psychology) 8. Himba (African people) 9. Interplanetary relations 10. Human/alien

encounters 11. Space opera 12. Science fiction 13. African American fiction 14. Afrofuturism and Afrofantasy

Series complete in 3 volumes.

Trilogy published together in one volume, 2019.

Binti has returned to her home planet, believing that the violence of the Meduse has been left behind. Unfortunately, although her people are peaceful on the whole, the same cannot be said for the Khoush, who fan the flames of their ancient rivalry with the Meduse. Far from her village when the conflicts start, Binti hurries home, but anger and resentment has already claimed the lives of many close to her. Once again it is up to Binti, and her intriguing new friend Mwinyi, to intervene--though the elders of her people do not entirely trust her motives--and try to prevent a war that could wipe out her people, once and for all.

Okorafor, Nnedi

* **Who** fears death / Nnedi Okorafor. Daw Books, 2010. 304 p.

ISBN 9780756406172

1. Genocide 2. Far future 3. Women shamans 4. Survival (after nuclear warfare) 5. Interethnic conflict 6. Post-apocalypse 7. Spirituality 8. Racism 9. Sexism 10. Magic 11. Africa 12. Science fantasy 13. Coming-of-age stories 14. Apocalyptic fiction 15. African American fiction 16. Afrofuturism and Afrofantasy

Prequel: The Book of Phoenix.

Amelia Bloomer List, 2011

World Fantasy Award, 2011.

Born into post-apocalyptic Africa by a mother who was raped after the slaughter of her entire tribe, Onyesonwu is tutored by a shaman and discovers that her magical destiny is to end the genocide of her people.

Okparanta, Chinelo

* **Under** the udala trees / Chinelo Okparanta. Houghton Mifflin Harcourt, 2015 328 p.

ISBN 9780544003446

1. Civil war 2. Lesbians 3. Interethnic romance 4. Prejudice 5. Household employees 6. Refugees 7. Religion and homosexuality 8. Women/women relations 9. Nigeria 10. Political fiction 11. Coming-of-age stories 12. LGBTQIA fiction 13. Literary fiction

LC 2014044506

Amelia Bloomer List, 2017

Lambda Literary Award for Lesbian Fiction, 2016

Shortlisted for the International Dublin Literary Award, 2017.

A young Nigerian girl, displaced during their civil war, begins a powerful love affair with another refugee girl from a different ethnic community until the pair are discovered and must learn the cost of living a lie amidst taboos and prejudices.

"The fact that Nigeria criminalized same-sex marriages in 2014 makes Okparanta's tale that much more sobering and urgent. It is especially gratifying that one of the defining tag lines of the feminist movement, 'a woman without a man,' just might be co-opted here in another time and place." Booklist.

Oksanen, Sofi, 1977-

When the doves disappeared : a novel / Sofi Oksanen ; translated from the Finnish by Lola Rogers. Knopf, 2015. 336 p.

ISBN 9780385350174

1. Soviet Union. Army. 2. Second World War era (1939-1945) 3. 1940s 4. 1960s 5. Cousins 6. Deserters 7. Communism 8. Nazis 9. Secrets 10. Survival 11. Betrayal 12. Deception 13. Totalitarianism 14. Military occupation 15. World War II 16. Estonia -- History -- 1944-1991 17. War stories 18. Historical fiction 19. Parallel narratives 20. Translations -- Finnish to English

LC 2014034970

Originally published as: Kun kyyhkyset katosivat. Helsinki : Like Kustannus Oy, 2012.

Two former deserters from the Red Army during World War II try to keep their past a secret in 1963 Communist Estonia.

"Oksanen captures both the futility of the citizens of a tiny country who yearn for freedom and the dark heart of an opportunist who would sell out his own family in order to survive. This is powerful fiction that stirs history, war crimes, and psychology into a compelling mix." Booklist.

Okuizumi, Hikaru, 1956-

The **stones** cry out / Hikaru Okuizumi ; translated from the Japanese by James Westerhoven. Harcourt Brace, 1998. 138 p.

ISBN 0151003653

1. World War II veterans -- Japan 2. Geologists -- Japan 3. Guilt in men -- Japan 4. Memory 5. Japan 6. Psychological fiction 7. Translations -- Japanese to English

LC 98-14434

Japanese World War II veteran Tsuyoshi Manase, troubled by memories of the war's end, returns to civilian life, marries, and has children. But when his eldest son is gouged to death in a cave, suspicion falls on Manase, and his life begins to unravel.

"A monstrous tale, The Stones Cry Out is written with a lyrical beauty that only underscores the horror Manase's life becomes. As Okuizumi elegantly plays Manase's nightmare out, Manase is compelled to reenact the real atrocities he has tried so desperately to forget." Booklist.

Olaf Olafsson

The **sacrament** : a novel / Olaf Olafsson. Ecco Press, 2019. 292 p.

ISBN 9780062899873

1. Nuns 2. Memory 3. Catholic schools 4. Clergymen child sexual abusers 5. Child sexual abuse 6. Catholics 7. Errors 8. Witnesses 9. Power (Social sciences) 10. Investigations 11. Life change events 12. Redemption 13. Iceland 14. France 15. Psychological fiction 16. Literary fiction 17. Translations -- Icelandic to English

LC bl2019028916

Tells the haunting, vivid story of a nun whose past returns to her in unexpected ways, all while investigating a mysterious death and a series of harrowing abuse claims.

"Emotionally gratifying and spiritually challenging?a compelling novel that grabs the reader's psyche and won't let go." Kirkus.

Older, Malka, 1977-

Infomocracy / Malka Ann Older. Tom Doherty, 2016. 368 p. Centenal cycle

ISBN 9780765385154

1. Dystopias 2. Corporate power 3. Corporate greed 4. Elections 5. Resistance to government 6. Intelligence officers 7. Conspiracies 8. Dystopian fiction 9. Science fiction 10. Cyberpunk

It's been twenty years and two election cycles since Information, a powerful search engine monopoly, pioneered the switch from warring nation-states to global microdemocracy. The corporate coalition party Heritage has won the last two elections. With another election on the horizon, the Supermajority is in tight contention, and everything's on the line.

LIST OF FICTIONAL WORKS

Oldham, Nick, 1956-

Fighting for the dead / Nick Oldham. Severn House, 2012. 224 p. Henry Christie mysteries

ISBN 9780727882134

1. Detectives 2. Murder investigation 3. Rape investigation 4. Crimes against teenage girls 5. Conspiracies 6. Drowning 7. Deception 8. Robbery 9. Police -- Blackpool, England 10. Lancashire, England 11. Mysteries

Tackling the murder case of a teen that is complicated by the drowning death of a local businessman's wife, Henry Christie finds himself targeted by the killer when he uncovers a complex conspiracy stretching across Eastern Europe.

Oleksiw, Susan

The **wrath** of Shiva / Susan Oleksiw. Five Star, 2012. 308 p. Anita Ray mysteries

ISBN 9781432825911

1. East Indian American women 2. Americans in India 3. Missing persons 4. Aunt and niece 5. Exorcism 6. Murder 7. Murder investigation 8. India 9. Mysteries

LC 2011051011

Anita Ray is featured in several of Susan Oleksiw's short stories.

Oliveras, Priscilla

Their **perfect** melody / Priscilla Oliveras. Zebra Books, 2018. 328 p. Matched to perfection

ISBN 9781420144307

1. Police 2. Victim services 3. Protectiveness in men 4. Hispanic American families 5. Family relationships 6. Communities 7. Sexual attraction 8. Men/women relations 9. Chicago, Illinois 10. Multicultural romances 11. Contemporary romances

Inspired by Chicago police officer Diego Reyes's passion for music, life, family--and her-- Lili Maria Fernandez, haunted by tragedy and loss, learns to embrace her wild side once more in his arms.

"Sexy, sassy, and overflowing with music, complex emotions, and family-loving Latinx American and Puerto Rican characters, this romance is a compelling, often joyful read and perfectly wraps up the Perfection trilogy." Library Journal.

Olmstead, Robert

* **Coal** black horse / Robert Olmstead. Algonquin Books of Chapel Hill, 2007. 224 p.

ISBN 1565125215

1. American Civil War era (1861-1865) 2. Civil war 3. Teenage boys and horses 4. Quests 5. Teenagers and war 6. Rescues 7. Fathers -- Death 8. United States Civil War, 1861-1865 9. United States -- History -- Civil War, 1861-1865 10. Historical fiction

LC 2006042914

When Robey Childs's mother experiences a premonition about her husband, a Civil War soldier, she sends her only son to retrieve his father from the battlefield, accompanied by a horse that becomes his only companion as he makes his way through the destruction of war.

"This novel is mostly memorable as an exquisite corpse, a fictive vision of war so vivid and gruesome that it remains in the memory--grotesque, stiff and gape-mouthed--after every other detail of Olmstead's tale fades away." Paste..

Olmstead, Robert

The **coldest** night : a novel / Robert Olmstead. Algonquin Books, 2012. 287 p.

ISBN 9781616200435

1. 1950s 2. Teenage boy/girl relations 3. Korean War, 1950-1953

4. Runaway teenagers 5. Marines 6. Social classes 7. West Virginia 8. Korea -- History -- 1945- 9. Historical fiction 10. War stories 11. Love stories 12. Literary fiction

When Henry Childs is threatened by his first love's father, he enlists in the Marines to escape.

Olmstead, Robert

Far bright star / Robert Olmstead. Algonquin Books of Chapel Hill, 2009. 207 p.

ISBN 9781565125926

1. Villa, Pancho, 1878-1923 2. United States. Army History Punitive Expedition into Mexico, 1916. 3. 1910s 4. Soldiers -- United States 5. Revolutionaries -- Mexico 6. Outlaws 7. Self-discovery in men 8. Violence 9. Mexican-American Border Region 10. Literary fiction 11. Historical fiction 12. War stories

LC 2008041858

Spur Award for Best Western Novel (Short Novel), 2010.

The year is 1916. The enemy, Pancho Villa, is elusive. The terrain is unforgiving, the intense heat and dust both relentless and overpowering. Through the mountains and across the long dry stretches of Mexico, Napoleon Childs, an aging cavalryman, leads an expedition of inexperienced horse soldiers on seemingly fruitless searches. Napoleon has weathered the storms of battle with a toughness that has become like a second skin, with the Rattler, a horse who's as flinty and seasoned as he. But this time, Napoleon can't control one of his young soldiers who has a penchant for reckless, dramatic actions--and who singlehandedly, in his desire to prove himself, makes a move that is the beginning of the end. Before long, Napoleon's patrol is at the mercy of an enemy who is intent not only on killing Napoleon's men but on something much bigger: avenging a brutal act.

"Gleaming, spellbinding fiction . . . . Terrifying and abruptly beautiful, the new novel gleams with a masculine intensity; it is hard to read and hard to put down." Cleveland Plain Dealer.

Olsen, Tillie

Tell me a riddle / Tillie Olsen. Laurel, 1976, c1961. 116 p.

ISBN 9780385290104

1. Short stories 2. Literary fiction

Four short stories.

Originally published: New York : Delacorte Press, 1961.

Four short stories set in the United States are concerned with the suffering and tragedy of human experience.

Olshan, Joseph

Black diamond fall / Joseph Olshan. Polis Books, 2018 304 p.

ISBN 9781947993341

1. Missing persons investigation 2. College students 3. Police 4. Truth 5. Suspicion 6. Vandalism 7. Dishonesty 8. Criminal investigation 9. Interpersonal relations 10. Vermont 11. Police procedurals 12. Mysteries

Some feel that Flanders left on his own accord and is deliberately out of touch. Others, including detectives Nick Jenkins and Helen Kennedy, suspect that harm may have come to him. As Luke Flanders disappears, the Robert Frost house near the Middlebury campus is vandalized. There seems to be a link between the two events that the police are determined to discover.

Olson, Neil, 1964-

Before the devil fell / Neil Olson. Hanover Square Press, 2019. 320 p.

ISBN 9781335217554

1. College teachers 2. Children of aging parents 3. Witchcraft

4. Spirits 5. Secrets 6. Mothers and sons 7. Childhood friends 8. Witchcraft -- Rites and ceremonies 9. Death 10. Family history 11. New England 12. Boston, Massachusetts 13. Supernatural mysteries

Returning to his Boston village hometown to care for an aging parent, Will is embroiled in the case of a mysterious death and the New England witchcraft traditions upheld by his mother's spirit circle.

Ondaatje, Michael, 1943-
  Anil's ghost / Michael Ondaatje. Alfred A. Knopf, 2000. 311 p.
  ISBN 9780375410536
  1. Women forensic anthropologists 2. Massacres -- Sri Lanka 3. Civil war -- Sri Lanka 4. Dead -- Identification 5. Human rights activists 6. Women archaeologists 7. Interethnic relations 8. Genocide 9. Sri Lanka -- History -- 20th century 10. Literary fiction 11. Psychological fiction

  LC 99059208
  Governor General's Literary Award for English-Language Fiction, 2000.
  Giller Prize, 2000.
  Kiriyama Prize for Fiction, 2000.
  ALA Notable Book, 2001.
  A young forensic anthropologist is sent by an international human rights group to her homeland, Sri Lanka, to discover the source of the organized campaigns of murder engulfing the island.
  "Anil comes with Western-bred investigative passion: the certainty that facts are there to be unearthed and that truth is to be constructed out of them. Sarath, a polymorphous spirit and the book's most memorable figure, cautions that the real truth of his country is ambiguous and unobtainable. . . . It is Ondaatje's extraordinary achievement to use magic in order to make the blood of his own country real." New York Times Book Review.

Ondaatje, Michael, 1943-
  The **cat's** table / Michael Ondaatje. Alfred A. Knopf, 2011. 288 p.
  ISBN 9780307700117
  1. 1950s 2. Ocean travel 3. Eleven-year-old boys 4. Passenger ships 5. Boys -- Friendship 6. Childhood 7. Growing up 8. Literary fiction 9. Coming-of-age stories
  ALA Notable Book, 2012.
  Shortlisted for the Giller Prize, 2011
  In the early 1950s, an eleven-year-old boy in Colombo boards a ship bound for England. Looking back from adulthood, the narrator relates a tale about the magical, often forbidden, discoveries of childhood and a lifelong journey that begins unexpectedly with a sea voyage.
  "The book tells the tale of an 11-year-old boy named Michael who is on a boat trip from Colombo, Sri Lanka, to England in 1954. In the sections that take place on the boat, we are entirely in a boy's head and feverish point of view. It is also told by a Michael 50 years later, when he has become a celebrated writer and lives in Canada. His long past is behind him, but emigration has marked him. He has never truly felt at home anywhere in the world. . . . [The novel] expertly strums these cords of autobiography without overdoing it. As a result this small, and beautifully minor book, vibrates with the borrowed intimacy of real life. It also never force-feeds its young hero with wisdom he could not have acquired or stolen at such an age." Boston Globe.

Ondaatje, Michael, 1943-
  * The **English** patient : a novel / Michael Ondaatje. A. A. Knopf, 1992. 307 p.
  ISBN 9780679416784
  1. Great Britain. Army East Indian troops. 2. Second World War era

(1939-1945) 3. Burn victims 4. Military nurses 5. World War II -- Italy 6. Thieves 7. Spies 8. Loss (Psychology) 9. Soldiers -- Great Britain 10. Men/women relations 11. Love triangles 12. Extramarital affairs 13. Survival (after airplane accidents, shipwrecks, etc) 14. Italy -- History -- 20th century 15. Literary fiction 16. Historical fiction

  LC 92053089
  Booker Prize, 1992.
  Governor General's Literary Award for English-Language Fiction, 1992.
  Trillium Book Award, 1992.
  ALA Notable Book, 1993.
  At the end of World War II, the lives of four people--a young American nurse; her dying English patient; a handless American thief; and an Indian soldier in the British army--intertwine in a deserted Italian villa.
  "This is a poetic and solemn narrative of the horrible process of war, the discipline, displacement, loss, and sudden, desperate love. Ondaatje seems to whisper, even confess each scene to his readers, handling them gingerly like shards of shattered glass." Booklist.

Ondaatje, Michael, 1943-
  In the skin of a lion : a novel / Michael Ondaatje. Knopf, 1987. 243 p.
  ISBN 9780394563633
  1. Small, Ambrose, 1866-1919 2. 1920s 3. Immigrant workers 4. Missing persons 5. Labor unions 6. Men -- Canada 7. Actors and actresses 8. Men/women relations 9. Millionaires 10. Bridges -- Design and construction 11. Toronto, Ontario -- History -- 20th century 12. Literary fiction

  LC 87045340
  Toronto Book Awards, 1988.
  Trillium Book Award, 1987.
  Governor General's Literary Awards, English-language Fiction finalist
  Arriving in Toronto in the 1920s from the Canadian wilderness, Patrick Lewis experiences a series of adventures as he makes a living searching for a missing millionaire, tunnels beneath Lake Ontario, and falls in love.
  "Ondaatje is a beautiful writer. What he writes about most beautifully is work. Mr. Ondaatje is passionate about process, the way work, particularly construction of all kinds, is done and how it feels to do it. This is, of course, a rarity in fiction at any time, and one can only be grateful for a man who is not focused on the classroom, the bedroom and the bar." New York Times Book Review.

Ondaatje, Michael, 1943-
  * **Warlight** / Michael Ondaatje. Alfred A Knopf, 2018. 288 p.
  ISBN 9780525521198
  1. 20th century 2. Postwar life 3. Brothers and sisters 4. Guardian and ward 5. Eccentrics and eccentricities 6. Mentors 7. Betrayal 8. Loss (Psychology) 9. Family secrets 10. Consequences 11. Growing up 12. London, England 13. Coming-of-age stories 14. Literary fiction
  ALA Notable Book, 2019.
  Longlisted for the Man Booker Prize, 2018.
  Shortlisted for the Walter Scott Prize for Historical Fiction, 2019.
  Years after growing up in the care of a group of mysterious protectors who served in unspecified ways during World War II, a young man endeavors to piece together the truth about his parents and the unconventional education he received.
  "The multi-award-winning author of The English Patient turns in a new novel both mysterious and dramatic, featuring 14-year-old Nathaniel and older sister Rachel, whose parents leave them in the care of

a shadowy and possibly criminal individual called the Moth when they move to Singapore in 1945. The Moth's friends, connected by wartime service, have lots to teach the siblings, who face more confusion when the siblings' mother returns, mum about their father." Library Journal.

Onyebuchi, Tochi

* **Riot** baby / Tochi Onyebuchi. Tor, 2020, c2019. 176 p.
ISBN 9781250214751

1. 20th century 2. 21st century 3. Violence against African Americans 4. Psychic ability 5. Brothers and sisters 6. African American families 7. Racism 8. Injustice 9. Prisoners 10. Police brutality 11. Social change 12. United States 13. Political fiction 14. Dystopian fiction 15. Literary fiction

LC 2019041049

Ella and Kev are brother and sister, both gifted with extraordinary power. Their childhoods are defined and destroyed by structural racism and brutality. Their futures might alter the world. When Kev is incarcerated for the crime of being a young black man in America, Ella-through visits both mundane and supernatural-tries to show him the way to a revolution that could burn it all down. --, Provided by publisher.

"Onyebuchi (War Girls) paints a grim, dystopian portrait of contemporary America shot through with elements of the supernatural in this urgent, brutal work." Publishers Weekly.

Orange, Tommy, 1982-

* There **there** / Tommy Orange. Alfred A. Knopf, 2018. 294 p.
ISBN 9780525520375

1. Native American families 2. Culture conflict 3. Multiracial persons 4. Indians of North America 5. Powwows 6. Family reunions 7. City life 8. Addiction 9. Prejudice 10. Indians of North America -- Urban residence 11. Interpersonal relations 12. Oakland, California 13. California 14. Literary fiction

LC 2017038125

ALA Notable Book, 2019.
Hemingway Foundation/PEN Award, 2019.
Society of American Historians Prize for Historical Fiction (formerly the James Fenimore Cooper Prize), 2019.
Andrew Carnegie Medal for Excellence in Fiction finalist, 2019.
Pulitzer Prize for Fiction finalist, 2019.

A novel which grapples with the complex history of Native Americans; with an inheritance of profound spirituality; and with a plague of addiction, abuse and suicide, follows 12 characters, each of whom has private reasons for traveling to the Big Oakland Powwow.

Orczy, Emmuska Orczy,, Baroness, 1865-1947

The **old** man in the corner / Baroness Orczy. Pushkin Vertigo, 2018, c1908. 284 p.
ISBN 9781782275237

1. Edwardian era (1901-1914) 2. Amateur detectives 3. Tearooms 4. London, England -- History -- 1800-1950 5. Great Britain -- History -- Edward VII, 1901-1910 6. Mysteries 7. Short stories 8. Anthologies

"This welcome reissue of a 1908 collection by Orczy (The Scarlet Pimpernel) opens with a story in which the eponymous lead, whose real name is never revealed, sits down uninvited at the table of reporter Polly Burton in a London tea shop. As arrogantly as Sherlock Holmes, the interloper proclaims that 'there is no such thing as a mystery in connection with any crime, provided intelligence is brought to bear upon its investigation.'" Publishers Weekly

Orczy, Emmuska, Baroness, 1865-1947

* The **Scarlet** Pimpernel / Baroness Orczy. Modern Library, 2002, c1905. xviii, 271 p. Scarlet Pimpernel series
ISBN 9780812966114

1. Revolutionary France (1789-1799) 2. 1790s 3. Rescues 4. Secret identity 5. Heroes and heroines, English 6. Dandies 7. Disguises 8. Nobility 9. French Revolution, 1789-1799 10. Husband and wife 11. Chivalry 12. France -- History -- Revolution, 1789-1799 13. England -- History -- 18th century 14. Adventure stories

LC 08015153

Originally published: Hutchinson, 1905.

In 1792, during the French Revolution's Reign of Terror, an English aristocrat known to be an ineffectual fop is actually a master of disguises who, with a small band of dedicated friends, undertakes dangerous missions to save members of the French nobility from the guillotine.

Orenstein, Hannah

Love at first like / Hannah Orenstein. Atria Books, 2019. 320 p.
ISBN 9781982117795

1. Instagram (Electronic resource) 2. Women business owners 3. Social media 4. Engagement rings 5. Deception 6. Sisters 7. Engaged persons 8. Jewelers 9. Men/women relations 10. Brooklyn, New York City 11. New York City 12. Romantic comedies

LC 2019005677

When her Instagram following skyrockets over a mistaken rumor about her mystery engagement, a young jewelry shop owner hires an actor to keep up the ruse, which is complicated by her growing feelings for someone else.

"Orenstein's (Playing With Matches, 2018) writing is quick, witty, and compulsively readable, even when Eliza's desperate actions evoke cringes. Although the story is over the top, the feelings are real, and readers will be able to relate to Eliza's struggle to find her soul mate in the age of apps and social media. A classic wacky rom-com and an ideal summer read." Kirkus.

Orner, Peter

Love and shame and love : a novel / Peter Orner. Little, Brown and Co., 2011. 439 p.
ISBN 9780316129398

1. 20th century 2. Families 3. Jewish families 4. Frustration 5. Shame 6. Humiliation 7. Chicago, Illinois 8. Family sagas 9. Literary fiction

LC 2011022547

The interactions of four generations of the Popper family reveal the ways in which love, memory, and connections can make individuals whole or completely unravel them.

"Orner anatomizes family relationships with precision in a novel that spans three--and touches on four--generations. At the center of the author's examination is Alexander Popper, a fiction writer manqué (he tries in vain to write a good, sad story) and reluctant law-school graduate who winds up handling misdemeanor cases for the Cook County Public Defender. . . . [This] is a masterful, multifaceted novel. Readers will find both love and shame in abundance in Orner's teeming fictional world." Kirkus.

Orringer, Julie

* The **flight** portfolio : a novel / Julie Orringer. Alfred A. Knopf, 2019. 448 p.
ISBN 9780307959409

1. Fry, Varian, 1908-1967 2. Second World War era (1939-1945) 3. Righteous Gentiles in the Holocaust 4. World War II -- Jews -- Rescue 5. World War II -- Refugees 6. Journalists -- United States 7. Jews, French 8. Holocaust (1933-1945) 9. Rescues 10. Personal

conduct 11. Americans in France 12. Artists 13. Intellectuals 14. Men/men relations 15. Intrigue 16. France 17. Vichy (France) 18. Biographical fiction 19. Historical fiction

LC 2018044985

"This is a Borzoi book."

Presents a long-anticipated novel based on the story of Varian Fry's extraordinary effort to save the lives and work of Jewish artists fleeing the Holocaust.

"Brilliantly conceived, impeccably crafted, and showcasing Orringer's extraordinary gifts, this is destined to become a classic." Publishers Weekly.

Orringer, Julie

* The **invisible** bridge : a novel / Julie Orringer. Alfred A. Knopf, 2010. x, 602 p.

ISBN 9781400041169

1. Second World War era (1939-1945) 2. 1930s 3. 1940s 4. World War II -- Europe 5. Students 6. Jews 7. Brothers 8. Jews -- Persecutions 9. Men/women relations 10. Antisemitism 11. Europe -- History -- 20th century 12. Budapest, Hungary 13. Paris, France 14. Historical fiction 15. Love stories 16. Literary fiction

LC 2009046498

Edward Lewis Wallant Award, 2010.
RUSA Reading List, 2011.

A story of three brothers, of history and love, of marriage tested by disaster, of a Jewish family's struggle against annihilation, and of the dangerous power of art in a time of war.

"Andras is a Hungarian Jew studying in Paris as Hitler's influence begins to spread across a continent already riddled with anti-Semitism and bloodlust. He falls for fellow émigré Klara, and their world is soon rocked by war. Other characters weave in and out of the story line, but it's the love tethering Andras and Klara that powers the narrative's massive machinery. The Invisible Bridge is without a doubt an ambitious slice of literature, but Orringer fulfills her ambitions with crisp writing that never wanders far from the story's path. World War II is hardly undiscovered literary territory. Still, this stunning work manages to feel both original and part and parcel of the well-blazed tradition of historical novels that came before it." Entertainment Weekly.

Orstavik, Hanne, 1969-

Love / Hanne Orstavik ; translated from the Norwegian by Martin Aitken. Archipelago Books, 2018., c2013. 125 p.

ISBN 9780914671947

1. Mothers and sons 2. Small towns 3. Winter 4. Single mothers 5. Birthdays 6. Loneliness in women 7. Selfishness in women 8. Norway 9. Psychological fiction 10. Translations -- Norwegian to English

LC 2017022875

Originally published: Oslo : Forl, 2013.

A mother and son move to a village in northern Norway, each ensconced in their own world. Their distance has fatal consequences.

Orullian, Peter Vance

The **unremembered** / Peter Orullian. Tor, 2011. 640 p. Vault of heaven

ISBN 9780765325716

1. Orphans 2. Quests 3. Good and evil 4. Gods and goddesses 5. Adventurers 6. Heroes and heroines 7. Magic 8. Imaginary kingdoms 9. Courts and courtiers 10. Intrigue 11. Epic fantasy

LC 2010036105

"A Tom Doherty Associates book."

Millennia after a god is condemned to live among the hateful creatures he has created, the magical veil entrapping the god and his mon-

sters weakens, compelling bow hunter Than Junell and his companions to undertake a dangerous and secret journey to protect their people.

Orwell, George, 1903-1950

* **Animal** farm / George Orwell. Signet Classics, 1996, c1945. 140 p.

ISBN 9780451526342

1. Totalitarianism 2. Dystopias 3. Farm animals 4. Talking animals 5. Domestic animals 6. Political fiction 7. Allegories 8. Satirical fiction 9. Dystopian fiction 10. Modern classics

Originally published: [London] : Martin Secker & Warburg, 1945.

A satire on totalitarianism in which farm animals overthrow their human owner and set up their own government.

Orwell, George, 1903-1950

* **1984** : a novel / George Orwell. Harcourt Brace Jovanovich, 1984, c1949. 314 p.

ISBN 9780151660384

1. Dystopias 2. Totalitarianism 3. Near future 4. Resistance (Psychology) 5. Identity (Psychology) 6. Dystopian fiction 7. Science fiction 8. Modern classics

LC 8318442

Originally published: London: Secker & Warburg, 1949.

Portrays life in a future time when a totalitarian government watches over all citizens and directs all activities.

Osborne, David, 1951-

The **coming** / David Osborne. Bloomsbury Publishing USA, 2017. 400 p.

ISBN 9781632863850

1. Daytime Smoke 2. American Westward Expansion (1803-1899) 3. Indians of North America 4. Government relations with indigenous peoples 5. Land claims 6. First contact of indigenous peoples with Europeans 7. Indians of North America -- Relations with missionaries, traders, etc 8. Indians of North America -- Social life and customs 9. Indians of North America -- Wars 10. Genocide 11. Nez Perce Indians 12. United States -- Territorial expansion 13. The West (United States) -- History 14. Historical fiction 15. Biographical fiction

Spur Awards, Best Western Historical Novel, 2018.

An epic novel of native-white relations in North America, intimately told through the life of Daytime Smoke--the real-life red-haired son of explorer William Clark and a Nez Perce woman.

Osborne, Lawrence, 1958-

The **forgiven** : a novel / Lawrence Osborne. Hogarth, 2012. 272 p.

ISBN 9780307889034

1. Married people 2. Cultural differences 3. Fatal traffic accidents 4. Upper class 5. Social classes 6. Deserts 7. British in Morocco 8. Parties 9. Prejudice 10. Muslims 11. Race relations 12. Morocco 13. Literary fiction

LC 2011025942

A couple in a deteriorating relationship are involved in a fatal car accident on their way to an annual wild party at a friend's house deep in the Moroccan desert and must deal with the repercussions.

Osborne, Lawrence, 1958-

Only to sleep : a Philip Marlowe novel / Lawrence Osborne. Hogarth, 2018. 256 p. Philip Marlowe mysteries

ISBN 9781524759612

1. 1980s 2. Retirees 3. Senior men 4. Private investigators 5.

Widows 6. Rich people 7. Staged deaths 8. Septuagenarians 9. Murder investigation 10. Marlowe, Philip (Fictional character) 11. California 12. United States -- Boundaries -- Mexico 13. Mysteries 14. Hardboiled fiction

LC 2018017511

In 1988, 72-year-old Philip Marlowe must come out of retirement to investigate the death of Donald Zinn--supposedly drowned off his yacht, and leaving behind a much younger and now very rich wife.

Osondu, E. C.

Voice of America : stories / E.C. Osondu. Harper, 2010. 215 p.

ISBN 9780061990861

1. Nigeria 2. United States 3. Short stories

LC 2010005729

Collects 18 short stories.

An acclaimed African writer offers a debut collection of stories set both in Nigeria and the United States, which moves from the fears and dreams of boys and girls in African villages and refugee camps, to the disillusionment and confusion of young married couples living in America.

"These richly shaded tales explore old ways and new, wealth and poverty, myth and misapprehension. Though there is sadness here, the tone is deadpan, and the reader can imagine the storyteller's eyes crinkled in a smile." Booklist.

Osondu, E. C.

This house is not for sale : a novel / E.C. Osondu. Harper, 2015. 182 p.

ISBN 9780061990885

1. Large families 2. Houses 3. Family problems 4. Family relationships 5. Extramarital affairs 6. Parent and child 7. Communities 8. Eccentrics and eccentricities 9. Africa 10. Domestic fiction 11. Literary fiction

LC 2014013856

A young member of an extraordinary African-American family observes the larger-than-life people who shape his house's vibrant history, from his contradictory grandfather to the longtime rival owners of competing convenience stores.

Otsuka, Julie, 1962-

The **Buddha** in the attic / Julie Otsuka. Alfred A. Knopf, 2011. 144 p.

ISBN 9780307700001

1. Second World War era (1939-1945) 2. Mail order brides 3. Japanese in the United States 4. Assimilation (Sociology) 5. Identity (Psychology) 6. World War II 7. Marriage 8. Prejudice 9. Culture conflict 10. Japanese Americans -- Forced removal and incarceration, 1942-1945 11. World War II home front 12. San Francisco, California -- History -- 20th century 13. Historical fiction 14. Literary fiction

David J. Langum, Sr. Prize in American Historical Fiction, 2011

PEN-Faulkner Award, 2012.

Shortlisted for the International IMPAC Dublin Literary Award, 2013

National Book Award for Fiction finalist, 2011

Presents the stories of six Japanese mail-order brides whose new lives in early twentieth-century San Francisco are marked by backbreaking migrant work, cultural struggles, children who reject their heritage, and the prospect of wartime internment.

Otsuka, Julie, 1962-

When the emperor was divine : a novel / Julie Otsuka. Knopf, 2002. 141 p.

ISBN 0375414290

1. Second World War era (1939-1945) 2. 1940s 3. Japanese Americans -- Forced removal and incarceration, 1942-1945 4. World War II -- California 5. Concentration camps -- California 6. Japanese American families 7. Family relationships 8. Loss (Psychology) 9. World War II home front 10. California 11. Historical fiction 12. War stories

LC 2002020814

A story told from five different points of view, chronicles the experiences of Japanese Americans caught up in the nightmare of the World War II internment camps.

"Otsuka demonstrates a breathtaking restraint and delicacy throughout this supple and devastating first novel." Booklist.

Otto, Whitney

Eight girls taking pictures : a novel / Whitney Otto. Scribner, 2012. 352 p..

ISBN 9781451682694

1. 20th century 2. Women photographers 3. Photography 4. Feminism 5. Women artists 6. Creativity in women 7. Ambition in women 8. Women's role 9. Literary fiction 10. Biographical fiction

LC 2012009167

Amelia Bloomer List, 2013

A tale inspired by the lives of famous twentieth-century female photographers traces the progression of feminism and photography in various world regions as each woman explores private and public goals while balancing the demands of family and creativity.

Otto, Whitney

How to make an American quilt / Whitney Otto. Villard Books, 1991. 179 p.

ISBN 9780679400707

1. Small town life 2. Quiltmakers 3. Group quilting 4. Women 5. California 6. Women's lives and relationships

LC 90048233

The various passages in a woman's life are revealed through the emotions, personalities, attitudes, struggles, tragedies and triumphs, and life stories of a group of women who are members of a quilting circle in a small California town.

"Otto has tremendous insight and compassion, understanding the rareness of a perfect marriage, the anger of thwarted lives, and the vagaries of love and motherhood." Booklist.

Overholser, Wayne D., 1906-1996

Death of a cattle king : a western story / Wayne D. Overholser. Five Star, 2011. 188 p.

ISBN 9781432825171

1. Cattle ranches 2. Ranchers 3. Land claims 4. Widowers 5. Indians of North America 6. Frontier and pioneer life 7. Greed 8. Family relationships 9. Pacific Northwest -- History -- 19th Century 10. Westerns

LC 2011015379

"The Holt family traveled the Oregon Trail from Pennsylvania to the Northwest, where they established the modest Rainbow Ranch. Even after Sam's wife, Helen, dies, leaving him with two kids, Mary and Bruce, the ranch continues to prosper. But trouble arrives in the form of Morgan Drew, son of Sam's late best friend. Drew's ambition and greed become plain as he allies himself with the valley's biggest rancher. Now he intends to absorb the Holt ranch as well as all the other small claims in the valley. If Sam doesn't accept Drew's offer, the implied threat is that the

Rainbow will be taken by force. An Indian uprising puts a temporary hold on the land grab as the ranchers form an uneasy alliance to ward off the threat . . . . Like most of [Overholser's] work, this novel is driven less by violence and more by the timeless human emotions of greed, jealousy, and love." Booklist.

Overholser, Wayne D., 1906-1996

Law at Angel's Landing : a western story / Wayne D. Overholser. Five Star, 2010. 164 p.

ISBN 9781594149078

1. Mines and mineral resources 2. Gold mines and mining 3. Sheriffs 4. Law enforcement 5. Colorado 6. Westerns

LC 2010008448

"Mark Girard moved to Angel's Landing in the Colorado foothills as a young boy with his mother and father, who was a chase-the-rainbow gold miner. When the strike played out and the town was destined to be abandoned, the elder Girard wanted to pick up stakes and move to the next big strike. Mark's mother refused, opting for stability in the soon to be very tiny village. Mother, son, and the town all survived, with Mark becoming county sheriff. Overholser tells two stories here: the melancholy saga of a broken family reunited too late and the pendulum-swinging life of a boom-and-bust gold town. . . . Overholser, a consummate western storyteller with an eye for character and dialogue, delivers another solid effort." Booklist.

Overton, Hollie

The **runaway** / Hollie Overton. Redhook Books/Orbit, 2019. 439 p.

ISBN 9780316482257

1. Missing teenage girls 2. Foster mothers 3. Manipulation by women 4. Teenage girls 5. Runaways 6. Psychologists 7. Homeless teenagers 8. Police 9. Mental health 10. Los Angeles, California 11. Thrillers and suspense

LC 2019002121

Originally published in England, 2018.

The search for a teenage runaway sends her foster mother, a psychologist working for the LAPD, on a dangerous journey through Los Angeles' criminal underworld.

"Readers will root for the deeply empathetic Becca, who's devoted to helping society's most vulnerable, and Overton shines a light on the plight of the mentally ill, foster children, and the homeless while building plenty of tension. Fans of bighearted thrillers will find a lot to like." Publishers Weekly.

Owen, Howard, 1949-

The **bottom** / Howard Owen. Permanent Press, 2015 240 p. Willie Black mysteries

ISBN 9781579623920

1. Journalists 2. Serial murders 3. Threat (Psychology) 4. Real estate development 5. Crimes against teenage girls 6. Tattooing 7. Frameups 8. Murder investigation 9. Multiracial men 10. Richmond, Virginia 11. Virginia 12. Mysteries 13. Southern fiction

LC 2015013684

"Willie Mays Black, reporter/drinker/police gadfly, searches for a serial killer in Owen's (Parker Field, 2014, etc.) fourth crime caper. . . . Owen has a solid grip on people and place and the social and racial tensions buzzing through a city haunted by history--a perfect milieu for nuanced crime capers." Kirkus

Owen, Howard, 1949-

The **devil's** triangle / Howard Owen. Permanent Press, 2017 240 p. Willie Black mysteries

ISBN 9781579624996

1. Airplane accidents 2. Stalking 3. Journalists 4. Murder suspects 5. Murder investigation 6. Murder 7. Stalkers 8. Richmond, Virginia 9. Virginia 10. Mysteries 11. Southern fiction

LC 2017008730

Willie Black tries to uncover the reason a man named David Biggio crashed a twin-engine Beechcraft airplane into a Richmond bar.

Owen, Howard, 1949-

Oregon Hill / Howard Owen. Permanent Press, 2012. 240 p. Willie Black mysteries

ISBN 9781579622084

1. Journalists 2. Murder investigation 3. Innocence (Law) 4. Multiracial men 5. Crimes against women 6. Beheading 7. Richmond, Virginia 8. Virginia 9. Mysteries 10. Southern fiction

Reporter Willie Black investigates when a student, who attends the same university as his daughter, is murdered, embarking on a one-man crusade to identify the killer even after the police and his bosses consider the case closed.

Owen, Howard, 1949-

Parker Field / Howard Owen. The Permanent Press, 2014. 224 p. Willie Black mysteries

ISBN 9781579623616

1. Journalists 2. Murder investigation 3. Baseball players 4. Innocence (Law) 5. Multiracial men 6. Minor league baseball 7. Richmond, Virginia 8. Virginia 9. Mysteries 10. Southern fiction

When his mother's boyfriend is severely wounded by a shooter, reporter Willie Black's investigation uncovers players from the 1964 Richmond Virginians are being targeted.

Owen, Lauren, 1985-

The **quick** : a novel / Lauren Owen. Random House, 2014. 544 p.

ISBN 9780812993271

1. Victorian era (1837-1901) 2. 19th century 3. Secret societies 4. Vampires 5. Brothers and sisters 6. Gay men 7. Poets 8. Diary writing 9. Deception 10. Men/women relations 11. Men/men relations 12. London, England 13. Historical horror 14. Gothic fiction 15. Horror 16. Literary fiction

LC 2013018600

When a shy aspiring poet disappears from late-19th-century London after falling in love, his sister's ensuing confrontation with an institution of powerful men is aided by three underworld helpers.

Owens, Delia

* **Where** the crawdads sing / Delia Owens. G.P. Putnam's Sons, 2018. 320 p.

ISBN 9780735219090

1. 1960s 2. Hermits 3. Marshes 4. Suspicion 5. Loners 6. Coasts 7. Prejudice 8. Xenophobia 9. Rural women 10. Murder suspects 11. Wilderness survival 12. North Carolina 13. Literary fiction 14. Coming-of-age stories

LC 2018010775

Viewed with suspicion in the aftermath of a tragedy, a beautiful hermit who has survived for years in a marsh becomes targeted by unthinkable forces.

"Owens memorably depicts the small-town drama and courtroom theatrics, but perhaps best of all is her vivid portrayal of the singular North Carolina setting." Publishers Weekly.

The **Oxford** book of science fiction stories / edited by Tom Shippey. Oxford University Press, 1992 xxvi, 587 p.
ISBN 9780192803818
1. Science fiction
LC 2003265368
A collection of classic science fiction short stories features tales by H. G. Wells, Arthur C. Clark, Frederik Pohl, Clifford Simak, Brian Aldiss, Ursala K. LeGuin, and many others.

Oyeyemi, Helen
Boy, Snow, Bird : a novel / Helen Oyeyemi. Riverhead Hardcover, 2014. 320 p.
ISBN 9781594631399
1. 1950s 2. 1960s 3. Mothers and daughters 4. Identity (Psychology) 5. Beauty 6. Mirrors 7. Passing (Identity) 8. African Americans 9. Multiracial girls 10. Stepmothers 11. Stepdaughters 12. Family secrets 13. Family relationships 14. Fairy tales 15. Adaptations, retellings, and spin-offs 16. Magical realism 17. Literary fiction
LC 2013025053
A reimagining of the Snow White story recast as a story of family secrets, race, beauty, and vanity set in the United States during the 1950s and 1960s.
"Dense with fully realized characters, startling images, original observations and revelatory truths, this masterpiece engages the reader's heart and mind as it captures both the complexities of racial and gender identity in the 20th century and the more intimate complexities of love in all its guises." Kirkus.

Oyeyemi, Helen
Gingerbread : a novel / Helen Oyeyemi. Riverhead Books, 2019. 258 p.
ISBN 9781594634659
1. Mothers and daughters 2. Family recipes 3. Characters and characteristics in fairy tales 4. Gingerbread 5. Family history 6. Female friendship 7. Family secrets 8. Storytelling 9. Family relationships 10. London, England 11. Literary fiction 12. Magical realism 13. Adaptations, retellings, and spin-offs
LC 2018019890
Draws on the classic fairy-tale element of gingerbread in the story of a British family whose surprising legacy and secret past are tied to a favorite recipe.
"Readers familiar with Oyeyemi's work will not be surprised to learn that her latest plot sets off in one direction and immediately takes a hairpin curve in another (and another, and still another). The effect is heady, surreal, and disarming--you have to be willing to surrender to Oyeyemi's vision and the delicious twists and turns of her prose." Kirkus.

Oyeyemi, Helen
Mr. Fox / Helen Oyeyemi. Riverhead Books, 2011. 324 p.
ISBN 9781594488078
1. Authors 2. Writing 3. Muses (Persons) 4. Heroes and heroines 5. Death 6. Imagination 7. Dishonesty 8. Metafiction 9. Love stories
LC 2011013747
Hurston/Wright Legacy Award: Fiction, 2012.
Unable to stop killing off the heroines of his novels, celebrated writer Mr. Fox is confronted by a living embodiment of his muse, Mary, who challenges him to join her in fairy-tale stories where they must stay together in spite of disparate character traits.

"Each character is so superbly formed, and they are believable people whose habits of thought and language are so perfectly pitched and entertaining that they become instantly lovable, that is until we learn more about them. The combination of intensity and changeability in all three characters reflect many of the archetypal baddies from myth and batty old fairy-fables, the most prominent of which is Bluebeard, with his many bloodbaths, and the Furies, with their readiness to punish crime." Chicago Sun-Times.

Oyeyemi, Helen
The **opposite** house / Helen Oyeyemi. Nan A. Talese, Doubleday, 2007. 257 p.
ISBN 9780385513845
1. Young women 2. Cubans in Great Britain 3. Identity (Psychology) 4. Faith 5. Magic 6. Immigrants, Cuban -- Great Britain 7. Pregnant women 8. Yoruba (African people) -- Religion 9. Family relationships 10. Lesbians 11. Female friendship 12. Gods and goddesses, Yoruba 13. Santeria 14. Self-perception 15. London, England 16. Psychological fiction 17. Mythological fiction
LC 2006036812
An exploration of the thin wall that exists between myth and reality chronicles the alternating stories of two young women--Maja Carmen Carrera, the daughter of a black Cuban couple living in England who longs for a connection to her African roots, and Yemaya Saramgua, a Yoruba goddess in the Somewherehouse--in search of the meaning of faith and identity.
"The novel is insightful, urgently and sometimes painfully so. What Oyeyemi shows us about cultural alienation, about what makes and marks a migrant, needs to be seen. . . . At times, it's true, Maja's skin feels thin, stretched, raw. We can feel Oyeyemi writing through her character. But those times are rare; on most of the pages in this novel Maja lives, and it matters that she lives. This is her life." Strange Horizons.

Oyeyemi, Helen
What is not yours is not yours : stories / Helen Oyeyemi. Riverhead Books, 2016. 325 p.
ISBN 9781594634635
1. Locks and keys 2. Literary fiction 3. Magical realism 4. Short stories
A collection of stories by the award-winning author of Boy, Snow, Bird features entries about literal and metaphorical keys that open or shut the fates of lovers, the heart of a puppeteering student and the doors of a house of locks that holds unobservable developments.

Oz, Amos
Don't call it night / Amos Oz ; translated from the Hebrew by Nicholas de Lange. Harcourt Brace, 1995. 199 p.
ISBN 0151001529
1. 1980s 2. Deserts 3. Engineers 4. Teachers 5. Small town life 6. Men/women relations 7. Negev 8. Israel 9. Historical fiction 10. Love stories 11. Translations -- Hebrew to English
LC 9614587
Set in a small Israeli settlement in the desert during the summer of 1989, a novel follows the difficult romance between a sixty-year-old engineer and a schoolteacher fifteen years his junior
"This novel is a piece of sweet but melancholy chamber music--light but not necessarily insubstantial. It belongs to a genre of restful novel that is ruled by an esthetic of peace and a yearning for peace. If one is looking for politics, there is that--clearly, if quietly." New York Times Book Review.

Oz, Amos

* Fima / Amos Oz ; translated from the Hebrew by Nicholas de Lange Harcourt, Brace, 1993. 322 p.

ISBN 0151898510

1. Poets, Israeli 2. Middle-aged men -- Israel 3. Jerusalem, Israel 4. Psychological fiction 5. Translations -- Hebrew to English

LC 92044200

"Not only does Mr. Oz strive toward a Chekhovian compassion for his characters, but his novel depends . . . on making us believe in the possibility of last-minute grace. When tragedy strikes, we watch Fima rise to the occasion and begin to tap his own resources of generosity, humility, common sense, and his sense of purpose." New York Times Book Review.

Oz, Amos

Judas / Amos Oz ; translated from the Hebrew by Nicholas De Lange. Houghton Mifflin Harcourt, 2016, c2014. 305 p.

ISBN 9780544464049

1. 1950s 2. Scholars and academics 3. Young men -- Relations with older women 4. Caregivers 5. Intellectual life 6. Senior men 7. Widows 8. Betrayal 9. Jews 10. Interpersonal relations 11. Men/women relations 12. Jerusalem, Israel 13. Israel -- Social life and customs -- 20th century 14. Coming-of-age stories 15. Literary fiction 16. Translations -- Hebrew to English

Originally published: 2014.

A biblical scholar finds himself falling for the daughter of a deceased Zionist leader after accepting a job as a caregiver for an irritable old man in 1959 Jerusalem.

Oz, Amos

Panther in the basement / Amos Oz ; translated from the Hebrew by Nicolas de Lange. Harcourt Brace, 1997. 147 p.

ISBN 0151002878

1. 1940s 2. Twelve-year-old boys -- Palestine 3. Jewish boys -- Palestine 4. British in Palestine 5. Intergenerational friendship -- Palestine 6. Palestine 7. Jerusalem, Israel -- History -- 1917-1948 8. Palestine -- History -- 1929-1948 9. Autobiographical fiction 10. Coming-of-age stories 11. Historical fiction 12. Translations -- Hebrew to English

LC 9720577

Book made into a movie called The little traitor.

Proffy, 12, tries to form his own underground resistance group in his family's basement as Israel prepares to fight for independence, but he becomes friends with a British police officer instead.

Oz, Amos

The **same** sea / Amos Oz; translated from the Hebrew by Nicholas de Lange in collaboration with the author. Harcourt, 2001. 201 p. ;

ISBN 0151005729

1. Families -- Israel 2. Widowers 3. Fathers and sons 4. Senior men -- Israel 5. Family relationships 6. Literary fiction 7. Metafiction 8. Translations -- Hebrew to English

LC 2001024121

Offers a lyrical novel whose characters include an elderly widower, the spirit of his dead wife, their son who has journeyed to Tibet to find truth, and his young, enticing girlfriend.

"Never has the author's writing been more controlled and polished. . . . His depictions of his characters' lives are tableaux vivants, succint and visual." Times Literary Supplement.

Ozeki, Ruth L.

* A tale for the time being / Ruth Ozeki. Viking, 2013. 432 p.

ISBN 9780670026630

1. Women authors 2. Diary writing 3. Compassion 4. Loneliness 5. Tsunamis 6. Zen Buddhism 7. Time 8. Unhappiness in women 9. Tohoku Earthquake and Tsunami, Japan, 2011 10. Teenage girls -- Japan 11. Buddhist nuns 12. Great-grandmothers 13. Bullying and bullies 14. Tokyo, Japan 15. Vancouver Island 16. Literary fiction 17. Metafiction

LC 2012039878

ALA Notable Book, 2014

Asian Pacific American Award for Literature: Adult Fiction, 2014.

Canada-Japan Literary Awards, 2014

Sunburst Award for Excellence in Canadian Literature of the Fantastic, 2014.

Shortlisted for the Man Booker Prize, 2013.

National Book Critics Circle Award for Fiction finalist, 2013

A novelist on a remote island in the Pacific is linked to a bullied and depressed Tokyo teenager after discovering a Hello Kitty lunchbox that washed ashore.

Ozick, Cynthia, 1928-

* Foreign bodies / Cynthia Ozick. Houghton Mifflin Harcourt, 2010. 272 p.

ISBN 9780547435572

1. 1950s 2. Divorced women 3. Americans in France 4. Nephews 5. Brothers and sisters 6. Fifties (Age) 7. Former husbands 8. Women teachers 9. Paris, France 10. Literary fiction 11. Psychological fiction

LC 2010005757

Shortlisted for The Orange Prize for Fiction, 2012

Presents a retelling of Henry James's "The Ambassadors" that follows the efforts of divorced schoolteacher Bea Nightingale to navigate a turbulent year spent with her estranged brother's family.

"Ozick is a craggy writer, with strenuous climbs, momentary slides and startling views. Some of Bea's confrontations, feeling out her new independence back in the United States, seem contrived, even stagy. But her vision of Europe and its tragic history is profound; and Lili is a creation of stunning depth. It is not Jamesian, it is Ozickian." Boston Globe.

Ozick, Cynthia, 1928-

* Heir to the glimmering world / Cynthia Ozick. Houghton Mifflin, 2004. 320 p.

ISBN 0618470492

1. Depression era (1929-1941) 2. 1930s 3. Children of authors 4. Refugees, Jewish 5. Young women 6. Jewish families 7. Benefactors 8. Rich people 9. Nannies 10. Orphans 11. Inheritance and succession 12. Faith 13. Independence in women 14. Identity (Psychology) 15. Family relationships 16. Secrets 17. Depressions, -- 1929-1941 18. New York City 19. Bronx, New York City 20. Historical fiction 21. Domestic fiction

LC 2004042723

James A'bair, whose father is the author of the popular series "The Bear Boy," has taken in the eccentric Mitwisser family and the orphaned Rose Meadows, who must resist the pull of the actual Bear Boy, in a novel of Depression-era New York.

"In 1933, the Mitwissers, a family of German Jews, arrive in America after a narrow and eccentric escape from Berlin. . . . After landing somewhat haphazardly in New York, they place an ad for help in a local paper. The only applicant for the job is an eighteen-year-old orphan, Rose Meadows, who narrates the story, and who observes the Mitwissers with the dry neutrality of an invisible servant. Her duties are vaguely defined--part nanny, part secretary--and her salary comes intermittently, the family's sole source of income being the whimsy of a troubled bene-factor. Ozick portrays this ramshackle household to dazzling effect, as it adjusts to its many states of exile--from a sense of security, from cherished ideas, and from the consolations of each other." The New Yorker.

Ozick, Cynthia, 1928-

* The **Puttermesser** papers / Cynthia Ozick. Alfred A. Knopf, 1997. 235 p.

ISBN 9780679454762

1. Jewish women 2. Women mayors 3. Life change events 4. Golem 5. Interpersonal relations 6. Bureaucracy 7. New York City 8. Picaresque fiction 9. Literary fiction

Shortlisted for the International IMPAC Dublin Literary Award, 1999

National Book Award for Fiction finalist, 1997

A female Don Quixote transplanted to modern-day Manhattan, Ruth Puttermesser yearns for a life of the mind, only to find herself hopelessly mired in the eternal circle of city bureaucracy when she is unexpectedly elected mayor of the Big Apple

"This entertaining fable is a social commentary as well as a comic tour de force, and it bristles with Ozick's formidable intelligence and wit." Publishers Weekly.

P

Packer, Ann, 1959-

The **children's** crusade / Ann Packer. Scribner, 2015. 464 p.

ISBN 9781476710457

1. Brothers and sisters 2. Women artists 3. Adult children of dysfunctional families 4. Mother-deserted children 5. Married people 6. Single men 7. Houses 8. Land acquisition 9. Family relationships 10. Family secrets 11. San Francisco Bay Area 12. California 13. Family sagas 14. Literary fiction

When their younger sibling returns, the three oldest Blair children find their lives disrupted in ways they could have never imagined as they each tell their story that is interwoven with portraits of their family at crucial points in their history.

"Packer fully captures the intimacy of this familys life and, by extension, the way the childrens interactions impact their adult lives. A masterful portrait of indelible family bonds." Booklist.

Packer, Ann, 1959-

The **dive** from Clausen's pier / Ann Packer. Alfred A. Knopf, 2002. 369 p.

ISBN 0375412824

1. Self-discovery 2. Engaged persons 3. Small town life 4. Self-fulfillment 5. Young women 6. Accident victims 7. Childhood friends 8. Wisconsin 9. New York City 10. Coming-of-age stories

LC 2001042522

Great Lakes Book Awards, Fiction category, 2002.

When her fiancé Mike is left paralyzed following a tragic accident, Carrie Bell begins to question her familiar world, from her everyday life in Wisconsin to her relationships, as she sets out to rediscover her own identity.

Packer, Ann, 1959-

Songs without words / Ann Packer. Knopf, 2007. 352 p.

ISBN 9780375412813

1. Friendship 2. Self-perception 3. Loss (Psychology) 4. Grief 5. Interpersonal relations 6. Tragedy 7. Happiness in women 8. Options,

alternatives, choices 9. Mothers and daughters 10. California 11. Domestic fiction

LC 2006100512

This chronicles the long-time friendship between Liz and Sarabeth, a relationship that is forged in childhood and sustained through the decades that follow, until both women are forced to reexamine their lives in the wake of a devastating crisis.

"[Packer] shows a deft touch in framing emotional dilemmas, such as whether it is the duty of those who have been raised with affection to compensate those who have gone without." The New Yorker.

Page, Katherine Hall

The **body** in the big apple / Katherine Hall Page. Morrow, 1999. 239 p. Faith Fairchild mysteries

ISBN 0380731304

1. Women caterers 2. Extortion 3. Murder investigation 4. Women amateur detectives 5. Secrets 6. Manhattan, New York City 7. Cozy mysteries 8. Gentle reads 9. Culinary mysteries

This title serves as a prequel to the series and is listed as the first title in the series

Includes recipes.

Caterer Faith Sibley becomes embroiled in her first mystery after Emma Stanstead, a former high-school classmate is threatened by an anonymous blackmailer.

Page, Katherine Hall

The **body** in the bog : a Faith Fairchild mystery / Katherine Hall Page. W. Morrow, 1996. 276 p. Faith Fairchild mysteries

ISBN 0688145736

1. Women caterers 2. Extortion -- Massachusetts 3. Anonymous letters 4. Hate mail 5. Spouses of clergy 6. Women amateur detectives 7. Small town life -- Massachusetts 8. Murder 9. Wetland conservation 10. Real estate developers -- Massachusetts 11. Massachusetts 12. Cozy mysteries 13. Gentle reads 14. Culinary mysteries

Includes recipes.

When a housing project protester is killed, Faith Fairchild launches an investigation in the middle of the town's Patriot's Day celebration and becomes a murderous stalker's next target

"Sleuth Faith Fairchild occupies her time in small-town Massachusetts with her husband, Tom, a preacher; their two small children; Have Faith, her catering business; and an occasional murder. When wetlands are converted into a chi-chi housing development, poison pen letters fly, one of the houses burns, and police discover murder. Faith's persistent quest for clues exposes many secrets, but the ultimate confrontation occurs in Have Faith's kitchen. Well-delineated action and characters mix easily with Faith's attendant domesticity." Library Journal.

Page, Katherine Hall

The **body** in the casket : a Faith Fairchild mystery / Katherine Hall Page. William Morrow, 2017 272 p. Faith Fairchild mysteries

ISBN 9780062439567

1. Caterers and catering 2. Actors and actresses 3. Women amateur detectives 4. Murder investigation 5. Amateur detectives 6. Women caterers 7. Birthday parties 8. Women in the food industry and trade 9. Savannah, Georgia 10. Cozy mysteries 11. Gentle reads 12. Culinary mysteries

Catering the lavish birthday party of a Broadway legend, Faith Fairchild is astonished when her client reveals that he hired her less for her culinary prowess and more for her skills as a detective and that one of his guests is trying to kill him. Includes recipes.

"Agatha-winner Page's 24th Faith Fairchild mystery (after 2016s Body in the Wardrobe) is a cracking good traditional manor house mystery....Realistic characters and a pair of intriguing side stories contribute to a satisfying read." Publishers Weekly.

Page, Katherine Hall

The **body** in the vestibule / Katherine Hall Page. St. Martin's Press, 1992. 211 p. Faith Fairchild mysteries

1. Women caterers 2. Murder investigation 3. Spouses of clergy 4. Women amateur detectives 5. Lyon, France 6. Cozy mysteries 7. Gentle reads 8. Culinary mysteries

LC 92018455

Includes recipes.

"With beautifully detailed descriptions of Lyons added to Faith's intelligent observations, Page . . . continues to hit the mark with this charming series." Publishers Weekly.

Page, Katherine Hall

The **body** in the wake : a Faith Fairchild mystery / Katherine Hall Page. William Morrow, 2019. 240 p. Faith Fairchild mysteries

ISBN 9780062863256

1. Caterers and catering 2. Women amateur detectives 3. Vacation homes 4. Murder investigation 5. Amateur detectives 6. Women caterers 7. Weddings 8. Women in the food industry and trade 9. Maine 10. Cozy mysteries 11. Gentle reads 12. Culinary mysteries

LC bl2019006116

Supporting her friends through a less-than-relaxing summer at Penobscot Bay, amateur detective and caterer Faith Fairchild helps prepare for an upcoming wedding before stumbling on a body with a mysterious tattoo and connections far from Sanpere Island.

Pajer, Bernadette

Capacity for murder : a Professor Bradshaw mystery / Bernadette Pajer. Poisoned Pen Press, 2013. 250 p. Professor Bradshaw mysteries

ISBN 9781464201288

1. 1900s (Decade) 2. Sick persons 3. Private investigators 4. College teachers 5. Electrical engineers 6. Physicians 7. Murder 8. Murder investigation 9. Sanatoriums 10. Electric shock 11. Interpersonal relations 12. Men/women relations 13. Washington (State) 14. Historical mysteries 15. Pacific Northwest fiction

When a mysterious death occurs at Healing Sands Sanitarium, Professor Bradshaw, summoned to investigate, must prove that this death was no accident.

Pajer, Bernadette

The **Edison** effect : a Professor Bradshaw mystery / Bernadette Pajer. Poisoned Pen Press, 2014. 246 p. Professor Bradshaw mysteries

ISBN 9781464202520

1. Edison, Thomas A (Thomas Alva), 1847-1931 2. 1900s (Decade) 3. Inventions 4. Private investigators 5. College teachers 6. Universities and colleges 7. Electrical engineers 8. Inventors 9. Electricians -- Death 10. Men/women relations 11. Washington (State) 12. Historical mysteries 13. Pacific Northwest fiction

When an electrician is found dead clutching Edison's new holiday bulbs, Professor Bradshaw, Henry Pratt, and Detective O'Brien investigate, uncovering the dead man's secrets and rivalries at the Bon Marche Department Store.

Pajer, Bernadette

Fatal induction : a Professor Bradshaw mystery / Bernadette Pajer. Poisoned Pen Press, 2012. 250 p. Professor Bradshaw mysteries

ISBN 9781590586129

1. 1900s (Decade) 2. Universities and colleges 3. Electricity -- History 4. College teachers 5. Murder 6. Murder investigation 7. Romanies 8. Girl murder witnesses 9. Inventions 10. Single fathers 11. Seattle, Washington 12. Historical mysteries 13. Pacific Northwest fiction 14. Mysteries

As Professor Bradshaw works toward winning a contest to design a telephonic system, he is drawn into a mystery involving a missing Gypsy peddler and a child that may have witnessed a murder.

Pajer, Bernadette

A **spark** of death / Bernadette Pajer. Poisoned Pen Press, 2011. 250 p. Professor Bradshaw mysteries

ISBN 9781590589052

1. 1900s (Decade) 2. Universities and colleges 3. Electricity -- History 4. College teachers 5. Murder 6. Murder investigation 7. Single fathers 8. Seattle, Washington 9. Historical mysteries 10. Pacific Northwest fiction 11. Mysteries

Professor Benjamin Bradshaw sets out to clear his name after becoming the only suspect in the murder of an unpopular colleague, whom he discovered electrocuted in a Faraday cage on campus.

" [This book] presents a good mystery, a clever detective and a fascinating look at the early days of electrical power." Kirkus.

Palahniuk, Chuck

Choke : a novel / Chuck Palahniuk. Doubleday, 2001. 293 p.

ISBN 0385501560

1. Get-rich-quick ventures 2. Women with Alzheimer's disease 3. Sex addiction in men 4. Mother and adult son 5. Swindlers and swindling 6. Choking 7. Men/women relations 8. Role playing 9. Historical reenactments 10. Attention-seeking 11. People with Alzheimer's disease 12. Sex addicts 13. Psychological fiction

LC 00063905

Medical school dropout Victor Mancini comes up with a complicated but ingenious scam to pay for his mother's elder care, cruises sex addiction groups for action, and visits his zany mother, whose Alzheimer's disease hides the bizarre truth about his parentage.

Palahniuk, Chuck

Fight Club / Chuck Palahniuk. W. W. Norton & Company, 1996. 208 p.

ISBN 0393039765

1. Secret societies 2. Violence 3. Men/women relations 4. Insurance investigators 5. Young men -- United States 6. Fist fights 7. Boxers (Sports) 8. Millennialism -- United States 9. Men's organizations 10. Insomnia 11. Support groups 12. Men with mental illnesses 13. Love triangles 14. Terrorism 15. Transgressive fiction

LC 95047591

Has a graphic novel sequel released in 2016, Fight Club 2.

In a confusing world poised on the brink of mayhem, Tyler Durden, a projectionist, waiter, and anarchic genius, comes up with an idea to create clubs in which young men can escape their humdrum existence and prove themselves in barehanded fights.

Palahniuk, Chuck

Lullaby : a novel / Chuck Palahniuk. Doubleday, 2002. 260 p.

ISBN 0385504470

1. Incantations 2. Journalists 3. Sudden Infant Death Syndrome 4. Widowers 5. Paranormal phenomena 6. Urban families 7. Good and evil 8. Spells (Magic) 9. Infant death 10. Mass media 11. Murder 12. Witches 13. Poetry 14. Horror 15. Transgressive fiction

LC 2001052979

Assigned to a story on sudden infant death syndrome, journalist Carl Streator finds a poetry anthology that contains an African chant that becomes lethal when spoken or thought in someone's direction.

"This is vintage Palahniuk: weird, creepy, twisted, upsetting, and ultimately a great read for anyone who wants to be scared for pleasure." Library Journal.

Palahniuk, Chuck

Pygmy / Chuck Palahniuk. Doubleday, 2009. 240 p.

ISBN 9780385526340

1. Foreign students 2. Terrorists 3. Terrorism 4. Young adults 5. International relations 6. Middle West -- Social life and customs 7. Satirical fiction 8. Thrillers and suspense

Pygmy--a young adult from a totalitarian state, disguised as an exchange student--plans a terrorist attack and depicts U.S. Midwestern life through the eyes of a hateful, indoctrinated little killer, in a satire of American xenophobia.

"The story unfolds in a series of dispatches from an unnamed 13-year-old agent, dubbed Pygmy by the locals. . . . The frisson around his internal, target-acquiring narrative, the locals' unwitting perception of him, and his outsider's view of the routine humiliations inflicted upon high-school youth is so spot-on it produces a sense of deja vu: surely someone would have thought of this before." Booklist.

Palaia, Marian

The **given** world / Marian Palaia. Simon & Schuster, 2015 224 p.

ISBN 9781476777931

1. Brothers and sisters 2. Vietnam War, 1961-1975 3. Missing in action 4. Farm life 5. Bereavement 6. Missing persons 7. War and society 8. Psychological fiction

Withdrawing and taking drugs to cope when her brother goes missing in Vietnam, Riley falls in love with a reservation youth who also goes to war, compelling a journey to Vietnam that introduces her to others affected by wartime losses.

Paley, Grace, 1922-

* The **collected** stories / Grace Paley. Farrar Straus Giroux, 1994 386 p.

ISBN 0374126364

1. Short stories 2. Literary fiction

LC 93042230

45 short stories

From The little disturbances of man, Enormous changes at the last minute, and Later the same day.

ALA Notable Book, 1995.

National Book Award for Fiction finalist, 1994.

Pulitzer Prize for Fiction finalist, 1995.

An introduction by Paley accompanies a comprehensive collection of short fiction by the author of "Later the same day," "Enormous changes at the last minute," and "The little disturbances of man"

Palliser, Charles, 1947-

The **quincunx** / Charles Palliser. Ballantine Books, 1990, c1989. 788 p.

ISBN 9780345364630

1. 19th century 2. Inheritance and succession 3. Identity (Psychology) 4. Revenge 5. Men -- Identity 6. England -- History -- 19th century 7. Historical mysteries 8. Literary fiction 9. Mysteries

LC 89091787

This meditation on the Victorian novel and sprawling epic tale of a man's quest for his identity follows John as he journeys to the heart of the Quincunx to reveal his elusive past.

"This is not an ironic parody à la Barth, not an echo of Eco, but a genuine reproduction of a full-bodied 19th-century page-turner of a novel, set in late Regency England, thick with characters of all classes, with plots, counterplots, fore-bodings, reversals and interpolated tales. . . . Mr. Palliser's re-creation of this period is absolutely convincing, his dialogue never jars, his command of details never falters." New York Times Book Review.

Palliser, Charles, 1947-

Rustication / Charles Palliser. W. W. Norton, 2013. 327 p.

ISBN 9780393088724

1. Victorian era (1837-1901) 2. Sex addicts 3. Opium addiction 4. Criminal behavior 5. Crime 6. Murder 7. Secrets 8. Mansions 9. Suspicion 10. Family secrets 11. Murder suspects 12. Great Britain -- Social life and customs -- Victoria, 1837-1901 13. England -- Social life and customs -- 19th century 14. Cambridge, England 15. Victorian mysteries 16. Gothic fiction 17. Historical mysteries

In 1863, a sexually obsessed opium addict is sent away from Cambridge to live in the country where he becomes the lead suspect in a series of threatening letters and crimes.

Palliser, Charles, 1947-

The **unburied** / Charles Palliser. Farrar, Straus and Giroux, 1999. 403 p., 25 cm.

ISBN 9780374280352

1. 19th century 2. College teachers 3. Manuscripts, Medieval 4. Cathedrals 5. Ghosts 6. Historians 7. Libraries 8. Murder 9. Witnesses 10. England 11. Historical mysteries 12. Literary fiction 13. Mysteries

LC 99014740

Invited to the spend the holidays with his old friend, Austin, in the cathedral close of Thurchester, unworldly academic Dr. Courtine becomes engrossed in a haunting, two-hundred-year-old mystery with ties to both a medieval manuscript and to terrifying events in the present.

"All the murders are puzzles, and Palliser constructs his plot like a maze and lures his readers into it. The book's ruthless consistency of style and the somewhat bleak view of humankind set it apart from the usual thriller." The New Yorker.

Palmer, Ada

Too like the lightning / Ada Palmer. Tor, 2016. 400 p. Terra Ignota

ISBN 9780765378002

1. 25th century 2. Far future 3. Criminals 4. Spirituality 5. Political science 6. Utopias 7. Dystopias 8. Science fiction

In the 25th century, human civilization is divided into philosophical sects based on technologically generated abundance and inspired by the 18th-century European Enlightenment. In this utopia, convicted felon Mycroft Canner serves his sentence by carrying out the orders of everyone he meets, while sensayer Carlyle Foster acts as a spiritual counselor in a world where organized religion has been outlawed. Their paths converge when they encounter Bridger, a young boy whose unusual abilities could destroy their hard-won world of peace and prosperity. -- Description by Gillian Speace.

"Although the primary plot centers around a stolen list ranking the most powerful people on the planet and its political ramifications, the overarching theme of the book is philosophy, from the debate about gendered pronouns to thoughts about the afterlife." Booklist.

Palmer, Daniel, 1962-

The **new** husband / D. J. Palmer. St. Martin's Press, 2020. 384 p.

ISBN 9781250107497

1. Single mothers 2. Control (Psychology) 3. Widowers 4. Deception 5. Teenage girls 6. Trust 7. Boyfriends 8. Teachers 9. Cohabitation 10. Missing men 11. Options, alternatives, choices 12. Family relationships 13. Men/women relations 14. New Hampshire 15. Psychological suspense

LC 2019048512

After meeting Simon Fitch, a teacher from her daughter Maggie's middle school, widow Nina Garrity has hopes of putting her shattered life back together, but her friends aren?t so sure that Simon has the best of intentions.

"A well-crafted, increasingly tense page-turner." Kirkus.

Palmer, Dexter Clarence, 1974-

The **dream** of perpetual motion / Dexter Palmer. St. Martin's Press, 2010. 352 p.

ISBN 9780312558154

1. Prisoners 2. Dystopias 3. Perpetual motion 4. Androids 5. Virtual reality 6. Inventors 7. Storytelling 8. Steampunk 9. Epistolary novels 10. Science fiction

LC 2009040231

With his only companions being his insane lover and her cryogenically frozen father, greeting card writer Harold Winslow must come to terms with the madness of a genius inventor and his quest to create a perpetual motion machine.

"Palmer takes elements from Nabokov, Neal Stephenson, Steven Millhauser and The Tempest, tosses them into a retro-futuristic blender and hits pure. The result is a singular riff on steampunk--sophisticated, subversive entertainment that never settles for escapism." New York Times Book Review.

Palmer, Dexter Clarence, 1974-

* **Mary** Toft; or, the rabbit queen : a novel / Dexter Palmer. Pantheon Books, 2019. 320 p.

ISBN 9781101871935

1. 18th century 2. Curiosities and wonders 3. Childbirth 4. Hoaxes 5. Rabbits 6. Apprentices 7. Surgeons 8. Deception 9. Eccentrics and eccentricities 10. London, England 11. Historical fiction 12. Psychological fiction

LC 2019013815

The award-winning author of Version Control presents a novel based on true events depicting a young woman who baffles the medical community of early 18th-century England when she begins giving birth to dead rabbits.

Palmer, Dexter Clarence, 1974-

* **Version** control / Dexter Palmer. Pantheon Books, 2016. viii, 495 p.

ISBN 9780307907592

1. Near future 2. Married people 3. Physics -- Experiments 4. Time machines 5. Consequences 6. Online dating 7. Time travel 8. Physicists 9. Inventions 10. Reality 11. New York City 12. Hard science fiction 13. Science fiction

Convinced that "nothing is as it should be; everything is upside down," Rebecca Wright struggles to explain her conviction to her husband, physicist Philip Steiner, who's skeptical to say the least. Could the "wrongness" that Rebecca perceives have something to do with Philip's work? Philip has spent the better part of ten years developing a causality violation device. The CVD is NOT a time machine, although the way it works (if it, in fact, works) seems remarkably similar to how a time machine might behave, disrupting the space-time continuum in subtle, yet powerful ways. -- Description by Gillian Speace.

"A Mobius strip of a novel in which time is more a loop than a path and various possibilities seem to exist simultaneously." Kirkus.

Palmer, Lindsey J.

Otherwise engaged / Lindsey J. Palmer. Skyhorse Publishing, 2019. 304 p.

ISBN 9781510732391

1. Couples 2. Engagement 3. Authors 4. Engaged persons 5. Wedding planning 6. Former girlfriends 7. Suspicion 8. Paranoia 9. Jealousy 10. Work-life balance 11. Female friendship 12. New York City 13. Chick lit

After her fiancé authors a sensational and best-selling novel loosely based on his torrid love affair with his ex-girlfriend, Molly's paranoia that she will come back and try to rekindle their romance sends her into a downward spiral.

Palmer, Michael, 1942-2013

The **fifth** vial / Michael Palmer. St. Martin's Press, 2007. 384 p.

ISBN 0312343515

1. Women medical students 2. Medical research 3. Blood -- Collection and preservation 4. Transplantation of organs, tissues, etc 5. Secret societies 6. Kidnapping 7. Murder 8. Private investigators 9. Women kidnapping victims 10. Organ donors 11. Human body parts industry and trade 12. Brazil 13. Africa 14. Medical thrillers 15. Thrillers and suspense

LC 2006050971

A suspended Harvard Medical School student is kidnapped and left for dead in Rio de Janeiro, while a terminally ill medical genius works on a potentially world-changing cure, and a Chicago detective struggles to identify a mysterious accident victim.

"Palmer is adept at tapping into people's natural fear of disease, doctors, and hospitals and converting that fear into unnerving suspense. In this . . . medical thriller, Palmer plays with the phenomenon of organ donation, forcing the reader to ask nervously, Where do donated organs come from? The answer comes slowly, in the best medical-thriller tradition." Booklist.

Palmer, Michael, 1942-2013

The **last** surgeon / Michael Palmer. St. Martin's Press, 2010. 384 p.

ISBN 9780312587499

1. Physicians 2. Psychopaths 3. Serial murders 4. Crimes against surgeons 5. Homeless persons 6. Political corruption 7. Conspiracies 8. Baltimore, Maryland 9. Medical thrillers 10. Thrillers and suspense

LC 2009039234

Dr. Nick Garrity and psych nurse Gillian Coates determine that one-by-one, each of those in the operating room for a fatally botched case is dying. Their discoveries pit them against genius Franz Koller--the highly-paid master of the "non-kill." As doctor and nurse move closer to finding the terrifying secret behind these killings, Koller has been given a new directive: his mission will not be complete until Gillian and Garrity, the last surgeon, are dead.

"Palmer's latest has an appealing couple at its center, plus good pacing and gritty action to keep the pages turning." Library Journal.

Palmer, Michael, 1942-2013

The **society** / Michael Palmer. Bantam, 2004. 400 p.
ISBN 0553802046
1. Managed care plans -- (Medical care) -- Moral and ethical aspects
2. Surgeons 3. Rookie police 4. Women detectives 5. Women executives 6. Health services administrators 7. Serial murderers
8. Serial murders 9. Massachusetts 10. Boston, Massachusetts 11. Medical thrillers 12. Thrillers and suspense

Working diligently at a trauma center, surgeon Will Grant, a member of a group that works against insurance companies to prevent unjust cost-cutting practices, is accused by detective Patty Moriarity of killing managed-care executives.

"This thriller begins with the murder of several loathsome CEOs of HMOs in Massachusetts. Dr. Will Grant is a talented and caring physician in the Boston area who works long hours and hates the unfair and obstructive practices of the big insurance companies. Patty Moriarity is a rookie state cop whose first big case is investigating the deaths of the health care vultures. After some early research, Patty suspects Will, but soon enough that's all straightened out and they're smooching on the couch. After Will is drugged and collapses during a delicate operation, things get rough: he's kicked out of his hospital for drug abuse and sued. Next he's being tortured, while Patty, shot after attempting to save the boorish chauvinist detective who has taken over her case, lies in a coma. The action is a bit preachy in the beginning, but once Palmer gets all his characters in place, the suspense builds." Publishers Weekly.

Palumbo, Dennis, 1951-

Night terrors : a Daniel Rinaldi mystery / Dennis Palumbo. Poisoned Pen Press, 2013. 250 p. Daniel Rinaldi mysteries
ISBN 9781464201318
1. Psychotherapists 2. Nightmares 3. Former FBI agents 4. Murder 5. Serial murderers 6. Police 7. Revenge 8. Professional/client relations 9. Men/women relations 10. Pittsburgh, Pennsylvania 11. Mysteries

In the midst of a brutally cold winter in Pittsburgh, Daniel Rinaldi is asked to treat Lyle Barnes, a retired FBI profiler whose terrifying nocturnal visions cause him to wake up screaming. Barnes, after twenty years spent inside the minds of the nation's worst serial killers, is not only falling apart psychologically but also finds himself the target of an unknown assassin, whose mounting list of victims is paralyzing the city. Hidden for his own protection by his former bureau colleagues, Barnes secretly escapes, drawing Daniel and a joint task force of the FBI and the Pittsburgh Police Department into a desperate manhunt. They must try to find the missing agent before the killer does.

Palwick, Susan

Mending the moon / Susan Palwick. Tor, 2013. 352 p.
ISBN 9780765327581
1. Friends' death 2. Loss (Psychology) 3. Mothers and sons 4. Bereavement 5. College teachers 6. Adoptive mothers 7. Friendship 8. Interpersonal relations 9. Comic book characters 10. Murder victims 11. Suicide victims 12. Seattle, Washington 13. Mexico 14. Psychological fiction 15. Mysteries
LC 2012043362
"A Tom Doherty Associates book."

When a charismatic champion of popular causes is murdered by a fellow tourist while vacationing in Mexico, her death poses profound implications for a circle of friends back home, the family of the killer and her adopted son, who struggles with torn feelings and identifies with a favorite comic-book hero before pursuing an unlikely path toward healing.

Palwick, Susan

The **necessary** beggar / Susan Palwick. Tor, 2005. 420 p.
ISBN 076531097X
1. Exiles 2. Refugees 3. Murder suspects 4. Suicide victims 5. Ghosts 6. Families 7. Beggars 8. Refugee camps 9. Family relationships 10. Cultural differences 11. Punishment 12. Men/women relations 13. Terrorism 14. Grief 15. Loss (Psychology) 16. Near future 17. Imaginary wars and battles 18. Reno, Nevada 19. Domestic fiction 20. Fantasy fiction 21. Middle Eastern-influenced fantasy
LC 2005041919
"A Tom Doherty Associates book."

When young Darroti is accused of murdering a holy woman, his entire family is forced into exile away from their peaceful home city, a situation that thrusts them into a hostile land where hatred and war threaten their survival.

Pamuk, Orhan, 1952-

My name is Red / Orhan Pamuk ; translated from the Turkish by Erdag Goknar. Alfred A. Knopf, 2001. xv, 417 p.
ISBN 9780375406959
1. 16th century 2. Illumination of books and manuscripts 3. Islam and art 4. Books and reading 5. Istanbul, Turkey 6. Translations -- Turkish to English 7. Literary fiction 8. Historical mysteries 9. Mysteries
LC 2001029866
Includes Historical chronology.
Originally published in Istanbul: Lletisim, 1998.
International IMPAC Dublin Literary Award, 2003.

In sixteenth-century Istanbul, a furor erupts when the Sultan hires a group of artists to illuminate a great book in the European style at a time in which all figurative art is considered Islamic heresy, but the situation becomes worse when one of the miniaturists vanishes.

Pamuk, Orhan, 1952-

The **museum** of innocence / Orhan Pamuk ; translated from the Turkish by Maureen Freely. Alfred A. Knopf, 2009. 535 p.
ISBN 9780307266767
1. 1970s 2. Obsession in men 3. Love triangles 4. Rich families 5. Men -- Turkey 6. Men/women relations 7. Virginity -- Social aspects 8. Breach of promise 9. Istanbul, Turkey 10. Translations -- Turkish to English 11. Literary fiction
LC 2009019475
Translated from the Turkish Masumiyet muzesi.

Ending his engagement to pursue a married cousin, Kemal unsuccessfully woos the woman over the course of nine years, during which he amasses personal effects that reflect his obsession and render him a laughingstock among his peers.

"Pamuk is brilliant at the human parade, and especially at humiliation in its masculine forms, frequently played out in Istanbul along East-West tensions." Cleveland Plain Dealer.

Pamuk, Orhan, 1952-

The **red-haired** woman / Orhan Pamuk ; translated from the Turkish by Ekin Oklap. Alfred A. Knopf, 2017, c2016. 253 p.
ISBN 9780451494429
1. Blue collar workers 2. Young men 3. Middle-aged men 4. Apprentices 5. Intergenerational friendship 6. Actors and actresses 7. Men/women relations 8. Wells 9. Digging 10. Accidents 11. Guilt 12. Istanbul, Turkey 13. Literary fiction 14. Translations -- Turkish to English
LC 2016057733

Originally published in Turkey as 'Kirmizi Sacli Kadin' by Yapi Kredi Yayinlari, Istanbul, in 2016.

Hired to find water on a barren plain during the hot summer, a master well digger and his young apprentice develop a filial bond neither has known until the boy becomes fatefully attracted to a red-haired actress from a traveling theatre company.

"As usual, Pamuk handles weighty material deftly, and the result is both puzzling and beautiful." Booklist.

Pamuk, Orhan, 1952-

* A **strangeness** in my mind : a novel / Orhan Pamuk ; translated by Ekin Oklap. Alfred A. Knopf, 2015, c2014. 599 p.

ISBN 9780307700292

1. 20th century 2. 21st century 3. Self-fulfillment in men 4. City life 5. Growing up 6. Men -- Psychology 7. Street vendors 8. Family relationships 9. Men/women relations 10. Turkey 11. Istanbul, Turkey 12. Coming-of-age stories 13. Literary fiction 14. Political fiction 15. Translations -- Turkish to English

LC 2015006769

Includes index.

Originally published in Turkish as Kafamda bir tuhaflik by Yapi Kredi Publications. First published in the UK in 2015.

Shortlisted for the International Dublin Literary Award, 2017

Selling Turkish spirits on the street and dreaming of becoming rich in a rapidly developing Istanbul, street youth Melvut Karatas elopes with the wrong woman and builds a family over decades marked by a series of dead-end jobs and an enduring sense of his unique destiny.

"If anything, Pamuk recalls the great Victorian novelists as he ranges confidently from near-documentary passages on real estate machinations and the privatization of electrical service to pensive meditations on the gap between people's public posturing and private beliefs. The oppression of women is quietly but angrily depicted as endemic... As Pamuk follows his believably flawed protagonist and a teeming cast of supporting players across five decades, Turkey's turbulent politics provide a thrumming undercurrent of unease. Rich, complex, and pulsing with urban life: one of this gifted writer's best." Kirkus.

Pamuk, Orhan, 1952-

Silent house / Orhan Pamuk ; translated from the Turkish by Robert Finn. Alfred A. Knopf, 2012. 334 p.

ISBN 9780307700285

1. 1980s 2. Widows -- Turkey 3. Families 4. Memories 5. Coups d'etat 6. Household employees 7. Nationalism -- Turkey 8. Turkey 9. Translations -- Turkish to English 10. Literary fiction

LC 2012005468

"This is a Borzoi book."

Awaiting the arrival of her grandchildren in her home outside Istanbul, bed-ridden widow Fatma shares memories and grievances with her late husband's illegitimate son until his cousin, a right-wing nationalist, involves the family in the Turkish military coup of 1980.

Pamuk, Orhan, 1952-

* **Snow** / Orhan Pamuk ; translated from the Turkish by Maureen Freely. Knopf, 2004. 448 p.

ISBN 9780375406973

1. Islam and women 2. Suicide 3. Poets, Turkish 4. Married women 5. Actors and actresses 6. Sisters 7. Culture conflict -- Turkey 8. Political science 9. Fundamentalism 10. Women's rights 11. Theater 12. Snow 13. Islam 14. Turkey -- Social life and customs 15. Translations -- Turkish to English 16. Political fiction 17. Literary fiction

LC 2003065935

After years of lonely political exile, Turkish poet Ka returns to Istanbul to attend his mother's funeral and learns about a series of suicides among pious girls forbidden to wear headscarves.

"Pamuk's sometimes exhaustive conversations and descriptions create a stark picture of a too-little-known part of the world, where politics, religion and even happiness can seem alternately all-consuming and irrelevant. A detached tone and some dogmatic abstractions make for tough reading, but Ka's rediscovery of God and poetry in a desolate place makes the novel's sadness profound and moving." Publishers Weekly.

Pandian, Gigi, 1975-

The **accidental** alchemist / Gigi Pandian. Midnight Ink, 2015 360 p. Accidental alchemist

ISBN 9780738741840

1. Alchemists 2. Gargoyles 3. Murder investigation 4. Poisoning 5. Murder suspects 6. Amateur detectives 7. Vegans 8. Portland, Oregon 9. Supernatural mysteries

LC 2014037546

Former alchemist Zoe, hoping to leave her old life behind her, is instead forced back into it when she discovers a dead man on her porch and a gargoyle stow-away in her new house.

Panowich, Brian

Bull Mountain / Brian Panowich. Putnam Adult, 2015. 304 p. Bull Mountain

ISBN 9780399173967

1. Sheriffs 2. Drug traffic 3. Mountain life 4. Outlaws 5. Brothers 6. Mountain people 7. Bootleggers 8. ATF agents 9. Family relationships 10. Georgia 11. Appalachian region 12. Rural noir 13. Literary fiction 14. Southern fiction 15. Family sagas

LC 2015002115

Sequel: Like lions.

Thriller Award for Best First Novel, 2016.

Taking a job as sheriff to distance himself from his drug-running family and keep the peace in their Georgia mountain territory, Clayton Burroughs is approached by a federal agent who claims he wants to help shut down the family's operations.

Panowich, Brian

Like lions / Brian Panowich. St Martins Pr, 2019 320 p. Bull Mountain

ISBN 9781250206947

1. Sheriffs 2. Organized crime 3. Family relationships 4. Crime 5. Criminals 6. Drug traffic 7. Grief in men 8. Mountain life 9. Gunshot victims 10. Mountain people 11. Georgia 12. Appalachian region 13. Rural noir 14. Literary fiction 15. Southern fiction

Sequel to: Bull Mountain.

A follow-up to the award-winning Bull Mountain finds sheriff and father Clayton Burroughs struggling to recover from the shooting that ended his brothers' lives before violent rivals compel his return to the criminal past he would leave behind.

Paretsky, Sara

Bitter medicine / Sara Paretsky. W. Morrow, 1987. 321 p. V. I. Warshawski mysteries

ISBN 9780688064488

1. Medical malpractice 2. Women private investigators 3. Hospitals 4. Criminal investigation 5. Murder 6. Murder investigation 7. Feminists 8. Chicago, Illinois 9. Mysteries

LC 86033238

V. I. Warshawski performs a favor when she drives her 16-year-old pregnant friend and her husband to a job interview. The next day the obstetrician is found murdered.

LIST OF FICTIONAL WORKS

Paretsky, Sara

Blacklist : a V.I. Warshawski novel / Sara Paretsky. G. P. Putnam's Sons, 2003. 416 p. V. I. Warshawski mysteries

ISBN 0399150854

1. FBI 2. Women private investigators 3. Terrorism 4. Missing persons 5. Egyptians in the United States 6. Secrets 7. Betrayal 8. September 11 Terrorist Attacks, 2001 9. Suburbs 10. Criminal investigation 11. Feminists 12. Chicago, Illinois 13. Mysteries

LC 2003043157

Gold Dagger Award for Best Crime Novel of the Year, 2004.

Checking up on empty family mansions for an old client, V.I. discovers the body of a missing reporter who disappeared during the McCarthy era, a find that has links to two prestigious Chicago families.

"As always, V. I.'s determined pursuit of the truth ensures at least a few heart-stopping moments." Library Journal.

Paretsky, Sara

Blood shot / Sara Paretsky. Delacorte Press, 1988. 328 p. V. I. Warshawski mysteries

ISBN 0440500354

1. Criminal investigation 2. Women private investigators 3. Murder 4. Murder investigation 5. Feminists 6. Chicago, Illinois 7. Mysteries

LC 88003861

Also published as Toxic Shock.

Silver Dagger Award for Fiction, 1988.

Returning to her South Side alma mater for a reunion, private detective V.I. Warshawski becomes involved in the search for a former classmate's long-lost father, a quest that uncovers a web of corruption, danger, and murder.

"Blood Shot takes [the detective-heroine V.I. Warshawski] back to the working-class Chicago neighbourhoods of her youth, where a callous industrialist lurks at the centre of a deadly web of violence and intrigue." Quill & Quire.

Paretsky, Sara

Breakdown / Sara Paretsky. G.P. Putnam's Sons, 2012. 448 p. V. I. Warshawski mysteries

ISBN 9780399157837

1. Women private investigators 2. Murder suspects 3. Murder investigation 4. Women politicians 5. Rich men 6. Feminists 7. Chicago, Illinois 8. Mysteries

When the teenage daughters of some of Chicago's most influential families discover the body of a ritually murdered victim, V.I. Warshawski explores theories that the killing is linked to a senatorial candidate or a wealthy patriarch's childhood in Lithuania.

Paretsky, Sara

* **Brush** back / Sara Paretsky. G. P. Putnam's Sons, 2015. 480 p. V. I. Warshawski mysteries

ISBN 9780399160578

1. Women private investigators 2. Innocence (Law) 3. Conspiracies 4. Murder suspects 5. Murder investigation 6. Women politicians 7. Private investigators 8. Feminists 9. Chicago, Illinois 10. Mysteries

LC 2015005018

First published: London : Hodder & Stoughton, 2015.

Reluctantly agreeing to help when an old boyfriend asks her to exonerate his mother for the murder of his sister, V. I. Warshawski is forced to confront ugly politics and violent elements in her hometown.

"Paretsky, who plots more conscientiously than anyone else in the field, digs deep, then deeper, into past and present until all is revealed. The results will be especially appealing to baseball fans, who'll appreciate the punning chapter titles and learn more than they ever imagined about Wrigley Field." Kirkus.

Paretsky, Sara

* **Burn** marks / Sara Paretsky. Delacorte Press, 1990. 340 p. V. I. Warshawski mysteries

ISBN 9780385298926

1. Arson 2. Women private investigators 3. Political corruption 4. Construction industry and trade 5. Criminal investigation 6. Murder 7. Murder investigation 8. Feminists 9. Chicago, Illinois 10. Mysteries

LC 89023418

When Chicago private eye V.I. Warshawski investigates a fire at a SRO hotel that leaves her aunt homeless, she becomes embroiled in a tangle of political corruption, arson, and murder.

"The 'whydunit' in Ms. Paretsky's books is often embedded in the fabric of problems that confront us all--the poisoned environment, for example, or urban blight. This extra dimension adds an immediacy to 'Burn Marks' that is not found in many private-eye novels." New York Times Book Review.

Paretsky, Sara

Critical mass / Sara Paretsky. Putnam Adult, 2013. 448 p. V. I. Warshawski mysteries

ISBN 9780399160561

1. Women private investigators 2. Secrets 3. Conspiracies 4. Murder suspects 5. Murder investigation 6. Women politicians 7. Holocaust survivors 8. Private investigators 9. Feminists 10. Chicago, Illinois 11. Mysteries

LC 2013025097

Assisting best friend Lotty Herschel to protect a fellow Holocaust survivor's daughter from dangerous adversaries, V. I. Warshawski uncovers a maelstrom of lies and secrets stemming from the competition to develop the first atomic bomb.

Paretsky, Sara

* **Dead** land / Sara Paretsky. William Morrow & Co, 2020. 304 p. V. I. Warshawski mysteries

ISBN 9780062435927

1. Women private investigators 2. Grandmother and granddaughter 3. Corruption 4. Land use 5. Real estate development 6. Murder 7. Conspiracies 8. Intrigue 9. Criminal investigation 10. Chicago, Illinois 11. Kansas 12. Mysteries

Dragged by her impetuous goddaughter into a legal battle over a clandestine deal that is threatening community land, V. I. Warshawski uncovers a developer scheme that ends the life of the young man her goddaughter is dating.

"A high point in Paretsky's long-running and much-loved series." Booklist.

Paretsky, Sara

Fallout / Sara Paretsky. HarperCollins, 2017. 304 p. V. I. Warshawski mysteries

ISBN 9780062435842

1. Women private investigators 2. Small towns 3. Race relations 4. Murder suspects 5. Murder investigation 6. Universities and colleges 7. Cold War 8. Private investigators 9. Feminists 10. Kansas 11. Mysteries

Savvy investigator Vic leaves her comfort zone in Chicago to investigate the disappearances of a young film student and a faded Hollywood star in Kansas, where a university town, the remnants of the Cold War and long-simmering racial tensions are stirred into violence by mysteries and murders.

"Paretsky is at the top of her game here, evidenced by the satisfying, layered puzzle peopled by a vividly described and intriguing cast." Booklist.

Paretsky, Sara

Fire sale / Sara Paretsky. G.P. Putnam's Sons, 2005. 416 p. V. I. Warshawski mysteries

ISBN 0399152792

1. Business sabotage 2. Women private investigators 3. Murder 4. High school basketball coaches 5. Family businesses 6. Inheritance and succession 7. Family relationships 8. Criminal investigation 9. Murder investigation 10. Feminists 11. Chicago, Illinois 12. Mysteries

LC 2005047601

Coaching the basketball team at her former South Chicago high school, V.I. Warshawski investigates sabotage at the site of the area's largest employer, where an explosion has killed the facility's owner and launched a dangerous family rivalry.

"Fast-paced and as entertaining." Library Journal.

Paretsky, Sara

Guardian angel / Sara Paretsky. Delacorte Press, 1992. 370 p. V. I. Warshawski mysteries

ISBN 9780385299312

1. Real estate 2. Political corruption 3. Women private investigators 4. Criminal investigation 5. Murder 6. Murder investigation 7. Feminists 8. Chicago, Illinois 9. Mysteries

LC 91024976

After her golden retriever has puppies, and her yuppie neighbors put them to sleep while dog-sitting, V.I. uncovers a corporate network of murder and corruption

Paretsky, Sara

* **Hard** time / Sara Paretsky. Delacorte Press, 1999. 385 p. V. I. Warshawski mysteries

ISBN 0385313632

1. Traffic accident victims 2. Criminal investigation 3. Women private investigators 4. Murder 5. Murder investigation 6. Feminists 7. Chicago, Illinois 8. Mysteries

LC 99022214

V.I. Warshawski takes on the entertainment industry when a fateful Good Samaritan act on behalf of a woman lying injured in the street plunges the plucky PI into a case involving dastardly deeds committed by the world's largest provider of security and prison services

Paretsky, Sara

Hardball / Sara Paretsky. G. P. Putnams Sons, 2009. 464 p. V. I. Warshawski mysteries

ISBN 9780399155932

1. Women private investigators 2. Missing persons 3. Racism 4. Gang members 5. Race relations 6. Kidnapping 7. Criminal investigation 8. Feminists 9. Chicago, Illinois 10. Mysteries

LC 2009020700

Hired to track down a man who has been missing for forty years, V.I. Warshawski inadvertently unearths old skeletons from Chicago's history and her own family, a situation marked by a young cousin she has never met and the untimely death of a nun.

"The thing about Sara Paretsky is, she's tough--not because she observes the bonebreaker conventions of the private-eye genre but because she doesn't flinch from examining old social injustices others might find too shameful (and too painful) to dig up." New York Times Book Review.

Paretsky, Sara

Indemnity only : a novel / Sara Paretsky. Dell, 1982. 244 p. V. I. Warshawski mysteries

ISBN 9780385272131

1. Labor unions -- Corrupt practices 2. Missing persons 3. Women private investigators 4. Criminal investigation 5. Murder 6. Insurance companies 7. Bankers 8. Murder investigation 9. Feminists 10. Chicago, Illinois 11. Mysteries

"Chicago private eye V. I. Warshawski is hired to locate a young woman and instead comes across the body of her boyfriend, a crooked union, and an insurance scam. Thugs beat V. I. up, and another man is murdered. This is all standard hard-boiled detective stuff, except that V. I. is a woman: independent, good looking, and believable. Paretsky has done an excellent job of presenting a real female private eye, without falling into parody." Library Journal.

Paretsky, Sara

Shell game / Sara Paretsky. William Morrow, 2018. 304 p. V. I. Warshawski mysteries

ISBN 9780062435866

1. Women private investigators 2. White collar crime 3. International intrigue 4. Law firms 5. Greed 6. Murder suspects 7. Organized crime 8. Criminals 9. Criminal investigation 10. Chicago, Illinois 11. Mysteries

LC 2018018513

Returning to Chicago to prevent an erroneous murder charge, V. I. Warshawski traces a stolen artifact with links to a network of international mobsters, terrorist financiers, scammers and art thieves.

Paretsky, Sara

* **Total** recall : a V.I. Warshawski novel / Sara Paretsky. Delacorte Press, 2001. xiii, 414 p. V. I. Warshawski mysteries

ISBN 9780385313667

1. Criminal investigation 2. Family secrets 3. Insurance -- Adjustment of claims 4. Women private investigators 5. Murder 6. Murder investigation 7. Feminists 8. Women Holocaust survivors 9. Holocaust (1933-1945) -- Reparations 10. Female friendship 11. Secrets 12. Extortion 13. Recovered memory 14. Chicago, Illinois 15. Mysteries

LC 2001028801

Private detective V.I. Warshawski is called in to assist her dear friend and mentor, Dr. Lotty Hershel, who is faced with the appearance of a mysterious man who may have a terrifying link to Lotty's past and dangerous implications for her present.

"This mystery is written with the stylistic verve and intellectual energy of a writer just coming into her own." New York Times Book Review.

Paretsky, Sara

Tunnel vision / Sara Paretsky. Delacorte Press, 1994. 432 p. V. I. Warshawski mysteries

ISBN 038529932X

1. Homeless persons 2. Political corruption 3. Criminal investigation 4. Women private investigators 5. Murder 6. Murder investigation 7. Feminists 8. Chicago, Illinois 9. Mysteries

LC 946050

Private investigator V.I. Warshawski pits her sleuthing skills against high-level government and financial powers when she investigates Home Free, a homeless advocates' group; financial fraud; and murder

"This principled private eye intimidates people because she doesn't know the meaning of compromise and won't tolerate moral slackers." New York Times Book Review.

LIST OF FICTIONAL WORKS

Paretsky, Sara

Windy city blues : V.I. Warshawski stories Delacorte Press, 1995. 258 p. V. I. Warshawski mysteries

ISBN 0385315023

1. Criminal investigation 2. Women private investigators 3. Murder 4. Murder investigation 5. Feminists 6. Chicago, Illinois 7. Short stories 8. Mysteries

LC 95008302

Nine stories feature Chicago's hard-nosed but tender-hearted private investigator V.I. Warshawski

"Although V.I.'s just as feisty and tough-talking as ever, she presents a somewhat softer side in this series of stories that gives a nostalgic nod to Vic's friends, family, and past." Booklist.

Parini, Jay

The **Damascus** road : a novel of Saint Paul / Jay Parini. Doubleday, 2019 368 p.

ISBN 9780385522786

1. Paul,, the Apostle, Saint 2. Luke,, Saint 3. 1st century 4. Apostles 5. Christianity 6. Conversion to Christianity 7. Church history -- Primitive and early church, ca 30-600 8. Voyages and travels 9. Life change events 10. Jewish men 11. Prophets 12. Visions 13. Bible novels 14. Christian historical fiction

The best-selling author of The Last Station presents a historical novel inspired by the Apostle Paul, who at the side of gospel writer Luke becomes Christianity's most influential messenger in an ancient world on the brink of epochal change.

Parini, Jay

The **passages** of H.M. : a novel of Herman Melville / Jay Parini. Doubleday, 2010. 464 p.

ISBN 9780385522779

1. Melville, Herman, 1819-1891 2. Authors, American 3. Alcoholism 4. Marital conflict 5. Husband and wife 6. Male friendship -- United States -- History 7. United States -- History -- 19th century 8. Biographical fiction 9. Historical fiction

LC 2010006291

A tale inspired by the life of Herman Melville finds the aging author's wife witnessing his descent into alcoholism and obscurity in the decades after the failure of "Moby Dick," a work of creative genius shaped by memories of youthful seafaring adventures.

Paris, B. A.

* **Behind** closed doors / B. A. Paris. St. Martin's Press, 2016. 293 p.

ISBN 9781250121004

1. Husband and wife 2. Suburban life 3. Deception 4. Married people 5. Newlyweds 6. Psychopaths 7. Abused women 8. Sisters 9. Psychological suspense

The friends of a seemingly perfect socialite couple begin to see cracks in the facade when they realize that the husband and wife are never apart and that there are bars on one of their upstairs windows.

Paris, B. A.

The **breakdown** / B. A. Paris. St. Martin's Press, 2017. 328 p.

ISBN 9781250122469

1. Murder witnesses 2. Memory 3. Stalking 4. Murder 5. Guilt 6. Paranoia 7. Dementia 8. Stalkers 9. Thrillers and suspense

LC 2017002673

Unable to forget a murder she witnessed when she was where she was not supposed to be, Cass struggles with an increasingly compromised memory before she begins receiving silent, sinister phone calls.

Paris, B. A.,

Bring me back : a novel / B.A. Paris. St. Martin's Press, 2018. 291 p.

ISBN 9781250151339

1. Missing women 2. Sisters 3. Former lovers 4. Loss (Psychology) 5. Deception 6. Engaged persons 7. Men/women relations 8. Psychological suspense

LC 2017060169

A decade after a man's wife disappears without a trace, his new fiancée makes a discovery that raises questions about what happened and whether his first wife may still be alive.

Parker, Lucy

The **Austen** playbook / Lucy Parker. Carina Press, 2019. 400 p. London celebrities

ISBN 9781335006899

1. Actors and actresses 2. Theater critics 3. Interpersonal attraction 4. Men/women relations 5. England 6. Romantic comedies 7. Contemporary romances

"In the delightful fourth in Parker's contemporary London Celebrities series (after Making Up), readers will easily immerse themselves into the passionate world of actor Frederica 'Freddy' Carlton and critic James 'Griff' Ford-Griffin. . . . There's more drama offstage than on, the writing is outstanding, and the bit of mystery blends well into the romance." Publishers Weekly

Parker, Robert B., 1932-2010

* **Appaloosa** / Robert B. Parker. G.P. Putnam's Sons, 2005. 288 p. Virgil Cole and Everett Hitch

ISBN 0399152776

1. United States deputy marshals 2. Wanderers and wandering 3. Honor in men 4. Ranchers 5. Male friendship 6. Fugitives 7. Escaped convicts 8. Gunfighters 9. Outlaws 10. Small town life -- The West (United States) 11. Gunfights 12. Manipulation by women 13. Men/women relations 14. The West (United States) -- History -- 19th century 15. Westerns

LC 2004058745

Arriving in a small nineteenth-century western town only to discover that its sheriff has been killed and its residents placed at the mercy of renegade rancher Randall Bregg, itinerant lawmen Virgil Cole and Everett Hitch find themselves facing an unusually challenging adversary who works by playing psychological games.

"The story gallops along to a surprise ending, but beneath the trappings of this gunfighter novel, Parker really has something to say about the nature of men and women in the Old West." Library Journal.

Parker, Robert B., 1932-2010

Back story / Robert B. Parker. G.P. Putnam's Sons, 2003. 320 p. Spenser novels

ISBN 0399149775

1. FBI 2. Cold cases (Criminal investigation) 3. Bank robberies 4. Mafia 5. Male friendship 6. Hippies 7. Revolutionaries 8. Children of murder victims 9. Murder investigation 10. Private investigators 11. Boston, Massachusetts 12. Massachusetts 13. Mysteries 14. Hardboiled fiction

LC 2002036901

Thirty years after an unsolved bank robbery leaves a woman dead, Paul Giacomin, whom Spenser regards like a son, and Daryl Gordon, the son of the robbery victim, turn to Spenser to seek out clues about the crime.

"The repartee between Spenser and Hawk is fast and funny; the sentiment between Spenser and Susan and the musings about Spenser's code are only occasionally cloying; and there's a scattering of remarkable action scenes including a tense shootout in Harvard Stadium." Publishers Weekly.

Parker, Robert B., 1932-2010

Blue-eyed devil / Robert B. Parker. G.P. Putnam's Sons, 2010. 288 p. Virgil Cole and Everett Hitch

ISBN 9780399156489

1. Police chiefs 2. Police corruption 3. Protection racket 4. Honor in men 5. Gunfighters 6. Outlaws 7. Small town life -- The West (United States) 8. Gunfights 9. The West (United States) -- History -- 19th century 10. Westerns

Refusing recruitment by ambitious new chief Amos Callico, itinerant lawmen Virgil Cole and Everett Hitch protect local merchants who the chief is harassing for protection money, a situation that escalates to the shooting of a politically connected landowner's son.

"More shifting allegiances, moral dilemmas and characters capable of change than Virgil and Everett's fans may be used to. It's a shame that this youngest of the late Parker's franchises has to end so soon." Kirkus.

Parker, Robert B., 1932-2010

Brimstone / Robert B. Parker. G. P. Putnam's Sons, 2009. 320 p. Virgil Cole and Everett Hitch

ISBN 9780399155710

1. Former lovers 2. Assassins 3. Love triangles 4. Brothels 5. Redemption 6. Change (Psychology) 7. Murder 8. Violence in men 9. Gunfights 10. Protectiveness in men 11. Small town life -- The West (United States) 12. The West (United States) -- History -- 19th century 13. Texas -- History -- 19th century 14. Westerns

LC 2009008107

Everett Hitch and Virgil Cole track down Virgil's sweetheart Allie and the three head north to start over in the town of Brimstone. Given their reputations as guns for hire, Everett and Virgil are able to secure positions as the town's deputies. But a sanctimonious leader of a local church stirs up trouble at the local saloons, and as the violence escalates into murder, the two struggle to keep the peace.

"The result is classic Parker--exciting, suspenseful, fast-moving and entertaining." Publishers Weekly.

Parker, Robert B., 1932-2010

Chance / Robert B. Parker. Berkley Books, 1996. 328 p. Spenser novels

ISBN 9780425157473

1. Missing persons investigation -- Las Vegas, Nevada 2. Gamblers -- Las Vegas, Nevada 3. Mafia -- Las Vegas, Nevada 4. Extramarital affairs 5. Women murder victims 6. Private investigators 7. Las Vegas, Nevada 8. Boston, Massachusetts 9. Massachusetts 10. Mysteries 11. Hardboiled fiction

Spenser and his sidekick, Hawk, become entangled in the affairs of the Mafia and in an internecine struggle for control of the Boston underworld when they set out to find the errant spouse of the daughter of big-time Boston hoodlum Julius Ventura

"Parker's stouthearted hero proves that he is still as tough and manly as they come, and more principled than ever in this punchy private-eye caper." New York Times Book Review.

Parker, Robert B., 1932-2010

Cold service / Robert B. Parker. G.P. Putnam's Sons, 2005. 320 p. Spenser novels

ISBN 9780399152405

1. Mafia 2. Police corruption 3. International intrigue 4. Bodyguards 5. Male friendship 6. Ukrainians in the United States 7. Gangsters 8. Independence in men 9. Pride and vanity in men 10. Revenge 11. Professional ethics 12. Private investigators 13. Boston, Massachusetts 14. Massachusetts 15. Mysteries 16. Hardboiled fiction

LC 2004056608

When his friend, Hawk, is brutally injured after helping protect another man, bookie Luther Gillespie, Boston private detective Spenser throws himself into Hawk's rehabilitation and investigates the Ukrainian mob he believes is responsible for the attack, a case that is complicated by local police force corruption.

"As the tale begins, the heretofore-indestructible Hawk is recovering from a near-death experience: shot in the back while protecting a bookie from the upstart Ukrainian Mob. It's payback time, of course, but not before Hawk nurses himself back to psychic and physical health. Meanwhile, Spenser does a bit of sleuthing on his own, determining that Hawk's assailants are the tip of a Ukrainian iceberg that has stuck its tentacles deep into Boston's underworld. Payback, Hawk style, requires eliminating not just the shooters but also the entire Mob. The action comes in a rush near the end, but the satisfying part here is watching Parker dig deeply into the remarkable friendship between two tough guys constitutionally averse to the whole touchy-feely side of life." Booklist.

Parker, Robert B., 1932-2010

Death in paradise / Robert B. Parker. G.P. Putnam's Sons, 2001 294 p. Jesse Stone mysteries

ISBN 9780399147791

1. Police chiefs 2. Small town life -- Massachusetts 3. Teenage girl murder victims 4. Murder investigation 5. Former baseball players 6. Recovering alcoholics 7. Divorced men 8. Massachusetts 9. Mysteries 10. Hardboiled fiction

LC 2001031874

Jesse Stone, Chief of Police in the quiet New England town of Paradise, is enjoying a beer when he receives a call for help. The body of a teenage girl has been found in a nearby lake. Stone must figure out who would want to kill her, all the while fighting to keep his personal life in order as he struggles with alcoholism and strong feelings for his ex-wife.

Parker, Robert B., 1932-2010

Double deuce / Robert B. Parker. Berkley Books, 1993, c1992. 244 p. Spenser novels

ISBN 9780425137932

1. Public housing 2. Gangs 3. Inner city violence 4. Shooting 5. Murder investigation 6. Private investigators 7. Boston, Massachusetts 8. Massachusetts 9. Mysteries 10. Hardboiled fiction

Originally published: New York : G.P. Putnam's Sons, 1992.

The Double Deuce is a Boston housing project. Good people live in poverty there. So do the Hobarts, a gang that relieves boredom by shooting pedestrians. To protect the residents of the Double Deuce, urban gunslinger Hawk enlists the aid of private investigator Spenser. Together, they try to track down Major Johnson, the gang leader responsible for a particularly tragic drive-by shooting.

Parker, Robert B., 1932-2010

Double play / Robert B. Parker. G.P. Putnam's Sons, 2004. 304 p.

ISBN 0399151885

1. Robinson, Jackie, 1919-1972 2. Brooklyn Dodgers (Baseball team) 3. 1940s 4. Bodyguards 5. African American baseball players 6. Baseball players 7. World War II veterans 8. Professional baseball players 9. Baseball 10. Gangsters 11. Race relations 12. Racism 13. Mafia 14. Memories 15. Interracial friendship 16. Trust 17. Brooklyn, New York City 18. Historical mysteries 19. Hardboiled fiction

LC 2004040029

Joseph Burke--ex-marine, ex-husband, ex-somebody--is hired as a bodyguard to protect Lauren Roach, twenty-five and spoiled rotten. The unlikely duo become entangled with Burke's boyhood hero, color barrier-breaking baseball player Jackie Robinson, in a story that is both thrilling and engaging. It is in the historical character of Jackie Robinson that Mr. Parker finds his inspiration, and Joseph Burke may find his redemption.

"Parker pretty much defies category altogether in this deeply felt and intimately told memory tale, which takes place during the historic baseball season of 1947, when Jackie Robinson broke the color bar in major-league baseball by playing first base for the Brooklyn Dodgers. Fusing this chapter of sports history with a hardboiled gangster plot and haunting recollections of his own Boston boyhood, Parker fashions a hugely entertaining fiction that also serves as a blueprint for the themes that preoccupy him as a writer and the code of values that sustains his work." New York Times Book Review.

Parker, Robert B., 1932-2010

Family honor : a Sunny Randall novel / Robert B. Parker. G. P. Putnam's Sons, 1999. 322 p. Sunny Randall mysteries

ISBN 0399145664

1. Runaway teenagers 2. Conspiracies 3. Attempted murder 4. Teenage prostitution 5. Politicians 6. Former policewomen 7. Women private investigators 8. Boston, Massachusetts 9. Mysteries

LC 99027488

Sunny Randall, a Boston private investigator, is hired by a wealthy family to locate their teenage daughter. When the difficult teenager refuses to return to her family, Sunny reluctantly becomes her bodyguard. Before long, Sunny finds herself battling a criminal conspiracy involving top state officials.

"Private detective Sunny Randall is hired by a powerful family to find their runaway daughter, Millicent, who, it transpires, is hooking and needs rescuing. . . . Millicent, it happens, witnessed a conspiracy to murder arising from her cold, ambitious parentsher father aims to be governorand the Italian mobsters who control them. The mobsters now want her dead, and Sunny, too, if need be. . . . The high suspense is equaled by the emotional power of Sunny's bonding with the damaged girl. A bravura performance." Publishers Weekly.

Parker, Robert B., 1932-2010

Gunman's rhapsody / Robert B. Parker. Putnam's, 2001. 289 p.

ISBN 0399147624

1. Earp, Wyatt, 1848-1929 2. Holliday, John H, 1851-1887 3. Masterson, Bat, 1853-1921 4. 1870s 5. United States marshals 6. Love triangles 7. Gunfighters 8. Feuds 9. Outlaws 10. Jealousy in men 11. Conspiracies 12. Dodge City, Kansas 13. Tombstone, Arizona 14. Westerns 15. Biographical fiction

LC 00053327

In 1879, lawman Wyatt Earp, accompanied by his wife and his brothers, leaves Dodge City and heads to Tombstone, Arizona, where he takes a job as deputy sheriff.

"The novel shows surprising fidelity to most of the known facts without letting them get in the way of a good story. Parker's strengths here, as in his crime novels, are plot and dialogue." New York Times Book Review.

Parker, Robert B., 1932-2010

Hugger Mugger / Robert B. Parker. G.P. Putnam's Sons, 2000. 307 p. Spenser novels

ISBN 9780399145872

1. Race horses 2. Thoroughbred horse farms 3. Dysfunctional families 4. Horse racing 5. Private investigators 6. Georgia 7. Boston, Massachusetts 8. Massachusetts 9. Mysteries 10. Hardboiled fiction

LC 9956105

Boston private detective Spenser journeys to Georgia to protect a young horse after he is hired by Walter Clive, the president of Three Fillies Stables, to uncover the creep who is threatening his prize horse, Hugger Mugger.

Parker, Robert B., 1932-2010

Hush money / Robert B. Parker. G. P. Putnam's Sons, 1999. 309 p. Spenser novels

ISBN 0399144587

1. African American political activists 2. Extortion 3. Gay men -- Outing 4. Women stalkers 5. Militia movement -- Maine 6. White supremacists -- Maine 7. Universities and colleges 8. African American college teachers 9. College teachers -- Tenure 10. Private investigators 11. Boston, Massachusetts 12. Massachusetts 13. Mysteries 14. Hardboiled fiction

LC 9837344

Popular Boston private investigator Spenser and his sidekick Hawk investigate untoward doings at a venerable university that involve politics, sex, and race and develop into a vast racial conspiracy.

Parker, Robert B., 1932-2010

Melancholy baby / Robert B. Parker. G. P. Putnam's Sons, 2004. 320 p. Sunny Randall mysteries

ISBN 0399152180

1. Family secrets 2. Gay men 3. Birthparents -- Identification 4. Divorced women 5. Women psychotherapy patients 6. Women psychiatrists 7. Former husbands 8. College students 9. Women college students 10. Birthmothers 11. Remarriage 12. Women and dogs 13. Former policewomen 14. Women private investigators 15. Boston, Massachusetts 16. Mysteries

LC 2004050377

First published in 2005.

Upset by her ex-husband Richie's upcoming marriage, private detective Sunny Randall takes the case of college student Sarah Markham, a troubled young woman searching for her birth parents, but her investigation uncovers dangerous secrets that could not only shatter Sarah's life but also lead to painful secrets about her own past.

"Boston P.I. Sunny Randall is unhappy to learn that the ex-husband she still loves is getting married to someone else. Her life seemingly a mess, Sunny seeks the help of psychiatrist Susan Silverman. In between sessions that probe her relationship with her insufferable mother and beloved father, Sunny works on the case of Sarah Markham, a distraught 21-year-old woman who wants to track down her biological parents. The only trouble is that the couple who raised her claim she's theirs but refuse to take a DNA test to prove it. Sunny soon learns that Sarah's parents have lied about their past. . . . Parker, as always, leavens his story with sly wit while relying on dialog to advance the plot and develop character." Library Journal.

Parker, Robert B., 1932-2010

Night passage / Robert B. Parker. G. P. Putnam's Sons, 1997. 322 p. Jesse Stone mysteries

ISBN 9780399143045

1. Organized crime 2. Small town life -- Massachusetts 3. Police chiefs -- Massachusetts 4. Divorced men 5. Alcoholic men 6. Militia movement 7. Massachusetts 8. Mysteries 9. Hardboiled fiction

LC 97-6901

Previous ed.: New York : G.P. Putnam's, 1997 ; Harpenden, Hertfordshire : No Exit Press, 1999.

An otherwise washed-up LAPD cop with a drinking problem gets a job offer from a small Massachusetts town that is too good to be true, and Jesse Stone finds himself with no one to trust and a town full of moral and political corruption.

"This mystery features complex, expertly shaded relationships, especially romantic, as Jesse flails and fails at loving both his ex-wife and his new girlfriend. The most powerful romance here, though, is between Parker and the written word." Publishers Weekly.

Parker, Robert B., 1932-2010

Now and then / Robert B. Parker. G. P. Putnam's Sons, 2007. 304 p. Spenser novels

ISBN 9780399154416

1. Extramarital affairs 2. Terrorists 3. Murder suspects 4. Murder 5. Murder investigation 6. Former lovers 7. Deception 8. Secrets 9. Dishonesty 10. Men/women relations 11. Private investigators 12. Boston, Massachusetts 13. Massachusetts 14. Mysteries 15. Hardboiled fiction

LC 2007023056

Investigating a new client's unfaithful wife, Boston private eye Spenser finds himself in trouble when the case goes terribly wrong and three people wind up dead, a situation that reveals the wife's lover's ties to a terrorist organization.

"The story itself makes compelling reading on its own, but Parker, as usual, spikes it with caustic wit and the interplay between Spenser and his longtime love, Susan. And here he ups the ante by calling on Spenser to use all his brain and brawn to protect Susan. Terrific." Booklist.

Parker, Robert B., 1932-2010

Painted ladies / Robert B. Parker. G.P. Putnam's Sons, 2010. 304 p. Spenser novels

ISBN 9780399156854

1. Private investigators 2. Art thefts 3. Bombing 4. Ransom 5. Secrets 6. Deception 7. Art museums 8. Boston, Massachusetts 9. Massachusetts 10. Mysteries 11. Hardboiled fiction

LC 2010020027

Hired by a museum to provide protection during a ransom exchange for a stolen painting, Spenser is personally outraged when the ransom fails and the painting is not recovered, a case that makes him suspect the innocence of the art scholar who retained him.

"The focus on Susan comes at the expense of the plot, which, as Spenser novels go, is fairly pedestrian. . . . The story gives us extended looks at two of the most-beloved Spenser side characters, homicide Capt. Martin Quirk and Sgt. Frank Belson, as well as brief nods to many of the others who have stood at Spenser's side in the past Hawk, Vinnie, Chollo, Lee Farrell, Epstein, Tedy Sapp, the Grey Man. Mostly, though, what Painted Ladies gives us is Spenser being Spenser. And he couldn't do that without Susan." Chicago Sun-Times.

Parker, Robert B., 1932-2010

Paper doll / Robert B. Parker. Berkley Books, 1993 279 p. Spenser novels

ISBN 9780425141557

1. Husband and wife 2. Women murder victims 3. Scandals 4. Politicians 5. Rich people 6. Private investigators 7. Boston, Massachusetts 8. Massachusetts 9. Mysteries 10. Hardboiled fiction

LC 92030528

Originally published: New York : G.P. Putnam's, 1993.

When Boston aristocrat Loudon Tripp hires Spenser to investigate his wife's murder, Spenser uncovers high-class scandals and a corpse that might not be dead after all.

"Mr. Parker has trimmed his language and characterizations right down to the knuckle to tell this poignant story about the false fronts that people put up to shield themselves from shame. There's no flab on Spenser, either." New York Times Book Review.

Parker, Robert B., 1932-2010

Potshot / Robert B. Parker. G.P. Putnam's Sons, 2001. 294 p. Spenser novels

ISBN 0399147101

1. Seniors 2. Small town life -- Arizona 3. Extortion 4. Swindlers and swindling 5. Coercion 6. Murder investigation 7. Gangs 8. Private investigators 9. Arizona 10. Mysteries 11. Hardboiled fiction

LC 00068342

Spenser heads to Potshot, Arizona, a former mining town reborn as a paradise for the wealthy of Los Angeles looking for a place to escape. Spenser has been hired by Mary Lou Buckman to investigate the murder of her husband. Mrs. Buckman believes that her husband was killed when he refused to pay a local gang, led by The Preacher, protection money for their outdoor tour service.

"Rounding up this posse of urban gunslingers--all hard-bitten veterans of previous Spenser novels--was pure inspiration on Parker's part, because another shrewd way of keeping a sleuth in shape over the long haul is to guarantee that he has some fun." New York Times Book Review.

Parker, Robert B., 1932-2010

Rough weather / Robert B. Parker. G.P. Putnam's Sons, 2008. 304 p. Spenser novels

ISBN 9780399155192

1. Weddings 2. Kidnapping 3. Enemies 4. Islands 5. Brides 6. Murder investigation 7. Hurricanes 8. Missing persons investigation 9. Private investigators 10. Boston, Massachusetts 11. Massachusetts 12. Mysteries 13. Hardboiled fiction

LC bl2008020411

Reluctantly escorting the gold-digging and recently separated Heidi Bradshaw to her daughter's wedding, Boston private investigator Spenser hopes to reconnect with his beloved Susan at the wedding, but becomes enmeshed in a kidnapping plot involving his nemesis Rugar.

Parker, Robert B., 1932-2010

School days / Robert B. Parker. G.P. Putnam's Sons, 2005. 304 p. Spenser novels

ISBN 0399153233

1. School shootings 2. Teenage murder suspects 3. Parent and teenager 4. Rich women 5. Grandmothers 6. Teenagers 7. Teenage boys 8. Grandmother and grandson 9. Private investigators 10. Mass shootings 11. Boston, Massachusetts 12. Massachusetts 13. Mysteries 14. Hardboiled fiction

LC 2005047690

Hired by a Massachusetts grand dame to prove the innocence of her grandson, who has been implicated in a school shooting,

Spenser wonders why the boy seems unconcerned about his possible wrongful imprisonment.

Parker, Robert B., 1932-2010

Sea change / Robert B. Parker. G.P. Putnam's Sons, 2006. 304 p. Jesse Stone mysteries

ISBN 0399152679

1. Police chiefs 2. Crimes against women 3. Small town life -- Massachusetts 4. Divorced men 5. Former wives 6. Families of murder victims 7. Sailboat racing 8. Sailing 9. Yachts 10. Murder 11. Murder investigation 12. Dead -- Identification 13. Men/women relations 14. Private investigators 15. Massachusetts 16. Mysteries 17. Hardboiled fiction

LC 2004043150

Features a cameo appearance by Spenser, the main character in the author's Spenser series.

When the body of a divorced Florida heiress washes ashore in Massachusetts, police chief Jesse Stone learns of the woman's past appearances in an erotic video and finds it suspicious that the victim's family seems unaffected by her death.

"The body of an unidentified woman is found in a cove off the Massachusetts village of Paradise, where Jesse Stone, former L.A. homicide detective, is now chief of police. With no clues and a bevy of nonlocals in town for the annual sailboat competition, Stone must use every resource at his disposal to find out who the woman was, what happened to her, and why no one has reported her missing. . . . Parker is a master at creating memorable characters and crime stories that are inevitably tied to social issues of some importance." Library Journal.

Parker, Robert B., 1932-2010

Shrink rap / Robert B. Parker. G.P. Putnam's Sons, 2002. 320 p. Sunny Randall mysteries

ISBN 0399149309

1. Stalkers 2. Women authors 3. Former husbands 4. Psychotherapists 5. Former policewomen 6. Women private investigators 7. Stalking 8. Boston, Massachusetts 9. Mysteries

LC 2002024826

Boston private detective Sunny Randall agrees to protect a touring writer from her abusive ex-husband, but she quickly learns that the stalker in question is much more sophisticated, intelligent, and potentially deadly than most.

"The Sunny Randall novel has the Boston private eye on a national book tour with a best-selling author who is being stalked by her former husband, an unethical and possibly unhinged psychiatrist. The situation proves ideal for Parker's patented brand of knowing humor, yielding glossary snapshots of dithering book dealers, dollar-driven publishers and awe-struck fans." New York Times Book Review.

Parker, Robert B., 1932-2010

Sixkill / Robert B. Parker. G. P. Putnam's Sons, 2011. 304 p. Spenser novels

ISBN 9780399157264

1. Private investigators 2. Murder investigation -- Boston, Massachusetts 3. Bodyguards 4. Actors and actresses 5. Women murder victims 6. Boston, Massachusetts 7. Massachusetts 8. Mysteries 9. Hardboiled fiction

LC 2010048041

When infamous actor Jumbo Nelson is accused of rape and murder, the Boston PD calls on Spenser to make heads or tails of the case. Although the evidence is mounting against Jumbo, Spenser makes a break when he teams up with Jumbo's bodyguard, Zebulon Sixkill, and uncovers some secrets involving the murder victim.

"The story has the depth of a puddle, but it's a well-designed puddle, so when it ripples, the clean, steady rolling of the waves is like a shimmering poem." Chicago Sun-Times.

Parker, Robert B., 1932-2010

Small vices / Robert B. Parker. G. P. Putnam's Sons, 1997. 308 p. Spenser novels

ISBN 0399142444

1. Judicial error 2. Frameups 3. Murder investigation 4. Women murder victims 5. Assassins 6. Private investigators 7. Boston, Massachusetts 8. Massachusetts 9. Mysteries 10. Hardboiled fiction

LC 969827

When a street kid with a rap sheet full of petty larcenies is convicted for the murder of a wealthy co-ed, Spenser delves into the bizarre world of the ultra-rich to prove his innocence.

"Mr. Parker has written a powerful piece about the defeat and reclamation of a hero, but I wouldn't say that Spenser's dance with death teaches the old knight to act his age. . . . By virtue of his mythic death and rebirth, he has defied mortality altogether and become like some fertility god who lowers himself into the ground each winter and comes roaring back to life each spring." New York Times Book Review.

Parker, Robert B., 1932-2010

Stone cold / Robert B. Parker. G.P. Putnam's Sons, 2003. 304 p. Jesse Stone mysteries

ISBN 0399150870

1. Rape 2. Serial murder investigation 3. Police chiefs 4. Recovering alcoholics 5. Divorced men 6. Serial murderers 7. Husband and wife 8. Former wives 9. Teenage rape victims 10. Men/women relations 11. Small town life -- Massachusetts 12. Massachusetts 13. Mysteries 14. Hardboiled fiction

LC 2003046730

Investigating a thrill-seeking pair of serial killers who are targeting the residents of an affluent suburban town, police chief Jesse Stone finds his job complicated by local politicians, the media, his drinking problem, and his ex-wife.

Parker, Robert B., 1932-2010

Stranger in paradise / Robert B. Parker. G.P. Putnam's Sons, 2008. 304 p. Jesse Stone mysteries

ISBN 9780399154607

1. Police chiefs 2. Kidnapping 3. Murder for hire 4. Former convicts 5. Organized crime 6. Gangs 7. Ethics 8. Massachusetts 9. Mysteries 10. Hardboiled fiction

LC 2007044773

Ten years after hit man Crow Cromartie escapes with the spoils of a lucrative heist, Massachusetts police officer Jesse Stone is astonished when the fugitive enlists his cooperation with a job gone bad involving a young woman whose father wants her killed.

Parker, Robert B., 1932-2010

Thin air / Robert B. Parker. Berkley Books, 1996, c1995. 293 p. Spenser novels

ISBN 9780425152904

1. Missing women 2. Mafia 3. Kidnapping 4. Missing persons investigation 5. Secrets 6. Private investigators 7. Boston, Massachusetts 8. Boston, Massachusetts 9. Massachusetts 10. Mysteries 11. Hardboiled fiction

LC 94039046 //r95

Originally published: New York : G.P. Putnam's, 1995.

When the bride of a Boston police detective vanishes, he hires Spenser to find her. His path leads from a New England college campus to glamorous L.A. sports clubs. When the trail turns to a world of prostitution, drug abuse, and self-destruction, Spenser must enter ghetto tenements to continue his search. Ultimately, Spenser must hire a Chicago hitman to help him free the girl from a sociopathic ex-lover. Working through gang leaders and corrupt cops, Spenser learns about humanity and justice as he strives to achieve his goal.

Parker, Robert B., 1932-2010

Trouble in Paradise / Robert B. Parker. G. P. Putnam's Sons, 1998. 324 p. Jesse Stone mysteries

ISBN 0399144331

1. Police chiefs 2. Former convicts 3. Small town life -- Massachusetts 4. Men/women relations 5. Recovering alcoholics 6. Divorced men 7. Criminals 8. Islands -- Massachusetts 9. Massachusetts 10. Mysteries 11. Hardboiled fiction

LC 987354

Jesse Stone, police chief of the Massachusetts coast town of Paradise, finds two of his lovers and an entire island threatened by a maniacal ex-convict

Parker, Robert B., 1932-2010

Valediction / Robert B. Parker. Dell, 1988, c1984. 284 p. Spenser novels

ISBN 9780440192466

1. Cults 2. Missing persons 3. Drug traffic 4. Money laundering 5. Heroin traffic 6. Private investigators 7. Boston, Massachusetts 8. Massachusetts 9. Mysteries 10. Hardboiled fiction

Originally published: New York : Delacorte Press, 1984.

Searching for a young woman who may or may not have been kidnapped, Spenser encounters a church militant and a heroin ring and struggles against his growing estrangement from the women he loves.

Parker, Robert B., 1932-2010

Walking shadow / Robert B. Parker. Berkley Books, 1995, c1994. 293 p. Spenser novels

ISBN 9780425147740

1. Stalking 2. Murder investigation 3. Gangs 4. Police misconduct 5. Police corruption 6. Repertory theater -- Massachusetts 7. Private investigators 8. Stalkers 9. Boston, Massachusetts 10. Massachusetts 11. Mysteries 12. Hardboiled fiction

Originally published: New York : Putnam, 1994.

"Boston PI Spenser encounters danger, venality and plenty of comic material in this . . . tale spanning the worlds of experimental theater and illegal immigration. While he'd rather be at work renovating the old farmhouse that he and his lover, psychiatrist Susan, have bought in nearby Concord, Spenser agrees to find out who is following the Artistic Director of the Port City Theater Company, on whose board of directors Susan sits." Publishers Weekly.

Parker, Robert B., 1932-2010

Widow's walk / Robert B. Parker. G. P. Putnam's Sons, 2002 320 p. Spenser novels

ISBN 0399148450

1. Murder investigation 2. Shooting 3. Women murder suspects 4. Widows 5. Private investigators 6. Boston, Massachusetts 7. Massachusetts 8. Mysteries 9. Hardboiled fiction

LC 2001048771

Spenser is getting nowhere investigating the gunshot murder of banker Nathan Smith. The police figure his unfaithful young wife, Mary, pulled the trigger. She denies it. Spenser is hired by former prosecutor Rita Fiore to help build Mary Smith's defense.

"The writing is as clean as fresh ice, and from the opening sentence (''I think she's probably guilty,' Rita Fiore said to me'), it's clear

that readers are in the hands of a vet who knows what he's doing." Publishers Weekly.

Parker, Samuel, 1974-

* Coldwater / Samuel Parker. Baker Pub Group, 2018 336 p.

ISBN 9780800727345

1. Former convicts 2. Revenge 3. Vigilantes 4. Enemies 5. Pariahs 6. Murderers 7. Demonic possession 8. Guilt 9. Justice 10. Thrillers and suspense 11. Christian suspense

LC 2017038473

An ex-con reluctantly moves back to his small hometown and must fight against both the vigilante group that is threatening him and the dark and destructive force that lives inside him.

Parker, Samuel, 1974-

Purgatory road / Samuel Parker. Revell, 2017. 304 p.

ISBN 9780800727338

1. Married people 2. Hermits 3. Desert survival 4. Kidnapping victims 5. Violence 6. Deception 7. Suffering 8. Mojave Desert 9. Nevada 10. Christian suspense

LC 2016029230

After Jack and his wife get lost on a day trip outside Las Vegas, they run into a desert hermit who has no intention of providing assistance, and also encounter a kidnapped runaway and her mentally unstable and possibly dangerous abductor.

"This is a skillfully written, gripping thriller, well supported by the author's fine eye for setting and ear for dialogue." Booklist.

Parker, T. Jefferson

Black water / T. Jefferson Parker. Hyperion, 2002. 352 p. Merci Rayborn mysteries

ISBN 078686804X

1. Police murders 2. Husband and wife 3. Revenge 4. Policewomen 5. Women detectives 6. Murder investigation 7. Southern California 8. Orange County, California 9. Mysteries 10. Police procedurals

LC 2001051903

Sequel to: Red light.

Detective Merci Rayborn must unravel a tangled web of murder, betrayal, and love when the attempted murder/suicide of young cop Archie Wildcraft, who is still alive with a bullet in his head, and his wife leads her in pursuit of the truth.

"Merci Rayborn, homicide detective for the Orange County, California, sheriff's department, has a crime scene that's a puzzler. And it's going to be very high profileit's in an upscale enclave of million-dollar estates, and one of the victims is a cop. Gwen Wildcraft is dead, and her husband, Archie, is unconscious with a severe head wound. Wildcraft is a patrol officer with the department, and his gun appears to be the murder weapon. Merci's superiors would prefer a quick call of murder-suicide, but her instincts tell her that's the wrong conclusion. . . . A thoughtful, multilayered tale in which crime is a catalyst rather than the centerpiece." Booklist.

Parker, T. Jefferson

The **blue** hour / T. Jefferson Parker. Hyperion, 1999. 359 p. Merci Rayborn mysteries

ISBN 0786862882

1. Former police 2. People with cancer 3. Serial murderers 4. Policewomen 5. Women detectives 6. Murder investigation 7. California 8. Southern California 9. Mysteries 10. Police procedurals

Sequel: Red light.

In a picturesque southern California beach community, a brutal serial killer is on the loose. His only victims are beautiful young women.

His only adversaries are two cops haunted by problems of their own: the tough Tim Hess who is batting a life threatening illness, and the brash Merci Rayborn who has a rep for causing trouble. Now this unlikely team must put aside their personal issues to stop a ruthless madman before he strikes again.

"Solid police work, beefed up with some ingenious devices from Parker's bottomless bag of tricks, makes it all come out rightbut not before the wondrously weird characters have taken this lurid plot to its outer limits." New York Times Book Review.

Parker, T. Jefferson

California girl : a novel / T. Jefferson Parker. William Morrow, 2004. 352 p.

ISBN 0060562366

1. 1960s 2. Cold cases (Criminal investigation) 3. Family secrets 4. Dysfunctional families 5. Police -- California 6. Clergy 7. Journalists 8. Brothers 9. Women murder victims 10. Murder investigation 11. California 12. Mexico 13. Mysteries

LC 2004042575

Edgar Allan Poe Award for Best Novel, 2005.

Living in Orange County, California, in the late 1960s, three brothers pursue leads relevant to their respective careers as a homicide detective, a minister, and a reporter when a woman from a childhood rival family is found murdered.

"Drenched in lust, love, betrayal, and unfulfilled promise, California Girl features masterly plotting, smart prose, and memorable characters." Library Journal.

Parker, T. Jefferson

Cold pursuit / T. Jefferson Parker. Hyperion, 2003. 384 p.

ISBN 0786868058

1. Police -- San Diego, California 2. Revenge 3. Assault and battery 4. Inheritance and succession 5. Murder 6. Murder investigation 7. Murder suspects 8. Octogenarians 9. Rich men 10. Home health care nurses 11. Feuds 12. California 13. San Diego, California 14. Mysteries

LC 2002032940

When the head of one of two feuding families is found murdered, homicide officer Tom McMichael, a member of the suspected family, is challenged to put aside his personal feelings in order to investigate.

"The murder of retired San Diego Port Commissioner and local politician Pete Braga falls in the lap of homicide detective Tom McMichael, whose family has a multigenerational feud going with the Bragas. Parker makes the most of a standard mystery device heremurder driven by a motive from the distant pastbut the real joy of the novel is its remarkably evocative prose, which flows seamlessly from lyrical descriptions of rainy San Diego to crisp, no-nonsense dialogue." Booklist.

Parker, T. Jefferson

The **fallen** : a novel / T. Jefferson Parker. William Morrow, 2006. 336 p.

ISBN 0060562382

1. Synesthesia 2. Political corruption 3. Police murders 4. Crimes against former police 5. Murder 6. Murder investigation 7. City life 8. Local government 9. Police -- San Diego, California 10. Secrets 11. Prostitution 12. Marital conflict 13. Organized crime 14. California 15. San Diego, California 16. Mysteries

LC 2005047934

After surviving a push from a sixth-floor hotel room, detective Robbie Brownlaw uses his new talent for synesthesia--seeing colorful shapes tied to emotions when someone speaks--to investigate the death of a fellow San Diego cop.

"This stand-alone classic police procedural, replete with its portrait of big-city crime and power-hungry politicians, follows a recognizable storyline. However, its lively writing, well-paced plot, rounded characters (from call girls to shady politicians), and twists stand out." Bookmarks Magazine.

Parker, T. Jefferson

The **famous** and the dead / T. Jefferson Parker. Dutton, 2013. 368 p. Charlie Hood thrillers

ISBN 9780525953173

1. United States. Bureau of Alcohol, Tobacco and Firearms Officials and employees 2. Undercover operations 3. Illegal arms transfers 4. Drug couriers 5. Cartels 6. Drug traffic 7. Police 8. Mexico 9. Southern California 10. Thrillers and suspense 11. Police procedurals

Charlie Hood struggles with the moral challenges of arresting his late love's cartel-connected son, Bradley Jones, while the enigmatic Mike Finnegan uses his unsettling knowledge to infiltrate both of their lives.

Parker, T. Jefferson

L.A. outlaws : a novel / T. Jefferson Parker. Dutton, 2008. 372 p. Charlie Hood thrillers

ISBN 9780525950554

1. Teachers 2. Criminals 3. Secret identity 4. Thieves 5. Police 6. Gangs 7. Secrets 8. Suspicion 9. Protectiveness in men 10. Criminal investigation 11. California 12. Los Angeles, California 13. Southern California 14. Thrillers and suspense

LC 2007033722

Investigating the latest crime scene of a celebrity thief who has been staging lucrative heists and donating the spoils to charity, rookie deputy Charlie Hood is forced to make an ethics-testing decision when the thief is targeted by a professional killer.

"Parker writes with an understanding of the West's essential character: in Outlaws, he casts Los Angeles as an eternally sprawling, brawling camp town, populated by bandits and bigots, the quick and the dead, where the poor who once rendered tallow now work the deep fryer at KFC. . . . His concise prose, at once low-key and lyrical, plays almost like cowboy poetry." Los Angeles Times.

Parker, T. Jefferson

Pacific beat : a novel / T. Jefferson Parker. St. Martin's Press, 1991. 364 p.

ISBN 9780312059439

1. Love triangles 2. Police 3. Revenge 4. Murder investigation 5. Brothers-in-law 6. Husband and wife 7. Frameups 8. Extramarital affairs 9. Adoptees -- Identity 10. Illegal hazardous waste disposal 11. Former police 12. California 13. Newport Beach, California 14. Mysteries

LC 90027411

A former detective's investigation into his pregnant sister's brutal murder is complicated by a clue implicating the police and by the bereaved husband's drive for revenge.

"This exciting, multidimensional plot should grab even the most demanding mystery reader." Library Journal.

Parker, T. Jefferson

The **renegades** : a novel / T. Jefferson Parker. Dutton, 2009. 416 p. Charlie Hood thrillers

ISBN 9780525950950

1. Police 2. Corruption investigation 3. Police murders 4. Police misconduct 5. Police corruption 6. Murder investigation 7. California 8. Southern California 9. Thrillers and suspense 10. Police procedurals

LC 2008029265

Patrolling a section of America's West that he finds just as untamed as those depicted in early pulp novels, Charlie Hood finds his preference for working alone overruled when he is assigned to partner with a popular county veteran whose subsequent murder reveals sinister truths behind the man's stellar reputation.

Parker, T. Jefferson

Storm runners : a novel / T. Jefferson Parker. William Morrow, 2007. 384 p.

ISBN 0060854235

1. Revenge 2. Organized crime 3. Stalking 4. Former police 5. Widowers 6. Stalkers 7. Weather forecasters 8. Prisoners 9. Bodyguards 10. Southern California 11. Thrillers and suspense

LC 2006046599

Includes index.

Hitting rock bottom after losing his family and ability to work after an explosion that was intended to kill him, former police officer Matt Stromsoe takes a job as a bodyguard for a television personality whose private life has rendered her a stalker's target.

"Parker's trademark is the ability to create real characters--tangible, flawed, and heroic--and Stromsoe follows the tradition." Library Journal.

Parkhurst, Carolyn, 1971-

The **dogs** of Babel / Carolyn Parkhurst. Little, Brown, 2003. 208 p.

ISBN 0316168688

1. Linguists 2. Widowers 3. Accident victims 4. Witnesses 5. Grief 6. Dogs 7. Human/animal communication 8. Virginia 9. New Orleans, Louisiana 10. Psychological fiction 11. Literary fiction

LC 2002043644

Also published in London as Lorelei's secret.

Discovering clues that indicate his beloved wife may not have died accidentally, Paul Iverson begins a perilous search for the truth while attempting to teach his dog, who witnessed the crime, to communicate.

"[W]hat had been a poignant, affecting tale turns truly frightening . . . . Parkhurst delivers a remarkable debut in quiet, authoritative prose." Library Journal.

Parks, Brad, 1974-

Closer than you know / Brad Parks. E.P. Dutton, 2018. 416 p.

ISBN 9781101985625

1. Foster care 2. Malicious accusation 3. Frameups 4. Cocaine 5. Rape victims 6. Mothers and sons 7. Married women 8. Women lawyers 9. Serial rapists 10. Deception 11. Virginia 12. Thrillers and suspense

Enduring a brutal foster-care upbringing, Melanie embarks on an adult life that she hopes will allow her to leave the past behind, only to be framed for drug charges that threaten her ability to keep her baby, a situation that is aided by an attorney who wants to solve the cold case of a serial rapist.

Parks, Brad, 1974-

The **girl** next door : a mystery / Brad Parks. Minotaur Books, 2012. 336 p. Carter Ross mysteries

ISBN 9780312667689

1. Journalists 2. Murder investigation 3. Crimes against women 4. Newspapers 5. Hit-and-run accidents 6. Newark, New Jersey 7. New Jersey 8. Mysteries

LC 2011040880

Gathering information for a heroic piece about the hit-and-run death of his newspaper carrier, reporter Carter Ross risks his reputation to investigate the victim's sister's claim that the death was not accidental.

Parks, Brad, 1974-

The **player** : a mystery / Brad Parks. Minotaur Books, 2014. 336 p. Carter Ross mysteries

ISBN 9781250044082

1. Investigative journalism 2. Environmental protection 3. Organized crime 4. Diseases 5. Real estate development 6. Building 7. Newspapers 8. Newark, New Jersey 9. New Jersey 10. Mysteries

LC 2013045900

Investigating an outbreak of a bizarre and occasionally fatal disease in a Newark neighborhood, investigative reporter Carter Ross contracts the illness himself before discovering mob ties to a local construction project.

Parks, Brad, 1974-

Say nothing : a novel / Brad Parks. Dutton, 2017. 448 p.

ISBN 9781101985595

1. Extortion 2. Child kidnapping victims 3. Families of kidnapping victims 4. Trials 5. Judges 6. Secrets 7. Coercion 8. Suspicion 9. Politicians 10. Drug dealers 11. Husband and wife 12. Legal thrillers 13. Thrillers and suspense

LC 2016018767

When their children are abducted by a man who blackmails them to follow instructions at the risk of the children's lives, a judge and his wife endure a terrorizing ordeal of no-holds-barred deceit and bond-breaking suspicions.

"The nerve-shredding never lets up for a minute as Parks picks you up by the scruff of the neck, shakes you vigorously, and repeats over and over again till a climax so harrowing that you'll be shaking with gratitude that it's finally over." Kirkus.

Parks, Gordon, 1912-2006

* The **learning** tree / Gordon Parks. Ballantine Books, 1989, c1963. 240 p.

ISBN 9780449215043

1. Growth (Psychology) 2. Teenage boys 3. African American boys -- Kansas 4. Racism -- Kansas 5. Murder witnesses 6. Kansas 7. African American fiction 8. Coming-of-age stories

A black youth in rural Kansas of the 1920's must make a difficult decision after he witnesses a murder.

Parks, Suzan-Lori

Getting mother's body : a novel / Suzan-Lori Parks. Random House, 2003. 288 p.

ISBN 1400060222

1. 1960s 2. African American women 3. African American families 4. Pregnant women 5. Treasure hunters 6. Poor families 7. Race relations 8. Voyages and travels 9. Treasure hunting 10. Jewelry 11. Burial 12. Exhumation 13. Southwest (United States) 14. Texas 15. African American fiction 16. Historical fiction 17. Domestic fiction

LC 2002031762

Learning that a company plans to dig up the area where her mother is buried, supposedly with a cache of jewels, Billy Beede, poor and pregnant, heads for Arizona to rescue her mother's body and search for the jewels that could bring her a new life.

"Set in the summer of 1963, and recounted in a slow, Southern drawl befitting the mood, the story unravels from a myriad of viewpoints, including the no-good custom coffin salesman who's fathered Billy's unborn baby, the one-legged neighbor in love with Billy, and her deceased mother's feisty lesbian lover." Publishers Weekly.

LIST OF FICTIONAL WORKS

Parmar, Priya, 1974-

Vanessa and her sister / Priya Parmar. Ballantine Books, 2014. 368 p.

ISBN 9780804176378

1. Bell, Vanessa, 1879-1961 2. Woolf, Virginia, 1882-1941 3. Edwardian era (1901-1914) 4. 1900s (Decade) 5. Intellectual life 6. Sisters 7. Bloomsbury group 8. Artists 9. Authors 10. Diary writing 11. Competition 12. Men/women relations 13. Family relationships 14. London, England 15. England -- Social life and customs -- 20th century 16. Biographical fiction 17. Historical fiction 18. Diary novels

Set in early 1900s London, this historical novel examines the adult lives of sisters Virginia Woolf and Vanessa Bell, focusing on the controversial and popular circle of artists and writers known as the Bloomsbury Group.

"Pamar's novel sparkles, intrigues, and attracts, just as the Stephen sisters must have done in their time. It should inspire readers to revisit the works of the Bloomsbury crowd in a new light, especially Virginia Woolf's." Booklist.

Parnell, Sean, 1981-

Man of war : an Eric Steele novel / Sean Parnell. William Morrow, 2018, 400 p. Eric Steele novels

ISBN 9780062668783

1. Special forces 2. Intelligence officers 3. Nuclear weapons thefts 4. Intelligence service 5. Nuclear weapons 6. National security 7. Military missions 8. CIA agents 9. Traitors 10. Techno-thrillers

LC 2017049082

An intelligence operative draws on the elite skills he learned as a Special Forces soldier when an adversary from his past steals a nuclear weapon.

Parris, S. J., 1974-

Sacrilege / S. J. Parris. Doubleday, 2012. 432 p. Giordano Bruno novels

ISBN 9780385535472

1. Bruno, Giordano, 1548-1600 2. Thomas,, a Becket, Saint, 1118?-1170 3. 16th century 4. Spies -- Great Britain -- History -- 16th century 5. Murder investigation 6. Cults 7. England -- History -- 16th century 8. Biographical fiction 9. Historical mysteries 10. Mysteries

Agreeing to help former paramour Sophia Underhill clear her name of a wrongful murder charge, 16th-century radical philosopher and spy Giordano Bruno uncovers secrets with ties to the cult of Thomas Becket and the legend surrounding the disappearance of the saint's body.

Parris, S. J., 1974-

Treachery / S.J. Parris. Pegasus Books, 2019, c2014. 592 p. Giordano Bruno novels

ISBN 9781643132242

1. Bruno, Giordano, 1548-1600 2. 16th century 3. Rulers 4. Conspiracies 5. Murder investigation 6. Secrecy 7. Spies 8. England -- History -- 16th century 9. Biographical fiction 10. Historical mysteries 11. Mysteries

Originally published: Toronto, Ontario : Doubleday Canada, 2014.

When Sir Francis Drake's daring 1585 expedition against the Spanish is sabotaged by an on-board murder, Giordano Bruno uncovers multiple deadly plots in Plymouth's murky underworld.

"Fans of the series will relish the violent and suspenseful adventures; believable relationships, both personal and political; and, especially, the author's skillful and unobtrusive re-creation of the historical period, filth and all." Booklist.

Parrish, Christa

Still life / Christa Parrish. Thomas Nelson, 2015. 352 p.

ISBN 9781401689032

1. Newlyweds 2. Married women 3. Airplane accidents 4. Life change events 5. Female friendship 6. Widows 7. Former cult members 8. Secrets 9. Grace (Christian theology) 10. Photographs 11. Photographers 12. Women's lives and relationships 13. Christian fiction

LC 2014029129

Five months after leaving her family's fringe religious sect to elope with a mysterious stranger, Ada is left widowed in a strange world, while Katherine struggles with a loveless marriage just as an artistic young man brings the two women together.

Parry, Ambrose

The **way** of all flesh / Ambrose Parry. Canongate, 2018. 407 p.

ISBN 9781786893789

1. Victorian era (1837-1901) 2. 1840s 3. Medical students 4. Housekeepers 5. Social classes 6. Women murder victims 7. Physicians 8. Gender role 9. Murder investigation 10. Medicine 11. Edinburgh, Scotland 12. Scotland -- Social life and customs -- 19th century 13. Historical mysteries

LC bl2018182031

An apprentice to a mid-19th-century anesthesia pioneer unexpectedly partners with a quick-witted housemaid in order to survive an investigation in the Edinburgh underworld to solve a string of grisly deaths.

"Parry provides a fascinating look at how medicine was practiced at a period when anesthetics were still not widely used or understood, as well as certain things that have changed little over time: mansplaining, the subservience expected of women of any social class, and religious leaders demanding their God-given right to control reproductive health." Publishers Weekly.

Parry, H. G.

The **unlikely** escape of Uriah Heep / H. G. Parry. Redhook Books/Orbit, 2019. 456 p.

ISBN 9780316452717

1. Characters and characteristics in literature 2. Superhuman abilities 3. Brothers 4. Family secrets 5. Books and reading 6. Contemporary fantasy 7. Fantasy fiction

LC 2019000762

A young scholar with a secret uncontrollable magical ability to bring literary characters into the world is overseen by a protective older sibling before an unknown stranger unleashes literary characters throughout their city.

" Fun, witty, and full of insights about the powerful effect of stories on our lives, this book is highly recommended. Give it to readers who devoured Jasper Fforde, Jim C. Hines' Libriomancer (2012), and Genevieve Cogman's The Invisible Library (2016), and to readers looking for adventurous fantasy with a soupçon of family drama." Booklist.

Parshall, Sandra

Bleeding through / Sandra Parshall. Poisoned Pen Press, 2012. 250 p. Rachel Goddard and Tom Bridger mysteries

ISBN 9781464200298

1. Law students 2. Stalkers 3. Murder investigation 4. Mountain life 5. Murder 6. Women veterinarians 7. Sheriffs 8. Stalking 9. Appalachian Region, Southern 10. Virginia 11. Mysteries

In rural Mason County, Virginia, Deputy Sheriff Tom Bridger investigates the murder of a young law school student, while veterinarian Rachel Goddard's sister Michelle visits and brings her stalker along with her.

Parshall, Sandra

Poisoned ground / Sandra Parshall. Poisoned Pen Press, 2014. 287 p. Rachel Goddard and Tom Bridger mysteries
ISBN 9781464202247

1. Murder 2. Real estate development 3. Sheriffs 4. Women veterinarians 5. Husband and wife 6. Small town life 7. Murder investigation 8. Secrets 9. Appalachian Region, Southern 10. Virginia 11. Mysteries

While her newly elected sheriff husband navigates growing hostilities about plans for a posh resort in their Blue Ridge Mountains community, newlywed veterinarian Rachel Goddard investigates the shooting deaths of a beloved local couple who refused to give up their farm.

"Rachel is a likable amateur sleuth who displays genuine affection for her neighbors and the animals she treats. Readers will enjoy seeing series regulars appear throughout the story and appreciate a peek at how Rachel and Tom are getting along as newlyweds." Booklist.

Parsons, Kelly

Doing harm / Kelly Parsons. St. Martin's Press, 2014. 351 p.
ISBN 9781250033475

1. Surgeons 2. Psychopaths 3. Hospitals 4. Ambition 5. Suspicion 6. Murder 7. Medical thrillers 8. Thrillers and suspense
LC 2013030121

Botching a major surgery when his ambition for a prestigious job gets the better of him, Steve Mitchell learns that a patient who died under mysterious circumstances was targeted by a sociopath who holds information capable of destroying Steve's family and career.

"[T]his skillfully wrought debut gets high marks for building tension to a breathtaking climax." Library Journal.

Pasternak, Boris Leonidovich, 1890-1960

* **Doctor** Zhivago / Boris Pasternak ; translation by Max Hayward and Manya Harrari. Pantheon Books, 1991, c1958. xxiii, 558 p.
ISBN 9780679774389

1. Russian Revolution and Civil War (1917-1921) 2. Physicians 3. Poets, Russian -- 20th century 4. Love triangles 5. Civil war 6. Idealism in men 7. War -- Psychological aspects 8. Men/women relations 9. Russia -- History -- 20th century 10. Soviet Union -- History -- Revolution, 1917-1921 11. Love stories 12. Translations -- Russian to English 13. Modern classics
LC 58008005

"The poems of Yurii Zhivago" translated by Bernard Guilbert Guerney.

Originally published in English: London : Collins, 1958.

Originally published: Milan : Feltrinelli, 1957.

Epic novel of post-revolutionary Russia focuses on the torments and dreams of a doctor-poet who attempts to avoid the struggles of his turbulent era.

Patchett, Ann

* **Bel** canto : a novel / Ann Patchett. HarperCollins, 2001. 304 p.
ISBN 0060188731

1. Hostages 2. Victims of terrorism 3. Diplomats 4. Women opera singers 5. Singing 6. Embassy buildings 7. Terrorism 8. South America 9. Psychological fiction 10. Literary fiction
LC 00053671

Book Sense Book of the Year Paperback, 2003.

Orange Prize for Fiction, 2002.

PEN-Faulkner Award, 2002.

Shortlisted for the International IMPAC Dublin Literary Award, 2003

National Book Critics Circle Award for Fiction finalist, 2001

When terrorists seize hostages at an embassy party, an unlikely assortment of people is thrown together, including American opera star Roxanne Coss, and Mr. Hosokawa--a Japanese CEO and her biggest fan.

"An impoverished South American country hosts a birthday extravaganza for a Japanese industrialist in the hope of securing new foreign investment. The lure? An internationally renowned lyric soprano. Indeed, when Roxane Coss sings, even the ragtag terrorists who are about to flood through the air-conditioning vents and take the guests hostage hold their breath, transported by the beauty of her voice. Patchett's tragicomic novela fantasia of guns and Puccini and Red Cross negotiations invokes the glorious, unreliable promises of art, politics, and love." The New Yorker.

Patchett, Ann

* **Commonwealth** / Ann Patchett. HarperCollins, 2016. 322 p.
ISBN 9780062491794

1. Extramarital affairs 2. Stepbrothers and stepsisters 3. Blended families 4. Family secrets 5. Family history 6. Authors 7. Loss (Psychology) 8. Family relationships 9. Men/women relations 10. California 11. Virginia 12. Family sagas

Australian Book Industry Awards, International Book of the Year, 2017.

National Book Critics Circle Award for Fiction finalist, 2016

A five-decade saga tracing the impact of an act of infidelity on the parents and children of two Southern California families traces their shared summers in Virginia and the disillusionment that shapes their lasting bond.

"A satisfying meat-and-potatoes domestic novel from one of our finest writers." Kirkus.

Patchett, Ann

* The **Dutch** house : a novel / Ann Patchett. Harper, 2019. 352 p.
ISBN 9780062963673

1. Houses 2. Brothers and sisters 3. Family relationships 4. Mother-deserted children 5. Stepmothers 6. Inheritance and succession 7. Poverty 8. Obsession 9. Forgiveness 10. Philadelphia, Pennsylvania 11. Pennsylvania 12. New York City 13. Literary fiction 14. Family sagas 15. Coming-of-age stories
LC 2019024072

"Ann Patchett, the New York Times bestselling author of Commonwealth and State of Wonder, returns with her most powerful novel to date: a richly moving story that explores the indelible bond between two siblings, the house of their childhood, and a past that will not let them go." --Publisher

Patchett, Ann

Run / Ann Patchett. Harper Collins Publishers, 2007. 304 p.
ISBN 9780061340635

1. Families 2. Adopted children 3. Adoptees 4. Protectiveness in men 5. Rich families 6. Poor families 7. Single mothers 8. African American men 9. Traffic accidents 10. Traffic accident victims 11. Family secrets 12. Boston, Massachusetts 13. Massachusetts 14. Domestic fiction 15. Psychological fiction
LC 2006041297

Bernadette and Bernard Doyle share a great love for family. Already blessed with a son, they adopt two black children, Teddy and Tip. Even after Bernadette dies, she continues to exert a profound influence over the family. And then Tip is pushed out of a car's path in a sudden act of heroism, and lives are bound by this selfless act.

"Ms. Patchett gives her readers much to contemplate when genetics, privilege, opportunity and nurture come into play. And to her credit she is neither vague nor reductive about any of these things; she creates a genuinely rich landscape of human possibility." New York Times.

Patchett, Ann

* **State** of wonder : a novel / Ann Patchett. Harper, 2011. 353 p.

ISBN 9780062049803

1. Change (Psychology) 2. Kinship-based society 3. Transformations, Personal 4. Fertility drugs 5. Pharmaceutical research 6. Missing persons 7. Extramarital affairs 8. Identity (Psychology) 9. Corporate greed 10. Scientists 11. Medical research 12. Jungles 13. Amazon Valley 14. Psychological fiction

LC 2010029229

Shortlisted for The Orange Prize for Fiction, 2012

A researcher at a pharmaceutical company, Marina Singh journeys into the heart of the Amazonian delta to check on a field team that has been silent for two years--a dangerous assignment that forces Marina to confront the ghosts of her past.

"The book's dreamlike claustrophobia weaves a spell even when farfetched plot twists tip toward absurdity. Though it ultimately can't match the subtler pleasures of Patchett's previous voyage to South America, 2001's gorgeous Bel Canto, it's still a trip well worth taking." Entertainment Weekly.

Paton, Alan

Ah, **but** your land is beautiful / Alan Paton. Scribner, 1982, c1981. 271 p.

ISBN 0684173360

1. 1950s 2. 1960s 3. Apartheid 4. Anti-apartheid movements 5. Race relations 6. Political parties -- South Africa -- History -- 20th century 7. South Africa -- Race relations 8. Political fiction 9. Historical fiction

LC 81013547

Dramatizes the public and private lives of contemporary South Africa, tracing the multifarious reactions of the human spirit to life in a racially divided society and perceptively sketching heroes, victims, and the self-absorbed ordinary citizen.

"Alan Paton's considerable practical life in South Africa aside, his place in the literature of social protest has been secured by his steady devotion to the ideal of the empathetic imagination in fiction." New York Times Book Review.

Paton, Alan

* **Cry,** the beloved country / Alan Paton. Scribner Classics, 2003, c1948. 316 p.

ISBN 9780743261951

1. 1940s 2. Apartheid 3. Race relations 4. South Africans 5. Fathers and sons 6. Clergymen 7. Clergymen's families 8. South Africa 9. South Africa -- Race relations 10. Johannesburg, South Africa 11. Political fiction 12. Literary fiction 13. Modern classics

LC 86009674

Originally published: New York : C. Scribner's and Sons, 1948.

A novel depicting the racial ferment in the beautiful country of South Africa in 1948.

Paton, Alan

Too late the phalarope / Alan Paton. Scribner, 1995, c1953. 253 p.

ISBN 9780684818955

1. Racism -- South Africa 2. Police -- South Africa 3. Race relations 4. Apartheid 5. South Africa -- Race relations 6. Political fiction

Originally published: J. Cape, 1953.

Portrays a police lieutenant's struggle with his conscience when he violates a strict South African law concerning relationships between Blacks and whites.

"The book is written with superb simplicity. It is cadenced but unaffected; it will inevitably be called Biblical and yet there is no conscious parodying of scriptural prose. It flows relentlessly to its crisis, and sometimes we cry out at its power. The people are all clear and real, the South African backgrounds are colorfully and deeply etched. The conflicts are diverse but they all contribute to the basic struggle; father and son, races, languages, prejudices." Christian Science Monitor.

Patric, A. S.

Black rock white city / A.S. Patric. Melville House, 2017, c2015 248 p.

ISBN 9781612196831

1. Refugees 2. Children -- Death 3. Loss (Psychology) 4. Grief 5. House cleaners 6. Genocide 7. Sarajevo (Bosnia and Hercegovina) -- History -- Siege, 1992-1996 8. Australian 9. Literary fiction

Originally published: Melbourne, Australia : Transit Lounge Publishing, 2015.

Miles Franklin Award, 2016

After losing everything and fleeing war-torn Sarajevo, Jovan and Suzana fight to start anew in Melbourne, but face tremendous pressures at work where Jovan must deal with the suspicion that he's being targeted by violent and racially charged vandals.

Patterson, James, 1947-

1st to die : a novel / James Patterson. Little Brown, 2001. 424 p. Women's Murder Club

ISBN 0316666009

1. Women detectives 2. Women coroners 3. Serial murderers 4. Female friendship 5. Serial murders 6. Women assistant district attorneys 7. Women journalists 8. Women serial murderers 9. Husband and wife 10. Women's Murder Club (Imaginary organization) 11. San Francisco, California 12. Mysteries

LC 00061123

Four women friends--a homicide detective, a medical examiner, an assistant DA, and a crime desk reporter--form a Women's Murder Club to stop a killer who has been stalking newlyweds in San Francisco.

"The story opens in San Francisco with the gruesome murder of a bride and groom on their wedding night. Detective Lindsay Boxer is called to the scene, just after learning she is suffering from a rare and potentially life-threatening blood disease. For help with the case, she calls on her best friend, Claire, a medical examiner, and, reluctantly at first, Cindy, a newspaper reporter who is covering the story. . . . Patterson keeps up the suspense until the very last page." Booklist.

Patterson, James, 1947-

* **Along** came a spider : a novel / James Patterson. Little, Brown, 1993. 435 p. Alex Cross novels

ISBN 0446364193

1. United States. Secret Service Officials and employees, Women 2. African American men 3. Kidnapping 4. Murder investigation 5. Men with dissociative identity disorder 6. Murder investigation 7. African American psychologists 8. Serial murderers 9. Teachers 10. Police psychologists 11. Detectives 12. Washington, D.C. 13.

Thrillers and suspense

LC 92024581

Washington, D.C., police detective Alex Cross becomes caught up in a kidnapping case that may involve Gary Soneji, a teacher at an elite private school who is also a schizophrenic psychopath and serial murderer.

"Patterson's storytelling talent is in top form in this grisly escapist yarn." Library Journal.

Patterson, James, 1947-

Kiss the girls : a novel / James Patterson. Little, Brown, 1995. 451 p. Alex Cross novels

ISBN 0316693707

1. Serial murderers 2. African American men 3. Police psychologists 4. Missing teenage girls 5. African American psychologists 6. Police -- Washington, D.C. 7. Detectives 8. North Carolina 9. Washington, D.C. 10. Thrillers and suspense

LC 94014177

As two serial killers terrorize different regions of America, the FBI begins to suspect that the two are competing with each other, and Washington, D.C., police detective Alex Cross embarks on a personal quest to find the perpetrators.

Patterson, James, 1947-

* Private / James Patterson and Maxine Paetro. Little, Brown and Co., 2010. 400 p. Private Detective Agency novels

ISBN 9780316096157

1. Scandals 2. Cold cases (Criminal investigation) 3. Murder investigation 4. Crimes against girls 5. Revenge 6. Private investigators 7. California 8. Thrillers and suspense

LC 2009052188

Former CIA agent Jack Morgan inherits his father's elite Los Angeles detective agency and along with it such cases as an NFL gambling scandal, eighteen unsolved schoolgirl slayings, and the murder of his best friend's wife.

Patterson, Molly

Rebellion / Molly Patterson. Harper, 2017. 548 p.

ISBN 9780062574046

1. 1890s 2. 1950s 3. Missionaries 4. Sisters 5. Married women 6. Widows 7. Extramarital affairs 8. Loss (Psychology) 9. Grief 10. Boxer Rebellion, 1899-1901 11. Farm life 12. Missing persons 13. Christians 14. China -- History -- 19th century 15. United States -- History -- 19th century 16. Historical fiction 17. Family sagas

A mid-20th-century widow struggles to manage her farm and raise her children while reflecting on the intertwined experiences of her farm wife mother, her missionary aunt and a Chinese student whose lives were shaped by the Boxer Rebellion.

Patterson, Richard North

Balance of power / Richard North Patterson. Ballantine Books, 2003. 624 p. Kerry Kilcannon trilogy

ISBN 9780345450173

1. Gun control 2. Presidents -- United States 3. Family violence 4. Presidents' spouses -- United States 5. Women journalists 6. Families of murder victims 7. Lobbyists 8. Gun industry and trade 9. Suing (Law) 10. Washington, D.C. 11. United States -- Politics and government 12. Political thrillers 13. Thrillers and suspense 14. Legal thrillers

LC 2003051848

The marriage of President Kerry Kilcannon and TV journalist Lara Costello is marred by a massacre of innocent civilians by gunfire, setting in motion events that reveal the hidden connections among guns, money, and power in Washington.

"This complex novel has a fascinating debate at its heart. To his credit, Patterson has done his research, and though it's clear which side he's on, he does a good job of presenting all the arguments." Booklist.

Patterson, Richard North

Dark lady / Richard North Patterson. Alfred A. Knopf, 1999. 371 p.

ISBN 0679450432

1. Political corruption 2. Cities and towns 3. Ruthlessness in women 4. Murder 5. Greed 6. Women public prosecutors 7. Baseball fields 8. Ambition in women 9. Middle West 10. Thrillers and suspense 11. Legal thrillers

LC 99023565

Two prominent men are found dead in Steelton, a small town struggling with an economic turnaround. Enter Assistant County Prosecutor Stella Marz, referred to as Dark Lady by her fellow lawyers. As she makes her way through the maze of corruption, deceit, and greed to get at the truth behind these murders, Stella comes to believe that the history of the small town is involved and may threaten her own life.

"Patterson is familiar with the civic shenanigans that can destroy a community, and he draws wisely on the history and geography of Cleveland to portray a city struggling to escape its bondage to organized crime, racial conflict and the entrenched corruption of its elected officials." New York Times Book Review.

Patterson, Richard North

Eclipse / Richard North Patterson. Henry Holt & Co., 2009. 384 p.

ISBN 9780805087727

1. Lawyers -- San Francisco, California 2. Oil -- Africa 3. Frameups 4. Murder -- West Africa 5. Divorced men 6. Former lovers 7. Oil industry and trade 8. Murder suspects 9. West Africa 10. San Francisco, California 11. Thrillers and suspense 12. Legal thrillers

LC 2008017386

An American lawyer takes on a nearly impossible case--the defense of an African freedom fighter against his corrupt government's charge of murdering three PetroGlobal workers.

"Eclipse aspires to be any number of books: a novel of political intrigue, an international conspiracy thriller, a courtroom drama, a romance, even a straightforward murder mystery. . . . To Patterson's credit, the novel succeeds on all counts." Washington Post Book World.

Patterson, Richard North

No safe place / Richard North Patterson. Alfred A. Knopf, 1998. 497 p. Kerry Kilcannon trilogy

ISBN 0679450424

1. Scandals 2. Pro-life Movement 3. Presidential candidates 4. Legislators -- United States 5. Elections -- United States 6. Presidents -- Election 7. Lawyers 8. Primaries -- California 9. Journalists 10. California 11. Political thrillers 12. Thrillers and suspense

LC 9814573

As Senator Kerry Kilcannon campaigns in the California presidential primary, he struggles to cope with memories of his older brother's assassination during his own run for the nomination twelve years before and becomes the target of a deranged anti-abortion activist on the ultimate mission.

"The main character, Kerry Kilcannon, is an Irish Catholic U.S. senator, reminiscent of the Kennedy brothers. Embroiled in a close campaign with the vice president for the Democratic presidential nomination, Kilcannon struggles to maintain his honesty and upright values in a sleazy world where everything depends on image and the proper spin. At the same time, a militant right-to-lifer vows to kill Kilcannon for his pro-choice stance on abortion. Throughout the constant twists and turns of the plot, Patterson builds realistic supporting characters and brings to life the surrealistic world of a presidential campaign." Library Journal.

Patterson, Richard North

Protect and defend / Richard North Patterson. Knopf, 2000 544 p. Kerry Kilcannon trilogy

ISBN 0679450440

1. Pro-life movement 2. Presidents -- United States 3. Abortion 4. Women lawyers 5. Secrets 6. Women Supreme Court justices 7. Washington, D.C. 8. United States -- Politics and government 9. Thrillers and suspense 10. Political thrillers

In San Francisco, a fifteen-year-old girl wants to sue for permission to have a late-term abortion over the opposition of her pro-life parents. In Washington, the President is about to nominate a woman as the next Chief Justice. She's shadowed by a personal secret. But the politics and medical dilemmas of abortion threatens to tear both women and the nation apart.

"Patterson skillfully juggles a large cast of characters and controversies." School Library Journal.

Pattison, Eliot

Beautiful ghosts / Eliot Pattison. St. Martin's Minotaur, 2004. 352 p. Shan Tao Yun mysteries

ISBN 9780312277598

1. Former police 2. Art thefts 3. Murder 4. Former police 5. Buddhists 6. Buddhist monks 7. Buddhist monasteries 8. Political persecution 9. Fathers and sons 10. Truth 11. Himalaya Mountains region 12. Tibet -- History -- Chinese occupation, 1950- 13. China 14. United States 15. Mysteries

LC 2003062543

Having lived a year in exile and disgrace since his unofficial release from a work camp, former Beijing inspector Shan Tao Yun is entreated by the officials who exiled him to help with a murder investigation involving missing art, his former gulag, and his son.

Pattison, Eliot

Blood of the oak : a novel / Eliot Pattison. Counterpoint, 2016., 304 p. Bone rattler mysteries

ISBN 9781619026155

1. Colonial America (1600-1775) 2. Scots in the United States 3. Indians of North America 4. Stealing 5. Material culture 6. Murder 7. Murder investigation 8. Voyages and travels 9. Enemies 10. United States -- History -- Colonial period, 1600-1775 11. Historical mysteries

LC 2015035581

Colonial America in 1765 is a place full of danger and anger as colonists make their first movements toward freedom. Amidst the Stamp Tax dissent, Scotsman Duncan McCallum is called to the deathbed of a highly respected Iroquois woman. She tells him about her dead grandson, whom she believes was murdered, a stolen Iroquois artifact, and a dream she had in which McCallum and his Nipmuc Indian best friend bring the artifact back. But before McCallum even reaches home, he discovers a dead Oneida Indian, and he knows more blood will be shed before he figures out what's going on. This atmospheric, authentic book is the excellent 4th entry in the Bone Rattler mysteries. -- Description by Dawn Towery.

Pattison, Eliot

Bones of the earth : an Inspector Shan Tao Yun mystery / Eliot Pattison. Minotaur Books, 2019. 320 p. Shan Tao Yun mysteries

ISBN 9781250169686

1. Corruption 2. Secrecy in government 3. Archaeological sites 4. Justice 5. Military occupation 6. Buddhism 7. Murder 8. Murder investigation 9. Dams 10. Tibet -- History -- Chinese occupation, 1950- 11. China 12. Mysteries

LC 2018050880

Bones of the Earth is Edgar Award-winning author Eliot Pattison's much anticipated tenth and final installment in the internationally acclaimed Inspector Shan series.

"Pattison's tenth and final Inspector Shan novel is a pitch-perfect series ending, leaving readers with a satisfying last look at the scrupulously ethical investigator as well as further insight into a recent era of Asian history little known in the West." Kirkus.

Pattison, Eliot

The **lord** of death / Eliot Pattison. Soho Press, 2009. 314 p. Shan Tao Yun mysteries

ISBN 9781569475799

1. Former police 2. Murder investigation 3. Gunshot victims 4. Exiles 5. Former police 6. Parolees 7. Buddhists 8. Buddhist monks 9. Himalaya Mountains region 10. Tibet -- History -- Chinese occupation, 1950- 11. China 12. Mysteries

Shan Tao Yun is an exiled Chinese national, a former Beijing Investigator, on parole from the Tibetan gulag to which he had been consigned as punishment. Leading a mule bearing a corpse at the request of a local wisewoman, he comes upon a traffic accident involving a government bus transporting illegal monks to prison. Two women in an approaching vehicle are shot, and one dies in his arms....

Pattison, Eliot

Mandarin gate / Eliot Pattison. Minotaur Books, 2012. 352 p. Shan Tao Yun mysteries

ISBN 9780312656041

1. Bounty hunters 2. Former police 3. Murder investigation 4. Exiles 5. Former police 6. Buddhists 7. Buddhist monks 8. Himalaya Mountains region 9. Tibet -- History -- Chinese occupation, 1950- 10. China 11. Mysteries

Stumbling across a murder scene on the grounds of an old Buddhist temple, Shan uncovers links to a police cover-up and activities at a new internment camp for Tibetan dissidents and is challenged to protect a key witness and navigate a precarious investigation on both sides of the law.

Pattison, Eliot

Prayer of the dragon / Eliot Pattison. Soho Crime, 2007. 416 p. Shan Tao Yun mysteries

ISBN 9781569474792

1. Murder investigation 2. Former police 3. Navajo Indians 4. Former police 5. Murder 6. Buddhists 7. Buddhist monks 8. Buddhist monasteries 9. Himalaya Mountains region 10. Tibet -- History -- Chinese occupation, 1950- 11. China 12. Mysteries

LC 2007006205

While living with Tibetan lamas since his release from a gulag, exiled Chinese national and former investigator Shan Tao Yun is asked to find the true killer of two men, whose arms had been severed and removed, after a comatose man is accused of the crime.

Pattison, Eliot

The **skull** mantra / Eliot Pattison. St. Martin's Minotaur, 1999 403 p. Shan Tao Yun mysteries

ISBN 9780312204785

1. Conspiracies 2. Murder investigation 3. Political prisoners 4. Forced labor 5. Former police 6. Former police 7. Buddhists 8. Buddhist monks 9. Himalaya Mountains region 10. Tibet -- History -- Chinese occupation, 1950- 11. China 12. Mysteries

Edgar Allan Poe Award for Best First Mystery Novel, 2000.

When a headless corpse turns up on a Tibetan mountainside, inspector Shan Tao Yun is released from prison to investigate the crime, and he quickly uncovers a conspiracy involving American mining interests, corrupt Party officials, and Tibetan sorcerers.

"Set against a background that is alternately bleak and blazingly beautiful, this is at once a topnotch thriller and a substantive look at Tibet under siege." Publishers Weekly.

Pattison, Eliot

Water touching stone / Eliot Pattison. St. Martin's Minotaur, 2001. 419 p. Shan Tao Yun mysteries

ISBN 0312206127

1. Political prisoners 2. Murder investigation 3. Crimes against children 4. Police misconduct 5. Police corruption 6. Missing persons investigation 7. Former police 8. Former police 9. Former convicts 10. Voyages and travels 11. Himalaya Mountains region 12. Tibet -- History -- Chinese occupation, 1950- 13. China 14. Mysteries

LC 2001019163

Includes glossary.

Former Beijing police investigator Shan Tao Yun heads for a remote Tibetan plateau to investigate the murder of a venerated teacher and the subsequent disappearance of a lama.

Paul, Bart

Under Tower Peak / Bart Paul. Arcade Publishing, 2013. 288 p. Under Tower Peak

ISBN 9781611458367

1. Guides (Persons) 2. Wilderness survival 3. Money-making projects 4. Snipers 5. Criminals 6. Deception 7. Veterans 8. Airplane accidents 9. Cowboys 10. Attempted assassination 11. Missing persons 12. The West (United States) 13. Thrillers and suspense 14. Modern Westerns

LC 2012043982

Sequel: Cheatgrass.

Military sniper Tommy Smith returns to his former life as a cowboy and wilderness guide in California's Sierra Nevada, but his peaceful life is compromised when he discovers a wrecked plane that draws him into a world of violence.

Paul, Gill, 1960-

* The **lost** daughter / Gill Paul. William Morrow & Company, 2019. 469 p.

ISBN 9780062843272

1. Maria Nikolaevna,, Grand Duchess, daughter of Nicholas II, Emperor of Russia, 1899-1918 2. Romanov, House of 3. 20th century 4. Princesses 5. Exile (Punishment) 6. Family relationships 7. Men/ women relations 8. Family secrets 9. Abusive men 10. Soviet Union -- History -- 20th century 11. Soviet Union -- History -- Revolution, 1917-1921 12. Historical fiction 13. Biographical fiction 14. Parallel narratives

LC 2018059051

Heartbreaking and gripping novel of a Russian princess and a journey to solve a mystery that might change everything we know about the tragic Romanov family."--, Provided by publisher.

Pava, Sergio de la,

Lost empress : a novel / Sergio De La Pava. Pantheon, 2018., 623 p.

ISBN 9781524747220

1. Football teams 2. Women business owners 3. Criminal justice system 4. Football team owners 5. Inheritance and succession 6. Criminals 7. Prisoners 8. Misfits (Persons) 9. Interpersonal relations

10. Satirical fiction 11. Literary fiction

LC 2017049323

Shocked when her brother inherits their father's NFL team in spite of her pivotal role in building the family dynasty, Nina takes over a small indoor football franchise and resolves to take the NFL by storm, an ambition that is challenged by a criminal mastermind who prepares to commit an audacious act.

Pava, Sergio de la.

A **naked** singularity / Sergio de la Pava. University of Chicago Press, 2012, c2008. 696 p.

ISBN 9780226141794

1. Children of immigrants 2. Public defenders 3. Judicial system 4. Existentialism 5. Lawyers 6. Death row prisoners 7. New York City 8. Experimental fiction 9. Satirical fiction

Originally self-published in 2008.

Casi, the child of Colombian immigrants, lives in Brooklyn but works in Manhattan as a public defender. Casi has never lost a trial, but then his world ruptures when a case goes bad. Increasingly disillusioned, the young lawyer finds himself involved in a scheme that might be the perfect crime--or his undoing.

Pava, Sergio de la

Personae : a novel / Sergio De La Pava. University of Chicago Press, 2013, c2011. 201 p.

ISBN 9780226078991

1. Detectives 2. Fate and fatalism 3. Ideas (Philosophy) 4. Women detectives 5. College teachers 6. Victims 7. Literary fiction 8. Experimental fiction 9. Mysteries

LC 2013016557

"Game readers should have as much fun with this clever experiment as the author seems to have had inventing it, and be challenged by his more serious and troubling questions." Publishers Weekly.

Pavone, Chris

* The **expats** : a novel / Chris Pavone. Crown, 2012. 336 p. Kate Moore novels

ISBN 9780307956354

1. Former CIA agents 2. Secrets 3. Married people 4. Deception 5. FBI agents 6. Security consultants 7. Embezzlement 8. Americans in Luxembourg 9. Betrayal 10. Luxembourg 11. Spy fiction 12. Thrillers and suspense

LC 2011046207

Anthony Award for Best First Novel, 2013.

Edgar Allan Poe Award for Best First Novel by an American Author, 2013.

An international spy thriller about a former CIA agent who moves with her family to Luxembourg where everything is suspicious and nothing is as it seems.

Pavone, Chris

The **Paris** diversion : a novel / Chris Pavone. Crown Publishing, 2019. 373 p. Kate Moore novels

ISBN 9781524761509

1. Former CIA agents 2. Terrorism 3. Suicide bombers 4. Deception 5. Undercover operations 6. Americans in France 7. Married people 8. Investments 9. Day trading 10. Secrets 11. Paris, France 12. Spy fiction 13. Thrillers and suspense

Sequel to: The expats.

Kate Moore partners with a French agent to investigate a bombing threat in Paris, a race against time that is complicated by her husband's missing nemesis and a suspicious absence of orders from Langley.

"Pavone gives us a fresh, pulsating, and introspective thriller that delivers on its tourist-heavy Parisian setting and expands and connects territory from his previous novels." Library Journal.

Pawel, Rebecca, 1977-

Death of a nationalist / Rebecca Pawel. Soho Press, 2003. 262 p. Carlos Tejada Alonso y Leon investigations

ISBN 1569473048

1. 1930s 2. Police -- Spain 3. Men -- Spain 4. Postwar life 5. Nationalists -- Spain 6. Communists -- Spain 7. Murder investigation 8. Violence 9. Revenge 10. Notebooks 11. Grief 12. Death 13. Postwar life 14. Madrid, Spain 15. Spain -- Political culture 16. Spain -- History -- Civil War, 1936-1939 -- Post-war aspects 17. Historical mysteries 18. Police procedurals 19. Mysteries

LC 2002026921

Edgar Allan Poe Award for Best First Mystery Novel, 2004.

"Madrid in 1939 is filled with bomb craters, desecrated churches and nearly abandoned streets, while black markets are just about the only markets with anything to sell. The hatreds and atrocities shared by the Nationalists (supported by the Communists) still simmer and erupt in sporadic violence. The Guardia Civil has the responsibility to maintain authority--and their enthusiasm and ruthlessnesss for enforcing order terrorizes the citizens. The intertwined fates of Sergeant Tejada Alonzo Leon of the Guardia Civil and that of Gonzalo Llorente, a wounded Republican in hiding are handled with unusual skill and subtlety." Publishers Weekly.

Peace, David

Occupied city / David Peace. Alfred A. Knopf, 2010, c2009. 288 p. Tokyo trilogy

ISBN 9780307263759

1. 1940s 2. Massacres 3. Bank robberies 4. Mass murder investigation 5. Murder suspects 6. Biological warfare 7. Japan 8. Tokyo, Japan 9. Japan -- History -- Allied occupation, 1945-1952 10. Noir fiction 11. Literary fiction

LC 2009043254

Originally published: London : Faber and Faber, 2009.

A tale inspired by a true story follows the murder of a dozen people in 1948 Tokyo by a man who claimed he was providing government-directed medical care, an event recounted from the disparate perspectives of the victims.

"Powerful and ambitious, this British import is deepened by a multiperspective, Rashomon-like approach. But reader be warned: The immensely talented Peace . . . is not in the business of making his work easy." Kirkus.

Peace, David

Tokyo year zero / David Peace. Alfred A. Knopf, 2007. 368 p. Tokyo trilogy

ISBN 9780307263742

1. 1940s 2. Serial murder investigation -- Tokyo, Japan 3. Police -- Tokyo, Japan 4. Serial murders -- Tokyo, Japan 5. Tokyo, Japan 6. Japan -- History -- Allied occupation, 1945-1952 7. Noir fiction 8. Literary fiction

LC 2007023813

When the bodies of two women, raped and strangled, turn up on the first anniversary of the Japanese surrender in American-occupied Tokyo, Detective Minami of the Tokyo Metropolitan Police, haunted by the atrocities of war, searches for the killer.

"Peace, whose complex style feels like a cross between Haruki Murakami and James Ellroy, delivers an expressionistic portrait of a harrowing, devastated time and place." Publishers Weekly.

Pearce, Michael, 1933-

A **dead** man in Barcelona / Michael Pearce. Soho Constable, 2008. 256 p. Seymour of Special Branch

ISBN 9781569475379

1. Scotland Yard 2. 1910s 3. Diplomatic and consular service 4. Murder investigation 5. British in Spain 6. Detectives 7. Police -- Great Britain 8. Barcelona, Spain -- History -- 20th century 9. Historical mysteries 10. Mysteries

LC 2008023622

Seymour goes to Barcelona to investigate the cold case of a successful English businessman, who suspiciously died in a Barcelona prison two years after "Tragic Week," a series of riots between reserve troops and the Spanish army.

Pearl, Matthew

The **Dante** Club : a novel / Matthew Pearl. Random House, 2003. 384 p. Dante Club novels (Matthew Pearl)

ISBN 0375505296

1. Dante Alighieri, 1265-1321 Appreciation 2. Holmes, Oliver Wendell, 1809-1894 3. Emerson, Ralph Waldo, 1803-1882 4. Longfellow, Henry Wadsworth, 1807-1882 5. 1860s 6. Authors 7. Banned books 8. Serial murder investigation 9. Censorship 10. Book clubs 11. African American police 12. Race relations 13. Secrets 14. Boston, Massachusetts -- History -- 19th century 15. Cambridge, Massachusetts -- History -- 19th century 16. Historical mysteries 17. Mysteries

LC 2002017886

Sequel: The Dante chamber, Penguin, 2018.

In 1865, the preparations of the Dante Club--led by Henry Wadsworth Longfellow and Oliver Wendell Holmes--to release the first translation of Dante's "The Divine Comedy" are threatened by a series of murders that re-create episodes from "Inferno."

"A literary thriller about a serial murderer who draws gory inspiration from the torments of Dante's Inferno. . . . The author sets this novel in Boston in 1865, when Henry Wadsworth Longfellow, James Russell Lowell, and Oliver Wendell Holmes were translating Dante into English. As they work through the cantos, the Dante-inspired corpses arrive on cue, and the versifiers must turn detective." The New Yorker.

Pearl, Matthew

The **Dante** chamber / Matthew Pearl. Penguin Press, 2018. 368 p. Dante Club novels (Matthew Pearl)

ISBN 9781594204937

1. Dante Alighieri, 1265-1321 Influence 2. Browning, Robert, 1812-1889 3. Tennyson, Alfred, 1809-1892 4. 1870s 5. Authors, English -- 19th century 6. Amateur detectives 7. Poets, English -- 19th century 8. Women poets 9. Serial murder investigation 10. Codes (Communication) 11. London, England 12. Historical mysteries

LC 2018006196

Sequel to The Dante Club.

Poets Robert Browning and Alfred Tennyson team up to decode literary clues after a murder victim is discovered in a London park with a verse from the Divine Comedy around his neck.

Pearl, Matthew

The **last** Dickens : a novel / Matthew Pearl. Random House, 2009. 400 p.

ISBN 9781400066568

1. Osgood, James R (James Ripley), 1836-1892 2. Dickens, Charles, 1812-1870 Manuscripts 3. 19th century 4. Publishers and publishing 5. Authors -- Death 6. London, England 7. Historical mysteries 8. Mysteries

LC 2008046962

The news of the untimely death of Charles Dickens reaches his American publisher. James R. Osgood, a junior partner there, suspicious of unscrupulous New York publishers and their ruthless agents intent on stealing Dickens' last novel "The Mystery of Edwin Drood," Osgood sends his trusted young clerk, Daniel Sands, to await its arrival.

"Pearl is too smart to hinge his plot on mere publishing rights. Like Dickens, he finds compelling stories in every social stratum, viewing the downtrodden with sympathy and the upper crust with a gimlet eye." New York Daily News.

Pearl, Matthew

The **Poe** shadow : a novel / Pearl Matthew. Random House, 2006. 384 p.

ISBN 1400061032

1. Poe, Edgar Allan, 1809-1849 2. 1840s 3. Authors, American -- 19th century 4. Fanaticism 5. Lawyers 6. Death 7. Impostors 8. Detectives 9. International intrigue 10. French in the United States 11. Murder 12. Virginia -- History -- 19th century 13. Baltimore, Maryland -- History -- 19th century 14. Historical mysteries 15. Mysteries

LC 2005057998

In 1849, the body of Edgar Allan Poe has been buried in an unmarked grave in Baltimore. Concluded by everyone as a second-rate writer who met a disgraceful end, one lone admirer, Quentin Clark, puts his own career and reputation at risk in a crusade to salvage Poe's. Quentin soon finds himself enmeshed in sinister machinations involving international political agents and the lost secrets of Poe's final hours, and must himself turn master investigator to escape Poe's grisly fate.

Pearl, Matthew

The **technologists** : a novel / Matthew Pearl. Random House, 2012. 480 p.

ISBN 9781400066575

1. Massachusetts Institute of Technology History 19th century 2. 1860s 3. 19th century 4. College students 5. Paranormal phenomena 6. Scholars and academics 7. Secret societies 8. Civil war veterans 9. Boston, Massachusetts 10. Cambridge, Massachusetts 11. Historical mysteries 12. Mysteries

LC 2011014628

Massachusetts Book Awards, Fiction Award, 2013.

The first graduating class at the Massachusetts Institute of Technology is thrown into turmoil by bizarre phenomena that cause instruments to inexplicably spin out of control, challenging enterprising students to protect lives while combating Harvard rivals.

Pearlman, Edith, 1936-

Binocular vision : new & selected stories / Edith Pearlman. Lookout Books/University of North Carolina Wilmington, 2011. 392 p.

ISBN 9780982338292

1. New England 2. Short stories 3. Literary fiction

LC 2010033376

Edward Lewis Wallant Award, 2011.

National Book Critics Circle Award for Fiction, 2011.

National Book Award for Fiction finalist, 2011

Presents a collection of short stories that focus on the trials and tribulations of a group of Northeasterners.

"Short stories are like miniatures: A delicate touch makes all the difference. In Edith Pearlman's world, that light hand means choosing the perfect phrase to capture a moment or a mood. Often it leaves the reader breathless. In Binocular Vision, a hefty collection of 34 stories, including 13 new ones, . . . Pearlman shows her unerring sense for the right words. . . . Set all over the world, in different times during the last

hundred years, and involving characters of all ages, these tales focus on the precise pivotal moments when life changes often for the worse. Death and dying are common themes, while ill-fated liaisons, frequently involving incest, occur with regularity." Boston Globe.

Pearlman, Edith, 1936-

Honeydew : stories / Edith Pearlman. Little Brown & Co., 2015. 279 p.

ISBN 9780316297226

1. Misfits (Persons) 2. Interpersonal relations 3. Loss (Psychology) 4. Identity (Psychology) 5. Teenage drug abusers 6. People with anorexia 7. Interpersonal attraction 8. Stowaways 9. Literary fiction 10. Short stories

This new collection of short stories from the National Book Critics Circle Award-winning author of Binocular Vision, who describes tales full of teenage drug use, anorexia, cruise-ship stowaways and a widowed nail tech who finds herself falling for a client.

"Ovid is a subtle influence throughout, as Pearlman imagines gentle metamorphoses catalyzed by longing, as in the ravishing title story about the headmistress of a private girls' day school and an anorexic, ant-loving student. Pearlman not only writes with bewitching clarity, she also fathoms much about our inner lives and relationships that is unexpectedly wondrous." Booklist.

Pears, Iain

Death and restoration / Iain Pears. Scribner, 1996. 223 p. Jonathan Argyll and Flavia DiStefano mysteries

ISBN 0684814617

1. Caravaggio, Michelangelo Merisi da, 1573-1610 2. Art historians 3. Art thefts 4. Monasteries 5. Art restorers 6. Engaged persons 7. Women thieves 8. Amateur detectives 9. Rome, Italy 10. Mysteries

LC 97-39932

Sequel to: Giotto's hand.

Sequel: The immaculate deception.

A tale of intrigue and murder set in the heart of Italy's art world pits Jonathan Argyll and art squad investigator Flavia de Stefano against a wily band of thieves that steals a painting reputed to have miraculous powers.

Pears, Iain

The **dream** of Scipio / Iain Pears. G. P. Putnam's Sons, 2002 608 p.

ISBN 157322202X

1. Roman Empire (27 BCE-476 CE) 2. Medieval period (476-1492) 3. Second World War era (1939-1945) 4. 14th century 5. World War II -- Provence, France 6. Black Death -- Provence, France 7. Nazi collaborators -- Provence, France 8. Aristocracy -- Provence, France 9. Cardinals -- Provence, France 10. Poets -- Provence, France 11. Provence, France -- History -- 14th century 12. Rome -- History -- Empire, 30 BC-476 AD 13. Historical fiction 14. Love stories 15. Parallel narratives

An ancient manuscript called "The Dream of Scipio" links three separate centuries--the fifth, the end of the Roman Empire; the fourteenth, the time of the Black Death; and the twentieth during World War II--and three stories of love, all set in Provence.

"Pears builds a multilayered tale of moral choice, love, danger and loss. Like an archaeologist, he uncovers worlds beneath worlds in a few square miles of Provecal earth." New York Times Book Review.

Pears, Iain

The **immaculate** deception / Iain Pears. Scribner, 2000. 221 p. Jonathan Argyll and Flavia DiStefano mysteries

ISBN 9780743212571

1. Art historians 2. Art thefts 3. Murder investigation 4. Husband-and-wife detectives 5. Women detectives 6. Amateur detectives 7. Rome, Italy 8. Italy 9. Mysteries

Sequel to: Death and restoration.

Flavia di Stefano, the acting head of Italy's Art Theft Squad, attempts to track down the thief who stole a politically sensitive painting on loan from a foreign museum, a search that soon becomes a hunt for a killer.

Pears, Iain

An **instance** of the fingerpost / Iain Pears. Riverhead Books, 1998. 691 p.

ISBN 1573220825

1. Restoration England (1660-1688) 2. 17th century 3. Stuart period (1603-1714) 4. Murder 5. Italians in England 6. Physicians 7. Mathematicians 8. Students 9. Historians 10. Household employees 11. Housekeepers 12. Oxford, England -- History -- 17th century 13. Great Britain -- History -- Charles II, 1660-1685 14. Great Britain -- History -- Restoration, 1660-1688 15. Historical mysteries 16. Literary fiction 17. Mysteries

LC 9723899

In the 1660s, as Charles II and the Church of England try to quell residual opposition, Robert Grove, fellow of New College, is murdered, and four different people give their versions of the incident.

"Robert Boyle, the devout chemist, and John Thurloe, Cromwell's inscrutable spymaster, are among the historical characters who figure in this richly imagined mystery set in Oxford in the sixteen-sixties, after Charles II has been restored to the throne. A Fellow of New College is found dead, and a woman accused of whoring and witchcraft is sentenced to hang for the murder. Three narrators--all unreliable and all self-self-interested--tell their versions of the story, which unfolds in a turbulent atmosphere of scientific, political, and religious dissent. Not until a fourth, and final, narrator speaks are the mysteries, including the meaning of the book's title, revealed." The New Yorker.

Pears, Iain

The **last** judgement / Iain Pears. Scribner, 1996, c1993. 224 p. Jonathan Argyll and Flavia DiStefano mysteries

ISBN 9780684814599

1. Art historians 2. French Resistance (World War II) 3. Murder investigation 4. Women detectives 5. Crimes of passion 6. Amateur detectives 7. World War II 8. Resistance to military occupation 9. Rome, Italy 10. Paris, France 11. Mysteries

LC 9538120

Sequel to: The Bernini bust.

Sequel: Giotto's hand.

Originally published: London : Gollancz, 1993.

Art dealer Jonathan Argyll has found a buyer for an 18th century painting of the death of Socrates. However when he arrives in Rome to deliver the painting, the purchaser, Mr. Muller seems disinterested in it and asks Jonathan to arrange its resale. But if he is no longer interested in the painting, someone else is--enough to commit murder to possess it.

"A sophisticated, adventurous, and gripping story that is sure to hold wide appeal." Booklist.

Pears, Iain

Stone's fall / Iain Pears. Spiegel & Grau, 2009. 608 p.

ISBN 9780385522847

1. 19th century 2. Capitalists and financiers 3. Arms transfers 4. International finance 5. Death 6. Europe -- History -- 1871-1918 7.

Historical mysteries

LC 2009000472

Shortlisted for the Walter Scott Prize for Historical Fiction, 2010

In this dazzling historical mystery, John Stone, financier and arms dealer, dies falling out of a window at his London home. The quest to uncover the truth behind his death plays out against the backdrop of high-stakes international finance, Europe's first great age of espionage, and the start of the twentieth century's arms race.

"Pears manages his complicated structure with a confidence and dexterity possible only to a master of the craft of fiction. It is a novel which frequently and daringly challenges credibility, skating on the thinnest of ice, and yet meets that challenge successfully every time." The Scotsman.

Pearson, Allison, 1960-

* How hard can it be? / Allison Pearson. St. Martin's Press, 2018. 352 p. Kate Reddy novels

ISBN 9781250086082

1. Middle-aged women 2. Working mothers 3. Menopause 4. Women employees 5. Husband and wife 6. Parent and teenager 7. Household activities 8. Investment advisers 9. Men/women relations 10. London, England 11. Chick lit 12. Diary novels

LC 2017059419

The heroine from I Don't Know How She Does It is forced by her husband's flaky unemployment to reinvent herself as a younger, hip professional to secure a job with the hedge fund she founded.

"Tackling sexism, growing older, and understanding ones needs when catering to those of so many others, Pearson writes realism with all the fun of escapism." Booklist.

Pearson, Ridley

Choke point / Ridley Pearson. G. P. Putnam's Sons, 2013. 416 p. Grace Chu and John Knox novels

ISBN 9780399158841

1. Rescues 2. Organized crime 3. Child trafficking 4. Child slaves 5. Security consultants 6. International intrigue 7. Sweatshops 8. Slavery 9. Netherlands 10. Amsterdam, Netherlands 11. Adventure stories 12. Thrillers and suspense 13. Spy fiction

LC 2013003706

Hired to investigate allegations of a sweat-shop operation in Amsterdam that is enslaving young girls, Knox and tech information expert Grace Chu embark on a rescue mission that is challenged by a crime organization that has seduced local neighborhoods with showy goodwill practices.

Pearson, Ridley

The **red** room / Ridley Pearson. G. P. Putnam's Sons, 2014. 304 p. Grace Chu and John Knox novels

ISBN 9780399163746

1. International intrigue 2. Intelligence service 3. Photographs 4. Surveillance 5. Insurance 6. Illegal arms transfers 7. Art 8. Istanbul, Turkey 9. Adventure stories 10. Thrillers and suspense 11. Spy fiction

LC 2013051019

"In the newest international thrill ride from New York Times-bestselling author Ridley Pearson, John Knox and Grace Chu, the incomparable and often incompatible duo, team up again, this time in the exotic "city between two worlds," Istanbul."--, Provided by publisher.

Pearson, Ridley

* The **risk** agent / Ridley Pearson. G.P. Putnam's Sons, 2012. 432 p. Grace Chu and John Knox novels

ISBN 9780399158834

1. Hostages 2. Hostage negotiations 3. Security consultants 4. Real estate development 5. International intrigue -- China 6. Hostage-taking 7. Americans in China 8. Shanghai, China 9. China 10. Adventure stories 11. Thrillers and suspense 12. Spy fiction

LC 2012001184

When a Chinese national working for an American-owned construction company is kidnapped along with his one-man security detail, Rutherford Risk, a firm specializing in hostage recovery, recruits two outsiders to aide in the victims return.

Pearson, Robin W.

A **long** time comin' / Robin W. Pearson. Tyndale House., 2020. 425 p.

ISBN 9781496441881

1. Grandmother and granddaughter 2. Family secrets 3. Women with terminal illnesses 4. Pregnant women 5. Faith (Christianity) 6. Letter writing 7. Forgiveness 8. African American families 9. Family relationships 10. North Carolina 11. Christian fiction 12. Southern fiction 13. African American fiction

LC 2019025105

To hear Beatrice Agnew tell it, she entered the world with her mouth tightly shut. Just because she finds out she's dying doesn't mean she can?t keep it that way. If any of her children have questions about their daddy and the choices she made after he abandoned them, they'd best take it up with Jesus. There's no room in Granny B's house for regrets or hand-holding. Or so she thinks.

"Though it is perhaps overlong, the writing is strong, and the story is engaging, and readers will be pleased to discover a new voice in southern inspirational fiction. Libraries with Christian-fiction collections will want to add this novel to their shelves." Booklist.

Peebles, Frances de Pontes

The **air** you breathe / Frances De Pontes Peebles. Penguin Group USA, 2018 464 p.

ISBN 9780735210998

1. 1930s 2. Female friendship 3. Ambition in women 4. Interclass friendship 5. Friendship 6. Samba music 7. Voyages and travels 8. Interpersonal relations 9. Brazil 10. Historical fiction 11. Coming-of-age stories

An orphaned kitchen maid and the reckless daughter of a sugar baron embark on a volatile friendship marked by their ambitions to escape, their changing fortunes and unexpected fame.

Peebles, Frances de Pontes

The **seamstress** / Frances de Pontes Peebles. Harper Collins, 2008. 656 p.

ISBN 9780060738877

1. 1920s 2. 1930s 3. Seamstresses 4. Outlaws 5. Villages 6. Sisters 7. Social classes 8. Rich families 9. Orphans 10. Brazil -- History -- 20th century 11. Historical fiction

Taquaritinga do Norte, Brazil, 1928. As seamstresses, the young sisters Emilia and Luzia dos Santos know how to cut, mend and conceal. These are useful skills in the backcountry of Brazil, where ruthless land barons feud with bands of outlaw cangaceiros. While Emilia dreams of falling in love with a gentleman and escaping to a big city, Luzia, scarred by a childhood accident that left her with a deformed arm, finds her escape in sewing and in secret prayers to the saints she believes once saved her life.

"Using as backdrop the populist revolt of 1930 and the push to develop Brazil's enormous resources at the expense of the subsistence farmers, Peebles creates a vast and diverse cast of characters. . . . However, the novel's true beauty is the exquisitely realized relationship between Emlia and Luzia, two strong women who, despite the separate paths their lives take, remain connected and committed to each other." Library Journal.

Peet, Mal

The **Murdstone** trilogy / Mal Peet. Candlewick Press, 2015. 313 p.

ISBN 9780763681845

1. Authors 2. Quests 3. Faustian bargains 4. Amulets 5. Literary agents 6. Writing 7. Drinking 8. Publishers and publishing 9. Fantasy fiction authors 10. England 11. Dartmoor, England 12. Satirical fiction 13. Fantasy fiction

Philip Murdstone's books are not selling, so his agent convinces him to write a high fantasy blockbuster, but Philip is totally unsuited to the task, until he meets a dwarfish stranger and makes a Faustian bargain.

"The resulting novel, which Philip calls Dark Entropy, is brilliant but incomplete.. Bitter and frothy as a pint of stout, this formula-thwarting satire will intoxicate fantasy fans with strong stomachs." Kirkus.

Peikoff, Kira

Mother knows best / Kira Peikoff. Crooked Lane Books, 2019. 288 p.

ISBN 9781643850405

1. Grief in mothers 2. Sons -- Death 3. Medical genetics 4. Physicians 5. Women scientists 6. Experiments 7. Medical innovations 8. Medical ethics 9. Daughters 10. Birthparents 11. Revenge 12. Medical thrillers

Claire Abrams's dreams became a nightmare when she passed on a genetic mutation that killed her little boy. Now she wants a second chance to be a mother, and finds it in Robert Nash, a maverick fertility doctor who works under the radar with Jillian Hendricks, a cunning young scientist bent on making her mark. Claire, Robert, and Jillian work together to create the world's first baby with three genetic parents--an unprecedented feat that could eliminate inherited disease. But when word of their illegal experiment leaks to the wrong person, Robert escapes into hiding with the now-pregnant Claire, leaving Jillian to serve out a prison sentence that destroys her future.

Pelecanos, George P.

* The **big** blowdown / George P St. Martin's Press, 1996. 313 p. Marcus Clay and Dimitri Karras novels

ISBN 0312142846

1. 1940s 2. 1950s 3. Immigrants -- Washington, D.C. 4. Mafia 5. Gangsters 6. Detectives -- Washington, D.C. 7. Prostitutes 8. Drug use 9. Friendship 10. World War II 11. Washington, D.C. 12. Hardboiled fiction 13. Mysteries

This novel features Nick Stefanos in a minor role.

Karras and Recevo face off when organized crime threatens their old friend's establishment in a story that explores the seamier side of life surrounding Nick's Grill

"Set in Washington, D.C. from the 1930s to the 1950s, Pelecanos's . . . novel traces a group of boyhood friends as they make their way in the richly detailed Greek and Italian neighborhoods of the city. Peter Karras, a Greek, and his friend Joe Recevo, an Italian, grow up together, serve separately in World War II, and reunite for a time after the war as Joe becomes involved in organized crime in the city. Peter cannot stomach the practice of shaking down immigrants for loan vigorish and is brutally cast out by the gangsters, as Joe stands by. The two friends will inevitably cross paths again." Library Journal.

Pelecanos, George P.

The **cut** : a novel / George Pelecanos. Little, Brown and Co., 2011. 304 p. Spero Lucas mysteries

ISBN 9780316078429

1. Private investigators 2. Organized crime -- Washington, D.C. 3. Violence in men 4. Stolen property recovery 5. Crime bosses 6. Washington, D.C. 7. Hardboiled fiction 8. Mysteries

LC 2010044937

After returning home from serving in Iraq, Spero Lucas makes a living doing special investigations for a defense attorney and catches the attention of a high-profile crime boss who offers Lucas a high paying job he cannot refuse.

"The novel's story is O.K., but nowhere near as heart-racing as the storytelling." New York Times Book Review.

Pelecanos, George P.

The **double** / George Pelecanos. Little, Brown and Company, 2013. 304 p. Spero Lucas mysteries

ISBN 9780316078399

1. Private investigators 2. Veterans 3. Art thefts 4. Lovers 5. Extramarital affairs 6. Murder investigation 7. Stolen property recovery 8. Lawyers 9. Men/women relations 10. Washington, D.C. 11. Hardboiled fiction 12. Mysteries

LC 2013017709

Detective Spero Lucas uses his knack for getting what he wants when he helps a woman retrieve a valuable painting stolen by her ex-boyfriend.

Pelecanos, George P.

Drama city : a novel / George Pelecanos. Little, Brown and Co., 2005. 304 p.

ISBN 0316608211

1. Former convicts 2. Dogfighting 3. Gangs 4. Drug traffic 5. Animal shelter workers 6. Criminals -- Rehabilitation 7. Women parole officers 8. Criminals 9. Enforcers (Criminals) 10. Men and dogs 11. Animal shelters 12. Animal fighting 13. Violence 14. Revenge 15. Men/women relations 16. Washington, D.C. 17. Noir fiction 18. Crime fiction

LC 2004016757

Hoping to start over after serving eight years in prison, Lorenzo Brown returns to the Washington, D.C., neighborhood of his youth to take a job as a Humane Society officer but finds challenges from a local drug boss.

"There is a fierce inevitability to the way George Pelecanos's new book unfolds. Drama City is unleashed, not simply set in motion. In the tough, imperiled parts of Washington, where his earlier books have been set, Mr. Pelecanos puts the forces of good and evil on a collision course, igniting the kind of suspense that hinges on heartbreak. As this lean, stirring, knife-edged novel escalates, the question is not whether one of its principals will become a casualty. The question is when." New York Times.

Pelecanos, George P.

Hard revolution : a novel / George Pelecanos. Little, Brown, 2004. 384 p. Derek Strange and Terry Quinn mysteries

ISBN 0316608971

1. King, Martin Luther,, Jr, 1929-1968 Assassination 2. 1960s 3. Race relations 4. Riots -- Washington, D.C. 5. African American police -- Washington, D.C. 6. Private investigators 7. Rookie police 8. Police -- Washington, D.C. 9. Vietnam veterans 10. Brothers -- Death 11. Criminals -- Washington, D.C. 12. Drug dealers 13. Drug traffic 14. Robbery 15. Race riots 16. Washington, D.C. 17.

Hardboiled fiction 18. Mysteries

LC 2003054501

Two brothers--rookie police officer Derek Strange, and his older brother, Dennis, a troubled Vietnam Veteran--become caught up in the riots engulfing Washington, D.C., in the wake of the assassination of Martin Luther King, Jr.

"Pelecanos's foray into Strange's past does not in the end diminish, but rather adds to, our sense of his complexity and humanity. In narrating Derek's buried crime story, Pelecanos has further tapped into an archetypal vein of family experience in the black community since the 1950's, as drugs, murder and prison cut a swath through three generations of young men." New York Times Book Review.

Pelecanos, George P.

Hell to pay : a novel / George P. Pelecanos. Little, Brown, 2002. 288 p. Derek Strange and Terry Quinn mysteries

ISBN 0316695068

1. Teenage prostitution 2. Race relations 3. African American police -- Washington, D.C. 4. Teenage prostitutes 5. Former police -- Washington, D.C. 6. Private investigators 7. Runaway teenagers 8. Interracial friendship 9. Hardboiled fiction 10. Mysteries

LC 2001038111

P.I.'s Derek Strange and Terry Quinn are hired to find a 14-year-old girl from the suburbs who has run away from home and is now working as a prostitute in Washington, D.C.

"Pelecanos's style is one of total-shock immersion in the sights, sounds and cultural codes of the dangerous world he roams." New York Times Book Review.

Pelecanos, George P.,

* The **man** who came uptown / George P. Pelecanos. Little, Brown and Company, 2018. 320 p.

ISBN 9780316479820

1. Corruption 2. Former convicts 3. Books and reading 4. Robbery 5. Librarians 6. Prison libraries 7. Criminal behavior 8. Private investigators 9. African American prisoners 10. Washington, D.C. 11. Crime fiction 12. Noir fiction

LC bl2018125748

Unexpectedly released from jail, Michael Hudson confronts profound changes in his Washington, D.C. home while struggling between loyalties to the person responsible for his freedom and the prison librarian who helped him develop a love of reading.

"A love letter to the power of reading and small acts of kindness, this novel focuses on Michael Hudson, a young man who discovers his passion for reading while awaiting sentencing on a gun charge." Library Journal.

Pelecanos, George P.

The **night** gardener : a novel / George Pelecanos. Little, Brown, 2006. 384 p.

ISBN 0316156507

1. Detectives 2. Serial murder investigation 3. Cold cases (Criminal investigation) 4. Police -- Washington, D.C. 5. Former detectives 6. Serial murders 7. Serial murderers 8. Cooperation 9. Teenagers -- Death 10. Community gardens 11. Washington, D.C. 12. Hardboiled fiction 13. Mysteries

LC 2006001286

When the body of a local teenager turns up in a community garden, veteran homicide detective Gus Ramone teams up with T. C. Cook, a legendary, now retired detective, and Dan "Doc" Holiday, his former partner who left the force under a cloud of suspicion.

"In 1985, the body of a 14-year-old girl turns up in a Washington, D.C. park, the latest in a series of murders by a killer the media dub

The Night Gardener. T.C. Cook, the aging detective on the case, works with a quiet, almost monomaniacal, focus. Also involved are two young uniformed cops, Gus Ramone, who's diligent, conscientious and unimpressed by heroics, and Dan Doc Holiday, an adrenaline junkie who's decidedly less straight. Fast forward 20 years. Detective Ramone, now married with kids of his own, investigates the murder of one of his teenage son's friends. The homicide closely resembles the earlier unsolved Night Gardener murders. Holiday, now an alcoholic chauffeur and bodyguard, follows the case on his own and tracks down Cook, long retired but still obsessed with the original murders." Publishers Weekly.

Pelecanos, George P.

Shame the devil : a novel / George P. Pelecanos. Little, Brown and Co., 2000. 299 p. Marcus Clay and Dimitri Karras novels

ISBN 0316695238

1. 1990s 2. Murder 3. Revenge 4. Robbery 5. Violence 6. Greek American men 7. Detectives 8. Police 9. Traffic accidents -- Washington, D.C. 10. Washington, D.C. 11. Noir fiction 12. Thrillers and suspense

LC 99029854

A restaurant robbery goes badly wrong in Washington, D.C., leaving a number of employees dead, the gunman's brother killed by police, and a young boy run over by the getaway car, a situation that rapidly worsens as the gunman vows to avenge his brother by killing every person involved in his death.

"Pelecanos is one of those dangerous writers who aren't afraid to take risks, so there's a merciless reality to his characters and a cold clarity about the way they talk, think and feel. Whatever their flaws, none of the people in this writer's world are ashamed to tell the truth." New York Times Book Review.

Pelecanos, George P.

Soul circus / George P. Pelecanos. Little, Brown, 2003. 352 p. Derek Strange and Terry Quinn mysteries

ISBN 0316608432

1. Drug traffic 2. Criminals -- Washington, D.C. 3. Private investigators 4. Former police -- Washington, D.C. 5. African American police -- Washington, D.C. 6. Detectives 7. Interracial friendship 8. Washington, D.C. 9. Hardboiled fiction 10. Mysteries

LC 2002016207

In the midst of a brutal courtroom battle during which a Washington, D.C., crime overlord faces the death penalty and his rivals vie for his territory, private investigator Derek Strange struggles to protect the life of a witness.

"Pelecanos is fascinated with the way things work, and he takes apart the gun trade like an urban anthropologist, fitting the pieces into the drug business and the gang culture with an exactness that is breathtaking--anddepressing. At the same time, he treats his criminals like human beings, talking their talk, driving their cars, listening to their music, getting into their world with something that can only be called sympathy." New York Times Book Review.

Pelecanos, George P.

* The **sweet** forever : a novel / George P. Pelecanos. Little, Brown, 1998. 298 p. Marcus Clay and Dimitri Karras novels

ISBN 0316691097

1. 1980s 2. Drug traffic 3. Police misconduct 4. Record store owners 5. African Americans 6. Vietnam veterans 7. Greek American men 8. African American communities 9. City life -- Washington, D.C. 10. Cocaine traffic 11. Drug dealers 12. Violence 13. Washington, D.C. 14. Noir fiction 15. Thrillers and suspense

LC 9741963

Marcus Clay and Dimitri Karras square off against drug lords and racists on the crime-ridden streets of the nation's capital in the midst of the 1980s.

"Pelecanos's kickback style works just as well when his characters put down their weapons to watch a ball game or to hit the music clubs on a Friday night. This may be a battleground, but it's also Pelecanos's home ground, and he knows the territory as well as any crime writer alive." New York Times Book Review.

Pelecanos, George P.

The **turnaround** : a novel / George Pelecanos. Little, Brown, and Co., 2008. 304 p.

ISBN 9780316156479

1. Crimes against minorities 2. Reconciliation 3. Racism 4. Violence 5. Restaurateurs 6. Physical therapists 7. Victims of crimes 8. Inner city 9. Poverty 10. Memories 11. Survival 12. Crime and race 13. Washington, D.C. 14. Psychological fiction 15. Noir fiction

LC 2007033276

Thirty-five years after a devastating accident that irrevocably shapes the lives of six people, a pair of redemption-seeking survivors reaches out to one another in an effort that is compromised by a fellow survivor's release from prison.

"Pelecanos does what few, if any, American writers do: He tells the truth. Twain told the truth; Faulkner toyed with the truth; Hemingway told his version of the truth and Chandler certainly told a cold, cynical truth. Pelecanos' truth is from deep in the heart, from places where red blood cells know more than all the sweet, heady words truth usually hides behind." Chicago Sun-Times.

Pelecanos, George P.

The **way** home : a novel / George Pelecanos. Little, Brown and Co., 2009. 368 p.

ISBN 9780316156493

1. Juvenile delinquents (Boys) 2. Stolen money -- Family relationships 3. Fathers and sons 4. Redemption 5. Conflict in families 6. Resentfulness in men 7. Disappointment 8. Options, alternatives, choices 9. Problem youth 10. Crime fiction

LC 2008054837

After years of trouble and rebellion that enraged his father and nearly cost him his life, Chris has a steady job in his father's company, he's seriously dating a woman he respects, and, aside from the distrust that lingers in his father's eyes, his mistakes are firmly in the past. One day on the job, Chris and his partner come across a temptation almost too big to resist. Chris does the right thing, but old habits and instincts rise to the surface, threatening this new-found stability with sudden treachery and violence. With his father and his most trusted friends, he takes one last chance to blast past the demons trying to pull him back.

"In a sense, The Way Home is a coming-of-age story, as Chris tries to find his place in the world. More fortunate than most of the boys who share his past, he can succeed, Pelecanos tells us but not everybody is quite so lucky." PopMatters.

Pelevin, Viktor

The **hall** of singing caryatids / Victor Pelevin ; translated from the Russian by Andrew Bromfield. New Directions, 2011. 105 p.

ISBN 9780811219426

1. Elite (Social sciences) 2. Nightclubs 3. Sexploitation 4. Upper class 5. Billionaires 6. Drug use 7. Sexuality 8. Murder 9. Praying mantis 10. Russia 11. Satirical fiction 12. Surrealist fiction 13. Allegories 14. Translations -- Russian to English

LC 2011023260

Twelve girls are hired to perform in a posh new nightclub for Russia's elite. There they find things are very strange.

"Pelevin's so funny, sharp and engaging that not only do you forgive him his excesses, you look forward to them." Salon.com.

Penelope, L., 1978-

Song of blood and stone / L. Penelope. St. Martin's Press, 2018. 384 p. Earthsinger chronicles

ISBN 9781250148070

1. Pariahs 2. Exiles 3. Spies 4. Magic 5. Soldiers 6. Singers 7. Prejudice 8. Women singers 9. Afrofuturism and Afrofantasy 10. Epic fantasy 11. Fantasy fiction 12. African American fiction

LC 2017055114

Enduring life as an outcast from a homeland where her Earthsong talents are feared, orphan Jasminda helps care for an injured spy, Jack, who enlists her help in protecting the protective mantle around two nations that are preparing for war.

Penelope, L., 1978-

Whispers of shadow & flame / L. Penelope. St. Martin's Griffin, 2019. 484 p. Earthsinger chronicles

ISBN 9781250148094

1. Singers 2. Women singers 3. Magic 4. Assassins 5. Rebels 6. Betrayal 7. Prophecies 8. Trust 9. Prejudice 10. Imaginary kingdoms 11. Afrofuturism and Afrofantasy 12. Epic fantasy 13. Fantasy fiction 14. African American fiction

LC 2019025385

Life in the kingdoms of Elsira and Lagrimar is about to change. Born with a deadly magic she cannot control, Kyara is forced to become an assassin, but secretly seeks freedom from both her untamed power and the blood spell that commands her. Darvyn ol-Tahlyro may be the most powerful Earthsinger in generations, but when he discovers Kyara can unlock the secrets of his past, he can't stay away. Kyara and Darvyn grapple with betrayal, old promises, and older prophecies. And when a new threat emerges, they must beat the odds to save both kingdoms.

"Despite an enticing cliff-hanger, this taut, suspenseful fantasy stands alone, and readers new to the series can comfortably start here. This is a wonderful integration of high-stakes epic fantasy intrigue with intimate personal connections." Publishers Weekly.

Penman, Sharon Kay

Cruel as the grave : a medieval mystery / Sharon Kay Penman. H. Holt, 1998. 242 p.. Justin de Quincy mysteries

ISBN 0805056084

1. Eleanor,, of Aquitaine, Queen, consort of Henry II, King of England, 1122?-1204 2. Richard I,, King of England, 1157-1199 3. John,, King of England, 1167-1216 4. Medieval period (476-1492) 5. Plantagenet period (1154-1485) 6. 12th century 7. Murder investigation 8. Royal houses 9. Royal pretenders 10. Spies 11. England -- History -- 12th century 12. London, England -- History -- 12th century 13. Historical mysteries 14. Medieval mysteries 15. Mysteries

LC 9813085

Steeped in political machinations, London in 1193 provides the setting for a new investigation by Justin de Quincy, the Queen's Man, who searches for the individual responsible for the brutal murder of a young girl in a churchyard.

"Penman's clear prose and engrossing plot, the skill with which she brings the politics, people, and ambience of medieval England alive, and her engaging characters make this a must-read, must-have mystery." Booklist.

Penman, Sharon Kay

Devil's brood / Sharon Kay Penman. G. P. Putnam's Sons, 2008. 752 p. Henry II novels

ISBN 9780399155260

1. Henry II,, King of England, 1133-1189 2. Eleanor,, of Aquitaine, Queen, consort of Henry II, King of England, 1122?-1204 3. Medieval period (476-1492) 4. Plantagenet period (1154-1485) 5. 12th century 6. Family relationships 7. Inheritance and succession 8. Marriages of royalty and nobility 9. Fathers and sons 10. Betrayal 11. Insurgency 12. Husband and wife 13. Great Britain -- History -- Henry II, 1154-1189 14. Great Britain -- Rulers -- Family relationships 15. Biographical fiction 16. Historical fiction

LC 2008029451

The third installment of a trilogy about Henry II and Eleanor of Aquitaine traces the collapse of the royal family in the aftermath of Henry's self-imposed exile to Ireland, as Eleanor and Henry's three eldest sons enter into a rebellion against him.

"The empathetic reader can't help but be both horrified by the machinations of this grievously dysfunctional family and filled with pity for the pain they inflict upon one another. Penman does a remarkable job of depicting passionate, dramatic characters and the perilous times in which they live. For those who like their historical fiction as complex and tightly woven as a medieval tapestry, this book cannot fail to please." Library Journal.

Penman, Sharon Kay

Dragon's lair : a medieval mystery / Sharon Kay Penman. G.P. Putnam's Sons, 2003. 304 p.. Justin de Quincy mysteries

ISBN 0399150773

1. Eleanor,, of Aquitaine, Queen, consort of Henry II, King of England, 1122?-1204 2. Richard I,, King of England, 1157-1199 3. John,, King of England, 1167-1216 4. Philippe II, Augustus, King of France, 1165-1223 5. Medieval period (476-1492) 6. Plantagenet period (1154-1485) 7. 12th century 8. Ransom 9. Kidnapping 10. Prisoners 11. Royal houses 12. England -- History -- 12th century 13. Great Britain -- History -- Richard I, 1189-1199 14. Wales 15. Austria -- History -- 12th century 16. Historical mysteries 17. Medieval mysteries 18. Mysteries

LC 2003046745

When her beloved son Richard is imprisoned and held for ransom in an Austrian dungeon and the hated Prince John plots with King Phillippe of France to prevent Richard's return, Queen Eleanor sends Justin de Quincy into Wales to recover a ransom payment that has gone missing.

"Despite a large cast of characters from every social class, Penman keeps them all clearly distinguishable." Publishers Weekly.

Penman, Sharon Kay

Falls the shadow / Sharon Kay Penman. H. Holt, 1988. 580 p. Welsh trilogy

ISBN 0805003002

1. Henry III,, King of England, 1207-1272 2. Montfort, Simon de, Earl of Leicester, 1208?-1265 3. Medieval period (476-1492) 4. Plantagenet period (1154-1485) 5. 13th century 6. Royal houses 7. Civilization, Medieval 8. Princesses 9. Great Britain -- History -- Henry III, 1216-1272 10. England -- History -- Medieval period, 1066-1485 11. Historical fiction 12. Biographical fiction

LC 87032255

Maps on lining papers.

In thirteenth-century England, King Henry III's sister Nell breaks tradition and marries Simon de Montfort, an outspoken nobleman who risks death in battle to preserve honor.

Penman, Sharon Kay

Here be dragons / Sharon Kay Penman. Holt, Rinehart, and Winston, 1985. xii, 704 p. Welsh trilogy

ISBN 0030627737

1. Llewelyn ap Iorwerth, d 1240 2. John,, King of England, 1167-1216 3. Medieval period (476-1492) 4. Plantagenet period (1154-1485) 5. 13th century 6. Rulers 7. Royal houses 8. Civilization, Medieval 9. Princesses 10. Marriages of royalty and nobility 11. Wales -- History -- To 1536 12. Great Britain -- History -- Plantagenets, 1154-1399 13. Wales -- History -- 1063-1284 14. Historical fiction 15. Biographical fiction

LC 84023480

Maps on lining papers.

King John arranges a marriage between his youngest daughter, Joanna, and his rival, Llewelyn, Prince of North Wales, a young leader who intends to unite all of Wales.

Penman, Sharon Kay

A **king's** ransom / Sharon Kay Penman. G. P. Putnam's Sons, 2014 448 p. Henry II novels

ISBN 9780399159220

1. Richard I,, King of England, 1157-1199 2. Medieval period (476-1492) 3. Plantagenet period (1154-1485) 4. 12th century 5. Rulers 6. Ambition 7. Imprisonment 8. Hostages 9. Family relationships 10. Great Britain -- History -- Richard I, 1189-1199 11. Historical fiction 12. Biographical fiction

LC 2013042663

"A Marian Wood Book"

Sequel to: Lionheart.

From the New York Times-bestselling author of Lionheart comes the dramatic sequel, telling of the last dangerous years of Richard, Coeur de Lion's life.

"Penman gives readers a well-researched and impressively detailed narrative displaying a strong commitment to historical accuracy and richly drawn, sympathetic characters." Library Journal.

Penman, Sharon Kay

Lionheart / Sharon Kay Penman. G. P. Putnam's Sons, 2011. 608 p. Henry II novels

ISBN 9780399157851

1. Richard I,, King of England, 1157-1199 2. Medieval period (476-1492) 3. Plantagenet period (1154-1485) 4. 12th century 5. Crusades -- Third, 1189-1192 6. Rulers 7. War 8. Conspiracies 9. Great Britain -- History -- Richard I, 1189-1199 10. Historical fiction 11. Biographical fiction

LC 2011013731

"A Marian Wood book."

Sequel: A king's ransom.

Richard, the second surviving son of Henry Plantagenet and Eleanor of Aquitaine, inherits the throne of England before embarking on the Third Crusade, a conflict that is complicated by the schemes of his usurping brother, John.

"Penman expertly weaves well-researched historical events into her fast-paced revisionist story. Certain to appeal to historical fiction fans interested in the medieval era." Library Journal.

Penman, Sharon Kay

The **Queen's** man : a medieval mystery / Sharon Kay Penman. H. Holt, 1996. 291 p.. Justin de Quincy mysteries

ISBN 080503885X

1. Eleanor,, of Aquitaine, Queen, consort of Henry II, King of England, 1122?-1204 2. John,, King of England, 1167-1216 3. Richard I,, King of England, 1157-1199 4. Medieval period (476-

1492) 5. Plantagenet period (1154-1485) 6. 12th century 7. Murder investigation 8. Royal pretenders 9. Goldsmiths 10. Royal houses 11. Secrets 12. Conspiracies 13. England -- History -- 12th century 14. Historical mysteries 15. Medieval mysteries 16. Mysteries

LC 9615027

In England in 1193, a dying man gives Justin de Quincy a letter that must be delivered to Eleanor of Aquitaine, a letter that tells the Queen if her son, Richard Lionheart, is living or dead.

"Penman's authentic period details, larger-than-life characters, and fast-paced plot add up to great reading for both mystery fans and history buffs." Booklist.

Penman, Sharon Kay

The **reckoning** / Sharon Kay Penman. H. Holt, 1991. 592 p. Welsh trilogy

ISBN 0805010149

1. Edward I, King of England, 1239-1307 2. Llewelyn ap Gruffudd, d 1282 3. Medieval period (476-1492) 4. Plantagenet period (1154-1485) 5. 13th century 6. Power (Social sciences) 7. Half-brothers 8. Princesses 9. Royal houses 10. Wales -- History -- 1063-1284 11. Great Britain -- History -- Plantagenets, 1154-1399 12. Great Britain -- History -- Medieval period, 1066-1485 13. Great Britain -- Rulers 14. Great Britain -- History -- 13th century 15. Historical fiction

LC 90027099

Five years after the slaying of Simon de Montfort has assured the throne for Henry III, Llewelyn ap Gruffydd--Simon's friend and ally--awaits the chaos he is certain will erupt in the land.

"The action involves religious and political intrigue, battles and plots. The players include well-researched historical personages and fictional characters. As with Penman's other historical novels, this one is both informative and enjoyable. Settings, events, and individuals are well drawn." Library Journal.

Penman, Sharon Kay

The **sunne** in splendour / Sharon Kay Penman. St. Martin's Griffin, 2008, c1982. 936 p.

ISBN 9780312375935

1. Richard III,, King of England, 1452-1485 2. Edward IV,, King of England, 1442-1483 3. Anne,, Queen, consort of Richard III, King of England, 1456-1485 4. Medieval period (476-1492) 5. Plantagenet period (1154-1485) 6. 15th century 7. Inheritance and succession 8. Rulers 9. Wars of the Roses, 1455-1485 10. Royal houses 11. Great Britain -- History -- Wars of the Roses, 1455-1485 12. Great Britain -- History -- Richard III, 1483-1485 13. England -- History -- 15th century 14. Historical fiction

LC 81020149

Includes map and family trees.

First published: New York : Holt, Rinehart and Winston, 1982.

Originally published: Ballantine Books, 1982.

Departing from the traditional Shakespearian and Tudor historical portraits, this saga depicts the love story of Richard III and Anne Neville against the backdrop of royal family intrigue.

"A historical novel of the first rank." Publishers Weekly.

Penman, Sharon Kay

Time and chance / Sharon Kay Penman. G. P. Putnam's Sons, 2002. 512 p. Henry II novels

ISBN 0399147853

1. Henry II,, King of England, 1133-1189 2. Thomas,, a Becket, Saint, 1118?-1170 3. Medieval period (476-1492) 4. Plantagenet period (1154-1485) 5. 12th century 6. Marriages of royalty and nobility 7. Women rulers 8. Royal houses 9. Civilization, Medieval 10. Great Britain -- History -- Henry II, 1154-1189 11. Great Britain

-- Rulers 12. Great Britain -- History -- Medieval period, 1066-1485 13. England -- History -- 12th century 14. Biographical fiction 15. Historical fiction

LC 2001048255

Recreates the tumultuous marriage of Eleanor of Aquitaine and Henry II, presenting a tale filled with love, ambition, betrayal, and murder.

"This second volume of the author's medieval trilogy re-creates the drama, the intrigue, and the passion that distinguished the lives of Henry Plantagenet, Eleanor of Aquitaine, and Thomas Becket. Though the subject has been exhaustively chronicled in both history and literature, this fictionalized account of the trials and tribulations of this prominent trio of historical figures manages to breathe new life into a familiar story." Booklist.

Penman, Sharon Kay

When Christ and his saints slept / Sharon Kay Penman. H. Holt, 1995. 746 p. Henry II novels

ISBN 0805010157

1. Maude, princess of England, 1102-1167 2. Medieval period (476-1492) 3. Norman period (1066-1154) 4. 12th century 5. Nobility 6. Battles 7. Cousins 8. Civilization, Medieval 9. Royal houses 10. Inheritance and succession 11. England -- History -- 12th century 12. England -- Rulers 13. Great Britain -- History -- Norman period, 1066-1154 14. Historical fiction 15. Biographical fiction

LC 94022593

Map on lining papers.

A novel depicting a dark period in English history follows the story of Maude, daughter of Henry I and England's uncrowned queen, and her cousin Stephen, as their battles for the crown of England lead to twenty years of anarchy.

"The author showcases her mastery of the historical novel in this long and thoroughly engrossing study of pragmatic politics, idealism, and the role of women during the 12th century. She brings to life a vast array of unforgettable characters, both historical and invented, all of whose loyalties are being constantly tested by the chaos of the times." Library Journal.

Penney, Stef

The **invisible** ones / Stef Penney. G. P. Putnam's Sons, 2012, c2011. 416 p.

ISBN 9780399157714

1. 1980s 2. Romanies 3. Missing women 4. Private investigators 5. Missing persons investigation 6. Rural families 7. Strangers 8. Family secrets 9. Multiracial men 10. Romani teenage boys 11. England -- Social life and customs -- 20th century 12. Mysteries

Includes glossary of gypsy terms used in the novel.

Originally published: London : Quercus, 2011.

Leon Wood, a Gypsy, hires London PI Ray Lovell to find his daughter Rose, who hasn't been seen in six years. Lovell is half Gypsy himself, but Rose proves a tough quarry and the family acts towards him with hostility, which leads Ray to suspect them of hiding a secret connected with Rose's disappearance.

Penney, Stef

The **tenderness** of wolves : a novel / Stef Penney. Simon & Schuster, 2007. 352 p.

ISBN 1416540741

1. 19th century 2. Missing persons 3. Voyages and travels 4. Teenage boys 5. Detectives 6. Murder suspects 7. Tracking and trailing 8. Men/women relations 9. Murder 10. Cold weather 11. Frontier and pioneer life -- Canada 12. Canada -- History -- 1841-1867 13. Historical mysteries 14. Literary fiction 15. Mysteries

LC 2006100796

First published in Great Britain: Quercus, 2006.

Costa First Novel Award, 2006.

Costa Book of the Year Award, 2006.

Theakston Old Peculier Crime Novel of the Year Award, 2008

When her teenage son disappears in the aftermath of a brutal murder, a determined mother sets out from her snow-covered nineteenth-century settlement to find him, an effort that is hampered by vigilante groups and the harrowing forces of nature.

"A confident and complex portrait of 1860s Ontario. . . . Between twists and turns of plot, Penney evokes the land--its shades of light and changes of weather, its marshes and treacherous waters. Rarely has winter seemed so febrile." Books in Canada.

Penney, Stef

Under a pole star / Stef Penney. Quercus, 2017., 580 p.

ISBN 9781681441177

1. 19th century 2. Women explorers 3. Independence in women 4. North Pole expeditions 5. Explorers 6. Competition 7. Lovers 8. Men/women relations 9. Greenland 10. Arctic regions 11. Historical fiction

LC 2016047484

Originally published: 2016.

A whaler's daughter, Flora Mackie first crossed the Arctic Circle at the age of 12 and fell in love with the unforgiving terrain, and, in 1889, despite those who believe that a woman has no place in this harsh world, she heads back to Greenland at the head of a British expedition.

"...[T]he icy Arctic setting comes alive in passages of shimmering beauty. Penney conveys both the elation and fear evoked when crossing into unfamiliar territory, be it geographical or emotional. She also delves into the customs and beliefs of the Inuit, whose generous hospitality to the Westerners is indispensable. An exceptional epic about an unconventional womans life and loves." Booklist.

Penny, Louise

* The **beautiful** mystery : a Chief Inspector Gamache novel / Louise Penny. Minotaur Books, 2012. 384 p. Inspector Armand Gamache mysteries

ISBN 9780312655464

1. Murder investigation -- Quebec (Province) 2. Monasteries 3. Choral conductors -- Death 4. Police -- Quebec (Province) 5. Detectives -- Quebec (Province) 6. Quebec (Province) 7. Police procedurals 8. Mysteries

Agatha Award for Best Novel, 2012.

Anthony Award for Best Novel, 2013.

Macavity Award for Best Mystery Novel, 2013.

When the choir director at the monastery of Saint-Gilbert-Entre-les-Loups is found murdered, Chief Inspector Gamache of the Surete du Quebec is called to investigate.

Penny, Louise

* A **better** man : a Chief Inspector Gamache novel / Louise Penny. Minotaur Books, 2019. 400 p. Inspector Armand Gamache mysteries

ISBN 9781250066213

1. Fathers 2. Missing persons 3. Small town life 4. Fathers and daughters 5. Missing persons investigation 6. Detectives 7. Murder 8. Murder investigation 9. Villages 10. Secrets 11. Quebec (Province) 12. Police procedurals 13. Mysteries

LC 2019012651

Searching for a missing woman amid a catastrophic flood and blistering social media attacks, a demoted Armand Gamache bonds with the victim's distraught father, who contemplates a murder of his own.

Penny, Louise

Bury your dead : a Chief Inspector Gamache novel / Louise Penny. Minotaur Books, 2010. 371 p. Inspector Armand Gamache mysteries

ISBN 9780312377045

1. Police -- Quebec (Province) 2. Winter carnivals 3. Murder investigation 4. Villages -- Quebec (Province) 5. Secrets 6. Murder 7. Murder suspects 8. Quebec (Province) 9. Canada 10. Mysteries 11. Police procedurals

Agatha Award for Best Novel, 2010.

Anthony Award for Best Novel, 2011.

Arthur Ellis Award for Best Novel, 2011.

Macavity Award for Best Mystery Novel, 2011.

RUSA Reading List, 2011.

Taking leave during Quebec's Winter Carnival after a case gone wrong, a disgruntled Chief Inspector Armand Gamache is unable to avoid assisting a politically charged investigation involving a historian's murder during a search for a famous figure's burial site.

"Hovering over both these present investigations is the case gone wrong in the past, the details of which are gradually revealed in perfectly placed flashbacks. Penny brilliantly juggles the three stories, which are connected only by a kind of psychological membrane." Booklist.

Penny, Louise

The **cruelest** month : a Three Pines mystery / Louise Penny. St. Martin's Minotaur, 2008. 320 p. Inspector Armand Gamache mysteries

ISBN 9780312352578

1. Spiritualism 2. Traitors 3. Small town life 4. Police -- Quebec (Province) 5. Detectives -- Quebec (Province) 6. Villages -- Quebec (Province) 7. Easter 8. Death 9. Murder investigation 10. Quebec (Province) 11. Canada 12. Police procedurals 13. Mysteries

LC 2007042422

Agatha Award for Best Novel, 2008.

Chief Inspector Armand Gamache of the Surete du Quebec is called to investigate the death of a villager at an Easter seance that was held at the Old Hadley House.

"Penny paints a vivid picture of the French-Canadian village, its inhabitants and a determined detective who will strike many Agatha Christie fans as a 21st-century version of Hercule Poirot." Publishers Weekly.

Penny, Louise

* **Glass** houses / Louise Penny. Minotaur Books, 2017. 400 p. Inspector Armand Gamache mysteries

ISBN 9781250066190

1. Murder suspects 2. Trials (Murder) 3. Police -- Quebec (Province) 4. Murder 5. Murder investigation 6. Secrets 7. Quebec (Province) 8. Police procedurals 9. Mysteries

Agatha Award for Best Novel, 2017.

When a mysterious figure travels through Three Pines and leaves a dead body in its wake, Armand Gamache pursues a difficult investigation that yields unexpected consequences and forces him into a battle with his own conscience.

"A meticulously built mystery that follows a careful ascent toward a breaking point that will leave you breathless." Kirkus.

Penny, Louise

* A **great** reckoning / Louise Penny. Minotaur Books, 2016. 384 p. Inspector Armand Gamache mysteries

ISBN 9781250022134

1. Murder suspects 2. Corruption 3. Maps 4. Police training 5. Teachers 6. Police -- Quebec (Province) 7. Murder 8. Murder investigation 9. Secrets 10. Quebec (Province) 11. Police procedurals 12. Mysteries

Agatha Award for Best Novel, 2016.

Anthony Award for Best Novel, 2017.

Macavity Award for Best Mystery Novel, 2017.

Receiving a mysterious old map that has been found stuffed in the walls of a bistro, former Quebec homicide investigator Armand Gamache follows clues to the site of a dead Sûreté academy professor and an unlikely cadet with whom he is implicated in a murder case.

"Young, learning minds are precious things, and Penny is here to make us aware of the evil out there, eager for a chance to mold--and poison--them. A chilling story that's also filled with hope--a beloved Penny trademark." Kirkus.

Penny, Louise

* **How** the light gets in : Chief Inspector Gamache novel / Louise Penny. Minotaur Books, 2013. 384 p. Inspector Armand Gamache mysteries

ISBN 9780312655471

1. Missing persons 2. Detectives -- Quebec (Province) 3. Senior women 4. Missing persons investigation 5. Quintuplets 6. Police -- Quebec (Province) 7. Quebec (Province) 8. Police procedurals 9. Mysteries

LC 2013013622

Struggling to maintain the Homicide group during the holiday season in the wake of interdepartmental estrangements, Chief Inspector Armand Gamache quietly investigates the disappearance of a once-famous mad poet while seeking a safe haven for his loyal colleagues in an increasingly hostile town.

Penny, Louise

* **Kingdom** of the blind / Louise Penny. Minotaur Books, 2018. 389 p. Inspector Armand Gamache mysteries

ISBN 9781250066206

1. Strangers 2. Wills 3. Women booksellers 4. Detectives 5. Murder 6. Murder investigation 7. Villages 8. Secrets 9. Small town life 10. Quebec (Province) 11. Police procedurals 12. Mysteries

LC 2018022773

Still coping with the events that led to his suspension, Armand Gamache is curious when he discovers that an elderly woman who was a complete stranger to him has named him as one of the executors of her will.

"Penny is a master at blending the modern evils affecting the big city and the hidden secrets of the almost mythical village of Three Pines. Well-known characters return and new faces add richness to a narrative that will keep readers intrigued until the last page." Library Journal.

Penny, Louise

The **long** way home : Chief Inspector Gamache novel / Louise Penny. Minotaur Books, 2014. 384 p. Inspector Armand Gamache mysteries

ISBN 9781250022066

1. Missing persons 2. Husband and wife 3. Artists 4. Retirees 5. Detectives -- Quebec (Province) 6. Missing persons investigation 7. Police -- Quebec (Province) 8. Quebec (Province) 9. Police procedurals 10. Mysteries

At first enjoying a peaceful retirement, former Quebec homicide detective Armand Gamache reluctantly agrees to help a neighbor search for her missing estranged husband and teams up with two former colleagues on a search that reveals the workings of a psychologically damaged mind.

"Over the course of the intriguing search, Penny offers real insight into the evolution of artistic style as well as the envy that artists feel about each other's success." Publishers Weekly.

Penny, Louise

* The **nature** of the beast : a Chief Inspector Gamache novel / Louise Penny. Minotaur Books, 2015. 376 p. Inspector Armand Gamache mysteries

ISBN 9781250022080

1. Murder investigation 2. Missing boys 3. Cold cases (Criminal investigation) 4. Missing persons investigation 5. Husband and wife 6. Detectives -- Quebec (Province) 7. Police -- Quebec (Province) 8. Quebec (Province) 9. Police procedurals 10. Mysteries

LC 2015017153

When a young boy prone to crying wolf goes missing, village new-comers Armand and Reine-Marie Gamache join a frantic search for the child only to stumble on a community secret about a long-ago betrayal and murder.

"Penny is an expert at pulling away the surface of her characters to expose their deeperand often uglylayers, always doing so with a direct but compassionate hand." Kirkus.

Penny, Louise

Still life / Louise Penny. St. Martin's Minotaur, 2006. 288 p. Inspector Armand Gamache mysteries

ISBN 9780312352554

1. Small town life 2. Victims of violent crimes 3. Murder investigation 4. Police -- Quebec (Province) 5. Detectives -- Quebec (Province) 6. Murder 7. Retired teachers 8. Thanksgiving Day 9. Quebec (Province) 10. Canada 11. Mysteries 12. Police procedurals

LC 2006041992

Anthony Award for Best First Novel, 2007.

Arthur Ellis Award for Best First Novel, 2006.

Chief Inspector Armand Gamache of Canada's Surete du Quebec is called to Three Pines, a tiny hamlet south of Montreal, just north of the U.S. border, to investigate the suspicious hunting "accident" that claimed the life of Jane Neal, a local fixture in the village.

"The residents of a tiny Canadian village called Three Pines are shocked when the body of Miss Jane Neal is found in the woods. Miss Neal, the village's retired schoolteacher and a talented amateur artist, has been a good friend to most of the townsfolk, so her loss is keenly felt. At first, her death appears to be a tragic accidentit's deer-hunting season, and it looks a stray hunter's arrow killed her. But some folks are suspicious, and Chief Inspector Armand Gamache of the Montreal Surete is called in to investigate." Booklist.

Penny, Louise

A **trick** of the light : a Chief Inspector Gamache novel / Louise Penny. Minotaur Boooks, 2011. 352 p. Inspector Armand Gamache mysteries

ISBN 9780312655457

1. Women painters 2. Art -- Exhibitions 3. Murder investigation 4. Murder 5. Women artists 6. Police -- Quebec (Province) 7. Detectives -- Quebec (Province) 8. Small town life 9. Quebec (Province) 10. Mysteries 11. Police procedurals

LC 2011020256

Anthony Award for Best Novel, 2012.

Investigating a murder at a solo artist's Quebec village home, Chief Inspector Gamache and his team encounter deceptive nuances in the art world that distort every clue they find with tales of duality and broken hearts.

"Penny, elevating herself to the pantheon that houses P.D. James, Ruth Rendell and Minette Walters, demonstrates an exquisite touch with characterization, plotting and artistic sensitivity. And there could be no better explanation of A.A. than you will find here." Kirkus.

Penrose, Andrea

Murder at half moon gate / Andrea Penrose. Kensington, 2018. 304 p. Wrexford and Sloane historical mysteries

ISBN 9781496710796

1. Scientists 2. Women artists 3. Murder suspects 4. Political cartoons 5. Inventors 6. Aristocracy 7. Murder investigation 8. London, England -- History -- 19th century 9. England -- History -- 19th century 10. Historical mysteries

A wealthy lord who happens to be a brilliant scientist . . . an enig-matic young widow who secretly pens satirical cartoons . . . a violent killing disguised as a robbery . . . Nothing is as it seems in Regency London, especially when the Earl of Wrexford and Charlotte Sloane join forces to solve a shocking murder.

Penrose, Andrea

* **Murder** at Kensington Palace / Andrea Penrose. Kens-ington, 2019. 304 pags Wrexford and Sloane historical mys-teries

ISBN 9781496722812

1. Regency period (1811-1820) 2. Scientists 3. Women artists 4. Murder investigation 5. Earls and countesses 6. Secret identity 7. Political cartoons 8. Murder 9. Cousins -- Death 10. Men/women relations 11. Interpersonal attraction 12. London, England -- History -- 19th century 13. England -- History -- 19th century 14. Historical mysteries

Wrexford and Sloane must unravel secrets within secrets - including a few that entangle their own hearts - when they reunite to solve a string of shocking murders that have horrified Regency London.

Penrose, Andrea

Murder on Black Swan Lane / Andrea Penrose. Kensing-ton, 2017. 304 p. Wrexford and Sloane historical mysteries

ISBN 9781496710772

1. Regency period (1811-1820) 2. Scientists 3. Women artists 4. Murder suspects 5. Political cartoons 6. Clergy 7. Aristocracy 8. Anonyms and pseudonyms 9. London, England -- History -- 19th century 10. England -- History -- 19th century 11. Historical mysteries

In Regency London, an unconventional scientist and a fearless fe-male artist form an unlikely alliance to expose unspeakable evil.

Percy, Benjamin

Red moon / Benjamin Percy. Grand Central Pub., 2013. 544 p.

ISBN 9781455501663

1. Werewolves 2. Terrorism 3. Civil rights 4. Resistance to government 5. Infection 6. Supernatural 7. Minority rights 8. Fugitives 9. Governors 10. Interpersonal relations 11. Men/women relations 12. Oregon 13. Horror 14. Literary fiction

LC 2012016127

First published: Great Britain: Hodder & Stoughton, 2013.

Dwelling among ordinary humans and suppressing their shape-shifting nature with drugs, lycans have been around for millennia -- but a new movement has emerged that presses for werewolf equal rights with increasing violence. Opposition to the lycan resistance movement has likewise escalated, and war has broken out in the Lupine Republic. A prion infection causes the condition known as lycanthropy, and ordi-nary humans never know when they might be infected, or who already has been! A sophisticated thriller for fans of Max Brooks' World War

Z and Glen Duncan's The Last Werewolf. - Description by Katherine Bradley Johnson.

Percy, Benjamin

The **wilding** / Benjamin Percy. Graywolf Press, 2010. 288 p.

ISBN 9781555975692

1. Hunters 2. Fathers and sons 3. Real estate development 4. Wilderness areas 5. Nature 6. Nature -- Effect of humans on 7. Marital conflict 8. Family relationships 9. Hunting 10. Oregon 11. Literary fiction

Returning to Echo Canyon for one last time before it is turned into a golf resort, Justin Caves and his father Paul must battle the physical demands of the terrain and the presence of bears along with each other, as Justin tries to come to terms with his rocky relationship with his father.

Percy, Walker, 1916-1990

Lancelot / Walker Percy. Picador, 1999, c1977. 257 p.

ISBN 9780312243074

1. Jesus Christ 2. Psychiatric hospital patients 3. Suicide -- Religious aspects 4. Murder -- Religious aspects 5. Extramarital affairs 6. Faith (Christianity) 7. Catholics 8. Lawyers 9. Priests 10. Belief and doubt 11. Southern States 12. Psychological fiction

Originally published: New York : Farrar, Straus and Giroux, 1977.

Confined in the Institute for Aberrant Behavior, Lancelot Andrewes Lamar, scion of a distinguished Southern family and disenchanted liberal lawyer, tells a psychiatrist-priest of his efforts to prove his wife's infidelity and his decision to begin life anew.

"In this novel the author knowledgeably fingers what he perceives as the rotting fabric of Southern aristocratic life, and describes it with vividness and a kind of affection, even as he starts to shred it." Christian Science Monitor.

Percy, Walker, 1916-1990

* The **last** gentleman / Walker Percy. Picador USA, 1999, c1966. 409 p.

ISBN 0679602720

1. Catholics 2. Suicide -- Religious aspects 3. Engineers 4. City life 5. Fathers and sons 6. Dysfunctional families 7. Alienation in men 8. Men/women relations 9. New York City 10. Louisiana 11. Picaresque fiction 12. Modern classics 13. Literary fiction 14. Southern fiction

LC 66018861

Sequel: The second coming.

Will Barrett, a Princeton graduate working as a janitor, meets Kitty when looking through his telescope at Central Park, and is drawn away from his remote lifestyle into the realities of her Southern family.

Percy, Walker, 1916-1990

Love in the ruins : the adventures of a bad Catholic at a time near the end of the world / Walker Percy. Picador USA, 1999, c1971. 403 p.

ISBN 9780312243111

1. Catholics 2. Alcoholic men 3. End of the world 4. Physicians 5. Inventions 6. Men/women relations 7. Priests 8. Apocalyptic fiction

LC 71143301

Originally published: New York : Farrar, Straus, and Giroux, 1971.

Amid the decadence and polarization of a future American society, a U.S. doctor discovers a promising cure for all the ills of the human psyche.

"A beautifully comic and humane work, the satirist's projection of a grotesque future world based on the realities of the present and stimulus to thought and evaluation and, hopefully, to improvement. Percy's style shows mastery of language." Choice.

Percy, Walker, 1916-1990

* The **moviegoer** / Walker Percy. Vintage International, 1998, c1961. 241 p.

ISBN 9780375701962

1. Self-discovery in men 2. Redemption 3. Purpose in life 4. Catholics 5. Young men 6. Mardi Gras 7. Hedonism 8. Films 9. Family relationships 10. Men/women relations 11. New Orleans, Louisiana 12. Louisiana 13. Psychological fiction 14. Modern classics 15. Literary fiction 16. Southern fiction

Originally published: New York : Knopf, 1961.

National Book Award for Fiction, 1962.

" ... the tale of Binx Bolling, a small-time stockbroker who lives quietly in suburban New Orleans, pursuing an interest in the movies, affairs with his secretaries, and living out his days. But soon he finds himself on a 'search' for something more important, some spiritual truth to anchor him. Binx's life floats casually along until one fateful Mardi Gras week, when a bizarre series of events leads him to his unlikely salvation. In his half-brother Lonnie, who is confined to a wheelchair and soon to die, and his stepcousin Kate, whose predicament is even more ominous, Binx begins to find the sort of 'certified reality' that had eluded him everywhere but at the movies"--Publisher's web site.

Percy, Walker, 1916-1990

The **second** coming / Walker Percy. Farrar, Straus, Giroux, 1980. 359 p.

ISBN 0374256748

1. Jesus Christ 2. People with mental illnesses 3. End of the world 4. Second coming of Christ 5. Catholics 6. Widowers 7. Rich men 8. Belief and doubt 9. Psychological fiction 10. Southern fiction

LC 80012899

Sequel to: The last gentleman.

National Book Critics Circle Award for Fiction finalist, 1980

National Book Award for Fiction finalist, 1981

Widower Will Barrett, with very little interest in money and much concern for all the unhappiness in the world, inherits forty million dollars from his late wife. Will, who has some episodes of blacking out, is drawn into a rewakening, "a second coming," with the help of a young escapee from a mental hospital. She becomes for him the light at the end of a long, dark tunnel. Some strong language. Sequel to : "The Last Gentleman" (RC 11597). Bestseller.

"A beautiful . . . exploration of Percy's recurrent themean individual man's search for the hand of God in the meaningless muddle of contemporary life." Booklist.

Perec, Georges, 1936-1982

Life : a user's manual / Georges Perec ; translated from the French by David Bellos. D. R. Godine, 1987. 581 p.

ISBN 9780879237516

1. Apartment houses 2. Apartment dwellers 3. Apartment house life 4. Life 5. Death 6. Painting 7. Eccentrics and eccentricities 8. Creation (Literary, artistic, etc) 9. Paris, France 10. Literary fiction 11. Translations -- French to English 12. Modern classics

LC 87008782

Originally published in French: Paris : Hachette litterature, 1978.

Represents an exploration of the relationship between imagination and reality as seen through the eyes of the dying Serge Valene, an inhabitant of a large Parisian apartment block.

"The inextricable incoherence of things is presumably the basic theme of the late Georges Perec's work, but this pessimistic view of life is dramatized with inventiveness, audacity, and even humor." The Atlantic.

Perez-Reverte, Arturo

Captain Alatriste / Arturo Perez-Reverte ; translated from the Spanish by Margaret Sayers Peden. G.P. Putnam's Sons, 2005, c1996. 272 p. Captain Alatriste adventures

ISBN 039915275X

1. 17th century 2. Swordfighters 3. Assassins 4. Veterans 5. Strangers 6. Travelers 7. Conspiracies 8. Attempted assassination 9. Inquisition -- Spain 10. Thirty Years' War, 1618-1648 11. Spain -- History -- 17th century 12. Madrid, Spain 13. Historical thrillers 14. Swashbuckling tales 15. Translations -- Spanish to English

LC 2004060210

Book made into a movie called Alatriste.

Originally published: Madrid : Alfaguara, 1996.

"Equipped with a quick-witted, charismatic hero and much to provoke and goad him, Mr. Prez-Reverte has the makings of a flamboyantly entertaining series. Captain Alatriste ends with a wicked flourish, an evil laugh and a strong likelihood that the best is yet to come." New York Times.

Perez-Reverte, Arturo

* The **Club** Dumas / Arturo Perez-Reverte ; translated from the Spanish by Sonia Soto. Harcourt Brace, 1997, c1993. 362 p.

ISBN 0151001820

1. Dumas, Alexander, 1802-1870 Three musketeers 2. Rare books 3. Demons 4. Book collectors 5. Antiquarian booksellers 6. Booksellers 7. Critics -- Spain 8. Satanism 9. Widows 10. Amateur detectives 11. Madrid, Spain 12. Paris, France 13. Portugal 14. Adventure stories 15. Mysteries 16. Literary fiction 17. Translations -- Spanish to English

This book was released as a movie entitled The ninth gate.

Originally published in Spanish under the title El Club Dumas: Madrid : Santillana, 1993.

"Corso, a tough-guy bibliophile living in Madrid, is hired by a wealthy client to track down a rare seventeenth-century book on how to summon the Devil. He soon finds himself in noir metafiction in which he's been cast as D'Artagnan and is threatened by characters suspiciously like Richelieu's agents--a menacing man with a scar and a blonde with a fleur-de-lis tattoo. Even a reader armed with a Latin dictionary and a copy of 'The Three Musketeers' cannot anticipate the thrilling twists of this stylish, Escher-like mystery." The New Yorker.

Perez-Reverte, Arturo

The **fencing** master / Arturo Perez-Reverte ; translated from the Spanish by Margaret Jull Costa. Harcourt Brace & Company, 1999, c1988. 245 p.

ISBN 9780151001811

1. 19th century 2. 1860s 3. Conspiracies 4. Fencers -- Spain 5. Fencing 6. Women fencers -- Spain 7. Murder -- Madrid, Spain 8. Madrid, Spain -- History -- 19th century 9. Spain -- Politics and government -- 19th century 10. Mysteries 11. Translations -- Spanish to English 12. Literary fiction

LC 98-35536

Originally published: Madrid: Mondadori, 1988.

"In lieu of snappy pater, Prez-Reverte provides artful, intricate conversation. Rather than send his characters on a relentless search, he provides them with an inexorable unfolding of revelation, increasingly ghastly. And instead of the clever puzzle that lies at the heart of many a lesser crime novel, he substitutes a subtle meditation on the deeper mysteries of fate and choice." New York Times Book Review.

Perez-Reverte, Arturo

The **painter** of battles : a novel / Arturo Perez-Reverte ; translated from the Spanish by Margaret Sayers Peden. Random House, 2008. 224 p.

ISBN 9781400065981

1. Painters 2. War photographers 3. Assassins 4. Painting 5. Mural painting and decoration 6. War 7. Artists 8. Love 9. Violence 10. Art 11. Psychological fiction 12. Literary fiction 13. Translations -- Spanish to English

LC 2007016997

Andrés Faulques, a world-renowned war photographer, has retired to a life of solitude on the Spanish coast. He spends his days painting a huge mural that pays homage to history's classic works of war art and that incorporates a lifetime of disturbing images. One night, an unexpected visitor arrives at Faulques' door and challenges the painter to remember him. As Faulques struggles to recall the face, the man explains that he was the subject of an iconic photo taken by Faulques in a war zone years ago. "And why have you come looking for me?" asks Faulques. The stranger answers, "Because I'm going to kill you."

"The character of the title is Andrs Faulques, a hermit who spends his time painting a colossal battle scene on the interior of a watchtower. Faulques was once a war photographer, famed for his ability to capture in a single image horror, beauty and geometry. One day he has a visitor, the subject of one of Faulques's most celebrated shots: a weary Croatian soldier in the hour of dejected defeat. The photograph helped to change Faulques's life, winning an award. It also changed the soldier's: its publication and his identification as the husband of a young woman sheltering in a Serbian village saw her raped and then, along with his son, tortured and murdered. Now he has come to pay Faulques back. What follows is a game of mental chess, an excursion into art, history and imagination, and both men's lives as Faulques realises that only the continuation of their discourse, and his painting, is keeping him alive." London Times

Perez-Reverte, Arturo

The **siege** : a novel / Arturo Perez-Reverte ; translated from the Spanish by Frank Wynne. Random House, 2014, c2010. 624 p.

ISBN 9781400069682

1. 1810s 2. War and society 3. Violence against women 4. War -- Psychological aspects 5. Police 6. Sieges 7. Bombs 8. Napoleonic Wars, 1800-1815 9. Military campaigns 10. Murder 11. Murder investigation 12. Men/women relations 13. Spain -- History -- 19th Century 14. Historical mysteries 15. Literary fiction 16. Translations -- Spanish to English

Translation from the Spanish of: El asedio.

Originally published: Madrid : Alfaguara, 2010.

Duncan Lawrie International Dagger, 2014.

A tale set during the Napoleonic siege of Cadiz finds unwavering police commissioner Rogelio Tizon investigating a series of murders committed by one of several possible suspects trapped within the bomb-stricken city.

"There may be a little too much going on here--the density of both the prose and the story lines can seem almost suffocating at times--but there is no denying the author's ability to build character, evoke landscape, and communicate the crush of history on individual lives... Prez-Reverte, an international best-seller and a favorite among booksellers and librarians, has not had a new book since 2010 and will attract plenty of attention with this one." Booklist.

Perez-Reverte, Arturo

* What we become / Arturo Perez-Reverte ; translated by Nick Caistor and Lorenza Garcia. Atria Books, 2016. 512 p.

ISBN 9781476751986

1. 1920s 2. 1930s 3. 1960s 4. Tango (Dance) 5. Extramarital affairs 6. Married women 7. Thieves 8. Upper class 9. Romantic love 10. Espionage 11. Intelligence officers 12. Men dancers 13. Buenos Aires, Argentina -- History -- 20th century 14. France -- History -- History -- 20th century 15. Italy -- History -- History -- 20th century 16. Love stories 17. Historical fiction 18. Translations -- Spanish to English

LC 2015037715

"Originally published in Spain in 2012 by Santillana Ediciones Generales, S. L. as El tango de la Guardia Vieja" -- Verso title page.

A dangerous and passionate love affair between an accomplished tango dancer turned elegant thief and a beautiful, intelligent society woman bursts off the page in this epic historical tale of romance and espionage.

"Prez-Reverte summons the romantic spirit of an old black-and-white movie: impossibly glamorous, undeniably wistful." Kirkus.

Perkins, S. C. (Stephanie C.)

Murder once removed / S.C. Perkins. Minotaur Books, 2019. 318 p. Ancestry detective novels

ISBN 9781250189035

1. Women genealogists 2. Ancestors 3. Women amateur detectives 4. Family secrets 5. Murder 6. Murder investigation 7. FBI agents 8. Men/women relations 9. Austin, Texas 10. Texas 11. Cozy mysteries 12. Gentle reads

LC 2018046203

When a high-profile billionaire makes a history-changing claim on live television, genealogist Lucy Lancaster of Austin, Texas begins an investigation dating back to the mid-19th century before she is confronted by a modern descendant who would protect family secrets.

"The winner of Minotaur's Malice Domestic Best First Traditional Mystery Novel competition, this debut features an intelligent genealogist detective, a strong supporting cast, some romantic tension, and information about Texas history that should appeal to readers of Rett MacPherson's genealogy mysteries as well as cozy lovers who prefer a dash of history in their mysteries." Library Journal.

Perkins-Valdez, Dolen

Wench / Dolen Perkins-Valdez. Amistad, 2010. 293 p.

ISBN 9780061706547

1. Women slaves 2. Resorts 3. Fugitive slaves 4. Mistresses 5. African American women -- Friendship 6. Slavery 7. Escapes 8. Men/women relations 9. Emotionally abused women 10. Sexually abused women 11. Ohio -- History -- 19th century 12. Historical fiction 13. African American fiction

BCALA Literary Award for First Novelist, 2011.

Slave mistresses Lizzie, Reenie, and Sweet travel to a resort in Ohio each year with their white masters, until Mawu shows up and encourages them to escape, forcing them to choose between freedom and leaving their friends and families.

"Readers of historical fiction centering on Southern women's stories like Lalita Tademy's Cane River or Lee Smith's On Agate Hill will be moved by the skillful portrayal of Lizzie's precarious situation and the tragic stories of her fellow slaves." Library Journal.

Perrotta, Tom, 1961-

The **abstinence** teacher / Tom Perrotta. St. Martin's Press, 2007. 336 p.

ISBN 9780312358334

1. High school teachers 2. Sex education for teenagers 3. Divorced parents 4. Fathers 5. Fathers and daughters 6. Soccer coaches 7. Small town life 8. Disagreement 9. Child rearing 10. Understanding (Personal quality) 11. Suburbs 12. Men/women relations 13. Sexuality 14. Culture conflict 15. Suburban life 16. Christianity 17. Fundamentalists 18. Mainstream fiction

LC 2007021961

Teaching human sexuality from a perspective that information and pleasure are top priorities, divorced mom Ruth Ramsey butts heads with the local soccer coach, a divorced former addict who became an evangelical Christian after hitting rock bottom.

"Perrotta, an accomplished satirist who has made the suburbs his personal stomping ground, turns Stonewood Heights . . . into a battleground for the hearts and minds (and, need I add, souls) of his characters. While Perrotta does do more than give lip service to both sides, it's pretty clear where his allegiance lies. . . . What keeps the book from getting too heavy-handed, besides the sharply written humor, is the fact that Perrotta makes his evangelical Christian protagonist less of a zealot than the atheist." Christian Science Monitor.

Perrotta, Tom, 1961-

Joe College / Tom Perrotta. St. Martin's Press, 2000. 306 p.

ISBN 0312261845

1. Yale University. 2. 1980s 3. College students 4. Family businesses 5. Hometowns 6. Young men 7. Spring Break 8. Men/women relations 9. New Haven, Connecticut 10. New Jersey 11. Humorous stories 12. Mainstream fiction

LC 00031722

Danny, a Yale student, who is spending his summer vacation working in his father's lunch wagon, tries to cope with an increasingly complicated love life and an incipient battle with a gang over his father's business.

"Perrotta's genius is his ability to depict student culture with dead-on accuracy. His satiric touch is like a light, but killing frost." Christian Science Monitor.

Perrotta, Tom, 1961-

* Little children / Tom Perrotta. St. Martin's Press, 2004. 368 p.

ISBN 0312315716

1. Suburban life 2. Married people 3. Stay-at-home fathers 4. Former police 5. Mothers 6. Fathers 7. Child sexual abusers 8. Parent and child 9. Husband and wife 10. Marriage 11. Extramarital affairs 12. Psychological fiction 13. Mainstream fiction 14. Domestic fiction

LC 2003015947

A group of young suburban parents, including a handsome stay-at-home dad, a former feminist, an internet surfer, and an over-structured mom, finds its sleepy existence shattered when a convicted child molester moves back into town and two of the parents have an affair.

"The eponymous children in this satirical novel are actually adults who, chafing at the burdens of parenthood, try to recreate their unencumbered youth. Sarah, an overeducated young homemaker, likens her tantrum-prone daughter to a brooding Russian epileptic out of Dostoevsky, and pines for lost college days of feminism and bisexuality. While her husband orders used panties online, she has furtive sex with a stay-at-home dad whose repeated failure to pass the bar has earned him the contempt of his gorgeous wife. The humor is sometimes cruel, but Perrotta never betrays the complexity of his characters." The New Yorker.

Perrotta, Tom, 1961-

The **leftovers** / Tom Perrotta. St. Martin's Press, 2011. 336 p.

ISBN 9780312358341

1. Life change events 2. Mayors 3. Conflict in families 4. Disappeared persons 5. Anxiety 6. Cults 7. New Jersey 8. Satirical fiction

First published: 2011.

"A new original series from HBO"--Cover.

When a bizarre phenomenon causes the cataclysmic disappearances of numerous people all over the world, Kevin Garvey, the new mayor of a once-comfortable suburban community, struggles to help his neighbors heal while enduring the fanatical religious conversions of his wife and son.

"Perrotta has a gifted ear for dialogue and a distinct appreciation for the particularities of suburban life." Minneapolis Star Tribune.

Perry, Anne

Bedford Square / Anne Perry. Fawcett Books, 1999. 330 p. Thomas and Charlotte Pitt mysteries

ISBN 0345432983

1. Victorian era (1837-1901) 2. 19th century 3. Husband-and-wife detectives 4. Murder investigation 5. Police 6. Police spouses 7. Extortion 8. Betrayal 9. Guilt in women 10. Orphanages 11. Orphans 12. London, England -- History -- 19th century 13. Historical mysteries 14. Victorian mysteries 15. Mysteries

LC 9829854

Thomas Pitt is called to the scene of a murder at a respectble house in Bedford Square. The house, and a snuffbox found on the body, belong to one of the pillars of the community and a friend of Pitt's wife, Charlotte. Pitt is dismayed to find that the man can barely recall the evening.

Perry, Anne

* **Belgrave** Square / Anne Perry. Fawcett Columbine, 1992. 361 p. Thomas and Charlotte Pitt mysteries

ISBN 9780449906781

1. Victorian era (1837-1901) 2. 19th century 3. Husband-and-wife detectives 4. Murder investigation 5. Extortion 6. Closeted gay men 7. Police 8. Police spouses 9. Women detectives 10. London, England -- History -- 19th century 11. Historical mysteries 12. Victorian mysteries 13. Mysteries

LC 91073144

The death of a petty moneylender leads Inspector Thomas Pitt and his well-connected wife, Charlotte, to the doorsteps of London's most powerful citizenry, and to shocking secrets and further death

"The author paints handsome portraits of . . . [Victorian] aristocratic society and provides luxurious details of the gala balls and garden parties, the fashionable outings at Covent Garden and the Royal Academy of Arts, where they congregate to preen themselves. But it isn't all done for show. The author has the eyes of a hawk for character nuance and her claws out for signs of the criminal injustices rampant among the privileged classes during this gilded historical period." New York Times Book Review.

Perry, Anne

Bethlehem Road / Anne Perry. St. Martin's Press, 1990. 309 p. Thomas and Charlotte Pitt mysteries

ISBN 9780312042660

1. Victorian era (1837-1901) 2. 19th century 3. Husband-and-wife detectives 4. Murder investigation 5. Suffrage 6. Women detectives 7. Police 8. Police spouses 9. London, England -- History -- 19th century 10. Historical mysteries 11. Victorian mysteries 12. Mysteries

LC 89078014

When three members of Parliament who voted against woman suffrage are crossing Westminster Bridge, their throats are slit, and Thomas Pitt needs Charlotte's help to solve the murder.

"The author's concern with presenting an unassailable argument for her feminist cause tends to drag the pace and dull the action. But her finely drawn characters couldn't be more comfortable within the customs and sensibility of their historical period." New York Times Book Review.

Perry, Anne

Blind justice : a William Monk novel / Anne Perry. Ballantine Books, 2013. 352 p. William Monk and Hester Latterly mysteries

ISBN 9780345536709

1. Victorian era (1837-1901) 2. 1860s 3. 19th century 4. Detectives 5. Extortion 6. Trials 7. Corruption 8. London, England -- History -- 1800-1950 9. Victorian mysteries 10. Historical mysteries 11. Police procedurals 12. Mysteries

LC bl2013029976

When his friend, judge Oliver Rathbone, rashly crosses a line and inadvertently causes the death of a charismatic minister, police superintendent William Monk and his wife, Hester, navigate the perilous case to expose the truth and clear Rathbone's name.

Perry, Anne

Blood on the water : a William Monk novel / Anne Perry. Ballantine Books, 2014. 256 p. William Monk and Hester Latterly mysteries

ISBN 9780345548436

1. Victorian era (1837-1901) 2. 1860s 3. 19th century 4. Police 5. Bombing investigation 6. Frameups 7. Conspiracies 8. International intrigue 9. Detectives 10. Boating accidents 11. London, England -- History -- 1800-1950 12. Great Britain -- Foreign relations -- Egypt 13. Thames River 14. Victorian mysteries 15. Historical mysteries 16. Police procedurals

Shut out of the investigation of a massive bombing he witnessed, William Monk takes over when evidence surfaces that the person executed for the crime was innocent, a situation that places him in the center of a violent power struggle for control of the Suez Canal.

Perry, Anne

Bluegate Fields / Anne Perry. St. Martin's Press, 1984. 308 p. Thomas and Charlotte Pitt mysteries

ISBN 9780312087180

1. Victorian era (1837-1901) 2. 19th century 3. Husband-and-wife detectives 4. Murder investigation 5. Women detectives 6. Police 7. Police spouses 8. London, England -- History -- 19th century 9. Historical mysteries 10. Victorian mysteries 11. Mysteries

LC 84011769

Inspector Pitt and his wife Charlotte uncover shocking depravity and unexpected decadence among the aristocracy when the body of a young gentleman turns up in the sewers of the Bluegate Fields slum.

Perry, Anne

A **breach** of promise / Anne Perry. Fawcett Columbine, 1998. 374 p. William Monk and Hester Latterly mysteries

ISBN 0449908496

1. Victorian era (1837-1901) 2. 19th century 3. 1850s 4. Police 5. Murder investigation 6. Lawyers 7. Breach of promise -- Great Britain 8. Abandoned children 9. Children with disfigurements 10. Nurses 11. Detectives 12. London, England -- History -- 19th century 13. Victorian mysteries 14. Historical mysteries 15. Police

procedurals 16. Mysteries

LC 9821212

Also published as: The whited sepulchres.

Investigator William Monk is involved in a breach of promise suit brought by wealthy social climbers on behalf of their daughter. The defendant declares that he will not and cannot marry the woman. Monk must search London for clues to this bizarre case.

"Aside from the jarring coincidence that sets up the resolution, the story is full of feeling and weighted with intelligent thought about the status of women in mid-Victorian society." New York Times Book Review.

Perry, Anne

Buckingham Palace gardens : a novel / Anne Perry. Ballantine Books, 2008. 320 p. Thomas and Charlotte Pitt mysteries

ISBN 9780345469311

1. Victorian era (1837-1901) 2. 19th century 3. Husband-and-wife detectives 4. Murder investigation 5. Women detectives 6. Police 7. Police spouses 8. Prostitutes 9. Murder 10. London, England -- History -- 19th century 11. Great Britain -- Politics and government -- 19th century 12. Historical mysteries 13. Victorian mysteries 14. Mysteries

LC 2007042767

Pitt investigates the murder of a maid at Buckingham Palace, narrowing his group of suspects down to several house guests who are meeting with the Prince of Wales to discuss the funding of a huge project: the Cape to Cairo railway. While the Prince might overlook the unfortunate loss of a maid, the Queen, who is due back soon, will likely veto any Royal support in the scheme if she finds out.

"A mystery featuring Perry's 19th-century police inspector, Thomas Pitt. Unlike so many detective series gliding on cruise control, this mature work provides a fine introduction to Perry's alluring world of Victorian crime and intrigue. Ever the master of her milieu, she delivers sumptuous descriptions of life among the gentry when England still basked in its imperial glory. And in an intricate plot about a murder at the palace while the Prince and Princess of Wales are in residence, she also marshals the series's major themes: the way crime reverberates throughout the social classes; the precarious status of women of every rank; and the need for honorable heroes to preserve and protect the Empire, sometimes from itself." New York Times Book Review.

Perry, Anne

Cain his brother / Anne Perry. Fawcett Columbine, 1995. 390 p. William Monk and Hester Latterly mysteries

ISBN 0804115079

1. Victorian era (1837-1901) 2. 19th century 3. 1850s 4. Police 5. Murder investigation 6. Missing persons 7. Twins 8. Nurses 9. Detectives 10. London, England -- History -- 19th century 11. Victorian mysteries 12. Historical mysteries 13. Police procedurals 14. Mysteries

LC 95008680

When the honorable Angust Stonefield disappears and suspicion falls on his depraved twin brother Caleb, William Monk steps into the shoes of the victim in order to find the truth behind his disappearance.

"This one deserves high marks for superb plotting, fine writing, intriguing characters, and outstanding historical detail." Booklist.

Perry, Anne

Cardington Crescent / Anne Perry. St. Martin's Press, 1987. 314 p. Thomas and Charlotte Pitt mysteries

ISBN 9780312001131

1. Victorian era (1837-1901) 2. 19th century 3. Husband-and-wife detectives 4. Murder investigation 5. Suspicion 6. Incest 7. Social

classes 8. Women detectives 9. Police 10. Police spouses 11. London, England -- History -- 19th century 12. Historical mysteries 13. Victorian mysteries 14. Mysteries

LC 86027942

Charlotte and Thomas Pitt discover corruption in Charlotte's sister's life when she is suspected of poisoning her womanizing husband.

"A detailed period puzzler suffused with atmosphere, emotion, and suspense." Booklist.

Perry, Anne

A **Christmas** message / Anne Perry. Ballantine Books, 2016. 176 p. Christmas mysteries (Anne Perry)

ISBN 9781101886380

1. 1900s (Decade) 2. Voyages and travels 3. Amateur detectives 4. Husband and wife 5. Travelers 6. Murder 7. Israel -- History -- 20th century 8. Historical mysteries 9. Christmas stories

The year is 1900, and Victor Narraway is giving his wife, Vespasia, an unforgettable Christmas present: a trip to Jerusalem for the holiday. Vespasia is enchanted by the exotic landscape of Palestine, and charmed by a fellow traveler they meet at their hotel in Jaffa. But when the man is murdered over a torn piece of ancient parchment he was taking to Jerusalem, Victor and Vespasia risk their lives to finish his mission and deliver the mysterious document to its home. Pursued by a shadowy figure with evil intent, they embark on a dangerous yet ultimately enlightening pilgrimage to the holy city, where the mysterious message on the parchment may finally be revealed.

Perry, Anne

A **Christmas** return / Anne Perry. Random House Inc, 2017 176 p. Christmas mysteries (Anne Perry)

ISBN 9780425285077

1. 1900s (Decade) 2. Christmas 3. Amateur detectives 4. Cold cases (Criminal investigation) 5. Voyages and travels 6. Murder investigation 7. Reconciliation 8. Former friends 9. Surrey, England 10. England 11. Historical mysteries 12. Christmas stories

Spurred by holiday cheer and a surprise hidden in Christmas pudding, an elderly aristocrat tries to right a past wrong by solving a decade-old murder.

Perry, Anne

A **dangerous** mourning / Anne Perry. Fawcett Columbine, 1991. 330p. William Monk and Hester Latterly mysteries

ISBN 9780747245261

1. Victorian era (1837-1901) 2. 19th century 3. Murder investigation 4. Police 5. Nurses 6. Women's role 7. Detectives 8. London, England -- History -- 19th century 9. Historical mysteries 10. Victorian mysteries 11. Police procedurals 12. Mysteries

LC 91070655

Inspector Monk returns to the scene of another Victorian era murder mystery when the daughter of an upper-crust family is stabbed in her own home.

Perry, Anne

Dark tide rising : a William Monk novel / Anne Perry. Ballantine Books, 2018. 289 p. William Monk and Hester Latterly mysteries

ISBN 9780399179914

1. Victorian era (1837-1901) 2. 1860s 3. 19th century 4. Police 5. Suspicion 6. Betrayal 7. Ransom 8. Loyalty 9. Secrets 10. Kidnappers 11. London, England -- History -- 1800-1950 12. Victorian mysteries 13. Historical mysteries 14. Police procedurals

LC 2018014439

A ransom exchange gone violently wrong forces Commander William Monk to investigate the unthinkable possibility that one of his own men has betrayed him.

"The 24th title in Perry's long-running William Monk series delivers an excellent atmospheric Victorian mystery. While astute readers will identify the villain long before Monk does, longtime fans will delight in the camaraderie among the series regulars and the return to the dark underbelly of polite British society." Library Journal.

Perry, Anne

Death in focus : an Elena Standish novel / Anne Perry. Ballantine Books, 2019. 305 p. Elena Standish

ISBN 9780525620983

1. Between the Wars (1918-1939) 2. 1930s 3. Women photographers 4. International intrigue 5. Families 6. Spies 7. Assassination plots 8. Women amateur detectives 9. Interpersonal attraction 10. Men/women relations 11. Diplomats 12. Secrets 13. England -- History -- 20th century 14. Italy 15. Germany 16. Historical mysteries

LC 2019011797

An intrepid young photographer carries her imperiled lover's final, urgent message into the heart of pre-World War II Berlin as Hitler is ascending to power.

"Obvious comparisons to Charles Todd's Bess Crawford and Jacqueline Winspear's Maisie Dobbs are warranted, but this novel also hearkens back to Helen MacInnes's classic spy thrillers and Mary Stewart's romantic suspense novels. At turns heartbreaking and action-packed, this gripping and superbly written story proves Perry still has what it takes." Library Journal.

Perry, Anne

Death of a stranger / Anne Perry. Ballantine Books, 2002. 320 p. William Monk and Hester Latterly mysteries

ISBN 0345440056

1. Victorian era (1837-1901) 2. 19th century 3. 1850s 4. Police 5. Murder investigation 6. Lawyers 7. Business -- Corrupt practices 8. Railroad owners 9. Nurses 10. Detectives 11. London, England -- History -- 19th century 12. Victorian mysteries 13. Historical mysteries 14. Police procedurals 15. Mysteries

LC 2002066735

Private detective William Monk is hired by a mysterious client who wants him to discover whether or not her fiancé, a railway firm executive, engages in fraudulent practices, a case that brings Monk face to face with his past.

"This Monk mystery opens with the murder of a wealthy railroad businessman in a brothel. Outraged by the crime, high society pressures the police into cracking down on prostitution. But a police presence is bad for business, and the pimps take out their frustration on the call girls. These battered women seek medical assistance at a Coldbath Square clinic rum by Monk's wife, Hester. . . . Meanwhile, a mysterious young socialite asks Monk to investigate her fiancé, a partner in a successful railroad company that, she fears, is involved in fraud and corruption." Library Journal.

Perry, Anne

Death on Blackheath : a Charlotte and Thomas Pitt novel / Anne Perry. Ballantine Books, 2014, c2013. 302 p. Thomas and Charlotte Pitt mysteries

ISBN 9780345548382

1. Victorian era (1837-1901) 2. 19th century 3. Criminal investigation 4. Missing persons 5. Murder 6. Conspiracies 7. Husband-and-wife detectives 8. Murder investigation 9. Murder 10. Women detectives 11. Police 12. Police spouses 13. London, England -- History -- 19th century 14. Great Britain -- Politics and government -- 19th century

15. Historical mysteries 16. Victorian mysteries 17. Mysteries Originally published: 2013.

Investigating evidence of a violent struggle at the home of Ministry of Defense member Dudley Kynaston, Pitt and the Special Branch discover the brutally murdered body of a young woman before realizing that Kynaston is not who he appears to be.

Perry, Anne

Defend and betray / Anne Perry. Fawcett Columbine, 1992. 385 p. William Monk and Hester Latterly mysteries

ISBN 9780747248705

1. Victorian era (1837-1901) 2. People with amnesia 3. Police 4. Murder investigation 5. Husband and wife 6. Defense attorneys 7. London, England -- History -- 19th century 8. Victorian mysteries 9. Historical mysteries 10. Police procedurals 11. Mysteries

LC 92052665

Investigator William Monk knows that the wife of General Carlyon is lying when she admits to killing her husband, but it takes a devastating courtroom confrontation to get at the truth.

"The climactic trial, and its ugly disclosures, are well wrought. . . . Throughout, the plight of the intelligent, educated woman who is not rich--her need for a meaningful independence, her culture's resistance to her fulfillment--is, while not deeply explored, frequently touched upon." New York Times Book Review.

Perry, Anne

The **face** of a stranger / Anne Perry. Fawcett Columbine, 1990. 328 p. William Monk and Hester Latterly mysteries

ISBN 9780449905302

1. Victorian era (1837-1901) 2. 19th century 3. 1850s 4. People with amnesia 5. Police 6. Murder investigation 7. Social classes 8. Nurses 9. Detectives 10. London, England -- History -- 19th century 11. Victorian mysteries 12. Historical mysteries 13. Police procedurals 14. Mysteries

LC 90034169

William Monk, a member of the London police force in 1856, develops amnesia after an accident, and, while trying to solve the murder of an aristocrat, he looks at his own character.

"The author understands her amnesiac sleuth so intimately that she knows he can rediscover himself only in moments of inspiration along the trail of his quarry. This, and the fact that Monk has more to learn about himself even as the story concludes, are brilliant touches that effectively blend contemporary understanding of character with a Victorian sensibility." New York Times Book Review.

Perry, Anne

Farriers' Lane / Anne Perry. Fawcett Columbine, 1993. 374 p. Thomas and Charlotte Pitt mysteries

ISBN 9780449905692

1. Victorian era (1837-1901) 2. 19th century 3. Husband-and-wife detectives 4. Murder investigation 5. Antisemitism 6. Judges 7. Police 8. Police spouses 9. London, England -- History -- 19th century 10. Historical mysteries 11. Victorian mysteries 12. Mysteries

LC 92054390

Investigating the poisoning death of a distinguished judge, Inspector Pitt finds himself haunted by a grisly murder committed in desolate Farrier's Lane five years before

Perry, Anne

* **Funeral** in blue / Anne Perry. Ballantine Books, 2001. 344 p. William Monk and Hester Latterly mysteries

ISBN 0345440013

1. Victorian era (1837-1901) 2. 1850s 3. 19th century 4. Police 5.

Murder investigation 6. Antisemitism -- Vienna, Austria 7. Nurses 8. Detectives 9. London, England -- History -- 19th century 10. Vienna, Austria -- History -- 19th century 11. Victorian mysteries 12. Historical mysteries 13. Police procedurals 14. Mysteries

LC 2001037481

Murder investigator William Monk and his wife Hester, investigate the murder of two women, and hope to clear Hester's colleague, a Viennese émigré, of suspicion.

"A mystery featuring Hester and William Monk. In the studio of a London artist, two women have been murdered, one of them the wife of Dr. Kristian Beck, a physician from Vienna with whom Hester's dear friend, Lady Callandra, is secretly in love. When Beck is charged with the murder, Callandra enlists the aid of Hester and William. . . . The author excels at re-creating the ambience of 1860s London streets." Publishers Weekly.

Perry, Anne

* **Half** Moon Street / Anne Perry. Ballantine, 2000. 312 p. Thomas and Charlotte Pitt mysteries

ISBN 0345433270

1. Victorian era (1837-1901) 2. 19th century 3. Husband-and-wife detectives 4. Murder investigation 5. Women detectives 6. Police 7. Police spouses 8. Theater 9. Photography 10. Pornography 11. London, England -- History -- 19th century 12. Historical mysteries 13. Victorian mysteries 14. Mysteries

Superintendent Pitt finds a dead man in a battered boat drifting through the morning mist on the Thames. He is clad in a torn green gown, and flowers bestrew his battered body. Pitt's search for answers lead him into London's bohemia.

Perry, Anne

Highgate Rise / Anne Perry. Fawcett Columbine, 1991. 330 p. Thomas and Charlotte Pitt mysteries

ISBN 9780449905678

1. Victorian era (1837-1901) 2. 19th century 3. Husband-and-wife detectives 4. Murder investigation 5. Social classes 6. Slums 7. Women detectives 8. Police 9. Police spouses 10. Arson 11. London, England -- History -- 19th century 12. Historical mysteries 13. Victorian mysteries 14. Mysteries

LC 90085131

In their eleventh mystery, Inspector Pitt and Charlotte investigate a mysterious fire in which a woman died, and uncover arson and murder.

"Ms. Perry gives Pitt a breather from his customary gutter research by confining his investigation to the victim's upper-class social circle. Following her own conscience, Charlotte insinuates her way into elegant drawing rooms where the author's satirical wit is free to spread its rather showy skirts." New York Times Book Review.

Perry, Anne

The **Hyde** Park headsman / Anne Perry. Fawcett Columbine, 1994. 392 p. Thomas and Charlotte Pitt mysteries

ISBN 0449906361

1. Victorian era (1837-1901) 2. 19th century 3. Husband-and-wife detectives 4. Murder investigation 5. Women detectives 6. Police 7. Police spouses 8. London, England -- History -- 19th century 9. Historical mysteries 10. Victorian mysteries 11. Mysteries

LC 9322124

Thomas Pitt uses Charlotte's help to work on a murder in Hyde Park that is followed by three more murders.

Perry, Anne

* **Midnight** at Marble Arch / Anne Perry. Ballantine Books, 2013, c2012. 352 p. Thomas and Charlotte Pitt mysteries

ISBN 9780345536662

1. Victorian era (1837-1901) 2. 19th century 3. Crimes against women 4. Rape 5. Murder suspects 6. International intrigue 7. Husband-and-wife detectives 8. Murder investigation 9. Murder 10. Women detectives 11. Police 12. Police spouses 13. London, England -- History -- 19th century 14. Great Britain -- Politics and government -- 19th century 15. Historical mysteries 16. Victorian mysteries 17. Mysteries

When the bodies of two high-profile women are discovered, bearing signs of rape, and an innocent man is accused of the crime, Thomas Pitt's quest for the truth forces him to play a dangerous game of international politics and murder.

Perry, Anne

No graves as yet : a novel of World War I / Anne Perry. Ballantine Books, 2003. 352 p. World War I novels

ISBN 0345456521

1. First World War era (1914-1918) 2. 1910s 3. World War I 4. Adult children of murder victims 5. Conspiracies 6. Young men 7. Secrets 8. Clergy 9. Grief in men 10. Loss (Psychology) 11. Great Britain -- History -- George V, 1910-1936 12. Cambridge, England 13. Historical fiction 14. War stories

LC 2003052233

In June of 1914, Cambridge professor Joseph Reavley learns that his father was carrying a vitally important secret document when he died, and that his best student has been murdered.

"Perry's melancholy evocation of the 'eternal afternoon' that would soon turn to night all over England is lovely." New York Times Book Review.

Perry, Anne

Paragon Walk / Anne Perry. St. Martin's Press, 1981. 204 p. Thomas and Charlotte Pitt mysteries

ISBN 9780312595982

1. Victorian era (1837-1901) 2. 19th century 3. Husband-and-wife detectives 4. Murder investigation 5. Crimes against women 6. Psychopaths 7. Women detectives 8. Police 9. Police spouses 10. London, England -- History -- 19th century 11. Historical mysteries 12. Victorian mysteries 13. Mysteries

LC 80023186

When Inspector Thomas Pitt investigates the murder of an upper-class 17-year-old girl, a crime that has terrorized the neighborhood, he finds surprising suspects.

Perry, Anne

* **Pentecost** Alley / Anne Perry. Fawcett Columbine, 1996. 405 p. Thomas and Charlotte Pitt mysteries

ISBN 0449906353

1. Victorian era (1837-1901) 2. 19th century 3. Husband-and-wife detectives 4. Murder investigation 5. Prostitutes 6. Women detectives 7. Police 8. Police spouses 9. Rich families 10. London, England -- History -- 19th century 11. Historical mysteries 12. Victorian mysteries 13. Mysteries

LC 95-43557

Thomas Pitt is relieved when a pimp confesses to the brutal slaying of a prostitute, but after the man is executed, another murder just like the first occurs.

"Perry has created a superbly plotted, grippingly suspenseful period piece filled with intriguing characters and fascinating descriptions of the manners and customs of Victorian London." Booklist.

Perry, Anne

Resurrection Row / Anne Perry. St. Martin's Press, 1981. 204 p. Thomas and Charlotte Pitt mysteries

ISBN 9780312677978

1. Victorian era (1837-1901) 2. 19th century 3. Husband-and-wife detectives 4. Murder investigation 5. Women detectives 6. Police 7. Police spouses 8. Grave robbing 9. London, England -- History -- 19th century 10. Historical mysteries 11. Victorian mysteries 12. Mysteries

LC 81008846

After a wonderful night at the theatre, Thomas and Charlotte find themselves confronted with a corpse in the driver's seat of a hansom cab. Even more shocking--it is the body of a peer of the realm who had been decently buried the week before. While the doctor insists Lord Fitzroy-Hammond died a natural death, the Pitts find the situation anything but natural.

Perry, Anne

***** **Seven** Dials / Anne Perry. Ballantine Books, 2003. 368 p. Thomas and Charlotte Pitt mysteries

ISBN 0345440072

1. Victorian era (1837-1901) 2. 19th century 3. Husband-and-wife detectives 4. Murder investigation 5. Women detectives 6. Police 7. Police spouses 8. Cabinet officers -- Great Britain 9. London, England -- History -- 19th century 10. Great Britain -- Politics and government -- 19th century 11. Historical mysteries 12. Victorian mysteries 13. Mysteries

LC 2002035605

Thomas Pitt of Her Majesty's Special Branch investigates the murder of a diplomat whose body turns up at a mansion inhabited by the notorious Egyptian woman Ayesha Zakhari and her rumored lover, Senior Cabinet Minister Saville Ryerson.

"Although the focus of the plot tends to drift, the visual panorama is voluptuous to behold." New York Times Book Review.

Perry, Anne

The **shifting** tide / Anne Perry. Ballantine Books, 2004. 352 p. William Monk and Hester Latterly mysteries

ISBN 0345440099

1. Victorian era (1837-1901) 2. 19th century 3. 1850s 4. Police 5. Murder investigation 6. Merchant ships 7. Ivory 8. Nurses 9. Detectives 10. London, England -- History -- 19th century 11. Victorian mysteries 12. Historical mysteries 13. Police procedurals 14. Mysteries

Reluctantly accepting an assignment to investigate an Ivory cargo theft along the Thames, Victorian sleuth William Monk wonders why his client elected not to report the crime to police.

"As the sailor says, River's full o' tales, and Perry knows how to bring them to life." New York Times Book Review.

Perry, Anne

Shoulder the sky / Anne Perry. Ballantine Books, 2004. 352 p. World War I novels

ISBN 0345456548

1. First World War era (1914-1918) 2. World War I 3. Adult children of murder victims 4. Conspiracies 5. Young men 6. Clergy 7. War correspondents 8. Intelligence officers 9. Chauffeurs 10. Soldiers 11. Secrets 12. Ethics 13. Belief and doubt 14. Secret identity 15. International intrigue 16. Great Britain -- History -- George V, 1910-1936 17. England 18. Belgium 19. Historical fiction 20. War stories

While tending to the soldiers in his care, chaplain Joseph Reavley stumbles upon the body of a war correspondent, while his brother Mat-thew, an intelligence officer, searches for the sinister criminal master-mind known as the Peacemaker.

"Questions about the morality of war resonate throughout this harrowing novel, which Perry has constructed with hallmark attention to period detail and sense of place. Her vivid evocations of the battlefield . . . are unforgettable." Booklist.

Perry, Anne

The **silent** cry / Anne Perry. Fawcett Columbine, 1997. 361 p. William Monk and Hester Latterly mysteries

ISBN 0449908488

1. Victorian era (1837-1901) 2. 19th century 3. 1850s 4. Police 5. Murder investigation 6. Slums 7. Rape 8. Prostitutes 9. Abused women 10. Lawyers 11. Male rape 12. Nurses 13. Detectives 14. London, England -- History -- 19th century 15. Victorian mysteries 16. Historical mysteries 17. Police procedurals 18. Mysteries

LC 9716848

In Victorian London, two middle-class men -- a solicitor and his adult son -- are discovered in a decidedly lower-class part of town: the father is dead, and the son, Rhys, has been so badly beaten that he can't speak. Former Crimean War nurse Hester Latterly takes care of Rhys, and her sometime-beau, PI William Monk, discovers a link between the two men and a case he's working on involving the brutal rapes of factory workers moonlighting as prostitutes. -- Description by Shauna Griffin.

"With her grimly detailed descriptions of the match factories, sweatshops, paupers hospitals and tenement 'rookeries' crowded into these slums, Perry brings a rank sense of reality to the wretched living conditions of the working poor." New York Times Book Review.

Perry, Anne

The **sins** of the wolf / Anne Perry. Fawcett Columbine, 1994. 374 p. William Monk and Hester Latterly mysteries

ISBN 0449906388

1. Victorian era (1837-1901) 2. 19th century 3. 1850s 4. Police 5. Murder investigation 6. Frameups 7. Trials (Murder) 9. Detectives 10. London, England -- History -- 19th century 11. Edinburgh, Scotland -- History -- 19th century 12. Victorian mysteries 13. Historical mysteries 14. Police procedurals 15. Mysteries

LC 94-12099

In a blend of Victorian courtroom drama and intricate mystery, William Monk frantically searches for the truth to save his trusted sidekick, Nurse Latterly--on trial for her life.

Perry, Anne

Slaves of obsession / Anne Perry. Ballantine Books, 2000. 344 p. William Monk and Hester Latterly mysteries

ISBN 0345433262

1. Victorian era (1837-1901) 2. American Civil War era (1861-1865) 3. 1850s 4. Police 5. Murder investigation 6. Lawyers 7. Americans in England 8. Arms transfers 9. Nurses 10. Detectives 11. Civil war 12. United States Civil War, 1861-1865 13. London, England -- History -- 19th century 14. Virginia -- History -- Civil War, 1861-1865 15. Victorian mysteries 16. Historical mysteries 17. Police procedurals 18. Mysteries

LC 00040375

William Monk and his wife Hester, track the man they believe to be a cold-blooded murderer all the way to Washington D.C., and the bloody battlefield at Manassas. When London arms dealer Daniel Albertson's entire inventory of weapons disappear.

"Perry's images of the carnage and confusion of battle are relentless in their intensity, unflinching in their truth-telling detail." New York Times Book Review.

Perry, Anne

* **Southampton** Row / Anne Perry. Ballantine Books, 2002 352 p. Thomas and Charlotte Pitt mysteries

ISBN 034544003X

1. Victorian era (1837-1901) 2. 19th century 3. Husband-and-wife detectives 4. Murder investigation 5. Women detectives 6. Police 7. Police spouses 8. Conspiracies 9. Elections 10. Women spiritualists 11. Politicians' spouses 12. Candidates for public office 13. London, England -- History -- 19th century 14. Great Britain -- Politics and government -- 19th century 15. Historical mysteries 16. Victorian mysteries 17. Mysteries

LC 2001052664

A general election is approaching and Thomas is called to monitor the bitter struggle for one crucial London seat.

"Thomas Pitt ventures into the world of spiritualism when, on the eve of a critical parliamentary election, the wife of the Liberal candidate is implicated in the murder of a clairvoyant. As she has done increasingly in recent books, Perry links the crime to a secret political cabal known as the Inner Circle and draws everyone into its machinations. . . . Perry's proto-feminists have the kind of intellectual radiance that eludes their spouses." New York Times Book Review.

Perry, Anne

A **sunless** sea / Anne Perry. Ballantine Books, 2012. 336 p. William Monk and Hester Latterly mysteries

ISBN 9780345510648

1. Victorian era (1837-1901) 2. 1860s 3. 19th century 4. Detectives 5. Violence against women 6. Murder investigation 7. Opium industry and trade 8. Political corruption 9. Scientists -- Death 10. London, England -- History -- 1800-1950 11. Victorian mysteries 12. Historical mysteries 13. Police procedurals 14. Mysteries

Monk discovers a shocking truth while investigating the murder of a high-end prostitute with ties to an opium-dispensing doctor's widow.

Perry, Anne

Traitors Gate / Anne Perry. Fawcett, 1995. 411 p. Thomas and Charlotte Pitt mysteries

ISBN 0449906345

1. Victorian era (1837-1901) 2. 19th century 3. Husband-and-wife detectives 4. Murder investigation 5. Conspiracies 6. Women detectives 7. Police 8. Police spouses 9. Treason 10. London, England -- History -- 19th century 11. Historical mysteries 12. Victorian mysteries 13. Mysteries

LC 94027624

When the father of Thomas Pitt's good friend is poisoned at his club, the investigation points to the Inner Circle, a group of aristocrats with a strong loyalty oath.

"In combination with her meticulous research, Ms. Perry's infallible feeling for the historical moment yields animated political debate over the colonization of Africa, glittering views of Victorian society at play and tantalizing glimpses of a confident, assertive creature known as the 'new woman.'" New York Times Book Review.

Perry, Anne

The **twisted** root / Anne Perry. Ballantine Books, 1999. 346 p. William Monk and Hester Latterly mysteries

ISBN 9780345433251

1. Victorian era (1837-1901) 2. 1850s 3. 19th century 4. Police 5. Murder investigation 6. Missing persons 7. Lawyers 8. Nurses 9. Detectives 10. London, England -- History -- 19th century 11. Victorian mysteries 12. Historical mysteries 13. Police procedurals 14. Mysteries

Victorian-era private detective William Monk and his new wife, Hester, investigate the mysterious disappearance of Miriam Gardiner, who vanishes from a croquet party at the sumptuous estate of her future in-laws, leaving behind the body of a murdered coachman.

Perry, Anne

* **Weighed** in the balance / Anne Perry. Fawcett Columbine, 1996. 355 p. William Monk and Hester Latterly mysteries

ISBN 0449910784

1. Victorian era (1837-1901) 2. 1850s 3. 19th century 4. Police 5. Murder investigation 6. Counts and countesses 7. Exiles 8. Lawyers 9. Princes 10. Princesses 11. Nurses 12. Detectives 13. London, England -- History -- 19th century 14. Victorian mysteries 15. Historical mysteries 16. Police procedurals 17. Mysteries

LC 9634824

As barrister Oliver Rathbone prepares to defend his client, Countess Zorah Rostova, against a charge of slander, private detective William Monk and nurse Hester Latterly become caught up in a notorious case of royal scandal and murder in nineteenth-century London.

"Monk, the dark and brooding hero who infuses this luxuriantly detailed series with its romantic soul, is not immune to the seductive appeal of this aristocratic crowd. . . . But he also comes to understand the human passions behind the political forces that transformed Europe in the mid-1800's." New York Times Book Review.

Perry, Anne

The **Whitechapel** conspiracy / Anne Perry. Ballantine Books, 2001. 341 p. Thomas and Charlotte Pitt mysteries

ISBN 0345433289

1. Victorian era (1837-1901) 2. 1890s 3. 19th century 4. Husband-and-wife detectives 5. Murder investigation 6. Undercover operations 7. Conspiracies 8. Women detectives 9. Police 10. Police spouses 11. London, England -- History -- 19th century 12. Historical mysteries 13. Victorian mysteries 14. Mysteries

LC 00064206

In the wake of a successful but unlikely sentencing of a distinguished soldier and murder suspect, Bow Street Station Superintendent Thomas Pitt is removed from office and forced to work undercover in the dangerous East End Special Branch.

"Perry's interpretation of the Jack the Ripper killings is a beauty, brilliantly presented, ingeniously developed and packed with political implications that reverberate on every level of British society." New York Times Book Review.

Perry, Sarah, 1979-

The **Essex** serpent / Sarah Perry. Custom House, 2017, c2016. 432 p.

ISBN 9780062666376

1. Victorian era (1837-1901) 2. Widows 3. Clergy 4. Belief and doubt 5. Social classes 6. Single mothers 7. Friendship 8. Searching 9. Mothers and sons 10. Children with autism 11. Married people 12. Men/women relations 13. Interpersonal attraction 14. England -- History -- Victoria, 1837-1901 15. Historical fiction

Originally published: London : Serpent's Tail, 2016.

Longlisted for The Baileys Women's Prize for Fiction, 2017.

Longlisted for the Walter Scott Prize for Historical Fiction, 2017

Freed from an unhappy marriage by her husband's death, Victorian widow Cora Seaborne settles in Colchester, where she pursues her interest in natural history by searching the Blackwater estuary for evidence of the Essex Serpent, a winged serpent dismissed as superstition by vicar Will Ransome, but greatly feared by the locals. With its heady atmosphere and lush descriptions, the novel vividly explores Victorian

English society and culture through the experiences of its ensemble cast. -- Description by Gillian Speace

"Stuffed with smarts and storytelling sorcery, this is a work of astonishing breadth and brilliance." Kirkus.

Perry, Sarah, 1979-

Melmoth : a novel / Sarah Perry. Custom House, 2018. 271 p.

ISBN 9780062856395

1. Characters and characteristics in fairy tales 2. Guilt 3. Superstition 4. Suffering 5. Women translators 6. British in the Czech Republic 7. Manuscripts 8. Friendship 9. Secrets 10. Prague, Czech Republic 11. Czech Republic 12. Gothic fiction 13. Horror 14. Literary fiction

LC 2018029870

RUSA Reading List Short List, 2019.

Helen, an English translator working in Prague, disregards an obscure local monster legend before a friend's disappearance reveals that Helen is being watched.

Perry, Thomas, 1947-

The **bomb** maker / Thomas Perry. Pgw, 2018 384 p.

ISBN 9780802127488

1. Bomb threats 2. Bombings 3. Police 4. Terrorism 5. Former police 6. Bomb squads 7. Men/women relations 8. Private security services 9. Los Angeles, California 10. Thrillers and suspense

LC 2017025438

A lethally clever designer of explosives tests the skills and collective strength of the highly skilled LAPD Bomb Squad.

Perry, Thomas, 1947-

The **boyfriend** / Thomas Perry. Grove Press, 2013. 288 p.

ISBN 9780802126061

1. Serial murderers 2. Serial murder investigation 3. Former police 4. Private investigators 5. Prostitution 6. Escort services (Prostitution) 7. Crimes against prostitutes 8. Thrillers and suspense

Jack Till must delve into the shadowy world of the online escort business to find a serial killer who hops from city to city.

Perry, Thomas, 1947-

Dead aim : a novel / Thomas Perry. Random House, 2002. 384 p.

ISBN 1400060036

1. Suicide investigation 2. Assassins 3. Women detectives 4. Young women 5. Suicide 6. Murder 7. Millionaires 8. Rich men 9. Police 10. Self-defense 11. Santa Barbara, California 12. Mysteries

LC 2002068100

When Robert Mallon and his ally, Detective Lydia Marks, investigate the life of a young murder victim found on the beach in Santa Barbara, the case brings them into conflict with Parish, an amoral predator who runs a training camp for killers.

"For someone who made millions in real estate and retired when he was 38, Robert Mallon lacks the wit and imagination to figure out how to enjoy his good fortune. Some nascent feelings are awakened in his anesthetized soul when he accepts a sexual favor from Catherine Broward, a young woman he pulls out of the ocean in front of his Santa Barbara beach house when she tries to drown herself. After Catherine turns around and kills herself anyway, the newly energized hero plays detective to determine the circumstances of her life and death." New York Times Book Review.

Perry, Thomas, 1947-

Death benefits : a novel / Thomas Perry. Random House, 2001. 384 p.

ISBN 0679453059

1. Insurance investigators 2. Fraud investigation 3. Insurance fraud 4. Missing women 5. Deception in men 6. Insurance companies 7. San Francisco, California 8. New Hampshire 9. Mysteries

LC 00041476

When gruff and intimidating security consultant Max Stillman appears without warning in the San Francisco office of McClaren Life and Casualty and begins asking questions and scrutinizing files, the employees can't help wondering just which of them he's been hired to investigate.

"San Francisco insurance data analyst John Walker is sleePublishers Weekly.alking through his young life when the boss assigns him to assist a private detective on an inside job involving Walker's ex-girlfriend, a claims adjuster who disappeared after being implicated in a New York Times Book Review.

Perry, Thomas, 1947-

Fidelity / Thomas Perry. Harcourt, 2008. 368 p.

ISBN 9780151012923

1. Murder investigation 2. Assassins 3. Secrets 4. Detectives 5. Assassins 6. Widows 7. Loyalty 8. Betrayal 9. Extortion 10. Crimes against married men 11. Extramarital affairs 12. Mysteries

LC 2007026507

"An Otto Penzler Book."

When Emily Kramer's husband Phil is murdered, she finds herself with an empty bank account and many questions. Jerry Hobart did not know why he was hired to kill Phil Kramer, but now being ordered to kill Kramer's widow, he has questions of his own. In searching for Phil's secret, both Hobart and Emily must decide where their loyalties are.

"Perry's characters are uncannily good at sizing one another up and anticipating what the next moves will be. Though he briefly equates Hobart's tactics to the ways a coyote slinks through a neighborhood, Mr. Perry need not even articulate this. It's always built into his storytelling, and it's already on the page." New York Times.

Perry, Thomas, 1947-

The **informant** / Thomas Perry. Houghton Mifflin Harcourt, 2011. 336 p. Butcher's boy

ISBN 9780547569338

1. Government investigators 2. Assassins 3. Attempted murder 4. Alliances 5. Informers 6. Mafia 7. Organized crime 8. Organized crime investigation 9. Crime bosses 10. Thrillers and suspense

LC 2010043566

Years after the Butcher's Boy wipes out several mobsters and disappears, Justice Department official Elizabeth Waring is approached by the mythical hit man, who asks her for crucial information in exchange for helping her to crack an unsolved murder case.

"Perry's immaculate style--clean, polished, uncluttered by messy emotion--suits the Butcher's Boy, who executes his kills with the same cool, dispassionate skill." New York Times Book Review.

Perry, Thomas, 1947-

The **old** man / Thomas Perry. Grove Press, 2017. 352 p.

ISBN 9780802125866

1. Seniors 2. Veterans 3. Fugitives 4. Assassins 5. Intelligence service 6. Stealing 7. Options, alternatives, choices 8. Widowers 9. Pretending 10. Vermont 11. United States 12. Thrillers and suspense

Decades after taking millions of dollars during a mission in Libya and starting over in Vermont under a new name, former Army intelligence offer Dan Chase is forced back on the run after eluding two attackers with an interest in obtaining the loot.

Perry, Thomas, 1947-

Pursuit : a novel / Thomas Perry. Random House, 2002,c2001. 370 p.

ISBN 0679453067

1. Serial murder investigation 2. Former police 3. Mass murder 4. Criminologists 5. Criminal profilers 6. Serial murderers 7. Mass murderers 8. Assassins 9. Psychopaths 10. Louisville, Kentucky 11. Psychological suspense 12. Mysteries

LC 2001040365

Originally published in 2001.

Thirteen bodies are found in a Louisville restaurant. When the police can find no suspect or motive, a victim's family seeks the services of the enigmatic and solitary specialist Roy Prescott, known for his ability to find people who don't want to be found. Working outside the law and willing to do what the police can't, Prescott hunts the killer, an elusive adversary who is as smart, as methodical, as deadly as he is. The only way to conduct this pursuit is to goad the killer into believing that he must kill Roy Prescott. It is a contest fought from one end of the country to the other, and both men understand that when it's over, only one of them will be alive.

Perry, Thomas, 1947-

Vanishing act / Thomas Perry. Random House, 1995. 289 p. Jane Whitefield novels

ISBN 0679435360

1. Protectiveness 2. New identities 3. Deception 4. Witnesses 5. Violence against women 6. Impostors 7. Malicious accusation 8. Seneca women 9. Seneca Indians 10. Fugitives 11. Multiracial women 12. Indians of North America 13. New York (State) 14. Thrillers and suspense

LC 94017413

Jane Whitefield helps people disappear by giving them a new identity--new appearance, new social security card--and her clientele ranges from bankrupt businessmen to fleeing wives. On this occasion, things backfire and she must resort to her Native American talents to track a dangerous customer she helped disappear.

"This is all very satisfying and quite scenic... ." New York Times Book Review.

Persson Giolito, Malin, 1969-

Beyond all reasonable doubt : a novel / Malin Persson Giolito ; translated from the Swedish by Rachel Willson-Broyles. Other Press, 2019, c2005. 452 p.

ISBN 9781590519196

1. Judicial error 2. Women lawyers 3. Criminal justice system 4. Teenage girl murder victims 5. Scientists 6. Crime 7. Guilt 8. Sweden 9. Legal thrillers 10. Scandinavian crime fiction 11. Translations -- Swedish to English

LC 2018049563

Originally published: 2005.

From the award-winning author of Quicksand, a gripping legal thriller that follows one woman's conflicted efforts to overturn what may be a wrongful conviction.

Persson Giolito, Malin, 1969-

Quicksand / Malin Persson Giolito ; translated from the Swedish by Rachel Willson-Broyles. Other Press, 2017, c2016. 512 p.

ISBN 9781590518571

1. High school girls 2. Teenage prisoners 3. School shootings 4. Prep schools 5. Prisons 6. Mass murder 7. High school students 8. Trials (Murder) 9. Racism 10. Refugees 11. Mass shootings 12. Stockholm, Sweden 13. Coming-of-age stories 14. Psychological fiction 15. Scandinavian crime fiction 16. Translations -- Swedish to English

LC 2016032468

Originally published: Sweden : Wahlstrom & Widstrand, 2016

After spending nine months in jail awaiting trial for her involvement in a mass shooting that took the lives of her boyfriend and best friend in a prep school in Stockholm's richest suburb, Maja finally reveals the circumstances that brought her there.

"Giolitos astonishing English-language debut . . . is a dark exploration of the crumbling European social order and the psyches of rich Swedish teens." Booklist.

Persson, Leif G. W.

Another; time, another life : the story of a crime / Leif GW Persson ; translated from the Swedish by Paul Norlen. Pantheon Books, 2012, c2003. 404 p. Story of a crime trilogy

ISBN 9780307377463

1. 1990s 2. Conspiracies 3. Secrets 4. Murder 5. Politicians 6. Secret service 7. Political corruption 8. Police 9. Sweden 10. Political thrillers 11. Translations -- Swedish to English 12. Thrillers and suspense 13. Scandinavian crime fiction

LC 2011017394

Translation from the Swedish.

Originally published: En annan tid, ett annat liv (2003).

An investigation into the murder of a Swedish civil servant is put on indefinite hold by a corrupt senior official before Swedish Security Police newcomer Lars Johansson reopens the case and follows leads to the highest levels of government.

Persson, Leif G. W.

The **dying** detective : a mystery / Leif G.W. Persson ; translated from the Swedish by Neil Smith. Pantheon Books, 2017, c2010. 426 p.

ISBN 9780307907639

1. Former police 2. People who have had strokes 3. Girl murder victims 4. Cold cases (Criminal investigation) 5. Retirees 6. Hospital patients 7. Hospitals 8. Sex crimes 9. Women amateur detectives 10. Orphans 11. Interpersonal relations 12. Sweden 13. Translations -- Swedish to English 14. Mysteries

LC oc2016039400

Originally published: Stockholm : Bonnier, 2010.

Duncan Lawrie International Dagger, 2017.

After suffering a stroke that reveals additional health problems, Swedish homicide detective Lars Martin Johansson launches an investigation into a cold case murder from his hospital bed with the help of a rebellious young woman.

"In the hands of a lesser storyteller, this novel, which takes more than 400 pages to tell, would collapse under the staggering amount of dialogue and detail, but, in Persson's telling, it is almost impossible to put down. An absolutely masterful crime novel." Booklist.

Persson, Leif G. W.

Free falling, as if in a dream : the story of a crime / Leif GW Persson ; translated from the Swedish by Paul Norlen. Pantheon Books, 2014, c2007. 592 p. Story of a crime trilogy

ISBN 9780307377470

1. Palme, Olof, 1927-1986 Assassination 2. Prime ministers 3. Assassination investigation 4. Cold cases (Criminal investigation) 5. Murder 6. Murder investigation 7. Detectives 8. Revenge 9. Spin control (Public relations) 10. Sweden 11. Political thrillers 12. Thrillers and suspense 13. Scandinavian crime fiction 14. Translations -- Swedish to English

LC 2012050987

Translation from the Swedish.

"Originally published in Sweden as Faller fritt som i en drom, by Albert Bonniers Forlag, Stockholm, in 2007"--Title page verso.

Lars Martin Johansson investigates the unsolved 1986 murder of Swedish prime minister Olof Palme, only to be seduced by his own ambitions and a shady political spin doctor.

"Strong characterization, a solid grasp of investigatory complexities, and an appreciation of the elusive, chimerical nature of truth make this a fine example of a conspiracy thriller." Publishers Weekly.

Pesci, David

Amistad : a novel / David Pesci. Marlowe, 1997. 292 p.

ISBN 156924748X

1. Adams, John Quincy, 1767-1848 2. Cinque, Joseph, died 1879? 3. 19th century 4. Antebellum America (1820-1861) 5. Amistad Case, 1839-1841 6. Slaves -- United States 7. Slavery -- Connecticut 8. Trials (Mutiny) 9. Slave trade 10. Slave resistance and revolts -- United States 11. Anti-slavery movements 12. Africans in the United States 13. Historical fiction

LC 9654050

Tells the story of an African farmer who is sold into slavery and stages a rebellion aboard the slave ship, the Amistad.

"Pesci deftly blends the facts of this fascinating historical episode with story." School Library Journal.

Pessl, Marisha

Night film : a novel / Marisha Pessl. Random House, 2013. 624 p.

ISBN 9781400067886

1. Suicide 2. Fathers and daughters 3. Subcultures 4. Investigative journalism 5. Murder 6. Investigative journalists 7. Filmmakers 8. Revenge 9. New York City 10. Psychological suspense 11. Literary fiction 12. Illustrated books

LC 2012041163

First published in Great Britain in 2013 by Hutchinson.

When the daughter of a cult horror film director is found dead in an abandoned Manhattan warehouse, investigative journalist Scott McGrath, disbelieving the official suicide ruling, probes into the strange circumstances of the young woman's death.

Pessl, Marisha

Special topics in calamity physics / Marisha Pessl. Viking, 2006. 528 p.

ISBN 067003777X

1. Fathers and daughters 2. Murder investigation 3. Teenage girls 4. Teenagers -- Death 5. Teachers -- Death 6. College teachers 7. Eccentrics and eccentricities 8. Cliques 9. Identity (Psychology) 10. Moving to a new city 11. Murder 12. North Carolina 13. Coming-of-age stories 14. Mysteries 15. Literary fiction

LC 2005058474

"Even the physics equation on the book's back cover has outsized verve. And what begins as a dubious proposition, in a world wholly without need for additions to its Prep School Confidential bibliography, becomes a whirling, glittering, multifaceted marvel, delivered in an irrepressibly smart and flamboyant new voice." New York Times.

Peters, Elizabeth, 1927-2013

Children of the storm / Elizabeth Peters. William Morrow, 2003. 416 p. Amelia Peabody mysteries

ISBN 9780066214764

1. Between the Wars (1918-1939) 2. 1910s 3. Sabotage 4. Kidnapping 5. Egyptologists 6. British in Egypt 7. Women archaeologists 8. Husband-and-wife detectives -- Egypt 9. Grandparents 10. Family reunions 11. Nationalism 12. Archaeological sites -- Egypt 13. Excavations (Archaeology) -- Egypt 14. Amateur detectives 15. Women amateur detectives 16. Postwar life 17. Egypt 18. Valley of the Kings, Egypt 19. Historical mysteries 20. Mysteries 21. Gentle reads

LC 2002041083

This title takes places in 1919-1920.

With her family in tow, successful archaeologist and amateur sleuth Amelia Peabody prepares for yet another Egyptian excavation with hopes of a quiet season without death-defying incidents, but old dangers bring fresh foes and Amelia finds herself and family in the throes of peril.

"This installment, set in 1919, finds Amelia Peabody back in Egypt, reunited with her extended brood of family and friends (a helpful preface sorts them all out) and anticipating an enriching season at the archaeological dig being excavated by her husband. In some respects, the story follows the formula of the 14 earlier books in this spirited series: precious tomb artifacts go missing and the logical suspect turns up dead, necessitating adventures filled with romance and fraught with peril." New York Times Book Review.

Peters, Elizabeth, 1927-2013

The **deeds** of the disturber / Elizabeth Peters. Atheneum, 1988. 389 p. Amelia Peabody mysteries

ISBN 9780689119071

1. Victorian era (1837-1901) 2. 19th century 3. Mummies 4. Curses 5. Women detectives 6. Murder investigation 7. Pyramids -- Egypt 8. Husband and wife 9. Egyptologists 10. Husband-and-wife detectives 11. Excavations (Archaeology) -- Egypt 12. Egypt 13. Historical mysteries 14. Mysteries 15. Gentle reads

This title takes places during the Summer of 1896.

Amerlia Peabody, her sexy archaeologist husband Emerson, and their precocious son Ramses find themselves caught up in an intrigue at the British Museum that includes a haunted mummy case, supernatural curses, and a lunatic murderer.

Peters, Elizabeth, 1927-2013

* **Guardian** of the horizon / Elizabeth Peters. William Morrow, 2004. 416 p. Amelia Peabody mysteries

ISBN 9780066214719

1. Edwardian era (1901-1914) 2. 1900s (Decade) 3. Desert survival 4. Excavations (Archaeology) -- Egypt 5. Deception 6. Women archaeologists 7. Egyptologists 8. Husband-and-wife detectives -- Egypt 9. British in Egypt 10. Loyalty 11. Deserts 12. Amateur detectives 13. Women amateur detectives 14. Egypt 15. England 16. Historical mysteries 17. Mysteries 18. Gentle reads

LC 2003067665

This title takes places in 1907-1908.

Recounts the adventures of Amelia Peabody and the Emerson family in 1907 and 1908, a period following their banishment from the Valley of the Kings, during which Ramses, hopelessly in love with Nefret, finds his plans interrupted by a plea for help from Prince Tarek from the Lost Oasis.

Peters, Elizabeth, 1927-2013

The **golden** one / Elizabeth Peters. William Morrow, 2002. 448 p. Amelia Peabody mysteries

ISBN 9780380978854

1. First World War era (1914-1918) 2. 1910s 3. Archaeological sites 4. Murder investigation 5. Women archaeologists 6. Egyptologists 7. British in Egypt 8. Husband-and-wife detectives -- Egypt 9. World War I -- Egypt 10. Excavations (Archaeology) -- Egypt 11. International intrigue -- Egypt 12. Amateur detectives 13. Women amateur detectives 14. Egypt 15. Luxor, Egypt 16. Historical mysteries 17. Mysteries 18. Gentle reads

LC 2001052169

This title takes places in 1916-1917.

Revisiting Egypt in 1917 with her husband, son, and daughter-in-law, Egyptologist Amelia Peabody stumbles across a murdered body, a situation that is complicated by an assignment by British intelligence and her daughter-in-law's troubling secret.

"On arriving in Luxor for a season of archaeological investigation, Amelia [Peabody Emerson] and her family discover that war (it's 1917) has taken its toll on their beloved Egypt. Before too long, the conflict intrudes on their plans and embroils them in an adventure, complete with double agents, Turkish spies, derring-do, and the ever-puzzling Sethos. At the same time, they must reckon with tomb robbers, killers, and antiquities fraud." Booklist.

Peters, Elizabeth, 1927-2013

He shall thunder in the sky / Elizabeth Peters W. Morrow, 2000. 400 p. Amelia Peabody mysteries

ISBN 9780380976591

1. First World War era (1914-1918) 2. 1910s 3. Spies 4. Excavations (Archaeology) -- Egypt 5. Women archaeologists 6. Egyptologists 7. Archaeological sites -- Egypt 8. British in Egypt 9. Husband-and-wife detectives 10. Amateur detectives 11. Women amateur detectives 12. Egypt 13. Historical mysteries 14. Mysteries 15. Gentle reads

LC 00025807

This title takes places in 1914-1915.

Amelia and Emerson Peabody travel to Egypt to continue their archaeological work, but a nationalist is stirring up trouble in the town where they are working, and Amelia's nemesis, Sethos, has apparently re-emerged.

"Peters works in drama galore, plus the usual shots of wry humor and local color." Booklist.

Peters, Elizabeth, 1927-2013

The **hippopotamus** pool / Elizabeth Peters. Warner Books, 1996. 384 p. Amelia Peabody mysteries

ISBN 9780446518338

1. Victorian era (1837-1901) 2. Excavations (Archaeology) 3. Kidnapping 4. Thieves 5. Egyptologists 6. British in Egypt 7. Women archaeologists -- Egypt 8. Husband-and-wife detectives 9. Amateur detectives 10. Women amateur detectives 11. Historical mysteries 12. Mysteries 13. Gentle reads

LC 95-31886

This title takes places in 1900.

Amelia, her husband Emerson, their son Ramses, and their ward Nefret return to Egypt for a royal excavation, only to encounter art thieves, jealous colleagues, looters, the press, and evil-doers.

Peters, Elizabeth, 1927-2013

The **last** camel died at noon / Elizabeth Peters. Warner Books, 1991. 352 p. Amelia Peabody mysteries

ISBN 9780446514835

1. Victorian era (1837-1901) 2. 19th century 3. Slaves 4. Missing persons 5. Women archaeologists 6. Betrayal 7. Egyptologists 8. Husband-and-wife detectives 9. Egyptologists 10. Amateur detectives 11. Women amateur detectives 12. Sudan 13. Historical mysteries 14. Mysteries 15. Gentle reads

LC 90026759

This title takes places during the winter of 1897

In the Sudan to search for Viscount Blacktower's son and his new bride, Egyptologist Amelia Peabody, her husband Emerson, and their son, Ramses, become caught in web of treachery, and their survival depends on Amelia's sleuthing skills.

"The Emersons are decidedly unstodgy Victorians--feminist, democratic, egalitarian, respectful of other cultures--and charming, witty, entertaining sleuths." Booklist.

Peters, Elizabeth, 1927-2013

* **Lion** in the valley / Elizabeth Peters. Atheneum, 1986. 370 p. Amelia Peabody mysteries

ISBN 9780689116193

1. Victorian era (1837-1901) 2. 19th century 3. Egyptologists 4. Criminals 5. Murder investigation 6. Pyramids 7. Excavations (Archaeology) -- Egypt 8. Husband-and-wife detectives 9. Egypt 10. Historical mysteries 11. Mysteries 12. Gentle reads

This title takes places in 1895-1896.

Amelia Peabody, the intrepid archaeologist, returns to the Nile with her Egyptologist husband Emerson and their entourage to track down a brilliant and dashing master criminal wreaking havoc among the excavations.

"Murder, mayhem . . . and a pair of distressed young lovers, not to mention a modicum of archaeological pursuits, round out a decided treat for fans of the indomitable duo--or, perhaps, with Ramses, it is now a trio." Booklist.

Peters, Elizabeth, 1927-2013

The **mummy** case / Elizabeth Peters. Congdon & Weed, 1985. 313 p. Amelia Peabody mysteries

ISBN 0865531404

1. Victorian era (1837-1901) 2. 19th century 3. Murder investigation 4. Mummies 5. Women detectives 6. Egyptologists 7. Husband-and-wife detectives 8. Archaeological sites -- Egypt 9. British in Egypt 10. Historical mysteries 11. Mysteries 12. Gentle reads

This title takes places in 1894.

Amelia Peabody, accompanied by her irascible archaeologist husband and their precocious son, Ramses, returns to Egypt and finds herself caught up in murder, danger, intrigue, and archaeological mystery

"Victorian Amelia Peabody with her virile husband Emerson and precocious son Ramses embarks on a . . . archaeological dig in Egypt-but not before the death of a dealer in stolen antiquities. A disappearing mummy case and missing Coptic Papyri are the clues in this slapstick comedy-mystery. The ample archaeological detail is vivid, albeit a bit confusing. The irresistable attraction of this story: the heroine's droll tone and intrepid spirit." Library Journal.

Peters, Elizabeth, 1927-2013

Night train to Memphis / Elizabeth Peters. Warner Books, 1994. 353 p. Vicky Bliss mysteries

ISBN 9780446515863

1. Archaeological thefts -- Egypt 2. Cruise ships -- Nile River 3. Undercover operations 4. Thieves 5. Women museum curators 6. Art

historians 7. Women amateur detectives 8. Mysteries

LC 94-3967

Offered a luxury Nile cruise if she will solve a murder and stop a heist of Egyptian antiquities, assistant curator Vicky Bliss jumps at the chance and is horrified when her investigations also unveil her lover's infidelities.

"This one is vintage Peters at her entertaining best." Booklist.

Peters, Elizabeth, 1927-2013

Seeing a large cat / Elizabeth Peters. Warner Books, 1997. 386 p. Amelia Peabody mysteries

ISBN 9780446518345

1. Edwardian era (1901-1914) 2. 1900s (Decade) 3. Excavations (Archaeology) 4. Assassins 5. British in Egypt 6. Egyptologists 7. Women archaeologists -- Egypt 8. Husband-and-wife detectives 9. Amateur detectives 10. Women amateur detectives 11. Valley of the Kings, Egypt 12. Egypt 13. Historical mysteries 14. Mysteries 15. Gentle reads

LC 9637998

This title takes places in 1903.

In 1903's Egypt, archaeologist Amelia Peabody and her husband, Emerson, encounter danger when they receive a warning not to enter the Valley of the Kings, where an assassin tries to halt their discoveries, and Amelia exposes a fraudulent spiritualist.

"Amelia's unquenchable joie de l'aventure continues to define the exuberant style of these mysteries, but Peters doesn't leave it at that. There are always grand views of Egyptian antiquities in her stories, as well as acidic caricatures of globe-trotting tourists and the endlessly entertaining spectacle of busy professional parents confounded by their own progeny." New York Times Book Review.

Peters, Elizabeth, 1927-2013

The snake, the crocodile, and the dog / Elizabeth Peters. Warner Books, 1992. 340 p. Amelia Peabody mysteries

ISBN 9780446515856

1. Victorian era (1837-1901) 2. 19th century 3. Deserts 4. Missing persons 5. Rescues 6. Secrets 7. Husband-and-wife detectives 8. Women archaeologists -- Egypt 9. Egyptologists 10. Amateur detectives 11. Women amateur detectives 12. Historical mysteries 13. Mysteries 14. Gentle reads

LC 92054096

This title takes places in 1898.

As she and her husband travel down the Nile to the remote desert site of Amarna, Amelia Peabody is forced to disclose a dangerous secret.

Peters, Elizabeth, 1927-2013

Trojan gold / Elizabeth Peters. Atheneum, 1987. 363 p. Vicky Bliss mysteries

ISBN 9780689116216

1. Treasure hunting 2. Murderers 3. Attempted murder 4. Art historians 5. Treasure troves 6. Women amateur detectives 7. Bavaria 8. Mysteries

After finding a recent bloodstained photograph of a woman wearing the legendary golden jewels of Troy, Vicky Bliss sets out into the Bavarian mountains to search for the lost Trojan Gold, where she finds herself competing with a devastatingly mysterious man and a ruthless killer.

"Art historian Vicky Bliss receives a photograph of a modern woman dressed in the gold jewelry that Schliemann discovered in his archaeological excavation of Troy. The gold has been missing since the night the Soviet Army marched into Munich in 1945. The usual assortment of male admirers gather round, all trying to out-maneuver Vicky; but she manages to side-step nicely and come out the winner in this scintillating, captivating tale." Library Journal.

Peters, Ellis, 1913-1995

Brother Cadfael's penance / Ellis Peters. Mysterious Press, 1994. 292 p. Brother Cadfael medieval mysteries

ISBN 9780892965991

1. Medieval period (476-1492) 2. Norman period (1066-1154) 3. 12th century 4. Monks 5. Prisoners of war 6. Fathers and sons 7. Rescues 8. Amateur detectives 9. Monasticism and religious orders for men -- Great Britain 10. Herbalists 11. Civilization, Medieval 12. Great Britain -- History -- Medieval period, 1066-1485 13. Great Britain -- History -- Stephen, 1135-1154 14. Shrewsbury, England -- History -- 12th century 15. Historical mysteries 16. Medieval mysteries 17. Mysteries

LC 94027140

Medieval Benedictine monk Brother Cadfael journeys to save his thirty-year-old-son, who has been taken prisoner in the Civil War between Empress Maud and King Stephen

Peters, Ellis, 1913-1995

Dead man's ransom / Ellis Peters. Mysterious Press, 1997, c1984. 275 p. Brother Cadfael medieval mysteries

ISBN 9780446405164

1. Medieval period (476-1492) 2. Norman period (1066-1154) 3. 12th century 4. Monks 5. Prisoners of war 6. Murder investigation -- Great Britain 7. Amateur detectives 8. Monasticism and religious orders for men -- Great Britain 9. Civilization, Medieval 10. Herbalists 11. Great Britain -- History -- Medieval period, 1066-1485 12. Great Britain -- History -- Stephen, 1135-1154 13. Shrewsbury, England -- History -- 12th century 14. Historical mysteries 15. Medieval mysteries 16. Mysteries

In the midst of a twelfth-century civil war between King Stephen and Empress Maud, a hostage exchange is put in jeopardy when one of the prisoners dies, and Brother Cadfael determines that he was murdered.

"A wonderfully atmospheric whodunit." Booklist.

Peters, Ellis, 1913-1995

Death to the landlords! / Ellis Peters. Headline, 1989, c1972. 224 p. Inspector George Felse mysteries

ISBN 9780747202325

1. 1960s 2. Terrorism 3. Landowners 4. Terrorists 5. Terrorism investigation 6. British in India 7. India 8. Mysteries

Originally published: London : Macmillan, 1972.

When a greedy, ruthless landlord is blown up on his boat, suspicion falls on the boat-boy who died with him. Dominic Felse, one of a party of tourists accidentally involved in the fatality, is not convinced of the boy's guilt. A very different landlord is killed where Dominic and his friends are guests, and death seems to follow them south to the tip of India....

"The setting is southern India, and the landlords are wealthy landholders who are the objectives of a terrorist murder gang. Dominic Felse . . . is at the center of the action, touring with a casual American acquaintance. The two young men meet up again and again with some of the same people as they travel India's Cape Comorin, among them a very intense English girl and a shy Indian nurse. Although the setting seems idyllic and the young people most attractive there is an undercurrent of brutal violence that hits home hard. The deaths are achieved by bombing. . . . Most effective of all is the interesting, perceptive, intuitive portrait of . . . problem-ridden India that emerges." Publishers Weekly.

Peters, Ellis, 1913-1995

Fallen into the pit / Ellis Peters. Mysterious Press, 1994, c1951. 324 p. Inspector George Felse mysteries

ISBN 9780446403184

1. World War II veterans 2. Murder suspects 3. Murder investigation

4. Villages -- Shropshire, England 5. Fathers and sons 6. Secrets 7. Shropshire, England 8. England 9. Mysteries

LC 9250656

A World War II Resistance hero and popular modern-day anti-violence speaker is accused of murdering a former German prisoner of war, and policeman George Felse must stop his son from getting too close to the investigation.

Peters, Ellis, 1913-1995

* The **hermit** of Eyton Forest / Ellis Peters. Mysterious Press, 1995, c1987. 224 p. Brother Cadfael medieval mysteries
ISBN 9780445403475
1. Medieval period (476-1492) 2. Norman period (1066-1154) 3. 12th century 4. Hermits 5. Amateur detectives 6. Monks 7. Missing boys 8. Monasticism and religious orders for men -- Great Britain 9. Abbeys 10. Civilization, Medieval 11. Herbalists 12. Great Britain -- History -- Medieval period, 1066-1485 13. Shrewsbury, England -- History -- 12th century 14. Historical mysteries 15. Medieval mysteries 16. Mysteries

Originally published: London : Headline, 1987

Brother Cadfael's tranquil life as a herbalist is disturbed by the arrival of a saintly hermit and the disappearance of a young boy.

Peters, Ellis, 1913-1995

* The **holy** thief / Ellis Peters. Mysterious Press, 1994, c1992. 237 p. Brother Cadfael medieval mysteries
ISBN 9780446403634
1. Medieval period (476-1492) 2. Norman period (1066-1154) 3. 12th century 4. Monks 5. Amateur detectives 6. Christian relic thefts 7. Stolen property recovery 8. Murder investigation -- Great Britain 9. Monasticism and religious orders for men -- Great Britain 10. Civilization, Medieval 11. Herbalists 12. Great Britain -- History -- Medieval period, 1066-1485 13. Shrewsbury, England -- History -- 12th century 14. Historical mysteries 15. Medieval mysteries 16. Mysteries

Originally published: London : Headline, 1992.

Brother Cadfael must solve a puzzling murder case and locate the sacred bones stolen from the Benedictine Abbey of Saint Peter and Saint Paul in Shrewsbury.

"Twelfth-century Shropshire comes vividly alive when peopled with Peters's aristocratic ladies, sturdy lawmen, eager squires and, above all, devout--and devious--monks." Publishers Weekly.

Peters, Ellis, 1913-1995

* **Monk's** hood / Ellis Peters. Mysterious Press, 1992, c1980. 210 p. Brother Cadfael medieval mysteries
ISBN 9780446403009
1. Medieval period (476-1492) 2. Norman period (1066-1154) 3. 12th century 4. Monks 5. Poisoning 6. Abbeys 7. Monasticism and religious orders for men -- Great Britain 8. Amateur detectives 9. Civilization, Medieval 10. Herbalists 11. Great Britain -- History -- Medieval period, 1066-1485 12. Shrewsbury, England -- History -- 12th century 13. Historical mysteries 14. Medieval mysteries 15. Mysteries

Originally published: London : Macmillan, 1980.

Silver Dagger Award for Fiction, 1980.

When Gervase Bonel, a guest at the Shrewsbury Abbey, takes ill, Brother Cadfael, an expert herbalist, runs to his side, only to discover that his patient has been poisoned by monk's hood oil taken from Cadfael's own laboratory.

"Peters' language has a full, rich cadence, and her story is wonderfully vivid." Booklist.

Peters, Ellis, 1913-1995

The **pilgrim** of hate / Ellis Peters. Mysterious Press, 1997, c1984. 247 p. Brother Cadfael medieval mysteries
ISBN 9780446405317
1. Medieval period (476-1492) 2. Norman period (1066-1154) 3. 12th century 4. Pilgrims and pilgrimages, Christian 5. Murder suspects -- Great Britain 6. Shrines 7. Monks 8. Amateur detectives 9. Murder investigation -- Great Britain 10. Monasticism and religious orders for men -- Great Britain 11. Civilization, Medieval 12. Herbalists 13. Great Britain -- History -- Medieval period, 1066-1485 14. Shrewsbury, England -- History -- 12th century 15. Historical mysteries 16. Medieval mysteries 17. Mysteries

Originally published: London : Macmillan, 1984.

As hundreds of pilgrims arrive at the shrine of St. Winifred, Brother Cadfael wonders if two of the pilgrims, obviously intensely bound to each other, are bound to the murder of a knight in Winchester.

Peters, Ellis, 1913-1995

* The **potter's** field / Ellis Peters. Mysterious Press, 1991, c1989. 217 p. Brother Cadfael medieval mysteries
ISBN 9780446400589
1. Medieval period (476-1492) 2. Norman period (1066-1154) 3. 12th century 4. Women murder victims 5. Monks 6. Murder investigation -- Great Britain 7. Monasticism and religious orders for men -- Great Britain 8. Civilization, Medieval 9. Amateur detectives 10. Herbalists 11. Great Britain -- History -- Medieval period, 1066-1485 12. Shrewsbury, England -- History -- 12th century 13. Historical mysteries 14. Medieval mysteries 15. Mysteries

Originally published: London : Headline, 1989.

When the monks inherit the field of a local potter and discover the corpse of a murdered woman while plowing, Brother Cadfael is called upon to solve the mystery.

"In place of the pretty romances with which the author often lightens her historically plausible fictions, Ms. Peters provides darker characters and a more somber view of Shrewsbury life. More than the brilliant detection of a crime, the true subject of her wintry tale is human misery, as it extends from the meanest peasant cottage to the grandest manor house." New York Times Book Review.

Peters, Ellis, 1913-1995

* A **rare** Benedictine / Ellis Peters. Mysterious Press, 1989. 118 p. Brother Cadfael medieval mysteries
ISBN 9780446400886
1. Medieval period (476-1492) 2. Norman period (1066-1154) 3. 12th century 4. Monks 5. Monasticism and religious orders for men -- Great Britain 6. Amateur detectives 7. Civilization, Medieval 8. Herbalists 9. Great Britain -- History -- Medieval period, 1066-1485 10. Shrewsbury, England -- History -- 12th century 11. Historical mysteries 12. Medieval mysteries 13. Mysteries

3 short stories.

These stories originally appeared in Winter's Crimes volumes 17, 11 and 13, published by Macmillan UK Ltd.

"Introducing the medieval sleuth Brother Cadfael"--Cover.

Twelfth-century monastic sleuth Brother Cadfael tracks down criminals in three tales of his life before he entered a Benedictine monastery.

"The author reveals for the first time how her medieval sleuth, Brother Cadfael, came to his calling at Shrewsbury Abbey. . . . For all his spirituality, mild Brother Cadfael once again impresses us with his practical grasp of the criminal side of human nature." New York Times Book Review.

LIST OF FICTIONAL WORKS

Peters, Ellis, 1913-1995

The **rose** rent / Ellis Peters. Mysterious Press, 1997, c1986. 230 p. Brother Cadfael medieval mysteries

ISBN 9780446405331

1. Medieval period (476-1492) 2. Norman period (1066-1154) 3. 12th century 4. Missing women 5. Monks 6. Amateur detectives 7. Missing persons investigation 8. Civilization, Medieval 9. Monasticism and religious orders for men -- Great Britain 10. Herbalists 11. Great Britain -- History -- Medieval period, 1066-1485 12. Shrewsbury, England -- History -- 12th century 13. Historical mysteries 14. Medieval mysteries 15. Mysteries

Originally published : London : Macmillan, 1986.

A late spring in 1142 has the Abbey monks dismayed, for there may be no roses by June 22nd. For three years, the wealthy young widow Judith Perle has rented her house to the monks for the price of a single rose each year. When nature finally complies, a pious monk is sent to pay the rent--and found murdered beside the hacked rose-bush. Without a rose, the monks' rental contract becomes void, adding greatly to the widow's dowry. But before Brother Cadfael can ponder if a greedy suitor has done this dreadful deed, another crime is committed. Now the good monk must thread his way through a tangle more tortuous than the widow's thorny bushes.

"When Judith Perle, a most generous benefactor of the abbey, vanishes without a trace, Cadfael immediately connects her disappearance with the vicious murder of a pious young monk and the seemingly senseless destruction of a rose bush. An accomplished whodunit meticulously wrought with a wealth of medieval detail." Booklist.

Peters, Ellis, 1913-1995

St. Peter's fair / Ellis Peters. Mysterious Press, 1992, c1981. 217 p. Brother Cadfael medieval mysteries

ISBN 9780446403016

1. Medieval period (476-1492) 2. Norman period (1066-1154) 3. 12th century 4. Monasticism and religious orders for men -- Great Britain 5. Murder investigation -- Great Britain 6. Monks 7. Civilization, Medieval 8. Amateur detectives 9. Herbalists 10. Great Britain -- History -- Medieval period, 1066-1485 11. Shrewsbury, England -- History -- 12th century 12. Historical mysteries 13. Medieval mysteries 14. Mysteries

Originally published: London : Macmillan, 1981.

Brother Cadfael, a medieval monk, attempts to solve the murder of Thomas of Bristol, a prosperous merchant who was stabbed just before the start of the fair.

"Brother Cadfael, who led an adventurous life in the world before becoming a monk, is on the side of young love, honor and truth as he investigates deaths taking place while a local fair is in full swing. A well-respected merchant is found murdered, and his lovely daughter takes it upon herself to keep secrets so she involves two young men, both of whom fancy her. Another death occurs. Peters has an authentic eye and ear for her 12th century way of life and death, and engages our interest all the way." Publishers Weekly.

Peters, Ellis, 1913-1995

The **sanctuary** sparrow / Ellis Peters. Mysterious Press, 1995, c1983. 221 p. Brother Cadfael medieval mysteries

ISBN 9780446404297

1. Medieval period (476-1492) 2. Norman period (1066-1154) 3. 12th century 4. Troubadours 5. Asylum, Right of 6. Murder investigation -- Great Britain 7. Monks 8. Civilization, Medieval 9. Monasticism and religious orders for men -- Great Britain 10. Amateur detectives 11. Herbalists 12. Great Britain -- History -- Medieval period, 1066-1485 13. Shrewsbury, England -- History -- 12th century 14. Historical mysteries 15. Medieval mysteries 16. Mysteries

Originally published: London : Macmillan, 1983.

Medieval Benedictine monk Brother Cadfael investigates the case of a boy, an itinerant acrobat and jongleur accused of assault and murder who seeks refuge from an angry mob in the monastery.

Peters, Ellis, 1913-1995

The **summer** of the Danes / Ellis Peters. Mysterious Press, 1995, c1991. 245 p. Brother Cadfael medieval mysteries

ISBN 9780446400183

1. Medieval period (476-1492) 2. Norman period (1066-1154) 3. 12th century 4. Monks 5. Diplomacy 6. Political prisoners 7. Kidnapping 8. Amateur detectives 9. Civilization, Medieval 10. Herbalists 11. Wales -- History -- 12th century 12. Great Britain -- History -- Stephen, 1135-1154 13. Shrewsbury, England -- History -- 12th century 14. Historical mysteries 15. Medieval mysteries 16. Mysteries

Originally published: London : Headline, 1991.

In the Summer of 1144, a strange calm has settled over England. The armies of King Stephen and Empress Maud, the two royal cousins contending for the throne, have temporarily exhausted each other. On the whole, Brother Cadfael considers peace a blessing. Still a little excitement never comes amiss to a former soldier, and Cadfael is delighted to accompany his young friend, Brother Mark, on a mission of church diplomacy to his native Wales. But shortly after their arrival, the two monks are caught up in yet another royal feud. The Welsh prince Owain Gwynedd has banished his brother Cadwaladi, accusing him of the treacherous murder of an ally. The reckless Cadwaladi has retaliated by landing an army of Danish mercenaries, poised to invade Wales and retake his lost lands. As the two armies teeter on the brink of bloody civil war, Cadfael is captured by the Danes. His fellow prisoner is a headstrong young woman fleeing an arranged marriage-or perhaps her involvement in a murder.

Peters, Ellis, 1913-1995

The **virgin** in the ice / Ellis Peters. Mysterious Press, 1995, c1982. 202 p. Brother Cadfael medieval mysteries

ISBN 9780446404280

1. Medieval period (476-1492) 2. Norman period (1066-1154) 3. 12th century 4. Nuns -- History -- Medieval period, 1066-1485 5. Missing persons -- Great Britain 6. Monks 7. Monasticism and religious orders for men -- Great Britain 8. Missing persons investigation 9. Amateur detectives 10. Abbeys 11. Civilization, Medieval 12. Herbalists 13. Great Britain -- History -- Medieval period, 1066-1485 14. Shrewsbury, England -- History -- 12th century 15. Historical mysteries 16. Medieval mysteries 17. Mysteries

Originally published: London : Macmillan, 1982.

Brother Cadfael sets out to find a young nun and her two wards, who have disappeared, and comes upon a desperate villain, an unusual affair of the heart, and the possible implication of his own abbey.

Peters, Ralph, 1952-

Hell or Richmond / Ralph Peters. Forge, 2013. 432 p. Battle hymn cycle

ISBN 9780765330482

1. Barlow, Francis C (Francis Channing), 1834-1896 2. Oates, William Calvin, 1835-1910 3. American Civil War era (1861-1865) 4. 1860s 5. Union soldiers 6. Battles 7. Civil war 8. United States Civil War, 1861-1865 9. United States -- History -- Civil War, 1861-1865 10. Virginia -- History -- 1775-1865 11. War stories 12. Historical fiction

LC 2012049720

"A Tom Doherty Associates book."

Sequel to: Cain at Gettysburg

W. Y. Boyd Literary Award, 2014.

A sequel to Cain at Gettysburg reimagines a brutal 30-day period of the Civil War as experienced by Harvard valedictorian Union general Francis Channing Barlow, brawling Rebel colonel William C. Oates and a simple laborer destined to win the Medal of Honor.

Peterson, Jerry A.

Early's fall / Jerry Peterson. Five Star, 2009. 304 p. James Early mysteries

ISBN 9781594146787

1. Sheriffs 2. Murder investigation 3. Women with bipolar disorder 4. Women murder victims 5. Marital conflict 6. Pregnant women 7. Diaries 8. Kansas -- History -- 20th century 9. Mysteries

Kansas sheriff James Early works to solve the murder of a teacher and pursues a bank robber, as his personal life unravels with his wife sinking into depression and risking the life of his unborn child.

Peterson, Tracie

What comes my way / Tracie Peterson. Bethany House, 2019. 384 p. Brookstone brides

ISBN 9780764233395

1. 1900s (Decade) 2. Trick riding 3. Wild West shows 4. Cowgirls 5. Independence in women 6. Alcoholism 7. Faith (Christianity) 8. Adult children of murderers 9. Secrets 10. Men/women relations 11. The West (United States) 12. Montana 13. Christian historical romances

Only while trick riding can Ella Fleming forget the truth about who she really is--the daughter of a murderer. Phillip DeShazer buries the guilt he feels for his father's death in work and drink, and his guilt continues to grow the more Ella Fleming comes to his rescue. Will they be able to overcome their pasts and trust God to guide their futures?

Petrie, Nicholas

Burning bright / Nicholas Petrie. G.P. Putnam's Sons, 2017. 432 p. Peter Ash novels

ISBN 9780399174575

1. Iraq war veterans 2. Journalists 3. Artificial intelligence 4. Veterans 5. Former marines 6. Wilderness areas 7. Computer scientists 8. Claustrophobia 9. Murder 10. Post-traumatic stress disorder 11. California 12. Thrillers and suspense

LC 2016011425

Afghan war veteran Peter Ash is hiking through northern California's redwoods when he's forced up a tree to escape a grizzly. What he finds in that tree is an elaborate network of ropes, with a pretty blonde on the platform at the top. June Cassidy is no treehugger, however -- she's an investigative journalist on the run from fake government agents who believe she's in possession of a powerful algorithm created by her mother, who'd recently been killed. June hires Peter to discover who's behind the threat, and they uncover far more than expected. The 2nd in a series that started with?The Drifter?(with promises of at least two more to come),?Burning?Bright?is a fast-paced, action-packed read that also addresses the effects of PTSD. -- Description by Shauna Griffin

Petrie, Nicholas

The **drifter** / Nicholas Petrie. G.P. Putnam's Sons, 2016. 384 p. Peter Ash novels

ISBN 9780399174568

1. Iraq war veterans 2. Post-traumatic stress disorder 3. Conspiracies 4. Claustrophobia 5. Widows 6. Former marines 7. Domestic terrorism 8. Milwaukee, Wisconsin 9. Thrillers and suspense

Thriller Award for Best First Novel, 2017.

Wisconsin Library Association Literary Award, 2017.

Like Jack Reacher, Marine Corps veteran Peter Ash stays constantly on the move. In Ash's case, however, PTSD prevents him from settling down -- or even staying indoors. When a close friend and fellow Marine commits suicide, Ash heads to Milwaukee to look after his family however he can. This includes home repair, which is when he finds a suitcase packed full of money -- and explosives. Figuring out his friend's last few days leads Ash straight into a complex situation that allows both a pulse-pounding plot and a sympathetic look at the challenges veterans face at home. -- Description by Shauna Griffin.

Petrie, Nicholas

Tear it down / Nick Petrie. G.P. Putnam's Sons, 2019 373 p. Peter Ash novels

ISBN 9780399575662

1. Iraq War veterans 2. Post-traumatic stress disorder 3. Death threats 4. Street musicians 5. Women photojournalists 6. Thieves 7. Criminal investigation 8. Violence against women 9. African Americans 10. Racism 11. Tennessee 12. Memphis, Tennessee 13. Thrillers and suspense

LC 2018018176

Peter Ash tackles two difficult cases in Memphis involving an attack on a war photographer, a homeless street musician, a stolen cache of watches, vengeful gangsters and a valuable Civil War heirloom.

"...[T]here's no denying that Petrie is hell on wheels at mounting lethal action face-offs. A close cousin to Lee Childs's more analytical Jack Reacher, Peter Ash is one of today's more exciting action heroes." Publishers Weekly.

Petrie, Nicholas

The **wild** one / Nick Petrie. G. P. Putnam's Sons, 2020. 400 p. Peter Ash novels

ISBN 9780525535447

1. Iraq War veterans 2. Post-traumatic stress disorder 3. Kidnapping 4. Fugitives 5. Child kidnapping victims 6. Missing children 7. Criminal investigation 8. Violence against women 9. Iceland 10. Tennessee 11. Thrillers and suspense

LC 2019046077

Traumatized war veteran Peter Ash tracks a murderer from a criminal family through the icy landscapes of Reykjavik, where he is confronted by government officials who would block his investigation.

"This kinetic, breathless masterpiece illustrates why Petrie is here to stay." Publishers Weekly.

Petry, Ann, 1908-1997

* The **street** / Ann Petry. Houghton Mifflin, 1998, c1946 435 p.

ISBN 9780395901496

1. 1940s 2. Ghettoes, African American -- Harlem, New York City 3. Single-parent families -- Harlem, New York City 4. Poverty -- Harlem, New York City 5. African American women 6. Inner city 7. Street life 8. African American community life -- Harlem, New York City 9. Mothers and sons -- Harlem, New York City 10. African Americans -- Harlem, New York City 11. Harlem, New York City 12. Urban fiction 13. Literary fiction 14. African American fiction 15. Modern classics

Explores the life and dreams of a young woman who struggles to raise her son in a suffocating ghetto world of racism, human degradation, and uncontrolled violence.

LIST OF FICTIONAL WORKS

Petterson, Per, 1952-

I curse the river of time / Per Petterson ; translated from the Norwegian by Charlotte Barslund. Farrar Straus & Giroux, 2010. 224 p.

ISBN 9781555975562

1. 1980s 2. Mothers with terminal illnesses 3. Life change events 4. Divorce 5. Family relationships 6. Guilt in men 7. Coping 8. Literary fiction 9. Psychological fiction 10. Translations -- Norwegian to English

English translation originally published: London : Harvill Secker, 2010.

First published with the title Jeg forbanner tidens elv by Forlaget Oktober, Oslo: 2008.

Anticipating a divorce against a backdrop of the fall of communism, Arvid Jansen is further dismayed by his mother's diagnosis with cancer, a situation that prompts his emotionally charged quest for understanding and balance.

"Needless to say, it's a sad book, and at times it'll feel alien to readers who've never been young Communists or hung out in, say, Nittedal or Eidsvoll. (The translation can also be quite a rickety bridge.) But there's no denying the novel's Raymond Carver-like power as Arvid and his mother come to terms with how life hands you hope just before it hands you disappointment and tragedy." Entertainment Weekly.

Petterson, Per, 1952-

I refuse / Per Petterson ; translated from the Norwegian by Don Bartlett. Graywolf Press, 2015, c2012. 224 p.

ISBN 9781555976996

1. Male friendship 2. Psychic trauma 3. Family problems 4. Adult children of dysfunctional families 5. Betrayal 6. Suicidal behavior 7. Guilt in men 8. Family relationships 9. Psychological fiction 10. Literary fiction 11. Translations -- Norwegian to English

Translation from the Norwegian of: Jeg nekter.

First published with the title Jeg nekter in 2012 by Forgalet Oktober, Oslo.

Originally published: 2012.

A chance encounter between two childhood friends, including one who escaped an abusive father, reveals how their fortunes have reversed.

"Without pyrotechnics, Petterson brings his characters and working-class Norway vividly, even passionately, to life; days after they finish the novel , readers may still have dreams of ice cracking." Kirkus.

Petterson, Per, 1952-

Out stealing horses : a novel / Per Petterson ; translated from the Norwegian by Anne Born. Graywolf Press, 2007, c2003. 288 p.

ISBN 1555974708

1. 1940s 2. Senior men 3. Neighbors 4. Memories 5. Fathers and sons 6. Boys -- Friendship 7. Life change events in children 8. Growing up 9. Norway -- History -- 20th century 10. Coming-of-age stories 11. Translations -- Norwegian to English 12. Literary fiction
LC 2006938263

Originally published: Oslo : Forlaget Oktober, 2003.

ALA Notable Book, 2008.

International IMPAC Dublin Literary Award, 2007.

Sixty-seven-year-old Trond Sander lives secluded in a far corner of Norway. Casting his mind back to 1948, he recalls a horse stealing prank with his best friend that turned tragic and changed his life forever.

"Petterson's spare and deliberate prose has astonishing force, and the narrative gains further power from the artful interplay of Trond's childhood and adult perspectives." The New Yorker.

Phillips, Arthur, 1969-

* The **king** at the edge of the world : novel / Arthur Phillips. Random House, 2020. 288 p.

ISBN 9780812995480

1. Elizabeth I,, Queen of England, 1533-1603 2. Elizabethan era (1558-1603) 3. Tudor period (1485-1603) 4. Physicians 5. Undercover operations 6. Inheritance and succession 7. Spies 8. Religion 9. Women rulers 10. Heirs and heiresses 11. Muslim men 12. Courts and courtiers 13. Intrigue 14. England 15. Historical thrillers 16. Spy fiction

A secret Muslim warrior from the height of England's religious battles is sent to Scotland to uncover the true nature of James VI's actual religious beliefs while an heirless Elizabeth I lies on her deathbed.

"Readers will flock to the latest from esteemed best-seller Phillips, whose signature literary prowess and nimble imagination remain ascendant." Booklist.

Phillips, Arthur, 1969-

Prague : a novel / Arthur Phillips. Random House, 2002. 448 p.

ISBN 0375507876

1. 1990s 2. Americans in Budapest, Hungary 3. Teenagers 4. Expatriates -- Budapest, Hungary 5. Budapest, Hungary 6. Historical fiction 7. Coming-of-age stories
LC 2001048975

In the 1990s, five young American expatriates meet in Budapest. As they seeks fortune and success, their lives reflect various facets of a city that is shaped by its history, culture, and the aftermath of Communism.

"In Phillips's wry and skillful telling, a sexual tryst or the renting of an apartment can become a tragicomic pantomime about East and West. . . . As 'Prague' progresses, each of the five foreigners at the cafe table becomes less and less attractive, and the satiric edge to Phillips's portrayal sharpens into something close to anger: at their solipsism, their savage cynicism, their detachment from their surrounding and from one another." New York Times Book Review.

Phillips, Arthur, 1969-

* The **tragedy** of Arthur : a novel / Arthur Phillips. Random House, 2011. 432 p.

ISBN 9781400066476

1. Shakespeare, William, 1564-1616 Authorship 2. Dramatists 3. Art forgeries 4. Fathers and sons 5. Family relationships 6. Writing 7. Satirical fiction 8. Metafiction
LC 2010021192

ALA Notable Book, 2012.

Shortlisted for the International IMPAC Dublin Literary Award, 2013

When their long-imprisoned con-artist father reaches the end of his life, Arthur and his twin sister become the owners of an undiscovered play by William Shakespeare that their father wants published, a final request that represents either a great literary gift or their father's last great heist.

Phillips, Caryl

Dancing in the dark / Caryl Phillips. Knopf, 2005. 224 p.

ISBN 1400043964

1. Williams, Bert, 1874-1922 2. Walker, George, 1873-1911 3. 1900s (Decade) 4. African American men -- Identity 5. African American entertainers 6. African American comedians 7. Bahamian Americans 8. Blackface entertainers 9. Entertainers 10. Comedians 11. Minstrels 12. Minstrel shows 13. Identity (Psychology) 14. Ethnic identity 15. Prejudice 16. Racism 17. Race relations 18. Family relationships 19. Harlem, New York City 20. Broadway, New York

City 21. Biographical fiction 22. Historical fiction

LC 2005044106

A fictional re-creation of the life and times of Bert Williams, the first black entertainer in the United States to achieve success, a man who dons blackface to become a headliner in the Ziegfeld Follies.

"As subjects for historical novels go, Bert Williams is an inspired choice; his strange career exemplified all the ironies and paradoxes that confronted the African-American performers of his time. . . . Dancing in the Dark is riveting when it recreates mores and social conventions our culture has done its best to forget." New York Times Book Review.

Phillips, Caryl

A **distant** shore / Caryl Phillips. Knopf, 2003. 256 p.

ISBN 1400041090

1. Retired teachers 2. Senior women 3. Refugees 4. Undocumented immigrants 5. Undocumented workers 6. Caretakers 7. Murder victims 8. Africans in Great Britain 9. Violence 10. Racism 11. Hate crimes 12. Secret identity 13. False imprisonment 14. African resistance and revolts 15. Africa 16. England 17. Psychological fiction 18. Literary fiction

National Book Critics Circle Award for Fiction finalist, 2003

Moving into a new bungalow in an English village, retired teacher Dorothy meets night watchman Solomon, an illegal immigrant, in a tale that recounts their experiences as solitary outsiders in a hostile world.

"This muted, sad novel breaks down the distinction between the placed and the displaced, dissolving our sense of security, if we had one, about safely belonging in the world, dispelling our illusion of being at home. We are all adrift, Phillips says, whether we know it or not: a fact not of race or nationality, but of the human condition." New York Times Book Review.

Phillips, Caryl

Foreigners / Caryl Phillips. Alfred A. Knopf, 2007. 256 p.

ISBN 9781400043972

1. Barber, Frank, d 1801 2. Turpin, Randolph 3. Oluwale, David, 1930-1969 4. Slaves 5. Boxers (Sports) 6. Africans in Great Britain 7. Stowaways 8. Racism 9. Prejudice 10. Race relations 11. Interpersonal relations 12. Identity (Psychology) 13. Ethnic identity 14. Hate crimes 15. England 16. Biographical fiction 17. Historical fiction 18. Psychological fiction

LC 2007029219

The life stories of three black men of different times and backgrounds reveals the place and role of the foreigner in English society.

"With great empathy, and through a collage of voices, Phillips has created three distinct portraits. All are superbly crafted and utterly absorbing . . . . As Phillips suggests, Englishness, like foreignness, is a complex and changeable thing. An important and sobering book, highly relevant today." The Daily Mail.

Phillips, Carly

Perfect fit / Carly Phillips. Berkley, 2012. 295 p. Serendipity's finest

ISBN 9780425259719

1. Homecomings 2. Police chiefs 3. Policewomen 4. Investigations 5. Family secrets 6. Police 7. Interpersonal attraction 8. Men/women relations 9. Small towns -- New York (State) 10. New York (State) 11. Contemporary romances

When Michael Marsden returns to Serendipity to take over his adopted father's job as police chief, he finds his desire to move on waning after he reconnects with Cara Hartley, a policewoman with whom he had a one night stand.

Phillips, Caryl

A **view** of the empire at sunset / Caryl Phillips. Farrar, Straus and Giroux, 2018. 324 p.

ISBN 9780374283612

1. Rhys, Jean 2. 20th century 3. Women authors 4. Colonialism 5. Misfits (Persons) 6. Cultural differences 7. Race relations 8. Identity (Psychology) 9. Exiles 10. Men/women relations 11. Great Britain 12. West Indies 13. Historical fiction 14. Biographical fiction

LC 2017047959

A reimagining of the life of Jean Rhys, author of Wide Sargasso Sea, traces her tempestuous life in Edwardian England and 1920s Paris before a brief visit transforms her views about colonization in the Caribbean of her childhood.

Phillips, Christi

The **Devlin** diary / Christi Phillips. Pocket Books, 2008. 448 p.

ISBN 9781416527398

1. Restoration England (1660-1688) 2. Stuart period (1603-1714) 3. College teachers -- Cambridge, England 4. Serial murders 5. Women physicians 6. Murder investigation -- Cambridge, England 7. Great Britain -- Court and courtiers 8. Great Britain -- History -- Restoration, 1660-1688 9. Mysteries

LC 2008021769

When a Trinity College history professor is found murdered with a torn page of a seventeenth-century diary in his hand, Claire Donovan and historian Andrew Kent believe his death may be linked to a series of unsolved killings in 1670s London.

Phillips, Christi

The **Rossetti** letter : a novel / Christi Phillips. Pocket Books, 2007. 352 p.

ISBN 9781416527374

1. Habsburg, House of 2. 17th century 3. Courtesans 4. Letters 5. Conspiracies 6. Women scholars and academics 7. Dissertation writing 8. Historians -- Great Britain 9. Research 10. Investigations 11. Truth 12. Venice, Italy -- History -- 17th century 13. Italy -- Foreign relations -- Spain 14. Historical mysteries 15. Parallel narratives 16. Mysteries

Fearing that her research will be rendered useless if a Cambridge professor proves his theory about seventeenth-century Venetian courtesan Alessandra Rossetti, Ph.D. candidate Claire Donovan agrees to chaperone a troubled teen in order to gain passage to the professor's presentation in Venice.

Phillips, Clyde

Unthinkable / Clyde Phillips. Thomas & Mercer, 2013. 367 p. Jane Candiotti mysteries

ISBN 9781611098112

1. Pregnant women 2. Mass murder 3. Murder investigation 4. Murder witnesses 5. Former convicts 6. Women detectives 7. San Francisco, California 8. Mysteries 9. Police procedurals

"Pregnant with her first child, homicide lieutenant Jane Candiotti is under strict doctor's orders to take it easy. But when a mass shooting claims the life of her teenage nephew, all bets are off. Jane will go to any lengths to bring down the monster who did this-- even enlisting the help of a dangerous ex-con. And when she uncovers a chilling connection between the shooting and a decades old murder case, she knows she cannot stop until the final horrifying pice of the puzzle falls into place."--p.4 of cover.

Phillips, Gin

Fierce kingdom : a novel / Gin Phillips. Viking, 2017. 288 p.

ISBN 9780735224278

1. Mothers and sons 2. Survival 3. Zoos 4. Protectiveness in women 5. Life change events 6. Fear in women 7. Motherhood 8. Thrillers and suspense

LC 2016057138

RUSA Reading List, 2018.

Trapped in a closed zoo after witnessing a life-shattering event, a woman and her 4-year-old son navigate the zoo's hidden pathways and under-renovation exhibits to stay ahead of a dangerous adversary who tests their survival and the limits of the mother-child bond.

"A searing exploration of motherhood at its most basic, this all-too-plausible horror story may haunt even readers with steely nerves and strong stomachs." Publishers Weekly.

Phillips, Helen, 1981-

The **beautiful** bureaucrat : a novel / Helen Phillips. Henry Holt and Co., 2015. 192 p.

ISBN 9781627793766

1. Married women 2. Conspiracies 3. Husband and wife 4. Bureaucracy 5. Data processing -- Data entry 6. Anagrams 7. Secrets 8. Office politics 9. Satirical fiction 10. Literary fiction

LC 2014045386

Becoming increasingly uneasy about suspicious activities at a new job she felt lucky to land, Josephine makes a terrible realization and is forced to confront dangerous and powerful elements in order to protect her loved ones.

"Phillips takes situations and sentiments that will be all too familiar to many readers--a soul-crushingly dull job that callously steals our youth and beauty, the desperate yearning to be free of it, the restoring power of love and food and intimacy and of shared language and laughter--and uses them to explore bigger universal themes of life and death and the choices and compromises they demand. Intense and enigmatic, tense and tender, this novel offers no easy answers--its deeper meanings may mystify--but it grabs you up, propels you along, and leaves you gasping, grasping, and ready to read it again." Kirkus.

Phillips, Helen, 1981-

The **need** : a novel / Helen Phillips. Simon & Schuster, 2019. 224 p.

ISBN 9781982113162

1. Working mothers 2. Parenting 3. Home invasions 4. Women scientists 5. Maternal love 6. Anxiety 7. Fear in women 8. Excavations (Paleontology) 9. Identity (Psychology) 10. Self-discovery in women 11. Literary fiction 12. Psychological suspense

LC 2018044381

Longlisted for the National Book Award for Fiction, 2019.

A woman grapples with the complex dualities of motherhood -- joy and dread, tenderness and anxiety -- after confronting a masked intruder in her home.

Phillips, Jayne Anne, 1952-

Lark and Termite : a novel / Jayne Anne Phillips. Alfred A. Knopf, 2009. 272 p.

ISBN 9780375401954

1. 1950s 2. Korean War, 1950-1953 3. Family secrets 4. Brothers and sisters 5. Family relationships 6. Aunts 7. West Virginia 8. Domestic fiction 9. Historical fiction

LC 2008033453

National Book Critics Circle Award for Fiction finalist, 2009
National Book Award for Fiction finalist, 2009

Set against the backdrop of the Korean War in the 1950s, a novel about family, the repercussions of war, and the bonds that sustain personal relationships focuses on a single family--Lark, her brother Termite, their mother Lola, and Termite's soldier father, Robert Leavitt.

"Phillips has done in Lark and Termite what she did in previous novels such as Machine Dreams (1984) and Shelter (1994), which is to take a relatively simple, straightforward tale and twist it into something luminous and haunting and singular. This is Phillips' first novel in almost a decade, but it doesn't feel tardy or excessively fussed over. It feels fresh. It feels as if it has been taken straight from the griddle and is still too hot to touch. And because it deals with issues over which people have been arguing for centuries--family and war--the novel's raw immediacy is really quite spectacular." PopMatters.

Phillips, Jayne Anne, 1952-

* **Quiet** dell : a novel / Jayne Anne Phillips. Scribner, 2013. 480 p.

ISBN 9781439172537

1. 1930s 2. Women journalists 3. Serial murderers 4. Swindlers and swindling 5. Trials 6. Widows 7. Murder investigation 8. Families -- Death 9. Secrets 10. Men/women relations 11. Chicago, Illinois 12. Illinois 13. Historical fiction

LC 2013016013

In 1931, Emily Thornhill, one of the few women in the Chicago press, covers the murders of Asta Eicher and her three children and, obsessed with finding out what happened to this beautiful family, allies herself with the man funding the investigation who is wracked with guilt for not saving Asta himself.

Phillips, Julia

* **Disappearing** earth / Julia Phillips. Alfred A Knopf, 2019. 304 p.

ISBN 9780525520412

1. Girl kidnapping victims 2. Loss (Psychology) 3. Communities 4. Missing girls 5. Women 6. Sisters 7. Race relations 8. Cultural relations 9. Russia 10. Literary fiction 11. Thrillers and suspense

National Book Award for Fiction finalist, 2019.

The shattering disappearance of two young girls from Russia's Kamchatka Peninsula compounds the isolation and fears of a tight-woven community, connecting the lives of neighbors, witnesses, family members and a detective throughout an ensuing year of tension.

Phillips, Susan Elizabeth

* **Call** me irresistible / Susan Elizabeth Phillips. HarperCollins, 2011 400 p. Wynette, Texas romances

ISBN 9780061351525

1. Mayors 2. Engaged persons 3. Small town life 4. Friendship 5. Weddings 6. Self-fulfillment 7. Men/women relations 8. Texas 9. Contemporary romances 10. Western romances

Ostracized for her role in halting best friend Lucy's wedding, Meg finds herself stranded without family support in a hostile Texas town where she unexpectedly falls for Ted Beaudine.

Phillips, Susan Elizabeth

The **great** escape / Susan Elizabeth Phillips. William Morrow, 2012. 432 p. Wynette, Texas romances

ISBN 9780062106063

1. Runaway wives, husbands, etc 2. Voyages and travels 3. Self-fulfillment in women 4. Children of presidents 5. Brides 6. Lakes 7. Men/women relations 8. Interpersonal attraction 9. Great Lakes 10. Texas 11. Contemporary romances

Lucy Jorik, the daughter of the former president of the United States, jilts her soon-to-be husband at the altar and embarks on the adventure she has been waiting for.

Phillips, Susan Elizabeth

First Lady / Susan Elizabeth Phillips. Avon Books, 1999 384 p. Wynette, Texas romances

ISBN 0380808072

1. Widows 2. Presidents' spouses -- United States 3. Secret identity 4. Disguises 5. Secret service -- United States 6. Journalists 7. Guardian and ward 8. Texas 9. Contemporary romances 10. Western romances

RITA Award for Best Contemporary Single Title, 2001.

The young widow of the United States President decides to escape for a few days, and heads out across the heartland of the country, in the company of a seductive stranger and two little girls.

Phillips, Susan Elizabeth

First star I see tonight / Susan Elizabeth Phillips. William Morrow, 2016. 384 p. Chicago Stars

ISBN 9780062405616

1. Former football players 2. Women private investigators 3. Fame 4. Nightclubs 5. Family businesses 6. Competition 7. Businesspeople 8. Sexual attraction 9. Men/women relations 10. Contemporary romances 11. Sports romances

Discovered by the former quarterback she was hired to tail, detective Piper Dove pretends to be the athlete's stalker and is subsequently hired by him, an arrangement threatened by their growing chemistry.

"This thoroughly enjoyable novel delivers a swift kick to the heartan essential summer read." Kirkus.

Phillips, Susan Elizabeth

Heroes are my weakness / Susan Elizabeth Phillips. William Morrow, 2014. 384 p.

ISBN 9780062106070

1. Authors 2. Actors and actresses 3. Men recluses 4. Horror story authors 5. Puppeteers 6. Men/women relations 7. Island life 8. Homecomings 9. Maine 10. Contemporary romances

LC 2014007547

A down-on-her-luck actress reduced to staging kids' puppet shows finds herself trapped on a remote island off the coast of Maine with a sexy horror novelist who knows a dozen ways to kill with his bare hands.

"Phillips takes all the iconic elements of those classic gothic novels of the 1960s and '70s and deftly combines them with her own signature literary calling cards of realistically quirky yet all too relatable characters, polished writing, tart humor, and an abundance of potent sexual chemistry." Booklist.

Phillips, Susan Elizabeth

* **It** had to be you / Susan Elizabeth Phillips. Avon Books, 1994. 376 p. Chicago Stars

ISBN 0380776839

1. Heirs and heiresses 2. Inheritance and succession 3. Professional football teams 4. Men/women relations 5. Fathers -- Death 6. Social acceptance 7. Self-discovery in women 8. Professional football coaches 9. Chicago, Illinois 10. Contemporary romances 11. Sports romances

LC 93-91031

Characters from this book also briefly appear in the author's book Match me if you can.

RITA Award for Best Romance of 1994.

Inheriting the Chicago Stars football team, trendy New Yorker Phoebe Somerville knocks heads with Coach Dan Calebow, who resents her

meddling as much as she despises his sexist jocularity, until they discover an unlikely attraction for each other

Phillips, Susan Elizabeth

Match me if you can / Susan Elizabeth Phillips. William Morrow, 2005. 400 p. Chicago Stars

ISBN 0060734558

1. Single men 2. Single women 3. Sports agents 4. Matchmakers 5. Women business owners 6. Matchmaking 7. Inheritance and succession 8. Dating services 9. Business competition 10. Dating (Social customs) 11. Mate selection for men 12. Mate selection 13. Chicago, Illinois 14. Contemporary romances

LC 2004065644

Includes appearances by characters from the author's books This heart of mine and It had to be you.

Anabelle Granger endeavors to promote her grandmother's matchmaking business by landing sports agent Heath Champion as a client, an effort that is challenged by Heath's arrogant nature and Annabelle's own unexpected feelings.

Phillips, Susan Elizabeth

* **Natural** born charmer / Susan Elizabeth Phillips. William Morrow, 2007. 400 p. Chicago Stars

ISBN 0060734574

1. Quarterbacks (Football) 2. Mothers and sons 3. Automobile travel 4. Single men 5. Single women 6. Football players 7. Men/women relations 8. Colorado 9. Tennessee 10. Contemporary romances 11. Sports romances

LC 2006049173

Sequel to: Match me if you can.

RUSA Reading List, 2008.

Taking to the road between seasons, attractive Chicago Stars quarterback Dean Robillard meets the beautiful and infuriating Blue under unusual circumstances and draws on his competitive skills to overcome her wariness of relationships.

"While the verbal sparring in this textbook case of opposites attracting feels stagy at first, the rough edges come together in an alluring way." Publishers Weekly.

Phillips, Susan Elizabeth

What I did for love / Susan Elizabeth Phillips. William Morrow, 2009. 416 p. Wynette, Texas romances

ISBN 9780061351501

1. Actors and actresses 2. Divorce 3. Remarriage 4. Celebrities -- Press coverage 5. Paparazzi 6. Film industry and trade 7. Men/women relations 8. Hollywood, California 9. Texas 10. Contemporary romances 11. Western romances

LC 2008037321

When actress Georgie York's film career hits rock bottom along with her marriage, the paparazzi has a field day with her misfortune, which is only complicated by the reappearance of her sexy, unscrupulous former costar, Bramwell Shepard.

Phoenix, Michele,

The **space** between words / Michele Phoenix. Harpercollins Christian Pub, 2017 336 p.

ISBN 9780718086442

1. Historic documents 2. Victims of terrorism 3. Religious persecution 4. Coping 5. Huguenots 6. Faith (Christianity) 7. Historical research 8. Translating and interpreting 9. France 10. Christian historical fiction 11. Parallel narratives

LC 2017013000

Michele Phoenix crafts a poignant story of a young woman recovering from the evils of this world through perseverance, hope, and the light in a centuries-old document.

Piatote, Beth H., 1966-

The **beadworkers** : stories / Beth Piatote. Counterpoint, 2019. 208 p.

ISBN 9781640092686

1. Indians of North America 2. Indians of North America -- Social life and customs 3. Indigenous peoples 4. Culture conflict 5. Pacific Northwest 6. Literary fiction 7. Historical fiction 8. Short stories

LC 2019017873

Told with humor, subtlety, and beautiful spareness, the mixed-genre works of Beth Piatote's first collection find unifying themes in the strength of kinship, the pulse of longing, and the language of return. Formally inventive, witty, and generous, The Beadworkers, a singular debut collection, draws on Indigenous aesthetics and forms to offer a powerful, sustaining vision of Native life in the Americas.

Piccirilli, Tom

The **last** kind words / Tom Piccirilli. Bantam Books, 2012. 352 p.

ISBN 9780553592481

1. Criminals 2. Brothers 3. Murder investigation 4. Families 5. Murder 6. Death row prisoners -- Family relationships 7. Redemption 8. Guilt in men 9. Long Island, New York 10. Thrillers and suspense 11. Crime fiction

Sequel: The Last Whisper in the Dark

Resolving to pursue an honest life after his brother goes on a murderous rampage and is sentenced to execution, Terrier Rand learns that his brother did not commit one of the killings for which he was sentenced and resolves to learn what really happened that day.

Piccirilli, Tom

The **last** whisper in the dark : a novel / Tom Piccirilli. Bantam Books, 2013. 336 p.

ISBN 9780345529008

1. Criminals 2. Brothers 3. Swindlers and swindling 4. Robbery 5. Enemies 6. Long Island, New York 7. Thrillers and suspense 8. Crime fiction

LC 2012043223

Sequel to: The Last Kind Words

A follow-up to The Last Kind Words finds youngest son Terry, a surviving member of the Rand family of cat burglars and con artists, endeavoring to go straight before becoming enmeshed in a heist gone wrong that pits him against an old nemesis and threatens to permanently estrange him from the woman he once loved.

Pickard, Nancy

The **scent** of rain and lightning : a novel / Nancy Pickard. Ballantine Books, 2010. 319 p.

ISBN 9780345471017

1. Family secrets 2. Dreams 3. Conspiracies 4. Families of murder victims 5. Greed 6. Best friends 7. Redemption 8. Precognition 9. Former convicts 10. City life 11. Mysteries

The man convicted of murdering Jody's father, Billy Crosby, is being released from prison and returning to the small town of Rose, Kansas. Crosby has been granted a new trial, thanks in large part to the efforts of his son, Collin, a lawyer who has spent most of his life trying to prove his father's innocence. As Jody revisits old wounds, startling revelations compel her to uncover the dangerous truth about her family's tragic past.

"Well-plotted, clearly written mystery novels are always welcome. A novel that simultaneously qualifies as a gripping read, a master character study and as literary is more than welcome--it is exceedingly rare." Kansas City Star.

Picoult, Jodi, 1966-

Change of heart : a novel / Jodi Picoult. Atria Books, 2008. 460 p.

ISBN 9780743496742

1. Death row prisoners 2. Transplantation of organs, tissues, etc 3. Repentance 4. Carpenters 5. Murderers 6. Murder 7. Helpfulness in men 8. Trust in women 9. Redemption 10. Medical ethics 11. Truth 12. Mainstream fiction

LC 2007035721

Her life shattered by a devastating act of violence, June Nealon is forced to make a pivotal choice that involves her twelve-year-old daughter and a salvation-seeking criminal.

"Picoult moves the story along with lively debates about prisoner rights and religion." Publishers Weekly.

Picoult, Jodi, 1966-

House rules : a novel / Jodi Picoult. Atria Books, 2010. 544 p.

ISBN 9780743296434

1. Asperger's syndrome 2. Children with autism 3. Forensic sciences 4. Murder investigation 5. Boys with autism 6. Murder suspects 7. Mental illness 8. Mainstream fiction 9. Psychological fiction

LC 2009026381

Unable to express himself socially but possessing a savant-like knack for investigating crimes, a teenage boy with Asperger's Syndrome is wrongly accused of killing his tutor when the police mistake his autistic tics for guilty behavior.

"Emma, a single mother, copes just fine with her teenage sons until the day Jacob is arrested for the murder of his tutor. Jacob has Asperger's, and the cops confuse his symptoms--such as avoiding eye contact--with guilt. Jodi Picoult loses points for ruining what could have been a riveting mystery by establishing Jacob's innocence at the outset. (The real story behind the tutor's death is obvious to the careful reader.) The author has delivered a sweet family drama that doubles as a handbook on Asperger's--not exactly a thrill, but hardly a bad thing." Entertainment Weekly.

Picoult, Jodi, 1966-

Keeping faith : a novel / Jodi Picoult. W. Morrow, 1999. 422 p.

ISBN 0688168256

1. Child custody 2. Mothers and daughters 3. Stigmatization 4. Miracles 5. Faith 6. Single mothers 7. Motherhood 8. Mainstream fiction

LC 98-43953

Faith, a seven-year-old girl whose family is torn apart by divorce, begins talking to God and performing miracles, and her family enters a media circus of believers, critics, medical professionals, and lawyers

Picoult, Jodi, 1966-

Leaving time : a novel / Jodi Picoult. Ballantine Books, 2014. 405 p.

ISBN 9780345544926

1. Mothers and daughters 2. Missing women 3. Animal welfare 4. Missing persons investigation 5. Teenage girls 6. Thirteen-year-old girls 7. Former police 8. Psychics 9. Grief 10. Elephants 11. Mainstream fiction

LC 2014023994

Abandoned by a grief-stricken father and accomplished-scientist mother who disappeared under mysterious circumstances, 13-year-old

Jenna Metcalf approaches a disgraced psychic and a jaded detective in the hopes of finding answers.

"A truly engaging read that crosses through the genres of mystery and the supernatural. The interspersing of elephant behavior information and Alice's journal entries about her subjects provide just the right amount of parallelism." Library Journal.

Picoult, Jodi, 1966-

Lone wolf : a novel / Jodi Picoult. Atria Books, 2012. 480 p.

ISBN 9781439102749

1. Accident victims 2. Parent and adult child 3. Terminal care 4. Families 5. Options, alternatives, choices 6. Fathers and sons 7. Conflict in families 8. Family relationships 9. Brothers and sisters 10. Mainstream fiction 11. Domestic fiction

LC 2011039017

When his father and sister are injured in an accident that has rendered his father comatose, estranged son Edward decides to stop his father's life support so that his organs can be donated, a choice his sister urges him to reconsider.

Picoult, Jodi, 1966-

My sister's keeper / Jodi Picoult. Atria Books, 2004. 432 p.

ISBN 0743454529

1. People with leukemia 2. Sisters 3. Suing (Law) 4. Donation of organs, tissues, etc 5. Thirteen-year-old girls 6. Sixteen-year-old girls 7. Lawyers 8. Young men 9. Former lawyers 10. Parent and child 11. Family relationships 12. Mainstream fiction 13. Domestic fiction

Originally published: London: Hodder & Stoughton, 2004.

Includes book club discussions questions.

First published: 2004.

Abraham Lincoln Illinois High School Book Award, 2006.

Black-Eyed Susan Book Award (Maryland), High School, 2007.

Heartland Award, 2006.

Pennsylvania Young Reader's Choice Awards, Young Adult, 2007.

Virginia Readers' Choice Award for High School, 2007.

Conceived to provide a bone marrow match for her leukemia-stricken sister, teenage Anna begins to question her moral obligations in light of countless medical procedures and decides to fight for the right to make decisions about her own body.

Picoult, Jodi, 1966-

Nineteen minutes : a novel / Jodi Picoult. Atria Books, 2007. 464 p.

ISBN 0743496728

1. Bullying and bullies 2. School shootings 3. Trials (Murder) 4. Seventeen-year-old boys 5. High school students 6. Lawyers 7. Crimes against teenagers 8. Women judges 9. Small-town life -- New Hampshire 10. Mass shootings 11. New Hampshire 12. Mainstream fiction

LC 2006049276

Originally published: New York: Simon & Schuster; London: Hodder & Stoughton, 2007.

Includes book club discussion questions.

Iowa High School Book Award, 2010.

In the aftermath of a small-town school shooting, lawyer Jordan McAfee finds himself defending a youth who desperately needs someone on his side, while detective Patrick Ducharme works with a primary witness, the daughter of the judge assigned to the case.

Picoult, Jodi, 1966-

Sing you home : a novel / Jodi Picoult. Pocket Books, 2011. 496 p.

ISBN 9781439102725

1. Embryo transfer -- Moral and ethical aspects 2. Lesbian couples 3. Reproductive technology 4. Music therapists 5. Lesbians -- Rights 6. LGBTQIA rights 7. Infertility 8. Divorced couples 9. Human embryo 10. Embryo freezing 11. Fundamentalists 12. Psychological fiction 13. Mainstream fiction 14. Domestic fiction

Ten years of infertility issues culminate in the destruction of music therapist Zoe Baxter's marriage, after which she falls in love with another woman, Vanessa, and wants to start a family; but her ex-husband, Max, in the grips of an anti-gay pastor, stands in the way.

"Picoult may have an agenda, but she has written an immensely entertaining melodrama with crackerjack dialogue." USA Today.

Picoult, Jodi, 1966-

A **spark** of light : a novel / Jodi Picoult. Ballantine Books, 2018. 352 p.

ISBN 9780345544988

1. Women's health centers and clinics 2. Pregnant women 3. Hostages 4. Women hostages 5. Hostage negotiations 6. Physicians 7. Nurses 8. Crime and guns 9. Police 10. Mainstream fiction

LC 2018018966

When a deranged gunman forces his way into the Center, a women's reproductive health services clinic, and takes hostages, the police hostage negotiator discovers his daughter is inside the clinic.

Picoult, Jodi, 1966-

The **storyteller** / Jodi Picoult. Atria Books, 2013. 460 p.

ISBN 9781439102763

1. Intergenerational friendship 2. Guilt in men 3. Holocaust (1933-1945) 4. Retired teachers 5. Former Nazis 6. Assisted suicide 7. Bakers 8. Friendship 9. Good and evil 10. Psychological fiction 11. Mainstream fiction 12. Parallel narratives

Becoming friends with Josef Weber, an old man who's particularly loved in her community, Sage Singer is shocked when one day he asks her to kill him and reveals why he deserves to die, causing her to question her beliefs--and to wonder if his request would be murder or justice.

Picoult, Jodi, 1966-

Vanishing acts : a novel / Jodi Picoult. Atria Books, 2005. 432 p.

ISBN 0743454545

1. Girl kidnapping victims 2. Recovered memory 3. Kidnapping 4. Adult children of divorced parents 5. Parental kidnapping 6. Senior men 7. Hopi Indians -- Spiritual life 8. Search dogs 9. Memories 10. Memory 11. Identity (Psychology) 12. Men/women relations 13. Love triangles 14. New Hampshire 15. Arizona 16. Mainstream fiction

LC 2004059454

Working with the Search and Rescue bloodhound team to find missing people, single mother Delia Hopkins anticipates her upcoming nuptials, until a series of unsettling flashbacks threatens to devastate her life and the lives of those she loves.

"Picoult weaves together plot and characterization in a landscape that is fleshed out in rich, journalistic detail, so that readers will come away with intriguing questions rather than pat answers." Publishers Weekly.

Piercy, Marge

Gone to soldiers : a novel / Marge Piercy. Summit Books/ Simon & Schuster, 1987. 703 p.

ISBN 9780671634216

1. Second World War era (1939-1945) 2. Women and war 3. World War II -- Women's participation 4. Jews 5. Jewish women 6. Lesbians 7. Women pilots 8. Historical fiction 9. War stories 10. Literary fiction

LC 86030118

Women serve in World War II in a variety of roles, and a female journalist is finally allowed to cover the war.

Piercy, Marge

Sex wars / Marge Piercy. William Morrow, 2005. 416 p.

ISBN 0060789832

1. Stanton, Elizabeth Cady, 1815-1902 2. Anthony, Susan B (Susan Brownell), 1820-1906 3. Woodhull, Victoria C (Victoria Claflin), 1838-1927 4. Vanderbilt, Cornelius, 1794-1877 5. Comstock, Anthony 6. Gilded Age (1865-1898) 7. American Civil War era (1861-1865) 8. Suffragists 9. Women's rights 10. Power (Social sciences) 11. Immigrants, Russian 12. Immigrants 13. Immigrants, Jewish 14. Women immigrants 15. Widows 16. Political science 17. Ethics 18. Scandals 19. Sexuality 20. Condoms 21. Birth control 22. Civil war 23. United States Civil War, 1861-1865 24. New York City 25. United States -- History -- Civil War, 1861-1865 -- Influence 26. Historical fiction 27. Literary fiction

LC 2005041499

Coming of age in a post-Civil War New York City tenement flat, Jewish-Russian Freydeh juggles multiple jobs to earn passage for her family, until she learns that her younger sister is adrift somewhere in the city.

"This is an enjoyable book--usually entertaining and, in its best sections, engrossing. In Woodhull and Freydeh, Piercy has created fascinating portraits of women determined to live on their own terms. As the freewheeling Gilded Age gives way to a growing conservatism that traps both women, observant readers will notice obvious parallels to our own time." Christian Science Monitor.

Piercy, Marge

Vida : a novel / Marge Piercy. Fawcett Crest, 1989, c1979. 477 p.

ISBN 0671401106

1. 1960s 2. 1970s 3. Marxism 4. Political activists 5. Women radicals 6. Men/women relations 7. Sexuality 8. Psychological fiction

LC 79019298

Vida, an antiwar activist during the 1960s, goes underground in 1970 after being associated with a bombing.

"This novel is not 'simply' a novel but a political brief. I have my differences with 'Vida,' but I think they are substantive rather than literary. It is an interesting--and challenging--book. . . . Marge Piercy has written about movement people before but never, I think, as lovingly as here." New York Times Book Review.

Pietroni, Anna Lawrence

Ruby's spoon : a novel / Anna Lawrence Pietroni. Spiegel & Grau, 2010. 366 p.

ISBN 9781400068685

1. 1930s 2. Factories 3. Eccentrics and eccentricities 4. Witchcraft 5. City life 6. England -- Social conditions -- 20th century 7. Black Country (England) -- Social conditions -- 20th century 8. Historical fiction

LC 2009034841

A depression-era factory town in England is turned upside-down by an enigmatic white-haired newcomer from the coast who particularly influences a motherless 13-year-old girl, a middle-aged bachelor and the factory's Oxford-educated spinster heir.

"The author knows her territory as thoroughly as Ruby, and she has created an evocative fairy tale that slowly pulls a reader under as surely as one of the mermaids the locals tell legends about. . . . The Black Country English dialect her characters speak takes some getting used to, but it's more than showboating. Lawrence Pietroni is able to conjure an entire lost world through their words, and the writing of Ruby's Spoon is one of its chief pleasures." Christian Science Monitor.

Pike, Signe

The **lost** queen / Signe Pike. Touchstone, 2018. 576 p. Lost queen (Signe Pike)

ISBN 9781501191411

1. 6th century 2. Medieval period (476-1492) 3. Women rulers 4. Civilization, Celtic 5. Druids and druidism 6. Twin brothers and sisters 7. Merlin (Legendary character) 8. Culture conflict -- Religious aspects 9. Christianity 10. Saxons 11. Political intrigue 12. Courage in women 13. Belief and doubt 14. Scotland -- History -- 6th century 15. Scotland -- History -- To 1057 16. Arthurian fantasy 17. Historical fantasy

LC 2018002985

Reveals the untold story of Languoreth--a forgotten queen of sixth-century Scotland and twin sister of the man who inspired the legend of Merlin--as her family fights for the survival of their kingdom against the encroaching forces of Christianity and the Anglo-Saxons.

"Pike's narrative blends court intrigue, romantic interludes, and gritty violence into a literary brew worth savoring to the dramatic finale. The elements of Celtic mysticism will appeal to fantasy fans looking for a Mists of Avalon-type experience, while the setting remains grounded in sixth-century Scotland's political realities. Enthusiastically recommended for readers of female-centered historical sagas and those enamored of Arthurian tales." Booklist.

Pilcher, Rosamunde

Coming home / Rosamunde Pilcher. St. Martin's Press, 1995. 728 p.

ISBN 0312958129

1. Second World War era (1939-1945) 2. 1930s 3. 1940s 4. Families -- Great Britain 5. Growing up 6. World War II -- Great Britain 7. Social classes 8. Great Britain -- History -- 20th century 9. Coming-of-age stories 10. War stories 11. Historical fiction 12. Gentle reads

LC 95021656

Later printing issued by St. Martin's Paperbacks.

Judith Dunbar comes of age while confronting her feelings about love and sadness and journeying back to her childhood home

"The book's heroine is Judith Dunbar, who is a schoolgirl of 13 when the tale begins in 1935. Sent to boarding school in Cornwall because her parents are posted to Singapore, Judith becomes friends with Loveday Carey-Lewis, who introduces her to a family and an estate, Nancherrow, that is to influence her for the rest of her life. Pilcher does a marvelous job of describing life in England before World War II." Booklist.

Pilcher, Rosamunde

* The **shell** seekers / Rosamunde Pilcher. St. Martin's Press, 1987. 530 p.

ISBN 9780312010584

1. Family relationships 2. Motherhood 3. Greed 4. Artists 5. Painting 6. Children of artists 7. Families 8. London, England 9. Cornwall, England 10. Family sagas 11. Gentle reads

LC 87028345

"It is a measure of this story's strength and success that a reader can be carried for more than 500 pages in total involvement with Penelope, her children, her past and the painting that hangs in her country cottage. 'The Shell Seekers' is a deeply satisfying story, written with love and confidence." New York Times Book Review.

Pinborough, Sarah, 1972-

* Behind her eyes : a novel / Sarah Pinborough. Flatiron Books, 2017. 320 p.

ISBN 9781250111173

1. Control (Psychology) 2. Secrets 3. Manipulation (Social sciences) 4. Psychologists 5. Husband and wife 6. Female friendship 7. Personal assistants 8. Single mothers 9. Mistresses 10. Flashbacks 11. London, England 12. Psychological suspense

LC 2016037630

The secretary of a successful psychiatrist is drawn into the seemingly picture-perfect life of her boss and his wife before discovering a complex web of controlling behaviors and secrets that gradually reveal profound and dangerous flaws in the couple's relationship.

Pinborough, Sarah, 1972-

* Cross her heart : a novel / Sarah Pinborough. William Morrow, 2018. 352 p.

ISBN 9780062856791

1. Promises 2. Betrayal 3. Obsession 4. Teenage girls 5. Single mothers 6. Female friendship 7. Mothers and daughters 8. Secrets 9. Overprotectiveness in parents 10. Honesty 11. Stalking 12. Stalkers 13. Psychological suspense

LC 2018002651

A devoted single parent hides the truth about her daughter's absent father and asks her best friend for help when challenges from her past threaten her teenage daughter.

Pinborough, Sarah, 1972-

Dead to her : a novel / Sarah Pinborough. William Morrow, 2020. 352 p.

ISBN 9780062856821

1. Newlyweds 2. Cheating (Interpersonal relations) 3. Upper class 4. Jealousy 5. Revenge 6. Mistresses 7. Seduction 8. Secrets 9. Remarriage 10. Savannah, Georgia 11. Psychological suspense 12. Thrillers and suspense

LC 2019032506

Navigating her new husband's complicated social circle and wandering eye, a mistress-turned-wife becomes ruthless when her husband begins an affair with his boss's own second wife.

"With Dead to Her, Pinborough plants her flag as the master of seductively sinister suspense. This absorbing tale will satisfy and even surprise fans of Jennifer McMahon and Gillian Flynn." Booklist.

Pineiro, Caridad, 1958-

One summer night / Caridad Pineiro. Sourcebooks Casablanca, 2017. 352 p. At the shore novels

ISBN 9781492649649

1. Family businesses 2. Real estate developers 3. Family feuds 4. Neighbors 5. Vacation homes 6. Beaches 7. Heirs and heiresses 8. Helpfulness in men 9. Businesspeople 10. Coastal towns 11. Sexual attraction 12. Men/women relations 13. New Jersey 14. Contemporary romances

To save her family's business, Jersey girl Maggie Sinclair is forced to ask Jax Pierce for help--despite the fact that the Sinclairs and Pierces have been feuding for nearly 30 years--a decision that causes them to both risk everything.

Pinsker, Sarah

* A song for a new day / Sarah Pinsker. Berkley, 2019. 372 p.

ISBN 9781984802583

1. Post-apocalypse 2. Women musicians 3. Social isolation 4. Terrorism 5. Epidemics 6. Virtual reality 7. Lesbians 8. Near future 9. Music 10. Concerts 11. Crowds 12. Social change 13. Social science fiction

LC 2019011852

Public gatherings are illegal making concerts impossible, except for those willing to break the law for the love of music, and for one chance at human connection.

Pinter, Jason

Hide away / Jason Pinter. Thomas & Mercer, 2020. 367 p. Rachel Marin novels

ISBN 9781542005906

1. Single mothers 2. Widows 3. Women vigilantes 4. Loss (Psychology) 5. Murder investigation 6. Protectiveness in women 7. Small towns 8. Illinois 9. Thrillers and suspense

From the bestselling author of the Henry Parker series comes a page-turning thriller about a vigilante who's desperate to protect her secrets--and bring a killer to justice.

"Pinter does a masterful job of ramping up suspense about the Marin family's past and the current case, spinning an absolutely riveting plot with a cast of full-bodied, fallible characters, in what seems the start of a promising series." Booklist.

Pintoff, Stefanie

Hostage taker : a novel / Stefanie Pintoff. Bantam Books, 2015. 448 p. Eve Rossi novels

ISBN 9780345531407

1. Hostages 2. Women FBI agents 3. Hostage taking 4. Guilt 5. Criminals 6. Cathedrals 7. Loss (Psychology) 8. New York City 9. Thrillers and suspense

LC 2015001375

FBI hostage negotiator Eve Rossi is burned out and on leave when a shooting in Manhattan turns into a hostage situation at the iconic St. Patrick's Cathedral. Called back to work, Eve is hampered by a hostage taker who won't identify himself -- and makes only bizarre demands. Also not helping: intense pressure from the Catholic Church, the media, and the mayor. The behind-the-scenes views of St. Patrick's add an unusual element to a well-paced and increasingly tense story (and likely series debut). -- Description by Shauna Griffin.

"Strong writing, a well-paced plot, and intriguing characters make this one of the best thrillers of the year." Library Journal.

Pintoff, Stefanie

In the shadow of Gotham / Stefanie Pintoff. Minotaur Books, 2009. 400 p. Simon Ziele mysteries

ISBN 9780312544904

1. Columbia University. 2. 1900s (Decade) 3. Police 4. Murder investigation 5. Women murder victims 6. Criminologists 7. Women college graduates 8. Fiances -- Death 9. Murder suspects 10. New York City -- History -- 20th century 11. Westchester County, New York 12. Historical mysteries 13. Mysteries

LC 2008045676

Edgar Allan Poe Award for Best First Novel by an American Author, 2010.

Having relocated to Westchester County after losing his fiancée, detective Simon Ziele investigates a young woman's brutal murder, follows leads to a local criminologist's violent subject, and wonders if someone is imitating the lead suspect.

"The author has inevitably been compared to Caleb Carr. . . . She does an outstanding job of blending historical detail with engaging characters and a suspenseful plot." Denver Post.

Pipkin, John
   Woodsburner : a novel / John Pipkin. Nan A. Talese, 2009. 384 p. cm.
   ISBN 9780385528658
   1. Thoreau, Henry David, 1817-1862 2. 1840s 3. Forest fires 4. Philosophers 5. Interpersonal relations 6. Walden Pond region, Massachusetts 7. Massachusetts 8. Biographical fiction 9. Historical fiction
                                             LC 2008033233
   Massachusetts Book Awards, Fiction Award, 2010.
   Henry Thoreau accidentally sets fire to three hundred acres near nineteenth-century Concord, Massachusetts and affects the lives of three people, a Norwegian farmhand, a bookseller and aspiring playwright, and a preacher, as they respond to the disaster.
   "Pipkin doesn't underplay Thoreau's horror at what he's done (or overplay the inherent irony of the author of Walden burning down the woods). Instead, he concentrates on the ability of a natural disaster to act as a catalyst in people's minds and lives. The result is, well, transcendent." Christian Science Monitor.

Pirie, David, 1946-
   The **patient's** eyes / David Pirie. St. Martin's Minotaur, 2002, c2001. ix, 244 p. Dark beginnings of Sherlock Holmes
   ISBN 0312290950
   1. Doyle, Arthur Conan,, Sir, 1859-1930 2. Bell, Joseph, 1837-1911 3. 19th century 4. Physicians 5. Forensic scientists 6. Amateur detectives 7. Heirs and heiresses 8. Women stalking victims 9. Visions in women 10. Criminal investigation 11. Stalking 12. Edinburgh, Scotland -- History -- 19th century 13. Scotland 14. Historical mysteries 15. Mysteries
   Young medical student Arthur Conan Doyle teams up with his mentor, Dr. Joseph Bell, to investigate a Victorian murder mystery involving a phantom cyclist and a rich Spanish businessman.
   "A 'fictional' account of Arthur Conan Doyle's early life that relates how his association with Edinburgh physician Joseph Bell was the inspiration for his Holmes character. Pirie vividly evokes the dark ambience of Victorian England, his prose is elegant, and his gift for mimicking the slightly haughty tone of Doyle's writing is uncanny." Booklist.

Pirro, Jeanine
   Sly fox : a Dani Fox novel / Jeanine Pirro. Hyperion, 2012. 304 p. Dani Fox mysteries
   ISBN 9781401324575
   1. 1970s 2. Women assistant district attorneys 3. Child sexual abuse 4. Trials 5. Family violence 6. Women lawyers 7. Public prosecutors 8. Westchester County, New York 9. Legal stories 10. Mysteries
                                             LC 2011038932
   While investigating a series of brutal crimes against women and children in 1978 New York, young Assistant District Attorney Dani Fox stumbles upon one of her most challenging cases yet when she goes after a successful businessman who has been secretly molesting his young daughter for years.

Pirrone, D. M.
   Shall we not revenge / D.M. Pirrone. Allium Press of Chicago, 2014. 334 p. Hanley & Rivka mysteries
   ISBN 9780989053532
   1. 1870s 2. Detectives 3. Religious communities 4. Political corruption 5. Murder investigation 6. Organized crime 7. Police

misconduct 8. Police corruption 9. Survival (after disaster) 10. Welfare 11. Orthodox Jews 12. Irish Americans 13. Chicago, Illinois -- History -- 19th century 14. Historical mysteries
                                             LC 2014011252
   Shortly after the Great Chicago Fire of 1871, Irish detective Frank Hanley is assigned the case of a murdered rabbi. He is aided in his investigation by the rabbi's daughter, Rivka. They uncover political corruption involving Irish gangsters and a prominent relief organization. Provided by publisher.

Pistalo, Vladimir, 1960-
   Tesla : a portrait with masks / Vladimir Pistalo ; translated from the Serbian by Bogdan Rakic and John Jeffries. Graywolf Press, 2015, c2008. 452 p.
   ISBN 9781555976972
   1. Tesla, Nikola, 1856-1943 2. Inventors 3. Eccentrics and eccentricities 4. Electrical engineers 5. Electrical engineering 6. Obsessive-compulsive disorder 7. Biographical fiction 8. Historical fiction 9. Translations -- Serbian to English
   Originally published: Zrenjanin : Agora, 2008.
   A historical novel attempts to capture the inner life of Nikola Tesla during the whirlwind years of the dawn of the electrical age, when his flair for showmanship kept him in the public eye, despite the loss of his older brother, his mistrust of institutional support and his flashes of madness.
   "This is the great empathetic work that fiction can do: taking a life from the past and making it relatable. A moving, inventive and poetic work of biographical fiction." Kirkus.

Pitoniak, Anna
   Necessary people / Anna Pitoniak. Little Brown & Co, 2019. 352 p.
   ISBN 9780316451703
   1. Ambition in women 2. Class conflict 3. Television industry and trade 4. Competition in women 5. Rich women 6. Best friends 7. Class consciousness 8. Interclass friendship 9. Television news 10. Television journalism 11. Women television newscasters and commentators 12. New York (State) 13. Psychological suspense
   In a novel set against the fast-paced backdrop of TV news, the author of The Futures offers a work of psychological suspense about ambition and privilege and the thin line between friendship and rivalry.

Pittman, Allison
   The **seamstress** / Allison Pittman. Tyndale House, 2019. 416 p.
   ISBN 9781496440181
   1. 1780s 2. French Revolution, 1789-1799 3. Orphans 4. Social change 5. Young women 6. Seamstresses 7. Revolutionaries 8. Poverty 9. Christians 10. Faith (Christianity) 11. Men/women relations 12. France -- History -- 18th century 13. Christian historical fiction 14. Adaptations, retellings, and spin-offs
                                             LC 2018027835
   "1788: In a tiny French village, during the waning days of peace, cousins Renee and Laurette live a peaceful, relatively contented life as the shepherdesses under the guardianship of the respectable Emile Gagnon. When Renee is given the chance to work as a seamstress at the Palace at Versailles, their lives take two very different paths straight into the heart of the Revolution. Based on a character who appears in the classic, A Tale of Two Cities"--Provided by publisher.

Pitts, Leonard

Freeman / Leonard Pitts. Agate, 2012. 432 p.

ISBN 9781932841640

1. Searching 2. Forced relocations 3. African American husband and wife 4. Loyalty 5. Slavery 6. Civil war 7. Teachers 8. Race relations 9. Fugitive slaves 10. Separated couples 11. Voyages and travels 12. United States -- History -- 1865-1898 13. Historical fiction 14. Love stories 15. War stories 16. African American fiction

BCALA Literary Award for Fiction, 2013.

"At the end of the Civil War, an escaped slave first returns to his old plantation and then walks across the ravaged South in search of his lost wife."--Provided by the publisher.

Plaidy, Jean, 1906-1993

The **captive** Queen of Scots / Jean Plaidy. G. P. Putnam's Sons, 1970, c1963. 410 p. Mary Queen of Scots novels

ISBN 0399101160

1. Mary,, Queen of Scots, 1542-1587 2. Medieval period (476-1492) 3. Scottish Stewart period (1371-1603) 4. 16th century 5. Elizabethan era (1558-1603) 6. Tudor period (1485-1603) 7. Women rulers 8. Treason 9. Women prisoners 10. Catholic women 11. Illegitimate children of royalty 12. Half-brothers and sisters 13. Inheritance and succession 14. Heirs and heiresses 15. Scandals 16. Conspiracies 17. Political corruption 18. Scotland -- History -- Mary Stuart, 1542-1567 19. Great Britain -- History -- Elizabeth I, 1558-1603 20. Biographical fiction 21. Historical fiction

LC 72105579

Originally published: London : Robert Hale, 1963.

"The story of the last 18 years of Queen Mary's life, during which she was first a prisoner of her Scottish enemies and later, after a dramatic escape and flight to England, the captive of her archenemy, Queen Elizabeth. Treated with at least some respect due a queen, Mary is pictured with her retinue of loyal friends and servants, living in varying degrees of discomfort and confinement as she moved from one castle to another at the whim of Elizabeth. She emerges as a generous, overly trustful, emotional victim, attractive even as she grew older though not wise, who met her tragic fate because she could not cope with the treachery and intrigue of both friends and enemies." Booklist.

Plaidy, Jean, 1906-1993

Murder most royal / Jean Plaidy. G. P. Putnam's Sons, 1972, c1949. 543 p. Tudor series (Jean Plaidy)

ISBN 039910934X

1. Anne Boleyn,, Queen, consort of Henry VIII, King of England, 1507-1536 2. Henry VIII,, King of England, 1491-1547 Wives 3. Jane Seymour,, Queen, consort of Henry VIII, King of England, 1509?-1537 4. Catherine Howard,, Queen, consort of Henry VIII, King of England, d 1542 5. Tudor period (1485-1603) 6. Executions and executioners 7. Women rulers 8. Royal houses 9. Rulers 10. Widowers 11. Courts and courtiers 12. Inheritance and succession 13. Heirs and heiresses 14. Mistresses 15. Remarriage 16. Extramarital affairs 17. Betrayal 18. Great Britain -- History -- Henry VIII, 1509-1547 19. Great Britain -- History -- Tudors, 1485-1603 20. England -- History -- 16th century 21. Historical fiction 22. Biographical fiction

LC 79189782

Originally published: London : Hale, 1949.

Anne Boleyn and her younger cousin Catherine Howard face similar fates in their lives at court.

"Concentrating on Anne Boleyn and her younger cousin Catherine Howard, the author follows the two from childhood to death on the block, with her usual thoroughness, sentimentality, and overdramati-

zation, sparing the reader few details of torture, violence, intrigue, or thwarted love affairs." Booklist.

Plaidy, Jean, 1906-1993

The **pleasures** of love : the story of Catherine of Braganza / Jean Plaidy. G. P. Putnam's Sons, 1992, c1991. 329 p. Queens of England

ISBN 0399137319

1. Catharine of Braganza,, Queen of England, 1638-1705 2. Charles II,, King of England, 1630-1685 3. Stuart period (1603-1714) 4. Women rulers 5. Childlessness 6. Royal houses 7. Rulers 8. Courts and courtiers 9. Catholic women 10. Mistresses 11. Inheritance and succession 12. Political corruption 13. Great Britain -- History -- Charles II, 1660-1685 14. Historical fiction 15. Biographical fiction

LC 91034593

Originally published: London : Hale, 1991.

Although Charles II continues to have affairs after marrying Catherine of Braganza, he loves her and refuses to divorce her merely because she is barren.

Plaidy, Jean, 1906-1993

William's wife / Jean Plaidy. G.P. Putnam's Sons, 1993, c1992. 276, 1] p. Queens of England

ISBN 0399138072

1. Mary II, Queen of Great Britain, 1662-1694 2. William III, King of Great Britain, 1650-1702 3. James II,, King of Great Britain, 1633-1701 4. Stuart period (1603-1714) 5. 17th century 6. Women rulers 7. Royal houses 8. Rulers 9. Courts and courtiers 10. Marriages of royalty and nobility 11. British in the Netherlands 12. Loyalty 13. Extramarital affairs 14. Political corruption 15. Great Britain -- History -- William and Mary, 1689-1702 16. Netherlands -- History -- 17th century 17. Historical fiction 18. Biographical fiction

LC 92032588

Originally published: London : Hale, 1992.

In an era shaped by a power struggle between Catholic and Protestant forces, Princess Mary, heir to the throne of England, is forced to marry the dour, power-hungry William of Orange, who is involved in a blatant affair with Elizabeth Villiers.

Plain, Belva

Crescent City : a novel / Belva Plain. Delacorte Press, 1984. 429 p.

1. American Civil War era (1861-1865) 2. 1860s 3. Jewish American women -- New Orleans, Louisiana 4. Jewish American families 5. Civil war 6. United States Civil War, 1861-1865 7. United States -- History -- Civil War, 1861-1865 8. New Orleans, Louisiana -- History -- Civil War, 1861-1865 9. New Orleans, Louisiana -- History -- 19th century 10. Family sagas 11. Historical fiction 12. Gentle reads

LC 84005045

Plain, Belva

The **golden** cup / Belva Plain. Delacorte Press, 1986. 399 p. Werner family saga

ISBN 0440130913

1. 1910s 2. Jewish American women 3. Suffragists 4. Marriage 5. Jewish families 6. Husband and wife 7. New York City 8. Love stories 9. Family sagas 10. Historical fiction 11. Gentle reads

LC 86008851

"The author invests her story with dignity and historical relevance while insightfully depicting the class consciousness of Progressive Era Americans." Publishers Weekly.

Plain, Belva

Harvest / Belva Plain. Delacorte Press, 1990. 409 p. Werner family saga

1. 1960s 2. Jewish American women 3. Jewish American families 4. Motherhood 5. Dysfunctional families 6. Love stories 7. Family sagas 8. Historical fiction 9. Gentle reads

LC 90034417

The Werner family saga continues as Iris and Theo's marriage dissolves, their son Steve is drawn to the charismatic son of Paul Werner's niece Meg, and Paul finds himself drawn to Theo.

Plain, Belva

Tapestry / Belva Plain. Dell Publishing, 1989, c1988. 554 p. Werner family saga

1. Second World War era (1939-1945) 2. 1940s 3. Jewish American families 4. Jewish American men 5. Extramarital affairs 6. World War II 7. Holocaust (1933-1945) 8. Bankers 9. New York City 10. Family sagas 11. Historical fiction 12. Gentle reads

LC 87022346

Previously issued by Delacorte Press, 1988.

"Paul Werner, the key figure of a powerful New York banking family, is the protagonist in this saga of one man's concerns with the impending doom of World War II and the plight of his German-Jewish relatives and friends. Paul is caught in a passionless, childless marriage, and he struggles for years with the memory and reality of his first love and subsequent affairs of the heart." Library Journal.

Plath, Sylvia

* The **bell** jar / Sylvia Plath ; foreword by Frances Mc-Cullough ; biographical note by Lois Ames ; drawings by Sylvia Plath. HarperCollins, 1996, c1948. xviii, 296 p.

ISBN 0060174900

1. Women with depression 2. Mental illness 3. Women with mental illnesses 4. Women authors, American 5. Nervous breakdown 6. Women college students 7. Women 8. Suicidal behavior 9. Psychological fiction 10. Autobiographical fiction 11. Modern classics 12. Literary fiction

LC 96211742

Originally published: New York : Harper & Row, 1948.

Presents the American poet's semi-autobiographical account of Esther Greenwood, a talented writer who struggles for intimacy and meaning in her artist life.

Pobi, Robert

City of windows / Robert Pobi. Minotaur Books, 2019. 336 p. Dr Lucas Page novels

ISBN 9781250293947

1. Astrophysicists 2. Former FBI agents 3. People who have had amputations 4. Crime scenes 5. College teachers 6. Snipers 7. Murder investigation 8. FBI agents 9. Families 10. City life 11. New York City 12. Mysteries

LC 2019006904

When his former partner is murdered by an unusually skilled sniper, a disabled former FBI agent with an exceptional ability for reading difficult crime scenes struggles to outmaneuver a killer during a historical blizzard.

"Relentless pacing, tight plotting, and a brainy, idiosyncratic new hero make this one a winner." Kirkus.

Pochoda, Ivy

These women / Ivy Pochoda. Ecco Press, 2020. 256 p. ISBN 9780062656384

1. Women -- Psychology 2. Violence against women 3. Serial murderers 4. Poverty 5. Street life 6. Sexism 7. Racism 8. Minorities 9. Loss (Psychology) 10. City life 11. Neighborhoods 12. Los Angeles, California 13. Thrillers and suspense 14. Literary fiction

Connected by the deadly obsessions of a single man, five very different women endure lives of danger and anguish, including a mother whose daughter's murder remains unsolved.

"This deep dive into the lives of women too often unseen in the shadows makes them vividly unforgettable." Publishers Weekly.

Pochoda, Ivy

Visitation Street : a novel / Ivy Pochoda. Ecco, 2013. 306 p.

ISBN 9780062249890

1. Missing persons investigation 2. Secrets 3. Life change events 4. Neighborhoods 5. Missing teenage girls 6. Interpersonal relations 7. City life -- Brooklyn, New York City 8. Brooklyn, New York City 9. New York City 10. Mysteries

When an adventure on the bay takes a tragic turn, resulting in her best friend's disappearance, Val, who was washed ashore semi-conscious, is left to deal with the aftermath, while their teacher, a Julliard drop-out and barfly, must confront a past riddled with sins of omission.

"The prose is so lyrical and detailed that readers will easily imagine themselves in Red Hook. A great read for those who enjoy urban mysteries and thrillers with a literary flair." Library Journal.

Poe, Edgar Allan, 1809-1849

* **Complete** stories and poems of Edgar Allan Poe Doubleday, 1966. ix, 821 p.

ISBN 9780385074070

1. Anthologies 2. Short stories 3. Horror 4. Mysteries 5. Classics 6. Gothic fiction 7. Poetry

LC 66024310

A complete collection of the writings of Poe, including his mysteries, fantasies, satires, and poems

Poe, Edgar Allan, 1809-1849

The **narrative** of Arthur Gordon Pym of Nantucket / Edgar Allan Poe. Dover Publications, 2005, c1838. ix, 155 p.

ISBN 0486440931

1. Survival (after airplane accidents, shipwrecks, etc) 2. Stowaways 3. Sailors 4. Whaling ships 5. Young men 6. Mutiny 7. Nantucket, Massachusetts 8. Sea stories 9. Classics 10. Gothic fiction

LC 2004061804

"This Dover edition, first published in 2005, is an unabridged republication of the first edition of the work originally published in 1838 by Harper & Brothers, New York"--T.p. verso.

Originally published: New York: Harper & Brothers, 1838.

A horror tale presented in journal form by Pym, a young man who is smuggled aboard the brig Grampus in 1827. Mutiny, cannibalism, fantastic animals and natives of Antarctica, and supernatural happenings comprise a story of adventure in the South Seas.

Poe's children : the new horror : [edited by] Peter Straub. Doubleday, 2008. 544 p.

ISBN 9780385522830

1. Ghosts 2. Obsession 3. Revenge 4. Horror 5. Ghost stories 6. Short stories

LC 2008003013

An anthology of modern horror fiction features tales from twenty-five masters of the genre, with such selections as Stephen King's "The Ballad of the Flexible Bullet," Dan Chaon's "The Bees," and Peter Straub's "Little Red."

"An impressive, highly personal assortment of perspectives and techniques. The result is a remarkably consistent, frequently unsettling book that does as much to blur the artificial boundary between genre fiction and literature as any anthology in living memory. . . . [The anthology] transcends genre labels and deserves to be recognized for what it is: first-rate fiction." Washington Post Book World.

Pohl, Frederik

Chernobyl : a novel / Frederik Pohl. Bantam Books, 1987. 355p.

ISBN 0553052101

1. Chernobyl Nuclear Accident, 1986

LC 86047896

Dramatizes the human stories of the Chernobyl disaster, and chronicles the accident's day-to-day impact on personal lives, the dreadful future toll on the world, and the effect the catastrophe has on Russian political policies

"The author re-creates in fiction the massive 1986 Ukrainian nuclear power plant disaster. The book opens during normal days just before the accident; suspense builds, as the reader expects the worst. Characters that would actually have been on the scene are seen being overwhelmed by berserk technology, their lives shattered. The tale is gripping, and the locale well established." Library Journal.

Pohl, Frederik

Gateway / Frederik Pohl. Ballantine Books, 1977. 313 p. Heechee saga

ISBN 0345346904

1. Alien artifacts 2. Space flight 3. Far future 4. Corporations 5. Voyages and travels 6. Space flight 7. Space vehicles 8. Asteroids 9. Chance 10. Technology 11. Robots 12. Aliens (Humanoid) 13. Space opera 14. Science fiction

LC 76-10561

Hugo Award for Best Novel, 1978.

John W. Campbell Memorial Award for Best Science Fiction Novel, 1978.

Locus Award for Best Science Fiction Novel, 1978.

Nebula Award for Best Novel, 1977.

The Heechee gateways, remnants of an ancient civilization, provide instantaneous passage to the far reaches of the universe but do not ensure destination, return, wealth, or survival.

Pohl, Frederik

The **space** merchants / Frederik Pohl and C. M. Kornbluth Thomas Dunne Books, 2011, c1953. 239 p.

ISBN 9781250000156

1. Space colonies 2. Advertising copywriters 3. Mass media and public opinion -- United States 4. Intrigue 5. Corruption 6. Identity theft 7. Overpopulation 8. Corporate power 9. Dystopias 10. Advertising 11. Scarcity -- Social aspects 12. Venus (Planet) -- Exploration 13. Science fiction

Sequel: The merchants' war.

Originally published: New York : Ballantine Books, 1953.

Mitchell Courtenay, an advertising copywriter of the future, is assigned to sway public support for the American colonization of Venus.

"Kornbluth later stated that he and Pohl packed into this story everything they hated about advertising, and it came out with Swiftian savagery. One of the first novels by writers with primary roots in the pulps to make an impact in mainstream circles." Anatomy of Wonder, 4th edition.

Polansky, Daniel

Low town : a novel / Daniel Polansky. Doubleday, 2011. 384 p. Low Town

ISBN 9780385534468

1. Drug dealers 2. Street life 3. Child murder victims 4. Black magic 5. Police corruption 6. Organized crime 7. Murder investigation 8. Drug use 9. Crime bosses 10. Urban fantasy 11. Noir fiction

Leading a life of crime in a back-alley region of the Thirteen Lands's finest city, the Warden discovers a murdered child and is catapulted back to his former life as a secret police agent before embarking on a dangerous game of deception between his former supervisor and dangerous underworld bosses.

Polk, C. L. (Chelsea L.)

Witchmark / C.L. Polk. Tor Books, 2018 318 p. Kingston cycle series

ISBN 9781250162687

1. Magic 2. Veterans 3. Aristocracy 4. Angels 5. Secrets 6. Staged deaths 7. Social classes 8. War and society 9. Men/men relations 10. Military physicians 11. Fantasy fiction 12. Steampunk

World Fantasy Award, 2019.

After going to war to escape his destiny, Miles Singer is unable to leave his past behind when he, after faking his own death, reinvents himself as a doctor at a cash-strapped veteran's hospital where he can no longer hide what he truly is.

Pollock, Donald Ray, 1954-

The **devil** all the time / Donald Ray Pollock. Random House Inc, 2011 304 p.

ISBN 9780385535045

1. 20th century 2. Veterans 3. Serial murderers 4. Violence 5. Fugitives 6. Religious fanaticism 7. Betrayal 8. Ohio -- Rural conditions 9. West Virginia -- Rural conditions 10. Rural noir 11. Crime fiction 12. Literary fiction

Presents a dark tale set in rural southern Ohio and West Virginia between World War II and the 1960s that follows the experiences of tormented and violent individuals whose respective struggles culminate in the adult patterns of an orphaned son.

"The flawless cadence of Pollock's gorgeous shadow-and-light prose plays against the heinous acts of his sorrowful and sometimes just sorry characters." Elle.

Pollock, Donald Ray, 1954-

Knockemstiff / Donald Ray Pollock. Doubleday, 2008. 206 p.

ISBN 9780385523820

1. Small town life -- Ohio 2. Ohio -- Social life and customs 3. Rural noir 4. Short stories 5. Literary fiction

Spanning the era from the mid-1960s to the late 1990s, a collection of stories journeys inside the world of the diverse inhabitants of Knockemstiff, a tough, Midwestern town, as their lives change and intertwine.

"Knockemstiff--real name, real town--is full of the sorriest group of people imaginable, a bunch of damaged souls with crass manners, greasy hair, sour breath, addictions galore and savage tendencies. ... Pollock underscores their struggles with vivid imagery and, at times, a tender touch. . . . Pollock's writing has been compared to that of Flannery O'Connor, Raymond Carver and Cormac McCarthy. He draws his readers in slowly, tangling them in the mundane toil of small-town life, before smacking them upside the head with something unexpected and primal. Small moments yield big surprises." The Oregonian.

Pomerantz, Sharon

* **Rich** boy / Sharon Pomerantz. Twelve, 2010. 528 p.
ISBN 9780446563185
1. Rich people 2. Self-fulfillment 3. Jewish American men 4. Hypocrisy 5. Ambition 6. Classism 7. Identity (Psychology) 8. American dream 9. Men/women relations 10. Manhattan, New York City 11. Philadelphia, Pennsylvania 12. Psychological fiction
LC 2009032386
After he rises from a working-class New York Jewish neighborhood in the 1970s to the cloistered universities of New England to the highest circles of Manhattan society during the Reagan boom, Robert Vishniak sees his carefully crafted identity start to unravel after he bumps into a beautiful woman from the old neighborhood.

"It would spoil Pomerantz's pleasingly soapy narrative to detail too much of Robert's subsequent journey, first in 1960s Boston and then in the go-go Manhattan of the '70s and '80s. But while his tale often feels allegorical . . . Rich Boy is told with such page-turning skill that its pleasures, if not deep, feel rich indeed." Entertainment Weekly.

Pontoppidan, Henrik, 1857-1943,

Lucky Per / Henrik Pontoppidan ; translated by Naomi Lebowitz ; introduction by Garth Risk Hallberg. Everyman's Library, 2019. 608 p.
ISBN 9781101908099
1. 20th century 2. Social change 3. Children of clergy 4. Ambition in men 5. Jewish women 6. Engineers 7. Fate and fatalism 8. Belief and doubt 9. Modernization (Social sciences) 10. Independence in men 11. Philosophy 12. Men/women relations 13. Interfaith couples 14. Copenhagen, Denmark 15. Denmark 16. Coming-of-age stories 17. Classics 18. Translations -- Danish to English
LC 2018053817
A (hbk.) edition of the 1904 novel by Nobel Prize-winning Danish author Henrik Pontoppidan, widely considered "the great Danish novel," but not available in English until recently. In a translation by Naomi Lebowitz, with a new introduction by novelist Garth Risk Hallberg, bibliography, and chronology.

Poole, Sara, 1951-

The **Borgia** mistress / Sara Poole. St. Martin's Griffin, 2012. 416 p. Poisoner mysteries
ISBN 9781250023520
1. Borgia family 2. Alexander VI,, Pope, 1431-1503 3. Renaissance (1300-1600) 4. 15th century 5. Women poisoners 6. Conspiracies 7. Secrets 8. Lovers 9. Alliances 10. Popes 11. Courage in women 12. European Renaissance 13. Italy -- History -- 15th century 14. Rome, Italy -- History -- 15th century 15. Historical mysteries 16. Mysteries
Francesca Giordano joins forces with her lover, Cesare Borgia, in order to decrypt a conspiracy against Pope Alexander VI, after he and the papal court is forced to flee from Rome.

"True to its characters and historical facts, Poole's novel immerses readers in a seductive Renaissance environment, full of danger and passion." Publishers Weekly.

Poore, Michael

Reincarnation blues / Michael Poore. Del Rey, 2017. 400 p.
ISBN 9780399178481
1. Men 2. Quests 3. Reincarnation 4. Death (Personification) 5. Metaphysics 6. Immortality 7. Perfection 8. Karma 9. Death 10. Love 11. Contemporary fantasy 12. Fantasy fiction
A man who has been reincarnated nearly ten thousand times, living lives in regions from ancient India and Renaissance Italy to outer space and the modern world, searches for the secret to immortality so that he can be with his beloved, the incarnation of Death.

"Poore (Up Jumps the Devil) addresses humans relationship to the universe through a clever, personal story filled with gentle humor, wry sweetness, and perhaps even some wisdom." Publishers Weekly.

Pope, Barbara Corrado

The **missing** Italian girl : a mystery in Paris / Barbara Corrado Pope. Pegasus Books, 2013 352 p. Bernard Martin novels
ISBN 9781605984087
1. Belle Epoque (1871-1914) 2. 19th century 3. 1890s 4. Murder 5. Mothers 6. Missing persons 7. Murder investigation 8. Italians in France 9. Judges 10. Detectives 11. Compassion 12. Helpfulness in women 13. Paris, France 14. France -- History -- Third Republic, 1870-1940 15. Historical mysteries 16. Mysteries
Bernard and Clarie Martin are on the case after two young women disappear after having assisted a Russian man throw a dead body into a canal in 1897 Paris.

Pope, Jamie

One warm winter / Jamie Pope. Dafina, 2019. 320 p. Sunny and warm
ISBN 9781496718273
1. Heirs and heiresses 2. Women adoptees 3. Bodyguards 4. Family secrets 5. Scandals 6. Sexual attraction 7. Islands 8. Contemporary romances 9. Multicultural romances
Wynter Bates, who was adopted as a child by a tech billionaire, tries to ignore her attraction to her bodyguard, Cullen Whelan, whom she is pretending to date, while investigating her true parentage after a scandal is exposed.

Porter, Chana, 1984-

The **seep** : a novel / Chana Porter. Soho, 2020 203 p.
ISBN 9781641290869
1. Aliens 2. Utopias 3. Trans women 4. Loss (Psychology) 5. Fifties (Age) 6. Change 7. Coping 8. Identity (Psychology) 9. Quests 10. Science fiction
LC 2019023457
Living in a utopian world shaped by alien invaders who make any dream possible, a 50-year-old trans woman is devastated by the end of her marriage before an unexpected quest pits her against the aliens? most avid supporters.

"Porter's gripping, subtly hopeful work of literary speculative fiction is shaped by remarkable world-building elements and acute observation of human frailties and impetus." Booklist.

Porter, Henry, 1953-

The **bell** ringers / Henry Porter. Atlantic Monthly Press, 2010, c2009. 288 p.
ISBN 9780802119315
1. Women intelligence officers 2. Conspiracies 3. Privacy -- Government policy 4. Terrorism 5. Inheritance and succession 6. Murder 7. Secrecy in government 8. England 9. Political thrillers 10. Thrillers and suspense 11. Spy fiction
Originally published as The dying light: London : Orion, 2009.
After her ex-boyfriend, a former head of intelligence, is killed, Kate Lockhart inherits his dangerous secrets, all having to do with the Orwellian reality this near-future England has become, and she soon finds herself on the run from the security-obsessed state.

"The tale is set in England, where cameras identify license plates and faces, computers catalog phone and financial records, and submitting an incomplete form can be a felony. What's to prevent a prime minister from abusing these powers? Just a few committed (if sometimes cliched) characters, some intricately complex plotting and gobs of local color. The world of The Bell Ringers isn't as dystopian as 1984, but it's not that far off." Cleveland Plain Dealer.

Porter, Henry, 1953-

Firefly / Henry Porter. The Mysterious Press, 2018, c2018. 480 p. Paul Samson novels

ISBN 9780802128959

1. M I 6 2. ISIS (Islamic State of Iraq and Syria) 3. Teenage refugees 4. Intelligence service 5. International intrigue 6. Terrorists 7. National security 8. Thirteen-year-olds 9. Intelligence officers 10. Spies -- Great Britain 11. North Macedonia 12. Syria 13. Europe 14. Spy fiction 15. Thrillers and suspense

LC 2018026964

Originally published by Quercus, 2018.

An ex-MI6 agent-turned-detective races to find a 13-year-old refugee in the mountains of Macedonia who holds vital intelligence about a terrorist threat targeting the center of Europe.

Porter, Henry, 1953-

White hot silence / Henry Porter. Mysterious Press, 2019. 448 p. Paul Samson novels

ISBN 9780802147530

1. Mafia 2. Kidnapping victims 3. International intrigue 4. Former lovers 5. Financial intrigue 6. Private investigators 7. Humanitarian assistance 8. Former spies -- Great Britain 9. Italy 10. Thrillers and suspense 11. Spy fiction

After being ambushed outside new African refugee centers built by her billionaire husband, a Greek aid worker is kidnapped by the Mafia and her life is threatened in exchange for some explosive information, in the sequel to Firefly.

Porter, Katherine Anne, 1890-1980

* The **collected** stories of Katherine Anne Porter / Katherine Anne Porter. Harcourt, Brace & World, 1979, c1965. viii, 495 p.

ISBN 0156188767

1. Short stories

Originally published: New York :

National Book Award for Fiction, 1966.

Pulitzer Prize for Fiction, 1966.

Twenty-seven short stories by the Pulitzer Prize-winning writer

"These are perfect examples of the short story and are representative not only of the best American writing but of the best in the world." School Library Journal.

Porter, Katherine Anne, 1890-1980

Pale horse, pale rider : three short novels / Katherine Anne Porter. Harcourt Brace Jovanovich, 1990, c1939. 208 p.

ISBN 9780151707553

1. Short stories 2. Modern classics

Three short novels deal with turn of the century family life, a new hired hand, and the World War I homefront and the influenza epidemic.

Porter, Katherine Anne, 1890-1980

Ship of fools / Katherine Anne Porter. Back Bay Books; Little Brown, 1962. 497 p.

ISBN 0316713902

1. 1930s 2. Voyages and travels 3. Middle-aged women 4. Ocean travel -- Atlantic Ocean 5. Ocean liners 6. Atlantic Ocean 7.

Allegories

LC 629557

An unforgettable voyage of discovery and self-delusion aboard the vessel sailing from Mexico to pre-Hitler Germany. These interlocking stories unfold and give us a cross-section view of humanity.

Porter, Max, 1981-

* **Grief** is the thing with feathers / Max Porter. Graywolf Press, 2016, c2015. 114 p.

ISBN 9781555977412

1. Fathers and sons 2. Grief 3. Loss (Psychology) 4. Coping 5. Men-headed families 6. Mothers -- Death 7. Widowers 8. London, England 9. Literary fiction

Originally published: London : Faber & Faber, 2015.

ALA Notable Book, 2017.

A recently widowed father of two has difficulty dealing with his grief and the overwhelming sadness of his children, until they are visited by Crow, an actual crow, who serves as an antagonist, protector, therapist and babysitter and helps them heal.

"Porter's daringly strange story skirts disbelief to speak, engagingly and effectively, of the pain this world inflicts, of where the ghosts go, and of how we are left to press on and endure it all." Kirkus.

Porter, Max, 1981-

* **Lanny** : a novel / Max Porter. Graywolf Press, 2019. 213 p.

ISBN 9781555978402

1. 21st century 2. Mythical creatures 3. Missing boys 4. Villages 5. Missing persons investigation 6. Eccentric boys 7. Mischief in boys 8. Families 9. Artists 10. Spirits 11. Supernatural 12. Blame 13. Mass media 14. Social conflict 15. England 16. Literary fiction

ALA Notable Book, 2020.

Longlisted for the Booker Prize, 2019.

Follows the awakening of a mythical being in a London village, where he observes the domestic dramas and creative energies surrounding a mischievous, ethereal young newcomer.

Porter, Regina

The **travelers** / Regina Porter. Random House Inc, 2019 320 p.

ISBN 9780525576198

1. 1950s 2. 2000s (Decade) 3. Families -- History 4. Interpersonal relations 5. Intergenerational relations 6. African Americans -- Social conditions 7. African American families 8. Interracial couples 9. Consequences 10. Race relations 11. United States -- Race relations 12. Literary fiction 13. African American fiction

A first novel by an award-winning playwright follows the experiences of two American families, one black and one white, against a backdrop of historical events from the 1950s through the first year of Barack Obama's presidency.

Portis, Charles

* The **dog** of the South Knopf, 1979. 245 p.

ISBN 9780394506142

1. Runaway wives, husbands, etc 2. Jilted men 3. Chases 4. Former journalists 5. Former husbands 6. Little Rock, Arkansas 7. Humorous stories 8. Picaresque fiction

LC 78067580

Ray Midge is on the trail of his wife Norma, who's headed for Mexico with her ex-husband. On the way Ray meets the eccentric Dr. Reo Symes, a man with more get-rich-quick schemes than common sense. Together, they'll have to overcome tropical storms, grifters, and plenty of car trouble en route to their destination--wherever that may be.

"Simultaneously hilarious and heart breakingly odd. . . you find yourself laughing so hard in sections that tears run down your face." Baltimore Sun.

Portis, Charles

* **Gringos** : a novel / Charles Portis. Simon and Schuster, 1991. 269 p.

ISBN 9780671724573

1. Swindlers and swindling 2. Expatriates 3. Cults 4. Archaeological thefts 5. New Age 6. Cult leaders 7. Americans in Mexico 8. Mayas -- Antiquities 9. Yucatan Peninsula 10. Humorous stories

LC 90042476

Follows the fortunes of Jimmy Burns, an American expatriate living a simple life in Mexico until his peace is shattered by the arrival of a band of hippies seeking psychic happenings and a woman tracking UFO landing sites

"'Gringos,' by far, is Portis's most inward-turning book, a story of a grownup trying to grow up, to keep it together with some dignity. Watching him pull it off is one of the finest pleasures afforded by any novel in a long time." Newsweek.

Portis, Charles

* **Masters** of Atlantis : a novel / Charles Portis. A. A. Knopf, 1985. 247 p.

ISBN 9780394546834

1. 1910s 2. Delusions 3. Secret societies 4. Occult centers, groups, etc 5. Americans in France 6. Atlantis (Legendary place) 7. Misfits (Persons) 8. France 9. Humorous stories

LC 85040212

When Lamar Jimmerson "comes across a little book crammed with Atlantean puzzles, Egyptian riddles, and extended alchemical metaphors," he's convinced that he is called to lead the Gnomon Society in the search for truth concerning the lost city of Atlantis.

"The plot spins dizzily along as sly Sydney Hen and antic Austin Popper are drawn into the society, engineer a farcical schism, and espouse assorted crackpot causes. . . . Those who enjoy deadpan comedy should get a good laugh here." Library Journal.

Portis, Charles

* **True** grit : a novel / Charles Portis. Simon and Schuster, 1968. 215 p.

ISBN 9780671203016

1. Texas Rangers. 2. 1870s 3. Revenge 4. Fathers -- Death 5. Outlaws 6. United States marshals 7. Independence in teenage girls 8. Alcoholic men 9. Fourteen-year-old girls 10. Reminiscing in old age 11. Pioneer teenagers -- The West (United States) 12. The West (United States) 13. Westerns

LC 200234552

With her papa's pistol tied to her saddlehorn and a supersized ration of audacity, fourteen-year-old Mattie Ross sets out to avenge her father's murder.

Potenza, Carol

Hearts of the missing / Carol Potenza. Minotaur Books, 2018. 368 p.

ISBN 9781250178282

1. Tribal police 2. Indians of North America 3. Missing persons 4. Suicide 5. Women detectives 6. Pueblo Indians 7. Murder investigation 8. Dead -- Desecration 9. Spirituality 10. Gambling on Indian reservations 11. New Mexico 12. Mysteries

LC 2018027002

A prize-winning debut novel follows the experiences of Pueblo Police Sergeant Nicky Matthews, who investigates a personally relevant case involving the serial murders of genetic members of the Fire-Sky tribe by a killer who also deliberately violates spiritual laws.

"Potenza's polished, page-turning debut shares Hillermans thoughtful exploration of Native identity, story-driving cultural tension, and evocative setting." Booklist.

Potok, Chaim

The **gift** of Asher Lev / Chaim Potok. Fawcett Columbine, 1997, c1990. 369 p.

ISBN 9780449001158

1. Jewish Americans -- Brooklyn, New York City 2. Hasidim -- Brooklyn, New York City 3. Artists 4. Cultural differences 5. Middle-aged men 6. Jewish American men 7. Homecomings -- New York (State) 8. New York City 9. Brooklyn, New York City 10. Domestic fiction

LC 89043401

Sequel to: My name is Asher Lev.

Originally published: New York : Knopf, 1990.

National Jewish Book Award for Fiction, 1991.

When the death of a beloved uncle brings him back to his native Brooklyn after two decades, painter Asher Lev is plunged into a conflict between the culture into which he was born and the life that he has forged for himself.

Potok, Chaim

* **My** name is Asher Lev / Chaim Potok. Anchor Books, 2003, c1972. 369 p.

ISBN 9781400031047

1. Jewish families -- Brooklyn, New York City 2. Culture conflict 3. Identity (Psychology) 4. Self-fulfillment in men 5. Art 6. Hasidim -- Brooklyn, New York City 7. Artists 8. Jewish Americans -- Brooklyn, New York City 9. New York City 10. Crown Heights, New York City 11. Brooklyn, New York City 12. Coming-of-age stories

LC 70171131

Sequel: The gift of Asher Lev.

Originally published: New York : Knopf, 1972.

Records the anguish and triumps of a young painter as he emerges into the great world of art and rejects all else.

Potzsch, Oliver

The **beggar** king / Oliver Potzsch ; translated from the German by Lee Chadeayne. Houghton Mifflin Harcourt, 2013, c2010. 544 p. Hangman's daughter tales

ISBN 9780547992198

1. 1660s 2. 17th century 3. Murder investigation 4. Innocence (Law) 5. Sisters -- Death 6. Men/women relations 7. Executions and executioners 8. Fathers and daughters 9. Poisoning 10. Villages 11. Germany -- History -- 17th century 12. Historical mysteries 13. Translations -- German to English 14. Mysteries

Originally published Henkerstochter und der Konig der Bettler: Berlin : Ullstein, 2010.

After the hangman Jakob Kuisl is framed for his sister's murder, his daughter Magdalena and her paramour, Simon, enlist the help of a network of beggars in order to save him from the noose.

Potzsch, Oliver

The **dark** monk : a hangman's daughter tale / Oliver Potzsch ; translated from the German by Lee Chadeayne. Mariner Books, 2012. 528 p. Hangman's daughter tales

ISBN 9780547807683

1. Knights Templar (Masonic order) 2. 1660s 3. 17th century 4. Murder investigation 5. Monks 6. Poisoning 7. Villages 8. Treasure

hunting 9. Thieves 10. Executions and executioners 11. Germany -- History -- 17th century 12. Historical mysteries 13. Translations -- German to English 14. Mysteries

LC 2012014848

Originally published Henkerstochter und der schwarze Monch: Berlin : Ullstein, 2009.

A follow-up to The Hangman's Daughter traces the 1648 investigation by hangman Jakob Kuisl, his headstrong daughter and the town physician into the poisoning murder of a priest whose demise is precariously linked to the Crusades and the Knights Templar treasure.

Potzsch, Oliver

The **hangman's** daughter : a historical novel / Oliver Potzsch ; translated from the German by Lee Chadeayne. AmazonCrossing, 2010, c2008. 435 p. Hangman's daughter tales

ISBN 9781935597056

1. 1660s 2. 17th century 3. Executions and executioners 4. Witchcraft 5. Pariahs 6. Murder investigation 7. Villages 8. Midwives 9. Magic (Occultism) 10. Torturers 11. Missing children 12. Germany -- History -- 17th century 13. Historical mysteries 14. Translations -- German to English 15. Mysteries

"First published in Germany in 2008 by Ullstein Buchverlage GmbH as Die henkerstochter"--T.p. verso.

Germany, 1659: When a dying boy is pulled from the river with a mark crudely tattooed on his shoulder, hangman Jakob Kuisl is called upon to investigate whether witchcraft is at play in his small Bavarian town. Whispers and dark memories of witch trials and the women burned at stake just seventy years earlier still haunt the streets of Schongau. When more children disappear and an orphan boy is found dead, marked by the same tattoo, the mounting hysteria threatens to erupt into chaos. Before the unrest forces him to torture and execute the very woman who aided in the birth of his children, Jakob must unravel the truth. With the help of his clever daughter, Magdalena, and Simon, the university-educated son of the town's physician, Jakob discovers that a devil is indeed loose in Schongau. But it may be too late to prevent bloodshed. A brilliantly detailed, fast-paced historical thriller, The Hangman's Daughter is the first novel from German television screenwriter Oliver Pötzsch, a descendent of the Kuisls, a famous Bavarian executioner clan.

Potzsch, Oliver

The **play** of death / Oliver Potzsch ; translated by Lee Chadeayne. Mariner Books, 2017, c2016. 544 p. Hangman's daughter tales

ISBN 9781328662088

1. 17th century 2. Executions and executioners 3. Murder investigation 4. Villages 5. Crucifixion 6. Passion-plays 7. Actors and actresses 8. Christianity -- Rites and ceremonies 9. Immigrant workers 10. Sons-in-law 11. Conspiracies 12. Germany -- History -- 17th century 13. Historical mysteries 14. Translations -- German to English

LC 2016051868

Originally published: Berlin : Ullstein, 2016.

Simon Fronwieser and his hangman father-in-law investigate the murder of the actor due to play Christ in a Passion Play, who was found nailed to the set's cross, in the latest addition to the series.

"A veritable Series of Unfortunate Events for adults and perfect for fans of bleak, folktale-laden landscapes and bogeyman heroes . . . ." Booklist.

Potzsch, Oliver

The **poisoned** pilgrim : a hangman's daughter tale / Oliver Potzsch ; translated by Lee Chadeayne. Mariner Books-Houghton Mifflin Harcourt, 2013. 496 p. Hangman's daughter tales

ISBN 9780544114609

1. 1660s 2. 17th century 3. Missing persons 4. Monks 5. Pilgrims and pilgrimages 6. Murder investigation 7. Families 8. Monasteries 9. Inventions 10. Germany -- History -- 17th century 11. Historical mysteries 12. Translations -- German to English 13. Mysteries

Translation from the German of: Hexer und die Henkerstochter.

Originally published: 2012.

In 1666, Magdalena and her physician husband arrive at Andechs Abbey where they, along with the hangman of Schongau, set out to find the mysterious Brother Virgilius, who disappeared after creating an eerie automaton.

Potzsch, Oliver

The **werewolf** of Bamberg / Oliver Potzsch ; translated by Lee Chadeayne. Houghton Mifflin Harcourt, 2015, c2014. 720 p. Hangman's daughter tales

ISBN 9780544610941

1. 1660s 2. 17th century 3. Murder investigation 4. Voyages and travels 5. Vacations 6. Amputation 7. Werewolves 8. Superstition 9. Families 10. Germany -- History -- 17th century 11. Historical mysteries 12. Translations -- German to English 13. Mysteries

Translation from the German of: Die henkerstochter und der teurfel von Bamberg.

Originally published: Germany : Ullstein Buchverlag, 2014.

A 1668 family vacation turns into a nightmare when a series of violent murders are thought to be the work of a werewolf.

Powell, Gareth

* **Embers** of war / Gareth L. Powell. Titan Books, 2018 411 p. Embers of war

ISBN 9781785655180

1. Veterans 2. Space vehicles 3. Artificial intelligence 4. Rescues 5. Atonement 6. Conspiracies 7. Missing persons 8. Intelligence officers 9. Imaginary wars and battles 10. Missing persons investigation 11. People with post-traumatic stress disorder 12. Military science fiction 13. Science fiction mysteries 14. Science fiction

BSFA Award for Best Novel, 2018.

The sentient warship Trouble Dog was built for violence, yet following a brutal war, she is disgusted by her role in a genocide. Stripped of her weaponry and seeking to atone, she joins the House of Reclamation, an organisation dedicated to rescuing ships in distress. When a civilian ship goes missing in a disputed system, Trouble Dog and her new crew of loners, captained by Sal Konstanz, are sent on a rescue mission. Meanwhile, light years away, intelligence officer Ashton Childe is tasked with locating the poet, Ona Sudak, who was aboard the missing spaceship. What Childe doesn't know is that Sudak is not the person she appears to be. A straightforward rescue turns into something far more dangerous, as Trouble Dog, Konstanz and Childe find themselves at the centre of a conflict that could engulf the entire galaxy. If she is to save her crew, Trouble Dog is going to have to remember how to fight... --Provided by publisher

Powell, Mark, 1976-

Firebird / Mark Powell. Haywire Books, 2020. 312 p.

ISBN 9781950182022

1. 2010s 2. Natural gas 3. Corporations 4. Political intrigue 5. International crime 6. Billionaires 7. Men with cancer 8. Illegal arms transfers 9. Money laundering 10. Ukraine 11. United States 12.

Eastern Europe 13. Political thrillers

An arms deal gone south takes you into the underground world of political operatives, Ivy League criminals, and a hedge fund billionaire with eyes on the presidency.

"Powell has created a cast of indelible characters, and he spins an action-packed story of political intrigue and corruption that could be torn from today's headlines." Booklist.

Powell, Padgett

* **Edisto** : a novel / Padgett Powell. Farrar, Straus, Giroux, 1984. 183 p.

ISBN 0374146519

1. Boys 2. Atlantic Coast (South Carolina) 3. Mainstream fiction 4. Coming-of-age stories

LC 83025334

Sequel: Edisto Revisited.

A twelve-year-old boy chronicles his coming of age on a rural strip of coast between Savannah and Charleston

"This is distinctly a tour de force. . . . Powell's ear is acute: one of the pleasures of the book is his ability to catch the nuances of Southern speech." New York Times Book Review.

Power, Susan, 1961-

The **grass** dancer / Susan Power. Putnam's, 1994. 300 p.

ISBN 9780399139116

1. Dakota Indians -- North Dakota 2. Powwows -- North Dakota 3. Seventeen-year-old boys 4. Spirits 5. Witches 6. Family secrets 7. Loss (Psychology) 8. Interpersonal relations 9. Intergenerational relations 10. Native American mysticism 11. North Dakota 12. Mythological fiction 13. Contemporary fantasy

LC 93047199

ALA Notable Book, 1995.

Hemingway Foundation/PEN Award, 1995.

From the 1860s, when two lovers are separated by death, the cosmic drama of the two spirits desperately seeking to be reunited molds the lives and fates of their descendants, in a lyrical debut novel shaped by the lore of the Sioux.

"This is a passionate portrayal of universal human emotions and a vivid account of Native American history and culture." School Library Journal.

Powers, Kevin

* The **yellow** birds : a novel / Kevin Powers. Little, Brown, 2012. 192 p.

ISBN 9780316219365

1. War -- Psychological aspects 2. Iraq War, 2003-2011 3. Soldiers -- United States 4. Military life 5. Stress in men 6. War neuroses 7. Companionship 8. Young men -- Psychology 9. Families of military personnel 10. Combat -- Psychological aspects 11. Basic training (Military education) 12. Iraq -- Military relations -- United States 13. United States -- Military relations -- Iraq 14. War stories 15. Literary fiction

LC 2012019435

Adapted into a film by the same name in 2017.

Guardian First Book Award, 2012.

Hemingway Foundation/PEN Award, 2013.

National Book Award for Fiction finalist, 2012

In the midst of a bloody battle in the Iraq War, two soldiers, bound together since basic training, do everything to protect each other from both outside enemies and the internal struggles that come from constant danger.

Powers, Richard, 1957-

The **echo** maker / Richard Powers. Farrar, Straus and Giroux, 2006. 464 p.

ISBN 0374146357

1. Brothers and sisters 2. People in comas 3. Cognitive disorders 4. Neurologists 5. Medicine 6. Twenties (Age) 7. Memories 8. Capgras syndrome 9. Accidents 10. Head injuries 11. Brain injury 12. Paranoia 13. Men/women relations 14. Interpersonal relations 15. Secrets 16. Reality 17. Nebraska 18. Psychological fiction 19. Literary fiction

LC 2006000093

National Book Award for Fiction, 2006.

Pulitzer Prize for Fiction finalist, 2007.

Twenty-seven-year-old Mark Schluter, suffering from a rare brain disorder that causes him to believe his sister to be an impostor, endeavors to discover the cause of the motor vehicle accident that resulted in his head injury.

"This novel--a kind of neuro-cosmological adventure--is an exhilarating narrative feat. The ease with which the author controls his frequently complex material is sometimes as thrilling to watch as the unfolding of the story itself." Washington Post Book World.

Powers, Richard, 1957-

Generosity : an enhancement / Richard Powers. Farrar, Straus and Giroux, 2009. 304 p.

ISBN 9780374161149

1. College teachers 2. Genetic research 3. Writing 4. Authors 5. Genetics 6. Happiness 7. Optimism 8. College students 9. Literary fiction

LC 2008054249

ALA Notable Book, 2010.

Intrigued by an Algerian woman whose blissful demeanor contrasts with the horrific environment of her home country, Chicago teacher Russell Stone brings her to the attention of others who become equally entranced.

"Depending on personal philosophy, readers will disagree as to whether Generosity has a happy ending. But few will fail to be moved by Thassadit's joyful vision of human life." Dallas Morning News

Powers, Richard, 1957-

The **Gold** Bug Variations / Richard Powers. W. Morrow, 1991. 639 p.

ISBN 9780688098919

1. 1960s 2. 1980s 3. Molecular biologists 4. Extramarital affairs 5. Music 6. Information science 7. Women librarians 8. Genetic code 9. Pattern perception 10. Computer programs 11. Computer viruses 12. Love stories 13. Psychological fiction 14. Literary fiction

LC 90020267

National Book Critics Circle Award for Fiction finalist, 1991

Stuart Ressler, an up-and-coming molecular biologist, finds his career sidetracked by the turmoil of the sixties, and a young couple of the 1980s tries to discover why the biologist abandoned his scientific pursuits.

Powers, Richard, 1957-

Orfeo : a novel / Richard Powers. W.W. Norton & Company, 2014. 352 p.

ISBN 9780393240825

1. Suspicion 2. Time travel 3. Music 4. Retirees 5. Composers 6. Former college teachers 7. Loneliness in men 8. Pennsylvania 9. Thrillers and suspense

LC 2013031952

ALA Notable Book, 2015.

An experimental composer becomes a fugitive after his home microbiology lab, set up to find music in surprising patterns, results in a Homeland Security raid.

Powers, Richard, 1957-

The **overstory** : a novel / Richard Powers. W. W. Norton & Co., 2018 502 p.

ISBN 9780393635522

1. Trees 2. Nature 3. Forests 4. Humans -- Effect of environment on 5. Women and nature 6. Environmentalism 7. Men and nature 8. Biosphere 9. Literary fiction

LC 2017051173

ALA Notable Book, 2019.

Pulitzer Prize for Fiction, 2019.

Pen/Faulkner Award Finalist, 2019

Shortlisted for the Man Booker Prize, 2018.

Presents an impassioned novel of activism and natural-world power that is comprised of interlocking fables about nine remarkable strangers who are summoned in different ways by trees for an ultimate, brutal stand to save the continent's few remaining acres of virgin forest.

"A magnificent achievement: a novel that is, by turns, both optimistic and fatalistic, idealistic without being nave." Kirkus.

Powning, Beth, 1949-

The **sea** captain's wife : a novel / Beth Powning. A.A. Knopf Canada, 2010. 372 p.

ISBN 9780307397102

1. 19th century 2. 1860s 3. Married women 4. Seafaring life 5. Ship captains' spouses 6. Ship captains 7. Children of ship captains 8. Ocean travel 9. Women and the sea 10. Love 11. Literary fiction 12. Historical fiction

As a new wife living on the Bay of Fundy in the 1860s, Azuba craves a life beyond the tea and sewing circles. When her husband, Nathaniel, allows her to join him abroad, she faces tests that only a woman with a tenacious spirit and boundless fortitude could conquer.

Poyer, David

A **country** of our own : a novel of the Civil War at sea / David Poyer. Simon & Schuster, 2003. 429 p. Civil War at sea

ISBN 0684871343

1. Confederate States of America. Navy History 2. United States. Navy History 3. American Civil War era (1861-1865) 4. 1860s 5. Abolitionists 6. Blockade running 7. Spies 8. Confederate soldiers 9. Naval battles 10. Shipwrecks 11. Soldiers 12. Civil war 13. United States Civil War, 1861-1865 14. New Orleans, Louisiana 15. Caribbean Area 16. Fort Sumter (Charleston, SC : Fort) -- Siege, 1861 17. United States -- History -- Civil War, 1861-1865 -- Naval operations 18. Sea stories 19. War stories 20. Historical fiction

LC 2003045435

Sequel to: Fire on the waters.

Reaching the agonizing decision to join the Confederate States Navy, abolitionist Lieutenant Ker Claiborne works to destroy a ship in order to undermine Union finances and experiences confrontations with fellow officers.

"Lt. Ker Claiborne has reluctantly relinquished his commission in the U.S. Navy and joined the Confederacy. He's an anomalya Virginian who opposes slavery. The plot follows Claiborne throughout the South and then across the Atlantic as captain of a highly successful and feared rebel commerce raider. There are enough spies, plots, battles, storms, and shipwrecks to satisfy any reader." Library Journal.

Poyer, David

Fire on the waters : a novel of the Civil War at sea / David Poyer. Simon & Schuster, 2001. 445 p. Civil War at sea

ISBN 0684871335

1. United States. Navy 2. American Civil War era (1861-1865) 3. 1860s 4. Rich men 5. Ships 6. Loyalty 7. Friendship 8. Union soldiers 9. Civil war 10. United States Civil War, 1861-1865 11. Fort Sumter (Charleston, SC : Fort) -- Siege, 1861 12. United States -- History -- Civil War, 1861-1865 -- Naval operations 13. Sea stories 14. War stories 15. Historical fiction

LC 2001020307

Sequel: A country of our own.

With the outbreak of the Civil War, New Yorker Eli Eaker enlists in the Union Navy against his father's wishes and joins the crew of Captain Parker Bucyrus Trezevant, who is sailing south to help protect Fort Sumter.

"An interesting character study of a young man's coming of age as well as an accurate historical novel." Library Journal.

Poyer, David

Overthrow : the war with China and North Korea--fall of an empire / David Poyer. St. Martin's Press, 2019. 320 p. Tales of the Modern Navy

ISBN 9781250220561

1. Strategic alliances (Military) 2. Nuclear weapons 3. Naval battles 4. War 5. International relations 6. Aggression (International relations) 7. High technology weapons 8. Battleships 9. Families 10. Secrets 11. United States -- Foreign relations -- China 12. China -- Foreign relations -- United States 13. Pacific Ocean 14. Sea stories 15. Techno-thrillers

LC 2019024272

Admiral Dan Lenson leads an allied invasion in South China in the hopes of ending World War III, while his wife conducts secret negotiations with Beijing rebels and his daughter fights against a dangerous new epidemic.

"Since this novel supplies little backstory, it will be difficult for newbies to connect the dots at various points in the narrative. Fans, however, will continue to enjoy the ride and will want to get their hands on the next one quickly." Booklist.

Poyer, David

The **whiteness** of the whale / David Poyer. St. Martin's Press, 2013. 320 p.

ISBN 9781250020567

1. Whaling 2. Whales 3. Environmentalists 4. Courage in women 5. Women primatologists 6. Seafaring life 7. Antarctica 8. Thrillers and suspense 9. Adventure stories

Joining six other activists to sail a racing yacht into Antarctic waters to expose a Japanese whaling fleet, disgraced primate behaviorist Sara Pollard finds her courage tested by brutal storms, hostile adversaries and romantic conflicts before encountering a sperm whale with a murderous agenda of its own.

Pratchett, Terry

* The **color** of magic / Terry Pratchett. Harper, 2005. 240 p. Discworld

ISBN 9780060855925

1. Magic 2. Voyages and travels 3. Monsters 4. Dragons 5. Heroes and heroines 6. Adventurers 7. Wizards 8. Fantasy fiction 9. Fantasy classics 10. Humorous stories

LC 83009698

A slightly disorganized and somewhat naive interplanetary tourist named Twoflower joins up with a bumbling wizard and embarks on a chaotic voyage through a world filled with monsters and dragons, heroes and knaves.

Pratchett, Terry

Equal rites / Terry Pratchett. Harper Paperbacks, 2000, c1987. 213 p. Discworld

ISBN 9780061020698

1. Wizards 2. Magic 3. Fantasy fiction 4. Humorous stories

A dying wizard hopes to pass his wisdom on to the eighth son of an eighth son, but when the child comes out female, the future of magic could be in jeopardy.

Pratchett, Terry

The **fifth** elephant : a novel of Discworld / Terry Pratchett. HarperPrism, 2000, c1999. 336 p. Discworld

ISBN 0061051578

1. Police 2. Inheritance and succession 3. Dwarves (Fantasy characters) 4. Werewolves 5. Vampires 6. Royal houses 7. Public officials 8. Fantasy fiction 9. Humorous stories

LC 99043960

Originally published: London: Doubleday,

A new visit to the satiric Discworld involves a search for the missing elephant from the five who support Discworld on their backs, as a stolen scone, a dwarf coronation, and ruby tights get into the act

"Pratchett cheerfully takes readers on an exuberant tale of mystery and invention. . . . Along the way, he skewers everything from monarchy to fascism, as well as communism and capitalism, oil wealth and ethnic identities, Russian plays, immigration, Publishers Weekly.

Pratchett, Terry

Going postal : a novel of Discworld / Terry Pratchett. Harper Collins, 2004. 320 p. Discworld

ISBN 0060013133

1. Swindlers and swindling 2. Magic 3. Postmasters 4. Postal service employees 5. Letter carriers 6. Golem 7. Civil service 8. Postal service 9. Corporations 10. Big business 11. Communication 12. Fantasy fiction 13. Humorous stories

LC 2004047391

Arch-swindler Moist Van Lipwig never believed his confidence crimes were hanging offenses-until he found himself with a noose tightly around his neck, dropping through a trapdoor, and falling into-a government job? By all rights, Moist should have met his maker. Instead, it's Lord Vetinari, supreme ruler of Ankh-Morpork, who promptly offers him a job as Postmaster. Since his only other option is a nonliving one, Moist accepts the position-and the hulking golem watchdog who comes along with it, just in case Moist was considering abandoning his responsibilities prematurely. Getting the moribund Postal Service up and running again, however, may be a near-impossible task, what with literally mountains of decades-old undelivered mail clogging every nook and cranny of the broken-down post office building; and with only a few creaky old postmen and one rather unstable, pin-obsessed youth available to deliver it. Worse still, Moist could swear the mail is talking to him.

"The author's inventiveness seems to know no end, his playful and irreverent use of language is a delight, and there is food for thought in his parody of fantasyland." School Library Journal.

Pratchett, Terry

Guards! Guards! / Terry Pratchett. V. Gollancz, 1989. 288 p. Discworld

ISBN 0575046066

1. Dragons 2. Police 3. Dwarves (Fantasy characters) 4. Fantasy

fiction 5. Humorous stories

LC 91172661

In Anhk-Morpork, the blissful alcoholic oblivion of Vimes is disrupted by the arrival of Carrot, an ambitious dwarf cop who goes on an arresting spree, freeing an enormous dragon in the process.

Pratchett, Terry

The **last** hero : a discworld fable / Terry Pratchett & illustrated by Paul Kidby. HarperCollins, 2001. 160 p. Discworld

ISBN 0061040967

1. Magic 2. Heroes and heroines 3. Good and evil 4. Wizards 5. End of the world 6. Fantasy fiction 7. Humorous stories

LC 2001039188

Cohen the Barbarian. He's been a legend in his own lifetime. He can remember the good old days of high adventure, when being a Hero meant one didn't have to worry about aching backs and lawyers and civilization. But these days, he can't always remember just where he put his teeth. So now, with his ancient (yet still trusty) sword and new walking stick in hand, Cohen gathers a group of his old -- very old -- friends to embark on one final quest. He's going to climb the highest mountain of Discworld and meet the gods. It's time the Last Hero in the world returns what the first hero stole. Trouble is, that'll mean the end of the world, if no one stops him in time.

Pratchett, Terry

Lords and ladies : a novel of Discworld / Terry Pratchett. HarperPrism, 1996, c1992. 281 p. Discworld

ISBN 0061056928

1. Witches 2. Good and evil 3. Dwarves (Fantasy characters) 4. Elves 5. Fantasy fiction 6. Humorous stories

Originally published: 1992.

Irresistibly cute but vicious elves infest the kingdom of Lancre, upsetting plans for a royal wedding and leaving the ordinary citizens helpless, and it is up to the witches, led by Granny Weatherwax, to handle the deadly brutes

Pratchett, Terry

Men at arms : a novel of Discworld / Terry Pratchett. HarperPrism, 1996, c1993. 341 p. Discworld

ISBN 0061092185

1. Police 2. Good and evil 3. Assassins 4. Affirmative action 5. Dwarves (Fantasy characters) 6. Fantasy fiction 7. Humorous stories

Placed in charge of the new recruits guarding Discworld's greatest city, Corporal Carrot investigates the discovery of an ancient document that reveals the existence of the city's secret sovereign, who is Carrot himself

Pratchett, Terry

Monstrous regiment / Terry Pratchett. HarperCollins, 2003. 368 p. Discworld

ISBN 006001315X

1. Dukes and duchesses 2. Patriotism 3. Women soldiers 4. Soldiers 5. Nobility 6. Secret identity 7. Passing (Identity) 8. Gender role 9. Propaganda 10. Magic 11. Imaginary wars and battles 12. Fantasy fiction 13. Humorous stories

LC 2003050800

Running the family inn despite dwindling resources while her brother is away at war, Polly cuts off her hair to join the army and notices that her fellow recruits seem to be hiding secrets of their own.

"Pratchett revels in pricking pomp and assurance, but it isn't going too far to say that of late his real subject, like Wilfred Owen's, is the pit of war. Pratchett's approach may be less lyrical, but he can move from farce to sadness in seconds." New York Times Book Review.

Pratchett, Terry

Pyramids : the book of going forth / Terry Pratchett. V. Gollancz, 1989. 272 p. Discworld

ISBN 9780575044630

1. Rulers 2. Inheritance and succession 3. Fantasy fiction 4. Humorous stories

LC 91155566

BSFA Award for Best Novel, 1989.

Magic and humor are combined in the whimsical story of the hard life of Teppic, a teenage pharaoh who does not have a clue about what he is supposed to do as the new ruler of the desert kingdom of Djelibeybi.

Pratchett, Terry

Reaper man / Terry Pratchett. Victor Gollancz, 1991. 253 p. Discworld

ISBN 0575049790

1. Wizards 2. Magic 3. Fantasy fiction 4. Humorous stories

LC 92231334

When Death is officially retired, chaos ensues on the planet Earth, and Dead Rights activist Reg Shoe is up to his neck in paperwork and poltergeists in his attempts to put Death back on the job.

Pratchett, Terry

Small gods : a novel of Discworld / Terry Pratchett. HarperPrism, 1994, c1992. 344 p. Discworld

ISBN 0061092177

1. Gods and goddesses 2. Magic 3. Fantasy fiction 4. Humorous stories

Originally published: 1992.

Brutha, a simple man leading a quiet life tending his garden, finds his life irrevocably changed when his god, speaking to him through a tortoise, sends him on a mission of peace.

Pratchett, Terry

Thief of time / Terry Pratchett. Harper Collins, 2001. 336 p. Discworld

ISBN 0060199563

1. Wizards 2. Time 3. Thieves 4. Sixteen-year-old boys 5. Clock and watch makers 6. Magic 7. Good and evil 8. End of the world 9. Fantasy fiction 10. Humorous stories

LC 00065347

Originally published: London: Doubleday, 2001.

Carefully reallocating the Time of Discworld to where it is most needed, Monk of History Lu Tze and his apprentice begin a literal race against time when the world's first truly accurate clock threatens to stop Time forever.

"This is Discworld, an adolescent Oz in which far fewer folks are immortal, but long life doesn't entail decrepitude; magic works; and politics and culture are fluid, far off, and mostly for old guys. Spun out of words and wit, it is as light and curiously tasty as cotton candy." Booklist.

Pratchett, Terry

Thud! : a novel of Discworld / Terry Pratchett. HarperCollins, 2005. 384 p. Discworld

ISBN 0060815221

1. Police 2. Murder investigation 3. Magic 4. Dwarves (Fantasy characters) 5. Trolls 6. Women vampires 7. Werewolves 8. Golem 9. Painting 10. Secrets 11. Mines and mineral resources 12. Political science 13. Vimes, Samuel 14. Prejudice 15. Superstition 16. Hate 17. Fear 18. Valleys 19. Fantasy fiction 20. Humorous stories

LC 2005046271

Where's My Cow? is a companion volume to Terry Pratchett's Discworld novel Thud.

A seemingly routine day in the life of City Watch commander Sam Vimes is abruptly interrupted by an unsolved murder, an impending war, an unwanted new recruit, and a pesky government inspector.

"It's all in a day's work for the City Watch in the latest novel set in the author's hilariously surreal Disc World." Library Journal.

Pratchett, Terry

The **truth** : a novel of Discworld / Terry Pratchett HarperCollins, 2000. 336 p. Discworld

ISBN 0380978954

1. Journalists 2. Investigative journalism 3. Newspaper publishers and publishing 4. Fantasy fiction 5. Humorous stories

LC 00031928

Originally published: London: Doubleday, 2000.

William de Worde plunges into the world of investigative journalism after a high official is impeached following a botched murder attempt.

"Pratchett's . . . Discworld novel takes on the press and investigative journalism in a hilarious romp that examines the fleeting nature of truth and lies." Library Journal.

Pratchett, Terry

Witches abroad / Terry Pratchett. V. Gollancz, 1991. 252 p. Discworld

ISBN 0575049804

1. Witches 2. Magic 3. Fantasy fiction 4. Humorous stories

LC 93136323

First published: 1991.

Discworld's own version of the three witches--Magrat Garlick, Granny Weatherwax, and Nanny Ogg--grab their broomsticks and journey to Genua to save Princess Emberella from an overzealous fairy godmother.

Pratchett, Terry

Wyrd sisters / Terry Pratchett. ROC Books, 1988. 319 p. Discworld

ISBN 0451450124

1. Witches 2. Spells (Magic) 3. Black magic 4. Fantasy fiction 5. Humorous stories

Starring three witches, also kings, daggers, crowns, storms, dwarfs, cats, ghosts, spectres, apes, bandits, demons, forests, heirs, jesters, tortures, trolls, turntables, general rejoicing, and divers alarums.

Prcic, Ismet

Shards : a novel / Ismet Prcic. Black Cat , 2011 392 p.

ISBN 9780802170811

1. 1990s 2. Young men -- California 3. Bosnians in the United States 4. Writing -- Psychological aspects 5. Memories -- Psychological aspects 6. Guilt in men 7. Bosnia and Hercegovina 8. California 9. Psychological fiction 10. Literary fiction

A young Bosnian, Ismet Prcic, who has fled his war-torn homeland for California, uses writing to come to terms with his past, while another Bosnian, Mustafa, stays in his country to fight.

"The author's debut is about a young Bosnian, also named Ismet Prcic, who has fled his wartorn homeland and is now struggling to reconcile his past with his present life in California. He is advised that in order to make peace with the corrosive guilt he harbors over leaving his family behind, he must write everything. The result is a great rattlebag of memories, confessions, and fictions: sweetly humorous recollections of Ismet's childhood in Tuzla appear alongside anguished letters to his mother about the challenges of life in this new world. As Ismet's foothold in the present falls away, his writings are further complicated by stories from the point of view of another young man--real or imagined-

-named Mustafa, who joined a troop of elite soldiers and stayed in Bosnia to fight. When Mustafa's story begins to overshadow Ismet's new-world identity, the reader is charged with piecing together the fragments of a life that has become eerily unrecognizable, even to the one living it." Bookreporter.com.

Prescott, Lara

The **secrets** we kept / Lara Prescott. Alfred A. Knopf, 2019. 304 p.

ISBN 9780525656159

1. Pasternak, Boris Leonidovich, 1890-1960 Doktor Zhivago 2. Invinskaya, Olga 3. CIA 4. Women CIA agents 5. Banned books 6. Authors, Russian -- 20th century 7. International intrigue 8. Men/women relations 9. Dissenters 10. Propaganda 11. Typists 12. Cold War 13. Spies 14. Women/women relations 15. Concentration camps -- Soviet Union 16. Soviet Union 17. Washington, D.C. 18. Historical fiction

A tale of spycraft, love and sacrifice inspired by the true story of Doctor Zhivago follows the efforts of two CIA agents to help publish Boris Pasternak's censored masterpiece against a backdrop of Cold War politics in Moscow.

Pressfield, Steven

36 righteous men : a novel / Steven Pressfield. W. W. Norton & Company, 2020, c2019. 320 p.

ISBN 9781324002895

1. Near future 2. End of the world 3. Detectives 4. Serial murder investigation 5. Scars 6. Rabbis 7. Climate change 8. Lamed-vavniks 9. Thrillers and suspense

LC 2019014779

Two New York homicide detectives make an apocalyptic discovery before racing to prevent the murder of a last surviving guardian who would protect the world from destruction.

Preston, Caroline

The **scrapbook** of Frankie Pratt / Caroline Preston. Ecco Press, 2011. 240 p.

ISBN 9780061966903

1. 1920s 2. Scrapbooks 3. Women authors 4. Men/women relations 5. Growing up 6. Moving to a new city 7. Independence in women 8. Historical fiction 9. Diary novels 10. Illustrated books

Using an array of vintage memorabilia, a novel told in the form of a scrapbook follows Frankie Pratt, who goes to Vassar in 1920 with dreams of becoming a writer, which becomes a stepping stone to an international adventure.

Preston, Douglas J.

City of endless night / Douglas Preston & Lincoln Child. Grand Central Publishing, 2018. 416 p. Pendergast novels

ISBN 9781455536948

1. FBI 2. Beheading 3. FBI agents 4. Serial murder investigation 5. Clues 6. Police 7. Billionaires 8. Murder investigation 9. Massachusetts 10. Thrillers and suspense

LC 2017031496

Heading an investigation into the murder of a wealthy tech billionaire's daughter, Lieutenant CDS Vincent D'Agosta teams up with FBI Special Agent A.X.L. Pendergast, only to uncover the work of a serial killer whose agenda threatens an entire city.

Preston, Douglas J.

The **codex** / Douglas Preston. Forge, 2004. 400 p.

ISBN 0765307006

1. Treasure hunting 2. Inheritance and succession 3. Brothers 4. Treasure hunters 5. Veterinarians 6. College teachers 7. Missing persons 8. Art -- Collectors and collecting 9. Fathers and sons 10. Herbal medicine 11. Drug industry and trade 12. Archaeological thefts 13. Manuscripts, Maya 14. Tombs 15. Quests 16. Honduras 17. Thrillers and suspense

LC 2003049427

Sequel: Tyrannosaur Canyon.

"A Tom Doherty Associates book."

The mysterious disappearance of treasure hunter and adventurer Maxwell Broadbent--along with his riches--sends his three sons on a search for their father, who has hidden himself and his treasures, in order to claim their inheritance.

"Fascinating characters, exotic jungle scenery, and surprising twists make this nonstop thrill ride well worth deciphering." Library Journal.

Preston, Douglas J.

Crooked river / Douglas Preston, Lincoln Child. Grand Central Publishing, 2020. 400 p. Pendergast novels

ISBN 9781538747254

1. FBI agents 2. Violence 3. Criminal investigation 4. Foot 5. Oceans 6. Thrillers and suspense

Racing to uncover the mystery of several light green-shoe-clad severed feet found floating in the Gulf of Mexico, Agent Pendergast is faced with the most inexplicable challenge of his career

"There is plenty of suspense, and the action gets bloody. Great storytelling, a quirky hero, and a quirkier plot make this a winner for adventure fans." Kirkus.

Preston, Douglas J.

The **Obsidian** chamber / Douglas Preston & Lincoln Child. Grand Central Publishing, 2016. 416 p. Pendergast novels

ISBN 9781455536917

1. Missing persons 2. Kidnapping 3. Kidnapping victims 4. Missing persons investigation 5. Clues 6. Massachusetts 7. Thrillers and suspense

LC 2016022192

With special agent Pendergast missing and presumed dead and his ward Constance taken captive by a shadowy figure from the past, Pendergast's bodyguard, Proctor, begins an international pursuit of Constance's kidnapper.

"This twisty and bizarre 16th series installment will puzzle and delight fans as well as readers who enjoy locked-room mysteries, international intrigue, shadowy characters with ambiguous moral compasses, and tales that confound and entertain." Library Journal.

Preston, Douglas J.

Old bones / Douglas Preston & Lincoln Child. Grand Central Publishing, 2019. 384 p. Nora Kelly novels (Preston & Child)

ISBN 9781538747223

1. Donner Party 2. Women archaeologists 3. Women FBI agents 4. Expeditions 5. Grave robbing 6. Bones 7. Secrets 8. Violence 9. Searching 10. Gold 11. Greed 12. California 13. Thrillers and suspense

LC 2019006977

Young curator Nora Kelly leads a team in search of the "Lost Camp" of the Donner Party, but as they expose the real truth of what happened, those ancient horrors lead to present-day violence in a case assigned to rookie FBI agent Corrie Swanson.

Preston, Douglas J.

Thunderhead / Douglas Preston & Lincoln Child. Warner Books, 1999. 483 p.

    ISBN 0446523372

    1. Women archaeologists 2. Stalking 3. Quests 4. Archaeologists 5. Anasazi Culture 6. Extinct cities 7. Stalkers 8. Thrillers and suspense 9. Adventure stories

                LC 98037557

Sixteen years after her father's mysterious disappearance, archaeologist Nora Kelly follows in his footsteps, guided by an enigmatic letter, as she embarks on an expedition into the remote canyon country of southeastern Utah to search for Quivira, the fabled Lost City of Gold.

Preston, Douglas J.

Verses for the dead / Douglas Preston, Lincoln Child. Grand Central Pub, 2018 368 p. Pendergast novels

    ISBN 9781538747209

    1. FBI agents 2. Serial murders 3. Serial murder investigation 4. Suicide 5. Letter writing 6. Cemeteries 7. Miami Beach, Florida 8. Thrillers and suspense

Notoriously rogue Agent Pendergast must accept two new challenges: a partner, and a serial killer leaving cryptic notes--along with his victims' hearts--at the graves of women who committed suicide. As he digs deeper, he realizes the brutal new crimes may be just the tip of the iceberg: a conspiracy of death that reaches back decades.

Price, Reynolds, 1933-2011

The **good** priest's son / Reynolds Price. Scribner, 2005. 288 p.

    ISBN 9780743254007

    1. September 11 Terrorist Attacks, 2001 2. Parent and adult child 3. Homecomings 4. Middle-aged men 5. Children of clergy 6. Families 7. Art restorers 8. Widowers 9. Episcopalians 10. Clergy 11. Sick persons 12. Multiple sclerosis 13. African American women 14. Women caregivers 15. North Carolina 16. New York City 17. Domestic fiction 18. Literary fiction 19. Psychological fiction 20. Southern fiction

                LC 2004065383

Visiting his aging Episcopal priest father when his own home is decimated by the September 11 attacks, art conservator Mabry Kincaid meets his father's caregiver, an ambitious African-American woman, and struggles with mixed feelings about his adult daughter.

"This novel is thematically rich--indeed, it is rather bowed by its meanings--and features many pleasing Southern voices, along with an impeccable depiction of the region's deep-rooted traditions." New York Times Book Review.

Price, Reynolds, 1933-2011

Roxanna Slade / Reynolds Price. Scribner, 1998. 301 p.

    ISBN 9780684832920

    1. Women with depression 2. Small town life 3. Family relationships 4. Women 5. Men/women relations 6. Husband and wife 7. Southern States 8. Literary fiction 9. Psychological fiction

                LC 9739167

Roxanna begins her story on her twentieth birthday - a day that introduces her to the harsh realities of adulthood and changes the course of her life forever. From this day on, Roxanna is quick to share with the reader the intimate details of ninety years of life in North Carolina. While she rarely leaves the small town of her youth, Roxanna's vision of the world is shaped by intense passions and loyalties and the certain tragedies of a life long lived.

Price, Richard, 1949-

Clockers / Richard Price. Houghton Mifflin, 1992. 599 p.

    ISBN 0395537614

    1. Crack traffic -- New Jersey 2. Detectives -- New Jersey 3. Drug dealers 4. Drug traffic 5. African American teenagers 6. Identity (Psychology) 7. Brothers 8. New Jersey 9. Mysteries

                LC 91043318

National Book Critics Circle Award for Fiction finalist, 1992

Certain that the young Black man who has confessed to a recent murder is covering for his drug-dealing half-brother, Striker, veteran cop Rocco Klein decides to make Striker's life a nightmare

"This is an incredible course in urban street life, particularly the crack culture." Booklist.

Price, Richard, 1949-

Freedomland / Richard Price. Broadway Books, 1998. 546 p.

    ISBN 9780767900249

    1. Carjacking 2. Public housing 3. Race relations 4. African American men 5. Detectives 6. Women -- Puerto Rico 7. Journalists 8. African Americans 9. Hispanic Americans 10. Working class 11. Minorities 12. Small town life 13. Amusement parks 14. Kidnapping 15. Child murders 16. Single mothers 17. Women journalists 18. New Jersey 19. Psychological fiction 20. Crime fiction

                LC 9810527

A white woman, her hands gashed and bloody, stumbles into an inner-city emergency room and announces that she has just been carjacked by a black man. But then comes the horrifying twist: Her young son was asleep in the back seat, and he has now disappeared into the night.

"Price's characters are, as usual, dead-on, and his eye for unflinchingly capturing humans at their very bestand their very worst is unrivaled." Library Journal.

Price, Richard, 1949-

Lush life / Richard Price. Farrar, Straus, and Giroux, 2008. 464 p.

    ISBN 9780374299255

    1. Police questioning 2. Child abuse and crime 3. Robbery 4. Teenagers 5. Teenage boys 6. Police 7. Child abuse victims 8. Thieves 9. Murder 10. Murder investigation 11. Lower East Side, New York City 12. New York City 13. Crime fiction

Still living on the Lower East Side and waiting tables, thirty-five-year-old Eric Cash has every reason to be jealous of Ike Marcus, an ambitious young man on the way to the top, until he is supposedly gunned down by street thugs while walking one night with Eric.

"Price has been around for what seems like forever, but there's a reason we still read him. Because every sentence is a pleasure. Because he never puts a foot wrong, and never lingers. He takes just enough time to make you care." Esquire.

Price, Richard, 1949-

Samaritan / Richard Price. Knopf, 2003. 377 p.

    ISBN 9781400041824

    1. Victims of violent crimes 2. Men and success 3. Criminal investigation 4. Public housing 5. Detectives 6. Victims of crimes 7. Assault and battery 8. Psychological suspense

Price, Steven, 1976-

By gaslight / Steven Price Farrar, Straus & Giroux, 2016 731 p.

    ISBN 9780374160531

    1. Scotland Yard 2. Victorian era (1837-1901) 3. 1850s 4. Americans in London, England 5. Hoboes 6. Detectives 7. Mutilation 8. Murder

investigation 9. London, England 10. Historical mysteries 11. Victorian mysteries

London, 1885. In a city of fog and darkness, the notorious thief Edward Shade exists only as a ghost, a fabled con, a thief of other men's futures - a man of smoke. William Pinkerton is already famous, the son of a brutal detective, when he descends into the underworld of Victorian London in pursuit of a new lead. His father died without ever tracing Shade; William, still reeling from his loss, is determined to drag the thief out of the shadows.

"Yet Price's novel is entirely contemporary, and assuredly his own: a sweeping tale of hunter and hunted in which the most-dangerous pursuer is always the human heart." Publishers Weekly.

Priest, Cherie

Boneshaker / Cherie Priest. Tor, 2009. 416 p. Clockwork century

ISBN 9780765318411

1. American Westward Expansion (1803-1899) 2. 19th century 3. 1880s 4. Mothers and sons 5. Zombies 6. Inventors 7. Rescues 8. Mad scientist (Concept) 9. Motherhood 10. Seattle, Washington 11. Pacific Northwest 12. Steampunk 13. Alternative histories 14. Horror 15. Pacific Northwest fiction 16. Historical horror

LC 2009018700

Locus Award for Best Science Fiction Novel, 2010.

Commissioned to build a machine that will promote gold-rush landbreaking efforts between Civil War-era Seattle and Alaska, inventor Leviticus Blue inadvertently triggers the release of a deadly gas that transforms people into the living dead, a situation that prompts his teenage son to restore the family reputation years later.

"Intelligent, exceptionally well written and showcasing a phenomenal strong female protagonist who embodies the complexities inherent in motherhood, this yarn is a must-read for the discerning steampunk fan." Publishers Weekly.

Priest, Cherie

Clementine / Cherie Priest. Subterranean, 2010. 208 p. Clockwork century

ISBN 9781596063082

1. 1880s 2. 19th century 3. Women spies 4. Fugitive slaves 5. Intelligence service 6. Conspiracies 7. Strategic alliances (Military) 8. Airships 9. Espionage 10. Race relations 11. Steampunk 12. Alternative histories 13. Spy fiction

Maria Isabella Boyd's success as a Confederate spy has made her too famous for further espionage work, and now her employment options are slim. Exiled, widowed, and on the brink of poverty...she reluctantly goes to work for the Pinkerton National Detective Agency in Chicago. Adding insult to injury, her first big assignment is commissioned by the Union Army. In short, a federally sponsored transport dirigible is being violently pursued across the Rockies and Uncle Sam isn't pleased. The Clementine is carrying a top secret load of military essentials--essentials which must be delivered to Louisville, Kentucky, without delay. Intelligence suggests that the unrelenting pursuer is a runaway slave who's been wanted by authorities on both sides of the Mason-Dixon for fifteen years. In that time, Captain Croggon Beauregard Hainey has felonied his way back and forth across the continent, leaving a trail of broken banks, stolen war machines, and illegally distributed weaponry from sea to shining sea. And now it's Maria's job to go get him.

Priest, Cherie

Dreadnought / Cherie Priest. Tor, 2010. 480 p. Clockwork century

ISBN 9780765325785

1. American Westward Expansion (1803-1899) 2. Nurses 3. Zombies

4. Widows 5. Overland journeys to the Pacific 6. Child-separated fathers 7. Railroad travel 8. Airships 9. United States -- History -- 1865-1898 10. Steampunk 11. Alternative histories 12. Horror 13. Historical horror

Mercy Lynch is just a frustrated nurse who wants to see her father before he dies. But she'll have to survive both Union intrigue and Confederate opposition if she wants to make it off the Union-operated, Tacoma-bound "Dreadnought" alive.

Priest, Cherie

Ganymede / Cherie Priest. Tor Books, 2011. 400 p. Clockwork century

ISBN 9780765329462

1. 1880s 2. Pilots 3. Submarines 4. Brothels 5. Zombies 6. Smuggling 7. New Orleans, Louisiana 8. Steampunk 9. Alternative histories 10. Horror 11. Historical horror

LC 2011021569

In a new steampunk adventure, air pilot Andan Cly and his crew must retrieve a dangerous submersible called Ganymede from the bottom of Lake Pontchartrain near New Orleans.

Priest, Cherie

The **inexplicables** / Cherie Priest. Tor, 2012. 320 p. Clockwork century

ISBN 9780765329479

1. Greed 2. Zombies 3. Monsters 4. Orphans 5. Drug dealers 6. Seattle, Washington 7. Steampunk 8. Alternative histories 9. Horror 10. Pacific Northwest fiction

LC 2012024853

Rector "Wreck 'em" Sherman, a drug dealer haunted by the ghost of a kid he used to know, sneaks over the wall into the wasteland of Seattle where he makes a shocking discovery that changes everything.

Pronzini, Bill

Blue lonesome / Bill Pronzini. Walker, 1995. 207 p.

ISBN 0802732682

1. Accountants 2. Obsession in men 3. Suicide 4. Incest 5. Sexually abused women 6. Murder -- Nevada 7. Amateur detectives 8. Nevada 9. Mysteries

LC 9513049

After a woman that he meets briefly at the Harmony Cafe commits suicide, CPA Jim Messenger uses one clue to uncover a series of lies and a horrible murder that will tear a quiet little town apart

"Two quotes that connect hell, the devil, and loneliness foreshadow the suicide of a woman known as Ms. Lonesome. The often-solitary James Messenger sets out in search of the aloof woman's identity even though he spoke to her only once. He finds himself in Beulah, Nevada, a harsh countryside dominated by embittered people, violent murder, and mulish sensibilities. Pronzini skillfully handles Messenger's quest. He uses jazz to accompany changes in mood, but is not verbose." Library Journal.

Pronzini, Bill

Bones St. Martin's Press, 1985. 196p. Nameless Detective mysteries

1. Private investigators 2. San Francisco, California 3. Mysteries 4. Hardboiled fiction

LC 85001708

"The 'Nameless Detective' is hired by Michael Kiskadon to find out why his father, pulp writer Harmon Crane, committed suicide 35 years ago. This proves to be a locked room puzzle. The twisting plot eventually turns up three murders. This is a crisply written mystery with perfect pacing; new clues are cunningly placed so that reader interest is constantly piqued." Library Journal.

Pronzini, Bill

Crazybone : a "Nameless Detective" novel. Carroll & Graf, 2000. 197 p. Nameless Detective mysteries

ISBN 0786707305

1. Mothers and daughters 2. Ten-year-old girls 3. Private investigators 4. San Francisco, California 5. California 6. Mysteries 7. Hardboiled fiction

The "nameless detective" journeys behind the lush facade of the affluent California community of Greenwood when he investigates an unusual case of insurance fraud and uncovers a complex web of larceny, adultery, betrayal, and murder.

"Pronzini's nameless detective lumbers down the San Francisco Peninsula to a private enclave of wooded estates and walled country clubs to find out why a grieving widow has refused a $50,000 insurance settlement for the accidental death of her husband. The look of 'raw terror' on the woman's face when he confronts her . . . suggests that she might have something to hide, and the nameless hero does a good job of ferreting out her secret. But the real fun comes from watching the old war horse plod through a hostile social environment, observing the swells at their selfish pursuits and making them regret every condescending sneer they threw in his face." New York Times Book Review

Pronzini, Bill

The **crimes** of Jordan Wise / Bill Pronzini. Walker & Co., 2006. 231 p.

ISBN 0802714935

1. 1970s 2. 20th century 3. Accountants -- San Francisco, California 4. Embezzlement 5. Greed 6. Men/women relations 7. Consequences 8. Money addiction 9. Betrayal 10. Violence 11. Authors 12. Virgin Islands 13. Thrillers and suspense 14. Crime fiction

LC 2006046115

Obsessed by the gorgeous Annalise Bonner, who cares only for adventure and the good life, accountant Jordan Wise uses his bookkeeping skills to embezzle half a million dollars from his company and plans an escape to the Virgin Islands.

"Like an expert fisherman, Pronzini spins out his yarn to its inevitable conclusion; there's only one way to end the old story of a lovesick sap and a dame whose appetites can never be satisfied. The Crimes of Jordan Wise is a neat piece of writing: James M. Cain by way of Jimmy Buffett." Washington Post Book World.

Pronzini, Bill

Fever : a Nameless Detective novel / Bill Pronzini. Forge, 2008. 288 p. Nameless Detective mysteries

ISBN 9780765318183

1. Husband and wife -- San Francisco, California 2. Missing persons 3. Abused women 4. Marital conflict 5. Organized crime and gambling 6. Criminal investigation 7. Innocence (Law) 8. Compulsive gambling 9. Gambling 10. Private investigators 11. San Francisco, California 12. California 13. Mysteries 14. Hardboiled fiction

LC 2008005228

"A Tom Doherty Associates book."

Nameless had told Mitchell Krochek that he'd do whatever he could to find his missing wife, Janice. She'd run away before--propelled by a gambling fever that rose ever higher--and Mitch had always taken her back. This time, when Nameless, his partner Tamara, and the agency's chief operative Jake Runyon finally found her in a sleazy San Francisco hotel, she demanded a divorce. A few days later, a beaten and bloody Janice stumbled into the agency begging to go home. No one is surprised when, soon after her homecoming, she disappears again. With Janice missing again, Mitchell is the prime suspect, and as Nameless searches for the truth behind her disappearance, he uncovers a vicious racket that preys on gambling fever victims.

"Mitchell Krochek, who's worried about the gambling addiction of his wife, Janice, hires Nameless to trace Janice, who's disappeared for the fourth time in four years. When Jake Runyon, Nameless's associate, traces Janice to an apartment hotel near their San Francisco office, Nameless and Jake decide to honor Janice's request not to reveal her location to her husband. Later, a battered Janice shows up at the detective agency's office, where she agrees to go home, only to vanish again amid circumstances strongly indicating foul play. . . . This insightful novel will appeal to those who like the mean streets portrayed with understatement and subtlety rather than gory violence." Publishers Weekly.

Pronzini, Bill

* Hardcase Delacorte Press, 1995. 215 p. Nameless Detective mysteries

ISBN 0385305060

1. Private investigators 2. Adoptees -- Identity 3. Family secrets 4. San Francisco, California 5. Mysteries 6. Hardboiled fiction

LC 95005723

Hired to locate a woman's biological parents, the Nameless Detective discovers that the woman's mother had been an emotionally unstable girl raped by a teenage delinquent who is determined to repeat his crime

"This mystery opens as the California PI, approaching 60, marries his longtime girlfriend, Kerry. After a civil ceremony marked by his nervous clumsiness, Nameless takes on a client who wants him to find her birthparents. Melanie Ann Aldrich has just discovered that she was adopted and is sure there's a reason her adoptive parents, who are deceased, kept this information from her. Nameless fairly quickly identifies the woman's birthparents, but that's just the beginning." Publishers Weekly.

Pronzini, Bill

Hellbox / Bill Pronzini. Forge, 2012. 320 p. Nameless Detective mysteries

ISBN 9780765325655

1. Missing persons investigation 2. Missing women 3. Private investigators 4. San Francisco, California 5. Sierra Nevada Mountains 6. California 7. Mysteries 8. Hardboiled fiction

LC 2012011650

"A Tom Doherty Associates book."

When his wife goes missing from their Sierra foothills cabin after spotting a suspicious man, Nameless Detective Bill and his associate, Jake Runyon, launch a search and rescue mission that stretches legal boundaries and pits them against uncaring locals and a brutal adversary.

Pronzini, Bill

Illusions : a "Nameless Detective" novel Carroll & Graf, 1997. 243 p. Nameless Detective mysteries

ISBN 0786704039

1. Private investigators 2. Suicide 3. Suicide investigation 4. Missing persons investigation -- California 5. San Francisco, California 6. Mysteries 7. Hardboiled fiction

LC 97-4274

The "Nameless Detective" investigates the suicide of his estranged friend and detective partner while searching for his missing ex-wife, who holds the secrets to his death.

"Shaken by the suicide of his former partner and onetime best friend, a pathetic figure whose life had shrunk to 'drinking, brooding, building his own private gallows day by day,' Nameless throws himself into a job for a Santa Fe businessman who wants to contact his former wife. The woman is easily found; but before the shamus can cash his check, a second suicide delivers another body blow to his code of ethics and deposits another load of guilt on his conscience. . . . The parallel investigations offer prime examples of Pronzini's ace plotting techniques . . . and if you can take the mood swings, Nameless is a good man to walk you through the noir landscape." New York Times Book Review.

Pronzini, Bill

In an evil time / Bill Pronzini. Walker & Company, 2001. 266 p.

ISBN 0802733530

1. Violence in men 2. Stalkers 3. Stalking 4. San Francisco, California 5. Mysteries

LC 00049996

Jack Hollis steeled himself for what he knew had to be done. His daughter and grandson were threatened. Restraining orders and the police could not help, so his choices were limited. David Rakubian was vicious, abusive and deadly; and he was married to Jack's daughter. Jack would have to succeed to save her, and he would need to hurry, before he lost his nerve.

"[Pronzini] has fashioned a nail-biter out of the issue of domestic abuse and the law's inability to deal with it effectively." Booklist.

Pronzini, Bill

Mourners : a nameless detective novel / Bill Pronzini. Forge, 2006. 288 p. Nameless Detective mysteries

ISBN 0765309327

1. Private investigators 2. Financial planners 3. Husband and wife 4. Sisters of murder victims 5. Grief 6. Funerals 7. San Francisco, California 8. California 9. Mysteries 10. Hardboiled fiction

LC 2005043510

"A Tom Doherty Associates book."

When a suspicious wife reports her husband's inexplicable attendance at the funerals of murdered strangers, the nameless detective and his companions, Tamara and Jake, find themselves compromised in the face of a stalled investigation.

"Pronzini's series becomes more layered and complex with each entry. This time the primary characters are all in one stage or another of mourning, but the only one who recognizes it is the initial subject of the investigation. He is also the only one who understands the timeless omnipresence of grief. . . . A dark, foreboding entry in a classic series." Booklist.

Pronzini, Bill

Nemesis / Bill Pronzini. A Tom Doherty Associates Book, 2013. 352 p. Nameless Detective mysteries

ISBN 9780765325662

1. Private investigators 2. Extortion 3. Frameups 4. Malicious accusation 5. California 6. Mysteries 7. Hardboiled fiction

LC 2013003644

"A Tom Doherty Associates book."

Agreeing to investigate threats by a mysterious extortionist against a newly rich young woman, Jake Runyon makes a series of surprise discoveries that cause him to be wrongfully accused of a crime and his employers to be subjected to a vicious legal vendetta.

Pronzini, Bill

Nightcrawlers / Bill Pronzini. Forge Books, 2005. 304 p. Nameless Detective mysteries

ISBN 0765309319

1. Private investigators 2. Seniors 3. African American women 4. Women kidnapping victims 5. Former police 6. Parents of gay men and lesbians 7. Crimes against gay men and lesbians 8. Violence

against gay men and lesbians 9. Hate crimes 10. Kidnapping 11. Families 12. San Francisco, California 13. Mysteries 14. Hardboiled fiction

LC 2004056323

"A Tom Doherty Associates book."

Unaware of links between a series of gay hate crimes and the kidnapping of a young girl, investigators Bill, Jake, and Tamara tackle difficult cases when Jake pursues leads related to an attack on his son's partner.

"The long-running Nameless series continues to evolve. With the novels no longer exclusively first-person narratives by Nameless, parallel plotlines have been introduced from multiple points of view, giving readers a chance to view Nameless as others see him. And, as always, the novels are never just about crime." Booklist.

Pronzini, Bill

* Quarry Delacorte Press, 1992. 216p. Nameless Detective mysteries

1. Private investigators 2. Arsonists 3. San Francisco, California 4. Mysteries 5. Hardboiled fiction

LC 91015284

"Pronzini can get a shade overwrought . . . but his detective is a welcome journey into yesterday, where a shamus could bend the law and not have to agonize about it for too long afterwards." Booklist.

Pronzini, Bill

Savages : a nameless detective novel / Bill Pronzini. Forge Books, 2007. 304 p. Nameless Detective mysteries

ISBN 0765309335

1. Private investigators 2. Husband and wife -- San Francisco, California 3. Partners of people with breast cancer 4. Sisters 5. Falls (Accidents) 6. Suspicion 7. Accidental death investigation 8. Wife-killing 9. Murder suspects -- San Francisco, California 10. Murder investigation -- San Francisco, California 11. San Francisco, California 12. California 13. Mysteries 14. Hardboiled fiction

Sequel: Fever.

"A Tom Doherty Associates book."

Investigating the death of a woman that has been ruled accidental by the police but that her sister insists was a murder by a known perpetrator, a reluctant Nameless begins to suspect that the victim's sister is telling the truth when he learns unsettling facts about her life.

"San Francisco detective Nameless is asked by a former client to look into the death of her sister, who was trapped in an unhappy marriage. Although the death had been ruled an accident, Nameless finds himself stymied by ethical questions and lack of evidence. Meanwhile, Jake Runyon, a partner in Nameless's agency, is trying to serve a subpoena and gets caught in a case of serial arson and murder. It is hard to find a better crime writer than Pronzini, and his understanding of feminine angst as well as male motivations has made this one of the best detective series ever." Library Journal.

Pronzini, Bill

Spook : a "Nameless Detective" novel / Bill Pronzini. Carroll & Graf, 2003. 240 p. Nameless Detective mysteries

ISBN 0786710861

1. Identity (Psychology) 2. Homeless men 3. Murder victims 4. Murder investigation 5. Homeless people with mental illnesses 6. Private investigators 7. San Francisco, California 8. California 9. Mysteries 10. Hardboiled fiction

LC BL2002012420

After a near brush with death, the Nameless Detective searches for the identity of a gentle, mentally disturbed homeless man who was brutally slain, a search that leads him to a small California town rife with murder and mayhem.

"The case seems simple enough. Spook, a homeless street person, becomes a fixture at a local business; its employees provide assistance as needed for the obviously mentally disturbed individual. He is murdered in an especially heinous assault. His unofficial 'family' wants San Francisco private investigator 'Nameless' to learn his real identity. Nameless hands the case over to his newly hired field operative, Jake Runyon, a former Seattle cop. . . . A fascinating entry in a series that continues to redefine noir fiction even as it honors its roots." Booklist.

Pronzini, Bill

Step to the graveyard easy / Bill Pronzini. Walker & Co., 2002. 165 p.

ISBN 0802733751

1. Gambling 2. Swindlers and swindling 3. Poker 4. Cheating at dice, roulette, etc 5. Deception 6. Redemption 7. San Francisco, California 8. Lake Tahoe (Calif and Nev) 9. Noir fiction

LC 2001055914

Matthew Cape runs into a pair of grifters named Boone and Tanya Judson and they lead him from San Francisco to Lake Tahoe, and just maybe to redemption.

"Compelling modern noir with a thought-provoking conclusion." Booklist.

Pronzini, Bill

The **stolen** gold affair / Bill Pronzini. Forge, 2019. 224 p. Carpenter and Quincannon novels

ISBN 9781250216489

1. 1890s 2. Private investigators 3. Undercover operations 4. Miners 5. Mines and mineral resources 6. Criminal investigation 7. Women private investigators 8. Secrets 9. Couples 10. Men/women relations 11. San Francisco, California 12. California 13. Historical mysteries

While Quincannon goes undercover to investigate a string of gold thefts in a lucrative mine, his bride-to-be, Sabina, tackles an audacious real-estate scam and an abusive young man's villainous secret.

"Attractive characters, a finely tuned plot, and fascinating snippets of California history distinguish this outing." Publishers Weekly.

Pronzini, Bill

The **violated** / Bill Pronzini. Bloomsbury USA, 2016. 256 p.

ISBN 9781632866608

1. Rapists 2. Small towns 3. Murder victims 4. Police 5. Murder 6. Detectives 7. Rape victims 8. Police chiefs 9. Sex offenders 10. Murder investigation 11. Spouses of murder victims 12. California 13. Mysteries

LC 2016025590

When a registered sex offender who has been implicated in a string of attacks is found murdered in a small California town, police chief Griffin Less and detective Robert Ortiz are pressured by a results-oriented mayor as they reconstruct events from the testimonies of the offender's wife and the irate husbands of women victims.

"This is a psychological novel dressed up in a thriller suit, which means the teeth are showing, and Pronzinis skill keeps things moving. Another satisfying tale from a crime master." Booklist.

Pronzini, Bill

A **wasteland** of strangers Walker, 1997. 257 p.

ISBN 0802733018

1. Strangers 2. Small town life 3. Murder suspects 4. Women murder victims 5. Northern California 6. Mysteries

LC 96-50927

The arrival of enigmatic stranger John Faith in Pomo, a small, isolated town in northern California, unleashes a series of ominous events that culminate in the murder of a beautiful and lonely woman, a crime in which Faith becomes the prime suspect.

"The story fairly tears along to the jolting climax. Even after everyone has his or her say in the epilogue, readers still don't know John Faith's secrets. But that mystery is more haunting than maddening. Pronzini's . . . story is a gem." Publishers Weekly.

Prose, Francine, 1947-

Blue angel : a novel / Francine Prose. HarperCollins, 2000. 314 p.

ISBN 006019541X

1. Universities and colleges 2. Teacher-student relationships 3. Scandals 4. Authors 5. College teachers 6. Creative writing teachers 7. Goth culture (Subculture) 8. Campus life 9. New England 10. Satirical fiction 11. Literary fiction

LC 99040564

National Book Award for Fiction finalist, 2000

An ironic look at modern academia offers the chronicle of the trials and tribulations of Swenson, a frustrated college professor who finds that Angela Argo, a post-punk, oft-pierced student, has a brilliant writing talent.

"An ironic gloss on Von Sternberg's tragedy of erotic abasement. . . . Prose's retelling focuses less on the ridiculous and self-destructive behavior of the professor . . . than on the far more laughable (and hazardous) rigidity of the politically correct behavior codes governing his tiny Vermont campus." The New Yorker.

Prose, Francine, 1947-

Goldengrove : a novel / Francine Prose. HarperCollins, 2008. 288 p.

ISBN 9780066214115

1. Grief 2. Sexuality 3. Teenage girls 4. Growing up 5. Loss (Psychology) 6. Thirteen-year-old girls 7. Sisters -- Death 8. Middle class families 9. New England 10. Psychological fiction 11. Coming-of-age stories 12. Literary fiction

LC 2008002112

Grieving after the drowning death of her sister, thirteen-year-old Nico falls into a seductive and dangerous relationship with her sister's enigmatic boyfriend during a summer when she realizes that she has moved beyond the help of her parents.

"Nico's introduction into adult situations is accelerated and scary, and Prose doesn't handle the topic with kid gloves. As Nico's relationship with Aaron progresses, her thoughts about physical intimacy run rampant. Prose expertly conveys the newfound sexual desires teenagers experience as they grow into adults." Deseret News.

Prose, Francine, 1947-

Household saints / Francine Prose. St. Martin's Press, 1981. 227 p.

ISBN 9780312393410

1. 1950s 2. Italian American families 3. Christian saints 4. Husband and wife 5. Marriage 6. Cardsharping 7. Mothers-in-law 8. Women with mental illnesses 9. New York City 10. Literary fiction 11. Magical realism

LC 80029116

In Little Italy during the 1950s, sausage-maker Joseph Santangelo wins a wife in a card game in an unusual story encompassing the lives of three generations of women.

"When Joseph Santangelo, the sausagemaker, wins the bride, Catherine, in a pinochle game, he sets in motion a pattern of events laced with ancient Mediterranean customs, superstition and religion that affect the women in his life. In addition to Catherine, there is his mother, a nonstop oracle of doom, and his Americanized daughter who seeks and perhaps finds Jesus in obsessive domesticity. A skillful fabulist, [the author] . . . not only captures the domestic scenes and smells of Little Italy but allows her 'naifs' to unfold in recognizable earthiness and warmth as they confront life's mysteries." Publishers Weekly.

Prose, Francine, 1947-

Primitive people / Francine Prose. Farrar, Straus, Giroux, 1992. 227 p.

ISBN 9780374237226

1. Rich families 2. Dysfunctional families 3. Au pairs 4. Suburban life 5. Haitians in the United States 6. Undocumented workers 7. Sexuality 8. Undocumented immigrants 9. Hudson Valley 10. Satirical fiction 11. Literary fiction

LC 91028692

The au pair for the Porter family, Haitian-born Simone, becomes witness to the family's casual cruelty, observing the activities of Rosemary, a sculptor, her philandering husband, her mercurial friends, and her strange children.

"This comedy of manners has a serious purpose but it is never earnest and provides a lot of shrewd and malicious fun. . . . The author finds it hard to write a dull sentence. Her gargoyles are sometimes gruesome. They are also witty and she has a perfect ear for the chatter of this particular set of rich Americans." The Economist.

Proulx, Annie

Accordion crimes / E. Annie Proulx. Scribners, 1996. 381 p.

ISBN 9780684195483

1. Accordion 2. Immigrants -- United States 3. Underclass -- United States 4. Poor people -- United States 5. Death 6. Bad luck 7. Historical fiction 8. Literary fiction

LC 96-16299

Shortlisted for The Orange Prize for Fiction, 1997

A tale of immigrants centered on an accordion brought to America in the 1880s. After its Italian owner is murdered, the instrument passes into the hands of other ethnic groups--German, French-Canadian, Mexican, Polish, Norwegian--and the novel describes their ceremonies, dreams and hates.

"Following successive owners of an accordion--this twelve-car pile-up of a book brims with the sort of disasters you read about on the inside pages of the paper." The New Yorker.

Proulx, Annie

Bad dirt : Wyoming stories 2 / Annie Proulx. Scribner, 2004. 240 p. Wyoming stories

ISBN 0743257995

1. Cowboys 2. Husband and wife 3. Family relationships 4. Ranch life -- Wyoming 5. Small town life -- Wyoming 6. Wyoming 7. Wyoming -- Social life and customs 8. Short stories 9. Westerns 10. Literary fiction

LC 2004056530

11 short stories.

An anthology of short stories, all set in Wyoming, features characters who have a profound effect on the people around them, in such tales as "The Trickle Down Effect," "The Contest," and "What Kind of Furniture Would Jesus Pick?"

"This poignant and often humorous collection is packed with well-drawn characters that linger in the mind and heart. As expected, the Wyoming landscape is the enduring character in each story, silently wielding its magical and brutal power." Library Journal.

Proulx, Annie

Barkskins : a novel / Annie Proulx. Scribner, 2016. 640 p.

ISBN 9780743288781

1. New France (1534-1763) 2. 17th century 3. 18th century 4. 19th century 5. 20th century 6. 21st century 7. Forests 8. Wilderness areas 9. Immigrants, French 10. Families 11. Colonialism 12. First Nations (Canada) 13. Lumber industry and trade 14. Voyages and travels 15. Survival 16. Interracial families 17. Ancestors 18. Loss (Psychology) 19. Indians of North America 20. Family sagas 21. Literary fiction 22. Historical fiction

LC 2015030152

Longlisted for The Baileys Women's Prize for Fiction, 2017.
Kirkus Prize for Fiction finalist, 2016.

Working as woodcutters under a feudal lord in 17th-century New France, two impoverished young Frenchmen follow separate journeys, one of extraordinary hardship, the other of wealth and craftiness, that shape their families throughout three centuries.

"Despite the length, nothing seems extraneous, and not once does the reader sense the story slipping from Proulx's grasp, resulting in the kind of immersive reading experience that only comes along every few years." Publishers Weekly.

Proulx, Annie

Fine just the way it is : Wyoming stories 3 / Annie Proulx. Scribner, 2008. 240 p. Wyoming stories

ISBN 9781416571667

1. Family relationships 2. Ranch life 3. Wyoming -- Social life and customs 4. Short stories 5. Westerns 6. Literary fiction

LC 2008013682

A collection of nine western-themed tales features an array of pioneer country inhabitants from different backgrounds.

"This collection of Wyoming tales, continues [Proulx's] Dickensian delight in memorable nomenclature. [r Proulx's writing can be as fine as anything being produced in America today." Times Literary Supplement.

Proulx, Annie

Postcards / E. Annie Proulx. Scribner, 1992. 308 p.

ISBN 9780684187181

1. Family relationships -- Vermont 2. Farm life 3. Poor families 4. Wanderers and wandering 5. Eccentric families 6. Fugitives 7. United States -- Rural conditions 8. Domestic fiction 9. Literary fiction

LC 91025089

PEN-Faulkner Award, 1993.

The story of a well-meaning fugitive-at-large provides a glimpse of America's past as it follows Loyal Blood from his home in Vermont, where he mistakenly commits a heinous crime, to the coast of California.

Proulx, Annie

That old ace in the hole : a novel / Annie Proulx. Scribner, 2002. xii, 361 p.

ISBN 9780684813073

1. Young men 2. Land development 3. Ranches 4. Farms 5. Cattle ranches 6. Land stewardship 7. Ranchers 8. Cattle ranchers 9. Pigs -- Breeding -- Environmental aspects 10. Environmental degradation 11. Texas Panhandle 12. The West (United States) 13. Oklahoma Panhandle 14. Coming-of-age stories 15. Literary fiction

LC 2002030462

Assigned to locate land in the panhandles of Texas and Oklahoma that can be purchased and converted into pig farms for his employer, Bob Dollar meets the residents of Woolybucket and comes to respect their fierce desire to retain their land.

Proulx, Annie

* The **shipping** news / E. Annie Proulx. Scribner, 1993. 337 p.

ISBN 9780684193373

1. Widowers 2. Families -- Newfoundland and Labrador 3. Small town life -- Newfoundland and Labrador 4. Redemption 5. Psychic trauma 6. Adult children of dysfunctional families 7. Second chances 8. Misfits (Persons) 9. Children with emotional illnesses 10. Journalists -- Newfoundland and Labrador 11. Newfoundland and Labrador 12. Literary fiction

LC 92030315

National Book Award for Fiction, 1993.

Pulitzer Prize for Fiction, 1994.

ALA Notable Book, 1994.

National Book Critics Circle Award for Fiction finalist, 1993

Quoyle retreats to Newfoundland with his daughters after the death of his unfaithful wife. There, as his family begins anew, Quoyle deals with his personal fears.

"The author blends Newfoundland argot, savage history, impressively diverse characters, fine descriptions of weather and scenery, and comic horseplay without ever lessening the reader's interest in Quoyle's progress from bumbling outsider to capable journalist." The Atlantic.

Proust, Marcel, 1871-1922

The **complete** short stories of Marcel Proust / Marcel Proust ; compiled and translated by Joachim Neugroschel ; foreword by Roger Shattuck. Cooper Square Press, 2001. xvii, 201 p.

ISBN 0815411367

1. Short stories 2. Translations -- French to English 3. Classics

LC 00065739

16 stories.

"This collection contains Proust's first literary endeavor, 'Pleasures and Days,' translated into English for the first time in 50 years, along with six additional stories, never before seen in English. . . . Delicately translated by Neugroschel . . . these early musings are priceless, insightful venturing into the mind of a maturing virtuoso." Booklist.

Proust, Marcel, 1871-1922

* **Remembrance** of things past / Marcel Proust ; translated by C.K. Scott Moncrieff and Terence Kilmartin. Random House, 1981. 3 v.

ISBN 0394506448

1. Memories 2. Introspection 3. France -- Social life and customs 4. Autobiographical fiction 5. Translations -- French to English 6. Classics

LC 79005542

Vol. 3's Time regained, translated by Andreas Mayor.

"This is the first complete English version of Proust's masterpiece, translated from the definitive 1954 Pliade edition, Terence Kilmartin has checked the Scott Moncrieff translation (which comprised the first 11 volumes of the English language version and was made from the uneven first French edition) against the impeccable Clarac-Ferre Pliade edition. The 12th volume, Andreas Mayor's 1970 translation of 'Time Regained' was the only English translation based on the Pliade edition prior to this one and has been incorporated into it with only minor changes." Library Journal.

Proust, Marcel, 1871-1922

* **Swann's** way / Marcel Proust ; translated by C. K. Scott Moncrieff and Terence Kilmartin. Modern Library, 1992, c1913. 615 p. In search of lost time

ISBN 0679600051

1. Villages -- France 2. Growing up 3. Memories 4. France -- Social life and customs -- 19th century 5. Coming-of-age stories 6. Autobiographical fiction 7. Translations -- French to English 8. Classics

LC 92025657

Originally published in 1913.

In this opening volume of Proust's great novel, the narrator seems at first to be launching a fairly traditional life-story. But after the prelude the narrator travels backwards rather than forwards in time, in order to tell the story of a love affair that had taken place before his own birth. Swann's jealous love for Odette, together with the comic antics of the Verdurins and the adoring members of their 'little clan', provide a prophetic model of the narrator's own love-relationships and peregrinations in salon society. All Proust's great themes - time and memory, love and loss, art and the artistic vocation - are here in kernel form.

Proust, Marcel, 1871-1922

Time regained / Marcel Proust ; translated by Andreas Mayor, Terence Kilmartin, and C.K. Scott-Moncrieff. Revised by D. J. Enright Modern Library, 1993. 749 p. In search of lost time

ISBN 0679424768

1. Memories 2. Introspection 3. Grief 4. Love 5. France -- History -- 20th century 6. Autobiographical fiction 7. Translations -- French to English 8. Classics

LC 93003628 //r94

"This translation is a revised edition of the 1981 translation of Time regained by Andreas Mayor and Terence Kilmartin."

The narrator returns to Paris after World War I, and reflects on his past life as the raw material for literature, in the final part of the author's cycle of autobiographical novels entitled: A la recherche du temps perdu (Remembrance of things past).

Proust, Marcel, 1871-1922

Within a budding grove / Marcel Proust ; translated from the French by C.K. Scott Moncrieff. The Modern Library, 1930. 356 p. In search of lost time

ISBN 067960006X

1. Girls 2. Boys 3. Growing up 4. Memories 5. Love 6. Villages -- France 7. Memories 8. Introspection 9. France -- Social life and customs 10. Paris, France 11. Autobiographical fiction 12. Coming-of-age stories 13. Translations -- French to English 14. Classics

Later English editions published under the title: In the shadow of young girls in flower.

Follows the narrator's transition from childhood to adolescence and first love on the beaches of Normandy.

Pryor, Mark, 1967-

Hollow man / Mark Pryor. Seventh Street Books, 2015. 260 p. Hollow man

ISBN 9781633880863

1. Psychopaths 2. Stealing 3. Personal conduct 4. Lawyers 5. Musicians 6. Murder 7. British in the United States 8. Austin, Texas 9. Texas 10. Noir fiction 11. Crime fiction

LC 2015011552

Dominic finds his plans of living a normal life unraveling when he, after being demoted at work, meets a beautiful woman who convinces him to unleash his dark side and embark on a life of crime and murder.

Pufahl, Shannon

On swift horses / Shannon Pufahl. Riverhead Books, 2019. 352 p.

ISBN 9780525538110

1. 1950s 2. Postwar life 3. Closeted gay men 4. Independence in women 5. Newlyweds 6. Brothers 7. Searching 8. Gambling 9. Military discharge 10. Horse race betting 11. Casinos 12. Sexuality 13. Men/men relations 14. Korean War, 1950-1953 15. San Diego, California 16. Las Vegas, Nevada 17. LGBTQIA fiction 18. Literary fiction

A lonely newlywed and her wayward brother-in-law follow divergent and dangerous paths through the postwar American West.

Puig, Manuel

Kiss of the spider woman / Manuel Puig ; translated from the Spanish by Thomas Colchie. Knopf, 1979. 281 p.

ISBN 039450366X

1. Prisoners 2. Friendship 3. Loyalty 4. Resistance to government 5. Gay prisoners 6. Torture 7. Gay men 8. Political prisoners 9. Gender identity 10. Film 11. Argentina 12. Psychological fiction 13. Translations -- Spanish to English

LC 78014307

Kiss of the Spider Woman is a graceful, intensely compelling novel about love and victimization. In an Argentine prison, two men share a cell: Molina, a gay window dresser who is self-centered, self-denigrating, yet charming as well; and Valentin, an articulate, fiercely dogmatic revolutionary haunted by memories of a woman he left for the cause. Both are gradually transformed by their guarded but growing friendship and by Molina's obsession with the fantasy and romance of the movies.

Pulley, Natasha

The **Bedlam** stacks / Natasha Pulley. Bloomsbury, 2017. 336 p.

ISBN 9781620409671

1. Victorian era (1837-1901) 2. 1850s 3. Smugglers 4. Expeditions 5. Forests 6. Adventure 7. British in South America 8. Quinine 9. Quests 10. Men with disabilities 11. Friendship 12. Loss (Psychology) 13. Secrets 14. Peru 15. England -- History -- 19th century 16. Historical fantasy 17. Steampunk

Longlisted for the Walter Scott Prize for Historical Fiction, 2018

Still recovering from his latest, near-lethal mission abroad, smuggler Merick Tremayne is tapped by the East India Company to acquire cinchona tree cuttings from Peru, thus breaking the country's monopoly on quinine. But Merrick's expedition to the Andes soon takes a unexpected turn. Although the plot of The Bedlam Stacks is not directly connected to the events of The Watchmaker of Filigree Street, readers can expect brief cameo appearances from some of the previous novel's characters. -- Description by Gillian Speace

"Pulley's beautifully descriptive language sets the stage for a mysterious and dangerous journey reminiscent of the grand scientific expeditions of the nineteenth century." Booklist.

Pulley, Natasha

The lost future of Pepperharrow / Natasha Pulley. Bloomsbury, 2020. 336 p. Watchmaker of Filigree Street series

ISBN 9781635573305

1. Victorian era (1837-1901) 2. 1880s 3. Precognition 4. Ghosts 5. Memory 6. Lovers 7. Clocks and watches 8. Men/men relations 9. Prejudice 10. Missing men 11. Xenophobia 12. Forced labor 13. Children with autism 14. England -- History -- 19th century 15. Historical fantasy 16. Steampunk

Sequel to: The Watchmaker of Filigree Street

Finds Thaniel's unexpected posting to the British legation in politically charged 1888 Tokyo complicated by ghostly sightings, Mori's sudden disappearance and bizarre activities at a frozen labor camp.

"Pulley's intricate plot, vibrant setting, entrancing magic, and dynamic ensemble of characters make for an un-put-downable historical fantasy. New readers will be pulled in and series fans will be delighted by this tour de force." Publishers Weekly.

Pulley, Natasha

The **watchmaker** of Filigree Street / Natasha Pulley. Bloomsbury, 2015. 318 p. Watchmaker of Filigree Street series

ISBN 9781620408339

1. Victorian era (1837-1901) 2. 1880s 3. Clocks and watches 4. Precognition 5. Male friendship 6. Bombs 7. Office workers 8. Clock and watch makers 9. Women scientists 10. Men/men relations 11. Prejudice 12. Suspicion 13. Xenophobia 14. Immigrants 15. Gender role 16. England -- History -- 19th century 17. Historical fantasy 18. Steampunk

Employed as a telegraph operator for the Home Office, synesthete Thaniel Steepleton sees colors in sound and dreams of becoming a musician. But just as Thaniel resigns himself to a dreary life as an underpaid civil servant, someone breaks into his boarding house and leaves a pocket watch on his pillow. The watch leads him to Filigree Street, where he meets gifted Japanese watchmaker Keita Mora who can "remember" the future. However, their budding friendship is complicated by the detonation of a terrorist's bomb, which contains a mechanism strikingly similar to Mori's clockwork creations. -- Description by Gillian Speace.

"The story thwarts expectations; whenever an outcome looks as predetermined as clockwork, it might well go another way. Clever and engaging, this impressive first novel will reward both casual readers looking for a fun period adventure and those fascinated by the tension between free will and fate." Kirkus.

Purcell, Laura

The **silent** companions : a ghost story / Laura Purcell. Penguin Books, 2018, c2017. 304 p.

ISBN 9780143131632

1. 17th century 2. 19th century 3. Mansions 4. Women with mental illnesses 5. Women murderers 6. Haunted houses 7. Pregnant women 8. Secrets 9. Guilt 10. London, England -- History 11. England -- History 12. Gothic fiction 13. Historical fiction 14. Parallel narratives 15. Horror

Originally published: London : Raven Books, 2017.

RUSA Reading List, 2019.

While residing in her late husband's crumbling estate to see out her pregnancy, newly widowed Elsie is met with resentment and hostility from both the servants and local villagers and soon discovers that she is not alone when she finds a wooden figure that bears a startling resemblance to her--and whose eyes seem to follow her where she goes.

"[Purcell's] novel is reminiscent of the work of all the greats, particularly Shirley Jackson and Daphne du Maurier, but Purcell has a style all her own. A must for all lovers of Gothic literature." Library Journal.

The **Pushcart** Prize 2020 XLIV: edited by Bill Henderson, with the Pushcart Prize editors. Pushcart Press, 2019. 600 p.

ISBN 9781888889956

1. Literary fiction 2. Short stories 3. Anthologies

A 44th edition high points presents 600 pages of literature from both new and established authors, featuring traditional and experimental work.

"Pushcart is a beacon and wellspring for aspiring writers and inquisitive readers. The list of indie presses which have contributed works to this, the forty-fourth triumphant Pushcart Prize volume, fills more than 20 pages, providing a unique resource." Booklist.

Putnam, Jonathan F.

These **honored** dead / Jonathan Putnam. Crooked Lane Books, 2016. 297 p. Lincoln and Speed novels

ISBN 9781629537771

1. Lincoln, Abraham, 1809-1865 2. 1830s 3. Lawyers 4. Women murder suspects 5. Women murder victims 6. Small town life -- Illinois 7. Murder investigation 8. Frontier and pioneer life 9. Male friendship 10. Slavery 11. Illinois -- History -- 19th century 12. Historical mysteries

Abraham Lincoln has just moved to Springfield, Illinois in 1837 to practice law, and since beds are sparse, he ends up rooming with store-keeper Joshua Speed. When an orphaned girl from a neighboring town is found murdered and suspicion falls on her aunt (Joshua's former lover), Joshua makes it his mission to clear her name and calls upon Lincoln to help. This well-researched, richly detailed debut novel will especially please readers who like a bit of courtroom drama. -- Description by Dawn Towery.

Putney, Mary Jo

The **burning** point / Mary Jo Putney. Berkley Books, 2000. 335 p. Circle of friends trilogy (Mary Jo Putney)

ISBN 9780425174289

1. Divorced couples 2. Family businesses 3. Second chances 4. Family violence 5. Wrecking 6. Men/women relations 7. Forgiveness 8. Redemption 9. Maryland 10. Contemporary romances

Sequel: The spiral path.

A story of family, love, and desire: Kate Corsi's lifelong dream has been to work for her family's world-famous explosive demolition business.

Putney, Mary Jo

A **kiss** of fate / Mary Jo Putney. Ballantine, 2004. 352 p. Guardian series (Mary Jo Putney)

ISBN 0345449169

1. Jacobite Rebellions (1689-1746) 2. 18th century 3. Widows 4. Magic 5. Paranormal phenomena 6. Psychics 7. Young women 8. Landowners 9. Weather control 10. Fate and fatalism 11. Men/women relations 12. England -- History -- 18th century 13. Scotland -- History -- 18th century 14. Paranormal romances 15. Historical romances

Hiding mystical powers that assist his efforts to end hostilities between Scotland and England, clan laird Duncan Macrae falls for English widow Gwyneth Owens, whose own latent powers are released when she experiences foreboding visions.

"Born into a legendary family of mages known as the Guardians, Gwyneth Owens believes that she has little inherited power. She does, however, have a destiny to fulfill. When the Guardian elders seek to forestall a coming disaster by invoking her Guardian oath and asking her to marry Duncan Macrae, Lord Ballister, the most powerful weather mage in the realm, she cannot honorably refuse. Although they are already attracted to each other, Gwyneth can't forget the single kiss from him that sent alarming visions of destruction flaming through her mind or the sword that he held in his hand. Intelligent, compelling characters that appeal to both heart and mind, a brilliant blending of history and fantasy, and a beautifully unfolding love relationship combine to produce a magical tale." Library Journal.

Putney, Mary Jo

Loving a lost lord / Mary Jo Putney. Zebra Books, 2009. 352 p. Lost lords (Mary Jo Putney)

ISBN 9781420103281

1. Regency period (1811-1820) 2. 19th century 3. Deception 4. Inheritance and succession 5. Nobility 6. People with amnesia 7. Interpersonal attraction 8. Mistaken identity 9. Sexuality 10. Regency romances 11. Historical romances

Mariah Clarke, desperate to escape the grasp of a bullying suitor, stumbles upon a man washed ashore on a desolate beach who has no memory of his past and convinces him that he is her husband.

Putney, Mary Jo

The **marriage** spell : a novel / Mary Jo Putney. Ballantine Books, 2006. 336 p.

ISBN 0345449185

1. 1810s 2. Wizards 3. Women wizards 4. Women healers 5. Nobility 6. Family secrets 7. Equestrianism 8. Accidents 9. Convalescence 10. Men/women relations 11. Magic 12. Classism 13. Shame 14. Taboo 15. England -- History -- 19th century 16. Paranormal romances 17. Historical romances

LC 2005057087

Jack Langdon has always suppressed his talent for sorcery. But his marriage to Abigail, a skilled wizard, ignites his passion and opens doorways he never imagined.

Putney, Mary Jo

Nowhere near respectable / Mary Jo Putney. Zebra Books, 2011. 352 p. Lost lords (Mary Jo Putney)

ISBN 9781420117226

1. Gamblers 2. Men/women relations 3. Rescues 4. Assassination plots 5. Secrets 6. Social classes -- 19th century 7. London, England -- History -- 19th century 8. Historical romances

Rescued from smugglers by notorious scoundrel Damien Mackenzie, Lady Kiri Laford finds herself falling in love with her brother's oldest friend as they work together to stop a deadly threat against England's crown.

Putney, Mary Jo

No longer a gentleman / Mary Jo Putney. Zebra Books, 2012. 352 p. Lost lords (Mary Jo Putney)

ISBN 9781420117233

1. Regency period (1811-1820) 2. Women spies 3. Prisoners 4. Rescues 5. Former spies -- Great Britain 6. Nobility 7. Men/women relations 8. Interpersonal attraction 9. Napoleonic Wars, 1800-1815 10. London, England -- History -- 19th century 11. England 12. Great Britain -- History -- George III, 1760-1820 13. France -- History -- Consulate and First Empire, 1799-1815 14. Regency romances 15. Historical romances

Cassie Fox, a spy determined to help destroy Napoleon's empire, is distracted from her mission to rescue Grey Sommers, Lord Wyndham, from a French dungeon by her unexpected attraction to him.

Putney, Mary Jo

Not quite a wife / Mary Jo Putney. Kensington, 2014. 352 p. Lost lords (Mary Jo Putney)

ISBN 9781617733093

1. Regency period (1811-1820) 2. Married people 3. Aristocracy 4. Second chances 5. Pregnant women 6. Kidnappers 7. Men/women relations 8. England -- Social life and customs -- 19th century 9. Regency romances 10. Historical romances

When Laurel Herbert witnessed her husband, James, Lord Kirkland, commit an act of shocking violence, she abandoned him, but a passionate encounter ten years later causes her to rethink their estrangement.

"RITA Award-winning Putney (Sometimes a Rogue, 2013) continues her Lost Lords series with a superbly written historical Regency that borrows a classic romance story line and imbues it with all the elements her readers love: simmering sensuality, subtle wit, a surfeit of danger, and a sophisticated flair for characterization." Booklist.

Putney, Mary Jo

Once a soldier / Mary Jo Putney. Kensington Books, 2016. 368 p. Rogues redeemed

ISBN 9781496703514

1. Georgian era (1714-1837) 2. Soldiers 3. Independence in women 4. Courage 5. Napoleonic Wars, 1800-1815 6. Heirs and heiresses 7. Men/women relations 8. Europe 9. Georgian romances 10. Historical romances

After shirking his title and great wealth, Will Masterson is hoping to wrap up his military years, spent fighting the French, until he meets fiercely loyal Athena Markham in the tiny mountain stronghold of San Gabriel.

Puzo, Mario, 1920-1999

The **family** : a novel / Mario Puzo; completed by Carol Gino. Regan Books, 2001 304 p.

ISBN 0060394455

1. Borgia family 2. Nobility -- Italy 3. Manipulation (Social sciences) 4. Power (Social sciences) 5. Greed 6. Italy -- History -- 1492-1559 7. Biographical fiction 8. Historical fiction 9. Family sagas

LC 2001031876

The story opens with Cardinal Rodrigo Borgia manipulating papal elections in 1492 to become the new Pope Alexander. Determined to establish a family dynasty, he appoints his son Cesare cardinal in his stead and, after a strategically engineered episode of incest between siblings Cesare and Lucrezia, begins ruthlessly eliminating rivals and marrying his children into alliances with the offspring of noble families of France and Spain.

"The saga is lush, full of detail, with characters who manage to be larger than life while seeming entirely realistic. The dialogue is slightly ornmented but never clumsy, and the plot is appropriately epic in scope, mixing fact and fiction seamlessly." Booklist.

Puzo, Mario, 1920-1999

* The **godfather** / Mario Puzo. G. P. Putnam's Sons, 1969. 446 p. Godfather series (Mario Puzo)

ISBN 9780399103421

1. Organized crime 2. Men-headed families 3. Fathers and sons 4. Violence 5. Gangsters 6. Change (Psychology) 7. Italian American criminals 8. Mafia 9. Italian Americans 10. New York (State) 11. Crime fiction 12. Family sagas

LC 69011465

The Godfather is an extraordinary novel which has become a modern day classic. Puzo pulls us inside the violent society of the Mafia and its gang wars. The leader, Vito Corleone, is the Godfather. He is a benevolent despot who stops at nothing to gain and hold power. His command post is a fortress on Long Island from which he presides over a vast underground empire that includes the rackets, gambling, bookmaking, and unions. His influence runs through all levels of American society, from the cop on the beat to the nation's mighty.

"Names, places, crimes have been changed, but the Mafia world remains true to fact. Here is Cosa Nostra: the wars of the competing families; their changing 'business enterprises'; their struggle for power and money; their weapons: graft, guns, spies, violence, murder. A wide variety of characters are colorfully drawn. The Don comes though as a person you will remember." Library Journal.

Puzo, Mario, 1920-1999

The **last** don / Mario Puzo. Random House, 1996. 482 p.

ISBN 0679401431

1. Mafia 2. Violence 3. Families 4. Cousins 5. Film industry and trade 6. Organized crime and gambling 7. Sexuality 8. Money 9. Hollywood, California 10. Las Vegas, Nevada 11. Crime fiction

LC 963401

Don Domenico has a surprise in store for his family--he wants them to create a life free from criminal activities for his grandchildren. There is nothing unusual about that, except that the Clericuzio are the last great Mafia family and there are seeds of evil in the family history, seeds sown by the Don himself. Killing is what the family does best.

"Mr. Puzo wraps up his intricate plot with the same ingenuity he exhibits throughout this satisfying novel." New York Times Book Review.

Puzo, Mario, 1920-1999

The **Sicilian** : a novel Linden Press/Simon and Schuster, 1984. 410 p. Godfather series (Mario Puzo)

ISBN 9780671435646

1. Organized crime 2. Men-headed families 3. Fathers and sons 4. Violence 5. Gangsters 6. Change (Psychology) 7. Italian American criminals 8. Mafia 9. Italian Americans 10. Sicily, Italy 11. Family sagas 12. Crime fiction

After his three-year exile in Sicily, Michael Corleone is charged to return to America with Salvatore Giuliano, a young Sicilian bandit whose activities have angered the head of the Sicilian Mafia.

"Perhaps only an American writer with deep Sicilian roots and passions could have succeeded as Mr. Puzo has in symbolizing a desperate society through the deeds of a desperado, and in revealing how thin is the line that often separates a freedom-fighter from a terrorist." New York Times Book Review.

Pym, Barbara, 1913-1980

An **academic** question / Barbara Pym. E. P. Dutton, 1986. 182p.

1. College teachers' spouses 2. Women volunteers 3. Universities and colleges 4. Manuscript thefts 5. Mysteries 6. Gentle reads

LC 86004509

"Based upon...Pym's first-personal early draft...Hazel Holt...prepared the novel for publication by amalgamating the author's original two drafts, and consulting...Pym's notes and the original holograph version."

It is 1970 and there is student unrest throughout England. In a small university in the West Country, Caroline Grimstone, the wife of an ambitious young historian, is also uneasy.

"Assembled by Pym's literary executor from two separate, discarded drafts, this tale . . . is slightly more acid than Pym's usual work but bears her characteristic wit." Newsweek.

Pym, Barbara, 1913-1980

* **Excellent** women / Barbara Pym. Plume Books, 1978, c1952. 256p.

ISBN 0452267307

1. Single women 2. England -- Social life and customs -- 20th century 3. Satirical fiction 4. Classics 5. Gentle reads

LC 88-70110

Originally published 1952 by Dutton.

"Mildred Lathbury, 30ish, a spinster, a clergyman's daughter, is an excellent woman, one who, with no life of her own to speak of, finds herself somewhat unwillingly a part of the lives of others. Her days are made up of small things: church, flowers, dinner with the bachelor vicar and his sister, brief encounters with neighbors. . . . Pym's singular world is a lonely, bittersweet familiar place. She travels it with rueful wit, views the human landscape with a wise, sharp, compassionate eye." Publishers Weekly.

Pynchon, Thomas, 1937-

Against the day : a novel / Thomas Pynchon. Penguin Press, 2006. 1085 p.

ISBN 9781594201202

1. Mexican Revolution (1910-1920) 2. 1890s 3. 20th century 4. Human behavior 5. Labor disputes -- History -- 20th century 6. Good and evil 7. Uncertainty 8. Sexuality 9. Silent films 10. Corporate greed 11. World War I -- Causes 12. World War I -- Influence 13. Tunguska explosion, 1908 14. United States -- History -- 1865-1921 15. Mexico -- History -- Revolution, 1910-1920 16. Paris, France -- History -- 1919-1939 17. Hollywood, California -- History -- 20th century 18. Historical fiction 19. Satirical fiction

LC 2006050714

An epic tale spanning the years between the Chicago World's Fair of 1893 and the end of World War I features a sizable cast of characters who are caught up by such events as the labor troubles of Colorado, the Mexican revolution, and the heyday of silent-movie Hollywood.

"For all its brilliant passages, this is the book that makes you wonder whether even Pynchon knows what lies behind all those veils he's always urging us to part. But wouldn't you know it? Even when he jumps the shark, he does it with an agility that can take your breath away." Time.

Pynchon, Thomas, 1937-

* **Bleeding** edge / Thomas Pynchon. The Penguin Press, 2013. 512 p.

ISBN 9781594204234

1. 2000s (Decade) 2. Women private investigators 3. High technology 4. Billionaires 5. Rich men 6. Businesspeople 7. Criminals 8. Murder 9. New York City 10. Literary fiction 11. Mysteries

LC 2013017173

National Book Award for Fiction finalist, 2013

An average mother of two working in investigation fraud gets drawn into a shady and eccentric underworld after looking into the finances of a billionaire computer geek.

Pynchon, Thomas, 1937-

* The **crying** of lot 49 / Thomas Pynchon. Perenial Library, 1986, c1966. 183 p.

ISBN 9780060913076

1. 1960s 2. Administration of estates 3. Conspiracies 4. Counterculture 5. Paranoia 6. Entropy 7. Southern California 8. Satirical fiction 9. Literary fiction 10. Modern classics

LC 85045221

Originally published: Philadelphia : Lippincott, 1966.

When Oedipa Maas is named as the executor of her late lover's will, she discovers that his estate is mysteriously connected with an underground organization.

Pynchon, Thomas, 1937-

Gravity's rainbow / Thomas Pynchon. Viking, 1973. 760 p.

ISBN 9780670348329

1. Second World War era (1939-1945) 2. Soldiers -- United States 3. Rockets (Ordnance) 4. Americans in Europe 5. Science -- Experiments 6. Conditioned response 7. Misadventures 8. World War II 9. Germany -- History -- 1933-1945 10. Literary fiction 11.

Modern classics 12. Science fiction

LC 72083804

National Book Award for Fiction, 1974.

Tyrone Slothrop, a GI in London in 1944, is under suspicion by his superiors and soon on the run from enemies through Germany.

"Fiction allows at last what was forbidden to the original suffering poets and novelists of 1914-18: the utmost in obscene description, the limit of masochistic pornography. If 'Gravity's Rainbow' is often nauseating it is in a good cause. This is the war book to end them all. Burgess." 99 Novels.

Pynchon, Thomas, 1937-

Inherent vice / Thomas Pynchon. Penguin Press, 2009. 384 p.

ISBN 9781594202247

1. 1960s 2. Private investigators 3. Kidnapping 4. Rich men 5. Criminals 6. Former girlfriends 7. Los Angeles, California -- History -- 20th century 8. Noir fiction 9. Experimental fiction 10. Literary fiction

LC 2009007705

Reluctantly investigating a kidnapping threat against his ex-girlfriend's billionaire beau, Doc Sportello tackles a bizarre tangle of nefarious characters before stumbling on a mysterious entity that may actually be a tax shelter for a dental group.

"An account of the adventures of a hippie private eye pursuing assorted nonlucrative commissions in a Southern California beach town around 1970, Inherent Vice is a sun-struck, pot-addled shaggy dog story that fuses the sulky skepticism of Raymond Chandler with the good-natured scrappiness of The Big Lebowski. It's an inspired formula; the mystery plot supplies the novel with a minimum of structure (as well as confidence that there's some point to the enterprise) and the genre provides ample cover for Pynchon's literary weaknesses." Salon.com.

Pynchon, Thomas, 1937-

Mason & Dixon / Thomas Pynchon. H. Holt, 1997. 773 p.

ISBN 9780805037586

1. Mason, Charles, 1728-1786 2. Dixon, Jeremiah, 1733-1779 3. Colonial America (1600-1775) 4. Mason-Dixon Line 5. Surveying -- United States -- History -- Colonial period, 1600-1775 6. Surveyors -- United States 7. Frontier and pioneer life -- Pennsylvania 8. Frontier and pioneer life -- Maryland 9. British in the United States 10. United States -- History -- Colonial period, 1600-1775 11. Biographical fiction 12. Historical fiction

LC 976467

Follows mismatched British surveyors Charles Mason and Jeremiah Dixon as they make their way through frontier hardships, Native Americans, warfare, conspiracies, and other perils of eighteenth-century, pre-Revolutionary America

"From historical odds and ends and the Field Journal they left behind, Pynchon re-imagines Mason and Dixon before, during and after the four-plus years, 1763-1767, they took to draw their 244-mile-long line through the American wilderness, dividing the proprietorships of the Penns of Pennsylvania and the Calverts of Maryland, ordaining our North and South. From his omnivorous reading, with his diabolical genius for mimicry, he also re-creates their tumultuous era." The Nation.

Pynchon, Thomas, 1937-

* **V** : a novel / Thomas Pynchon. Perennial Library, 1986, c1963. 492 p.

ISBN 9780060913083

1. 20th century 2. Losers (Persons) 3. Women -- Identity 4. Imperialism 5. British in the United States 6. Sewer workers 7. Misadventures 8. Travelers 9. Femmes fatales 10. New York City

11. Literary fiction 12. Modern classics

LC 8545222

Originally published: Philadelphia : Lippincott, 1963.

The search for the mysterious V ranges from New York to Cairo to Alexandria to Malta. Apart from its strange heroine, the book's characters include sailors, spies, priests, philosophers, bums and bawds.

Pynchon, Thomas, 1937-

Vineland / Thomas Pynchon. Little, Brown, 1990. 385 p.
ISBN 9780316724449
1. 1960s 2. 1980s 3. The Sixties generation 4. Hippies -- Influence 5. Counterculture 6. Obsession in men 7. Northern California 8. Satirical fiction

LC 89013025

Ex-hippie and unemployed FBI sting specialist Frenesi Gates must confront her past when former commune-mates start disappearing and an old lover turns up after fifteen years

"This is manifestly the work of a man of quick intelligence and quirky invention. Many of its episodes flicker with an appealingly far-flung humor. And Pynchon displays throughout Vineland what might be called an internal loyalty: he keeps the faith with the generally feckless and almost invariably inarticulate misfits he assembles, tracking their looping thoughts and indecisive actions with a patience that seems grounded in affection." The New York Review of Books.

Pyne, Daniel

Catalina eddy : a novel in three decades / Daniel Pyne. Blue Rider Press, 2017 560 p.
ISBN 9780399171659
1. Crime 2. Police 3. Criminal investigation 4. Lawyers 5. Corruption 6. Drug lords 7. Crime bosses 8. Undercover operations 9. Southern California 10. California 11. Los Angeles, California 12. San Diego, California 13. Long Beach, California 14. Crime fiction 15. Noir fiction

LC 2016041986

Presents three interconnected novellas about crime and corruption in Southern California's underworld.

Pyne, Daniel

Twentynine Palms : a novel / Daniel Pyne. Counterpoint, 2010. 320 p.
ISBN 9781582435732
1. Love triangles 2. Revenge 3. Missing persons 4. Murder 5. Extramarital affairs 6. Actors and actresses 7. California 8. Noir fiction 9. Thrillers and suspense

LC 2010005454

After having an affair with his friend's wife, Jack lies low at a small-town hotel, but he becomes the prime suspect when a family disappears from the motel and must clear his name while trying to evade his vengeful friend.

"Marginal Hollywood actor Jack Baylor ends an affair with the wife of his best friend, Tory, and knowing Tory's anger-management issues, he retreats to the California desert town of Twentynine Palms to let the metaphorical dust settle. There he promptly begins an affair with Mona, a young mother of two. But Tory arrives in the town bent on revenge, Mona and her kids disappear, and Jack's motel room is awash with blood. Jack is promptly arrested and must escape to clear himself. Character is everything in this desert-noir debut, and Jack is the embodiment of fecklessness; without a script, he's simply lost. Rachel, a clever 14-year-old runaway, saves him repeatedly. . . . Great fun." Booklist.

Pyper, Andrew

The damned : a novel / Andrew Pyper. Simon & Schuster, 2015. 304 p.
ISBN 9781476755113
1. Twin brothers and sisters 2. Ghosts 3. Life after death 4. Good and evil 5. Near-death experience 6. Psychopaths 7. Death 8. Detroit, Michigan 9. Horror

LC 2014016217

Twenty years after his death and resuscitation following a fire, Danny Orchard is still haunted by his twin, Ashleigh, who didn't survive. A psychopath before her death, Ash's ghost proves even more malicious. When Danny gets engaged, Ash (who has sabotaged all of Danny's relationships) threatens mayhem. Canadian author Andrew Pyper enhances this chiller -- set in modern Detroit -- with a vivid sense of place and realistic character development. -- Description by Katherine Bradley Johnson.

"Pyper's pacing, as well as the novel's length, is perfect, and his evocative description of Detroit, a city desolate in its decline, comes off as both sad and poetic at the same time. A treat for fans of intelligent treatments of the supernatural and rock-solid writing." Kirkus.

Pyper, Andrew

The homecoming : a novel / Andrew Pyper. Simon & Schuster, 2019 353 p.
ISBN 9781982108977
1. Wills 2. Family secrets 3. Social isolation 4. Family relationships 5. Fathers -- Death 6. Family estates 7. Eccentric men 8. Survival 9. Secrets 10. Pacific Northwest 11. Psychological suspense 12. Thrillers and suspense

After learning from their father's will that to claim their inheritance they must stay at the family estate for thirty days with their troubled mother and sister, two brothers are drawn into a world of dark revelations and long-kept secrets.

"Pyper fairly lays the groundwork for the truth behind their experiences, and readers will be invested in the thoughtfully constructed characters." Publishers Weekly.

Pywell, Sharon L.

What happened to Henry / Sharon Pywell. G.P. Putnam's Sons, 2004. 272 p.
ISBN 0399151680
1. 1950s 2. 1960s 3. Boys 4. Brothers and sisters 5. Boys and spirits 6. Hibakusha 7. Radiation victims 8. Spirits 9. Dysfunctional families 10. Infant death 11. Bereavement 12. Grief 13. Love 14. Belief and doubt 15. Religion 16. Paranormal phenomena 17. Spirit possession 18. Family relationships 19. United States -- History -- 20th century 20. Hiroshima, Japan -- Atomic bombing, 1945 21. Psychological fiction 22. Historical fiction

LC 2003062239

Idolizing her older brother throughout their childhoods, young Lauren Cooper witnesses his transformation in the aftermath of a sudden tragedy and a compromising, but strangely enlightening, disorder.

Q

Qashu, Sayed, 1975-

Second person singular / Sayed Kashua ; translated from the Hebrew by Mitch Ginsburg. Grove Press, 2012. 346 p.
ISBN 9780802120199
1. Lawyers 2. Extramarital affairs 3. Palestinians 4. Identity (Psychology) 5. Social workers 6. Jews 7. Betrayal 8. Jerusalem, Israel 9. Literary fiction 10. Translations -- Hebrew to English

Follows the experiences of a highly respected Jerusalem attorney who embarks on a jealous search upon finding a love letter in his wife's handwriting.

Qiu, Xiaolong, 1953-
    Death of a red heroine / Qiu Xiaolong. Soho, 2000. 463 p. Inspector Chen Cao mysteries
    ISBN 9781569471937
    1. Police -- Shanghai, China 2. Murder investigation -- Shanghai, China 3. Detectives -- Shanghai, China 4. Poets 5. Murder -- Shanghai, China 6. Translators 7. Interpreters 8. Propaganda 9. Communists 10. Shanghai, China 11. China -- Social life and customs -- 20th century 12. Mysteries 13. Police procedurals
                          LC 00020362
    Anthony Award for Best Novel, 2001.
    Inspector Chen must battle the political climate of Shanghai and seek the help of a former lover in order to solve the murder of a National Model Worker.
    "An engrossing first novel set in China during the 1990s that begins as a simple police procedural and then just keeps on getting more complex. . . . Chen is an irresistible protagonist, likable and determined to make the honorable choices, no matter how dangerous." Kirkus.

Qiu, Xiaolong, 1953-
    Don't cry Tai Lake : an Inspector Chen novel / Qiu Xiaolong. Minotaur Books, 2011. 336 p. Inspector Chen Cao mysteries
    ISBN 9780312550646
    1. Police -- Shanghai, China 2. Murder investigation -- China 3. Manufacturing industry and trade 4. Murder -- China 5. Crimes against men 6. Pollution 7. Shanghai, China 8. China 9. Mysteries 10. Police procedurals
    Offered a luxury vacation near Lake Tai, Chief Inspector Chen Cao is drawn into the murder investigation of a manufacturing plant director who had been accused of polluting the once-beautiful lake, a case that implicates the leader of a local ecological group.

Qiu, Xiaolong, 1953-
    Enigma of China / Xiaolong Qiu. St. Martin's Minotaur, 2013. 277 p. Inspector Chen Cao mysteries
    ISBN 9781250025807
    1. Police -- Shanghai, China 2. Suicide investigation -- China 3. Murder -- China 4. Crimes against men 5. Political intrigue 6. Shanghai, China 7. China 8. Mysteries 9. Police procedurals
    In line for the top politic position of the Shanghai Police Department, Chief Inspector Chen Cao is drawn into the investigation of a major party member's son, whose suspicious suicide in the face of corruption charges forces Chen to make a difficult choice.

Qiu, Xiaolong, 1953-
    Red mandarin dress : an Inspector Chen novel / Qiu Xiaolong. St. Martin's Minotaur, 2007. 310 p. Inspector Chen Cao mysteries
    ISBN 9780312371074
    1. Police -- Shanghai, China 2. Corruption investigation 3. Murder -- Shanghai, China 4. Serial murderers 5. Young women 6. Organized crime 7. Shanghai, China 8. China 9. Mysteries 10. Police procedurals
                          LC 2007044109
    Chief Inspector Chen Cao of the Shanghai Police Department finds himself caught up in a dangerous case when the bodies of two young

women dressed in identical red mandarin dresses turn up, igniting fears of the city's first sexual serial killer.
    "The suspense, and the way Qiu weaves in the human wreckage caused by Mao Zedong's Cultural Revolution, gives one of contemporary fiction's best pictures yet of the wrenching changes facing China as it struggles with its recent, wretched past." St. Louis Post-Dispatch.

Qiu, Xiaolong, 1953-
    * **Shanghai** redemption : an Inspector Chen novel / Xiaolong Qiu. Minotaur Books, 2015. 308 p. Inspector Chen Cao mysteries
    ISBN 9781250065278
    1. Investigations 2. Reputation 3. Political corruption 4. Deception 5. Police 6. Communists 7. Assassins 8. Shanghai, China 9. China 10. Mysteries 11. Police procedurals
    Given a bogus promotion and targeted by an assassin after a controversial case, former Shanghai detective and Communist Party secretary Chen Cao risks his life to investigate an increasingly corrupt Party leader.
    "Chen's 10th outing is another complex, methodical police procedural as well as a multifaceted look at a powerful society in flux." Kirkus.

Qiu, Xiaolong, 1953-
    When red is black / Qiu Xiaolong. Soho Press, 2004. 309 p. Inspector Chen Cao mysteries
    ISBN 9781569473696
    1. Police -- Shanghai, China 2. Murder investigation -- Shanghai, China 3. Crimes against women 4. Translators 5. Real estate developers 6. Translating and interpreting 7. Shanghai, China 8. China -- Social life and customs -- 21st century 9. Mysteries 10. Police procedurals
                          LC 2003023436
    When Inspector Chen is made an offer by a triad-connected businessman, he takes a vacation, leaving his partner to investigate a novelist's death, only to apprehend the culprit after Chen returns, who then discovers how the triad has played him.
    "This mystery offers a complex and riveting portrait of Shanghai, a city in transition from a proletarian dictatorship to a capitalist playground." Washington Post Book World.

Quade, Kirstin Valdez
    Night at the fiestas : stories / Kirstin Valdez Quade. W.W. Norton & Company, 2015 288 p.
    ISBN 9780393242980
    1. Parent and child 2. Growing up 3. Families 4. Catholics 5. Interpersonal relations 6. New Mexico 7. Literary fiction 8. Short stories
                          LC 2014038352
    Exploring the themes of race, class and coming-of-age, a stunning collection of stories about growing up in a land shaped by love, loss and violence introduces a cast of unforgettable characters who protect, betray, wound, undermine, bolster, define and, ultimately, save each other.
    "A piercingly perfect debut collection from a young writer who's already arrived; highly recommended." Library Journal.

Quartey, Kwei
    Children of the street : a novel / Kwei Quartey. Random House Trade Paperbacks, 2011. x, 335 p. Inspector Darko Dawson mysteries
    ISBN 9780812981674
    1. Teenage murder victims 2. Serial murder investigation 3. Street

life 4. Detectives 5. Marijuana use 6. Ghana 7. Mysteries 8. Police procedurals

"A follow-up to Wife of the Gods finds Inspector Darko Dawson investigating a string of murders targeting the street teens of Ghana in a case that takes him through the city's underground, where he is forced to come to terms with the brutal world of the urban poor."--publisher's description.

"A must-read for anyone who follows African crime fiction." Booklist.

Quartey, Kwei

Gold of our fathers / Kwei Quartey. Soho Crime, 2016. 368 p. Inspector Darko Dawson mysteries

ISBN 9781616956301

1. Gold mines and mining 2. Murder 3. Police 4. Corruption 5. Detectives 6. Rural crimes 7. Business -- Corrupt practices 8. Murder investigation 9. Ghana 10. Mysteries 11. Police procedurals

LC 2015028758

A body has been unearthed in one of the remote Obuasi gold quarries. The list of potential suspects is a long one, and Dawson must pursue it alone, because he can't trust his sergeant partner. He learns very quickly how dangerous it is to pursue justice in this kingdom of illegal gold mines, where the worst offenders have so much money they have no fear of the law.

Quartey, Kwei

The **missing** American / Kwei Quartey. Soho Crime, 2020. 432 p. Emma Djan novels

ISBN 9781641290708

1. Private investigators 2. Women private investigators 3. Missing persons investigation 4. Computer crimes 5. Widowers 6. Missing persons 7. Deception 8. Organized crime 9. Impostors 10. Swindlers and swindling 11. Accra, Ghana 12. Ghana 13. Mysteries

LC 2019019288

Accra private investigator Emma Djan's first missing persons case will lead her to the darkest depths of the email scams and fetish priests in Ghana, the world's Internet capital.

"This promising series debut from the acclaimed Quartey ('Darko Dawson' mysteries) introduces the formidable Emma, and most important, the culture and politics of Ghana. Recommended for readers of mystery, African American and African fiction, and international crime/mystery." Library Journal.

Quartey, Kwei

Murder at Cape Three Points / Kwei Quartey. Soho Crime, 2014 336 p. Inspector Darko Dawson mysteries

ISBN 9781616953898

1. Crimes against rich people 2. Murder investigation 3. Oil industry and trade 4. Real estate development 5. Beheading 6. Detectives 7. Police -- Ghana 8. Coastal towns 9. Ghana 10. Mysteries 11. Police procedurals

LC 2013038337

"When a prominent couple is found murdered on the Ghanaian coast, Detective Inspector Darko Dawson of the Accra police force is separated from his family while investigating an increasingly dangerous case involving the efforts of real estate and oil interests to force out local fishing villages."--Provided by publisher.

Quartey, Kwei

Wife of the gods : a novel / Kwei J. Quartey. Random House, 2009. 336 p. Inspector Darko Dawson mysteries

ISBN 9781400067596

1. Murder 2. Missing persons 3. Detectives 4. Murder suspects 5.

Villages 6. Marijuana use 7. Cold cases (Criminal investigation) 8. Mothers 9. Ghana 10. Mysteries 11. Police procedurals

LC 2008032579

Investigating the murder of an AIDS worker in an African community from which his mother went missing years earlier, Detective Inspector Darko Dawson collects details about the killing and realizes that he is close to solving the truth about his mother's disappearance.

Queen, Ellery

The **best** of Ellery Queen : four decades of stories from the mystery masters / edited by Francis M. Nevins, Jr., and Martin H. Greenberg Beaufort Books, 1985. 238 p.

1. Short stories 2. Mysteries

LC 84021572

Stories deal with a dead man's coded message, a surprise party, a poisoning, a murdered boxer, the death of an alumni, the theft of an antique doll, and a tontine.

Quick, Amanda

Crystal gardens / Amanda Quick. G. P. Putnam's Sons, 2012. 352 p. Ladies of Lantern Street

ISBN 9780399159084

1. 19th century 2. Women psychics 3. Women amateur detectives 4. Death threats 5. Cottage gardens 6. Psychic ability 7. Murderers 8. Rental housing 9. Men/women relations 10. Paranormal romances

LC 2011049449

Moving to a country cottage where she seeks refuge in a paranormally charged garden, Evangeline Ames is rescued from a would-be assassin by the garden's owner, Lucas Sebastian, who taps Evangeline's detective skills to solve a buried-treasure mystery and stop a common enemy.

Quick, Amanda

* **Garden** of lies / Amanda Quick. G.P. Putnam Sons, 2015 359 p.

ISBN 9780399165153

1. Victorian era (1837-1901) 2. 19th century 3. Murder investigation 4. Amateur detectives 5. Secretaries 6. Crimes against secretaries 7. Widows 8. Archaeologists 9. Men/women relations 10. London, England -- History -- 19th century 11. Victorian mysteries 12. Historical mysteries

Refusing to believe that her star employee's death was not accidental, Ursula Kern, the owner of a secretarial agency for wealthy clients, hires skeptical adventurer Slater Roxton to investigate the dark side of cultured society.

"The end result is another top-drawer historical romance that delivers the perfect fusion of witty dialogue, intriguing characters, and seductive passion." Booklist.

Quick, Amanda

The **girl** who knew too much / Amanda Quick. Berkley, 2017. 352 p. Burning Cove, California

ISBN 9780399174476

1. 1930s 2. Women journalists 3. Magicians 4. Hotel owners 5. Gossiping and gossips 6. Film industry and trade 7. Murder investigation 8. Interpersonal attraction 9. Men/women relations 10. Hollywood, California 11. Romantic suspense 12. Historical romances

LC 2016050066

Discovering the body of a beautiful actress at the bottom of a pool at an exclusive California hotel, rookie reporter Irene Glasson investigates the victim's secret about an up-and-coming man and becomes drawn to a once-famous master magician whose career was mysteriously cut short.

"Quick (Jayne Ann Krentz, who also writes as Jayne Castle) transports readers back to the 1930s, showing the grimy truth behind Hollywoods glamorous facades and proving that she is a titan of historical romantic thrillers." Publishers Weekly.

Quick, Amanda

I thee wed / Amanda Quick. Bantam Books, 1999. 341 p.
ISBN 9780553100846
1. Regency period (1811-1820) 2. Single women 3. Men/women relations 4. Book thefts 5. Independence in women -- 19th century 6. Businesspeople 7. England 8. Great Britain -- History -- Regency, 1811-1820 9. Regency romances 10. Romantic suspense 11. Historical romances

LC 9837168

Emma Greyson has a position as a companion to Lady Mayfield. But when Emma meets the darkly handsome Edison Stokes, a guest at her employer's estate, she is lured into a dangerous quest for an ancient book of potions.

"Strong-willed, and with a redhead's combustible temper, paid companion Emma Greyson finds herself embroiled in a dangerous adventure with the dashing Edison Stokes. A wealthy member of Regency England's 'Polite World,' Stokes follows the clue in a dying man's last words to arrive at Ware Castle, where he suspects a dark plot is underway. At the castle he encounters Emma, who stands out among the era's decadent and depraved society as a woman of sharp intelligence. . . . Attractive protagonists, loose bodices, thwarted love and odds overcome prove themselves once again the ingredients for success in this genre." Publishers Weekly.

Quick, Amanda

The **mystery** woman / Amanda Quick. G.P. Putnam's Sons, 2013. 371 p. Ladies of Lantern Street
ISBN 9780399159091
1. Women psychics 2. Spies 3. Extortion 4. Mad scientist (Concept) 5. Psychic ability 6. Murderers 7. Assassins 8. Resurrection 9. Men/women relations 10. Women psychics 11. Women amateur detectives 12. Paranormal romances

Targeted by a disabled former spy for the Crown who wrongly believes she is blackmailing his sister, Beatrice Lockwood offers her assistance in tracking down the real culprit and eventually falls for the spy only to find herself hunted by a mad scientist who would resurrect a dead lover.

Quick, Amanda

The **other** lady vanishes / Amanda Quick. Berkley, 2018. 340 p. Burning Cove, California
ISBN 9780399585326
1. 1930s 2. Coastal towns 3. Escapes 4. Secret identity 5. Undercover operations 6. Swindlers and swindling 7. Magicians 8. Gossiping and gossips 9. Murder investigation 10. Interpersonal attraction 11. Men/women relations 12. Hollywood, California 13. Romantic suspense 14. Historical romances

After escaping from a private sanitarium, Adelaide Blake arrives in Burning Cove, California, desperate to start over. Working at an herbal tea shop puts her on the radar of those who frequent the seaside resort town: Hollywood movers and shakers always in need of hangover cures and tonics. One such customer is Jake Truett, a recently widowed businessman in town for a therapeutic rest. But unbeknownst to Adelaide, his exhaustion is just a cover. In Burning Cove, no one is who they seem. Behind facades of glamour and power hide drug dealers, gangsters, and grifters. Into this make-believe world comes psychic to the stars Madame Zolanda. Adelaide and Jake know better than to fall for her kind of con. But when the medium becomes a victim of her own dire

prediction and is killed, they'll be drawn into a murky world of duplicity and misdirection. Neither Adelaide nor Jake can predict that in the shadowy underground they'll find connections to the woman Adelaide used to be--and uncover the specter of a killer who's been real all along. Provided by publisher.

Quick, Amanda

Otherwise engaged / Amanda Quick. G. P. Putnam's Sons, 2014. 342 p. Ladies of Lantern Street
ISBN 9780399165146
1. Spies 2. Voyages and travels 3. Murderers 4. Obsession 5. Kidnappers 6. Women travelers 7. Men/women relations 8. Interpersonal attraction 9. Romantic suspense 10. Spy fiction

LC 2013042660

Barely escaping a would-be abductor who has left a trail of victims in his wake, world traveler Miss Amity Doncaster discovers that her attacker has become obsessed with gossip that ties Amity to scientist Benedict Stanbridge, a spy for the throne who resolves to bring the killer to justice.

Quick, Amanda

Slightly shady / Amanda Quick. Bantam Books, 2001. 343 p. Lavinia Lake and Tobias March series
ISBN 9780553801880
1. Regency period (1811-1820) 2. Private investigators 3. Extortion 4. Men/women relations 5. Women antique dealers 6. Spies 7. Thieves 8. Independence in women 9. British women in Italy 10. London, England -- History -- 19th century 11. Regency romances 12. Historical romances

LC 00058528

Sequel: Don't look back.

Beseiged by gambling debts, a desperate gentleman purchases a diary as a tool for blackmail. But he does not live to carry out his plans. He is murdered, and the diary is stolen. Now Tobias March, discrete private investigator, has been hired to find the incriminating diary. Tobias is famliar with danger, but when his inquiries lead him to the beautiful entrepreneur Lavinia Lake, his emotions are sidetracked.

"Arch humor and the expert removal of bodices are Quick's stock in trade, and the old formula still works splendidly." Publishers Weekly.

Quick, Amanda

'Til death do us part / Amanda Quick. Berkley Books, 2016. 342 p.
ISBN 9780399174469
1. Victorian era (1837-1901) 2. Matchmakers 3. Mystery story writers 4. Men recluses 5. Women stalking victims 6. Stalking 7. Obsession in men 8. Threat (Psychology) 9. Murder 10. Interpersonal attraction 11. Men/women relations 12. Stalkers 13. London, England 14. England -- Social life and customs -- 19th century 15. Great Britain -- History -- Victoria, 1837-1901 16. Romantic suspense 17. Historical romances 18. Victorian romances

LC 2015037168

Operating an exclusive matchmaking service for nobles in Victorian London, Calista is stalked by a dangerously obsessed individual and turns to a reclusive author, who is fighting mysterious demons from his past, for help.

Quincy, D. M. (Diana)

Murder at the opera / D. M. Quincy. Crooked Lane Books, 2019. 304 p. Atlas Catesby mysteries
ISBN 9781643852355
1. Regency period (1811-1820) 2. 1810s 3. Aristocracy 4. Amateur detectives 5. Competition 6. Theater 7. Sisters -- Death 8. Murder

9. Murder investigation 10. Interclass romance 11. Interpersonal attraction 12. Men/women relations 13. Historical mysteries

In 1815 London, amateur sleuth Atlas Catesby investigates the murder of a notorious courtesan and discovers a link between this crime and the death of his own sister years ago, leading him down a dark and dangerous path of violence and revenge.

Quincy, D. M. (Diana)

* Murder in Mayfair : an Atlas Catesby mystery / D. M. Quincy. Crooked Lane Books, 2017. 304 p. Atlas Catesby mysteries

ISBN 9781683312253

1. Regency period (1811-1820) 2. 1810s 3. Rescues 4. Frameups 5. Abusive men 6. Small town life 7. Murder 8. Murder investigation 9. Adventurers 10. Amateur detectives 11. Secrets 12. Auctions 13. Extortion 14. Historical mysteries

After rescuing a woman, Lilliana, who was being auctioned off by her husband in a small country village in 1810 England, Atlas Catesby must work to help her to clear her name after the husband is found murdered.

Quindlen, Anna

Every last one / Anna Quindlen. Random House, 2010. 299 p.

ISBN 9781400065745

1. Mothers 2. Teenagers with depression 3. Coping 4. Violence 5. Healing 6. Hope 7. Determination (Personal quality) 8. Families 9. Teenagers 10. Gardeners 11. Psychological fiction

Mary Beth Latham is first and foremost a mother, whose three teenaged children come first, before her career as a landscape gardener, or even her life as the wife of a doctor. Caring for her family and preserving their everyday life is paramount. And so, when one of her sons, Max, becomes depressed, Mary Beth becomes focused on him, and is blindsided by a shocking act of violence.

"Quindlen has a talent for gently, almost imperceptibly, setting the stage for what happens. The narrative of life with the Lathams is subtly prophetic regarding the impending doom. All the while, we come to love this family, because Quindlen makes their ordinary lives so fascinating, their mundane interactions engaging and important. Every Last One is about excruciating grief. It's about how people treat victims of violence, survivors' guilt, random blame and figuring out how to go on living." USA Today.

Quindlen, Anna

Miller's Valley / Anna Quindlen. Random House, 2016. 257 p.

ISBN 9780812996081

1. Girls 2. Farm life 3. Family relationships 4. Families 5. Growing up 6. Floodplains 7. Self-fulfillment 8. Home (Concept) 9. Men/women relations 10. Pennsylvania 11. Domestic fiction 12. Coming-of-age stories

LC 2015025157

Coming of age in a dwindling 1960s farming community in eastern Pennsylvania, Mimi struggles with profound family secrets and the pain of falling in love with the wrong person against a backdrop of dynamic historical periods.

Quindlen, Anna

Object lessons / Anna Quindlen. Random House, 1991. 262 p.

ISBN 9780394569659

1. 1960s 2. Mothers and daughters 3. Self-discovery in women 4. Large families -- Westchester County, New York 5. Family relationships 6. Thirteen-year-old girls 7. Girls -- Westchester

County, New York 8. Irish American families -- Westchester County, New York 9. Italian American families 10. Suburbs 11. Coming-of-age stories 12. Mainstream fiction

LC 90048656

During a pivotal summer, young Maggie Scanlan struggles to deal with the realities of the adult world as she wrestles with the approaching death of her grandfather, parental conflict, and the other trials of her Irish-Italian family

"Quindlen's social antennae are acute: she conveys the fierce ethnic pride that distinguishes Irish and Italian communities, their rivalry and mutual disdain. Her character portrayal is empathetic and beautifully dimensional, not only of Maggie but of her mother, who experiences her own wrenching rite of passage." Publishers Weekly.

Quinn, Julia, 1970-

The **lady** most willing : a novel in three parts / Julia Quinn, Eloisa James, Connie Brockway. Avon Books, 2012. 371 p.

ISBN 9780062107381

1. Regency period (1811-1820) 2. Uncle and nephew 3. Nobility -- Scotland 4. Kidnapping 5. Castles 6. Blizzards 7. Balls (Parties) 8. Men/women relations 9. Dukes and duchesses 10. Inheritance and succession 11. England -- Social life and customs -- 19th century 12. Regency romances 13. Historical romances

Follows the authors' The lady most likely.

When both of his nephews refuse to wed, Taran Ferguson, laird of his clan, takes matters into his own hands by raiding a ball and kidnapping four likely brides--an heiress and her sister, an English beauty and a woman without name or fortune--in hopes that one of them will want to marry a Scottish lord.

"Clever, engaging, funny, and guaranteed to keep the pages turning, this well-written Regency 'novel in three parts' by popular authors Quinn, Eloisa James, and Connie Brockway is a pure delight." Library Journal.

Quinn, Julia, 1970-

An **offer** from a gentleman / Julia Quinn. Avon Books, 2001. 377 p. Bridgerton series

ISBN 0380815583

1. Regency period (1811-1820) 2. Stepmothers 3. Earls and countesses 4. Fathers -- Death 5. Household employees 6. Rescues 7. Classism 8. Men/women relations 9. Balls (Parties) 10. Families 11. Brothers 12. Housekeepers 13. England -- History -- 19th century 14. England -- Social life and customs -- 19th century 15. Regency romances 16. Historical romances

While searching for a mysterious beauty he met at a masquerade party, Benedict Bridgerton meets Sophie Beckett, a servant in need of his help, and as passion flares between them, he must choose between Sophie and the woman of his dreams.

Quinn, Julia, 1970-

The **secrets** of Sir Richard Kenworthy / Julia Quinn. Avon Books, 2015. 453 p. The Smythe-Smith quartet

ISBN 9780062370211

1. Regency period (1811-1820) 2. Mate selection 3. Courtship 4. Women musicians 5. Interpersonal attraction 6. Men/women relations 7. England -- Social life and customs -- 19th century 8. Regency romances 9. Historical romances

Sir Richard Kenworthy has married Iris Smythe-Smith for a secret reason--he wants to pretend that she is pregnant so his 17-year-old unmarried, pregnant sister does not become a pariah once the baby is born--but when he actually begins to have feelings for Iris, things get complicated.

Quinn, Kate

The **huntress** / Kate Quinn. William Morrow & Co., 2019. 400 p.

ISBN 9780062884343

1. Soviet Union. Air Force. Night Witches regiment 2. Women pilots 3. Nazi hunters 4. Postwar life 5. War correspondents 6. Justice 7. Deception 8. Teenage girls 9. Families 10. Historical thrillers

Stranded behind enemy lines, brave bomber pilot Nina Markova becomes the prey of a lethal Nazi murderess known as the Huntress and joins forces with a Nazi hunter and British war correspondent to find her before she finds them.

Quinn, Kate

Ribbons of scarlet : a novel of the French Revolution's women / Kate Quinn, Stephanie Dray, Laura Kamoie, Sophie Perinot, Heather Webb, E. Knight ; foreword by Allison Pataki. William Morrow & Company, 2019. 400 p.

ISBN 9780062952196

1. Revolutionary France (1789-1799) 2. 1790s 3. French Revolution, 1789-1799 4. Women and politics 5. Gender role 6. Insurgency 7. Women revolutionaries 8. Royal houses 9. Monarchy 10. Class conflict 11. Revolutions 12. Aristocracy 13. Poor women 14. Political violence 15. Revenge 16. France -- History -- Revolution, 1789-1799 17. Paris, France -- History -- Revolution, 1789-1799 18. Historical fiction 19. Political fiction

Six bestselling and award-winning authors bring to life a breathtaking epic novel illuminating the hopes, desires, and destinies of princesses and peasants, harlots and wives, fanatics and philosophers'six unforgettable women whose paths cross during one of the most tumultuous and transformative events in history: the French Revolution.

"The disparate social and political views presented make this an excellent choice for a lively book discussion, and readers of historical fiction will appreciate this unique take on an era not often covered in English-language popular fiction." Booklist.

Quinn, Spencer

Dog on it : a Chet and Bernie mystery / Spencer Quinn. Atria Books, 2008. 320 p. Chet and Bernie mysteries

ISBN 9781416585831

1. Dogs 2. Missing persons investigation 3. Private investigators 4. Missing teenagers 5. Dog owners 6. Organized crime 7. Lost dogs 8. Rescues 9. Mysteries 10. Stories told by animals

LC 2008015370

Copyright page from the original book.

Chet and Bernie investigate the disappearance of Madison, a teenage girl who may or may not have been kidnapped, but who has definitely gotten mixed up with some very unsavory characters.

"Chet the Jet is a dog who failed K-9 school (cats in the open country played a role in his demise), but now he is a dedicated PI and works with Bernie, owner of the Little Detective Agency. The story is told entirely from Chet's point of view, which will delight dog-loving mystery readers, but the book is also an excellent PI tale, dogs aside, as Chet and Bernie investigate the disappearance of a teenage girl whose developer dad may be up to no good. . . . Excellent and fully fleshed primary and secondary characters, a consistently doggy view of the world, and a sprightly pace make this a not-to-be-missed debut." Booklist.

Quinn, Spencer

The **right** side : a novel / Spencer Quinn. Atria Books, 2017. 336 p.

ISBN 9781501118401

1. Women veterans 2. Human/animal relationships 3. Mother-

separated children 4. Dogs 5. Veterans 6. Missing children 7. Missing persons investigation 8. Mothers and daughters 9. Scars 10. Amnesia 11. Afghanistan 12. Maryland 13. Mysteries

LC 2017001680

Disfigured from a war injury incurred during an operation she barely remembers, a woman veteran of the war in Afghanistan embarks on an obsessive search for her missing daughter before forging a deep bond with a stray dog and discovering new perils beyond the combat zone.

Quinonez, Ernesto

Bodega dreams / Ernesto Quinonez. Vintage Contemporaries, 2000. 213 p.

ISBN 0375705899

1. Puerto Ricans 2. Drug lords 3. Spanish Harlem, New York City 4. Urban fiction

LC 99033380

In a stunning narrative combining the gritty rhythms of Junot Diaz with the noir genius of Walter Mosley, Bodega Dreams pulls us into Spanish Harlem, where the word is out: Willie Bodega is king. Need college tuition for your daughter? Start-up funds for your fruit stand? Bodega can help. He gives everyone a leg up, in exchange only for loyalty-and a steady income from the drugs he pushes. Lyrical, inspired, and darkly funny, this powerful debut novel brilliantly evokes the trial of Chino, a smart, promising young man to whom Bodega turns for a favor.

Quirk, Matthew

Cold barrel zero / Matthew Quirk. Mulholland Books, 2016. 373 p. John Hayes novels

ISBN 9780316259217

1. Former Special Forces members 2. Malicious accusation 3. Terrorism 4. Intrigue 5. Physicians 6. High technology 7. Innocence (Law) 8. Techno-thrillers

Returning from exile to win back his family and take revenge on his accusers, a disgraced Black Ops soldier plots escalating attacks on U.S. soil and is targeted by doctor and former comrade-in-arms Thomas Byrne, who struggles with his loyalties during an explosive confrontation.

"Characters, most known only by their last names, are well drawn and motivated, and their exploits are hair raising. Another hard-to-put-down adventure from Quirk, this is even more chilling for its air of plausibility. A fine thriller." Booklist.

Quirk, Matthew

Dead man switch / Matthew Quirk. Mulholland Books, 2017. 368 p. John Hayes novels

ISBN 9780316259231

1. Former Special Forces members 2. Malicious accusation 3. Assassins 4. Murder 5. Intrigue 6. Special forces 7. High technology 8. Innocence (Law) 9. Women assassins 10. Undercover operations 11. Techno-thrillers

The suspicious deaths of two members of an elite undercover military team are investigated by Special Ops legend Captain John Hayes, who is horrified to discover that his protege, a brilliant assassin, is the prime suspect.

R

Rabb, Jonathan

Among **the** living / Jonathan Rabb. Other Press, 2016. 288 p.

ISBN 9781590518038

1. 1940s 2. Holocaust survivors 3. Jewish families 4. Communities

5. Postwar life 6. Refugees 7. Race relations 8. Reform Judaism 9. Conservative Judaism 10. Racism 11. Widows 12. Engaged persons 13. Men/women relations 14. Georgia 15. Savannah, Georgia 16. Historical fiction

LC 2016008314

A moving novel about a Holocaust survivor's unconventional journey back to a new normal in 1940s Savannah, Georgia. In late summer 1947, thirty-one-year-old Yitzhak Goldah, a camp survivor, arrives in Savannah to live with his only remaining relatives. They are Abe and Pearl Jesler, older, childless, and an integral part of the thriving Jewish community that has been in Georgia since the founding of the colony. There, Yitzhak discovers a fractured world, where Reform and Conservative Jews live separate lives distinctions, to him, that are meaningless given what he has been through. He further complicates things when, much to the Jeslers' dismay, he falls in love with Eva, a young widow within the Reform community. When a woman from Yitzhak's past suddenly appears--one who is even more shattered than he is--Yitzhak must choose between a dark and tortured familiarity and the promise of a bright new life. Set amid the backdrop of America's postwar south, Among the Living grapples with questions of identity and belonging, and steps beyond the Jewish experience as it situates Yitzhak's story during the last gasp of the Jim Crow era. Yitzhak begins to find echoes of his own experience in the lives of the black family who work for the Jeslers--an affinity he does not share with the Jeslers themselves. This realization both surprises and convinces Yitzhak that his choices are not as clear-cut as he might have thought. Provided by publisher.

"This stirring, powerful novel never sugarcoats its themes or characters; what emerges is a hard-won realism and a compelling look at one corner of the postwar world." Booklist.

Rabe, Peter, 1921-

* **Anatomy** of a killer ; A shroud for Jesso / Peter Rabe. Stark House Press, 2008, c1955-1960. 308 p.

ISBN 9781933586229

1. Gangsters 2. Organized crime 3. Criminals 4. Spies -- United States 5. Assassins 6. Men/women relations 7. Germany 8. Noir fiction

Originally published by Abelard-Schuman in 1960 (Anatomy of a killer) and Fawcett in 1955 (A shroud for Jesso).

Anatomy of a Killer (1960) is the story of a hitman who learns, too late, what it is to be human. A Shroud for Jesso (1955) is the story of a crime boss who is hijacked on a steamer to Europe, where he quickly learns what it takes to stay alive.

Racculia, Kate

* **Bellweather** rhapsody / Kate Racculia. Houghton Mifflin Harcourt, 2014. 304 p.

ISBN 9780544129917

1. 1990s 2. Hotels 3. Blizzards 4. Missing teenage girls 5. Fear 6. Murder 7. Music festivals 8. Missing persons 9. High school students 10. Teenage boy prodigies 11. Eccentrics and eccentricities 12. Ghosts 13. Mysteries 14. Supernatural mysteries

LC 2013026339

A young music prodigy goes missing from a hotel room that was the site of an infamous murder-suicide 15 years earlier, renewing trauma for a bridesmaid who witnessed the first crime and rallying an eccentric cast of characters during a snowstorm that traps everyone on the grounds.

"[A] novel of dueling wills, marked by textured characterization and an ebullient storytelling style." Publishers Weekly.

Racculia, Kate

Tuesday Mooney talks to ghosts : a novel / Kate Racculia. Houghton Mifflin Harcourt, 2019. 368 p.

ISBN 9780358023937

1. Poe, Edgar Allan, 1809-1849 Influence 2. Treasure hunts (Games) 3. Clues 4. Misfits (Persons) 5. Billionaires 6. Women volunteers 7. Women amateur detectives 8. Scavenger hunts 9. Contests 10. Research 11. Men/women relations 12. Interpersonal relations 13. Ghosts 14. Boston, Massachusetts 15. Adventure stories 16. Mainstream fiction

LC 2018046444

A dying billionaire sends one woman and a cast of dreamers and rivals on a citywide treasure hunt.

Rachman, Tom

The **imperfectionists** : a novel / Tom Rachman. The Dial Press, 2010. 288 p.

ISBN 9780385343664

1. Journalists 2. Newspaper publishers and publishing 3. Newspaper editors 4. Americans in Italy 5. Jealousy 6. Competition 7. Interpersonal relations 8. Italy 9. Psychological fiction 10. Literary fiction

LC 2009033148

Canadian Authors Association Literary Awards, MOSAID Technologies Inc. Award for Fiction, 2011.

Preoccupied by personal challenges while running a struggling newspaper in Rome, an obituary writer confronts mortality, an eccentric publisher obsesses over his dog, and other staff members uncover the paper's founding by an impulsive millionaire.

"Rachman's strength lies in his rendering of the characters all 11 are believable, flawed and loveable. The narrative works and forms a coherent whole." The Scotsman.

Rachman, Tom

The **Italian** teacher / Tom Rachman. Viking, 2018. 341 p.

ISBN 9780735222694

1. 20th century 2. 21st century 3. Fathers and sons 4. Father-deserted families 5. Genius 6. Ambition 7. Artists 8. Art 9. Genius 10. Self-fulfillment 11. Growing up 12. Family relationships 13. Europe 14. Literary fiction 15. Historical fiction

LC 2017032493

An Italian youth raised to revere the genius artist father who abandoned their family strives to become worthy of his father's attentions through a series of failed career pursuits before he hatches a scheme to secure his father's legacy.

"Rachman's ... haunting addition to the list of novels about children overshadowed by famous parents is a momentous drama of a volatile relationship and the fundamental will to survive." Booklist.

Radcliffe, Ann Ward, 1764-1823

* The **mysteries** of Udolpho / Ann Radcliffe ; edited by Bonamy Dobree ; with an introduction and notes by Terry Castle. Oxford University Press, 1998. xxxiii, 693 p.

ISBN 9780192825230

1. Guardian and ward 2. Orphans 3. Women prisoners 4. Castles -- Italy 5. Gothic fiction 6. Classics

First published in 1794.

Fresh with grief for her recently-deceased father and forced to live with an aunt who doesn't want her, Emily is plunged into a nightmarish world in this terrifying gothic classic by Ann Radcliffe. Steeped in atmosphere and full of dark sweeping landscapes, Radcliffe offers a disturbing tale couched in beautiful language.

Rademacher, Cay

Deadly Camargue : a Provence mystery / Cay Rademacher ; translated from the French by Peter Millar. Minotaur Books, 2018, c2015. 293 p. Provence mysteries

ISBN 9781250110725

1. Cold cases (Criminal investigation) 2. Art thefts 3. Rural life 4. Journalists 5. Detectives 6. Provence, France 7. France 8. Translations -- French to English 9. Mysteries

LC 2018013875

Roger Blanc and Marius Tonon investigate after a Parisian political reporter and to personality is discovered gored to death by a fighting bull in Camargue.

Rader-Day, Lori, 1973-

The **black** hour / Lori Rader-Day. Seventh Street Books, 2014. 330 p.

ISBN 9781616148850

1. Sociology 2. Gunshot victims 3. Women college teachers 4. Graduate students 5. Former boyfriends 6. Student teachers 7. Academic rivalry 8. Campus life 9. Obsession 10. Scholars and academics 11. Violence 12. Chicago, Illinois 13. Psychological suspense

LC 2014003653

Anthony Award for Best First Novel, 2015.

"For Chicago sociology professor Amelia Emmet, violence was a research topic-until a student she'd never met shot her"--, Provided by publisher.

"Chapters that alternate between Amelia and Nath's viewpoints provide an irresistible combination of menace, betrayal, and self-discovery." Publishers Weekly.

Rader-Day, Lori, 1973-

The **day** I died / Lori Rader-Day. William Morrow, 2017. 408 p.

ISBN 9780062560292

1. Family violence 2. Criminal profiling 3. Missing boys 4. Graphologists 5. Kidnapping investigation 6. Ransom 7. Small towns 8. Single mothers 9. Mothers and sons 10. Parental kidnapping 11. Missing persons investigation 12. Indiana 13. Psychological suspense

Anthony Award for Best Paperback Original, 2018.

Using her skills as a handwriting analyst to assist a local murder case, Anna identifies disturbing parallels between the crime and her own struggles to protect her troubled teen son from an abusive ex.

"Beautiful prose and tack-sharp observations round out this slow-burning but thought-provoking meditation on the ravages of domestic violence." Publishers Weekly.

Rader-Day, Lori, 1973-

Little pretty things / Lori Rader-day. Random House Inc., 2015. 298 p.

ISBN 9781633880047

1. Best friends 2. Friends' death 3. Women amateur detectives 4. Hotels 5. Secrets 6. Reunions 7. High schools 8. Murder suspects 9. Amateur detectives 10. Murder investigation 11. Mysteries

Edgar Allan Poe Awards: Mary Higgins Clark Award, 2016.

"OLD RIVALRIES NEVER DIE. BUT SOME RIVALS DO. Juliet Townsend is used to losing. Back in high school, she lost every track team race to her best friend, Madeleine Bell. Ten years later, she's still running behind, stuck in a dead-end job cleaning rooms at the Mid-Night Inn, a one-star motel that attracts only the cheap or the desperate. But what life won't provide, Juliet takes. Then one night, Maddy checks in.

Well-dressed, flashing a huge diamond ring, and as beautiful as ever, Maddy has it all. By the next morning, though, Juliet is no longer jealous of Maddy--she's the chief suspect in her murder. To protect herself, Juliet investigates the circumstances of her friend's death. But what she learns about Maddy's life might cost Juliet everything shedidn't realize she had"--, Provided by publisher.

Ragan, Theresa

Buried deep / T. R. Ragan. Thomas & Mercer, 2019. 275 page Jessie Cole novels

ISBN 9781542091480

1. Women private investigators 2. Men with amnesia 3. Missing women 4. Missing persons investigation 5. Heirs and heiresses 6. New identities 7. Journalists 8. Murder 9. Suicide 10. Family secrets 11. Mothers and daughters 12. Sacramento, California 13. California 14. Thrillers and suspense

Two missing persons. One apparent suicide. Three cases pushing PI Jessie Cole and crime reporter Ben Morrison closer to the edge. As the mysteries, puzzles, and lies of three investigations are unearthed, Jessie and Ben will risk everything to bring all that is hidden into the light.

Ragan, Theresa

Deadly recall / T. R. Ragan. Thomas & Mercer, 2018. 286 p. Jessie Cole novels

ISBN 9781503949232

1. Women private investigators 2. Journalists 3. Revenge 4. Girl kidnapping victims 5. Kidnapping investigation 6. Blame 7. Men with amnesia 8. Sacramento, California 9. California 10. Thrillers and suspense

PI Jessie Cole is about to discover that there's no revenge too wicked as New York Times bestselling author T.R. Ragan's gripping series continues.

Ragan, Theresa

Deranged / T. R. Ragan. Thomas & Mercer, 2018. 288 p. Jessie Cole novels

ISBN 9781503904293

1. Women private investigators 2. Men with amnesia 3. Fathers and sons 4. Prisoners 5. Surveillance 6. Cheating (Interpersonal relations) 7. Murder investigation 8. Serial murderers 9. Sacramento, California 10. California 11. Thrillers and suspense

Ever since a car accident left reporter Ben Morrison with amnesia, he's been trying to rebuild a future as he puts together the pieces of his past. With the help of PI Jessie Cole, he's getting closer. But few who remember Ben's troubled childhood want to talk. Then Jessie is sidetracked by a surveillance request from a suspicious husband. An ordinary case, until the cheating wife and lover are found murdered. They bear the trademark wounds of an elusive serial killer who's now leading Jessie down a chilling path--one that's about to put a dangerous twist in the search for Ben's identity.

Ragan, Theresa

Her last day / T. R. Ragan. Thomas & Mercer, 2017. 305 p. Jessie Cole novels

ISBN 9781542046060

1. Women private investigators 2. Missing women 3. Sisters 4. Journalists 5. Men with amnesia 6. Nieces 7. Serial murderers 8. Sacramento, California 9. California 10. Thrillers and suspense

Ten years ago, PI Jessie Cole and reporter Ben Morrison each suffered a tragedy that changed their lives--and now these two strangers are about to share a nightmare.

Raheem, Zara

The **marriage** clock : a novel / Zara Raheem. William Morrow Paperbacks, 2019. 342 p.

ISBN 9780062877925

1. Arranged marriage 2. Dating (Social customs) 3. Muslim American families 4. Young women 5. East Indian Americans 6. Men/women relations 7. Parent and adult child 8. Los Angeles, California 9. India 10. Chick lit

LC 2018059052

Given three months by her traditional parents to find a husband or agree to an arranged marriage, a Muslim-American woman with dreams of Bollywood romance starts dating in hopes of finding love on her own terms.

"Raheem's debut uses chick-lit tropes to smartly skewer modern ways of dating and to bring humor to more traditional South Asian ones." Booklist.

Rai, Alisha

* **Hate** to want you / Alisha Rai. Avon Books, 2017 384 p. Forbidden hearts

ISBN 9780062566737

1. One-night stands (Interpersonal relations) 2. Enemies 3. Business competition 4. Family feuds 5. Sexual attraction 6. Men/women relations 7. Interpersonal attraction 8. Contemporary romances RUSA Reading List Short List, 2018.

Meeting once a year for a single, illicit night of pleasure, parting ways before dawn, sworn enemies Nicholas Chandler and Olivia Tanaka cannot stop wanting each other as secrets from the past threaten to come to light.

Rai, Alisha

* The **right** swipe / Alisha Rai. Avon Books, 2019. 384 p. Modern love

ISBN 9780062878090

1. Professional athletes 2. Former lovers 3. Second chances 4. Women entrepreneurs 5. Online dating 6. Business competition 7. African American women 8. Men/women relations 9. Interpersonal attraction 10. Ambition in women 11. Contemporary romances 12. Multicultural romances

Cynical dating app creator Rhiannon Hunter must decide whether or not to give former pro-football player Samson Lima, who wooed her during one magical night and then disappeared, a second chance despite the fact that his in league with a business rival.

Rai, Alisha

Wrong to need you / Alisha Rai. Avon Books, 2017 384 p. Forbidden hearts

ISBN 9780062566751

1. Widows 2. Single mothers 3. Former convicts 4. Malicious accusation 5. First loves 6. Reunions 7. Sexual attraction 8. Men/women relations 9. Interpersonal attraction 10. Contemporary romances

Returning home 10 years after being accused of a crime he did not commit, Jackson Kane helps his brother's widow, the only woman he has ever loved, with the cafe she's inherited, and must decide if he is strong enough to face the past in order to have a future with this woman he cannot live without.

Raichev, R. T.

Assassins at Ospreys / R.T. Raichev. Soho Press, 2008. 224 p. Country house crime novels

ISBN 9781569475058

1. Women mystery story writers 2. Inheritance and succession 3. Missing persons 4. Murder investigation 5. Secret identity 6. Country homes 7. Men/women relations 8. Women authors 9. Librarians 10. Women amateur detectives 11. England 12. Cozy mysteries 13. Gentle reads

LC 2007039248

When one of mystery writer Antonia Darcy's admiring readers, Bee Ardleigh, becomes over friendly, Antonia finds it just a bit of a bore, but when she and husband Major Hugh Payne are persuaded to visit Bee at Millbrook House, they begin to suspect it's something more sinister.

Raimondo, Lynne, 1957-

* **Dante's** dilemma : a Mark Angelotti novel / Lynne Raimondo. Seventh Street Books, 2015. 290 p. Mark Angelotti novels

ISBN 9781633880429

1. Psychiatrists 2. People who are blind 3. Women murderers 4. Frameups 5. College teachers 6. Murder 7. Murder investigation 8. Winter 9. Chicago, Illinois 10. Mysteries

LC 2015004945

After his testimony against the wife of a murdered professor seems to establish her guilt, blind psychiatrist Mark Angelotti becomes unsure of his role when new evidence points to another killer and he discovers that his own life may be in danger.

Raimondo, Lynne, 1957-

Dante's poison : a Mark Angelotti novel / Lynne Raimondo. Seventh Street Books, 2014. 271 p. Mark Angelotti novels

ISBN 9781616148799

1. Psychiatrists 2. People who are blind 3. Pharmaceutical research 4. Pharmacology 5. Murder investigation 6. Murder suspects 7. Innocence (Law) 8. Belief and doubt 9. Journalists 10. Chicago, Illinois 11. Mysteries

LC 2013045364

While enrolling in a drug trial that could restore his eyesight, blind psychiatrist Mark Angelotti helps an attorney discredit the testimony of a crucial eyewitness in a case involving Big Pharma and a powerful antipsychotic drug that may have been responsible for the death of an investigative journalist.

Raimondo, Lynne, 1957-

Dante's wood : a Mark Angelotti novel / Lynne Raimondo. Seventh Street Books, 2013. 350 p. Mark Angelotti novels

ISBN 9781616147181

1. Women murder victims 2. Child sexual abuse 3. Murder investigation 4. Psychologists 5. Teenagers with developmental disabilities 6. Paternity 7. Pregnant women -- Death 8. Chicago, Illinois 9. Mysteries

LC 2012031725

After looking into a case of possible sexual abuse of a mentally handicapped teen named Charlie Dickerson, psychiatrist Mark Angelotti soon has to testify on Charlie's behalf when the boy's teacher is found murdered.

Rajaniemi, Hannu

The **fractal** prince / Hannu Rajaniemi. Tor Books, 2012. 320 p. Quantum thief novels

ISBN 9780765329509

1. Thieves 2. Criminals 3. Fugitives 4. Escapes 5. Prisoners 6. Far future 7. Mars (Planet) 8. Space 9. Hard science fiction 10. Science fiction mysteries 11. Science fiction

A sequel to The Quantum Thief finds a physicist receiving mysterious information about how to enable immortality in a city torn by the agendas of "fast ones," shadow players, jinni and two revolution-minded sisters; while a thief on the edges of reality is aided by a sardonic ship to risk his freedom and find his patron.

Rajaniemi, Hannu

The **quantum** thief / Hannu Rajaniemi. Tor, 2011. 330 p. Quantum thief novels

ISBN 9780765329493

1. Thieves 2. Criminals 3. Fugitives 4. Escapes 5. Prisoners 6. Far future 7. Posthumanism 8. Mars (Planet) 9. Space 10. Science fiction mysteries 11. Hard science fiction 12. Science fiction

Broken free from a nightmarish distant-future prison by a mysterious woman who offers him his life back if he will complete the ultimate heist he left unfinished, con man Jean le Flambeur is pursued in worlds where people communicate through shared memories.

"Liberated from the infamous Dilemma Prison run by the Archons of the Sobornost collective of the Inner Solar System, master thief Jean le Flambeur agrees to accompany his rescuer, a mysterious woman named Mieli who owns a sentient spaceship with a taste for flirtation, to the Oubliette, a moving city of Mars that traffics in time as currency. Flambeur's tale intersects with that of detective Isidore Beautrelet in an intricately woven, highly charged pas de deux that brings both men to a startling discovery that reinvents the story of their experiences." Library Journal.

Ramadan, Ahmad Danny

The **clothesline** swing / Ahmad Danny Ramadan. Nightwood Editions, 2017. 288 p.

ISBN 9780889713321

1. Storytelling 2. Death 3. Memories 4. Gay couples 5. Men with terminal illnesses 6. Last days 7. Storytellers 8. Immigrants 9. War 10. Violence against gay men and lesbians 11. Homophobia 12. Political persecution 13. Religious persecution 14. Arab countries 15. Syria 16. Egypt 17. Literary fiction

Tells the epic story of two lovers anchored to the memory of a dying Syria. One is a Hakawati, a storyteller, keeping life in forward motion by relaying remembered fables to his dying partner.

Ramos, Joanne

The **farm** : a novel / Joanne Ramos. Random House, 2019. 326 p.

ISBN 9781984853752

1. Women immigrants 2. Surrogate mothers 3. Money-making projects 4. Human reproduction 5. American dream 6. Filipino American women 7. Class struggle 8. Racism 9. Surrogate motherhood 10. Pregnancy 11. Health resorts 12. Social isolation 13. New York (State) 14. Mainstream fiction

Ensconced within a Hudson Valley retreat where expectant birth mothers are given luxurious accommodations and lucrative rewards to produce perfect babies, a Filipino immigrant is forced to choose between a life-changing payment and the outside world.

Ramqvist, Karolina, 1976-

The **white** city / Karolina Ramqvist ; translated from the Swedish by Saskia Vogel. Black Cat, 2017. 161 p.

ISBN 9780802125958

1. Organized crime 2. New mothers 3. Despair 4. Motherhood 5. Life change events 6. Infants 7. Criminals 8. Deception 9. Memories 10. Men/women relations 11. Interpersonal relations 12. Sweden 13. Scandinavian crime fiction 14. Translations -- Swedish to English
LC 2016030009

Originally published: Stockholm : Norstedts, 2015.

Karen must take drastic measures to claim what is rightfully hers when the shady legacy of her high-flying criminal boyfriend sends the authorities after the only thing she has left, the home she lives in with her young daughter.

"The ghostly Scandinavian setting and Karen's closely narrated sense of impending doom, baby cooing patiently at her hip, make Swedish star Ramqvists English-language debut an atmospheric and suspenseful read." Booklist.

Ramsay, Frederick

Countdown / Frederick Ramsay. Poisoned Pen Press, 2018. 196 p. Jesse Sutherlin mysteries

ISBN 9781464210594

1. 1920s 2. Fathers -- Death 3. Amateur detectives 4. Murder investigation 5. Sheriffs 6. Stolen property recovery 7. Cold cases (Criminal investigation) 8. Virginia 9. Historical mysteries

Features characters from the author's's Copper Kettle.

Sheriff Privette doesn't take a deep interest in this cold crime, but Jesse is not letting it go. His father's body has been found with a money belt fat with fifty dollars, a small fortune. Twenty of the seventy dollars that Sutherlin Sr. was carrying when he was reported dead of the Spanish flu in 1918 is missing. His heirloom watch given to him for "thirty years' service in the AM and O Railroad which is now the Norfolk and Western is also missing. It was gold and big as an onion." What happened to the money and to "the onion"? Was all this the work of a thief? Who was the man who showed up at the Sutherlins' door? There's not much to work with. But that won't stop Jesse who investigates as the 1928 boom progresses relentlessly toward 1929.

Ramsay, Frederick

Scone Island : an Ike Schwartz mystery / Frederick Ramsay. Ingram Pub Services, 2012. 250 p. Ike Schwartz mysteries

ISBN 9781464200557

1. Engaged persons 2. Vacations 3. Islands 4. Murder investigation 5. Sheriffs -- Virginia 6. Former CIA agents 7. Small towns -- Virginia 8. Maine 9. Virginia 10. Mysteries

When sheriff and former CIA agent Ike Schwartz and his fiancée, Ruth Dennis, vacation on Scone Island, a small piece of land off the coast of Maine with no electricity or phone service, Ike's CIA past comes back to haunt them.

Ramsay, Frederick

Stranger room / Frederick Ramsay. Poisoned Pen Press, 2008. 256 p. Ike Schwartz mysteries

ISBN 9781590585351

1. Murder 2. Family secrets 3. Sheriffs 4. Family relationships 5. Mansions 6. Drug traffic 7. Racism 8. Small towns -- Virginia 9. Former CIA agents 10. Virginia 11. Mysteries

Elderly Jonathan Lydell III is proud of his family history and his house, which he is committed to restoring to its antebellum configuration, complete with a stranger room. Found in many family homes in the

1800s, an attached room with its own entrance, separately locked and kept for use by unknown travelers, it was intended to protect the family from unsavory guests. Nearly 150 years ago, an inexplicable murder took place in the locked stranger room of the Lydell house. The murderer was never caught. But when a new, identical murder is committed in the same room, not even sheriff Ike Schwartz and FBI agent Karl Hedrick can explain it. Why would history repeat itself? What could explain these identical murders? Could the Lydell family history hold the key?

Ramsay, Hope

Summer on Moonlight Bay / Hope Ramsay. Forever, 2019. 368 p. Moonlight Bay

ISBN 9781538732496

1. Women veterans 2. Veterinarians 3. Dogs 4. Moving, Household 5. Guilt 6. Options, alternatives, choices 7. Small towns 8. Interpersonal attraction 9. Men/women relations 10. South Carolina 11. Contemporary romances

"2-in-1 special! Includes a bonus novel by Miranda Liasson." -- cover

From USA Today bestselling author Hope Ramsay comes a small-town romance filled with love, laughter, and friendship!

Ramzipoor, E. R.

The **ventriloquists** / E. R. Ramzipoor. Park Row, 2019. 544 p.

ISBN 9780778308157

1. Second World War era (1939-1945) 2. Resistance to military occupation 3. Journalists 4. Dissenters 5. World War II 6. Anti-Nazi movement 7. Newspapers 8. Nazis 9. Propaganda 10. Brussels, Belgium 11. Belgium 12. Historical fiction

A tale based on true events finds a misfit journalist, a forger and a street urchin joining a band of resistance fighters who risk their lives to publish a satiric newspaper mocking the Nazis.

Rand, Ayn

* The **fountainhead** / Ayn Rand. Plume, 1994, c1943. xiii, 736 p.

ISBN 9780452273337

1. Architects -- United States 2. Individualism 3. Creativity 4. Self-interest 5. Egotism 6. Trials 7. Collectivism 8. May-December romance 9. Individuality 10. Objectivism (Philosophy) 11. Psychological fiction

LC 86008760

Originally published: New York: Bobbs-Merrill, 1943.

The story of an intransigent young architect, Howard Roark, of his violent battle against a mindless status quo, and of his explosive love affair with a beautiful woman who worships him yet struggles to defeat him. In order to build his kind of buildings according to his own standards, Roark must fight against every variant of human corruption.

Rand, Ayn

We the living / Ayn Rand. Dutton, 1995, c1936. xix, 433 p.

ISBN 9780525940548

1. Communism 2. Freedom 3. Political corruption 4. Government ownership of industry and trade 5. Totalitarianism 6. Love triangles 7. Men/women relations 8. Communists 9. Communism and society 10. Soviet Union -- Social conditions -- 1917-1936 11. Soviet Union -- Politics and government -- 1917-1936 12. Political fiction

Originally published: New York : Macmillan, 1936.

We the Living portrays the impact of the Russian Revolution on three people who demand the right to live their own lives. At its center is a girl whose passionate love is her fortress against the cruelty and oppression of a totalitarian state.

Randel, Weina Dai

The **empress** of bright moon / Weina Dai Randel. Sourcebooks Landmark, 2016 368 p.

ISBN 9781492613596

1. Wu hou,, Empress of China, 624-705 2. Women rulers 3. Inheritance and succession 4. Political intrigue 5. Power (Social sciences) 6. Rulers -- Death 7. Married women 8. Lovers 9. Ambition in women 10. Concubinage 11. Courts and courtiers 12. China -- History -- Tang dynasty, 618-907 13. Historical fiction 14. Biographical fiction

LC 2015022864

Sequel to: Moon in the palace.

At the moment of the Emperor's death, everything changes in the palace. Mei, his former concubine, is free, and Pheasant, the heir and Mei's lover, is proclaimed as the new Emperor, heralding a new era in China. But just when Mei believes she's closer to her dream, Pheasant's chief wife, Lady Wang, powerful and unpredictable, turns against Mei and takes unthinkable measures to stop her. The power struggle that ensues will determine Mei's fate and that of China.

"A must-read for fans of historical fiction set in ancient China, this novel offers a compelling look at a woman's unprecedented rise to power and a fresh take on the often vilified Empress Wu." Library Journal.

Randisi, Robert J.

Hey there (you with the gun in your hand) : a Rat Pack mystery / Robert J. Randisi. Minotaur Books, 2008. 272 p. Rat pack mysteries

ISBN 9780312376420

1. Sinatra, Frank, 1915-1998 2. Davis, Sammy, 1925-1990 3. Rat Pack 4. 1960s 5. Entertainers 6. Film actors and actresses 7. Extortion 8. Casino employees 9. Murder 10. Celebrities 11. Gangsters 12. Investigations 13. Casinos 14. Amateur detectives 15. Las Vegas, Nevada 16. Mysteries

LC 2008030119

In 1961 Las Vegas, Eddie Gianelli, pit boss at the Sands Casino and a friend of members of the Rat Pack, is called in by Frank Sinatra to stop an extortionist targeting Sammy Davis, Jr., only to find himself and New York torpedo Jerry Epstein caught in a conspiracy involving treachery, murder, and the Secret Service.

Rankin, Ian

The **beat** goes on : the complete Rebus stories / Ian Rankin. Little, Brown & Co., 2015, c2014. 240 p. Inspector John Rebus mysteries

ISBN 9780316296830

1. Detectives 2. Police 3. Criminal investigation 4. Crime 5. Crime bosses 6. Edinburgh, Scotland 7. Short stories 8. Mysteries 9. Police procedurals 10. Anthologies

First published: London : Orion Books, 2014.

A complete anthology of the author's John Rebus short stories as well as two previously unpublished tales.

Rankin, Ian

* **Black** and blue : an Inspector Rebus novel / Ian Rankin. St. Martin's Press, 1997. 394 p. Inspector John Rebus mysteries

ISBN 9780312167837

1. Detectives 2. Malicious accusation 3. Serial murder investigation 4. Police -- Edinburgh, Scotland 5. Police -- Scotland 6. Serial murderers -- Scotland 7. Edinburgh, Scotland 8. Aberdeen, Scotland 9. Scotland 10. Mysteries 11. Police procedurals

LC 9725381

Gold Dagger Award for Best Crime Novel of the Year, 1997.

Already tackling a murder in Edinburgh, Inspector John Rebus becomes involved when a copy-cat serial rapist called "Bible Johnny" begins striking in Aberdeen and must keep his wits about him in the center of the media circus surrounding the case.

"Rankin has a point to make about the corrosive effects of human wickedness that, if left unchecked, seeps into the bloodstream and poisons the national body--a point well made in his blunt and bruising style." New York Times Book Review.

Rankin, Ian.

The **black** book / Ian Rankin. O. Penzler books, 1994, c1993. 278 p. Inspector John Rebus mysteries

ISBN 1883402778

1. Detectives 2. Murder investigation 3. Cold cases (Criminal investigation) 4. Police -- Edinburgh, Scotland 5. Missing persons 6. Arson 7. Edinburgh, Scotland 8. Mysteries 9. Police procedurals

LC 948929

Originally published in 1993.

"Rankin's compelling and original plot is almost as intriguing as the gruff, tough, rebellious Rebus, whose rough exterior hides a charming, funny, tenderhearted human being we'd all like to know." Booklist.

Rankin, Ian

Blood hunt : a novel / Ian Rankin. Little, Brown and Company, 2006, c1995. 400 p.

ISBN 0316009113

1. Revenge 2. Murder investigation 3. Former Special Forces members 4. Survivalists 5. Crimes against journalists 6. Brothers of murder victims 7. Families of murder victims 8. Murder 9. Brothers -- Death 10. Mad cow disease 11. Scotland 12. San Diego, California 13. Mysteries

LC 2005050419

The main character, Gordon Reeve, first appeared in Rankin's book Knots and crosses.

Originally published by Ian Rankin writing as Jack Harvey: England : Headline, 1995.

Determined to exact revenge in the aftermath of his brother's unlikely suicide, professional assassin Gordon Reeve becomes increasingly enraged by a local cop who thwarts his attempts to talk with a friend who last saw Reeve's brother alive.

"Gordon Reeve is an ex-SAS soldier who now makes his living training weekend warriors in rural Scotland. Told that his brother has committed suicide in California, Reeve goes to the funeral and quickly decides that the investigative reporter was murdered. Trying to get the story and then revenge, he finds himself pitted against both an amoral chemical conglomerate and an unwelcome face from his own past. . . . Not Rankin's best but still awfully good." Booklist.

Rankin, Ian

The **complaints** / Ian Rankin. Orion, 2009. 381 p. Malcolm Fox mysteries

ISBN 9780752889511

1. Police 2. Police internal affairs investigation 3. Police misconduct 4. Detectives 5. Edinburgh, Scotland 6. Mysteries 7. Police procedurals

LC 2009510086

Sequel: The impossible dead.

Nobody likes The Complaints--they're the cops who investigate other cops. It's a department known within the force as "The Dark Side," and it's where Malcolm Fox works. His new case: investigate a cop named Jamie Breck. As Fox takes on the job, he learns that there's more

to Breck than anyone thinks--dangerous knowledge, especially when a vicious murder takes place far too close to home.

"This novel is part mystery, part buddy story, part morality essay. Mr. Rankin never lets the reader down for a single page." Pittsburgh Post-Gazette.

Rankin, Ian

Dead souls : an Inspector Rebus novel / Ian Rankin. St. Martin's Minotaur, 1999. 406 p. Inspector John Rebus mysteries

ISBN 0312202938

1. Detectives 2. Pedophiles 3. Missing persons investigation 4. Police -- Edinburgh, Scotland 5. Serial murderers 6. Suicide investigation 7. Edinburgh, Scotland 8. Mysteries 9. Police procedurals

LC 99044276

John Rebus has trouble in the form of a paroled murderer, a pedophile, and the missing son of a former sweetheart, all coming together in a mystery that could cost him everything.

Rankin, Ian

Exit music / Ian Rankin. Little, Brown and Co., 2008. 432 p. Inspector John Rebus mysteries

ISBN 9780316057585

1. Detectives 2. Murder investigation 3. Conspiracy theories 4. Retirement 5. Police 6. Murder 7. Edinburgh, Scotland 8. Scotland 9. Mysteries 10. Police procedurals

LC 2008001888

First published in Great Britain: Orion, 2007.

It's late autumn in Edinburgh and late autumn in the career of Detective Inspector John Rebus. As he tries to tie up some loose ends before retirement, a murder case intrudes. A dissident Russian poet has been found dead in what looks like a mugging gone wrong. By apparent coincidence, a high-level delegation of Russian businessmen is in town - and everyone is determined that the case should be closed quickly and clinically. But the further they dig, the more Rebus and DS Siobhan Clarke become convinced that they are dealing with something more than a random attack - especially after a particularly nasty second killing. Meanwhile, a brutal and premeditated assault on a local gangster sees Rebus in the frame. Has the Inspector taken a step too far in tying up those loose ends? Only a few days shy of the end to his long, inglorious career, will Rebus even make it that far?.

"The final novel in Rankins Inspector Rebus series is set during the Edinburgh detective's final week at work. (He is nearing the mandatory retirement age of sixty.) The novel begins with a dissident Russian poet beaten to death, and expands to take in smalltime drug dealers, cloak-wearing women who act in walking mystery tours of the city, international oligarchs, and Scottish bank executives. A contemporary artist who makes sound installations may be in league with politicians agitating for Scotlands independence. Rebus is as gruffly mischievous as ever, and the novel ends in a cliffhanger scene with his archenemy that will have readers gasping into the blank space that follows. Rankins work is crime fiction at its most consuming, cerebral best." The New Yorker.

Rankin, Ian

The **falls** : an Inspector Rebus novel / Ian Rankin. St. Martin's Minotaur, 2001, c2000. 399 p. Inspector John Rebus mysteries

ISBN 0312206100

1. Detectives 2. Missing persons investigation 3. Internet games 4. Missing girls 5. Police -- Edinburgh, Scotland 6. Missing persons -- Edinburgh, Scotland 7. Edinburgh, Scotland 8. Mysteries 9. Police procedurals

LC 2001041946

LIST OF FICTIONAL WORKS

Originally published, 2000.

When a young student mysteriously disappears, Inspector John Rebus comes up with two bizarre clues--a carved wooden doll in a coffin and an Internet role-playing game--and must follow a deadly trail from Edinburgh's past to a modern-day killer.

"Rankin combines complicated multiple plot lines with finely drawn characters and fascinating Scottish lore and settings." Library Journal.

Rankin, Ian

The **hanging** garden : an Inspector Rebus novel / Ian Rankin. St. Martin's Press, 1998. 335 p. Inspector John Rebus mysteries

ISBN 0312192789

1. Detectives 2. Gangsters -- Edinburgh, Scotland 3. Organized crime 4. People in comas 5. War criminals 6. Police -- Edinburgh, Scotland 7. Edinburgh, Scotland 8. Mysteries 9. Police procedurals
"A Rebus omnibus"--Cover.

The hanging garden: DI Rebus is buried under a pile of paperwork but an escalating dispute between the upstart Tommy Telford and Big Ger Cafferty's gang gives Rebus an escape clause. Telford is known to have close links with a Chechen gangster bringing refugees into Britain as prostitutes. When Rebus takes under his wing a distraught Bosnian call girl, it gives him a personal reason to make sure Telford goes back to Paisley and pronto. Then Rebus's daughter is the victim of an all too professional hit-and-run and Rebus knows that there is now nothing he won't do to bring down prime suspect Tommy Telford - even if it means cutting a deal with the devil. Dead souls: A call from an old friend brings back memories and more than a little guilt for DI John Rebus. An old schoolfriend's son has gone missing, the ghost of Jack Morton is inhabiting Rebus' dreams, a part-time poisoner is terrorising the local zoo and a freed paedophile rouses the vigilantes.

"John Rebus, an Edinburgh detective-inspector and father of a 24-year-old daughter, feels especially protective of a young Serbian woman coerced into prostitution by a local mobster. The woman's inability to communicate adds to the frustration of an unproductive, ongoing police surveillance and the continuation of crimes associated with the mobster. At the same time, Rebus investigates a local ex-Nazi's alleged role in a French war crime." Library Journal.

Rankin, Ian

The **impossible** dead / Ian Rankin. Little Brown & Co, 2011. 384 p. Malcolm Fox mysteries

ISBN 9780316039772

1. Police corruption 2. Politicians 3. Suicide 4. Police 5. Police internal affairs investigation 6. Detectives 7. Conspiracies 8. Edinburgh, Scotland 9. Mysteries 10. Police procedurals
Sequel to: The Complaints.

A major inquiry into a neighboring police force sees Malcolm Fox and his colleagues cast adrift, unsure of territory, protocol, or who they can trust. An entire station-house looks to have been compromised, but as Fox digs deeper he finds the trail leads him back in time to the suicide of a prominent politician and activist. There are secrets buried in the past, and reputations on the line.

"Edinburgh Internal Affairs cop Malcolm Fox and his two colleagues receive a frosty reception in Kirkcaldy, where they must decide whether a disgraced officer's three fellow cops helped cover up his misdeeds. Det. Constable Paul Carter, found guilty of sexual misconduct, intrigues Fox because it was Carter's ex-copper uncle, Alan, who turned him in. Since interviewing the belligerent Carter and his mates leads nowhere, Fox turns to Alan for insight. He discovers the elder Carter was hired by a prestigious lawyer to look into the 1985 suicide--or possible murder--of Francis Vernal, a fellow attorney, well-known orator, and vocal supporter of the fringe Scottish separatist movement. Soon Fox's attention is divided between following up scant leads in the Carter investigation and unearthing decades-old secrets about Vernal's life and associates. Rankin elegantly weaves together the two story lines without forcing a connection." Publishers Weekly.

Rankin, Ian

The **naming** of the dead : an Inspector Rebus novel / Ian Rankin. Little, Brown and Co., 2007, c2006. 432 p. Inspector John Rebus mysteries

ISBN 0316057576

1. Group of Eight (Organization) 2. Detectives 3. Murder investigation 4. Organized crime 5. Police -- Edinburgh, Scotland 6. Summit meetings -- Scotland 7. Protests, demonstrations, vigils, etc -- Scotland 8. Anti-globalization movement 9. Suicide 10. Murder 11. Serial murderers 12. London Terrorist Bombings, London, England, 2005 13. Edinburgh, Scotland 14. Scotland 15. Mysteries 16. Police procedurals

LC 2006031495

Originally published: London : Orion, 2006.
British Book Award for Crime Thriller of the Year, 2007.

Sent to man an abandoned police station during an international conference between the leaders of the free world, officer John Rebus investigates the suspicious falling death of a delegate at an Edinburgh banquet.

"In his backhanded, reluctant way Rebus winds up uniting all the book's loose ends, and seeing how he accomplishes this is a pleasure. Besides, The Naming of the Dead isn't really about its detective plot. It's about Rebus's taking stock, not only of his own past but also of the world around him." New York Times.

Rankin, Ian

* A **question** of blood : an inspector Rebus novel / Ian Rankin. Little, Brown and Co., 2004, c2003. 416 p. Inspector John Rebus mysteries

ISBN 0316095648

1. Detectives 2. Murder investigation 3. School shootings 4. Police -- Edinburgh, Scotland 5. Loners 6. Veterans 7. Teenage boys 8. Police internal affairs investigation 9. Forensic science 10. Mass shootings 11. Edinburgh, Scotland 12. Mysteries 13. Police procedurals

LC 2003059549

First published in Great Britain in 2003 by Orion Books.
Originally published: London : Orion Books, 2003.

At a private school, two teenagers are killed by an ex-Army loner who then turned the gun on himself. Finding the truth will take Detective Inspector John Rebus into the heart of a shattered community. Ex-Army himself, Rebus becomes fascinated by the killer, and finds he is not alone. It seems the man had friends in high places and enemies to spare. And Rebus has secrets of his own. He's fresh out of hospital, with newly bandaged hands, and won't say what happened. But after the death of a criminal he visited, who had been stalking DS Siobhan Clarke, Rebus is the prime suspect.

Rankin, Ian

* **Rather** be the devil / Ian Rankin. Little Brown & Co, 2017, c2016. 400 p. Inspector John Rebus mysteries

ISBN 9780316342575

1. Organized crime 2. Women murder victims 3. Cold cases (Criminal investigation) 4. Violence against men 5. Murder 6. Aging 7. Extortion 8. Detectives 9. City life 10. Scotland 11. Edinburgh, Scotland 12. Police procedurals

Originally published: London : Orion, 2016.

Maverick investigator John Rebus gains dangerous enemies upon reopening a cold case from the 1970s involving the murder of a wealthy socialite.

Rankin, Ian

Resurrection men : an Inspector Rebus novel / Ian Rankin. Little, Brown, 2003, c2002. 448 p. Inspector John Rebus mysteries

ISBN 0316766844

1. Detectives 2. Police internal affairs investigation 3. Police misconduct 4. Police corruption 5. Police -- Edinburgh, Scotland 6. Organized crime 7. Murder investigation 8. Edinburgh, Scotland 9. Mysteries 10. Police procedurals

LC 2002016271

Originally published in 2002.

Edgar Allan Poe Award for Best Mystery Novel, 2004.

Sent to a rehabilitation school after a serious mistake, Inspector John Rebus discovers that his classmates are plotting a drug heist and joins forces with Detective Sergeant Siobhan Clarke to investigate ties to an art dealer's murder.

"We are well and truly in Rankin country--a shady world where good and evil are relative terms and truth is an arbitrary concept." New York Times Book Review.

Rankin, Ian

Set in darkness : an Inspector Rebus novel / Ian Rankin. Minotaur Books, 2000. 320 p. Inspector John Rebus mysteries

ISBN 0312206097

1. Detectives 2. Conspiracy theories 3. Stalkers 4. Murder 5. Suicide 6. Police -- Edinburgh, Scotland 7. Stalking 8. Edinburgh, Scotland 9. Scotland 10. Mysteries 11. Police procedurals

Inspector John Rebus investigates a body found in a Queensbury House fireplace, the suicide of a homeless man in possession of a fortune, and the murder of an ambitious politician--three deaths with ties to one of Scotland's most notorious criminals.

"Rebus has been assigned to a bogus task force called the Policing of Parliament Liaison Committee. Things liven up, though, when a body is found inside a bricked-up fireplace in one of the buildings under construction for the new Scottish Parliament. That's a tantalizing enough mystery, but when a top politico is found dead at the construction site, Rebus has something he can sink his teeth into: a decades-old crime whose tentacles touch the present and lead to a new confrontation with Rebus' longtime nemesis, Edinburgh crime boss Big Ger Cafferty. . . . Nobody writes darker than Rankin." Booklist.

Ranney, Karen

The **Scottish** duke / Karen Ranney. Avon Books, 2016. 368 p. Duke series (Karen Ranney)

ISBN 9780062466877

1. Victorian era (1837-1901) 2. 1860s 3. Dukes and duchesses 4. Household employees 5. One-night stands (Interpersonal relations) 6. Masquerades 7. Unplanned pregnancy 8. Trust in men 9. Secret identity 10. Interpersonal attraction 11. Men/women relations 12. Highlands, Scotland 13. Scotland 14. Highland romances 15. Victorian romances 16. Historical romances

Lorna Gordon, an upstairs maid at Blackhall Castle, finds Alex Russell, the Duke of Kinross, to be the most tempting man she's ever seen--and completely unattainable--until, at a fancy dress ball, Lorna disguises herself as Marie Antoinette and pursues an illicit tryst.

Rao, Shobha

* **Girls** burn brighter / Shobha Rao. Flatiron Books, 2018. 307 p.

ISBN 9781250074256

1. 21st century 2. Female friendship 3. Poor women 4. Ambition in women 5. Arranged marriage 6. Human trafficking 7. Voyages and travels 8. Violence against women 9. Sexual slavery 10. Loss (Psychology) 11. India 12. United States 13. Literary fiction

LC 2017045149

Forging a deep friendship with impoverished but passionate fellow weaver Savitha, motherless Poornima begins to reconnect with the beauty of the world before a devastating act of cruelty drives her friend away, compelling her to leave behind everything she knows to search for her friend in the darkest corners of India's underworld and beyond.

Rash, Ron, 1953-

Above the waterfall / Ron Rash. Ecco, 2015. 288 p.

ISBN 9780062349316

1. Sheriffs 2. Small town life -- North Carolina 3. Drug traffic 4. Park rangers 5. Methamphetamine 6. Poisoning 7. Retirement 8. Betrayal 9. Men/women relations 10. Mountain life 11. North Carolina 12. Appalachian Region 13. Rural noir 14. Literary fiction 15. Southern fiction

Enduring the mistakes and tragedies that have shaped their lives in contemporary Appalachia, a sheriff on the brink of retirement and a haunted park ranger confront violent forces when an elderly local is accused of poisoning a trout stream.

Rash, Ron, 1953-

Burning bright : stories / Ron Rash. Ecco, 2010. 205 p.

ISBN 9780061804113

1. Poverty 2. Small town life -- Appalachian region 3. Appalachian Region 4. Rural noir 5. Short stories 6. Literary fiction 7. Southern fiction

Captures the eerie beauty, stark violence, and rugged character of Appalachia in a collection of stories that spans the Civil War to the present day.

"The stories in this collection are set in the rural, meth-addled hills of North Carolina. Pervaded with desperation pawn shops, gravediggers, arson and a sense of impending death these are not uplifting stories. . . . Burning Bright is a collection to be read for the quality of the prose, which reflects Rash's intimate knowledge of this region and its history. His heart is clearly in this place the dialect is pitch-perfect and he is a skillful translator of the inner worlds and difficult lifestyles of the unique, hardened-by-necessity breed of people who have populated the area, past and present." The Oregonian.

Rash, Ron, 1953-

* The **cove** / Ron Rash. HarperCollins, 2012. 255 p.

ISBN 9780061804199

1. First World War era (1914-1918) 2. 1910s 3. Loneliness 4. Misfits (Persons) 5. Men/women relations 6. Small town life -- Appalachian region 7. World War I 8. Men who are mute 9. Secrets 10. Veterans 11. Superstition 12. Mountain people 13. Patriotism 14. World War I home front 15. Appalachian Region 16. North Carolina -- History -- 20th century 17. Historical fiction 18. Rural noir 19. Literary fiction 20. Southern fiction

David J. Langum, Sr. Prize in American Historical Fiction, 2012

Living deep within a cove in the Appalachians of North Carolina during World War I, Laurel Shelton finally finds the happiness she deserves in Walter, a mysterious stranger who's mute, but their love can't protect them from a devastating secret.

Rash, Ron, 1953-

Nothing gold can stay : stories / Ron Rash. Ecco Press, 2013. 239 p.

ISBN 9780062202710

1. Change (Psychology) 2. Violence 3. North Carolina 4. Appalachian Region 5. Rural noir 6. Short stories 7. Literary fiction 8. Southern

fiction

This collection of stories navigates the emotionally harsh terrain of Appalachia and includes The Trusty, in which a convict sent to fetch water for the chain gang tries to convince a farmer's young wife to help him escape, but she is trapped in her own prison.

Rash, Ron, 1953-
Serena : a novel / Ron Rash. Ecco, 2008. 384 p.
ISBN 9780061470851
1. 1930s 2. Husband and wife 3. Lumber industry and trade 4. Greed 5. Infertility 6. Environmentalism 7. Ambition 8. North Carolina -- History -- 20th century 9. Historical fiction 10. Southern fiction
LC 2008000712
Film tie-in.
Originally published: New Yorks : Ecco, 2008.
Sir Walter Raleigh Award for Fiction, 2009.

Traveling to the mountains of 1929 North Carolina to forge a timber business with her new husband, Serena Pemberton champions her mastery of harsh natural and working conditions but turns murderous when she learns she cannot bear children.

"Set in 1929, in the rugged mountains of North Carolina, Rash's novel is a tightly knit tale of industrial development, greed, and betrayal. George Pemberton and his new bride, Serena, maintain a close watch over a burgeoning logging empire, dealing with their workers while fighting off the efforts of environmental activists to expand the country's network of national parks. As the title character -- a Depression-era Lady Macbeth wholly comfortable in the wilderness -- drives her husband to commit increasingly malevolent acts, he must also contend with the reemergence of a woman with whom he had an illegitimate child years earlier. Rash's evocative rendering of the blighted landscape and the tough characters who inhabit it recalls both John Steinbeck and Cormac McCarthy, while the malignant character of Serena, who projects a stark unflinching certainty about her actions, propels his finely paced story." The New Yorker.

Rash, Ron, 1953-
Something rich and strange : selected stories / Ron Rash. Ecco, 2014 288 p.
ISBN 9780062349347
1. City life 2. Mountain life 3. Men and nature 4. Men/women relations 5. Appalachian region 6. Southern states 7. Rural noir 8. Short stories 9. Literary fiction 10. Southern fiction
Collects thirty stories from his previously published collections: Nothing Gold Can Stay, Burning Bright, Chemistry, and The Night New Jesus Fell to Earth.
ALA Notable Book, 2015.
A collection of stories set in Appalachia illuminates the tensions between the traditional and the modern, the old and new south, tenderness and violence and man and nature.
"These superbly suspenseful stories evoke a world of hurt, but what makes them so deeply satisfying is that they enlarge our capacity for empathy." Booklist.

Rashan, Nikki
You make me wanna / Nikki Rashan. Urban Books., 2009. 259 p.
ISBN 9781601621634
1. African American lesbians 2. Women -- Sexuality 3. Romantic love 4. Cousins 5. Breaking up (Interpersonal relations) 6. Lesbian couples 7. Coming out (Sexual or gender identity) 8. Atlanta, Georgia 9. LGBTQIA romances 10. Urban erotica 11. Erotic romances 12. LGBTQIA fiction 13. African American fiction
LC 2010277068

Sequel to: Double Pleasure, Double Pain.
Kyla tries to move forward in her relationship despite pain from her past.

Ratner, Vaddey
Music of the ghosts / Vaddey Ratner. Touchstone, 2017. 324 p.
ISBN 9781476795782
1. Khmer Rouge 2. Refugees 3. Genocide -- Cambodia 4. Homecomings 5. Musicians 6. Memories 7. Missing persons 8. Loss (Psychology) 9. Atrocities 10. Justice 11. Forgiveness 12. Atonement 13. Interpersonal relations 14. Cambodian genocide, 1975-1979 15. Cambodia -- History -- 20th century 16. Literary fiction
LC 2016026793

Returning to the Cambodian homeland she fled as a child refugee decades earlier, Teera finds herself in a country of survivors and perpetrators of the Khmer Rouge holocaust before bonding with a mysterious musician who claims to have known her late father.

"Ratner's descriptions of Teeras confrontation with her past, even as she experiences, once again, the beauty of her homeland, alternate with the old mans memories of his life in captivity with his old friend, Teera's father. The juxtaposition is unnerving and powerful as the reader is transported from scenes of unbearable torture to glimpses of monks arriving at a temple, their saffron robes like a row of candle flames moving across the land. Ratner, herself a Cambodian refugee, has penned another haunting, unforgettable novel." Booklist.

Rawle, Graham
Woman's world : a novel / Graham Rawle. Counterpoint, 2008. 469 p.
ISBN 9781593761837
1. Femininity 2. Gender role 3. Women's periodicals 4. Clippings (Books, newspapers, etc) 5. Personal conduct 6. Irony 7. Brothers and sisters 8. Mother and adult child 9. Interpersonal relations 10. Family secrets 11. Humorous stories 12. Mysteries 13. Experimental fiction
LC 2007047418

Measuring her life in accordance with the standards set in women's magazines, Norma Fontaine is challenged to forfeit her beliefs when she discovers dark secrets that threaten her brother's blossoming romance, in a tale told through an assemblage of 40,000 magazine text fragments.

Rawles, Nancy, 1958-
My Jim : a novel / Nancy Rawles. Crown Publishers, 2004. 176 p.
ISBN 1400054001
1. Antebellum America (1820-1861) 2. 19th century 3. Reminiscing in old age 4. Fugitive slaves -- United States 5. Characters and characteristics in literature 6. Separated friends, relatives, etc 7. Slaves 8. African Americans 9. Senior women 10. Husband and wife 11. Grandparent and child 12. Loss (Psychology) 13. Plantation life -- Southern States 14. Slavery 15. Southern States 16. United States -- History -- 19th century 17. Adaptations, retellings, and spin-offs 18. Historical fiction 19. African American fiction
LC 2004011606
Hurston/Wright Legacy Award: Fiction, 2006.

Pens a moving story about Huck Finn's slave friend Jim, told through the eyes of the wife Jim was forced to leave behind. Sadie shares her story of loss with her granddaughter as they weave Sadie's most treasured items--her mother's knife, a piece of a bowl from Africa, a piece of Jim's hat found when he was thought to be dead--into a quilt.

Rawlings, David, 1971-

The **baggage** handler : a novel / David Rawlings. Thomas Nelson, 2019. 240 p.

ISBN 9780785224938

1. Attitude (Psychology) 2. Change (Psychology) 3. Personal conduct 4. Belief and doubt 5. Faith (Christianity) 6. Spiritual journeys 7. Luggage 8. Christian fiction 9. Allegories

LC 2018033737

Christy Award for First Novel Category, 2019.

When David, Gillian, and Michael all take the wrong suitcase in baggage claim, they are directed to a mysterious facility where the Baggage Handler shows them that their baggage represents larger problems in their lives.

Ray, Kalyan

No country / Kalyan Ray. Simon & Schuster, 2014 553 p.

ISBN 9781451635997

1. 19th century 2. 20th century 3. Voyages and travels 4. Family relationships 5. Family sagas 6. Historical fiction

Spanning two centuries and three continents, from famine-stricken Ireland to colonial India to modern-day upstate New York, this is a riveting, enchanting melting pot of a story about history, family, fate, and the enduring ties of friendship.

"Told from multiple perspectives, this thoughtful novel offers a panoramic view of the way personal and national destinies collide, sometimes ending in tragedy, sometimes in triumph." Booklist.

Raybourn, Deanna

A **curious** beginning : a Veronica Speedwell mystery / Deanna Raybourn. Obsidian, 2015 352 p. Veronica Speedwell novels

ISBN 9780451476012

1. Victorian era (1837-1901) 2. 1880s 3. Independence in women 4. Orphans 5. Young women 6. Nobility 7. Kidnapping 8. Rescues 9. Secrets 10. England -- History -- Victoria, 1837-1901 11. Historical mysteries

LC 2015009286

Receiving a warning from a mysterious baron after suffering a home invasion, Veronica Speedwell accepts the baron's shelter and teams up with an ill-tempered naturalist when her host is subsequently murdered.

Raybourn, Deanna

A **dangerous** collaboration / Deanna Raybourn. Berkley, 2019. 328 p. Veronica Speedwell novels

ISBN 9780451490711

1. Victorian era (1837-1901) 2. 1880s 3. Women amateur detectives 4. Upper class 5. Butterflies 6. Pretending 7. Missing women 8. Missing persons investigation 9. Parties 10. Mansions 11. Secrets 12. England -- History -- Victoria, 1837-1901 13. Historical mysteries

LC 2018043155

Sequel to: A treacherous curse.

Attending a party in remote Cornwall as a favor to a colleague, Victorian adventuress Veronica Speedwell races to uncover her host's true agenda when suspicious accidents plague the guests.

"A brooding castle, rain-lashed windows, hidden passages, and a seance all contribute to a delightfully creepy tale with twists that would make Daphne Du Maurier proud." Publishers Weekly.

Raybourn, Deanna

A **murderous** relation / Deanna Raybourn. Berkley, 2020. 336 p. Veronica Speedwell novels

ISBN 9780451490742

1. Jack,, the Ripper 2. Victorian era (1837-1901) 3. 1880s 4. Women amateur detectives 5. Nobility 6. Royal houses 7. Naturalists 8. Undercover operations 9. Scandals 10. Murder 11. Murder investigation 12. City life 13. Sexual attraction 14. Men/women relations 15. London, England -- Social life and customs -- 19th century 16. England -- History -- Victoria, 1837-1901 17. Historical mysteries

LC 2019043282

Tasked to prevent a royal scandal involving the prince and a brothel madam, Veronica and Stoker go undercover, only to become embroiled in the Jack the Ripper killings.

"The charming characters and involving story, together with the smoldering heat between Stoker and Veronica, make this one a highlight in a very popular series." Booklist.

Raybourn, Deanna

A **perilous** undertaking : a Veronica Speedwell mystery / Deanna Raybourn. Berkley Books, 2017. 352 p. Veronica Speedwell novels

ISBN 9780451476159

1. Victorian era (1837-1901) 2. 1880s 3. Women amateur detectives 4. Upper class 5. Malicious accusation 6. Murder investigation 7. Secrets 8. England -- History -- Victoria, 1837-1901 9. Historical mysteries

LC 2016019601

Visiting a ladies-only club for intrepid women, Victorian adventuress Veronica Speedwell is challenged to save a society art patron from execution.

"Another exciting installment in Raybourn's promising historical-mystery series, starring a fun heroine who defies convention and embraces intrigue." Booklist.

Raybourn, Deanna

Silent in the grave / Deanna Raybourn. MIRA, 2007. 512 p. Lady Julia Grey novels

ISBN 0778324109

1. 1880s 2. Murder investigation 3. Secrets 4. Widows 5. Aristocracy 6. Husband and wife 7. Death 8. Detectives 9. Men/women relations 10. Clues 11. Murder suspects 12. London, England -- History -- 19th century 13. Historical romances 14. Romantic suspense

Sequel : Silent in the sanctuary.

RITA Award for Novel with Strong Romantic Elements, 2008.

After the sudden death of her husband, Edward, Lady Julia Grey enlists the help of private sleuth Nicholas Brisbane to unravel the mystery of Edward's death and the threats that he had been receiving.

"At its best, historical fiction is an insight into a bygone era, giving flesh to the bones of dates, events and customs. At worst, it's got bugger all to do with history--the temporal location is a tool, an escapist device to generate automatic glamour and mystique without any of the hard work of plot and character nuance. While Silent in the Grave does not provide completely new insights into Victorian England, it makes the most of its location and provides enough thrills, surprises, and wit to avoid this undignified company. Raybourn has the potential to take her novels beyond genre constraints." PopMatters.

Raybourn, Deanna

A **treacherous** curse : a Veronica Speedwell mystery / Deanna Raybourn. Berkley, 2018. 308 p. Veronica Speedwell novels

ISBN 9780451476173

1. Victorian era (1837-1901) 2. 1880s 3. Women amateur detectives 4. Upper class 5. Antiquities thefts 6. Murder investigation 7. Conspiracies 8. Archaeological sites -- Egypt 9. Curses 10. Secrets 11. England -- History -- Victoria, 1837-1901 12. Historical mysteries

LC 2017013413

Sequel to: A perilous undertaking.

Sequel: A dangerous collaboration.

When the enigmatic Stoker's former expedition partner goes missing from an archaeological dig with a priceless Egyptian diadem, Victorian adventurer Veronica Speedwell investigates mishaps that have plagued the expedition as well as malevolent enemies that threaten Stoker's career.

"A Victorian Phryne Fisher, Veronica is an irresistible, modern, engaging woman who uses scientific observation and natural charm to guide her investigations. Details about Egyptian relics, myths, and curses add an extra layer of intrigue to an already fun, rollicking puzzle. Though A Treacherous Curse can be read on its own, recommend the whole series to fans of upbeat, savvy, historical mysteries." Booklist.

Rayfiel, Thomas, 1958-

In pinelight : a novel / Thomas Rayfiel. TriQuarterly Books, 2013. 320 p.

ISBN 9780810152366

1. Senior men 2. Reminiscing in old age 3. Small town life 4. Memories 5. Older men 6. New York (State) -- Social life and customs -- 20th century 7. Literary fiction 8. Psychological fiction

LC 2013002127

As the elderly hero of Thomas Rayfiel's daring new novel, In Pinelight, sits in an old folks' home responding to the questions of an unseen interrogator, the fragments he supplies form the portrait of a man's life in upstate New York. Losses, loves, destructive family relationships, sexual entanglements, and moments of mystical awareness filter through the seeming minutiae of small-town gossip to confront the reader with their cumulative power.

Raymond, Jonathan

The **half-life** : a novel / Jonathan Raymond. Bloomsbury, 2004. 368 p.

ISBN 1582344485

1. 1820s 2. 1980s 3. Teenage girls -- Friendship 4. Women filmmakers 5. Filmmakers 6. Young men -- Friendship 7. Cooks 8. Trappers 9. Pioneer men 10. Best friends 11. Communes 12. Communes and children 13. Amateur films 14. Frontier and pioneer life 15. Money-making projects 16. Friendship 17. Skeleton 18. Portland, Oregon 19. Oregon 20. Pacific Northwest 21. China 22. Psychological fiction 23. Pacific Northwest fiction 24. Historical fiction

LC 2003022602

"Raymond, in his first novel, seamlessly links the two narratives with elegant and often haunting prose. The characters are finely drawn, and Raymond poses them against a seductively beautiful landscape." Booklist.

Rayne, Sarah

Music macabre / Sarah Rayne. Severn House Pub Ltd, 2019. 256 p. Phineas Fox mysteries

ISBN 9780727888969

1. Liszt, Franz, 1811-1886 2. Jack,, the Ripper 3. Research 4.

Musicologists 5. Amateur detectives 6. Secrets 7. Serial murderers 8. Restaurants 9. Music 10. Investigations 11. London, England 12. Mysteries 13. Parallel narratives

Music researcher Phineas Fox has been enjoying gathering background material for a biography of Franz Liszt. But matters take a decidedly unexpected turn when his investigations lead to Linklighters, a new restaurant built on the site of a Victorian music hall, and unearth evidence of a possible murder involving a performer known as Scaramel.

Rayne, Sarah

Property of a lady / Sarah Rayne. Severn House, 2011. 252 p. Nell West and Michael Flint novels

ISBN 9780727880284

1. Haunted houses 2. Ghosts 3. Secrets 4. Widows 5. Mothers and daughters 6. Diaries 7. Supernatural 8. England 9. Shropshire, England 10. Supernatural mysteries

Michael Flint is asked to be the caretaker of Charect House, a haunted place with past secrets that could endanger present occupants.

"Rayne's crisp and fast-paced writing deftly combines sharp characters, obscure legend, the panorama of 20th-century history, subtle romance, and even subtler melancholy, turning the picked-over bones of the haunted house story into something fresh and frequently terrifying." Publishers Weekly.

Read, Cornelia

The **crazy** school / Cornelia Read. Warner Books, 2008. 326 p. Madeline Dare mysteries

ISBN 9780446582599

1. Problem youth 2. Boarding schools 3. Classroom management 4. Women teachers 5. Teenagers 6. Murder 7. Murder suspects 8. Upper class 9. Women journalists 10. Women amateur detectives 11. Berkshire Hills, Massachusetts 12. Massachusetts 13. Mysteries

LC 2007010282

Sequel to: A field of darkness.

Madeline Dare goes to work as a teacher at Santangelo Academy, a boarding school for emotionally disturbed teenagers in the Berkshires. Once there she finds a disturbing realm where students and teachers must follow the dean's bizarre therapies. She quickly discovers that many of her colleagues are devout followers of the dean. Maddie forms an unlikely alliance with a small group of rebellious students whose constant resistance to authority may be her only salvation.

Read, Cornelia

Invisible boy / Cornelia Read. Grand Central Pub., 2010. 320 p. Madeline Dare mysteries

ISBN 9780446511346

1. Cold cases (Criminal investigation) 2. Social conflict 3. Missing children 4. Murder investigation 5. Child abuse 6. Volunteers 7. Socialites 8. Upper class 9. Women journalists 10. Women amateur detectives 11. New York City 12. Mysteries

LC 2009017205

Outspoken socialite Madeline Dare is prompted by the discovery of a 3-year-old's body to examine her own troubled history in the public class and racial warfare of 1990s New York City society.

"Read expertly evokes the New York City of the period, from the nearly palpable grime of Chelsea to disturbing undertones of racism and classism in the justice system. Equal parts toughness and vulnerability, Madeline is always a bracing heroine." Publishers Weekly.

Read, Cornelia

Valley of ashes / Cornelia Read. Grand Central Pub., 2012. 368 p. Madeline Dare mysteries

ISBN 9780446511360

1. Marital conflict 2. Life change events 3. Arson investigation 4. Autism 5. Arson -- Boulder, Colorado 6. Women journalists 7. Women amateur detectives 8. New York City 9. Boulder, Colorado 10. Mysteries

LC 2011049675

Madeline Dare, a recently transplanted New Yorker and stay-at-home mom, takes on a freelance position for a Boulder, Colorado, newspaper and must protect her family when her investigative coverage of a local serial arsonist gets a bit too hot.

Read, Piers Paul, 1941-

Alice in exile / Piers Paul Read. Thomas Dunne, 2002, c2001. 344 p.

ISBN 9780312303983

1. First World War era (1914-1918) 2. Young women 3. British in Russia 4. Governesses 5. Pregnant women 6. World War I -- Russia 7. London, England 8. Russia 9. Love stories 10. Historical fiction

Originally published: London : Weidenfeld & Nicolson, 2001.

Alice Fry, a free-thinking woman who is rejected by Edward Cobb, the eligible son of an ambitious baronet, builds a new life for herself in Russia during the Russian Revolution and World War I.

"As striking in her beauty as she is shocking in her behavior, Alice Fry has an uninhibited sexuality that makes her attractive to two very different men. Pregnant with fiancé Edward Cobb's child, Alice is abandoned by him when her father becomes embroiled in a sexual scandal that threatens Cobb's political ambition. With no one to turn to and nowhere to go, Alice is rescued by Baron von Rettenberg, a womanizing Russian nobleman who hires her as his children's governess. . . .To read Read is to be caught up in an epic wonder of passion, scandal, adn international intrigue." Booklist.

Reay, Katherine, 1970-

The Brontë plot / Katherine Reay. Thomas Nelson, 2015 336 p.

ISBN 9781401689759

1. Brontë, Emily, 1818-1848 Influence 2. Brontë, Charlotte, 1816-1855 Influence 3. Brontë, Anne, 1820-1849 Influence 4. Booksellers 5. Business ethics 6. Consequences 7. Rare books 8. Christian life 9. Women travelers 10. Personal conduct 11. Books and reading 12. Men/women relations 13. Souvenirs (Keepsakes) 14. Women -- Interpersonal relations 15. Great Britain 16. Chicago, Illinois 17. Love stories 18. Christian fiction

LC 2015022374

When Lucy Alling's secret is unearthed, her world begins to crumble, but it may be the best thing that has ever happened to her after discovering that she is not the only one with ghosts and that she can prevail even in the midst of change.

"The moral ambiguity makes the story more modern than its premise would suggest and proves how well its source material holds up over time." Kirkus.

Recacoechea S., Juan

American visa / Juan De Recacoechea ; translated by Adrian Althoff ; with an afterword by Ilan Stavans. Akashic Books, 2007, c1994. 257 p.

ISBN 1933354208

1. Middle-aged men -- Bolivia 2. Teachers -- Bolivia 3. Fathers and sons 4. Visas 5. Identification cards -- Forgeries 6. Quests 7. Immigration and emigration 8. Prostitutes -- La Paz, Bolivia 9. Men/women relations 10. Robbery 11. Crime -- Economic aspects 12. Bribery 13. La Paz, Bolivia 14. Bolivia 15. Noir fiction 16. Translations -- Spanish to English

LC 2006936532

Translated from the Spanish

Originally published: Cochabamba, Bolivia : Editorial "Los Amigos del Libro", 1994.

"In this 1994 Bolivian bestseller, written as an antidote to what de Recacoechea considered an overdose of magical-realism in Latin literature, a schoolteacher with a taste for American crime fiction sees the underside of La Paz as he awaits a visa to enter the United States. . . . A serious novel made palatable by humor as dry as the Andean uplands in which it is set." Kirkus

Reddi, Rishi

Passage west : a novel / Rishi Reddi. Ecco, 2020. 432 p.

ISBN 9780060898793

1. 20th century 2. Immigrants, East Indian 3. Sharecroppers 4. Farm life 5. Agriculture 6. Friendship 7. Xenophobia 8. Prejudice 9. Families 10. California -- History -- 20th century 11. Historical fiction

LC 2019050704

Follows a family of Indian sharecroppers at the onset of World War I, revealing a little-known part of California history.

"Reddi's Steinbeck-ian tale adds a valuable contribution to the stories of immigrants in California." Publishers Weekly.

Redfern, Elizabeth

The music of the spheres / Elizabeth Redfern. G.P. Putnam's Sons, 2001. 420 p.

ISBN 9780399147630

1. Georgian era (1714-1837) 2. 1790s 3. Intelligence officers 4. Astronomers 5. Murder investigation 6. Loss (Psychology) 7. Astronomical societies 8. Families of murder victims 9. Spies -- France 10. Murder 11. London, England -- History -- 18th century 12. Historical mysteries 13. Spy fiction 14. Mysteries

LC 00068343

England is at war with France in 1795, and espionage is rampant. Jonathan Absey of the Home Office must do his best to apprehend spies while haunted by the unsolved murder of his fifteen-year-old daughter. Pursuing both investigations, he stumbles upon a strange society of astronomers whose quest for a long-lost star begins to merge with his own.

"A tale of murder and intrigue set in 1795 London. Jonathan Absey is a clerk at the Home Office whose job is to search out spies in the war with France. Instead, he spends much of his time trying to discover who murdered his daughter, a red-haired prostitute. In his quest for justice, he enlists the reluctant help of half-brother Alexander. An amateur astronomer, Alexander ingratiates himself with an unusual group of French emigres who are searching the skies for an elusive new planet they call Selene. Secret agents, murdered prostitutes, and the love of science all combine in an enjoyable if slow-paced story." Library Journal.

Redfield, James

The celestine prophecy : an adventure / James Redfield. Warner Books, 1993. 246 p. Celestine series (James Redfield)

ISBN 9780446518628

1. Quests -- Peru 2. Manuscripts, Peruvian 3. Prophecies (Occultism) 4. Spiritual life 5. New Age 6. Peru 7. Adventure stories 8. Spiritual fiction

LC 93-61754

The unnamed hero takes on the Peruvian government, priests, guerrillas and drug dealers to find an ancient manuscript whose nine insights prophesy New Age spirituality. An adventure story replete with energy transfers and other psychic phenomena.

"Redfield has a real talent for page-turning action." Publishers Weekly.

Redhill, Michael, 1966-
Bellevue square / Michael Redhill Doubleday Canada, 2017 272 p.
ISBN 9780385684842
1. Doppelgangers 2. Moving to a new city 3. Obsession 4. Searching 5. City life 6. Misfits (Persons) 7. Toronto, Ontario 8. Thrillers and suspense
Scotiabank Giller Prize, 2017.

Jean Mason has a doppelganger. At least, that's what people tell her. With the aid of a small army of locals, Jeans begins her investigation at a city park called Bellevue Square. But when some of them start disappearing, it becomes apparent that her alleged double has a sinister agenda.

Redhill, Michael, 1966-
Consolation / Michael Redhill. Little, Brown and Co., 2007. 352 p.
ISBN 0316734985
1. 1990s 2. Widows 3. Sons-in-law 4. Mothers and daughters 5. Photographers 6. Historians 7. Grief in women 8. Secrets 9. Photographs 10. Salvage 11. Family relationships 12. Fathers -- Death 13. Ontario 14. Toronto, Ontario -- History -- 19th century 15. Lake Ontario 16. Historical fiction 17. Domestic fiction 18. Parallel narratives
Toronto Book Awards, 2007.

With the help of her daughter's fiancé, widow Marianne Hollis sets out to make her husband's last dream a reality by uncovering a treasure trove of missing glass negatives that represent the earliest pictures ever taken of Toronto, in a novel that moves back and forth between the present and the past, into the life of the photographer who took the pictures more than a century and a half earlier.

"A gentle but unfaltering cadence, a well-tempered voice, and a highly resolved sense of detail bring readers back and forth smoothly between these two eras." Quill & Quire.

Redondo, Dolores, 1969-
The **invisible** guardian / Dolores Redondo ; translated from the Spanish by Isabelle Kaufeler. Atria Books, 2016, c2013. 384 p. Baztan trilogy
ISBN 9781501102134
1. Homecomings 2. Women detectives 3. Serial murder investigation 4. Murder 5. Secrets 6. Superstition 7. Policewomen 8. Villages -- Spain 9. Human sacrifice 10. Legends 11. Murder investigation 12. Basque Provinces -- Social life and customs 13. Spain 14. Police procedurals 15. Mysteries 16. Translations -- Spanish to English
Originally published by Destino, 2013.

Homicide investigator Amaia Salazar returns to her hometown in Basque Country in Spain after a murdered teenage girl is found along the riverbank, and must determine if the crime is a result of a ritual killer or a mythological creature known as the Basajuan.

Reed, Ishmael, 1938-
* **Flight** to Canada / Ishmael Reed. Random House, 1976. 179 p.
ISBN 9780394487540
1. 1960s 2. Fugitive slaves -- United States 3. Civil war 4. Slavery 5. African Americans 6. Escapes 7. Slaves 8. Racism 9. Human rights 10. Civil rights 11. United States Civil War, 1861-1865 12. United States -- History -- Civil War, 1861-1865 13. Southern States -- History -- 19th century 14. Canada -- History -- 19th century 15. Satirical fiction 16. Literary fiction 17. African American fiction
LC 76015598

Raven Quickskill runs away from his master during the Civil War but cannot reach the Canadian border until the war has ended because his master is determined to capture him.

Reed, Ishmael, 1938-
* **Mumbo** jumbo / Ishmael Reed. Doubleday, 1972. 223 p.
ISBN 0684824779
1. 1920s 2. Harlem Renaissance 3. African American men 4. African Americans 5. African Americans -- Social life and customs -- 20th century 6. Epidemics 7. Jazz music 8. Dancing 9. Hoodoo 10. African American arts 11. New Orleans, Louisiana 12. Harlem, New York City 13. United States -- Race relations -- History -- 20th century 14. African American fiction 15. Afrofuturism and Afrofantasy 16. Historical fiction 17. Satirical fiction
LC 73171314

A strange psychic epidemic called "Jes Grew" is spreading through the country, affecting millions. People start doing stupid sensual things with abandon, and civilization itself is threatened. PaPa LaBas, a HooDoo detective, is trying to find out the origins of the Jes Grew-- not because he wants to cure it, but because he's ready for a new kind of society.

Rees, Matt, 1967-
The **fourth** assassin / Matt Beynon Rees. Soho, 2009. 336 p. Omar Yussef mysteries
ISBN 9781569476192
1. Fathers and sons 2. Murder suspects 3. Beheading 4. Murder investigation 5. History teachers 6. Palestinian men 7. Palestinian women 8. Christians -- Palestine 9. Crimes against roommates 10. Palestinians in New York City 11. Brooklyn, New York City 12. Mysteries
LC 2009041044

Arriving to visit his son in a heavily Palestinian area of Bay Ridge, Brooklyn, Omar Yussef discovers the beheaded body of one of the boy's roommates; and when his son is arrested as a suspect, Omar must prove his innocence.

Reich, Christopher, 1961-
Rules of deception / Christopher Reich. Doubleday, 2008. 320 p. Jonathan Ransom novels
ISBN 9780385524063
1. Physicians 2. Grief in men 3. Assassins 4. Husband and wife 5. Loss (Psychology) 6. Secrets 7. Terrorism 8. Switzerland 9. Thrillers and suspense 10. Spy fiction
LC 2007036368

Sequel : Rules of vengeance.

Following the death of his wife in a mountaineering accident, Dr. Jonathan Ransom receives a mysterious message that makes him the subject of an international manhunt as he struggles to unravel the truth behind his wife's secrets.

"Reich's everyman hero, Jonathan Ransom, is plunged into a world of intrigue when his wife dies in an accident. Growing questions about her true identity dig him deeper into trouble. Ransom is unaware that he is interrupting the endgame of an enormous and long-running conspiracy that he--and the Swiss cop tracking him--could derail. Reich . . . throws readers off the scent but never loses control of the plot. He skillfully handles the pacing, and this results in a suspenseful story balanced by cinematic action scenes. . . . Fans of early Ludlum will particularly enjoy it." Library Journal.

Reich, Christopher, 1961-

The **take** / Christopher Reich. Little Brown & Co, 2018. 336 p. Simon Riske novels

ISBN 9780316342353

1. CIA 2. Spies 3. Espionage 4. Stolen property recovery 5. International intrigue 6. Gangsters 7. Secrets 8. Princes 9. Letters 10. Paris, France 11. London, England 12. Spy fiction 13. Political thrillers

Preferring work that allows him to stay under the radar, freelance industrial spy Simon Riske reluctantly takes a high-profile job from the CIA involving a gangster's theft of millions from a visiting Saudi prince and a stolen letter containing highly sensitive information.

Reichs, Kathy

206 Bones / Kathy Reichs. Simon & Schuster, 2009. 320 p. Temperance Brennan mysteries

ISBN 9780743294393

1. Women forensic anthropologists 2. Crimes against women 3. Sabotage 4. Murder -- Montreal, Quebec 5. Bones 6. Forensic sciences 7. Chicago, Illinois 8. Montreal, Quebec 9. Mysteries

Forensic anthropologist Tempe Brennan regains consciousness to discover herself bound and trapped in a small enclosed space before remembering an autopsy case that resulted in a murder and an attempt on her life.

Reichs, Kathy

* **Bare** bones / Kathy Reichs. Scribner, 2003. 320 p. Temperance Brennan mysteries

ISBN 0743233468

1. Women forensic anthropologists -- North Carolina 2. Murder investigation 3. Drug smuggling 4. Forensic sciences 5. Rare and endangered animals 6. Wild animal smuggling 7. Vacations 8. Bones 9. Dead -- Identification 10. Mother and child 11. Infant death 12. Murder 13. Charlotte, North Carolina 14. Mysteries

LC 2003040725

Sequel to: Grave secrets.

Sequel: Monday mourning.

First published: London: William Heinemann, 2003.

Her plans for a romantic vacation interrupted by the discoveries of two murdered bodies and a small plane crash, Tempe Brennan traces leads to an isolated North Carolina farm.

Reichs, Kathy

Bones of the lost : a Temperance Brennan novel / Kathy Reichs. Simon & Schuster, 2013. 304 p. Temperance Brennan mysteries

ISBN 9781439102459

1. Women forensic anthropologists 2. Murder 3. Bones 4. Forensic sciences 5. Murder investigation 6. Human trafficking 7. Montreal, Quebec 8. Mysteries

While examining a bundle of Peruvian dog mummies confiscated by U.S. Customs, forensic anthropologist Tempe Brennan finds herself in the center of a human trafficking conspiracy when she investigates the murder of a teenage girl.

Reichs, Kathy

Bones to ashes / Kathy Reichs. Scribner, 2007. 320 p. Temperance Brennan mysteries

ISBN 9780743294379

1. Women forensic anthropologists 2. Missing girls 3. Forensic sciences 4. Missing persons 5. Murder 6. Forensic anthropology 7. Leprosy 8. People with leprosy 9. Forensic medicine 10.

Women forensic scientists 11. Loss (Psychology) 12. Excavations (Archaeology) 13. Canada 14. Mysteries

LC 2007002405

Discovering the skeleton of a young girl in the neighborhood of a childhood best friend who had gone missing thirty years earlier, Tempe Brennan investigates suspicions that the victim and her friend are one and the same.

Reichs, Kathy

Break no bones / Kathy Reichs. Scribner, 2006. 352 p. Temperance Brennan mysteries

ISBN 0743233492

1. Women forensic anthropologists 2. Missing persons 3. Murder investigation 4. Cemeteries 5. Excavations (Archaeology) 6. Former husbands 7. Murder 8. Forensic sciences 9. Dead -- Identification 10. Charleston, South Carolina 11. Mysteries

LC 2006045038

Struggling with a lackluster teaching position at an archaeology field school in South Carolina, Tempe Brennan discovers a fresh skeleton among ancient bones and traces leads to a free street clinic where patients are going missing.

"Reichs's down-to-earth heroine is an appealing creation, who deftly juggles personal problems with professional challenges." Publishers Weekly.

Reichs, Kathy

* A **conspiracy** of bones / Kathy Reichs. Scribner, 2020. 336 p. Temperance Brennan mysteries

ISBN 9781982138882

1. Women forensic anthropologists 2. Forensic sciences 3. Brain aneurysms 4. Murder victims 5. Supervisors 6. Secrets 7. Text messaging 8. Missing children 9. Cold cases (Criminal investigation) 10. Law enforcement 11. Men/women relations 12. Charlotte, North Carolina 13. North Carolina 14. Mysteries

Forensic anthropologist Temperance Brennan struggles to identify a faceless murder victim in possession of her cell number, a mystery that is entangled with a decade-old missing-child case.

"The novel shows us a more vulnerable side of Brennan, and Reichs' writing style is subtly different, too, as though she were trying to make us feel ever so slightly off-kilter. A complete success." Booklist.

Reichs, Kathy

Deadly decisions / Kathy Reichs. Scribner, 2000. 333 p. Temperance Brennan mysteries

ISBN 0684859718

1. FBI 2. Women forensic anthropologists 3. Murder investigation 4. Motorcycle gangs 5. Bombing 6. Explosions 7. Identical twins -- Death 8. DNA fingerprinting 9. Murder 10. Drive-by shootings 11. Gun accidents 12. Outlaws 13. Montreal, Quebec 14. North Carolina 15. Mysteries

LC 00022220

Sequel to: Death du jour.

Sequel: Fatal voyage.

Forensic anthropologist Temperance Brennan divides her time between North Carolina and Montreal. In Canada, a motorcycle gang war claims the life of a nine-year-old girl. Back in the states, the body of a long-missing teenager is found hundreds of miles from her home. Are the two cases related? If so, how? That's what Tempe wonders even as she faces surprising trouble in her love life and with her nephew. -- Description by Dawn Towery.

"The author doesn't dumb down the scientific stuff, delivering the full textbook version of subjects like hydrocephalus, blood-spatter analysis, ground-penetrating radar devices and the history of outlaw motor-cycle clubs in North America." New York Times Book Review.

Reichs, Kathy

Death du jour / Kathy Reichs. Scribner, 1999. 379 p. Temperance Brennan mysteries

ISBN 0684841185

1. Women forensic anthropologists 2. Burn victims -- Montreal, Quebec 3. Cults -- Texas 4. Women cult leaders -- Texas 5. Women with mental illnesses -- Texas 6. Arson 7. Fires -- Montreal, Quebec 8. Forensic sciences 9. Montreal, Quebec 10. Texas 11. North Carolina 12. Mysteries

LC 98048763

Sequel to: Deja dead.

Sequel: Deadly decisions.

Forensic anthropologist Temperance Brennan investigates an occurance of arson, which leads to the work of a controversial professor, a commune, and a primate colony.

Reichs, Kathy

Deja dead / Kathy Reichs. Scribner, 1997. 411 p. Temperance Brennan mysteries

ISBN 0684841177

1. Women forensic anthropologists 2. Women murder victims 3. Serial murder investigation 4. Serial murderers -- Montreal, Quebec 5. Stalkers -- Montreal, Quebec 6. Bones 7. Monasteries 8. Detectives -- Montreal, Quebec 9. Best friends 10. Mothers and daughters 11. Forensic sciences 12. Stalking 13. Montreal, Quebec 14. Mysteries

LC 97002990

Sequel: Death du jour.

Arthur Ellis Award for Best First Novel, 1998.

Temperance Brennan leaves a shaky marriage behind and heads to Quebec on an assignment as director of forensic anthropology that leads her to track down a killer on the loose.

"Except for imparting an excess of lab information, Reichs, also a forensic anthropologist, drives the pace at a heady clip. A first-class writer, she dazzles readers with sensory imagery that is apt, fresh, and funny." Library Journal.

Reichs, Kathy

Grave secrets / Kathy Reichs. Scribner, 2002. 416 p. Temperance Brennan mysteries

ISBN 0684859734

1. Women forensic anthropologists 2. Massacres -- Guatemala 3. Murder investigation 4. Forensic sciences 5. Dead -- Identification 6. Americans in Guatemala 7. Mayas 8. Women murder victims 9. Murder 10. Missing girls 11. Missing persons -- Guatemala 12. Stem cells 13. Greed 14. Guatemala 15. Mysteries

LC 2002022695

Sequel to: Fatal voyage.

Sequel: Bare bones.

First published: London: William Heinemann, 2002.

Summer, 1982: Soldiers enter a Guatemalan village and massacre its women and children. Today, families refer to their lost members as the disappeared. Enter Temperance Brennan, about to confront the most heartbreaking case of her careeer. Out of shallow graves fading clues emerge. Something savage happened in the highlands two decades ago. Is it happening again? Four girls are missing and a human rights investigator is murdered as Tempe listens to her screams on the phone. Will Tempe be the next victim?

Reichs, Kathy

Monday mourning / Kathy Reichs. Scribner, 2004. 320 p. Temperance Brennan mysteries

ISBN 0743233476

1. Women forensic anthropologists 2. Murder investigation 3. Teenage girl murder victims 4. Forensic sciences 5. Murder 6. Restaurants 7. Pizza industry and trade 8. Bones 9. Dead -- Identification 10. Montreal, Quebec 11. Mysteries

LC 2004045263

Sequel to: Bare bones.

Journeying to wintry Montreal to testify at a murder trial, forensic anthropologist Tempe Brennan discovers three skeletons in the basement of a pizza parlor and realizes that she has stumbled into a crime from the past.

"This Temperance Brennan mystery finds the forensic anthropologist in Montreal to testify in a murder case. Arriving a day early to prepare, she becomes caught up in a new investigation when three sets of human bones are discovered in the basement of a pizza parlor. Examining the remains, she discovers that the victims were Caucasian and female. Antique buttons found near the bodies lead Homicide Detective Claudel to believe that the remains are over a century old, but Tempe is not so convinced and investigates with the help of her friend Anne, who has come to visit while contemplating her marriage. Readers of the series will be pleased to see the relationship between Tempe and Detective Andrew Ryan develop further." Library Journal.

Reid, Iain, 1981-

I'm thinking of ending things / Iain Reid. Scout Press, 2016. 224 p.

ISBN 9781501126925

1. Automobile travel 2. Abandonment (Psychology) 3. Couples 4. Solitude 5. Threat (Psychology) 6. Identity (Psychology) 7. Purpose in life 8. Psychological suspense

LC 2015031094

ALA Notable Book, 2017.

A thriller about a young woman who is considering what to do about Jake, the man with whom she is driving for hours to and from his parents house in the country.

"Reid's tightly crafted tale toys with the nature of identity and comes by its terror honestly, building a wall of intricately layered psychological torment." Kirkus.

Reid, Kiley

* Such a fun age / Kiley Reid. G.P. Putnam's Sons, 2019. 310 p.

ISBN 9780525541905

1. Babysitters 2. African American women -- Identity 3. Whiteness (Concept) 4. Children 5. Racism 6. Race relations 7. Malicious accusation 8. Self-doubt 9. Consequences 10. Interracial romance 11. Former lovers 12. Interpersonal relations 13. Philadelphia, Pennsylvania 14. Literary fiction 15. African American fiction

A story about race and privilege is centered around a young black babysitter, her well-intentioned employer and a surprising connection that threatens to undo them both.

"In her smart and timely debut, Reid has her finger solidly on the pulse of the pressures and ironies inherent in social media, privilege, modern parenting, racial tension, and political correctness." Booklist.

Reid, Taylor Jenkins

Daisy Jones & the Six : a novel / Taylor Jenkins Reid. Ballantine Books, 2019. 336 p.

ISBN 9781524798628

1. 1970s 2. Women singers 3. Rock groups 4. Fame 5. Addiction

6. Drug use 7. Rock music 8. Rock musicians 9. Interviews 10. Pregnant women 11. Interpersonal relations 12. Literary fiction

LC 2018051135

Goodreads Choice Award, 2019

When singer Daisy Jones meets Billy Dunne of the band The Six, the two rising 70s rock-and-roll artists are catapulted into stardom when a producer puts them together, a decision that is complicated by a pregnancy and the seductions of fame.

"Framed as a tell-all biography compiled through interviews and articles, Reid's (The Seven Husbands of Evelyn Hugo, 2017) novel so resembles a memoir of a real band and conjures such true-to-life images of the seventies music scene that readers will think they're listening to Fleetwood Mac or Led Zeppelin." Booklist.

Reid, Taylor Jenkins

Forever, interrupted : a novel / Taylor Jenkins Reid. Washington Square Press, 2013. 320 p.

ISBN 9781476712826

1. Grief 2. Loss (Psychology) 3. Friendship 4. Husband and wife 5. Widowers 6. Mothers-in-law 7. Intergenerational friendship 8. Accidents 9. Love stories

LC 2012035073

After her newlywed husband, Ben, is killed while riding his bike, Elsie realizes the only family she has left is a mother-in-law she does not meet until after Ben's death, and whom she is instantly at odds with, and must forge a bond with the woman if she is ever going to get over the grief.

Reiken, Frederick

Day for night / Frederick Reiken. Little, Brown and Co., 2010. 326 p.

ISBN 9780316077569

1. Middle-aged women 2. Rock musicians 3. Brothers and sisters 4. People with cancer 5. Family relationships 6. Single mothers 7. Motorcycle accidents 8. People in comas 9. Fugitives 10. Vacations 11. Literary fiction

LC 2009038597

In a novel that spans time and space, a middle-aged woman on vacation in Florida is linked to an elusive Sixties-era fugitive, as well as dozens of other characters whose lives seem mysteriously intertwined.

"An entrancing and profoundly complicated tale Reiken tells as he slowly reveals the submerged connections among his intriguing characters while sustaining psychological sophistication, suspense, shrewd humor, and many-tiered compassion." Booklist.

Reimringer, John

Vestments / John Reimringer. Milkweed Editions, 2010. 304 p.

ISBN 9781571310804

1. Catholic Church 2. Priests -- Minnesota 3. Self-fulfillment -- Religious aspects 4. Temptation 5. Faith in men 6. Minnesota 7. Literary fiction

LC 2010007143

Just a few years after his ordination as a priest in the Catholic Church, James Dressler finds himself attracted again to his first love, Betty Garcia, and is torn by his opposing desires for the Church and for Betty.

"Just a few years after his ordination and his first assignment as a parish priest, James Dressler is placed on leave. His housekeeper found some letters from a woman and turned them into the archdiocese. For little more than a kiss, he is relegated to a parish in a backwater burg. He opts instead to live back home with his mother in St. Paul until he can come up with a better game plan. But his gritty hometown has its own temptations, and, broke and in need of work, James finds himself renovating apartments and butting heads with his tough, bad-tempered father and attracted once again to his old highschool lover, Betty Garcia. Through his thoughtful themes and lyrical prose, Reimringer effortlessly restores a measure of dignity to the priesthood even as he pays tender homage to the working-class roots of St. Paul." Booklist.

Reisman, Nancy, 1961-

The **first** desire / Nancy Reisman. Pantheon Books, 2004. 320 p.

ISBN 0375423087

1. 1930s 2. 1940s 3. Jews 4. Jewelers 5. Widowers 6. Jewish families 7. Father and child 8. Brothers and sisters 9. Missing persons 10. Families of missing persons 11. Dysfunctional families 12. Family relationships 13. Responsibility 14. Resentfulness 15. Loneliness 16. Love 17. Mental illness 18. Family and mental illness 19. Depressions, -- 1929-1941 20. World War II 21. Buffalo, New York 22. Historical fiction

LC 2004044665

The lives of the four Cohen siblings--Sadie, Jo, Goldie, and Irving--are turned upside down by the secrets that they have kept hidden, even from themselves, as the sudden disappearance of Goldie sparks revelations about their family.

"The novel is both lovely and heartbreaking in its vision of family ties at their most inevitable." New York Times.

Remarque, Erich Maria, 1898-1970

* All quiet on the western front / Erich Maria Remarque ; translated from the German by A. W. Wheen. Fawcett Columbine, 1996, c1929. 295 p.

ISBN 0449911497

1. First World War era (1914-1918) 2. Trench warfare 3. War and society 4. Soldiers 5. Teenage boys 6. War -- Psychological aspects 7. Growing up 8. Duty 9. Justice 10. Teenagers and death 11. Germans in France 12. Life change events 13. Friends' death 14. Loss (Psychology) 15. World War I 16. Survival -- Psychological aspects 17. Germany -- Social life and customs -- 20th century 18. War stories 19. Modern classics 20. Literary fiction 21. Translations -- German to English

LC 96096745

Sequel: The road back.

This translation originally published: London: Jonathan Cape, 1994. "Complete & unabridged"

Originally published: London : Bodley Head, 1929.

Originally published: Berlin : Propylaen-Verlag, 1929.

The testament of Paul Baumer, who enlists with his classmates in the German army of World War I, illuminates the savagery and futility of war.

Remarque, Erich Maria, 1898-1970

The **road** back / Erich Maria Remarque ; translated from the German by A.W. Wheen. Ballantine Books, 1998, c1931. 313 p.

ISBN 9780449912461

1. 1910s 2. Survival -- Psychological aspects 3. Postwar life 4. Veterans 5. Food supply 6. Justice 7. Life change events 8. Loss (Psychology) 9. World War I 10. Germany -- Social life and customs -- 20th century 11. War stories 12. Translations -- German to English

Sequel to: All quiet on the Western Front.

Also published under the title "The Way Back" in the UK.

Originally published in 1931 under the title Weg zuruck.

In a sequel to " All quiet on the Western Front," Ernst and the few survivors of his company return home after the war to find food in short supply and their families changed.

"A profoundly moving, a painfully moving, document. Unlike tragedy, it has no katharsis, but, like a tragedy, it has to be looked at open-eyed, honestly, courageously." The Spectator.

Remarque, Erich Maria, 1898-1970

A **time** to love and a time to die / Erich Maria Remarque; translated from the German by Denver Lindley. Fawcett Columbine ;, 1998, c1954. 378 p.

ISBN 9780449912508

1. Second World War era (1939-1945) 2. Soldiers -- Germany 3. Loss (Psychology) 4. World War II 5. Bombing victims 6. Disillusionment 7. Germans in the Soviet Union 8. Parents -- Death 9. Soviet Union 10. Love stories 11. War stories 12. Historical fiction 13. Translations -- German to English

LC 98096094

"The whole story is told with great restraint, with little sentimentality for those in misery and with little open rage at those who caused it." Chicago Tribune.

Renault, Mary, 1905-1983

* The **bull** from the sea / Mary Renault. Vintage Books, 1975, c1962. 343 p.

ISBN 9780394715049

1. Theseus (Greek mythology) 2. Interpersonal attraction 3. Men/women relations 4. Minotaur (Greek mythology) 5. Heroes and heroines, Greek 6. Historical fiction

LC 62008924

Slaying the Minotaur was only the beginning. Theseus's legendary exploits continue in this magnificent novel of mythological adventure in classical Greece. Esteemed author Mary Renault picks up where her classic The King Must Die left off, relating the tale of Theseus's triumphant return from Crete to become King of Athens. Plunge into the thrilling world of the continuing adventures of this mythic ruler, from his famous capture of the Amazon Hippolyta to the bitter twist of fate that loosened the bull from the sea. Renault's writing is rich with color and drama, vividly capturing the heroism and uniquely Greek sense of destiny that characterize this classic tale of a royal ruler who looms larger than life.

Renault, Mary, 1905-1983

Funeral games / Mary Renault. Pantheon Books, 1981. 335p. Alexander the Great trilogy (Mary Renault)

ISBN 9780394520681

1. Alexander,, the Great, 356-323 BC 2. Ancient Greece (800 BCE-640 CE) 3. Rulers 4. Conspiracies 5. Heirs and heiresses 6. Betrayal 7. Power (Social sciences) 8. Rulers 9. Ambition in women 10. Widows 11. Generals 12. Ancient Greece -- History -- Hellenistic Period, 323-146 BC 13. Biographical fiction 14. Historical fiction

LC 81047273

Sequel to The Persian boy (1972)

After the death of Alexander the Great, an extraordinary power struggle, involving intrigue and a series of murders, takes place among the various successors to his reign.

Renault, Mary, 1905-1983

The **king** must die / Mary Renault. Vintage Books, 1988, c1958. 339 p.

ISBN 9780394751047

1. Minotaur (Greek mythology) 2. Heroes and heroines, Greek 3. Theseus (Greek mythology) 4. Men/women relations 5. Crete 6.

Historical fiction

An adaptation of the legend of Theseus who masters the art of bull leaping and slays the Minotaur in the process of fulfilling his destiny.

"Retold by its hero, the legend of Theseus becomes a logical sequence of adventures that befell a slight, wiry, quick-witted youth impelled to prove his manhood in a semibarbaric society that put a premium on size and brawn. Although, at seventeen, he was already a king and a seasoned warrior, Theseus obeyed his patron god's prompting and voluntarily joined a company of young people conscripted for the bull-dances in Crete, became a renowned bull-leaper, and took advantage of an earthquake to overthrow the Cretan kingdom." Booklist.

Renault, Mary, 1905-1983

* The **last** of the wine / Mary Renault. Vintage Books, 1975, c1956. 446 p.

ISBN 0394716531

1. Socrates, 469-399 BC 2. Ancient Greece (800 BCE-640 CE) 3. Gay men -- Ancient Greece 4. Peloponnesian War, 431-404 BC 5. Interpersonal attraction 6. Interpersonal relations 7. Men/men relations 8. Ancient Greece -- History 9. Historical fiction 10. LGBTQIA fiction

LC 754841

Illustrated with map of Greece and the Aegean.

Includes chronological table and glossary.

Originally published by Pantheon Books, New York. 1956

Two young Athenians, Alexias and Lysis compete in the palaestra, take part in the Olympic games, fight in the wars against Sparta, and grow to manhood influenced by the friendship of Alkibiades and the wise guidance of Socrates.

Renault, Mary, 1905-1983

The **Persian** boy / Mary Renault. Vintage Books, 1988, c1972. 419 p. Alexander the Great trilogy (Mary Renault)

ISBN 9780394751016

1. Alexander,, the Great, 356-323 BC 2. Bagoas 3. Hephaestion 4. Gay men 5. Rulers 6. Eunuchs 7. Lovers 8. Battles 9. Gay rulers -- Macedon (Empire) 10. Men/men relations 11. Iran -- History -- To 640 A D 12. Biographical fiction 13. Historical fiction 14. LGBTQIA fiction

LC 72003407

Sequel to: Fire from heaven.

Sequel: Funeral games.

Includes map, and sources for the general reader.

A slave-boy in the household of Alexander the Great tells about the adventures of the Macedonian king during the last seven years of his life.

"This sequel to Fire from heaven continues the story of Alexander the Great, focusing upon his momentous expedition into Asia. This time we observe events through the eyes of Bagoas, a beautiful Persian eunuch who was loved by King Darius and then by Alexander himself. The multiple facets of Renault's art, familiar to a host of admirers, are once again apparent: a particularly sensitive depiction of boyhood and youth; an astounding grasp of the facts and the spirit of the ancient world; an unerring sense of the dramatic which, along with her superb descriptive powers, brings to life a great historical period." Library Journal.

Rendell, Ruth, 1930-2015

The **babes** in the wood : a Chief Inspector Wexford mystery / Ruth Rendell. Crown, 2002. 368 p. Chief Inspector Wexford mysteries

ISBN 140004930X

1. Dysfunctional families 2. Murder investigation 3. Family secrets 4. Police 5. Teenage girls 6. Babysitters 7. Missing persons 8. Drug use 9. Small town life 10. England 11. Mysteries 12. Police

procedurals

LC 2003001575

The mysterious disappearance of two local teenagers and their baby-sitter draws Inspector Wexford into a baffling case involving dark family secrets, violence, a religious cult, adultery, and murder.

Rendell, Ruth, 1930-2015

Blood lines : long and short stories / Ruth Rendell. Crown Publishers, 1996. 215 p.

ISBN 0517703238

1. Mysteries 2. Short stories

LC 96-852

Eleven stories deal with murder, complex family relationships, and the psychology of killers.

"In this collection of short stories, Rendell is at her best, using her own quixotic brand of dark humor and an often heartwrenching poignancy to produce 11 mini-masterpieces." Booklist.

Rendell, Ruth, 1930-2015

* The **bridesmaid** / Ruth Rendell. Mysterious Press, 1989. 259 p.

ISBN 9780892963881

1. Women with mental illnesses 2. Obsession in men 3. Murder 4. Men/women relations 5. Bridesmaids 6. Psychological suspense

LC 88043471

Philip Wardman, a young man with an abnormal fear of violence and death, meets beautiful and mysterious Senta, a bridesmaid in his sister's wedding, who insists that he prove his love to her by committing a murder.

"Ms. Rendell is a diabolically subtle writer. For much of this claustrophobic study of mutual obsession, she has us peering into Senta's mind through Philip's eyes, suspiciously analyzing her bizarre statements and mysterious behavior. But, like a cunning old spider, the author has caught two flies in her web; and in the end, Philip proves the more interesting study, with his phobia about violence and his fanaticism for propriety." New York Times Book Review.

Rendell, Ruth, 1930-2015

Collected stories / Ruth Rendell. Pantheon Books, 1987. 536 p.

ISBN 0394569423

1. Murder 2. Obsession 3. Mental illness 4. Psychological suspense 5. Short stories 6. Mysteries

LC 87035949

Collected stories from the author's early career.

Includes nearly forty stories from the author's first four short story collections, among them five Inspector Wexford tales and two Edgar award winners

Rendell, Ruth, 1930-2015

End in tears : a Chief Inspector Wexford mystery / Ruth Rendell. Crown Publishers, 2005. 336 p. Chief Inspector Wexford mysteries

ISBN 0307339769

1. Crimes against teenage girls 2. Stalking 3. Murder investigation 4. Serial murderers 5. Teenage girls 6. Young women 7. Stalkers 8. Class conflict 9. Race relations 10. Gender role 11. Police 12. England 13. Mysteries 14. Police procedurals

LC 2005026619

A lump of concrete dropped deliberately from a little stone bridge over a relatively unfrequented road kills the wrong person. The driver behind is spared. But only for a while ... One particular member of the local press is gunning for the Chief Inspector, distinctly unimpressed

with what he regards as old-fashioned police methods. But Wexford, with his old friend and partner, Mike Burden, along with two new recruits to the Kingsmarkham team, pursue their inquiries with a diligence and humanity that make Ruth Rendell's detective stories enthralling, exciting and very touching.

Rendell, Ruth, 1930-2015

The **face** of trespass / Ruth Rendell. Crime Club by Doubleday, 1974. 184 p.

ISBN 0385016778

1. Obsession in men 2. Social isolation 3. Manipulation by women 4. Breaking up (Interpersonal relations) 5. Men/women relations 6. Psychological suspense

LC 73010817

When his affair with beautiful, young Drusilla Jones abruptly ends, Graham Lanceton withdraws from the world, obsessed by her memory.

"The author conveys the derelict half-dream, half-nightmare life Gray is leading in an Essex hovel far better than a crime-writer need, and through this . . . makes credible the blindness that allows him to be led to total disaster." Times Literary Supplement.

Rendell, Ruth, 1930-2015

Harm done / Ruth Rendell. Crown Publishers, 1999. 346 p. Chief Inspector Wexford mysteries

ISBN 060960547X

1. Child sexual abusers 2. Missing persons 3. Murder investigation 4. Violence against women 5. Police 6. Small town life 7. Father and adult daughter 8. Women social workers 9. England 10. Mysteries 11. Police procedurals

LC 9920432

Inspector Wexford must solve the mysterious disappearances of young girls, protect a pedophile and catch the killer of a wealthy executive found stabbed to death shortly after his child disappears.

Rendell, Ruth, 1930-2015

Heartstones / Ruth Rendell ; illustrations by George Underwood. Harper & Row, 1987. 80 p.

ISBN 9780060157579

1. Teenagers with mental illnesses 2. Fathers and daughters 3. Dysfunctional families 4. Sisters 5. Sixteen-year-old girls 6. Haunted houses 7. England 8. Psychological suspense

LC 86046098

The world of two young girls is threatened when an attractive young woman becomes engaged to their widowed father.

"Such is Rendell's mastery of psychological suspense that throughout we remain unsure of the seriousness of Elvira's intentions." Library Journal.

Rendell, Ruth, 1930-2015

* A **judgement** in stone / Ruth Rendell. Doubleday, 1978, c1977. 188 p.

ISBN 9780385132237

1. Rich families 2. Household employees 3. Mass murder 4. Classism 5. Former prostitutes 6. Religious fanaticism 7. Housekeepers 8. Psychological suspense 9. Thrillers and suspense

LC 77076961

When a housekeeper carries out a modern "Valentine's Day Massacre" on the family that employs her, Detective Chief Superintendent William Vetch investigates to uncover evidence of a personal tragedy that precipitated the crime.

Rendell, Ruth, 1930-2015

Kissing the gunner's daughter / Ruth Rendell. Mysterious Press, 1992. 378 p. Chief Inspector Wexford mysteries

ISBN 9780892963904

1. Father and adult daughter 2. Murder investigation 3. Family relationships 4. Police 5. England 6. Mysteries 7. Police procedurals

LC 91050615

Detective Chief Inspector Reginald Wexford remains cool in the face of massive media attention as he sets out to investigate the stabbing death of celebrity writer Davina Flory and her husband and daughter.

"This is an intricate story that hinges on vanity and self-deception, a story in which the most minor and seemingly innocent relationships are charged with meaning and malice." New York Times Book Review.

Rendell, Ruth, 1930-2015

Live flesh / Ruth Rendell. Pantheon Books, 1986. 272 p.

ISBN 9780394555447

1. Rapists 2. Obsession in men 3. Love triangles 4. Former convicts 5. Men with disabilities 6. People with paraplegia 7. Murder 8. Psychological suspense

LC 86004922

Gold Dagger Award for Best Crime Novel of the Year, 1986.

After fourteen years in prison, rapist Victor Jenner attempts to pick up the pieces of his life but finds himself involved in an awkward triangle whose conflicts resurrect the buried demons of his violent past.

"The obvious way to write this novel would have been to tell it through the eyes of the crippled policeman; Rendell takes the bolder path of getting inside the mind of Jenner. . . . [This] is a frightening, resonant novel--an extraordinary achievement." New Statesman.

Rendell, Ruth, 1930-2015

Not in the flesh : a Wexford novel / Ruth Rendell. Crown Publishers, 2008, c2007. 304 p. Chief Inspector Wexford mysteries

ISBN 9780307406811

1. Murder investigation 2. Dead 3. Missing persons investigation 4. Police -- Sussex, England 5. Burial 6. England 7. Mysteries 8. Police procedurals

LC 2007040945

Searching for truffles in a wood, a man and his dog unearth something less savoury - a human hand. The body, as Chief Inspector Wexford is informed later, has lain buried for ten years or so, wrapped in a purple cotton sheet. The post mortem cannot reveal the precise cause of death. The only clue is a crack in one of the dead man's ribs.

"Rendell has been documenting change in her imaginary Kingsmarkham for 44 years; Not in the Flesh continues to hold a mirror to British society. . . . [She] also weaves into the story Wexford's heartbreaking attempts to address the tradition of female genital mutilation within the Somali community of Kingsmarkham." Los Angeles Times Book Review.

Rendell, Ruth, 1930-2015

Road rage / Ruth Rendell. Crown Publishers, 1997 344 p. Chief Inspector Wexford mysteries

ISBN 0609600567

1. Hostages 2. Green movement 3. Murder investigation 4. Resistance to road construction, powerlines, etc 5. Police 6. England 7. Mysteries 8. Police procedurals

LC 97-1200

Chief Inspector Wexford confronts a group of environmental radicals who attempt to stop a highway project by taking five people hostage, including Wexford's wife

"Taking what he vows will be his last walk in the deep woods that border his Sussex village, Chief Inspector Reginald Wexford contemplates with dread the new superhighway that will soon plow it all under. . . . But whatever sympathy he feels for the militant conservationists who pitch camp in Framhurst Great Wood to protest the highway is lost when a radical splinter group calling itself Sacred Globe kidnaps five innocent people--including Wexford's wife--and threatens to kill them unless the road is stopped." New York Times Book Review.

Rendell, Ruth, 1930-2015

Simisola / Ruth Rendell. Crown Publishers, 1995. 327 p. Chief Inspector Wexford mysteries

ISBN 0440222028

1. Racism 2. Sexual violence 3. Serial murders 4. Nigerians in England 5. Missing persons 6. Police 7. England 8. Kingsmarkham, England 9. Mysteries 10. Police procedurals

Chief Inspector Wexford's sixteenth case centers on a teenaged African girl, the child of a prosperous doctor, who is found in a shallow grave in her quiet English suburb.

"Rendell's long acquaintance with her characters has not diminished the freshness of her work, nor her consummate storytelling. Rather, in Simisola, she offers a finely tuned moral tale that raises questions as it solves crimes." Times Literary Supplement.

Rendell, Ruth, 1930-2015

A sleeping life / Ruth Rendell. Vintage Books, 1978. 180 p. Chief Inspector Wexford mysteries

ISBN 0375704930

1. Murder investigation 2. Secret identity 3. Police 4. England 5. Mysteries 6. Police procedurals

LC 99-87718

An expensive leather wallet is Inspector Wexford's only clue to the death of a woman whose body is found on the outskirts of Kingsmarkham and whose past is completely dark.

Rendell, Ruth, 1930-2015

Speaker of Mandarin / Ruth Rendell. Random House, 1990, c1983. 212 p. Chief Inspector Wexford mysteries

ISBN 9780345302748

1. Murder investigation 2. Voyages and travels 3. British in China 4. Police 5. China 6. Mysteries 7. Police procedurals

LC 83047745

Previous printing issued by Pantheon Books.

The suspects in the murder of wealthy Adela Knighton are the group of travellers with whom, along with Inspector Wexford, the dead woman had recently toured mainland China.

Rendell, Ruth, 1930-2015

The tree of hands / Ruth Rendell. Pantheon Books, 1984. 271 p.

ISBN 0394530985

1. Murder 2. Mental illness 3. Kidnapping 4. Missing children 5. Mother and child 6. Single parents 7. Grief in women 8. Loss (Psychology) 9. Child abuse 10. England 11. Psychological suspense

LC 84019002

Silver Dagger Award for Fiction, 1984.

Benet Archdale's erratic mother Mapsa casts Benet, her baby son James, Carol Stratford, another young single mother, and her son into a maelstrom of kidnapping, fraud, family violence, and death.

"The story explores spectrum of parental feeling against a background of pervasive anxiety and impending doom. This is not a mystery, really, but rather an engrossing psychological thriller." Library Journal.

Restrepo, Laura

Delirium : a novel / Laura Restrepo ; translated from the Spanish by Natasha Wimmer. Nan A. Talese, 2007. 336 p.

ISBN 0385519907

1. 1980s 2. Mental illness 3. Personality change 4. Family secrets 5. Husband and wife 6. Married women 7. Drug lords 8. Adult child abuse victims 9. Investigations 10. Denial (Psychology) 11. Corruption 12. Despair 13. Social classes 14. Colombia 15. Bogota, Colombia 16. Political fiction 17. Psychological fiction 18. Literary fiction 19. Translations -- Spanish to English

Originally published: Madrid: Alfaguara, 2004.

Aguilar returns from a brief business trip to find that his wife, Agustina, has had a complete mental breakdown, and as he struggles to help her regain her sanity, he begins to realize how little he knows about his wife's troubled past.

"Restrepo manages her tricky, time-hopping, polyphonic structure with uncommon grace. Everything in 'Delirium' flows, like tributaries into a river. And where that mighty stream is meant to take us, I think, is back to that large body of passionate, history-obsessed literature that is, (or was) Latin American fiction. Restrepo's techniques in this novel recall the favored narrative methods of the so-called Boom years, invoking the spirits of Juan Rulfo, Jose Donoso, Manuel Puig and many others." New York Times Book Review.

Restrepo, Laura

No place for heroes : a novel / Laura Restrepo ; translated from the Spanish by Ernesto Mestre-Reed. Nan A. Talese/ Doubleday, 2010. 304 p.

ISBN 9780385519915

1. 1980s 2. 1990s 3. Journalists 4. Revolutionaries 5. Resistance to government 6. Teenage boys 7. Father-separated teenage boys 8. Mothers and sons 9. Birthfathers 10. Ideology 11. Military government 12. Argentina -- History -- Dirty War, 1976-1983 13. Buenos Aires, Argentina 14. Political fiction 15. Literary fiction 16. Parallel narratives

LC 2009047858

Originally published in Spain as Demasiados heroes in 2009.

Lorenza and her son, Mateo, return to Buenos Aires as they try to find Ramon, Mateo's father, who was a political radical with Lorenza in Argentina's "Dirty War," as Lorenza deals with her memories of the past and Mateo, who is not interested in politics, only wants to find his father.

"Ultimately, this coming-of-age dance, the winding stories of Lorenza's past and the search for Ramon all converge in a climax as unexpected as it is moving." San Francisco Chronicle.

Reuss, Frederick, 1960-

Mohr : a novel / Frederick Reuss. Unbridled Books, 2006. 320 p.

ISBN 1932961178

1. Mohr, Max, b 1891 2. Between the Wars (1918-1939) 3. Authors, German 4. Authors, Jewish -- Germany 5. Physicians -- Shanghai, China 6. Immigrants 7. Germany 8. Shanghai, China 9. Biographical fiction 10. Historical fiction

LC 2005037958

"Reuss's prose rarely if ever impresses through sheer imagery or wordplay or beauty, but it's concise and solidly-constructed, and it conveys his meaning well. The strength of Reuss's writing is more in his observations, the way he builds emotions out of little details like the objects in the clutter of a room or the way a certain person moves. The writing and the photographs play off of one another, illustrating each other. And the images seem to perfectly capture the mood of the story as it goes on." PopMatters.

Reynolds, Alastair, 1966-

Permafrost / Alastair Reynolds. Tor, 2019. 192 p.

ISBN 9781250303561

1. World Health Organization 2. Climate change 3. Consciousness transfer 4. Time travel (Past) 5. Women teachers 6. Global warming 7. Scientists 8. Paradoxes 9. Arctic Regions 10. Science fiction

Fix the past. Save the present. Stop the future. Master of science fiction Alastair Reynolds unfolds a time-traveling climate fiction adventure in Permafrost.

Reynolds, Alastair, 1966-

The **prefect** / Alastair Reynolds. Ace Books, 2008, c2007. 416 p. Revelation space universe

ISBN 9780441015917

1. Police 2. Life on other planets 3. Criminal investigation 4. Adventurers 5. Space colonies 6. Aliens 7. Murder 8. Alien artifacts 9. Posthumanism 10. Hard science fiction 11. Space opera 12. Science fiction

LC 2008060017

According to the author, this book can be read at any point in the Revelation space universe

Prefect Tom Dreyfus investigates a murderous attack on one of the space habitats of the Glitter Band--a crime that has left nine hundred people dead--and uncovers a plot by a mysterious entity seeking total control of the region.

"As a prefect working for the Panoply, Tom Dreyfus enforces the law in the utopian society of the Glitter Band, a collection of space habitats that orbit the planet Yellowstone. When an attack on one of the habitats leaves nearly 1000 people dead, Dreyfus uncovers a plot that threatens the freedom of the entire Glitter Band. Reynolds . . . returns to the universe of Revelation Space as he demonstrates his powerful ability to blend futuristic suspense/intrigue with personal drama in a tale of one man's search for truth, however unpleasant or demanding it may be. . . . Action-packed hard sf." Library Journal.

Reynolds, Alastair, 1966-

Revelation space / Alastair Reynolds. Ace Books, 2001, c2000. 476 p. Revelation space universe

ISBN 0441008356

1. 26th century 2. Artificial intelligence 3. Life on other planets 4. Far future 5. Space colonies 6. Aliens 7. Cyborgs 8. Alien artifacts 9. Posthumanism 10. Hard science fiction 11. Space opera 12. Science fiction

LC 00050260

Originally published: 2000.

Resurgam, Delta Pavonis system; 2551. Dr. Daniel Sylveste discovers the puzzling remains of a civilization annihilated nine hundred thousand years ago. Believing that the truth will save humanity, he seeks answers aboard a starship despite its dangerous cyborg crew.

Reynolds, Alastair, 1966-

Revenger / Alastair Reynolds. Orbit, 2017. 560 p. Revenger novels

ISBN 9780316555562

1. Far future 2. Treasure hunters 3. Spaceship captains 4. Life on other planets 5. Revenge in women 6. Alien artifacts 7. Adventurers 8. Adventure 9. Revenge 10. Solar system 11. Space 12. Science fiction 13. Space opera

LC 2016037813

Locus Young Adult Book Award, 2017.

Adrana and Fura Ness are new on Captain Rackamore's ship, and they are using their Bone Reader abilities to their advantage while trying to avoid the feared Bosa Sennen.

"The award-winning Reynolds newest action-packed science fiction novel is a tale of sisterly devotion, heartbreaking loss, and brutal vengeance." Booklist.

Reynolds, Marjorie, 1944-

The **Starlite** Drive-in : a novel / Marjorie Reynolds. W. Morrow, 1997. 282 p.

ISBN 0688153895

1. Drive-in theaters 2. Agoraphobia in women 3. Rural life 4. Daughters 5. Drifters 6. Extramarital affairs 7. Husband and wife 8. Murder 9. Indiana 10. Mysteries

LC 97728

The discovery of human bones at the site of an old drive-in leads Callie Anne Benton to recall the eventful summer of 1956 when her agoraphobic mother developed a strong bond with a drifter named Charlie Memphis.

Rhodes, Jewell Parker

Voodoo dreams : a novel of Marie Laveau / Jewell Parker Rhodes. St. Martin's Press, 1993. 436 p.

ISBN 0312098693

1. Laveau, Marie, 1794-1881 2. Voodoo 3. African American women 4. Family secrets 5. Mambos (Voodooism) 6. Slavery 7. Supernatural 8. African American grandmother and granddaughter 9. Visions 10. Gender role 11. Marriage 12. Independence in African American women 13. Self-discovery in women 14. New Orleans, Louisiana -- History -- 19th century 15. Historical fiction 16. Biographical fiction 17. African American fiction

LC 93024283

Followed by the author's contemporary Voodoo trilogy.

In mid 19th-century New Orleans, Marie Laveau was the notorious queen of voodoo -- worshiped and feared by blacks and whites alike. Voodoo Dreams reimagines the woman behind this legend, a mesmerizing combination of history and storytelling.

Rhodes, Jewell Parker

Yellow moon : a novel / Jewell Parker Rhodes. Atria Books, 2008. 288 p. Voodoo trilogy

ISBN 9781416537106

1. Voodoo 2. Vampires 3. Magic (Occultism) 4. Ghosts 5. Good and evil 6. African American women 7. Women physicians 8. New Orleans, Louisiana -- History -- 21st century 9. Louisiana -- History -- 21st century 10. Supernatural mysteries 11. African American fiction

LC 2008015221

Marie Levant, a doctor who is a descendant of a legendary voodoo queen, struggles with an increasing number of violence victims in her New Orleans hospital, a situation that is complicated by her nightmares about an African vampire.

Rhys, Jean

Quartet / Jean Rhys. Harper, 1971, c1957. 186 p.

1. 1920s 2. Love triangles 3. Married people 4. British in France 5. Women 6. Men/women relations 7. Extramarital affairs 8. Paris, France 9. Literary fiction

LC 77138795

First published in London in 1928 under title: Postures.

Set against a background of winter-wet streets, Pernod in smoky cafes and cheap hotel rooms, Marya tries to make something substantial of her life in order to withstand the unreality of her surroundings. Alone, her Polish husband in prison, she is taken up by an English couple who slowly overwhelm her with their passions.

Rhys, Jean

* **Wide** Sargasso Sea / Jean Rhys. W.W. Norton, 1999, c1966. xiii, 270 p.

ISBN 9780393960129

1. 1830s 2. 19th century 3. Women with mental illnesses 4. Race relations 5. Forced marriage 6. Married people 7. Women -- West Indies 8. Men/women relations 9. West Indies -- History -- 19th century 10. Historical fiction 11. Literary fiction 12. Adaptations, retellings, and spin-offs 13. Modern classics

Beautiful and wealthy Antoinette Cosway's passionate love for an English aristocrat threatens to destroy her idyllic West Indian island existence and her very life; accompanied by notes and criticism

Rhys, Rachel, 1963-

Fatal inheritance / Rachel Rhys. Washington Square Press, 2019. 400 p.

ISBN 9781982111571

1. 1940s 2. Married women 3. Inheritance and succession 4. Mansions 5. Wills 6. Family secrets 7. Postwar life 8. Rich people 9. Strangers 10. Families 11. French Riviera 12. France 13. Historical mysteries

She didn't have an enemy in the world--until she inherited a fortune.

Ricciardi, David

Warning light / David Ricciardi. Berkley, 2018. 323 p. Jake Keller novels

ISBN 9780399585739

1. CIA agents 2. Intrigue 3. Undercover operations 4. Nuclear weapons 5. Torture 6. International relations 7. Life change events 8. Soldiers 9. Middle East 10. Thrillers and suspense

LC 2017006920

A routine surveillance job becomes a do-or-die mission in the Middle East for CIA analyst Zac Miller, who, in the wake of an agent's blown cover and an emergency landing, makes his way over the mountains of Iran and through the Persian Gulf while outmaneuvering Islamic Revolutionary Guards and former teammates who believe he has gone rogue.

"Ricciardi's debut thriller is a slow and steady adrenaline flow. Zac's ability to think or fight his way out of seemingly hopeless situations hints at Lee Child's Jack Reacher and Dan Brown's Robert Langdon, while his solo status adds Robert Ludlum's Jason Bourne and John le Carre's George Smiley to the mix. The author does a nice job of highlighting local culture and settings. ... Readers of le Carre, Ludlum, Len Deighton, and other authors of Cold War-era espionage thrillers will enjoy this action-packed adventure." Library Journal.

Rice, Anne, 1941-

Angel **time** : a novel / Anne Rice. Alfred A. Knopf, 2009. 288 p. Songs of the seraphim

ISBN 9781400043538

1. Catholic Church Relations Judaism 2. Medieval period (476-1492) 3. Angels 4. Antisemitism 5. Assassins 6. Human sacrifice 7. Civilization, Medieval 8. Time travel (Past) 9. England -- History -- 13th century 10. Thrillers and suspense

LC 2009015470

Sequel: Of love and evil.

"This is a Borzoi book."

A seraph offers contract killer Toby O'Dare a chance to save rather than destroy lives. Carried back through the ages to thirteenth-century England, to dark realms where accusations of ritual murder have been made against Jews, where children suddenly die or disappear, O'Dare begins his perilous quest for salvation.

"Angelically inspiring. Devilishly clever." Kirkus.

Rice, Anne, 1941-

Blackwood farm / Anne Rice. A.A. Knopf, 2002 528 p. Vampire chronicles

ISBN 0375411992

1. Ancient Greece (800 BCE-640 CE) 2. Vampires 3. Good and evil 4. Immortality 5. Mortality 6. Doppelgangers 7. Southern States 8. New Orleans, Louisiana 9. Ancient Greece 10. Gothic fiction

Haunted since birth by a mysterious doppelganger known as Goblin, Quinn Blackwood seeks out the legendary vampire Lestat to free him from the horrifying specter that draws him back to Sugar Devil Swamp and its dark secrets.

"Slowly, the dark, Gothic settings and eccentric characters that make Rice's fiction so fascinating emerge." Library Journal.

Rice, Anne, 1941-

Blood canticle / Anne Rice. A.A. Knopf, 2003. 320 p. Vampire chronicles

ISBN 037541200X

1. Vampires 2. Good and evil 3. Immortality 4. Mortality 5. Witches 6. Redemption 7. Loyalty 8. New Orleans, Louisiana 9. Gothic fiction

LC 2002192475

Continues the crossover events of "Blackwood Farm," pitting the vampire Lestat against the ghost of Julian Mayfair, who is out to evenge the transformation of Mona Mayfair, and chronicling Rowan Mayfair's dangerous attraction to Lestat.

Rice, Anne, 1941-

Blood communion : a tale of Prince Lestat / Anne Rice. Alfred A. Knopf, 2018. 272 p. Vampire chronicles

ISBN 9781524732646

1. Vampires 2. Leadership 3. Power (Social sciences) 4. Demons 5. Supernatural 6. Social conflict 7. Spirit possession 8. Atlantis (Legendary place) 9. Gothic fiction

LC 2017058218

Navigating his new leadership of the vampire world, Lestat uncovers the story of a mysterious outcast demon who he traces to 18th-century Petersburg and the court of Empress Catherine.

Rice, Anne, 1941-

Blood and gold : or, The story of Marius / Anne Rice. A. A. Knopf, 2001. 471 p. Vampire chronicles

ISBN 0679454497

1. Vampires 2. Good and evil 3. Immortality 4. Mortality 5. Gothic fiction

LC 2001029869

Marius, the former mentor to the vampire Lestat, tells his story, which begins in the ancient Roman Empire when he is made a "blood god" by the Druids and follows him through the darkest, bloodiest centuries of European history.

"[A] rollicking vampire adventure through time." Booklist.

Rice, Anne, 1941-

Christ the Lord: out of Egypt : Anne Rice. Knopf, 2005. 336 p. Christ the Lord

ISBN 0375412018

1. Jesus Christ 2. Jesus Christ Childhood and youth 3. Jesus Christ Family 4. Mary,, Blessed Virgin, Saint 5. Joseph, Husband of Mary 6. Bible. New Testament History of Biblical events 7. Jews 8. Healers 9. Jewish families 10. Identity (Psychology) 11. Questions and answers 12. Truth 13. Riots 14. Egypt 15. Israel 16. Bible novels

LC 2005044077

Sequel: Christ the Lord: the road to Cana.

Adapted into film in 2016 under the title: The Young Messiah.

Republished in 2016 as The young messiah.

A novel about the childhood of Christ the Lord based on the Gospels and on the most respected New Testament scholarship.

"Rice is a first-rate writer. There are no purple patches in this narrative, and no attempts to sermonize. There is a story to tell, and since we know the story on which it is based, Rice adroitly forces us to think about how she is going to weave in the gospel stories without sounding contrived or forced." Commonwealth.

Rice, Anne, 1941-

Christ the Lord: the road to Cana : Anne Rice Knopf, 2008. 256 p. Christ the Lord

ISBN 9781400043521

1. Jesus Christ 2. Jesus Christ Family 3. Mary,, Blessed Virgin, Saint 4. Joseph, Husband of Mary 5. Bible. New Testament History of Biblical events 6. Jews 7. Healers 8. Jewish families 9. Identity (Psychology) 10. Truth 11. Temptation 12. Devil 13. Israel 14. Christian fiction 15. Bible novels

Sequel to: Christ the Lord: out of Egypt.

A second volume in the author's chronicle of the life of Christ begins prior to his baptism in the Jordan River and concludes with the miracle at Cana, as he leaves Nazareth to confront his destiny and the call to be Israel's liberator from Roman occupation.

"One of the great achievements of Rice's undertaking, thus far, is to reveal Christ's Jewish roots in all their strength and complexity. . . . Rice has achieved a prose style that is much simpler, much more straightforward, than that of her earlier works. Yet, in moments of revelation, her old breathless rapture serves her well." New Orleans Times-Picayune.

Rice, Anne, 1941-

* Interview with the vampire / Anne Rice. A.A. Knopf, 1976. 371 p. Vampire chronicles

ISBN 9780394498218

1. Vampires 2. Good and evil 3. Immortality 4. Redemption 5. Mortality 6. Gothic fiction

LC 75036792

Confessions from a vampire of his first two hundred years as one of the living dead.

Rice, Anne, 1941-

Memnoch the devil / Anne Rice. A.A. Knopf, 1995. 353 p. Vampire chronicles

ISBN 0679441018

1. Devil 2. Purgatory 3. Vampires 4. Good and evil 5. Immortality 6. Mortality 7. Gothic fiction

LC 95-77866

Visited by two beings who claim to be God and the Devil, the vampire Lestat is offered an ultimate chance at redemption when he is invited to be a witness at the Creation in a purgatorial land beyond death.

"The author boldly probes the significance of death, belief in the afterlife and other spiritual matters." Publishers Weekly.

Rice, Anne, 1941-

Merrick : a novel / Anne Rice. A.A. Knopf, 2000. 307 p. Vampire chronicles

ISBN 9780679454489

1. Vampires 2. Good and evil 3. Immortality 4. Mortality 5. Witches 6. Witchcraft -- New Orleans, Louisiana 7. Gothic fiction

LC 9988556

David Talbot, an adventurer and near-mortal vampire, narrates the saga of Merrick, a descendant of the Mayfair witches, from whom she inherits her magical gifts, and of a mixed African and French background that is steeped in traditions and lore of voodoo.

"This volume merges several long-running plots. . . . Merrick must revisit the Guatemalan rainforest, where she traveled as a young girl, to locate a secret treasure trove of ominous ancient runes. Displaying her imaginative talents for atmosphere and suspense, Rice creates a riveting scene that shows Merrick's awesome magic at work." Publishers Weekly.

Rice, Anne, 1941-

Of love and evil / Anne Rice. Alfred A. Knopf, 2010. 160 p. Songs of the seraphim

ISBN 9781400043545

1. Former assassins 2. Angels 3. Poisoning 4. Atonement 5. Salvation (Christianity) 6. Rome, Italy 7. Thrillers and suspense

Sequel to: Angel time.

In fifteenth century Rome, Toby O'Dare, a recently retired government assassin, receives a visit from the angel Malchiah. The heavenly figure instructs O'Dare to solve a grisly murder. But during the investigation, O'Dare discovers that the city is being haunted by an ancient demon and that solving the murder may have disastrous consequences for all of Rome.

"If this kinder, gentler Rice has you rattled, fear not, for the scenes in the seething cesspool of sin that typify Pope Leo X's Rome prove the author hasn't lost her verve for the seamier side of life." Minneapolis Star Tribune.

Rice, Anne, 1941-

The **queen** of the damned / Anne Rice. A. A. Knopf, 1988. 448 p. Vampire chronicles

ISBN 9780394558233

1. Vampires 2. Good and evil 3. Immortality 4. Mortality 5. Women vampires 6. Damned persons 7. Gothic fiction

LC 88045310

Sequel to: The vampire Lestat.

The third novel in the Chronicle of the Vampires intertwines the stories of rockstar Lestat, beautiful twins haunted by a gruesome tragedy, and Akasha, mother of all vampires, who dreams of godhood

"Don't let the title or the subject matter fool you; this is quality fiction written with care and intelligence. There are no false steps or wasted words in the multilayered plot, and the many characters each have a distinct voice. It's not absolutely necessary to have read the other 'Chronicles' to understand this one, but it would add greatly to the richness of the whole." Library Journal.

Rice, Anne, 1941-

Prince Lestat : the vampire chronicles / Anne Rice. Knopf, 2014. 464 p. Vampire chronicles

ISBN 9780307962522

1. Vampires 2. Good and evil 3. Immortality 4. Mortality 5. Redemption 6. Loyalty 7. New Orleans, Louisiana 8. Gothic fiction

LC 2014009319

Goodreads Choice Award, 2014.

A tale spanning periods from the ancient to the modern world reunites fans with beloved characters, from Louis de Pointe Lac and the eternally young Armand to David Talbot and Marius, who hear a mysterious voice urging ancients to destroy increasing populations of maverick vampires.

"Featuring beloved characters from previous installments and spanning continents and centuries, Rice's exciting return to the Vampire Chronicles is bound to please her legions of fans." Booklist.

Rice, Anne, 1941-

The **tale** of the body thief / Anne Rice. A. A. Knopf, 1992. 430 p. Vampire chronicles

ISBN 9780345419637

1. Vampires 2. Good and evil 3. Immortality 4. Mortality 5. Gothic fiction

LC 92053085

"Readers who crave a happy ending, a justice and a moral coherence that transcend the muddle they really live in, may feel [the author] has broken faith with them. After all, isn't that what escapist fiction is supposed to provide? Grown-ups, on the other hand, will be intelligently entertained, and no more disquieted than usual." Newsweek.

Rice, Anne, 1941-

The **vampire** Armand / Anne Rice. A. A. Knopf, 1998. 387 p. Vampire chronicles

ISBN 0679454470

1. Vampires 2. Good and evil 3. Immortality 4. European Renaissance 5. Sexuality 6. Reunions 7. Kievan Rus 8. Paris, France 9. New Orleans, Louisiana 10. Venice, Italy 11. Gothic fiction

LC 9814579

Follows the story of Armand across the centuries, from his boyhood in ancient Kiev to his relationship with the great vampire Marius, as he struggles to choose between immortality and his eternal soul

"The sixth volume of the Vampire chronicles follows the vampire Armand from his boyhood in Kiev Rus, a conquered city under the rule of the Mongols, to ancient Constantinople, where he is sold into slavery by vicious Tartars, to the palazzo in Renaissance Venice, where he meets the great vampire Marius, who gives him the gift of the vampire blood and shows him how to be an 'ethical' vampire. . . . As always, Rice paints a fascinating and dazzling historical tapestry, providing a beautifully written and incredibly absorbing tale." Booklist.

Rice, Anne, 1941-

The **vampire** Lestat / Anne Rice. A. A. Knopf, 1985. 481 p. Vampire chronicles

ISBN 9780394534435

1. Vampires 2. Good and evil 3. Immortality 4. Mortality 5. Gothic fiction

LC 85040123

Lestat is a vampire, but not one of the conventional undead. He is vivid, ecstatic, stagestruck, and in this extravagant story he plunges from the Rome of Augustus to the demonic Egypt of prehistory, and from fin-de-siecle New Orleans to the frenetic world of 20th-century rock stardom.

"This novel is ornate and pungently witty. In the classic tradition of Gothic fiction, it teases and tantalizes us into accepting its kaleidoscopic world. Even when they annoy us or tell us more than we want to know, its undead characters are utterly alive. Their adventures and frustrations are funny, frightening and surprising at once." New York Times Book Review.

Rice, Anne, 1941-

The **witching** hour : a novel / Anne Rice. A. A. Knopf, 1990. 965 p. Mayfair witches

ISBN 9780394587868

1. Witchcraft -- New Orleans, Louisiana 2. Secret societies 3. Psychic ability 4. Witches 5. Secrets 6. Men/women relations 7. Magic 8. Family sagas 9. Gothic fiction

LC 90053103

Sequel: Lasher.

Locus Award for Dark Fantasy-Horror Novel, 1991.

Demonstrating once again her gift for spellbinding storytelling, Anne Rice makes real for us a great dynasty of four centuries of witches--a family given to poetry and incest, murder and philosophy, a family that over the ages is itself haunted by a powerful, dangerous, and seductive being called Lasher who haunts the Mayfair women.. Moving in time from today's New Orleans and San Francisco to long-ago Amsterdam and the France of Louis XIV, from the coffee plantations of Port-au-Prince to Civil War New Orleans and back to today, Anne Rice has spun a mesmerizing tale that challenges everything we believe in.

"Rice tells the story of the prominent and wealthy Mayfair family who, for five centuries, has cavorted with a supernatural entity that has brought them both great bounty as well as abject misery. Neurosurgeon Rowan Mayfair inherits the family fortune, along with the sinister attentions of this entity. When Rowan saves the life of Michael Curry their fates become entwined, and together they seek to understand and destroy the terrible force that holds her family in its power. Helping them in this dangerous task is occult investigator Aaron Lightner. . . . Although a bit long-winded at times, this is still a compelling novel." Library Journal.

Rice, Craig, 1908-1957

Home sweet homicide / Craig Rice ; introduction by Otto Penzler. American Mystery Classics, 2018, c1944. 295 p.

ISBN 9781613161036

1. Amateur detectives 2. Children of authors 3. Crime scenes 4. Women mystery story writers 5. Neighbors 6. Murder investigation 7. Mysteries

Originally published: New York : Simon & Schuster, 1944.

The children of a mystery writer play amateur sleuths and matchmakers.

Rice, Luanne

* **Last** day / Luanne Rice. Thomas & Mercer, 2020. 412 p.

ISBN 9781542018203

1. Art thefts 2. Women murder victims 3. Sisters 4. Loss (Psychology) 5. Detectives 6. Women pilots 7. Art 8. Murder investigation 9. Family secrets 10. Friendship 11. Coastal towns 12. Connecticut 13. Thrillers and suspense

When her sister is murdered amid the theft of a valuable painting, an eerie echo of their mother's murder 20 years earlier, pilot Kate teams up with the case's original detective and childhood friends to identify a killer.

"Strong love overcomes pain in this latest from Rice (Pretend She's Here), which combines suspense with stories of survivors, sisterhood, best friends, and small communities shaken by violence or death." Library Journal.

Rice, Luanne

Last kiss / Luanne Rice. Bantam Books, 2008. 352 p.

ISBN 9780553805123

1. Mothers and sons 2. Grief 3. Sons -- Death 4. Film producers and directors 5. Bereavement 6. Detectives 7. Unrequited love 8. Connecticut 9. New York City 10. Mysteries

LC 2007052179

Hubbard's Point, Connecticutt. Nearly a year after the death of eighteen-year-old Charlie, singer-songwriter Sheridan Rosslare still hasn't played a note of the music that was once her life's passion. Tucked away in the beach house where she raised her only child, she lives with her memories of him and a grief too big to share even with her beloved sisters or her dear friend Stevie Moore. Nor can Stevie comfort Charlie's heartbroken girlfriend, Nell Kilvert, whom she regards as a daughter. Nell won't rest until she finds out what really happened to the boy she loved. Out of the past she summons a man she believes cares enough,

and is tough enough, to uncover the truth--Sheridan's long-ago soul mate, Gavin Dawson.--From publisher description.

"An element of supernatural whimsy, a dark secret involving a trust fund and a disturbing question related to Charlie's estranged father, Randy, add complexity, while cameos from other Beach Girls characters contribute an engaging, homey touch." Publishers Weekly.

Rice, Luanne

Little night / Luanne Rice. Pamela Dorman Books/Viking, 2012. 336 p.

ISBN 9780670023561

1. Sisters 2. Family relationships 3. Aunt and niece 4. Nieces 5. Forgiveness 6. Protectiveness in women 7. Former convicts 8. Betrayal 9. Family reunions 10. New York City 11. Women's lives and relationships

LC 2011049237

Estranged from the sister who refused to testify against an abusive husband, Clare pursues a quiet life as a nature blogger in Manhattan only to be approached by her niece, Grit, with whom she confronts a painful shared history.

Rice, Luanne

The **lemon** orchard / Luanne Rice. Pamela Dorman Books, 2013. 352 p.

ISBN 9780670025275

1. Grief in women 2. Loss (Psychology) 3. Interracial romance 4. Healing 5. Men/women relations 6. Interpersonal attraction 7. Immigrants 8. California 9. Southern California 10. Mainstream fiction

LC 2013009690

House-sitting a family home in Malibu where she hopes for peace and healing in the aftermath of her daughter's death, Julia is unexpectedly drawn to a handsome man who oversees a lemon orchard, sends his earnings to an extended family in Mexico and hides the pain of his own daughter's loss.

Rice, Waubgeshig, 1979-

Moon of the crusted snow : a novel / Waubgeshig Rice. ECW Press, 2018. 224 p.

ISBN 9781770414006

1. First Nations (Canada) 2. Threat (Psychology) 3. Survival 4. Winter 5. Indians of North America 6. Communities 7. Wilderness areas 8. Ojibwa Indians 9. Ontario 10. Canada 11. Apocalyptic fiction

Evergreen Award (Ontario), 2019.

Moon of the Crusted Snow imagines a small community on the precipice of winter without power or communication where leaders must grapple with control, restore order, and save their people from a grave fate.

Rice-Gonzalez, Charles

Chulito / Charles Rice-Gonzalez. Magnus Books, 2011. 317 p.

ISBN 9781936833030

1. Hispanic Americans 2. Coming out (Sexual or gender identity) 3. Young gay men 4. Homophobia 5. Bronx, New York City 6. Coming-of-age stories 7. LGBTQIA fiction

Rainbow List, 2013.

Chulito rejects his childhood friend Carlos after Carlos comes out and goes away to college, but when Carlos returns for a visit, Chulito cannot continue to bury his romantic feelings for his old friend.

Rich, Nathaniel, 1980-

Odds against tomorrow / Nathaniel Rich. Farrar, Straus and Giroux, 2013. 304 p.

ISBN 9780374224240

1. Mathematicians 2. Disaster forecasting 3. Survival (after hurricanes) 4. Pen pals 5. Disasters 6. Hurricanes 7. Near future 8. Disaster relief 9. Rural life -- Maine 10. City dwellers 11. New York City 12. Science fiction

LC 2012028928

While working for a financial consulting firm that offers insurance against catastrophic events, a young mathematician becomes increasingly obsessed with doomsday scenarios until one of his worst-case scenarios unfolds in Manhattan.

Rich, Virginia

The **baked** bean supper murders / Virginia Rich. E. P. Dutton, 1983. 267 p. Eugenia Potter mysteries

1. Cooking, American 2. Fishing villages 3. Death threats 4. Murder investigation 5. Women cooks 6. Women detectives 7. Women amateur detectives 8. Maine 9. Culinary mysteries

LC 83070156

Includes recipes.

"While Mrs. Potter goes about discovering who is responsible for what she determines to be murder, we get to sample Maine cooking, complete with recipes." Publishers Weekly.

Rich, Virginia

The **cooking** school murders / Virginia Rich. Dutton, 1982. 207 p. Eugenia Potter mysteries

ISBN 9780525241102

1. Cooking schools 2. Women cooks 3. Cooking, American 4. Murder investigation 5. Women cooks 6. Women detectives 7. Women amateur detectives 8. Iowa 9. Culinary mysteries

LC 81022162

Includes recipes.

In Harrington, Iowa, for her yearly hometown visit, dignified and down-to-earth Mrs. Potter becomes involved in the slashed-throat murder of a student in an advanced cooking class attended by Harrington's elite.

Rich, Virginia

The **Nantucket** diet murders / Virginia Rich. Delacorte Press, 1985. 276 p. Eugenia Potter mysteries

1. Weight loss 2. Cooking schools 3. Women cooks 4. Cooking, American 5. Women detectives 6. Women amateur detectives 7. Culinary mysteries

LC 84021501

Includes recipes.

"Fans of Nantucket and haute cuisine will find and enjoy both in this somewhat over-long, but well-written book." Publishers Weekly.

Richards, Dusty

The **mustanger** and the lady/ Dusty Richards. Galway Press, 2017. 211 p.

ISBN 9781633731073

1. American Westward Expansion (1803-1899) 2. Mustangs 3. Cowboys 4. Fugitives 5. Frontier and pioneer life 6. Outlaws 7. Protectiveness in men 8. Interpersonal attraction 9. Men/women relations 10. The West (United States) -- History -- 19th century 11. Westerns

Spur Awards, Best Western Traditional Novel, 2017.

Richards, Linda, 1960-

* **Death** was in the blood / Linda L. Richards. Five Star, 2013. 332 p. Kitty Pangborn novels

ISBN 9781432827168

1. Depression era (1929-1941) 2. 1930s 3. Murder investigation 4. Private investigators 5. Women private investigators 6. Rich families 7. Olympic athletes 8. Detectives 9. Murder 10. Depressions -- 1929-1941 11. Los Angeles, California 12. Hardboiled fiction 13. Historical mysteries 14. Mysteries

LC 2013005470

Richardson, C. S.

The **end** of the alphabet / C.S. Richardson. Doubleday, 2007. 139 p.

ISBN 038552255X

1. Men 2. Women 3. Men/women relations 4. Husband and wife 5. Romantic love 6. Friendship 7. Alphabet 8. Emotions 9. Perception 10. Art 11. Memories 12. Men with terminal illnesses 13. Trips around the world 14. Voyages and travels 15. Home (Concept) 16. Death 17. Literary fiction

LC 2006036823

Reeling from the news that his doctor is giving him only one month to live, fifty-year-old Ambrose Zephyr and his loving wife, Zipper, embark on a whirlwind tour from A to Z of all the places he has ever loved or has ever wanted to visit.

"The surprise of this little book is not that it is poignant but that it is delightful: graceful, stylish, humorous, intelligent and lacking even the faintest whiff of sanctimony." Washington Post Book World.

Richardson, Kat

Greywalker / Kat Richardson. Roc, 2006. 352 p. Greywalker

ISBN 045146107X

1. Women private investigators 2. Vampires 3. Dead 4. Supernatural 5. Paranormal phenomena 6. Witches 7. Ghosts 8. Missing persons 9. College students 10. Life after death 11. Men/women relations 12. Seattle, Washington 13. Urban fantasy

LC 2006011233

"Recovering from a brutal assault that had left her clinically dead for two minutes, private investigator Harper Blaine finds her perceptions have changed. Now she sees people that others can't and often struggles against a grayish mist that seems to permeate her world. A friendly couple with experience in the paranormal explain to her that she is a Greywalker, someone with the ability to cross between the living and the ghostly worlds. Suddenly, her life and her business grow a lot more interesting and much more dangerous. Richardson's first novel features a genuinely likable and independent heroine with a unique view of reality." Library Journal.

Richardson, Samuel, 1689-1761

* **Clarissa,** or, The history of a young lady / Samuel Richardson ; edited with an introduction and notes by Angus Ross. Penguin Books, 1985. 1533 p.

ISBN 9780140432152

1. 18th century 2. Young women -- 18th century 3. Captives 4. Nobility 5. Marriage 6. Deception 7. Seduction 8. Idealism 9. Rape victims 10. Rape 11. Self-deception in women 12. England -- Social life and customs -- 18th century 13. Epistolary novels 14. Classics 15. Literary fiction

A rakish city gentleman determines to seduce the youngest daughter of the Harlowe household.

Richardson, Samuel, 1689-1761

* Pamela or, Virtue rewarded / Samuel Richardson ; edited with explanatory notes by Thomas Keymer and Alice Wakely ; with an introduction by Thomas Keymer. Oxford University Press, c2001, 1740. xxlv, 546 p.

ISBN 0192829602

1. 18th century 2. Household employees 3. Seduction 4. Families 5. Marriage 6. Gender role 7. Honor 8. Values 9. Extramarital affairs 10. Women prisoners 11. Letter writing 12. Housekeepers 13. England -- Social life and customs -- 18th century 14. Epistolary novels 15. Classics

LC 2001021704

First published 1740-1741.

A country gentleman attempts to seduce his maidservant and ends up falling in love with her in this literary landmark, first published in 1740 and regarded as the English language's first novel.

Richler, Mordecai, 1931-2001

Barney's version : a novel / Mordecai Richler. A. A. Knopf, 1997. 355 p.

ISBN 067940418X

1. Immigrants, Jewish 2. Septuagenarians 3. Bohemianism 4. Extremism 5. Jewish Canadians 6. City life 7. Television producers and directors 8. Montreal, Quebec 9. Literary fiction 10. Satirical fiction

LC 9737033

Giller Prize, 1997.

Quebec Writers' Federation Literary Awards, Hugh MacLennan Prize for Fiction, 1998.

Stephen Leacock Medal for Humour, 1998.

The urban sensibility of immigrant Jewish Montreal is chronicled in this darkly satirical portrait of 67-year-old Barney Panofsky, who decides to set the record straight about his Bohemian days in Paris and London in the 1950s, his circle of famous and infamous friends, his career as a television producer, and his wildly unsuccessful relationships with women.

"What entertains and affects us in 'Barney's Version' is the headlong, spendthrift passage of a life, redeemed from oblivion in the unbridled telling. The edge of the grave makes a lively point vantage." The New Yorker.

Richler, Mordecai, 1931-2001

Solomon Gursky was here / Mordecai Richler. Knopf, 1990, c1989. 413 p.

ISBN 0394539958

1. Alcoholic men 2. Authors 3. Wanderers and wandering 4. Airplane accidents 5. Suing (Law) 6. Jewish Canadian families 7. Montreal, Quebec 8. Literary fiction 9. Family sagas

LC 88094762

Originally published: Markham, Ont. : Penguin Books Canada, 1989.

Quebec Writers' Federation Literary Awards, Hugh MacLennan Prize for Fiction, 1990.

Shortlisted for the Booker-McConnell Prize, 1990.

While researching a biography of Solomon Gursky, the blacksheep scion of an influential Jewish family in Montreal, Moses Berger becomes obsessed with uncovering the secret and momentous life of his subject

"Richler is a ringmaster, making his performers do dazzling backflips without missing a beat. At the same time he is a moralist, recoiling from those who would sentimentalize the Holocaust or make power a sacrament." Time.

Richler, Nancy, 1957-

Your mouth is lovely : a novel / Nancy Richler. Ecco, 2002. 357 p.

ISBN 0060096772

1. Romanov Dynasty (1613-1917) 2. Political prisoners -- Siberia 3. Political prisons -- Siberia 4. Single mothers 5. Women prisoners 6. Women murderers 7. Jewish women 8. Revolutionaries -- Russia 9. Jews 10. Kiev, Ukraine 11. Russia -- History -- 1904-1914 12. Russia -- History -- 19th century 13. Russia -- History -- 20th century 14. Siberia 15. Belarus 16. Historical fiction 17. Diary novels

LC 2002023521

Canadian Jewish Book Award

A story told through a series of letters to the main character's daughter follows her upbringing in a Russian shtetl by her stepmother after her mother's mysterious suicide, her isolation as an outcast, and her exile to Siberia.

"This novel summons up the lost world of the Russian shtetls around the Pripet marshe's in Ukraine, and shows how those communities were first changed and then annihilated by the events that led, ultimately, to the Russian Revolution. At the center of Richler's tale is Miriam Lev, whose mother drowned herself when she was a day old, and who at age six is taken in hand by her father's new wife, Tsila, a harsh, beautiful seamstress who teaches Miriam the alphabet and dreams of another life. After an ill-starred and and painful series of events, Miriam ends up, at nineteen, in Siberia, having shot an officer of the Tsar at point-blank range. Miriam's hegira is told here as a letter to her own daughter, whom she hasn't seen since she gave birth to her, in prison. Richler's work recalls the stories of Isaac Babel, in which the knowable is charged with mystery." The New Yorker.

Richman, Alyson

The **secret** of clouds / Alyson Richman. Berkley, 2019. 371 p.

ISBN 9781984802620

1. Children of immigrants 2. Women teachers 3. Sick children 4. Teacher-student relationships 5. Tutoring 6. Immigrant families 7. Decision-making 8. Memories 9. Interpersonal relations 10. Men/women relations 11. Long Island, New York 12. Mainstream fiction

LC 2018016371

An English teacher with haunting childhood memories gains perspective and inspiration while tutoring a young Ukrainian immigrant whose serious health issues prevent him from taking any day for granted.

Richmond, Michelle, 1970-

No one you know / Michelle Richmond. Delacorte Press, 2008. 320 p.

ISBN 9780385340137

1. Sisters -- Death 2. Secrets 3. Family relationships 4. Mathematics 5. Murder 6. Murder investigation 7. Lovers 8. Men/women relations 9. San Francisco, California 10. Mysteries 11. Domestic fiction

LC 2008013508

Twenty years after the unsolved murder of her sister Lila, Ellie's chance meeting with the man accused of the crime leads to the discovery of Lila's secret notebook, filled with mathematical equations that lead to other enigmas in her sister's life.

"As complex and beautiful as a mathematical proof, this gripping, thought-provoking novel will keep you thinking long after the last page has been turned." Family Circle.

Richter, Conrad, 1890-1968

The **awakening** land / Conrad Richter. A. A. Knopf, 1966. 630 p.

1. 18th century 2. Frontier and pioneer life -- Ohio 3. Pioneer

families -- Ohio 4. Ohio -- History -- 18th century 5. Family sagas

LC 66021362

Sayward, a pioneer in Ohio's forest, helps clear and farm the land and watches the town develop.

Richter, Conrad, 1890-1968

The **sea** of grass / Conrad Richter. Knopf, 1937. 149 p.

1. 19th century 2. Ranchers 3. Cattle ranchers 4. Farmers 5. Pioneers 6. Husband and wife 7. Ambition 8. Ambition in men 9. Love triangles 10. Frontier and pioneer life -- New Mexico 11. Southwest (United States) 12. New Mexico 13. Westerns

LC 37027107

Lutie Brewton leaves her husband and children on the cattle ranch to return to the city, but 20 years later, after desperadoes kill her son, she returns.

Rickards, John

Winter's end / John Rickards. Thomas Dunne Books, 2003. 297 p.

ISBN 0312310978

1. Sheriffs 2. Private investigators 3. Former FBI agents 4. Murder suspects 5. Psychopaths 6. Police questioning 7. Hometowns 8. Small town life -- Maine 9. Maine 10. Mysteries

LC 2003046874

Discovering a knife-wielding young man standing over a woman's murdered body, sheriff Dale Townsend wonders at the enigmatic suspect's refusal to answer questions and a lack of forensic evidence linking him to the crime.

"An attention-getting plot, riveting prose, calculated suspense, and tense, human-interest subplotting mark this noteworthy first novel." Library Journal.

Ridgway, Keith, 1965-

Hawthorn & Child / Keith Ridgway. New Directions, 2013, c2012. 288 p.

ISBN 9780811221665

1. Detectives 2. City life 3. Interpersonal relations 4. Eccentrics and eccentricities 5. Criminal investigation 6. Sexuality 7. Gay men 8. Gangs 9. London, England -- Social life and customs 10. England -- Social life and customs 11. Mysteries

"Originally published in English by Granta Publications under the title Hawthorn & Child, copyright Keith Ridgway 2012."

Hawthorn and his partner, Child, are called to the scene of a mysterious shooting in North London. The only witness is unreliable, the clues are scarce, and the victim, a young man who lives nearby, swears he was shot by a ghost car. While Hawthorn battles with fatigue and strange dreams, the crime and the narrative slip from his grasp and the stories of other Londoners take over.

Ridpath, Michael

Far north / Michael Ridpath. Minotaur Books, 2012, c2011. 376 p. Fire and ice

ISBN 9780312675042

1. Murder -- Iceland 2. Conspiracies 3. Crimes against politicians 4. Murder investigation 5. Detectives -- Boston, Massachusetts 6. Americans in Iceland 7. Iceland 8. Scandinavian crime fiction 9. Police procedurals 10. Mysteries

Originally published under the title, 66 degrees north (London: Corvus, 2011).

Generations after two boys from isolated farmsteads witness a haunting act in the Icelandic lava fields, a grassroots revolution sparked by the economic crisis of 2009 challenges Magnus Jonson to unravel a web of conspirators who are killing off blamed bankers and politicians.

Rigosi, Giampiero, 1962-

Night bus / Giampiero Rigosi ; translated from the Italian by Ann Goldstein. Bitter Lemon Press, 2006. 348 p.

ISBN 1904738117

1. Young men 2. Swindlers and swindling 3. Debtor and creditor 4. Gamblers 5. Bus drivers 6. Crime 7. Police 8. Stealing 9. Extortion 10. Chases 11. Secret Service -- Italy 12. Men/women relations 13. Violence 14. Murder 15. Torture 16. Bologna, Italy 17. Italy 18. Caper novels 19. Translations -- Italian to English 20. Crime fiction

Translation from the Italian of: Notturno bus.

"Francesco is a gambling-addicted bus driver in Bologna, with a thuggish debt collector on his trail; Leila is a smart dame with a great pair of legs, who each night looks for a man to bed, drug, and rob. In perfect noir fashion, the two become uneasy allies, trying to escape a pair of vicious intelligence agents after Leila unknowingly swipes a mysterious document from a victim's apartment. Rigosi somewhat overdoes character quirks--one agent has a condition that leads him to constantly leak tears as he slices apart his victims--but an ever-expanding cast of creeps and criminals keeps the plot accelerating, and he describes the dripping of blood and the angle of a broken neck as lovingly as the preparation of a nice eggplant parmigiana." The New Yorker.

Riley, Judith Merkle

In pursuit of the green lion / Judith Merkle Riley. Delacorte Press, 1990. 440 p. Margaret of Ashbury trilogy

ISBN 0385300891

1. Medieval period (476-1492) 2. 14th century 3. Alchemy 4. Alchemists 5. Widows 6. Women -- History -- 14th century 7. Remarriage 8. Inheritance and succession 9. Courage in women 10. Missing persons 11. British in France 12. Hundred Years' War, 1339-1453 13. England -- History -- 14th century 14. France -- History -- 14th century 15. Historical fiction

LC 90032498

"The year is 1356..."

Sequel: The Water-Devil.

In 1356, Margaret of Ashbury marries Brother Gregory, and when he is taken prisoner by the French, she and two friends embark on a quest to rescue him

"In this non-stop picaresque adventure quips fly as thickly as a barrage of arrows; a steady stream of drunken noblemen, corrupt priests, scheming ladies and truculent ghosts keep the action white-hot." Booklist.

Riley, Judith Merkle

The **serpent** garden / Judith Merkle Riley. Viking, 1996. 467 p.

ISBN 067086661X

1. Henry VIII,, King of England, 1491-1547 2. 16th century 3. Women -- History -- 16th century 4. Women painters -- 16th century 5. Women artists 6. Widows 7. Angels 8. Arranged marriage -- France 9. Women's role 10. Married men -- Death 11. Extramarital affairs 12. Good and evil 13. Spirits 14. Demons 15. Men/women relations 16. Brothers and sisters 17. Royal houses 18. Courts and courtiers 19. France -- Rulers -- History -- 16th century 20. Great Britain -- History -- Henry VIII, 1509-1547 21. Historical fiction

LC 95036067

Set in "the intrigue-ridden courts of sixteenth-century England and France."

When Henry VIII arranges a marriage between his sister and the aging French king, widowed painter Susanna Dallet joins the entourage of the princess-bride, unwittingly carrying a perilous secret that will embroil her in the dark intrigues of the French court.

"Riley . . . creates a stunning period fantasy that combines historical detail with magical realism." Library Journal.

Riley, Judith Merkle

A **vision** of light / Judith Merkle Riley. Delacorte Press, 1989. 442 p. Margaret of Ashbury trilogy

ISBN 0440501091

1. 14th century 2. Midwives 3. Married women 4. Women authors, English -- 14th century 5. Women -- History -- 14th century 6. Women mystics 7. Women healers 8. Women's role 9. Courage in women 10. Great Britain -- History -- 14th century 11. Historical fiction

LC 88017514

In 1355, Margaret of Ashbury depends on renegade friar Brother Gregory to record her life story and state of Mystic Union, and he is forced to accept the state of grace of this "mere woman."

"This is a chronicle rich with the ambience and flavor of the Middle Ages, but it is a 14th-century story told with a 20th-century sensibility." New York Times Book Review.

Riley, Lucinda

The **girl** on the cliff : a novel / Lucinda Riley. Atria Books, 2012, c2011. 407 p.

ISBN 9781451655827

1. First World War era (1914-1918) 2. World War I 3. Family secrets 4. Feuds 5. Breaking up (Interpersonal relations) 6. Miscarriage 7. Grief in women 8. Household employees 9. Mothers and daughters 10. Rich families 11. Ireland 12. Family sagas

Originally published: Great Britain: Penguin Books, 2011.

Grania Ryan returns home to Ireland and forms a close friendship with a young girl whose family history is intertwined with Grania's own.

Rimmer, Kelly

Before I let you go / Kelly Rimmer. Graydon House, 2018. 379 p.

ISBN 9781525820847

1. Sisters 2. Drug addicts 3. Pregnant women 4. Child welfare 5. Infants 6. Physicians 7. Child custody 8. Australia 9. Australian 10. Women's lives and relationships

Librarians' Choice (Australia), 2018.

When Lexie Vidler hears from her drug addict sister, Annie, for the first time in years, she finds out that Annie is strung-out, pregnant, and in premature labor, leaving Lexie to help her troubled sister once again, as they face ghosts from the past that neither wants to face.

"Rimmer's timely novel captures the unbreakable bond of two sisters and humanizes the difficult intersection of the opioid epidemic and the justice system." Publishers Weekly.

Rimmer, Kelly

Truths I never told you / Kelly Rimmer. Graydon House, 2020. 352 p.

ISBN 9781525804656

1. 1950s 2. 1990s 3. Postpartum depression 4. Family secrets 5. New mothers 6. Diary writing 7. Family relationships 8. Seattle, Washington 9. Women's lives and relationships 10. Epistolary novels

Uncovering disturbing evidence that her mother did not die in a car accident when her sisters and she were toddlers, a woman on maternity leave pieces together journal entries to uncover harrowing truths about her father.

"With a mix of engrossing mystery and deep feeling, Rimmer offers a harrowing account of a doomed mother's experience in the 1950s and a family grappling with the truth." Publishers Weekly.

Rindell, Suzanne

The **other** typist / Suzanne Rindell. G. P. Putnam's Sons, 2013. 368 p.

ISBN 9780399161469

1. 1920s 2. Prohibition 3. Obsession in women 4. Typists 5. Police 6. Crime 7. Criminals 8. Gender role 9. Women's role 10. Historical thrillers

Working as a typist for the NYC Police Department in 1923, Rose Baker documents confessions of harrowing crimes and struggles with changing gender roles while clinging to her Victorian ideals and searching for nurturing companionship before becoming obsessed with a glamorous newcomer and her world of bobbed hair, smoking and speakeasies.

Rinehart, Mary Roberts, 1876-1958

The **circular** staircase / Mary Roberts Rinehart. Dover Publications, 1997, c1908. ix, 178 p.

ISBN 9780486297132

1. Securities 2. Default (Finance) 3. Middle-aged women 4. Crime 5. Murder 6. Stealing 7. Single women 8. Vacation homes 9. Household employees 10. Murder investigation 11. Mysteries

LC 971445

Originally published: New York :

The Circular Staircase is perhaps Mary Roberts Rinehart's most famous story. Wealthy spinster Rachel Innes is persuaded by her niece and nephew Gertrude and Halsey to take a house in the country for the summer. Rachel is unaware that the house holds a secret, and soon unexplained happenings and murder follow.

Rinehart, Mary Roberts, 1876-1958

Miss Pinkerton / Mary Roberts Rinehart. Kensington Books, 1998, c1932. 272 p.

ISBN 9781575662558

1. Informers 2. Nurses 3. Gunshot victims 4. Aunts 5. Detectives 6. Murder 7. Senior women 8. Serial murders 9. Murder suspects 10. Live-in companions 11. Murder investigation 12. Mysteries

Republished by American Mystery Classics in 2019.

Originally published: New York : International Readers League, 1932.

When Herbert Wynne supposedly commits suicide, Miss Pinkerton poses as a private nurse to his aunt Juliet and discovers that his "bedridden" aunt takes midnight jaunts, a stranger skulks about the stairs, and the other nurse on duty is scared of her own shadow, and Miss Pinkerton must unmask a killer before he strikes again.

Ripley, Mike

Mr Campion's fault / Mike Ripley. Severn House, 2016. 243 p. Albert Campion mysteries

ISBN 9780727886255

1. 1960s 2. Amateur detectives 3. Boys' schools 4. Class conflict 5. Small town life 6. Social classes 7. Families 8. Teaching 9. Murder investigation 10. Voyages and travels 11. Communities 12. Secrets 13. England 14. Yorkshire, England 15. Mysteries

Featuring Margery Allingham's character Albert Campion.

Following the death of the senior English master in a tragic road accident, Mr Campion's son Rupert and daughter-in-law Perdita are helping out at Ash Grange School for Boys in Yorkshire. When Rupert is arrested, Albert Campion heads to Denby Ash to find out what's going on. Was the English master's death really an accident?

"A charming, courtly, slightly eccentric hero; an intricate and unusual plot; and plenty of gentle humor make this an enticing read for old-school cozy fans." Booklist.

LIST OF FICTIONAL WORKS

Ripley, Mike

Mr. Campion's war / Mike Ripley. Severn House, 2018. 243 p. Albert Campion mysteries

ISBN 9780727888099

1. 1970s 2. Second World War era (1939-1945) 3. Senior men 4. Former intelligence officers 5. Amateur detectives 6. British in France 7. Espionage 8. England 9. France -- History -- German occupation, 1940-1945 10. Mysteries

Featuring Margery Allingham's character Albert Campion.

It's Albert Campion's seventieth birthday, and he has decided to enthral his guests at the Dorchester Hotel with his account of his wartime experiences in Vichy France more than twenty-five years before. But in doing so he unveils a series of extraordinary events, the repercussions of which put one of his guests in deadly danger...

Ripley, Nathan

Find you in the dark / Nathan Ripley Atria Books, 2018. 368 p.

ISBN 9781501178207

1. Anonymous persons 2. Missing persons 3. Serial murderers 4. Serial murder investigation 5. Women detectives 6. Police corruption 7. Obsession in men 8. Thrillers and suspense

Martin Reese has a hobby, he digs up murder victims. He buys stolen police files on serial killers, and uses them to find and dig up missing bodies. Calls in the results anonymously, taunting the police for their failure to do their job. Detective Sandra Whittal takes that a little personally. She's suspicious of the mysterious caller, who she names the Finder. Maybe he's the one leaving the bodies behind. If not, who's to say he won't start soon? As Whittal begins to zero in on the Finder, Martin makes a shocking discovery. It seems someone, someone lethal is very unhappy about the bodies he's been digging up. Hunted by a cop, hunted by a killer. To escape and keep his family safe, Martin may have to go deeper into the world of murder than he ever imagined.

Ritter, Todd

* Devil's night / Todd Ritter. Minotaur Books, 2013. 368 p. Kat Campbell mysteries

ISBN 9781250028532

1. Arson 2. Women detectives 3. Small town life -- Pennsylvania 4. Museums 5. Policewomen 6. Murder investigation 7. Pennsylvania 8. Mysteries

LC 2013009831

Summoned in the middle of the night to the site of an arson fire at the Perry Hollow museum, Police Chief Kat Campbell examines the murdered body of the curator before glimpsing nemesis Henry Goll in the crowd, a discovery that prompts a harrowing race against time.

Rivero, Melissa

The **affairs** of the Falcons / Melissa Rivero. Ecco, 2019. 277 p.

ISBN 9780062872357

1. 1990s 2. Undocumented immigrants 3. Immigrant families 4. Husband and wife 5. Marital conflict 6. Taxicab drivers 7. Blue collar workers 8. Peruvian Americans 9. Money lenders 10. New York City 11. Peru 12. Literary fiction

Fleeing the economic and political strife of 1990s Peru, undocumented factory worker Ana struggles to support her family while fending off the challenges of discrimination, sexual harassment and a loan shark's criminal enforcers.

Rivers, Francine, 1947-

And the shofar blew / Francine Rivers. Tyndale House Publishers, 2003. 439 p.

ISBN 0842365826

1. 1980s 2. 1990s 3. 2000s (Decade) 4. Ambition in men 5. Architects -- California 6. Clergy -- California 7. Spouses of clergy 8. Husband and wife -- California 9. Married people -- California 10. Alcoholics -- California 11. Recovering alcoholics -- California 12. Churches -- California 13. California 14. Christian fiction

LC 2002156552

Includes discussion questions.

Commited to building his new church, dynamic young preacher Paul Hudson loses sight of the purer intentions of his ministry and struggles to choose between his own will and God's plan.

Rivers, Francine, 1947-

Bridge to haven / Francine Rivers. Tyndale House Publishers, 2014. 500 p.

ISBN 9781414368184

1. Actors and actresses 2. Redemption (Christianity) 3. Christian life 4. Belonging 5. Abandoned infants 6. Adopted children 7. Alienation (Social psychology) 8. Rejection (Psychology) 9. Northern California 10. California -- Social life and customs -- 20th century 11. Hollywood, California 12. Christian historical fiction

LC 2013040115

Having been abandoned as a newborn and found and raised by Pastor Ezekiel Freeman in the small California town of Haven, Abra Matthews feels like she doesn't belong and at the age of seventeen runs off to Hollywood, becoming starlet Lena Scott.

"Rivers nicely evokes 1950s Hollywood, with its gossip columnists, high-wattage movie stars, and ladder-climbing aspirants; Elvis Presley and Lana Turner put in cameos. This story arc will be particularly resonant for Christian readers, but Rivers has the writing ability to reel in others who enjoy a well-told tale of redemption." Publishers Weekly.

Rivers, Francine, 1947-

The **masterpiece** / Francine Rivers. Tyndale House Publishers, 2018 500 p.

ISBN 9781496407900

1. Artists 2. Personal assistants 3. Single mothers 4. Christian women 5. Atheists 6. Graffiti artists 7. Secrets 8. Faith (Christianity) 9. Christian life 10. Redemption 11. Interpersonal attraction 12. Men/women relations 13. Los Angeles, California 14. Christian romances

LC 2017033594

Struggling to make a home for herself and her five-month old son Samuel, Grace Moore accepts a position as a personal assistant to Roman Velasco, a temperamental successful artist.

Rivers, Francine, 1947-

* Redeeming love / Francine Rivers. Multnomah, 1997, c1991. 464 p.

ISBN 1576738167

1. Bible. Old Testament Hosea Adaptations. 2. 1850s 3. Desire 4. Belief and doubt 5. Forgiveness 6. Redemption 7. Pioneer women 8. Men/women relations 9. Prostitutes 10. Christian men 11. Marriage 12. Husband and wife 13. Fear in women 14. Runaway wives, husbands, etc 15. Gold rush -- San Francisco, California 16. San Francisco, California 17. Christian historical romances

LC 97014694

"This is the 'redeemed' version of Redeeming Love, published by Bantam Books in 1991. The original edition is no longer available."

Originally published: Colorado Springs, Colorado : Multnomah, 1997.

After being beaten, Angel, a young prostitute, decides to accept devout Christian Michael Hosea's offer of marriage and falls in love not only with him, but also with God.

Rizzuto, Rahna R.

Shadow child / Rahna Reiko Rizzuto. Grand Central Publishing, 2018. 341 p.

ISBN 9781538711453

1. 1970s 2. Second World War era (1939-1945) 3. Twin sisters 4. Families -- History 5. World War II -- Japan 6. Japanese Americans -- Forced removal and incarceration, 1942-1945 7. Separated twin sisters 8. Concentration camps 9. Mothers -- Death 10. Hawaii 11. Japan 12. Historical fiction

LC 2017053601

Raised in a postwar Hawaiian town and estranged in the wake of a violent betrayal, mixed-race twins Hana and Kei are reunited years later by a life-changing secret.

"National Book Critics Circle finalist Rizzuto (Why She Left Us; Hiroshima in the Morning) blends historical fiction and mystery into a haunting examination of identity and family in this perfect book club choice." Library Journal.

The **road** ahead : fiction from the forever war / edited by Adrian Bonenberger, and Brian Castner. Pegasus Books, 2017 xvii, 349 p.

ISBN 9781681773070

1. Veterans 2. Afghan War, 2001- 3. Iraq War, 2003-2011 4. War on Terrorism, 2001-2009 5. Soldiers -- United States 6. Homecomings 7. Loneliness 8. Loss (Psychology) 9. Violence 10. Courage 11. Death 12. Guilt 13. War 14. Short stories 15. War stories

Twenty-five veterans describe and meditate on the way combat has changed in the decade since U.S. forces arrived in Iraq and Afghanistan through this collection of short stories.

"Bonenberger and Castners treasury captures the contemporary American soldiers experience in intimate and harrowing detail, touching on everything from loneliness to pride, death to brotherhood, and paranoia to compassion." Booklist.

Roanhorse, Rebecca

* **Trail** of lightning / Rebecca Roanhorse. Saga Press, 2018 352 p. Sixth world

ISBN 9781534413498

1. Native American women 2. Monsters 3. Navajo Indians 4. Shamans 5. Magic (Occultism) 6. Missing persons 7. Superhuman abilities 8. Legends, Native American 9. Gods and goddesses, Native American 10. Post-apocalypse 11. Navajo Indian Reservation 12. Apocalyptic fiction 13. Fantasy fiction

LC 2017034119

Locus Award for First Novel, 2019.

RUSA Reading List Short List, 2019.

When a small town needs her help in finding a missing girl, Maggie Hoskie, a Dinetah monster hunter, reluctantly enlists the help of an unconventional medicine man to uncover the terrifying truth behind the disappearance and her own past.

"This exciting postapocalyptic debut, with its heady combination of smartly drawn characters, Wild West feel, and twisty plot, is a must-read for fantasy enthusiasts." Library Journal.

Robards, Karen

Ghost moon / Karen Robards. Delacorte Press, 2000. 320 p.

ISBN 038531972X

1. Single mothers 2. Blended families 3. Serial murderers 4. Men/ women relations 5. Rich families 6. Eight-year-old girls 7. Mothers and daughters 8. Single fathers 9. Louisiana 10. Romantic suspense

LC 99047420

Ten years after her elopement with a cowboy, Olivia Morrison returns to the Louisiana estate of her wealthy stepfather as a prodigal daughter, with an eight-year-old daughter in tow, uncertain of her reception, only to come face to face with her hostile family, her devastatingly attractive step-cousin Seth, and dark secrets concerning her mother's death.

"Robards has crafted a mossy modern gothic drenched in gore. . . . [She] conveys the dusty heat of the Louisiana summer, and has an ear for the nuances of dialogue." Publishers Weekly.

Robards, Karen

The **last** victim / Karen Robards. Ballantine Books, 2012. 336 p. Charlotte Stone novels

ISBN 9780345535405

1. Women psychics 2. Serial murders 3. Family killing 4. Serial murderers 5. Criminal profilers 6. Ghosts 7. FBI agents 8. Missing teenagers 9. Virginia 10. Virginia Beach, Virginia 11. Paranormal romances 12. Romantic suspense

Investigating the brutal murders of two vacationing families in sunny Virginia Beach, FBI agents Ryan Sinclair and Buzz Crane suspect the work of a notorious serial killer and tap the skills of preeminent clinical expert Charlotte Stone, who is also the culprit's only known survivor.

Robards, Karen

The **ultimatum** / Karen Robards. Mira Books, 2017. 330 p. Guardian (Karen Robards)

ISBN 9780778330707

1. Women swindlers 2. Women thieves 3. Swindlers and swindling 4. Fathers and daughters 5. Men/women relations 6. Security consultants 7. Personal assistants 8. Family businesses 9. Criminals 10. Thieves 11. Secrets 12. Romantic suspense

A talented master of disguise who devotes herself to conning thieves and returning stolen money to its rightful owners hides her Robin Hood activities behind a day job as a personal assistant to her thief father's alluring former partner.

Robb, Candace M.

* The **cross-legged** knight : an Owen Archer mystery / Candace Robb. Mysterious Press, 2003. 321 p. Owen Archer mysteries

ISBN 9780892967728

1. William,, of Wykeham, Bishop of Winchester, 1324-1404 2. Medieval period (476-1492) 3. Plantagenet period (1154-1485) 4. 14th century 5. Political intrigue 6. Government investigators 7. Bishops 8. Husband and wife 9. Civilization, Medieval 10. Grief in women 11. Nobility 12. Murder 13. Murder investigation 14. Men/women relations 15. Great Britain -- History -- Edward III, 1327-1377 16. York, England 17. Historical mysteries 18. Medieval mysteries

LC 2002027248

Owen Archer investigates a suspicious accident that threatened the life of William of Wykeham, the recently deposed Lord Chancellor of England, who has been scheming to get back in the king's good graces despite a feud with the Duke of Lancaster.

"Once again, Robb provides the reader with an evocative and suspenseful whodunit thoroughly bolstered by a wealth of authentic historical detail." Booklist.

Robb, Candace M.

* A **gift** of Sanctuary : an Owen Archer mystery / Candace Robb. St. Martin's Press, 1998. 303 p. Owen Archer mysteries
ISBN 0312192665

1. Chaucer, Geoffrey, d 1400 2. Dafydd ap Gwilym, 1320?-1380? 3. Medieval period (476-1492) 4. Plantagenet period (1154-1485) 5. 14th century 6. Civilization, Medieval 7. Murder investigation -- Wales 8. Great Britain -- History -- Edward III, 1327-1377 9. Wales -- History -- 14th century 10. Historical mysteries 11. Medieval mysteries 12. Mysteries

LC 9841394

"Robb deftly interweaves a complex story of love, passion and murder into the troubled and tangled fabric of Welsh history, fashioning a rich and satisfying novel." Publishers Weekly.

Robb, Candace M.

* A **murdered** peace / Candace M. Robb. Pegasus Books, 2018. 400 p. Kate Clifford novels
ISBN 9781681778624

1. Medieval period (476-1492) 2. Plantagenet period (1154-1485) 3. Women amateur detectives 4. Independence in women 5. Political intrigue 6. Resistance to government 7. Friendship 8. Murder suspects 9. Murder investigation 10. Helpfulness in women 11. Secrets 12. Great Britain -- History -- Henry IV, 1399-1413 13. York, England 14. Medieval mysteries 15. Historical mysteries

Kate defends a friend who may be involved in an uprising against the king and who is also implicated in the murder of a spice seller in 1400 York.

Robb, Candace M.

* The **riddle** of St. Leonard's : an Owen Archer mystery. St. Martin's Press, 1997. 303 p. Owen Archer mysteries
ISBN 0312169833

1. Medieval period (476-1492) 2. Plantagenet period (1154-1485) 3. 14th century 4. Hospitals -- Great Britain 5. Civilization, Medieval 6. Great Britain -- History -- Edward III, 1327-1377 7. Historical mysteries 8. Medieval mysteries 9. Mysteries

LC 9716231

When there is a spate of deaths and thefts at St. Leonard's Hospital in York that are not related to the plague, the Master of the hospital calls upon one-eyed master spy Owen Archer to solve the mystery

"An evocative historical mystery steeped in authentically gritty period detail." Booklist.

Robb, Candace M.

A **twisted** vengeance / Candace Robb. Pegasus Books, 2017. 297 p. Kate Clifford novels
ISBN 9781681774527

1. Plantagenet period (1154-1485) 2. Widows 3. Independence in women 4. Political intrigue 5. Women amateur detectives 6. Knights and knighthood 7. Military occupation 8. Household employees 9. Missing women 10. Suspicion 11. Mothers and daughters 12. Family relationships 13. Family secrets 14. York, England 15. Great Britain -- History -- 14th century 16. Medieval mysteries 17. Historical mysteries

As the fourteenth century comes to a close, York seethes on the brink of civil war, and young widow Kate Clifford, struggling to keep her business afloat, realizes that her mother is harboring a dangerous secret?

Robb, J. D., 1950-

Fantasy in death / J.D. Robb. G.P. Putnam's Sons, 2010. 368 p. In Death series
ISBN 9780399156243

1. 21st century 2. Women detectives 3. Murder investigation 4. Virtual reality 5. Rich men 6. Policewomen 7. Electronic games industry and trade 8. New York City 9. Romantic suspense 10. Police procedurals

LC 2009041114

Investigating the bizarre murder of a millionaire video game maven within a locked room, NYPSD Lieutenant Eve Dallas is baffled by a lack of suspects and the victim's demise in spite of his considerable resources.

Robb, J. D., 1950-

Innocent in death / J.D. Robb. G.P. Putnam's Sons, 2007. 400 p. In Death series
ISBN 0399154019

1. 21st century 2. Women detectives 3. Murder investigation 4. Poisoning 5. Policewomen 6. Teachers 7. Husband and wife 8. Women murder suspects 9. Murder 10. New York City 11. Romantic suspense 12. Police procedurals

LC 2006025431

Sequel to: Born in death.

Investigating the baffling murder case of an ordinary and much-loved private school teacher, New York City lieutenant Eve Dallas struggles to identify who may have wanted the death of an innocent man.

Robb, J. D., 1950-

Naked in death / J.D. Robb. Berkley Books, 1995. 313 p. In Death series
ISBN 0425148297

1. 21st century 2. Women detectives 3. Murder suspects 4. Murder investigation 5. Policewomen 6. Women murder victims 7. Murder 8. Billionaires 9. Irish in New York City 10. New York City 11. Romantic suspense 12. Police procedurals

New York City police lieutenant Eve Dallas pursues a romantic relationship with a mysterious and wealthy Irishman while investigating a murder case.

"Naked in Death features Lt. Eve Dallas of the NYPD as she searches for a serial killer of prostitutes. It hints at the isolation, neglect, and sexual abuse that Eve suffered as a child, memories that she tries to suppress. The adult Eve is slow to trust and awkward when faced with affection and kindness. Yet over the course of this series, she acquires a husband, Roark; a partner, Peabody; and a varied host of friends: hardboiled reporter Nadine, humanitarian doctor Louise, and worldly wise, bursting with life, rock star Mavis." Library Journal.

Robbins, David L., 1954-

Last citadel : a novel of the Battle of Kursk / David L. Robbins. Bantam Books, 2003. 421 p. World War II (David L. Robbins)
ISBN 0553801775

1. S. S. Officers 2. Second World War era (1939-1945) 3. Soldiers 4. Intelligence Service 5. Battles 6. Bomber pilots 7. Violence 8. World War II 9. Kursk, Battle of, Russia, 1943 10. Tanks (Military science) 11. Revenge 12. Kursk, Russia 13. Soviet Union -- History -- German occupation, 1941-1944 14. War stories 15. Historical fiction

LC 2003044304

During the greatest tank battle in armored warfare, the Battle of Kursk, Dimitri Berko and Luis de Vega find themselves in the tensions of deadly battle.

"The battle for the Soviet city of Kursk in July 1943 during World War II involved two million soldiers. Code-named Citadel, it was Hitler's frenzied--and final--attempt to defeat Russia on the eastern front and was the largest buildup of German armed power of the war. Robbins re-creates the battle in this rousing novel: its characters being Hitler; his generals and advisers; Russian, German, and Spanish foot soldiers and tank drivers; fighter pilots (both men and women); partisans; and even elderly men and women digging trenches." Booklist.

Robbins, David L., 1954-
War of the rats : a novel / David L. Robbins. Bantam Books, 1999. 392 p. World War II (David L. Robbins)

ISBN 9780553108170

1. Second World War era (1939-1945) 2. Snipers 3. Women assassins 4. World War II 5. Undercover operations 6. Americans in Russia 7. Violence 8. Battles 9. Stalingrad, Battle of, 1942-1943 10. Soviet Union -- History -- German occupation, 1941-1944 11. War stories 12. Historical fiction

LC 98043918

During the siege of Stalingrad at the height of World War II, two master snipers--Chief Master Sergeant Vasily Zaitsev and German marksman Heinz Thorvald--embark on a deadly and calculating competition to destroy each other.

"The final confrontation takes a while to play out, but once Robbins . . . gets to the heart of the matter, he presents a riveting account of a battle within a battle, and the sniper motif proves an ideal vehicle to analyze the strengths and weaknesses of both sides." Publishers Weekly.

Robbins, Tom, 1932-
Fierce invalids home from hot climates / Tom Robbins. Bantam Books, 2000. 415 p.

ISBN 0553107755

1. Former CIA agents 2. International intrigue 3. Eccentrics and eccentricities 4. Inca shamans 5. Pedophiles 6. Wheelchair users 7. Men/women relations 8. Peru 9. Middle East 10. Humorous stories

LC 99051683

Follows the adventures, across four continents, of a man who is a contradiction for all seasons, as he falls in and out of love and danger.

"In true Robbins style, the writing throughout is lush and sexy, containing a great deal of witty social and political commentary." Publishers Weekly.

Robbins, Tom, 1932-
Jitterbug perfume / Tom Robbins. Bantam Books, 1984. 342 p.

ISBN 0553348981

1. Perfumes 2. Immortalism 3. Eccentrics and eccentricities 4. Men/women relations 5. Gods and goddesses 6. Seattle, Washington 7. Washington (State) 8. Humorous stories 9. Pacific Northwest fiction

LC 84045233

This philosophical epic, with a large cast of characters, addresses the fervent desire of the human race to overcome the tyranny of aging and physical death

"Robbins is still in top form, still mixing the lunatic and the thoughtful--or rather, doing a literary watusi up every page and jitterbugging back down." Publishers Weekly.

Robbins, Tom, 1932-
Skinny legs and all / Tom Robbins. Bantam Books, 1990. 422 p.

ISBN 9780553057751

1. Eccentrics and eccentricities 2. Terrorism -- Jerusalem, Israel 3. End of the world 4. Restaurants 5. Sculptors 6. Evangelists 7.

Husband and wife 8. Men/women relations 9. Belly dancers 10. Women artists 11. Manhattan, New York City 12. Humorous stories

LC 89018309

When an Arab and a Jew open a restaurant across the street from the U.N., a host of tragic and triumphant characters descend on the strange establishment.

"A painter's struggle with her art, a restaurant opened as an experiment in brotherhood, the journey of several inanimate objects to Jerusalem, a preacher's scheme to hasten Armageddon, and a performance of a legendary dance: these are the diverse elements around which Robbins has built this wild, controversial novel. Ellen Cherry Charles, one of the 'Daughters of the Daily Special' in Jitterbug Perfume, takes center stage. She has married Boomer Petway and moved to New York, hoping to make it as a painter. Instead, she winds up a waitress at the Isaac and Ishmael, a restaurant co-owned by an Arab and a Jew. . . . Few contemporary novelists mix tomfoolery and philosophy so well." Library Journal.

Robbins, Tom, 1932-
* **Still** life with Woodpecker / Tom Robbins. Bantam Books, 2003, c1980. x, 277 p.

ISBN 0553348973

1. Eccentrics and eccentricities 2. Men/women relations 3. Revolutionaries 4. Anarchists 5. Humorous stories 6. Pacific Northwest fiction

LC 2005281899

Originally published: New York : Bantam Books, 1980.

A love story that takes place inside a pack of cigarettes reveals the moon's purpose, differentiates between outlaws and criminals, and presents portraits of powerful Arabs, exiled royalty, and pregnant cheerleaders.

"The author's prose, as spasmodic as his heroine's sex life, is marbled with limping puns heavily splattered with recurrent motifs and a boyish zeal for the scatological." School Library Journal.

Roberts, Gillian, 1939-
* **Adam** and evil : an Amanda Pepper mystery / Gillian Roberts. Ballantine Books, 1999. 248 p. Amanda Pepper mysteries

ISBN 0345429346

1. Teachers 2. Midlife crisis 3. Murder investigation 4. Women teachers 5. Women amateur detectives 6. Teenage boys with emotional illnesses 7. Teacher-student relationships 8. Missing teenagers 9. Philadelphia, Pennsylvania 10. Cozy mysteries 11. Gentle reads

LC 99014225

Schoolteacher and sleuth Amanda Pepper takes her class to Philadelphia's public library only to find a young woman murdered and one of her students the prime suspect.

"Although the mystery is somewhat implausible, book lovers will enjoy Roberts' detours into the pricey hobby of book collecting. The story also gives libraries the acclaim they deserve, with many vivid descriptions of the majestic Free Library." Booklist.

Roberts, Gillian, 1939-
* The **bluest** blood : an Amanda Pepper mystery / Gillian Roberts. Ballantine Books, 1998. 230 p. Amanda Pepper mysteries

ISBN 0345403266

1. Teachers 2. Murder investigation 3. Book burning 4. Women teachers 5. Women amateur detectives 6. Rich people -- Philadelphia, Pennsylvania 7. Upper class -- Philadelphia, Pennsylvania 8. Hanging 9. Philadelphia, Pennsylvania 10. Cozy mysteries 11.

Gentle reads

LC 9726868

When English teacher and amateur sleuth Amanda Pepper attends an extravagant gala in honor of the local prep school's library and hosted by some of Philadelphia's ultrarich socialites, murder is on the menu

"A swift and intriguing spin through the sometimes murderous precincts of Philadelphia." Publishers Weekly.

Roberts, Michele

Ignorance / Michele Roberts. Bloomsbury USA, 2012. 240 p.

ISBN 9781608197712

1. Second World War era (1939-1945) 2. Young women 3. World War II -- France 4. Jewish women 5. Prejudice 6. Household employees 7. Holocaust (1933-1945) 8. Catholic schools 9. Poverty 10. Small towns -- France 11. France -- History 12. Historical fiction

LC 2011042283

Growing up side by side in the Catholic village of Ste. Madeleine, pious grocer's daughter Marie Angele aspires to a life of comfort and influence while impoverished laundress' daughter Jeanne hides her Jewish heritage and steals food to survive until the outbreak of war inadvertently binds the girls together.

Roberts, Nora

Chesapeake blue / Nora Roberts. G.P. Putnam's Sons, 2002. 384 p. Chesapeake Bay saga

ISBN 0399149392

1. Extortion 2. Men/women relations 3. Adult child abuse victims 4. Poor families 5. Young men 6. Adopted children 7. Artists 8. Stepbrothers and stepsisters 9. Chesapeake Bay Region 10. Eastern Shore, Maryland 11. Maryland 12. Contemporary romances

LC 2002024827

Sequel to: Inner harbor.

Returning as a successful artist to the home of the family that adopted him, Seth Quinn is intrigued by independent newcomer Dru Whitcomb Banks, who is hesitant to trust Seth, while dark secrets from the past threaten the entire Quinn family.

Roberts, Nora

Come sundown / Nora Roberts. St. Martin's Press, 2017. 432 p.

ISBN 9781250123077

1. Ranches 2. Family businesses 3. Murder 4. Ranchers 5. Family relationships 6. Missing persons 7. Resorts 8. Men/women relations 9. Interpersonal attraction 10. Montana 11. Romantic suspense

LC 2017002672

When danger lurks in the mountains around Bo's idyllic ranch and resort in western Montana, she turns to new hire Callen Skinner after they discover her estranged aunt badly injured and another woman murdered.

Roberts, Nora

* **Dance** upon the air / Nora Roberts. Jove Books, 2001. 386 p. Three Sisters Island trilogy

ISBN 9780515131222

1. Witches -- Massachusetts 2. Abused women 3. Magic 4. Islands 5. Men/women relations 6. Fate and fatalism 7. Curses 8. Violence against women 9. Husband and wife 10. Massachusetts 11. Paranormal romances

Sequel: Heaven and earth.

Includes excerpt from sequel: Heaven and earth.

After a year on the run, Nell Channing feels that she can make a home for herself on Three Sisters Island and, aided by Mia, the pro-

prietor of the Island's small book store and Ripley, the town's assistant sherriff, she finally dares to envision a brighter future.

Roberts, Nora

Dark witch / Nora Roberts. Berkley Books, 2013. 368 p. Cousins O'Dwyer trilogy

ISBN 9780425259856

1. Americans in Ireland 2. Cousins 3. Curses 4. Family secrets 5. Women -- Family relationships 6. Women and horses 7. Stables 8. Paranormal phenomena 9. Good and evil 10. Interpersonal attraction 11. Men/women relations 12. Ireland 13. Paranormal romances 14. Romantic suspense

LC 2013006292

American Iona Sheehan searches for her Irish ancestors, the O'Dwyers, to learn more about her powers and break an ancient curse, and meets Boyle McGrath.

Roberts, Nora

Honest illusions / Nora Roberts. Berkley Trade, 2002, c1992. 383 p.

ISBN 0425186199

1. Revenge 2. Jewel thieves 3. Magicians 4. Women jewel thieves 5. Adopted teenagers 6. Entertainers 7. Men/women relations 8. Interpersonal attraction 9. Romantic suspense

LC 92000277

Originally published in 1992.

Roxy Nouvelle and Luke Callahan, two accomplished illusionists who double as jewel thieves, team up as partners in crime and passion until Luke's mysterious past forces them apart.

"Max Nouvelle is the patriarch of a family of magicians and jewel thieves made up of Lily, his partner in love; Roxanne, his headstrong, beautiful daughter; and Luke, the abused runaway Max had taken in years ago, now a charming young man. They join Max in elaborate performances onstage and in equally elaborate robberies. For years Roxanne and Luke battle constantly, but as young adults they finally realize they are deeply in love. Luke, haunted by the fear that his past will hurt his adopted family, is the target of coldblooded Sam Wyatt, driven by a vow of revenge on the Nouvelles." Publishers Weekly.

Roberts, Nora

Midnight Bayou / Nora Roberts Putnam's, 2001. 432 p.

ISBN 0399148248

1. Haunted houses -- New Orleans, Louisiana 2. Lawyers 3. Interpersonal attraction 4. Home ownership 5. Bayous -- Louisiana 6. Mansions -- New Orleans, Louisiana 7. Visions 8. Secrets 9. Bar owners 10. Men/women relations 11. Houses -- Remodeling 12. New Orleans, Louisiana 13. Romantic suspense

LC 2001041643

While renovating an old mansion on the outskirts of New Orleans, Declan Fitzgerald begins seeing visions of days from a century past. Local legend has it that the house is haunted but he uncovers the reason for the strange sensations of terror and unbearable grief.

"Roberts has cleverly crafted an enticing tangle of times and relationship." Booklist.

Roberts, Nora

The **obsession** / Nora Roberts. Berkley, 2016 464 p.

ISBN 9780399175169

1. Women photographers 2. Adult children of murderers 3. Threat (Psychology) 4. Automobile mechanics 5. Family secrets 6. Trust in women 7. Stalking 8. Loyalty 9. Murder 10. Small towns 11. Houses -- Remodeling 12. Men/women relations 13. Stalkers 14. Washington (State) 15. Romantic suspense

Years after discovering her father's predatory double life, successful photographer Naomi Bowes struggles to hide her painful past from her fellow residents in a community thousands of miles away, a situation that introduces her to a new relationship andforces her to confront her demons.

"Roberts retains her impeccably high standards in this excellently executed tale, once again dazzling readers with a sophisticated blend of edge-of-your-seat suspense and sexy romance." Booklist.

Roberts, Nora
* **Sea** swept / Nora Roberts. Jove Books, 1998. 342 p. Chesapeake Bay saga

ISBN 0515121843

1. Brothers 2. Social workers 3. Interpersonal attraction 4. Men/women relations 5. Boys 6. Sailboat racing 7. Guardian and ward 8. Adopted boys 9. Chesapeake Bay Region 10. Maryland 11. Contemporary romances

Sequel: Rising tides.

Cameron, a champion boat racer, returns home to the Maryland shore at the behest of his dying father to care for Seth, a troubled young boy.

Roberts, Nora
Shelter in place / Nora Roberts. St. Martin's Press, 2018. 432 p.

ISBN 9781250161598

1. Post-traumatic stress disorder 2. Gunshot victims 3. Mass shootings 4. Serial murders 5. Threat (Psychology) 6. Survivor guilt 7. Massacres 8. Maine 9. Thrillers and suspense

A group of survivors navigate trauma and recovery challenges in the aftermath of a mass shooting at a movie theater, an event that inspires a career in law enforcement, triggers devastating PTSD and gives way to an escaped killer's plot to orchestrate an event with an even higher death toll.

Robertson, Imogen, 1973-
* **Anatomy** of murder / Imogen Robertson. Pamela Dorman Books, 2012. 384 p. Crowther and Westerman mysteries

ISBN 9780670023172

1. Georgian era (1714-1837) 2. 1780s 3. Women amateur detectives 4. Murder investigation 5. Anatomists -- History -- 18th century 6. Drowning victims 7. Murder -- History 8. London, England -- History -- 18th century 9. England -- History -- 18th century 10. Great Britain -- History -- George III, 1760-1820 11. Historical mysteries 12. Mysteries

LC 2011036291

Originally published: [London] : Headline Review, 2010.

The streets of London seethe with rumour and conspiracy as the King's navy battles the French at sea. And while the banks of the Thames swarm with life, a body is dragged from its murky waters. In another part of town, where the air seems sweeter, the privileged enjoy a brighter world of complacent wealth and intoxicating celebrity. But as society revels in its pleasures, a darker plot is played out. Yet some are willing to look below the surface to the unsavoury depths. Mrs Harriet Westerman believes passionately in justice. Reclusive anatomist Gabriel Crowther is fascinated by the bones beneath the skin. Invited to seek the true nature of the dead man, they risk censure for an unnatural interest in murder. But when the safety of a nation is at stake, personal reputation must give way to the pursuit of reason and truth.

Robertson, Imogen, 1973-
* **Circle** of shadows / Imogen Robertson. Viking, 2013. 384 p. Crowther and Westerman mysteries

ISBN 9780670026289

1. Georgian era (1714-1837) 2. Secret societies 3. Murder investigation 4. Poisoning 5. Widows 6. Anatomists 7. Women amateur detectives 8. Nobility 9. London, England 10. England -- History -- 18th century 11. Great Britain -- History -- George III, 1760-1820 12. Historical mysteries

LC 2013009688

"Pamela Dorman Books."

When a beautiful aristocrat is murdered during a Shrove Tuesday masked ball in 1784, the forthright Mrs. Harriet Westerman and her reclusive companion, anatomist Gabriel Crowther, struggle with reluctant witnesses to clear the name of a falsely accused suspect who is facing execution.

Robertson, Imogen, 1973-
Instruments of darkness : a novel / Imogen Robertson. Pamela Dorman Books, 2011. 384 p. Crowther and Westerman mysteries

ISBN 9780670022427

1. Georgian era (1714-1837) 2. 1780s 3. 18th century 4. Women amateur detectives 5. Murder investigation -- Sussex, England 6. Anatomists 7. Family secrets 8. Murder -- Sussex, England 9. Sussex, England -- History -- 18th century 10. England -- History -- 18th century 11. Great Britain -- History -- George III, 1760-1820 12. Historical mysteries 13. Mysteries

Discovering a dead neighbor from a menacing local estate, the unconventional Mrs. Westerman of 1780 Sussex enlists a reclusive local anatomist to uncover the family's secrets, which include ties to the American Revolution and links to the murder of a music shop owner.

Robertson, Imogen, 1973-
* **Island** of bones / Imogen Robertson. Pamela Dorman Books, 2012. 384 p. Crowther and Westerman mysteries

ISBN 9780670026272

1. Georgian era (1714-1837) 2. 18th century 3. Anatomists 4. Men recluses 5. Tombs 6. Dead 7. Investigations 8. Family estates 9. Women amateur detectives 10. Nobility 11. Gravestones, mausoleums, etc 12. Family secrets 13. Lake District (England) 14. England -- History -- 18th century 15. Great Britain -- History -- George III, 1760-1820 16. Historical mysteries 17. Mysteries

LC 2012003378

Originally published: 2011.

Cumbria, 1783. A broken heritage; a secret history. The tomb of the first Earl of Greta should have lain undisturbed on its island of bones for three hundred years. When idle curiosity opens the stone lid, however, inside is one body too many. Gabriel Crowther's family bought the Greta's land long ago, and has suffered its own bloody history. His brother was hanged for murdering their father, the Baron of Keswick, and Crowther has chosen comfortable seclusion and anonymity over estate and title for thirty years. But the call of the mystery brings him home at last. Travelling with forthright Mrs Harriet Westerman, who is escaping her own tragedy, Crowther finds a little town caught between new horrors and old, where ancient ways challenge modern justice. And against the wild and beautiful backdrop of fells and water, Crowther discovers that his past will not stay buried.

Robertson, Imogen, 1973-

The **Paris** winter / Imogen Robertson. St. Martin's Press, 2014. 360 p.

ISBN 9781250051837

1. Belle Epoque (1871-1914) 2. 1910s 3. Women painters 4. Revenge 5. Opium addiction 6. Poverty 7. Brothers and sisters 8. Secrets 9. Art 10. Paris, France -- History -- 1870-1940 11. Historical fiction

British painter Maud Heighton, seduced by the elegance and luxury of Paris, is unknowingly caught in a web of deception and revenge at the height of La Belle Epoque.

"For readers of historical fiction looking for a complex story, this is a sure bet." Library Journal.

Robertson, Michael, 1951-

The **Baker** Street letters / Michael Robertson. Minotaur Books, 2009. 320 p. Baker Street brothers

ISBN 9780312538125

1. 1990s 2. Brothers 3. Letter writing 4. Missing persons investigation 5. Murder investigation 6. Cold cases (Criminal investigation) 7. Characters and characteristics in literature 8. Lawyers 9. Missing persons 10. Offices 11. London, England 12. Los Angeles, California 13. Mysteries

LC 2008045668

Reggie is thrilled when he learns that his new office is in the same space where famous sleuth Sherlock Holmes used to ply his trade. However, when he starts to receive mysterious mail, written for Holmes, his excitement soon turns into intrigue. As Reggie's brother, Nigel, begins to investigate one of these letters, he inexplicably disappears. Now, Reggie must find his brother while simultaneously solving a murder case.

Robertson, Michael, 1951-

The **Baker** Street translation : a mystery / Michael Robertson. Minotaur Books, 2013. 288 p. Baker Street brothers

ISBN 9781250016454

1. 1990s 2. Wills 3. Heirs and heiresses 4. Inheritance and succession 5. Kidnappers 6. Murder investigation 7. Lawyers 8. Lawyers 9. Brothers 10. Innocence (Law) 11. Letter writing 12. Characters and characteristics in literature 13. London, England 14. England 15. Mysteries

When new letters misaddressed to famous former tenant Sherlock Holmes embroil them in a tangle of new cases, brothers Reggie and Nigel Heath are compelled to sort out an American heiress's unconventional will, translate a nursery rhyme and find a missing rival while preventing an attack on an upcoming royal event.

Robertson, Michael, 1951-

The **brothers** of Baker Street / Michael Robertson. Minotaur Books, 2011. 288 p. Baker Street brothers

ISBN 9780312538132

1. 1990s 2. Murder investigation 3. Lawyers 4. Murder suspects 5. Crimes against tourists 6. Lawyers 7. Brothers 8. Innocence (Law) 9. Letter writing 10. Characters and characteristics in literature 11. London, England 12. England 13. Mysteries

LC 2010042020

When Reggie and Nigel Heath set up their law office at the famed 221B Baker Street, they are forced to respond to letters mailed to Sherlock Holmes, the most famous previous tenet at that address. As the brothers investigate their current case where a cabbie is accused of murdering two American tourists, the letters begin to pile up.

"According to the terms of their lease, . . . Reggie and Nigel Heath were able to set up their modern-day law practice in the desirable 200 block of Baker Street by agreeing to answer all correspondence addressed to Sherlock Holmes at 221B. Reggie, the less whimsical of the pair, has been neglecting that responsibility, so . . . that task falls to Nigel, freeing up Reggie to concentrate on defending a young cab driver accused of robbing and killing two American tourists. An anonymous letter to Holmes gives Reggie a valuable tip, but the communications from a certain Professor Moriarty add a more sinister twist to this breezy and entertaining legal mystery." New York Times Book Review.

Robertson, Michael, 1951-

Moriarty returns a letter : a Baker Street mystery / Michael Robertson. Minotaur Books, 2014. 288 p. Baker Street brothers

ISBN 9781250016461

1. 1990s 2. Brothers 3. Enemies 4. Voyages and travels 5. Lawyers 6. Letter writing 7. Characters and characteristics in literature 8. London, England 9. Los Angeles, California 10. Mysteries

LC 2013033400

"A Thomas Dunne book for Minotaur Books"--T.p. verso.

After an exhibition of vintage Sherlock Holmes letters opens at the Marylebone Hotel, lawyers Reggie and Nigel Heath, who are charged with answering letters to Holmes that arrive at their office, are faced with a whole new set of problems as an enemy from their past returns.

Robertson, Robin, 1955-

The **long** take : a noir narrative / Robin Robertson. Alfred A. Knopf, 2018. 236 p.

ISBN 9780525655213

1. 1940s 2. 1950s 3. Postwar life 4. Social change 5. World War II veterans 6. Journalists 7. Homelessness 8. Urban problems 9. House demolition 10. Canadians in the United States 11. World War II -- Canadian participation 12. People with post-traumatic stress disorder 13. Los Angeles, California -- History -- 20th century 14. Novels in verse 15. Literary fiction

Also published as The Long Take : Or A Way To Lose More Slowly.

Walter Scott Prize for Historical Fiction, 2019.

Longlisted for the Man Booker Prize, 2018.

A D-Day veteran with post-traumatic stress disorder makes his way from New York to Los Angeles and San Francisco and as a journalist explores the social and racial divisions, spiraling corruption, and collapse of inner cities in America.

"Robertson transforms the long take into an epic taking of life, liberty, reason, and hope in this saga of a good man broken by war and a city savaged by greed, an arresting and gorgeously lyrical and disquieting tale of brutal authenticity, hard-won compassion, and stygian splendor." Booklist.

Robinson, Kim Stanley

2312 : a novel / Kim Stanley Robinson. Orbit, 2012. 576 p.

ISBN 9780316098120

1. 24th century 2. Space colonies 3. High technology 4. Mercury (Planet) 5. Solar system 6. Science fiction 7. Space opera

LC 2011044805

Nebula Award for Best Novel, 2012.

A tale set in a technologically sophisticated solar system three hundred years in the future follows the experiences of former world designer Swan, who in the wake of an unexpected death is led into a plot to destroy everything she has helped to create.

Robinson, Kim Stanley

* **Antarctica** / Kim Stanley Robinson. Bantam Books, 1998. 511 p.

ISBN 0553100637

1. 21st century 2. Conservation of natural resources 3. Greed 4.

Sabotage 5. Environmentalists 6. Environmental crimes 7. Ecology 8. Oil industry and trade 9. Voyages and travels 10. Antarctica 11. Science fiction

LC 97041701

When the treaty protecting Antarctica from profiteers is about to dissolve--sending politicians and corporations scrambling to plunder its resources--a radical environmental group embarks on a campaign of sabotage to protect the land's pristine beauty

"This is an exhilarating addition to a body of work distinguished by two elements all too rare in modern science fiction: a sense of character and a sense of place. Robinson brings the two together by writing about people who are in love with where they are." New York Times Book Review.

Robinson, Kim Stanley

Aurora / Kim Stanley Robinson. Orbit, 2015. 466 p.
ISBN 9780316098106

1. Far future 2. Space vehicles 3. Communities 4. Space travelers 5. High technology 6. Mothers and daughters 7. Space flight 8. Women engineers 9. Family relationships 10. Interpersonal relations 11. Space 12. Hard science fiction 13. Science fiction

The starship is headed for Tau Ceti, approximately 12 light years away. Launched from Earth in the 26th century, the vessel is nearing its destination after nearly 160 years. Charged with creating a comprehensive narrative of the voyage by chief engineer Devi, the ship's AI narrates this moving, thought-provoking novel, seamlessly blending the technical aspects of the spacecraft with the more personal stories of its passengers -- particularly Devi's daughter, Freya, who's expected to succeed her mother as chief engineer just as they reach their new home. -- Description by Gillian Speace.

"Robinson's latest well-researched novel exposes the fundamental flaws in one of science fiction's most beloved tropes: the multigenerational space ark traveling at sub-light speed to colonize a planet around a distant star." Kirkus.

Robinson, Kim Stanley

* **Blue** Mars / Kim Stanley Robinson. Bantam Books, 1996. 609 p. Mars trilogy
ISBN 9780553573350

1. Overpopulation 2. Immigration and emigration 3. Planets -- Colonization 4. Human settlements 5. Terraforming 6. Cooperation 7. Ice age (Geology) 8. Climate change 9. Life on other planets 10. Mars (Planet) -- Colonization 11. Hard science fiction 12. Science fiction

LC 9546700

Hugo Award for Best Novel, 1997.
Locus Award for Best Science Fiction Novel, 1997.

After declaring independence from Earth, Mars still faces problems: an impending ice age, a search for religious meaning, and immigration. New medical discoveries enable people to live 200 years, causing overpopulation on Earth and the Martians object to being swamped by Earthmen. A replay of New World problems in space.

Robinson, Kim Stanley

Galileo's dream / Kim Stanley Robinson. Bantam Spectra, 2009. 416 p.
ISBN 9780553806595

1. Galilei, Galileo 2. Astronomers 3. Time travel (Future) 4. Religion and science 5. Consulting 6. Space colonies 7. Scientific discoveries 8. Alternative histories 9. Science fiction

From the summit of their distant future, a charismatic renegade named Ganymede travels to the past to bring Galileo forward in an attempt to alter history and ensure the ascendancy of science over religion.

Yet between his brief and jarring visitations to this future, Galileo must struggle against the ignorance and superstition of his own time.

Robinson, Kim Stanley

* **Green** Mars / Kim Stanley Robinson. Bantam Books, 1994. 535 p. Mars trilogy
ISBN 0553096400

1. 22nd century 2. Revolutionaries 3. Life on other planets 4. Human settlements 5. Planets -- Colonization 6. Conservation of natural resources 7. Technology -- Social aspects 8. Mars (Planet) -- Colonization 9. Hard science fiction 10. Science fiction

LC 93039516

Hugo Award for Best Novel, 1994.
Locus Award for Best Science Fiction Novel, 1994.

One generation after the first pioneers begin to transform Mars into an Earthlike planet, the first grown children born on Mars, led by Peter Clayborne, rebel against colonization in an effort to preserve Mars' natural state.

Robinson, Kim Stanley

The **Martians** / Kim Stanley Robinson. Bantam Books, 1999. 336 p. Mars trilogy
ISBN 0553801171

1. Life on other planets 2. Space colonies -- Mars (Planet) 3. Revolutions 4. Martians 5. Space flight 6. Men/women relations 7. Political corruption 8. Imaginary wars and battles 9. Antarctica 10. Mars (Planet) -- Colonization 11. Short stories 12. Science fiction 13. Hard science fiction

LC 99013115

Companion to: Mars trilogy.
Locus Award for Best Collection, 2000.

A collection of stories set in the universe of Red Mars, Green Mars, and Blue Mars, tells the story of the colonists of the red planet and their experiences during its terraformation.

"Also included is Green Mars, a previously published novella about climbing Olympus Mons, the highest mountain in the solar system. . . . Some of the pieces here will be of interest only to those who have already read the trilogy, but the finest of the short fiction stands firmly on its own. As is the norm with Robinson's work, the stories are beautifully written, the characters are well developed and the author's passion for ecology manifests on every page." Publishers Weekly.

Robinson, Kim Stanley

New York 2140 / Kim Stanley Robinson. Orbit, 2017. 480 p.
ISBN 9780316262347

1. 22nd century 2. Near future 3. Social change 4. Climate change 5. City life 6. Sea level 7. Global warming 8. Adaptability (Psychology) 9. New York City 10. Hard science fiction 11. Apocalyptic fiction 12. Science fiction

LC 2016039922

Librarians' Choice (Australia), 2017

When a New York City of the near future is submerged by rising waters, the residents rapidly adapt the thriving metropolis until it becomes a vibrant, though permanently changed, canal region of island skyscrapers and remarkable inhabitants.

"A post-disaster fairy tale that's light on plot...but a thoroughly enjoyable exercise in worldbuilding, written with a cleareyed love for the city's past, present, and future." Kirkus.

Robinson, Kim Stanley

* **Red** Mars / Kim Stanley Robinson. Bantam Books, 1993. 572 p. Mars trilogy

ISBN 9780553560732

1. 21st century 2. Planets -- Colonization 3. Cooperation 4. Human settlements 5. Colonies 6. Revolutionaries 7. Interpersonal conflict 8. Exploitation 9. Life on other planets 10. Disagreement 11. Mars (Planet) -- Colonization 12. Hard science fiction 13. Science fiction

LC 92021607

BSFA Award for Best Novel, 1992.

Nebula Award for Best Novel, 1993.

For centuries, the red planet has enticed the people of Earth. Now an international group of scientists has colonized Mars. Leaving Earth forever, there 100 people have traveled nine months to reach their new home. This is the remarkable story of the world they create.

"A novel fully inhabited both by detailed technical processes and by people whose careers those processes are; it is also a novel with a complex sense of political reality. . . . This is one of the finest works of American SF because it is one of the few that aspire to the dignity of the genuinely tragic." Times Literary Supplement.

Robinson, Kim Stanley

The **years** of rice and salt / Kim Stanley Robinson. Bantam Books, 2002. 658 p.

ISBN 9780553109207

1. 14th century 2. Black Death 3. War 4. Islam 5. Buddhists 6. Eastern religions 7. China 8. Asia 9. Alternative histories

LC 2001043492

Locus Award for Best Science Fiction Novel, 2003.

In an alternate history world in which the population of Europe is almost completely wiped out by the Black Death during the fourteenth century, three superpowers--China, India, and the nations of Islam--battle for supremacy in a World War destined to create a new world order.

"Because this alternate history is set in the same lawful universe as ours, its science must be the same. Because its people have the same basic human needs, their societies resemble ours. However, as events march toward the alternative year of 2002, some of his characters come to believe, despite much evidence to the contrary, that they can change the way they live. The reader is left to ponder whether this is an illusion." New York Times Book Review.

Robinson, Lynda Suzanne

Murder at the feast of rejoicing : a Lord Meren mystery Walker, 1996. 229 p. Lord Meren mysteries

ISBN 0802732747

1. Ancient Egypt (3100 BCE-640 CE) 2. 14th century BCE 3. Courts and courtiers -- Egypt 4. Murder investigation 5. Political corruption 6. Secrets 7. Tombs 8. Adopted boys 9. Murder 10. Ancient Egypt -- History -- Eighteenth dynasty, ca 1570-1320 BC 11. Ancient Egypt -- Civilization -- To 332 BC 12. Ancient Egypt -- History -- To 332 BC 13. Egypt -- Rulers 14. Historical mysteries 15. Mysteries

LC 95-33190

Lord Meren, ordered to take some time off by the pharaoh, is dismayed to learn that one of his friends or relatives may be a murderer, when the body of a shrewish cousin is discovered.

"Good scholarship authenticates the historical setting; imagination provides the sense of danger and romance to make it come alive." New York Times Book Review.

Robinson, Lynda Suzanne

Murder at the god's gate Walker, 1995. 236 p. Lord Meren mysteries

ISBN 0802731988

1. Tutankhamen,, King of Egypt 2. Ancient Egypt (3100 BCE-640 CE) 3. 14th century BCE 4. Courts and courtiers -- Egypt 5. Political corruption 6. Priests 7. Murder investigation 8. Murder 9. Jealousy 10. Thebes (Egypt : Extinct city) 11. Ancient Egypt -- Civilization -- To 332 BC 12. Ancient Egypt -- History -- To 332 BC 13. Egypt -- Rulers 14. Historical mysteries 15. Mysteries

LC 9428806

When the life of the fourteen-year-old Pharaoh Tutankhamun is endangered, his agent, Lord Meren, embarks on a deadly mission, challenging the priests who threaten the young pharaoh and protecting him from the traitors in his own court

"Robinson . . . surrounds Meren with palace and temple intrigue, authentic details of daily life, and frequent mention of a wide assortment of indigenous animals." Library Journal.

Robinson, Marilynne

* **Gilead** / Marilynne Robinson. Farrar, Straus and Giroux, 2004. 256 p.

ISBN 0374153892

1. 1950s 2. Fathers and sons 3. Reminiscing in old age 4. May-December romance 5. Slavery 6. Faith (Christianity) 7. Septuagenarian men 8. Senior men 9. Clergy 10. Military chaplains 11. Abolitionists 12. Pacifists 13. Family relationships 14. Letters 15. United States Civil War, 1861-1865 16. Iowa 17. Kansas -- History -- Civil war, 1861-1865 18. United States -- History -- 19th century 19. Literary fiction 20. Historical fiction 21. Epistolary novels 22. Family sagas 23. Gentle reads

LC 2004047063

Originally published: New York, N.Y. : Farrar, Straus and Giroux, 2004.

"Winner of the 2005 Pulitzer prize for fiction"--Cover.

ALA Notable Book, 2006.

National Book Critics Circle Award for Fiction, 2004.

Pulitzer Prize for Fiction, 2005.

As the Reverend John Ames approaches the hour of his own death, he writes a letter to his son chronicling three previous generations of his family, a story that stretches back to the Civil War and reveals uncomfortable family secrets.

"Gilead possesses the quiet ineluctable perfection of Flaubert's A Simple Heart as well as the moral and emotional complexity of Robert Frost's deepest poetry. There's nothing flashy in these pages, and yet one regularly pauses to reread sentences, sometimes for their beauty, sometimes for their truth." Washington Post Book World.

Robinson, Marilynne

Home / Marilynne Robinson. Farrar, Straus and Giroux, 2008. 336 p.

ISBN 9780374299101

1. 1950s 2. Clergy 3. Homecomings 4. Families 5. Generation gap 6. Reminiscing in old age 7. Alcoholic men 8. Family secrets 9. Fathers and sons 10. Brothers and sisters 11. Fathers and daughters 12. Faith (Christianity) 13. Children of clergy 14. Iowa 15. Literary fiction 16. Domestic fiction 17. Gentle reads

LC 2008018301

Orange Prize for Fiction, 2009.

National Book Award for Fiction finalist, 2008

National Book Critics Circle Award for Fiction finalist, 2008

Shortlisted for the International IMPAC Dublin Literary Award, 2010

Returning to Gilead to care for her dying father, Glory Boughton is joined by her long-absent brother, with whom she bonds throughout his struggles with alcoholism, unemployment, and their father's traditionalist values.

"There is almost no first-rate American fiction about what happens in a household where religion is the family business, but if you ever wondered what it's like to be a preacher's kid, you can't do better than Home. Robinson's greatest achievement is that she manages to introduce the notions of belief and religious mystery without ever seeming vague. She never shies from uncomfortable truths." Newsweek.

Robinson, Marilynne

* **Lila** / Marilynne Robinson. Farrar Straus & Giroux, 2014. 261 p.

ISBN 9780374187613

1. Drifters 2. Adult child abuse victims 3. Clergy 4. Calvinism 5. Life change events 6. Faith (Christianity) 7. Marriage 8. Belief and doubt 9. May-December romance 10. Men/women relations 11. Iowa 12. Literary fiction 13. Gentle reads

National Book Critics Circle Award for Fiction, 2014.

National Book Award for Fiction finalist, 2014.

Shortlisted for the International Dublin Literary Award, 2016.

Triggering a romance and debate by seeking shelter in a church and becoming a minister's wife, homeless Lila reflects on her hardscrabble life on the run with a canny young drifter and her efforts to reconcile her painful past with her husband's gentle Christian worldview.

"A passionate and learned moral and spiritual inquiry, a paean to the earth, and a witty and transcendent love story." Booklist.

Robinson, Peter, 1950-

All the colors of darkness / Peter Robinson. William Morrow, 2009. 351 p. Inspector Alan Banks mysteries

ISBN 9780061362934

1. Police -- Yorkshire, England 2. Spies 3. Murder investigation 4. Detectives -- Yorkshire, England 5. Murder 6. Suicide 7. Theatrical costume designers 8. Men with paranoia 9. Yorkshire, England 10. London, England 11. Mysteries 12. Police procedurals

LC 2008019015

Originally published: Toronto : McClelland & Stewart, c2008.

When the body of a man is discovered hanging from a tree in the woods near Eastvale, all signs point toward suicide. Inspector Banks finds himself plunged into a case where nothing is as it seems.

Robinson, Peter, 1950-

Careless love / Peter Robinson. William Morrow, 2019, c2018. 432 p. Inspector Alan Banks mysteries

ISBN 9780062847522

1. Suicide investigation 2. Murder suspects 3. Police 4. Crime scenes 5. Criminal evidence 6. Murder investigation 7. Police procedurals 8. Mysteries

Originally published: London : Hodder & Stoughton, 2018.

Detective Superintendent Alan Banks and his crack investigation team investigate two suspicious deaths that are complicated by a shocking revelation and the return of an old enemy.

Robinson, Peter, 1950-

Children of the revolution / Peter Robinson. McClelland & Stewart, 2013. 387 p. Inspector Alan Banks mysteries

ISBN 0771076304

1. Murder suspects 2. College teachers 3. Scandals 4. Police 5. Murder investigation 6. England 7. Yorkshire, England 8. Mysteries 9. Police procedurals

Inspector Banks investigates the death of a disgraced college professor.

Robinson, Peter, 1950-

Cold is the grave / Peter Robinson. W. Morrow, 2000. 369 p. Inspector Alan Banks mysteries

ISBN 0380978083

1. Villages -- Yorkshire, England 2. Runaway teenage girls 3. Murder investigation -- Yorkshire, England 4. Murder -- Yorkshire, England 5. Police -- Yorkshire, England 6. England 7. Yorkshire, England 8. Mysteries 9. Police procedurals

LC 00037231

Sequel to: In a dry season.

Arthur Ellis Award for Best Novel, 2001.

Maverick police inspector Alan Banks finds himself drawn into London's underworld when he aids his archrival Chief Constable Riddle, after the chief's missing daughter turns up on a pornographic website.

"A cunningly constructed plot, enhanced by Robinson's engaging descriptions and insights." Booklist.

Robinson, Peter, 1950-

* **Close** to home / Peter Robinson. William Morrow, 2016, 396 p. Inspector Alan Banks mysteries

ISBN 9780062431271

1. Missing persons 2. Missing persons investigation 3. Murder 4. Murder investigation 5. Missing teenage boys 6. Detectives 7. Police 8. England 9. Yorkshire, England 10. Mysteries 11. Police procedurals

LC 2002071901

Also published under the title The summer that never was.

When the remains of a childhood friend of Alan Banks are discovered, who disappeared more then 35 years ago, Banks is drawn into an investigation.

"A moody chap on the sunniest of days, Peter Robinson's Yorkshire copper, Inspector Alan Banks, slips into a melancholy funk. . . when he returns to his boyhood homeindeed, to his own narrow bed in his old room in his parents' houseto help with an investigation into the death of a former schoolmate. Graham Marshall was 14 when he disappeared in 1965, and the belated discovery of his skeletal remains brings a rush of painful memories to the middle-aged detective who had been his best friend and the keeper of their secrets." New York Times Book Review.

Robinson, Peter, 1950-

The **first** cut / Peter Robinson. Perennial Dark Alley, 2004, 310 p.

ISBN 9780060735357

1. Victims of violent crimes 2. Women with amnesia 3. Serial murders 4. Women college graduates 5. Women impostors 6. Women authors 7. Authors 8. Fiction writing 9. Obsession in women 10. Memories 11. England 12. Whitby, England 13. Yorkshire, England 14. Psychological suspense

LC 2003067660

Previously published as: Caedmon's song (1990).

Originally published: Canada: Penguin, 1990; London: Pan, 2004.

"Recent university graduate Kirsten survives a brutal Jack the Ripper-style attack of which she has no memory. As Kirsten recovers, she becomes fixated on finding the man who nearly killed her. Miles away, Martha has come to the coastal town of Whitby, where she is doing research for a book. Or is she? Carefully surveying her surroundings, Martha grows more obsessed with the object of her trip. The women's stories are told in alternate chapters until the unsettling end. This atmospheric tale of suspense will keep readers wondering what's really going on." Library Journal.

LIST OF FICTIONAL WORKS

Robinson, Peter, 1950-

* **Friend** of the devil / Peter Robinson. William Morrow, 2008. 400 p. Inspector Alan Banks mysteries

ISBN 9780060544379

1. Women murder victims 2. Secret identity 3. Identity (Psychology) 4. Teenage murder victims 5. Police -- Yorkshire, England 6. Detectives -- Yorkshire, England 7. Murder 8. Women with disabilities 9. Murder investigation 10. Secrets 11. Revenge 12. England 13. Yorkshire, England 14. Mysteries 15. Police procedurals

LC 2007021678

Chief Inspector Alan Banks and Detective Inspector Annie Cabbot must work together to solve two chilling crimes. On loan to a sister precinct, Cabbot draws the first case. Karen Drew seems to have lived a quiet and nearly invisible life for the past seven years. Try as she might, Annie turns up nothing in the woman's past that might have prompted someone to wheel her out to the sea and to her death. Meanwhile, in the Hayley Daniels murder, Banks has suspects galore. Then a breakthrough spins Annie's case in a shocking and surprising new direction, straight toward Banks.

Robinson, Peter, 1950-

In the dark places / Peter Robinson. William Morrow, 2014. 336 p. Inspector Alan Banks mysteries

ISBN 9780062240545

1. Murder suspects 2. Crime scenes 3. Missing persons 4. Police 5. Murder investigation 6. Mysteries 7. Police procedurals

Originally published as Abattoir blues, Toronto: McClelland & Stewart, 2014.

"As Banks and his team follow what few clues they have, desperate to find the missing boy, who holds the key to the puzzle, they find themselves branching out in different directions. As the end game becomes a race against time, even Banks's team isn't safe from the rage of the hunted animal."--Provided by publisher.

Robinson, Peter, 1950-

* **Innocent** graves : an Inspector Banks mystery / Peter Robinson. Berkley Prime Crime, 1996. 346 p. Inspector Alan Banks mysteries

ISBN 0425153150

1. Murder investigation -- Yorkshire, England 2. Crimes against teenage girls 3. Murder suspects 4. Police -- Yorkshire, England 5. Villages -- Yorkshire, England 6. England 7. Yorkshire, England 8. Mysteries 9. Police procedurals

LC 95-38218

Arthur Ellis Award for Best Novel, 1997.

When the brutal murder of a teenage girl shatters the peace of the small village of Eastvale, Inspector Banks and his colleague, Susan Gay, dig beneath the surface of small-town secrets to uncover the guilty party

"Although the story follows the classical form of a whodunit, the characters have complexity and the issues range broad and deep, raising interesting moral questions about bigotry, class privilege and the terrible crime of being different." New York Times Book Review.

Robinson, Peter, 1950-

Piece of my heart / Peter Robinson. William Morrow, 2006. 378 p. Inspector Alan Banks mysteries

ISBN 006054435X

1. Murder investigation 2. Rock concerts 3. Power failures 4. Fathers and daughters 5. Fathers and sons 6. Journalists 7. Police -- Yorkshire, England 8. Detectives -- Yorkshire, England 9. Murder 10. England 11. Yorkshire, England 12. Mysteries 13. Police procedurals

LC 2005058363

First published: London: Hodder & Stoughton, 2006.

"DCI Banks" -- Cover.

TV tie-in.

As he probes the killing of a freelance music journalist, Detective Inspector Alan Banks finds his investigation journeying back in time more than thirty years and into the heart of the mystery surrounding a decades-old crime.

"The author invokes the most disturbing aspects of the 60's to the point at which even the Manson murders have repercussions in Yorkshire to sustain the book's ominous mood. There is pathos too, as Banks winds up revisiting characters who were young and energetic in 1969 but are now tea-sipping retirees." New York Times.

Robinson, Peter, 1950-

Playing with fire / Peter Robinson. W. Morrow, 2004. 384 p. Inspector Alan Banks mysteries

ISBN 006019877X

1. Art forgeries 2. Arson 3. Former lovers 4. Former wives 5. Women heroin addicts 6. Artists 7. Murder 8. Murder investigation 9. Barges 10. Canals 11. Police -- Yorkshire, England 12. Detectives -- Yorkshire, England 13. Policewomen -- Yorkshire, England 14. Women detectives -- Yorkshire, England 15. England 16. Yorkshire, England 17. Mysteries 18. Police procedurals

LC 2003056569

Investigating a dual arson case that has claimed three lives on an English canal, Detective Inspector Banks teams up with fellow investigator Annie Cabot and discovers that the victims are linked to an art forgery operation.

"Characterization is Robinson's real strength. Virtually every character is etched with care, precision and emotional insight." Publishers Weekly.

Robinson, Peter, 1950-

Strange affair / Peter Robinson. William Morrow, 2005. 352 p. Inspector Alan Banks mysteries

ISBN 0060544333

1. Families of missing persons 2. Missing persons 3. Lovers 4. Murder 5. Murder investigation 6. Policewomen -- Yorkshire, England 7. Women detectives -- Yorkshire, England 8. Brothers 9. Police -- Yorkshire, England 10. Detectives -- Yorkshire, England 11. England 12. Yorkshire, England 13. Mysteries 14. Police procedurals

LC 2004053633

Inspector Alan Banks heads to London after receiving a disturbing call from his estranged brother, while back in Eastvale, detective Annie Cabbot's investigation of a young woman's death uncovers a connection to someone close to Annie.

Robinson, Roxana

Cost / Roxana Robinson. Farrar, Straus & Giroux, 2008. 432 p.

ISBN 9780374271879

1. College teachers 2. Women college teachers 3. Heroin addicts 4. Parent and adult child 5. Children of aging parents 6. People with Alzheimer's disease 7. Middle-aged women 8. Sandwich generation 9. Heroin addiction 10. Helpfulness 11. Coping 12. Family relationships 13. Dysfunctional families 14. Interpersonal conflict 15. Conflict in families 16. Families 17. Maine 18. Mainstream fiction

LC 2007047954

"Sarah Crichton Books."

Settling into her parents' home in Maine hoping to help them with their respective health challenges, art professor Julie Lambert is shattered by the discovery of her son's heroin addiction.

"It's a nice touch that no one much likes Carpenter, the bossy and authoritative purveyor of unwelcome information. One of Robinson's most impressive achievements is to show that even in extreme situations, individual personalities come into play, and people respond in characteristic ways. . . . Bleak though it undeniably is, Cost is also a warmly human and deeply satisfying book, marking a new level of ambition and achievement for this talented author." Chicago Tribune.

Robotham, Michael, 1960-
Close your eyes / Michael Robotham. Little Brown & Co., 2016, c2015. vii, 392 p. Joseph O'Loughlin and Vincent Ruiz novels
ISBN 9780316267946
1. Clinical psychologists 2. Death -- Psychological aspects 3. Murder investigation 4. Serial murders 5. London, England 6. Australian 7. Psychological suspense 8. Thrillers and suspense
Originally published: London : Sphere, 2015.
When a former student bungles the investigation of a mother-daughter double murder, clinical psychologist Joseph O'Loughlin discovers a link between the case and a series of escalating attacks.

Robotham, Michael, 1960-
* Good girl, bad girl : a novel / Michael Robotham. Scribner, 2019 352 p.
ISBN 9781982103606
1. Secret identity 2. Deception 3. Crime 4. Emancipation of minors 5. Forensic psychologists 6. Women murder victims 7. Secrets 8. Thrillers and suspense
LC 2019012944
A dangerous young woman with a unique ability to detect lies sues for her emancipation from a secure children's home, while the psychologist on her case finds herself in a battle of wits for survival.

Robotham, Michael, 1960-
Life or death / Michael Robotham. Mulholland Books, 2015. 432 p.
ISBN 9780316252058
1. Fugitives 2. Escaped convicts 3. Greed 4. Money 5. Flashbacks 6. Bank robberies 7. Crime 8. Secrets 9. Men/women relations 10. Texas 11. Crime fiction
LC 2014024896
"Due to be released tomorrow. Why escape today?"--Cover.
Gold Dagger Award for Best Crime Novel of the Year, 2015.
Brutalized in prison for a decade for his alleged knowledge about where a fortune in stolen money is hidden, Audie mysteriously escapes the day before his scheduled release in a determined effort to save someone else's life.

Robotham, Michael, 1960-
The **night** ferry : a novel / Michael Robotham. Doubleday, 2007. 384 p.
ISBN 9780385517904
1. Sikh women 2. Detectives 3. Murder investigation 4. Police 5. Immigrants 6. Adoption racket 7. Pregnant women 8. Deception 9. Class reunions 10. Murder 11. London, England 12. England 13. Amsterdam, Netherlands 14. Netherlands 15. Mysteries
LC 2006019771
The main character in The night ferry,Ali Barba, made her first appearance as Inspector Ruiz's colleague in Michael Robotham's novel Lost.

First published: 2007.
When a murder suspect broke her back across a brick wall, Allisha's dreams of being a detective were shattered. Now on her feet again, but her career in limbo, she receives a message from a schoolfriend, Cate, who is pregnant and in trouble. She travels to the the murky underworld of sex trafficking, slavery and exploitation.

Robotham, Michael, 1960-
The **other** wife / Michael Robotham. Sphere, 2018. 400 p. Joseph O'Loughlin and Vincent Ruiz novels
ISBN 9780751562828
1. Clinical psychologists 2. Family secrets 3. Deception 4. Husband and wife 5. London, England 6. Australian 7. Psychological suspense 8. Thrillers and suspense
Originally published: Sydney, NSW : Hachette Australia, 2018.
Librarians' Choice (Australia), 2018.
When his father, a celebrated surgeon, is brutally attacked and a strange woman shows up at his bedside covered in blood, Joe O'Loughlin is forced to question everything he has always believed about his father and soon discovers that the truth comes with a high price.

Robotham, Michael, 1960-
Say you're sorry / Michael Robotham. Mulholland Books, 2012. 448 p. Joseph O'Loughlin and Vincent Ruiz novels
ISBN 9780316221245
1. Clinical psychologists 2. Murder investigation 3. Crimes against married people 4. Murder suspects 5. Missing girls 6. London, England 7. Psychological suspense 8. Thrillers and suspense
LC 2012020772
Two young girls. Both taken. Dead? Or alive? When best friends Piper and Tash disappear one Sunday morning, the investigation captivates a nation but the teenage girls are never found. Three years later, during the worst blizzard in a century, a husband and wife are brutally killed in the farmhouse where Tash McBain once lived. A suspect is in custody, a troubled young man who can hear voices and claims that he saw a girl that night being chased by a snowman. Convinced that Piper or Tash might still be alive, clinical psychologist Joe O'Loughlin persuades police to reopen the investigation, but the closer he gets to the truth, the more dangerous it becomes...

Robotham, Michael, 1960-
* Suspect / Michael Robotham. Doubleday :, 2005, c2004. 368 p. Joseph O'Loughlin and Vincent Ruiz novels
ISBN 9780385508612
1. Psychiatrists 2. People with Parkinson's disease 3. Middle-aged men 4. Murder suspects 5. Married people 6. Fugitives 7. Psychotherapist and patient 8. Crimes against nurses 9. Revenge 10. Secrets 11. London, England 12. Psychological suspense 13. Thrillers and suspense
LC 2004050156
Originally published: London : Time Warner, 2004.
Joe O'Loughlin, a successful psychologist faced with a recent diagnosis of Parkinson's disease, confronts a dangerous conspiracy against him after he becomes the prime suspect in the brutal murder of a woman who turns out to be a woman with whom he once had a relationship and must deal with the betrayal and abandonment of those he trusts the most.

Robotham, Michael, 1960-
The **wreckage** / Michael Robotham. Mulholland Books, 2011. 320 p. Joseph O'Loughlin and Vincent Ruiz novels
ISBN 9780316126403
1. Former police 2. Banks and banking 3. Bombings 4. Missing persons 5. Swindlers and swindling 6. Executives 7. Conspiracies 8.

International intrigue 9. Thrillers and suspense

After being robbed of his briefcase, ex-cop Vincent Ruiz tracks down the thieves, who had mistaken him for someone else, and becomes unwittingly involved unraveling plots involving bank bombings in Baghdad and a missing VP at an international finance powerhouse.

"This fast-paced, gritty, and violent tale of international crime and investigation, with a sharp political edge, will appeal to readers seeking summer fiction with depth." Library Journal.

Rock, Peter, 1967-

The **shelter** cycle / Peter Rock. Houghton Mifflin Harcourt, 2013. 224 p.

ISBN 9780547859088

1. Church Universal and Triumphant. 2. Missing girls 3. Christian churches 4. Mysticism -- Christianity 5. Eccentrics and eccentricities 6. People with mental illnesses 7. Married women 8. Former friends 9. Childhood 10. Memories 11. Reunions 12. Magical realism 13. Literary fiction

LC 2012016429

Two friends who grew up together as part of an extreme doomsday-prepping religion are reunited twenty years later in a search for an abducted child.

Rockaway, Kristin

How to hack a heartbreak / Kristin Rockaway. Graydon House, 2019 384 p.

ISBN 9781525834257

1. Women computer programmers 2. Sexism in employment 3. Dating (Social customs) 4. Self-fulfillment in women 5. Men/women relations 6. Female friendship 7. Entrepreneurship 8. Office romance 9. Misogyny 10. Chick lit

A help-desk tech who supports inept "genius" male co-workers tires of sexual harassment and uses her elite coding skills to create a viral app before she is forced to choose between her relationships and career.

Rodale, Maya

Lady Bridget's diary / Maya Rodale. Avon Books, 2016. 384 p. Keeping up with the Cavendishes

ISBN 9780062386731

1. Regency period (1811-1820) 2. Heirs and heiresses 3. Americans in England 4. Nobility 5. Diaries 6. Misadventures 7. Transformations, Personal 8. Mate selection 9. Titles of honor and nobility 10. Families 11. Love triangles 12. Interpersonal attraction 13. Men/women relations 14. London, England 15. England 16. Great Britain 17. Regency romances 18. Historical romances 19. Romantic comedies

American heiress Lady Bridget Cavendish keeps a diary that documents her disastrous attempts to assimilate in London high society, her adoration of the dashing rogue next door, her hatred for the Dreadful Lord Darcy and some scandalous secrets that could ruin them all.

Rodrigues Fowler, Yara, 1992-

Stubborn archivist / Yara Rodrigues Fowler. Mariner Books, 2019. 320 p.

ISBN 9780358006084

1. Brazilians 2. Children of immigrants 3. British in Brazil 4. Difference (Psychology) 5. Identity (Psychology) 6. Family relationships 7. Self-acceptance 8. Belonging 9. London, England 10. Brazil 11. Literary fiction 12. Psychological fiction 13. Autobiographical fiction

LC 2018042566

A young Brazilian woman from South London, growing up between two cultures, takes us through first love and loss, losing and finding home, trauma and healing and various awakenings of sexuality and identity.

Rodriguez, Linda

Every broken trust : a mystery / Linda Rodriguez. Minotaur Books, 2013. viii, 294 p. Marquitta Skeet Bannion mysteries

ISBN 9781250030351

1. Women detectives 2. Politicians 3. Murder 4. Detectives 5. Universities and colleges 6. Former police 7. Adoption 8. Murder investigation 9. Human trafficking 10. Mysteries

When a party celebrating the arrival of a Kansas City politician is thrown into turmoil by an attack on a friend that left another person dead, half-Cherokee chief of campus police Skeet Bannion investigates allegations that the survivor's husband's accidental death years earlier was actually a murder.

Rodriguez, Linda

Every hidden fear : a Skeet Bannion mystery / Linda Rodriguez. St. Martin's Press, 2014. viii, 292 p. Marquitta Skeet Bannion mysteries

ISBN 9781250049155

1. Women detectives 2. Murder 3. Universities and colleges 4. Detectives 5. Indians of North America 6. Frameups 7. Real estate developers 8. Revenge 9. Murder investigation 10. Mysteries

Adjusting to a household that includes her Cherokee grandmother and teenage ward, Skeet struggles to keep the peace when a wealthy developer makes a shocking paternity claim and announces plans to build a community-devastating mall.

"This is a strong series featuring a multidimensional heroine." Booklist.

Rodriguez, Linda

Every last secret : a mystery / Linda Rodriguez. Minotaur Books, 2012. 304 p. Marquitta Skeet Bannion mysteries

ISBN 9781250005458

1. Native American women 2. Universities and colleges 3. Policewomen 4. Murder investigation 5. Multiracial persons 6. College student newspapers and periodicals 7. Mysteries

LC 2012005484

Leaving her position as the highest-ranking woman officer in the Kansas City Police Department for what she hopes will be a less-stressful job as the chief of a small-town campus police force, half-Cherokee Skeet Bannion investigates the murder of a student editor and untangles ugly involvements at the highest levels of the college.

Rogan, Charlotte

The **lifeboat** / Charlotte Rogan. Little Brown & Co., 2012. 256 p.

ISBN 9780316185905

1. 1910s 2. Shipwrecks -- Atlantic Ocean 3. Young widows 4. Survival (after airplane accidents, shipwrecks, etc) 5. Ocean liners 6. Manipulation by women 7. Historical fiction 8. Psychological suspense

Forced into an overcrowded lifeboat after a mysterious explosion on their trans-Atlantic ocean liner, newly widowed Grace Winter battles the elements and her other survivors and remembers her husband, Henry, who set his own safety aside to ensure Grace's.

Rogues

Rogues / edited by George R.R. Martin and Gardner Dozois.

Bantam, 2014. 832 p. Song of ice and fire prequel stories
ISBN 9780345537263

1. Crime 2. Tricks 3. Rogues 4. Spies 5. Crime 6. Mischief 7. Deception 8. Cleverness 9. Fantasy fiction 10. Short stories

LC 2014010317

Gillian Flynn's What Would You Do? published in 2015 as a separate volume of 64 pages under the name The Grownup by Crown. ISBN 9780804188975.

'The Rogue Prince, or, A King's Brother' is a prequel story to George R. R. Martin's series 'A Song of Ice and Fire.'

Locus Award for Best Anthology, 2015.

A collection of 21 original stories by an all-star list of contributors looks at the more shady denizens of the fantasy world.

"The wide array of styles and genres mean that this is easiest to dip in and out of rather than read cover to cover, but there is not a single bad story in the bunch. Perhaps inevitable owing to Martin's coediting (with skilled anthologist Dozois), some of the most exquisitely written are the fantasy descriptions." Library Journal.

Roiphe, Anne, 1935-

An **imperfect** lens : a novel / Anne Roiphe. Shaye Areheart Books, 2006. 296 p.

ISBN 1400082110

1. Pasteur, Louis, 1822-1895 2. 1880s 3. 19th century 4. French in Egypt 5. Scientists 6. Epidemics 7. Cholera 8. Men/women relations 9. Medicine 10. Medicine 11. Alexandria, Egypt 12. Historical fiction

LC 2005011250

"Roiphe does an incredible job of painting paradoxical portraits of collective fear and coolheaded reason as she painstakingly reconstructs the life cycle of a deadly epidemic. This authentically detailed blend of fact and fiction gift wraps the history of an astonishing medical and scientific breakthrough inside an irresistible love story, providing a little something for everyone across a wide spectrum of readers." Booklist.

Rojas Contreras, Ingrid,

* **Fruit** of the drunken tree : a novel / Ingrid Rojas Contreras. Doubleday, 2018. 304 p.

ISBN 9780385542722

1. 1990s 2. Families 3. Sisters 4. Household employees 5. Gated communities 6. Teenage girls 7. Drug traffic 8. Cartels 9. Violence -- Psychological aspects 10. Bogota, Colombia 11. Colombia 12. Domestic fiction 13. Coming-of-age stories

LC 2017039664

Follows a sheltered girl and a teen maid, who forge an unlikely friendship that threatens to undo them both amid the violence of 1990s Columbia.

Rojstaczer, Stuart

The **mathematician's** shiva : a novel / Stuart Rojstaczer. Penguin Books, 2014. 384 p.

ISBN 9780143126317

1. Mathematicians 2. Mathematics 3. Jewish mourning customs 4. Mathematics teachers 5. Mourning customs 6. Loss (Psychology) 7. Jewish Americans 8. Jewish American families 9. Wisconsin 10. Literary fiction 11. Humorous stories

LC 2014012521

"A comic, bittersweet tale of family evocative of The Yiddish Policemen's Union and Everything Is Illuminated. Alexander "Sasha" Karnokovitch and his family would like to mourn the passing of his mother, Rachela, with modesty and dignity. But Rachela, a famous Polish émigré, mathematician, and professor at the University of Wisconsin, is rumored to have solved the million-dollar, Navier-Stokes Millennium Prize Problem. Rumor also has it that she spitefully took the solution to her grave. To Sasha's chagrin, a ragtag group of socially challenged mathematicians arrives in Madison and crashes the shiva, vowing to do whatever it takes to find the solution-even if it means prying up the floorboards for Rachela's notes. Written by a trained geophysicist, this hilarious and multi-layered debut novel brims with colorful characters and brilliantly captures humanity's drive not just to survive, but to solve the impossible."--Provided by publisher.

"Though Rojstaczer doesn't have the spikey wit of Gary Shteyngart or the inventiveness of Michael Chabon, his steadiness and empathy are appealing in their own ways. A geophysicist, he brings an added dimension to the book's discussions of scientific matters. He's very good at exploring the apparent divide between genius and happiness as well as the intersection of cultures. An enjoyable debut, the book is distinguished by a fluid, lyrical style that is equally at home with serious and comic matters." Kirkus.

Rollins, James, 1961-

Crucible / James Rollins. William Morrow & Co., 2019. xiv, 461 p. Sigma Force novels

ISBN 9780062381781

1. Elite operatives 2. Inquisition 3. Rare books 4. Violence against women 5. Women kidnapping victims 6. Pregnant women 7. Sigma Force (Imaginary organization) 8. Adventure stories

After his home is attacked and his pregnant girlfriend is kidnapped, Commander Gray Pierce and the Sigma Force confront deep spiritual mysteries tracing back to the Spanish Inquisition.

Rollins, James, 1961-

The **demon** crown : a Sigma Force novel / James Rollins. Morrow, 2017 448 p. Sigma Force novels

ISBN 9780062381736

1. Plague 2. Antiquities 3. Secrets 4. Secret societies 5. Enemies 6. Alliances 7. Epidemics 8. Sigma Force (Imaginary organization) 9. Elite operatives 10. Brazil 11. Adventure stories

The members of Sigma Force reluctantly join forces with their most hated enemy to stop a primordial threat with ties to the American Civil War and the secret work of Alexander Graham Bell.

"Rollins's latest Sigma Force novel is one of the best in the series.... The mix of science, history, and high-concept adventure is always first-rate in a Rollins novel, and thats true here as well, even with killer wasps in the mix.." Booklist.

Rollins, James, 1961-

The **devil** colony / James Rollins. William Morrow, 2011. xvi, 480 p. Sigma Force novels

ISBN 9780061784781

1. United States. Department of Defense 2. Alliances 3. Conspiracies 4. Secrets 5. Criminal investigation 6. Deception 7. National security 8. Massacres 9. Sigma Force (Imaginary organization) 10. Violence 11. Elite operatives 12. United States -- Covert operations 13. Adventure stories

After a mountainside massacre yields a grim message, Painter Crowe, director of Sigma Force, must join with Commander Grayson Pierce and an unlikely ally if he is going to get to the root of a conspiracy that stretches back to a lost prehistoric colony in America.

Rollins, James, 1961-

The **eye** of God / James Rollins. William Morrow, 2013. xviii, 410 p. Sigma Force novels

ISBN 9780061784804

1. United States. Department of Defense 2. Murder 3. Codes (Communication) 4. National security 5. Prophecies 6. Antiquities

7. Murder investigation 8. Sigma Force (Imaginary organization) 9. Elite operatives 10. Adventure stories

Commander Gray Pierce and Sigma Force set out to uncover the truth tied to the fall of the Roman Empire, to a mystery going back to the birth of Christianity, and to a weapon hidden for centuries that holds the fate of humanity.

Rollins, James, 1961-

The **sixth** extinction : a Sigma Force novel / James Rollins. William Morrow, 2014. 448 p. Sigma Force novels

ISBN 9780061784811

1. Murder 2. Codes (Communication) 3. National security 4. Prophecies 5. Antiquities 6. Murder investigation 7. Sigma Force (Imaginary organization) 8. Elite operatives 9. Adventure stories

When a remote military research station is decimated, Commander Gray Pierce and the Sigma Force must solve a mystery from Antarctica's distant past using an ancient map that leads them to a new form of death, which could result in mankind's extinction.

Rolvaag, O. E. (Ole Edvart), 1876-1931

* **Giants** in the Earth : a saga of the prairie / O.E. Rolvaag ; translated from the Norwegian by Lincoln Colcord and the author ; with an introduction by Lincoln Colcord. HarperPerennial, 1999, c1927. 531 p. Norwegian pioneers trilogy

ISBN 9780060931933

1. Norwegians in the United States 2. Immigrants 3. Frontier and pioneer life 4. Prairie life 5. South Dakota -- History -- 19th century 6. Historical fiction 7. Translations -- Norwegian to English

After settling in South Dakota, Per Hansa, a Norwegian, tries to change his wife's attitudes about their new life.

Romain, Theresa

Fortune favors the wicked / Theresa Romain. Zebra Books, 2016. 368 p. Royal rewards

ISBN 9781420138658

1. Regency period (1811-1820) 2. Courtesans 3. Sailors 4. Treasure hunting 5. Men who are blind 6. Treasure troves 7. Gold coins 8. Napoleonic Wars veterans 9. Interpersonal attraction 10. Men/women relations 11. Derbyshire, England 12. England -- Social life and customs -- 19th century 13. Great Britain -- History -- Regency, 1811-1820 14. Regency romances 15. Historical romances

The London papers call it the theft of the century. Someone has robbed the Royal Mint of 50,000 pounds and the Crown is offering a substantial reward for its return. Courtesan Charlotte Perry wants the money to start a new life. A chance encounter in a tavern leads to an alliance with blind Royal Navy lieutenant Benedict Frost, who wishes to use the funds to augment his sister's meager dowry. As they join forces to track down the stolen sovereigns, Charlotte and Benedict discover a love more precious than gold. -- Description by Gillian Speace.

Romano-Lax, Andromeda, 1970-

The **Spanish** bow / Andromeda Romano-Lax. Harcourt, 2007. 560 p.

ISBN 0151015422

1. 19th century 2. Cellists 3. Child prodigies 4. Competition in men 5. Musicians 6. Happiness 7. Music 8. Small towns -- Spain 9. Friendship 10. Men/women relations 11. Madrid, Spain 12. Spain 13. Historical fiction

LC 2006100937

Chronicles the lifelong friendship and rivalry between Feliu Delargo, a Catalan cellist, and eccentric piano prodigy Justo Al-Cerraz, a relationship that is dramatically transformed by the arrival in their lives of Aviva, an Italian violinist with a haunted past.

"Expertly woven throughout the book are cameo appearances by Pablo Picasso, Adolf Hitler, Francisco Franco, Bertolt Brecht, and others, but it is the fictional Feliu, Justo, and Aviva who will keep you mesmerized to the last page." Christian Science Monitor.

Rooney, Kathleen, 1980-

* **Lillian** Boxfish takes a walk / Kathleen Rooney. St. Martin's Press, 2017. 304 p.

ISBN 9781250113320

1. 20th century 2. 1980s 3. City life 4. Social change 5. Octogenarians 6. Aging 7. Marriage 8. Memories 9. City dwellers 10. Senior women 11. Women executives 12. Nervous breakdown 13. Women advertising executives 14. New York City 15. Manhattan, New York City 16. Historical fiction 17. Psychological fiction

RUSA Reading List Short List, 2018.

Embarking on a walk across Manhattan on New Year's Eve in 1984, eighty-five-year-old Lillian Boxfish recalls her long and eventful life, which included a brief reign as the highest-paid advertising woman in America, whose career was cut short by marriage and loss.

"Elegantly written, Rooney creates a glorious paean to a distant literary life and time and an unabashed celebration of human connections that bridge the past and future." Publishers Weekly.

Rooney, Sally

* **Conversations** with friends / Sally Rooney. Hogarth Press, 2017. 309 p.

ISBN 9780451499059

1. Best friends 2. Women college students 3. Female friendship 4. Women journalists 5. Poets 6. Young women 7. Extramarital affairs 8. Interpersonal relations 9. Former lovers 10. Married people 11. Actors and actresses 12. Dublin, Ireland 13. Ireland 14. Psychological fiction 15. Mainstream fiction

Shortlisted for the International Dublin Literary Award, 2019.

Devoting herself to an intellectual life and the self-possessed lover with whom she performs spoken-word poetry readings, a college student is drawn into the lives of a sophisticated journalist and her husband before the increasingly intimate relationship tests the boundaries of her resolve.

Rooney, Sally

Normal people : a novel / Sally Rooney. Hogarth Press, 2019, c2018. 272 p.

ISBN 9781984822178

1. Trinity College, Dublin, Ireland. 2. Social classes 3. College students 4. First loves 5. Emotional abuse 6. Universities and colleges 7. Life change events 8. Misfits (Persons) 9. Lovers 10. Sexual attraction 11. Men/women relations 12. Dublin, Ireland 13. Ireland 14. Literary fiction

This book is being made into a TV show on Hulu in 2020.

"Originally published in (hbk.) in the United Kingdom by Faber & Faber, London, in 2018"--Title page verso

ALA Notable Book, 2020.

Costa Novel Award, 2018.

Longlisted for the Man Booker Prize, 2018.

Longlisted for The Women's Prize for Fiction, 2019.

The unconventional secret childhood bond between a popular boy and a lonely, intensely private girl is tested by character reversals in their first year at a Dublin college that render one introspective and the other social, but self-destructive.

Roorbach, Bill

Life among giants : a novel / Bill Roorbach. Algonquin Books of Chapel Hill, 2012. 352 p.

ISBN 9781616200763

1. Children of murder victims 2. Murder investigation 3. Quarterbacks (Football) 4. Women ballet dancers 5. Mansions 6. Brothers and sisters 7. Loss (Psychology) 8. Business -- Corrupt practices 9. Connecticut 10. Mysteries

LC 2012016965

A star quarterback and his sister spend decades trying to figure out who murdered their parents, uncovering the involvement and possible motives of a ballerina and her rock star husband who lived in a mansion across the street.

Roosevelt, Elliott, 1910-1990

The **Hyde** Park murder / Elliott Roosevelt. St. Martin's Press, 1985. 231 p. Eleanor Roosevelt mysteries

1. Roosevelt, Eleanor, 1884-1962 2. 1930s 3. Women detectives 4. Presidents' spouses -- United States 5. Suicide investigation 6. Murder investigation 7. Stock market -- Corrupt practices 8. Hyde Park, New York 9. Historical mysteries 10. Cozy mysteries 11. Gentle reads

LC 85001752

"The author's fascinating glimpses into history, into the Roosevelts at home, and into corrupt politics are delivered in a measured and sure-footed manner." Booklist.

Roosevelt, Elliott, 1910-1990

* **Murder** and the First Lady / Elliott Roosevelt. St. Martin's Press, 1984. 227 p. Eleanor Roosevelt mysteries

ISBN 9780312552800

1. Roosevelt, Eleanor, 1884-1962 2. 1930s 3. Women detectives 4. Presidents' spouses -- United States 5. Poisoning 6. Murder investigation 7. Washington, D.C. 8. Historical mysteries 9. Cozy mysteries 10. Gentle reads

LC 83024659

First Lady Eleanor Roosevelt embarks on an undercover investigation into the White House murder of a crooked New Jersey congressman's son after her young British secretary becomes the prime suspect.

"This historical mystery is set just before World War II, when international tensions are at a peak. Philip Garber, a lowly bookkeeper and assistant to the chief usher at the White House, is found murdered. Eleanor Roosevelt turns sleuth when it's discovered that Garber was found dead in the room of her British secretary, Pamela Rush-Hodgeborne." Booklist.

Roosevelt, Elliott, 1910-1990

Murder at midnight / Elliott Roosevelt. St. Martin's Press, 1997. 216 p. Eleanor Roosevelt mysteries

ISBN 0312965540

1. Roosevelt, Eleanor, 1884-1962 2. Women detectives 3. Presidents' spouses 4. Murder investigation 5. Sadists 6. Sadism 7. Judges -- Death 8. Washington, D.C. 9. Historical mysteries 10. Cozy mysteries 11. Gentle reads

LC 96-53530

"Judge Horace Blackwell, friend and adviser to the president, is stabbed to death in his White House suite, and Sara Carter, a black maid, is arrested after finding the body. After promising the girl a fair hearing and gaining the confidence of lead investigator Lawrence Pickering, Eleanor takes an active role. Her doubts about Sara's guilt lead to some disturbing discoveries, not least of which is that the judge appears to have been a sadistic womanizer. . . . Peopled with famous lights of 1933, including Babe Ruth, William Faulkner and Gertrude Stein,

Washington, D.C. is bought to life in the mirror of the White House." Publishers Weekly.

Roosevelt, Elliott, 1910-1990

Murder at the palace / Elliott Roosevelt. St. Martin's Press, 1988. 232 p. Eleanor Roosevelt mysteries

1. Roosevelt, Eleanor, 1884-1962 2. Buckingham Palace 3. 1940s 4. Women detectives 5. Presidents' spouses -- United States 6. Murder investigation 7. Politicians 8. Deception in men 9. Great Britain -- History -- 20th century 10. Historical mysteries 11. Cozy mysteries 12. Gentle reads

LC 87027961

Mrs. Roosevelt goes to Buckingham Palace during World War II and lends support to Sir Alan Burton when he is associated with an embarrassing murder.

Roosevelt, Elliott, 1910-1990

Murder in the Blue Room / Elliott Roosevelt. St. Martin's Press, 1990. 215 p. Eleanor Roosevelt mysteries

1. Roosevelt, Eleanor, 1884-1962 2. White House, Washington, D.C. 3. 1940s 4. Women detectives -- Washington, D.C. 5. Presidents' spouses -- United States 6. Murder investigation 7. Women murder victims 8. Washington, D.C. -- History -- 20th century 9. Historical mysteries 10. Cozy mysteries 11. Gentle reads

LC 89077677

"Set in 1942 during Soviet Foreign Minister Molotov's secret visit to FDR, [this] mystery . . . finds the author's mother, Eleanor Roosevelt, solving a double murder and combating racial discrimination in the armed forces. A droll, yet affectionate, portrait that is standard but intriguing fare." Booklist.

Roosevelt, Elliott, 1910-1990

Murder in the map room : an Eleanor Roosevelt mystery / Elliott Roosevelt. St. Martin's Press, 1998. 251 p. Eleanor Roosevelt mysteries

ISBN 031218168X

1. Roosevelt, Eleanor, 1884-1962 2. Chiang, May-ling Soong, 1897-2003 3. White House, Washington, D.C. 4. Second World War era (1939-1945) 5. Presidents' spouses -- United States 6. Women detectives -- Washington, D.C. 7. Murder investigation 8. Shoe sellers -- Washington, D.C. 9. Chinese in Washington, D.C. 10. World War II -- Washington, D.C. 11. Secret Service -- United States 12. World War II home front 13. Washington, D.C. -- History -- 1933-1945 14. Historical mysteries 15. Cozy mysteries 16. Gentle reads

LC 97-37243

In 1943, First Lady Eleanor Roosevelt finds herself becoming immersed in the dark world of opium trading when, during a visit from Madame Chiang Kai-Shek, a Chinese shoe salesman is found murdered in the White House map room.

"As usual, Elliot Roosevelt's respectfully playful portrayal of his down-to-earth mother as a clever sleuth is enough to keep the pages turning." Booklist.

Roosevelt, Elliott, 1910-1990

Murder in the Oval Office / Elliott Roosevelt. St. Martin's Press, 1989. 247 p. Eleanor Roosevelt mysteries

ISBN 9780312022594

1. Roosevelt, Eleanor, 1884-1962 2. Roosevelt, Franklin D (Franklin Delano), 1882-1945 3. White House, Washington, D.C. 4. 1930s 5. Presidents' spouses -- United States 6. Women detectives -- Washington, D.C. 7. Murder investigation 8. Politicians 9. Historical

mysteries 10. Cozy mysteries 11. Gentle reads

LC 88018848

An apparent suicide in the Oval Office of the White House leaves a number of unanswered questions and a long list of people who wanted the victim dead, and Eleanor Roosevelt must once again investigate.

Roosevelt, Elliott, 1910-1990

Murder in the Rose Garden / Elliott Roosevelt. St. Martin's Press, 1989. 232 p. Eleanor Roosevelt mysteries

1. Roosevelt, Eleanor, 1884-1962 2. White House, Washington, D.C. 3. 1930s 4. Women detectives -- Washington, D.C. 5. Presidents' spouses -- United States 6. Murder investigation 7. Historical mysteries 8. Cozy mysteries 9. Gentle reads

LC 89035326

"During the summer of 1936, popular Washington hostess Vivian Taliafero is strangled in the White House Rose Garden. . . . The First Lady helps the Secret Service and the D.C. police gather information about the murdered woman who was, it turns out, an extortionist. . . . Vivian's partner in blackmail, photographer Joe Bob Skaggs, is killed, as is one of their victims, while Mrs. Roosevelt strives to solve the mystery." Publishers Weekly.

Roosevelt, Elliott, 1910-1990

The **White** House pantry murder / Elliott Roosevelt. St. Martin's Press, 1987. 231 p. Eleanor Roosevelt mysteries

1. Roosevelt, Eleanor, 1884-1962 2. Roosevelt, Franklin D (Franklin Delano), 1882-1945 3. Churchill, Winston, 1874-1965 4. White House, Washington, D.C. 5. 1940s 6. Presidents' spouses -- United States 7. Women detectives -- Washington, D.C. 8. Murder investigation 9. Historical mysteries 10. Cozy mysteries 11. Gentle reads

LC 86026249

While Winston Churchill is visiting the White House in 1941, someone finds an unidentified man in the freezer and weapons in a storm sewer, spurring Mrs. Roosevelt into action.

Rose, Heather, 1964-

The **museum** of modern love / Heather Rose. Algonquin Books of Chapel Hill, 2018, c2016. 288 p.

ISBN 9781616208523

1. Abramovic, Marina Exhibitions 2. Composers 3. Creativity 4. Self-discovery 5. Personal conduct 6. Sick persons 7. Art 8. Husband and wife 9. Grief 10. Australian 11. Literary fiction

Originally published: Crows Nest, NSW : Allen & Unwin, 2016.

Stella Prize, 2017.

Tasmania Book Prizes, Margaret Scott Prize, 2017.

Arky Levin has reached a creative dead end. Guilty and restless after an unexpected separation from his wife, almost by chance he stumbles upon an art exhibit that will change his life. Based on a real piece of performance art, the installation that the fictional Arky Levin discovers is inexplicably powerful. Visitors to the Museum of Modern Art sit across a table from artist Marina Abramovi for as short or long a period of time as they choose. Although some go in skeptical, almost all leave moved. And the participants are not the only ones to find themselves changed by this unusual experience: Arky finds himself returning daily to watch others with Abramovi. As the performance unfolds over the course of 75 days, so too does Arky. As he bonds with other peopledrawn to the exhibit, he slowly starts to understand what might be missing in his life and what he must do. Provided by publisher.

"This captivating work explores the meaning of art in our lives and the ways in which it deepens our understanding of ourselves. As Hannah Rothschild did in The Improbability of Love, Australian author Rose also combines intriguing characters with a laser-sharp focus on art to produce a gem of a novel." Library Journal.

Rose, Joel

The **blackest** bird : a novel of murder in nineteenth-century New York / Joel Rose. W.W. Norton, 2007. 479 p.

ISBN 9780393062311

1. Rogers, Mary, 1820-1841 2. Poe, Edgar Allan, 1809-1849 3. 1840s 4. Murder 5. Missing women 6. Women sales personnel 7. Women murder victims 8. Murder investigation 9. Murder suspects 10. Sensationalism in journalism 11. Police 12. New York City -- History -- 1775-1865 13. Historical mysteries 14. Mysteries

LC 2006031703

During the summer of 1841, High Constable Jacob Hays, New York City's first detective, finds himself investigating a series of brutal crimes, including the rape and murder of Mary Rogers, a young clerk at a Manhattan tobacco shop.

"Rose does a scrupulous and impressive job of mustering the pace and mood of the rapidly expanding city, its still pastoral fringes and its customs." PopMatters.

Rose, M. J., 1953-

* **Cartier's** hope / M. J. Rose. Atria Books, 2020. 334 p.

ISBN 9781501173639

1. 1910s 2. Women journalists 3. Women's role 4. Hope Diamond 5. Extortion 6. Intrigue 7. Fathers -- Death 8. Jewelers 9. Diamonds 10. Deception 11. Men/women relations 12. Interpersonal attraction 13. New York City -- Social life and customs -- 20th century 14. Historical fiction

Determined to make her mark in Gilded Age New York, a woman journalist investigates rumors and curses swirling around Pierre Cartier's recently acquired Hope Diamond, before attracting the attention of the blackmailer behind her father's death.

"The narrative cleverly explores highlights of early 20-century history and heaps on plenty of intrigue. Rose irresistibly combines elements of mystery, romance, and historical events in this memorable novel." Publishers Weekly.

Rose, M. J., 1953-

Tiffany blues : a novel / M.J. Rose. Atria Books, 2018. 336 p.

ISBN 9781501173592

1. Tiffany, Louis Comfort, 1848-1933 2. 1920s 3. Artists 4. Secrets 5. Artists' colonies 6. Women artists 7. Forbidden love 8. Women painters 9. Men/women relations 10. Interpersonal attraction 11. Long Island, New York 12. Historical fiction

LC 2017058991

A candidate at Tiffany's Jazz Age artist colony navigates her attraction to her host's grandson and competes for a gallery spot before an unknown rival exposes her traumatic past.

Rosen, Leonard J.

The **Kortelisy** escape / Leonard Rosen. The Permanent Press, 2018. 302 p.

ISBN 9781579625429

1. Parolees 2. Magic tricks 3. Grandfather and granddaughter 4. Criminal evidence 5. Child custody 6. Brothers 7. Human trafficking 8. Sex crimes 9. Organized crime 10. Sexually abused children 11. Eastern Europeans in the United States 12. Secrets 13. Loss (Psychology) 14. New England 15. Crime fiction 16. Literary fiction

LC 2018027960

After negotiating with prosecutors for an early prison release for testifying against his brother, Nate Larson takes in his orphaned teenage granddaughter, Grace, and starts a traveling magic show in New England.

"Distinctive characters, a tightly woven plot, and polished prose make this a winner." Publishers Weekly.

Rosen, Leonard J.

The **tenth** witness / Leonard Rosen. The Permanent Press, 2013. 288 p. Henri Poincare mysteries

ISBN 9781579623197

1. 1970s 2. Salvage 3. Murder investigation 4. Shipwrecks 5. Engineers 6. Heirs and heiresses 7. Loyalty 8. Racism 9. Netherlands 10. Waddenzee (Netherlands) 11. Mysteries

LC 2013019229

Prequel to: All cry chaos.

"This prequel to the acclaimed All Cry Chaos (2011) goes back in time to show how Henri Poincaré became an Interpol agent. . . . This is a complex, dark, and disturbing story, beautifully told and based in part on history." Booklist

Rosen, Renee

* **Dollface** : a novel of the roaring twenties / Renee Rosen. New American Library, 2013. 416 p.

ISBN 9780451419200

1. 1920s 2. Young women 3. Organized crime 4. Murder 5. Flappers 6. Gangsters 7. Prohibition 8. Men/women relations 9. Love triangles 10. St Valentine's Day Massacre, Chicago, Illinois, 1929 11. Chicago, Illinois -- Social life and customs -- 20th century 12. Historical fiction 13. Crime fiction

LC 2012051794

Also released under the title A Living Doll.

Touring the nightclubs of 1920s Chicago in the hopes of enjoying an exciting life, beautiful Vera captures the attentions of two high rollers who admit her into an underworld of jazz, gambling and bootleg bourbon before Vera discovers that they are actually mobsters from rival Beer Wars gangs.

Rosenberg, Jordy,

* **Confessions** of the fox : a novel / Jordy Rosenberg. One World, 2018. 329 p.

ISBN 9780399592270

1. Sheppard, Jack, 1702-1724 2. 18th century 3. 21st century 4. Transgender persons 5. Subcultures 6. Gender identity 7. Manuscripts 8. Scholars and academics 9. College teachers 10. Thieves 11. Sexuality 12. Prostitutes 13. Lovers 14. City life 15. London, England 16. Literary fiction 17. Historical fiction 18. LGBTQIA fiction

LC 2017059886

A love story set in the eighteenth-century London of notorious thieves and queer subcultures, this genre-bending debut tells a profound story of gender, desire, and liberation.

Rosenberg, Nancy Taylor

Interest of justice / Nancy Taylor Rosenberg. Dutton, 1993. 368 p.

ISBN 9780525936800

1. Murder investigation -- Orange County, California 2. Sisters -- Death 3. Aunts -- Orange County, California 4. Prostitutes -- Orange County, California 5. Murder -- Orange County, California 6. Pedophiles -- Orange County, California 7. Fourteen-year-old boys -- Orange County, California 8. People with amyotrophic lateral sclerosis 9. Women judges -- Orange County, California 10. Orange County, California 11. Mysteries

LC 93013005

Judge Lara Sanderstone searches for the murderer of her sister and brother-in-law and is stalked by the killer whose attacks leave no clue or motive.

"Lara Sanderstone is such an intelligent, finely detailed character that even the unlikeliest plot twists work in this absorbing legal thriller." Publishers Weekly.

Rosenfelt, David

Bark of night / David Rosenfelt. Minotaur Books, 2019. 304 p. Andy Carpenter novels

ISBN 9781250133090

1. Lawyers 2. Men and dogs 3. Animal welfare 4. Dogs 5. Abandoned dogs 6. Murder victims 7. Dog owners 8. Murder investigation 9. New Jersey 10. Mysteries

LC 2019018214

Rescuing a dog who was abandoned at a veterinarian's office by a stranger, defense lawyer Andy Carpenter, with help from his loyal golden retriever Tara, searches for answers upon learning that the dog's real owner has been found murdered.

Rosenfelt, David

Black and blue : a Doug Brock thriller / David Rosenfelt. Minotaur Books, 2019. 290 p. Doug Brock novels

ISBN 9781250133144

1. Men with amnesia 2. Cold cases (Criminal investigation) 3. Murder suspects 4. Murder investigation 5. Police 6. Secrets 7. New Jersey 8. Thrillers and suspense

LC 2018050881

Struggling with amnesia after surviving a shooting, Doug Brock re-investigates a cold case involving the DNA of a man he eliminated as a suspect, but can no longer remember.

"Dead ends and red herrings abound as the action builds to a jaw-dropping reveal. Rosenfelt knocks it out of the park with this fiendishly twisty serial killer thriller." Publishers Weekly.

Rosenfelt, David

Blackout / David Rosenfelt. St. Martin's Press, 2016. 304 p. Doug Brock novels

ISBN 9781250055316

1. Police 2. Amnesia 3. Terrorism -- Prevention 4. Terrorists 5. Gunshot wounds 6. New Jersey 7. Thrillers and suspense

In the next thrilling standalone from David Rosenfelt, policeman Doug Brock races against the clock to recover his memory after a gunshot to the head before a terror plot can be put into action.

Rosenfelt, David

Don't tell a soul / David Rosenfelt. St. Martin's Minotaur, 2008. 320 p.

ISBN 9780312373955

1. Murder suspects 2. Frameups 3. Police 4. Confession (Law) 5. Crimes against married women 6. Widowers 7. Murder 8. Murder investigation 9. Suspicion 10. Truth 11. Innocence (Law) 12. Boating accidents 13. New Jersey 14. Thrillers and suspense

LC 2008014777

Tim Wallace's wife died in a boating accident several months ago. Tim was the only eye witness, and one New Jersey cop is sure he killed her.

"Rosenfelt keeps the plot hopping and popping as he reveals a complex frameup of major proportions with profound political ramifications both terrifying and enlightening." Publishers Weekly.

Rosenthal, Pam

The **bookseller's** daughter / Pam Rosenthal. Brava Books, 2004. 384 p.

ISBN 0758204450

1. 1780s 2. Household employees 3. Working class 4. Aristocracy 5. Booksellers 6. Smugglers 7. Mistresses 8. Books and reading 9. Writing 10. Murder 11. Betrayal 12. Dishonesty 13. Independence in women 14. Seduction 15. Housekeepers 16. France -- History -- 18th century 17. Historical romances 18. Erotic romances

LC bl2004004545

Events in France on the eve of the Revolution have forced Marie-Laure Vernet into service as a maid and into the eye of Viscomte Joseph d'Auvers-Raimond, a book smuggler, and passion unfolds amid murder and betrayal.

Rosenthal, Pam

The **edge** of impropriety / Pam Rosenthal. Signet Eclipse, 2008. 352 p.

ISBN 9780451222305

1. Regency period (1811-1820) 2. 19th century 3. Women authors 4. Widows 5. Interpersonal attraction 6. Sexuality 7. Men/women relations 8. Extortion 9. Italy -- History -- 19th century 10. Regency romances 11. Historical romances

LC 2008019614

RITA Award for Best Historical Romance, 2009.

The scandalous private life of novelist Countess Marina Wyatt takes a dramatic turn when she becomes embroiled in a torrid and dangerous love affair with Jasper James Hedges, a renowned art appraiser and the uncle of a former lover.

Roslund, Anders, 1961-

Cell 8 / Anders Roslund and Borge Hellstrom ; translated from the original Swedish by Kari Dickson. SilverOak, 2012, c2006. 370 p. Ewert Grens thrillers

ISBN 9781402787157

1. Murderers 2. Criminal evidence 3. Detectives 4. Capital punishment 5. Death row prisoners 6. Police -- Sweden 7. People with heart disease 8. Sweden 9. Ohio 10. Thrillers and suspense 11. Translations -- Swedish to English 12. Scandinavian crime fiction

Originally published as Edward Finnigans upprattelse, Stockholm : Piratforlaget, 2006.

Six years after a seventeen-year-old death-row inmate dies unexpectedly of heart disease, his case is disturbingly linked to that of a man using a false identity who has been arrested for attacking a fellow ferry passenger.

Roslund, Anders, 1961-

Pen 33 / Anders Roslund & Borge Hellstrom ; translated by Elizabeth Clark Wessel. Quercus, 2017, 311 p. Ewert Grens thrillers

ISBN 9781681440132

1. Escaped convicts 2. Vigilantes 3. Child murder investigation 4. Detectives 5. Pedophiles 6. Child murders 7. Loss (Psychology) 8. Revenge 9. Sweden 10. Mysteries 11. Translations -- Swedish to English 12. Scandinavian crime fiction

First published in English under the title The beast, translated by Anna Paterson.

First published in Swedish: Sweden : Piratforlaget, 2004. First published in English as "The beast": Great Britain : Little, Brown, 2005. This translation first published: 2016.

Originally published: 2004.

The murderer of two children escapes from prison. Another child is murdered in the nearby town of Strengnas. The father of the murdered child decides he must take revenge. Anger spreads across the whole country and the case is assigned to two detectives. This novel is an exploration of what can happen when we take the law into our own hands.

Rosnay, Tatiana de, 1961-

Sarah's key / Tatiana de Rosnay. St. Martin's Press, 2007. 288 p.

ISBN 9780312370831

1. World War II -- France 2. Family secrets 3. Women journalists 4. Americans in France 5. Antisemitism 6. Jews -- Persecutions -- France 7. Family relationships 8. France -- History -- German occupation, 1940-1945 9. Paris, France 10. Psychological fiction 11. Historical fiction 12. Parallel narratives

LC 2007010080

First published in the United States of America in 2007.

On the sixtieth anniversary of the 1942 roundup of Jews by the French police in the Vel d'Hiv section of Paris, American journalist Julia Jarmond is asked to write an article on this dark episode during World War II and embarks on investigation that leads her to long-hidden family secrets and to the ordeal of Sarah, a young girl caught up in the raid.

Rosner, Jennifer

* The **yellow** bird sings / Jennifer Rosner. Flatiron Books, 2020. 224 p.

ISBN 9781250179760

1. Second World War era (1939-1945) 2. Jews 3. Mothers and daughters 4. Girl prodigies 5. Hiding 6. Persecution by Nazis 7. Music 8. Storytelling 9. Separated friends, relatives, etc 10. Birds 11. Holocaust (1933-1945) 12. World War II 13. Poland 14. Historical fiction

LC 2019045279

A mother who goes into hiding when Nazis begin arresting Jewish citizens in Poland considers an impossible choice while struggling to keep her 5-year-old daughter, a musical prodigy, from being overheard.

"This stunning debut novel sings with the power of a mother's love and the heartbreaking risks she'll endure." Booklist.

Ross, Adam, 1967-

Ladies and gentlemen / Adam Ross. Alfred A. Knopf, 2011. 256 p.

ISBN 9780307270719

1. Young adults 2. Loners 3. Brothers 4. Lovers 5. Short stories

LC 2011006960

A follow-up to Mr. Peanut includes the stories of a guilt-burdened lawyer who is rendered a pawn by his irresponsible kid brother, a lonely professor who fears he is being made an accessory to murder and an adolescent who uses his brief career as a child actor to attract a girl.

Ross, Adam, 1967-

Mr. Peanut / Adam Ross. Alfred A. Knopf, 2010. 304 p.
ISBN 9780307270702

1. Married people 2. Marital conflict 3. Murder investigation 4. Crimes against women 5. Widowers 6. Marriage 7. Assassins 8. Mysteries

LC 2009041693

Having imagined his beloved wife's death in many ways (you name it, he probably thought of it), video game designer David is eventually charged with killing her after she dies from anaphylactic shock. But the New York investigators dealing with David have their own experiences with marital problems and murder. -- Description by Shauna Griffin.

"Ross is a sorcerer with words, whose David Foster Wallace-like descriptive powers have given him the ability to conjure everything from a pretty Hawaiian beachscape to the slow-motion horror of a car accident with color and lan." New York Times.

Ross, Ann B.

Miss Julia delivers the goods : a novel / Ann B. Ross. Viking, 2009. 352 p. Miss Julia series

ISBN 9780670020652

1. Conflict resolution 2. Pregnant women 3. Archives 4. Robbery 5. Love triangles 6. Women amateur detectives 7. Senior women 8. North Carolina 9. Cozy mysteries 10. Gentle reads

LC 2008045609

Miss Julia reckons Mr. J.D. Pickens is the key to solving all of Hazel Marie's problems, especially the female kind. But how can Miss Julia coax the savvy PI back to town--and back into the arms of her 40-something friend Hazel Marie?

Ross, Ann B.

Miss Julia takes the wheel / Ann B. Ross. Viking, 2019 320 p. Miss Julia series

ISBN 9780525560487

1. Physicians 2. Small town life 3. Women amateur detectives 4. Funeral homes 5. Female friendship 6. North Carolina 7. Cozy mysteries 8. Gentle reads

LC 2018051406

Miss Julia's efforts to understand mysteries surrounding an unscrupulous new doctor and his painfully shy wife are complicated by Lloyd's first car and a newly divorced LuAnne's makeover in accordance with a new funeral home job.

Ross, Ann B.

Miss Julia throws a wedding / Ann B. Ross. Viking, 2002. 308 p. Miss Julia series

ISBN 0670031054

1. Sheriffs 2. Women lawyers 3. Weddings 4. Widows 5. Small town life 6. Senior women 7. Women amateur detectives 8. North Carolina 9. Cozy mysteries 10. Gentle reads

LC 2001056798

Septuagenarian Julia Springer is back. This time out, Sheriff Coleman Bates and busy attorney Binkie Enloe's casual announcement that they plan to get married spurs Miss Julia, the only person in Abbotsville who knows or cares how things should be done, into action. She's determined to put together a proper and dignified wedding but faces many hurdles, people being what they are. Will Miss Julia be able to pull this wedding off?

"The inimitable Miss Julia pushes an indecisive couple toward matrimong in this Southern comedy-of-manners, . . . which begins with the protagonist frustrated at the inability of her friend, Miss Hazel, to get her beau to propose. But another opportunity surfaces when Sheriff Coleman Bates proposes to his lawyer girlfriend Binkie Enloe. . . . Ross gets a bit carried away with wedding details, but her cheeky style works flawlessly once Miss Julia digs into the romantic intrigue and begins to ply her unique combination of common sense and old-fashioned, smalltown wisdom." Publishers Weekly.

Rossner, Judith

Looking for Mr. Goodbar / Judith Rossner. Simon and Schuster, 1975. 284 p.

1. Single women 2. Teachers 3. Bars (Drinking establishments) 4. Men/women relations 5. Women murder victims 6. New York City 7. Mainstream fiction

LC 75002317

"The tale is stark, capably told, believable; Rossner's prose is a delight, and her sense of the inner life of her characters, all tortured, is deft and sure. This is a very good novel." Booklist.

Rotert, Rebecca, 1971-

Last night at the blue angel : a novel / Rebecca Rotert. William Morrow, 2014. 328 p.

ISBN 9780062315281

1. 1960s 2. Mothers and daughters 3. Women singers 4. Jazz singers 5. Single mothers 6. Fame 7. Friendship 8. Ten-year-old girls 9. Flashbacks 10. Men/women relations 11. Chicago, Illinois 12. Psychological fiction 13. Historical fiction

LC 2013036555

In early 1960s Chicago, Naomi Hill, a fiercely ambitious, yet extremely self-destructive jazz singer at the Blue Angel club, embarks on a desperate journey to stardom, while her ten-year-old daughter Sophia becomes even more anxious as she struggles for her mother's love.

"Though the characters are very different, the author's interpretation of both emerges spot-on. And, while Naomi's journey is interesting, Sophia's story hooks the reader from the beginning and dominates." Kirkus.

Roth, Henry

* Call it sleep / Henry Roth ; with an introduction by Alfred Kazin and an afterword by Hana Wirth-Nesher. Picador, 2005, c1934. 462 p.

ISBN 9780312424121

1. 1910s 2. Immigrants, Jewish 3. Jewish way of life -- Lower East Side, New York City 4. Jewish American boys 5. Slums 6. Jewish families 7. Family relationships 8. Culture conflict 9. Lower East Side, New York City 10. Lower East Side, New York City -- Social life and customs -- 20th century 11. New York City -- Social life and customs -- 20th century 12. Coming-of-age stories 13. Modern classics

Originally published: 1934.

An imaginative young boy, David Schearl grows up and comes of age in a candid portrayal of Jewish life in the immigrant tenements of New York, in a novel first published in 1934.

Roth, Henry

A **diving** rock on the Hudson / Henry Roth. St. Martin's Press, 1995. 418 p. Mercy of a rude stream

ISBN 9780312140854

1. 1920s 2. Jewish American teenage boys 3. Immigrant families 4. Teenage boys -- Psychology 5. Shame 6. Self-hate (Psychology) 7. Incest 8. Reminiscing in old age 9. Senior men 10. Coming-of-age stories

Includes "Glossary of Yiddish and Hebrew words and phrases."

"Simultaneously, we are inside the mind of a troubled adolescent and that of an aged but still mentally vital man, a man engaged with words, with concepts, obsessively reconsidering the role of the artist and in particular his own responsibility in portraying events truthfully." Booklist.

Roth, Henry

From bondage / Henry Roth. St. Martin's Press, 1996. 397 p. Mercy of a rude stream

ISBN 9780312143411

1. 1920s 2. Jewish American men 3. Men -- Psychology 4. Immigrant families 5. Creativity 6. Shame 7. Self-hate (Psychology) 8. Culture conflict 9. Young men 10. Men/women relations 11. Reminiscing in old age 12. Senior men 13. Intellectual life 14. New York City 15. Coming-of-age stories

Includes "Glossary of Yiddish and Hebrew words and phrases."

LIST OF FICTIONAL WORKS

National Book Critics Circle Award for Fiction finalist, 1996

"This third volume of Roth's autobiographical cycle continues the story of Ira Stigman, son of East European Jewish immigrant parents and now college-aged, as he struggles to find his way in 1920s New York. But, like the previous volumes, it is also the story of Ira the octogenarian writer who, nearing the end of his life, is trying to come to terms with both the forces and the choices that shaped it. Paralleling Roth's own experience, this volume focuses on the beginnings of what was to become a decade-long affair between Ira and NYU professor Edith Welles." Library Journal.

Roth, Henry

Requiem for Harlem / Henry Roth. St. Martin's Press, 1998. 291 p. Mercy of a rude stream

ISBN 9780312169800

1. 1920s 2. Jewish American men 3. College students 4. Immigrant families 5. Young men -- Relations with older women 6. Young men -- Family relationships 7. Jewish American families 8. Incest 9. Selfishness in men 10. Guilt in men 11. Social mobility 12. Creativity 13. Reminiscing in old age 14. Senior men 15. Harlem, New York City -- Social life and customs -- 20th century 16. New York City 17. Coming-of-age stories

LC 9717824

Includes a "Glossary of Yiddish and Hebrew words and phrases."

"Even as we see the older writer commenting ruefully on all that has come to pass, we see the young artist taking in every detail of the world. . . . And if it is hard to sympathize with either the egocentric youth or the rueful old man, taken together they meld into a living whole. This is Roth's achievement, this double vision of the artist as both young and old man, hungry and regretful, flawed and penitent." New York Times Book Review.

Roth, Henry

A **star** shines over Mt. Morris Park / Henry Roth. St. Martin's Press, 1994. 290 p. Mercy of a rude stream

ISBN 0312104995

1. 1910s 2. Jewish American boys 3. Immigrant families 4. Identity (Psychology) 5. Jewish Americans 6. Antisemitism 7. Culture conflict 8. Assimilation (Sociology) 9. Reminiscing in old age 10. Senior men 11. Harlem, New York City -- Social life and customs -- 20th century 12. Coming-of-age stories

LC 93037270

"Mr. Roth remains an admirable craftsman, and the scenes of immigrant life in the second decade of the century are evoked with persuasive concreteness." New York Times Book Review.

Roth, Joseph, 1894-1939

* The **collected** stories of Joseph Roth / translated from the German with an introduction by Michael Hofmann. W. W. Norton, 2002. 281 p.

ISBN 0393043207

1. Short stories 2. Translations -- German to English

LC 2001044747

Seventeen short stories.

"Combining a shrewd reportorial eye with a taste for the fantastic and droll, Roth portrays characters living materially and spiritually impoverished lives in isolated Eastern European villages and those left homeless in their own homes in the tumultuous aftermath of World War I." Booklist.

Roth, Philip, 1933-2018

* **American** pastoral / Philip Roth. Houghton Mifflin, 1997. 423 p. Zuckerman novels

ISBN 9780395860212

1. Roth, Philip, 1933- 2. 1960s 3. Women fugitives 4. Fathers and daughters 5. American dream 6. Jewish American families 7. Bombings 8. Jewish American men -- Identity 9. Women radicals 10. Interfaith marriage 11. Glove industry and trade 12. Generation gap 13. Newark, New Jersey 14. Literary fiction 15. Autobiographical fiction 16. Modern classics

LC 9649368

Film under the same title released in 2016.
Pulitzer Prize for Fiction, 1998.
National Book Critics Circle Award for Fiction finalist, 1997

A former athletic star, devoted family man, and owner of a thriving glove factory, Seymour "Swede" Levov finds his life coming apart during the social disorder of the 1960s, when his beloved daughter turns revolutionary terrorist out to destroy her father's world

"This cultural horror story is deepened by Roth's genius for blending humor, pathos, sympathy and rage. . . . You will search the shelf of contemporary fiction long and hard to find a parental nightmare projected with the emotional force and verbal energy that Roth brings to American Pastoral." Time.

Roth, Philip, 1933-2018

* The **anatomy** lesson / Philip Roth. Vintage International, 1996, c1983. 291 p. Zuckerman novels

ISBN 9780679749028

1. Roth, Philip, 1933- 2. 1970s 3. Jewish American authors 4. Pain 5. Family relationships 6. Self-discovery in men 7. Middle-aged men 8. Jewish American men -- Identity 9. Writing 10. Artists -- Social responsibility 11. Humorous stories 12. Literary fiction 13. Psychological fiction 14. Autobiographical fiction

Originally published: New York : Farrar, Straus, and Giroux, 1983.
National Book Critics Circle Award for Fiction finalist, 1983
National Book Award for Fiction finalist, 1984

In 1973, Nathan Zuckerman, a writer who has lost the ability to create, attempts to console himself with women as he decides to abandon writing and become a doctor.

"A ferocious, heartfelt book. . . . One might venture to say that, like a goodly number of Roth's previous works, 'The Anatomy Lesson' revolves around the paradox of incarnation--the astonishing coexistence in one life of infantilism and intelligence, of selfishness and altruism, of sexual appetite and social conscience--and has the form and manner of a monologue conducted under psychoanalysis." The New Yorker.

Roth, Philip, 1933-2018

The **dying** animal / Philip Roth. Houghton Mifflin, 2001. 156 p. Kepesh novels

ISBN 0618135871

1. Senior men -- Sexuality 2. Aging 3. Desire 4. Teacher-student relationships 5. Women college students 6. College teachers 7. Lovers' reunions 8. Jealousy 9. May-December romance 10. New York City 11. Erotic fiction 12. Psychological fiction 13. Literary fiction

LC 00054225

This book was released as a movie entitled Elegy.
Sequel to: The professor of desire.

A prominent TV culture critic and lecturer, sixty-plus David Kepesh finds his world thrown into erotic turmoil by Consuela Castillo, a twenty-four-year-old beauty who ignites in him sexual possessiveness, unreasoning jealousy, and obsessive passion.

"Like many works of modern literature, The Dying Animal ends on a note of radical ambiguity and indeterminacy. What is rather unusual about it is the way it challenges the reader at every point to define and defend his own ethical position toward the issues raised by the story. It is a small, disturbing masterpiece." The New York Review of Books.

Roth, Philip, 1933-

* Everyman / Philip Roth. Houghton Mifflin, 2006. 162 p.

ISBN 061873516X

1. Roth, Philip, 1933- 2. Aging 3. Mortality 4. Senior men 5. Jewish American men 6. Brothers 7. Health 8. Families 9. Jewish families 10. Compulsive behavior in men 11. Regret in senior men 12. Newark, New Jersey 13. Psychological fiction 14. Literary fiction 15. Autobiographical fiction

LC 2005031538

PEN-Faulkner Award, 2007.

"From a distance, Everyman looks like a shaggy dog storya long, quotidian story whose meaning resides in its final pointlessness. Up close, though, it is a parable that captures, as few works of fiction have, the pathos of Being, as it's manifested even in the favored precincts of affluent America." Washington Post Book World.

Roth, Philip, 1933-

Exit ghost / Philip Roth. Houghton Mifflin, 2007. 304 p. Zuckerman novels

ISBN 9780618915477

1. Roth, Philip, 1933- 2. Jewish American authors 3. Self-fulfillment in men 4. Aging 5. Jewish American men -- Identity 6. Senior men -- Sexuality 7. Men's fantasies 8. Interpersonal relations 9. Men/women relations 10. New York City 11. Psychological fiction 12. Literary fiction 13. Autobiographical fiction

LC 2006102467

After eleven years of solitude working on his New England mountain as a writer, Nathan Zuckerman returns to New York to confront a turbulent city in the wake of September 11, as well as the aging Amy Bellette, one-time muse to his first literary hero, E.I. Lonoff.

"Mr. Roth has created a melancholy, if occasionally funny, meditation on aging, mortality, loneliness and the losses that come with the passage of time. . . . For fans of the Zuckerman books, it provides a poignant coda to Nathan's story, putting a punctuation point to his journey from youthful idealism and passion through midlife confusion and angst toward elderly renunciation." New York Times.

Roth, Philip, 1933-2018

The **ghost** writer / Philip Roth. Vintage Books, 1995, c1979. 179 p. Zuckerman novels

ISBN 9780679748984

1. Roth, Philip, 1933- 2. 1950s 3. Jewish American authors 4. Writing 5. Self-discovery in men 6. Jewish American men -- Identity 7. Role models 8. Fiction -- Appreciation 9. Fiction writing 10. Extramarital affairs 11. Husband and wife 12. Artists -- Social responsibility 13. Berkshire Hills, Massachusetts 14. Humorous stories 15. Literary fiction 16. Autobiographical fiction

Originally published: New York : Farrar Straus Giroux, 1979.

National Book Award for Fiction finalist, 1980

National Book Critics Circle Award for Fiction finalist, 1979

Pulitzer Prize for Fiction finalist, 1980.

A young writer in search of a spiritual father, Nathan Zuckerman views E. I. Lonoff, who lives with his wife and his student-mistress in rural Massachusetts, as an embodiment of the ideal of artistic integrity and independence.

Roth, Philip, 1933-2018

* Goodbye, Columbus, and five short stories / Philip Roth. Modern Library, 1995, c1959. xii, 298 p.

ISBN 9780679601593

1. 1950s 2. Jewish American men -- Identity 3. Assimilation (Sociology) 4. Social classes 5. Identity (Psychology) 6. Self-discovery in men 7. Jewish Americans 8. United States -- Social life and customs -- 20th century 9. Literary fiction 10. Short stories

Originally published: Boston : Houghton Mifflin, 1959.

National Book Award for Fiction, 1960.

The contemporary writer provides insight into varied aspects of Jewish-American life.

"The title story in this collection is about a young Radcliffe girl and a Rutgers boy who learn that there is more to love than exuberance and passion. All of the stories dramatize the dilemma of modern American Jews, torn between two worlds." Publishers Weekly.

Roth, Philip, 1933-2018

The **great** American novel / Philip Roth. Vintage Books, 1995, c1973. 400 p.

ISBN 0679749063

1. Baseball players 2. Baseball teams 3. Scandals 4. Baseball 5. Humorous stories 6. Picaresque fiction 7. Literary fiction

LC 94041584

Originally published: New York : Holt, Rinehart and Winston, 1973.

A third major baseball league tries to survive, but World War II decimates it by 1943.

Roth, Philip, 1933-2018

* The human stain / Philip Roth. Houghton Mifflin, 2000. 361 p. Zuckerman novels

ISBN 9780618059454

1. Roth, Philip, 1933- 2. 1990s 3. African Americans -- Identity 4. Passing (Identity) 5. Scandals 6. Prejudice 7. African American men 8. Jewish American men -- Identity 9. Men college teachers 10. American dream 11. Racism 12. New England -- Social conditions -- 20th century 13. United States -- Social conditions -- 1997- 14. Psychological fiction 15. Literary fiction 16. Autobiographical fiction 17. Modern classics

LC 99089867

National Jewish Book Award for Fiction, 2000.

PEN-Faulkner Award, 2001.

A college professor with a sexual indiscretion in his past is hounded from his job by academic enemies who label him a racist

"Roth is clearly enjoyed himself. The Human Stain is as fresh, as angry and as bitterly amused as his early fiction. It vibrates with mockery, disapproval, poetry, and a healthy dose of personal vindictiveness that one would be tempted to dismiss as unworthy if it weren't so funny." The New Leader.

Roth, Philip, 1933-2018

I married a Communist / Philip Roth. Houghton Mifflin, 1998. 323 p. Zuckerman novels

ISBN 9780395933466

1. Roth, Philip, 1933- 2. 1940s 3. McCarthyism 4. Communists 5. Betrayal 6. Husband and wife 7. Jewish American men -- Identity 8. Jewish Americans 9. Radio personalities 10. Blacklisting of entertainers 11. American dream 12. Brothers 13. Mother and adult daughter 14. Political persecution 15. Newark, New Jersey 16. Domestic fiction 17. Literary fiction 18. Autobiographical fiction

LC 9816797

ALA Notable Book, 1999.

Shortlisted for the International IMPAC Dublin Literary Award, 2000

During the McCarthy era, a wife revenges herself on her husband by denouncing him as a Communist. It happens to Iron Rinn, a radio commentator, after he told her he did not want her daughter in the house.

"What Zuckerman/Roth does with this imagined material is constantly mesmerizing. Library shelves groan under the weight of books published about the witch hunts and blacklistings during the Truman and Eisenhower presidencies, but it would be hard to find one among them that presents as nuanced, as humanly complex an account of those years as I Married a Communist." Time.

Roth, Philip, 1933-
    Indignation / Philip Roth. Houghton Mifflin Company, 2008. 256 p.
    ISBN 9780547054841
    1. 1950s 2. Self-fulfillment in men 3. Interclass romance 4. Interpersonal conflict 5. First loves 6. College students 7. Jewish Americans 8. Men/women relations 9. Antisemitism 10. Fear in men 11. Growing up 12. Young men 13. Sexuality 14. Suicide 15. Ohio 16. New Jersey 17. Coming-of-age stories 18. Literary fiction
                                                            LC 2008011431
    In 1951 America, during the second year of the Korean War, Marcus Messner, a studious young man from Newark, New Jersey, escapes his butcher father's fears about the potential dangers facing his beloved son, by attending college at Ohio's pastoral, conservative Winesburg College, where he confronts the confusing customs and constrictions of a different world.

    "We are back in nineteen-fifties Newark, and nineteen-year-old Marcus Messner, the son of a kosher butcher, attempts to escape his father's stifling influence by enrolling at a college in Ohio farm country. Messner is a scholarly type, while his new classmates are an unfriendly bunch of churchgoing, beer-swilling louts. Stubbornly disregarding overtures of friendship from members of the school's only Jewish fraternity, Messner devotes his attentions to a troubled Gentile named Olivia Hutton. There's something of Portnoy in the masturbation-filled high jinks that follow, but Messner, fearful that he might wind up a rifleman in Korea, is a far darker creation." The New Yorker.

Roth, Philip, 1933-2018
    Letting go / Philip Roth. Vintage Books, 1997, c1962. 630 p.
    ISBN 9780679764175
    1. 1950s 2. Jewish American men -- Identity 3. Family relationships 4. Korean War veterans 5. Jewish men 6. Mortality 7. College teachers 8. Abortion 9. Chicago, Illinois 10. New York City 11. Iowa City, Iowa 12. Psychological fiction 13. Literary fiction

    Originally published: New York : Random House, 1962.
    An affluent young man struggles to maintain a healthy balance between his sympathy for less fortunate friends and his instinct for self protection.

Roth, Philip, 1933-2018
    My life as a man / Philip Roth. Vintage Books, 1993, c1974. 334 p.
    ISBN 9780679748274
    1. Roth, Philip, 1933- 2. Married people 3. Dysfunctional families 4. Husband and wife 5. Jewish American men 6. Jewish American authors 7. Self-destructive behavior in women 8. Women with mental illnesses 9. Men/women relations 10. Psychological fiction 11. Literary fiction 12. Autobiographical fiction
    Originally published: New York : Holt, Rinehart and Winston, 1974.

A young novelist's obsession with proving his manhood is transferred to his fiction and echoed in his tempestuous marriage

"The novel consists of three stories: a long autobiographical narrative told by the novelist Peter Tarnopol, preceded by two of Peter's stories, 'useful fictions' in which elements of his 'true story' are metamorphosed. Peter's alter ego, Nathan Zuckerman, is, like his author, a highly self-conscious intellectual urban Jew, adept at eliciting astonishing sexual performances from teen-age girls, but fatally drawn into a disastrous marriage with an older, damaged woman who is incapable of sexual response." Newsweek.

Roth, Philip, 1933-2018
    * **Nemesis** / Philip Roth. Houghton Mifflin Harcourt, 2010. 304 p.
    ISBN 9780547318356
    1. 1940s 2. Young men -- Personal conduct 3. Poliomyelitis 4. Epidemics 5. Playgrounds 6. Newark, New Jersey 7. New Jersey 8. Historical fiction
    In 1944 Newark, devoted playground director Bucky Cantor, sidelined from the war due to his poor eyesight, watches in horror as the city's polio epidemic begins to ravage the children on his playground.

Roth, Philip, 1933-2018
    * The **plot** against America / Philip Roth. Houghton Mifflin Co., 2004. 400 p.
    ISBN 0618509283
    1. Lindbergh, Charles A (Charles Augustus), 1902-1974 2. Roth, Philip, 1933- 3. 1940s 4. Presidents -- United States -- Election -- 1940 5. Antisemitism 6. Isolationism 7. Jewish Americans 8. Jewish American families 9. Jews -- Persecutions 10. Prejudice 11. Discrimination 12. Reminiscing in old age 13. Newark, New Jersey 14. Alternative histories 15. Political fiction 16. Literary fiction
                                                            LC 2004047490
    ALA Notable Book, 2005.
    James Fenimore Cooper Prize, 2005
    Sidewise Awards for Alternate History, 2004.
    National Book Critics Circle Award for Fiction finalist, 2004
    In a novel of alternative history, aviation hero and isolationist Charles A. Lindbergh defeats Franklin Roosevelt in the 1940 presidential election, negotiating a cordial accord with Adolf Hitler, accepting his conquest of Europe and anti-Semitic policies, and igniting a storm of fear for Jewish families throughout America.

    "Philip Roth has written a terrific political novel, though in a style his readers might never have predicted. . . . The novel is sinister, vivid, dreamlike, preposterous and, at the same time, creepily plausible." New York Times Book Review

Roth, Philip, 1933-2018
    * **Portnoy's** complaint / Philip Roth. Vintage International, 1994, c1969. 289 p.
    ISBN 9780679756453
    1. 1940s 2. 1950s 3. Jewish American men 4. Masturbation 5. Compulsive behavior in men 6. Family relationships 7. Expectation (Psychology) 8. Sexuality 9. Men/women relations 10. Picaresque fiction 11. Literary fiction 12. Modern classics
    Originally published: New York : Random House, 1969.
    A New York lawyer, dominated by a demanding Jewish mother, plays out a sexual revenge in fact and fantasy

Roth, Philip, 1933-2018

The **professor** of desire / Philip Roth. Vintage International, 1994, c1977. 263 p. Kepesh novels

ISBN 9780679749004

1. Emotional maturity 2. Desire 3. Middle-aged men -- Sexuality 4. College teachers 5. Men -- Identity 6. Men/women relations 7. Self-discovery in men 8. London, England 9. New York City 10. Humorous stories 11. Erotic fiction 12. Literary fiction

Sequel to: The breast.

Sequel: The dying animal.

Originally published: New York : Farrar Straus Giroux, 1977.

National Book Critics Circle Award for Fiction finalist, 1977

A chronicle of the passion and desire of David Kepesh and of his endeavors, from adolescent accession to middle-aged ebb, to realize and sustain erotic happiness and domestic security

"Like most writers who prove they have enough talent for the long haul of a career, Roth has found the story he will tell until either he or it is exhausted. It is a good story and, as The Professor of Desire proves, it gets better with each telling." Time.

Roth, Philip, 1933-2018

Sabbath's theater / Philip Roth. Houghton Mifflin, 1995. 451 p.

ISBN 0395739829

1. Senior men -- Sexuality 2. Compulsive behavior in men 3. Aging 4. Men/women relations 5. Reminiscing in old age 6. Former puppeteers 7. Jewish American senior men 8. Sexuality 9. Death 10. Sexagenarians 11. Humorous stories 12. Literary fiction

LC 95000914

National Book Award for Fiction, 1995.

Pulitzer Prize for Fiction finalist, 1996.

The death of his mistress sends Mickey Sabbath, an audacious libertine and onetime puppeteer, on a psychic journey into his past.

"There is plenty of the nasty in this virtuoso performance by our best literary stand-up comic. . . . The verbal play is almost tactile, like slaps, as the narrative moves from third-person comic to first-person perverse confession, but there is a polemical energy that lifts it beyond verbal playfulness; at times the message is painful." New York Times Book Review.

Roth, Philip, 1933-2018

When she was good / Philip Roth. Vintage, 1995, c1967. 306 p.

ISBN 9780679759256

1. Married women 2. Alcoholism 3. Dysfunctional families 4. Fathers and daughters 5. Women 6. Family relationships 7. Middle West 8. Family sagas 9. Literary fiction

Originally published: New York : Random House, 1967.

"Roth knows exactly what he's doing. With unerring fidelity, he records the flat surface of provincial American life, the look and feel and sound of it, and then penetrates it to the cesspool of its invisible dynamisms. Beneath the 'good,' and impelling it, he says, lies the horrid." Newsweek.

Roth, Philip, 1933-2018

Zuckerman bound / Philip Roth. Farrar, Straus and Giroux, 1985. 784 p. Zuckerman novels

ISBN 9780374299439

1. Roth, Philip, 1933- 2. Jewish American authors 3. Writing 4. Self-discovery in men 5. Jewish American men -- Identity 6. Artists -- Social responsibility 7. Humorous stories 8. Psychological fiction 9. Literary fiction 10. Autobiographical fiction

LC 84023265

Collects the Zuckerman trilogy and its epilogue: The Ghost Writer, Zuckerman Unbound, The Anatomy Lesson, and The Prague Orgy.

A new novella, "The Prague Orgy," takes Nathan Zuckerman to Prague to rescue the stories of an unknown Yiddish writer from oblivion and also forms a startling epilogue to "The Ghost Writer," "Zuckerman Unbound," and "The Anatomy Lesson," all included in this volume.

Roth, Philip, 1933-2018

* **Zuckerman** unbound / Philip Roth. Vintage International, 1995, c1981. 225 p. Zuckerman novels

ISBN 9780679748991

1. Roth, Philip, 1933- 2. 1960s 3. Jewish American authors 4. Family relationships 5. Self-discovery in men 6. Writing 7. Fame 8. Celebrities 9. Jewish American men -- Identity 10. Artists -- Social responsibility 11. Humorous stories 12. Literary fiction 13. Autobiographical fiction

Originally published: New York : Farrar, Straus, Giroux, 1981.

"After three marriages and a respected body of fiction, Nathan Zuckerman has suddenly struck free with the scandalous and subversive success of a book about a Portnoyish complainer called Carnovsky. The promising apprentice of The Ghost Writer who engaged in biographical fantasy, has himself become a creature of public fantasy who cannot cope comfortably even with material success. The consequences range from bizarre comedy (the plague of a ruined quiz show contestant who claims his life has been plagiarized) to the distortion of family relations." Library Journal.

Rothfuss, Patrick, 1973-

* The **name** of the wind / Patrick Rothfuss. DAW, 2007. 896 p. Kingkiller chronicles

ISBN 075640407X

1. Wizards 2. Magic 3. Demons 4. Quests 5. Loss (Psychology) 6. Fate and fatalism 7. Voyages and travels 8. Heroes and heroines 9. Orphans 10. Murder 11. Rulers 12. Gods and goddesses 13. Good and evil 14. Storytelling 15. Truthfulness and falsehood 16. Epic fantasy

RUSA Reading List, 2008.

A hero named Kvothe, now living under an assumed name as the humble proprietor of an inn, recounts his transformation from a magically gifted young man into the most notorious wizard, musician, thief, and assassin in his world.

Rothfuss, Patrick, 1973-

* The **wise** man's fear / Patrick Rothfuss. DAW Books, 2011. 1008 p. Kingkiller chronicles

ISBN 9780756404734

1. Heroes and heroines 2. Magicians 3. Fairies 4. Mercenaries 5. Quests 6. Loss (Psychology) 7. Fate and fatalism 8. Attempted assassination 9. Epic fantasy

Sequel to: The name of the wind.

Kvothe takes his first steps on the path of the hero as he attempts to uncover the truth about the mysterious Amyr, the Chandrian, and the death of his parents. Along the way, Kvothe is put on trial by the legendary Adem mercenaries, forced to reclaim the honor of the Edema Ruh, and travels into the Fae realm where he meets Felurian, the faerie woman no man can resist.

"This breathtakingly epic story is heartrending in its intimacy and masterful in its narrative essence, and will leave fans waiting on tenterhooks for the final installment." Publishers Weekly.

Rothmann, Ralf

To die in spring : a novel / Ralf Rothmann ; translated from the German by Shaun Whiteside. Farrar, Straus and Giroux, 2017. 211 p.

ISBN 9780374278144

1. First World War era (1914-1918) 2. Farmers 3. War -- Psychological aspects 4. Atrocities 5. Soldiers 6. Teenage boys 7. World War II 8. Suffering 9. Consequences 10. Responsibility 11. Life change events 12. Fathers and sons 13. Germany -- History -- 1933-1945 14. War stories 15. Literary fiction 16. Historical fiction 17. Translations -- German to English

LC 2017012724

Originally published in 2015 as Im fruling sterben by Suhrkamp Verlag, Berlin.

The son of an alcoholic World War II veteran pieces together the story of his father's experiences as a young apprentice milker on a northern German farm who, along with his outspoken friend, was tricked into becoming an army volunteer and committing an unthinkable act.

Rothschild, Hannah, 1962-

The improbability of love : a novel / Hannah Rothschild. Knopf, 2015. 416 p.

ISBN 9781101874141

1. Single women 2. Painting -- Collectors and collecting 3. Art dealers 4. Concentration camp survivors 5. Men/women relations 6. World War II -- Art and the war 7. Intrigue 8. Artists 9. Art 10. Literary fiction 11. Satirical fiction

LC 2014047753

Shortlisted for the Baileys Women's Prize for Fiction, 2016.
Longlisted for the Baileys Women's Prize for Fiction, 2016.

"Annie McMorrow, 31 and not recovered from the end of her long-term relationship, is an assistant to film producer Carlo Spinetti and then to his chilling wife Rebecca Winkleman Spinetti whose father started Winkleman Fine Art in Curzon St. Annie has spent her meagre savings on a dusty painting from a junk shop to give to her new, unsuitable, boyfriend who never shows up for his birthday dinner. The painting now hers, talks, but only to us. Shrewd, spoiled, charming, world weary and cynical, he comments perceptively on Annie, and the modern world and tells tales about his previous owners: Louis XV, Voltaire, Catherine the Great among others. The story unfolds through this voice and many others--unexpected, entertaining, and strangely authentic. Annie will have her apartment ransacked and be pursued by dealers, buyers and an auctioneer in an attempt to get back the painting. With The Improbability of Love, Rothschild has spun a dazzling tale--both irreverant and entertainng--of a many-layered, devious world where, in the end, love triumphs."--, Provided by publisher.

"For readers anticipating the next irresistible blend of art, mystery, and intrigue along the lines of Donna Tartt's The Goldfinch, the wait is over. This compulsively readable, immensely enjoyable novel will deeply satisfy that craving." Library Journal.

Rouda, Kaira Sturdivant, 1963-

Best day ever : a novel / Kaira Rouda. Graydon House Books, 2017. 342 p.

ISBN 9781525811401

1. Husband and wife 2. Marital conflict 3. Vacations 4. Secrets 5. Deception in men 6. Weekends 7. Ohio 8. Psychological suspense 9. Thrillers and suspense

Paul Strom has the perfect life: a glittering career as an advertising executive, a beautiful wife, two healthy boys and a big house in a wealthy suburb. And he's the perfect husband: breadwinner, protector, provider. That's why he's planned a romantic weekend for his wife, Mia, at their lake house, just the two of them. And he's promised today will be the best day ever.

Rouda, Kaira Sturdivant, 1963-

The favorite daughter / Kaira Rouda. Graydon House Books, 2019. 384 p.

ISBN 9781525835148

1. Grief in women 2. Mothers and daughters 3. Gated communities 4. Marital conflict 5. Daughters -- Death 6. Control (Psychology) 7. Change (Psychology) 8. Revenge 9. Manipulation by women 10. Social classes 11. Rich people 12. Dysfunctional families 13. Secrets 14. Orange County, California 15. California 16. Psychological suspense

Emerging from a year grieving the tragic death of her older daughter, a woman in a California oceanfront gated community observes the changes in her family while uncovering disturbing truths about her late daughter's final days.

Rourke, Lee

The canal / Lee Rourke. Melville House, 2010. 199 p.

ISBN 9781935554011

1. Men 2. Boredom 3. Secrets 4. Canals 5. Modernization (Social sciences) 6. Young women 7. London, England 8. Literary fiction

The unnamed narrator not only admits his life is a drag; he embraces banality. Disgusted by his inane office job, he quits and spends every morning on a bench along a London canal, watching waterfowl in the park and aircraft above, and commuters headed to and from their death-trap jobs. When a mysterious young woman begins to join him on the bench, recounting strange stories and confessing lies, and a gang of thugs begins to pester him, the narrator questions the meaning of love, violence, and nature.

"You have to salute Rourke he has written a novel about boredom and how it saturates modernity, which is a ballsy thing to do. But The Canal also takes in urban renewal, technology and violence as it questions the manner in which we live our lives in the 21st century. . . . For a book about urban ennui it's one hell of a page-turner." GQ (UK).

Roussel, Raymond, 1877-1933,

Locus solus / Raymond Roussel. New Directions, 2017, c1914. 256 p.

ISBN 9780811226455

1. Inventors 2. Scientists 3. Inventions 4. Curiosities and wonders 5. Manors 6. Paris, France 7. France 8. Experimental fiction 9. Literary fiction 10. Translations -- French to English

LC 2016048024

Originally published in 1914.

"The wealthy scientist Martial Canterel guides a group of visitors through his expansive estate, Locus Solus, where he displays his various deranged inventions, each more spectacular than the last."--Provided by the publisher.

"Both a guide to a deranged scientist's estate and a prism for refracting Roussel's diverse stories, this incredible novel is somehow both Gothic and modern at the same time." Publishers Weekly.

Row, Jess

Your face in mine : a novel / Jess Row. Penguin Group USA, 2014. 384 p.

ISBN 9781594488344

1. Male friendship 2. Surgery patients 3. Race relations 4. Identity (Psychology) 5. Belonging 6. Alienation in men 7. Secret identity 8. Grief in men 9. Baltimore, Maryland 10. Literary fiction

LC 2013038938

"A novel about a grieving man who reconnects with a high-school friend who has undergone racial reassignment surgery and finds their chance encounter has potentially devastating consequences for him"--, Provided by publisher.

"Row has outdone himself in a first novel that offers great quantities of food for thought and discussion involving, for starters, questions of race and identity. Plunging deeper than common notions of the self and racial distinctions, Row presents wholly credible, if not thoroughly trustworthy, characters and complicated circumstances that will inspire serious reflection." Booklist.

Rowell, Rainbow

Landline / Rainbow Rowell. St Martin's Press, 2014. 320 p.

ISBN 9781250049377

1. Magic telephones 2. Marital conflict 3. Women television writers 4. Families 5. Christmas 6. Workaholics 7. Married women 8. Discontent in men 9. Antique telephones 10. Men/women relations 11. Los Angeles, California 12. Nebraska 13. Mainstream fiction

Goodreads Choice Award, 2014.

"In New York Times bestselling author Rainbow Rowell's Landline, Georgie McCool knows her marriage is in trouble. That it's been in trouble for a long time. She still loves her husband, Neal, and Neal still loves her, deeply -- but that almost seems besides the point now.Maybe that was always besides the point.Two days before they're supposed to visit Neal's family in Omaha for Christmas, Georgie tells Neal that she can't go. She's a TV writer, and something's come up on her show; she has to stay in Los Angeles. She knows that Neal will be upset with her -- Neal is always a little upset with Georgie -- but she doesn't expect him to pack up the kids and go home without her. When her husband and the kids leave for the airport, Georgie wonders if she's finally done it. If she's ruined everything. That night, Georgie discovers a way to communicate with Neal in the past. It's not time travel, not exactly, but she feels like she's been given an opportunity to fix her marriage before it starts.Is that what she's supposed to do? Or would Georgie and Neal be better off if their marriage never happened?"--, Provided by publisher.

"Rowell knows romance writing and executes many conventions well: Christmastime setting, romantic triangle, and barriers to vital communication. Yet her tinkering with genre to explore love already in progress is the true gem." Booklist.

Rowland, Laura Joh

Bedlam : the further secret adventures of Charlotte Brontë / Laura Joh Rowland. The Overlook Press, 2010. 349 p. Secret adventures of Charlotte Brontë

ISBN 9781590202715

1. Brontë, Charlotte, 1816-1855 2. Victorian era (1837-1901) 3. 19th century 4. 1840s 5. Psychiatric hospitals 6. Missing persons 7. Former lovers 8. Secrets 9. Women authors 10. England -- Social life and customs -- 19th century 11. Great Britain -- History -- Victoria, 1837-1901 12. Historical mysteries 13. Mysteries

Finds Charlotte Bront struggling with the losses of family members and her growing literary prominence before recognizing her ex-lover at a famous London asylum and uncovering a global conspiracy.

Rowland, Laura Joh

The **hangman's** secret / Laura Joh Rowland. Crooked Lane Books, 2019. 304 p. Victorian mysteries (Laura Joh Rowland)

ISBN 9781683319023

1. Victorian era (1837-1901) 2. 19th century 3. Women photographers 4. Women private investigators 5. Crime scenes 6. Private investigators 7. Murder 8. Murder investigation 9. Newspapers 10. Secrets 11. Women serial murderers 12. Gay men 13. Coworkers 14. London, England -- History -- 19th century 15. Victorian mysteries 16. Historical mysteries

From award-winning author Laura Joh Rowland, a story about the darkness that lurks within and the deadly secrets that beg to be revealed.

Rowland, Laura Joh

The **incense** game : a novel of feudal Japan / Laura Joh Rowland. Minotaur Books, 2012. 304 p. Sano Ichiro mysteries

ISBN 9780312658533

1. 18th century 2. Detectives -- Japan 3. Murder investigation -- Japan 4. Women murder victims 5. Shoguns 6. Murder -- Japan 7. Samurai 8. Japan -- History -- Genroku period, 1688-1704 9. Historical mysteries 10. Mysteries

When the shogun's carefully regulated court is thrown into chaos by a massive earthquake in 1703 Japan, Sano Ichiro investigates the poisoning murders of a nobleman's daughters to prevent the regime's takeover.

Rowland, Laura Joh

The **iris** fan : a novel of feudal Japan / Laura Joh Rowland. Minotaur Books, 2014. 352 p. Sano Ichiro mysteries

ISBN 9781250047069

1. Shoguns 2. Heirs and heiresses 3. Rulers 4. Samurai 5. Japan -- History -- Genroku period, 1688-1704 6. Historical mysteries 7. Mysteries

LC 2014027065

In 1709 Japan, Sano Ichiro, dedicated to the samurai code of honor, is restored to the rank of chief investigator when the shogun is stabbed with a fan made of painted silk with sharp-pointed iron ribs?a case that, if the shogun's heir is displeased with the outcome, will result in his death.

"Rowland's 18th and final mystery set in feudal Japan showcases the series' strengths and weaknesses. ... Rowland offers the usual high-stakes suspense, convincing period detail, and nuanced characters you care about. Readers will be sorry to see the last of Sano." Publishers Weekly.

Rowland, Laura Joh

The **Ripper's** shadow / Laura Joh Rowland. Crooked Lane Books, 2017. 358 p. Victorian mysteries (Laura Joh Rowland)

ISBN 9781683310051

1. Jack,, the Ripper 2. Victorian era (1837-1901) 3. Women photographers 4. Women murder victims 5. Prostitutes 6. Erotic photographs 7. Sex crimes 8. Police 9. Violence against women 10. Amateur detectives 11. Serial murder investigation 12. London, England -- History -- 19th century 13. Victorian mysteries 14. Historical mysteries

Supplementing her meager income by shooting illicit "boudoir photographs" of the local ladies of the night, photographer Miss Sara Bain and her motley crew of friends are embroiled in the crime of the century when two of her clients are murdered by Jack the Ripper.

Rowland, Laura Joh

The **secret** adventures of Charlotte Brontë / Laura Joh Rowland. Penguin, 2008 320 p. Secret adventures of Charlotte Brontë

ISBN 1590200330

1. Brontë, Charlotte, 1816-1855 2. Brontë, Emily, 1818-1848 3. Brontë, Anne, 1820-1849 4. Victorian era (1837-1901) 5. 1840s 6. 19th century 7. Women authors 8. Kidnapping 9. Revenge 10. Women murder victims 11. Murder investigation 12. Brothers and sisters 13. Men/women relations 14. Interpersonal attraction 15. Voyages and travels 16. England -- Social life and customs -- 19th

century 17. Great Britain -- History -- Victoria, 1837-1901 18. Historical mysteries 19. Mysteries

Setting out for London to clear her name when she is falsely accused of plagiarism, Charlotte Brontë inadvertently stumbles on a murder scene and becomes involved in a chain of events that forces her to confront past demons while following a trail of clues.

Rowland, Laura Joh

The **Shogun's** daughter : a novel of Feudal Japan / Laura Joh Rowland. St. Martin's Minotaur, 2013. 336 p. Sano Ichiro mysteries

ISBN 9781250028617

1. 18th century 2. Detectives -- Japan 3. Shoguns 4. Heirs and heiresses 5. Death 6. Smallpox 7. Samurai 8. Japan -- History -- Genroku period, 1688-1704 9. Historical mysteries 10. Mysteries

LC 2013013933

When the shogun is forced to claim an illegitimate son as his heir after the death of his only child, Sano Ichiro, believing the malevolent youth to be part of a plot to seize power, risks the safety and honor of his family to uncover the truth.

Rowland, Laura Joh

The **snow** empress / Laura Joh Rowland. St. Martin's Minotaur, 2007. 293 p. Sano Ichiro mysteries

ISBN 9780312365424

1. 17th century 2. Boy kidnapping victims 3. Fathers and sons 4. Warlords 5. Samurai 6. Detectives -- Japan 7. Kidnapping 8. Kidnapping investigation 9. Husband-and-wife detectives 10. Murder 11. Samurai 12. Japan -- History -- Genroku period, 1688-1704 13. Historical mysteries 14. Mysteries

In 1699 Japan, when their son is kidnapped by dangerous rivals jealous over his influence in the shogun's court, Sano Ichiro and his wife, Reiko, search desperately for the boy, only to be trapped by Lord Matsumae, who has been driven mad by the murder of his mistress.

Rowland, Russell

Cold country : a novel / Russell Rowland. Dzanc Books, 2019. 232 p.

ISBN 9781945814921

1. 1960s 2. Ranchers 3. Single men 4. Murder 5. Murder suspects 6. Small town life 7. Murder investigation 8. Dysfunctional families 9. Former teachers 10. Moving, Household 11. Police 12. Secrets 13. Suspicion 14. Rural life 15. Bullying and bullies 16. Montana 17. Mysteries 18. Modern Westerns

LC 2019013630

A small 1968 Montana community is thrown into turmoil over the murder of a notorious bachelor rancher, a crime that implicates an innocent newcomer and reveals a dangerous secret.

Rowling, J. K.

The **casual** vacancy / J.K. Rowling. Little Brown & Co., 2012. 480 p.

ISBN 9780316228534

1. Social classes 2. Interpersonal conflict 3. Deception 4. Elections 5. City council members 6. Small town life 7. Men -- Death 8. Consequences 9. Interpersonal relations 10. Intergenerational relations 11. Political campaigns 12. England -- Social life and customs -- 21st century 13. Mainstream fiction

Goodreads Choice Award, 2012.

The early death of a small town councilman reveals deep-rooted conflicts in the seemingly idyllic community of Pagford, which rapidly deteriorates in the face of cultural disputes, generation clashes, and a volatile election.

Rowson, Pauline

Death lies beneath / Pauline Rowson. Severn House, 2012. 224 p. Marine mystery crime novels

ISBN 9780727882028

1. Former convicts 2. Murder investigation 3. Detectives 4. Death threats 5. Police 6. Portsmouth, England 7. England 8. Mysteries 9. Police procedurals

Detective Inspector Horton questions Intelligence Directorate theories on the death of an ex-convict and soon finds himself pursuing a complex and frustrating investigation that is complicated by a second body and a chilling personal message.

Rowson, Pauline

Undercurrent / Pauline Rowson. Severn House, 2013. 224 p. Marine mystery crime novels

ISBN 9780727882684

1. Murder investigation 2. Police cover-ups 3. Police misconduct 4. Murder 5. Suicide 6. Detectives 7. Police 8. Portsmouth, England 9. England 10. Mysteries 11. Police procedurals

When naval historian Dr Douglas Spalding is found dead in Portsmouth's Historic Dockyard, the Major Crime Team is adamant it is suicide. When another body is found in similar circumstances, Horton is convinced they're looking at murder; but not so his bosses. The deaths have all the hallmarks of a cover-up at the highest level, but who is behind it and why? As Horton gets closer to the truth and uncovers a personal twist, someone is determined to stop him from finding the killer.

Roy, Anuradha

All the lives we never lived : a novel / Anuradha Roy. Atria Books, 2018. 272 p.

ISBN 9781982100513

1. 20th century 2. Mothers and sons 3. World War II 4. Mother-deserted children 5. Artists 6. Quests 7. War and society 8. Children of artists 9. Identity (Psychology) 10. Reminiscing in old age 11. India -- History -- 20th century 12. Literary fiction 13. Historical fiction 14. Parallel narratives

LC 2018026734

A novel set from World War II India through the present day and following a son's quest to uncover the story of his freedom-craving, rebellious artist mother.

"Roy (Sleeping on Jupiter, 2016) peppers her novel with intricate descriptions of small-town India and weaves an eloquent and tragic story of straitjacketed lives upended when history and personal ambition intersect." Booklist.

Roy, Anuradha

An **atlas** of impossible longing / Anuradha Roy. Free Press, 2011. 320 p.

ISBN 9781451608625

1. Orphans 2. Families 3. Women with mental illnesses 4. Family relationships 5. Familial love 6. Husband and wife 7. Home (Concept) 8. India -- Social life and customs -- 20th century 9. India -- History -- Partition, 1947 10. Bengal (India) 11. Family sagas 12. Love stories

LC 2010019362

First published: 2008.

Growing up in the Bengal region of India, motherless daughter Bakul and Mukunda, an orphan, are inseparable, but after they grow older and their relationship turns into something more than friendship, Mukunda is banished to Calcutta, where he prospers during India's Partition, yet yearns to be back with Bakul.

"An incandescently evocative debut novel filled with wrenching tragedy as well as abiding passion, Roy's panoramic, multigenerational tale of desire, revenge, and loss is filled with the rhythms and values of India's rich and varied subcultures." Booklist.

Roy, Arundhati

* The **god** of small things / Arundhati Roy. Random House, 1997. 321 p.

ISBN 9780679457312

1. Twins 2. Family visits 3. Social classes 4. Families 5. Cousins 6. Accidents 7. Murder 8. Drowning 9. India 10. Literary fiction

LC 96-39190

Booker Prize, 1997.

In 1969, in Kerala, India, Rahel and her twin brother, Estha, struggle to forge a childhood for themselves amid the destruction of their family life, as they discover that the entire world can be transformed in a single moment.

"If the symbolism is a trifle overdone, the lush local color and the incisive characterizations give the narrative power and drama." Publishers Weekly.

Roy, Arundhati

* The **ministry** of utmost happiness : a novel / Arundhati Roy. Alfred A. Knopf, 2017. 449 p.

ISBN 9781524733155

1. Interpersonal relations 2. Misfits (Persons) 3. Unrequited love 4. Self-fulfillment 5. People who are intersex 6. Abandoned children 7. Quality of life 8. Identity (Psychology) 9. Social isolation 10. Coping 11. Emotions 12. Jammu and Kashmir, India 13. Delhi 14. India 15. Literary fiction

LC 2017002124

Librarians' Choice (Australia), 2017.

Longlisted for the Man Booker Prize, 2017.

Longlisted for the Andrew Carnegie Medal for Excellence in Fiction, 2018.

Longlisted for The Women's Prize for Fiction, 2018.

National Book Critics Circle Award for Fiction finalist, 2017.

A provocative love story meanders through a spectrum of powerful emotions experienced by diverse protagonists, including a grieving father who writes a letter profiling the people who came to his 5-year-old daughter's funeral and two longtime friends at a guest house who sleep wrapped around each other like newlyweds.

"Roy joins Dickens, Naipaul, Garca Mrquez, and Rushdie in her abiding compassion, storytelling magic, and piquant wit as she questions our perceptions of gender, family, home, country, war, freedom, love, and death in this righteous and tender illumination of humankinds paradoxical capacities for cruelty and kindness." Booklist.

Roy, Lori

Bent Road / Lori Roy. Dutton, 2011. 368 p.

ISBN 9780525951834

1. 1960s 2. Cold cases (Criminal investigation) 3. Rural families 4. Crimes against girls 5. Secrets -- Kansas 6. Rural life -- Kansas 7. Farm life -- Kansas 8. Kansas 9. Psychological suspense

LC 2010037239

Edgar Allan Poe Award for Best First Novel by an American Author, 2012.

Celia Scott and her family move back to her husband's hometown in Kansas, where his sister died under mysterious circumstances twenty years before and where Celia and two of her children struggle to adjust--especially when a local girl disappears.

"Like Michael Chabon's work, which sometimes crosses genres, Roy's novel could be called literary fiction or mystery. Whatever the label, Bent Road is written with the care and craft of standout storytelling. There's inevitability to the novel's crisis and denouement but plenty of surprise. Psychological acuity, tight plot and in-depth character development keep the reader trying to resist the urge to read ahead." Kansas City Star.

Roy, Lori

* **Gone** too long : a novel / Lori Roy. Dutton, 2019 320 p.

ISBN 9781524741969

1. Ku-Klux Klan 2. Missing children 3. Family secrets 4. Hate groups 5. Former captives 6. Captives 7. Survival 8. Racism 9. Georgia 10. Thrillers and suspense

LC 2018053742

Seven years after a girl with unusual skills goes missing amid a Klan uprising in Georgia, an estranged daughter confronts community secrets when she discovers a child in her father's basement.

Royal, Priscilla

Covenant with hell : a medieval mystery / Priscilla Royal. Poisoned Pen Press, 2013. 250 p. Prioress Eleanor of Tyndal mysteries

ISBN 9781464201936

1. Medieval period (476-1492) 2. Plantagenet period (1154-1485) 3. 13th century 4. Nuns 5. Political intrigue 6. Pilgrims and pilgrimages 7. Murder 8. Women amateur detectives 9. Civilization, Medieval 10. Great Britain -- History -- Medieval period, 1066-1485 11. East Anglia, England 12. Medieval mysteries 13. Historical mysteries

Going on a pilgrimage in the spring of 1277 to a famous East Anglian shrine where King Edward is rumored to be seeking God's blessing for a war, Prioress Eleanor investigates the suspicious falling death of a nun whose demise is linked to several pilgrims and a canny street child.

Royal, Priscilla

Sanctity of hate / Priscilla Royal. Poisoned Pen Press, 2012. 250 p. Prioress Eleanor of Tyndal mysteries

ISBN 9781464200182

1. Medieval period (476-1492) 2. Plantagenet period (1154-1485) 3. 13th century 4. Jews 5. Murder suspects 6. Murder investigation 7. Priories 8. Nuns 9. Women amateur detectives 10. Antisemitism 11. Monasticism and religious orders 12. Civilization, Medieval 13. Great Britain -- History -- Medieval period, 1066-1485 14. East Anglia, England 15. Medieval mysteries 16. Historical mysteries 17. Mysteries

In the summer of 1276 a villager's corpse is found floating in the millpond, and though the victim was a newcomer to the village and greatly disliked, the investigation soon becomes divisive, especially when Eleanor's maid Gytha joins the list of suspects.

Royal, Priscilla

Satan's lullaby : a medieval mystery / Priscilla Royal. Poisoned Pen Press, 2015. 300 p. Prioress Eleanor of Tyndal mysteries

ISBN 9781464203541

1. Medieval period (476-1492) 2. Plantagenet period (1154-1485) 3. 13th century 4. Nuns 5. Political intrigue 6. Murder 7. Women amateur detectives 8. Civilization, Medieval 9. Great Britain -- History -- Medieval period, 1066-1485 10. East Anglia, England 11. Medieval mysteries 12. Historical mysteries

Past relationships, dark secrets and religious fervor shape Tyndal Priory in 1278 France when an inspection ordered by Abbess Isabeau is overshadowed by the suspicious death of a clerk and a threat on the priest inspector's life.

Rozan, S. J.

Paper son / S. J. Rozan. Minotaur Books, 2019. 352 p. Lydia Chin and Bill Smith mysteries

ISBN 9781643131290

1. Women private investigators 2. Chinese American women 3. Cousins 4. Murder suspects 5. Innocence (Law) 6. Extended families 7. Chinese American families 8. Private investigators 9. Asian American women 10. Mississippi 11. Delta Region, Mississippi 12. Mysteries

Informed that an unknown cousin is in jail, Chinese-American private detective Lydia Chin and her partner, Bill Smith, travel to the Mississippi Delta, where they confront river-levee disputes, computer scams and questions about her cousin's innocence.

Rozan, S. J.

The **Shanghai** Moon : a Lydia Chin/ Bill Smith novel / St. Martin's Minotaur, 2009. 384 p. Lydia Chin and Bill Smith mysteries

ISBN 9780312245566

1. Private investigators 2. Women private investigators 3. International intrigue 4. Jewelry theft 5. Stolen property recovery 6. Chinese American women 7. Asian American women 8. Shanghai, China 9. New York City 10. Mysteries

LC 2008033941

Chinese-American P. I. Lydia Chin is brought in by former mentor Joel Pilarsky to help with a case that crosses continents, cultures, and decades. In Shanghai, excavation has unearthed a cache of European jewelry dating back to World War II. The jewelry was immediately stolen by a Chinese official who fled to New York City. Hired by a lawyer specializing in the recovery of Holocaust assets, Chin and Pilarsky are to find any and all leads to the missing jewels. Lydia soon learns that there is much more to the story than they've been told.

Rozan, S. J.

Winter and night / S.J. Rozan. Minotaur Books, 2002 338 p. Lydia Chin and Bill Smith mysteries

ISBN 9780312245559

1. Secrets 2. Runaway teenagers 3. Private investigators 4. Women private investigators 5. Chinese American women 6. Small town life 7. High school football 8. Asian American women 9. Anabolic steroid abuse 10. Uncles 11. Nephews 12. New Jersey 13. Mysteries

LC 2001048659

Republished in the U.K. under the title, Blood ties, (Ebury Press, Edgar Allan Poe Award for Best Mystery Novel, 2003.

Macavity Award for Best Mystery Novel, 2003.

Private detective Bill Smith is hurtled headlong into the most provocative -- and personal -- case of his career when he receives a chilling late night phone call from the NYPD, who is holding his fifteen-year-old nephew Gary.

Rubart, James L.

The **long** journey to Jake Palmer / James L. Rubart. Thomas Nelson, 2016. 400 p.

ISBN 9781401686130

1. Life change events 2. Loss (Psychology) 3. Lakes 4. Self-fulfillment 5. Vacation homes 6. Friendship 7. Faith (Christianity) 8. Forgiveness 9. Christian fiction

LC 2016006264

Christy Award for Allegory/Fantasy/Visionary Category, 2017.

On his annual lake-house vacation with friends, Jake Palmer meets an elderly man who tells him about a hidden corridor at the far end of the lake that leads to answers for their deepest questions of loss, and must decide if he really wants to find it.

Rubart, James L.

* The **man** he never was / James L. Rubart. Harpercollins Christian Pub, 2018 371 p.

ISBN 9780718099398

1. Anger in men 2. Men -- Spiritual life 3. Transformations, Personal 4. Former football players 5. Husband and wife 6. Attitude change 7. Married people 8. Self-discovery 9. Missing men 10. Christian life 11. Christian suspense 12. Adaptations, retellings, and spin-offs

LC 2017038970

"Includes discussion questions"--Page 4 of cover.

Christy Award for Allegory/Fantasy/Visionary Category, 2018.

When Toren Daniels resurfaces after an eight-month disappearance, his wife and children discover that his violent temper is completely gone, and Toren goes in search of where he has been and how he has transformed so radically.

Rubenfeld, Jed, 1959-

The **interpretation** of murder : a novel / Jed Rubenfeld. H. Holt, 2006. 384 p.

ISBN 0805080988

1. Freud, Sigmund, 1856-1939 2. Jung, C G (Carl Gustav), 1875-1961 3. 1900s (Decade) 4. Psychoanalysts 5. Murder investigation 6. Women murder victims 7. Conspiracies 8. Murder 9. Heirs and heiresses 10. Escapes 11. Hysteria in women 12. Psychoanalysis 13. Secrets 14. Manhattan, New York City 15. New York City -- History -- 20th century 16. New York City -- Social life and customs -- 20th century 17. Historical mysteries 18. Mysteries

LC 2006043434

British Book Award for the Richard & Judy Best Read of the Year, 2007.

In 1909, as a sadistic killer stalks Manhattan's wealthiest heiresses, Sigmund Freud is called in by American analyst Dr. Stratham Younger to assist him in interviewing Nora Acton, a hysterical survivor of the killer who can recall nothing about the attack.

"As The Interpretation of Murder races past ravished damsels, sinister aristocrats, architectural marvels (the building of the Manhattan Bridge), hysterical symptoms, a Hamlet-Freud nexus and downright criminal wordplay . . . , it cobbles together its own brand of excitement. That excitement is as palpable as it is peculiar. In a book that pays too much homage to contemporary suspense templates, there are still deep reserves of insight, data, wit and anecdote upon which the author ingeniously draws." New York Times.

Rucker, Rudy v. B. (Rudy von Bitter), 1946-

Hylozoic / Rudy Rucker. Tor, 2009. 336 p.

ISBN 9780765320742

1. Newlyweds 2. Telepathy 3. Exploitation 4. Aliens (Non-humanoid) 5. Teenagers 6. Earth 7. Cyberpunk 8. Science fiction 9. Humorous stories

LC 2008053399

"A Tom Doherty Associates book."

When aliens discover that everything on Earth has become sentient and telepathic, they invade the planet--some to enslave humanity, some to help--and Founders Thuy and Jayjay must save the Earth from the alien threat.

"Serious, uproarious fun, with brain-teasers and brilliant ideas tossed about like confetti." Kirkus.

Rucker, Rudy v. B. (Rudy von Bitter), 1946-

Postsingular / Rudy Rucker. Tor, 2007. 320 p.
ISBN 9780765317414

1. Billionaires 2. Boys with autism 3. Fathers and sons 4. Artificial intelligence 5. Parallel universes 6. Aliens (Humanoid) 7. Nanotechnology 8. Dystopias 9. Posthumanism 10. California 11. Cyber-thrillers 12. Science fiction

LC 2007020210

Sequel: Hylozoic.

"A Tom Doherty Associates Book."

After a bizarre scheme on the part of a ruthless computer billionaire and a wacky U.S. president to radically alter the world through sentient nanotechnology goes awry, mysterious giant humanoids from another quantum universe arrive on Earth with plans to tidy up humankind's mess.

"Rucker . . . excels in mind-bending premises and thought-stretching stories peopled with appealingly flawed characters that resonate with familiarity despite their eccentricities." Library Journal.

Ruff, Matt

* **88** names / Matt Ruff. HarperCollins, 2020. 320 p.
ISBN 9780062854674

1. Role-playing games 2. Virtual reality 3. Avatars (Virtual reality) 4. Dictators 5. Spies 6. Secret identity 7. Rich people 8. Power (Social sciences) 9. International intrigue 10. Popular culture 11. Former girlfriends 12. Cyber-thrillers

A romantic cyberthriller set in a world of fluid identities follows the experiences of a paid guide to online role-playing games who comes to believe that an anonymous wealthy new client is actually a violent dictator.

"Whether it's delving into Afro-futurism and historical horror in Lovecraft Country (2016) or taking readers on a twisty sf thriller in Bad Monkeys (2007), Ruff is an expert at keeping readers off-balance and providing entertaining stories that cross genres." Booklist.

Ruiz Zafon, Carlos, 1964-

The **angel's** game / Carlos Ruiz Zafon ; translated by Lucia Graves. Doubleday, 2009. 464 p. Cemetery of forgotten books
ISBN 9780385528702

1. 1920s 2. Obsession in men 3. Journalists 4. Secrets 5. Authors -- Spain 6. Antiquarian booksellers 7. Murder 8. Friendship 9. Supernatural 10. Books and reading 11. Men/women relations 12. Barcelona, Spain 13. Spain 14. Magical realism 15. Historical fiction 16. Literary fiction 17. Translations -- Spanish to English

This book is set in 1920-1930s.

Translated from the Spanish: Juego del angel.

Offered a career-making writing deal from an enigmatic publisher in turbulent 1960s Barcelona, David Martín wonders about his capacity for writing a book for which the publisher claims others will live and die.

"As the book opens in 1917, David Martín is 17, a down-on-his-luck Barcelona writer and budding journalist. An orphan since his father was murdered, David is forced by necessity to subvert his lofty literary ambitions in the service of writing a series of pulp novels in the macabre Grand Guignol tradition. Then a mysterious stranger named Andreas Corelli, a close relative of the stranger in Mark Twain's book of the same name and every other deal-with-the-devil tale you've ever read, presents a proposal to Martn write a book that will create a perfect narrative for a religion. In essence, his assignment is to create a mythical story that will seduce the masses into belief. The mortal medical condition Martn suffers from goes into remission, and a fortune is placed in his bank account. And off we go. This novel operates on so many levels, a brief review can't quite do justice to its many layers." Seattle Times.

Ruiz Zafon, Carlos, 1964-

The **labyrinth** of the spirits / Carlos Ruiz Zafon. HarperCollins, 2018. 848 p. Cemetery of forgotten books
ISBN 9780062668691

1. 1950s 2. Women detectives 3. Books and reading 4. Political corruption 5. State-sponsored terrorism 6. Rare books 7. Bookstores 8. Booksellers 9. Conspiracies 10. Missing men 11. Revenge 12. Authors 13. Family secrets 14. Barcelona, Spain 15. Spain -- History -- 1939-1975 16. Spain -- History -- Civil War, 1936-1939 17. Historical fiction 18. Magical realism 19. Literary fiction 20. Translations -- Spanish to English

Originally published: Barcelona, Spain : Planeta, 2016.

A conclusion to the best-selling series finds enigmatic Alicia Gris, supported by the Sempere family, uncovering one of the most shocking conspiracies in Spanish history.

"Compelling if unevenly paced, this is for readers who savor each word and scene, soaking in the ambience of Barcelona, Zafn's greatest character (after, perhaps, the irrepressible Fermn Romero de Torres)." Booklist.

Ruiz Zafon, Carlos, 1964-

The **prisoner** of heaven / Carlos Ruiz Zafon. HarperCollins, 2012. 416 p. Cemetery of forgotten books
ISBN 9780062206282

1. 1950s 2. Booksellers 3. Rare books 4. Inscriptions 5. Enemies 6. Fathers and sons 7. Imprisonment 8. Eccentrics and eccentricities 9. Secrets 10. Magic 11. Bookstores 12. Barcelona, Spain 13. Historical fiction 14. Magical realism 15. Translations -- Spanish to English 16. Literary fiction

Includes Reading group notes.

First published in Spain as 'El prisionero del cielo' by Editorial Planeta, 2011.

This translation originally published: London: Weidenfeld & Nicolson, 2012.

In 1957 Barcelona, Daniel Semper and his close friend Fermin Romero de Torres find their lives violently disrupted by the arrival of a mysterious stranger who threatens to divulge a terrible secret that has been buried for two decades in the city's dark past.

Ruiz Zafon, Carlos, 1964-

The **shadow** of the wind / Carlos Ruiz Zafon ; translated by Lucia Graves. Penguin Press, 2004. 480 p. Cemetery of forgotten books
ISBN 9780143126393

1. 1940s 2. Rare books 3. Obsession in men 4. Magic 5. Fathers and sons 6. Books and reading 7. Rare book libraries 8. Men/women relations 9. Boys -- Barcelona, Spain 10. Eccentrics and eccentricities 11. Barcelona, Spain 12. Historical fiction 13. Magical realism 14. Translations -- Spanish to English 15. Literary fiction

LC 2003062376

This book is set in 1945-1950s.

First published as La sombra del viento: Barcelona : Editorial Planeta, 2001. This edition published 2006.

This edition includes an interview with the author, discussion notes, and an illustrated 'Shadow of the Wind' walk through the streets of Barcelona.

A literary mystery set in 1945 Barcelona where David Sempere finds a book that will change the course of his life and throw him into a labyrinth of intrigues and buried secrets in the heart of the city.

"[T]he setting--Spain under Franco--injects an air of sobriety into some plot elements that might otherwise seem soap operatic. Part detective story, part boy's adventure, part romance, fantasy, and gothic horror, the intricate plot is urged on by extravagant foreshadowing and nail-nibbling tension." Booklist.

Runcie, James, 1959-

Canvey Island / James Runcie. Other Press, 2008. 301 p.
ISBN 9781590512937

1. 1950s 2. Communication in families 3. Loss (Psychology) 4. Men 5. Floods 6. Tragedy 7. Mothers -- Death 8. Guilt in men 9. Fathers and sons 10. Resentfulness 11. Men/women relations 12. Marital conflict 13. England -- Social life and customs -- 20th century 14. Canvey Island, England 15. Historical fiction 16. Literary fiction
LC 2007052431

On 1953 Canvey Island, in the aftermath of a tragic flood that claims his mother's life, Martin abandons his home to study at Cambridge and take up with Claire, a bohemian feminist and radical activist, until her actions drive him back to Canvey Island, into the arms of a teenage love and back into his old life, in a novel set against the backdrop of post-war Britain.

"In highly readable chapters narrated by each family member, the book manages to address class and generational conflict as it travels through the decades." Booklist.

Runcie, James, 1959-

The **road** to Grantchester / James Runcie. Bloomsbury, 2019. 320 p. Grantchester mysteries
ISBN 9781635570588

1. 20th century 2. Belief and doubt 3. Postwar life 4. World War II veterans 5. World War II 6. Loss (Psychology) 7. Christian life 8. Romantic love 9. Friendship 10. Clergy 11. England -- History -- 20th century 12. Historical mysteries 13. TV tie-ins

A prequel to the Grantchester series follows the life, loves and losses of young Sidney Chambers in postwar London, where, as a traumatized veteran, he navigates devastating survivor guilt and a haphazard religious calling.

"A must for fans and a good starting point for others." Booklist.

Runcie, James, 1959-

Sidney Chambers and the forgiveness of sins / James Runcie. Bloomsbury, 2015. 405 p. Grantchester mysteries
ISBN 9781632861030

1. 1950s 2. Amateur detectives 3. Clergymen 4. Forgiveness 5. Betrayal 6. Deception 7. Revenge 8. Murder investigation 9. Murder 10. Detectives 11. Scholars and academics 12. England -- History -- 20th century 13. Grantchester, England 14. Mysteries

Collects six new stories featuring the priest and part-time detective Sidney Chambers, in which a stranger seeks sanctuary believing he murdered his wife, a group of school boys blow up the science block, and Sidney is accused of stealing a painting while on holiday.

"Chambers is a winning protagonist, fervid in his faith yet prone to human frailty, and his exploits provide multiple pleasures for readers of cozies and beyond. The full Grantchester mystery series, projected to include six novels, will have a new entry in each of the next two years, and readers, as well as fans of the PBS show based on this series, should treasure them." Booklist.

Runcie, James, 1959-

Sidney Chambers and the perils of the night / James Runcie. Bloomsbury USA, 2013. 256 p. Grantchester mysteries
ISBN 9781608199518

1. 1950s 2. Investigations 3. Amateur detectives 4. Clergymen 5. Murder 6. Arson 7. International intrigue 8. Detectives 9. Scholars and academics 10. Men/women relations 11. England -- History -- 20th century 12. Grantchester, England 13. Mysteries 14. Short

stories
LC 2012050017

Originally published: 2013.

Canon Sidney Chambers investigates the unexpected fall of a Cambridge don from the roof of King's College Chapel; a case of arson at a glamour photographer's studio; and a poisoning in the middle of a crucial game of cricket.

Runcie, James, 1959-

Sidney Chambers and the persistence of love / James Runcie. Bloomsbury, 2017. 344 p. Grantchester mysteries
ISBN 9781632867940

1. 1970s 2. Clergymen 3. Amateur detectives 4. Hippies 5. Rare books 6. Husband and wife 7. Fathers and daughters 8. Poisonous plants 9. Detectives 10. Murder investigation 11. Love triangles 12. Stealing 13. England -- History -- 20th century 14. Grantchester, England 15. Mysteries

Discovering the body of a man in the Cambridgeshire woods, priest and detective Sidney Chambers immerses himself in the 1970s counterculture of psychedelic plants; while his longtime friend, Detective Inspector Geordie Keating, investigates the disappearance of a historic religious text.

Runcie, James, 1959-

Sidney Chambers and the problem of evil / James Runcie. Bloomsbury, 2014. 352 p. Grantchester mysteries
ISBN 9781608199525

1. 1950s 2. Amateur detectives 3. Clergymen 4. Investigations 5. Murder 6. Detectives 7. Scholars and academics 8. Men/women relations 9. England -- History -- 20th century 10. Grantchester, England 11. Mysteries 12. Short stories
LC 2013043690

Our favorite clerical detective is back with four longer mysteries in which Canon Sidney Chambers attempts to stop a serial killer with a grievance against the clergy; investigates the disappearance of a famous painting after a distracting display of nudity by a French girl in an art gallery; uncovers the fact that an "accidental" drowning on a film shoot may have been something more sinister; and discovers the reasons behind the theft of a baby from a hospital just before Christmas 1963. In the meantime, Sidney wrestles with the problem of evil, attempts to fulfill the demands of his faithful Labrador, Dickens, and contemplates, as always, the nature of love.

Runcie, James, 1959-

Sidney Chambers and the shadow of death / James Runcie. Bloomsbury USA, 2012. 256 p. Grantchester mysteries
ISBN 9781608198566

1. 1950s 2. Murder investigation 3. Amateur detectives 4. Clergymen 5. Vicars 6. Detectives 7. Suicide 8. Jewelry theft 9. Art forgeries 10. Single men 11. England -- History -- 20th century 12. Grantchester, England 13. Mysteries

Introduces unconventional clergyman Sidney Chambers, who teams up with roguish Inspector Harry Keating to investigate a suspicious suicide, a jewelry theft, the unexplained demise of a jazz promoter, and a shocking art forgery.

Rush, Norman

* **Mating** / Norman Rush. Knopf, 1991. 477 p.
ISBN 0394544722

1. Americans in Africa 2. Women anthropologists -- Africa 3. Courtship 4. Women -- Botswana 5. Men/women relations 6. Botswana 7. Kalahari Desert 8. Literary fiction
LC 90025752

Includes end paper maps.

National Book Award for Fiction, 1991.

National Book Critics Circle Award for Fiction finalist, 1991

Two Americans--a thirtyish anthropologist in the pursuit of a man, and a late-forties utopian who has set up a modern-day Eden--search for love in 1980s Botswana, Africa, a land full of political turmoil and local color.

"Mr. Rush has created one of the wiser and wittier fictive meditations on the subject of mating. His novel illuminates why we yield when we don't have to. It seeks to illuminate the nature of true intimacyhow to define it, how to know when one has achieved it. And few books evoke so eloquently that state of love at its apogee." New York Times Book Review.

Rush, Norman

Mortals : a novel / Norman Rush. Alfred A. Knopf, 2003. 592 p.

ISBN 0679406220

1. 1990s 2. Apartheid 3. Americans in Botswana 4. African American physicians 5. Government investigators 6. CIA agents 7. Revolutionaries 8. Husband and wife 9. Brothers 10. Gay men 11. Jealousy in men 12. Religion 13. Commitment (Psychology) 14. Military maneuvers 15. Botswana 16. Political fiction 17. Literary fiction

LC 2002043289

In the heart of Botswana, the lives of three Americans--an undercover CIA agent, his disaffected wife, and an iconoclastic black holistic physician--entangle with that of a local populist leader as a violent insurrection erupts in the area.

"The richness of Rush's vision, and its stringent moral clarity, sweep the reader into his brilliantly observed world." Publishers Weekly.

Rush, Norman

Subtle bodies / Norman Rush. Alfred A. Knopf, 2013. 224 P.

ISBN 9781400042500

1. Reunions 2. Friends' death 3. Marriage 4. Middle-age 5. Husband and wife 6. Catskill Mountains Region, New York 7. Literary fiction 8. Psychological fiction

LC 2013013813

When the ringleader of a group of former college friends dies suddenly, the survivors gather at his Catskills estate to memorialize his life, pitting Iraq war protestor Ned against his wife, who believes that the deceased did not truly value Ned's friendship.

Rushdan, Juno

Every last breath / Juno Rushdan. Sourcebooks Casablanca, 2019. 384 p. Final hour

ISBN 9781492686088

1. Elite operatives 2. Women CIA agents 3. Former lovers 4. Biological terrorism 5. Absence and presumption of death 6. Terrorism -- Prevention 7. Assassins 8. Undercover operations 9. Sexual attraction 10. Men/women relations 11. Romantic suspense

Maddox Kinkade is an expert at managing the impossible. Tasked with neutralizing a lethal bioweapon, she has everything under control... until she collides with the former love of her life, back from the dead. Recruiting Cole to save millions may be harder than resisting the attraction still burning between them, but Maddox will do whatever it takes--and the clock is ticking. When Maddox crashes back into Cole Matthews' life nine years after she left him for dead, he wants nothing more than to turn her away. But the threat of pandemic looms, and soon the former lovers find themselves working side-by-side to stop a world-class assassin with a secret that could destroy everything...

Rushdie, Salman

East, West : stories / Salman Rushdie. Pantheon Books, 1994. 214 p.

ISBN 067943965X

1. Options, alternatives, choices 2. Violence 3. East-West relations 4. Short stories 5. Fantasy fiction 6. Literary fiction

LC 94028277

"Rushdie's brilliant style reinforces his stories' marvelous combination of dignity and poignancy. Though these stories were originally published in such periodicals as the New Yorker and the Atlantic, the collection will serve for many readers as an introduction to Rushdie's talent in the short story form." Booklist.

Rushdie, Salman

The **enchantress** of Florence : a novel / Salman Rushdie. Random House, 2008. 368 p.

ISBN 9780375504334

1. Storytellers 2. Illegitimate children of royalty 3. Women -- Mughal Empire 4. Women -- Florence, Italy 5. Women rulers 6. Kidnapping victims 7. Kidnapping 8. Secrets 9. Betrayal 10. Desire 11. Mughal Empire -- History 12. Mughal Empire -- Social conditions 13. Florence, Italy -- Social conditions 14. Italy 15. Historical fiction 16. Literary fiction

LC 2008000070

Originally published: London: Jonathan Cape, 2008.

First published in Great Britain in 2008 by Jonathan Cape.

A traveler from Italy arrives at the court of Emperor Akbar, lord of the Mughal empire, and entertains him with a story about Akbar's great aunt, Qara Kz, the enchantress of Florence: a tale which suggests a larger, secret history interconnecting East and West.

Rushdie, Salman

* The **golden** house / Salman Rushdie. Penguin, 2017. 368 p.

ISBN 9780399592805

1. Rich families 2. Family secrets 3. Ambition 4. Corruption 5. Filmmakers 6. Presidential candidates 7. Real estate developers 8. Immigrants 9. Satirical fiction 10. Political fiction 11. Literary fiction

Longlisted for the Andrew Carnegie Medal for Excellence in Fiction, 2018.

A real estate tycoon and his mysterious, corrupt family become the subjects of an aspiring filmmaker's project before revelations of their criminal past activities give way to the rise of a mad presidential candidate.

"A sort of Great Gatsby for our time: everyone is implicated, no one is innocent, and no one comes out unscathed, no matter how well padded with cash." Kirkus.

Rushdie, Salman

The **ground** beneath her feet : a novel / Salman Rushdie. H. Holt, 1999. 575 p.

ISBN 0805053085

1. Women singers 2. Rock music 3. Friendship 4. Photographers 5. Photojournalists 6. Romantic love 7. Celebrities 8. Mumbai, India 9. England 10. New York City 11. India 12. Literary fiction

LC 9842407

The romance of two Indian musicians who form a band. He is Ormus, a composer, she is Vina, an American-raised singer, and their romance plays out across continents, parallel universes and different lives--she dying and returning for a second life.

"Vina and Ormus are icons, not fully formed characters. But that's the point. And Rai . . . is the most moving character Rushdie's ever created." Newsweek.

LIST OF FICTIONAL WORKS

Rushdie, Salman

Haroun and the sea of stories / Salman Rushdie. Granta Books, 1990. 218 p.

ISBN 9780670838042

1. Fathers and sons 2. Storytellers 3. Storytelling 4. Allegories 5. Literary fiction

LC 90045496

Mythopoeic Award for Children's Literature.

The author of The Satanic Verses returns with his most humorous and accessible novel yet. This is the story of Haroun, a 12-year-old boy whose father Rashid is the greatest storyteller in a city so sad that it has forgotten its name. When the gift of gab suddenly deserts Rashid, Haroun sets out on an adventure to rescue his print.

Rushdie, Salman

* **Midnight's** children : a novel / Salman Rushdie. A. A. Knopf, 1981, c1980. 446 p.

ISBN 9780394514703

1. Children 2. Infants switched at birth 3. Supernatural 4. Islam -- Relations -- Hinduism 5. Hinduism -- Relations -- Islam 6. Children of rich people 7. Poor children 8. India -- Politics and government -- 1947-1971 9. India -- History -- 1947-1971 10. Literary fiction 11. Magical realism 12. Modern classics

LC 80002712

First published: London : Jonathan Cape, 1980.
Booker Prize, 1981.
James Tait Black Memorial Prize for Fiction, 1981.

Born at the stroke of midnight on August 15, 1947, the exact moment of India's independence, Saleem Sinai becomes inextricably linked to that of his nation and is a whirlwind of disasters and triumphs that mirror modern India's course.

Rushdie, Salman

The **moor's** last sigh / Salman Rushdie. Pantheon Books, 1995. 435 p.

ISBN 0679420495

1. Families 2. Mothers and sons 3. Spice industry and trade 4. India -- Interfaith relations 5. India 6. Satirical fiction 7. Family sagas 8. Literary fiction

LC 95024392

Whitbread Book Award for Novel, 1995.
Shortlisted for the Booker-McConnell Prize, 1995.

A family saga reflecting the troubled state of India. The protagonists are four generations of the da Gama, who became wealthy in the spice trade before declining into gangsterism. Their tale is narrated by the family's last descendant and he attributes their fall to bickering, a reflection of Hindu-Moslem strife plaguing India today.

"This is a marvellously inventive display of verbal dexterity; an exuberant, entertaining, zestful novel which proves, if proof were needed, that Mr Rushdie's spirit remains undiminshed." The Economist.

Rushdie, Salman

* **Quichotte** : a novel / Salman Rushdie. Random House, 2019. 396 p.

ISBN 9780593132982

1. 21st century 2. Traveling sales personnel 3. Quests 4. Television programs 5. Automobile travel 6. Fathers and sons 7. Authors 8. Characters and characteristics in fairy tales 9. Characters and characteristics in literature 10. Popular culture 11. United States 12. Literary fiction 13. Metafiction 14. Adaptations, retellings, and spin-offs

LC 2019016494

Shortlisted for the Booker Prize, 2019.

Presents a modern adaptation of Don Quixote that finds a courtly, addled salesman embarking on a cross-country journey with his imaginary son after falling impossibly in love with a television star.

Rushdie, Salman

* The **satanic** verses / Salman Rushdie. Viking, 1989, c1988. 546 p.

ISBN 0670825379

1. East Indians 2. Good and evil 3. Islam 4. Survival (after airplane accidents, shipwrecks, etc) 5. London, England 6. Magical realism 7. Literary fiction 8. Modern classics

LC 88040266

First published in Great Britain in 1988.
Whitbread Book Award for Novel, 1988.
Shortlisted for the Booker-McConnell Prize, 1988.

Just before dawn one winter's morning, a hijacked aeroplane blows apart high above the English Channel and two figures tumble, clutched in an embrace, towards the sea: Gibreel Farishta, India's legendary movie star, and Saladin Chamcha, the man of a thousand voices. Washed up, alive, on an English beach, their survival is a miracle. But there is a price to pay. Gibreel and Saladin have been chosen as opponents in the eternal wrestling match between Good and Evil. But chosen by whom? And which is which? And what will be the outcome of their final confrontation?

Rushdie, Salman

Shalimar the Clown : a novel / Salman Rushdie. Random House, 2005. 416 p.

ISBN 0679463356

1. Extremism 2. Revenge 3. Guilt 4. Muslim men 5. Clowns 6. Extramarital affairs 7. Chauffeurs 8. Ambassadors 9. Americans in India 10. Love triangles 11. Paternity 12. Flashbacks 13. Resistance to government 14. Jammu and Kashmir, India -- Politics and government 15. Strasbourg, France 16. Los Angeles, California 17. Psychological fiction 18. Literary fiction

LC 2005042796

Originally published: London : Jonathan Cape, c2005.
Shortlisted for the International IMPAC Dublin Literary Award, 2007

In 1991, Ambassador Maximilian Ophuls--ex-ambassador to India, and America's counterterrorism chief--is murdered on the Los Angeles doorstep of his illegitimate daughter's home by his Kashmiri Muslim driver, who calls himself Shalimar the Clown.

"Rushdie has written an intensely political novel, infused with recent events, but its emotional scope reaches so far beyond our current crisis and its vision into the vagaries of the heart is so perceptive that one can imagine Shalimar the Clown being read long after this age of sacred terror has faded into history." Washington Post Book World.

Rushdie, Salman

Two years eight months and twenty-eight nights : a novel / Salman Rushdie. Random House, 2015. 304 p.

ISBN 9780812998917

1. Genies 2. Imaginary wars and battles 3. Superhuman abilities 4. Half-human hybrids 5. Fundamentalism 6. Belief and doubt 7. Good and evil 8. Secularism 9. Religion 10. Magic 11. New York City 12. Literary fiction 13. Fantasy fiction 14. Satirical fiction 15. Middle Eastern-influenced fantasy

LC 2015008158

A modern fairy tale by the award-winning author of Midnight's Children is set in a world of religious dominance where mystical acts and supernatural abilities shape a war over control of Fairyland.

"Rushdie scatters intriguing allusions (Beckett, Magritte, Gogol, Obama) about like fairy dust and coins of the realm while sustaining swiftly flowing, incisive, piercingly funny commentary on everything from religious extremists to reality TV, anti-Semitism and racism, and economic injustice." Booklist.

Ruskovich, Emily

Idaho : a novel / Emily Ruskovich. Random House, 2017 336 p.

ISBN 9780812994049

1. Women murderers 2. Husband and wife 3. Memories 4. Dementia 5. Women prisoners 6. Life change events 7. Loss (Psychology) 8. Forgiveness 9. Violence in men 10. Secrets 11. Idaho 12. Literary fiction

LC 2016006621

International IMPAC Dublin Literary Award, 2019.

A tale told from multiple perspectives traces the complicated relationship between Ann and Wade on a rugged landscape and how they came together in the aftermath of his first wife's imprisonment for a violent murder.

"Shocking and heartbreaking, Ruskovich has crafted a remarkable love story and a narrative that will stay with readers." Publishers Weekly.

Russell, Karen, 1981-

Orange world and other stories / Karen Russell. Alfred A. Knopf, 2019. 320 p.

ISBN 9780525656135

1. Short stories 2. Literary fiction

LC 2018054561

"This is a Borzoi book published by Alfred A. Knopf."

A latest collection of short fiction by the award-winning author of Swamplandia! includes the title story, in which a desperate new mother strikes a bargain to breastfeed the devil in exchange for his protection over her baby.

"Heir to Shirley Jackson and a compatriot of T. C. Boyle, virtuoso Russell, gifted with acute insights, compassion, and a daring, free-diving imagination, explores the bewitching and bewildering dynamic between the voracious appetite of nature and its yawning indifference and humankinds relentless profligacy and obliviousness." Booklist.

Russell, Karen, 1981-

* Swamplandia! / Karen Russell. Alfred A. Knopf, 2011. 304 p.

ISBN 9780307263995

1. Family relationships 2. Quests 3. Swamps 4. Mother-separated families 5. Amusement parks 6. Girls 7. Mothers -- Death 8. Alligators 9. Missing teenage girls 10. Grief in teenage girls 11. Everglades, Florida 12. Ten Thousand Islands, Florida 13. Coming-of-age stories 14. Magical realism 15. Literary fiction

LC 2010036708

ALA Notable Book, 2012.

Andrew Carnegie Medal for Excellence in Fiction finalist, 2012.

Pulitzer Prize for Fiction finalist, 2012.

Shortlisted for the International IMPAC Dublin Literary Award, 2013

The Bigtree children struggle to protect their Florida Everglades alligator-wrestling theme park from a sophisticated competitor after losing their parents.

"When Hilola Bigtree, professional alligator wrestler and star attraction at a Florida venue that calls itself 'the Number One Gator-Themed Park and Swamp Caf in the area,' dies in the vise grip not of some prehistoric behemoth but of unglamorous cancer, the family-owned tourist destination shrivels into insolvency. Likewise, the remaining Bigtree

clan unspools in her absence, and Ava, the youngest of three children, can only watch as they drift apart. Her sister, Ossie, obsessed with the afterlife, carries out furtive relationships with the spirits of dead boys she claims possess her. Her brother, Kiwi, runs off to work for the World of Darkness, an amusement park designed to resemble hell. The plot of Swamplandia! tilts toward the odd. Kiwi toils in his ersatz inferno; Ava goes on a quest to save Ossie after she elopes into the otherworldly wetlands with one of her phantom paramours. But Russell isn't a magic realist. In fact, the only truly magical things about this book are its effortless prose and its small, beautifully drawn cast of characters." Entertainment Weekly.

Russell, Karen, 1981-

Vampires in the lemon grove : stories / Karen Russell. Alfred A. Knopf, 2013. 256 p.

ISBN 9780307957238

1. Short stories 2. Literary fiction

LC 2012027415

"This is a Borzoi book."

Award-winning author Karen Russell's latest short story collection blends whimsy and horror in equal measure. Her daringly inventive characters range from centuries-old vampires with surprisingly touching human desires, to a former U.S. president now reincarnated as a horse. Russell's dry humor and keen eye for relatable emotional experiences will lure readers deeply into these surreal vignettes. - Description by Shauna Griffin.

Russell, Kate Elizabeth

* My dark Vanessa / Kate Elizabeth Russell. William Morrow & Co., 2020. 372 p.

ISBN 9780062941503

1. Teenage girls -- Relations with older men 2. Teacher-student relationships 3. High school teachers 4. Sex crimes 5. Memories 6. Boarding schools 7. Sexual consent 8. Manipulation (Social sciences) 9. Maine 10. Psychological fiction 11. Parallel narratives

Asked to help defend an older high-school English teacher with whom she had an affair at age 15, Vanessa struggles to choose between her romantic teen illusions and harrowing adult perceptions.

"Russell offers readers an introspective narrative that fully captures the complexity and necessity of the #MeToo movement in her powerful debut." Publishers Weekly.

Russell, Mary Doria, 1950-

Children of God : a novel / Mary Doria Russell. Villard, 1998. 438 p. Sparrow novels (Mary Doria Russell)

ISBN 067945635X

1. Jesuits 2. 21st century 3. Religion 4. Life on other planets 5. Revolutions 6. Linguists 7. Space flight 8. Priests 9. Disillusionment in men 10. Misunderstanding 11. Aliens (Non-humanoid) 12. Social science fiction 13. Science fiction 14. Literary fiction

LC 97-42160

Sequel to: The sparrow.

A priest named Emilio Sandoz embarks on a quest to demystify God's providence that leads him to question the possibility of faith.

"Russell succeeds in painting an alien culture with remarkably detailed verisimilitude." New York Times Book Review.

Russell, Mary Doria, 1950-

Dreamers of the day : a novel / Mary Doria Russell. Random House, 2008. 256 p.

ISBN 9781400064717

1. Lawrence, T E (Thomas Edward), 1888-1935 2. Churchill, Winston, 1874-1965 3. Bell, Gertrude Lowthian, 1868-1926 4. Spies

-- Germany 5. World War I 6. Independence in women 7. Love 8. Inheritance and succession 9. Voyages and travels 10. Women teachers 11. Self-discovery in women 12. Middle East -- History -- 20th century 13. Cairo, Egypt 14. Historical fiction 15. Political fiction

LC 2007024665

A forty-year-old schoolteacher from Ohio still reeling from the tragedies of the Great War and the influenza epidemic comes into a modest inheritance that allows her to take the trip of a lifetime to Egypt and the Holy Land. Arriving at the Semiramis Hotel, site of the 1921 Cairo Peace Conference, she meets Winston Churchill, T. E. Lawrence, and Lady Gertrude Bell. With her plainspoken American opinions, she becomes a sounding board for these historic luminaries who will, in the space of a few days, invent the nations of Iraq, Syria, Lebanon, Israel, and Jordan. While neither a pawn or a participant at the conference, she is drawn into the geopolitical intrigue surrounding the conference.

"Russell perfectly captures the political and social milieus of the 1920s, driving home how important it is to consider history when dealing with present-day issues. . . . The fact that Agnes is telling her story after she has--yes--already died does not come across as a literary conceit but as perfectly fitting for this perfectly enchanting tale." BookPage.

Russell, Mary Doria, 1950-

* **Doc** : a novel / Mary Doria Russell. Random House, 2011. 400 p. Doc novels (Mary Doria Russell)

ISBN 9781400068043

1. Holliday, John H, 1851-1887 2. Earp, Wyatt, 1848-1929 3. American Westward Expansion (1803-1899) 4. Male friendship 5. Peace officers 6. Dentists 7. Frontier and pioneer life 8. Boy murder victims 9. Gambling 10. Prostitutes 11. Murder investigation 12. Dodge City, Kansas 13. Biographical fiction 14. Westerns

LC 2010015062

RUSA Reading List, 2012.

After the burned body of mixed-blood boy Johnnie Sanders is discovered in 1878 Dodge City, Kansas, part-time policeman Wyatt Earp enlists the help of his professional-gambler friend Doc Holliday, in a novel that also features Doc's girlfriend, the Hungarian prostitute Kate Katarina Harony.

"An engaging bit of de-mythology, a vivid re-imagining of a more authentic, slightly less wild West than the one we've come to know through dime-store novels." Cleveland Plain Dealer.

Russell, Mary Doria, 1950-

Epitaph : a novel of the O.K. Corral / Mary Doria Russell. Ecco Press, 2015. 581 p. Doc novels (Mary Doria Russell)

ISBN 9780062198761

1. Earp, Wyatt, 1848-1929 2. Holliday, John H, 1851-1887 3. American Westward Expansion (1803-1899) 4. 1880s 5. Gunfights 6. Frontier and pioneer life 7. Competition 8. Gunfighters 9. Greed 10. Jewish women 11. Men/women relations 12. Arizona (Territory) -- History -- 19th century 13. O K Corral, Arizona -- History 14. Biographical fiction 15. Westerns 16. Literary fiction

A sequel to Doc is based on the true events of the gunfight at the O.K. Corral and Wyatt Earp's survival against a backdrop of volatile politics in 1881 America.

"The multitude of points of view exemplifies the best of third-person omniscience, revealing innermost secrets, hopes, and fears. Readers of Lyndsay Faye's Gods of Gotham are sure to enjoy this novel, and fans of Westerns ready to branch out beyond Louis L'Amour and Max Brand might see it as a breath of fresh air." Library Journal.

Russell, Mary Doria, 1950-

* The **sparrow** / Mary Doria Russell. Villard, 1996. 408 p. Sparrow novels (Mary Doria Russell)

ISBN 0679451501

1. Jesuits 2. 21st century 3. Life on other planets 4. Priests 5. Change (Psychology) 6. Near future 7. Linguists 8. Space flight 9. Jesuit missionaries 10. Faith (Christianity) 11. Aliens 12. Religion 13. Social science fiction 14. Science fiction 15. Literary fiction

Sequel: Children of God (1998).

Arthur C. Clarke Award, 1998.

BSFA Award for Best Novel, 1997.

James Tiptree, Jr. Award, 1996.

The sole survivor of a crew sent to explore a new planet, Jesuit priest Emilio Sandoz discovers an alien civilization that raises questions about the very essence of humanity, an encounter that leads Sandoz to a public inquisition and the destruction of his faith.

Russell, Mary Doria, 1950-

A **thread** of grace : a novel / Mary Doria Russell. Random House, 2005. 448 p.

ISBN 0375501843

1. Second World War era (1939-1945) 2. 1940s 3. Catholics 4. Resistance to military occupation 5. Nazis 6. World War II -- Jews -- Rescue 7. Holocaust (1933-1945) 8. Holocaust survivors 9. Jews, Italian 10. Refugees, Jewish 11. Priests 12. Communists 13. Former fighter pilots 14. Righteous Gentiles in the Holocaust 15. Former Nazis 16. Italy -- History -- German occupation, 1943-1945 17. Historical fiction 18. War stories

LC 2004050942

In September 1943, Claudette Blum and her father flee across the Alps into Italy with other Jews seeking refuge, only to find an open battle ground among the Nazis, Allied forces, resistance fighters, and ordinary Italians struggling to survive.

"This is a morality play that at times uses black humor, and then shifts to solemn reflection or moving portraiture. A Thread of Grace is deft, sensate, ruthless in its moral incisiveness, and affirming in that even in the worst of times, the lamp of humanity cannot be completely extinguished." The Hudson Review.

Russell, Mary Doria, 1950-

The **women** of the copper country : a novel / Mary Doria Russell. Atria Books, 2019. 339 p.

ISBN 9781982109585

1. Clemenc, Ana K, 1888-1956 2. 1910s 3. Copper Miners' Strike, Mich, 1913-1914 4. Women labor leaders 5. Labor movement 6. Young women 7. Coal mines and mining 8. Coal mining towns 9. Social classes 10. Social advocacy 11. Miners 12. Labor organizing 13. Strikes 14. Michigan 15. United States -- History -- 20th century 16. Historical fiction 17. Biographical fiction

LC 2018051007

Presents a story inspired by the life of Annie Clements, retelling in historically authentic detail how in 1913 she led a courageous strike against the world's largest copper-mining company.

"The painstakingly comprehensive narrative and omniscient point of view make for a deliberate pace, but they also ensure readers completely understand what happened. The tale is often bleak, but it serves as a worthwhile counterpoint to historical writing centered on "great men."" Publishers Weekly.

Russell, Sheldon

The **insane** train / Sheldon Russell. Minotaur Books, 2010. 304 p. Hook Runyon mysteries

ISBN 9780312566715

1. 1940s 2. People with mental illnesses 3. Railroads 4. Murder 5. Revenge 6. Railroad police 7. Veterans 8. People who have had amputations 9. Men and dogs 10. Historical mysteries 11. Mysteries

LC 2010032672

Railroad security worker Hook Runyon and a crew of damaged World War II veterans find themselves facing murder when they escort a group of mental patients and their doctors to a new home after the Baldwin Insane Asylum burns to the ground.

"The author imbues even bit characters with personality, and presents a rough-edged view of the world that will be familiar to fans of classic hardboiled writers such as Chandler and Hammett." Publishers Weekly.

Russo, Richard, 1949-

Bridge of sighs / Richard Russo. Alfred A. Knopf, 2007. 544 p.

ISBN 9780375414954

1. Small towns 2. Small town life 3. Community life 4. Interpersonal relations 5. Senior men 6. Family relationships 7. Male friendship 8. Painters 9. Artists 10. Husband and wife 11. Father and adult son 12. Expatriate artists 13. Expatriates 14. New York (State) 15. Literary fiction

LC 2007027970

After sixty years of living in the upstate New York town of Thomaston, Louis Charles and his wife of forty years, Sarah, prepare for a trip to Italy to visit Louis' childhood friend, an artist who had fled his hometown many years earlier.

"Whatever the scale of their lives, Russo's characters--the stars and the walk-ons are gorgeously drawn. The writing is always in service of illuminating them--with one exception. The black characters speak in a corny-sounding dialect, which can make the reader stop to decode sentences. In this case, the reach for authenticity doesn't work. But everything else works brilliantly. . . . That Russo manages to juggle so many characters, themes, places, and time periods through 528 delicious pages is an astounding achievement. From its lovely beginning to its exquisite, perfect end, Russo has written a masterpiece." Boston Globe.

Russo, Richard, 1949-

* **Chances** are... : a novel / Richard Russo. Alfred A. Knopf, 2019. 304 p.

ISBN 9781101947746

1. Sixties (Age) 2. Male friendship 3. Vacations 4. Missing women 5. Secrets 6. Memories 7. Social classes 8. Martha's Vineyard, Massachusetts 9. Literary fiction

LC 2019010992

One beautiful September day, three 66-year-old men convene on Martha's Vineyard, friends ever since meeting in college, and must puzzle out a lingering mystery from the summer of 1971.

Russo, Richard, 1949-

* **Empire** Falls / Richard Russo. Knopf, 2001. 483 p.

ISBN 9780679432470

1. Small town life 2. Working class 3. Diners (Restaurants) 4. Divorce 5. Family businesses 6. Men -- Family relationships 7. Middle-aged men 8. Plant closings 9. Restaurateurs 10. Maine 11. Literary fiction

LC 01088568

Pulitzer Prize for Fiction, 2002.

Milo Roby tries to hold his family together while working at the Empire Grill in the once-successful logging town of Empire Falls, Maine,

with his partner, Mrs. Whiting, who is the heir to a faded logging and textile legacy.

"Miles Roby is a typical Russo hero: wry, unlucky in love and money; and just a little bit smarter than the people who populate his run-down industrial town. In this case, the town is Empire Falls, Maine, where Miles manages a restaurant that serves as a kind of meeting hall for the novel's large cast of characters. There's David, Miles's recovering-alcoholic brother; Walt, the health-club entrepreneur who has stolen Miles's estranged wife; Tick, Miles's precocious, befuddled teen-age daughter; and Francine Whiting, the rich widow who runs everything. Russo is preoccupied with the death of a certain version of the American dream, but his belief in the power of comedy--sometimes low, sometimes high--rescues his work from bathos and elvates it into the realm of literature." The New Yorker.

Russo, Richard, 1949-

* **Everybody's** fool / Richard Russo. Alfred A. Knopf, 2016. 480 p. Nobody's fool

ISBN 9780307270641

1. 1990s 2. Small town life 3. Police chiefs 4. Misadventures 5. Obsession 6. Crime 7. Loss (Psychology) 8. Interpersonal relations 9. New York (State) 10. Literary fiction

LC 2015043451

Returns to the setting of "Nobody's Fool" to find Sully confronting a daunting health prognosis, which he hides from his loved ones, including his longtime mistress, an increasingly distant best friend, and an obsessive chief of police.

"Russos reunion with these beloved characters is genius: silly slapstick and sardonic humor play out in a rambling, rambunctious story that poignantly emphasizes that particular brand of loyalty and acceptance that is synonymous with small-town living." Booklist.

Russo, Richard, 1949-

* **Nobody's** fool / Richard Russo. Random House, 1993. 549 p. Nobody's fool

ISBN 0394577787

1. Bad luck 2. Unemployed persons -- New York (State) 3. Blue collar workers 4. Small town life 5. Literary fiction

LC 92056844

First published in USA in 1993 by Random House.

ALA Notable Book, 1994.

Follows the unexpected operation of grace in a deadbeat, upstate New York town--and in the lives of the unluckiest of its citizens.

"A grand read sparkling with witty dialogue and memorable characters, Russo's novel is a rollicking tale of a born loser on a downward slide. An economically depressed upper New York State community is the setting, and its lower-middle-class and blue-collar inhabitants are portrayed with empathy and a shrewd understanding of human nature." Publishers Weekly.

Russo, Richard, 1949-

The **risk** pool / Richard Russo. Random House, 1988. 479p.

ISBN 0394565274

1. Small town life -- New York (State) 2. Fathers and sons -- New York (State) 3. Misadventures 4. Drifters 5. New York (State) 6. Domestic fiction 7. Literary fiction

LC 88042666

Ned, the introspective son of the freewheeling World War II veteran Sam Hall struggles for acceptance from his father while trying to avoid adopting the same hedonistic lifestyle.

"A superbly original, maliciously funny book, peopled by characters that most of us would back away from plenty fast if they ever lurched toward our barstool. It is Mr. Russo's brilliant, deadpan writing that gives their wasted lives and miserable little town such haunting power and insidious charm." New York Times Book Review.

Russo, Richard, 1949-
Straight man / Richard Russo. Random House, 1997. 391 p.
ISBN 0679432469
1. Middle-aged men 2. Small town life -- Pennsylvania 3. Universities and colleges -- Faculty 4. College teachers 5. Communities 6. Budget 7. Geese 8. Pennsylvania 9. Humorous stories 10. Literary fiction
LC 9648578
During one tortuous week, Hank Devereaux, head of the English department at the state university in Railton, Pennsylvania, has his nose slashed by a feminist poet, finds his secretary is a better writer than he is, suspects his wife is having an affair, threatens wild fowl, and confronts his father

Rutherfurd, Edward
The **forest** : a novel / Edward Rutherfurd. Crown Publishers, 2000. 598 p.
ISBN 0609603825
1. Families 2. Poor families 3. Smugglers 4. Clergy 5. Nobility 6. Forests 7. Foresters 8. Men/women relations 9. Rulers 10. Battles 11. England -- History 12. New Forest, England 13. Historical fiction 14. Family sagas 15. Epic fiction
LC 00022219
Chronicles the lives of 5 families over four centuries of British history, set on the southern coast of England.
"This historical saga focuses on the New Forest, part of the southern coast of England bounded by the English Channel. Rutherfurd traces the lives of peasants, smugglers, churchmen, woodsmen, and upper-class families from the 11th to the 20th centuries. These assorted men and women take part in the events surrounding the death of King Rufus (William the Conqueror's son), the failure of the Spanish Armada, England's Civil War, and more." Library Journal.

Rutherfurd, Edward
London / Edward Rutherfurd. Crown, 1997. 829 p.
ISBN 0517591812
1. Shakespeare, William, 1564-1616 2. Newgate Prison 3. Westminster Abbey. 4. Roman Britain (55 BCE-449 CE) 5. Anglo-Saxon period (449-1066) 6. Norman period (1066-1154) 7. Plantagenet period (1154-1485) 8. Tudor period (1485-1603) 9. Elizabethan era (1558-1603) 10. Stuart period (1603-1714) 11. Georgian era (1714-1837) 12. Victorian era (1837-1901) 13. Edwardian era (1901-1914) 14. 20th century 15. City life 16. Families 17. Normans in England 18. Bombings 19. Black Death 20. Marriage 21. Historic buildings 22. Influenza Epidemic, 1918-1919 23. Great Fire, London, England, 1666 24. London, England -- History 25. Historical fiction 26. Family sagas 27. Epic fiction
LC 97010176
Illustrated with maps
"A novel"--Cover.
First published in the United Kingdom in 1997 by Century.
The triumphs and failures of seven individual family clans span the history of a city from the third-century Roman occupation of Londinium through such eras as the Norman conquest and the Elizabethan period
"This fictional history of London is told through the experiences of a group of diverse families who, over the generations, meet, mingle, intermarry, and feud. Beginning with prehistory and continuing to the present, Rutherfurd combines geological details, historical events, real people, and his fictional characters to bring London to life." Library Journal.

Rutherfurd, Edward
Paris / Edward Rutherfurd. Doubleday, 2013. 528 p.
ISBN 9780385535304
1. Notre Dame (Cathedral), Chartres, France 2. Cities and towns 3. City life 4. Hundred Years' War, 1339-1453 5. Revolutions 6. Eiffel Tower, Paris, France 7. Paris, France -- History 8. France -- History 9. Historical fiction 10. Family sagas 11. Epic fiction
Taking readers on a journey through Parisian history, this sweeping multigenerational saga, filled with romance, danger and rich detail, beautifully illuminates the City of Lights, from its founding under the Romans to the hotbed of cultural activity during the 1920s and 1930s that included Picasso.

Rutherfurd, Edward
* The **princes** of Ireland : the Dublin saga / Edward Rutherfurd. Doubleday :, 2004. 752 p. Dublin saga
ISBN 0385502869
1. Henry II,, King of England, 1133-1189 2. Princes 3. Nobility 4. Families 5. Monks 6. Soldiers 7. Authors 8. Love 9. War 10. Family relationships 11. Ireland -- History 12. Dublin, Ireland 13. Great Britain -- History 14. Historical fiction 15. Family sagas 16. Epic fiction
LC 2003070005
Sequel: The Rebels of Ireland: The Dublin Saga.
A fictional account of the history of Ireland recreates such events as the mission of Saint Patrick, the Viking invasion, and the trickery of Henry II that led to England's establishment in Ireland.
"Beginning in the tribal, pre-Christian times of the warrior kings at Tara, this first book in a two-part novelized history of Ireland sweeps readers through the early centuries of Druids, chieftains, monks, Vikings, noblemen, merchants, and mercenaries, ending with the disastrous invasion of England that tragically changed the course of Irish history. Through the eyes of the men and women who built the mighty city that became Dublin, the unfolding of a colorful and turbulent history is told with energy and a meticulous attention to historical detail." Library Journal.

Rutherfurd, Edward
The **rebels** of Ireland : the Dublin saga / Edward Rutherfurd. Doubleday :, 2006. 800 p. Dublin saga
ISBN 0385512899
1. Families 2. Famines -- Ireland 3. Immigration and emigration 4. Family relationships 5. British in Ireland 6. Catholics -- Ireland 7. Protestants -- Ireland 8. Irish resistance and revolts 9. Aristocracy -- Ireland 10. Nationalism -- Ireland 11. Dublin, Ireland 12. Ireland -- History 13. Ireland -- Social conditions 14. Historical fiction 15. Family sagas 16. Epic fiction
Sequel to: The Princes of Ireland: The Dublin Saga.
Published in the UK as Ireland awakening.
Follows the lives and destinies of several Dublin families, both Catholic and Protestant, from all strata of society, from the sixteenth-century colonization of Ireland by the English to the founding of the Irish Free State in 1922.
"Beginning with Elizabeth's ascendancy to the English throne and the plantation period of the English conquest of Ireland and ending with the founding of the Irish republic in 1922, this sequel to Princes of Ireland vividly tells the history of Irish suppression through the lives of ordinary people on both sides of the turmoil. It is a story of bitter and tragic contrast. Rutherfurd casts the Irish, thought to be savages by England's Protestant elite, against a backdrop of a vibrant, intellectual Dublin, deeply divided by religion and politics yet aglow with the literary renaissance of Yeats, Shaw, and Joyce." Library Journal.

Rutherfurd, Edward

Russka : the novel of Russia / Edward Rutherfurd. Crown Publishers, 1991. viii, 760 p.

ISBN 0517580489

1. Ivan IV,, the Terrible, Czar of Russia, 1530-1584 2. Peter I,, the Great, Emperor of Russia, 1672-1725 3. Catherine II,, Empress of Russia, 1729-1796 4. Families 5. Farm life 6. Nobility 7. Crimean Tatars 8. Cossacks 9. Refugees, Russian 10. Human settlements 11. Communism 12. Small town life -- Soviet Union 13. Villages -- Russia 14. Soviet Union -- History 15. Russia -- History 16. Historical fiction 17. Family sagas 18. Epic fiction

LC 90034457

Includes map and family tree.

The triumphs, tragedies, passions, and struggles of successive generations of four families are shaped by the turbulent events and forces of Russian history, from ancient times to the twentieth century

"The book does provide a sweeping overview of the land whose very vastness and complexity make it overwhelming and fascinating." Christian Science Monitor.

Rutherfurd, Edward

Sarum : the novel of England / Edward Rutherfurd. Gramercy Books, 2004. 897 p.

ISBN 0517223546

1. Families 2. Technology and civilization 3. Human evolution 4. Human settlements 5. Hunters 6. Farmers 7. Civilization, Stone age 8. Christianity 9. Men/women relations 10. Industrial revolution 11. Women rulers 12. Cathedrals 13. Stonehenge, England 14. England -- Civilization -- History 15. England -- History 16. Salisbury Plain, England 17. Historical fiction 18. Family sagas 19. Epic fiction

LC 2003067523

"Rutherfurd is strong on the explication of trends and the narration of events. But he relies heavily on the repetition of character types. Nevertheless, 'Sarum' is fascinating and will appeal to Anglophiles, history buffs, and fans of epic-style novels." Christian Science Monitor.

Rutland, Eva

No crystal stair / Eva Rutland. Mira, 2000. 474 p.

ISBN 9781551665191

1. United States. Army Air Forces 2. African Americans -- History 3. Civil rights 4. Racism 5. Women's lives and relationships 6. African American fiction

Growing up in Atlanta during the 1920s and 1930s as a member of the black privileged class, Ann Elizabeth Carter, the daughter of a doctor and granddaughter of a slave, comes face to face with the realities of prejudice and segregation when she marries Robert Metcalf, a black pilot stationed at Tuskegee, Alabama, in a story that follows the life of one African American woman through the turbulent history of the twentieth century.

Ryan, Anthony

The **waking** fire / Anthony Ryan. Ace Books, 2016. 582 p. Draconis memoria

ISBN 9781101987858

1. Imaginary empires 2. Dragons 3. Voyages and travels 4. Adventure 5. Blood 6. Elixirs 7. Thieves 8. Magic 9. Espionage 10. Women spies 11. Women assassins 12. Sailors 13. Interpersonal relations 14. Fantasy fiction 15. Steampunk

LC 2015039369

With their lines weakening, the drakes, whose prized blood is used to make a powerful elixir, pose a threat to the supremacy of the Ironship Syndicate.

"Ryan handily juggles draconic fantasy, espionage, and steampunk naval fiction with realism and effortless skill." Publishers Weekly.

Ryan, Hank Phillippi

The **other** woman / Hank Phillippi Ryan. Forge, 2012. 416 p. Jane Ryland mysteries

ISBN 9780765332578

1. Elections 2. Women journalists 3. Serial murder investigation 4. Police 5. Governors 6. Serial murders 7. Missing women 8. Women politicians 9. Political corruption 10. Extramarital affairs 11. Government cover-ups 12. Women amateur detectives 13. Boston, Massachusetts 14. Mysteries

LC 2012019932

"A Tom Doherty Associates book."

Edgar Allan Poe Awards: Mary Higgins Clark Award, 2013.

Tracking down a candidate's secret mistress days before a pivotal Senate election, reporter Jane Ryland discovers links between her story and a serial killer investigation by detective Jake Brogan, with whom she partners to stop a killer in the face of dirty politics and betrayal.

Ryan, Hank Phillippi

Say no more / Hank Phillippi Ryan. Forge, 2016. 384 p. Jane Ryland mysteries

ISBN 9780765385352

1. Women journalists 2. Date rape 3. Violence against women 4. Violence in universities and colleges 5. Universities and colleges 6. Threat (Psychology) 7. Rape 8. Hit-and-run accidents 9. Alibi 10. Boston, Massachusetts 11. Mysteries

Discovering that she has witnessed the collapse of an alibi after reporting a hit and run, Boston reporter Jane Ryland convinces a date rape victim to come forward as part of an expose on college campus sexual assaults, an assignment that is complicated by an ominous threat.

Ryan, Hank Phillippi

Truth be told / Hank Phillippi Ryan. Forge, 2014. 400 p. Jane Ryland mysteries

ISBN 9780765374936

1. Foreclosure 2. Women journalists 3. Business -- Corrupt practices 4. Police 5. Eviction 6. Detectives 7. Conspiracies 8. Confession (Law) 9. Murder investigation 10. Women amateur detectives 11. Cold cases (Criminal investigation) 12. Boston, Massachusetts 13. Mysteries

Agatha Award for Best Novel, 2014.

In digging up the facts on the heartbreaking story of a middle-class family evicted from their suburban home, and on other foreclosures, reporter Jane Ryland soon learns the truth behind a big-bucks scheme and the surprising players who will stop at nothing, including murder, to keep their goal a secret.

Ryan, Hank Phillippi

What you see / Hank Phillippi Ryan. Forge Books, 2015. 400 p. Jane Ryland mysteries

ISBN 9780765374950

1. Women journalists 2. Parental kidnapping 3. Conspiracies 4. Stepfathers 5. Murder investigation 6. Stabbing victims 7. Detectives 8. Extortion 9. Police 10. Boston, Massachusetts 11. Mysteries

LC 2015023330

While reporter Jane Ryland searches for a 9-year-old flower girl who has been kidnapped by her stepfather, detective Jake Brogan investigates a public stabbing, only to uncover a dark conspiracy of extortion and stolen lives.

Ryan, Hank Phillippi

The **wrong** girl / Hank Phillippi Ryan. St. Martin's Press, 2013. 366 p. Jane Ryland mysteries

ISBN 9780765332585

1. Adoption agencies 2. Birthparents -- Identification 3. Child welfare 4. Crimes against women 5. Murder investigation 6. Missing children 7. Women journalists 8. Women amateur detectives 9. Boston, Massachusetts 10. Mysteries

Agatha Award for Best Novel, 2013.

Investigating allegations against an adoption agency that is suspected of reuniting adopted children with the wrong birth parents, Jane Ryland finds her efforts suspiciously tied to Jake Brogan's case involving a young woman's brutal murder and the disappearance of a baby.

Ryan, Jennifer, 1973-

Restless rancher : Wild Rose Ranch / Jennifer Ryan. Avon Books, 2019. 384 p. Wild Rose Ranch

ISBN 9780062952646

1. Ranches 2. Cowboys 3. Single women 4. Women accountants 5. Alcoholics 6. Spendthrifts 7. Inheritance and succession 8. Personal finance 9. Children of prostitutes 10. Responsibility in women 11. Protectiveness in men 12. Family feuds 13. Family secrets 14. Sexual attraction 15. Men/women relations 16. Montana 17. Western romances 18. Contemporary romances

One minute down-on-his-luck rancher Austin Hubbard slept soundly, the next, a sassy spitfire dumped a pitcher of water on his head and woke him up--in more ways than one. Hired to help him rebuild his ranch, Sonya Tucker ends up helping him put the tattered pieces of his life back together. The capable, all-business accountant is on a mission to get the ranch up and running, but can he convince the temptingly beautiful woman to take a chance on him?

Ryan, Jennifer (Jennifer L.)

* The **spies** of Shilling Lane : a novel / Jennifer Ryan. Crown Publishing, 2019 355 p.

ISBN 9780525576495

1. Second World War era (1939-1945) 2. Family secrets 3. Women and war 4. World War II -- Great Britain 5. Women -- Family relationships 6. World War II home front 7. Mothers and daughters 8. Divorced women 9. Missing women 10. War and society 11. Social classes 12. London, England -- History -- Bombardment, 1940-1941 13. England 14. Great Britain 15. Historical fiction

A follow-up to The Chilbury Ladies' Choir finds scandalous divorc?e Mrs. Braithwaite traveling to World War II London in search of her missing daughter, an effort that is complicated by a difficult secret.

"Even with sometimes-vivid descriptions of the horrors of the Blitz, there is a good deal of fun in this cozy caper, and fans of The Chilbury Ladies' Choir will eat it up." Booklist.

Ryan, Kennedy

* **Long** shot / Kennedy Ryan. Scribechick Media, 2018. 460 p. Hoops (Kennedy Ryan)

ISBN 9781732144309

1. College athletes 2. Multiracial persons 3. Engaged persons 4. Abused women 5. Love triangles 6. Basketball players 7. Sexual attraction 8. Men/women relations 9. Sports romances 10. Contemporary romances 11. Multicultural romances

RITA Award, 2019.

Ryan, William, 1965-

The **darkening** field / William Ryan. Minotaur Books, 2012. viii, 322 p. Investigations of Captain Korolev

ISBN 9780312586515

1. Soviet Union. Narodnyi komissariat vnutrennikh del 2. 1930s 3. Crimes against women 4. Murder investigation 5. Conspiracies 6. Detectives 7. Moscow, Russia -- Politics and government 8. Soviet Union -- Politics and government -- 1936-1953 9. Historical mysteries 10. Mysteries

Originally published as: The bloody meadow, London : Mantle, 2011.

In 1937, Captain Korolev of Moscow's Criminal Investigation Division looks into the suicide of a young loyal party member who was intimately involved with a party director, a case that is unexpectedly linked to a treasonous plot.

Ryan, William, 1965-

The **twelfth** department / William Ryan. Minotaur Books, 2013. 336 p. Investigations of Captain Korolev

ISBN 9780312586522

1. Soviet Union. Narodnyi komissariat vnutrennikh del 2. 1930s 3. Murder investigation 4. Conspiracies 5. Detectives 6. Missing persons 7. Political corruption 8. Communism 9. Moscow, Russia -- Politics and government 10. Soviet Union -- Politics and government -- 1936-1953 11. Historical mysteries 12. Mysteries

LC 2013011923

Originally published: London : Mantle, 2013.

Captain Alexei Korolev endures threats against his family when a high-level murder is tied to corruption in State Security and the NKVD.

S

Sa'dawi, Ahmad

Frankenstein in Baghdad / Ahmed Saadawi ; translated from the Arabic by Jonathan Wright. Penguin Books, 2018, c2013. 304 p.

ISBN 9780143128793

1. Junk dealers 2. Iraq War, 2003-2011 3. Dead 4. War casualties 5. Monsters 6. Revenge 7. Journalists 8. Murder 9. Terrorism 10. Military occupation 11. Violence 12. Baghdad, Iraq 13. Horror 14. Literary fiction 15. Translations -- Arabic to English

LC 2017008182

Originally published: Beirut : Al Kamel, 2013.

Shortlisted for the Man Booker International Prize, 2018.

From the rubble-strewn streets of U.S.-occupied Baghdad, Hadi?a scavenger and an oddball fixture at a local caf??collects human body parts and stitches them together to create a corpse. His goal, he claims, is for the government to recognize the parts as people and to give them proper burial. But when the corpse goes missing, a wave of eerie murders sweeps the city, and reports stream in of a horrendous-looking criminal who, though shot, cannot be killed.

"A haunting and startling mix of horror, mystery, and tragedy." Booklist.

Sabatini, Rafael, 1875-1950

Captain Blood / Rafael Sabatini. Dover Publications, 2004, 1922. vi, 242 p.

ISBN 0486436543

1. 17th century 2. Physicians 3. Pirates 4. Sailing ships 5. Seafaring life 6. British in the Caribbean Area 7. Buccaneers 8. Caribbean Area 9. Adventure stories 10. Sea stories 11. Swashbuckling tales

12. Historical fiction

LC 2004055142

Originally published as Captain Blood, His Odyssey: New York :

Wrongfully arrested following the Monmouth rebellion of 1685, Peter Blood, country physician and former soldier, escapes the hangman's noose only to be exiled to the tropical colonies. Sold into slavery to a cruel plantation owner, his moral fortitude and medical ability soon earn him the favour of the island's governor, and the attentions of Arabella, his master's niece. When the town is attacked by marauding Spanish buccaneers, Blood springs to the rescue, and with a motley yet loyal band of shipmates escapes to begin a life of noble piracy and adventure on the caribbean seas.

"Peter Blood was many things in his timesoldier, country doctor, slave, pirate, and finally Governor of Jamaica. Incidentally, he was an Irishman. Round his humorous-heroic figure Mr. Sabatini has written an exciting romance of the Spanish Main, the facts of which he alleges to have been found in the diary and log books of one Jeremiah Pitt, a follower of Monmouth in 1685 and Blood's faithful companion in adventure." Times Literary Supplement.

Sabatini, Rafael, 1875-1950

Scaramouche : a romance of the French Revolution / Rafael Sabatini. Norton, 2002, c1921. x, 406 p.

ISBN 9780393323306

1. Revolutionary France (1789-1799) 2. 1780s 3. Actors and actresses 4. Traveling theater 5. Disguises 6. French Revolution, 1789-1799 7. Swordfighters 8. Swordplay 9. Nobility 10. Injustice 11. Revenge 12. Class conflict 13. France -- History -- Revolution, 1789-1799 14. Historical fiction 15. Adventure stories

Originally published: Boston: Houghton Mifflin Co., 1921.

When his best friend is struck down by an uncaring aristocrat, French lawyer Andre-Louis Moreau disguises himself as the clown Scaramouche to speak out against an unjust nobility, in a novel of romance and adventure set during the French Revolution.

Saberhagen, Fred, 1930-2007

Coinspinner's story / Fred Saberhagen. T. Doherty Associates, 1989. 244 p. Book of Lost Swords

ISBN 9780312932213

1. Magic swords 2. Quests 3. Princes 4. Swords 5. Magic 6. Fantasy fiction 7. Sword and sorcery

LC 89039878

A host of strange characters--Prince Nurat of Culm, the evil macrowizard Wood, Prince Adrian, and Trilby--become involved in a desperate struggle to possess a sword of chance known as Coinspinner.

Saberhagen, Fred, 1930-2007

Farslayer's story / Fred Saberhagen. T. Doherty Associates, 1989. 252 p. Book of Lost Swords

ISBN 9780312931704

1. Magic swords 2. Good and evil 3. Family feuds 4. Quests 5. Swords 6. Magic 7. Fantasy fiction 8. Sword and sorcery

LC 89011638

"Two rival families wage a war of attrition and vengeance for possession of 'Farslayer,' one of the 12 Lost Swords made by the gods and imbued with unearthly powers. A grim sense of fatality underlies the deceptive simplicity of the author's style." Library Journal.

Saberhagen, Fred, 1930-2007

Mindsword's story / Fred Saberhagen. Tor Books, 1990. 250 p. Book of Lost Swords

ISBN 9780312851286

1. Magic swords 2. Quests 3. Princes 4. Good and evil 5. Magic 6.

Swords 7. Fantasy fiction 8. Sword and sorcery

LC 90038899

When the long-lost Mindsword--which gives mindless devotion to the one who wields it--falls into the hands of Prince Murat, Kristen, the beautiful wife of Prince Mark, falls under its spell, and it is up to Mark and his companions to save his wife and his kingdom.

"Saberhagen treads a fine line between fantasy and moral fable in his latest addition to a popular series." Library Journal.

Saberhagen, Fred, 1930-2007

Shieldbreaker's story / Fred Saberhagen. TOR, 1994. 255 p. Book of Lost Swords

ISBN 0312850018

1. Magic swords 2. Princes 3. Good and evil 4. Quests 5. Demons 6. Magicians 7. Swords 8. Magic 9. Fantasy fiction 10. Sword and sorcery

An unsuspecting fourteen-year-old warrior, Prince Stephen, is forced into manhood, when he uses Sheildbreaker to protect the universe from the greedy hands of Vikata the Dark King

Saberhagen, Fred, 1930-2007

Sightblinder's story / Fred Saberhagen. T. Doherty Associates, 1987. 248 p. Book of Lost Swords

ISBN 0312930321

1. Magic swords 2. Adventure 3. Wizards 4. Swords 5. Magic 6. Fantasy fiction 7. Sword and sorcery

LC 87050477

When Prince Mark and the good wizard Honan-Fu are cast into a hellish enchantment by the Ancient One, Ben and young Zoltan need the help of Sightbinder, the Sword of Power that causes to appear that which a person most desires, or fears

Saberhagen, Fred, 1930-2007

Stonecutter's story / Fred Saberhagen. Tor, 1988. 247 p. Book of Lost Swords

ISBN 9780312930738

1. Magic swords 2. Quests 3. Black magic 4. Adventure 5. Swords 6. Magic 7. Fantasy fiction 8. Sword and sorcery

LC 87051397

Four very different people--Prince al-Farabi, Kasimir, a young physician, the wise magistrate Wen Chang, and Natalia, an inhabitant of a House of Pleasure in the city of Eylan--pursue the stolen Stonecutter, the Sword of Siege.

"The book's virtues include a cast of well-drawn characters and some vividly realized societies, as well as Saberhagen's usual spare prose and sound narrative technique." Booklist.

Saberhagen, Fred, 1930-2007

Wayfinder's story / Fred Saberhagen. TOR, 1992. 251 p. Book of Lost Swords

ISBN 9780312850005

1. Magic swords 2. Quests 3. Wisdom 4. Wizards 5. Swords 6. Magic 7. Fantasy fiction 8. Sword and sorcery

LC 92000858

When Wayfinder, the Sword of Wisdom, turns up in the hut of Valdemar, a simple grower of grapes, it leads Valdemar on his quest to find a wife.

"One of 12 magical swords forged by the Gods, Wayfinder has the power to guide its possessor to whatever the seeker wants. Chance brings Wayfinder to Ben of Purkinje, who uses it to find Woundhealer, the sword with powers to cure the injured wife of Prince Mar of Sarykam. The evil magician Wood also wants the swords; his attack on Ben brings Mark, and even more swords, into the fray. . . . Saberhagen keeps the plot moving, providing a pleasurable light reading experience." Publishers Weekly.

Saberhagen, Fred, 1930-2007

Woundhealer's story / Fred Saberhagen. TOR, 1986. 281 p. Book of Lost Swords

ISBN 9780312932435

1. Magic swords 2. Healing 3. Good and evil 4. Quests 5. Princes 6. Adventure 7. Boys who are blind 8. Wizards 9. Swords 10. Magic 11. Fantasy fiction 12. Sword and sorcery

LC 86050319

Prince Mark of Tasavalta sets out to find the Sword Woundhealer--the only cure for his ill son--but the evil wizard Berslam and Baron Amnitor have other ideas

"A pleasant adventure that benefits greatly from Saberhagen's narrative gifts as the various strands leapfrog forward, keeping the reader off balance but constantly intrigued." Publishers Weekly.

Sackville-West, V. (Victoria), 1892-1962

All passion spent / Vita Sackville-West. Vintage Books, 2017, c1931. 169 p.

ISBN 9780525433972

1. Senior women 2. England -- Social life and customs -- 20th century 3. Modern classics 4. Psychological fiction

Originally published: Great Britain: Hogarth Press, 1931.

After the death of elder statesman Lord Slane--a former prime minister of Great Britain and viceroy of India--everyone assumes that his eighty-eight-year-old widow will slowly fade away in her grief, remaining as proper, decorative, and dutiful as she has been her entire married life. But the deceptively gentle Lady Slane has other ideas. First she defies the patronizing meddling of her children and escapes to a rented house in Hampstead. There, to her offspring's utter amazement, she revels in her new freedom, recalls her youthful ambitions, and gathers some very unsuitable companions, who reveal to her just how much she had sacrificed under the pressure of others' expectations.

"Gentle, charming Lady Slane, her family, and her friends, drawn with wit and skill in this tale of graceful old age, create an impression of subtlety and beauty." Booklist.

Sackville-West, V. (Victoria), 1892-1962

The **Edwardians** / Vita Sackville-West ; new introduction by Victoria Glendinning. Virago, 2003., c1930. 349 p.

ISBN 9780860683599

1. Edwardian era (1901-1914) 2. Upper class 3. Aristocracy 4. Generation gap 5. Young men -- Relations with older women 6. Freedom 7. Manners and customs 8. Brothers and sisters 9. Discontent 10. Explorers 11. Great Britain -- History -- Edward VII, 1901-1910 12. England -- History -- 20th century 13. England -- Social life and customs -- 20th century 14. Literary fiction

Originally published: London : Hogarth Press, 1930.

At nineteen, Sebastian is a duke and heir to a vast country estate. A deep sense of tradition binds him to his inheritance, though he loathes the social circus he is a part of. Deception, infidelity and greed hide beneath the glittering surface of good manners. Among the guests at a lavish party are two people who will change Sebastian's life: Lady Roehampton, who will initiate him in the art of love; and Leonard Anquetil, a polar explorer who will lead Sebastian and his free-spirited sister Viola to question their destiny.

Sada, Daniel, 1953-2011

Almost never / Daniel Sada ; translated by Katherine Silver. Graywolf, 2012. 320 p.

ISBN 9781555976095

1. 1940s 2. Prostitutes 3. Love triangles 4. Lust 5. Men/women relations 6. Pregnancy 7. Mexico -- History -- 1910-1946 8. Historical fiction 9. Love stories 10. Translations -- Spanish to English

In 1945 Oaxaca, an agronomist named Demetrio Sordo regularly visits a prostitute named Mireya even as he pursues a more pure form of love in his correspondence with a girl from his hometown named Renata, until problems arise with the arrangement.

Saer, Juan Jose, 1937-2005

The **sixty-five** years of Washington / Juan Jose Saer ; translated from the Spanish by Steve Dolph. Open Letter, 2010, c1986. 203 p.

ISBN 9781934824207

1. 1960s 2. Walking 3. Memories 4. Coups d'etat 5. Birthday parties 6. Male friendship 7. Argentina -- History -- 20th century 8. Literary fiction 9. Metafiction 10. Translations -- Spanish to English

LC 2010029041

Originally published in Spanish as Glosa: Buenos Aires : Alianza, 1986.

"In this novel, the Argentine writer Saer packs several decades of his country's history into a single hour. The premise is deceptively simple. On a fall morning in 1961 a pair of young men take a stroll in the city of Santa Fe. Angel Leto, a skinny man who lives with his mother, skips work and runs into a tall, white-clad acquaintance known among friends as the Mathematician, a chemical engineer distributing press releases about a recent trip to Europe. In three sections covering seven blocks each, Saer flits between his protagonists' minds, relating their fleeting sensations, memories, epiphanies and distractions in exquisite detail. As they speculate about the events of a recent party that neither attended (for the 65th birthday of Jorge Washington Noriega, the Washington of the title) the reader begins to grasp the web of relationships that bind their circle of intellectuals and activists. . . . With meticulous prose, rendered by Dolph's translation into propulsive English, Saer's novel captures the wilderness of human experience in all its variety." New York Times Book Review.

Sagan, Carl, 1934-1996

Contact : a novel / Carl Sagan. Simon and Schuster, 1985. 432 p.

ISBN 0671434004

1. Life on other planets 2. Women scientists 3. Interstellar communication 4. Mathematics 5. Aliens 6. Women astronomers 7. Space flight 8. Transportation 9. Human/alien encounters 10. Hard science fiction 11. Science fiction

LC 85014645

Locus Award for First Novel, 1986.

Astrophysicist Dr. Rebecca Blake deciphers a message from outer space and finds that the message contains directions for the construction of a complicated machine.

"A serious blend of science fact and speculation with a fast-paced and well-crafted story . . . suggesting that Sagan is more interested in illustrating human relations and human response than depicting alien creatures. . . . Sagan has provided a novel of ideas, and finds drama in how people interact with them in a situation of challenge and discovery." Christian Science Monitor.

Sagan, Francoise, 1935-2004

* **Bonjour** tristesse / Francoise Sagan ; translated from the French by Irene Ash ; introduction by Diane Johnson. Harper-Collins, 2001, c1955. x, 130 p.

ISBN 0066211697

1. Teenage romance 2. Seventeen-year-old girls 3. Fathers and daughters 4. Mistresses 5. Jealousy in teenage girls 6. French Riviera 7. Translations -- French to English 8. Coming-of-age stories 9. Modern classics 10. Literary fiction

Bonjour tristesse first published by Editions Rene Julliard 1954 ; first published in Great Britain by John Murray 1955.

Cecile is the spoiled 17-year-old daughter of Raymond, a wealthy Parisian widower vacationing in a villa on the French Riviera. Their pleasure-seeking existence is threatened when Raymond decides to marry Cecile's straitlaced godmother, Anne, who disapproves of the teenager's steamy summer affair with Philippe.

Sager, Riley,

Final girls : a novel / Riley Sager. Dutton, 2017. 352 p.

ISBN 9781101985366

1. Young women 2. Violence against women 3. Victims of violent crimes 4. Murder 5. Coping in women 6. Recovered memory 7. Repression (Psychology) 8. Survival -- Psychological aspects 9. Manhattan, New York City 10. New York City 11. Psychological suspense

LC 2016034340

Librarians' Choice (Australia), 2017

Thriller Award for Best Novel, 2018.

Emerging a lone survivor of a serial killer's massacre a decade earlier, a former college student struggles to ignore traumatic memories and move on as one of a group of other survivors who look to her for answers when one of them is found dead in a suspicious suicide.

"Sager does an excellent job throughout of keeping the audience guessing until the final twist. A fresh voice in psychological suspense." Kirkus.

Sager, Riley

The **last** time I lied : a novel / Riley Sager. Dutton, 2018. 370 p.

ISBN 9781524743079

1. Witnesses 2. Young women 3. Summer camps 4. Artists 5. Missing girls 6. Missing persons investigation 7. Cold cases (Criminal investigation) 8. Psychological suspense

LC 2017060923

An artist who witnessed the disappearance of her bunkmates at summer camp as a young girl accepts an opportunity to return to Camp Nightingale as a painting instructor and tries to discover what really happened to her friends.

"Sager's second thriller is as tense and twisty as his best-selling Final Girls (2017), but this one is even more polished, with gut-wrenching plot surprises skillfully camouflaged by Emma's paranoia and confusion, the increasingly creepy setting, and a cast of intriguingly secretive characters." Booklist.

Sager, Riley

Lock every door : a novel / Riley Sager. Dutton, 2019. 368 p.

ISBN 9781524745141

1. Apartment house life 2. Housesitting 3. Secrets 4. Missing women 5. Rules 6. Apartment dwellers 7. Manhattan, New York City 8. New York City 9. Psychological suspense

LC 2018058455

Follows a young woman whose new job apartment sitting in one of New York's oldest and most glamorous buildings may cost more than it pays.

"Sager (Final Girls) delivers a psychological, creepy, and unputdownable thriller. Likable characters, great writing, just enough twists, and a Rosemary's Baby vibe will make this a summer hit. Purchase for Stephen King and Gillian Flynn fans." Library Journal.

Sahota, Sunjeev, 1981-

The **year** of the runaways / Sunjeev Sahota. Alfred A. Knopf, 2016, c2015. 484 p.

ISBN 9781101946107

1. Undocumented immigrants 2. Life change events 3. Communities 4. East Indians in England 5. Immigration and emigration 6. Options, alternatives, choices 7. England 8. Sheffield, England 9. India 10. Political fiction 11. Literary fiction

Originally published: London : Picador, 2015.

Shortlisted for the Man Booker Prize, 2015.

Follows three young men and a woman who journey together from India to England to fulfill respective goals while hiding painful secrets from the past and struggling with financial limitations and the punishing realities of immigrant life.

"Quarrelling, parting, and finding solace in one another in unexpected ways, Sahota's characters are wonderfully drawn, and imbued with depth and feeling." Publishers Weekly.

Saint-Exupery, Antoine de, 1900-1944

* The **little** prince / written and drawn by Antoine de Saint-Exupery. Harcourt, 1943. 91 p.

ISBN 0152023984

1. Princes 2. Pride and vanity 3. Pilots 4. Purpose in life 5. Boy adventurers 6. Aliens (Humanoid) 7. Voyages and travels 8. Life on other planets 9. Sahara 10. Allegories 11. Translations -- French to English 12. Illustrated books 13. Classics

LC 82011968

Translated from the French by Katherine Woods.

"This many-dimensional fable of an airplane pilot who has crashed in the desert is for readers of all ages. The pilot comes upon the little prince soon after the crash. The prince tells of his adventures on different planets and on Earth as he attempts to learn about the universe in order to live peacefully on his own small planet. A spiritual quality enhances the seemingly simple observations of the little prince. Shapiro. Fic for Youth. 3d edition

Saint-Exupery, Antoine de, 1900-1944

Night flight / Antoine de Saint Exupery ; translated from the French by Stuart Gilbert. Harcourt Brace Jovanovich, 1974, c1932. 87 p.

ISBN 0156656051

1. 1930s 2. Pilots 3. Night flying 4. Air mail service 5. Flight 6. Aviation 7. Courage 8. Airplanes 9. Husband and wife 10. Airplane accidents 11. Argentina -- History -- 20th century 12. Adventure stories 13. Translations -- French to English

Reprint of the translation of Vol de nuit, originally published by Reynal & Hitchcock, New York, 1932.

A group of pilots must conquer the savage Andean weather as well as the mechanical shortcomings of early aircraft to establish an air-mail service to South America.

Saintcrow, Lilith

The **Iron** Wyrm Affair / Lilith Saintcrow. Little, Brown & Co., 2012. 320 p. Bannon and Clare

ISBN 9780316201261

1. Victorian era (1837-1901) 2. Dragons 3. Serial murders 4. Women wizards 5. Detectives 6. Gods and goddesses 7. Women rulers 8. Magic 9. Shapeshifters 10. Conspiracies 11. Assassins 12. Great Britain -- History -- Victoria, 1837-1901 13. Steampunk 14. Historical fantasy

The last remaining mentath in Londoninium, Archibald Clare, teams up with the Prime sorceress, Emma Bannon, to uncover who is behind the treachery, conspiracies and black magic claiming lives all over the city.

Saintcrow, Lilith

The **ripper** affair / Lilith Saintcrow. Orbit, 2014. 320 p.. Bannon and Clare

ISBN 9780316183727

1. Victorian era (1837-1901) 2. Assassination plots 3. Women wizards 4. Detectives 5. Accident victims 6. Women rulers 7. Secrets 8. Magic 9. Shapeshifters 10. Conspiracies 11. Assassins 12. Great Britain -- History -- Victoria, 1837-1901 13. Steampunk 14. Historical fantasy

LC 2014933834

"A shattering accident places Archibald Clare, mentath in the service of Britannia, in the care of Emma Bannon, sorceress Prime. Clare needs a measure of calm to repair his faculties of Logic and Reason. Without them, he is not his best. At all. Unfortunately, calm and rest will not be found. There is a killer hiding in the sorcerous steam-hells of Londinium, murdering poor women of a certain reputation. A handful of frails murdered on cold autumn nights would make no difference...but the killings echo in the highest circles, and threaten to bring the Empire down in smoking ruins. Once more Emma Bannon is pressed into service; once more Archibald Clare is determined to aid her. The secrets between these two old friends may give an ambitious sorcerer the means to bring down the Crown. And there is still no way to reliably find a hansom when one needs it most"--P. [4] of cover.

Saintcrow, Lilith

Trailer park fae / Lilith Saintcrow. Orbit, 2015. 320 p. Gallow and ragged

ISBN 9780316277853

1. Fairies 2. Rulers 3. Plague 4. Weapons 5. Construction workers 6. Widowers 7. Deception 8. Urban fantasy

LC 2014046001

After the death of his wife, construction worker Jeremiah Gallow wants to leave the fairy world behind, but a woman with special powers who resembles his wife manages to involve him with that world when a plague breaks out and the fullborn-fae begin dying.

"Saintcrow's excellent tale will immerse readers in a complex and eerily familiar world of fae-inhabited trailer parks and diners and find definite appeal among fans of Seanan Maguire's October Daye series. Try this for Charles de Lint aficionados who want something a touch lighter but still with profound worldbuilding and characters." Library Journal.

Sainz Borgo, Karina, 1982-

* **It** would be night in Caracas / Karina Sainz Borgo ; translated from the Spanish by Elizabeth Bryer. HarperCollins Publishers, 2019. 224 p.

ISBN 9780062936868

1. Mothers -- Death 2. Revolutionaries 3. Survival 4. Options, alternatives, choices 5. Anarchism 6. Pillage 7. Loss (Psychology) 8. Memories 9. Venezuela 10. Caracas (Venezuela) 11. Political fiction 12. Translations -- Spanish to English

LC 2019013246

Originally published: Barcelona : Lumen, 2019.

A woman tests the limits of what she is willing to do to secure her future in turbulent modern Venezuela overrun by violent revolutionaries.

Sakey, Marcus

A **better** world / Marcus Sakey. Thomas & Mercer, 2014. 380 p. Brilliance saga

ISBN 9781477823941

1. 21st century 2. Terrorism 3. Antiterrorists 4. Superhuman abilities 5. Families 6. Genius 7. Justice 8. Equality 9. Paranoia 10. Government investigators 11. Dystopian fiction 12. Political thrillers 13. Science fiction

In a world where one percent of the population is born with special abilities, a terrorist network led by these "brilliants" devastates three cities, and presidential adviser Nick Cooper must stop the oncoming war between brilliants and humans.

"Sakey's series has been taken as an allegory of America devouring its own. Could be. But recommend it, too, as a first-rate actioner forever pulsing forward, told in vivid, even poetic prose." Booklist.

Sakey, Marcus

The **blade** itself / Marcus Sakey. St. Martin's Minotaur, 2007. 320 p.

ISBN 0312360312

1. Irish Americans 2. Criminals 3. Former convicts 4. Kidnapping 5. Robbery 6. Male friendship 7. Revenge 8. Extortion 9. Options, alternatives, choices 10. Personal conduct 11. Manipulation by men 12. Childhood friends 13. Chicago, Illinois 14. Thrillers and suspense 15. Crime fiction

LC 2006050562

Leaving his past as a professional thief behind after his best friend and partner Evan is sent to prison, Danny Carter feels safe in his new life, until Evan returns, out on early parole and determined to draw Danny back into a criminal career.

"As the author takes Danny apart and looks to see what the man is really worth, the novel delivers some implicit social commentary about the shaky foundation on which Danny's new life has been built. . . . Not until the very end of the story is it clear who Danny is or where he stands. His ability to churn these questions so vigorously will bring Mr. Sakey attention." New York Times.

Sakey, Marcus

Brilliance / Marcus Sakey. Thomas & Mercer, 2013. 439 p. Brilliance saga

ISBN 9781611099690

1. 21st century 2. Terrorism 3. Antiterrorists 4. Superhuman abilities 5. Families 6. Genius 7. Justice 8. Equality 9. Paranoia 10. Government investigators 11. Dystopian fiction 12. Political thrillers 13. Science fiction

Starting in 1980, about 1% of all children born in the U.S. were gifted with unusual abilities. Thirty-three years later, these "brilliants" (also called "abnormals" or "abs") are leaders in various fields -- including terrorism. Nick Cooper's one of them, though he works for a government agency charged with stopping ab terrorists. To stop them, Nick will have to demolish most of his beliefs about the world he lives in -- and maybe most of that world itself. The too-close-for-comfort possibilities of this near-future thriller will linger long after the last page. -- Description by Shauna Griffin.

Sala, Sharon

Forever my hero / Sharon Sala. Sourcebooks Casablanca, 2019 384 p. Blessings, Georgia

ISBN 9781492663539

1. Widows 2. Widowers 3. Hurricanes 4. Loss (Psychology) 5. Small town life 6. Storms 7. Neighbors 8. Small towns 9. Communities 10. Men/women relations 11. Georgia 12. Contemporary romances

Having both tragically lost their spouses, Dan Amos and Alice Conroy find their aversion to new love being swept away when a tropical storm brings them together.

Salinger, J. D. (Jerome David), 1919-2010

* The **catcher** in the rye / J. D. Salinger. Little, Brown and Company, 2001, c1951. 288 p.

ISBN 0316769533

1. Alienation in teenagers 2. Runaway teenagers 3. Sensitivity in teenagers 4. Sixteen-year-old boys 5. New York City 6. Psychological fiction 7. Modern classics 8. Coming-of-age stories

LC 00108915

First published in serial form in the USA, 1945-46 ; first published in book form in the USA, 1951.

Orginally published: 1951.

After leaving prep school Holden Caulfield spends three days on his own in New York City.

Salinger, J. D. (Jerome David), 1919-2010

* **Franny** and Zooey / J. D. Salinger Little, Brown, 1991, c1961. 202 p.

ISBN 9780316769495

1. Teenagers -- Religious life 2. Brothers and sisters 3. Compulsive behavior in women 4. Prayer 5. College seniors 6. Young women 7. Family relationships 8. Psychological fiction 9. Modern classics

Two stories, first published in the New Yorker, "about the Glass family of 20th century New York."

Two children of the Glass family appear in separate stories laid in twentieth-century New York.

Salinger, J. D. (Jerome David), 1919-2010

* **Nine** stories / J.D. Salinger. Little, Brown, 1991, c1953. 198 p.

ISBN 9780316769501

1. Loss (Psychology) 2. Interpersonal relations 3. Short stories

Originally published: Boston : Little, Brown and Co., 1953.

"DeDaumier-Smith's Blue Period," "Teddy," and "A Perfect Day for Bananafish" are among the nine works in a collection of Salinger's perceptive and realistic short stories.

Salinger, J. D. (Jerome David), 1919-2010

Raise high the roof beam, carpenters, and Seymour--an introduction. / J. D. Salinger. Little, Brown, 1963. 248 p.

ISBN 9780316769570

1. Jewish Americans 2. Brothers 3. Weddings 4. Psychological fiction

LC 63008969

The first of these two stories was originally published in the New Yorker in 1955. The second was originally published in 1959 in the same magazine.

Sallis, James, 1944-

Drive / James Sallis. Poisoned Pen Press, 2005. 158 p. Drive novels

ISBN 9781590581810

1. Automobile driving 2. Stunt performers 3. Betrayal 4. Criminals 5. Fugitives 6. Thieves 7. Stunt driving 8. Revenge in men 9. Loners 10. Los Angeles, California 11. Arizona 12. Noir fiction

LC 2005925325

The story of a man who works as a stunt driver by day and a getaway driver by night. He drives, that's all, until a heist goes sour and a contract is put on his head.

"Sallis gives us his most tightly written mystery to date, worthy of comparison to the compact, exciting oeuvre of French noir giant Jean-Patrick Manchette." Publishers Weekly.

Sallis, James, 1944-

* **Driven** / James Sallis. Poisoned Pen Press, 2012. 154 p. Drive novels

ISBN 9781464200106

1. Fiances -- Death 2. Revenge in men 3. Former criminals 4. Stunt performers 5. Thieves 6. Fugitives 7. Change (Psychology) 8. Automobile driving 9. Los Angeles, California 10. Arizona 11. Noir fiction

Driver thinks he has settled into a normal life, but after his fiancée is killed, he must confront his criminal past.

"The language is plain, the action is brutal, and the characters are memorably and briefly etched... This gritty, gristly tale will rivet Sallis's growing audience." Library Journal.

Sallis, James, 1944-

The **killer** is dying : a novel / James Sallis. Walker Pub. Co., 2011. 240 p.

ISBN 9780802779458

1. Assassins 2. Detectives 3. Abandoned teenagers 4. Women with terminal illnesses 5. Phoenix, Arizona 6. Arizona 7. Mysteries

LC 2010038548

A hired assassin searching for a rival killer, a burned-out detective with a terminally ill wife and an abandoned youth surviving by his wits follow inextricably linked paths toward community acceptance in the unforgiving sunlight and sprawl of Phoenix.

"Sallis takes his time weaving together the lives of these lost souls, each apparently as aimless as the bugs and birds they can't help noticing. The payoff is a moment of well-nigh miraculous consolation." Kirkus.

Sallis, James, 1944-

Others of my kind : a novel / James Sallis. Bloomsbury, 2013. 128 p.

ISBN 9781620402092

1. Captives 2. Crimes against girls 3. Post-traumatic stress disorder 4. Rehabilitation counseling 5. Memory 6. Near future 7. Thrillers and suspense

LC 2013012215

Agreeing to help a young woman who, like her many years before, has been abducted and traumatized, Jenny Rowan, a production editor for the local public TV station, finds long-buried memories coming to the surface, which sets in motion an unexpected chain of events in a world of political turmoil.

Sallis, James, 1944-

* **Sarah** Jane / James Sallis. Soho Crime, 2019. 216 p.

ISBN 9781641290807

1. Women sheriffs 2. Missing men 3. Rural life 4. Independence

in women 5. Small towns 6. Secrets 7. Former sheriffs 8. Abused women 9. Memories 10. Southwest (United States) 11. Rural noir 12. Psychological fiction

LC 2019016070

Sarah Jane Pullman is a good cop with a complicated past. Her life takes an unexpected turn when she is named the de facto sheriff of a rural town, investigating the mysterious disappearance of the sheriff whose shoes she's filling--and the even more mysterious realities of the life he was hiding from his own colleagues and closest friends.

Salter, James

All that is : a novel / James Salter. Alfred A. Knopf, 2013. 304 p.

ISBN 9781400043132

1. Editors 2. Men/women relations 3. Betrayal 4. World War II veterans 5. Book industry and trade 6. Literary fiction 7. Love stories

LC 2012020914

Returning to America after World War II, former naval officer Philip Bowman finds a position as a book editor and loses himself in a world of intimate connections and surprising triumphs until he is betrayed by the woman he loves, which sets him on a course he could never have imagined for himself.

Salter, James

Last night / James Salter. Knopf, 2005. 144 p.

ISBN 1400043123

1. Interpersonal relations 2. Men/women relations 3. Short stories

LC 2004057793

Ten short stories.

A compilation of short fiction explores the themes of love, honor, friendship, sacrifice, memory, and abandon through the lives of a translator assisting in his wife's suicide, a rare books collector, a profoundly lonely married woman, and other characters.

"All of the stories in Last Night are superb, but the title story is the tautest and most memorable. . . . This story about the consequences of adultery gives new meaning to the phrase the morning after. Despite its shocking plot twist, the story maintains the exacting, calm narrative voice that has distinguished all of Salter's work. His characters may be haunted by death and disappointment, but Salter never judges them, never even pretends to have them neatly pegged. He lets them stay elliptical, in shadow." New York Times Book Review.

Salvalaggio, Karin

Bone dust white / Karin Salvalaggio. Minotaur Books, 2014. 288 p. Macy Greeley novels

ISBN 9781250046185

1. Women detectives 2. Murder investigation 3. Cold cases (Criminal investigation) 4. Missing persons 5. Murder witnesses 6. Abandoned girls 7. Teenage girls 8. Families of murder victims 9. Pregnant women 10. Small towns -- Montana 11. Montana 12. Police procedurals 13. Mysteries

LC 2013050958

"Someone is knocking at the door to Grace Adams' house, and he won't stop. Grace thinks she knows who it is, but when she goes to her second floor window for a look she sees a woman she doesn't recognize. The woman isn't alone for long before a man emerges from the dark of the surrounding woods, stabs her, and leaves her for dead. Trying to help, Grace goes to the woman and is shocked to find that it's her mother Leanne--a woman who abandoned her 11 years before. There's nothing she can do, and Leanne is already past the point where she can tell Grace what happened all those years ago or why she came back now. While Grace was only a child when Leanne left her, Detective Macy Greeley has been waiting for Leanne ever since she disappeared from Collier,

MT. She's looking to close a case that has been haunting the town for far too long, but Collier is a hard-bitten place where the people are fierce when it comes to keeping their feuds between themselves and keeping secrets hidden in the past. Karin Salvalaggio's outstanding crime fiction debut Bone Dust White is an absolutely stunning work that signals the entrance of a major new talent."--, Provided by publisher.

Sanchez, Thomas

King Bongo : a novel of Havana / Thomas Sanchez. Alfred A. Knopf, 2003. 304 p.

ISBN 0679406964

1. 1950s 2. Insurance investigators 3. Brothers and sisters 4. Bombings 5. Nightclubs 6. New Year's Eve 7. Cuba -- History -- 1933-1959 8. Havana, Cuba 9. Historical fiction

LC 2002040770

Bongo finds his life as an insurance agent in 1957 Havana, Cuba in turmoil after a New Year's Eve bomb goes off in front of the Tropicana nightclub's center stage where his sister, the island's most famous showgirl, is performing.

"The byzantine plot is neatly constructed and thoroughly involving but never an end in itself. Sanchez shows us a city and a people on the eve of revolution but filters it all through the emotions of a conflicted hero, sympathetic to the cause but loyal only to himself and those he loves. Havana is both setting and soul in this pulsing bolero of a novel." Booklist.

Sand, George, 1804-1876

Marianne / George Sand ; edited and translated by Sian Miles. Carrol and Graf Publishers, 1988, c1987. 171 p..

ISBN 0881844152

1. 19th century 2. Young women -- Relations with older men 3. Matchmakers 4. Independence in women 5. Love triangles 6. Men/women relations 7. France 8. Translations -- French to English 9. Love stories

LC 88007308

"While very much a period piece, this last scrap of Sand's tremendous oeuvre is a charming bit of entertainment." Publishers Weekly.

Sanders, Dori, 1934-

Clover : a novel / Dori Sanders. Algonquin Books of Chapel Hill, 1990. 183 p.

ISBN 9780945575269

1. Interracial parenting 2. Ten-year-old girls -- South Carolina 3. African American girls -- South Carolina 4. Stepmothers -- South Carolina 5. South Carolina -- Race relations 6. South Carolina 7. African American fiction 8. Mainstream fiction

LC 89039072

After her father dies within hours of being married to a white woman, a ten-year-old black girl learns with her new mother to overcome grief and to adjust to a new place in their rural black South Carolina community.

"The author has staked out an impressive new territory here, replete with peach farmers, textile workers, drunks and crazy people, with the newly middle class as well as the terminally poor. As a specimen of the new realism in regional fiction, 'Clover' is very much the genuine item." New York Times Book Review.

Sanders, J. Aaron

Speakers of the dead / J. Aaron Sanders. Plume, 2016. 320 p.

ISBN 9780143128717

1. Whitman, Walt, 1819-1892 2. 1840s 3. Body snatching 4. Journalists 5. Murder investigation 6. Legislation 7. Murder suspects

8. Poets 9. Gay men 10. New York City -- History -- 19th century 11. Historical mysteries

LC 2015022268

Lambda Literary Award for Gay Mystery, 2017.

In 1843, reporter Walt Whitman, after his friend Lena is hanged for a murder she did not commit, vows to exonerate her with the help of his estranged boyfriend and they descend into a dangerous underworld of resurrection men.

Sanders, Lawrence, 1920-1998

* The **first** deadly sin / Lawrence Sanders. G.P. Putnam's Sons, 1973. 566 p. Edward X. Delaney mysteries

ISBN 9780399112287

1. Police 2. Serial murder investigation 3. Upper class 4. Secrets 5. Serial murders 6. Businesspeople 7. New York City 8. Mysteries 9. Psychological fiction

LC 73082018

Captain Ed Delaney of the New York City police is out to stop a well-dressed man from depopulating Manhattan's priciest neighborhoods with an ice pick, in an early thriller by the author of McNally's Gamble.

Sanders, Lawrence, 1920-1998

* The **fourth** deadly sin / Lawrence Sanders. G. P. Putnam's Sons, 1985. 313 p. Edward X. Delaney mysteries

ISBN 9780399130625

1. Psychiatric hospital patients 2. Murder suspects 3. Extramarital affairs 4. Deception 5. Violence 6. Psychiatrists 7. Former police 8. New York City 9. Psychological fiction 10. Mysteries

When saintly New York psychiatrist Simon Ellerbee is murdered, retired Chief of Detectives Edward X. Delaney pursues the murderer on a list of the doctor's six most potentially violent patients, obtained from his beautiful psychologist wife.

"Delaney displays that combination of computerlike efficiency and human touch that make him such an appealing detective. It's a masterly performance, not only chilling, but thought-provoking and often touching." Publishers Weekly.

Sanders, Lawrence, 1920-1998

McNally's dilemma / Lawrence Sanders and Vincent Lardo. G. P. Putnam's Sons, 1999. 309 p. Archy McNally mysteries

ISBN 0399144900

1. Private investigators 2. Extortion 3. Murder 4. Rich women 5. Husband killing 6. Palm Beach, Florida 7. Mysteries

LC 99-20988

McNally is hired to find out about thefts from the wealth Forsythe estate, and becomes involved in a family power struggle that can lead to death.

Sanders, Lawrence, 1920-1998

* **McNally's** gamble / Lawrence Sanders. G. P. Putnam's Sons, 1997. 307 p. Archy McNally mysteries

ISBN 0399142487

1. Greed 2. Widows 3. Lust 4. Murder 5. Private investigators 6. Faberge eggs 7. Rich families 8. Palm Beach, Florida 9. Mysteries

LC 9650369

When well-to-do widow Edythe Westmore is urged to buy a Faberge Imperial egg, her children oppose the investment and hire Archy McNally to stop the deal. Archy is thrust into a whirling vortex of greed, passion, and murder that even he must fight to rise above.

"A comic whodunit featuring Archy McNally, the foppish but likable head of 'discreet inquiries' at his father's law firm in Palm Beach, Fla. This time Archy's task is to investigate the credentials of a suspicious investment adviser, Frederick Clemens, and his secretary, Felix Katz. . .

. Mr. Sanders clearly delights in playing up the bumbling, spoof aspects of this detective yarn, especially during its climactic but unavoidably funny denouement." New York Times Book Review.

Sanders, Lawrence, 1920-1998

McNally's luck / Lawrence Sanders. G. P. Putnam's Sons, 1992. 319 p. Archy McNally mysteries

ISBN 9780399137624

1. Women psychics 2. Murder 3. Lust 4. Private investigators 5. Murder investigation 6. Greed 7. Violence against women 8. Palm Beach, Florida 9. Mysteries

LC 921394

It's hazy, hot and humid in the Palm Beach world of the rich and famous, but charming, sophisticated--and street-smart--investigator Archibald McNally keeps his cool, solving discreet cases for a select group of posh clients.

Sanders, Lawrence, 1920-1998

McNally's puzzle / Lawrence Sanders. G. P. Putnam's Sons, 1996. 311 p. Archy McNally mysteries

ISBN 9780399141355

1. Private investigators 2. Death threats 3. Heirs and heiresses 4. Father and adult child 5. Murder 6. Murder investigation 7. Kidnapping 8. Pet shop owners 9. Palm Beach, Florida 10. Mysteries

LC 96-5398

A pet store owner turns to McNally and Son for answers when he believes his life is in danger, but then he is murdered in his sleep and Archy McNally's manic depressive son is the prime suspect.

Sanders, Lawrence, 1920-1998

McNally's secret / Lawrence Sanders. G. P. Putnam's Sons, 1992. 317 p. Archy McNally mysteries

ISBN 9780399136757

1. Robbery 2. Extortion 3. Private investigators 4. Deception 5. Men/women relations 6. Murder 7. Stamp thefts 8. Robbery investigation 9. Palm Beach, Florida 10. Mysteries

LC 91009803

Beneath the glaring sun of Palm Beach--and behind the lowest crimes of high society--McNally is paid to keep family secrets in the closet.

"Four priceless U.S. airmail stamps issued in 1918 and known as 'inverted Jennies' have been stolen from a wealthy matron's mansion in Palm Beach. . . . McNally's task is to find the thief 'without the barest hint of scandal coming to light.' There are lots of suspects, a couple of deaths, and a fine romance." Booklist.

Sanders, Lawrence, 1920-1998

McNally's trial G.P. Putnam's Sons, 1995. 309 p. Archy McNally mysteries

ISBN 1568952082

1. Private investigators 2. Business -- Corrupt practices 3. Funeral homes 4. Deception 5. Rich families 6. Palm Beach, Florida 7. Mysteries

LC 95-5417

At the request of the nubile treasurer of a posh funeral home, Archy McNally and his partner, Binky Watrous, investigate suspicious goings-on and uncover family scandal, criminal conspiracy, business intrigue, and other sinister surprises.

"The novel boasts a delightful assembly of supporting characters, especially Archy's pal, the totally dissolute, utterly inept would-be detective Binky Watrous. A pleasant diversion." Booklist.

Sanders, Lawrence, 1920-1998

The **second** deadly sin / Lawrence Sanders. G. P. Putnam's Sons, 1977. 443 p. Edward X. Delaney mysteries

ISBN 9780399120237

1. Former police 2. Greed 3. Murder investigation 4. Murder 5. New York City 6. Mysteries 7. Psychological fiction

LC 77003652

Coming out of retirement to investigate the stabbing murder of acclaimed and hated artist Victor Maitland, ex-Chief of Detectives Edward X. Delaney is faced with a mob of greedy suspects and a tangle of possible motives.

Sanders, Lawrence, 1920-1998

The **sixth** commandment : a novel G. P. Putnam's Sons, 1978. 312 p.

ISBN 9780399123054

1. Cancer research 2. Scientists 3. Deception 4. Human experimentation in medicine 5. Small towns 6. Private investigators 7. Violence 8. Secrets 9. Extramarital affairs 10. Mysteries

LC 78013158

"This gloomy escapade about a hard-drinking, chain-smoking, world-pitying investigator . . . is brimful of juice and excitement, with some insight and much foolishnessa genuinely riveting diversion." The New Yorker.

Sanders, Lawrence, 1920-1998

The **tenth** commandment : a novel G. P. Putnam's Sons, 1980. 385 p.

ISBN 9780425050019

1. Revenge 2. Private investigators 3. Millionaires 4. Law firms 5. Suicide 6. Widows 7. Police 8. Swindlers and swindling 9. New York City 10. Mysteries

LC 80013002

Joshua Bigg, the very short chief investigator for a very offbeat law firm, finds that the link between one client's apparent suicide and the disappearance of another is a widow-loving lay minister.

Sanders, Lawrence, 1920-1998

* The **third** deadly sin / Lawrence Sanders. G. P. Putnam's Sons, 1981. 444 p. Edward X. Delaney mysteries

ISBN 9780399126147

1. Former police 2. Violence 3. Women murderers 4. Violence against men 5. Psychopaths 6. New York City 7. Psychological fiction 8. Mysteries

LC 80026325

The murders of out-of-town businessmen in large Manhattan hotels, by a bizarre, brilliant psychopath, hurls retired Chief of Detectives Edward X. Delaney into an elusive, horrifying, tragic manhunt.

Sanders, Lawrence, 1920-1998

The **Timothy** files G. P. Putnam's Sons, 1987. 380 p. Timothy Cone mysteries

ISBN 9780399132612

1. Private investigators 2. Violence 3. Stock market 4. Drug addiction 5. Vietnam veterans 6. Wall Street, New York City 7. New York City 8. Mysteries

LC 86025496

Timothy Cone, a detective who works for a firm that investigates companies with whom its clients are contemplating big business deals, becomes involved with three baffling cases.

Sanders, Lawrence, 1920-1998

Timothy's game / Lawrence Sanders. G. P. Putnam's Sons, 1988. 382 p. Timothy Cone mysteries

ISBN 9780399133688

1. Private investigators 2. Violence 3. Scandals 4. Stock market 5. Vietnam veterans 6. Wall Street, New York City 7. New York City 8. Mysteries

LC 87029073

Detective Timothy Cone wanders Wall Street seeking mobsters, murderers, and shady Market operators, in a quest to solve a baffling mystery.

"This novel is set on Wall Street, where clever detective Timothy Cone dresses in Salvation Army chic, chain-smokes Camels, and drinks too much. Cone has a cat named Cleo who eats ham hocks, potato salad, and garlic salami, and a girlfriend named Samantha who sports long, auburn hair. Throw in a foul-mouthed woman who owns a garbage-hauling firm controlled by the mob, an insider-trading leak, murder, and a tong war in Chinatown, and you have the usual brand of Sanders' readable fiction." Booklist.

Sandford, John, 1944 February 23-

Bloody genius / John Sandford. G. P. Putnam's Sons, 2019. 372 p. Virgil Flowers mysteries

ISBN 9780525536611

1. Campus murders 2. Culture wars 3. Scholars and academics 4. Murder investigation 5. Universities and colleges 6. Detectives 7. Murder 8. Minnesota 9. Police procedurals

When a culture war between rival departments at a local state university culminates in the death of a renowned scholar, Virgil Flowers struggles to identify a killer among a group of wildly passionate, diametrically opposed zealots.

Sandford, John, 1944 February 23-

Broken prey / John Sandford. G.P. Putnam's Sons, 2005. 400 p. Prey series

ISBN 0399152725

1. Detectives -- Minneapolis, Minnesota 2. Serial murder investigation 3. Deception 4. Serial murderers 5. Sex offenders 6. Serial murders 7. Imitation 8. Minnesota 9. Minneapolis, Minnesota 10. Thrillers and suspense 11. Police procedurals

LC 2005042981

After a series of killings that disturbingly emulate the works of a trio of inmates currently being held at the Minnesota Security Hospital, Lucas Davenport investigates a missing man who was released from the hospital weeks earlier.

"Lucas Davenport, a Minnesota State Bureau of Criminal Apprehension investigator, had lately been doing political fix-it jobs for the governor, but this time he's got a psychopathic serial killer on his hands. . . . The first victim, a young woman, was scourged with a wire whip; number two, a young man, had his penis cut off. Evidence first points to recently released sex offender Charlie Pope. Though Charlie is pretty dumb and the killer is extremely smart, it takes Davenport and his series partner, Detective Sloan, a while to realize they're chasing the wrong guy. Sandford introduces some lighter moments, the most entertaining about Davenport's new iPod and his quest to compile a list of the 100 best rock songs ever recorded, which every cop on the force gives him suggestions for. These moments allow readers to catch their breath amid the otherwise nonstop tension." Publishers Weekly.

Sandford, John, 1944 February 23-

Buried prey / John Sandford. G.P. Putnam's Sons, 2011. 390 p. Prey series

ISBN 9780399157387

1. Police 2. Detectives 3. Cold cases (Criminal investigation) 4.

Serial murders 5. Serial murder investigation 6. Minnesota 7. St Paul, Minnesota 8. Thrillers and suspense 9. Police procedurals

Investigating the discovery of two bodies in a house demolition, Lucas Davenport identifies the victims as two girls who disappeared in 1985, a cold case that overshadowed the early years of his career.

Sandford, John, 1944 February 23-

Certain prey / John Sandford. G. P. Putnam's Sons, 1999. 339 p. Prey series

ISBN 039914496X

1. Police -- Minneapolis, Minnesota 2. Women assassins -- Minneapolis, Minnesota 3. Women defense attorneys -- Minneapolis, Minnesota 4. Women serial murderers -- Minneapolis, Minnesota 5. Serial murders -- Minneapolis, Minnesota 6. Minnesota 7. Minneapolis, Minnesota 8. Thrillers and suspense 9. Police procedurals

LC 9919048

2011 TV movie also known as John Sandford's Certain prey.

Clara Rinker is the best hit woman in the business. She's been hired by an attorney in Minnesota who wants a rival eliminated. But the witness survives, the attorney starts acting strangely and a big cop named Lucas Davenport gets on her case. There are loose ends popping up everywhere and Lucas is in for the run of his life.

"Sandford keeps the level of suspense dizzyingly high as he shifts viewpoints between the women and Davenport." Booklist.

Sandford, John, 1944 February 23-

Chosen prey / John Sandford. G.P. Putnam's Sons, 2001. 416 p. Prey series

ISBN 0399147284

1. Art history teachers 2. Murder investigation -- Minneapolis, Minnesota 3. Police -- Minneapolis, Minnesota 4. Serial murderers -- Twin Cities metropolitan area 5. Serial murders -- Minneapolis, Minnesota 6. Obsession 7. Sex addiction in men 8. Fetishism (Sexuality) 9. Minnesota 10. Minneapolis, Minnesota 11. Thrillers and suspense 12. Police procedurals

LC 2001018594

Deputy Chief Lucas Davenport takes on a murder case involving an art history professor who is a suspect in a serial murder case involving the murder of women who have modeled for photographs.

Sandford, John, 1944 February 23-

* Deadline / John Sandford. G.P Putnam's Sons, 2014. 388 p. Virgil Flowers mysteries

ISBN 9780399162374

1. Government investigators -- Minnesota 2. Murder 3. Journalists 4. Detectives 5. Intelligence service 6. Minnesota 7. Police procedurals

In the aftermath of a school board's secret decision to have a local reporter murdered, Virgil Flowers' investigation of a sinister dognapping is interrupted by a suspicious death.

"Sanford's balances straight-talking Virgil Flowers often hilariously folksy tone and Trippton's dark core of methamphetamine manufacturers and sociopaths; the result is pure reading pleasure for thriller fans." Booklist.

Sandford, John, 1944 February 23-

Deep freeze / John Sandford. Penguin Group USA, 2017. 400 p. Virgil Flowers mysteries

ISBN 9780399176067

1. Teachers 2. Serial murderers 3. Girl murder victims 4. Murder investigation 5. Detectives 6. High schools 7. Minnesota 8. Police procedurals

When a woman, with connections to a high school class of twenty years ago, is found frozen in a block of ice, Virgil Floweres returns to Trippton, Minnesota to investigate, uncovering years of traumas, feuds, and bad blood.

Sandford, John, 1944 February 23-

Easy prey / John Sandford. G. P. Putnam's Sons, 2000. 407 p. Prey series

ISBN 039914613X

1. Police -- Minneapolis, Minnesota 2. Murder investigation -- Minneapolis, Minnesota 3. Fashion models 4. Murder 5. Murderers 6. Minnesota 7. Minneapolis, Minnesota 8. Thrillers and suspense 9. Police procedurals

LC 00023962

Police Chief Lucas Davenport hunts two separate murderers tied together by one victim, a model who was on the fast-track to superstardom at the time of her murder.

"Although Lucas makes his own strong fashion statement . . . his smooth professional moves are the best feature of his style. A shrewd gamester who made his personal fortune designing computer games, he follows sound police procedures and devises one intricate ploy after another to draw out the killers." New York Times Book Review.

Sandford, John, 1944 February 23-

Field of prey / John Sandford. G. P. Putnam's Sons, 2014. 416 p. Prey series

ISBN 9780399162381

1. Serial murder investigation 2. Serial murders 3. Detectives 4. Murder investigation 5. Minnesota 6. St Paul, Minnesota 7. Thrillers and suspense 8. Police procedurals

LC 2014006595

Lucas Davenport investigates the discovery of several bodies in an abandoned Minnesota farmyard, discovering the work of a local serial killer who has been murdering one victim every summer for years.

Sandford, John, 1944 February 23-

* Golden prey / John Sandford. Penguin Group USA, 2017. 416 p. Prey series

ISBN 9780399184574

1. Gangs 2. Robbery investigation 3. United States marshals 4. Robbery 5. Drug cartels 6. Murder investigation 7. North Dakota 8. Thrillers and suspense 9. Police procedurals

A series of audacious robberies compels newly appointed U.S. marshal Lucas Davenport to investigate the possible return of a gang leader who once killed two FBI agents.

"Sandfords trademark blend of rough humor and deadly action keeps the pages turning until the smile-inducing wrap-up, which reveals the fates of a number of his quirky, memorable characters." Publishers Weekly.

Sandford, John, 1944 February 23-

Heat lightning / John Sandford. G.P. Putnam's Sons, 2008. 384 p. Virgil Flowers mysteries

ISBN 9780399155277

1. Vietnam War, 1961-1975 2. Serial murders 3. Murder investigation 4. Murder 5. Detectives 6. Intelligence service 7. Minnesota 8. Police procedurals

LC 2008028339

Sequel to: Dark of the moon.

Sequel: Rough country.

Summoned by Lucas Davenport to investigate a pair of murders in which the victims are found with lemons in their mouths, Minnesota

Bureau of Criminal Apprehension investigator Virgil Flowers struggles to find a connection that could prevent additional killings.

Sandford, John, 1944 February 23-

Hidden prey / John Sandford. G. P. Putnam's Sons, 2004. 400 p. Prey series

ISBN 039915180X

1. Detectives -- Minneapolis, Minnesota 2. Russians in the United States 3. Murder investigation 4. Murder 5. Murderers 6. Minnesota 7. Minneapolis, Minnesota 8. Lake Superior region 9. Thrillers and suspense 10. Police procedurals

LC 2004044351

"Readers will be pleased with this relaxed version of the moody Minneapolis investigator. In past novels, the womanizing Davenport would have romanced the good-looking Russian lady, but the new Davenport is content to play the part of friend and protector and go back to his cozy family with an unstained and remarkably contented soul." Publishers Weekly.

Sandford, John, 1944 February 23-

Holy ghost / John Sandford. Putnam Pub Group, 2018. 400 p. Virgil Flowers mysteries

ISBN 9780735217324

1. Apparitions 2. Mayors 3. Fraud 4. Tourists 5. Murder 6. Murder investigation 7. Shrines 8. Detectives 9. Money 10. Small town life 11. Minnesota 12. Police procedurals

A mayor's half-baked scheme to revive a floundering Minnesota community by turning it into a religious shrine is thrown into chaos by the discovery of a body.

Sandford, John, 1944 February 23-

* Invisible prey / John Sandford. G. P. Putnam's Sons, 2007. 384 p. Prey series

ISBN 0399154213

1. Senior murder victims 2. Sex crimes 3. Murder investigation 4. Crimes against seniors 5. Murder 6. Senior women 7. Clues 8. Detectives -- Minneapolis, Minnesota 9. Minnesota 10. Minneapolis, Minnesota 11. Thrillers and suspense 12. Police procedurals

Investigating the seemingly open-and-shut double homicide case involving a pair of wealthy elderly women, Lucas Davenport begins to suspect that the handful of small items that were stolen from the crime scene may have had more significant values.

Sandford, John, 1944 February 23-

Mad River / John Sandford. G.P. Putnam's Sons, 2012. 400 p. Virgil Flowers mysteries

ISBN 9780399157707

1. Government investigators -- Minnesota 2. Teenage murderers 3. Mass murder 4. Murder investigation -- Minnesota 5. Detectives 6. Intelligence service 7. Minnesota 8. Police procedurals

LC 2012025454

When three teenagers with dead-end prospects begin a killing and robbery spree through rural Minnesota, Bureau of Criminal Apprehension investigator Virgil Flowers joins a growing number of cops trying to stop them.

Sandford, John, 1944 February 23-

* Mind prey / John Sandford. G.P. Putnam's Sons, 1995. 323 p. Prey series

ISBN 9780399140099

1. Women psychiatrists 2. Psychopaths 3. Women kidnapping victims 4. Mothers and daughters 5. Minnesota 6. Minneapolis,

Minnesota 7. Thrillers and suspense 8. Police procedurals

LC 95003790

1999 TV movie also known as John Sandford's Mind prey.

Lucas Davenport is back on a case involving a therapist who's been kidnapped by a former patient. The kidnapper has also taken the therapist's two young daughters. Deeply ill, he acts out his violent sexual fantasies on the therapist first and is about to go after the daughters so Davenport must figure out the clues to the kidnapper's identity.

"Sandford expertly ratchets up the suspense from beginning to the brutal finish." Publishers Weekly.

Sandford, John, 1944 February 23-

Mortal prey / John Sandford. G. P. Putnam's Sons, 2002. 368 p. Prey series

ISBN 0399148639

1. Police -- Minneapolis, Minnesota 2. Murder investigation 3. Women assassins 4. Revenge 5. Drug lords 6. Murder 7. Minnesota 8. Minneapolis, Minnesota 9. Thrillers and suspense 10. Police procedurals

Lucas Davenport and Clara Rinker, a hitwoman are tangled together again. It seems the hitwoman is the target of a hit and vows vengeance against a Mexican drug lord who murders her boyfriend and her unborn child. Davenport is supposed to find Rinker before she kills again.

Sandford, John, 1944 February 23-

* Naked prey / John Sandford. G.P. Putnam's Sons, 2003. 352 p. Prey series

ISBN 0399150439

1. Police 2. Murder investigation 3. Lynching 4. Murder 5. Murderers 6. Detectives -- Minneapolis, Minnesota 7. Race relations 8. Marriage 9. New fathers 10. Minnesota 11. Minneapolis, Minnesota 12. Thrillers and suspense 13. Police procedurals

LC 2003041364

Moving with his boss to state-level cases, Lucas Davenport, having recently become the head of a family, investigates the hanging deaths of an African American man and a white woman, a case that proves more complicated than it appears.

"Lucas Davenport is now Director of Regional Studies in the Minnesota Bureau of Criminal Apprehension, which is a fancy name for the job of investigating difficult crimes as quickly as possible and answering to the governor of the state. Known for his ability to solve the unsolvable, he goes to a remote area of the state to discover why a black man and a white woman were hanged in a groove of trees. . . . Fast paced and full of surprises, this may be Sandford's best novel yet." Library Journal.

Sandford, John, 1944 February 23-

* Night prey / John Sandford. G.P. Putnam's Sons, 1994. 336 p. Prey series

ISBN 0399139141

1. Women police chiefs -- Minneapolis, Minnesota 2. Murder investigation 3. Murder 4. Murderers 5. Police 6. Minnesota 7. Carlos Avery State Wildlife Management Area, Minnesota 8. Thrillers and suspense 9. Police procedurals

LC 9407564

Lucas Davenport is asked by a female game warden to investigate a mysterious murder in a Minnesota wildlife refuge, in a case that leads to a confrontation with a skillful and elusive killer

"Despite its length, Night Prey is a tight, fast-moving thriller with appealing good guys and a suitably evil villain. Especially fascinating among the characters is Policewoman Connell." Library Journal.

Sandford, John, 1944 February 23-

* **Phantom** prey / John Sandford. G. P. Putnam's Sons, 2008. 384 p. Prey series

ISBN 9780399155000

1. Goth culture (Subculture) 2. Murder investigation 3. Missing persons investigation 4. Detectives -- Minneapolis, Minnesota 5. Heirs and heiresses 6. Missing persons 7. Goths 8. Murder 9. Minnesota 10. Minneapolis, Minnesota 11. Thrillers and suspense 12. Police procedurals

Convinced a missing heiress is dead, Lucas Davenport searches for her body. His hunt connects him to the Twin Cities' Goth community, a group of young people fascinated by death and darkness. The deeper he digs, the closer he gets to the killer.

Sandford, John, 1944 February 23-

* **Rules** of prey / John Sanford. G. P. Putnam's Sons, 1989. 317 p. Prey series

ISBN 9780399134654

1. Serial murder investigation 2. Serial murderers -- Twin Cities metropolitan area 3. Crimes against women 4. Lawyers 5. Police -- Minneapolis, Minnesota 6. Murder 7. Murder investigation 8. Detectives 9. Minnesota 10. Twin Cities metropolitan area 11. Thrillers and suspense 12. Police procedurals

LC 89004040

Lieutenant Lucas Davenport is determined to track down a diabolically clever serial killer who leads a double life, carefully picks out his female victims, and taunts the police with notes signed "Maddog."

"A killer who calls himself the 'maddog' has been murdering Minneapolis women, seemingly without pattern or motive. The crimes are linked only by their brutality and by the slayer's 'signature': at each scene, he leaves a written rule of crime, such as 'Never kill anyone you know,' or, 'Never carry a weapon after it has been used.' Into the case comes Lucas Davenport, a policeman with five kills in the line of duty, a surefire sense of how to handle the thirsty media and strong instincts about the killer's psyche." Publishers Weekly.

Sandford, John, 1944 February 23-

Shock wave / John Sandford. G.P. Putnam's Sons, 2011. 400 p. Virgil Flowers mysteries

ISBN 9780399157691

1. Government investigators 2. Bombing 3. Building 4. Small town life 5. Real estate development 6. Minnesota 7. Police procedurals

LC 2011027848

When protests about a superstore chain's plans to build a location in a Minnesota river town escalate into bombing attacks at the construction site and the company's headquarters, Virgil Flowers races against time to find and stop the bomber.

"Virgil Flowers is a pretty mellow guy. If he isn't casting off in some quiet trout stream, John Sandford's Minnesota crimestopper might be found behind Bob's Bad Boy Barbeque & Bar, watching some well-nourished farm girls playing a cutthroat game of beach volleyball. But when Virgil's troubleshooting skills are called for, as they are . . . when a bomb-maker initiates a wave of industrial terrorism against the small-town incursions of a big-box chain store, he can move as fast as the next action hero. For someone who casually saunters onto a crime scene in a pink T-shirt, jeans and cowboy boots, Virgil can think on his feet, a valuable asset when the bomber steps up his deadly campaign against Willard Pye's PyeMart empire, which threatens to destroy the small-town character of Butternut Falls." New York Times Book Review.

Sandford, John, 1944 February 23-

* **Silent** prey / John Sandford. G. P. Putnam's Sons, 1992. 320 p. Prey series

ISBN 9780399137426

1. Serial murderers 2. Serial murder investigation 3. Vigilantes 4. Murder 5. New York City 6. Thrillers and suspense 7. Police procedurals

LC 91043696

A brilliant but insane pathologist flees to New York to continue his research on death, and the police call on Lucas Davenport, who merges his investigative talents with an old flame to put an end to the madness.

"Mad pathologist Bekker's face is battered and broken after his encounter with unorthodox Minneapolis cop Lucas Davenport in Eyes of Prey. Now Bekker's on the loose again, having escaped during his trial and landed in New York City. Even more nutso than ever, he's determined to exact revenge on Lucas and to continue his evil experiments, in which he searches the eyes of his victims in the few, pain-creased seconds before death." Booklist.

Sandford, John, 1944 February 23-

* **Silken** prey / John Sandford. G.P. Putnam's Sons, 2013. 406 p. Prey series

ISBN 9780399159312

1. Political corruption 2. Political campaigns 3. Extortion 4. Heirs and heiresses 5. Police 6. Campaigning 7. Murder investigation 8. Detectives 9. Minnesota 10. St Paul, Minnesota 11. Thrillers and suspense 12. Police procedurals

Investigating the murder of a political fixer who had blackmailed his ambitious heiress employer during a vicious smear campaign, Lucas Davenport follows disturbing leads to the Minneapolis police department and a ruthless woman who threatens his life.

Sandford, John, 1944 February 23-

Storm Front / John Sandford. G. P. Putnam's Sons, 2013 400 p. Virgil Flowers mysteries

ISBN 9780399159305

1. Government investigators -- Minnesota 2. Relics 3. Thieves 4. Detectives 5. Intelligence service 6. Minnesota 7. Police procedurals

LC 2013024514

Approached by an Israeli police officer who is tailing a man in possession of a stolen relic, Virgil Flowers learns that the artifact reveals details about the biblical King Solomon and that rivals are killing everyone who would protect it.

Sandford, John, 1944 February 23-

* **Storm** prey / John Sandford. G. P. Putnam's Sons, 2010. 408 p. Prey series

ISBN 9780399156496

1. Detectives 2. Robbery -- Minnesota 3. Women witnesses 4. Robbery investigation 5. Criminals 6. Police 7. Minnesota 8. St Paul, Minnesota 9. Thrillers and suspense 10. Police procedurals

Witnessing a robbery gone wrong that has caused the death of a pharmacy employee, Lucas Davenport's surgeon wife, Weather Karkinnen, is targeted by the thieves when they become fearful that she can identify them.

Sandford, John, 1944 February 23-

Sudden prey / John Sandford. G. P. Putnam's, 1996. 360 p. Prey series

ISBN 0399141383

1. Police -- Minneapolis, Minnesota 2. Revenge -- Minneapolis, Minnesota 3. Death 4. Minnesota 5. Minneapolis, Minnesota 6.

Thrillers and suspense 7. Police procedurals

Lucas Davenport and his men have been tracking a dangerous woman bank robber. When they finally catch her, she does not go quietly and they are forced to kill her. Now her ex-husband swears revenge: he will find out who's responsible for her death and kill those near and dear to them.

"This Lucas Davenport adventure opens with the Candy LaChaise gang's robbery of a Minnesota credit union. When Candy is ambushed and killed by Davenport and his men, Candy's husband, Dick LaChaise, swears vengeance on the spouses and families of all officers involved. A series of attacks ensue in which spouses are killed at work. With the lives of Davenport's own daughter and his fiance threatened, he quickly metamorphoses into a hunting machine himself." Library Journal.

Sandford, John, 1944 February 23-
* **Winter** prey / John Sandford. G. P. Putnam's Sons, 1993. 338 p. Prey series
ISBN 9780399138157
1. Psychopaths 2. Serial murderers 3. Serial murder investigation 4. Former police 5. Winter 6. Small towns 7. Wisconsin 8. Thrillers and suspense 9. Police procedurals
LC 92042072
Twin Cities detective Lucas Davenport faces his most determined foe yet, the savage serial killer called Iceman.

"Davenport, a cool, cynical man of action, is entirely in his element in this harsh terrain--so bitter that it turns animals against men, so brutal that it turns men into beasts." New York Times Book Review.

Sandlin, Lisa
The **bird** boys : a Delpha Wade and Tom Phelan mystery / Lisa Sandlin. Cinco Puntos Press, 2019. 306 p. Delpha Wade and Tom Phelan novels
ISBN 9781947627130
1. 1970s 2. Women former convicts 3. Private investigators 4. Personal assistants 5. Missing men 6. Brothers 7. Deception 8. Investigations 9. Texas 10. Beaumont, Texas 11. Hardboiled fiction
LC 2018049003
Sequel to: The Do-Right
Finds Delpha questioned for her attack on the man who nearly killed her; while her boss, neophyte private detective Tom, tries to determine which of two brothers is a murderer.

Sankaran, Lavanya
The **hope** factory : a novel / Lavanya Sankaran. Dial Press, 2013. 384 p.
ISBN 9780385338196
1. Factories 2. Social classes 3. Industrialists 4. Teenage boys 5. Land acquisition 6. Household employees 7. Political corruption 8. Family relationships 9. Generation gap 10. Bangalore, India 11. India 12. Political fiction
LC 2012023483
Anand, the proud owner of a small factory, finds his future uncertain when it collides with urban forces out of his control and a woman named Kamala who is determined to make a better life for her son.

Sansom, C. J.
* **Lamentation** / C.J. Sansom. Mullholland, 2015. 592 p. Matthew Shardlake novels
ISBN 9780316254960
1. Tudor period (1485-1603) 2. 16th century 3. Political corruption 4. Manuscripts 5. Lost articles 6. Criminal investigation 7. Rulers 8. Inheritance and succession 9. Secrets 10. Lawyers 11. Great Britain -- History -- Henry VIII, 1509-1547 12. Historical mysteries 13.

Mysteries
First published: [London] : Mantle, 2014.
While King Henry VIII lies on his deathbed, Queen Catherine Parr searches for the person who murdered the London printer who had her shocking, confessional memoir.

Sansom, C. J.
Revelation / C.J. Sansom. Macmillan, 2008. 549 p. Matthew Shardlake novels
ISBN 9781405092722
1. Tudor period (1485-1603) 2. 16th century 3. Religious fanatics 4. Serial murderers 5. Lawyers 6. Friends' death 7. Men with disfigurements 8. Great Britain -- History -- Henry VIII, 1509-1547 9. Historical mysteries 10. Mysteries
LC 2008411769
Defending a young religious zealot who is being held in the infamous Bedlam hospital for the insane, Matthew Shardlake investigates a series of murders with disturbing ties to Lady Catherine Parr, a reform sympathizer and future wife of Henry VIII.

Sansom, C. J.
* **Sovereign** / C.J. Sansom. Viking, 2007. 592 p. Matthew Shardlake novels
ISBN 0670038318
1. Henry VIII,, King of England, 1491-1547 2. Tudor period (1485-1603) 3. 16th century 4. Conspiracies 5. Nobility 6. Rulers 7. Murder 8. Men with disfigurements 9. Lawyers 10. Murder investigation 11. Great Britain -- History -- Henry VIII, 1509-1547 12. Historical mysteries 13. Mysteries
LC 2006048686
First published: [London] : Macmillan, 2006.
When Henry VIII sets out to quell rebellion in the north and transport a dangerous conspirator back to London for questioning, lawyer Matthew Shardlake finds himself investigating the murder of a local glazier with unsettling ties to the royal family.

"The skill with which C.J. Sansom is able to conjure up the sights, smells, and sounds of Tudor England is unrivalled." Birmingham Post

Sansom, C. J.
Tombland / C.J. Sansom. Mulholland Books, 2019, c2018. 866 p. Matthew Shardlake novels
ISBN 9780316412421
1. Edward VI,, King of England, 1537-1553 2. Elizabeth I,, Queen of England, 1533-1603 3. Tudor period (1485-1603) 4. 16th century 5. Lawyers 6. Political intrigue 7. Murder 8. Kett's Rebellion, England, 1549 9. Murder investigation 10. Rulers 11. Inheritance and succession 12. Secrets 13. Great Britain -- History -- Edward VI, 1547-1553 14. Great Britain -- History -- Tudors, 1485-1603 15. Historical mysteries 16. Mysteries
Originally published: London : Mantle, 2018.
When a distant relative of Princess Elizabeth is found dead, Matthew Shardlake is sent to investigate the murder, which may have connections reaching to a peasant rebellion sweeping the country.

Sansom, Ian
The **case** of the missing books / Ian Sansom. Harper Paperbacks, 2007, c2006. 352 p. Mobile library mysteries
ISBN 0060822503
1. Book thefts 2. Misadventures 3. Small town life -- Ireland 4. Librarians 5. Amateur detectives 6. Bookmobiles 7. Traveling libraries 8. Northern Ireland 9. Mysteries
Originally published in the UK in 2006

Israel Armstrong, a new Emerald Isle bookmobile attendant, discovers that the roving library's 15,000 books have disappeared and that he cannot resign from his job until he finds them.

"This title launches a new series set in Tumdrum, Northern Ireland, the small village that transplanted Londoner Israel Armstrong reluctantly makes his home. The nebbishy Jewish vegetarian shows up at the Tumdrum and District Public Library eager to assume his post as the new librarian, only to find the place boarded up and that it's his job to steward the beat-up mobile library instead. When he finally gets inside the library building, he discovers its 15,000 books are missing. Less astute than the detective characters in the novels he has devoured, Israel blunders through an investigation, making startling discoveries while suffering some hard knocks along the way." Publishers Weekly.

Santiago, Danny, 1911-1988

Famous all over town / Danny Santiago. Plume, 1984, c1983. 284 p.

ISBN 9780671432492

1. Mexican American boys 2. Mexican American families 3. Values 4. Street life 5. Los Angeles, California 6. Urban fiction

LC 83-22020

Originally published: New York : Simon & Schuster, c1983.

A fourteen-year-old Mexican American boy struggles to resolve the conflict between the traditional values of his family and life on the streets of Los Angeles.

Santiago, Esmeralda

Conquistadora : a novel / Esmeralda Santiago. Alfred A. Knopf, 2011. 416 p.

ISBN 9780307268327

1. 19th century 2. Plantation life 3. Independence in women 4. Love triangles 5. Twin brothers 6. Slavery 7. Determination in women 8. Ambition in women 9. Women plantation owners 10. Sugar plantations 11. Spaniards in Puerto Rico 12. Puerto Rico -- History -- 19th century 13. Historical fiction

LC 2010051324

Drawn to the exotic island of Puerto Rico by the diaries of an ancestor who traveled there with Ponce de León, Ana Cubillas becomes involved with enamored twin brothers Ramón and Inocente before convincing them to claim a sugar plantation they have inherited.

"The book's greatest strength lies in its dissection of the systematic enslavement and oppression of people without which the large-scale planting, harvesting, processing, and transporting of sugar was impossible. Santiago's language is most animated in her depiction of slavery. . . . In Ana, Santiago creates a woman consciously at odds with her culture, chafing at her own oppression, and reluctant but willing to oppress others in order to achieve her own freedom. Though the plot of Conquistadora is thin and the characterizations are flat, in Ana's uneasy rationalization of the brutal, unsustainable system on which these dreams depend, Santiago fleetingly achieves the hallmark of great historical fiction she makes her protagonist a woman of her times." Boston Globe.

Santopolo, Jill

More than words / Jill Santopolo. G. P. Putnam's Sons, 2019 336 p.

ISBN 9780735218307

1. Fathers and daughters 2. Family secrets 3. Self-fulfillment in women 4. Fathers -- Death 5. Hotel owners 6. Grief in women 7. Loss (Psychology) 8. Heirs and heiresses 9. Rich women 10. Couples 11. Men/women relations 12. New York City 13. Mainstream fiction

LC 2018041586

A woman mourning the death of her hotel owner father and reeling from an astounding secret finds herself caught between the world of her longtime boyfriend and her passionate boss.

Santora, Nick, 1970-

Fifteen digits / Nick Santora. Mulholland Books / Little, Brown and Company, 2012. 288 p.

ISBN 9780316176316

1. Law firms 2. Blue collar workers 3. White collar crime 4. Legal documents 5. Bank accounts 6. Corruption 7. Greed 8. Trust 9. New York City 10. Crime fiction

LC 2011038283

A 15-digit bank account number holds the key to a plot involving five behind-the-scenes employees at a white shoe law firm who use discarded documents full of sensitive legal information to get rich.

Sapphire, 1950-

American dreams / Sapphire. Vintage Books, 1996, c1994. 177 p.

ISBN 9780679767992

1. City life 2. Violence 3. Street life 4. African American lesbians 5. Dysfunctional families 6. Race relations 7. African American fiction 8. African American poetry 9. Poetry

Originally published: New York : High Risk Books/Serpent's Tail, 1994.

A collection of poetry and prose pieces captures an angry teenager who goes "wilding" in Central Park, a young African American girl gunned down by a Korean storeowner, a sexually abused child, and the power of art to bear witness and heal its creators.

Sapphire, 1950-

* The **kid** : a novel / Sapphire. Penguin Press, 2011. 384 p.

ISBN 9781594203046

1. African American boys -- Identity 2. Orphans 3. Sexually abused boys 4. Dancing 5. Mothers -- Death 6. Masculinity 7. African Americans 8. Child abusers 9. Harlem, New York City 10. New York City 11. African American fiction 12. Coming-of-age stories

LC 2011001739

Sequel to: Push

After his mother dies when he is nine years old, Abdul Jones finds his way toward adulthood by overcoming the legacy of physical and sexual abuse he carries with him from his time in a foster home and at a boys' Catholic school.

Sapphire, 1950-

* **Push** : a novel / Sapphire. A.A. Knopf, 1996. 141 p.

ISBN 0679446265

1. 1980s 2. Sixteen-year-old girls 3. Incest 4. Teacher-student relationships 5. Teenage mothers 6. African Americans 7. African American teenage mothers 8. Child abusers 9. Child abuse victims 10. Illiterate women 11. Overweight teenagers 12. Street life 13. Redemption 14. New York City 15. African American fiction 16. Urban fiction

LC 9616516

This novel was made into film called Precious: based on the novel Push by Sapphire in 2009, starring Gabourey Sidibe, Mo'Nique, Paula Patton, and Mariah Carey and directed by Lee Daniels.

Includes unpaged section "Life stories".

Sequel: The kid

BCALA Literary Award for First Novelist, 1997.

A courageous and determined young teacher opens up a new world of hope and redemption for sixteen-year-old Precious Jones, an abused young African American girl living in Harlem who was raped and left pregnant for the second time by her father.

Saramago, Jose

All the names / Jose Saramago ; translated from the Portuguese by Margaret Jull Costa. Harcourt, 1999. 238 p.

ISBN 9780151004218

1. Obsession in men 2. Loneliness 3. Office workers 4. Birth and death records 5. Vital statistics 6. Portugal 7. Lisbon, Portugal 8. Translations -- Portuguese to English 9. Literary fiction

When a clerk in the Central Registry discovers a stray unfiled birth certificate, he decides to investigate the identity of the woman--the first step in an obsession that will lead him to her.

Saramago, Jose

* **Blindness** / Jose Saramago ; translated from the Portuguese by Giovanni Pontiero. Harcourt Brace, 1997, c1995. 294 p.

ISBN 0151002517

1. People who are blind 2. Epidemics 3. Survival 4. Loss (Psychology) 5. Disorientation 6. Dystopias 7. Translations -- Portuguese to English 8. Literary fiction 9. Modern classics 10. Modern classics Translation of: Ensaio sobre a cegueira (1995).

A city is hit by an epidemic of "white blindness" whose victims are confined to a vacant mental hospital, while a single eyewitness to the nightmare guides seven oddly assorted strangers through the barren urban landscape.

"A man waiting in his car for a red light to turn green is the first of an entire city's population--with one exception--to be blinded by a 'milky sea' of dazzling whiteness. The inexplicably disabled victims grope and stumble their way through nightmarish landscapes: first an asylum where those initially afflicted are quarantined, and then the chaotic, squalid streets to which they return. Saramago's surreal allegory explores the ability of the human spirit to prevail in even the most absurdly unjust of conditions, yet he reinvents this familiar struggle with the stylistic eccentricity of a master." The New Yorker.

Saramago, Jose

Cain / Jose Saramago ; translated from the Portuguese by Margaret Jull Costa. Houghton Mifflin Harcourt, 2011, c2009. 208 p.

ISBN 9780547419893

1. Cain, (Biblical figure) 2. Bible. Old Testament History of Biblical events 3. God 4. Fugitives 5. Murderers 6. Voyages and travels 7. Brothers 8. Literary fiction 9. Bible novels 10. Translations -- Portuguese to English

LC 2011028600

First published in 2009 by Editorial Caminho, Lisbon. This translation originally published: London: Harvill Secker, 2011.

In a reimagining of the Old Testament, Cain, condemned to wander forever for murdering his brother, journeys through time and space to witness key biblical events that impress upon him the unjust nature of God's edicts.

"This is the author's final novel, but the story it tells is among the world's first. In this version of several biblical tales, characters lose their initial capitals, and readers follow the adventures and misadventures of adam and eve, cain and abel, lilith and joshua and job--plus those of the lord, also known as god--with new eyes. Typographical diminution is the first of many wonderful acts of estrangement. Like a postmodern Creator of sorts, Saramago crafts a new world by recycling a series

of well-known episodes and interpreting them from the viewpoint of a common reader." San Francisco Chronicle.

Saramago, Jose

* The **cave** / Jose Saramago; translated from the Portuguese by Margaret Jull Costa. Harcourt, 2002. 320 p.

ISBN 0151004145

1. Senior men 2. Potters 3. Extinction (Biology) 4. Septuagenarians 5. Translations -- Portuguese to English 6. Literary fiction

LC 2002002355

English translation of: La Caverna.
ALA Notable Book, 2004.

Informed that his clay pots and jugs are no longer needed, elderly potter Cipriano applies his craft to the making of ceramic dolls, but his family's subsequent successes are compromised by a terrible discovery.

"As a further warning against the urge to seek safety on common gound--moving to the center, as it were--the writer highlights the menaces of cliche by parodying the worldly-wise narrative interventions of an earlier era. . . . Such deft manipulations in Saramago's style are brilliantly rendered in Margaret Jull Costa's agile English version of his Portuguese." New York Times Book Review.

Saramago, Jose

Death with interruptions / Jose Saramago ; translated from the Portuguese by Margaret Jull Costa. Harcourt, 2008. 256 p.

ISBN 9780151012749

1. Death 2. Immortality 3. Romantic love 4. Love 5. Philosophy 6. People with terminal illnesses 7. Chaos 8. Psychological fiction 9. Translations -- Portuguese to English 10. Satirical fiction 11. Literary fiction

LC 2008010088

While Death sits in her apartment wondering what would happen if she became human and fell in love, no one dies, raising concerns among politicians, religious leaders, doctors, morticians, and others as they confront the harsh realities of eternal life.

"Starting at the stroke of midnight on New Year's, in an unidentified country in an undetermined year, in Jose Saramago's new novel, death goes on strike. Nobody dies from illness or suicide or, Mr. Saramago writes, from a car accident, so frequent on festive occasions, when blithe irresponsibility and an excess of alcohol jockey for position on the roads to decide who will reach death first. Thus the Saramago sentence: conversational but a conversation with oneself; portentous yet ludicrous, like a solemn address delivered by someone who has forgotten to wear pants. Thus too the Saramago plot: an impossible event like universal blindness, or Portugal's history altered because of a proofreader's error in a history book. Or, as here, death feeling unappreciated and refusing to oblige. . . . Mr. Saramago, one of the last of the old-line Communists, has written an atheist's religious parable; a story abounding in sentiment and purged of it." New York Times.

Saramago, Jose

* The **Elephant's** journey / Jose Saramago ; translated from the Portuguese by Margaret Jull Costa. Houghton Mifflin Harcourt, 2010, c2008. 288 p.

ISBN 9780547352589

1. 16th century 2. Elephants 3. Wedding presents 4. Voyages and travels 5. Friendship 6. Adventure 7. Historical fiction 8. Translations -- Portuguese to English

"First published with the title A Viagem do Elefante in 2008 by Editorial Caminho, SA, Lisbon"--T.p. verso.

A tale inspired by a true story follows the adventures of a neglected elephant who is given by King Joao of Portugal to Archduke Maximilian as a wedding gift and who travels with the archduke through the war-torn storied cities of 16th-century Europe.

"[This] is a tale rich in irony and empathy, regularly interrupted by witty reflections on human nature and arch commentary on the powerful who insult human dignity." Los Angeles Times.

Saramago, Jose

The **history** of the siege of Lisbon / Jose Saramago ; translated by Giovanni Pontiero. Harcourt Brace, 1996. 314 p.

ISBN 015100238X

1. Proofreading 2. Single men 3. Men/women relations 4. Authors 5. Writing 6. Imagination in men 7. Lisbon, Portugal -- History 8. Translations -- Portuguese to English 9. Literary fiction

LC 96-46826

An editor at a Portuguese publishing house, Raimundo Silva, undertakes to rewrite a crucial episode in Portuguese history as a romantic saga, with the amorous encouragement of his supervisor.

"Although the novel's stream-of-consciousness technique, baroque prose and paragraphs that run on for pages may daunt some readers, this hypnotic tale is a great comic romp through history, language and the imagination." Publishers Weekly.

Saramago, Jose

The **manual** of painting and calligraphy / Jose Saramago ; translated from the Portuguese by Giovanni Pontiero. Mariner Books, 2012, c1994. 224 p.

ISBN 9780547640228

1. Artists 2. Creativity in men 3. Self-discovery in men 4. Political prisoners 5. Totalitarianism -- Psychological aspects 6. Portrait painters 7. Portugal 8. Political fiction 9. Literary fiction 10. Translations -- Portuguese to English

Translation first published: Manchester : Carcanet Press, 1994.

In the last years of Salazar's dictatorship, a struggling young artist is commissioned to paint the portrait of a wealthy client and struggles to capture his likeness while acknowleging his artistic limitations.

Sargent, Colin, 1954-

Museum of human beings / Colin Sargent. McBooks Press, 2008. 352 p.

ISBN 9781590131671

1. Charbonneau, Jean-Baptiste, 1805-1866 2. Sacagawea 3. Clark, William, 1770-1838 4. Lewis and Clark Expedition, (1804-1806) 5. Native American boys 6. Mother-separated boys 7. Expeditions 8. Sexually abused boys 9. Mothers -- Death 10. Cultural differences 11. Native Americans in Europe 12. The West (United States) -- History -- To 1848 13. Historical fiction

LC 2008037492

"Explores the fantastic life and times of Baptiste Charbonneau, the son of Sacagawea, the Indian woman who guided the Lewis and Clark Expedition. Raised in many cultures but belonging to none, Baptiste travels deep into the heart of the American wilderness on an epic quest for ultimate identity."--Provided by publisher.

"With wit, humor, detailed understanding of the time, imagination and uncomplicated storytelling, Sargent opens a door on an era." Maine Sunday Telegram

Sarginson, Saskia

* The **wonderful** / Saskia Sarginson. Flatiron Books, 2019, c2018. 376 p.

ISBN 9781250083517

1. 1950s 2. Misfits (Persons) 3. Families -- Death 4. Twins 5. Americans in England 6. Cold War 7. Paranoia 8. Families of military personnel 9. Loss (Psychology) 10. Writing 11. Authors 12.

Psychic trauma 13. Secrets 14. England 15. Historical fiction 16. Coming-of-age stories

LC 2019032728

Originally published as How it ends: London : Little, Brown Book Group, 2018.

Losing her military family to a sudden mysterious tragedy on a 1957 airbase, young Hedy tries to piece together what happened by reading stories written by her intellectually gifted late twin.

"Set against a historical backdrop that will surprise many readers, Sarginson's novel movingly captures the private and at times painful evolution of a resilient and inventive protagonist." Publishers Weekly.

Saroyan, William, 1908-1981

* The **human** comedy / William Saroyan. Dell, 1971, c1943. 192 p.

ISBN 9780440339335

1. 1940s 2. Teenage boys -- California 3. Families -- California 4. Small towns 5. World War II -- United States 6. Brothers -- California 7. California 8. Historical fiction 9. Coming-of-age stories

Originally published: New York : Harcourt, Brace and Co., 1943.

Homer is a night messenger for the Postal Telegraph Office in a small California town during World War II after his father dies and his brother serves in the army.

Sarton, May, 1912-1995

* A **reckoning** : a novel / May Sarton. W. W. Norton, 1978. 254 p.

ISBN 9780393088281

1. Terminal illness 2. Women -- Family relationships 3. Lesbians 4. Mothers and daughters 5. Death 6. People with cancer 7. Senior women 8. Literary fiction

LC 78009691

When Laura Spelman learns that she will not get well, she looks on this last illness as a journey during which she must reckon up her life, give up the nonessential, and concentrate on what she calls "the real connections."

"Sarton incorporates . . . the issues of mother/daughter relationships, what it is to be a woman (and a man), and the conflict of art and life." Library Journal.

Sartre, Jean Paul, 1905-1980

* The **age** of reason / Jean Paul Sartre ; translated from the French by Eric Sutton. Vintage Books, 1973, c1947. 397 p.. Roads to freedom

1. 1930s 2. College teachers -- France 3. Philosophy teachers -- France 4. Freedom 5. Existentialism 6. France -- History -- 1914-1940 7. Historical fiction 8. Translations -- French to English

LC 72004476

Sequel: The reprieve.

L'Age de raison first published 1945.

This translation published in Hamish Hamilton 1947.

Following a Parisian philosophy teacher through the cafes and bars of Montparnasse over two days in the sweltering summer of 1938, Sartre's searing novel explores what it truly means to be free.

Sartre, Jean Paul, 1905-1980

* **Nausea** / Jean Paul Sartre ; translated from the French by Lloyd Alexander ; introduction by Hayden Carruth. Bentley, 1979, c1964. 178 p..

ISBN 0837604435

1. Existentialism 2. Self-awareness 3. Emotions 4. Authors 5. Diary novels 6. Translations -- French to English 7. Psychological fiction

8. Modern classics

LC   79017598

The diary of Antoine Roquentin follows his thoughts as he gradually sinks into a metaphysical crisis of despair, in this the first novel by the leader of French Existentialism.

Sartre, Jean Paul, 1905-1980

Reprieve / Jean Paul Sartre ; translated from the French by Eric Sutton. Hamish Hamilton, 1973, c1947. 398 p.. Roads to freedom

1. Munich Four-Power Agreement, 1938 2. France -- Politics and government 3. Great Britain -- Foreign relations -- Germany 4. Germany -- Foreign relations -- Great Britain 5. Translations -- French to English 6. Historical fiction

"This sequel to The age of reason confines itself to the eight frenetic days that led to the Munich Pact and the rape of Czechoslovakia. The original characters reappear merging now with many others as a shocked France mobilizes for war. Sartre, the leading exponent of Existentialism manages in this kaleidoscope novel to re-create the confusion, even the odor of the fear that gripped Europe in September, 1938." Library Journal.

Sartre, Jean Paul, 1905-1980

Troubled sleep / Jean Paul Sartre ; translated from the French by Gerard Hopkins. Vintage Books, 1992, c1950. 421 p.. Roads to freedom

ISBN 9780679740797

1. Second World War era (1939-1945) 2. World War II -- France 3. France -- HIstory -- German occupation, 1940-1945 4. Historical fiction 5. War stories 6. Translations -- French to English 7. Modern classics

LC   91050896

Sequel to: The reprieve.

Sartre portrays the emotional and intellectual impact of the fall of France on one group of citizens

Sarvas, Mark

Memento Park / Mark Sarvas. Farrar, Straus and Giroux, 2018. 272 p.

ISBN 9780374206376

1. Family secrets 2. Fathers and sons 3. Hungarian Americans 4. Painting 5. Nazi plunder 6. World War II 7. Jews -- Identity 8. Families -- History 9. Jewish Americans 10. Actors and actresses 11. Hollywood, California 12. Hungary -- History -- 1939-1945 13. Literary fiction

LC 2017038321

Learning that a painting that was stolen from his family during World War II has been found, Hungarian native Matt Santos is challenged to repair complicated relationships, uncover important family history and restore his own connection to Judaism in order to recover the artwork.

Satyal, Rakesh

No one can pronounce my name : a novel / Rakesh Satyal. Picador, 2017. 320 p.

ISBN 9781250112118

1. Suburban life 2. Immigrant families 3. Culture shock 4. East Indian Americans 5. Identity (Psychology) 6. Self-acceptance 7. Loneliness 8. Friendship 9. Communities 10. Closeted gay men 11. Married women 12. Students 13. Interpersonal relations 14. Cleveland, Ohio 15. Ohio 16. Literary fiction

LC 2016058277

Struggling with cultural divisions in a Cleveland suburb mostly populated by Indian Americans, lonely forty-something Harit dresses up in a sari to comfort his grief-stricken mother before befriending a woman who writes paranormal romances to manage her fears about her husband's affair.

"Satyal captures his characters experiences within a close-knit Indian community, rounded out with excellent supporting characters like Harit's mother and Ranjana's husband, who have their own stories to tell, resulting in a vivid, complex tale." Publishers Weekly.

Saul, John

Midnight voices Ballantine, 2002 320 p.

ISBN 0345433319

1. Widows 2. Apartment house life 3. Secrets 4. Mother and child 5. Demons 6. Remarriage 7. Manhattan, New York City 8. Horror 9. Thrillers and suspense

Cheryl Evans is a recently widowed mother of two. Things seem to have fallen into place when she meets Anthony Fleming and they are quickly married. She and her two children move into Fleming's luxury apartment on Central Park West despite her son's misgivings about the building and the people who dwell there. The building is home to a monstrously evil secret.

"This is good, drafty atmospheric horror stuff unafraid to indulge in not-at-all subtle gory bits." Booklist.

Saums, Mary

* **Thistle** & Twigg / Mary Saums. St. Martin's Minotour, 2007. 288 p. Thistle & Twigg

ISBN 0312360630

1. Widows 2. Female friendship 3. Eccentrics and eccentricities 4. Women amateur detectives 5. Murder suspects 6. Murder 7. Murder investigation 8. Conspiracies 9. Alabama 10. Cozy mysteries 11. Gentle reads

LC 2006048684

Sequel: Mighty old bones.

Two widows living in sleepy Tullulah, Alabama, newcomer Jane Thistle and lifelong resident Phoebe Twigg, quickly bond after they stumble upon a corpse during a walk in the woods near Jane's new house, discover that someone may be threatening Jane's reclusive neighbor, and a firebomb explodes in Phoebe's kitchen.

Saunders, George, 1958-

In persuasion nation : stories / George Saunders. Riverhead Books, 2006. 240 p.

ISBN 159448922X

1. Popular culture 2. Mass media 3. Materialism 4. Consumerism 5. Advertising 6. Literary fiction 7. Satirical fiction 8. Short stories

LC 2005057715

"The most unnerving fiction boldly envisions the dire consequences of our most hubristic tendencies: our bottomless greed, maniacal competitiveness, hyper-materialism, environmental obliviousness, spiritual callousness, and fear of being different. Following in the footsteps of Orwell, Bradbury, and Atwood, Saunders writes shrewd, off-the-charts speculative fiction. . . . In his third savagely imaginative collection, his most riveting to date, he considers various forms of diabolical persuasion in a techno-colonized world in which advertising governs every aspect of life." Booklist.

Saunders, George, 1958-

* **Lincoln** in the bardo : a novel / George Saunders. Random House, 2017. 343 p.

ISBN 9780812995343

1. Lincoln, Abraham, 1809-1865 2. 1860s 3. Loss (Psychology) 4.

Presidents -- United States 5. Grief 6. Spiritual journeys 7. Family relationships 8. Spirits 9. Cemeteries 10. Purgatory 11. United States Civil War, 1861-1865 12. Biographical fiction 13. Historical fiction 14. Literary fiction

LC 2016004993

ALA Notable Book, 2018.

Man Booker Prize, 2017.

Andrew Carnegie Medal for Excellence in Fiction finalist, 2018.

Shortlisted for the International Dublin Literary Award, 2019.

Traces a night of solitary mourning and reflection as experienced by the sixteenth president after the death of his eleven-year-old son at the dawn of the Civil War.

"With this book, Saunders asserts a complex and disturbing vision in which society and cosmos blur." Kirkus.

Saunders, George, 1958-

* **Tenth** of December : stories / George Saunders. Random House, 2013. 208 p.

ISBN 9780812993806

1. Soldiers 2. Kidnapping 3. People with cancer 4. Misfits (Persons) 5. Short stories 6. Literary fiction

LC 2012013782

National Book Award for Fiction finalist, 2013

A collection of stories includes "Home," a wryly whimsical account of a soldier's return from war; "Victory Lap," a tale about an inventive abduction attempt; and the title story, in which a suicidal cancer patient saves the life of a young misfit.

Saunders, Kate, 1960-

The **case** of the wandering scholar / Kate Saunders. Bloomsbury, 2019. 352 p. Laetitia Rodd mysteries

ISBN 9781632868381

1. Victorian era (1837-1901) 2. 1850s 3. Widows 4. Women private investigators 5. Middle-aged women 6. Missing men 7. Friendship 8. Missing persons investigation 9. Secrets 10. Murder 11. Rural life 12. England -- Social life and customs -- 19th century 13. Victorian mysteries 14. Historical mysteries

Finds Victorian detective Laetitia Rodd assisting a terminally ill gentleman in a search for his long-missing Oxford academic brother, before uncovering a formidable adversary lurking in the English countryside.

"Saunders's exquisite prose and patient storytelling build a convincing Victorian voice, while Mrs. Rodd's shrewd, energetic narration adds further appeal to the rich depiction of 19th-century landscapes and attitudes." Publishers Weekly.

Saunders, Kate, 1960-

The **secrets** of Wishtide / Kate Saunders. Bloomsbury USA, 2016. 334 p. Laetitia Rodd mysteries

ISBN 9781632864499

1. Victorian era (1837-1901) 2. Widows 3. Women private investigators 4. Middle-aged women 5. Lawyers 6. Scandals 7. Governesses 8. Murder investigation 9. London, England -- Social life and customs -- 19th century 10. Victorian mysteries 11. Historical mysteries

Archdeacon's widow and private investigator Laetitia Rodd goes undercover as a governess in order to assist her barrister brother during a case involving the illicit affairs of a nobleman's son.

"The book is a sheer delight, with its deliciously intricate puzzle and well-drawn characters whom readers are sure to continue to enjoy in volumes to come." Booklist.

Savage, Sam, 1940-2019

Firmin : adventures of a metropolitan lowlife / Sam Savage. Coffee House Press, 2006. 162 p.

ISBN 1566891817

1. Science fiction authors 2. Books and reading 3. Identity (Psychology) 4. Rats 5. Bookstores 6. Alienation (Social psychology) 7. Wrecking 8. Readers 9. Fate and fatalism 10. Loneliness 11. Urban renewal 12. Human/animal relationships 13. Boston, Massachusetts 14. Coming-of-age stories 15. Stories told by animals 16. Fantasy fiction

LC 2005035803

ALA Notable Book, 2007.

"Blending philosophy and abundant literary references with originality, Savage crafts a small comic gem about the costs and rewards of literary illusions." Booklist.

Savage, Sam, 1940-2019

Glass : a novel / Sam Savage. Coffee House Press, 2011. 223 p.

ISBN 9781566892735

1. Widows 2. Introspection 3. Thought and thinking 4. Authors 5. Writing 6. Housesitting 7. Literary fiction

Asked by a publisher to write a preface to her late husband's novel, Edna defiantly sets out to write a separate book telling her own story of their marriage.

Savage, Sam, 1940-2019

The **way** of the dog : a novel / Sam Savage. Coffee House Press, 2013. 152 p.

ISBN 9781566893121

1. Senior men 2. Artists 3. Alienation in men 4. Regret in men 5. Father and adult son 6. Death -- Psychological aspects 7. Psychological fiction 8. Literary fiction

LC 2011046604

A disillusioned artist looks for meaning in the wreckage of his life, and finds it in unexpected places.

Savas, Aysegul

Walking on the ceiling / Aysegul Savas. Penguin Group USA, 2019 208 p.

ISBN 9780525537410

1. Women -- Identity 2. Friendship 3. Memories 4. Belonging 5. Authors, British 6. Guilt in women 7. Conflict in families 8. Fathers -- Death 9. Identity (Psychology) 10. Paris, France 11. Istanbul, Turkey 12. Literary fiction 13. Coming-of-age stories

A novel set in Paris and a changing Istanbul follows a young Turkish woman grappling with the past?her country's and her own?and her complicated relationship with the famous British writer who longs for her memories.

Saville, Laurel

* **Henry** and Rachel / Laurel Saville. Lake Union Publishing , 2013. 271 p.

ISBN 9781611099669

1. Widowers 2. Loss (Psychology) 3. Romantic love 4. Secrets 5. Courtship 6. West Indies 7. Historical fiction 8. Love stories

Brought to live with the George family as a child, all anyone knew about enigmatic Rachel was that she worked hard, making herself indispensable to the plantation. And she remained a mystery until the day she disappeared, even to her husband. Especially to her husband. Henry was Rachel's opposite, gregarious where she was quiet, fanciful where she was pragmatic. After years of marriage, Rachel left Henry and their oldest son without explanation and set off on a steamer for New York City with their other four children. Was her flight the ultimate act of betrayal or one of extraordinary courage? Eight characters connected by blood and circumstance reconstruct Rachel's inexplicable vanishing act.

Sayers, Dorothy L. (Dorothy Leigh), 1893-1957
   * **Busman's** honeymoon / Dorothy L. Sayers. Harper and Row, 1995, c1937. 403 p. Lord Peter Wimsey mysteries
      ISBN 9780061043512
      1. Murder investigation 2. Newlyweds 3. Honeymoons 4. Amateur detectives 5. Husband and wife 6. Nobility 7. Villages 8. Murder 9. England 10. Mysteries
      "A love story with detective interruptions."
      "A Lord Peter Wimsey mystery with Harriet Vane."
      Originally published in 1937.
      When their plans for a private and romantic honeymoon are disrupted by the untimely murder of their estate's former owner, newlyweds Lord Peter and Harriet Vane are baffled by the strange clues that they discover.

Sayers, Dorothy L. (Dorothy Leigh), 1893-1957
   * **Clouds** of witness / Dorothy L. Sayers. HarperCollins, 1995, c1927. 279 p. Lord Peter Wimsey mysteries
      ISBN 9780061043536
      1. 1920s 2. Murder investigation 3. Brothers and sisters 4. Amateur detectives 5. Nobility 6. Engaged persons 7. Murder 8. Trials (Murder) 9. Hunting lodges 10. Mysteries
                                                    LC 86045689
      Originally published in 1927.
      When his future brother-in-law is murdered during a country retreat, Lord Peter Wimsey is shocked when his brother is accused and seeks the truth in a letter from Egypt, a suitcase-bearing fiancée, and a second murder attempt.

Sayers, Dorothy L. (Dorothy Leigh), 1893-1957
   * The **documents** in the case / Dorothy L. Sayers and Robert Eustace. Avon, 1968, c1930. 221 p.
      ISBN 0061043605
      1. 1920s 2. Poisonous mushrooms 3. Murder investigation 4. Murder 5. Toxins 6. Mycotoxicoses 7. Fathers and sons 8. London, England 9. Mysteries
      The clues to the death of a fungi expert who had died after eating enough poisonous mushrooms to kill thirty people, lie in a series of seemingly unimportant documents that nevertheless intrigue the victim's son.

Sayers, Dorothy L. (Dorothy Leigh), 1893-1957
   * The **five** red herrings / Dorothy L. Sayers. Harpercollins, 1995, c1931. 306 p. Lord Peter Wimsey mysteries
      ISBN 9780061043635
      1. 1930s 2. Murder investigation 3. Artists 4. Murder 5. Painting 6. Amateur detectives 7. Nobility 8. Crimes against painters 9. Scotland 10. Mysteries
      Originally published under the title Suspicious characters : New York : Harper, 1931.
      When an artist is found dead at the bottom of a cliff where he had been painting, a masterpiece in mystery arises, with six artists as suspects, five of them "red herrings" and one a murderer who baffles even Lord Peter Wimsey.

Sayers, Dorothy L. (Dorothy Leigh), 1893-1957
   * **Gaudy** night / Dorothy L. Sayers. Harpercollins, 1995, c1936. 501 p. Lord Peter Wimsey mysteries
      ISBN 9780061043499
      1. 1930s 2. Universities and colleges 3. Murder investigation 4. Class reunions 5. Amateur detectives 6. Women college teachers 7. Nobility 8. Revenge 9. Men/women relations 10. Oxford, England 11. England 12. Mysteries
      Originally published in 1936.
      Harriet Vane's Oxford reunion is shadowed by a rash of bizarre pranks and malicious mischief that include beautifully worded death threats, burnt effigies, and vicious poison-pen letters, and Harriet finds herself and Lord Peter Wimsey challenged by an elusive set of clues.

Sayers, Dorothy L. (Dorothy Leigh), 1893-1957
   Hangman's holiday / Dorothy L. Sayers. Harpercollins, 1995, c1961. 209 p. Lord Peter Wimsey mysteries
      ISBN 9780061043628
      1. Nobility 2. Murder 3. Amateur detectives 4. Murder investigation 5. Short stories 6. Mysteries
      "A collection of short mysteries."
      Originally published: Victor Gollancz, 1933.
      First published 1933.
      Poisoned port ...Pet cats in peril ...Purloined pearls ...Lord Peter Wimsey solves the mysteries of the man who was blown into the fourth dimension and the murder in fancy dress. He pursues miscreants across several countries and into unexpected hiding places. Dorothy L. Sayers' other detective, Montague Egg, encounters a fugitive murderer and uncovers a killer in an Oxford cloister. The travelling salesman extraordinaire solves puzzles with a unique combination of matter-of-fact practicality and brilliant deduction.

Sayers, Dorothy L. (Dorothy Leigh), 1893-1957
   Have his carcase / Dorothy L. Sayers. Harper and Row, 1986, c1932. 448p. Lord Peter Wimsey mysteries
      ISBN 9780061043529
      1. 1930s 2. Murder investigation 3. Nobility 4. Soviets in England 5. Mystery story writers 6. Amateur detectives 7. Murder 8. Men/women relations 9. England 10. Mysteries
      Originally published in 1932.
      Retreating to a barren beach in order to console her broken heart, mystery writer Harriet Vane is alarmed when she discovers the dead body of a young man and appeals to her friend Lord Peter for assistance in solving the mystery.

Sayers, Dorothy L. (Dorothy Leigh), 1893-1957
   In the teeth of the evidence / Dorothy L. Sayers. Harpercollins, 1987, c1968. 265 p. Lord Peter Wimsey mysteries
      ISBN 9780061043567
      1. Nobility 2. Murder 3. Murder investigation 4. Amateur detectives 5. Mysteries 6. Short stories
      Previously published 1940 as: In the teeth of the evidence, and other stories.
      First published in Great Britain in 1939 by Victor Gollancz.
      All that was left of the garage was a heap of charred and smouldering beams. In the driving seat of the burnt-out car were the remains of a body. This is a vintage collection of Sayers' crime and detection stories featuring Lord Peter Wimsey.

Sayers, Dorothy L. (Dorothy Leigh), 1893-1957
   * **Lord** Peter / Dorothy L. Sayers ; compiled and with an introduction by James Sandoe ; coda by Carolyn Heilbrun ; co-

detta by E.C. Bentley. Harper, 1972. 487 p. Lord Peter Wimsey mysteries

ISBN 038001694X

1. Nobility 2. Murder 3. Murder investigation 4. Amateur detectives 5. Short stories 6. Mysteries

LC 86045694

"A collection of all the Lord Peter Wimsey stories."

Sayers, Dorothy L. (Dorothy Leigh), 1893-1957

Murder must advertise / Dorothy L. Sayers. Harpercollins, 1995, c1933. 344 p. Lord Peter Wimsey mysteries

ISBN 9780061043550

1. 1930s 2. Murder investigation 3. Advertising agencies 4. Drug traffic 5. Nobility 6. Amateur detectives 7. Advertising copywriters 8. Undercover operations 9. Accidental death investigation 10. England 11. Mysteries

Originally published in 1933.

When an ad man dies after an apparent accident, Lord Peter Wimsey goes undercover as an advertising copywriter and discovers a suspicious set of clues that involve cocaine dealing, blackmail, and wanton women.

Sayers, Dorothy L. (Dorothy Leigh), 1893-1957

The **nine** tailors / Dorothy L. Sayers. Harcourt Brace Jovanovich, 1989, c1934. 397 p. Lord Peter Wimsey mysteries

ISBN 0156658992

1. 1930s 2. Murder investigation 3. Jewelry theft 4. Churches 5. Amateur detectives 6. Nobility 7. Valets 8. Clergy 9. Villages 10. Murder 11. Influenza 12. England 13. Mysteries

LC 89038102

Tale of suspense in which the famous Lord Peter Wimsey is called upon to solve the murder of an unknown man in East Anglia.

Sayers, Dorothy L. (Dorothy Leigh), 1893-1957

* **Strong** poison / Dorothy L. Sayers. Harper, 1930. 252p. Lord Peter Wimsey mysteries

1. 1930s 2. Arsenic poisoning 3. Women murder suspects 4. Murder investigation 5. Amateur detectives 6. Nobility 7. Women mystery story writers 8. Innocence (Law) 9. Scotland 10. Mysteries

LC 86045144

Dashing detective Lord Peter Wimsey is caught up in the murder trial of mystery writer Harriet Vane. Her fiance has died of poisoning exactly as described in one of Harriet's novels -- so naturally she is the prime suspect. As Peter looks on, he not only falls in love with the accused but eagerly helps with Harriet's defense when the first trial ends in a hung jury. Will she be convicted and executed for the crime, or can he save her life and win her hand in marriage? Strong Poison is the first of a series of Lord Peter Wimsey and Harriet Vane mysteries in which their complex romantic relationship is revealed in detail. This superb classic was originally published in 1930.

Sayers, Dorothy L. (Dorothy Leigh), 1893-1957

Thrones, dominations / Dorothy L. Sayers & Jill Paton Walsh. St. Martin's Press, 1998. 312 p. Lord Peter Wimsey mysteries

ISBN 0312181965

1. 1930s 2. Murder investigation 3. Newlyweds 4. Amateur detectives 5. Husband and wife 6. Marriage 7. Women mystery story writers 8. Theatrical producers and directors 9. Aristocracy 10. Murder 11. England 12. Mysteries

Dorothy Sayers' unfinished Lord Peter Wimsey novel, Thrones, Dominations, completed sixty years later by Jill Paton Walsh.

Newlyweds Lord Peter Wimsey and Harriet Vane explore another mysterious turn of events during the short-lived reign of Edward VIII, in a novel left unfinished and unpublished for almost sixty years.

"Paton Walsh has made a valiant and resourceful stab at mimicry. No devotee of Lord Peter and his novelist wife Harriet Vane will want to miss it." New Statesman.

Sayers, Dorothy L. (Dorothy Leigh), 1893-1957

The **unpleasantness** at the Bellona Club / Dorothy L. Sayers. Harper and Row, 1928. 345 p. Lord Peter Wimsey mysteries

ISBN 0060550260

1. 1920s 2. Murder investigation 3. Poisoning 4. Inheritance and succession 5. Amateur detectives 6. Nobility 7. Heirs and heiresses 8. Wills 9. Libraries 10. Murder 11. Mysteries

Originally published : New York : Harper and Row, 1928.

A ninety-year-old man's time of death becomes pivotal in deciding upon his half-million-pound estate, and Lord Peter Wimsey must search through such clues as an artificial poppy and an unsolicited telephone repair.

Sayers, Dorothy L. (Dorothy Leigh), 1893-1957

* **Whose** body? : a Lord Peter Wimsey novel / Dorothy L. Sayers. Harper, 1994, c1923. 212 p. Lord Peter Wimsey mysteries

ISBN 9780061043574

1. 1920s 2. Murder investigation 3. Nobility 4. Amateur detectives 5. Veterans 6. Upper class 7. Valets 8. Brothers 9. Dukes and duchesses 10. Eccentrics and eccentricities 11. Murder 12. England 13. Mysteries

Originally published: New York : Harper & Row, 1923.

Sayers's most renowned amateur detective, the engaging and amusing Lord Peter Wimsey, sets out to unravel a puzzling case involving the disappearance of a wealthy financier and the discovery of a nude corpse, wearing a golden pince-nez, in a bathtub.

Sayers, Valerie

The **powers** : a novel / Valerie Sayers. Northwestern University Press, 2013. 312 p.

ISBN 9780810152298

1. DiMaggio, Joe, 1914-1999 2. Second World War era (1939-1945) 3. 1940s 4. Baseball players 5. World War II 6. Marital conflict 7. Friendship 8. Photographers 9. Peace activists 10. World War II home front 11. Baseball players -- United States 12. Baseball stories -- United States 13. World War, 1939-1945 -- United States 14. Historical fiction

LC 2012036262

Presents a fictionalized account of Joe DiMaggio's hitting streak in 1941 and his gift of being able to see the future.

Sayles, John, 1950-

A **moment** in the sun / John Sayles. McSweeney's, 2011. 600 p.

ISBN 9781936365180

1. 1890s 2. 1900s (Decade) 3. Race relations 4. War and society 5. Gold rush 6. Assassination 7. Colonialism 8. United States -- History -- 19th century 9. Philippines -- History -- 19th century 10. Historical fiction 11. Epic fiction

Traces the tales of America and its events in 1897, months before the start of the Spanish American War, and follows the different lives of men at the turn of the century.

"At times, Sayles' research for A Moment in the Sun makes the writing absolutely vivid: His description of a difficult childbirth is so precise that it will have you flinching. But at other times, the historical trivia overcrowds the book: The novel's world can be so cluttered with exterior detail that it feels as though there is insufficient space for its characters' interior lives. This might seem a natural pitfall for a filmmaker writing a novel. Persnickety fans and critics point out any accidental anachronism that slips into a film's frames, and, so, perhaps, he transfers this anxiety to his fiction. But it is wrongheaded to look at Sayles as just a filmmaker writing a book. If anything, his career has been so interesting because it has demonstrated the opposite: how a novelist would think about and make films." Daily Beast

Saylor, Steven, 1956-

The **house** of the Vestals : the investigations of Gordianus the Finder / Steven Saylor. St. Martin's Press, 1997. 260 p. Roma Sub Rosa series

ISBN 0312154445

1. Roman Republic (509-27 BCE) 2. 1st century BCE 3. Slaves 4. Private investigators 5. Criminal investigation 6. Rome -- History -- Republic, 265-30 BC 7. Historical mysteries 8. Short stories 9. Mysteries

LC 977597

Nine stories featuring the Roman sleuth Gordianus the Finder, set between the end of Sulla's dictatorship and the Spartacus slave revolt, detail the relationship between Gordianus and his adopted son

"Saylor serves up a collection of short stories designed to fill in some of the gaps that have piqued the curiosity of devoted fans of his popular Roma Sub Rosa series. Set between the years 80 and 72 B.C., these nine tales document some of the early adventures of Gordianus the Finder. . . . While each brief mystery presented is a gem in and of itself, readers will delight in the informational overview provided by the collection as a whole. As usual, Saylor does a superb job of seamlessly incorporating the tumultuous history of the Roman Republic into the narrative flow." Booklist.

Saylor, Steven, 1956-

The **judgment** of Caesar : a novel of Ancient Rome / Steven Saylor. St. Martin's Minotaur, 2004. 288 p. Roma Sub Rosa series

ISBN 0312271190

1. Cleopatra, Queen of Egypt, 69-30 BC 2. Pompey,, the Great, 106-48 BC 3. Caesar, Julius, 100-44 BC 4. Roman Republic (509-27 BCE) 5. Ancient Egypt (3100 BCE-640 CE) 6. 1st century BCE 7. Battles 8. Innocence (Law) 9. Poisoning 10. Private investigators 11. Romans in Egypt 12. Sick women 13. Husband and wife 14. Egypt -- Rulers 15. Rome -- History -- Civil War, 49-45 BC 16. Ancient Egypt -- History -- 332-30 BC 17. Historical mysteries 18. Mysteries

LC 2003069548

Heading to Egypt in search of a cure for the mysterious illness of his ailing wife, Bethesda, Gordianus the Finder arrives in a country torn by war and power struggles, a situation that worsens when Bethesda vanishes.

"Readers will be equally absorbed by the bloody history unfolding (Saylor's description of the beheading of Pompey is both suspenseful and wrenching); by the historical figures depicted (Ptolemy listening to his flute player with the head of Pompey in a clay jar at his feet is a miniature study in royal pathology); and by the mysteries Gordianus must solve to keep his own head. Wonderful reading." Booklist.

Saylor, Steven, 1956-

A **mist** of prophecies / Steven Saylor. St. Martin's Minotaur, 2002. x, 270 p. Roma Sub Rosa series

ISBN 0312271212

1. Roman Republic (509-27 BCE) 2. 1st century BCE 3. Civil war 4. Murder investigation 5. Insurgency 6. Slaves 7. Private investigators 8. Women prophets 9. Rome -- History -- Civil War, 49-45 BC 10. Rome -- History -- Republic, 265-30 BC 11. Historical mysteries 12. Mysteries

LC 2001058901

When a beautiful seeress is murdered while Julius Caesar and Pompey make war for control of the Roman Empire, Gordianus the Finder investigates the murder amid the larger intrigues of ancient Rome.

"A mystery set in Rome during the Civil War. A beautiful young woman, given the street name Cassandra for her habit of delivering prophesies, is found murdered. Gordianus is disturbed that no one claims her body--even though, he reflects, someone cared enough to murder her. Yet, at Cassandra's funeral pyre, seven of the most powerful women in Rome, including the wives of Caesar, Cicero, and Marc Antony, attend. Gordianus sorts out the tangled motives of the women who watched Cassandra burn, believing one of them to be her murderer. Saylor brings a wealth of historical information lightly to bear on a chilling mystery." Booklist.

Saylor, Steven, 1956-

Raiders of the Nile : a novel of the ancient world / Steven Saylor. Minotaur Books, 2014. 384 p. Roma Sub Rosa series

ISBN 9781250015976

1. Roman Republic (509-27 BCE) 2. Ancient Egypt (3100 BCE-640 CE) 3. Romans 4. Kidnapping 5. Young men 6. Slaves 7. Tombs -- Egypt 8. Rome -- History -- Republic, 265-30 BC 9. Ancient Egypt -- History -- 332-30 BC 10. Historical mysteries 11. Mysteries

LC 2013032463

Finds Gordianus struggling to rescue Bethesda, who has been mistakenly kidnapped as part of a plot to steal the golden sarcophagus of Alexander the Great.

"Gordianus leaps from the pages as a modern trope--a wisecracking, good-hearted charmer--and Saylor frames him against an entrancing interpretation of ancient Egypt." Kirkus.

Saylor, Steven, 1956-

Roma : the novel of ancient Rome / Steven Saylor. St. Martin's Press, 2007. 555 p.

ISBN 0312328311

1. Caesar, Julius, 100-44 BC 2. Roman Empire (27 BCE-476 CE) 3. Roman Republic (509-27 BCE) 4. Romans 5. Families 6. Insurgency 7. Generations 8. Romulus (Roman mythology) 9. Remus (Roman mythology) 10. Roman emperors 11. Slaves 12. Amulets 13. Rome -- History 14. Epic fiction 15. Historical fiction

LC 2006051179

Sequel: Empire.

"Spanning a thousand years, and following the shifting fortunes of two families though the ages, this is the epic saga of Rome, the city and its people."--From source other than the Library of Congress

"Livy's Early History of Rome offers fertile material for a crime writer. The body count is high, and Saylor adds plenty more along the way. Even Livy smelt a 'whodunit' in the sudden apotheosis of Romulus in a thunderclap in the middle of a Senatorial meeting. Saylor illuminates the mystery in gory detail as, with unfailing efficiency, he unravels the enigmas. There is plenty of instruction here for students of classical civilization but sometimes the period detail founders in bathos when characters explain to each other facts they must already know, for the reader's benefit. Sometimes, though, with the scalpel-like deftness of a

Hollywood director, Saylor puts his finger on the very essence of Roman history." Times Literary Supplement.

Saylor, Steven, 1956-

Rubicon / Steven Saylor. St. Martin's Press, 1999 276 p. Roma Sub Rosa series

ISBN 9780312205768

1. Pompey,, the Great, 106-48 BC 2. Caesar, Julius, 100-44 BC 3. Roman Republic (509-27 BCE) 4. 1st century BCE 5. Murder investigation 6. Insurgency 7. Self-sacrifice 8. Murder 9. Civil war 10. Private investigators 11. Rome -- History -- Republic, 265-30 BC 12. Historical mysteries 13. Mysteries

A story of murder and double-cross during the Roman Civil War puts Gordianus the Finder in a tough spot when Pompey takes his son-in-law hostage, and to save both their lives, Gordianus must prove that his son, who works for Pompey's enemy Caesar, did not kill Pompey's beloved cousin

"This novel is an excellent blending of mystery and history." Library Journal.

Saylor, Steven, 1956-

The **seven** wonders : a novel of the ancient world / Steven Saylor. Minotaur Books, 2012. 336 p. Roma Sub Rosa series

ISBN 9780312359843

1. Roman Republic (509-27 BCE) 2. Voyages and travels 3. Tutors 4. Eighteen-year-old men 5. Divination 6. Rome -- History -- Republic, 265-30 BC 7. Europe 8. Historical mysteries 9. Mysteries

LC 2012005475

A prequel to the Roma Sub Rosa series finds 18-year-old Gordianus embarking on a quest in politically restless 92 B.C. to see the world's Seven Wonders and accompanied by a celebrated poet who fakes his own death to travel under an assumed identity.

Saylor, Steven, 1956-

The **triumph** of Caesar : a novel of ancient Rome / Steven Saylor. St. Martin's Minotaur, 2008. 320 p. Roma Sub Rosa series

ISBN 9780312359836

1. Caesar, Julius, 100-44 BC 2. Pisonis, Calpurnia 3. Roman Republic (509-27 BCE) 4. 1st century BCE 5. Assassination 6. Betrayal 7. Attempted murder 8. Private investigators 9. Divination 10. Rome -- History -- Republic, 265-30 BC 11. Europe 12. Historical mysteries 13. Mysteries

LC 2008003668

Sequel to: The judgment of Caesar.

Rome, 46 BC: the Roman civil war has come to its conclusion and Caesar is now dictator for life. Cleopatra is making a state visit to the city in order to convince Caesar to acknowledge their son as his heir. Marc Antony and Caesar are at odds; Cicero is making a fool of himself with a new teenage bride; and Caesar's wife Calpurnia is troubled by prophesies of disaster and fears for her husband's life. To uncover the truth, Calpurnia calls on Gordianus the Finder, recently returned from Egypt with his wife Bethesda. Although essentially retired, and doubting whether Caesar's life is worth saving, he begins the search, hoping to find the murderer of the friend who was first sent out to investigate the plot.

Saylor, Steven, 1956-

Wrath of the furies : a novel of the ancient world / Steven Saylor. Minotaur Books, 2015. 320 p. Roma Sub Rosa series

ISBN 9781250015983

1. Roman Republic (509-27 BCE) 2. Ancient Egypt (3100 BCE-640 CE) 3. Romans 4. Rescues 5. International relations 6. Civilization,

Ancient 7. Rome -- History -- Republic, 265-30 BC 8. Ancient Egypt -- History -- 332-30 BC 9. Historical mysteries 10. Mysteries

LC 2015022081

To rescue an old friend, Gordianus must go behind enemy lines, facing unspeakable danger in the greatest war of the ancient world.

Scalzi, John, 1969-

The **collapsing** empire / John Scalzi. Tor Books, 2017. 336 p. Interdependency novels

ISBN 9780765388889

1. Interplanetary relations 2. Imaginary empires 3. Teleportation 4. Life on other planets 5. Spaceship captains 6. Interstellar relations 7. Space exploration 8. Political intrigue 9. Women rulers 10. Space flight 11. Space opera 12. Science fiction

Locus Award for Best Science Fiction Novel, 2018.

RUSA Reading List, 2018.

When humanity discovers the existence of an extra-dimensional field capable of transporting travelers to different worlds instantly, a significantly depopulated Earth is threatened by a subsequent finding that the field is unstable and may be cutting travelers off on the wrong side of Earth-friendly worlds.

"Fans of Game of Thrones and Dune will enjoy this bawdy, brutal, and brilliant political adventure.." Booklist.

Scalzi, John, 1969-

Head on / John Scalzi. Tor Books, 2018. 335 p. Lock in novels

ISBN 9780765388919

1. Virus diseases 2. Near future 3. FBI agents 4. Murder investigation 5. Professional athletes 6. Professional sports 7. Science fiction

Finds the near-future world reveling in a violent but seemingly harmless, robot-bodied sport until a star athlete dies unexpectedly on the field, prompting an investigation by two FBI agents into the game's increasingly lucrative competition.

Scalzi, John, 1969-

* **Lock** in / John Scalzi. Tor Books, 2014. 320 p. Lock in novels

ISBN 9780765375865

1. Virus diseases 2. Near future 3. FBI agents 4. Murder investigation 5. Epidemics 6. Virtual reality 7. Paralysis 8. Science fiction

LC 2014015247

When a new virus causes one percent of the population to become completely paralyzed in body but not in mind, America pursues a scientific initiative to develop a virtual-reality world for victims, with unexpected consequences.

"[C]ontains plenty of action, great character development, vivid and believable worldbuilding and a thought-provoking examination of disability culture and politics." Kirkus.

Scalzi, John, 1969-

* **Old** man's war / John Scalzi. Tor Books, 2005. 320 p. Old Man's War universe

ISBN 0765309408

1. Life on other planets 2. Senior men 3. Space warfare 4. Space colonies 5. Septuagenarians 6. Widowers 7. Soldiers 8. Aliens 9. Human/alien encounters 10. Land claims 11. Military science fiction 12. Science fiction

LC 2004057953

Sequel: The ghost brigades.

Enlisting in the army on his seventy-fifth birthday, John Perry joins an interstellar war between Earth and alien enemies who would stake claims on the few existing inhabitable planets, unaware that the conflict involves much more than he understands.

Scalzi, John, 1969-

Redshirts : a novel with three codas / John Scalzi. Tor, 2012. 304 p.

ISBN 9780765316998

1. Space warfare 2. Aliens (Humanoid) 3. Interplanetary relations 4. Betrayal 5. Interstellar relations 6. Near future 7. Human/alien encounters 8. Metafiction 9. Science fiction 10. Humorous stories

LC 2012009383

"A Tom Doherty Associates book."

Hugo Award for Best Novel, 2013.

Locus Award for Best Science Fiction Novel, 2013.

Enjoying his assignment with the Xenobiology lab on board the prestigious Intrepid, ensign Andrew Dahl worries about casualties suffered by low-ranking officers during away missions before making a shocking discovery about the starship's actual purpose.

Scapellato, Joseph, 1982-

Big lonesome / Joseph Scapellato. Mariner Books, 2017. 192 p.

ISBN 9780544769809

1. Cowboys 2. The West (United States) 3. Short stories 4. Westerns 5. Surrealist fiction

LC 2016029360

Reinventing a great American tradition through an absurdist, discerning eye, Joseph Scapellato uses these twenty-five stories to conjure worlds, themes, and characters who are at once unquestionably familiar and undeniably strange. Big Lonesome navigates through the American West--from the Old West to the modern-day West to the Midwest, from cowboys to mythical creatures to everything in between--exploring place, myth, masculinity, and what it means to be whole or to be broken.

"Scapellato's debut is unpredictable, witty, and self-aware while remaining heartfelt in the most unexpected ways." Kirkus.

Scego, Igiaba, 1974-

Adua / Igiaba Scego ; translated by Jamie Richards. New Vessel Press, 2017, c2015. 185 p.

ISBN 9781939931450

1. Married women 2. Refugees 3. Fathers and daughters 4. African diaspora 5. Immigrants 6. Racism 7. Young men -- Relations with older women 8. Fathers -- Death 9. Intergenerational communication 10. Conflict in families 11. Inheritance and succession 12. Options, alternatives, choices 13. Civil war -- Somalia 14. Colonialism 15. Rome, Italy 16. Somalia 17. Literary fiction 18. Family sagas 19. Translations -- Italian to English

Originally published: Florence : Giunti, 2015.

Adua, an immigrant from Somalia to Italy, has lived in Rome for nearly forty years. She came seeking freedom from a strict father and an oppressive regime, but her dreams of becoming a film star ended in shame. Now that the civil war in Somalia is over, her homeland beckons. Yet Adua has a husband who needs her, a young man, also an immigrant, who braved a dangerous crossing of the Mediterranean Sea. When her father, who worked as an interpreter for Mussolini's fascist regime, dies, Adua inherits the family home. She must decide whether to make the journey back to reclaim her material inheritance, but also how to take charge of her own story and build a future.

Scerbanenco, Giorgio, 1911-1969

A **private** Venus / Giorgio Scerbanenco ; translated by Howard Curtis ; with an autobiographical essay, I, Vladimir

Scerbanenko. Hersilia Press, 2012, c1966. 285 p. Milano quartet

ISBN 9780956379641

1. 1960s 2. Murder investigation 3. Women murder victims 4. Drinking 5. Murder 6. Kidnapping 7. Pornography 8. Prostitution 9. Organized crime 10. Former physicians 11. Milan, Italy 12. Mysteries 13. Translations -- Italian to English

Originally published as Venere privata: Milano : Garzanti, 1966.

Duca Lamberti's a doctor who's just been released from prison, where he's spent the last three years for having practiced euthanasia. Unable to work in medicine, he takes a job helping Davide, a young and depressed alcoholic, whose past seems to involve prostitution, pornography, and murder.

Scerbanenco, Giorgio, 1911-1969

Traitors to all / Giorgio Scerbanenco ; translated from the Italian by Howard Curtis. Melville House, 2014 256 p. Milano quartet

ISBN 9781612193663

1. 1960s 2. Drowning victims 3. Accidental death investigation 4. Former physicians 5. Amateur detectives 6. Antiheroes and antiheroines 7. Conspiracies 8. Drowning investigation 9. Milan, Italy 10. Mysteries 11. Translations -- Italian to English

Originally published: Milano : Garzanti Editore, 1966.

A lawyer who has spent time in prison with Duca is found drowned in one of the Milanese canals. Duca is contacted by a friend of the dead lawyer to perform surgery on a woman who after the operation confesses that although she is due to marry a wealthy butcher, is really in love with another man, the friend of the lawyer. Shortly afterwards, she is killed together with her lover. Duca discovers that the two events are linked and starts to unravel an arms and drugs trafficking business, centered in an understated trattoria, of which the two were part.

Schaefer, Jack, 1907-1991

The **collected** stories of Jack Schaefer / Jack Schaefer ; with an introduction by Winfield Townley Scott Houghton Mifflin, 1966. 520 p.

1. Short stories 2. Westerns

LC 66022612

"The author's mastery of narrative technique, his excellent character development, and his consistently concise description combine in avoiding the unfortunate aspects of typical 'Western' fiction and melodrama." Library Journal.

Schaefer, Jack, 1907-1991

Monte Walsh / Jack Schaefer. University of Nebraska Press, 1981, c1963 vii, 442 p.

ISBN 9780803241244

1. Cowboys -- New Mexico 2. Westerns

LC 80025036

Originally published: Boston : Houghton Mifflin, 1963.

Times change. Monte Walsh doesn't. For him, being a cowboy isn't a job, it's a life. And that's something the fenced-in, corporate-bean-counting ways of the onrushing 20th century must never alter.

"His characters seem real, and, according to the author, the characters and the episodes are based upon historical accounts. This is not just another 'Western.' It is worthy of a place alongside the writing of Will James and Eugene Manlove Rhodes." Library Journal.

Schaefer, Jack, 1907-1991

* **Shane** / Jack Schaefer ; illustrated by John McCormack Houghton, 1982, c1949. 214 p.

ISBN 9780395070901

1. 19th century 2. Gunfighters 3. Fifteen-year-old boys 4. Ranches 5. Ranchers 6. Wyoming 7. Westerns

A mysterious stranger dressed in black rides into the Wyoming valley where Bob Starrett lives with his parents.

Schaitkin, Alexis, 1985-

* **Saint** X / Alexis Schaitkin. Celadon Books, 2020. viii, 343 p.

ISBN 9781250219596

1. Sisters -- Death 2. Murder suspects 3. Families of murder victims 4. Loss (Psychology) 5. Social classes 6. Taxicab drivers 7. Young women 8. Stalking 9. Suspicion 10. Obsession 11. Immigrants 12. Race relations 13. Whiteness (Concept) 14. New York City 15. Caribbean Area 16. Psychological suspense

When a brief but fateful encounter brings her together with one of the men originally suspected of killing her sister, Claire, hoping to gain his trust and learn the truth, forms an unlikely attachment with this man whose life is forever marked by the same tragedy.

"This killer debut is both a thriller with a vivid setting and an insightful study of race, class, and obsession." Kirkus.

Schami, Rafik, 1946-

Sophia : or the beginning of all tales / Rafik Schami ; translated by Monique Arav and John Hannon. Interlink Books, 2018, c2017. 480 p.

ISBN 9781566560313

1. First loves 2. Social change 3. Exiles 4. Loyalty 5. Mothers and sons 6. Malicious accusation 7. Lovers 8. Interfaith romance 9. Men/women relations 10. Interpersonal relations 11. Damascus, Syria 12. Rome, Italy 13. Literary fiction 14. Political fiction 15. Translations -- German to English

LC 2017031326

Originally published: 2017.

A murder in Damascus, a love with the power to save a young man's life... In his latest novel, Rafik Schami ventures to the land of his childhood, where he is now unable to safely return: Syria.

Schanbacher, Gary Lester

Crossing Purgatory / Gary Schanbacher. Pegasus Books, 2013. 336 p.

ISBN 9781605984438

1. American Westward Expansion (1803-1899) 2. 1850s 3. Families -- Death 4. Guilt 5. Frontier and pioneer life 6. Loss (Psychology) 7. Widowers 8. Wagon trains 9. Voyages and travels 10. Disasters 11. Interpersonal relations 12. The West (United States) 13. Westerns

David J. Langum, Sr. Prize in American Historical Fiction, 2013

Spur Awards, Best Western Traditional Novel, 2014.

A young farmer in 1858 sets out across the American frontier in an attempt to deal with his guilt at not being home to prevent a devastating family tragedy and finds himself tested in ways he hadn't imagined.

Scharer, Whitney

The **age** of light / Whitney Scharer. Little Brown & Co, 2019. 384 p.

ISBN 9780316524087

1. Miller, Lee, 1907-1977 2. Man Ray, 1890-1976 3. 20th century 4. Women photographers 5. Ambition in women 6. Intellectual life 7. Fashion models 8. Artists 9. Lovers 10. Creativity 11. Men/women

relations 12. Biographical fiction 13. Historical fiction

Inspired by the life of the Vogue model-turned-renowned photographer, Lee Miller relocates to 1929 Paris, where she becomes the muse and colleague of the mercurial Surrealist, Man Ray.

Schine, Cathleen

The **Grammarians** / Cathleen Schine. Sarah Crichton Books/Farrar, Straus and Giroux, 2019. 256 p.

ISBN 9780374280116

1. Sisters 2. Sibling rivalry 3. Language and languages -- Grammars 4. English language 5. Identical twins 6. Family relationships 7. Dictionaries 8. Women editors 9. Women poets 10. Women journalists 11. Obsession 12. Women's lives and relationships 13. Literary fiction

LC 2018060805

Follows the experiences of identical twins whose respective literary careers are upended by their battle to claim an heirloom dictionary.

Schlink, Bernhard

The **reader** : a novel / Bernhard Schlink ; translated from the German by Carol Brown Janeway. Pantheon Books, 1997. 218 p.

ISBN 9780679442790

1. S. S. 2. Former Nazis 3. War crime trials 4. Law students 5. Teenage boys -- Germany 6. Women prison guards 7. Books and reading 8. Young men -- Relations with older women 9. Coming-of-age stories 10. Literary fiction 11. Translations -- German to English

LC 971511

Shortlisted for the International IMPAC Dublin Literary Award, 1999

Schoolboy Michael Berg, 15, meets an older woman and they have an affair, which she breaks off and disappears. Seven years later Berg, now a law student attending a trial, sees her in the dock, accused in a crime dating back to World War II and the death camp at Auschwitz.

"This novel raises provocative questions about guilt and responsibility, as well as the power of literature to heal and bind." Publishers Weekly.

Schlink, Bernhard

Self's deception / Bernhard Schlink ; translated from the German by Peter Constantine. Vintage Crime/Black Lizard, 2007, c1992. 334 p. Gerhard Self mysteries

ISBN 9780375709081

1. Private investigators 2. Missing persons investigation -- Germany 3. Secrecy in government 4. Missing women 5. Psychiatric hospitals 6. Conspiracies 7. Germans 8. Terrorism -- Germany 9. Former Nazis 10. Former lawyers 11. Senior men 12. Germany 13. Mysteries 14. Translations -- German to English

LC 2006042169

Sequel to: Self's punishment.

Sequel: Self's murder.

Originally published: Zurich : Diogenes, 1992.

Hired to find Leo Salger, private detective Gerhard Self traces the girl to the psych ward of a local hospital where he is told she died following a fatal fall, only to discover that Leo is very much alive.

Schlink, Bernhard

Self's murder / Bernhard Schlink ; translated from the German by Peter Constantine. Vintage Crime/Black Lizard, 2009. 262 p. Gerhard Self mysteries

ISBN 9780375709098

1. Private investigators 2. Money laundering 3. Business partners 4. Banks and banking -- Germany 5. Private banks -- Germany

6. Accidental death investigation 7. Germans 8. Senior men 9. Former lawyers 10. Former Nazis 11. Germany 12. Mysteries 13. Translations -- German to English

Sequel to: Self's deception.

Originally published: Zurich : Diogenes, 2001.

When septuagenarian sleuth Gerhard Self is hired by a German bank owner to track down the silent partner in his business, the detective tangles with Nazi youth and uncovers a money laundering ring with connections to the Russian mafia.

Schlink, Bernhard

Self's punishment / Bernhard Schlink with Walter Popp. Vintage Books, 2005. 256 p. Gerhard Self mysteries

ISBN 037570907X

1. 1980s 2. Private investigators 3. Hackers 4. Guilt in men 5. Murder 6. Justice 7. Senior men 8. Former lawyers 9. Germans 10. Former Nazis 11. Germany 12. Mysteries 13. Translations -- German to English

LC 2004057166

Sequel: Self's deception.

"This mystery features former Nazi prosecutor turned investigator Gerhard Self. It's the early 1980s, and Self has been hired by a boyhood friend to smoke out a hacker who's playing havoc with the computers at Rhineland Chemical Works. But after Self springs a trap that gets the troublemaker murdered, he gradually faces the guilt he still carries for his youthful embrace of National Socialism. His simple refusal to let himself off the hook and step back into his old public prosecutor's role after the war doesn't seem like penance enough anymore. . . . Self's unwitting participation in the new crime drives him to pursue the path of justice wherever it may lead. A fascinating exploration of how people often manage to carve out normal lives even after being complicit in terrible acts." Booklist.

Schmidt, Sarah

See what I have done / Sarah Schmidt. Atlantic Monthly Press, 2017. 324 p.

ISBN 9780802126597

1. Borden, Lizzie, 1860-1927 2. 1890s 3. Murder investigation 4. Sisters 5. Single women 6. Murder 7. Family relationships 8. Memory 9. Dysfunctional families 10. United States -- History -- 19th century 11. Massachusetts -- History -- 19th century 12. Australian 13. Historical fiction

Originally published: Sydney: Hachette Australia, 2017.

Australian Book Industry Awards, Literary Fiction Book of the Year, 2018.

Librarians' Choice (Australia), 2017

Longlisted for The Women's Prize for Fiction, 2018.

Lizzie Borden took an axe... and, well, we all know what happened next. Or do we? This unsettling debut by Australian author Sarah Schmidt tells the story from the (conflicting) perspectives of Lizzie, her elder sister, a maid in the Borden household, and a stranger whose surprising connection to the crime is gradually revealed. With its creeping dread and unreliable narrators,?See What I Have Done?may appeal to fans of Margaret Atwood's?Alias Grace. -- Description by Gillian Speace

"Equally compelling as a whodunit, 'whydunit,' and historical novel, the book honors known facts yet fearlessly claims its own striking vision." Publishers Weekly.

Schofield, Douglas

Time of departure / Douglas Schofield. Minotaur, 2015. 320 p.

ISBN 9781250072757

1. Women lawyers 2. Women public prosecutors 3. Cold cases

(Criminal investigation) 4. Detectives 5. Murder investigation 6. Men/women relations 7. Sexism in employment 8. Kidnapping investigation 9. Florida 10. Mysteries

LC 2015022092

Discriminated against because of her youth and gender, newly promoted Florida Felony Division Chief Claire Talbot links the discovery of a pair of skeletons to a decades-old string of abductions while questioning the agenda of a retired cop with suspicious knowledge of the case.

Schulberg, Budd

Waterfront : a novel / Budd Schulberg. R. Bentley, 1979, c1955. 320 p.

1. Labor unions -- Corrupt practices 2. Priests 3. Crime 4. Stevedores 5. Labor unions -- Stevedores 6. New York City 7. Literary fiction

LC 79011704

Terry Malloy, a minor hood and would-be boxer, and Father Barry, a Catholic priest raised in the slums, struggle to survive in and reform the corrupt, violent life on the New York waterfront.

Schulberg, Budd

What makes Sammy run? R. Bentley, 1979, c1941. 303 p.

1. Jewish Americans 2. Hollywood, California 3. Modern classics

LC 79010457

Sammy Glick, obsessed by his ambition, lies and cheats his way to the front office of a major Hollywood studio.

Schulman, Helen

Come with me / Helen Schulman. HarperCollins, 2018 320 p.

ISBN 9780062459138

1. Family relationships 2. Computer algorithms 3. Options, alternatives, choices 4. Technology -- Social aspects 5. Married people 6. Regret 7. Palo Alto, California 8. California 9. Literary fiction

A part-time employee of a tech company owned by her friend's 19-year-old son acts as his guinea pig to test an algorithm that allows people to access their "multiverses" and see their alternative life choices and paths.

Schumacher, Julie, 1958-

Dear committee members / Julie Schumacher. Doubleday, 2014. 176 p. Dear committee members

ISBN 9780385538138

1. Creative writing teachers 2. Employment references 3. Letters 4. Passive-aggressive personality 5. Teacher-student relationships 6. Discontent in men 7. College teachers 8. Academic rivalry 9. Divorced men 10. Office politics 11. Authors 12. Satirical fiction 13. Epistolary novels

LC 2013043014

Sequel: The Shakespeare Requirement.

Thurber Prize for American Humor, 2015.

Enduring budget cuts and the favoritism of other departments at his small liberal arts college, literature professor Jason Fitger despairs of his writing ambitions and imposed role in a star pupil's would-be opus while writing wryly comic, passive-aggressive letters to students and colleagues.

"Schumacher's warm satire of the peculiarities of the Ivory Tower will be recognizable to anyone who has encountered the bureaucracy and internal politics of higher education." Booklist.

Schutt, Bill

The **Darwin** strain : an R. J. MacCready novel / Bill Schutt, J. R. Finch. William Morrow & Co, 2019. 384 p. R. J. MacCready novels

ISBN 9780062835475

1. Cryptozoology 2. Mutation (Biology) 3. Cold War 4. International intrigue 5. Cryptozoologists 6. Miracles 7. Springs 8. Islands 9. Greece 10. Historical thrillers

Sent to a remote Greek island by the Pentagon in the early days of the Cold War, MacCready and Thorne investigate rumors of the healing properties of a volcanic spring connected to an ancient sea monster legend.

Schwab, Victoria

A **conjuring** of light / V. E. Schwab. Tor Books, 2017 624 p. Darker shade of magic

ISBN 9780765387462

1. Magic 2. Parallel universes 3. Power (Social sciences) 4. Enemies 5. Magicians 6. Thieves 7. Pirates 8. Royal houses 9. London, England 10. Historical fantasy 11. Gateway fantasy 12. Fantasy fiction

Series complete in 3 volumes.

Londons fall and kingdoms rise while darkness sweeps the Maresh Empire, and the fraught balance of magic blossoms into dangerous territory while heroes struggle.

"Schwab has fully delivered on the promise of this inventive and captivating series." Kirkus.

Schwab, Victoria

A **darker** shade of magic / V. E. Schwab. Tom Doherty Associates, 2015 400 p. Darker shade of magic

ISBN 9780765376459

1. Magic 2. Parallel universes 3. Intrigue 4. Thieves 5. Enemies 6. Magicians 7. Smugglers 8. Royal houses 9. Material culture 10. London, England 11. Historical fantasy 12. Gateway fantasy 13. Fantasy fiction

Republished by Tor Books in 2017 as a special collector's edition.

RUSA Reading List Short List, 2016.

Prepare to be dazzled by a world of parallel Londons -- where magic thrives, starves, or lies forgotten, and where power can destroy just as quickly as it can create.

"The brisk plot makes this a page-turner that confronts darkness but is never overwhelmed by it. Fantasy fans will love this fast-paced adventure, with its complex magic system, thoughtful hero and bold heroine." Kirkus.

Schwab, Victoria

A **gathering** of shadows / V.E. Schwab. Tom Doherty Associates, 2016. 512 p. Darker shade of magic

ISBN 9780765376473

1. Magic 2. Contests 3. Parallel universes 4. Pirates 5. Enemies 6. Magicians 7. Prophetic dreams 8. International relations 9. London, England 10. Historical fantasy 11. Gateway fantasy 12. Fantasy fiction

LC 2015031510

Experiencing ominous dreams four months after the events of A Darker Shade of Magic, Kell watches Red London excitedly preparing for the Element Games international magic competition only to realize that the threat of Black London is returning.

"New touches such as a bustling magical market enliven already-rich worldbuilding. Tensions rise steadily, culminating with the exciting Element Games, and the finale will leave readers breathless." Publishers Weekly.

Schwab, Victoria

Vengeful / V. E. Schwab. Tor, 2018. 400 p. Villains (V. E. Schwab)

ISBN 9780765387523

1. Superhuman abilities 2. Enemies 3. Revenge 4. Superheroes 5. Former friends 6. Villains 7. Betrayal 8. Survival 9. Resurrection 10. Good and evil 11. Superhero stories

Goodreads Choice Award, 2018

A conclusion to the story that began with Vicious finds Marcella Riggins targeting the city of Merit while manipulating Victor Vale and Eli Ever into a battle against one another.

Schwab, Victoria

Vicious / V. E. Schwab. Tor, 2013. 364 p. Villains (V. E. Schwab)

ISBN 9780765335340

1. Superhuman abilities 2. Former friends 3. Enemies 4. Villains 5. Revenge 6. Supernatural 7. Good and evil 8. College students 9. Ambition 10. Escaped convicts 11. Near-death experience 12. Superhero stories

LC 2013023963

"A Tom Doherty Associates Book."

RUSA Reading List, 2014.

Ten years after a thesis experiment designed to tap a human's supernatural abilities goes terribly wrong, Victor breaks out of prison and resolves to track down his former roommate, Eli, who is accompanied by a girl with astonishing abilities and who resolves to eradicate the world's super-powered people.

"In a genre that tends toward the flippant or pretentious, this is a rare superhero novel as epic and gripping as any classic comic. Schwab's tale of betrayal, self-hatred, and survival will resonate with superhero fans as well as readers who have never heard of Charles Xavier or Victor von Doom." Publishers Weekly.

Schwartz, John Burnham

The **commoner** : a novel / John Burnham Schwartz. Nan A. Talese, 2008. 304 p.

ISBN 9780385515719

1. Nobility -- Japan 2. Women -- Japan 3. Young women -- Japan 4. Class conflict 5. Social classes 6. Gender role 7. Rulers 8. Mothers and sons 9. Women rulers -- Japan 10. Heirs and heiresses 11. Inheritance and succession 12. Japan -- History -- 1945- 13. Domestic fiction 14. Historical fiction

LC 2007015391

In 1959, Haruko marries the Crown Prince of Japan, becoming the first commoner to enter the mysterious and reclusive world of Japanese royalty,

"An American taking on a fictional memoir about a living Japanese empress is a gutsy move, but Schwartz makes it work. . . . While the external details of life in the palace remain stunning, it's Schwartz's grasp of [Haruko's] internal struggle that resonates after the last page is turned." Denver Post.

Schwartz, John Burnham

Northwest corner : a novel / John Burnham Schwartz. Random House, 2011. 304 p.

ISBN 9781400068456

1. Fathers and sons 2. Family secrets 3. Redemption 4. Former convicts 5. Family relationships 6. Guilt in men 7. Family reunions

8. Men/women relations 9. California 10. Psychological fiction

LC 2010045784

Sequel to: Reservation road.

"A follow-up to Reservation Road finds 50-year-old Dwight Arno's new start in California thrown into turmoil by the unexpected arrival of college-age Sam, who is fleeing a devastating incident in his own life, a parallel struggle that dramatically transforms the lives of the women around them."--From publisher.

"Multiple viewpoints are usually jarring, interrupting the flow of a novel, but not here: In Schwartz's hands, the narrative unfolds delicately, each chapter a puzzle piece that fits seamlessly into the whole. It's painful to watch the two men confront their lives but it's also exhilarating." Entertainment Weekly.

Schwartz, John Burnham,

The **red** daughter : a novel / John Burnham Schwartz. Random House Inc, 2019 288 p.

ISBN 9781400068463

1. Allilueva, Svetlana, 1926-2011 2. 1960s 3. Defectors 4. Women -- Psychology 5. Children of heads of state 6. Marriage 7. Cold War 8. Belonging 9. Culture shock 10. Culture conflict 11. Women immigrants 12. Interpersonal relations 13. United States -- Foreign relations -- Soviet Union 14. Soviet Union -- Foreign relations -- United States 15. Biographical fiction 16. Literary fiction

LC 2018040604

Defecting to America at the height of the Cold War, the daughter of Joseph Stalin finds her quiet existence upended by controversial associates, CIA suspicion and her relationship with a young lawyer.

Schwarz, Christina

All is vanity / Christina Schwarz. Doubleday, 2002. 400 p.
ISBN 0385499728

1. Social mobility 2. Self-fulfillment 3. Fiction writing 4. Debt 5. Friendship 6. Greed 7. Egotism in women 8. Childhood friends 9. Psychological fiction

LC 2002067583

Friends since childhood and living on opposite coasts, Margaret and Letty find themselves dissatisfied with their lives now that they are in their mid-thirties and set out to rectify the situation.

"Schwarz's portrait of the talentless, self-absorbed Margaret is surgically accurate. . . . Anyone who has ever tried to write and been blocked will howl with recognition at the indignities that befall the novelist. . . . The novel is both a page turner and a cautionary tale of consumerism run amok." New York Times Book Review.

Schwarz, Christina

Drowning Ruth / Christina Schwarz. Doubleday, 2000. 338 p.

ISBN 0385502532

1. Drowning victims 2. Family secrets 3. Farm life 4. Nurses 5. Mothers and daughters 6. Sisters 7. Aunts 8. Nieces 9. Women with mental illnesses 10. Wisconsin 11. Psychological fiction

LC 00029523

Worn out from nursing soldiers at a Milwaukee hospital and struggling to recover from a traumatic love affair, Amanda Starkey returns to her family's rural Wisconsin farm to stay with her beloved sister, Mattie, and young niece, Ruth.

"The vivid realism of the novel's setting adds depth to an already gripping plot. . . . Schwarz maintains her mystery with an expert hand, arriving at far more than a simple determination of guilt." New York Times Book Review.

Schwarz, Christina

The **edge** of the Earth / Christina Schwarz. Atria Books, 2013. 288 p.

ISBN 9781451683677

1. 1890s 2. Lighthouses 3. Husband and wife 4. Selfishness in men 5. Native American women 6. Ambition in men 7. Self-discovery in women 8. California 9. Historical fiction

Feeling restless in spite of her accomplishments and imminent marriage to a respectable young man, Trudy is ostracized by her late 19th-century Milwaukee community when she falls in love with an enigmatic man and relocates to a California lighthouse, where she uncovers a life-changing secret.

Schwarz-Bart, Andre, 1928-2006

The **last** of the just : a novel / Andre Schwarz-Bart ; translated from the French by Stephen Becker. Overlook Press, 2000. 374 p.

ISBN 1585670162

1. Ghettoes, Jewish -- Eastern Europe 2. Jews, Eastern European 3. Jewish families 4. Jews -- Persecutions 5. Jews, German 6. France -- History -- 20th century 7. Historical fiction 8. Translations -- French to English

LC 99059550

Originally published: New York :

"On March 11, 1185, in the old Anglican city of York, the Jews of the city were brutally massacred by their townsmen. As legend has it, God blessed the only survivor of this medieval pogrom, Rabbi Yom Tov Levy, as one of the Lamed-Vov, the thirty-six Just Men of Jewish tradition, a blessing which extended to one Levy of each succeeding generation. This terrifying and remarkable legacy is traced over eight centuries, from the Spanish Inquisition, to expulsions from England, France, Portugal, Germany, and Russia, and to the small Polish village of Zemyock, where the Levys settle for two centuries in relative peace. It is in the twentieth century that Ernie Levy emerges, The Last of the Just, in 1920s Germany, as Hitler's sinister star is on the rise and the agonies of Auschwitz loom on the horizon." Provided by publisher

Schweblin, Samanta, 1978-

Fever dream : a novel / Samanta Schweblin ; translated from the Spanish by Megan McDowell. Riverhead Books, 2017, c2002. 192 p.

ISBN 9780399184598

1. Women with terminal illnesses 2. Rural life 3. Intergenerational relations 4. Memories 5. Hazardous waste 6. Last days 7. Clinics 8. Mothers 9. Neighbors 10. Death 11. Interpersonal relations 12. Argentina 13. Literary fiction 14. Psychological suspense 15. Translations -- Spanish to English

LC 2016026585

Originally published: Buenos Aires : Ediciones Destino, c2002.

Follows the nightmarish experiences of a dying woman and a boy beside her hospital bed, who explore the dynamics of broken souls, toxic relationships and the power and desperation of family.

"A taut, exquisite page-turner vibrating with existential distress and cumulative dread." Kirkus.

Schweblin, Samanta, 1978-

Mouthful of birds : stories / Samanta Schweblin ; translated from the Spanish by Megan McDowell. Riverhead Books, 2019 228 p.

ISBN 9780399184628

1. Psychology 2. Human behavior 3. Interpersonal relations 4. Interpersonal conflict 5. Discontent 6. Competition 7. Argentina

8. Short stories 9. Literary fiction 10. Horror 11. Translations -- Spanish to English

"Originally published in Spanish in 2010 as Pájaros en la boca by Random House Mondadori."

A first English-language collection of stories by the Man Booker International Prize-finalist author incorporates themes of high suspense, psychological tension, unearthly restlessness and distortions in reality.

"These 20 tales have a visceral effect as Schweblin navigates the extremes of her characters actions and thoughts, both healing and destructive." Booklist.

Scibona, Salvatore

The **volunteer** : a novel / Salvatore Scibona. Penguin Press, 2019. 432 p.

ISBN 9780525558521

1. Fathers and sons 2. Vietnam veterans 3. Secrecy 4. War -- Psychological aspects 5. Intelligence service 6. Abandoned children 7. Life change events 8. Interpersonal relations 9. Literary fiction

LC 2018046079

The abandonment of a child at an international airport is tied to the Vietnam War experiences of a restless recruit into a clandestine branch of the U.S. government.

Scoppettone, Sandra

Everything you have is mine / Sandra Scoppettone. Little, Brown, 1991. 261 p. Lauren Laurano mysteries

ISBN 0316776467

1. Murder investigation 2. Rape investigation 3. Lesbians 4. Feminists 5. Women private investigators 6. Rape 7. Former FBI agents 8. Women/women relations 9. New York City 10. Greenwich Village, New York City 11. Mysteries 12. LGBTQIA fiction

LC 90048889

Lauren Laurano, a gay private detective, and her psychotherapist lover, Kip, join forces to solve the brutal murder of a wealthy young woman who had a penchant for computer dating services, in a mystery set in New York's Greenwich Village

"Lauren Laurano, a bighearted, wisecracking lesbian who makes her debut here as a Manhattan private eye, brings cunning as well as caring to her investigation of the murder of a young rape victim who might have met her killer by hooking into a dating service on her personal computer." New York Times Book Review.

Scoppettone, Sandra

Gonna take a homicidal journey / Sandra Scoppettone. Little, Brown and Co., 1998. 229 p. Lauren Laurano mysteries

ISBN 0316776653

1. Murder investigation 2. Vacations 3. Cheating (Interpersonal relations) 4. Lesbians 5. Feminists 6. Women private investigators 7. Resorts 8. Women/women relations 9. Conspiracies 10. Land development 11. Child pornography 12. New York City 13. Long Island, New York 14. Mysteries 15. LGBTQIA fiction

LC 9744247

Lesbian sleuth Lauren Laurano is hoping she can regain Kep's trust while they are on vacation together, but she does not have much time for her lover after someone hires her to investigate a brutal murder made to look like a suicide.

"The wide-ranging, all-encompassing case may seem shallow or far-fetched, but Scoppettone's tongue-in-cheek attitude makes the book work." Library Journal.

Scoppettone, Sandra

My sweet untraceable you / Sandra Scoppettone. Little, Brown, 1994. 275 p. Lauren Laurano mysteries

ISBN 0316776483

1. Filmmaking 2. Cold cases (Criminal investigation) 3. Murder investigation 4. Lesbians 5. Feminists 6. Women private investigators 7. Women/women relations 8. New York City 9. Greenwich Village, New York City 10. Mysteries 11. LGBTQIA fiction

LC 93047426

In the most puzzling case of her career, lesbian detective Lauren Laurano finds herself sorting through three decades of bad memories and fending off a succession of all-too-present dangers

"Scoppettone is a highly entertaining writer with her fingers on current political and commercial pulses. So she ably transmits the modish urban-grit feel of Laurano's encounters with Manhattan's winos, weirdos, and wise guys as she counterpoints the complex case her sleuth is solving with the deterioration from AIDS of the brother of Laurano's lesbian partner of 14 years." Booklist.

Scoppettone, Sandra

* **Too** darn hot : a novel / Sandra Scoppettone. Ballantine Books, 2006. 288 p. Faye Quick novels

ISBN 0345478126

1. Second World War era (1939-1945) 2. 1940s 3. Missing persons 4. Women detectives 5. World War II 6. Murder investigation 7. Independence in women 8. Men/women relations 9. World War II home front 10. New York City 11. Manhattan, New York City 12. Historical mysteries 13. Cozy mysteries 14. Gentle reads

LC 2005053093

In 1943 New York City, private detective Faye Quick is hired by a distraught, young salesgirl to find her missing boyfriend, an AWOL Army private, only to be drawn into a bizarre murder investigation.

"Set in 1943 Manhattan, this mystery features Faye Quick, the semi-tough New York steno who turns private eye after her boss goes off to fight in WWII. . . . Claire Turner, a blonde beauty who works as a salesgirl at Wanamaker's department store, plays on Faye's sympathies to get her to agree to spend some of her time looking for Claire's missing GI boyfriend, Charlie Ladd. . . . Of course, the too-good-to-be-true Charlie turns out to be just that, murders are committed both coolly and in hot blood, and all the while our very interesting Faye does a great imitation of the sort of dame Ida Lupino was born to play." Publishers Weekly.

Scotch, Allison Winn

In twenty years / Allison Winn Scotch. Lake Union Publishing, 2016. 332 p.

ISBN 9781503935242

1. Friendship 2. Reunions 3. Loss (Psychology) 4. Marital conflict 5. Coping 6. Disappointment 7. Change 8. Pennsylvania 9. Mainstream fiction 10. Women's lives and relationships

Twenty years ago, six Penn students shared a house, naively certain that their friendships would endure?until the death of their ringleader and dear friend Bea splintered the group for good. Now, mostly estranged from one another, the remaining five reluctantly gather at that same house on the eve of what would have been Bea's fortieth birthday.

Scott, A. D.

* **Beneath** the abbey wall : a novel / A. D. Scott. Atria Books, 2012. 384 p. Joanne Ross novels

ISBN 9781451665772

1. 1950s 2. Journalists -- Scotland 3. Murder 4. Innocence (Law) 5. Newspaper employees 6. Single mothers 7. Interpersonal attraction 8. Crimes against middle-aged women 9. Murder investigation 10.

Secrets 11. Highlands, Scotland 12. Scotland 13. Mysteries

LC 2012030071

On a dark, damp Sunday evening, a man taking a shortcut home sees a hand reaching out in supplication from a bundle of sacks. In an instant he knows something terrifying has happened. In the Highlands in the late 1950s, much of the local newspaper's success was due to Mrs. Smart, the no-nonsense office manager who kept everything and everyone in line. Her murder leaves her colleagues in shock and the Highland Gazette office in chaos. Joanne Ross, a budding reporter and shamefully separated mother, assumes Mrs. Smart's duties, but an intriguing stranger provides a distraction not only from the job and the investigation but from everything Joanne believes in.

Scott, A. D.

A **double** death on the Black Isle : a novel / A. D. Scott. Atria Paperback, 2011. 384 p. Joanne Ross novels

ISBN 9781439154946

1. 1950s 2. Journalists -- Scotland 3. Murder investigation 4. Betrayal 5. Murder 6. Newspaper employees 7. Highlands, Scotland 8. Scotland 9. Mysteries

"Set against the bleak beauty of the Highlands, . . . [this book explores] the slow transformation of Scotland from a highly ordered society while presenting a fine mystery with engaging characters." Kirkus.

Scott, A. D.

* A **kind** of grief : a novel / A.D. Scott. Atria Paperback, 2015. 336 p. Joanne Ross novels

ISBN 9781476756189

1. 1950s 2. Journalists -- Scotland 3. Small town life -- Scotland 4. Superstition 5. Witchcraft 6. Trials (Witchcraft) 7. Murder 8. Murder investigation 9. Suicide investigation 10. Highlands, Scotland 11. Scotland 12. Mysteries

LC 2015025918

Joanne Ross investigates the death of an artist and alleged witch, who was found dead in her home on a remote glen in Scotland

Scott, A. D.

* The **low** road / A.D. Scott. Atria, 2014. 336 p.. Joanne Ross novels

ISBN 9781476756165

1. 1950s 2. Journalists -- Scotland 3. Gangs 4. Missing persons investigation 5. Murder investigation 6. Small town life -- Scotland 7. Murder 8. Feuds 9. Engagement 10. Options, alternatives, choices 11. Highlands, Scotland 12. Scotland 13. Mysteries

LC 2014005047

Joanne Ross' fiancé, John McAllister, is on a fast-paced hunt for his good friend Jimmy McPhee, who is involved in a blood feud with a murderous razor gang in 1950s Glasgow.

Scott, Caroline

The **poppy** wife : a novel of the Great War / Caroline Scott. William Morrow Paperbacks, 2019. 448 p.

ISBN 9780062955326

1. First World War era (1914-1918) 2. 1920s 3. World War I 4. Missing in action 5. Brothers 6. Veterans 7. Married women 8. Loss (Psychology) 9. Psychic trauma 10. Western Front (World War I) 11. Voyages and travels 12. Cemeteries 13. Photographs 14. War casualties 15. Great Britain 16. France 17. Belgium 18. Historical fiction

LC 2019013072

Hired by other families looking for MIA soldiers, a grieving man searches for his own missing brother along the Western Front, where he photographs soldier graves while making life-changing discoveries.

Scott, James, 1977

* The **kept** / James Scott. HarperCollins, 2014. 336 p.

ISBN 9780062236739

1. 19th century 2. Revenge 3. Widows 4. Loss (Psychology) 5. Midwives 6. Kidnapping 7. Guilt in women 8. Male impersonators 9. Historical fiction

LC 2013027875

After her husband and four of her children are brutally murdered in the winter of 1897, midwife Elspeth Howell, along with her surviving son, 12-year-old Caleb, takes on the frozen wilderness to find the men responsible for shattering their family.

"Scott writes with sustained intensity and strong descriptive powers, whether evoking the pair's dangerous trudge through high snowdrifts, the rough lake town where many answers lie, or his characters' complex lives and motivations." Booklist.

Scott, Joanna, 1960-

Follow me / Joanna Scott. Little Brown & Co., 2009. 400 p.

ISBN 9780316051651

1. Grandmothers 2. Family secrets 3. Family relationships 4. Memories 5. Grandmother and child 6. Fathers and daughters 7. Truth 8. Women -- Decision-making 9. Self-fulfillment in women 10. Pennsylvania 11. Historical fiction

Sally Werner entrusts the secrets of her early life to her grandaughter, telling her how, after an affair with her cousin, she abandoned their baby and drifted from town to town assuming new identities.

"Scott . . . excels in her stream-of-consciousness descriptions of the mysterious Tuskee that provides Sally's true north." Washington Post Book World.

Scott, Joanna, 1960-

* **Tourmaline** : a novel / Joanna Scott. Little, Brown, 2002. 288 p.

ISBN 9780316776189

1. Napoleon I,, Emperor of the French, 1769-1821 Elba and the Hundred Days, 1814-1815 2. 1950s 3. Families 4. Brothers 5. Fathers 6. Mothers 7. Youngest child 8. Failure (Psychology) 9. Gems 10. Islands 11. Americans in Italy 12. Missing persons 13. Eccentric girls 14. Expatriates 15. Money-making projects 16. Treasure hunting 17. Tourmaline 18. Mediterranean region 19. Elba, Italy 20. Domestic fiction 21. Historical thrillers

LC 2002067111

A family heads for an island off the coast of Italy hoping to make a fortune in jewels, but instead is embroiled in a mystery surrounding the disappearance of a local girl.

"Book reviewers are fond of calling belletristic novels 'poetic.' 'Tourmaline' isn't poetic because of its pretty writing but because of its sympathetic ordering and reordering of ideas, its philosophical probing." New York Times Book Review.

Scott, Justin

Mausoleum / Justin Scott. Poisoned Pen Press, 2007. 244 p. Ben Abbott mysteries

ISBN 9781590584682

1. Real estate agents 2. Former convicts 3. Murder 4. Murder investigation 5. Amateur detectives 6. Tombs 7. Immigrants 8. Murder suspects 9. Small town life -- Connecticut 10. Connecticut 11. Mysteries

Angered when Newbury, Connecticut's three-hundred-year-old cemetery is invaded by an eyesore of a mausoleum belonging to newcomer Brian Groses, Ben Abbott launches a personal investigation when Brian's body is found in his monument, the victim of a shooting.

Scott, Kim, 1957-

That deadman dance / Kim Scott. Picador Australia, 2010. 400 p.

ISBN 9781405040433

1. Colonial Australia (1788-1901) 2. Aboriginal Australians -- Western Australia -- History 3. Colonized peoples -- Australia 4. Aboriginal Australians -- Relations with whites -- 19th century 5. Aboriginal Australians, Treatment of 6. Nyunga (Australian people) 7. Australia -- History -- 19th century 8. Western Australia -- Race relations 9. Australia -- Race relations 10. Great Britain -- Colonies 11. Historical fiction 12. Historical fiction

Previously published: 2010.

Australian Literature Society Gold Medal, 2011.

Miles Franklin Award, 2011.

Western Australian Premier's Book Awards, Fiction category, 2010.

Western Australian Premier's Book Awards, Premier's Prize, 2010.

Bobby Wabalanginy is a young Nyunga man, smart, resourceful, and eager to please. He befriends the European arrivals, joining them as they hunt whales, till the land, and establish their new colony. He is welcomed into a prosperous white family, and eventually finds himself falling in love with the daughter, Christine. But slowly -by design and by hazard-things begin to change. Not everyone is happy with how the colony is progressing. "Told through the eyes of black and white, young and old, this is a story about fledgling Western Australian community in the early 1800s known as the 'friendly frontier'. Poetic, warm-hearted and bold, it is a story which shows that first contact did not have to lead to war."--Back cover.

Scott, Paul, 1920-1978

* **Staying** on : a novel / Paul Scott. University of Chicago Press, 1998, c1977. 215 p.

ISBN 9780226743493

1. British in India 2. Culture conflict 3. Race relations 4. Senior couples 5. Husband and wife 6. Marital conflict 7. Villages 8. India -- History -- 20th century 9. Historical fiction 10. Literary fiction

Originally published: London: Heinemann, 1977.

Booker Prize, 1977.

Tusker and Lily Smalley stayed on in India. Given the chance to return 'home' when Tusker, once a Colonel in the British Army, retired, they chose instead to remain in the small hill town of Pangkot, with its eccentric inhabitants and archaic rituals left over from the days of the Empire. Only the tyranny of their landlady, the imposing Mrs Bhoolab-hoy, threatens to upset the quiet rhythm of their days.

Scott, Rion Amilcar

* The **world** doesn't require you : stories / Rion Amilcar Scott. Liveright, 2019. 304 p.

ISBN 9781631495380

1. African American communities 2. African Americans 3. Race relations 4. Local history 5. Communities 6. Maryland 7. Short stories 8. Literary fiction 9. Surrealist fiction 10. African American fiction

This collection of short stories, set in fictional Cross River, Maryland, includes the tales of a struggling musician who is God's last son and a Ph.D. candidate whose dissertation about a childhood game sparks a riot in a once-segregated town.

"Mordantly bizarre and trenchantly observant, these stories stake out fresh territory in the nation's literary landscape." Kirkus.

Scott, Walter, Sir, 1771-1832

The **bride** of Lammermoor / Walter Scott ; preface by W.M. Parker. Dent; Dutton, 1966, c1819. 342 p. Waverley novels

ISBN 023110572X

1. 1700s (Decade) 2. Arranged marriage 3. Heirs and heiresses 4. Murder 5. Stabbing victims 6. Husband and wife 7. Women murderers 8. Interclass romance 9. Nobility -- Scotland 10. Family relationships 11. Scotland -- History -- 18th century 12. Historical fiction 13. Classics

Originally published, 1819.

Scott, Walter, Sir, 1771-1832

* **Ivanhoe** / Walter Scott ; edited with an introduction by Graham Tulloch. Penguin, 2000, c1820. xlv, 496 p. Waverley novels

ISBN 9780140436587

1. Richard I,, King of England, 1157-1199 2. John,, King of England, 1167-1216 3. Medieval period (476-1492) 4. Plantagenet period (1154-1485) 5. 12th century 6. Chivalry 7. Knights and knighthood 8. Coups d'etat 9. Jews, English 10. Romantic love 11. Inheritance and succession 12. Crusades -- Third, 1189-1192 13. Robin Hood (Legendary character) 14. Great Britain -- History -- Richard 1, 1189-1199 15. Epic fiction 16. Historical fiction 17. Adventure stories 18. Classics

Based on the acclaimed Edinburgh edition of the Waverley novels.

Adapted into several theatrical and television films and miniseries.

Originally published: London : A. Constable, 1820.

Scott's classic historical romance, set in the twelfth-century England of Richard I, depicts the adventures of the heroic Wilfred of Ivanhoe in winning the hand of beautiful Lady Rowena.

Scott, Walter, Sir, 1771-1832

* **Rob** Roy / Walter Scott. Tom Doherty Associates, 1998, c1817. lxix, 465 p. Waverley novels

ISBN 9780812580433

1. Rob Roy, 1671-1734 2. Jacobite Rebellions (1689-1746) 3. 1710s 4. Jacobites 5. Uncle and nephew 6. Rebels 7. Battles 8. Religion 9. Christian sects 10. Revolutionaries 11. Nobility -- Scotland 12. Scottish resistance and revolts 13. Scotland -- Social conditions -- 18th century 14. Historical fiction 15. Classics

Originally published: Edinburgh : A. Constable, 1817.

An English gentleman, involved in Jacobite intrigues, journeys to the Trossachs to meet a famous Scottish outlaw.

Scottoline, Lisa

After Anna / Lisa Scottoline. St. Martin's Press, 2018. 352 p.

ISBN 9781250099655

1. Widowers 2. Blended families 3. Trials (Murder) 4. Manipulation by teenage girls 5. Mothers and daughters 6. Murder 7. Murder suspects 8. Secrets 9. Psychological suspense

LC 2017053395

Marrying a wonderful woman after years of loneliness and single fatherhood, John finds his newfound happiness turned upside-down by the arrival of his beautiful sociopath teen daughter, whose campaign to destroy their family and untimely murder force John to prove his innocence in the face of malevolent discoveries.

Scottoline, Lisa

* **Come** home / Lisa Scottoline. St. Martin's Press, 2012. 384 p.

ISBN 9780312380823

1. Divorced women 2. Motherhood 3. Murder investigation 4. Former husbands -- Death 5. Stepdaughters 6. Thrillers and suspense

LC 2011046492

Rebalancing her life and career after a painful divorce, pediatrician Jill learns that her ex has died from an alleged overdose that her former stepdaughter believes was actually murder, a situation that forces Jill to choose between her duty to past circumstances and her future happiness.

Scottoline, Lisa

Don't go / Lisa Scottoline. St. Martin's Press, 2013. 384 p.

ISBN 9781250010070

1. Military physicians 2. Married women -- Death 3. Grief in men 4. Fathers and daughters 5. Family secrets 6. Murder investigation 7. Post-traumatic stress disorder 8. Thrillers and suspense

Fleeing home from his military service in Afghanistan when his wife dies in an apparent freak household accident, Dr. Mike Scanlon struggles with the tragedy, his inability to bond with his new baby daughter and a downsizing in his medical practice only to discover a shocking secret that changes his understanding of everything.

Scottoline, Lisa

* **Every** fifteen minutes / Lisa Scottoline. St. Martin's Press, 2015 352 p.

ISBN 9781250010117

1. Frameups 2. Murder suspects 3. Obsessive-compulsive disorder 4. Single fathers 5. Hospitals 6. Physicians 7. Murder 8. Divorced men 9. Sexual harassment 10. Psychopaths 11. Missing persons 12. Philadelphia, Pennsylvania 13. Thrillers and suspense

LC 2014042835

A single father and head of a successful Philadelphia psychiatric care unit sees his life begin to crumble when a teen patient is implicated in a murder and the doctor himself is wrongly accused of sexual harassment.

"Scottoline casts an unflinching eye on the damaged world of sociopaths in this exciting page-turner. . . . Many characters who seem to be gunning for Eric are likely candidates for a sociopathic diagnosis. Once the red herrings are dispatched, the identity of the culprit who plots his downfall is a genuine surprise." Publishers Weekly.

Scottoline, Lisa,

Feared / Lisa Scottoline. St. Martin's Press, 2018. 386 p. Rosato and Associates novels

ISBN 9781250099594

1. Law firms 2. Suing (Law) 3. Women lawyers 4. Enemies 5. Revenge in women 6. Malicious accusation 7. Philadelphia, Pennsylvania 8. Pennsylvania 9. Legal thrillers 10. Thrillers and suspense

LC 2018022095

When nemesis Nick Machiavelli targets her family with frivolous legal claims and slander that escalate to an unthinkable tragedy, Mary DiNunzio discovers her own unsettling capacity for dark retaliation.

Scottoline, Lisa

Legal tender / Lisa Scottoline. HarperCollins, 1996. 452 p. Rosato and Associates novels

ISBN 006017658X

1. Women lawyers 2. Animal rights advocates 3. Murder 4. Police corruption 5. Women murder suspects 6. Lawyers 7. Italian American women 8. Rosato & Associates (Imaginary organization)

9. Philadelphia, Pennsylvania 10. Legal thrillers 11. Thrillers and suspense

LC 967165

When her former lover and partner, Mark Biscardi, turns up murdered and she becomes the prime suspect in the crime, Philadelphia lawyer Benedetta "Bennie" Rosato finds herself framed for murder, on the run from the cops, and searching for the real killer

Scottoline, Lisa

One perfect lie / Lisa Scottoline. St. Martin's Press, 2017. 355 p.

ISBN 9781250099563

1. Single mothers 2. Teenage boys 3. Deception 4. Mothers and sons 5. Teachers 6. Secret identity 7. Peer pressure 8. Rich people 9. Conspiracies 10. Murder 11. Thrillers and suspense 12. Parallel narratives

A single mom's efforts to support her shy star athlete son's recruitment into a Division I college are violently complicated by a secretly disturbed young man from an affluent family and a new teacher with a mysterious agenda.

"Scottoline keeps the pace relentless as she drops a looming threat into the heart of an idyllic suburban community, causing readers to hold their breath in anticipation." Booklist.

Searles, John

Help for the haunted / John Seales. William Morrow, 2013. 368 p.

ISBN 9780060779634

1. Parents -- Death 2. Family secrets 3. Demons 4. Christian men 5. Sisters 6. Murder 7. Teenage girls 8. Ostracism 9. Grief in teenagers 10. Secrets 11. Psychic ability 12. Psychological suspense

Struggling with the loss of her parents, who helped haunted souls find peace, Sylvie Mason pursues the mystery, moving closer to the truth of what happened that night as she comes to terms with her family's past.

Sears, Michael, 1950-

Black Fridays / Michael Sears. G. P. Putnam's Sons, 2012. 352 p. Jason Stafford novels

ISBN 9780399158667

1. Financial services industry and trade -- Corrupt practices 2. Former convicts 3. Self-fulfillment 4. Parents of children with autism 5. Corporate crime 6. Child custody 7. Divorced men 8. Wall Street, New York City 9. Financial thrillers

LC 2012011085

Shamus Award for Best First P.I. Novel, 2013.

Struggling to rebuild his life after a two-year prison term for unscrupulous choices, former Wall Street hotshot Jason Stafford is tapped by an investment firm to investigate the suspicious death of a junior trader, a dangerous assignment that is complicated by his efforts to reclaim his young autistic son from his unstable ex-wife.

Seay, Martin

The **mirror** thief / Martin Seay. Melville House, 2016. 582 p.

ISBN 9781612195148

1. 1950s 2. Mirrors 3. Identity (Psychology) 4. Conspiracies 5. Secrets 6. Truth 7. Swindlers and swindling 8. Venice, Italy -- History -- 16th century 9. Venice Beach, Florida 10. Las Vegas, Nevada 11. Literary fiction 12. Parallel narratives

Three schemers hatch plans to outwit others and steal secrets in interconnected stories that are set in three Venices--in Italy, California, and the casino in Las Vegas-- during different eras.

"In sum, this is a splendid masterpiece, to be loved like a long-lost friend, an epic with near-universal appeal." Publishers Weekly.

Sebald, Winfried Georg, 1944-2001

* **Austerlitz** /   W.G. Sebald ; translated from the German by Anthea Bell. Random House, 2001. 298 p.

ISBN 0375504834

1. Holocaust (1933-1945) 2. Refugees, Jewish 3. Orphans -- Europe 4. Exiles -- Germany 5. World War II 6. Memory 7. Europe 8. Literary fiction 9. Translations -- German to English

LC 2001019785

Originally published: Munchen : C. Hanser, 2001.

ALA Notable Book, 2002.

National Book Critics Circle Award for Fiction, 2001.

In 1939, five-year-old Jacques Austerlitz is sent to England on a Kindertransport and placed with foster parents. This childless couple promptly erase from the boy all knowledge of his identity and he grows up ignorant of his past. Later in life, after a career as an architectural historian, Austerlitz - having avoided all clues that might point to his origin - finds the past returning to haunt him and he is forced to explore what happened fifty years before.

"As so often in Sebald's fiction, direct connections are never highlighted in the vast loops and sudden knottings of his rhetoric, but the reader cannot escape the inference that in the long sweep of history the Nazis were not alone, but that an inquirer searching for meaning is." New York Times Book Review.

Sebald, Winfried Georg, 1944-2001

The **emigrants** ;, W. G. Sebald ; translated by Michael Hulse. New Directions, 1996. 237 p.

ISBN 0811213382

1. Exiles 2. World War II 3. Holocaust (1933-1945) 4. Germany 5. Literary fiction 6. Psychological fiction 7. Translations -- German to English

LC 96-22223

Four narratives weave history and fiction together as refugees from the holocaust remember their experiences

"A profound and original work . . . . W. G. Sebald has created an end-of-century meditation that explores the most delicate, most painful, most nervously repressed and carefully concealed lesions of the last hundred years. Illuminatingly engaged with the history and literature of the modern era, Mr. Sebald's book gains power through its poetic obsessions with the past." New York Times Book Review.

Sebald, Winfried Georg, 1944-2001

Vertigo / W.G. Sebald ; translated by Michael Hulse. New Directions Pub., 2000. 263 p.

ISBN 0811214303

1. Travelers 2. Voyages and travels 3. Venice, Italy -- History 4. Bavaria -- History 5. France -- History 6. Literary fiction 7. Translations -- German to English

LC 99058955

First-person narrative describes a journey from Italy during Napoleon's invasion to a Bavarian village, drawing in the memories of notable thinkers such as Franz Kafka and Casanova.

"W.G. Sebald is unusual for a literary star. He fuses genres (travelogue, biography, the novel, meditation, myth), confounding the categories most readers are used to. The narrator of 'Vertigo' offers a fair account of Mr. Sebald's intricate methods. . . . This is poetic or philosophical fiction for readers content to follow the path of a remarkable author's thoughts without the guard-rail of an overarching story." The Economist.

Sebastian, Cat

It takes two to tumble / Cat Sebastian. Avon Impulse, 2018. 304 p. Seducing the Sedgwicks

ISBN 9780062821577

1. Regency period (1811-1820) 2. Clergy 3. Ship captains 4. Gay men 5. Single fathers 6. Tutors 7. Families 8. Engaged persons 9. Options, alternatives, choices 10. Sexual attraction 11. Men/men relations 12. England -- Social life and customs -- 19th century 13. Regency romances 14. LGBTQIA romances 15. Historical romances

"Sebastian's latest elegantly and eloquently written Regency historical, which puts a clever, same-sex spin on the classic employer/governess trope, slowly unfolds into an unforgettable love story that manages to be both sweetly romantic and sizzlingly sensual at the same time." Booklist

Sebastian, Cat

The **Lawrence** Browne affair / Cat Sebastian. Avon Impulse, 2017. 336 p. Turner series (Cat Sebastian)

ISBN 9780062642516

1. Regency period (1811-1820) 2. Earls and countesses 3. Gay men 4. Men/men relations 5. Manors 6. Scientists 7. False personation 8. Interclass romance 9. Personal assistants 10. Interpersonal attraction 11. Swindlers and swindling 12. Men with mental illnesses 13. Cornwall, England 14. Regency romances 15. LGBTQIA romances 16. Historical romances

RUSA Reading List Short List, 2018.

Hiding from the world in his family's crumbling estate, Lawrence Browne, brilliant scientist and the Earl of Radnor, finds his life turned upside down when Georgie Turner arrives at Penkellis claiming to be his new secretary.

Sebastian, Tim

Fatal ally / Tim Sebastian. Severn House, 2019. 240 p.

ISBN 9780727889522

1. M I 6 2. Women spies 3. Double agents 4. Defectors 5. Betrayal 6. International intrigue 7. Russia 8. Syria 9. Spy fiction 10. Thrillers and suspense

After five years' silence, a British intelligence asset has made contact from Moscow. Claiming to be in possession of an explosive piece of information, he wishes to defect to the West. The carefully-planned operation however goes catastrophically wrong, the would-be defector ruthlessly betrayed by a rogue element at the highest level of US government.

"Posing difficult questions about loyalty and morality, this unputdownable novel boasts a taut and suspenseful plot, vividly drawn characters, and an eye-opening look inside the dirty world of spying." Booklist.

Sebold, Alice

The **almost** moon : a novel / Alice Sebold. Little, Brown and Co., 2007. 304 p.

ISBN 9780316677462

1. Parricide 2. Women with mental illnesses 3. Mother and adult daughter 4. Middle-aged women 5. Divorced women 6. Mothers -- Death 7. Detachment (Psychology) 8. Family relationships 9. Murder 10. Childhood innocence (Concept) 11. Mothers and daughters 12. Parent and child 13. Senior women 14. Psychological fiction

LC 2007009917

Having set aside her own life in her support of her parents, husband, and children, Helen Knightly confronts the realities of the choices that were imposed upon her during a harrowing twenty-four-hour period of death and revelation.

"This novel is brilliantly paced, it's brutally honest, and the Gordian knot at its core an abusive mother and her traumatically attached daughter is depicted with such generous intelligence that the fineness of the novel more than surpasses its own horror show of circumstance. Sebold has managed to give us a sympathetic protagonist who smothers her mother in the opening pages, and yet the decades that led up to this black moment are delivered without a shred of sentimentality or melodramatic overkill. It's a tightrope walk of character building." Boston Globe.

Sebold, Alice

* The **lovely** bones / Alice Sebold. Little, Brown, 2002. 288 p.

ISBN 9780316666343

1. Families of murder victims 2. Crimes against teenage girls 3. Murder victims 4. Teenage girl murder victims 5. Rape victims 6. Grief 7. Loss (Psychology) 8. Heaven 9. Spirits 10. Life after death 11. Psychological fiction 12. Literary fiction

LC 2001050622

Bram Stoker Award for Best First Novel, 2002.

Book Sense Book of the Year Adult Fiction, 2003.

British Book Award for the Richard & Judy Best Read of the Year, 2004.

Eliot Rosewater Indiana High School Book Award (Rosie Award), 2005.

Gateway Readers Award (Missouri), 2005.

Iowa High School Book Award, 2005.

Kentucky Bluegrass Award for Grades 9-12, 2004.

South Carolina Book Award, Young Adult Books, 2005.

Looking down from heaven, 14-year-old Susie Salmon recounts her rape and murder and watches her family as they cope with their grief and "the lovely bones" growing around her absence.

"As pleasant as Susie's heaven is, there's no God there, and certainly no Jesus. This is spirituality for an age that's ecumenical to a fault. But emotionally, it's faultless. Sebold never slips as she follows this family. The risks she walks are enough to give you vertigo." Christian Science Monitor.

Sedaris, David

Holidays on ice / David Sedaris. Little, Brown and Co., 2008, c1997. 192 p.

ISBN 9780316035903

1. Families -- United States 2. Holidays -- United States 3. Americans in France 4. Family relationships 5. Christmas stories 6. Short stories 7. Essays 8. Life stories General

LC 2008925927

A classic collection of stories features six additional works on the joys and embarrassments of favorite holidays, including tales of tardy trick-or-treaters, the difficulties of explaining the Easter Bunny to another culture, and a barnyard Secret Santascheme gone awry.

An anthology of humorous Christmas tales and essays features excerpts from the author's "Barrel Fever" and "Naked," as well as "The Santaland Diaries," "Season's Greetings to Our Friends and Family," and a new tale of holiday mayhem.

"For those dreading the holiday season, bestseller Sedaris (When You Are Engulfed In Flames) makes life a little easier with this re-release of his uproarious essay collection, newly expanded from the original 1997 edition." Publishers Weekly.

Sedgwick, Marcus

Mister Memory : a novel / Marcus Sedgwick. Pegasus Crime, 2017. 327 p.

ISBN 9781681773407

1. Belle Epoque (1871-1914) 2. 1890s 3. Murder suspects 4.

Psychiatric hospitals 5. Photographic memory 6. Police 7. Dancers 8. Corruption 9. Obsession 10. Physicians 11. Wife-killing 12. Conspiracies 13. Murder investigation 14. Paris, France -- History -- 19th century 15. France -- History -- 19th century 16. Historical mysteries

Transferred to a famous asylum after being arrested for his wife's murder at the end of the 19th century, a man with an eidetic memory is investigated by a doctor and a police officer who discover links between the bizarre crime and the highest and lowest establishments in France.

"Marvelously imagined and sure to appeal to readers who enjoy an intelligent thriller." Kirkus.

Sedley, Kate

* The **Tintern** treasure / Kate Sedley. Severn House, 2012. 256 p. Roger the Chapman tales

ISBN 9780727881649

1. Plantagenet period (1154-1485) 2. Medieval period (476-1492) 3. 15th century 4. Murder investigation 5. Robbery 6. Nobility 7. Insurgency 8. Robbery investigation 9. Murder 10. Civilization, Medieval 11. Peddlers 12. Amateur detectives 13. London, England -- History -- 15th century 14. Great Britain -- History -- Edward IV, 1461-1483 15. Medieval mysteries 16. Historical mysteries

Roger the Chapman discovers the treasure that was stolen from Tintern Abbey the night he took refuge there during the Duke of Buckingham's rebellion, and his knowledge of the treasure quickly puts his and a family member's lives in danger.

See, Carolyn

The **handyman** : a novel / Carolyn See. Random House, 1999. 220 p.

ISBN 9780375501555

1. Artists -- California 2. Blue collar workers 3. Interpersonal relations 4. Repairers 5. Psychological fiction

LC 98-21098

A twenty-eight-year-old aspiring painter, Bob Hampton is discouraged by his lack of artistic vision, drops out of art school, and sets out to earn money as a handyman, but he soon discovers his real talent lies in repairing the mixed-up lives of his clients.

"Bob Hampton, a future great artist, leads a quintessentially California life as a freelance handyman before he answers his true calling; in the course of a hot Los Angeles summer, he worries about his lack of aesthetic sophistication, comforts lonely housewives in the time-honored way, and rescues a drowning child and an AIDS patient. Despite a confusing start, the novel quickly takes on the brightness of a sun-dazzled swimming pool and makes a case for shadowless livinga state its hero achieves through an unlikely combination of application and hedonism." The New Yorker.

See, Carolyn

There will never be another you : a novel / Carolyn See. Random House, 2006. 256 p.

ISBN 0679463178

1. Widows 2. Volunteer hospital workers 3. Mother and adult son 4. Crisis management 5. Dysfunctional families -- Los Angeles, California 6. Dermatologists 7. Hospitals -- Los Angeles, California 8. War 9. Terrorism 10. Eco-terrorism 11. Secrets 12. Marital conflict 13. Breaking up (Interpersonal relations) 14. Los Angeles, California -- History -- 21st century 15. Southern California 16. Psychological fiction 17. Domestic fiction

LC 2005044932

In an unstable world of the near future, as three generations of a Southern California family confront a series of personal and international crises, Phil, a physician at the UCLA hospital, deals with a grieving mother, belligerent children, and disinterested wife while taking on leadership of a top-secret emergency response team.

"Among the most potent and poignant new novels to address post-9/11 America. . . . It is potent because the sense of dread and unease that mark almost every moment in the book is palpable; it is poignant because See, who in previous books has proven eminently capable of skewering her characters when they misbehave, has such compassion for the largely villain-less ensemble that populates this tale." Washington Post Book World.

See, Lisa

Dragon bones : a novel / Lisa See. Random House, 2003. xv, 348 p. Red princess mysteries

ISBN 0679463208

1. Three Gorges Project, China 2. Policewomen -- China 3. Archaeological sites -- China 4. Cults -- China 5. Murder investigation 6. Antiquities -- Collection and preservation 7. Dams -- Design and construction -- China 8. Interracial marriage 9. Archaeological thefts 10. Husband-and-wife detectives 11. Americans in China 12. China -- Antiquities 13. Yangtze River 14. Yangtze River Gorges (China) 15. Yangtze River Valley, China 16. China -- Social life and customs -- 1976- 17. Mysteries

LC 2002024871

When the body of an American archaeologist turns up in the Yangtze, Liu Hulan, an agent for the Chinese government, and her American husband, David Stark, investigate and find that the murder may be tied to a missing priceless artifact.

"The novel flows beautifully, engaging readers in the mystery while gently introducing them to China's rich cultural history." Library Journal.

See, Lisa

Dreams of joy : a novel / Lisa See. Random House, 2011. 336 p.

ISBN 9781400067121

1. 1950s 2. Family relationships 3. Mothers and daughters 4. Family secrets 5. Birthfathers 6. Communism 7. Reconciliation 8. China -- History -- 20th century 9. Historical fiction

LC 2011003891

Sequel to: Shanghai girls.

Finds a devastated Joy fleeing to China to search for her real father while her mother, Pearl, desperately pursues her, a dual quest marked by their encounters with the nation's intolerant Communist culture.

"Although the ending betrays Sees roots in genre fiction, this is a riveting, meticulously researched depiction of one of the worlds worst human-engineered catastrophes." Kirkus.

See, Lisa

The **island** of sea women / Lisa See. Scribner, 2019 320 p.

ISBN 9781501154850

1. 20th century 2. Women divers 3. Fishers 4. Female friendship 5. Family secrets 6. Islands 7. Villages 8. Traitors 9. Insurgency 10. Jeju Island, South Korea 11. South Korea 12. Historical fiction

While working as divers with the all-female diving collective on a small Korean island, Mi-ja and Young-sook find their friendship challenged by their differences and forces outside their control.

See, Lisa

Peony in love : a novel / Lisa See. Random House, 2007. 304 p.

ISBN 9781400064663

1. 17th century 2. Women -- China 3. Operas 4. Love 5. Men/women relations 6. Interpersonal attraction 7. Sexual freedom 8. Self-fulfillment in women 9. Happiness in women 10. Gender role 11.

China -- History -- Ming dynasty, 1368-1644 12. Love stories 13. Historical fiction

LC 2007001623

In seventeenth-century China, three women become emotionally involved with "The Peony Pavilion," a famed opera rumored to cause lovesickness and even death.

"This novel, isfor the reader willing to venture a crucial suspension of disbeliefa complex period tapestry inscribed with the age-old tragedy of love and death and bordered round with vignettes from Chinese metaphysics, dynastic history and the intimate chamber tales of women's friendship and rivalry. . . . See is gifted with a lucid, graceful style and a solid command of her many motifs." New York Times Book Review.

See, Lisa

Shanghai girls : a novel / Lisa See. Random House, 2009. 336 p.

ISBN 9781400067114

1. 1930s 2. Chinese American women 3. Immigrants -- United States 4. Sisters 5. Immigrants, Chinese 6. Fathers and daughters 7. Husband and wife 8. Family secrets 9. Betrayal 10. Loyalty 11. United States -- Social life and customs -- 20th century 12. China -- History -- 20th century 13. Historical fiction

LC 2008049245

Sequel: Dreams of joy.

Forced to leave Shanghai when their father sells them to California suitors, sisters May and Pearl struggle to adapt to life in 1930s Los Angeles while still bound to old customs, as they face discrimination and confront a life-altering secret.

"Pearl and May Chin are Beautiful Girls, models in 1930s Shanghai whose images grace calendars and ads and who party with the young and restless in the Paris of Asia. But the party is soon over. . . . Their father sells them into arranged marriages with the sons of a Chinese family that emigrated to Los Angeles. The daughters rebel and literally miss the boat until the Japanese attack on Shanghai in 1937 forces them on an Odyssean journey to America. In this moving historical novel, Lisa See explores her Chinese-American roots and those of the Chinese who headed to California in the early 20th century in hopes of a better life, only to find hardship and discrimination." USA Today.

See, Lisa

The **tea** girl of Hummingbird Lane / Lisa See. Scribner, 2017. 352 p.

ISBN 9781501154829

1. Adopted girls 2. International adoption 3. Chinese American girls 4. Tea 5. Families 6. Cultural differences 7. Identity (Psychology) 8. Mother-separated girls 9. Mothers and daughters 10. Adoption of Chinese children 11. Akha (Southeast Asian people) 12. China 13. California 14. Literary fiction

Explores the lives of a Chinese mother and her daughter, who has been adopted by an American couple, tracing the very different cultural factors that compel them to consume a rare native tea that has shaped their family's destiny for generations.

"With vivid and precise details about tea and life in rural China, Li-Yans gripping journey to find her daughter comes alive." Publishers Weekly.

Segal, Erich, 1937-2010

* **Love** story / Erich Segal. Bantam Books, 1970. 115 p.

ISBN 9780380017607

1. Harvard University Students 2. College students 3. Interclass romance 4. Women with terminal illnesses 5. Boston, Massachusetts 6. Love stories

LC 71096003

Sequel: Oliver's story (1977).

"A very professionally crafted short first novel. The author makes no great claims of insight for his work. Indeed, the story is all on the surface. But it is funny and sad and generally recommended." Library Journal.

Seiffert, Rachel

A **boy** in winter : a novel / Rachel Seiffert. Pantheon, 2017 224 p.

ISBN 9780307908834

1. S. S. 2. Second World War era (1939-1945) 3. 1940s 4. Nazis 5. Jews, Ukrainian -- History -- 20th century 6. Military occupation 7. Holocaust (1933-1945) 8. Fathers 9. Missing boys 10. Conscientious objectors 11. Fear 12. Courage 13. Survival 14. War 15. World War II -- Ukraine 16. Ukraine -- History -- German occupation, 1941-1944 17. Historical fiction

LC 2017008889

Longlisted for The Women's Prize for Fiction, 2018.

Shortlisted for the International Dublin Literary Award, 2019.

In a small Ukrainian town that is overrun by the SS in 1941, the lives of its residents--including Ephraim, a Jew under the threat of deportation who awaits word of his missing sons; Yasia, who has come in search of her lover only to confront new and harsh truths about those closest to her; and a young boy determined to survive--become intertwined.

Sekaran, Shanthi, 1977-

* **Lucky** boy / Shanthi Sekaran. G.P. Putnam's Sons, 2016 480 p.

ISBN 9781101982242

1. Undocumented immigrants 2. Determination in women 3. Motherhood 4. Single mothers 5. Foster mothers 6. Mexicans in the United States 7. East Indian-American women 8. Infertility 9. Marital conflict 10. Child custody 11. Undocumented workers 12. Berkeley, California 13. Literary fiction 14. Domestic fiction

LC 2016008418

A wrenching emotional battle ensues between Soli, an undocumented Mexican single mother, and Kavya, an Indian-American chef who cannot have children, when Soli's infant son is placed in Kavya's care during an immigration detention.

"Sekaran is a master of drawing detailed, richly layered characters and relationships; here are the subtly nuanced lines of love and expectation between parents and children; here, too are moments of great depth and insight. A superbly crafted and engrossing novel." Kirkus.

Self, Will

The **book** of Dave : a revelation of the recent past and the distant future / Will Self. Bloomsbury Pub. : 2006. 512 p.

ISBN 1596911239

1. 21st century 2. Taxicab drivers 3. Dystopias 4. Rulers 5. Near future 6. Books 7. Divorced couples 8. Heresy 9. Prophets 10. Fathers and sons 11. Sacred books 12. Regression (Civilization) 13. London, England 14. Satirical fiction 15. Satirical fiction

LC 2006004750

"Self achieves an elaborate vision of vicious superstition and hopeless struggle." The New Yorker.

Self, Will

Shark / Will Self. Grove Press, 2014. 466 p.

ISBN 9780802123107

1. 1970s 2. Psychiatrists 3. Veterans 4. Memory 5. Survival 6. World War II 7. Literary fiction

Sequel/prequel to: Umbrella.

In 1975, five years after being tricked into going on an ill-advised LSD trip, maverick psychiatrist Dr. Zack Busner realizes the true nature of the events that transpired on that dread-soaked day, when a survivor of the World War II sinking of the USS Indianapolis[/i] came face-to-face with the British Royal Air Force observer on the Enola Gay's mission to bomb Hiroshima.

"This jumbled structure is the platform from which Self explores society's judgments of and effects on sanity and mental health. Self's style pays homage to the modernism of writers such as Joyce and Cline and the black humor of Vonnegut and Heller in this challenging but exceptional read." Booklist.

Self, Will

Umbrella / Will Self. Grove Press, 2012. 397 p.

ISBN 9780802120724

1. Psychiatrists 2. Psychiatric hospitals 3. People in comas 4. Consciousness 5. Memory 6. Epidemic encephalitis 7. Physician and patient 8. Photographic memory 9. World War I 10. Literary fiction

Originally published: London : Bloomsbury, 2012.

Shortlisted for the Man Booker Prize, 2012.

A psychiatrist at a mental hospital in London's northern suburb of Friern Barnet, Zachary Busner, investigating a group of unconscious patients called enkies who exhibit a peculiar type of physical tic, stumbles upon a miracle drug that could save these patients, but the hospital has other, darker ideas.

Sem-Sandberg, Steve, 1958-

* The **chosen** ones : a novel / Steve Sem-Sandberg ; translated from the Swedish by Anna Paterson. Farrar, Straus and Giroux, 2016, c2014. 512 p.

ISBN 9780374122805

1. Spiegelgrund (Children's institution) 2. Second World War era (1939-1945) 3. Euthanasia 4. Persecution by Nazis 5. Children with chronic illnesses 6. Nazis 7. Murder 8. Nazism 9. Nazi scientists 10. Children's hospitals 11. Holocaust (1933-1945) 12. Children -- Institutional care 13. Vienna, Austria -- History -- 20th century 14. Austria -- History -- 20th century 15. Historical fiction 16. Literary fiction 17. Translations -- Swedish to English

LC 2015042554

"Originally published in Swedish in 2014 by Albert Bonniers Forlag, Sweden, as De utvalda. English translation originally published in 2016 by Faber and Faber Ltd., Great Britain" -- Verso title page.

A tale inspired by a devastating, forgotten incident from annexed Vienna follows the experiences of a young inmate at a reform school for chronically ill children who become subject to the Nazi regime's euthanasia program on the eve of World War II.

"With a gift for finding humanity in even the darkest of stories, Sem-Sanberg has written an indelible, moving novel." Publishers Weekly.

Semple, Maria

Where'd you go, Bernadette : a novel / Maria Semple. Little, Brown and Co., 2012. 330 p..

ISBN 9780316204279

1. Women architects -- Seattle, Washington 2. Missing persons investigation 3. Phobias 4. Mothers and daughters 5. Agoraphobia in women 6. Antarctica 7. Seattle, Washington 8. Humorous stories 9. Mainstream fiction 10. Pacific Northwest fiction

LC 2011040639

Shortlisted for The Women's Prize for Fiction, 2013

When her notorious, hilarious, volatile, talented, troubled and agoraphobic mother goes missing, teenage Bee begins a trip that takes her to the ends of the earth to find her.

Senna, Danzy

New people / Danzy Senna. Riverhead Books, 2017. 288 p.

ISBN 9781594487095

1. 1990s 2. Multiracial persons 3. Doctoral students 4. Race relations 5. Poets 6. City life 7. Couples 8. Young women 9. Wedding planning 10. Documentary films 11. Crushes in women 12. Brooklyn, New York City 13. New York City 14. Literary fiction 15. African American fiction

LC 2016045954

Working on her dissertation while planning her wedding to her college sweetheart as the 20th century draws to a close, Maria, a young woman from Brooklyn being featured in a documentary about mixed-heritage couples, risks the life she has worked so hard to achieve by fantasizing about a poet she barely knows.

"Senna combines the clued-in status details you'd find in a New York magazine article with the narrative invention of big-league fiction. Every detail and subplot, including Maria's dissertation on the Jonestown massacre and her buried secret about a college prank gone awry, is resonant." Kirkus.

Seo, Mi-ae

The **only** child / Mi-ae Seo. HarperCollins, 2020. 288 p.

ISBN 9780062905048

1. Psychologists 2. Stepchildren 3. Serial murderers 4. Koreans 5. Children with behavioral disorders 6. Husband and wife 7. Child rearing 8. Violence in children 9. Women psychologists 10. Girls 11. Stepmothers 12. Korea 13. Thrillers and suspense

When serial killer Yi Byeongdo asks to speak to her, and her husband's 11-year-old daughter from a previous marriage shows up at their door, criminal psychologist Seonkyeong starts to unravel the pasts of the two new arrivals in her life and begins to see startling similarities.

"This strong addition to the growing collection of Asian crime fiction available in English shares unflinching narration and the unsettling atmosphere of a horror film with the work of Kanae Minato, Natsuo Kirino, and Masako Togawa." Booklist.

Sepetys, Ruta

Out of the Easy / Ruta Sepetys. Philomel Books, 2013. 288 p.

ISBN 9780399256929

1. 1950s 2. Children of prostitutes 3. Murder investigation 4. Teenage romance 5. Seventeen-year-old girls 6. Teenage girls 7. New Orleans, Louisiana -- History -- 20th century 8. French Quarter (New Orleans, La) 9. Historical mysteries 10. Mysteries

LC 2012016062

Josie, the seventeen-year-old daughter of a French Quarter prostitute, is striving to escape 1950 New Orleans and enroll at prestigious Smith College when she becomes entangled in a murder investigation.

Serafim, Leta

The **devil** takes half / Leta Serafim. Coffeetown Press, 2014 256 p. Greek Islands mysteries

ISBN 9781603819657

1. Archaeological sites 2. Murder investigation 3. Police 4. Islands of the Aegean 5. Greece 6. Police procedurals 7. Mysteries

"At an archeological dig on the idyllic Greek Island of Chios, a severed hand is found lying in a blood-filled trench. Could it belong to Eleni Argentis, a beautiful archeologist who is also the wealthy daughter of a local ship owner. She and her young assistant, Petros, are both missing. The chief officer of the local police force, Yiannis Patronas, suspects that Eleni and Petros happened upon something of real value. However, his search turns up nothing but handfuls of broken clay, and then, another body--that of Petros, whose throat has been brutally cut. More body parts belonging to Eleni are left behind on a remote beach, confirming her demise. Then an old priest with a fondness for TV detective shows is attacked and left for dead. The dig site is located near the monastery where he was the only resident. Patronas interviews Petros' longsuffering grandmother, his flighty mother and her money-grubbing boyfriend, as well as Eleni's greedy stepmother and her charming son. He also confronts two archeologists, one British and one American... If Eleni's find is, as they insist, worthless, what are these men doing on Chios? Although Patronas has little experience with homicide, he is determined to conquer the evil that threatens this formerly peaceful island."--Page 4 of cover.

Serafim, Leta

* **When** the devil's idle / Leta Serafim. Coffeetown Press, 2015. 180 p. Greek Islands mysteries

ISBN 9781603819985

1. Murder investigation 2. Tourists 3. Murder suspects 4. Murder 5. Secrets 6. Germans in Greece 7. Swastikas 8. Police 9. Islands of the Aegean 10. Greece 11. Police procedurals 12. Mysteries

Chief officer Yiannis Patronas brings in detective Giorgos Tembelos and amateur sleuth Papa Michalis to investigate the murder of a German tourist in the garden of an estate on Patmos.

Serle, Rebecca

In five years : a novel / Rebecca Serle Atria Books, 2020. 240 p.

ISBN 9781982137441

1. Fate and fatalism 2. Women lawyers 3. Ambition 4. Marriage proposals 5. Type A personality 6. Goals and objectives 7. Time travel (Future) 8. Men/women relations 9. Manhattan, New York City 10. Women's lives and relationships 11. Mainstream fiction 12. Love stories

LC 2019027133

An ambitious young lawyer on the brink of having it all disregards a vivid dream about how different her life will be in five years, before meeting the man in her vision nearly five years later.

"While the plot hinges on well-worn tropes, the deadpan prose highlights the author's keen sense of irony. Serle's whimsical tale is book club catnip." Publishers Weekly.

Serpell, Namwali, 1980-

* The **old** drift / Namwali Serpell. Hogarth Press, 2019. 640 p.

ISBN 9781101907146

1. 20th century 2. 21st century 3. Race relations 4. Family curses 5. Social change 6. Families 7. Families -- History 8. Colonialism 9. Postcolonialism 10. Interracial romance 11. Romantic love 12. Life change events 13. Zambia 14. Africa 15. Epic fiction 16. Family sagas 17. Magical realism 18. Literary fiction

Three generations of a cursed family traverse from India and Italy to England and ultimately a fantastical Zambia of the near future, where an interstitial Greek chorus of mosquitoes traces their vibrant human experiences as children, parents and grandparents.

Seth, Vikram, 1952-

* A **suitable** boy : a novel / Vikram Seth. Harper Collins, 1993. 1349 p.

ISBN 0060170123

1. 1950s 2. Family relationships 3. Extended families 4. Mothers and daughters 5. Rich families 6. Upper class 7. Land reform 8. Gentry 9. India -- History -- 1947 10. Love stories 11. Historical fiction

LC 92054744

While a widowed mother agonizes over her daughter's future, the newly independent India of the early 1950s struggles through a time of great crisis when its varied cultures clash

"This novel is, at its heart an elegy as well as a comedy of manners, about a traditional society in a time of change, and about a leisurely world of graces giving way to a new, more democratic time." Times Literary Supplement.

Seton, Anya

Avalon / Anya Seton. Chicago Review Press, 2006, c1965. 440 p.

ISBN 9781556526008

1. Anglo-Saxon period (449-1066) 2. 10th century 3. Princes 4. Shipwreck survivors 5. Voyages and travels 6. Men/women relations 7. Avalon (Legendary place) 8. Great Britain -- History -- Anglo-Saxon period, 449-1066 9. Historical fiction

Originally published: Boston : Houghton Mifflin, 1965.

During the period of conflict and exploration in the late-tenth century, a shipwreck brings a French prince into the life of a Cornish peasant.

"Late tenth- and early eleventh-century life in England and in the lands colonized by the Norsemen [i.e. Iceland] is re-created from early Anglo-Saxon chronicles, French manuscripts, and secondary sources. . . . The action and milieu are vivid and though the characterization is not strong the psychological and historical motivations are believable. An honest historical novel for enthusiasts of the genre." Booklist.

Seton, Anya

* Dragonwyck / Anya Seton. Chicago Review Press, 2005, c1944. 342 p.

ISBN 9781556525810

1. 19th century 2. Governesses 3. Family estates 4. Violence 5. Narcissism 6. Men/women relations 7. Dysfunctional families 8. New York City 9. Hudson River 10. Gothic fiction

Originally published: Boston : Houghton Mifflin, 1944.

It was on an afternoon in May 1844 when the letter came from Dragonwyck. Tired of life on her father's farm in Connecticut, Miranda Wells happily accepts the invitation to the luxurious estate of her distant relative, the dashing and mysterious Nicholas Van Ryn. Introduced to a way of life she has only ever dreamed of, the innocent farm girl becomes a great lady. But soon the dark secrets of Dragonwyck begin to unfold.

Seton, Anya

Green darkness / Anya Seton. Chicago Review Press, 2005, c1972. 591 p.

ISBN 9781556525766

1. Time travel (Past) 2. Reincarnation 3. Visions 4. Fear in women 5. Household employees 6. Americans in England 7. Husband and wife 8. Men/women relations 9. Reformation 10. Great Britain -- History -- Tudors, 1485-1603 11. Gothic fiction

Originally published: Boston : Houghton Mifflin, 1972.

After a young American woman named Celia moves to England with her new husband, she finds herself haunted by a strange dread, a fear she can only escape by traveling four hundred years into the past and reliving her life as a beautiful servant in the sixteenth century.

"Reincarnation is the theme of [this] . . . novel. A 16th-century Benedictine monk, Stephen Marsdon, falls prey to a consuming passion for alluring Celia de Bohun and forsakes his vows. The tragic end of the lovers, involving murder and suicide, brings, nearly 400 years later, madness and near death to their reincarnations, newlyweds Celia and Richard Marsdon. Fortunately, a Hindu doctor (himself a reincarnated Italian physician in Tudor England who longed for warmer climates) hovers nearby to monitor the proceedings and brings the souls to rest." Library Journal.

Seton, Anya

Katherine / Anya Seton. Chicago Review Press, 2004, c1954. 500 p.

ISBN 9781556525322

1. Katharine, duchess of Lancaster, 1350-1403 2. John,, of Gaunt, Duke of Lancaster, 1340-1399 3. Plantagenet period (1154-1485) 4. 14th century 5. Knights and knighthood 6. Extramarital affairs 7. Redemption 8. Love triangles 9. Murder 10. Nobility 11. Loneliness 12. Dukes and duchesses 13. Great Britain -- History -- Plantagenets, 1154-1399 14. Biographical fiction 15. Historical fiction 16. Love stories

Originally published: Boston : Houghton Mifflin, 1954.

"It is a story that demands no intellectual or emotional effort from the reader. . . . But Miss Seton presents her facts accurately. Her research extends as far as visiting what remains of any of John of Gaunt's 30 castles and her zest for her subject communicates itself to the reader." San Francisco Chronicle.

Seton, Anya

* The Winthrop woman / Anya Seton. Chicago Review Press, 2006, c1958. 586 p.

ISBN 9781556526442

1. Winthrop, Elizabeth, ca 1610-ca 1668 2. Hutchinson, Anne Marbury, 1591-1643 3. Colonial America (1600-1775) 4. 17th century 5. Puritan women -- Massachusetts 6. Prejudice 7. Independence in women 8. Governors' spouses 9. Theocracy 10. Female friendship 11. Massachusetts -- History -- Colonial period, 1600-1775 12. Biographical fiction 13. Historical fiction

Originally published: Boston : Houghton Mifflin, 1958.

A biographical novel of Elizabeth Winthrop, a courageous woman who defied Puritan conventions and beliefs.

Setterfield, Diane

The **thirteenth** tale : a novel / Diane Setterfield. Atria Books, 2006. 406 p.

ISBN 0743298020

1. Books and reading 2. Twins 3. Women recluses 4. Women authors 5. Booksellers 6. Secrets 7. Storytellers 8. Exaggeration 9. Family secrets 10. Ghosts 11. Supernatural 12. Paranormal phenomena 13. Gothic fiction

LC 2006042906

When her health begins failing, the mysterious author Vida Winter decides to let Margaret Lea, a biographer, write the truth about her life, but Margaret needs to verify the facts since Vida has a history of telling outlandish tales.

Settle, Mary Lee

O Beulah land / Mary Lee Settle. C. Scribner's Sons, 1987, c1956. 368 p. Beulah series

ISBN 9780684188461

1. Virginia -- History -- Colonial period, 1600-1775 2. West Virginia 3. Family sagas 4. Historical fiction

LC 87023336

Johnny Lacey, on the eve of the Revolution, builds a valuable estate in the Virginia Territory, despite the threat from Indians and frontier bandits

Sexton, Margaret Wilkerson

A **kind** of freedom / Margaret Wilkerson Sexton. Counterpoint Press, 2017. 256 p.

ISBN 9781619029224

1. African American families 2. Middle class 3. Racism 4. Matriarchs

5. Single mothers 6. Father-deserted families 7. Drug addiction 8. Creoles (Louisiana) 9. Color of African Americans 10. Marijuana growing 11. African American young men 12. African American former convicts 13. Intergenerational relations 14. New Orleans, Louisiana 15. Family sagas 16. African American fiction 17. Literary fiction

LC 2017015331

BCALA Literary Award for First Novelist, 2018.

Longlisted for the National Book Award for Fiction, 2017.

Explores the legacy of racial disparity in the South through the story of three generations of an African American family in New Orleans.

"This novel sparked a competition among literary agents, and for good reason. This family is worth every minute of a readers time." Booklist.

Sexton, Margaret Wilkerson

The **revisioners** : a novel / Margaret Wilkerson Sexton. Counterpoint, 2019. 288 p.

ISBN 9781640092587

1. Women 2. Race relations 3. African American families 4. Interracial friendship 5. Freed slaves 6. Women farmers 7. Female friendship 8. Racism 9. White supremacists 10. Family history 11. Multiracial women 12. Single mothers 13. Grandmothers 14. Extended families 15. People with dementia 16. New Orleans, Louisiana 17. Family sagas 18. Literary fiction 19. African American fiction 20. Parallel narratives

LC 2019008282

Explores the impact of racism and interracial relationships between women through the story of an early 20th-century farmer and her unemployed single mother descendant.

Seymour, Gerald, 1941-

Vagabond / Gerald Seymour. Thomas Dunne Books, 2016, c2014. 448 p.

ISBN 9781250075659

1. M I 5. 2. Spies 3. Illegal arms transfers 4. Special operations (Military science) 5. Political violence 6. Special forces 7. Double agents 8. Dissenters 9. Terrorism 10. Espionage 11. Revenge 12. Prague, Czech Republic 13. Northern Ireland 14. Spy fiction 15. Thrillers and suspense

LC 2015037442

Originally published in 2014 by Hodder.

Living in quiet isolation after a brutal military career, elite spy handler Danny Curnow is summoned by his former boss to resume the work he tried to leave behind while helping a double agent broker an arms deal between Northern Ireland and Russia.

Shaara, Jeff, 1952-

Gods and generals : a novel of the Civil War / Jeff Shaara. Ballantine Books, 1996. 498 p. Civil War trilogy (Jeff Shaara)

ISBN 0345404920

1. Jackson, Stonewall, 1824-1863 2. Hancock, Winfield Scott, 1824-1886 3. Chamberlain, Joshua Lawrence, 1828-1914 4. Lee, Robert E (Robert Edward), 1807-1870 5. American Civil War era (1861-1865) 6. 1860s 7. Generals 8. Battles 9. Command of troops 10. Fredericksburg, Battle of, 1862 11. Chancellorsville, Battle of, 1863 12. Confederate soldiers 13. Union soldiers 14. Civil war 15. United States Civil War, 1861-1865 16. United States -- History -- Civil War, 1861-1865 17. Confederate States of America -- History, Military 18. Historical fiction 19. War stories 20. Biographical fiction

LC 95-53360

A prequel to Michael Shaara's The killer angels.

W. Y. Boyd Literary Award, 1997.

The lives and careers of four great military leaders--Stonewall Jackson, Winfield Scott Hancock, Joshua Chamberlain, and Robert E. Lee--reach a climax as Union and Confederate forces clash on the battlefields of the Civil War

"As should be the case with good historical fiction, Shaara, in taking actual figures from the past, rekindles them; he uses the personal experiences of these four men to meaningfully explore the political and military issues of the day." Booklist.

Shaara, Jeff, 1952-

Gone for soldiers / Jeff Shaara. Ballantine Books, 2000. xix, 424 p.

ISBN 0345427505

1. Lee, Robert E (Robert Edward), 1807-1870 2. Scott, Winfield, 1786-1866 3. Santa Anna, Antonio Lopez de, 1794-1876 4. 19th century 5. Revolutionaries 6. Revolutions 7. Soldiers -- United States 8. Generals 9. Command of troops 10. Mexican-American War, 1845-1848 11. Mexico -- History -- 1821-1867 12. United States -- History -- 1815-1865 13. Mexico -- History -- 1821-1861 14. United States -- History, Military -- 19th century 15. Historical fiction 16. War stories

LC 00022745

Eight thousand marines land in Vera Cruz bound for a war against the Mexican army, including Winfield Scott, a general who made history in the War of 1812, and Robert E. Lee, a forty-year-old engineer as yet untested in battle

"The book is simply wonderful, populated with eminently human heroes who are called upon to perform Herculean tasks in a war muddied beyond redemption by the ambitions of back-home and battlefield politicians." Library Journal.

Shaara, Jeff, 1952-

The **last** full measure / Jeff Shaara. Ballantine Books, 1998. 560 p. Civil War trilogy (Jeff Shaara)

ISBN 0345404912

1. Chamberlain, Joshua Lawrence, 1828-1914 2. Grant, Ulysses S, 1822-1885 3. Lee, Robert E (Robert Edward), 1807-1870 4. American Civil War era (1861-1865) 5. 1860s 6. Battles 7. Generals 8. Command of troops 9. Civil war 10. United States Civil War, 1861-1865 11. Confederate soldiers 12. Union soldiers 13. Confederate States of America -- History, Military 14. United States -- History -- Civil War, 1861-1865 15. Historical fiction 16. War stories 17. Biographical fiction

LC 97-49383

Illustrated with maps.

A second companion novel to "The Killer Angels" follows the continuing showdown between Grant and Lee on the battlefields of the Civil War

"As characters, Grant and Lee dominate this book. . . . Civil War buffs will find Shaara nodding on some small details, but they generally will be delighted with this book." Library Journal.

Shaara, Jeff, 1952-

The **rising** tide : a novel of World War II / Jeff Shaara. Ballantine Books, 2006. 576 p. World War II novels

ISBN 034546141X

1. Eisenhower, Dwight D (Dwight David), 1890-1969 Military leadership 2. Patton, George S, 1885-1945 Military leadership 3. Rommel, Erwin, 1891-1944 Military leadership 4. United States. Air Force Parachute troops. 5. Germany. Army. Afrika Korps. 6. Second World War era (1939-1945) 7. 1940s 8. World War II 9. Commando operations 10. Military aircraft -- United States -- History -- World War II 11. Tanks (Military science) 12. Soldiers 13. Nazism 14.

Military art and science -- United States -- History -- 20th century 15. Military history -- 20th century 16. Military strategy -- United States -- History -- World War II 17. Air warfare 18. Military campaigns 19. Europe -- History -- 1918-1945 20. Sicily, Italy -- History -- 1870-1945 21. North Africa -- History, Military -- 20th century 22. United States -- History -- 1933-1945 23. Historical fiction 24. War stories 25. Biographical fiction

LC 2006042936

As the forces of Nazi Germany overrun the nations of Europe and America is drawn into the war by the Japanese attack on Pearl Harbor, American troops and their British allies launch a campaign to stop Hitler on battlefields ranging from the deserts of North Africa to the rugged mountains of Sicily.

"Shaara opens this first volume of a projected trilogy in the deserts of North Africa, where Allied troops attempt to match wits and forces with the Desert Fox, wily German commander Field Marshall Erwin Rommel, and his formidable Afrika Korps. After Hitler overruns France, solidifying his position in Western Europe, he turns his attention eastward toward the vast Russian expanse. With the German focus split, the Allies sense the time is right to launch a united second front in North Africa, setting their sights on an eventual invasion of southern Italy. As plans for Operation Torch become a reality, Shaara vividly recreates a cast of military and political heroes and villains, including General Dwight D. Eisenhower, General George Marshall, General George Patton, British general Bernard Montgomery, German field marshal Erwin Rommel, Adolf Hitler, Winston Churchill, and Franklin Roosevelt." Booklist.

Shaara, Jeff, 1952-

The **steel** wave : a novel of World War II / Jeff Shaara. Ballantine Books, 2008. 576 p. World War II novels

ISBN 9780345461421

1. Bradley, Omar N, 1893-1981 Military leadership 2. Rommel, Erwin, 1891-1944 3. Eisenhower, Dwight D (Dwight David), 1890-1969 Military leadership 4. Patton, George S, 1885-1945 Military leadership 5. Second World War era (1939-1945) 6. 1940s 7. World War II 8. Soldiers 9. Nazism 10. Leadership -- United States 11. Normandy Invasion, June 6, 1944 12. Military art and science -- United States -- History -- 20th century 13. Military history -- 20th century 14. Military strategy -- United States -- History -- World War II 15. World War II -- Aerial operations, American 16. Commando operations 17. World War II -- France 18. Europe -- History -- 1918-1945 19. United States -- History -- 1933-1945 20. Historical fiction 21. War stories 22. Biographical fiction

LC 2008004813

RUSA Reading List, 2009.

A fictional account of D-Day and the Allied invasion of Europe chronicles the events of the campaign and the personalities who took part, from the ordinary soldiers on the land and in the air, to such leaders as Dwight Eisenhower and George Patton.

"The muscular prose, deft sense of military drama and relentless pacing are well suited for this crackerjack saga." Publishers Weekly.

Shaara, Michael

* The **killer** angels : a novel / Michael Shaara. David McKay Co., 1974. 374 p. Civil War trilogy (Jeff Shaara)

ISBN 0679504664

1. Longstreet, James, 1821-1904 2. Lee, Robert E (Robert Edward), 1807-1870 3. Buford, John, 1826-1863 4. Chamberlain, Joshua Lawrence, 1828-1914 5. United States. Army History Civil War, 1861-1865 6. American Civil War era (1861-1865) 7. Gettysburg, Battle of, 1863 8. Confederate soldiers 9. Civil war 10. United States Civil War, 1861-1865 11. United States -- History -- Civil War,

1861-1865 12. War stories 13. Historical fiction

LC 73091120

Pulitzer Prize for Fiction, 1975.

"Shaara's version of private reflections and conversations are based on his reading of documents and letters. Although some of his judgments are not necessarily substantiated by historians, he demonstrates a knowledge of both the battle and the area. The writing is vivid and fast moving." Library Journal.

Shacochis, Bob

The **woman** who lost her soul / Bob Shacochis. Atlantic Monthly Press, 2013. 715 p.

ISBN 9780802119827

1. Espionage 2. Women photojournalists 3. Incest 4. Lawyers 5. Investigations 6. Murder 7. Spies 8. Revenge 9. Flashbacks 10. War 11. Family relationships 12. Men/women relations 13. Literary fiction

Pulitzer Prize for Fiction finalist, 2014.

This novel spans five decades and three continents; it traces a global lineage of political, cultural, and personal tumult from World War II to the present. During a time of brutal guerrilla warfare and civilian kidnappings, the humanitarian lawyer Tom Harrington travels to Haiti to investigate the murder of a beautiful, seductive photojournalist, Jackie Scott. There he is confronted with a dangerous landscape of poverty, corruption, and voodoo. The story brings to life an intricate portrait of catastrophic events that led up to the war on terror and the America we are today.-- Publisher's website.

Shafak, Elif, 1971-

* **10** minutes 38 seconds in this strange world / Elif Shafak Bloomsburg Publishing, 2019. 311 p.

ISBN 9781635574470

1. Sex workers 2. Memories 3. Sexual violence victims 4. Psychic trauma 5. Women -- Social conditions 6. City life 7. Istanbul, Turkey 8. Turkey 9. Psychological fiction 10. Literary fiction

Shortlisted for the Booker Prize, 2019.

In the moments after she has been murdered and left in a dumpster outside Istanbul, Tequila Leila enters a state of heightened awareness. Her heart has stopped beating but her brain is still active?for 10 minutes 38 seconds. While the Turkish sun rises and her friends sleep soundly nearby, she remembers her life?and the lives of others, outcasts like her. In Tequila Leila's death, the secrets and wonders of modern Istanbul come to life, painted vividly by the captivating tales of how Leila came to know and be loved by her friends. As her epic journey to the afterlife comes to an end, it is her chosen family who brings her story to a buoyant and breathtaking conclusion.

"Shafak's motley and compassionate cast embodies both the brutal consequences of tyranny and the power of individuals to undermine it in a full-tilt novel set in a fabled city, a swirling microcosm of human complexity and paradox." Booklist.

Shafak, Elif, 1971-

The **bastard** of Istanbul / Elif Shafak. Viking, 2007. 368 p.

ISBN 0670038342

1. Single mothers 2. Tattooing 3. Mothers and daughters 4. Armenians in Turkey 5. Armenian Americans 6. Women -- Istanbul, Turkey 7. Women's role 8. Multiracial women 9. Nineteen-year-old women 10. Female friendship 11. Family secrets 12. Culture conflict 13. Mysticism 14. Brothers and sisters 15. Armenian massacres, 1915-1923 16. Istanbul, Turkey 17. San Francisco, California 18. Satirical fiction 19. Domestic fiction

LC 2006042116

From one of Turkey's most acclaimed and outspoken writers comes a novel about the tangled histories of two families.

"Shafak's writing is seductive; each chapter of her novel is named for a food, and the warmth of the Turkish kitchen lies at the center of its wide-ranging plot. The Bastard of Istanbul portrays family as more than merely a function of genetics and fate, folding together history and fiction, the personal and the political into a thing of beauty." Elle.

Shafak, Elif, 1971-

Honor : a novel / Elif Shafak. Viking, 2013. 342 p.

ISBN 9780670784837

1. 1970s 2. 1990s 3. Muslims 4. Culture conflict 5. Mothers -- Death 6. Father-deserted families 7. Child immigrants 8. Honor 9. Betrayal 10. Life change events 11. Kurds 12. Interethnic relations 13. Parricide 14. Honor killings 15. London, England 16. Literary fiction

LC 2012039761

Follows the destinies of twin sisters born in a Kurdish village. While Jamila stays to become a midwife, Pembe follows her Turkish husband, Adem, to London, where they hope to make new lives for themselves and their children.

Shaffer, Mary Ann

The **Guernsey** Literary and Potato Peel Pie Society / Mary Ann Shaffer & Annie Barrows. Dial Press, 2008. 288 p.

ISBN 9780385340991

1. Second World War era (1939-1945) 2. Women authors 3. Book clubs 4. Letter writing 5. Interpersonal relations 6. Memories 7. Island life 8. World War II 9. Letters 10. England -- History -- 20th century 11. Guernsey (Channel Islands) 12. Epistolary novels 13. Historical fiction 14. Gentle reads

LC 2007047869

In 1946, writer Juliet Ashton finds inspiration for her next book in her correspondence with a native of Guernsey, who tells her about the Guernsey Literary and Potato Peel Pie Society, a book club born as an alibi during German occupation.

"Juliet's ready wit is enchanting, as are the discussion of authors from Catullus to Shakespeare. . . . There is the occasional false note. . . . However, The Guernsey Literary and Potato Peel Pie Society is a labor of love, and it shows on almost every page." Christian Science Monitor.

Shakar, Alex, 1968-

Luminarium / Alex Shakar. Soho Press, 2011. 438 p.

ISBN 9781569479759

1. 2000s (Decade) 2. Twin brothers 3. Virtual reality 4. Spirituality 5. Human experimentation in medicine 6. Corporate acquisitions 7. Technology 8. Loss (Psychology) 9. Desire in men 10. Purpose in life 11. People in comas 12. New York City 13. Literary fiction

LC 2011013331

Struggling with the loss of his computer software company and his twin brother's coma, a despairing Fred becomes a test subject in a neurological study promising a new spiritual outlook before he begins receiving bizarre e-mails and texts from someone claiming to be his comatose twin.

"The novel's most impressive aspect is that it always seems to be grounded. It's about the possibility of life after death, spiritualism through technology, Lord Of The Rings, 9/11, and the societal potential of videogames, and yet it mostly doesn't feel like it's overreaching." A.V. Club.

Shalev, Meir

Two she-bears : a novel / Meir Shalev ; translated from the Hebrew by Stuart Schoffman. Schocken Books, 2016. 304 p.

ISBN 9780805243291

1. Women high school teachers 2. Family history 3. Storytelling 4. Rural life 5. Loss (Psychology) 6. Farms 7. Children -- Death 8. Suicide 9. Murder 10. Forgiveness 11. Families 12. Palestine -- History -- 1917-1948 13. Israel 14. Literary fiction 15. Translations -- Hebrew to English

LC 2016001663

Originally published: 2013.

A U.S. release of a best-seller from Israel follows the efforts of teacher Ruta Tavori to promote independent thinking in a small British Palestine farming community by revealing the true story behind the suicides of three 1930s farmers.

"This tale of love and bloodshed resonates with the primal passions of the biblical texts it invokes, while opening provocative new perspectives on modern questions about Israeli politics and gender identity." Booklist.

Shalvis, Jill

Second chance summer / Jill Shalvis. Grand Central, 2015. 354 p. Cedar Ridge novels

ISBN 9781455586738

1. Former lovers 2. Second chances 3. Homecomings 4. Wildfire fighters 5. Search and rescue operations 6. Rescue work 7. Hometowns 8. Colorado 9. Contemporary romances

Despite hating her home town, Lily Danville must stay where the work is--in this case, a job at the hottest resort in Cedar Ridge, Colorado--and when rescue worker and firefighter Aidan Kincaid regrets letting her walk out of his life, it's all he can do to get her to give Cedar Ridge--and him--a second chance.

Shalvis, Jill

* **Simply** irresistible / Jill Shalvis. Forever, 2010. 326 p. Lucky Harbor novels

ISBN 9780446571616

1. Inheritance and succession 2. Abused women 3. Men/women relations 4. Interpersonal attraction 5. Trust in women 6. Sisters 7. Hotels 8. Transformations, Personal 9. Washington (State) 10. Contemporary romances

RITA Award for Best Contemporary Single Title Romance, 2011.

After losing both her boyfriend and her job, Maddie Moore, claiming the inheritance left by her free-spirited mother, arrives in the town of Lucky Harbor, Washington where she must convince her two half-sisters to join her in a business venture as well as convince herself to take a chance on love.

Shalvis, Jill

Sweet little lies / Jill Shalvis. Avon Books, 2016. 384 p. Heartbreaker Bay novels

ISBN 9780062448026

1. Women ship captains 2. Bar owners 3. Neighbors 4. Secrets 5. Wishing and wishes 6. Interpersonal attraction 7. Men/women relations 8. San Francisco, California 9. California 10. Contemporary romances

When she makes a wish in a wishing well for Finn to fall in love and find the happiness he deserves, Pru finds herself way in over her head--and heart--when he sets his sights on her and she realizes she must tell him the truth, which could ruin everything.

"Shalvis has created a love story romance fans can't help but root for and grounds it in an affable community they'll adore." Kirkus.

Shalvis, Jill

The **sweetest** thing / Jill Shalvis. Forever, 2011. 370 p. Lucky Harbor novels

ISBN 9780446571623

1. Sisters 2. Divorced women 3. Second chances 4. Coastal towns 5. Interpersonal attraction 6. Hotels 7. Sailors 8. Love triangles 9. Washington (State) 10. Contemporary romances

LC bl2011007482

When she returns home to Lucky Harbor, Washington, to help her sisters get their newly renovated inn up and running, Tara unexpectedly finds herself torn between two men--her sexy ex-husband and handsome sailor Ford Walker.

Shames, Terry

A **risky** undertaking for Loretta Singletary : a Samuel Craddock mystery / Terry Shames. Seventh Street Books, 2019. 272 p. Samuel Craddock mysteries

ISBN 9781633884908

1. Police chiefs 2. Online dating 3. Seniors 4. Missing women 5. Missing persons investigation 6. Small towns 7. Small town life 8. Secrets 9. Texas 10. Mysteries

LC 2018034389

After using an online dating site for senior citizens, town favorite Loretta Singletary--maker of cinnamon rolls and arbiter of town gossip--goes missing.

Shames, Terry

* An **unsettling** crime for Samuel Craddock / Terry Shames. Seventh Street Books, 2017. 270 p. Samuel Craddock mysteries

ISBN 9781633882096

1. Small town life -- Texas 2. Police chiefs 3. Hate crimes 4. Racism 5. Crimes against African Americans 6. Racism in law enforcement 7. Murder investigation 8. Young men 9. Police 10. Texas 11. Mysteries

"In this prequel, a young Samuel Craddock, as the newly elected chief of police in Jarrett Creek, must investigate the murder of five black residents and confront the ingrained prejudices in the small Texas town."--Provided by the publisher.

Shamsie, Kamila, 1973-

Home fire : a novel / Kamila Shamsie. Riverhead Books, 2017. 240 p.

ISBN 9780735217683

1. Brothers and sisters 2. Muslims 3. Politicians 4. Women graduate students 5. Loyalty 6. British in the United States 7. Lovers 8. Secrets 9. Families 10. Men/women relations 11. Family relationships 12. Great Britain -- Politics and government -- 21st century 13. London, England 14. Massachusetts 15. Syria 16. Political fiction 17. Literary fiction

LC 2017003238

Baileys Women's Prize for Fiction, 2018.

Longlisted for the Man Booker Prize, 2017.

Shortlisted for the International Dublin Literary Award, 2019.

Given a chance to resume a deferred dream years after raising her troubled siblings, Isma worries about the influence of a powerful politician's son who drives the family to choose between love and loyalty, with devastating consequences.

"In accessible, unwavering prose and without any heavy-handedness, Shamsie addresses an impressive mix of contemporary issues . . ." Booklist.

Shan, Sa, 1972-

The **girl** who played Go / Shan Sa ; translated by Adriana Hunter. Alfred A. Knopf, 2003. 288 p.

ISBN 1400040256

1. 1930s 2. Teenage girls 3. Obsession 4. Go (Game) 5. Board games 6. Love 7. War 8. Manchuria -- History -- 20th century 9. Translations -- French to English 10. Historical fiction

LC 2003044679

Kiriyama Prize for Fiction, 2004.

"The alternating parallel tales add an extra spark of energy to this swift-moving novel, as Sa portrays tenderness and brutality with equal clarity." Publishers Weekly.

Shanbhag, Vivka

Ghachar ghochar / Vivek Shanbhag ; translated from the Kannada by Srinath Perur. Penguin Books, 2017, c2013. 128 p.

ISBN 9780143111689

1. Families 2. Spice industry and trade 3. Wealth 4. Success (Concept) 5. Poverty 6. Slums 7. Businesspeople 8. Poor people 9. Identity (Psychology) 10. Transformations, Personal 11. Interpersonal relations 12. India -- Social conditions 13. Domestic fiction 14. Translations -- Kannada to English

LC 2016027137

Originally published: Heggodu : Aksara Prakasana, 2013

Follows the changing dynamics of an impoverished Bangalorean family who lived in a bug-infested shack until their family's spice company became an overnight success and ushered them into a new way of life and a brand new set of challenges.

"Absorbing, insightful, and altogether a wonderful read." Publishers Weekly.

Shannon, Dell, 1921-1988

* **Chaos** of crime / Dell Shannon. Morrow, 1985. 190 p. Luis Mendoza mysteries

ISBN 9780688022976

1. Robbery 2. Heat waves (Meteorology) 3. Crimes against prostitutes 4. Police 5. Criminals 6. Murderers 7. Murder investigation 8. Criminal investigation 9. Detectives 10. Mexican Americans 11. Los Angeles, California 12. Hardboiled fiction 13. Mysteries

Luis Mendoza and the L.A.P.D. pursue a psychotic sex killer, a gas station heister with an unusual MO, and an escaped convict

"A maniac is loose on the streets of Los Angeles, tying prostitutes to their beds, beheading them, disemboweling them, and then surgically dissecting them like laboratory animals. Detective Luis Mendoza and the Los Angeles Police Department are sufficiently stumped in trying to locate this madman who never leaves a clueuntil finally the discovery of a rare French wristwatch helps to reveal a seemingly unlikely killer." Booklist.

Shannon, Dell, 1921-1988

The **Manson** curse / Dell Shannon. W. Morrow, 1990. 262 p.

1. Family curses 2. Men with mental illnesses 3. Wakes (Funeral rites and ceremonies) 4. Families 5. Murder 6. Journalists 7. Supernatural 8. Murder investigation 9. Americans in England 10. Cornwall, England 11. Supernatural mysteries

LC 90036989

During a visit to England, American journalist Johnny Harkness becomes embroiled in a bizarre mystery involving an ancient family curse, the supernatural, and cold-blooded murder.

Shannon, Samantha, 1991-

The **bone** season / Samantha Shannon. Bloomsbury, 2013. 466 p. Bone season

ISBN 9781620401392

1. 21st century 2. Clairvoyance 3. Women psychics 4. Women prisoners 5. Mentors 6. Enemies 7. Criminals 8. Dystopias 9. Near future 10. Supernatural 11. Concentration camps 12. Interpersonal attraction 13. London, England 14. Oxford, England 15. England 16. Dystopian fiction 17. Science fantasy

LC 2012038358

Paige Mahoney is a Dreamwalker, a rare type of clairvoyant employed by the Seven Seals, the powerful criminal syndicate that operates within a dystopian 21st-century London controlled by the Scion government. When she's captured by Scion agents and turned over to the otherworldly Rephaim, Paige -- renamed XX-59-40 -- ends up in Sheol I, a prison camp where she and her fellow "voyants" will be trained to battle the flesh-eating Emim. Placed under the guardianship of Arcturus, Warden of the Mesarthim, Paige must develop her gifts if she wants to survive, let alone escape. This fast-paced, action-packed fantasy boasts extensive world-building, a complex system of magic, and a well-developed cast of characters. - Description by Gillian Speace.

Shannon, Samantha, 1991-

The **mime** order / Samantha Shannon. St. Martin's Press, 2015. 320 p. Bone season

ISBN 9781620408933

1. 21st century 2. Clairvoyance 3. Women fugitives 4. Women psychics 5. Intrigue 6. Secrets 7. Mentors 8. Criminals 9. Dystopias 10. Insurgency 11. Near future 12. Supernatural 13. London, England 14. Oxford, England 15. England 16. Dystopian fiction 17. Science fantasy

Fugitive Paige Mahoney flees Scion while Jaxon Hall and his Seven Seals prepare for a rare assembly of the clairvoyant community that is clouded by dark secrets, the emergence of the Rephaim, and an elusive Warden.

"Shannon creates vividly dilapidated, macabre, and mysterious worlds both urban and within the dreamscapes Paige valiantly enters. The motley, elaborately costumed characters are compelling; the non-stop, often eerie action is riveting." Booklist.

Shannon, Samantha, 1991-

The **priory** of the orange tree / Samantha Shannon. Bloomsbury USA, 2019 830 p.

ISBN 9781635570298

1. Royal houses 2. Dragons 3. Women assassins 4. Political intrigue 5. Women rulers 6. Secret societies 7. Courts and courtiers 8. Women wizards 9. Wizards 10. Magic 11. Good and evil 12. Imaginary kingdoms 13. Epic fantasy

A queen who would survive assassination attempts to continue her ruling line is protected with forbidden magic by a court outsider, while a secret society works to prevent a dragon war.

"A well-drawn feminist fantasy with broad appeal for fans of the epic and readers of Zen Cho, Naomi Novik, and V. E. Schwab." Booklist.

Shapiro, Barbara A., 1951-

The **muralist** / B. A. Shapiro. Algonquin Books of Chapel Hill, 2015 336 p.

ISBN 9781616203573

1. 1940s 2. Artists 3. Missing persons 4. Jewish women 5. Aunts 6. Muralists 7. Refugees 8. World War II 9. New York City -- Social life and customs -- 20th century 10. Historical fiction

Auction-house employee Danielle Abrams investigates the unsolved disappearance of her famous-artist great-aunt when she discovers enigmatic paintings hidden behind Abstract Expressionist works created decades earlier.

"Mystery and historical fiction lovers who can accept that many lives and tragic histories can indeed intersect and converge around works of art in New York and France will find this a riveting read." Library Journal.

Sharfeddin, Heather

Mineral spirits : a novel / Heather Sharfeddin. Bridge Works Pub. Co., 2006. 264 p..

ISBN 1882593987

1. Sheriffs 2. Ten-year-old boys 3. Women murder victims 4. Murder 5. Widows 6. Missing women 7. Self-defense 8. Courage in boys 9. Murder investigation 10. Men/women relations 11. Missing persons investigation 12. Montana 13. Mysteries 14. Pacific Northwest fiction

LC 2006000762

"The author blends Western and mystery genres into a fine, heady concoction." Library Journal.

Sharp, Zoe, 1966-

Fox hunter / Zoe Sharp. Pegasus Books, 2017. 336 p. Charlie Fox novels

ISBN 9781681774381

1. Women veterans 2. Private security services 3. Rape victims 4. Missing men 5. Rapists 6. Former Special Forces members 7. Lovers 8. Revenge 9. Iraq 10. Thrillers and suspense

In the latest novel in this energetic series, ex-special forces soldier Charlie Fox finds herself on a mission to the Iraqi countryside to track down a missing comrade-in-arms.

Sharp, Zoe, 1966-

Second shot : a Charlie Fox thriller / Zoe Sharp. Thomas Dunne Books/St. Martin's Minotaur, 2007. 320 p. Charlie Fox novels

ISBN 9780312358952

1. Women bodyguards 2. Murder 3. Secrets 4. Bodyguards 5. Former Special Forces members 6. Women motorcyclists 7. Women veterans 8. Protectiveness in women 9. Lotteries 10. New England 11. Mysteries

LC 2007019016

Hired to protect the beautiful Simone and her little girl while searching for Simone's long-lost father, female bodyguard Charlie Fox confronts a ruthless enemy who will do anything to stop her, including leaving her alone and wounded in the middle of a frozen New England woods.

Sharpe, Tess

Barbed wire heart / Tess Sharpe. Grand Central Publishing, 2018. 400 p.

ISBN 9781538744093

1. Organized crime 2. Young women 3. Drug traffic 4. Crime 5. Violence 6. Revenge 7. Rural families 8. Family violence 9. Methamphetamine 10. Northern California 11. California 12. Rural noir 13. Crime fiction

LC 2017041580

RUSA Reading List Short List, 2019.

In a book set in rural northern California, Harley McKenna has had to work for her North County-criminal father since she was 16, and as she is trying to decide whether to stay in the family business or get out, her family's biggest rivals, the Springfields, come gunning for her.

Sharratt, Mary, 1964-

Daughters of the Witching Hill / Mary Sharratt. Houghton Mifflin Harcourt, 2010. 352 p.

ISBN 9780547069678

1. Widows 2. Witchcraft -- Lancashire, England 3. Trials (Witchcraft) -- Lancashire, England 4. Witchcraft -- History -- 17th century 5. England -- History -- 17th century 6. Lancashire, England -- History -- 17th century 7. Historical fiction

LC 2009042057

A tale inspired by the Pendle witch hunt of 1612 finds the granddaughter of a folk healer targeted by an ambitious local magistrate who plays neighbors and family members against one another until paranoia reaches frenzied levels.

"Based on the infamous 1612 Lancashire witch trials, Sharratt's . . . novel vividly portrays the religious turmoil and hardscrabble life of 17th-century rural England. It's a familiar premise: an old beggar woman accused of witchcraft is sentenced to hang, along with others of her ilk. What makes this story stand out are the strong voices of the two main characters, stalwart Bess Southerns (aka Demdike) and her feisty granddaughter Alizon Device. Demdike is a cunning woman, able to heal animals and people with herbal folk magic. She strives to do only good, but when she teaches her dear friend the craft, she releases a Pandora's box of resentment, revenge, and evil." Library Journal.

Sharratt, Mary, 1964-

Illuminations : a novel of Hildegard von Bingen / Mary Sharratt. Houghton Mifflin Harcourt, 2012. 272 p.

ISBN 9780547567846

1. Hildegard von Bingen,, Saint, 1098-1179 2. Medieval period (476-1492) 3. 12th century 4. Nuns 5. Courage in women 6. Christianity 7. Civilization, Medieval 8. Benedictine nuns 9. Abbesses 10. Lifestyle change 11. Germany -- History -- 12th century 12. Biographical fiction 13. Historical fiction 14. Psychological fiction

LC 2012014252

A tale inspired by the life of the 12th-century abbess, composer and prophet depicts a young girl who upon being given to the Church rejects the order's masochistic piety and finds grace in studying books, growing herbs and rejoicing in divine visions before finding ways to liberate her sisters and herself.

Shaw, Irwin, 1913-1984

Beggarman, thief Delacorte, 1977. 436 p.

ISBN 0440006732

1. Families 2. Family sagas

LC 77024523

Sequel to Rich man, poor man.

"Scenes from the earlier novel are interwoven allowing the unfamiliar reader to complete enjoyment and understanding." Booklist.

Shaw, Irwin, 1913-1984

* **Rich** man, poor man / Irwin Shaw. Delacorte, 1970. 723 p.

ISBN 9780385288583

1. Immigrant families 2. Family sagas

LC 74120463

Sequel: Beggarman, thief.

Traces the fortunes of a first generation German-American family who pursue their dreams in a post-World War II United States.

"Each member of the clan is doomed in one way or another. They fight, love, live hard and their fortunes are inevitably intertwined. Mr. Shaw has juxtaposed their rise and fall against a panoramic picture of the times. . . . This may not be great literature but it certainly has popular appeal." Publishers Weekly.

Shaw, L. C.

The **network** : a Jack Logan thriller / L. C. Shaw. HarperCollins, 2019. 304 p. Jack Logan novels

ISBN 9780062955852

1. Investigative journalists 2. Former fiances 3. Political corruption 4. Politicians 5. Widows 6. Political intrigue 7. Power (Social sciences) 8. Secrets 9. Men/women relations 10. Political thrillers

Investigating the suspicious death of a senator who had predicted his murder days before, investigative journalist Jack Logan and the victim's wife, Taylor, uncover a dangerous plot by a powerful political influencer.

Shaw, M. B.

* **Murder** at the mill : a mystery / M. B. Shaw. Minotaur Books, 2018. 448 p. Iris Grey novels

ISBN 9781250189295

1. Women amateur detectives 2. Murder 3. Artists 4. Portrait painting 5. Separated women (Marital relations) 6. Villages 7. Christmas 8. Authors 9. Gossiping and gossips 10. Intrigue 11. Secrets 12. Amateur detectives 13. Holiday mysteries 14. Cozy mysteries

LC 2018027004

Renting a cottage in picturesque Hampshire village to escape her crumbling marriage, Iris Grey is commissioned to paint the portrait of a celebrated crime writer before a tension-filled Christmas Eve party is thrown into turmoil by an untimely death.

Shaw, Vivian

* **Dreadful** company / Vivian Shaw. Orbit, 2018. 431 p. Greta Helsing novels

ISBN 9780316434638

1. Physicians 2. Supernatural 3. Imaginary creatures 4. Women physicians 5. Undead 6. Murder 7. Vampires 8. Paris, France 9. France 10. Supernatural mysteries 11. Urban fantasy

LC 2018010014

When Greta Helsing, doctor to the undead, is called to Paris to present at a medical conference, she must navigate the darkest corners of the city to escape a coven of bloodthirsty vampires.

Shaw, Vivian

* **Strange** Practice / Vivian Shaw. Orbit, 2017. 320 p. Greta Helsing novels

ISBN 9780316434607

1. Physicians 2. Supernatural 3. Imaginary creatures 4. Women physicians 5. Undead 6. Monks 7. Murder 8. Vampires 9. Mummies 10. London, England 11. England 12. Supernatural mysteries 13. Urban fantasy

Meet Greta Helsing, fast-talking doctor to the undead. Keeping the supernatural community not-alive and well in London has been her family's specialty for generations. Greta Helsing inherited the family's highly specialized, and highly peculiar, medical practice. In her consulting rooms, Dr. Helsing treats the undead for a host of ills - vocal strain in banshees, arthritis in barrow-wights, and entropy in mummies. Although barely making ends meet, this is just the quiet, supernatural-adjacent life Greta's been groomed for since childhood. Until a sect of murderous monks emerges, killing human and undead Londoners alike. As terror takes hold of the city, Greta must use her unusual skills to stop the cult if she hopes to save her practice, and her life.

"In this comic supernatural mystery debut, Wright assembles an appealing, amusing collection of London's modern undead and the humans who care for them." Publishers Weekly.

Shaw, William, 1959-

The **birdwatcher** / William Shaw. Mulholland Books, 2017. 336 p.

ISBN 9780316316248

1. Detectives 2. Bird watchers 3. Secrets 4. Murder investigation 5. Neighbors 6. Police 7. Memories 8. Childhood 9. Guilt 10. Kent, England 11. Northern Ireland 12. Police procedurals 13. Mysteries

First published in Great Britain in 2016 by riverrun.

When a fellow birdwatcher is found murdered in his remote home, Police Sergeant William South, who may have murdered a man when he was a child in Northern Ireland, finds his world turned upside down.

Shaw, William, 1959-

* **Salt** lane / William Shaw. Mulholland Books, 2018. 336 p. Alexandra Cupidi novels

ISBN 9780316563505

1. Policewomen 2. Marshes 3. Rural life 4. Adoptees 5. Single mothers 6. Mothers and daughters 7. Peace activists 8. Murder 9. Murder investigation 10. Coastal towns 11. England 12. Police procedurals

Misfit London metro police officer Alexandra Cupidi investigates the case of a woman who is found dead in a marshland and a homeless woman claiming to be the same person in search of the son she gave up for adoption.

Shaw, William, 1959-

* A **song** for the brokenhearted / William Shaw. Mulholland Books, 2016. 403 p. Breen and Tozer novels

ISBN 9780316246910

1. 1960s 2. Police 3. Detectives 4. Cold cases (Criminal investigation) 5. Murder investigation 6. Sisters -- Death 7. Class conflict 8. Rich men 9. London, England -- History -- 1960-1969 10. Police procedurals 11. Historical mysteries

LC 750274410

The earthshaking year of 1968 comes to sweeping and dangerous close, as Detectives Breen and Tozer battle the most powerful members of London society.

Shaykh, Hanan

* **One** thousand and one nights : a sparkling retelling of the beloved classic / Hanan al-Shaykh ; with an introduction by Mary Gaitskill. Pantheon Books, 2013. 328 p.

ISBN 9780307958860

1. Storytelling 2. Young women 3. Rulers 4. Independence in women 5. Power (Social sciences) 6. Supernatural 7. Magic 8. Interpersonal relations 9. Adaptations, retellings, and spin-offs

LC 2012039272

A reimagining of 19 tales from the classic story about young queen Shahrazad's efforts to save her life from a brutal husband focuses on female characters at the heart of each tale in a woven sequence that incorporates humor and sensuality.

Shefchik, Rick

* **Amen** corner / Rick Shefchik. Poisoned Pen Press, 2007. 270 p. Sam Skarda mysteries

ISBN 1590584112

1. Augusta National Golf Club. 2. Masters Golf Tournament 3. Detectives 4. Golfers 5. Murder 6. Rehabilitation 7. Gender equity 8. Protests, demonstrations, vigils, etc 9. Privacy 10. Men/women relations 11. Married women 12. Augusta, Georgia 13. Mysteries

LC 2006932882

Arriving at the Augusta National Golf Club to play in his first Masters tournament, amateur golfer Sam Skarda, a Minneapolis police detective, finds himself tapped to investigate the killing of a Masters official whose body is found in the middle of the fairway.

Shelley, Mary Wollstonecraft, 1797-1851

* **Frankenstein** : or, The modern Prometheus / Mary Shelley. Penguin Classics, 2014, c1818. 273 p.

ISBN 9780141393391

1. 19th century 2. Monsters 3. Scientists 4. Ethics 5. Regeneration (Biology) 6. Social acceptance 7. Mad scientist (Concept) 8. Self-control 9. Murder 10. Guilt in men 11. Revenge 12. Grief in men 13. Horror 14. Gothic fiction 15. Classics 16. Science fiction

LC 97061744

Obsessed by creating life itself, Victor Frankenstein plunders graveyards for the material to fashion a new being, which he shocks into life by electricity. But his botched creature, rejected by Frankenstein and denied human companionship, sets out to destroy his maker and all that he holds dear.

Shelton, Paige

Thin ice : a mystery / Paige Shelton. Minotaur Books, 2019. 320 p. Alaska mysteries (Paige Shelton)

ISBN 9781250295217

1. Women kidnapping victims 2. Moving to a new state 3. Women authors 4. Criminals 5. Murder 6. Murder investigation 7. Women amateur detectives 8. Kidnappers 9. Secrets 10. Small town life 11. Alaska 12. Mysteries

LC 2019019598

A best-selling writer escapes from an obsessed fan by hiding in Alaska, where she is embroiled in a local murder case.

Shepard, Jim

* The **book** of Aron / Jim Shepard. Alfred A. Knopf, 2015. 259 p.

ISBN 9781101874318

1. Holocaust (1933-1945) 2. Children 3. Jews 4. Ghettoes, Jewish -- Warsaw, Poland 5. Physicians 6. War and society 7. Orphans 8. Antisemitism 9. Poland 10. Historical fiction

ALA Notable Book, 2016.

PEN New England Award for Fiction, 2016.

Sophie Brody Medal, 2016.

Andrew Carnegie Medal for Excellence in Fiction finalist, 2016.

Kirkus Prize for Fiction finalist, 2015.

Aron and a handful of boys and girls in the Warsaw Ghetto smuggle and trade things through the "quarantine walls" to keep their people alive until he is rescued by a Jewish-Polish doctor and advocate of children's rights who instills within him the importance of letting the world know the atrocities they have all suffered at the hands of the enemy.

"Aron proves to be engaging company as he describes the selfishness that will help him survive as the world becomes increasingly hellish. The horrors are so incremental that Aron--and the reader--might be compared to the lobster dropped into the pot as the temperature keeps rising past the boiling point." Kirkus

Shepard, Jim

The **world** to come : stories / Jim Shepard. Alfred A. Knopf, 2017. 256 p.

ISBN 9781524731809

1. Ambition 2. Interpersonal relations 3. Literary fiction 4. Short stories

LC 2016038353

An anthology of 10 stories by the author of The Book of Aron reflects the personal and political challenges of protagonists ranging from English Arctic explorers during one of history's most nightmarish expeditions to 18th-century French balloonists who would invent manned flight.

"With the release of his fifth story collection, Shepard . . . continues to weave interlacing narrative threads that imaginatively evoke time and place." Library Journal.

Shepard, Karen

The **Celestials** : a novel / Karen Shepard. Tin House Books, 2013. 320 p.

ISBN 9781935639558

1. 1870s 2. Culture conflict 3. Communities 4. Supervisors 5. Industrialists 6. Labor unions 7. Shoe industry and trade 8. Teenage boys 9. Identity (Psychology) 10. Chinese Americans 11. English as a second language -- Study and teaching 12. Massachusetts -- History -- 19th century 13. New England 14. Historical fiction

LC 2012050808

In 1870, seventy-five Chinese laborers are unwittingly brought in as strikebreakers at a shoe factory in the town of North Adams, Massachusetts, setting off a conflict with the locals.

Shepard, Sam, 1943-2017

The **one** inside / Sam Shepard. Alfred A. Knopf, 2017 172 p.

ISBN 9780451494580

1. Memories 2. Life change events 3. Extortion 4. Visions 5. Actors and actresses 6. Authors 7. Writing 8. Literary fiction

The One Inside is a narrative in which an actor/writer explores and revisits key moments and people from his life--all the while attempting to negotiate with a young woman who threatens to publish recordings of their darkly revealing phone conversations. In his dreams and in visions he sees his late father, sometimes in miniature, sometimes flying planes, sometimes at war. In his childhood memories he sees his father's young girlfriend, with whom the narrator also became involved, setting into motion a tragedy that continues to haunt him.

"Shepard is a master of conflicting emotions and haunting regrets, andgraced with a foreword by Patti Smith (M Train, 2015)this is a ravishing tale of deep-dark cosmic humor, complex tragedy, and self-inflicted exile." Booklist.

Shepard, Sara, 1977-

* **Reputation** / Sara Shepard. E.P. Dutton, 2019. 368 p.

ISBN 9781524742904

1. Universities and colleges 2. Scandals 3. Hacking 4. College towns 5. Murder victims 6. Women 7. Secrets 8. Revenge 9. Options, alternatives, choices 10. Sisters 11. Pennsylvania 12. Psychological suspense

Told in multiple points of view, a story of intrigue, sabotage and secrets follows a tight-knit college community as it is rocked to its core when a hacker dumps 40,000 people's emails onto an easily searchable database, which results in murder.

"From chapter to chapter, Shepard's plotting breathlessly careens between characters, with each cliffhanger swiftly answered by another, ratcheting up the stakes until the killer is finally unmasked." Kirkus.

Shepherd, Lynn, 1964-

A **fatal** likeness : a novel / Lynn Shepherd. Delacorte Press, 2013. 384 p. Charles Maddox novels

ISBN 9780345532442

1. Shelley, Percy Bysshe, 1792-1822 2. Shelley family 3. Victorian era (1837-1901) 4. 1850s 5. Murder investigation 6. Inheritance and succession 7. Family secrets 8. Poets, English -- 19th century 9. Private investigators 10. Suicide 11. Conspiracies 12. Former police 13. Great Britain -- History -- Victoria, 1837-1901 14. London, England -- Social conditions -- 19th century 15. Historical mysteries 16. Victorian mysteries

LC 2012038988

Also published as: A treachurous likeness.

Commissioned to negotiate the release of papers linked to the celebrated poet Percy Bysshe Shelley, London detective Charles Maddox must determine if the papers are authentic, but his disturbing investigation uncovers signs of foul play.

Shepherd, Lynn, 1964-

The **Solitary** House : a novel / Lynn Shepherd. Delacorte Press, 2012. 352 p. Charles Maddox novels

ISBN 9780345532428

1. Victorian era (1837-1901) 2. 1850s 3. Private investigators 4. Young women 5. Former police 6. Lawyers 7. Death threats 8. Great Britain -- History -- Victoria, 1837-1901 9. London, England -- Social conditions -- 19th century 10. Historical mysteries 11. Victorian mysteries

LC 2011029728

Also published as: Tom-All-Alone's.

Summoned to the offices of Victorian London's most powerful and dangerous solicitors, disgraced police officer turned independent detective Charles Maddox turns to his famous but aging investigator uncle to identify who has been sending threatening letters to a client.

Shepherd, Peng

The **book** of M : a novel / Peng Shepherd. William Morrow, 2018 485 p.

ISBN 9780062669605

1. Near future 2. Memory 3. Epidemics 4. Identity (Psychology) 5. Husband and wife 6. Shadows 7. Amnesia 8. Voyages and travels 9. Apocalyptic fiction 10. Literary fiction

LC 2017050120

In a dangerous near-future world where an unknown phenomenon causes people to gain strange new powers but lose their memories, Ory and his wife Max journey through a perilous, unrecognizable world in a search for answers.

Sherrill, Steven, 1961-

The **minotaur** takes his own sweet time : a novel / Steven Sherrill. John F. Blair, 2016. 288 p. Minotaur novels (Steven Sherrill)

ISBN 9780895876737

1. Minotaur (Greek mythology) 2. Working class 3. Identity (Psychology) 4. Loss (Psychology) 5. Alienation (Social psychology) 6. Social isolation 7. Misfits (Persons) 8. Mythical creatures 9. Eccentrics and eccentricities 10. Historical reenactments 11. Battlefields 12. Interpersonal relations 13. Pennsylvania 14. Contemporary fantasy 15. Mythological fiction

LC 2016026939

Sixteen years have passed since Steven Sherrill first introduced us to "M," the selfsame Minotaur from Greek mythology, transplanted to the modern American South. M has moved north now, from a life of kitchens and trailer parks, to that of Civil War re-enactor at a run-down living history park in the dying blue-collar rustbelt of central Pennsylvania. Though he dies now, in uniform, on a regular basis, M's world, his daily struggles, remain unchanged.

"This novels juxtaposition of magical realism and the mundane allows for a number of haunting and contemplative moments." Kirkus.

Sherwood, Frances, 1940-

The **book** of splendor / Frances Sherwood. Norton, 2002. 348 p.

ISBN 0393021386

1. Judah Loew ben Bezalel, ca 1525-1609 2. Rudolf II,, Holy Roman Emperor, 1552-1612 3. Brahe, Tycho, 1546-1601 4. Dee, John, 1527-1608 5. 17th century 6. Jewish women 7. Alchemists 8. Religious persecution 9. Golem 10. Courts and courtiers 11. Prejudice 12. Love triangles 13. Seamstresses 14. Poverty 15. Rabbis 16. Jews -- Persecutions 17. Immortality 18. Rulers with mental illnesses 19. Prague, Czech Republic -- History 20. Holy Roman Empire -- History -- Rudolf II, 1576-1612 21. Historical fantasy

LC 2002000520

Map on lining papers.

Rochel, an illegitimate seamstress, escapes the travails of poverty through an arranged marriage to the tailor Zev, but finds herself falling in love with Yossel, the Golem created by Rabbi Loew to protect the Jewish community of Prague.

Sherwood, Frances, 1940-

Night of sorrows / Frances Sherwood. W.W. Norton & Co., 2006. 384 p.

ISBN 0393058255

1. Cortes, Hernan, 1485-1547 2. Marina, ca 1505-ca 1530 3. Conquest of Mexico (1519-1540) 4. 16th century 5. Aztecs -- History -- 16th century 6. Conquistadors 7. Women slaves 8. Mayan women 9. Translators 10. Men/women relations 11. Tenochtitlan (Extinct city) 12. Mexico -- History -- Conquest, 1519-1540 13. Historical fiction 14. Biographical fiction

LC 2006000420

Sold as a love slave to Hernan Cortes in the early sixteenth century, Aztec princess Malintzin accompanies him on a journey to Tenochtitlan, while Cortes and his compadres engage in a battle that marks the end of the Aztec empire.

"An account of conquest and dehumanization, [this novel] is also a story of survival in the midst of a harsh cultural clash. The linguistic and narrative riches of the book enhance its moral complexity: Sherwood has refused to settle for the black-and-white thinking that so often mars this sort of historical fiction." New York Times Book Review.

Shields, Carol

The **republic** of love / Carol Shields. Viking, 1992. 366 p.

ISBN 9780670838752

1. Women folklorists 2. Radio talk show hosts and guests 3. Self-discovery in men 4. Love 5. Divorced men 6. Men/women relations 7. Canada 8. Love stories

LC 91016154

A story of the persistence of love in modern times follows Fay, a fickle folklorist falling hard for her neighbor Tom, an all-night disc jockey three times divorced.

"Not only are Fay and Tom exceptionally likable and capable of arresting insights, their worlds are complete and organic. Secondary characters are respectfully but economically drawn via short monologues, and the city of Winnipeg bustles in the background." Publishers Weekly.

Shields, Carol

* The **stone** diaries / Carol Shields. Viking, 1994. 361 p.

ISBN 0670853097

1. 20th century 2. Women 3. Middle class families 4. Families 5. Quarries and quarrying 6. Growing up 7. Change (Psychology) 8. Fathers and daughters 9. Marriage 10. Life change events 11. Winnipeg, Manitoba 12. Ottawa, Ontario 13. Indiana 14. Florida 15.

Literary fiction

LC 9330239

Governor General's Literary Award for English-Language Fiction, 1993.

Manitoba Writing and Publishing Awards, McNally Robinson Book of the Year Award, 1993.

National Book Critics Circle Award for Fiction, 1994.

Pulitzer Prize for Fiction, 1995.

Shortlisted for the Booker-McConnell Prize, 1993.

From her birth in rural Manitoba, to her journey with her father to southern Indiana, to her years as a wife, mother, and widow, to her old age, Daisy Stone Goodwill struggles to find a place for herself in her own life

"This book is a miraculous meeting of intellectual rigour and imaginative flow. On the one hand, it's a sharp-as-tacks investigation into the limits of the autobiographical form; on the other, a novel of effortless pleasure and sensuality. Daisy Goodwill . . . attempts intermittently to tell the story of a life remarkable only in its large tracts of ordinariness." New Statesman.

Shields, Carol

Unless / Carol Shields. Fourth Estate, 2002. 213 p.

ISBN 9780007141074

1. Teenage girls with mental illnesses 2. Feminism 3. Social advocacy 4. Family problems 5. Women authors 6. Mothers and daughters 7. Middle-aged women 8. Ontario 9. Literary fiction

BC Book Prizes, Ethel Wilson Fiction Prize, 2003.

Governor General's Literary Awards, English-language Fiction finalist, 2002.

Shortlisted for the Giller Prize, 2002

Shortlisted for the James Tait Black Memorial Prize for Fiction, 2002

Shortlisted for the Man Booker Prize, 2002.

Shortlisted for The Orange Prize for Fiction, 2003

A mother's grief over a daughter's break with the family revises her feminist outlook and pushes her craft as a writer in a new direction.

"Shields's ability to use Reta's darkest fears to reveal the order lurking in chaos, without ever losing her light touch . . . is nothing short of astonishing." The New Yorker.

Shields, Kieran

A **study** in revenge / Kieran Shields. Crown Publishers, 2013. 372 p. Archie Lean and Perceval Grey mysteries

ISBN 9780307985767

1. Gilded Age (1865-1898) 2. 19th century 3. 1890s 4. Detectives 5. Grave robbing 6. Relics 7. Murder investigation -- Maine 8. Abenaki Indians 9. Multiracial men 10. United States deputy marshals 11. Private police 12. Portland, Maine 13. Historical mysteries 14. Mysteries

Sequel to: The truth of all things

Finds late-19th century police detective Archie Lean and his half-Native American partner, Perceval Grey, investigating the theft of a recently buried body and the staging of a bizarre occult scene that is linked to a centuries-old magical relic.

Shields, Kieran

The **truth** of all things / Kieran Shields. Crown, 2012. 416 p. Archie Lean and Perceval Grey mysteries

ISBN 9780307720276

1. Gilded Age (1865-1898) 2. 19th century 3. 1890s 4. Detectives 5. Human sacrifice 6. Serial murder investigation 7. Abenaki Indians 8. United States deputy marshals 9. Racism 10. Indians of North America 11. Witchcraft 12. Private police 13. Maine 14. Portland,

Maine 15. Historical mysteries 16. Mysteries

Sequel: A study in revenge

Investigating the murder of a prostitute in 1892 Portland, Maine, newly appointed Deputy Marshal Archie Lean discovers that the victim was ritually executed as a witch, prompting him to enlist the help of a historian and a brilliant criminologist with whom he follows a trail to the spiritual societies and asylums of gothic New England.

Shields, Sharma

The **Cassandra** : a novel / Sharma Shields. Henry Holt and Company, 2019. 304 p.

ISBN 9781250197412

1. Second World War era (1939-1945) 2. Women psychics 3. Prophetic dreams 4. Nuclear weapons 5. Military secrets 6. Prophecies (Occultism) 7. World War II home front 8. Misogyny 9. Violence against women 10. Sexism 11. War and society 12. Washington (State) 13. Historical fiction 14. Adaptations, retellings, and spin-offs

LC 2018022670

The Cassandra follows a woman who goes to work in a top secret research facility during WWII, only to be tormented by visions of what the mission will mean for humankind.

Shimotakahara, Leslie

After the bloom / Leslie Shimotakahara. Dundurn, 2017 321 p.

ISBN 9781459737433

1. Japanese Canadians 2. Families 3. World War II 4. Mothers and daughters 5. Missing persons 6. Immigrants 7. Concentration camps 8. Family secrets 9. Toronto, Ontario 10. California -- History -- 1850-1950 11. United States -- History -- 20th century 12. Historical fiction

Lily Takemitsu goes missing from her home in Toronto in the mid-1980s. Her daughter, Rita sets out to find her. In the course of searching for her mom, Rita is forced to confront a labyrinth of secrets surrounding the family's internment at a camp in the California desert during the Second World War, their postwar immigration to Toronto, and the father she has never known.

Shipman, Viola

The **heirloom** garden / Viola Shipman. Graydon House, 2020. 384 p.

ISBN 9781525804649

1. Widows 2. Loss (Psychology) 3. Gardens 4. Female friendship 5. Intergenerational friendship 6. Senior women 7. Recluses 8. Flower gardening 9. Families 10. Mothers and daughters 11. Iraq War veterans 12. Post-traumatic stress disorder 13. Healing 14. Michigan 15. Women's lives and relationships

Moving to Grand Haven with her traumatized veteran husband, Abby bonds with her reclusive next-door neighbor over a shared love of flowers that they cultivate together, discovering hope and healing along the way.

"Shipman's tale successfully captures these women's resilience and their hopeful desire for new beginnings." Publishers Weekly.

Shoham, Liad, 1971-

Asylum city : a novel / Liad Shoham ; translated from the Hebrew by Sara Kitai. Harper, 2014, c2013. 336 p.

ISBN 9780062237538

1. Policewomen 2. Violence against women 3. Political activists 4. City life 5. Criminals 6. Murder investigation 7. Murder 8. Refugees 9. Tel Aviv, Israel 10. Israel 11. Mysteries 12. Translations -- Hebrew

to English

LC 2014011217

Translation from the Hebrew of: Ir Miklat.

"Originally published as Ir Miklat in a different form in Israel in 2013 by Kinneret Zmora-Bitan"--Title page verso.

A Tel Aviv police officer isn't convinced the case is closed when an African man confesses to the murder of a social activist.

Sholem Aleichem, 1859-1916

Tevye the dairyman and the railroad stories / Sholem Aleichem ; translated from the Yiddish and with an introduction by Hillel Halkin Schocken Books, 1987. 309 p.

ISBN 9780805240269

1. Shtetl 2. Jews, Eastern European 3. Literary fiction 4. Short stories 5. Translations -- Yiddish to English

LC 86024835

The movie Fiddler on the roof was based on the Tevye stories in this collection.

Tells the stories of a milkman and his daughters and a salesman's encounters with fellow Jews while riding the train

"In the first eight stories of this collection, Tevye, the Russian Jew so familiar from Fiddler on the Roof, bemoans his fate. In these as well as the following 21 tales, the author displays his splendid storytelling skills." Booklist.

Sholem Aleichem, 1859-1916

Tevye's daughters / Sholem Aleichem ; translated from the Yiddish by Frances Butwin ; with illustrations by Ben Shahn. Crown, 1949. 302 p.

ISBN 9780517507100

1. Fathers and daughters 2. Jews, Eastern European 3. Shtetl 4. Literary fiction 5. Translations -- Yiddish to English

The movie Fiddler on the roof was based on the stories in this collection.

"Translated from the Yiddish, many of these stories are about the seven daughters of Tevye the Dairyman and the life each chooses as she comes of age in Russia during the years preceding the first World War." Publishers Weekly.

Sholokhov, Mikhail Aleksandrovich, 1905-1984

* And quiet flows the Don / Mikhail Sholokhov ; translated from the Russian by Stephen Garry. A. A. Knopf, 1969, c1934. 554p.

1. Cossacks 2. Soviet Union 3. Soviet Union -- History -- Revolution, 1917-1921 4. Translations -- Russian to English 5. Modern classics

LC 89040101

Gregor Melekhov, a young married Cossack, lives along the Don River where he engages in military adventures while having a torrid love affair.

Sholokhov, Mikhail Aleksandrovich, 1905-1984

The **Don** flows home to the sea / Mikhail Sholokhov ; translated from the Russian by Stephen Garry. Alfred A. Knopf, 1965, c1940. 777 p.

1. Russian Revolution and Civil War (1917-1921) 2. Social change 3. Historical fiction 4. Literary fiction

A group of Cassacks find themselves torn between loyalty to their culture and the ideals of the ongoing Russian Revolution.

Showalter, Gena

Shadow and ice / Gena Showalter. Hqn Books, 2018. 384 p. Gods of war

ISBN 9781335080943

1. Gods and goddesses 2. Imaginary wars and battles 3. Warriors 4. Protectiveness in men 5. Mate selection 6. Sexual attraction 7. Men/women relations 8. Paranormal romances

The most ruthless Earth-defending warrior in All War history risks his lifetime struggle for freedom from slavery in his unlikely alliance with a street-tough human who is inadvertently drawn into an ancient war.

Shreve, Anita

Eden Close : a novel / Anita Shreve. Harcourt Brace Jovanovich, 1989. 265 p.

ISBN 0151275823

1. Friendship 2. Rape victims 3. Secrets 4. Coping in women 5. Women who are blind 6. Violence against women 7. Divorced men 8. Secrets 9. Men/women relations 10. New York (State) 11. Love stories

LC 89034712

"Eden Close' is not a novel of suspense but one of sensibility. Its insights are keen, its language measured and haunting. In it, a sense of loss and then of rupture is everywhere." New York Times Book Review.

Shreve, Anita

Fortune's rocks : a novel / Anita Shreve. Little, Brown, 2000. 453 p.

ISBN 9780316781015

1. 19th century 2. Young women -- Sexuality 3. Extramarital affairs 4. Sex scandals -- History 5. Mills and millwork 6. Trials (Child custody) 7. Classism 8. Young women -- Relations with older men 9. Illegitimacy 10. Mill workers 11. Pariahs 12. New England -- Social life and customs -- 19th century 13. New England -- Social conditions -- 19th century 14. Coming-of-age stories 15. Historical fiction

Set in the late 1890s in New England, a passionate and idealistic young woman tries to put her life back together after she has been made an outcast because of an affair she had with an older, married man.

"The level of suspense never falters, but becomes breathtaking during a custody court battle. . . . The astounding denouement of cascading events will leave no reader unmoved." Publishers Weekly.

Shreve, Anita

The **last** time they met : a novel / Anita Shreve. Little, Brown, 2001. 313 p.

ISBN 0316781142

1. Men/women relations 2. Romantic love 3. Forgiveness 4. Married people 5. Widows 6. Divorced men 7. Women poets 8. Extramarital affairs 9. Poets 10. Former lovers 11. Teenage boys 12. Teenage girls 13. Traffic accidents 14. Teenage romance 15. Kenya 16. Massachusetts 17. Toronto, Ontario 18. Love stories 19. Mainstream fiction

LC 00053496

At a literary festival, poet Linda Fallon meets, for the first time in years, fellow poet Thomas Janes. Thomas has arranged to be there hoping to reestablish contact with the woman he passionately pursued years earlier, in an affair that ended disastrously. As the story moves backward, it examines their love affair.

"Romantic regret is Anita Shreve's subject in this instantly captivating novel. . . . Fiction writers could go to school on Shreve's command of scene." The Atlantic.

Shreve, Anita

The **pilot's** wife : a novel / Anita Shreve. Little, Brown, 1998. 293 p.

ISBN 9780316789080

1. Married people and secrets 2. Widows 3. Secrets 4. Women high school teachers 5. Fifteen-year-old girls 6. Mothers and daughters 7. Airplane bombings -- Ireland 8. Bigamists -- Ireland 9. New Hampshire 10. London, England 11. Mainstream fiction

LC 9751647

When her husband, a pilot, dies in an airplane crash off the Irish coast, Kathryn Lyons finds herself in the media spotlight as rumors abound of her husband's shocking secret past.

"The climax, less dramatic than meditative, may strike some readers as too muted: understatement is one of this novel's strengths. What haunts us is the way Jack's secret life gradually weakens its hold on Kathryn's imagination and ours." Publishers Weekly.

Shreve, Anita

Sea glass : a novel / Anita Shreve. Little, Brown, 2002. 378 p.

ISBN 0316780812

1. Depression era (1929-1941) 2. 1920s 3. Labor movement -- United States -- History -- 20th century 4. Purpose in life 5. Massacres -- History 6. Depressions -- 1929-1941 7. Husband and wife 8. Mill workers 9. New Hampshire 10. Historical fiction

When Honora and Sexton Beecher are rendered penniless by the crash of the stock market, Sexton is forced to work in a nearby mill that is plagued by violence, and as they try to reconstruct their lives, they are confronted by passions of every kind.

"Shreve does not use her characters frivolously. They reveal who they are through their actions, with the author--who writes with admirable economy--rarely having to point a finger or underline the obvious. The true power of her novel comes from the appalling social conditions she describes so vividly, the grim but heroic lives her characters live." New York Times Book Review.

Shreve, Anita

Testimony : a novel / Anita Shreve. Little, Brown, 2008. 320 p.

ISBN 9780316059862

1. Boarding schools 2. Scandals 3. Sexuality 4. Students 5. Life change events 6. Personal conduct 7. Social classes 8. Teenagers -- Sexuality 9. Ethics 10. Vermont -- Social life and customs 11. New England -- Social life and customs 12. Literary fiction

LC 2008005027

A New England boarding school is rocked in the wake of a sex scandal in which participants were caught on videotape, a situation that derails the innocence and best intentions of students, parents, and others in life-shattering ways.

"Shreve arrows in on many targets--underage drinking, instant exposure via the Internet, familial expectations, youthful insecurities, and peer pressure, among them--as she flawlessly weaves a tale that is mesmerizing, hypnotic, and compulsive." Library Journal.

Shreve, Anita

The **weight** of water / Anita Shreve. Little, Brown, 1997. 246 p.

ISBN 0316789976

1. Women photographers -- New Hampshire 2. Women murder victims 3. Boat living -- New Hampshire 4. Norwegian Americans 5. Fishers -- New Hampshire 6. Husband and wife -- New Hampshire 7. Island life -- New Hampshire 8. Marriage -- New Hampshire 9. Murder -- New Hampshire 10. Norwegian American women 11.

Women immigrants -- New Hampshire 12. New Hampshire 13. Literary fiction 14. Parallel narratives

LC 9621326

L. L. Winship/PEN New England Award, 1997.

Shortlisted for The Orange Prize for Fiction, 1998

A photographer who has come to a small island off the coast of New Hampshire to shoot a photo-essay about a double murder that took place there over a century ago, notices parallels between her own life and the lives of the murder victims.

"Deftly moving among almost as many plot lines as there are islands and employing at least two distinct voices, Ms. Shreve unravels themes of adultery, jealousy, crimes of passion, incest, negligence, loss and guilt, and then manages somehow to knit them all together into an engrossing tale." New York Times Book Review.

Shrier, Howard

* **Boston** cream / Howard Shrier. Vintage Canada, 2012. 336 p. Jonah Geller novels

ISBN 9780307359568

1. Missing persons investigation 2. Organized crime 3. Missing persons 4. Former assassins 5. Surgeons 6. Jewish Canadians 7. Private investigators 8. Boston, Massachusetts 9. Mysteries

LC oc2011034137

PI Jonah Geller investigates a missing persons case that leads him on the trail of a Boston crime boss.

Shriver, Lionel

The **post-birthday** world / Lionel Shriver. Harper Collins Publishers, 2007. 528 p.

ISBN 0061187844

1. Boredom in women 2. Women's fantasies 3. Extramarital affairs 4. Couples 5. Unmarried couples 6. Women illustrators 7. Men/women relations 8. Temptation 9. Snooker players 10. Desire 11. Monogamy 12. London, England 13. Parallel narratives 14. Mainstream fiction

LC 2006049233

A tale told from the parallel perspectives of two possible timelines considers the life of American expatriate Irena McGovern, who in one reality stays faithful to her disciplined American intellectual partner, and in the other runs off with an exuberant British long-time friend.

"Lawrence often verges on being a parody of a judgmental, snobbish prig, while Ramsey often verges on being a parody of a hard-living, irresponsible celebrity. . . . That we're able to overlook the flaws of Ramsey and Lawrence is, in the end, a testament to Ms. Shriver's ability to make Irina into a thoroughly compelling character, an idiosyncratic yet recognizable heroine about whom it's impossible not to care." New York Times.

Shriver, Lionel

So much for that / Lionel Shriver. Harper, 2010. 436 p.

ISBN 9780061458583

1. Husband and wife 2. Women with cancer 3. Medical care -- Costs 4. Mesothelioma 5. Retirement 6. Women with terminal illnesses -- Family relationships 7. Life change events 8. Mainstream fiction

National Book Award for Fiction finalist, 2010

After his wife is diagnosed with cancer, Shep Knacker sees his dream of retiring to a developing country slip away, along with all the money in his once-plentiful bank account, as he tries to navigate America's labyrinthine health-care system.

"Though there is one farcical plot development that is poorly woven into the emotional fabric of the story, and though some of the asides about health care feel shoehorned into the narrative, the author's understanding of her people is so intimate, so unsentimental that it lofts the novel over such bumpy passages, insinuating these characters permanently into the readers imagination." New York Times.

Shriver, Lionel

We need to talk about Kevin / Lionel Shriver. Counterpoint, 2003. 400 p.

ISBN 9781582432670

1. School shootings 2. Teenage murderers 3. Mass shootings 4. Violence in schools 5. Parents of criminals 6. Mass murder 7. Teenage boys 8. High school students 9. Teenagers and violence 10. Parent and child 11. Husband and wife 12. High schools 13. Massacres 14. New York (State) 15. Psychological fiction

LC 2002152753

First published: New York :

Orange Prize for Fiction, 2005.

The mother of a teenage boy who killed seven fellow students and two adults in a high-school shooting writes a series of letters to her estranged husband on their son's upbringing and questions what she fears may be her own part in the tragedy.

"It's a harrowing, psychologically astute, sometimes even darkly humorous novel, with a clear-eyed, hard-won ending and a tough-minded sense of the difficult, often painful human enterprise." Publishers Weekly.

Shteyngart, Gary, 1972-

* **Lake** Success : a novel / Gary Shteyngart. Random House, 2018. 338 p.

ISBN 9780812997415

1. Midlife crisis 2. Transcontinental journeys 3. Self-discovery in men 4. Marital conflict 5. Rich men 6. Buses 7. Life change events 8. Former girlfriends 9. Governmental investigations 10. Antique clocks and watches 11. Fathers and sons 12. Success (Concept) 13. Mainstream fiction 14. Satirical fiction

LC 2017043962

A self-made Wall Street millionaire, baffled by the implosion of his seemingly perfect life, takes a cross-country bus trip in search of his college sweetheart and the ideals of his youth.

Shteyngart, Gary, 1972-

The **Russian** debutante's handbook / Gary Shteyngart. Riverhead Books, 2002. 452 p.

ISBN 1573222135

1. 1990s 2. Immigrants, Russian 3. Expatriates 4. Russian Americans 5. Young men 6. Immigrants 7. Men -- Identity 8. Ethics 9. Family relationships 10. Suburban families 11. Men/women relations 12. Organized crime 13. Expectation (Psychology) 14. New York City 15. Coming-of-age stories 16. Satirical fiction

LC 2001047676

National Jewish Book Award for Fiction, 2002-2003.

ALA Notable Book, 2003.

"Shteyngart's playful, carnivalesque sensibility fits within a Russian satirical-fantastic tradition that stretches from Nikolai Gogol in the 19th century to Mikhail Bulgakov in the Stalin period and Vassily Aksyonov in the Soviet twilight. The sturdy conventions of the traditional novel . . . are blithely disregarded in favor of digressive, madcap inventiveness." New York Times Book Review.

Shteyngart, Gary, 1972-

* **Super** sad true love story : a novel / Gary Shteyngart. Random House, 2010. 352 p.

ISBN 9781400066407

1. Equality 2. Pride and vanity 3. Eccentric men 4. Immortality 5. Death 6. Dystopias 7. Transformations, Personal 8. Men/women relations 9. Recession (Economics) 10. Class conflict 11. Satirical

fiction

LC 2009037971

In a novel set in the near future, when a beautiful, yet cruel, woman that Lenny Abramov met in Italy says she his coming to stay with him in New York, even the tanks and soldiers stationed in the city and the ongoing war with Venezuela can't get him down.

"Full-tilt and fulminating satirist Shteyngart . . . is mordant, gleeful, and embracive as he funnels today's follies and atrocities into a devilishly hilarious, soul-shriveling, and all-too plausible vision of a ruthless and crass digital dystopia in which techno-addled humans are still humbled by love and death." Booklist.

Shumway, Charity

Ten girls to watch : a novel / Charity Shumway. Washington Square Press, 2012. 320 p.

ISBN 9781451673418

1. Self-discovery in women 2. Single women 3. Women authors 4. Women college graduates 5. Self-acceptance 6. New York City 7. Chick lit

LC 2011048888

When she lands a job tracking down the past winners of Charm magazine's "Ten Girls to Watch" contest, Dawn West is excited to interview hundreds of fascinating women and discovers that success, love and friendship can be found in the most unexpected of places.

Shupe, Joanna

The **courtesan** duchess / Joanna Shupe. Zebra, 2015. 352 p. Wicked deceptions

ISBN 9781420135527

1. 1810s 2. Dukes and duchesses 3. Separated couples 4. Secret identity 5. Seduction 6. Courtesans 7. Debt 8. Betrayal 9. Inheritance and succession 10. Reconciliation in marriage 11. Sexual attraction 12. Men/women relations 13. Venice, Italy 14. Historical romances

Disguising herself as a courtesan to get the attention of her husband, who she has not seen in eight years, the Duchess of Colton arrives in Venice where she sets her plan of seduction in motion and is shocked to discover that the man she married just could be the love of her life.

Shupe, Joanna

The **prince** of Broadway / Joanna Shupe. Avon Books, 2019. 384 p. Uptown girls

ISBN 9780062906830

1. Gilded Age (1865-1898) 2. Casinos 3. Young women 4. Casino owners 5. Mentoring 6. Upper class 7. Families 8. Revenge 9. Ambition in women 10. Sexual attraction 11. Men/women relations 12. New York City -- Social life and customs -- 19th century 13. Historical romances

Using each other for their own means, Clayton Madden, the owner of the city's most exclusive casino, and heiress Florence Greene's finds their mutually beneficial relationship taking a romantic turn, which forces both their hands.

"Shupe . . . continues her lusciously detailed Gilded Age-set series with a dynamic duo determined to get what they want at any cost. Sensual and passionate and with an unconventional, intriguing story line, this second in the series (after The Rogue of Fifth Avenue) is one readers will clamor for." Library Journal.

Shupe, Joanna

The **rogue** of Fifth Avenue / Joanna Shupe. Avon Books, 2019. 384 p. Uptown girls

ISBN 9780062906816

1. Gilded Age (1865-1898) 2. Lawyers 3. Rich families 4. Helpfulness in women 5. City life 6. Independence in women 7. Sexual attraction

8. Men/women relations 9. New York City -- Social life and customs -- 19th century 10. Historical romances

Determined to help struggling families in the tenements, Mamie Greene, the daughter of a wealthy New York City powerbroker, matches wits with her father's lawyer who threatens her efforts.

Sidhu, Ranbir Singh

Good Indian girls : stories / Ranbir Singh Sidhu. Soft Skull, 2013, c2012. 240 p.

ISBN 9781593765316

1. Identity (Psychology) 2. Self 3. East Indians 4. Interpersonal relations 5. Family relationships 6. Literary fiction 7. Short stories

LC 2013017908

Presents a collection of twelve short stories about the complicated lives of Indian immigrants in the United States.

Sidor, Steven

* The **mirror's** edge / Steven Sidor. St. Martin's Minotaur, 2008. 287 p.

ISBN 9780312354138

1. Journalists 2. Missing children 3. Cold cases (Criminal investigation) 4. Brothers 5. Small towns 6. Middle West 7. Mysteries

LC 2007051830

Years after two boys are abducted from their home, the unresolved disappearance still resonates with the inhabitants of a small Midwestern town, including a reporter who had covered the case, which bears an eerie similarity to the disappearance of his own brother.

"Sidor is a master of the unsettling, and each twist is more grisly and unexpected than the last." Publishers Weekly.

Sidor, Steven

Skin River / Steven Sidor. St. Martin's Minotaur, 2004. 256 p.

ISBN 0312329490

1. Bar owners 2. Amateur detectives 3. Waitresses 4. Bars (Drinking establishments) 5. Serial murders -- Wisconsin 6. Serial murderers -- Wisconsin 7. Crimes against young women 8. Small town life -- Wisconsin 9. Small towns -- Wisconsin 10. Second chances 11. Wisconsin 12. Chicago, Illinois 13. Mysteries

LC 2004046784

Hoping to escape his dark past by working as a tavern keeper in a small Wisconsin town, Buddy Bayes stumbles into a brutal missing-persons case and makes a wrongful conclusion that has disturbing consequences.

"Deft descriptions, slick prose, and growing tension mark this first novel." Library Journal.

Siegel, Jan

Prospero's children / Jan Siegel. Del Rey, 2000, c1999. 350 p.

ISBN 0345439015

1. Atlantis (Legendary place) 2. Fantasy fiction

LC 00190160

Sixteen-year-old Fern Chapel rediscovers the secret and powerful magic of Atlantis

Sienkiewicz, Henryk, 1846-1916

* **Quo** vadis : a story of faith in the last days of the Roman Empire / Henryk Sienkiewicz ; introduction and afterword by Joe Wheeler. Tyndale House Publishers, 2000. 606 p.

ISBN 1561797952

1. Nero,, Emperor of Rome, 37-68 2. Petronius Arbiter 3. Roman Empire (27 BCE-476 CE) 4. Christians 5. Men/women relations 6.

Church history -- Primitive and early church, ca 30-600 7. Rome -- History -- Nero, 54-68 8. Rome -- Rulers 9. Historical fiction 10. Translations -- Polish to English

LC 00036463

Marcus, a Roman officer in Nero's army, risks his career, his family, and even his life when he falls in love with a Christian woman named Callina. In order to win Callina's love, Marcus must come to understand the true meaning of her religion, even as Rome sinks under the excesses of Nero and Christians are thrown to the lions.

Siger, Jeffrey

Mykonos after midnight : a Chief Inspector Kaldis Mystery / Jeffrey Siger. Poisoned Pen, 2013. 250 p. Greek mysteries (Jeffrey Siger)

ISBN 9781464201813

1. Murder investigation 2. Murder 3. Rich people 4. Nightclubs 5. Detectives 6. Mykonos (Island) -- Social life and customs 7. Greece 8. Mysteries

The murder of a legendary nightclub owner who helped transform Mykonos from an impoverished Greek island into a wealthy, world-renown tourist paradise puts politically explosive secrets into play and Chief Inspector Andreas Kaldis into battle with a powerful, clandestine international force intent on doing whatever necessary to dominate the island.

Siger, Jeffrey

Target Tinos : an Inspector Kaldis mystery / Jeffrey Siger. Poisoned Pen Press, 2012. 250 p. Greek mysteries (Jeffrey Siger)

ISBN 9781590589786

1. Romanies 2. Secret societies 3. Hate crimes 4. Organized crime 5. Murder investigation 6. Immigrants 7. Engaged persons 8. International intrigue 9. Detectives 10. Police chiefs 11. Tenos, Greece 12. Greece 13. Mysteries

Andreas Kaldis's investigation into the murder of two gypsies on the Aegean island of Tinos leads him to more bodies, a secret society, and questions about the growing number of non-Greeks and gypsies flocking to the island.

Silber, Joan

Improvement / Joan Silber. Counterpoint Press, 2017 227 p.

ISBN 9781619029606

1. Interpersonal relations 2. Consequences 3. Smuggling 4. Prisoners 5. Single mothers 6. Decision-making 7. Family relationships 8. New York City 9. Literary fiction

LC 2017025010

National Book Critics Circle Award for Fiction, 2017.
PEN-Faulkner Award, 2018.

A young single mother living with her concerned eccentric aunt in New York makes fateful decisions that have unexpected implications, including her relationship with a Rikers Island inmate who draws her into a cigarette smuggling scheme.

"In Silber's (Fools, 2013) latest, big events in characters lives play out on a small stage in quiet and reflective ways. ... Silber's decision to write events of great magnitude from everyday points of view lends realism and universality to her story. Fans of character-driven, literary fiction should be on the lookout for Improvement." Booklist.

Silko, Leslie Marmon, 1948-

Almanac of the dead / Leslie Marmon Silko. Simon and Schuster, 1991. 763 p.

ISBN 0140173196

1. Prophecies 2. Native American resistance and revolts 3. Indians of North America -- Relations with missionaries, traders, etc 4. Political corruption 5. Race relations 6. Clairvoyance 7. Secretaries 8. Drug traffic 9. Revolutions 10. Real estate 11. Tucson, Arizona 12. Southwest (United States) -- Race relations 13. Magical realism 14. Literary fiction

LC 91019978

Includes endpaper illustrations.

Seese, a survivor of the dangerous world of drug dealing, takes a job as a secretary to Lecha, an old woman who is suspected of being a witch.

Silko, Leslie Marmon, 1948-

* Ceremony / Leslie Marmon Silko ; introduction by Larry McMurtry ; with a new preface by the author. Penguin Books, 2006. xxiii, 243 p.

ISBN 9780143104919

1. Native American men 2. Culture conflict 3. Despair 4. World War II veterans 5. Pueblo Indians -- New Mexico 6. Former prisoners of war 7. Indian reservations 8. Alienation (Social psychology) 9. Identity (Psychology) 10. Belief and doubt 11. Rites and ceremonies 12. Laguna Pueblo Reservation, New Mexico 13. Historical fiction 14. Literary fiction

LC 76046936

Originally published: New York :

On a New Mexico reservation, one Navajo family--including Tayo, a World War II veteran deeply scarred by his experiences as a Japanese POW and by the rejection of his own people--struggles to survive in a world no longer theirs in the years just before and after World War II.

Silko, Leslie Marmon, 1948-

Gardens in the dunes : a novel / Leslie Marmon Silko. Simon & Schuster, 1999. 479 p.

ISBN 0684811545

1. 19th century 2. Native American girls 3. Assimilation (Sociology) 4. Identity (Psychology) 5. Indians of North America -- Relations with missionaries, traders, etc 6. Race relations 7. Adopted girls 8. Color 9. Dreams 10. Desert life 11. Frontier and pioneer life 12. Southwest (United States) 13. Historical fiction 14. Literary fiction

LC 98-51987

An Indian girl left orphaned after soldiers raid and destroy her village is adopted by a well-meaning American family, but she cannot forget her past and accept the white traditions and education they expect her to embrace.

"Set in the 19th century this is the tale of two sisters, the last remaining members of the ancient Sand Lizard tribe. Sister Salt, so called for her light skin, and her younger sister, Indigo, learn all about the hidden, life-sustaining plants of the desert from Grandma Fleet, who teaches them how to live happily with a minimum of material goods and a wealth of knowledge. Such self-sufficiency is essential if they are to stay free from the misery of reservation life, but even so their liberty is put at risk when they travel to the mean little town of Needles, Arizona, where hundreds of Indians gather to dance in anticipation of the arrival of the Messiah. In the chaotic aftermath of the miraculous visitation, the girls lose their mother and grandmother and then are cruelly separated by the authorities." Booklist.

Sillitoe, Alan

* The **loneliness** of the long-distance runner / Alan Sillitoe. New American Library, 1959. 144 p.

1. Working class 2. Nottinghamshire, England 3. Short stories

LC 60008227

Nine stories deal with members of England's young working class as they struggle against poverty.

Sillitoe, Alan

Saturday night and Sunday morning / Alan Sillitoe. Knopf, 1959, c1958. 239 p.

1. Working class 2. Iron and steel workers 3. Young men 4. Machinists 5. Extramarital affairs 6. Pregnant women 7. Love triangles 8. Nottingham, England 9. England 10. Coming-of-age stories 11. Modern classics 12. Literary fiction

Alan Sillitoe was an integral part of the Angry Young Men movement of the fifties that focused on its authentic depiction of real working class people. This book is true to their ideals in its raw sharp writing of the story of a young man framed by his brutal experience in the army and as a factory worker. Fuelled by a bleak aggressive outlook on life the book centres around a boozy, philandering weekend which is graphically captured by Sillitoe's clever prose.

Silone, Ignazio, 1900-1978

Bread and wine / Ignazio Silone ; a new version translated from the Italian by Harvey Fergusson II, with a new preface by the author. Atheneum, 1962. 331 p., 21 cm. Abruzzo trilogy

1. Catholic Church Clergy 2. Priests 3. Secret identity 4. Fascism -- Italy 5. Communism -- Italy 6. Peasantry -- Italy 7. Villages -- Italy 8. Italy -- History -- 1922-1945 9. Abruzzo, Italy 10. Political fiction 11. Translations -- Italian to English

LC 62017288

After 15 years of exile, Pietro Spina returns to Italy disguised as a monk in order to help Italian peasants fearful of the Fascist dictatorship.

Silva, Daniel, 1960-

* The **black** widow / Daniel Silva. Harper, 2016. 528 p. Gabriel Allon novels

ISBN 9780062320223

1. Intelligence officers 2. International intrigue 3. Spies 4. Bombings 5. Assassination 6. Intelligence service 7. Thrillers and suspense 8. Spy fiction

Art restorer, assassin, and spy Gabriel Allon finds himself poised to become the chief of Israel's secret intelligence service, but not before answering the French government's request to eliminate the person responsible for detonating a massive bomb in Paris.

"Silva proves once again that he can rework familiar genre material and bring it to new life." Publishers Weekly.

Silva, Daniel, 1960-

* The **kill** artist : a novel / Daniel Silva. Random House, 2000. 428 p. Gabriel Allon novels

ISBN 0375500901

1. Art restorers 2. Fashion models 3. Intelligence officers 4. International intrigue 5. Secret service -- Israel 6. Mossad agents 7. Terrorism 8. Palestinians 9. Israel 10. Middle East 11. Thrillers and suspense 12. Spy fiction

LC 00055308

The Israeli intelligence chief recalls two former agents to eliminate a top Palestinian terrorist. The former agents were once lovers and their pasts and their enemies come back to haunt them as the terrorist begins his campaign of murder.

Silva, Daniel, 1960-

The **new** girl / Daniel Silva. Harper, 2019. 496 p. Gabriel Allon novels

ISBN 9780062834836

1. Intelligence officers 2. International intrigue 3. Teenage girl kidnapping victims 4. Enemies 5. Spies 6. Secrecy 7. Thrillers and suspense 8. Spy fiction

The kidnapping of a mysterious girl from her Swiss boarding school ignites a secret war between Israeli intelligence chief Gabriel Allon and an old enemy who would transform the future of the Middle East.

Silva, Daniel, 1960-

The **other** woman / Daniel Silva. Harper, 2018. 476 p. Gabriel Allon novels

ISBN 9780062834829

1. Intelligence officers 2. International intrigue 3. Spies 4. Revenge 5. Terrorism 6. Thrillers and suspense 7. Spy fiction

After his asset inside Russian intelligence is assassinated, Gabriel's search for the truth leads him to the twentieth century's greatest act of treason.

Silver, Elizabeth L., 1978-

The **execution** of Noa P. Singleton : a novel / Elizabeth L. Silver. Crown Publishers, 2013. 304 p.

ISBN 9780385347433

1. Death row prisoners 2. Women prisoners 3. Attorney and client 4. Women lawyers 5. Murder investigation 6. Envy in women 7. Clemency 8. Guilt in women 9. Former convicts 10. Mothers and daughters 11. Dysfunctional families 12. Legal thrillers 13. Psychological suspense

LC 2012040204

Visited by a high-powered attorney who has initiated a clemency petition on her behalf and who is also the mother of her victim, death-row inmate Noa is slowly persuaded to share the events surrounding the murder in spite of her reluctance to reveal the whole story or have her life extended.

Silver, Marisa

Mary Coin : a novel / Marisa Silver. Blue Rider Press, 2013. 336 p.

ISBN 9780399160707

1. Depression era (1929-1941) 2. Poor people 3. Depressions -- 1929-1941 4. Photographers 5. Women migrant workers 6. Women photographers 7. Photojournalism -- United States -- History -- 20th century 8. Rural poor people 9. Mothers 10. College teachers 11. Indians of North America 12. Divorced men 13. Genealogy 14. Farms 15. Widows 16. Men/women relations 17. Historical fiction 18. Parallel narratives 19. Women's lives and relationships

LC 2012039861

Imagines the lives of the subject of the photograph, photographer, and a college professor who finds a connection to a family legacy in the image of the iconic "Migrant Mother."

Silvis, Randall, 1950-

Two days gone : a novel / Randall Silvis. Sourcebooks Landmark, 2017. 400 p. Ryan DeMarco novels

ISBN 9781492639732

1. Murder suspects 2. Family killing 3. Friendship 4. Murder investigation 5. Police 6. College towns 7. Authors 8. Pennsylvania 9. Police procedurals 10. Mysteries

LC 2016008657

When a woman and her children are murdered, Sergeant Ryan De-Marco doubts the prime suspect, the woman's fugitive husband, was capable of killing his family and wonders if the half-finished manuscript he left behind contains clues to the killer.

Simenon, Georges, 1903-1989

Maigret and the black sheep / Georges Simenon ; translated from the French by Helen Thomson Harcourt Brace Jovanovich, 1976, c1962. 158 p. Jules Maigret mysteries

ISBN 9780151551460

1. Police -- Paris, France 2. Murder 3. Extramarital affairs 4. Letter writing 5. Murder investigation 6. Detectives 7. Paris, France 8. France 9. Mysteries 10. Translations -- French to English 11. Police procedurals

LC 75028384

"A Helen and Kurt Wolff book."

"The victim is a retired carton manufacturer who has been shot, without apparent motive, while sitting at home in his favorite armchair. To [Chief Inspector Maigret's] chagrin, he can find no crack or crevice in the utter respectability of the dead man's life. . . . The season is the end of summer. Parisians are drifting back to the city from their vacations, there is a nip in the air. . . . Maigret sips his beer in several cafs, confers with his faithful colleague Lapointe, and ponders the many facts of this . . . case." The New Yorker.

Simenon, Georges, 1903-1989

Maigret and the fortuneteller / Georges Simenon ; translated by Geoffrey Sainsbury. Harcourt Brace Jovanovich, 1989, c1944. 140 p. Jules Maigret mysteries

ISBN 9780151555710

1. Police -- Paris, France 2. Murder 3. Fortune-tellers 4. Murder investigation 5. Detectives 6. Paris, France 7. France 8. Mysteries 9. Translations -- French to English 10. Police procedurals

LC 88016301

Previously published as: To any lengths.

Inspector Maigret investigates the death of fortuneteller Mademoiselle Jeanne, a case remarkable for its wealth of unconnected suspects and fragmentary clues.

"Maigret is forewarned of a murder but fails to prevent it. He tracks down the villain by exercising his famous 'capacity for putting himself in other people's shoes.' In this case, the shoes belong to a woebegone old man, apparently senile, who was found at the scene of the crime. Obviously more terrified of his wife and daughter than he is of the thunderous Maigret, the old man piques the policeman's interest and so leads him to the solution." Booklist.

Simenon, Georges, 1903-1989

* **Maigret** and the killer / Georges Simenon ; translated by Lyn Moir. Harcourt Brace Jovanovich, 1971, c1969. 165 p. Jules Maigret mysteries

ISBN 9780151551279

1. Murder 2. Murder investigation 3. Detectives 4. Police -- Paris, France 5. Criminal investigation 6. Paris, France 7. France 8. Mysteries 9. Translations -- French to English 10. Police procedurals

LC 91017180

"The witty pace featuring kidnappings and shootings, is effectively sustained throughout." Booklist.

Simenon, Georges, 1903-1989

Maigret and the madwoman / Georges Simenon ; translated from the French by Eileen Ellenbogen. Harcourt, 1972, c1970. 176 p. Jules Maigret mysteries

ISBN 9780151551385

1. Murder 2. Detectives 3. Police -- Paris, France 4. Murder investigation 5. Criminal investigation 6. Paris, France 7. France 8. Mysteries 9. Translations -- French to English 10. Police procedurals

LC 72075421

2019 reprint by Penguin Classics, London, was translated by Sian Reynolds.

A kind but seemingly paranoid old lady turns to Inspector Maigret for help. Against the judgement of his subordinates, he decides to pay a visit to her Parisian apartment to investigate, but is he already too late?

Simenon, Georges, 1903-1989

* **Maigret** and the Saturday caller / Georges Simenon ; translated by Tony White Harcourt Brace Jovanovich, 1991, c1962. 124 p. Jules Maigret mysteries

ISBN 9780151555666

1. Police -- Paris, France 2. Murder 3. Extramarital affairs 4. Detectives 5. Crimes of passion 6. Love triangles 7. Murder investigation 8. Paris, France 9. France 10. Mysteries 11. Translations -- French to English 12. Police procedurals

LC 90046032

Slow-moving psychological detective Jules Maigret is hot on the trail of a crime that has not even happened yet after being visited by Leonard Planchon, a man who confesses that he intends to murder his wife and her lover.

"Maigret is visited by a harelipped man who confesses that he wants to murder his wife and her lover but hasn't yet done so. Needless to say, Maigret cannot dismiss the man's plans as the fantasy of a harmless lunatic and begins to probe around the edges, irritated by the handicaps imposed by the public prosecutor's recent restrictions on police powers." Booklist.

Simenon, Georges, 1903-1989

* **Maigret** and the toy village / Georges Simenon ; translated by Eileen Ellenbogen Harcourt, 1979, c1944. 139 p. Jules Maigret mysteries

ISBN 9780151555543

1. Police -- Paris, France 2. Murder 3. Murder investigation 4. Sailors 5. Household employees 6. Detectives 7. Villages -- France 8. Housekeepers 9. France 10. Mysteries 11. Translations -- French to English 12. Police procedurals

LC 79001843

"A Helen and Kurt Wolff book."

Investigating the murder of Jules Lapie, a sailor nicknamed Peg Leg, Maigret finds Lapie's young housekeeper the most difficult obstacle to solving the case.

Simenon, Georges, 1903-1989

Maigret and the wine merchant / Georges Simenon ; translated from the French by Eileen Ellenbogen Harcourt Brace Jovanovich, 1971, c1970. 187 p. Jules Maigret mysteries

ISBN 9780151551361

1. Murder 2. Detectives 3. Criminal investigation 4. Wine and wine making 5. Murder investigation 6. Police -- Paris, France 7. Paris, France 8. France 9. Mysteries 10. Translations -- French to English 11. Police procedurals

LC 73142097

"A Helen and Kurt Wolff book."

"When a wealthy wine merchant is shot and killed in Paris, Inspector Maigret must investigate a long list of family, colleagues and lovers to uncover just who could have committed the crime. Delving into the depths of the man's personality, Maigret discovers that the victim may have made one too many enemies on his way to the top." Provided by publisher

Simenon, Georges, 1903-1989

* **Maigret** bides his time / Georges Simenon ; translated by Alastair Hamilton Harcourt Brace Jovanovich, 1985, c1965. 155 p. Jules Maigret mysteries

ISBN 9780151555635

1. Police -- Paris, France 2. Jewelry theft 3. Murder 4. Murder investigation 5. Detectives 6. Paris, France 7. France 8. Mysteries 9. Translations -- French to English 10. Police procedurals

"This novel combines a delight in the sensual world with an exploration of the horrors of human cruelty. Vintage Simenon." Booklist.

Simenon, Georges, 1903-1989

* **Maigret** goes home / Georges Simenon ; translated by Robert Baldick. Harcourt Brace Jovanovich, 1989, c1932. 139 p. Jules Maigret mysteries

ISBN 9780151551507

1. Police -- Paris, France 2. Hometowns -- France 3. Murder 4. Murder investigation 5. Detectives 6. Villages -- France 7. Widows 8. Inheritance and succession 9. Paris, France 10. France 11. Translations -- French to English 12. Mysteries 13. Police procedurals

LC 89002011

Also published as: Maigret on Home Ground, The Saint-Fiacre Affair, Death of a countess, and Maigret and the Countess

Chief Inspector Maigret returns to the village of Saint-Fiacre, where he was born, after a note to the police warns that a crime will take place, and soon after he arrives the Countess de Saint-Fiacre dies, leaving Maigret to find the killer.

"The countess of the estate where Maigret grew up drops dead during early mass on All Souls' Day, shocked to death by a fake newspaper report falsely reporting the suicide of her son. Although the estate had been heavily mortgaged to pay for the son's debts and the countess' young lovers, the inheritance is still not inconsiderable, and, of course, there are at least three likely suspects." Booklist.

Simenon, Georges, 1903-1989

Maigret in Holland / Georges Simenon ; translated by Geoffrey Sainsbury. Harcourt Brace, 1993, c1940. 165 p. Jules Maigret mysteries

ISBN 0151551596

1. Police -- Paris, France 2. Murder 3. Murder investigation 4. Detectives 5. Teachers -- Death 6. Secrets 7. Netherlands 8. Mysteries 9. Translations -- French to English 10. Police procedurals
LC 92030504

Previously published as A Crime in Holland

When Inspector Maigret arrives in Delfzijl to investigate the murder of Conrad Popinga, he finds a long list of suspects, including a giggling, man-hungry farmer's daughter and a pompous criminologist found holding the murder weapon.

"Although Maigret speaks no Dutch, he is called to Holland to assist a compatriot, Jean Duclos. Unfortunately, Duclos was present when Conrad Popinga, a former captain in the merchant marine, was murdered, and the Dutch police think Duclos, along with Popinga's wife and sister-in-law, a young sailor, and a local farm girl, is a prime suspect. Once the capable but long-suffering Maigret arrives, he methodically

reviews the evidence and questions suspects. . . . Readers will marvel at the inspector's brilliant logic." Booklist.

Simenon, Georges, 1903-1989

Maigret's memoirs / Georges Simenon ; translated from the French by Jean Stewart. Harcourt Brace Jovanovich, 1985, c1951. 134 p. Jules Maigret mysteries

ISBN 9780151551484

1. Police -- Paris, France 2. Memories 3. Courtship 4. Detectives 5. Paris, France 6. France 7. Translations -- French to English 8. Mysteries 9. Police procedurals

LC 85008591

Inspector Maigret shows the ways of police work to a young writer and reveals his rural upbringing, his first assignment as a bicycle messenger, and how he wooed and won Madame Maigret.

"Inspector Maigret, upset by writer Georges Simenon's 'caricature' of him, decides to correct the world's misconception of his personality and his cases by writing his memoirs. . . . Maigret outlines a few criminal cases, digresses about the Parisian weather, explains his dislike for Simenon, and presents his views on the criminal mind and on life in general in this odd but marvelous 'autobiographical' account." Booklist.

Simenon, Georges, 1903-1989

My friend Maigret / Georges Simenon ; translated by Nigel Ryan. Penguin Books, 2008, c1949. 176 p. Jules Maigret mysteries

ISBN 9780143112846

1. Detectives 2. Murder 3. Murder investigation 4. Police -- Paris, France 5. France 6. Mysteries 7. Translations -- French to English 8. Police procedurals

LC 2007025931

Translated from the French of: Mon ami Maigret (1949).

First published in French as Mon ami Maigret by Presses de la Cite 1949.

A small time crook has been murdered on a Mediterranean island - a thug, drunk, pimp and thief - yet just before he died he was heard boasting about his friend Maigret! Maigret, who is mentoring a Scotland Yard detective, Inspector Pike, travels to sun-drenched Porquerolles Island to investigate.

Simmons, Dan

The **abominable** : a novel / Dan Simmons. Little, Brown and Company, 2013. 704 p.

ISBN 9780316198837

1. 1920s 2. Missing persons 3. Mountaineering -- Mount Everest 4. Mountaineers 5. Friendship 6. Secrets 7. Mountain survival 8. Mount Everest 9. Horror 10. Historical horror

LC 2013017754

Four climbers travel to Mount Everest in 1924 in an attempt to recover the body of a missing adventurer but find themselves being pursued by someone or something.

Simmons, Dan

Drood : a novel / Dan Simmons. Little, Brown and Co., 2009. 784 p.

ISBN 9780316007023

1. Dickens, Charles, 1812-1870 2. 1860s 3. Authors, English 4. Railroad travel 5. Accidents 6. Railroad accidents -- Psychological aspects 7. Secrets 8. London, England -- History -- 19th century 9. Biographical fiction 10. Historical mysteries

LC 2008024501

A tale inspired by the mysterious final years of Charles Dickens finds the fifty-three-year-old literary master irrevocably changed when a train journey with his mistress ends in violence.

"The narrative is overlong, with discarded subplots and red herrings, but Simmons, a master of otherworldly suspense, cleverly explores envy's corrosive effects." The New Yorker.

Simmons, Dan

Endymion / Dan Simmons. Bantam Books, 1996. 468 p. Hyperion series

ISBN 0553100203

1. Catholic Church 2. 32nd century 3. Androids 4. Artificial intelligence 5. Messiahs 6. Time travel (Future) 7. Space flight 8. Eleven-year-old girls 9. Science fiction 10. Space opera

LC 95033191

Trapped in an orbiting prison that will kill him at the slightest sign of tampering, the narrator looks back on events leading up to his impending death.

"The protagonist, a good-hearted soldier named Raul Endymion, sets off on a quest with historic consequences: he must keep from harm a young girl who holds the key to a rebirth of human civilization. Arrayed against him is the power of the Pax, a militarized Catholic Church that offers its adherents a literal resurrection of the body. It is Mr. Simmons's inspiration to embody the Pax in the person of Father Captain Federico de Soya, a starship commander who pursues Endymion and the young girl from one exotic planet to the next." New York Times Book Review.

Simmons, Dan

The **fall** of Hyperion / Dan Simmons. Doubleday, 1990. 517 p. Hyperion series

ISBN 0385249500

1. 28th century 2. Pilgrims and pilgrimages 3. Space warfare 4. Imaginary empires 5. Priests 6. Detectives 7. Poets 8. Scholars and academics 9. Soldiers 10. Spaceship captains 11. Space opera 12. Science fiction

LC 89037438

"A Foundation book."

BSFA Award for Best Novel, 1991.

Locus Award for Best Science Fiction Novel, 1991.

Seven pilgrims continue their fateful mission to Hyperion, a planet that may be humankind's only hope in a galaxy threatened by an all-encompassing war.

"In this sequel to Hyperion, Simmons weaves together many strands of a complex plot with lucidity and poetic imagination." Library Journal.

Simmons, Dan

The **fifth** heart / Dan Simmons. Little, Brown and Company, 2015. 640 p.

ISBN 9780316198820

1. James, Henry, 1843-1916 2. Gilded Age (1865-1898) 3. 1890s 4. Private investigators 5. Authors, American 6. Characters and characteristics in literature 7. Murder investigation 8. Reality 9. Manipulation by men 10. National security 11. British in the United States 12. Historical mysteries 13. Adaptations, retellings, and spin-offs

LC 2014021881

Originally published: 2015.

While in America to solve the mystery of the 1885 death of Clover Adams, wife of the esteemed historian Henry Adams, Sherlock Holmes and Henry James find themselves involved in matters of national importance possibly orchestrated by Moriarty. By the author of The Abominable.

Simmons, Dan

* **Hyperion** / Dan Simmons. Doubleday, 1989. 481 p. Hyperion series

ISBN 9780385249492

1. 28th century 2. Pilgrims and pilgrimages 3. Imaginary empires 4. Space warfare 5. Priests 6. Soldiers 7. Detectives 8. Poets 9. Scholars and academics 10. Spaceship captains 11. Space opera 12. Science fiction

LC 88033407

Hugo Award for Best Novel, 1990.

Locus Award for Best Science Fiction Novel, 1990.

A pilgrimage to the realm of the Shrike, a part-god/part-killing machine, provides the travellers the forum to tell their incredible stories.

Simmons, Dan

The **rise** of Endymion / Dan Simmons. Bantam Books, 1997. 579 p. Hyperion series

ISBN 055310652X

1. Messiahs 2. Androids 3. Artificial intelligence 4. Religion 5. Space flight 6. Time travel (Past) 7. Science fiction 8. Space opera

LC 97-5658

Locus Award for Best Science Fiction Novel, 1998.

The conclusion of the author's Hyperion series follows Aenea's emergence as a messiah and her relationship to Raul Endymion and the poet, Martin Silenius.

Simmons, Dan

* The **Terror** : a novel / Dan Simmons. Little, Brown and Co., 2007. 784 p.

ISBN 9780316017442

1. John Franklin Arctic Expedition, (1845-1851?) 2. 1840s 3. Survival (after airplane accidents, shipwrecks, etc) 4. Shipwrecks 5. Sea monsters 6. Ship captains 7. Inuit women 8. Rescues 9. Mental illness 10. Mutiny 11. Adventurers 12. Explorers 13. Wilderness survival 14. Voyages and travels 15. Arctic regions -- Exploration 16. Northwest Passage 17. Sea stories 18. Horror 19. Historical horror

LC 2006014608

Adapted into a television series by AMC network in 2017.

International Horror Guild Award for Best Novel, 2007.

Captain Crozier must find a way for his crew to survive the deadly attacks of a sea monster, in a novel loosely based on the mid-nineteenth-century Arctic expedition originally led by Sir John Franklin.

"A deeply absorbing story that combines awe-inspiring myth, grinding horror and historically accurate adventure." Seattle Times.

Simon, Clea

Dogs don't lie / Clea Simon. Poisoned Pen Press, 2011. 250 p. Pru Marlowe pet noir

ISBN 9781590588604

1. Human/animal communication 2. Women psychics 3. Murder investigation 4. Psychic ability 5. Pit bull terriers 6. Secrets 7. Small town life -- Massachusetts 8. Women and cats 9. Women amateur detectives 10. Massachusetts 11. Cozy mysteries 12. Supernatural mysteries 13. Mysteries

Animal psychic and behaviorist Pru Marlowe investigates after one of her clients is killed and the prime suspect is the victim's dog, a pitbull named Lily.

Simon, Clea

Grey dawn / Clea Simon. Severn House, 2013. 224 p. Dulcie Schwartz feline-filled mysteries

ISBN 9780727882615

1. Harvard University Students 2. Murder investigation 3. Graduate students 4. Innocence (Law) 5. Murder suspects 6. Women graduate students 7. Animal ghosts 8. Women and cats 9. Cambridge, Massachusetts 10. Cozy mysteries 11. Gentle reads 12. Supernatural mysteries

When grad student Dulcie Schwartz hears a wolf late one night she tries to dismiss it, but the noises, the dark building, and an unnerving sighting of her adviser all combine to give her the creeps. Next morning Dulcie learns that a university student was savagely attacked that very night. A woman who looks like Dulcie. Aided by the cryptic advice from her kitten Esme and the ghost of her late, great cat Mr. Grey, Dulcie investigates.

Simon, Clea

Panthers play for keeps : a Pru Marlowe pet mystery / Clea Simon. Poisoned Pen Press, 2014. 250 p. Pru Marlowe pet noir

ISBN 9781590588727

1. Human/animal communication 2. Murder witnesses 3. Women amateur detectives 4. Psychic ability 5. Murder investigation 6. Women psychics 7. Dogs 8. Women and birds 9. Small town life -- Massachusetts 10. Women and cats 11. Massachusetts 12. Cozy mysteries 13. Supernatural mysteries 14. Mysteries

Pru Marlowe investigates the death of a young woman who appears to have been mauled by a wild cat even though there have been no sightings of mountain lions in the Berkshires for years.

Simon, Clea

Stages of Grey / Clea Simon. Severn House, 2014. 224 p. Dulcie Schwartz feline-filled mysteries

ISBN 9780727883933

1. Harvard University Students 2. Women graduate students 3. Theater companies 4. Graduate students 5. Theater 6. Murder 7. Murder investigation 8. Animal ghosts 9. Women and cats 10. Cambridge, Massachusetts 11. Cozy mysteries 12. Gentle reads 13. Supernatural mysteries

When Dulcie Schwartz attends a disco version of Ovid's Metamorphosis by a local theater company, she witnesses the murder of a performer and must uncover the truth while determining whether the troupe's cat Gus played a role in the affair.

Simon, Michael, 1963-

The **last** Jew standing : a novel / Michael Simon. Viking, 2007. xii, 289 p. Dan Reles novels

ISBN 9780670063246

1. 1990s 2. Detectives -- Austin, Texas 3. Police -- Austin, Texas 4. Fathers and sons 5. Jewish men 6. Prostitutes 7. Mafia 8. Organized crime 9. Options, alternatives, choices 10. Escapes 11. Crime bosses 12. Austin, Texas 13. Mysteries

As his solid family life and career as the head of Austin Homicide are disturbed by the arrivals of his mob-connected father and an escaped prostitute, Dan Reles also contends with a sociopath mobster who forces him to question his priorities.

Simon, Misty

Cremains of the day / Misty Simon. Kensington Books, 2017 300 p. Tallie Graver mysteries

ISBN 9781496712219

1. Household employees 2. Murder investigation 3. Former husbands 4. Rich people 5. Funeral homes 6. Women amateur detectives 7. Mysteries 8. Cozy mysteries

Cleaning houses to make ends meet, former socialite Tallulah Graver is plagued by a series of strange events that end in murder and she must clean up this mess before another victim is swept under the rug.

Simonson, Helen

Major Pettigrew's last stand : a novel / Helen Simonson. Random House, 2010. 368 p.

ISBN 9781400068937

1. Rural life 2. Retirees 3. Interracial friendship 4. Widowers 5. Widows 6. Seniors 7. Aging 8. Villages 9. Reading 10. Shopkeepers 11. Pakistanis in Great Britain 12. Men/women relations 13. England 14. Mainstream fiction 15. Gentle reads

LC 2009022231

Forced to confront the realities of life in the twenty-first century when he falls in love with Pakistani widow Mrs. Ali, Major Pettigrew finds the relationship challenged by local prejudices that view Mrs. Ali, a Cambridge native, as a perpetual foreigner.

"As with the polished work of Alexander McCall Smith, there is never a dull moment but never a discordant note either. Still, this book feels fresh despite its conventional blueprint. Its main characters are especially well drawn, and Ms. Simonson makes them as admirable as they are entertaining." New York Times.

Simonson, Helen

The **summer** before the war : a novel / Helen Simonson. Random House, 2016. 479 p.

ISBN 9780812993103

1. Edwardian era (1901-1914) 2. Women teachers 3. Rural life 4. Villages 5. War and society 6. Life change events 7. World War I 8. Men/women relations 9. England -- History -- 1900-1945 10. England -- History -- 20th century 11. Historical fiction

LC 2015016554

Arriving in the village of Rye, England, in 1914, Beatrice Nash, a young woman of good family, becomes the first female teacher of Latin at the local school and falls in love with her sponsor's nephew.

"Aficionados of Downton Abbey and The Guernsey Literary and Potato Peel Pie Society will sigh with pleasure." Kirkus.

Simpson, Dorothy, 1933-

Dead and gone : an Inspector Luke Thanet novel. Scribner, 1999. 247 p. Inspector Luke Thanet mysteries

ISBN 0684863367

1. Detectives 2. Police 3. Murder investigation 4. Families 5. England 6. Mysteries

LC 99-39091

Inspector Luke Thanet and Detective Sergeant Mike Lineham unravel the intricate events leading up to the drowning of Victoria Mintaur, the wife of a renowned barrister

"A perfect puzzle, perfectly solved." New York Times Book Review.

Simpson, Dorothy, 1933-

Dead by morning / Dorothy Simpson. C. Scribner's Sons, 1989. 277 p. Inspector Luke Thanet mysteries

ISBN 9780684191232

1. Detectives 2. Murder investigation 3. Suspicion 4. Sisters 5.

Police 6. Hotels 7. Kent, England 8. Mysteries

LC 89006270

Delia and her husband may lose their posh country hotel if her brother, Leo, who has reappeared after a twenty-year absence reclaims his inheritance.

"Inspector Thanet is faced with a murder at a luxurious English country inn and an overzealous superintendent who is busily reorganizing with all the annoying haste of the newly promoted." Booklist.

Simpson, Dorothy, 1933-

* **Doomed** to die / Dorothy Simpson. C. Scribner's Sons, 1991. 245 p. Inspector Luke Thanet mysteries

ISBN 9780684193816

1. Detectives 2. Women artists 3. Murder investigation 4. Police -- Kent, England 5. Mysteries

LC 91004185

Inspector Luke Thanet investigates the murder of Perdita Master--a woman who, before her death, had felt a sense of impending doom

"Confirmed clue-sniffers should be ready for a surprise here: both the solution and the sinner are shockers, though eminently fair ones." Booklist.

Simpson, Dorothy, 1933-

* **Last** seen alive : a Luke Thanet mystery / Dorothy Simpson. Scribner, 1985. 220 p. Inspector Luke Thanet mysteries

ISBN 9780684184357

1. Detectives 2. Resorts 3. Motive (Law) 4. Murder investigation 5. Police -- Kent, England 6. Kent, England 7. Mysteries

LC 85014530

Silver Dagger Award for Fiction, 1985.

Police Inspector Luke Thanet investigates the apparently motiveless murder of Alice Parnall, a guest at the luxurious Black Swan hotel in England's Sturrenden village.

Simpson, Dorothy, 1933-

* **No** laughing matter / Dorothy Simpson. Scribner, 1993. 262 p. Inspector Luke Thanet mysteries

ISBN 0684196263

1. Detectives 2. Murder investigation 3. Police -- Kent, England 4. Kent, England 5. Mysteries

LC 93019799

"Simpson turns out her usual high-caliber tale and gives the reader more to ponder than a simple mystery. Her shrewd understanding of what makes humans tick results in a story that is both entertaining and thought-provoking." Booklist.

Simpson, Dorothy, 1933-

* **Once** too often : an Inspector Luke Thanet novel / Dorothy Simpson. Scribner, 1998. 223 p. Inspector Luke Thanet mysteries

ISBN 0684845784

1. Detectives 2. Police -- Kent, England 3. Fathers and daughters -- Kent, England 4. Murder investigation -- Kent, England 5. Kent, England 6. Mysteries

LC 9732513

Jessica Manifest's questionable death spirits Inspector Luke Thanet away from his daughter's wedding preparations to investigate the victim's supposedly accidental death, and as he delves into her secretive past, he realizes that there are many people with motives for murdering her

Simpson, Mona

Anywhere but here / Mona Simpson. A. A. Knopf, 1987, 406 p.

ISBN 9780394552835

1. Mothers and daughters 2. Moving to a new city 3. Eccentric women 4. Ambition 5. Families 6. Runaway wives, husbands, etc 7. Hope 8. Selfishness in women 9. Los Angeles, California 10. Domestic fiction

LC 86045282

Adapted in 1999 into a film of the same name starring Susan Sarandon and Natalie Portman.

Sequel: The lost father.

This novel about the dreams of three generations of a Midwestern family begins with twelve-year-old Ann August and her ambitious mother, as they travel to California in search of fame and fortune.

"Any single episode could stand on its own, but Simpson keeps piling them on, building with strength and grace." Booklist.

Simpson, Rosemary, 1942-

* **Let** the dead keep their secrets / Rosemary Simpson. Kensington Books, 2018 304 p. Gilded Age mysteries (Rosemary Simpson)

ISBN 9781496715739

1. Gilded Age (1865-1898) 2. 1890s 3. Heirs and heiresses 4. Undercover operations 5. Women amateur detectives 6. Murder investigation 7. Amateur detectives 8. Opera singers 9. Rich people 10. Wife-killing 11. Gamblers 12. Lawyers 13. New York City -- History -- 19th century 14. Historical mysteries

Heiress Prudence MacKenzie and former Pinkerton agent Geoffrey Hunter attempt to discover the truth behind the death of opera singer Claire Buchanan's twin sister and newborn niece when Claire confides her belief that they were murdered.

Simpson, Rosemary, 1942-

* **What** the dead leave behind / Rosemary Simpson. Kensington Books, 2017. 390 p. Gilded Age mysteries (Rosemary Simpson)

ISBN 9781496709080

1. Pinkerton's National Detective Agency 2. Gilded Age (1865-1898) 3. 1890s 4. Heirs and heiresses 5. Blizzards 6. Engaged persons 7. Murder victims 8. Women amateur detectives 9. Amateur detectives 10. Rich people 11. New York City -- History -- 19th century 12. Histo rical mysteries

When her beloved fiancée is found dead after the Great Blizzard of 1888 in New York City, heiress Prudence MacKenzie, suspecting foul play, turns to her fiancée best friend, a former Pinkerton agent, to discover the truth and find protection from sinister forces.

"Launching an atmospheric new series set in Gilded Age New York, Simpson...incorporates historical events and figures to add verisimilitude to this tension-filled story." Library Journal.

Simsion, Graeme C.

The **Rosie** effect / Graeme Simsion. Simon & Schuster, 2014. 304 p. Rosie novels (Graeme Simsion)

ISBN 9781476767314

1. Geneticists 2. Marriage 3. Fatherhood 4. Pregnant women 5. Husband and wife 6. Marital conflict 7. New York City 8. Mainstream fiction 9. Romantic comedies

"The highly anticipated sequel to the New York Times bestselling novel The Rosie Project, starring the same extraordinary couple now living in New York and unexpectedly expecting their first child. Get ready to fall in love all over again. Don Tillman and Rosie Jarman are back.

The Wife Project is complete, and Don and Rosie are happily married and living in New York. But they're about to face a new challenge because-- surprise!--Rosie is pregnant. Don sets about learning the protocols of becoming a father, but his unusual research style gets him into trouble with the law. Fortunately his best friend Gene is on hand to offer advice: he's left Claudia and moved in with Don and Rosie. As Don tries to schedule time for pregnancy research, getting Gene and Claudia to reconcile, servicing the industrial refrigeration unit that occupies half his apartment, helping Dave the Baseball Fan save his business, and staying on the right side of Lydia the social worker, he almost misses the biggest problem of all: he might lose Rosie when she needs him the most. Graeme Simsion first introduced these unforgettable characters in The Rosie Project, which NPR called "sparkling entertainment along the lines of Where'd You Go Bernadette and When Harry Met Sally." The SanFrancisco Chronicle said, "sometimes you just need a smart love story that will make anyone, man or woman, laugh out loud." If you were swept away by the book that's captivated a million readers worldwide, you will love The Rosie Effect."--, Provided by publisher.

Simsion, Graeme C.

* The **Rosie** project / Graeme Simsion. Simon & Schuster, 2013. 329 p. Rosie novels (Graeme Simsion)

ISBN 9781476729084

1. Geneticists 2. Dating (Social customs) 3. Birthfathers -- Identification 4. Interpersonal attraction 5. Men/women relations 6. Women bartenders 7. Mate selection 8. Personality 9. Prejudice 10. Marriage 11. Australia 12. Mainstream fiction 13. Romantic comedies

Originally published: Melbourne : Text Publishing, 2013.

Australian Book Industry Awards, Book of the Year, 2014.

Australian Book Industry Awards, General Fiction Book of the Year, 2014.

A socially awkward genetics professor who has never been on a second date sets out to find the perfect wife, but instead finds Rosie Jarman, a fiercely independent barmaid who is on a quest to find her biological father.

"The story lurches from one set piece of deadpan nudge-nudge, wink-wink humor to another: We laugh at, and with, Don as he tries to navigate our hopelessly emotional, nonliteral world, learning as he goes." Kirkus.

Simsion, Graeme C.

The **Rosie** result / Graeme Simsion. Text Publishing, 2019. 368 p. Rosie novels (Graeme Simsion)

ISBN 9781925773811

1. Geneticists 2. Marriage 3. Fatherhood 4. Husband and wife 5. Marital conflict 6. Happiness 7. New York City 8. Mainstream fiction 9. Romantic comedies

Series complete in 3 volumes.

Don and Rosie help their eleven-year-old son who is struggling at school and having trouble fitting in while trying to open a cocktail bar.

"Charming, eloquent, and insightful, The Rosie Result is a triumphant conclusion to Dons story, one that celebrates this remarkable father, husband, and friend in all his complexity and brilliance." Booklist.

Sinclair, Upton, 1878-1968

* The **jungle** / Upton Sinclair. Penguin Books, 1985, c1906. xxxv, 411 p.

ISBN 9780140390315

1. 1900s (Decade) 2. Immigrants 3. Capitalism 4. Meat industry and trade -- Corrupt practices 5. Meat workers -- Health and safety 6. Corporate accountability 7. Poverty 8. Lithuanian Americans 9. Immigrant families 10. Labor exploitation 11. Stockyards 12.

Socialism 13. Chicago, Illinois -- Social conditions 14. United States -- Social conditions -- 20th century 15. Political fiction 16. Classics

Originally published: New York : Doubleday, Jabber & Co., 1906.

A documentary novel portraying industry's conditions at the end of the 19th and beginning of the 20th century. Sinclair's novel prompted public outrage which led President Theodore Roosevelt to demand an official investigation. This eventually led to the passage of the Pure Food and Drug laws.

Singer, I. J., 1893-1944

The **brothers** Ashkenazi / Israel Joshua Singer; a new translation from the Yiddish by Joseph Singer. Atheneum, 1980, c1936. 426 p.

ISBN 9780689111020

1. Jews, Polish 2. Brothers 3. Jewish families 4. Social classes 5. Lodz, Poland 6. Poland -- History -- 1864-1918 7. Translations -- Yiddish to English 8. Family sagas 9. Literary fiction

LC 80066017

Originally published in Warsaw, Poland as Di brider Ashkenazi by Farlag H. Bzshoza, in 1936.

With a large cast of characters, this is a social novel, a family saga set against the rise of capitalism and of a Jewish bourgeoisie in Lodz. It tells the story, through an interwoven plot, of the clash between old traditions and growing desires.

"What gives the book its significance is not the picture of nineteenth-century Jewish family life, and not the characterizations of the two brothers, but the clear exposition of the class struggle of which Max and Jacob form unconscious parts." The New Yorker.

Singer, Isaac Bashevis, 1904-1991

Collected stories : A friend of Kafka to Passions / Isaac Bashevis Singer. Library of America, 2004. x, 856 p.

ISBN 1931082626

1. Jews 2. Families 3. Jewish way of life 4. Hope 5. Belonging 6. Jews, Eastern European 7. Short stories 8. Translations -- Yiddish to English

LC 2003066057

"Ilan Stavans is the editor of this volume"--Page [vii].

Singer, Isaac Bashevis, 1904-1991

Collected stories : Gimpel the fool to the Letter writer / Isaac Bashevis Singer. Library of America, 2004. 789 p.

ISBN 1931082618

1. Jews 2. Families 3. Jewish way of life 4. Hope 5. Belonging 6. Jews, Eastern European 7. Short stories 8. Translations -- Yiddish to English

LC 2003066055

"Ilan Stavans is the editor of this volume"--page after t.p. verso.

Presents a collection of fifty-four short stories, including "Gimpel the Fool," "Yentl the Yeshiva Boy," and "The Mirror."

Singer, Isaac Bashevis, 1904-1991

Enemies, a love story / Isaac Bashevis Singer. Farrar, Straus, 1972, c1966. 280 p.

ISBN 9780374148300

1. 1940s 2. Guilt in men 3. Love triangles 4. Holocaust survivors 5. Concentration camp survivors 6. Jewish Americans 7. Dishonesty 8. Men/women relations 9. Extramarital affairs 10. Reunions 11. Belief and doubt 12. Jews, Eastern European 13. New York City 14. Literary fiction 15. Translations -- Yiddish to English

LC 78189337

"First published in The Jewish daily forward in 1966 under the title 'Sonim, di Geshichte fun a Liebe.'"

"The book has the surface gaiety, ribaldry and surprise of a medieval fabliau. Yet the New York subways, telephone calls, Bronx Zoo, bus trip to the Adirondacks are solidly, meticulously real. Herman's three women expand into mythic dimension. . . . Whether or not you accept its ending, [this] is a brilliant, unsettling novel." Newsweek.

Singer, Isaac Bashevis, 1904-1991

The **family** Moskat / Isaac Bashevis Singer. Knopf, 1950. 611 p. Family chronicles

1. Family relationships 2. Jews 3. Jewish way of life 4. Antisemitism 5. Family traditions 6. Change 7. Shtetl 8. Jews, Eastern European 9. Poland -- History -- 20th century 10. Family sagas 11. Literary fiction 12. Translations -- Yiddish to English

Reb Meshulam Moskat's wealthy family represents the thoughts and concerns of Jews from the end of the 19th century until the beginning of World War II.

Singer, Isaac Bashevis, 1904-1991

* The **magician** of Lublin / Isaac Bashevis Singer ; translated from the Yiddish by Elaine Gottlieb and Joseph Singer. Farrar Straus & Giroux, 2010, c1960. 256 p.

ISBN 9780374532543

1. 1870s 2. Escape artists 3. Jewish way of life 4. Extramarital affairs 5. Jews 6. Shtetl 7. Magicians 8. Jews, Eastern European 9. Poland -- History -- 19th century 10. Literary fiction 11. Historical fiction 12. Translations -- Yiddish to English

LC 2010926163

Originally published in Yiddish, 1960.

Caught between his eagerness to win fame and fortune as a performer and his reluctance to give up his easy life of pleasure, a late-nineteenth-century Polish magician and holy man finds himself on the brink of disaster.

Singh, Nalini, 1977-

A **madness** of sunshine / Nalini Singh. Berkley, 2019. 352 p.

ISBN 9780593099131

1. Homecomings 2. Hometowns 3. Women pianists 4. Missing women 5. Maori (New Zealand people) 6. Detectives 7. Poverty 8. Missing persons investigation 9. Small town life 10. Coastal towns 11. New Zealand 12. Thrillers and suspense

LC 2019014381

Returning to her impoverished New Zealand hometown to reconnect with familiar things after a personal tragedy, Anahera Rawiri bonds with detective Will Gallagher to uncover the community secrets behind a missing-persons case.

"Popular romance author Singh shifts to a new genre, New Zealand gothic, in which nearly every character including the dense, ferocious landscape has something to hide, and studying them is nearly as fascinating and compelling as solving the multifaceted mystery." Kirkus.

Singh, Nalini, 1977-

* **Silver** silence / Nalini Singh. Berkley, 2017. 496 p. Psy-Changeling trinity

ISBN 9781101987797

1. Negotiation 2. Shapeshifters 3. Assassination plots 4. Imaginary wars and battles 5. Protectiveness 6. Shapeshifting 7. Lust 8. Bears 9. Psychic ability 10. Sexual attraction 11. Men/women relations 12. Paranormal romances

LC 2016058705

Australian Romance Readers Awards, Favourite Paranormal Romance, 2017.

A first entry in a story arc tied to the Psy-Changeling series finds Silver Mercant, a negotiator for peace for a fledgling Trinity Accord, targeted by an assassination plot and finding protection from Valentin Nikolaev, alpha of the wild StoneWater Bears.

Sinha, Indra

Animal's people / Indra Sinha. Simon & Schuster, 2008, c2005. 384 p.

ISBN 9781416578789

1. Bhopal Union Carbide Plant Disaster, Bhopal, India, 1984 2. Chemical spills 3. Accident victims 4. Men with disfigurements 5. Orphans 6. Musicians 7. Interpersonal relations 8. Physicians 9. Reparations 10. Love triangles 11. Frustration 12. Secrets 13. Betrayal 14. Kindness 15. Slums 16. Lawyers 17. Americans in India 18. India -- Social conditions -- 20th century 19. Humorous stories

LC 2007042118

Shortlisted for the Man Booker Prize, 2007.

Shortlisted for the International IMPAC Dublin Literary Award, 2009

Ever since That Night, the residents of Khaufpur have lived a perilous existence. Their world is poisoned. Nobody has received compensation or help for the chemical leak, least of all Animal, as he is known, whose spine twisted at a young age, leaving him to walk on all fours. Though he inhabits a dark kind of half-life, he knows what love is. He has long harboured feelings for his friend Nisha but since she is enamoured of his friend Zafar he cannot even allow himself to hope. When Elli Barber arrives, an "Amrikan" keen to set up a free clinic to help the victims of the disaster, deep suspicion arises amongst the community. Animal resolves to turn the situation to his advantage and starts to investigate Elli's motives.

"Animal is a teenage boy who lives on the streets of the Indian city of Khaufpur. He goes around on all fours since his spine is badly damaged; he cannot walk normally. As an infant, he was one of the thousands of victims of a poison gas leak at an American-owned company, here just called the Kampani. Animal also lost his parents that night (as the local people refer to the horrible event). Animal has a lively mind and a way with words, some of them angry and profane, some of them bitterly funny, as he gets caught up in the struggle of those in Khaufpur who seek long-delayed justice from the Kampani. Sinha . . . has clearly based his story on the human and environmental disaster at the Union Carbide factory in Bhopal in 1984. The result is a gripping novel that also reminds us of a continuing real-life tragedy." Library Journal.

Sisters of the revolution : a feminist speculative fiction anthology / edited by Ann and Jeff VanderMeer. PM Press, 2015. 341 p.

ISBN 9781629630359

1. Feminism 2. Social science fiction 3. Science fiction 4. Fantasy fiction 5. Horror 6. Anthologies 7. Short stories

A collection of short speculative fiction explores feminism.

"This fascinating collection illustrates how writing trends from new-wave sf and feminist speculative fiction reflect changes in culture and in perspectives on women and feminism. It also provides a valuable primer on women writers in the sf, fantasy, and horror genres." Booklist.

Sittenfeld, Curtis

Eligible : a novel / Curtis Sittenfeld. Random House, 2016. 384 p.

ISBN 9781400068326

1. Sisters 2. Dysfunctional families 3. Family relationships 4. Mate selection 5. Single women 6. Families 7. Family problems 8. Periodical writers 9. Surgeons 10. Reality television programs 11. Thirties (Age) 12. Men/women relations 13. Cincinnati, Ohio 14.

New York City 15. Romantic comedies 16. Mainstream fiction 17. Adaptations, retellings, and spin-offs

LC 2015027778

A modern retelling of Jane Austen's "Pride and Prejudice".

Returning with her sister, Jane, to their Ohio hometown when their father falls ill, New York magazine editor Lizzy Bennett confronts her younger sisters' football fangirl antics, a creepy cousin's unwanted attentions, and the infuriating standoffish manners of a handsome neurosurgeon.

"Sittenfeld's style is endlessly amusing and, at times, gut-wrenchingly painful. Her take on Austen's iconic characters is skillful, her pacing excellent, and her dialog highly entertaining." Library Journal.

Sittenfeld, Curtis

Prep : a novel / Curtis Sittenfeld. Random House, 2005. 416 p.

ISBN 1400062314

1. Fourteen-year-old girls 2. Middle class teenage girls 3. Prep school students 4. Boarding school students 5. New students 6. Teenage girls -- Friendship 7. Loners 8. Misfits (Persons) 9. Rich teenagers 10. Teenage children of rich people 11. Teenagers -- Interpersonal relations 12. Self-destructive behavior 13. Alienation in teenagers 14. Self-consciousness in teenage girls 15. Private schools 16. Boarding schools 17. Schools 18. Social classes 19. Teenage boy/girl relations 20. Memories 21. Massachusetts 22. Indiana 23. Coming-of-age stories 24. Chick lit

LC 2004046858

"Lee Fiora, a scholarship student at the prestigious Ault School (not Ault Academy, as her parents embarrassingly refer to it), negotiates her days there in a blaze of self-consciousness that is, by turns, hilarious and excruciating... And yet she becomes an expert on the rituals that govern the rarefied microenvironment in which she finds herself: the students fondness for catchphrases like therein lies the paradox and LMC (lower middle class); the taboo against enthusiasm for anything other than sports; the fact that the school always sings God be with you till we meet again at chapel before breaks. In the end, Lees incisive vision of herself and others is her downfall but also--as this richly textured narrative suggests--her greatest gift." The New Yorker.

Sittenfeld, Curtis

Sisterland : a novel / Curtis Sittenfeld. Random House, 2013. 448 p.

ISBN 9781400068319

1. Twin sisters 2. Psychic ability 3. Earthquakes 4. Sisters 5. Identical twins 6. Women psychics 7. Marital conflict 8. Family relationships 9. Mainstream fiction

LC 2012043726

When the strongest earthquake in U.S. history occurs just north of their St. Louis home, Kate and Jeremy find the disaster further complicated by Kate's self-proclaimed-medium twin's prediction about a more powerful earthquake, a situation that places Kate under public scrutiny and reveals her own psychic abilities.

"The author turns conventions on their collective head and creates a world that is familiar, maddening, alluring, and, ultimately, guardedly hopeful." Library Journal.

Sittenfeld, Curtis,

* You think it, I'll say it : stories / Curtis Sittenfeld. Random House, 2018. 226 p.

ISBN 9780399592867

1. Short stories 2. Literary fiction

LC 2017020945

The best-selling author of Eligible presents a collection of 10 short stories that features both original pieces and two previously published in the New Yorker.

Sjon, 1962-

The blue fox / Sjón ; translated from the Icelandic by Victoria Cribb. Farrar, Straus and Giroux, 2013, c2004. 128 p.

ISBN 9780374114459

1. 19th century 2. Hunting 3. Priests 4. People with Down syndrome 5. Natural history 6. Guardian and ward 7. Winter 8. Shipwrecks 9. Searching 10. Naturalists 11. Mysteries 12. Translations -- Icelandic to English

LC 2012039701

Translation from the Icelandic of: Skugga-Baldur.
Originally published: 2004.

An elusive fox leads a hunter on a transformative quest, while a naturalist endeavors to build a life for a young woman with Down syndrome whom he rescued from a shipwreck years earlier.

Sjowall, Maj, 1935-

* Cop killer : the story of a crime / Maj Sjowall and Per Wahloo ; translated from the Swedish by Thomas Teal. Pantheon Books, 1975, c1974. 296 p. Martin Beck mysteries

ISBN 9780394485317

1. 1960s 2. Crimes against police 3. Murder investigation 4. Detectives 5. Crimes against women 6. Murder 7. Police -- Stockholm, Sweden 8. Stockholm, Sweden 9. Mysteries 10. Translations -- Swedish to English 11. Police procedurals 12. Scandinavian crime fiction

LC 74026197

Translation from the Swedish of: Polismordaren.
Originally published: Stockholm : Norstedt, 1974.

"In a country town, a woman is brutally murdered and left buried in a swamp. There are two main suspects: her closest neighbor and her ex-husband. Meanwhile, on a quiet suburban street a midnight shootout takes place between three cops and two teenage boys. Dead, one cop and one kid. Wounded, two cops. Escaped, one kid. Martin Beck and his partner Lenart Kollberg are called in to investigate. As Beck digs deeper into the murky waters of the young girl's murder, Kollberg scours the town for the teenager, and together they are forced to examine the changing face of crime." Provided by publisher

Sjowall, Maj, 1935-

* The laughing policeman / By Maj Sjowall and Per Wahloo ; translated from the Swedish by Alan Blair Vintage Books, 1992, c1968. 211 p. Martin Beck mysteries

ISBN 9780679742234

1. 1960s 2. Mass murder 3. Gunshot victims 4. Detectives 5. Police -- Stockholm, Sweden 6. Stockholm, Sweden 7. Mysteries 8. Translations -- Swedish to English 9. Police procedurals 10. Scandinavian crime fiction

LC 92050005

Translation from the Swedish of: Den skrattande polisen.
Originally published: Stockholm : Norstedt, 1968.
Edgar Allan Poe Award for Best Mystery Novel, 1971.

Superintendent Martin Beck seeks the murderer of nine passengers on a Stockholm bus, one of whom was his best detective

Sjowall, Maj, 1935-

* The locked room : the story of a crime / By Maj Sjowall and Per Wahloo. Translated from the Swedish by Paul Britten

Austin Vintage Crime/Black Lizard, 1973, c1972. 311 p. Martin Beck mysteries

ISBN 9780394485331

1. 1960s 2. Bank robberies 3. Murder investigation 4. Detectives 5. Police -- Stockholm, Sweden 6. Stockholm, Sweden 7. Mysteries 8. Translations -- Swedish to English 9. Police procedurals 10. Scandinavian crime fiction

LC 73007027

Translation from the Swedish of: Slutna rummet

Originally published: Stockholm : Norstedt, 1972.

The eighth classic installment in this genre-changing series of novels starring Detective Inspector Martin Beck.

Sjowall, Maj, 1935-

The **man** on the balcony : the story of a crime / Maj Sjowall and Per Wahloo ; translated from the Swedish by Alan Blair. Vintage Books, 1993, c1967. 180 p. Martin Beck mysteries

ISBN 0679745963

1. 1960s 2. Serial murder investigation 3. Murder witnesses 4. Detectives 5. Women murder victims 6. Police -- Stockholm, Sweden 7. Stockholm, Sweden 8. Mysteries 9. Translations -- Swedish to English 10. Police procedurals 11. Scandinavian crime fiction

LC 92050693

Translation from the Swedish of: Mannen pa balkongen.

Originally published: Stockholm : Norstedt, 1967.

Swedish police superintendent Martin Beck conducts a thorough investigation of a series of brutal muggings and child sex murders

"The chief problem is child murder in Stockholm, and it is a macabre race with death when the only clues are disturbing and intangible for Beck and for the 75-man force assigned to help him." Library Journal.

Sjowall, Maj, 1935-

* **Murder** at the Savoy / Maj Sjowall and Per Wahloo ; translated from the Swedish by Joan Tate. Harper Perennial, 2007, c1971. xi, 238 p. Martin Beck mysteries

ISBN 9780007242962

1. 1960s 2. Industrialists 3. Assassination 4. Detectives 5. Shooting 6. Arms dealers 7. Police -- Stockholm, Sweden 8. Stockholm, Sweden 9. Mysteries 10. Translations -- Swedish to English 11. Police procedurals 12. Scandinavian crime fiction

This translation originally published: New York: Pantheon, 1971.

Originally published: Stockholm : Norstedt, 1970.

"When Viktor Palmgren, a powerful Swedish industrialist is shot during his after-dinner speech in the luxurious Hotel Savoy, it sends a shiver down the spine of the international money markets and terrifies the tiny town of Malmo. No one in the restaurant can identify the gunman, and local police are sheepishly baffled. That's when Beck takes over the scene and quickly picks through Palmgren's background. What he finds is a web of vice so despicable that it's hard for him to imagine who wouldn't want Palmgren dead, but that doesn't stop him and his team of dedicated detectives from tackling one of their most intriguing cases yet." Provided by publisher

Skarmeta, Antonio

The **dancer** and the thief : a novel / Antonio Skarmeta ; translated from the Spanish by Katherine Silver. W. W. Norton, 2008. 320 p.

ISBN 9780393064940

1. Revenge 2. Thieves 3. Stealing 4. Dancers 5. Entertainers 6. Interpersonal attraction 7. Men/women relations 8. Love 9. Former convicts 10. Chile 11. South America 12. Love stories 13. Crime

fiction 14. Translations -- Spanish to English

LC 2007033340

Granted amnesty along with other non-violent Chilean prisoners, Ángel Santiago plots revenge against those who abused him in jail, teaming up with bank robber Nicolás Vergara Grey during a heist that is complicated by the presence of a talented dancer.

"Though Skarmeta scarcely ranks at the very top of Latin America's remarkably distinguished and varied literary elite, he is a serious writer to whom the death and rebirth of democracy in his native Chile is an endlessly compelling subject. . . . Though the ending that Skarmeta gives his characters falls well short of happy, the Chile that he portrays herein is vibrant and strong." Washington Post Book World.

Skibell, Joseph

A **curable** romantic : a novel / Joseph Skibell. Algonquin Books of Chapel Hill, 2010. 608 p.

ISBN 9781565129290

1. Freud, Sigmund, 1856-1939 2. Zamenhof, L L (Ludwik Lazar), 1859-1917 3. Jewish men 4. Identity (Psychology) 5. Psychoanalysis 6. Self-discovery in men 7. Men/women relations 8. Voyages and travels 9. Esperanto -- History 10. Vienna, Austria 11. Warsaw, Poland 12. Historical fiction 13. Satirical fiction

LC 2010018605

When Dr. Jakob Josef Sammelsohn arrives in Vienna in the 1890s, he happens to meet Sigmund Freud, has a series of affairs, is haunted by the ghost of his abandoned wife, and eventually ends up in the Warsaw Ghetto in 1940. His Candide-like adventures illuminate a Europe moving between a new scientific age and age-old superstitions and beliefs.

"Skibell Skibell plays fast and loose with the intermingling of historical fact and fiction, giving Sigmund Freud his own resurrection, as well as Esperanto founder Dr. L.L. Zamenhof, and others. The past here is bathed in a soft-focus filter, cloaked in gaslights and cigar smoke, brought to life with stylistic flair and linguistic pizazz, complete with multilingual translations and breathless enthusiasm. Sammelsohn, like Zelig, is there to see it all." Dallas Morning News.

Skyhorse, Brando

* **Madonnas** of Echo Park : a novel / Brando Skyhorse. Free Press, 2010. 224 p.

ISBN 9781439170809

1. Mexican Americans 2. Identity (Psychology) 3. Undocumented immigrants 4. American dream 5. Murder witnesses 6. Cultural differences 7. Drive-by shootings 8. Undocumented workers 9. Los Angeles, California 10. Echo Park, Los Angeles, California 11. Psychological fiction

LC 2009034403

Hemingway Foundation/PEN Award, 2011.

Revolving around the random shooting of a young girl, this novel interweaves stories from the barrios of Los Angeles to coalesce into a powerful examination of the Mexican-American experience.

Slaughter, Karin, 1971-

Cop Town : a novel / Karin Slaughter. Delacorte Press, 2014. 402 p.

ISBN 9780345547491

1. 1970s 2. Policewomen 3. Serial murder investigation 4. Police murders 5. Race relations 6. Violence 7. Widows 8. Family relationships 9. Atlanta, Georgia 10. Georgia 11. Mysteries

LC 2014005076

Ian Fleming Steel Dagger Award, 2015.

Finds reluctant rookie cop Kate Murphy teamed with agenda-seeking Maggie Lawson in a manhunt for a cop killer in 1974 Atlanta.

"Slaughter's first stand-alone thriller is a superb, very gritty look at both a city and era in social and political flux. It's also a searing portrait of family ties and how our pasts can shape our futures, as well as a gripping procedural, with some genuinely terrifying moments. ... [T]his title is sure to win over readers new to Slaughter's work while reminding old fans of her enormous talent." Library Journal.

Slaughter, Karin, 1971-
   Criminal : a novel / Karin Slaughter. Delacorte Press, 2012. 416 p. Will Trent series
   ISBN 9780345528506
   1. Detectives 2. Murder investigation 3. Death threats 4. Secrets 5. Men/women relations 6. Georgia 7. Atlanta, Georgia 8. Thrillers and suspense
                                                        LC 2012001504
A Georgia Bureau of Investigation search into a shocking crime from 1975 poses unprecedented personal and professional challenges for top agent Will Trent, who encounters threats against his life and everything he thought he understood about his past.

Slaughter, Karin, 1971-
   * **Fallen** : a novel / Karin Slaughter. Delacorte, 2011. 416 p. Georgia series (Karin Slaughter)
   ISBN 9780345528209
   1. Missing persons 2. Mother and adult daughter 3. Women hostages 4. Policewomen 5. Police corruption 6. Women coroners 7. Women pediatricians 8. Murder investigation 9. Violence 10. Georgia 11. Atlanta, Georgia 12. Georgia 13. Thrillers and suspense 14. Police procedurals
   This novel involves characters from her "Will Trent series."
Georgia Bureau of Investigations Detective Faith Mitchell, her partner Will Trent, and trauma doctor Sara Linton join forces to find Faith's mother, missing after a deadly hostage situation that leaves Faith a murder suspect -- and the scapegoat for police corruption, bribery, and murder.
   "Family--biological, professional, and everything in between-plays a key role in a thriller sure to please Slaughter's many fans." Publishers Weekly.

Slaughter, Karin, 1971-
   The **good** daughter / Karin Slaughter. William Morrow, 2017 515 p.
   ISBN 9780062430243
   1. Cold cases (Criminal investigation) 2. Small town life 3. Women lawyers 4. Secrets 5. Home invasions 6. School shootings 7. Sisters 8. Family relationships 9. Mass shootings 10. Georgia 11. Psychological suspense
   Librarians' Choice (Australia), 2017
Decades after a shattering confrontation that left her mother dead and her sister traumatized, a New York-based lawyer returns to her Atlanta hometown to help her father save the life of a young woman accused of a school shooting.

Slaughter, Karin, 1971-
   The **kept** woman / Karin Slaughter. William Morrow & Co., 2016. 400 p. Will Trent series
   ISBN 9780062430212
   1. Government investigators 2. Professional basketball players 3. Rich people 4. Building sites 5. Former police 6. Murder 7. Murder investigation 8. Family violence 9. Divorced persons 10. Men/women relations 11. Atlanta, Georgia 12. Thrillers and suspense
   Georgia detective Will Trent faces off against the dark forces of a case that threatens to destroy him.

Slaughter, Karin, 1971-
   * The **last** widow / Karin Slaughter. William Morrow & Co., 2019. 400 p. Will Trent series
   ISBN 9780062858085
   1. Epidemics 2. Conspiracies 3. Kidnapping victims 4. Couples 5. Government investigators 6. Women coroners 7. National security 8. Atlanta, Georgia 9. Thrillers and suspense
   Finds Will and Sara pitted against a mysterious group that would unleash a deadly epidemic.

Slaughter, Karin, 1971-
   * **Pieces** of her / Karin Slaughter. HarperCollins, 2018 400 p.
   ISBN 9780062430274
   1. 1980s 2. 2010s 3. Secrets 4. Family secrets 5. Mothers and daughters 6. Domestic terrorism 7. Violence in women 8. Consequences 9. Secret identity 10. Georgia 11. Thrillers and suspense 12. Parallel narratives
   The daughter of a woman who has wanted nothing more than a quiet life in her small beachside home embarks on a desperate search for answers when she discovers the explosive truth about her mother's true identity.
   "Readers will find themselves totally immersed in the suspenseful, alternating story lines and wont want either of them to end." Booklist.

Slaughter, Karin, 1971-
   * **Pretty** girls : a novel / Karin Slaughter. William Morrow, 2015. 396 p.
   ISBN 9780345547521
   1. Corruption 2. Stalkers 3. Murderers 4. Lawyers 5. Sisters 6. Small towns 7. Women lawyers 8. Stalking 9. Thrillers and suspense
   The prepublication title of this novel was The truth about pretty girls. RUSA Reading List, 2016.
   The story of estranged sisters -- Claire and Lydia -- reunited by the murder of Claire's husband, whom Lydia had accused of harassment years ago. Hidden computer files pique Claire's interest and provoke suspicion that he may have known something about the disappearance of their oldest sister, Julia, decades previously. Realistic characters, unexpected humor, poignant chapters from their father's perspective, ample suspense, and the slow healing of damaged relationships make for a tense, unsettling, and utterly compelling read. -- Description by Shauna Griffin.
   "Slaughter (Cop Town, 2014, etc.) is so uncompromising in following her blood trails to the darkest places imaginable that she makes most of her high-wire competition look pallid, formulaic, or just plain fake." Kirkus.

Slaughter, Karin, 1971-
   * **Undone** : a novel / Karin Slaughter. Delacorte Press, 2009. 448 p. Georgia series (Karin Slaughter)
   ISBN 9780385341967
   1. Women physicians 2. Accidents 3. Violence against women 4. Kidnapping 5. Torture 6. Hospitals -- Emergency service 7. Atlanta, Georgia 8. Thrillers and suspense 9. Psychological fiction 10. Police procedurals
                                                        LC 2009013477
This novel involves characters from her "Will Trent series."
   Published in the United Kingdom by Century in 2009 under the title: Genesis.
   Fleeing to Atlanta to seek refuge in the aftermath of a violent act, Sara Linton becomes unwittingly enmeshed in a case involving a tortured young ER patient, a situation that is investigated by special agents Will Trent and Faith Mitchell.

Sloan, Robin, 1979-

Mr. Penumbra's 24-hour bookstore / Robin Sloan. Farrar, Straus and Giroux, 2012. 288 p.

ISBN 9780374214913

1. Google (Firm) 2. Bookstores 3. Codes (Communication) 4. Secret societies 5. Displaced workers 6. Website designers 7. Books and reading 8. Conspiracies 9. Cryptographers 10. Immortality 11. California 12. San Francisco, California 13. Science fiction 14. Literary fiction

LC 2012012357

First published: New York :

First published: New York: Farrar, Straus & Giroux, 2012.

The Great Recession has shuffled Clay Jannon out of his life as a San Francisco web-design drone and landed him a new gig working the night shift at Mr. Penumbra's 24-Hour Bookstore. But after just a few days on the job, Clay begins to realize that this store is even more curious than the name suggests. There are only a few customers, but they come in repeatedly and never seem to actually buy anything. Soon he embarks on a complex analysis of the customers' behaviour and ropes his friends into helping him figure out just what's going on.

Sloin, Hilary, 1963-2019

Art on fire / Hilary Sloin. Bywater Books, 2012 289 p.

ISBN 9781612940311

1. Women painters 2. Women artists 3. Lesbians 4. Family relationships 5. Rejection (Psychology) 6. Art -- Psychological aspects 7. Literary fiction 8. LGBTQIA fiction

Stonewall Book Award for the Barbara Gittings Literature Award, 2014.

Seeking to emerge from her prodigy sister's shadow and reeling from her grandmother's rejection due to her sexuality, Francesca deSilva escapes to a ramshackle cabin in Massachusetts, where she unwittingly becomes an overnight art sensation.

Slouka, Mark

God's fool / Mark Slouka. Alfred A. Knopf, 2002. 271 p.

ISBN 9780375402166

1. Chang, 1811-1874 2. Eng, 1811-1874 3. Barnum, P T (Phineas Taylor), 1810-1891 4. Conjoined twins 5. Brothers 6. Freak shows 7. Thai-Americans 8. Civil war 9. United States Civil War, 1861-1865 10. North Carolina -- History -- Civil War, 1861-1865 11. Historical fiction

LC 2001053975

ALA Notable Book, 2003.

A fictional biography of Chang and Eng, the first Siamese twins in recorded history, describes how these two men transcended their physical abnormality to live lives of remarkable grace, suffering, and love.

"Slouka, a gifted stylist, eschews much of the freak-show energy that thrust Chang and Eng onto the stage of world history, in favor of an alluring balance between the elegiac and the ironic." Publishers Weekly.

Smiley, Jane

Early warning / Jane Smiley. Knopf, 2015. 384 p. Last hundred years trilogy

ISBN 9780307700322

1. 20th century 2. Family relationships 3. Joy and sorrow 4. Families 5. Farm life 6. Farms 7. Moving to a new city 8. Growing up 9. Family secrets 10. United States -- History -- 20th century 11. Iowa 12. Family sagas

Follows the Langdon family after the sudden death of their patriarch, Walter, as the five Langdon children, now adults, navigate the Cold War years of the 1950s and the social revolution of the '60s and '70s.

Smiley, Jane

Golden age / Jane Smiley. Random House, 2015. 384 p. Last hundred years trilogy

ISBN 9780307700346

1. 20th century 2. 21st century 3. Family relationships 4. Joy and sorrow 5. Family secrets 6. Growing up 7. Farmers 8. Change 9. Families 10. Farms 11. Postwar life 12. United States -- History -- 20th century 13. Iowa 14. Family sagas

"The third book of a trilogy about a farm family from Iowa, which takes them from the late 1980s through the present and into the future"--, Provided by publisher.

"As for Smileys cantering, far-reaching, yet intimate trilogy, it is both timely in the issues it so astutely raises, especially as Iowa is once again in the presidential election spotlight, and timeless in the rapture of its storytelling and the humanness of its insights into family, self, and our connection to the land. Readers will be reading and rereading Smileys Last Hundred Years far into the next." Booklist.

Smiley, Jane

Horse heaven / Jane Smiley. Knopf, 2000. 561 p.

ISBN 037540600X

1. Horse racing 2. Race horses 3. Humans and horses 4. Equestrians 5. Jack Russell terriers 6. Satirical fiction 7. Mainstream fiction 8. Stories told by animals

Shortlisted for The Orange Prize for Fiction, 2001

A novel set in the world of thoroughbred racing follows a group of trainers, jockeys, and "track brats" on a two-year journey through the racing cycle.

"What's remarkable about Smiley's handling of horses as characters is that she manages to bring it off at alland more, she does it brilliantly." New York Times Book Review.

Smiley, Jane

* A thousand acres / Jane Smiley. Knopf, 1991. 371 p.

ISBN 0394577736

1. Sisters 2. Family problems 3. Farm life 4. Farmers 5. Family farms 6. Family secrets 7. Interpersonal relations 8. Interpersonal conflict 9. Inheritance and succession 10. Alcoholic men 11. Retirement 12. Decision-making 13. Fathers and daughters 14. Iowa 15. Adaptations, retellings, and spin-offs 16. Literary fiction 17. Domestic fiction

LC 91052720

ALA Notable Book, 1993.

National Book Critics Circle Award for Fiction, 1991.

Pulitzer Prize for Fiction, 1992.

Larry Cook, an Iowan farmer who has worked a thousand acre plot owned by his family for generations, abruptly decides to leave his farm to his three daughters and retire. His two eldest daughters are pleased with the decision but his youngest daughter has been cut out by her father and is angry. As the daughters' activity on the land progresses, they notice a change in their father. Events begin to unfold that will threaten and destroy the family and their farm.

"What makes this novel such a triumph is Smiley's brilliant twist on the Lear story: she tells it not from Larry's point of view but from his eldest daughter's. . . . In the end Smiley does what Shakespeare himself never did: she creates a female heroine who grows through her own anguish until she towers over the hero and conquers him." Newsweek.

Smiley, Jane

Some luck / Jane Smiley. Alfred A. Knopf, 2014. 395 p.
Last hundred years trilogy

ISBN 9780307700315

1. 20th century 2. 1920s 3. 1930s 4. 1940s 5. Farm life 6. Rural families 7. World War I veterans 8. Family relationships 9. Joy and sorrow 10. Farmers 11. Families 12. United States -- History -- 20th century 13. Iowa 14. Family sagas

Follows the triumphs and tragedies of a farm family from post-World War I America through the early 1950s.

"An expansive, episodic tale showing this generally flinty author in a mellow mood: surprising, but engaging." Kirkus.

Smith, Ali, 1962-

The **accidental** / Ali Smith. Pantheon Books, 2006. 320 p.
ISBN 0375422250

1. Strangers 2. Twelve-year-old girls 3. Teenage boys 4. Women biographers 5. College teachers 6. Married men -- Relations with single women 7. Married people 8. Families 9. Houseguests 10. Transformations, Personal 11. Interpersonal relations 12. Family relationships 13. Summer resorts 14. Truthfulness and falsehood 15. Honesty 16. Family problems 17. Norfolk, England 18. Psychological fiction 19. Domestic fiction

LC 2005051031

Whitbread Book Award for Novel, 2005.

Shortlisted for the Man Booker Prize, 2005.

Shortlisted for The Orange Prize for Fiction, 2006

Shortlisted for the James Tait Black Memorial Prize for Fiction, 2005

Talking her way into the Norfolk cottage that the Smart family is renting for the summer, Amber, an enigmatic, lying con artist insinuates herself into the lives of Eve, her husband Michael, and their children, forcing them to reexamine the events of their lives through her perceptions and forever altering the world around them.

"Smith is a wonderful ventriloquist, adept at throwing her voice into an astonishing array of characters. . . . [She] can do suicidal teenage angst and middle-aged ennui, a 12-year-old's sardonic innocence and an aging Lothario's randy daydreams with equal aplomb. And in riffing on the stream of consciousness form, pioneered by such highbrow litterateurs as Joyce and Woolf, she manages to make it as accessible and up to the minute (if vastly more entertaining) as talk radio or an Internet chat room." New York Times.

Smith, Ali, 1962-

* **Autumn** / Ali Smith. Pantheon Books, 2017, c2016. 208 p. Seasonal (Ali Smith)

ISBN 9781101870730

1. Time 2. Aging 3. Intergenerational friendship 4. Interpersonal relations 5. Social change 6. Human nature 7. Art historians 8. Xenophobia 9. Senior men 10. History 11. Brexit, 2016-2020 12. Great Britain 13. Literary fiction 14. Psychological fiction

Originally published: London : Hamish Hamilton, 2016.

Shortlisted for the Man Booker Prize, 2017.

A debut installment in a series about aging, time, love and the nature of stories examines the dynamics of pop culture, meditation and harvests in a world growing more bordered and exclusive.

"Smith's book is a kaleidoscope whose suggestive fragments and insights don't easily render a pleasing pattern, yet it's compelling in its emotional and historical freight, its humor, and keen sense of creativity and loss." Kirkus.

Smith, Ali, 1962-

* **How** to be both / Ali Smith. Pantheon Books, 2014, c2014. 384 p.

ISBN 9780375424106

1. Cossa, Francesco del, approximately 1435-approximately 1477 2. Art and society 3. Romantic love 4. Injustice 5. Painters 6. Teenage girls 7. Gender identity 8. Mothers and daughters 9. Second chances 10. Literary fiction 11. Parallel narratives

Originally published in UK (London: Hamish Hamilton, 2014).

Baileys Women's Prize for Fiction, 2015.

Costa Novel Award, 2014.

Shortlisted for the Man Booker Prize, 2014.

How to be both is a novel all about art's versatility. Borrowing from painting's fresco technique to make an original literary double-take, it's a fast-moving genre-bending conversation between forms, times, truths and fictions. Two tales of love and injustice twist into a singular yarn where time gets timeless, structural gets playful, knowing gets mysterious, fictional gets real--and all life's givens get given a second chance.

"The narratives are captivating, challenging, and often puzzling, as the prose varies among contemporary vernacular English, archaic 15th-century rhetoric interposed with fragments of poetry, and unpunctuated stream-of-consciousness narration. . . . Smith's two-in-one novel is a provocative reevaluation of the form." Publishers Weekly.

Smith, Ali, 1962-

* **Spring** / Ali Smith. Pantheon Books, 2019. 339 p. Seasonal (Ali Smith)

ISBN 9781101870778

1. 2010s 2. Spring 3. Social change 4. Social values 5. Political values 6. Pretending 7. Voyages and travels 8. Nationalism 9. Friendship 10. Regret 11. Immigration and emigration 12. Entertainment industry and trade 13. Brexit, 2016-2020 14. Great Britain -- Social life and customs -- 21st century 15. Literary fiction 16. Psychological fiction

"Smith's work is always challenging and always rewarding." Kirkus.

Smith, Ali, 1962-

There but for the : a novel / Ali Smith. Pantheon Books, 2011. 256 p.

ISBN 9780375424090

1. Houseguests 2. Social interaction 3. Identity (Psychology) 4. Middle-aged men 5. Personal space 6. Dinners and dining 7. England 8. Greenwich, England 9. Literary fiction

LC 2010051377

Hawthornden Prize, 2012.

Shortlisted for the James Tait Black Memorial Prize for Fiction, 2011

When Miles Garth locks himself in an upstairs room during a dinner party and communicates only through notes slipped under the door, his involuntary hosts beg help from childhood friend Anna, who is unwittingly thrust into the family's surreal world.

"The novel is ostensibly about a dinner-party guest who locks himself in a spare bedroom and refuses to come out, inadvertently sparking a media frenzy. But the book--packed with jokes and random facts--is really about small stuff like life and death and the meaning of human existence, all told with sharp humor and real insight. The novel itself is a riddle with no solution, which is exactly the point: When you reluctantly come to the end, you can't help going back to the beginning, trying to unravel this beautifully elusive book's mysterious spell." Entertainment Weekly.

LIST OF FICTIONAL WORKS

Smith, Ali, 1962-

* **Winter** / Ali Smith. Pantheon Books, 2018. 208 p. Seasonal (Ali Smith)

ISBN 9781101870754

1. 2010s 2. Social change 3. Winter 4. Christmas 5. Memory 6. Sisters 7. Family relationships 8. Art 9. Secrets 10. Brexit, 2016-2020 11. Cornwall, England 12. Great Britain -- Social life and customs -- 21st century 13. Literary fiction 14. Psychological fiction

Winter? Bleak. Frosty wind, earth as iron, water as stone, so the old song goes. The shortest days, the longest nights. The trees are bare and shivering. The summer's leaves? Dead litter. The world shrinks; the sap sinks. But winter makes things visible. And if there's ice, there'll be fire.

Smith, B. J. (Brad J.)

All hat : a novel / Brad Smith. Henry Holt and Co., 2003. 308 p.

ISBN 0805072179

1. Former convicts 2. Farms 3. Cowboys 4. Swindlers and swindling 5. Male friendship 6. Race horse owners 7. Women jockeys 8. Race horses 9. Former lovers 10. Ontario 11. Canada 12. Caper novels 13. Crime fiction

LC 2002027307

Ex-convict Ray Dokes heads to the farm of his friend, Pete Culpepper, a Texas cowboy, and he eventually finds himself up against Sonny Stanton, the rich heir of a thoroughbred dynasty, after a ten-million-dollar thoroughbred goes missing. Stanton is also creating trouble by buying up large amounts of farmland, and threatening family farms.

"Set in rural Ontario and featuring an ensemble cast of delightfully eccentric, even downright loopy, characters, this big-hearted caper novel mixes laugh-out-loud-comedy with streaks of country noir that call to mind Daniel Woodrell." Booklist.

Smith, B. J. (Brad J.)

Crow's landing : a novel / Brad Smith. Scribner, 2012. 320 p. Virgil Cain mysteries

ISBN 9781451678536

1. Police misconduct 2. Drug traffic 3. Evidence (Law) 4. Fishing 5. Ranchers 6. Murder investigation 7. Mysteries 8. Black humor

LC 2012015809

Drawing the attention of a crooked city cop when he fishes up a mysterious steel cylinder linked to an old crime, Virgil Cain finds his boat and the cylinder confiscated and teams up with an attractive single mom to solve a case involving a cache of pure cocaine, a violent dealer and a wild Russian cowboy.

Smith, B. J. (Brad J.)

The **return** of Kid Cooper : a novel / Brad Smith. Arcade Publishing, 2018. 296 p.

ISBN 9781628728712

1. 1910s 2. Former convicts 3. Cowboys 4. Personal conduct 5. Values 6. Innocence (Law) 7. Kainah Indians 8. Indians of North America 9. Corruption 10. Justice 11. Social change 12. Montana -- History 13. Westerns

LC 2017045572

Spur Awards, Best Western Traditional Novel, 2019.

After spending thirty years in prison for a wrongful conviction, Nate Cooper returns to a changed Northern Montana where his search for justice stirs up controversy.

Smith, B. J. (Brad J.)

Shoot the dog : a Virgil Cain mystery / Brad Smith. Scribner, 2013. 320 p. Virgil Cain mysteries

ISBN 9781439197561

1. Actors and actresses 2. Horses 3. Kidnapping 4. Horse farms 5. Detectives 6. Murder 7. Casinos 8. Murder investigation 9. New York (State) 10. Mysteries 11. Black humor

LC 2013017221

Finds Virgil Cain renting his draft horses to a film crew only to discover the director's irresponsible nature and a casino owner's agenda to replace the film's star, a situation that is further complicated by two murders.

Smith, Betty, 1896-1972

* **Joy** in the morning Harper, 1963. 308 p.

1. 1920s 2. Young women 3. College students 4. Married people 5. Universities and colleges -- Middle West 6. Marriage 7. Middle West 8. Love stories

LC 62014560

Annie McGairy, 18, elopes with a young law student in the late 1920s, and her husband continues to attend school.

Smith, Betty, 1896-1972

* A **tree** grows in Brooklyn / Betty Smith. Harper Collins Publishers, 2001, c1943. xi, 493 p.

ISBN 0060001941

1. 1900s (Decade) 2. Poor families 3. Children of immigrants 4. Children of alcoholic fathers 5. City life 6. Girls 7. Growing up 8. Neighbors 9. Family relationships 10. Brooklyn, New York City 11. Coming-of-age stories 12. Literary fiction 13. Modern classics

LC 2001039509

Originally published: New York : Harper, 1943.

A young girl in a shabby neighborhood lives with dreams in an innocent time before the war.

Smith, Carrie

* **Silent** city / Carrie Smith. Crooked Lane Books, 2015. 304 p. Claire Codella mysteries

ISBN 9781629533100

1. Policewomen 2. Detectives 3. Murder investigation 4. School principals 5. Public schools 6. Women cancer survivors 7. Gay men 8. New York City 9. Police procedurals 10. Mysteries

After successfully overcoming cancer, NYPD detective Claire Codella is welcomed back with a case of a murdered public school principal that draws her into a dangerous world of dirty politics and dark secrets.

Smith, Dan, 1970-

The **darkest** heart / Dan Smith. Pegasus Crime, 2015. 387 p.

ISBN 9781605988184

1. Criminals 2. Assassination 3. Organized crime 4. Smuggling 5. Nuns 6. Brazil 7. Crime fiction

Accepting a potentially lucrative final job before leaving his life of violence, a killer-for-hire journeys through the Brazilian underworld while contemplating dark choices between survival and abandoning a loved one.

Smith, Dodie, 1896-1990

* **I** capture the castle / Dodie Smith. St. Martin's Press, 1998, c1948. 343 p.

ISBN 9780312181109

1. 1930s 2. Poor families 3. Eccentric families 4. Teenage girls 5. Men/women relations 6. Unrequited love 7. Castles 8. Americans in England 9. England -- Social life and customs -- 1910-1936 10. Diary novels 11. Coming-of-age stories

LC 9737231

Originally published: Boston : Little, Brown, 1948.

The 1934 journal of seventeen-year-old Cassandra Mortmain reveals her perspective on six stormy months in the eccentric and poverty-stricken life of her family in a ruined Suffolk castle, ending with the revelation that Cassandra is deeply in love.

Smith, Dominic

Bright and distant shores / Dominic Smith. Washington Square Press, 2011. 470 p.

ISBN 9781439198865

1. Gilded Age (1865-1898) 2. Collectors and collecting 3. Voyages and travels 4. Orphans 5. Ship captains 6. Ethnological museums 7. Insurance executives 8. Compulsive behavior in men 9. Chicago, Illinois -- History -- 19th century 10. Oceania 11. Historical fiction 12. Literary fiction

Originally published: Crows Nest, N.S.W. : Allen & Unwin, 2011.

When a late-19th-century Chicago insurance magnate sponsors a South Seas expedition to collect various Melanesian artifacts, his schemes ensnare two orphans including a recently engaged itinerant trader and a mission houseboy who longs to be reunited with his sister.

"Beautifully researched and ripe with symbolisman enthralling narrative peopled by characters both exotic and real." Kirkus.

Smith, Dominic

* The **electric** hotel / Dominic Smith. Sarah Crichton Books/Farrar, Straus and Giroux, 2019. 400 p.

ISBN 9780374146856

1. 1960s 2. Cinematographers 3. Films -- History 4. Silent films 5. Film industry and trade 6. Reminiscing in old age 7. Filmmakers 8. Lost films 9. Hotels 10. Hollywood, California -- History -- 20th century 11. Historical fiction 12. Parallel narratives

LC 2018045335

A French pioneer of silent films who has lived for half a century in a Hollywood hotel is forced to reckon with the reappearance of the lost movie masterpiece that left him bankrupt.

Smith, Dominic

* The **last** painting of Sara De Vos / Dominic Smith. Sarah Crichton Books, 2016. 288 p.

ISBN 9780374106683

1. Baalbergen, Sarah van, 1607- approximately 1638 2. 1950s 3. 17th century 4. Women artists 5. Painting, Dutch -- 17th century 6. Art forgeries 7. Art historians 8. Art forgers 9. Art 10. Deception 11. Netherlands -- History -- 17th century 12. Brooklyn, New York City -- History -- 20th century 13. Biographical fiction 14. Historical fiction 15. Parallel narratives

Australian Book Industry Awards, Literary Fiction Book of the Year, 2017.

Longlisted for the Walter Scott Prize for Historical Fiction, 2017

Parallel narratives unfold and eventually converge in this multi-layered novel, which explores the legacy of fictional 17th-century Dutch painter Sara de Vos. The artist's masterpiece,?At the Edge of a Wood, is stolen from Manhattan attorney Marty de Groot's Upper East Side residence in 1957 and replaced with a skillfully executed forgery that

remains a secret for decades -- until museum curator Ellie Shipley, who created the fake, is confronted by the two versions of the painting. Don't miss this richly detailed and complex meditation on art and identity by the author of?Bright and Distant Shores. -- Description by Gillian Speace.

"Rich in historical detail, the novel explores the immense challenges faced by women in the arts (past and present), provides a glimpse into the seedy underbelly of the art world across the centuries, and illustrates the transformative power and influence of great art." Booklist.

Smith, Donald, 1941-

The **constable's** tale : a novel of Colonial America / Donald Smith. Pegasus Books, 2015. xiv, 287 p.

ISBN 9781605988610

1. Colonial America (1600-1775) 2. Voyages and travels 3. Self-discovery in men 4. Political intrigue 5. Murder 6. Murder investigation 7. Married men 8. Extramarital affairs 9. Indians of North America 10. Suspicion 11. French in North America 12. Men/women relations 13. North Carolina -- History -- 18th century 14. United States -- History -- French and Indian War, 1754-1763 15. Historical mysteries

A former volunteer constable travels the Atlantic seacoast, searching for the murderer of a colonial farm family in North Carolina while refusing to believe it was the result of an Indian attack.

Smith, Frank, 1927-

* **Night** fall / Frank Smith. Severn House, 2013. 240 p. Detective Chief Inspector Neil Paget mysteries

ISBN 9780727882714

1. Murder investigation 2. Detectives 3. Murder victims 4. Photographers 5. Clues 6. Murder 7. Police 8. Shropshire, England 9. Mysteries

When a body is found having been bound, gagged, thrown off a bridge, and with the letter 'A' carved into his forehead, Detective Inspector Neil Paget has nothing to go on until another body appears in a similar condition.

Smith, Gregory Blake

* The **maze** at Windermere : a novel / Gregory Blake Smith. Viking, 2018. 352 p.

ISBN 9780735221925

1. James, Henry, 1811-1882 2. 17th century 3. 18th century 4. 19th century 5. 21st century 6. Cities and towns 7. Social classes 8. Personal conduct 9. Ambition 10. Self-fulfillment 11. Manipulation (Social sciences) 12. Inequality 13. Secrets 14. Race relations 15. Interpersonal relations 16. Newport, Rhode Island 17. Rhode Island 18. Literary fiction 19. Parallel narratives 20. Historical fiction

LC 2017025390

A reckless, high-stakes wager between a fading tennis pro and a drunken party guest launches a narrative odyssey that brings three centuries of ambition and adversity full circle.

"Taken individually, each story is dramatic and captivating, but as the author makes ever-increasing connections among the stories and shuffles them all into one unbroken narrative, the novel becomes a moving meditation on love, race, class, and self-fulfillment in America across the centuries." Publishers Weekly.

Smith, J. P., 1949-

If she were dead / J. P. Smith. Poisoned Pen Press, 2020. 336 p.

ISBN 9781492669036

1. Divorced women 2. Extramarital affairs 3. Women authors 4. Obsession 5. Married women 6. Betrayal 7. Secrets 8. Men/women

relations 9. Psychological suspense

A successful novelist pursues an obsessive affair with a married man before the line between the fiction she writes and the reality she lives begins to blur, in a psychologically twisted thriller by the author of The Drowning.

"In clear prose, Smith spins out a sensuous, sinuous psychological thriller that compels attention to the final line." Booklist.

Smith, Jill Eileen, 1958-

Star of Persia : Esther's story / Jill Eileen Smith. Revell, 2020. 368 p.

ISBN 9780800734718

1. Esther, Queen of Persia 2. Xerxes I,, King of Persia, 519-465 or 4 BC 3. Bible. Esther 4. Bible. Old Testament History of Biblical events. 5. Women rulers 6. Jewish women 7. Courage in women 8. Faith 9. Women in the Old Testament 10. Women in the Bible 11. Jews -- Rulers 12. Men/women relations 13. Persian Empire 14. Christian fiction 15. Bible novels

Esther is poised to save her people from annihilation. Relying on a fragile trust in a silent God, can she pit her wisdom against a vicious enemy and win?

"Smith's latest will be of great interest to fans of historical fiction, especially those interested in biblical times, as well as readers who enjoy new perspectives on women figures of the past." Booklist.

Smith, Julie, 1944-

82 Desire : a Skip Langdon novel / Julie Smith. Fawcett Columbine, 1998. 309 p. Skip Langdon mysteries

ISBN 0449000605

1. Missing persons investigation 2. Murder 3. Revenge 4. Police -- New Orleans, Louisiana 5. Policewomen 6. Women detectives 7. New Orleans, Louisiana 8. Mysteries 9. Southern fiction

LC 98022259

Introduces Talba Wallis (aka Baroness Pontalba) who is featured in Smith's Baroness Pontalba novels.

Police Detective Skip Langdon investigates the disappearance of a New Orleans councilwoman's husband

"Russell Fortier, a prominent businessman, has vanished. His wife asks Langdon, a New Orleans detective, to look into his disappearance. Later, a private detective who was investigating Fortier turns up dead, and one of his employees, a poet and freelance computer expert, wants to know how Fortier's disappearance is connected with the murder. . . . The novel is intricately constructed, and while Smith keeps nothing important unfairly hidden from her readers, she manages to spring some nice little surprises." Booklist.

Smith, Julie, 1944-

Crescent City kill : a Skip Langdon novel / Julie Smith. Fawcett Columbine, 1997. 326 p. Skip Langdon mysteries

ISBN 0804112738

1. Vigilantes -- New Orleans, Louisiana 2. Swindlers and swindling -- New Orleans, Louisiana 3. Murder investigation 4. Assassination 5. Women detectives -- New Orleans, Louisiana 6. Policewomen -- New Orleans, Louisiana 7. New Orleans, Louisiana 8. Mysteries 9. Southern fiction

LC 9722099

"The New Orleans ambiance is less pronounced than in most Skip Langdon mysteries, but Smith's colorful characterizations and the showdown with Jacomine make this an excellent addition to the series." Publishers Weekly.

Smith, Julie, 1944-

House of blues / Julie Smith Fawcett Columbine, 1995. 343 p. Skip Langdon mysteries

ISBN 0449909360

1. Missing persons -- New Orleans, Louisiana 2. Murder investigation 3. Restaurateurs 4. Policewomen -- New Orleans, Louisiana 5. Women detectives -- New Orleans, Louisiana 6. New Orleans, Louisiana 7. Mysteries 8. Southern fiction

LC 9448823

Finding local pressures rising when a crime wave peaks with the murder of a prominent restauranteur, New Orleans homicide detective Skip Langdon begins a detailed search for the killer, as well as for the victim's missing heirs

"Arthur Hebert, a prominent restaurateur and domineering patriarch hated by his children, doesn't attend the opening of his restaurant in New Orleans' first casinobecause he's been gunned down at home while enjoying his usual Monday evening meal of red beans and rice. Hebert's daughter, his son-in-law and his baby granddaughter have vanished. In the race to find the killer and the missing family, Skip calls on the denizens of the New Orleans underworld. . . . Smith carries off a tricky balancing act, rendering Skip heroic while imbuing her with a credibly textured emotional life. But the real star of this superb effort is New Orleans, which has never seemed more dangerous or alluring." Publishers Weekly.

Smith, Julie, 1944-

Jazz funeral / Julie Smith. Fawcett Columbine, 1993. 365p. Skip Langdon mysteries

ISBN 0449907422

1. Runaways 2. Street musicians 3. Murder investigation 4. Policewomen -- New Orleans, Louisiana 5. Women detectives -- New Orleans, Louisiana 6. New Orleans, Louisiana 7. Mysteries 8. Southern fiction

LC 92054997

Policewoman Skip Langdon is drawn to the New Orleans Jazz Festival in her search for the cold-blooded murderer of a music producer.

Smith, Julie, 1944-

The **kindness** of strangers : a Skip Langdon novel / Julie Smith. Fawcett Columbine, 1996. 338 p. Skip Langdon mysteries

ISBN 0449909379

1. Mayoral candidates -- New Orleans, Louisiana 2. Political corruption 3. Campaigning 4. Women detectives -- New Orleans, Louisiana 5. Policewomen -- New Orleans, Louisiana 6. Political campaigns 7. New Orleans, Louisiana 8. Mysteries 9. Southern fiction

LC 95-52460

Traces Police Detective Skep Langdon's ongoing struggle to expose Errol Jacomine, a candidate for mayor of New Orleans with a reputation for civic spirit, as a psychopath

"Langdon takes on the Big Easy's corrupt political machine, as three 'pick the best of the worst' candidates line up for the mayoral race. New Orleans voters, tired of years of corruption and scandal, are leaning toward Errol Jacomine, a Christian right-winger who appears to have the right stuff. But Skip senses evil lurking behind Jacomine's jovial facade, and she figures to discredit him before he gains control of the city. . . . Smith serves up a gritty, gripping story along with a big helping of action and a pinch of humor." Booklist.

Smith, Julie, 1944-

Louisiana hotshot / Julie Smith. Forge, 2001. 335 p.
Baroness Pontalba novels

ISBN 0765300583

1. Crimes against teenage girls 2. Family relationships 3. Rape 4. Women private investigators 5. African American women -- New Orleans, Louisiana 6. African American women poets -- New Orleans, Louisiana 7. New Orleans, Louisiana 8. Mysteries 9. Southern fiction

LC 2001018958

Sequel: Louisiana bigshot.

Talba Wallis (aka Baroness Pontalba) is first introduced in Smith's 82 Desire.

Talba Wallis--African American poet, leader of New Orleans' café society, and fledgling private detective--is hired by veteran sleuth Eddie Valentino to find a dangerous lothario who seduces teenage black girls who then mysteriously vanish.

"A mystery set in New Orleans featuring Talba Wallis (aka Baroness de Pontalba), the black poet/computer expert and would-be investigator. . . . Answering an unlikely ad with her customary bravado lands her a job as assistant to aging PI Eddie Valentino. The young black female and 65-year-old Italian male have striking similarities that offset their obvious differences. Both are stubborn and strongly attached to, if somewhat alienated from, their families. Throw in a vulnerable young girl, Cassandra, being preyed on by a rap star's hanger-on identified only by the nickname 'Toes,' and you have a story that spans generations, races and lifestyles." Publishers Weekly.

Smith, Julie, 1944-

* **Mean** woman blues / Julie Smith. Forge, 2003. 304 p.
Skip Langdon mysteries

ISBN 0765305526

1. Evangelists 2. Politicians 3. Attempted murder 4. Television talk show hosts and guests 5. Murder 6. Policewomen 7. Police -- New Orleans, Louisiana 8. Women detectives 9. Men/women relations 10. New Orleans, Louisiana 11. Mysteries 12. Southern fiction

LC 2003040018

"A Tom Doherty Associates book."

Having chased corrupt evangelist and dangerous presidential hopeful Errol Jacomine for years, New Orleans detective Skip Langdon finds her loved ones targeted and realizes that Jacomine is so carefully disguised that nobody recognizes him.

"The Formosan termites that infest new Orleans every May haunt police detective Skip Langdon's dreams, an apt image for the gnawing fear that her happiness will collapse. That happiness is based on the fact that her long distance lover, a documentary filmmaker, has moved to New Orleans. Her fear is that her enemy, an evangelical fanatic who aspires to the mind control of Jim Jones, is coming back to kill her, after a disappearance of two years." Booklist.

Smith, Julie, 1944-

New Orleans beat / Julie Smith. Fawcett Columbine, 1994. 359 p. Skip Langdon mysteries

ISBN 0449907430

1. Electronic bulletin boards 2. Murder investigation 3. Murder witnesses 4. Women detectives -- New Orleans, Louisiana 5. Policewomen -- New Orleans, Louisiana 6. New Orleans, Louisiana 7. Mysteries 8. Southern fiction

LC 93046506

Detective Skip Langdon believes that TOWN, a computer bulletin board community, holds the key to the "accidental" death of Geoff, a computer genius

"Smith is a skilled writer who can evoke the steamy, mysterious ambience of New Orleans while simultaneously proving that computer jargon can be comprehensible even to the 'computer-challenged.' This is a humorous, suspenseful mystery." Booklist.

Smith, Lee, 1944-

* **Fair** and tender ladies / Lee Smith. G. P. Putnam's Sons, 1988. 316 p.

ISBN 0399133828

1. Mountain life -- Appalachian Region, Southern 2. Family secrets 3. Death 4. Mothers and daughters 5. Sisters 6. Mental illness 7. Women with mental illnesses 8. Women -- Virginia 9. Families -- Appalachian Region, Southern 10. Virginia 11. Epistolary novels 12. Southern fiction

LC 88010915

Sir Walter Raleigh Award for Fiction, 1989.

A series of letters, written to family and friends, reveals the life and times of Ivy Rowe, as she grows from girlhood to old age, finds love, dreams great visions, and raises a family, in an evocative portrait of Appalchia.

"An exquisite novel. . . . Through Ivy's curiously spelled and situated letters, we see the growth not only of her own family, but also of wider Appalachia." Christian Science Monitor.

Smith, Lee, 1944-

Family linen / Lee Smith G. P. Putnam's Sons, 1985. 272 p.

ISBN 0399130802

1. Families -- Virginia 2. Small town life -- Virginia 3. Mother and adult child 4. Brothers and sisters 5. Death 6. Virginia 7. Mysteries 8. Southern fiction

LC 85003664

Gathered at Miss Elizabeth's deathbed, the whole Hesse family learns unexpected secrets about Elizabeth and each other

"This is a companionable, chatty book populated by people who tell us about themselves in a rambling style and with good humor." New York Times Book Review.

Smith, Lee, 1944-

On Agate Hill : a novel / Lee Smith. Algonquin Books of Chapel Hill, 2006. 416 p.

ISBN 1565124529

1. 19th century 2. 1860s 3. Orphans -- North Carolina 4. Plantation life -- North Carolina 5. Plantations -- North Carolina 6. Uncles 7. Widows 8. Teacher-student relationships 9. Stillbirth 10. Parents of stillborn infants 11. Malicious accusation 12. Murder 13. Reconstruction (United States history) 14. North Carolina -- History -- 1865-1918 15. Southern States -- History -- 19th century 16. Coming-of-age stories 17. Historical fiction 18. Southern fiction

LC 2006045859

"A Shannon Ravenel book."

"Molly is like a grown-up, Southern version of Louisa May Alcott's Jo, only she is thrown into circumstances that test her essentially wholesome nature. For the most part, she battles back not with sasswhich modern novels seem to think is universally charmingbut pluck. As this is Smith's first historical novel, she deserves credit for understanding this subtle, but essential period point." Denver Post.

Smith, Lee, 1944-

Oral history / Lee Smith. G. P. Putnam's Sons, 1983. 286p.

ISBN 0399127941

1. Oral histories 2. Rural life 3. Mountain life 4. Family relationships

5. Interpersonal relations 6. Virginia 7. Family sagas 8. Southern fiction

LC 82018081

Sir Walter Raleigh Award for Fiction, 1983.

"Smith is excellent at making the separate voices distinctive. . . . Serious fiction readers will be interested in Smith's techniques and will appreciate her decision to utilize this 'oral history' format to best achieve her intentions." Booklist.

Smith, Mark Haskell

Baked / Mark Haskell Smith. Black Cat, 2010. 288 p.
ISBN 9780802170767

1. Botanists 2. Marijuana 3. Gunshot victims 4. Inventions 5. Quests 6. Greed 7. Sexuality 8. Belief and doubt 9. Los Angeles, California 10. Crime fiction

Miro Basinas is an experimental botanist who sells his rarefied product to a discerning clientele. Only Miro's not growing heirloom tomatoes or making organic wine--he's growing weed. And when Miro hits the big time by winning Amsterdam's famed Cannabis Cup,

"As cockeyed and riotous as Carl Hiaasen on really good dope." Kirkus.

Smith, Martin Cruz, 1942-

December 6 / Martin Cruz Smith. Simon & Schuster, 2002. 352 p.

ISBN 0684872536

1. Second World War era (1939-1945) 2. 1940s 3. Pearl Harbor, Attack on, 1941 4. World War II -- Tokyo, Japan 5. Americans in Japan 6. Swindlers and swindling 7. Pearl Harbor, Hawaii -- History -- 20th century 8. Tokyo, Japan 9. Historical thrillers

Harry Niles, a disreputable American businessman with an unknown agenda, seeks to abandon his life in Tokyo while fleeing to the west on the last flight out before the Pearl Harbor attack.

"Smith's plot is more than slightly reminiscent of 'Casablanca' and the spectre of the Second World War seems, at this distance, almost quaint, but the characters are so well drawn and the local color so colorful that these quibbles hardly interfer with the novel's pleasures." The New Yorker.

Smith, Martin Cruz, 1942-

* Gorky Park / Martin Cruz Smith. Random House, 1981. 365 p. Arkady Renko novels
ISBN 0394517482

1. Detectives 2. Murder 3. Government cover-ups 4. FBI agents 5. KGB agents 6. Police -- Soviet Union 7. Moscow, Russia 8. Thrillers and suspense 9. Police procedurals

LC 80006022

Gold Dagger Award for Best Crime Novel of the Year, 1981.

In contemporary Moscow, Chief Homicide Investigator Arkady Renko unravels the mystery of a triple murder complicated by the shadowy and uncooperative presence of the KGB and by his falling in love.

"The author has succeeded in rendering very believable, realistic, and gripping portrayals of certain segments of Soviet society and of one man's search for meaning." Christian Science Monitor.

Smith, Martin Cruz, 1942-

Havana Bay / Martin Cruz Smith. Random House, 1999. 329 p. Arkady Renko novels
ISBN 9780679426622

1. International intrigue 2. Detectives 3. Murder investigation 4. Murder 5. Russians in Cuba 6. Havana, Cuba 7. Thrillers and suspense 8. Police procedurals

When the body of a Russian embassy official turns up floating in Havana Bay, detective Arkady Renko is sent to Cuba to identify it, only to find himself caught up in a dangerous conspiracy that will do anything to seize control of Cuba.

"His earnest unsentimentality and calm tenaciousness on the hunt are what make Renko one of the most interesting detectives in modern fiction. What a clever stroke for Smith to dispatch him to Havana, where sentimentality and passion are in rare abundance." New York Times Book Review.

Smith, Martin Cruz, 1942-

Polar Star / Martin Cruz Smith. Random House, 1989. 386 p. Arkady Renko novels
ISBN 9780394578194

1. Detectives 2. International intrigue 3. Murder 4. Murder investigation 5. Food processing plants 6. Ships 7. Former police -- Soviet Union 8. Soviet Union 9. Thrillers and suspense 10. Police procedurals

LC 88043232

Former Moscow Police Inspector Arkady Renko escapes from a psychiatric "hospital" to Siberia, where he becomes embroiled in an investigation into the death of a female crew member of a fish-processing ship.

"Rich in humor, generous in spirit, endlessly entertaining and deeply serious, 'Polar Star' is not merely the work of our best writer of suspense, but of one of our best writers, period." New York Times Book Review.

Smith, Martin Cruz, 1942-

Red Square / Martin Cruz Smith. Random House, 1992. 418p. Arkady Renko novels

1. Organized crime -- Russia 2. International intrigue 3. Detectives 4. Murder investigation 5. Police 6. Exiles 7. Murder 8. Moscow, Russia 9. Russia 10. Thrillers and suspense 11. Police procedurals

LC 92050166

With the fall of Soviet Communism, Inspector Arkady Renko returns from exile and once again takes up his career with the police, only to find himself embroiled in a perilous confrontation with Moscow's new crime elite.

"Just prior to the 1991 attempted coup, [Arkady Renko] finds himself reestablished as an investigator with the Moscow police and struggling to contain a flourishing underworld in the newly democratic Soviet Union. . . . A seemingly straightforward murder investigation leads Arkady first to corruption in high places, then to official censure, and finally to Munich, where he is reunited with Irina, the lover who got him in . . . trouble back in the early 1980s." Booklist.

Smith, Martin Cruz, 1942-

Rose / Martin Cruz Smith. Random House, 1996. 364 p.
ISBN 0679426612

1. 1870s 2. 19th century 3. Coal mine accidents 4. Coal miners 5. Men/women relations 6. Mining engineers 7. Missing persons 8. Women coal miners 9. Americans in England 10. England -- History -- 19th century 11. Lancashire, England -- History -- 19th century 12. Historical fiction

LC 95037914

In 1872, Jonathan Blair wants only to return to Africa, but his employer demands that he go to Lancashire to find out about a missing minister, which leads to information on a recent mining disaster.

"Rose has everthing a compelling novel needs: Blair is a fascinating protagonist, by turns a hero and a boor; other significant characters are complex and as multifaceted as a chunk of coal; the mystery is gripping. But it is the horrific, mesmerizing portrayal of the dark, hellish Wigan, the mines themselves, and the lives of miners that makes this novel much more than a good read." Booklist.

Smith, Martin Cruz, 1942-

The **Siberian** dilemma / Martin Cruz Smith. Simon & Schuster, 2019. 288 p. Arkady Renko novels

ISBN 9781439140253

1. Detectives 2. Women journalists 3. Undercover operations 4. Missing women 5. Missing persons investigation 6. Candidates for public office 7. Business partners 8. Murder 9. Rich people 10. Police 11. Political corruption 12. Political intrigue 13. Police -- Soviet Union 14. Moscow, Russia 15. Thrillers and suspense 16. Police procedurals

When his lover fails to return from a deep-cover assignment, Moscow investigator Arkady Renko embarks on a dangerous journey involving the rise of a political dissident who threatens Putin's rule.

"This is Smith at his absolute best: black humor, brown bears, and gray souls." Booklist.

Smith, Martin Cruz, 1942-

Stalin's ghost / Martin Cruz Smith. Simon & Schuster, 2007. 352 p. Arkady Renko novels

ISBN 0743276728

1. Detectives 2. Police corruption 3. Murder investigation 4. Police -- Moscow, Russia 5. Ghosts 6. Subways 7. Adopted boys 8. Fathers and sons 9. Men/women relations 10. Love triangles 11. Murder 12. Chess 13. Moscow, Russia 14. Thrillers and suspense 15. Police procedurals

A high-stakes tale set in Moscow follows the machinations of a group of reactionaries who harbor a nostalgic loyalty to the regime of Joseph Stalin and who plot to create a groundswell for a new dictatorship.

"Every page reeks of Moscow: dirty snow, the stink of cigarette and vodka fumes, the cynicism and tasteless opulence of the mafia, the all-pervasive corruption. . . . Like the Red Army facing the Nazis, Renko refuses to give up, surrendering neither his investigation nor those he loves. In this subtle, moving book, he is an everyman, whose loyalty and courage speak to all of us." The Economist.

Smith, Martin Cruz, 1942-

Stallion Gate / Martin Cruz Smith. Random House, 1986. 321 p.

ISBN 9780394530062

1. Oppenheimer, J Robert, 1904-1967 2. Groves, Leslie Richard, 1896-1970 3. Fuchs, Klaus, 1911-1988 4. Native American soldiers 5. Atomic bomb -- Testing 6. Interracial romance 7. Jewish American women 8. Women mathematicians 9. Pueblo Indians -- New Mexico 10. New Mexico 11. Los Alamos, New Mexico 12. Historical mysteries

LC 85024444

Dr. Robert Oppenheimer; General Groves, the director of the Manhattan project; Klaus Fuchs, a German-born British scientist; and Sergeant Joe Pena, a Pueblo Indian, figure in this imagined account of the creation of the first atomic bomb.

"Obviously Stallion Gate is not meant to be taken too literally. There is a touch of the folk hero about Pea as he moves across the New Mexican landscape. A conscious stylist, Smith relies strongly on emotional echoes and calibrated suspense." Time.

Smith, Martin Cruz, 1942-

* **Tatiana** : an Arkady Renko novel / Martin Cruz Smith. Simon & Schuster, 2013. 304 p. Arkady Renko novels

ISBN 9781439140215

1. Government cover-ups 2. Detectives 3. Organized crime 4. Police 5. Women journalists 6. Political corruption 7. Murder 8. FBI agents 9. KGB agents 10. Police -- Soviet Union 11. Moscow, Russia 12.

Thrillers and suspense 13. Police procedurals

LC 2013026426

When investigative reporter Tatiana Petrovna falls to her death from a sixth-floor window in Moscow the same week that a mob billionaire is shot and buried, investigator Arkady Renko connects the two cases, which leads him to a Cold War secret city and a teenage chess hustler to find the truth.

Smith, Martin Cruz, 1942-

Three stations : an Arkady Renko novel / Martin Cruz Smith. Simon & Schuster, 2010. 352 p. Arkady Renko novels

ISBN 9780743276740

1. Detectives 2. Police corruption 3. Murder investigation 4. Police -- Moscow, Russia 5. Kidnapping 6. Trains 7. Women murder victims 8. Men/women relations 9. Murder 10. Chess 11. Moscow, Russia 12. Thrillers and suspense 13. Police procedurals

LC bl2010001966

Struggling with a prosecutor's refusal to send work his way, investigator Arkady Renko of Moscow finds his efforts to watch out for teen chess prodigy Zhenya challenged by a case involving a kidnapped baby, a dead prostitute, and police corruption.

"The main investigation underpinning Three Stations doesn't carry the full force of past adventures. . . . The denouement, in particular, feels rushed and half-hearted. Smith does, however, nail the key to the structure of a detective novel, when Renko thinks there was still time for [him] to walk away from a case he did not fathom and a woman he did not understand. One can trace that very essence back to Hammett and Chandler, who imbued their respective gumshoes with dogged determination no matter what price they paid later. So too must Arkady, who is doomed to repeat this existential cycle in book after book?" Los Angeles Times Book Review.

Smith, Martin Cruz, 1942-

Wolves eat dogs : a novel / Martin Cruz Smith. Simon & Schuster, 2004. 352 p. Arkady Renko novels

ISBN 0684872544

1. Detectives 2. Radiation victims 3. Nuclear accidents 4. Police -- Moscow, Russia 5. Russians in Ukraine 6. Chernobyl Nuclear Accident, 1986 -- Influence 7. Murder investigation 8. Radioactive pollution 9. Ukraine 10. Moscow, Russia 11. Thrillers and suspense 12. Police procedurals

LC 2004052585

In the wake of a businessman's suicide, Moscow detective Arkady Renko investigates secrets and international plots that may have driven him to his death, in a case that leads Renko to discover crimes in the area surrounding Chernobyl.

"Senior Investigator Arkady Renko must determine whether the defenestration death of a Russian tycoon was suicide or murder. The discovery of radioactive salt in the dead man's apartment leads Renko to the abandoned Ukrainian towns of Chernobyl and Pripyat, still dangerously contaminated 18 years after the world's deadliest nuclear accident. There he finds a ghostly world inhabited by scavengers, elderly villagers, and a small group of Russian militia and scientists. As Renko pursues his investigation, he uncovers a greater crime, the sad legacy of Soviet ineptitude and corruption." Library Journal.

Smith, Mary-Ann Tirone, 1944-

Love her madly : a novel / Mary-Ann Tirone Smith. Henry Holt & Co., 2002. 507 p., 25 cm. Poppy Rice mysteries

ISBN 9780805066487

1. Women death row prisoners 2. Judicial error 3. Innocence (Law) 4. Revenge 5. Women FBI agents 6. Government investigators 7.

LIST OF FICTIONAL WORKS

Texas 8. Washington, D.C. 9. Mysteries

LC 2001039306

Poppy Rice decides to reopen the investigation of convicted ax-murderer Rona Leigh Glueck after she views a newscast and sees Rona's delicate, child-like hands. Rona is due to be executed in 10 days, becoming the first woman executed in Texas since the Civil War.

"Smith delivers a smart, irreverent heroine; pitch-perfect Texan dialogue; gasp-worthy plot twists; and quite a bit of substance along with the action. Poppy has some serious and scathing things to say about the death penalty, religion, and Texas politics." Booklist.

Smith, Mary-Ann Tirone, 1944-

She smiled sweetly : a Poppy Rice mystery / Mary-Ann Tirone Smith. H. Holt, 2004. 288 p. Poppy Rice mysteries
ISBN 0805072241
1. Crimes against young women 2. Politicians 3. Crime laboratories 4. Irish American women 5. DNA testing 6. Murder investigation 7. Women FBI agents 8. Government investigators 9. Boston, Massachusetts 10. Mysteries

LC 2003055757

The discovery of an unidentified pregnant woman whose body washes ashore on a rocky Boston beach sends FBI agent Poppy Rice on a quest to uncover the truth about the crime, which is linked by DNA to a similar drowning thirty years earlier.

Smith, Mary-Ann Tirone, 1944-

She's not there : a Poppy Rice novel / Mary-Ann Tirone Smith. H. Holt, 2003. 336 p. Poppy Rice mysteries
ISBN 0805072233
1. Overweight teenagers 2. Serial murders 3. Weight loss camps 4. Lovers 5. Murder investigation 6. Women FBI agents 7. Government investigators 8. Block Island, Rhode Island 9. Mysteries

LC 2002068592

When her vacation on Block Island is interrupted by her discovery of the body of a murder victim, FBI agent Poppy Rice investigates, which leads her to discover another body and strange clues that link the two deaths.

"The ease with which Poppy gets technical support from Washington and manpower from the Rhode Island mainland is some stretch, but that doesn't take away from her shrewd analysis of the isolationist island mentality or her understanding of teenage behavior." New York Times Book Review.

Smith, Michael F. (Michael Farris), 1970-

Blackwood / Michael Farris Smith. Little, Brown and Co., 2020. 293 p.
ISBN 9780316529815
1. 1970s 2. Homecomings 3. Family history 4. Artists 5. Rural life 6. Small towns 7. Psychic trauma 8. Good and evil 9. Forests 10. Invasive plants 11. Mississippi 12. Southern gothic 13. Southern fiction

LC 2019946516

In this timeless, mythical tale of unforgiving justice and elusive grace, rural Mississippi townsfolk shoulder the pain of generations as something dangerous lurks in the enigmatic kudzu of the woods.

"Smith's meditation on the darkness of the human heart offers a moving update to the Southern gothic tradition." Publishers Weekly.

Smith, Michael F. (Michael Farris), 1970-

The **fighter** : a novel / Michael Farris Smith. Little Brown & Co., 2018 243 p.
ISBN 9780316432344
1. Foster mothers 2. Middle-aged men 3. Bare knuckle boxing

4. Circus performers 5. Boxers (Sports) 6. Foster children 7. Repossession 8. Gambling 9. Addiction 10. Poverty 11. Debt 12. Mississippi 13. Delta Region, Mississippi 14. Southern gothic 15. Literary fiction 16. Southern fiction

His mind failing from the effects of decades of bare-knuckle fighting, his foster mother's family legacy in the hands of strangers, and overwhelmed with gambling debts, Jack's only chance at redemption is to step into the fighting pit one last time.

Smith, Scott, 1965 July 13-

A **simple** plan : a novel / Scott Smith. Knopf, 1993. 335 p.
ISBN 9780679419853
1. Airplane accidents 2. Money 3. Greed in men 4. Fathers 5. Brothers 6. Murder 7. Extortion 8. Ohio 9. Thrillers and suspense

LC 92042478

When a young man finds a suitcase with a million dollars in cash, his life is changed forever.

"This novel is so cunningly imagined that for the most part Mr. Smith drags us willingly through what in less deft hands could be a morally repugnant story." New York Times Book Review.

Smith, Scott, 1965 July 13-

The **ruins** : a novel / Scott Smith. Alfred A. Knopf, 2006. 336 p.
ISBN 1400043875
1. Tourists 2. Jungle survival 3. Mayas 4. Jungles -- Mexico 5. Americans in Mexico 6. Travelers -- United States 7. Brothers 8. Excavations (Archaeology) 9. Missing persons 10. Cancun, Mexico 11. Horror

LC 2005057782

Best friends Amy and Stacy (and their boyfriends Jeff and Eric) travel to Cancun, Mexico for a summer they'll never forget. On arrival, the Americans meet German tourist Mathias, whose brother Heinrich is missing. Last seen heading into the jungle with a beautiful woman to join an archaeological expedition to some Mayan ruins, Heinrich hasn't been heard from since-- although he did leave behind a crudely drawn map. -- Description by Dawn Towery.

Smith, Tom Rob

* **Agent** 6 / Tom Rob Smith. Grand Central Pub., 2012. 448 p. Leo Demidov thrillers
ISBN 9780446550765
1. 1950s 2. Former spies 3. Conspiracies 4. Secret service -- Soviet Union 5. Daughters -- Death 6. Communism 7. Betrayal 8. Murder 9. Married women -- Death 10. Grief in men 11. New York City 12. Soviet Union -- History -- 1925-1953 13. Historical thrillers

Former secret police agent Leo Demidov is thrown into a foreign conflict and is forced to question and confront everything he ever thought he knew about his country, his family, and himself.

Smith, Tom Rob

Child 44 / Tom Rob Smith. Grand Central Pub., 2008. 439 p. Leo Demidov thrillers
ISBN 0446402389
1. Trans-Siberian Railway 2. 1950s 3. Secret service -- Soviet Union 4. Serial murder investigation 5. Political crimes and offenses 6. Police 7. Serial murderers 8. Innocence (Law) 9. Crimes against children 10. Redemption 11. Nationalism 12. Soviet Union -- History -- 1925-1953 13. Historical thrillers

LC 2007028272

Sequel : The secret speech.
Ian Fleming Steel Dagger Award, 2008.

Thriller Award for Best First Novel, 2009.

Rising Soviet state security force officer Leo Demidov encounters the test of his career when a serial killer challenges his beliefs about the paradise of the working world, resulting in his demotion and threats against the lives of his family members.

"Smith captures the rhythm of day-today paranoia in Stalinist Russia and the ways that personal jealousies can balloon into ruthless vendettas. It's hard to fathom which is more grisly, the descriptions of the serial murders or the scenes of torture perpetrated by Leo's colleagues in the MGB. Throughout, Smith's prose is propulsive but plain; his real genius is his careful plotting." Entertainment Weekly.

Smith, Tom Rob

The **secret** speech / Tom Rob Smith. Grand Central Pub., 2009. 416 p. Leo Demidov thrillers

ISBN 9780446402408

1. 1950s 2. Secret service -- Soviet Union 3. Political oratory 4. Revenge 5. Murder 6. Political crimes and offenses 7. Nationalism 8. Soviet Union -- History -- 1925-1953 9. Historical thrillers

LC 2008048329

Sequel to : Child 44.

Honored as a hero for his role in stopping a serial killer three years earlier, post-Stalinist Soviet Union MGB officer Leo Demidov is placed at the head of a newly formed Moscow homicide department and is forced to undertake a personal mission in the criminal underworld when dark elements from his past catch up with him.

"Based on real events, The Secret Speech is jam-packed with action the near-sinking of a prison ship, a violent takeover at a Kolyma gulag, and a rebellion in Hungary--and Smith explores pertinent questions of revenge, morality and responsibility." PopMatters.

Smith, Wilbur A.

Birds of prey / Wilbur A. Smith. St. Martin's Press, 1997 554 p. Courtney novels

ISBN 0312157916

1. 17th century 2. Fathers -- Death 3. Betrayal 4. Revenge 5. Deception 6. Fathers and sons 7. Piracyn Ocean 8. Sailors 9. Caravels 10. Indian Ocean 11. Adventure stories 12. Historical fiction 13. Sea stories

LC 978192

1667, Sir Francis Courteney and his son Hal are on patrol in their fighting caravel off the Agulhas Cape of South Africa. They are lying in wait there for one of the treasure-laden galleons of the Dutch East India Company returning from the Orient. So begins a quest for adventure and the spoils of war. They are swept from the settlement of Good Hope at the southern tip of Africa to the Great Horn of Ethiopia far to the north at a time when international maritime law permitted acts of piracy, rape, and murder otherwise punishable by death. In this book the author presents a generation of the indomitable Courtney's and thrillingly recreates their part in the struggle for supremacy and riches on the high seas.

"Smith's depiction of the African coast, and of life aboard ship, is vivid and believable. He handles the action sequences well, opting for short, trenchant paragraphs to sustain momentum. . . . Smith knows what his readers want, and once again he delivers the goods." Publishers Weekly.

Smith, Wilbur A.

Monsoon / Wilbur A. Smith. St. Martin's Press, 1999. 613 p. Courtney novels

ISBN 031220339X

1. 18th century 2. Sibling rivalry 3. Kidnapping 4. Fathers and sons 5. Sailors 6. Africa -- Exploration -- British 7. Sea stories 8.

Adventure stories 9. Historical fiction

LC 9924554

"This sequel to Birds of Prey finds Sir Hal Courtney and his sons up to their bloody sword arms in piracy, intrigue, treachery and civil war in late 17th and early 18th century East Africa and Arabia. ... Clever plot twists and lavish historical detail attend the siblings' adventures." Publishers Weekly.

Smith, Zadie

The **autograph** man : a novel / Zadie Smith. Random House, 2002. 347 p.

ISBN 037550186X

1. Jewish men -- Identity 2. Ethnicity 3. Autographs -- Collectors and collecting 4. Friendship 5. Misadventures 6. Forgery 7. Loss (Psychology) 8. Actors and actresses 9. Fame 10. Obsession in men 11. London, England 12. Picaresque fiction

LC 2002069705

Originally published: London: Hamish Hamilton, 2002.

Shortlisted for The Orange Prize for Fiction, 2003

Alex-Li Tandem is a 27-year-old, half-Jewish, half-Chinese man in search of himself. In his own words, he has "no love, no transportation, no ambitions, no faith," and not much else. An autograph peddler, he hunts down the signatures people want and sells them.

"Smith's pen portraits of the shabby, yobbish autograph trading circle are intermittently funny, but her prose is so busy being clever that the laughter never builds. This is disappointing but, even with its faults, the novel points to a literary talent of a high order." Publishers Weekly.

Smith, Zadie

* **Grand** union : stories / Zadie Smith. Penguin Press, 2019. 256 p.

ISBN 9780525558996

1. Identity (Psychology) 2. Legacies 3. Interpersonal relations 4. Short stories 5. Literary fiction

The award-winning author of <I>White Teeth</I> presents a first collection of 10 original short stories and selections from her most-lauded pieces as first published in The New Yorker and other prestigious literary magazines.

Smith, Zadie

* **NW** : a novel / Zadie Smith. Penguin Press, 2012. 320 p.

ISBN 9781594203978

1. Young adults 2. Planned communities 3. Social isolation 4. City life 5. Adulthood 6. Public housing 7. Social classes 8. Social behavior 9. Life change events 10. Options, alternatives, choices 11. London, England 12. Literary fiction 13. Coming-of-age stories 14. Psychological fiction

LC 2012015114

National Book Critics Circle Award for Fiction finalist, 2012.

Shortlisted for The Women's Prize for Fiction, 2013.

Growing up in the same 1970s urban planning development in Northwest London, four young people pursue independent and reasonably successful lives until one of them is abruptly drawn out of her isolation by a stranger who is seeking her help.

Smith, Zadie

On beauty / Zadie Smith. Penguin Press, 2005. 320 p.

ISBN 1594200637

1. Rembrandt Harmenszoon van Rijn, 1606-1669 Influence 2. Extramarital affairs 3. Family relationships 4. Ethnic identity 5. Interracial families 6. College teachers 7. British in the United States 8. Husband and wife 9. Intellectuals 10. Generation gap 11. Religion 12. Men/women relations 13. Deception 14. Universities and

colleges 15. Massachusetts 16. New England 17. Domestic fiction 18. Literary fiction

Includes author's note.

Originally published: London: Hamish Hamilton, 2005.

Orange Prize for Fiction, 2006.

Somerset Maugham Award, 2006.

Shortlisted for the Man Booker Prize, 2005.

Howard Belsey, a Rembrandt scholar who doesn't like Rembrandt, is an Englishman abroad and a long-suffering Professor at Wellington College. He has been married for thirty years to Kiki, an American woman who no longer resembles the sexy activist she once was. Their three children passionately pursue their own paths, and faced with the oppressive enthusiasms of his children, Howard feels that the first two acts of his life are over and he has no clear plans for the finale. Then Jerome, Howard's oldest son, falls for Victoria, the stunning daughter of the right-wing icon Monty Kipps. Increasingly, the two families find themselves thrown together in a beautiful corner of America, enacting a cultural and personal war against the background of real wars that they barely register.

"Ms Smith has her shortcomings. The novel's first half is under-edited; surely we do not need to meet every guest at an anniversary party. . . . Nevertheless, the book gathers momentum, and the second half gallops along." The Economist.

Smith, Zadie

* **Swing** time / Zadie Smith. Penguin Press, 2016. 416 p.

ISBN 9781594203985

1. Female friendship 2. Dancing 3. Multiracial women 4. Competition 5. Race relations 6. Social classes 7. Popular culture 8. Dancers 9. Celebrities 10. Voyages and travels 11. Family relationships 12. London, England 13. West Africa 14. Literary fiction

Andrew Carnegie Medal for Excellence in Fiction Finalist, 2017

National Book Critics Circle Award for Fiction finalist, 2016

Longlisted for the Man Booker Prize, 2017.

Two dark-skinned dancers with very different talents share a complicated childhood friendship that ends abruptly in early adulthood in a story that transitions from northwest London to West Africa.

"Moving, funny, and grave, this novel parses race and global politics with Fred Astaire's or Michael Jackson's grace." Kirkus.

Smith, Zadie

* **White** teeth : a novel / Zadie Smith. Random House, 2000. 448 p.

ISBN 0375501851

1. 1970s 2. Immigrants 3. Interracial friendship 4. Families 5. Muslim families 6. Gender role 7. Race relations 8. Social classes 9. Popular culture -- History -- 20th century 10. London, England 11. Great Britain -- Social conditions -- 1945- 12. Satirical fiction 13. Literary fiction

LC 99043658

ALA Notable Book, 2001.

Betty Trask Award, 2001.

Guardian First Book Award, 2000.

James Tait Black Memorial Prize for Fiction, 2000.

Whitbread Book Award for First Novel, 2000.

Shortlisted for The Orange Prize for Fiction, 2000

National Book Critics Circle Award for Fiction finalist, 2000

White Teeth is a comic epic of multicultural Britain by one of the most exciting young writers of 2000. It tells the story of immigrants in England over a period of 40 years.

"Hopscotching through several continents and 150 years of history, 'White Teeth' encompasses a teeming family saga, a sly inquiry into race and identity and a tender-hearted satire on religious antagonism and cultural bemusement. . . . Smith holds it all together with a raucous energy and confidence." New York Times Book Review.

Snipes, Wesley

Talon of God / Wesley Snipes with Ray Norman. Harper Voyager, 2017. 368 p.

ISBN 9780062668165

1. Demons 2. Good and evil 3. Warriors 4. Physicians 5. Demonic possession 6. Survival 7. Women physicians 8. Belief and doubt 9. Drug traffic 10. Devil 11. Chicago, Illinois 12. Christian fantasy 13. Urban fantasy 14. African American fiction

A fiction debut by the acclaimed actor depicts a holy warrior in a fantastical urban world where he must convince a doctor with no faith to help stop a powerful demon and his minions from establishing a hell on earth.

Snow, C. P. (Charles Percy), 1905-1980

* **Strangers** and brothers / C.P. Snow. Scribner, 1960 309 p. Strangers and brothers

1. 1930s 2. Men 3. Lawyers 4. Fraud 5. Families 6. Helpfulness in men 7. Friendship 8. Classism 9. England -- Social life and customs -- 20th century 10. Historical fiction

LC 60012605

"Essentially the tragedy of a good man defeated by the mediocrity of his world, the story of George Passant is completed in the novel 'Homecoming.' . . . Like all the novels in the series, 'Strangers and Brothers' is distinguished by virtue of its analysis of motive and character and its anatomization of a world in which a smooth mediocrity is the greatest virtue." Library Journal.

Snow, Jennifer

An **Alaskan** Christmas / Jennifer Snow. HQN Books, 2019. 384 p. Wild River

ISBN 9781335041500

1. Women surgeons 2. Search and rescue operations 3. Vacations 4. Best friends 5. Christmas 6. Fathers and daughters 7. Workaholics 8. Men/women relations 9. Interpersonal attraction 10. Alaska 11. Contemporary romances 12. Holiday romances

Arriving in Wild River, Alaska for a much-needed break, workaholic surgeon Erika Sheraton is reunited with her best friend's brother, Reed Reynolds, who makes it his mission to prove to her just how much his search-and-rescue team -- and he -- needs her.

Soderberg, Alexander

The **other** son : a Sophie Brinkmann novel / Alexander Soderberg ; translated from the Swedish by Neil Smith. Crown Publishing, 2015, c2014. 388 p. Sophie Brinkman trilogy

ISBN 9780770436087

1. People in comas 2. Organized crime 3. Single mothers 4. Kidnapping 5. Police corruption 6. Murder 7. Nurses 8. Voyages and travels 9. Drug cartels 10. Europe 11. Scandinavian crime fiction 12. Crime fiction 13. Translations -- Swedish to English

Translation from the Swedish of: Den Andre Sonen.

Originally published as: Den Andre Sonen. Stockholm : Norstedts, 2014.

Originally published: Stockholm : Norstedts, 2014.

A follow-up to The Andalucian Friend finds Sophie Brinkmann using a family murder to plot a daring escape from comatose Hector Guzman's crime family, an effort that compels her to forge dubious alliances and tap darker aspects of her own nature.

Sofer, Dalia

The **Septembers** of Shiraz / Dalia Sofer. Ecco Press, 2007. 336 p.

ISBN 0061130400

1. 1980s 2. Jews, Iranian 3. Jewish families -- Iran 4. Revolutions -- Iran 5. Religious persecution 6. Imprisonment 7. Political prisoners -- Iran 8. Prisoners' families 9. Social change -- Psychological aspects 10. Coping 11. Escapes 12. Tehran, Iran 13. Iran -- Social conditions -- 20th century 14. Iran -- History -- Islamic revolution, 1979-1997 15. Domestic fiction 16. Historical fiction

Their serene villa life devastated by a wrongful imprisonment, the wife and children of Tehran gentleman Isaac Amin face potential betrayals within their own household and eventually plan a dangerous escape.

"Sofer paints a complicated picture of postrevolutionary Iran: The Amins (and especially their relatives) aren't entirely innocent, having shut their eyes to brutality and corruption under the shah, but [the author] recoils from the idea of justice by 'collective retribution' voiced by Farnaz's formerly docile housekeeper. While the dialogue can feel overly formal at times, the impression the reader is left with at the end is that of a powerful story honestly told." Christian Science Monitor.

Solares, Martin

The **black** minutes / Martin Solares ; translated by Aura Estrada and John Pluecker. Grove Press, 2010. 436 p.

ISBN 9780802170682

1. Detectives -- Mexico 2. Murder -- Mexico 3. Crimes against journalists 4. Murder investigation -- Mexico 5. Mexico 6. Mysteries 7. Translations -- Spanish to English

Translation form the Spanish of: Minutos negros.

Follows the investigation of police officer Ramon Cabrera into the murder of a journalist that has unsettling links to a corruption-tainted multiple homicide case from years earlier.

Solares, Martin, 1970-

Don't send flowers / Martin Solares ; translated by Heather Cleary. Black Cat, 2018, c2015 288 p.

ISBN 9780802128157

1. Former police 2. Police corruption 3. Missing persons investigation 4. Cartels 5. Corruption 6. Police chiefs 7. Businesspeople 8. Missing teenage girls 9. Mexico 10. Literary fiction 11. Noir fiction 12. Translations -- Spanish to English

LC 2018015205

Originally published in 2015 by Literatura Random House.

A twisty, darkly captivating novel about a police detective hired to investigate the disappearance of a rich businessman's daughter several years after rampant corruption forced him to retire and made him a target of everyone still on the force in cartel-controlled, northern Mexico.

Soli, Tatjana

The **lotus** eaters / Tatjana Soli. St. Martin's Press, 2010. 400 p.

ISBN 9780312611576

1. Women war photographers 2. Vietnam War, 1961-1975 3. Lovers 4. Americans in Vietnam 5. War -- Psychological aspects 6. Women photojournalists 7. Women war correspondents 8. Ho Chi Minh City (Vietnam) 9. Vietnam 10. War stories 11. Historical fiction 12. Love stories 13. Literary fiction

LC 2009045697

James Tait Black Memorial Prize for Fiction, 2010.

ALA Notable Book, 2011.

Helen Adams, an American combat photographer during the Vietnam War, captures the wrenching chaos of battle on film and finds herself torn between the love of two men, one an American war correspondent and the other his Vietnamese underling.

"Soli is at her best in conveying the day-to-day mix of adventure, tedium, and violence in wartime. Her descriptions are visceral, almost cinematic. . . . And she captures the camaraderie and tension among soldiers in a way that seems authentic." Boston Globe.

Soli, Tatjana

The **removes** / Tatjana Soli. Sarah Crichton Books/Farrar, Straus and Giroux, 2018. 288 p.

ISBN 9780374249311

1. Custer, Elizabeth Bacon, 1842-1933 2. Custer, George A (George Armstrong), 1839-1876 3. American Westward Expansion (1803-1899) 4. Frontier and pioneer life 5. Cheyenne Indians 6. Gender role 7. Captives 8. Violence in men 9. Ambition in men 10. Indians of North America -- Wars -- 1866-1895 11. Great Plains (United States) 12. Westerns 13. Literary fiction

LC 2017052980

Traces the intertwining stories of Civil War hero George Armstrong Custer, his frontierswoman wife Libbie and a teen who became a member of the Cheyenne tribe after surviving a homestead attack.

Solomita, Stephen

A **good** day to die O. Penzler Books, 1993. 297 p.

ISBN 9781883402037

1. Police 2. Serial murders 3. African-American policewomen 4. Violence against male prostitutes 5. Manhattan, New York City 6. New York City 7. Noir fiction 8. Thrillers and suspense

LC 93-19400

Sparks fly when Roland Means, a native American street cop, and Vanessa Bouton, an African-American sergeant, team up to solve two seemingly unrelated cases

"As Means researches the profiled backgrounds of serial killers, he recognizes his own abused childhood; his search for the killer becomes a search for himself. This multiethnic thriller vividly depicts the gritty streets of the city, the dark and feral forest, and the danger lurking in both." Library Journal.

Solomon, Anna

Leaving Lucy Pear / Anna Solomon. Viking Press, 2016. 336 p.

ISBN 9781594632655

1. Between the Wars (1918-1939) 2. 1920s 3. Life change events 4. Abandoned children 5. Gender role 6. Mothers and daughters 7. Identity (Psychology) 8. Social classes 9. Catholic women 10. Jewish women 11. Birthmothers 12. Motherhood 13. Secrets 14. New England -- Social life and customs -- 20th century 15. Historical fiction

Inadvertently reunited with the daughter she secretly abandoned and the girl's Irish-Catholic adoptive mother during the height of America's xenophobic Prohibition era, the adult daughter of a Jewish industrialist finds her life turned upside down by her daughter's bold and unconventional personality.

"A beautifully rendered tale of discovering one's true nature." Library Journal.

Solomon, Asali

Disgruntled : a novel / Asali Solomon. Farrar, Straus & Giroux, 2015. 304 p.

ISBN 9780374140342

1. 1980s 2. African American girls 3. Ethnic identity 4. Bullying and bullies 5. Racism 6. Vigilantes 7. Black power 8. Belonging 9. Philadelphia, Pennsylvania 10. Psychological fiction 11. Coming-of-

age stories 12. African American fiction

LC 2014027442

In a powerful coming-of-age tale that also doubles as a portrait of Philadelphia in the late 80s and early 90s, Kenya Curtis, who knows that she is different, but can't put her finger on why, grows increasingly disgruntled by her inability to find any place, thing or person that feels like home.

"Solomon's cultural references resound, her dialogue stings, and the intricate and surprising relationships she choreographs are saturated with racial, sexual, and political quandaries of intimate and epochal repercussions. A deft, knowing, bold, and witty debut." Booklist.

Solomon, Burt

The **attempted** murder of Teddy Roosevelt / Burt Solomon. Forge, 2019. 304 p.

ISBN 9780765392671

1. Hay, John, 1838-1905 2. Roosevelt, Theodore, 1858-1919 3. Bly, Nellie, 1864-1922 4. United States. Secretary of State. 5. 1900s (Decade) 6. Amateur detectives 7. Politicians 8. Attempted assassination 9. Women journalists 10. Investigations 11. Death threats 12. Murder 13. Married men 14. Intrigue 15. Massachusetts -- History -- 20th century 16. United States -- Politics and government -- 1865-1933 17. Historical mysteries

A historical tale based on true events finds Secretary of State John Hay teaming up with journalist Nellie Bly to investigate a suspicious accident that nearly ended the life of the 26th President.

Solomon, Burt

* The **murder** of Willie Lincoln / Burt Solomon. Forge, 2017. 302 p.

ISBN 9780765385833

1. Lincoln, Abraham, 1809-1865 2. Hay, John, 1838-1905 3. Lincoln, William Wallace, 1850-1862 4. American Civil War era (1861-1865) 5. Murder investigation 6. Conspiracies 7. Anonymous letters 8. Children -- Death 9. Children of presidents 10. Washington, D.C. -- Social life and customs -- 19th century 11. Historical mysteries

LC 2016043547

A grief stricken Abraham Lincoln, in the midst of raging civil war, enlists the help of his aide, John Hay, in investigating the death of the president's beloved son, Willie. While it appears the boy died from typhoid fever, a mysterious message suggests this might not be the case. What Hay discovers has the potential of not only destroying Lincoln, but a nation.

"For fans of historical mysteries with a "what if?" bent, this enjoyable look back in time to another presidency suggests a political landscape just as plagued with controversy as our current one." Library Journal.

Solomon, Rivers

The **deep** / Rivers Solomon, with Daveed Diggs, William Hutson, Jonathan Snipes. Saga Press, 2019. 166 p.

ISBN 9781534439863

1. Underwater cities 2. Memories 3. Mermaids 4. Women -- Africa 5. Slave trade 6. Slavery 7. Historians 8. Freedom 9. Communities 10. Collective memory 11. Psychic trauma 12. Afrofuturism and Afrofantasy 13. Fantasy fiction 14. African American fiction

LC 2020275363

The historian of the water-dwelling descendants of pregnant African slaves thrown overboard by slavers keeps all the memories of her people both painful and miraculous, until she discovers that their future lies in returning to the past.

Solomon, Rivers

An **unkindness** of ghosts / Rivers Solomon. Akashic Books, 2017. 340 p.

ISBN 9781617755880

1. Misfits (Persons) 2. Space vehicles 3. Racism 4. Race relations 5. Social classes 6. Gender role 7. Extremists 8. Slavery 9. Slums 10. Discrimination 11. Dystopias 12. Social science fiction 13. Literary fiction

Aster lives in the lowdeck slums of the HSS Matilda, a space vessel organized much like the antebellum South. For generations, Matilda has ferried the last of humanity to a mythical Promised Land. On its way, the ship's leaders have imposed harsh moral restrictions and deep indignities on dark-skinned sharecroppers like Aster. Embroiled in a grudge with a brutal overseer, Aster learns there may be a way to improve her lot--if she's willing to sow the seeds of civil war.

"Infused with the spirit of Octavia Butler . . . an Unkindness of Ghosts will appeal to a wide variety of readers. Solomon's impassioned, speculative, literary book is sorely needed on library shelves." Booklist.

Solomons, Natasha

House of Gold / Natasha Solomons. G.P. Putnam's Sons, 2018 432 p.

ISBN 9780735212978

1. 20th century 2. Heirs and heiresses 3. War and society 4. Rich families 5. Jewish families 6. Husband and wife 7. Women and war 8. Nationalism 9. World War I 10. Austrians in England 11. Options, alternatives, choices 12. Family relationships 13. England -- Social life and customs -- 20th century 14. Austria -- History -- 20th century 15. Historical fiction

LC 2018002308

The outbreak of World War I forces a headstrong Austrian heiress to choose between the family she built and the family she left behind.

Solzhenitsyn, Aleksandr Isaevich, 1918-2008

* **Cancer** ward / Alexander Solzhenitsyn ; translated by Nicholas Bethell and David Burg. Modern library, 1995, c1968. vii, 536 p.

ISBN 0679601635

1. 1950s 2. Medical care -- Corrupt practices -- Soviet Union 3. Socialism -- Soviet Union 4. Collectivism -- Soviet Union 5. Men/ women relations 6. Communism -- Soviet Union 7. People with cancer 8. Uzbekistan 9. Soviet Union 10. Translations -- Russian to English 11. Political fiction

LC 95003798

Solzhenitsyn's celebrated novel describes the lives of people in the Soviet Union under Stalin who were condemned on health grounds to "internment" or death. It also give a psychological insight into the intensified experience of people under varying degrees of pressure and deprivation.

Solzhenitsyn, Aleksandr Isaevich, 1918-2008

In the first circle : a novel : Aleksandr I. Solzhenitsyn ; translated by Harry T. Willetts. Harper Perennial Modern Classics, 2009. xxx, 741 p.

ISBN 9780061479014

1. 1940s 2. Mathematicians 3. Political prisoners -- Soviet Union 4. Political persecution -- Soviet Union 5. Soviet Union -- Politics and government -- 1936-1953 6. Political fiction 7. Translations -- Russian to English

Previously published (1968) in a shortened and altered ed., with title: The first circle.

"The first uncensored edition."--Cover.

The government orders an imprisoned mathematician and his fellow genius inmates to figure out a turncoat's identity, forcing the prisoners to choose between helping the Stalinist regime that jailed them or being sent to certain death in the Siberian Gulags, in an edition that restores a significant amount of text originally cut by Soviet censors.

"It has taken a half-century for English-language readers to receive the definitive text of In the First Circle... Such is the fate of art created under a totalitarian regime. But now it is finally available in the West as the author envisioned it. The English translator is Harry T. Willetts, renowned for combining fidelity to Aleksandr Solzhenitsyn's rich, complex Russian with supple equivalents in English prose and the only person Solzhenitsyn fully trusted to render his fiction into English." The Wall Street Journal.

Solzhenitsyn, Aleksandr Isaevich, 1918-2008

One day in the life of Ivan Denisovich / Aleksandr Solzhenitsyn ; translated from the Russian by H. T. Willetts ; with an introduction by John Bayley. A. A. Knopf, 1995, c1963. 159 p.

ISBN 0679444645

1. Forced labor -- Soviet Union 2. Concentration camps -- Soviet Union 3. Political prisoners -- Soviet Union 4. Communism 5. Soviet Union 6. Translations -- Russian to English 7. Literary fiction 8. Modern classics

LC 96121678

Presents a new translation of the fictional account of the daily hardships a prisoner endures in a Stalinist labor camp

Somer, Mehmet Murat, 1959-

The **serenity** murders / Mehmet Murat Somer. Penguin Books, 2012. 256 p. Hop-Ciki-Yaya mysteries

ISBN 9780143121220

1. Cross-dressers 2. Murder investigation 3. Television programs 4. Death threats 5. Murder 6. Amateur detectives 7. Gay culture -- Turkey 8. Turkey 9. Istanbul, Turkey 10. Mysteries 11. Translations -- Turkish to English 12. LGBTQIA fiction

LC 2012030581

During a television show appearance, transvestite Burçak Veral receives a call from an irate man who threatens to kill everyone close to her and then murders the show's host, prompting Burçak to put her sleuthing skills to the test.

Soniah Kamal

Unmarriageable : a novel / Soniah Kamal. Ballantine Books, 2019. 342 p.

ISBN 9781524799717

1. Marriage 2. Teachers 3. Families -- Pakistan 4. Men/women relations 5. Mate selection 6. Weddings 7. Sisters 8. Pakistan 9. Chick lit 10. Romantic comedies 11. Adaptations, retellings, and spin-offs

LC 2018036398

A retelling of *Pride and Prejudice*, set in modern-day Pakistan, finds a practical-minded teacher from a family of sisters evaluating her resolve never to marry after encountering a brusque but compelling man during a series of lavish wedding parties.

"This love letter to Austen reexamines sisterhood, society, and marriage in Pakistani culture and includes a fleshed-out epilogue that will satisfy today's readers." Booklist.

Sontag, Susan, 1933-2004

* **In** America / Susan Sontag. Farrar, Straus and Giroux, 2000. 387 p.

ISBN 9780374175405

1. 1870s 2. 19th century 3. Polish Americans 4. Actors and actresses 5. Frontier and pioneer life 6. Theater -- United States -- 19th century 7. Utopias 8. Ranches -- California -- 19th century 9. Marriage 10. Lovers 11. Independence in women 12. Creativity in women 13. Historical fiction 14. Biographical fiction 15. Literary fiction

LC 99054641

National Book Award for Fiction, 2000.

Poland's greatest living actress leads a utopian community to the wilds of 1876 California, where she will struggle to maintain love, hope, and idealism in the harsh reality of the American West.

"This novel displays Sontag in a relaxed, pleasure-seeking mode, guiding her characters through a long travelogue in time, specifically the beginnings of the gilded age in the brave new world." Time.

Sontag, Susan, 1933-2004

The **volcano** lover : a romance / Susan Sontag. Farrar Straus Giroux, 1992. 419 p.

ISBN 9780374285166

1. Nelson, Horatio Nelson, Viscount, 1758-1805 2. Hamilton, William, 1730-1803 3. Hamilton, Emma, 1761?-1815 4. Great Britain. Royal Navy Officers 5. 18th century 6. Love triangles 7. Extramarital affairs 8. Mistresses 9. Men/women relations 10. Married people 11. Husband and wife 12. Volcanoes 13. Naples, Italy 14. Vesuvius 15. Mediterranean region -- History 16. Historical fiction 17. Love stories 18. Biographical fiction 19. Literary fiction

LC 92071738

A romance set in eighteenth-century Naples follows the fortunes of a British ambassador, the ravishing woman he marries, and the young British admiral with whom she falls in love

"Sontag's narrative deftly blends the magnetism of personality and the suspense of event with shrewd commentary and sly mockery as she contrasts the habits of thought in that age with ours and reflects on the meaning of mercy and vengeance, self-invention and praise, love and obsession. In all, a memorable group portrait and a brilliant, fresh improvisation on classically grand themes." Booklist.

Sorenson, Jill

Aftershock / Jill Sorenson. Harlequin Books, 2012. 384 p. Aftershock (Jill Sorenson)

ISBN 9780373777327

1. Earthquakes 2. Rescues 3. Secrets 4. Paramedics 5. Veterans 6. Men/women relations 7. Sexual attraction 8. Escaped convicts 9. Courage 10. Sexuality 11. San Diego, California 12. Romantic suspense 13. Category romances

When she is trapped by an earthquake underneath the freeway with a group of strangers, including Iraq war veteran Garrett Wright, emergency paramedic Lauren Boyer turns to Garrett for help in saving the others when a gang of escaped convicts goes on the attack.

Sosa, Mia

* **Acting** on impulse / Mia Sosa. HarperCollins, 2017. 400 p. Love on cue

ISBN 9780062690340

1. Vacations 2. Disguises 3. Sexual attraction 4. Personal trainers 5. Actors and actresses 6. Film industry and trade 7. Trust in women 8. Privacy 9. Caribbean Area 10. Aruba 11. Contemporary romances

Sparks fly during their vacations when fitness trainer Tori Alvarez and Hollywood heartthrob Carter Stone meet on their way to Aruba for rest & relaxation.

Sosa, Mia

* The **worst** best man / Mia Sosa. Avon Books, 2020. 359 p.

ISBN 9780062909879

1. Wedding consultants 2. Jilted women 3. Brothers 4. Business competition 5. Interpersonal attraction 6. African American women 7. Advertising executives 8. Interracial couples 9. Family problems 10. Jilted brides 11. African-Latin Americans 12. Business presentations 13. Men/women relations 14. Romantic comedies

A wedding planner left at the altar? Yeah, the irony isn't lost on Carolina Santos, either. But despite that embarrassing blip from her past, Lina's offered an opportunity that could change her life. There's just one hitch: she has to collaborate with the best (make that worst) man from her own failed nuptials.

"Sosa (Acting on Impulse) delivers a steamy and witty enemies-to-lovers romance. Lina and Max's relationship grows against a rich background of Lina's Afro-Latinx culture, and readers will enjoy the complex cast of side characters." Library Journal.

Sosin, Danielle, 1959-

The **long-shining** waters / Danielle Sosin. Milkweed Editions, 2011. 320 p.

ISBN 9781571310835

1. 2000s (Decade) 2. 20th century 3. 17th century 4. Self-acceptance 5. Dreams 6. Purpose in life 7. Ojibwa Indians 8. Women bar owners 9. Lakes 10. Change (Psychology) 11. Lake Superior 12. Historical fiction

LC 2011002077

Lake Superior, the north country, the great fresh-water expanse. Frigid. Lethal. Wildly beautiful. The Long-Shining Waters gives us three stories whose characters are separated by centuries and circumstance, yet connected across time by a shared geography. In 1622, Grey Rabbit-an Ojibwe woman, a mother and wife-struggles to understand a dream-life that has taken on fearful dimensions. As she and her family confront the hardship of living near the "big water," her psyche and her world edge toward irreversible change. In 1902, Berit and Gunnar, a Norwegian fishing couple, also live on the lake. Berit is unable to conceive, and the lake anchors her isolated life, testing the limits of her endurance and spirit. And in 2000, when Nora, a seasoned bar owner, loses her job and is faced with an open-ended future, she is drawn reluctantly into a road trip around the great lake. As these narratives unfold and overlap with the mesmerizing rhythm of waves, a fourth mysterious character gradually comes into stark relief. Rich in historical detail, and universal in its exploration of the human desire for meaning when faced with uncertainty, The Long-Shining Waters is an unforgettable and singular debut.

"Lake Superior proves to be more than a bucolic backdrop for Sosin's debut novel. It swallows fishing nets, boats, and even men, and shapes the lives of three women from different eras: Grey Rabbit, an Ojibwe woman following seasonal routes with her family in 1622 and struggling to feed her children; Berit Kleiven, who lives in a lonely cove with her husband, Gunnar, in 1902; and Nora Truneau, a Duluth bar owner who explores the lake in 2000 after a crisis. . . . Sosin writes sensuously detailed prose and distills the emotions of her characters into a profound and universal need for acceptance and love." Publishers Weekly.

Soule, Charles

* **Anyone** / Charles Soule. Perennial, 2019. 400 p.

ISBN 9780062890634

1. Women scientists 2. Consciousness 3. Mind transfers 4. Human body 5. High technology 6. Women spies 7. Control (Psychology) 8. Identity (Psychology) 9. Black market 10. Near future 11. Techno-thrillers 12. Parallel narratives

When a botched experiment leads to the unexpected development of consciousness-transferring technology, a scientist witnesses the havoc of her innovation throughout two subsequent decades of body-rental violence, entertainment and warfare.

"Soule s uncomfortable vision of the future will please readers of cutting-edge speculative fiction." Publishers Weekly.

Soule, Maris

The **crows** / Maris Soule. Five Star, 2007. 263 p. P. J. Benson mysteries

ISBN 9781594146053

1. Murder 2. Interpersonal attraction 3. Women murder suspects 4. Murder investigation 5. Certified public accountants 6. Detectives 7. Men/women relations 8. Women accountants 9. Michigan 10. Mysteries

LC 2007030667

Beware the menace posed by a dying man, a sniper in the woods and killer ladybugs. Accountant P.J. Benson recently inherited her grandfather's farm in rural Michigan. During tax season, she has no time for outside interests, but when she's suspected in the murder of a stranger who dies in her dining room she's forced to turn sleuth.

Souljah,, Sister

* The **coldest** winter ever : a novel / Sister Souljah. Pocket Books, 1999. 337 p.

ISBN 9780671025366

1. African American women 2. Street life 3. Drug traffic 4. Inner city 5. City life 6. Drug use 7. Violence 8. Seventeen-year-old girls 9. Drug dealers 10. African American teenagers 11. African American fathers and daughters 12. Mothers -- Death 13. Imprisonment 14. FBI agents 15. Love triangles 16. Extramarital affairs 17. Anger in teenage girls 18. Rap musicians 19. Brooklyn, New York City 20. African American fiction 21. Urban fiction

LC 99012242

Sequel: A deeper love inside

Street Lit Book Award Medal: Adult Fiction, 2000

Winter Santiaga, the daughter of one of Brooklyn's most powerful drug czars, uses her own weapons--including sex and an aggressive attitude--to stay on top, after her father's empire is threatened by a drug war.

Souljah, Sister

* A **deeper** love inside : the Porsche Santiaga story, by Sister Souljah. Emily Bestler Books/Atria, 2012. 432 p.

ISBN 9781439165317

1. Street life 2. Problem youth 3. African American teenagers 4. Growing up 5. Inner city 6. Mother-separated children 7. Juvenile delinquency 8. City life 9. Escapes 10. New York City 11. Brooklyn, New York City 12. Coming-of-age stories 13. African American fiction 14. Urban fiction

LC 2012029222

Sequel to: The Coldest Winter Ever

Natural-born hustler Porsche Santiaga refuses to accept her new life in juvenile detention after her family is torn apart and fights to regain what she has lost.

Souljah, Sister

Midnight and the meaning of love / Sister Souljah. Atria Books, 2011. 608 p. Midnight series (Sister Souljah)

ISBN 9781439165355

1. African American men 2. Family relationships 3. Protectiveness in men 4. Martial artists 5. Family fortunes 6. Kidnapping 7. Ninja 8. Brooklyn, New York City 9. Love stories 10. Urban fiction 11. African American fiction

Midnight's efforts to rescue his wife trigger unexpected consequences that mark his journey into adulthood.

Spain, Jo

With our blessing : an Inspector Tom Reynolds mystery / Jo Spain. Crooked Lane Books, 2019, c2015. 368 p. Inspector Tom Reynolds novels

ISBN 9781683314363

1. Convents 2. Revenge 3. Women murder victims 4. Detectives 5. Murder 6. Murder investigation 7. Crime 8. Winter storms 9. Small towns 10. Secrets 11. Ireland 12. Police procedurals 13. Mysteries
Originally published: London : Quercus, 2015.

After the corpse of a nun is found in a public Dublin park, Detective Inspector Tom Reynolds investigates its connection in this American debut from the best-selling Irish author.

Spann, Susan

Blade of the Samurai : a Shinobi mystery / Susan Spann. Minotaur Books, 2014. 293 p. Shinobi mysteries

ISBN 9781250027054

1. 16th century 2. Political intrigue 3. Ninja 4. Assassination 5. Murder 6. Murder investigation 7. Samurai 8. Priests 9. Assassins 10. Japan -- History -- 16th century 11. Kyoto, Japan -- History -- 16th century 12. Historical mysteries 13. Mysteries

LC 2014008766

Learning that the shogun's cousin has been murdered within palace walls, master ninja Hiro Hattori and Father Mateo learn of an assassination plot by a usurping clan and begin to doubt a friend's innocence.

"There are already a couple of good mystery series set in feudal-era Japan, one at the beginning of the historical period and the other at the end; this one's set in between, meaning the been-there-done-that factor is reduced to background noise. A strong second entry in a very promising series." Booklist.

Spann, Susan

* **Claws** of the cat : a Shinobi mystery / Susan Spann. Minotaur Books, 2013. 288 p. Shinobi mysteries

ISBN 9781250027023

1. 16th century 2. Ninja 3. Murder 4. Samurai 5. Priests 6. Assassins 7. Secrets 8. Women murder suspects 9. Japan -- History -- 16th century 10. Kyoto, Japan -- History -- 16th century 11. Historical mysteries 12. Mysteries

In sixteenth-century Japan, master ninja Hiro and the Jesuit priest he is sworn to protect race against time to prevent a wrongful execution by solving the murder of a samurai whose death is linked to numerous possible suspects.

Spann, Susan

Trial on Mount Koya : a Hiro Hattori novel / Susan Spann. Seventh Street Books, 2018 256 p. Shinobi mysteries

ISBN 9781633884151

1. 16th century 2. Ninja 3. Samurai 4. Buddhism 5. Priests 6. Sacred space 7. Buddhist priests 8. Portuguese in Japan 9. Serial murder investigation 10. Japan -- History -- 16th century 11. Kyoto, Japan -- History -- 16th century 12. Historical mysteries 13. Mysteries

LC 2018006388

November, 1565: Master ninja Hiro Hattori and Portuguese Jesuit Father Mateo travel to a Buddhist temple at the summit of Mount Koya, carrying a secret message for an Iga spy posing as a priest on the sacred mountain. When a snowstorm strikes the peak, a killer begins murdering the temple's priests and posing them as Buddhist judges of the afterlife--the Kings of Hell. Hiro and Father Mateo must unravel the mystery

before the remaining priests--including Father Mateo--become unwilling members of the killer's grisly council of the dead.

Spark, Muriel

Aiding & abetting / Muriel Spark. Doubleday, 2001, c2000. viii, 166 p.

ISBN 0385501536

1. Lucan, Richard John Bingham, 1934- 2. Deception 3. Extortion 4. Murderers 5. Fugitives 6. Missing persons 7. Psychotherapist and patient 8. Stigmatization 9. Upper class 10. Women embezzlers 11. Women psychiatrists 12. Women swindlers 13. England 14. Paris, France 15. France 16. Mysteries 17. Literary fiction

LC 00055559

Originally published: London: Viking, 2000.

Psychiatrist Hildegard Wolf is intrigued when two patients begin therapy with her--both claiming to be the notorious Lord Lucan. Lucan disappeared in 1974, shortly after murdering his children's nanny in a botched attempt to kill his wife. It's not just the patients who have secrets, as the doctor has also abandoned a previous life.

"The unsettling wit of 'Aiding and Abetting' hits the funny bone as hard it pricks the conscience. . . . It's kiln-dried wit that never cracks, with a smile that dares you to laugh. As always [Spark is] breathtakingly deft with the anxieties of well-bred people, people who know how to dress, where to eat, and how to commit the most heinous cruelty. If satire is your cup of tea, . . . [this is a] perfectly seeped book to be savored." Christian Science Monitor.

Spark, Muriel

The **driver's** seat / Muriel Spark. Knopf, 1970. 117 p.

ISBN 9789997405333

1. Self-destructive behavior 2. Deception 3. Women travelers 4. Women -- Psychology 5. Sexuality 6. Mental illness 7. Murder 8. Manipulation by women 9. Men/women relations 10. Italy 11. Psychological fiction 12. Mysteries

LC 79111242

"This novel first appeared in the New Yorker."

Originally published: London : Macmillan, 1970.

"The author's perspective is cosmically cool and fantastic: she knows no more about her protagonist, Lise, than does the reader. . . . She follows this woman, another of her slightly bizarre lunatics, through a day's grotesque project, narrating only its circumstances, leaving all motive, all emotion, all inner plan to be inferred. The result is a long, elusive joke that casts as deep an irony on life's arbitrariness as do the more 'compassionate' ironies of, say, E. M. Forster." The Nation.

Spark, Muriel

* A **far** cry from Kensington / Muriel Spark. New Directions, 2000, c1988. 189 p.

ISBN 9780811214575

1. 1950s 2. Boarding houses 3. Widows 4. Reminiscing in old age 5. Extortion 6. Eccentrics and eccentricities 7. Dieting 8. Publishers and publishing 9. Women editors 10. London, England 11. England 12. Psychological fiction

LC 88005904

Originally published: New York : Houghton Mifflin, 1988.

In a post-war London boarding house, kindly Mrs. Hawkins, adept at handling other people's problems, finds herself a player in some very strange events.

"Spark balances devastatingly eccentric characters and funny situations with darker elements, even pathos. Her well-constructed novel has no loose ends and few contrived situations." Library Journal.

LIST OF FICTIONAL WORKS

Spark, Muriel

* The **girls** of slender means / Muriel Spark. New Directions, 1998, c1963. 141 p.

ISBN 9780811213790

1. 1940s 2. Single women 3. War and society 4. Young women 5. Poor women 6. Boarding houses for women 7. World War II 8. Interpersonal relations 9. Men/women relations 10. London, England 11. Satirical fiction 12. Modern classics 13. Literary fiction
LC 89091877

Originally published: London : Macmillan, 1963.

Just after World War II in a London ladies' hostel its lady inhabitants do their best to act as if the world were back to normal, practicing elocution and jostling over suitors and a single Schiaparelli gown.

Spark, Muriel

* The **Mandelbaum** gate / Muriel Spark Welcome Rain Pub., 2001, c1965. 329 p.

ISBN 9781566492263

1. 1960s 2. Young women 3. British in Israel 4. Jewish women 5. Pilgrims and pilgrimages, Christian 6. Interethnic conflict 7. Diplomats -- Great Britain 8. Converts to Catholicism from Judaism 9. Jerusalem, Israel -- Social conditions -- 20th century 10. West Bank (Jordan River) 11. Literary fiction

Originally published: London: Macmillan, 1965.

James Tait Black Memorial Prize for Fiction, 1965.

The Mandelbaum Gate divides the conflict-torn realm of Jerusalem, separating Israel from Jordan. Barbara Vaughan, a stubborn young Englishwoman and half-Jewish Catholic convert, insists upon crossing the divide in order to rendezvous with her fiance, in spite of the very real danger. Not even the threat of bodily harm and fearful admonishments of staid British diplomat Freddy Hamilton can dissuade Barbara from her ill-timed pilgrimage. Her quest sets off a series of bizarre situations and adventures, set against the backdrop of the Eichmann trial of 1961.

Spark, Muriel

* **Memento** mori / Muriel Spark. New Directions, 2000, c1959. 224 p.

ISBN 9780811214384

1. 1950s 2. Seniors 3. Mortality 4. Extortion 5. Secrets 6. Extramarital affairs 7. Upper class 8. Telephone calls 9. Interpersonal relations 10. London, England 11. England 12. Satirical fiction 13. Modern classics 14. Literary fiction
LC 90093171

Originally published: London : Macmillan, 1959.

In late 1950s London, a group of aging eccentrics is brought together by a series of uncanny events. Lettie Colston is the first to receive an anonymous phone call from an insinuating voice reminding her that she must die. Soon, ten of Lettie's friends also receive the call. In the flurry that results from these seemingly supernatural messages, a bizarre investigation is launched that reveals a network of deception binding the group, including such dark secrets as blackmail and adultery.

Spark, Muriel

* The **prime** of Miss Jean Brodie / Muriel Spark. Harper Perennial, 1999, c1961. 150 p.

ISBN 9780060931735

1. 1930s 2. Middle-aged women 3. Teacher-student relationships 4. Women teachers 5. Nonconformists 6. Teenage girls 7. Betrayal 8. Egotism in women 9. Edinburgh, Scotland 10. Scotland -- Social life and customs -- 20th century 11. Modern classics 12. Psychological fiction 13. Literary fiction

First published in the USA by the New Yorker 1961. First published in Great Britain by Macmillan 1961. Published in Penguin, 1965.

A teacher at a girl's school in Edinburgh during the 1930s comes into conflict with school authorities because of her unorthodox teaching methods.

Sparks, Nicholas

Every breath / Nicholas Sparks. Grand Central Publishing, 2018. 496 p.

ISBN 9781538728529

1. Beaches 2. Strangers 3. Birthparents 4. Safari guides 5. Sick fathers 6. Coastal towns 7. Life change events 8. Secrets 9. Interpersonal attraction 10. Men/women relations 11. North Carolina 12. Love stories
LC 2018012865

A chance encounter becomes a transcendent turning point for two very different people, including the conflicted surgeon daughter of an ALS patient and a Sunset Beach newcomer from Zimbabwe who aims to meet his birth father.

"Sparks confirms his gifts as he spans the last two decades and transports readers to the bush of Zimbabwe and the Carolina coast in this thoughtfully researched and spellbinding story of love that defies time, a tale both heartbreaking and heartwarming." Booklist.

Sparks, Nicholas

The **guardian** / Nicholas Sparks. Warner Books, 2003. 384 p.

ISBN 0446527793

1. Love triangles 2. Men/women relations 3. Stalking victims 4. Possessiveness 5. Courtship 6. Great Danes 7. Widows 8. Antisocial personality disorders 9. Stalkers 10. North Carolina 11. Romantic suspense
LC 2002192411

Four years after losing her husband, twenty-nine-year-old Julie Barenson considers falling in love again and wonders if she should choose sophisticated Richard, who treats her like a queen, or down-to-earth Mike, who is her best friend.

"On Christmas Eve, Julie Barenson, 25 years old and newly widowed, finds an unexpected present: a Great Dane pup that her late husband, Jim, had arranged for her to receive after he died from a brain tumor. . . . Julie's new dog, Singer, turns out to be a better judge of character than she, which is unfortunate because the dog nearly gives away the book's ending when he growls warily at Richard Franklin, the new man in Julie's life." Publishers Weekly.

Sparks, Nicholas

* The **notebook** / Nicholas Sparks. Warner, 1996. 214 p.

ISBN 0446520802

1. Senior romance 2. Men/women relations 3. Single men 4. World War II veterans 5. Former lovers 6. Engaged persons 7. Plantation houses 8. Octogenarians 9. Nursing home patients 10. Women with Alzheimer's disease 11. North Carolina 12. Love stories 13. Mainstream fiction
LC 9633815

Sequel: The wedding

An elderly man reads a story from a not(ebk.) to a woman who does not know him; the story is of young lovers kept apart by disapproving parents.

"At 80, Noah Calhoun reads daily from a not(ebk.) containing the love story of Noah and Allie. We learn of the teenaged lovers, their 14-year separation and reunion in New Bern, North Carolina, just weeks before Allie is to marry another man. Back in the present, we learn that Noah and Allie did marry and were happy for more than 40 years. Now, they are residents of a nursing home, separated both by rooms and, more profoundly, by Allie's Alzheimer's. Noah's daily reading from the notebook is not to himself; he reads aloud to Allie, hoping that the power of their love story will reach her." Library Journal.

Sparks, Nicholas

A **walk** to remember / Nicholas Sparks. Warner Books, 1999. 240 p.

ISBN 0446525537

1. 1950s 2. First loves 3. Teenage boy/girl relations 4. People with cancer 5. Middle-aged men 6. Teenagers 7. High school students 8. Christmas plays 9. Love 10. Memories 11. Homecoming (School) 12. North Carolina 13. Love stories 14. Mainstream fiction

LC 99012079

Colorado Blue Spruce YA Book Award, 2003.
Iowa High School Book Award, 2004.

A nostalgic look back at the 1950s in a story of first love set in a small North Carolina town.

"The author is a master at pulling heartstrings and bringing a tear to his readers' eyes. . . . Told in Landon's down-home voice, this bittersweet tale will enthrall Sparks' numerous fans." Booklist.

Spear, Terry

A **billionaire** wolf for Christmas / Terry Spear. Sourcebooks, 2018. 352 p. Billionaire wolf (Terry Spear)

ISBN 9781492655848

1. Billionaires 2. Werewolves 3. Physicians 4. Women werewolves 5. Wolf packs 6. Brothers and sisters 7. Shapeshifters 8. Mate selection 9. Secrets 10. Sexual attraction 11. Men/women relations 12. Paranormal romances

Wolf shifter Dr. Aidan Denali has been working day and night to find a cure for werewolves' alarmingly sudden decline in lifespan. The key to the problem eludes him. But when Aidan grudgingly leaves his work to do some holiday shopping, he meets a remarkable she-wolf whose mysterious pack could bring him one step closer to the answer.

Speight, Shameek A.

The **pleasure** of pain / Shameek A. Speight ; editor Kelly Klem. Createspace : 2011. 228 p. Pleasure of pain novels (Shameek A. Speight)

ISBN 9781463526245

1. Drug dealers 2. African American women 3. Women criminals 4. Street life 5. Men/women relations 6. New York City 7. Urban fiction 8. African American fiction

Speller, Elizabeth

The **strange** fate of Kitty Easton / Elizabeth Speller. Virago, 2011. 416 p. Laurence Bartram novels

ISBN 9781844086313

1. 1920s 2. World War I veterans 3. Missing girls 4. Missing persons investigation 5. War and society 6. War -- Psychological aspects 7. Villages 8. Wiltshire, England 9. England -- Social conditions -- 20th century 10. Historical mysteries 11. Mysteries

Sequel to: The return of Captain John Emmett.
Originally published: 2011.

When former infantry officer Laurence Bartram is called to the small village of Easton Deadall, he is struck by the beauty of the place: a crumbling stately home; a centuries-old church; and a recently planted maze, a memorial to the men of the village, almost all of whom died in one heroic battle in 1916. But it soon becomes clear to Laurence that while rest of the country is alight with hope for the first time since the end of the War, as the first Labour government takes power, the Wiltshire village is haunted by its tragic past. In 1911, five-year-old Kitty Easton disappeared from her bed and has not been seen since: only her fragile mother believes still she is alive. When a family trip to the Empire Exhi-

bition in London ends in disaster and things take an increasingly sinister turn, Laurence struggles to find out what has happened as it seems that the fate of the house, the men and of Kitty herself may be part of a much longer, darker story of love, betrayal and violence.

Speller, Elizabeth

The **return** of Captain John Emmett / Elizabeth Speller. Houghton Mifflin Harcourt, 2011, c2010. 384 p. Laurence Bartram novels

ISBN 9780547511696

1. 1920s 2. World War I veterans 3. Suicide investigation 4. War -- Psychological aspects 5. War and society 6. Soldiers 7. London, England -- History -- 20th century 8. England -- Social conditions -- 20th century 9. Historical mysteries 10. Mysteries

LC 2010052590

Sequel: The strange fate of Kitty Easton.
Originally published: 2010.

"An absorbing mystery set in postwar London, . . . [this book] is brimming with historical details of the period and doesn't shy away from war's atrocities." Library Journal.

Spencer, Elizabeth, 1921-

The **southern** woman : new and selected fiction / Elizabeth Spencer. Modern Library, 2001. 462 p.

ISBN 0679642188

1. Women -- Southern States 2. Women -- Italy 3. Southern States -- Social life and customs 4. Italy -- Social life and customs 5. Short stories

LC 00054612

The author's most masterful stories and novellas plus more than ten new stories. This collection celebrates a six-decade career devoted to the art of the story and the novella.

"This collection offers selections from the Mississippi native's earlier short fiction together with several new stories. Best known of the earlier fiction is her stunning novella, The Light in the Piazza (1960), the deceptively simple tale of an American mother and daughter in Florence." Library Journal.

Spencer, Elizabeth, 1921-

The **stories** of Elizabeth Spencer / Elizabeth Spencer ; with a foreword by Eudora Welty Doubleday, 1981. 429 p.

ISBN 0385156979

1. Short stories

LC 79006601

An award-winning Southern writer includes thirty-three short stories spanning four decades of her life, portraying her homeland, Mississippi, and other places she has come to love

Spencer, Minerva

Barbarous / Minerva Spencer. Zebra Books, 2018. 304 p. Outcasts (Minerva Spencer)

ISBN 9781420147216

1. Pirates 2. Widows 3. Independence in women 4. Aristocracy 5. Thirties (Age) 6. Inheritance and succession 7. Heirs and heiresses 8. Sexual attraction 9. Men/women relations 10. England 11. Historical romances

When the man whom she thought was dead returns, Lady Daphne Davenport, who secretly cheated him of his title, lands and fortune, must find a way to makes things right despite an unknown enemy standing in her way.

"Deft writing and astute character development sustain a complex plot and a huge cast of characters that could flounder in less accomplished hands, while a touch of humor tempers some darker edges of the nuanced story." Kirkus.

Spencer, Minerva

Dangerous / Minerva Spencer. Zebra Books, 2018. 304 p. Outcasts (Minerva Spencer)

ISBN 9781420147193

1. Former captives 2. Misfits (Persons) 3. Widowers 4. Aristocracy 5. Independence in women 6. Thirties (Age) 7. Secrets 8. Sexual attraction 9. Men/women relations 10. England 11. Historical romances

What sort of lady doesn?t make her debut until the age of thirty-two? A timeless beauty with a mysterious past?and a future she intends to take into her own hands . . .

Spencer, Minerva

Scandalous / Minerva Spencer. Zebra Books, 2019. 304 p. Outcasts (Minerva Spencer)

ISBN 9781420147209

1. Women missionaries 2. Ship captains 3. Privateers 4. Virgins 5. Rescues 6. Slave ships 7. Extortion 8. Sexual attraction 9. Men/women relations 10. Historical romances

When straight-laced missionary Sarah Fisher makes him an outrageous offer, Captain Martin Bouchard is captivated by this brazen beauty and must confront his scandalous past in order to have a future with the first woman to steal his heart.

Spencer, Sally

Backlash / Sally Spencer. Severn House, 2011. 224 p. Monika Paniatowski mysteries

ISBN 9780727880550

1. 1970s 2. Policewomen 3. Missing persons investigation 4. Missing women 5. Police spouses 6. Women murder victims 7. Mutilation 8. Police 9. England 10. Mysteries

DCI Monika Paniatowski tries to balance searching for both Chief Superintendent Kershaw's wife, Elaine, and young prostitute Grace Meade, who suddenly disappear.

Spencer, Sally

Best served cold / Sally Spencer. Severn House, 2015. 224 p. Monika Paniatowski mysteries

ISBN 9780727885074

1. 1970s 2. Policewomen 3. Murder investigation 4. Actors and actresses 5. Secrets 6. Revenge 7. Police 8. Murder 9. England 10. Mysteries 11. Police procedurals

DCI Monika Paniatowski investigates the death of a member of a theater company and discovers everyone in the company had a reason to want the victim dead.

Spencer, Sally

Dead end / Sally Spencer. Severn House, 2019. 240 p. Monika Paniatowski mysteries

ISBN 9780727888747

1. 1970s 2. Policewomen 3. Cold cases (Criminal investigation) 4. Murder investigation 5. England 6. Lancashire, England 7. Mysteries 8. Police procedurals

When a body is discovered on a local allotment after lying buried for years, Monika Paniatowski has no real leads - until she sees possible links with a case she closed four years earlier. Are the two cases connected? All she knows is that she is being watched by an old enemy, and will be killed if she shares her information with her team...

Spencer, Sally

The **dead** hand of history / Sally Spencer. Severn House, 2009. 224 p. Monika Paniatowski mysteries

ISBN 9780727868053

1. 1970s 2. Extramarital affairs 3. Murder suspects 4. Gender role 5. Single mothers 6. England 7. Mysteries

On her first day in a new job, DCI Monika Paniatowski finds herself in the middle of a mystery after a severed female hand is found on the riverbank.

Spencer, Sally

Death's dark shadow / Sally Spencer. Severn House, 2013 208 p. Monika Paniatowski mysteries

ISBN 9780727883476

1. 1970s 2. Policewomen 3. Murder investigation 4. Crimes against women 5. Police 6. Murder 7. England 8. Mysteries

Before she can even begin to track down the killer of the old woman dumped on the lonely canalside, Monika Paniatowski needs to find out who she is--but no one seems to know.

Spencer, Sally,

* A **dying** fall / Sally Spencer. Severn House, 2008. 248 p. Chief Inspector Woodend mysteries

ISBN 9780727866097

1. 1960s 2. Detectives 3. Women detectives 4. Women journalists 5. Politicians 6. Murder 7. Murder investigation 8. Interpersonal relations 9. Interpersonal conflict 10. Deception 11. England 12. Mysteries

When a charred body is discovered at an abandoned mill, DCI Woodend must attempt to solve a crime with virtually no clues while also fighting against police authority that blocks him at every turn.

Spencer, Sally

* **Echoes** of the dead / Sally Spencer. Severn House, 2011. 218 p. Monika Paniatowski mysteries

ISBN 9780727869807

1. 1970s 2. Police 3. Cold cases (Criminal investigation) 4. False imprisonment 5. Police corruption 6. Policewomen 7. England 8. Mysteries

LC oc2010056413

When a recently released prisoner claims in a deathbed confession that he is innocent of the rape and murder of a young girl for which he was convicted twenty-two years earlier, DCI Monika Paniatowski is tasked to lead an unofficial investigation into his claims. At first she is reluctant, but when she learns that her old mentor Charlie Woodend was the lead detective in the case, she knows she must do everything she can to protect his reputation.

Spencer, Sally

* The **hidden** / Sally Spencer. Severn House, 2017. 186 p. Monika Paniatowski mysteries

ISBN 9780727887078

1. Policewomen 2. Murder investigation 3. Murder suspects 4. Secret societies 5. Murder 6. England 7. Mysteries 8. Police procedurals

DCI Paniatowski's team are increasingly convinced that the girl found dead in the woods is the victim of a ritual killing, carried out by a secret society which has been established in the very heart of Whitebridge. Their problem is that without Paniatowski there to back them up, they find it impossible to persuade the ambitious DCI ?Rhino? Dixon that treating it as a mere domestic murder will get them nowhere. And so Meadows, Crane and Beresford find themselves out on a limb - cutting corners, ignoring procedure, and running the very real risk that their careers could be brought to an abrupt and dramatic end.

Spencer, Sally

Lambs to the slaughter / Sally Spencer. Severn House, 2012. 208 p. Monika Paniatowski mysteries

ISBN 9780727881922

1. 1970s 2. Policewomen 3. Murder investigation 4. Small towns 5. Strikes 6. Mines and mineral resources 7. Miners 8. Police 9. England 10. Mysteries

Inspector Monika Paniatowski investigates the murder of retired miner Len Hopkins, but progress is hindered by the unwelcoming nature of the mining industry and concerns for the behavior of her partner, Inspector Colin Beresford.

Spencer, Sally

The **ring** of death / Sally Spencer. Severn House, 2010. 240 p. Monika Paniatowski mysteries

ISBN 9780727868688

1. 1970s 2. Police 3. Serial murder investigation 4. Serial murderers 5. Policewomen 6. England 7. Mysteries

Originally published: 2010.

DCI Monika Paniatowski finds herself handicapped by a colleague she doesn't trust and being watched by an old enemy as she tries to unravel a series of clues left by a deranged murderer.

Spencer, Sally

The **shivering** turn / Sally Spencer. Severn House, 2017. 218 p. Jennie Redhead novels

ISBN 9780727886675

1. 1970s 2. Women private investigators 3. Missing teenage girls 4. Secret societies 5. Upper class 6. Poetry 7. Former policewomen 8. Missing persons investigation 9. Oxford, England 10. Mysteries

Seventeen-year-old Linda Corbet is missing and Jennie is hired to investigate. The only clue Jennie has is a fragment of a 17th century poem she finds in Linda's room. But from that one clue her investigations will lead her to a secret Oxford society ? and a hidden world of violence, excess and desire which lies behind the city's dreaming spires.

Spencer, Sally

* **Thicker** than water : a Monika Paniatowski British police procedural / Sally Spencer. Severn House, 2016. 224 p. Monika Paniatowski mysteries

ISBN 9780727885616

1. Policewomen 2. Murder investigation 3. Murder suspects 4. New mothers 5. Politicians 6. Murder 7. England 8. Mysteries 9. Police procedurals

Just back from maternity leave, DCI Monika Paniatowski is called in to investigate the murder of a wealthy politician's wife, who is the mother of three small children, a case in which she must make a quick arrest or her career may be on the line.

Spencer, Sally

* A **walk** with the dead / Sally Spencer. Severn House, 2013. 208 p. Monika Paniatowski mysteries

ISBN 9780727882424

1. 1970s 2. Policewomen 3. Murder investigation 4. Crimes against girls 5. Guilt in women 6. Police 7. England 8. Mysteries

DCI Monica Paniatowski becomes emotionally invested in finding the murderer of a wedding guest who was killed just hours after the investigator saw her alive.

Spencer, Scott

* **Endless** love / Scott Spencer. Knopf, 1979. 417 p.

ISBN 9780394506050

1. 1960s 2. 1970s 3. People with mental illnesses 4. Obsession 5. Arson 6. Lovers 7. Men/women relations 8. Accidental death 9. Love stories

LC 79002089

This book was made into film twice -- in 1981 directed by Franco Zeffirelli, starring Brooke Shields and Martin Hewitt and in 2014, directed by Shana Feste and staring Alex Pettyfer and Gabriella Wilde.

National Book Award for Fiction finalist, 1980

"The author has achieved something quite remarkable in this unabashedly romantic and often harrowing novel. He has created an adolescent love that is believably endless. . . . Mr. Spencer has an acute grasp of character and situation. He gives us details that make these often tormented people uncommonly convincing." New York Times Book Review.

Spencer, Scott

Man in the woods / Scott Spencer. Ecco Press, 2010. 288 p.

ISBN 9780061466557

1. Murder 2. Guilt in men 3. Animal welfare 4. Carpenters 5. Women authors 6. Faith (Christianity) 7. Recovering alcoholics 8. New York (State) 9. Psychological fiction

Two characters from A Ship Made of Paper, Kate Ellis and her daughter, Ruby, meet a wandering adventurer and offer him stability if he is willing to forgo his deep convictions and make compromises to get along with others.

"A novel about what happens to a couple when the man, Paul Phillips, impulsively decides to stop a stranger from beating his dog. . . . Paul's partner, Kate Ellis, is successful, sober and blissfully happy in love, a hard-won trifecta. Her collection of essays, Prays Well With Others, chronicling her years as an alcoholic and wayward mother, has become a best seller; Kate's brand of honesty, humor and religion has found a wide audience. She and her young daughter Ruby (both characters from Spencer's novel, A Ship Made of Paper) are living with Paul, a carpenter. . . . After a stressful meeting with a Manhattan client one day, Paul stops off at a state park to clear his head before driving on to Kate's home in rural New York. He spots the man and the dog. One life-altering moment isn't new in fiction, of course, but Spencer makes it fresh, and compelling." Cleveland Plain Dealer.

Spencer-Fleming, Julia

All mortal flesh / Julia Spencer-Fleming. St. Martin's Minotaur, 2006. 320 p. Reverend Clare Fergusson mysteries

ISBN 0312312644

1. Episcopal Church. 2. Gossiping and gossips 3. Separation (Marital relations) 4. Innocence (Law) 5. Murder investigation 6. Betrayal 7. Extramarital affairs 8. Small town life -- Adirondack Mountains, New York 9. Clergywomen 10. Women amateur detectives 11. Adirondack Mountains, New York 12. Mysteries

Police Chief Russ Van Alstyne and Reverend Clare Fergusson have long fought their passion in deference to his marriage, but it's difficult keeping secrets in the small Adirondack town of Millers Kill. When his wife is found brutally murdered in their home, the state police think it's an open-and-shut-case of a disaffected husband, silencing first his wife, then the investigation he controls. But nothing is as it seems in Millers Kill, where betrayal twists old friendships and evil waits inside white-clapboard farmhouses. Russ and Clare struggle against the reach of the law, the authority of the church, and their own guilty hearts.

LIST OF FICTIONAL WORKS

"In a story as unpredictable as its characters, the resolution takes this series in a direction that should give the good bishop heart palpitations." New York Times Book Review.

Spencer-Fleming, Julia

Hid from our eyes / Julia Spencer-Fleming. Minotaur Books, 2020. 336 p. Reverend Clare Fergusson mysteries

ISBN 9780312606855

1. Clergywomen 2. Police chiefs 3. Women murder victims 4. Husband and wife 5. Copycat murderers 6. Cold cases (Criminal investigation) 7. Trans women 8. Alcoholic women 9. New parents 10. Infants 11. Small towns 12. Episcopalians 13. Murder investigation 14. Adirondack Mountains, New York 15. New York (State) 16. Mysteries

LC 2019049217

Police chief Russ van Alstyne races to solve a baffling murder that eerily resembles two unsolved killings from decades earlier for which he was the prime suspect.

"Spencer-Fleming combines a first-rate mystery with flawed but endearing characters." Publishers Weekly.

Spencer-Fleming, Julia

*** I** shall not want : a Clare Fergusson/ Russ Van Alstyne mystery / Thomas Dunne Books, 2008. 336 p. Reverend Clare Fergusson mysteries

ISBN 9780312334871

1. Migrant workers 2. Drug traffic 3. Separated couples 4. Serial murderers 5. Clergywomen 6. Women amateur detectives 7. Small town life -- Adirondack Mountains, New York 8. Adirondack Mountains, New York 9. Mysteries

LC 2008012281

Russ's balance between duty and desire was broken by his wife's tragic death. Now, Russ and Episcopal priest Clare Fergusson are separated by a wall of guilt and grief. When a Mexican farmhand stumbles over a Latino man killed with a single shot to the back of his head, Clare is drawn into the investigation. The discovery of two more bodies ignites fears that a serial killer is loose in the rural town and Russ is plagued by the media hysteria, conflict within the police department, and a series of baffling assaults. Throughout the escalating tensions, he and Clare find themselves seeking each other out even as they intend to keep distant.

Spencer-Fleming, Julia

In the bleak midwinter / Julia Spencer-Fleming. St. Martin's Minotaur, 2002. 308 p. Reverend Clare Fergusson mysteries

ISBN 9780312288471

1. Episcopal Church. 2. Abandoned infants 3. Police chiefs 4. Moving to a new city 5. Women murder victims 6. Clergywomen 7. Women amateur detectives 8. Small town life 9. Adirondack Mountains, New York 10. Mysteries

LC 2001051303

Agatha Award for Best First Novel, 2003.
Anthony Award for Best Novel, 2003.
Macavity Award for Best First Mystery Novel, 2003.

Trying to acclimate herself to her new parish and surroundings, Clare Fergusson, the first female priest of an Episcopal church in Millers Kill, New York, finds herself immersed in murder when a newborn baby is abandoned and a young mother is brutally slain, forcing her to dig deeply into the town's secrets, while fighting her attraction to the married police chief.

"[A] freshly conceived and meticulously plotted whodunit ..." New York Times Book Review.

Spencer-Fleming, Julia

Through the evil days : a Clare Fergusson/ Russ van Alstyne mystery / Minotaur Books, 2013. 320 p. Reverend Clare Fergusson mysteries

ISBN 9780312606848

1. Fires 2. Clergywomen 3. Police chiefs 4. Murder 5. Kidnapping 6. Pregnant women 7. Murder investigation 8. Missing persons 9. Episcopalians 10. Adirondack Mountains, New York 11. Mysteries

LC 2013025276

When a raging fire quickly becomes a double homicide and kidnapping, expectant parents Chief of Police Russ Van Alstyne and the Reverend Clare Fergusson must deal with personal and professional issues they never before encountered.

Spiegelman, Peter

Black maps / Peter Spiegelman. Alfred A. Knopf, 2003. 304 p. John March novels

ISBN 1400040752

1. Private investigators 2. Extortion 3. Capitalists and financiers 4. White collar crime 5. Financial intrigue 6. Millionaires 7. Former police 8. Recovering alcoholics 9. Missing persons 10. Lawyers 11. New York (State) 12. Manhattan, New York City 13. Mysteries 14. Hardboiled fiction 15. Financial thrillers

Shamus Award for Best First P.I. Novel, 2004.

Manhattan P.I. John March takes on the case of Rick Pierro, a successful banker, who is on the verge of losing everything to a blackmail attempt that threatens to engulf him in a money-laundering scheme under federal investigation.

Spillane, Mickey, 1918-2006

The **Consummata** / Mickey Spillane and Max Allan Collins. Hardcase Crime, 2011. 256 p.

ISBN 9780857682888

1. 1960s 2. Double agents 3. Stolen property recovery 4. Rescues 5. Criminals 6. Violence against women 7. Sadomasochism 8. Exiles 9. Cubans in the United States 10. Mistaken identity 11. Miami, Florida 12. Mysteries 13. Hardboiled fiction

In a tale completed from an unfinished Spillane outline, Morgan the Raider sets out to clear his name after he is accused of being the mastermind behind a forty million dollar heist and finds himself hiding out in the middle of Miami's Little Havana neighborhood.

"Spillane decided to introduce a new series featuring a master criminal called Morgan the Raider. The first entry, The Delta Factor, came out in '67. So far, so good. Then the business intervened in the form of Hollywood, which decided to make a movie out of the first Morgan book. But the experience left Spillane so upset that he stopped work on the already announced second installment. . . . Collins finishes this project seamlessly. It is impossible to tell where one great writer left off and another begins." BookReporter.com.

Spillane, Mickey, 1918-2006

The **Goliath** bone / Mickey Spillane ; with Max Allan Collins. Harcourt, 2008. 288 p. Mike Hammer mysteries

ISBN 9780151014545

1. Goliath, (Biblical giant) Relics 2. Relics 3. Terrorists 4. Right-wing extremists 5. Bones 6. Archaeological thefts 7. Thieves 8. Private investigators 9. New York City 10. Mysteries 11. Hardboiled fiction

LC 2008010091

"An Otto Penzler Book."

After preventing the violent robbery of two college sweethearts who stumbled onto a priceless archaeological find, P.I. Mike Hammer takes on Islamic terrorists and Israeli extremists out to seize the relic for their own purposes.

"Much of the jargon is vintage, as is the indomitable Hammer as he strives to protect the kids and prevent the Goliath bone from setting off the next big war. While not on a par with early Spillane classics, this is a fitting capstone to Hammer's career." Publishers Weekly.

Spillane, Mickey, 1918-2006

Kill me, darling / Mickey Spillane, Max Allan Collins. Titan Books, 2015. 296 p. Mike Hammer mysteries

ISBN 9781783291380

1. Private investigators 2. Organized crime 3. Automobile travel 4. Crimes against police 5. Murder 6. Murder investigation 7. Criminals 8. Long Island, New York 9. Miami, Florida 10. Hardboiled fiction 11. Mysteries

An inebriated Mike Hammer investigates the murder of an aging police officer who once worked with Mike Hammer's ex-partner Velda, who is reputed to be involved with a powerful Florida gangster.

Spillane, Mickey, 1918-2006

A **long** time dead : a Mike Hammer cas(ebk.) / Mickey Spillane, Max Allan Collins. Open Road Media, 2016. 250 p. Mike Hammer mysteries

ISBN 9781504036092

1. Private investigators 2. Crime 3. Criminal investigation 4. New York City 5. Hardboiled fiction 6. Mysteries

The first Mike Hammer short story collection from the twentieth-century bestselling American mystery writer Mickey Spillane.

"Collins has published several Hammer novels, completions of Spillanes original unfinished manuscripts, and, as with those novels, the writing here is so fluid, so very much in Spillanes voice, that its impossible to tell where the original writers words end and the coauthors begin. A must for anyone interested in the history of hard-boiled mysteries." Booklist.

Spufford, Francis, 1964-

* **Golden** hill / Francis Spufford. Simon & Schuster, 2017, c2016. 336 p.

ISBN 9781501163876

1. Colonial America (1600-1775) 2. 1740s 3. Misadventures 4. Escapes 5. Swindlers and swindling 6. Deception 7. New York City -- History -- Colonial period, 1600-1775 8. Historical fiction

Originally published: London : Faber, 2016.

Costa First Novel Award, 2016.

RSL Ondaatje Prize, 2017.

RUSA Reading List Short List, 2018.

Shortlisted for the Walter Scott Prize for Historical Fiction, 2017

When a mysterious man shows up at the countinghouse in 1746 New York with an order for a huge sum of money, the local colonial merchants can't decide if they should trust him, befriend him, arrest him or seduce him.

"Spuffords . . . spirited 'novel of Old New York,' playfully rendered in simulated eighteenth-century prose, pays homage to the literature of the colonial era." Booklist.

St. Aubyn, Edward, 1960-

At last / Edward St. Aubyn. Farrar, Straus and Giroux, 2012. 264 p. Patrick Melrose novels

ISBN 9780374298890

1. Mothers -- Death 2. Mother and adult son 3. Funerals 4. Dysfunctional families 5. Self-destructive behavior in men 6. Recovering alcholics 7. Family relationships 8. Family secrets 9. Inheritance and succession 10. Upper class 11. London, England 12.

Psychological fiction

LC 2011034964

First published: 2011.

Friends, relatives, and foes trickle in to pay final respects to Patrick's mother, Eleanor. An American heiress, Eleanor married into the British aristocracy, giving up the grandeur of her upbringing for "good works" freely bestowed on everyone but her own son, who finds himself questioning whether his transition to a life without parents will indeed be the liberation he had so long imagined.

St. James, Simone

The **broken** girls / Simone St. James. Berkley, 2018. 336 p.

ISBN 9780451476203

1. Boarding schools 2. Women journalists 3. Murder investigation 4. Sisters 5. Ghosts 6. Small towns 7. Missing girls 8. Child neglect 9. Boarding school students 10. Cold cases (Criminal investigation) 11. Vermont 12. Horror 13. Mysteries 14. Ghost stories 15. Parallel narratives

LC 2017004873

RUSA Reading List Short List, 2019.

More than 60 years after one of four friends in a reputedly haunted boarding school goes missing, journalist Fiona Sheridan resolves to learn her sister's fate before a harrowing discovery is made.

St. James, Simone

The **haunting** of Maddy Clare / Simone St. James. New American Library, 2012. 336 p.

ISBN 9780451235688

1. 1920s 2. Ghosts 3. Suicide victims 4. Revenge 5. Paranormal phenomenon investigation 6. Haunted places 7. Exorcism 8. Hallucinations and illusions 9. Obsession in women 10. England 11. Ghost stories 12. Historical fiction

LC 2011033391

Arthur Ellis Award for Best First Novel, 2013.

RITA Award for Best First Book, 2013.

RITA Award for Best Novel with Strong Romantic Elements, 2013.

In 1920s England, Sarah Piper is sent by her temporary agency to assist a ghost hunter, Alistair Gellis, as he investigates the spirit of Maddy Clare, a young serving maid said to haunt the barn where she committed suicide. The ghost is no hoax, and Sarah is soon caught up in trying to discover who Maddy was, where she came from, and why she is desperate for revenge.

St. James, Simone

The **Sun** Down motel / Simone St. James. Berkley, 2020. 336 p.

ISBN 9780440000174

1. Young women 2. Motels 3. Missing persons 4. Serial murders 5. Aunts 6. Crimes against women 7. Small towns 8. Haunted hotels 9. Paranormal phenomena 10. New York (State) 11. United States 12. Horror 13. Parallel narratives

LC 2019026692

A young woman takes a night-clerk job at the same roadside motel from where her aunt went missing decades earlier before uncovering the work of a serial killer.

"Booktalk this one to your mystery-loving readers until you run out of superlatives. What a story!" Booklist.

Stabenow, Dana

* A **deeper** sleep : a Kate Shugak novel / Dana Stabenow. St. Martin's Minotaur, 2007. 240 p. Kate Shugak mysteries
ISBN 0312343221

1. District attorneys 2. Women murder victims 3. Shooting 4. Former lawyers 5. Park rangers 6. Aleut women 7. Husband and wife 8. Mothers and sons 9. State police -- Alaska 10. Murder -- Alaska 11. Murder investigation -- Alaska 12. Trials (Murder) 13. Women private investigators 14. Alaska 15. Anchorage, Alaska 16. Mysteries 17. Pacific Northwest fiction

Previously published in Great Britain in 2013.

Anchorage private detective Kate Shugak and Alaska state trooper Jim Chopin pursue Louis Deem, a man arrested for and acquitted of the murder of his wife, after a witness to the shooting of a woman and her son places Deem at the scene of the crime.

"Private investigator Kate Shugak is determined to find the evidence to convict Louis Deem, who has been arrested and tried for several serious crimes but never convicted. When a double homicide occurs after his latest acquittal, Kate investigates. A witness places Deem at the scene, but Kate wants additional evidence to convince the jury. Deem is a dangerous character who intimidates witnesses, and Kate and her family won't be safe until he is in jail." Booklist.

Stabenow, Dana

* A **fine** and bitter snow : a Kate Shugak novel / Dana Stabenow. St. Martin's Minotaur, 2002. 211 p. Kate Shugak mysteries
ISBN 9780312205485

1. Oil well drilling 2. Park rangers 3. State police 4. Women private investigators 5. Former lawyers 6. Aleut women 7. Murder 8. Murder investigation 9. Alaska 10. Mysteries 11. Pacific Northwest fiction
LC 2002022863

Aleutian private detective Kate Shugak becomes caught up in a vicious battle between conservationists and developers of Alaska's pristine wilderness when an environmentalist protesting plans for drilling for oil in a nearby wildlife preserve is found poisoned.

"Rich with details about life in this snowbound culture, the story moves at a steady pace to a classic ending." Publishers Weekly.

Stabenow, Dana

* A **grave** denied / Dana Stabenow. St. Martin's Minotaur, 2003. 304 p. Kate Shugak mysteries
ISBN 0312306814

1. Guardian and ward 2. Arson 3. Glaciers 4. Former lawyers 5. Park rangers 6. Aleut women 7. Teenagers 8. Fourteen-year-old boys 9. State police 10. Repairers 11. Murder investigation 12. Revenge 13. Women private investigators 14. Alaska 15. Pacific Northwest fiction 16. Mysteries
LC 2003050605

When the body of a murdered town handyman is discovered, frozen and in the path of a receding glacier, Alaska state trooper Jim Chopin asks Kate Shugak to investigate the victim's background in the hope of finding the killer.

Stabenow, Dana

* **Hunter's** moon / Dana Stabenow. G. P. Putnam's Sons, 1999. 239 p. Kate Shugak mysteries
ISBN 0425172597

1. Big game hunters 2. Hunting 3. Wilderness areas 4. Park rangers 5. Aleut women 6. Big game hunting 7. Former lawyers 8. Women private investigators 9. Alaska 10. Mysteries 11. Pacific Northwest fiction
LC 98-33465

Kate Shugak and her boyfriend, Jack, lead a group of German tourists into the wilds of Alaska on a hunting trip, but the expedition begins to go horribly wrong when several of the hunters turn up dead, and Kate discovers that bears are not the only animals being hunted in the bush

Stabenow, Dana

Killing grounds : a Kate Shugak mystery / Dana Stabenow. G. Putnam's Sons, 1998. 273 p. Kate Shugak mysteries
ISBN 0399143564

1. Fisheries 2. Fishers 3. Undercover operations 4. Former lawyers 5. Park rangers 6. Aleut women 7. Women private investigators 8. Alaska 9. Mysteries 10. Pacific Northwest fiction
LC 97-23900

While deckhanding on board a salmon tender, Kate Shugak hauls up the body of a widely disliked fisherman whose apparent murder is greeted with great rejoicing. Drafted by State Trooper Jim Chopin to assist in the investigation, Kate draws up a long list of suspects. Meanwhile, Kate's Aleut aunties are mixed up in some shady dealings of their own, which Kate must prove do not include murder.

Stabenow, Dana

* **Less** than a treason / Dana Stabenow. Head of Zeus, 2017. 336 p. Kate Shugak mysteries
ISBN 9781786695697

1. Wolfdogs 2. Aleut women 3. Women private investigators 4. Aleuts 5. Survival 6. Gunshot victims 7. Wilderness areas 8. Women and dogs 9. Wilderness survival 10. Indians of North America 11. Alaska 12. Mysteries 13. Pacific Northwest fiction

Native Aleut private investigator Kate Shugak finds her and her trusty half-wolf, half-husky dog Mutt in trouble in the Alaskan wilds when they both wind up shot.

"The book is sprinkled with wit, studded with exquisite descriptions of the rugged landscape, and filled with opinionated and endearing characters, including reality TV show producers, park rangers, geologists, and barkeeps." Publishers Weekly.

Stabenow, Dana

* A **night** too dark : a Kate Shugak novel / Dana Stabenow. Minotaur Books, 2010. 336 p. Kate Shugak mysteries
ISBN 9780312559090

1. Murder investigation 2. Gold mines and mining 3. State parks -- Alaska 4. Murder 5. Park rangers 6. Aleut women 7. Women private investigators 8. Former lawyers 9. Alaska 10. Mysteries 11. Pacific Northwest fiction
LC 2009039815

When a man believed to have committed suicide reappears from the wilderness, Aleut private investigator Kate Shugak and Trooper Jim Chopin struggle to identify the remains of a mysterious victim, a case that is complicated by political factors at the local gold mine.

Stabenow, Dana

No fixed line / Dana Stabenow. Head of Zeus, 2020. 336 p. Kate Shugak mysteries
ISBN 9781788549110

1. Aleut women 2. Women private investigators 3. Wilderness areas 4. Blizzards 5. Airplane accidents 6. Wilderness survival 7. Former police 8. Winter 9. Indians of North America 10. Alaska 11. Mysteries 12. Pacific Northwest fiction

When a New Year's Eve blizzard blocks access to the site of a plane crash in the Quilak mountains, former trooper Jim Chopin struggles to rescue two child survivors, before Kate Shugak receives an unwelcome accusation from beyond the grave.

"Stabenow's affection for her characters, in particular Chopin, shines through, as does her fondness for the Alaskan country she knows so well. Fans will hope this series goes on forever." Publishers Weekly.

Stabenow, Dana

Restless in the grave / Dana Stabenow. Minotaur Books, 2012. 368 p. Kate Shugak mysteries

ISBN 9780312559137

1. Sabotage 2. Murder investigation 3. Undercover operations 4. State police 5. Conspiracies 6. Family secrets 7. Entrepreneurs 8. Former lawyers 9. Park rangers 10. Aleut women 11. Women private investigators 12. Alaska 13. Mysteries 14. Pacific Northwest fiction

LC 2011037662

Aleut private investigator Kate Shugak and Alaska State Trooper Liam Campbell--the heroes of "New York Times" bestseller Stabenow's most beloved series--team up for the first time ever when Liam needs Kate's help to clear his wife of the murder of a wealthy aviation entrepreneur.

Stabenow, Dana

The **singing** of the dead / Dana Stabenow. St. Martin's Minotaur Books, 2000. 272 p. Kate Shugak mysteries

ISBN 0312209576

1. Women politicians 2. Senatorial candidates 3. Park rangers 4. Aleut women 5. Former lawyers 6. Men/women relations 7. Women private investigators 8. Alaska 9. Mysteries 10. Pacific Northwest fiction

Kate Shugak joins the staff of a Native woman running for the Alaska State Senate to work security. The candidate has been receiving anonymous threats and Kate's job will be to shadow the candidate. The campaign is rocked when a staff researcher is murdered and it appears linked to a ninety-year-old unsolved murder.

"With well-drawn characters, splendid scenery and an insider's knowledge of Alaskan history and politics, this fine novel ranks as one of Stabenow's best." Publishers Weekly.

Stabenow, Dana

So sure of death : a Liam Campbell mystery / Dana Stabenow. Dutton, 1999. 275 p. Liam Campbell mysteries

ISBN 9780525945192

1. Excavations (Archaeology) 2. Fishing villages 3. State police 4. Murder investigation 5. Men/women relations 6. Father and adult son 7. Alaska 8. Mysteries 9. Pacific Northwest fiction

LC 99025121

When the brutally murdered bodies of a local family are found adrift at sea, Alaska State Trooper Liam Campbell suddenly is drawn into a nasty homicide case involving forbidden romance, family scandal, tribal taboos, and adultery.

Stabenow, Dana

* A **taint** in the blood / Dana Stabenow. St. Martin's Minotaur, 2004. 305 p. Kate Shugak mysteries

ISBN 9780312306830

1. Women with cancer 2. Families of murder victims 3. Arson investigation 4. State police -- Alaska 5. Former lawyers 6. Park rangers 7. Aleut women 8. Frameups 9. Sexuality 10. Men/women relations 11. Women private investigators 12. Alaska 13. Anchorage, Alaska 14. Pacific Northwest fiction 15. Mysteries

LC 2004046856

Hired by Charlotte Mauravieff, who wants to clear her mother's name of the arson fire that killed one of her brothers, private investiga-

tor Kate Shugak finds the case complicated by someone who wants the truth to stay hidden.

Stabenow, Dana

Though not dead : a Kate Shugak novel / Dana Stabenow. Minotaur Books, 2011. 480 p. Kate Shugak mysteries

ISBN 9780312559113

1. Wills 2. Family secrets 3. Fathers and sons 4. Material culture 5. Attempted murder 6. Gold mines and mining 7. Park rangers 8. Aleut women 9. Women private investigators 10. Former lawyers 11. Alaska 12. Mysteries 13. Pacific Northwest fiction

LC 2010039080

"First published in the UK in 2013 by Head of Zues, Ltd."--Title page verso.

Inheriting a homestead from her late uncle, a stunned Kate Shugak receives a cryptic letter from him imploring her to discover his father's fate, a mystery involving a priceless tribal artifact for which Kate is targeted by murderous attacks.

Stabenow, Dana

Whisper to the blood : a Kate Shugak novel / Dana Stabenow. Minotaur Books, 2009. 368 p. Kate Shugak mysteries

ISBN 9780312369743

1. Foster family 2. Mines and mineral resources 3. Robbery 4. Park rangers 5. Aleut women 6. Wilderness areas 7. Widows 8. Former lawyers 9. Women private investigators 10. Murder investigation 11. Alaska 12. Mysteries 13. Pacific Northwest fiction

LC 2008033959

The inhabitants of Niniltna are uneasy about the gold-mining company buying up tracts of land nearby, an unease shared by P.I. Kate Shugak as she probes the killings of a mine opponent and a popular ski champion-turned-company spokesperson.

"A dynamite combination of atmosphere, action, and character." Booklist.

Stachniak, Eva, 1952-

The **chosen** maiden: a novel / Eva Stachniak Doubleday Canada, 2017 432 p.

ISBN 9780385678568

1. Russian Revolution and Civil War (1917-1921) 2. Between the Wars (1918-1939) 3. Ballet dancers 4. Sibling rivalry 5. Brothers and sisters 6. Determination (Personal quality) 7. Kiev, Ukraine 8. St Petersburg, Russia 9. London, England 10. Paris, France 11. Historical fiction

Born on the road to dancer parents, the Nijinsky children seem destined for the stage. Vaslav is an early prodigy, and through single-minded pursuit will grow into arguably the greatest--and most infamous--Russian ballet dancer of the 20th century. His talented younger sister Bronia, however, also longs to dance. Overshadowed by Vaslav, plagued by a body deemed less than ideal and struggling against the constraints of her gender, Bronia will have to work triply hard to prove herself worthy.

"A memorable literary rendering of a remarkable womans life." Booklist.

Stachniak, Eva, 1952-

The **Winter** Palace : a novel of Catherine the Great / Eva Stachniak. Bantam Books, 2012. 384 p.

ISBN 9780553808124

1. Catherine II,, Empress of Russia, 1729-1796 2. Romanov Dynasty (1613-1917) 3. 18th century 4. Women rulers 5. Courts and courtiers 6. Heirs and heiresses 7. Arranged marriage 8. Household employees 9. Women spies 10. Germans in Russia 11. Loyalty 12. Betrayal 13. Deception 14. Extramarital affairs 15. Housekeepers 16. Russia

-- History -- Catherine II, 1762-1796 17. Historical fiction 18. Biographical fiction

A reimagining of the early years of Catherine the Great traces the story of two young women: Barbara, a servant who will become one of Russia's most cunning royal spies, and Sophia, a pretty, naive German duchess who will become Catherine the Great.

Stage, Zoje

* **Baby** teeth : a novel / Zoje Stage. St. Martin's Press, 2018. 304 p.

ISBN 9781250170750

1. People who are mute 2. Mothers and daughters 3. Manipulation (Social sciences) 4. Motherhood -- Psychological aspects 5. Seven-year-old girls 6. Violence in children 7. Psychopaths 8. Parenting 9. Psychological suspense

LC 2017056740

An ailing woman fights to protect her family from her mute daughter's psychologically manipulative schemes, which are complicated by her doting husband's denial about their daughter's true nature.

Stanley, Michael

A **carrion** death / Michael Stanley. Harper Collins, 2008. 480 p. Detective Kubu mysteries

ISBN 0061252409

1. Detectives 2. Murder investigation 3. Corruption investigation 4. Overweight men 5. Diamond mines and mining 6. Dead 7. Murder 8. Crime 9. Politicians 10. Botswana 11. Africa 12. Mysteries

Michael Sears and Stanley Trollip writing under the pseudonym, Michael Stanley.

In the aftermath of the murder of an anonymous victim, assistant superintendent David Bengu begins his career in Botswana, where his convivial passions and determined methods earn him a local nickname that likens him to a hippopotamus.

"Readers may be lured to Africa by the landscape, but it takes a great character like Kubu to win our loyalty." New York Times Book Review.

Stanley, Michael

Deadly harvest / Michael Stanley. Bourbon Street Books, 2013. xiv, 477 p. Detective Kubu mysteries

ISBN 9780062221520

1. Detectives 2. Serial murder investigation 3. Missing persons 4. Missing persons investigation 5. Politicians 6. Serial murders 7. Botswana 8. Africa 9. Mysteries

Detecive Kubu searches for a possible serial killer targeting girls in Botswana in order to use their bodies in muti, a witch doctor's potion that can be made more potent with the addition of human remains.

"The real-life phenomenon of African witch doctors committing murder to get ingredients for their spells drives the richly atmospheric fourth Detective Kubu mystery (after 2011's Death of the Mantis) ... Their investigation takes place during a time of political instability in the country when the prospect that an opposition party could finally be gaining traction spawns violence. The gritty depiction of corruption and obsession serves as a striking counterpoint to Alexander McCall Smith's blood-free No. 1 Ladies' Detective Agency series, also set in Botswana." Publishers Weekly.

Stanley, Michael

* A **death** in the family / Michael Stanley. Minotaur Books, 2015. 304 p. Detective Kubu mysteries

ISBN 9781250070890

1. Mineral industry and trade 2. Public officials 3. Corruption 4. Murder investigation 5. Detectives 6. Botswana 7. Africa 8. Mysteries

Just as Detective Kubu, against orders, begins to inspect the murder of his father in modern-day Africa, a senior official at the Department of Mines is found dead amid a Chinese-owned company's effort to take over part of a village.

Stanley, Michael

Death of the mantis / Michael Stanley. Harper Paperbacks, 2011. 448 p. Detective Kubu mysteries

ISBN 9780062000378

1. Murder investigation 2. Innocence (Law) 3. Detectives 4. Police 5. New fathers 6. Game parks and ranches 7. San (African people) 8. Botswana 9. Africa 10. Kalahari Desert 11. Mysteries

LC 2011022154

Michael Sears and Stanley Trollip writing under the pseudonym, Michael Stanley.

In the southern Kalahari area of Botswana, three Bushmen are found standing around a ranger who is dying from a severe head wound in a dry ravine and Dectective David "Kubu" Bengu must figure out, with the help of an old school friend, if the Bushmen were there to help -- or were the murderers.

Stanley, Michael

Dying to live / Michael Stanley. Minotaur Books, 2017. 324 p. Detective Kubu mysteries

ISBN 9781250070906

1. Detectives 2. Indigenous peoples 3. Senior murder victims 4. Murder investigation 5. San (African people) 6. Dead 7. Shamans 8. Botswana 9. Africa 10. Minnesota 11. Mysteries

LC 2017024858

A Bushman is discovered dead near the Central Kalahari Game Reserve in Africa. Although the man looks old enough to have died of natural causes, the police suspect foul play. Pathologist Ian MacGregor confirms the cause of death as a broken neck, and calls in Assistant Superintendent David "Kubu" Bengu. When the Bushman's corpse is stolen from the morgue, suddenly the case takes on a new dimension.

Stansel, Ian

The **last** cowboys of San Geronimo / Ian Stansel. Houghton Mifflin Harcourt, 2017. 186 p.

ISBN 9780544963399

1. Fratricide 2. Brothers 3. Widows 4. Horse trainers 5. Sibling rivalry 6. Revenge 7. California 8. Modern Westerns 9. Crime fiction

LC 2016047296

A justice-fueled race across the wilds of Northern California reveals the hardscrabble youth and fateful experiences of a preeminent horse trainer who has been murdered by his jealous brother.

Staples, Dennis E.

This town sleeps / Dennis E. Staples. Counterpoint, 2020. 224 p.

ISBN 9781640092846

1. Gay men 2. Ojibwa Indians 3. Prejudice 4. Small town life 5. Urban legends 6. Secrets 7. Closeted gay men 8. Native American men 9. Murder investigation 10. Ghosts 11. Family history 12. Indian reservations 13. Men/men relations 14. Minnesota 15. Mysteries 16. Literary fiction 17. LGBTQIA fiction

Engaging in a secret affair with a closeted white man, an Ojibwe from a northern Minnesota reservation navigates small-town discrimination before a ghost leads him to the grave of a basketball star whose murder becomes linked to a local legend.

"With its multiple narrators and stories of ghosts, this debut will find its audience in those searching for #ownvoices authors with an authentic view of reservation life and the tragedies that haunt the communities." Library Journal.

Stapley, Marissa

The **last** resort / Marissa Stapley. Graydon House, 2019. 384 p.

ISBN 9781525823541

1. Married people 2. Marital conflict 3. Marriage counseling 4. Resorts 5. Hurricanes 6. Secrets 7. Celebrities 8. Husband and wife 9. Men/women relations 10. Mexico 11. Psychological suspense

When two couples head to an intensive marriage therapy program at the Harmony Resort, it soon becomes clear that the getaway is not what it seems, and neither are its celebrity owners.

Stark, Richard, 1933-2008

Ask the parrot : a Parker novel / Richard Stark. Mysterious Press, 2006. 279 p. Parker thrillers

ISBN 9780892960682

1. Bank robberies 2. Criminals 3. Race tracks 4. Former convicts 5. Thieves 6. Thieves 7. Police 8. Escapes 9. Conspiracies 10. Deception 11. Money laundering 12. Crime fiction

LC 2006927625

Racing through the backwoods of Massachusetts and on the verge of being taken down for one of the biggest and most disastrous bank heists the state has ever seen, Parker runs right into the barrel of a gun pointed from the wrong side of the law. A quiet and angry recluse with only a silent parrot for company in his seclusion, Tom Lindahl saves Parker from the police dogs, but enmeshes him in yet another in a long line of dubious, highly dangerous, but seriously profitable jobs. Far more than some aimless indigent, holed up in a shack in the woods, Lindahl is a man built on rage and driven by a thirst for revenge. A whistleblower whom nobody heard, a man tossed aside by a corrupt political establishment, Lindahl plans to rob them of their lucre and needs Parker's help.

Stark, Richard, 1933-2008

Breakout / Richard Stark. Mysterious Press, 2002. 299 p., 20 cm. Parker thrillers

ISBN 089296779X

1. Criminals 2. Escapes 3. Robbery 4. Thieves 5. Crime fiction

LC 2002023492

"Richard Stark (the name that Donald E. Westlake uses when he lets Parker off the leash) writes with ruthless efficiency. His bad guys are polished pros who think hard, move fast and turn on a dime in moments of crisis. And because talk doesn't come cheap, every bit of dialogue counts." New York Times Book Review.

Stark, Richard, 1933-2008

Comeback / Richard Stark. Mysterious Press, 1997. 292 p. Parker thrillers

ISBN 0892966610

1. Thieves 2. Robbery 3. Betrayal 4. Evangelists 5. Revivals 6. Crime fiction

LC 977019

The robbery of a Christian crusade comes off without a hitch, but it seems that the evangelist, the cops, the criminals, and the church's security officer are all after the loot, in a dark world where no one can be trusted

Stark, Richard, 1933-2008

Dirty money / Richard Stark. Grand Central Pub., 2008. 276 p. Parker thrillers

ISBN 9780446178587

1. Bank robberies 2. Criminals 3. Deception 4. Churches 5. Noir fiction 6. Crime fiction

LC 2007931314

Master criminal Parker takes another turn for the worse as he tries to recover loot from a heist gone terribly wrong. Parker and two cohorts stole the assets of a bank in transit, but the police heat was so great they could only escape if they left the money behind. Now Parker and his associates plot to reclaim the loot, which they hid in the choir loft of an unused country church. As they implement the plan, people on both sides of the law use the forces at their command to stop Parker and grab the goods for themselves. Though Parker's new getaway van is an old Ford Econoline with "Holy Redeemer Choir" on its doors, his gang is anything but holy, and Parker will do whatever it takes to redeem his prize, no matter who gets hurt in the process.

Stark, Richard, 1933-2008

The **hunter** : a Parker novel / Richard Stark. University of Chicago Press, 2008, 199 p. Parker thrillers

ISBN 9780226770994

1. Thieves 2. Revenge 3. Criminals 4. New York City 5. Crime fiction

Title of later film version: Point blank.

Parker, a professional thief, comes to New York City seeking revenge on a woman who betrayed him and a man who stole his money.

Stark, Richard, 1933-2008

The **jugger** : a Parker novel / Richard Stark. University of Chicago Press, 2009, c1965. x, 211 p. Parker thrillers

ISBN 9780226771021

1. Criminals 2. Inheritance and succession 3. Murder 4. Nebraska 5. Crime fiction

Originally published: New York :

Parker is in Sagamore, Nebraska, at the request of Joe Sheer, a retired safe cracker who carries many of Parker's criminal secrets.

Starling, Caitlin

The **luminous** dead / Caitlin Starling. Harper Voyager, 2019. 352 p.

ISBN 9780062846907

1. Spelunkers 2. Planets 3. Caves 4. Exploration 5. Caving 6. Women employees 7. Manipulation (Social sciences) 8. Deception in women 9. Life on other planets 10. Light and darkness 11. Near future 12. Science fiction

When Gyre Price lied her way into this expedition, she thought she'd be mapping mineral deposits, and that her biggest problems would be cave collapses and gear malfunctions. She also thought that the fat paycheck -- enough to get her off-planet and on the trail of her mother- -meant she'd get a skilled surface team, monitoring her suit and environment, keeping her safe. Instead, she got Em.

"Starling's riveting near-future debut depicts an intense psychological battle of wills between two damaged, deeply flawed women who forge an unbreakable connection in the dark." Publishers Weekly.

Starnone, Domenico, 1943-

Ties / Domenico Starnone, Jhumpa Lahiri. Europa Editions, 2017, c2014. 144 p.

ISBN 9781609453855

1. Abandoned wives 2. Marital conflict 3. Marriage 4. Cheating

(Interpersonal relations) 5. Forgiveness 6. Second chances 7. Men/women relations 8. Naples, Italy 9. Italy 10. Domestic fiction 11. Translations -- Italian to English

Originally published: Torino : Einaudi, 2014

When her husband, who left her for a younger woman, returns home for the sake of the children, a woman, forced to carry on as if nothing ever came between them, wonders if she has the strength to overcome the betrayal or the courage to start over.

"A slim, stunning meditation on marriage, fidelity, honesty, and truth." Kirkus.

Starnone, Domenico, 1943-

Trick / Domenico Starnone, translated from the Italian by Jhumpa Lahiri. Europa Editions, 2018, c2016. 191 p.

ISBN 9781609454449

1. Grandfather and grandson 2. Four-year-old boys 3. Solitude 4. Babysitting 5. Interpersonal relations 6. Illustrators 7. Naples, Italy 8. Translations -- Italian to English

Originally published: Torino : Giulio Einaudi, 2016

A grandfather, used to living in solitude and obsessively focusing on his illustrating career, and his 4-year-old grandson match wits during a 72-hour babysitting stay in Naples.

Starr, Jason, 1966-

Lights out / Jason Starr. Vintage Books, 2006. 240 p.
ISBN 1400075076

1. Baseball players 2. Rich men 3. Poor men 4. House painters 5. Homecomings 6. Celebrities 7. Engaged persons 8. Love triangles 9. Men/women relations 10. Secrets 11. Scandals 12. Women -- Decision-making 13. Baseball 14. Competition in men 15. Brooklyn, New York City 16. Canarsie, New York City 17. Noir fiction

LC 2005043481

"[This novel] sizzles with streetwise dialog and furious emotional energy." Library Journal.

Starr, Melvin R.

* **Unhallowed** ground / Mel Starr. Monarch, 2012. 240 p. Chronicle of Hugh de Singleton, surgeon

ISBN 9780857210586

1. Medieval period (476-1492) 2. Plantagenet period (1154-1485) 3. 14th century 4. Surgeons 5. Murder investigation 6. Suicide investigation 7. Amateur detectives 8. Oxfordshire, England -- History -- 14th century 9. England -- History -- 14th century 10. Great Britain -- History -- 14th century 11. Medieval mysteries 12. Historical mysteries 13. Mysteries

While renovating her house, Sarah McKinley finds the remains of dozens of bodies that are linked to current missing-persons cases as well as a long-ago murder, which points toward a killer who has the ability to transcend time.

Stead, Christina, 1902-1983

* The **man** who loved children / Christina Stead ; introduction by Randall Jarrell. Picador USA, 2001, c1940. xli, 527 p.

ISBN 9780312280444

1. Father and child 2. Marriage -- Psychological aspects 3. Married women -- Psychology 4. Idealism in men 5. Contempt 6. Marital conflict 7. Washington, D.C. 8. Domestic fiction

Originally published: New York : Simon and Schuster, 1940.

Introduction by Michael Schmidt.

Originally published: New York : Simon and Schuster, 1940.

After ten years of marriage, Sam and Henny Pollit find themselves with too many children, insufficient money, and an abundant loathing for each other.

Steadman, Catherine

Mr. Nobody : a novel / Catherine Steadman. Ballantine Books, 2020. 320 p.

ISBN 9781524797683

1. Men with amnesia 2. Women psychiatrists 3. Physician and patient 4. Secrets 5. New identities 6. Memories 7. Small towns 8. Rural life 9. England 10. Psychological suspense

LC 2019035576

Treating a man found on the beach with no memory of his identity, a neuropsychologist who would hide her own past is confronted by her patient's mysterious knowledge of her secrets.

"Steadman (Something in the Water) strikes an engaging balance between character development and action in this satisfying, intricately plotted thriller that will appeal to fans of Sarah Pinborough and Ruth Ware." Library Journal.

Steadman, Catherine

Something in the water / Catherine Steadman. Ballantine Books, 2018. 352 p.

ISBN 9781524797188

1. Married people 2. Honeymoons 3. Scuba diving 4. Options, alternatives, choices 5. Greed 6. Bora-Bora (French Polynesia) 7. Psychological suspense

LC 2018005086

Erin is a documentary filmmaker on the brink of a professional breakthrough, Mark a handsome investment banker with big plans. Passionately in love, they embark on a dream honeymoon to the tropical island of Bora Bora, where they enjoy the sun, the sand, and each other. Then, while scuba diving in the crystal blue sea, they find something in the water. . . .

Stedman, M. L.

* The **light** between oceans : a novel / M.L. Stedman. Scribner, 2012. 345 p.

ISBN 9781451681734

1. Social isolation 2. Loss (Psychology) 3. Grief in women 4. Lighthouse keepers 5. Lighthouses 6. Island life 7. Orphans 8. Birthmothers 9. Childlessness 10. Australia 11. Literary fiction 12. Historical fiction 13. Domestic fiction

Originally published: North Sydney, N.S.W. : Vintage Australia, 2012.

Australian Book Industry Awards, Book of the Year, 2013.

Australian Book Industry Awards, Literary Fiction Book of the Year, 2013.

Australian Book Industry Awards, Newcomer of the Year, 2013.

Goodreads Choice Award, 2012.

Nielsen BookData Australian Booksellers? Choice Award, 2013.

After moving with his wife to an isolated Australian lighthouse where they suffer miscarriages and a stillbirth, Tom allows his wife to claim an infant that has washed up on the shore, a decision with devastating consequences.

Steel, Danielle

First sight / Danielle Steel. Delacorte Press, 2013. 384 p.
ISBN 9780385338301

1. Clothing industry and trade 2. Fashion 3. Women executives 4. Physicians 5. Married men 6. Extramarital affairs 7. Divorced women 8. Contemporary romances

LC 2006042666

Running a successful fashion empire in Paris and New York that hides the pain of a failed marriage, Timmie O endures a sequence of meaningless relationships before a surprise bout of appendicitis places her under the care of alluring but married French doctor, Jean-Charles Vernier.

Steele, Allen M.

Coyote : a novel of interstellar exploration / Allen M. Steele. Ace Books, 2002. 390 p. Coyote novels

ISBN 0441009743

1. 21st century 2. Space colonies 3. Dissenters 4. Time travel 5. Life on other planets 6. Space flight 7. Space vehicles 8. Space exploration 9. Space opera 10. Science fiction 11. Political fiction

LC 2002074517

Sequel: Coyote Rising: A Novel of Interstellar Revolution.

Coyote marks a dramatic new turn in the career of Allen Steele, Hugo Award-winning author of Chronospace. Epic in scope, passionate in its conviction, and set against a backdrop of plausible events, it tells the brilliant story of Earth's first interstellar colonists--and the mysterious planet that becomes their home.

"A much-foreshadowed 'surprise' ending is by far the least of the surprises in Steele's bag of tricks. But each page of this novel bears evidence of fresh thought about the opportunities inherent in science fiction to take the familiar and make it new." New York Times Book Review.

Stegner, Wallace, 1909-1993

* **Angle** of repose / Wallace Stegner. Penguin Books, 1992, c1971. 569 p.

ISBN 9780140169300

1. Grandsons 2. Grandmothers 3. Marital conflict 4. Extramarital affairs 5. The West (United States) 6. California 7. Family sagas 8. Literary fiction 9. Modern classics

LC 72144301

Originally published: Garden City, N.Y. : Doubleday, 1971.

Pulitzer Prize for Fiction, 1972.

Traces the fortunes of four generations of one family as they attempt to build a life for themselves in the American West

"This novel is set mainly in the West in the late 1800's; but the central characters cannot be confined to the West nor to the 19th Century. They have a healing effect on the narrator, their grandson and biographer. . . . The beautiful, talented, charming Susan and her inarticulate engineer husband Oliver Ward rough it in mining camps and desolate, unfinished irrigation project camps. Their lives are hard and their marriage is strained past redemption. Yet their suffering and their strength do redeem." Library Journal.

Stegner, Wallace, 1909-1993

* The **Big** Rock Candy Mountain / Wallace Stegner. Penguin Books, 1995, c1943. 563 p.

ISBN 9780140139396

1. Violence in men 2. Poor families 3. Liquor smuggling 4. Family relationships 5. Ruthlessness in men 6. Fathers and sons 7. The West (United States) 8. Northwestern States -- History -- 1848-1950 9. Autobiographical fiction 10. Domestic fiction

Sequel: Recapitulation

"First published in 1943."

"A well-written study of the footloose family. . . . The life of the household is a misery of continual cruelty and often crushing poverty, alternating with occasional scenes of simple family happiness which stand out beautifully and unforgettably." The New Yorker.

Stegner, Wallace, 1909-1993

Crossing to safety / Wallace Stegner ; introduction by Terry Tempest Williams ; afterword by T.H. Watkins. Modern Library, 2002, c1987. xviii, 335 p.

ISBN 037575931X

1. Universities and colleges 2. Married people 3. Friendship 4. Women with poliomyelitis 5. Couples 6. Memories 7. Best friends 8. Authors 9. Vermont 10. Domestic fiction 11. Literary fiction

LC 2001057942

Originally published: New York : Random House, 1987.

National Book Critics Circle Award for Fiction finalist, 1987

Two young couples, Sid and Charity and Larry and Sally, from different backgrounds--East and West, rich and poor--befriend each other in 1937 Madison, Wisconsin.

Stein, Garth

The **art** of racing in the rain : a novel / Garth Stein. Harper Collins, 2008. 336 p..

ISBN 0061537934

1. Dogs 2. Humans and dogs 3. Automobile racing drivers 4. Automobile racing 5. Wishing and wishes 6. Persistence 7. Philosophy 8. Washington (State) 9. Literary fiction 10. Stories told by animals 11. Pacific Northwest fiction

LC 2007033890

First published: 2008.

Movie version to be released August 2019.

Enzo knows he is different from other dogs: a philosopher with a nearly human soul (and an obsession with opposable thumbs), he has educated himself by watching television and by listening closely to the words of his master, Denny Swift, an up-and-coming race car driver. On the night before his death, Enzo takes stock of his life, recalling all that he and his family have been through, hoping, in his next life, to return as a human.

"Enzo narrates his life story, beginning with his impending death. Enzo's not afraid of dying, as he's seen a television documentary on the Mongolian belief that a good dog will reincarnate as a man. Yes, Enzo is a dog. And he belongs to Denny: husband, father, customer service technician. Denny's dream is to be a professional race-car driver, and Enzo recounts the triumphs and tragedies-medical, financial, and legal-they share in this quest, the dangers of the racetrack being the least of their obstacles. . . . [Stein] creates a patient, wise, and doggish narrator that is more than just fluff and collar." Library Journal.

Stein, Gertrude, 1874-1946

* **Three** lives Vintage Books, 1936, c1909. 279 p.

ISBN 9780394701530

1. Women 2. Short stories

First published : 1909.

A kindly housekeeper, a German servant, and a young black girl seek happiness within the strict confines of their lives

Steinbeck, John, 1902-1968

Cannery Row / John Steinbeck. Penguin Books, 1994, c1945. xxx, 185 p.

ISBN 9780140187373

1. Community life -- Monterey, California 2. Loneliness 3. Homeless persons 4. Misfits (Persons) 5. Marine biologists -- Monterey, California 6. Coastal towns 7. Fishing villages 8. Working class 9. Friendship 10. California 11. Monterey, California 12. Cannery Row (Monterey, Calif) 13. Literary fiction 14. Modern classics

LC 93-11713

Sequel : Sweet Thursday.

Vividly depicts the colorful, sometimes disreputable, inhabitants of a run-down area in Monterey, California.

Steinbeck, John, 1902-1968
  * **East** of Eden / John Steinbeck. Viking, 1986, c1952. 778 p.
    ISBN 9780670287383
    1. Good and evil 2. Brothers 3. Sibling rivalry 4. Fathers and sons -- Salinas Valley, California 5. World War I 6. Children of prostitutes 7. Twins 8. California 9. Salinas Valley, California 10. Modern classics 11. Family sagas 12. Literary fiction
                LC 86001526
    Originally published: New York : Viking Press, 1952.
    California's fertile Salinas Valley is home to two families whose destinies are fruitfully, and fatally, intertwined. Over generations, between the beginning of the twentieth century and the end of the First World War, the Trasks and the Hamiltons will helplessly replay the fall of Adam and Eve and the murderous rivalry of Cain and Abel.
    "The saga of more than half a century in the lives of two American families: the Trasks, a mixture of gentleness and brutality doled out in unequal measure and the Hamiltons, Steinbeck's own forebears, a well adjusted, lovable group who provide a tranquil background for the turbulent careers of the Trasks. The scene is chiefly Salinas, California from the turn of the century through the first World War, and thanks to a great wealth of fascinating detail woven through the plot, we are given a complete and unforgettable picture of country and small town life during the period." Library Journal.

Steinbeck, John, 1902-1968
  * The **grapes** of wrath / John Steinbeck. Penguin Books, 2002, c1939. 455 p.
    ISBN 0142000663
    1. Rural families -- Oklahoma 2. Depressions 3. Migrant agricultural laborers 4. Poor people -- California 5. Labor camps -- California 6. Working class 7. Dust Bowl (South Central United States) 8. California 9. Oklahoma 10. Domestic fiction 11. Modern classics 12. Literary fiction
                LC 2001056103
    Originally published: New York : Viking, 1939.
    Pulitzer Prize for Fiction, 1940.
    Depicts the hardships and suffering endured by the Joads as they journey from Oklahoma to California during the Depression.

Steinbeck, John, 1902-1968
  The **long** valley / John Steinbeck ; with an introduction and notes by John H. Timmerman. Penguin Books, 1995, c1938. 233 p.
    ISBN 0140187456
    1. Growing up 2. Interpersonal relations 3. Aging 4. Salinas Valley, California 5. Short stories 6. Literary fiction 7. Modern classics
    15 short stories.
    Includes the O. Henry Prize winning story "The murder ... and the classic tales of The red pony."
    First published in 1938.
    Presents a collection of short stories, including "The Murder," "The Chrysanthemums," "Flight," and "The Red Pony."

Steinbeck, John, 1902-1968
  * **Of** mice and men / John Steinbeck. Penguin Books, 1994, xxviii, 105 p.
    ISBN 0140186425
    1. Men with developmental disabilities 2. Migrant workers -- California 3. Ranch life -- California 4. People with developmental disabilities -- California 5. Male friendship 6. Agricultural laborers 7. California 8. Salinas River Valley (Calif) 9. Psychological fiction 10. Literary fiction 11. Modern classics
                LC 93011712
    Originally published: New York .: Covici, Friede, 1937.
    The tragic story of two itinerant ranch hands on the run--one is the lifelong companion to the other, a developmentally disabled man.

Steinbeck, John, 1902-1968
  The **pearl** / John Steinbeck. Penguin Books, 2002, c1945. 87 p.
    ISBN 0142000698
    1. Husband and wife -- Mexico 2. Poor people -- Mexico 3. Greed 4. Fishers -- Mexico 5. Pearls 6. Pearl divers 7. Mexico 8. Literary fiction 9. Modern classics
                LC 2001056113
    "Originally published in Woman's home companion as 'The pearl of the world'"--T.p. verso.
    Originally published in book form: New York : Viking Press, 1947.
    A poor fisherman dreams of wealth and happiness for his family when he finds a priceless pearl.

Steinbeck, John, 1902-1968
  Tortilla Flat / John Steinbeck. Penguin Books, 1986, c1935. 207 p.
    ISBN 9780140042405
    1. 1930s 2. Gangs -- Monterey, California 3. Poor people 4. Loyalty 5. Misadventures 6. Rogues 7. Mexican American women -- Monterey, California 8. California 9. Monterey, California 10. Literary fiction 11. Modern classics
    In the shabby district called Tortilla Flat above Monterey, California lives a gang whose exploits compare to those of King Arthur's knights.

Steiner, Susie, 1971-
  Missing, presumed : a novel / Susie Steiner. Random House, 2016 350 p. DS Manon
    ISBN 9780812998320
    1. Women detectives 2. Missing persons investigation 3. Women college students 4. Missing persons 5. Online dating 6. England 7. Mysteries
                LC 2015037112
    Assigned to the high-profile case of a missing graduate student, brilliant detective and lonelyheart Manon Bradshaw uncovers the abductee's erratic behavior, a close friend's secrets and the role of a sex offender while struggling to maintain a professional distance.

Steiner, Susie, 1971-
  * **Persons** unknown : a novel / Susie Steiner. Random House, 2017. 272 p. DS Manon
    ISBN 9780812998344
    1. Women detectives 2. Pregnant women 3. Cold cases (Criminal investigation) 4. Murder 5. Murder investigation 6. Detectives 7. England 8. Mysteries
                LC 2016057332
    Sequel to: Missing, Presumed
    Having left the Met police for Cambridgeshire in order to give her adopted 12-year-old son a new start, detective Manon Bradshaw finds things aren't going as planned. Her black son is being bullied, she's single and pregnant, and most troubling, someone close to her family has been murdered and the police think her son may be involved. The case pits her against colleagues, but Manon will do whatever she can to find the real killer and prove her son's innocence. Told from multiple points of view, this thought-provoking 2nd book to feature Manon (after Miss-

ing, Presumed) slowly builds momentum and addresses timely topics. -- Description by Dawn Towery

"With its multiple viewpoints, this follow-up to the acclaimed Missing Presumed is another engrossing stunner, incorporating social justice issues into the narrative along with superb plotting, dark humor, and excellent characterizations." Library Journal.

Steinhauer, Olen

* **All** the old knives / Olen Steinhauer. Minotaur Books, 2015. viii, 294 p.

ISBN 9781250045423

1. CIA Agents 2. Former lovers 3. Dinners and dining 4. Terrorists 5. Intelligence service 6. Betrayal 7. Married women 8. International intrigue 9. Secrets 10. Men/women relations 11. Spy fiction

After a failed rescue attempt of a hijacked plane in Vienna, two retired spies, former lovers, can't help but relive the past and determine if the mission went wrong because of a compromised agent on the inside.

"It's an understatement to say that nothing is as it seems, but even readers well-versed in espionage fiction will be pleasantly surprised by Steinhauer's plot twists and double backs." Kirkus.

Steinhauer, Olen

An **American** spy / Olen Steinhauer. Minotaur Books, 2012. 416 p. Milo Weaver trilogy

ISBN 9780312622893

1. CIA Officials and employees 2. Elite operatives 3. Kidnapping 4. Secrecy 5. Loyalty in men 6. Intelligence service 7. Separated men (Marital relations) 8. Spy fiction 9. Thrillers and suspense

LC 2011040874

When the CIA's Department of Tourism is dismantled by an elaborate Chinese intelligence scheme that has caused numerous agent deaths, survivor Milo Weaver is placed at risk by his former boss, Alan Drummond, who uses one of Milo's aliases to exact revenge.

Steinhauer, Olen

The **Bridge** of Sighs / Olen Steinhauer. St. Martin's Minotaur, 2003. 278 p. Eastern European crime series

ISBN 0312302452

1. Second World War era (1939-1945) 2. 1940s 3. Murder investigation 4. Political corruption 5. Police 6. Suspicion 7. Rookie police 8. Extortion 9. World War II -- Eastern Europe -- Post-war aspects 10. Soviets in Eastern Europe 11. Postwar life 12. Eastern Europe 13. Berlin, Germany 14. Psychological suspense 15. Historical thrillers 16. Political thrillers

LC 2002068127

Investigating murders for the post-World War II People's Militia, Emil Brod suspects political motives behind the killing of a state songwriter and finds himself accused of spying by his corrupt colleagues in the homicide department.

"This is an intelligent, finely polished debut, loaded with atmospheric detail that effortlessly re-creates the rubble-strewn streets of the postwar period in an Eastern state 'liberated' from German occupation by the Russians." Library Journal.

Steinhauer, Olen

The **Cairo** affair / Olen Steinhauer. Minotaur Books, 2014. 400 p.

ISBN 9781250036131

1. Extramarital affairs 2. Diplomats 3. Marriage 4. Husband and wife 5. Former lovers 6. Spies 7. Murder investigation 8. Espionage 9. Cairo (Egypt) 10. Thrillers and suspense 11. Spy fiction

LC 2013033452

The assassination of an American diplomat in Hungary places a Cairo-based CIA agent in love with the victim's wife, an Egyptian intelligence agent and an American analyst at the mercy of a dangerous political game of shifting allegiances.

"A complex tale of the Arab Spring, WikiLeaks, the CIA, and a marriage, this leaves us with the unsettling feeling that, despite all the information won, lost, hoarded, and put to use, the world of intelligence is no stronger than the fragile, fallible humans who navigate it." Booklist.

Steinhauer, Olen

The **last** tourist / Olen Steinhauer. Minotaur Books, 2020. 416 p. Milo Weaver trilogy

ISBN 9781250036216

1. Former CIA agents 2. Intelligence service 3. Terrorists 4. Espionage 5. Intrigue 6. CIA agents 7. Spy fiction 8. Thrillers and suspense

LC 2019048501

Retired agent Milo Weaver has his hideout in the Western Sahara invaded by a young CIA analyst who questions him about suspicious deaths and the possible return of the Tourists.

"Steinhauer reinforces his position at the top of the espionage genre." Publishers Weekly.

Steinhauer, Olen

The **middleman** / Olen Steinhauer. Minotaur Books, 2018. 416 p.

ISBN 9781250036179

1. 2010s 2. Undercover operations 3. Domestic terrorism 4. Terrorists 5. FBI agents 6. Revolutionaries 7. Left-wing extremists 8. United States -- Politics and government -- 21st century 9. Thrillers and suspense

LC 2018004424

The rise and fall of a domestic left-wing terrorist group is traced from the perspectives of an FBI agent, an undercover agent, a convert and a writer on the sidelines.

Steinhauer, Olen

The **nearest** exit / Olen Steinhauer. Minotaur Books, 2010. 416 p. Milo Weaver trilogy

ISBN 9780312622879

1. CIA Officials and employees 2. Undercover operations 3. Elite operatives 4. Secrecy 5. Loyalty in men 6. Intelligence service 7. Separated men (Marital relations) 8. Spy fiction 9. Thrillers and suspense

LC 2009047486

RUSA Reading List, 2011.

Now faced with the end of his quiet, settled life, reluctant spy Milo Weaver has no choice but to turn back to his old job as a 'tourist.' Before he can get back to the CIA's dirty work, he has to prove his loyalty to his new bosses, who know little of Milo's background and less about who is really pulling the strings in the government above the Department of Tourism - or in the outside world, which is beginning to believe the legend of its existence. Milo is suddenly in a dangerous position, between right and wrong, between powerful self-interested men, between patriots and traitors - especially as a man who has nothing left to lose.

Steinhauer, Olen

The **tourist** / Olen Steinhauer. Minotaur Books, 2009. 416 p. Milo Weaver trilogy

ISBN 9780312369729

1. CIA Officials and employees 2. Undercover operations 3. Innocence (Law) 4. Betrayal 5. Spies 6. Paranoia 7. Trust 8. International intrigue 9. Intelligence service 10. Elite operatives 11.

Spy fiction 12. Thrillers and suspense

LC 2008033958

Milo Weaver is drawn into a conspiracy that links riots in the Sudan, an assassin committing suicide and an old friend who's been accused of selling secrets to the Chinese. Once the CIA and Homeland Security are after him, the only way for him to survive is to return, headfirst, into Tourism.

"As rich and intriguing as the best of Le Carre, Deighton or Graham Greene, Steinhauer's complex, moving spy novel is perfect for our uncertain, emotionally fraught times." Los Angeles Times Book Review.

Steinke, Rene

Holy skirts / Rene Steinke. William Morrow, 2005. 368 p.
ISBN 0688176941
1. Freytag-Loringhoven, Elsa von, 1874-1927 2. 1910s 3. 1900s (Decade) 4. Germans in New York State 5. Women poets 6. Women artists 7. Women performance artists 8. Artists' models 9. Barons and baronesses 10. Eccentric women 11. Women's clothing 12. Bohemianism 13. Dadaism 14. Creativity 15. Creativity in women 16. Men/women relations 17. Marriage 18. Independence in women 19. Sexuality 20. New York City -- Social life and customs -- 20th century 21. Greenwich Village, New York City -- Social life and customs -- 20th century 22. Europe 23. Biographical fiction 24. Historical fiction

LC 2004052783

National Book Award for Fiction finalist, 2005

"Steinke's writing is vivid and wonderful, and she can make even a sorrowful story entertaining because she never allows the character's melancholy to infect the prose. The baroness might have been sad, but not tragic. The heroism of her spirit is expressed in a way that transcends the shroud of misfortune." The Hudson Review.

Stephens, Alice, 1967-

Famous adopted people / Alice Stephens. Unnamed Press, 2018. 331 p.
ISBN 9781944700744
1. Best friends 2. Adoptees 3. Birthparents -- Identification 4. Korean Americans 5. Quarreling 6. Self-destructive behavior in women 7. Kidnapping 8. Palaces 9. Captivity 10. Ethnic identity 11. Family relationships 12. Eccentrics and eccentricities 13. South Korea 14. North Korea 15. Mainstream fiction 16. Domestic fiction

LC 2018033188

Lisa Pearl and her best friend, Mindy, both Koreans adopted as children into white American families, are in Seoul where Mindy hopes to find her birthmother and tries to persuade Lisa to search for hers, until Lisa wakes up in captivity.

Stephenson, Neal

Anathem / Neal Stephenson. William Morrow, 2008. 928 p.
ISBN 9780061474095
1. Intellectual life 2. Life on other planets 3. Monasteries 4. Mathematics 5. Disasters 6. Philosophy 7. Intellectuals 8. Words 9. Technology 10. Material culture 11. Intelligence 12. Planets 13. Hard science fiction 14. Science fiction

LC 2008013175

Locus Award for Best Science Fiction Novel, 2009.

Having lived in a monastery since childhood, away from the violent upheavals of the outside world, Raz becomes one of a group of formerly cloistered scholars who are appointed by a fear-driven higher power to avert an impending catastrophe.

"The novel is beautifully written (fans of Adam Roberts? ornately written science fiction will see some similarities), and, even though it runs to nearly 1,000 pages, it feels somehow too short, as though we?re made to leave this carefully constructed world and return to our own before we're quite ready. A magnificent achievement." Booklist.

Stephenson, Neal

Cryptonomicon / Neal Stephenson. Avon Press, 1999. 918 p.
ISBN 0380973464
1. Conspiracies 2. Cryptographers -- United States 3. Deception 4. Secrecy 5. Drug addicts 6. Computer programmers 7. Data encryption (Computer science) 8. World War II 9. Cryptography 10. Codes (Communication) 11. United States 12. Hard science fiction 13. Science fiction

LC 99-11685

Cryptonomicon features characters descended from those who appear in Stephenson's Baroque cycle series, and takes place about 300 years after the storyline of the cycle.

Locus Award for Best Science Fiction Novel, 2000.

More than fifty years after Lawrence Pritchard Waterhouse and Sergeant Bobby Shaftoe are assigned to Detachment 2702, a secret cryptographic mission, their grandchildren--Randy and Amy--join forces to create a "data haven" in the South Pacific, only to uncover a massive conspiracy with roots in Detachment 2702

"This fast-paced, genre-transcending novel is full of absorbing action, witty dialogue and well-drawn characters. Amazingly, it is also, even at its tremendous length, only the first volume in what promises to be one of the most extravagant literary creations of the turn of the millenniumand beyond." Publishers Weekly.

Stephenson, Neal

The diamond age, : or, a young lady's illustrated primer / Neal Stephenson. Bantam Books, 1995. 455 p.
ISBN 9780553096095
1. 21st century 2. Girl heroes 3. Social classes 4. Nanotechnology 5. Far future 6. Computers 7. Mass media 8. Social control 9. Nanotechnologists 10. Shanghai, China 11. Hard science fiction 12. Cyberpunk 13. Science fiction

LC 0679416021

Hugo Award for Best Novel, 1996.
Locus Award for Best Science Fiction Novel, 1996.

The story of an engineer who creates a device to raise a girl capable of thinking for herself reveals what happens when a young girl of the poor underclass obtains the device.

"With breathtaking vision and insight, Stephenson establishes himself as not only a major voice in contemporary sf but also a prophet of technology's future." Booklist.

Stephenson, Neal

* **Fall** or, Dodge in hell : a novel / Neal Stephenson. William Morrow, 2019. 883 p. Dodge novels
ISBN 9780062458711
1. Life after death 2. High technology 3. Cyberspace 4. Soul 5. Cryonics 6. Rich men 7. Near future 8. Intrigue 9. Artificial intelligence 10. Science fiction

When a routine procedure gone wrong renders a gaming billionaire brain dead, his stunned family and friends cryopreserve and digitally transfer his consciousness into an immortal tech-driven existence.

"Best-selling Stephenson is cutting edge and his followers and all readers intrigued by shrewd speculative fiction will queue up." Booklist.

Stephenson, Neal

Reamde / Neal Stephenson. William Morrow, 2011. 1044 p. Dodge novels

ISBN 9780061977961

1. Entrepreneurs 2. Computer games 3. Money laundering 4. Virtual reality 5. Technology 6. Cyber-thrillers 7. Science fiction

When his own high-tech start up turns into a Fortune 500 computer gaming group, Richard Forthrast, the black sheep of an Iowa family who has amassed an illegal fortune, finds the line between fantasy and reality becoming blurred when a virtual war for dominance is triggered.

"Stephenson's novels have always been a little nuts, but thoughtfully nuts. That he is even able to keep this big, careening, recreational-vehicular novel on the road during its hairpin narrative turns says a lot about him as a plot juggler and information wrangler." New York Times Book Review.

Stephenson, Neal

The **rise** and fall of D.O.D.O. : a novel / Neal Stephenson and Nicole Galland. William Morrow, 2017 800 p.

ISBN 9780062409164

1. Time travel (Past) 2. Linguists 3. Intelligence officers 4. Magic 5. Language and languages 6. History 7. Contemporary fantasy 8. Fantasy fiction

LC 2016043352

A discreet translation assignment enmeshes a linguistics expert and a military intelligence operator in the world-shattering revelation that magic was once widely practiced and can be reactivated if they travel back in time to make historical changes that are complicated by human treachery.

"A departure for both authors and a pleasing combination of much appeal to fans of speculative fiction." Kirkus.

Stephenson, Neal

Seveneves / Neal Stephenson. William Morrow, 2015 1056 p.

ISBN 9780062190376

1. Disasters 2. Survival 3. Space exploration 4. Space colonies 5. Far future 6. Earth 7. Moon 8. Hard science fiction 9. Apocalyptic fiction 10. Science fiction

RUSA Reading List Short List, 2016.

When a catastrophic event dooms the planet, nations around the world band together to devise an ambitious survival plan in outer space 5,000 years before their progeny organize an audacious return.

"Stephensons remarkable novel is deceptively complex, a disaster story and transhumanism tale that serves as the delivery mechanism for a series of technical and sociological visions. . . . There's a ton to digest, but Stephensons lucid prose makes it worth the while." Publishers Weekly.

Stephenson, Neal

* **Snow** crash / Neal Stephenson. Bantam Books, 1992. 440 p.

ISBN 9780553088533

1. 21st century 2. Computer viruses 3. Virtual reality 4. Hackers 5. Dystopias 6. Technology 7. Conspiracies 8. Cyberpunk 9. Science fiction

LC 91045453

With the strange new designer drug, Snow Crash, making zombies of nearly everyone and a deadly computer virus striking down hackers, Hiro Protagonist, the last of the free-lance hackers, comes to the rescue.

Sterling, Bruce

Pirate Utopia / Bruce Sterling ; art by John Coulthart ; introduction by Warren Ellis. Tachyon Publications, 2016. 187 p.

ISBN 9781616962364

1. Political intrigue 2. Pirates 3. Ideology 4. Futurists 5. Revolutionaries 6. Technology 7. Anarchism 8. Imaginary wars and battles 9. Alternative histories 10. Science fiction 11. Satirical fiction

At the end of the Great War, the Futurists, a group of utopian pirate warriors, rampage through Europe with the help of a sinister American to establish world domination.

Stern, Steve, 1947-

The **Pinch** : a history : Steve Stern. Graywolf Press, 2015. 349 p.

ISBN 9781555977153

1. 1960s 2. 1910s 3. Immigrants 4. Jewish men 5. Women folklorists 6. Clerks (Retail industry and trade) 7. Authors 8. Bookstores 9. Communities 10. Memphis, Tennessee 11. Historical fiction 12. Mainstream fiction 13. Metafiction 14. Parallel narratives

The last Jewish tenant on North Main Street in Memphis, Lenny Sklarew, makes the startling discovery that he's a character in a book about his neighborhood, and the stories he finds within the book transform both himself and the fate of the Pinch.

"With a motley cast, including blues musicians, a folklorist, an ogre, levitating Hasidim, and a limping tightrope walker, Stern, an ebullient maestro of words and mayhem, wonder and conscience, orchestrates a cacophonous, whirling, gritty, tender, time-warping saga that encompasses a cavalcade of horror, stubborn love, cosmic slapstick, burlesque humor, and a scattering of miracles." Booklist.

Sternbergh, Adam

The **blinds** / Adam Sternbergh. HarperCollins, 2017 304 p.

ISBN 9780062661340

1. Criminals 2. Memories 3. Sheriffs 4. Rural life 5. Communities 6. Secrets 7. Suicide 8. Murder investigation 9. Second chances 10. Texas 11. Crime fiction 12. Modern Westerns

Helping maintain an uneasy peace in The Blinds, a rural Texas community of criminal misfits who were given a chance at a new life after having their memories altered, sheriff Calvin Cooper struggles with personal secrets in the wake of a suicide and murder.

Stevens, Chevy

Never let you go / Chevy Stevens. St. Martin's Press, 2017. 406 p.

ISBN 9781250034564

1. Abused women 2. Life change events 3. Violence in men 4. Former convicts 5. Stalkers 6. Teenage girls 7. Single mothers 8. Obsession 9. Secrets 10. Small towns 11. Men/women relations 12. Stalking 13. British Columbia 14. Canada 15. Psychological suspense

When someone begins stalking her, intimidating her boyfriend, and shadowing her daughter, Lindsey Nash is convinced it's her abusive ex-husband, but his claims of innocence have her wondering if the threat is closer to home.

"Stevens's taut writing and chilling depiction of love twisted beyond recognition make this a compelling read from the first page to the last." Publishers Weekly.

Stevens, Chevy

Still missing / Chevy Stevens. St. Martin's Press, 2010. 352 p.

ISBN 9780312595678

1. Self-fulfillment in women 2. Captives 3. Identity (Psychology) 4. Survival 5. Real estate agents 6. Crimes against women 7. British Columbia 8. Canada 9. Psychological suspense

LC 2009047037

Thriller Award for Best First Novel, 2011.

Interwoven with the story of the year Annie spent captive in a remote mountain cabin, which unfolds through sessions with her psychiatrist, is a second narrative recounting the nightmare that follows her escape and her struggle to piece her shattered life back together.

"As Annie's experience as an abductee prompts her to explore hidden corners of her former life and dredge up old secrets, Still Missing risks sounding extremely generic. This, after all, is the template for countless current novels in which a single shattering event leads to shocking revelations about the past. But Still Missing runs deeper than that in the chills it delivers, the surprises it holds and the resilience of its main character." New York Times.

Stevens, Francis

The **heads** of Cerberus / Francis Stevens ; introduction by Naomi Alderman. Modern Library, 2019. 208 p.

ISBN 9781984854209

1. 1910s 2. Friendship 3. Time travel (Future) 4. Dictatorship 5. Women rulers 6. Competition 7. Class struggle 8. Gladiators 9. Loyalty 10. Philadelphia, Pennsylvania 11. Fantasy classics 12. Dystopian fiction

Originally published in serial form in The thrill book by Street & Smith Pulications, 1919.

Philadelphia, 1918: Three friends--brave, confident Viola Trenmore, clever but shy Robert Drayton, and Viola's strong and hot-tempered brother, Terry--discover a mysterious powder that transports them two hundred years into the future. The Philadelphia of 2118 is no longer a bustling metropolis but instead a completely isolated city recovering from an unknown disaster. Citizens are issued identification tags instead of having names, and society is split between a wealthy, powerful minority and a downtrodden lower class. The position of supreme authority is held by a woman, and once a year she oversees competitions to the death to determine who rules alongside her.

Stevenson, Robert Louis, 1850-1894

* The **strange** case of Dr. Jekyll and Mr. Hyde / Robert Louis Stevenson ; wood engravings by Barry Moser ; foreword by Joyce Carol Oates. University of Nebraska Press, 1990, c1886. 157 p.

ISBN 0803242123

1. Physicians 2. Scientists 3. Dissociative identity disorder 4. Self medication 5. Human experimentation in medicine 6. Mad scientist (Concept) 7. Virtues 8. Vices 9. Good and evil 10. Personal conduct 11. Self-control 12. Self-destructive behavior in men 13. Secret identity 14. Secrets 15. London, England 16. Horror 17. Gothic fiction 18. Classics

LC 90030544

First published in 1886.

This book has inspired movies called Dr. Jekyll and Mr. Hyde, Jekyll and Hyde, and Mary Reilly.

Wood engravings accompany this edition of the story of Dr. Jekyll, who becomes transformed into the horrifying Mr. Hyde after conducting a scientific experiment.

Stewart, Amy

* **Girl** waits with gun / Amy Stewart. Houghton Mifflin Harcourt, 2015. 408 p. Kopp sisters novels

ISBN 9780544409910

1. 1910s 2. Policewomen 3. Organized crime 4. Silk Workers' Strike, Paterson, New Jersey, 1913 5. Black Hand (United States) 6. Extortion 7. Sheriffs 8. Strikes 9. Sisters 10. Families 11. Farms 12. New Jersey -- History -- 20th century 13. Historical fiction

LC 2014045223

RUSA Reading List Short List, 2016.

Living in virtual isolation years after the revelation of a painful family secret, Constance Kopp is terrorized by a belligerent silk factory owner and fights back in ways outside the norm for early twentieth-century women.

"A sheer delight to read and based on actual events, this debut historical mystery packs the unexpected, the unconventional, and a serendipitous humor into every chapter." Booklist.

Stewart, Amy

Kopp sisters on the march / Amy Stewart. Houghton Mifflin Harcourt, 2019. 355 p. Kopp sisters novels

ISBN 9781328736529

1. First World War era (1914-1918) 2. Sisters 3. Military service 4. World War I home front 5. Military training camps 6. Women murder suspects 7. Gender role 8. Secret identity 9. Maryland 10. United States -- Social life and customs -- 1910-1919 11. Historical mysteries

LC 2019002553

In 1917, as the U.S. prepares to enter World War I, the Kopp sisters arrive at Camp Chevy Chase training camp where they are faced with scandal, betrayal, the skepticism of the War Department, the double standards of a scornful public and the very real perils of war.

"Told in Stewart's nimble, witty prose, this fifth in the popular series is based largely on fact and offers a paean to patriotism and the role women have played in war, even a century ago. Devoted fans will be pleased with the tantalizing hint Stewart provides about what lies ahead for Constance." Booklist.

Stewart, Amy

Lady cop makes trouble / Amy Stewart. Houghton Mifflin Harcourt, 2016. 272 p. Kopp sisters novels

ISBN 9780544409941

1. First World War era (1914-1918) 2. Policewomen 3. Sisters 4. Swindlers and swindling 5. Germans in the United States 6. Sexism 7. Prisoners 8. Sheriffs 9. New York City -- History -- 20th century 10. Historical mysteries

LC 2016004634

"The best-selling author of Girl Waits with Gun returns with another adventure featuring the fascinating, feisty, and unforgettable Kopp sisters."--, Provided by publisher.

"Stewart adeptly introduces details of early twentieth-century life in Hackensack, New Jersey, a burgeoning city on the outskirts of New York, and timely concerns such as jail reform and womens rights, rounding out this immensely satisfying mystery." Booklist.

Stewart, Amy

* **Miss** Kopp just won't quit / Amy Stewart. Houghton Mifflin Harcourt, 2018. 336 p. Kopp sisters novels

ISBN 9781328736512

1. First World War era (1914-1918) 2. Women sheriffs 3. Elections 4. Psychiatric hospitals 5. Deception 6. Criminal investigation 7. Justice 8. Sisters 9. Gender role 10. New Jersey 11. United States

-- Social life and customs -- 1865-1918 12. Historical mysteries

LC 2017061492

In 1916, New Jersey's first female deputy, Constance Kopp, while trying to investigate two cases involving the same asylum, finds her controversial career on the line.

"This entry is more suspenseful than its predecessors and boasts a deeper emphasis on character, politics, and social issues. A must for Constance's growing fan base." Booklist.

Stewart, Amy

Miss Kopp's midnight confessions / Amy Stewart. Houghton Mifflin Harcourt, 2017. 304 p. Kopp sisters novels

ISBN 9780544409996

1. First World War era (1914-1918) 2. Policewomen 3. Sisters 4. Sexism 5. Prisoners 6. Sheriffs 7. New York City -- History -- 20th century 8. United States -- Social life and customs -- 1865-1918 9. Historical mysteries

LC 2017007453

RUSA Reading List Short List, 2018.

Deputy Sheriff Constance Kopp and her sister Fleurette defend the young women being brought into the 1916 Hackensack jail under dubious charges like waywardness and incorrigibility.

"Collectively, the story lines intersect to create an intriguing window into women's rights and the social mores that women challenged on the eve of World War I." Library Journal.

Stewart, Ann Marie, 1971-

Stars in the grass / Ann Marie Stewart Shiloh Run Press, 2017. 305 p.

ISBN 9781634099509

1. 1970s 2. Loss (Psychology) 3. Nine-year-old girls 4. Families 5. Grief in families 6. Faith (Christianity) 7. Family relationships 8. Christian fiction

Christy Award for First Novel Category, 2017.

Set in 1970, a story told through the eyes of nine-year-old Abby relates how she, her older brother, her mother, and her father take very different paths to cope with the horrendous loss of her baby brother.

Stewart, David O.

The **Babe** Ruth deception / David O. Stewart. Kensington Books, 2016. 304 p. Fraser and Cook mysteries

ISBN 9781496702005

1. Ruth, Babe, 1895-1948 2. 1920s 3. Between the Wars (1918-1939) 4. Amateur detectives 5. Former baseball players 6. Fathers 7. Baseball 8. Prejudice 9. Physicians 10. Interracial couples 11. Corruption investigation 12. Historical mysteries

Under scrutiny for his participation in the 1918 World Series, Babe Ruth calls in Speed Cook and Dr. Jamie Fraser to clear his name, but Fraser and Cook's own family troubles may cloud their eyes from the truth.

"The third from Stewart (The Wilson Deception, 2015, etc.) cleverly mixes real-life people and historical events. The problems of the unlikely sleuths will particularly appeal to baseball fans." Kirkus.

Stewart, George R., 1895-1980

Earth abides / George R. Stewart. Del Rey, 2006, c1949. xiv, 345 p.

ISBN 9780345487131

1. Plague 2. Virus diseases 3. Epidemics 4. Survival (after environmental catastrophe) 5. Disasters 6. Post-apocalypse 7. Apocalyptic fiction 8. Science fiction

Originally published: New York : Random House, 1949.

Returning from a field trip, Isherwood Williams discovers that a mysterious plague has destroyed human civilization during his absence

and makes his way to San Francisco, where he finds a few survivors who build a small community, living like their pioneer ancestors.

Stewart, Mary, 1916-2014

* The **crystal** cave / Mary Stewart. Eos, 2003, c1970. 494 p. Merlin, the enchanter series

ISBN 9780060548254

1. 5th century 2. Misfits (Persons) 3. Illegitimate children of royalty 4. Prophecies 5. Merlin (Legendary character) 6. Wizards 7. Magic 8. Great Britain -- History -- Anglo-Saxon period, 449-1066 9. Arthurian fantasy 10. Historical fantasy

Originally published: New York : Morrow, 1970.

Later collected in Mary Stewart's Merlin trilogy: New York : Morrow, 1980.

Mythopoeic Award for Adult Literature, 1971.

Born the bastard son of a Welsh princess, Myridden Emrys -- or as he would later be known, Merlin -- leads a perilous childhood, haunted by portents and visions. But destiny has great plans for this no-man's-son, taking him from prophesying before the High King Vortigern to the crowning of Uther Pendragon . . . and the conception of Arthur -- king for once and always.

Stewart, Mary, 1916-2014

* The **hollow** hills / Mary Stewart Eos, 2003, c1973. 475 p. Merlin, the enchanter series

ISBN 9780060548261

1. Arthur,, King 2. 5th century 3. Rulers 4. Swords 5. Fate and Fatalism 6. Merlin (Legendary character) 7. Wizards 8. Magic 9. Great Britain -- History -- Anglo-Saxon period, 449-1066 10. Arthurian fantasy 11. Historical fantasy

Map on lining paper.

Originally published: New York : Morrow, 1973.

Later collected in Mary Stewart's Merlin trilogy: New York : Morrow, 1980.

Mythopoeic Award for Adult Literature, 1974.

Keeping watch over the young Arthur Pendragon, the prince and prophet Merlin Ambrosius is haunted by dreams of the magical sword Caliburn, which has been hidden for centuries. When Uther Pendragon is killed in battle, the time of destiny is at hand, and Arthur must claim the fabled sword to become the true High King of Britain.

Stewart, Mary, 1916-2014

The **last** enchantment / Mary Stewart. Eos, 2003, c1979. 513 p. Merlin, the enchanter series

ISBN 9780060548278

1. Arthur,, King 2. 5th century 3. Enchantment 4. Witches 5. Lust 6. Merlin (Legendary character) 7. Wizards 8. Magic 9. Great Britain -- History -- Anglo-Saxon period, 449-1066 10. Arthurian fantasy 11. Historical fantasy

Originally published: New York : Morrow, 1979.

Later collected in Mary Stewart's Merlin trilogy: New York : Morrow, 1980.

Merlin the Enchanter recounts the events of Arthur's formative years as he grew from young warrior to king and reveals the horrible consequences of Arthur's incestuous relationship with Morgause, his half-sister.

Stewart, Mary, 1916-2014

Nine coaches waiting / Mary Stewart. HarperCollins, 2001, c1959. 391 p.

ISBN 9780380820764

1. Boy orphans -- France 2. Governesses 3. Attempted murder 4. Uncles -- France 5. Nobility 6. Men/women relations 7. Paris,

France 8. Gothic romances

Originally published: New York : M. S. Mill and W. Morrow, 1959.

Charmed in spite of herself, English governess Linda Martin is baffled by the increasingly strange behavior of the de Valmys.

"Intelligent, spirited Linda Martin comes to Valmy, an isolated chateu in the French Alps, as English governess to nine-year-old Philippe, the orphaned Comte de Valmy. After several frightening 'accidents' Linda discovers that her pupil is the object of a murder plot which apparently involves his crippled uncle and the latter's handsome son Raoul, with whom she is in love." Booklist.

Stewart, Mary, 1916-2014

The **wicked** day / Mary Stewart. Eos, 2003, c1983. 417 p. Merlin, the enchanter series

ISBN 9780060548285

1. Arthur,, King 2. 5th century 3. Fate and fatalism 4. Family secrets 5. Incest 6. Illegitimacy 7. Children of incest victims 8. Imaginary wars and battles 9. Mordred (Legendary character) 10. Camelot (Legendary place) 11. Merlin (Legendary character) 12. Wizards 13. Magic 14. Great Britain -- History -- Anglo-Saxon period, 449-1066 15. Arthurian fantasy 16. Historical fantasy

Originally published: New York : Morrow, 1983.

Mordred, the son of King Arthur and his treacherous half-sister, the enchantress Morgause, unwittingly becomes caught up in a scheme to destroy Arthur and his kingdom.

"The author returns to the Arthurian world she portrayed . . . in her Merlin trilogy. The principal character is Mordred, born of the incestuous liaison between Arthur the High King and his half-sister, the evil sorceress and northern queen Morgause. Mordred is summoned to Camelot by the formidable warrior king, along with Morgause and her four legitimate but ungovernable sons, and told of his true parentage. After growing to manhood in Arthur's court . . . Mordred is left in charge of the kingdom, and of Queen Guinevere, while Arthur is off fighting the Romans in Brittany. Reported dead, the king returns to Britain and there ensues the fulfillment of the 'wicked day' that has been prophesied by Merlin." Publishers Weekly.

Sthers, Amanda, 1978-

Holy lands : a novel / Amanda Sthers. Bloomsbury Publishing, 2019. 161 p.

ISBN 9781635572834

1. Physicians 2. Letter writing 3. Lifestyle change 4. Pig farming 5. Jewish men 6. Cardiologists 7. Jews -- Identity 8. Conflict in families 9. Long-distance friendship 10. Separated friends, relatives, etc 11. Israel 12. Epistolary novels 13. Humorous stories 14. Translations -- French to English

LC 2018015184

Leaving a thriving medical practice in Paris to raise pigs in Israel, a Jewish cardiologist disconnects himself from modern technology, forcing his gay playwright son, heartbroken daughter and cancer-stricken wife to correspond strictly through written letters.

"Her slim, swiftly moving novel describes the complicated relationships between siblings, a married couple, a man and his rabbi and still has room for a light critique of Israel's policies toward Palestine. This is a book you can read in an afternoon, but it'll stick with you for much longer than that. Comic, moving, and occasionally profound, Sthers' novel is a delight." Kirkus.

Stibbe, Nina

Reasons to be cheerful / Nina Stibbe. Little Brown & Co, 2019. 240 p. Man at the helm novels (Nina Stibbe)

ISBN 9780316309370

1. 1980s 2. Eccentrics and eccentricities 3. Gender role 4. Crushes

(Interpersonal relations) 5. Dentists 6. Dental assistants 7. Young women 8. Love 9. Growing up 10. Small town life 11. Family relationships 12. England 13. Coming-of-age stories 14. Satirical fiction

Taking a job as an assistant to an eccentric dental surgeon, 18-year-old Lizzie pursues a fantasy relationship with her crush before realizing that he is not quite as imagined.

Stirling, S. M.

Dies the fire / S.M. Stirling. New American Library, 2004. 496 p. Dies the fire trilogy

ISBN 0451459792

1. Regression (Civilization) 2. Technology and civilization 3. Determination (Personal quality) 4. Power failures 5. Survival (after disaster) 6. Wilderness survival 7. Farm life 8. Power (Social sciences) 9. Civilization 10. Post-apocalypse 11. Pacific Northwest 12. Oregon 13. Idaho 14. Science fiction 15. Apocalyptic fiction 16. Science fantasy

LC 2004004363

Sequel: The protector's war.

Set in the world that was left behind in the author's book Island in the Sea of Time.

The change occurred when an electrical storm centered over the island of Nantucket produced a blinding white flash that rendered all electronic devices and fuels inoperable. What follows is the most terrible global catastrophe in the history of the human race - and a Dark Age more universal and complete than could possibly be imagined.

Stirling, S. M.

A **meeting** at Corvallis / S.M. Stirling. Roc, 2006. 512 p. Dies the fire trilogy

ISBN 0451461118

1. Exiles 2. Communities 3. Kidnapping 4. Regression (Civilization) 5. Technology and civilization 6. Rescues 7. Power (Social sciences) 8. Conflict of interests 9. Social conflict 10. Civilization 11. Imaginary wars and battles 12. Determination (Personal quality) 13. Post-apocalypse 14. Oregon 15. Pacific Northwest 16. Science fiction 17. Apocalyptic fiction 18. Science fantasy

LC 2006002080

Tensions continue among Mike Havel's Bearkillers and their allies, Clan Mackenzie under the leadership of Juniper Mackenzie and Norman Arminger, the warlord of Portland, after Arminger's daughter falls into the hands of Clan Mackenzie.

Stirling, S. M.

The **protector's** war / S. M. Stirling. ROC, 2005. 486 p. Dies the fire trilogy

ISBN 0451460464

1. Civilization 2. Determination (Personal quality) 3. Imaginary wars and battles 4. Regression (Civilization) 5. Witches 6. Exiles 7. Communities 8. Technology and civilization 9. Power (Social sciences) 10. Post-apocalypse 11. Oregon 12. Great Britain 13. Science fiction 14. Apocalyptic fiction 15. Science fantasy

LC 2005008432

Sequel to: Dies the fire.

Ten years after all of Earth's technology had been rendered useless by the Change, two thriving communities in Oregon's Willamette Valley are confronted by a dangerous new challenge when the totalitarian Protectorate prepares to seek control over their priceless farmland.

Stockett, Kathryn

* The **help** / Kathryn Stockett. Amy Einhorn Books/G.P. Putnam's Sons, 2009. 464 p.

ISBN 9780399155345

1. 1960s 2. Interracial friendship 3. Determination in women 4. African American women 5. Household employees 6. Unemployed persons 7. College graduates 8. Civil Rights Movement 9. Life change events 10. Race relations 11. Housekeepers 12. Jackson, Mississippi 13. Women's lives and relationships 14. Historical fiction 15. Southern fiction

LC 2008030185

Goodreads Choice Award, 2009.

Amelia Bloomer List, 2010

Limited and persecuted by racial divides in 1962 Jackson, Mississippi, three women, including an African-American maid, her sassy and chronically unemployed friend, and a recently graduated white woman, team up for a clandestine project.

Stoker, Bram, 1847-1912

* **Dracula** / Bram Stoker ; edited with an introduction and notes by Maurice Hindle ; preface by Christopher Frayling. Penguin Books, 2003, c1897. xlvii, 454 p.

ISBN 9780141439846

1. 19th century 2. Vampires 3. British in Romania 4. Good and evil 5. Men/women relations 6. Virtues 7. Husband and wife 8. Quests 9. Transylvania, Romania 10. London, England -- Social life and customs -- 19th century 11. Gothic fiction 12. Horror 13. Epistolary novels

Inspired the movie entitled Nosferatu.

Having discovered the double identity of the wealthy Transylvanian nobleman, Count Dracula, a small group of people vow to rid the world of the evil vampire.

Stoker, Bram, 1847-1912

The **new** annotated Dracula / Bram Stoker ; edited with a foreword and notes by Leslie S. Klinger ; additional research by Janet Byrne ; introduction by Neil Gaiman. W.W. Norton, 2008. 672 p.

ISBN 9780393064506

1. Stoker, Bram, 1847-1912 Dracula 2. 19th century 3. Vampires 4. British in Romania 5. Good and evil 6. Men/women relations 7. Virtues 8. Husband and wife 9. Quests 10. Popular culture 11. Transylvania, Romania 12. London, England -- Social life and customs -- 19th century 13. Gothic fiction 14. Horror

LC 2008025919

Inspired the movie entitled Nosferatu.

An illustrated tribute to Bram Stoker's classic shares additional insights into the historical plausibility of vampire lore, in an edition that surveys more than two centuries of popular culture and myth while providing a detailed examination of the book's original typescript and different ending.

"An introduction by Neil Gaiman, numerous illustrations, essays on topics ranging from Dracula in the movies to the academic response, and much more enhance the package." Publishers Weekly.

Stoker, Dacre

Dracul / Dacre Stoker, J. D. Barker. Putnam Pub Group, 2018. 512 p.

ISBN 9780735219342

1. Stoker, Bram, 1847-1912 2. Vampires 3. Brothers and sisters 4. Nannies 5. Secrets 6. Memories 7. Intrigue 8. Families 9. Letter writing 10. Diary writing 11. Historical horror 12. Horror

A prequel to Dracula, based on original author notes and co-written by a family descendant, reveals the iconic vampire's origin story, the early years of Bram Stoker and the tale of the enigmatic woman who connected them.

Stone, Irving, 1903-1989

* The **agony** and the ecstasy : a biographical novel of Michelangelo / Irving Stone. Signet, 1987, c1961. 776 p.

ISBN 0451171357

1. Michelangelo Buonarroti, 1475-1564 2. Renaissance (1300-1600) 3. Artists -- Italy 4. Creativity in men 5. Men and success 6. European Renaissance -- Italy 7. Sexuality 8. Genius 9. Family relationships 10. Greed in men 11. Competition in men 12. Failure (Psychology) 13. Social acceptance 14. Italy 15. Florence, Italy 16. Biographical fiction 17. Historical fiction

Originally published: Garden City, N.Y. : Doubleday, 1961.

The great best seller about Michelangelo.

Dramatizes the life of the artistic genius Michelangelo, recalls his love affairs, his disputes with cardinals and popes, and his years of working on the Sistine Chapel.

Stone, Irving, 1903-1989

Lust for life : a novel of Vincent van Gogh / Irving Stone. Penguin, 1989, c1934. x, 489 p.

ISBN 0452262496

1. Gogh, Vincent van, 1853-1890 2. Purpose in life 3. Artists -- Netherlands 4. Determination in men 5. Painters -- Netherlands 6. Brothers 7. Violence in men 8. First loves 9. Unrequited love 10. Men/women relations 11. Men with depression 12. Netherlands -- History -- 19th century 13. London, England -- History -- 19th century 14. Biographical fiction 15. Historical fiction

LC 83024666

Lust for Life inspired the film Lust for Life in 1956.

Companion book: Dear Theo.

Originally published: New York : Longmans, Green, 1934.

A Novel of the life of the tormented genius who put so much of himself into his art that he found it difficult to maintain himself in ordinary society.

Stone, Nick, 1966-

The **verdict** / Nick Stone. Pegasus Crime, 2015. 499 p.

ISBN 9781605989235

1. Trials (Murder) 2. Former friends 3. Law firms 4. Law clerks 5. Conspiracies 6. Millionaires 7. Personal conduct 8. Secrets 9. London, England 10. Legal thrillers

Leaping at a chance to make his career by taking a high-profile murder case, Terry Flynt is forced to make a terrible choice and confront secrets from the past when he discovers that his millionaire client is a former friend who brutally betrayed him years earlier.

"The suspense never lets up in this terrific courtroom drama. Fans of John Grisham will love it. It's definitely movie material." Kirkus.

Stories : all-new tales / edited by Neil Gaiman and Al Sarrantonio. William Morrow & Co., 2010. 432 p.

ISBN 9780061230929

1. Supernatural 2. Consequences 3. Imagination 4. Magic 5. Death 6. Good and evil 7. Revenge 8. Imaginary creatures 9. Gods and goddesses 10. Curiosities and wonders 11. Fantasy fiction 12. Short stories 13. Short stories 14. Anthologies

Shirley Jackson Awards, Edited Anthology, 2010.

"An ambitious anthology with a pleasing mix of modes and moods. Stories has a little something for everyone who appreciates the possibilities of short fiction." San Francisco Chronicle.

Stott, Rebecca

The **coral** thief : a novel / Rebecca Stott. Spiegel & Grau, 2009. 304 p.

ISBN 9780385531467

1. 19th century 2. 1810s 3. Evolution -- Philosophy 4. Thieves 5. Men/women relations 6. Anatomists 7. Paris, France 8. Historical fiction

LC 2009012846

In 1815 France, a young medical student discovers that the beauty who shared his coach has stolen the rare coral specimens he carried and soon he encounters a ring of philosopher thieves determined to sabotage pre-Darwinian theories of evolution.

"Aside from her graceful writing style and believable characters, Stott also delights with her grasp of history. Romantic, full of twists and turns and glimpses of the past, The Coral Thief is an unlikely page-turner." BookPage.

Stott, Rebecca

Ghostwalk / Rebecca Stott. Spiegel & Grau, 2007. 320 p.

ISBN 0385521065

1. Newton, Isaac, 1642-1727 2. College teachers 3. Biographers 4. Historians 5. Alchemy 6. Supernatural 7. Murder 8. Conspiracies 9. Secrets 10. Cambridge, England 11. England 12. Mysteries

LC 2006022326

When the death of a Cambridge historian leaves her opus on Sir Isaac Newton unfinished, Lydia Brooke is called in to finish the book, only to find herself embroiled in a mystery in which the present becomes entangled with a past based on Newton's life.

"Stott brings a nervy intelligence to her work, skillfully linking the war on terror, quantum physics, alchemy, serial murder, ghosts, and thwarted romance." Miami Herald.

Stout, Dan

* **Titanshade** / Dan Stout. DAW Books, 2019. 400 p. Carter archives

ISBN 9780756414863

1. Detectives 2. Cities and towns 3. Energy resources 4. Oil executives 5. Diplomats 6. Corruption 7. Rich families 8. Half-human hybrids 9. Imaginary creatures 10. Murder investigation 11. Fantasy mysteries 12. Urban fantasy

In Titanshade, a metropolis on the edge of disaster, homicide cop Carter is led into a conflict with the city's elite while investigating the brutal murder of a Squib diplomat and must solve the case quickly to protect those closest to him.

Stout, Rex, 1886-1975

The **doorbell** rang / Rex Stout ; introduction by Stuart M. Kaminsky. ImPress Mystery, 2000, c1965. 207 p. Nero Wolfe mysteries

ISBN 076218857X

1. Murder investigation 2. FBI agents 3. Secrecy in government 4. Rich women 5. Private investigators 6. Eccentric men 7. Gourmets 8. Orchid growers 9. Agoraphobia 10. New York City 11. Mysteries

LC 00061464

Originally published: New York :

"Nero Wolfe tangles with the FBI, on behalf of a wealthy woman who has sent as gifts to prominent people 10,000 copies of Fred Cook's book criticizing the FBI. . . . She is being shadowed and spied on by the FBI. To the surprise of Wolfe and of Archie Goodwin, they have the good will of the New York Police Department. The New York Police believe that FBI agents have murdered a magazine writer who was doing an article on the FBI. The police are powerless to prove anything or to prosecute. Clever and ingenious, this ranks among the best Rex Stout mysteries." Publishers Weekly.

Stout, Rex, 1886-1975

* **Gambit** / Rex Stout. Bantam Books, 1973, c1962. 155 p. Nero Wolfe mysteries

ISBN 9780553251722

1. Murder investigation 2. Poisoning 3. Murder suspects 4. Chess 5. Private investigators 6. Eccentric men 7. Gourmets 8. Orchid growers 9. Agoraphobia 10. New York City 11. Mysteries

Originally published: New York : Viking Press, 1962.

Master sleuth Nero Wolfe and his confidential assistant Archie Goodwin match wits with a deadly adversary to solve a bizarre murder that takes place during a chess game at a private club.

"Nero Wolfe, with his usual witty, urbane, conversational approach, looks into a case of arsenic poisoning in a Manhattan chess club." Publishers Weekly.

Stowe, Harriet Beecher, 1811-1896

* **Uncle** Tom's cabin / Harriet Beecher Stowe ; with a new introduction by Charles Johnson. Oxford University Press, 2002. xv, 456 p.

ISBN 0195158164

1. Slavery -- United States 2. Fugitive slaves 3. African Americans 4. Master and servant 5. Plantation life 6. Slaves 7. Southern States 8. Classics

LC 2002068424

First published in the National era at Washington from June 1851 to April 1852.

Originally published in two volumes: Boston : John P. Jewett & company ; Cleveland : Jewett, Proctor & Worthington, 1852.

Originally published as Uncle Tom's cabin or, life among the lowly.

Uncle Tom's master sells him, separating him from his wife, and he becomes attached to the gentle daughter of his new owner, but after her death, he is sold to the evil Simon Legree.

Stradal, J. Ryan

* The **lager** queen of Minnesota / J. Ryan Stradal. Pamela Dorman Books / Viking, 2019 384 p.

ISBN 9780399563058

1. Women-owned businesses 2. Breweries 3. Family businesses 4. Sisters 5. Inheritance and succession 6. Senior women 7. Grandmother and granddaughter 8. Women brewers 9. Women bakers 10. Beer 11. Women business owners 12. Family relationships 13. Minnesota 14. Middle West 15. Mainstream fiction 16. Women's lives and relationships

LC 2018057023

A talented baker running a business out of her nursing home reconnects with her master brewer sister at the same time her pregnant granddaughter launches an IPA brewpub.

Straight, Susan

A **million** nightingales / Susan Straight. Pantheon Books, 2006. 352 p.

ISBN 0375423648

1. Antebellum America (1820-1861) 2. 1800s (Decade) 3. 19th century 4. Women slaves 5. Slavery -- Louisiana 6. Plantations -- Louisiana 7. Multiracial teenagers 8. Multiracial women 9. Slaves 10. Teenage slaves 11. Mothers and daughters 12. Slaveholders -- Louisiana 13. Plantation life 14. Sugar plantations 15. Louisiana -- History -- 19th century 16. Historical fiction 17. Literary fiction 18. Coming-of-age stories

LC 2005050052

When she is sold away from her family, Moinette begins to prepare herself for an escape to freedom, journeying through a world of brutality, sexual violence, loss, and struggle to find her way out of the bonds of slavery.

"Straight's book is a deep consideration of the servitude all women experienced then--and, in some ways and some places, continue to experience even now. . . . But her novel is, besides, a powerful and moving story, written in language so beautiful you can almost believe the words themselves are capable of salving history's wounds." New York Times Book Review.

Straley, John, 1953-

The **big** both ways / John Straley. Alaska Northwest Books, 2008. 350 p. Cold storage novels

ISBN 9780882407395

1. 1930s 2. Women labor organizers 3. Revenge 4. Survival 5. Labor movement 6. Aunt and niece 7. Lumber workers 8. Police 9. Organized crime 10. Inside Passage (Pacific Northwest) 11. Alaska 12. British Columbia 13. Washington (State) 14. Mysteries 15. Pacific Northwest fiction 16. Historical mysteries

LC 2007051440

Fleeing a logging camp after an accident kills a coworker, Slip Wilson's life changes forever when he meets Ellie Hobbes, an anarchist from Seattle who is on the run with a dead body in the trunk of her car.

Strange, Marc

Follow me down : an Orwell Brennan mystery / Marc Strange. ECW Press, 2010. 260 p. Orwell Brennan mysteries

ISBN 9781550229264

1. Police 2. Small towns -- Ontario 3. Murder 4. Murder investigation 5. Sexuality 6. Robbery 7. Greed 8. Police chiefs 9. Ontario 10. Mysteries

LC oc2009074290

A man, hanging from a tree at the edge of the forest that surrounds Dockerty, has been shot with arrows. Orwell Brennan, Dockerty's chief of police, is determined to find out what really happened, no matter whose toes he steps on.

Stratford, Sarah-Jane

Red letter days / Sarah-Jane Stratford. Berkley, 2020. 384 p.

ISBN 9780451475572

1. McCarthy, Joseph, 1908-1957 2. 1950s 3. McCarthyism 4. Women screenwriters 5. Americans in England 6. Women television producers and directors 7. Female friendship 8. Sexism 9. Hollywood Blacklist 10. Anti-communist movements 11. Anti-Communism -- United States 12. Independence in women 13. Men/women relations 14. England 15. London, England 16. Hollywood, California 17. New York City 18. Historical fiction

LC 2019022993

When two brave women flee from the Communist Red Scare, they soon discover that no future is free from the past.

"A...thoroughly fascinating and too-little-known story of Hannah Weinstein and her role in supporting blacklisted Americans, regardless of gender or race." Booklist.

Straub, Emma

* **Modern** lovers / Emma Straub. Riverhead Books, 2016. 320 p.

ISBN 9781594634673

1. Friendship 2. Growing up 3. Parenthood 4. Identity (Psychology) 5. Aging 6. Secrets 7. Neighbors 8. Ambition 9. Brooklyn, New York City 10. Domestic fiction 11. Coming-of-age stories

Three friends and former college bandmates struggle with the midlife difficulties of managing the sexuality, independence, and secrets of their young-adult children against painful memories of a friend who soared and fell without them.

"Straub's handful of characters, followed with alternating close third-person narratives, are honestly and devilishly observed with clarity and kindness." Booklist.

Straub, Emma

The **vacationers** / Emma Straub. Riverhead Books, 2014. 304 p.

ISBN 9781594631573

1. Family vacations 2. Couples 3. Change (Psychology) 4. Americans in Spain 5. Friendship 6. Voyages and travels 7. Secrets 8. Marital conflict 9. Young women 10. Competition 11. Family relationships 12. Majorca, Spain 13. Spain 14. Mainstream fiction 15. Coming-of-age stories

LC 2013037110

Celebrating their thirty-fifth anniversary and their daughter's high-school graduation during a two-week vacation in Mallorca, Franny and Jim Post confront old secrets, hurts, and rivalries that reveal sides of themselves they try to conceal.

"Spongy and dear, sharply observed and funny, Straub's domestic-drama-goes-abroad is a delightful study of the complexities of family and love, and the many distractions from both." Booklist.

Straub, Peter, 1943-

* A **dark** matter : a novel / Peter Straub. Doubleday, 2010. 416 p.

ISBN 9780385516389

1. 1960s 2. High school students 3. Rites and ceremonies 4. Supernatural 5. Teenagers 6. Psychic trauma 7. Murder 8. Consequences 9. Good and evil 10. Madison, Wisconsin 11. Horror 12. Psychological suspense

LC 2009020028

Bram Stoker Award for Best Novel, 2010.

Old friends try to come to grips with the darkness of the past--a secret ritual that left behind a gruesomely dismembered body--and find themselves face-to-face with the evil they helped create.

"A multiple-perspective take on a murky collegiate misadventure in 1966. Spencer Mallon, campus-flitting intellectual and seducer of coeds, is compared in the early pages to a host of flattering figures: a god, a hero, a guru. What Mallon feels most like to us, though, is a Manson-like charmer who lures several young people out to a field, where one of them dies. How, though? Straub expertly weaves a Rashmon-crazy quilt of varying and sometimes conflicting recollections of the incident, left purposefully vague, as we shuttle through the intervening yearsunkind ones in which his characters are struck by blindness, become criminals and, in an especially sad case, go insane. A slight slackness in the story's middle game will have some readers exhorting, Get over it already! whatever it is. But ambitiously, the author mounts his referendum on a wild, unpredictable moment of the 1960s, saluting the era's competing urges of decadence and justice." Time Out New York.

Straub, Peter, 1943-

* **Ghost** story / Peter Straub. Pocket Books, 1980, c1979. 567 p.

ISBN 9780671826857

1. Ghosts 2. Secret societies 3. Seniors 4. Brothers 5. Authors 6. Death 7. Storytelling 8. Small town life -- New York (State) 9. New York (State) 10. Horror 11. Ghost stories

Questions arise concerning the connections between a strangely detached young girl's captivity in a seedy Florida motel, a death that occurs at a party for a visiting actress, and a young California instructor's obsession with one of his students.

"With considerable technical skill, Peter Straub has constructed an extravagant entertainment which, though flawed, achieves in its second half some awesome effects." Newsweek.

Straub, Peter, 1943-

Lost boy lost girl : a novel / Peter Straub. Random House, 2003. 320 p.

ISBN 1400060923

1. Suicide victims 2. Haunted houses 3. Missing persons 4. Vietnam veterans 5. Teenage boys 6. Girls 7. Mothers -- Death 8. Family and suicide 9. Abandoned houses 10. Secrets 11. Crime scenes 12. Serial murders 13. Illinois 14. Horror

LC 2003046689

Bram Stoker Award for Best Novel, 2003.
International Horror Guild Award for Best Novel, 2003.

The suicide of a woman and the disappearance of her teenage son, Mark, draws the boy's uncle, Timothy Underhill, back to his hometown of Millhaven, where his investigation uncovers a neighborhood haunted by a serial killer.

"Inquisitive and open-minded as Tim is, he makes it easy for Mr. Straub to move from conventionally hair-raising effects . . . to the more happening teenage world of cyberscares. Strongly visual without resorting to secondhand cinematic imagery, the book is equally well equipped to play both kinds of tricks." New York Times.

Straub, Peter, 1943-

Mr. X / Peter Straub. Random House, 1999. 482 p.

ISBN 9780679401384

1. Father-separated children 2. Serial murderers 3. Nightmares 4. Paranormal phenomena 5. Horror

LC 98047688

Bram Stoker Award for Best Novel, 1999.

Every year on his birthday, Ned Dunstan experiences a seizure in which he is forced to witness scenes of ruthless slaughter perpetrated by a mysterious and malevolent figure in black whom Ned calls Mr. X. This year Ned learns from his mother, who is on her death bed, the name of his long-absent father and other disturbing information about his own identity and that of his entire fantastic family.

"[Straub's] evocative prose, a seamless splice of clipped hard-boiled banter and poetic reflection, contributes to the thick atmosphere of apprehension that makes this one of the most invigorating horror reads of the year." Publishers Weekly.

Straub, Peter, 1943-

* **Mystery** / Peter Straub. E. P. Dutton, 1990. 548 p. Blue rose

ISBN 9780525248187

1. 1960s 2. Cold cases (Criminal investigation) 3. Murder investigation 4. Murder 5. Deception 6. Upper class 7. Traffic accidents 8. Obsession in men 9. Government cover-ups 10. Former detectives 11. Wisconsin 12. Caribbean Area 13. Mysteries

LC 89007734

A near-fatal traffic accident and a resulting obsession with death drive Tom Pasmore to join his neighbor, famous retired detective Lamont von Heilitz, in investigating two very different murders.

"The remarkable depth of characterization make apparent the fact that Mystery is meant to be much more than a conventional shocker. For the most part, Straub delivers the goods." Booklist.

Street, Karen Lee

Edgar Allan Poe and the jewel of Peru / Karen Lee Street. W W Norton & Co Inc., 2018. 352 p. Poe and Dupin mysteries

ISBN 9781681776675

1. Poe, Edgar Allan, 1809-1849 2. 1840s 3. Murder investigation 4. Private investigators 5. Kidnapping investigation 6. Gems 7. Ornithologists 8. Social conflict 9. Immigrants, Irish 10. Women kidnapping victims 11. Philadelphia, Pennsylvania 12. Historical mysteries

Edgar Allan Poe and C. Auguste Dupin strive to unravel a mystery involving old enemies, lost soul-mates, ornithomancy, and the legendary jewel of Peru.

Stridsberg, Sara, 1972-

Valerie : or the faculty of dreams : Sara Stridsberg ; translated from the Swedish by Deborah Bragan-Turner. Farrar, Straus and Giroux, 2019. 384 p.

ISBN 9780374151911

1. Solanas, Valerie 2. 20th century 3. Feminists 4. Women with mental illnesses 5. Women radicals 6. Women -- Psychology 7. Paranoid schizophrenia 8. Dead 9. Interpersonal relations 10. United States -- Social life and customs -- 20th century 11. Experimental fiction 12. Biographical fiction 13. Translations -- Swedish to English

LC 2018060814

In April 1988, Valerie Solanas, the writer, radical feminist and would-be assassin of Andy Warhol, was discovered dead in her hotel room, in a grimy corner of San Francisco. She was only 52; alone, penniless and surrounded by the typed pages of her last writings. In The Faculty of Dreams, Sara Stridsberg revisits the hotel room where Solanas died, the courtroom where she was tried and convicted of attempting to murder Andy Warhol, the Georgia wastelands where she spent her childhood, and the mental hospitals where she was interned. Through imagined conversations and monologues, reminiscences and rantings, Stridsberg reconstructs this most intriguing and enigmatic of women, articulating the thoughts and fears that she struggled to express in life and giving a powerful, heartbreaking voice to the writer of the infamous SCUM Manifesto.

Stringer, Vickie M.

Dirty Red : a novel / Vickie M. Stringer. Atria Books, 2006 238 p. Dirty Red novels

ISBN 0743493486

1. African American women 2. Swindlers and swindling 3. Pregnancy 4. Violence 5. Sexuality 6. Greed in women 7. African Americans 8. African American men/women relations 9. Child sexual abuse 10. Men/women relations 11. Interpersonal relations 12. Manipulation by women 13. Seduction 14. Fraud 15. Deception 16. Street life 17. African American fiction 18. Drama lit

Having tricked her boyfriend into believing she is pregnant, eighteen-year-old Red enjoys his lavish attentions until she becomes pregnant for real by an ex-boyfriend who is in jail, a situation that leads her into a successful new career.

Stringer, Vickie M.

* **Let** that be the reason / Vickie M. Stringer. Upstream, 2002, c1999. 247 p. Let that be the reason novels

ISBN 9781886433854

1. Women drug dealers 2. Street life 3. Prostitution 4. Drug traffic 5. African American women 6. African Americans 7. Inner city 8. City life 9. Love 10. Men/women relations 11. African American single mothers 12. Sexuality 13. Husband and wife 14. Money 15. New York City 16. Columbus, Ohio 17. African American fiction

18. Drama lit

Prequel: The reason why.

Originally published: Columbus, Ohio : Triple Crown Publications, c1999.

Street Lit Book Award Medal: Adult Fiction, 2003

Abandoned by a drug-dealing boyfriend who leaves her with a stack of bills and nothing to her name, Pamela Xavier assumes a tough alter ego, Carmen, to survive on the streets as the head of a call-girl operation.

Stringer, Vickie M.

Still dirty : a novel / Vickie M. Stringer. Atria Books, 2008. 226 p. Dirty Red novels

ISBN 9781416563587

1. Manipulation by women 2. Street life 3. Former convicts 4. Former boyfriends 5. African American women 6. Swindlers and swindling 7. Violence 8. Sexuality 9. Greed 10. Men/women relations 11. African American fiction 12. Drama lit

The hustler Red and her companions Bacon and Q face such challenges as a double-dealing boyfriend, a friend's betrayal, and an unscrupulous business partner.

Stroby, Wallace

Some die nameless / Wallace Stroby. Mulholland Books, 2018 352 p.

ISBN 9780316440202

1. Mercenaries 2. Journalists 3. Survival 4. Murder 5. Dictators 6. Political corruption 7. Florida 8. Pennsylvania 9. South America 10. Thrillers and suspense

An ex-mercenary and an embattled journalist find themselves unlikely allies against a corrupt defense contractor.

Stross, Charles

Accelerando / Charles Stross. Ace Books, 2005. 390 p.

ISBN 0441012841

1. 21st century 2. Entrepreneurs 3. Dysfunctional families 4. Family relationships 5. Parent and adult child 6. Artificial intelligence 7. Technological innovations 8. Technology and civilization 9. Nanotechnology 10. Life on other planets 11. Near future 12. Posthumanism 13. Space 14. Hard science fiction 15. Science fiction

LC 2005042815

Locus Award for Best Science Fiction Novel, 2006.

Trying to cope with the unchecked technological innovations that have rendered humankind nearly obsolete, the members of the Macx family are confronted by an unknown enemy that is systematically attempting to annihilate all biological lifeforms.

"Expanded from several stories originally published in Asimov's Science Fiction, . . . [this] novel follows several generations of the Macx family through the rapidly transforming, Internet-enabled global economy of the early twenty-first century to the human and transhuman populated worlds of the outer solar system a half century later. . . . Stross has his thumb squarely on the pulse of technology's leading edge and exults in extrapolating mere glimmers of ideas out to their mind-bending limits." Booklist.

Stross, Charles

Empire Games / Charles Stross. Tor, 2017. 336 p. Empire Games

ISBN 9780765337566

1. Near future 2. Espionage 3. Drone aircraft 4. Spies 5. Political intrigue 6. National security 7. Nuclear weapons 8. International intrigue 9. Parallel universes 10. United States 11. Science fiction 12. Spy fiction 13. Political thrillers

Empire Games is set after and in the same world as the author's Merchant Princes novels.

Includes main time lines, character profiles, cast list and glossary.

A tale set in an alternate world of the immediate future follows the efforts of the head of a paratime espionage agency to prepare for an upcoming drone war at the same time her estranged spy daughter attempts to protect national security during an ominous succession crisis.

"Stross handles the story well enough that you dont need to have read the previous six books. Of course, those who have will be overjoyed to renew their acquaintance with Miriam and her associates . . ." Booklist.

Stross, Charles

Glasshouse / Charles Stross. Ace Books, 2006. 335 p.

ISBN 0441014038

1. 27th century 2. Men with amnesia 3. Volunteers 4. Identity (Psychology) 5. Resistance to government 6. Recovered memory 7. Censorship 8. Experiments 9. Men/women relations 10. Far future 11. Posthumanism 12. Human evolution 13. Social science fiction 14. Science fiction

LC 2006004358

When Robin wakes up in a clinic with most of his memories missing, it doesn't take him long to discover that someone is trying to kill him. It's the 27th century, when interstellar travel is by teleport gate and conflicts are fought by network worms that censor refugees' personalities and target historians. The civil war is over and Robin has been demobilized, but someone wants him out of the picture because of something his earlier self knew. On the run from a ruthless pursuer, he volunteers to participate in a unique experimental polity, the Glasshouse, constructed to simulate a pre-accelerated culture. Participants are assigned anonymized identities: it looks like the ideal hiding place for a posthuman on the run. But in this escape-proof environment,Robin will undergo an even more radical change, placing him at the mercy of the experimenters--and the mercy of his own unbalanced psyche.--From publisher description.

Stross, Charles

Neptune's brood / Charles Stross. ACE BOOKS, 2013. 336 p.

ISBN 9780425256770

1. Androids 2. Assassins 3. Life on other planets 4. Space flight 5. Robots 6. Financial intrigue 7. Sisters 8. Space opera 9. Science fiction

LC 2013002384

After being stalked across the galaxy by an assassin, post-human Krina Alzon-114 journeys to the water-world Shin-Tethys in search of her sister in this new space opera.

Stross, Charles

Saturn's children : a space opera / Charles Stross. Ace Books, 2008. 323 p.

ISBN 9780441015948

1. 23rd century 2. Androids 3. Space flight 4. Life on other planets 5. Robots 6. Sexuality 7. Posthumanism 8. Space opera 9. Science fiction

LC 2008008228

Sometime in the twenty-third century, humanity went extinct leaving only androids behind. Freya Nakamichi 47 is a femmebot, one of the last of her kind still functioning. With no humans left to pay for the pleasures she provides, she agrees to transport a mysterious package from Mercury to Mars. Unfortunately for Freya, she has just made herself a moving target for some very powerful, very determined humanoids who will stop at nothing to possess the contents of the package.

"Stross tosses out ideas aplenty. Since his robots know they were created by humans, for example, they consider evolution heretical. It isn't a relaxing bedtime read, but it is the sort of mind-expanding adventure that made hard science fiction famous." The New Scientist.

Stroud, Carsten, 1946-

The **shimmer** / Carsten Stroud. MIRA Books, 2018. 384 p.

ISBN 9780778331223

1. Serial murderers 2. Time travel 3. Widowers 4. Detectives 5. Serial murder investigation 6. Life change events 7. Loss (Psychology) 8. Thrillers and suspense

Craving to bathe in the shimmering afterglow that sometimes emanates when the soul leaves the body, a traveling female serial killer finds a way to slip into the past to right a wrong, changing the lives of two families in two different time periods.

Strout, Elizabeth

Amy and Isabelle : a novel / Elizabeth Strout. Random House, 1998. 303 p.

ISBN 9780375501340

1. Mothers and daughters 2. Teacher-student relationships 3. Family secrets 4. Teenage girls 5. Extramarital affairs 6. High school teachers 7. Teachers 8. Single mothers 9. Children of single parents 10. Small town life 11. Alienation in women 12. Shame in women 13. Shyness in teenage girls 14. Mill towns 15. Birthmothers 16. Adoptees 17. New England 18. Literary fiction 19. Coming-of-age stories

LC 9819995

Shortlisted for The Orange Prize for Fiction, 2000

When Amy Goodrow, a shy high school student, falls in love with her math teacher, the love affair threatens the intimate relationship between Amy and her mother, Isabelle, whose feelings are influenced by the shame of her own past.

"As the cacophony of disaster grows ever louder in contemporary culture, Strout has written an excellent novel about enduring the banalities of ordinary life." The New Yorker.

Strout, Elizabeth

* **Anything is** possible : fiction / Elizabeth Strout. Random House, 2017. 254 p.

ISBN 9780812989403

1. Mothers and daughters 2. Brothers and sisters 3. Families 4. Small town life 5. Interpersonal relations 6. Family relationships 7. Poor families 8. Illinois 9. Domestic fiction 10. Literary fiction

LC 2016020620

Featuring the setting and characters from Elizabeth Strout's 2016 novel My Name Is Lucy Barton.

Librarians' Choice (Australia), 2017

Two sisters, one who trades self-respect for a wealthy husband and one who discovers a kindred spirit in the pages of a book, struggle with intimate human dramas at the sides of their community members and a returned Lucy Barton.

"A radiant collection of stories linked to Strout's previous novel, My Name Is Lucy Barton...but moving beyond its first-person narration to limn small-town life from multiple perspectives." Kirkus.

Strout, Elizabeth

* The **Burgess** boys : a novel / Elizabeth Strout. Random House, 2013. 320 p.

ISBN 9781400067688

1. Homecomings 2. Brothers 3. Guilt in men 4. Fathers -- Death 5. Deception 6. Lawyers 7. Brothers and sisters 8. Maine 9. Literary fiction

LC 2012035132

Catalyzed by a nephew's thoughtless prank, a pair of brothers confront painful psychological issues surrounding the freak accident that killed their father when they were boys, a loss linked to a heartbreaking deception that shaped their personal and professional lives.

Strout, Elizabeth

My name is Lucy Barton / Elizabeth Strout. Random House, 2016. 193 p.

ISBN 9781400067695

1. 1980s 2. Mothers and daughters 3. Family relationships 4. Motherhood 5. Hospital care 6. Appendix (Anatomy) -- Surgery 7. Surgery 8. Family secrets 9. Family reunions 10. Women authors 11. Poverty 12. Forgiveness 13. Self-discovery in women 14. New York City 15. Domestic fiction

Longlisted for the Baileys Women's Prize for Fiction, 2016.

Longlisted for the Man Booker Prize, 2016

Shortlisted for the International Dublin Literary Award, 2018.

After an appendix operation puts her in the hospital, New York writer Lucy Barton reconnects with her estranged mother as the pair reminisce about the past.

"In a compact novel brimming with insight and emotion, Strout relays with great tenderness and sadness the way family relationships can both make and break us." Booklist.

Strout, Elizabeth

Olive Kitteridge / Elizabeth Strout. Random House, 2007. 288 p. Olive novels

ISBN 9781400062089

1. Teachers 2. Mothers and sons 3. Change (Psychology) 4. Coastal towns 5. Small town life 6. Junior high school teachers 7. Middle schools 8. Loneliness in women 9. Loss (Psychology) 10. Jealousy 11. Despair 12. Interpersonal relations 13. Men/women relations 14. Maine 15. Literary fiction 16. Short stories

13 linked stories

Sequel: Olive, again

ALA Notable Book, 2009.

Pulitzer Prize for Fiction, 2009.

National Book Critics Circle Award for Fiction finalist, 2008

The world of Olive Kitteridge, a retired school teacher in a small coastal town in Maine, is revealed in stories that explore her diverse roles in many lives, including a lounge singer haunted by a past love, her stoic husband, and her own resentful son.

"These linked stories introduce the inhabitants of Crosby, Maine, where the pull of domestic tragedy is stronger for rarely being spoken of. ... Strout makes us experience not only the terrors of change but also the terrifying hope that change can bring: she plunges us into these churning waters and we come up gasping for air." The New Yorker.

Strout, Elizabeth

* **Olive,** again : a novel / Elizabeth Strout. Random House, 2019. 304 p. Olive novels

ISBN 9780812996548

1. Former teachers 2. Mothers and sons 3. Change (Psychology) 4. Coastal towns 5. Small town life 6. Senior women 7. Widows 8. Remarriage 9. Loneliness in women 10. Loss (Psychology) 11. Beauty in nature 12. Interpersonal relations 13. Men/women relations 14. Maine 15. Literary fiction 16. Short stories

LC 2019004792

Sequel to: Olive Kitteridge

A sequel to Olive Kitteridge finds Olive struggling to understand herself while bonding with a teen suffering from loss, a woman who gives birth unexpectedly, a nurse harboring a longtime crush and a lawyer who resists an unwanted inheritance.

Stuart, Douglas, 1976-

* **Shuggie** Bain / Douglas Stuart. Grove Press, 2020. 448 p.

ISBN 9780802148049

1. 1980s 2. Working class families 3. Alcoholism 4. Mothers 5. Family violence 6. Working class boys 7. Social isolation 8. Psychic trauma 9. Families 10. Coming out (Sexual or gender identity) 11. Cheating (Interpersonal relations) 12. Abandonment (Psychology) 13. Glasgow, Scotland 14. Literary fiction 15. Coming-of-age stories
LC 2019037882

A young boy growing up in a rundown 1980s Glasgow public housing facility pursues some semblance of a normal life as his older siblings move on and his mother increasingly succumbs to alcoholism.

"Perfect for getting lost in, Stuart's richly wrought coming-of-age saga is a trenchant portrayal of poverty and addiction, true to life and steeped in its era, setting, and dialect." Booklist.

Styles, Toy, 1974-

Black and ugly / T. Styles. Triple Crown Publications, 2006. vi, 241 p. Black and ugly novels

ISBN 9780977880416

1. African American women 2. Friendship 3. Self-esteem in women 4. Street life 5. Appearances 6. Drug use 7. Secrets 8. Women with HIV 9. Secrets 10. Prostitution 11. Cross-dressers 12. Hyattsville, Maryland 13. Maryland 14. African American fiction 15. Drama lit
LC 2006937037

Sequel: Black and ugly as ever.

The tale of four totally different friends from the same block, whose friendship is tested during a seemingly innocent game of Truth or Dare.

Styles, Toy, 1974-

A **hustler's** son : a novel / T. Styles. Triple Crown Publications, 2006. 210 p. Hustler's son

ISBN 9780976789499

1. Mothers and sons 2. African American teenage boys 3. Street life 4. Violence 5. Drug traffic 6. Dishonesty 7. Women murderers 8. Murder 9. Family secrets 10. Maryland 11. Bladensburg, Maryland 12. Urban fiction 13. African American fiction

Trying to shield her son, Kelsi, from the realities of life on the streets, Janet Stayley realizes it is too late after Kelsi murders a fellow high school student and he finds out about his mother's past.

Styles, Toy, 1974-

Raunchy / T. Styles ; [edited by] Advanced Editorial Services. Cartel Publications, 2010. 338 p. Making of a mother monster

ISBN 9780982391372

1. Family secrets 2. Mothers and daughters 3. Child abuse victims 4. African American women 5. Sexuality 6. Single mothers 7. Inheritance and succession 8. Street life 9. Drug traffic 10. Betrayal 11. Maryland 12. Urban fiction 13. African American fiction
LC 2010936906

Raunchy is a heartbreaking, explicit story of failed mother and daughter relationships. Provided by publisher

Styles, Toy, 1974-

Raunchy 2 : Mad's love / T. Styles ; [edited by] Advanced Editorial Services. Cartel Publications, 2011. 324 p. Making of a mother monster

ISBN 9780984303069

1. Mothers and daughters 2. Revenge 3. Betrayal 4. African American women 5. Inheritance and succession 6. Street life 7. Drug traffic 8. Maryland 9. Urban fiction 10. African American fiction

Styles, Toy, 1974-

Redbone / T. Styles. Urban Books ; 2012. 484 p. Redbone novels

ISBN 9781601624932

1. Roommates 2. Obsession in women 3. African American women -- Interpersonal relations 4. Privacy 5. Secrets 6. Revenge 7. Rent and renting 8. Multiracial persons 9. Interpersonal conflict 10. Self-perception in women 11. Washington, D.C. 12. Urban fiction 13. African American fiction

LC bl2012009756

When her new roommate Farah Cotton becomes obsessed with her and her personal life, Lesa Carmine tries to sever ties immediately, but Farah has other ideas, forcing Lesa to investigate Farah's past, which leads to a shocking discovery that could end her life.

Styron, William, 1925-2006

The **confessions** of Nat Turner / William Styron. Random House, 1967. 428 p.

ISBN 0679601015

1. Turner, Nat, 1800?-1831 2. Antebellum America (1820-1861) 3. African American clergy 4. Slavery -- Virginia 5. Slave resistance and revolts 6. Race relations 7. Turner's Slave Revolt, Southampton, Virginia, 1831 8. Biographical fiction 9. Historical fiction 10. Literary fiction

Pulitzer Prize for Fiction, 1968.

Gives an account, based on the true story of a slave rebellion in 1831, of a noble man's moral decline.

Styron, William, 1925-2006

Lie down in darkness / William Styron. Vintage Books, 1992, c1951. 400 p.

ISBN 9780679735977

1. Dysfunctional families 2. Suicide 3. Fathers and daughters 4. Daughters -- Death 5. Loss (Psychology) 6. Grief in men 7. Southern States -- Race relations 8. Domestic fiction 9. Psychological fiction 10. Southern Gothic 11. Southern fiction

Originally published in 1951.

As Milton Loftis follows the hearse in which his beautiful daughter, Peyton, is being carried to the grave, a story unfolds about the degeneration of a tormented Southern family submerged in infidelity and vengeful love.

"The book is not bleakly written. On the contrary, it is richly and even (in the best sense) poetically written. . . . If the parts seem to succeed each other with no apparent logic or dialectic, each part is brilliantly made and lovingly accomplished." The Atlantic.

Styron, William, 1925-2006

* **Sophie's** choice / William Styron. Random House, 1979. 515 p.

ISBN 9780394461090

1. Authors, American -- 20th century 2. Concentration camp survivors 3. Women Holocaust survivors 4. Jewish men 5. Men/women relations 6. Guilt in women 7. Jealousy in men 8. Dating

violence 9. Love triangles 10. Suicide pacts 11. Historical fiction 12. Modern classics

LC 78021835

National Book Award for Fiction, 1980.

National Book Critics Circle Award for Fiction finalist, 1979

As the fierce lovemaking and fights of Nathan, a paranoiac Jewish intellectual, and Sophie, a Polish-Catholic concentration-camp survivor, intensify, Stingo, a writer who lives below them in a cheap rooming house, becomes more and more involved in their lives

Suarez, Daniel, 1964-

Change agent : a novel / Daniel Suarez. Dutton, 2017. 416 p.

ISBN 9781101984666

1. Interpol 2. 21st century 3. Interpol agents 4. Human evolution 5. Genetic engineering 6. Identity (Psychology) 7. Human trafficking 8. Black market 9. Near future 10. Fugitives 11. Singapore 12. Science fiction

LC 2016030244

Drugged and abducted while standing on a crowded train platform, Kenneth Durand, an Interpol agent working against black-market labs that perform illegal embryo augmentation, awakens to discover he has been genetically transformed into his most wanted suspect.

"This outstanding speculative thriller from bestseller Suarez (Kill Decision) imagines a future of 'living technologya fourth industrial revolution of synthetic biology and genetic editing,' as the author puts it in an opening note to the reader." Publishers Weekly.

Sullivan, Michael J., 1961-

Theft of swords / Michael J. Sullivan. Orbit, 2011, c2008. 688 Riyria revelations

ISBN 9780316187749

1. Thieves 2. Swordplay 3. Adventure 4. Extortion 5. Rulers 6. Kidnapping 7. Rescues 8. Monsters 9. Princesses 10. Monks 11. Wizards 12. Churches 13. Fantasy fiction 14. Sword and sorcery

LC 2011008814

Originally published as two books, under the titles, The Crown Conspiracy and Avempartha.

Two thieves, Royce Melborn and Hadrian Blackwater, become the unwitting scapegoats in a plot to murder the king after taking on too many dangerous assignments for machinating and conspiring noble people.

Sundaresan, Indu

The splendor of silence : a novel / Indu Sundaresan. Atria Books, 2006. 416 p.

ISBN 0743283678

1. Second World War era (1939-1945) 2. Nobility 3. Interracial romance 4. Intelligence service -- United States 5. Americans in India 6. Romantic love 7. Men/women relations 8. World War II 9. Soldiers 10. Deserts 11. Secret service 12. Spies 13. Missing persons 14. Brothers 15. Search and rescue operations 16. Rulers 17. Brothers and sisters 18. India 19. Love stories 20. Historical fiction

LC 2006042884

In 1942, Sam Hawthorne, a young U.S. Army captain, arrives in a tiny princely state in western India. He carries combat wounds and several secrets, one of which is the real reason behind his visit: to find his brother Mike, an idealistic American soldier who disappeared after joining the local struggle for independence from the British. But Sam's mission is soon threatened when he falls in love with Mila, daughter of the local political agent. Betrothed to the local prince, Mila draws Sam into a doomed affair that places them both in the path of dynastic intrigue, racial prejudice, and the explosive circumstances of a country torn between imperialism and nationalism.

"Flashbacks to 1940s India occur when Olivia receives a mysterious trunk that promises to explain who she is. The trunk arrives on the same day that her father, Sam, dies and contains information about her biological mother, Mila. Through a letter hidden among the keepsakes in the box, Olivia learns that her father spent time in India searching for his missing brother. While there, he fell in love with Mila, the daughter of the local political agent and fiance of a prince. It was also there that he got to know Mila's brothers, who knew the whereabouts of his own brother. A series of events leads to the arrival of the trunk for Olivia years later. Sundaresan's descriptive writing style makes for a colorful, engrossing read, and while the story does hop between time periods and locations, the reader is never lost along the way." Library Journal.

Sundin, Sarah

Through waters deep : a novel / Sarah Sundin. Revell, 2015 368 p. Waves of freedom

ISBN 9780800723422

1. United States. Navy Officers 2. Second World War era (1939-1945) 3. Secretaries 4. Destroyers (Warships) 5. Sabotage 6. Criminal investigation 7. Men/women relations 8. Christian historical romances

LC 2015000435

A World War II naval officer and a Boston Navy Yard secretary investigate evidence on board the officer's destroyer that implicates someone in their personal lives.

"Providing readers with an immersive experience, Sundin (In Perfect Time) vividly re-creates the atmosphere of a country on the brink of entering World War II. The tender romance at the story's center keeps readers rooting for Jim and Mary to realize their true feelings for each other. In the wake of the popularity of Anita Diamant's The Boston Girl, this book holds local interest for those who have lived in or loved the city.." Library Journal.

Sundstol, Vidar, 1963-

The land of dreams / Vidar Sundstol ; translated from the Norwegian by Tiina Nunnally. University of Minnesota Press, 2013, c2008. 284 p. Minnesota trilogy

ISBN 9780816689408

1. United States. Forest Service 2. Family secrets 3. Crimes against tourists 4. Norwegians in the United States 5. Brothers 6. Guilt 7. Murder investigation 8. Murder 9. Tourists 10. Gay men 11. Ancestors 12. FBI agents 13. Ojibwa Indians 14. Violence against Native Americans 15. Violence against gay men and lesbians 16. Lake Superior 17. Minnesota 18. Scandinavian crime fiction 19. Mysteries

Translation from the Norwegian of: Drommenes Land.

Originally published: Oslo : Tiden Norsk Forlag, c2008.

Lance Hansen, forest service officer and grandson of Norwegian immigrants, lives a quiet life working and pursuing the hobby of genealogy, until he finds a Norwegian tourist's dead body near a stone cross on the shore of Lake Superior.

"The landscape is a big part of the story, as is the history of the area, making this a fascinating look at Minnesota as well as a suspenseful thriller." Booklist.

Suri, Manil

The age of Shiva : a novel / Manil Suri. W.W. Norton, 2008. 448 p.

ISBN 9780393065695

1. Husband and wife 2. Conflict in families 3. Politics and culture 4. Men/women relations 5. Marital conflict 6. Love 7. Family relationships 8. Happiness in women 9. Young women 10. Maternal love -- Fiction 11. Mothers and sons 12. India 13. Domestic fiction

14. Historical fiction 15. Political fiction

LC 2007037322

Marrying in order to escape an overbearing father, Meera is further victimized by her physically demanding husband and lustful brother-in-law, a circumstance from which she finds fleeting escape through her relationships with her sister-in-law and young son.

"Suri's . . . novel is a sensuous, nuanced portrait of motherhood, but it also sparks with the frictions of being female in an India where television soaps and political slogans compete noisily with Hindu myth." The New Yorker.

Suri, Tasha

* **Empire** of sand / Tasha Suri. Orbit, 2018. 480 p. Books of Ambha

ISBN 9780316449717

1. Aristocracy 2. Rulers 3. Gods and goddesses 4. Imperialism 5. Young women 6. Deserts 7. Arranged marriage 8. Deception 9. Asian-influenced fantasy 10. Fantasy fiction

LC 2018027281

The illegitimate daughter of an imperial governor and an Amrithi, an outcast nomad with magic in her blood, must fight the plans of the Emperor's mystics to use her ability to manipulate the dreams of gods to alter the shape of the world.

"The desert setting, complex characters, and epic mythology will captivate readers of Suri's debut fantasy." Booklist.

Suri, Tasha

* **Realm** of ash / Tasha Suri. Orbit, 2019. 496 p. Books of Ambha

ISBN 9780316449755

1. Young widows 2. Princes 3. Imaginary empires 4. Curses 5. Magic 6. Inheritance and succession 7. Rulers 8. Illegitimate children of royalty 9. Gods and goddesses 10. Demons 11. Deserts 12. Dreams 13. Asian-influenced fantasy 14. Fantasy fiction

LC 2019027766

The Ambhan Empire is crumbling. A terrible war of succession hovers on the horizon. The only hope for peace lies in the mysterious realm of ash, where mortals can find what they seek in the echoes of their ancestors' dreams. But to walk there requires a steep price.

"Those with a penchant for lyrical prose, intricate world building, beautifully imagined characters, compelling immersive folklore, and a fascinating look into a setting reminiscent of the Mughal Empire need look no further." Booklist.

Suskind, Patrick

Perfume : the story of a murderer / Patrick Suskind ; translated from the German by John E. Woods. A.A. Knopf, 1986. 255 p.

ISBN 0394550846

1. 18th century 2. 1730s 3. Perfumes 4. Murderers 5. Women murder victims 6. Serial murders 7. Smell 8. Psychopaths 9. France -- History -- 18th century 10. Horror 11. Translations -- German to English 12. Historical horror

LC 86045419

Translation from the German of: Das Parfum.

First published as: Das Parfum by Diogenes Verlag, AG, Zurich, 1985.

This translation first published: Great Britain: Hamish Hamilton, 1986.

World Fantasy Award, 1987.

Survivor, genius, perfumer, killer: this is Jean-Baptiste Grenouille. He was abandoned on the filthy streets of Paris as a child, but grows up to discover he has an extraordinary gift: a sense of smell more powerful

than any other human's. Soon, he is creating the most sublime fragrances in all the city. Yet there is one odour he cannot capture. It is exquisite, magical: the scent of a young virgin. And to get it he must kill.

"Those readers who feel they are wasting their time with novels unless they are picking up facts will welcome Suskind's encyclopedic overview of the methods of making perfume. Like the best scents, there is something fundamentally formulaic about this novel, but its effects will linger long after it has been stoppered." Time.

Sutcliff, Rosemary

Sword at sunset / Rosemary Sutcliff. Tom Doherty Associates, 1987, c1963. 498 p.

ISBN 9780812588521

1. Arthur,, King 2. Rulers 3. Great Britain -- History -- Anglo-Saxon period, 449-1066 4. Arthurian fantasy 5. Historical fantasy 6. Celtic fantasy

"A Tor book."

Originally published: New York : Coward-McCann, 1963.

"A novel based on historical facts about the legendary Arthur. The time is the century after the last Roman legions leave Britain, and Arthur is desperately striving to hold Britain against the Saxons, Picts, and other invading savage tribes. [This is] the story of his tragic fate, his good times and bad." Publishers Weekly.

Sveistrup, Soren, 1968-

* The **chestnut** man : a novel / Soren Sveistrup ; translated from the Danish by Caroline Waight. Harper, 2019, c2018. 516 p.

ISBN 9780062895363

1. Serial murder investigation 2. Detectives 3. Missing persons 4. Serial murder investigation 5. Murder victims 6. Politicians 7. Scandinavian crime fiction 8. Translations -- Danish to English 9. Police procedurals

When a serial killer begins leaving handmade dolls at his murder scenes, two detectives struggle to put aside their differences and follow forensic clues linking the case to a politician's kidnapped daughter.

Svevo, Italo, 1861-1928

Zeno's conscience / Italo Svevo ; translated from the Italian by William Weaver. Alfred A. Knopf, 2001. xlix, 437 p.

ISBN 9780375413308

1. Psychoanalysis -- Italy 2. Married men -- Italy 3. Psychiatric hospital patients -- Italy 4. Guilt 5. Autobiography -- Therapeutic use -- Italy 6. Italy 7. Translations -- Italian to English 8. Modern classics

LC 2001040821

After being advised by his doctor to write his memoirs as a form of therapy, Zeno sets out in search of truth, health, and happiness.

"This is a highly human story and its material is fundamentally as sound as its method. . . . The work of a man who wrote to please himself, it has an individuality and originality you cannot escape noticing, and it has, too, a fine and comprehensive knowledge of its character." New York Times Book Review.

Swanson, Peter, 1968-

Eight perfect murders : a novel / Peter Swanson. William Morrow & Co, 2020. 270 p.

ISBN 9780062838209

1. Booksellers 2. Women FBI agents 3. Serial murderers 4. Murder suspects 5. Murder victims 6. Serial murder investigation 7. Secrets 8. Widowers 9. Books and reading 10. Winter 11. Boston, Massachusetts 12. Psychological suspense

Years after establishing a literary career through his compilation of the mystery genre's most unsolvable classics, an unsuspecting bookseller is tapped by the FBI for help solving murders that eerily mimic the books on his list.

"The wintry New England setting and eerily cool narration, together with trust-no-one twists and garish murders, will satisfy thriller readers; fans of classic mysteries by Agatha Christie, Ira Levin, and John D. MacDonald will enjoy how Swanson (Before She Knew Him) repurposes the plots." Library Journal.

Swanson, Peter, 1968-

Her every fear : a novel / Peter Swanson. William Morrow, 2017. 304 p.

ISBN 9780062427021

1. Art students 2. Fear in women 3. Apartment dwellers 4. Murder 5. Cousins 6. Suspicion 7. Neighbors 8. Former boyfriends 9. Kidnapping victims 10. Trading and swapping 11. British in the United States 12. Boston, Massachusetts 13. London, England 14. Psychological suspense

LC 2016007758

A woman prone to panic attacks in the aftermath of a violent kidnapping relocates to a cousin's home in Boston, where a neighbor's murder embroils her in speculation about her cousin's nature and the intentions of an appealing stranger.

"Psychological thriller devotees should block time to read Swanson's (The Kind Worth Killing) novel in one sitting, preferably in the daylight. Readers can expect the hairs on their necks to stand straight up as they are consumed with a full-blown case of heebie-jeebies." Library Journal.

Swanson, Peter, 1968-

The kind worth killing : a novel / Peter Swanson. William Morrow, 2015. 352 p.

ISBN 9780062267528

1. Strangers 2. Married men 3. Women murderers 4. Wife-killing 5. Deception 6. Conspiracies 7. Murder 8. Psychological suspense

LC 2014019249

Engaging in an intimate sharing of secrets with a mysterious woman on an airplane, an unhappily married businessman is tangled in a psychologically twisted game of cat-and-mouse involving a plot to kill the man's wife.

Swanwick, Michael

Bones of the Earth / Michael Swanwick. EOS, 2002. 335 p.

ISBN 9780380978366

1. Dinosaurs 2. Time travel 3. Paleontologists 4. Science fiction

LC 2001040196

A paleontologist who discovers the secret of time travel is initially thrilled at the prospect of conducting research on live dinosaurs, but his frequent trips into the past soon begin to have negative consequences on the present.

Swarthout, Glendon, 1918-1992

Bless the beasts and children / Glendon Swarthout. Pocket Books, 1970. 192 p.

ISBN 9780385033626

1. 1960s 2. Misfits (Persons) 3. Summer camps 4. Animal liberation 5. Rejection (Psychology) 6. Children of rich people 7. Teenage boys 8. Arizona 9. Southwest (United States) 10. Coming-of-age stories

LC 79094331

The neglected attendees of the Box Canyon Boys Camp find their lives turned around by Cotton, who, in a hot-wired pickup, challenges them to join efforts to save a herd of buffalo and rediscover themselves in the process.

Swarthout, Glendon, 1918-1992

* The **shootist** / Glendon Swarthout. Berkley, 1998, c1975. xvi, 215 p. Shootist

ISBN 9780425164198

1. 1900s (Decade) 2. Gunfighters 3. Death 4. Cancer 5. The West (United States) 6. Westerns

Sequel: The last shootist.

Originally published: Garden City, N.Y. : Doubleday, 1975.

Spur Award for Best Western Novel (Short Novel), 1976.

John Bernard Books rides into El Paso in 1901 only to be told by a doctor that he will soon confront the greatest shootist of all: Death.

"This is definitely more than a Western; the characterization is flawless, the plot absorbing and convincing." Library Journal.

Swift, Graham, 1949-

* **Here** we are / Graham Swift. Alfred A. Knopf, 2020. 192 p.

ISBN 9780525658054

1. 1950s 2. Vaudeville performers 3. Magicians 4. Friendship 5. Engaged persons 6. Secrets 7. Memories 8. Postwar life 9. Men/women relations 10. Love triangles 11. Brighton, England 12. Great Britain 13. Literary fiction

It's the summer of 1959, and something magical can be witnessed at the end of the pier in beach town Brighton, England. Jack Robbins, Ronnie Deane, and Evie White are performing in a seaside variety show, starring as Jack Robinson the compere comedian, and The Great Pablo and Eve: a magic act. By the end of the summer, Evie's glinting engagement ring will be flung to the bottom of the ocean and one of the trifecta will vanish forever.

"Swift's brief, magical tale demonstrates one more brilliant example of his talent for pulling universal themes out of the hats of ordinary lives." Publishers Weekly.

Swift, Graham, 1949-

* **Last** orders : a novel / Graham Swift. Knopf, 1996. 294 p.

ISBN 9780679412243

1. World War II veterans 2. Senior men -- Friendship 3. Betrayal 4. Male friendship 5. Parents of children with developmental disabilities 6. Friends' death 7. Friendship 8. Family relationships 9. England 10. Psychological fiction 11. Literary fiction

ALA Notable Book, 1997.

Booker Prize, 1996.

James Tait Black Memorial Prize for Fiction, 1996.

Shortlisted for the International IMPAC Dublin Literary Award, 1998

In England three working-class buddies, united by pub-drinking and World War II experiences, drive the ashes of the fourth to the sea. In the process emerge the lives of four families and the reason no wife came.

"The narrative is parceled out among . . . four men, as well as Amy, the widow, Vince's wife, Mandy, and Jack, the dead man. The accent is flat London vernacular, and the tone varies between mordant humor, gentle regret, and deep sorrow. Swift carries off this feat of ventriloquism with admirable skill." The New York Review of Books.

Swift, Graham, 1949-

* **Mothering** Sunday : a romance / Graham Swift. Alfred A. Knopf, 2016. 208 p.

ISBN 9781101947524

1. Between the Wars (1918-1939) 2. 1920s 3. Self-discovery in women 4. Social classes 5. Household employees 6. Lovers 7. Grief in women 8. Flashbacks 9. Orphans 10. Secrets 11. Men/women

relations 12. Historical fiction 13. Literary fiction

LC 2015033402

Hawthornden Prize, 2017.

Shortlisted for the Walter Scott Prize for Historical Fiction, 2017

Sharing what she believes will be a last tryst with a longtime secret lover on the eve of his marriage, a woman reflects on the years they have spent together and her journey of self-discovery against a backdrop of 20th-century history.

"Swift has fun with language, with class conventions, and with narrative expectations in a novel where nothing is as simple or obvious as it seems at first." Kirkus.

Swift, Graham, 1949-

Wish you were here / Graham Swift. Vintage Canada, 2011. 352 p.

ISBN 9780307360106

1. Brothers 2. Grief in men 3. Loss (Psychology) 4. Funerals 5. Soldiers 6. Husband and wife 7. Marital conflict 8. Farm life 9. Rural families 10. Family relationships 11. England 12. Iraq 13. Psychological fiction 14. Literary fiction

First published in 2011.

Originally published: London : Picador, 2011.

Jack must travel to bring the body of his brother, who has been killed in the Iraq War, home to England. The process of doing this has a terrible impact on Jack and on his relationship with his wife.

Swift, Jonathan, 1667-1745

* **Gulliver's** travels / Jonathan Swift. Dover Publications, 1996, c1735. xiii, 226 p.

ISBN 9780486292731

1. 19th century 2. Voyages and travels 3. Giants 4. Sailing 5. Miniature persons (Imaginary characters) 6. Fantasy classics 7. Fantasy fiction 8. Satirical fiction 9. Classics

Gullible ship's doctor Lemuel Gulliver experiences extraordinary travels, in which he goes through a series of apparently child-like fantasy worlds of tiny people and giants, floating islands and talking horses.

Swinson, Kiki

A **gangster** and a gentleman / Kiki Swinson, De'nesha Diamond. Dafina, 2012. 295 p.

ISBN 9780758251824

1. African American women 2. Protectiveness in men 3. Extramarital affairs 4. Organized crime 5. Gunfights 6. Revenge 7. Interpersonal conflict 8. Couples 9. African American couples 10. Men/women relations 11. African American men/women relations 12. African American fiction 13. Drama lit

LC bl2012021793

Two stories about women and their bad men, featuring Melody, who hires Scotty to take care of her cheating husband, but winds up seeking revenge, and Blake, who turns to her kingpin father's enforcer for protection from his employer.

Swinson, Kiki

I'm New York's finest / Kiki Swinson. K S Publicatons, 2017. 238 p.

ISBN 9780986203794

1. FBI 2. Drug dealers 3. Brothers and sisters 4. Families 5. Drug traffic 6. Suspicion 7. Freedom 8. Urban fiction 9. African American fiction

Naomi is a hustler at heart. And she loves her family. Put the two together and you'll end up with a very profitable drug enterprise.

Swinson, Kiki

Lifestyles of the rich and shameless / Kiki Swinson, Noire. Dafina, 2012. 264 p.

ISBN 9780758251800

1. Street life 2. Heirs and heiresses 3. African American women 4. Police 5. Wealth 6. Sexuality 7. Seduction 8. Life change events 9. Men/women relations 10. Urban erotica 11. African American fiction

In "Shamelessly rich," heiress Megan Rich suddenly loses her inheritance and must make a life-changing choice; and in "Puttin' Shame In The Game," three women scheme to seduce New York police officer Noble for his riches.

Swinson, Kiki

The **safe** house / Kiki Swinson. Kensington Books, 2019 256 p. Black market (Kiki Swinson)

ISBN 9781496720023

1. Cartels 2. Fugitives 3. African American women 4. Drug enforcement agents 5. Missing persons investigation 6. Missing persons 7. Crime bosses 8. Drug traffic 9. Crime 10. Virginia 11. Urban fiction 12. African American fiction

With the local police closing in on her as the prime suspect in her abusive boyfriend's disappearance, a fierce, strong woman has no choice but to ditch the feds and take down a cartel leader on her own.

Swinson, Kiki

Who's wife extraordinaire now / Kiki Swinson. K. S. Publications, 2014. 240 p. Wife extraordinaire

ISBN 9780985349554

1. African-American women 2. Power (Social sciences) 3. Married women 4. Extramarital affairs 5. Secrets 6. African American men/women relations 7. Sexuality 8. African American fiction 9. Drama lit

Swinson, Kiki

* **Wifey** / Kiki Swinson. Dafina, 2008. 294 p. Wifey

ISBN 9780758229014

1. African American women 2. Drug traffic 3. Street life 4. Husband and wife 5. Sexuality 6. City life 7. Men/women relations 8. Washington, D.C. 9. Urban fiction 10. African American fiction 11. Urban fiction

Street Lit Book Award Medal: Adult Fiction, 2005

Tired of his hustling and cheating, Kira tries to leave her drug-dealing husband Ricky as federal charges mount against him, but she faces complications along the way.

Swinson, Kiki

Wifey's next sticky situation / Kiki Swinson. KS Publications, 2017. 238 p. Wifey

ISBN 9780986203756

1. African American women 2. Drug traffic 3. Revenge 4. Murderers 5. Street life 6. Sexuality 7. City life 8. Men/women relations 9. New Jersey 10. Washington, D.C. 11. Urban fiction 12. African American fiction

Kira is the on the homicide detectives' radar once again. Right now, she's clueless as to how she's going to fix this situation but with Dylan now dead, things are going to get even stickier.

Swyler, Erika

* **Light** from other stars : a novel / Erika Swyler. Bloomsbury Publishing, 2019. 352 p.

ISBN 9781635573169

1. 1980s 2. 21st century 3. Women astronauts 4. Space and time 5.

Ambition 6. Inventions 7. Loss (Psychology) 8. Physicists 9. Space flight 10. Grief 11. Scientists 12. Parent and child 13. Family secrets 14. Family relationships 15. Florida 16. Space 17. Coming-of-age stories 18. Science fiction 19. Parallel narratives

LC 2018034280

Decades after her grieving father, a laid-off NASA scientist, triggers chaotic changes in his pursuit of life-extending technology, an astronaut confronts dangerous family secrets to stop a world-threatening crisis.

Szabo, Magda, 1917-2007

Abigail / Magda Szabo ; translated from Hungarian by Len Rix. New York Review Books, 2020, 360 p.

ISBN 9781681374031

1. Second World War era (1939-1945) 2. World War II 3. Boarding schools 4. Teenage girls 5. Spoiled children 6. Statues 7. Secrets 8. Schools 9. Resistance (Psychology) in teenage girls 10. Fathers and daughters 11. Hungary 12. Historical fiction 13. Coming-of-age stories 14. Translations -- Hungarian to English

LC 2019025320

Originally published: Budapest : Europa , 1970.

Fourteen-year-old Gina, the spoiled daughter of a Hungarian general, rails against being sent to boarding school far from Budapest when war breaks out, but finds help in a statue of Abigail and her new "sisters."

"This infectious coming-of-age novel from Szab (1917 2007), released in 1970 and translated into English for the first time, is a rollicking delight." Publishers Weekly.

T

T. I., (Rapper)

Power & Beauty : a love story of life on the streets / T.I. ; TIP "T.I." Harris with David Ritz. William Morrow, 2011. 352 p.

ISBN 9780062067654

1. African American men 2. Fashion 3. Drug traffic 4. Men/women relations 5. Street life 6. African American women 7. Violence 8. Loss (Psychology) 9. Atlanta, Georgia 10. New York City 11. Urban fiction 12. African American fiction

Sequel: Trouble & Triumph

After the death of his mother, Paul "Power" Clay allows himself to be guided by Slim, a local businessman. Power is sure that if he learns Slim's ways, he'll make something of himself-- and perhaps be worthy of Tanya "Beauty" Long. From Chicago to Miami to New York, through drugs, women, and violence, Power makes the difficult transition from boy to man and, in doing so, begins to question if those who have taught him truly have his best interests at heart.

T. I., (Rapper)

Trouble & triumph : a novel of Power & Beauty / TIP "T.I." Harris with David Ritz. HarperCollins, 2012. 288 p.

ISBN 9780062067685

1. African American men 2. Fashion 3. Drug traffic 4. Street life 5. Men/women relations 6. African American women 7. Violence 8. Atlanta, Georgia 9. Urban fiction 10. African American fiction

Sequel to: Power & Beauty.

Leaving Power, the boy she's come to love, behind, Tanya "Beauty" Long makes a name for herself in New York City's fashion industry, while Power becomes trapped in a world of drugs, women and money where he makes a shocking discovery that brings Tanya back to him.

Tademy, Lalita

Cane River / Lalita Tademy. Warner Books, 2001. 418 p. Tademy family chronicles

ISBN 0446527327

1. Tademy family 2. 19th century 3. 20th century 4. Race relations 5. Family relationships 6. Women slaves 7. African American families 8. African American women 9. Creoles (Louisiana) 10. Multiracial persons 11. Slavery -- Louisiana 12. Rape victims 13. Ambition 14. Plantations 15. Reconstruction (United States history) 16. Cane River Region, Louisiana 17. Louisiana -- History -- 19th century 18. Louisiana -- Race relations 19. African American fiction 20. Historical fiction 21. Family sagas 22. Southern fiction

LC 00043682

Cane River is an isolated community that lies on a small river in central Louisiana. There in the early 19th century, slaves, free people of color, and Creole French planters lived and worked, loved and bore children. The author discovered her amazing heritage there and chronicles four generations of strong, determined black women.

"Five generations and a hundred years in the life of a matriarchal black Louisiana family are encapsulated in this . . . novel that is based in part upon the lives, as preserved in both historical record and oral tradition, of the author's ancestors. . . . Her frank observations about black racism add depth to the tale, and she demonstrates that although the practice of slavery fell most harshly upon blacks, and especially women, it also constricted the lives and choices of white men. Photos of and documents relating to Tademy's ancestors add authenticity to a fascinating story." Publishers Weekly.

Tallis, Frank

Vienna blood : a Max Liebermann mystery / Frank Tallis. Random House, 2007, c2006. 496 p. Liebermann papers

ISBN 9780812977769

1. Belle Epoque (1871-1914) 2. 1900s (Decade) 3. Secret societies 4. Mutilation 5. Prostitutes 6. Detectives 7. Serial murders 8. Psychoanalysts 9. Serial murderers 10. Marital conflict 11. Men/women relations 12. Police 13. Vienna, Austria -- History -- 20th century 14. Austria -- History -- 20th century 15. Historical mysteries 16. Mysteries

LC 2007019605

In the sequel to "A Death in Vienna," 1902 Vienna is terrorized by a serial killer targeting prostitutes and leaving strange crosslike symbols in his wake, and Detective Oscar Rheinhardt and Dr. Max Liebermann reunite to find a murderer.

Tamirat, Nafkote

The **parking** lot attendant : a novel / Nafkote Tamirat. Henry Holt & Company, 2018 225 p.

ISBN 9781250128508

1. Ethiopians 2. Immigrants 3. Fathers and daughters 4. Teenage girls -- Relations with older men 5. Swindlers and swindling 6. Fifteen-year-old girls 7. African Americans 8. Communes 9. Islands 10. Boston, Massachusetts 11. Coming-of-age stories 12. Literary fiction 13. African American fiction

LC 2017019274

A reviled member of a dysfunctional Ethiopian immigrant community in Boston reflects on the experiences that brought her and her introverted father to America and traces her growing bond with the community's charismatic con-man leader, whose schemes embroil her in a plot with unanticipated repercussions.

"Tamirat's razor-sharp prose fashions a magnificently dimensional and emotionally resonant narrator, herself a storyteller who frames her own tale with beguiling skill. This debut is remarkable in every way." Booklist.

Tan, Amy

The **bonesetter's** daughter / Amy Tan. G.P. Putnam's, 2001. 333 p.

ISBN 0399146431

1. Mothers and daughters 2. Generation gap 3. Chinese American families 4. Chinese American women 5. Women immigrants 6. Women with Alzheimer's disease 7. Memory in senior women 8. Women ghostwriters 9. Widows 10. Healers 11. China -- Social life and customs 12. San Francisco, California 13. Women's lives and relationships

LC 00062673

First published in Great Britain by Flamingo, 2001.

Set in Contemporary San Francisco and in a Chinese village where Peking Man is being unearthed, The Bonesetter's Daughter is an excavation of the human spirit: the past, its deepest wounds, its most profound hopes. The story conjures the pain of broken dream, the power of myths, and the strength of love that enables us to recover in memory what we have lost in grief. Over the course of one fog-shrouded year, between one season of falling stars and the next, mother and daughter find what they share in their bones through heredity, history, and inexpressible qualities of love.

"A fine and highly readable novel, The Bonesetter's Daughter is essentially about writing and the act of writing, what fuels it and how it is created. More specifically still, it is about how we, as women creatively express ourselves via language." Women's Review of Books.

Tan, Amy

The **hundred** secret senses / Amy Tan. G.P. Putnam's Sons, 1995. 358 p.

ISBN 0399141146

1. Chinese American women 2. Sisters -- United States 3. Senses and sensation 4. Half-sisters 5. Chinese Americans in China 6. Husband and wife 7. Chinese in California 8. Reincarnation 9. Ghosts 10. China 11. Ghost stories 12. Magical realism 13. Literary fiction

LC 95031791

Shortlisted for The Orange Prize for Fiction, 1996

Kwan, a seventeen-year-old half-sister from China, turns young Olivia's world upside-down with her stories of ghosts of another time, tales that have a profound impact on Olivia's life and imagination, until she discovers a way to reconcile the ghosts of the past with her dreams of the future

"Nearing divorce from her husband, Simon, Olivia Yee is guided by her elder half-sister, the irrepressible Kwan, into the heart of China. Olivia was five when 18-year-old Kwan first joined her family in the United States, and though always irritated by Kwan's oddities, Olivia was entranced by her eerie dreams of the ghost World of Yin. Only when visiting Kwan's home in Changmian does Olivia realize the dreams are, in Kwan's mind, memories from past lives. . . . Tan tells a mysterious, believable story and delivers Kwan's clipped, immigrant voice and engaging personality with charming clarity." Library Journal.

Tan, Amy

* The **Joy** Luck Club / Amy Tan. Putnam's, 1989. 288 p.

ISBN 9780399134203

1. Chinese American women -- Identity 2. Generation gap 3. Mothers and daughters -- San Francisco, California 4. Friendship 5. Female friendship 6. Immigrants, Chinese 7. Chinese in California 8. Immigrants 9. San Francisco, California 10. Women's lives and relationships 11. Historical fiction

LC 88026492

ALA Notable Book, 1990.

National Book Critics Circle Award for Fiction finalist, 1989

National Book Award for Fiction finalist, 1989

After being drawn together by the shadows of their past, four women start meeting every week in San Francisco to engage in hobbies they all enjoy. After one of the four members dies, her daughter takes her place to fulfill her mother's dying wish. After the revelation of a secret, the women are forced to think back to their pasts and remember the sometimes painful events of their lives.

Tan, Amy

* The **kitchen** god's wife / Amy Tan. G. P. Putnam's Sons, 1991. 415 p.

ISBN 0399135782

1. Mothers and daughters -- Los Angeles, California 2. Generation gap 3. Chinese American women 4. Secrets 5. Family secrets 6. Interracial marriage 7. Women with multiple sclerosis 8. Chinese Americans -- Interracial marriage 9. Los Angeles, California 10. China -- History -- 20th century 11. Women's lives and relationships

LC 91007828

ALA Notable Book, 1992.

For forty years, in China and in San Francisco, Winnie Louie and Helen Kwong have kept certian confidences. Suddenly, those shattering secrets are about to be revealed. So begins a series of comic misunderstandings and heartbreaking realizations about luck, loss, and trust; about the things a mother cannot tell her daughter, the secrets daughters keep, and the miraculous resiliency of love.

"Within the peculiar construction of Amy Tan's second novel is a harrowing, compelling and at times bitterly humorous tale in which an entire world unfolds in a Tolstoyan tide of event and detail." New York Times Book Review.

Tan, Amy

The **Valley** of Amazement / Amy Tan. Ecco Press, 2013. 608 p.

ISBN 9780062107312

1. Mothers and daughters 2. Prostitution 3. Identity (Psychology) 4. Kidnapping 5. Art 6. Family secrets 7. Americans in China 8. Courtesans 9. Men/women relations 10. Family relationships 11. Shanghai, China 12. San Francisco, California 13. China 14. California 15. Family sagas 16. Historical fiction

Violet Minturn, a half-Chinese/half-American courtesan who deals in seduction and illusion in Shanghai, struggles to find her place in the world, while her mother, Lucia, tries to make sense of the choices she has made and the men who have shaped her.

Tan, Lucy

What we were promised / Lucy Tan. Little Brown & Co, 2018 336 p.

ISBN 9780316437189

1. Rich families 2. Immigrants 3. Discontent 4. Secrets 5. Jewelry theft 6. Family problems 7. Nouveaux riches 8. Arranged marriage 9. Immigrants, Chinese 10. Household employees 11. Chinese Americans in China 12. Shanghai, China 13. Literary fiction

Returning home to Shanghai after years of chasing the American dream, Wei Zhen and his newly wealthy family, including his wife, Lina, and their daughter, Karen, must each confront painful secrets and unfulfilled promises.

Tan, Twan Eng, 1972-

The **garden** of evening mists / Tan Twan Eng. Weinstein Books, 2012. 352 p.

ISBN 9781602861800

1. 1950s 2. Former prisoners of war 3. Loss (Psychology) 4. Survival (in concentration camps, prisons, etc) 5. World War II 6. Tea plantations -- Malaysia 7. Plantations -- Malaysia 8. Men -- Japan 9.

Women -- Malaysia 10. Gardens 11. Gardening 12. Coping 13. Grief in women 14. Memorials 15. Guerrilla warfare 16. Communism 17. Malaysia -- History -- 20th century 18. Malaya -- History -- 20th century 19. Malaya -- History -- Japanese occupation, 1942-1945 20. Historical fiction 21. Literary fiction
Man Asian Literary Prize, 2012.
Walter Scott Prize for Historical Fiction, 2013.
Shortlisted for the Man Booker Prize, 2012.
Shortlisted for the International IMPAC Dublin Literary Award, 2014
Seeking solace in the Malaysian plantations of her childhood after grueling World War II experiences, criminal prosecutor Yun Ling Teoh discovers a Japanese garden and its enigmatic tender, an exiled Japanese royal gardener who reluctantly accepts her as an apprentice.

Taneja, Preti,
We that are young : a novel / Preti Taneja. Knopf, 2018, c2017. 512 p.
ISBN 9780525521525
1. 2010s 2. Families 3. Family businesses 4. Power (Social sciences) 5. Inheritance and succession 6. Family relationships 7. Arranged marriage 8. Rich families 9. Corruption 10. India 11. Delhi 12. Literary fiction 13. Adaptations, retellings, and spin-offs
LC 2018015399
A reissue of the 2017 edition published by Galley Beggar Press (Norwich, England).
A modern-day *King Lear*, set in contemporary India, traces the power struggles of a turbulent family that becomes painfully subject to the anti-corruption riots of 2011 and 2012, a father's advancing dementia and an unwanted arranged marriage.

Tanen, Sloane
There's a word for that / Sloane Tanen. Little, Brown and Company, 2019. 375 p.
ISBN 9780316437165
1. Dysfunctional families 2. Addiction 3. Rehabilitation 4. Rehabilitation centers 5. Celebrities 6. Seniors 7. Divorced couples 8. Parent and adult child 9. Family relationships 10. Los Angeles, California 11. California 12. Domestic fiction 13. Humorous stories
The wildly flawed and dysfunctional Kessler family--retired film producer Marty; his daughter Janine, a former child star; granddaughter Hailey; and long-forgotten first wife, Bunny--comes together in Malibu's most exclusive rehab center.
"With equal parts humor and empathy, Tanen's first novel for adults employs multiple narrators and a skillfully drawn cross-generational family to examine how relatives impact one another." Booklist.

Tarkington, Booth, 1869-1946
* **Alice** Adams / Booth Tarkington ; illustrated by Arthur William Brown ; introduction by Donald Gray. Indiana University Press, 2003, c1921. xix, 434 p.
ISBN 0253215935
1. Young women 2. Social classes 3. Middle-class families 4. Indiana 5. Coming-of-age stories 6. Modern classics
Originally published: New York : Grosset & Dunlap, 1921.
Pulitzer Prize for Fiction, 1922.
This is the story of a middle-class family living in the industrialized "midland country" at the turn of the 20th century. It is against this dingy backdrop that Alice Adams seeks to distinguish herself. She goes to a dance in a used dress, which her mother attempts to renew by changing the lining and adding some lace. She adorns herself not with orchids sent by the florist but with a bouquet of violets she has picked herself. Because her family cannot afford to equip her with the social props or "background" so needed to shine in society. Alice is forced to make do. Ultimately, her ambitions for making a successful marriage must be tempered by the realities of her situation.

Tarkington, Booth, 1869-1946
* The **magnificent** Ambersons / Booth Tarkington. Tor, 2001, c1918. 346 p.
ISBN 081259004X
1. Rich families 2. Fathers and daughters 3. Mothers and sons 4. Social classes 5. Family relationships 6. Change 7. Indiana 8. Family sagas 9. Modern classics
Originally published: New York : Grosset & Dunlap, 1918.
Pulitzer Prize for Fiction, 1919.
The rise and fall of a prominent Hoosier family centers around the life and experiences of George Amberson Menafer, a spoiled young man.

Tartt, Donna
* The **goldfinch** / Donna Tartt. Little Brown & Co, 2013. 771 p.
ISBN 9780316055437
1. Misfits (Persons) 2. Obsession 3. Loss (Psychology) 4. Art 5. Mothers -- Death 6. Friendship 7. Drug use 8. Grief 9. Crime 10. Antique dealers 11. Criminals 12. Men/women relations 13. Manhattan, New York City 14. New York City 15. Las Vegas, Nevada 16. Psychological fiction 17. Literary fiction 18. Coming-of-age stories
Movie version to be released September 2019.
ALA Notable Book, 2014
Andrew Carnegie Medal for Excellence in Fiction, 2014.
Pulitzer Prize for Fiction, 2014.
Shortlisted for The Baileys Women's Prize for Fiction, 2014
National Book Critics Circle Award for Fiction finalist, 2013
Taken in by a wealthy family friend after surviving an accident that killed his mother, thirteen-year-old Theo Decker tries to adjust to life on Park Avenue.
"The novel is slow to build but eloquent and assured, with memorable characters. . . . A standout." Kirkus.

Tartt, Donna
* The **secret** history / Donna Tartt. Alfred A. Knopf, 1992. 523 p.
ISBN 9780679410324
1. College students 2. Guilt in men 3. Intellectuals 4. Cliques 5. Friendship 6. Campus life 7. Murder 8. Responsibility in men 9. Universities and colleges 10. College teachers 11. Deception 12. Suicide 13. Vermont 14. Psychological suspense 15. Literary fiction
LC 92053053
A transfer student from a small town in California, Richard Papen is determined to affect the ways of his Hampden College peers, and he begins his intense studies under the tutelage of eccentric Julian Morrow.
"Tartt records the aftereffects of unpunished crime with great skill." The New Republic.

Taseer, Aatish, 1980-
The **way** things were : a novel / Aatish Taseer. Faber & Faber, 2015. 496 p.
ISBN 9780865478244
1. Families 2. Fathers and sons 3. Scholars and academics 4. Voyages and travels 5. Family relationships 6. Culture 7. India -- History -- 20th century 8. India -- Social conditions -- 20th century 9. India -- Social life and customs -- 20th century 10. Domestic fiction 11. Historical fiction
LC 2014049064

"Authors often attempt to frame a given period of a country's history through a single family's story, but Taseer's book is a cut above the rest. Colonialism, racism, sectarian violence, class tension, and the rise of the Indian nouveau riche are all handled with a delicate touch. This is a difficult book to put down, and readers will enjoy every minute of it, as well as learning about contemporary Indian culture." Publishers Weekly.

Tata, A. J. (Anthony J.), 1959-

Dark winter / A. J. Tata. Kensington, 2018. 464 p. Jake Mahegan thrillers

ISBN 9781496717900

1. National security 2. International intrigue 3. Hackers 4. Power (Social sciences) 5. Terrorism -- Prevention 6. Nuclear weapons 7. Couples 8. Elite operatives 9. Political thrillers 10. Thrillers and suspense

In a blistering scenario almost too close to the headlines, former Brigadier General Anthony J. Tata delivers a chillingly authentic glimpse of tomorrow's wars--and the anonymous hackers who hold the fate of the world at their fingertips . . .

Tatlock, Ann

Promises to keep / Ann Tatlock. Bethany House, 2011. 368 p.

ISBN 9780764208096

1. Escapes 2. Senior women -- Friendship 3. Mothers and daughters 4. Secrets 5. Courage in women 6. Determination in women 7. Faith (Christianity) 8. Helpfulness in women 9. Families 10. Single-parent families 11. Abusive men 12. Illinois 13. Christian fiction 14. Gentle reads

LC 2010037083

Christy Award for Contemporary (Stand Alone) Category, 2012.

The Anthony family, on the run from their alcoholic husband and father, leaves Minneapolis for the small town of Mills River, Ill. But they've barely begun to acclimate when sassy old lady Tillie Monroe shows up at their doorstep explaining that the house once belonged to her and her late husband.

Tawada, Yoko, 1960-

* The **emissary** / Yoko Tawada ; translated by Margaret Mitsutani. New Directions, 2018, c2014. 128 p.

ISBN 9780811227629

1. Dystopias 2. Post-apocalypse 3. Intergenerational relations 4. Aging 5. Longevity 6. Near future 7. Sick children 8. Grandfather and grandson 9. Japan 10. Literary fiction 11. Apocalyptic fiction 12. Dystopian fiction 13. Translations -- Japanese to English

LC 2017041786

Originally published in Japanese as Kentoshi in 2014.

Also published as The last children of Tokyo.

In Japan, which has cut itself off from the world after suffering a massive irreparable disaster, Yoshiro cares for his grandson, Mumei, a strangely wonderful boy and ancient soul whom he believes is a beacon of hope for the world in this time of darkness.

"An ebullient meditation on language and time that feels strikingly significant in the present moment." Kirkus.

Taylor, Brad, 1965-

* **Daughter** of war : a novel / Brad Taylor. Dutton, 2019 416 p. Pike Logan thrillers

ISBN 9781101984840

1. Weapons of mass destruction 2. Special forces 3. Military missions 4. International relations 5. Military intelligence 6. Thrillers and suspense

LC 2018031286

Pike Logan and the Taskforce uncover a Syrian plot to create a weapon of mass destruction against American and Kurdish forces, a situation that is complicated by a violent North Korean retaliation against western sanctions.

Taylor, Brad, 1965-

Ring of fire / Brad Taylor. E.P. Dutton, 2017. 416 p. Pike Logan thrillers

ISBN 9781101984765

1. Special forces 2. Special operations (Military science) 3. Terrorism -- Prevention 4. Secrets 5. News leaks 6. Crime 7. Thrillers and suspense

Learning of an imminent terrorist attack on the U.S., Pike Logan, Jennifer Cahill and the Taskforce race against time to stop catastrophic events in multiple locations.

"Taylors background in Special Forces gives his story lines authenticity, and his uncanny sense of tomorrows headlines makes him seem almost psychic. Fine work from a thriller writer at the very top of his game." Booklist.

Taylor, Brandon (Brandon L. G.)

* **Real** life / Brandon Taylor. Riverhead Books, 2020. 288 p.

ISBN 9780525538882

1. Gay men 2. African American gay men 3. African American men 4. Introverts 5. Graduate students 6. Sexuality 7. Fathers -- Death 8. Men/men relations 9. Biochemistry 10. Racism 11. Loneliness 12. Homophobia 13. Race relations 14. Middle West 15. Literary fiction 16. African American fiction

LC 2019022438

Keeping his head down at a lakeside Midwestern university where the culture is in sharp contrast to his Alabama upbringing, an introverted African-American biochem student endures unexpected encounters that bring his orientation and defenses into question.

"He works a needle through Wallace's knots of race, class, and love, stopping after loosening their loops and making hidden intricacies visible, before neatly untying them." Booklist.

Tepper, Sheri S.

The **gate** to Women's Country / Sheri S. Tepper. Foundation Books, 1988. 278 p.

ISBN 9780385247092

1. Dystopias 2. Men/women relations 3. Survival (after nuclear warfare) 4. Warriors 5. Men psychics 6. Women physicians 7. Imaginary wars and battles 8. Social science fiction 9. Science fiction

LC 88000387

In a futuristic society where the sexes are separated, men are warriors, and women cultivate the arts, Stavia disobeys the group's prohibitions by loving a man forbidden to her, setting the stage for a momentous decision.

"A feminist fable set somewhere in the Pacific Northwest 300 years after a nuclear holocaust. Men and women now live in separate but adjacent communities. Although the men are organized into military garrisons, the women appear to have the upper hand in government, deciding matters of trade and law and, most important, reproduction. . . . The elaborate society that the author takes such pains to describe is based on a big lie; the story she tells is part of the deception. Some will find this narrative strategy as distasteful as the secret it conceals. But Ms. Tepper is not afraid to ask hard questions, beginning with this: If biology is destiny, how can society hope to control its self-destructive tendencies without controlling biology as well?" New York Times Book Review.

Tepper, Sheri S.
  * Grass / Sheri S. Tepper. Doubleday, 1989. 426 p. Marjorie Westriding trilogy
    ISBN 9780385260121
    1. Interplanetary relations 2. Human/alien encounters 3. Plague 4. Space flight 5. Space vehicles 6. Aliens (Non-humanoid) 7. Space warfare 8. Religion 9. Investigations 10. Space colonies 11. Social science fiction 12. Science fiction
                                                LC   89030105
    Sequel: Raising the stones.
    Sent to the land of Grass to find out how that planet has escaped the deadly plague that threatens the rest of the galaxy, a strong-willed woman makes some unexpected and frightening discoveries.
    "This is a beautifully written novel with well-developed characters and a number of very interesting aliens." Anatomy of Wonder, 4th edition.

Tepper, Sheri S.
  Singer from the sea / Sheri S. Tepper. Eos, 1999. 426 p.
    ISBN 9780380974801
    1. Longevity 2. Mothers and daughters 3. Class conflict 4. Social classes 5. Heirs and heiresses 6. Arranged marriage 7. Gender role 8. Women's role 9. Social science fiction 10. Science fiction
                                                LC 99-10231
    The heiress to a great title on the isolated planet of Haven, Genevieve is torn between the rigid teachings of the Covenants, inflexible laws that govern women of her class, and the secret knowledge learned from her late mother, only to discover that she alone holds the key to the salvation of her world.
    "Despite her status as a young noblewoman of the planet Haven, Genevieve rebels against the strict regulations concerning highborn women. Defying her father's wishes, she seeks her own forbidden destiny and discovers the dark secrets that lie at the heart of her world and its forgotten history. Tepper . . . continues to explore the intricacies of human societal structures and the complex connections between humans and their environment, combining stylistic grace with imaginative insight." Library Journal.

Tepper, Sheri S.
  The **visitor** / Sheri S. Tepper. EOS, 2002. 407 p.
    ISBN 9780380979059
    1. Dystopias 2. Asteroids -- Collisions with Earth 3. Religious fanatics 4. Ancestors 5. Magic 6. Books and reading 7. Far future 8. Mythology 9. Stepdaughters 10. Superstition 11. Women scientists 12. Young women 13. Social science fiction 14. Science fiction 15. Science fantasy
                                                LC 2001040197
    Civilization has survived--barely--in the wake of a twenty-first century collision with an asteroid, but when Disme, an orphan, begins to read a fascinating book by one of her ancestors from before the dark times, she is compelled to search out a mystery.

Tesh, Emily
  Silver in the wood / Emily Tesh. Tom Doherty Associates, 2019. 112 p. Greenhollow duology
    ISBN 9781250229793
    1. Victorian era (1837-1901) 2. Forests 3. Men/men relations 4. Dryads 5. Cats 6. Gay men 7. Mother and adult son 8. Fantasy fiction 9. Mythological fiction 10. LGBTQIA fiction 11. Folklore General.
    There is a Wild Man who lives in the deep quiet of Greenhollow, and he listens to the wood. Tobias, tethered to the forest, does not dwell on his past life, but he lives a perfectly unremarkable existence with his cottage, his cat, and his dryads. When Greenhollow Hall acquires a handsome, intensely curious new owner in Henry Silver, everything changes. Old secrets better left buried are dug up, and Tobias is forced to reckon with his troubled past, both the green magic of the woods, and the dark things that rest in its heart.

Tey, Josephine, 1896 or 1897-1952
  The **daughter** of time / Josephine Tey. Scribner Paperback Fiction, 1995, c1951. 218 p. Alan Grant mysteries
    ISBN 9780684803869
    1. Richard III,, King of England, 1452-1485 2. Scotland Yard. 3. 15th century 4. 20th century 5. Hospital patients 6. Portraits 7. Conspiracies 8. Detectives -- Great Britain 9. Criminal investigation 10. Murder 11. Murder victims 12. Great Britain -- History -- 20th century 13. Mysteries
    A hospitalized English policeman reconstructs historical evidence concerning Richard III's role in the murder of Edward IV's two sons.
    "The author not only reconstructs the probably historical truth, she re-creates the intense dramatic excitement of the scholarly research necessary to unveil it." New York Times Book Review.

Thackeray, William Makepeace, 1811-1863
  * Vanity fair : a novel without a hero / William Makepeace Thackeray ; edited with an introduction and notes by John Carey. Penguin Books, 2001, c1848. xl, 866 p.
    ISBN 9780141439839
    1. 19th century 2. Young women 3. Upward mobility 4. Manipulation by women 5. Men/women relations 6. Social status 7. England -- Social life and customs -- 19th century 8. Literary fiction 9. Satirical fiction 10. Classics
    Originally serialized in Punch magazine, January 1847-July 1848.
    Chronicles the exploits of Becky Sharp, an unscrupulous young woman who is determined to achieve wealth and social success, and her sentimental companion, Amelia, who has fallen for a caddish soldier, in the classic novel set against the backdrop of English society in the early 1800s.

Thelen, Albert Vigoleis, 1903-1989
  The **island** of second sight : from the applied recollections of Vigoleis / Albert Vigoleis Thelen ; translated from the German by Donald O. White. Overlook Press, 2012, c1953. 730 p.
    ISBN 9781468301168
    1. 1930s 2. Authors 3. Husband and wife 4. Fugitives 5. Civil War 6. Brothers 7. Majorca, Spain 8. Spain -- History -- Civil War, 1936-1939 9. Literary fiction 10. Historical fiction 11. Translations -- German to English
    First published in German as Die Insel des zweiten Gesichts: Dusseldorf : Diederichs, 1953.
    An English-language release of a German award-winner originally published in 1953 traces the largely autobiographical experiences of inventor Vigoleis, who with his wife scrapes out an existence in 1930s Mallorca and befriends literary figures and Jewish neighbors before making Nazi enemies and plotting a daring escape during the Spanish Civil War.

Theroux, Marcel, 1968-
  Far north / Marcel Theroux. Farrar, Straus and Giroux, 2009. 320 p.
    ISBN 9780374153533
    1. Refugees 2. Post-apocalypse 3. Dystopias 4. Murder -- Siberia 5. Redemption 6. Quests 7. Survival 8. Siberia 9. Apocalyptic fiction
                                                LC 2008049224
    National Book Award for Fiction finalist, 2009

A last of a group of settlers in a hardscrabble abandoned western town, self-declared sheriff Makepeace decides to reconnect with others after a visit from a traveling refugee but finds his sense of the world unraveling through his encounters with other ghost towns, stockade villages that enforce a dubious sense of the law, and mysterious slave camps.

"Theroux's haunting meditation on annihilation gives his novel the power of grief-stricken mourning." Booklist.

Theroux, Marcel, 1968-

Strange bodies : a novel / Marcel Theroux. Farrar, Straus and Giroux, 2014, c2013. 352 p.

ISBN 9780374270650

1. Johnson, Samuel, 1709-1784 2. Consciousness 3. Identity (Philosophical concept) 4. Forgery 5. Psychotherapy patients 6. Authors 7. Scholars and academics 8. Literary fiction 9. Gothic fiction

LC 2013034018

John W. Campbell Memorial Award for Best Science Fiction Novel, 2014.

Locked in a notorious psychiatric hospital, a man claiming to be the deceased Dr. Nicholas Slopen eventually uncovers a dark conspiracy between Silicon Valley and Russia that created new technology known as the Malevin Procedure.

"Observations about science, medicine, psychology, love, madness, and literature result in a thought-provoking and engaging fusion of comedy and horror, irony and insight." Publishers Weekly.

Theroux, Paul

The **Elephanta** suite / Paul Theroux. Houghton Mifflin, 2007. 256 p.

ISBN 9780618943326

1. Americans in India 2. Culture conflict 3. Husband and wife 4. Vacations 5. Men/women relations 6. Rich people 7. Young women 8. Stalkers 9. Stalking 10. India 11. Literary fiction 12. Psychological fiction

LC 2007013978

Three intertwining novellas portray Westerners in India, as a middle-aged couple travel on vacation, a lawyer discovers Mumbai's slums, and a woman befriends an elephant in Bangalore.

Theroux, Paul

* The **Lower** River / Paul Theroux. Houghton Mifflin Harcourt, 2012. 320 p.

ISBN 9780547746500

1. Self-discovery in men 2. Divorced men 3. Life change events 4. Idealism in men 5. Villages -- Africa 6. Travelers -- United States 7. Voyages and travels 8. Malawi 9. Africa 10. Political fiction 11. Literary fiction

LC 2011036975

Idealizing the four years he spent in Malawi with the Peace Corps, Ellis Hock is abruptly divorced by his wife and decides to return to Africa only to find the region devastatingly transformed by poverty and apathy.

Theroux, Paul

* The **Mosquito** Coast : a novel / Paul Theroux ; with woodcuts by David Frampton. Houghton Mifflin, 1982, c1981. 374 p.

ISBN 0395318378

1. Americans in Honduras 2. Inventors -- United States 3. Fathers and sons 4. Ideology 5. Utopians 6. Family problems 7. Family relationships 8. Americans in South America 9. Honduras 10.

Literary fiction

LC 81006787

Originally published: London : Hamilton, 1981.

James Tait Black Memorial Prize for Fiction, 1981.

National Book Award for Fiction finalist, 1983

An eccentric American inventor moves his family to the jungles of Central America in hopes of finding a better life.

Thien, Madeleine, 1974-

* **Do** not say we have nothing / Madeleine Thien. W. W. Norton & Co., 2016. 473 p.

ISBN 9780393609882

1. 1960s 2. 1980s 3. Families -- History 4. Social conflict 5. Social change -- China 6. Family relationships 7. Politics and culture -- China 8. Musicians 9. Shanghai, China 10. China -- Politics and government -- 20th century 11. Vancouver, British Columbia 12. Literary fiction

First published in Canada in 2016 by Alfred A. Knopf Canada.

Governor General's Literary Award for English-Language Fiction, 2016

Scotiabank Giller Prize, 2016.

Shortlisted for the Man Booker Prize, 2016.

Shortlisted for The Baileys Women's Prize for Fiction, 2017.

Marie endeavors to piece together the story of her fractured family's past and its connection to her friend Ai-Ming, uncovering information about how both women's fathers were forced to reimagine their identities during Mao's Cultural Revolution.

"Mythic yet realistic, panoramic yet intimate, intellectual yet romantic--Thien has written a concerto dauntingly complex and deeply haunting." Kirkus.

This way to the end times : classic tales of the apocalypse / edited by Robert Silverberg. Three Rooms Press, 2016. xvii, 452 p.

ISBN 9781941110478

1. End of the world 2. Post-apocalypse 3. Survival (after disaster) 4. Civilization 5. Apocalyptic fiction 6. Science fiction 7. Short stories 8. Anthologies

LC 2016936893

A collection of stories about the not-too-distant demise of the earth as we know it.

"With its range of contributors, this is a much-needed volume that will both satisfy the high demand for apocalyptic tales and remind readers of the actual breadth and depth of this literature of the end of the world." Booklist.

Thom, James Alexander

Panther in the sky : a novel based on the life of Tecumseh / James Alexander Thom. Ballantine Books, 1989. 655 p.

ISBN 9780345305961

1. Tecumseh,, Shawnee Chief, 1768-1813 2. Early America (1784-1819) 3. Indians of North America 4. Freedom 5. War 6. Shawnee Indians -- Wars -- 1750-1815 7. Shawnee Indians 8. Warriors 9. Native American men 10. United States -- History -- 1783-1815 11. Westerns 12. Biographical fiction

LC 88048012

Maps on lining papers.

Spur Award for Best Novel of the West (Long Novel), 1990.

A fictional biography of the legendary Native American chief and warrior Tecumseh.

Thomas, Bev

A **good** enough mother : a novel / Bev Thomas. Pamela Dorman Books, 2019. 384 p.

ISBN 9780525561255

1. Mothers and sons 2. Missing men 3. Psychotherapist and patient 4. Women psychotherapists 5. Loss (Psychology) 6. Sexual violence victims 7. Marital conflict 8. Motherhood 9. Violence in men 10. London, England 11. Psychological suspense

LC 2018039700

When a new patient, Dan--unstable and traumatized-- looks exactly like her missing son, psychotherapist Ruth Hartland is determined to help him, but soon, her own complicated feelings cloud her professional judgement, and she begins to cross some dangerous boundaries.

Thomas, D. M.

The **white** hotel / D.M. Thomas. Penguin Books, 1993, c1981. x, 274 p.

ISBN 9780140231731

1. Freud, Sigmund, 1856-1939 2. 20th century 3. Psychoanalysis 4. Women -- Sexuality 5. Opera singers 6. Sexual fantasies 7. Psychic trauma 8. Holocaust (1933-1945) 9. Historical fiction 10. Literary fiction

LC 80052004

Originally published: London: Gollancz, 1981.

Shortlisted for the Booker-McConnell Prize, 1981.

This is a story of eroticism and inexplicable violence, recounted by a young woman to her analyst, Sigmund Freud. It is a vision of the wounds of the 20th century, and an attempt to heal them.

Thomas, Dylan, 1914-1953

* The **collected** stories / Dylan Thomas. New Directions Books, 1984. 362 p.

ISBN 9780811209984

1. Manners and customs 2. Wales -- Social life and customs 3. Short stories

LC 84006822

This edition of Dylan Thomas's collected stories is published to co-incide with the 50th anniversary of his death.

Thomas, Matthew, 1975-

We are not ourselves : a novel / Matthew Thomas. Simon & Schuster, 2014. 620 p.

ISBN 9781476756660

1. 20th century 2. Irish Americans 3. Children of immigrants 4. Ambition in women 5. Husband and wife 6. American dream 7. Family relationships 8. Men/women relations 9. Queens, New York City 10. New York City 11. Family sagas

LC 2013044414

Shortlisted for the James Tait Black Memorial Prize for Fiction, 2014

Raised by her Irish immigrant parents in a 1940s Queens apartment where alcohol and company combine in mercurial ways, Eileen marries an unambitious scientist with whom she endures an increasingly psycho-logically dark family life.

"Thomas works on a large canvas to create a memorable depiction of Eileen's vibrant spirit, the intimacy of her love for Ed, and the desperate stoicism she exhibits as reality narrows her dreams." Publishers Weekly.

Thomas, Russ, 1975-

* **Firewatching** / Russ Thomas. G. P. Putnam's Sons, 2020 320 p.

ISBN 9780525542025

1. Detectives 2. Cold cases (Criminal investigation) 3. One-night stands (Interpersonal relations) 4. Murder investigation 5. Murder suspects 6. Gay men 7. Heirs and heiresses 8. Family secrets 9. Arson 10. Manipulation (Social sciences) 11. England 12. Great Britain 13. Mysteries 14. Police procedurals

LC 2019042363

"A taut and ambitious police procedural debut introducing Detec-tive Sergeant Adam Tyler, a cold case reviewer who lands a high-profile murder investigation only to find the main suspect is a recent one-night stand."--, Provided by publisher.

"Red herrings and uncovered family secrets abound. This stun-ning police procedural marks Thomas as an author to watch." Publishers Weekly.

Thomas, Scarlett

Oligarchy / Scarlett Thomas. Counterpoint, 2020. 208 p.

ISBN 9781640093065

1. Boarding schools 2. Conspiracies 3. Teenage girls 4. Eating disorders 5. Weight control 6. Rich girls 7. Murder 8. Perfectionism 9. Gender role 10. Obsession in girls 11. Girls -- Russia 12. Literary fiction 13. Coming-of-age stories

Arriving at her English boarding school, the daughter of a Russian oligarch is enmeshed in her classmates' thin-obsessed world of pecking orders, eating disorders and online drama, before a friend goes missing amid rumors of a dormitory ghost.

"Though Thomas's characters get a lot of flak for being insufferable rich girls from outsiders in the novel--and they are--she's captured with an empathetic eye all the brutal, visceral, and surprisingly funny aspects of teenage girlhood." Publishers Weekly.

Thomas, Sherry (Sherry M.)

Beguiling the beauty / Sherry Thomas. Berkley Sensation, 2012. viii, 296 p. Fitzhugh trilogy

ISBN 9780425246962

1. Victorian era (1837-1901) 2. Dukes and duchesses 3. Widows 4. Secret identity 5. Transatlantic voyages 6. Interpersonal attraction 7. Revenge 8. Men/women relations 9. Great Britain -- Social life and customs -- Victoria, 1837-1901 10. England -- Social life and customs -- 19th century 11. Victorian romances 12. Historical romances

Venetia Easterbrook pretends to be a wealthy baroness in order to take revenge on the Duke of Lexington, but she ends up falling in love with him.

Thomas, Sherry (Sherry M.)

* The **luckiest** lady in London / Sherry Thomas. Berkley, 2013. 304 p. London novels (Sherry Thomas)

ISBN 9780425268889

1. Victorian era (1837-1901) 2. 19th century 3. Mate selection 4. Nobility 5. Aristocracy 6. Men/women relations 7. Interpersonal attraction 8. England -- History -- 19th century 9. Victorian romances 10. Historical romances

Louisa Cantwell must marry rich to support her sisters, but dare she fall in love with a man of so many dark and devastating secrets as the Marquess of Wrenworth?

Thomas, Sherry (Sherry M.)

My beautiful enemy / Sherry Thomas. Berkley, 2014. 304 p.

ISBN 9780425268896

1. Victorian era (1837-1901) 2. 1890s 3. Independence in women 4. Reunions 5. Betrayal 6. Second chances 7. Espionage 8. Forgiveness 9. Trust 10. Men/women relations 11. Great Britain -- Social life and customs -- Victoria, 1837-1901 12. England -- Social life and customs -- 19th century 13. Victorian romances 14. Historical romances

When she arrives in London on a mission for her stepfather, Catherine Blade is plunged into a web of espionage and treachery, forcing her to work with a man from her past--the only man she's ever loved, and the only person to ever betray her.

"A thought-provoking exploration of gender roles in the East and West and in the historical romance genre. It's also a darn good read." Kirkus.

Thomas, Sherry (Sherry M.)

Not quite a husband / Sherry Thomas. Bantam Books, 2009. viii, 341 p.

ISBN 9780553592436

1. British Raj (1858-1947) 2. 19th century 3. Women physicians 4. British in India -- History 5. Marital conflict 6. Husband and wife 7. Sisters 8. Gender role 9. Interpersonal attraction 10. Men/women relations 11. India -- History -- 19th century 12. Historical romances
LC bl2009013572

RITA Award for Best Historical Romance, 2010.

When her estranged husband, Leo Marsden, arrives at her clinic in India to deliver an urgent message from her sister, Byrony Asquith, who rebelled against London society by becoming a doctor, risks both her life and her heart by returning home.

Thomas, Sherry (Sherry M.)

Private arrangements / Sherry Thomas. Bantam Books, 2008. 384 p.

ISBN 9780440244318

1. Regency period (1811-1820) 2. Nobility 3. Marital conflict 4. Love triangles 5. Extramarital affairs 6. Betrayal 7. Pregnancy 8. Secrets 9. Men/women relations 10. Desire 11. London, England -- Social life and customs -- 19th century 12. Regency romances 13. Historical romances

After ten years of marriage and living on separate continents following a betrayal on the day after their wedding, Lord and Lady Tremaine are reunited when Gigi decides that she wants a divorce, and Camden comes up with an outrageous demand in exchange for her freedom.

"Camden Saybrook, Lord Tremaine, returns to late 19th-century England to confront his wife, Gigi, about her petition for divorce. Still bitter from Gigi's machinations to snare him as her husband, Camden will grant the divorce under one condition: must give him an heir within a year. Sparks fly as the two embark on heated attempts to put the bun in the oven, despite Gigi's fear that her next conquest, the insipid Lord Frederick, will discover her duplicitously lusty reunion. A captivating subplot emerges when Gigi's mother, Mrs. Rowland, sets her own plan in motion for Gigi's next nuptials. Thomas propels the plot forward with revealing repartee and gives the leads real nuance." Publishers Weekly.

Thomas, Sherry (Sherry M.)

Ravishing the heiress / Sherry Thomas. Berkley Sensation, 2012. 304 p. Fitzhugh trilogy

ISBN 9780425250877

1. Victorian era (1837-1901) 2. 19th century 3. Love triangles 4. Unrequited love 5. Nobility 6. Interpersonal attraction 7. Men/women relations 8. Great Britain -- Social life and customs -- Victoria, 1837-1901 9. England -- Social life and customs -- 19th century 10. Victorian romances 11. Historical romances

First published: New York : Berkley Sensation, 2012.

When her arranged marriage to the Earl Fitzhugh leads to a lasting friendship, but nothing more, Millicent, who has fallen head over heels in love with her husband, vows to prove to him that there is something between them that is worth fighting for.

Thomas, Sherry (Sherry M.)

Tempting the bride / Sherry Thomas. Berkley Sensation, 2012. 296 p. Fitzhugh trilogy

ISBN 9780425251027

1. Victorian era (1837-1901) 2. Women with amnesia 3. Husband and wife 4. Betrayal 5. Romantic love 6. Marriage 7. Viscounts and viscountesses 8. Interpersonal attraction 9. Love/hate relationships 10. Men/women relations 11. Great Britain -- Social life and customs -- Victoria, 1837-1901 12. England -- Social life and customs -- 19th century 13. Victorian romances 14. Historical romances

First published: New York : Berkley Sensation, 2012.

When he elopes with Helena Fitzhugh, who has despised him since they were children, to save her reputation, Viscount Hastings gets a second chance to prove his love after a carriage accident robs Helena of her memory.

Thompson, Jim, 1906-1977

The **killer** inside me / Jim Thompson. Vintage Books/ Black Lizard, 1991, c1952. 244 p.

ISBN 0679733973

1. Sheriffs -- Texas 2. Murderers -- Texas 3. Teachers 4. Deception 5. Psychopaths 6. Antisocial personality disorders 7. Men with mental illnesses 8. Murder 9. Subconsciousness 10. Secrets 11. Small town life 12. Texas 13. Psychological suspense 14. Modern classics
LC 90050472

Lou Ford, an easy-going deputy sheriff in Central City, hides his psychotic nature as he plans a double murder

Thompson, Tade

* **Rosewater** / Tade Thompson. Orbit, 2018, c2016. 423 p. Wormwood trilogy

ISBN 9780316449052

1. Aliens 2. Human/alien encounters 3. Government investigators 4. Secrecy in government 5. Aliens (Non-humanoid) 6. Revolutionaries 7. Former thieves 8. Psychic ability 9. Alien artifacts 10. Near future 11. Telepathy 12. Nigeria 13. West Africa 14. Afrofuturism and Afrofantasy 15. Science fiction

Originally published by Apex Publications in 2016.

Arthur C. Clarke Award, 2019.

Rosewater is a town on the edge. A community formed around the edges of a mysterious alien biodome, its residents comprise the hopeful, the hungry and the helpless - people eager for a glimpse inside the dome or a taste of its rumored healing powers. Kaaro is a government agent with a criminal past. He has seen inside the biodome, and doesn't care to again -- but when something begins killing off others like himself, Kaaro must defy his masters to search for an answer, facing his dark history and coming to a realization about a horrifying future.

"Never fails to intrigue and entertain. A captivating, cerebral work of science fiction that may very well signal a new definitive voice in the genre." Kirkus.

Thompson, Tade

The **Rosewater** insurrection / Tade Thompson. Orbit, 2019. 400 p. Wormwood trilogy

ISBN 9780316449083

1. Aliens 2. Human/alien encounters 3. Government investigators 4. Secrecy in government 5. Aliens (Non-humanoid) 6. Revolutionaries 7. Former thieves 8. Psychic ability 9. Alien artifacts 10. Near future 11. Telepathy 12. Nigeria 13. West Africa 14. Afrofuturism and Afrofantasy 15. Science fiction

Amidst a secret invasion, government agent Aminat must capture a woman who is the key to the survival of the human race but her mission is endangered by the Mayor of Rosewater and the emergence of an old enemy of Wormwood.

Thompson, Tade

The **Rosewater** redemption / Tade Thompson. Orbit, 2019. 416 p. Wormwood trilogy

ISBN 9780316449090

1. Aliens 2. Human/alien encounters 3. War 4. Undead 5. Aliens (Non-humanoid) 6. Mayors 7. Revolutionaries 8. Former thieves 9. Hackers 10. Psychic ability 11. Alien artifacts 12. Near future 13. Telepathy 14. Nigeria 15. West Africa 16. Afrofuturism and Afrofantasy 17. Science fiction

Operating across spacetime, the xenosphere, and international borders, it is up to a small group of hackers and criminals to prevent the extra-terrestrial advance. The fugitive known as Bicycle Girl, Kaaro, and his former handler Femi may be humanity's last line of defense.

Thompson-Spires, Nafissa

Heads of the colored people : stories / Nafissa Thompson-Spires. Atria/37 INK, 2018. 209 p.

ISBN 9781501167997

1. African Americans 2. Race relations 3. Identity (Psychology) 4. Interpersonal relations 5. Human behavior 6. Short stories 7. African American fiction 8. Literary fiction

LC 2017050727

Hurston/Wright Legacy Award: Fiction, 2019.

Shortlisted for the James Tait Black Memorial Prize for Fiction, 2018

Kirkus Prize for Fiction finalist, 2018.

In a collection of boundary-pushing stories that are touching, contemporary and darkly humorous, the author illuminates the simmering tensions and precariousness of black citizenship and the concept of black identity in this so-called post-racial era.

Thomson, E. S.

Beloved poison / E.S. Thomson. Pegasus Crime, 2016. 390 p. Jem Flockhart novels

ISBN 9781681772141

1. Victorian era (1837-1901) 2. 1850s 3. Hospitals 4. Medicine 5. Intrigue 6. Secrets 7. Pharmacists 8. Investigations 9. Historic buildings 10. Amateur detectives 11. Male impersonators 12. London, England -- History -- 19th century 13. Victorian mysteries 14. Historical mysteries

After the discovery of six tiny coffins filled with dried flowers and rags in the old chapel of a crumbling 1850s London infirmary, apothecary Jem Flockhart begins a quest to understand their meaning and is forced to make impossible choices.

"A debut mystery chock full of mysterious doings, riveting historical detail, and so many horrifying anecdotes about the state of medicine in the mid-1800s that you can almost feel the evil miasma rising from the pages." Kirkus.

Thomson, E. S.

The **blood** / E. S. Thomson. Pegasus Books, 2018. 384 p. Jem Flockhart novels

ISBN 9781681778754

1. Victorian era (1837-1901) 2. 1850s 3. Hospitals 4. Amateur detectives 5. Medicine 6. Docks 7. Sailors 8. Dissection 9. Secret identity 10. Male impersonators 11. Crimes against prostitutes 12. London, England -- History -- 19th century 13. Victorian mysteries 14. Historical mysteries

In a hunt that takes Jem Flockhart and Will Quartermain through the harrowing streets of Victorian London to the dangers of the seamen's floating hospital, The Blood, they will endeavor to solve a dark and terrible new mystery.

Tidhar, Lavie

Central Station / Lavie Tidhar. Tachyon Publications, 2016 288 p.

ISBN 9781616962142

1. Far future 2. Virtual reality 3. Space colonies 4. Posthumanism 5. Space stations 6. Communities 7. Families 8. Cyborgs 9. Viruses 10. Robots 11. Israel 12. Science fiction

John W. Campbell Memorial Award for Best Science Fiction Novel, 2017.

A worldwide diaspora has left a quarter of a million people at the foot of a space station. Cultures collide in real life and virtual reality. The city is literally a weed, its growth left unchecked. Life is cheap, and data is cheaper. When Boris Chong returns to Tel Aviv from Mars, much has changed. Boris' ex-lover is raising a strangely familiar child who can tap into the datastream of a mind with the touch of a finger. His cousin is infatuated with a robotnik--a damaged cyborg soldier who might as well be begging for parts. His father is terminally-ill with a multigenerational mind-plague. And a hunted data-vampire has followed Boris to where she is forbidden to return. Rising above them is Central Station, the interplanetary hub between all things: the constantly shifting Tel Aviv; a powerful virtual arena, and the space colonies where humanity has gone to escape the ravages of poverty and war. Everything is connected by the Others, powerful alien entities who, through the Conversation--a shifting, flowing stream of consciousness--are just the beginning of irrevocable change. At Central Station, humans and machines continue to adapt, thrive ... and even evolve.

"Tidhar (A Man Lies Dreaming; The Violent Century) changes genres with every outing, but his astounding talents guarantee something new and compelling no matter the story he tells." Library Journal.

Tidhar, Lavie

A **man** lies dreaming : a novel / Lavie Tidhar. Melville House, 2016, c2014. 307 p.

ISBN 9781612195049

1. Auschwitz (Concentration camp) 2. Dictators 3. Men's dreams 4. Private investigators 5. Survival (in concentration camps, prisons, etc) 6. Criminal investigation 7. Pulp fiction 8. Imagination in men 9. Holocaust victims 10. Antisemitism 11. Authors 12. Slavery 13. Nazis 14. London, England 15. Noir fiction 16. Alternative histories 17. Parallel narratives

Originally published: London : Hodder & Stoughton, 2014.

To escape the brutality of Auschwitz, a former pulp fiction author imagines an alternate history where Hitler was toppled in a coup and is forced to eke out a living as a low-rent private investigator on the grimiest streets of London.

"Everything in this genre-bender works; intriguing historical characters are worked into expertly managed plots, and the visceral noir atmosphere is juxtaposed nicely against the drawing-room world of Londons political scene." Booklist.

Tie, Ning

The **bathing** women / Tie Ning ; translated from the Chinese by Hongling Zhang and Jason Sommer. Scribner, 2012, c2000. 361 p.

ISBN 9781451694840

1. Friendship 2. Women 3. Self-discovery in women 4. Sisters 5. Sibling rivalry 6. Interpersonal relations 7. Family relationships 8. Family secrets 9. Female friendship 10. China -- Social life and customs -- 21st century 11. Political fiction 12. Women's lives and relationships 13. Translations -- Chinese to English

Originally published as Da yu nu: Shenyang Shi : Chun feng wen yi chu ban she, 2000.

Traces the lives of four women in China from their shared childhoods during the Cultural Revolution to adulthood in the new market economy of the 1990s, from children's book editor Tiao and her America-idealizing sister Fan to the self-destructive hedonist Fei and the chef Youyou.

Tinti, Hannah

The **twelve** lives of Samuel Hawley : a novel / Hannah Tinti. The Dial Press, 2017. 480 p.

ISBN 9780812989885

1. Former criminals 2. Twelve-year-old girls 3. Fathers and daughters 4. Fishers 5. Villages 6. Overfishing 7. Mothers -- Death 8. Organized crime 9. Gunshot victims 10. Family relationships 11. Children of criminals 12. New England 13. Coming-of-age stories 14. Crime fiction 15. Literary fiction

LC 2016021409

Librarians' Choice (Australia), 2017.

A once-professional killer protects his daughter from the legacy of his criminal past, an effort that is challenged by his daughter's struggles with the death of her mother and the reckoning of old enemies.

"An accomplished if overstuffed merger of coming-of-age tale and literary thriller." Kirkus.

Title, Sarah

The **undateable** / Sarah Title. Zebra Books, 2017. 352 p. Librarians in love

ISBN 9781420141832

1. Women librarians 2. Single women 3. Journalists 4. Matchmaking 5. Dating (Social customs) 6. Social media 7. Marriage proposals 8. Academic libraries 9. Interpersonal attraction 10. Men/women relations 11. San Francisco, California 12. Contemporary romances

Rendered as a love-hating, undateable librarian after a video of her rolling her eyes at a marriage proposal goes viral, Melissa "Bernie" Bernard, who doesn't believe in happily-ever-afters, but never backs down from a challenge, agrees to let reporter Colin Rodriguez find her the perfect match.

Toews, Miriam, 1964-

A **complicated** kindness : a novel / Miriam Toews. Counterpoint, 2004. 256 p.

ISBN 1582433216

1. Mennonites 2. Life change events in teenagers 3. Mother-separated teenage girls 4. Family problems 5. Fathers and daughters 6. Despair 7. Teenage boy/girl relations 8. Small town life -- Canada 9. Partying 10. Manitoba 11. Coming-of-age stories 12. Psychological fiction

LC 2004007960

Canadian Library Association Young Adult Book Award, 2005.

CBA Libris Award for Fiction Book of the Year, 2005.

Governor General's Literary Award for English-Language Fiction, 2004.

Manitoba Writing and Publishing Awards, Margaret Laurence Award for Fiction, 2004.

Manitoba Writing and Publishing Awards, McNally Robinson Book of the Year Award, 2004.

Shortlisted for the Giller Prize, 2004

Doomed to work at the Happy Family Farm, a chicken slaughterhouse in a town run by religious fundamentalists, sixteen-year-old Nomi Nickel nevertheless manages to bear witness to the dissolution of her family with a dark, sly wit.

"Nomi's hunger for life prevents the novel from being as bleak as her situation might suggest; her account of her trials is veined with a dark humor that glints with the glee of payback." New York Times Book Review.

Toews, Miriam, 1964-

* **Women** talking : a novel / Miriam Toews. Bloomsbury Publishing, 2019, c2018. 216 p.

ISBN 9781635572582

1. Mennonite women 2. Rape victims 3. Patriarchy 4. Sex crimes 5. Mennonites 6. Religious communities 7. Women 8. Decision-making 9. Violence against women 10. Belief and doubt 11. South America 12. Literary fiction

Originally published: Toronto, Ont. : Knopf Canada, 2018.

After learning the men in the community have been drugging and attacking more than a hundred women, eight Mennonite women meet in secret to decide whether they should escape to a place outside the colony or stay in the only world they've ever known.

"An exquisite critique of patriarchal culture...Stunningly original and altogether arresting." Kirkus.

Toibin, Colm, 1955-

The **blackwater** lightship / Colm Toibin. Scribner, 2000, c1999. 273 p.

ISBN 9780684873893

1. Women 2. Families -- Ireland 3. Intergenerational relations 4. Men with terminal illnesses 5. Death -- Psychological aspects 6. People with AIDS 7. Family relationships 8. Alienation (Social psychology) 9. Gay men 10. Ireland 11. Wexford County, Ireland 12. Domestic fiction 13. Psychological fiction

LC 00021036

Originally published: London : Picador, 1999.

Shortlisted for the Booker-McConnell Prize, 1999.

Shortlisted for the International IMPAC Dublin Literary Award, 2001

With AIDS about to claim a well-loved young man, three generations of his family are reunited at his bedside in Ireland, in a novel that explores the nature of love and the complex interrelationships among family members.

"The novel shows us discreetly what a practical, complicated matter dying is, how much logistics and paraphernalia it requires, and its unflinchingly exact style is a kind of respect paid to this. The commonplace and the catastropic lie cheek-by-jowl." London Review of Books.

Toibin, Colm, 1955-

Brooklyn : a novel / Colm Toibin. Scribner, 2009. 256 p.

ISBN 9781439138311

1. 1950s 2. Irish in the United States 3. Women immigrants 4. Social isolation 5. Immigration and emigration 6. Brooklyn, New York City -- History -- 20th century 7. Ireland -- History -- 20th century 8. Psychological fiction

LC 2009001548

Adapted into a movie in 2015.

Originally published: Viking, 2009.

Originally published the United Kingdom by Penguin Books, 2009.
Costa Novel Award, 2009.
ALA Notable Book, 2010.
Shortlisted for the International IMPAC Dublin Literary Award, 2011

Young Eilis Lacey dreams of life beyond the confines of her tiny Irish village, but unlike her beautiful sister, Rose, Eili's gifts are of a more practical nature: she has a head for numbers, and is a loving and dutiful daughter. Yet her ambition cannot be hidden and soon is noted by the Parish Priest, Father Flood. Via a church contact, he arranges for Eilis to travel to America where a job opportunity has arisen in New York with a reputable "merchant of Italian origin". Eilis finds lodgings in an eccentric boarding house and ekes out an existence in the cosmopolitan melting pot that is 1950s Brooklyn, impressing her employer, outwitting her landlady, and even falling in love. It seems her dream is truly becoming a reality. But then fate intervenes: a family crisis back home forces Eilis to make a choice between the past and the future, the old world and the new.

"A diligent young woman with few opportunities in nineteen-fifties Ireland is packed off by her family to Brooklyn, where she works in a department store, goes to church and night school, and acquires a boyfriend, before a family crisis presents her with a stark choice between her new life and her old one. Within these confines, Toibin creates a narrative of remarkable power, writing with a spareness and intensity that give the minutest shades of feeling immense emotional impact. Seen through his protagonist's cautious eyes, even hackneyed tropes of Brooklyn life, such as trips to Ebbets Field and Coney Island, take on a subtle strangeness. Purging the immigrant novel of all swagger and sentimentality, Toibin leaves us with a renewed understanding that to emigrate is to become a foreigner in two places at once." The New Yorker.

Toibin, Colm, 1955-
 * The **empty** family : stories / Colm Toibin. Simon & Schuster, 2011 288 p.
   ISBN 9781439138328
   1. Loss (Psychology) 2. Interpersonal relations 3. Homosexuality 4. Short stories 5. Literary fiction
   Silence -- The empty family -- Two women -- One minus one -- The pearl fishers -- Barcelona, 1975 -- The new Spain -- The colour of shadows -- The street.
   Lambda Literary Award for Gay Men's Fiction, 2011
   A collection of stories portraying mute emotion and intense intimacies that remain unarticulated.
   "The slow deletion of personal relationships is at the core of the nine stories in this collection, as Tibn projects a slideshow of reclusive figures, many of whom have found that a life well-hid is a life sufficient. With a spare, eloquent style, he guides us through hotel lobbies and pensines from Dublin to Barcelona. He directs our attention to estranged family members, divorces and Muslim immigrants, catching each of them at the moment in which they are forced to reckon with their pasts." Los Angeles Times Book Review.

Toibin, Colm, 1955-
 The **heather** blazing / Colm Toibin. Viking, 1993, c1992. 245 p.
   ISBN 9780670847891
   1. Judges 2. Middle-aged men 3. Alienation in men 4. Men -- Psychology 5. Emotions in men 6. Married men 7. Wexford County, Ireland 8. Ireland -- Social life and customs -- 20th century 9. Psychological fiction
                                                             LC 92050350
   Originally published: London : Picador, 1992.

The sea is slowly eating into the land and the hill with the old watchtower has completely disappeared. The nearest house has crumbled and fallen into the sea. It is Ireland in the late twentieth century. Eamon Redmond is a judge in the Irish High Court. Obsessed all his life by the letter and spirit of the law, he is just beginning to discover how painfully unconnected he is from other human beings.

Toibin, Colm, 1955-
 House of names / Colm Toibin. Scribner, 2017. 288 p.
   ISBN 9781501140211
   1. Ancient Greece (800 BCE-640 CE) 2. Revenge in women 3. Women murderers 4. Husband-killing 5. Human sacrifice 6. Family violence 7. Revenge 8. Mythology, Greek 9. Atreus, House of (Greek mythology) 10. Clytemnestra (Greek mythology) 11. Agamemnon (Greek mythology) 12. Orestes (Greek mythology) 13. Electra (Greek mythology) 14. Mycenae (Extinct city) 15. Ancient Greece 16. Adaptations, retellings, and spin-offs 17. Mythological fiction 18. Literary fiction
   A retelling of the Greek myth Agememnon, in which Clytemnestra and her children become involved in revenge schemes because of Agamemnon's actions.
   "This extraordinary book reads like a pristine translation rather than a retelling, conveying both confounded strangeness and timeless truths about love's sometimes terrible and always exhilarating energies." Library Journal.

Toibin, Colm, 1955-
 * The **master** : a novel / Colm Toibin. Scribner, 2004. 352 p.
   ISBN 9780743250405
   1. James, Henry, 1843-1916 2. 1890s 3. Authors 4. Dramatists, American 5. Closeted gay men 6. Americans in England 7. Failure (Psychology) 8. Men -- Sexuality 9. Social isolation 10. Identity (Psychology) 11. England 12. Biographical fiction 13. Historical fiction 14. Literary fiction 15. Psychological fiction
                                                   LC 2003067376
   International IMPAC Dublin Literary Award, 2006.
   Lambda Literary Award for Gay Men's Fiction, 2004.
   Stonewall Book Award for the Barbara Gittings Literature Award, 2005.
   Shortlisted for the Man Booker Prize, 2004.
   Tells the story of Henry James, the famous novelist born into one of America's intellectual first families two decades before the Civil War, and who left his country to live in Paris, Rome, Venice, and London among privileged artists and writers. Toibin captures the exquisite anguish of a man who circulated in the grand parlours and palazzos of Europe, who was astonishingly vibrant and alive in his art, and yet whose attempts at intimacy inevitably failed him and those he tried to love.
   "What Toibin has so boldly done--and so brilliantly and successfully--is forge a sympathetic imagining of James' interior life. . . . Even the reader who knows little about Henry James or his work can enjoy this marvelously intelligent and engaging novel, which presents not on a silver platter but in tender, opened hands a beautifully nuanced psychological portrait." Booklist.

Toibin, Colm, 1955-
 * **Nora** Webster : a novel / Colm Toibin. Scribner, 2014. 373 p.
   ISBN 9781439138335
   1. Catholic Church Ireland. 2. 1970s 3. Widows 4. Mothers and sons 5. Self-fulfillment in women 6. Small town life 7. Family and death 8. Single mothers 9. Grief in women 10. Singing 11. Families 12.

Ireland 13. Wexford, Ireland 14. Literary fiction

LC 2014008519

Hawthornden Prize, 2015.

Andrew Carnegie Medal for Excellence in Fiction finalist, 2015.

Struggling with grief and financial hardships after the death of her beloved husband, widow Nora struggles to support her four children and clings to secrecy in the intrusive community of her childhood before finding her voice.

"The Ireland of four decades ago is beautifully evoked through events in the three-year widowhood of fortysomething Nora Webster, left by the early death of her beloved Maurice with four children and scarcely enough money to cover the family expenses. A character-portrait novel in the full definition of that type--which means as meticulous in detail and as sound in psychological understanding as a biography--Irishman Toibin's latest rich novel ... is self-assured in its authenticity, daring in the male author's presumption of inhabiting a female protagonist, and all this is achieved through prose at once alive and understated." Booklist.

Toibin, Colm, 1955-

The **testament** of Mary / Colm Toibin. Scribner, 2012. 81 p.

ISBN 9781451688382

1. Mary,, Blessed Virgin, Saint 2. Jesus Christ 3. Apostles 4. Guilt in women 5. Belief and doubt 6. Faith (Christianity) 7. Bible novels 8. Historical fiction 9. Literary fiction

LC 2012007578

Originally published: London: Viking, 2012.

Shortlisted for the Man Booker Prize, 2013.

A provocative imagining of the later years of the mother of Jesus finds her living a solitary existence in Ephesus years after her son's crucifixion and struggling with guilt, anger and feelings that her son is not the son of God and that His sacrifice was not for a worthy cause.

"A stunning interpretation that is as beautiful in its presentation as it is provocative in its intention." Booklist.

Tokarczuk, Olga, 1962-

Drive your plow over the bones of the dead / Olga Tokarczuk ; translated from the Polish by Antonia Lloyd-Jones. Riverhead Books, 2019, c2009. 288 p.

ISBN 9780525541332

1. Women recluses 2. Villages 3. Winter 4. Dead 5. Rural life 6. Murder investigation 7. Astrology 8. Women amateur detectives 9. Theories 10. Neighbors 11. Mysteries 12. Literary fiction 13. Translations -- Polish to English

Originally published: Krakow : Wydawn. Literackie, 2009.

Longlisted for the National Book Award for Translated Literature, 2019.

When her neighbor turns up dead, and then other bodies turn up under strange circumstances, Janine, a recluse in a remote Polish village who prefers the company of animals over humans, inserts herself into the investigation, certain she knows whodunit.

Tokarczuk, Olga, 1962-

* **Flights** / Olga Tokarczuk ; translated from the Polish by Jennifer Croft. Riverhead Books, 2018, c2017, c2007. 416 p.

ISBN 9780525534198

1. Voyages and travels 2. Eccentrics and eccentricities 3. Death 4. Travelers 5. Museums 6. Culture 7. Airports 8. Senses and sensation 9. Australian 10. Literary fiction 11. Translations -- Polish to English Includes index.

Originally published in Poland by Wydawnictwo Literackie, Krakow in 2007.

First published in English by Fitzcarraldo Editions in 2017.

Man Booker International Prize, 2018.

A meditative collection from Poland explores themes of travel, movement and existentialism in stories that feature protagonists who question their shifting perspectives in time and space as they tackle extreme agendas.

Tolkien, J. R. R. (John Ronald Reuel), 1892-1973

Beren and Luthien / J. R. R. Tolkien ; edited by Christopher Tolkien ; illustrated by Alan Lee. Houghton Mifflin Harcourt, 2017. 304 p.

ISBN 9781328791825

1. Elves 2. Immortalism 3. Heroes and heroines 4. Good and evil 5. Mortality 6. Quests 7. Lovers 8. Magic 9. Love 10. Epic fantasy Originally written in 1917.

An important chapter in the saga of The Silmarillion, first conceived by Tolkien at the end of his service in World War I, follows the romance between an immortal elf and a mortal whose worthiness is put to an impossible test.

Tolkien, J. R. R. (John Ronald Reuel), 1892-1973

The **children** of Hurin / J.R.R. Tolkien ; edited by Christopher Tolkien ; illustrated by Alan Lee. Houghton Mifflin, 2007. 313 p., 8 leaves of plates, 1 fold-out leaf

ISBN 9780618894642

1. Elves 2. Imaginary wars and battles 3. Good and evil 4. Dwarves (Fantasy characters) 5. Wizards 6. Magic 7. Brothers 8. Epic fantasy

A fantasy adventure saga set in the early days of Middle-Earth features humans and elves, dwarves and dragons, orcs and dark sorcerers clashing in an epic battle between good and evil.

"If anyone still labors under the delusion that J. R. R. Tolkien was a writer of twee fantasies for children, this novel should set them straight. A bleak, darkly beautiful tale played out against the background of the First Age of Tolkien's Middle Earth, The Children of Hurin possesses the mythic resonance and grim sense of inexorable fate found in Greek tragedy." Washington Post Book World.

Tolkien, J. R. R. (John Ronald Reuel), 1892-1973

The **fall** of Gondolin / J. R. R. Tolkien ; edited by Christopher Tolkien ; illustrated by Alan Lee. Houghton Mifflin Harcourt, 2018. 320 p.

ISBN 9781328613042

1. Elves 2. Wizards 3. Rulers 4. Good and evil 5. Gods and goddesses 6. Neutrality 7. Betrayal 8. Storytelling 9. Epic fantasy

Following his presentation of Beren and Luthien, Christopher Tolkien has used the same "history in sequence" mode in the writing of this edition of The Fall of Gondolin. In the words of J.R.R. Tolkien, it was "the first real story of this imaginary world" and, together with Beren and Luthien and The Children of Hurin, he regarded it as one of the three ?Great Tales? of the Elder Days.

Tolkien, J. R. R. (John Ronald Reuel), 1892-1973

The **fellowship** of the ring : being the first part of The lord of the rings / J.R.R. Tolkien. Houghton Mifflin, 2001, c1965. viii, 423 p. Lord of the rings

ISBN 0618153985

1. Heroes and heroines 2. Magic rings 3. Quests 4. Good and evil 5. Dwarves (Fantasy characters) 6. Elves 7. Wizards 8. Friendship 9. Magic 10. Epic fantasy 11. Fantasy classics

LC 2001276576

Sequel: The two towers.

Originally published: London : Allen & Unwin, 1954.

First published in the United States as part one of The Lord of the rings: Boston : Houghton Mifflin, 1965.

Frodo the hobbit and his companions set out to deliver the One Ring of Power to the dark land of Mordor in order to destroy the ring in the forge of its creation.

"Elves, dwarfs, hobbits, men, and sundry evil beings, each as real as the other, populate an allegorical tale that shows how power corrupts." Booklist.

Tolkien, J. R. R. (John Ronald Reuel), 1892-1973

* The **hobbit,** or, there and back again / J. R. R. Tolkien. Ballantine, 1996, c1937. 306 p. Lord of the rings

ISBN 9780345339683

1. Adventurers 2. Quests 3. Dragons 4. Wizards 5. Dwarves (Fantasy characters) 6. Heroes and heroines 7. Magic 8. Self-discovery 9. Travelers 10. Epic fantasy 11. Fantasy classics

LC 77-8025

Prelude to: The lord of the rings.

Book made into three feature motion pictures called The Hobbit: An unexpected journey ; The Hobbit: There and back again ; and The Hobbit: The battle of the Five Armies.

Originally published: London: Allen & Unwin, 1937.

Bilbo Baggins, a respectable, well-to-do hobbit, lives comfortably in his hobbit-hole until the day the wandering wizard Gandalf chooses him to take part in an adventure from which he may never return.

Tolkien, J. R. R. (John Ronald Reuel), 1892-1973

* The **lord** of the rings / J.R.R. Tolkien. Houghton Mifflin, 2004. xxv, 1157 p.

ISBN 9780618517657

1. Dwarves (Fantasy characters) 2. Magic rings 3. Quests 4. Good and evil 5. Elves 6. Wizards 7. Friendship 8. Magic 9. Epic fantasy 10. Fantasy classics

LC 2004275215

Presents the epic depicting the Great War of the Ring, a struggle between good and evil in Middle-earth, following the odyssey of Frodo the hobbit and his companions on a quest to destroy the Ring of Power.

Tolkien, J. R. R. (John Ronald Reuel), 1892-1973

The **return** of the king : being the third part of The lord of the rings / J.R.R. Tolkien ; illustrated by Alan Lee. Houghton Mifflin, 2004, c1965. 544 p. Lord of the rings

ISBN 0618574972

1. Heroes and heroines 2. Magic rings 3. Quests 4. Good and evil 5. Dwarves (Fantasy characters) 6. Elves 7. Wizards 8. Friendship 9. Magic 10. Epic fantasy 11. Fantasy classics

LC 2005278030

Sequel to: The two towers.

Includes index.

Originally published: London: George Allen & Unwin, 1955. 2nd ed. originally published: 1966.

Originally published: Allen & Unwin, 1955. This large print edition first published by Clio Press 1990.

First published in the United States as part three of The Lord of the rings: Boston : Houghton Mifflin, 1965.

Originally published: London : Allen & Unwin, 1955.

In the concluding volume of the trilogy, Frodo and Sam make a terrible journey to the heart of the Land of the Shadow in a final reckoning with the power of Sauron.

Tolkien, J. R. R. (John Ronald Reuel), 1892-1973

The **Silmarillion** / J.R.R. Tolkien ; edited by Christopher Tolkien. Houghton Mifflin, 1977. 365 p.

ISBN 0395257301

1. Elves 2. Creation 3. Gems 4. Magic 5. Good and evil 6. Fantasy fiction 7. Fantasy classics

Includes index.

Some copies have folded map in rear.

Locus Award for Fantasy Novel, 1978.

Hugo Awards: Gandalf Award for Best Book-Length Fantasy, 1978.

The Silmarillion tells of the Elder Days, or the First Age of the World, and is the history of the rebellion of Fëanor, the most gifted of the Elves, and his people against the gods, their exile in Middle-earth, and their war against the first Dark Lord, Morgoth, for the recovery of the Silmarils, the jewels containing the pure light of Valinor.

"Tolkien began writing these introductory legends in 1917 and, sporadically throughout his life, continued adding to them; his son Christopher has edited and compiled the various versions into a single cohesive work. Two brief tales, which outline the origin of the world and describe the gods who create and rule, precede the title story about the Silmarilsthree brilliant, jewel-like creatures who are desired and fought over, setting up a clash between good and evil." Booklist.

Tolkien, J. R. R. (John Ronald Reuel), 1892-1973

The **two** towers : being the second part of The lord of the rings / J.R.R. Tolkien ; illustrated by Alan Lee. Houghton Mifflin, 2002, c1965. x, 415-750 p. Lord of the rings

ISBN 0618260595

1. Heroes and heroines 2. Magic rings 3. Quests 4. Good and evil 5. Dwarves (Fantasy characters) 6. Elves 7. Wizards 8. Friendship 9. Magic 10. Epic fantasy 11. Fantasy classics

LC 2003542568

Sequel to: The fellowship of the ring.

Sequel: The return of the king.

Originally published: London : Allen & Unwin, 1954.

First published in the United States as part two of The Lord of the rings: Boston : Houghton Mifflin, 1965.

Tells of the quest to destroy Sauron's mighty Ring of Power and the struggle against the Darkness of Mordor.

"Here the Companions of the Ring, separated, meet Saruman the wizard, cross the Dead Marshes, and prepare for the Great War in which the power of the Ring will be undone." Library Journal.

Tolstaya, Tatyana, 1951 May 3-

Aetherial **worlds** : stories / Tatyana Tolstaya ; translated from the Russian by Anya Migdal. Alfred A. Knopf, 2018. 256 p.

ISBN 9781524732776

1. Love 2. Interpersonal relations 3. Human nature 4. Literary fiction 5. Short stories 6. Translations -- Russian to English

LC 2017032042

"Borzoi book."

Tolstaya, Tatyana, 1951-

The **slynx** / Tatyana Tolstaya ; translated by Jamey Gambrell. Houghton Mifflin, 2003. 288 p.

ISBN 0618124977

1. Survival (after disaster) 2. Rulers 3. Banned books 4. Moscow, Russia 5. Dystopian fiction 6. Literary fiction 7. Translations -- Russian to English

LC 2002027627

In the ruins of Moscow two centuries after the apocalypse, inhabitants dwell in primitive, frequently brutal conditions in which mice are a source of food, clothing, and commerce and books are banned by the ruling tyrant.

"It takes some time for a plot to develop, but Tolstaya sketches a vivid picture of life in this permanent winter. . . . In this extended fable, she captures the Russian yearning for culture, even in desperate circumstances. Gambrell ably translates the mix of neologisms and plain speech with which Tolstaya describes this devastated world." Publishers Weekly.

Tolstoy, Leo,, graf, 1828-1910

* **Anna** Karenina / Leo Tolstoy ; translated by Richard Pevear and Larissa Volokhonsky. Penguin Books, 2002, c1877. xxi, 837 p.

ISBN 9780142000274

1. Romanov Dynasty (1613-1917) 2. Married people 3. Extramarital affairs 4. Men/women relations 5. Russia -- Social life and customs -- 19th century 6. Literary fiction 7. Classics 8. Translations -- Russian to English

Originally serialized in The Russian Messenger, 1873-1877.

A movie called Love was inspired by the book.

Beautiful and charming, Anna lives in a splendid world of her own making. She smokes, rides horseback, plays tennis, takes opium, practices birth control, and--although she is already married--falls in love with a handsome army officer. Anna's life is played out against a backdrop of dazzling balls and the vastness of Russia's landscape.

Tolstoy, Leo,, graf, 1828-1910

Divine and human and other stories / Leo Tolstoy ; translated from the Russian and with an introduction and notes by Gordon Spence. Northwestern University Press, 2000. xxi, 112 p.

ISBN 9780810117624

1. Short stories 2. Christian fiction 3. Translations -- Russian to English 4. Classics

"These 16 selections from Tolstoy's final eclectic collection of tales titled The Sunday Reading Stories represent the Russian novelist's turn away from the troubling human condition in Anna Karenina toward a growing preoccupation with moral issues." Publishers Weekly.

Tolstoy, Leo,, graf, 1828-1910

War and peace / Leo Tolstoy ; translated from the Russian by Richard Pevear and Larissa Volokhonsky. Alfred A. Knopf, 2007, c1869. xviii, 1273 p.

ISBN 9780307266934

1. Romanov Dynasty (1613-1917) 2. Napoleonic Wars, 1800-1815 3. Military campaigns 4. Aristocracy -- Russia 5. Russia -- History -- Alexander I, 1801-1825 6. Literary fiction 7. Classics 8. War stories 9. Translations -- Russian to English 10. Historical fiction

Adapted into a 1956 theatrical film and television series.

Presents a new translation of the classic reflecting the life and times of Russian society during the Napoleonic Wars, in a book accompanied by an index of historical figures, textual annotation, a chapter summary, and an introduction.

"Stressing that their War and Peace sticks more closely to the Russian text than any other, including Louise and Aylmer Maude's semi-canonical 1923 version, Pevear and Volokhonsky retain the considerable amount of French used by Tolstoy's counts and princesses, preserve the author's penchant for word repetition and aim to match his tidy syntactic conciseness. The result certainly reads smoothly, its English being neither egregiously contemporary nor inappropriately old-fashioned." Washington Post Book World.

Toole, F. X., 1930-

Pound for pound : a novel / F.X. Toole. Ecco, 2006. 384 p.

ISBN 006088133X

1. African American senior men 2. African American grandfathers 3. Grandsons -- Death 4. Families 5. Hispanic American teenage boys 6. Boxing 7. Interracial friendship 8. Intergenerational friendship 9. Redemption 10. Forgiveness 11. Persistence 12. Loss (Psychology) 13. Grief in men 14. Men with depression 15. Self-discovery in teenage boys 16. Self-discovery in men 17. Los Angeles, California 18. San Antonio, Texas 19. Domestic fiction 20. Coming-of-age stories

LC 2005049508

The lives of Dan Cooley, a legendary L.A. trainer, and Chicky Garza, a young man battling to make a name for himself on the San Antonio boxing circuit, intertwine as both men struggle to cope with the pain of the past and their individual demons.

"This is the story of Eduardo Chicky Garza, a young San Antonio fighter and grandson of onetime contender Eloy Texas Wolf Garza. When Chicky is cheated out of a shot at the Olympic team, his grandfather encourages him to move to Los Angeles and find trainer Dan Cooley, a former boxer who lost to the grandfather 40 years earlier in a fixed fight. Though struggling with a deep depression brought on by the accidental death of his young grandson, Cooley decides to take Chicky on, paving the way for him to face the fighter who cheated him. The result is powerful and very readable, if somewhat sentimental, and Toole's deep love of boxing's rituals, traditions, and code of honor shines through." Library Journal.

Toole, John Kennedy, 1937-1969

* A **confederacy** of dunces / John Kennedy Toole ; foreword by Walker Percy. Louisiana State University Press, 1980. vii, 338 p.

ISBN 9780807106570

1. Alienation in men 2. Mothers and sons 3. Social reformers 4. Self-fulfillment in men 5. New Orleans, Louisiana 6. Satirical fiction 7. Literary fiction 8. Southern fiction

LC 79020190

Pulitzer Prize for Fiction, 1981.

Ignatius J. Reilly of New Orleans, --selfish, domineering, deluded, tragic and larger than life-- is a noble crusader against a world of dunces. He is a modern-day Quixote beset by giants of the modern age. In magnificent revolt against the twentieth century, Ignatius propels his monstrous bulk among the flesh posts of the fallen city, documenting life on his Big Chief tablets as he goes, until his maroon-haired mother decrees that Ignatius must work.

"At the heart of this splendid mock-heroic with its blundering and canniness, its falstaffian excesses and 'Alice in Wonderland' wit, lies a profound sense of solitude. Like everything else in Ignatuis J. Reilly's world, the absence of love is larger than life." Newsweek.

Torday, Daniel

The **last** flight of Poxl West : a novel / Daniel Torday. St. Martin's Press, 2015. 304 p.

ISBN 9781250051684

1. 1980s 2. World War II veterans 3. Revenge 4. Loss (Psychology) 5. Jewish men 6. Autobiography 7. Uncles 8. Fighter pilots 9. Love 10. Memory 11. War -- Psychological aspects 12. Literary fiction 13. Parallel narratives

LC 2014036360

National Jewish Book Award for Fiction, 2015.

Worshipping his charismatic and cultured uncle Poxl, young Elijah finds his carefully constructed illusions shattering when he learns about the violent, vengeance-driven missions his uncle performed during World War II.

"After each section of the memoir, Eli returns to fill us in on reviews in the Times and the Economist, the book signings and the things we will not be discussing in this review. A richly layered, beautifully told and somehow lovable story about war, revenge and loss." Kirkus.

Toro, Guillermo del, 1964-

The **strain** / Guillermo Del Toro and Chuck Hogan. William Morrow, 2009. 416 p. Strain trilogy

ISBN 9780061558238

1. Vampires 2. Virus diseases 3. Epidemics 4. Infection 5. Physicians 6. Holocaust survivors 7. Battles 8. New York City 9. Horror 10. Apocalyptic fiction

LC 2008043520

A vampiric virus infects New York and spreads outward, threatening the city and then the world, as a CDC doctor and a Holocaust survivor fight to save humanity.

Torres, Justin, 1980-

* **We** the animals : a novel / Justin Torres. Houghton Mifflin Harcourt, 2011. 144 p.

ISBN 9780547576725

1. Brothers -- New York (State) 2. Growing up 3. Dysfunctional families -- New York (State) 4. Family relationships 5. Identity (Psychology) 6. New York (State) 7. Coming-of-age stories

ALA Notable Book, 2012.

Rainbow List, 2012.

Follows the intense family life of three brothers living in the shadow of their parents' passionate love, and their own profound sense of family unity and belonging.

"Though partially autobiographical, the novel evokes the exhilaration and violence of boyhood with such authenticity, the reader wonders how the author accessed his memories with such accuracy. Torres . . . brings a poet's attention to the placement and rhythm of words. His lyrical language sustains an almost trancelike reading experience--that is, until an abrupt chronological leap late in the novel finds the narrator transformed from boy to adolescent. Despite this jarring effect, the picture of the narrator's messy upbringing feels complete. His relationships with his brothers and his parents veer off in unexpected, often unwanted, directions, and the force of the book's final emotional punch surprises." Time Out New York.

Towles, Amor

* A **gentleman** in Moscow / Amor Towles. Viking, 2016. 448 p.

ISBN 9780670026197

1. 1920s 2. Aristocracy 3. Home confinement (Corrections) 4. Hotels 5. Counts and countesses 6. Interpersonal relations 7. Moscow, Russia 8. Russia -- History -- 20th century 9. Historical fiction 10. Literary fiction

Kirkus Prize for Fiction finalist, 2016.

Deemed unrepentant by a Bolshevik tribunal in 1922, Count Alexander Rostov is sentenced to house arrest in a hotel across the street from the Kremlin, where he lives in an attic room while some of the most tumultuous decades in Russian history unfold.

"Count Rostovs long transformation occurs against a lightly sketched background of upheaval, repression, and war. Gently but dauntlessly, like his protagonist, Towles is determined to chart the course of the individual." Publishers Weekly.

Towles, Amor

Rules of civility : a novel / Amor Towles. Viking, 2011. 334 p.

ISBN 9780670022694

1. 1930s 2. Young women 3. Fate and fatalism 4. Upper class 5. Ambition in women 6. Upward mobility 7. Friendship 8. Wall Street, New York City 9. New York City 10. Historical fiction 11. Literary fiction

LC 2011004118

A chance encounter with a handsome banker in a jazz bar on New Year's Eve 1938 catapults Wall Street secretary Katey Kontent into the upper echelons of New York society, where she befriends a shy multi-millionaire, an Upper East Side ne'er-do-well, and a single-minded widow.

"On New Year's Eve 1937, at a jazz bar in New York's Greenwich Village, Katey and Eve are charmed by the handsome and successful Tinker Grey. The three become fast friends and spend early 1938 exploring the town together, until a car accident permanently injures Eve. Feeling guilty, Tinker, the driver, takes care of Eve and unsuccessfully tries to love her. Despite the presence and initial impact of Tinker and Eve, though, this first novel is about Katey's 1938." Library Journal.

Townsend, Sue

* The **Adrian** Mole diaries / Sue Townsend. HarperPerennial, 2010. 342 p.

ISBN 9780062004697

1. Identity (Psychology) 2. Family relationships 3. Teenage boys -- Great Britain 4. Great Britain 5. Humorous stories 6. Diary novels 7. Coming-of-age stories

LC 86000226

Adrian Mole, a thirteen-year-old budding intellectual beset with worries about his complexion, his untried sexuality, and his parents's unsteady marriage, meets Pandora, a new student in his class, and decides to fall in love.

"Adrian's pithy commentary records the ludicrousness of school and state bureaucracy and the aberrations of the nuclear age." Booklist.

Townsend, Sue

Number 10 / Sue Townsend. Soho, 2003. 277 p.

ISBN 1569473498

1. Prime ministers 2. Public opinion 3. Disguises 4. Politicians' spouses 5. Families 6. Automobile travel 7. Social classes 8. Edinburgh, Scotland 9. East Midlands, England 10. London, England 11. Great Britain 12. Political fiction 13. Satirical fiction

LC 2003050562

"In Townsend's latest British farce . . . the prime minister, known by much of his public as 'that prat Edward Clare,' sets out to get in touch with the masses. . . . The three story lines are masterfully and hilariously interwoven, and the book's delightfully absurd characters (especially Edward, and Jack's mother, Norma) are unforgettable." Publishers Weekly

Tracy, P. J

Ice cold heart / P. J. Tracy. Crooked Lane Books, 2019. 320 p. Monkeewrench

ISBN 9781643851327

1. Computer software developers 2. Detectives 3. Conspiracies 4. Art 5. Murder investigation 6. Winter 7. Computer crimes 8. Violence against women 9. Women murder victims 10. Secrets 11. Minnesota 12. Thrillers and suspense

With the help of Grace MacBride and her partners at Monkeewrench Software, Detectives Magozzi and Rolseth investigate a grisly murder that exactly mirrors a previous homicide.

Tracy, P. J

Monkeewrench / P.J. Tracy. G.P. Putnam's Sons, 2003. 373 p. Monkeewrench

ISBN 9780399149788

1. Women computer programmers 2. Serial murders -- Minnesota 3. Computer software developers 4. Detectives -- Minneapolis, Minnesota 5. Police 6. Computer software industry and trade 7. Computer games 8. Murder -- Wisconsin 9. Murder investigation -- Wisconsin 10. Minneapolis, Minnesota 11. Wisconsin 12. Thrillers and suspense

LC 2002068139

Sequel: Live Bait.

Also published as: Want to play?

Anthony Award for Best Novel, 2004.

"Haunted by a series of horrifying and violent episodes in their past, Grace McBride and the oddball crew of her software company, Monkeewrench, create a computer game where the killer is always caught, where the good guys always win. But their game becomes a nightmare when someone starts duplicating the fictional murders in real life, down to the last detail. By the time the police realize what's happening, three people are dead, and with seventeen more murder scenarios available online, there are seventeen more potential victims. While the authorities scramble to find the killer in a city paralyzed by fear, the Monkeewrench staff are playing their own game, analyzing victim profiles in a frantic attempt to discover the murderer's next target. In a thriller populated by characters both hilarious and heartbreaking, a rural Wisconsin sheriff, two Minneapolis police detectives, and Grace's gang are caught in a web of decades-old secrets that could get them all killed"--Front flap.

"Unlike the conventionally dimwitted cops and hick sheriff's deputies, Grace and her four geek partners in the software company . . . add real flavor to the proceedings with their colorful jargon and quirky personas. These techno-nerds may be freaks--and one of them may even be a killer--but they have style." New York Times Book Review.

Tran, Vu, 1975-

Dragonfish : a novel / Vu Tran. W. W. Norton & Company, 2015. 320 p.

ISBN 9780393077803

1. Missing women 2. Divorced persons 3. Loss (Psychology) 4. Vietnamese Americans 5. Violence in men 6. Extortion 7. Refugees 8. Gamblers 9. Flashbacks 10. Police 11. Criminals 12. Secrets 13. Mother-deserted children 14. Las Vegas, Nevada 15. Vietnam -- History -- 20th century 16. Malaysia -- History -- 20th century 17. Noir fiction 18. Crime fiction

LC 2015005764

Unable to forget the mysterious Vietnamese wife who left him and blackmailed by her second husband into searching for her, a rugged Oakland cop infiltrates the sleazy gambling dens of Las Vegas to uncover his ex's painful past in a Malaysian refugee camp.

"This haunting and mesmerizing debut is filled with all the noir elements: a dark and seedy underworld, damsels in distress, tarnished heroes, and a blurring of moral boundaries. It examines such themes as culture, desperation, memory, mental illness, love, loss, and redemption. Highly recommended for mystery fans." Library Journal.

Transgressions / edited by Ed McBain. Forge, 2005. 784 p.

ISBN 0765308517

1. Police 2. Detectives 3. Criminals 4. Assassins 5. Murder 6. September 11 Terrorist Attacks, 2001 7. Mysteries 8. Psychological suspense

LC 2004061960

10 previously unpublished novellas.

"A Tom Doherty Associates book."

Traven, B.

* The **treasure** of the Sierra Madre / B. Traven. Farrar, Straus and Giroux, 2010, c1967. 308 p.

ISBN 9780809092970

1. Americans in Mexico 2. Gold mines and mining -- Mexico 3. Mexico 4. Westerns 5. Translations -- German to English

LC 6723519

Two hard-luck drifters and a grizzled prospector seek gold in the mountains in Mexico. They start off as friends, but after they discover the lode the greed and paranoia set in.

Tregillis, Ian

The **mechanical** / Ian Tregillis. Orbit, 2015. 471 p. Alchemy wars

ISBN 9780316248006

1. 20th century 2. Robots 3. Artificial intelligence 4. Slavery 5. Inventions 6. Civil rights 7. Women spies 8. Free will and determinism 9. Imaginary wars and battles 10. Netherlands 11. France 12. North America 13. Steampunk 14. Alternative histories

LC 2014018728

Built by humans and powered by alchemy, Clakkers are mechanical servants invented by 17th-century Dutch clockmaker Christiaan Huygens. With their strength, longevity, and ability to follow orders in lockstep, the Clakkers are largely responsible for the Netherlands' rise to global dominance -- although perhaps not for much longer. When Clakker Jax takes advantage of an unexpected opportunity to escape from bondage, he flees to the New World, determined to remain free at all costs. -- Description by Gillian Speace.

"Although he keeps the pace moving at a brisk clip, the author is able to work in some Big Ideas, asking us to think about what we mean when we speak about souls and free will." Booklist.

Tremain, Rose

The **colour** / Rose Tremain. Farrar, Straus and Giroux, 2003. 382 p.

ISBN 9780374126056

1. 19th century 2. Gold rush -- New Zealand 3. Frontier and pioneer life -- New Zealand 4. Newlyweds 5. Married people 6. British in New Zealand 7. Husband and wife 8. Gold mines and mining 9. Immigrants 10. Greed 11. Men/women relations 12. New Zealand -- History -- 19th century 13. Historical fiction

LC 2002192528

Shortlisted for The Orange Prize for Fiction, 2004

An epic of life in New Zealand during the nineteenth century explores the relationship between two newlyweds as they encounter the harsh realities of their chosen home in the South Pacific.

"As the story gathers momentum, it widens . . . . Tremain's excursions into the minds of her Maori and Chinese characters are written with a blend of sympathy and irony that sabotages our expectations of things exotic and inscrutable." New York Times Book Review.

Tremain, Rose

The **Gustav** sonata : a novel / Rose Tremain. W. W. Norton & Company, 2016 288 p.

ISBN 9780393246698

1. Male friendship 2. Pianists 3. Prejudice 4. Growing up 5. Jews 6. Antisemitism 7. Mothers and sons 8. World War II 9. Small town life 10. Postwar life 11. Switzerland -- History -- 20th century 12. Literary fiction

LC 2016012494

National Jewish Book Award for Fiction, 2016.

Longlisted for The Baileys Women's Prize for Fiction, 2017.

Shortlisted for the Walter Scott Prize for Historical Fiction, 2017

Growing up in a small town in Switzerland where he is sheltered from the echoes of World War II, only child Gustav forges an intense relationship with a mercurial Jewish boy, Anton, a talented pianist who introduces him to the harsh realities of racism, tolerance and cruelty during a friendship spanning more than half a century.

Tremain, Rose

Music & silence / Rose Tremain. Farrar, Straus, and Giroux, 2000, c1999. 485 p.

ISBN 9780374199890

1. Christian IV,, King of Denmark and Norway, 1577-1648 2. Renaissance (1300-1600) 3. Court musicians 4. Favorites, Royal 5. Courts and courtiers 6. Music -- Psychological aspects 7. Romantic love 8. Men/women relations 9. British in Denmark 10. Orchestras 11. Denmark -- History -- 17th century 12. Denmark -- Rulers 13. Historical fiction

LC 99042880

Originally published: London : Chatto & Windus, 1999.

Whitbread Book Award for Novel, 1999.

Brought to the Danish court in 1629 to serve in the king's orchestra, English lutenist Peter Claire soon finds himself caught up in royal intrigue when he falls for a young woman who is the companion of the queen.

"So hypnotic are Rose Tremain's seductive paragraphs that we are borne along without effort in a world which is neither fact nor fiction but has the strengths of both, with a uniquely sensitive imagination at work." The New York Review of Books.

Tremblay, Paul

* The **cabin** at the end of the world : a novel / Paul Tremblay. William Morrow, 2018 272 p.

ISBN 9780062679109

1. End of the world 2. Home invasions 3. Strangers 4. Violence 5. Cabins 6. Married people 7. Adopted children 8. Paranoia 9. Families 10. Rural life 11. New Hampshire 12. Horror 13. Psychological suspense

LC 2017048369

Bram Stoker Award for Best Novel, 2018.

Locus Award for Dark Fantasy-Horror Novel, 2019.

RUSA Reading List Short List, 2019.

A family vacationing at a remote cabin on a quiet New Hampshire lake faces a home invasion by four strangers carrying menacing but unidentifiable objects who claim to be acting to save the world.

"Alternating between unreliable narrators, Tremblay captures the intense emotional struggle, especially in flashbacks into the lives of the odds-defying family of Wen, Andrew, and Eric, while dread and terror permeate every sentence." Booklist.

Tremblay, Paul

Disappearance at Devil's Rock : a novel / Paul Tremblay. William Morrow, 2016 288 p.

ISBN 9780062363268

1. Missing teenage boys 2. Ghosts 3. Supernatural 4. Secrets 5. Devil 6. Parks 7. Horror 8. Psychological suspense

LC 2015042759

Late one summer night, Elizabeth Sanderson receives the devastating news that every mother fears: her 13-year-old son, Tommy, has vanished in the woods of a local park. Riddled with worry, pain and guilt, Elizabeth is wholly unprepared for the strange series of events that follow. She believes a wraithlike apparition of Tommy materializes in her bedroom, while Kate and other local residents claim to see a shadowy figure peering through their windows in the dead of night. Then, random pages torn from Tommy's journals begin to mysteriously appear--entries that reveal an introverted teenager obsessed with the loss of his father, killed in a drunk-driving accident a decade earlier, a folktale involving the devil and the woods of Borderland a horrific incident that Tommy believed connected them all.

"This tense, quick-moving story, part mystery and part folktale with a dash of police procedural, moves between points of view that offer tantalizing clues and moments of discomfort. The result is a satisfying piece of fiction that shifts genres underneath the reader." Booklist.

Tremblay, Paul

Growing things and other stories / Paul Tremblay. William Morrow, 2019. 336 p.

ISBN 9780062679130

1. Short stories 2. Horror

LC 2018051852

Tremblay, Paul

A **head** full of ghosts / Paul Tremblay. William Morrow & Co., 2015. 288 p.

ISBN 9780062363237

1. Demonic possession 2. Reality television programs 3. Sisters 4. Memory 5. Priests 6. Teenage girls 7. Suburban life 8. Exorcism 9. Mental illness 10. Popular culture 11. Blogs 12. Family secrets 13. Family relationships 14. New England 15. Horror

Bram Stoker Award for Best Novel, 2015.

Massachusetts Book Awards, Fiction Award, 2016.

RUSA Reading List Short List, 2016.

The lives of the Barretts, a normal suburban New England family, are torn apart when 14-year-old Marjorie begins to display signs of what at first seems to be acute schizophrenia, a condition which only gets worse, leading them believe its actually demonic possession, as they become the center of a reality TV show.

"The novel is stylishly written and well-conceived, with lifelike characters and an air of plausibility about it, as if all this really could happen." Booklist.

Treuer, David

Prudence / David Treuer. Riverhead Books, 2015. 272 p.

ISBN 9781594633089

1. Second World War era (1939-1945) 2. Life change events 3. Secrets 4. Interpersonal relations 5. World War II 6. Soldiers 7. Romantic love 8. Race relations 9. Gun accidents 10. Indian reservations 11. Minnesota 12. Literary fiction 13. Historical fiction

When his farewell departure for World War II is shattered by an act of violence involving an escaped German soldier, bombardier Frankie Washburn witnesses the unfolding of consequences that reverberate for several years.

"Clearness and precision are what Ojibwa writer Treuer (The Translation of Dr Apelles, 2006) so evocatively attains in this magnetizing and richly original novel. As he cycles in and out of his extraordinarily affecting characters lives of deprivation and stoicism, he elucidates stygian emotions and annihilating psychological traumas incited by brutal, even genocidal conflicts over sexuality, race, and religion. Treuer's trenchant and compassionate novel glimmers with natures potent beauty, fresh historical detail, and scrupulous insight." Booklist.

Trevanian

Incident at Twenty-mile St. Martin's Press, 1998. 308 p.

ISBN 0312192339

1. Small town life -- Wyoming 2. Drifters -- Wyoming 3. Escaped convicts -- Wyoming 4. Wyoming 5. Westerns

LC 9819401

The arrival of a mysterious young stranger at Twenty Mile, a remote and fading town in the middle of nowhere, sets in motion a series of events leading to a dramatic showdown, in a novel exploring the myths of the American West.

"Matthew Dubcheck wanders into the dying silver-mining town of Twenty-Mile, Wyoming, and declares himself the Ringo Kid, after the hero of his favorite dime novels. The romanticized West clashes with the real West when an escaped con comes to town, befriends Matthew, and the wheels begin to turn toward an inevitably tragic conclusion. The anti-western is also a staple of the genre, and this tragicomic tale takes its place alongside such similar efforts as True Git and poet David Waggoner's delightful Where Is My Wandering Boy Tonight?". Booklist.

Trevanian

The **summer** of Katya : a novel / Trevanian. Three Rivers Press, 2005, c1983. 275 p.

ISBN 1400098041

1. Twins 2. Physicians 3. Brothers and sisters -- France 4. Basques 5. France 6. Love stories 7. Historical fiction

LC 83001790

Originally published: New York : Crown, 1983.

Twenty years after the outbreak of World War I, Dr. Jean-Marc Montjean remembers his love for Katya, a woman he met in a French Basque village.

Trevor, William, 1928-2016

Last stories / William Trevor. Viking, 2018. 212 p.

ISBN 9780525558101

1. Interpersonal relations 2. Short stories 3. Literary fiction

Collects ten short stories that illuminate the human condition

"The situations behind Trevors (Selected Stories, 2010) beautifully composed stories revolve around themes of personal cruelty, romantic and marital heartbreak, lover betrayal, and even violent death, and he has long established himself as a writer of great charity for the ordinary person and sympathy for the hard knocks of unheralded lives." Booklist.

Trigiani, Adriana

Big Cherry Holler : a Big Stone Gap novel / Adriana Trigiani. Random House, 2001. 272 p. Big Stone Gap novels

ISBN 0375506179

1. 1980s 2. Italian American women 3. Grief in women 4. Loss (Psychology) 5. Sons -- Death 6. Women pharmacists 7. Husband and wife 8. Married women 9. Men/women relations 10. Marital conflict 11. Employees -- Dismissal 12. Mountain life -- Appalachian Region 13. Small towns -- Virginia 14. Rural life -- Virginia 15. Eccentrics and eccentricities 16. Virginia 17. Big Stone Gap, Virginia 18. Blue Ridge Mountains Region 19. Gentle reads 20. Mainstream fiction 21. Domestic fiction 22. Southern fiction

LC 2001018599

Sequel to: Big Stone Gap.

Revisits the marriage of Ave Maria and Jack MacChesney, eight years after their wedding, amid the eccentric inhabitants in the small Virginia mountain town of Big Stone Gap.

"Although readers of Big Stone Gap are going to find this novel more serious, they should rest assured that most of the old favorite small town characters are still there. Catching an earful, usually unsolicited, of their views and advice on life, marriage, and love is a part of the charm of both the predecessor and this follow-up." Booklist.

Trigiani, Adriana

Big Stone Gap : a novel / Adriana Trigiani. Random House, 2000. 272 p. Big Stone Gap novels

ISBN 0375504036

1. 1970s 2. Women pharmacists 3. Single women 4. Italian American women 5. Family secrets 6. Pharmacists 7. Women librarians 8. Mountain life -- Appalachian Region 9. Small towns -- Virginia 10. Rural life -- Virginia 11. Eccentrics and eccentricities 12. Men/women relations 13. Virginia 14. Big Stone Gap, Virginia 15. Blue Ridge Mountains Region 16. Romantic comedies 17. Gentle reads 18. Mainstream fiction 19. Southern fiction

LC 99043306

Sequel: Big Cherry Holler.

The 35-year-old self-proclaimed spinster of a small Virginia village discovers a skeleton in her family's formerly tidy closet that completely unravels her quiet, conventional life.

"One chapter, which is based on a real-life campaign visit from John Warner and his then-wife Elizabeth Taylor is a hoot. And you don't want to miss Ave Maria's friend, the sexy Iva Lou Wade, one of the best fictional librarians to come along in years." Library Journal.

Trollope, Anthony, 1815-1882

* Barchester Towers / Anthony Trollope. A.A. Knopf, 1992. 277 p. Chronicles of Barsetshire

ISBN 0679405879

1. Church of England Clergy 2. Victoriana 3. Rural life -- 19th century 4. Small town life -- 19th century 5. Clergy 6. England -- Social life and customs -- 19th century 7. Literary fiction 8. Classics

LC 91053197

Originally published in 1857.

Citizens enjoy their daily lives in Barchester, an English cathedral town, during the 19th century.

Trollope, Anthony, 1815-1882

Doctor Thorne / Anthony Trollope ; introduction by N. John Hall. A. A. Knopf, 1929, c1858. various pagings. Chronicles of Barsetshire

ISBN 0679423044

1. 19th century 2. Rural physicians -- 19th century 3. Heirs and heiresses -- 19th century 4. Rural life -- 19th century 5. Gentry -- 19th century 6. Nieces and nephews -- 19th century 7. Small town life -- 19th century 8. England -- Social life and customs -- 19th century 9. Psychological fiction 10. Classics

LC 93001853 //r94

Includes chronology.

First published in 1858.

Frank Gresham, son of the impoverished squire of Greshambury, has fallen in love with penniless Mary Thorne. Despite the promptings of his family to consider a Miss Dunstable, heiress to a fortune, Frank's affections persist and the humane Doctor Thorne, as Mary's protector, must confront the prejudices of the mid-Victorian society.

Trollope, Anthony, 1815-1882

* The Eustace diamonds / Anthony Trollope. Oxford University Press, 1998, c1873. 832 p. The Palliser novels

ISBN 9780192834669

1. Widows 2. Greed in women 3. Diamonds 4. Jewelry 5. Politicians -- Great Britain 6. Inheritance and succession 7. Victoriana 8. England -- Social life and customs -- 19th century 9. Great Britain -- Politics and government -- 19th century 10. Psychological fiction 11. Classics

First published in 1873.

Young and widowed, Lizzie Eustace makes bold to keep a family necklace given to her by her late husband. The in-laws consolidate against her.

Trollope, Anthony, 1815-1882

Framley parsonage / Anthony Trollope ; with an introduction by Graham Handley. A. A. Knopf, 1994. 587 p. Chronicles of Barsetshire

ISBN 0679431330

1. Church of England Clergy 2. Clergy 3. Classism 4. Small town life -- 19th century 5. Rural life -- 19th century 6. Victoriana 7. England -- Social life and customs -- 19th century 8. Psychological fiction 9. Classics

LC 93-81320

Originally published in 1861.

Mark Robarts the new vicar of Framley, with ambitions to further his career, seeks connections in the county's high society. He agrees guarantee a substantial loan for a local member of parliament which brings him to the brink of ruin. Lord Lufton has proposed to Mark's sister Lucy, but his mother Lady Lufton is against the marriage, preferring that her son choose the coldly beautiful Griselda Grantly.

Trollope, Anthony, 1815-1882

The **last** chronicle of Barset / Anthony Trollope. Knopf, 1995, c1867. xxix, 983 p. Chronicles of Barsetshire

ISBN 0679443665

1. Courtship 2. Classism 3. Small town life -- 19th century 4. Rural life -- 19th century 5. England -- Social life and customs -- 19th century 6. Psychological fiction 7. Classics

LC 68112673

Originally published in 1867.

Barsetshire's latest scandal involves Mr. Crawley, the impoverished curate of Hogglestock, accused of theft when he uses a large check to pay off his debts. Unables to remember how he came by the money, he feels himself shames in the eyes of the community and even begins question his own sanity. The scandal fiercely divides the citizens of Barsetshire and threatens to tear apart Mr. Crawley's family.

Trollope, Anthony, 1815-1882

* The **Prime** Minister / Anthony Trollope ; edited with an introduction and notes by David Skilton. Penguin Books, 1996, c1876. 702 p. The Palliser novels

ISBN 9780140433494

1. Prime Ministers -- Great Britain 2. Politicians -- Great Britain 3. Dukes and duchesses 4. Marriage 5. Victoriana 6. Great Britain -- Politics and government -- 19th century 7. England -- Social life and customs -- 19th century 8. Political fiction 9. Psychological fiction 10. Classics

First published in eight monthly parts, from November 1875 to June 1876, reissued in four volumes in 1876.

Plantaganet Palliser, Prime Minister of England--a man of power and prestige, with all the breeding and inherited wealth that goes with it--is appalled at the inexorable rise of Ferdinand Lopez. An exotic impostor, seemingly from nowhere, Lopez has society at his feet, while well-connected ladies vie with each other to exert influence on his behalf--even Palliser's own wife, Lady Glencora...

Trollope, Anthony, 1815-1882

The **warden** / Anthony Trollope. Oxford University Press, 2008, c1855. 294 p. Chronicles of Barsetshire

ISBN 9780199537785

1. Church of England Clergy 2. 19th century 3. Small town life 4.

Clergy 5. Social reformers 6. Charities 7. England -- Social life and customs -- 19th century 8. Psychological fiction 9. Classics

Originally published in 1855.

"Set in the world of the Victorian professional and landed classes, the book centres on Mr. Harding, a clergyman of great personal integrity who is nevertheless in possession of an income from a charity far in excess of the sum devoted to the purposes of the foundation. On discovering such an apparent abuse of privilege, and despite the fact that he is in love with Mr. Harding's daughter, John Bold turns his reforming zeal to the matter." -- Back cover.

Trollope, Joanna

The **best** of friends / Joanna Trollope. Viking, 1998, c1995. 293 p.

ISBN 0670879738

1. Love triangles 2. Extramarital affairs 3. Betrayal 4. Divorce 5. Friendship 6. Families 7. Men/women relations 8. Best friends 9. England 10. Mainstream fiction

LC 9749162

Gina and Laurence, friends since childhood, turn to each other for solace when their marriages fail

"Trollope's facility at spinning an intricate story is enhanced by light-fingered dialogue, and the lesson she spins in this tale of easy pleasure and its complicated aftermath is both sobering and hopeful." Publishers Weekly.

Trollope, Joanna

Brother and sister : a novel / Joanna Trollope. Bloomsbury, 2004. 320 p.

ISBN 1582344000

1. Birthparent/adoptee relations 2. Identity (Psychology) 3. Adoption reunions 4. Life-change events 5. Adopted children 6. Adoptees 7. Women adoptees 8. Birthmothers -- Identification 9. Brothers and sisters 10. Married people 11. Families 12. Family relationships 13. Loyalty 14. Mainstream fiction 15. Domestic fiction

LC 2003062649

Brought up by the same parents, but born to two different mothers, adopted siblings decide, in their late thirties, to embark upon the journey to find their birth mothers.

"Trollope is a pointillist of domestic relationships, and she has built an impressive body of work addressing powerful tensions like those that animate Brother and Sister. With well-placed strokes, she brings to life all of her characters, including the complex lives of the birth mothers. She's especially accomplished in her portrayals of children by turns humorous, frustrating or heartbreaking, but never precious." Washington Post Book World.

Trollope, Joanna

Marrying the mistress / Joanna Trollope. Viking, 2000. 293 p.

ISBN 0670891509

1. Remarriage 2. Self-acceptance in women 3. Marital conflict 4. Judges 5. Mistresses 6. Extramarital affairs 7. May-December romance 8. Middle-aged men 9. Young women 10. Stepmothers 11. Stepchildren -- Family relationships 12. Mainstream fiction 13. Domestic fiction

LC 99462175

Judge Stockdale decides to leave his wife of 40 years and marry a woman with whom he has been having an affair for seven years.

"None of the themes here . . . are terribly unusual, but Trollope's proven ability to present them intelligently, as moral and emotional tangles faced by thinking, interesting people, satisfyingly combines the universally recognizable and the intellectually engaging." Publishers Weekly.

Trollope, Joanna

The **men** and the girls / Joanna Trollope. Random House, 1992. 248 p.

ISBN 067942587X

1. Senior men 2. Young women -- Relations with older men 3. Marital conflict 4. Generation gap 5. Television actors and actresses 6. May-December romance 7. England 8. Mainstream fiction 9. Domestic fiction

LC 9318421

"One of the pleasures in good contemporary British fiction like 'The Men and the Girls' is the writing itself--deft, fluid, perceptive and concise. Another is the wonderfully wry humor, particularly when its objects are sacred cows. Like Muriel Spark, Joanna Trollope is hilarious about old people, for instance." New York Times Book Review.

Trollope, Joanna

Next of kin / Joanna Trollope. Viking, 2001. 304 p.

ISBN 0670899992

1. Rural families 2. Farm life 3. Widowers 4. Married people 5. Women photographers 6. Adopted girls 7. Families 8. Blended families 9. Grief 10. Bereavement 11. England 12. Love stories 13. Mainstream fiction

LC 2001017743

Caro Meredith, originally from California, led the life of an English farmer's wife for more than twenty years. Yet after her death, her grieving husband, Robin, wonders how well he really knew her. But Robin is not the only one left vulnerable; his brother, parents, and Judy, his daughter and Caro's step-daughter, are all thrown by the absence of the woman who had become a central figure in their lives. As they each struggle to cope with Caro's death, Judy's friend Zoe arrives from London and brings with her hope for a new beginning. All recognize that she is a catalyst for change.

"In addition to crafting an absorbing narrative, Trollope charms with her depiction of several young children, whose speech and behavior are captured with clarity and endearing fidelity." Publishers Weekly.

Tropper, Jonathan

One last thing before I go / Jonathan Tropper. Dutton, 2012. 352 p.

ISBN 9780525952367

1. Heart -- Disease 2. Second chances 3. Men -- Psychology 4. Former wives 5. Terminal illness 6. Middle aged men 7. Life change events 8. Fathers and daughters 9. Unplanned pregnancy 10. Former rock musicians 11. Transformations, Personal 12. Mainstream fiction

LC 2012019370

ALA Notable Book, 2013

Struggling with his ex-wife's imminent marriage to a nice guy and his Princeton-bound daughter's unplanned pregnancy, a bewildered Drew Silver tackles difficult family dynamics and refuses to undergo a life-saving operation.

Trollope, Joanna

The **other** family : a novel / Joanna Trollope. Simon & Schuster, 2010. 336 p.

ISBN 9781439129838

1. Bereavement 2. Inheritance and succession 3. Families 4. Death 5. Half-brothers 6. Grief 7. Pianists 8. Extended families 9. Abandonment (Psychology) 10. England -- Social life and customs 11. Mainstream fiction 12. Domestic fiction

LC 2010000529

"A Touchstone book."

Originally published: London: Doubleday, 2010.

Two families must confront love and loss as an inheritance hangs in the balance.

"Richie Rossiter is an aging crooner with a shrinking yet substantial fan base. He lives in London with Chrissie, his beautiful, common-law wife, 20 years his junior. Chrissie has been managing his career for 25 years, ever since they embarked on the affair that demolished his marriage. Only Richie never legally ended his marriage. Even after raising three daughters with Chrissie, he has refused to propose. Chrissie has been comforting herself with the knowledge that he hardly thinks of his wife and their son. But when Richie dies suddenly of a heart attack, she learns the truth. Richie has left his first family the lion's share of his musical estate, which includes a beautiful Steinway piano, his prized possession. The novel brilliantly explores the fallout of Richie's will." Globe and Mail (Toronto)

Trollope, Joanna

* **Other** people's children / Joanna Trollope. Viking, 1999, c1998. 294 p.

ISBN 0670885134

1. Remarriage 2. Divorce 3. Blended families 4. Stepmothers 5. Stepchildren 6. Stepchildren -- Family relationships 7. Stepfathers 8. Stepfathers -- Family relationships 9. Stepmothers -- Family relationships 10. England 11. Mainstream fiction 12. Domestic fiction

LC 9840004

An exploration into that ever-expanding unit--the step-family--and how to cope with present and former husbands and wives, but most of all other people's children.

"Falling in love with a man does not mean falling in love with his children: that is the premise of this story of linked and sundered families. Josie's second marriage includes three stepchildren, whose loyalty to their inadequate mother makes them hate Josie for her very competence; Elizabeth's beloved fiancé comes with a son she adores and a grown daughter determined to oust her. Trollope may not aim high, but she aims for the heart, and she hits it." The New Yorker.

Trollope, Joanna

Second honeymoon : a novel / Joanna Trollope. Bloomsbury, 2006. 320 p.

ISBN 1596910380

1. Middle-aged women 2. Adult children 3. Empty nesters 4. Husband and wife 5. Middle-aged men 6. Self-fulfillment in middle-aged women 7. Parents 8. Adult children living with parents 9. Family relationships 10. Homecomings 11. Debt 12. Financial crises 13. London, England 14. Mainstream fiction 15. Domestic fiction

LC 2005057011

Distraught when her youngest son, twenty-two-year-old Ben, plans to leave home, Edie, an actress, and her theatrical agent husband, Russell, are faced with an empty nest for the first time, until their two older children plan to move back in.

"The author excels at middle-class family dramas, and [this] is a welcome entry in her canon. Like an overzealous housewife who just can't step away from the vacuum, she succumbs to the impulse to tidy up all the subplots. But Edie, Russell, and their brood are winning enough that fans will want to move in right along with the kids." Christian Science Monitor.

Trollope, Joanna

A **Spanish** lover / Joanna Trollope. Random House, 1997, c1993. 334 p.

ISBN 0679425861

1. Twin sisters -- Spain 2. Extramarital affairs 3. Family relationships 4. Sisters 5. Life change events 6. Spain 7. Love stories 8. Mainstream

fiction

Follows the divergent paths of Lizzie and Frances, a pair of nearly identical twin sisters, one of whom shocks the family by taking a married lover.

"Lizzie has been rather smug about her thriving marriage, her four children, her successful shop, and her big house, but she becomes unconscionably jealous when Frances, her quiet, devoted twin, finds love with the sexy, supportive, but marriedand foreignLuis. This British author excels at setting up the stuff of female fantasy and, from those worn materials, making something that draws you in and slams you with a thud of emotion so authentic it becomes your own." The New Yorker.

Trueblood, Valerie

Seven loves : a novel / Valerie Trueblood. Little, Brown and Co., 2006. 240 p.

ISBN 0316058939

1. Female friendship 2. Lovers 3. Sons -- Death 4. Children -- Death 5. Grief in women 6. Coping 7. Interpersonal relations 8. Men/women relations 9. Families 10. Love 11. Loss (Psychology) 12. Husband and wife 13. Mothers and daughters 14. Extramarital affairs 15. Seattle, Washington 16. Washington (State) 17. Domestic fiction 18. Pacific Northwest fiction

LC 2005026604

May Nilsson experiences seven pivotal relationships throughout the course of her life, from a passionate lover who changes her future and a risk-taking son who resists intervention to an eccentric mother and a beautiful young co-worker.

"Gently told, Trueblood's first work is poetic, contemplative, and tender." Booklist.

Trumbo, Dalton, 1905-1976

* **Johnny** got his gun / Dalton Trumbo. L. Stuart, 1970, c1959. 309 p.

ISBN 0818401109

1. World War I 2. Disabled veterans -- United States 3. World War I veterans 4. War -- Psychological aspects 5. Violence 6. Soldiers -- United States 7. Families 8. Fathers and sons 9. Psychological fiction

LC 71115416

First published 1939.

During World War I, an American soldier awakens in a hospital and realizes his arms, legs, ears, and face have been destroyed by an artillery shell. After nine years of lying in bed, he begins to tap messages in Morse code by moving his head. He communicates with a nurse and asks for someone to help him leave the hospital or die.

Truong, Monique T. D.

The **book** of salt, Monique Truong. Houghton Mifflin, 2003. 261 p.

ISBN 0618304002

1. Stein, Gertrude, 1874-1946 2. Toklas, Alice B, 1877-1967 3. Robeson, Paul, 1898-1976 4. Ho, Chi Minh, 1890-1969 5. 1920s 6. 1930s 7. Vietnamese in France 8. Cooks -- Vietnam 9. Household employees 10. Cooking 11. Americans in France 12. Women authors 13. Lesbians -- Paris, France 14. Gay men 15. Housekeepers 16. Paris, France 17. Vietnam 18. Biographical fiction 19. Historical fiction

LC 2002192152

Stonewall Book Award for the Barbara Gittings Literature Award, 2004.

In deciding if he should accompany his employers to America, stay in France, or go back to his native Vietnam, Binh recalls his life in Vietnam, the jobs he's held since leaving there, and the people it has helped him meet.

"Truong is tapping some trendy territory here: the postcolonial perspective; the book derived from a minor character in another well-known book. . .; the gay novel; the novel of exile. And Truong's central character, the gay Asian houseboy, is something of a stereotype in itself. But nothing in this distinctive novel feels secondhand." New York Times Book Review.

Truong, Monique T.D.

The **sweetest** fruits / Monique Truong. Viking Press, 2019 304 p.

ISBN 9780735221017

1. Hearn, Lafcadio 2. 19th century 3. Life change events 4. Voyages and travels 5. Influence (literary, artistic, etc) 6. Freed slaves 7. Authors 8. Former wives 9. Travelers 10. Men/women relations 11. Marriage 12. Motherhood 13. Nonconformists 14. Independence in women 15. Biographical fiction

A reimagining of Greek-Irish writer Lafcadio Hearn's migratory life through the voices of the women who knew him best, and who testify to their own remarkable journeys.

Truss, Lynne

The **man** that got away : a Constable Twitten mystery / Lynne Truss. Bloomsbury Pub Plc USA, 2019. 304 p. Constable Twitten mysteries

ISBN 9781635570731

1. 1950s 2. Detectives 3. Coastal towns 4. Witnesses 5. Nightlife 6. Murder investigation 7. Waxworks 8. Brighton, England 9. England 10. Great Britain 11. Historical mysteries

A sequel to A Shot in the Dark finds the murder of a young man at a 1957 Brighton beach party challenging Constable Twitten to seek clues in a notorious nightspot.

Tsao, Tiffany

The **majesties** / Tiffany Tsao. Atria Books, 2020. 256 p.

ISBN 9781982115500

1. Rich families 2. Poisoning 3. Family violence 4. Family problems 5. Family secrets 6. Sisters 7. People in comas 8. Mass murder 9. Elite (Social sciences) 10. Stereotypes (Social psychology) 11. Family relationships 12. Indonesia 13. Paris, France 14. California 15. Literary fiction

A sole survivor of a Chinese-Indonesian family struggles on the edge of a coma to regain consciousness while reexamining tragic elements in her family that may have driven a beloved sister to a shocking act of violence.

"This is a bold and dramatic portrayal of characters on the cusp of an impossible choice between complicit self-preservation and total annihilation." Publishers Weekly.

Tsukiyama, Gail

Dreaming water / Gail Tsukiyama. St. Martin's Press, 2002. 288 p.

ISBN 0312206070

1. Werner's syndrome 2. Mothers and daughters 3. Best friends 4. Sick children 5. Female friendship 6. Women with terminal illnesses 7. California 8. Psychological fiction 9. Women's lives and relationships

LC 2001058896

Cate and her adult daughter, Hana, who has Werner's Syndrome, a disease which speeds aging to twice the normal rate, find their lives changed irrevocably by the arrival of Hana's childhood friend, Laura, and her two energetic daughters.

"At 38, Hana Murayama is dying of Werner's syndrome, a genetic defect that causes premature aging. Hana is almost totally dependent on her mother, Cata, who at 62 is still recovering from the sudden death of her husband, Max. . . . Over the course of two days, Hana and Cate retrace in memory their lives and Max's. Their scattered and sometimes conflicting expectations are brought into sharp focus when Hana's best friend, Laura, now a successful East Coast lawyer, arrives with her two daughters, Hana's godchildren, allowing Hana and Cate to find a measure of the reconciliation that has eluded them." Publishers Weekly.

Tsukiyama, Gail

The **street** of a thousand blossoms / Gail Tsukiyama. St. Martin's Press, 2007. 432 p.

ISBN 9780312274825

1. Brothers 2. Orphans 3. World War II -- Influence 4. Grandparents 5. Sumo wrestling 6. Theater 7. Japan -- Social life and customs -- 20th century 8. Historical fiction 9. Domestic fiction

LC 2007021012

Raised by loving and traditionally minded grandparents, Japanese youths Hiroshi and Kenji are forced to put their dreams on hold in the wake of World War II and find their destinies intertwining with those of a famous sumo master's daughters.

"Set in Japan and spanning over 25 years (1939-66), the novel unravels the hardships and triumphs of two brothers raised by their loving maternal grandparents following the loss of their parents in a tragic accident. The dreams of older brother Hiroshi of becoming a sumotori (a sumo wrestler) and younger brother Kenji of becoming a Noh theater mask artisan are quelled by the onset of World War II. Passages describing the devastation wrought by the atomic bombings upon their lives and of those close to them, particularly the family of sisters Haru and Aki, who later becomes Hiroshi's wife, are well written and emotionally gripping." Library Journal.

Tsypkin, Leonid, 1926-1982

Summer in Baden-Baden : a novel / Leonid Tsypkin ; introduction by Susan Sontag ; translated from the Russian by Roger and Angela Keys. New Directions, 2001, c1987. xxi, 146 p.

ISBN 0811214842

1. Dostoyevsky, Fyodor, 1821-1881 Travel Europe 2. 1860s 3. Gambling 4. Self-destructive behavior 5. Authors, Russian -- 19th century 6. Poverty 7. Jews -- Identity 8. Women 9. Husband and wife 10. Voyages and travels 11. Jews, Soviet 12. Compulsive behavior in men 13. Germany -- Social life and customs -- 19th century 14. Baden-Baden (Germany) 15. Biographical fiction 16. Historical fiction 17. Literary fiction 18. Translations -- Russian to English

LC 2001032658

Translation of Leto v Badene, originally published: London : Quartet, 1987.

The narrator recounts his journey to Leningrad as the story of the 1867 travels of Fyodor Dostoyevsky and his new wife, Anna Grigoryevna, also unfolds.

"Tsypkin's stream-of-consciousness prose style is associative, inclusive, allusive, detached and yet humane." New York Times Book Review.

Tudor, C. J.

The **chalk** man : a novel / C J Tudor. Crown Publishers, 2018. 288 p.

ISBN 9781524760984

1. 1980s 2. 2010s 3. Games 4. Childhood 5. Dismemberment 6. Friendship 7. Chalk drawing 8. Villages 9. Murder 10. Small town life 11. Psychic trauma 12. Secrets 13. Flashbacks 14. England 15. Thrillers and suspense

LC 2016058866

"A mystery set in 1986 and 2016" -- Publisher's note.

Thriller Award for Best First Novel, 2019.
Librarians' Choice (Australia), 2017.

Three decades after his circle of friends is traumatized by the discovery of a murder victim while passing secret messages through a chalk-figure code of their invention, Eddie finds himself targeted by an unknown adversary who is using their former communication methods to torment and kill his friends.

Tudor, C. J.

The **other** people / C.J. Tudor. Ballantine Books, 2020. 288 p.

ISBN 9781984824998

1. Missing children 2. Fathers 3. Threat (Psychology) 4. Mothers and daughters 5. Kidnapping 6. Child kidnapping victims 7. Great Britain 8. Thrillers and suspense

Gabe desperately looks for his missing daughter, who most people believe is dead. Fran and her daughter also put in a lot of miles on the road--running from the people who want to hurt them. Because Fran knows what really happened to Gabe's daughter.

"A breathless escape story with hints of the supernatural and the promise of redemption dangling just out of reach." Booklist.

Turansky, Carrie

No ocean too wide : a novel / Carrie Turansky. Multnomah, 2019. 320 p. McAlister family novels

ISBN 9780525652939

1. Edwardian era (1901-1914) 2. Poor families 3. Brothers and sisters 4. Orphanages 5. Immigration and emigration 6. Interclass romance 7. Household employees 8. Lawyers 9. Secrecy 10. Helpfulness in men 11. Sick mothers 12. Faith (Christianity) 13. Interpersonal attraction 14. Men/women relations 15. England 16. Christian historical romances

LC 2018058174

When Edna McAlister falls gravely ill and is hospitalized, twins Katie and Garth and eight-year-old Grace are forced into an orphans' home before oldest daughter, Laura--who works at an estate more than an hour away--is notified about her family's unfortunate turn of events in 1908 London.

Turgenev, Ivan Sergeevich, 1818-1883

* **Fathers** and sons / Ivan Turgenev ; a new translation by Michael R. Katz. W.W. Norton, 1994, c1862. 157 p.

ISBN 9780393035599

1. Romanov Dynasty (1613-1917) 2. Fathers and sons -- Russia 3. Generation gap -- Russia 4. Russia -- Social life and customs -- 19th century 5. Russia -- Social conditions -- 19th century 6. Translations -- Russian to English 7. Classics

LC 92040010

Bazarov, a nihilist, advocates a materialistic view of life and disappoints his adoring parents.

Turgenev, Ivan Sergeevich, 1818-1883

First love, and other stories / Translated by Isaiah Berlin and Leonard Schapiro. Introduced by V. S. Pritchett. A. A. Knopf, 1994. 253 p.

ISBN 0679435948

1. Translations -- Russian to English 2. Classics

LC 946233

Includes chronology of Turgenev's life.

Turnbull, Cadwell, 1987-

* The **lesson** / Cadwell Turnbull. Blackstone Publishing, 2019. 290 p.

ISBN 9781538584644

1. Human/alien encounters 2. Aliens 3. Violence -- Psychological aspects 4. Ambassadors 5. Research 6. Murder 7. Healers 8. Cohabitation 9. Postcolonialism 10. Cultural memory 11. Virgin Islands of the United States 12. Caribbean Area 13. Science fiction 14. Afrofuturism and Afrofantasy

The people of the U.S. Virgin Islands tensely coexist with an alien species on an undisclosed research mission on Earth, until the death of a boy plunges three families into a conflict that will touch everyone and teach a terrible lesson.

Turner, Bethany, 1979-

The **secret** life of Sarah Hollenbeck / Bethany Turner. Revell, 2017. 296 p.

ISBN 9780800727666

1. Romance writers 2. Women -- Religious life 3. Divorced women 4. Women authors 5. Christian life 6. Clergy 7. Life change events 8. Faith (Christianity) 9. Interpersonal attraction 10. Men/women relations 11. Christian romances

LC 2017024938

Sarah Hollenbeck is torn between her Christian faith and her future as a writer of steamy romance novels and things become even more complicated when she finds herself falling in love with her pastor.

Turner, Bethany, 1979-

Wooing Cadie McCaffrey / Bethany Turner. Revell, 2019. 352 p.

ISBN 9780800736309

1. Jilted men 2. Former girlfriends 3. Breaking up (Interpersonal relations) 4. Romantic comedy films 5. Romantic love 6. Commitment (Psychology) 7. Regret 8. Second chances 9. Interpersonal relations 10. Men/women relations 11. Faith (Christianity) 12. Christian romances

LC 2018049157

"When Cadie McCaffrey breaks up with her adorably oblivious boyfriend, he determines to win her back by pulling out every "foolproof" romantic comedy tactic he's ever seen. What could go wrong" --, Provided by publisher.

Turner, Nancy E., 1953-

My name is Resolute : a novel / Nancy E. Turner. Thomas Dunne Books, 2014. 560 p.

ISBN 9781250036599

1. Revolutionary America (1775-1783) 2. 18th century 3. Young women 4. Kidnapping 5. Slavery 6. Families 7. Secrets 8. Weaving 9. Textile industry and trade 10. American Revolution, 1775-1783 11. Massachusetts 12. United States -- History -- Revolution, 1775-1783 13. Historical fiction

LC 2013031729

Only nine years old when she's kidnapped from her family's home in 1729 Jamaica by pirates, aristocrat's daughter Resolute Talbot is sold into slavery in New England, then taken prisoner by Native Americans, and finally sent to a Catholic orphanage in Quebec, where she learns to spin and weave. Although she regains her freedom, Resolute discovers that -- for a penniless young woman alone in the world -- survival may prove even more difficult than captivity. Starring a resourceful, resilient heroine whose adventurous life encompasses, among other momentous events, the Seven Years' War and the American Revolution, My Name is Resolute takes readers on an engrossing journey through Colonial North America. -- Description by Gillian Speace.

"Throughout the narrative, Turner skillfully keeps her main characters in the forefront and reveals historical events through their eyes and actions rather than by means of long, explanatory passages that stall the plot. The novel is lengthy and somewhat repetitious as so many characters are introduced, disappear and then are reunited multiple times, but the author convincingly conveys a pivotal time in American history and provides a rewarding reading experience. A fitting story about resiliency, ingenuity and heroism." Kirkus.

Turner, Nikki

The **Banks** sisters / Nikki Turner. Urban Books, 2015 288 p. Banks sisters

ISBN 9781601626479

1. Sisters 2. African American women 3. Grandmothers 4. Family relationships 5. People with cancer 6. Debt 7. Crime 8. Urban fiction 9. African American fiction

New York Times bestselling author Nikki Turner returns with her most spellbinding story to date: Meet the Banks sisters:Simone, Bunny, Tallhya, and Ginger. The four beauties are living under the same roof by force, but they can't stand each other. Their only common denominator is their loving grandmother, Me-Ma. When she's not at work trying to make ends meet, she's home with her girls, trying to keep them from killing each other.

Turner, Nikki

Black widow : a novel / Nikki Turner. One World / Ballantine Books, 2008. xi, 285 p.

ISBN 9780345493873

1. African American women 2. City life 3. Loss (Psychology) 4. Betrayal 5. Criminals 6. Men/women relations 7. African Americans 8. Women jewelry designers 9. Street life 10. Virginia 11. Urban fiction 12. African American fiction

LC 2007043351

Chronicles the saga of Isis Tatum, a woman marked forever by the tough world of street life and love as she is transformed from an innocent and sweet young girl into "The Black Widow" by the desertion, betrayal, and deaths of the men in her life.

Turner, Nikki

* **Forever** a hustler's wife : a novel / Nikki Turner. One World/Ballantine Books, 2007. 304 p.

ISBN 0345493850

1. Swindlers and swindling 2. Street life 3. African Americans 4. African American men 5. African American women 6. Women lawyers 7. Married women 8. Pimps 9. Frameups 10. Innocence (Law) 11. Murder 12. Betrayal 13. Deception 14. Urban fiction 15. African American fiction

LC 2006046947

Yarni is reunited with her husband, Des, after he is freed from prison, but finds her loyalty--and her religious faith--tested when he takes on the role of preacher in order to pursue his thirst for money, power, and respect.

Turner, Nikki

Heartbreak of a hustler's wife / Nikki Turner. One World, 2011. 212 p.

ISBN 9780345511089

1. Women lawyers 2. Clergy 3. Attempted murder 4. Fathers and daughters 5. Husband and wife 6. African Americans 7. Street life 8. Criminal behavior 9. Mysteries 10. Urban fiction 11. African American fiction

Sequel to: Natural Born Hustler.

Corporate attorney Yarni Taylor has her hands full when someone tries to kill her husband Des and Desember Day, the eighteen-year-old daughter Des never knew he had, shows up at their door.

Turner, Nikki

* A **hustler's** wife / Nikki Turner. Urban Books, 2013, c2003. 288 p.

ISBN 9781601625779

1. Prostitution 2. African American young women 3. Drug abuse and crime 4. African Americans 5. Street life 6. City life 7. Women drug dealers 8. Organized crime 9. Drug dealers 10. Drug traffic 11. Prisoners 12. African American men/women relations 13. Prisoners' spouses 14. Betrayal 15. Greed 16. Money addiction 17. Revenge 18. Richmond, Virginia 19. Virginia 20. Urban fiction 21. African American fiction

Originally published: Columbus, Ohio : Triple Crown Publications, 2003

Coming from a well-to-do family, Yarni knows life with her new love--Richmond, Virginia's notorious drug kingpin Des--will be quite a change, but the innocent girl can't imagine what is in store for her when Des is sentenced to life in prison.

Turner, Nikki

Natural born hustler : a novel / Nikki Turner. One World Trade Paperbacks/Ballantine Books, 2010. xi, 114 p.

ISBN 9780345523600

1. Father-deserted families 2. Birthfathers 3. Women sales personnel 4. African Americans 5. Street life 6. Men/women relations 7. Drug traffic 8. Urban fiction 9. African American fiction

LC 2010022021

Sequel: Heartbreak of a hustler's wife.

Desember Day loves basketball, money, and her boyfriend, but a shooting changes her life and leads her to Richmond, Virginia, and a father she has never known.

Turow, Scott

Ordinary heroes / Scott Turow. Farrar, Straus and Giroux, 2005. 384 p.

ISBN 0374184216

1. Second World War era (1939-1945) 2. Family secrets 3. Fathers -- Death 4. World War II 5. World War II veterans 6. Military lawyers 7. Soldiers -- United States 8. Women concentration camp survivors 9. Former fiances 10. Fathers and sons 11. Options, alternatives, choices 12. Dilemmas 13. Battles 14. Ardennes, Battle of the, 1944-1945 15. Courts-martial and courts of inquiry 16. Letters 17. Europe 18. Domestic fiction 19. War stories 20. Parallel narratives

LC 2005011824

Stewart Dubinsky plunges into the mystery of his family's secret history when he discovers his deceased father's wartime letters to his former fiancée, revealing his court-martial and imprisonment during World World II.

"Stewart Dubinsky is not especially close to his father, David Dubin. Even their names are different, yet David's death prompts Stewart to try and find out more about this enigmatic man. He uncovers some startling information: that his father was engaged to another woman before his mother, and that he was court-martialed during the Battle of the Bulge. Dubinsky decides to write a family history, starts digging, and uncovers a manuscript his father wrote about his war experiences that is alternately moving and horrifying, vindicating, and vilifying and shines light on a side of his parents that he never knew. While some of the historical facts presented are not 100 percent accurate, the book's emotional wallop more than justifies the literary license and should secure its place in the canon of World War II literature." Library Journal.

Turow, Scott

* **Presumed** innocent / Scott Turow. Farrar, Straus, Giroux, 1987. 431 p. Kindle County novels

ISBN 0374237131

1. Public prosecutors 2. Extramarital affairs 3. Murder investigation 4. Former lovers 5. Innocence (Law) 6. Lawyers 7. Rape victims 8. Manipulation by women 9. Middle-aged men 10. Guilt 11. Trials (Murder) 12. Middle West 13. Legal thrillers

LC 87000368

Silver Dagger Award for Fiction, 1987.

Rusty Sabich, a prosecuting attorney investigating the murder of Carolyn Polhemus, his former lover and a prominent member of his boss's staff, finds himself accused of the crime.

"This novel contains high drama and suspense, as scenes in and out of the courtroom crackle with the amazing interactions of complex, fascinating characters. This is a great book." Library Journal.

Turow, Scott

Testimony / Scott Turow. Grand Central Pub, 2017. 416 p. Kindle County novels

ISBN 9781455553549

1. Lawyers 2. Refugees 3. Refugee camps 4. Missing persons 5. Survival 6. War crimes 7. Atrocities 8. Paramilitary forces 9. Organized crime 10. Murder investigation 11. Kosovo, Serbia -- History -- 20th century 12. Bosnia and Hercegovina -- History -- 1991- 13. Legal thrillers

Assigned to investigate the unsolved disappearance of an entire Gypsy refugee camp during the Bosnian War, a disillusioned American prosecutor navigates a host of suspects while uncovering disturbing alliances and betrayals.

Tursten, Helene, 1954-

Hunting game / Helene Tursten ; translated from the Swedish by Paul Norlen. Soho Crime, 2019. 288 p. Embla Nystrom investigations

ISBN 9781616956509

1. Women detectives 2. Hunting 3. Vacations 4. Murder investigation 5. Anxiety in women 6. Hunters 7. Women hunters 8. Murder 9. Moose hunting 10. Sweden 11. Scandinavian crime fiction 12. Police procedurals 13. Translations -- Swedish to English

LC 2018016750

Translations of: Jaktmark.

When an annual moose hunt leads to murder, 28-year-old Swedish Detective Inspector Embla Nyström must delve into the dark pasts of her fellow hunters to expose a killer.

Tursten, Helene, 1954-

Winter grave / Helene Tursten ; translated from the Swedish by Marlaine Delargy. Soho Crime, 2019, c2018. 336 p. Embla Nyström investigations

ISBN 9781641290760

1. Missing children 2. Violent crimes 3. Suspicion 4. Women detectives 5. Christmas 6. Winter 7. Small towns 8. Teenagers with developmental disabilities 9. Extramarital affairs 10. Investigations 11. Sweden 12. Scandinavian crime fiction 13. Police procedurals 14. Translations -- Swedish to English

LC 2019014169

Originally published in Sweden, 2018.

When a mentally disabled boy is wrongly targeted with suspicion in the wake of a child's disappearance, Detective Inspector Embla uncovers suspicious links to an unsolved missing-persons case from her childhood.

Turtledove, Harry

Into the darkness / Harry Turtledove. TOR, 1999. 540 p. Derlevai novels

ISBN 0312868952

1. Dragons 2. Magic 3. Sabotage 4. Rulers -- Death 5. War and civilization 6. Imaginary wars and battles 7. Military fantasy 8. Fantasy fiction

LC 98-43610

In a world dominated by magic, the sudden death of the Duke of Bari leads to international conflict as the nation of Algarve seeks to annex his country, while the nations surrounding Algarve strive to prevent it

"First title in the author's Alternate world fantasy series. In the beginning, militarily efficient Algarve occupies the Duchy of Bari . . . and is quickly followed by one of Algarve's traditional foes, Unkerlant. . . . Throughout, World War II buffs will search for further reflections in Turtledove's fantastic mirror, but they will also, like other readers, be quickly caught up in the sheer ingenuity of the tale, in which dragons provide airpower, behemoths (think rhinoceroses the size of elephants) are tanks, magic wands take the place of rifles, and submarine warfare is in the hands of leviathan-riders." Booklist.

Turtledove, Harry

Rulers of the darkness / Harry Turtledove. Tom Doherty Associates Book, 2002 656 p. Derlevai novels

ISBN 0765300362

1. Violence 2. Genocide 3. Magic 4. Dragons 5. Scholars and academics 6. Sabotage 7. War and civilization 8. Imaginary wars and battles 9. Military fantasy 10. Fantasy fiction

LC 2001058465

The war for the continent of Derlavi reaches its climax as the mages of Kuusamo and Lagoas race against time to come up with a new magic to stop the Algarve invaders.

"The fourth volume of the alternate-history saga Darkness deals with the fourth year of a World War II. . . . Kuusamo's sorcerous Manhattan Project has the potential to generate destructive energy by drawing on the past and the future, which is the same way the Algarvians use the life energy of murdered Kaunians. Meanwhile, more conventional counteroffensives against Algarve are in progress, with Unkerlant and Algarve reaching a gigantic confrontation in a battle recognizable as a re-imagining of the Battle of Kursk. One need not, however, be able to run down all of Turtledove's real-world parallels to appreciate how well he presents the human dilemmas of global warfare." Booklist.

Turton, Stuart

The **7** 1/ 2 deaths of Evelyn Hardcastle / Sourcebooks Landmark, 2018. 435 p.

ISBN 9781492657965

1. Women murder victims 2. Reincarnation 3. Consciousness transfer 4. Country homes 5. Murder investigation 6. Amateur detectives 7. Murder 8. Second chances 9. England 10. Mysteries

Costa First Novel Award, 2018.

Librarians' Choice (Australia), 2018.

Doomed to repeat the same day over and over, Aiden Bishop must solve the murder of Evelyn Hardcastle in order to escape the curse in a world filled with enemies where nothing and no one are quite what they seem.

Twain, Mark, 1835-1910

* **Adventures** of Huckleberry Finn : Tom Sawyer's comrade ... / Mark Twain ; illustrated by E.W. Kemble and John Harley ; editors, Victor Fischer and Lin Salamo with Harriet Eli-

nor Smith and the late Walter Blair. University of Calif.Press, 2001. 561 p.

ISBN 0520228065

1. Twain, Mark, 1835-1910 Adventures of Huckleberry Finn Criticism and interpretation 2. 19th century 3. Boys -- Friendship 4. Fugitive slaves -- United States 5. Boy adventurers -- Mississippi Valley 6. Slavery 7. Personal conduct 8. Racism 9. Boys -- Missouri 10. Mississippi River 11. Missouri -- History -- 19th century 12. Picaresque fiction 13. Coming-of-age stories 14. Classics 15. Southern fiction

LC 2001027448

The book has been made into a movie called Tom and Huck, Huckleberry Finn, and one called Adventures of Huck Finn.

First published in 1885.

Complete and unabridged.

Includes a short biography of the author.

Rather than be 'sivilized' by the Widow Douglas, Huckleberry Finn sets off with Jim, an escaped slave, to find freedom on the Mississippi river. With the law on their tail, they navigate a world of robbers, slave hunters and con men, and Huck must choose between what society says is right and his own burgeoning understanding of Jim's friendship and humanity, in a razor-sharp satire of the antebellum South that is one of the most important of all American novels.

Twain, Mark, 1835-1910

The **complete** short stories of Mark Twain / edited with an introduction by Charles Neider. Bantam Books, 2005. xxii, 814 p.

ISBN 9780553211955

1. Short stories 2. Anthologies

Gathers all sixty of Twains stories, including tall tales, mysteries, sketches, and tales of travel.

"The sixty pieces which are here hospitably called short stories illustrate both the weaknesses and the strengths of Mark Twain as a writer of fiction." New York Times Book Review.

Twain, Mark, 1835-1910

* A **Connecticut** Yankee in King Arthur's Court / Mark Twain ; introduction by Roy Blount, Jr. ; illustrations by Daniel Carter Beard. Modern Library, 2001, c1889. xxx, 465 p.

ISBN 9780375757808

1. Arthur,, King 2. 6th century 3. 19th century 4. Time travel (Past) 5. Camelot (Legendary place) 6. Knights and knighthood 7. Feudalism 8. Merlin (Legendary character) 9. Wizards 10. Americans in Great Britain 11. Technology 12. Monarchy 13. Democracy 14. Education 15. England -- Social life and customs -- 6th century 16. Satirical fiction 17. Classics

The films A Kid in King Arthur's Court (1995) and Black Knight (2001) were inspired by A Connecticut Yankee in King Arthur's Court.

Originally published: New York : Charles L. Webster & Co., 1889

This satirical novel tells the story of Hank Morgan, the quintessential self-reliant New Englander, who brings to King Arthur's Age of Chivalry the "great and beneficent" miracles of nineteenth-century engineering and Yankee ingenuity.

Twain, Mark, 1835-1910

Personal recollections of Joan of Arc / Mark Twain. Dover Publications, 2002, c1896. xvi, 329 p.

ISBN 0486424596

1. Joan of Arc,, Saint, 1412-1431 2. Conte, Louis de, 1835-1910 3. Women saints 4. Courage in women 5. Leadership in women 6. Women -- Spiritual life 7. Religious persecution 8. France -- History

-- Charles VII, 1422-1461 9. Biographical fiction 10. Historical fiction 11. Classics

LC 2002067628

Originally published: New York :

Offers a fictional account of the 15th century saint as a paragon of honesty, unselfishness, and innocence.

Twain, Mark, 1835-1910

Pudd'nhead Wilson ; and, Those extraordinary twins / Mark Twain ; introduction by Ron Powers ; illustrations by F.M. Senior and C.H. Warren. Modern Library, 2002, c1899. xvi, 263 p.

ISBN 0812966228

1. Passing (Identity) 2. Trials (Murder) 3. Impostors 4. Race relations 5. Mistaken identity 6. Infants switched at birth 7. Role reversal 8. Slavery -- Missouri 9. Conjoined twins 10. Small town life -- Missouri 11. Human nature 12. Missouri -- History -- 19th century 13. Satirical fiction 14. Legal thrillers 15. Classics

LC 2002066002

David Wilson is called "Pudd'nhead" by the townspeople, who fail to understand his combination of wisdom and eccentricity. He redeems himself by simultaneously solving a murder mystery and a case of transposed identities. Two children, a white boy and a mulatto, are born on the same day. Roxy, mother of the mulatto, is given charge of the children; in fear that her son will be sold, she exchanges the babies. The mulatto, though he grows up as a white boy, turns out to be a scoundrel. He sells his mother and murders and robs his uncle. He accuses Luigi, one of a pair of twins, of the murder. Pudd'nhead, a lawyer, undertakes Luigi's defense. On the basis of fingerprint evidence, he exposes the real murderer, and the white boy takes his rightful place.

Twardoch, Szczepan, 1979-

The **king** of Warsaw / Szczepan Twardoch ; translated from the Polish by Sean Gasper Bye. Amazon Crossing, 2020. 384 p.

ISBN 9781542044462

1. 1930s 2. 1980s 3. Jews, Polish 4. Gangsters 5. Fascists 6. Antisemitism 7. Anti-fascism 8. City life 9. Social conflict 10. Revenge 11. Warsaw, Poland 12. Poland 13. Israel 14. Historical thrillers 15. Translations -- Polish to English

"Twardoch's willingness to stare into the abyss elevates this racing work to sublime heights." Publishers Weekly.

Tyers, Kathy

* **Shivering** world / Kathy Tyers. Bethany House, 2004. 398 p.

ISBN 0764226762

1. Women scientists 2. Mothers and daughters 3. Space colonies 4. Women with terminal illnesses 5. Immortalism 6. Ethics 7. Medical genetics 8. Healing 9. Christian men 10. Men/women relations 11. Secrets 12. Attempted murder 13. Prejudice 14. Christianity 15. Faith (Christianity) 16. Christian science fiction

LC 2003022940

Christy Award for Allegory/Fantasy/Visionary Category, 2019.

Graysha Brady-Phillips moves to the planet Goddard, where she hopes colonists will find a cure for her genetic disorder even though genetic engineering has been banned for decades.

Tyler, Anne

* The **accidental** tourist : a novel / Anne Tyler. Ballantine Books, 2002, c1985. 329 p.

ISBN 9780345452009

1. Separated men (Marital relations) 2. Coping in men 3. Men/women relations 4. Women dog trainers -- Baltimore, Maryland 5. Separated women (Marital relations) 6. Travel writers -- Baltimore, Maryland 7. Separation (Marital relations) 8. Baltimore, Maryland 9. Love stories 10. Mainstream fiction 11. Gentle reads

Originally published: New York : Knopf, 1985.

National Book Critics Circle Award for Fiction, 1985.

Pulitzer Prize for Fiction finalist, 1986.

A travel writer who hates to travel, and to whom "things just happen," becomes involved with an unusual woman following the desertion of his wife.

"After 20 years of marriage, Macon and Sarah separate. Thus, a man used to intense order in his life finds his existence thrown into disorder; forced to create a new life for himself, Macon must overcome numerous obstacles--particularly his inability to communicate, to relate to other people's needs and problems." Booklist.

Tyler, Anne

* The **amateur** marriage : a novel / Anne Tyler. Knopf, 2004. 306 p.

ISBN 9781400042074

1. Marital conflict 2. Married people 3. Husband and wife 4. Runaway teenagers 5. Teenage mothers 6. Grandparent and child 7. Guardian and ward 8. Mate selection 9. Family relationships 10. Baltimore, Maryland 11. San Francisco, California 12. Mainstream fiction 13. Domestic fiction 14. Gentle reads

LC 2003059536

Marrying quickly during World War II after falling in love at first sight, a mismatched couple discovers that their very different personalities and approaches to life are taking a toll on their lives, their relationship, and their family.

"Although Tyler's prose occasionally slips into banality, she never falters in creating vivid characters whose weaknesses are both credible and compelling." The New Yorker.

Tyler, Anne

Back when we were grownups : a novel / Anne Tyler. Alfred A. Knopf, 2001. 273 p.

ISBN 0375412530

1. Midlife crisis in women 2. Self-confidence 3. Widows 4. Middle-aged women 5. Middle-aged women -- Identity 6. Married women 7. Stepmothers 8. Parties 9. Baltimore, Maryland 10. Women's lives and relationships 11. Mainstream fiction 12. Gentle reads

LC 00108810

Beck Davitch looks back on her thirty-year marriage to Joe and her role as a mother and manager of the Open Arms, wondering if she is living the life she was meant to live and reconsidering her dedication to the family business.

"This is as perceptive, as full of gentle comedy and human warmth as any of Ms. Tyler's previous novels. She manages her quirky, engagingly named characters (Patch, Biddy, NoNo, Jeep, Zeb) beautifully, spinning a web of family tensions with a wonderful lightness of touch in this, Ms. Tyler is matchless." The Economist.

Tyler, Anne

The **beginner's** goodbye : a novel / Anne Tyler. Alfred A. Knopf, 2012. 197 p.

ISBN 9780307957276

1. Middle-aged men 2. Coping in men 3. Grief 4. Married women

-- Death 5. Bereavement 6. Men with disabilities 7. Widowers 8. Life after death 9. Loss (Psychology) 10. Spirits 11. Good-byes 12. Baltimore, Maryland 13. Mainstream fiction 14. Gentle reads

LC 2011033507

Sharing a happy marriage with the plain and outspoken Dorothy, Aaron, a physically disabled man who spent his youth avoiding a controlling sister, is devastated by his wife's sudden death and moves through the grieving process with the help of her apparition.

Tyler, Anne

* **Breathing** lessons / Anne Tyler. Knopf, 1988. 327 p.

ISBN 0394572343

1. Automobile travel 2. Communication in marriage 3. Husband and wife 4. Marriage 5. Self-fulfillment 6. Middle-age 7. Mainstream fiction 8. Domestic fiction 9. Gentle reads

LC 88045260

Pulitzer Prize for Fiction, 1989.

National Book Award for Fiction finalist, 1988

During a ninety-mile drive to her best friend's husband's funeral, Maggie and her husband, Ira, recall and revaluate the details of their twenty-eight-year marriage.

"This novel has irresistibly funny passages you want to read out loud and poignant insights that illuminate the serious business of sharing lives in an unsettling world." Publishers Weekly.

Tyler, Anne

Celestial navigation / Anne Tyler. A. A. Knopf, 1974. 273 p.

1. Men/women relations 2. Boarding houses 3. Single men 4. Mothers -- Death 5. Artists 6. Boarding house owners 7. Baltimore, Maryland 8. Love stories 9. Mainstream fiction 10. Gentle reads

LC 73018189

"The author is especially gifted in the art of freeing her characters and then keeping track of them as they move in their unique and often solitary orbits. . . . She has a way of transcribing their peculiarities with such loving wholeness that when we examine them we keep finding more and more pieces of ourselves." New York Times Book Review.

Tyler, Anne,

* **Clock** dance : a novel / Anne Tyler. Alfred A. Knopf, 2018. 288 p.

ISBN 9780525521228

1. Families 2. Senior women 3. Single mothers 4. Marriage 5. Married women 6. Community life 7. Gunshot victims 8. Mothers and sons 9. Family relationships 10. Interpersonal relations 11. Baltimore, Maryland 12. Literary fiction 13. Gentle reads

LC 2017043200

Librarians' Choice (Australia), 2018.

A lifetime of painful milestones and fading grandchild prospects compel a woman to help her son's ex, whose 9-year-old daughter needs protection from violent local dynamics.

"Tyler's bedazzling, yet fathoms-deep, feel-good novel is wrought with nimble humor, intricate understanding of emotions and family, place and community--and bounteous pleasure in quirkiness, discovery, and renewal." Booklist.

Tyler, Anne

The **clock** winder / Anne Tyler. Knopf, 1972. 312 p.

1. Dysfunctional families 2. Family relationships 3. Widows -- Baltimore, Maryland 4. Baltimore, Maryland 5. Mainstream fiction 6. Gentle reads

LC 70178960

"The author has a remarkable understanding of the intricacies of family life, a sympathy for odd-ball characters who never become merely southern grotesques . . . but are observed so gently that the term 'neurotic' seems equally inappropriate for them." The New Republic.

Tyler, Anne

Digging to America : a novel / Anne Tyler. Alfred A. Knopf, 2006. 288 p.

ISBN 0307263940

1. Americanization 2. International adoption 3. Belonging 4. Interethnic friendship 5. Interracial adoption 6. Interracial families 7. Interethnic families 8. Family traditions 9. Reunions 10. Interethnic relations 11. Race relations 12. Culture conflict 13. Independence in women 14. Identity (Psychology) 15. Baltimore, Maryland 16. Mainstream fiction 17. Domestic fiction 18. Gentle reads

LC 2005052963

Shortlisted for The Orange Prize for Fiction, 2007

A chance encounter between two families--the Donaldsons, and the Iranian-born Yasdans--at the Baltimore airport, as both couples await the arrival of an adopted daughter from Korea, prompts an examination about what it means to be an American while the lives of the two families intertwine over the years.

"With this novel, Tyler has delivered something startlingly fresh while retaining everything we love about her work . . . . Her success at portraying culture clash and the complex longings and resentments of those new to America confirms what we knew, or should have known, all along: There's nothing small about Tyler's world, nothing precious about her attention to the hopes and fears of ordinary people." Washington Post Book World.

Tyler, Anne

Dinner at the Homesick Restaurant / Anne Tyler. A. A. Knopf, 1982. 303 p.

ISBN 9780394523811

1. Perspective, Personal 2. Conflict in families 3. Parent and child 4. Mothers and sons 5. Mothers and daughters 6. Brothers and sisters 7. Father-separated children 8. Father-deserted families 9. Jealousy in men 10. Interpersonal conflict 11. Baltimore, Maryland 12. Mainstream fiction 13. Gentle reads

LC 81013694

National Book Award for Fiction finalist, 1983

National Book Critics Circle Award for Fiction finalist, 1982

Pulitzer Prize for Fiction finalist, 1983.

Eighty-five-year-old Perla Tull recalls the desertion of her husband and her solo attempts to raise three children--Cody, Ezra, and Jenny--who must come to terms with themselves and their father after their mother's death.

Tyler, Anne

Earthly possessions / Anne Tyler. Knopf, 1977. 197 p.

ISBN 0394411471

1. 1970s 2. Kidnapping 3. Women hostages 4. Women -- Identity 5. Crimes against women 6. Thieves 7. Maryland 8. Mainstream fiction 9. Gentle reads

LC 76041222

"The book is contrapuntal, alternating chapters of the present action with chapters of first-person flashback. . . . The dialogue has perfect pitch, the visual detail seems astonishing yet apt." The New Republic.

Tyler, Anne

Ladder of years / Anne Tyler. Knopf, 1995. 325 p.

ISBN 0679441557

1. Middle-aged women -- Maryland 2. Runaway wives, husbands,

etc -- Maryland 3. Self-acceptance in women 4. Physicians' spouses -- Maryland 5. Married women -- Identity 6. Maryland 7. Women's lives and relationships 8. Mainstream fiction 9. Gentle reads

LC 94038909

Shortlisted for The Orange Prize for Fiction, 1996

Forty-year-old Delia Grinstead, mother of three almost-grown children, impulsively walks away from her marriage and sets off into the unknown to begin an entirely new life, but suddenly she discovers that she is accumulating fresh responsibilities.

"Ladder of Years' feels, indeed, like the story of a woman who thought she could prune her life down to a short story, only to find it blooming, unexpectedly, into an Anne Tyler novel. There can be few more delightful revelations." The New Yorker.

Tyler, Anne

Morgan's passing / Anne Tyler. Knopf, 1980. 311 p.
ISBN 9780385691031

1. Obsession in men 2. Middle-aged men -- Identity 3. Midlife crisis in men 4. Married men 5. Extramarital affairs 6. Baltimore, Maryland 7. Mainstream fiction 8. Domestic fiction 9. Gentle reads

LC 79020272

National Book Critics Circle Award for Fiction finalist, 1980

While lost in the dreams he wished for his life, Morgan Gower becomes entangled in the lives of newlyweds Emily and Leon and dreads the return to his own dreary life.

Tyler, Anne

Noah's compass : a novel / Anne Tyler. Alfred A. Knopf, 2009. 288 p.
ISBN 9780307272409

1. Senior men 2. Retirees 3. Amnesia 4. Aging -- Psychological aspects 5. Divorced men 6. Men/women relations 7. Mainstream fiction 8. Gentle reads

LC 2009014925

Preparing to retire early from an unfulfilling teaching job, Liam Pennywell struggles to recall missing memories of the night before he awoke in the hospital with a head injury, an effort that leads to unexpected discoveries.

"Tyler's acutely perceptive observations of family interactions are dead on." BookPage.

Tyler, Anne

A **patchwork** planet / Anne Tyler. A. A. Knopf, 1998. 287 p.
ISBN 037540256X

1. Divorced men 2. Emotional maturity 3. Eccentrics and eccentricities 4. Men/women relations 5. Mother and adult son 6. Rich families 7. Baltimore, Maryland 8. Mainstream fiction 9. Gentle reads

A troubled boy with a compulsion to break into other people's houses to read their mail is not able to break free of it until he is almost thirty, when he meets Sophia, a woman of unshakeable goodness who little by little transforms him into the good man he wants to be.

"For some readers, the story may indeed be too quiltlike-cozy and cute. But unlike the patchwork it depicts, it is a wonder of construction: everything fits; it's seamless." The New Yorker.

Tyler, Anne

* **Saint** Maybe / Anne Tyler. A. A. Knopf, 1991. 337 p.
ISBN 0679403612

1. Single fathers 2. Adoptive fathers 3. Teenage fathers 4. Seventeen-year-old boys -- Baltimore, Maryland 5. Seventeen-year-old boys 6. Brothers -- Death 7. Guilt in teenage boys 8. Atonement 9.

Fundamentalists 10. Christianity 11. Baltimore, Maryland 12. Mainstream fiction 13. Domestic fiction 14. Gentle reads

LC 91052704

In 1965, the Bedloe family is living an ideal life in Baltimore. But an accident shatters their peace forever, and seventeen year-old Ian Bedloe is guilt-wracked over the accidental death of his brother. Unable to live under the weight of his self-punishment, he espies a second chance in a stereotypical, and therefore, unlikely, place.

"Tyler's remarkable novel pulls at the heart strings and jogs the memories of forgotten youth. . . . While the majority of YA readers lack enough life experiences to appreciate the pure joy of Tyler's descriptions and thoughts, not to steer them in her direction would be a shame." School Library Journal.

Tyler, Anne

Searching for Caleb / Anne Tyler. A. A. Knopf, 1976, c1975. 309 p.

ISBN 0394498488

1. Missing persons 2. Housing relocation 3. Grandfathers 4. Runaways 5. Fortune-tellers 6. Moving, Household 7. Family sagas 8. Mainstream fiction 9. Gentle reads

LC 75008251

The lives and secrets of four generations of the Peck family of Roland Park intertwine as forty-year-old fortune teller Justine accompanies her deaf, ex-judge grandfather in search of his maverick half-brother Caleb, who vanished in the spring of 1912.

Tyler, Anne

A **slipping-down** life / Anne Tyler. Berkley Books, 1983, c1970. 222 p.

ISBN 9780425061428

1. Rock musicians 2. Crushes (Interpersonal relations) 3. Teenage girls 4. Overweight teenagers 5. Obsession 6. Boy/girl relations 7. Mainstream fiction 8. Gentle reads

Anne Tyler's third novel is the story of Evie Decker, one of the most overweight girls in her high school in Pulqua, North Carolina. Evie, who has always been on the outskirts of the popular crowd, falls in love with a rock and roll singer and guitar player named Bertram "Drumstrings" Casey. To demonstrate her absolute devotion to him, Evie uses a pair of nail scissors to carve his name on her forehead--but because she does it while looking in the mirror, the word is spelled YESAC. Although her father wants her to go to a plastic surgeon, Evie refuses. Tyler explores the relationship between Drum and Evie with compassion and grace. -- Description by: Nancy Pearl.

Tyler, Anne

* A **spool** of blue thread / Anne Tyler. Knopf, 2015. 357 p.
ISBN 9781101874271

1. Seniors 2. Houses 3. Decision-making 4. Families 5. Reminiscing in old age 6. Secrets 7. Family relationships 8. Domestic fiction 9. Gentle reads

Shortlisted for The Baileys Women's Prize for Fiction, 2015
Shortlisted for the Man Booker Prize, 2015

A Baltimore family gathers on the porch to talk about their lives in the past, present and future.

"Using her signature gifts for brilliant dialog and for intricately framing the complex messiness of parental and spousal relationships, Tyler beautifully untangles the threads that bind and sometimes choke all of them." Library Journal.

Tyler, Anne

The **tin** can tree / Anne Tyler. Knopf, 1965. 273 p.

1. Children -- Death 2. Bereavement 3. Coping 4. Grief 5. Accidental

death 6. Family relationships 7. Mainstream fiction 8. Domestic fiction 9. Gentle reads

LC 65018762

"Six-year-old Janie Rose Pike was killed in a fall from a tractor, an accident which shook but does not really change the little world in which she lived. Mrs. Pike, left stunned and silent by her daughter's death, is too apathetic to pay attention to her 10-year-old son, Simon. Her grown-up niece, who lives with the family, tries to take care of Simon and at the same time to cope with her own problems. It is Simon himself . . . who finally awakens his mother to the need for life to continue." Library Journal.

Tyler, Anne
Vinegar girl : The taming of the shrew retold / Anne Tyler. Hogarth Shakespeare, 2016 237 p. Hogarth Shakespeare
ISBN 9780804141260
1. Fathers and daughters 2. Independence in women 3. Women's role 4. Scientists 5. Gender role 6. Family relationships 7. Marriage 8. Immigrants 9. Husband and wife 10. Men/women relations 11. Domestic fiction 12. Adaptations, retellings, and spin-offs 13. Gentle reads

LC 2015040137

A modern retelling of The Taming of the Shrew follows the experiences of a preschool teacher who alienates others by speaking her mind and who manages her family's home before she is expected by her eccentric father to marry his assistant to prevent the young man's deportation.

"The Taming of the Shrew meets Green Card in this delightful reinvention that owes as much to Tyler's quirky sensibilities as it does to its literary forebear. Come for the Shakespeare, stay for the wonderful Tyler." Library Journal.

Tyree, Omar
* **Flyy** girl / Omar Tyree. Simon & Schuster, 1996. 415 p. Tracy Ellison novels
ISBN 9780684829289
1. 1980s 2. African American teenage girls 3. Casual sex 4. Street life 5. African American girls 6. Philadelphia, Pennsylvania 7. Germantown (Philadelphia, Pa) 8. African American fiction 9. Coming-of-age stories 10. Urban fiction

LC 96024834

Sequel: For the love of money.

As a young black woman motivated by material things, Tracey plunges into a world of violence, gratuitous sex, and lies, until heartbreak forces her to take a closer look at her own life, sexuality, and dreams.

Tyree, Omar
For the love of money : a novel / Omar Tyree. Simon & Schuster, 2000. 416 p. Tracy Ellison novels
ISBN 0684872919
1. African American women screenwriters 2. Moving to a new state -- California 3. Homecomings 4. Young women -- California 5. African American actors and actresses 6. Fame 7. Street life 8. African American women film producers and directors 9. African American women -- Philadelphia, Pennsylvania 10. Philadelphia, Pennsylvania 11. California 12. African American fiction 13. Coming-of-age stories 14. Urban fiction

LC 00037166

Sequel to: Flyy girl.

After making it in Hollywood, twenty-eight-year-old "Flyy Girl" Tracy Ellison returns to her old Philadelphia neighborhood, but her homecoming is bittersweet as she confronts the things and people she left behind.

Tyree, Omar
Leslie : a novel / Omar Tyree. Simon & Schuster, 2002. 352 p.
ISBN 0743228669
1. African American women college students 2. Murder suspects 3. Voodoo 4. African American universities and colleges 5. Haitian American families 6. Children of immigrants 7. Poor African American families 8. Young women 9. Revenge 10. Street life 11. New Orleans, Louisiana 12. Thrillers and suspense 13. African American fiction 14. Urban fiction

LC 2002066790

Idolized by her family and admired by her peers and teachers at Dillard University, New Orleans native Leslie Beaudet becomes the center of a disturbing murder mystery that reveals her misunderstood personal struggles and craving for power.

U

Udall, Brady
The **lonely** polygamist : a novel / Brady Udall. W.W. Norton, 2010. 576 p.
ISBN 9780393062625
1. Middle-aged men 2. Polygamy 3. Bereavement -- Psychological aspects 4. Families 5. Mormons 6. Family secrets 7. Utah 8. Domestic fiction

LC 2009052226

ALA Notable Book, 2011.

Golden Richards, a polygamist with four wives and twenty-eight children has a midlife crisis affair that threatens to destroy his family's future, in this tale of a dysfunctional American family.

"Udall's control over his complex plot, and his psychological insight into his characters, are admirable and impressive. But perhaps the most pleasing thing about The Lonely Polygamist is the way it avoids giving in to the prurient interests that could easily have dominated a novel about polygamy." Chicago Tribune

Ugresic, Dubravka
Fox / Dubravka Ugresic ; translated from the Croatian by Ellen Elias-Bursa and David Williams. Open Letter, 2018, c2017 308 p.
ISBN 9781940953762
1. Writing 2. Women 3. Storytelling 4. Literature 5. Foxes 6. Literary fiction 7. Translations -- Croatian to English

LC 2017055368

Originally published by Nijgh & van Ditmar, 2017.

"Using the duplicitous and shape-shifting fox of Eastern folklore as a motif, Ugresic constructs a novel that reinvents itself over and over, blending nuggets of literary trivia (like how Nabokov named the Neonympha Dorothea Dorothea butterfly after the woman who drove him cross country), with the timeless story of a woman trying to escape her hometown and find love to magical effect." --Provided by publisher

Ulinich, Anya, 1973-
Petropolis / Anya Ulinich. Viking, 2007. 336 p.
ISBN 9780670038190
1. Teenage girls -- Siberia 2. Father-separated teenage girls 3. Teenage boy/girl relations 4. Unplanned pregnancy 5. Teenage mothers 6. Escapes 7. Mail order brides 8. Immigrants, Russian 9. Russians in the United States 10. Quests 11. Culture shock 12. Misadventures 13. Siberia 14. United States 15. Coming-of-age

stories 16. Satirical fiction

LC 2006041356

Abandoned by her father and struggling under the shadow of her overbearing mother, Jewish-Siberian teen Sasha has a baby with a homeless alcoholic and becomes a mail-order bride as part of her quest to find her father in America.

"In the end, [the author] ties a neat bow around Sasha's serious coming-of-age problems, but bittersweetness lingers. Petropolis bursts with artful details of an immigrant's peripatetic youth and quest for home-- the grappling for the strong woman inside of the lost girl." Ms.

Ullman, Ellen

By blood / Ellen Ullman. Farrar Straus & Giroux, 2012. 400 p.

ISBN 9780374117559

1. 1970s 2. Psychotherapy 3. Birthparents -- Identification 4. College teachers 5. Eavesdropping 6. Obsession in men 7. Compulsive behavior in men 8. Psychologists 9. World War II -- Influence 10. Lesbians 11. San Francisco, California 12. Psychological suspense

1970s San Francisco. A disgraced professor takes a downtown office to plot his return. But the walls are thin and he's distracted by voices from next door. His neighbor is a psychologist, and one of her patients dislikes the hum of the white-noise machine. And so he begins to hear about the patient's troubles with her female lover, her conflicts with her adoptive WASP family, and her quest to track down her birth mother.

Ullmann, Linn, 1966-

* **Unquiet** : a novel / Linn Ullmann ; translated from the Norwegian by Thilo Reinhard. W. W. Norton & Co., 2019, c2015. 392 p.

ISBN 9780393609943

1. Bergman, Ingmar, 1918-2007 2. Memories 3. Family relationships 4. Fathers and daughters 5. Aging 6. Authors 7. Interviewing 8. Parent and child 9. Families -- History 10. Reminiscing in old age 11. Literary fiction 12. Autobiographical fiction 13. Translations -- Norwegian to English

Originally published by Oktober forlag, 2015.

Presents a genre-bending novel about time, memory and the author's extraordinary childhood as the daughter of a genius filmmaker and his muse.

"To examine the soul of Ingmar Bergman, a man so private and so iconic, requires much deconstruction and reconstruction, not unlike the careful editing of a film. Ullman succeeds on every level, blending time, memory, and emotion into a fascinating and intimate portrait that easily evokes the universal sense of love and loss." Library Journal.

Umrigar, Thrity N.

Everybody's son / Thrity Umrigar. HarperCollins, 2017. 352 p.

ISBN 9780062442246

1. Race relations 2. Identity (Psychology) 3. Power (Social sciences) 4. Social classes 5. Politicians 6. Poverty 7. Drug abusers 8. Mothers and sons 9. Unconscious bias 10. Rape victims 11. Kidnapping 12. Children of prisoners 13. Foster children 14. Birthmothers 15. Adopted children 16. Families 17. Literary fiction

The bestselling, critically acclaimed author of The Space Between Us and The World We Found deftly explores issues of race, class, privilege, and power and asks us to consider uncomfortable moral questions in this probing, ambitious, emotionally wrenching novel of two families:one black, one white.

Umrigar, Thrity N.

The **secrets** between us / Thrity Umrigar. HarperCollins, 2018. 352 p.

ISBN 9780062442208

1. Female friendship 2. Inequality 3. Poor women 4. Senior women 5. Women business owners 6. Poverty 7. Slums 8. India 9. Mumbai, India 10. Literary fiction

Features the character Bhima who previously appeared in "The Space Between Us".

After being fired from her job as a servant, Bhima forms a partnership with Parvati to sell produce at the local market and makes her first true friend, in a follow up to The Space Between Us.

Umrigar, Thrity N.

The **space** between us : a novel / Thrity Umrigar. William Morrow, 2006. 321 p.

ISBN 9780060791551

1. Widows 2. Homemakers 3. Master and servant 4. Middle class women 5. Household employees 6. Women 7. Female friendship 8. Women -- Interpersonal relations 9. Families 10. Grandmother and granddaughter 11. Women college students 12. Social classes 13. Social classes and family 14. Classism 15. Friendship 16. Interclass friendship 17. Family relationships 18. Loss (Psychology) 19. Disappointment in women 20. Housekeepers 21. India 22. Mumbai, India 23. Domestic fiction 24. Psychological fiction

LC 2005050510

Set in modern-day India, this evocative novel follows upper-middle-class Parsi housewife Sera Dubash and 65-year-old illiterate household worker Bhima as they make their way through life. Though separated by their stations in life, the two women share bonds of womanhood that prove far stronger than the divisions of class or culture.

"The life of the privileged is harshly measured against the life of the powerless, but empathy and compassion are evoked by both strong women, each of whom is forced to make a separate choice. Umrigar is a skilled storyteller, and her memorable characters will live on for a long time." Washington Post Book World.

Umrigar, Thrity N.

The **weight** of heaven : a novel / Thrity Umrigar. Harper, 2009. 365 p.

ISBN 9780061472541

1. Married people 2. Bereavement 3. Americans in India 4. Marital conflict 5. Grief -- Psychological aspects 6. Murder 7. Sons -- Death 8. Obsession 9. India 10. Ann Arbor, Michigan 11. Psychological fiction

LC 2008032950

Having lost their beloved only child to a sudden illness, Frank and Ellie Benton hope to rebuild their lives by accepting a job offer in India but find their new home compromised by Frank's efforts to heal his grief through a friendship with a young boy.

"This is is a bold, beautifully rendered tale of cultures that clash and coalesce." Booklist.

Unger, Lisa, 1970-

Crazy love you / Lisa Unger. Touchstone, 2015. 338 p. Hollows novels (Lisa Unger)

ISBN 9781451691207

1. Adult children of dysfunctional families 2. Self-destructive behavior 3. Best friends 4. Young men 5. Men/women relations 6. Change (Psychology) 7. Love triangles 8. New York (State) 9. Psychological suspense

Enjoying a successful career with his best friend Priss, a destructive friend who helped him escape bullies in childhood, Ian fears for his life when she becomes irrationally angry about Ian's new relationship.

Unger, Lisa, 1970-

The **red** hunter / Lisa Unger. Touchstone, 2017. 358 p. ISBN 9781501101670

1. Revenge 2. Houses -- Conservation and restoration 3. Rape victims 4. Martial arts 5. Bloggers 6. Single mothers 7. Mothers and daughters 8. Identity (Psychology) 9. Loss (Psychology) 10. Coping 11. New York City 12. New Jersey 13. Psychological suspense

LC 2016029518

Tackling a house restoration project and blog in the hopes of escaping a traumatic event that ended her marriage, Claudia uncovers an ugly history in the crumbling house, where another woman, Zoey, survived a home invasion and pursued the martial arts to find security and healing.

"Unger's knack for blending encroaching danger with complex relationship themes is as sharp as ever here, as she creates characters facing the tangle of betrayals and mistakes that have shaped their identities." Booklist.

Unger, Lisa, 1970-

* The **stranger** inside / Lisa Unger. Harlequin Books, 2019 336 p.

ISBN 9780778308720

1. Women journalists 2. Recovered memory 3. Vigilantes 4. Psychic trauma 5. Suburban life 6. Kidnapping victims 7. Murder 8. Investigations 9. Kidnapping 10. Stay-at-home mothers 11. New York state 12. Psychological suspense

A woman is forced to confront the dark secrets of her past when a serial killer strikes too close to home. By the award-winning author of Under My Skin.

Unger, Lisa, 1970-

Under my skin / Lisa Unger. Park Row, 2018. 368 p. ISBN 9780778308409

1. Widows 2. Loss of consciousness 3. Married men -- Death 4. Loss (Psychology) 5. Murder 6. Investigations 7. Women with amnesia 8. Nightmares 9. Secrets 10. New York City 11. Psychological suspense

Emerging from grief a year after her beloved husband's unsolved murder, a haunted widow has nightmares and blackouts before realizing she is trapped in a surreal game of cat and mouse.

Unsworth, Barry, 1930-2012

After Hannibal / Barry Unsworth. Doubleday, 1997, c1996. 250 p.

ISBN 9780385486514

1. Expatriates 2. Manipulation by men 3. Betrayal 4. Gay men 5. Lawyers 6. Retirees 7. Americans in Italy 8. British in Italy 9. Germans in Italy 10. Interpersonal relations 11. Italy 12. Umbria, Italy 13. Domestic fiction

LC 96-20856

Originally published: London: H. Hamilton, c1996.

A group of very different people--including a retired American couple, a feuding British family, two gay lovers, and a manipulative lawyer--is brought together and overwhelmed by local chicanery and the byzantine circuitry of Italian life.

Unsworth, Barry, 1930-2012

Land of marvels : a novel / Barry Unsworth. Nan A. Talese, 2009. 304 p.

ISBN 9780385520072

1. 1910s 2. Archaeologists -- Great Britain 3. Excavations (Archaeology) -- Mesopotamia 4. Oil prospecting 5. Violence in men 6. British in Mesopotamia 7. Geologists -- United States 8. Impostors 9. Greed 10. Americans in Mesopotamia 11. Oil industry and trade -- Middle East -- History 12. Mesopotamia -- History -- 20th century 13. Great Britain -- Foreign relations -- 1910-1936 14. Historical fiction

LC 2008009201

In 1914, as the nations of the West are making a play for political power and oil in the Middle East, Somerville, a British archaeologist, finds his excavation of a long-buried Assyrian palace threatened by construction of a new railroad to Baghdad.

"There is something of E. M. Forster in Unsworths knowing depiction of a decaying empire run by upper-class incompetents, and in his generous and sympathetic portrayal of women caught between cultures." The New Yorker.

Unsworth, Barry, 1930-2012

The **quality** of mercy : a novel / Barry Unsworth. Nan A. Talese, 2012, c2011. 319 p.

ISBN 9780385534772

1. Coal mines and mining 2. Abolitionists 3. Slave ships 4. Social classes 5. Social change 6. Sailors 7. Villages 8. Industrialists 9. Slave trade 10. Trials (Mutiny) 11. Durham, England -- Social life and customs -- 18th century 12. London, England -- Social life and customs -- 18th century 13. England -- History -- 18th century 14. Historical fiction

LC 2011010110

Sequel to: Sacred hunger.

Originally published: London : Hutchinson, 2011.

Shortlisted for the Walter Scott Prize for Historical Fiction, 2012

A sequel to the Sacred Hunger finds Irish fiddler Sullivan escaping from prison after being implicated in the loss of Erasmus Kemp's ship only to reencounter his nemesis in an epic struggle that pits Kemp's desire for wealth against Sullivan's passionate advocacy for the disadvantaged.

"Unsworth's finely crafted plot brings together a vivid cast of seamen, miners, and landowners at a moment in history when crimes of property were considered more serious than crimes against persons and a more enlightened future lay just around the corner." Library Journal.

Unsworth, Barry, 1930-2012

Sacred hunger / Barry Unsworth. Doubleday, 1992. 629 p. ISBN 0385265301

1. 18th century 2. Greed 3. Mutiny 4. Slave traders 5. Equality 6. Slave ships 7. Middle passage (Atlantic slave trade) 8. Slavery 9. Cousins 10. Utopias 11. Historical fiction

LC 91033237

Sequel: The quality of mercy.

Booker Prize, 1992.

En route to America with a cargo of African slaves, the crew of the "Liverpool Merchant," enraged at the captain's impotence in the face of disease, carry out a mutiny that pits two cousins against each other.

"Deftly utilizing a flood of period detail, Unsworth has written a book whose stately pace, like the scope of its meditations, seems accurately to evoke the age. Tackling here a central perversity of our historythe keeping of slaves in a land where 'all men are created equal'Unsworth illuminates the barbaric cruelty of slavery, as well as the subtler habits of politics and character that it creates." Publishers Weekly.

Unsworth, Barry, 1930-2012

The **songs** of the kings / Barry Unsworth. Nan A. Talese/ Doubleday, 2003. 338 p.

ISBN 9780385501149

1. Ancient Greece (800 BCE-640 CE) 2. Heroes and heroines, Greek 3. Manipulation by men 4. Power (Social sciences) 5. Human sacrifice 6. Greed 7. Iphigenia (Mythological character) 8. Agamemnon (Greek mythology) 9. Trojan War 10. Ancient military history -- Greece 11. Strategic alliances (Military) 12. Superstition 13. Gods and goddesses, Greek 14. Odysseus (Greek mythology) 15. Ancient Greece 16. Historical fiction 17. Mythological fiction

LC 2002066845

Includes bibliographical references (p. 337-338).

A thoroughly modern tale of politics, spin-doctoring, and media manipulation. As the harsh wind holds the Greek fleet trapped in the straits at Aulis, frustration and political impotence turn into a desire for the blood of a young and innocent woman...

"Unsworths' retelling of the story, familiar from Euripides, of the sacrifice of Iphigeneia to appease the gods so that the boats can sail is a bold, modern tale with cynical riffs on the themes of duty and power, truth and fiction. His Greek warriors are schemers and media-savvy self-promoters who are desperate to look good in the sung reports that are their equivalent of the news mediasongs that are, we realize, the seeds of the Homeric tradition." The New Yorker.

Upadhyay, Samrat

The **guru** of love / Samrat Upadhyay. Houghton Mifflin, 2003. 290 p.

ISBN 9780618247271

1. Love triangles 2. Mathematics teachers 3. Tutors 4. Married people 5. Extramarital affairs 6. Nepal 7. Psychological fiction 8. Domestic fiction

LC 2002032234

A math teacher and tutor earning a low wage and living in a small apartment with his wife and children, Ramchandra becomes involved in an illicit affair with one of his students, Malati, a beautiful, impoverished young new mother.

"The author excels at depicting the thousand small cuts that afflict a middle-class married man having an affair. . . . The writing is emotionally restrained and doesn't call attention to itself. There are no lyrical bursts of exuberance over the country's beauty or the torments of love. At points the novel is excessively terse; when three words would have sufficed, Upadhyay uses two. In spite of that it is gripping, because you like the characters so much, and wish them well." New York Times Book Review.

Updike, John

The **afterlife** and other stories / John Updike. A. A. Knopf, 1994. 316 p.

ISBN 0679435832

1. Middle-aged persons 2. Marriage 3. Mortality 4. Married people 5. Literary fiction 6. Short stories

LC 949818

22 short stories.

An anthology of short fiction features twenty-two tales that explore the magical fragility, memory, nostalgia, and translucent quality of life beyond middle age

"In these mellow, reflective stories, where parents die and grandchildren are born, Updike's heroes are acutely aware of lost glory yet discover the strength to persevere." Library Journal.

Updike, John

Brazil : a novel / John Updike. Knopf, 1994. 260 p.

ISBN 9780679430711

1. Interracial romance 2. Interclass romance 3. Racism 4. African Brazilians 5. Classism 6. Young adults 7. Sexuality 8. Enchantment 9. Tristan (Legendary character) 10. Iseult (Legendary character) 11. Brazil -- Social life and customs 12. Love stories 13. Magical realism 14. Literary fiction

LC 9328632

Tristao, an African-Brazilian street kid, and Isabel, an upper-class teen fresh from convent school, fall in love and flee from her rich father and the toughs he has sent in pursuit of them.

"This novel, for all its political incorrectness, seems good-natured and bent on self-parody. . . . If the book's surface is sometimes a little sticky, its allegorical underpinnings are graceful and firm." New York Times Book Review.

Updike, John

Gertrude and Claudius / John Updike. A.A. Knopf, 2000. 212 p.

ISBN 0375409084

1. Brothers 2. Betrayal 3. Remarriage 4. Fratricide 5. Rulers 6. Women rulers 7. Extramarital affairs 8. Mothers and sons 9. Men/ women relations 10. Denmark -- History -- 1241-1397 11. Historical fiction 12. Literary fiction 13. Adaptations, retellings, and spin-offs

LC 99033436

Set before the action begins in Shakespeare's "Hamlet," this speculative novel follows the lives of Gertrude and Claudius, King and Queen of Denmark, as they wend their way towards adultery and treachery to ascend the throne

"Updike turns to Shakespeare's 'Hamlet,' exploring the origin of Gertrude and Claudius' 'reechy kisses.' When the sixteen-year-old Gertrude is unwillingly betrothed to the elder Hamlet, Horwendil, by her father . . . she quickly falls for his brother, Claudius. The two honorably resist their feelings until they are beset by the anxieties of aging; as it turns out, the murder of Horwendil is an act of emotional (and political) desperation rather than cold calculation. Likewise, Updike's portrayal of Gertrude and Claudius' thwarted affections is not just a deft literary exercise but an affecting--and funny--invocation of the abundant desires of what Hamlet called 'this too too solid flesh." The New Yorker.

Updike, John

In the beauty of the lilies / John Updike. A.A. Knopf, 1996. 491 p.

ISBN 0679446400

1. God 2. Belief and doubt 3. Faith 4. Families 5. Family relationships 6. Clergy 7. Cults 8. Film industry and trade 9. United States -- Social life and customs -- 20th century 10. Family sagas

LC 95-23467

Through four generations--from Clarence Wilmot, a lapsed minister-turned-encyclopedia salesman, in 1910, to the present day--one family pursues the American obsession with God and the unreal world of the motion picture

"The novel opens in Paterson, New Jersey, in 1910. 'At the moment Mary Pickford fainted' while making a movie close by, Presbyterian minister Clarence Wilmot loses his faith. That loss precipitates another loss: his job. Since 'now he was freefree to sink,' he turns to selling encyclopedias door to door and to an addictive habit of watching the fabulous new medium, moving pictures. Updike then tells of the following three generations of Clarence's family. . . . Updike's soaring novel becomes an extended yet taut metaphor for the secularization of religion and the concomitant infatuation with movies as a substitute for religion." Booklist.

Updike, John

Licks of love : short stories and a sequel / John Updike. Alfred A. Knopf, 2000. 359 p.

ISBN 0375411135

1. Aging 2. Regret 3. Married men 4. Men/women relations 5. Extramarital affairs 6. United States -- Social life and customs -- 20th century 7. Literary fiction 8. Short stories

LC 00034906

Twelve short stories and a sequel, "Rabbit remembered."

Twelve short stories revisit the locales of the author's previous works of fiction and focus on a theme of love, in an anthology that is complemented by a novella-length sequel, "Rabbit Remembered," to his Harry Angstrom series.

Updike, John

Memories of the Ford administration : a novel / John Updike. Alfred A. Knopf, 1992. 371 p.

ISBN 0679416811

1. Ford, Gerald R, 1913-2006 2. Buchanan, James, 1791-1868 3. 1970s 4. Historians -- United States 5. Presidents -- United States 6. Extramarital affairs 7. Separated men (Marital relations) 8. Men/women relations 9. Sexuality 10. United States -- Politics and government -- 1974-1977 11. Political fiction 12. Satirical fiction

LC 92052955

Alfred Clayton, a history instructor at Wayward Junior College in New Hampshire, juxtaposes his memories of Gerald Ford's administration with pages from his unpublished biography of James Buchanan

"Updike's elegant, yet slangy portrait of the Ford era demonstrates considerable finesse. Even more impressive is his authentic, yet unstilted, evocation of Buchanan's era." Christian Science Monitor.

Updike, John

My father's tears and other stories / John Updike. Alfred A. Knopf, 2009. 304 p.

ISBN 9780307271563

1. Men -- Identity 2. Senior men 3. Small town life 4. Aging 5. Voyages and travels 6. Americans in foreign countries 7. Pennsylvania -- Social life and customs 8. Literary fiction 9. Short stories

LC 2008054376

A collection of short fiction includes tales set in the author's native Pennsylvania, the New England suburbs, and foreign countries, all depicting different facets of the American experience from the Depression through the aftermath of 9/11.

"A perfect bookend to Pigeon Feathers, the precocious collection of stories that nearly five decades ago announced their 30-year-old writer's discovery of his own inimitable voice. . . . Mr. Updike writes in these stories . . . with the quiet assurance of someone in complete control of his craft." New York Times.

Updike, John

* **Rabbit** is rich : a novel / John Updike A. A. Knopf, 1981. 467 p. Rabbit Angstrom novels

ISBN 9780394520872

1. 1970s 2. Middle-aged men 3. Small town life 4. Father and child 5. Men/women relations 6. Married men 7. Automobile sales personnel 8. Pennsylvania -- Social life and customs -- 20th century 9. Literary fiction 10. Modern classics

LC 81001287

National Book Award for Fiction, 1982

National Book Critics Circle Award for Fiction, 1981.

Pulitzer Prize for Fiction, 1982.

Harry Angstrom, now middle-aged and the chief sales representative of a Toyota dealership, attempts to cope with such problems as inflation, governmental ineffectiveness, the return of his prodigal son, and a chance encounter with an old girlfriend.

"A superlative comic novel that is also an American romance." Time.

Updike, John

* **Rabbit,** run / John Updike. A. A. Knopf, 1960. 308 p. Rabbit Angstrom novels

ISBN 0394442067

1. 1950s 2. Self-perception in men 3. Runaway wives, husbands, etc 4. Disillusionment in men 5. Small town life 6. Married men 7. Alcoholic women 8. Automobile sales personnel 9. Former basketball players 10. Unhappiness 11. Extramarital affairs 12. Pennsylvania -- Social life and customs -- 20th century 13. Literary fiction 14. Modern classics

LC 60012552

Tired of the responsibility of married life, Harry Angstrom leaves his wife and home

Updike, John

Seek my face / John Updike. Alfred A. Knopf, 2002. 276 p.

ISBN 9780375414909

1. Reminiscing in old age 2. Women painters 3. Art appreciation 4. Interviewing 5. Autobiographical memory 6. Aging 7. Artists -- Psychology 8. Senior women 9. Vermont 10. Psychological fiction 11. Literary fiction

LC 2002018442

During an interview with a New York writer, seventy-nine-year-old artist Hope Chafetz describes her eventful life and her integral place in the saga of postwar American art, as the evolving relationship between the interviewer and subject subtly evolves in and out of the roles of mother and daughter, patient and therapist, prey and predator.

"Despite its uncomplicated premise, the novel achieves a remarkable depth of characterization and a glowing beauty in its articulation of the artistic sensibility." Booklist.

Updike, John

The **widows** of Eastwick / John Updike. Alfred A. Knopf, 2008. 308 p.

ISBN 9780307269607

1. Widows 2. Supernatural 3. Guilt 4. Voyages and travels 5. Consequences 6. Spells (Magic) 7. Witches -- Rhode Island 8. Female friendship 9. Middle aged women 10. Redemption 11. Rhode Island 12. Satirical fiction 13. Contemporary fantasy

LC 2008018513

Sequel to: The witches of Eastwick.

Alexandra, Jane, and Sukie, all now widowed, return to the Rhode Island seaside town of Eastwick after many years away and find themselves dealing with the legacy of their evil deeds, the shocks of a mysterious counterspell, and the inroads of aging.

"One wonders whether anybody has ever described the small physical indignities of the aging process with as much tenderness and good humor as Updike. . . . Now the witches' sex lives are over, but their lives aren't, and you sense Updike's twinkly eyes peering cautiously into the darkness, beyond the glow of the merely fleshly, trying to make out what the world beyond might look like." Time.

Updike, John

* The **witches** of Eastwick / John Updike. A. A. Knopf, 1984. 307 p.

ISBN 9780394537603

1. 1960s 2. Witches -- Rhode Island 3. Suburban life 4. Divorced women 5. Female friendship 6. Devil 7. Witchcraft 8. Feminism 9. Revenge 10. Rhode Island 11. Satirical fiction 12. Contemporary fantasy

LC 83049048

Sequel : The widows of Eastwick.

Alexandra, Jane, and Sukie ply their individual witcheries in contemporary Eastwick, Rhode Island, and are themselves bewitched by a dark, wealthy, decadent stranger

"While not a typical Updike narrative, the author's glittering wit, pungent observations, and fabled legerdemain at tabulating mundane particulars reach their peaks in the first half of the novel. Only in the last sections does the reader's attention flag." Booklist.

Uris, Leon, 1924-2003

Armageddon : a novel of Berlin / Leon Uris. Doubleday, 1964. 632 p.

ISBN 9780385003568

1. Cold War 2. East-West relations 3. Men/women relations 4. Communism 5. World War II -- Influence 6. Berlin, Germany -- History -- 1945- 7. Berlin, Germany -- Blockade, 1948-1949 8. War stories 9. Historical fiction

LC 64016837

The struggle to limit Communist control in Berlin underlies this story of the romances and personal conflicts of American, British, and Russian officers.

"The author provides a broad and moving panorama of the rebuilding of postwar Germany at the time when the Allies and the Russians first came to clash over Berlin and its routes of access." The Atlantic.

Uris, Leon, 1924-2003

Battle cry / Leon Uris. HarperCollins, 2005, c1953. 505 p.

ISBN 9780060751869

1. United States Marine Corps 2. Second World War era (1939-1945) 3. Marines 4. World War II 5. Battles 6. War stories

First published 1953 by G. P. Putnam's Sons.

Follows the fortunes of a marine outfit from boot camp to Guadalcanal, Tarawa, and elsewhere in the Pacific during World War II.

"Taking an average group of American boys from their home environment through the ordeal of boot camp, to the battlefields of Guadalcanal, Tarawa, and Saipan, the author fills in a detailed picture of Marine training and traditions." Booklist.

Uris, Leon, 1924-2003

* **Exodus** / Leon Uris. Doubleday, 1958. 626 p.

ISBN 9780385050821

1. Exodus 1947 (Ship) 2. Jews 3. Israel-Arab War, 1948-1949 4. Americans in Israel 5. Zionism 6. Holocaust survivors 7. Refugees, Jewish 8. Nurses 9. Antisemitism 10. Israel -- History -- 1948-1967 11. Palestine -- History -- 1929-1948 12. Historical fiction

LC 58011328

Sequel: The Haj.

National Jewish Book Award for Fiction, 1959.

Describes the flight of Jews from areas such as the ghettos of Russia and Poland to find haven and a homeland in Israel

Uris, Leon, 1924-2003

Mila 18 / Leon Uris. Bantam Books, 1983, c1961. 563 p.

ISBN 9780553241600

1. Warsaw ghetto uprising, 1943 2. Holocaust (1933-1945) 3. Jews 4. Nazis 5. Ghettoes, Jewish 6. Courage 7. Warsaw, Poland 8. War stories 9. Historical fiction

"Uris' major talent is that he is a master storyteller. And in 'Mila 18' he uses this talent fully and unhampered, in a straight narrative that generates an almost unbelievable dramatic intensity." San Francisco Chronicle.

Uris, Leon, 1924-2003

Redemption : a novel / Leon Uris. HarperCollins, 1995. 827 p.

ISBN 9780060183332

1. Churchill, Winston, 1874-1965 2. 20th century 3. Families 4. Tragedy 5. Interpersonal relations 6. Loss (Psychology) 7. Grief in women 8. Easter Rising, 1916 9. Irish resistance and revolts 10. World War I 11. Military campaigns 12. Gallipoli Campaign, Turkey, 1915 13. Gallipoli, Turkey 14. Ireland -- Social conditions 15. New Zealand 16. Family sagas 17. Historical fiction

LC 95010834

Sequel to Trinity (1976)

A dramatic saga set against the backdrop of growing unrest in Ireland and a world on the brink of the First World War, Redemption From the magnificence of New Zealand's green mountains, to the bloody beaches and cliffs of Gallipoli, to the streets of Dublin and the shipyards of Belfast, Redemption follows three Irish patriots on their odysseys of freedom and passion -- in a monumental tale of the men and women who loved, fought, and died for the chance to live free.

"The focus of this sequel is the conflict between two of the three dominant families of Trinity, the tempestuous Larkins and their staid British counterparts, the Hubbles. . . . Uris begins by tracing the Larkin legacy from patriarch Liam's exile to New Zealand, where he becomes squire of a sheep farm; his brother, Conor, becomes a legendary Irish revolutionary. Another Larkin progeny, Liam's son Rory, is acclaimed as a war hero after fighting with the British at Gallipoli, while Rory's brother Dary takes Catholic clerical vows, only to have a powerful love drive him to question both celibacy and his calling. Uris balances the struggles of the Larkins with the more repressed travails of Caroline Hubble, who battles the efforts of her husband to oppress the Irish after losing a pair of sons in the disastrous British battle against the Turks." Publishers Weekly.

Uris, Leon, 1924-2003

* **Trinity** / Leon Uris. Doubleday, 1976. 751 p.

ISBN 9780385034586

1. Irish Potato Famine (1845-1852) 2. 19th century 3. 1840s 4. 20th century 5. Famines 6. Disasters 7. Families 8. Tragedy 9. Irish resistance and revolts 10. Ireland -- Social conditions -- 1837-1901 11. Ireland -- History -- Easter Rising, 1916 12. Historical fiction 13. Family sagas

LC 75014844

Sequel: Redemption (1995)

Recounts the interrelationships, clashes, and common concerns of the Catholic, hill-farming Larkins of Donegal, the aristocratic and British Hubbles, and the Scottish-Presbyterian MacLeods of Belfast during the years from the 1840's famine to the 1916 Easter Rising.

"The story has a kind of relentless power, based on the real tragedy of Ireland, and Uris's achievement is that he has neither cheapened nor trivialized that tragedy." New York Times Book Review.

Urquhart, Jane

Away : a novel / Jane Urquhart. Viking, 1994, c1993. 356 p.

ISBN 9780670855049

1. 1840s 2. Immigrants, Irish 3. Fairies 4. Unrequited love 5. Supernatural 6. Famines 7. Men/women relations 8. Irish Canadians 9. Canada 10. Historical fantasy 11. Family sagas

Originally published: Toronto : McClelland & Stewart, 1993.

Trillium Book Award, 1993.

Shortlisted for the International IMPAC Dublin Literary Award, 1996

A chronicle of the lives, loves, and passions of four generations of women begins near Lake Ontario as Esther O'Malley Robertson reminisces about her family's past, from its origin in Ireland where her great-grandmother had a daemon lover.

"Urquhart's blending of the spiritual and political sides of the Irish makes an amazing story told in a language that is melodious and laden with complex imagery." Booklist.

Urquhart, Jane

The **night** stages : a novel / Jane Urquhart. Farrar, Straus and Giroux, 2015. 401 p.

ISBN 9780374222192

1. 1950s 2. Women pilots 3. City life 4. Men/women relations 5. Bicycle racing 6. Extramarital affairs 7. Ireland 8. Historical fiction

LC 2015010123

Leaving Ireland behind after being abandoned by her lover, Tamara, an auxiliary pilot in World War II, during a layover in Gander, Newfoundland, takes stock of her life and the events that forced her into exile while searching to find the truth about the man who betrayed her.

"Canadian author Urquharts (Sanctuary Line, 2013) elegiac prose evokes metaphors of arrivals and departures as she weaves together Tam and Niall's love story, Kieran's history, and a fictionalized account of Lochhead's creation of the enigmatic mural that serves as the narrative centerpiece." Booklist.

Urquhart, Rachel

The **visionist** / Rachel Urquhart. Little, Brown & Co., 2014. 345 p.

ISBN 9780316228114

1. Shakers 2. Antebellum America (1820-1861) 3. 19th century 4. Deception 5. Secrets 6. Teenage girls 7. Suspicion 8. Indentured servants 9. Private investigators 10. New England -- History -- 19th century 11. Historical fiction

After killing her abusive father in an intentionally-set fire, Polly Kimball and her younger brother seek refuge in a Shaker community in 1840s Massachusetts and unexpectedly become involved in a wave of mystical visions sweeping the Northeast religious communities.

"For historical fiction fans wanting to immerse themselves in a setting they may know little about, this novel fits the bill." Library Journal.

Urrea, Luis Alberto

The **water** museum : stories / Luis Alberto Urrea. Little, Brown & Co., 2015 258 p.

ISBN 9780316334372

1. Hispanic Americans 2. Culture shock 3. Small towns 4. Short stories

"Urrea's well-recommended collection leads readers to feel empathy for each character, deserving or not, and provides a gut-wrenching view of life along the sidelines." Library Journal.

Urrea, Luis Alberto

* The **house** of broken angels / Luis Alberto Urrea. Little, Brown & Co, 2018 326 p.

ISBN 9780316154888

1. Mexican American families 2. Families -- History 3. Birthday parties 4. Hispanic American families 5. Family relationships 6. Family and death 7. Large families 8. Celebrations 9. Immigrants 10. San Diego, California 11. Mexican-American Border Region 12. Literary fiction

ALA Notable Book, 2019.

National Book Critics Circle Award for Fiction finalist, 2018

Across one bittersweet weekend in their San Diego neighborhood, revelers mingle among the palm trees and cacti, celebrating the lives of family patriarch Miguel "Big Angel" De La Cruz and his mother, and recounting the many tales that have passed into family lore.

Urrea, Luis Alberto

The **hummingbird's** daughter : a novel / Luis Alberto Urrea. Little, Brown, 2005. 499 p.

ISBN 9780316745468

1. 19th century 2. Teenage girls 3. Young women 4. Women healers 5. Women saints 6. Ranchers 7. Families 8. Sixteen-year-old girls 9. Paternity 10. Near-death experience 11. Faith 12. Mexico -- History -- 1867-1910 13. Historical fiction 14. Coming-of-age stories 15. Magical realism 16. Literary fiction

LC 2004027849

Sequel: Queen of America

ALA Notable Book, 2006.

Kiriyama Prize for Fiction, 2006.

When sixteen-year-old Teresita, the illegitimate daughter of a late-nineteenth-century rancher, arises from death possessing the power to heal, she is declared a saint and finds her faith tested by the impending Mexican civil war.

Urrea, Luis Alberto

Into the beautiful North : a novel / Luis Alberto Urrrea. Little, Brown and Company, 2009. 352 p.

ISBN 9780316025270

1. Young women -- Mexico 2. City life -- Mexico 3. Thieves 4. Return migration -- Mexico 5. Undocumented immigrants 6. Gender role 7. Nineteen-year-old women 8. Mexico -- Immigration and emigration 9. LGBTQIA fiction 10. Mainstream fiction

LC 2008039962

Rainbow List, 2010.

In recent years, the tiny Mexican village of Tres Camarones has been losing its men to the lure of good jobs in the U.S. Inspired by the film The Magnificent Seven, beautiful 19-year-old Nayeli decides to leave her home for "el Norte," where she plans to find and ultimately bring home seven men to repopulate and protect Tres Camarones. With encouragement from the women left behind and accompanied by three friends, Nayeli marches north, where she finds far more than she'd been looking for. -- Description by Shauna Griffin.

Urrea, Luis Alberto

Queen of America : a novel / Luis Alberto Urrea. Little, Brown, 2011. 384 p.

ISBN 9780316154864

1. 1890s 2. 19th century 3. Women healers 4. Women saints 5. Mexicans in the United States 6. Fathers and daughters 7. Assassins 8. Frontier and pioneer life 9. Young women 10. Faith 11. Arizona -- History -- 19th century 12. United States -- History -- 1865-1921 13. Historical fiction 14. Magical realism 15. Literary fiction

LC 2011023065

Sequel to: The Hummingbird's Daughter

The sequel to The Hummingbird's Daughter finds Teresita Urrea fleeing to Arizona with her father after the Tomochic Rebellion but is inundated with visits from pilgrims seeking her skills as a healer until she is chased to New York by assassins.

V

Vachss, Andrew H.

Two trains running / Andrew Vachss. Pantheon Books, 2005. 464 p.

ISBN 1400043816

1. 1950s 2. Mafia 3. Illegal arms transfers 4. Gangs 5. Racism 6. Strategic alliances (Military) 7. Assassins 8. Black power 9. Wheelchair users 10. Political corruption 11. Men/women relations 12. Southern States -- History -- 20th century 13. Crime fiction 14. Political thrillers 15. Historical thrillers

LC 2004060127

"Locke City, a Southern mill town turned tourist mecca, is controlled by the firm but benevolent hand of local crime tsar Royal Beaumont. When the New York mafia arrives, he hires former undercover FBI agent Walker Dett to protect his interests. In short snippets of action and dialog, Vachss . . . creates a broad picture of crime in Locke City, from teenage street gangs to crooked national politicians, with the Ku Klux Klan, militant African Americans, and other factions woven into a shocking climax. A riveting page-turner that marks a definite change of direction from the author's dark Burke thrillers." Library Journal.

Valdes, Alisa

Dirty Girls on top / Alisa Valdes-Rodriguez. St. Martin's Press, 2008. 336 p. Dirty Girls Social Club

ISBN 9780312349677

1. Hispanic American women 2. Friendship 3. Self-acceptance in women 4. Thirties (Age) 5. Men/women relations 6. Young women 7. Interpersonal relations 8. Self-esteem in women 9. Boston, Massachusetts 10. New Mexico 11. Women's lives and relationships

LC 2008012930

Sequel to : The Dirty Girls Social Club.

A follow-up to The Dirty Girls Social Club takes place five years after the first tale and finds Lauren still struggling to find love in spite of her career successes, Usnavys's seeking fun away from her husband and baby daughter, and Rebecca's facing the prospect of a life without children.

"The six sucias (dirty girls) return with hilarious and raunchy tales of Latina-tinged love, marriage, and sex told from each character's point of view. Pop star Cuicatl likens the touch of one of her groupie lovers to uncooked tofu from the refrigerator, while man-izer Usnavys describes her husband's wardrobe style as like a college student on welfare cheese. Despite a plot full of guilty-pleasure material, Dirty Girls admirably dives into darker areas like infidelity, mortality, addiction, and abuse. Hey, life can't be a fiesta 24/7." Entertainment Weekly.

Valente, Catherynne M., 1979-

Radiance / Catherynne M. Valente. Tor, 2015. 352 p.

ISBN 9780765335296

1. Filmmaking 2. Space flight 3. Aliens 4. Documentary films 5. Colonies 6. Venus (Planet) 7. Science fiction 8. Space opera

In the shadow of her father's movie-directing fame, Severin Unck blazes her own artistic trail making documentaries about obscure and overlooked cultures within the solar system. However, her latest project, a film about a lost colony on Venus, becomes her controversial final work when she disappears during the shoot. In a "found footage" nar-

rative style that compiles transcripts, news items, eyewitness accounts, and more, Radiance is a must-read for SF fans seeking a lush, lyrical outer space adventure. -- Description by Gillian Speace.

"The splendiferous prose swirls and twirls in a manic, vocabulary-enhancing dance in a world where silent black-and-white movies have never gone out of vogue. Expect Valentes hugely imaginative, retro adventure on multiple science-fiction- and fantasy-award short lists." Booklist.

Valente, Catherynne M., 1979-

Space opera / Catherynne M. Valente. Saga Press, 2018 304 p.

ISBN 9781481497497

1. Music -- Competitions 2. Interplanetary relations 3. Human/alien encounters 4. Singing contests 5. Aliens 6. Friendship 7. Space opera 8. Science fiction 9. Humorous stories

LC 2017028788

"A band of human musicians, dancers, and roadies have been chosen to represent Earth on the greatest stage in the galaxy. And the fate of their species lies in their ability to rock."--Provided by the publisher.

Valentine, Genevieve

Mechanique : a tale of the Circus Tresaulti / Genevieve Valentine. Prime Books, 2011. 320 p.

ISBN 9781607012535

1. Circus 2. Circus performers 3. Dystopias 4. Imaginary wars and battles 5. Steampunk 6. Dystopian fiction

As a circus of performers recreated with mechanical parts treks across a chaotic world, a government man asks for the ringmaster's help in building a world of order, while two performers desire a pair of cursed magical wings.

"The author raises the novel above the ordinary through her ability to convey the richness of the circus performers' emotional lives, coupled with impressive writing--as in a description of Alec's surgically attached wings, 'every bone-and-brass feather jigsawed and hammered and smoothed so thin that when it strikes another feather it rings out a clear note.'" New York Times Book Review.

Van Booy, Simon

The **illusion** of separateness / Simon Van Booy. HarperCollins, 2013 224 p.

ISBN 9780062112248

1. Second World War era (1939-1945) 2. 1940s 3. World War II 4. War wounds 5. Friendship 6. Nazis 7. Aging 8. Regret 9. Social isolation 10. France -- History -- 20th century 11. Historical fiction

One by one, through seemingly random acts of selflessness, the lives of several individuals, including a deformed German infantryman, a lonely British film director, and a young, blind museum curator, become intertwined, shattering the illusion of their separateness.

Van Meter, Crissy

Creatures : a novel / Crissy Van Meter. Algonquin Books of Chapel Hill, 2020. 256 p.

ISBN 9781616208592

1. Island life 2. Brides 3. Fathers and daughters 4. Memories 5. Nature 6. Childhood 7. Mothers 8. Whales 9. Missing men 10. Drug dealers 11. Weddings 12. Southern California 13. California 14. Literary fiction

LC 2019010469

A bride explores the complexities of love, abandonment and forgiveness when her California wedding is upended by a trapped whale carcass, the groom's disappearance at sea and the unexpected return of her long-absent mother.

"Heavily influenced by the weather and wildlife of this ruggedly beautiful place, Van Meter's wonderfully un-ordinary debut is rather like the ocean itself: layered, deep, and happening all at once." Booklist.

Van Vogt, A. E. (Alfred Elton), 1912-2000
    * **Slan** / A.E. Van Vogt. Tom Doherty, 2007, c1940. 255 p. ISBN 0312852363
    1. Genocide 2. Human evolution 3. Psychic ability 4. Adaptation (Biology) 5. Mutation (Biology) 6. Telepathy 7. Race (Biology) 8. Mothers -- Death 9. Intelligence 10. Children 11. Posthumanism 12. Pulp fiction 13. Science fiction

LC 97-38438

Sequel: Slan hunter.
    After escaping extermination by the humans, young Jommy Cross searches for the meaning of the Slans' great mental superiority.
    "One of the landmark novels of the genre, Van Vogt's 1940 tale follows the Slan, a new breed of telepathic humans and their search for a society free from persecution. Essential for all libraries." Library Journal.

Van der Vliet Oloomi, Azareen
    Call me Zebra / Azareen Van der Vliet Oloomi. Houghton Mifflin Harcourt, 2018. 292 p.
    ISBN 9780544944602
    1. Self-discovery in women 2. Identity (Psychology) 3. Young women 4. Exiles 5. Refugees 6. Voyages and travels 7. Literature and society 8. Books and reading 9. Men/women relations 10. Interpersonal attraction 11. Purpose in life 12. Fathers -- Death 13. Loss (Psychology) 14. Grief 15. New York City 16. Spain 17. Literary fiction 18. Picaresque fiction

LC 2017044915

PEN-Faulkner Award, 2019.
    The last surviving member of a line of exiled, bookish anarchists, atheists and autodidacts leaves her New York home for Barcelona to retrace the journey she made years earlier with her father, only to forge an unexpected connection with a man with very different perspectives.

Vandelly, T. Marie
    Theme music / T. Marie Vandelly. Dutton, 2019. 384 p. ISBN 9781524744700
    1. Family-killing 2. Moving, Household 3. Nightmares 4. Murder investigation 5. Demons 6. Former detectives 7. Massacre survivors 8. Interpersonal relations 9. Men/women relations 10. Virginia 11. Psychological suspense 12. Horror

LC 2018048002

An only survivor of her family's massacre, Dixie impulsively moves into her early childhood home, where she begins to question her sanity and the haunted shadows of the past that threaten her future.
    "Vandelly shows a deft touch at creating characters and spinning plots, leading to an almost unbearably terrifying and bloody climax in this gripping debut." Booklist.

Vanderbes, Jennifer
    Easter Island : a novel / Jennifer Vanderbes. Dial Press, 2003. 320 p.
    ISBN 9780385336734
    1. 1910s 2. 1970s 3. Women -- Easter Island 4. Widows 5. British in Easter Island 6. Americans in Easter Island 7. Anthropologists' spouses 8. Women botanists 9. Voyages and travels 10. Easter Island 11. Psychological fiction 12. Historical fiction

LC 2002031588

The centuries-old mysteries and haunting past of Easter Island become catalysts for the parallel quests of two young women, separated by sixty years of history--Elsa Pendleton, who travels to Easter Island with her anthropologist husband in 1913, and widowed American botanist Dr. Greer Faraday--as they confront discoveries about themselves and the people they love.
    "Vanderbes knows how to craft suspense, and the narrativeswhile packed with vivid historical and scientific detailmove forward on the strength of her fully realized characters." Publishers Weekly.

Vanderbes, Jennifer
    Strangers at the feast : a novel / Jennifer Vanderbes. Scribner, 2010. 352 p.
    ISBN 9781439166956
    1. Families 2. Crime 3. Social classes 4. Consequences 5. Middle class 6. Thanksgiving Day 7. American dream 8. Family relationships 9. Literary fiction

LC 2009049756

A riveting second novel that unfolds over the course of Thanksgiving Day as two families are connected by a horrific crime.
    "Vanderbes lays on the cultural ironies a little too thickly in what is otherwise an inventively plotted, highly readable novel about white Americans' overweening sense of entitlement." Booklist.

Vanderhaeghe, Guy, 1951-
    The **last** crossing / Guy Vanderhaeghe. Alantic Monthly Press, 2004, c2002. 393 p. Western trilogy
    ISBN 9780871139122
    1. American Westward Expansion (1803-1899) 2. 1870s 3. Separated brothers 4. British in Canada 5. Overland journeys to the Pacific 6. Multiracial men 7. Missing persons 8. Pioneers 9. Frontier and pioneer life 10. Revenge 11. British in the United States 12. The West (Canada) 13. The West (United States) 14. Oxford, England 15. Westerns 16. Literary fiction

LC 2002503479

Originally published: Toronto : McClelland & Stewart, 2002.
CBA Libris Award for Fiction Book of the Year, 2003.
Saskatchewan Book Awards, Book of the Year Award, 2002.
Saskatchewan Book Awards, Fiction Award, 2002.
Saskatchewan Book Awards, Saskatoon Book Award, 2002.
Set in the 1870s, Charles and Addington Gaunt travel from England to the Western frontier of the U.S. and Canadian border in search of their brother, encountering a number of colorful characters battling with their own personal problems along the way.
    "Centered on three English brothers who venture to the American Westone as a missionary, the two others in pursuit when he disappearsthis saga encompasses a wide range of characters through alternating narrative voices. In a panorama of late-nineteenth-century Montana and western Canada, Vanderhaeghe details the lawlessness of the early frontier towns and the desperate ferocity of the dying indigenous tribes. He dwells with particular pathos on the children of white traders and Native American women, who are caught between two cultures. The prose can be overripe, particularly in the opening chapters, and moments of historical exposition are clumsily inserted. However, the sweep of the narrative gradually overcomes these missteps, and as the various searches for revenge or redemption get under way the writing achieves unforced grace and power." The New Yorker.

VanderMeer, Jeff
    Acceptance : a novel / Jeff VanderMeer. FSG Originals, 2014. 240 p. Southern Reach novels
    ISBN 9780374104115
    1. Scientists 2. Expeditions 3. Psychic ability 4. Threat (Psychology) 5. Missing persons 6. Exploration 7. Secrets 8. Science fiction
    Sequel to: Authority.

It is winter in Area X. A new team embarks across the border on a mission to find a member of a previous expedition who may have been left behind. As they press deeper into the unknown, navigating new terrain and new challenges, the threat to the outside world becomes more daunting. In Acceptance, the last installment of Jeff VanderMeer's Southern Reach Trilogy, the mysteries of Area X may have been solved, but their consequences and implications are no less profound or terrifying.

"The series is less about a straight throughline of plot and more about constructing a fully realized portrait of peculiar, often alienated people and the odd landscapes they inhabit, both inside and outside of their skulls; and this the author has decidedly achieved." Kirkus.

VanderMeer, Jeff

* **Annihilation :** a novel / Jeff Vandermeer. Farrar, Straus & Giroux, 2014. 195 p. Southern Reach novels

ISBN 9780374104092

1. Scientists 2. Expeditions 3. Survival 4. Women scientists 5. Psychic ability 6. Threat (Psychology) 7. Missing persons 8. Science fiction

Nebula Award for Best Novel, 2014.

Shirley Jackson Awards, Novel, 2014.

Four women -- a biologist, a psychologist, a surveyor, and an anthropologist -- set out on a scientific expedition to Area X, a quarantined zone that defies all attempts to map its terrain or understand its nature. Eleven previous missions have failed; is the twelfth time the charm, or will these intrepid explorers join their predecessors as casualties of Area X? -- Description by Gillian Speace.

"A gripping fantasy thriller.... VanderMeer weaves together an otherworldly tale of the supernatural and the half-human." Booklist.

VanderMeer, Jeff

Authority : a novel / Jeff VanderMeer. Farrar, Straus and Giroux, 2014. 341 p. Southern Reach novels

ISBN 9780374104108

1. Scientists 2. Expeditions 3. Psychic ability 4. Threat (Psychology) 5. Secrecy in government 6. Intelligence service 7. Secrets 8. Science fiction

LC 2013041337

John Rodriguez, the new head of a secret agency tasked to monitor Area X--a lush and remote terrain mysteriously sequestered from civilization--is faced with disturbing truths about himself and the agency he has sworn to serve when the secrets of Area X begin to reveal themselves.

"The new director of the Southern Reach is in over his head. His predecessor disappeared on the last mission that the agency sent across the border into Area X, and all that John Rodriguez, aka 'Control,' has to go on to understand the mysterious zone are cryptic notes, disturbing videos, unreliable colleagues, and the interviews he conducts with one of the survivors who made it out. . . . [VanderMeer] carefully ladles out just enough information to keep readers hooked and the truth shadowed." Library Journal.

VanderMeer, Jeff

* **Borne** : a novel / Jeff VanderMeer. Farrar, Straus and Giroux, 2017. 323 p. Borne novels

ISBN 9780374115241

1. Biotechnology 2. Post-apocalypse 3. Genetically engineered organisms 4. Couples 5. Survival 6. Deception 7. Near future 8. Scavenging 9. Drug dealers 10. Shapeshifters 11. Life change events 12. Apocalyptic fiction 13. Science fiction

LC 2016033244

Animal, mineral, or vegetable? When scavenger Rachel rescues Borne, the discarded creation of a defunct biotech company, she has no idea what she's discovered. That doesn't stop her from taking it home

and raising it. To her surprise, the shapeshifting Borne is not only sentient, but intelligent. But Rachel's partner, Wick, is not enchanted with the new arrival. With its dark dystopian setting and non-human(oid) characters, author Jeff VanderMeer's latest novel has more in common with his Ambergris series than his more recent Southern Reach novels. -- Description by Gillian Speace

"VanderMeer marries bildungsroman, domestic drama, love story, and survival thriller into one compelling, intelligent story centered not around the gee-whiz novelty of a flying bear but around complex, vulnerable characters struggling with what it means to be a person." Booklist.

VanderMeer, Jeff

Dead astronauts : a novel / Jeff Vandermeer. MCD/Farrar, Straus and Giroux, 2019. 224 p. Borne novels

ISBN 9780374276805

1. Biotechnology 2. Genetically engineered organisms 3. Near future 4. Creation 5. Post-apocalypse 6. Space and time 7. Cities and towns 8. Literary fiction 9. Dystopian fiction 10. Science fiction

LC 2019022186

lives human and otherwise, from a demon-haunted homeless woman to a messianic blue fox, converge in terrifying and miraculous ways in a nameless city that is overshadowed by a brutally powerful company.

"The varied points of view and stylistic shifts of the narrative allow the reader to experience reality through the eyes of different characters, human and otherwise, and the struggle of different forms of life trying to survive unites the vignettes that form the bulk of the novel. Highly recommended for those interested in sf invested in ecological concerns and speculative fiction that plays with narrative form." Booklist.

VanderMeer, Jeff

Finch / Jeff Vandermeer. Underland Press, 2009. 339 p.

ISBN 9780980226010

1. Martial law 2. Counterculture 3. Murder 4. Murder investigation 5. Fungi 6. Detectives 7. Rebels 8. Deception 9. Fantasy fiction

Ruled by sentient fungi, the human inhabitants of the city of Ambergris spend their days constructing a tower for their "gray cap" overlords -- or, in the case of detective Finch, keeping societal disruption to a minimum. When Finch is tasked with investigating a double homicide involving a human and a gray cap, his life gets infinitely more complicated and dangerous. -- Description by Gillian Speace.

"Surreal and at times intoxicating, Finch is ambitious in a way that few genre novels ever are. VanderMeer has tried and, often, succeeded in blending fantasy, science fiction, and crime fiction into something delightfully evil and strange. He's converted the traditional hard edges of noir fiction into the foggy, fungal shapes of magical science realism." io9.

Vandermeer, Jeff

The **third** bear / Jeff Vandermeer. Tachyon, 2010. 273 p.

ISBN 9781892391988

1. Fantasy fiction 2. Short stories

"These 15 elegantly crafted stories ably demonstrate VanderMeer's skill at telling tales of wonder in language that enhances the reading experience. Fans of imaginative literature and true speculative fiction should appreciate this groundbreaking collection by a World Fantasy Award winner that calls to mind the works of Borges, Kafka, and Stanislaw Lem." Library Journal.

LIST OF FICTIONAL WORKS

Vann, David

Aquarium / David Vann. Atlantic Monthly Press, 2015. 266 p.

ISBN 9780802123527

1. 1990s 2. Mothers and daughters 3. Fishes 4. Senior men 5. Aquariums 6. Twelve-year-old girls 7. Poverty 8. Growing up 9. Stevedores 10. Family secrets 11. Seattle, Washington 12. Coming-of-age stories 13. Literary fiction

First published: London: William Heinemann, 2015.

Immersing herself in a fantasy life inspired by the Seattle aquarium, a preadolescent girl living in subsidized housing befriends an elderly fellow enthusiast before making a shattering discovery about a family secret.

"By pulling no punches in this explicit exploration of family, forgiveness, duty, acceptance, parent-child relationships, and what constitutes abuse, Vann has outdone himself." Booklist.

Vann, David

Caribou Island : a novel / David Vann. Harper, 2011. 320 p.

ISBN 9780061875724

1. Marital conflict 2. Social isolation 3. Wilderness survival 4. Marriage 5. Mother and adult daughter 6. Husband and wife 7. Family relationships 8. Violence 9. Alaska 10. Psychological fiction

LC 2010015703

David Vann, author of "Legend of a suicide," presents a new novel that is set against the majestic scenery of Alaska. Now that their children are grown, Gary is determined to carry out his dream of building a log cabin. Although wife Irene doesn't care for the idea, she helps him out anyway. Their already strained marriage is stretched even thinner as there are setbacks in the cabin's construction and Irene begins to suffer from strange headaches.

"Vann locates his characters in an utterly convincing Alaska, but the natural world provides no ease for human anguish nor is nature anything except a mirror in which these characters see what they wish to see. . . . [His] writing is confident concrete and efficient. His characters' emotions and experiences bleed directly into the reader." Los Angeles Times Book Review.

Vann, David

Goat Mountain / David Vann. Harper, 2013. 304 p.

ISBN 9780062121097

1. 1970s 2. Boy murderers 3. Intergenerational relations 4. Eleven-year-old boys 5. Deer hunting 6. Poachers 7. Violence 8. California 9. Literary fiction

In the fall of 1978, an 11-year-old boy joins his grandfather, his father and his father's best friend on the family's annual deer hunt during which a simple act leads to tragedy, transforming them all and forcing them to question themselves and everything they thought they knew.

Vargas Llosa, Mario, 1936-

Aunt Julia and the scriptwriter / Mario Vargas Llosa ; translated from the Spanish by Helen R. Lane Farrar/Straus/Giroux, 1982. 374 p.

ISBN 9780380700462

1. 1950s 2. Aunt and nephew 3. Scandals 4. Divorced women 5. Men/women relations 6. Radio playwriting 7. Authors 8. Creativity in men 9. Lima, Peru 10. Literary fiction 11. Parallel narratives 12. Translations -- Spanish to English

LC 82005159

Translation fo La Tia Julia y el escribidor (1977).

Mario falls in love with and and embarks on a secret love affair with his recently divorced Aunt Julia, scandalizing the town of Lima, Peru, while Mario's friend Pedro Camacho becomes more and more obsessed with the soap operas he writes.

Vargas Llosa, Mario, 1936-

The **bad** girl / Mario Vargas Llosa ; translated from the Spanish by Edith Grossman. Farrar, Straus and Giroux, 2007. 304 p.

ISBN 9780374182434

1. Expatriates 2. Crushes (Interpersonal relations) 3. Lovers 4. Men/women relations 5. Interpersonal attraction 6. Love 7. Independence in women 8. Voyages and travels 9. Ethics 10. France 11. Peru 12. South America 13. Literary fiction 14. Translations -- Spanish to English

LC 2007004941

Presents the story of a love affair between a Peruvian translator and an adventurous and independent woman, "the bad girl," as it unfolds over the course of forty years, from Lima to London, Paris, Tokyo, and Madrid.

"Each chapter in Ricardo's life, in Edith Grossman's tart, fluent translation, is a small novel unto itself with its own amiable or striking protagonists, offering a whole fabric of reality waiting to be shredded to pieces by the reappearance of the bad girl. In this way, Vargas Llosa lures us into the world of Latin American revolutionaries; the tony equestrian crowd of Norfolk, England; the denizens of sex clubs in Tokyo; and much more. . . . Vargas Llosa, pulling back one illusory screen after another, eventually reveals the bad girl's true story in a manner that couldn't be more satisfying." Seattle Times.

Vargas Llosa, Mario, 1936-

* The **discreet** hero / Mario Vargas Llosa ; translated from the Spanish by Edith Grossman. Farrar, Straus and Giroux, 2015, c2013. 288 p.

ISBN 9780374146740

1. Fathers and sons 2. Personal conduct 3. Businesspeople 4. Men -- Psychology 5. Extortion 6. Insurance executives 7. Greed 8. Senior men 9. Crime 10. Flashbacks 11. Men/women relations 12. Family relationships 13. Peru 14. Literary fiction 15. Translations -- Spanish to English

LC 2014031209

Translation from the Spanish of: El heroe discreto.

Originally published: Lima, Peru : Alfaguara, 2013.

A successful insurance company owner whose two lazy sons want him permanently out of the way crosses paths with a blackmail victim in Peru.

"Vargas Llosa, a soaring storyteller, mixes humor with solemnity, farce with seriousness, to arrive at novels that maintain a perfect balance between rigorous literary standards and free-for-all fun." Booklist.

Vargas Llosa, Mario, 1936-

The **dream** of the Celt / Mario Vargas Llosa ; translated from the Spanish by Edith Grossman. Farrar Straus & Giroux, 2012, c2010. 480 p.

ISBN 9780374143466

1. Casement, Roger, 1864-1916 2. Class conflict 3. Treason 4. Nationalism 5. Nationalism and social classes 6. Capital punishment 7. Biographical fiction 8. Literary fiction 9. Historical fiction

Originally published in Spanish in 2010 by Alfaguara Ediciones, Spain, as El sueno del Celta.

A Nobel Prize-winning author offers a work of historical fiction that centers around real-life Irish nationalist Roger Casement, who was hanged for treason after he challenged the British authority in Northern Ireland.

Vargas Llosa, Mario, 1936-

The **feast** of the Goat / Mario Vargas Llosa ; translated from the Spanish by Edith Grossman. Farrar, Straus, and Giroux, 2001. 404 p.

ISBN 9780374154769

1. Trujillo Molina, Rafael Leonidas, 1891-1961 Assassination 2. 1960s 3. Presidents -- Dominican Republic 4. Fathers and daughters 5. Women lawyers 6. Dictators 7. Assassination 8. Dominican Republic -- Politics and government 9. Literary fiction 10. Political fiction 11. Translations -- Spanish to English 12. Modern classics

LC 2001033480

Returning to her native Dominican Republic, forty-nine-year-old Urania Cabral, discovers that Rafael Trujillo, the depraved dictator called the Goat by the Domincans, still reigns over his inner circle, which includes Urania's father, with brutality and blackmail, but soon an uprising against him will result in a revolution that will have profound consequences.

Vargas Llosa, Mario, 1936-

Green house / Mario Vargas Llosa ; translated from the Spanish by Gregory Rabassa. Harper Perennial, 2005, c1968. 416 p.

ISBN 9780060732790

1. Brothels 2. Prostitution 3. Small towns -- Peru 4. Jungles 5. Prostitutes 6. Arson 7. Priests 8. Nuns 9. Soldiers 10. Peru 11. Literary fiction 12. Translations -- Spanish to English

Originally published under the title La Casa Verde. Copyright 1965 by Editorial Seix Barral, S.A., Barcelona, Spain.

Known as the Green House, the brothel founded by the enigmatic stranger Don Anselmo on the outskirts of Puira affects both the Latin American city and the mission deep in the jungle.

Vargas Llosa, Mario, 1936-

The **time** of the hero / Mario Vargas Llosa. Faber and Faber, 2004, c1967. 379 p.

ISBN 9780571173204

1. Military cadets 2. Students -- Personal conduct 3. Hazing 4. Armed forces and society -- Latin America 5. Peru 6. Satirical fiction 7. Literary fiction 8. Translations -- Spanish to English

Originally published in English: New York : Grove Press, 1967.

At a military academy in Peru in which savage initiation ceremonies, lewdness, and bullying take place, one of the most put-upon cadets reveals the name of the perpetrator of a minor crime and is shot during maneuvers shortly afterward.

"This novel is a remarkably mature (and, one imagines, highly autobiographical) account. . . . In a sense Llosa is too clever a writer, for his novel gets swamped in places with unnecessary attempts at literary sophistication, repeated flashbacks, multiple viewpoints, and so on. The first hundred pages or so are inordinately prolix, but it is worth making an effort. . . . If [the] novel had been severely edited at an early stage its dramatic core would, I think, have emerged more effectively: despite its prolixity, it is still a harsh and honest piece of fiction." New York Review of Books.

Vargas Llosa, Mario, 1936-

The **war** of the end of the world / Mario Vargas Llosa ; translated from the Spanish by Helen R. Lane. Farrar Straus Giroux, 1984. 568 p.

ISBN 9780374286514

1. 19th century 2. Utopias 3. Prophets 4. Religious fanaticism 5. Revolutionaries 6. Brazil -- History -- Conselheiro Revolt, 1896-1897 7. Literary fiction 8. Epic fiction 9. Historical fiction 10. War stories 11. Translations -- Spanish to English

LC 84010187

Originally published in Spanish under the title: La guerra del fin del mundo.

In nineteenth-century Brazil, just after the establishment of the Republic, an apocalyptic movement, led by a mysterious prophet, establishes another republic of prostitutes, bandits, and beggars, who reject every aspect of the modern state.

"Vargas Llosa depicts a clash not only between two opposing factions but also between two societies inhabiting the same nation, who share only one thing in common: their ignorance of one another. This work represents his most ambitious novel to date in terms of the vastness of the world it portrays and the intensity of its epic action. Helen R. Lane's superb translation now makes this novel available to the English-speaking reader who will find the book to be a memorable literary experience." Choice.

Vargas Llosa, Mario, 1936-

* The **way** to paradise / Mario Vargas Llosa ; translated from the Spanish by Natasha Wimmer. Farrar Straus and Giroux, 2003. 373 p.

ISBN 9780374228033

1. Tristan, Flora, 1803-1844 2. Gauguin, Paul, 1848-1903 3. 19th century 4. Independence (Personal quality) 5. Painters 6. Feminists 7. Women labor organizers 8. Travelers 9. Terminal illness 10. Sexuality 11. France 12. Oceania 13. Literary fiction 14. Biographical fiction 15. Historical fiction 16. Parallel narratives 17. Translations -- Spanish to English

LC 2003056379

Recounts the stories of civil rights campaigner Flora Tristan and Paul Gauguin, the artist grandson who was born after her death, in a tale that follows Flora's struggles with class imbalances and her grandson's effort to escape civilization.

"A whiff of the lecture hall is detectable all through this book. (Some passages have more dates than an almanac.) But the juxtaposition of Tristan's and Gauguin's stories is fascinating all the same. In their different ways, both were moralists and proselytizers." New York Times Book Review.

Varley, John, 1947 August 9-

Dark lightning / John Varley. Ace Books , 2014 344 p. Thunder and lightning (John Varley)

ISBN 9780425274071

1. Space vehicles 2. Mutiny 3. Twins 4. Suspended animation 5. Eccentrics and eccentricities 6. Space colonies 7. Space flight 8. Inventors 9. Belief and doubt 10. Science fiction 11. Space opera

LC 2014009515

Awakening from his cryogenic sleep, Jubal Broussard, the inventor of a strange energy that powers his starship, announces that the current mission must stop or everyone on board will die.

Varley, John, 1947 August 9-

Demon / John Varley. Ace Books, 1987, c1984. 464 p. Gaea trilogy

ISBN 9781101623299

1. Aliens (Non-humanoid) 2. Human-alien encounters 3. Nuclear warfare 4. Sexuality 5. Aliens 6. Gods and goddesses 7. Science fiction

LC 84004814

Previously published: New York : G. P. Putnam's Sons, 1984.

"The author concludes his trilogy about Gaea, the sentient asteroid circling Titan. Cirocco Jones and her allies, including various Titanides and a Terran bodybuilder, struggle to provide the last refuge for fugitives from an Earth devastated by nuclear war." Booklist.

Varley, John, 1947 August 9-
Red lightning / John Varley. Ace Books, 2006 330 p. Thunder and lightning (John Varley)
ISBN 0441013643
1. Martians 2. Teenagers 3. Teenage boys 4. Celebrities 5. Eccentrics and eccentricities 6. Children of celebrities 7. Asteroids 8. Tsunamis 9. Space vehicles 10. Space flight 11. Collisions (Astrophysics) 12. Rescues 13. Questioning 14. Missing persons 15. Teenage boy/girl relations 16. Time machines 17. Mars (Planet) 18. Earth 19. Space opera 20. Science fiction
Sequel to: Red thunder
Sequel: Rolling thunder.
The son of one of the first explorers of Mars, Ray Garcia-Strickland is tired of the overdevelopment and tourists there, and when Earth is struck by a mysterious object, he is forced to return to Earth to help solve the mystery.
"Drawing unabashedly on current events from 9/11 to Hurricane Katrina, the author mixes space opera-esque adventure and merriment with uncensored images of disaster areas and teenage sex. At his Heinlein-channeling best, Varley preaches the gospel of individual responsibility with all the fervor of a space-age libertarian revival preacher." Publishers Weekly.

Varley, John, 1947 August 9-
Red thunder / John Varley. Ace Books, 2003. 411 p. Thunder and lightning (John Varley)
ISBN 0441010156
1. Young adults 2. Space vehicles 3. Space programs 4. Space flight 5. Astronauts 6. Alcoholics 7. Mars (Planet) -- Exploration 8. Space opera 9. Science fiction
LC 2002038231
An unlikely group of seven suburban misfits band together to construct a spaceship built out of old tanker cars that they call Red Thunder, determined to beat the Chinese in a race to become the first humans to set foot on Mars.
"With hilarious, well-drawn characters, extraordinary situations presented plausibly, plus exciting action and adventure, this book should do thunderously well." Publishers Weekly.

Varley, John, 1947 August 9-
Rolling thunder / John Varley. Ace Books., 2008. 344 p. Thunder and lightning (John Varley)
ISBN 9780441015634
1. Martians 2. Celebrities 3. Young women 4. Children of celebrities 5. Singers 6. Women entertainers 7. Family reunions 8. Space vehicles 9. Space flight 10. Space colonies 11. Europa (Satellite) 12. Mars (Planet) 13. Space opera 14. Science fiction
LC 2007046581
Sequel to: Red Lightning.
A third generation Martian, Lieutenant Patricia Kelly Elizabeth Strickland joins the Music, Arts, and Drama Division of the Martian Navy and is sent to Europa, one of Jupiter's moons, as an entertainer, but she soon discovers that hidden dangers lurk everywhere.
"Varley's style of future sf is immediate and gritty, filled with realistic details and believable characters. His conclusion to a trilogy begun with Red Lightning and Red Thunder demonstrates his skill as both raconteur and master of science-based fiction." Library Journal.

Varley, John, 1947 August 9-
* **Titan** / John Varley ; illustrated by Freff. Berkley, 1979. 302 p. Gaea trilogy
ISBN 9780441813049
1. Space flight 2. Aliens (Non-humanoid) 3. Human-alien encounters 4. Sexuality 5. Aliens 6. Space vehicles 7. Science fiction
LC 78023865
Sequel: Wizard (1980).
Locus Award for Best Science Fiction Novel, 1980.
When Cirrocco Jones, captain of the spaceship Ringmaster, and his crew are captured by Gaea, a planet-sized creature that orbits around Saturn, they find themselves inside a bizarre world inhabited by centaurs, harpies, and constantly shifting environment.
"Conscientiously nonsexist action-adventure SF." Anatomy of Wonder, 3rd edition.

Varley, John, 1947 August 9-
Wizard / John Varley. Ace Books, 1987, c1980. 354 p. Gaea trilogy
ISBN 9780441900671
1. Aliens (Non-humanoid) 2. Gods and goddesses 3. Human-alien encounters 4. Lesbians 5. Sexuality 6. Science fiction
LC 79024871
Previously published : Berkley Publishing; distributed by G. P. Putnam's Sons, 1980.
"In this sequel to . . . 'Titan,' Varley continues his exploration of the sentient, wheel-shaped world called Gaea. Twenty years have passed, and now that Earth is aware of her, Gaea has tried to protect herself by becoming valuable to humanityoffering us 'miracles' based on her immense scientific knowledge. Two supplicants for such boons are the central characters: Chris, a man from Earth, and Robin, a woman from the Coven, an all-female orbital colony. To earn their miracles, Gaea requires them to become heroes. To achieve this, they accompany Rocky and Gaby (heroines of the first book, back in supporting roles) on a dangerous odyssey through Gaea's rebellious regions and learn that Gaea herself is the real enemy." Publishers Weekly.

Vasquez, Juan Gabriel, 1973-
* The **shape** of the ruins / Juan Gabriel Vasquez ; translated by Anne McLean. Riverhead Books, 2018. 560 p.
ISBN 9780735211148
1. Assassination 2. Political violence 3. Conspiracy theories 4. Memories 5. Secrecy in government 6. Violence -- Psychological aspects 7. Corruption 8. Obsession 9. Authors 10. Colombia 11. Political fiction 12. Metafiction 13. Literary fiction 14. Translations -- Spanish to English
Originally published: 2015.
A sweeping tale of conspiracy theories, assassinations, and twisted obsessions -- the much anticipated masterpiece from Juan Gabriel Vasquez.

Vasquez, Juan Gabriel, 1973-
The **sound** of things falling / Juan Gabriel Vasquez ; translated from the Spanish by Anne McLean. Riverhead Books, 2013, c2011. 270 p.
ISBN 9781594487484
1. 1960s 2. Drug traffic -- Colombia 3. Violence 4. Male friendship 5. Friendship 6. Murder witnesses 7. Murder 8. Colombia -- History 9. Bogota, Colombia 10. Thrillers and suspense 11. Literary fiction 12. Translations -- Spanish to English
LC 2013009330
This translation originally published: 2012.

"Originally published in Spain 2011 by Alfaguara (Santillana Ediciones Generales) as El ruido de las cosas al caer."

International IMPAC Dublin Literary Award, 2014.

Bogota resident Antonio Yammara reflects on a mid-20th-century uprising between Pablo Escobar's drug cartel and government forces that trapped Pablo's community in a nightmarish existence and culminated in a friend's murder.

Vatner, Jonathan

Carnegie Hill : a novel / Jonathan Vatner. Thomas Dunne Books/St. Martin's Press, 2019. 352 p.

ISBN 9781250174765

1. Apartment house life 2. Marital conflict 3. Rich people 4. Upper class 5. Marriage 6. Neighbors 7. Secrets 8. Power (Social sciences) 9. Prejudice 10. Couples 11. Families 12. Upper East Side, New York City 13. New York City 14. Mainstream fiction

LC 2018055679

Urged by her overprotective parents to call off her wedding at the same time she discovers suspicious texts, an aimless woman in her early 30s turns for advice to her neighbors, who reveal their own marital crises.

Vaughan, Sarah, 1972-

* Anatomy of a scandal : a novel / Sarah Vaughan. Atria/Emily Bestler Books, 2018. 256 p.

ISBN 9781501172168

1. Women lawyers 2. Elite (Social sciences) 3. Trials (Rape) 4. Politicians 5. Married women 6. Power (Social sciences) 7. Upper class 8. Rape victims 9. Secrets 10. England 11. Legal thrillers

LC 2017010834

Librarians' Choice (Australia), 2017.

Desperate to clear the name of her loving and charismatic public figure husband in the wake of scandalous accusations, Sophie clashes with a determined prosecution lawyer, Kate, who resolves to uncover the truth and bring Sophie's husband to justice.

"Vaughan, a former political correspondent, offers gripping insight into a political scandal's hidden machinations and the tension between justice and privilege. An absorbing, polished debut mystery." Booklist.

Vaughn, Carrie

Bannerless / Carrie Vaughn. Houghton Mifflin Harcourt, 2017. 352 p. Bannerless novels (Carrie Vaughn)

ISBN 9780544947306

1. Dystopias 2. Post-apocalypse 3. Survival (after environmental catastrophe) 4. Sustainability 5. Near future 6. Financial crises 7. Mediators 8. Misfits (Persons) 9. Murder 10. Murder investigation 11. Families 12. Small town life 13. Apocalyptic fiction 14. Science fiction mysteries

LC 2017000816

"A John Joseph Adams Book."

Philip K. Dick Award for Science Fiction, 2018.

An investigator must discover the truth behind a mysterious death in a world where small communities struggle to maintain a ravaged civilization decades after environmental and economic collapse.

Veletzos, Roxanne

The **girl** they left behind / Roxanne Veletzos. Atria Books, 2018. 368 p.

ISBN 9781501187681

1. Adopted girls 2. Jewish girls 3. Rich families 4. Young men 5. Communism -- Romania 6. Jews -- Persecutions 7. Political persecution 8. Postwar life 9. Family secrets 10. Men/women relations 11. Options, alternatives, choices 12. Bucharest, Romania 13. Romania -- Social conditions -- 1945-1989 14. Historical fiction

15. Love stories

LC 2018005009

On a freezing night in January 1941, a little Jewish girl is found on the steps of an apartment building in Bucharest. The girl is placed in an orphanage and eventually adopted by a wealthy childless couple who name her Natalia. As she assimilates into her new life, she all but forgets the parents who were forced to leave her behind. Yet, as Natalia comes of age in a bleak and hopeless world, traces of her identity pierce the surface of her everyday life, leading gradually to a discovery that will change her destiny.

Verble, Margaret

* Cherokee America / Margaret Verble. Houghton Mifflin Harcourt, 2019. 384 p.

ISBN 9781328494221

1. 1870s 2. 19th century 3. Native American women 4. Missing persons 5. Culture conflict 6. Crimes against Native Americans 7. Cherokee Indians 8. Indians of North America 9. Indians of North America 10. Women farmers 11. Communities 12. Murder 13. Secrets 14. Family relationships 15. Historical fiction 16. Literary fiction

LC 2018006352

In the Spring of 1875 in the Cherokee Nation, Check, a wealthy farmer and mother of five boys, must protect her mixed-race family and tight-knit community at all costs when violence erupts.

"This complicated, engrossing story of the post-Civil War West is a prequel to Verble's Pulitzer Prize finalist, Maud's Line (2016), but stands on its own." Booklist.

Verghese, A. (Abraham), 1955-

Cutting for stone : a novel / Abraham Verghese. Alfred A. Knopf, 2009. 560 p.

ISBN 9780375414497

1. Physicians 2. Brothers 3. Adoption 4. Fathers and sons 5. Medicine -- Practice 6. Conjoined twins 7. Ethiopia 8. Bronx, New York City 9. Family sagas

LC 2008028252

Marion and Shiva Stone, twin brothers born from a secret love affair between an Indian nun and a British surgeon in Addis Ababa, come of age in an Ethiopia on the brink of revolution, where their love for the same woman drives them apart.

"A novel about identical twin boys born in Addis Ababa in 1954 and instantly orphaned--their mother dies, their father flees. Raised by doctors at the hospital, Shiva and Marion soon begin practicing medicine themselves, but their lives unhappily diverge. . . . Verghese, a doctor, has an affinity for unstinting detail and unscientific intuition. The exhaustive gore of the medical procedures is matched by a poetic perception of the outside world: arriving in New York, Marion misses the cacophony of Addis Ababa's roads, observing that in America the cars were near silent, like a school of fish. Verghese bends history and coincidence to his narrative needs--characters cross paths when they should and find the information they seek--creating a story much like the human bodies Marion painstakingly describes: beautiful, amazing, and a bit of a mess." The New Yorker.

Verne, Jules, 1828-1905

* Around the world in eighty days / Jules Verne ; translated with an introduction and notes by William Butcher. Oxford University Press, 2008. xlv, 247 p.

ISBN 9780199552511

1. 19th century 2. Bets 3. Trips around the world -- 19th century 4. Travelers 5. Voyages and travels 6. Adventure stories 7. Translations

-- French to English 8. Classics

LC 2008482138

In 1872 Phileas Fogg wins a bet by traveling around the world in seventy-nine days, twenty-three hours, and fifty-seven minutes.

Verne, Jules, 1828-1905

* Journey to the centre of the Earth / Jules Verne ; translated by Frank Wynne and edited by Peter Cogman, with an introduction by Jane Smiley. Penguin, 2009. 252 p.

ISBN 9780141441979

1. Adventurers 2. Volcanoes 3. Scientific expeditions 4. Imaginary journeys 5. Adventure 6. Exploration 7. Geologists 8. College teachers 9. Uncles 10. Nephews 11. Teenage boys 12. Iceland 13. Earth -- Core 14. Science fiction 15. Classics 16. Translations -- French to English

First published in Paris in 1864 as Voyage au centre de la terre.

First published in the United Kingdom in 1871 by Griffith and Farran.

Follows Professor Lidenbrock, his nephew Axel, and their guide Hans as they venture deep into a volcanic crater in Iceland on a journey that leads them to the center of the earth and to incredible and horrifying discoveries.

"More than half the book is given to the preliminaries before the actual descent begins, the first two chapters relying on a standard point of departure, the discovery of a manuscript giving the location of the caverns in Iceland. The narrative shows Verne's intense care in presenting the latest scientific thought of his age, while the sighting of the plesiosaurus and the giant humanoid shepherding mammoths indicates how well he incorporated lengthy imaginary episodes to flesh out the factual report." Anatomy of Wonder, 4th edition.

Verne, Jules, 1828-1905

The **mysterious** island / Jules Verne ; pictures by N. C. Wyeth Scribner's, 1946, c1875. viii, 493 p.

ISBN 9780684189574

1. Castaways -- Pacific Ocean 2. Escapes 3. Islands 4. Survival 5. Adventurers 6. Islands of the Pacific 7. Adventure stories 8. Sea stories 9. Translations -- French to English

The book The mysterious island was the inspiration for the movie "Journey 2 : the mysterious island".

Text originally published : Paris : Hetzel, 1874.

After using a helium-filled balloon to escape from the Confederate Army, five men find themselves being swept across the ocean by hurricane winds.

Vernon, Olympia

A **killing** in this town / Olympia Vernon. Grove Press, 2006. 256 p.

ISBN 0802118135

1. Boys 2. African Americans -- Mississipi 3. Ku-Klux Klan -- Mississippi 4. European American men 5. Factories -- Safety measures 6. Working class 7. Initiation rites for boys 8. Violence against African-Americans 9. Race relations 10. Hate 11. Reconciliation 12. Lynching 13. Racism 14. Injustice 15. Mississippi 16. Coming-of-age stories 17. African American fiction 18. Southern fiction

LC 2005052547

A horrific period from the annals of the American South is resurrected in this novel that exposes the fragile hierarchy of a society poisoned by racism and hatred and shows the power of an individual to defy tradition.

"The novel shows the debilitating cancer of hatred and prejudice and the beauty of the effort to stop the violence. In language reminiscent of Toni Morrison and William Faulkner, Vernon weaves a powerful yet dreamlike story of our not-too-distant past." Booklist.

The **very** best of the best : 35 years of The year's best science fiction / Gardner R. Dozois. St. Martin's Griffin, 2019 ix, 686 p. Year's best science fiction (Gardner Dozois)

ISBN 9781250296191

1. Science fiction 2. Anthologies 3. Short stories

An ultimate science fiction anthology compiles the best short stories from the last 35 annual collections.

"The 38 stories in this culling of the last 15 annual anthologies edited by the late Dozois testify to the breathtaking scope of science fiction and the diversity and talent of its writers." Publishers Weekly.

Vestal, Shawn

Daredevils / Shawn Vestal. Penguin Press, 2016. 320 p.

ISBN 9781101979891

1. 1970s 2. Mormons 3. Teenage girls 4. Mormon polygamy 5. Polygamy 6. Runaway wives, husbands, etc 7. Escapes 8. Freedom 9. Self-discovery in teenage girls 10. Independence in teenage girls 11. Idaho 12. Arizona 13. Coming-of-age stories 14. Pacific Northwest fiction

1974: Fifteen-year-old Loretta slips out of her bedroom window to meet her "Gentile" boyfriend. This time, however, her strict Mormon parents catch her returning at dawn and quickly arrange for her to marry the upstanding Dean Harder, a devout yet materialistic fundamentalist who already has a wife and a brood of kids, some not much younger than Loretta herself. Trapped in her role as a "sister wife," Loretta dreams of another, better future, of a world glimpsed in magazines and ads. Her chance comes when Dean uproots the family to Idaho, and she meets Jason, Dean's teenage nephew, who worships Evel Knievel and longs to leave his small town--and the Mormon faith--behind. As Jason's parents clash with Dean and struggle to come to terms with his unconventional family living next door, Loretta and Jason make their plans to escape. Vestal delivers a dizzying jolt of teenage freedom as the two drive off into the starry night, with hopes of recovering Dean's cache of "Mormon gold." But someone Loretta left behind is on their trail.

"Vestal has created a riveting, rollicking thrill ride about throwing caution to the wind." Publishers Weekly.

Vida, Vendela

Let the Northern Lights erase your name : a novel / Vendela Vida. Ecco, 2007. 226 p.

ISBN 9780060828370

1. Young women 2. Mother-separated children 3. Abandoned children 4. Dysfunctional families 5. Fathers -- Death 6. Family secrets 7. Quests 8. Voyages and travels 9. Mothers and daughters 10. Sami (European people) 11. Self-discovery in women 12. Lapland 13. Psychological fiction

LC 2006045030

Raised by her father after the disappearance of her mother, twenty-eight-year-old Clarissa discovers upon her father's death that he was not her father at all, a finding that drives her to leave her fiancé and travel to the Arctic to discover the truth about her heritage.

"Vida gives the icy landscape an eerie, forbidding beauty, and her writing has moments of great emotional acuity. Her heroine is inexplicable and often unlikable, but Vida skillfully draws a parallel between her harsh and thoughtless behavior and that of her mother." The New Yorker.

Vidal, Gore, 1925-2012

1876 : a novel / Gore Vidal. Random House, 1976. 364 p. American chronicle (Gore Vidal)

ISBN 9780394497501

1. Hayes, Rutherford B, 1822-1893 2. Tilden, Samuel J (Samuel Jones), 1814-1886 3. Presidents -- United States -- Election -- 1876 4. Political corruption 5. Elections 6. Political campaigns 7. Journalists 8. Father and adult daughter 9. United States -- History -- 1865-1898 10. United States -- Politics and government -- 1865-1877 11. Historical fiction 12. Political fiction 13. Literary fiction

LC 75034311

Returning to America after his long European sojourn, Charlie Schuyler, Aaron Burr's unacknowledged son, and Charlie's widowed daughter seek financial and political advancement in the centennial power centers, as republican idealism is giving way to imperial expediency.

"As in 'Burr,' Charles Schuyler, hinted-at as the illegitimate son of Aaron Burr, again narrates. Now a respected and popular journalist-historian, Schuyler at 63 has returned, after years abroad, to the U.S. in the company of his widowed daughter, the Princess d'Agrigente, who is in need of a well-connected husband--thereby giving Vidal another occasion to crash society's party as he follows Schuyler on his journalistic assignments through New York, the city of Washington, later to Philadelphia for the Centennial, then Cincinnati for the Republican Convention." Publishers Weekly.

Vidal, Gore, 1925-2012

Burr : a novel / Gore Vidal. Random House, 1973. 430 p., 25 cm. American chronicle (Gore Vidal)

ISBN 9780394480244

1. Burr, Aaron, 1756-1836 2. 19th century 3. Ambition in men 4. Conspiracies -- United States -- History 5. Vice-presidents -- United States 6. United States -- History -- 1783-1865 7. United States -- Politics and government -- 1783-1809 8. Historical fiction 9. Biographical fiction 10. Political fiction 11. Literary fiction

LC 73003985

Aaron Burr tells his biographer details of his life, including his duel with Alexander Hamilton and his two marriages.

"Burr is a novel in the form of a memoir told in part by Burr and in part by the young journalist Charles Schuyler, a fictional creation and Vidal's strongest character." Choice.

Vidal, Gore, 1925-2012

Empire : a novel / Gore Vidal. Vintage International, 2000, c1987. 486 p. American chronicle (Gore Vidal)

ISBN 9780394561233

1. Roosevelt, Theodore, 1858-1919 2. Hearst, William Randolph, 1863-1951 3. Hay, John, 1838-1905 4. James, Henry, 1843-1916 5. Adams, Henry, 1838-1918 6. 1900s (Decade) 7. Rich women 8. Ambition 9. Half-brothers 10. United States -- History -- 1901-1909 11. United States -- Politics and government -- 1898-1920 12. Historical fiction 13. Political fiction 14. Literary fiction

LC 86029782

An historical novel with portraits of Teddy Roosevelt, William Randolph Hearst, and others, this story illuminates Roosevelt's Washington, America's Gilded Age, and the expanding American empire.

Vidal, Gore, 1925-2012

The **golden** age : a novel / Gore Vidal Doubleday, 2000. 467 p. American chronicle (Gore Vidal)

ISBN 9780385500753

1. 1940s 2. 1950s 3. Newspaper publishers and publishing 4. Women newspaper employees 5. Authors and publishers 6. Aunt and nephew 7. United States -- History -- 20th century 8. Washington, D.C. 9.

New York City 10. Historical fiction 11. Political fiction 12. Literary fiction

LC 00043071

A fictional narrative of American history from 1939 to 1954 follows the events and personalities that transformed America from a republic to an empire through the eyes of Caroline Sanford, a Washington newspaper publisher.

"Vidal is best on the surface. His account of the 1940 conventions is a real romp. He depicts F.D.R. with irreverent skill. . . . It's good to know how badly Wendell Willkie could give a public speech; and there are some wonderful scenes in which Eleanor Roosevelt skillfully manipulates her husband and the bosses of the old Democratic Party." New York Times Book Review.

Vidal, Gore, 1925-2012

Hollywood : a novel of America in the 1920s / Gore Vidal. Random House, 1990. 437 p. American chronicle (Gore Vidal)

ISBN 9780394576596

1. Hearst, William Randolph, 1863-1951 2. Harding, Warren G, 1865-1923 3. Wilson, Woodrow, 1856-1924 4. 1920s 5. Film industry and trade -- Hollywood, California -- History 6. Scandals 7. Propaganda films 8. Film actors and actresses 9. Women film producers and directors 10. Hollywood, California 11. Historical fiction 12. Literary fiction

LC 89042834

Follows the career of Caroline Sanford, a brilliant and beautiful newspaper publisher who leaves Washington to become a Hollywood producer and movie star.

"Vidal's highly polished prose style, in part the fruit of his classical training, is a constant delight." New York Times Book Review.

Vidal, Gore, 1925-2012

* Lincoln : a novel / Gore Vidal. Random House, 1984. 657 p. American chronicle (Gore Vidal)

ISBN 9780394528953

1. Lincoln, Abraham, 1809-1865 2. Presidents 3. Character in men 4. Politics and culture 5. Slavery 6. United States -- History -- 1815-1861 7. United States -- Politics and government -- 1815-1865 8. Biographical fiction 9. Historical fiction 10. Political fiction 11. Literary fiction

LC 83043185

The character of President Lincoln, unremittingly tested by the trials of the war years, is reflected through the eyes of the diverse and colorful denizens of Washington, including his wife Mary and his political rivals and disciples.

"This novel is not so much an imaginative reconstruction of an era as an intelligent, lucid and highly informative transcript of it, never less than workmanlike in its blocking out of scenes and often extremely compelling." New York Times Book Review.

Vidal, Gore, 1925-2012

Washington, D. C. : a novel / Gore Vidal. Vintage International, 2000, c1967. 374 p. American chronicle (Gore Vidal)

ISBN 9780375708770

1. 1940s 2. Ambition in men 3. Political corruption 4. Journalists 5. Washington, D.C. 6. United States -- Politics and government -- 1933-1953 7. Historical fiction 8. Political fiction 9. Literary fiction

A new age of media politics emerges when conservative senator Clay Overbury begins his quest for the Presidency during World War II, and receives help from liberal newspaper tycoon Blaise Sanford.

"Set from the New Deal to the McCarthy years this political novel features the ambitions of both a senator and his young secretary for the Presidency. The senator loses his chance for the Democratic nomination when Roosevelt decides to run for a third term. The secretary, mapping his course to the top, with the help of a journalist invents a non-happening which makes him a national hero. He then blackmails the senator into withdrawing from the race and wins the senatorial seat for himself." Booklist.

Vidich, Paul

The **coldest** warrior / Paul Vidich. Pegasus Books, 2020. 256 p.

ISBN 9781643133355

1. Espionage 2. Government cover-ups 3. CIA agents 4. Experiments 5. Criminal investigation 6. Scientists 7. Secrets 8. Thrillers and suspense

When the release of the Rockefeller Commission report implicates the CIA in the death of a bioweapons scientist decades earlier, agent Jack Gabriel confronts a life-threatening cover-up at the highest levels of government.

"With this outing, Vidich enters the upper ranks of espionage thriller writers." Publishers Weekly.

Vine, Barbara, 1930-2015

Anna's book / Ruth Rendell, writing as Barbara Vine. Harmony Books, 1993. 394 p.

ISBN 0517587963

1. 1900s (Decade) 2. Family secrets 3. Murder 4. Missing children 5. Diaries 6. Mothers and daughters 7. London, England 8. Psychological suspense

LC 92034309

Also published under the title: Asta's Book.

An entry torn from the diary of a dead Englishwoman of Scandinavian descent holds the key to the identity of the woman's daughter.

"Vine's story is utterly riveting, rich and multifaceted in its complexity. Her characters are wonderfully real and fascinatingly unconventional." Booklist.

Vine, Barbara, 1930-2015

The **chimney** sweeper's boy : a novel / Barbara Vine. Harmony Books, 1998. 344 p.

ISBN 060960287X

1. Impostors 2. Authors, English 3. Murder 4. Children of authors 5. Heart attack 6. Men -- Identity 7. New identities 8. Fathers and daughters 9. Men -- Sexuality 10. England 11. Devon, England 12. Psychological suspense

LC 9810567

An Englishwoman writing a biography of her father, a famous novelist, discovers that as a young man he changed names, taking the name of a boy who died in infancy. She goes looking for the reason and discovers murder.

"This novel revolves around the sudden death of Gerald Candless, a celebrated English novelist who lived on the Devon coast with his wife, Ursula, and two daughters to whom he was conspicuously devoted. When one daughter, Sarah, starts researching her father's early history for the biography she has been asked to write, she discovers that he was living under a false identity for most of his life. As more facts emerge from Sarah's research, they both illuminate and contradict the dark views of Gerald's personality supplied by his bitter wife and the deep, if ambiguous, insights contained in his own novels." New York Times Book Review.

Vine, Barbara, 1930-2015

Grasshopper / Barbara Vine Harmony Books, 2000 332 p.

ISBN 0609607898

1. Young women 2. Kidnapping 3. Secrets 4. Altitudes -- Psychological aspects 5. Claustrophobia 6. Mental illness 7. Roofs 8. London, England 9. Psychological suspense 10. Coming-of-age stories

LC 00038281

Clodagh Brown was nineteen when her parents packed her off to college and a relative's house in Maida Vale, two years after the death on the pylon. They blamed her for it, everyone did. It was hardly surprising that she fell into the arms of Silver. In his flat at the top of his parents' house he played host to a strange crew of young drop-outs whose pleasure was to range the rooftops. It was a happy, heady time until the moment when on a trek fifty feet above the street, they looked into a window and saw a scene that was to lead to tragedy.

"Only a handful of writers, in any genre, can match Barbara Vine for imaginative originality and ingenuity. . . . Grasshopper is about good intentions gone wrong, violence, innocence and an encounter with true evil. . . . To say that a book can open your eyes to a different world is a cliche, but rarely has it been more apt than in describing this novel." New Statesman.

Vine, Barbara, 1930-2015

The **House** of Stairs / Ruth Rendell writing as Barbara Vine. Harmony Books, 1989, c1988. 277 p.

ISBN 0517572524

1. Former convicts 2. Murder 3. Women authors 4. Female friendship 5. Nieces and nephews 6. Aunts 7. England 8. Psychological suspense

LC 88038303

"Originally published in Great Britain in 1988 by Viking"-- T.p. verso.

Elizabeth Vetch and her recently widowed aunt Cosette move into the mysterious House of Stairs and find that troubled souls often come to roost there, and that murder lurks on the premises.

"A complex, eloquent novel sure to retain Vine's large readership and undoubtedly gain her even more followers." Booklist.

Vine, Barbara, 1930-2015

The **minotaur** : a novel / Barbara Vine. Shaye Areheart Books, 2006. 352 p.

ISBN 0307237605

1. 1960s 2. Murder 3. Dysfunctional families 4. People with autism 5. Nurses 6. People with schizophrenia 7. Swedes in England 8. Rich families 9. Widows 10. Mothers and daughters 11. Administration of estates 12. Family estates 13. Country homes 14. Inheritance and succession 15. Autism 16. England 17. Essex, England 18. Psychological suspense

LC 2005010837

Swedish nurse Kirsten Kvist has no idea what to expect when she takes a job with the Cosway family at their estate deep in the Essex countryside, but she discovers a divided family in which secrets, sexual obsession, and betrayal lead to murder.

"This is very satisfying reading, a sort of blend of Edgar Allan Poe and Anthony Trollope." Booklist.

Vinge, Joan D.

* The **snow** queen / Joan D. Vinge. Dial Press, 1980. 536 p.

ISBN 0803777396

1. Women rulers 2. Clones and cloning 3. Oracles 4. Interstellar

relations 5. Environmental degradation 6. Science fiction

LC 79020555

"A Quantum novel"

Sequel: The Summer Queen.

Hugo Award for Best Novel, 1981.

Locus Award for Best Science Fiction Novel, 1981.

"An amalgam of SF and heroic fantasy borrowing the structure of Hans Christian Andersen's famous story, set on a barbarian world exploited by technologically superior outworlders, against the background of a fallen galactic empire." Anatomy of Wonder, 4th edition.

Vinge, Joan D.

The **summer** queen / Joan D. Vinge. Warner Books, 1991. 670 p.

ISBN 0446513970

1. Science fiction

LC 90050521

Moon, reigning as the Snow Queen, tries to keep her people from the tyranny of the Hegemony, while solving the mystery of the otherworldly Mers.

"Plots and subplots proliferate, and although the prose is sometimes florid and the romance and sex scenes overly sentimental, the book is so full of drama, conflict and tragedy that it justifies its length." Publishers Weekly.

Vinge, Joan D.

World's end / Joan D. Vinge. Bluejay Books, 1984. 230 p.

ISBN 0312944683

1. Science fiction

LC 83021324

BZ Gundhalinu ventures into the bizarre land of World's End where he struggles to retain his sanity, find his lost brothers, uncover the secret of Fire Lake, and be reunited with Moon.

Vinge, Vernor

The **children** of the sky / Vernor Vinge. Tor Books, 2011. 448 p. Zones of thought

ISBN 9780312875626

1. Life on other planets 2. Survival (after disaster) 3. Librarians 4. Teenagers 5. Greed 6. Power (Social sciences) 7. Space warfare 8. Aliens (Non-humanoid) 9. Intelligence 10. Refugees 11. Knowledge 12. Human/alien encounters 13. Posthumanism 14. Space opera 15. Hard science fiction 16. Science fiction

LC 2011024210

Ten years after a disaster that nearly obliterated humankind throughout the galaxy, Ravna Bergnsdot must try to prevent power-seeking humans and intelligent pack animals called Tines from dragging the fledgling civilization on Tines World into chaos.

"Vinge has crafted a tale that should captivate his fans and win for him a larger and well-deserved audience. Libraries should anticipate demand." Library Journal.

Vinge, Vernor

A **deepness** in the sky / Vernor Vinge. TOR, 1999. 606 p. Zones of thought

ISBN 0312856830

1. Life on other planets 2. Aliens (Non-humanoid) 3. Slavery 4. Pirates 5. Trading and swapping 6. Far future 7. Space warfare 8. Intelligence 9. Space opera 10. Hard science fiction 11. Science fiction

LC 98-43457

Prequel to: A fire upon the deep

Hugo Award for Best Novel, 2000.

John W. Campbell Memorial Award for Best Science Fiction Novel, 2000.

The story of the Spiders, inhabitants of a planet where the sun regularly stops shining for periods of 200 years, during which they are frozen in ice. The novel picks them up emerging from their most recent hibernation in a frenzy of activity and innovation to make up for lost time.

"Vinge is among the very best of the current crop of hard SF writers, producing work that is not only fast-paced and intellectually challenging, but also stylishly written and centered on carefully drawn characters." Publishers Weekly.

Vinge, Vernor

* A **fire** upon the deep / Vernor Vinge. TOR, 1992. 391 p. Zones of thought

ISBN 0312851820

1. Space warfare 2. Aliens (Non-humanoid) 3. Space flight 4. Refugees 5. Knowledge 6. Accidents 7. Human/alien encounters 8. Intelligence 9. Posthumanism 10. Space opera 11. Hard science fiction 12. Science fiction

LC 91039020

Prequel: A deepness in the sky

Hugo Award for Best Novel, 1993.

When scientists of the Straumli realm use an ancient Transcendent artifact as a weapon, they unwittingly unleash an awesome power that destroys thousands of worlds and enslaves all natural and artificial intelligence.

"Thoughtful space opera at its best, this book delivers everything it promises in terms of galactic scope, audacious concepts and believable characters both human and nonhuman." New York Times Book Review.

Vinge, Vernor

Rainbows end / Vernor Vinge. TOR, 2006. 364 p.

ISBN 0312856849

1. 21st century 2. Conspiracies 3. Technology 4. Biological weapons 5. Near future 6. Viruses 7. Chinese American men 8. People with Alzheimer's disease 9. Poets 10. College teachers 11. Computer technology 12. Protests, demonstrations, vigils, etc 13. Manipulation (Social sciences) 14. San Diego, California 15. California 16. Hard science fiction 17. Science fiction

Hugo Award for Best Novel, 2007.

Locus Award for Best Science Fiction Novel, 2007.

In a near-future western civilization that is threatened by corruptive practices within its technologically advanced information networks, a recovered Alzheimer's victim and his family are caught up in a dangerous maelstrom beyond their worst imaginings.

"Vinge's world is saturated with the logical extensions of current R&D. He has thought long and hard about how pervasive and ubiquitous information technology will transform our lives." Science Fiction Weekly.

Vlautin, Willy

Don't skip out on me / Willy Vlautin. Perennial, 2018. 288 p.

ISBN 9780062684455

1. Identity (Psychology) 2. Abandonment (Psychology) 3. Boxers (Sports) 4. Orphans 5. Ranches 6. Ambition in men 7. Coping 8. Purpose in life 9. Mexico 10. Las Vegas, Nevada 11. Literary fiction

ALA Notable Book, 2019.

Pen/Faulkner Award Finalist, 2019

Determined to prove his worth as a son abandoned by his biological parents, a half-Paiute, half-Irish ranch hand leaves his aging caregivers to become a champion boxer before matches organized in Mexico and

Las Vegas lead to his realization that he cannot change his identity or outrun his destiny.

Vlautin, Willy

Lean on Pete : a novel / Willy Vlautin. Harper Perennial, 2010. 304 p.

ISBN 9780061456534

1. Teenage boys 2. Race horses 3. Friendship 4. Stable hands 5. Single fathers 6. Hope in boys 7. Oregon 8. Portland, Oregon 9. Pacific Northwest fiction 10. Coming-of-age stories

LC 2009020460

Shortlisted for the International IMPAC Dublin Literary Award, 2012

Left homeless by the death of his father, fifteen-year-old Charley Thompson sets off with a racehorse, Lean on Pete, on a perilous treck from Portland, Oregon to Wyoming to find a distant aunt, hoping to regain stability in his life.

"Charley Thompson is a 15-year-old boy who dreams of a normal home and the chance to play high-school football. Newly arrived in Portland with a mostly absent father, Charley hopes for the best and gets the worst. Suddenly homeless, he hangs out on the backstretch at Portland Meadows racetrack and finds a friend: an aging Thoroughbred named Lean on Pete. That's exactly what Charley does, at least for a while, until Pete, bound for the slaughterhouse, needs to lean on Charley. The perilous journey on which Charley and Pete embark must end badly--think of Kirk Douglas and another loyal horse on the run from civilization in Lonely Are the Bravebut on the road Charley tells Pete the story of his life, and in this young boy's flatly descriptive but heartbreaking words, reprising a lifetime of barely getting by . . . , Vlautin transforms what might have been a weepy, unbelievable TV-movie of a novel into a tough-and-tender account of a boy, a big-hearted horse, and a mostly unforgiving world." Booklist.

Vollmann, William T.

The **rainbow** stories / William T. Vollmann. Atheneum, 1989. 541 p.

ISBN 9780689119613

1. Pariahs 2. Prostitutes 3. Neo-Nazis 4. Alcoholics 5. Homeless persons 6. Gangs 7. Punk culture 8. Short stories

LC 88032628

A collection of short stories, including "Red Hands," "Yellow Sugar," "The Green Dress," "The Indigo Engineers," and "Violet Hair".

Vollmann, William T.

Europe central / William T. Vollmann. Viking, 2005. 832 p.

ISBN 9780670033928

1. Shostakovich, Dmitrii Dmitrievich, 1906-1975 2. Composers 3. Artists 4. Poets 5. Generals 6. Authoritarianism 7. Censorship 8. Ethics 9. World War II 10. Germany -- Social life and customs 11. Soviet Union -- Social life and customs 12. Short stories 13. Historical fiction 14. Literary fiction

LC 2004061170

A collection of paired stories.

Includes index.

National Book Award for Fiction, 2005.

National Book Critics Circle Award for Fiction finalist, 2005

Vollmann presents a mesmerizing series of intertwined paired stories that compare and contrast the moral decisions made by various figures (some famous, some infamous, some unknown) associated with the warring authoritarian cultures of Germany and the USSR from 1900-1968.

"What sets Europe Central apart from Vollmann's other large-scale historical productions is its strong narrative lines. The pieces are dated and arranged chronologically to give the book a plot that arcs from prewar political machinations to Germany's surge east to Russia's counteroffensive, and that ends with cold war politics in divided Berlin." New York Times Book Review.

Vollmann, William T.

Last stories and other stories / William T. Vollmann. Viking, 2014. xvii, 677 p.

ISBN 9780670015979

1. Sexuality 2. Death 3. Love 4. Life after death 5. Ghosts 6. Memory 7. Fantasy fiction 8. Short stories

LC 2013047856

A collection of connected ghost stories includes tales about a farmer's deceased wife who returns, a geisha who becomes a cherry tree, and a man who romances the ghost of his high school girlfriend.

"The writing is atmospheric, otherworldly, and highly accessible." Library Journal.

Voltaire, 1694-1778

Candide and other stories / Voltaire ; translated from the French, with an introduction and notes, by Roger Pearson. A. A. Knopf, 1990, c1759. 307 p.

ISBN 067941746X

1. Happiness 2. Rationalism 3. Optimism 4. Short stories 5. Satirical fiction 6. Translations -- French to English 7. Classics

LC 92522911

Includes chronology of Voltaire's life and works.

Candide also published as: Candide, or Optimism.

Originally published in French: Geneve : Cramer, 1759.

A classic, satiric novel by the eighteenth century author and philosopher chronicles the misadventures of Candide, who continues to manifest his belief that "all is for the best" despite life's injustice, despair, and suffering.

Vonnegut, Kurt

Armageddon in retrospect : and other new and unpublished writings on war and peace / Kurt Vonnegut   G. P. Putnams Sons, 2008. 232 p.

ISBN 9780399155086

1. Popular culture 2. Peace 3. War 4. Violence 5. World War II 6. United States -- Social life and customs -- 20th century 7. Essays 8. Arts and Entertainment Writing and Publishing

LC 2008921969

Includes non-fiction and short stories.

Twelve previously unpublished writings on war and peace include such pieces as an essay on the destruction of Dresden, a story about the first-meal fantasies of three soldiers, and a meditation on the impossibility of shielding children from the temptations of violence.

"Only a few of the . . . stories rely on the twists of reality and narrative present in Vonnegut's novels; the majority are carried by the characters' struggle with the absurdities of war and peace. Vonnegut's World War II experience as a prisoner of war in Dresden haunts the work, with multiple stories featuring American POWs in Germany. . . . Readers of Vonnegut's books won't find any surprises here, but because he is at his sardonic best when working in short form, they won't be let down by his humor and poignancy, either." Library Journal.

Vonnegut, Kurt

Bagombo snuff box : uncollected short fiction / Kurt Vonnegut. G.P. Putnam's Sons, 1999. 295 p.

ISBN 0399145052

1. United States -- Social life and customs -- 20th century 2. Short

stories

LC 99013665

This is vintage Vonnegut: short stories never-before collected or published in book form. They are from the era of the Golden Age of magazines: a pre-television time when publications such as The Saturday evening post, Collier's, Argosy and others reigned supreme as Americans' entertainment choice.

"The 23 stories in this collection were published in magazines . . . during the Fifties and are collected here for the first time. The topics covered include space travel (Thanasphere), which describes the first manned orbit of Earth; finding the American dream (The package), about a new home full of the latest accessories; and an attempt to impress an old girlfriend (the title story). . . . Although many of the stories are topically dated, the ironic insights and illumination of character are timeless, and no one does it better than Vonnegut." Library Journal.

Vonnegut, Kurt

* **Breakfast** of champions : or, Goodbye blue Monday! / Kurt Vonnegut, Jr. ; with drawings by the author. Delacorte Press, 1973. 295 p.

ISBN 0224008889

1. 1970s 2. Purpose in life 3. Human nature 4. Reality 5. Automobile dealers 6. Men with mental illnesses 7. Science fiction writing 8. Mental illness 9. Fate and fatalism 10. Racism 11. Success (Concept) 12. Satirical fiction 13. Literary fiction

LC 72013086

The author questions the condition of modern man in this novel depicting a science fiction writer's struggle to find peace and sanity in the world.

"In this novel Vonnegut is . . . clearing his head by throwing out acquired ideas, and also liberating some of the characters from his previous books. . . . This explosive meditation ranks with Vonnegut's best." New York Times Book Review.

Vonnegut, Kurt

* **Cat's** cradle / Kurt Vonnegut. Delta Trade Paperbacks, 1998, c1963. xiii, 287 p.

ISBN 038533348X

1. Human nature 2. Fate and fatalism 3. End of the world 4. Disasters 5. Scientists 6. Ice 7. Chases 8. Dishonesty 9. Islands 10. Atomic bomb 11. Religion 12. Politics and culture 13. Satirical fiction 14. Literary fiction 15. Modern classics

LC 2004557124

A young writer decides to interview the children of a scientist primarily responsible for the creation of the atomic bomb.

Vonnegut, Kurt

Complete stories / Kurt Vonnegut ; collected and introduced by Jerome Klinkowitz and Dan Wakefield ; foreword by Dave Eggers. Seven Stories Press, 2017. 1024 p.

ISBN 9781609808082

1. Short stories 2. Literary fiction

LC 2017013594

A complete volume of the 20th century literary master's short fiction is organized thematically under such headers as "War," "Women" and "Fortune" and includes five previously unpublished stories as well as several that were published only online.

Vonnegut, Kurt

* **Galapagos** : a novel / Kurt Vonnegut. Delacorte Press/ Seymour Lawrence, 1985. 295 p.

ISBN 0385294166

1. 1980s 2. Human evolution 3. Adaptation (Biology) 4. Purpose in life 5. Ghosts 6. Voyages and travels 7. Survival (after airplane accidents, shipwrecks, etc) 8. Ship passengers 9. Island life 10. Islands 11. Human nature 12. Individuality 13. Fate and fatalism 14. End of the world 15. Galapagos Islands 16. Satirical fiction 17. Literary fiction 18. Science fiction

LC 85004581

Also published in omnibus titled Kurt Vonnegut : novels 1976-1985. Observed by a ghost of the Vietnam War for one million years, the descendants of survivors of a cruise to the Galapagos Archipelago prove Darwin's Theory of Evolution.

Vonnegut, Kurt

God bless you, Mr. Rosewater : or, Pearls before swine / Kurt Vonnegut. Delacorte, 1965. 217 p.

1. Human nature 2. Rich men 3. Greed 4. Hypocrisy 5. Satirical fiction 6. Modern classics 7. Literary fiction

LC 70154036

"With a satirist's eye for the meanness of man, especially his greed, Vonnegut tells the story of Eliot Rosewater, president of the Rosewater Foundation, who uses his position to help all petitioners. Discovering a plot to remove him from authority Rosewater gives all his money to over 50 children he is falsely accused of fathering." Booklist.

Vonnegut, Kurt

Hocus pocus / Kurt Vonnegut. G. P. Putnam's Sons, 1990. 302 p.

ISBN 9780425130216

1. 21st century 2. Fate and fatalism 3. Veterans 4. Vietnam veterans 5. Prisoners 6. Satirical fiction

LC 90034535

Tarkington College, a small, exclusive college in upstate New York, is turned upside down when ten thousand prisoners from the maximum security prison across Lake Mohiga break out and head for the college.

"Vonnegut remains an effectual stylist, combining deadpan irony and faux naivet. As usual, his central narrative winds through a mosaic of aphorisms, verbal tics, digressions, homilies, obscure facts. . . . This compendium of devices and concerns may have hardened into a formula, but it has not yet ceased to be a diverting one." Times Literary Supplement.

Vonnegut, Kurt

Jailbird : a novel / Kurt Vonnegut. Doubleday, 1979. 246 p.

ISBN 9780385286275

1. 1970s 2. Political corruption 3. Bureaucracy 4. Selfishness 5. Watergate Scandal 6. Satirical fiction

LC 79012881

Also published in omnibus titled Kurt Vonnegut : novels 1976-1985 (2014).

Recently released from a prison for white-collar criminals, Walter Starbuck tries to rebuild the life that was ruined during the Communist witchhunt of the 1950s.

Vonnegut, Kurt

* **Player** piano / Kurt Vonnegut, Jr. Delacorte Press, 1952. 295 p.

ISBN 0385333781

1. Far future 2. Conformity 3. Dystopias 4. Rebels 5. Machines and labor 6. Automation -- Social aspects 7. Engineers 8. Satirical fiction 9. Dystopian fiction 10. Science fiction

LC 73154037

"A Seymour Lawrence book."

Kurt Vonnegut's first novel spins the chilling tale of engineer Paul Proteus, who must find a way to live in a world dominated by a super-computers and run completely by machines. Paul's rebellion is vintage Vonnegut: wildly funny, deadly serious, and terrifyingly close to reality.

"Incisive satire; a classic modern dystopia." Anatomy of Wonder, 3rd edition.

Vonnegut, Kurt

* The **sirens** of Titan / Kurt Vonnegut, Jr Houghton Mifflin, 1961, c1959. 319 p.

ISBN 0385289235

1. Rich men 2. Space flight to Mars 3. Space vehicles 4. Life on other planets 5. Martians 6. Human nature 7. Space warfare 8. Men/women relations 9. Purpose in life 10. Fate and fatalism 11. Religion 12. Ethics 13. Personal conduct 14. Satirical fiction 15. Science fiction

LC 61006895

America's wealthiest man succumbs to the irresistible charms of a lunar siren.

Vonnegut, Kurt

Slapstick : or, Lonesome no more! a novel / Kurt Vonnegut. Delacorte/S. Lawrence, 1976. 243 p.

ISBN 9780385334235

1. Loneliness 2. Presidents -- United States 3. Near future 4. End of the world 5. Diseases 6. Grandfather and granddaughter 7. Imaginary wars and battles 8. New York City 9. Fantasy fiction 10. Black humor

LC 76015605

Book inspired a 1980's film called: Slapstick of another kind.

Also published in omnibus titled Kurt Vonnegut : novels 1976-1985 (2014).

Flying to a favorite uncle's funeral, a middle-aged Kurt Vonnegut daydreams of one-hundred-year-old Wilbur Oriole-11 Swain, pediatrician and past United States President, who wrote history's most popular child-rearing manual and sold the original Louisiana Purchase

"Slapstick is a deceptively short and simple book. Its readability should not distract one from the fact that Vonnegut has found a fictional situation which considers serious human problems." The New Republic.

Vonnegut, Kurt

* **Slaughterhouse-five** : or, The children's crusade : Kurt Vonnegut, Jr. Delacorte Press/Seymour Lawrence, 1994, c1969. xiii, 205 p.

ISBN 9780099800200

1. Second World War era (1939-1945) 2. Life on other planets 3. Space flight 4. Prisoners of war, American 5. World War II 6. Time travel 7. UFO abductions 8. Kidnapping victims 9. Fate and fatalism 10. Purpose in life 11. Husband and wife 12. Human nature 13. Germany 14. Dresden, Germany -- Bombing, 1945 15. Literary fiction 16. Modern classics 17. Science fiction

LC 94171120

Billy Pilgrim, a chaplain's assistant during the Second World War, returns home only to be kidnapped by aliens from the planet Tralfamadore, who teach him that time is an eternal present.

Vonnegut, Kurt

Timequake / Kurt Vonnegut. G. P. Putnam's Sons, 1997. 219 p.

ISBN 0399137378

1. 1990s 2. Deja vu 3. Free will and determinism 4. Time 5. Satirical fiction 6. Literary fiction 7. Metafiction 8. Science fiction

LC 9714508

After the universe decides to back up ten years and all humans must live through the 1990s again, author Kurt Vonnegut finds himself trying to write a book called Timequake, which he knows he will never finish since he already did not finish it.

"The cataclysm of the title--in 2001, time undergoes a tremor, and everyone must relive the nineties--provides an excuse for Vonnegut and his longtime alter ego, Kilgore Trout, to trade rants: on desert camouflage, thirties socialism, the joys of waiting in line at the post office, the traitorousness of Dillinger's Hungarian girlfriend, semicolons. The resulting quilt of snippets is equal parts memoir, literary charm, self-congratulation, humanist sermon, randy geriatric fantasy, and toastmasterly jokefest." The New Yorker.

Vonnegut, Kurt

Welcome to the monkey house / Kurt Vonnegut. Delta, 1998, c1968. 352 p.

ISBN 0385333501

1. Near future 2. Religion 3. Birth control 4. Censorship 5. Human nature 6. Short stories 7. Satirical fiction 8. Science fiction

Originally published: New York : Delacorte, 1968.

Tender stories of love, incisive esays on human greed and misery, and imaginative tales of futuristic happenings reveal Vonnegut's versatility and vision.

Vonnegut, Kurt

While mortals sleep : unpublished short fiction / Kurt Vonnegut. Delacorte Press, 2011. xii, 253 p.

ISBN 9780385343732

1. Social isolation 2. Technology 3. Ethics 4. Short stories

LC 2010033817

An anthology of sixteen previously unpublished works includes selections from the iconic writer's early literary career and is complemented by more than a dozen of his original works of art.

"In well over a dozen novels and hundreds of short stories, Vonnegut wrote about the madness of war and about alienation in the modern machine age. When he died in 2007, he was acclaimed as a great American writer with a signature style. [This] is the second collection of his previously unpublished short stories. Written early in his career, they are concerned less with war and corporate malfeasance than with the pursuit of success, happiness and love. Vintage Vonnegut, for better and worse, they put characters, settings and stories in the service of moral messages. At their best, these messages achieve a simple and powerful eloquence." Pittsburgh Post-Gazette.

Vreeland, Susan

Clara and Mr. Tiffany : a novel / Susan Vreeland. Random House, 2011. xiii, 405 p.

ISBN 9781400068166

1. Driscoll, Clara, 1861-1944 2. Tiffany, Louis Comfort, 1848-1933 3. Tiffany and Company, New York 4. Gilded Age (1865-1898) 5. 19th century 6. Women glass artists 7. Widows 8. Glass artists 9. Women employees 10. Gender role 11. Historical fiction 12.

Biographical fiction

LC 2010007758

Hoping to honor his father and the family business with innovative glass designs, Louis Comfort Tiffany launches the Tiffany lamp as designed by women's division head Clara Driscoll, who struggles with the mass production of her creations.

"Vreeland traces the secret history of an objet d'art . . . the iconic Tiffany lamp. Her heroine is Clara Driscoll, head of the all-female glass-cutting department at Tiffany Studios, who designed many of the fanciful, nature-inspired leaded-glass lamps for which Louis Comfort Tiffany earned fame. . . . Through Driscoll's life, Vreeland offers a fascinating look at turn-of-the-century New York City." People

Vreeland, Susan

Girl in hyacinth blue / Susan Vreeland MacMurray & Beck, 1999. 242 p.

ISBN 9781878448903

1. Vermeer, Johannes, 1632-1675 2. 20th century 3. 19th century 4. 18th century 5. 17th century 6. Artists -- Netherlands -- History -- 17th century 7. Jewish girls 8. Art thefts 9. Children of artists 10. College teachers 11. Children of Nazis 12. Fathers and daughters 13. Ownership 14. Memories 15. Men/women relations 16. Netherlands -- Social life and customs 17. Amsterdam, Netherlands 18. Delft, Netherlands 19. Biographical fiction 20. Literary fiction

LC 99027405

Chronicles the history of a painting and the lives with which it intersects, from the artist's inspiration to its admiration by two art scholars three hundred years later.

"Vreeland strikes a pleasing balance between the timeless world of the painting as a work of art and the finite worlds of its possessors and admirers--not to mention the world of its subject and its creator. Intelligent, searching and unusual, the novel is filled with luminous moments; like the painting it describes so well, it has a way of lingering in the reader's mind." New York Times Book Review.

Vreeland, Susan

Luncheon of the boating party / Susan Vreeland. Viking, 2007. xii, 434 p.

ISBN 9780670038541

1. Renoir, Auguste, 1841-1919 2. Renoir, Auguste, 1841-1919 Luncheon of the boating party 3. Belle Epoque (1871-1914) 4. 19th century 5. Painters -- France 6. Impressionism (Art) 7. Upper class 8. Artists -- 19th century 9. Men/women relations 10. Love 11. Love triangles 12. Engaged persons 13. Interpersonal attraction 14. Love stories 15. Historical fiction

LC 2006035324

Meeting his closest friends for a summer lunch on a cafe terrace along the Seine, master Impressionist painter Auguste Renoir undertakes the most challenging project of his career while struggling with the issues that are polarizing post-Franco-Prussian War France.

"In this novel Vreeland turns to French impressionist master Auguste Renoir's famous painting Luncheon of the Boating Party , which depicts a group of people (in 1880) enjoying leisure time on the terrace of a riverside restaurant. The current conditions in the life of the painter himself launch the author on an amazingly engrossing reinvigoration of the lives of the individuals who modeled for Renoir for that work, all of whom were actual people, and all are given a third dimension in Vreeland's lovely prose." Booklist.

Vreeland, Susan

The **passion** of Artemisia / Susan Vreeland. Viking, 2002. 288 p.

ISBN 0670894494

1. Gentileschi, Artemisia, 1593-1652 or 3 2. 17th century 3. Art, Baroque -- Italy 4. Women painters 5. Fathers and daughters 6. Rape 7. Trials 8. Ambition in women 9. Anger in women 10. Art and society 11. Women artists 12. Italy -- History -- 17th century 13. Biographical fiction 14. Historical fiction

LC 2001026119

From patronage by the Medicis, friendship with Galileo and beautiful and original paintings, to rape by her father's colleague, torture by the Inquisition, struggles for acceptance by the artistic establishment and betrayal by the men she loved, Susan Vreeland brings Artemisia's intensely moving story to vivid life.

"Vreeland palpably captures Artemisia's joy as she blends colors and watches her artistic imaginings take shape. . . . Although her final confrontation with her father, artist Orazio Gentileschi, feels forced, the novel brilliantly captures the life of an extraordinary artist." Library Journal.

Vuong, Ocean, 1988-

* **On** Earth we're briefly gorgeous : a novel / Ocean Vuong. Penguin Press, 2019. 246 p.

ISBN 9780525562023

1. Mothers and sons 2. Immigration and emigration 3. Vietnamese Americans 4. Teenage boy/boy relations 5. Single mothers 6. Adult child abuse victims 7. Letter writing 8. Growing up 9. Vietnam War, 1961-1975 10. Refugees, Vietnamese 11. Loss (Psychology) 12. Extended families 13. Mental illness 14. Authors 15. Poets 16. Literary fiction 17. Coming-of-age stories 18. Epistolary novels

LC 2018046290

ALA Notable Book, 2020.

Kirkus Prize for Fiction finalist, 2019.

Longlisted for the National Book Award for Fiction, 2019.

A letter from a son to a mother who cannot read reveals the impact of the Vietnam War on their family history and provides a view into parts of the son's life that his mother has never known.

Vyleta, Dan

Smoke : a novel / Dan Vyleta. Doubleday, 2016. 431 p. Smoke

ISBN 9780385540162

1. Victorian era (1837-1901) 2. Social classes 3. Power (Social sciences) 4. Friendship 5. Political intrigue 6. Good and evil 7. Violence in men 8. Life change events 9. Quests 10. Love triangles 11. Aristocracy 12. Boarding schools 13. Class conflict 14. Secrets 15. England 16. Historical fantasy

LC 2015037301

A tale set in an alternate 19th-century England where the lower classes emit smoke from their bodies that is believed to reflect wicked natures, three students at an elite boarding school for future leaders make discoveries that could cost them their lives.

"Vyleta imagines an alternative turn-of-the-century England where the proletariat and aristocratic classes are further divided by the relationship to Smoke, the manifestation of sin that flows from the body as blackened breath or ashen sweat whenever someone thinks or acts immorally." Booklist.

W

Wade, Becky

Falling for you / Becky Wade. Bethany House, 2018. 368 p. Bradford sisters

ISBN 9780764219375

1. Mate selection 2. Innkeepers 3. Missing persons investigation 4. Fashion models 5. Quarterbacks (Football) 6. Inns 7. Women innkeepers 8. Cold cases (Criminal investigation) 9. Single women 10. Men/women relations 11. Interpersonal attraction 12. Christian romances 13. Contemporary romances

LC 2017963578

Christy Award for Contemporary Romance Category, 2019.

Willow Bradford is content taking a break from modeling to run her family's inn until she comes face-to-face with NFL quarterback Corbin Stewart, the man who broke her heart--and wants to win her back. When a decades-old family mystery brings them together, they're forced to decide whether they can risk falling for one another all over again.

Wade, Becky

* **True** to you / Becky Wade. Bethany House, 2017. 368 p. Bradford sisters

ISBN 9780764219368

1. Single women 2. Genealogy 3. Former Navy SEALs 4. Veterans 5. Birthparents 6. Sisters 7. Men/women relations 8. Interpersonal attraction 9. Mate selection 10. Christian romances

LC 2016050049

Christy Award for Book of the Year, 2018.
Christy Award for Contemporary Romance Category, 2018.

Genealogist and historical village owner Nora Bradford throws herself into her work following a heartbreak, until she meets former Navy SEAL John Lawson, who seeks her out when he suddenly needs to find his birth parents.

Wagers, K. B.

After the crown / K.B. Wagers. Orbit, 2016. 432 p. Indranan war

ISBN 9780316308632

1. Smugglers 2. Space vehicles 3. Conspiracies 4. Alliances 5. Betrayal 6. Trust 7. Rulers 8. Women rulers 9. Heirs and heiresses 10. Assassination 11. Space opera 12. Science fiction

Former gunrunner-turned-Empress Hail Bristol discovers the work of a traitor when peaceful alliance efforts with neighboring worlds turn violent.

Wagers, K. B.

There before the chaos / K. B. Wagers. Orbit, 2018. 465 p. Farian war

ISBN 9780316411219

1. Women rulers 2. Political intrigue 3. Imaginary empires 4. Aliens 5. Rulers 6. Interplanetary relations 7. Imaginary wars and battles 8. Space opera 9. Science fiction

LC 2018026314

Retiring her gun to rebuild her Empire, former runaway princess and infamous galactic gunrunner Hail Bristol finds her hard-won peace short-lived when she is asked to intervene in an interstellar military crisis between two alien civilizations.

"This series launch provides an exciting dose of space opera and political intrigue peppered with hard choices. Highly recommended for fans of science fiction with assertive female characters." Booklist.

Waite, Olivia

* The **lady's** guide to celestial mechanics / Olivia Waite. Avon Impulse, 2019. 322 p.

ISBN 9780062931795

1. Regency period (1811-1820) 2. Widows 3. Women scientists 4. Interpersonal attraction 5. Astronomy 6. Celestial mechanics 7. Mathematics 8. Nobility 9. Women/women relations 10. Great Britain -- History -- Regency, 1811-1820 11. England -- Social life and customs -- 19th century 12. Great Britain -- History -- 19th century 13. Regency romances 14. LGBTQIA romances 15. Historical romances

Hired to translate a French treatise on celestial mechanics, aspiring astronomer Lucy Muchelney finds herself drawn to her employer, the widowed Catherine St. Day, Countess of Moth. -- Description by Gillian Speace.

Wakefield, Dan

* **Starting** over Delacorte Press, 1973. 290 p.

1. Divorce 2. Literary fiction

LC 73001930

"A powerful, naturalistic depiction of the agony suffered by a man whose affluence merely conceals an utter absence of value and direction." Library Journal.

Walbert, Kate, 1961-

She was like that : new and selected stories / Kate Walbert. Scribner, 2019. 288 p.

ISBN 9781476799421

1. Maternal love 2. Motherhood 3. Anxiety in women 4. Female friendship 5. Single mothers 6. Short stories 7. Literary fiction

From the National Book Award finalist and national best-selling author of A Short History of Women and His Favorites comes a career-spanning collection of new and selected stories.

Waldman, Amy, 1969-

A **door** in the earth / Amy Waldman. Little Brown & Company, 2019. 400 p.

ISBN 9780316451574

1. Women college graduates 2. War and society 3. Deception 4. Clinics 5. Voyages and travels 6. Rural life 7. Afghan Americans 8. Afghan War, 2001- 9. Villages 10. Options, alternatives, choices 11. Afghanistan 12. Political fiction 13. Literary fiction

An Afghan-American college student in California travels to a remote village in Afghanistan to work for a professor's charitable foundation and after surviving a horrific bombing must side with either the villagers or the American soldiers.

Walker, Alice, 1944-

* The **color** purple : a novel / Alice Walker. Harcourt Brace Jovanovich, 1982. 245 p.

ISBN 9780151191536

1. African American women -- Southern States 2. Separated friends, relatives, etc 3. Loyalty in women 4. African American lesbians -- Southern States 5. Sisters -- Southern States 6. Husband and wife 7. Family relationships 8. Southern States 9. Epistolary novels 10. African American fiction 11. Literary fiction 12. Modern classics 13. Southern fiction

LC 81048242

National Book Award for Fiction, 1983.
Pulitzer Prize for Fiction, 1983.
National Book Critics Circle Award for Fiction finalist, 1982

The lives of two sisters--Nettie, a missionary in Africa, and Celie, a southern woman married to a man she hates--are revealed in a series of letters exchanged over thirty years.

Walker, Alice, 1944-

Possessing the secret of joy / Alice Walker Harcourt Brace Jovanovich, 1992. 286 p.

ISBN 0151731527

1. African American women -- Psychotherapy 2. Clitoridectomy 3. Grief in women 4. African American women with mental illnesses 5. Revenge 6. Anger in women 7. African American women 8. Infibulation -- Africa 9. African American fiction 10. Literary fiction
LC 92006883

Severely traumatized after suffering genital mutilation in her native Africa, Tashi Johnson spends much of her adult life in North America seeking help through psychoanalysis and desperate to regain the ability to feel.

"The people in Ms. Walker's book are archetypes rather than characters as we have come to expect them in the 20th-century novel, and this is by defiant intention. . . . When the novel is operating genuinely on this archetypal level, it has a mythic strength. Its many voices are not rendered as stream-of-consciousness monologues, nor are they made to belong to distinct individuals. Instead, they are highly stylized, operatic, prophetic -- and powerfully poetic." New York Times Book Review.

Walker, Alice, 1944-

The **temple** of my familiar / Alice Walker. Washington Square Press, 1997, c1989. 417 p.

ISBN 0671003763

1. African American women 2. Ethnic identity 3. Self-discovery 4. African Americans 5. Men/women relations 6. African American seniors 7. African American musicians 8. African American men/women relations 9. African Americans -- Identity 10. Africa 11. England 12. North Carolina 13. San Francisco, California 14. Epic fiction 15. African American fiction 16. Literary fiction
LC 96042427

Originally published: San Diego : Harcourt Brace Jovanovich, 1989.

In a story that moves through America, England, and Africa, men, women, and animals share a spiritual world and learn the intricacies of their connecting lives.

"This is a novel only in a loose sense. Rather, it is a mixture of mythic fantasy, revisionary history, exemplary biography and sermon. It is short on narrative tension, long on inspirational message." New York Times Book Review.

Walker, Alice, 1944-

The **third** life of Grange Copeland / Alice Walker. Pocket Books, 1988, c1970. 346 p.

ISBN 9780671745882

1. Family violence 2. African American families 3. Fathers and sons 4. African-American tenant farmers 5. African American men 6. Family relationships 7. Georgia 8. Family sagas 9. Literary fiction 10. African American fiction 11. Southern fiction
LC 79117577

In Georgia during the 1920s, Grange Copeland creates and sustains a dream for his granddaughter in the midst of African American dehumanization.

Walker, Alice, 1944-

You can't keep a good woman down : stories / Alice Walker Harcourt Brace Jovanovich, 1981. 167 p.

ISBN 0151997543

1. Women 2. African American women 3. African American fiction

4. Short stories
LC 80008761

Thirteen short stories, including a political dialogue between two young black women as they meet over the years, explore the African-American experience in contemporary America, probing into relations between races and between sexes.

Walker, Caroline Louise

Man of the year / Caroline Louise Walker. Gallery Books, 2019. 256 p.

ISBN 9781982100452

1. Married people 2. Fathers and sons 3. Jealousy 4. Physicians 5. Suspicion 6. Personal conduct 7. Men with paranoia 8. Dishonesty 9. Trust 10. Self-destructive behavior 11. Houseguests 12. College friends 13. Dysfunctional families 14. Identity (Psychology) 15. Awards, prizes, honors, etc 16. New York (State) 17. Sag Harbor, New York 18. Psychological suspense
LC 2018049693

Offering shelter to a former college roommate, a doctor who has just been named Sag Harbor's Man of the Year reveals a dark inner nature when he develops paranoid suspicions about his wife's fidelity.

Walker, Karen Thompson

* The **age** of miracles : a novel / Karen Thompson Walker. Random House, 2012. 320 p.

ISBN 9780812992977

1. Teenage girls 2. Climate change 3. Environmental disasters 4. Teenage boy/girl relations 5. Family problems 6. Near future 7. California 8. Earth -- Rotation 9. Coming-of-age stories 10. Apocalyptic fiction 11. Science fiction
LC 2011040664

Julia's world is thrown into upheaval when it is discovered that the Earth's rotation has suddenly begun to slow, posing a catastrophic threat to all life.

Walker, Karen Thompson

The **dreamers** / Karen Thompson Walker. Random House, 2019 303 p.

ISBN 9780812994162

1. Epidemics 2. Sleep disorders 3. College students 4. Universities and colleges 5. Interpersonal relations 6. Dreams 7. Sleep 8. California 9. Southern California 10. Apocalyptic fiction 11. Literary fiction

Presents the story of a student in an isolated Southern California college town who witnesses a strange sleeping illness that subjects patients to life-altering, heightened dreams.

"Walker jolts the narrative with surprising twists, ensuring it keeps its energy until the end. This is a skillful, complex, and thoroughly satisfying novel about a community in peril." Publishers Weekly.

Walker, Margaret, 1915-1998

* **Jubilee** Houghton, 1966. 497 p.

1. African Americans 2. Plantation life 3. Civil war 4. United States Civil War, 1861-1865 5. United States -- History -- Civil War, 1861-1865 6. Georgia -- History -- Civil War, 1861-1865 7. African American fiction 8. Modern classics 9. Southern fiction
LC 66011218

In the South, freed people, poor whites, and landowners survive the Civil War and begin Reconstruction.

Walker, Nico,

* **Cherry** : a novel / Nico Walker. Knopf, 2018. 272 p.
ISBN 9780525520139

1. Veterans 2. Drug addicts 3. Bank robberies 4. Iraq War veterans 5. Iraq War, 2003-2011 6. Identity (Psychology) 7. Post traumatic stress disorder 8. Ohio 9. Literary fiction 10. Autobiographical fiction

LC 2017056634

Rashly marrying his college girlfriend to keep their relationship active during his tour of duty, a college dropout turned army soldier is overwhelmed by the realities of war, PTSD and opioid addiction before forging a desperate plan.

"A raging, agonized scream of a novel and a tremendously powerful debut." Library Journal.

Walker, Sarai

Dietland / Sarai Walker. Houghton Mifflin Harcourt, 2015. 272 p.

ISBN 9780544373433

1. Overweight women 2. Self-esteem in women 3. Women radicals 4. Nonconformists 5. Revenge 6. Violence 7. Feminists 8. Obesity -- Surgery 9. Femininity 10. Beauty 11. Satirical fiction

LC 2014026803

Biding her time alone until she can have weight-loss surgery, Plum joins an underground community of empowered women and agrees to a series of challenges, including work with a group that stages anti-misogyny terrorist acts.

"Through her protagonist, debut novelist Walker gives a plaintive yet powerful voice to anyone who has struggled with body image, feelings of marginalization, and sexual manipulation. Her robust satire also vibrantly redefines what it means to be a woman in contemporary society." Booklist.

Walker, Walter

Crime of privilege / Walter Walker. Ballantine Books, 2013. 416 p.

ISBN 9780345541536

1. Murder 2. Rape 3. Power (Social sciences) 4. Crime 5. Lawyers 6. Secrets 7. Rich families 8. Cold cases (Criminal investigation) 9. Police corruption 10. Palm Beach, Florida 11. Cape Cod, Massachusetts 12. Thrillers and suspense 13. Legal thrillers

Pitted against a powerful family when he reopens the scandalous case of a young woman's unsolved murder, George Becket is forced to confront a haunting mistake from his own past while outmaneuvering wealth-driven corruption.

Walker, Wendy, 1967-

All is not forgotten / Wendy Walker. St. Martin's Press, 2016. 352 p.

ISBN 9781250097910

1. Psychiatrists 2. Rape 3. Amnesia 4. Memory 5. Rich families 6. Assault and battery 7. Psychotherapy 8. Young women 9. Obsession in men 10. Connecticut 11. Psychological suspense

LC 2016000031

"In the small, affluent town of Fairview, Connecticut, everything seems picture perfect. Until one night when young Jenny Kramer is attacked at a local party. In the hours immediately after, she is given a controversial drug to medically erase her memory of the violent assault. But, in the weeks and months that follow, as she heals from her physical wounds, and with no factual recall of the attack, Jenny struggles with her raging emotional memory. Her father, Tom, becomes obsessed with his inability to find her attacker and seek justice while her mother, Charlotte, prefers to pretend this horrific event did not touch her perfect country club world. As they seek help for their daughter, the fault lines

within their marriage and their close-knit community emerge from the shadows where they have been hidden for years, and the relentless quest to find the monster who invaded their town - or perhaps lives among them - drive this psychological thriller to a shocking and unexpected conclusion."--, Provided by publisher.

Walker, Wendy, 1967-

Emma in the night / Wendy Walker. St Martin's Press, 2017. 320 p.

ISBN 9781250141439

1. Sisters 2. Missing teenage girls 3. Missing persons investigation 4. Dysfunctional families 5. Kidnapping victims 6. Former captives 7. Psychiatrists 8. Narcissism 9. Pedophilia 10. Deception 11. Psychological suspense

"One night three years ago, the Tanner sisters disappeared: fifteen-year-old Cass and seventeen-year-old Emma. Three years later, Cass returns, without her sister Emma. Her story is one of kidnapping and betrayal, of a mysterious island where the two were held. But to forensic psychiatrist Dr. Abby Winter, something doesn't add up. Looking deep within this dysfunctional family Dr. Winter uncovers a life where boundaries were violated and a narcissistic parent held sway. And where one sister's return might just be the beginning of the crime."--, Provided by publisher.

"Walkers second thriller (following All Is Not Forgotten, 2016) delves into dark territory, pitting a fully dimensional cast of clever, damaged characters against each other in high-stakes mind games." Booklist.

Wall, Cara

The **dearly** beloved : a novel / Cara Wall. Simon & Schuster, 2019. 342 p.

ISBN 9781982104528

1. 20th century 2. Clergy 3. Husband and wife 4. Individual differences 5. Social change 6. Faith (Christianity) 7. Romantic love 8. Friendship 9. Change (Psychology) 10. Marriage 11. Families 12. Belief and doubt 13. Greenwich Village, New York City 14. New York City 15. Historical fiction 16. Literary fiction

LC 2019000251

In a novel that spans decades, two young couples' lives become intertwined when the husbands are appointed co-ministers of a venerable New York City church in the 1960s.

Wallace, Carey, 1974-

The **blind** contessa's new machine / Carey Wallace. Pamela Dorman Books/Viking, 2010. 224 p.

ISBN 9780670021895

1. 19th century 2. Love triangles 3. Women who are blind 4. Inventors 5. Counts and countesses 6. Nobility 7. Typewriters 8. Eccentrics and eccentricities 9. Extramarital affairs 10. Italy -- History -- 19th century 11. Historical romances 12. Love stories

LC 2010003332

Unable to convince her family and desirable fiancé that she is going blind, early 19th-century Italian contessa Carolina Fantoni turns to her dreams and an eccentric local inventor when she loses her sight, inspiring the inventor's development of the first typewriter.

"The time is the late 19th century, the place the northern Italian countryside, where minor aristocrats flourish as abundantly as grapevines. A blooming rose, Contessa Carolina Fantoni is about to marry Pietro, a neighboring landowner. Neither Pietro nor her parents take her seriously, however, when Carolina tells them she is going blind. With a love deeper than Pietro's fickle infatuation, Carolina's devoted admirer, Turri, a local eccentric and amateur inventor, gives her a precious gift, the ability to communicate with an outside world locked out by her blindness and her overprotective husband. He invents a machine, the typewriter, which

Carolina uses to arrange their increasingly indiscreet and ill-fated assignations. A small gem of sensuality." Boston Globe.

Wallace, Daniel, 1959-

* **Big** fish : a novel of mythic proportions / Daniel Wallace. Algonquin Books Of Chapel Hill, 1998. 180 p.

ISBN 1565122178

1. Father and adult son 2. Family storytelling 3. Eccentrics and eccentricities 4. Men with terminal illnesses 5. Joking relationships 6. Fathers -- Death 7. Sales personnel 8. Alabama 9. Picaresque fiction

LC 9826216

When his attempts to get to know his dying father fail, William Bloom makes up stories that recreate his father's life in heroic proportions.

"In a plainspoken style dotted with transcendent passages, Wallace mixes the mundane and the mythical. His chapters have the transformative quality of fable and fairy tale, and the novel's roomy structure allows the mystery and lyricism of the story to coalesce." Publishers Weekly.

Wallace, Daniel, 1959-

Mr. Sebastian and the Negro magician / Daniel Wallace. Doubleday, 2007. 272 p.

ISBN 9780385521093

1. 1950s 2. Faustian bargains 3. Circus 4. Magicians 5. African Americans 6. African American men 7. Brothers and sisters 8. Magic 9. Storytelling 10. Loss (Psychology) 11. Southern States 12. Coming-of-age stories

LC 2006028103

Sir Walter Raleigh Award for Fiction, 2008.

Traveling through the Deep South in 1950 with Jeremiah Musgrove's Chinese Circus, magician Henry Walker finds himself in deep trouble with three angry white teenagers, while his friends from the circus describe how Henry received the gift of magic from the devil himself.

"The unraveling of a man's myth to illuminate the essence of his life is the charm of this accomplished and inventive novel." Paste.

Wallace, Daniel, 1959-

The **watermelon** king / Daniel Wallace. Houghton Mifflin, 2003. 226 p.

ISBN 0618221387

1. 1980s 2. 2000s (Decade) 3. Small town life -- Alabama 4. Fertility rites -- Alabama 5. Eccentrics and eccentricities 6. Watermelons -- Alabama 7. Young men -- Alabama 8. Grandfathers -- Death 9. Maternal deprivation 10. Alabama 11. Coming-of-age stories

LC 2002075941

Thomas Rider heads for Ashland, Alabama, to uncover the truth about his parents, and discovers a bizarre place whose fate is intertwined with that of their watermelon crop as well as the mysteries of his own identity.

"This is a unique and spellbinding novel, an unforgettable southern tall tale with extraordinary characters." Booklist.

Wallace, David Foster

* **Brief** interviews with hideous men / David Foster Wallace. Little, Brown, 1999. 273 p.

ISBN 9780316925419

1. Men/women relations 2. Men -- Sexuality 3. Sexuality 4. Short stories 5. Literary fiction

LC 9850944

23 short stories.

Twenty-two stories tell of a frightened boy frozen on a diving board, a depressed woman trying to find help, and a group of men who try to rationalize their relationships with women

Wallace, David Foster

* **Infinite** jest : a novel / David Foster Wallace. Little, Brown, 1996. xv, 1079 p.

ISBN 9780316920049

1. Films -- Influence 2. Addiction 3. Pleasure 4. Fathers -- Suicide 5. Dysfunctional families 6. Compulsive behavior 7. Halfway houses (for alcoholics, drug addicts, runaways, etc) 8. Group homes 9. Twelve-step programs 10. Tennis 11. Boston, Massachusetts 12. Quebec (Province) -- History -- Autonomy and independence movements 13. Satirical fiction

LC 2006934927

The story of an intelligent but zany dysfunctional family is set in a drug-and-alcohol addicts' halfway house and a tennis academy and follows such themes as heartbreak, philosophy, and advertising

"This novel is set sometime in the next century, on the grounds of a New England tennis academy and in a rehab clinic. Among other things, the book contains perhaps the most moving and hypnotic writing on the psychology of addiction and recovery to be found in modern fiction. There are obsessive riffs on sports, on drugs, and on the hidden horrors of entertainment: the title of the novel refers to the title of a movie that is said to be so 'terminally compelling' that viewers will watch it passively and repeatedly to the point of death. Comparisons with Pynchon are inevitable, and in this case they are fully justified." The New Yorker.

Wallace, David Foster

Oblivion : stories / David Foster Wallace. Little, Brown, 2004. 384 p.

ISBN 0316919810

1. Self-consciousness 2. Interpersonal relations 3. Short stories

LC 2003027135

8 short stories

A collection of short stories includes "The Soul Is Not a Smithy," in which a father distracts his son from noticing a teacher's breakdown; and "The Suffering Channel," in which a sculpture artist's profile is influenced by office politics.

"Unpacking our inner lives with empathy and care, Oblivion showcases the incredibly rich textures and crystalline clarity of Wallace's prose, confirming the singular genius of his expansive imagination and resonating with the complexities of minds in motion. American Book Review

Wallace, David Foster

* The **pale** king : an unfinished novel / David Foster Wallace. Little, Brown and Co., 2011. 432 p.

ISBN 9780316074230

1. United States. Internal Revenue Service Officials and employees 2. Boredom 3. Meaning (Psychology) 4. Happiness 5. Interpersonal relations 6. Occupations 7. Purpose in life 8. Illinois 9. Satirical fiction 10. Literary fiction

LC 2010045489

Pulitzer Prize for Fiction finalist, 2012.

Partially written before his death, author David Foster Wallace presents a fictitious version of himself as the protagonist in his final novel. When Wallace arrives for training at the IRS Regional Examination Center in Peoria, Illinois, everything appears normal. However, as Wallace quickly learns, normal just isn't the case. From the bizarre boredom-survival training to the wild personalities among his co-workers, Wallace is convinced the IRS is determined to dehumanize and humiliate him.

Wallace, Lew, 1827-1905

* Ben-Hur / Lew Wallace ; edited and with an introduction and notes by David Mayer. Oxford University Press, 1998. 530 p.

ISBN 0192831992

1. Jesus Christ 2. Bible. New Testament History of Biblical events. 3. Roman Empire (27 BCE-476 CE) 4. 1st century 5. Jews -- History -- To 70 AD 6. Slaves -- Rome 7. Chariot-racing 8. Revenge 9. Judaea (Region) 10. Palestine -- History -- To 70 AD 11. Rome -- History -- Tiberius, 14-37 12. Historical fiction 13. Bible novels 14. Classics

First published 1880.

Includes chronology.

Details how a wealthy young Jewish man and his family, who are all experiencing changing fortunes under Roman tyranny, are affected by the life and teachings of a Nazarene named Jesus Christ.

Wallace, Melanie, 1949-

The **girl** in the garden / Melanie Wallace. Houghton Mifflin Harcourt, 2017. 240 p.

ISBN 9780544784666

1. 1970s 2. Abandoned women 3. Single mothers 4. Coastal towns 5. Small town life 6. Motels 7. Loss (Psychology) 8. Secrets 9. Interpersonal relations 10. New England 11. Mainstream fiction

LC 2015043036

Abandoned in a seaside motel and offered shelter in the home of the manager's friend, a young woman with an infant son is integrated into the lives of long-time locals and starts over amid revelations of loves and crimes from the past.

"Wallace's (The Housekeeper, 2006) poignant novel is, at once, a portrait of a small, coastal, New England town; a bit of a mystery; and a completely engaging study of an odd mix of characters whose lives become intricately intertwined." Booklist.

Wallant, Edward Lewis, 1926-1962

The **pawnbroker** / Edward Lewis Wallant. Harcourt Brace Jovanovich, 1978, c1961. 279 p.

ISBN 0156714221

1. Holocaust (1933-1945) 2. Holocaust survivors 3. Jewish men 4. Loss (Psychology) 5. Pawnbrokers 6. Ethics 7. Indifference (Personal quality) 8. Psychological fiction

LC 78007101

Left as an emotional zombie after witnessing the murder of his family during the Nazi Holocaust, a Harlem pawnbroker runs his shop as a front for organized crime.

Waller, Robert James, 1939-2017

* The bridges of Madison County / Robert James Waller. Warner Books, 1992. 171 p.

ISBN 044651652X

1. 1960s 2. Extramarital affairs 3. Lovers 4. Romantic love 5. Photographers 6. Middle-aged women 7. Italian American women 8. Farms 9. Covered bridges 10. Men/women relations 11. Iowa 12. Love stories 13. Mainstream fiction

LC 91050416

Sequel: A thousand country roads.

Book Sense Book of the Year Adult Trade, 1993.

A novel about the profound love between a photographer and an Iowa farmer's wife. They spend only four days together while he is on location to photograph covered bridges for National Geographic magazine, yet they never lose their feelings for each other.

"An erotic, bittersweet tale of lingering memories and forsaken possibilities." Publishers Weekly.

Walls, Jeannette

Half broke horses : a true-life novel / Jeannette Walls. Scribner, 2009. 288 p.

ISBN 9781416586289

1. Smith, Lily Casey, 1901-1968 2. Growing up 3. Determination (Personal quality) 4. Survival 5. Teachers 6. Marriage 7. Ranches 8. Family relationships 9. The West (United States) 10. Biographical fiction

LC 2009018781

Presents a novel based on the life of the author's grandmother, Lily Casey Smith, who learned to break horses in childhood, journeyed five hundred miles as a teen to become a teacher, and ran a vast ranch in Arizona with her husband while raising two children.

"Walls novelizes the life of her grandmother. Lily Casey Smith is one astonishing woman, tough enough to trot her pony across several hundred miles of desert to her first job when she's only a teenager. After a brief stint in Chicago and marriage to a flimflam man, she's back in the West, teaching again and eventually remarrying, helping her fine new husband at the gas station, raising her children, and running hootch if she must to make ends meet during the Depression. Her story is at once simple and utterly remarkable. . . . Told in a natural, offhand voice that is utterly enthralling, this is essential reading for anyone who loves good fiction--or any work about the American West." Library Journal.

Walls, Jeannette

The **silver** star : a novel / Jeannette Walls. Scribner, 2013. 288 p.

ISBN 9781451661507

1. 1970s 2. Mother-deserted children 3. Sisters 4. Self-discovery in teenagers 5. Small towns -- Virginia 6. Mothers and daughters 7. Uncle and niece 8. Family secrets 9. Women artists 10. Widowers 11. Virginia 12. Coming-of-age stories 13. Mainstream fiction

LC 2012050790

First published: Great Britain: Simon & Schuster UK Ltd., 2013.

Abandoned by their artist mother at the age of 12, Bean and her older sister, Liz, are sent to live in the decaying antebellum mansion of their widowed uncle, where they learn the truth about their parents and take odd jobs to earn extra money before an increasingly withdrawn Liz has a life-shattering experience.

"[A] captivating, read-in-one-sitting, coming-of-age adventure." Booklist.

Walser, Robert, 1878-1956

The **assistant** / Robert Walser ; translated from the German by Susan Bernofsky ; with an afterword by the translator. New Directions, 2007, c1908. 320 p.

ISBN 9780811215909

1. Coworkers 2. Business partners 3. Inventors 4. Interpersonal relations 5. Helpfulness in men 6. Men/women relations 7. Financial crises 8. Helplessness (Psychology) 9. Psychological fiction 10. Translations -- German to English

LC 2007006865

Originally published in 1908.

Joseph, hired to become an inventor's new assistant, arrives one rainy Monday morning at Technical Engineer Karl Tobler's splendid hilltop villa: he is at once pleased and terribly worried, a state soon followed by even stickier psychological complexities. He enjoys the beautiful view over Lake Zurich, in the company of the proud wife, Frau Tobler, and the delicious savory meals. But does he deserve any of these pleasures?

Walsh, Helen

Brass / Helen Walsh. Canongate, 2004. 292 p.
ISBN 1841954845

1. College students 2. Women college students 3. College students -- Sexuality 4. Self-destructive behavior in women 5. Men/women relations 6. Drug use 7. Drugs 8. Street life 9. Women -- Sexuality 10. Prostitution 11. Lesbians -- Sexuality 12. Hedonism 13. Children of divorced parents 14. Liverpool, England 15. Psychological fiction 16. Erotic fiction

"What sets this first novel apart within a burgeoning subgenre is Walsh's lyrical prose. Her evocative phrasing both contains and stands in direct contrast to incredibly graphic scenes of depravity, and the result is both disturbing and compelling." Booklist.

Walsh, M. O. (Milton O'Neal)

My sunshine away / M. O. Walsh. G. P. Putnam's Sons, 2015. 320 p.
ISBN 9780399169526

1. 1980s 2. Rape victims 3. First loves 4. Neighborhoods 5. Teenagers 6. Families 7. Rape 8. Suspicion 9. Obsession 10. Memory 11. Baton Rouge, Louisiana 12. Louisiana 13. Coming-of-age stories 14. Literary fiction 15. Southern fiction

A man reflects on the summer of his fourteenth year, where in Baton Rouge he fell in love with a golden-haired girl across the street before an unspeakable crime shattered illusions in his seemingly idyllic neighborhood.

"Suspenseful, compassionate, and absorbing, Walsh's word-perfect rendering of the doubts, insecurities, bravado, and idealism of teens deserves to be placed in the hands of readers of Tom Franklin, Hannah Pittard, and Jeffrey Eugenides." Booklist.

Walter, Jess, 1965-

* Beautiful ruins : a novel / Jess Walter. Harper, 2012. 337 p.
ISBN 9780061928123

1. 1960s 2. 21st century 3. Film actors and actresses 4. Hotels 5. Unrequited love 6. Screenwriters 7. Italy 8. Mainstream fiction 9. Parallel narratives

The story of an almost-love affair that begins on the Italian coast in 1962 ... and is rekindled in Hollywood fifty years later, featuring an Italian housekeeper and his long-lost American starlet, the producer who once brought them together, and his assistant.

Walter, Jess, 1965-

Citizen Vince : a novel / Jess Walter. ReganBooks, 2004. 320 p.
ISBN 0060394412

1. Carter, Jimmy, 1924- 2. Reagan, Ronald 3. Gotti, John 4. 1980s 5. Criminals 6. Voting 7. Federal Witness Protection Program 8. Informers 9. Bakers 10. Redemption 11. Presidents -- United States -- Election -- 1980 12. Mafia 13. Police -- Spokane, Washington 14. Crime 15. Men/women relations 16. Spokane, Washington 17. New York City 18. Noir fiction 19. Crime fiction 20. Pacific Northwest fiction

LC 2004046828

Edgar Allen Poe Award for Best Mystery Novel, 2006.

Beginning his witness-protection job at a doughnut restaurant in the week before the 1980 presidential election, small-time thief Vince Camden finds himself unwittingly embroiled in a local politician's troubles.

Walter, Jess, 1965-

The financial lives of the poets : a novel / Jess Walter. Harper, 2009. 290 p.
ISBN 9780061916045

1. Personal finance 2. Entrepreneurs 3. Debt 4. Husband and wife 5. Money-making projects 6. Family relationships 7. Mainstream fiction

Matt Prior is losing his job, his wife, and his house, and he's about to lose his mind--until he discovers a way that he might possibly be able to save it all.

Walters, Minette

The last hours : a novel / Minette Walters. MIRA, 2018, c2017. 608 p. Last hours
ISBN 9780778369318

1. Medieval period (476-1492) 2. Civilization, Medieval 3. Black death 4. Plague 5. Women rulers 6. Independence in women 7. Aristocracy 8. Intrigue 9. Church and state 10. England -- History -- Medieval period, 1066-1485 11. Historical fiction

Originally published: Sydney : Allen & Unwin, 2017.

When the Black Death enters England in June of 1348, Lady Anne decides to quarantine her estate of Develish, including two hundred bonded serfs she must bring inside the walls. But with this sudden overturning of the accepted social order, where serfs exist only to serve their lords, conflicts soon arise and a dreadful event threatens the safety of everyone inside the walls.

Walton, Jo

* Among others / Jo Walton. Tor, 2011. 304 p.
ISBN 9780765321534

1. Young women 2. Mothers and daughters 3. Spells (Magic) 4. Books and reading 5. Enchantment 6. Magic 7. England 8. Contemporary fantasy 9. Fantasy fiction

LC 2010036108

"A Tom Doherty Associates book."

Hugo Award for Best Novel, 2012.

Nebula Award for Best Novel, 2011.

Seeking refuge in fantasy novel worlds throughout a youth under the shadow of a dubiously sane mother who dabbled in magic, Mori Phelps is forced to confront her in a tragic battle and gains unwanted attention when she attempts to perform spells herself.

Walton, Jo

Farthing / Jo Walton. Tor, 2006. 320 p. Small change
ISBN 0765314215

1. 1940s 2. 20th century 3. Police -- Great Britain 4. Country homes 5. Nobility 6. Murder 7. World War II 8. Jewish men 9. Prejudice 10. Interfaith marriage 11. Antisemitism 12. Murder suspects 13. Malicious accusation 14. Men/women relations 15. Fascism 16. London, England 17. Alternative histories 18. Mysteries

LC 2005034487

"A Tom Doherty Associates book."

Sequel : Ha'penny.

In an alternate post-World War II London in which an upper-crust political group has overthrown Churchill and negotiated peace with Hitler, Lucy, ostracized since her marriage to a Jewish man, is unexpectedly invited to a family gathering only to find her husband framed for a ritualistic murder.

"An excellent example of alternate history." Library Journal.

Walton, Jo,

* **Lent** / Jo Walton. Tor Book, 2019. 320 p.

ISBN 9780765379061

1. Savonarola, Girolamo, 1452-1498 2. Medici, Lorenzo de', 1449-1492 3. Renaissance (1300-1600) 4. Priests 5. Demons 6. Prophecy 7. God (Christianity) 8. Spirituality 9. Magic rocks 10. Redemption 11. Heresy 12. Philosophy 13. European Renaissance 14. Florence, Italy -- History -- 15th century 15. Italy -- History -- 15th century 16. Europe -- History -- 1492-1648 17. Historical fantasy

LC 2019006678

"A Tom Doherty Associates Book."

Possessing the supernatural ability to see and cast out demons, Girolamo Savanarola of 15th-century Florence organizes seemingly miraculous peace initiatives and delivers soul-transforming sermons before enthralled crowds, inciting the wrath of the pope.

Walton, Jo

My real children / Jo Walton. Tor, 2014. 320 p.

ISBN 9780765332653

1. 20th century 2. 2010s 3. Senior women 4. Near future 5. Memories 6. Options, alternatives, choices 7. Identity (Psychology) 8. Parallel universes 9. Nuclear warfare 10. Uncertainty 11. Change 12. Moon -- Colonization 13. Social science fiction 14. Alternative histories 15. Science fiction

James Tiptree, Jr. Award, 2014.

RUSA Reading List, 2015.

Ninety-year-old Patricia Cowan has two sets of memories, not to mention two different families who come to visit her in the nursing home (where her room sometimes has navy blue curtains, sometimes pale green blinds). Although her caregivers believe that she suffers from dementia, Patricia suspects that her life decisions may, in fact, have changed history and created two distinct, branching timelines. In one reality, "Trish" becomes an unhappily married mother of four with an abiding interest in local politics; in the other, "Pat" becomes a writer, finding love and happiness with a woman named Bee. Which world, if any, is "real" -- and does it even matter? -- Description by Gillian Speace.

"[A] quiet triumph, not least because whatever life Patricia happens to be living at any given moment, she remains deeply and recognizably herself. Good novels show us a character's destiny as an expression of who they fundamentally are. What most novels do only once, My Real Children does twice." Publishers Weekly.

Walton, Jo

* **Necessity** / Jo Walton. Tor, 2016. 320 p. Just city novels

ISBN 9780765379023

1. Gods and goddesses, Greek 2. Fathers and daughters 3. Social conflict 4. Voyages and travels 5. Civilization, Ancient 6. Grief in men 7. Time travel 8. Humanists 9. Athena (Greek deity) 10. Apollo (Greek deity) 11. Thera (Islands) 12. Ancient Greece 13. Mythological fiction 14. Science fiction

"The conclusion to The Just City and The Philosopher Kings" --, Dust cover.

"As before, Walton has done a superb job of world building and character development, giving readers a novel that both stimulates and satisfies." Booklist.

Wambaugh, Joseph

The **blue** knight / Joseph Wambaugh. Little, 1972. 338p.

ISBN 0316921467

1. Police 2. Criminals 3. Crime 4. Retirement 5. Los Angeles, California 6. California 7. Thrillers and suspense 8. Police procedurals

LC 79175474

"An Atlantic Monthly Press book."

Three days before Bumper Morgan is to retire from the police force, he becomes caught up in a series of crimes and finds easy decisions difficult to make.

"The caricature is deliberate; the author means to endow a stereotype with complexity and sentiment. Bumper has his own street ethics. . . . The book tends to be a bit ostentatious in such honesties, as if they established Bumper's credibility. In the end, Wambaugh sentimentalizes Bumper as a sort of repellently lovable super-cop who, whenever he is not strongarming 'pukepots,' is bantering in Yiddish, Spanish or Arabic with the ethnics on the beat." Time.

Wambaugh, Joseph

Finnegan's week / Joseph Wambaugh. W. Morrow, 1993. 348 p.

ISBN 9780688128012

1. Hazardous materials -- Transportation 2. Environmental crimes 3. Police 4. Women detectives 5. San Diego, California 6. Mysteries 7. Police procedurals

LC 93024890

Seeking two truckers hauling a drum of lethal chemicals, San Diego detective Finbar Finnegan joins forces with two strong-willed female cops to investigate a deadly toxic waste scam.

"There is a boyish excessiveness to Mr. Wambaugh's writing that produces an odd synergy with his carefully constructed plots and his colorful characters." New York Times Book Review.

Wambaugh, Joseph

Floaters / Joseph Wambaugh. Bantam Books, 1996. 293 p.

ISBN 0553103512

1. Yacht racing 2. Murder investigation 3. Police 4. Harbors 5. Regattas 6. Murder 7. Extortion 8. America's Cup races 9. San Diego, California 10. Mysteries 11. Police procedurals

LC 95-26625

With the America's Cup sailing regattas coming to San Diego, water cops Mickey Fortney and his partner, Leeds, have their hands full with international yacht fans, tourists, con artists, and a gorgeous redhead who leads them along a bizarre criminal trail to murder.

Wambaugh, Joseph

The **new** centurions / Joseph Wambaugh. Dell, 1987, c1970. 358 p.

ISBN 9780440164173

1. 1960s 2. Police 3. Crime 4. Criminals 5. Justice 6. Los Angeles, California 7. Thrillers and suspense 8. Police procedurals

Depicts the brutal experiences and rigorous training endured by three Los Angeles policemen.

"The author shows us the excitement, danger and sordidness found in the daily work of three young Los Angeles policemen. From the police academy to the first foot patrol, from the first patrol-car duty to the first promotion, Wambaugh follows his three main characters in their professional and personal lives, and shows us that police work, like the ministry, medicine or the military, is a profession demanding 24-hour dedication, determination, discipline and often a frustrating acceptance of defeat." The National Review.

Wang, Kathy

Family trust : a novel / Kathy Wang. William Morrow, 2018 400 p.

ISBN 9780062855251

1. 21st century 2. Chinese Americans 3. Rich families 4. Inheritance and succession 5. Ambition 6. Sick men 7. Rich people 8.

Intergenerational communication 9. Goals and objectives 10. Asian Americans 11. Family relationships 12. Silicon Valley, California 13. California 14. Domestic fiction

LC 2018029406

Struggling to fulfill a terminally ill father's final bequest, a privileged Chinese-American family in Silicon Valley is forced to contend with the realities of their ambitions and actual desires.

Ward, Amanda Eyre, 1972-

Forgive me : a novel / Amanda Eyre Ward. Random House, 2007. 256 p.

ISBN 9780345494467

1. Women journalists 2. Murder 3. Women foreign correspondents 4. Love 5. Motherhood 6. Loss (Psychology) 7. Regret 8. Grief in women 9. Guilt in women 10. Forgiveness 11. Betrayal 12. Redemption 13. South Africa 14. Psychological fiction

LC 2006050436

Haunted by memories of an assignment in Cape Town that ended in tragedy, foreign correspondent Nadine becomes involved in an American couple's odyssey to South Africa for the hearing in which their son's murderer is planning to confess.

Ward, Jesmyn

Salvage the bones : a novel / Jesmyn Ward. Bloomsbury USA, 2011. 256 p.

ISBN 9781608195220

1. Hurricane Katrina, 2005 2. Rural poor -- Mississippi 3. African American teenage girls 4. Teenage pregnancy 5. African American families 6. Brothers and sisters 7. Mother-separated families 8. Mississippi 9. Gulf Coast, Mississippi 10. Coming-of-age stories 11. Literary fiction 12. African American fiction 13. Southern fiction

LC 2010053025

National Book Award for Fiction, 2011.

Enduring a hardscrabble existence as the children of alcoholic and absent parents, four siblings from a coastal Mississippi town prepare their meager stores for the arrival of Hurricane Katrina while struggling with such challenges as a teen pregnancy and a dying litter of prize pups.

"Ward uses fearless, toughly lyrical language to convey this familys close-knit tenderness [and] the sheer bloody-minded difficulty of rural African American life... Its an eye-opening heartbreaker that ends in hope You owe it to yourself to read this book." Library Journal.

Ward, Jesmyn

* **Sing,** unburied, sing / Jesmyn Ward. Scribner, 2017. 288 p.

ISBN 9781501126062

1. Multiracial children 2. Extended families 3. Automobile travel 4. Women drug abusers 5. Former convicts 6. Grandparents 7. Farm life 8. Rural poor people 9. Race relations 10. Poverty 11. Suffering 12. Ghosts 13. African American families 14. Family relationships 15. Mississippi 16. Gulf Coast, Mississippi 17. Literary fiction 18. Southern fiction 19. African American fiction

ALA Notable Book, 2018.

Librarians' Choice (Australia), 2017

National Book Award for Fiction, 2017.

Finalist for the Hurston/Wright Legacy Awards for Fiction, 2018.

Kirkus Prize for Fiction finalist, 2017.

Andrew Carnegie Medal for Excellence in Fiction finalist, 2018.

Shortlisted for The Women's Prize for Fiction, 2018.

National Book Critics Circle Award for Fiction finalist, 2017

Pen/Faulkner Award Finalist, 2018

A story of how the past affects the present, and of deeply entrenched racism, Sing Unburied Sing describes the life of a biracial boy, his

addicted, grieving black mother, and his incarcerated white father. A road trip to Dad's prison kick-starts the novel, which offers deeply affecting characters, a strong sense of place (rural Mississippi), and a touch of magical realism in appearances by the dead. -- Description by Shauna Griffin

"Lyrical yet tough, Ward's distilled language effectively captures the hard lives, fraught relationships, and spiritual depth of her characters." Library Journal.

Ware, Ruth,

The **death** of Mrs. Westaway / Ruth Ware. Gallery/Scout Press, 2018. 384 p.

ISBN 9781501156212

1. Inheritance and succession 2. False personation 3. Young women 4. Wills 5. Tarot 6. Impostors 7. Deception 8. Rich families 9. Family secrets 10. Brighton, England 11. Penzance, England 12. England 13. Psychological suspense 14. Gothic fiction

LC 2018004355

Librarians' Choice (Australia), 2018.

"From the #1 New York Times bestselling author of In a Dark, Dark Wood, The Woman in Cabin 10, and The Lying Game comes Ruth Ware's highly anticipated fourth novel. On a day that begins like any other, Hal receives a mysterious letter bequeathing her a substantial inheritance. She realizes very quickly that the letter was sent to the wrong person--but also that the cold-reading skills she's honed as a tarot card reader might help her claim the money. Soon, Hal finds herself at the funeral of the deceased...where it dawns on her that there is something very, very wrong about this strange situation and the inheritance at the center of it. Full of spellbinding menace and told in Ruth Ware's signature suspenseful style, this is an unputdownable thriller from the Agatha Christie of our time."--, Provided by publisher.

Ware, Ruth

In a dark, dark wood / Ruth Ware. Scout Press, 2015. 310 p.

ISBN 9781501112317

1. Women authors 2. Female friendship 3. Hospital patients 4. Recluses 5. Country homes 6. Bachelorette parties 7. Memory 8. Murder 9. Secrets 10. England 11. Psychological suspense

LC 2015005077

Reluctantly accepting an old friend's invitation to spend a weekend on the English countryside, reclusive writer Leonora awakens in a hospital badly injured, unable to recall what happened and confronting a growing certainty that someone involved has died.

Ware, Ruth

The **lying** game / Ruth Ware. Gallery Books, 2017. 320 p.

ISBN 9781501156007

1. Dishonesty 2. Consequences 3. Boarding school students 4. Dead 5. Cliques 6. Secrets 7. Student expulsion 8. Female friendship 9. Life change events 10. Great Britain 11. England 12. Psychological suspense

"Four friends. One promise. But someone isn't telling the truth" --Cover.

On a cool June morning, a woman is walking her dog in the idyllic coastal village of Salten along a tidal estuary known as the Reach. Before she can stop him, the dog charges into the water to retrieve what first appears to be a wayward stick, but to herhorror, turns out to be something much more sinister. The next morning, three women in and around London -- Fatima, Thea, and Isabel -- receive the text they had always hoped would never come, from the fourth in their formerly inseparable clique, Kate, that says only, "I need you." The four girls were best friends at Salten, a second rate boarding school set near the cliffs of the English Channel. Each different in their own way, the four became inseparable and were notorious for playing the Lying Game, telling lies at every turn to both fellow boarders and faculty, with varying states of serious and flippant nature that were disturbing enough to ensure that everyone steered clear of them. The myriad and complicated rules of the game are strict: no lyingto each other -- ever. Bail on the lie when it becomes clear it is about to be found out. But their little game had consequences, and the girls were all expelled in their final year of school under mysterious circumstances surrounding the death of the school's eccentric art teacher, Ambrose, who also happened to be Kate's father...

"Alternating between the past and present, Ware builds up a rock-solid cast of intriguing characters and spins a mystery that will keep readers turning pages to the end." Publishers Weekly.

Ware, Ruth

* The **turn** of the key / Ruth Ware. Scout Press, 2019. 352 p.

ISBN 9781501188770

1. 21st century 2. Nannies 3. Technology 4. Child murder victims 5. Women murder suspects 6. Women prisoners 7. Letters 8. Social isolation 9. Children 10. Secrets 11. Surveillance 12. Household employees 13. Mansions 14. Rich families 15. Highlands, Scotland 16. Scotland 17. Gothic fiction 18. Psychological suspense 19. Epistolary novels

LC 2019021733

When a high-paying nanny job at a luxurious Scottish Highlands home ends with her imprisonment for a child's murder, a young woman struggles to explain to her lawyer the unravelling events that led to her incarceration.

"Ware's [Henry] James-like embroidery of the strange and sinister produces a Turn of the Screw with cellphones and Teslas that will enthrall today's readers." Booklist.

Ware, Ruth

The **woman** in cabin ten / Ruth Ware. Gallery, 2016. 288 p.

ISBN 9781501132933

1. Journalists 2. Pleasure cruises 3. Murder witnesses 4. Murder 5. Missing persons 6. North Sea 7. Psychological suspense

Assigned to review an exclusive North Sea luxury cruise, travel journalist Lo Blacklock witnesses a woman being thrown overboard and is baffled when all passengers remain unruffled and accounted for, a nightmare that unravels as Lo struggles to convince everyone that what she saw was real.

"Ware's follow-up to her best-selling debut, In a Dark, Dark Wood, is a gripping maritime psychological thriller that will keep readers spellbound. The intense final chapters just might induce heart palpitations." Library Journal.

Warren, Robert Penn, 1905-1989

All the king's men / Robert Penn Warren. Harcourt, 2005, c1946. 661 p.

ISBN 9780151011636

1. 1930s 2. Political corruption 3. Journalists 4. Politicians 5. Personal conduct 6. Race relations 7. Extortion 8. Power (Social sciences) 9. Southern States -- Politics and government 10. Literary fiction 11. Political fiction 12. Modern classics 13. Southern fiction

LC 2005004239

Originally published: New York : Harcourt, Brace, 1946.

Pulitzer Prize for Fiction, 1947.

Louisiana governor Willie Stark's obsession with political power leads to the ultimate corruption of his gubernatorial administration, in the story of the rise and fall of a Southern politician and demagogue in the 1930s.

Warren, Robert Penn, 1905-1989

Band of angels / Robert Penn Warren. Louisiana State University Press, 1994, c1955. 375 p.

ISBN 0807119466

1. American Civil War era (1861-1865) 2. Multiracial women 3. Identity (Psychology) 4. Freedom 5. Slavery 6. Multiracial persons -- Identity 7. Slave traders 8. Plantations 9. Self-discovery in women 10. Children of slaves 11. Civil war 12. United States Civil War, 1861-1865 13. Kentucky 14. New Orleans, Louisiana -- History -- Civil War, 1861-1865 15. United States -- History -- Civil War, 1861-1865 16. Historical fiction 17. Southern fiction

LC 94213598

Originally published: New York : Random House, 1955.

Returning to Kentucky upon her father's sudden death, sixteen-year-old Amantha Starr learns that she is to be sold into slavery to appease her father's creditors.

Warren, Robert Penn, 1905-1989

World enough and time : a romantic novel / Robert Penn Warren. Louisiana State University Press, 1999, c1950. 465 p.

ISBN 0807124788

1. 1820s 2. 19th century 3. Married people 4. Betrayal 5. Love triangles 6. Frontier and pioneer life 7. Murder 8. Revenge 9. Misadventures 10. Politicians 11. Idealism 12. Kentucky 13. Historical fiction 14. Literary fiction 15. Southern fiction

LC 99015675

Originally published: New York : Random House, 1950.

Jeremiah Beaumont, accused of murder, tries to justify the murder before he repents of it.

Warren, Susan May, 1966-

Rescue me / Susan May Warren. Baker Pub Group, 2017. 336 p. Montana rescue

ISBN 9780800727444

1. Search and rescue operations 2. Small towns 3. Sisters 4. Rescues 5. Sisters 6. Love triangles 7. Christian life 8. Men/women relations 9. Montana 10. Christian romantic suspense

LC 2016036310

Deputy Sam Brooks, a member of the PEAK rescue team, faces a life-and-death situation, causing him to spill his heart to his girlfriend. Except the room was dark and it was actually Sierra's sister, flower child Willow, he talked to... and kissed. Willow, who's hoping to be named her church's youth pastor, has loved Sam for years, but wants her sister to be happy, and they agree to never mention what happened. But when the two of them lead a youth group trip in Glacier National Park, disaster strikes and they must work together to save themselves and the teens in their care -- and they might just find a way to understand their feelings for each other. Buckle up for outdoor adventures, suspense, and a fast-paced plot. -- Description by Dawn Towery

Warren, Tiffany L.

Her secret life / Tiffany L. Warren. Dafina, 2017. 320 p.

ISBN 9781496708724

1. African American women 2. Second chances 3. Women's shelters 4. Self-fulfillment in women 5. Homelessness 6. Men/women relations 7. Interpersonal attraction 8. Women's lives and relationships 9. Drama lit 10. African American fiction

Scarred by poverty and life with a crackhead mother, Onika Lewis had a rough start. Still, thanks to her sharp mind, and hard work, she graduated with honors from a prestigious college. But her achievements weren't enough to earn her the elite status she craved. So she leveraged her gorgeous looks to become a rich man's trophy?and was eventually dumped her for a younger model. Now Onika is unemployed, broke?and homeless. She's making a fresh start through a unique women's shelter, but when she meets Graham, a kind-hearted commuter with whom she has an instant connection, she can?t bring herself to tell him her secret?

Warren, Tiffany L.

The **replacement** wife / Tiffany L. Warren. Dafina Books, 2014. 320 p.

ISBN 9780758280602

1. Widowers 2. Single fathers 3. Rich men 4. Mate selection 5. Fortune hunters 6. Manipulation by women 7. Faith (Christianity) 8. Nannies 9. Christians 10. Love triangles 11. African-American men/women relations 12. Atlanta, Georgia 13. Mainstream fiction 14. African American fiction

LC bl2014000558

Gold digger Chloe, growing impatient as she awaits widower Quentin Chambers' decision about whether to marry her or his new nanny, Montana, decides to take matters into her own hands.

Warren, Tiffany L.

The **pastor's** husband / Tiffany L. Warren. Dafina Books, 2016. 266 p.

ISBN 9781617732027

1. Clergy 2. Married people 3. Marital conflict 4. Betrayal 5. Temptation 6. Deception 7. Dallas, Texas 8. Drama lit

Felicia Caldwell has a great job, a healthy bank account, and stunning good looks, and when charismatic superstar pastor Nya Hempstead declares that partnership is on its way, Felicia is elated-- until her life becomes filled with more curses than blessings. Five years later, someone has to pay.... Felicia moves from Atlanta to Dallas and joins the church led by Nya and her co-pastor husband, Gregory. In public they have a perfect life, but their marriage is feeling the strain of Nya's success. As Felicia infiltrates the pastors' lives it will take a team of prayer warriors and heavenly intervention to save their relationship-- and their ministry.

Warrington, Freda, 1956-

Elfland / Freda Warrington. Tor, 2009. 464 p. Aetherial tales

ISBN 9780765318695

1. Elves 2. Doorways 3. Interdimensional travel 4. Magic 5. Alliances 6. Parallel universes 7. Family relationships 8. Men/women relations 9. Dysfunctional families 10. Interpersonal attraction 11. Love triangles 12. England 13. Gateway fantasy 14. Contemporary fantasy 15. Fantasy fiction

LC 2009012918

"A Tom Doherty Associates book."

When the passage to the Other World fails to open on the designated Night of the Summer Stars due to great danger in the realm, Aetherials Auberon and Rose form a forbidden alliance to breach the gates.

"Solid wordplay, great pacing and a thrilling conclusion." Publishers Weekly.

Warrington, Freda, 1956-

Grail of the summer stars / Freda Warrington. Tor, 2013. 368 p. Aetherial tales

ISBN 9780765318718

1. Painting 2. Orphans 3. Amnesia 4. Elves 5. Magic 6. Doorways 7. Parallel universes 8. Museum curators 9. Men/women relations 10. Interdimensional travel 11. Interpersonal attraction 12. England 13. Gateway fantasy 14. Contemporary fantasy 15. Fantasy fiction

LC 2012042626

"A Tom Doherty Associates book."

A conclusion to the trilogy that includes Elfland follows the arrival of a mysterious painting of a red-haired goddess in an art gallery, where the curator and an ancient member of the fey Aetherial folk discover a profound connection to one another.

Warrington, Freda, 1956-

Midsummer night / Freda Warrington. Tor, 2010. 480 p. Aetherial tales

ISBN 9780765318701

1. Elves 2. Doorways 3. Interdimensional travel 4. World War I veterans 5. Loss (Psychology) 6. Athletes -- Health 7. Sports injuries 8. Redemption 9. Betrayal 10. Magic 11. Parallel universes 12. England 13. Gateway fantasy 14. Contemporary fantasy 15. Fantasy fiction

LC 2010036680

"A Tom Doherty Associates book."

A young woman studying art at a vast country estate near the site where a child was snatched by fairies decades earlier, stumbles onto the portal to the Otherworld through which a handsome, charming, and innocent young man emerges and captures her heart.

Wascom, Kent, 1986-

The **blood** of heaven / Kent Wascom. Grove Press, 2013. 432 p.

ISBN 9780802121189

1. Burr, Aaron, 1756-1836 2. Early America (1784-1819) 3. 19th century 4. Children of clergy 5. Revolutionaries 6. Social classes 7. Slavery 8. Frontier and pioneer life 9. Florida -- History -- To 1821 10. Historical fiction 11. Southern fiction

The son of an itinerant preacher, Angel Woolsack is just a boy in 1799 when his father embarks on a mission to save the sinners of the Louisiana Territory. Under the influence of his adoptive brother, Samuel Kemper, Angel commits murder and flees to Natchez, Mississippi, where the two bible-brandishing bandits rob merchants while spreading the gospel. A fateful encounter with a young prostitute, Red Kate, changes the trajectory of Angel's life -- though not necessarily for the better. All end up in lawless West Florida, embroiled in events that will change history. Bleak, violent, and richly detailed, The Blood of Heaven is a sprawling story of life on the American frontier. - Description by Gillian Speace.

Washington, Bryan, 1993-

Lot : stories / Bryan Washington. Riverhead Books, 2019. 240 p.

ISBN 9780525533672

1. Multiracial boys 2. City life 3. Neighborhoods 4. Working class 5. Identity (Psychology) 6. Race relations 7. Gay boys 8. Family relationships 9. Houston, Texas 10. Short stories 11. Literary fiction 12. African American fiction

In the city of Houston - a sprawling, diverse microcosm of America - the son of a black mother and a Latino father is coming of age. He's working at his family's restaurant, weathering his brother's blows, resenting his older sister's absence. And discovering he likes boys.

"Washington debuts with a stellar collection in which he turns his gaze onto Houston, mapping the sprawl of both the city and the relationships within it, especially those between young black and brown boys." Publishers Weekly.

LIST OF FICTIONAL WORKS

Waters, Sarah, 1966-

Fingersmith / Sarah Waters. Riverhead Books, 2002. 511 p.

ISBN 1573222038

1. 1860s 2. Swindlers and swindling 3. Betrayal 4. Thieves 5. Orphans 6. Lesbians 7. Prisons 8. Psychiatric hospitals 9. Women/women relations 10. London, England -- History -- 19th century 11. England -- Social life and customs -- 19th century 12. Gothic fiction 13. Literary fiction 14. Historical fiction 15. LGBTQIA fiction

LC 2001051053

Ellis Peters Historical Dagger Award, 2002.
Lambda Literary Award for Lesbian Fiction, 2002.
Shortlisted for the Man Booker Prize, 2002.
Shortlisted for The Orange Prize for Fiction, 2002

Growing up as a foster child among a family of thieves, orphan Sue Trinder hopes to pay back that kindness by playing a key role in a swindle scheme devised by their leader, Gentleman, who is planning to con a fortune out of the naive Maud Lily, but Sue's growing pity for their helpless victim could destroy the plot.

"Sue Trinder, who also goes by a number of other names, appears to be a foundling, left for safekeeping at Mrs. Sucksby's baby farm by her thieving mother. . . . Raised by Mrs. Sucksby as her own, Sue picks up a few tricks from a crooked locksmith. . . . One day a young man, Richard Rivers, known as Gentleman, comes knocking at the door with a scheme to marry himself off to a lonely heiress, Maud Lily, then have her shut up in a madhouse once her money is his. He enlists Sue to be the young woman's maid, promising her a cut of the proceeds. But having attached herself to Maud for the sake of the money, Sue finds herself drawn into an unexpected and fearful intimacy." New York Times Book Review.

Waters, Sarah, 1966-

The **little** stranger / Sarah Waters. Riverhead Books, 2009. 466 p.

ISBN 9781594488801

1. 1940s 2. Haunted houses 3. Physicians 4. Classism 5. World War II veterans 6. Misadventures 7. Envy in men 8. Ghosts 9. Supernatural 10. Warwickshire, England 11. Ghost stories 12. Horror 13. Historical fiction 14. Literary fiction

Shortlisted for the Man Booker Prize, 2009.

After being summoned to treat a patient at dilapidated Hundreds Hall, Dr. Faraday finds himself becoming entangled in the lives of the owners, the Ayres family, and the supernatural presences in the house.

"This spooky, satisfying read has the added pleasure of effectively detailing postwar village life, with its rationing, social strictures, and gossip." Library Journal.

Waters, Sarah, 1966-

The **night** watch / Sarah Waters. Riverhead Books, 2006. 464 p.

ISBN 159448905X

1. Second World War era (1939-1945) 2. 1940s 3. Female friendship 4. World War II -- Women 5. Women and war 6. Lovers 7. Lesbians 8. Sexuality 9. Extramarital affairs 10. Men/women relations 11. Women ambulance drivers 12. London, England -- History -- Bombardment, 1940-1945 13. England -- History -- 20th century 14. Psychological fiction 15. Historical fiction 16. War stories 17. LGBTQIA fiction 18. Literary fiction

LC 2005044927

Lambda Literary Award for Lesbian Fiction, 2006.
Shortlisted for the James Tait Black Memorial Prize for Fiction, 2006
Shortlisted for the Man Booker Prize, 2006.
Shortlisted for The Orange Prize for Fiction, 2006

A tale set in World War II London finds a rescue worker struggling for composure after a bombing, a young woman longing for her soldier lover, and a convict who watches a battle through the bars of his window.

"[T]his historical novel begins at the end and moves backward, tracing the lives of its characters from peacetime Britain to the early years of the war. The centerpiece of the book is set in 1944, when the characters come fully alive, creeping through blackout Londonan apocalyptic landscape of rubble and ash, searchlights and fires. Waters, acclaimed for her Victorian-era romps, has done meticulous research, and renders wartime scenes with unnerving authenticity." The New Yorker.

Waters, Sarah, 1966-

The **paying** guests / Sarah Waters. Riverhead Books, 2014. 496 p.

ISBN 9781594633119

1. 1920s 2. Widows 3. Boarding houses 4. Hospitality 5. Lesbian couples 6. Single women 7. Lesbians -- Identity 8. Sexuality 9. Murder 10. Women/women relations 11. Interpersonal relations 12. World War I veterans 13. London, England -- History -- 20th century 14. Historical fiction 15. Literary fiction 16. LGBTQIA fiction

LC 2014016148

Shortlisted for The Baileys Women's Prize for Fiction, 2015
Kirkus Prize for Fiction finalist, 2014.

It is 1922, and London is tense. Ex-servicemen are disillusioned, the out-of-work and the hungry are demanding change. And in South London, in a genteel Camberwell villa, a large silent house now bereft of brothers, husband and even servants, life is about to be transformed, as impoverished widow Mrs Wray and her spinster daughter, Frances, are obliged to take in lodgers.

"Waters is a master of pacing, and her metaphor-laced prose is a delight. . . . As life-and-death questions are answered, new ones come up, and until the last page, the reader will have no idea what's going to happen." Kirkus.

Waters, Sarah, 1966-

Tipping the velvet / Sarah Waters. Riverhead Books, 1999. 472 p.

ISBN 9781573221368

1. 1890s 2. Lesbian couples 3. Lesbians -- Identity 4. Sexuality 5. Misadventures 6. Socialism 7. Women/women relations 8. Drag kings 9. London, England -- Social life and customs -- 19th century 10. England -- Social life and customs -- 19th century 11. Erotic fiction 12. Historical fiction 13. Literary fiction 14. LGBTQIA fiction

LC 98043836

Lambda Literary Award for Lesbian Fiction, 1999.

Nan, a poor oyster girl, is captivated by the music hall phenomenon that is Kitty Butler, a male impersonator extraordinaire treading the boards in Canterbury. Through a friend at the box office, Nan manages to visit all her shows and meet her heroine. Soon after, she becomes Kitty's dresser, and the two head for the bright lights of Leiscester Square ...

"A perfect fictional equivalent to such eye-opening standard works as Frank Harris's My Life and Loves and Steven Marcus's The Other Victorians and a rather formidable debut." Kirkus.

Watkins, Claire Vaye

* **Gold** fame citrus / Claire Vaye Watkins. Riverhead Books, 2015. 352 p.

ISBN 9781594634239

1. Squatters 2. Near future 3. Water supply 4. Cults 5. Surfers 6. Droughts 7. Dowsers 8. Social control 9. Environmentalists 10. Concentration camps 11. Men/women relations 12. Southern California 13. Dystopian fiction 14. Literary fiction

LC 2015013564

First published: [New York] : Riverhead Books, 2015.

In the wake of a devastating Southern California drought, two idealistic holdouts fall in love and scavenge for their needs before taking charge of a mysterious child and embarking on a perilous journey in search of water.--Publisher's description.

"In Margaret Atwood mode, Watkins spikes this fast-moving, high-tension, sexy, ecocrisis saga with caustic parodies and resounding allusions that cohere into a knowing and elegiac tale of scrappy adaptation and epic loss." Booklist.

Watkins, Jessica N.

Secrets of a side bitch / Jessica N. Watkins. Femistry Press, 2013. 259 p. Secrets of a side bitch novels

ISBN 9781492747895

1. Organized crime 2. African American couples 3. Drug dealers 4. Men/women relations 5. African Americans 6. Murder 7. Love triangles 8. Fugitives 9. Police 10. Sexuality 11. Chicago, Illinois 12. Urban fiction 13. African American fiction

At head of title: David Weaver presents.

"No matter how hard [Omari] works at his job at UPS, it is never enough to take care of himself and his long-term girlfriend. After continuous pressure from his older cousin, Ching, Omari finally traded in busting his ass for working under Ching hustling three major blocks on the Westside. All is good as Omari juggles work and the drug game. That is, until Ching involves him in the murder of who ends up being the governor's nephew. As he dodges homicide detectives, Omari is also trying to dodge getting caught between two loves." Provided by publisher

Watkins, Jessica N.

Secrets of a side bitch 2 / Jessica N. Watkins. Femistry Press, 2013. 250 p. Secrets of a side bitch novels

ISBN 9781493713400

1. Drug dealers 2. Organized crime 3. Women criminals 4. Love triangles 5. African American women 6. Men/women relations 7. African Americans 8. Sexuality 9. Murder 10. Chicago, Illinois 11. Urban fiction 12. African American fiction

At head of title: David Weaver presents.

"Simone is struggling to keep together the web of lies that she has woven, all in attempts to be the number one woman in Omari Sutton's life." Provided by publisher

Watson, Brad

Miss Jane : a novel / Brad Watson. W. W. Norton & Co., 2016. 224 p.

ISBN 9780393241730

1. Birth defects 2. Gender role 3. Misfits (Persons) 4. Women and nature 5. Loneliness in women 6. Self-fulfillment in women 7. Farm life 8. Physicians 9. Interpersonal relations 10. Mississippi -- Social life and customs -- 20th century 11. Southern gothic 12. Historical fiction 13. Southern fiction

LC 2016011032

A tale inspired by the story of the author's great-aunt explores the life of a woman in early 20th-century rural Mississippi whose genital birth defect prevents her marriage ability as she endures the hardships of farm life, observes the erotic qualities of nature and shares a relationship with a boy who loves but is forced to leave her.

"As Watson arcs through the story of Jane's life in sensitive, beautifully precise prose, we are both absorbed and humbled. Highly recommended." Library Journal.

Watson, Jan Elizabeth, 1972-

Asta in the wings / Jan Elizabeth Watson. Tin House Books, 2009. 336 p.

ISBN 9780980243611

1. 1970s 2. Brothers and sisters 3. Emotionally abused children 4. Girls 5. Mothers and daughters 6. Rural families 7. Deception 8. Social isolation 9. Maine 10. Psychological fiction

LC 2008040525

Growing up in an isolated house in woodland Maine, seven-year-old Asta Hewitt exists as one of a three-person society including a delusional mother and a bookish older brother before circumstances push her into the outside world, where she struggles to assimilate while remaining true to her fractured family.

"Watson hasn't set herself an easy task for her debut. The success of the novel rests entirely on her main character's sparrow-sized shoulders. Fortunately, Asta has reserves of intelligence and resourcefulness to spare and her voice is unforgettable." Christian Science Monitor.

Watson, Larry, 1947-

As good as gone : a novel / Larry Watson. Algonquin Books of Chapel Hill, 2016. 400 p.

ISBN 9781616205713

1. 1960s 2. Grandparent and child 3. Dysfunctional families 4. Ranchers 5. Cowboys 6. Widowers 7. Grandfathers -- Family relationships 8. Montana 9. Domestic fiction

LC 2015034265

One of the last cowboys, Calvin Sidney--a steely, hardened man with his own personal code who lives off the grid in a trailer on the prairie--agrees to help his adult son out and stay with his grandchildren for a week during which he solves problems the Old West way, which has a powerful effect on those around him.

"This is a very well done novel in which every character faces an individual conflict, resulting in a rich, suspenseful read." Publishers Weekly.

Watson, Larry, 1947-

Let him go : a novel / Larry Watson. Milkweed Editions, 2013. 256 p.

ISBN 9781571311023

1. 1950s 2. Grandparent and child 3. Families 4. Violence 5. Child custody 6. Visitation rights (Domestic relations) 7. North Dakota 8. Montana 9. The West (United States) 10. Rural noir 11. Historical fiction 12. Pacific Northwest fiction 13. Literary fiction

LC 2013006976

Wisconsin Library Association Literary Award, 2014.

In 1951 North Dakota, years after losing her son in a horse riding accident, Margaret Blackledge seeks to retrieve her grandson from the daughter-in-law who ran off with another man but finds her efforts challenged by her reluctant husband and the boy's stepfamily.

Watson, Martine Fournier

The **dream** peddler / Martine Fournier Watson. Penguin Books, 2019. 336 p.

ISBN 9780143133179

1. Dreams 2. Missing children 3. Loss (Psychology) 4. Sales personnel 5. Grief 6. Scandals 7. Desire 8. Rural life 9. Small towns 10. Psychological fiction

In early 20th-century America, traveling salesman Robert Owens arrives to sell dreams to a rural town rocked by a child's disappearance.

Watson, S. J. (Steven J.)

Before I go to sleep : a novel / S.J. Watson. Harper, 2011. 360 p.

ISBN 9780062060556

1. Women authors 2. Memory disorders 3. Life change events 4. Identity (Psychology) 5. Neurologists 6. Psychological suspense
LC 2010043159

British Book Award for Crime Thriller of the Year, 2011.

New Blood Dagger Award, 2011.

RUSA Reading List, 2012.

An accident in her 20s severely damaged her memory, so although Christine Lucas is now 47, she doesn't recall anything that has happened since the accident. Each morning, her husband has to tell her who she is, and who he is. But each morning after he leaves for work, she receives a phone call and is prompted by a doctor to retrieve her secret journal. -- Description by Shauna Griffin.

"One can't help but be impressed by Watson's skill. This British writer's attention to detail and empathy are impressive. No story is so compelling that it can't survive a bad telling; no concept is so clichéd that it can't benefit from a new, fresh and gifted voice." Los Angeles Times Book Review.

Watt, Holly

To the lions / Holly Watt. Dutton, 2019 400 p.

ISBN 9781524745455

1. Women investigative journalists 2. Hunting 3. International intrigue 4. Undercover operations 5. Journalism 6. Politicians 7. Refugees 8. Power (social sciences) 9. Personal conduct 10. Options, alternatives, choices 11. Rich men 12. North Africa 13. Thrillers and suspense

Ian Fleming Steel Dagger Award, 2019.

After she stumbles upon a dark conspiracy having to do with an extreme and secret hunt in North Africa, journalist Casey Benedict is determined to follow the clues, no matter how far it takes her.

Watts, Peter, 1958-

Starfish / Peter Watts. TOR Books, 1999. 317 p. Rifter series (Peter Watts)

ISBN 0312868553

1. 21st century 2. Hydrothermal vents 3. Marine animals 4. Hydrothermal vent ecology 5. Monsters 6. Geothermal energy 7. Underwater exploration 8. Misfits (Persons) 9. Criminals 10. Cyborgs 11. Marine engineers 12. Survival 13. Body modification 14. Biotechnology 15. Juan de Fuca Ridge 16. Science fiction 17. Cyberpunk
LC 9922967

Attempting to exploit the geothermal energy of the deepest rifts in the Pacific Ocean, a group of volunteers journeys to an ocean-floor experimental base, where their psychoses become rampant and a deadly foe approaches from the deep.

"Watts's first novel elegantly captures the isolation and claustrophobia of the lightless ocean depths, smoothly blending psychological suspense with high-tech sf adventure." Library Journal.

Watts, Peter, 1958-

Blindsight / Peter Watts. Tor, 2006. 384 p.

ISBN 0765312182

1. Misfits (Persons) 2. Diplomats 3. Interstellar relations 4. Aliens (Non-humanoid) 5. Consciousness 6. Alien artifacts 7. Expeditions 8. Engineers 9. Vampires 10. Linguists 11. Space 12. Earth -- Invasions 13. Hard science fiction 14. Science fiction
LC 2006005917

"A Tom Doherty Associates book."

Sequel: Echopraxia.

An odd assortment of diplomats--including a linguist with a multiple personality disorder, a biologist spliced to machinery, a pacifist warrior, and a vampire--journey to the far edges of the solar system to seek out a mysterious alien presence that may or may not want to meet with them and that may or may not be friendly toward Earth.

Watts, Stephanie Powell

No one is coming to save us / Stephanie Powell Watts. Ecco Press, 2017. 352 p.

ISBN 9780062472984

1. African American families 2. Small town life 3. Disillusionment 4. Intergenerational communication 5. Desire in men 6. Rich African American men 7. Family relationships 8. American dream 9. Wishing and wishes 10. African Americans 11. Interpersonal relations 12. Furniture industry and trade 13. North Carolina 14. Literary fiction 15. Southern fiction 16. Domestic fiction 17. Adaptations, retellings, and spin-offs 18. African American fiction

A tale inspired by The Great Gatsby is set in the contemporary South and follows the difficulties endured by an extended black family with colliding visions of the American dream.

"Watts lyrical writing and seamless floating between characters viewpoints make for a harmonious narrative chorus. This feels like an important, largely missing part of our ongoing American story." Booklist.

Waugh, Evelyn, 1903-1966

* **Brideshead** revisited / Evelyn Waugh ; with an introduction by Frank Kermode. A. A. Knopf, 1993, c1945. 315 p.

ISBN 0679423001

1. University of Oxford 2. 1920s 3. Rich people 4. Catholics 5. Male friendship 6. Men/women relations 7. Religion -- Social aspects 8. Country homes -- Great Britain 9. Catholic families 10. Faith -- Psychology 11. Family relationships 12. England -- Social life and customs -- 20th century 13. Great Britain -- Social life and customs -- 20th century 14. Literary fiction 15. Modern classics
LC 93-1854

Originally published: London: Chapman & Hall, 1945.

Set in 1920's England, the story examines the wealthy Flyte family through the eyes of Sebastian Flyte's less wealthy school friend Charles Ryder, who is eventually tempted into an extramarital affair with Sebastian's sister, Lady Julia. The novel is a story of faith and disillusionment in a glamorous upper-class world.

Waugh, Evelyn, 1903-1966

* The **complete** stories of Evelyn Waugh / Evelyn Waugh Little, Brown & Company, 1999 535 p.

ISBN 9780316925464

1. Manners and customs 2. England -- Social life and customs -- 20th century 3. Short stories 4. Literary fiction 5. Modern classics

A brilliant collection of thirty-nine stories spans the entire career of the literary master and comic genius, from his earliest character sketches and barbed portraits of the British upper class to Brideshead Revisited and Black Mischief.

"These 39 stories span Waugh's writing career, and to a one they demonstrate his trademark wit and sophistication." Booklist.

Waugh, Evelyn, 1903-1966

Decline and fall / Evelyn Waugh. Back Bay Books, 1999, c1928. 293 p.

ISBN 9780316926072

1. Young men 2. Upper class 3. Manners and customs 4. Misadventures 5. Boarding schools 6. England -- Social life and

customs -- 20th century 7. Satirical fiction 8. Modern classics

Originally published: London : Chapman & Hall, 1928.

Sent down from Oxford in outrageous circumstances, Paul Pennyfeather is oddly unsurprised to find himself qualifying for the position of schoolmaster at Llanabba Castle, where his colleagues turn out to be an assortment of misfits, rascals and fools.

Waugh, Evelyn, 1903-1966

The **loved** one : an Anglo-American tragedy / Evelyn Waugh. Back Bay Books, 1999, c1948. 164 p.

ISBN 9780316926089

1. Expatriates -- Hollywood, California 2. Undertakers 3. Film industry and trade -- Hollywood, California 4. Funeral homes 5. Poets, English 6. Survivors of suicide victims 7. Love triangles -- Hollywood, California 8. Hollywood, California -- Social life and customs 9. Satirical fiction 10. Modern classics

Originally published: Boston : Little, Brown, 1948.

Mr. Joyboy, the embalmer at a full-service funeral home for Hollywood's departed greats, and Aimee Thanatogenos, the crematorium cosmetician, find their romance complicated with the appearance of a young English poet.

Waugh, Evelyn, 1903-1966

* **Vile** bodies / Evelyn Waugh. Back Bay Books, 1999, c1930. 321 p.

ISBN 9780316926119

1. 1920s 2. Young men 3. Socialites 4. Rich people 5. Parties 6. Men/women relations 7. England -- Social life and customs -- 1910-1936 8. London, England -- Social life and customs -- 1901-1910 9. Satirical fiction 10. Modern classics

Originally published: Boston : Little, Brown, 1930.

The comic aspects of London society during the thirties are presented in Waugh's early novel.

Waxman, Abbi

The **bookish** life of Nina Hill / Abbi Waxman. Berkley, 2019. 320 p.

ISBN 9780451491879

1. Women -- Family relationships 2. Life change events 3. Introverts 4. Families 5. Bookstores 6. Single mothers 7. Attitude change 8. Family relationships 9. Southern California 10. California 11. Chick lit

LC 2018057848

A confirmed introvert finds her simple life upended when the father she never knew passes away, revealing an enormous extended family that overwhelms her budding relationship with a fellow trivia buff.

Wayne, Teddy

Apartment : a novel / Teddy Wayne. Bloomsbury Publishing, 2020. 240 p.

ISBN 9781635574005

1. 1990s 2. Male friendship 3. Apartments 4. Social isolation 5. Authors 6. Insecurity (Psychology) 7. Secrets 8. Loneliness in men 9. Anonymous persons 10. Class conflict 11. Graduate students 12. New York City 13. Literary fiction 14. Satirical fiction

LC 2019024893

A man who offers a rent-free spare bedroom in his illegal sublet of a rent-stabilized NYC apartment to a working-class, Midwestern student on scholarship at Columbia develop a friendship that eventually clashes over politics, socioeconomic identity and privilege in 1996.

"A near-anthropological study of male insecurity." Kirkus.

Wayne, Teddy

Loner : a novel / Teddy Wayne. Simon & Schuster, 2016. 224 p.

ISBN 9781501107894

1. College students 2. Crushes (Interpersonal relations) 3. Personal conduct 4. Loners 5. Obsession 6. Sexuality 7. Popularity 8. Stalkers 9. Universities and colleges 10. Ambition 11. Men/women relations 12. Stalking 13. Cambridge, Massachusetts 14. Satirical fiction

LC 2015044742

A painfully overlooked, academically gifted Harvard freshman resigns himself to anonymity before falling head-over-heels for a beautiful Manhattan glamour girl who compels him to compromise his moral standards and get in touch with his true identity.

"Wayne (The Love Song of Jonny Valentine) offers a witty and fascinating peek into today's youth culture, and delivers an enthralling portrait of male narcissism and voyeuristic obsession through the literary device of an unreliable, though brilliant, narrator." Library Journal.

Wayne, Teddy

* The **love** song of Jonny Valentine : a novel / Teddy Wayne. Free Press, 2013. 256 p.

ISBN 9781476705859

1. Child celebrities 2. Fame -- Psychological aspects 3. Mothers and sons 4. Eleven-year-old boys 5. Boy singers 6. Celebrity promotion 7. Mass media 8. Consumer society 9. Father-separated boys 10. United States -- Social life and customs -- 21st century 11. Coming-of-age stories 12. Satirical fiction

LC 2012038331

A tale about America's obsession with fame follows the experiences of preadolescent pop idol Jonny Valentine, who hides behind his megastar success the bitterness and innocence of a child who feels manufactured by his LA label and hard-partying manager mother.

Weatherspoon, Rebekah

A **cowboy** to remember / Rebekah Weatherspoon. Dafina, 2020. 320 p. Cowboys of California

ISBN 9781496725400

1. Cowboys 2. Women cooks 3. Amnesia 4. Dude ranches 5. Former rodeo performers 6. Reality television programs 7. Childhood friends 8. African American men 9. Contemporary romances 10. Western romances 11. Multicultural romances 12. African American fiction

When an accident leaves her with no memory, chef Evie Buchanan gets her own happily-ever-after when former rodeo champion Zach Pleasant walks into her hospital and awakens feelings long dormant.

"The amnesia trope gets a pop culture-infused update in this second-chance romance featuring reality-star chefs, ranch resorts, Instagram feuds, and Hollywood royalty." Publishers Weekly.

Weatherspoon, Rebekah

Haven / Rebekah Weatherspoon. CreateSpace, 2017. 256 p. Beards and bondage

ISBN 9781545487273

1. Bondage (Sexual behavior) 2. Sexuality 3. Sexual dominance and submission 4. Protectiveness in men 5. Wilderness areas 6. Sexual attraction 7. Interpersonal attraction 8. Erotic romances 9. African American fiction

"City girl Claudia Cade's carefree life is plunged into chaos when a camping trip with her brother in the national forests of Northern California turns into a deadly dash for her survival. . . . Nature photographer Shepard Olsen has resigned himself to a quiet existence, with only his dog by his side, until a woman in need of his protection shows up on his doorstep and throws his universe into disarray." Provided by publisher

Weatherspoon, Rebekah

Rafe : a buff male nanny / Rebekah Weatherspoon. Rebekah Weatherspoon, 2018. 252 p. Loose ends

ISBN 9781724106506

1. Divorced women 2. Single mothers 3. Nannies 4. Women physicians 5. African American women 6. Interracial romance 7. Sexual attraction 8. Men/women relations 9. California 10. Los Angeles, California 11. Contemporary romances 12. Multicultural romances

"After a nasty divorce and a thousand mile move, Dr. Sloan Copeland and her twin daughters are finally getting the hang of their new life in Los Angeles. When their live-in nanny bails with no warning, Sloan is left scrambling to find a competent caretaker to wrangle her smart, sensitive girls. Nothing less will do. Enter Rafe Whitcomb. He's all of those things, not to mention good-natured and one heck of a whiz in the kitchen. He's also tall, and handsome, and bearded, and ripped, and tatted, wrist to neck. It doesn't take long for the Copelands to invite Rafe into their home. Just as quickly, both Sloan and Rafe find themselves succumbing to a heady mutual attraction, neither of them wants to deny. With every minute they spend under the same roof, this working mom can't help but wonder if Rafe can handle all her needs?"--Publisher's description.

Weatherspoon, Rebekah

* Xeni : a marriage of inconvenience / Rebekah Weatherspoon. Rebekah Weatherspoon Presents, 2019. 275 p. Loose ends

ISBN 9780578592077

1. Inheritance and succession 2. Musicians 3. African American women 4. Married people 5. Interracial romance 6. Sexual attraction 7. Bisexual couples 8. Scots in the United States 9. Men/women relations 10. Contemporary romances 11. Multicultural romances

"Xeni Everly-Wilkins has ten days to clean out her recently departed aunt's massive colonial in Upstate New York. With the feud between her mom and her sisters still raging even in death, she knows this will be no easy task, but when the will is read Xeni quickly discovers the decades old drama between the former R&B singers is just the tip of the iceberg. The secrets, lies, and a crap ton of cash spilled on her lawyer's conference room table all come with terms and conditions. Xeni must marry before she can claim the estate that will set her up for life and her aunt has just the groom in mind. The ruggedly handsome and deliciously thicc Scotsman who showed up at her aunt's memorial, bagpipes at the ready. When his dear friend and mentor Sable Everly passed away, Mason McInroy knew she would leave a sizable hole in his heart. He never imagined she'd leave him more than enough money to settle the debt that's keeping him from returning home to Scotland. He also never imagined that Sable would use her dying breaths to play match-maker, trapping Mason and her beautiful niece in a marriage scheme that comes with more complications than either of them need. With no choice but to say I do, the unlikely pair try to make the best of a messy situation. They had no plans to actually fall in love."--Back cover.

Weber, Carl, 1964-

Man on the run / Carl Weber. Grand Central Pub., 2017. 320 p.

ISBN 9781455505272

1. Escaped convicts 2. Judicial error 3. African American men 4. Male friendship 5. Trust 6. Injustice 7. Betrayal 8. Fugitives 9. African American men/women relations 10. Thrillers and suspense 11. African American fiction

Sent to jail for a crime he did not commit, Jay Crawford escapes from prison and calls on his three best friends--Wil, Kyle, and Allan--to help clear his name.

Weber, David, 1952-

By schism rent asunder / David Weber. TOR, 2008. 512 p. Safehold series

ISBN 9780765315014

1. Androids 2. Religion and science 3. Civilization, Medieval 4. Secrecy in government 5. Government cover-ups 6. Space colonies 7. Technology 8. Secrets 9. Rulers 10. Aliens 11. Military science fiction 12. Science fiction

LC 2008016957

Sequel to: Off Armageddon Reef.
Sequel: By heresies distressed.
"A Tom Doherty Associates book."

The mercantile kingdom of Charis evaluates the agenda of a mysterious being who calls himself Merlin, a person who is playing a pivotal role in humanity's struggle against the oppressive forces of the Church of God Awaiting.

Weber, David, 1952-

The **honor** of the queen / David Weber. Baen Books, 1993. 448 p. Honor Harrington novels. Main series

ISBN 9780743435727

1. Women spaceship captains 2. Diplomacy 3. Interplanetary relations 4. Sexism in politics and government 5. Space warfare 6. Imaginary kingdoms 7. Misogyny 8. Space opera 9. Science fiction

On the planet Grayson to participate in diplomatic talks between the Kingdom of Manticore and the Republic of Haven, Honor Harrington discovers that she is stuck on a fiercely patriarchal, misogynist planet.

Weber, David, 1952-

* Off Armageddon reef / David Weber. Tor, 2007. 608 p. Safehold series

ISBN 0765315009

1. Androids 2. Religion and science 3. Civilization, Medieval 4. Secrecy in government 5. Government cover-ups 6. Medieval science 7. Space colonies 8. Aliens 9. Military science fiction 10. Science fiction

LC 2006025838

Sequel: By schism rent asunder.

With humankind reduced to a single colony on the distant world of Safehold by a ruthless alien enemy, the human rulers of the planet will do anything to preserve the remnants of their industrial civilization, including building a religion designed to hide the colony by keeping its society medieval, until the awakening of an android signals a chance for humankind to regain its place.

Weber, David, 1952-

On Basilisk Station / David Weber. Baen, 1993. 422 p. Honor Harrington novels. Main series

ISBN 9780671721633

1. Space stations 2. Space vehicles 3. Women spaceship captains 4. Space warfare 5. Imaginary kingdoms 6. Space opera 7. Science fiction

Instead of remaining out of sight during her assignment to a forlorn outpost, spaceship commander Honor Harrington, along with her vessel, the Fearless, performs incredible flying maneuvers to stop a foreign takeover of a major space station.

Weber, David, 1952-

Shadow of freedom / David Weber. Baen Books, 2013. 400 p. Honor Harrington novels. Saganami Island

ISBN 9781451637823

1. Space warfare 2. Frameups 3. Women soldiers 4. Secret societies

5. Insurgency 6. Courage in women 7. Enemies 8. Women spaceship captains 9. Good and evil 10. Imaginary empires 11. Imaginary wars and battles 12. Space opera 13. Science fiction

Receiving a suspicious warning about a rising rebellion against an oppressive leader, Manticore Tenth Fleet commander Michelle Henke believes that she is being set up by the shadowy Mesan Alignment.

Weber, David, 1952-

The **short** victorious war / David Weber. Baen Books, 1994. 376 p. Honor Harrington novels. Main series

ISBN 9780671875961

1. Women spaceship captains 2. Space warfare 3. Imaginary wars and battles 4. Imaginary kingdoms 5. Space opera 6. Science fiction

Banking on a short, victorious war to replenish their depleted treasury, the ruling class of the People's Republic of Haven do not count on coming up against Captain Honor Harrington and the Royal Manticoran Navy.

Wecker, Helene

* The **golem** and the jinni / Helene Wecker. Harper, 2013. 486 p.

ISBN 9780062110831

1. Gilded Age (1865-1898) 2. 1890s 3. Golem 4. Genies 5. Magicians 6. Immigrants 7. Power (Social sciences) 8. Freedom 9. Rabbis 10. Mythical creatures 11. New York City -- History -- 19th century 12. Historical fantasy 13. Middle Eastern-influenced fantasy

Mythopoeic Award for Adult Literature, 2014.

After her creator dies en route to America, Chava, a golem from a Polish shtetl, must navigate the streets of 1899 New York City by herself -- her only ally is a rabbi unsure whether to destroy her, or allow her to fulfill her destiny as the harbinger of destruction. Ahmad, a jinni from Syria's deserts has been released from his thousand-year-old glass bottle by a tinsmith but has little intention of remaining a metalworker, despite his uncanny talent for it. Chava and Ahmad meet and discover that they're soul mates, but a dangerous adversary threatens their future. This vibrant blend of myth, adventure, and romance will enchant fans of stories based on folklore. - Description by Gillian Speace.

Weinberg, Kate

The **truants** / Kate Weinberg. G. P. Putnam & Sons, 2020, c2019 320 p.

ISBN 9780525541967

1. Christie, Agatha, 1890-1976 2. Women college students 3. Women college teachers 4. Creativity 5. Hedonism 6. Obsession 7. Love triangles 8. Friendship 9. Betrayal 10. Universities and colleges 11. Campus life 12. Secrets 13. England 14. Psychological suspense

LC 2019021290

Originally published in Great Britain, 2019.

Jess Walker has come to a concrete campus under the flat grey skies of East Anglia for one reason: To be taught by the mesmerizing and rebellious Dr Lorna Clay, whose seminars soon transform Jess? thinking on life, love and Agatha Christie.

"With intrigue sparking throughout, Weinberg's immensely compelling debut novel explores the years-long reverberations of a fractured friend group and echoes Donna Tartt's The Secret History." Booklist.

Weiner, Jennifer

Good in bed : a novel / Jennifer Weiner. Pocket Books, 2001. 376 p.

ISBN 9780743418164

1. Overweight women 2. Jewish American women 3. Former lovers 4. Family relationships 5. Men/women relations 6. Fathers and daughters 7. Women journalists 8. Female friendship 9. Father-

separated families 10. Philadelphia, Pennsylvania 11. Chick lit

LC 00068212

Humiliated to discover that her ex-boyfriend has been chronicling their former sex life in a series of articles called "Loving a Larger Woman" in a popular women's magazine, pop-culture journalist Cannie Shapiro embarks on an adventure-filled odyssey as she confronts her losses, makes peace with the past, and comes to terms with herself, her dreams, and her goals in life.

"Cannie Shapiro is in her late twenties, funny, independent, and a talented reporter for the Philadelphia Inquirer. After a temporary break-up with her boyfriend of three years, she reads his debut column, Good in Bed, in the women's magazine Moxie. Titled Loving a Larger Woman, this very personal piece triggers events that completely transform her and those around her. Cannie's adventures will strike a chord with all young women struggling to find their place in the world, especially those larger than a size eight." Library Journal.

Weiner, Jennifer

In her shoes : a novel / Jennifer Weiner. Atria Books, 2002. 424 p.

ISBN 0743418190

1. Retirement communities 2. Self-fulfillment in women 3. Sibling rivalry 4. Grandmothers 5. Sisters 6. Women lawyers 7. Women -- Family relationships 8. Family relationships 9. Dysfunctional families 10. Single women -- Interpersonal relations 11. Men/women relations 12. Florida 13. Philadelphia, Pennsylvania 14. Women's lives and relationships

Meet Rose Feller. She's thirty years old and a high-powered attorney with a secret passion for romance novels. She dreams of a man who will slide off her glasses, gaze into her eyes, and tell her that she's beautiful. She also dreams of getting her fantastically screwed-up little sister to get her life together. Meet Rose's sister, Maggie. Twenty-eight years old, drop-dead gorgeous and only occasionally employed.

"Meet plump, dependable Rose Feller and her gorgeous, out-of-control sister, Maggie. As children, they lost their mother and contact with grandmother Ella. Now, 20 years later, we follow their struggles to forgive the past, reclaim each other's love, and become their best selves. . . . Reworking the age-old theme that self-knowledge and acceptance are needed before love and happiness can be achieved, Weiner embroiders serious matters with threads of humor to produce a novel full of memorable characters and situations." Library Journal.

Weiner, Jennifer

Little earthquakes / Jennifer Weiner. Atria, 2004. 432 p.

ISBN 0743470095

1. Pregnant women 2. Infant death 3. Husband and wife 4. Mothers-in-law 5. Mothers and daughters 6. Motherhood 7. Grief 8. Loss (Psychology) 9. Paternity 10. Family relationships 11. Men/women relations 12. Weight control 13. Homecomings 14. Pennsylvania 15. Philadelphia, Pennsylvania 16. Women's lives and relationships

A chef, an event planner, and a basketball player's wife find their marriages and careers in Philadelphia challenged by new motherhood, difficult schedules, and infidelity.

"This is the story of four women in Philadelphia who bond over pregnancy and motherhood. Becky, Kelly, and Ayinde meet in yoga class, and the three become friends when Ayinde's water breaks one day after class and they take her to the hospital. Becky is a chef with an adoring husband and an annoying mother-in-law; Kelly is frustrated when her husband loses his job and drags his feet looking for another; Ayinde's husband is a famous basketball player whom she suspects of infidelity. What brings the women together is their love for their new-borns. The fourth woman, Lia, watches the group from afar; she's an actress who walked out on her husband after a devastating tragedy. Weiner seamlessly and gracefully weaves the four women's stories together." Booklist.

Weiner, Jennifer

* Mrs. Everything : a novel / Jennifer Weiner. Atria Books, 2019. 416 p.

ISBN 9781501133480

1. 20th century 2. Sisters 3. Family relationships 4. Identity (Psychology) 5. Jewish families 6. Women's role 7. Loss (Psychology) 8. Child sexual abuse 9. Eating disorders 10. Closeted lesbians 11. Psychic trauma 12. Self-esteem in women 13. Women's dreams 14. Ambition in women 15. Michigan 16. Detroit, Michigan 17. Women's lives and relationships 18. Historical fiction

LC 2018056036

Two sisters struggle to find their place, be true to themselves and adapt to rapid changes happening throughout the latter half of 20th-century America.

"It's been a while since Weiner explored the complicated terrain of sisterhood, and readers will flock to this ambitious, nearly flawless novel." Booklist.

Weinstein, Alexander

Children of the new world : stories / Alexander Weinstein. Picador, 2016. 272 p.

ISBN 9781250098993

1. Social media 2. Memories 3. Virtual reality 4. Robots 5. Artificial intelligence 6. High technology 7. Science fiction 8. Short stories

LC 2016019224

A collection of short stories explores the near-future world of social-media implants, immersive virtual reality games, and frighteningly intuitive robots.

"Complete with footnotes from fictional future publications and technology that is just one leap away, this is mind-bending stuff. Weinsteins collection is full of spot-on prose, wicked humor, and heart." Publishers Weekly.

Weir, Alison, 1951-

Anna of Kleve : the princess in the portrait / Alison Weir. Ballantine Books, 2019. 288 p. Six Tudor queens

ISBN 9781101966570

1. Anne,, of Cleves, Queen, consort of Henry VIII, King of England, 1515-1557 2. Henry VIII,, King of England, 1491-1547 3. Tudor period (1485-1603) 4. Marriages of royalty and nobility 5. Courts and courtiers 6. Germans in Great Britain 7. Marital conflict 8. Nobility 9. Intrigue 10. Extramarital affairs 11. Secrets 12. Great Britain -- History -- Henry VIII, 1509-1547 13. England -- History -- 16th century 14. Great Britain -- History -- Tudors, 1485-1603 15. Biographical fiction 16. Historical fiction

Arranged in a doomed marriage to England's infamous Henry VIII, a princess from a small German duchy hides a desperate secret in a hostile foreign court.

Weir, Alison, 1951-

A **dangerous** inheritance : a novel of Tudor rivals and the secret of the tower / Alison Weir. Ballantine Books, 2012. 307 p.

ISBN 9780345511898

1. Tower of London (London, England) 2. Political prisoners 3. Nobility 4. Men/women relations 5. Treason 6. Secrets 7. Great Britain -- Court and courtiers 8. London, England 9. Historical fiction 10. Biographical fiction

Originally published: London: Hutchinson, 2012.

A tale inspired by the life of Lady Jane Gray's younger sister, Katherine, interweaves the tragic story of her imprisonment in the Tower of London with the fates of three other innocent political prisoners including Kate Plantagenet and boy princes Edward and Richard.

Weir, Alison., 1951-

Innocent traitor / Alison Weir. Ballantine Books, 2007. 416 p.

ISBN 0345494857

1. Grey, Jane,, Lady, 1537-1554 2. Tudor period (1485-1603) 3. Rulers 4. Aristocracy 5. Courts and courtiers 6. Inheritance and succession 7. Greed 8. Manipulation by parents 9. Treason 10. Men/women relations 11. England -- History -- 16th century 12. Great Britain -- History -- Tudors, 1485-1603 13. Great Britain -- History -- Edward VI, 1547-1553 14. Great Britain -- History -- Mary I, 1553-1558 15. Coming-of-age stories 16. Historical fiction 17. Biographical fiction

LC 2006049860

Lady Jane Grey was born into times of extreme danger. Child of a scheming father and a ruthless mother, for whom she was merely a pawn in a dynastic power game with the highest stakes, she lived a live in thrall to political machinations and lethal religious fervour. Jane's astonishing and essentially tragic story was played out during one of the most momentous periods of English history. As a great-niece of Henry VIII, and the cousin of Edward VI, Mary I and Elizabeth I, she grew up to realize that she could never throw off the chains of her destiny. Her honesty, intelligence and strength of character carry the reader through all the vicious twists of Tudor power politics, to her nine-day reign and its unbearably poignant conclusion.

"Lady Jane, known to history as the Nine Days Queen, is a tragic and appealing figure. Abused by her parents, this talented and intelligent girl was bullied into a hateful marriage and pushed into accepting the Crown after the death of King Edward VI. Edward's older sister, Princess Mary (later known as Bloody Mary, and for good reason), rightfully claimed the Crown as her own, and Jane was sent to the Tower of London and eventually executed. Weir tells the story of Jane's short life from multiple viewpoints, which might initially confuse readers unfamiliar with the history, but this is a small fault in an otherwise entertaining and moving novel." Library Journal.

Weir, Alison., 1951-

The **Lady** Elizabeth : a novel / Alison Weir. Ballantine Books, 2008. 416 p.

ISBN 9780345495358

1. Elizabeth I,, Queen of England, 1533-1603 Childhood and youth 2. Grey, Jane,, Lady, 1537-1554 3. Tudor period (1485-1603) 4. Rulers -- Great Britain 5. Courts and courtiers 6. Inheritance and succession 7. Greed 8. Aristocracy -- 16th century 9. Manipulation by parents 10. Treason 11. Men/women relations 12. Great Britain -- History -- Edward VI, 1547-1553 13. Great Britain -- History -- Mary I, 1553-1558 14. England -- History -- 16th century 15. Great Britain -- History -- Tudors, 1485-1603 16. Coming-of-age stories 17. Historical fiction 18. Biographical fiction

LC 2008000284

First published in the United Kingdom in 2008 by Hutchinson.

A vivid fictional portrait of the tumultuous early life of Queen Elizabeth I describes her perilous path to the throne of England and the scandal, political intrigues, and religious turmoil she confronted along the way, from the deaths of her parents, Anne Boleyn and Henry VIII, to the fanaticism of her sister, Mary I.

"A novel about the life of the young Elizabeth Tudor before she ascended to the throne. From the time of her mother's death when she was three to her inheritance of the throne in her twenties, danger always came at Elizabeth from some corner. Early in her life, she was stripped of her title of princess; later, she had to defend her virtue from the roving eyes and hands of her stepfather; and, finally, she had to navigate the deadly waters between her Protestant faith and her sister's fanatical Catholicism. Several times Elizabeth barely escaped alive; hers was not a life that could be borne by the average person. Weir successfully depicts this extraordinary young woman who beat the odds to become one of the world's greatest rulers." Library Journal.

Weir, Andy

Artemis / Andy Weir. Crown Publishing, 2017 384 p.
ISBN 9780553448122

1. Smugglers 2. Near future 3. Conspiracies 4. Space colonies 5. Organized crime 6. Gangsters 7. Lunar bases 8. Moon -- Colonization 9. Crime fiction 10. Science fiction 11. Hard science fiction
Goodreads Choice Award, 2017
Librarians' Choice (Australia), 2017.

Augmenting his limited income by smuggling contraband to survive on the moon's wealthy city of Artemis, Jazz agrees to commit what seems to be a perfect, lucrative crime, only to find herself embroiled in a conspiracy for control of the city.

Weir, Andy

* The **Martian** / Andy Weir. Crown Publishers, 2014. 368 p.
ISBN 9780804139021

1. Survival 2. Astronauts 3. Space flight to Mars 4. Extreme environments 5. Planets -- Exploration 6. Determination in men 7. Resourcefulness 8. Dust storms 9. Mars (Planet) -- Exploration 10. Hard science fiction 11. Science fiction 12. Diary novels
"Originally self-published as an (ebk.) in 2011"--Title page verso.
Goodreads Choice Award, 2014.
RUSA Reading List, 2015.

Stranded on Mars by a duststorm that compromised his space suit and forced his crew to leave him behind, astronaut Mark Watney struggles to survive in spite of minimal supplies and harsh environmental challenges that test his ingenuity in unique ways.

"[A] tightly constructed and completely believable story of a man's ingenuity and strength in the face of seemingly insurmountable odds." Booklist.

Weir, Meghan MacLean

The **book** of Essie : a novel / Meghan MacLean Weir. Alfred A. Knopf, 2018. 319 p.
ISBN 9780525520313

1. Reality television programs 2. Teenage pregnancy 3. Evangelicalism 4. Fundamentalists 5. High school students 6. Fame 7. Weddings 8. Family secrets 9. Mainstream fiction
LC 2017032041

A debut novel of family, fame, and religion that tells the emotionally stirring, wildly captivating story of the seventeen-year-old daughter of an evangelical preacher, star of the family's hit reality show, and the secret pregnancy that threatens to blow their entire world apart.

Weisgall, Deborah

The **world** before her / Deborah Wisgall. Houghton Mifflin, 2008. 304 p.
ISBN 9780618746576

1. Eliot, George, 1819-1880 2. Women sculptors 3. Husband and wife 4. Married people 5. Venice, Italy 6. Italy 7. Biographical fiction 8. Domestic fiction
LC 2008004734

Two parallel stories, set in Venice a century apart, follow two women and their marriages--Marian Evans, better known as famed English author George Eliot, who is newly married to a man twenty years her junior and in the city on her honeymoon; and sculptor Caroline Spingold, coming unwillingly to the city with her older, wealthy husband to celebrate their tenth anniversary.

"Describing the stories of Mary Ann and Caroline in alternate chapters, Weisgall draws parallel portraits of marital dissatisfaction and the attraction of the fleeting past to nullify the dreariness of the present. Her writing is tender, drowning you in its drunken energy, with the city of Venice providing a tasteful backdrop." St. Petersburg Times (Florida).

Weiss, Leah, 1947-

If the creek don't rise : a novel / Leah Weiss. Sourcebooks Landmark, 2017 320 p.
ISBN 9781492647454

1. 1970s 2. Rural life 3. Mountain life 4. Abused women 5. Teachers 6. Abusive men 7. Pregnant women 8. Female friendship 9. Extramarital affairs 10. Women -- Interpersonal relations 11. North Carolina 12. Appalachian Region 13. Appalachian Region, Southern 14. Southern gothic 15. Southern fiction 16. Women's lives and relationships

"In a North Carolina mountain town filled with moonshine and rotten husbands, Sadie Blue is only the latest girl to face a dead-end future at the mercy of a dangerous drunk. She's been married to Roy Tupkin for fifteen days, and she knows now that she should have listened to the folks who said he was trouble. But when a stranger sweeps in and knocks the world off-kilter for everyone in town, Sadie begins to think there might be more to life than being Roy's wife. As stark and magnificent as Appalachia itself, If the Creek Don't Rise is a bold and beautifully layered debut about a dusty, desperate town finding the inner strength it needs to outrun its demons. The folks of Baines Creek will take you deep into the mountains with heart, honesty, and homegrown grit."--, Provided by publisher

"In this tender but powerful debut, Weiss paints both the bright and the dark in the lives of her fictional Appalachian communitys denizens." Publishers Weekly.

Welch, James, 1940-

* The **heartsong** of Charging Elk : a novel / James Welch. Doubleday, 2000. 440 p.
ISBN 0385496745

1. Buffalo Bill's Wild West Show 2. Oglala Indians -- Marseille 3. Native Americans in France 4. Prostitutes -- Marseille 5. Murder -- Marseille 6. Oglala Indians in France 7. Marseille -- History -- 19th century 8. France -- History -- 19th century 9. Historical fiction
LC 99058875

Charging Elk, an Oglala Sioux, is recruited by Buffalo Bill Cody to join his Wild West show, which creates a sensation in Europe, until he is left behind--because of illness and a bureaucratic mix-up--in the unfamiliar world of Marseilles.

"The author estranges our vision. We have no choice but to feel, as we look through Charging Elk's eyes, what it is like to live in a no man's land forever." New York Times Book Review.

Weldon, Fay,

Chalcot Crescent / Fay Weldon. Europa Editions, 2010, c2009. 269 p.
ISBN 9781933372792

1. 2010s 2. Dystopias 3. Women authors 4. Families 5. Change 6. Rationing 7. Food supply 8. Conspiracies 9. Totalitarianism 10. Revolutionaries 11. Octogenarian women 12. London, England -- History -- 20th century 13. Alternative histories 14. Family sagas

Originally published: London : Corvus, 2009.

By 2013, capitalism has collapsed in Europe, and England has turned to protectionist policies, communal farms, and an intrusive National Unity Government that feeds its citizens National Meat Loaf and monitors people by street-corner CiviCams. In this bleak near-future, Frances Prideaux, once a successful writer of feminist novels and a proud product of the era of sexual liberation, is rehashing the sins of her past. As bailiffs try to repossess her house, Frances tells the story of her life--how she married her sister's boyfriend; rejected her stepson Henry, the revolution's creepily austere leader; and squandered her fortune and influence--and tries to keep tabs on her grandson, Amos, who is busy plotting against the government with his cohorts from Redpeace.

"[T]his is Orwellian nightmare recast for the Twittering classes. There is more skewed memoir than grim future or alternate universe, but you'll be entertained if you enjoy Weldon's trademark barbed frivolity." The New Scientist.

Weldon, Fay,

* The **life** and loves of a she-devil / Fay Weldon. Pantheon Books, 1983. 241 p.

ISBN 9780394539201

1. Anger in women 2. Revenge 3. Homemakers 4. Beauty 5. Mistresses 6. Superficiality 7. Husband and wife 8. Revenge in women 9. Extramarital affairs 10. Women -- Psychology 11. Tallness and shortness 12. Literary fiction

LC 84007070

Book made into a movie called She-devil.

Humble and unassuming Ruth, long-suffering wife and mother is ditched by her husband and decides to get what she wants--power, money, sex, and revenge.

Weldon, Fay

Worst fears : a novel / Fay Weldon. Atlantic Monthly Press, 1996. 200 p.

ISBN 087113635X

1. Husband and wife 2. Widows 3. Extramarital affairs 4. Narcissism in women 5. Black humor

LC 95-52367

A woman investigates the conflicting reports regarding her husband's recent death, and begins to dread the ominous implications in the story of suspense and black humor.

"Fay Weldon is the quintessential anti-romance novelist and always will be. But she's filed down a few sharp edges in 'Worst Fears,' and that makes it one of her best novels yet." New York Times Book Review.

Wellington, David

Positive / David Wellington. HarperCollins, 2015 416 p.

ISBN 9780062315373

1. Zombies 2. Exiles 3. Post-apocalypse 4. Concentration camps 5. Infection 6. Survival 7. Nineteen-year-old men 8. Murder 9. Horror

"Anyone can be positive. Acclaimed author David Wellington delivers his most ambitious, breakout novel yet a huge zombie novel in the bestselling vein of Guillermo Del Toro and Justin Cronin."--, Provided by publisher.

"Like The Walking Dead, the book uses the zombie apocalypse as a backdrop for a gripping story about the shattering of human society--the real villains here aren't the zombies but rather the road pirates, looters, religious cultists, and other groups that have sprung up in the 20 years since the 'crisis.' Wellington's most ambitious book is also his best, written with a maturity and compassion indicative of a writer who's found the story he was made to tell. Zombie groupies will eat this one up, but it should also be recommended to readers of all epic-scale fantasy,

including Justin Cronin's best-selling epic vampire novel The Passage (2010)." Booklist.

Wells, Benedict, 1984-

The **end** of loneliness : a novel / Benedict Wells ; translated from the German by Charlotte Collins. Penguin Books, 2019, c2016. 240 p.

ISBN 9780143134008

1. Grief 2. Orphans 3. Brothers and sisters 4. Memories 5. Life change events 6. Familial love 7. Romantic love 8. Friendship 9. Loss (Psychology) 10. Growing up 11. Writing 12. Family relationships 13. Germany 14. Translations -- German to English 15. Literary fiction

LC 2018033281

Originally published in German: Diogenes Verlag, Zurich 2016.

Follows the struggles of a directionless young man who, after a childhood overshadowed by the loss of his family, seeks to reconnect with a boarding-school friend and his own literary ambitions

Wells, H. G. (Herbert George), 1866-1946

The **complete** short stories of H. G. Wells / Edited by John Hammond. Phoenix Giant, 1999, c1998. 883 p.

ISBN 0753808722

1. Science fiction 2. Short stories

"A fat, heavy volume packed with humour, strangeness, horror and imaginative stimulus." Telegraph (London, UK).

Wells, H. G. (Herbert George), 1866-1946

* The **invisible** man / H. G. Wells. Signet Classic, 2002, c1897. xvi, 176 p.

ISBN 9780451528520

1. Invisibility 2. Human experimentation in medicine 3. Mad scientist (Concept) 4. Scientists 5. Men with mental illnesses 6. Classism 7. Social classes 8. Social acceptance 9. Self-acceptance 10. Privacy 11. Freedom 12. Neighbors 13. Murder 14. Good and evil 15. Classics 16. Science fiction

First published 1897.

First published by C.A. Pearson, 1897.

A scientist who has discovered a way to make himself invisible unleashes his growing madness and frustrations by terrorizing a small town.

Wells, H. G. (Herbert George), 1866-1946

* The **island** of Dr. Moreau / H. G. Wells. Signet Classics, 2005, c1896. vi, 224 p.

ISBN 0451529898

1. Survival (after airplane accidents, shipwrecks, etc) 2. Animal experimentation 3. Mad scientist (Concept) 4. Islands 5. Shipwrecks 6. Scientists 7. Physicians 8. Human/animal relationships 9. Horror 10. Classics 11. Science fiction

LC 2005008127

Originally published: 1896.

The sole survivor of a shipwreck, Edward Prendick, a young naturalist, finds himself stranded on a remote Pacific island run by the sinister Dr. Moreau, a mad scientist intent on creating a strain of beast men.

Wells, H. G. (Herbert George), 1866-1946

* The **time** machine / H.G. Wells ; with a new introduction by Greg Bear. Signet Classic, 2014, c1895. xix, 123 p.

ISBN 9780451470706

1. Time travel 2. Far future 3. Scientists 4. Inventions 5. Class conflict 6. Utopias 7. Dystopias 8. Time machines 9. Good and evil 10. Classics 11. Dystopian fiction 12. Social science fiction 13.

Science fiction

LC 2002066963

Originally published: London : Heinemann, 1895. First American edition: New York : H. Holt and company, 1895.

A classic novel of the future follows the Time Traveller as he hurtles one million years into the future and encounters a world populated by two distinct races, the childlike Eloi and the disgusting Morlocks who prey on the Eloi.

Wells, H. G. (Herbert George), 1866-1946

* The **war** of the worlds / H.G. Wells ; introduction by Arthur C. Clarke. Modern Library, 2002, c1898. 190 p.

ISBN 0375759239

1. Aliens (Non-humanoid) -- Sightings and encounters 2. Human/alien encounters 3. Martians 4. Life on other planets 5. Space vehicles 6. Diseases 7. Earth -- Invasions 8. Classics 9. Science fiction

First serialized in Pearson's Magazine, 1897.

Originally published: London : Heninemann, 1898.

The ultimate tale of Earth's invasion, written by one of the fathers of the science fiction genre. They came from a depleted, dying planet. Their target: the riches of a moist, green Earth. With horrifyingly advanced machines of destruction, they began their inexorable conquest. The war for Earth seemed destined to be ... but was it?

Wells, Martha

All systems red / Martha Wells. Tor, 2017. 144 p. Murderbot diaries

ISBN 9780765397539

1. Androids 2. Artificial intelligence 3. Scientists 4. High technology 5. Robots 6. Robotics 7. Investigations 8. Life on other planets 9. Scientific expeditions 10. Human/computer interaction 11. Science fiction

"As a heartless killing machine, I was a terrible failure," confesses the AI narrator of this fast-paced SF adventure. After hacking its own governor module and overriding its programming, security droid "Murderbot" ends up saving lives instead of ending them -- but only because letting all the humans die would interfere with its favorite activity: binge-watching some 35,000 hours' worth of entertainment media.?All Systems Red's snarky protagonist and suspenseful, action-packed plot should have readers eagerly anticipating future installments of the Murderbot Diaries. -- Description by Gillian Speace

"Wells gives depth to a rousing but basically familiar action plot by turning it into the vehicle by which SecUnit engages with its own rigorously denied humanity. The creepy panopticon of SecUnits multiple interfaces allows a hybrid first-person/omniscient perspective that contextualizes its experience without ever giving center stage to the humans." Publishers Weekly.

Wells, Rebecca, 1952-

Divine secrets of the Ya-Ya Sisterhood : a novel / Rebecca Wells. Harper Collins, 1996. 400 p. Ya-Yas

ISBN 0060173289

1. Forgiveness 2. Mother and adult daughter 3. Small town life -- Louisiana 4. Middle-aged women -- Friendship 5. Girls -- Friendship 6. Women theatrical producers and directors 7. Individual differences 8. Women -- Louisiana 9. Louisiana 10. Women's lives and relationships 11. Southern fiction

LC 964151

Sequel to: Little Altars Everywhere.

Sequel: Ya-Yas in Bloom.

Book Sense Book of the Year Adult Trade, 1999.

When Siddi inadvertently reveals some revealing things about her Southern childhood in a newspaper interview, her mother, Vivi, virtually disowns her. Vivi's lifelong friends, the Ya-Ya's, set in motion a plan to bring the mother and daughter back together using a scrapbook of childhood memories that they ask Vivi to put together.

"She has written an entertaining and engrossing novel filled with humor and heartbreak." Library Journal.

Welsh, Irvine

Dead men's trousers / Irvine Welsh. Melville House, 2019, c2018 419 p. Trainspotting

ISBN 9781612197555

1. Human body parts industry and trade 2. Men and success 3. Art 4. Drug addicts -- Edinburgh, Scotland 5. Sexuality 6. Drugs 7. Violence 8. Edinburgh, Scotland 9. Black humor

Originally published: London : Jonathan Cape, 2018.

Somewhat matured, international jet-setter Mark Renton and psychotic artist Frank Begbie accidentally reunite with Sick Boy and Spud in Scotland for one last scheme involving organ harvesting.

"Raunchy, profane, violent, and frequently hilarious in its epic descriptions of drug and alcohol abuse, the continued saga is remarkable for the way it delivers the anarchic goods to Trainspotting fans while touching on the ultimate obsessions of middle age: death and the purpose of life. The zenith of these books may well be the powerful prequel, Skagboys (2012), and nothing will match the intensity with which Welsh announced himself, but Dead Men's Trousers delivers a strangely life-affirming dose of dark absurdity, ensuring that, if this is the last we see of these characters, they won't soon be forgotten." Booklist.

Welsh, Irvine

Porno / Irvine Welsh. W. W. Norton, 2002. 483 p. Trainspotting

ISBN 0393057232

1. Pornographic films 2. Drug addicts -- Edinburgh, Scotland 3. Working class -- Edinburgh, Scotland 4. Young men -- Edinburgh, Scotland 5. Young women -- Edinburgh, Scotland 6. Heroin addicts 7. Sexuality 8. Drugs 9. Violence 10. Edinburgh, Scotland 11. Black humor

LC 2002026362

Sequel to: Trainspotting.

Adapted into the film entitled T2 trainspotting in 2017.

Originally published: London : Jonathan Cape, 2002.

Ten years on from "Trainspotting", Sick Boy is back in Edinburgh to realize his dream of making a pornographic movie with old pal, Mark Renton. Sick Boy and Renton find that they have unresolved issues to address, concerning Frank Begbie, the drug-addled Spud, but most of all, with each other.

"This novel signals, if not a return to form, then at least a return to enthusiastic formlessness to something like the raw, jagged energy of old." New York Times Book Review.

Welsh, Irvine

Skagboys / Irvine Welsh. W. W. Norton, 2012. 560 p. Trainspotting

ISBN 9780393088731

1. Drug addicts -- Edinburgh, Scotland 2. Working class -- Edinburgh, Scotland 3. Young men -- Edinburgh, Scotland 4. Young women -- Edinburgh, Scotland 5. Heroin addicts 6. Sexuality 7. Drugs 8. Violence 9. Edinburgh, Scotland 10. Great Britain -- Politics and government -- 1979-1997 11. Black humor

LC 2012018043

Prequel to Trainspotting.

Mark Renton seems to have it all: he's the first in his family to go to university, he's young, has a pretty girlfriend and a great social life. But Thatcher's government is destroying working-class communities across Britain, and the post-war certainties of full employment, educational opportunity and a welfare state are gone. When his badly handicapped younger brother dies the family bonds start to weaken, his life flips out of control, and he succumbs to the defeatism and the heroin which has taken hold in Edinburgh's grimmer areas. His friends face similar challenges. Spud Murphy is paid off from his job and faces long-term unemployment, while Tommy Lawrence feels that only love can save him from being sucked into a life of petty crime and violence, exemplified respectively by the thieving Matty Connell and psychotic Franco Begbie. And then there is Sick Boy, the supreme manipulator of the opposite sex, scamming and hustling his way through life. Skagboys charts their journey from likely lads to young men addicted to the heroin which has flooded their disintegrating community. This is the 1980s: not the sanitised version, of upbeat pop music, mullets, shoulder-pads and MTV, but a time of drugs, poverty, AIDS, violence, political strife and hatred and maybe just a little love; a decade which changed Britain for ever. The prequel to the world-renowned Trainspotting, this is an exhilarating and moving book, full of the scabrous humour, salty vernacular and appalling behaviour that has made Irvine Welsh a household name.

Welsh, Irvine

Trainspotting / Irvine Welsh. W. W. Norton, 1996, c1993. 348 p. Trainspotting
ISBN 0393314804
1. Drug addicts -- Edinburgh, Scotland 2. Working class -- Edinburgh, Scotland 3. Young men -- Edinburgh, Scotland 4. Young women -- Edinburgh, Scotland 5. Heroin addicts 6. Sexuality 7. Drugs 8. Violence 9. Edinburgh, Scotland 10. Great Britain -- Politics and government -- 1979-1997 11. Black humor
LC 9615044
Sequel: Porno.
Originally published: London: Secker & Warburg, 1993.
The story of a group of working-class junkies in Edinburgh, Rents, Sick Boy, Mother Superior, Swanney, Spuds, and Begbie. Violent, rude, sexually explicit, and very, very black.
"This novel is set in a working class neighborhood in Edinburgh. Narrator Mark Renton tells the story of young junkies in their 20s living on the dole, fending off adulthood and trying to escape from a world of AIDS, death and national despair." The New Republic.

Welsh, Kaite

The **unquiet** heart / Kaite Welsh. Pegasus Crime, 2019. 281 p. Sarah Gilchrist series
ISBN 9781681777498
1. Victorian era (1837-1901) 2. 1890s 3. Women medical students 4. Ambition in women 5. Autopsy 6. College teachers 7. Murder suspects 8. Murder investigation 9. Misogyny 10. Engaged persons 11. Independence in women 12. Men/women relations 13. Edinburgh, Scotland 14. Scotland -- Social life and customs -- 19th century 15. Great Britain -- History -- Victoria, 1837-1901 16. Historical mysteries
In this sequel to the acclaimed The Wages of Sin--and once again set in moody fin de siecle Edinburgh--Sarah Gilchrist finds herself trying to prove her fiancé's innocence in the midst of his murder trial.
"This excellent mix of historical mystery and romance should be recommended to fans of Deanna Raybourn's Lady Julia Grey's Victorian mysteries." Booklist.

Welsh, Kaite

The **wages** of sin / Kaite Welsh. Pegasus Crime, 2017. 290 p. Sarah Gilchrist series
ISBN 9781681773322
1. Victorian era (1837-1901) 2. Women medical students 3. Pariahs 4. Public hospitals 5. Murder investigation 6. Rape victims 7. Prostitutes 8. Crimes against women 9. Edinburgh, Scotland 10. Scotland 11. Great Britain -- History -- Victoria, 1837-1901 12. Historical mysteries
Despite numerous barriers, Sarah Gilchrist is determined to become a doctor in 1882, the first year the University of Edinburgh admitted women, but is drawn into a murder mystery when a former acquaintance turns up as a corpse in the dissecting room.
"Welshs deeply feminist novel is an engaging, fast-paced tale full of twists and turns." Booklist.

Welty, Eudora, 1909-2001

* The **collected** stories of Eudora Welty / Eudora Welty. Harcourt Brace Jovanovich, 1980. xvi, 622 p.
ISBN 9780151189946
1. Southern States -- Social life and customs -- 20th century 2. Short stories 3. Modern classics 4. Southern fiction
LC 80007947
National Book Award for Fiction finalist, 1981
All forty-one stories published by the distinguished writer are brought together, displaying her insights into the American South and including her most famous work, "Death of a Traveling Salesman"

Welty, Eudora, 1909-2001

* **Delta** wedding / Eudora Welty. Harcourt, 1946. 247 p.
ISBN 9781784971663
1. 1920s 2. Orphans 3. Weddings 4. Family relationships 5. Girls -- Mississippi 6. Cousins 7. Families 8. Social classes 9. Plantations 10. Southern States -- Social life and customs -- 20th century 11. Mississippi 12. Delta Region, Mississippi 13. Domestic fiction 14. Modern classics 15. Southern fiction
Set in 1923, on the Mississippi Delta, this story captures the mind and manners of a large aristocratic family.

Welty, Eudora, 1909-2001

Losing battles / Eudora Welty. Random House, 1970. 436 p.
1. 1930s 2. Family reunions 3. Grandmothers 4. Rural life -- Mississippi 5. Families -- Mississippi 6. Mississippi 7. Domestic fiction 8. Modern classics 9. Southern fiction
LC 74102304
On a hot August weekend in the 1930s, family members attend Granny Vaughan's 90th birthday on Sunday and the funeral of a former teacher on Monday.

Welty, Eudora, 1909-2001

The **optimist's** daughter / Eudora Welty. Random House, 1972. 180 p.
ISBN 0394480171
1. Funerals 2. Reunions 3. Young women -- Mississippi 4. Families -- Mississippi 5. Middle-aged women -- Southern States 6. Reminiscing in old age 7. Women -- Mississippi 8. Fathers -- Death 9. Second wives 10. Stepmothers 11. Mississippi 12. Psychological fiction 13. Domestic fiction 14. Modern classics 15. Southern Gothic 16. Southern fiction
LC 76039769
Pulitzer Prize for Fiction, 1973.

Laurel Hand is forced to face her Southern past when she returns to Mississippi for her father's funeral.

Welty, Eudora, 1909-2001

* The **ponder** heart / Eudora Welty ; drawings by Joe Krush. Harcourt Brace Jovanovich, 1954. 156 p.

1. Husband and wife -- Southern States 2. Small town life -- Southern States 3. Rich men -- Southern States 4. Marriage -- Southern States 5. Seventeen-year-old girls -- Southern States 6. Trials (Murder) -- Southern States 7. Uncles -- Southern States 8. Nieces -- Southern States 9. Senior men -- Southern States 10. Modern classics 11. Southern fiction

Edna Earle, a person of large distinction in Clay County, and the talkative owner of the Beulah Hotel, tells the story of her Uncle Daniel Ponder, a local hero whose over-affection for society compels him to give everything he owns away. The disappearance of Uncle Daniel's second wife, the waifish and willowy Bonnie Dee Peacock, leads to his arrest for murder. The trial, which comprises the second half of the novel, is a masterpiece of courtroom anarchy.

Welty, Eudora, 1909-2001

* The **robber** bridegroom / Eudora Welty ; designed and illustrated by Barry Moser. Harcourt Brace Jovanovich, 1987, c1942. 134 p.

ISBN 0151783187

1. Thieves 2. Merchants 3. Frontier and pioneer life 4. Mississippi 5. Historical fiction 6. Modern classics 7. Southern Gothic 8. Southern fiction

LC 87021195

Welty, Eudora, 1909-2001

Stories, essays & memoir / Eudora Welty. Library of America, 1998. x, 976 p.

ISBN 1883011558

1. Welty, Eudora, 1909- Childhood and youth 2. Welty, Eudora, 1909- Authorship 3. Authors, American -- 20th century 4. Racism 5. Violence 6. Family reunions 7. Southern States -- Social life and customs -- 20th century 8. Mississippi -- Social life and customs -- 20th century 9. Short stories 10. Essays 11. Modern classics 12. Southern fiction

LC 97046691

Gathers all of the short stories, published between 1941 and 1954, by the influential Southern writer, along with two nonfiction pieces from the 1960s and a perennially popular memoir, One Writer's Beginnings, from 1984.

Wendig, Chuck

* **Wanderers** : a novel / Chuck Wendig. Del Rey, 2019. xii, 782 p.

ISBN 9780399182105

1. Epidemics 2. Sleep walkers 3. Wanderers and wandering 4. Rock musicians 5. Radio personalities 6. Teenage girls 7. Survival (after epidemics) 8. Epidemiologists 9. Interpersonal relations 10. Artificial intelligence 11. Fear 12. Hysteria (Social psychology) 13. Civilization 14. Right and wrong 15. Militias and irregular armies 16. Science fiction 17. Apocalyptic fiction

When her little sister is afflicted by a bizarre sleepwalking disorder that begins to affect people all across the country, Shana is embroiled in an apocalyptic epidemic involving a decadent rock star, a religious radio host and a disgraced scientist.

"Wendig is clearly wrestling with some of the demons of our time, resulting in a story that is ambitious, bold, and worthy of attention." Kirkus.

Werfel, Franz, 1890-1945

* The **forty** days of Musa Dagh / Franz Werfel. Carroll & Graf, 1990, c1962. xviii, 824 p.

ISBN 0881846686

1. Armenian genocide, 1915-1923 2. Armenians in Turkey -- History -- 20th century 3. Persecution -- Turkey 4. Musa Dagh, Defense of, Turkey, 1915 5. Revolutions -- Turkey 6. Turkey -- History -- 1918-1960 7. Historical fiction 8. Translations -- German to English

Originally published: London : Jarrolds, Ltd., 1934.

Wealthy Armenian Gabriel Bagradian returns to Syria from Paris in 1915 and becomes caught in the Turkish campaign against the Armenians of Musa Dagh.

West, Dorothy, 1907-1998

* The **wedding** / Dorothy West. Doubleday, 1995. 240 p.

ISBN 9780385471435

1. 1950s 2. African American families 3. Weddings 4. African American intellectuals -- Martha's Vineyard, Massachusetts 5. Family relationships 6. Middle class African Americans 7. African American women 8. Marriage 9. Interracial marriage 10. Human skin color -- Social aspects 11. African Americans 12. Martha's Vineyard, Massachusetts 13. African American fiction 14. Family sagas

LC 9427285

Shelby Coles' marriage to a white jazz musician sends shockwaves through her upper class African American community on Martha's Vineyard in the 1950s.

"Through the ancestral histories of the Coles family, West . . . subtly reveals the ways in which color can burden and codify behavior. The author makes her points with a delicate hand, maneuvering with confidence and ease through a sometimes incendiary subject." Publishers Weekly.

West, Jessamyn, 1907-1984

The **friendly** persuasion / Jessamyn West. Harcourt Brace Jovanovich, 1991, c1945. 214 p.

ISBN 0156336065

1. Society of Friends Indiana 2. American Civil War era (1861-1865) 3. Quaker families 4. Families 5. Quakersna 6. United States Civil War, 1861-1865 7. Indiana -- Social life and customs 8. United States -- History -- Civil war, 1861-1865 9. Historical fiction 10. War stories

LC 91006468

Jess Birdwell, a Quaker with a fondness for fast horses, his wife Eliza, and their children struggle to deal with the turmoil, violence, and challenges of the Civil War in their own way.

West, Kathleen, 1978-

Minor dramas & other catastrophes / Kathleen West. Berkley, 2020. 377 p.

ISBN 9780593098400

1. Overprotectiveness in parents 2. Women teachers 3. Obsession 4. High schools 5. Gossiping and gossips 6. Stay-at-home mothers 7. Social justice 8. Virtual community 9. Progressive education 10. Minnesota 11. Literary fiction

Targeted by privileged families for her progressive educational approaches, a beloved teacher discovers unexpected common ground with a meddling parent whose inadvertent encounter with a drama student has had dangerous consequences for her family.

"An excellent, nuanced exploration of the world of high school and the students and adults who live within it." Kirkus.

West, Nathanael, 1903-1940

Novels and other writings / Nathanael West. Library of America, 1997 829 p.

ISBN 1883011280

1. Advice columnists 2. Film industry and trade 3. Los Angeles, California 4. Satirical fiction 5. Short stories 6. Letters 7. Essays 8. Modern classics 9. Anthologies

The first comprehensive, authoritative edition of the work of America's prince of black humor and social satire includes his most famous novels of the thirties, along with his poetry, essays, plays, film scripts, and letters.

Westerfeld, Scott

The **killing** of worlds / Scott Westerfeld. Tor, 2003. 336 p. Succession

ISBN 0765308509

1. Cyborgs 2. Immortalism 3. Space warfare 4. Immortality 5. Life after death 6. Imperialism 7. Cybernetics 8. Artificial intelligence 9. Rulers 10. Imaginary empires 11. Science fiction 12. Military science fiction

LC 2003056304

"A Tom Doherty Associates book."

Captain Laurent Zai embarks on a suicide mission to stop the next invasion of the Rix, machine-augmented humans dedicated to the destruction of the immortal Emperor, while his lover, Senator Nara Oxham, faces off against the Emperor himself.

"Captain Laurent Zai demonstrates his strategic cleverness as well as an unusual amount of luck, when he unexpectedly defeats the Rix ship he was sent to destroy an assignment intended to be a suicide mission. Meanwhile, in the imperial senate, Nara Oxham walks a fine line between treason and her party's agenda as she fights the emperor himself. . . . [This is] a rip-roaring space opera, with its strength residing in the characters, all of them involved in believable dilemmas." Booklist.

Westerfeld, Scott

The **risen** empire / Scott Westerfeld. Tor, 2003. 304 p. Succession

ISBN 9780765305558

1. Cyborgs 2. Hostages 3. Immortalism 4. Hostage taking 5. Rulers 6. Imaginary empires 7. Cybernetics 8. Life after death 9. Imperialism 10. Space warfare 11. Imaginary empires 12. Science fiction 13. Military science fiction

LC 2002042952

"A Tom Doherty Associates book."

When the empire is challenged by a band of machine-augmented humans who seek to put their own gods in control by kidnapping the Immortal Child Empress, captain Laurent Zal of the Imperial Frigate Lynx is charged with her rescue.

"Westerfeld's speculations about the rise and fall of civilizations are appealingly quirky . . . and his action scenes have a breathless realism that does not gloss over the bloody nature of combat. Perhaps most important, his moral calculus never lapses into Q.E.D. As the narrative jumps from intimate glimpses of the Empire to the Rix Cult and back again, we grow less and less clear about whom we are rooting for." New York Times Book Review.

Westheimer, David

* **Von** Ryan's express / David Westheimer. Doubleday, 1964. 327 p.

ISBN 9780385025478

1. Escapes 2. World War II 3. Prisoners of war, American 4. Italy 5. War stories

LC 63020513

Sequel: Von Ryan's return.

An Air Force colonel unwittingly delivers a group of British and American officers into the hands of the Germans and then plans an escape.

Westlake, Donald E.

Bad news / Donald Westlake. Mysterious Press, 2001. 352 p. Dortmunder novels

ISBN 089296717X

1. Swindlers and swindling 2. Criminals 3. Burglary 4. Gambling on Indian reservations 5. Casinos 6. New York City 7. New York (State) 8. Caper novels 9. Farcical fiction

LC 00045592

A criminal mastermind offers Dortmunder one thousand dollars to help him dig up a grave in Queens and switch the corpses of two Indians in order to illegally inherit one-third of the largest casino in the east.

"Westlake has a genius for comic strategy, and the complications he devises when the casino operators initiate a counterplot to discredit Little Feather have a lunatic brilliance worthy of Abbott and Costello. But Westlake is also a card with characters, and he flashes that talent to terrific effect here." New York Times Book Review.

Westlake, Donald E.

* **Bank** shot / Donald E. Westlake. Simon and Schuster, 1972. 224 p. Dortmunder novels

ISBN 0671211803

1. Swindlers and swindling 2. Criminals 3. Bank robberies 4. Burglary 5. Banks and banking 6. Former FBI agents 7. Police 8. Criminals 9. Caper novels 10. Farcical fiction

LC 72183763

When John Dortmunder sets out to rob a bank, he really means it. He steals the whole thing. With the help of a sophomoric ex-FBI man, a militant safe-cracker, and old standbys Andy Kelp, Stan Murch, and Murch's Mom, Dortmunder puts a set of wheels under a trailer that just happens to be the temporary site of the Capitalists' & Immigrants' Trust ("Just Watch Us Grow!"). But when the safe won't open and the cops get close, Dortmunder realizes he's got a bigger problem than robbing a bank. He's got to find a place--somewhere in the suburban wasteland of Long Island--to put it.

"It is Westlake's triumph that whereas on one hand the reader knows he simply can't take the characters and situations seriously, those characters are so deftly drawn that they are eminently believable." New York Times Book Review.

Westlake, Donald E.

Brothers keepers / Donald E. Westlake. M. Evans, 1975. 254 p.

ISBN 9780446401357

1. Greed 2. Monasticism and religious orders for men 3. Eviction 4. Benedictine monasteries 5. Real estate 6. Manhattan, New York City 7. Caper novels

LC 75011831

What will a group of monks do when their two-century-old monastery in New York City is threatened with demolition to make room for a new high-rise? Anything they have to. "Thou Shalt Not Steal" is only the first of the Commandments to be broken as the saintly face off against the unscrupulous over that most sacred of relics, a Park Avenue address.

Westlake, Donald E.

Don't ask / Donald E. Westlake. Mysterious Press, 1993. 327 p. Dortmunder novels

ISBN 0892964693

1. Christian relic thefts 2. Criminals 3. Thieves 4. Relic thefts 5. Art

thefts 6. Art thefts 7. Caper novels

LC 92053721

John Dortmunder has a job offer. He's been hired by third parties to pull off heists in the past, but never to lay his hands on anything this peculiar. Frankly, it's a bone. A femur which, 800 years ago, was part of a 16-year-old girl who, having been killed and eaten by her own family, was made a saint by the Church. Now, two small eastern European countries--Tsergovia and Votskojek--are fighting over the bone. There's only room for one of them in the United Nations General Assembly, and the choice is in the hands of a powerful Catholic prelate. The country that tosses him the bone is sure to be in like Flynn. Dortmunder rounds up his gang and cases the Votskojekian mission, a former tramp steamer parked in the East River. The current repository of the bone, it will be the target of a heist carried out by land and sea, with the team displaying the finesse and split-second timing for which they're famous.

"If the plot is of no great concern, it is the effortlessness, wit, and sheer good-heartedness of the telling that make 'Don't Ask' such a consistent delight." New York Times Book Review.

Westlake, Donald E.

Drowned hopes / Donald E. Westlake. Mysterious Press, 1990. 418 p. Dortmunder novels

ISBN 0892961783

1. Criminals 2. Thieves -- Albany, New York 3. Dams -- New York (State) 4. Former criminals 5. Reservoirs -- New York (State) 6. New York (State) 7. Caper novels

LC 89035859

John Dortmunder strikes it unlucky again when he gets a visit from an old cellmate, Tom Jimson. During Jimson's long stretch in the pen, the State of New York decided to turn a certain valley near Albany into a reservoir and it just so happens that the loot from Tom's last bank job was buried in that valley. Now the cash is under fifty feet of water and Dortmunder has to find a way to retrieve it--or else Tom will dynamite the reservoir dam and flood the countryside. One botched attempt follows another, and Jimson's blasting finger is getting mighty itchy. Will Dortumunder muddle through?

Westlake, Donald E.

Forever and a death / Donald E. Westlake. Hard Case Crime, 2017 463 p.

ISBN 9781785654237

1. 1990s 2. Revenge in men 3. Businesspeople 4. Bank robberies 5. Inventors 6. Espionage 7. Gold thefts 8. Terrorism -- Prevention 9. High technology weapons 10. Women environmentalists 11. Hong Kong -- History -- 1997- 12. Thrillers and suspense 13. Pulp fiction

A formerly wealthy businessman who loses everything to Hong Kong's new Chinese authorities vengefully plots to use a construction technology to destroy the city and steal its gold, a heist that is countered by the technology's developer and a beautiful young environmental activist.

Westlake, Donald E.

Get real / Donald E. Westlake. Grand Central Pub., 2009. 288 p. Dortmunder novels

ISBN 9780446178600

1. Thieves 2. Reality television programs 3. Organized crime 4. Criminals 5. Rich men 6. Television actors and actresses 7. Crime bosses 8. New York City 9. Caper novels

LC bl2009012454

Reluctantly agreeing to allow his gang to appear in a reality television cop show that promises a lucrative payout and legal protection, luckless thief John Dortmunder and his partner, Kelp, devise a secondary plot to deceive case-cracking television viewers.

"A rollicking crime caper that pulls the pants right off the reality TV industry." New York Times Book Review.

Westlake, Donald E.

Good behavior / Donald E. Westlake. Mysterious Press, 1985, c1986. 244 p. Dortmunder novels

ISBN 0892962402

1. Criminals 2. Kidnapping -- Manhattan, New York City 3. Nuns -- Manhattan, New York City 4. Kidnappers 5. Convents -- Manhattan, New York City 6. Thieves -- Manhattan, New York City 7. Manhattan, New York City 8. Caper novels

LC 85043178

Master burglar John Dortmunder returns in the unlikely role of a modern-day Manhattan Robin Hood. When a bungled burglary drops Dortmunder through a skylight into an impoverished Tribeca convent, he finds himself at the mercy of a congregation of hard-nosed but devout nuns, who need the sort of aid that only a man of his peculiar talents can provide. One of their group, Sister Mary Grace, has been kidnapped by a brutal deprogrammer in the employ of her father, a business tycoon who rules his empire (and his family) with an iron hand. She is being held, Rapunzel-like, on the heavily-guarded upper floor of a midtown skyscraper. Dortmunder, threatened with exposure by the Holy Sisters, is charged with the seemingly impossible task of stealing back Sister Mary.

"The author manages to create characters who are a curious mixture of stereotypes and archetypes. If he is a master of the comic crime caper, and he is, he also does what the best comic writers throughout history have donemake a comment on society." New York Times Book Review.

Westlake, Donald E.

* The **hot** rock / Donald E. Westlake. Mysterious Press, 2001, c1970. 287 p. Dortmunder novels

ISBN 9780671205416

1. Jewelry theft 2. Jewel thieves 3. Former convicts 4. Criminals 5. Emeralds 6. Caper novels

LC 70107263

John Dortmunder proves he has what it takes to be an habitual offender. Dortmunder steals the same jewel not just once, not twice, but again, and again, and again. Dortmunder didn't want to steal the Balabomo Emerald, but when one of two competing African countries--the nation of Talabwo--finances the scheme, he can be persuaded. Talabwo has purchased a fiasco. As Dortmunder's gang strikes by car, helicopter, and train, one heist after another goes wrong. The gem keeps slipping away, fast becoming an emerald with a sense of humor.

"This novel comes awesomely close to the ultimate in comic, big-caper novels; it's . . . filled with mocking style and action and imagination." New York Times Book Review.

Westlake, Donald E.

* **Memory** / Donald E. Westlake. Leisure Books, 2010. 336 p.

ISBN 9780843963755

1. Life change events 2. Memory 3. Amnesia 4. Actors and actresses 5. Extramarital affairs 6. Voyages and travels 7. Psychological fiction

Hospitalized after a liaison with another man's wife ends in violence, Paul Cole has just one goal: to rebuild his shattered life. But with his memory damaged, the police hounding him, and no way even to get home, Paul's facing steep odds--and a bleak fate if he fails.

"In this novel that Westlake wrote in the early 1960s and never published, Paul Cole suffers from partial amnesia his past is just beyond the reach of his mind. He keeps moving, like a fugitive, through a succession of working-class jobs; he falls in love; he gets in trouble with the law. Westlake never again dabbled in social realism, which is a shame:

Memory is terse and bleak and low-key emotional, and as indelible as Westlake's other books." Entertainment Weekly.

Westlake, Donald E.

The **road** to ruin / Donald E. Westlake. Mysterious Press, 2004. 342 p. Dortmunder novels

ISBN 089296801X

1. Criminals 2. Swindlers and swindling 3. Kidnapping 4. Impostors 5. Chief executive officers 6. Venture capitalists 7. Business -- Corrupt practices 8. Labor unions 9. Automobile thefts 10. Antique and classic cars 11. Caper novels

LC 2003065007

"Ingenuity fuels the plot, but what puts the match to the comedy is the moral outrage of the furiously funny characters." New York Times Book Review.

Westlake, Donald E.

Watch your back! / Donald E. Westlake. Mysterious Press, 2005. 320 p. Dortmunder novels

ISBN 0892968028

1. Criminals 2. Organized crime 3. Robbery 4. Rich men 5. Mafia 6. Bars 7. Islands 8. New York City 9. Caribbean Area 10. Caper novels

LC 2004061064

Dortmunder's trusted fence Arnie Albright is onto the score of a life-time: easy access to one of the most lavish apartments in New York, but when the gang round up to plan the heist they find their beloved gin joint in the mob's clutches.

"Arnie Albright, a fence so obnoxious his family intervened and sent him to Club Med in hopes he'd become more likable, has returned from the resort minimally improved, but having met the man of his dreams Preston Fareweather, a millionaire who's as comically distasteful as Arnie and who, more importantly, plans to be away from his art-filled New York penthouse indefinitely, on the run from hordes of furious ex-wives. Albright calls in Dortmunder and his pals to take advantage of Fareweather's absence. . . . Events unfold in a delicious sequence, and every step is complemented by great writing." Publishers Weekly.

Westlake, Donald E.

What's so funny? / Donald E. Westlake. Warner Books, 2007. 320 p. Dortmunder novels

ISBN 9780446582407

1. Criminals 2. Chess sets 3. Robbery 4. Thieves 5. Rich men 6. Mafia 7. Organized crime 8. Caper novels

LC 2006933789

Tempted to find a highly valuable, seven-hundred-pound chess set, hapless crook John Dortmunder musters his merry band of fellow ne'er-do-wells on a haphazard treasure hunt that prompts his investigation of Russia's last czar, an effort in which he enlists the assistance of tough former cop Johnny Eppick.

"This caper has an ending so laden with irony it almost has you thinking that crime doesn't pay. But of course it does pay, in those laughs that land on every page." New York Times Book Review.

Westlake, Donald E.

What's the worst that could happen? / Donald E. Westlake. Mysterious Press, 1996. 373 p. Dortmunder novels

ISBN 089296586X

1. Criminals 2. Burglary 3. Good luck charms 4. Billionaires 5. Rings 6. Thieves 7. Caper novels

LC 96-12770

It started with a ring. The yellow metal said brass, not gold, and the sparkly bits were certainly not diamonds. But the ring belonged to May's horseplaying uncle, who swore it brought good luck. Dort-munder, who wouldn't kick a little good luck out of bed, put it to the test when he goes to burglarize Long Island billionaire Max Fairbanks. As luck would have it, Dortmunder is greeted by Fairbanks himself--and a loaded gun--as soon as he strolls through the door. When the cops arrive, the mogul adds insult to injury by claiming that Dortmunder's lucky ring is actually his. As soon as Dortmunder can give the cops the slip, the world's most single-minded burglar goes after the fat cat with a vengeance and a team of crooks that only he can assemble.

"Although the gang's dirty tricks are wonderfully ingenious, the characters deliver the real razzle-dazzle. A grandiose guy like Max is cut to order for Mr. Westlake's droll comic style, which reflects a kind of gleeful horror at the schlocky esthetics of the rich and the morally damned." New York Times Book Review.

Westward : a fictional history of the American West : edited by Dale L. Walker. Forge, 2003. 432 p.

ISBN 0765304511

1. Frontier and pioneer life -- The West (United States) 2. The West (United States) 3. Short stories 4. Westerns 5. Anthologies

LC 2002045481

"A Tom Doherty Associates book."

"The collection reveals both the vitality and the diversity of the west-ern genre as well as the enduring appeal of the short story." Booklist.

Wharton, Edith, 1862-1937

The **children** / Edith Wharton ; with an introduction by Marilyn French. Virago, 2006, c1928. 368 p.

ISBN 9781844082926

1. Stepbrothers and stepsisters 2. Eccentric families 3. Single men and children 4. Children of divorced parents 5. Loss (Psychology) 6. Middle-aged men 7. Child neglect 8. Families 9. Domestic fiction 10. Modern classics

Originally published: 1998.

Originally published: New York : D. Appleton & Co., 1928.

On a cruise ship between Algiers and Venice Martin Boyne, a bach-elor in his forties, befriends a band of ebullient, precocious children. With humour and drama, the author portrays a world of intrigues and infidelities, skewering the manners and mores of Americans abroad.

Wharton, Edith, 1862-1937

Collected stories, 1891-1910 / Edith Wharton ; selected and with notes by Maureen Howard. Library of America , 2001. x, 928 p.

ISBN 1883011930

1. Manners and customs 2. United States -- Social life and customs -- 1865-1918 3. United States -- Social life and customs -- 19th century 4. United States -- Social life and customs -- 20th century 5. Short stories 6. Modern classics

LC 00057596

Contains thirty-eight short stories exploring the author's themes of relations between the sexes, satire of social class, character, and moral-ity.

Wharton, Edith, 1862-1937

Collected stories, 1911-1937 / Edith Wharton ; selected and with notes by Maureen Howard. Library of America, 2001. x, 848 p.

ISBN 9781883011949

1. Manners and customs 2. United States -- Social life and customs -- 20th century 3. Short stories 4. Anthologies 5. Modern classics

LC 00057595

Contains twenty-nine short stories exploring the author's themes of relations between the sexes, satire of social class, character, and morality.

Wharton, Edith, 1862-1937

* **Ethan** Frome / Edith Wharton. Scribner, 1997, c1911. 150 p.

ISBN 9780684825915

1. Farmers -- Massachusetts 2. Married men 3. Single women -- Massachusetts 4. Farm life -- Massachusetts 5. Accident victims 6. Men with disfigurements 7. Love triangles 8. Rural poor people 9. Husband and wife -- Massachusetts 10. Women cousins 11. Villages -- Massachusetts 12. Massachusetts 13. New England 14. Literary fiction 15. Modern classics

Originally published: New York : C. Scribner's Sons, 1911.

Ethan Frome works his unproductive farm and struggles to maintain a bearable existence with his difficult, suspicious, and hypochondriac wife, Zeenie. But when Zeenie's vivacious cousin enters their household as a "hired girl", Ethan finds himself obsessed with her and with the possibilities for happiness she comes to represent.

Wheeler, Richard S.

The **canyon** of bones / Richard S. Wheeler. Forge, 2007. 336 p. Skye's West

ISBN 9780765313249

1. 1850s 2. Guides (Persons) 3. Explorers -- Great Britain 4. Shoshoni Indians 5. Mountain men 6. Frontier and pioneer life 7. Voyages and travels 8. Quests 9. Wilderness survival 10. The West (United States) -- History -- 19th century 11. Westerns 12. Adventure stories

LC 2006102846

"A Tom Doherty Associates Book."

Working as a guide for wealthy Englishman Graves Duplessis Mercer, mountain man Barnaby Skye soon discovers that his employer is only interested in salacious and weird tales to write up for the British tabloids, a situation that endangers all of their lives when they visit a Missouri River valley filled with gigantic fossils of ancient monsters, a region sacred to local tribes.

"Overall, this is genial, character-driven western writing with plenty of action and appreciation for Native American customs. Skye's foul-mouthed Crow wife, Victoria, is absolutely delightful, and even his cantankerous horse, Jawbone, has more personality than most western leads. Not just for fans of the series, this will appeal to anyone in search of solidly adventuresome tales." Booklist.

Wheeler, Richard S.

North star / Richard S. Wheeler. Forge, 2009. 320 p. Skye's West

ISBN 9780765316639

1. 19th century 2. Senior men 3. Guides (Persons) 4. Native American women 5. Frontier and pioneer life 6. Mountain men 7. Voyages and travels 8. The West (United States) -- History -- 19th century 9. Westerns

Pursuing a new life away from Montana's Crazy Mountains, Barnaby Skye, his Indian wives, and his son search for missing family members while the government and settlers continually push their tribe through Missouri and Wyoming.

Whelan, Julia, 1984-

My Oxford year / Julia Whelan. William Morrow & Co., 2018. 329 p.

ISBN 9780062740649

1. Women graduate students 2. College teachers 3. Studying abroad 4. People with cancer 5. Americans in Great Britain 6. Secrets 7. Universities and colleges 8. Sexual attraction 9. Men/women relations 10. England 11. Oxford, England 12. Contemporary romances

Offered a fantastic job in a rising star's political campaign on condition that she will work abroad and return to Washington after spending a dream year at Oxford, Ella clashes with, and then falls for, an outspoken literature professor with a life-changing secret that forces her to rethink her ambitions.

Whitaker, Kayla Rae

The **animators** : a novel / Kayla Rae Whitaker. Random House, 2016. 372 p.

ISBN 9780812989281

1. Female friendship 2. Animation (Cinematography) 3. Women animators 4. Women artists 5. Women film producers and directors 6. Obsession 7. Ambition 8. Secrets 9. Love 10. Business partners 11. Life change events 12. Mainstream fiction 13. Psychological fiction

LC 2015049662

Two women, who met in an art class in college and instantly became best friends, try to salvage their relationship after their successful animated filmmaking partnership nearly destroys their personal lives nearly a decade later.

"Highly recommended for fiction readers, the LBGTQ community, those with an interest in cartooning, and anyone interested in the variability of the human condition." Library Journal.

White, Bailey

Quite a year for plums : a novel / Bailey White. A. A. Knopf, 1998. 220 p.

ISBN 0679445315

1. Women wildlife artists 2. Plant pathologists 3. Eccentrics and eccentricities 4. Small town life 5. Horticulture 6. Wildlife 7. Interpersonal relations 8. Men/women relations 9. Georgia -- Social life and customs 10. Mainstream fiction 11. Short stories 12. Gentle reads

LC 9741124

Introduces the colorful and offbeat inhabitants of a sleepy, southern Georgia town, including Roger, a studious peanut virologist; Della, a newcomer and painter of chickens; and Louise, who is trying to summon Martian invaders.

"The women in town are worried about Roger, the peanut virologist. Hilma and Meade discuss him at their weekly readings. Eula frets over his welfare--not to mention his appetite. And everyone else just seems to be content with giving opinions on his budding romance with the strange bird artist, Della. . . . [The author] will make the reader care about this nurturing gaggle of women and other community members in a small, sleepy town in southern Georgia." Library Journal.

White, Christian

The **wife** and the widow / Christian White Minotaur Books, 2020, c2019. 320 p.

ISBN 9781250194374

1. Widows 2. Married women 3. Secrets 4. Married men -- Death 5. Murderers 6. Grief 7. Island life 8. Thrillers and suspense

Originally published in Australia, 2019.

On an eerie island town in the middle of winter, two women join forces to uncover the secret life of one's dead husband and the guilt of the other's.

"White exceeds readers' expectations after his supersuccessful debut, with strong, complex protagonists in Abby and Kate and notable secondary characters who are well developed. The plot never stops and the clever twist is thrilling." Library Journal.

LIST OF FICTIONAL WORKS

White, Edmund, 1940-

The **beautiful** room is empty / Edmund White. Knopf, 1988. 227 p.

ISBN 9780394564449

1. Gay men 2. Identity (Psychology) 3. Self-awareness in men 4. Homosexuality 5. Gay men -- Sexuality 6. Gay men -- Psychotherapy 7. LGBTQIA fiction 8. Coming-of-age stories

LC 87040495

Sequel to: A boy's own story.

Sequel: The farewell symphony.

Lambda Literary Award for Gay Men's Fiction, 1988.

A young gay man experiences the pain of growing out of adolescence and struggles to come to terms with his homosexuality and his desire for power as society moves from the constrained 1950s to the expressive 1960s.

"[S]equel to A boy's own story. ... What emerges is the picture of a young man desperately struggling to come to terms with himself, a struggle that is a universal even if the context for every individual is different. Artfully constructed, this work clearly transcends its theme." Library Journal.

White, Edmund, 1940-

* A **boy's** own story / Edmund White. Penguin, 2009, c1982. 217 p.

ISBN 9780143114840

1. Gay teenagers 2. Homosexuality 3. Identity (Psychology) 4. Growing up 5. Coming-of-age stories 6. LGBTQIA fiction

Sequel: The beautiful room is empty.

Originally published: New York : Dutton, 1982.

At home, in school, and on the streets, a homosexual teenager moves through comic sexual experiments, isolation, fear, and exciting expectations toward an escape from childhood and a firm sense of self.

"This first-person novel is written with the flourish of a master stylist. . . . It is an endearing portrait of a child's longing to be charming, popular, powerful, and loved, and of his struggles with adults . . . [told with] sensitivity and elegance." Harper's..

White, Edmund, 1940-

Jack Holmes and his friend : a novel / Edmund White. Bloomsbury, 2012. 392 p.

ISBN 9781608197033

1. 1960s 2. 1970s 3. 1980s 4. Male friendship 5. Homosexuality 6. Sexuality 7. Love triangles 8. Married men 9. Unrequited love 10. Friendship 11. New York City 12. LGBTQIA fiction

LC 2011014728

A tale set against a backdrop of the sexual revolution in America traces the decades-long friendship of Jack Holmes and Will Wright, which is marked by Jack's secret love for Will, Will's marriage in spite of conflicted sexual feelings and the devastating rise of AIDS.

White, Elle Katharine, 1991-

Dragonshadow / Elle Katharine White. Harper Voyager, 2018. 352 p. Heartstone

ISBN 9780062747969

1. Quests 2. Dragons 3. Married people 4. Monsters 5. Newlyweds 6. Aristocracy 7. Missing girls 8. Men/women relations 9. Epic fantasy 10. Adaptations, retellings, and spin-offs

A second Austen-inspired romantic fantasy continues of the story of warrior newlyweds Aliza and Alastair, who journey through the Tekari-infested Old Wilds of Arle to assist the mysterious Lord Selwyn amid rumors of an unseen monster.

White, Elle Katharine, 1991-

Heartstone / Elle Katharine White. Harper Voyager, 2017. 336 p. Heartstone

ISBN 9780062451941

1. Dragons 2. Courtship 3. Young women 4. Griffins 5. Marriage 6. Social classes 7. Men/women relations 8. Epic fantasy 9. Adaptations, retellings, and spin-offs

LC 2016018398

In a retelling of "Pride and Prejudice," Aliza Bentaine agrees when the people of Merybourne Manor hire Riders to fight the monsters threatening their kingdom, but is thrown off guard by her romantic attraction to the proud dragonrider Alastair Daired.

"Referencing Austen just enough to ground her characters, White fills her unusual fantasy world with plenty of interesting conflicts to fuel this tale of romance and heroism." Publishers Weekly.

White, Randy Wayne

Salt river / Randy Wayne White. G. P. Putnam's Sons, 2020. 384 p. Doc Ford novels

ISBN 9780735212725

1. Marine biologists 2. Male friendship 3. Sperm donors 4. Single men 5. Adult children 6. Deception 7. Florida 8. Gulf Coast, Florida 9. Thrillers and suspense

LC 2019050880

When his reckless bachelor friend reveals that he has fathered numerous children through sperm-bank donations, Doc Ford races to prevent his friend's past misdeeds from turning deadly during an impromptu family reunion.

White, Roseanna M., 1982-

A **lady** unrivaled / Roseanna M. White. Bethany House Publishing, 2016. 384 p. Ladies of the manor

ISBN 9780764213526

1. Edwardian era (1901-1914) 2. Extortion 3. Aristocracy 4. Independence in women 5. Hope (Christianity) 6. Protectiveness in men 7. Faith (Christianity) 8. Fathers and daughters 9. Intrigue 10. Manors 11. Mate selection 12. Men/women relations 13. Cotswolds, England -- History -- 20th century 14. England -- History -- 20th century 15. Christian historical romances

Lady Ella Myerston knows of the danger that haunts her brother, and she intends to put an end to it. While visiting her friend Brook, the true owner of the Fire Eyes diamonds, Ella accidentally gets entangled in an attempt to blackmail the dashing, newly reformed Lord Cayton. Will she become the next casualty of the alleged curse?

"Readers will be kept guessing through the final page, thrilled by the butterflies of Ella and Caytons courtship and abuzz in the series heart-pounding finale." Booklist.

White, Silk

* **Tears** of a hustler / Silk White. Good2Go Pub., 2008. 398 p. Tears of a hustler

ISBN 9780615211626

1. Street life 2. Drug dealers 3. African American men 4. Police corruption 5. Pregnant women 6. Men/women relations 7. African Americans 8. New York City 9. African American fiction 10. Urban fiction

Drug kingpin Pauleena must use all of her talents to defend her empire when Marvin, a rising hustler, sets out to take it over.

White, Silk

Tears of a hustler 2 / Silk White. Good2Go Pub., 2010. 303 p. Tears of a hustler

ISBN 9780578040110

1. Street life 2. African American men 3. Drug dealers 4. Organized crime 5. Police 6. Police corruption 7. Men/women relations 8. African Americans 9. African American fiction 10. Urban fiction

G-money is back, but this time he's on a mission: not only is he running things all by himself now, but he still has unfinished business that needs to be settled with Detective Nelson, Rell, and Big Mel.

White, Stephen (Stephen Walsh), 1951-

Compound fractures / Stephen White. Dutton, 2013. 384 p. Alan Gregory novels

ISBN 9780525952602

1. Clinical psychologists 2. Psychotherapist and patient 3. Murder witnesses 4. Psychologists 5. Secrets 6. Secrecy 7. Detectives 8. Wife killing 9. Murder suspects 10. Boulder, Colorado 11. Thrillers and suspense

LC 2013016252

Boulder psychologist Alan Gregory discovers that the obstacles threatening his personal and professional arenas are being orchestrated by unrecognized enemies who force him to reconsider what he has long believed about trust and love.

White, Stephen (Stephen Walsh), 1951-

Dry ice : a novel / Stephen White. Dutton, 2007. 416 p. Alan Gregory novels

ISBN 0525949976

1. Psychopaths 2. Escapes 3. Former psychiatric hospital patients 4. Psychologists 5. Forensic psychology 6. Men with mental illnesses 7. Revenge 8. Family secrets 9. Men -- Decision making 10. Consequences 11. Men/women relations 12. Boulder, Colorado 13. Thrillers and suspense

LC 2006026771

Alan Gregory finds his family targeted by brilliant murderer Michael McClelland when the latter is released from the Colorado State Mental Hospital, a situation that is complicated by McClelland's detailed knowledge about Alan's innermost secrets.

"Contemporary cerebral thrillers don't get much better than . . . [this novel], which deftly combines complex characterization and intricate plotting." Publishers Weekly.

White, Stephen (Stephen Walsh), 1951-

Kill me / Stephen White. Dutton, 2006. 352 p. Alan Gregory novels

ISBN 0525949305

1. Assisted suicide 2. Men with terminal illnesses 3. Mortality 4. Euthanasia 5. Businesspeople 6. Assassins 7. Forensic psychology 8. Psychologists 9. Boulder, Colorado 10. Thrillers and suspense

LC 2005024296

Dr. Alan Gregory confronts the case of a man who, having survived a near-fatal accident, makes an agreement with a shadowy organization that ends the lives of clients who do not want to be a burden in the event of dire illnesses or injuries.

"Bizarre, thrilling, and oh so much fun." Booklist.

White, Stephen (Stephen Walsh), 1951-

Line of fire / Stephen White. Dutton, 2012. 384 p. Alan Gregory novels

ISBN 9780525952527

1. Clinical psychologists 2. Psychotherapist and patient 3. Suicide investigation 4. Psychologists 5. Secrets 6. Detectives 7. Boulder, Colorado 8. Thrillers and suspense

LC 2011042217

Alan Gregory hopes for a quieter life involving his clinical psychology practice only to be thrown into upheaval by a challenging patient, Diane's imminent emotional collapse and the possible exposure of his involvement in a woman's suicide.

White, Stephen (Stephen Walsh), 1951-

The **siege** / Stephen White. Dutton, 2009. 416 p. Alan Gregory novels

ISBN 9780525951223

1. Yale University 2. Detectives -- Connecticut 3. Missing persons 4. Secret societies -- New Haven, Connecticut 5. Missing persons investigation 6. Kidnappers 7. Psychologists 8. Forensic psychology 9. New Haven, Connecticut 10. Connecticut 11. Thrillers and suspense

LC 2009007586

The popular character Dr. Alan Gregory takes a backseat as his long-time friend, suspended Boulder police detective Sam Purdy, investigates a number of high-profile disappearances at Yale University that may have ties to a campus secret society.

White, T. H. (Terence Hanbury), 1906-1964

* The **once** and future king / T.H. White. G. P. Putnam's Sons, 1958. 677 p. Once and future king

ISBN 0399105972

1. Arthur, King 2. Knights and knighthood -- Great Britain 3. Grail 4. Merlin (Legendary character) 5. Wizards 6. Magic 7. Betrayal 8. Quests 9. Rulers 10. Great Britain -- History -- Anglo-Saxon period, 449-1066 11. Arthurian fantasy 12. Historical fantasy 13. Modern classics

LC 58010760

Part 1 was the inspiration for the movie The sword in the stone.

Part 2,The Queen of air and darkness, also known as The witch in the wood.

The once and future king (comprising four books) first published by Collins, 1958. The book of Merlyn first published by Voyager, 1996.

Merlyn instructs Arthur and his brother Sir Kay in the ways of the world. One of them will need it-- the king has died leaving no heir, and a rightful one must be found by pulling a sword from an anvil resting on a stone. In the second and third parts of the novel, Arthur has become king and the kingdom is threatened from the north. In the final two books, the aging king faces his greatest challenge, when his own son threatens to overthrow him. In The Book of Merlyn, Arthur's tutor Merlyn reappears, and teaches him that, even in the face of apparent ruin, there is hope.

Whitehead, Colson, 1969-

Apex hides the hurt / Colson Whitehead. Doubleday :, 2006. 224 p.

ISBN 038550795X

1. Consultants 2. Identity (Psychology) 3. Marketing 4. Name-brand products -- Marketing 5. City life 6. Cities and towns 7. Local government 8. Marketing 9. Names, Geographical 10. Names 11. Small towns 12. Satirical fiction 13. African American fiction

LC 2005049391

A small Midwestern town is having an identity crisis--should they have a new techno-savvy name or a name honoring the freedmen who founded the town? Or is the current name just fine? They call in a professional naming consultant, famous for naming Apex bandages--guaranteed to match any skin color. But even he is losing his faith in monikers.

LIST OF FICTIONAL WORKS

"A secretive narrator often means the story is weak and has to be puffed up with mystery, but Whitehead's gorgeous, expertly crafted sentences help the reader past the novel's slow start. . . . We are slowly filled in on the limp, the misfortune, the meaning of the titleland we're treated to an eloquent novel about racial identity in America. . . . What could have been an academic exercise becomes a smart tale about who we are under our labels." Newsweek.

Whitehead, Colson, 1969-
The **intuitionist** / Colson Whitehead. Anchor Books, 1999. 255 p.
ISBN 9780385492997
1. African American women -- Identity 2. Race relations 3. Intrigue 4. City life 5. Sects 6. Intuition 7. Labor unions 8. Elevators 9. Labor unions -- Elections 10. Afrofuturism and Afrofantasy 11. Literary fiction 12. Contemporary fantasy 13. African American fiction 14. Afrofuturism and Afrofantasy
LC 986756
A black female elevator inspector must prove that her method of inspection by intuition, as opposed to visual observation, is not at fault when an elevator in a new city building crashes.
"Whitehead's prose is graceful and often lyrical and his elevator underworld is a complex, lovingly realized creation." The New Yorker.

Whitehead, Colson, 1969-
John Henry Days : a novel / Colson Whitehead. Doubleday, 2001. 389 p.
ISBN 0385498195
1. John Henry 2. African American journalists -- West Virginia 3. African American men 4. Festivals -- West Virginia 5. West Virginia 6. Psychological fiction 7. African American fiction
LC 00043143
National Book Critics Circle Award for Fiction finalist, 2001
Pulitzer Prize for Fiction finalist, 2002
An assignment for a travel website takes J. Sutter, a young black journalist, to West Virginia for the first annual "John Henry Days" festival, where history and popular culture are juxtaposed as the real story of John Henry unfolds.
"Whitehead relishes slashing through the mindlessness of the age in a voice so intelligent and an idiom so imaginative that it can lift a reader right out of his chair. But he is not remorseless. He likes these people and respects their longings. They have no moral compass, but he has, so we can laugh at them but still grieve for the loss of so much possiblility." New York Times Book Review.

Whitehead, Colson, 1969-
* The **Nickel** boys : a novel / Colson Whitehead. Doubleday, 2019. 213 p.
ISBN 9780385537070
1. King, Martin Luther,, Jr, 1929-1968 Influence 2. 1960s 3. African American teenage boys 4. Juvenile correctional institutions 5. Racism 6. Corruption 7. Teenage abuse victims 8. Torture 9. Emotional abuse 10. Sex crimes 11. Psychic trauma 12. Friendship 13. Resistance (Psychology) in teenage boys 14. African Americans -- Identity 15. Life change events 16. Florida 17. Southern States -- Race relations -- History -- 20th century 18. Historical fiction 19. African American fiction
ALA Notable Book, 2020.
BCALA Literary Award for Fiction, 2020.
Kirkus Prize for Fiction, 2018.
National Book Critics Circle Award for Fiction finalist, 2019
Longlisted for the National Book Award for Fiction, 2019.

Follows the harrowing experiences of two African-American teens at an abusive reform school in Jim Crow-era Florida.
"Whitehead's magnetic characters exemplify stoicism and courage, and each supremely crafted scene smolders and flares with injustice and resistance, building to a staggering revelation. Inspired by an actual school, Whitehead's potently concentrated drama pinpoints the brutality and insidiousness of Jim Crow racism with compassion and protest." Booklist.

Whitehead, Colson, 1969-
Sag Harbor : a novel / Colson Whitehead. Doubleday, 2009. 288 p.
ISBN 9780385527651
1. 1980s 2. African American teenage boys 3. Prep schools 4. Teenagers 5. Identity (Psychology) 6. Misfits (Persons) 7. Summer 8. Brothers 9. Adaptability (Psychology) 10. Interpersonal relations 11. Manhattan, New York City 12. Sag Harbor, New York 13. Coming-of-age stories 14. African American fiction
Benji, one of the only black kids at an elite prep school in Manhattan, tries desperately to fit in, but every summer, he and his brother, Reggie, escape to the East End of Sag Harbor, where a small community of African American professionals has built aworld of is own.
"The author serves up whole sundaes worth of riffs on the quotidian, all hung on the skinny frame of a 15-year-old everyman virgin and his marginally less distinct friends, give or take a repressive father and a particularly evocative shoreline landscape." Village Voice.

Whitehead, Colson, 1969-
* The **underground** railroad : a novel / Colson Whitehead. Doubleday, 2016. 304 p.
ISBN 9780385542364
1. Antebellum America (1820-1861) 2. Underground Railroad 3. Fugitive slaves 4. Race (Social sciences) 5. Racism 6. African Americans -- Social conditions -- 19th century 7. Escapes 8. Freedom 9. Slavery 10. Southern States -- Race relations -- History -- 19th century 11. United States -- History -- 19th century 12. Literary fiction 13. Historical fiction 14. African American fiction
LC 2016000643
Includes extract from: The Intuitionist.
First published: 2016.
ALA Notable Book, 2017.
Andrew Carnegie Medal for Excellence in Fiction, 2017.
Arthur C. Clarke Award, 2017.
Goodreads Choice Award, 2016
Hurston/Wright Legacy Award: Fiction, 2017.
National Book Award for Fiction, 2016.
Pulitzer Prize for Fiction, 2017.
Longlisted for the Man Booker Prize, 2017.
Kirkus Prize for Fiction finalist, 2016.
After Cora, a pre-Civil War Georgia slave, escapes with another slave, Caesar, they seek the help of the Underground Railroad as they flee from state to state and try to evade a slave catcher, Ridgeway, who is determined to return them to the South.
"Everything Whitehead describes is vividly, often joltingly realistic, even the novel's most fantastic element, his vision of this secret transport network as an actual railroad running through tunnels dug beneath the blood-soaked fields of the South, a jolting and resounding embodiment of heroic efforts and colossal risks." Booklist.

Whitehead, Colson, 1969-

Zone one : a novel / Colson Whitehead. Doubleday, 2011. 240 p.

ISBN 9780385528078

1. End of the world 2. Zombies 3. Coping 4. Virus diseases 5. Loneliness in men 6. New York City 7. Manhattan, New York City 8. Satirical fiction 9. Horror 10. African American fiction

LC 2011008339

In a post-apocalyptic world decimated by zombies, the U.S. government has retreated to Buffalo, New York, and survivor efforts to rebuild are focused on lower Manhattan. With several others, Mark Spitz works as a "sweeper" -- eliminating zombie stragglers as he struggles with PASD (Post-Apocalyptic Stress Disorder) and recalls humanity before the apocalypse. -- Description by Dawn Towery.

"It's a book you want to read rather than one you should read. Sure, there are familiar paradigms: the pandemic subsides behind a foreground of chase scenes, us-or-them admonitions, even the occasional bite sequence. But Zone One is mercilessly free of cookie-cutter social commentaries--office culture is for mindless drones; technology destroys our ability to connect while still providing the chilling, fleshy pleasures of zombies who lurch, pursue, hunger." Esquire.

Whitlow, Robert, 1954-

A **time** to stand / Robert Whitlow. Harpercollins Christian Pub, 2017 400 p.

ISBN 9780718083038

1. African American women lawyers 2. Race relations 3. Police brutality 4. Trials (Murder) 5. Defense attorneys 6. Small town life 7. Small towns 8. Faith (Christianity) 9. Unemployment 10. Christian fiction 11. Legal stories

LC 2017012470

Adisa Johnson, a young African American attorney, is living her dream of practicing law with a prestigious firm in downtown Atlanta. Then a split-second mistake changes the course of her career. Left with no other options, Adisa returns to her hometown where a few days earlier a white police officer shot an unarmed black teen who is now lying comatose in the hospital. Adisa is itching to jump into the fight as a special prosecutor, but feels pulled to do what she considers unthinkable--defend the officer. As the court case unfolds, everyone in the small community must confront their own prejudices.

Whittall, Zoe

Holding still for as long as possible / Zoe Whittall. House of Anansi, 2009. 301 p.

ISBN 9780887842344

1. Accidents 2. Paramedics 3. Singers 4. Filmmakers 5. Interpersonal relations 6. Men/women relations 7. Toronto, Ontario 8. Psychological fiction

Lambda Literary Award for Transgender/Bisexual, 2010.

Follows three twenty somethings living in Toronto. Josh, a female-to-male transgender works as a paramedic and tries to erase from his mind the atrocities he witnesses daily; Amy, his ex-girlfriend and an amateur filmmaker, lives off of her wealthy parents; and Billy, a former child pop star, now endures extreme anxiety attacks.

Whittle, Tina

The **dangerous** edge of things / Tina Whittle. Poisoned Pen Press, 2011. 250 p. Tai Randolph mysteries

ISBN 9781590588178

1. Murder investigation 2. Women detectives 3. Murder suspects 4. Women murder victims 5. Brothers and sisters 6. Stalkers 7. Revenge 8. Gun industry and trade 9. Women shopkeepers 10. Bodyguards 11. Stalking 12. Atlanta, Georgia 13. Mysteries

LC 2010932102

The week after Teresa Ann (Tai) Randolph moves from Savannah to Atlanta--to run a gun shop she and her brother, Eric, just inherited--she finds the body of a young woman, Eliza Compton, shot in a car across the street from Eric's house. The exclusive and secretive corporate security firm Phoenix, for which industrial psychologist Eric consults, attempts to take Tai in hand, offering the protective services of Trey Seaver, a crackerjack agent whose brain trauma suffered in a car accident left him emotionally insensitive but with an uncanny ability to detect lying. But Tai will not be restrained, with both herself and Eric of interest to police, she's in full investigative mode looking for Eliza's murderer.

Wibberley, Leonard, 1915-1983

* The **mouse** that roared / Leonard Wibberly. Little, Brown, 1955. 279 p.

1. Imaginary wars and battles 2. Grand Fenwick 3. Imperialism 4. International relations 5. Economic assistance, American 6. Small countries 7. Nuclear weapons 8. Humorous stories 9. Political fiction

LC 54008294

The Tiny Duchy of Grand Fenwick undertakes to rehabilitate its national economy by declaring war on the U.S., since that nation takes tender care of its defeated enemies. The story tells how the Fenwickian invasion Force of 23 longbowmen not only won the war, but seized the newly invented quadium bomb and by virtue of its possession compelled the cessation of the armament race.

Wickersham, Joan

The **news** from Spain : seven variations on a love story / Joan Wickersham. Alfred A. Knopf, 2012. 208 p.

ISBN 9780307958884

1. Love 2. Loss (Psychology) 3. Family relationships 4. Men/women relations 5. Interpersonal relations 6. Love stories 7. Short stories

LC 2012005073

"This is a Borzoi book."

Collects seven short stories connected by the theme of love.

Wideman, John Edgar

* **American** histories : stories / John Edgar Wideman. Scribner, 2018. 227 p.

ISBN 9781501178344

1. Douglass, Frederick, 1818-1895 2. Brown, John, 1800-1859 3. Turner, Nat, 1800?-1831 4. Interpersonal relations 5. Family relationships 6. African Americans 7. Abolitionists 8. Race relations 9. Loss (Psychology) 10. United States -- Race relations 11. Literary fiction 12. Short stories 13. African American fiction

Collects short stories about love, death, and struggle.

Wideman, John Edgar

Fanon / John Edgar Wideman. Houghton Mifflin, 2007. 288 p.

ISBN 9780618942633

1. Fanon, Frantz, 1925-1961 2. African Americans 3. African American authors 4. Racism 5. Intellectuals -- Algeria 6. Revolutionaries -- Algeria 7. Psychiatrists -- Algeria 8. Brothers 9. Prisoners 10. Purpose in life 11. African American prisoners 12. Psychological fiction 13. Biographical fiction 14. Literary fiction 15. African American fiction

LC 2007009420

A fictional portrait of Frantz Fanon, a philosopher and political activist, chronicles Fanon's life, from his Martinique upbringing through the publication of his influential work, as seen through the eyes of the African-American novelist writing his biography.

"This is Wideman's mulligan stew--on the one hand, the Homewood boy who went on scholarship to Penn, and from Penn to Oxford, and from Oxford to the Iowa Writers' Workshop, nods his head to Marx, Freud, Yeats, Sartre, Joyce, Nabokov, and Baudelaire; on the other, the novelist and college professor who still feels guilty about going to Europe instead of jail signifies his solidarity with W.E.B. DuBois, James Baldwin, and Frantz Fanon by riff, scat, and Igbo. How this mixture works is mysterious, but it always has." Harper's

Wieland, Liza

Paris, 7 a.m. / Liza Wieland. Simon & Schuster, 2019. 352 p.

ISBN 9781501197215

1. Bishop, Elizabeth, 1911-1979 2. Between the Wars (1918-1939) 3. 1930s 4. Women poets 5. Americans in France 6. Mothers and daughters 7. Women/women relations 8. Loss (Psychology) 9. Vacations 10. College roommates 11. Diary writing 12. Jewish children 13. French Resistance (World War II) 14. Holocaust (1933-1945) -- France 15. Righteous Gentiles in the Holocaust -- France 16. Paris, France 17. Normandy 18. Historical fiction 19. Biographical fiction

The award-winning author of A Watch of Nightingales reimagines the experiences of pre-fame poet Elizabeth Bishop during three life-changing weeks spent in Paris on the eve of World War II.

Wiesel, Elie, 1928-2016

* Dawn / Elie Wiesel ; translated from the French by Frances Frenaye. Bantam Books, 1982, c1960. 102 p.

ISBN 9780553225365

1. Holocaust survivors -- Palestine 2. Executions and executioners -- Palestine 3. Murder 4. Ethics 5. Jewish men 6. Violence 7. Victims -- Psychology 8. British in Palestine 9. Soldiers 10. Militants 11. Men -- Decision-making 12. Options, alternatives, choices 13. Separated friends, relatives, etc 14. Israel -- History -- 1948-1967 15. Autobiographical fiction 16. Translations -- French to English

First published in 1960 in French.

Sequel to: Night.

Sequel: The accident, which is also known as Day.

Deals with the conflicts and thoughts of a young Jewish concentration-camp veteran as he prepares to assassinate a British hostage in occupied Palestine.

Wiesel, Elie, 1928-2016

Hostage / Elie Wiesel ; translated from the French by Catherine Temerson. Alfred A. Knopf, 2012. 224 p.

ISBN 9780307599582

1. 1970s 2. Hostages 3. Hostage taking 4. Jewish men 5. Storytelling 6. Thrillers and suspense 7. Political thrillers 8. Translations -- French to English

LC 2011050747

"This is a Borzoi book."

Traces the experiences of an innocent Jewish writer from Brooklyn who endures a nightmarish abduction by Arab and Italian captors by sharing poignant stories from the time he spent hiding from the Nazis.

Wiesel, Elie, 1928-2016

The **judges** : a novel / Elie Wiesel ; translated from the French by Geoffrey Strachan. Knopf, 2002. 209 p.

ISBN 0375409092

1. Self-perception 2. Jews 3. Judgment 4. Guilt 5. Innocence (Psychology) 6. Strangers 7. Blizzards 8. Self-discovery in men 9. Executions and executioners 10. Secrets 11. Memories 12. Right and wrong 13. Connecticut 14. Psychological fiction 15. Translations --

French to English

LC 2002025462

A plane headed from New York to Tel Aviv is forced to crash land at a small airport, and five survivors are given shelter in a nearby home. Once they are locked in, their enigmatic host tells them he is their judge, and they must reveal their lives to him. Shockingly, he announces the least worthy of them will be sentenced to death.

"As the characters talk about themselves and remember crucial turning points in their lives, Wiesel weaves in Jewish history and mysticism with the characters' personal memories, and he raises the big existential questions about life and death and memory and guilt and forgiveness, with lots of metaphors about scapegoat, fellow traveler, messenger, etc." Booklist.

Wiesel, Elie, 1928-2016

A **mad** desire to dance : a novel / Elie Wiesel ; translated from the French by Catherine Temerson. Alfred A. Knopf, 2009. 288 p.

ISBN 9780307266507

1. Men with depression 2. Holocaust survivors 3. Death 4. Loneliness 5. Orphans 6. Senior men 7. Judaism 8. Family relationships 9. Immigrants, Jewish 10. Literary fiction 11. Translations -- French to English

LC 2008038951

A European orphan transplanted to New York, Doriel is shaped by the pain of the deaths of his parents following World War II and the horrors of the Holocaust, and seeks solace in an intense study of Judaism and a search for the secrets of his mother's life.

Wiesel, Elie, 1928-2016

* Night, Dawn, The accident : three tales / Elie Wiesel. Hill and Wang, 1972 318 p.

ISBN 0809073528

1. Wiesel, Elie, 1928-2016 2. God (Judaism) 3. Jews -- Identity 4. Holocaust survivors -- Palestine 5. Jewish men 6. Holocaust (1933-1945) 7. Concentration camp survivors 8. Good and evil 9. Separated friends, relatives, etc 10. Guilt 11. Belief and doubt 12. Loss (Psychology) 13. Memories 14. Autobiographies and memoirs 15. Translations -- French to English 16. History writing Wars and conflicts World War II Holocaust 17. Life stories Facing adversity War and oppression War survivors

LC 72081290

Translations of: Un di velt hot geshvign, L'aube, and Le jour, respectively.

Later editions published under the title: Night, Dawn, Day.

A terrifying account of Auschwitz that turns a young Jewish boy into an agonized witness to the death of his family, a member of the Israeli underground has to face the prospect of murder, and a near-fatal auto accident changes a man's outlook on life.

Wiggins, Marianne

Evidence of things unseen: Marianne Wiggins. Simon & Schuster, 2003. 383 p.

ISBN 0684869691

1. Second World War era (1939-1945) 2. Lovers 3. World War I veterans 4. Men/women relations 5. World War II 6. Radiation 7. Atomic bomb 8. Tennessee 9. Historical fiction 10. Literary fiction

LC 2003045611

National Book Award for Fiction finalist, 2003

Pulitzer Prize for Fiction finalist, 2004.

Falling in love during the Second World War, a soldier and a glass-blower's daughter eventually have a son, who in adulthood finds his own love affair impacted by the fallout of the atomic age.

Wiggins, Marianne

The **shadow** catcher / Marianne Wiggins. Simon and Schuster, 2007 336 p.

ISBN 0743265203

1. Curtis, Edward S, 1868-1952 2. 20th century 3. 21st century 4. Photographers 5. Men/women relations 6. Father and adult daughter 7. Redemption 8. Photographs 9. Family relationships 10. Love 11. Identity (Psychology) 12. Psychological fiction 13. Novels-within-novels 14. Parallel narratives

National Book Critics Circle Award for Fiction finalist, 2007

A series of tales about a photographer's developing relationship with the Native Americans he astonishes by showing them pictures of themselves is interspersed with parallel tales about an unsung soldier, a husband, and a father.

Wiggs, Susan

The **beekeeper's** ball / Susan Wiggs. Mira Books, 2014. 360 p. Bella Vista

ISBN 9780778314486

1. Family secrets 2. Women cooks 3. Journalists 4. Small towns 5. Cooking schools 6. Cooking 7. Interpersonal attraction 8. Men/women relations 9. Families 10. California 11. Contemporary romances

While transforming Bella Vista, her childhood home, into a destination cooking school, chef Isabel Johansen finds her plans interrupted by war-torn journalist Cormac O'Neill who has arrived to dig up old history.

Wiggs, Susan

The **ocean** between us / Susan Wiggs. Mira, 2004. 382 p.

ISBN 0778320359

1. United States. Navy Officers 2. Military life 3. Husband and wife 4. Marital conflict 5. Navy spouses 6. Separation (Psychology) 7. Parent and child 8. Teenagers 9. Family secrets 10. Family relationships 11. Men/women relations 12. Washington (State) 13. Domestic fiction 14. Pacific Northwest fiction 15. Gentle reads

After eighteen years of marriage, Grace Bennett is tired of her Navy captain husband Steve's lack of emotional support for her and their children, and Grace must decide whether or not to make a new life for herself.

"Steve Bennett is a perfect navy officer with a perfect navy family, and he's confident that his world is just the way it should be. But his son wants to be an artist instead of attending the U.S. Naval Academy, and his stalwart and capable wife of 20 years, Grace, is tired of being the perfect navy wife. She wants her own home, and she wants her own career. She's feeling altogether unsettled, but nothing is more unsettling than the secret her husband has hidden from her their entire marriage. Nothing, that is, until the accident on the carrier. Wiggs has done an excellent job of depicting what lies beneath the surfaces of relationshipsassumptions, misunderstandings, and expectations." Booklist.

Wiggs, Susan

* The **Oysterville** sewing circle / Susan Wiggs. William Morrow & Co, 2019. 320 p.

ISBN 9780062425584

1. Homecomings 2. Guardian and ward 3. Sewing 4. Family violence victims 5. Undocumented immigrants 6. Female friendship 7. Clubs 8. Fashion designers 9. Orphans 10. Life change events 11. Multiracial children 12. Loss (Psychology) 13. Small town life 14. Washington (State) 15. Women's lives and relationships

Forced by scandal to return to her Pacific coast childhood home, a Manhattan fashionista assumes guardianship over two orphans and bonds with a circle of fellow seamstresses before an unexpected challenge tests her courage and heart.

Wilde, Oscar, 1854-1900

* The **picture** of Dorian Gray / Oscar Wilde. Modern Library, 1998, c1890. xii, 254 p.

ISBN 9780375751516

1. Victorian era (1837-1901) 2. Portraits 3. Personal conduct 4. Immortality 5. Aging 6. Great Britain -- History -- Victoria, 1837-1901 7. London, England 8. England 9. Gothic fiction 10. Classics

Originally published as a story in Lippincott's Monthly Magazine (Philadelphia, Pa.) on June 20, 1890. A revised and expanded version was published as a novel in April 1891 by Ward and Lock (London).

An exquisitely beautiful young man in Victorian England retains his youthful and innocent appearance over the years while his portrait reflects both his age and evil soul as he pursues a life of decadence and corruption.

Wilder, Thornton, 1897-1975

* **Theophilus** North / Thornton Wilder. Harper & Row, 1973. 374 p.

ISBN 9780060146368

1. 1920s 2. Former teachers 3. Tutors 4. Cities and towns 5. City life 6. Octogenarians 7. Octogenarian men 8. Scholars and academics 9. Politicians 10. Widows 11. Gossiping and gossips 12. Newport, Rhode Island 13. Rhode Island 14. Coming-of-age stories

LC 73004165

Later published as: Mr. North. New York : Carroll & Graf, 1988.

Banta Award (Wisconsin), 1974.

A twenty-nine-year-old teacher attempts to achieve his nine life ambitions while passing the summer in Newport, Rhode Island.

Wilhelm, Kate

The **good** children / Kate Wilhelm. St. Martin's Press, 1998. 246 p.

ISBN 0312179146

1. Brothers and sisters 2. Life change events 3. Orphans 4. Families 5. Family secrets 6. Moving to a new state 7. Parents -- Death 8. Truthfulness and falsehood in children 9. Oregon 10. Psychological fiction 11. Pacific Northwest fiction

LC 9737101

It started with a promise, a pact. It became a secret that no one must tell: that their parents were dead and gone, including the one they'd buried in the backyard. Now the McNair children are growing older, discovering love, college, and careers. But their lie haunts them. Their home holds them captive. Only the horrifying truth of their mother's death can set the children free. And only the truth can destroy them all.

"Brilliantly plotted, lyrically written, alluring and magical, mesmerizing, terrifying, and heartbreakingly funny, Wilhelm's story is a wrenching masterpiece about love, loyalty, and lies that will lodge itself in readers' psyches long after they've finished the last, stunning chapter." Booklist.

Wilkins, Kim

Veil of gold / Kim Wilkins. Tor Books, 2008. 496 p.

ISBN 0765320061

1. Material culture 2. Voyages and travels 3. Parallel universes 4. Missing persons 5. Princesses 6. Secrets 7. Wizards 8. Magic 9. Russia 10. St Petersburg, Russia 11. Gateway fantasy 12. Fantasy fiction

Originally published: Rosa and the veil of gold. Pymble, N.S.W. : Harper Collins, 2005.

RUSA Reading List, 2009.

Setting out for the university in Arkhangelsk to investigate the authenticity of a recently discovered ancient artifact, researcher Daniel St. Clair and his frosty colleague, Em Hayward, go missing in the wake of a series of otherworldly mishaps, a situation that prompts Daniel's lost love, Rosa, to set out to rescue him.

"Wilkins's human characters are endearing and her mythic monsters spring into vibrant life. Adult fairy tales don't come any better than this." Publishers Weekly.

Wilhelm, Kate

* Where late the sweet birds sang / Kate Wilhelm. Harper & Row, 1976. 251 p.

ISBN 0060146540

1. Clones and cloning 2. Survivalism 3. Individuality 4. Disasters 5. Catastrophism 6. Genetic engineering 7. Genetics 8. Reproductive technology 9. Drug addiction 10. Identity (Psychology) 11. Virginia 12. Apocalyptic fiction 13. Science fiction

LC 75006379

Hugo Award for Best Novel, 1977.

Locus Award for Best Science Fiction Novel, 1977.

Having foreseen and planned for the worldwide devastation of war and pestilence, the landed Sumner family of Virginia have assured themselves physical survival but are hard-put to provide for a meaningful human future.

Wilkinson, Lauren, 1984-

* American spy : a novel / Lauren Wilkinson. Random House, 2019. 292 p.

ISBN 9780812998955

1. Sankara, Thomas, 1949-1987 2. FBI. 3. 1980s 4. Cold War 5. Undercover operations 6. Spies 7. Espionage 8. Loyalty 9. Betrayal 10. African American women 11. Intelligence officers 12. Sisters -- Death 13. International relations 14. Coups d'etat 15. Presidents -- Burkina Faso 16. Burkina Faso -- History -- Coup d'etat, 1987 17. Burkina Faso -- Politics and government -- 1960-1987 18. Sub-Saharan Africa -- Politics and government -- 1960- 19. Literary fiction 20. African American fiction 21. Spy fiction 22. Historical thrillers

A Cold War FBI intelligence officer joins an undercover task force to seduce a revolutionary African Communist president she secretly admires and comes to love.

"Written in the form of a lengthy missive from a mother to her young sons, this intriguing first novel blends literary fiction with a Cold War-era spy story." Library Journal.

Williams, Amanda Kyle, 1957-

The **stranger** you seek : a novel / Amanda Kyle Williams. Bantam Books, 2011. 304 p. Keye Street novels

ISBN 9780553808070

1. Women detectives 2. Serial murder investigation 3. Second chances 4. Former FBI agents 5. Recovering alcoholics 6. Atlanta, Georgia 7. Psychological suspense

Offered a second chance by the Atlanta Police Department to catch a serial killer who has eluded them for years, former FBI profiler and alcoholic Keye Street begins a deadly cat-and-mouse chase with an adversary who has taken a personal interest in her.

"Lt. Aaron Rauser needs help catching what seems to be a new serial killer in his Atlanta stomping ground. He knows that the woman for the job is his old friend and crime-solving compatriot Keye Street. Keye's not the kind of woman you mess around with, and while the folks on the force don't like that she's freelancing in their department, there's not much they can do about it. Keye was on track to be a well-respected FBI profiler before an inconvenient addiction to booze got in the way. Now that she's back on her feet, this tough and whip-smart investigator has opened her own small-time business. Although chasing bail jumpers keeps Keye and her hacker sidekick Neil in modest money,

hunting down the deranged psychopath the Atlanta papers have dubbed the Wishbone Killer is just Keye's piece of pie. . . . [Williams] creates a frightening and occasionally witty novel, perfect for those who can sleep with one eye open. Think Mary Higgins Clark with an edge." Kirkus.

Williams, Beatriz

All the ways we said goodbye : a novel of the Ritz Paris / Beatriz Williams, Lauren Willig, Karen White. William Morrow & Co, 2020. 368 p.

ISBN 9780062931092

1. Ritz Hotel (Paris, France) 2. First World War era (1914-1918) 3. Second World War era (1939-1945) 4. 1960s 5. Hotels 6. Family history 7. Family secrets 8. Romantic love 9. Women and war 10. Resistance to military occupation 11. Families 12. Men/women relations 13. Paris, France -- History -- 20th century 14. Parallel narratives 15. Historical fiction

An heiress, a Resistance fighter and a widow find their lives intertwined by their wartime experiences and the turbulent 1960s when they seek refuge at Paris-legendary Ritz hotel.

"Full of heart and intrigue, the authors' latest collaboration captures women's perseverance and how history connects us all." Booklist.

Williams, Beatriz

The **golden** hour / Beatriz Williams. William Morrow, 2019. 384 p.

ISBN 9780062834751

1. Windsor, Edward,, Duke of, 1894-1972 2. Windsor, Wallis Warfield,, Duchess of, 1896-1986 3. Second World War era (1939-1945) 4. Dukes and duchesses 5. Women journalists 6. Scientists 7. Social classes 8. Race relations 9. Espionage 10. Corruption 11. Governors 12. Murder 13. Nazis 14. World War II -- Prisoners and prisons 15. Family secrets 16. Interpersonal attraction 17. Men/women relations 18. Postpartum depression 19. Bahamas 20. Nassau, Bahamas 21. Historical fiction 22. Parallel narratives

Traveling to World War II Nassau to interview the infamous Duke and Duchess of Windsor, an investigator for a New York society magazine uncovers a treasonous plot that is complicated by her romance with an unscrupulous scientist.

Williams, Beatriz

The **summer** wives / Beatriz Williams. William Morrow, 2018 367 p.

ISBN 9780062660343

1. 1950s 2. Secrecy 3. Upper class 4. Judicial error 5. Interclass romance 6. Murder suspects 7. Vacation homes 8. Lobster fishers 9. Rich families 10. Redemption 11. Island life 12. New England 13. Historical fiction 14. Love stories

LC bl2018072167

Drawn into and then banished from exclusive Winthrop Island when a complex relationship between her stepsister and a working-class college youth ends in violence, a Shakespearean actress returns after 20 years to pursue justice.

Williams, Charlie, 1971-

Stairway to hell / Charlie Williams. Serpent's Tail, 2010. 281 p.

ISBN 9781846686894

1. Singers 2. Misadventures 3. Soul 4. Reincarnation 5. Celebrities 6. Rock music 7. Black magic 8. England 9. Humorous stories

Warchester pub singer Rik Suntan's slot is axed at the local nightclub, his girlfriend has dumped him for a ginger bloke, and he finds out he is the reincarnation of David Bowie.

"This is one of those rare books when, really, anything might happen in the next few pages. Rather than feeling contrived, Williams manages to create a milieu in which even the wackiest developments are both seamlessly logical and thoroughly unexpected, not to mention funny. Pop music, time travel, soul displacement? You bet!" PopMatters.

Williams, Drew, (Science fiction author)

The **stars** now unclaimed / Drew Williams. Tor Books, 2018 447 p. Universe after

ISBN 9781250186119

1. Child psychics 2. Psychokinesis 3. Disasters -- Prevention 4. Cults 5. Aliens 6. Extremists 7. Space warfare 8. Interplanetary relations 9. Regression (Civilization) 10. Space opera 11. Science fiction

Recruiting supernaturally gifted kids to help stop a cataclysmic force from decimating countless worlds, agent Jane Kamali teams up with a telekinetic teen to navigate the madcap schemes of a power-hungry fascist cult.

"This cast of memorable characters, particularly Jane, who wears her heart on her sleeve, and the sacrifices they make to save the universe is not to be missed." Booklist.

Williams, Joy, 1944-

Ninety-nine stories of God / Joy Williams. Tin House Books, 2016. 220 p.

ISBN 9781941040355

1. God 2. Spirituality 3. Short stories

LC 2016006741

A collection from the Pulitzer Prize and National Book Award finalist author feature stories about humans' daily, random interactions with the divine in the most unlikely of places.

"Each story is brief, with some less than a paragraph. Some amaze, some are quietly powerful, some gracefully absurd. Much like the divine, Williams prose is simple and brutal, thoughtful and haunting." Booklist.

Williams, Karen (Karen Lynn)

Dirty to the grave / Karen Williams. Urban, 2010. vii, 216 p.

ISBN 9781601622693

1. Street life 2. Dysfunctional families 3. African American women -- Friendship 4. Murder 5. Betrayal 6. Violence 7. Inner city 8. Sexuality 9. Adult child abuse victims 10. African American men/women relations 11. California 12. Urban fiction 13. African American fiction

In Long Beach, California, Cha and Goldie are desperate to escape the street life, while their friend Red, stepping deeper into the game to get what she wants, betrays them both, which leads to tragic consequences.

Williams, Karen (Karen Lynn)

Harlem on lock : a novel / Karen Williams. Q-Boro Books, 2008. x, 259 p.

ISBN 9781933967349

1. Drug addiction 2. Teenage prostitution 3. Children of drug abusers 4. Pimps 5. Gangs 6. Betrayal 7. Street life 8. African Americans 9. Fathers and daughters 10. Men/women relations 11. Love triangles 12. Los Angeles, California 13. Urban fiction 14. African American fiction

LC bl2008010772

At head of title on cover: Q-Boro Books presents.

When her mother dies and her father forces her into prostitution, Harlem becomes the property of a vicious drug lord and caught in the middle of a deadly turf war, forcing her to call upon her inner strength in order to survive.

Williams, Karen (Karen Lynn)

Sweet Giselle / Karen Williams. Urban Books ; 2012. 275 p.

ISBN 9781601624895

1. Secrecy 2. Child sex industry and trade 3. African American men/women relations 4. Seduction 5. Kidnapping 6. Drug traffic 7. Pornography 8. African Americans 9. Innocence (Personal quality) 10. Love triangles 11. Urban fiction 12. African American fiction

LC bl2012009286

When she is kidnapped by a vicious drug lord named Bryce, who, instead of torturing her, falls in love with her, Giselle is shocked to discover the truth about her husband's porn business and soon finds herself torn between two men.

Williams, Katie, 1978-

Tell the machine goodnight / Katie Williams. Riverhead Books, 2018. 287 p.

ISBN 9780525533122

1. Women professional employees 2. Happiness 3. Mothers and sons 4. Near future 5. Teenage boys 6. Family relationships 7. Purpose in life 8. Teenagers with eating disorders 9. Rejection (Psychology) 10. Technology -- Social aspects 11. Domestic fiction 12. Mainstream fiction

Republished in 2019 as "The happiness machine".

Kirkus Prize for Fiction finalist, 2018.

A woman whose job it is to help people find happiness finds a challenge in her own son, who seems to get the most joy out of being unhappy.

"Following the trajectory of today's preoccupation with self-help and our perhaps not-entirely-justified faith that technology can fix everything, Williams explores the way machines and screens can both disconnect us, launching us into loneliness, and connect us, bringing us closer to one another. In this imaginative, engaging, emotionally resonant story, she reveals how the devices we depend on can both deprive us of our humanity and deliver us back to it. With its clever, compelling vision of the future, deeply human characters, and delightfully unpredictable story, this novel is itself a recipe for contentment." Kirkus.

Williams, Lara, (Writer of Treats)

A **selfie** as big as the Ritz : stories / Lara Williams. Flatiron Books, 2017. 160 p.

ISBN 9781250126627

1. Short stories 2. Literary fiction

LC 2017025683

A collection of short stories focuses on women trying to navigate their lives, including a woman whose relationship goes sour in the most romantic city on earth and another woman who supports her best friend through an abortion.

"Williams can limn huge swaths of a character's life in a handful of pages by zeroing in on details that communicate everything about everything, all in an instant. Williams' painstakingly, pointillistically composed portraits capture the small moments that can change the trajectory of a life." Kirkus.

Williams, Lara, (Writer of Treats)

Supper club : a novel / Lara Williams. G. P. Putnams Sons, 2019. 304 p.

ISBN 9780525539582

1. Young women 2. Clubs 3. Dinners and dining 4. Women's organizations 5. Secret societies 6. Female friendship 7. Hunger 8. Food 9. Desire 10. Enjoyment 11. Resistance (Psychology) 12. Self-discovery in women 13. Self-acceptance in women 14. Literary fiction

LC 2018046714

A woman confronts her personal limits and repressed past after forming a nighttime collective of women who gorge themselves passionately and embrace their bodies.

Williams, Niall, 1958-

John : a novel / Niall Williams. Bloomsbury, 2008. 276 p.
ISBN 9781596914674

1. John,, the Apostle, Saint 2. Jesus Christ Friends and associates 3. Apostles 4. Church history -- Primitive and early church, ca 30-600 5. Biographical fiction 6. Christian fiction

A tale based on John the Apostle's final years places the elderly, blind John in exile on the island of Patmos, until the Roman emperor lifts the ban against Christianity, enabling John's return to the religiously torn region of Ephesus.

"This novel will appeal to readers who like imaginative and gritty sagas of the lives of key Christians in the early church as well as those who value lyricism." Publishers Weekly.

Williams, Niall, 1958-

This is happiness / Niall Williams. Bloomsbury, 2019. 368 p.
ISBN 9781635574203

1. 1950s 2. Reminiscing in old age 3. Villages 4. Electricity 5. Boarders 6. Jilted women 7. Teenage boys 8. Small town life 9. Spring 10. Friendship 11. Romantic love 12. Forgiveness 13. Loss (Psychology) 14. Change (Psychology) 15. Men/women relations 16. Ireland 17. Literary fiction

A young man's first experiences of falling in and out of love are shaped by the arrival of electricity in his small western seaboard village, an enigmatic woman and a mysterious drought.

"Warm and whimsical, sometimes sorrowful, but always expressed in curlicues of Irish lyricism, this charming book makes varied use of its electrical metaphor, not least to express the flickering pulse of humanity. A story both little and large and one that pulls out all the Irish stops." Kirkus.

Williams, Synithia

Forbidden promises / Synithia Williams. HQN Books, 2020. 368 p. Jackson Falls
ISBN 9781335013248

1. Women violinists 2. Divorced men 3. Campaigning 4. Families 5. Brothers and sisters 6. African American families 7. Lawyers 8. Secrets 9. Loyalty 10. Sexual attraction 11. Men/women relations 12. Multicultural romances 13. Contemporary romances 14. African American fiction

Recruited by her politician brother to work with her older sister's ex-husband, with whom she is in love, violinist India Robidoux and Travis Strickland have a secret affair that neither of them wants to stop until family loyalties and desperate enemies threaten to tear them apart.

"With skillful characterization and sizzling chemistry, Williams succeeds at capturing the allure of this taboo connection. Even skeptical readers will be hard-pressed not to root for India and Travis." Publishers Weekly.

Williams, Tennessee, 1911-1983

* **Collected** stories / Tennessee Williams ; with an introduction by Gore Vidal New Directions, 1985. 57p.
ISBN 9780811209526

1. Manners and customs 2. Short stories

LC   85010642

49 short stories.

Williams, Tennessee, 1911-1983

* The **Roman** spring of Mrs. Stone / Tennessee Williams. New Directions, 1993, c1950. 111 p.
ISBN 9780811212496

1. 1950s 2. Middle-aged women 3. Young men -- Relations with older women 4. Men/women relations 5. Resentfulness 6. Female friendship 7. Extramarital affairs 8. May-December romance 9. Actors and actresses 10. Rome, Italy 11. Literary fiction 12. Italy

This is the story of a 50-ish wealthy American widow who was most recently a famous stage beauty but is now drifting after the death of her husband. With poignant wit and his own particular brand of relish, Williams charts her drift into an affair with a cruel young gigolo.

"There are many superb moments, scenes which move with a dramatist's ease. There is a hard candor about Mrs. Stone, about all people who fail at real living and attempt a life of fantasy and fail at that, leaving them vulnerable to annihilation. . . . This different version of Mr. Williams' repeated theme has resulted in a sharp, witty and moving novel." Chicago Tribune.

Willig, Lauren

The **Ashford** affair / Lauren Willig. St. Martin's Press, 2013. 352 p.
ISBN 9781250014498

1. 1920s 2. Women lawyers 3. Family secrets 4. Self-discovery in women 5. Senior women 6. World War I 7. Grandmother and granddaughter 8. England -- History -- 20th century 9. Kenya -- History -- 20th century 10. New York City 11. Family sagas 12. Parallel narratives

LC 2012037787

Feeling unfulfilled in the face of an imminent legal partnership and a broken engagement, Manhattan lawyer Clementine Evans learns of a long-buried family secret that leads her to the inner circles of World War I British society and the red hills of Kenya.

Willig, Lauren

The **betrayal** of the blood lily / Lauren Willig. Dutton, 2010. 416 p. Pink Carnation novels
ISBN 9780525951506

1. Georgian era (1714-1837) 2. 19th century 3. Women spies 4. British in India 5. Protectiveness in men 6. Men/women relations 7. Nobility 8. Forced marriage 9. Espionage 10. Women graduate students 11. Americans in England 12. India 13. London, England -- History -- 19th century 14. Hyderabad, India 15. Adventure stories 16. Georgian romances 17. Parallel narratives 18. Novels-within-novels 19. Historical romances

LC 2009036179

As Lady Frederick Staines, Penelope Deveraux plunges into the treacherous waters of the court of the Nizam of Hyderabad and with the assistance of Captain Alex Reid draws out the deadly plans of the spy known as the Marigold.

Willig, Lauren

The **deception** of the emerald ring / Lauren Willig. Dutton, 2006. 400 p. Pink Carnation novels
ISBN 0525949771

1. Georgian era (1714-1837) 2. Mistaken identity 3. Spies -- Great Britain 4. Love triangles 5. Women spies 6. Women graduate students 7. Americans in England 8. Elopement 9. Secret identity 10. Espionage 11. Dissertation writing 12. Men/women relations 13. Napoleonic Wars, 1800-1815 14. London, England -- History -- 19th century 15. France -- History -- Consulate and First Empire, 1799-1815 16. Ireland -- History -- 19th century 17. Adventure stories 18. Georgian romances 19. Parallel narratives 20. Novels-within-novels

21. Historical romances

LC 2006025304

The top spies of England and France contend with one another in 1803 Ireland, while Letty Alsworthy finds herself forcibly married to her sister's undesirable fiancé.

Willig, Lauren

The **garden** intrigue / Lauren Willig. Dutton, 2012. 388 p. Pink Carnation novels

ISBN 9780525952541

1. Georgian era (1714-1837) 2. Socialites 3. Espionage 4. Intelligence officers 5. Undercover operations 6. Americans in France 7. Men/women relations 8. Nobility 9. Napoleonic Wars, 1800-1815 10. France -- History -- Consulate and First Empire, 1799-1815 11. Parallel narratives 12. Historical romances 13. Georgian romances

An atrocious poet teams up with an American widow to prevent Napoleon's invasion of England.

Willig, Lauren

The **lure** of the moonflower : a Pink Carnation novel / Lauren Willig. New American Library, 2015. 515 p. Pink Carnation novels

ISBN 9780451473028

1. Georgian era (1714-1837) 2. 1800s (Decade) 3. Women spies 4. Intelligence officers 5. Napoleonic Wars, 1800-1815 6. Alliances 7. Government missions 8. Women rulers 9. Rescues 10. Interpersonal attraction 11. Men/women relations 12. Portugal -- History -- Maria I, 1777-1816 13. Parallel narratives 14. Historical romances 15. Georgian romances

LC 2015012935

Series complete in 12 volumes.

To stop the French from getting their hands on Queen Maria, who was spirited away by a group of loyalists, Jane Wooliston, the Pink Carnation, must team up with a rogue agent named Moonflower, who is brilliant--and insubordinate.

Willig, Lauren

The **masque** of the Black Tulip / Lauren Willig. Dutton, 2005. 400 p. Pink Carnation novels

ISBN 0525949208

1. Georgian era (1714-1837) 2. Women spies 3. Secret identity 4. Men/women relations 5. Women graduate students 6. Americans in England 7. Spies -- Great Britain 8. Spies -- France 9. Espionage 10. Napoleonic Wars, 1800-1815 11. London, England -- History -- 19th century 12. France -- History -- Consulate and First Empire, 1799-1815 13. Adventure stories 14. Georgian romances 15. Parallel narratives 16. Novels-within-novels 17. Historical romances

Sequel to: The secret history of the Pink Carnation.

When a London War Office courier is murdered for the confidential dispatch he carried for a known as the Pink Carnation, Henrietta Uppington and Miles Dorrington work with the War Office to prevent the Pink Carnation's assassination.

Willig, Lauren

The **orchid** affair / Lauren Willig. E. P. Dutton, 2011. 405 p. Pink Carnation novels

ISBN 9780525951995

1. Georgian era (1714-1837) 2. 19th century 3. Women spies 4. Governesses 5. Conspiracies 6. Men/women relations 7. Nobility 8. Espionage 9. India 10. London, England -- History -- 19th century 11. Adventure stories 12. Georgian romances 13. Parallel narratives 14. Novels-within-novels 15. Historical romances

Joining the Selwick Spy School to pursue an adventurous life, governess Laura Grey is assigned to the home of Bonaparte police insider Andre Jaouen, who is investigating a suspected Royalist plot.

Willig, Lauren

The **secret** history of the Pink Carnation / Lauren Willig. Dutton, 2005. 384 p. Pink Carnation novels

ISBN 9780525948605

1. Georgian era (1714-1837) 2. Women spies 3. Secret identity 4. Men/women relations 5. Women graduate students 6. Americans in England 7. Spies -- Great Britain 8. Espionage 9. Dissertation writing 10. Napoleonic Wars, 1800-1815 11. London, England -- History -- 19th century 12. France -- History -- Consulate and First Empire, 1799-1815 13. Adventure stories 14. Georgian romances 15. Parallel narratives 16. Novels-within-novels 17. Historical romances

LC 2004021334

Sequel: The masque of the Black Tulip.

Leaving Harvard to complete her dissertation on the Scarlet Pimpernel and the Purple Gentian in England, Eloise Kelly discovers information about the most elusive spy of all time, a figure who single-handedly saved England from Napoleon's invasion.

Willig, Lauren

The **seduction** of the Crimson Rose / Lauren Willig. Dutton, 2008. 400 p. Pink Carnation novels

ISBN 9780525950332

1. Georgian era (1714-1837) 2. Women spies 3. Secret identity 4. Men/women relations 5. Spies -- France 6. Seduction 7. Deception 8. Espionage 9. Napoleonic Wars, 1800-1815 10. Women graduate students 11. Americans in England 12. London, England -- History -- 19th century 13. France -- History -- Consulate and First Empire, 1799-1815 14. Adventure stories 15. Georgian romances 16. Parallel narratives 17. Novels-within-novels 18. Historical romances

LC 2007043044

Determined to secure another London season without assistance from her new brother-in-law, Mary Alsworthy accepts a secret assignment from Lord Vaughn on behalf of the Pink Carnation: to infiltrate the ranks of the dreaded French spy, the Black Tulip, before he and his master can stage their planned invasion of England. Every spy has a weakness, and for the Black Tulip that weakness is black-haired women--his "petals" of the Tulip. A natural at the art of seduction, Mary easily catches the attention of the French spy, but Lord Vaughn never anticipates that his own heart will be caught as well.--From publisher description.

"The flower-named spies of Regency England return as Willig's smart, sassy style cleverly incorporates a modern-day historian's hunt for information with Regency characters and events. Willig switches from a historical voice to a modern tone with ease, drawing readers back and forth in time as they hold their breath to see what happens next." Romantic Times.

Willig, Lauren

The **summer** country : a novel / Lauren Willig. William Morrow, 2019. 384 p.

ISBN 9780062839022

1. Victorian era (1837-1901) 2. Regency period (1811-1820) 3. Inheritance and succession 4. Family secrets 5. Sugar plantations 6. Race relations 7. Interracial romance 8. Families 9. Neighbors 10. Women plantation owners 11. Sugar plantation owners 12. Plantation life 13. Slaves 14. Slave resistance and revolts 15. Freed slaves 16. Colonialism 17. Local history 18. West Indies 19. Barbados 20. Family sagas 21. Historical fiction 22. Parallel narratives

LC 2018044474

Inheriting the ruins of a Barbados sugar plantation, a young woman from Victorian Bristol is seduced by the region's dark tropical beauty at the same time her new neighbors take steps to acquire the property for themselves.

Willig, Lauren

The **temptation** of the night jasmine / Lauren Willig. Dutton, 2009. 400 p. Pink Carnation novels

ISBN 9780525950967

1. Georgian era (1714-1837) 2. 19th century 3. Women spies 4. Secret identity 5. Revenge 6. Men/women relations 7. Nobility 8. Women rulers 9. Espionage 10. Spies -- Great Britain 11. Women graduate students 12. Americans in England 13. London, England -- History -- 19th century 14. Adventure stories 15. Georgian romances 16. Parallel narratives 17. Novels-within-novels 18. Historical romances

LC 2008028938

Returning to his English estate to avenge his mentor's murder during the 1803 Battle of Assaye, the Duke of Dovedale infiltrates a secretive club where he encounters Lady Charlotte, who has loved him since childhood.

Willis, Connie

Blackout / Connie Willis. Spectra Ballantine Books, 2010. 528 p. Oxford time travel novels

ISBN 9780553803198

1. 1940s 2. 21st century 3. Time travel (Past) 4. Historians 5. Computer errors 6. College students 7. Research 8. World War II 9. Oxford, England 10. Science fiction 11. Parallel narratives

Sequel: All clear

Hugo Award for Best Novel, 2011.

Locus Award for Best Science Fiction Novel, 2011.

Nebula Award for Best Novel, 2010.

Stranded in the past during World War II, three researchers from the future investigate period behavior and seek each other out in a shared effort to return to their own time.

"Despite the conceit of time travel, the book shows the attention to period detail that defines historical novels." Cleveland Plain Dealer.

Willis, Connie

Crosstalk / Connie Willis. Del Rey, 2016. 384 p.

ISBN 9780345540676

1. Near future 2. Young women 3. Interpersonal communication 4. Couples 5. Empathy 6. Telepathy 7. Social media 8. Irish Americans 9. Misunderstanding 10. Men/women relations 11. Interpersonal relations 12. Satirical fiction 13. Science fiction

RUSA Reading List Short List, 2017

"One of science fiction's premiere humorists turns her eagle eye to the crushing societal implications of telepathy. In a not-too-distant future, a simple outpatient procedure that has been promised to increase empathy between romantic partners has become all the rage. So when Briddey Flannigan's fiancé proposes that he and Briddey undergo the procedure, she is delighted! Only...the results aren't quite as expected. Instead of gaining an increased empathetic link with her fiancé Briddey finds herself hearing the actual thoughts of one of the nerdiest techs in her office. And that's the least of her problems."--, Provided by publisher.

"In other hands this novel could have been mere cliche, but Willis exuberant humor and warmhearted, fast-paced plotting transform it into a satisfying, if old-fashioned, romantic comedy." Kirkus.

Willis, Connie

* Doomsday book / Connie Willis. Bantam Books, 1992. 445 p. Oxford time travel novels

ISBN 0553081314

1. Medieval period (476-1492) 2. 14th century 3. 21st century 4. Time travel (Past) 5. Plague -- Europe -- History -- 14th century 6. Civilization, Medieval -- Europe 7. Women college students 8. Historians 9. Epidemics -- 14th century 10. Europe -- History -- 476-1492 11. Science fiction

LC 91042819

Hugo Award for Best Novel, 1993.

Locus Award for Best Science Fiction Novel, 1993.

Nebula Award for Best Novel, 1992.

A crisis linking the past and future, strands an Oxford student in the most dangerous year of the Middle Ages.

Willis, Connie

Passage / Connie Willis. Bantam Books, 2001. 594 p.

ISBN 0553111248

1. Near-death experience 2. Human experimentation in medicine 3. Medical research 4. Near-death experience -- Research 5. Neurologists 6. Women psychologists 7. Science fiction 8. Medical thrillers

LC 00068052

Locus Award for Best Science Fiction Novel, 2002.

Joanna Lander, a clinical psychologist obsessed with near-death experiences, joins forces with Dr. Richard Wright, a neurologist who has discovered a way to manufacture NDEs with the help of a mind-altering drug.

"With memorable characters, believable science, and convincing hospital ambiance, an initially slow-moving yarn turns into a page-turner whose explosive climax will rock readers back on their heels." Booklist.

Willis, Connie

To say nothing of the dog : or, how we found the bishop's bird stump at last / Connie Willis. Bantam Books, 1997. 434 p. Oxford time travel novels

ISBN 0553099957

1. University of Oxford 2. Time travel (Past) 3. Material culture 4. Chaos theory 5. Men/women relations 6. Coventry Cathedral -- History 7. World War II 8. Nazis 9. Rest 10. Victoriana 11. England -- History -- 19th century 12. England -- History -- 20th century 13. Oxford, England -- History 14. Coventry, England -- History 15. Science fiction 16. Humorous stories

Hugo Award for Best Novel, 1999.

Locus Award for Best Science Fiction Novel, 1999.

Ned Henry goes back in time to 1889 to study the Coventry Cathedral for a wealthy American who wants to build an exact replica before it is destroyed.

"No one mixes scientific mumbo jumbo and comedy of manners with more panache than Willis." New York Times Book Review.

Willocks, Tim, 1957-

Memo from Turner / Tim Willocks. Blackstone Pub, 2019, c2018. 334 p.

ISBN 9781538519615

1. Traffic accidents 2. Police corruption 3. Murder investigation 4. Secrets 5. Classism 6. Detectives 7. Corruption 8. Rich families 9. Racism -- South Africa 10. Power (Social sciences) 11. Mines and mineral resources 12. South Africa 13. Cape Town, South Africa 14. Thrillers and suspense

Originally published: London : Jonathan Cape, 2018.

During a weekend spree in Cape Town a young, rich Afrikaner fatally injures a teenage street girl with his Range Rover but is too drunk to know that he has hit her. His companions-who do know-leave the girl to die. The driver's mother, a self-made mining magnate named Margot Le Roux, intends to keep her son in ignorance of his crime. By chance the case falls to the relentless Warrant Officer Turner of Cape Town Homicide.

Willocks, Tim, 1957-

The **religion** / Tim Willocks. Farrar, Straus and Giroux, 2007, c2006. 618 p. Tannhauser trilogy

ISBN 9780374248659

1. Knights of Malta. 2. 16th century 3. Mercenaries 4. Counts and countesses 5. Birthmothers 6. Rulers 7. Monks 8. Violence 9. War 10. Quests 11. Ambition in men 12. Sieges 13. Religion and politics 14. War -- Religious aspects 15. Mediterranean Islands 16. Mediterranean Region 17. Malta -- History -- 1530-1798 18. Turkey -- History -- Ottoman Empire, 1288-1918 19. War stories 20. Historical fiction

LC 2006030419

"Originally published in 2006 by Jonathan Cape, Great Britain"--T.p. verso.

RUSA Reading List, 2008.

A French countess seeks passage to Malta from Sicily in a quest to find the son taken from her at his birth, in a historical novel set in 1565 during the last great medieval conflict between East and West.

"The author is especially convincing on the battle lust which overtakes both sides, and vividly places us among the besieged. If you don't mind a bit of romance tacked around the fighting, it is a gripping story with reliable factual underpinnings: history as heroics." Times Literary Supplement.

Wilson, Carter, (Novelist)

Dead girl in 2A / Carter Wilson. Sourcebooks Landmark, 2019 384 p.

ISBN 9781492686033

1. Amnesia 2. Experiments 3. Change (Psychology) 4. Memory 5. Flights 6. Guilt 7. Suicide 8. Loss (Psychology) 9. Interpersonal relations 10. Colorado 11. Psychological suspense

LC 2019000366

This flight will take them somewhere they never expected to go...

Wilson, Daniel H. (Daniel Howard), 1978-

The **Andromeda** evolution : a novel / Daniel H. Wilson. Harper, 2019. 448 p. Andromeda novels

ISBN 9780062473271

1. Human/alien encounters 2. Microorganisms 3. Evolution 4. Pathogenic microorganisms 5. Molecular evolution 6. Quarantine 7. Viruses 8. Epidemics 9. Scientists 10. People with paraplegia 11. Rain forests 12. Military bases, American 13. Washington (State) 14. Brazil 15. Bio-thrillers 16. Science fiction

LC 2019023408

A 50th-anniversary sequel to The Andromeda Strain finds a Brazilian drone detecting a bizarre anomaly in the middle of the jungle with the same chemical signature of the microparticle that nearly ended all life on Earth.

"Wilson takes one of Crichton's most durable story structures a group of specialists ventures into the unknown and works numerous variations, some small, some devastatingly large, on the theme." Booklist.

Wilson, Daniel H. (Daniel Howard), 1978-

The **clockwork** dynasty : a novel / Daniel H. Wilson. Doubleday, 2017. 352 p.

ISBN 9780385541787

1. 18th century 2. 21st century 3. Automata 4. Immortalism 5. Secret societies 6. Robots 7. Secrets 8. Androids 9. Scientists 10. Women scientists 11. Artificial intelligence 12. Imaginary wars and battles 13. Europe 14. Russia 15. Steampunk 16. Science fiction 17. Parallel narratives

LC 2016053069

A young anthropologist specializing in ancient technology makes the astonishing discovery that a race of human-like machines has been hiding among people for untold centuries.

"This is science fiction at its bestthoughtful, challenging, beautifully written, and astonishing." Booklist.

Wilson, Daniel H. (Daniel Howard), 1978-

Robogenesis : a novel / Daniel H. Wilson. Random, 2014. 361 p. Robopocalypse novels

ISBN 9780385537094

1. Robots 2. Artificial intelligence 3. Technology and civilization 4. Revolutions 5. Science fiction 6. Apocalyptic fiction

A sequel to Robopocalypse is told through a series of narratives that finds new and former characters fighting to rebuild a war-stricken world under threat of the surviving Archos machine code.

"This Hollywood-ready techno-thriller is packed to the brim with enough tough characters and brutal conflict to satisfy the most hardcore video gamers and action movie fans." Publishers Weekly.

Wilson, Daniel H. (Daniel Howard), 1978-

Robopocalypse : a novel / Daniel H. Wilson. Doubleday, 2011. 304 p. Robopocalypse novels

ISBN 9780385533850

1. Robots 2. Artificial intelligence 3. Technology and civilization 4. Revolutions 5. Science fiction 6. Apocalyptic fiction

LC 2010043134

A tale set in the near future finds the world thrown into chaos by rebelling artificial intelligences under the leadership of a murderous technology called Archos that kills its creator and takes over the global network, triggering an unprecedented united front among all human cultures.

"In this story of a global robotic revolution, Wilson's malevolent machines have surprisingly nuanced motives, and a few of the vignettes, particularly one about the chilling fate of an Alaskan drill team, could even stand alone as great horror short fiction." Entertainment Weekly.

Wilson, G. Willow, 1982-

* **Alif** the unseen / G. Willow Wilson. Grove Press, 2012. 433 p.

ISBN 9780802120205

1. Hackers 2. Computer technology 3. Death threats 4. Magic 5. Surveillance 6. Middle East 7. Urban fantasy 8. Middle Eastern-influenced fantasy

World Fantasy Award, 2013.

Forced underground when his ex-lover's new fiancé breaches his computer, putting him and his clients in jeopardy, young Arab-Indian hacker and shielder Alif discovers the secret book of the jinn and uses its insights to enable life-threatening developments in information technology.

"Wilson skillfully weaves a story linking modern-day technologies and computer languages to the folklore and religion of the Middle East." Library Journal.

Wilson, G. Willow, 1982-

* The **bird** king / G. Willow Wilson. Grove Press, 2019 403 p.

ISBN 9780802129031

1. 15th century 2. Inquisition -- Spain 3. Cartographers 4. Concubinage 5. Malicious accusation 6. Muslims 7. Fugitives 8. Imaginary creatures 9. Friendship 10. Platonic love 11. Young women 12. Magic 13. Good and evil 14. Spain -- History -- 15th century 15. Historical fantasy 16. Literary fiction 17. Middle Eastern-influenced fantasy

LC 2018045952

A concubine in the royal court of Granada at the height of the Spanish Inquisition and her mapmaker friend risk their lives to escape when the latter is accused of sorcery.

Wilson, Kevin, 1978-

The **family** Fang : a novel / Kevin Wilson. Ecco Press, 2011 256 p.

ISBN 9780061579035

1. Performance artists 2. Parent and child 3. Families 4. Adult children living with parents 5. Growing up 6. Dysfunctional families 7. Missing persons 8. Manipulation by men 9. Literary fiction 10. Satirical fiction

Performance artists Caleb and Camille Fang dedicated themselves to making great art. But when an artist's work lies in subverting normality, it can be difficult to raise well-adjusted children. Just ask Buster and Annie Fang. For as long as they can remember, they starred (unwillingly) in their parents' madcap pieces. But now that they are grown up, the chaos of their childhood has made it difficult to cope with life outside the fishbowl of their parents' strange world. When the lives they've built come crashing down, brother and sister have nowhere to go but home, where they discover that Caleb and Camille are planning one last performance-- their magnum opus-- whether the kids agree to participate or not. Soon, ambition breeds conflict, bringing the Fangs to face the difficult decision about what's ultimately more important: their family or their art. The novel displays a keen sense of the complex performances that unfold in the relationships of people who love one another.

"Caleb and Camille Fang are gallery darlings of a particularly discomfiting sort, staging public confrontations to provoke an extreme reaction from unwitting bystanders and recording the results for posterity. In a move that Dr. Spock would never endorse, they've raised their two young children to be accomplices in their work. They take their Santa-fearing daughter, Annie, to every mall they can find so she'll wail the moment she touches the jolly man's lap. They enter their son, Buster, in the Little Miss Crimson Clover pageant disguised as a girl. And so on. As you might imagine, the kids flee the first moment they can. Annie heads to Hollywood and takes up acting; Buster becomes a freelance writer and sometime novelist. But the Fang umbilical cord proves oddly bungee-like, and the offspring soon return for adult-size doses of psychological torment. Wilson writes with the studied quirkiness of George Saunders or filmmaker Wes Anderson, and there's some genuine warmth beneath all the surface eccentricity." Entertainment Weekly.

Wilson, Kevin, 1978-

Nothing to see here / Kevin Wilson. Ecco, 2019. 288 p.

ISBN 9780062913463

1. Women caregivers 2. Child care 3. Spontaneous human combustion 4. Twins 5. Familial love 6. Superhuman abilities 7. College roommates 8. Mainstream fiction 9. Domestic fiction 10. Humorous stories

LC 2019008256

Agreeing to help her former college roommate care for two step-children who possess the ability to spontaneously combust when agitated, Lillian endeavors to keep her young charges cool in the face of an astonishing revelation.

Wilson, Robert Charles, 1953-

Blind Lake / Robert Charles Wilson. Tor, 2003. 399 p.

ISBN 0765302624

1. Scientists 2. Human/alien encounters 3. Communication 4. Quarantine 5. Life on other planets 6. Aliens 7. Divorced couples 8. Minnesota 9. Science fiction

LC 2003047345

"A Tom Doherty Associates book."

Prix Aurora: Best Novel, 2004.

Working with an unfamiliar technology at a federal research installation, Marguerite, alongside the man she recently divorced, studies a distant alien race and deals with a military cordon that has cut off all communication.

"No one knows better than Wilson how to manipulate the language of science to suggest the essential unknowability of the universe. . . . The drama at Blind Like gradually expands to encompass humans and aliens in entirely unforeseen ways." New York Times Book Review.

Wilson, Robert Charles, 1953-

Julian Comstock : a story of 22nd-century America / Robert Charles Wilson. Tor, 2009. 416 p.

ISBN 9780765319715

1. 22nd century 2. Dystopias 3. Aristocracy 4. Fame 5. Small town life 6. United States 7. Social science fiction 8. Science fiction

LC 2008053400

"A Tom Doherty Associates book."

As the United States struggles back to prosperity in the 22nd Century, the dashing Captain Commongold faces treachery and intrigue while being at fatal odds with the hierarchy of the Dominion for his beliefs in the doctrines of the Secular Ancients.

"The narrative is beautifully written, populated with engaging and sympathetic, if conflicted, characters, and unlike anything else [Wilson's] done to date . . . . It's also a fascinating example of SF's ongoing negotiations with ideas of history and identity, and a good deal more complex than its faux-naif narrative voice and boys'- book adventure plotting would seem to suggest." Locus.

Wilson, Robert Charles, 1953-

Spin / Robert Charles Wilson. Tor Books, 2005. 368 p. Spin novels (Robert Charles Wilson)

ISBN 0765309386

1. End of the world (Astronomy) 2. Human/alien encounters 3. Space and time 4. Best friends 5. Physicians 6. Scientists 7. Time 8. Friendship 9. Alien artifacts 10. Sun 11. Mars (Planet) -- Colonization 12. Apocalyptic fiction 13. Science fiction

LC 2004058862

Sequel: Axis.

"A Tom Doherty Associates book."

Hugo Award for Best Novel, 2006

After witnessing the onset of an astronomical event that has caused the sun to go black and the stars and moon to disappear, Tyler, Jason, and Diane learn that the darkness has been caused by a time-altering, alien-created artificial barrier and that the sun will be extinguished in less than forty years.

"The narrative time oscillates effortlessly between Tyler Dupree's early adolescence and his near-future young manhood haunted by the impending death of the sun and the earth. Tyler's best friends, twins Diane and Jason Lawton, take two divergent paths: Diane into a troubling religious cult of the end, Jason into impassioned scientific research to discover the nature of the galactic Hypotheticals whose Spin suddenly sealed Earth in a cosmic baggie, making one of its days equal to a hundred million years in the universe beyond. As convincing as Wilson's scientific hypothesizing is--biological, astrophysical, medical--he excels even more dramatically with the infinitely intricate, minutely nuanced relationships among Jason, Diane and Tyler, whose older self tries to save them both with medicines from Mars, terraformed through Jason's genius into an incubator for new humanity." Publishers Weekly.

Wilson, Sloan, 1920-2003

* The **man** in the gray flannel suit / Sloan Wilson. Four Walls Eight Windows, 2002, c1955. 276 p.

ISBN 9781568582467

1. 1950s 2. World War II veterans 3. Suburban life -- Connecticut 4. Corporate culture 5. Marriage 6. Businesspeople 7. Self-discovery in men 8. Identity (Psychology) 9. Job satisfaction 10. Connecticut 11. Psychological fiction 12. Domestic fiction 13. Modern classics

LC 2002-69297

Originally published: New York : Simon and Schuster, 1955.

After returning from World War II, Tom Rath enters the corporate world to face the pressures and demands of the rat race.

Wilson, Susan, 1951-

The **fortune** teller's daughter / Susan Wilson. Atria Books, 2002. 342 p.

ISBN 074344230X

1. Psychic ability 2. Rural life 3. Love stories

LC 2002104271

Stunning her free-spirited mother by settling down in a quiet New England community, Sabine, a possessor of psychic abilities, helps unravel a local mystery with the help of Dan Smith, who has returned to the town of his childhood to claim the family business.

Winawer, Melodie

The **scribe** of Siena : a novel / Melodie Winawer. Touchstone, 2017. 352 p.

ISBN 9781501152252

1. 14th century 2. Medieval period (476-1492) 3. Time travel (Past) 4. Artists 5. Women physicians 6. Loss (Psychology) 7. Conspiracies 8. Options, alternatives, choices 9. Men/women relations 10. Interpersonal attraction 11. Black Death 12. Time travel 13. Historical fiction

LC 2016025826

The story of a brilliant woman's passionate affair with a time and a place that captures her in an impossibly romantic and dangerous trap--testing the strength of fate and the bonds of love.

"Winawers debut is a detailed historical novel, a multifaceted mystery, and a moving tale of improbable love." Publishers Weekly.

Winer, Jeanne, 1950-

Her kind of case / Jeanne Winer. Bancroft Press, 2018. 308 p. Lee Isaacs, Esq. novels

ISBN 9781610882286

1. Lawyers 2. Hate crimes 3. Public defenders 4. Crimes against gay men and lesbians 5. Teenage murder suspects 6. Defense attorneys 7. Violence in gangs 8. Innocence (Law) 9. Women lawyers 10. Trials (Murder) 11. Senior women 12. Martial artists 13. Boulder, Colorado 14. Legal stories

A legal drama that centers on Lee Isaacs, a female defense attorney on the cusp of turning 60, who, out of curiosity, determination, and desire for a big, even impossible, professional challenge, chooses to take on a tough murder case in which a largely uncooperative young man is accused of helping kill a gay gang member.

"Winer...who was a criminal defense attorney for decades, brings vivid, insider knowledge of all things legal, from lawyers' black humor to the importance of details to a jury. Unlike many dull legal novels, though, this is filled with witty dialogue, believable characters, and quick pacing." Kirkus.

Winfrey, Kerry

Waiting for Tom Hanks : a novel / Kerry Winfrey. Jove, 2019. viii, 274 p.

ISBN 9781984804020

1. Screenplay writing 2. Single women 3. Obsession 4. Film industry and trade 5. Actors and actresses 6. Female friendship 7. Sexual attraction 8. Men/women relations 9. Ohio 10. Romantic comedies

A rom-com-obsessed romantic waiting for her perfect leading man learns that life doesn't always go according to a script.

"The chemistry between Annie and Drew is irresistible, and the plots many moving pieces add complexity. Chloe, lovable Uncle Don, and the local coffee shops colorful characters provide humor and heart in just the right places." Publishers Weekly.

Wingate, Lisa

Before we were yours / Lisa Wingate. Ballantine Books, 2017. 368 p.

ISBN 9780425284681

1. Tann, Georgia, 1891-1950 2. 1930s 3. Adoption racket 4. Brothers and sisters 5. Child kidnapping victims 6. Crimes against children 7. Human trafficking 8. Poor children 9. Orphanages 10. Kidnappers 11. Adoption 12. Tennessee 13. Historical fiction 14. Parallel narratives

Goodreads Choice Award, 2017

Librarians' Choice (Australia), 2017

A tale inspired by firsthand accounts about the notoriously corrupt Tennessee Children's Home Society follows the efforts of a Baltimore assistant D.A. to uncover her parents' fateful secrets in the wake of a political attack and a chance encounter with a stranger.

Winkler, Anthony C.

Dog war / Anthony C. Winkler. Akashic Books, 2007. 195 p.

ISBN 9781933354286

1. Christian women 2. Widows 3. Jamaicans in the United States 4. Christian widows 5. Family relationships 6. Household employees 7. Families 8. Women and dogs 9. East Indian immigrants 10. East Indians in the United States 11. Interpersonal attraction 12. Men/women relations 13. Christian women -- Sexuality 14. Change (Psychology) 15. Housekeepers 16. Jamaica 17. Florida 18. Humorous stories

LC 2006936538

After Precious Higginson's husband suddenly passes away, she is forced to move in with her son, then her daughter, and on from there, always finding herself in one insulting situation after another.

"Newly widowed, Precious, an upstanding Jamaican with practical ideas and a conversational relationship with Jesus, becomes a maid in a Miami mansion for a pampered dog, who soon develops overfond feelings for her person. The dog belongs to the spiritually questing Mistress Lucy, a multimillionaire among whose most pressing concerns is whether to have her Rolls decowed--the leather removed on moral grounds. Winkler has a fine ear for patois and dialogue, and a love of language that makes bawdy jokes crackle." The New Yorker.

Winman, Sarah, 1964-

Tin man : a novel / Sarah Winman. G.P. Putnam's Sons, 2018, c2017 224 p.

ISBN 9780735218727

1. 20th century 2. Love triangles 3. Growing up 4. Men/men relations 5. Widowers 6. Art 7. Friendship 8. AIDS (Disease) 9. Gay men 10. Bisexual men 11. Loneliness 12. Homophobia 13. Gay teenagers 14. Life change events 15. Interpersonal relations 16. Men/women relations 17. England 18. Literary fiction 19. LGBTQIA fiction

LC 2018005873

Originally published: London : Tinder Press, 2017.

A heartbreaking celebration of love in all its forms gradually reveals a fallout between two longtime friends and Oxford students over the course of a decade marked by the marriage of one and the disappearance of the other.

Winslow, De'Shawn Charles

* **In** West Mills / De'Shawn Charles Winslow. Bloomsbury Publishing, 2019. 272 p.

ISBN 9781635573404

1. 20th century 2. African American women 3. Independence in women 4. African American communities 5. Small town life 6. Eccentric women 7. Neighbors 8. Women teachers 9. Dysfunctional families 10. Ostracism 11. Toleration 12. Unplanned pregnancy 13. Secrets 14. North Carolina 15. Literary fiction 16. Historical fiction 17. African American fiction

LC 2018034737

A woman in mid-20th-century rural North Carolina, determined to live on her own terms in spite of community gossip, finds unexpected support from a veteran fixer who struggles with an inability to correct his own troubled past.

Winslow, Don, 1953-

The **border** / Don Winslow. William Morrow, 2019. 750 p. Art Keller novels

ISBN 9780062664488

1. Drug enforcement agents 2. Drug cartels 3. Organized crime 4. Redemption 5. Heroin addiction 6. Drug traffic 7. Corruption 8. Criminals 9. Revenge 10. Violence 11. New Mexico 12. Mexico 13. Mexican-American Border Region 14. Crime fiction

LC 2018037648

Promoted by the DEA after a crucial victory, Art Keller is targeted by the power-hungry traffickers behind an American heroin epidemic.

"An action-filled, sometimes even instructive look at the world of the narcos and their discontents." Kirkus.

Winslow, Don, 1953-

The **cartel** / Don Winslow. Alfred A. Knopf, 2015 592 p. Art Keller novels

ISBN 9781101874998

1. Drug cartels 2. Organized crime 3. Drug enforcement agents 4. Redemption 5. Drug traffic 6. Corruption 7. Prisoners 8. Criminals 9. Revenge 10. New Mexico 11. Mexico 12. Mexican-American Border Region 13. Crime fiction

LC 2015006233

Ian Fleming Steel Dagger Award, 2016

RUSA Reading List Short List, 2016.

This long-awaited sequel to The Power of the Dog catches us up on DEA agent Art Keller's life: he's become a beekeeper for a New Mexico monastery. But when his nemesis, cartel leader Adán Barrera, escapes from a Mexican prison, Keller is drawn back into the world to stop the escalating violence between cartels. At nearly 600 pages, this is an epic tale, not only taking on personal vendettas but incorporating the very real damage done to bystanders in Mexican drug wars. -- Description by Shauna Griffin.

"The staggering body count will be a challenge for many readers to get past, but the payoffs for those who persevere are immense. Winslow's two-novel project about this still-raging conflict is entertaining, well researched, and difficult to process, a jarring glimpse into a reality about which many Americans remain blissfully unaware." Library Journal.

Winslow, Don, 1953-

The **dawn** patrol / Don Winslow. Alfred A. Knopf, 2008. 320 p. Boone Daniels mysteries

ISBN 9780307266200

1. Surfers 2. Redemption 3. Guilt in men 4. Arson investigation 5. Private investigators 6. Former police 7. Women lawyers 8. Men/women relations 9. California 10. Mysteries

LC 2008006531

Boone Daniels lives to surf. Every morning he's out in the break off Pacific Beach with the other members of The Dawn Patrol: four men and one woman as single-minded about surfing as he is. But Boone is also obsessed with the unsolved case of a young girl named Rain who was abducted back when he was on the San Diego police force. He blames himself--just as almost everyone in the department does--for not being able to save her. Now he's unexpectedly staring at a chance to make some amends.

"Winslow transforms his blithe trifle into an elegiac riff on the Pacific Coast's paradise lost, and produces a classic. If you haven't read Winslow yet, get to it." San Francisco Chronicle.

Winslow, Don, 1953-

The **kings** of cool / Don Winslow. Simon & Schuster, 2012. 322 p.

ISBN 9781451665321

1. Friendship 2. Generation gap 3. Drug dealers 4. Marijuana smuggling 5. Extortion 6. Kidnapping -- California 7. Cartels 8. Drug traffic 9. Laguna Beach, California 10. California 11. Thrillers and suspense

LC 2012010619

A prequel to Savages shares the formative stories of Ben, Chon, and O in California, describing how while battling a cabal of drug dealers and corrupt cops, the trio finds that their futures are linked with their parents' histories.

Winslow, Don, 1953-

Satori / Don Winslow. Grand Central Pub., 2010. 352 p.

ISBN 9780446561921

1. 1950s 2. Assassins 3. Fugitives 4. International intrigue 5. Terrorism 6. International businesses 7. China 8. Thrillers and suspense

LC 2010012415

Sequel: Shibumi.

Prequel to: Shibumi / Trevanian.

In a prequel to Trevanian's "Shibumi," amid the chaos of the Korean War, the CIA offers Nicholai Hel his freedom only if he kills the Soviet Union's Commissioner to China in Beijing, a mission that draws on all his strengths.

"Perfect for Shibumi fans and anyone else who likes their espionage over the top." Kirkus.

Winslow, Don, 1953-

* **Savages** : a novel / Don Winslow. Simon & Schuster, 2010. 302 p.

ISBN 9781439183366

1. Drug dealers 2. Marijuana smuggling 3. Extortion 4. Kidnapping

-- California 5. Cartels 6. Drug traffic 7. Laguna Beach, California 8. California 9. Thrillers and suspense

Running a lucrative marijuana operation in Laguna Beach, sometime environmentalist Ben and mercenary Chon confront a dangerous adversary in the Mexican Baja Cartel, which kidnaps their playmate confidante Ophelia, compelling the duo to plot ingenious negotiations.

"[Winslow] dispenses short chapters that drive his plot breathlessly forward. He also serves up plenty of savage wit." Booklist.

Winspear, Jacqueline, 1955-

The **American** agent / Jacqueline Winspear. Harper, 2019 352 p. Maisie Dobbs novels

ISBN 9780062436665

1. Second World War era (1939-1945) 2. 1930s 3. World War II 4. Women private investigators 5. Women journalists 6. Americans in England 7. Organized crime 8. Murder investigation 9. Secrecy in government 10. Great Britain -- History -- George VI, 1936-1952 11. Historical mysteries 12. Mysteries

When Catherine Saxon, an American correspondent reporting on the war in Europe, is found murdered in her London digs, news of her death is concealed by British authorities. Serving as a linchpin between Scotland Yard and the Secret Service, Robert MacFarlane pays a visit to Maisie Dobbs, seeking her help. Accompanied by an agent from the US Department of Justice--Mark Scott, the American who helped Maisie escape Hitler's Munich in 1938--he asks Maisie to work with Scott to uncover the truth about Saxon's death. As the Germans unleash the full terror of their blitzkrieg upon the citizens of London, raining death and destruction from the skies, Maisie must balance the demands of solving this dangerous case with her need to protect the young evacuee she has grown to love. Entangled in an investigation linked to the power of wartime propaganda and American political intrigue being played out in Britain, Maisie will face losing her dearest friend-and the possibility that she might be falling in love again.

Winspear, Jacqueline, 1955-

Birds of a feather / Jacqueline Winspear. Soho Press, 2004. 360 p. Maisie Dobbs novels

ISBN 1569473684

1. Between the Wars (1918-1939) 2. 1930s 3. Women private investigators 4. World War I veterans 5. Missing persons 6. Women psychologists 7. Former nurses 8. Crimes against young women 9. Meditation 10. Inheritance and succession 11. World War I 12. London, England 13. Historical mysteries 14. Mysteries

LC 2003025732

Agatha Award for Best Novel, 2005.

Amelia Bloomer List, 2005

When Maisie Dobbs is hired to find the missing daughter of a wealthy grocery magnate, she discovers that three of the heiress's friends have died violently, leading her to investigate the connection between the disappearance and the murders.

"The period touches, from clothing to manners, are not only elegantly presented but unostentatious." Booklist.

Winspear, Jacqueline, 1955-

Maisie Dobbs / Jacqueline Winspear. Soho Press, 2003. 294 p. Maisie Dobbs novels

ISBN 1569473307

1. 1910s 2. 1920s 3. Women private investigators 4. Extramarital affairs 5. Household employees 6. Nurses 7. Human nature 8. Women psychologists 9. Murder 10. World War I veterans 11. World War I 12. Housekeepers 13. London, England 14. France 15. Historical mysteries 16. Mysteries

LC 2002044656

Agatha Award for Best First Novel, 2004.

Macavity Award for Best First Mystery Novel, 2004.

Maisie Dobbs entered domestic service in 1910 at thirteen, working for Lady Rowan Compton. When her remarkable intelligence is discovered by her employer, Maisie becomes the pupil of Maurice Blanche, a learned friend of the Comptons. In 1929, following an apprenticeship with Blanche, Maisie hangs out her shingle: M. Dobbs, Trade and Personal Investigations.

"For a clever and resourceful young woman who has just set herself up in business as a private investigator, Maisie seems a bit too sober and much too sad. Romantic readers sensing a story-within-a-story won't be disappointed. But first, they must prepare to be astonished at the sensitivity and wisdom with which Maisie resolves her first professional assignment." New York Times Book Review.

Winter, Evan

* The **rage** of dragons / Evan Winter. Orbit, 2019. 544 p. The burning

ISBN 9780316489768

1. Warriors 2. Revenge 3. Determination in men 4. Class conflict 5. Social classes 6. Imaginary wars and battles 7. War and society 8. Options, alternatives, choices 9. Magic 10. Dragons 11. Demons 12. Loss (Psychology) 13. Men/women relations 14. Afrofuturism and Afrofantasy 15. Sword and sorcery

Born into a never ceasing war dominated by women who summon dragons and magically strong men, Tau has no gifts, but pledges to do all in his power to avenge his murdered family members.

"Winter's secondary characters support his heros story and amplify its themes of brotherhood, but it is Tau himself, far more nuanced than a simple underdog, who will move readers to eagerly seek the next volume." Publishers Weekly.

Winter, Kathleen

Annabel / Kathleen Winter. House of Anansi Press, 2010. 465 p.

ISBN 9780802170828

1. 1960s 2. People who are intersex 3. Gender role and children 4. Surgery 5. Social acceptance in children 6. Identity (Psychology) 7. Social structure 8. Rural life -- Canada 9. Newfoundland and Labrador 10. Literary fiction

Thomas Head Raddall Atlantic Fiction Prize, 2011.

Governor General's Literary Awards, English-language Fiction finalist

Shortlisted for the Giller Prize, 2010

Shortlisted for The Orange Prize for Fiction, 2011

Born a boy and a girl but raised as a boy, Wayne or "Annabel" struggles with his identity growing up in a small Canadian town and seeks freedom by moving to the city.

Winters, Ben H.

Countdown City / Ben H. Winters. Quirk, 2013. 288 p. Last policeman trilogy

ISBN 9781594746260

1. End of the world 2. Asteroids 3. Detectives 4. Police 5. Suicide 6. Murder investigation 7. New Hampshire 8. Science fiction mysteries 9. Apocalyptic fiction 10. Science fiction

Philip K. Dick Award for Science Fiction, 2014.

Having lost his job in the wake of an imminent asteroid collision, Detective Hank Palace agrees to help a woman from his past find her missing husband in a world that is rapidly descending into apocalyptic chaos.

Winters, Ben H.

The **last** policeman / Ben H. Winters. Quirk Books, 2012. 288 p. Last policeman trilogy

ISBN 9781594745768

1. End of the world 2. Asteroids 3. Detectives 4. Police 5. Suicide 6. Murder investigation 7. New Hampshire 8. Science fiction mysteries 9. Apocalyptic fiction 10. Science fiction

Edgar Allan Poe Award for Best Paperback Original Mystery, 2013.

When the Earth is doomed by an imminent and unavoidable asteroid collision, New Hampshire homicide detective Hank Palace considers the worth of his job in a world destined to end in six months and investigates a suspicious suicide that nobody else cares about.

Winters, Ben H.

World of trouble / Ben H. Winters. Quirk, 2014. 320 p. Last policeman trilogy

ISBN 9781594746857

1. End of the world 2. Asteroids 3. Detectives 4. Police 5. Suicide 6. New Hampshire 7. Science fiction mysteries 8. Apocalyptic fiction 9. Science fiction

"With the doomsday asteroid looming, Detective Hank Palace has found sanctuary in the woods of New England, secure in a well-stocked safe house with other onetime members of the Concord police force. But with time ticking away before the asteroid makes landfall, Hank's safety is only relative, and his only relative--his sister Nico--isn't safe. Soon, it's clear that there's more than one earth-shattering revelation on the horizon, and it's up to Hank to solve the puzzle before time runs out . . . for everyone." --, from publisher's web site.

"The bleak premise of this series could be too much, but, instead, it gives a certain clarity to the action of people who become their most real selves when the end of the world arrives." Library Journal.

Winterson, Jeanette, 1959-

The **daylight** gate / Jeanette Winterson. Grove Press, 2013, c2012. 240 p.

ISBN 9780802121639

1. Stuart period (1603-1714) 2. 17th century 3. Witchcraft 4. Trials (Witchcraft) 5. Hysteria (Social psychology) 6. Secrets 7. Superstition 8. Single women 9. Magic (Occultism) 10. Women entrepreneurs 11. Catholics 12. Color in the textile industry and trade 13. Great Britain -- History -- James I, 1603-1625 14. Historical horror

Includes author's introduction.

Originally published: London : Random House, 2012.

Can a man be maimed by witchcraft? Can a severed head speak? Based on the most notorious of English witch-trials, this is a tale of magic, superstition, conscience and ruthless murder. It is set in a time when politics and religion were closely intertwined; when, following the Gunpowder Plot of 1605, every Catholic conspirator fled to a wild and untamed place far from the reach of London law. This is Lancashire. This is Pendle. This is witch country.

Winterson, Jeanette, 1959-

* **Frankissstein** / Jeanette Winterson. Grove Press, 2019 340 p.

ISBN 9780802129499

1. Shelley, Mary Wollstonecraft, 1797-1851 2. 19th century 3. 21st century 4. Posthumanism 5. Artificial intelligence 6. Trans men 7. Cryonics 8. Sexuality 9. Physicians 10. Gender fluid 11. Brexit, 2016-2020 12. Resuscitation 13. Science fiction 14. Literary fiction 15. Adaptations, retellings, and spin-offs

Longlisted for the Booker Prize, 2019.

A transgender doctor falls in love with a celebrated professor who is leading the debate about artificial intelligence and conducting controversial experiments impacting cryogenics and the sex trade.

Winterson, Jeanette, 1959-

The **passion** / Jeanette Winterson. Atlantic Monthly Press, 1988, c1987. 160p.

ISBN 9780802135223

1. Soldiers 2. Married women 3. Bisexuality 4. Gambling 5. Men/women relations 6. Napoleonic Wars, 1800-1815 7. Women/women relations 8. Men/women relations 9. Venice, Italy 10. Moscow, Russia 11. Historical fiction 12. LGBTQIA fiction

LC 88003427

Passion consumes Henri, a chef with Napoleon's army, and Villanelle, who has lost her heart to a married noblewoman, until the two meet at the gates of Moscow and form a bond based on bitter loss.

Winthrop, Elizabeth Hartley, 1979-

The **mercy** seat : a novel / Elizabeth Hartley Winthrop. Grove Press, 2018 240 p.

ISBN 9780802128188

1. 1940s 2. Racism 3. Race relations 4. Small town life 5. Trials (Rape) 6. Judicial error 7. Capital punishment 8. Executions and executioners 9. Racism in the judicial system 10. Louisiana 11. Literary fiction 12. Historical fiction

LC 2017051039

Set during the hours leading up to the scheduled execution of a black teen for the alleged rape of a white woman in 1943 Louisiana, a meticulous portrait of race, racism and injustice in the Jim Crow era South traces the experiences of the convicted boy; his father, the District Attorney; the convict truck driver delivering the executioner's chair and a couple grappling with grief and secrets.

"This potent novel about prejudice and the constraints of challenging the status quo will move and captivate readers, especially those looking for socially conscious historical fiction." Publishers Weekly.

Winthrop, Elizabeth Hartley, 1979-

* The **why** of things / Elizabeth Hartley Winthrop. Simon & Schuster, 2013. 256 p.

ISBN 9781451695755

1. Murder investigation 2. Family and suicide 3. Family relationships 4. Dog adoption 5. Grief in families 6. Loss (Psychology) 7. Mainstream fiction

LC 2012041122

Arriving in their summer home less than a year after the suicide of a teenage daughter, Joan and her family stumble on the death of a local young man and adopt his homeless dog before bonding with his grieving mother and learning that the victim's death was not accidental.

Winton, Tim, 1960-

The **shepherd's** hut / Tim Winton. Farrar, Straus and Giroux, 2018. 272 p.

ISBN 9780374262327

1. Hermits 2. Deserts 3. Teenage boys 4. Accidental death 5. Survival 6. Fathers and sons 7. Trust 8. Solitude 9. Friendship 10. Western Australia 11. Australia 12. Literary fiction

Librarians' Choice (Australia), 2018.

A brutalized rural youth flees his father's violent death to live in exile in Australia's harsh saltlands, where his life comes to depend on a ruined priest he is not sure he trusts.

Wiseman, Beth, 1962-

Listening to love / Beth Wiseman. Zondervan, 2019. 320 p. Amish journey

ISBN 9780529118714

1. Amish 2. Faith (Christianity) 3. Interfaith romance 4. Expectation (Psychology) 5. Men/women relations 6. Interpersonal attraction 7. Options, alternatives, choices 8. Indiana 9. Christian romances

LC 2019013783

Lucas, a member of the Old Order Amish, falls in love with Natalie, a woman pursuing a veterinary medicine career, and both of their families are against their relationship, making it hard for the couple to stay true to themselves.

Wodehouse, P. G. (Pelham Grenville), 1881-1975

The **best** of Wodehouse : an anthology / P.G. Wodehouse ; with an introduction by John Mortimer. Alfred A. Knopf, 2007. xli, 796 p.

ISBN 9780307266613

1. Anthologies 2. Humorous stories 3. Short stories 4. Gentle reads

LC bl2007014198

A compilation of works by one of the twentieth century's leading humorists features two novels, The Code of the Woosters and Uncle Fred in the Springtime, as well as fourteen short stories and three autobiographical pieces.

Wodehouse, P. G. (Pelham Grenville), 1881-1975

* The **inimitable** Jeeves / P.G. Wodehouse. Overlook Hardcover, 2007, c1923. 272 p. Jeeves and Wooster

ISBN 1585679224

1. Single men 2. Butlers 3. Marriage 4. Upper class 5. Misadventures 6. England 7. Farcical fiction 8. Short stories 9. Gentle reads

Typical, just when Bertie thinks that God's in his heaven and all's right with the world, things start to go wrong again. There's young Bingo Little, who's in love for the umpteenth time and needs Bertie to put in a good word for him with his uncle. Aunt Agatha, who forces Bertie to get engaged to the formidable Honoria Glossop, and the troublesome twins, Claude and Eustace, whose antics when let loose in London knows no bounds. Add to that some friction in the Wooster home over a red cummerbund, purple socks and some snazzy old Etonian spats, and poor Bertie's really in the soup. Only one man can save the day, the inimitable Jeeves.

Wodehouse, P. G. (Pelham Grenville), 1881-1975

* **My** man Jeeves / P. G. Wodehouse. Overlook Press, 2006. 185 p. Jeeves and Wooster

ISBN 9781585678754

1. Rich people 2. Single men 3. Misadventures 4. Butlers 5. Valets 6. England 7. Humorous stories 8. Short stories 9. Gentle reads

LC 2006938089

Originally published in the U.K. in 1919.

The story of the relationship between Bertie Wooster and his valet Jeeves.

Wojtas, Olga

* **Miss** Blaine's prefect and the golden samovar / Olga Wojtas. Felony & Mayhem Press, 2018. 264 p.

ISBN 9781631941702

1. Spark, Muriel Prime of Miss Jean Brodie 2. 19th century 3. Librarians 4. Time travel (Past) 5. Murder investigation 6. Aristocracy -- Russia 7. Middle-aged women 8. Time travel 9. Scots 10. Edinburgh, Scotland 11. Russia -- History -- 19th century 12.

Historical mysteries 13. Humorous stories

LC 2018025061

Skills in everything from martial arts to quantum physics make Shona McMonagle the perfect recruit for a new and interesting project: Time-travel to Tzarist Russia, prevent a gross miscarriage of romance, and-- in any spare time--see to it that only the right people get murdered.

"Firmly set in Russia with fascinating details of the life and times of the people, from princesses to serfs, woven through the story, and with Shona cleverly using historical clues gained from conversations to piece together facts about her new environment, this humorous romp includes plot twists and well-delineated, quirky, characters." Booklist.

Wolf, Dick

The **execution** / Dick Wolf. William Morrow, 2014. 335 p. Jeremy Fisk novels

ISBN 9780062064851

1. Police 2. Assassins 3. International intrigue 4. Detectives 5. Intelligence service 6. New York City 7. Thrillers and suspense

LC 2013031972

After a Mexican assassin leaves behind 23 beheaded bodies on the United States border, Detective Cecilia Garza of the Mexican intelligence agency follows him to New York City where she teams up with NYPD Detective Jeremy Fisk to stop this ruthless killer from adding to his body count.

Wolf, Dick

The **intercept** / Dick Wolf. William Morrow, 2012. 387 p. Jeremy Fisk novels

ISBN 9780062064837

1. Terrorism 2. Intelligence service 3. International intrigue 4. Conspiracies 5. New York City 6. Thrillers and suspense

When the hijacking of a commercial jet over the Atlantic Ocean is thwarted, iconoclastic New York Police detective Jeremy Fisk and his partner Krina Gersten match wits with opponents who are smarter and more agile than any they have ever faced.

Wolf, Dick

The **ultimatum** / Dick Wolf. William Morrow, 2015. 341 p. Jeremy Fisk novels

ISBN 9780062286833

1. Assassins 2. International intrigue 3. Snipers 4. Detectives 5. Intelligence service 6. New York City 7. Thrillers and suspense

When sensitive NYPD intelligence including his home address is released to WikiLeaks, Detective Jeremy Fisk is attacked by mysterious assailants linked to a serial sniper who is using cutting edge drone technology to murder innocent civilians.

Wolfe, Gene

* The **best** of Gene Wolfe : a definitive retrospective of his finest short fiction / Gene Wolfe. St. Martins Press, 2009. 480 p.

ISBN 9780765321350

1. Short stories 2. Science fiction 3. Fantasy fiction

Locus Award for Best Collection, 2010.

An anthology of thirty-one signature short works by the winner of the World Fantasy Award for Life Achievement includes "Petting Zoo," "The Tree Is My Hat," and "The Island of Dr. Death and Other Stories."

"This is a highly flattering career retrospective of a postmodern fabulist disguised as a mild-mannered SF writer." Publishers Weekly.

Wolfe, Gene

The **citadel** of the Autarch / Gene Wolfe. Timescape Books, 1983. 317 p. Book of the new sun

ISBN 0671452517

1. Exiles 2. Gems 3. Torturers 4. Parallel universes 5. Time travel 6. Imaginary wars and battles 7. Science fantasy 8. Science fiction

LC 82005964

John W. Campbell Memorial Award for Best Science Fiction Novel, 1984.

Severian the Torturer, possessor of the miracle-producing gem, the Claw of the Conciliator, experiences strange adventures as he journeys across the savage land of Urth.

Wolfe, Gene

The **claw** of the conciliator / Gene Wolfe. Timescape Books, 1981. 301 p. Book of the new sun

ISBN 0671413708

1. Exiles 2. Gems 3. Monsters 4. Torturers 5. Executions and executioners 6. Alliances 7. Mercy 8. Imprisonment 9. Imaginary wars and battles 10. Science fantasy 11. Science fiction

Sequel to: The shadow of the torturer.

Sequel: The sword of the Lictor.

Locus Award for Fantasy Novel, 1982.

Nebula Award for Best Novel, 1981.

Continues the tale of an Earth one million years in the future, following the cross-continent journey of Severian, owner of the Claw of the Conciliator, a miracle-producing gem.

Wolfe, Gene

Home fires / Gene Wolfe. Tor, 2011. 304 p.

ISBN 9780765328182

1. Married people 2. Space warfare 3. Hijacking of ships 4. Lawyers 5. Women veterans 6. Human/alien encounters 7. Imaginary wars and battles 8. Science fiction

LC 2010036106

"A Tom Doherty Associates book."

Chelle and Skip have been separated by Chelle's tour of duty in a war against aliens from distant solar systems. They find their relationship complicated by time differentials that cause an injured and war-weary Chelle to age only a few months while Skip reaches his forties.

"With complications involving spies, murderers, cyborgs and pirates, Wolfe cross-examines his characters with a subtle, intelligent series of psychological and logical challenges. A somber, almost brooding tone permeates this compelling work from one of the genre's grandmasters." Kirkus.

Wolfe, Gene

The **land** across / Gene Wolfe. Tor Books, 2013. 286 p.

ISBN 9780765335951

1. Travel writers 2. Espionage 3. Supernatural 4. Political corruption 5. Spies 6. Americans in Europe 7. Kidnapping 8. Secrets 9. Eastern Europe 10. Noir fiction 11. Horror

LC 2013022126

In need of a new location, an American writer of travel guides journeys to a small and obscure Eastern European country where it soon becomes evident that there are supernatural forces at work, but they are not as threatening as the country's corruption and brute forces of bureaucracy.

"Mirroring the absurdist novels of Franz Kafka and the surreal stories of Stanislaw Lem and Jorge Luis Borges, Wolfe's latest novel begins quietly and grows stranger and more whimsical by the page. In the end, the author's creative genius brings everything together with twists and turns that are both surprising and immensely satisfying." Library Journal.

Wolfe, Gene

Pirate freedom / Gene Wolfe. Tor, 2007. 320 p.

ISBN 9780765318787

1. Priests 2. Time travel (Past) 3. Pirates 4. Buccaneers 5. Identity (Psychology) 6. Treasure troves 7. Seafaring life 8. Dueling 9. Caribbean Area 10. Fantasy fiction 11. Sea stories

LC 2007014348

A young priest fresh out of seminary, Father Christopher finds himself inexplicably swept back in time to the Golden Age of Piracy, where he finds himself caught up in the life of a buccaneer and trolling the waters of the Caribbean in search of Spanish gold.

"Wolfe's writing is reminiscent of Carol Emshwiller. . . . There's the same concrete level of detail mixed with an occasionally hazy sense of time and events. The novel is as simple as Wolfe's straightforward, lean prose and easily pulls the reader through to an enjoyable circular ending." BookPage.

Wolfe, Gene

The **shadow** of the torturer / Gene Wolfe. Simon and Schuster, 1980 303 p. Book of the new sun

ISBN 0671253255

1. Dystopias 2. Quests 3. Far future 4. Torture victims 5. Love 6. Torturers 7. Euthanasia 8. Guilds 9. Elite (Social sciences) 10. Voyages and travels 11. Gems 12. Science fantasy 13. Science fiction

LC 79022371

Sequel: The claw of the conciliator.

BSFA Award for Best Novel, 1981.

World Fantasy Award, 1981.

In a thoroughly decadent world of the future, Severian the torturer is cast out from the torturer's guild when he falls in love with one of his victims and allows her to die.

"The book combines elements of fantasy and sf, and the slow pacing is balanced by the excellent characterization and the richly detailed, thoroughly compelling future world." Booklist.

Wolfe, Gene

The **sword** of the Lictor / Gene Wolfe. Timescape Books, 1981. 302 p. Book of the new sun

ISBN 0671435957

1. Exiles 2. Monsters 3. Gems 4. Voyages and travels 5. Torturers 6. Mercy 7. Aliens (Non-humanoid) 8. Revenge 9. Far future 10. Imaginary wars and battles 11. Science fantasy 12. Science fiction

LC 81009427

Sequel to: The claw of the conciliator.

Locus Award for Fantasy Novel, 1982.

When Severian, the Torturer, sets a woman free from prison, he is forced to flee and experiences many strange adventures in the distant future of Earth.

Wolfe, Gene

The **urth** of the new sun / Gene Wolfe. St. Martin's Press, 1987. 372 p. Book of the new sun

ISBN 0312863942

1. Quests 2. Aliens 3. Time travel 4. Torturers 5. Stars 6. Far future 7. Imaginary wars and battles 8. Science fantasy 9. Science fiction

LC 87050478

"For all its obvious unity, the book also has a strongly picaresque quality, with many episodes and characters developed as lovingly and skillfully as Wolfe can manage--which is very well indeed." Booklist.

Wolfe, Paul, 1947-

The **lost** diary of M / Paul Wolfe. HarperCollins, 2020. 304 p.

ISBN 9780062910660

1. Kennedy, John F (John Fitzgerald), 1917-1963 2. Meyer, Mary, 1920-1964 3. CIA 4. 1960s 5. Conspiracy theories 6. Presidents 7. Mistresses 8. Murder 9. Political intrigue 10. Men/women relations 11. Extramarital affairs 12. Hallucinogenic drugs 13. Historical fiction 14. Biographical fiction 15. Literary fiction 16. Diary novels

A reimagining of the life of Georgetown socialite Mary Pinchot Meyer traces her marriage to a CIA chief, presidential affair and LSD experiments before her baffling murder a year after JFK's assassination.

"Wolfe's inspired study of a cryptic woman is credible and haunting." Booklist.

Wolfe, Suzanne M.

The **course** of all treasons / Suzanne M. Wolfe. Crooked Lane Books, 2019. 272 p. Elizabethan spy novels

ISBN 9781643851785

1. Elizabeth I,, Queen of England, 1533-1603 2. Tudor period (1485-1603) 3. Elizabethan era (1558-1603) 4. Spies 5. Political intrigue 6. Treason 7. Catholic families 8. Undercover operations 9. Courts and courtiers 10. Women rulers 11. Historical mysteries

Working directly for Sir Francis Walsingham in 1586 England, Nicholas Holt, a spy for Queen Elizabeth I, tries to figure out who is attacking his loved ones.

"Wolfe vividly brings London to life, from the raunchy taverns to the stages offering plays by Will Shakespeare. But the book's greatest strength is its characters, starting with the clever but flawed Holt, and including a twin brother and sister team of Jewish healers and a young Irish woman with a talent for disguise." Publishers Weekly.

Wolfe, Thomas, 1900-1938

* **Look** homeward, angel : a story of a buried life / Thomas Wolfe. Scribner's, 2006, c1929. 512 p.

ISBN 9780743297318

1. Authors, American -- 20th century 2. Small town life 3. Dysfunctional families 4. Children of alcoholic fathers 5. Small town families 6. North Carolina 7. Coming-of-age stories 8. Autobiographical fiction 9. Modern classics 10. Southern fiction

First published in the United States of America, 1929.

Wolfe's largely autobiographical novel features Eugene Gant, who pines for a more expansive life after being born to a father whose bouts of maniacal raving are fueled by a prodigious appetite for drink.

Wolfe, Thomas, 1900-1938

* **Of** time and the river : a legend of man's hunger in his youth / Thomas Wolfe. C. Scribner's Sons, 1935. 912 p.

ISBN 0684147394

1. Authors, American 2. Coming-of-age stories

LC 35027095

The second novel by the great American novelist, Thomas Wolfe, and now the subject of a major new film, Genius, starring Jude Law, Colin Firth, Dominic West and Nicole Kidman. It is 1920 and Eugene Gant leaves the American South for Harvard, New York and Europe, determined to make his way as a writer. On the boat home, he meets Esther Jack, the woman who is to dominate his life. Autobiographical, vital and passionate, this novel blazes with energy and life.

Wolfe, Thomas, 1900-1938

* The **web** and the rock / Thomas Wolfe. Harper, 1939. 695 p.

1. Literary fiction

As George Webber grows up and attends college, he tries to understand the meaning of life, but is unsuccessful.

Wolfe, Thomas, 1900-1938

* **You** can't go home again / Thomas Wolfe. Harper, 1940. 743 p.

1. Wolfe, Thomas, 1900-1938 2. Depression era (1929-1941) 3. Truth 4. Depressions -- 1929-1941 5. Authors, American 6. Autobiographical fiction 7. Modern classics

LC 40027633

Novelist George Webber is driven from his hometown when his successful autobiographical novel infuriates the family and friends he has depicted in it.

Wolfe, Tom

* **Back** to blood : a novel / Tom Wolfe. Little, Brown, 2012. 608 p.

ISBN 9780316036313

1. Police -- Miami, Florida 2. Mayors 3. Journalists 4. Immigration and emigration 5. Ambition in men 6. Sex addiction 7. Artists 8. City life 9. Cuban American men 10. Psychiatrists 11. Miami, Florida 12. Satirical fiction

LC 2012019545

A colorful cast of residents and visitors to Miami go about their daily activities, both legal and illegal.

"Wolfe is back to some old tricks, including an ever-shifting, sometimes untrustworthy point of view, dizzying pans from one actor to another and rat-a-tat prose...a welcome pleasure from an old master and the best from his pen in a long while." Kirkus.

Wolfe, Tom

The **bonfire** of the vanities / Tom Wolfe. Farrar, Straus Giroux, 1987. 659 p.

ISBN 0374115346

1. 1980s 2. City life 3. Social classes 4. Traffic accidents 5. Brokers 6. District attorneys 7. Bankers 8. Trials (Murder) 9. Rich people 10. Yuppies 11. Scandals 12. Race relations 13. New York City 14. Satirical fiction 15. Modern classics

LC 87017691

National Book Critics Circle Award for Fiction finalist, 1987

Sherman McCoy, a young investment banker in Manhattan, finds himself arrested following a freak accident and becomes involved with prosecutors, politicians, the press, and assorted hustlers.

Wolfe, Tom

I am Charlotte Simmons / Tom Wolfe. Farrar, Straus and Giroux, 2004. 608 p.

ISBN 0374281580

1. Women college students 2. Campus life 3. Social status 4. Race relations 5. College freshmen 6. Social acceptance 7. Difference (Psychology) 8. Innocence (Personal quality) 9. Drinking 10. Drug use 11. Universities and colleges 12. Men/women relations 13. Sexuality 14. New England 15. Coming-of-age stories 16. Satirical fiction

LC 2004047131

As Charlotte encounters the paragons of Dupont University's privileged elite, she is seduced by the heady glamour of acceptance, betraying her values and upbringing before she grasps the power of being different and the exotic allure of her innocence.

"Tom Wolfe can make words dance and sing and perform circus tricks, he can make the reader sigh with pleasure before his arias of coloratura description, he can do just about anything in these pages with words, including exaggerate, distort and rant." Washington Post Book World.

Wolfe, Tom

* A **man** in full : a novel / Tom Wolfe. Farrar, Straus, Giroux, 1998. 742 p.

ISBN 0374270325

1. Real estate developers 2. Debtor and creditor 3. Race relations 4. Rape 5. African American college football players 6. Rich people 7. Senior men 8. Mayoral candidates 9. Former football players 10. College football players 11. Rape victims 12. Atlanta, Georgia -- Race relations 13. Georgia 14. Satirical fiction

LC 9829842

National Book Award for Fiction finalist, 1998

Charles Croker, a middle-aged, egotistical former college football star turned tycoon, finds his life turned upside down and the delicate racial balance of Atlanta threatened when star running back Fareek Fanon, a product of the city's slums, is accused of raping an Atlanta aristocrat's daughter.

"Among all the animal appetites that are slaked or comically thwarted during the novel there appears one new to Wolfe's fiction. For all their affluence, or their pained lack of same, his chief characters hunger for a code of conduct or a framework of beliefs that will make sense of their lives right now, a blink before the millennium. At its heart, A Man in Full is a cliff-hanging morality tale." Time.

Wolff, Tobias, 1945-

Old school : a novel / Tobias Wolff. Knopf, 2003. 208 p.

ISBN 9780375401466

1. Prep schools 2. Social classes 3. Belonging 4. Teenage boys 5. Prep school students 6. Authors 7. Creative writing 8. New England 9. New England -- Social life and customs 10. Psychological fiction 11. Literary fiction

LC 2003052930

ALA Notable Book, 2005.

National Book Critics Circle Award for Fiction finalist, 2003

During his senior year at an elite New England prep school, a young man who had struggled to fit in with his contemporaries finds his life unraveling due to the school's obsession with literary figures and their work.

Wolff, Tobias, 1945-

Our story begins : new and selected stories / Tobias Wolff. Alfred A. Knopf, 2008. xii, 379 p.

ISBN 9781400044597

1. Short stories

Ten potent new stories that, along with twenty-one classics, display Wolff's mastery over a quarter century.

"It does not seem coincidental that Wolff's most protean narratives draw heavily upon his autobiographical experiences. Wolff, at his best, is truly a novelist of himself. His feats of self-invention offer a compelling rebuttal both to the fabulists whose stories fall so short of reality that they have to borrow the truth guarantee of memoirif the lies rang truer, they could be published as fiction--and to those who denounce the faking of memoir as some sort of heinous crime, rather than the failed act of literature it is." Slate.

Wolitzer, Hilma

Hearts / Hilma Wolitzer. Farrar, Straus and Giroux, 1980. 324 p.

ISBN 9780374168704

1. Widows 2. Blended families 3. Thirteen-year-old girls 4. Families 5. Secrecy 6. Stepchildren 7. Automobile travel 8. Single-parent families 9. Mothers and daughters 10. Interpersonal relations 11. California 12. New Jersey 13. Psychological fiction

LC 80018556

Sequel: Tunnel of Love.

"This is a comedy about the heart-wrenching process of growth; it is written with great skill and no condescension. Few readers will fail to be moved." The New Republic.

Wolitzer, Meg

* The **female** persuasion / Meg Wolitzer. Riverhead Books, 2018. 456 p.

ISBN 9781594488405

1. Ambition in women 2. Feminists 3. Mentors 4. Couples 5. Self-fulfillment in women 6. Women radicals 7. Men/women relations 8. Coming-of-age stories

LC 2017031394

A shy college freshman finds her perspectives transformed by a mentor activist at the center of the women's movement who challenges her to discover herself in ways that take her far from the traditional life she envisioned at the side of her boyfriend.

Wolitzer, Meg

The **Interestings** / Meg Wolitzer. Riverhead Books, 2013. 468 p.

ISBN 9781594488399

1. Marriage 2. Friendship 3. Success (Concept) 4. Actors and actresses 5. Jealousy in women 6. Ambition in women 7. Creativity 8. Gay men 9. Secrets 10. Mainstream fiction

Forging a powerful bond in the mid-1970s that lasts throughout subsequent decades, six individuals pursue respective challenges into their midlife years, including an aspiring actress who harbors jealousy toward friends who achieve successful creative careers.

Wolitzer, Meg

Surrender, Dorothy : a novel / Meg Wolitzer. Scribner, 1999. 224 p.

ISBN 0684848449

1. Fatal traffic accidents 2. Grief 3. Loss (Psychology) 4. Gay men 5. Married people 6. Interpersonal relations 7. Mothers 8. Long Island, New York 9. Mainstream fiction

LC 9847007

A group of friends who share a summer house every year on Long Island are knit together primarily by the vivacious Sara, but when she is killed in a tragic accident, they must all learn to redefine their lives, and their feelings, without her

"Buried within this affecting novel is the troubling question of whether close friendships and close family ties can keep a person from finding romantic intimacy. Wolitzer's Sara didn't live long enough to explore that possibility; perhaps her survivors will be luckier." New York Times Book Review.

Wolitzer, Meg

The **wife** : a novel / Meg Wolitzer. Scribner, 2003. 219 p.

ISBN 0684869403

1. Authors' spouses 2. Extramarital affairs 3. Married women 4. Husband and wife 5. Marriage 6. Authors 7. Fame 8. Secrets,

9. Sixties (Age) 10. New York City 11. Mainstream fiction 12. Domestic fiction

LC 2002036660

On the eve of her husband's receipt of a prestigious literary award, Joan Castleman, who has put her own writing ambitions on hold to support her husband, evaluates her choices and decides to end the marriage.

"Wolitzer's crisp pacing and dry wit carry us headlong into a devastating message about the price of love and fame." Publishers Weekly.

Wong, David, 1975

* **Futuristic** violence and fancy suits / David Wong. Thomas Dunne Books, 2015. 374 p.

ISBN 9781250040190

1. Near future 2. Superheroes 3. Supervillains 4. Young women 5. Secrets 6. Survival 7. Income distribution 8. Life change events 9. Fathers and daughters 10. Baristas 11. Superhero stories 12. Satirical fiction

LC 2015025817

RUSA Reading List Short List, 2016.

The pseudonymous author of John Dies at the End forays into science fiction with this fast-paced, darkly humorous novel. After barista Zoey Ashe survives a live-streamed assassination attempt, she discovers that her deceased biological father was not the deadbeat she always assumed; he's actually the billionaire founder of Tabula Ra$a, a Mob-ruled metropolis in the Utah desert. Her dead dad's associates, the Suits, offer to protect her from future attacks in exchange for help defeating cyborg crime boss Molech. Staying alive is Zoey's top priority, so she has no choice but to take their deal. -- Description by Gillian Speace.

"Well-timed humor and explosive thrills, a smart backbone, and witty wordsmithing make this new release by Cracked.com's pseudonym-wielding Jason Pargin (John Dies at the End, 2009) as fun as it gets. Steer this one toward readers of sf with a sense of humor, and fans of Max Barry's satirical futuristic novels." Booklist.

Wong, David, 1975

John dies at the end / David Wong. Thomas Dunne Books/St. Martin's Press, 2009. 384 p. John dies at the end

ISBN 9780312555139

1. Paranormal phenomena 2. Monsters 3. Space and time 4. Fear 5. Friendship 6. Middle west 7. Horror 8. Satirical fiction

LC 2009016944

Sequel: This Book Is Full of Spiders

A full-length tale based on the cult online serial finds an increasing number of people changed into threatening inhuman creatures by a hallucinogen, a situation that places the fate of the world in the hands of a pair of anti-heroes.

Wong, David, 1975

This book is full of spiders : seriously, dude, don't touch it / David Wong. St. Martin's Press, 2012. 384 p. John dies at the end

ISBN 9780312546342

1. Paranormal phenomena 2. Zombies 3. Quakers 4. Slackers 5. Shapeshifters 6. Horror 7. Humorous stories

Sequel to: John Dies At the End

A sequel to John Dies at the End finds heroes David and John embroiled in a new set of horrific but absurd challenges when movie-induced zombie phobia enables a nefarious shape-shifter race to take over the world.

Woo, Sung J.

Everything Asian / Sung J. Woo. St. Martin's Press, 2009. 328 p.

ISBN 9780312538859

1. Immigrants 2. Cultural differences 3. Immigrant families 4. Acculturation 5. Korean American boys 6. Twelve-year-old boys 7. Koreans in the United States 8. Family relationships 9. New Jersey 10. Coming-of-age stories

LC 2008037673

Asian Pacific American Award for Literature: Young Adult Literature, 2010.

Young David Kim reunites with the father he has not seen in five years while working in the family strip-mall gift shop, an endeavor during which he harbors a secret shame about what he believes to be his father's character flaws.

"A charming tale of family, community and the struggle for understanding. . . . Woo eschews immigrant cliches to focus on complicated familial relationships and surprising, sympathetic characters. Alternating between humor and melancholy, Woo's text strikes a true chord." Publishers Weekly.

Woo, Sung J.

Love love : a novel / Sung J. Woo. Soft Skull Press, 2015. 256 p.

ISBN 9781593766177

1. Brothers and sisters 2. Divorced persons 3. Parent and adult child 4. Identity (Psychology) 5. Adopted children 6. Loss (Psychology) 7. Sick fathers 8. Former professional tennis players 9. Family relationships 10. Men/women relations 11. Mainstream fiction

LC 2015009333

Two siblings try to deal with the disappointments they have encountered in their lives, as Judy Lee tries to find love and her brother Kevin, hoping to help his father by donating a kidney, discovers that he was adopted.

"Woos narrative takes serendipitous turns--he has a knack for making these twists seem organic, like things that would happen in life. Scenes recounting memories of family and lost love are also skillfully interspersed." Publishers Weekly.

Wood, James, 1965-

Upstate / James Wood. Farrar, Straus & Giroux, 2018. 214 p.

ISBN 9780374279530

1. Widowers 2. Real estate developers 3. Family relationships 4. Fathers and daughters 5. Sisters 6. Women with depression 7. Couples 8. British in the United States 9. Happiness 10. Purpose in life 11. Saratoga Springs, New York 12. New York (State) 13. Domestic fiction

A British property developer faces philosophical questions about family and suffering when one of his estranged daughters falls into a severe depression.

Wood, Shelley, 1971-

The **Quintland** sisters / Shelley Wood. William Morrow & Co., 2019. 384 p.

ISBN 9780062839091

1. Dionne quintuplets 2. 1930s 3. Depression era (1929-1941) 4. Quintuplets 5. Child custody 6. Midwives 7. Nurses 8. Exploitation 9. Tourists 10. Fame 11. Rural life 12. Premature infants 13. Parents' rights 14. French Canadians 15. Politicians 16. Ontario 17. Canada 18. Coming-of-age stories 19. Historical fiction

Attending the birth of the Dionne quintuplets in 1934 Ontario, a teen midwife witnesses an explosive custody dispute between the government and family members involving the quintuplets' exploitation as curiosities.

"Blending historical fact with a fictional coming-of-age story, Wood has crafted an ambitious, meticulously researched, and imaginative debut novel that is engrossing and compelling." Booklist.

Wood, Tracey Enerson

The **engineer's** wife : a novel / Tracey Enerson Wood. Sourcebooks Landmark, 2020 352 p.

ISBN 9781492698135
1. Roebling, Emily Warren, 1843-1903 2. Roebling, Washington Augustus, 1837-1926 3. 1870s 4. Bridges 5. Husband and wife 6. Married women -- Identity 7. Helpfulness in women 8. Life change events 9. Engineers 10. Sexism 11. City life 12. Men/women relations 13. New York City -- Social life and customs -- 19th century 14. Brooklyn Bridge, New York City 15. Historical fiction 16. Biographical fiction

LC 2019032996
When her happy domestic life is turned upside-down by her husband's work as the chief engineer on an under-construction Brooklyn Bridge, Emily Warren Roebling gradually takes over the project to advocate on behalf of worker safety.

"This important work of historical fiction brings to life the strength and resolve of a nineteenth-century woman overshadowed by men and overlooked by history books." Booklist.

Woodrell, Daniel

The **Maid's** Version : a novel / Daniel Woodrell. Little, Brown and Company, 2013. 164 p.

ISBN 9780316205856
1. Grandmother and grandson 2. Housekeepers 3. Justice 4. Explosions 5. Death 6. Secrets 7. Small towns 8. Suspicion 9. Families 10. Extramarital affairs 11. Dance halls 12. Missouri 13. Literary fiction 14. Historical fiction 15. Southern fiction

In 1929, Alma DeGeer Dunahew, the maid for a prominent family in Missouri, chases down justice after her younger sister is one of forty-two people killed in a mysterious explosion at a local dance hall.

Woodrell, Daniel

Winter's bone : a novel / Daniel Woodrell. Little, Brown and Co., 2006. 208 p.

ISBN 031605755X
1. Fathers and daughters 2. Rural families 3. Drug traffic 4. Sixteen-year-old girls 5. Mothers with mental illnesses 6. Fugitives 7. Missing persons 8. Brothers and sisters 9. Arrest 10. Dysfunctional families 11. Repossession 12. Drug culture 13. Methamphetamine 14. Small town life -- Ozark Mountain Region 15. Mountain life 16. Ozark Mountain region 17. Southern States 18. Rural noir 19. Coming-of-age stories 20. Literary fiction 21. Southern fiction

LC 2005017349
Ree Dolly's father has skipped bail on charges that he ran a crystal meth lab, and the Dollys will lose their house if he doesn't show up for his next court date. With two young brothers depending on her, 16-year-old Ree knows she has to bring her father back, dead or alive. Living in the harsh poverty of the Ozarks, Ree learns quickly that asking questions of the rough Dolly clan can be a fatal mistake. But, as an unsettling revelation lurks, Ree discovers unforeseen depths in herself and in a family network that protects its own at any cost.

"Like his characters, and especially his teen characters, Woodrell's prose mixes tough and tender so thoroughly yet so delicately that we never taste even a hint of false bravado, on the one hand, or sentimentality, on the other. And Ree is one of those heroines whose courage and vulnerability are both irresistible and completely believable--think of not just Mattie Ross in True Grit but also Scout in To Kill a Mockingbird or even Eliza Naumann in Bee Season. One runs out of superlatives to describe Woodrell's fiction." Booklist.

Woods, Chavisa

Things to do when you're goth in the country : and other stories / Chavisa Woods. Seven Stories Press, 2017. 221 p.

ISBN 9781609807450
1. 21st century 2. Misfits (Persons) 3. United States -- Social life and customs -- 21st century 4. Short stories 5. Literary fiction

LC 2016043180
Things to Do When You're Goth in the Country introduces us to Chavisa Woods's people. They are smart and poor, lost and hoping not to be found, a people of faith who have no god, and of high hopes but few if any expectations--inhabitants, mostly young, of a third world country without a name that exists within America, mostly hidden.

"This book is tight, intelligent, and important, and sure to secure Woods a seat in the pantheon of critical twenty-first-century voices." Booklist.

Woods, Rita

* **Remembrance** / Rita Woods. Forge, 2020, c2019. 352 p.

ISBN 9781250298454
1. 1790s 2. 1850s 3. 2010s 4. Slavery 5. Racism 6. Supernatural 7. Protectiveness 8. Freedom 9. Magic 10. Race relations 11. Underground Railroad 12. Women psychics 13. Psychic ability 14. Haiti 15. New Orleans, Louisiana 16. Ohio 17. Historical fantasy 18. Literary fiction

LC 2019041000
Looks at present-day Ohio, 1791 Haiti, and 1857 New Orleans, in which house girl Margot is sold just before her 18th birthday and her promised freedom, and, desperate, she escapes and tries to find Remembrance, a rumored stop on the Underground Railroad.

"This book deserves to be a breakout hit. Woods's magical realist take on the black female experience will have huge appeal to readers of Marlon James and Tara Conklin." Library Journal.

Woods, Stuart

Below the belt / Stuart Woods. G.P. Putnam's Sons, 2017. 320 p. Stone Barrington novels

ISBN 9780399573972
1. Former police 2. Law firms 3. Power (Social sciences) 4. Ambition 5. Intrigue 6. Lovers 7. Santa Fe, New Mexico 8. Thrillers and suspense

Stone Barrington and the gang are back in the line of fire, but with his usual unflappable aplomb, Stone always comes out on top.

"Woods brings back several recurring characters in this political novel in which art comes to imitate life. ... Woods is compulsively readable, even as he churns out three novels a year, so a slip on the last page is easy to forgive and doesn't really lessen the pleasure of the journey in this easy-reading page-turner." Booklist.

Woods, Stuart

Chiefs / Stuart Woods. W. W. Norton, 1981. 427 p. Lee family saga

ISBN 0039014614
1. 1920s 2. Small towns 3. Political corruption 4. Secrets 5. Missing persons 6. Police chiefs 7. Deception 8. Murder investigation 9. Racism 10. Murder 11. African American men 12. Small town life 13. Georgia 14. Thrillers and suspense

LC 80027350
Edgar Allan Poe Award for Best First Mystery Novel, 1982.

Beginning in 1920, the experiences of three Georgia police chiefs, who watch the world, their town, and their jobs change. At the heart of this is a 40-year-old mystery each chief must try to crack.

Woods, Stuart

A **delicate** touch / Stuart Woods. G. P. Putnam's Sons, 2018. 320 p. Stone Barrington novels

ISBN 9780735219250

1. Private investigators 2. Law firms 3. Scandals 4. Upper class 5. Secrets 6. Criminals 7. Protectiveness in men 8. Crime 9. City life 10. Men/women relations 11. New York City 12. Thrillers and suspense

LC 2018041585

Asked by an old acquaintance with help solving a tricky puzzle, Stone Barrington unwittingly stirs up a decades-old scandal in high-society New York and must risk his life to protect innocent lives.

Woods, Stuart

Fast & loose / Stuart Woods. G.P. Putnam's Sons, 2017. 357 p. Stone Barrington novels

ISBN 9780399574191

1. Former police 2. Law firms 3. Power (Social sciences) 4. Ambition 5. Intrigue 6. Lovers 7. Men/women relations 8. Manhattan, New York City 9. Thrillers and suspense

Stone Barrington, a New York City cop turned rainmaker for a white-shoe Manhattan law firm, tackles a formidable case that challenges the boundaries of his talents.

"In Barrington, Woods has created a rich man who could walk through the needles eye into heaven and then have St. Peter waiting for him with Stone's favorite drink on the bar. Pure fantasy, to be sure, but a thoroughly entertaining escapist read." Booklist.

Woods, Stuart

The **money** shot / Stuart Woods, Parnell Hall. G.P. Putnam's Sons, 2018 320 p. Teddy Fay novels

ISBN 9780735218598

1. Extortion 2. Actors and actresses 3. Criminal investigation 4. Disguises 5. Stunt performers 6. Former assassins 7. Intelligence officers 8. Hollywood, California 9. Thrillers and suspense

LC 2018000922

Disguising himself as a stuntman to investigate blackmail threats against an actress starring in a new production, Teddy Fay discovers that the perpetrators are looking for something other than money, in a novel that also features fan-favorite Stone Barrington.

Woods, Stuart

New York dead / Stuart Woods. HarperCollins Publishers, 1991. 303 p. Stone Barrington novels

ISBN 9780060179250

1. Murder 2. Police 3. Sexuality 4. Women television newscasters and commentators 5. Secrets 6. Missing persons 7. Frameups 8. Men/women relations 9. Private investigators 10. New York City 11. Thrillers and suspense

LC 90056374

On disability leave from the New York City Police Department, Detective Sergeant Stone Barrington witnesses the murder of network news star Sasha Nijinsky, who is pushed from her penthouse terrace.

"A mystery set in Manhattan's Upper East Side, the stomping ground of Stone Barrington, a well-bred but unpretentious detective. . . . Late one evening, as Stone trudges home from Elaine's Restaurant, popular TV newscaster Sasha Nijinsky plummets 12 stories from her terrace and lands on a heap of dirt 20 yards away from himremarkably, still alive. Stone fails to apprehend the person who flees Sasha's penthouse and,

after the ambulance carrying her collides with a fire truck, Sasha herself disappears. Despite the fact that no corpse is in evidence, the baffled NYPD eagerly pins a murder rap on Sasha's distraught lesbian lover. Stone refuses to accept his colleagues' pat solution." Publishers Weekly.

Woods, Stuart

Orchid beach / Stuart Woods. Harper Collins, 1998. 325 p. Holly Barker novels

ISBN 9780060191818

1. Murder 2. Conspiracies 3. Drug smuggling 4. Small town life 5. Women deputy police chiefs 6. Murder investigation 7. Doberman pinschers 8. Women and dogs 9. Florida 10. Thrillers and suspense

Military policewoman Holly Barker lost a harassment case against her superior and quit the army. On arriving for a new job as deputy of a Florida town she finds the chief shot, a case which will lead to an assault by the FBI on a compound of the very rich.

"The story gets extra bite from Holly's intriguing relationship with an inherited canine named Daisy, the clairvoyant Doberman that belonged to her mentor." Publishers Weekly.

Woods, Stuart

Palindrome / Stuart Woods. Harper Collins Publishers, 1991. 344 p.

ISBN 0060179112

1. Abused women 2. Solitude 3. Revenge 4. Women photographers 5. Men/women relations 6. Abusive men 7. Murder 8. Second chances 9. Divorced women 10. Identical twins 11. Serial murderers 12. Men with mental illnesses 13. Cumberland Island, Georgia 14. Atlanta, Georgia 15. Thrillers and suspense

LC 90055587

For years, Liz Barwick, a talented photographer, has been battered by her husband, a pro football player. This time, it takes an emergency room to keep her from death. Liz retreats to an island off Georgia's coast to find solitude and herself. She becomes involved with the strange and handsome Drummond twins and begins to leave her past behind. Then, a series of gruesome murders occur, and Liz realizes that there's no place to hide.

"When Liz Barwick is beaten nearly to death by her steroid-crazed husband, Baker Ramsey, a star NFL running back, she quickly divorces him, takes a large cash settlement and disappears from public view. Liz, whose book of sports photographs has just been released, takes advantage of her publisher's offer to live in his cottage on an isolated private island off the Georgia coast. But when Ramsey goes on a murderous rampage, Liz's lawyer and publisher and his wife are among his victims. Meanwhile other events are unfolding on Cumberland Island, where Liz becomes involved with the Drummond family." Publishers Weekly.

Woods, Stuart

Santa Fe rules / Stuart Woods. HarperCollins, 1992. 303 p. Ed Eagle novels

ISBN 0060179635

1. Husband and wife 2. Innocence (Law) 3. Secrets 4. Native American lawyers 5. Film producers and directors -- United States 6. Sisters 7. Murder 8. Love triangles 9. Mistaken identity 10. Married women -- Death 11. Santa Fe, New Mexico 12. Thrillers and suspense

LC 91058476

Sequel: Short straw.

Learning that his wife and partner have died suspiciously while he was away, successful Hollywood producer Wolf Willett returns home and hires ace criminal defense lawyer Ed Eagle to clear his name of the murder charge.

LIST OF FICTIONAL WORKS

Woods, Stuart,

Skin game / Stuart Woods and Parnell Hall. Penguin Group USA, 2019 320 p. Teddy Fay novels

ISBN 9780735219168

1. Treason 2. Rare and endangered animals 3. Double agents 4. Espionage 5. Undercover operations 6. Criminal investigation 7. Disguises 8. Former CIA agents 9. Scientists 10. Former assassins 11. Intelligence officers 12. Paris, France 13. Thrillers and suspense

LC 2018049556

When former CIA operative Teddy Fay travels to Paris in search of a treasonous criminal, his trail of clues leads to complicated secrets, evildoers making power grabs, and a global threat.

Woods, Stuart

Smooth operator / Stuart Woods, with Parnell Hall. G.P. Putnam's Sons, 2016. 320 p. Teddy Fay novels

ISBN 9780399185267

1. Assassination 2. Former assassins 3. Intelligence officers -- United States 4. Intrigue 5. Snipers 6. Politicians 7. Moles (Spies) 8. Former CIA agents 9. Kidnapping victims 10. Politicians' families 11. Washington, D.C. 12. Thrillers and suspense

LC 2016008414

"When President Kate Lee calls Stone Barrington to Washington on an urgent matter, it's soon clear that a potentially disastrous situation requires the kind of help more delicate than even he can provide. and he knows just the right man for the job. Teddy Fay: ex-CIA, master of disguise, and a gentleman not known for abiding by legal niceties in the pursuit of his own brand of justice."--Provided by publisher.

Woods, Stuart

Stealth / Stuart Woods. Putnam Pub Group, 2019. 320 p. Stone Barrington novels

ISBN 9780593083161

1. Private investigators 2. Lawyers 3. Sabotage 4. Attempted murder 5. Intelligence service 6. Americans in Great Britain 7. Women physicians 8. Military physicians 9. Men/women relations 10. Enemies 11. Sexual attraction 12. Great Britain 13. Scotland 14. Thrillers and suspense

Abruptly dispatched to a remote region of the U.K., Stone Barrington teams up with two brilliant colleagues only to land in a trap that reveals a rival power's lethal agenda and the larger conspiracy of a criminal mastermind.

Woods, Teri

Alibi / Teri Woods. Grand Central Pub., 2009. viii, 257 p.

ISBN 9780446581691

1. Robbery 2. African American drug dealers 3. Witnesses 4. Criminals 5. Murder 6. Violence 7. Alibi 8. African Americans 9. Philadelphia, Pennsylvania 10. Urban fiction 11. Thrillers and suspense 12. African American fiction

LC 2008048145

Two men think they've found the perfect opportunity--a chance to rob the stash house of Simon Shuller, one of Philadelphia's biggest drug lords. But their plans are spoiled when one of Shuller's men catches them as they break into the stash house. Temperatures flare as the men capture Shuller's worker, Poncho, and force him to show them the goods. What they didn't expect was for Poncho's partner to be armed and very dangerous. An altercation breaks out and when the smoke clears, Nard, Poncho's accomplice, is the only one left standing. Thinking quickly, Nard cleans shop and makes his escape, but not before being spotted by a few neighbors. Not wanting to kill anyone else, he makes a mad dash for the streets but wonders if the witnesses will give up his identity.

What he needs now is a plausible alibi. If he doesn't come up with one fast, it could mean life in prison, or death on the streets.

Woods, Teri

Dutch : the first of a trilogy / Teri Woods. Grand Central Pub., 2009, c2003. 242 p. Dutch novels

ISBN 9780446551533

1. Gangsters 2. Organized crime 3. Street life 4. Former convicts 5. Muslims 6. Hispanic American women 7. African American men 8. Mafia 9. Murder 10. Vigilantes 11. Power (Social sciences) 12. Dutch 13. Newark, New Jersey 14. New Jersey 15. Urban fiction 16. African American fiction

LC bl2009027971

Originally self-published: New York : Teri Woods Pub., c2003.

Street Lit Book Award Medal: Adult Fiction, 2004

James Bernard Jr., also known as "Dutch," makes his rise in New Jersey's world of organized crime from a car thief to successful heroin trafficker.

Woods, Teri

* True to the game : a Teri Woods fable / Teri Woods. Teri Woods Publishing, 2003, 244 p. True to the game

ISBN 096722490X

1. 1980s 2. 20th century 3. African American drug dealers 4. Drug abuse and crime 5. Men/women relations 6. African American men 7. African American women 8. Drug dealers 9. Inner city 10. Extortion 11. African American young women 12. Money addiction 13. Love 14. Street life 15. City life 16. Organized crime 17. Drug traffic 18. Philadelphia, Pennsylvania 19. Pennsylvania 20. African American fiction 21. Urban fiction

Sequel: True to the game II.

Street Lit Book Award Medal: Adult Fiction, 2000

Gena, a street-smart Philadelphian, finds her life turned upside down by a whirlwind romance with Quadir, a wealthy man who can give her whatever she wants but whose connections with a powerful drug cartel could threaten both their lives.

Woods, Teri

* True to the game II / Teri Woods. Warner, 2007. 232 p. True to the game

ISBN 9780446581660

1. 1980s 2. 20th century 3. African American drug dealers 4. Men/women relations 5. Drug abuse and crime 6. African American men 7. African American women 8. Drug dealers 9. Inner city 10. Men/women relations 11. African American young women 12. Money addiction 13. African American men/women relations 14. Street life 15. City life 16. Organized crime 17. Drug traffic 18. Philadelphia, Pennsylvania 19. Pennsylvania 20. Urban fiction 21. African American fiction

Sequel to: True to the game.

After Quadir's death, Gena has fallen head-over-heels for her new man, Jay. Little does she know, however, that her new flame is really Jerrell Jackson, Quadir's rival who would like nothing more than to exact revenge on Quadir's crew, starting with Gena.

Woods, Teri

True to the game III / Teri Woods. Grand Central Pub., 2008. 224 p. True to the game

ISBN 9780446581684

1. 1980s 2. 20th century 3. African American drug dealers 4. Drug abuse and crime 5. Organized crime 6. Men/women relations 7. African American men 8. African American women 9. Drug dealers 10. Inner city 11. Men/women relations 12. African American young

women 13. Stalkers 14. Protectiveness in men 15. Police corruption 16. African American men/women relations 17. Street life 18. City life 19. Drug traffic 20. Stalking 21. Philadelphia, Pennsylvania 22. Pennsylvania 23. Urban fiction 24. African American fiction

LC 2007039788

Sequel to: True to the game II.

Saved from Jerrell's clutches by her enigmatic stalker, Gena is ready to get her life back on track. However, there's a new killer on the streets. To make matters worse, Gena and her family are targeted by some crooked cops who are hoping to score her drug money.

Woodson, Jacqueline

* **Another** Brooklyn / Jacqueline Woodson. Amistad, 2016. 192 p.

ISBN 9780062359988

1. 1970s 2. Female friendship 3. African Americans -- Identity 4. Memories 5. Violence in men 6. Sexual violence 7. Growing up 8. African American girls 9. Identity (Psychology) 10. African American families 11. Loss (Psychology) 12. City life 13. Race relations 14. Family relationships 15. Brooklyn, New York City 16. New York City 17. Coming-of-age stories 18. Literary fiction 19. African American fiction

BCALA Literary Award for Fiction, 2017.

Finalist for the Hurston/Wright Legacy Awards for Fiction, 2017.

August is 35 the year she returns to Brooklyn to bury her father, and a chance encounter with a friend in her old neighborhood prompts a flood of memories from her youth. Having moved to Brooklyn at eight, August's coming of age was marked by a search for belonging, close friendships, freedom, and the little-understood absence of her mother. Her memories explore what it was like to be an African-American girl (and teen) in the 1970s, what possibilities existed -- and what challenges. This tale of friendship, love, and loss cuts back and forth through time. -- Description by Shauna Griffin.

Woodson, Jacqueline

* **Red** at the bone / Jacqueline Woodson. Riverhead Books, 2019 176 p.

ISBN 9780525535270

1. 20th century 2. Family celebrations 3. Social classes 4. Unplanned pregnancy 5. Mothers and daughters 6. Gentrification of cities 7. Racism 8. Growing up 9. African American families 10. Extended families 11. Generation gap 12. Brooklyn, New York City 13. New York City 14. African American fiction 15. Coming-of-age stories 16. Literary fiction

As Melody celebrates a coming of age ceremony at her grandparents' house in 2001 Brooklyn, her family remembers 1985, when Melody's own mother prepared for a similar party that never took place in this novel about different social classes.

Woolf, Virginia, 1882-1941

Between the acts / Virginia Woolf. Harcourt Brace Jovanovich, 1969, c1941. 219 p.

ISBN 9780156118705

1. 1930s 2. Husband and wife 3. Villages 4. Pageants 5. Manors 6. Women dramatists 7. Psychological fiction 8. Modern classics

LC 41017876

Isa and her husband must confront each other after a day of pageantry and emotional tension

Woolf, Virginia, 1882-1941

Jacob's room / Virginia Woolf. Harcourt Brace Jovanovich, 1976, c1922. 176 p.

ISBN 9780156457422

1. Young men 2. Soldiers 3. Men/women relations 4. Growing up 5. Social classes 6. World War I 7. Experimental fiction 8. Psychological fiction 9. Modern classics

An extraordinary departure from traditional forms of the novel, Jacob's Room is both an elegiac and experimental tale told in pieces and fragments and a paean to the slaughter and loss of the First World War.

Woolf, Virginia, 1882-1941

* **Mrs.** Dalloway / Virginia Woolf. Harcourt Brace & Company, 1997, c1925. 212 p.

ISBN 0156005557

1. Middle-aged women 2. Social classes 3. Feminism 4. Politicians' spouses 5. Social conflict 6. Depression 7. Alienation (Social psychology) 8. England 9. Psychological fiction 10. Modern classics

LC 97-13622

First published in Great Britain: Hogarth, 1925.

During one day of arranging for her party Mrs. Dalloway remembers her youth, considers the crushing effects of the Great War, and reexamines her marriage.

Woolf, Virginia, 1882-1941

Orlando : a biography / Virginia Woolf. Harcourt Brace Jovanovich, 1973, c1928. ix, 333 p.

ISBN 9780156701600

1. Young men 2. Nobility -- History -- 16th century 3. Sex (Psychology) 4. Metamorphosis 5. Transgender persons 6. Transformations (Magic) 7. Gender role 8. Immortalism 9. Centenarians 10. Trans women 11. Satirical fiction 12. Modern classics

Originally published: London : Hogarth Press, 1928.

Orlando emerges as a young man at the court of Queen Elizabeth I and progresses, with breathtaking ease, through three centuries until, by now a woman, she arrives in the bustle and diversions of the 1920s ... Orlando's journey, from wondrous youth barbed by love, to feted writer, settled in her femininity, is a wild and curiously relevant fable.

Woolf, Virginia, 1882-1941

* **To** the lighthouse / Virginia Woolf. Harcourt Brace Jovanovich, 1981, c1927. xii, 209 p.

ISBN 9780151907366

1. 1920s 2. Women 3. Human behavior 4. Men/women relations 5. Nature 6. Husband and wife 7. Mothers 8. Family relationships 9. Vacations 10. Psychological fiction 11. Modern classics

"The text of this edition is based on that of the original Hogarth Press edition, published by Leonard and Virginia Woolf on 5 May 1927"-- Page facing colophon.

Originally published: London : Hogarth, 1927.

The Ramsay family and the one summer spent with their friends in their holiday home in Scotland. Offshore stands the lighthouse; remote, inaccessible, and an external presence in a changing world.

Woolf, Virginia, 1882-1941

The **voyage** out / Virginia Woolf ; edited, with an introduction and notes, by Jane Wheare. Penguin Books, 1992, c1915. 382 p.

ISBN 9780140185638

1. Young women 2. Self-discovery in women 3. Women travelers 4. Men/women relations 5. Ocean travel 6. Feminists 7. British women in South America 8. Authors 9. Coming-of-age stories 10. Modern

classics

Standard print edition originally published: London : Duckworth, 1915.

Disillusioned with her life, Rachel Vinrace embarks on a journey to South America aboard her father's vessel. During the long voyage, Rachel discovers the true plight of women during the early 20th century and becomes determined to reinvent herself.

Woolf, Virginia, 1882-1941

The **waves** / Virginia Woolf ; annotated and with an introduction by Molly Hite ; Mark Hussey, general editor. Harcourt, 2006, c1931. lxvii, 270 p.

ISBN 9780156031578

1. Identity (Psychology) 2. Friendship 3. Aging 4. Growing up 5. Purpose in life 6. Psychological fiction 7. Experimental fiction 8. Literary fiction 9. Modern classics

LC 2005037770

First published in the U.K. : Hogarth Press,

As they move from childhood to maturity, the personalities of six friends are revealed through interior monologues. Elliptical, but deeply poetic, the strands of their experiences emerge gently and reflectively in a stream of consciousness, illuminating the meaning of life itself.

Woolf, Virginia, 1882-1941

* The **years** / Virginia Woolf. Harcourt Brace Jovanovich, 1965, c1937. 435 p.

ISBN 9780156997010

1. Rich families 2. Family relationships 3. Death 4. Families 5. England -- Social life and customs -- 20th century 6. Domestic fiction 7. Modern classics

LC 37027268

Originally published: The Hogarth Press, 1937.

Three generations of the Pargiters, an upper-class English family, are caught up in the changes, burdens, and promises of life from 1880 to the 1930's.

Wouk, Herman, 1915-2019

* The **Caine** mutiny : a novel of World War II / Herman Wouk. Back Bay Books, 2003, c1951. xii, 537 p.

ISBN 0316955108

1. Second World War era (1939-1945) 2. Mutiny 3. Courts-martial and courts of inquiry 4. Leadership in men 5. World War II -- Naval operations, American 6. Sailors 7. Pacific Ocean 8. War stories 9. Sea stories 10. Historical fiction 11. Modern classics

LC 2003109473

Originally published: Garden City, N.Y. : Doubleday,

Pulitzer Prize for Fiction, 1952.

"When Lieutenant Commander Philip Queeg becomes captain of the destroyer-minesweeper USS Caine, Ensign Willie Keith believes that the tough Naval Academy graduate will bring much needed discipline to the Caine's rough crew. But Queeg soon reveals himslef to be a cowardly, paranoid man. When his actions begin to endanger not just the crew but the war effort itself, Keith finds himself faced with a terrible choice: obey Queeg, and risk the lives of his shipmates and allies -- or mutiny".

Wouk, Herman, 1915-2019

A **hole** in Texas : a novel / Herman Wouk. Little, Brown, 2004. 224 p.

ISBN 0316525901

1. Scientific discoveries 2. National security 3. Former lovers 4. Physicists 5. Married men 6. Celebrities 7. Women physicists -- China 8. Political science 9. Mass media 10. News media 11. Scandals 12. Temptation 13. International intrigue 14. Texas 15.

Washington, D.C. 16. Satirical fiction

LC 2003020148

Physicist Guy Carpenter finds his peaceful life with a prestigious career at NASA turned upside down by a Chinese scientific discovery that raises serious questions about possible military implications, an old love affair, and national security.

"The plot is busy but secondary to Carpenter's banter and romantic escapades. Occasionally corny but also playful, thoughtful and passionate." Publishers Weekly.

Wouk, Herman, 1915-2019

* **Marjorie** Morningstar : a novel / Herman Wouk. Doubleday, 1955. 565 p.

1. Jewish American women 2. Identity (Psychology) 3. Self-fulfillment 4. Actors and actresses 5. Jewish Americans 6. New York City 7. Coming-of-age stories

LC 55006485

A young Jewish girl experiences love, pain, and disappointment in the struggle to become an actress.

Wouk, Herman, 1915-2019

* **War** and remembrance : a novel / Herman Wouk. Little, Brown, 1978. 1042 p.

ISBN 0316955019

1. Hitler, Adolf, 1889-1945 2. Stalin, Joseph, 1879-1953 3. Mussolini, Benito, 1883-1945 4. Churchill, Winston, 1874-1965 5. Roosevelt, Franklin D (Franklin Delano), 1882-1945 6. United States. Navy 7. Second World War era (1939-1945) 8. 1940s 9. Family relationships 10. World War II 11. Jews 12. Holocaust (1933-1945) 13. Men/women relations 14. War stories 15. Historical fiction

LC 78017746

Sequel to The winds of war.

"America at war, from Pearl Harbor to Hiroshima."

"Wouk's work is a journey of extraordinary emotional riches. Quantity in time becomes quality, movement becomes scope, and history becomes human yearning." New York Times Book Review.

Wouk, Herman, 1915-2019

* The **winds** of war : a novel / Herman Wouk. Little, Brown, 1971. 885 p.

ISBN 9781444779264

1. Hitler, Adolf, 1889-1945 2. Stalin, Joseph, 1879-1953 3. Mussolini, Benito, 1883-1945 4. Churchill, Winston, 1874-1965 5. Roosevelt, Franklin D (Franklin Delano), 1882-1945 6. United States. Navy 7. Second World War era (1939-1945) 8. 1940s 9. Family relationships 10. World War II 11. Holocaust (1933-1945) 12. Atrocities 13. Jews 14. War stories 15. Historical fiction

LC 72161857

Sequel: War and remembrance.

As the war escalates in Europe, the Henry clan, a family of American naval heroes, finds itself drawn into the center of the conflict and must send its patriarch and several sons into the fray.

"On the broadest of tapestries, Wouk weaves the effect of the preparation and the actual outbreak of World War II upon the family of Commander Pug Henry. The affairs of the Henry family became intertwined with those of others, in such varying scenes as Washington, Berlin, Rome, London, and Moscow. . . . Despite the novel's breadth, the development of Henry's character as the middle-class military leader America needed in the 1940's is surprisingly credible." Choice.

Wright, Alexis, 1950-

Carpentaria / Alexis Wright. Giramondo, 2006. 519 p.
ISBN 1920882170

1. Mayors 2. Murderers 3. Religious fanatics 4. Eccentrics and eccentricities 5. Police 6. Families 7. Mines and mineral resources 8. Race relations 9. Storytelling 10. Kinship-based society 11. Political science 12. Landfills 13. Social classes and family 14. Cyclones 15. Natural disasters 16. Oceans 17. Coastal towns 18. Queensland 19. Australia -- Race relations 20. Literary fiction

LC 2007367834

Australian Book Industry Awards, Literary Fiction Book of the Year, 2007.

Australian Literature Society Gold Medal, 2007.

Miles Franklin Award, 2007.

Queensland Premier's Literary Awards, Fiction Book Award, 2007.

Centred on the precariously settled coastal town of Desperance, a township shaped by cyclones, monsoonal floods and a river that spurns human endeavour with its incomprehensible tides, it tells the story of the powerful Phantom family. Led by Norm Phantom, the great fish-embalming king of time, legendary storyteller, suspected murderer and leader of the Pricklebush people, the Phantoms battle to retain sovereignty over a country where "legends and ghosts live side by side". Sovereignty depends on stories. The official version of the region's history makes no mention of the Phantoms or the Great War of the Dump that burst the Pricklebush people apart and set Eastsider against Westsider. Nor does it mention the old tribal tensions that resurfaced and the search for lost ancestral stories that lay claim to traditional ownership.

"This book is a sprawling, surreal anti-Odyssey in which time and space contract and expand and experience takes place in the Dreamtime, on the sea, and on and under the continent of Australia. . . . [This novel] will surely stand as a masterpiece of modern English-language literature." Library Journal.

Wright, Jaime Jo

The **house** on Foster Hill / Jaime Jo Wright. Bethany House, 2017. 352 p.
ISBN 9780764230288

1. 21st century 2. 1900s (Decade) 3. Abandoned houses 4. Family secrets 5. Widows 6. Ancestors 7. Stalkers 8. Faith (Christianity) 9. Women murder victims 10. Threat (Psychology) 11. Small towns 12. Stalking 13. Wisconsin 14. Christian suspense 15. Parallel narratives

LC 2017030033

Christy Award for Suspense Category, 2018.

In an attempt to hide from a stalker, Kaine buys an old house in Wisconsin where an unidentified woman was found dead a century prior, and Kaine soon learns about her ancestor, Ivy Thorpe, who had tried to uncover the truth about the crime.

Wright, John C. (John Charles), 1961-

The **golden** age : a romance of the far future / John C. Wright. Tor/Tom Doherty Associates Book, 2002. 336 p. Golden age series
ISBN 0312848706

1. Immortality 2. Memory 3. Identity (Psychology) 4. Far future 5. Dystopias 6. Posthumanism 7. Science fiction

LC 2001058468

Sequel: The phoenix exultant.

Phaethon Prime Rhadamanth Humodified encounters an old man who accuses him of being an imposter and an alien from Neptune who reveals that he has had essential parts of his memory removed.

"The author chooses simple pulp-fiction plots to drive us through the technological complexities of Phaethon's world. The hero's quest to regain his lost memories, learn his true identity and reach the stars is undeniably compelling. As a result, having to wait for the next volume is frustrating. Wright's ornate and conceptually dense prose will not be to everyone's taste but, for those willing to be challenged, this is a rare and mind-blowing treat." Publishers Weekly.

Wright, Richard, 1908-1960

Eight men : stories / Richard Wright; introduction by Paul Gilroy. Harper Perennial, 1996. xxi, 242 p.
ISBN 0060976810

1. African American men 2. Race relations 3. United States 4. Short stories 5. Literary fiction 6. African American fiction 7. Modern classics

LC 96021614

Tells the stories of a young farm worker deep in debt, a flood, murder, a fugitive, exile, and a railroad porter.

Wright, Richard, 1908-1960

* **Native** son / Richard Wright ; with an introduction by Arnold Rampersad. Harper Perennial Modern Classics, 2005, c1940. xxii, 504 p.
ISBN 9780060837563

1. 1930s 2. Murderers 3. Racism 4. Poverty 5. African Americans 6. Ghettoes, African American 7. Trials (Murder) 8. Death row prisoners 9. Chicago, Illinois -- Race relations 10. Literary fiction 11. Modern classics 12. African American fiction

LC 79086654

"The restored text, established by the Library of America."

Right from the start, Bigger Thomas had been headed for jail. It could have been for assault or petty larceny; by chance, it was for murder and rape. Native Son tells the story of this young black man caught in a downward spiral after he kills a young white woman in a brief moment of panic. Set in Chicago in the 1930s, Richard Wright's novel is just as powerful today as when it was written -- in its reflection of poverty and hopelessness, and what it means to be black in America.

Wright, Richard, 1908-1960

Uncle Tom's children / Richard Wright. Harper and Row, 1965, c1938. 215 p.
ISBN 9780060800550

1. African American authors -- 20th century 2. Racism 3. Political persecution 4. Discrimination 5. African Americans -- Southern States 6. Short stories 7. Literary fiction 8. African American fiction 9. Modern classics

An autobiographical sketch and five short stories by the author, who was born on a Mississippi plantation, which focus on the plight of his people.

Wrobel, Stephanie

Darling Rose Gold / Stephanie Wrobel. Berkley, 2020. 320 p.
ISBN 9780593100066

1. Munchausen syndrome by proxy 2. Mothers and daughters 3. Deception 4. Child abuse 5. Former convicts 6. Life change events 7. Single mothers 8. Manipulation by women 9. Hometowns 10. Secrets 11. Former convicts 12. Psychological suspense

Enduring decades of serious illness as a victim of Munchausen Syndrome by Proxy before exposing her mother's behavior, Rose Gold invites her unrepentant mother back into her life to secretly settle the score.

"Propulsive pacing, a claustrophobic setting, and vividly sketched characters who are equal parts victim and villain conspire to create an anxious, unsettling narrative. Psychological suspense fans will be well satisfied." Publishers Weekly.

LIST OF FICTIONAL WORKS

Wroblewski, David

The **story** of Edgar Sawtelle / David Wroblewski. Ecco Press, 2008. 480 p.

ISBN 9780061374227

1. Guilt in men 2. Human/animal communication 3. Murder suspects 4. Families 5. Dog breeders 6. Fathers and sons 7. Uncles 8. Boys who are mute 9. Dog breeding 10. Fathers -- Death 11. Grief 12. Suspicion 13. Wisconsin 14. Literary fiction 15. Coming-of-age stories 16. Adaptations, retellings, and spin-offs

A tale reminiscent of "Hamlet" that also celebrates the alliance between humans and dogs follows speech-disabled Wisconsin youth Edgar, who bonds with three yearling canines and struggles to prove that his sinister uncle is responsible for his father's death.

"Set in rural nineteen-seventies Wisconsin, this loose retelling of Hamlet focusses on Edgar, a boy born mute and with a preternatural ability to commune with the dogs whose breeding and training is his family's business. ... In this debut novel, Wroblewski illustrates the relationship between man and canine (at times, from the dog's point of view) in a way that is both lyrical and unsentimental, and demonstrates an ability to create a coherent, captivating fictional world in which even supernatural elements feel entirely persuasive." The New Yorker.

Wuertz, Yoojin Grace

Everything belongs to us : a novel / Yoojin Grace Wuertz. Random House, 2016. 368 p.

ISBN 9780812998542

1. Sul Taehakkyo 2. 1970s 3. College students 4. Friendship 5. Ambition 6. Despotism 7. Postwar life 8. Class conflict 9. Young women 10. Family problems 11. Interclass friendship 12. Protests, demonstrations, vigils, etc 13. Motivation (Psychology) 14. South Korea 15. Seoul, Korea 16. Psychological fiction 17. Historical fiction

LC 2016012226

Attending the elite Seoul National University in 1970s South Korea during the final years of a repressive and transformative regime, a tycoon's daughter and her impoverished best friend are drawn to a social-climbing boy who would find his place in a cutthroat world.

"Wuertz is an important new voice in American fiction." Kirkus.

Wurlitzer, Rudolph

* The **drop** edge of yonder / Rudolph Wurlitzer. Two Dollar Radio, 2007. 304 p.

ISBN 9780976389552

1. Trappers 2. Curses 3. Spirits 4. Dreams 5. Brothers 6. Voyages and travels 7. Outlaws 8. Adventurers 9. Gold rush 10. Westerns

LC 2007924062

Cursed by a Native American woman for unknowingly killing her lover, Zebulon travels across the American West wondering which world--real, spirit, or imagined--he roams in and partaking in different escapades and tragedies.

Wyld, Evie

After the fire, a still small voice / Evie Wyld. Pantheon Books, 2009. 304 p.

ISBN 9780307378460

1. Fathers and sons 2. Veterans 3. Family secrets 4. Solitude 5. Small town life 6. Seashore 7. Family relationships 8. Australia 9. Psychological fiction 10. Parallel narratives

LC 2009014832

Shortlisted for the International IMPAC Dublin Literary Award, 2011.

Fleeing to an ocean shack to escape painful memories and a relationship gone bad, Frank is unable to find the solitude he craves; while Vietnam veteran Leon explores the ways in which war destroyed both his and his Korean veteran father's family lives.

"Frank last visited his family's shack, on a Queensland beach, as a gas-huffing teenager, battered by his mother's death and his father's abusive neglect. He returns an alcoholic man, . . . having lashed out at his girlfriend until she left. The shack has served as a retreat before: for Frank's grandfather, reeling from the Korean War, and for his father, who holed up there after serving in Vietnam. The stories of these wounded forebears are layered into Frank's tormented recovery, trauma seeping from one man into the next. Wyld has a feel both for beauty and for the ugliness of inherited pain. The mood is creepy--strange creatures in the sugar cane, grieving neighbors, a missing local girl--and the sentiment is plain." The New Yorker.

Y

Yan, Lianke, 1958-

Dream of Ding Village / Yan Lianke ; translated from the Chinese by Cindy Carter. Grove/Atlantic, 2011, c2005 341 p.

ISBN 9780802119322

1. AIDS (Disease) 2. Blood -- Transfusion -- Social aspects 3. Epidemics 4. Criminals 5. Death 6. Villages 7. Communities 8. China 9. Henan Sheng, China 10. Satirical fiction 11. Translations -- Chinese to English

Originally published: Xianggang : Wen hua yi shu chu ban she, 2005.

A previously banned work based on a true scandal finds an impoverished village targeted by a blood-selling operation that leads to a catastrophic outbreak of AIDS and decimates an entire community.

"Ding Village, a town of 800 people located in the Henan province, finds a quick fix to its dire needs in the form of a plasma-selling scheme promoted by county officials. Money flows the way the Yellow River once did before changing course and leaving the village parched. But exposed to dirty syringes and tainted cotton, and eager to give blood more frequently than their bodies can tolerate, townspeople in increasing numbers come down with the fever and face certain death. Told from the grave by a 12-year-old boy whose grandfather is the deposed town leader and conscience, and whose father buys blood and resells it for a profit, the novel details the contamination of the town's moral as well as physical being. . . . A sorrowful but captivating novel about the price of progress in modern China. The book, which was censored in that country, builds to an act of violence that resonates with the impact of Greek tragedy or Shakespearean drama." Kirkus.

Yanagihara, Hanya

* A **little** life : a novel / Hanya Yanagihara. Doubleday, 2015. 728 p.

ISBN 9780385539258

1. 21st century 2. Male friendship 3. Psychic trauma 4. Ambition 5. City life 6. Self-destructive behavior 7. Actors and actresses 8. Artists 9. Architects 10. Lawyers 11. New York City 12. Literary fiction 13. Psychological fiction

LC 2014027379

ALA Notable Book, 2016.
Kirkus Prize for Fiction, 2015.
Andrew Carnegie Medal for Excellence in Fiction finalist, 2016.
National Book Award for Fiction finalist, 2015
Shortlisted for The Baileys Women's Prize for Fiction, 2016
Shortlisted for the International Dublin Literary Award, 2017
Shortlisted for the Man Booker Prize, 2015.

Moving to New York to pursue creative ambitions, four former classmates share decades marked by love, loss, addiction and haunting elements from a brutal childhood.

"This is a novel that values the everyday over the extraordinary, the push and pull of human relationshipsand the book's effect is cumulative. There is real pleasure in following characters over such a long period, as they react to setbacks and successes, and, in some cases, change." Publishers Weekly.

Yanagihara, Hanya

The **people** in the trees / Hanya Yanagihara. Doubleday, 2013. 384 p.

ISBN 9780385536776

1. Nobel Prize winners 2. Child sexual abuse 3. Smuggling 4. Interethnic relations 5. Culture conflict 6. Mortality 7. Aging 8. Micronesia 9. Literary fiction

LC 2012034034

Joining an anthropologist's 1950 expedition to discover a lost tribe on a remote Micronesian island, a young doctor investigates and proves a theory that the tribe's considerable longevity is linked to a rare turtle, a finding that brings worldwide fame and unexpected consequence.

Yang, JY

The **ascent** to godhood / J. Y. Yang. St Martins Press, 2019. 112 p. Tensorate novellas

ISBN 9781250165886

1. Women rulers 2. Resistance to government 3. Power (Social sciences) 4. Psychic ability 5. Loss (Psychology) 6. Secrets 7. Conspiracies 8. Magic 9. Asian-influenced fantasy 10. Steampunk 11. Fantasy fiction

The Protector is dead. For fifty years, the world turned around her as she built her armies, trained her Tensors, and grasped at the reins of fate itself. Now she is dead. Her followers will quiver, her enemies rejoice. But in one tavern, deep in rebel territory, her greatest enemy drowns her sorrows. Lady Han raised a movement that sought the Protector's head, yet now she can only mourn her loss. She remembers how it all began, when the Protector was young, not yet crowned, and a desperate dancing girl dared to fall in love with her.

Yang, JY

The **black** tides of heaven / J. Y. Yang. Tor.com, 2017. 160 p. Tensorate novellas

ISBN 9780765395412

1. Twins 2. Psychic ability 3. Resistance to government 4. Power (Social sciences) 5. Secrets 6. Conspiracies 7. Magic 8. Steampunk 9. Asian-influenced fantasy 10. Fantasy fiction

The Black Tides of Heaven is one of a pair of unique, standalone introductions to JY Yang's Tensorate Series, which Kate Elliott calls "effortlessly fascinating." For more of the story you can read its twin novella The Red Threads of Fortune, available simultaneously.

"Yang's world is imbued with magic, yet a burgeoning rebellion eschews that magic for technology. The other striking bit of worldbuilding is that children in this world do not have gender until they choose which sex they wish to be, and the stories are full of fascinating gender explorations." Library Journal.

Yang, JY

The **descent** of monsters / J. Y. Yang. St Martins Pr, 2018. 160 p. Tensorate novellas

ISBN 9781250165855

1. Criminal investigation 2. Political corruption 3. Secrets 4. Experiments 5. Monsters 6. Massacres 7. Dystopias 8. Terrorists 9. Government cover-ups 10. Biological stations 11. Twins 12. Nightmares 13. Fantasy mysteries 14. Asian-influenced fantasy 15. Steampunk 16. Fantasy fiction

An investigation into atrocities committed at a classified research facility threaten to expose secrets that the Protectorate will do anything to keep hidden.

Yang, JY

The **red** threads of fortune / J. Y. Yang. Tor.com, 2017. 160 p. Tensorate novellas

ISBN 9780765395399

1. Psychic ability 2. Loss (Psychology) 3. Women psychics 4. Women hunters 5. Monsters 6. Secrets 7. Conspiracies 8. Magic 9. Steampunk 10. Asian-influenced fantasy 11. Fantasy fiction

The Red Threads of Fortune is one of a pair of unique, standalone introductions to JY Yang's Tensorate Series, which Kate Elliott calls "effortlessly fascinating." For more of the story you can read its twin novella The Black Tides of Heaven, available simultaneously.

Yanique, Tiphanie

Land of love and drowning : a novel / Tiphanie Yanique. Riverhead Books, 2014. 368 p.

ISBN 9781594488337

1. Brothers and sisters 2. Magic 3. Shipwrecks 4. Racism 5. Islands 6. African Americans 7. African American families 8. Virgin Islands 9. Saint Thomas, Virgin Islands 10. Magical realism 11. Family sagas 12. Historical fiction 13. Literary fiction

LC 2013044381

Chronicles the families of three siblings who survived a shipwreck off the Virgin Islands in 1916 and raised three generations on the islands, adapting to the unique language, rhythm and magic of island life over 60 years.

"This is a beautifully conceived and written tale of frustrated and forbidden love, beauty, aging, and family secrets." Booklist.

Yap, Felicia

Yesterday / Felicia Yap. Mulholland Books, 2017. 352 p.

ISBN 9780316465250

1. Social classes 2. Memory 3. Self-deception 4. Revenge 5. Married people 6. Detectives 7. Authors 8. Extramarital affairs 9. Women murder victims 10. Murder suspects 11. Murder investigation 12. Diary writing 13. Secrets 14. England 15. Psychological suspense 16. Science fiction

LC 2016056953

A tale set in a stratified world where classes are divided by their members' ability to recall one or two days of memory follows a rare mixed marriage that is shattered by the secrets and murder of the husband's mistress, a situation that is further complicated by the perpetually erased memories of both investigator and suspect.

"For readers seeking a new spin on the unreliable narrator or fans of stories of self-deception." Library Journal.

Yarbrough, Steve, 1956-

* **Safe** from the neighbors / Steve Yarbrough. Alfred A. Knopf, 2010. 272 p.

ISBN 9780307271709

1. History teachers 2. African Americans -- Civil rights 3. Family secrets 4. Race relations 5. Cold cases (Criminal investigation) 6. Murder investigation 7. Husband and wife 8. Mississippi 9. Delta Region, Mississippi 10. Psychological fiction

LC 2009022311

A high school history teacher looks into his own past and begins to discover secrets from his childhood in Mississippi during the 1960s, secrets that he didn't know existed and connect him to the violence of the Civil Rights movement.

"There are moments in Safe from the Neighbor--squiet observations about a gesture or a scene frozen in Luke's memory--that will stick with the reader long after the book is finished. The murder mystery and the tension created by Luke's adultery will draw readers in to this novel. But it is Yarbrough's beautifully crafted sentences that will keep them riveted to the end." BookPage.

Yates, Christopher J.
Black chalk / Christopher J. Yates. Picador, 2015, c2014 346 p.

ISBN 9781250075550

1. College students 2. Humiliation 3. Games 4. Friendship 5. Secret societies 6. Oxford, England 7. Psychological suspense
Originally published: London : Trafalgar Square, 2014.

One game. Six students. Five survivors. It was only ever meant to be a game. A game of consequences, of silly forfeits, childish dares. A game to be played by six best friends in their first year at Oxford University. But then the game changed: the stakes grew higher and the dares more personal, more humiliating, finally evolving into a vicious struggle with unpredictable and tragic results. Now, fourteen years later, the remaining players must meet again for the final round.

Yates, Christopher J.
Grist Mill Road : a novel / Christopher J. Yates. Picador, 2018, c2017. 342 p.

ISBN 9781250150288

1. 1980s 2. 2000s (Decade) 3. Violence against teenage girls 4. Crime 5. Witnesses 6. Life change events 7. Married people 8. Violence -- Psychological aspects 9. Consequences 10. Memories 11. Interpersonal relations 12. New York City 13. New York (State) 14. Psychological suspense 15. Literary fiction

LC 2017028306

Years after three friends from an idyllic hamlet 90 miles north of New York City are bound and then separated by a devastating, seemingly senseless crime, the trio revisits their painful pasts in even more traumatizing ways.

"Mesmerizing and impossible to put down, this novel demands full attention, full empathy, and full responsibility; in return it offers poignant insight into human fragility and resilience." Kirkus.

Yates, Richard, 1926-1992
* The **collected** stories of Richard Yates / Richard Yates ; introduction by Richard Russo. Henry Holt and Co., 2001. xx, 472 p.

ISBN 0805066934

1. United States -- Social life and customs 2. Short stories

LC 00061400

Collects the stories of Richard Yates, featuring nine new stories as well as works from the anthologies "Eleven Kinds of Loneliness" and "Liars in Love."

"Bitterness, loneliness and lack of fulfillment are the central themes of this grim posthumous collection." Publishers Weekly.

The **year's** best science fiction : thirty-fifth annual collection / Gardner R. Dozois. St. Martin's Griffin, 2018. 720 p.
Year's best science fiction (Gardner Dozois)
ISBN 9781250164636

1. Science fiction 2. Short stories

Yellin, Jessica
Savage news / Jessica Yellin. Mira Books, 2019. 384 p.
ISBN 9780778308423

1. White House, Washington, D.C. 2. Women journalists 3. Competition 4. Television industry and trade 5. Sexism 6. Politicians 7. Misogyny 8. Presidents -- United States 9. Washington, D.C. 10. Satirical fiction

A first novel by the award-winning former CNN chief White House correspondent follows the career of a woman cable news journalist who navigates ratings wars, sexual harassment and impossible standards throughout a precarious diplomatic and political incident.

Yi, Chong-myong
The **investigation** / J.M. Lee ; translated by Chi-Young Kim. Pegasus, 2015, c2014. 336 p.
ISBN 9781605988467

1. Dong-ju, Yun 2. Second World War era (1939-1945) 3. 1940s 4. Prisons 5. Poets 6. Censorship 7. Colonialism 8. Prison guards 9. Conspiracies 10. Prisoners 11. Murder 12. Murder investigation 13. Koreans in Japan 14. Japan -- History -- 20th century 15. Historical mysteries 16. Literary fiction 17. Translations -- Korean to English
This translation originally published: London : Mantle, 2014.
Originally published as: Byureul seuchineun baram. EunTlaeng NaMu Publishing Co., 2012.

Ordered to investigate the murder of an unpopular fellow guard in a 1944 Korean prison, Watanbe Yuichi is unconvinced by a powerful inmate's confession and examines clues to piece together the victim's poetic nature and final months.

"Based on the true story of one of Korea's most revered poets, Lee'sU.S. debut is a breathtakingly beautiful novel that boasts a cerebral murder mystery and a rare look at the human impact of Japan's colonialism in Korea. David Guterson's Snow Falling on Cedars (1994) makes an excellent pairing, providing a contrasting but also beautifully portrayed exploration of the impact of Japan's role in WWII." Booklist.

Yocum, Robin
A **welcome** murder / Robin Yocum. Seventh Street Books, 2017. 280 p.
ISBN 9781633882638

1. Murder investigation 2. Small towns 3. Drug dealers 4. Murder suspects 5. Former convicts 6. Former baseball players 7. Police 8. FBI agents 9. Ohio 10. Mysteries

LC 2016051813

Meet Johnny Earl, a washed-up former professional baseball player and ex-con who is the best athlete Steubenville, Ohio has ever produced. He'd like to find the drug money he's hidden there and get out of town, but a Neo Nazi also wants the money... and the high-school friend and FBI informant who sent Johnny up the river has been murdered. Johnny's a suspect, of course, but he's not the only one. Turns out plenty of people are happy Rayce Daubner is dead, including Johnny Earl's high-school girlfriend, her current husband, the local sheriff, and his unhappy wife. Told from the first-person point of view of several people, this lively, violent, funny novel provides an intimate look at an eccentric cast of memorable characters. -- Description by Dawn Towery

"Yocum (A Brilliant Death) has produced a rollicking tale sure to appeal to Donald Westlake and Elmore Leonard fans." Publishers Weekly.

Yoon, Paul
* The **mountain** : stories / Paul Yoon. Simon & Schuster, 2017. 224 p.
ISBN 9781501154089

1. Loneliness 2. Belonging 3. Purpose in life 4. Immigrants 5. Short

stories 6. Literary fiction

LC 2016054159

A collection of six thematically linked stories set in locales ranging from the Hudson Valley to the Russian Far East in the tumultuous years following World War II.

Yoon, Paul

* **Run** me to earth / Paul Yoon. Simon & Schuster, 2020. 272 p.

ISBN 9781501154041

1. 1960s 2. 2010s 3. Orphans 4. Children and war 5. Physicians 6. Friendship 7. War -- Psychological aspects 8. Couriers 9. Refugees 10. Voyages and travels 11. Life change events 12. Laos 13. Historical fiction 14. Literary fiction

Three children orphaned in 1960s Laos meet a dedicated doctor who enlists them as motorcycle couriers in his effort to rescue civilians and find medical supplies in a novel from the award-winning author of Snow Hunters.

"Yoon again exemplifies his unparalleled ability to create a quietly spectacular narrative that reveals the unfathomable worst and unwavering best of humanity; the result here provides mesmerizing gratification." Booklist.

Yoshimoto, Banana, 1964-

Goodbye Tsugumi / Banana Yoshimoto ; translated from the Japanese by Michael Emmerich. Grove Press, 2002. 186 p.

ISBN 0802116388

1. Teenagers 2. Fathers and daughters 3. Cousins 4. Family relationships 5. Summer 6. Female friendship 7. Women college students 8. Coastal towns 9. Japan 10. Translations -- Japanese to English 11. Coming-of-age stories 12. Psychological fiction

Having grown up by the sea with her invalid cousin Tsugumi, Maria moves to Tokyo and encounters university life and impending adulthood, and spending a last summer with her cousin, she comes to a new understanding about home and family.

"Maria Shirakawa is a thoughtful young woman thrown by family circumstance (her parents never married; with her mother, she is waiting for her father's divorce from his current wife) into growing up with her cousin, Tsugumi Yamamoto, in her aunt and uncle's small inn. Tsugumi, who is chronically ill, possesses a mischievous charm that both maddens and amuses her family. . . . Tsugumi's tenuous health seems to free her from the behavioral norms that govern Maria and Tsugumi's long-suffering older sister, Yoko, allowing her to curse, flirt with boys, concoct elaborate pranks and shock adults in a way Maria resents, envies and admires." Publishers Weekly.

Yoshimoto, Banana, 1964-

The **lake** / Banana Yoshimoto ; translated from the Japanese by Michael Emmerich. Melville House, 2011, c2010. 128 p.

ISBN 9781933633770

1. Friendship 2. Growing up 3. Men/women relations 4. Mothers -- Death 5. Artists 6. Solitude 7. Identity (Psychology) 8. College students 9. Shame in women 10. Cults 11. Brainwashing 12. Childhood 13. Tokyo, Japan 14. Japan 15. Translations -- Japanese to English 16. Psychological fiction 17. Literary fiction

LC 2011006711

Originally published: Mizuumi (2010).

"Chihiro, an artist, and Nakajima, a graduate student in genetics, finally meet after watching and waving to each other from their respective apartment windows across a Tokyo street. They're both unconventional and seemingly untethered souls; they've both lost their beloved mothers. They meander into a sweet, simple life together, although past secrets involving a mysterious brother and sister who live by an ethereal lake

threaten to create an emotional divide. . . . Yoshimoto aficionados . . . will recognize her signature crisp, clipped style (thanks to exacting translator Emmerich's constancy) and revel in her latest cast of quirky characters." Library Journal.

Yoshimoto, Banana, 1964-

Moshi-moshi / Banana Yoshimoto ; translated from the Japanese by Asa Yoneda. Counterpoint Press, 2016, c2010. 206 p.

ISBN 9781619027862

1. Survivors of suicide victims 2. Loss (Psychology) 3. Fathers -- Death 4. Grief 5. Spirits 6. Coping 7. Families 8. Nightmares 9. Suicide pacts 10. Family and death 11. Fathers and daughters 12. Tokyo, Japan 13. Coming-of-age stories 14. Mainstream fiction 15. Translations -- Japanese to English

Originally published as Moshi moshi Shimokitazawa, 2010.

"In Moshi-Moshi, Yoshie's much-loved musician father has died in a suicide pact with an unknown woman. It is only when Yoshie and her mother move to Shimo-kitazawa, a traditional Tokyo neighborhood of narrow streets, quirky shops, and friendly residents that they can finally start to put their painful past behind them. However, despite their attempts to move forward, Yoshie is haunted by nightmares in which her father is looking for the phone he left behind on the day he died, or on which she is trying-unsuccessfully-to call him. Is her dead father trying to communicate a message to her through these dreams? With the lightness of touch and surreal detachment that are the hallmarks of her writing, Banana Yoshimoto turns a potential tragedy into a poignant coming-of-age ghost story and a life-affirming homage to the healing powers of community, food, and family. Published in 2010 in Japanese in Tokyo, it has sold over 29,000 copies there so far."--, Provided by publisher.

"Prolific novelist Yoshimoto (The Lake, 2011, etc.) offers another story of youth, grief, and redemption in this ephemeral yet lovely portrait of an unformed woman." Kirkus.

Young, William P.

* The **shack** : a novel / William P. Young. Windblown Media, 2007. 266 p.

ISBN 9780964729247

1. God (Christianity) 2. Missing children 3. Loss (Psychology) 4. Suffering -- Religious aspects -- Christianity 5. Family relationships 6. Life change events 7. Theodicy 8. Belief and doubt 9. Murder -- Religious aspects 10. Oregon 11. Christian fiction 12. Pacific Northwest fiction

LC 2008274723

Four years after his daughter is abducted and evidence of her murder is found in an abandoned shack, Mackenzie Allen Philips returns to the shack in response to a note claiming to be from God, and has a life-changing experience.

Youngson, Anne

Meet me at the museum / Anne Youngson. Flatiron Books, 2018 224 p.

ISBN 9781250295163

1. Heaney, Seamus, 1939-2013 2. Friendship 3. Museum curators 4. Farmers' spouses 5. Seniors 6. Widowers 7. Bog bodies 8. Letter writing 9. Men/women relations 10. Poetry -- Appreciation 11. Interpersonal relations 12. Interpersonal attraction 13. Denmark 14. England 15. Literary fiction 16. Epistolary novels

RUSA Reading List Short List, 2019.

A disenchanted farmer's wife and a widowed museum curator begin a correspondence over their mutual fascination with poet Seamus Heaney's "The Tollund Man" and gradually share details from their lives, forging an unexpected bond along the way.

Yourcenar, Marguerite

* **Memoirs** of Hadrian : and reflections on the composition of memoirs of Hadrian / Marguerite Yourcenar ; translated from the French by Grace Frick in collaboration with the author Modern Library, 1984, c1951. 393 p.

ISBN 0394605055

1. Hadrian,, Emperor of Rome, 76-138 2. Roman Empire (27 BCE-476 CE) 3. Rulers 4. Personal conduct 5. Letter writing 6. Roman emperors 7. Humanists 8. Spiritual life 9. Purpose in life 10. Meaning (Psychology) 11. Men/men relations 12. Men/women relations 13. Rome -- History -- Hadrian, 117-138 14. Modern classics 15. Psychological fiction 16. Biographical fiction 17. Historical fiction 18. Translations -- French to English

LC 83022065 //r93

Illustrated with black-and-white unpaged photos.

Originally published in French: Paris : Plon, 1951.

In a letter to his adopted grandson (later Marcus Aurelius), Hadrian tells about his life.

Yu, Charles, 1976-

* **How** to live safely in a science fictional universe : a novel / Charles Yu. Pantheon Books, 2010. 240 p.

ISBN 9780307379207

1. Time travel 2. Missing persons 3. Fathers and sons 4. Time machines 5. Science fiction 6. Humorous stories

LC 2010001837

In a world transformed by time-travel technology, counselor Charles Yu searches for the father who invented time travel and vanished, a quest marked by quirky pseudo-companions.

"Yu is fond of meta-narrative, and packs the novel with adventures that take place entirely in theoretical universes, nostalgia-altered pasts, fictional worlds, and inside the protagonist's own time-looped mind." io9.

Yu, Charles, 1976-

* **Interior** Chinatown / Charles Yu. Pantheon Books, 2020. 240 p.

ISBN 9780307907196

1. Actors and actresses 2. Asian-Americans 3. Stereotypes (Social psychology) 4. Families 5. Kung fu 6. Immigrants 7. Racism 8. Literary fiction 9. Family sagas

A stereotyped character actor stumbles into the spotlight before uncovering surprising links between his family and the secret history of Chinatown.

"An acid indictment of Asian stereotypes and a parable for outcasts feeling invisible in this fast-moving world." Kirkus.

Yu, Hua, 1960-

Brothers / Yu Hua ; translated from the Chinese by Eileen Chow and Carlos Rojas. Pantheon Books, 2009. 656 p.

ISBN 9780375424991

1. Chinese Cultural Revolution (1966-1976) 2. 20th century 3. Stepbrothers 4. Difference (Psychology) 5. Revolutions -- China 6. Love triangles 7. Interpersonal attraction 8. Teenagers 9. Men/women relations 10. Coping 11. Self-discovery in men 12. Change (Psychology) 13. China -- History -- Cultural Revolution, 1966-1976 14. China -- Social life and customs -- 20th century 15. Translations -- Chinese to English 16. Domestic fiction

LC 2008021617

Set against the backdrop of a modern-day China caught in the midst of a growing capitalism, Baldy Li, a teenage ne'er-do-well, and Song Gang, his bookish stepbrother, vow to preserve their close relationship despite their personal differences.

"This novel, a family history documenting four decades of profound social and cultural transformation in China, begins on a toilet. In a sleepy rural outpost known as Liu Town, fourteen-year-old Baldy Li is caught peeping at women's bottoms in a latrine. He becomes known as a compulsive public masturbator, and his obsession continues into adulthood: he ends up hosting a beauty pageant for virgins (all of whom rely on doctored hymens to gain entrance). The book has sold more than a million copies in China, despite its irreverent take on everything from the Cultural Revolution to the capitalist boom." The New Yorker.

Z

Zahn, Timothy

Dark force rising / Timothy Zahn. Bantam Books, 1992. 376 p. Star Wars novels. Thrawn trilogy

ISBN 9780553085747

1. Space warfare 2. Resistance to government 3. Soldiers 4. Deception 5. Good and evil 6. Imaginary wars and battles 7. Star Wars fiction 8. Science fiction 9. Space opera 10. Franchise books

LC 92000743

With Luke trapped by the Dark Jedi, Han pursuing a missing battle fleet, and Princess Leia occupied with influencing an alien race heretofore loyal to Thrawn, the fate of the Republic is threatened.

Zahn, Timothy

Heir to the empire / Timothy Zahn. Ballantine, 2011, c1991. 400 p. Star Wars novels. Thrawn trilogy

ISBN 9780345528292

1. Space warfare 2. Resistance to government 3. Soldiers 4. Deception 5. Good and evil 6. Imaginary empires 7. Imaginary wars and battles 8. Star Wars fiction 9. Movie tie-ins 10. Franchise books 11. Science fiction 12. Space opera

Five years after they defeated Darth Vader and the Emperor, Princess Leia and Han Solo are married and expecting children, and Luke is a Jedi knight, unaware that the last of the Emperor's warlords plan to reclaim the empire.

Zahn, Timothy

The **last** command / Timothy Zahn. Bantam Books, 1993. 407 p. Star Wars novels. Thrawn trilogy

ISBN 0553564927

1. Space warfare 2. Resistance to government 3. Soldiers 4. Deception 5. Good and evil 6. Imaginary wars and battles 7. Star Wars fiction 8. Science fiction 9. Space opera 10. Franchise books

LC 92-43876

While Han and Chewbacca struggle to form a coalition of smugglers for the last-ditch attack against the Empire, Leia prepares for the birth of her Jedi twins and Luke Skywalker enters Thrawn's stronghold.

Zailckas, Koren

Mother, mother : a novel / Koren Zailckas. Crown Publishers, 2013. 352 p.

ISBN 9780385347235

1. Family relationships 2. Dysfunctional families 3. Narcissism 4. Manipulation by women 5. Self-control 6. Addiction 7. Matriarchs 8. Sisters 9. Runaways 10. Loss (Psychology) 11. Mothers and daughters 12. New York City 13. Psychological suspense

LC 2013010450

First published: New York : Crown Publishing Group, 2013.

With two beautiful daughters, a brilliantly intelligent son, a tech-guru of a husband and a historical landmark home, her life is picture perfect. She has everything she wants; all she has to do is keep it that way. But living in this matriarch's determinedly cheerful, yet subtly controlling domain hasn't been easy for her family, and when her oldest daughter, Rose, runs off with a mysterious boyfriend, Josephine tightens her grip, gradually turning her flawless home into a darker sort of prison.

Zaman, Nadeem

Up in the main house & other stories / Nadeem Zaman. Unnamed Press, 2019. 176 p.

ISBN 9781944700980

1. Social classes 2. Class conflict 3. City dwellers 4. Working class 5. City life 6. Interpersonal relations 7. Dhaka, Bangladesh 8. Bangladesh 9. Short stories 10. Literary fiction

LC 2019030045

Set in modern Dhaka, a brand-new collection of eight stories explores the inner lives of the cooks and butlers, nightwatchmen and peons who have spent decades working for the same family.

Zamyatin, Yevgeny Ivanovich, 1884-1937

* We / Yevgeny Zamyatin ; translated and with an introduction by Clarence Brown. Penguin Books, 1993, c1924. xxxii, 221 p.

ISBN 0140185852

1. Mathematicians 2. Men -- Identity 3. Men 4. Dystopias 5. Totalitarianism 6. Isolationism 7. Men/women relations 8. Sexuality 9. Seduction 10. Political corruption 11. Dictatorship 12. Space vehicles 13. Censorship 14. Creativity 15. Freedom 16. Technology and civilization 17. Conformity 18. Rules 19. Diary novels 20. Translations -- Russian to English 21. Modern classics 22. Dystopian fiction 23. Social science fiction 24. Science fiction

LC 92044187

Originally published: New York : Dutton, 1924.

The narrator describes a state in which the individuals have given up their freedom for materialistic rewards, in this utopian satire

Zan, Koethi

The **never** list / Koethi Zan. Pamela Dorman Books/Viking, 2013. 320 p.

ISBN 9780670026517

1. Friendship 2. Captivity 3. Sadism 4. Captives 5. Female friendship 6. Fear in women 7. Murder 8. Post-traumatic stress disorder 9. Brainwashing 10. Thrillers and suspense

LC 2013007348

Having lived lives of careful prudence, best friends Sarah and Jennifer are abducted from a cab and held captive for three years in a dungeon-like cellar by a sadistic man, a trauma Sarah endeavors to understand a decade later as she pursues healing and unravels a horrifying mystery. --Provided by publisher.

Zander, Joakim

The **swimmer** / Joakim Zander. Harper, 2015, c2013. 417 p. Klara Walldeen novels

ISBN 9780062337245

1. Former CIA agents 2. Military intelligence 3. International intrigue 4. Conspiracies 5. Fathers and daughters 6. Family secrets 7. Thrillers and suspense 8. Spy fiction 9. Translations -- Swedish to English

First published in Sweden in 2013 as: Simmaren.

A former spy whose career forced him to give up his infant daughter must come to her rescue years later when she is targeted by powerful international adversaries who would kill her for discovering volatile intelligence.

"Skillfully moving between the past and the present, from Sweden to Syria to Washington and back again, Zander weaves an increasingly tight web of intrigue and suspense with Klara at the center. And if the novel occasionally veers toward spy-movie cliches, it's quickly reanchored by the strength of its characters. Beyond the blood-pumping chase sequences and requisite shootouts, there is real humanity here. A compulsively readable page-turner with unexpected heart." Kirkus.

Zane, 1967-

Addicted / Zane. Strebor Books International, 2001, c1998. xiii, 250 p. Addicted novels (Zane)

ISBN 0967460174

1. African Americans 2. African American women 3. Art dealers 4. Adult child sexual abuse victims 5. African American men 6. African American men/women relations 7. Husband and wife 8. Married women 9. Extramarital affairs 10. Sex addicts 11. Sexuality 12. Dishonesty 13. Secrets 14. Stalkers 15. Murder 16. Sex counselors and therapists 17. Stalking 18. Urban erotica 19. African American fiction

LC 2001086308

Originally published: New York :

Zoe Reynard's perfect life--marriage to her childhood sweetheart, a thriving business, and three wonderful children--begins to unravel as she begins to lose control, fails to get her husband to open up to her sexually, and embarks on three extramarital affairs.

Zapata, Mike

The **lost** book of Adana Moreau / Michael Zapata. Hanover Square Press, 2020. 336 p.

ISBN 9781335010124

1. Women authors 2. Manuscripts 3. Voyages and travels 4. Immigrants 5. Lawyers 6. Last words 7. Dominicans (Dominican Republic) 8. Hurricane Katrina, 2005 9. Hurricanes 10. Lost books 11. New Orleans, Louisiana 12. Literary fiction

Decades after a 1929 Dominican immigrant writer passes away believing her final manuscript was destroyed, a Chicago lawyer discovers the book and endeavors to learn the woman's remarkable story against a backdrop of Hurricane Katrina.

"In a lyrical tale spanning a century and veering from the colonized Caribbean to revolutionary Russia, from mid-twentieth-century Chicago to Katrina-besieged New Orleans, Zapata spins an iridescent web of grief, loss, and memory." Booklist.

Zelazny, Roger

Donnerjack / Roger Zelazny and Jane Lindskold. Avon Books, 1997. 503 p.

ISBN 038097326X

1. 22nd century 2. Virtual reality 3. Parallel universes 4. Artificial intelligence 5. Gods and goddesses 6. Interdimensional travel 7. Death 8. World Wide Web 9. Science fantasy 10. Cyberpunk 11. Science fiction

LC 9648705

One century after the World Net crashes and creates Virtu, a virtual world with its own beliefs and laws, the restless gods of Virtu plot to cross over to the real world and take over.

"The late Zelazny's last novel, completed by Lindskold, is one of his largest and most ambitious. . . . All the mythic resonances we have come to expect from Zelazny are here in abundance." Booklist.

Zelazny, Roger
  * **Lord** of light / Roger Zelazny. EOS, 2004, c1967. 296 p.
  ISBN 9780060567231
  1. Clones and cloning 2. Gods and goddesses, Hindu 3. Immortality 4. Reincarnation 5. Technology 6. Interpersonal conflict 7. Space flight 8. Space vehicles 9. Buddhism 10. Demons 11. Religion 12. Mythological fiction 13. Science fantasy 14. Science fiction 15. Asian-influenced fantasy
  Originally published: Garden City, N.Y.: Doubleday, 1967.
  Hugo Award for Best Novel, 1968.
  In a post-Apocalyptic world where a few technology-endowed immortal humans rule the Earth as the pantheon of Hindu gods, one among them, Siddhartha, dares to oppose their tyranny.

Zevin, Gabrielle
  The **hole** we're in / Gabrielle Zevin. Black Cat, 2010. 283 p.
  ISBN 9780802119230
  1. Seventh-Day Adventists 2. Financial crises 3. Debt 4. Family relationships 5. Compulsive shopping 6. Extramarital affairs 7. Consequences 8. Personal conduct 9. Christianity 10. Fundamentalists 11. Domestic fiction
  Roger and George Pomeroy's struggles with financial troubles lead to a series of poor choices that affect their three children, especially Patsy, the youngest, who will spend her life fighting to overcome the decisions' consequences.
  "All five Pomeroys--flawed, devoted, cranky, impetuous, utterly relatable--come blazingly alive on the page." Entertainment Weekly.

Zevin, Gabrielle
  The **storied** life of A. J. Fikry : a novel / Gabrielle Zevin. Algonquin Books of Chapel Hill, 2014. 320 p.
  ISBN 9781616203214
  1. Booksellers 2. Bookstores 3. Abandoned children 4. Healing 5. Book thefts 6. Attitude change 7. Men with depression 8. Widowers 9. Life change events 10. Men/women relations 11. New England 12. Mainstream fiction
  LC 2013043144
  Published in Great Britain in 2014 by Little, Brown as The collected works of A.J. Fikry.
  When his most prized possession, a rare collection of Poe poems, is stolen, bookstore owner A. J. Fikry begins isolating himself from his friends, family and associates before receiving a mysterious package that compels him to remake his life.
  "Filled with interesting characters, a deep knowledge of bookselling, wonderful critiques of classic titles, and very funny depictions of book clubs and author events, this will prove irresistible to book lovers everywhere." Booklist.

Zevin, Gabrielle,
  Young Jane Young : a novel / Gabrielle Zevin. Algonquin Books of Chapel Hill, 2017. 272 p.
  ISBN 9781616205041
  1. Interns 2. Shame 3. Identity (Psychology) 4. Life change events 5. Young women 6. Self-fulfillment in women 7. Mistresses 8. Mothers and daughters 9. Women -- Social conditions 10. Family relationships 11. Florida 12. Maine 13. Women's lives and relationships 14. Mainstream fiction
  LC 2017002944
  Cruelly branded for her affair with her congressman boss, an intern and blogger changes her name and moves to a remote town in Maine with her young daughter before local prompting to run for public office forces her to reckon with the past.

"This book will not only thoroughly entertain everyone who reads it; it is the most immaculate takedown of slut-shaming in literature or anywhere else. Cheers, and gratitude, to the author." Kirkus.

Zhang, Jenny
  Sour heart : stories / Jenny Zhang. Lenny, 2017 240 p.
  ISBN 9780399589386
  1. 1990s 2. Children of immigrants 3. Cultural differences 4. Teenage girls -- Sexuality 5. Communities 6. Immigrant families 7. Poverty 8. New York City 9. Short stories 10. Literary fiction
  LC 2016058411
  "A debut collection of stories that plunge readers into the tender and chaotic hearts of adolescent girls growing up in New York City, from celebrated poet and National Magazine Award nominee Jenny Zhang"-- Provided by publisher.
  "Taken as a whole, these linked stories illuminate the complexities and contradictions of first-generation life in America. Zhang has a gift for sharp, impactful endings, and a poets ear for memorable detail." Publishers Weekly.

Zhou, Haohui, 1977-
  Death notice : a novel / Zhou Haohui ; translated from the Chinese by Zac Haluza. Doubleday, 2018. 301 p.
  ISBN 9780385543323
  1. Police 2. Revenge 3. Vigilantes 4. Justice 5. Murderers 6. Punishment 7. Death threats 8. Murder investigation 9. Executions and executioners 10. Cold cases (Criminal investigation) 11. China 12. Chengdu (China) 13. Thrillers and suspense 14. Translations -- Chinese to English
  LC 2017048812
  Originally published in Chinese as "Si wang tong zhi dan: an hei zhe" in 2014.
  An elite police squad hunts a manipulative mastermind out to publically execute criminals the law cannot reach.

Zimler, Richard
  The **last** Kabbalist of Lisbon / Richard Zimler. Overlook Press, 1998 318 p.
  ISBN 9780879518349
  1. Jews, Portuguese 2. Secrets 3. Murder 4. Uncles 5. Inquisition 6. Converts to Christianity from Judaism 7. Judaism 8. Philosophers 9. Jewish way of life 10. Mysticism 11. Portugal -- History -- 16th century 12. Lisbon, Portugal -- History -- 16th century 13. Historical mysteries
  Sequel: Guardian of the dawn.
  Berekiah Zarco, a young manuscript illustrator, searches for the killer of his uncle Abraham, a renowned kabbalist discovered murdered in a secret synagogue.
  "This novel first published in Portuguese, vividly re-creates the world of ancient Lisbon, presenting Berekiah's mysticism in graceful, albeit occasionally florid, prose. Zimler's portrait of the city (and the New Christians' uneasy place within it) enriches his many-layered narrative, in which a suitably complex cast of characters plays a dangerous game with fate." New York Times Book Review.

Zimler, Richard
  The **seventh** gate / Richard Zimler. Overlook Press, 2012, c2007. 400 p.
  ISBN 9781590207130
  1. 1930s 2. Resistance to government 3. Murder investigation 4. Nazis 5. Teenage girls 6. Antisemitism 7. Holocaust (1933-1945) 8. Secret societies 9. Germany -- History -- 1933-1945 10. Coming-of-age stories 11. Historical mysteries 12. Mysteries

Originally published: London : Constable, 2007.

Coming of age in 1932 Berlin during Hitler's rise, precocious and promiscuous Sophie dreams of becoming an actress and is forced to hide her Jewish friendships when her father and boyfriend become Nazi collaborators, a situation that turns dangerous when a friend is sent to the Dachau concentration camp.

Zimmer, Michael, 1955-

The **long** hitch : a western story / Michael Zimmer. Five Star, 2011. 364 p.

ISBN 9781432825249

1. Stagecoach drivers 2. Murder investigation -- Utah 3. Friends' death 4. Murder -- Utah 5. Freight and freightage 6. Utah -- History -- 19th century 7. Westerns

Buck leads a wagon train heading to Montana for a contract with a mining company after the last leader, his mentor Mase, is murdered, but he faces obstacles that include a competitor vying for the same contract, a mole within his crew, and Mase's killer.

"Zimmer has put together a believable, gritty, and action-packed tale of the real Old West." Publishers Weekly.

Zimmer, Michael, 1955-

Wild side of the river : a western story / Michael Zimmer. Five Star, 2011. 216 p.

ISBN 9781594149467

1. Ranchers 2. Murder 3. Revenge 4. Murder investigation 5. Fathers -- Death 6. Westerns

LC 2010043349

"A man's single-minded quest for vengeance is a traditional western theme, but this one doesn't feel like a traditional western. It's darker, harder around the edges, a noir crime drama wearing western clothing." Booklist.

Zimmerman, David

The **sandbox** / David Zimmerman. Soho Press, 2010. 368 p.

ISBN 9781569476284

1. Iraq War, 2003-2011 2. Soldiers 3. Americans in Iraq 4. Military life 5. Iraq 6. War stories

LC 2009043994

In Iraq, a roadside ambush puts a young American soldier on the trail of a high-reaching conspiracy.

"Set at a remote military base in the Iraqi desert, this debut novel unsparingly portrays the experience of fighting in the Iraq War. ... [A] seemingly minor infraction draws [an American soldier] into a complex conspiracy that involves the base's senior officers, an Iraqi translator, and many of his fellow soldiers." Library Journal.

Zimmerman, Jean

The **orphanmaster** / Jean Zimmerman. Viking, 2012. 448 p.

ISBN 9780670023646

1. Colonial America (1600-1775) 2. 1660s 3. 17th century 4. Dutch American women 5. Missing children 6. Orphans 7. Superstition 8.

Spies -- Great Britain 9. Serial murder investigation 10. Criminal investigation 11. New York City -- History -- Colonial period, 1600-1775 12. New Amsterdam -- History 13. Historical mysteries 14. Mysteries

LC 2011038593

In 17th-century New Amsterdam, today Manhattan, 22-year-old trader Blandine von Couvering and British spy Edward Drummond investigate the mysterious disappearance of orphan children.

Zola, Emile, 1840-1902

* **Germinal** / Emile Zola ; translated from the French with an introduction by Havelock Ellis. Dutton, 1946, c1885. viii, 404 p. Rougon-Macquart

ISBN 9780460008976

1. Coal miners 2. Revolutionaries 3. Strikes -- Coal miners 4. Working class 5. Class struggle 6. Human nature 7. Labor disputes 8. Unemployed persons 9. Industrial Revolution 10. Coal mines and mining 11. France -- Social conditions -- 19th century 12. Political fiction 13. Translations -- French to English 14. Classics

LC 37018102

Originally published in French: Paris : G. Charpentier, 1885 ; originally translated by Havelock Ellis, 1894 ; first published in this edition, 1933. Revised and reset 1946.

Etienne Lenier works in the mines and leads an ultimately unsuccessful strike against the low wages and fines.

Zola, Emile, 1840-1902

* **Nana** / Emile Zola ; translated from the French with an introduction by Douglas Parmee. Oxford University Press, 1992, c1880. 430 p.. Rougon-Macquart

ISBN 9780192826749

1. 19th century 2. Prostitutes 3. Brothels 4. Actors and actresses 5. Pornography 6. Women -- Social conditions -- 19th century 7. Upper class -- History 8. Paris, France -- Social life and customs -- 19th century 9. Classics 10. Historical fiction 11. Translations -- French to English

LC 91022416

Nana, daughter of Gervaise and Coupeau, is beautiful enough to attract the attention of a theatrical producer of pornography.

Zumas, Leni, 1972-

Red clocks / Leni Zumas. Little Brown & Co, 2018. 356 p.

ISBN 9780316434812

1. Near-future 2. Misogyny 3. Women's role 4. Small towns 5. Homeopathic physicians 6. Trials 7. Social change 8. Sexism 9. Women 10. Oregon 11. Literary fiction 12. Dystopian fiction

Five women--including a high-school teacher, a biographer, a frustrated mom, a pregnant adopted teen and a forest-dwelling homeopath--struggle with changes in a near-future America where abortion and assisted fertility have been outlawed and where the homeopath is targeted by a modern-day witch hunt.

"Dark humor further enhances the novel, making this a thoroughly affecting and memorable political parable." Publishers Weekly.

NAME INDEX

This index of author names and pseudonyms provides a quick reference for finding authors who have written under multiple names. Included, also, are name listings that may require clarification with regard to accurate alphabetization (e.g. Honore de Balzac is filed under *Balzac, Honore de.*) The names are arranged alphabetically, and are listed according to Library of Congress name authority files. Furthermore, this list provides a two-way reference point for pseudonyms. For example, Mark Twain can be found under both *Twain, Mark, 1835-1910,* and *Clemens, Samuel Langhorne.* Works by authors included in this index may be found in Part 1 of this collection, listed under the name used in the responsibility statement of the work. As only authors listed in the *Fiction Core Collection* are included in this index, it should not be considered an exhaustive listing of current and past pseudonyms.

Abrahams, Peter, 1947-
    See also Quinn, Spencer
Agnon, Shmuel Yosef, 1888-1970
    See Czaczkes, Shmuel Josef
Ahmadou Kourouma
    See Kourouma, Ahmadou
Ahndoril, Alexander
    See also Kepler, Lars
Akunin, Boris, 1956-
    See also Chkhartishvili, Grigory
Alba, Alicia Gaspar de
    See Gaspar de Alba, Alicia, 1958-
Aleas, Richard
    See also Ardai, Charles, 1969-
Alexander, Margaret Walker
    See also Walker, Margaret, 1915-1998
Allen, Conrad, 1940-
    See also Marston, Edward
Anatoli, A., 1929-1979
    See also Kuznetsov, Anatolii Vasil'evich
Anderson, Sherwood, 1876-1941
    See also Fever, Buck
Andrews, Cecily Isabel Fairfield
    See also West, Rebecca, 1892-1983
Andrews, Colin
    See also Wilson, F. Paul
Anthony, Evelyn, 1928-
    See also Stephens, Eve
Ardai, Charles, 1969-
    See also Aleas, Richard
Arends, Marthe
    See also MacAlister, Katie
Aristides
    See also Epstein, Joseph, 1937-
Armitage, G. E.
    See also Edric, Robert, 1956-
Arouet, Francois Marie
    See also Voltaire, 1694-1778
Arslan Veronese, Antonia
    See Arslan, Antonia
Asimov, Isaac, 1920-1992
    See also French, Paul
Aubert, Rosemary, 1946-

    See also Snow, Lucy
Auster, Paul, 1947-
    See also Benjamin, Paul
Awlinson, Richard
    See Denning, Troy
Bachman, Richard
    See also King, Stephen, 1947-
Baldwin, Margaret
    See also Weis, Margaret, 1948-
Bales, Susan Ford Vance, 1957-
    See also Ford, Susan
Balzac, Honore de, 1799-1850
    See also Saint-Aubin, Horace de
Bancroft, Stephanie
    See Bond, Stephanie; Hauck, Stephanie
Bannister, Patricia V., 1923-
    See Veryan, Patricia
Banville, John
    See also Black, Benjamin
Barbash, Thomas
    See Barbash, Tom
Barger, Ralph
    See also Barger, Sonny
Barger, Sonny
    See also Barger, Ralph
Barlett, Alica Gimenez
    See Gimenez Barlett, Alicia,1951-
Barnes, Djuna, 1892-1982
    See also Steptoe, Lydia
Barnes, Julian, 1946-
    See also Kavanagh, Dan
Bart, Andre Schwarz
    See Schwarz-Bart, Andre, 1928-
Bayley, Iris
    See also Murdoch, Iris
Beauman, Sally
    See also James, Vanessa
Beaton, M.C.
    See also Chesney, Marion; Tremaine, Jennie; Chesterton, G. K.
Becerra, Michael Jaime
    See Jaime-Becerra, Michael
Bell, Acton

See also Bronte, Anne, 1820-1849

Bell, Currer
    See also Bronte, Charlotte, 1816-1855

Bell, Ellis
    See also Bronte, Emily, 1818-1848

Ben Jelloun, Tahar, 1944-
    See Jelloun, Tahar ben

Benjamin, Paul
    See also Auster, Paul, 1947-

Beyle, Marie Henri
    See also Brulard, Henry; Stendhal, 1783-1842

Bienes, Nick
    See also Gould, Judith

Birdwell, Cleo
    See also DeLillo, Don

Black, Benjamin
    See also Banville, John

Blair, Eric
    See also Orwell, George, 1903-1950

Bleeck, Oliver, 1926-1995
    See also Thomas, Ross

Block, Lawrence, 1938-
    See also Kavanagh, Paul

Bolton, S. J.
    See also Bolton, Sharon J.

Bolton, Sharon J.
    See Bolton, S. J.

Bond, Stephanie
    See also Bancroft, Stephanie; Hauck, Stephanie

Bostwick, Marie
    See also Skinner, Marie Bostwick

Boucolon, Maryse
    See also Conde, Maryse, 1937-

Bowen-Judd, Sara Hutton
    See also Woods, Sara

Box, Edgar
    See also Vidal, Gore, 1925-

Boyd, Jerry
    See also Toole, F. X., 1930-2002

Boz
    See also Dickens, Charles, 1812-1870; Sparks, Timothy

Bradley, Alan, 1938-
    See Bradley, C. Alan

Bradley, C. Alan
    See Bradley, Alan, 1938-

Bragi Olafsson, 1962-
    See Olafsson, Bragi

Brand, Max, 1892-1944
    See also Evans, Evan; Faust, Frederick

Braybrooke, June, 1920-1994
    See also English, Isobel; Jolliffe, June

Brennan, John
    See also Welcome, John, 1914-

Bronte, Anne, 1820-1849
    See also Bell, Acton

Bronte, Charlotte, 1816-1855
    See also Bell, Currer

Bronte, Charlotte, 1816-1855
    See also Wellesley, Charles

Bronte, Emily, 1818-1848
    See also Bell, Ellis

Brooks-Davies, Douglas
    See Davies, Douglas Brooks-

Brown, Elizabeth Inness
    See Inness-Brown, Elizabeth, 1954-

Brown, James Willie Jr.
    See also Komunyakaa, Yusef

Brown, Sandra, 1948-
    See also Jordan, Laura; Ryan, Rachel

Brulard, Henry
    See also Stendhal, 1783-1842

Buchan, John, 1875-1940
    See also Tweedsmuir, John Buchan

Buck, Pearl S. (Pearl Sydenstricker), 1892-1973
    See also Hedge, John; Walsh, Pearl S.

Bulwer-Lytton, Edward
    See Lytton, Edward Bulwer Lytton, 1803-1873

Buntline, Ned, 1822 or 3-1886
    See also Judson, Edward Zane Carroll

Burgess, Anthony, 1917-1993
    See also Wilson, John Anthony Burgess

Butler, Samuel, 1835-1902
    See also Owen, John Pickard

Butters, Dorothy Gilman
    See also Gilman, Dorothy, 1923-

Byatt, Antonia Susan
    See Byatt, A. S., 1936-

Campbell, R. Wright, 1927-2000
    See Campbell, Robert

Campbell, Robert
    See Campbell, R. Wright, 1927-2000

Cannon, Curt, 1926-2005
    See also Collins, Hunt, 1926-2005; Hannon, Ezra, 1926-2005; Hudson, Dean, 1926-2005; Hunter, Evan, 1926-2005 Marsten, Richard, 1926-2005; McBain, Ed, 1926-2005

Can Xue
    See also Tsan-hsueh, 1953-; Deng Xiaohua

Carlyle, Liz, 1958-
    See also Woodhouse, Susan T.

Carr, Alex
    See also Siler, Jenny

Cary, Arthur Joyce Lunel
    See also Cary, Joyce, 1888-1957

Cary, Joyce, 1888-1957
    See Cary, Arthur Joyce Lunel

Cassirer, Nadine Gordimer
    See Gordimer, Nadine, 1923-

Cauwelaert, Didier van, 1960-
    See Van Cauwelaert, Didier

Cavallo, Evelyn
    See also Spark, Muriel

Celine, Louis-Ferdinand, 1894-1961
    See also Destouches, Henri-Louis

Challans, Mary

See also Awlinson, Richard

Dennis, Patrick, 1921-1976
> *See also* Tanner, Edward Everett

Destouches, Henri-Louis
> *See* Celine, Louis-Ferdinand, 1894-1961

Di Lampedusa, Giuseppe Tomasi
> *See* Tomasi di Lampedusa, Giuseppe, 1896-1957

Diago, Evelio Rosero
> *See* Rosero Diago, Evelio, 1958-

Dick, R. A.
> *See also* Leslie, Josephine Aimee Campbell, 1898-1979

Dickens, Charles, 1812-1870
> *See also* Boz; Sparks, Timothy

Dikty, Julian May
> *See* May, Julian, 1931-

Ditzen, Rudolf
> *See also* Fallada, Hans, 1893-1947

Dominic, R. B.
> *See also* Lathen, Emma

Dos Passos, John
> *See* Passos, John Dos

Dostoevskii, Fedor Mikhailovich
> *See* Dostoyevsky, Fyodor, 1821-1881

Douglas, Michael
> *See also* Crichton, Michael, 1942-2008; Hudson, Jeffery; Lange, John

Douglass, Billie
> *See* Delinsky, Barbara; Drake, Bonnie

Doyle, Conan
> *See* Doyle, Sir Arthur Conan, 1859-1930

Drabble, Margaret, 1939-
> *See also* Swift, Margaret

Drake, Bonnie
> *See* Delinsky, Barbara; Douglass, Billie

Drawcansir, Alexander
> *See also* Fielding, Henry, 1707-1754

Ducornet, Rikki
> *See also* Rikki

Dudevant, Amantine Lucile Aurore Dupin
> *See also* Dudevant, Mme; Dupin, Amantine Aurore Lucile; Sand, George, 1804-1876; Sand, Jules

Dudevant, Mme
> *See also* Dudevant, Amantine Lucile Aurore Dupin; Dupin, Amantine Aurore Lucile; Sand, George, 1804-1876; Sand, Jule

Dukes, Carol Muske, 1945-
> *See* Muske-Dukes, Carol

Dunn, Kathleen
> *See also* Fleming, Irene, 1939-

Dupin, Amantine Aurore Lucile, 1804-1876
> *See also* Dudevant, Amantine Lucile Aurore Dupin; Dudevant, Mme; Sand, George; Sand, Jules

Eagles, Cynthia Harrod
> *See* Harrod-Eagles, Cynthia

Echevarria, Roberto Gonzalez
> *See* Gonzalez Echevarria, Roberto

Edric, Robert, 1956-

See also Armitage, G. E.

Eliot, Alice C.
> *See also* Jewett, Sarah Orne, 1849-1909

Eliot, George, 1819-1880
> *See also* Cross, Mary Ann Evans

Elliot, Jessie
> *See also* Grodstein, Lauren

English, Isobel
> *See also* Braybrooke, June, 1920-1994; Jolliffe, June

Ephron, Hallie
> *See also* Touger, Hallie Ephron

Epstein, Joseph, 1937-
> *See also* Aristides

Escobar, Marisol
> *See also* Marisol, 1930-

Evanovich, Janet
> *See also* Hall, Steffie

Evans, Evan
> *See also* Brand, Max, 1892-1944; Faust, Frederick

Evelyn, John Michael
> *See also* Underwood, Michael, 1916-

Exupery, Antoine de Saint
> *See* Saint-Exupery, Antoine de, 1900-1944

Fair, A. A.
> *See also* Gardner, Erle Stanley, 1889-1970; Kendrake, Carleton; Kenny, Charles J.

Fairbairn, Ann, 1901 or 2-1972
> *See also* Tait, Dorothy

Fallada, Hans, 1893-1947
> *See also* Ditzen, Rudolf

Fallon, Martin
> *See also* Graham, James; Higgins, Jack, 1929-; Marlowe, Hugh; Patterson, Harry

Fast, Howard, 1914-2003
> *See also* Cunningham, E. V.

Faust, Frederick
> *See also* Brand, Max, 1892-1944; Evans, Evan

Feige, Hermann Albert Otto Max
> *See also* Marut, Ret; Torsvan, Berick Traven; Torsvan, Traven; Traven, B.

Fever, Buck
> *See also* Anderson, Sherwood, 1876-1941

Fielding, Henry, 1707-1754
> *See also* Drawcansir, Alexander

Finlay, Peter Warren
> *See also* Pierre, D. B. C.

Finney, Patricia
> *See also* Chisholm, P. F., 1958-

Fitzgerald, Conor
> *See also* Deane, Conor Fitzgerald

Fleming, Irene, 1939-
> *See also* Dunn, Kathleen

Fleming, Oliver
> *See also* Lawless, Anthony; Macdonald, Filip; MacDonald, Philip, 1899-1981; Porlock, Martin

Flying Officer X
> *See also* Bates, H. E., 1905-1974

Foe, Daniel
    See also Defoe, Daniel, 1661?-1731; Morton, Andrew
Ford, Ford Madox, 1873-1939
    See also Hueffer, Ford Madox
Ford, Susan
    See also Bales, Susan Ford Vance, 1957-
Frank, Pat, 1907-1964
    See also Hart, HarryFranklin, Ariana
    See also Norman, Diana
Franklin, Miles, 1879-1954
    See also Franklin, Stella Maria Miles Lampe
Franklin, Stella Maria Miles Lampe
    See also Franklin, Miles, 1879-1954
French, Paul
    See also Asimov, Isaac, 1920-1992
Freundlich, Jeffry P.
    See also Lindsay, Jeffry P., 1952-; Lindsay, Jeff
Fujiwara, Murasaki
    See also Murasaki Shikibu, b. 978?; Shikibu, Murasaki
Fyfield, Frances, 1948-
    See also Hegarty, Frances
Galbraith, Robert
    See also Rowling, J.K.
Gallaher, Rhea
    See also Gould, Judith
Gao Xingjian
    See also Kao, Hsing-chien, 1940-
Gardner, Erle Stanley, 1889-1970
    See also Fair, A. A.; Kendrake, Carleton; Kenny, Charles J.
Gardner, Lisa
    See also Scott, Alicia
Gash, Joe
    See also Granger, Bill; Griffith, Bill
Gash, Jonathan, 1933-
    See also Grant, John
Gill, Bartholomew, 1943-2002
    See also McGarrity, Mark
Gilman, Dorothy, 1923-
    See also Butters, Dorothy Gilman
Goff, Annabel Davis
    See Davis-Goff, Annabel
Goldsher, A. M.
    See Goldsher, Alan, 1966-
Goodjohn, Bunny
    See also Goodjohn, B. A.
GoodWeather, Hartley
    See also King, Thomas, 1943-
Gopaleen, Myles
    See also Knowall, George; Na Gopaleen, Myles; O'Brien, Flann, 1911-1966; O'Nolan, Brian
Gordimer, Nadine, 1923-
    See also Cassirer, Nadine Gordimer
Gores, Joe
    See Gores, Joseph N.
Gorky, Maksim, 1868-1936
    See also Gorky, Maxim; Peshkov, Alexei Maximovich
Gorky, Maxim

    See also Gorky, Maksim, 1868-1936; Peshkov, Alexei Maximovich
Gould, Judith
    See also Bienes, Nick; Gallaher, Rhea
Graham, James
    See also Fallon, Martin; Higgins, Jack, 1929-; Marlowe, Hugh; Patterson, Harry
Graham, Tom
    See Lewis, Sinclair, 1885-1951
Granger, Bill
    See also Gash, Joe; Griffith, Bill
Grant, John
    See also Gash, Jonathan, 1933-
Grant, Linda
    See also Williams, Linda Verlee
Grant, Mira
    See also McGuire, Seanan
Green, Hannah
    See also Greenberg, Joanne, 1932-
Greenberg, Joanne, 1932-
    See also Green, Hannah
Griffith, Bill
    See also Granger, Bill; Gash, Joe
Grodstein, Lauren
    See also Elliot, Jessie
Hall, Oakley M.
    See also Manor, Jason
Hall, Steffie
    See also Evanovich, Janet
Hamilton, Clive
    See also Lewis, C. S., 1898-1963
Hammett, Samuel Dashiell
    See Hammett, Dashiell, 1894-1961
Hannon, Ezra, 1926-2005
    See also Cannon, Curt, 1926-2005; Collins, Hunt, 1926-2005; Hannon, Ezra, 1926-2005; Hudson, Dean, 1926-2005; Hunter, Evan, 1926-2005; Marsten, Richard, 1926-2005; McBain, Ed, 1926-2005
Harding, John Wesley, 1965-
    See also Stace, Wesley Harding
Harris, Mark, 1922-2007
    See also Wiggen, Henry W.
Hart, Harry
    See also Frank, Pat, 1907-1964
Hartog, Jan de
    See De Hartog, Jan, 1914-2002
Harvey, Caroline
    See also Trollope, Joanna
Harvey, Jack
    See also Rankin, Ian, 1960-
Hauck, Stephanie
    See also Bancroft, Stephanie; Bond, Stephanie
Hawk, Alex
    See also Kelton, Elmer, 1926-2009; McElroy, Lee
Hawkins, Anthony Hope
    See Hope, Anthony, 1863-1933
Haynes, Conrad

See also Haynes, Dana

Haynes, Dana
See also Haynes, Conrad

Haywood, Gar Anthony
See also Shannon, Ray

Head, Ann
See also Morse, Anne Christensen

Hedge, John
See also Buck, Pearl S., 1892-1973; Walsh, Pearl S.

Hegarty, Frances
See also Fyfield, Frances, 1948-

Heilbrun, Carolyn G., 1926-2003
See also Cross, Amanda, 1926-2003

Helgason, Hallgrimur
See Hallgrimur Helgason, 1959-

Henry, O., 1862-1910
See also Porter, William Sydney

Hervey, Evelyn
See also Keating, H. R. F., 1926-2011; Keating, Henry Reymond Fitzwalter

Higgins, Jack, 1929-
See also Fallon, Martin; Graham, James; Marlowe, Hugh; Patterson, Harry

Highet, Helen MacInnes
See also MacInnes, Helen, 1907-1985

Highsmith, Patricia, 1921-1995
See also Morgan, Claire

Hill, Joe
See also King, Joseph Hillstrom

Hill, John, 1945-
See also Koontz, Dean R.

Hill, Reginald, 1936-
See also Morland, Dick; Ruell, Patrick; Underhill, Charles

Hiraoka, Kimitake
See also Mishima, Yukio, 1925-1970

Hobb, Robin
See also Lindholm, Megan; Ogden, Margaret Astrid Lindholm

Holton, Leonard
See also O'Connor, Patrick; Wibberley, Leonard, 1915-1983

Hope, Anthony, 1863-1933
See also Hawkins, Anthony Hope

Horowitz, James
See also Salter, James

Hudson, Dean, 1926-2005
See also Cannon, Curt, 1926-2005; Collins, Hunt, 1926-2005; Hannon, Ezra, 1926-2005; Hunter, Evan, 1926-2005; Marsten, Richard, 1926-2005; McBain, Ed, 1926-2005

Hudson, Jeffery
See also Crichton, Michael, 1942-2008; Douglas, Michael; Lange, John

Hueffer, Ford Madox
See Ford, Ford Madox, 1873-1939

Hulme, Juliet
See also Perry, Anne, 1938-

Humphreys, C. C.

See also Humphreys, Chris

Humphreys, Chris
See also Humphreys, C. C.

Hunter, Evan, 1926-2005
See also Cannon, Curt, 1926-2005; Collins, Hunt, 1926-2005; Hannon, Ezra, 1926-2005; Hudson, Dean, 1926-2005; Marsten, Richard, 1926-2005; McBain, Ed, 1926-2005

Ibanez, Vicente Blasco
See Blasco Ibanez, Vicente, 1867-1928

Irving, Clifford
See also Luckless, John

Irving, Washington, 1783-1859
See also Crayon, Geoffrey; Knickerbocker, Diedrich

Isherwood, Christopher, 1904-1986
See also Bradshaw-Isherwood, Christopher William

Jaber, Diana Abu-
See Abu-Jaber, Diana

James, P. D.
See also White, Phyllis Dorothy James

James, Vanessa
See also Beauman, Sally

Jefferies, William, 1950-
See also Deaver, Jeffery

Jelloun, Taharben
See also Ben Jelloun, Tahar, 1944-

Jensen, Mrs. Oliver
See also Stafford, Jean, 1915-1979

Jewett, Sarah Orne, 1849-1909
See Eliot, Alice C.

Jiang Rong, 1946-
See also Lu Jiamin

Jin, Ha
See Ha Jin, 1956-

Jolliffe, June
See also Braybrooke, June, 1920-1994; English, Isobel

Jong, Erica
See also Mann, Erica

Jonge, Peter de
See also De Jonge, Peter

Jordan, Laura
See also Brown, Sandra, 1948-; Ryan, Rachel

Judson, Edward Zane Carroll
See also Buntline, Ned, 1822 or 3-1886

Kao, Hsing-chien
See also Gao Xingjian, 1940-

Katayev, Evgenii Petrovich
See also Petrov, Evgenii, 1903-1942

Kava, Alex
See also Kava, Sharon M.

Kava, Sharon M.
See also Kava, Alex

Kavanagh, Dan
See also Barnes, Julian, 1946-

Kavanagh, Paul
See also Block, Lawrence, 1938-

Keating, H. R. F., 1926-2011

See also Hervey, Evelyn; Keating, Henry Reymond Fitzwalter

Keating, Henry Reymond Fitzwalter
See Keating, H. R. F., 1926-2011; Hervey, Evelyn

Kells, Susannah
See Cornwell, Bernard

Kelman, Nic, 1971-
See also Kelman, Nicholas L.

Kelman, Nicholas L.
See also Kelman, Nic, 1971-

Kelton, Elmer, 1926-2009
See also Hawk, Alex; McElroy, Lee

Kendrake, Carleton
See also Gardner, Erle Stanley, 1889-1970; Fair, A. A.;
Kenny, Charles J.

Kenny, Charles J.
See also Gardner, Erle Stanley, 1889-1970;
Fair, A. A.; Kendrake, Carleton

Kepler, Lars
See also Ahndoril, Alexander

Kerouac, Jack, 1922-1969
See also Kerouac, Jean; Kerouac, Jeanlouis

Kerouac, Jean
See Kerouac, Jack, 1922-1969; Kerouac, Jeanlouis

Kerouac, Jeanlouis
See Kerouac, Jack, 1922-1969; Kerouac, Jean

Khadra, Yasmina
See also Moulessehoul, Mohammed, 1955-

Khoury, Elias
See also Khuri, Ilyas

Khuri, Ilyas
See also Khoury, Elias

King, Joseph Hillstrom
See also Hill, Joe

King, Stephen, 1947-
See also Bachman, Richard

King, Thomas, 1943-
See also GoodWeather, Hartley

Kinsella, Sophie
See also Wickham, Madeleine, 1969-

Knickerbocker, Diedrich
See also Irving, Washington, 1783-1859; Crayon, Geoffrey

Knowall, George
See also Gopaleen, Myles; Na Gopaleen, Myles; O'Brien,
Flann, 1911-1966; O'Nolan, Brian

Komunyakaa, Yusef
See also Brown, James Willie Jr.

Koontz, Dean R., 1945-
See also Hill, John; North, Anthony

Kosinski, Jerzy N., 1933-1991
See also Novak, Joseph

Kourouma, Ahmadou
See also Ahmadou Kourouma

Krentz, Jayne Ann
See also Quick, Amanda

Kuznetsov, Anatolii Vasil'evich
See also Anatoli, A., 1929-1979

Lambrecht, Patricia
See Tracy, P. J.; Lambrecht, Traci

Lambrecht, Traci
See Tracy, P. J.; Lambrecht, Patricia

Lampedusa, Giuseppe Tomasi di
See Tomasi di Lampedusa, Giuseppe, 1896-1957

Lange, John
See also Crichton, Michael, 1942-2008; Douglas, Michael;
Hudson, Jeffrey

Larminie, Margaret Beda
See also Nicholson, Margaret Beda; Yorke, Margaret

Lathen, Emma
See also Dominic, R. B.

Lawhead, Stephen R.
See Lawhead, Steve, 1950-

Lawless, Anthony
See also Fleming, Oliver; Macdonald, Filip; MacDonald,
Philip, 1899-1981; Porlock, Martin

Lax, Andromeda Romano-
See Romano-Lax, Andromeda, 1971-

Le Carre, John, 1931-
See also Cornwell, David John Moore

Lear, Peter
See also Lovesey, Peter

Lee, Lilian
See also Li, Pi-hua

Lennon, J. Robert, 1970-
See also Lennon, John Robert

Lennon, John Robert
See also Lennon, J. Robert, 1970-

Leslie, Josephine Aimee Campbell, 1898-1979
See also Dick, R. A.

Lessing, Doris May, 1919-
See also Somers, Jane

Leventhal, Alice Walker
See also Walker, Alice, 1944-

Lewis, C. S. (Clive Staples), 1898-1963
See also Hamilton, Clive

Lewis, M. G. (Matthew Gregory), 1775-1818
See also Lewis, Monk

Lewis, Monk
See Lewis, M. G., 1775-1818

Lewis, Sinclair, 1885-1951
See also Graham, Tom

Li, Pi-hua
See also Lee, Lilian

Lindsay, Jeffry P., 1952-
See also Freundlich, Jeffry P.; Lindsay, Jeff

Lindsay, Jeff
See also Lindsay, Jeffry P., 1952-; Freundlich, Jeffry P.

Lindholm, Megan
See also Hobb, Robin; Ogden, Margaret Astrid Lindholm

Linmark, R. Zamora
See also Zamora Linmark, R.

Litwos
See also Sienkiewicz, Henryk, 1846-1916

Llosa, Mario Vargas

See Vargas Llosa, Mario, 1936-

Loo, Tessa de
    See also De Loo, Tessa

Lovesey, Peter
    See also Lear, Peter

Lu Jiamin
    See also Jiang Rong, 1946-

Lucas, Victoria
    See also Plath, Sylvia

Luckless, John
    See also Irving, Clifford

Ludlum, Robert, 1927-2001
    See also Ryder, Jonathan; Shepherd, Michael

Lynch, James Mitchell
    See Lynch, Jim, 1961-

Lynch, Jim, 1961-
    See also Lynch, James Mitchell

Lytton, Edward Bulwer Lytton, 1803-1873
    See Bulwer-Lytton, Edward

MacAlister, Katie
    See also Arends, Marthe; Maxwell, Katie

Macdonald, Filip
    See MacDonald, Philip, 1899-1981
    Lawless, Anthony; Porlock, Martin; Fleming, Oliver

Macdonald, John
    See Macdonald, John Ross; Macdonald, Ross, 1915-1983;
    Millar, Kenneth

Macdonald, John Ross
    See Macdonald, John; Macdonald, Ross, 1915-1983; Millar, Kenneth

Macdonald, Malcolm, 1932-
    See also Ross-Macdonald, Malcolm

MacDonald, Philip, 1899-1981
    See also Fleming, Oliver; Lawless, Anthony; Macdonald,
    Filip; Porlock, Martin

Macdonald, Ross, 1915-1983
    See also Macdonald, John; Macdonald, John Ross; Millar,
    Kenneth

MacInnes, Helen, 1907-1985
    See also Highet, Helen MacInnes

Mackintosh, Elizabeth
    See also Tey, Josephine, 1896-1952

MacLean, Alistair, 1922-1987
    See also Stuart, Ian

MacLeod, Charlotte
    See also Craig, Alisa

MacNeil, Duncan
    See also McCutchan, Philip, 1920-

Mahfouz, Naguib
    See Mahfuz, Najib, 1911-2006

Malraux, Georges Andre
    See Malraux, Andre, 1901-1976

Mandel, Emily St. John
    See St. John Mandel, Emily, 1979-

Mankind (Wrestler)
    See Foley, Mick, 1965-

Mann, Erica

    See also Jong, Erica

Manor, Jason
    See also Hall, Oakley M.

Mansfield, Kathleen Beauchamp
    See Mansfield, Katherine, 1888-1923

Marchant, Catherine
    See also Cookson, Catherine

Marisol, 1930-
    See also Escobar, Marisol

Markandaya, Kamala, 1924-2004
    See also Taylor, Kamala Purnaiya

Marlowe, Hugh
    See also Fallon, Martin; Graham, James; Higgins, Jack,
    1929-; Patterson, Harry

Marlowe, Ralph
    See Manheim, Ralph, 1907-1992

Marquez, Gabriel Garcia
    See Garcia Marquez, Gabriel, 1928-

Marshall, Sarah Catherine Wood
    See Marshall, Catherine, 1914-1983

Marsten, Richard, 1926-2005
    See also Cannon, Curt, 1926-2005; Collins, Hunt, 1926-
    2005; Hannon, Ezra, 1926-2005; Hudson, Dean, 1926-
    2005; Hunter, Evan, 1926-2005; Marsten, Richard, 1926-
    2005; McBain, Ed, 1926-2005

Marston, Edward
    See also Allen, Conrad, 1940-

Martin, Peter
    See Melville, James, 1931-; Martin, Roy Peter

Martin, Roy Peter
    See Melville, James, 1931-; Martin, Peter

Marut, Ret
    See also Feige, Hermann Albert Otto Max; Torsvan, Berick
    Traven; Torsvan, Traven; Traven, B.

Matas, Enrique Vila-
    See Vila-Matas, Enrique, 1948-

Maugham, Somerset
    See Maugham, W. Somerset (William Somerset), 1874-
    1965

Maxwell, Katie
    See also MacAlister, Katie

May, Julian, 1931-
    See also Dikty, Julian May

McBain, Ed, 1926-2005
    See also Cannon, Curt, 1926-2005; Collins, Hunt, 1926-
    2005; Hannon, Ezra, 1926-2005; Hudson, Dean, 1926-
    2005; Hunter, Evan, 1926-2005; Marsten, Richard, 1926-
    2005; McBain, Ed, 1926-2005

McCall Smith, Alexander, 1948-
    See also McCall Smith, R. A. (R. Alexander)

McCall Smith, R. A. (R. Alexander),
    See also McCall Smith, Alexander, 1948-

McCutchan, Philip, 1920-
    See also MacNeil, Duncan

McElroy, Lee
    See also Kelton, Elmer, 1926-2009; Hawk, Alex

McGarrity, Mark

Myles; O'Brien, Flann, 1911-1966

Orwell, George, 1903-1950
    See also Blair, Eric

Owen, John Pickard
    See also Butler, Samuel, 1835-1902

Parker, K. J.
    See also Parker, Kenneth John

Parker, Kenneth John
    See also Parker, K. J.

Passos, John Dos
    See Dos Passos, John

Paterson, James Hamilton-
    See Hamilton-Paterson, James

Patterson, Henry
    See also Fallon, Martin; Graham, James; Higgins, Jack, 1929-; Marlowe, Hugh

Perry, Anne, 1938-
    See also Hulme, Juliet

Peshkov, Alexei Maximovich
    See also Gorky, Maksim, 1868-1936; Gorky, Maxim

Peters, Elizabeth, 1927-
    See also Mertz, Barbara Gross; Michaels, Barbara

Petrov, David Shrayer-
    See Shrayer-Petrov, David, 1936-

Pierre, D. B. C.
    See also Finlay, Peter Warren

Pincherle, Alberto
    See also Moravia, Alberto, 1907-1990

Plath, Sylvia
    See also Lucas, Victoria

Porlock, Martin
    See also MacDonald, Philip, 1899-1981; Fleming, Oliver; Lawless, Anthony; Macdonald, Filip

Porter, William Sydney
    See Henry, O., 1862-1910

Pramoedya Ananta Toer
    See Toer, Pramoedya Ananta, 1925-2006

Quick, Amanda
    See also Krentz, Jayne Ann

Quinn, Spencer
    See also Abrahams, Peter, 1947-

Quoirez, Francoise
    See Sagan, Francoise, 1935-2004

Rabinovitch, Sholem
    See Rabinowitz, Solomon; Sholem Aleichem, 1859-1916

Rabinowitz, Solomon
    See Rabinovitch, Sholem; Sholem Aleichem, 1859-1916

Ramirez, Sergio
    See Ramirez Mercado, Sergio, 1942-

Rampling, Anne
    See also Rice, Anne, 1941-; Roquelaure, A. N.

Rankin, Ian, 1960-
    See also Harvey, Jack

Read, 1913-
    See also Miss Read; Saint, Dora Jessie

Reed, Ernesto Mestre-
    See Mestre-Reed, Ernesto, 1964-

Reed, Kit, 1932-
    See also Reed, Lillian Craig

Reed, Lillian Craig
    See also Reed, Kit, 1932-

Renault, Mary, 1905-1983
    See also Challans, Mary

Rendell, Ruth, 1930-
    See also Vine, Barbara, 1930-

Reverte, Arturo Perez-
    See Perez-Reverte, Arturo

Rhodes, Daniel
    See also McMahon, Neil

Riboud, Barbara Chase-
    See Chase-Riboud, Barbara, 1939-

Rice, Anne, 1941-
    See also Rampling, Anne; Roquelaure, A. N.

Richardson, C. S.
    See also Richardson, Charles Scott

Richardson, Charles Scott
    See also Richardson, C. S.

Rikki
    See also Ducornet, Rikki

Robb, J. D., 1950-
    See also Roberts, Nora

Roberts, Nora
    See also Robb, J.D., 1950-

Robertson, R. Garcia y
    See Garcia y Robertson, R.

Rodriguez, Alisa Valdes-
    See Valdes-Rodriguez, Alisa

Roquelaure, A. N.
    See also Rampling, Anne; Rice, Anne, 1941-

Ross, Leonard Q.
    See Rosten, Leo, 1908-1997

Ross-Macdonald, Malcolm
    See also Macdonald, Malcom, 1932-

Rowling, J.K.
    See also Galbraith, Robert

Roza, Luiz Alfredo Garcia-
    See Garcia-Roza, Luiz Alfredo, 1936-

Ruell, Patrick
    See also Hill, Reginald, 1936-; Morland, Dick; Underhill, Charles

Rule, Ann
    See also Stack, Andy

Runyon, Damon, 1884-1946
    See Runyon, Alfred Damon

Russell, Sean Thomas
    See also Russell, S. Thomas, 1952-

Ryan, Rachel
    See also Brown, Sandra, 1948-; Jordan, Laura

Ryder, Jonathan
    See also Ludlum, Robert, 1927-2001; Shepherd, Michael

Saavedra, Miguel de Cervantes
    See Cervantes Saavedra, Miguel de, 1547-1616

Sagan, Francoise, 1935-2004
    See also Quoirez, Francoise

Tan Twan Eng
    See Eng, Tan Twan
Tanner, Edward Everett
    See Dennis, Patrick, 1921-1976
Taylor, Kamala Purnaiya
    See Markandaya, Kamala, 1924-2004
Templeton, Edith, 1916-
    See also Walbrook, Louise
Tey, Josephine, 1896-1952
    See also Mackintosh, Elizabeth
Thackeray, William Makepeace, 1811-1863
    See also Titmarsh, Michael Angelo
Thomas, Ross, 1926-1995
    See also Bleeck, Oliver
Thompson, Margaret Cezair
    See Cezair-Thompson, Margaret
Titmarsh, Michael Angelo
    See also Thackeray, William Makepeace, 1811-1863
Toer, Pramoedya Ananta, 1925-2006
    See Pramoedya Ananta Toer
Toole, F. X., 1930-2002
    See also Boyd, Jerry
Torsvan, Berick Traven
    See also Feige, Hermann Albert Otto Max; Marut, Ret; Traven, B.; Torsvan, Traven
Torsvan, Traven
    See also Feige, Hermann Albert Otto Max; Marut, Ret; Traven, B.; Torsvan, Berick Traven;
Touger, Hallie Ephron
    See Ephron, Hallie
Tracy, P. J.
    See also Lambrecht, Patricia; Lambrecht, Traci
Traven, B.
    See also Feige, Hermann Albert Otto Max; Marut, Ret; Torsvan, Berick Traven; Torsvan, Traven
Traver, Robert, 1903-1991
    See also Voelker, John Donaldson
Tremaine, Jennie
    See also Chesney, Marion; Beaton, M.C.; Chesterton, G. K.
Trevanian
    See also Whitaker, Rodney
Trollip, Stanley
    See also Stanley, Michael; Sears, Michael
Trollope, Joanna
    See also Harvey, Caroline
Truman, Margaret, 1924-2008
    See also Daniel, Margaret Truman
Tsan-hsueh, 1953-
    See also Can Xue; Deng Xiaohua
Twain, Mark, 1835-1910
    See also Clemens, Samuel Langhorne
Tweedsmuir, John Buchan
    See Buchan, John, 1875-1940
Underhill, Charles
    See also Hill, Reginald, 1936-
Underwood, Michael, 1916-
    See also Evelyn, John Michael

Unischewski, Rene
    See also Stevens, Chevy
Van Cauwelaert, Didier
    See Cauwelaert, Didier van, 1960-
Van Gulik, Robert
    See Gulik, Robert Hans van, 1910-1967
Vasilikos, Vasiles
    See Vassilikos, Vassilis, 1934-
Veronese, Antonia Arslan
    See Arslan, Antonia
Veryan, Patricia, 1923-
    See also Bannister, Patricia V.
Vian, Boris, 1920-1959
    See also Sullivan, Vernon
Vidal, Gore, 1925-
    See also Box, Edgar
Vine, Barbara, 1930-
    See also Rendell, Ruth, 1930-
Voelker, John Donaldson
    See also Traver, Robert, 1903-1991
Voltaire, 1694-1778
    See also Arouet, Francois Marie
Von Goethe, Johann Wolfgang
    See Goethe, Johann Wolfgang von, 1749-1832
Wahloo, Maj Sjowall
    See also Sjowall, Maj, , 1935-
Walbrook, Louise
    See also Templeton, Edith, 1916-
Walker, Margaret, 1915-1998
    See also Alexander, Margaret Walker
Walsh, Jill Paton
    See Paton Walsh, Jill, 1937-
Walsh, Pearl S.
    See Buck, Pearl S., 1892-1973; Hedge, John
Wayshak, Deborah
    See Noyes, Deborah, 1965-
Webb, James H.
    See also Webb, Jim
Webb, Jim
    See also Webb, James H.
Weis, Margaret, 1948-
    See also Baldwin, Margaret
Welcome, John, 1914-
    See also Brennan, John
Wellesley, Charles
    See also Bronte, Charlotte, 1816-1855
West, Bing
    See also West, Francis J., 1940-
West, Francis J., 1940-
    See also West, Bing;
West, Jessamyn, 1902-1984
    See also McPherson, Jessamyn West; West, Mary Jessamyn
West, Mary Jessamyn
    See also McPherson, Jessamyn West; West, Jessamyn, 1902-1984
West, Dame Rebecca, 1892-1983
    See also Andrews, Cecily Isabel Fairfield

TITLE, SERIES, AND SUBJECT INDEX

This index to the books listed in part 1 includes title, series, and subject entries, arranged in one alphabet. Full information for each book is given in part 1 under the main entry, which is usually the author.

Title entries. Novels are listed under title. The entries include the author's last name and first initial.

Subject entries. Subject headings are printed in capital letters. The listing of a work under a subject indicates that a major portion of the work is about that subject. In addition to topical headings and proper names, subject headings include genres, locations, and historical eras or time periods. Under these headings, such as SCIENCE FICTION, BANGLADESH, or 10TH CENTURY, works of that genre, era or location are listed.

Series entries. Series names are listed alphabetically, in bold, followed by the author name. To find the entries in the series that are included in Core Collections, go to that author's portion of part 1.

10 minutes 38 seconds in this strange world Shafak, E.
100 year old man novels [series] Jonasson, J.
10TH CENTURY
  Cornwell, B. Sword of kings
  Cornwell, B. War of the wolf
  Kay, G. The last light of the sun
  Seton, A. Avalon
11 King, S.
11TH CENTURY
  Hertmans, S. The convert
  Lyndon, R. Hawk quest
12TH CENTURY
  Eco, U. Baudolino
  Follett, K. The pillars of the earth
  Franklin, A. Mistress of the art of death
  Franklin, A. The serpent's tale
  Holland, C. Jerusalem
  Penman, S. Cruel as the grave
  Penman, S. Devil's brood
  Penman, S. Dragon's lair
  Penman, S. A king's ransom
  Penman, S. Lionheart
  Penman, S. The Queen's man
  Penman, S. Time and chance
  Penman, S. When Christ and his saints slept
  Peters, E. Brother Cadfael's penance
  Peters, E. Dead man's ransom
  Peters, E. The hermit of Eyton Forest
  Peters, E. The holy thief
  Peters, E. Monk's hood
  Peters, E. The pilgrim of hate
  Peters, E. The potter's field
  Peters, E. A rare Benedictine
  Peters, E. The rose rent
  Peters, E. St. Peter's fair
  Peters, E. The sanctuary sparrow
  Peters, E. The summer of the Danes
  Peters, E. The virgin in the ice
  Scott, W. Ivanhoe
  Sharratt, M. Illuminations
13 ways of looking at a fat girl Awad, M.
1356 Cornwell, B.
13TH CENTURY
  Jones, S. Four sisters, all queens
  Nicholas, D. Throne of darkness

  Nicholas, D. The wicked
  Penman, S. Falls the shadow
  Penman, S. Here be dragons
  Penman, S. The reckoning
  Royal, P. Covenant with hell
  Royal, P. Sanctity of hate
  Royal, P. Satan's lullaby
The **13th** valley Del Vecchio, J.
14TH CENTURY
  Arden, K. The bear and the nightingale
  Arden, K. The girl in the tower
  Arden, K. The winter of the witch
  Cornwell, B. 1356
  Cornwell, B. The archer's tale
  Druon, M. The iron king
  Eco, U. The name of the rose
  Flynn, M. Eifelheim
  Follett, K. World without end
  Fortier, A. Juliet
  Gear, K. People of the mist
  Kadare, I. The three-arched bridge
  Pears, I. The dream of Scipio
  Riley, J. In pursuit of the green lion
  Riley, J. A vision of light
  Robb, C. The cross-legged knight
  Robb, C. A gift of Sanctuary
  Robb, C. The riddle of St. Leonard's
  Robinson, K. The years of rice and salt
  Seton, A. Katherine
  Starr, M. Unhallowed ground
  Willis, C. Doomsday book
  Winawer, M. The scribe of Siena
14TH CENTURY BCE
  Robinson, L. Murder at the feast of rejoicing
  Robinson, L. Murder at the god's gate
15TH CENTURY
  Dunant, S. The birth of Venus
  Dunnett, D. Niccolo rising
  Penman, S. The sunne in splendour
  Poole, S. The Borgia mistress
  Sedley, K. The Tintern treasure
  Tey, J. The daughter of time
  Wilson, G. The bird king
1660S
  Brooks, G. Caleb's crossing

Koen, K. Before Versailles
Potzsch, O. The beggar king
Potzsch, O. The dark monk
Potzsch, O. The hangman's daughter
Potzsch, O. The poisoned pilgrim
Potzsch, O. The werewolf of Bamberg
Zimmerman, J. The orphanmaster

16TH CENTURY

Amirrezvani, A. Equal of the sun
Andersen, L. The Boleyn deceit
Andersen, L. The Boleyn king
Andersen, L. The Boleyn reckoning
Baker, K. In the garden of Iden
Bear, E. Ink and steel
Black, B. Wolf on a string
Brandreth, B. The assassin of Verona
Brandreth, B. The spy of Venice
Buckley, F. The doublet affair
Buckley, F. The siren queen
Cervantes Saavedra, M. Don Quixote
Clements, R. Martyr
Clements, R. Revenger
Dunant, S. Blood and beauty
Dunant, S. In the company of the courtesan
Dunant, S. Sacred hearts
George, M. Elizabeth I
Gregory, P. The Boleyn inheritance
Gregory, P. The constant princess
Gregory, P. The last Tudor
Gregory, P. The taming of the queen
Harkness, D. Shadow of night
Harper, K. The poyson garden
Levack, S. Demon of the air
Lovett, C. The bookman's tale
Maalouf, A. Leo Africanus
Mantel, H. Bring up the bodies
Mantel, H. Wolf Hall
Marston, E. The bawdy basket
Marston, E. The devil's apprentice
Marston, E. The roaring boy
Marston, E. The vagabond clown
Marston, E. The wanton angel
Maxwell, R. The secret diary of Anne Boleyn
Maxwell, R. The wild Irish
Morgan, J. The secret life of William Shakespeare
Newman, S. The heavens
Pamuk, O. My name is Red
Parris, S. Sacrilege
Parris, S. Treachery
Plaidy, J. The captive Queen of Scots
Riley, J. The serpent garden
Sansom, C. Lamentation
Sansom, C. Revelation
Sansom, C. Sovereign
Sansom, C. Tombland
Saramago, J. The Elephant's journey
Sherwood, F. Night of sorrows

Spann, S. Blade of the Samurai
Spann, S. Claws of the cat
Spann, S. Trial on Mount Koya
Willocks, T. The religion

1700S (DECADE)

Hart, E. City of ink
Scott, W. The bride of Lammermoor

1710S

Kearsley, S. The firebird
Scott, W. Rob Roy

1720S

Green, J. The mark of the king
Hodgson, A. The last confession of Thomas Hawkins

1730S

Nickson, C. At the dying of the year
Nickson, C. Cold cruel winter
Nickson, C. Come the fear
Nickson, C. The constant lovers
Suskind, P. Perfume

1740S

Blake, R. A dark anatomy
Spufford, F. Golden hill

1760S

Beverley, J. Devilish
Beverley, J. My lady notorious
Beverley, J. Something wicked
Beverley, J. Tempting fortune

1770S

Gabaldon, D. A breath of snow and ashes
Gabaldon, D. An echo in the bone
Gabaldon, D. The fiery cross
Gabaldon, D. Written in my own heart's blood
Heyer, G. These old shades

1780S

Lawrence, M. Hearts and bones
Pittman, A. The seamstress
Robertson, I. Anatomy of murder
Robertson, I. Instruments of darkness
Rosenthal, P. The bookseller's daughter
Sabatini, R. Scaramouche

1790S

Hollingshead, G. Bedlam
Hunter, M. The conquest of Lady Cassandra
Hunter, M. The surrender of Miss Fairbourne
Lambdin, D. King's captain
Orczy, E. The Scarlet Pimpernel
Quinn, K. Ribbons of scarlet
Redfern, E. The music of the spheres
Woods, R. Remembrance

17TH CENTURY

Amirrezvani, A. The blood of flowers
Brooks, G. Caleb's crossing
Burton, J. The miniaturist
Chevalier, T. Girl with a pearl earring
Crichton, M. Pirate latitudes
Dumas, A. The man in the iron mask
Dumas, A. Twenty years after

McCarthy, C. Blood meridian, or, The evening redness in the West

Moran, M. Rebel queen

Morrell, D. Murder as a fine art

Perry, A. A breach of promise

Perry, A. Cain his brother

Perry, A. Death of a stranger

Perry, A. The face of a stranger

Perry, A. Funeral in blue

Perry, A. The shifting tide

Perry, A. The silent cry

Perry, A. The sins of the wolf

Perry, A. Slaves of obsession

Perry, A. The twisted root

Perry, A. Weighed in the balance

Price, S. By gaslight

Pulley, N. The Bedlam stacks

Rivers, F. Redeeming love

Saunders, K. The case of the wandering scholar

Schanbacher, G. Crossing Purgatory

Shepherd, L. A fatal likeness

Shepherd, L. The Solitary House

Thomson, E. Beloved poison

Thomson, E. The blood

Wheeler, R. The canyon of bones

Woods, R. Remembrance

1860S

Burnet, G. His bloody project

Cobbs Hoffman, E. The Tubman command

Coover, R. Huck out west

Doctorow, E. The march

Finch, C. A beautiful blue death

Finch, C. The September Society

Fowles, J. The French lieutenant's woman

Frazier, C. Cold Mountain

Gingrich, N. Gettysburg

Gingrich, N. Grant comes east

Gleason, C. Murder at the capitol

Groot, T. The sentinels of Andersonville

Haldane, S. The devil's making

Harte, B. The best short stories of Bret Harte

Hicks, R. The widow of the South

Horn, D. All other nights

Hunt, L. Neverhome

Jakes, J. Love and war

Jakes, J. On secret service

Jakes, J. Savannah, or, A gift for Mr. Lincoln

Jenkins, B. Rebel

Kelton, E. Badger boy

Kelton, E. The way of the coyote

Kolpan, G. Magic words

Lock, N. American meteor

Mason, T. The Darwin affair

McCabe, E. I shall be near to you

Milan, C. The duchess war

Pearl, M. The Dante Club

Pearl, M. The technologists

Perez-Reverte, A. The fencing master

Perry, A. Blind justice

Perry, A. Blood on the water

Perry, A. Dark tide rising

Perry, A. A sunless sea

Peters, R. Hell or Richmond

Plain, B. Crescent City

Powning, B. The sea captain's wife

Poyer, D. A country of our own

Poyer, D. Fire on the waters

Ranney, K. The Scottish duke

Saunders, G. Lincoln in the bardo

Shaara, J. Gods and generals

Shaara, J. The last full measure

Simmons, D. Drood

Smith, L. On Agate Hill

Tsypkin, L. Summer in Baden-Baden

Waters, S. Fingersmith

1870S

Abdul-Jabbar, K. The empty birdcage

Abdul-Jabbar, K. Mycroft and Sherlock

Abdul-Jabbar, K. Mycroft Holmes

Beams, C. The illness lesson

Brooks, B. Blood storm

Buchanan, C. The painted girls

Clark, P. The black god's drums

Coover, R. Huck out west

Donoghue, E. Frog music

Estleman, L. The adventures of Johnny Vermillion

Everett, P. God's country

Fowler, K. Sarah Canary

Jenkins, B. Forbidden

Jiles, P. News of the world

Kelton, E. Texas vendetta

Letts, E. Finding Dorothy

Lock, N. American meteor

McCrea, G. Mrs. Engels

Parker, R. Gunman's rhapsody

Pearl, M. The Dante chamber

Pirrone, D. Shall we not revenge

Portis, C. True grit

Shepard, K. The Celestials

Singer, I. The magician of Lublin

Smith, M. Rose

Sontag, S. In America

Vanderhaeghe, G. The last crossing

Verble, M. Cherokee America

Wood, T. The engineer's wife

1876 Vidal, G.

1880S

Anderson, A. The summer guest

Archer, Z. Dangerous seduction

Ashley, J. Lady Isabella's scandalous marriage

Ashley, J. The madness of Lord Ian Mackenzie

Bahr, H. The Judas Field

Benton, J. Lilli de Jong

Bonner, C. Lily

Levine, D. Arabella of Mars
Liss, D. A spectacle of corruption
Miller, A. Pure
Miller, R. Jacob's folly
Murphy, Y. Signed, Mata Hari
Naslund, S. The fountain of St. James Court
Natt och Dag, N. The wolf and the watchman
Neville, K. The eight
Nicholson, C. The elephant keeper
Nickson, C. The constant lovers
Palmer, D. Mary Toft; or, the rabbit queen
Proulx, A. Barkskins
Putney, M. A kiss of fate
Richardson, S. Clarissa, or, The history of a
  young lady
Richardson, S. Pamela
Richter, C. The awakening land
Robertson, I. Instruments of darkness
Robertson, I. Island of bones
Rosenberg, J. Confessions of the fox
Rowland, L. The incense game
Rowland, L. The Shogun's daughter
Smith, G. The maze at Windermere
Smith, W. Monsoon
Sontag, S. The volcano lover
Stachniak, E. The Winter Palace
Suskind, P. Perfume
Turner, N. My name is Resolute
Unsworth, B. Sacred hunger
Vreeland, S. Girl in hyacinth blue
Wilson, D. The clockwork dynasty

1900S (DECADE)

Adamson, G. The outlander
Agee, J. The bones of paradise
Burns, O. Cold Sassy tree
Cussler, C. The cutthroat
Cussler, C. The wrecker
Doctorow, E. Ragtime
Doig, I. The whistling season
Faulkner, W. The reivers
Goldstone, L. Assassin of shadows
Hoffman, A. The Museum of Extraordinary Things
Hoover, M. The quickening
Jakeman, J. In the kingdom of mists
Jones, J. The silence
Keane, M. Fever
Kibler, J. Home for erring and outcast girls
Kimani, P. Dance of the Jakaranda
Lawrence, D. Women in love
Macdonald, M. Tamsin Harte
Machart, B. The wake of forgiveness
Marlantes, K. Deep river
Martel, Y. The high mountains of Portugal
Meyer, N. The adventure of the peculiar protocols
Oates, J. The accursed
Oates, J. I lock my door upon myself
Pajer, B. Capacity for murder

Pajer, B. The Edison effect
Pajer, B. Fatal induction
Pajer, B. A spark of death
Parmar, P. Vanessa and her sister
Perry, A. A Christmas message
Perry, A. A Christmas return
Peters, E. Guardian of the horizon
Peters, E. Seeing a large cat
Peterson, T. What comes my way
Phillips, C. Dancing in the dark
Pintoff, S. In the shadow of Gotham
Rubenfeld, J. The interpretation of murder
Sayles, J. A moment in the sun
Sinclair, U. The jungle
Smith, B. A tree grows in Brooklyn
Solomon, B. The attempted murder of Teddy Roosevelt
Steinke, R. Holy skirts
Swarthout, G. The shootist
Tallis, F. Vienna blood
Vidal, G. Empire
Vine, B. Anna's book
Wright, J. The house on Foster Hill

1910S

Bainbridge, B. Every man for himself
Barker, P. The eye in the door
Barnett, L. Jam on the Vine
Bohjalian, C. The sandcastle girls
Boyden, J. Three day road
Buchan, J. The thirty-nine steps
Burdick, S. The girls with no names
Burns, O. Leaving Cold Sassy
Butler, R. The hot country
Coldsmith, D. The long journey home
Cussler, C. The chase
Cussler, C. The Titanic secret
Fredericks, M. Death of a new American
Gallagher, S. The bedlam detective
Gilman, C. Herland
Gloss, M. The hearts of horses
Groom, W. El Paso
Hammad, I. The Parisian, or, Al-Barisi
Hand, E. Curious toys
Hollinghurst, A. The stranger's child
Hood, A. The obituary writer
House, S. A parchment of leaves
Itani, F. Tell
Jones, S. The uninvited guests
Katsu, A. The deep
King, L. The beekeeper's apprentice
Lee, M. Pachinko
Lehane, D. The given day
Marshall, C. Christy
Matthiessen, P. Killing Mister Watson
McCann, C. Transatlantic
Meek, J. The people's act of love
Morris, M. Man in the blue moon
Moyes, J. The girl you left behind

Speller, E. The return of Captain John Emmett
Speller, E. The strange fate of Kitty Easton
St. James, S. The haunting of Maddy Clare
Stewart, D. The Babe Ruth deception
Swift, G. Mothering Sunday
Towles, A. A gentleman in Moscow
Truong, M. The book of salt, Monique Truong.
Vidal, G. Hollywood
Waters, S. The paying guests
Waugh, E. Brideshead revisited
Waugh, E. Vile bodies
Welty, E. Delta wedding
Wilder, T. Theophilus North
Willig, L. The Ashford affair
Winspear, J. Maisie Dobbs
Woods, S. Chiefs
Woolf, V. To the lighthouse

1921 Llywelyn, M.

1930S

Abbott, M. Bury me deep
Albert, S. The Darling Dahlias and the cucumber tree
Algren, N. A walk on the wild side
Allen, J. I lost my girlish laughter
Apelfeld, A. Badenheim 1939
Archer, J. Only time will tell
Baldwin, J. Go tell it on the mountain
Barr, M. Watershed
Bassani, G. The garden of the Finzi-Continis
Blake, S. The guest book
Bloom, A. White houses
Bolano, R. Monsieur Pain
Chandler, R. The annotated Big sleep
Chandler, R. The big sleep
Chevalier, T. A single thread
Chiaverini, J. Resistance women
Choo, Y. The night tiger
Clayton, M. The last train to London
Dallas, S. The Persian Pickle Club
Danticat, E. The farming of bones
Deaver, J. Garden of beasts
Depestre, R. Hadriana in all my dreams
Doctorow, E. Billy Bathgate
Doctorow, E. World's Fair
Duenas, M. The time in between
Faulkner, W. Pylon
Fitzgerald, F. The last tycoon
Flagg, F. Fried green tomatoes at the Whistle Stop Cafe
Ford, J. Songs of Willow Frost
French, A. Billy
Furnivall, K. The red scarf
Furst, A. The foreign correspondent
Furst, A. Mission to Paris
Furst, A. The spies of Warsaw
Gardam, J. God on the rocks
Gaynor, H. The lighthouse keeper's daughter
Golden, A. Memoirs of a geisha
Greaves, C. Hard twisted

Greene, A. Long Man
Greene, G. The power and the glory
Gross, A. Button man
Harman, P. The midwife of Hope River
Harrison, N. Montauk
Hegi, U. Children and fire
Hemingway, E. To have and have not
Holland, T. The archivist's story
Hunt, A. City of saints
Hurston, Z. Their eyes were watching God
Isherwood, C. The Berlin stories
Ishiguro, K. When we were orphans
Jin, H. Nanjing requiem
Johnson, M. Incognegro
Joinson, S. The photographer's wife
Kennedy, W. Ironweed
Kerr, P. Field gray
Kerr, P. March violets
King, L. Euphoria
Kittredge, W. The willow field
Koestler, A. Darkness at noon
Krueger, W. This tender land
Lanchester, J. Fragrant Harbor
Lansdale, J. The bottoms
Lansdale, J. Edge of dark water
Lansdale, J. The thicket
Leonard, E. The Hot Kid
Lessing, D. Martha Quest
Lessing, D. A proper marriage
Letts, E. Finding Dorothy
Lewis, S. It can't happen here
Littell, R. The Stalin epigram
Lowry, M. Under the volcano
Martel, Y. The high mountains of Portugal
Mathews, B. The world of tomorrow
McCann, C. Zoli
McCarthy, C. The crossing
McCullers, C. Reflections in a golden eye
McEwan, I. Atonement
McLain, P. Love and ruin
McPherson, C. A step so grave
Meadows, R. I will send rain
Mengiste, M. The shadow king
Miller, H. Tropic of Cancer
Moore, S. The life of objects
Mosher, H. On Kingdom Mountain
Mosley, W. Gone fishin'
Moyes, J. The giver of stars
Norman, H. The museum guard
O'Farrell, M. The vanishing act of Esme Lennox
O'Hara, J. Appointment in Samarra
O'Hara, J. Butterfield 8
Oates, J. A garden of earthly delights
Orringer, J. The invisible bridge
Ozick, C. Heir to the glimmering world
Pawel, R. Death of a nationalist
Peebles, F. The air you breathe

Iles, G. Black cross
Jakes, J. North and South
Jenoff, P. The lost girls of Paris
Jio, S. The last camellia
Jones, J. The thin red line
Jordan, H. Mudbound
Kaminsky, S. Dancing in the dark
Kaminsky, S. A fatal glass of beer
Kaminsky, S. To catch a spy
Kaminsky, S. Tomorrow is another day
Kanon, J. Los Alamos
Kelly, S. The wages of desire
Kerr, P. Hitler's peace
Kerr, P. The lady from Zagreb
Kerr, P. A man without breath
Kittredge, W. The willow field
Knowles, J. A separate peace
Kutsukake, L. The translation of love
Kuznetsov, A. Babi Yar
Leavitt, D. The two Hotel Francforts
Leithauser, B. The art student's war
Lessing, D. A ripple from the storm
Levy, A. Small island
Llywelyn, M. 1949
Loigman, L. The two-family house
Lourie, R. A hatred for tulips
Majmudar, A. Partitions
Mankell, H. The return of the dancing master
Mawer, S. The fall
McCarthy, C. All the pretty horses
McCullers, C. The heart is a lonely hunter
McLain, P. Love and ruin
Meloy, M. Liars and saints
Momaday, N. House made of dawn
Montclair, A. The right sort of man
Moore, C. Noir
Morgan, R. The road from Gap Creek
Mosley, W. Devil in a blue dress
Mullen, T. Darktown
Muller, H. The hunger angel
Munro, A. Lives of girls and women
Naylor, G. Bailey's Cafe
Nemirovsky, I. Fire in the blood
Nemirovsky, I. Suite Francaise
Nesbo, J. The redbreast
Nicholson, W. Motherland
Norman, H. What is left the daughter
Oksanen, S. When the doves disappeared
Orringer, J. The invisible bridge
Otsuka, J. When the emperor was divine
Oz, A. Panther in the basement
Parker, R. Double play
Paton, A. Cry, the beloved country
Peace, D. Occupied city
Peace, D. Tokyo year zero
Pelecanos, G. The big blowdown
Petry, A. The street

Petterson, P. Out stealing horses
Pilcher, R. Coming home
Plain, B. Tapestry
Rabb, J. Among the living
Reisman, N. The first desire
Rhys, R. Fatal inheritance
Robertson, R. The long take
Roosevelt, E. Murder at the palace
Roosevelt, E. Murder in the Blue Room
Roosevelt, E. The White House pantry murder
Roth, P. I married a Communist
Roth, P. Nemesis
Roth, P. The plot against America
Roth, P. Portnoy's complaint
Ruiz Zafon, C. The shadow of the wind
Russell, M. A thread of grace
Russell, S. The insane train
Sada, D. Almost never
Saroyan, W. The human comedy
Sayers, V. The powers
Scoppettone, S. Too darn hot
Seiffert, R. A boy in winter
Shaara, J. The rising tide
Shaara, J. The steel wave
Shapiro, B. The muralist
Singer, I. Enemies, a love story
Smiley, J. Some luck
Smith, M. December 6
Solzhenitsyn, A. In the first circle
Spark, M. The girls of slender means
Steinhauer, O. The Bridge of Sighs
Van Booy, S. The illusion of separateness
Vidal, G. The golden age
Vidal, G. Washington, D. C.
Walton, J. Farthing
Waters, S. The little stranger
Waters, S. The night watch
Willis, C. Blackout
Winthrop, E. The mercy seat
Wouk, H. War and remembrance
Wouk, H. The winds of war
Yi, C. The investigation

1949 Llywelyn, M.

1950S

Allison, D. Bastard out of Carolina
Amis, K. Lucky Jim
Atkins, A. Wicked city
Baldwin, J. Giovanni's room
Baldwin, J. Just above my head
Barth, J. The end of the road
Bartlett, N. The disappearance boy
Bates, J. Midnight at the Dragon Cafe
Bauer, C. Frances and Bernard
Berg, G. The operator
Black, B. Christine Falls
Blake, S. The guest book
Blume, J. In the unlikely event

Roth, P. Indignation
Roth, P. Letting go
Roth, P. Portnoy's complaint
Ruiz Zafon, C. The labyrinth of the spirits
Ruiz Zafon, C. The prisoner of heaven
Runcie, J. Canvey Island
Runcie, J. Sidney Chambers and the forgiveness of sins
Runcie, J. Sidney Chambers and the perils of the night
Runcie, J. Sidney Chambers and the problem of evil
Runcie, J. Sidney Chambers and the shadow of death
Sanchez, T. King Bongo
Sarginson, S. The wonderful
Scott, A. Beneath the abbey wall
Scott, A. A double death on the Black Isle
Scott, A. A kind of grief
Scott, A. The low road
Scott, J. Tourmaline
Seay, M. The mirror thief
See, L. Dreams of joy
Sepetys, R. Out of the Easy
Seth, V. A suitable boy
Smith, D. The last painting of Sara De Vos
Smith, T. Agent 6
Smith, T. Child 44
Smith, T. The secret speech
Solzhenitsyn, A. Cancer ward
Spark, M. A far cry from Kensington
Spark, M. Memento mori
Sparks, N. A walk to remember
Stratford, S. Red letter days
Swift, G. Here we are
Tan, T. The garden of evening mists
Toibin, C. Brooklyn
Truss, L. The man that got away
Updike, J. Rabbit, run
Urquhart, J. The night stages
Vachss, A. Two trains running
Vargas Llosa, M. Aunt Julia and the scriptwriter
Vidal, G. The golden age
Wallace, D. Mr. Sebastian and the Negro magician
Watson, L. Let him go
West, D. The wedding
Williams, B. The summer wives
Williams, N. This is happiness
Williams, T. The Roman spring of Mrs. Stone
Wilson, S. The man in the gray flannel suit
Winslow, D. Satori

1960S

Acevedo, C. The distant marvels
Adichie, C. Half of a yellow sun
Alexander, V. The Magdalen girls
Alther, L. Kinflicks
Alvarez, J. How the Garcia girls lost their accents
Auster, P. Invisible
Ausubel, R. Sons and daughters of ease and plenty
Baldwin, J. Another country
Baldwin, J. Just above my head

Barnes, K. In the kingdom of men
Barth, J. Giles Goat-Boy ;
Bausch, R. Rebel powers
Bellow, S. Mr. Sammler's planet
Berg, E. The art of mending
Berg, E. We are all welcome here
Binchy, M. Firefly summer
Bird, S. The Yokota Officers Club
Bisson, T. Any day now
Block, L. Killing Castro
Blum, J. The lost family
Bolano, R. Amulet
Bowman, D. Big bang
Boyle, T. Outside looking in
Buckley, W. Mongoose, R.I.P.
Butler, N. The hearts of men
Byatt, A. Babel Tower
Byatt, A. A whistling woman
Carter, S. Back channel
Castellani, C. Leading men
Cheever, J. Bullet Park
Cheever, J. The Wapshot scandal
Childress, M. Crazy in Alabama
Cline, E. The girls
Collins, M. Ask not
Conroy, P. South of Broad
Crandall, S. Whistling past the graveyard
Cruz, A. Dominicana
DeLillo, D. Libra
Dick, P. The man in the high castle
Didion, J. Play it as it lays
Doig, I. The bartender's tale
Doyle, R. Paddy Clarke, ha-ha-ha
Dunmore, H. Exposure
Dybek, S. I sailed with Magellan
Ellroy, J. American tabloid
Ellroy, J. Blood's a rover
Ellroy, J. The cold six thousand
Faulks, S. On Green Dolphin Street
Flint, E. Little deaths
Ford, J. The shadow year
Fowler, C. Bryant & May
Frazier, C. Nightwoods
Fuller, C. Bitter orange
Gifford, B. The stars above Veracruz
Gorman, E. Bad moon rising
Grant, L. Arcadia
Groff, L. We had it so good
Gunesekera, R. Suncatcher
Herlihy, J. Midnight cowboy
Hilderbrand, E. Summer of '69
Hill, N. The nix
Hoffman, A. The third angel
Hood, A. The obituary writer
Jiang, R. Wolf totem
Johnson, D. Tree of smoke
Joyce, G. The limits of enchantment

1970S

Abani, C. GraceLand
Abbott, P. Concrete angel
Aciman, A. Harvard square
Aguilar Camin, H. Death in Veracruz
Allende, I. In the midst of winter
Allio, K. Buddhism for Western children
Amis, M. The pregnant widow
Ammaniti, N. I'm not scared
Antunes, A. The return of the caravels
Ausubel, R. Sons and daughters of ease and plenty
Baldwin, J. If Beale Street could talk
Baldwin, J. Just above my head
Beattie, A. Chilly scenes of winter
Bender, T. The last ghost dancer
Benedetti, M. Springtime in a broken mirror
Blau, J. The summer of naked swim parties
Block, L. When the sacred ginmill closes
Bolano, R. The savage detectives
Brundage, E. All things cease to appear
Burns, A. Milkman
Burns, C. Black hole
Campbell, B. Once upon a river
Canty, K. The underworld
Carlson, S. Almost Graceland
Childress, M. One Mississippi
Clark, M. Death wears a beauty mask and other stories
Coe, J. The rotters' club
Coetzee, J. Summertime
Cotterill, C. The coroner's lunch
Cotterill, C. Disco for the departed
Cotterill, C. The second biggest nothing
Cotterill, C. Slash and burn
Couto, M. Sleepwalking land
Cumming, C. A colder war
Cumming, C. A foreign country
D'Souza, T. The Konkans
Daughters, A. You cannot mess this up
Davis, F. The masterpiece
DePoy, P. Sidewalk saint
Dean, P. Tam Lin
Deb, S. The point of return
Diehl, H. Lifelines
Echlin, K. The disappeared
Eskens, A. Nothing more dangerous
Eugenides, J. The virgin suicides
Faletti, G. A pimp's notes
Ferrante, E. The story of the lost child
Fesperman, D. Safe houses
French, M. The women's room
Fu, K. For today I am a boy
Fuqua, J. Gone and back again
Gaines, E. A gathering of old men
Ghaffari, R. To keep the sun alive
Gordimer, N. The conservationist
Gordon, J. Lord of misrule
Gorman, E. Riders on the storm
Green, N. The angel of Montague Street

Greer, R. First of state
Grisham, J. The last juror
Hage, R. Beirut Hellfire Society
Hallberg, G. City on fire
Hannah, K. The great alone
Harvey, M. Pulse
Hay, E. Late nights on air
Heller, J. Good as Gold
Ishiguro, K. Never let me go
James, P. Innocent blood
Johnson, D. Tree of smoke
Kennedy, R. Presidio
Kinder, C. Honeymooners
Kostova, E. The historian
Kunzru, H. My revolutions
Le Carre, J. The honourable schoolboy
Lewis, T. GBH
Li, Y. The vagrants
Limon, M. The line
Limon, M. Mr. Kill
Lopez, J. A beautiful young woman
MacDonald, J. The lonely silver rain
MacDonald, J. The scarlet ruse
Makine, A. The woman who waited
Mallon, T. Watergate
Matar, H. In the country of men
Matheson, R. I am legend
Maupin, A. Tales of the city
McCann, C. Let the great world spin
McClure, J. The steam pig
McDermott, A. After this
McEwan, I. Sweet tooth
McPhee, M. Gorgeous lies
Meloy, M. Liars and saints
Morrison, T. Paradise
Murdoch, I. A fairly honourable defeat
Murphy, D. Tiny Americans
Nesbo, J. Blood on snow
Nesbo, J. Macbeth
Neville, K. The eight
Ng, C. Everything I never told you
Nguyen, V. The sympathizer
Norman, H. Next life might be kinder
Pamuk, O. The museum of innocence
Piercy, M. Vida
Pirro, J. Sly fox
Pronzini, B. The crimes of Jordan Wise
Reid, T. Daisy Jones & the Six
Ripley, M. Mr. Campion's war
Rizzuto, R. Shadow child
Rosen, L. The tenth witness
Roth, P. The anatomy lesson
Runcie, J. Sidney Chambers and the persistence of love
Sandlin, L. The bird boys
Self, W. Shark
Shafak, E. Honor
Slaughter, K. Cop Town

Powers, R. The Gold Bug Variations
Pynchon, T. Vineland
Raymond, J. The half-life
Restrepo, L. Delirium
Restrepo, L. No place for heroes
Rivers, F. And the shofar blew
Rooney, K. Lillian Boxfish takes a walk
Sapphire, 1. Push
Schlink, B. Self's punishment
Slaughter, K. Pieces of her
Sofer, D. The Septembers of Shiraz
Solomon, A. Disgruntled
Stibbe, N. Reasons to be cheerful
Strout, E. My name is Lucy Barton
Stuart, D. Shuggie Bain
Swyler, E. Light from other stars
Thien, M. Do not say we have nothing
Torday, D. The last flight of Poxl West
Trigiani, A. Big Cherry Holler
Tudor, C. The chalk man
Twardoch, S. The king of Warsaw
Tyree, O. Flyy girl
Vonnegut, K. Galapagos
Wallace, D. The watermelon king
Walsh, M. My sunshine away
Walter, J. Citizen Vince
White, E. Jack Holmes and his friend
Whitehead, C. Sag Harbor
Wilkinson, L. American spy
Wolfe, T. The bonfire of the vanities
Woods, T. True to the game
Woods, T. True to the game II
Woods, T. True to the game III
Yates, C. Grist Mill Road
1984 Orwell, G.
1990S
Abraham, T. Black Sunday
Al Rawi, S. The Baghdad clock
Alenyikov, M. Ivan and Misha
Ali, M. Brick Lane
Aliu, X. Brass
Amis, M. London fields
Aramburu, F. Homeland
Bacon, C. There is room for you
Bandi, 1. The accusation
Barr, N. The rope
Batuman, E. The idiot
Benaron, N. Running the rift
Black, C. Murder in the Bastille
Black, C. Murder in the rue de Paradis
Bock, C. Alice & Oliver
Boyle, T. The Terranauts
Boyle, W. City of margins
Brockmeier, K. The truth about Celia
Campbell, A. On the floor
Carter, M. Further out than you thought
Cassara, J. The house of impossible beauties

Castillo, E. America is not the heart
Chariandy, D. Brother
Child, L. The enemy
Cleage, P. What looks like crazy on an ordinary day
Coupland, D. Microserfs
Coupland, D. Eleanor Rigby
Dahl, A. Bad Blood
Dahl, A. Misterioso
Darnielle, J. Universal harvester
Dennis-Benn, N. Here comes the sun
Eco, U. Numero zero
Edugyan, E. Half-blood blues
Ellis, M. Keeping bedlam at bay in the Prague Cafe
Faye, G. Small country
Frear, C. Sweet little lies
Gabel, A. The ensemble
Harrison, M. Light
Heller, Z. What was she thinking?
Higashino, K. Malice
Higashino, K. Newcomer
Hoffman, A. The third angel
Holbert, B. Whiskey
Ishiguro, K. Never let me go
Kelly, E. The poison tree
King, L. Writers & lovers
Lerner, B. The Topeka school
Levy, D. Swimming home
Lippman, L. Sunburn
Lordan, B. But come ye back , Beth Lordan
Lovett, C. The bookman's tale
Lowe, K. The furies
Mankell, H. The dogs of Riga
Mankell, H. The return of the dancing master
Marlette, D. Magic time
Mawer, S. The fall
McCann, C. Transatlantic
McFadden, B. Gathering of waters
McGahan, A. The white earth
McLean, F. The Van Apfel girls are gone
Mehta, R. No other world
Meloy, M. Liars and saints
Meno, J. Marvel and a wonder
Murakami, H. After the quake
Myers, A. Continental divide
Novic, S. Girl at war
O'Nan, S. Henry, himself
Obioma, C. The fishermen
Pelecanos, G. Shame the devil
Persson, L. Another time, another life
Phillips, A. Prague
Prcic, I. Shards
Racculia, K. Bellweather rhapsody
Redhill, M. Consolation
Restrepo, L. No place for heroes
Rimmer, K. Truths I never told you
Rivero, M. The affairs of the Falcons
Rivers, F. And the shofar blew

Ghosh, A. Flood of fire

Ghosh, A. River of smoke

Guthrie, A. The big sky

Gyasi, Y. Homegoing

Hand, E. Mortal love

Harris, R. An officer and a spy

Hijuelos, O. Twain & Stanley enter paradise

Hill, R. Hanta Yo

Hodder, M. The strange affair of Spring Heeled Jack

Hoffman, A. The marriage of opposites

James, H. Complete stories, 1874-1884

James, H. Complete stories, 1884-1891

James, H. Complete stories, 1892-1898

Jeffries, S. Project Duchess

Johnson, C. Middle Passage

Jones, D. The court-martial of George Armstrong Custer

Kidd, S. The invention of wings

Kingsolver, B. Unsheltered

Kinsale, L. Lessons in French

Lambdin, D. Hostile shores

Laurens, S. The pursuits of Lord Kit Cavanaugh

Leonard, E. The complete Western stories of Elmore Leonard.

Leveen, L. The secrets of Mary Bowser

Lock, N. A fugitive in Walden Woods

Lorret, V. How to forget a duke

Lovesey, P. Bertie and the seven bodies

Maguire, G. Hiddensee

Malerman, J. Unbury Carol

Mann, T. Buddenbrooks

Martin, V. Property

Matthiessen, P. Bone by bone

Matthiessen, P. Shadow country

Maupassant, G. Like death

McBride, J. Song yet sung

McCarthy, C. Blood meridian, or, The evening redness in the West

McMurtry, L. Dead man's walk

McMurtry, L. Lonesome Dove

Meyer, N. The seven-per-cent solution

Mitchell, D. The thousand autumns of Jacob De Zoet

Moore, C. Sacre bleu

Morgenstern, E. The night circus

Morrell, D. Murder as a fine art

Morrison, T. Beloved

Murphy, Y. Signed, Mata Hari

Nash, S. Between the Duke and the deep blue sea

Naslund, S. Ahab's wife, or, the star gazer

North, C. The pursuit of William Abbey

Novik, N. His majesty's dragon

O'Connor, J. Star of the Sea

Owen, L. The quick

Palliser, C. The quincunx

Palliser, C. The unburied

Pearl, M. The last Dickens

Pearl, M. The technologists

Pears, I. Stone's fall

Penney, S. The tenderness of wolves

Penney, S. Under a pole star

Perez-Reverte, A. The fencing master

Perry, A. Bedford Square

Perry, A. Belgrave Square

Perry, A. Bethlehem Road

Perry, A. Blind justice

Perry, A. Blood on the water

Perry, A. Bluegate Fields

Perry, A. Buckingham Palace gardens

Perry, A. A breach of promise

Perry, A. Cain his brother

Perry, A. Cardington Crescent

Perry, A. A dangerous mourning

Perry, A. Dark tide rising

Perry, A. Death of a stranger

Perry, A. Death on Blackheath

Perry, A. The face of a stranger

Perry, A. Farriers' Lane

Perry, A. Funeral in blue

Perry, A. Half Moon Street

Perry, A. Highgate Rise

Perry, A. The Hyde Park headsman

Perry, A. Midnight at Marble Arch

Perry, A. Paragon Walk

Perry, A. Pentecost Alley

Perry, A. Resurrection Row

Perry, A. Seven Dials

Perry, A. The shifting tide

Perry, A. The silent cry

Perry, A. The sins of the wolf

Perry, A. Southampton Row

Perry, A. A sunless sea

Perry, A. Traitors Gate

Perry, A. The twisted root

Perry, A. Weighed in the balance

Perry, A. The Whitechapel conspiracy

Pesci, D. Amistad

Peters, E. The deeds of the disturber

Peters, E. The last camel died at noon

Peters, E. Lion in the valley

Peters, E. The mummy case

Peters, E. The snake, the crocodile, and the dog

Pirie, D. The patient's eyes

Pope, B. The missing Italian girl

Powning, B. The sea captain's wife

Priest, C. Boneshaker

Priest, C. Clementine

Proulx, A. Barkskins

Purcell, L. The silent companions

Putney, M. Loving a lost lord

Quick, A. Crystal gardens

Quick, A. Garden of lies

Rawles, N. My Jim

Ray, K. No country

Rhys, J. Wide Sargasso Sea

Richter, C. The sea of grass

Aliu, X. Brass
Allende, I. In the midst of winter
Aramburu, F. Homeland
Bartz, A. The lost night
Camp, B. The city of lost fortunes
Dahl, K. The courier
Daughters, A. You cannot mess this up
Glynn, A. Receptor
Gray, A. The care and feeding of ravenously hungry girls
Hill, N. The nix
Kamali, M. The stationery shop
Lasdun, J. Afternoon of a faun
Le Carre, J. Agent running in the field
Ma, L. Severance
Makkai, R. The great believers
Markley, S. Ohio
Meuleman, S. Find me gone
Murphy, D. Tiny Americans
Powell, M. Firebird
Slaughter, K. Pieces of her
Smith, A. Spring
Smith, A. Winter
Steinhauer, O. The middleman
Taneja, P. We that are young
Tudor, C. The chalk man
Walton, J. My real children
Weldon, F. Chalcot Crescent
Woods, R. Remembrance
Yoon, P. Run me to earth
206 Bones Reichs, K.
20TH CENTURY
Abbott, M. Queenpin
Alharthi, J. Celestial bodies
Allende, I. A long petal of the sea
Archer, J. Nothing ventured
Artson, B. Odessa, Odessa
Atkinson, K. Transcription
Auster, P. 4 3 2 1
Bailey, P. Uncle Rudolf
Ballard, J. The kindness of women
Banner, C. The house at the edge of night
Bauman, B. Broken sleep
Beauman, N. Madness is better than defeat
Belfer, L. And after the fire
Benedict, M. Lady Clementine
Benedict, M. The only woman in the room
Benjamin, M. The aviator's wife
Benn, J. Billy Boyle
Bloom, A. White houses
Boyle, T. The women
Boyne, J. The heart's invisible furies
Boyne, J. The house of special purpose
Brennert, A. Daughter of Moloka'i
Cheever, J. The Wapshot chronicle
Chen, D. Brothers
Coe, J. Number 11
Colvin, J. Africaville

Craig, C. Miss Burma
Darznik, J. Song of a captive bird
Davis, F. The Chelsea girls
De Robertis, C. Cantoras
Del Amo, J. Animalia
Diamant, A. The Boston girl
Dupont, E. The American fiancee
Epstein, J. Wunderland
Follett, K. Edge of eternity
Follett, K. Fall of giants
Follett, K. Winter of the world
Forbes, C. A tall history of sugar
Gabaldon, D. Drums of autumn
Gage, E. The ladies of Managua
Gaines, E. The autobiography of Miss Jane Pittman
Ghosh, A. The glass palace
Gilman, S. The ice cream queen of Orchard Street
Goldberg, M. Feast your eyes
Gyasi, Y. Homegoing
Han, K. Human acts
Hegi, U. Stones from the river
Hollinghurst, A. The Sparsholt affair
James, M. A brief history of seven killings
Johnston, W. The colony of unrequited dreams
Kim, E. The kinship of secrets
Kracht, C. Imperium
Krivak, A. The signal flame
Kuang, R. The dragon republic
Kuang, R. The poppy war
Lahiri, J. The namesake
Lebrecht, N. The song of names
Lee, M. Pachinko
Lessing, D. The good terrorist
Liardet, F. We must be brave
Makkai, R. The hundred-year house
McCracken, E. Bowlaway
McDermott, A. The ninth hour
McEwan, I. On Chesil Beach
Meloy, M. Liars and saints
Miller, K. Augustown
Mitchell, D. The bone clocks
Morris, H. Cilka's journey
Murphy, T. Correspondents
Nemirovsky, I. Suite Francaise
Nguyen, P. The mountains sing
Nguyen, V. The sympathizer
North, C. The pursuit of William Abbey
Oates, J. The accursed
Oates, J. The falls
Oates, J. We were the Mulvaneys
Offutt, C. Country dark
Ondaatje, M. Warlight
Onyebuchi, T. Riot baby
Orner, P. Love and shame and love
Otto, W. Eight girls taking pictures
Pamuk, O. A strangeness in my mind
Paul, G. The lost daughter

Smith, G. The maze at Windermere
Steele, A. Coyote
Stephenson, N. The diamond age,
Stephenson, N. Snow crash
Stross, C. Accelerando
Suarez, D. Change agent
Swyler, E. Light from other stars
Vinge, V. Rainbows end
Vonnegut, K. Hocus pocus
Walter, J. Beautiful ruins
Wang, K. Family trust
Ware, R. The turn of the key
Watts, P. Starfish
Wiggins, M. The shadow catcher
Willis, C. Blackout
Willis, C. Doomsday book
Wilson, D. The clockwork dynasty
Winterson, J. Frankissstein
Woods, C. Things to do when you're goth in the country
Wright, J. The house on Foster Hill
Yanagihara, H. A little life
22 Britannia Road Hodgkinson, A.
22ND CENTURY
Clarke, A. Rendezvous with Rama
Cunningham, M. Specimen days
Gibson, W. Agency
Hamilton, P. Great North Road
Lai, L. The tiger flu
Morgan, R. Thirteen
Robinson, K. Green Mars
Robinson, K. New York 2140
Wilson, R. Julian Comstock
Zelazny, R. Donnerjack
2312 Robinson, K.
23RD CENTURY
Stross, C. Saturn's children
24TH CENTURY
Baker, K. In the garden of Iden
Hamilton, P. Pandora's star
Robinson, K. 2312
25TH CENTURY
Harrison, M. Light
Lafferty, M. Six wakes
Morgan, R. Altered carbon
Morgan, R. Broken angels
Palmer, A. Too like the lightning
2666 Bolano, R.
26TH CENTURY
Huxley, A. Brave new world
Reynolds, A. Revelation space
27TH CENTURY
Stross, C. Glasshouse
28TH CENTURY
Simmons, D. The fall of Hyperion
Simmons, D. Hyperion
2ND CENTURY
Downie, R. Caveat emptor

Downie, R. Medicus
Downie, R. Terra incognita
32ND CENTURY
Simmons, D. Endymion
34TH CENTURY
Hamilton, P. The dreaming void
36 arguments for the existence of God Goldstein, R.
36 righteous men Pressfield, S.
4 3 2 1 Auster, P.
The **42nd** parallel Dos Passos, J.
The **47th** samurai Hunter, S.
5TH CENTURY
Corby, G. The Pericles Commission
Llywelyn, M. After Rome
Stewart, M. The crystal cave
Stewart, M. The hollow hills
Stewart, M. The last enchantment
Stewart, M. The wicked day
5TH CENTURY BCE
Andrews, M. Of fire and lions
61 hours Child, L.
6TH CENTURY
Pike, S. The lost queen
Twain, M. A Connecticut Yankee in King Arthur's Court
The **7** 1 Turton, S.
7TH CENTURY
Griffith, N. Hild
82 Desire Smith, J.
87th Precinct mysteries [series] McBain, E.
88 names Ruff, M.
8TH CENTURY
Kay, G. Under heaven
9TH CENTURY
Cornwell, B. The last kingdom
Iggulden, C. The abbot's tale
Kay, G. The last light of the sun
Kay, G. River of stars

A

"**A**" is for alibi Grafton, S.
& sons Gilbert, D.
A **+** e 4ever Merey, I.
The **A** B C murders Christie, A.
Aaron Falk novels [series] Harper, J.
Abaddon's gate Corey, J.
ABANDONED BOYS
Greene, G. The captain and the enemy
Murr, N. The perfect man
ABANDONED CHILDREN
Bloom, A. Lucky us
Bronte, C. Emma
Chen, D. Brothers
Edwards, K. The memory keeper's daughter
Eliot, G. Silas Marner
Erdrich, L. The beet queen
Fielding, H. The history of Tom Jones, a foundling

Franck, J. Blindness of the heart
French, N. Blue Monday
Goonan, K. This shared dream
Hadley, T. The past
Holt, V. The black opal
Kingsolver, B. The bean trees
Lambert, C. The children's home
Livesey, M. Criminals
Lovesey, P. Diamond solitaire
McCaffrey, A. Acorna
Mosley, W. Blonde faith
Munier, P. A borrowing of bones
Perry, A. A breach of promise
Roy, A. The ministry of utmost happiness
Scibona, S. The volunteer
Solomon, A. Leaving Lucy Pear
Vida, V. Let the Northern Lights erase your name
Zevin, G. The storied life of A. J. Fikry

ABANDONED CHILDREN -- EASTERN EUROPE
Kosinski, J. The painted bird

ABANDONED DOGS
Cameron, W. The dogs of Christmas
Rosenfelt, D. Bark of night

ABANDONED GIRLS
Durrow, H. The girl who fell from the sky
Gilman, S. The ice cream queen of Orchard Street
Grey, Z. Woman of the frontier
Salvalaggio, K. Bone dust white

ABANDONED HOUSES
Jewell, L. The family upstairs
Straub, P. Lost boy lost girl
Wright, J. The house on Foster Hill

ABANDONED INFANTS
Armstrong, K. Alone in the wild
Burrowes, G. Lady Sophie's Christmas wish
Carr, R. Virgin river
Rivers, F. Bridge to haven
Spencer-Fleming, J. In the bleak midwinter

ABANDONED TEENAGERS
Butler, S. Cygnet
Sallis, J. The killer is dying

ABANDONED WIVES
Berg, E. We are all welcome here
Haigh, J. Mrs. Kimble
Kelly, S. The wages of desire
Starnone, D. Ties

ABANDONED WOMEN
Conde, M. The story of the cannibal woman
Long, J. The legend of Lyon Redmond
Wallace, M. The girl in the garden

ABANDONMENT (PSYCHOLOGY)
Brinkman, K. Up high in the trees
Donoghue, E. Frog music
Erdrich, L. The beet queen
Hart, J. Down river
Higgins, K. Life and other inconveniences
Hodgen, C. Elegies for the brokenhearted

Ko, L. The leavers
Lundrigan, N. Glass boys
Moore, A. The lighthouse
Nunez, E. Grace
Reid, I. I'm thinking of ending things
Stuart, D. Shuggie Bain
Trollope, J. The other family
Vlautin, W. Don't skip out on me

ABBESSES
Sharratt, M. Illuminations

Abbeville Fuller, J.

ABBEYS
Dean, A. A woman of consequence
Faber, M. The courage consort
Peters, E. The hermit of Eyton Forest
Peters, E. Monk's hood
Peters, E. The virgin in the ice

ABBEYS -- ITALY -- HISTORY
Eco, U. The name of the rose

The **abbot's** tale Iggulden, C.

ABDUCTION
James, E. Seven minutes in heaven
Lopez, J. A beautiful young woman

ABENAKI INDIANS
Shields, K. A study in revenge
Shields, K. The truth of all things

ABERDEEN, SCOTLAND
MacBride, S. Blind eye
MacBride, S. Close to the bone
MacBride, S. Cold granite
MacBride, S. Dying light
MacBride, S. Flesh house
MacBride, S. Shatter the bones
Rankin, I. Black and blue

Abigail Szabo, M.

ABILITY
Berger, T. Being invisible

ABOLITIONISTS
Banks, R. Cloudsplitter
Jakes, J. Love and war
Jakes, J. North and South
Johnson, T. Engraved on the heart
McBride, J. The good lord bird
Poyer, D. A country of our own
Robinson, M. Gilead
Unsworth, B. The quality of mercy
Wideman, J. American histories

The **abominable** Simmons, D.

ABORIGINAL AUSTRALIANS
Howarth, P. Only killers and thieves

ABORIGINAL AUSTRALIANS -- QUEENSLAND
Malouf, D. Remembering Babylon

ABORIGINAL AUSTRALIANS -- RELATIONS WITH WHITES -- 18TH CENTURY
Grenville, K. The lieutenant

ABORIGINAL AUSTRALIANS -- RELATIONS WITH WHITES -- 19TH CENTURY

Acorna McCaffrey, A.
Acorna series [series] McCaffrey, A.
Acting on impulse Sosa, M.
ACTING TEACHERS
  Choi, S. Trust exercise
ACTORS AND ACTRESSES
  Acampora, L. The paper wasp
  Alarcon, D. At night we walk in circles
  Allen, J. I lost my girlish laughter
  Antopol, M. The UnAmericans
  Armstrong, R. The don con
  Bagshawe, T. Adored
  Banville, J. Eclipse
  Banville, J. Ancient light
  Barnes, J. The somnambulist
  Benedict, M. The only woman in
    the room
  Bishop, A. Written in red
  Blatty, W. The exorcist
  Bradley, C. I am half-sick of shadows
  Bram, C. Lives of the circus animals
  Brandreth, B. The assassin of Verona
  Brandreth, B. The spy of Venice
  Brett, S. Murder unprompted
  Brookner, A. Brief lives
  Brunkhorst, A. The gilded Life of Matilda Duplaine
  Byrne, K. The hunter
  Castellani, C. Leading men
  Castile, Z. Flashed
  Davis, F. The Chelsea girls
  DeLuca, J. Well met
  Delaney, J. Believe me
  Dev, S. The Bollywood bride
  Dreiser, T. Sister Carrie
  Drury, T. Pacific
  Feeney, A. I know who you are
  Ford, J. Songs of Willow Frost
  Francis, D. Smokescreen
  Gallagher, S. The kingdom of bones
  Garrett, K. Hollywood homicide
  Goldberg, L. Fake truth
  Haddam, J. Cheating at solitaire
  Helprin, M. In sunlight and in shadow
  Jakes, J. On secret service
  James, P. The skull beneath the skin
  Kellerman, J. Private eyes
  Kerr, P. The lady from Zagreb
  Kitt, S. Celluloid memories
  L'Engle, M. Certain women
  Lee, J. The starlet and the spy
  Lessing, D. Love, again
  Lloyd, C. Death comes to the nursery
  Long, J. Hot in Hellcat Canyon
  Lovesey, P. Bertie and the seven bodies
  Mallon, T. Bandbox
  Mandel, E. Station Eleven
  Marsh, N. Light thickens

  Marston, E. The bawdy basket
  Marston, E. The devil's apprentice
  Marston, E. The roaring boy
  Marston, E. The vagabond clown
  Marston, E. The wanton angel
  Miller, A. Oxygen
  Newton, C. Start shooting
  O'Brien, T. The Lincoln conspiracy
  O'Connor, J. Ghost light
  Ondaatje, M. In the skin of a lion
  Page, K. The body in the casket
  Pamuk, O. The red-haired woman
  Pamuk, O. Snow
  Parker, L. The Austen playbook
  Parker, R. Sixkill
  Phillips, S. Heroes are my weakness
  Phillips, S. What I did for love
  Potzsch, O. The play of death
  Pyne, D. Twentynine Palms
  Rivers, F. Bridge to haven
  Rooney, S. Conversations with friends
  Sabatini, R. Scaramouche
  Sarvas, M. Memento Park
  Shepard, S. The one inside
  Smith, B. Shoot the dog
  Smith, Z. The autograph man
  Sontag, S. In America
  Sosa, M. Acting on impulse
  Spencer, S. Best served cold
  Westlake, D. Memory
  Williams, T. The Roman spring of Mrs. Stone
  Winfrey, K. Waiting for Tom Hanks
  Wolitzer, M. The Interestings
  Woods, S. The money shot
  Wouk, H. Marjorie Morningstar
  Yanagihara, H. A little life
  Yu, C. Interior Chinatown
  Zola, E. Nana
ACTORS AND ACTRESSES -- GREAT BRITAIN
  Marsh, N. False scent
Actress Enright, A.
Acts of faith Caputo, P.
Ada Nabokov, V.
Adam and evil Roberts, G.
Adam Bede Eliot, G.
Adam Dalgliesh mysteries [series] James, P.
ADAMS, HENRY, 1838-1918
  Vidal, G. Empire
ADAMS, JOHN QUINCY, 1767-1848
  Pesci, D. Amistad
ADAPTABILITY (PSYCHOLOGY)
  Levy, A. Small island
  Robinson, K. New York 2140
  Whitehead, C. Sag Harbor
ADAPTATION (BIOLOGY)
  Van Vogt, A. Slan
  Vonnegut, K. Galapagos

Bauermeister, E. The scent keeper

ADMINISTRATION OF ESTATES

Pynchon, T. The crying of lot 49

Vine, B. The minotaur

Admiral Hornblower in the West Indies Forester, C.

ADMIRATION IN MEN

Gander, F. As a friend

ADOPTED BOYS

Gander, F. As a friend

Kelton, E. The way of the coyote

Maxwell, R. The queen's bastard

Roberts, N. Sea swept

Robinson, L. Murder at the feast of rejoicing

Smith, M. Stalin's ghost

ADOPTED CHILDREN

Brown, R. Rubyfruit jungle

Eco, U. Baudolino

Forbes, C. A tall history of sugar

Ivey, E. The snow child

Mosley, W. Six Easy pieces

Patchett, A. Run

Rivers, F. Bridge to haven

Roberts, N. Chesapeake blue

Tremblay, P. The cabin at the end of the world

Trollope, J. Brother and sister

Umrigar, T. Everybody's son

Woo, S. Love love

ADOPTED CHILDREN -- JAPAN

Mishima, Y. The decay of the angel

ADOPTED GIRLS

Brennert, A. Daughter of Moloka'i

Doan, A. The summer list

Gestern, H. The people in the photo

Kittredge, W. The willow field

Morgan, S. The Christmas sisters

Muller, M. Cyanide Wells

See, L. The tea girl of Hummingbird Lane

Silko, L. Gardens in the dunes

Trollope, J. Next of kin

Veletzos, R. The girl they left behind

ADOPTED TEENAGE GIRLS

Joyce, G. The limits of enchantment

ADOPTED TEENAGERS

Roberts, N. Honest illusions

ADOPTEES

Carlson, S. Almost Graceland

Coupland, D. Eleanor Rigby

Cross-Smith, L. Whiskey & ribbons

Jacobs, N. The last equation of Isaac Severy

O'Connell, C. Mallory's oracle

Patchett, A. Run

Shaw, W. Salt lane

Stephens, A. Famous adopted people

Strout, E. Amy and Isabelle

Trollope, J. Brother and sister

ADOPTEES -- IDENTITY

James, P. Innocent blood

Parker, T. Pacific beat

Pronzini, B. Hardcase

ADOPTION

Archer, J. Best kept secret

Erdrich, L. Future home of the living god

Forman, G. Leave me

Gaitskill, M. Don't cry

Gaspar de Alba, A. Desert blood

Gilmore, J. The mothers

Ludwig, B. Ginny Moon

Lynn, A. Now you see it

Moore, L. A gate at the stairs

Ng, C. Little fires everywhere

Rodriguez, L. Every broken trust

Verghese, A. Cutting for stone

Wingate, L. Before we were yours

ADOPTION AGENCIES

Ryan, H. The wrong girl

ADOPTION OF CHINESE CHILDREN

See, L. The tea girl of Hummingbird Lane

ADOPTION POLICY

Leon, D. Unto us a son is given

ADOPTION RACKET

Atkins, A. The lost ones

Robotham, M. The night ferry

Wingate, L. Before we were yours

ADOPTION REUNIONS

Lombardo, C. The most fun we ever had

Trollope, J. Brother and sister

ADOPTIVE FAMILIES

Bauman, B. Broken sleep

Brennert, A. Daughter of Moloka'i

Ko, L. The leavers

ADOPTIVE FATHERS

Tyler, A. Saint Maybe

ADOPTIVE MOTHERS

Kingsolver, B. Pigs in heaven

O'Connell, C. Crime school

Palwick, S. Mending the moon

ADOPTIVE PARENTS

Gilmore, J. The mothers

Kohnstamm, T. Lake City

Adored Bagshawe, T.

The **Adrian** Mole diaries Townsend, S.

Adua Scego, I.

ADULT CHILD ABUSE VICTIMS

Bausch, R. Hello to the cannibals

Carlyle, C. A duke changes everything

Conroy, P. The prince of tides

Grossman, D. A horse walks into a bar

Gunday, H. The few

Harris, T. Red dragon

Koontz, D. Intensity

Monroe, M. God still don't like ugly

Oates, J. Blonde

Restrepo, L. Delirium

Roberts, N. Chesapeake blue

Cussler, C. The wrecker
Defoe, D. Robinson Crusoe
Diaz, H. In the distance
Dickens, C. Martin Chuzzlewit
Dumas, A. The count of Monte Cristo
Dumas, A. The man in the iron mask
Dumas, A. The three musketeers
Dumas, A. Twenty years after
Dunnett, D. Niccolo rising
Engelmann, K. The Stockholm octavo
Fay, K. The map of lost memories
Fleming, I. Casino royale
Fleming, I. Doctor No
Fleming, I. From Russia with love
Fleming, I. Goldfinger
Fleming, I. The man with the golden gun
Fleming, I. On Her Majesty's secret service
Fleming, I. You only live twice
Forester, C. Admiral Hornblower in the West Indies
Forester, C. The African Queen
Forester, C. Beat to quarters
Forester, C. Commodore Hornblower
Forester, C. Flying colours
Forester, C. Hornblower and the Atropos
Forester, C. Hornblower and the Hotspur
Forester, C. Lieutenant Hornblower
Forester, C. Lord Hornblower
Forester, C. Mr. Midshipman Hornblower
Forester, C. Ship of the line
Fortier, A. The lost sisterhood
Hackwith, A. The library of the unwritten
Hall, A. The quiller memorandum
Heacox, K. Jimmy Bluefeather
Hemingway, E. The snows of Kilimanjaro and other stories
Hilton, J. Lost horizon
Hope, A. The prisoner of Zenda
Johnson, C. Middle Passage
Joinson, S. A lady cyclist's guide to Kashgar
Krueger, W. This tender land
L'Amour, L. The last of the breed
L'Amour, L. May there be a road
Lambdin, D. Hostile shores
Lambdin, D. King's captain
Lansdale, J. The thicket
London, J. The call of the wild
London, J. The sea-wolf
London, J. White Fang
Lyndon, R. Hawk quest
McMurtry, L. Dead man's walk
Melville, H. Omoo
Monsarrat, N. The cruel sea
Neville, K. The eight
O'Brian, P. Blue at the mizzen
O'Brian, P. The commodore
O'Brian, P. The golden ocean
O'Brian, P. The hundred days
O'Brian, P. Master and commander

O'Brian, P. The unknown shore
O'Brian, P. The wine-dark sea
O'Brian, P. The yellow admiral
Orczy, E. The Scarlet Pimpernel
Paulits, J. Kemosabe
Pearson, R. Choke point
Pearson, R. The red room
Pearson, R. The risk agent
Perez-Reverte, A. The Club Dumas
Poyer, D. The whiteness of the whale
Preston, D. Thunderhead
Racculia, K. Tuesday Mooney talks to ghosts
Redfield, J. The celestine prophecy
Rollins, J. Crucible
Rollins, J. The demon crown
Rollins, J. The devil colony
Rollins, J. The eye of God
Rollins, J. The sixth extinction
Sabatini, R. Captain Blood
Sabatini, R. Scaramouche
Saint-Exupery, A. Night flight
Scott, W. Ivanhoe
Smith, W. Birds of prey
Smith, W. Monsoon
Verne, J. Around the world in eighty days
Verne, J. The mysterious island
Wheeler, R. The canyon of bones
Willig, L. The betrayal of the blood lily
Willig, L. The deception of the emerald ring
Willig, L. The masque of the Black Tulip
Willig, L. The orchid affair
Willig, L. The secret history of the Pink Carnation
Willig, L. The seduction of the Crimson Rose
Willig, L. The temptation of the night jasmine

ADVENTURERS
Guthrie, A. The big sky
James, E. Too Wilde to wed
James, E. Wilde in love
Kehlmann, D. Tyll
Orullian, P. The unremembered
Pratchett, T. The color of magic
Quincy, D. Murder in Mayfair
Reynolds, A. The prefect
Reynolds, A. Revenger
Simmons, D. The Terror
Tolkien, J. The hobbit, or, there and back again
Verne, J. Journey to the centre of the Earth
Verne, J. The mysterious island
Wurlitzer, R. The drop edge of yonder

ADVENTURERS -- ITALY
Calvino, I. The baron in the trees

ADVENTURERS -- SPAIN
Cervantes Saavedra, M. Don Quixote

ADVENTURERS -- UNITED STATES
Delany, S. Dhalgren

Adventures of Arabella Ashby [series] Levine, D.
The **adventures** of Augie March Bellow, S.

Tyree, O. For the love of money

AFRICAN AMERICAN ARTS

Reed, I. Mumbo jumbo

AFRICAN AMERICAN AUTHORS

Baldwin, J. Tell me how long the train's been gone

Everett, P. Erasure

Iles, G. Mississippi blood

K'wan Gangsta

Miller, K. An angry-ass black woman

Wideman, J. Fanon

AFRICAN AMERICAN AUTHORS -- 20TH CENTURY

Wright, R. Uncle Tom's children

AFRICAN AMERICAN BAIL BOND AGENTS

Greer, R. First of state

AFRICAN AMERICAN BASEBALL PLAYERS

Parker, R. Double play

AFRICAN AMERICAN BASKETBALL PLAYERS

K'wan Hoodlum

AFRICAN AMERICAN BLUES MUSICIANS

Kunzru, H. White tears

Mosley, W. RL's dream

AFRICAN AMERICAN BOOKSELLERS

Mosley, W. Fearless Jones

AFRICAN AMERICAN BOYS

Brinkley, J. A lucky man

French, A. Billy

Mosley, W. Fortunate son

AFRICAN AMERICAN BOYS -- IDENTITY

Sapphire The kid

AFRICAN AMERICAN BOYS -- KANSAS

Hughes, L. Not without laughter

Parks, G. The learning tree

AFRICAN AMERICAN BROTHERS

K'wan Hoodlum

AFRICAN AMERICAN BROTHERS AND SISTERS

Noire G-Spot

AFRICAN AMERICAN BUSINESSPEOPLE

Clark, W. Thug matrimony

Ervin, K. Mina's joint

Faye, L. The Paragon Hotel

AFRICAN AMERICAN CHIEF EXECUTIVE OFFICERS

Noire Candy licker

AFRICAN AMERICAN CHURCHES

Harris, E. I say a little prayer

AFRICAN AMERICAN CLERGY

Ellison, R. Three days before the shooting . . .

Neely, B. Blanche cleans up

Styron, W. The confessions of Nat Turner

AFRICAN AMERICAN COLLEGE FOOTBALL PLAYERS

Wolfe, T. A man in full

AFRICAN AMERICAN COLLEGE TEACHERS

Carter, S. New England white

Johnson, M. Pym

Parker, R. Hush money

AFRICAN AMERICAN COMEDIANS

Phillips, C. Dancing in the dark

AFRICAN AMERICAN COMMUNITIES

Bambara, T. The salt eaters

Bambara, T. Those bones are not my child

Bennett, B. The mothers

Cleage, P. What looks like crazy on an ordinary day

McKinney-Whetstone, D. Leaving Cecil Street

Morrison, T. Paradise

Pelecanos, G. The sweet forever

Scott, R. The world doesn't require you

Winslow, D. In West Mills

AFRICAN AMERICAN COMMUNITY LIFE

McKinney-Whetstone, D. Leaving Cecil Street

Naylor, G. The men of Brewster Place

AFRICAN AMERICAN COMMUNITY LIFE -- HARLEM, NEW YORK CITY

Petry, A. The street

AFRICAN AMERICAN COUPLES

Swinson, K. A gangster and a gentleman

Watkins, J. Secrets of a side bitch

AFRICAN AMERICAN COWBOYS

Lansdale, J. Paradise sky

AFRICAN AMERICAN COWBOYS -- THE WEST (UNITED STATES)

Durham, D. Gabriel's story

AFRICAN AMERICAN CRIMINALS

Clark, W. Honor thy thug

Clark, W. Justify my thug

Clark, W. Thug lovin'

AFRICAN AMERICAN DEFENDANTS

Faulkner, W. Intruder in the dust

AFRICAN AMERICAN DEFENDANTS -- MISSISSIPPI

Grisham, J. A time to kill

AFRICAN AMERICAN DRUG ABUSERS

JaQuavis The dopefiend

AFRICAN AMERICAN DRUG DEALERS

Woods, T. Alibi

Woods, T. True to the game

Woods, T. True to the game II

Woods, T. True to the game III

AFRICAN AMERICAN ENTERTAINERS

Phillips, C. Dancing in the dark

AFRICAN AMERICAN FAMILIES

Arnoult, D. Sufficient grace

Baldwin, J. Go tell it on the mountain

Baldwin, J. If Beale Street could talk

Baldwin, J. Just above my head

Bandele, A. Daughter

Burke, M. Team seven

Cha, S. Your house will pay

Collins, K. Notes from a black woman's diary

Collins, K. Whatever happened to interracial love?

Cross-Smith, L. Whiskey & ribbons

Dickey, E. The business of lovers

Everett, P. Suder

Flournoy, A. The Turner house

Goodwin, B. Revelation

Gray, A. The care and feeding of ravenously hungry girls

Greenidge, K. We love you, Charlie Freeman
Holmes, S. B-more careful
Hubbard, L. The talented Ribkins
Jones, T. An American marriage
Jones, T. Silver sparrow
K'wan Hoodlum
Mathis, A. The twelve tribes of Hattie
McKinney-Whetstone, D. Leaving Cecil Street
McMillan, T. It's not all downhill from here
Miller, K. An angry-ass black woman
Morrison, T. Jazz
Mosley, W. The last days of Ptolemy Grey
Onyebuchi, T. Riot baby
Parks, S. Getting mother's body
Pearson, R. A long time comin'
Porter, R. The travelers
Sexton, M. A kind of freedom
Sexton, M. The revisioners
Tademy, L. Cane River
Walker, A. The third life of Grange Copeland
Ward, J. Salvage the bones
Ward, J. Sing, unburied, sing
Watts, S. No one is coming to save us
West, D. The wedding
Williams, S. Forbidden promises
Woodson, J. Another Brooklyn
Woodson, J. Red at the bone
Yanique, T. Land of love and drowning

AFRICAN AMERICAN FAMILIES -- HISTORY
Mosley, W. The man in my basement

AFRICAN AMERICAN FAMILIES -- KANSAS
Durham, D. Gabriel's story

AFRICAN AMERICAN FAMILIES -- MISSISSIPPI
Campbell, B. Your blues ain't like mine

AFRICAN AMERICAN FATHERS AND DAUGHTERS
Monroe, M. God still don't like ugly
Mosley, W. Cinnamon kiss
Souljah,. The coldest winter ever

AFRICAN AMERICAN FATHERS AND SONS
Baldwin, J. Go tell it on the mountain
Morrison, T. Song of Solomon
Noire G-Spot

AFRICAN AMERICAN FICTION
50 Cent, (. Blow
Abdul-Jabbar, K. The empty birdcage
Abdul-Jabbar, K. Mycroft and Sherlock
Abdul-Jabbar, K. Mycroft Holmes
Anthony, M. Diary of a young girl
Antoinette, A. Butterfly
Antoinette, A. The Cartel
Antoinette, A. The Cartel 2
Antoinette, A. The Cartel 3
Antoinette, A. Murderville
Atakora, A. Conjure women
Baldwin, J. Another country
Baldwin, J. Early novels and stories
Baldwin, J. Giovanni's room

Baldwin, J. Go tell it on the mountain
Baldwin, J. Going to meet the man
Baldwin, J. If Beale Street could talk
Baldwin, J. Just above my head
Baldwin, J. Tell me how long the train's been gone
Bambara, T. Gorilla, my love
Bambara, T. The salt eaters
Bambara, T. Those bones are not my child
Bandele, A. Daughter
Barnes, S. Domino Falls
Barnett, L. Jam on the Vine
Beatty, P. The sellout
Beatty, P. Slumberland
Bennett, B. The mothers
Billingsley, R. The secret she kept
Bond, C. Ruby
Booth, C. Bronxwood
Booth, C. Kendra
Brinkley, J. A lucky man
Bryant, N. Christmas with the billionaire
Bryant, N. Madam, may I
Bryant, N. Message from a mistress
Bump, G. Everywhere you don't belong
Burke, M. Team seven
Butler, O. Adulthood rites
Butler, O. Bloodchild
Butler, O. Dawn
Butler, O. Imago
Butler, O. Kindred
Butler, O. Parable of the sower
Butler, O. Parable of the talents
Ca$h Thugs cry
Ca$h Trust no man
Ca$h Trust no man 2
Ca$h Trust no man 3
Campbell, B. Brothers and sisters
Campbell, B. Your blues ain't like mine
Capri, N. The pussy trap
Clark, W. Honor thy thug
Clark, W. Justify my thug
Clark, W. Payback ain't enough
Clark, W. Payback is a mutha
Clark, W. Payback with ya life
Clark, W. Thug lovin'
Clark, W. Thug matrimony
Clark, W. Thugs and the women who love them
Cleage, P. Some things I never thought I'd do
Cleage, P. What looks like crazy on an ordinary day
Clemmons, Z. What we lose
Coates, T. The water dancer
Cole, A. A duke by default
Cole, A. An extraordinary union
Cole, A. A hope divided
Cole, A. A prince on paper
Cole, A. A princess in theory
Cole, A. An unconditional freedom
Collins, K. Notes from a black woman's diary

Collins, K. Whatever happened to interracial love?

Crafts, H. The bondwoman's narrative

Cross-Smith, L. Whiskey & ribbons

De Leon, A. Side chick nation

Delany, S. Dhalgren

Delany, S. Stars in my pocket like grains of sand

Delany, S. Aye, and Gomorrah

Diamond, D. Boss divas

Diamond, D. Gangsta divas

Diamond, D. King divas

Diamond, D. Street divas

Dickey, E. Bad men and wicked women

Dickey, E. Before we were wicked

Dickey, E. The blackbirds

Dickey, E. The business of lovers

Dickey, E. Finding Gideon

Draper, S. Forged by fire

DuPree, K. Shattered

Due, T. Ghost summer

Durham, D. Gabriel's story

Ellison, R. Invisible man

Ellison, R. Three days before the shooting . . .

Ervin, K. Gunz and roses

Ervin, K. Mina's joint

Everett, P. Erasure

Everett, P. God's country

Everett, P. I am Not Sidney Poitier

Everett, P. Percival Everett by Virgil Russell

Everett, P. Suder

Flournoy, A. The Turner house

French, A. Billy

Gaines, E. The autobiography of Miss Jane Pittman

Gaines, E. A gathering of old men

Garrett, K. Hollywood homicide

Gay, R. Ayiti

Goodwin, B. Revelation

Gray, A. The care and feeding of ravenously hungry girls

Gray, E. Love & a gangsta

Greenidge, K. We love you, Charlie Freeman

Greer, R. First of state

Guillory, J. The proposal

Guillory, J. Royal holiday

Guillory, J. The wedding date

Guillory, J. The wedding party

Gyasi, Y. Homegoing

Hampton, B. Stalker

Hannaham, J. Delicious foods

Harris, E. Basketball Jones

Harris, E. I say a little prayer

Harris, E. Invisible life

Harris, E. Not a day goes by

Haywood, G. Cemetery Road

Himes, C. Cotton comes to Harlem

Hobbs, A. Stealing candy

Hodges, C. Rumor has it

Holmes, J. How are you going to save yourself

Holmes, S. B-more careful

Holmes, S. Bad girlz

Howard, R. Driving the king

Hughes, L. Not without laughter

Hughes, L. Short stories

Hughes, L. Simple speaks his mind

Hurston, Z. Hitting a straight lick with a crooked stick

Hurston, Z. Their eyes were watching God

JaQuavis The dopefiend

JaQuavis The dopeman's wife

JaQuavis The streets have no king

Jackson, B. Forged in desire

Jemisin, N. The fifth season

Jemisin, N. How long 'til black future month?

Jemisin, N. The hundred thousand kingdoms

Jemisin, N. The killing moon

Jemisin, N. The obelisk gate

Jemisin, N. The stone sky

Jenkins, B. Breathless

Jenkins, B. Forbidden

Jenkins, B. Rebel

Jenkins, B. Tempest

Johnson, A. The first part last

Johnson, C. Middle Passage

Johnson, R. No one in the world

Jones, E. The known world

Jones, T. An American marriage

Jones, T. Silver sparrow

Joseph, F. Niya

K'wan Animal

K'wan Animal II

K'wan The Diamond empire

K'wan Gangsta

K'wan Gutter

K'wan Hoodlum

K'wan Lawless

K'wan Revelations

K'wan Section 8

K'wan Street dreams

K'wan Welfare wifeys

King, D. Bitch

Kitt, S. Celluloid memories

LaValle, V. The devil in silver

Little, T. Where there's smoke

Locke, A. Bluebird, bluebird

Locke, A. Heaven, my home

McBride, J. Deacon King Kong

McBride, J. Five-carat soul

McBride, J. The good lord bird

McBride, J. Song yet sung

McKinney-Whetstone, D. Leaving Cecil Street

McMillan, T. How Stella got her groove back

McMillan, T. It's not all downhill from here

McMillan, T. Waiting to exhale

Mengestu, D. The beautiful things that heaven bears

Mengestu, D. How to read the air

Mengiste, M. The shadow king

Miller, K. An angry-ass black woman

Thompson-Spires, N. Heads of the colored people
Turner, N. The Banks sisters
Turner, N. Black widow
Turner, N. Forever a hustler's wife
Turner, N. Heartbreak of a hustler's wife
Turner, N. A hustler's wife
Turner, N. Natural born hustler
Tyree, O. Flyy girl
Tyree, O. For the love of money
Tyree, O. Leslie
Vernon, O. A killing in this town
Walker, A. The color purple
Walker, A. Possessing the secret of joy
Walker, A. The temple of my familiar
Walker, A. The third life of Grange Copeland
Walker, A. You can't keep a good woman down
Walker, M. Jubilee
Ward, J. Salvage the bones
Ward, J. Sing, unburied, sing
Warren, T. Her secret life
Warren, T. The replacement wife
Washington, B. Lot
Watkins, J. Secrets of a side bitch
Watkins, J. Secrets of a side bitch 2
Watts, S. No one is coming to save us
Weatherspoon, R. A cowboy to remember
Weatherspoon, R. Haven
Weber, C. Man on the run
West, D. The wedding
White, S. Tears of a hustler
White, S. Tears of a hustler 2
Whitehead, C. Apex hides the hurt
Whitehead, C. John Henry Days
Whitehead, C. The intuitionist
Whitehead, C. The Nickel boys
Whitehead, C. Sag Harbor
Whitehead, C. The underground railroad
Whitehead, C. Zone one
Wideman, J. American histories
Wideman, J. Fanon
Wilkinson, L. American spy
Williams, K. Dirty to the grave
Williams, K. Harlem on lock
Williams, K. Sweet Giselle
Williams, S. Forbidden promises
Winslow, D. In West Mills
Woods, T. Alibi
Woods, T. Dutch
Woods, T. True to the game
Woods, T. True to the game II
Woods, T. True to the game III
Woodson, J. Another Brooklyn
Woodson, J. Red at the bone
Wright, R. Eight men
Wright, R. Native son
Wright, R. Uncle Tom's children
Zane Addicted

AFRICAN AMERICAN FOOTBALL PLAYERS
Martin, A. Blitzed
AFRICAN AMERICAN FORMER CONVICTS
K'wan Street dreams
Sexton, M. A kind of freedom
AFRICAN AMERICAN FOSTER CHILDREN
Bohjalian, C. The buffalo soldier
AFRICAN AMERICAN FUGITIVES
Crumley, J. The final country
AFRICAN AMERICAN GANGS
K'wan Gangsta
K'wan Gutter
AFRICAN AMERICAN GAY MEN
Baldwin, J. Another country
Baldwin, J. Early novels and stories
Everett, P. Erasure
Harris, E. Basketball Jones
Harris, E. I say a little prayer
Lansdale, J. Honky tonk samurai
Lansdale, J. Vanilla Ride
Mathis, A. The twelve tribes of Hattie
Taylor, B. Real life
AFRICAN AMERICAN GIRLS
Bambara, T. Gorilla, my love
Finley, J. The dark above
Monroe, M. God don't like ugly
Morrison, T. The bluest eye
Morrison, T. A mercy
Solomon, A. Disgruntled
Tyree, O. Flyy girl
Woodson, J. Another Brooklyn
AFRICAN AMERICAN GIRLS -- SOUTH CAROLINA
Sanders, D. Clover
AFRICAN AMERICAN GRANDFATHERS
Toole, F. Pound for pound
**AFRICAN AMERICAN GRANDMOTHER AND GRAND-
DAUGHTER**
Rhodes, J. Voodoo dreams
AFRICAN AMERICAN HOUSEHOLD EMPLOYEES
Neely, B. Blanche cleans up
AFRICAN AMERICAN HUSBAND AND WIFE
Pitts, L. Freeman
**AFRICAN AMERICAN INTELLECTUALS -- MARTHA'S
VINEYARD, MASSACHUSETTS**
West, D. The wedding
AFRICAN AMERICAN JANITORS
Mosley, W. A little yellow dog
Mosley, W. Six Easy pieces
AFRICAN AMERICAN JOURNALISTS
Johnson, M. Incognegro
Mosley, W. Down the river unto the sea
**AFRICAN AMERICAN JOURNALISTS -- WEST VIR-
GINIA**
Whitehead, C. John Henry Days
AFRICAN AMERICAN LAWYERS
Harris, E. Invisible life
Noire Candy licker

Dickey, E. The blackbirds
Ervin, K. Gunz and roses
Harris, E. Not a day goes by
Hodges, C. Rumor has it
Hurston, Z. Their eyes were watching God
JaQuavis The dopeman's wife
K'wan Street dreams
McMillan, T. Waiting to exhale
Monroe, M. God still don't like ugly
Morrison, T. Jazz
Morrison, T. Love
Morrison, T. Paradise
Noire Candy licker
Noire G-Spot
Stringer, V. Dirty Red
Swinson, K. A gangster and a gentleman
Swinson, K. Who's wife extraordinaire now
Turner, N. A hustler's wife
Walker, A. The temple of my familiar
Weber, C. Man on the run
Williams, K. Dirty to the grave
Williams, K. Sweet Giselle
Woods, T. True to the game II
Woods, T. True to the game III
Zane, 1. Addicted

AFRICAN AMERICAN MOTHERS
Morrison, T. Sula

AFRICAN AMERICAN MOTHERS AND DAUGHTERS
Butler, O. Parable of the sower
Butler, O. Parable of the talents

AFRICAN AMERICAN MURDER SUSPECTS
Brooks, B. Frontier justice
Mosley, W. A little yellow dog

AFRICAN AMERICAN MUSICIANS
McKinney-Whetstone, D. Leaving Cecil Street
Walker, A. The temple of my familiar

AFRICAN AMERICAN NEIGHBORHOODS
Anderson, K. Green sun

AFRICAN AMERICAN NEWSPAPERS
Barnett, L. Jam on the Vine

AFRICAN AMERICAN PHYSICIANS
Rush, N. Mortals

AFRICAN AMERICAN PLANTATION OWNERS
Jones, E. The known world

AFRICAN AMERICAN POETRY
Sapphire, 1. American dreams

AFRICAN AMERICAN POLICE
Ball, J. In the heat of the night
Cross-Smith, L. Whiskey & ribbons
Pearl, M. The Dante Club

AFRICAN AMERICAN POLICE -- WASHINGTON, D.C.
Pelecanos, G. Hard revolution
Pelecanos, G. Hell to pay
Pelecanos, G. Soul circus

AFRICAN AMERICAN POLICEWOMEN
Grecian, A. The saint of wolves and butchers

AFRICAN AMERICAN POLITICAL ACTIVISTS

Parker, R. Hush money

AFRICAN AMERICAN PRISONERS
Grisham, J. The guardians
Hunter, S. Pale horse coming
Pelecanos, G. The man who came uptown
Wideman, J. Fanon

AFRICAN AMERICAN PSYCHOLOGISTS
Patterson, J. Along came a spider
Patterson, J. Kiss the girls

AFRICAN AMERICAN SCIENTISTS
Kingsolver, B. Flight behavior

AFRICAN AMERICAN SENIOR MEN
Gaines, E. A gathering of old men
Toole, F. Pound for pound

AFRICAN AMERICAN SENIOR WOMEN
Naylor, G. Mama Day
Odell, J. The healing

AFRICAN AMERICAN SENIORS
Mosley, W. The last days of Ptolemy Grey
Walker, A. The temple of my familiar

AFRICAN AMERICAN SINGERS
Harris, E. I say a little prayer
Howard, R. Driving the king

AFRICAN AMERICAN SINGLE MOTHERS
Bambara, T. Those bones are not my child
K'wan Section 8
Stringer, V. Let that be the reason

AFRICAN AMERICAN SISTERS
Cleage, P. What looks like crazy on an ordinary day

AFRICAN AMERICAN SLAVEHOLDERS
Jones, E. The known world

AFRICAN AMERICAN SOLDIERS
Burdett, J. Bangkok 8
Cobbs Hoffman, E. The Tubman command

AFRICAN AMERICAN STEPBROTHERS AND STEPSIS-TERS
Draper, S. Forged by fire

AFRICAN AMERICAN STEPFATHERS
Draper, S. Forged by fire

AFRICAN AMERICAN TEENAGE BOYS
Booth, C. Bronxwood
Bump, G. Everywhere you don't belong
DeLillo, D. Underworld
Draper, S. Forged by fire
Johnson, A. The first part last
Styles, T. A hustler's son
Whitehead, C. The Nickel boys
Whitehead, C. Sag Harbor

AFRICAN AMERICAN TEENAGE BOYS -- MISSISSIPPI
Campbell, B. Your blues ain't like mine

AFRICAN AMERICAN TEENAGE GIRLS
Booth, C. Kendra
Johnson, K. Little black girl lost
Johnson, K. Little black girl lost 2
Jones, T. Silver sparrow
McKinney-Whetstone, D. Leaving Cecil Street
Morrison, T. Jazz

Swinson, K. Lifestyles of the rich and shameless
Swinson, K. The safe house
Swinson, K. Wifey
Swinson, K. Wifey's next sticky situation
T. I. Power & Beauty
T. I. Trouble & triumph
Tademy, L. Cane River
Turner, N. The Banks sisters
Turner, N. Black widow
Turner, N. Forever a hustler's wife
Walker, A. Possessing the secret of joy
Walker, A. The temple of my familiar
Walker, A. You can't keep a good woman down
Warren, T. Her secret life
Watkins, J. Secrets of a side bitch 2
Weatherspoon, R. Rafe
Weatherspoon, R. Xeni
West, D. The wedding
Wilkinson, L. American spy
Winslow, D. In West Mills
Woods, T. True to the game
Woods, T. True to the game II
Woods, T. True to the game III
Zane, Addicted

AFRICAN AMERICAN WOMEN -- FRIENDSHIP
Clark, W. Payback ain't enough
Clark, W. Payback is a mutha
Clark, W. Payback with ya life
Hurston, Z. Their eyes were watching God
McMillan, T. How Stella got her groove back
McMillan, T. Waiting to exhale
Morrison, T. Sula
Perkins-Valdez, D. Wench
Williams, K. Dirty to the grave

AFRICAN AMERICAN WOMEN -- IDENTITY
Hurston, Z. Their eyes were watching God
Larsen, N. Passing
Reid, K. Such a fun age
Whitehead, C. The intuitionist

AFRICAN AMERICAN WOMEN -- INTERPERSONAL RELATIONS
Styles, T. Redbone

AFRICAN AMERICAN WOMEN -- NEW ORLEANS, LOUISIANA
Smith, J. Louisiana hotshot

AFRICAN AMERICAN WOMEN -- PHILADELPHIA, PENNSYLVANIA
Holmes, S. Bad girlz
Tyree, O. For the love of money

AFRICAN AMERICAN WOMEN -- PSYCHOLOGY
Deon, N. Grace

AFRICAN AMERICAN WOMEN -- PSYCHOTHERAPY
Walker, A. Possessing the secret of joy

AFRICAN AMERICAN WOMEN -- SOUTH CAROLINA
Kidd, S. The secret life of bees

AFRICAN AMERICAN WOMEN -- SOUTHERN STATES
Walker, A. The color purple

AFRICAN AMERICAN WOMEN -- SPIRITUAL LIFE
Hurston, Z. Their eyes were watching God

AFRICAN AMERICAN WOMEN COLLEGE STUDENTS
Tyree, O. Leslie

AFRICAN AMERICAN WOMEN FILM PRODUCERS AND DIRECTORS
Tyree, O. For the love of money

AFRICAN AMERICAN WOMEN INVESTMENT ADVISERS
McMillan, T. How Stella got her groove back

AFRICAN AMERICAN WOMEN JOURNALISTS
Barnett, L. Jam on the Vine

AFRICAN AMERICAN WOMEN LAWYERS
Clark, W. Thug matrimony
Whitlow, R. A time to stand

AFRICAN AMERICAN WOMEN POETS -- NEW ORLEANS, LOUISIANA
Smith, J. Louisiana hotshot

AFRICAN AMERICAN WOMEN SCREENWRITERS
Tyree, O. For the love of money

AFRICAN AMERICAN WOMEN WITH HIV
Cleage, P. What looks like crazy on an ordinary day

AFRICAN AMERICAN WOMEN WITH MENTAL ILLNESSES
Walker, A. Possessing the secret of joy

AFRICAN AMERICAN WORLD WAR II VETERANS
Mosley, W. Bad boy Brawly Brown
Mosley, W. Devil in a blue dress

AFRICAN AMERICAN YOUNG MEN
50 Cent Blow
Ca$h Trust no man
Ca$h Trust no man 2
Ca$h Trust no man 3
K'wan Hoodlum
K'wan Street dreams
Mosley, W. Gone fishin'
Sexton, M. A kind of freedom

AFRICAN AMERICAN YOUNG WOMEN
Holmes, S. B-more careful
K'wan Street dreams
Monroe, M. God still don't like ugly
Turner, N. A hustler's wife
Woods, T. True to the game
Woods, T. True to the game II
Woods, T. True to the game III

AFRICAN AMERICANS
Adjei-Brenyah, N. Friday black
Antoinette, A. Murderville
Aswani, A. Chicago
Atakora, A. Conjure women
Baldwin, J. Another country
Baldwin, J. Early novels and stories
Baldwin, J. Going to meet the man
Bambara, T. Gorilla, my love
Bambara, T. The salt eaters
Bambara, T. Those bones are not my child

Bandele, A. Daughter
Beatty, P. The sellout
Beatty, P. Slumberland
Benz, C. The gone dead
Berg, E. We are all welcome here
Bond, C. Ruby
Booth, C. Kendra
Bryant, N. Message from a mistress
Ca$h Thugs cry
Capri, N. The pussy trap
Carter, S. Back channel
Clark, W. Payback ain't enough
Collins, K. Whatever happened to interracial love?
Cush, J. Endangered
DeLillo, D. Underworld
Dickey, E. Bad men and wicked women
Doctorow, E. Ragtime
DuPree, K. Shattered
Ellison, R. Invisible man
Ervin, K. Gunz and roses
Eskens, A. Nothing more dangerous
Everyday people
Faulkner, W. The sound and the fury
Faye, L. The Paragon Hotel
Flournoy, A. The Turner house
Garrett, K. Hollywood homicide
Gray, E. Love & a gangsta
Gyasi, Y. Homegoing
Harris, E. I say a little prayer
Holmes, S. B-more careful
Hughes, L. Simple speaks his mind
Hurston, Z. Hitting a straight lick with a crooked stick
Ide, J. Hi five
JaQuavis The dopeman's wife
Jackson, B. Forged in desire
Jemisin, N. How long 'til black future month?
Jen, G. The resisters
Jenkins, B. Breathless
Jenkins, B. Forbidden
Jenkins, B. Rebel
Jenkins, B. Tempest
Johnson, A. The first part last
Johnson, M. Pym
Johnson, R. No one in the world
Jones, E. The known world
Jones, T. An American marriage
K'wan Animal
K'wan Animal II
K'wan The Diamond empire
K'wan Diamonds and Pearl
K'wan The fix
K'wan Gangsta
K'wan Hoodlum
K'wan Lawless
K'wan Revelations
K'wan Welfare wifeys
LaValle, V. The changeling

Lee, H. To kill a mockingbird
Leveen, L. The secrets of Mary Bowser
Luesse, V. Missing Isaac
McFadden, B. The Book of Harlan
Monroe, M. Bad blood
Morrison, T. The bluest eye
Morrison, T. Home
Morrison, T. Paradise
Mullen, T. Darktown
Mullen, T. Lightning men
Mychea He loves me, he loves you not
Naylor, G. Bailey's Cafe
Nelscott, K. Stone cribs
Newman, S. The country of Ice Cream Star
Oates, J. Because it is bitter, and because it is my heart
Oyeyemi, H. Boy, Snow, Bird
Pelecanos, G. The sweet forever
Petrie, N. Tear it down
Price, R. Freedomland
Rawles, N. My Jim
Reed, I. Flight to Canada
Reed, I. Mumbo jumbo
Sapphire Push
Sapphire The kid
Scott, R. The world doesn't require you
Stowe, H. Uncle Tom's cabin
Stringer, V. Dirty Red
Stringer, V. Let that be the reason
Tamirat, N. The parking lot attendant
Thompson-Spires, N. Heads of the colored people
Turner, N. Black widow
Turner, N. Forever a hustler's wife
Turner, N. Heartbreak of a hustler's wife
Turner, N. A hustler's wife
Turner, N. Natural born hustler
Walker, A. The temple of my familiar
Walker, M. Jubilee
Wallace, D. Mr. Sebastian and the Negro magician
Watkins, J. Secrets of a side bitch
Watkins, J. Secrets of a side bitch 2
Watts, S. No one is coming to save us
West, D. The wedding
White, S. Tears of a hustler
White, S. Tears of a hustler 2
Wideman, J. Fanon
Wideman, J. American histories
Williams, K. Harlem on lock
Williams, K. Sweet Giselle
Woods, T. Alibi
Wright, R. Native son
Yanique, T. Land of love and drowning
Zane Addicted

AFRICAN AMERICANS -- CIVIL RIGHTS
Naslund, S. Four spirits
Yarbrough, S. Safe from the neighbors
AFRICAN AMERICANS -- CIVIL RIGHTS -- HISTORY
Gaines, E. The autobiography of Miss Jane Pittman

AFRICAN AMERICANS -- DRUG USE
Little, T. Where there's smoke

AFRICAN AMERICANS -- HARLEM, NEW YORK CITY
Petry, A. The street

AFRICAN AMERICANS -- HISTORY
Rutland, E. No crystal stair

AFRICAN AMERICANS -- IDENTITY
Ellison, R. Three days before the shooting . . .
Morrison, T. Song of Solomon
Naylor, G. Linden Hills
Roth, P. The human stain
Walker, A. The temple of my familiar
Whitehead, C. The Nickel boys
Woodson, J. Another Brooklyn

AFRICAN AMERICANS -- MIGRATIONS
Colvin, J. Africaville

AFRICAN AMERICANS -- MIGRATIONS -- HISTORY -- 20TH CENTURY
Mathis, A. The twelve tribes of Hattie

AFRICAN AMERICANS -- MISSISSIPI
Vernon, O. A killing in this town

AFRICAN AMERICANS -- NORTH CAROLINA
Maron, M. Storm track

AFRICAN AMERICANS -- SOCIAL CONDITIONS
Collins, K. Notes from a black woman's diary
Porter, R. The travelers

AFRICAN AMERICANS -- SOCIAL CONDITIONS -- 19TH CENTURY
Coates, T. The water dancer
Lansdale, J. Paradise sky
Whitehead, C. The underground railroad

AFRICAN AMERICANS -- SOCIAL CONDITIONS -- TO 1964
Howard, R. Driving the king

AFRICAN AMERICANS -- SOCIAL LIFE AND CUSTOMS
Hughes, L. Short stories

AFRICAN AMERICANS -- SOCIAL LIFE AND CUSTOMS -- 20TH CENTURY
Reed, I. Mumbo jumbo

AFRICAN AMERICANS -- SOUTH CAROLINA
Naylor, G. Mama Day

AFRICAN AMERICANS -- SOUTHERN STATES
Wright, R. Uncle Tom's children

AFRICAN AMERICANS -- SOUTHERN STATES -- HISTORY -- 20TH CENTURY
Johnson, M. Incognegro

AFRICAN AMERICANS IN GERMANY
Beatty, P. Slumberland

AFRICAN BRAZILIANS
Updike, J. Brazil

AFRICAN DIASPORA
Gay, R. Ayiti
Scego, I. Adua
The **African** Queen Forester, C.

AFRICAN RESISTANCE AND REVOLTS
Phillips, C. A distant shore

AFRICAN WEST INDIAN WOMEN
Conde, M. I, Tituba, Black witch of Salem

AFRICAN-AMERICAN ACTORS AND ACTRESSES
Mosley, W. Debbie doesn't do it anymore

AFRICAN-AMERICAN COLLEGE PRESIDENTS
Carter, S. New England white

AFRICAN-AMERICAN DEATH ROW PRISONERS
Katzenbach, J. Just cause

AFRICAN-AMERICAN HOMELESS WOMEN
McKinney-Whetstone, D. Leaving Cecil Street

AFRICAN-AMERICAN MEN/WOMEN RELATIONS
Warren, T. The replacement wife

AFRICAN-AMERICAN MOTIVATIONAL SPEAKERS
Cleage, P. Some things I never thought I'd do

AFRICAN-AMERICAN NEIGHBORHOODS
Miller, K. An angry-ass black woman

AFRICAN-AMERICAN POLICEWOMEN
Solomita, S. A good day to die

AFRICAN-AMERICAN SPORTS AGENTS
Harris, E. Not a day goes by

AFRICAN-AMERICAN TENANT FARMERS
Walker, A. The third life of Grange Copeland

AFRICAN-AMERICAN WOMEN
Hampton, B. Stalker
Swinson, K. Who's wife extraordinaire now

AFRICAN-AMERICAN WOMEN BEEKEEPERS -- SOUTH CAROLINA
Kidd, S. The secret life of bees

AFRICAN-AMERICAN WOMEN COOKS
Lansdale, J. A fine dark line

AFRICAN-LATIN AMERICANS
Sosa, M. The worst best man

AFRICAN-NATIVE AMERICAN GIRLS
Dorris, M. Cloud chamber
Dorris, M. A yellow raft in blue water

AFRICANS
Couto, M. Sleepwalking land

AFRICANS IN FOREIGN COUNTRIES
Erpenbeck, J. Go, went, gone

AFRICANS IN GREAT BRITAIN
Phillips, C. A distant shore
Phillips, C. Foreigners

AFRICANS IN ITALY
Leon, D. Blood from a stone

AFRICANS IN THE UNITED STATES
Bulawayo, N. We need new names
Mengestu, D. All our names
Pesci, D. Amistad

Africaville Colvin, J.

AFRICVILLE (HALIFAX, NS)
Colvin, J. Africaville

AFRIKANER MEN
McClure, J. The steam pig

AFRIKANERS
Michener, J. The covenant

AFRIKANERS -- SOUTH AFRICA
Nunn, M. A beautiful place to die

LaPlante, A. Turn of mind

Leithauser, B. The promise of elsewhere

Lessing, D. The sweetest dream

Mann, T. The black swan

Maupassant, G. Like death

McFarlane, F. The night guest

McMillan, T. It's not all downhill from here

Mosley, W. The last days of Ptolemy Grey

O'Nan, S. Emily, alone

O'Nan, S. Henry, himself

Rankin, I. Rather be the devil

Rooney, K. Lillian Boxfish takes a walk

Roth, P. The dying animal

Roth, P. Everyman

Roth, P. Exit ghost

Roth, P. Sabbath's theater

Simonson, H. Major Pettigrew's last stand

Smith, A. Autumn

Steinbeck, J. The long valley

Straub, E. Modern lovers

Tawada, Y. The emissary

Ullmann, L. Unquiet

Updike, J. Licks of love

Updike, J. My father's tears and other stories

Updike, J. Seek my face

Van Booy, S. The illusion of separateness

Wilde, O. The picture of Dorian Gray

Woolf, V. The waves

Yanagihara, H. The people in the trees

AGING -- PREVENTION
Ludlum, R. The Sigma protocol

AGING -- PSYCHOLOGICAL ASPECTS
McMurtry, L. The evening star

Tyler, A. Noah's compass

The **agony** and the ecstasy Stone, I.

AGORAPHOBIA
Finn, A. The woman in the window

Stout, R. The doorbell rang

Stout, R. Gambit

AGORAPHOBIA IN WOMEN
Hoffman, A. Illumination night

Lehane, D. Since we fell

Reynolds, M. The Starlite Drive-in

Semple, M. Where'd you go, Bernadette

AGRIBUSINESS
Bacigalupi, P. The windup girl

Hiaasen, C. Skinny dip

AGRICULTURAL LABORERS
Daisley, S. Coming rain

Goldman, W. The princess bride

Steinbeck, J. Of mice and men

AGRICULTURE
Reddi, R. Passage west

The **Aguero** sisters Garcia, C.

Ah, but your land is beautiful Paton, A.

Ahab's wife, or, the star gazer Naslund, S.

Aiding & abetting Spark, M.

AIDS (DISEASE)
Brunt, C. Tell the wolves I'm home

Cassara, J. The house of impossible beauties

Kramer, L. Search for my heart

Lessing, D. The sweetest dream

Makkai, R. The great believers

Nava, M. Carved in bone

Winman, S. Tin man

Yan, L. Dream of Ding Village

AIDS (DISEASE) -- STUDY AND TEACHING
D'Souza, T. Whiteman

AIDS AND SEXUALITY
Irving, J. In one person

AIDS CAREGIVERS
Cunningham, M. The hours

Aimee Leduc investigations [series] Black, C.

AIR BASES -- GREECE
Cussler, C. The Mediterranean caper

AIR FORCE SPOUSES
Bausch, R. Rebel powers

AIR MAIL SERVICE
Saint-Exupery, A. Night flight

AIR TRAVEL
Flight or fright

AIR WARFARE
Michener, J. The bridges at Toko-Ri

Shaara, J. The rising tide

The **air** you breathe Peebles, F.

AIRLINES
Lathen, E. Something in the air

AIRMEN
Cotterill, C. Slash and burn

Heller, J. Catch-22

AIRPLANE ACCIDENT INVESTIGATION
Haynes, D. Crashers

AIRPLANE ACCIDENTS
Blume, J. In the unlikely event

Bohjalian, C. The night strangers

Center, K. How to walk away

Hawley, N. Before the fall

Kelly, J. The fire baby

L'Amour, L. The last of the breed

MacDonald, P. The list of Adrian Messenger

Michener, J. The bridges at Toko-Ri

Muller, M. Both ends of the night

Napolitano, A. Dear Edward

Owen, H. The devil's triangle

Parrish, C. Still life

Paul, B. Under Tower Peak

Richler, M. Solomon Gursky was here

Saint-Exupery, A. Night flight

Smith, S. A simple plan

Stabenow, D. No fixed line

AIRPLANE BOMBINGS -- IRELAND
Shreve, A. The pilot's wife

AIRPLANES
Flight or fright

Morris, M. Songs in ordinary time

ALCOHOLIC MEN

Baker, D. Young man with a horn
Bayard, L. The pale blue eye
Block, L. All the flowers are dying
Block, L. A drop of the hard stuff
Block, L. Eight million ways to die
Block, L. The sins of the fathers
Block, L. A ticket to the boneyard
Block, L. When the sacred ginmill closes
Box, C. The highway
Breslin, J. Table money
Bronte, A. The tenant of Wildfell Hall
Bruen, K. The guards
Deutermann, P. Pacific glory
Dovlatov, S. Pushkin Hills
Fowler, E. The road to Cardinal Valley
Geagley, B. Year of the hyenas
Karunatilaka, S. The legend of Pradeep Mathew
Kennedy, W. Ironweed
King, S. Cujo
Lansdale, J. A fine dark line
MacLaverty, B. Midwinter break
McDermott, A. Charming Billy
Meyer, D. Devil's peak
Nesbo, J. The redbreast
Parker, R. Night passage
Percy, W. Love in the ruins
Portis, C. True grit
Richler, M. Solomon Gursky was here
Robinson, M. Home
Smiley, J. A thousand acres

ALCOHOLIC MOTHERS

Crane, S. Maggie
Lodato, V. Mathilda Savitch

ALCOHOLIC POLICE

Nesbo, J. The redbreast

ALCOHOLIC PRIESTS

Greene, G. The power and the glory

ALCOHOLIC VETERANS

Chandler, R. The long goodbye

ALCOHOLIC WOMEN

Barnes, J. The only story
Blackstock, T. Smoke screen
Bohjalian, C. The flight attendant
Clement, J. Prayers for the stolen
Doyle, R. The woman who walked into doors
Haigh, J. Mrs. Kimble
Hawkins, P. The girl on the train
Hiaasen, C. Star Island
Jerkins, G. The ninth step
Johnson, D. Nobody move
Mda, Z. The whale caller
Merbeth, K. Fortuna
Mortimer, J. Quite honestly
Spencer-Fleming, J. Hid from our eyes
Updike, J. Rabbit, run

ALCOHOLICS

Cheever, J. The Wapshot scandal
Crumley, J. Bordersnakes
Crumley, J. The final country
Crumley, J. The last good kiss
Crumley, J. The wrong case
Doiron, P. The poacher's son
Fitzgerald, F. The beautiful and damned
Geagley, B. Year of the hyenas
Harrison, J. The great leader
Jackson, C. The lost weekend
King, S. The shining
Lowry, M. Under the volcano
McDermott, A. Charming Billy
Ryan, J. Restless rancher
Varley, J. Red thunder
Vollmann, W. The rainbow stories

ALCOHOLICS -- CALIFORNIA

Rivers, F. And the shofar blew

ALCOHOLISM

Burke, J. Robicheaux
Ellis, B. Lunar Park
Ford, J. The shadow year
Fowler, T. Z
Holbert, B. Whiskey
Jackson, C. The lost weekend
Jones, S. The outcast
Parini, J. The passages of H.M.
Peterson, T. What comes my way
Roth, P. When she was good
Stuart, D. Shuggie Bain

ALCOHOLISM -- INTERVENTION

Fowler, E. The road to Cardinal Valley

ALEPPO, SYRIA

Demirtas, S. Dawn

ALEUT WOMEN

Stabenow, D. A deeper sleep
Stabenow, D. A fine and bitter snow
Stabenow, D. A grave denied
Stabenow, D. Hunter's moon
Stabenow, D. Killing grounds
Stabenow, D. Less than a treason
Stabenow, D. A night too dark
Stabenow, D. No fixed line
Stabenow, D. Restless in the grave
Stabenow, D. The singing of the dead
Stabenow, D. A taint in the blood
Stabenow, D. Though not dead
Stabenow, D. Whisper to the blood

ALEUTS

Stabenow, D. Less than a treason

Alex Benedict novels [series] McDevitt, J.
Alex Cross novels [series] Patterson, J.
Alex Delaware novels [series] Kellerman, J.
Alex Morrow novels [series] Mina, D.
Alexander Cleave trilogy [series]
Banville, J.

Alexander Hawke thrillers [series] Bell, T.
Alexander the Great trilogy (Mary Renault) [series] Renault, M.
ALEXANDER VI,, POPE, 1431-1503
 Poole, S. The Borgia mistress
ALEXANDER,, THE GREAT, 356-323 BC
 Lyon, A. The sweet girl
 Renault, M. Funeral games
 Renault, M. The Persian boy
Alexandra Cooper novels [series] Fairstein, L.
Alexandra Cupidi novels [series] Shaw, W.
Alexandria quartet [series] Durrell, L.
ALEXANDRIA, EGYPT
 Durrell, L. Justine
 Roiphe, A. An imperfect lens
ALEXANDRIA, EGYPT -- HISTORY -- 1900-1945
 Durrell, L. Balthazar
 Durrell, L. Clea
 Durrell, L. Mountolive
ALFRED,, KING OF ENGLAND, 849-899
 Cornwell, B. The last kingdom
 Iggulden, C. The abbot's tale
ALGAE
 Bunn, T. Outbreak
ALGERIA
 Adimi, K. Our riches
 Boudjedra, R. The Barbary figs
 Camus, A. The plague
 Camus, A. The stranger
 Daoud, K. The Meursault investigation
 Neville, K. The eight
ALGERIA -- HISTORY -- REVOLUTION, 1954-1962
 Boudjedra, R. The Barbary figs
ALGIERS, ALGERIA
 Adimi, K. Our riches
ALGONQUIAN INDIANS -- CHESAPEAKE BAY REGION -- HISTORY -- 14TH CENTURY
 Gear, K. People of the mist
ALGONQUIAN INDIANS -- SOCIAL LIFE AND CUSTOMS -- 14TH CENTURY
 Gear, K. People of the mist
Alias Grace Atwood, M.
ALIBI
 Harper, J. The dry
 Ryan, H. Say no more
 Woods, T. Alibi
Alibi Woods, T.
Alice & Oliver Bock, C.
Alice Adams Tarkington, B.
Alice I have been Benjamin, M.
Alice in exile Read, P.
Alice in jeopardy McBain, E.
Alice Vega novels [series] Luna, L.
ALIEN ARTIFACTS
 Brin, D. Existence
 Clarke, A. 2001
 Clarke, A. The collected stories of Arthur C. Clarke

 Clarke, A. Rendezvous with Rama
 Corey, J. Babylon's ashes
 McDevitt, J. The Cassandra Project
 McDevitt, J. The engines of God
 McDevitt, J. A talent for war
 Morgan, R. Broken angels
 Pohl, F. Gateway
 Reynolds, A. The prefect
 Reynolds, A. Revelation space
 Reynolds, A. Revenger
 Thompson, T. Rosewater
 Thompson, T. The Rosewater insurrection
 Thompson, T. The Rosewater redemption
 Watts, P. Blindsight
 Wilson, R. Spin
ALIEN CHILDREN (HUMANOID)
 McCaffrey, A. Acorna
ALIENATION (SOCIAL PSYCHOLOGY)
 Abe, K. The woman in the dunes
 Aboulela, L. Elsewhere, home
 Baldwin, J. Another country
 Baldwin, J. Giovanni's room
 Brockmeier, K. The illumination
 Burns, C. Black hole
 Burroughs, W. Naked lunch
 Castel-Bloom, O. Textile
 Deb, S. The point of return
 Donohue, K. The stolen child
 Dos Passos, J. Manhattan transfer
 Gaige, A. Schroder
 Hale, B. The evolution of Bruno Littlemore
 Hemingway, E. The sun also rises
 Itani, F. Tell
 Joyce, J. Ulysses
 Kafka, F. The trial
 Kawabata, Y. The sound of the mountain
 Kincaid, J. Lucy
 Lahiri, J. The namesake
 Lee, D. Country of origin
 Lim, E. Dear cyborgs
 Mengestu, D. All our names
 Moshfegh, O. My year of rest and relaxation
 Mukherjee, N. A life apart
 Murakami, H. After dark
 Murakami, H. South of the border, west of the sun
 Murakami, H. The wind-up bird chronicle
 Murata, S. Convenience store woman
 Rivers, F. Bridge to haven
 Savage, S. Firmin
 Sherrill, S. The minotaur takes his own sweet time
 Silko, L. Ceremony
 Toibin, C. The blackwater lightship
 Woolf, V. Mrs. Dalloway
ALIENATION IN FAMILIES
 Austin, L. All she ever wanted
 Bank, M. The wonder spot
 Burke, A. The better sister

Haruf, K. Benediction

ALIENATION IN MEN

Auster, P. The Brooklyn follies
Beagle, P. A fine and private place
Begley, L. About Schmidt
Bellow, S. Herzog
Bellow, S. Seize the day
Conrad, J. Lord Jim
Conrad, J. Victory
Cooley, M. The archivist
Darnielle, J. Wolf in white van
DeLillo, D. The names
Deb, S. The point of return
Flaubert, G. Sentimental education
Hesse, H. Steppenwolf
Kafka, F. The castle
Millet, L. Ghost lights
Naipaul, V. Magic seeds
Percy, W. The last gentleman
Row, J. Your face in mine
Savage, S. The way of the dog
Toibin, C. The heather blazing
Toole, J. A confederacy of dunces

ALIENATION IN TEENAGERS

Salinger, J. The catcher in the rye
Sittenfeld, C. Prep

ALIENATION IN WOMEN

Didion, J. Play it as it lays
Strout, E. Amy and Isabelle

The **alienist** Carr, C.

ALIENS

Anders, C. The city in the middle of the night
Barnes, S. Domino Falls
Bradbury, R. The illustrated man
Brin, D. Existence
Chambers, B. A closed and common orbit
Chambers, B. The long way to a small, angry planet
Chambers, B. Record of a spaceborn few
Clarke, A. 2001
Delany, S. Aye, and Gomorrah
Faber, M. The book of strange new things
Foster, A. Relic
Gilman, C. Dark orbit
Gunn, J. Transcendental
Haig, M. The humans
Haldeman, J. The forever war
Hamilton, P. Great North Road
Harrison, M. Light
Harrison, M. Nova swing
Kress, N. After the fall, before the fall, during the fall
Kress, N. If tomorrow comes
Kress, N. Tomorrow's kin
Leckie, A. Ancillary justice
Leckie, A. Ancillary mercy
Leckie, A. Ancillary sword
Lem, S. His master's voice
Liu, C. The dark forest

Liu, C. Death's end
Liu, C. The three-body problem
Morgan, R. Broken angels
Not one of us
New suns
Okorafor, N. Binti
Porter, C. The seep
Reynolds, A. The prefect
Reynolds, A. Revelation space
Russell, M. The sparrow
Sagan, C. Contact
Scalzi, J. Old man's war
Thompson, T. Rosewater
Thompson, T. The Rosewater insurrection
Thompson, T. The Rosewater redemption
Turnbull, C. The lesson
Valente, C. Radiance
Valente, C. Space opera
Varley, J. Demon
Varley, J. Titan
Wagers, K. There before the chaos
Weber, D. By schism rent asunder
Weber, D. Off Armageddon reef
Williams, D. The stars now unclaimed
Wilson, R. Blind Lake
Wolfe, G. The urth of the new sun

ALIENS (HUMANOID)

Adams, D. The hitchhiker's guide to the galaxy
Adams, D. Life, the universe, and everything
Adams, D. The restaurant at the end of the universe
Asher, N. The skinner
Banks, I. The hydrogen sonata
Banks, I. Matter
Card, O. Ender's game
Chu, W. The lives of tao
Egan, G. Phoresis
Emshwiller, C. The secret city
Herbert, F. Dune
Le Guin, U. The birthday of the world
Le Guin, U. The left hand of darkness
Le Guin, U. The telling
Not one of us
Pohl, F. Gateway
Rucker, R. Postsingular
Saint-Exupery, A. The little prince
Scalzi, J. Redshirts

ALIENS (HUMANOID) -- SIGHTINGS AND ENCOUNTERS

Cherryh, C. Foreigner

ALIENS (INSECTOID)

Flynn, M. Eifelheim

ALIENS (NON-HUMANOID)

Anders, C. The city in the middle of the night
Bear, G. Anvil of stars
Bear, G. The forge of God

Eason, K. How Rory Thorne destroyed the multiverse
French, J. The true Bastards
Gladstone, M. Empress of forever
Lee, F. Jade war
Lee, Y. Ninefox gambit
Limon, M. Mr. Kill
Martin, G. A dance with dragons
Martin, G. A feast for crows
McDonald, L. The battle sylph
McGuire, S. Night and silence
Novik, N. His majesty's dragon
Perry, T. The informant
Poole, S. The Borgia mistress
Rollins, J. The demon crown
Rollins, J. The devil colony
Wagers, K. After the crown
Warrington, F. Elfland
Willig, L. The lure of the moonflower
Wolfe, G. The claw of the conciliator

ALLIGATORS

Russell, K. Swamplandia!

ALLILUEVA, SVETLANA, 1926-2011

Schwartz, J. The red daughter

Almanac of the dead Silko, L.

Almost famous women Bergman, M.

Almost Graceland Carlson, S.

Almost midnight Doiron, P.

The **almost** moon Sebold, A.

Almost never Sada, D.

The **almost** sisters Jackson, J.

Alone Gardner, L.

Alone in the crowd Garcia-Roza, L.

Alone in the wild Armstrong, K.

Along came a duke Boyle, E.

Along came a spider Patterson, J.

ALPHABET

Richardson, C. The end of the alphabet

Alphabet of thorn McKillip, P.

ALPS

Mawer, S. The fall

Altered carbon Morgan, R.

Altered states Chayefsky, P.

ALTERED STATES OF CONSCIOUSNESS

Chayefsky, P. Altered states

ALTERNATIVE COMICS

Cruse, H. The complete Wendel

ALTERNATIVE ENERGY DEVELOPMENT

Cussler, C. Sea of greed

ALTERNATIVE HISTORIES

Andersen, L. The Boleyn deceit
Andersen, L. The Boleyn king
Andersen, L. The Boleyn reckoning
Atkinson, K. Life after life
Bisson, T. Any day now
Chabon, M. The Yiddish Policemen's Union
Clark, P. The black god's drums
Dick, P. The man in the high castle

Evaristo, B. Blonde roots
Flynn, M. Eifelheim
Gingrich, N. Gettysburg
Gingrich, N. Grant comes east
Goonan, K. In war times
Goonan, K. This shared dream
Harris, R. Fatherland
Kerr, P. Hitler's peace
Khoury, R. Empire of lies
King, S. 11
Kowal, M. The calculating stars
Kowal, M. The fated sky
Levine, D. Arabella of Mars
Means, D. Hystopia
Newitz, A. The future of another timeline
Priest, C. Boneshaker
Priest, C. Clementine
Priest, C. Dreadnought
Priest, C. Ganymede
Priest, C. The inexplicables
Robinson, K. Galileo's dream
Robinson, K. The years of rice and salt
Roth, P. The plot against America
Sterling, B. Pirate Utopia
Tidhar, L. A man lies dreaming
Tregillis, I. The mechanical
Walton, J. Farthing
Walton, J. My real children
Weldon, F. Chalcot Crescent

ALTERNATIVE LIFESTYLES

Ffitch, M. Stay and fight

ALTERNATIVE MEDICINE

Davies, R. The cunning man

ALTERNATIVE SCHOOLS

McPherson, C. The child garden

ALTITUDES -- PSYCHOLOGICAL ASPECTS

Vine, B. Grasshopper

ALTRUISM

Butler, N. The hearts of men

ALZHEIMER'S DISEASE

LaPlante, A. Turn of mind
Moore, L. The unseen world

Amanda Jaffe novels [series] Margolin, P.

Amanda Pepper mysteries [series] Roberts, G.

AMATEUR DETECTIVES

Adams, E. The secret, book & scone society
Berry, S. The Templar legacy
Blake, R. A dark anatomy
Bowen, P. Badlands
Braun, L. The cat who ate Danish modern
Braun, L. The cat who went underground
Brett, S. Murder unprompted
Brown, R. The litter of the law
Cameron, W. Repo madness
Cantero, E. Meddling kids
Clark, M. My gal Sunday

Runcie, J. Sidney Chambers and the problem of evil

Runcie, J. Sidney Chambers and the shadow of death

Sansom, I. The case of the missing books

Sayers, D. Busman's honeymoon

Sayers, D. Clouds of witness

Sayers, D. The five red herrings

Sayers, D. Gaudy night

Sayers, D. Hangman's holiday

Sayers, D. Have his carcase

Sayers, D. In the teeth of the evidence

Sayers, D. Lord Peter

Sayers, D. Murder must advertise

Sayers, D. The nine tailors

Sayers, D. Strong poison

Sayers, D. Thrones, dominations

Sayers, D. The unpleasantness at the Bellona Club

Sayers, D. Whose body?

Scerbanenco, G. Traitors to all

Scott, J. Mausoleum

Sedley, K. The Tintern treasure

Shaw, M. Murder at the mill

Sidor, S. Skin River

Simpson, R. Let the dead keep their secrets

Simpson, R. What the dead leave behind

Solomon, B. The attempted murder of Teddy Roosevelt

Somer, M. The serenity murders

Starr, M. Unhallowed ground

Stewart, D. The Babe Ruth deception

Thomson, E. Beloved poison

Thomson, E. The blood

Turton, S. The 7 1

AMATEUR FILMS

Raymond, J. The half-life

The **amateur** marriage Tyler, A.

The **amazing** adventures of Kavalier & Clay Chabon, M.

AMAZON VALLEY

Patchett, A. State of wonder

The **ambassador's** daughter Jenoff, P.

AMBASSADORS

Jenoff, P. The ambassador's daughter

Martine, A. A memory called empire

Rushdie, S. Shalimar the Clown

Turnbull, C. The lesson

AMBASSADORS -- UNITED STATES

Clancy, T. Clear and present danger

Amberville Davys, T.

AMBITION

50 Cent, (. Blow

Adiga, A. The white tiger

Angelo, M. Followers

Archer, J. The prodigal daughter

Benedict, M. Lady Clementine

Bloom, A. Lucky us

Carter, M. The strangler vine

Castellani, C. Leading men

De Leon, A. Side chick nation

De la Motte, A. MemoRandom

Dunant, S. Blood and beauty

Ervin, K. Mina's joint

Follett, K. A column of fire

Follett, K. World without end

Gabel, A. The ensemble

Gregory, P. The Boleyn inheritance

Gregory, P. The kingmaker's daughter

Gregory, P. The lady of the rivers

Gregory, P. The other Boleyn girl

Gregory, P. The red queen

Gregory, P. The white princess

Haigh, J. Baker Towers

Harvey, M. The governor's wife

Helprin, M. Winter's tale

Hoffman, A. Skylight confessions

Holmes, J. How are you going to save yourself

Howrey, M. The wanderers

K'wan Street dreams

Kadrey, R. The grand dark

Lewis, S. Elmer Gantry

Lindsay, J. Just watch me

Llywelyn, M. After Rome

Martin, G. A clash of kings

Martin, G. A dance with dragons

Martin, G. A feast for crows

Martin, G. A game of thrones

Martin, G. A storm of swords

Maugham, W. The moon and sixpence

McKenzie, E. The portable Veblen

Morgan, C. The sport of kings

Muller, M. The broken promise land

Nesbo, J. Macbeth

Ng, C. Everything I never told you

Nickson, C. The constant lovers

Parsons, K. Doing harm

Penman, S. A king's ransom

Pomerantz, S. Rich boy

Rachman, T. The Italian teacher

Rash, R. Serena

Richter, C. The sea of grass

Rushdie, S. The golden house

Schwab, V. Vicious

Serle, R. In five years

Shepard, J. The world to come

Simpson, M. Anywhere but here

Smith, G. The maze at Windermere

Straub, E. Modern lovers

Swyler, E. Light from other stars

Tademy, L. Cane River

Vidal, G. Empire

Wang, K. Family trust

Wayne, T. Loner

Whitaker, K. The animators

Woods, S. Below the belt

Woods, S. Fast & loose

Wuertz, Y. Everything belongs to us

Yanagihara, H. A little life

Alexander, T. With this pledge
Bahr, H. The Judas Field
Brown, T. Fallen land
Cobbs Hoffman, E. The Tubman command
Cole, A. An extraordinary union
Cole, A. A hope divided
Cole, A. An unconditional freedom
Crane, S. The red badge of courage
Doctorow, E. The march
Frazier, C. Cold Mountain
Frazier, C. Varina
Gleason, C. Murder at the capitol
Harris, C. Good time coming
Hicks, R. The widow of the South
Horn, D. All other nights
Humphreys, J. Nowhere else on earth
Hunt, L. Neverhome
Jakes, J. Love and war
Jakes, J. On secret service
Jakes, J. Savannah, or, A gift for Mr. Lincoln
Johnson, T. Engraved on the heart
Kantor, M. Andersonville
Kelton, E. Badger boy
Lent, J. A slant of light
McCabe, E. I shall be near to you
Mitchell, M. Gone with the wind
Newman, J. Mary
Olmstead, R. Coal black horse
Perry, A. Slaves of obsession
Peters, R. Hell or Richmond
Piercy, M. Sex wars
Plain, B. Crescent City
Poyer, D. A country of our own
Poyer, D. Fire on the waters
Shaara, J. Gods and generals
Shaara, J. The last full measure
Shaara, M. The killer angels
Solomon, B. The murder of Willie Lincoln
Warren, R. Band of angels
West, J. The friendly persuasion
American dervish Akhtar, A.

AMERICAN DREAM

Baca, J. The importance of a piece of paper
Evison, J. Lawn boy
Fitzgerald, F. The last tycoon
Herlihy, J. Midnight cowboy
Pomerantz, S. Rich boy
Ramos, J. The farm
Roth, P. American pastoral
Roth, P. The human stain
Roth, P. I married a Communist
Skyhorse, B. Madonnas of Echo Park
Thomas, M. We are not ourselves
Vanderbes, J. Strangers at the feast
Watts, S. No one is coming to save us
American dreams Sapphire, 1.
American elsewhere Bennett, R.

American fantastic tales
American fantastic tales [series]
The **American** fiancee Dupont, E.
American gods Gaiman, N.
The **American** heiress Goodwin, D.
American histories Wideman, J.
American housewife Ellis, H.

AMERICAN INDIAN MOVEMENT.

Cook, D. Reservation nation
American innovations Galchen, R.
An **American** marriage Jones, T.
American meteor Lock, N.
American novels (Norman Lock) [series] Lock, N.
American pastoral Roth, P.
American people [series] Kramer, L.

AMERICAN REVOLUTION, 1775-1783

Calvi, M. Dear George, Dear Mary
Cobbs Hoffman, E. The Hamilton affair
Gabaldon, D. A breath of snow and ashes
Gabaldon, D. An echo in the bone
Gabaldon, D. Written in my own heart's blood
Harkness, D. Time's convert
Hill, L. Someone knows my name
Turner, N. My name is Resolute
American rust Meyer, P.
American salvage Campbell, B.

AMERICAN SIGN LANGUAGE

Gruen, S. The ape house
An **American** spy Steinhauer, O.
American spy Wilkinson, L.
American tabloid Ellroy, J.
An **American** tragedy Dreiser, T.
American visa Recacoechea S., J.
American war El Akkad, O.
American West

AMERICAN WESTWARD EXPANSION (1803-1899)

Bird, S. Daughter of a daughter of a queen
Bittner, R. Logan's lady
Dallas, S. The last midwife
Dallas, S. Westering women
Davies, C. West
Diaz, H. In the distance
Gilman, L. The cold eye
Gilman, L. Silver on the road
Guthrie, A. The big sky
Jenkins, B. Tempest
Jiles, P. The color of lightning
Jiles, P. News of the world
Katsu, A. The hunger
Kirkpatrick, J. One more river to cross
Kirkpatrick, J. This road we traveled
Larison, J. Whiskey when we're dry
Lock, N. American meteor
Malerman, J. Unbury Carol
Michener, J. Centennial
Obreht, T. Inland
Osborne, D. The coming

Bellow, S. Ravelstein
Black, C. Three hours in Paris
Butler, R. Paris in the dark
Chee, A. The queen of the night
Child, L. The enemy
Dean, L. The idea of love
Groot, T. Flame of resistance
Harmel, K. The room on Rue Amelie
Kay, G. Ysabel
Lauren, C. Sweet filthy boy
McLain, P. The Paris wife
Miller, H. Tropic of Cancer
Orringer, J. The flight portfolio
Ozick, C. Foreign bodies
Pavone, C. The Paris diversion
Portis, C. Masters of Atlantis
Rosnay, T. Sarah's key
Sedaris, D. Holidays on ice
Truong, M. The book of salt, Monique Truong.
Wieland, L. Paris, 7 a.m.
Willig, L. The garden intrigue

AMERICANS IN GERMANY
Belfer, L. And after the fire
Chiaverini, J. Resistance women
Deaver, J. Garden of beasts
Ford, F. The good soldier

AMERICANS IN GREAT BRITAIN
Berry, C. A legacy of murder
Freeman, D. A lady's guide to etiquette and murder
Guillory, J. Royal holiday
Higgins, J. Flight of eagles
Johnson, M. Smitten by the Brit
McCall Smith, A. The comforts of a muddy Saturday
Twain, M. A Connecticut Yankee in King Arthur's Court
Whelan, J. My Oxford year
Woods, S. Stealth

AMERICANS IN GREECE
DeLillo, D. The names

AMERICANS IN GUATEMALA
Reichs, K. Grave secrets

AMERICANS IN HONDURAS
Theroux, P. The Mosquito Coast

AMERICANS IN ICELAND
Ridpath, M. Far north

AMERICANS IN INDIA
Bacon, C. There is room for you
Oleksiw, S. The wrath of Shiva
Rushdie, S. Shalimar the Clown
Sinha, I. Animal's people
Sundaresan, I. The splendor of silence
Theroux, P. The Elephanta suite
Umrigar, T. The weight of heaven

AMERICANS IN IRAQ
Zimmerman, D. The sandbox

AMERICANS IN IRELAND
Binchy, M. Firefly summer
Connolly, S. The lost traveller

Hart, E. Haunted ground
Lordan, B. But come ye back , Beth Lordan
O'Farrell, M. This must be the place
Roberts, N. Dark witch

AMERICANS IN ISRAEL
Kemelman, H. Monday the rabbi took off
Krauss, N. Forest Dark
Uris, L. Exodus

AMERICANS IN ITALY
Dyer, G. Jeff in Venice, death in Varanasi
Elkins, A. Unnatural selection
Fortier, A. Juliet
Hemingway, E. A farewell to arms
Hersey, J. A bell for Adano
Langton, J. The thief of Venice
Rachman, T. The imperfectionists
Scott, J. Tourmaline
Unsworth, B. After Hannibal

AMERICANS IN JAPAN
Lee, D. Country of origin
Murakami, R. In the miso soup , Ryu Murakami ; translated by Ralph McCarthy.
Smith, M. December 6

AMERICANS IN KOREA
Limon, M. The line
Limon, M. Mr. Kill

AMERICANS IN LAOS
Cotterill, C. Slash and burn

AMERICANS IN LONDON, ENGLAND
Lurie, A. Foreign affairs
Price, S. By gaslight

AMERICANS IN LUXEMBOURG
Pavone, C. The expats

AMERICANS IN MESOPOTAMIA
Unsworth, B. Land of marvels

AMERICANS IN MEXICO
Doerr, H. Stones for Ibarra
Fuentes, C. The old gringo
Gaspar de Alba, A. Desert blood
L'Amour, L. May there be a road
McCarthy, C. All the pretty horses
McCarthy, C. Cities of the plain
McCarthy, C. The crossing
Michener, J. Mexico
Portis, C. Gringos
Smith, S. The ruins
Traven, B. The treasure of the Sierra Madre

AMERICANS IN MOROCCO
Bowles, P. The sheltering sky

AMERICANS IN MOSCOW, RUSSIA
Harris, R. Archangel

AMERICANS IN NORTHERN IRELAND
McKinty, A. In the morning I'll be gone

AMERICANS IN PANAMA
Le Carre, J. The tailor of Panama

AMERICANS IN PARIS, FRANCE
Avery, E. The last nude

Amos Walker novels [series] Estleman, L.

AMPUTATION

Potzsch, O. The werewolf of Bamberg

Amreekiya Mahmoud, L.

Amsterdam McEwan, I.

AMSTERDAM, NETHERLANDS

Burton, J. The miniaturist

Camus, A. The fall

Groen, H. On the bright side

Grunberg, A. Tirza

Kostova, E. The historian

MacLaverty, B. Midwinter break

McEwan, I. Amsterdam

Pearson, R. Choke point

Robotham, M. The night ferry

Vreeland, S. Girl in hyacinth blue

AMSTERDAM, NETHERLANDS -- HISTORY -- 17TH CENTURY

Moggach, D. Tulip fever

Amulet Bolano, R.

AMULETS

Norton, A. Golden trillium

Peet, M. The Murdstone trilogy

Saylor, S. Roma

AMUSEMENT PARK RIDES

Albom, M. The five people you meet in heaven

AMUSEMENT PARKS

Albom, M. The five people you meet in heaven

Albom, M. The next person you meet in Heaven

Barnes, J. England, England

Hand, E. Curious toys

Price, R. Freedomland

Russell, K. Swamplandia!

AMUSEMENT RIDES

Albom, M. The next person you meet in Heaven

Amy and Isabelle Strout, E.

AMYOTROPHIC LATERAL SCLEROSIS -- PATIENTS

Genova, L. Every note played

An American heiress in London [series] Guhrke, L.

ANABOLIC STEROID ABUSE

Rozan, S. Winter and night

ANAGRAMS

Phillips, H. The beautiful bureaucrat

The **analyst** Katzenbach, J.

ANANSI (LEGENDARY CHARACTER)

Gaiman, N. Anansi boys

Anansi boys Gaiman, N.

ANARCHISM

Delany, S. Dhalgren

Manchette, J. Fatale

Sainz Borgo, K. It would be night in Caracas

Sterling, B. Pirate Utopia

ANARCHISTS

Aswani, A. Chicago

Auster, P. Leviathan

Barthelme, F. Painted desert

Boyle, T. The harder they come

Goldstone, L. Assassin of shadows

Keneally, T. Shame and the captives

Le Guin, U. The dispossessed

Robbins, T. Still life with Woodpecker

ANASAZI CULTURE

Preston, D. Thunderhead

Anathem Stephenson, N.

ANATOMISTS

Robertson, I. Circle of shadows

Robertson, I. Instruments of darkness

Robertson, I. Island of bones

Stott, R. The coral thief

ANATOMISTS -- HISTORY -- 18TH CENTURY

Robertson, I. Anatomy of murder

ANATOMY

Kidd, J. Things in jars

The **anatomy** lesson Roth, P.

Anatomy of a disappearance Matar, H.

Anatomy of a killer ; Rabe, P.

Anatomy of a miracle Miles, J.

Anatomy of a scandal Vaughan, S.

Anatomy of murder Robertson, I.

ANCESTORS

Butler, O. Kindred

Coates, T. The water dancer

Djavadi, N. Disoriental

Fine, J. What should be wild

Gyasi, Y. Homegoing

Hill, R. The stranger house

Lukas, M. The last watchman of Old Cairo

Maturin, C. Melmoth the wanderer

Moore, A. Jerusalem

Perkins, S. Murder once removed

Proulx, A. Barkskins

Sundstol, V. The land of dreams

Tepper, S. The visitor

Wright, J. The house on Foster Hill

Ancestry detective novels [series] Perkins, S.

ANCHORAGE, ALASKA

Stabenow, D. A deeper sleep

Stabenow, D. A taint in the blood

ANCIENT AEGEAN CIVILIZATIONS (3000?1000 BCE)

Barker, P. The silence of the girls

Miller, M. Circe

Miller, M. The song of Achilles

The **ancient** child Momaday, N.

ANCIENT EGYPT (3100 BCE-640 CE)

Geagley, B. Year of the hyenas

Greenwood, K. Out of the Black Land

Mailer, N. Ancient evenings

Robinson, L. Murder at the feast of rejoicing

Robinson, L. Murder at the god's gate

Saylor, S. The judgment of Caesar

Saylor, S. Raiders of the Nile

Saylor, S. Wrath of the furies

ANCIENT EGYPT -- CIVILIZATION -- TO 332 BC

Greenwood, K. Out of the Black Land

Le Carre, J. Agent running in the field
Lelic, S. The child who

ANGER IN MEN
Boyle, T. The harder they come
Carlson, R. Five skies
Iles, G. Third degree
Rubart, J. The man he never was

ANGER IN TEENAGE BOYS
Howarth, P. Only killers and thieves

ANGER IN TEENAGE GIRLS
Souljah,. The coldest winter ever

ANGER IN WOMEN
Blundell, J. The high season
Ellis, H. American housewife
Giordano, P. The solitude of prime numbers
Hashemzadeh Bonde, G. What we owe
Hustvedt, S. The blazing world
Kincaid, J. See now then
Lessing, D. The good terrorist
Vreeland, S. The passion of Artemisia
Walker, A. Possessing the secret of joy
Weldon, F. The life and loves of a she-devil

Angle of repose Stegner, W.

ANGLO-IRISH RELATIONS -- HISTORY -- 20TH CENTURY
Llywelyn, M. 1949

ANGLO-SAXON PERIOD (449-1066)
Cornwell, B. The last kingdom
Cornwell, B. Sword of kings
Cornwell, B. War of the wolf
Griffith, N. Hild
Iggulden, C. The abbot's tale
Ishiguro, K. The buried giant
Rutherfurd, E. London
Seton, A. Avalon

ANGLO-SAXONS
Kay, G. The last light of the sun
An **angry-ass** black woman Miller, K.
Anil's ghost Ondaatje, M.
Animal K'wan

ANIMAL ATTACKS
Box, C. Long range
King, S. Cujo

ANIMAL BEHAVIOR
Duncan, G. By blood we live
Duncan, G. The last werewolf
Duncan, G. Talulla rising

ANIMAL CULTURE
Del Amo, J. Animalia

ANIMAL DETECTIVES
Brown, R. The litter of the law
Brown, R. Murder at Monticello, or, Old sins
Brown, R. Wish you were here

ANIMAL EXPERIMENTATION
Fowler, K. We are all completely beside ourselves
Wells, H. The island of Dr. Moreau

Animal farm Orwell, G.

ANIMAL FIGHTING
Pelecanos, G. Drama city

ANIMAL GHOSTS
Simon, C. Grey dawn
Simon, C. Stages of Grey

Animal II K'wan

ANIMAL INTELLIGENCE
Hale, B. The evolution of Bruno Littlemore

ANIMAL LIBERATION
Koontz, D. The darkest evening of the year
Swarthout, G. Bless the beasts and children

ANIMAL MIGRATION
Bakker, R. Raptor red

ANIMAL MUTILATIONS
Box, C. Trophy hunt
McGarrity, M. Everyone dies
Murakami, H. Kafka on the shore

Animal novels (K'wan) [series] K'wan

ANIMAL RESCUE
Cabot, M. No judgments
Cameron, W. The dogs of Christmas
Cooney, E. The mountaintop school for dogs and other second chances
Dare, T. The wallflower wager
Kerr, L. Wild on my mind

ANIMAL RIGHTS
Fowler, K. We are all completely beside ourselves
Geni, A. The wildlands
Leon, D. Beastly things

ANIMAL RIGHTS ADVOCATES
Follett, K. Whiteout
Freed, D. Hot start
Geni, A. The wildlands
Gruen, S. The ape house
Scottoline, L. Legal tender

ANIMAL SANCTUARIES
Koryta, M. The ridge

ANIMAL SHELTER WORKERS
Cameron, W. The dogs of Christmas
Pelecanos, G. Drama city

ANIMAL SHELTERS
Pelecanos, G. Drama city

ANIMAL STEALING
Gruen, S. The ape house

ANIMAL WELFARE
Cooney, E. The mountaintop school for dogs and other second chances
Del Amo, J. Animalia
Gruen, S. The ape house
Koontz, D. The darkest evening of the year
London, J. White Fang
Meyers, K. The work of wolves
Picoult, J. Leaving time
Rosenfelt, D. Bark of night
Spencer, S. Man in the woods

Animal's people Sinha, I.
Animalia Del Amo, J.

Coover, R. Going for a beer
Dangerous women
Everyday people
Flight or fright
Gaiman, N. Fragile things
Gaiman, N. Trigger warning
Gogol, N. The collected tales of Nikolai Gogol
Henry, O. The complete works of O. Henry
Hesse, H. The fairy tales of Hermann Hesse
It occurs to me that I am America
James, H. Complete stories, 1864-1874
Kafka, F. Collected stories
Kiernan, C. The very best of Caitlin R. Kiernan
It occurs to me that I am America
Leonard, E. When the women come out to dance
Liu, K. Invisible planets
The living dead
MatchUp
Moody, R. Right livelihoods
More deadling than the male
Nabokov, V. Novels and memoirs, 1941-51
Nebula Awards showcase 2017
New Cthulhu
The new voices of fantasy
Nightmares
Nin, A. Cities of the interior
The Norton book of science fiction
Not one of us
O. Henry prize stories 2019
O'Connor, F. Collected works
Orczy, E. The old man in the corner
A people's future of the United States
Poe, E. Complete stories and poems of Edgar Allan Poe
The Pushcart Prize 2020 XLIV
Rankin, I. The beat goes on
Sisters of the revolution
Stories
This way to the end times
Twain, M. The complete short stories of Mark Twain
The very best of the best
West, N. Novels and other writings
Wharton, E. Collected stories, 1911-1937
Wodehouse, P. The best of Wodehouse
Anthony Gethryn mysteries [series] MacDonald, P.
ANTHONY, SUSAN B (SUSAN BROWNELL), 1820-1906
  Piercy, M. Sex wars
ANTHROPOLOGISTS
  Elkins, A. Unnatural selection
  King, L. Euphoria
  Levy, D. Hot milk
  McCarthy, T. Satin Island
ANTHROPOLOGISTS' SPOUSES
  Vanderbes, J. Easter Island
ANTHROPOLOGY STUDENTS
  Lee, D. Country of origin
ANTHROPOMORPHISM
  Brown, R. Murder at Monticello, or, Old sins

Brown, R. Wish you were here
Murphy, S. Cat pay the devil
ANTI-APARTHEID ACTIVISTS
  Flanery, P. Absolution
ANTI-APARTHEID MOVEMENT SOUTH AFRICA
  Mda, Z. The Madonna of Excelsior
ANTI-APARTHEID MOVEMENTS
  Paton, A. Ah, but your land is beautiful
ANTI-CATHOLICISM
  Faye, L. The gods of Gotham
ANTI-COMMUNISM -- UNITED STATES
  Stratford, S. Red letter days
ANTI-COMMUNIST MOVEMENTS
  Jin, H. War trash
  Stratford, S. Red letter days
ANTI-FASCISM
  Hemingway, E. For whom the bell tolls
  Twardoch, S. The king of Warsaw
ANTI-GLOBALIZATION MOVEMENT
  Rankin, I. The naming of the dead
ANTI-HATE GROUP ACTION
  Brown, S. The witness
ANTI-NAZI MOVEMENT
  Black, C. Three hours in Paris
  Chiaverini, J. Resistance women
  Clayton, M. The last train to London
  Ramzipoor, E. The ventriloquists
ANTI-NAZIS
  Chiaverini, J. Resistance women
ANTI-NAZIS -- FRANCE
  Faulks, S. Charlotte Gray
ANTI-SLAVERY MOVEMENTS
  Kidd, S. The invention of wings
  Pesci, D. Amistad
ANTI-SLAVERY MOVEMENTS -- GREAT BRITAIN
  Hill, L. Someone knows my name
ANTIAIRCRAFT GUNS
  Kelly, J. The light over London
ANTICHRIST
  Levin, I. Rosemary's baby
ANTIETAM, BATTLE OF, MD, 1862
  Gurganus, A. Oldest living Confederate widow tells all
ANTIGUA AND BARBUDA
  Kincaid, J. Annie John
  Le Carre, J. Our kind of traitor
ANTIGUA AND BARBUDA -- SOCIAL CONDITIONS
  Kincaid, J. Annie John
ANTIHEROES AND ANTIHEROINES
  Morgan, R. Thirteen
  Scerbanenco, G. Traitors to all
ANTIQUARIAN BOOKSELLERS
  Berry, S. The Templar legacy
  Dunning, J. Booked to die
  Dunning, J. The bookman's wake
  Eco, U. The mysterious flame of Queen Loana
  Ghosh, A. Gun Island
  Grossman, D. Be my knife

Anything for you Black, S.
Anything is possible Strout, E.
Anywhere but here Simpson, M.

APACHE INDIANS
Grey, Z. Woman of the frontier
Leonard, E. The complete Western stories of Elmore Leonard.
Luiselli, V. Lost children archive
McCarthy, C. Blood meridian, or, The evening redness in the West

APALACHICOLA, FLORIDA
Morris, M. Man in the blue moon

APARTHEID
Abani, C. The secret history of Las Vegas
Cartwright, J. To heaven by water
Coetzee, J. Age of Iron
Flanery, P. Absolution
Gordimer, N. The conservationist
Gordimer, N. July's people
Greene, G. The human factor
McClure, J. The steam pig
Michener, J. The covenant
Nunn, M. A beautiful place to die
Nunn, M. Blessed are the dead
Nunn, M. Present darkness
Paton, A. Ah, but your land is beautiful
Paton, A. Cry, the beloved country
Paton, A. Too late the phalarope
Rush, N. Mortals

APARTHEID -- INFLUENCE
Matlwa, K. Evening primrose

APARTHEID -- SOUTH AFRICA
Mda, Z. The Madonna of Excelsior

Apartment Wayne, T.

APARTMENT DWELLERS
Link, C. The watcher
Loigman, L. The two-family house
Perec, G. Life
Sager, R. Lock every door
Swanson, P. Her every fear

APARTMENT HOUSE LIFE
Barbery, M. The elegance of the hedgehog
Gilb, D. The Flowers
O'Leary, B. The flatshare
Perec, G. Life
Sager, R. Lock every door
Saul, J. Midnight voices
Vatner, J. Carnegie Hill

APARTMENT HOUSES
Adiga, A. Last man in tower
Levin, I. Rosemary's baby
Mistry, R. A fine balance
Perec, G. Life

APARTMENTS
Nadel, B. The Ottoman cage
Wayne, T. Apartment

APATHY

Garcia Marquez, G. Chronicle of a death foretold
Hunter, E. The blackboard jungle

The **ape** house Gruen, S.

Apeirogon McCann, C.

APES
Crichton, M. Next
Gruen, S. The ape house

Apex hides the hurt Whitehead, C.

APOCALYPTIC FICTION
Atwood, M. Maddaddam
Anders, C. All the birds in the sky
Anders, C. Rock Manning goes for broke
Atwood, M. Oryx and Crake
Atwood, M. The year of the flood
Auster, P. In the country of last things
Brooks, M. World War Z
Buxton, K. Hollow kingdom
Cronin, J. The city of mirrors
Cronin, J. The passage
Cronin, J. The twelve
Currie, R. Everything matters!
Delany, S. Dhalgren
Egan, G. Perihelion summer
Elison, M. The book of Etta
Elison, M. The book of Flora
Elison, M. The book of the unnamed midwife
Erdrich, L. Future home of the living god
French, J. The Grey Bastards
French, J. The true Bastards
Grant, M. Blackout
Grant, M. Deadline
Grant, M. Feed
Grant, M. Feedback
Harkaway, N. The gone-away world
Harkaway, N. Tigerman
Harris, R. The second sleep
Heller, P. The dog stars
Hill, J. The Fireman
Jemisin, N. The fifth season
Jemisin, N. The obelisk gate
Jemisin, N. The stone sky
King, S. Sleeping beauties
King, S. The stand
Kress, N. After the fall, before the fall, during the fall
Krivak, A. The bear
Lai, L. The tiger flu
Lunde, M. The end of the ocean
Ma, L. Severance
Malerman, J. Bird box
Mandel, E. Station Eleven
Matheson, R. I am legend
McCarthy, C. The road
Melamed, J. Gather the daughters
Miller, W. A canticle for Leibowitz
Montag, K. After the flood
Moody, D. Hater
Newman, S. The country of Ice Cream Star

ARISTOCRACY -- PROVENCE, FRANCE

Pears, I. The dream of Scipio

ARISTOCRACY -- RUSSIA

Tolstoy, L. War and peace

Wojtas, O. Miss Blaine's prefect and the golden samovar

ARISTOTLE

Lyon, A. The sweet girl

ARIZONA

Baldacci, D. Long road to mercy

Beck, H. Here and gone

Boyle, T. The Terranauts

Caputo, P. Crossers

Chancellor, B. Sycamore

Dimberg, K. Girl in the rearview mirror

Harrison, J. The great leader

Jance, J. Queen of the night

Jance, J. Skeleton Canyon

Krentz, J. White lies

Leonard, E. The complete Western stories of Elmore Leonard.

Parker, R. Potshot

Picoult, J. Vanishing acts

Sallis, J. Drive

Sallis, J. Driven

Sallis, J. The killer is dying

Swarthout, G. Bless the beasts and children

Vestal, S. Daredevils

ARIZONA (TERRITORY)

Grey, Z. Woman of the frontier

Jenkins, B. Breathless

Obreht, T. Inland

ARIZONA (TERRITORY) -- HISTORY -- 19TH CENTURY

Russell, M. Epitaph

ARIZONA -- HISTORY -- 19TH CENTURY

Urrea, L. Queen of America

Arkady Renko novels [series] Smith, M.

ARKANSAS

Belle, K. Dear wife

Davidson, A. The boatman's daughter

Hess, J. Maggody and the moonbeams

Hunter, S. Hot springs

Arly Hanks mysteries [series] Hess, J.

Armageddon Uris, L.

The **armageddon** file Coonts, S.

Armageddon in retrospect Vonnegut, K.

ARMED FORCES

Campbell, R. Treason

ARMED FORCES -- FOREIGN COUNTRIES

Fuentes, C. The eagle's throne

ARMED FORCES -- OFFICERS

Deutermann, P. The Iceman

Moore, C. The serpent of Venice

ARMED FORCES AND SOCIETY -- LATIN AMERICA

Vargas Llosa, M. The time of the hero

ARMENIAN AMERICAN MEN

Haddam, J. Cheating at solitaire

Haddam, J. Hardscrabble road

Haddam, J. True believers

ARMENIAN AMERICANS

Shafak, E. The bastard of Istanbul

ARMENIAN GENOCIDE, 1915-1923

Bohjalian, C. The sandcastle girls

Werfel, F. The forty days of Musa Dagh

ARMENIAN MASSACRES, 1915-1923

Shafak, E. The bastard of Istanbul

ARMENIANS IN TURKEY

Nadel, B. The Ottoman cage

Shafak, E. The bastard of Istanbul

ARMENIANS IN TURKEY -- HISTORY -- 20TH CENTURY

Werfel, F. The forty days of Musa Dagh

ARMIES

Liu, K. The wall of storms

ARMISTICES

Hurley, K. The stars are legion

ARMORERS

Cole, A. A duke by default

ARMS DEALERS

Burke, J. House of the rising sun

Cameron, M. Oath of office

Child, L. The hard way

Le Carre, J. A delicate truth

Mina, D. The red road

Sjowall, M. Murder at the Savoy

ARMS TRANSFERS

Pears, I. Stone's fall

Perry, A. Slaves of obsession

ARMY SPOUSES

Ivey, E. To the bright edge of the world

ARMY TOWNS

Boll, H. The silent angel

Around the world in eighty days Verne, J.

ARRANGED MARRIAGE

Ali, M. Brick Lane

Antoinette, A. Murderville

Anton, M. Apprentice

Ashford, J. Heir to the duke

Banks, M. Never seduce a Scot

Boyle, E. Along came a duke

Callihan, K. Firelight

Craddock, C. An alchemy of masques and mirrors

Cruz, A. Dominicana

Dev, S. A Bollywood affair

Dunant, S. The birth of Venus

Fielding, H. The history of Tom Jones, a foundling

Florio, G. Silent hearts

Frampton, M. Put up your duke

Freudenberger, N. The newlyweds

Garriott, L. Promised

Garwood, J. The bride

Gregory, P. The constant princess

Gregory, P. The white princess

Hammad, I. The Parisian, or, Al-Barisi

Banville, J. The book of evidence
Bell, L. For the duke's eyes only
Bilal, P. The burning gates
Braun, L. The cat who ate Danish modern
Cussler, C. Golden Buddha
Elkins, A. A long time coming
Finch, C. The vanishing man
Horn, D. The world to come
Mason, J. The hidden things
Muller, M. The cavalier in white
Nesbo, J. Headhunters
Parker, R. Painted ladies
Pattison, E. Beautiful ghosts
Pears, I. Death and restoration
Pears, I. The immaculate deception
Pelecanos, G. The double
Rademacher, C. Deadly Camargue
Rice, L. Last day
Vreeland, S. Girl in hyacinth blue
Westlake, D. Don't ask

ART THEFTS -- PARIS, FRANCE
Morton, C. Stealing Mona Lisa

ART TREASURES IN WAR
Dean, D. The madonnas of Leningrad

Art trilogy [series] Cary, J.

ART, BAROQUE -- ITALY
Vreeland, S. The passion of Artemisia

ART, PREHISTORIC
Crace, J. The gift of stones

Artemis Weir, A.

Arthur Cathcart novels [series] Knopf, C.

ARTHUR,, KING
Cornwell, B. Enemy of God
Cornwell, B. Excalibur
Cornwell, B. The winter king
Griffiths, E. A dying fall
Stewart, M. The hollow hills
Stewart, M. The last enchantment
Stewart, M. The wicked day
Sutcliff, R. Sword at sunset
Twain, M. A Connecticut Yankee in King Arthur's Court
White, T. The once and future king

ARTHUR,, PRINCE OF WALES, 1486-1502
Gregory, P. The constant princess

ARTHURIAN FANTASY
Cornwell, B. Enemy of God
Cornwell, B. Excalibur
Cornwell, B. The winter king
Ishiguro, K. The buried giant
Pike, S. The lost queen
Stewart, M. The crystal cave
Stewart, M. The hollow hills
Stewart, M. The last enchantment
Stewart, M. The wicked day
Sutcliff, R. Sword at sunset
White, T. The once and future king

ARTIFICIAL INSEMINATION

Jewell, L. The making of us

ARTIFICIAL INTELLIGENCE
Asimov, I. I, robot
Beckett, L. Gamechanger
Card, O. Speaker for the dead
Chiang, T. The lifecycle of software objects
Clarke, A. 2001
Gibson, W. Agency
Gladstone, M. Empress of forever
Gunn, J. Transcendental
Hall, L. Speak
Heinlein, R. The moon is a harsh mistress
Iles, G. The footprints of God
Jen, G. The resisters
Moore, L. The unseen world
O'Keefe, M. Velocity weapon
Petrie, N. Burning bright
Powell, G. Embers of war
Reynolds, A. Revelation space
Rucker, R. Postsingular
Simmons, D. Endymion
Simmons, D. The rise of Endymion
Stephenson, N. Fall or, Dodge in hell
Stross, C. Accelerando
Tregillis, I. The mechanical
Weinstein, A. Children of the new world
Wells, M. All systems red
Wendig, C. Wanderers
Westerfeld, S. The killing of worlds
Wilson, D. The clockwork dynasty
Wilson, D. Robogenesis
Wilson, D. Robopocalypse
Winterson, J. Frankissstein
Zelazny, R. Donnerjack

ARTIFICIAL LIFE
Crichton, M. Prey

ARTIFICIAL LIMBS
O'Dell, C. A study in honor

ARTIFICIAL SATELLITES
Brown, D. The Kremlin strike

ARTISANS
Carlson, M. A Christmas by the sea
Golden, A. Memoirs of a geisha

An **artist** of the floating world Ishiguro, K.

ARTISTS
Alison, J. The marriage of the sea
Allende, I. The Japanese lover
Ashley, J. Lady Isabella's scandalous marriage
Banville, J. The blue guitar
Bauman, B. Broken sleep
Beukes, L. Broken monsters
Bialosky, J. The prize
Brenner, J. Drawing home
Brown, D. The Da Vinci code
Chabon, M. The amazing adventures of Kavalier & Clay
Diehl, H. Lifelines
Erdrich, L. Shadow tag

Forbes, C. A tall history of sugar

Gainza, M. The optic nerve

Ganek, D. The summer we read Gatsby

Gran, S. The infinite blacktop

Hand, E. Curious toys

Hand, E. Generation loss

Hand, E. Mortal love

Hawley, N. Before the fall

Heller, P. Celine

Heller, P. The painter

Hesse, H. Narcissus and Goldmund

Hibbert, T. Get a life, Chloe Brown

Houellebecq, M. The map and the territory

Ishiguro, K. An artist of the floating world

Jeffries, S. The art of sinning

Joyce, J. A portrait of the artist as a young man

Kay, G. Children of earth and sky

Kerley, J. The death collectors

King, R. Domino

Levine, J. Bingo's run

Lipsyte, S. The ask

Martin, S. Shopgirl

Maugham, W. The moon and sixpence

Maugham, W. Of human bondage

Maum, C. Costalegre

Murakami, H. Killing commendatore

Murdoch, I. Nuns and soldiers

Ng, C. Little fires everywhere

Orringer, J. The flight portfolio

Parmar, P. Vanessa and her sister

Penny, L. The long way home

Perez-Reverte, A. The painter of battles

Pilcher, R. The shell seekers

Porter, M. Lanny

Potok, C. The gift of Asher Lev

Potok, C. My name is Asher Lev

Rachman, T. The Italian teacher

Rivers, F. The masterpiece

Roberts, N. Chesapeake blue

Robinson, P. Playing with fire

Rose, M. Tiffany blues

Rothschild, H. The improbability of love

Roy, A. All the lives we never lived

Russo, R. Bridge of sighs

Sager, R. The last time I lied

Saramago, J. The manual of painting and calligraphy

Savage, S. The way of the dog

Sayers, D. The five red herrings

Scharer, W. The age of light

Shapiro, B. The muralist

Shaw, M. Murder at the mill

Smith, M. Blackwood

Tyler, A. Celestial navigation

Vollmann, W. Europe central

Winawer, M. The scribe of Siena

Wolfe, T. Back to blood

Yanagihara, H. A little life

Yoshimoto, B. The lake

ARTISTS -- 19TH CENTURY

Vreeland, S. Luncheon of the boating party

ARTISTS -- CALIFORNIA

See, C. The handyman

ARTISTS -- GREAT BRITAIN

Cusset, C. Life of David Hockney

ARTISTS -- HISTORY

Dean, M. I, Hogarth

ARTISTS -- ITALY

Stone, I. The agony and the ecstasy

ARTISTS -- NETHERLANDS

Stone, I. Lust for life

**ARTISTS -- NETHERLANDS -- HISTORY -- 17TH CEN-
TURY**

Chevalier, T. Girl with a pearl earring

Moggach, D. Tulip fever

Vreeland, S. Girl in hyacinth blue

ARTISTS -- PSYCHOLOGY

Murphy, D. Tiny Americans

Updike, J. Seek my face

ARTISTS -- SOCIAL RESPONSIBILITY

Roth, P. The anatomy lesson

Roth, P. The ghost writer

Roth, P. Zuckerman bound

Roth, P. Zuckerman unbound

ARTISTS' COLONIES

Makkai, R. The hundred-year house

Rose, M. Tiffany blues

ARTISTS' MODELS

Avery, E. The last nude

Jeffries, S. The art of sinning

Macneal, E. The doll factory

Mda, Z. The Madonna of Excelsior

Steinke, R. Holy skirts

ARTISTS' MODELS -- FRANCE

Buchanan, C. The painted girls

ARTISTS' MODELS -- NETHERLANDS

Chevalier, T. Girl with a pearl earring

ARTISTS' RETREATS

Bourland, B. Fake like me

ARTISTS' SPOUSES -- FRANCE

Cowell, S. Claude & Camille

**ARTS AND ENTERTAINMENT WRITING AND PUB-
LISHING**

Coetzee, J. Summertime

Nabokov, V. Novels and memoirs, 1941-51

Vonnegut, K. Armageddon in retrospect

ARTS FUND RAISING

Lipsyte, S. The ask

Arturo's island Morante, E.

ARUBA

Sosa, M. Acting on impulse

As a friend Gander, F.

As chimney sweepers come to dust Bradley, C.

As good as gone Watson, L.

As husbands go Isaacs, S.

Persson, L. Free falling, as if in a dream

The **assassination** of Jesse James by the coward Robert Ford
Hansen, R.

ASSASSINATION PLOTS
Child, L. Without fail
Kuang, R. The dragon republic
Moore, C. The serpent of Venice
Perry, A. Death in focus
Putney, M. Nowhere near respectable
Saintcrow, L. The ripper affair
Singh, N. Silver silence

ASSASSINS
Bacigalupi, P. The water knife
Baker, K. The bird of the river
Bennett, R. City of blades
Binet, L. HHhH
Black, C. Murder in the rue de Paradis
Blau, J. The Wonder Bread summer
Block, L. Hit me
Block, L. Killing Castro
Bohjalian, C. The flight attendant
Box, C. Long range
Box, C. Wolf pack
Brandreth, B. The assassin of Verona
Brandreth, B. The spy of Venice
Brekke, J. The fifth element
Brown, S. Ricochet
Burton, J. The eulogist
Byrne, K. The hunter
Child, L. 61 hours
Child, L. Echo burning
Child, L. The hard way
Child, L. Make me
Child, L. Night school
Child, L. No middle name
Child, L. Personal
Child, L. Without fail
Clements, R. Martyr
Coes, B. The Russian
Coleman, R. What you break
Collins, M. The wrong Quarry
Coonts, S. The Russia account
Costello, M. Big if
Crownover, J. Honor
Cussler, C. Serpent
DeMille, N. The deserter
Deaver, J. Garden of beasts
Dickey, E. Finding Gideon
Dugoni, R. The eighth sister
Eisler, B. The god's eye view
Eisler, B. The killer collective
Ellroy, J. The cold six thousand
Estleman, L. Something borrowed, something black
Finder, J. The switch
Fleming, I. Casino royale
Fleming, I. The man with the golden gun
Forsyth, F. The kill list

Gavin, R. Beluga
Goldberg, T. Gangsterland
Goldstone, L. Assassin of shadows
Gunn, J. Transcendental
Haydon, E. Prophecy
Higgins, G. The friends of Eddie Coyle
Higgins, J. Confessional
Higgins, J. Edge of danger
Higgins, J. Eye of the storm
Higgins, J. Rough justice
Hunter, S. Game of snipers
Hunter, S. Havana
Hunter, S. Time to hunt
Hurwitz, G. Hellbent
Hurwitz, G. The Nowhere Man
Hurwitz, G. Orphan X
Hurwitz, G. Out of the dark
Hurwitz, G. You're next
Iles, G. Black cross
Iles, G. The footprints of God
James, M. A brief history of seven killings
Knopf, C. Dead anyway
Koryta, M. If she wakes
Lake, J. Endurance
Lake, J. Green
Lansdale, J. Devil red
Leonard, E. Killshot
Leonard, E. Mr. Paradise
Lin, J. The dragon and the pearl
Lock, N. American meteor
Ludlum, R. The Bourne identity
Ludlum, R. The Bourne supremacy
Ludlum, R. The Bourne ultimatum
Malerman, J. Unbury Carol
Martin, G. A feast for crows
Martineau, M. Kingdom of exiles
Mathews, B. The world of tomorrow
Mayor, A. Tag man
Meltzer, B. The zero game
Morgan, R. Thirteen
Mosley, W. Trouble is what I do
Nesbo, J. Blood on snow
Nesbo, J. Headhunters
Nesbo, J. Midnight sun
Neville, S. The ghosts of Belfast
O'Brien, T. The Lincoln conspiracy
Parker, R. Brimstone
Parker, R. Small vices
Penelope, L. Whispers of shadow & flame
Perez-Reverte, A. Captain Alatriste
Perez-Reverte, A. The painter of battles
Perry, T. Dead aim
Perry, T. Fidelity
Perry, T. The informant
Perry, T. The old man
Perry, T. Pursuit
Peters, E. Seeing a large cat

At his mercy Bell, S.

At home in Mitford Karon, J.

At last St. Aubyn, E.

At night we walk in circles Alarcon, D.

At swim, two boys O'Neill, J.

At the dying of the year Nickson, C.

At the end of the century Jhabvala, R.

At the shore novels [series] Pineiro, C.

At weddings and wakes McDermott, A.

ATATURK, KEMAL, 1881-1938

De Bernieres, L. Birds without wings

ATF AGENTS

Panowich, B. Bull Mountain

ATHEISTS

Nesbo, J. Midnight sun

Rivers, F. The masterpiece

ATHENA (GREEK DEITY)

Walton, J. Necessity

Athenian mysteries [series] Corby, G.

ATHENS, GREECE

Corby, G. The Marathon conspiracy

Corby, G. The Pericles Commission

Cusk, R. Outline

ATHLETES

Benaron, N. Running the rift

ATHLETES -- HEALTH

Warrington, F. Midsummer night

ATHLETES WITH DISABILITIES

Abbott, M. You will know me

ATHLETIC TRAINERS

Loren, R. The one you fight for

ATLANTA, GEORGIA

Bambara, T. Those bones are not my child

Ca$h Trust no man

Ca$h Trust no man 2

Ca$h Trust no man 3

Cleage, P. Some things I never thought I'd do

Harris, E. I say a little prayer

Jones, T. An American marriage

Jones, T. Silver sparrow

K'wan Lawless

Mullen, T. Darktown

Mullen, T. Lightning men

Rashan, N. You make me wanna

Slaughter, K. Cop Town

Slaughter, K. Criminal

Slaughter, K. Fallen

Slaughter, K. The kept woman

Slaughter, K. The last widow

Slaughter, K. Undone

T. I. Power & Beauty

T. I. Trouble & triumph

Warren, T. The replacement wife

Whittle, T. The dangerous edge of things

Williams, A. The stranger you seek

Woods, S. Palindrome

ATLANTA, GEORGIA -- RACE RELATIONS

Wolfe, T. A man in full

ATLANTA, GEORGIA -- SOCIAL LIFE AND CUSTOMS -- 19TH CENTURY

Guinn, M. The scribe

ATLANTIC CITY, NEW JERSEY

Leonard, E. Glitz

ATLANTIC COAST (SOUTH CAROLINA)

Powell, P. Edisto

ATLANTIC OCEAN

Benchley, P. Jaws

Child, L. Deep storm

Clancy, T. The hunt for Red October

Golding, W. Close quarters

Golding, W. Rites of passage

Porter, K. Ship of fools

ATLANTIS (LEGENDARY PLACE)

Child, L. Deep storm

Portis, C. Masters of Atlantis

Rice, A. Blood communion

Siegel, J. Prospero's children

Atlas Catesby mysteries [series] Quincy, D.

An **atlas** of impossible longing Roy, A.

Atlee Pine novels [series] Baldacci, D.

ATOMIC BOMB

Cussler, C. Sacred stone

Follett, K. Winter of the world

Kanon, J. Los Alamos

Lawton, J. Hammer to fall

Nesbit, T. The wives of Los Alamos

Vonnegut, K. Cat's cradle

Wiggins, M. Evidence of things unseen

ATOMIC BOMB -- TESTING

Smith, M. Stallion Gate

ATONEMENT

Cash, W. This dark road to mercy

Erdrich, L. LaRose

Hawthorne, N. The scarlet letter

Mosley, W. The man in my basement

Powell, G. Embers of war

Ratner, V. Music of the ghosts

Rice, A. Of love and evil

Tyler, A. Saint Maybe

Atonement McEwan, I.

ATREUS, HOUSE OF (GREEK MYTHOLOGY)

Toibin, C. House of names

ATROCITIES

Apelfeld, A. To the edge of sorrow

Beah, I. Radiance of tomorrow

D'Eramo, L. Deviation

El Akkad, O. American war

Howarth, P. Only killers and thieves

Jones, S. Small wars

Kerr, P. A man without breath

Kerr, P. The lady from Zagreb

Konar, A. Mischling

Kuang, R. The poppy war

Kuang, R. The dragon republic

AUGUSTUS, EMPEROR OF ROME, 63 BC-14 AD
Graves, R. I, Claudius

AUNT AND NEPHEW
Boyden, J. Three day road
Godwin, G. Grief cottage
Miller, K. Augustown
Vargas Llosa, M. Aunt Julia and the scriptwriter
Vidal, G. The golden age

AUNT AND NIECE
Bergstrom, H. Steal the north
Bulawayo, N. We need new names
Cleage, P. Some things I never thought I'd do
Coomer, J. One vacant chair
Curran, K. My lady's choosing
Deveraux, J. A willing murder
Du Maurier, D. Jamaica Inn
Gilbert, E. City of girls
Godwin, G. Flora
Gray, A. The care and feeding of ravenously hungry girls
Hunt, S. Mr. Splitfoot
Itani, F. Tell
Maron, M. High country fall
McCall Smith, A. The forgotten affairs of youth
Monroe, M. Beach house reunion
Neubauer, E. Murder at the Mena House
O'Farrell, M. The vanishing act of Esme Lennox
Oleksiw, S. The wrath of Shiva
Rice, L. Little night
Straley, J. The big both ways
Aunt Julia and the scriptwriter Vargas Llosa, M.
Auntie Poldi and the Vineyards of Etna Giordano, M.
Auntie Poldi novels [series] Giordano, M.

AUNTS
Cheever, J. The Wapshot chronicle
Cheever, J. The Wapshot scandal
Coomer, J. One vacant chair
Dean, A. A place of confinement
Frazier, C. Nightwoods
Ganek, D. The summer we read Gatsby
Heyer, G. Black sheep
Hoffman, A. Practical magic
Phillips, J. Lark and Termite
Rinehart, M. Miss Pinkerton
Schwarz, C. Drowning Ruth
Shapiro, B. The muralist
St. James, S. The Sun Down motel
Vine, B. The House of Stairs

AUNTS -- ORANGE COUNTY, CALIFORNIA
Rosenberg, N. Interest of justice

AUNTS AND UNCLES
Jones, S. Mongrels

AURAS
Castle, J. The lost night
Aurelio Zen mysteries [series] Dibdin, M.
Aurora Robinson, K.

AUSCHWITZ (CONCENTRATION CAMP)
Amis, M. Time's arrow, or The nature of the offense

Amis, M. The zone of interest
Gross, A. The one man
Konar, A. Mischling
Krall, H. Chasing the king of hearts
Matthiessen, P. In paradise
Morris, H. Cilka's journey
Tidhar, L. A man lies dreaming
The **Aussie** next door London, S.
The **Austen** playbook Parker, L.

AUSTEN, JANE, 1775-1817 APPRECIATION
Fowler, K. The Jane Austen book club
Austenland Hale, S.
Austenland novels [series] Hale, S.
Austerlitz Sebald, W.

AUSTIN, TEXAS
Abbott, J. Blame
Hynes, J. Next
Loren, R. The one you fight for
Perkins, S. Murder once removed
Pryor, M. Hollow man
Simon, M. The last Jew standing

AUSTRALIA
Bail, M. Eucalyptus
Carey, P. My life as a fake
Carey, P. His illegal self
Clarke, M. Foreign soil
Cleary, J. The sundowners
Coetzee, J. Elizabeth Costello
Coetzee, J. Slow man
Daisley, S. Coming rain
Dalton, T. Boy swallows universe
Disher, G. Under the cold bright lights
Egan, G. Perihelion summer
Flanagan, R. The unknown terrorist
Fox, C. Crimson Lake
Fox, C. Redemption point
Fox, C. Gone by midnight
Francis, D. Wedding Bush Road
Greenwood, K. Death by water
Greenwood, K. Unnatural habits
Grenville, K. The idea of perfection
Harper, J. The dry
Harper, J. The lost man
Howarth, P. Only killers and thieves
Irwin, S. The dead path
Kate, J. A girl's guide to the Outback
Keneally, T. Woman of the inner sea
London, J. The golden age
London, S. The Aussie next door
Lowell, E. Pearl Cove
McFarlane, F. The night guest
McGahan, A. The white earth
McLean, F. The Van Apfel girls are gone
Moriarty, J. Gravity is the thing
Moriarty, L. The husband's secret
Moriarty, L. Nine perfect strangers
Moriarty, L. Truly madly guilty

Durrell, L. Clea
Durrell, L. Justine
Everett, P. Percival Everett by Virgil Russell
Fernandez, M. The museum of eterna's novel
Fox, C. Crimson Lake
Fuentes, C. The old gringo
Furst, A. Under occupation
Gessen, K. All the sad young literary men
Ginzburg, N. A family lexicon
Goldberg, L. Fake truth
Greer, A. Less
Gunday, H. The few
Hand, E. Mortal love
Handke, P. Crossing the Sierra de Gredos
Harkaway, N. Gnomon
Henry, P. Becoming Mrs. Lewis
Hijuelos, O. Twain & Stanley enter paradise
Horowitz, A. The sentence is death
Horowitz, A. The word is murder
Hurwitz, G. The crime writer
King, S. Finders keepers
Knausgaard, K. My struggle.
Kotzwinkle, W. The bear went over the mountain
Landis, J. Heartbreak hotel
Lovesey, P. The vault
Mann, T. Death in Venice and seven other stories
Martel, Y. Beatrice and Virgil
Maugham, W. Cakes and ale
McCall Smith, A. The Limpopo Academy of Private Detection
McEwan, I. Sweet tooth
McLain, P. Love and ruin
McLarty, R. Art in America
Means, D. Hystopia
Miller, H. Tropic of Cancer
Moore, G. The Sherlockian
Moore, M. The islanders
Mootoo, S. Moving forward sideways, like a crab
Mortimer, J. Felix in the underworld
Morton, B. Florence Gordon
Mosby, S. You can run
Murray, P. The mark and the void
Nabokov, V. Look at the harlequins!
Naipaul, V. Half a life
Novey, I. Ways to disappear
Oates, J. Jack of spades
Oe, K. The changeling
Oe, K. Death by water
Offill, J. Dept. of speculation
Ogawa, Y. The memory police
Ohlsson, K. The disappeared
Oyeyemi, H. Mr. Fox
Palmer, L. Otherwise engaged
Parmar, P. Vanessa and her sister
Patchett, A. Commonwealth
Pearl, M. The Dante Club
Peet, M. The Murdstone trilogy

Phillips, S. Heroes are my weakness
Powers, R. Generosity
Pronzini, B. The crimes of Jordan Wise
Prose, F. Blue angel
Richler, M. Solomon Gursky was here
Robinson, P. The first cut
Ruiz Zafon, C. The labyrinth of the spirits
Rushdie, S. Quichotte
Rutherfurd, E. The princes of Ireland
Saramago, J. The history of the siege of Lisbon
Sarginson, S. The wonderful
Sartre, J. Nausea
Savage, S. Glass
Schumacher, J. Dear committee members
Shaw, M. Murder at the mill
Shepard, S. The one inside
Silvis, R. Two days gone
Stegner, W. Crossing to safety
Stern, S. The Pinch
Straub, P. Ghost story
Thelen, A. The island of second sight
Theroux, M. Strange bodies
Tidhar, L. A man lies dreaming
Toibin, C. The master
Truong, M. The sweetest fruits
Ullmann, L. Unquiet
Vargas Llosa, M. Aunt Julia and the scriptwriter
Vasquez, J. The shape of the ruins
Vuong, O. On Earth we're briefly gorgeous
Wayne, T. Apartment
Wolff, T. Old school
Wolitzer, M. The wife
Woolf, V. The voyage out
Yap, F. Yesterday

AUTHORS -- DEATH
Cook, T. The crime of Julian Wells
Galbraith, R. The silkworm
James, P. The lighthouse
Pearl, M. The last Dickens

AUTHORS -- MAINE
King, S. Salem's lot

AUTHORS -- SPAIN
Ruiz Zafon, C. The angel's game

AUTHORS AND PUBLISHERS
Vidal, G. The golden age

AUTHORS' SPOUSES
Fowler, T. Z
Maugham, W. Cakes and ale
Morgan, J. The secret life of William Shakespeare
Wolitzer, M. The wife

AUTHORS' SPOUSES -- UNITED STATES
McLain, P. The Paris wife

AUTHORS, AMERICAN
Bellow, S. Humboldt's gift
Bellow, S. Ravelstein
Berger, T. Being invisible
Chabon, M. Wonder boys

Proust, M. Remembrance of things past
Proust, M. Swann's way
Proust, M. Within a budding grove
Rodrigues Fowler, Y. Stubborn archivist
Roth, P. American pastoral
Roth, P. The anatomy lesson
Roth, P. Everyman
Roth, P. Exit ghost
Roth, P. The ghost writer
Roth, P. The human stain
Roth, P. I married a Communist
Roth, P. My life as a man
Roth, P. Zuckerman bound
Roth, P. Zuckerman unbound
Stegner, W. The Big Rock Candy Mountain
Ullmann, L. Unquiet
Walker, N. Cherry
Wiesel, E. Dawn
Wolfe, T. Look homeward, angel
Wolfe, T. You can't go home again

AUTOBIOGRAPHICAL MEMORY
Drabble, M. The sea lady
Updike, J. Seek my face

AUTOBIOGRAPHIES AND MEMOIRS
Coetzee, J. Summertime
Nabokov, V. Novels and memoirs, 1941-51
Wiesel, E. Night, Dawn, The accident

AUTOBIOGRAPHY
Cohen, J. Book of numbers
Dufresne, J. Requiem, Mass.
Everett, P. Percival Everett by Virgil Russell
Grossman, D. A horse walks into a bar
Torday, D. The last flight of Poxl West

AUTOBIOGRAPHY -- THERAPEUTIC USE -- ITALY
Svevo, I. Zeno's conscience
The **autobiography** of Miss Jane Pittman Gaines, E.
The **autobiography** of my mother Kincaid, J.
The **autograph** man Smith, Z.

AUTOGRAPHS -- COLLECTORS AND COLLECTING
Smith, Z. The autograph man

AUTOMATA
Bear, E. The red-stained wings
Wilson, D. The clockwork dynasty

AUTOMATION -- SOCIAL ASPECTS
Vonnegut, K. Player piano

AUTOMOBILE DEALERS
Vonnegut, K. Breakfast of champions

AUTOMOBILE DRIVERS
Adiga, A. The white tiger

AUTOMOBILE DRIVING
Sallis, J. Drive
Sallis, J. Driven

AUTOMOBILE INDUSTRY AND TRADE -- UNITED STATES
Lewis, S. Dodsworth

AUTOMOBILE LICENSE PLATES
Greer, R. First of state

AUTOMOBILE MECHANICS
McCall Smith, A. In the company of cheerful ladies
Roberts, N. The obsession

AUTOMOBILE RACING
Carey, P. A long way from home
Gray, J. A lady never lies
Stein, G. The art of racing in the rain

AUTOMOBILE RACING DRIVERS
Stein, G. The art of racing in the rain

AUTOMOBILE RALLIES
Carey, P. A long way from home

AUTOMOBILE SALES PERSONNEL
Updike, J. Rabbit is rich
Updike, J. Rabbit, run

AUTOMOBILE THEFTS
Faulkner, W. The reivers
Kennedy, R. Presidio
Westlake, D. The road to ruin

AUTOMOBILE THIEVES
Cussler, C. The Gray Ghost

AUTOMOBILE TRAVEL
Barthelme, F. Painted desert
Clegg, B. Did you ever have a family
Coe, J. The terrible privacy of Maxwell Sim
Crumley, J. Bordersnakes
Danielewski, M. Only revolutions
Dicks, M. The perfect comeback of Caroline Jacobs
Downing, S. He started it
Evison, J. The revised fundamentals of caregiving
Faulkner, W. The reivers
Gifford, B. Wyoming
Gilman, S. Donna has left the building
Kennedy, R. Presidio
Kerouac, J. On the road
Kingsolver, B. The bean trees
Makkai, R. The borrower
Martel, Y. The high mountains of Portugal
Meno, J. Marvel and a wonder
Mina, D. Conviction
Nadzam, B. Lamb
O'Connell, C. Find me
Olafsdottir, A. Butterflies in November
Phillips, S. Natural born charmer
Reid, I. I'm thinking of ending things
Rushdie, S. Quichotte
Spillane, M. Kill me, darling
Townsend, S. Number 10
Tyler, A. Breathing lessons
Ward, J. Sing, unburied, sing
Wolitzer, H. Hearts

AUTOMOBILES
Buehlman, C. The Suicide Motor Club
Connelly, M. The Lincoln lawyer

AUTOMOBILES -- DESIGN AND CONSTRUCTION
Gray, J. A lady never lies
Autonomous Newitz, A.

AUTONOMOUS VEHICLES

Marrs, J. The passengers

AUTONOMY
McGhee, A. The opposite of fate

AUTOPSY
Martel, Y. The high mountains of Portugal
Welsh, K. The unquiet heart

AUTUMN
Allen, S. First frost

Autumn Smith, A.

The **autumn** of the patriarch Garcia Marquez, G.

Ava's place Cogburn, E.

Available dark Hand, E.

Avalon Seton, A.

AVALON (LEGENDARY PLACE)
Seton, A. Avalon

AVANT-GARDE (AESTHETICS)
Beatty, P. Slumberland

AVATARS (VIRTUAL REALITY)
Cline, E. Ready player one
Ruff, M. 88 names

Avenue of mysteries Irving, J.

AVERSION
Guillory, J. The wedding party

AVERSION THERAPY
Burgess, A. A clockwork orange

Avery & Blake novels [series] Carter, M.

AVIATION
Saint-Exupery, A. Night flight

The **aviator's** wife Benjamin, M.

The **awakening** land Richter, C.

AWARDS, PRIZES, HONORS, ETC
Coetzee, J. Elizabeth Costello
Walker, C. Man of the year

AWARENESS
Erpenbeck, J. The book of words

Away Urquhart, J.

AYATOLLAHS
Dowlatabadi, M. The colonel

Aye, and Gomorrah Delany, S.

Ayesha at last Jalaluddin, U.

Ayiti Gay, R.

Aztec mysteries [series] Levack, S.

AZTECS
Levack, S. Demon of the air

AZTECS -- HISTORY -- 16TH CENTURY
Sherwood, F. Night of sorrows

AZTECS -- RELIGION
Bowles, D. Feathered serpent, dark heart of sky

B

B-52 BOMBER
Brown, D. Flight of the Old Dog

B-more careful Holmes, S.

BAALBERGEN, SARAH VAN, 1607- APPROXIMATELY 1638
Smith, D. The last painting of Sara De Vos

Babbitt Lewis, S.

The **Babe** Ruth deception Stewart, D.

Babel Tower Byatt, A.

BABEL, I (ISAAK), 1894-1941 MANUSCRIPTS
Holland, T. The archivist's story

The **babes** in the wood Rendell, R.

Babi Yar Kuznetsov, A.

BABI YAR MASSACRE, 1941
Kuznetsov, A. Babi Yar

BABY BOOM GENERATION
Grant, L. We had it so good

Baby Ganesh Agency investigations [series] Khan, V.

BABY STEALING
Barton, F. The child

Baby teeth Stage, Z.

BABYLON (EXTINCT CITY)
Andrews, M. Of fire and lions
Anton, M. Apprentice

Babylon's ashes Corey, J.

BABYSITTERS
Arsenault, E. In search of the Rose notes
Haigh, J. Mrs. Kimble
McDermott, A. Child of my heart
Reid, K. Such a fun age
Rendell, R. The babes in the wood

BABYSITTING
Starnone, D. Trick

BACCARAT
Fleming, I. Casino royale

BACH, JOHANN SEBASTIAN, 1685-1750
Belfer, L. And after the fire

BACHELORETTE PARTIES
Ware, R. In a dark, dark wood

BACK BAY, BOSTON, MASSACHUSETTS
Lehane, D. Mystic river
Lehane, D. Prayers for rain

Back channel Carter, S.

Back roads O'Dell, T.

Back story Parker, R.

Back talk Lazarin, D.

Back to blood Wolfe, T.

Back when we were grownups Tyler, A.

Backlash Spencer, S.

Bad Blood Dahl, A.

Bad blood Malone, M.

Bad blood Monroe, M.

Bad boy Brawly Brown Mosley, W.

Bad company Higgins, J.

The **bad** daughter Fielding, J.

A **bad** day for sunshine Jones, D.

BAD DAYS
Barry, D. Lunatics

Bad dirt Proulx, A.

Bad dreams and other stories Hadley, T.

The **bad** girl Vargas Llosa, M.

Bad Girl Creek Mapson, J.

Bad Girl Creek trilogy [series] Mapson, J.

Bad girlz Holmes, S.

Bad girlz novels [series] Holmes, S.

Bad intentions Fossum, K.

Bad Little Falls Doiron, P.

BAD LUCK

Amirrezvani, A. The blood of flowers

Dexter, P. Spooner

Proulx, A. Accordion crimes

Russo, R. Nobody's fool

Bad luck and trouble Child, L.

Bad men and wicked women Dickey, E.

Bad monkey Hiaasen, C.

Bad moon rising Gorman, E.

BAD MOTHER (CONCEPT)

Flint, E. Little deaths

BAD NAUHEIM, GERMANY

Ford, F. The good soldier

Bad news Westlake, D.

The **bad** seed March, W.

Bad signs Ellory, R.

Bad things happen Dolan, H.

BADEN-BADEN (GERMANY)

Tsypkin, L. Summer in Baden-Baden

Badenheim 1939 Apelfeld, A.

Badger boy Kelton, E.

BADGERS

Kerr, L. Wild on my mind

Badlands Bowen, P.

Badlands Box, C.

BADMINTON (GAME)

Le Carre, J. Agent running in the field

The **baggage** handler Rawlings, D.

The **Baghdad** clock Al Rawi, S.

BAGHDAD, IRAQ

Barth, J. The last voyage of somebody the sailor

Sa'dawi, A. Frankenstein in Baghdad

BAGOAS

Renault, M. The Persian boy

Bagombo snuff box Vonnegut, K.

BAHAMAS

Williams, B. The golden hour

BAHAMIAN AMERICANS

Phillips, C. Dancing in the dark

BAHIA, BRAZIL

Amado, J. Dona Flor and her two husbands

BAIL BOND AGENTS

Koryta, M. The prophet

Leonard, E. Rum punch

Bailey Ruth mysteries [series] Hart, C.

Bailey's Cafe Naylor, G.

Baked Smith, M.

The **baked** bean supper murders Rich, V.

Baker Street brothers [series] Robertson, M.

The **Baker** Street letters Robertson, M.

The **Baker** Street translation Robertson, M.

Baker Towers Haigh, J.

BAKERS

Allen, S. The girl who chased the moon

Picoult, J. The storyteller

Walter, J. Citizen Vince

BAKING

Berg, E. Night of miracles

BALANCE (PSYCHOLOGY)

Cogburn, E. Ava's place

Balance of power Patterson, R.

BALDER (NORSE DEITY)

Gaiman, N. Norse mythology

BALKAN PENINSULA

Furst, A. Spies of the Balkans

Obreht, T. The tiger's wife

BALKAN PENINSULA -- HISTORY -- TO 1501

Kadare, I. The three-arched bridge

Ball lightning Liu, C.

Ballad novels [series] McCrumb, S.

The **ballad** of Frankie Silver McCrumb, S.

The **ballad** of Tom Dooley McCrumb, S.

BALLADS, AMERICAN -- HISTORY AND CRITICISM

McCrumb, S. The ballad of Tom Dooley

BALLADS, SCOTTISH

Dean, P. Tam Lin

BALLARD, J G, 1930-2009

Ballard, J. Empire of the sun

Ballard, J. The kindness of women

BALLET DANCERS

Brayden, M. First position

Buchanan, C. The painted girls

Matthews, J. Red sparrow

Stachniak, E. The chosen maiden

BALLISTIC MISSILES

Church, J. Bamboo and blood

BALLS (PARTIES)

Baker, J. Longbourn

Dare, T. Do you want to start a scandal

Fowler, T. A well-behaved woman

Quinn, J. An offer from a gentleman

Quinn, J. The lady most willing

Balthasar's odyssey Maalouf, A.

Balthazar Durrell, L.

Baltimore novels (Millie Criswell) [series] Criswell, M.

BALTIMORE, MARYLAND

Constantine, L. The last time I saw you

Holmes, S. B-more careful

JaQuavis The dopeman's wife

Lippman, L. After I'm gone

Lippman, L. Hush hush

Lippman, L. No good deeds

Lippman, L. What the dead know

Palmer, M. The last surgeon

Row, J. Your face in mine

Tyler, A. The accidental tourist

Tyler, A. The amateur marriage

Tyler, A. Back when we were grownups

Tyler, A. The beginner's goodbye

Tyler, A. Celestial navigation

Bannerless novels (Carrie Vaughn) [series] Vaughn, C.
Bannon and Clare [series] Saintcrow, L.
A **banquet** of consequences George, E.
BANSHEES
  Griffin, K. The glass god
  Griffin, K. Stray souls
BAPTISM
  O'Connor, F. The violent bear it away
BAPTISTS
  Kingsolver, B. The Poisonwood Bible
BAR OWNERS
  Carr, R. Virgin river
  Dell, K. Fearless in Texas
  Murakami, H. South of the border, west of the sun
  Roberts, N. Midnight Bayou
  Shalvis, J. Sweet little lies
  Sidor, S. Skin River
BARBADOS
  Edugyan, E. Washington Black
  Jackson, N. The star side of Bird Hill
  Willig, L. The summer country
Barbara Devane novels [series] Koen, K.
Barbarous Spencer, M.
The **Barbary** figs Boudjedra, R.
BARBECUES
  Moriarty, L. Truly madly guilty
Barbed wire heart Sharpe, T.
BARBER, FRANK, D 1801
  Phillips, C. Foreigners
BARBERS
  Berry, W. Jayber Crow
  Danticat, E. The dew breaker
BARCELONA, SPAIN
  Hill Gumbao, T. The good suicides
  Hill Gumbao, T. The summer of dead toys
  Ruiz Zafon, C. The angel's game
  Ruiz Zafon, C. The labyrinth of the spirits
  Ruiz Zafon, C. The prisoner of heaven
  Ruiz Zafon, C. The shadow of the wind
BARCELONA, SPAIN -- HISTORY -- 20TH CENTURY
  Pearce, M. A dead man in Barcelona
Barchester Towers Trollope, A.
Bare bones Reichs, K.
BARE KNUCKLE BOXING
  Smith, M. The fighter
Bareknuckle bastards [series] MacLean, S.
BARGES
  Robinson, P. Playing with fire
BARISTAS
  Ellis, M. Keeping bedlam at bay in the Prague Cafe
  Wong, D. Futuristic violence and fancy suits
Bark of night Rosenfelt, D.
Barkskins Proulx, A.
BARLOW, FRANCIS C (FRANCIS CHANNING), 1834-1896
  Peters, R. Hell or Richmond
BARNARD'S CROSSING, MASSACHUSETTS

  Kemelman, H. Monday the rabbi took off
  Kemelman, H. One fine day the rabbi bought a cross
  Kemelman, H. Thursday the Rabbi walked out
Barney's version Richler, M.
BARNUM, P T (PHINEAS TAYLOR), 1810-1891
  Slouka, M. God's fool
The **baron** in the trees Calvino, I.
Baroness Pontalba novels [series] Smith, J.
BARONS AND BARONESSES
  Higgins, J. Flight of eagles
  Steinke, R. Holy skirts
  deWitt, P. Undermajordomo Minor
BARONS AND BARONESSES -- ITALY
  Calvino, I. The baron in the trees
Barrytown novels [series] Doyle, R.
BARS
  Grimes, M. The Old Wine Shades
  Westlake, D. Watch your back!
BARS (DRINKING ESTABLISHMENTS)
  Alexis, A. The hidden keys
  Banner, C. The house at the edge of night
  Bruen, K. The guards
  Daoud, K. The Meursault investigation
  Koenig, M. Nine days
  Martin, A. Blitzed
  Rossner, J. Looking for Mr. Goodbar
  Sidor, S. Skin River
BARS -- MONTANA
  Doig, I. The bartender's tale
The **bartender's** tale Doig, I.
BARTENDERS
  Danler, S. Sweetbitter
  Drury, T. The driftless area
  Huston, C. Caught stealing
  Koontz, D. Velocity
  Mandel, E. The glass hotel
  Moore, C. Noir
BASEBALL
  Jen, G. The resisters
  Malamud, B. The natural
  Parker, R. Double play
  Roth, P. The great American novel
  Starr, J. Lights out
  Stewart, D. The Babe Ruth deception
BASEBALL -- HISTORY -- 20TH CENTURY
  DeLillo, D. Underworld
BASEBALL FANS
  DeLillo, D. Underworld
BASEBALL FIELDS
  Patterson, R. Dark lady
BASEBALL PLAYERS
  Everett, P. Suder
  Holmes, L. Evvie Drake starts over
  Owen, H. Parker Field
  Parker, R. Double play
  Roth, P. The great American novel
  Sayers, V. The powers

Andrews, M. Sunset Beach
Baldacci, D. One summer
Foster, L. Sisters of summer's end
Goodman, C. The sea of lost girls
Pineiro, C. One summer night
Sparks, N. Every breath
The **beadworkers** Piatote, B.
BEAGLE EXPEDITION, 1831-1836
McDonald, R. Mr. Darwin's shooter
The **bean** trees Kingsolver, B.
The **bear** Krivak, A.
The **bear** and the nightingale Arden, K.
BEAR ATTACKS
Heller, P. Celine
The **bear** went over the mountain Kotzwinkle, W.
Beards and bondage [series] Weatherspoon, R.
BEARS
Kotzwinkle, W. The bear went over the mountain
Krivak, A. The bear
McLaughlin, J. Bearskin
Singh, N. Silver silence
BEARS -- APPALACHIAN TRAIL
King, S. The girl who loved Tom Gordon
Bearskin McLaughlin, J.
Beartown Backman, F.
Beartown [series] Backman, F.
Beast Charmer [series] Martineau, M.
Beastly things Leon, D.
BEAT CULTURE
Bisson, T. Any day now
Joyce, G. The limits of enchantment
Kerouac, J. The dharma bums
Kerouac, J. On the road
Kerouac, J. Road novels 1957-1960
BEAT GENERATION
Kerouac, J. Road novels 1957-1960
The **beat** goes on Rankin, I.
Beat to quarters Forester, C.
Beatrice and Virgil Martel, Y.
BEATRICE,, OF PROVENCE, QUEEN OF SICILY, CON-
SORT OF CHARLES I, KING OF NAPLES, 1234-1267
Jones, S. Four sisters, all queens
Beau death Lovesey, P.
BEAUFORT, MARGARET,, COUNTESS OF RICHMOND
AND DERBY, 1443-1509
Gregory, P. The red queen
BEAUMONT, TEXAS
Sandlin, L. The bird boys
The **beautiful** and damned Fitzgerald, F.
A **beautiful** blue death Finch, C.
The **beautiful** bureaucrat Phillips, H.
Beautiful children Bock, C.
A **beautiful** corpse Daugherty, C.
The **beautiful** dead Bauer, B.
Beautiful ghosts Pattison, E.
Beautiful Maria of my soul Hijuelos, O.
The **beautiful** mystery Penny, L.

A **beautiful** place to die Nunn, M.
The **beautiful** room is empty White, E.
Beautiful ruins Walter, J.
The **beautiful** things that heaven bears Mengestu, D.
A **beautiful** young woman Lopez, J.
BEAUTY
George, M. Helen of Troy
Gowdy, B. Helpless
James, E. When Beauty tamed the Beast
Maupassant, G. Like death
McDermott, A. Child of my heart
Mishima, Y. The temple of the golden pavilion
Morris, H. Cilka's journey
Oyeyemi, H. Boy, Snow, Bird
Walker, S. Dietland
Weldon, F. The life and loves of a she-devil
BEAUTY CONTESTANTS
Butler, K. Pretty ugly
BEAUTY CONTESTS
Butler, K. Pretty ugly
BEAUTY IN NATURE
Strout, E. Olive, again
BEAUTY SHOPS
Ervin, K. Mina's joint
Because I'm watching Dodd, C.
Because it is bitter, and because it is my heart Oates, J.
Because the rain Buckman, D.
Becoming Madame Mao Min, A.
Becoming Mrs. Lewis Henry, P.
BED-AND-BREAKFAST
Block, L. The burglar in the library
McPherson, C. Go to my grave
Bedding Lord Ned MacKenzie, S.
Bedford Square Perry, A.
Bedlam Hollingshead, G.
Bedlam Rowland, L.
The **bedlam** detective Gallagher, S.
The **Bedlam** stacks Pulley, N.
BEDOUINS
Barnes, K. In the kingdom of men
The **beekeeper** of Aleppo Lefteri, C.
The **beekeeper's** apprentice King, L.
The **beekeeper's** ball Wiggs, S.
BEEKEEPERS
Frank, D. Queen bee
Kellerman, F. Milk and honey
Lefteri, C. The beekeeper of Aleppo
BEEKEEPERS -- SOUTH CAROLINA
Kidd, S. The secret life of bees
BEER
Stradal, J. The lager queen of Minnesota
The **beet** queen Erdrich, L.
Before and after Brown, R.
Before I go to sleep Watson, S.
Before I let you go Rimmer, K.
Before the devil fell Olson, N.
Before the fall Hawley, N.

Harris, R. An officer and a spy
Horrocks, C. The vexations
Inbinder, G. The hanged man
Jones, J. The silence
Maupassant, G. Like death
Moore, C. Sacre bleu
Pope, B. The missing Italian girl
Robertson, I. The Paris winter
Sedgwick, M. Mister Memory
Tallis, F. Vienna blood
Vreeland, S. Luncheon of the boating party
Bellevue square Redhill, M.
Bellfield Hall Dean, A.
Bellweather rhapsody Racculia, K.
BELLY DANCERS
Robbins, T. Skinny legs and all
Belmont mansion novels [series] Alexander, T.
BELMONT, ALVA, 1853-1933
Fowler, T. A well-behaved woman
BELONGING
Ahmad, J. The wandering falcon
Allende, I. A long petal of the sea
Awad, M. Bunny
Carey, P. His illegal self
Cauwelaert, D. One-way
Chai, M. Useful phrases for immigrants
Clemmons, Z. What we lose
Cline, E. The girls
Coster, N. Halsey Street
Cusset, C. Life of David Hockney
Deb, S. The point of return
Donohue, K. The stolen child
Eggers, D. What is the what
Fridlund, E. History of wolves
Hesse, H. The fairy tales of Hermann Hesse
Hodgen, C. Elegies for the brokenhearted
Iweala, U. Speak no evil
Jacobson, H. The Finkler question
Kafka, F. Collected stories
Kingsbury, K. A Baxter family Christmas
Krueger, W. This tender land
Kwok, J. Searching for Sylvie Lee
Lee, D. Country of origin
McCullers, C. The heart is a lonely hunter
McCullers, C. The member of the wedding
Mirza, F. A place for us
Mozley, F. Elmet
Myers, A. Continental divide
Netzer, L. Shine shine shine
Rivers, F. Bridge to haven
Rodrigues Fowler, Y. Stubborn archivist
Row, J. Your face in mine
Savas, A. Walking on the ceiling
Schwartz, J. The red daughter
Singer, I. Collected stories
Solomon, A. Disgruntled
Tyler, A. Digging to America

Wolff, T. Old school
Yoon, P. The mountain
Beloved Morrison, T.
Beloved poison Thomson, E.
Below the belt Woods, S.
Beluga Gavin, R.
Ben Abbott mysteries [series] Scott, J.
Ben Walker novels [series] Golden, C.
Ben Webster novels [series] Morgan Jones, C.
Ben-Hur Wallace, L.
A **bend** in the river Naipaul, V.
Bendigo Shafter L'Amour, L.
Beneath the abbey wall Scott, A.
Beneath the sugar sky McGuire, S.
BENEDICTINE MONASTERIES
Westlake, D. Brothers keepers
BENEDICTINE NUNS
Sharratt, M. Illuminations
BENEDICTINES ITALY.
Eco, U. The name of the rose
Benediction Haruf, K.
BENEFACTORS
Dickens, C. Great expectations
Lipsyte, S. The ask
Ozick, C. Heir to the glimmering world
BENGAL (INDIA)
Roy, A. An atlas of impossible longing
BENGALI (SOUTH ASIAN PEOPLE) IN ENGLAND
Ali, M. Brick Lane
BENGALI (SOUTH ASIAN PEOPLE) IN INDIA
Deb, S. The point of return
BENGALI AMERICANS
Ghosh, A. Gun Island
Benjamin January mysteries [series] Hambly, B.
Benjamin Weaver novels [series] Liss, D.
Benny Griessel novels [series] Meyer, D.
Bent Road Roy, L.
BEREAVEMENT
Adkins, M. When you read this
Bilenchi, R. The chill
Brockmeier, K. The brief history of the dead
Brockmeier, K. The illumination
Brockmeier, K. The truth about Celia
Byrne, T. Ghosts and lightning
Clarke, L. A single breath
Collins, C. The gamal
Drake, L. The sweet spot
Erdrich, L. The painted drum
Grossman, D. Falling out of time
Hemmings, K. The possibilities
Hill, S. The pure in heart
Krentz, J. River road
McAllister, T. The young widower's handbook
McPherson, C. Quiet neighbors
Meno, J. The boy detective fails
Meyers, K. Twisted tree
Palaia, M. The given world

Pitoniak, A. Necessary people
Rader-Day, L. Little pretty things
Raymond, J. The half-life
Reichs, K. Deja dead
Rooney, S. Conversations with friends
Snow, J. An Alaskan Christmas
Stegner, W. Crossing to safety
Stephens, A. Famous adopted people
Trollope, J. The best of friends
Tsukiyama, G. Dreaming water
Unger, L. Crazy love you
Wilson, R. Spin

BEST FRIENDS -- DEATH
Bellow, S. Humboldt's gift

BEST FRIENDS -- ILLINOIS
Bradbury, R. Something wicked this way comes

Best horror of the year (Ellen Datlow) [series]

Best kept secret Archer, J.

The **best** kind of trouble Dane, L.

The **best** man Higgins, K.

BEST MAN (WEDDINGS)
Johnson, M. Smitten by the Brit

The **best** of Ellery Queen Queen, E.

The **best** of friends Trollope, J.

The **best** of Gene Wolfe Wolfe, G.

Best of my love Mallery, S.

The **best** of the best horror of the year

The **best** of Wodehouse Wodehouse, P.

The **best** of youth Dahlie, M.

BEST SELLERS (BOOKS)
Carpenter, E. The weight of lies
Kotzwinkle, W. The bear went over the mountain

Best served cold Spencer, S.

The **best** short stories of Bret Harte Harte, B.

The **best** short stories of Dostoevsky Dostoyevsky, F.

BESTIALITY
Hale, B. The evolution of Bruno Littlemore

Bethlehem Road Perry, A.

BETHLEM ROYAL HOSPITAL (LONDON, ENGLAND)
Hollingshead, G. Bedlam

BETRAYAL
50 Cent Blow
Abani, C. The secret history of Las Vegas
Abbott, S. The future of love
Akunin, B. Sister Pelagia and the white bulldog
Allende, I. Portrait in sepia
Andersen, L. The Boleyn deceit
Andersen, L. The Boleyn king
Andersen, L. The Boleyn reckoning
Asimov, I. Second foundation
Atwood, M. The blind assassin
Auster, P. Leviathan
Baca, J. The importance of a piece of paper
Bagshawe, T. Adored
Banville, J. The blue guitar
Barclay, L. No safe house
Bear, E. Range of ghosts

Bear, E. Shattered pillars
Bezmozgis, D. The betrayers
Binchy, M. Circle of friends
Birmingham, S. Carriage trade
Blau, J. The summer of naked swim parties
Block, L. Killing Castro
Box, C. The bitterroots
Boyden, J. Through black spruce
Boyle, T. World's end
Boyne, J. A ladder to the sky
Brink, A. Philida
Brkic, C. The first rule of swimming
Bryant, N. Message from a mistress
Carlson, R. Five skies
Carpenter, E. Until the day I die
Ca$h Trust no man
Ca$h Trust no man 2
Ca$h Trust no man 3
Center, K. Things you save in a fire
Cheek, C. Cape May
Church, J. Bamboo and blood
Clark, W. Payback is a mutha
Cleeves, A. The crow trap
Clinch, J. Marley
Cobbs Hoffman, E. The Hamilton affair
Cogman, G. The burning page
Coleridge, N. Godchildren
Cook, T. Instruments of night
Cornwell, B. Enemy of God
Cornwell, B. The last kingdom
Cornwell, B. War of the wolf
Coulter, C. The sixth day
Craig, C. Miss Burma
Cumming, C. The Moroccan girl
De Leon, A. Side chick nation
De la Motte, A. Ultimatum
Deane, S. Reading in the dark
Diamant, A. The red tent
Dicks, M. The perfect comeback of Caroline Jacobs
Dimon, H. Mercy
Doan, A. The summer list
Doig, I. Dancing at the Rascal Fair
Dunant, S. Sacred hearts
Eason, K. How Rory Thorne destroyed the multiverse
Edugyan, E. Half-blood blues
Edugyan, E. Washington Black
Enright, A. The gathering
Epstein, J. Wunderland
Estleman, L. Gas City
Feeney, A. Sometimes I lie
Finder, J. Suspicion
Flanery, P. Absolution
Fleming, I. From Russia with love
Follett, K. Eye of the needle
Follett, K. The pillars of the earth
Follett, K. Whiteout
Francis, P. The orphans of Race Point

Renault, M. Funeral games
Rice, L. Little night
Rosenthal, P. The bookseller's daughter
Roth, P. I married a Communist
Runcie, J. Sidney Chambers and the forgiveness of sins
Rushdie, S. The enchantress of Florence
Sallis, J. Drive
Salter, J. All that is
Saylor, S. The triumph of Caesar
Scalzi, J. Redshirts
Schwab, V. Vengeful
Scott, A. A double death on the Black Isle
Sebastian, T. Fatal ally
See, L. Shanghai girls
Shafak, E. Honor
Shupe, J. The courtesan duchess
Sinha, I. Animal's people
Smith, J. If she were dead
Smith, T. Agent 6
Smith, W. Birds of prey
Spark, M. The prime of Miss Jean Brodie
Spencer-Fleming, J. All mortal flesh
Stachniak, E. The Winter Palace
Stark, R. Comeback
Steinhauer, O. All the old knives
Steinhauer, O. The tourist
Styles, T. Raunchy
Styles, T. Raunchy 2
Swift, G. Last orders
Thomas, S. My beautiful enemy
Thomas, S. Private arrangements
Thomas, S. Tempting the bride
Tolkien, J. The fall of Gondolin
Trollope, J. The best of friends
Turner, N. Black widow
Turner, N. Forever a hustler's wife
Turner, N. A hustler's wife
Unsworth, B. After Hannibal
Updike, J. Gertrude and Claudius
Wagers, K. After the crown
Ward, A. Forgive me
Warren, R. World enough and time
Warren, T. The pastor's husband
Warrington, F. Midsummer night
Waters, S. Fingersmith
Weber, C. Man on the run
Weinberg, K. The truants
White, T. The once and future king
Wilkinson, L. American spy
Williams, K. Dirty to the grave
Williams, K. Harlem on lock
The **betrayal** of the blood lily Willig, L.
The **betrayers** Bezmozgis, D.

BETS
Drayson, N. A guide to the birds of East Africa
Gray, J. A lady never lies
Lanchester, J. Fragrant Harbor

Noble, K. The game and the governess
Verne, J. Around the world in eighty days
The **better** liar Jones, T.
A **better** man Penny, L.
The **better** sister Burke, A.
A **better** world Sakey, M.
Between my father and the king Frame, J.
Between the acts Woolf, V.
Between the devil and the duke Bowen, K.
Between the Duke and the deep blue sea Nash, S.

BETWEEN THE WARS (1918-1939)
Chevalier, T. A single thread
Clark, C. In the full light of the sun
Clayton, M. The last train to London
Dunmore, H. The lie
Durrell, L. Justine
Dybek, N. The Verdun affair
Gross, A. Button man
Hannah, S. The mystery of three quarters
Joinson, S. The photographer's wife
Kerr, P. Metropolis
Mamet, D. Chicago
Mathews, B. The world of tomorrow
Mawer, S. The glass room
McPherson, C. A step so grave
Moore, S. The life of objects
Morante, E. Arturo's island
Nemirovsky, I. Fire in the blood
Neubauer, E. Murder at the Mena House
Perry, A. Death in focus
Peters, E. Children of the storm
Reuss, F. Mohr
Solomon, A. Leaving Lucy Pear
Stachniak, E. The chosen maiden
Stewart, D. The Babe Ruth deception
Swift, G. Mothering Sunday
Wieland, L. Paris, 7 a.m.
Winspear, J. Birds of a feather
Beulah series [series] Settle, M.

BEVERLY HILLS, CALIFORNIA
Connelly, M. The Lincoln lawyer
Martin, S. Shopgirl
Beyond absolution Harrison, C.
Beyond all reasonable doubt Persson Giolito, M.
Beyond reason Martin, K.
Beyond recall Goddard, R.
Beyond the limit Dees, C.
Beyond the outposts Brand, M.
Beyond the pale O'Donohue, C.
Beyond the point Gibson, C.

BHOPAL UNION CARBIDE PLANT DISASTER, BHOPAL, INDIA, 1984
Sinha, I. Animal's people

BIAFRA (1967-1970)
Adichie, C. Half of a yellow sun

BIBLE HISTORY OF BIBLICAL EVENTS.
Andrews, M. Of fire and lions

BILLIONAIRES -- CALIFORNIA
Cussler, C. Blue gold

Billy French, A.

Billy Bathgate Doctorow, E.

Billy Boyle Benn, J.

Billy Boyle World War II mysteries [series] Benn, J.

Billy Budd, foretopman Melville, H.

Billy Lynn's long halftime walk Fountain, B.

Billy, come home Callaghan, M.

BILLY,, THE KID
Momaday, N. The ancient child

Biloxi Miller, M.

BILOXI, MISSISSIPPI
Barthelme, F. Bob the gambler

Brown, L. Fay

Miles, J. Anatomy of a miracle

Miller, M. Biloxi

BIN LADEN, OSAMA, 1957-2011
Berenson, A. The faithful spy

BINGE-DRINKING
Bohjalian, C. The flight attendant

Bingo's run Levine, J.

Binocular vision Pearlman, E.

Binti Okorafor, N.

Binti [series] Okorafor, N.

BIO-THRILLERS
Crichton, M. Next

Grant, M. Parasite

Koepp, D. Cold storage

Kosmatka, T. The games

Wilson, D. The Andromeda evolution

BIOCHEMISTRY
Taylor, B. Real life

BIODIVERSITY
Elkins, A. Unnatural selection

The **biographer's** tale Byatt, A.

BIOGRAPHERS
Auster, P. The book of illusions

Barnes, J. Flaubert's parrot

Bellow, S. Ravelstein

Byatt, A. The biographer's tale

Cameron, P. The city of your final destination

Coetzee, J. Summertime

Flanery, P. Absolution

Hollinghurst, A. The stranger's child

Maugham, W. Cakes and ale

Stott, R. Ghostwalk

BIOGRAPHICAL FICTION
Adimi, K. Our riches

Alcott, K. A touch of stardust

Anstruther, E. A perfect explanation

Banks, R. Cloudsplitter

Barnes, J. Flaubert's parrot

Barnes, J. The noise of time

Benedict, M. Lady Clementine

Benedict, M. The only woman in the room

Benioff, D. City of thieves

Benjamin, M. Alice I have been

Benjamin, M. The aviator's wife

Bergman, M. Almost famous women

Bernhard, T. Wittgenstein's nephew

Bird, S. Daughter of a daughter of a queen

Bloom, A. White houses

Boyle, T. The women

Brooks, G. Caleb's crossing

Calvi, M. Dear George, Dear Mary

Carey, E. Little

Chiaverini, J. Resistance women

Cobbs Hoffman, E. The Hamilton affair

Cobbs Hoffman, E. The Tubman command

Cowell, S. Claude & Camille

Coyne, J. The caddie who played with hickory

Cusset, C. Life of David Hockney

Darznik, J. Song of a captive bird

DeLillo, D. Libra

Dean, M. I, Hogarth

Doctorow, E. Homer and Langley

Donoghue, E. Slammerkin

Druon, M. The iron king

Dunant, S. Blood and beauty

Ebershoff, D. The Danish girl

Echenoz, J. Lightning

Eggers, D. What is the what

Erdrich, L. The night watchman

Fallada, H. Every man dies alone

Fowler, T. A well-behaved woman

Fowler, T. Z

Frazier, C. Varina

Freedman, B. Mrs. Mike

Fuentes, C. The old gringo

Garcia Marquez, G. The general in his labyrinth

George, M. The confessions of young Nero

George, M. Elizabeth I

George, M. Helen of Troy

George, M. The splendor before the dark

Graves, R. I, Claudius

Gregory, P. The Boleyn inheritance

Gregory, P. The constant princess

Gregory, P. The kingmaker's daughter

Gregory, P. The lady of the rivers

Gregory, P. The last Tudor

Gregory, P. The other Boleyn girl

Gregory, P. The red queen

Gregory, P. The taming of the queen

Gregory, P. The white princess

Griffith, N. Hild

Hansen, R. The assassination of Jesse James by the coward
   Robert Ford

Henry, P. Becoming Mrs. Lewis

Hensher, P. Scenes from early life

Hicks, R. The widow of the South

Hijuelos, O. Twain & Stanley enter paradise

Hoffman, A. The marriage of opposites

Horan, N. Loving Frank

Walls, J. Half broke horses
Weir, A. Anna of Kleve
Weir, A. A dangerous inheritance
Weir, A. Innocent traitor
Weir, A. The Lady Elizabeth
Weisgall, D. The world before her
Wideman, J. Fanon
Wieland, L. Paris, 7 a.m.
Williams, N. John
Wolfe, P. The lost diary of M
Wood, T. The engineer's wife
Yourcenar, M. Memoirs of Hadrian

BIOGRAPHICAL FILMS
Hall, P. Lights! Camera! Puzzles!
Norman, H. Next life might be kinder

BIOGRAPHY
Byatt, A. The biographer's tale
Cameron, P. The city of your final destination
Maugham, W. Cakes and ale

BIOLOGICAL INVASIONS
McCaffrey, A. Dragonflight

BIOLOGICAL RESEARCH
Byatt, A. A whistling woman
Follett, K. Whiteout

BIOLOGICAL RESEARCHERS
McDonald, R. Mr. Darwin's shooter

BIOLOGICAL STATIONS
Yang, J. The descent of monsters

BIOLOGICAL TERRORISM
Bacigalupi, P. The windup girl
Dekker, T. Black
Dekker, T. Red
Dekker, T. White
Follett, K. Whiteout
Harvey, M. We all fall down
Koepp, D. Cold storage
Rushdan, J. Every last breath

BIOLOGICAL WARFARE
Kava, A. Hotwire
Peace, D. Occupied city

BIOLOGICAL WEAPONS
Dazieri, S. Kill the angel
Vinge, V. Rainbows end

BIOLOGISTS
Craig, P. A shoot on Martha's Vineyard
Gestern, H. The people in the photo
McLaughlin, J. Bearskin

BIOMEDICAL ENGINEERING
Fairstein, L. Blood oath

BIOSPHERE
Powers, R. The overstory

BIOSPHERE 2 (PROJECT)
Boyle, T. The Terranauts

BIOTECHNOLOGY
Asaro, C. Primary inversion
Atwood, M. Oryx and Crake
Cook, R. Pandemic

Crichton, M. Micro
Crichton, M. Next
Gonzales, L. Lucy
Grant, M. Parasite
VanderMeer, J. Borne
VanderMeer, J. Dead astronauts
Watts, P. Starfish

BIOTECHNOLOGY -- SOCIAL ASPECTS
Naam, R. Nexus

BIOTIC COMMUNITIES
Boyle, T. The Terranauts

BIPLANES
Follett, K. Hornet flight

BIPOLAR DISORDER
Garey, J. Too bright to hear too loud to see
Hiaasen, C. Nature girl

The **bird** artist Norman, H.

BIRD ARTISTS
Norman, H. The bird artist

Bird box Malerman, J.

The **bird** boys Sandlin, L.

BIRD CARVING
Kearsley, S. The firebird

The **bird** keeper Festing, I.

The **bird** king Wilson, G.

The **bird** of the river Baker, K.

BIRD SANCTUARIES
Festing, I. The bird keeper

BIRD WATCHERS
Shaw, W. The birdwatcher

BIRD WATCHING
Drayson, N. A guide to the birds of East Africa

Birdman Hayder, M.

BIRDS
Beams, C. The illness lesson
Rosner, J. The yellow bird sings

BIRDS AS PETS
Bourdeaut, O. Waiting for Bojangles

Birds of a feather Winspear, J.

Birds of paradise Abu-Jaber, D.

Birds of prey Jance, J.

Birds of prey Smith, W.

Birds without wings De Bernieres, L.

Birdsong Faulks, S.

The **birdwatcher** Shaw, W.

BIRMINGHAM, ALABAMA
Carpenter, E. Until the day I die

BIRMINGHAM, ALABAMA -- RACE RELATIONS
Naslund, S. Four spirits

BIRMINGHAM, ENGLAND
Coe, J. The rotters' club

BIRTH AND DEATH RECORDS
Saramago, J. All the names

BIRTH CONTROL
Piercy, M. Sex wars
Vonnegut, K. Welcome to the monkey house

BIRTH DEFECTS

BISHOP, ELIZABETH, 1911-1979
Wieland, L. Paris, 7 a.m.

BISHOPS
Robb, C. The cross-legged knight

Bitch King, D.

Bitter Eden Afrika, T.

A **bitter** feast Crombie, D.

Bitter medicine Paretsky, S.

Bitter orange Fuller, C.

Bitter spirits Bennett, J.

The **bitterroots** Box, C.

Bittersweet Albert, S.

Black Dekker, T.

Black and blue Rankin, I.

Black and blue Rosenfelt, D.

Black and ugly Styles, T.

Black and ugly novels [series] Styles, T.

Black Betty Mosley, W.

The **black** book Rankin, I.

BLACK BRITISH
Charles, K. Wanted, a gentleman
Evaristo, B. Girl, woman, other

BLACK CANADIAN WOMEN
Hill, L. Someone knows my name

BLACK CANADIANS
Colvin, J. Africaville

The **Black** Cathedral Gala, M.

Black chalk Yates, C.

Black cherry blues Burke, J.

**BLACK COUNTRY (ENGLAND) -- SOCIAL CONDI-
TIONS -- 20TH CENTURY**
Pietroni, A. Ruby's spoon

Black cross Iles, G.

BLACK DEATH
Follett, K. World without end
Robinson, K. The years of rice and salt
Rutherfurd, E. London
Winawer, M. The scribe of Siena

BLACK DEATH
Walters, M. The last hours

BLACK DEATH -- PROVENCE, FRANCE
Pears, I. The dream of Scipio

Black diamond fall Olshan, J.

Black dogs McEwan, I.

Black Fridays Sears, M.

The **black** god's drums Clark, P.

BLACK HAND (UNITED STATES)
Stewart, A. Girl waits with gun

The **black** hawk Bourne, J.

Black hole Burns, C.

BLACK HOLES (ASTRONOMY)
Egan, G. Perihelion summer

Black horizon Grippando, J.

The **black** hour Rader-Day, L.

BLACK HUMOR
Amdahl, G. I am death
Awad, M. Bunny

Bragi Olafsson, 1. The pets

Braithwaite, O. My sister, the serial killer

Breslin, J. I don't want to go to jail

Burns, A. Little constructions

Celine, L. Journey to the end of the night

Clarke, B. An arsonist's guide to writers' homes in New England

Coover, R. Noir

Crews, H. A feast of snakes

DeLillo, D. White noise

Dermansky, M. Very nice

Dostoyevsky, F. Notes from underground

Dunn, K. Geek love

Gass, W. Middle C

Harrison, J. The great leader

Heller, J. Catch-22

Hiaasen, C. Skin tight

Hynes, J. Kings of infinite space

Jin, H. The boat rocker

Lutz, L. The swallows

McMurtry, L. The evening star

O'Connor, R. Buffalo soldiers

O'Donnell, L. The death of bees

O'Connell, C. Killing critics

Smith, B. Crow's landing

Smith, B. Shoot the dog

Vonnegut, K. Slapstick

Weldon, F. Worst fears

Welsh, I. Dead men's trousers

Welsh, I. Porno

Welsh, I. Skagboys

Welsh, I. Trainspotting

The **black** ice Connelly, M.

Black leopard, red wolf James, M.

Black light Hunter, S.

BLACK LIVES MATTER MOVEMENT
Carty-Williams, C. Queenie

BLACK MAGIC
Bulgakov, M. The master and Margarita
Butcher, J. Proven guilty
Davidson, A. The boatman's daughter
French, J. The Grey Bastards
Garcia, C. Dreaming in Cuban
Polansky, D. Low town
Pratchett, T. Wyrd sisters
Saberhagen, F. Stonecutter's story
Williams, C. Stairway to hell

Black maps Spiegelman, P.

BLACK MARKET
Cook, R. Coma
Cook, R. Pandemic
Corey, J. Babylon's ashes
Cotterill, C. Don't eat me
Lee, F. Jade City
Lehane, D. Live by night
Soule, C. Anyone
Suarez, D. Change agent

Cross-Smith, L. Whiskey & ribbons
Farrow, J. The storm murders
Foley, L. The hunting party
Golden, C. Ararat
Knott, R. Robert B. Parker's Buckskin
Lyons, J. The name of all things
Mizushima, M. Stalking ground
Nelson, C. If we make it home
Quinn, J. The lady most willing
Racculia, K. Bellweather rhapsody
Simpson, R. What the dead leave behind
Stabenow, D. No fixed line
Wiesel, E. The judges

BLIZZARDS -- MAINE

Doiron, P. Bad Little Falls

BLOCH, EDUARD, 1872-1945

Neugeboren, J. 1940

BLOCK ISLAND, RHODE ISLAND

Moore, M. The islanders
Smith, M. She's not there

**BLOCK, LAWRENCE CRITICISM AND INTERPRETA-
TION**

Block, L. The sins of the fathers

BLOCKADE RUNNING

Poyer, D. A country of our own

BLOGGERS

Brookmyre, C. Black widow
Ma, L. Severance
Unger, L. The red hunter

BLOGS

Adkins, M. When you read this
Grant, M. Deadline
Grant, M. Feed
Tremblay, P. A head full of ghosts
Blonde Oates, J.
Blonde faith Mosley, W.
Blonde roots Evaristo, B.

BLOOD

Ryan, A. The waking fire
The **blood** Thomson, E.

BLOOD -- COLLECTION AND PRESERVATION

Palmer, M. The fifth vial

BLOOD -- DISEASES

Coulter, C. The sixth day

BLOOD -- TRANSFUSION -- SOCIAL ASPECTS

Yan, L. Dream of Ding Village
Blood and beauty Dunant, S.
Blood and gold Rice, A.
Blood and iron Bear, E.
Blood canticle Rice, A.
Blood communion Rice, A.
Blood defense Clark, M.
Blood from a stone Leon, D.
Blood hunt Rankin, I.
Blood lines Rendell, R.
Blood memory Coel, M.
Blood meridian, or, The evening redness in the West McCar-

thy, C.
Blood mud Constantine, K.
Blood oath Fairstein, L.
Blood of an exile Naslund, B.
Blood of angels Arvin, R.
The **blood** of flowers Amirrezvani, A.
The **blood** of heaven Wascom, K.
Blood of the oak Pattison, E.
Blood of victory Furst, A.
Blood on snow [series] Nesbo, J.
Blood on snow Nesbo, J.
Blood on the water Perry, A.
Blood shot Paretsky, S.
Blood storm Brooks, B.
Blood's a rover Ellroy, J.
Bloodchild Butler, O.

BLOODHOUNDS

Buxton, K. Hollow kingdom
Bloodroot Greene, A.

BLOODS (GANG)

K'wan Gutter
Bloody genius Sandford, J.
Bloody Sunday Coes, B.
Blooms of darkness Apelfeld, A.

BLOOMSBURY GROUP

Parmar, P. Vanessa and her sister
Blow 50 Cent

BLUE (COLOR)

Moore, C. Sacre bleu
Blue angel Prose, F.
Blue Ant trilogy [series] Gibson, W.
Blue at the mizzen O'Brian, P.
The **blue** between sky and water Abulhawa, S.

BLUE COLLAR FAMILIES

Lehane, D. Mystic river

BLUE COLLAR WOMEN

Erdrich, L. The night watchman

BLUE COLLAR WORKERS

Banks, R. Continental drift
Bolano, R. 2666
Breslin, J. Table money
Pamuk, O. The red-haired woman
Rivero, M. The affairs of the Falcons
Russo, R. Nobody's fool
Santora, N. Fifteen digits
See, C. The handyman
The **blue** flower Fitzgerald, P.
The **blue** fox Sjon, 1.
Blue gold Cussler, C.
The **blue** guitar Banville, J.
Blue heaven Box, C.
Blue Heron romances [series] Higgins, K.
The **blue** hour Parker, T.
The **blue** knight Wambaugh, J.
Blue light Yokohama Obregon, N.
Blue lonesome Pronzini, B.
Blue Mars Robinson, K.

BODY MODIFICATION
Watts, P. Starfish
Body of lies Ignatius, D.
Body slam Burns, R.
BODY SNATCHING
Blake, R. A dark anatomy
Sanders, J. Speakers of the dead
BODY WEIGHT
King, S. Elevation
BODYBUILDERS
Evison, J. All about Lulu
BODYGUARDS
Buchman, M. The night is mine
Carey, J. Starless
Foster, L. Under pressure
Fowler, C. Bryant & May
Gaiman, N. American gods
Galen, S. Third son's a charm
Huston, C. Skinner
Jackson, B. Forged in desire
Malpas, J. Leave me breathless
Meyer, D. Trackers
Parker, R. Cold service
Parker, R. Double play
Parker, R. Sixkill
Parker, T. Storm runners
Pope, J. One warm winter
Sharp, Z. Second shot
Whittle, T. The dangerous edge of things
BODYGUARDS -- RUSSIA
Boyne, J. The house of special purpose
BOER WAR, 1899-1902
Jakeman, J. In the kingdom of mists
BOG BODIES
Hart, E. Haunted ground
Hart, E. Lake of sorrows
Youngson, A. Meet me at the museum
BOGNOR REGIS, ENGLAND
Lovesey, P. The house sitter
BOGOTA, COLOMBIA
Restrepo, L. Delirium
Rojas Contreras, I. Fruit of the drunken tree
Vasquez, J. The sound of things falling
BOGS
Griffiths, E. The crossing places
Hart, E. Haunted ground
Hart, E. Lake of sorrows
BOHEMIANISM
Cortazar, J. Hopscotch
Kelly, E. The poison tree
Leavitt, D. The two Hotel Francforts
Miller, H. Tropic of Cancer
Miller, H. Tropic of Capricorn
Richler, M. Barney's version
Steinke, R. Holy skirts
BOKO HARAM
O'Brien, E. Girl

BOLANO, ROBERTO, 1953-2003
Bolano, R. Last evenings on Earth
The **Boleyn** deceit Andersen, L.
BOLEYN FAMILY
Gregory, P. The Boleyn inheritance
Gregory, P. The other Boleyn girl
The **Boleyn** inheritance Gregory, P.
The **Boleyn** king Andersen, L.
The **Boleyn** reckoning Andersen, L.
BOLEYN, JANE,, VISCOUNTESS ROCHFORD, D 1542
Gregory, P. The Boleyn inheritance
BOLEYN, MARY, 1508-1543
Gregory, P. The other Boleyn girl
BOLIVAR, SIMON, 1783-1830
Garcia Marquez, G. The general in his labyrinth
BOLIVIA
Ferencik, E. Into the jungle
Recacoechea S., J. American visa
A **Bollywood** affair Dev, S.
The **Bollywood** bride Dev, S.
BOLOGNA, ITALY
Rigosi, G. Night bus
The **bomb** maker Perry, T.
BOMB SQUADS
Crais, R. Demolition angel
Lutz, J. Final seconds
Perry, T. The bomb maker
BOMB THREATS
Perry, T. The bomb maker
BOMBER PILOTS
Atkinson, K. A god in ruins
Robbins, D. Last citadel
BOMBERS (PERSONS)
Crais, R. Demolition angel
Muller, M. A wild and lonely place
BOMBING
Hulse, S. Eden mine
Marlette, D. Magic time
Michener, J. The bridges at Toko-Ri
Parker, R. Painted ladies
Reichs, K. Deadly decisions
Sandford, J. Shock wave
BOMBING INVESTIGATION
Crais, R. Demolition angel
Muller, M. The ever-running man
Perry, A. Blood on the water
BOMBING SUSPECTS
Muller, M. The ever-running man
BOMBING VICTIMS
Ganshert, K. Life after
Remarque, E. A time to love and a time to die
BOMBINGS
Al Rawi, S. The Baghdad clock
Auster, P. Leviathan
Bisson, T. Any day now
Butler, R. Paris in the dark
Coughlin, J. In the crosshairs

Book of Lost Swords [series] Saberhagen, F.

The **book** of lost things Connolly, J.

The **book** of M Shepherd, P.

The **book** of night women James, M.

Book of numbers Cohen, J.

The **book** of salt, Monique Truong. Truong, M.

The **book** of splendor Sherwood, F.

The **book** of strange new things Faber, M.

Book of the new sun [series] Wolfe, G.

The **book** of the unnamed midwife Elison, M.

The **book** of words Erpenbeck, J.

Book Tea Shop novel [series] Avon, J.

BOOK THEFTS

Block, L. The burglar in the library

Cogman, G. The burning page

Cogman, G. The invisible library

Cogman, G. The masked city

Cogman, G. The mortal word

Quick, A. I thee wed

Sansom, I. The case of the missing books

Zevin, G. The storied life of A. J. Fikry

Booked to die Dunning, J.

The **bookish** life of Nina Hill Waxman, A.

The **bookman's** tale Lovett, C.

The **bookman's** wake Dunning, J.

BOOKMOBILES

Bennett, A. The uncommon reader

Sansom, I. The case of the missing books

BOOKS

George, N. The little Paris bookshop

Gruber, M. The book of air and shadows

Hackwith, A. The library of the unwritten

Jacobs, N. The last equation of Isaac Severy

Kostova, E. The historian

Lovett, C. The bookman's tale

McKillip, P. Alphabet of thorn

Morgenstern, E. The starless sea

Self, W. The book of Dave

BOOKS -- CONSERVATION AND RESTORATION

Brooks, G. People of the book

Hackwith, A. The library of the unwritten

BOOKS AND READING

Adams, E. The secret, book & scone society

Adams, L. The bromance book club

Alameddine, R. An unnecessary woman

Avon, J. In peppermint peril

Bennett, A. The uncommon reader

Bivald, K. The readers of Broken Wheel recommend

Callanan, L. Paris by the book

Calvino, I. If on a winter's night a traveler

Carlino, R. Swear on this life

Chase, L. A duke in shining armor

Connolly, J. The book of lost things

Cosse, L. A novel bookstore

Extence, G. The universe versus Alex Woods

Fernandez, M. The museum of eterna's novel

Fowler, K. The Jane Austen book club

Horowitz, A. Magpie murders

Jaswal, B. Erotic stories for Punjabi widows

King, S. Finders keepers

Krauss, N. The history of love

Krentz, J. Copper Beach

Lelchuk, S. Save me from dangerous men

Lovett, C. The lost book of the Grail

Makkai, R. The borrower

Pamuk, O. My name is Red

Parry, H. The unlikely escape of Uriah Heep

Pelecanos, G. The man who came uptown

Reay, K. The Bronte plot

Rosenthal, P. The bookseller's daughter

Ruiz Zafon, C. The angel's game

Ruiz Zafon, C. The labyrinth of the spirits

Ruiz Zafon, C. The shadow of the wind

Savage, S. Firmin

Schlink, B. The reader

Setterfield, D. The thirteenth tale

Sloan, R. Mr. Penumbra's 24-hour bookstore

Swanson, P. Eight perfect murders

Tepper, S. The visitor

Van der Vliet Oloomi, A. Call me Zebra

Walton, J. Among others

BOOKS FOR RELUCTANT READERS

Booth, C. Bronxwood

Booth, C. Kendra

Draper, S. Forged by fire

Johnson, A. The first part last

Books of Ambha [series] Suri, T.

Books of history chronicles. Circle trilogy [series] Dekker, T.

The **books** of the dead Bernhard, E.

The **bookseller's** daughter Rosenthal, P.

BOOKSELLERS

Auster, P. The Brooklyn follies

Berry, S. The Templar legacy

Block, L. The burglar in the closet

Block, L. The burglar in the library

Dunning, J. Booked to die

Dunning, J. The bookman's wake

George, N. The little Paris bookshop

Gruber, M. The book of air and shadows

Hart, C. Death walked in

Hart, C. Murder walks the plank

Hart, C. White elephant dead

Hart, C. Yankee Doodle dead

Lovett, C. The bookman's tale

Perez-Reverte, A. The Club Dumas

Reay, K. The Bronte plot

Rosenthal, P. The bookseller's daughter

Ruiz Zafon, C. The labyrinth of the spirits

Ruiz Zafon, C. The prisoner of heaven

Setterfield, D. The thirteenth tale

Swanson, P. Eight perfect murders

Zevin, G. The storied life of A. J. Fikry

BOOKSTORES

Higgins, G. The friends of Eddie Coyle
Higgins, K. Now that you mention it
Hill, E. Little comfort
Hogan, C. Devils in exile
Hoover, C. It ends with us
Kamali, M. The stationery shop
King, L. Father of the rain
Lathen, E. Something in the air
Lehane, D. Mystic river
Lehane, D. Prayers for rain
Lehane, D. Sacred
Lehane, D. Since we fell
Lightman, A. The diagnosis
Lipman, E. The pursuit of Alice Thrift
Minot, S. Evening
Moore, L. The unseen world
Mosley, W. Fortunate son
Neely, B. Blanche cleans up
O'Malley, T. We were kings
Olson, N. Before the devil fell
Palmer, M. The society
Parker, R. Back story
Parker, R. Chance
Parker, R. Cold service
Parker, R. Double deuce
Parker, R. Family honor
Parker, R. Hugger Mugger
Parker, R. Hush money
Parker, R. Melancholy baby
Parker, R. Now and then
Parker, R. Painted ladies
Parker, R. Paper doll
Parker, R. Rough weather
Parker, R. School days
Parker, R. Shrink rap
Parker, R. Sixkill
Parker, R. Small vices
Parker, R. Thin air
Parker, R. Valediction
Parker, R. Walking shadow
Parker, R. Widow's walk
Patchett, A. Run
Pearl, M. The technologists
Racculia, K. Tuesday Mooney talks to ghosts
Ryan, H. The other woman
Ryan, H. Say no more
Ryan, H. Truth be told
Ryan, H. What you see
Ryan, H. The wrong girl
Savage, S. Firmin
Segal, E. Love story
Shrier, H. Boston cream
Smith, M. She smiled sweetly
Swanson, P. Eight perfect murders
Swanson, P. Her every fear
Tamirat, N. The parking lot attendant
Valdes, A. Dirty Girls on top

Wallace, D. Infinite jest

BOSTON, MASSACHUSETTS -- HISTORY -- 19TH CENTURY
Horowitz, A. The House of Silk
Horowitz, A. Moriarty
Johnson, S. Blaze
Pearl, M. The Dante Club

BOSTON, MASSACHUSETTS -- HISTORY -- 20TH CENTURY
Lehane, D. The given day
O'Malley, T. Serpents in the cold

BOTANISTS
Bellow, S. More die of heartbreak
Ghosh, A. River of smoke
Smith, M. Baked

Both ends of the night Muller, M.

BOTSWANA
McCall Smith, A. Blue shoes and happiness
McCall Smith, A. The Double Comfort Safari Club
McCall Smith, A. The full cupboard of life
McCall Smith, A. The good husband of Zebra Drive
McCall Smith, A. The Limpopo Academy of Private Detection
McCall Smith, A. The Kalahari typing school for men
McCall Smith, A. In the company of cheerful ladies
McCall Smith, A. The No. 1 Ladies' Detective Agency
McCall Smith, A. The Saturday big tent wedding party
Rush, N. Mating
Rush, N. Mortals
Stanley, M. A carrion death
Stanley, M. Deadly harvest
Stanley, M. A death in the family
Stanley, M. Death of the mantis
Stanley, M. Dying to live

The **bottom** Owen, H.
The **bottoms** Lansdale, J.

BOULDER, COLORADO
Read, C. Valley of ashes
White, S. Dry ice
White, S. Kill me
White, S. Line of fire
White, S. Compound fractures
Winer, J. Her kind of case

BOUNCERS
Colfer, E. Plugged

BOUNTY HUNTERS
The plot thickens
Bittner, R. Logan's lady
Brooks, B. Frontier justice
Deaver, J. The empty chair
Dick, P. Do androids dream of electric sheep?
Evanovich, J. Look alive twenty-five
Evanovich, J. Turbo twenty-three
Greer, R. First of state
Lansdale, J. The thicket
Pattison, E. Mandarin gate

BOUNTY HUNTERS -- THE WEST (UNITED STATES)

Hart, J. Redemption road
Haruf, K. Eventide
Holdstock, P. Here I am!
Knowles, J. A separate peace
Llewellyn, R. How green was my valley
Lourie, R. A hatred for tulips
Makkai, R. The borrower
Napolitano, A. Dear Edward
Powell, P. Edisto
Proust, M. Within a budding grove
Pywell, S. What happened to Henry
Roberts, N. Sea swept
Vernon, O. A killing in this town

BOYS -- AFRICA
Faye, G. Small country

BOYS -- ALABAMA
McCammon, R. Boy's life

BOYS -- AUSTRALIA
McGahan, A. The white earth

BOYS -- BARCELONA, SPAIN
Ruiz Zafon, C. The shadow of the wind

BOYS -- DEATH
Erdrich, L. LaRose

BOYS -- FRIENDSHIP
Bradbury, R. Something wicked this way comes
Butler, N. The hearts of men
Frayn, M. Spies
Lebrecht, N. The song of names
Mosley, W. Fortunate son
Ondaatje, M. The cat's table
Petterson, P. Out stealing horses
Twain, M. Adventures of Huckleberry Finn

BOYS -- FRIENDSHIP -- AFGHANISTAN
Hosseini, K. The kite runner

BOYS -- MISSOURI
Twain, M. Adventures of Huckleberry Finn

BOYS -- NORTH CAROLINA
Earley, T. Jim the boy

BOYS -- PERU
Alarcon, D. Lost City Radio

BOYS AND HORSES
McCarthy, C. All the pretty horses

BOYS AND MEN
Brown, L. Joe
Coetzee, J. The childhood of Jesus
Faulkner, W. The reivers
Harkaway, N. Tigerman

BOYS AND NATURE
Bradbury, R. Dandelion wine

BOYS AND SPIRITS
Pywell, S. What happened to Henry

BOYS AND WOLVES
McCarthy, C. The crossing

BOYS AND WOMEN
McCracken, E. The giant's house
The **boys** from Brazil Levin, I.

BOYS WHO ARE BLIND

O'Connell, C. Blind sight
Saberhagen, F. Woundhealer's story

BOYS WHO ARE MUTE
Dalton, T. Boy swallows universe
Jimenez, S. The vanished birds
Wroblewski, D. The story of Edgar Sawtelle

BOYS WITH AUTISM
Brinkman, K. Up high in the trees
Dazieri, S. Kill the king
Dicks, M. Memoirs of an imaginary friend
Kim, A. Miracle Creek
Picoult, J. House rules
Rucker, R. Postsingular

BOYS WITH CLUBFOOT
Maugham, W. Of human bondage

BOYS WITH DISABILITIES
Mosley, W. Fortunate son

BOYS WITH LEARNING DISABILITIES
Box, C. Paradise Valley

BOYS' BOARDING SCHOOLS
Dickens, C. Nicholas Nickleby

BOYS' FANTASIES
Flagg, F. Standing in the rainbow

BOYS' SCHOOLS
Hilton, J. Good-bye, Mr. Chips
Ripley, M. Mr Campion's fault

BP DEEPWATER HORIZON EXPLOSION AND OIL SPILL, 2010
Cooper, T. The marauders

Bradbury stories Bradbury, R.
Braddock-Black Absarokee series [series] Johnson, S.
Bradford sisters [series] Wade, B.
BRADLEY, OMAR N, 1893-1981 MILITARY LEADER-SHIP
Shaara, J. The steel wave
Brady Coyne and J. W. Jackson mysteries [series] Craig, P.
BRAHE, TYCHO, 1546-1601
Sherwood, F. The book of splendor
BRAHMINS
Collins, W. The moonstone
Hesse, H. Siddhartha
The **braid** Colombani, L.
BRAIN
Doctorow, E. Andrew's brain
BRAIN -- TUMORS
Mackintosh, C. After the end
BRAIN ANEURYSMS
Reichs, K. A conspiracy of bones
BRAIN IMPLANTS
Gibson, W. The peripheral
BRAIN INJURY
Anderton, J. Debris
Dundas, C. The blaze
Powers, R. The echo maker
BRAINWASHING
Ballard, J. Millennium people
Lehane, D. Shutter Island

Rendell, R. The bridesmaid
Bridge of sighs Russo, R.
The **Bridge** of Sighs Steinhauer, O.
The **bridge** on the Drina Andric, I.
The **bridge** over the River Kwai Boulle, P.
Bridge series (Evan S. Connell) [series] Connell, E.
Bridge to haven Rivers, F.
Bridgerton series [series] Quinn, J.
BRIDGES
   Boulle, P. The bridge over the River Kwai
   Hair, D. Mage's blood
   Hair, D. Scarlet tides
   Michener, J. The bridges at Toko-Ri
   Wood, T. The engineer's wife
BRIDGES -- DESIGN AND CONSTRUCTION
   Andric, I. The bridge on the Drina
   Kadare, I. The three-arched bridge
   Ondaatje, M. In the skin of a lion
The **bridges** at Toko-Ri Michener, J.
The **bridges** of Madison County Waller, R.
Bridget Jones [series] Fielding, H.
Bridget Jones's diary Fielding, H.
A **brief** history of seven killings James, M.
The **brief** history of the dead Brockmeier, K.
Brief interviews with hideous men Wallace, D.
Brief lives Brookner, A.
The **brief** wondrous life of Oscar Wao Diaz, J.
Bright and distant shores Smith, D.
A **brightness** long ago Kay, G.
Brighton Harvey, M.
Brighton novels [series] Guttridge, P.
Brighton Rock Greene, G.
BRIGHTON, ENGLAND
   Greene, G. Brighton Rock
   Guttridge, P. The thing itself
   Swift, G. Here we are
   Truss, L. The man that got away
   Ware, R. The death of Mrs. Westaway
Brilliance Sakey, M.
Brilliance saga [series] Sakey, M.
Brimstone Parker, R.
Bring me back Paris, B.
Bring up the bodies Mantel, H.
Bringing down the duke Dunmore, E.
BRISBANE, QUEENSLAND
   Dalton, T. Boy swallows universe
BRISEIS
   Barker, P. The silence of the girls
BRISTOL, ENGLAND
   Freeman, A. The fair fight
   Hayder, M. Gone
   Hayder, M. Poppet
   Hayder, M. Ritual
   Hayder, M. Skin
Brit in the FBI [series] Coulter, C.
BRITANNIC (SHIP)
   Katsu, A. The deep

BRITISH AMERICANS
   Oates, J. The accursed
BRITISH COLUMBIA
   Haldane, S. The devil's making
   Kamal, S. It all falls down
   Munro, A. Runaway
   Stevens, C. Never let you go
   Stevens, C. Still missing
   Straley, J. The big both ways
BRITISH IN AFRICA
   Forester, C. The African Queen
   Kimani, P. Dance of the Jakaranda
   Lessing, D. A ripple from the storm
   McLain, P. Circling the sun
BRITISH IN ASIA
   Harkaway, N. Tigerman
BRITISH IN AUSTRALIA
   Carey, P. My life as a fake
   Grenville, K. The lieutenant
BRITISH IN BRAZIL
   Rodrigues Fowler, Y. Stubborn archivist
BRITISH IN BURMA
   Mason, D. The piano tuner
BRITISH IN CANADA
   Haldane, S. The devil's making
   Vanderhaeghe, G. The last crossing
BRITISH IN CENTRAL AFRICA
   Lessing, D. A ripple from the storm
BRITISH IN CHINA
   Ishiguro, K. When we were orphans
   Rendell, R. Speaker of Mandarin
BRITISH IN CROATIA
   Forna, A. The hired man
BRITISH IN CUBA
   Greene, G. Our man in Havana
BRITISH IN CYPRUS
   Jones, S. Small wars
BRITISH IN DENMARK
   Tremain, R. Music & silence
BRITISH IN EASTER ISLAND
   Vanderbes, J. Easter Island
BRITISH IN EGYPT
   Peters, E. Children of the storm
   Peters, E. The golden one
   Peters, E. Guardian of the horizon
   Peters, E. He shall thunder in the sky
   Peters, E. The hippopotamus pool
   Peters, E. The mummy case
   Peters, E. Seeing a large cat
BRITISH IN ETHIOPIA
   Gibb, C. Sweetness in the belly
BRITISH IN EUROPE
   Fleming, I. From Russia with love
BRITISH IN FOREIGN COUNTRIES
   Alexander, V. The Lady Travelers Guide to scoundrels and
     other gentlemen
BRITISH IN FRANCE

Sabatini, R. Captain Blood

BRITISH IN THE CZECH REPUBLIC

Perry, S. Melmoth

BRITISH IN THE MIDDLE EAST

Miller, D. The girl in green

BRITISH IN THE NETHERLANDS

Plaidy, J. William's wife

BRITISH IN THE UNITED STATES

Bittner, R. Logan's lady

Coulter, C. The devil's triangle

Coulter, C. The end game

Coulter, C. The final cut

Coulter, C. The last second

Coulter, C. The lost key

Coulter, C. The sixth day

Delaney, J. Believe me

Dickens, C. Martin Chuzzlewit

Ellison, J. Good girls lie

Faulks, S. On Green Dolphin Street

Higgins, K. The perfect match

L'Amour, L. To the far blue mountains

Pryor, M. Hollow man

Pynchon, T. Mason & Dixon

Pynchon, T. V

Shamsie, K. Home fire

Simmons, D. The fifth heart

Smith, Z. On beauty

Swanson, P. Her every fear

Vanderhaeghe, G. The last crossing

Wood, J. Upstate

BRITISH IN THE WEST (UNITED STATES)

McMurtry, L. Sin killer

BRITISH IN THE WEST INDIES

Forester, C. Admiral Hornblower in the West Indies

Naipaul, V. Guerrillas

BRITISH IN VIETNAM

Greene, G. The quiet American

BRITISH IN WEST AFRICA

Forna, A. The memory of love

Greene, G. The heart of the matter

BRITISH JAMAICANS

Carty-Williams, C. Queenie

BRITISH RAJ (1858-1947)

Forster, E. A passage to India

Massey, S. The Satapur moonstone

Mehta, G. Raj

Mukherjee, A. A necessary evil

Mukherjee, A. A rising man

Mukherjee, A. Smoke and ashes

Thomas, S. Not quite a husband

BRITISH WOMEN IN INDIA

Jhabvala, R. Heat and dust

BRITISH WOMEN IN ITALY

Hemingway, E. A farewell to arms

Quick, A. Slightly shady

BRITISH WOMEN IN SOUTH AMERICA

Woolf, V. The voyage out

Britt Montero novels [series] Buchanan, E.

Britt-Marie was here Backman, F.

BRITTANY, FRANCE

Bannalec, J. Death in Brittany

Bannalec, J. The killing tide

BROADCAST JOURNALISTS

Flanagan, R. The unknown terrorist

Broadchurch Kelly, E.

BROADWAY, NEW YORK CITY

Bram, C. Lives of the circus animals

Phillips, C. Dancing in the dark

Broke heart blues Oates, J.

Broken angels Morgan, R.

Broken Earth novels [series] Jemisin, N.

The **broken** girls St. James, S.

Broken harbor French, T.

Broken homes Aaronovitch, B.

Broken monsters Beukes, L.

The **broken** ones Irwin, S.

Broken open Dane, L.

The **broken** places Atkins, A.

Broken prey Sandford, J.

Broken promise Barclay, L.

The **broken** promise land Muller, M.

Broken sleep Bauman, B.

Broken stars

The **broken** teaglass Arsenault, E.

BROKERS

Wolfe, T. The bonfire of the vanities

The **bromance** book club Adams, L.

Bromance book club [series] Adams, L.

The **Bronte** plot Reay, K.

Bronte sisters mystery [series] Ellis, B.

BRONTE, ANNE, 1820-1849

Ellis, B. The vanished bride

Rowland, L. The secret adventures of Charlotte Bronte

BRONTE, ANNE, 1820-1849 INFLUENCE

Reay, K. The Bronte plot

BRONTE, CHARLOTTE, 1816-1855

Ellis, B. The vanished bride

Rowland, L. Bedlam

Rowland, L. The secret adventures of Charlotte Bronte

BRONTE, CHARLOTTE, 1816-1855 INFLUENCE

Reay, K. The Bronte plot

BRONTE, EMILY, 1818-1848

Ellis, B. The vanished bride

Rowland, L. The secret adventures of Charlotte Bronte

BRONTE, EMILY, 1818-1848 INFLUENCE

Reay, K. The Bronte plot

BRONX, NEW YORK CITY

Alvarez, J. How the Garcia girls lost their accents

Booth, C. Bronxwood

Neugeboren, J. 1940

Ozick, C. Heir to the glimmering world

Rice-Gonzalez, C. Chulito

Verghese, A. Cutting for stone

Finder, J. Vanished
Fisher, K. The silent wife
Fitzpatrick, L. Lights all night long
Gaiman, N. Anansi boys
Green, N. The angel of Montague Street
Gregory, P. The constant princess
Gross, A. Button man
Harper, J. The lost man
Hart, J. Iron house
Haruf, K. Eventide
Haruf, K. Plainsong
Harvey, M. Pulse
Hatcher, R. Cross my heart
Hijuelos, O. The mambo kings play songs of love
Hockensmith, S. Holmes on the range
Hockensmith, S. On the wrong track
Holbert, B. Whiskey
Howarth, P. Only killers and thieves
Hunting, H. Handle with care
Johnson, D. Tree of smoke
Johnson, M. Incognegro
K'wan Hoodlum
Kennedy, R. Presidio
Kerley, J. The death collectors
Kerstan, L. Heart of the tiger
Klassen, J. The painter's daughter
Koryta, M. The prophet
L'Amour, L. The Californios
Lahiri, J. The lowland
Larsen, R. The selected works of T. S. Spivet
Lennon, J. Familiar
Leonard, E. Raylan
Longworth, M. Death at the Chateau Bremont
MacLean, S. Brazen and the Beast
Martin, G. A clash of kings
Mathews, B. The world of tomorrow
McEwan, I. Nutshell
McInerny, R. Celt and pepper
McInerny, R. Irish coffee
Murdoch, I. The green knight
Mysliwski, W. Stone upon stone
Nesbo, J. The redeemer
Obioma, C. The fishermen
Orringer, J. The invisible bridge
Panowich, B. Bull Mountain
Parker, T. California girl
Parry, H. The unlikely escape of Uriah Heep
Piccirilli, T. The last kind words
Piccirilli, T. The last whisper in the dark
Preston, D. The codex
Price, R. Clockers
Pufahl, S. On swift horses
Quinn, J. An offer from a gentleman
Roberts, N. Sea swept
Robertson, M. The Baker Street letters
Robertson, M. The Baker Street translation
Robertson, M. The brothers of Baker Street

Robertson, M. Moriarty returns a letter
Robinson, P. Strange affair
Rosen, L. The Kortelisy escape
Ross, A. Ladies and gentlemen
Roth, P. Everyman
Roth, P. I married a Communist
Rush, N. Mortals
Salinger, J. Raise high the roof beam, carpenters,
Sandlin, L. The bird boys
Saramago, J. Cain
Sayers, D. Whose body?
Scott, C. The poppy wife
Scott, J. Tourmaline
Sidor, S. The mirror's edge
Singer, I. The brothers Ashkenazi
Slouka, M. God's fool
Smith, S. The ruins
Smith, S. A simple plan
Sosa, M. The worst best man
Stansel, I. The last cowboys of San Geronimo
Steinbeck, J. East of Eden
Stone, I. Lust for life
Straub, P. Ghost story
Strout, E. The Burgess boys
Sundaresan, I. The splendor of silence
Sundstol, V. The land of dreams
Swift, G. Wish you were here
Thelen, A. The island of second sight
Tolkien, J. The children of Hurin
Tsukiyama, G. The street of a thousand blossoms
Updike, J. Gertrude and Claudius
Verghese, A. Cutting for stone
Whitehead, C. Sag Harbor
Wideman, J. Fanon
Wurlitzer, R. The drop edge of yonder
deWitt, P. The Sisters brothers
Brothers Chen, D.
Brothers Yu, H.
BROTHERS -- CALIFORNIA
Saroyan, W. The human comedy
BROTHERS -- DEATH
Aslam, N. Maps for lost lovers
Bobotis, A. The last list of Miss Judith Kratt
Boswell, R. Century's son
Broun, B. Night of the animals
Brown, S. White hot
Child, L. Killing floor
Collins, M. A good rake is hard to find
Daoud, K. The Meursault investigation
Enright, A. The gathering
Goonan, K. In war times
Hayder, M. The treatment
Higgins, J. Midnight runner
McHugh, L. The wolf wants in
Michaels, F. Deep harbor
Pelecanos, G. Hard revolution
Rankin, I. Blood hunt

Tyler, A. Saint Maybe

BROTHERS -- NEW HAMPSHIRE

Banks, R. Affliction

BROTHERS -- NEW MEXICO

McCarthy, C. The crossing

BROTHERS -- NEW YORK (STATE)

Torres, J. We the animals

BROTHERS -- OREGON

Kesey, K. Sometimes a great notion

BROTHERS -- THE WEST (UNITED STATES)

L'Amour, L. Bendigo Shafter

BROTHERS AND SISTERS

Abbott, P. Concrete angel

Abraham, T. Black Sunday

Abu-Jaber, D. Birds of paradise

Adelman, M. Piece of mind

Albert, E. The book of Dahlia

Arden, K. The girl in the tower

Arden, K. The winter of the witch

Auster, P. In the country of last things

Baca, J. The importance of a piece of paper

Bayard, L. The pale blue eye

Beattie, A. The doctor's house

Benjamin, C. The immortalists

Berg, E. The art of mending

Beverley, J. Something wicked

Bond, C. Ruby

Bordas, C. How to behave in a crowd

Boswell, R. Century's son

Bragg, M. A son of war

Bram, C. Lives of the circus animals

Brookmyre, C. Black widow

Brown, S. White hot

Callaghan, M. Billy, come home

Card, O. Ender's game

Cather, W. O pioneers!

Clark, W. Payback with ya life

Conroy, P. The prince of tides

Cook, T. Instruments of night

Costello, M. Big if

Crombie, D. Water like a stone

Crumley, J. The wrong case

Crummey, M. The innocents

D'Agostino, K. The antiques

Dev, S. Pride, prejudice, and other flavors

Doig, I. The whistling season

Downing, S. He started it

Dunant, S. Blood and beauty

Eliot, G. The mill on the Floss

Fay, J. The shortest way home

Faye, G. Small country

Ferraris, Z. Finding Nouf

Flynn, G. Dark places

Ford, J. The shadow year

Fowler, E. The road to Cardinal Valley

Freeman, A. The fair fight

Fu, K. For today I am a boy

Galbraith, R. The cuckoo's calling

Garcia Marquez, G. Chronicle of a death foretold

Garwood, J. Wired

Geni, A. The wildlands

Gibson, W. The peripheral

Goenawan, C. Rainbirds

Gohlke, C. Promise me this

Goonan, K. This shared dream

Gregory, P. The other Boleyn girl

Hadley, T. The past

Haigh, J. Baker Towers

Hart, J. The last child

Hazzard, S. The great fire

Hilderbrand, E. Summer of '69

Hoffman, A. The rules of magic

Hoffman, A. Skylight confessions

Holthe, T. When the elephants dance

Horn, D. The world to come

Horrocks, C. The vexations

Hosking, J. Three years with the rat

Hulse, S. Eden mine

Hunter, E. The moment she was gone

Jewell, L. I found you

Kelly, E. The poison tree

Khalfah, K. Death is hard work

Kleypas, L. Christmas Eve at Friday Harbor

Lansdale, J. The bottoms

Lansdale, J. The thicket

Larison, J. Whiskey when we're dry

Laurens, S. A rake's vow

Lawrence, D. The rainbow

Lawson, M. Crow Lake

Lee, F. Jade war

Lessing, D. The fifth child

Lipman, E. The dearly departed, Elinor Lipman.

Lippman, L. Wilde Lake

Livesey, M. Criminals

Llywelyn, M. 1916

Loren, R. The one you fight for

Maaren, K. Weave a circle round

MacDonald, A. When we were Vikings

Macdonald, M. The Trevarton inheritance

Mailer, N. The castle in the forest

Makkai, R. The great believers

Mandanipour, S. Moon brow

Mandel, E. The glass hotel

Marillier, J. Daughter of the forest

Marlantes, K. Deep river

McBride, E. A girl is a half-formed thing

McCullers, C. The member of the wedding

McDermott, A. After this

McDermott, A. At weddings and wakes

McDermott, A. Someone

McDonald, I. New moon

Meek, J. The heart broke in

Merbeth, K. Fortuna

Miller, D. American by day

Miller, S. For love
Millhauser, S. Martin Dressler
Moore, A. Jerusalem
Moriarty, J. Gravity is the thing
Morrison, T. Home
Morrow, J. The last witchfinder
Murphy, D. Tiny Americans
Nabokov, V. Ada
Naipaul, V. Magic seeds
Newman, S. The country of Ice Cream Star
Noire G-Spot
O'Brien, E. Wild Decembers
O'Keefe, M. Velocity weapon
Ondaatje, M. Warlight
Onyebuchi, T. Riot baby
Owen, L. The quick
Ozick, C. Foreign bodies
Packer, A. The children's crusade
Palaia, M. The given world
Patchett, A. The Dutch house
Phillips, J. Lark and Termite
Picoult, J. Lone wolf
Powers, R. The echo maker
Pywell, S. What happened to Henry
Rawle, G. Woman's world
Reiken, F. Day for night
Reisman, N. The first desire
Riley, J. The serpent garden
Robertson, I. The Paris winter
Robinson, M. Home
Roorbach, B. Life among giants
Rowland, L. The secret adventures of Charlotte Bronte
Sackville-West, V. The Edwardians
Salinger, J. Franny and Zooey
Sanchez, T. King Bongo
Sayers, D. Clouds of witness
Shafak, E. The bastard of Istanbul
Shamsie, K. Home fire
Smith, L. Family linen
Spear, T. A billionaire wolf for Christmas
Stachniak, E. The chosen maiden
Stoker, D. Dracul
Strout, E. Anything is possible
Strout, E. The Burgess boys
Sundaresan, I. The splendor of silence
Swinson, K. I'm New York's finest
Trollope, J. Brother and sister
Turansky, C. No ocean too wide
Tyler, A. Dinner at the Homesick Restaurant
Wallace, D. Mr. Sebastian and the Negro magician
Ward, J. Salvage the bones
Watson, J. Asta in the wings
Wells, B. The end of loneliness
Whittle, T. The dangerous edge of things
Wilhelm, K. The good children
Williams, S. Forbidden promises
Wingate, L. Before we were yours

Woo, S. Love love
Woodrell, D. Winter's bone
Yanique, T. Land of love and drowning
Brothers and sisters Campbell, B.
BROTHERS AND SISTERS -- DEATH
  Adler-Olsen, J. The absent one
BROTHERS AND SISTERS -- FRANCE
  Trevanian The summer of Katya
BROTHERS AND SISTERS -- JAPAN
  Oe, K. A quiet life
BROTHERS AND SISTERS -- PENNSYLVANIA
  O'Dell, T. Back roads
BROTHERS AND SISTERS OF CHILDREN WITH AUTISM
  Greenfeld, K. True
The **brothers** Ashkenazi Singer, I.
The **brothers** Karamazov Dostoyevsky, F.
Brothers keepers Westlake, D.
The **brothers** of Baker Street Robertson, M.
BROTHERS OF MURDER VICTIMS
  Rankin, I. Blood hunt
BROTHERS-IN-LAW
  Cruz, A. Dominicana
  House, S. A parchment of leaves
  King, L. The game
  Muller, M. The broken promise land
  Oe, K. The changeling
  Parker, T. Pacific beat
BROWN, JOHN, 1800-1859
  Banks, R. Cloudsplitter
  McBride, J. The good lord bird
  Wideman, J. American histories
BROWN, OWEN, 1824-1889
  Banks, R. Cloudsplitter
BROWNING, ROBERT, 1812-1889
  Pearl, M. The Dante chamber
BRUNO, GIORDANO, 1548-1600
  Parris, S. Sacrilege
  Parris, S. Treachery
Brush back Paretsky, S.
BRUSSELS, BELGIUM
  Ramzipoor, E. The ventriloquists
Bryant & May Fowler, C.
Bryant and May mysteries [series] Fowler, C.
BUCCANEERS
  Sabatini, R. Captain Blood
  Wolfe, G. Pirate freedom
Buchanan novels (Julie Garwood) [series] Garwood, J.
BUCHANAN, JAMES, 1791-1868
  Updike, J. Memories of the Ford administration
BUCHAREST, ROMANIA
  Veletzos, R. The girl they left behind
Buck Schatz mysteries [series] Friedman, D.
The **bucket** list Clark, G.
BUCKINGHAM PALACE
  Roosevelt, E. Murder at the palace
Buckingham Palace gardens Perry, A.

O'Donovan, G. Dublin dead
O'Donovan, G. The priest
Ozick, C. The Puttermesser papers
Phillips, H. The beautiful bureaucrat
Vonnegut, K. Jailbird

The **Burgess** boys Strout, E.

The **burglar** in the closet Block, L.

The **burglar** in the library Block, L.

BURGLARY

Bauer, B. Snap
Hubbard, L. The talented Ribkins
McCall Smith, A. In the company of cheerful ladies
Mosley, W. A little yellow dog
Westlake, D. Bad news
Westlake, D. Bank shot
Westlake, D. What's the worst that could happen?

BURIAL

Gardner, L. Alone
Hage, R. Beirut Hellfire Society
Krivak, A. The bear
Ma, J. Stick out your tongue
Parks, S. Getting mother's body
Rendell, R. Not in the flesh

Burial rites Kent, H.

Buried Cooper, E.

Buried deep Ragan, T.

The **buried** giant Ishiguro, K.

Buried prey Sandford, J.

Buried secrets Finder, J.

BURKINA FASO -- HISTORY -- COUP D'ETAT, 1987

Wilkinson, L. American spy

BURKINA FASO -- POLITICS AND GOVERNMENT -- 1960-1987

Wilkinson, L. American spy

BURMA -- HISTORY

Ghosh, A. The glass palace

BURMA -- HISTORY -- 19TH CENTURY

Mason, D. The piano tuner

BURMA -- HISTORY -- 20TH CENTURY

Craig, C. Miss Burma

BURMA-SIAM RAILROAD

Boulle, P. The bridge over the River Kwai
Flanagan, R. The narrow road to the deep north

The **burn** Kent, K.

Burn Lutz, J.

Burn marks Paretsky, S.

Burn out Muller, M.

BURN VICTIMS

Ackerman, E. Waiting for Eden
Bolano, R. The Third Reich
Golding, W. Darkness visible
Lupton, R. Afterwards
Martin, C. Long way gone
Ondaatje, M. The English patient

BURN VICTIMS -- MONTREAL, QUEBEC

Reichs, K. Death du jour

The **burning** air Kelly, E.

Burning bright Petrie, N.

Burning bright Rash, R.

Burning Cove, California [series] Quick, A.

The **burning** gates Bilal, P.

The **burning** page Cogman, G.

The **burning** point Putney, M.

Burning ridge Mizushima, M.

The **burning** room Connelly, M.

The **burning** soul Connolly, J.

Burning your boats Carter, A.

BURNS AND SCALDS

Davidson, A. The gargoyle
Golding, W. Darkness visible

BURNS, LIZZIE, 1827-1878

McCrea, G. Mrs. Engels

Burr Vidal, G.

BURR, AARON, 1756-1836

Vidal, G. Burr
Wascom, K. The blood of heaven

BURR-HAMILTON DUEL, WEEHAWKEN, NJ, 1804

Cobbs Hoffman, E. The Hamilton affair

Burton & Swinburne [series] Hodder, M.

BURTON, RICHARD F, 1821-1890

Hodder, M. The strange affair of Spring Heeled Jack

BURUNDI

Faye, G. Small country

Bury me deep Abbott, M.

Bury your dead Penny, L.

BUS DRIVERS

Rigosi, G. Night bus

BUS TRAVEL

Doig, I. Last bus to wisdom

BUSES

Shteyngart, G. Lake Success

BUSH PILOTS

Boyden, J. Through black spruce

BUSH, GEORGE W (GEORGE WALKER), 1946-

Mallon, T. Landfall

BUSINESS

Bing, S. You look nice today

BUSINESS -- CORRUPT PRACTICES

Andrew, S. The Satanic mechanic
Archer, Z. Dangerous seduction
Barbash, T. The last good chance
Borjlind, C. Spring tide
Crichton, M. Micro
Deaver, J. The never game
Dee, J. A thousand pardons
Gross, A. Reckless
Hagberg, D. Abyss
Hart, R. The warehouse
Hawley, N. Before the fall
Hill Gumbao, T. The good suicides
Knopf, C. You're dead
Lathen, E. East is east
Lee, P. Signal
Muller, M. Both ends of the night

Perry, A. Death of a stranger
Quartey, K. Gold of our fathers
Roorbach, B. Life among giants
Ryan, H. Truth be told
Sanders, L. McNally's trial
Westlake, D. The road to ruin

BUSINESS -- CORRUPT PRACTICES -- KENYA
Le Carre, J. The constant gardener

BUSINESS COMPETITION
Chabon, M. Telegraph Avenue
K'wan The Diamond empire
K'wan Hoodlum
Lathen, E. East is east
Laurens, S. The pursuits of Lord Kit Cavanaugh
MacLean, S. Brazen and the Beast
Mallon, T. Bandbox
McDonald, I. New moon
Phillips, S. Match me if you can
Rai, A. Hate to want you
Rai, A. The right swipe
Sosa, M. The worst best man

BUSINESS CONSULTANTS
Modesitt, L. The one-eyed man

BUSINESS ETHICS
Cook, R. Nano
Reay, K. The Bronte plot

BUSINESS FAILURES
Bradford, B. Master of his fate

BUSINESS FAILURES -- ILLINOIS
Fuller, J. Abbeville

BUSINESS INTELLIGENCE
Grippando, J. Money to burn
Hart, R. The warehouse
Lelchuk, S. Save me from dangerous men
Morgan Jones, C. The jackal's share
Morgan Jones, C. The silent oligarch
The **business** of lovers Dickey, E.

BUSINESS PARTNERS
Carpenter, E. Until the day I die
Clinch, J. Marley
Hammett, D. The Maltese falcon
Hunter, M. The surrender of Miss Fairbourne
Schlink, B. Self's murder
Smith, M. The Siberian dilemma
Walser, R. The assistant
Whitaker, K. The animators

BUSINESS PARTNERSHIP
Crownover, J. Honor

BUSINESS PRESENTATIONS
Sosa, M. The worst best man

BUSINESS SABOTAGE
Muller, M. Dead midnight
Paretsky, S. Fire sale

BUSINESS SUCCESS
Bradford, B. Master of his fate

BUSINESS TRAVEL
Lathen, E. East is east

BUSINESSPEOPLE
Balogh, M. Someone to wed
Bellow, S. The Bellarosa connection
Billingsley, R. The secret she kept
Bing, S. You look nice today
Bradford, B. Just rewards
Bradford, B. Master of his fate
Bradford, B. A woman of substance
Chabon, M. Telegraph Avenue
Clark, M. Final judgment
Clark, M. Kiss the girls and make them cry
Cook, R. Pandemic
Crombie, D. Kissed a sad goodbye
Cussler, C. Golden Buddha
Cussler, C. Sacred stone
Dee, J. A thousand pardons
Dickens, C. Dombey and Son
Dickens, C. Our mutual friend
Dimon, H. Mercy
Eggers, D. A hologram for the king
Fisher, T. The wives
FitzGerald, G. Redemption Mountain
Foster, L. Sisters of summer's end
Fuentes, C. The death of Artemio Cruz
Grimes, L. In a fix
Gruber, M. Night of the jaguar
Keilson, H. Life goes on
Kleypas, L. Marrying Winterborne
Lackberg, C. The lost boy
Lanchester, J. Fragrant Harbor
Lehane, D. Since we fell
Lightman, A. The diagnosis
Manning, K. My notorious life
Matthiessen, P. Bone by bone
Meyer, D. Icarus
Moore, G. The last days of night
Morgan Jones, C. The jackal's share
Morgan Jones, C. The silent oligarch
Nelscott, K. Days of rage
Phillips, S. First star I see tonight
Pineiro, C. One summer night
Pynchon, T. Bleeding edge
Quick, A. I thee wed
Sanders, L. The first deadly sin
Shanbhag, V. Ghachar ghochar
Solares, M. Don't send flowers
Vargas Llosa, M. The discreet hero
Westlake, D. Forever and a death
White, S. Kill me
Wilson, S. The man in the gray flannel suit

BUSINESSPEOPLE -- FLORIDA
Garcia, C. The Aguero sisters
Busman's honeymoon Sayers, D.
But come ye back , Beth Lordan Lordan, B.

BUTCHER SHOPS
Erdrich, L. The beet queen
Butcher's boy [series] Perry, T.

BUTCHERS

Erdrich, L. The Master Butchers Singing Club

BUTLERS

Faulks, S. Jeeves and the wedding bells

Finch, C. A beautiful blue death

Ishiguro, K. The remains of the day

Wodehouse, P. The inimitable Jeeves

Wodehouse, P. My man Jeeves

Butterfield 8 O'Hara, J.

BUTTERFLIES

Bowman, C. Horace Winter says goodbye

Kingsolver, B. Flight behavior

Raybourn, D. A dangerous collaboration

Butterflies in November Audur A. Olafsdottir, 1.

Butterfly Ashley Antoinette, 1.

Butterfly novels [series] Ashley Antoinette, 1.

Butterfly tattoo Knight, D.

Button man Gross, A.

Buzz cut Hall, J.

By blood Ullman, E.

By blood we live Duncan, G.

By gaslight Price, S.

By night in Chile Bolano, R.

By nightfall Cunningham, M.

By schism rent asunder Weber, D.

By winter's light Laurens, S.

BYRON, GEORGE GORDON BYRON,, BARON, 1788-1824

Crowley, J. Lord Byron's novel

Evans, J. The white devil

Friedman, D. Riot most uncouth

C

C' series [series] Layton, E.

C. J. Floyd mysteries [series] Greer, R.

C. W. Sughrue mysteries [series] Crumley, J.

The **cabin** at the end of the world Tremblay, P.

CABINET OFFICERS -- GREAT BRITAIN

Perry, A. Seven Dials

CABINS

Cohen, T. The summer we lost her

Malpas, J. Leave me breathless

Nesbo, J. Midnight sun

Tremblay, P. The cabin at the end of the world

CABLE TELEVISION INDUSTRY AND TRADE

McBain, E. The frumious bandersnatch

Cabot Sisters [series] London, J.

CACTUS

Jance, J. Queen of the night

The **cactus** Haywood, S.

The **caddie** who played with hickory Coyne, J.

CADDIES

Coyne, J. The caddie who played with hickory

CAESAR, JULIUS, 100-44 BC

Saylor, S. The judgment of Caesar

Saylor, S. Roma

Saylor, S. Rubicon

Saylor, S. The triumph of Caesar

Caged Cooper, E.

Cain Saramago, J.

Cain his brother Perry, A.

CAIN, (BIBLICAL FIGURE)

Saramago, J. Cain

The **Caine** mutiny Wouk, H.

CAIRO (EGYPT)

Steinhauer, O. The Cairo affair

The **Cairo** affair Steinhauer, O.

Cairo trilogy [series] Mahfuz, N.

CAIRO, EGYPT

Bilal, P. The burning gates

Bilal, P. The ghost runner

Hassib, R. A pure heart

Hertmans, S. The convert

Lukas, M. The last watchman of Old Cairo

Mahfuz, N. Palace walk

Mahfuz, N. Sugar Street

Matar, H. Anatomy of a disappearance

Neubauer, E. Murder at the Mena House

Russell, M. Dreamers of the day

CAIRO, EGYPT -- HISTORY

Chakraborty, S. The city of brass

Chakraborty, S. The empire of gold

Chakraborty, S. The kingdom of copper

CAJUN MEN

Burke, J. Black cherry blues

Burke, J. Heaven's prisoners

CAJUNS -- LOUISIANA

Gaines, E. A gathering of old men

Cakes and ale Maugham, W.

CALAMITY JANE, 1852-1903

Dexter, P. Deadwood

McMurtry, L. Buffalo girls

The **calculating** stars Kowal, M.

CALCUTTA, INDIA

Carter, M. The strangler vine

Mukherjee, N. The lives of others

Mukherjee, A. A necessary evil

Mukherjee, A. A rising man

Mukherjee, A. Smoke and ashes

Caleb's crossing Brooks, G.

CALGARY, ALBERTA

Kittredge, W. The willow field

Caliban's war Corey, J.

CALIFORNIA

Albert, E. The book of Dahlia

Anderson, K. Green sun

Barnes, S. Domino Falls

Blau, J. The Wonder Bread summer

Boyle, T. The harder they come

Brennert, A. Daughter of Moloka'i

Brownrigg, S. Morality tale

Butler, O. Parable of the sower

Cander, C. The weight of a piano

Pronzini, B. Crazybone
Pronzini, B. Fever
Pronzini, B. Hellbox
Pronzini, B. Mourners
Pronzini, B. Nemesis
Pronzini, B. Savages
Pronzini, B. Spook
Pronzini, B. The stolen gold affair
Pronzini, B. The violated
Pyne, D. Catalina eddy
Pyne, D. Twentynine Palms
Ragan, T. Buried deep
Ragan, T. Deadly recall
Ragan, T. Deranged
Ragan, T. Her last day
Rice, L. The lemon orchard
Rivers, F. And the shofar blew
Rouda, K. The favorite daughter
Rucker, R. Postsingular
Saroyan, W. The human comedy
Schulman, H. Come with me
Schwarz, C. The edge of the Earth
Schwartz, J. Northwest corner
See, L. The tea girl of Hummingbird Lane
Shalvis, J. Sweet little lies
Sharpe, T. Barbed wire heart
Sloan, R. Mr. Penumbra's 24-hour bookstore
Stansel, I. The last cowboys of San Geronimo
Stegner, W. Angle of repose
Steinbeck, J. Cannery Row
Steinbeck, J. East of Eden
Steinbeck, J. The grapes of wrath
Steinbeck, J. Of mice and men
Steinbeck, J. Tortilla Flat
Tan, A. The Valley of Amazement
Tanen, S. There's a word for that
Tsao, T. The majesties
Tsukiyama, G. Dreaming water
Tyree, O. For the love of money
Van Meter, C. Creatures
Vann, D. Goat Mountain
Vinge, V. Rainbows end
Walker, K. The age of miracles
Walker, K. The dreamers
Wambaugh, J. The blue knight
Wang, K. Family trust
Waxman, A. The bookish life of Nina Hill
Weatherspoon, R. Rafe
Wiggs, S. The beekeeper's ball
Williams, K. Dirty to the grave
Winslow, D. The dawn patrol
Winslow, D. The kings of cool
Winslow, D. Savages
Wolitzer, H. Hearts

CALIFORNIA -- HISTORY -- 1846-1850
Allende, I. Daughter of fortune

CALIFORNIA -- HISTORY -- 1850-1950

Cussler, C. The chase
Shimotakahara, L. After the bloom

CALIFORNIA -- HISTORY -- 19TH CENTURY
Harte, B. The best short stories of Bret Harte

CALIFORNIA -- HISTORY -- 20TH CENTURY
Reddi, R. Passage west

CALIFORNIA -- HISTORY -- TO 1846
L'Amour, L. The Californios

CALIFORNIA -- SOCIAL LIFE AND CUSTOMS -- 19TH CENTURY
Allende, I. Daughter of fortune

CALIFORNIA -- SOCIAL LIFE AND CUSTOMS -- 20TH CENTURY
Newitz, A. The future of another timeline
Rivers, F. Bridge to haven

California girl Parker, T.
California girls Mallery, S.
The **Californios** L'Amour, L.

CALIGULA, EMPEROR OF ROME, 12-41
Graves, R. I, Claudius

CALIPHATE
Khoury, R. Empire of lies

The **call** Murphy, Y.
Call it sleep Roth, H.
Call me by your name Aciman, A.
Call me irresistible Phillips, S.
Call me Zebra Van der Vliet Oloomi, A.
The **call** of the toad Grass, G.
The **call** of the wild London, J.
Calm sea and prosperous voyage Howland, B.
Calumet City Newton, C.

CALVINISM
Robinson, M. Lila

CAMBODIA
Fay, K. The map of lost memories
Long, J. The reckoning, Jeff Long.

CAMBODIA -- HISTORY -- 20TH CENTURY
Echlin, K. The disappeared
Ratner, V. Music of the ghosts

CAMBODIAN AMERICANS
Jen, G. World and town

CAMBODIAN CANADIANS
Echlin, K. The disappeared

CAMBODIAN GENOCIDE, 1975-1979
Echlin, K. The disappeared
Ratner, V. Music of the ghosts

CAMBRIDGE, ENGLAND
Atkinson, K. Case histories
Cumming, C. The Trinity Six
Franklin, A. Mistress of the art of death
Friedman, D. Riot most uncouth
Hannah, S. Perfect little children
Harvey, J. Gone to ground
James, P. An unsuitable job for a woman
Palliser, C. Rustication
Perry, A. No graves as yet
Stott, R. Ghostwalk

CARACAS (VENEZUELA)
Sainz Borgo, K. It would be night in Caracas

CARAVAGGIO, MICHELANGELO MERISI DA, 1573-1610
Pears, I. Death and restoration

CARAVELS
Smith, W. Birds of prey

CARBON DIOXIDE EMISSIONS -- CONTROL
McDonald, I. The Dervish House

CARD DEALERS
Bell, M. The color of night
Bowen, K. Between the devil and the duke
The **cardinal** of the Kremlin Clancy, T.

CARDINALS -- PROVENCE, FRANCE
Pears, I. The dream of Scipio

Cardington Crescent Perry, A.

CARDIOLOGISTS
Sthers, A. Holy lands

CARDSHARPING
Bowen, K. Between the devil and the duke
Prose, F. Household saints
The **care** and feeding of ravenously hungry girls Gray, A.
Career of evil Galbraith, R.
Careful what you wish for Ephron, H.

CAREGIVERS
Barclay, L. Trust your eyes
Berg, E. We are all welcome here
Boyle, W. The lonely witness
Brown, R. Tender mercies
Coupland, D. Eleanor Rigby
Drabble, M. The dark flood rises
Evison, J. The revised fundamentals of caregiving
Genova, L. Every note played
McFarlane, F. The night guest
Moyes, J. Me before you
Oz, A. Judas
Careless in red George, E.
Careless love Robinson, P.

CARETAKERS
Dillard, A. The Maytrees
Ellison, R. Three days before the shooting . . .
Erpenbeck, J. Visitation
Genova, L. Left neglected
Jin, H. The crazed
King, S. The shining
Lodge, D. Paradise news
Long, J. Dirty dancing at Devil's Leap
Phillips, C. A distant shore
Caribbean Michener, J.

CARIBBEAN AMERICANS
Nunez, E. Anna in-between

CARIBBEAN AREA
Buffett, J. A salty piece of land
Carpenter, E. Until the day I die
Danticat, E. Everything inside
De Leon, A. Side chick nation
Matthiessen, P. Far Tortuga

Morrison, T. Tar baby
Muller, M. A wild and lonely place
Nunez, E. Anna in-between
Poyer, D. A country of our own
Sabatini, R. Captain Blood
Schaitkin, A. Saint X
Sosa, M. Acting on impulse
Straub, P. Mystery
Turnbull, C. The lesson
Westlake, D. Watch your back!
Wolfe, G. Pirate freedom

CARIBBEAN AREA
Crichton, M. Pirate latitudes

CARIBBEAN AREA -- HISTORY
Michener, J. Caribbean
Caribou Island Vann, D.

CARICATURISTS
Jarvis, S. Death and Mr. Pickwick

CARJACKING
Hayder, M. Gone
Manning, M. The victim
Price, R. Freedomland

CARLOS AVERY STATE WILDLIFE MANAGEMENT AREA, MINNESOTA
Sandford, J. Night prey
Carlos Tejada Alonso y Leon investigations [series] Pawel, R.

CARLOS, 1949-
Ludlum, R. The Bourne ultimatum
Carmen Merimee, P.
Carnegie Hill Vatner, J.

CARNEGIE, ANDREW, 1835-1919
Dos Passos, J. 1919

CARNIVALS
Beagle, P. The last unicorn
Blackstock, T. Shadow in Serenity
Dunn, K. Geek love

CARNIVALS -- ILLINOIS
Bradbury, R. Something wicked this way comes

CARNTON MANSION (FRANKLIN, TENN.)
Hicks, R. The widow of the South
Carnton novels [series] Alexander, T.

CARPATHIAN MOUNTAINS
Feehan, C. Dark illusion
Carpentaria Wright, A.
Carpenter and Quincannon novels [series] Pronzini, B.

CARPENTERS
Braun, L. The cat who went underground
Eliot, G. Adam Bede
Knopf, C. The last refuge
Moore, K. Sexy Lexy
Picoult, J. Change of heart
Spencer, S. Man in the woods
Carriage trade Birmingham, S.
Carrie King, S.

CARRIER PILOTS
Coonts, S. Flight of the Intruder

Goddard, R. Never go back
Castles ever after [series] Dare, T.
CASTRATI
King, R. Domino
CASTRO, FIDEL, 1926-2016
Buckley, W. Mongoose, R.I.P.
Hunter, S. Havana
CASTRO, FIDEL, 1926-2016 ATTEMPTED ASSASSINA-TION
Block, L. Killing Castro
CASUAL SEX
Amis, M. London fields
Brodesser-Akner, T. Fleishman is in trouble
Carty-Williams, C. Queenie
Flint, E. Little deaths
Tyree, O. Flyy girl
The **casual** vacancy Rowling, J.
Cat and mouse Grass, G.
CAT DETECTIVES
Braun, L. The cat who ate Danish modern
Braun, L. The cat who went underground
Brown, R. Murder at Monticello, or, Old sins
Brown, R. Wish you were here
Murphy, S. Cat pay the devil
CAT GHOSTS
Hynes, J. Kings of infinite space
Cat Kinsella [series] Frear, C.
CAT OWNERS
Braun, L. The cat who ate Danish modern
Braun, L. The cat who went underground
Cat pay the devil Murphy, S.
The **cat** who ate Danish modern Braun, L.
Cat Who mysteries [series] Braun, L.
The **cat** who went underground Braun, L.
Cat's cradle Vonnegut, K.
Cat's eye Atwood, M.
The **cat's** table Ondaatje, M.
CATACOMBS
Castle, J. Illusion Town
Catalina eddy Pyne, D.
CATASTROPHISM
McCarthy, C. The road
Wilhelm, K. Where late the sweet birds sang
Catch-22 Heller, J.
The **catcher** in the rye Salinger, J.
Catching Christmas Blackstock, T.
CATEGORY ROMANCES
Bryant, N. Christmas with the billionaire
Lin, J. The dragon and the pearl
Lohmann, J. Winning Ruby Heart
Sorenson, J. Aftershock
A **catered** Christmas cookie exchange Crawford, I.
CATERERS AND CATERING
Crawford, I. A catered Christmas cookie exchange
Davidson, D. Killer pancake
Davidson, D. The last suppers
Page, K. The body in the casket

Page, K. The body in the wake
CATERPILLARS
Mieville, C. Perdido Street Station
CATHARINE OF BRAGANZA,, QUEEN OF ENGLAND, 1638-1705
Plaidy, J. The pleasures of love
CATHARINE PARR,, QUEEN, CONSORT OF HENRY VIII, KING OF ENGLAND, 1512-1548
Gregory, P. The taming of the queen
CATHARINE,, OF ARAGON, QUEEN, CONSORT OF HENRY VIII, KING OF ENGLAND, 1485-1536
Gregory, P. The constant princess
Gregory, P. The other Boleyn girl
Cathedral of the sea Falcones de Sierra, I.
CATHEDRALS
Chevalier, T. A single thread
Gala, M. The Black Cathedral
Lovett, C. The lost book of the Grail
Palliser, C. The unburied
Pintoff, S. Hostage taker
Rutherfurd, E. Sarum
CATHEDRALS -- FRANCE
Kay, G. Ysabel
CATHEDRALS -- GREAT BRITAIN
Follett, K. A column of fire
Follett, K. The pillars of the earth
Follett, K. World without end
CATHERINE HOWARD,, QUEEN, CONSORT OF HENRY VIII, KING OF ENGLAND, D 1542
Gregory, P. The Boleyn inheritance
Plaidy, J. Murder most royal
CATHERINE II,, EMPRESS OF RUSSIA, 1729-1796
Rutherfurd, E. Russka
Stachniak, E. The Winter Palace
Catherine McLeod novels (Margaret Coel) [series] Coel, M.
CATHOLIC BOYS
Doyle, R. Paddy Clarke, ha-ha-ha
CATHOLIC CHURCH
Berry, S. The Templar legacy
Brown, D. The Da Vinci code
Guterson, D. Our Lady of the Forest
Hewson, D. A season for the dead
Lescroart, J. Guilt
MacLaverty, B. Midwinter break
Reimringer, J. Vestments
Simmons, D. Endymion
CATHOLIC CHURCH AND CHILD SEXUAL ABUSE
Boyne, J. A history of loneliness
CATHOLIC CHURCH CLERGY
Greene, G. The power and the glory
McInerny, R. Requiem for a realtor
O'Hagan, A. Be near me
Silone, I. Bread and wine
CATHOLIC CHURCH IRELAND
McInerney, L. The glorious heresies
Toibin, C. Nora Webster

Starling, C. The luminous dead
Cedar Ridge novels [series] Shalvis, J.
CELEBRATIONS
Kelly, C. Secrets of a happy marriage
Urrea, L. The house of broken angels
CELEBRITIES
Angelo, M. Followers
Bagshawe, T. Adored
Beyda, E. The body double
Bowman, D. Big bang
Bram, C. Lives of the circus animals
Coben, H. The boy from the woods
Cole, A. A prince on paper
Drabble, M. The sea lady
Enright, A. Actress
Galbraith, R. The cuckoo's calling
Gilman, S. The ice cream queen of Orchard Street
Haddam, J. Cheating at solitaire
Hiaasen, C. Star Island
James, E. Wilde in love
Knight, R. The secretary
Lethem, J. Chronic city
Moore, K. Sexy Lexy
Oates, J. Broke heart blues
Randisi, R. Hey there (you with the gun in your hand)
Roth, P. Zuckerman unbound
Rushdie, S. The ground beneath her feet
Smith, Z. Swing time
Stapley, M. The last resort
Starr, J. Lights out
Tanen, S. There's a word for that
Varley, J. Red lightning
Varley, J. Rolling thunder
Williams, C. Stairway to hell
Wouk, H. A hole in Texas
CELEBRITIES -- EUROPE
Ishiguro, K. The unconsoled
CELEBRITIES -- PRESS COVERAGE
Phillips, S. What I did for love
CELEBRITY PROMOTION
Wayne, T. The love song of Jonny Valentine
Celestial bodies Alharthi, J.
CELESTIAL MECHANICS
Waite, O. The lady's guide to celestial mechanics
Celestial navigation Tyler, A.
The **Celestials** Shepard, K.
The **celestine** prophecy Redfield, J.
Celestine series (James Redfield) [series] Redfield, J.
Celine Heller, P.
Cell Cook, R.
Cell 8 Roslund, A.
CELLISTS
Helprin, M. Paris in the present tense
Romano-Lax, A. The Spanish bow
Celluloid memories Kitt, S.
Celt and pepper McInerny, R.
Celtic empire Cussler, C.

CELTIC FANTASY
Bear, E. Blood and iron
Kay, G. The last light of the sun
Marillier, J. Daughter of the forest
Sutcliff, R. Sword at sunset
CELTIC MAGIC (OCCULTISM)
Kay, G. Ysabel
CELTS
Kay, G. The last light of the sun
CELTS -- HISTORY
Kay, G. Ysabel
CELTS -- MATERIAL CULTURE
Hart, E. Lake of sorrows
CEMETERIES
Beagle, P. A fine and private place
Grass, G. The call of the toad
Khalfah, K. Death is hard work
Miller, A. Pure
Preston, D. Verses for the dead
Reichs, K. Break no bones
Saunders, G. Lincoln in the bardo
Scott, C. The poppy wife
CEMETERIES -- MAINE
King, S. Pet sematary
CEMETERY MANAGERS
Hicks, R. The widow of the South
Cemetery of forgotten books [series] Ruiz Zafon, C.
Cemetery Road Haywood, G.
Cemetery road Iles, G.
CENSORSHIP
Bandi, 1. The accusation
Bradbury, R. Fahrenheit 451
Fforde, J. The Eyre affair
Littell, R. The Mayakovsky tapes
Littell, R. The Stalin epigram
Pearl, M. The Dante Club
Stross, C. Glasshouse
Vollmann, W. Europe central
Vonnegut, K. Welcome to the monkey house
Yi, C. The investigation
Zamyatin, Y. We
CENSORSHIP -- HISTORY -- 20TH CENTURY
Byatt, A. Babel Tower
CENSUS
Ball, J. Census
Census Ball, J.
Centenal cycle [series] Older, M.
CENTENARIANS
De la Roche, M. Jalna
Gaines, E. The autobiography of Miss Jane Pittman
Jonasson, J. The accidental further adventures of the hundred-year-old man
Woolf, V. Orlando
Centennial Michener, J.
CENTRAL AFRICA
Ballard, J. The day of creation
CENTRAL AFRICA -- RACE RELATIONS

Iles, G. The footprints of God
Neville, K. The eight
Smith, M. Stalin's ghost
Smith, M. Three stations
Stout, R. Gambit

CHESS PLAYERS

James, E. Desperate duchesses

CHESS SETS

Westlake, D. What's so funny?

The **chestnut** man Sveistrup, S.

Chet and Bernie mysteries [series] Quinn, S.

CHEYENNE INDIANS

Berger, T. Little Big Man
Brown, D. Creek Mary's blood
Johnson, C. Death without company
Soli, T. The removes

CHIANG, CH'ING, 1914-1991

Min, A. Becoming Madame Mao

CHIANG, MAY-LING SOONG, 1897-2003

Roosevelt, E. Murder in the map room

Chicago Aswani, A.

Chicago Mamet, D.

Chicago Stars [series] Phillips, S.

The **Chicago** way Harvey, M.

CHICAGO, ILLINOIS

Algren, N. The man with the golden arm
Aswani, A. Chicago
Bellow, S. The adventures of Augie March
Bellow, S. The dean's December
Bellow, S. Herzog
Bing, S. You look nice today
Blackwell, J. Letters from Paris
Buckman, D. Because the rain
Bump, G. Everywhere you don't belong
Butcher, J. Proven guilty
Cather, W. The song of the lark
Child, L. Die trying
Child, L. A wanted man
Cisneros, S. The house on Mango Street
Crouch, B. Dark matter
Dev, S. The Bollywood bride
Devon, C. Sleeping with the entity
Epstein, J. The love song of A. Jerome Minkoff, and other
  stories
Feehan, C. Shadow rider
Ferber, E. So big
Finder, J. Judgment
Ganshert, K. Life after
Goldberg, T. Gangsterland
Gonzales, L. Lucy
Hale, B. The evolution of Bruno Littlemore
Hamilton, S. The second life of Nick Mason
Hand, E. Curious toys
Harvey, M. The Chicago way
Harvey, M. The fifth floor
Harvey, M. The governor's wife
Harvey, M. We all fall down

James, J. Something about you
Johnson, M. Smitten by the Brit
Just, W. An unfinished season
Kubica, M. Pretty baby
Lancaster, J. Here I go again
Larsen, N. Passing
Lombardo, C. The most fun we ever had
Macomber, D. If not for you
Makkai, R. The great believers
Mamet, D. Chicago
Martinson, T. The reign of the Kingfisher
Meader, K. Playing with fire
Mitchard, J. The deep end of the ocean
Mitchard, J. No time to wave goodbye
Moore, E. The Supremes sing the happy heartache blues
Nelscott, K. Days of rage
Newton, C. Calumet City
Newton, C. Start shooting
Niffenegger, A. The time traveler's wife
Nussbaum, S. Good kings, bad kings
O'Connell, C. Dead famous
Oliveras, P. Their perfect melody
Orner, P. Love and shame and love
Paretsky, S. Bitter medicine
Paretsky, S. Blacklist
Paretsky, S. Blood shot
Paretsky, S. Breakdown
Paretsky, S. Brush back
Paretsky, S. Burn marks
Paretsky, S. Critical mass
Paretsky, S. Dead land
Paretsky, S. Fire sale
Paretsky, S. Guardian angel
Paretsky, S. Hard time
Paretsky, S. Hardball
Paretsky, S. Indemnity only
Paretsky, S. Shell game
Paretsky, S. Total recall
Paretsky, S. Tunnel vision
Paretsky, S. Windy city blues
Phillips, J. Quiet dell
Phillips, S. It had to be you
Phillips, S. Match me if you can
Rader-Day, L. The black hour
Raimondo, L. Dante's dilemma
Raimondo, L. Dante's poison
Raimondo, L. Dante's wood
Reay, K. The Bronte plot
Reichs, K. 206 Bones
Rotert, R. Last night at the blue angel
Roth, P. Letting go
Sakey, M. The blade itself
Sidor, S. Skin River
Snipes, W. Talon of God
Watkins, J. Secrets of a side bitch
Watkins, J. Secrets of a side bitch 2

CHICAGO, ILLINOIS -- HISTORY -- 19TH CENTURY

Sears, M. Black Fridays
Sekaran, S. Lucky boy
Watson, L. Let him go
Wood, S. The Quintland sisters
The **child** garden McPherson, C.

CHILD IMMIGRANTS

Alvarez, J. How the Garcia girls lost their accents
Luiselli, V. Lost children archive
Shafak, E. Honor
The **child** in time McEwan, I.

CHILD KIDNAPPING VICTIMS

Aira, C. The seamstress and the wind
Armstrong, K. Wherever she goes
Bambara, T. Those bones are not my child
Barber, L. A girl named Anna
Cain, C. One Kick
Geni, A. The wildlands
George, E. Just one evil act
Hayder, M. The treatment
Hill, L. Someone knows my name
McKinty, A. The chain
Parks, B. Say nothing
Petrie, N. The wild one
Tudor, C. The other people
Wingate, L. Before we were yours

CHILD LABOR

Dickens, C. David Copperfield

CHILD MURDER INVESTIGATION

Grimes, M. The winds of change
Roslund, A. Pen 33

CHILD MURDER VICTIMS

Bambara, T. Those bones are not my child
Crombie, D. Water like a stone
Dixon, S. Interstate
Flint, E. Little deaths
Franklin, A. Mistress of the art of death
Griffiths, E. The Janus stone
Johnson, C. Hell is empty
Kelly, E. Broadchurch
Mina, D. Field of blood
Nickson, C. At the dying of the year
Polansky, D. Low town
Ware, R. The turn of the key

CHILD MURDER WITNESSES

Nelscott, K. Stone cribs

CHILD MURDERERS

March, W. The bad seed
Mina, D. Field of blood

CHILD MURDERS

Faulkner, W. Requiem for a nun
Landay, W. Defending Jacob
MacBride, S. Cold granite
Morrison, T. God help the child
Price, R. Freedomland
Roslund, A. Pen 33

CHILD NEGLECT

Brownmiller, S. Waverly Place

Gardam, J. God on the rocks
St. James, S. The broken girls
Wharton, E. The children
Child of my heart McDermott, A.

CHILD PORNOGRAPHY

Koontz, D. The husband
Lackberg, C. The stonecutter
Scoppettone, S. Gonna take a homicidal journey

CHILD PORNOGRAPHY VICTIMS

Cain, C. One Kick

CHILD PRODIGIES

Leon, S. Wanderer
O'Neill, H. The Lonely Hearts Hotel
Romano-Lax, A. The Spanish bow

CHILD PSYCHICS

Hoeg, P. The quiet girl
Williams, D. The stars now unclaimed

CHILD PSYCHOLOGY

March, W. The bad seed

CHILD REARING

Perrotta, T. The abstinence teacher
Seo, M. The only child

CHILD REFUGEES

Byatt, A. Ragnarok
Clayton, M. The last train to London
El Akkad, O. American war
Hosseini, K. Sea prayer

CHILD SACRIFICE

Cornell, P. London falling

CHILD SEX INDUSTRY AND TRADE

Williams, K. Sweet Giselle

CHILD SEXUAL ABUSE

Boyne, J. A history of loneliness
Grimes, M. The winds of change
Jensen, N. The sisters
Lourey, J. Unspeakable things
Ma, J. Stick out your tongue
Melamed, J. Gather the daughters
Neely, B. Blanche cleans up
Olafur Johann Olafsson The sacrament
Pirro, J. Sly fox
Raimondo, L. Dante's wood
Stringer, V. Dirty Red
Weiner, J. Mrs. Everything
Yanagihara, H. The people in the trees

CHILD SEXUAL ABUSERS

Perrotta, T. Little children
Rendell, R. Harm done

CHILD SLAVES

Pearson, R. Choke point

CHILD SOLDIERS

El Akkad, O. American war

CHILD SUPPORT

Mortimer, J. Felix in the underworld

CHILD TRAFFICKING

Greenwood, K. Unnatural habits
Harvey, J. Cold in hand

Van Vogt, A. Slan
Ware, R. The turn of the key
Fftch, M. Stay and fight
The **children** Wharton, E.

CHILDREN -- AFRICA
Akpan, U. Say you're one of them

CHILDREN -- DEATH
Banks, R. The sweet hereafter
Betts, D. Souls raised from the dead
Black, L. Suffer the children
Coake, C. You came back
Cohen, L. The grief of others
Crombie, D. Water like a stone
DeBoard, P. The fragile world
Drake, L. The sweet spot
Erdrich, L. The painted drum
Lennon, J. Familiar
Odell, J. The healing
Patric, A. Black rock white city
Shalev, M. Two she-bears
Solomon, B. The murder of Willie Lincoln
Trueblood, V. Seven loves
Tyler, A. The tin can tree

CHILDREN -- DEATH -- PSYCHOLOGICAL ASPECTS
Banks, R. The sweet hereafter
Morrison, T. Beloved

CHILDREN -- FRIENDSHIP
Drabble, M. The sea lady
Lehane, D. Mystic river
Murakami, H. South of the border, west of the sun
Murr, N. The perfect man

CHILDREN -- INSTITUTIONAL CARE
Sem-Sandberg, S. The chosen ones

CHILDREN -- INTERPERSONAL RELATIONS
Lippman, L. The most dangerous thing
The **children** act McEwan, I.

CHILDREN AND ADULTS
Byatt, A. The children's book
McBride, J. The good lord bird

CHILDREN AND ADULTS -- 19TH CENTURY
Dickens, C. Oliver Twist, or The parish boy's progress

CHILDREN AND DEATH
Grodstein, L. Our short history
Children and fire Hegi, U.

CHILDREN AND SENIOR WOMEN
Backman, F. Britt-Marie was here

CHILDREN AND WAR
Couto, M. Sleepwalking land
Downing, D. Diary of a dead man on leave
Hosseini, K. Sea prayer
Lebrecht, N. The song of names
Yoon, P. Run me to earth

CHILDREN IN COMAS
Murphy, Y. The call
Children in Reindeer Woods Kristin Omarsdottir, 1.

CHILDREN OF ACTORS AND ACTRESSES
Enright, A. Actress

CHILDREN OF AFRICAN AMERICAN DRUG ABUSERS
Draper, S. Forged by fire

CHILDREN OF AGING PARENTS
Gelman, L. You've been volunteered
Olson, N. Before the devil fell
Robinson, R. Cost

CHILDREN OF ALCOHOLIC FATHERS
Smith, B. A tree grows in Brooklyn
Wolfe, T. Look homeward, angel

CHILDREN OF ALCOHOLICS
Gibbons, K. Ellen Foster

CHILDREN OF ANTHROPOLOGISTS
Faber, M. The courage consort

CHILDREN OF ARTISTS
Murphy, D. Tiny Americans
Pilcher, R. The shell seekers
Roy, A. All the lives we never lived
Vreeland, S. Girl in hyacinth blue

CHILDREN OF AUTHORS
Oe, K. A quiet life
Ozick, C. Heir to the glimmering world
Rice, C. Home sweet homicide
Vine, B. The chimney sweeper's boy

CHILDREN OF CELEBRITIES
Varley, J. Red lightning
Varley, J. Rolling thunder

CHILDREN OF CLERGY
Baldwin, J. Go tell it on the mountain
Cather, W. The song of the lark
Dos Passos, J. 1919
Fabry, C. The promise of Jesse Woods
Kate, J. Love and other mistakes
Lewis, B. The brethren
Lewis, B. The preacher's daughter
Mortimer, J. Quite honestly
Pontoppidan, H. Lucky Per
Price, R. The good priest's son
Robinson, M. Home
Wascom, K. The blood of heaven

CHILDREN OF CRIMINALS
DePoy, P. Sidewalk saint
K'wan Diamonds and Pearl
Malik, T. Three bargains
Mychea He loves me, he loves you not
Tinti, H. The twelve lives of Samuel Hawley

CHILDREN OF DISAPPEARED PERSONS
Lopez, J. A beautiful young woman

CHILDREN OF DIVORCED PARENTS
Allende, I. Ripper
Candlish, L. Our house
Fuqua, J. Gone and back again
Hawley, N. The good father
Moniz, T. Big familia
Walsh, H. Brass
Wharton, E. The children

CHILDREN OF DIVORCED PARENTS -- MAINE
King, S. The girl who loved Tom Gordon

Warren, R. Band of angels

CHILDREN OF SUICIDE VICTIMS

Durrow, H. The girl who fell from the sky

McDermott, A. The ninth hour

Nesbo, J. The son

Children of the new world Weinstein, A.

Children of the revolution Robinson, P.

The **children** of the sky Vinge, V.

Children of the storm Peters, E.

Children of the street Quartey, K.

CHILDREN OF VETERANS

Bragg, M. A son of war

CHILDREN OF VETERINARIANS

Deb, S. The point of return

Children of violence series [series] Lessing, D.

CHILDREN OF WIDOWERS

Abani, C. GraceLand

CHILDREN OF WIDOWS

Haigh, J. Baker Towers

CHILDREN OF WIDOWS -- AUSTRALIA

McGahan, A. The white earth

CHILDREN OF WIDOWS -- OHIO

Bialosky, J. House under snow

CHILDREN OF WOMEN COCAINE ADDICTS

Cleage, P. What looks like crazy on an ordinary day

CHILDREN OF WORLD WAR II VETERANS

McCarthy, C. All the pretty horses

Children of wrath Grossman, P.

CHILDREN WHO ARE DEAF AND MUTE

Audur A. Olafsdottir, 1. Butterflies in November

CHILDREN WHO ARE MUTE

Frazier, C. Nightwoods

CHILDREN WITH AUTISM

Brinkman, K. Up high in the trees

Kunzru, H. Gods without men

Lovesey, P. Diamond solitaire

Perry, S. The Essex serpent

Picoult, J. House rules

Pulley, N. The lost future of Pepperharrow

CHILDREN WITH BEHAVIORAL DISORDERS

Seo, M. The only child

CHILDREN WITH CANCER

Cleave, C. Gold

CHILDREN WITH CHRONIC ILLNESSES

Sem-Sandberg, S. The chosen ones

CHILDREN WITH DEPRESSION

Dennis-Benn, N. Patsy

Fuqua, J. Gone and back again

CHILDREN WITH DEVELOPMENTAL DISABILITIES

Nussbaum, S. Good kings, bad kings

CHILDREN WITH DISABILITIES

Drabble, M. The pure gold baby

Lawrence, M. Hearts and bones

Lessing, D. The fifth child

Nussbaum, S. Good kings, bad kings

CHILDREN WITH DISFIGUREMENTS

Perry, A. A breach of promise

CHILDREN WITH DOWN SYNDROME

Edwards, K. The memory keeper's daughter

Koontz, D. The darkest evening of the year

O'Connor, F. The violent bear it away

CHILDREN WITH EMOTIONAL ILLNESSES

Proulx, A. The shipping news

CHILDREN WITH TERMINAL ILLNESSES

Hazzard, S. The great fire

The **children's** book Byatt, A.

The **children's** crusade Packer, A.

The **children's** home Lambert, C.

CHILDREN'S HOSPITALS

Sem-Sandberg, S. The chosen ones

CHILDREN'S HOSPITALS -- CALIFORNIA

Kellerman, J. Devil's waltz

CHILDREN'S LITERATURE AUTHORS, ENGLISH

McEwan, I. The child in time

CHILDREN'S RIGHTS

Dare, A. The girl with the louding voice

CHILDREN'S SECRETS

Ammaniti, N. I'm not scared

CHILE

Allende, I. In the midst of winter

Berlin, L. Evening in paradise

Skarmeta, A. The dancer and the thief

CHILE -- FOREIGN RELATIONS -- GREAT BRITAIN

O'Brian, P. Blue at the mizzen

CHILE -- HISTORY

Allende, I. The house of the spirits

CHILE -- HISTORY -- 1973-1988

Bolano, R. By night in Chile

CHILE -- HISTORY -- 19TH CENTURY

Allende, I. Portrait in sepia

CHILE -- HISTORY -- 20TH CENTURY

Allende, I. A long petal of the sea

CHILE -- HISTORY -- COUP D'ETAT, 1973

Bolano, R. Distant star

CHILE -- HISTORY -- WAR OF INDEPENDENCE, 1810-1824

O'Brian, P. Blue at the mizzen

The **chill** Bilenchi, R.

Chilly scenes of winter Beattie, A.

Chimera Barth, J.

Chimes at midnight McGuire, S.

The **chimney** sweeper's boy Vine, B.

CHIMPANZEES

Fowler, K. We are all completely beside ourselves

Greenidge, K. We love you, Charlie Freeman

Hale, B. The evolution of Bruno Littlemore

Martel, Y. The high mountains of Portugal

CHINA

Ballard, J. Empire of the sun

Buck, P. The good Earth

Chen, Q. Waste tide

Church, J. A drop of Chinese blood

Davies, P. The fortunes

Freudenberger, N. The dissident

CHINESE AMERICAN GIRLS
See, L. The tea girl of Hummingbird Lane
CHINESE AMERICAN MEN
Vinge, V. Rainbows end
CHINESE AMERICAN MEN -- WASHINGTON (STATE)
Fowler, K. Sarah Canary
CHINESE AMERICAN WOMEN
Jen, G. World and town
Jin, H. A map of betrayal
Jin, M. Little gods
Kwan, K. Crazy rich Asians
Lee, C. On such a full sea
Rozan, S. Paper son
Rozan, S. The Shanghai Moon
Rozan, S. Winter and night
See, L. Shanghai girls
Tan, A. The bonesetter's daughter
Tan, A. The hundred secret senses
Tan, A. The kitchen god's wife
CHINESE AMERICAN WOMEN -- IDENTITY
Tan, A. The Joy Luck Club
CHINESE AMERICANS
Chai, M. Useful phrases for immigrants
Davies, P. The fortunes
Lim, R. Natalie Tan's book of luck and fortune
Ma, L. Severance
Ng, C. Everything I never told you
Shepard, K. The Celestials
Wang, K. Family trust
CHINESE AMERICANS -- CALIFORNIA
Allende, I. Daughter of fortune
CHINESE AMERICANS -- INTERRACIAL MARRIAGE
Tan, A. The kitchen god's wife
CHINESE AMERICANS IN CHINA
Tan, A. The hundred secret senses
Tan, L. What we were promised
CHINESE CANADIAN FAMILIES
Bates, J. Midnight at the Dragon Cafe
CHINESE CANADIAN GIRLS
Bates, J. Midnight at the Dragon Cafe
CHINESE CANADIANS
Fu, K. For today I am a boy
CHINESE CULTURAL REVOLUTION (1966-1976)
Chen, D. Brothers
Li, Y. The vagrants
Liu, C. The three-body problem
Min, A. Becoming Madame Mao
Yu, H. Brothers
CHINESE IN CALIFORNIA
Freudenberger, N. The dissident
Tan, A. The hundred secret senses
Tan, A. The Joy Luck Club
CHINESE IN CANADA
Bates, J. Midnight at the Dragon Cafe
Fu, K. For today I am a boy
CHINESE IN GREAT BRITAIN
Abdul-Jabbar, K. The empty birdcage

Abdul-Jabbar, K. Mycroft and Sherlock
CHINESE IN KOREA
Jin, H. War trash
CHINESE IN MALAYSIA
Choo, Y. The ghost bride
CHINESE IN MONGOLIA
Jiang, R. Wolf totem
CHINESE IN ONTARIO
Bates, J. Midnight at the Dragon Cafe
CHINESE IN SINGAPORE
Loh, V. Breaking the tongue , by Vyvyane Loh.
CHINESE IN THE UNITED STATES
Davies, P. The fortunes
Jin, H. The boat rocker
Jin, H. A free life
Jin, H. A good fall
Kwok, J. Searching for Sylvie Lee
CHINESE IN WASHINGTON, D.C.
Roosevelt, E. Murder in the map room
Chinook Brand, M.
CHIVALRY
Cervantes Saavedra, M. Don Quixote
Orczy, E. The Scarlet Pimpernel
Scott, W. Ivanhoe
Chocolat Harris, J.
Chocolat novels (Joanne Harris) [series] Harris, J.
CHOCOLATE
Harris, J. Chocolat
CHOCOLATE INDUSTRY AND TRADE
Bell, L. How the duke was won
Choke Palahniuk, C.
Choke hold Faust, C.
Choke point Pearson, R.
CHOKING
Palahniuk, C. Choke
CHOLERA
Roiphe, A. An imperfect lens
CHOLESTEATOMA
McGahan, A. The white earth
CHORAL CONDUCTORS -- DEATH
Penny, L. The beautiful mystery
Chorus of dragons [series] Lyons, J.
The **chosen** maiden Stachniak, E.
The **chosen** ones Sem-Sandberg, S.
Chosen prey Sandford, J.
Christ the Lord Rice, A.
Christ the Lord Rice, A.
Christ the Lord [series] Rice, A.
Christchurch novels [series] Cleave, P.
CHRISTCHURCH, NEW ZEALAND
Cleave, P. The cleaner
Cleave, P. Joe Victim
CHRISTIAN AFRICAN AMERICAN WOMEN
Gaines, E. The autobiography of Miss Jane Pittman
CHRISTIAN BROTHERS
Doyle, R. Smile
CHRISTIAN CHURCH CONTROVERSIES

Tyers, K. Shivering world

CHRISTIAN MISSIONARIES
Endo, S. Silence
Kingsolver, B. The Poisonwood Bible
Michener, J. Hawaii

CHRISTIAN MISSIONARIES -- NEW MEXICO
Cather, W. Death comes for the archbishop

CHRISTIAN MISSIONS -- CHINA
Cronin, A. The keys of the kingdom

CHRISTIAN MISSIONS -- HAWAII
Michener, J. Hawaii

CHRISTIAN RELIC THEFTS
Peters, E. The holy thief
Westlake, D. Don't ask

CHRISTIAN RELICS
Berry, S. The Warsaw protocol

CHRISTIAN RELICS -- VENICE, ITALY
Langton, J. The thief of Venice

CHRISTIAN ROMANCES
Blackstock, T. Catching Christmas
Blackstock, T. Shadow in Serenity
Hatcher, R. Cross my heart
Hauck, R. How to catch a prince
Hauck, R. Once upon a prince
Hauck, R. The wedding chapel
Hatcher, R. Who I am with you
Isaac, K. Then there was you
Johnson, L. A sparkle of silver
Kate, J. A girl's guide to the Outback
Kate, J. Love and other mistakes
Laureano, C. The Saturday Night Supper Club
Lewis, B. The ebb tide
Martin, C. Send down the rain
Rivers, F. The masterpiece
Turner, B. The secret life of Sarah Hollenbeck
Turner, B. Wooing Cadie McCaffrey
Wade, B. Falling for you
Wade, B. True to you
Wiseman, B. Listening to love

CHRISTIAN ROMANTIC SUSPENSE
Irvin, K. Tell her no lies
Warren, S. Rescue me

CHRISTIAN SAINTS
Davies, R. Fifth business
Griffith, N. Hild
Prose, F. Household saints

CHRISTIAN SCIENCE
Anstruther, E. A perfect explanation

CHRISTIAN SCIENCE FICTION
Locke, T. Enclave
Tyers, K. Shivering world

CHRISTIAN SCIENTISTS
Fridlund, E. History of wolves

CHRISTIAN SECTS
Meek, J. The people's act of love
Scott, W. Rob Roy

CHRISTIAN SUSPENSE
Blackstock, T. Smoke screen
Bunn, T. Outbreak
Dekker, T. Black
Dekker, T. The girl behind the red rope
Dekker, T. Red
Dekker, T. White
Mehl, N. Mind games
Nelson, C. If we make it home
Parker, S. Coldwater
Parker, S. Purgatory road
Rubart, J. The man he never was
Wright, J. The house on Foster Hill

CHRISTIAN TEACHERS
Marshall, C. Christy

CHRISTIAN WIDOWS
Winkler, A. Dog war

CHRISTIAN WOMEN
Benton, J. Lilli de Jong
Clayton, M. The last train to London
Ganshert, K. No one ever asked
Griffith, N. Hild
Marshall, C. Christy
Rivers, F. The masterpiece
Winkler, A. Dog war

CHRISTIAN WOMEN -- SEXUALITY
Winkler, A. Dog war

CHRISTIAN, FLETCHER, 1764-1793
Nordhoff, C. Men against the sea
Nordhoff, C. Pitcairn's Island

CHRISTIANITY
Baldwin, J. Go tell it on the mountain
Cather, W. Death comes for the archbishop
Greene, G. The last word and other stories
Karon, J. At home in Mitford
Karon, J. In this mountain
Karon, J. A new song
Karon, J. Out to Canaan
Nunez, S. Salvation city
O'Connor, F. Wise blood
Parini, J. The Damascus road
Perrotta, T. The abstinence teacher
Pike, S. The lost queen
Rutherfurd, E. Sarum
Sharratt, M. Illuminations
Tyers, K. Shivering world
Tyler, A. Saint Maybe
Zevin, G. The hole we're in

CHRISTIANITY -- HISTORY
Berry, S. The Templar legacy

CHRISTIANITY -- RELATIONS -- ISLAM
De Bernieres, L. Birds without wings

CHRISTIANITY -- RITES AND CEREMONIES
Potzsch, O. The play of death

CHRISTIANITY AND CULTURE
Achebe, C. Things fall apart

CHRISTIANITY AND INDIGENOUS PEOPLES
Achebe, C. Things fall apart

Abraham, T. Black Sunday
Harris, J. Chocolat
Sayers, D. The nine tailors
Stark, R. Dirty money
Sullivan, M. Theft of swords

CHURCHES -- CALIFORNIA
Rivers, F. And the shofar blew

CHURCHILL, CLEMENTINE, 1885-1977
Benedict, M. Lady Clementine

CHURCHILL, WINSTON, 1874-1965
Benedict, M. Lady Clementine
Higgins, J. The eagle has flown
Higgins, J. The eagle has landed
Kerr, P. Hitler's peace
Roosevelt, E. The White House pantry murder
Russell, M. Dreamers of the day
Uris, L. Redemption
Wouk, H. War and remembrance
Wouk, H. The winds of war

CIA
Berenson, A. The deceivers
Berenson, A. The prisoner
Clancy, T. The hunt for Red October
Coughlin, J. In the crosshairs
Ellroy, J. American tabloid
Fesperman, D. Safe houses
Hunter, S. Time to hunt
Huston, C. Skinner
Ignatius, D. Body of lies
Ignatius, D. A firing offense
Ignatius, D. The increment
Littell, R. The company
Ludlum, R. The Sigma protocol
MacInnes, H. The Venetian affair
Prescott, L. The secrets we kept
Reich, C. The take
Wolfe, P. The lost diary of M

CIA AGENTS
Berenson, A. The deceivers
Berenson, A. The faithful spy
Beauman, N. Madness is better than defeat
Berenson, A. The prisoner
Coes, B. Bloody Sunday
Coes, B. The Russian
Coonts, S. The armageddon file
Coonts, S. The art of war
Coonts, S. The Russia account
Coughlin, J. In the crosshairs
Coughlin, J. Long shot
Cussler, C. Golden Buddha
DeLillo, D. Libra
Dimon, H. Mercy
Dugoni, R. The eighth sister
Farnsworth, C. Flashmob
Farnsworth, C. Killfile
Littell, R. The company
Ludlum, R. The Prometheus deception

Matthews, J. The Kremlin's candidate
Matthews, J. Red sparrow
Matthews, J. Palace of treason
Parnell, S. Man of war
Ricciardi, D. Warning light
Rush, N. Mortals
Steinhauer, O. All the old knives
Steinhauer, O. The last tourist
Vidich, P. The coldest warrior

CIA CUBAN OPERATIONS
Buckley, W. Mongoose, R.I.P.

CIA EUROPEAN OPERATIONS
Clancy, T. Patriot games

CIA OFFICIALS AND EMPLOYEES
Steinhauer, O. An American spy
Steinhauer, O. The nearest exit
Steinhauer, O. The tourist

CIA SOVIET OPERATIONS
Clancy, T. The cardinal of the Kremlin

CIA.
Hunter, S. Havana

Cibola burn Corey, J.

The **Cider** House rules Irving, J.

Ciel Halligan novels [series] Grimes, L.

Cilka's journey Morris, H.

CINCINNATI, OHIO
Draper, S. Forged by fire
Foster, L. Under pressure
Sittenfeld, C. Eligible

CINEMATOGRAPHERS
Smith, D. The electric hotel

Cinnamon kiss Mosley, W.

Cinnamon skin MacDonald, J.

CINQUE, JOSEPH, DIED 1879?
Pesci, D. Amistad

Circe Miller, M.

CIRCE (GREEK MYTHOLOGY)
Miller, M. Circe

The **circle** Eggers, D.

Circle of friends Binchy, M.

Circle of friends trilogy (Mary Jo Putney) [series] Putney, M.

Circle of shadows Robertson, I.

A **circle** of wives LaPlante, A.

Circling the sun McLain, P.

The **circular** staircase Rinehart, M.

CIRCUS
Carter, A. Nights at the circus
Davis, A. Wonder when you'll miss me
Gruen, S. Water for elephants
Littlejohn, E. Inherit the bones
Mayer, M. Aerialists
Morgenstern, E. The night circus
Valentine, G. Mechanique
Wallace, D. Mr. Sebastian and the Negro magician

CIRCUS ANIMALS
Gruen, S. Water for elephants

K'wan Welfare wifeys
Kamal, S. It all falls down
Kroese, R. The last iota
Lauren, C. Roomies
Lebrecht, N. The song of names
Little, T. Where there's smoke
MacNeal, S. The king's justice
Macneal, E. The doll factory
Mamet, D. Chicago
Mandel, E. The glass hotel
Martel, Y. Beatrice and Virgil
Martin, S. An object of beauty
Martinson, T. The reign of the Kingfisher
Mason, T. The Darwin affair
Maupin, A. Tales of the city
McBain, E. The big bad city
McBain, E. Fat Ollie's book
McBain, E. The frumious bandersnatch
McBain, E. Hark!
McBain, E. The last dance
McBain, E. Nocturne
McCann, C. Let the great world spin
McDermott, A. The ninth hour
Mieville, C. The city & the city
Mina, D. The long drop
Mistry, R. A fine balance
Molloy, A. The perfect mother
Mosley, W. RL's dream
Mosley, W. Trouble is what I do
Mukherjee, B. Miss new India
Naylor, G. The men of Brewster Place
Naylor, G. The women of Brewster Place
O'Hara, J. Butterfield 8
O'Malley, T. We were kings
O'Nan, S. The night country
Obregon, N. Blue light Yokohama
Orange, T. There there
Pamuk, O. A strangeness in my mind
Parker, T. The fallen
Percy, W. The last gentleman
Pickard, N. The scent of rain and lightning
Pietroni, A. Ruby's spoon
Pobi, R. City of windows
Pochoda, I. These women
Rankin, I. Rather be the devil
Rash, R. Something rich and strange
Raybourn, D. A murderous relation
Redhill, M. Bellevue square
Richler, M. Barney's version
Ridgway, K. Hawthorn & Child
Robinson, K. New York 2140
Rooney, K. Lillian Boxfish takes a walk
Rosenberg, J. Confessions of the fox
Rutherfurd, E. London
Rutherfurd, E. Paris
Sapphire, 1. American dreams
Senna, D. New people

Shafak, E. 10 minutes 38 seconds in this strange world
Shoham, L. Asylum city
Shupe, J. The rogue of Fifth Avenue
Smith, B. A tree grows in Brooklyn
Smith, Z. NW
Souljah, S The coldest winter ever
Souljah, S. A deeper love inside
Stringer, V. Let that be the reason
Swinson, K. Wifey
Swinson, K. Wifey's next sticky situation
Turner, N. Black widow
Turner, N. A hustler's wife
Twardoch, S. The king of Warsaw
Urquhart, J. The night stages
Washington, B. Lot
Whitehead, C. Apex hides the hurt
Whitehead, C. The intuitionist
Wilder, T. Theophilus North
Wolfe, T. Back to blood
Wolfe, T. The bonfire of the vanities
Wood, T. The engineer's wife
Woods, S. A delicate touch
Woods, T. True to the game
Woods, T. True to the game II
Woods, T. True to the game III
Woodson, J. Another Brooklyn
Yanagihara, H. A little life
Zaman, N. Up in the main house & other stories

CITY LIFE -- BERLIN, GERMANY
Isherwood, C. The Berlin stories
CITY LIFE -- BROOKLYN, NEW YORK CITY
Pochoda, I. Visitation Street
CITY LIFE -- DUBLIN, IRELAND
Joyce, J. Ulysses
CITY LIFE -- FRANCE
Jenoff, P. The ambassador's daughter
CITY LIFE -- LOS ANGELES, CALIFORNIA
Ellis, B. Imperial bedrooms
CITY LIFE -- MEXICO
Urrea, L. Into the beautiful North
CITY LIFE -- PHILADELPHIA, PENNSYLVANIA
Holmes, S. Bad girlz
CITY LIFE -- WASHINGTON, D.C.
Pelecanos, G. The sweet forever
City of blades Bennett, R.
City of Bohane Barry, K.
The city of brass Chakraborty, S.
City of dark magic Flyte, M.
City of dark magic [series] Flyte, M.
City of endless night Preston, D.
City of girls Gilbert, E.
City of ink Hart, E.
City of lost dreams Flyte, M.
The city of lost fortunes Camp, B.
City of margins Boyle, W.
City of miracles Bennett, R.
The city of mirrors Cronin, J.

O'Dell, C. A study in honor
Okparanta, C. Under the udala trees
Olmstead, R. Coal black horse
Pasternak, B. Doctor Zhivago
Perry, A. Slaves of obsession
Peters, R. Hell or Richmond
Piercy, M. Sex wars
Pitts, L. Freeman
Plain, B. Crescent City
Poyer, D. A country of our own
Poyer, D. Fire on the waters
Reed, I. Flight to Canada
Saylor, S. A mist of prophecies
Saylor, S. Rubicon
Shaara, J. Gods and generals
Shaara, M. The killer angels
Shaara, J. The last full measure
Slouka, M. God's fool
Thelen, A. The island of second sight
Walker, M. Jubilee
Warren, R. Band of angels

CIVIL WAR -- CHECHNYA, RUSSIA
Marra, A. A constellation of vital phenomena
CIVIL WAR -- POST-WAR ASPECTS
Alarcon, D. At night we walk in circles
CIVIL WAR -- SOMALIA
Scego, I. Adua
CIVIL WAR -- SRI LANKA
Arudpragasam, A. The story of a brief marriage
Bala, S. The boat people
Ondaatje, M. Anil's ghost
CIVIL WAR -- SUDAN
Caputo, P. Acts of faith
Civil War at sea [series] Poyer, D.
Civil War trilogy (Jeff Shaara) [series] Shaara, J.
CIVIL WAR VETERANS
Bahr, H. The Judas Field
Cole, A. A hope divided
Estleman, L. The master executioner
Jenkins, B. Forbidden
Lent, J. A slant of light
Pearl, M. The technologists
CIVILIAN CONSERVATION CORPS
Barnett, K. Ever faithful
CIVILIANS IN WAR
Harris, C. Good time coming
CIVILIZATION
Khoury, R. Empire of lies
Mandel, E. Station Eleven
Martine, A. A memory called empire
McCormack, M. Solar bones
Miller, W. A canticle for Leibowitz
Stirling, S. Dies the fire
Stirling, S. A meeting at Corvallis
Stirling, S. The protector's war
 This way to the end times
Wendig, C. Wanderers

CIVILIZATION, ANCIENT
Barker, P. The silence of the girls
Corby, G. The Marathon conspiracy
Corby, G. The Pericles Commission
George, M. The confessions of young Nero
George, M. The splendor before the dark
Harris, R. Pompeii
Kidd, S. The book of longings
Long, J. The reckoning, Jeff Long.
Saylor, S. Wrath of the furies
Walton, J. Necessity
CIVILIZATION, CELTIC
Pike, S. The lost queen
CIVILIZATION, MEDIEVAL
Falcones de Sierra, I. Cathedral of the sea
Follett, K. World without end
Griffith, N. Hild
Harris, R. The second sleep
Hesse, H. Narcissus and Goldmund
Lin, J. The lotus palace
Lyndon, R. Hawk quest
Nicholas, D. Something red
Nicholas, D. Throne of darkness
Nicholas, D. The wicked
Penman, S. Falls the shadow
Penman, S. Here be dragons
Penman, S. Time and chance
Penman, S. When Christ and his saints slept
Peters, E. Brother Cadfael's penance
Peters, E. Dead man's ransom
Peters, E. The hermit of Eyton Forest
Peters, E. The holy thief
Peters, E. Monk's hood
Peters, E. The pilgrim of hate
Peters, E. The potter's field
Peters, E. A rare Benedictine
Peters, E. The rose rent
Peters, E. St. Peter's fair
Peters, E. The sanctuary sparrow
Peters, E. The summer of the Danes
Peters, E. The virgin in the ice
Rice, A. Angel time
Robb, C. A gift of Sanctuary
Robb, C. The cross-legged knight
Robb, C. The riddle of St. Leonard's
Royal, P. Covenant with hell
Royal, P. Sanctity of hate
Royal, P. Satan's lullaby
Sedley, K. The Tintern treasure
Sharratt, M. Illuminations
Walters, M. The last hours
Weber, D. By schism rent asunder
Weber, D. Off Armageddon reef
CIVILIZATION, MEDIEVAL -- EUROPE
Willis, C. Doomsday book
CIVILIZATION, PRE-COLUMBIAN
Bowles, D. Feathered serpent, dark heart of sky

Austen, J. Pride and prejudice
Austen, J. Sense and sensibility
Balzac, H. The country doctor
Balzac, H. Cousin Bette
Balzac, H. Eugenie Grandet
Blackmore, R. Lorna Doone
Bronte, A. The tenant of Wildfell Hall
Bronte, C. Emma
Bronte, C. Jane Eyre
Bronte, E. Wuthering Heights
Buchan, J. The thirty-nine steps
Bunyan, J. The pilgrim's progress
Camus, A. The fall
Cather, W. Death comes for the archbishop
Cather, W. A lost lady
Cather, W. My Antonia
Cather, W. O pioneers!
Cather, W. The song of the lark
Cervantes Saavedra, M. Don Quixote
Cisneros, S. The house on Mango Street
Collins, W. The moonstone
Collins, W. The woman in white
Conrad, J. Complete short fiction of Joseph Conrad
Conrad, J. Heart of darkness
Conrad, J. Lord Jim
Conrad, J. Nostromo
Conrad, J. Victory
Cooper, J. The last of the Mohicans
Crane, S. The red badge of courage
Defoe, D. Moll Flanders
Defoe, D. Robinson Crusoe
Dickens, C. Bleak House
Dickens, C. A Christmas carol
Dickens, C. David Copperfield
Dickens, C. Dombey and Son
Dickens, C. Great expectations
Dickens, C. Little Dorrit
Dickens, C. Martin Chuzzlewit
Dickens, C. Nicholas Nickleby
Dickens, C. The old curiosity shop
Dickens, C. Oliver Twist, or The parish boy's progress
Dickens, C. Our mutual friend
Dickens, C. The Pickwick papers
Dickens, C. A tale of two cities
Dostoyevsky, F. The best short stories of Dostoevsky
Dostoyevsky, F. The brothers Karamazov
Dostoyevsky, F. Crime and punishment
Dostoyevsky, F. Notes from underground
Doyle, A. The complete Sherlock Holmes
Dreiser, T. An American tragedy
Dreiser, T. Sister Carrie
Dumas, A. Camille
Dumas, A. The count of Monte Cristo
Dumas, A. The man in the iron mask
Dumas, A. The three musketeers
Dumas, A. Twenty years after
Eliot, G. Adam Bede

Eliot, G. Middlemarch
Eliot, G. The mill on the Floss
Eliot, G. Silas Marner
Fielding, H. The history of Tom Jones, a foundling
Flaubert, G. Madame Bovary
Flaubert, G. Sentimental education
Ford, F. The good soldier
Gaskell, E. Cranford
Gaskell, E. North and South
Godden, R. The greengage summer
Gogol, N. The collected tales of Nikolai Gogol
Gogol, N. Dead souls
Goldman, W. The princess bride
Hardy, T. Far from the madding crowd
Hardy, T. Jude the obscure
Hardy, T. The return of the native
Hardy, T. Tess of the d'Urbervilles
Hawthorne, N. The house of the seven gables
Hawthorne, N. The scarlet letter
Hilton, J. Good-bye, Mr. Chips
Hilton, J. Lost horizon
Hugo, V. The hunchback of Notre Dame
Hugo, V. Les miserables
Jackson, S. The lottery
James, H. Complete stories, 1874-1884
James, H. Complete stories, 1884-1891
James, H. Complete stories, 1892-1898
James, H. Complete stories, 1898-1910
James, H. Daisy Miller
James, H. The golden bowl
James, H. The portrait of a lady
James, H. The turn of the screw
James, H. The wings of the dove
Jewett, S. The country of the pointed firs and other stories
Lewis, M. The monk
London, J. The call of the wild
London, J. Martin Eden
London, J. White Fang
Maturin, C. Melmoth the wanderer
Maupassant, G. Like death
Melville, H. Billy Budd, foretopman
Melville, H. The complete shorter fiction
Melville, H. The confidence-man
Melville, H. Moby-Dick; or, The whale
Melville, H. Omoo
Norris, F. McTeague
Poe, E. Complete stories and poems of Edgar Allan Poe
Poe, E. The narrative of Arthur Gordon Pym of Nantucket
Pontoppidan, H. Lucky Per
Proust, M. The complete short stories of Marcel Proust
Proust, M. Remembrance of things past
Proust, M. Swann's way
Proust, M. Time regained
Proust, M. Within a budding grove
Pym, B. Excellent women
Radcliffe, A. The mysteries of Udolpho
Richardson, S. Clarissa, or, The history of a young lady

Boyne, J. A history of loneliness
Dallas, S. Westering women
Davidson, A. The boatman's daughter
Edvardsson, M. A nearly normal family
Faber, M. The book of strange new things
Faulkner, W. Light in August
Golding, W. Rites of passage
Guterson, D. Our Lady of the Forest
Harrison, C. Beyond absolution
Hawthorne, N. The scarlet letter
Iggulden, C. The abbot's tale
Karon, J. At home in Mitford
Karon, J. In this mountain
Karon, J. A new song
Karon, J. Out to Canaan
Kate, J. A girl's guide to the Outback
Kienzle, W. The rosary murders
Krauss, N. Forest Dark
Leine, K. The prophets of Eternal Fjord
Malliet, G. A demon summer
Malliet, G. A fatal winter
Malliet, G. Pagan spring
Malliet, G. Wicked autumn
Mathews, B. The world of tomorrow
McBride, J. Deacon King Kong
Miller, S. While I was gone
Nesbo, J. Midnight sun
Oates, J. The accursed
Parker, T. California girl
Penrose, A. Murder on Black Swan Lane
Perry, A. No graves as yet
Perry, A. Shoulder the sky
Perry, S. The Essex serpent
Price, R. The good priest's son
Robinson, M. Gilead
Robinson, M. Home
Robinson, M. Lila
Runcie, J. The road to Grantchester
Rutherfurd, E. The forest
Sayers, D. The nine tailors
Sebastian, C. It takes two to tumble
Trollope, A. Barchester Towers
Trollope, A. Framley parsonage
Trollope, A. The warden
Turner, B. The secret life of Sarah Hollenbeck
Turner, N. Heartbreak of a hustler's wife
Updike, J. In the beauty of the lilies
Wall, C. The dearly beloved
Warren, T. The pastor's husband

CLERGY -- CALIFORNIA
Rivers, F. And the shofar blew
The **clergyman's** wife Greeley, M.

CLERGYMEN
Austen, J. Northanger Abbey
Block, L. The sins of the fathers
Bohjalian, C. Secrets of Eden
Leigh, E. Temptations of a wallflower

Mortimer, J. Quite honestly
Paton, A. Cry, the beloved country
Runcie, J. Sidney Chambers and the forgiveness of sins
Runcie, J. Sidney Chambers and the perils of the night
Runcie, J. Sidney Chambers and the persistence of love
Runcie, J. Sidney Chambers and the problem of evil
Runcie, J. Sidney Chambers and the shadow of death

CLERGYMEN -- ILLINOIS
McInerny, R. Requiem for a realtor

CLERGYMEN CHILD SEXUAL ABUSERS
Olafur Johann Olafsson The sacrament

CLERGYMEN'S FAMILIES
Brooks, G. Caleb's crossing
Paton, A. Cry, the beloved country

CLERGYWOMEN
Baldwin, J. Just above my head
Eliot, G. Adam Bede
McPherson, C. Strangers at the gate
Spencer-Fleming, J. All mortal flesh
Spencer-Fleming, J. Hid from our eyes
Spencer-Fleming, J. I shall not want
Spencer-Fleming, J. In the bleak midwinter
Spencer-Fleming, J. Through the evil days

CLERKS (RETAIL INDUSTRY AND TRADE)
Link, K. Magic for beginners
Martin, S. Shopgirl
Stern, S. The Pinch

CLEVELAND, GROVER, 1837-1908
Oates, J. The accursed

CLEVELAND, OHIO
Black, L. Let justice descend
Black, L. Suffer the children
Black, L. That darkness
Koryta, M. Tonight I said goodbye
Ng, C. Little fires everywhere
Satyal, R. No one can pronounce my name
Clever girl Hadley, T.

CLEVERNESS
Rogues
The **client** Grisham, J.
Cliff Janeway mysteries [series] Dunning, J.
Clifton Chronicles [series] Archer, J.
CLIMACTERIC, MALE
Lewis, S. Dodsworth
CLIMATE CHANGE
Anders, C. All the birds in the sky
Egan, G. Perihelion summer
Ghosh, A. Gun Island
Kowal, M. The calculating stars
Lunde, M. The end of the ocean
Nemett, A. We can save us all
Pressfield, S. 36 righteous men
Reynolds, A. Permafrost
Robinson, K. Blue Mars
Robinson, K. New York 2140
Walker, K. The age of miracles
Climate novels [series] Lunde, M.

Harris, S. The color of Bee Larkham's murder
Horowitz, A. The House of Silk
Horowitz, A. Moriarty
Ide, J. Hi five
Jacobs, N. The last equation of Isaac Severy
Preston, D. City of endless night
Preston, D. The Obsidian chamber
Racculia, K. Tuesday Mooney talks to ghosts
Raybourn, D. Silent in the grave
Sandford, J. Invisible prey
Smith, F. Night fall

CLYTEMNESTRA (GREEK MYTHOLOGY)
Toibin, C. House of names
Coal black horse Olmstead, R.
COAL MINE ACCIDENTS
Coover, R. The origin of the Brunists
Cussler, C. The Titanic secret
Smith, M. Rose
COAL MINERS
Lawrence, D. Sons and lovers
Montgomery, J. The widows
Smith, M. Rose
Zola, E. Germinal
COAL MINERS -- WALES
Llewellyn, R. How green was my valley
COAL MINERS' FAMILIES
Llewellyn, R. How green was my valley
COAL MINES AND MINING
Adamson, G. The outlander
Cussler, C. The Titanic secret
Haigh, J. Baker Towers
Russell, M. The women of the copper country
Unsworth, B. The quality of mercy
Zola, E. Germinal
COAL MINING TOWNS
Haigh, J. Baker Towers
Hunter, S. Hot springs
Russell, M. The women of the copper country
COAL MINING TOWNS -- PENNSYLVANIA
O'Dell, T. Back roads
COASTAL TOWNS
Abe, K. The woman in the dunes
Andrews, M. Sunset Beach
Atkinson, K. Big sky
Bannalec, J. The killing tide
Beattie, A. The state we're in
Brenner, J. Drawing home
Brett, S. The torso in the town
Carlson, M. A Christmas by the sea
Carr, R. The wanderer
Cheek, C. Cape May
Cheever, J. The Wapshot chronicle
Danticat, E. Claire of the sea light
Dare, T. A night to surrender
Dodd, C. Virtue Falls
Doerr, A. All the light we cannot see
Donoghue, E. Akin

Gerritsen, T. The shape of night
Goodman, C. The sea of lost girls
Harris, R. Pompeii
Hensher, P. King of the badgers
Holmes, L. Evvie Drake starts over
Jewell, L. I found you
Kandasamy, M. When I hit you, or, A portrait of the writer as a young wife
Kubica, M. The other Mrs.
Lewis, T. GBH
Link, C. The other child
London, S. The Aussie next door
McPherson, C. Go to my grave
Millet, L. Sweet lamb of heaven
Miranda, M. The last house guest
Murphy, S. Cat pay the devil
Nichols, P. The rocks
Pineiro, C. One summer night
Quartey, K. Murder at Cape Three Points
Quick, A. The other lady vanishes
Rice, L. Last day
Shalvis, J. The sweetest thing
Shaw, W. Salt lane
Singh, N. A madness of sunshine
Sparks, N. Every breath
Steinbeck, J. Cannery Row
Strout, E. Olive Kitteridge
Strout, E. Olive, again
Truss, L. The man that got away
Wallace, M. The girl in the garden
Wright, A. Carpentaria
Yoshimoto, B. Goodbye Tsugumi
COASTAL TOWNS -- TURKEY
De Bernieres, L. Birds without wings
COASTS
Owens, D. Where the crawdads sing
COBAIN, KURT, 1967-1994
Crosbie, L. Where did you sleep last night?
COCAINE
Blau, J. The Wonder Bread summer
Parks, B. Closer than you know
COCAINE ABUSE
Meyer, N. The seven-per-cent solution
COCAINE ADDICTS
Little, T. Where there's smoke
COCAINE SMUGGLING
MacDonald, J. The lonely silver rain
COCAINE TRAFFIC
Ashley, 1. The Cartel
Ashley, 1. The Cartel 2
Ashley, 1. The Cartel 3
Pelecanos, G. The sweet forever
COCHISE COUNTY, ARIZONA
Jance, J. Skeleton Canyon
COCKROACHES
Knox, T. Kockroach
Cockroaches Nesbo, J.

Harvey, M. The fifth floor
Heller, P. Celine
Hill Gumbao, T. The good suicides
Hillerman, T. The shape shifter
Holt, V. The black opal
Hunt, A. City of saints
Hunter, S. Black light
Iles, G. Natchez burning
Ishiguro, K. When we were orphans
Jance, J. Queen of the night
Jewell, L. Then she was gone
Johnston, T. The current
Kellerman, J. The genius
Kelly, J. The moon tunnel
Kelly, S. The wages of desire
Kepler, L. The sandman
Krueger, W. Vermilion drift
Lansdale, J. Devil red
Lansdale, J. Honky tonk samurai
Larsson, S. The girl with the dragon tattoo
Lippman, L. After I'm gone
Lippman, L. What the dead know
Lippman, L. Wilde Lake
Lovesey, P. Beau death
Lovesey, P. Skeleton Hill
Lutz, L. The Spellman files
Marlette, D. Magic time
McCrumb, S. If I'd killed him when I met him
McDermid, V. The distant echo
McPherson, C. The child garden
McPherson, C. Scot & soda
Muller, M. Point Deception
Muller, M. Vanishing point
Murr, N. The perfect man
Nesbo, J. Police
Nesbo, J. The redbreast
Nesbo, J. The thirst
Newton, C. Start shooting
O'Connell, C. The chalk girl
Parker, R. Back story
Parker, T. California girl
Patterson, J. Private
Pelecanos, G. The night gardener
Penny, L. The nature of the beast
Perry, A. A Christmas return
Persson, L. The dying detective
Persson, L. Free falling, as if in a dream
Quartey, K. Wife of the gods
Rademacher, C. Deadly Camargue
Ramsay, F. Countdown
Rankin, I. The black book
Rankin, I. Rather be the devil
Read, C. Invisible boy
Reichs, K. A conspiracy of bones
Robertson, M. The Baker Street letters
Rosenfelt, D. Black and blue
Roy, L. Bent Road

Ryan, H. Truth be told
Sager, R. The last time I lied
Salvalaggio, K. Bone dust white
Sandford, J. Buried prey
Schofield, D. Time of departure
Scoppettone, S. My sweet untraceable you
Shaw, W. A song for the brokenhearted
Sidor, S. The mirror's edge
Slaughter, K. The good daughter
Spencer, S. Dead end
Spencer, S. Echoes of the dead
Spencer-Fleming, J. Hid from our eyes
St. James, S. The broken girls
Steiner, S. Persons unknown
Straub, P. Mystery
Thomas, R. Firewatching
Wade, B. Falling for you
Walker, W. Crime of privilege
Yarbrough, S. Safe from the neighbors
Zhou, H. Death notice
Cold country Rowland, R.
Cold cruel winter Nickson, C.
The **cold** eye Gilman, L.
Cold granite MacBride, S.
Cold in hand Harvey, J.
Cold is the grave Robinson, P.
Cold Mountain Frazier, C.
Cold pursuit Parker, T.
Cold Sassy series [series] Burns, O.
Cold Sassy tree Burns, O.
Cold service Parker, R.
The **cold** six thousand Ellroy, J.
Cold storage Koepp, D.
Cold storage novels [series] Straley, J.
COLD WAR
    Burdick, E. Fail-safe
    Cumming, C. The Trinity Six
    DeLillo, D. Underworld
    Deighton, L. Berlin game
    Deighton, L. London match
    Dunmore, H. Exposure
    Faulks, S. On Green Dolphin Street
    Fesperman, D. Safe houses
    Follett, K. Edge of eternity
    Greene, G. The human factor
    Kennedy, D. The moment
    Le Carre, J. The honourable schoolboy
    Le Carre, J. The spy who came in from the cold
    Lem, S. His master's voice
    Littell, R. The company
    Mallon, T. Finale
    Mankell, H. The troubled man
    McEwan, I. Sweet tooth
    Paretsky, S. Fallout
    Prescott, L. The secrets we kept
    Sarginson, S. The wonderful
    Schutt, B. The Darwin strain

Crucet, J. Make your home among strangers
Cumyn, A. Losing it
Dickey, E. Before we were wicked
Faulkner, W. Sanctuary
Finch, C. The September Society
Fitzgerald, P. The blue flower
Friedman, D. Riot most uncouth
Goenawan, C. The perfect world of Miwako Sumida
Johnston, T. The current
Kay, G. The summer tree
Koryta, M. If she wakes
Lahiri, J. The namesake
Lewis, B. The ebb tide
Longworth, M. Murder in the Rue Dumas
Lukas, M. The last watchman of Old Cairo
Mankell, H. One step behind
McEwan, I. On Chesil Beach
Moore, L. A gate at the stairs
Moss, S. Ghost wall
Munoz Molina, A. A manuscript of ashes
Naslund, S. Four spirits
Nemett, A. We can save us all
Olshan, J. Black diamond fall
Parker, R. Melancholy baby
Pearl, M. The technologists
Perrotta, T. Joe College
Powers, R. Generosity
Richardson, K. Greywalker
Rooney, S. Normal people
Roth, H. Requiem for Harlem
Roth, P. Indignation
Schwab, V. Vicious
Segal, E. Love story
Smith, B. Joy in the morning
Tartt, D. The secret history
Walker, K. The dreamers
Walsh, H. Brass
Wayne, T. Loner
Willis, C. Blackout
Wuertz, Y. Everything belongs to us
Yates, C. Black chalk
Yoshimoto, B. The lake

COLLEGE STUDENTS -- CAMBRIDGE, ENGLAND
James, P. An unsuitable job for a woman

COLLEGE STUDENTS -- NEW JERSEY
Fitzgerald, F. Novels and stories, 1920-1922
Fitzgerald, F. This side of paradise

COLLEGE STUDENTS -- SCOTLAND
McDermid, V. The distant echo

COLLEGE STUDENTS -- SEXUALITY
Amis, M. The pregnant widow
Walsh, H. Brass

COLLEGE TEACHERS
Abu-Jaber, D. Crescent
Albahari, D. Gotz and Meyer
Albert, E. After birth
Allende, I. In the midst of winter

Amis, K. Lucky Jim
Aswani, A. Chicago
Balasubramanyam, R. Professor Chandra follows his bliss
Banks, R. Lost memory of skin
Barclay, L. A noise downstairs
Barth, J. The end of the road
Barthelme, F. Elroy Nights
Bell, S. At his mercy
Bellow, S. Herzog
Bellow, S. Ravelstein
Brown, K. The clairvoyants
Butler, R. Perfume River
Buwalda, P. Bonita Avenue
Byatt, A. Possession
Choi, S. My education
Coetzee, J. Disgrace
Cook, T. Sandrine's case
Coover, R. Pinocchio in Venice
Crouch, B. Dark matter
Davies, R. The rebel angels
DeLillo, D. White noise
Dean, P. Tam Lin
Delaney, J. Believe me
Dermansky, M. Very nice
Dexter, C. The daughters of Cain
Elkins, A. Unnatural selection
Elkins, A. Dying on the vine
Farah, N. Crossbones
Freudenberger, N. Lost and wanted
Gaddis, W. A frolic of his own
Gass, W. Middle C
Goodman, C. The night villa
Gordimer, N. No time like the present
Henry, P. Becoming Mrs. Lewis
Higgins, K. The perfect match
Houellebecq, M. Submission
JaQuavis The streets have no king
Jin, H. The crazed
Kotzwinkle, W. The bear went over the mountain
Langton, J. Murder at Monticello
Langton, J. The thief of Venice
Langton, J. The deserter
Le Carre, J. Our kind of traitor
Leithauser, B. The promise of elsewhere
Longworth, M. Murder in the Rue Dumas
Lovett, C. The lost book of the Grail
Lurie, A. Foreign affairs
Matthiessen, P. In paradise
McInerny, R. Celt and pepper
McInerny, R. Irish coffee
Mosley, W. John Woman
Nabokov, V. Pale fire
Nabokov, V. Pnin
Nunez, E. Grace
O'Donohue, C. Beyond the pale
O'Farrell, M. This must be the place
Offill, J. Dept. of speculation

Naipaul, V. A bend in the river
Phillips, C. A view of the empire at sunset
Proulx, A. Barkskins
Sayles, J. A moment in the sun
Scego, I. Adua
Serpell, N. The old drift
Willig, L. The summer country
Yi, C. The investigation

COLONIALISM -- AFRICA
Antunes, A. The return of the caravels
Kimani, P. Dance of the Jakaranda
Ngugi wa Thiong'o, 1. Minutes of glory, and other stories

COLONIALISM -- BURMA
Mason, D. The piano tuner

COLONIALISM -- NIGERIA
Achebe, C. Things fall apart

COLONIALISM -- SOUTH AFRICA
Michener, J. The covenant

COLONIES
Leine, K. The prophets of Eternal Fjord
Robinson, K. Red Mars
Valente, C. Radiance

COLONIES -- AFRICA
Naipaul, V. Half a life

COLONISTS
Clements, R. Revenger
Green, J. The mark of the king
Haldane, S. The devil's making

COLONIZED PEOPLES
Boudjedra, R. The Barbary figs
Gappah, P. Out of darkness, shining light
Grenville, K. The secret river
Ngugi wa Thiong'o, 1. Minutes of glory, and other stories

COLONIZED PEOPLES -- AUSTRALIA
Scott, K. That deadman dance

The **colony** of unrequited dreams Johnston, W.

COLOR
Fforde, J. Shades of grey
Silko, L. Gardens in the dunes

COLOR BLINDNESS
Fforde, J. Shades of grey

COLOR IN THE TEXTILE INDUSTRY AND TRADE
Winterson, J. The daylight gate

COLOR OF AFRICAN AMERICANS
Johnson, M. Incognegro
Morrison, T. God help the child
Sexton, M. A kind of freedom

The **color** of Bee Larkham's murder Harris, S.
The **color** of lightning Jiles, P.
The **color** of magic Pratchett, T.
The **color** of night Bell, M.
The **color** purple Walker, A.

COLORADO
Black, S. The killing lessons
Black, S. Lovemurder
Borland, H. When the legends die
Cameron, W. The dogs of Christmas

Carr, R. What we find
Cather, W. The song of the lark
Child, L. Nothing to lose
Cussler, C. The Titanic secret
Dallas, S. Tallgrass
Davidson, D. Killer pancake
Dunning, J. The bookman's wake
Dunning, J. Booked to die
Ellison, J. Tear me apart
Goodman, J. A touch of forever
Haruf, K. Plainsong
Haruf, K. Benediction
Haruf, K. Eventide
Haruf, K. Our souls at night
Heller, P. Celine
Hemmings, K. The possibilities
Holsinger, B. The gifted school
King, S. The shining
Les Becquets, D. Breaking wild
Littlejohn, E. Inherit the bones
Littlejohn, E. Lost Lake
Martin, C. Long way gone
McLarty, R. Art in America
Michener, J. Centennial
Mizushima, M. Burning ridge
Mizushima, M. Killing trail
Mizushima, M. Stalking ground
Overholser, W. Law at Angel's Landing
Phillips, S. Natural born charmer
Shalvis, J. Second chance summer
Wilson, C. Dead girl in 2A

COLORADO -- SOCIAL LIFE AND CUSTOMS -- 19TH CENTURY
Dallas, S. The last midwife

COLORADO RIVER
Bacigalupi, P. The water knife

Colorless Tsukuru Tazaki and his years of pilgrimage Murakami, H.

The **colour** Tremain, R.

Colter Shaw novels [series] Deaver, J.

COLUMBIA UNIVERSITY.
Pintoff, S. In the shadow of Gotham

COLUMBUS, OHIO
Coake, C. You came back
Stringer, V. Let that be the reason

A **column** of fire Follett, K.

COLUMNISTS
Landvik, L. Chronicles of a radical hag

COMA
Malerman, J. Unbury Carol

Coma Cook, R.

COMA -- PATIENTS
Feeney, A. Sometimes I lie

COMANCHE INDIANS
Kelton, E. Badger boy
Kelton, E. The way of the coyote

Butler, N. The hearts of men

Butler, S. Cygnet

Byatt, A. The biographer's tale

Byatt, A. The children's book

Bynum, S. Ms. Hempel chronicles

Campbell, B. Once upon a river

Campbell, B. Your blues ain't like mine

Carr, B. Opioid, Indiana

Cather, W. A lost lady

Cather, W. My Antonia

Cather, W. The song of the lark

Chacon, D. And the shadows took him

Chang, A. Days of distraction

Chatterjee, U. English, August

Chevalier, T. Girl with a pearl earring

Childress, M. Crazy in Alabama

Childress, M. One Mississippi

Choi, A. Kay's lucky coin variety

Cisneros, S. The house on Mango Street

Cleary, J. The sundowners

Clement, J. Gun love

Clinch, J. Finn

Cline, E. The girls

Cline, E. Ready player one

Coe, J. The rotters' club

Coetzee, J. The childhood of Jesus

Cognetti, P. The eight mountains

Colette, 1. The complete Claudine

Conroy, P. South of Broad

Crandall, S. Whistling past the graveyard

Crowell, J. Etched on me

Crucet, J. Make your home among strangers

Cruz, A. Dominicana

Dahlie, M. The best of youth

Dalton, T. Boy swallows universe

Danler, S. Sweetbitter

Dare, A. The girl with the louding voice

Davis, A. Wonder when you'll miss me

De Robertis, C. The gods of tango

De Robertis, C. Perla

DeWoskin, R. Big girl small

Dean, M. The time it takes to fall

Deane, S. Reading in the dark

Dennis-Benn, N. Here comes the sun

Diachenko, S. Vita nostra

Dickens, C. David Copperfield

Dickens, C. Great expectations

Dickens, C. Martin Chuzzlewit

Dickens, C. Nicholas Nickleby

Dickens, C. Oliver Twist, or The parish boy's progress

Dicks, M. Memoirs of an imaginary friend

Dimechkie, K. Lifted by the great nothing

Divakaruni, C. Oleander girl

Doctorow, E. Billy Bathgate

Doig, I. The bartender's tale

Doig, I. Last bus to wisdom

Doig, I. The whistling season

Doyle, R. Paddy Clarke, ha-ha-ha

Dreiser, T. Sister Carrie

Drury, T. The driftless area

Drury, T. Pacific

Dugoni, R. The extraordinary life of Sam Hell

Durham, D. Gabriel's story

Durrow, H. The girl who fell from the sky

Earley, T. Jim the boy

Echlin, K. The disappeared

Ehirim, N. Prince of monkeys

Erdrich, L. The beet queen

Erdrich, L. The round house

Eskens, A. Nothing more dangerous

Eugenides, J. Middlesex

Eugenides, J. The virgin suicides

Evans, J. The white devil

Evison, J. All about Lulu

Evison, J. Lawn boy

Extence, G. The universe versus Alex Woods

Fabry, C. The promise of Jesse Woods

Fagan, J. The Panopticon

Faulkner, W. The reivers

Faye, G. Small country

Ferber, E. So big

Fine, J. What should be wild

Fitzgerald, F. This side of paradise

Fitzpatrick, L. Lights all night long

Frazier, C. Thirteen moons

Fridlund, E. History of wolves

Fu, K. For today I am a boy

Fuller, C. Our endless numbered days

Fuqua, J. Gone and back again

Gabel, A. The ensemble

Gaitskill, M. The mare

Galloway, G. As simple as snow

Gardam, J. The flight of the maidens

Gardam, J. God on the rocks

Gessen, K. All the sad young literary men

Gibbons, K. Ellen Foster

Gibbons, K. The life all around me by Ellen Foster

Gilb, D. The Flowers

Gilman, L. Flesh and fire

Godwin, G. Flora

Godwin, G. Grief cottage

Grames, J. The seven or eight deaths of Stella Fortuna

Grant, H. The vanishing of Katharina Linden

Green, H. An absolutely remarkable thing

Greenfeld, K. True

Greenidge, K. We love you, Charlie Freeman

Groff, L. Arcadia

Gunday, H. The few

Gunesekera, R. Suncatcher

Hamill, S. A cosmology of monsters

Harris, T. Hannibal rising

Hemingway, E. The Nick Adams stories

Hemingway, E. The old man and the sea

Herbert, F. Dune

Prose, F. Goldengrove
Proulx, A. That old ace in the hole
Proust, M. Swann's way
Proust, M. Within a budding grove
Quindlen, A. Miller's Valley
Quindlen, A. Object lessons
Rice-Gonzalez, C. Chulito
Rojas Contreras, I. Fruit of the drunken tree
Roth, H. Call it sleep
Roth, H. A diving rock on the Hudson
Roth, H. From bondage
Roth, H. Requiem for Harlem
Roth, H. A star shines over Mt. Morris Park
Roth, P. Indignation
Russell, K. Swamplandia!
Sagan, F. Bonjour tristesse
Salinger, J. The catcher in the rye
Sapphire The kid
Sarginson, S. The wonderful
Saroyan, W. The human comedy
Savage, S. Firmin
Savas, A. Walking on the ceiling
Schlink, B. The reader
Shreve, A. Fortune's rocks
Shteyngart, G. The Russian debutante's handbook
Sillitoe, A. Saturday night and Sunday morning
Sittenfeld, C. Prep
Smith, B. A tree grows in Brooklyn
Smith, D. I capture the castle
Smith, L. On Agate Hill
Smith, Z. NW
Solomon, A. Disgruntled
Souljah, S. A deeper love inside
Stibbe, N. Reasons to be cheerful
Straight, S. A million nightingales
Straub, E. Modern lovers
Straub, E. The vacationers
Strout, E. Amy and Isabelle
Stuart, D. Shuggie Bain
Swarthout, G. Bless the beasts and children
Swyler, E. Light from other stars
Szabo, M. Abigail
Tamirat, N. The parking lot attendant
Tarkington, B. Alice Adams
Tartt, D. The goldfinch
Thomas, S. Oligarchy
Tinti, H. The twelve lives of Samuel Hawley
Toews, M. A complicated kindness
Toole, F. Pound for pound
Torres, J. We the animals
Townsend, S. The Adrian Mole diaries
Twain, M. Adventures of Huckleberry Finn
Tyree, O. Flyy girl
Tyree, O. For the love of money
Ulinich, A. Petropolis
Urrea, L. The hummingbird's daughter
Vann, D. Aquarium

Vernon, O. A killing in this town
Vestal, S. Daredevils
Vine, B. Grasshopper
Vlautin, W. Lean on Pete
Vuong, O. On Earth we're briefly gorgeous
Walker, K. The age of miracles
Wallace, D. Mr. Sebastian and the Negro magician
Wallace, D. The watermelon king
Walls, J. The silver star
Walsh, M. My sunshine away
Ward, J. Salvage the bones
Wayne, T. The love song of Jonny Valentine
Weir, A. Innocent traitor
Weir, A. The Lady Elizabeth
White, E. The beautiful room is empty
White, E. A boy's own story
Whitehead, C. Sag Harbor
Wilder, T. Theophilus North
Wolfe, T. I am Charlotte Simmons
Wolfe, T. Look homeward, angel
Wolfe, T. Of time and the river
Wolitzer, M. The female persuasion
Woo, S. Everything Asian
Wood, S. The Quintland sisters
Woodrell, D. Winter's bone
Woodson, J. Another Brooklyn
Woodson, J. Red at the bone
Woolf, V. The voyage out
Wouk, H. Marjorie Morningstar
Wroblewski, D. The story of Edgar Sawtelle
Yoshimoto, B. Goodbye Tsugumi
Yoshimoto, B. Moshi-moshi
Zimler, R. The seventh gate
deWitt, P. Undermajordomo Minor

COMMAND OF TROOPS
Cobbs Hoffman, E. The Tubman command
Gingrich, N. Grant comes east
Lee, Y. Ninefox gambit
Shaara, J. Gods and generals
Shaara, J. Gone for soldiers
Shaara, J. The last full measure

Commandant Camille Verhoeven trilogy [series] Lemaitre, P.

COMMANDO OPERATIONS
Shaara, J. The rising tide
Shaara, J. The steel wave

COMMITMENT (PSYCHOLOGY)
Hijuelos, O. The mambo kings play songs of love
Hijuelos, O. Beautiful Maria of my soul
Hoover, C. It ends with us
Moniz, T. Big familia
Oakley, C. You were there too
Rush, N. Mortals
Turner, B. Wooing Cadie McCaffrey

Commodore Hornblower Forester, C.
The **commodore** O'Brian, P.
The **commoner** Schwartz, J.

COMMUNISTS -- CHINA
Jin, H. War trash
COMMUNISTS -- SOVIET UNION
Bulgakov, M. The master and Margarita
COMMUNISTS -- SPAIN
Pawel, R. Death of a nationalist
COMMUNITIES
Abbott, M. The fever
Alharthi, J. Celestial bodies
Allio, K. Buddhism for Western children
Backman, F. A man called Ove
Backman, F. Beartown
Bambara, T. The salt eaters
Banner, C. The house at the edge of night
Berne, S. The dogs of Littlefield
Bolton, S. A dark and twisted tide
Brown, T. Gods of Howl Mountain
Butler, S. Cygnet
Carey, L. The stolen child
Cha, S. Your house will pay
Chevalier, T. A single thread
Coben, H. The boy from the woods
Colgan, J. The endless beach
Dallas, S. The last midwife
De Bernieres, L. Birds without wings
De Robertis, C. Cantoras
Dennis-Benn, N. Here comes the sun
Doiron, P. Stay hidden
Erdrich, L. Tracks
Gaines, E. The autobiography of Miss Jane Pittman
Gaitskill, M. The mare
Goldbloom, G. On division
Gray, A. The care and feeding of ravenously hungry girls
Haigh, J. Baker Towers
Hannah, K. The great alone
Harris, R. The second sleep
Haruf, K. Eventide
Heacox, K. Jimmy Bluefeather
Henderson, S. The flicker of old dreams
Jalaluddin, U. Ayesha at last
Jaswal, B. Erotic stories for Punjabi widows
Kate, J. Love and other mistakes
Kirkpatrick, J. One more river to cross
Lalli, S. The matchmaker's list
Leine, K. The prophets of Eternal Fjord
MacDonald, A. When we were Vikings
McBride, J. Deacon King Kong
McDermott, A. The ninth hour
McGregor, J. The reservoir tapes
Mirvis, T. The outside world
Montgomery, J. The widows
Nahai, G. The luminous heart of Jonah S.
O'Brien, E. In the forest
Oliveras, P. Their perfect melody
Osondu, E. This house is not for sale
Phillips, J. Disappearing earth
Rabb, J. Among the living

Rice, W. Moon of the crusted snow
Ripley, M. Mr Campion's fault
Robinson, K. Aurora
Russo, R. Straight man
Sahota, S. The year of the runaways
Sala, S. Forever my hero
Satyal, R. No one can pronounce my name
Scott, R. The world doesn't require you
Shepard, K. The Celestials
Solomon, R. The deep
Stern, S. The Pinch
Sternbergh, A. The blinds
Stirling, S. A meeting at Corvallis
Stirling, S. The protector's war
Tidhar, L. Central Station
Verble, M. Cherokee America
Yan, L. Dream of Ding Village
Zhang, J. Sour heart
COMMUNITIES -- HAITI
Danticat, E. Claire of the sea light
COMMUNITY CENTERS
Cleeves, A. The long call
COMMUNITY GARDENS
Pelecanos, G. The night gardener
COMMUNITY LIFE
Baxter, C. The feast of love
Berg, E. Night of miracles
Berry, W. Jayber Crow
Berry, W. That distant land
Chancellor, B. Sycamore
Danticat, E. Claire of the sea light
Jewett, S. The country of the pointed firs and other stories
Morrison, T. Love
Morrison, T. Paradise
Morrison, T. Tar baby
Oates, J. The falls
Russo, R. Bridge of sighs
Tyler, A. Clock dance
COMMUNITY LIFE -- MONTEREY, CALIFORNIA
Steinbeck, J. Cannery Row
COMMUNITY NEWSPAPERS
Landvik, L. Chronicles of a radical hag
COMMUNITY ORGANIZATION
Bump, G. Everywhere you don't belong
COMMUNITY POLICING
Anderson, K. Green sun
COMMUNITY SERVICE (PUNISHMENT)
Kline, C. Orphan train
COMMUTERS
Hawkins, P. The girl on the train
COMPANIONSHIP
Couto, M. Sleepwalking land
Diaz, J. This is how you lose her
Kerouac, J. On the road
Nicholson, C. The elephant keeper
Powers, K. The yellow birds
The **company** Littell, R.

Compound fractures White, S.

COMPREHENSION

Lem, S. Eden

COMPROMISE

Danticat, E. The dew breaker

Muller, M. Vanishing point

COMPULSIVE BEHAVIOR

Abbott, P. Concrete angel

Burton, T. Social creature

Erdrich, L. Shadow tag

Ferris, J. The unnamed

Healey, E. Elizabeth is missing

McCullers, C. Reflections in a golden eye

Moses, K. Wintering

Norman, H. What is left the daughter

Oates, J. Little bird of heaven

Wallace, D. Infinite jest

COMPULSIVE BEHAVIOR IN MEN

Doctorow, E. Homer and Langley

Eugenides, J. The marriage plot

Ferris, J. To rise again at a decent hour

Grunberg, A. Tirza

Maugham, W. The moon and sixpence

Moore, A. The lighthouse

Roth, P. Everyman

Roth, P. Portnoy's complaint

Roth, P. Sabbath's theater

Smith, D. Bright and distant shores

Tsypkin, L. Summer in Baden-Baden

Ullman, E. By blood

COMPULSIVE BEHAVIOR IN WOMEN

Attenberg, J. The Middlesteins

Carey, P. My life as a fake

Lupton, R. Sister

Oates, J. Blonde

Salinger, J. Franny and Zooey

COMPULSIVE GAMBLERS -- BILOXI, MISSISSIPPI

Barthelme, F. Bob the gambler

COMPULSIVE GAMBLING

Pronzini, B. Fever

COMPULSIVE HOARDING

Ephron, H. Careful what you wish for

COMPULSIVE SHOPPING

Zevin, G. The hole we're in

COMPULSIVE SHOPPING IN WOMEN

Newman, J. Mary

COMPUTER ALGORITHMS

Schulman, H. Come with me

COMPUTER CRIMES

Forsyth, F. The fox

Quartey, K. The missing American

Tracy, P. Ice cold heart

COMPUTER ERRORS

Willis, C. Blackout

COMPUTER GAME DESIGNERS

Costello, M. Big if

COMPUTER GAMES

Costello, M. Big if

Stephenson, N. Reamde

Tracy, P. Monkeewrench

COMPUTER INDUSTRY AND TRADE

Connelly, M. The scarecrow

COMPUTER PROGRAMMERS

Coupland, D. Microserfs

Daniel, R. Hacked

Evanovich, S. Under the table

Frankel, L. Goodbye for now

Garwood, J. Wired

Gentry, A. Last woman standing

Stephenson, N. Cryptonomicon

COMPUTER PROGRAMS

Crichton, M. Prey

Powers, R. The Gold Bug Variations

COMPUTER SCIENTISTS

Moore, L. The unseen world

Petrie, N. Burning bright

COMPUTER SOFTWARE

Costello, M. Big if

Crichton, M. Prey

COMPUTER SOFTWARE -- TESTING

Gibson, W. The peripheral

COMPUTER SOFTWARE DEVELOPERS

Chiang, T. The lifecycle of software objects

Costello, M. Big if

Tracy, P. Ice cold heart

Tracy, P. Monkeewrench

COMPUTER SOFTWARE INDUSTRY AND TRADE

Tracy, P. Monkeewrench

COMPUTER TECHNOLOGY

Vinge, V. Rainbows end

Wilson, G. Alif the unseen

COMPUTER VIRUSES

Powers, R. The Gold Bug Variations

Stephenson, N. Snow crash

COMPUTERIZED MAPPING SYSTEMS

Barclay, L. Trust your eyes

COMPUTERS

Carcaterra, L. Tin badges

Clarke, A. 2001

Gibson, W. Neuromancer

Heinlein, R. The moon is a harsh mistress

O'Connell, C. The man who cast two shadows

Stephenson, N. The diamond age,

COMSTOCK, ANTHONY

Piercy, M. Sex wars

Con ed Klein, M.

CONCENTRATION CAMP INMATES

Amis, M. The zone of interest

Gross, A. The one man

Matthiessen, P. In paradise

Morris, H. Cilka's journey

CONCENTRATION CAMP SURVIVORS

Bohjalian, C. Skeletons at the feast

Konar, A. Mischling

Martin, C. Long way gone
Mosley, W. All I did was shoot my man
Mukherjee, N. The lives of others
O'Connor, F. The violent bear it away
Pelecanos, G. The way home
Perrotta, T. The leftovers
Picoult, J. Lone wolf
Robinson, R. Cost
Savas, A. Walking on the ceiling
Scego, I. Adua
Sthers, A. Holy lands
Suri, M. The age of Shiva
Tyler, A. Dinner at the Homesick Restaurant

CONFLICT OF INTERESTS
McLarty, R. Art in America
Stirling, S. A meeting at Corvallis

CONFLICT RESOLUTION
Adams, D. Life, the universe, and everything
McLarty, R. Art in America
Okorafor, N. Binti
Ross, A. Miss Julia delivers the goods

CONFORMITY
Bellow, S. Dangling man
Bellow, S. Novels, 1944-1953
Bradbury, R. Fahrenheit 451
Camus, A. The stranger
Harkaway, N. Gnomon
Karlsson, J. The room
Lee, D. Country of origin
Lewis, S. Babbitt
Vonnegut, K. Player piano
Zamyatin, Y. We

CONFRONTATION (INTERPERSONAL RELATIONS)
Baxter, C. Saul and Patsy
Berg, E. The art of mending
Blackstock, T. Smoke screen
Hulse, S. Black River

CONGO (BRAZZAVILLE)
Gonzales, L. Lucy
Mabanckou, A. Black Moses

CONGO (DEMOCRATIC REPUBLIC)
Kingsolver, B. The Poisonwood Bible

CONGO (DEMOCRATIC REPUBLIC) -- EXPLORATION -- BRITISH
Conrad, J. Heart of darkness

CONGRESSIONAL AIDES
Meltzer, B. The zero game
Michaels, F. Deep harbor

CONJOINED TWINS
Abani, C. The secret history of Las Vegas
Dufresne, J. Deep in the shade of paradise
Slouka, M. God's fool
Twain, M. Pudd'nhead Wilson ;
Verghese, A. Cutting for stone
Conjure women Atakora, A.
A **conjuring** of light Schwab, V.
CONNECTICUT

Acampora, L. The wonder garden
Aliu, X. Brass
Amidon, S. Human capital
Arsenault, E. In search of the Rose notes
Bardugo, L. Ninth house
Brown, K. The clairvoyants
Constantine, L. The last Mrs. Parrish
Gertler, S. Drifting
Grames, J. The seven or eight deaths of Stella Fortuna
Kennedy, D. The big picture
Knopf, C. Dead anyway
Knopf, C. You're dead
O'Nan, S. The night country
Rice, L. Last day
Rice, L. Last kiss
Roorbach, B. Life among giants
Scott, J. Mausoleum
Walker, W. All is not forgotten
White, S. The siege
Wiesel, E. The judges
Wilson, S. The man in the gray flannel suit
A **Connecticut** Yankee in King Arthur's Court Twain, M.
The **conquest** of Lady Cassandra Hunter, M.

CONQUEST OF MEXICO (1519-1540)
Sherwood, F. Night of sorrows
Conquistadora Santiago, E.

CONQUISTADORS
Sherwood, F. Night of sorrows

CONSCIENCE
Amis, M. Time's arrow, or The nature of the offense
Camus, A. The fall
Dostoyevsky, F. Crime and punishment

CONSCIENTIOUS OBJECTORS
Kelly, S. The wages of desire
MacNeal, S. The king's justice
Seiffert, R. A boy in winter

CONSCIOUSNESS
Ackerman, E. Waiting for Eden
Alexis, A. Fifteen dogs
Feeney, A. Sometimes I lie
Grant, M. Parasite
Lem, S. Solaris
Self, W. Umbrella
Soule, C. Anyone
Theroux, M. Strange bodies
Watts, P. Blindsight

CONSCIOUSNESS TRANSFER
Harrison, M. Nova swing
Morgan, R. Altered carbon
Morgan, R. Broken angels
Reynolds, A. Permafrost
Turton, S. The 7 1

CONSENT (LAW)
McGhee, A. The opposite of fate

CONSEQUENCES
50 Cent Blow
Alarcon, D. At night we walk in circles

CONSERVATION OF NATURAL RESOURCES

CONSERVATIVE JUDAISM

CONSERVATIVES

CONSPIRACIES

Bunn, T. Outbreak

Caputo, P. Acts of faith

Carpenter, E. Until the day I die

Child, L. The affair

Child, L. Bad luck and trouble

Child, L. The enemy

Child, L. Killing floor

Child, L. Make me

Child, L. Never go back

Child, L. Night school

Child, L. Nothing to lose

Child, L. A wanted man

Church, J. Bamboo and blood

Ciotta, B. Her sky cowboy

Ciotta, B. His clockwork canary

Clark, M. The Jezebel remedy

Clements, R. Martyr

Clements, R. Revenger

Cleveland, K. Keep you close

Coben, H. The stranger

Coel, M. Blood memory

Collins, M. Ask not

Connelly, M. Echo Park

Cook, R. Nano

Cook, R. Pandemic

Coonts, S. The armageddon file

Coonts, S. Liberty's last stand

Coonts, S. The Russia account

Corby, G. The Pericles Commission

Corey, J. Abaddon's gate

Corey, J. Caliban's war

Corey, J. Leviathan wakes

Crompton, R. Hell's gate

Crompton, R. Hour of the red god

Cumming, C. A foreign country

DeLillo, D. Libra

DeMille, N. Wild fire

Doctorow, C. Rapture of the nerds

Dodd, C. Because I'm watching

Dodd, C. Obsession Falls

Doetsch, R. Half-past dawn

Doiron, P. Almost midnight

Downie, R. Caveat emptor

Dumas, A. The man in the iron mask

Eco, U. Numero zero

Eisler, B. The killer collective

Eisler, B. The night trade

Ellis, B. Imperial bedrooms

Ellis, D. In the company of liars

Ellroy, J. Blood's a rover

Engelmann, K. The Stockholm octavo

Fesperman, D. Safe houses

Fforde, J. Shades of grey

Finder, J. Guilty minds

Finder, J. Judgment

Finder, J. The switch

Fleming, I. On Her Majesty's secret service

Flores, F. Tears of the trufflepig

Foster, L. Under pressure

Furst, A. The spies of Warsaw

Furst, A. Spies of the Balkans

Geagley, B. Year of the hyenas

Glynn, A. Paradime

Goddard, R. Never go back

Goss, T. The sinister mystery of the mesmerizing girl

Grant, M. Blackout

Grant, M. Deadline

Grant, M. Feed

Grant, M. Feedback

Gregory, P. The red queen

Gross, A. Reckless

Guttridge, P. The thing itself

Harkaway, N. The gone-away world

Hart, E. The book of Killowen

Hoeg, P. Smilla's sense of snow

Horowitz, A. The House of Silk

Huang, S. Zero sum game

Hunter, S. Black light

Hunter, S. Dead zero

Hunter, S. I, sniper

Hunter, S. Pale horse coming

Hunter, S. Time to hunt

James, M. The book of night women

Jemisin, N. The killing moon

Johnson, D. Detroit shuffle

Kadrey, R. The grand dark

Kava, A. Hotwire

Kerley, J. The death collectors

Koen, K. Before Versailles

Kramer, L. Search for my heart

Krentz, J. When all the girls have gone

Krentz, J. White lies

Kroese, R. The last iota

Larsson, S. The girl who kicked the hornet's nest

Le Carre, J. The constant gardener

Le Carre, J. A delicate truth

Le Carre, J. The tailor of Panama

Lee, P. Runner

Lee, P. Signal

Lehane, D. Shutter Island

Levin, I. The boys from Brazil

Liss, D. A spectacle of corruption

Ludlum, R. The Prometheus deception

Lyons, J. The ruin of kings

Mantel, H. Bring up the bodies

Mason, T. The Darwin affair

McCarthy, T. Satin Island

McDevitt, J. The Cassandra Project

Meltzer, B. The escape artist

Meltzer, B. The inner circle

Merbeth, K. Fortuna

Meyer, N. The adventure of the peculiar protocols

Meyer, N. The seven-per-cent solution

Mina, D. Gods and beasts

CONSPIRACIES -- GERMANY
CONSPIRACIES -- GREAT BRITAIN
CONSPIRACIES -- GREECE
CONSPIRACIES -- UNITED STATES
CONSPIRACIES -- UNITED STATES -- HISTORY
CONSPIRACY THEORIES

The **constant** lovers Nickson, C.
The **constant** princess Gregory, P.
A **constellation** of vital phenomena Marra, A.

CONSTRUCTION INDUSTRY AND TRADE
Paretsky, S. Burn marks

CONSTRUCTION WORKERS
Carlson, R. Five skies
Saintcrow, L. Trailer park fae

CONSULS
Lowry, M. Under the volcano

CONSULTANTS
Whitehead, C. Apex hides the hurt

CONSULTING
Robinson, K. Galileo's dream

CONSUMER SOCIETY
Butler, H. The new me
Wayne, T. The love song of Jonny Valentine

CONSUMERISM
Ballard, J. Kingdom come
Saunders, G. In persuasion nation

The **Consummata** Spillane, M.
Contact Sagan, C.

CONTE, LOUIS DE, 1835-1910
Twain, M. Personal recollections of Joan of Arc

CONTEMPORARY CHRISTIAN MUSIC
Isaac, K. Then there was you

CONTEMPORARY FANTASY
Beagle, P. A fine and private place
Beagle, P. In Calabria
Beagle, P. Summerlong
Bear, E. Blood and iron
Broder, M. The pisces
Dean, P. Tam Lin
Donohue, K. The stolen child
Gaiman, N. American gods
Gaiman, N. The ocean at the end of the lane
Grant, M. Into the drowning deep
Grossman, L. The magician king
Grossman, L. The magicians
Grossman, L. The magician's land
Harkness, D. The book of life
Harkness, D. A discovery of witches
Joyce, G. The limits of enchantment
Kay, G. Ysabel
Kiernan, C. The drowning girl
King, S. Elevation
LaValle, V. The changeling
Link, K. Magic for beginners
Mitchell, D. The bone clocks
Murphy, S. The possessions
Parry, H. The unlikely escape of Uriah Heep
Poore, M. Reincarnation blues
Power, S. The grass dancer
Sherrill, S. The minotaur takes his own sweet time
Stephenson, N. The rise and fall of D.O.D.O.
Updike, J. The widows of Eastwick
Updike, J. The witches of Eastwick

Walton, J. Among others
Warrington, F. Elfland
Warrington, F. Grail of the summer stars
Warrington, F. Midsummer night
Whitehead, C. The intuitionist

CONTEMPORARY ROMANCES
Adams, L. The bromance book club
Anders, A. Under her skin
Anderson, C. Mulberry moon
Bailey, T. Fix her up
Billingsley, R. The secret she kept
Brayden, M. First position
Bryant, N. Christmas with the billionaire
Bybee, C. Staying for good
Cabot, M. No judgments
Cameron, C. Just a summer fling
Carr, R. Virgin river
Carr, R. The wanderer
Carr, R. What we find
Castile, Z. Flashed
Castille, S. In your corner
Christopher, A. Not the girl you marry
Cleage, P. Some things I never thought I'd do
Cole, A. A duke by default
Cole, A. A prince on paper
Cole, A. A princess in theory
Criswell, M. What to do about Annie?
Crownover, J. Honor
Dane, L. The best kind of trouble
Dane, L. Broken open
DeLuca, J. Well met
Dell, K. Fearless in Texas
Dell, K. Mistletoe in Texas
Dell, K. Reckless in Texas
Dev, S. A Bollywood affair
Dev, S. The Bollywood bride
Dev, S. A distant heart
Dev, S. Pride, prejudice, and other flavors
Deveraux, J. Someone to love
Dimon, H. Her other secret
Dimon, H. Mercy
Drake, L. The sweet spot
Force, M. Five years gone
Foster, L. Sisters of summer's end
Guillory, J. The proposal
Guillory, J. Royal holiday
Guillory, J. The wedding date
Guillory, J. The wedding party
Hall, A. For real
Henson, P. Into the blue
Hibbert, T. A girl like her
Hibbert, T. Get a life, Chloe Brown
Higgins, K. The best man
Higgins, K. The perfect match
Hoang, H. The bride test
Hoang, H. The kiss quotient
Hodges, C. Rumor has it

CONTEMPT

CONTESTED WILLS

CONTESTS

CONTEXT EFFECTS (PSYCHOLOGY)

Continental divide Myers, A.
Continental drift Banks, R.

CONTRACEPTION

The **contract** surgeon O'Brien, D.

CONTRACTORS

CONTROL (PSYCHOLOGY)

Palmer, D. The new husband
Pinborough, S. Behind her eyes
Rouda, K. The favorite daughter
Soule, C. Anyone

CONVALESCENCE
Genova, L. Left neglected
Leithauser, B. The art student's war
Livesey, M. The missing world
London, J. The golden age
Putney, M. The marriage spell

Convenience store woman Murata, S.

CONVENIENCE STORES
Link, K. Magic for beginners
Mengestu, D. The beautiful things that heaven bears
Murata, S. Convenience store woman

CONVENTS
Hansen, R. Mariette in ecstasy
Murdoch, I. The bell
Spain, J. With our blessing

CONVENTS -- ITALY
Dunant, S. Sacred hearts

CONVENTS -- MANHATTAN, NEW YORK CITY
Westlake, D. Good behavior

CONVERSATION
Bailey, P. Chapman's odyssey
Boudjedra, R. The Barbary figs
Cusk, R. Outline
Doctorow, E. Andrew's brain
Hughes, L. Simple speaks his mind
Littell, R. The Mayakovsky tapes

Conversations with friends Rooney, S.

CONVERSION
Cunningham, M. The snow queen

CONVERSION TO CHRISTIANITY
Hulse, S. Black River
Parini, J. The Damascus road

CONVERSION TO ISLAM
Berenson, A. The faithful spy

CONVERSION TO JUDAISM
Hertmans, S. The convert

The convert Hertmans, S.

CONVERTS TO CATHOLICISM FROM JUDAISM
Spark, M. The Mandelbaum gate

CONVERTS TO CHRISTIANITY
Flynn, M. Eifelheim

CONVERTS TO CHRISTIANITY FROM JUDAISM
Zimler, R. The last Kabbalist of Lisbon

The conviction Dugoni, R.

Conviction Dahl, J.

Conviction Mina, D.

CONVULSIONS
Abbott, M. The fever

The cook Kerangal, M.

The cookbook collector Goodman, A.

COOKING
Andrew, S. Recipes for love and murder
Andrew, S. The Satanic mechanic

Bijan, D. The last days of Cafe Leila
Kerangal, M. The cook
Truong, M. The book of salt, Monique Truong.
Wiggs, S. The beekeeper's ball

COOKING CONTESTS
Beaton, M. Agatha Raisin and the quiche of death
The **cooking** school murders Rich, V.

COOKING SCHOOLS
Bauermeister, E. The school of essential ingredients
Rich, V. The cooking school murders
Rich, V. The Nantucket diet murders
Wiggs, S. The beekeeper's ball

COOKING, AMERICAN
Davidson, D. The last suppers
Rich, V. The baked bean supper murders
Rich, V. The cooking school murders
Rich, V. The Nantucket diet murders

COOKING, CHINESE
Lim, R. Natalie Tan's book of luck and fortune

COOKING, ENGLISH -- HISTORY -- 17TH CENTURY
Norfolk, L. John Saturnall's feast

COOKING, FRENCH
Kerangal, M. The cook

COOKING, LEBANESE
Abu-Jaber, D. Crescent

COOKING, MEXICAN
Esquivel, L. Like water for chocolate

COOKS
Bailey, M. An appetite for violets
Berger, T. Reinhart's women
Blackstock, T. Catching Christmas
Blum, J. The lost family
Cogburn, E. Ava's place
Dev, S. Pride, prejudice, and other flavors
Fitten, M. Elza's kitchen
Grass, G. The flounder
Keane, M. Fever
Kerangal, M. The cook
Mukherjee, N. A state of freedom
Norfolk, L. John Saturnall's feast
Raymond, J. The half-life

COOKS -- FRANCE
Handke, P. Don Juan

COOKS -- MEXICO
Fuentes, C. The crystal frontier

COOKS -- VIETNAM
Truong, M. The book of salt, Monique Truong.

COOL (PERSONAL QUALITY)
Leonard, E. Be cool

COOPERATION
Anders, C. All the birds in the sky
K'wan Animal II
Mosley, W. Fortunate son
Pelecanos, G. The night gardener
Robinson, K. Blue Mars
Robinson, K. Red Mars

Cop killer Sjowall, M.

COPYCAT MURDERERS

Bolton, S. Now you see me

Cleave, P. The cleaner

Downing, S. My lovely wife

North, A. The Whisper Man

Spencer-Fleming, J. Hid from our eyes

COPYCAT MURDERS

Black, S. Lovemurder

Cole, D. Hangman

COPYRIGHT

Gaddis, W. A frolic of his own

The **coral** thief Stott, R.

Cordelia Gray mysteries [series] James, P.

Cordell Logan mysteries [series] Freed, D.

COREY, DORIAN, 1937-1993

Cassara, J. The house of impossible beauties

CORINTH, GREECE

Afshar, T. Thief of Corinth

CORK COUNTY, IRELAND

Connolly, S. The lost traveller

Cork O'connor mysteries [series] Krueger, W.

CORK, IRELAND

Harrison, C. Beyond absolution

McInerney, L. The glorious heresies

Cormoran Strike novels [series] Galbraith, R.

Cornish trilogy (Robertson Davies) [series] Davies, R.

CORNWALL, ENGLAND

Du Maurier, D. Rebecca

George, E. Careless in red

Goddard, R. Beyond recall

McQuiston, J. The spinster's guide to scandalous behavior

Pilcher, R. The shell seekers

Sebastian, C. The Lawrence Browne affair

Shannon, D. The Manson curse

Smith, A. Winter

CORNWALL, ENGLAND -- HISTORY

Kelly, J. The light over London

CORNWALL, ENGLAND -- HISTORY -- 17TH CENTURY

Du Maurier, D. Frenchman's creek

CORNWALL, ENGLAND -- HISTORY -- 19TH CENTURY

Du Maurier, D. Jamaica Inn

CORNWALL, ENGLAND -- SOCIAL LIFE AND CUSTOMS -- 19TH CENTURY

Macdonald, M. The Trevarton inheritance

CORNWALL, ENGLAND -- SOCIAL LIFE AND CUSTOMS -- 20TH CENTURY

Macdonald, M. Tamsin Harte

The **coronation** Akunin, B.

CORONATIONS

Akunin, B. The coronation

The **coroner's** lunch Cotterill, C.

CORONERS

Blake, R. A dark anatomy

Cook, R. Genesis

Cook, R. Pandemic

Cornwell, P. Chaos

Cotterill, C. The coroner's lunch

Cotterill, C. Disco for the departed

Cotterill, C. Don't eat me

Cotterill, C. The second biggest nothing

Cotterill, C. Slash and burn

Disher, G. Under the cold bright lights

McCarthy, R. A handful of ashes

Nadel, B. The Ottoman cage

CORPORATE ACCOUNTABILITY

Sinclair, U. The jungle

CORPORATE ACQUISITIONS

Birmingham, S. Carriage trade

Shakar, A. Luminarium

CORPORATE CRIME

Sears, M. Black Fridays

CORPORATE CULTURE

Baker, C. Whisper network

Bing, S. You look nice today

Finder, J. Vanished

Hart, R. The warehouse

Wilson, S. The man in the gray flannel suit

CORPORATE GREED

Doctorow, C. Radicalized

Hurley, K. The light brigade

Older, M. Infomocracy

Patchett, A. State of wonder

Pynchon, T. Against the day

CORPORATE INTRIGUE

Lathen, E. Brewing up a storm

Lathen, E. East is east

Lathen, E. Something in the air

Lelchuk, S. Save me from dangerous men

McDonald, I. New moon

Modesitt, L. The one-eyed man

CORPORATE LAWYERS

Conklin, T. The house girl

Dugoni, R. Murder one

CORPORATE MERGERS

Lathen, E. East is east

CORPORATE POWER

Doctorow, C. Radicalized

Hurley, K. The light brigade

McDonald, I. New moon

Older, M. Infomocracy

Pohl, F. The space merchants

CORPORATIONS

Aalborg, G. River of porcupines

Bacigalupi, P. The windup girl

Bing, S. You look nice today

Carpenter, E. Until the day I die

Faber, M. The book of strange new things

Farnsworth, C. Flashmob

Farnsworth, C. Killfile

Finder, J. Buried secrets

Grant, M. Parasite

Hamilton, P. Great North Road

Hart, R. The warehouse

Heacox, K. Jimmy Bluefeather

Cotton Malone novels [series] Berry, S.
Coughlin novels [series] Lehane, D.
COUNSELING
  Higashino, K. The miracles of the Namiya General Store
The **count** of Monte Cristo Dumas, A.
Countdown Ramsay, F.
Countdown City Winters, B.
COUNTERCULTURE
  Boyle, T. Outside looking in
  Byatt, A. A whistling woman
  Cline, E. The girls
  Dektar, M. The Ash family
  Kerouac, J. The dharma bums
  Kerouac, J. On the road
  Kerouac, J. Road novels 1957-1960
  Nunez, S. The last of her kind
  Pynchon, T. The crying of lot 49
  Pynchon, T. Vineland
  Vandermeer, J. Finch
  Fftch, M. Stay and fight
COUNTERFEITS AND COUNTERFEITING
  MacDonald, J. The scarlet ruse
COUNTERINTELLIGENCE
  Ludlum, R. The Prometheus deception
Countess of Harleigh mysteries [series] Freeman, D.
COUNTRY CLUBS
  Coyne, J. The caddie who played with hickory
Country dark Offutt, C.
The **country** doctor Balzac, H.
Country girls trilogy [series] O'Brien, E.
The **country** girls trilogy and epilogue O'Brien, E.
COUNTRY HOMES
  Byatt, A. The children's book
  Collins, W. The woman in white
  Dare, T. Do you want to start a scandal
  Foley, L. The hunting party
  Fowler, C. Bryant & May
  Goodwin, D. The American heiress
  Ishiguro, K. The remains of the day
  Joss, M. Half broken things
  Kelly, E. The burning air
  Leigh, E. Scandal takes the stage
  Lovesey, P. Bertie and the seven bodies
  Morton, K. The house at Riverton
  Nash, S. Between the Duke and the deep blue sea
  Raichev, R. Assassins at Ospreys
  Turton, S. The 7 1
  Vine, B. The minotaur
  Walton, J. Farthing
  Ware, R. In a dark, dark wood
COUNTRY HOMES -- GREAT BRITAIN
  Waugh, E. Brideshead revisited
Country house crime novels [series] Raichev, R.
COUNTRY MUSIC
  Creech, S. The whole way home
COUNTRY MUSIC INDUSTRY AND TRADE
  Muller, M. The broken promise land

COUNTRY MUSICIANS
  Creech, S. The whole way home
  Muller, M. The broken promise land
The **country** of Ice Cream Star Newman, S.
Country of origin Lee, D.
A **country** of our own Poyer, D.
The **country** of the pointed firs and other stories Jewett, S.
COUNTS AND COUNTESSES
  Beverley, J. Devilish
  Bowman, V. Secrets of a wedding night
  Dumas, A. Camille
  Fortier, A. Juliet
  Freeman, D. A lady's guide to etiquette and murder
  Gilman, D. Kaleidoscope
  Kay, G. A brightness long ago
  Long, J. Lady Derring takes a lover
  Maupassant, G. Like death
  McGuire, S. Chimes at midnight
  Perry, A. Weighed in the balance
  Towles, A. A gentleman in Moscow
  Wallace, C. The blind contessa's new machine
  Willocks, T. The religion
County Cork mysteries [series] Connolly, S.
COUPLES
  Acker, J. The limits of the world
  Archer, J. Nothing ventured
  Atwood, M. Stone mattress
  Beagle, P. Summerlong
  Bohjalian, C. The red lotus
  Bolano, R. The Third Reich
  Childs, L. Lavender blue murder
  Clark, M. Final judgment
  Colgan, J. The endless beach
  Connolly, S. The lost traveller
  Crosbie, L. Where did you sleep last night?
  Crouch, B. Recursion
  Davis, K. Duplex
  Earley, T. Mr. Tall
  French, T. The likeness
  Gage, E. The ladies of Managua
  Hamid, M. Exit west
  Hilderbrand, E. The perfect couple
  Jones, S. The other woman
  Lauren, C. Roomies
  Lawrence, D. Women in love
  Livesey, M. The missing world
  MacNeal, S. The king's justice
  McGuire, S. Night and silence
  McMahon, J. The invited
  Mizushima, M. Burning ridge
  Mychea My boyfriend's wife
  Newman, S. The heavens
  O'Hara, J. Appointment in Samarra
  Palmer, L. Otherwise engaged
  Pronzini, B. The stolen gold affair
  Reid, I. I'm thinking of ending things
  Santopolo, J. More than words

Andersen, L. The Boleyn deceit
Andersen, L. The Boleyn king
Andersen, L. The Boleyn reckoning
Bear, E. Blood and iron
Black, B. Wolf on a string
Boyne, J. The house of special purpose
Buckley, F. The siren queen
Campisi, M. Sin eater
Clements, R. Revenger
Craddock, C. A labyrinth of scions and sorcery
Dumas, A. The three musketeers
Dunant, S. In the company of the courtesan
Eco, U. Baudolino
George, M. Elizabeth I
Ghosh, A. The glass palace
Gregory, P. The Boleyn inheritance
Gregory, P. The constant princess
Gregory, P. The other Boleyn girl
Gregory, P. The last Tudor
Jones, S. Four sisters, all queens
Kay, G. A brightness long ago
Lin, J. The dragon and the pearl
Mailer, N. Ancient evenings
Massey, S. The Satapur moonstone
Maxwell, R. The queen's bastard
Maxwell, R. The secret diary of Anne Boleyn
Maxwell, R. The wild Irish
Min, A. Empress Orchid
Orullian, P. The unremembered
Phillips, A. The king at the edge of the world
Plaidy, J. Murder most royal
Plaidy, J. The pleasures of love
Plaidy, J. William's wife
Randel, W. The empress of bright moon
Riley, J. The serpent garden
Shannon, S. The priory of the orange tree
Sherwood, F. The book of splendor
Stachniak, E. The Winter Palace
Tremain, R. Music & silence
Weir, A. Anna of Kleve
Weir, A. Innocent traitor
Weir, A. The Lady Elizabeth
Wolfe, S. The course of all treasons

COURTS AND COURTIERS -- EGYPT
Robinson, L. Murder at the feast of rejoicing
Robinson, L. Murder at the god's gate

COURTS AND COURTIERS -- FRANCE
Laker, R. To dance with kings
Naslund, S. Abundance

**COURTS AND COURTIERS -- HISTORY -- 16TH CEN-
TURY**
Mantel, H. Bring up the bodies
Mantel, H. Wolf Hall

COURTS-MARTIAL AND COURTS OF INQUIRY
Jones, D. The court-martial of George Armstrong Custer
Turow, S. Ordinary heroes
Wouk, H. The Caine mutiny

COURTSHIP
Amis, M. The zone of interest
Austen, J. Emma
Austen, J. Pride and prejudice
Austen, J. Sense and sensibility
Bail, M. Eucalyptus
Balogh, M. The arrangement
Balogh, M. The escape
Balogh, M. Only enchanting
Balogh, M. Someone to remember
Balogh, M. Someone to wed
Bateman, K. This earl of mine
Bowman, V. The unexpected duchess
Calvi, M. Dear George, Dear Mary
Fitzgerald, P. The blue flower
Garcia Marquez, G. Love in the time of cholera
Hardy, T. Far from the madding crowd
Heath, L. Falling into bed with a duke
Helprin, M. In sunlight and in shadow
Lackey, M. The fairy godmother
Lipman, E. The pursuit of Alice Thrift
Long, J. Angel in a devil's arms
McCall Smith, A. The full cupboard of life
Mishima, Y. The sound of waves
Quinn, J. The secrets of Sir Richard Kenworthy
Rush, N. Mating
Saville, L. Henry and Rachel
Simenon, G. Maigret's memoirs
Sparks, N. The guardian
Trollope, A. The last chronicle of Barset
White, E. Heartstone

Courtyards of the Others [series] Bishop, A.
Cousin Bette Balzac, H.
COUSINS
Ahlborn, A. The devil crept in
Austen, J. Mansfield Park
Boudjedra, R. The Barbary figs
Bowman, V. The accidental countess
Chabon, M. The amazing adventures of Kavalier & Clay
Coe, J. The rain before it falls
Daniel, R. Hacked
Egan, J. The keep
Evanovich, J. One for the money
George, M. Elizabeth I
Hardy, T. Jude the obscure
Heyer, G. The grand Sophy
Jalaluddin, U. Ayesha at last
Johnson, D. Detroit shuffle
Kim, C. If you leave me
Klaussmann, L. Tigers in red weather
Lasdun, J. The fall guy
Llywelyn, M. After Rome
London, J. The year of living scandalously
Mandel, E. The singer's gun
McCarry, C. Old boys
McCullers, C. The member of the wedding
McDermott, A. Child of my heart

Hart, C. Resort to murder
Hart, C. White elephant dead
Hart, C. Yankee Doodle dead
Hollis, L. Poppy Harmon investigates
Lathen, E. Brewing up a storm
Lathen, E. East is east
Lathen, E. Something in the air
Malliet, G. A demon summer
Malliet, G. A fatal winter
Malliet, G. Pagan spring
Malliet, G. Wicked autumn
McCall Smith, A. Blue shoes and happiness
McCall Smith, A. The Double Comfort Safari Club
McCall Smith, A. The full cupboard of life
McCall Smith, A. The good husband of Zebra Drive
McCall Smith, A. In the company of cheerful ladies
McCall Smith, A. The Kalahari typing school for men
McCall Smith, A. The Limpopo Academy of Private Detection
McCall Smith, A. The No. 1 Ladies' Detective Agency
McCall Smith, A. The Saturday big tent wedding party
McKevett, G. Murder in her stocking
McKevett, G. Murder in the corn maze
Meier, L. Silver anniversary murder
O'Donohue, C. The lover's knot
Page, K. The body in the big apple
Page, K. The body in the bog
Page, K. The body in the casket
Page, K. The body in the vestibule
Page, K. The body in the wake
Perkins, S. Murder once removed
Raichev, R. Assassins at Ospreys
Roberts, G. Adam and evil
Roberts, G. The bluest blood
Roosevelt, E. The Hyde Park murder
Roosevelt, E. Murder and the First Lady
Roosevelt, E. Murder at midnight
Roosevelt, E. Murder at the palace
Roosevelt, E. Murder in the Blue Room
Roosevelt, E. Murder in the map room
Roosevelt, E. Murder in the Oval Office
Roosevelt, E. Murder in the Rose Garden
Roosevelt, E. The White House pantry murder
Ross, A. Miss Julia delivers the goods
Ross, A. Miss Julia takes the wheel
Ross, A. Miss Julia throws a wedding
Saums, M. Thistle & Twigg
Scoppettone, S. Too darn hot
Shaw, M. Murder at the mill
Simon, C. Dogs don't lie
Simon, C. Grey dawn
Simon, C. Panthers play for keeps
Simon, C. Stages of Grey
Simon, M. Cremains of the day
Crabwalk Grass, G.
CRACK TRAFFIC -- NEW JERSEY
 Price, R. Clockers

The **cradle** in the grave Hannah, S.
CRAFTS, HANNAH
 Crafts, H. The bondwoman's narrative
The **craftsman** Bolton, S.
Cranford Gaskell, E.
Crashed Hallinan, T.
Crashers Haynes, D.
Crashers [series] Haynes, D.
Crave all, lose all novels [series] Gray, E.
The **crazed** Jin, H.
Crazy cupid love Heger, A.
CRAZY HORSE, APPROXIMATELY 1842-1877
 O'Brien, D. The contract surgeon
Crazy in Alabama Childress, M.
Crazy love you Unger, L.
Crazy rich Asians Kwan, K.
The **crazy** school Read, C.
Crazy thing called love O'Keefe, M.
Crazybone Pronzini, B.
CREATION
 Tolkien, J. The Silmarillion
 VanderMeer, J. Dead astronauts
CREATION (LITERARY, ARTISTIC, ETC)
 Hand, E. Mortal love
 Jarvis, S. Death and Mr. Pickwick
 Perec, G. Life
CREATION (LITERARY, ARTISTIC, ETC)
 Lim, E. Dear cyborgs
CREATION (NORSE RELIGION)
 Gaiman, N. Norse mythology
CREATION (RELIGION)
 Bowles, D. Feathered serpent, dark heart of sky
CREATIVE WRITING
 Baker, J. The body lies
 Dermansky, M. Very nice
 Egan, J. The keep
 Wolff, T. Old school
CREATIVE WRITING TEACHERS
 Chabon, M. Wonder boys
 Cusk, R. Outline
 Lutz, L. The swallows
 Prose, F. Blue angel
 Schumacher, J. Dear committee members
CREATIVITY
 Davis, F. The Chelsea girls
 Groff, L. Fates and furies
 Ishiguro, K. The unconsoled
 Jaswal, B. Erotic stories for Punjabi widows
 Murray, P. The mark and the void
 Rand, A. The fountainhead
 Roth, H. From bondage
 Rose, H. The museum of modern love
 Roth, H. Requiem for Harlem
 Scharer, W. The age of light
 Steinke, R. Holy skirts
 Weinberg, K. The truants
 Wolitzer, M. The Interestings

Palliser, C. Rustication
Panowich, B. Like lions
Persson Giolito, M. Beyond all reasonable doubt
Pyne, D. Catalina eddy
Rankin, I. The beat goes on
Rigosi, G. Night bus
Rindell, S. The other typist
Rinehart, M. The circular staircase
Robotham, M. Good girl, bad girl
Robotham, M. Life or death
  Rogues
Russo, R. Everybody's fool
Schulberg, B. Waterfront
Sharpe, T. Barbed wire heart
Spain, J. With our blessing
Spillane, M. A long time dead
Stanley, M. A carrion death
Swinson, K. The safe house
Tartt, D. The goldfinch
Taylor, B. Ring of fire
Turner, N. The Banks sisters
Vanderbes, J. Strangers at the feast
Vargas Llosa, M. The discreet hero
Walker, W. Crime of privilege
Walter, J. Citizen Vince
Wambaugh, J. The blue knight
Wambaugh, J. The new centurions
Woods, S. A delicate touch
Yates, C. Grist Mill Road

CRIME -- BRIGHTON, ENGLAND
Guttridge, P. The thing itself

CRIME -- ECONOMIC ASPECTS
Recacoechea S., J. American visa

CRIME -- NEW ORLEANS, LOUISIANA
Castro, J. Hell or high water

CRIME AND GUNS
Picoult, J. A spark of light
Crime and punishment Dostoyevsky, F.

CRIME AND RACE
Pelecanos, G. The turnaround

CRIME BOSSES
Abbott, M. Queenpin
Beukes, L. Zoo city
Breslin, J. I don't want to go to jail
Carr, C. The alienist
Colfer, E. Plugged
Cornell, P. London falling
Davys, T. Amberville
DeSilva, B. A scourge of vipers
Estleman, L. Gas City
Faletti, G. A pimp's notes
Goldberg, T. Gangsterland
Hallinan, T. Crashed
Hunter, S. Hot springs
Hurwitz, G. Into the fire
Lehane, D. Live by night
Lehane, D. World gone by

MacBride, S. Blind eye
Montero, M. Dancing to "Almendra"
Pelecanos, G. The cut
Perry, T. The informant
Polansky, D. Low town
Pyne, D. Catalina eddy
Rankin, I. The beat goes on
Simon, M. The last Jew standing
Swinson, K. The safe house
Westlake, D. Get real

CRIME FICTION
Abbott, M. Queenpin
Barry, K. City of Bohane
  The best American noir of the century
Beverly, W. Dodgers
Blake, J. The house of Wolfe
Block, L. Hit me
Burke, J. The jealous kind
Burns, A. Little constructions
Colfer, E. Plugged
Cooper, T. The marauders
Doctorow, E. Billy Bathgate
Ellroy, J. L.A. confidential
Estleman, L. Gas City
Faletti, G. A pimp's notes
Faust, C. Choke hold
Faust, C. Money shot
Gavin, R. Beluga
Gifford, B. The stars above Veracruz
Goldberg, T. Gangsterland
Goodis, D. Nightfall
Greaves, C. Hard twisted
Green, N. The angel of Montague Street
Greene, G. Brighton Rock
Hamill, P. Tabloid city
Hamilton, S. The lock artist
Hamilton, S. The second life of Nick Mason
Hansen, R. A wild surge of guilty passion
Hart, J. Iron house
Harvey, M. Brighton
Hiaasen, C. Bad monkey
Hilton, L. Maestra
Hoeg, P. Smilla's sense of snow
Huston, C. Caught stealing
Johnson, D. Nobody move
Kennedy, R. Presidio
Klein, M. Con ed
Lange, R. Angel baby
Lawton, J. Then we take Berlin
Lehane, D. Live by night
Lehane, D. World gone by
Lemaitre, P. Inhuman resources
Leonard, E. Be cool
Leonard, E. Get Shorty
Leonard, E. Killshot
Leonard, E. Pagan babies
Leonard, E. Raylan

Nickson, C. On Copper Street

Ohlsson, K. Unwanted

Pattison, E. Water touching stone

Smith, T. Child 44

Wingate, L. Before we were yours

CRIMES AGAINST CLERGY

Kienzle, W. The rosary murders

CRIMES AGAINST COWBOYS

Hockensmith, S. Holmes on the range

CRIMES AGAINST CRIMINALS

Mankell, H. The dogs of Riga

CRIMES AGAINST FAMILY

Flynn, G. Dark places

CRIMES AGAINST FORMER POLICE

Parker, T. The fallen

CRIMES AGAINST GAY MEN AND LESBIANS

McGarrity, M. Everyone dies

Pronzini, B. Nightcrawlers

Winer, J. Her kind of case

CRIMES AGAINST GENERALS

Child, L. The enemy

CRIMES AGAINST GIRLS

Danticat, E. Claire of the sea light

Gallagher, S. The bedlam detective

Grimes, M. The winds of change

Krentz, J. Secret sisters

McLean, F. The Van Apfel girls are gone

Patterson, J. Private

Roy, L. Bent Road

Sallis, J. Others of my kind

Spencer, S. A walk with the dead

CRIMES AGAINST HUMANITY

Gass, W. Middle C

CRIMES AGAINST IMMIGRANTS

Aw, T. We, the survivors

CRIMES AGAINST JEWISH WOMEN

Black, C. Murder in the Marais

CRIMES AGAINST JOURNALISTS

Harrod-Eagles, C. Game over

Mina, D. Slip of the knife

Rankin, I. Blood hunt

Solares, M. The black minutes

CRIMES AGAINST JUDGES

Grisham, J. The pelican brief

CRIMES AGAINST LAWYERS

Connelly, M. The brass verdict

CRIMES AGAINST MALE PROSTITUTES

Carr, C. The alienist

CRIMES AGAINST MARRIED MEN

Perry, T. Fidelity

CRIMES AGAINST MARRIED PEOPLE

Crais, R. The first rule

Robotham, M. Say you're sorry

CRIMES AGAINST MARRIED WOMEN

Boyne, J. Crippen

Rosenfelt, D. Don't tell a soul

CRIMES AGAINST MEN

Qiu, X. Don't cry Tai Lake

Qiu, X. Enigma of China

CRIMES AGAINST MIDDLE-AGED WOMEN

Scott, A. Beneath the abbey wall

CRIMES AGAINST MINORITIES

Pelecanos, G. The turnaround

CRIMES AGAINST MOTHERS

Hannah, S. The cradle in the grave

CRIMES AGAINST MUSICIANS

Elias, G. Death and transfiguration

CRIMES AGAINST NATIVE AMERICAN WOMEN

Erdrich, L. Four souls

CRIMES AGAINST NATIVE AMERICANS

Verble, M. Cherokee America

CRIMES AGAINST NURSES

Robotham, M. Suspect

CRIMES AGAINST PAINTERS

Sayers, D. The five red herrings

CRIMES AGAINST POETS

Morton, K. The house at Riverton

CRIMES AGAINST POLICE

Atkins, A. The ranger

Koryta, M. Tonight I said goodbye

Nunn, M. A beautiful place to die

Sjowall, M. Cop killer

Spillane, M. Kill me, darling

CRIMES AGAINST POLITICIANS

Faletti, G. A pimp's notes

Ridpath, M. Far north

CRIMES AGAINST PREGNANT WOMEN

Gaspar de Alba, A. Desert blood

CRIMES AGAINST PROSTITUTES

Block, L. Eight million ways to die

Brooks, B. Blood storm

Connelly, M. The gods of guilt

Crompton, R. Hour of the red god

Garcia-Roza, L. December heat

Hill, S. The shadows in the street

Kerr, P. Metropolis

Lippman, L. And when she was good

MacBride, S. Dying light

McBain, E. Nocturne

Perry, T. The boyfriend

Shannon, D. Chaos of crime

Thomson, E. The blood

CRIMES AGAINST REAL ESTATE AGENTS -- ILLINOIS

McInerny, R. Requiem for a realtor

CRIMES AGAINST RICH PEOPLE

Dahl, A. Misterioso

Guinn, M. The scribe

Jenkins, V. An unattended death

Laukkanen, O. The professionals

Mayor, A. Tag man

Quartey, K. Murder at Cape Three Points

CRIMES AGAINST ROOMMATES

Rees, M. The fourth assassin

CRIMES AGAINST SCHOLARS

Martini, S. Compelling evidence
Robinson, P. Careless love
Rosen, L. The Kortelisy escape
Roslund, A. Cell 8

CRIMINAL EVIDENCE TAMPERING
Black, B. Christine Falls
Brown, R. Before and after

CRIMINAL INVESTIGATION
Archer, J. Nothing ventured
Atkinson, K. Big sky
Bardugo, L. Ninth house
Barton, F. The child
The big book of Sherlock Holmes stories
The best American mystery stories 2018
The best American mystery stories 2019
Box, C. Savage run
Brown, S. Ricochet
Carcaterra, L. Tin badges
Catton, E. The luminaries
Christie, A. Three blind mice, and other stories
Clare, A. The woman who spoke to spirits
Clark, M. My gal Sunday
Conlon, E. Red on red
Connolly, J. The burning soul
Crace, J. Harvest
Craig, P. Third strike
Crombie, D. A bitter feast
Crumley, J. The last good kiss
Cussler, C. The Gray Ghost
DeMille, N. The deserter
Doyle, A. The complete Sherlock Holmes
Dunning, J. The bookman's wake
Faye, L. The whole art of detection
Finch, C. The vanishing man
Finder, J. Buried secrets
Finder, J. Guilty minds
Freeman, B. Marathon
George, E. A banquet of consequences
Golding, M. Little darlings
Griffiths, E. The crossing places
Griffiths, E. The Janus stone
Harvey, J. A darker shade of blue
Harvey, J. Gone to ground
Hill, S. The risk of darkness
Hillerman, T. The wailing wind
Hillerman, T. The shape shifter
Hillerman, T. The sinister pig
Hodder, M. The strange affair of Spring Heeled Jack
Houellebecq, M. The map and the territory
Kellerman, F. The forgotten
Kellerman, F. Jupiter's bones
Kellerman, F. Prayers for the dead
Kellerman, F. Serpent's tooth
Kemelman, H. Monday the rabbi took off
Kemelman, H. One fine day the rabbi bought a cross
Kemelman, H. Thursday the Rabbi walked out
Leon, D. Trace elements

Leon, D. Unto us a son is given
Leonard, E. Raylan
London, J. The year of living scandalously
MacDonald, J. The scarlet ruse
Mandel, E. The singer's gun
MatchUp
McCall Smith, A. The Department of Sensitive Crimes
Mortimer, J. Rumpole's return
Nava, M. Carved in bone
Newton, C. Calumet City
Olshan, J. Black diamond fall
Paretsky, S. Bitter medicine
Paretsky, S. Blacklist
Paretsky, S. Blood shot
Paretsky, S. Burn marks
Paretsky, S. Dead land
Paretsky, S. Fire sale
Paretsky, S. Guardian angel
Paretsky, S. Hardball
Paretsky, S. Hard time
Paretsky, S. Indemnity only
Paretsky, S. Shell game
Paretsky, S. Tunnel vision
Paretsky, S. Windy city blues
Paretsky, S. Total recall
Parker, T. L.A. outlaws
Perry, A. Death on Blackheath
Petrie, N. Tear it down
Petrie, N. The wild one
Pirie, D. The patient's eyes
Preston, D. Crooked river
Price, R. Samaritan
Pronzini, B. Fever
Pronzini, B. The stolen gold affair
Pyne, D. Catalina eddy
Rankin, I. The beat goes on
Reynolds, A. The prefect
Ridgway, K. Hawthorn & Child
Rollins, J. The devil colony
Sansom, C. Lamentation
Saylor, S. The house of the Vestals
Shannon, D. Chaos of crime
Simenon, G. Maigret and the killer
Simenon, G. Maigret and the madwoman
Simenon, G. Maigret and the wine merchant
Spillane, M. A long time dead
Stewart, A. Miss Kopp just won't quit
Sundin, S. Through waters deep
Tey, J. The daughter of time
Tidhar, L. A man lies dreaming
Vidich, P. The coldest warrior
Woods, S. The money shot
Woods, S. Skin game
Yang, J. The descent of monsters
Zimmerman, J. The orphanmaster

CRIMINAL INVESTIGATION
Dolan, H. Very bad men

Rabe, P. Anatomy of a killer ;
Rajaniemi, H. The fractal prince
Rajaniemi, H. The quantum thief
Ramqvist, K. The white city
Rindell, S. The other typist
Robards, K. The ultimatum
Sakey, M. The blade itself
Sallis, J. Drive
Sandford, J. Storm prey
Shannon, D. Chaos of crime
Shannon, S. The bone season
Shannon, S. The mime order
Shelton, P. Thin ice
Shoham, L. Asylum city
Smith, D. The darkest heart
Spillane, M. The Consummata
Spillane, M. Kill me, darling
Stark, R. Ask the parrot
Stark, R. Breakout
Stark, R. Dirty money
Stark, R. The hunter
Stark, R. The jugger
Sternbergh, A. The blinds
Tartt, D. The goldfinch
Tran, V. Dragonfish
Transgressions
Turner, N. Black widow
Walter, J. Citizen Vince
Wambaugh, J. The blue knight
Wambaugh, J. The new centurions
Watts, P. Starfish
Westlake, D. Bad news
Westlake, D. Bank shot
Westlake, D. Bank shot
Winslow, D. The border
Winslow, D. The cartel
Westlake, D. Don't ask
Westlake, D. Drowned hopes
Westlake, D. Get real
Westlake, D. Good behavior
Westlake, D. The hot rock
Westlake, D. The road to ruin
Westlake, D. Watch your back!
Westlake, D. What's so funny?
Westlake, D. What's the worst that could happen?
Woods, S. A delicate touch
Woods, T. Alibi
Yan, L. Dream of Ding Village
Criminals Livesey, M.
CRIMINALS -- REHABILITATION
Pelecanos, G. Drama city
CRIMINALS -- UNITED STATES
Ellroy, J. American tabloid
Higgins, G. The friends of Eddie Coyle
CRIMINALS -- WASHINGTON, D.C.
Pelecanos, G. Hard revolution
Pelecanos, G. Soul circus

CRIMINALS WITH MENTAL ILLNESSES
Lehane, D. Shutter Island
CRIMINOLOGISTS
Jones, J. The silence
Nelscott, K. Days of rage
Perry, T. Pursuit
Pintoff, S. In the shadow of Gotham
CRIMINOLOGY
French, N. The day of the dead
Crimson Empire (Alex Marshall) [series] Marshall, A.
Crimson Lake Fox, C.
Crimson Lake [series] Fox, C.
The **crimson** petal and the white Faber, M.
Crippen Boyne, J.
CRIPPEN, HAWLEY HARVEY, 1862-1910
Boyne, J. Crippen
CRIPS (GANG)
K'wan Gangsta
K'wan Gutter
Crisis Francis, F.
CRISIS MANAGEMENT
See, C. There will never be another you
Critical mass Paretsky, S.
CRITICISM
Nabokov, V. Pale fire
CRITICS
Bolano, R. 2666
Cosse, L. A novel bookstore
Laureano, C. The Saturday Night Supper Club
Lethem, J. Chronic city
CRITICS -- SPAIN
Perez-Reverte, A. The Club Dumas
CROATIA
Brkic, C. The first rule of swimming
Forna, A. The hired man
Novic, S. Girl at war
CROATS
Coetzee, J. Slow man
The **crocodile** De Giovanni, M.
CROMWELL, THOMAS,, EARL OF ESSEX, 1485?-1540
Mantel, H. Bring up the bodies
Mantel, H. Wolf Hall
Crooked Creek Ranch [series] O'Keefe, M.
Crooked letter, crooked letter Franklin, T.
Crooked numbers O'Mara, T.
Crooked river Preston, D.
Cross Bruen, K.
Cross her heart Pinborough, S.
Cross my heart Hatcher, R.
CROSS-COUNTRY AUTOMOBILE TRIPS
Bloom, A. Lucky us
Crumley, J. The final country
Drury, T. The driftless area
Luiselli, V. Lost children archive
CROSS-DRESSERS
Grebe, C. After she's gone
Somer, M. The serenity murders

Harris, R. Enigma
MacNeal, S. The king's justice
Stephenson, N. Cryptonomicon
Cryptonomicon Stephenson, N.
CRYPTOZOOLOGISTS
Schutt, B. The Darwin strain
CRYPTOZOOLOGY
Schutt, B. The Darwin strain
The **crystal** cave Stewart, M.
The **crystal** frontier Fuentes, C.
Crystal gardens Quick, A.
CUBA
Acevedo, C. The distant marvels
Cleeton, C. Next year in Havana
Cussler, C. Golden Buddha
Cussler, C. Havana storm
DeMille, N. The Cuban affair
Gala, M. The Black Cathedral
Garcia, C. The Aguero sisters
Hemingway, E. The old man and the sea
McLain, P. Love and ruin
CUBA -- CIVILIZATION
Garcia, C. Dreaming in Cuban
CUBA -- HISTORY -- 1933-1959
Hunter, S. Havana
Kennedy, W. Chango's beads and two-tone shoes
Latour, J. The Havana World Series
Sanchez, T. King Bongo
CUBA -- HISTORY -- 19TH CENTURY
Hijuelos, O. Twain & Stanley enter paradise
CUBA -- HISTORY -- 20TH CENTURY
Block, L. Killing Castro
Lehane, D. World gone by
The **Cuban** affair DeMille, N.
CUBAN AMERICAN MEN
Gruber, M. Night of the jaguar
Gruber, M. Valley of bones
Wolfe, T. Back to blood
CUBAN AMERICAN WOMEN
Buchanan, E. You only die twice
Cleeton, C. Next year in Havana
Garcia, C. The Aguero sisters
Garcia, C. Dreaming in Cuban
Hijuelos, O. Beautiful Maria of my soul
CUBAN AMERICANS
DeMille, N. The Cuban affair
Gruber, M. Night of the jaguar
Hijuelos, O. Beautiful Maria of my soul
Hijuelos, O. The mambo kings play songs of love
Makkai, R. The great believers
CUBAN RESISTANCE AND REVOLTS
Michener, J. Caribbean
CUBAN-AMERICANS
Crucet, J. Make your home among strangers
CUBANS
DeMille, N. The Cuban affair
Garcia, C. Dreaming in Cuban

CUBANS IN GREAT BRITAIN
Oyeyemi, H. The opposite house
CUBANS IN THE UNITED STATES
Garcia, C. King of Cuba
Hijuelos, O. Beautiful Maria of my soul
Hijuelos, O. The mambo kings play songs of love
Spillane, M. The Consummata
The **cuckoo's** calling Galbraith, R.
Cujo King, S.
CULINARY MYSTERIES
Andrew, S. Recipes for love and murder
Andrew, S. The Satanic mechanic
Bailey, M. An appetite for violets
Childs, L. Lavender blue murder
Crawford, I. A catered Christmas cookie exchange
Davidson, D. Killer pancake
Davidson, D. The last suppers
Page, K. The body in the big apple
Page, K. The body in the bog
Page, K. The body in the casket
Page, K. The body in the vestibule
Page, K. The body in the wake
Rich, V. The baked bean supper murders
Rich, V. The cooking school murders
Rich, V. The Nantucket diet murders
CULLODEN, BATTLE OF, 1746
Gabaldon, D. Dragonfly in amber
Gabaldon, D. Voyager
Culper Ring novels (Brad Meltzer) [series] Meltzer, B.
CULT BEHAVIOR
Dektar, M. The Ash family
CULT LEADERS
Byatt, A. A whistling woman
Dektar, M. The Ash family
Heinlein, R. Stranger in a strange land
Merullo, R. The talk-funny girl
Oe, K. Somersault
Portis, C. Gringos
CULTS
Adler-Olsen, J. The hanging girl
Allio, K. Buddhism for Western children
Barnes, S. Domino Falls
Bell, M. The color of night
Bird, S. The flamenco academy
Bowen, P. Badlands
Box, C. Winterkill
Broun, B. Night of the animals
Byatt, A. A whistling woman
Carter, M. The strangler vine
Chanter, C. The well
Coover, R. The origin of the Brunists
Darnielle, J. Universal harvester
Davis, L. One virgin too many
DeLillo, D. The names
Dekker, T. The girl behind the red rope
Gilman, D. Kaleidoscope
Goodman, C. The night villa

Momaday, N. House made of dawn

Murakami, R. In the miso soup , Ryu Murakami ; translated by Ralph McCarthy.

Okorafor, N. Binti

Orange, T. There there

Otsuka, J. The Buddha in the attic

Perrotta, T. The abstinence teacher

Piatote, B. The beadworkers

Potok, C. My name is Asher Lev

Roth, H. From bondage

Roth, H. Call it sleep

Roth, H. A star shines over Mt. Morris Park

Schwartz, J. The red daughter

Scott, P. Staying on

Shafak, E. The bastard of Istanbul

Shafak, E. Honor

Shepard, K. The Celestials

Silko, L. Ceremony

Theroux, P. The Elephanta suite

Tyler, A. Digging to America

Verble, M. Cherokee America

Yanagihara, H. The people in the trees

CULTURE CONFLICT -- RELIGIOUS ASPECTS
Pike, S. The lost queen

CULTURE CONFLICT -- TURKEY
Pamuk, O. Snow

CULTURE SHOCK
Bowles, P. The sheltering sky

Fitzpatrick, L. Lights all night long

Kincaid, J. Lucy

Miller, D. American by day

Satyal, R. No one can pronounce my name

Schwartz, J. The red daughter

Ulinich, A. Petropolis

Urrea, L. The water museum

Culture Universe series [series] Banks, I.

CULTURE WARS
Sandford, J. Bloody genius

CUMBERLAND ISLAND, GEORGIA
Woods, S. Palindrome

CUMBRIA, ENGLAND
Hill, R. The stranger house

Hill, R. The woodcutter

The **cunning** man Davies, R.

CUPCAKES
Devon, C. Sleeping with the entity

CUPID (ROMAN DEITY)
Lewis, C. Till we have faces

A **curable** romantic Skibell, J.

CURIOSITIES AND WONDERS
Borges, J. Collected fictions

Drury, T. The driftless area

Kidd, J. Things in jars

Kingsolver, B. Flight behavior

Macneal, E. The doll factory

McCarthy, T. Satin Island

Palmer, D. Mary Toft; or, the rabbit queen

Roussel, R. Locus solus

Stories

CURIOSITY IN BOYS
Ajvide Lindqvist, J. Let the right one in

CURIOSITY IN GIRLS
Gardam, J. God on the rocks

CURIOSITY IN TEENAGE GIRLS
Lyon, A. The sweet girl

A **curious** beginning Raybourn, D.

The **curious** incident of the dog in the night-time Haddon, M.

Curious toys Hand, E.

The **current** Johnston, T.

The **current** that carries Graley, L.

Curse of the Spellmans Lutz, L.

CURSES
Atakora, A. Conjure women

Atkinson, K. Human croquet

Bender, A. The particular sadness of lemon cake

Bennett, J. Bitter spirits

Bennett, R. City of miracles

Bledsoe, A. Wisp of a thing

Bledsoe, A. Gather her round

Bledsoe, A. Long black curl

Callihan, K. Firelight

Carey, L. The stolen child

Cheng, B. Southern cross the dog

Christie, A. Endless night

Cussler, C. The oracle

Druon, M. The iron king

Extence, G. The universe versus Alex Woods

Gear, K. People of the masks

Grames, J. The seven or eight deaths of Stella Fortuna

Gray, J. A duke never yields

Hawthorne, N. The house of the seven gables

Johnson, D. Train dreams

Long, J. The legend of Lyon Redmond

Lopez Barrio, C. The house of the impossible loves

Martineau, M. Kingdom of exiles

McGuire, S. Rosemary and rue

North, C. The pursuit of William Abbey

Novik, N. Uprooted

Oates, J. The accursed

Peters, E. The deeds of the disturber

Raybourn, D. A treacherous curse

Roberts, N. Dance upon the air

Roberts, N. Dark witch

Suri, T. Realm of ash

Wurlitzer, R. The drop edge of yonder

Curtain Christie, A.

CURTIS, EDWARD S, 1868-1952
Wiggins, M. The shadow catcher

CUSTER, ELIZABETH BACON, 1842-1933
Soli, T. The removes

CUSTER, GEORGE A (GEORGE ARMSTRONG), 1839-1876
Jones, D. The court-martial of George Armstrong Custer

Soli, T. The removes

DAIRY FARMS
Kate, J. A girl's guide to the Outback
Daisy Jones & the Six Reid, T.
Daisy Miller James, H.
DAKOTA INDIANS
Barry, S. Days without end
Brand, M. Beyond the outposts
Hill, R. Hanta Yo
DAKOTA INDIANS -- NORTH DAKOTA
Power, S. The grass dancer
DAKOTA INDIANS -- WARS, 1876
O'Brien, D. The contract surgeon
DAKOTA MEN
Hill, R. Hanta Yo
DAKOTA TERRITORY
Brooks, B. Blood storm
DALAI LAMAS
Cussler, C. Golden Buddha
DALEY, FRANK
Mackall, D. With love, wherever you are
DALEY, HELEN EBERHART
Mackall, D. With love, wherever you are
DALLAS, TEXAS
Baker, C. Whisper network
Fountain, B. Billy Lynn's long halftime walk
Kent, K. The burn
Kent, K. The dime
King, S. 11
O'Keefe, M. Crazy thing called love
Warren, T. The pastor's husband
DALLAS, TEXAS -- HISTORY
DeLillo, D. Libra
Damage Hart, J.
The **Damascus** road Parini, J.
DAMASCUS, SYRIA
Schami, R. Sophia
The **damned** Pyper, A.
DAMNED PERSONS
Butler, R. Hell
Rice, A. The queen of the damned
DAMS
Evison, J. West of here
Greene, A. Long Man
Pattison, E. Bones of the earth
DAMS -- DESIGN AND CONSTRUCTION
Barr, M. Watershed
DAMS -- DESIGN AND CONSTRUCTION -- CHINA
See, L. Dragon bones
DAMS -- NEW YORK (STATE)
Westlake, D. Drowned hopes
Dan Reles novels [series] Simon, M.
DANCE CONTESTS
Bird, S. The Yokota Officers Club
DANCE HALLS
Woodrell, D. The Maid's Version
Dance of the Jakaranda Kimani, P.
Dance upon the air Roberts, N.

A **dance** with dragons Martin, G.
The **dancer** and the thief Skarmeta, A.
A **dancer** in the dust Cook, T.
DANCERS
O'Connell, C. Killing critics
Sedgwick, M. Mister Memory
Skarmeta, A. The dancer and the thief
Smith, Z. Swing time
DANCING
Bird, S. The flamenco academy
Kaminsky, S. Dancing in the dark
Reed, I. Mumbo jumbo
Sapphire, 1. The kid
Smith, Z. Swing time
DANCING -- STUDY AND TEACHING
McCall Smith, A. In the company of cheerful ladies
Dancing at the Rascal Fair Doig, I.
Dancing in the dark Kaminsky, S.
Dancing in the dark Phillips, C.
Dancing to "Almendra" Montero, M.
Dandelion dynasty [series] Liu, K.
Dandelion wine Bradbury, R.
DANDELIONS
Bradbury, R. Dandelion wine
DANDIES
Orczy, E. The Scarlet Pimpernel
Dandy Gilver murder mysteries [series] McPherson, C.
Dangerous Spencer, M.
A **dangerous** collaboration Raybourn, D.
The **dangerous** edge of things Whittle, T.
The **dangerous** hour Muller, M.
A **dangerous** inheritance Weir, A.
A **dangerous** man Crais, R.
A **dangerous** mourning Perry, A.
Dangerous seduction Archer, Z.
Dangerous women
Dangling man Bellow, S.
Dani Fox mysteries [series] Pirro, J.
Daniel Hawthorne novels [series] Horowitz, A.
Daniel Jacobus mysteries [series] Elias, G.
Daniel Rinaldi mysteries [series] Palumbo, D.
DANIEL, (BIBLICAL FIGURE)
Andrews, M. Of fire and lions
The **Danish** girl Ebershoff, D.
Danse macabre Elias, G.
DANTE ALIGHIERI, 1265-1321 APPRECIATION
Pearl, M. The Dante Club
DANTE ALIGHIERI, 1265-1321 INFERNO
Brown, D. Inferno
DANTE ALIGHIERI, 1265-1321 INFLUENCE
Pearl, M. The Dante chamber
The **Dante** chamber Pearl, M.
The **Dante** Club Pearl, M.
Dante Club novels (Matthew Pearl) [series] Pearl, M.
Dante's dilemma Raimondo, L.
Dante's poison Raimondo, L.
Dante's wood Raimondo, L.

DAUGHTERS

Barry, K. Night boat to Tangier
Corman, A. Prized possessions
Craig, C. Miss Burma
Danticat, E. The dew breaker
Egan, J. Manhattan Beach
Ellison, J. Tear me apart
Lange, R. Angel baby
Lombardo, C. The most fun we ever had
Peikoff, K. Mother knows best
Reynolds, M. The Starlite Drive-in

DAUGHTERS -- DEATH

Bohjalian, C. The buffalo soldier
Diamond, E. An accidental light
Dixon, S. Interstate
Dowlatabadi, M. The colonel
Higgins, J. Midnight runner
Ng, C. Everything I never told you
Rouda, K. The favorite daughter
Smith, T. Agent 6
Styron, W. Lie down in darkness
The **daughters** of Cain Dexter, C.
The **daughters** of Mars Keneally, T.
Daughters of the Witching Hill Sharratt, M.

DAUGHTERS-IN-LAW

Arnoult, D. Sufficient grace
Lessing, D. The sweetest dream
Dave Robicheaux novels [series] Burke, J.
David Copperfield Dickens, C.
David Loogan mysteries [series] Dolan, H.
David Sloane thrillers [series] Dugoni, R.

DAVID,, KING OF ISRAEL

Edghill, I. Queenmaker
L'Engle, M. Certain women

DAVIDMAN, JOY, 1915-1960

Henry, P. Becoming Mrs. Lewis

DAVIS, SAMMY, 1925-1990

Randisi, R. Hey there (you with the gun in your hand)

DAVIS, VARINA, 1826-1906

Frazier, C. Varina
Dawn Butler, O.
Dawn Demirtas, S.
Dawn Wiesel, E.
The **dawn** patrol Winslow, D.
Day for night Reiken, F.
The **day** I died Rader-Day, L.
A **day** in the life of a smiling woman Drabble, M.
The **day** of creation Ballard, J.
Day of reckoning Higgins, J.
The **day** of the dead French, N.

DAY TRADING

Pavone, C. The Paris diversion
The **daylight** gate Winterson, J.
Days of awe Fox, L.
Days of distraction Chang, A.
Days of rage Nelscott, K.
Days without end Barry, S.

DAYTIME SMOKE

Osborne, D. The coming

DAYTON, OHIO

Daughters, A. You cannot mess this up
De Niro's game Hage, R.

DE QUINCEY, THOMAS, 1785-1859

Morrell, D. Murder as a fine art
Morrell, D. Ruler of the night
Deacon King Kong McBride, J.

DEAD

Ackerman, E. Waiting for Eden
Amis, M. The zone of interest
Beukes, L. Broken monsters
Bonnaffons, A. The regrets
Bradley, C. The grave's a fine and private place
Brockmeier, K. The brief history of the dead
Card, O. Speaker for the dead
Chancellor, B. Sycamore
Choo, Y. The ghost bride
Clinch, J. Finn
Cocco, G. Shadows on the lake
Cooper, E. Buried
Cotterill, C. Don't eat me
Deveraux, J. A willing murder
Dugoni, R. My sister's grave
Gappah, P. Out of darkness, shining light
Harvey, J. Darkness, darkness
Hiaasen, C. Nature girl
Kelly, J. The moon tunnel
Richardson, K. Greywalker
The living dead
Lourey, J. January thaw
Lovesey, P. Beau death
Miller, A. Pure
Moore, A. Jerusalem
Moore, C. You suck
Newton, C. Calumet City
Nickson, C. On Copper Street
Rendell, R. Not in the flesh
Richardson, K. Greywalker
Robertson, I. Island of bones
Sa'dawi, A. Frankenstein in Baghdad
Stanley, M. A carrion death
Stanley, M. Dying to live
Stridsberg, S. Valerie
Tokarczuk, O. Drive your plow over the bones of the dead
Ware, R. The lying game

DEAD -- DESECRATION

Potenza, C. Hearts of the missing

DEAD -- IDENTIFICATION

Brown, R. Murder at Monticello, or, Old sins
Elkins, A. Dying on the vine
Elkins, A. Unnatural selection
Macmillan, G. The nanny
Ondaatje, M. Anil's ghost
Parker, R. Sea change
Reichs, K. Bare bones
Reichs, K. Break no bones

Hoffman, A. The river king
Horn, D. Eternal life
Hustvedt, S. The blazing world
Kadare, I. The general of the dead army
Khadra, Y. The swallows of Kabul
Kleypas, L. Christmas Eve at Friday Harbor
Knowles, J. A separate peace
L'Engle, M. Certain women
Le Guin, U. The other wind
Mandel, E. Station Eleven
McDermott, A. Charming Billy
McKillip, P. Ombria in shadow
Millet, L. How the dead dream
Moore, C. A dirty job
Mott, J. The returned
Nelson, C. More than we remember
Noire Candy licker
Oates, J. Wild nights
Obioma, C. The fishermen
Ocampo, S. Forgotten journey
Olson, N. Before the devil fell
Oyeyemi, H. Mr. Fox
Pawel, R. Death of a nationalist
Pearl, M. The Poe shadow
Pears, I. Stone's fall
Penny, L. The cruelest month
Perec, G. Life
Poore, M. Reincarnation blues
Proulx, A. Accordion crimes
Pyper, A. The damned
Ramadan, A. The clothesline swing
Raybourn, D. Silent in the grave
Richardson, C. The end of the alphabet
  The road ahead
Roth, P. Sabbath's theater
Rowland, L. The Shogun's daughter
Sandford, J. Sudden prey
Saramago, J. Death with interruptions
Sarton, M. A reckoning
Schweblin, S. Fever dream
Shteyngart, G. Super sad true love story
Smith, L. Fair and tender ladies
Smith, L. Family linen
Straub, P. Ghost story
  Stories
Swarthout, G. The shootist
Tokarczuk, O. Flights
Trollope, J. The other family
Vollmann, W. Last stories and other stories
Wiesel, E. A mad desire to dance
Woodrell, D. The Maid's Version
Woolf, V. The years
Yan, L. Dream of Ding Village
Zelazny, R. Donnerjack

DEATH (PERSONIFICATION)
Camp, B. Gather the fortunes
Malerman, J. Unbury Carol

Moore, C. A dirty job
Poore, M. Reincarnation blues

DEATH -- PSYCHOLOGICAL ASPECTS
Brautigan, R. An unfortunate woman
Camus, A. The stranger
Fitch, J. Paint it black
Garcia Marquez, G. The general in his labyrinth
Garner, H. The spare room
Hemingway, E. For whom the bell tolls
Hemingway, E. The snows of Kilimanjaro and other stories
O'Brien, T. The things they carried
Robotham, M. Close your eyes
Savage, S. The way of the dog
Toibin, C. The blackwater lightship
Death and Mr. Pickwick Jarvis, S.
Death and other happy endings Cantor, M.
Death and restoration Pears, I.
Death and transfiguration Elias, G.
Death at the Chateau Bremont Longworth, M.
Death benefits Perry, T.
Death by water Greenwood, K.
Death by water Oe, K.
The **death** collectors Kerley, J.
Death comes for the archbishop Cather, W.
Death comes to the nursery Lloyd, C.
Death du jour Reichs, K.

DEATH IN ART
Kerley, J. The death collectors
Death in Brittany Bannalec, J.
Death in focus Perry, A.
Death in her hands Moshfegh, O.
Death in holy orders James, P.
Death in paradise Parker, R.
Death in Paris mysteries [series] Bernhard, E.
A **death** in the family Agee, J.
A **death** in the family Stanley, M.
Death in Venice and seven other stories Mann, T.
Death in Veracruz Aguilar Camin, H.
Death is hard work Khalfah, K.
Death lies beneath Rowson, P.
Death lives next door Butler, G.
Death notice Zhou, H.
Death of a cattle king Overholser, W.
Death of a literary widow Barnard, R.
Death of a macho man Beaton, M.
Death of a nationalist Pawel, R.
Death of a new American Fredericks, M.
Death of a red heroine Qiu, X.
Death of a stranger Perry, A.
Death of an expert witness James, P.
The **death** of Artemio Cruz Fuentes, C.
The **death** of bees O'Donnell, L.
The **death** of Mrs. Westaway Ware, R.
Death of the mantis Stanley, M.
Death on Blackheath Perry, A.
Death on Demand mysteries [series] Hart, C.
DEATH ROW

Deceived by desire Force, M.
The **deceivers** Berenson, A.
December 6 Smith, M.
December heat Garcia-Roza, L.
The **decent** inn of death Airth, R.
DECEPTION
  Abbott, P. Concrete angel
  Abrams, M. Meadowlark
  Alexander, V. The Lady Travelers Guide to larceny with a
    dashing stranger
  Alexander, V. What happens at Christmas
  Angelo, M. Followers
  Arden, K. The girl in the tower
  Arden, K. The winter of the witch
  Armstrong, K. Wherever she goes
  Atkinson, K. Big sky
  Bailey, M. An appetite for violets
  Ball, J. The way through doors
  Barber, L. A girl named Anna
  Bear, G. The forge of God
  Beck, H. Lost you
  Bell, L. How the duke was won
  Beverley, J. Tempting fortune
  Beyda, E. The body double
  Billingham, M. Their little secret
  Block, L. Hit me
  Bohjalian, C. The flight attendant
  Bohjalian, C. The red lotus
  Bourne, J. My lord and spymaster
  Bowman, V. The accidental countess
  Box, C. Blue heaven
  Boyne, J. A history of loneliness
  Brockway, C. The golden season
  Brown, S. Mean streak
  Bruni, S. The night Gwen Stacy died
  Buckley, F. The siren queen
  Camus, A. The fall
  Carpenter, E. The weight of lies
  Carter, S. New England white
  Child, L. Past tense
  Chizmar, R. A long December
  Choi, A. Kay's lucky coin variety
  Christopher, A. Not the girl you marry
  Clark, C. In the full light of the sun
  Clarke, L. A single breath
  Clinch, J. Marley
  Coben, H. Don't let go
  Coben, H. Fool me once
  Coben, H. The stranger
  Cole, A. A princess in theory
  Collins, W. The woman in white
  Connolly, J. The burning soul
  Constantine, L. The last Mrs. Parrish
  Corry, J. My husband's wife
  Coughlin, J. Long shot
  Coulter, C. Labyrinth
  Crais, R. The first rule

  Crouch, B. Recursion
  Currie, R. Flimsy little plastic miracles
  Dare, T. A week to be wicked
  Delaney, J. The perfect wife
  Dickens, C. Our mutual friend
  Dimberg, K. Girl in the rearview mirror
  Draven, G. Phoenix unbound
  Eason, K. How Rory Thorne destroyed the multiverse
  Edwards, K. The memory keeper's daughter
  Elkins, A. Dying on the vine
  Ellison, J. Tear me apart
  Essbaum, J. Hausfrau
  Faye, L. Jane Steele
  Finch, C. A beautiful blue death
  Finder, J. Suspicion
  Flynn, G. Dark places
  Flynn, G. Gone girl
  Flynn, G. Sharp objects
  Fowler, C. Bryant & May
  Frear, C. Sweet little lies
  French, N. The lying room
  French, T. The likeness
  Fuller, C. Bitter orange
  Furst, A. Dark voyage
  Gardner, L. Fear nothing
  Gardner, L. Find her
  Gass, W. Middle C
  George, E. Believing the lie
  Gibson, W. The peripheral
  Goddard, R. Beyond recall
  Goddard, R. Into the blue
  Gogol, N. Dead souls
  Goldberg, T. Gangsterland
  Goldin, M. The escape room
  Gordon, J. Lord of misrule
  Grecian, A. The saint of wolves and butchers
  Greenwood, T. Rust & stardust
  Gregory, P. The red queen
  Grippando, J. Money to burn
  Gruber, M. The forgery of Venus
  Guhrke, L. Governess gone rogue
  Hammett, D. The Maltese falcon
  Hannah, S. Keep her safe
  Hannah, S. The wrong mother
  Harper, J. The dry
  Harris, R. The ghost
  Harvey, M. The Chicago way
  Hegi, U. The vision of Emma Blau
  Hill, R. The stranger house
  Horowitz, A. The sentence is death
  Horowitz, A. The word is murder
  Howatch, S. The heartbreaker
  Hunt, L. Neverhome
  Hustvedt, S. The blazing world
  Ignatius, D. Body of lies
  Jackson, J. Never have I ever
  James, H. The golden bowl

Urquhart, R. The visionist
VanderMeer, J. Borne
Vandermeer, J. Finch
Waldman, A. A door in the earth
Walker, W. Emma in the night
Ware, R. The death of Mrs. Westaway
Warren, T. The pastor's husband
Watson, J. Asta in the wings
White, R. Salt river
Willig, L. The seduction of the Crimson Rose
Woods, S. Chiefs
Wrobel, S. Darling Rose Gold
Zahn, T. Dark force rising
Zahn, T. Heir to the empire
Zahn, T. The last command
Deception Cove Laukkanen, O.

DECEPTION IN MEN
Livesey, M. The missing world
Matar, H. In the country of men
Perry, T. Death benefits
Roosevelt, E. Murder at the palace
Rouda, K. Best day ever

DECEPTION IN WOMEN
Erdrich, L. Four souls
Erdrich, L. The last report on the miracles at Little No Horse
Starling, C. The luminous dead
The **deception** of the emerald ring Willig, L.

DECISION-MAKING
Adam, C. Golden child
Bartels, E. We hope for better things
Brown, K. The life Lucy knew
Dickey, E. The business of lovers
Gilman, S. Donna has left the building
Jimenez, S. The vanished birds
Kirkpatrick, J. One more river to cross
Mackintosh, C. After the end
Manning, M. The victim
Richman, A. The secret of clouds
Silber, J. Improvement
Smiley, J. A thousand acres
Toews, M. Women talking
Tyler, A. A spool of blue thread
Decline and fall Waugh, E.

DECOYS
Hammett, D. The Maltese falcon

DEE, JOHN, 1527-1608
Sherwood, F. The book of splendor
The **deeds** of the disturber Peters, E.
The **deep** Katsu, A.
The **deep** Solomon, R.
The **deep** end of the ocean Mitchard, J.
Deep freeze Sandford, J.
Deep harbor Michaels, F.
Deep in the shade of paradise Dufresne, J.
Deep river Endo, S.
Deep river Marlantes, K.
Deep storm Child, L.

DEEP-SEA SOUNDING
Laukkanen, O. Gale force
A **deeper** love inside Souljah,.
A **deeper** sleep Stabenow, D.
A **deepness** in the sky Vinge, V.

DEER HUNTING
Vann, D. Goat Mountain

DEFAULT (FINANCE)
Rinehart, M. The circular staircase

DEFECTION
DeLillo, D. Libra
Deighton, L. Berlin game
Deighton, L. London match
Greene, G. The human factor
Le Carre, J. Our kind of traitor

DEFECTORS
Coughlin, J. Long shot
Deighton, L. Berlin game
Deighton, L. London match
Greene, G. The human factor
Le Carre, J. Our kind of traitor
Schwartz, J. The red daughter
Sebastian, T. Fatal ally

DEFECTORS -- UNITED STATES
DeLillo, D. Libra
Defend and betray Perry, A.
Defending Jacob Landay, W.

DEFENSE ATTORNEYS
Brown, S. Fat Tuesday
Clark, M. Blood defense
Clark, M. Final judgment
Connelly, M. The brass verdict
Connelly, M. The fifth witness
Connelly, M. The gods of guilt
Connelly, M. The Lincoln lawyer
Edvardsson, M. A nearly normal family
Hannah, K. Home front
Hart, J. The king of lies
Lashner, W. A killer's kiss
Lescroart, J. The first law
Lescroart, J. The hearing
Lescroart, J. Nothing but the truth
Lescroart, J. The oath
Margolin, P. Wild justice
Martini, S. Compelling evidence
Moore, G. The holdout
Mortimer, J. Rumpole's return
Perry, A. Defend and betray
Whitlow, R. A time to stand
Winer, J. Her kind of case

DEFENSE ATTORNEYS -- MISSISSIPPI
Grisham, J. A time to kill

DEFIANCE
Benton, J. Lilli de Jong
Calvino, I. The baron in the trees

DEGAS, EDGAR, 1834-1917
Buchanan, C. The painted girls

Leithauser, B. The promise of elsewhere
Locascio, L. Open me
Pontoppidan, H. Lucky Per
Youngson, A. Meet me at the museum

DENMARK -- HISTORY

Hoeg, P. The history of Danish dreams

DENMARK -- HISTORY -- 1241-1397

Updike, J. Gertrude and Claudius

DENMARK -- HISTORY -- 17TH CENTURY

Tremain, R. Music & silence

DENMARK -- HISTORY -- 19TH CENTURY

MacAlister, K. The truth about Leo

DENMARK -- HISTORY -- GERMAN OCCUPATION, 1940-1945

Follett, K. Hornet flight

DENMARK -- RULERS

Tremain, R. Music & silence

DENTAL ASSISTANTS

Stibbe, N. Reasons to be cheerful

DENTISTS

Block, L. The burglar in the closet
Ferris, J. To rise again at a decent hour
Norris, F. McTeague
Russell, M. Doc
Stibbe, N. Reasons to be cheerful

DENVER, COLORADO

Burns, R. Body slam
Coel, M. Blood memory
Crownover, J. Honor
Dekker, T. Black
Dunning, J. Booked to die
Dunning, J. The bookman's wake
Fajardo-Anstine, K. Sabrina & Corina
Greer, R. First of state
Laureano, C. The Saturday Night Supper Club
Martin, A. Blitzed
Martin, A. Fumbled

The **Department** of Sensitive Crimes McCall Smith, A.

Department Q [series] Adler-Olsen, J.

DEPARTMENT STORE EMPLOYEES

Martin, S. Shopgirl

DEPARTMENT STORES

Martin, S. Shopgirl

DEPENDENCY (PSYCHOLOGY)

Coetzee, J. Slow man

DEPORTATION

Cauwelaert, D. One-way
Cleave, C. Little Bee
Grippando, J. The girl in the glass box
Kutsukake, L. The translation of love

DEPRESSION

Dean, L. The idea of love
Dodd, C. Because I'm watching
Greer, R. First of state
Haslett, A. Imagine me gone
Jackson, C. The lost weekend
Levy, D. Swimming home

Meno, J. The boy detective fails
Murdoch, I. The good apprentice
Nicholls, O. Love, unscripted
Woolf, V. Mrs. Dalloway

DEPRESSION ERA (1929-1941)

Albert, S. The Darling Dahlias and the cucumber tree
Barnett, K. Ever faithful
Barr, M. Watershed
Brown, J. Addie Pray
Earley, T. Jim the boy
Greaves, C. Hard twisted
Harman, P. The midwife of Hope River
Koryta, M. The Cypress House
Krueger, W. This tender land
Lansdale, J. Edge of dark water
Lansdale, J. Sunset and sawdust
Leonard, E. The Hot Kid
Meadows, R. I will send rain
Moyes, J. The giver of stars
O'Neill, H. The Lonely Hearts Hotel
Ozick, C. Heir to the glimmering world
Richards, L. Death was in the blood
Shreve, A. Sea glass
Silver, M. Mary Coin
Wolfe, T. You can't go home again
Wood, S. The Quintland sisters

DEPRESSIONS

Steinbeck, J. The grapes of wrath

DEPRESSIONS -- 1929-1941

Baldwin, J. Go tell it on the mountain
Barr, M. Watershed
Bellow, S. The adventures of Augie March
Bellow, S. Novels, 1944-1953
Brown, J. Addie Pray
Caldwell, E. Tobacco Road
Doctorow, E. World's Fair
Egan, J. Manhattan Beach
Gibbons, K. Charms for the easy life
Greaves, C. Hard twisted
Gruen, S. Water for elephants
Harman, P. The midwife of Hope River
Keilson, H. Life goes on
Koryta, M. The Cypress House
Lansdale, J. The bottoms
Lansdale, J. Edge of dark water
Leonard, E. The Hot Kid
Oates, J. A garden of earthly delights
Richards, L. Death was in the blood
Shreve, A. Sea glass
Silver, M. Mary Coin
Wolfe, T. You can't go home again

DEPRESSIONS -- 1929-1941 -- ALABAMA

Albert, S. The Darling Dahlias and the cucumber tree

DEPRESSIONS -- 1929-1941 -- NORTH CAROLINA

Earley, T. Jim the boy

DEPRESSIONS -- 1929-1941 -- SOUTHERN STATES

Adams, A. A southern exposure

Keller, J. Bone on bone
Lunde, M. The end of the ocean
McGregor, J. Even the dogs
Meyer, P. American rust
Montag, K. After the flood
Ramqvist, K. The white city
Restrepo, L. Delirium
Silko, L. Ceremony
Strout, E. Olive Kitteridge
Toews, M. A complicated kindness

DESPAIR IN MEN
Cleave, P. Joe Victim
Goodis, D. Nightfall
Desperate duchesses James, E.
Desperate duchesses by the numbers [series] James, E.
Desperate duchesses series [series] James, E.
A **desperate** fortune Kearsley, S.

DESPOTISM
Elison, M. The book of Etta
Garcia Marquez, G. The autumn of the patriarch
Wuertz, Y. Everything belongs to us
Destiny Haydon, E.
Destiny and desire Fuentes, C.
Destroyer angel Barr, N.

DESTROYERS (WARSHIPS)
Sundin, S. Through waters deep

DETACHMENT (PSYCHOLOGY)
Jin, H. A free life
Sebold, A. The almost moon
Detective Anders Knutas mysteries [series] Jungstedt, M.
Detective Betty [series] Kent, K.
Detective by day novels [series] Garrett, K.
Detective Chief Inspector Neil Paget mysteries [series]
Smith, F.
Detective D. D. Warren novels [series] Gardner, L.
Detective Emmanuel Cooper mysteries [series] Nunn, M.
Detective Galileo mysteries [series] Higashino, K.
Detective Gemma Monroe novels [series] Littlejohn, E.
Detective Harry Hole [series] Nesbo, J.
Detective Inspector Jack Caffery mysteries [series] Hayder,
M.
Detective Inspector Joona Linna mysteries [series] Kepler,
L.
Detective Kubu mysteries [series] Stanley, M.
Detective Mollel mysteries [series] Crompton, R.
Detective Sunderson novels [series] Harrison, J.
Detective Varg novels [series] McCall Smith, A.

DETECTIVES
Aaronovitch, B. Broken homes
Aaronovitch, B. Midnight riot
Aaronovitch, B. Moon over Soho
Aaronovitch, B. Whispers under ground
Abani, C. The secret history of Las Vegas
Adler-Olsen, J. The scarred woman
Alexis, A. The hidden keys
Archer, J. Nothing ventured
Arnaldur Indridason, 1. Strange shores

Ball, J. In the heat of the night
Bannalec, J. Death in Brittany
Bannalec, J. The killing tide
Bannister, J. Kindred spirits
Barclay, L. Elevator pitch
Barclay, L. Parting shot
Barclay, L. The twenty-three
Bateman, K. This earl of mine
Bauer, B. Snap
Bayard, L. The black tower
Beaton, M. Death of a macho man
Belle, K. Dear wife
The best American mystery stories 2017
The best American mystery stories 2018
Billingham, M. Their little secret
Black, L. Let justice descend
Black, L. Suffer the children
Bohjalian, C. The sleepwalker
Borjlind, C. Spring tide
Box, C. Badlands
Bradley, C. I am half-sick of shadows
Bradley, C. The weed that strings the hangman's bag
Brandt, H. The Whites
Brekke, J. The fifth element
Brett, S. Murder unprompted
Brooks, B. Blood storm
Brooks, B. Frontier justice
Brooks, B. Winter kill
Bruen, K. Cross
Burke, J. Black cherry blues
Burke, J. Heaven's prisoners
Burke, J. The New Iberia blues
Burnet, G. The disappearance of Adele Bedeau
Bussi, M. Black water lilies
Carver, T. The surrogate
Chabon, M. The Yiddish Policemen's Union
Church, J. Bamboo and blood
Church, J. A corpse in the Koryo
Church, J. Hidden moon
Clark, M. Blood defense
Cleave, P. Joe Victim
Cleeves, A. The long call
Cleeves, A. Raven black
Cleeves, A. Thin air
Cleeves, A. Wild fire
Coben, H. Don't let go
Cole, A. An extraordinary union
Cole, D. Ragdoll
Collins, W. The moonstone
Conlon, E. Red on red
Connelly, M. The burning room
Connelly, M. The crossing
Connelly, M. The night fire
Connolly, J. A book of bones
Connolly, J. The woman in the woods
Coover, R. Noir
Corey, J. Leviathan wakes

Kellerman, F. Jupiter's bones
Kellerman, F. Milk and honey
Kellerman, J. Monster
Kellerman, F. Prayers for the dead
Kellerman, J. Private eyes
Kellerman, J. Self-defense
Kellerman, F. Serpent's tooth
Kellerman, J. Therapy
Kellerman, J. Time bomb
Kelly, E. Broadchurch
Kelly, S. The wages of desire
Kepler, L. The hypnotist
Kepler, L. The rabbit hunter
Kepler, L. The sandman
Kepler, L. Stalker
Khan, A. Among the ruins
Khan, A. The unquiet dead
Kidd, J. Things in jars
King, L. The beekeeper's apprentice
King, L. The game
Koontz, D. The husband
L'Amour, L. May there be a road
Lackberg, C. The hidden child
Lackberg, C. The ice princess
Lackberg, C. The lost boy
Lackberg, C. The preacher
Lackberg, C. The stonecutter
Lehane, D. Mystic river
Lemaitre, P. Irene
Leon, D. Trace elements
Leon, D. Uniform justice
Leon, D. Unto us a son is given
Lescroart, J. The first law
Lescroart, J. The hearing
Lescroart, J. The oath
Lim, E. Dear cyborgs
Limon, M. Mr. Kill
Lippman, L. No good deeds
Littlejohn, E. Inherit the bones
Locke, A. Bluebird, bluebird
Locke, A. Heaven, my home
Lovesey, P. Beau death
Lovesey, P. The tooth tattoo
Lovesey, P. Waxwork
Lupton, R. Sister
Lutz, J. Burn
Lutz, J. Lightning
MacBride, S. Cold granite
MacBride, S. Dying light
MacBride, S. Flesh house
MacDonald, P. The list of Adrian Messenger
Mackintosh, C. I let you go
Macmillan, G. The nanny
Mankell, H. Before the frost
Mankell, H. The dogs of Riga
Mankell, H. Firewall
Mankell, H. The man who smiled

Mankell, H. One step behind
Mankell, H. The troubled man
Mark, D. Cruel mercy
Mark, D. The dark winter
Mark, D. Original skin
Mark, D. Sorrow bound
Marsh, N. Dead water
Marsh, N. False scent
Marsh, N. Grave mistake
Marsh, N. Last ditch
Marsh, N. Light thickens
Marsh, N. When in Rome
Mason, T. The Darwin affair
MatchUp
McBain, E. The big bad city
McBain, E. Fat Ollie's book
McBain, E. The frumious bandersnatch
McBain, E. Hark!
McBain, E. The last dance
McBain, E. Nocturne
McCall Smith, A. The Department of Sensitive Crimes
McCall Smith, A. The good husband of Zebra Drive
McClure, J. The steam pig
McDermid, V. How the dead speak
McKinty, A. The cold, cold ground
McKinty, A. In the morning I'll be gone
Meyer, D. Devil's peak
Meyer, D. Icarus
Moore, J. The night market
Morgan Jones, C. The jackal's share
Morgan Jones, C. The silent oligarch
Morrell, D. Ruler of the night
Mosby, S. You can run
Mukherjee, A. A necessary evil
Mukherjee, A. A rising man
Mukherjee, A. Smoke and ashes
Nabb, M. Some bitter taste
Nesbo, J. The devil's star
Nesbo, J. Nemesis
Nesbo, J. The redbreast
Neuhaus, N. Snow White must die
Neville, S. The ghosts of Belfast
Nickson, C. Gods of gold
Nickson, C. On Copper Street
North, A. The Whisper Man
Nykanen, H. Nights of awe
O'Connell, C. Blind sight
O'Connell, C. It happens in the dark
O'Donovan, G. Dublin dead
O'Donovan, G. The priest
O'Malley, T. We were kings
Obregon, N. Blue light Yokohama
Oldham, N. Fighting for the dead
Patterson, J. Along came a spider
Patterson, J. Kiss the girls
Pava, S. Personae
Pearce, M. A dead man in Barcelona

Simmons, D. Hyperion
Simpson, D. Last seen alive
Simpson, D. No laughing matter
Simpson, D. Once too often
Singh, N. A madness of sunshine
Sjowall, M. Cop killer
Sjowall, M. The laughing policeman
Sjowall, M. The locked room
Sjowall, M. The man on the balcony
Sjowall, M. Murder at the Savoy
Slaughter, K. Criminal
Smith, B. Shoot the dog
Smith, C. Silent city
Smith, F. Night fall
Smith, M. Gorky Park
Smith, M. Havana Bay
Smith, M. Polar Star
Smith, M. Red Square
Smith, M. Stalin's ghost
Smith, M. The Siberian dilemma
Smith, M. Three stations
Smith, M. Tatiana
Smith, M. Wolves eat dogs
Soule, M. The crows
Spain, J. With our blessing
Spencer, S. A dying fall
Stanley, M. A carrion death
Stanley, M. Deadly harvest
Stanley, M. A death in the family
Stanley, M. Death of the mantis
Stanley, M. Dying to live
Steiner, S. Persons unknown
Stout, D. Titanshade
Stroud, C. The shimmer
Sveistrup, S. The chestnut man
Tallis, F. Vienna blood
Thomas, R. Firewatching
Tracy, P. Ice cold heart
Transgressions
Truss, L. The man that got away
Vandermeer, J. Finch
White, S. Compound fractures
White, S. Line of fire
Willocks, T. Memo from Turner
Winters, B. Countdown City
Winters, B. The last policeman
Winters, B. World of trouble
Wolf, D. The execution
Wolf, D. The ultimatum
Yap, F. Yesterday

DETECTIVES -- AUSTIN, TEXAS
Simon, M. The last Jew standing
DETECTIVES -- BALTIMORE, MARYLAND
Lippman, L. What the dead know
DETECTIVES -- BOSTON, MASSACHUSETTS
Ridpath, M. Far north
DETECTIVES -- CONNECTICUT

White, S. The siege
DETECTIVES -- DETROIT, MICHIGAN
Johnson, D. Detroit shuffle
Leonard, E. Mr. Paradise
DETECTIVES -- GREAT BRITAIN
Tey, J. The daughter of time
DETECTIVES -- JAPAN
Rowland, L. The incense game
Rowland, L. The Shogun's daughter
Rowland, L. The snow empress
DETECTIVES -- LOS ANGELES, CALIFORNIA
Connelly, M. The black ice
Connelly, M. The brass verdict
Connelly, M. Echo Park
Mosley, W. Blonde faith
Mosley, W. Charcoal Joe
Mosley, W. Cinnamon kiss
Mosley, W. Little green
Mosley, W. Little Scarlet
Mosley, W. Rose gold
DETECTIVES -- MEXICO
Solares, M. The black minutes
DETECTIVES -- MINNEAPOLIS, MINNESOTA
Sandford, J. Broken prey
Sandford, J. Hidden prey
Sandford, J. Invisible prey
Sandford, J. Naked prey
Sandford, J. Phantom prey
Tracy, P. Monkeewrench
DETECTIVES -- MONTREAL, QUEBEC
Reichs, K. Deja dead
DETECTIVES -- MOSCOW, RUSSIA
Akunin, B. The coronation
DETECTIVES -- NEW JERSEY
Price, R. Clockers
DETECTIVES -- OSLO, NORWAY
Nesbo, J. The leopard
Nesbo, J. The redeemer
Nesbo, J. The snowman
DETECTIVES -- QUEBEC (PROVINCE)
Penny, L. The beautiful mystery
Penny, L. The cruelest month
Penny, L. How the light gets in
Penny, L. The long way home
Penny, L. The nature of the beast
Penny, L. Still life
Penny, L. A trick of the light
DETECTIVES -- RIO DE JANEIRO, BRAZIL
Garcia-Roza, L. December heat
DETECTIVES -- SAVANNAH, GEORGIA
Brown, S. Ricochet
DETECTIVES -- SCOTLAND
MacBride, S. Close to the bone
MacBride, S. Shatter the bones
May, P. The blackhouse
DETECTIVES -- SEATTLE, WASHINGTON
Jance, J. Birds of prey

TITLE, SERIES, AND SUBJECT INDEX

Butler, R. Hell
Gilman, L. The cold eye
Gilman, L. Silver on the road
Hill, J. Horns
Hurley, A. Devil's Day
Jones, D. Second grave on the left
Mailer, N. The castle in the forest
Mann, T. Doctor Faustus
Rice, A. Christ the Lord
Rice, A. Memnoch the devil
Snipes, W. Talon of God
Tremblay, P. Disappearance at Devil's Rock
Updike, J. The witches of Eastwick
The **devil** all the time Pollock, D.
The **devil** colony Rollins, J.
The **devil** crept in Ahlborn, A.
Devil in a blue dress Mosley, W.
The **devil** in silver LaValle, V.
Devil in spring Kleypas, L.
Devil red Lansdale, J.
The **devil** takes half Serafim, L.
The **devil** tree Kosinski, J.
Devil you know [series] Byrne, K.
The **devil's** alphabet Gregory, D.
The **devil's** apprentice Marston, E.
Devil's bride Laurens, S.
Devil's brood Penman, S.
Devil's Day Hurley, A.
Devil's duke novels [series] Ashe, K.
The **devil's** making Haldane, S.
Devil's night Ritter, T.
Devil's peak Meyer, D.
The **devil's** punchbowl Iles, G.
The **devil's** star Nesbo, J.
The **devil's** triangle Coulter, C.
The **devil's** triangle Owen, H.
Devil's wake [series] Barnes, S.
Devil's waltz Kellerman, J.
Devil's West [series] Gilman, L.
Devilish Beverley, J.
Devils in exile Hogan, C.
Devils of Dover [series] Bowen, K.
The **Devlin** diary Phillips, C.
DEVON, ENGLAND
Bowen, R. The victory garden
Christie, A. And then there were none
Cleeves, A. The long call
Vine, B. The chimney sweeper's boy
DEVOTEDNESS
Abbott, S. The future of love
Cornwell, B. War of the wolf
MacLaverty, B. Midwinter break
The **devotion** of suspect X Higashino, K.
The **dew** breaker Danticat, E.
Dewey Andreas thrillers [series] Coes, B.
DHAKA, BANGLADESH
Zaman, N. Up in the main house & other stories

Dhalgren Delany, S.
DHARMA (BUDDHISM)
Kerouac, J. The dharma bums
The **dharma** bums Kerouac, J.
DIAGNOSIS
Cantor, M. Death and other happy endings
Cook, R. Cell
The **diagnosis** Lightman, A.
The **diamond** age, Stephenson, N.
Diamond dust Lovesey, P.
The **Diamond** empire K'wan
DIAMOND INDUSTRY AND TRADE
Goddard, R. Long time coming
DIAMOND MINES AND MINING
Stanley, M. A carrion death
Diamond solitaire Lovesey, P.
DIAMONDS
Collins, W. The moonstone
Epperson, T. Sailor
Khan, V. The perplexing theft of the jewel in the crown
Leon, D. Blood from a stone
Lindsay, J. Just watch me
Rose, M. Cartier's hope
Trollope, A. The Eustace diamonds
Diamonds and Pearl K'wan
Diamonds and Pearl [series] K'wan
**DIANA,, PRINCESS OF WALES, 1961-1997 ATTEMPTED
ASSASSINATION**
Clancy, T. Patriot games
DIARIES
Anderson, A. The summer guest
Bacon, C. There is room for you
Bowen, R. The victory garden
Collins, K. Notes from a black woman's diary
Douglas, L. Magnificent obsession
Ghosh, A. The hungry tide
Kearsley, S. A desperate fortune
Kelly, J. The light over London
Mankell, H. The man from Beijing
McQuiston, J. The spinster's guide to scandalous behavior
Peterson, J. Early's fall
Rayne, S. Property of a lady
Rodale, M. Lady Bridget's diary
Vine, B. Anna's book
DIARY NOVELS
Bellow, S. Dangling man
Bernhard, T. Frost
Bolano, R. The savage detectives
Brautigan, R. An unfortunate woman
Butler, O. Parable of the sower
Colette, 1. The complete Claudine
Downing, D. Diary of a dead man on leave
Erdrich, L. Shadow tag
Fielding, H. Bridget Jones's diary
Groen, H. On the bright side
Hijuelos, O. Twain & Stanley enter paradise
Horlock, M. The book of lies

Mychea He loves me, he loves you not
Olshan, J. Black diamond fall
Oyeyemi, H. Mr. Fox
Parker, R. Now and then
Rosenthal, P. The bookseller's daughter
Singer, I. Enemies, a love story
Styles, T. A hustler's son
Vonnegut, K. Cat's cradle
Walker, C. Man of the year
Ware, R. The lying game
Zane Addicted

DISHONESTY IN MEN
Cauwelaert, D. One-way

DISILLUSIONMENT
Amidon, S. Human capital
Hemingway, E. The sun also rises
James, H. The portrait of a lady
Jin, H. A free life
Le Carre, J. Agent running in the field
Lessing, D. Landlocked
Ma, J. Beijing coma
Remarque, E. A time to love and a time to die
Watts, S. No one is coming to save us

DISILLUSIONMENT IN MEN
Banks, R. Continental drift
Flaubert, G. Sentimental education
Greene, G. The quiet American
Hemingway, E. For whom the bell tolls
London, J. Martin Eden
Maugham, W. The razor's edge
Naipaul, V. A bend in the river
Naipaul, V. Magic seeds
Russell, M. Children of God
Updike, J. Rabbit, run

Dismas Hardy novels [series] Lescroart, J.

DISMEMBERMENT
Brown, R. Wish you were here
Cole, D. Ragdoll
Cotterill, C. Grandad, there's a head on the beach
Tudor, C. The chalk man

Disoriental Djavadi, N.

DISORIENTATION
Garcia Marquez, G. Strange pilgrims
Saramago, J. Blindness

DISPLACED WORKERS
Sloan, R. Mr. Penumbra's 24-hour bookstore

The **dispossessed** Le Guin, U.

DISSECTION
Thomson, E. The blood

DISSENTERS
Bandi, 1. The accusation
Djavadi, N. Disoriental
Gao, X. Soul mountain
Goldberg, L. Fake truth
Han, K. Human acts
Harkaway, N. Gnomon
Kadare, I. The three-arched bridge

Kostova, E. The shadow land
Lopez, J. A beautiful young woman
Prescott, L. The secrets we kept
Ramzipoor, E. The ventriloquists
Seymour, G. Vagabond
Steele, A. Coyote

DISSENTERS -- SOVIET UNION
Holland, T. The archivist's story

DISSENTING OPINIONS
Bowman, V. Secrets of a wedding night

DISSERTATION WRITING
Broder, M. The pisces
Phillips, C. The Rossetti letter
Willig, L. The deception of the emerald ring
Willig, L. The secret history of the Pink Carnation

The **dissident** Freudenberger, N.

Dissident gardens Lethem, J.

DISSOCIATIVE IDENTITY DISORDER
Carey, M. Someone like me
Chung, M. The eighth girl
Ide, J. Hi five
McCall Smith, A. The No. 1 Ladies' Detective Agency
Stevenson, R. The strange case of Dr. Jekyll and Mr. Hyde

The **distant** echo McDermid, V.

A **distant** heart Dev, S.

The **distant** hours Morton, K.

The **distant** marvels Acevedo, C.

A **distant** shore Phillips, C.

Distant star Bolano, R.

DISTRESS (PSYCHOLOGY)
Demirtas, S. Dawn

DISTRICT ATTORNEYS
Doetsch, R. Half-past dawn
Johnson, R. No one in the world
Lippman, L. Wilde Lake
Stabenow, D. A deeper sleep
Wolfe, T. The bonfire of the vanities

Divas (De'nesha Diamond) [series] Diamond, D.

The **dive** from Clausen's pier Packer, A.

DIVERS
Egan, J. Manhattan Beach
Leonard, E. Tishomingo blues

A **divided** spy Cumming, C.

DIVINATION
Levack, S. Demon of the air
Saylor, S. The seven wonders
Saylor, S. The triumph of Caesar

Divine and human and other stories Tolstoy, L.

Divine cities [series] Bennett, R.

Divine secrets of the Ya-Ya Sisterhood Wells, R.

DIVING
Jackson, J. Never have I ever

A **diving** rock on the Hudson Roth, H.

DIVORCE
Anstruther, E. A perfect explanation
Bellow, S. Herzog
Bellow, S. Humboldt's gift

Cogburn, E. Ava's place
Corry, J. The dead ex
Davidson, D. Killer pancake
Davidson, D. The last suppers
Davis, F. The masterpiece
Dee, J. A thousand pardons
Dermansky, M. Very nice
Didion, J. Play it as it lays
Erdrich, L. The painted drum
Ferrante, E. The lost daughter
Fitten, M. Elza's kitchen
Gerritsen, T. The bone garden
Hampton, B. Stalker
Hawkins, P. The girl on the train
Hayder, M. Hanging hill
Henry, P. Becoming Mrs. Lewis
Higashino, K. The devotion of suspect X
Higashino, K. Newcomer
Jewell, L. Then she was gone
Lessing, D. The sweetest dream
Majors, I. Penelope Lemon
McKinty, A. The chain
McPherson, C. The child garden
McPherson, C. Scot free
McPherson, C. Scot & soda
Meier, L. Silver anniversary murder
Miller, S. The good mother
Miller, S. For love
Morgan, S. One summer in Paris
Naslund, S. The fountain of St. James Court
Ozick, C. Foreign bodies
Parker, R. Melancholy baby
Ryan, J. The spies of Shilling Lane
Scottoline, L. Come home
Sebold, A. The almost moon
Shalvis, J. The sweetest thing
Smith, J. If she were dead
Steel, D. First sight
Turner, B. The secret life of Sarah Hollenbeck
Updike, J. The witches of Eastwick
Vargas Llosa, M. Aunt Julia and the scriptwriter
Weatherspoon, R. Rafe
Woods, S. Palindrome
DIVORCED WOMEN -- VERMONT
Morris, M. Songs in ordinary time
DIXON, JEREMIAH, 1733-1779
Pynchon, T. Mason & Dixon
Djinn patrol on the purple line Anappara, D.
DNA
Chaon, D. Ill will
Cook, R. Genesis
Kosmatka, T. The games
DNA FINGERPRINTING
Dow, D. Confessions of an innocent man
Reichs, K. Deadly decisions
DNA TESTING
Anthony, M. Diary of a young girl

McDermid, V. The distant echo
Smith, M. She smiled sweetly
Do androids dream of electric sheep? Dick, P.
Do not become alarmed Meloy, M.
Do not say we have nothing Thien, M.
Do you want to start a scandal Dare, T.
DOBERMAN PINSCHERS
Woods, S. Orchid beach
Doc Russell, M.
Doc Ford novels [series] White, R.
Doc novels (Mary Doria Russell) [series] Russell, M.
DOCKS
Thomson, E. The blood
Doctor Faustus Mann, T.
Doctor No Fleming, I.
Doctor Sleep King, S.
Doctor Thorne Trollope, A.
Doctor Zhivago Pasternak, B.
The **doctor's** house Beattie, A.
DOCTORAL STUDENTS
Broder, M. The pisces
Senna, D. New people
Doctorow Doctorow, E.
DOCUMENTARY FILMMAKERS
Lipman, E. Good riddance
DOCUMENTARY FILMMAKERS -- CENTRAL AFRICA
Ballard, J. The day of creation
DOCUMENTARY FILMS
Danielewski, M. House of leaves
Koryta, M. So cold the river
Mitchard, J. No time to wave goodbye
Senna, D. New people
Valente, C. Radiance
**DOCUMENTARY FILMS -- PRODUCTION AND DIREC-
TION**
North, A. The life and death of Sophie Stark
The **documents** in the case Sayers, D.
DODD, MARTHA, 1908-1990
Chiaverini, J. Resistance women
DODGE CITY, KANSAS
Parker, R. Gunman's rhapsody
Russell, M. Doc
Dodge novels [series] Stephenson, N.
Dodgers Beverly, W.
Dodsworth Lewis, S.
DOG ADOPTION
Miller, M. Biloxi
Winthrop, E. The why of things
DOG BABY SITTERS
Broder, M. The pisces
DOG BREEDERS
Wroblewski, D. The story of Edgar Sawtelle
DOG BREEDING
Wroblewski, D. The story of Edgar Sawtelle
The **dog** of the South Portis, C.
Dog on it Quinn, S.
DOG OWNERS

Cather, W. O pioneers!
Cather, W. The song of the lark
Chabon, M. Moonglow
Cleary, J. The sundowners
Cline, R. My liar
Coe, J. The rain before it falls
Cohen, L. The grief of others
Cohen, T. The summer we lost her
Coleridge, N. Godchildren
Coleridge, N. A much married man
Colwin, L. Goodbye without leaving
Cook, D. Reservation nation
Cookson, C. The year of the virgins
Coomer, J. One vacant chair
Corman, A. Prized possessions
Cross-Smith, L. Whiskey & ribbons
Crummey, M. Sweetland
D'Agostino, K. The antiques
D'Souza, T. The Konkans
De los Santos, M. The precious one
DeBoard, P. The fragile world
DeCarlo, M. The art of crash landing
Dee, J. The locals
Dickens, C. The old curiosity shop
Diehl, H. Lifelines
Dillard, A. The Maytrees
Doerr, H. Stones for Ibarra
Doig, I. Mountain time
Edgarian, C. Three stages of amazement
Edwards, K. The memory keeper's daughter
Eliot, G. Middlemarch
Eliot, G. Silas Marner
Ellis, B. Lunar Park
Enger, L. Undiscovered country
Ephron, H. Careful what you wish for
Erdrich, L. LaRose
Erdrich, L. The Master Butchers Singing Club
Erdrich, L. The painted drum
Erdrich, L. The plague of doves
Evans, H. A place for us
Fabry, C. War room
Ferber, E. So big
Ferrante, E. The lost daughter
Ferris, J. The unnamed
Flaubert, G. Madame Bovary
Flournoy, A. The Turner house
Foer, J. Here I am
Ford, J. The shadow year
Forster, E. Howards End
Fowler, E. The road to Cardinal Valley
Fowler, T. A good neighborhood
Fox, L. Days of awe
Francis, D. Wedding Bush Road
Frank, D. Folly Beach
Frank, D. Queen bee
Frankel, L. This is how it always is
Friedland, E. The floating Feldmans

Friedland, E. The intermission
Fuller, C. Bitter orange
Gainza, M. The optic nerve
Gelman, L. Class mom
Genova, L. Inside the O'Briens
Gertler, S. Drifting
Gessen, K. All the sad young literary men
Gibbons, K. Ellen Foster
Gibbons, K. The life all around me by Ellen Foster
Gilb, D. The Flowers
Ginzburg, N. A family lexicon
Glass, J. The whole world over
Gordimer, N. Get a life
Grames, J. The seven or eight deaths of Stella Fortuna
Gray, A. The care and feeding of ravenously hungry girls
Griffin, A. When all is said
Grodstein, L. Our short history
Groff, L. Fates and furies
Hadley, T. The past
Hannah, K. The great alone
Hannah, K. Home front
Haruf, K. Eventide
Haruf, K. Plainsong
Hashemzadeh Bonde, G. What we owe
Heller, J. Good as Gold
Hill, N. The nix
Hoffman, A. Local girls
Hoffman, A. The probable future
Holsinger, B. The gifted school
House, S. A parchment of leaves
Jackson, J. The almost sisters
Jackson, N. The star side of Bird Hill
Jones, T. An American marriage
Joyce, G. The limits of enchantment
Just, W. An unfinished season
Kantra, V. Meg and Jo
Kenney, J. Talk to me
Kimmel, F. No good asking
Kincaid, J. Annie John
Kneale, M. When we were Romans
Leroy, M. Postcards from Berlin
Lessing, D. Landlocked
Lessing, D. A proper marriage
Levitt, P. Come with me to Babylon
Lewis, B. The brethren
Lewis, B. The preacher's daughter
Lewis, S. Dodsworth
Lipman, E. The family man
Llywelyn, M. 1949
Lodato, V. Edgar and Lucy
Loh, V. Breaking the tongue , by Vyvyane Loh.
Loigman, L. The two-family house
Lordan, B. But come ye back , Beth Lordan
MacLaverty, B. Midwinter break
Mahmoud, L. Amreekiya
Markandaya, K. Nectar in a sieve
Mason, B. Patchwork

DOMESTIC TERRORISM

DOMINANCE (PSYCHOLOGY)

Morrison, T. Love

DOMINICA

Kincaid, J. The autobiography of my mother

DOMINICAN AMERICAN FAMILIES

Alvarez, J. How the Garcia girls lost their accents

DOMINICAN AMERICAN WOMEN

Alvarez, J. How the Garcia girls lost their accents

DOMINICAN AMERICANS

Diaz, J. The brief wondrous life of Oscar Wao

DOMINICAN REPUBLIC

Alvarez, J. How the Garcia girls lost their accents

Coster, N. Halsey Street

Cruz, A. Dominicana

Danticat, E. The farming of bones

DOMINICAN REPUBLIC -- POLITICS AND GOVERN-MENT

Vargas Llosa, M. The feast of the Goat

DOMINICAN-HAITIAN CONFLICT, 1937

Danticat, E. The farming of bones

Dominicana Cruz, A.

DOMINICANS (DOMINICAN REPUBLIC)

Zapata, M. The lost book of Adana Moreau

Dominika Egorova and Nathaniel Nash novels [series] Matthews, J.

Domino King, R.

Domino Falls Barnes, S.

The **don** con Armstrong, R.

The **Don** flows home to the sea Sholokhov, M.

Don Juan Handke, P.

DON JUAN (LEGENDARY CHARACTER)

Handke, P. Don Juan

Don Quixote Cervantes Saavedra, M.

Don't ask Westlake, D.

Don't call it night Oz, A.

Don't cry Gaitskill, M.

Don't cry Tai Lake Qiu, X.

Don't eat me Cotterill, C.

Don't ever get old Friedman, D.

Don't go Scottoline, L.

Don't let go Coben, H.

Don't send flowers Solares, M.

Don't skip out on me Vlautin, W.

Don't tell a soul Rosenfelt, D.

Don't tempt me Chase, L.

Don't turn around Barry, J.

Don't wake up Lawler, L.

Don't you forget about me McFarlane, M.

Dona Flor and her two husbands Amado, J.

DONATION OF ORGANS, TISSUES, ETC

Cleave, P. A killer harvest

Cook, R. Coma

Ishiguro, K. Never let me go

Picoult, J. My sister's keeper

DONG-JU, YUN

Yi, C. The investigation

Donna has left the building Gilman, S.

DONNER PARTY

Katsu, A. The hunger

Preston, D. Old bones

Donnerjack Zelazny, R.

Donovan Family [series] Lowell, E.

Doomed to die Simpson, D.

DOOMSAYERS

Coover, R. The origin of the Brunists

Doomsday book Willis, C.

A **door** in the earth Waldman, A.

DOOR-TO-DOOR SALES FRAUD

Brown, J. Addie Pray

DOOR-TO-DOOR SELLING

Morrison, T. Jazz

The **doorbell** rang Stout, R.

DOORWAYS

Warrington, F. Elfland

Warrington, F. Grail of the summer stars

Warrington, F. Midsummer night

The **dopefiend** JaQuavis

Dopeman's trilogy [series] JaQuavis

The **dopeman's** wife JaQuavis

DOPING IN SPORTS

Lohmann, J. Winning Ruby Heart

DOPPELGANGERS

Conrad, J. Heart of darkness

Donohue, K. The stolen child

Glynn, A. Paradime

Redhill, M. Bellevue square

Rice, A. Blackwood farm

DORCHESTER, BOSTON, MASSACHUSETTS

Lehane, D. Prayers for rain

DORSET, ENGLAND

James, P. The black tower

James, P. The private patient

Kelly, E. Broadchurch

Dortmunder novels [series] Westlake, D.

DOSTOYEVSKY, FYODOR, 1821-1881 TRAVEL EUROPE

Tsypkin, L. Summer in Baden-Baden

The **double** Pelecanos, G.

DOUBLE AGENTS

Bourne, J. Rogue spy

Coughlin, J. Long shot

Follett, K. Eye of the needle

Furst, A. The spies of Warsaw

Greene, G. The human factor

Kerr, P. Prussian blue

Le Carre, J. The spy who came in from the cold

Matthews, J. The Kremlin's candidate

Matthews, J. Palace of treason

Nguyen, V. The sympathizer

Sebastian, T. Fatal ally

Seymour, G. Vagabond

Spillane, M. The Consummata

Woods, S. Skin game

The **double** bind Bohjalian, C.

The **Double** Comfort Safari Club McCall Smith, A.

Antoinette, A. The Cartel 3
Anthony, M. Diary of a young girl
Bryant, N. Madam, may I
Bryant, N. Message from a mistress
Dickey, E. Bad men and wicked women
Dickey, E. Before we were wicked
Dickey, E. The blackbirds
Dickey, E. Finding Gideon
Ervin, K. Gunz and roses
Ervin, K. Mina's joint
Hampton, B. Stalker
Harris, E. Basketball Jones
Harris, E. Not a day goes by
Hobbs, A. Stealing candy
King, D. Bitch
Monroe, M. Bad blood
Monroe, M. God don't like ugly
Monroe, M. God still don't like ugly
Mosley, W. Debbie doesn't do it anymore
Murray, V. Lust
Mychea He loves me, he loves you not
Mychea My boyfriend's wife
Stringer, V. Dirty Red
Stringer, V. Let that be the reason
Stringer, V. Still dirty
Styles, T. Black and ugly
Swinson, K. A gangster and a gentleman
Swinson, K. Who's wife extraordinaire now
Warren, T. Her secret life
Warren, T. The pastor's husband

DRAMATISTS
Groff, L. Fates and furies
Miller, A. Oxygen
Morgan, J. The secret life of William Shakespeare
O'Connell, C. It happens in the dark
Phillips, A. The tragedy of Arthur

DRAMATISTS, AMERICAN
Bram, C. Lives of the circus animals
Toibin, C. The master

DRAMATISTS, AMERICAN -- 20TH CENTURY
Gaddis, W. A frolic of his own

DRAMATISTS, ENGLISH
Brandreth, B. The assassin of Verona
Brandreth, B. The spy of Venice

DRAMATISTS, IRISH
O'Connor, J. Ghost light

DRAWING
Brenner, J. Drawing home
Kawakami, M. Ms. Ice Sandwich

DRAWING -- PSYCHOLOGICAL ASPECTS
Kellerman, J. The genius
Drawing conclusions Leon, D.
Drawing home Brenner, J.
Dreadful company Shaw, V.
Dreadful young ladies and other stories Barnhill, K.
Dreadnought Priest, C.
Dream of Ding Village Yan, L.

The **dream** of perpetual motion Palmer, D.
The **dream** of Scipio Pears, I.
The **dream** of the Celt Vargas Llosa, M.
The **dream** peddler Watson, M.
The **dream-quest** of Vellitt Boe Johnson, K.
Dreamblood duology [series] Jemisin, N.
The **dreamers** Walker, K.
Dreamers of the day Russell, M.
Dreaming in Cuban Garcia, C.
The **dreaming** void Hamilton, P.
Dreaming water Tsukiyama, G.

DREAMS
Apelfeld, A. The man who never stopped sleeping
Bailey, P. Chapman's odyssey
Boyden, J. Through black spruce
Brinkman, K. Up high in the trees
Burns, C. Black hole
Chariandy, D. Brother
Coelho, P. The alchemist
Dekker, T. Black
Dekker, T. Red
Dekker, T. White
Enard, M. Compass
Fforde, J. Early riser
Frei, M. The stranger's magic
Helprin, M. Winter's tale
Hoffman, A. The probable future
Iles, G. The footprints of God
Irving, J. Avenue of mysteries
Jemisin, N. The killing moon
Johnson, K. The dream-quest of Vellitt Boe
Jones, D. Second grave on the left
Joyce, J. Finnegans wake
Kiernan, C. The drowning girl
Le Guin, U. The lathe of heaven
Le Guin, U. The other wind
Levack, S. Demon of the air
Lightman, A. Einstein's dreams
Ma, J. China dream
Newman, S. The heavens
Oakley, C. You were there too
Pickard, N. The scent of rain and lightning
Silko, L. Gardens in the dunes
Sosin, D. The long-shining waters
Suri, T. Realm of ash
Walker, K. The dreamers
Watson, M. The dream peddler
Wurlitzer, R. The drop edge of yonder
Dreams of a dark warrior Cole, K.
Dreams of joy See, L.
Dreams of my Russian summers Makine, A.
Dresden files [series] Butcher, J.

DRESDEN, GERMANY -- BOMBING, 1945
Vonnegut, K. Slaughterhouse-five

DRESDEN, GERMANY -- BOMBING, 1945 -- INFLU-ENCE
Foer, J. Extremely loud and incredibly close

Gregory, D. Afterparty
Hayder, M. Ritual
Meyer, N. The seven-per-cent solution
Nelson, C. More than we remember
Newman, J. Mary

DRUG ABUSE AND CRIME
Holmes, S. B-more careful
Turner, N. A hustler's wife
Woods, T. True to the game
Woods, T. True to the game II
Woods, T. True to the game III

DRUG ABUSE TREATMENT CENTERS AND CLINICS
Haddam, J. Hardscrabble road

DRUG ABUSERS
Anshaw, C. Carry the one
Ellis, M. Keeping bedlam at bay in the Prague Cafe
Koryta, M. How it happened
Kushner, R. The Mars room
McBain, E. The big bad city
Umrigar, T. Everybody's son

DRUG ABUSERS -- REHABILITATION
Meyer, N. The seven-per-cent solution

DRUG ADDICTION
Butler, K. Pretty ugly
Chaon, D. Ill will
Cunningham, M. The snow queen
Gregory, D. Afterparty
Hannaham, J. Delicious foods
Keller, J. Bone on bone
Markley, S. Ohio
Sanders, L. The Timothy files
Sexton, M. A kind of freedom
Williams, K. Harlem on lock
Wilhelm, K. Where late the sweet birds sang

DRUG ADDICTS
Algren, N. The man with the golden arm
Beagin, J. Vacuum in the dark
Burroughs, W. Naked lunch
Cash Trust no man
Cheever, J. Falconer
Crosbie, L. Where did you sleep last night?
Fossum, K. Bad intentions
Hallinan, T. Crashed
Himes, C. Cotton comes to Harlem
JaQuavis The dopefiend
K'wan The fix
Keller, J. Bone on bone
Little, T. Where there's smoke
Meno, J. Marvel and a wonder
O'Malley, T. We were kings
Rimmer, K. Before I let you go
Stephenson, N. Cryptonomicon
Walker, N. Cherry

DRUG ADDICTS -- EDINBURGH, SCOTLAND
Welsh, I. Dead men's trousers
Welsh, I. Porno
Welsh, I. Skagboys

Welsh, I. Trainspotting
DRUG CARTELS
Atkins, A. The lost ones
Gruber, M. The return
Kent, K. The burn
Kent, K. The dime
McLaughlin, J. Bearskin
Sandford, J. Golden prey
Soderberg, A. The other son
Winslow, D. The border
Winslow, D. The cartel

DRUG CONTROL
Gregory, D. Afterparty
Huston, C. The shotgun rule

DRUG COURIERS
Levine, J. Bingo's run
Parker, T. The famous and the dead

DRUG CULTURE
Boyle, T. Outside looking in
Woodrell, D. Winter's bone

DRUG DEALERS
50 Cent, (. Blow
Atkins, A. The sinners
Barker, N. Darkmans
Bouman, T. Dry bones in the valley
Brekke, J. The fifth element
Brookmyre, C. Where the bodies are buried
Brookmyre, C. When the devil drives
Capri, N. The pussy trap
Carcaterra, L. Tin badges
Child, L. Persuader
Clark, W. Payback ain't enough
Clark, W. Payback with ya life
Connelly, M. The night fire
Connelly, M. The scarecrow
Corry, J. The dead ex
Dalton, T. Boy swallows universe
Diamond, D. Boss divas
Diamond, D. Gangsta divas
Diamond, D. King divas
Diamond, D. Street divas
Doiron, P. Bad Little Falls
Ervin, K. Gunz and roses
Everett, P. Suder
Hand, E. Curious toys
Hayder, M. Birdman
Haywood, G. Cemetery Road
Holmes, S. B-more careful
Huston, C. The shotgun rule
Ibrahim, A. Season of crimson blossoms
JaQuavis The dopeman's wife
JaQuavis The streets have no king
K'wan Diamonds and Pearl
Keller, J. Fast falls the night
Lange, R. Angel baby
Lansdale, J. Vanilla Ride
Leonard, E. Raylan

James, M. A brief history of seven killings
K'wan The Diamond empire
K'wan Diamonds and Pearl
K'wan Section 8
K'wan Street dreams
Kamal, S. It all falls down
Keller, J. Fast falls the night
Keller, J. A killing in the hills
Kent, K. The burn
Kent, K. The dime
Lee, F. Jade City
Mark, D. Original skin
Mark, D. Sorrow bound
Martin, K. Beyond reason
McBride, J. Deacon King Kong
McCarthy, C. No country for old men
Mcdonald, G. Fletch
Mizushima, M. Killing trail
Muller, M. A walk through the fire
Nesbo, J. Phantom
Noire Candy licker
Noire G-Spot
O'Donovan, G. Dublin dead
Panowich, B. Bull Mountain
Panowich, B. Like lions
Parker, R. Valediction
Parker, T. The famous and the dead
Pelecanos, G. Drama city
Pelecanos, G. Hard revolution
Pelecanos, G. Soul circus
Pelecanos, G. The sweet forever
Price, R. Clockers
Ramsay, F. Stranger room
Rash, R. Above the waterfall
Rojas Contreras, I. Fruit of the drunken tree
Sayers, D. Murder must advertise
Sharpe, T. Barbed wire heart
Silko, L. Almanac of the dead
Smith, B. Crow's landing
Snipes, W. Talon of God
Souljah, S. The coldest winter ever
Spencer-Fleming, J. I shall not want
Stringer, V. Let that be the reason
Styles, T. A hustler's son
Styles, T. Raunchy
Styles, T. Raunchy 2
Swinson, K. I'm New York's finest
Swinson, K. The safe house
Swinson, K. Wifey
Swinson, K. Wifey's next sticky situation
T. I. Power & Beauty
T. I. Trouble & triumph
Turner, N. A hustler's wife
Turner, N. Natural born hustler
Williams, K. Sweet Giselle
Winslow, D. The border
Winslow, D. The cartel

Winslow, D. The kings of cool
Winslow, D. Savages
Woodrell, D. Winter's bone
Woods, T. True to the game
Woods, T. True to the game II
Woods, T. True to the game III

DRUG TRAFFIC -- COLOMBIA
Vasquez, J. The sound of things falling
DRUG TRAFFIC INVESTIGATION
Carcaterra, L. Tin badges
DRUG USE
Blau, J. The Wonder Bread summer
Boyle, T. Outside looking in
Buntin, J. Marlena
Byrne, T. Ghosts and lightning
Canin, E. A doubter's almanac
Cooper, T. The marauders
Crumley, J. Bordersnakes
Crumley, J. The final country
Didion, J. Play it as it lays
Doyle, R. Threshold
Drury, T. Pacific
DuPree, K. Shattered
Goldberg, T. Gangsterland
Gran, S. Claire DeWitt and the city of the dead
Higgins, J. Midnight runner
Holmes, S. Bad girlz
K'wan The fix
Kinder, C. Honeymooners
Lethem, J. Chronic city
Lowe, K. The furies
Naam, R. Nexus
Nemett, A. We can save us all
Oates, J. Blonde
Pelecanos, G. The big blowdown
Pelevin, V. The hall of singing caryatids
Polansky, D. Low town
Reid, T. Daisy Jones & the Six
Rendell, R. The babes in the wood
Souljah,. The coldest winter ever
Styles, T. Black and ugly
Tartt, D. The goldfinch
Walsh, H. Brass
Wolfe, T. I am Charlotte Simmons
DRUG WITHDRAWAL SYMPTOMS
Burroughs, W. Naked lunch
DRUGS
Box, C. Badlands
Clark, W. Honor thy thug
Clark, W. Justify my thug
Clark, W. Thug lovin'
Conlon, E. Red on red
Hannaham, J. Delicious foods
Moody, R. Right livelihoods
Moshfegh, O. My year of rest and relaxation
Naam, R. Nexus
Nesbo, J. Phantom

Dare, T. The wallflower wager
Dunmore, E. Bringing down the duke
Force, M. Deceived by desire
Frampton, M. The duke's guide to correct behavior
Frampton, M. Put up your duke
Galen, S. Third son's a charm
Goodwin, D. The American heiress
Gray, J. A duke never yields
Gray, J. How to tame your duke
Guhrke, L. How to lose a duke in ten days
Guhrke, L. The truth about love and dukes
Harrington, A. An inconvenient duke
Heath, L. Falling into bed with a duke
Herbert, F. Dune
Heyer, G. These old shades
Hunter, J. Forbidden to love the duke
James, E. Desperate duchesses
James, E. Four nights with the duke
James, E. Seven minutes in heaven
James, E. The ugly duchess
Jeffries, S. Project Duchess
Jeffries, S. What the duke desires
Johnson, M. Smitten by the Brit
Kerstan, L. Heart of the tiger
Laurens, S. Devil's bride
London, J. The trouble with honor
Lorret, V. How to forget a duke
MacLean, S. No good duke goes unpunished
MacLean, S. Wicked and the wallflower
Milan, C. The duchess war
Moore, K. To seduce an angel
Nash, S. Between the Duke and the deep blue sea
Pratchett, T. Monstrous regiment
Quinn, J. The lady most willing
Ranney, K. The Scottish duke
Sayers, D. Whose body?
Seton, A. Katherine
Shupe, J. The courtesan duchess
Thomas, S. Beguiling the beauty
Trollope, A. The Prime Minister
Williams, B. The golden hour
Dukes behaving badly [series] Frampton, M.
DULA, TOM, 1843 OR 4-1868
McCrumb, S. The ballad of Tom Dooley
Dulcie Schwartz feline-filled mysteries [series] Simon, C.
DULUTH, MINNESOTA
Freeman, B. Goodbye to the dead
Freeman, B. Marathon
DUMAS, ALEXANDER, 1802-1870 THREE MUSKE-TEERS
Perez-Reverte, A. The Club Dumas
Duncan Kincaid and Gemma James mysteries [series]
  Crombie, D.
Dune Herbert, F.
Dune novels. Main series [series] Herbert, F.
Duplex Davis, K.

DURHAM, ENGLAND -- SOCIAL LIFE AND CUSTOMS -- 18TH CENTURY
Unsworth, B. The quality of mercy
DUSSELDORF, GERMANY
Diehl, H. Lifelines
DUST BOWL (SOUTH CENTRAL UNITED STATES)
Steinbeck, J. The grapes of wrath
DUST BOWL ERA, 1931-1939
Meadows, R. I will send rain
DUST STORMS
Weir, A. The Martian
DUTCH
Woods, T. Dutch
Dutch Woods, T.
DUTCH AMERICAN WOMEN
Zimmerman, J. The orphanmaster
DUTCH AMERICANS
Boyle, T. World's end
The **Dutch** house Patchett, A.
DUTCH IN JAPAN
Mitchell, D. The thousand autumns of Jacob De Zoet
DUTCH IN SOUTH AFRICA
Michener, J. The covenant
DUTCH IN SWEDEN
Furst, A. Dark voyage
DUTCH IN THE UNITED STATES
O'Neill, J. Netherland
Dutch novels [series] Woods, T.
DUTY
Balogh, M. The secret mistress
Bausch, R. Peace
Bouchet, A. Breath of fire
Bouchet, A. A promise of fire
Burrowes, G. The bridegroom wore plaid
Cornwell, B. Sword of kings
Cornwell, B. War of the wolf
Cruz, A. Dominicana
Esquivel, L. Like water for chocolate
Hauck, R. Once upon a prince
Iles, G. The bone tree
Iles, G. Natchez burning
Jin, H. Waiting
Kadare, I. The general of the dead army
Long, J. Lady Derring takes a lover
Lukas, M. The last watchman of Old Cairo
McCullough, C. An indecent obsession
Remarque, E. All quiet on the western front
DWARVES (FANTASY CHARACTERS)
Kay, G. The summer tree
Pratchett, T. The fifth elephant
Pratchett, T. Guards! Guards!
Pratchett, T. Lords and ladies
Pratchett, T. Men at arms
Pratchett, T. Thud!
Tolkien, J. The children of Hurin
Tolkien, J. The fellowship of the ring
Tolkien, J. The hobbit, or, there and back again

Walker, W. Emma in the night
Wallace, D. Infinite jest
Warrington, F. Elfland
Watson, L. As good as gone
Weiner, J. In her shoes
Williams, K. Dirty to the grave
Wilson, K. The family Fang
Winslow, D. In West Mills
Wolfe, T. Look homeward, angel
Woodrell, D. Winter's bone
Zailckas, K. Mother, mother

DYSFUNCTIONAL FAMILIES -- LOS ANGELES, CALI-FORNIA

See, C. There will never be another you

DYSFUNCTIONAL FAMILIES -- NEW YORK (STATE)

Torres, J. We the animals

DYSFUNCTIONAL FAMILIES -- SOUTH CAROLINA

Conroy, P. The prince of tides

DYSTOPIAN FICTION

Angelo, M. Followers
Atwood, M. The handmaid's tale
Atwood, M. The testaments
Bacigalupi, P. The water knife
Bacigalupi, P. The windup girl
Barry, K. City of Bohane
Bradbury, R. Fahrenheit 451
Broun, B. Night of the animals
Brown, P. Golden son
Brown, P. Morning star
Brown, P. Red rising
Burgess, A. A clockwork orange
Butler, O. Parable of the sower
Butler, O. Parable of the talents
Chanter, C. The well
Chen, Q. Waste tide
Doctorow, C. Radicalized
El Akkad, O. American war
Erdrich, L. Future home of the living god
Fforde, J. Early riser
Graedon, A. The word exchange
Haig, F. The fire sermon
Harkaway, N. Gnomon
Hart, R. The warehouse
Heinlein, R. The moon is a harsh mistress
Huxley, A. Brave new world
Jen, G. The resisters
Kafka, F. The castle
Koestler, A. Darkness at noon
Le Guin, U. The dispossessed
Lee, C. On such a full sea
Locke, T. Enclave
Melamed, J. Gather the daughters
Ogawa, Y. The memory police
Older, M. Infomocracy
Onyebuchi, T. Riot baby
Orwell, G. 1984
Orwell, G. Animal farm

A people's future of the United States
Sakey, M. A better world
Sakey, M. Brilliance
Shannon, S. The bone season
Shannon, S. The mime order
Stevens, F. The heads of Cerberus
Tawada, Y. The emissary
Tolstaya, T. The slynx
Valentine, G. Mechanique
VanderMeer, J. Dead astronauts
Vonnegut, K. Player piano
Watkins, C. Gold fame citrus
Wells, H. The time machine
Zamyatin, Y. We
Zumas, L. Red clocks

DYSTOPIAS

Anders, C. The city in the middle of the night
Atwood, M. The handmaid's tale
Atwood, M. Maddaddam
Atwood, M. Oryx and Crake
Atwood, M. The year of the flood
Auster, P. In the country of last things
Bacigalupi, P. The windup girl
Banks, I. The hydrogen sonata
Banks, I. Matter
Bradbury, R. Fahrenheit 451
Broun, B. Night of the animals
Brown, P. Golden son
Brown, P. Morning star
Brown, P. Red rising
Burgess, A. A clockwork orange
Butler, O. Adulthood rites
Butler, O. Parable of the sower
Butler, O. Parable of the talents
Cline, E. Ready player one
Dick, P. Do androids dream of electric sheep?
Fforde, J. Shades of grey
Gibson, W. Neuromancer
Gibson, W. The peripheral
Gilman, F. The half-made world
Gladstone, M. Empress of forever
Graedon, A. The word exchange
Grant, M. Blackout
Grant, M. Feed
Grant, M. Feedback
Grant, M. Deadline
Haig, F. The fire sermon
Harkaway, N. The gone-away world
Harkaway, N. Gnomon
Hart, R. The warehouse
Heinlein, R. The moon is a harsh mistress
Heinlein, R. Starship troopers
Huxley, A. Brave new world
Jordan, H. When she woke
Le Guin, U. The dispossessed
Lee, C. On such a full sea
Liu, K. Invisible planets

EAST AND WEST
Mitchell, D. The thousand autumns of Jacob De Zoet

EAST ANGLIA, ENGLAND
Gash, J. The rich and the profane
James, P. Death in holy orders
Royal, P. Covenant with hell
Royal, P. Sanctity of hate
Royal, P. Satan's lullaby

EAST GERMANY
Grass, G. Too far afield

EAST INDIA COMPANY (ENGLISH)
Carter, M. The strangler vine

EAST INDIAN AMERICAN MEN
Mehta, R. Quarantine

EAST INDIAN AMERICAN WOMEN
Oleksiw, S. The wrath of Shiva

EAST INDIAN AMERICANS
Dev, S. The Bollywood bride
Dev, S. Pride, prejudice, and other flavors
Ghosh, A. Gun Island
Mehta, R. No other world
Mirza, F. A place for us
Mukherjee, N. A state of freedom
Raheem, Z. The marriage clock
Satyal, R. No one can pronounce my name

EAST INDIAN AMERICANS -- SOCIAL LIFE AND CUS-TOMS
Lahiri, J. The namesake

EAST INDIAN BRITISH MEN
Balasubramanyam, R. Professor Chandra follows his bliss

EAST INDIAN IMMIGRANTS
Winkler, A. Dog war

EAST INDIAN-AMERICAN IMMIGRANTS
Lahiri, J. The namesake

EAST INDIAN-AMERICAN WOMEN
Sekaran, S. Lucky boy

EAST INDIANS
Anappara, D. Djinn patrol on the purple line
Kunzru, H. The impressionist
Mukherjee, N. A life apart
Naipaul, V. A house for Mr. Biswas
Rushdie, S. The satanic verses
Sidhu, R. Good Indian girls

EAST INDIANS IN AFRICA
Kimani, P. Dance of the Jakaranda
Naipaul, V. A bend in the river

EAST INDIANS IN CANADA
Lalli, S. The matchmaker's list

EAST INDIANS IN ENGLAND
Collins, W. The moonstone
Keating, H. The soft detective
Kunzru, H. The impressionist
Naipaul, V. Magic seeds
Sahota, S. The year of the runaways

EAST INDIANS IN GREAT BRITAIN
Mukherjee, N. A state of freedom

EAST INDIANS IN LONDON, ENGLAND

Naipaul, V. Half a life

EAST INDIANS IN THE UNITED STATES
D'Souza, T. The Konkans
Desai, K. The inheritance of loss
Dev, S. A Bollywood affair
Divakaruni, C. Oleander girl
Murr, N. The perfect man
Winkler, A. Dog war

East is east Lathen, E.

EAST MIDLANDS, ENGLAND
Townsend, S. Number 10

East of Eden Steinbeck, J.

EAST TENNESSEE
Bledsoe, A. Gather her round
Bledsoe, A. The hum and the shiver
Bledsoe, A. Long black curl
Bledsoe, A. Wisp of a thing

EAST TEXAS
Lansdale, J. Sunset and sawdust
Lansdale, J. The thicket

EAST TEXAS -- RACE RELATIONS
Lansdale, J. The bottoms

EAST VILLAGE, NEW YORK CITY
Epstein, J. Wunderland

East, West Rushdie, S.

EAST-WEST RELATIONS
Rushdie, S. East, West
Uris, L. Armageddon

EASTER
Penny, L. The cruelest month

EASTER ISLAND
Vanderbes, J. Easter Island

Easter Island Vanderbes, J.

EASTER RISING, 1916
Doyle, R. A star called Henry
Llywelyn, M. 1916
O'Neill, J. At swim, two boys
Uris, L. Redemption

EASTERN EUROPE
Egan, J. The keep
Kostova, E. The shadow land
Le Guin, U. Orsinian tales
Mieville, C. The city & the city
Powell, M. Firebird
Steinhauer, O. The Bridge of Sighs
Wolfe, G. The land across

Eastern European crime series [series] Steinhauer, O.

EASTERN EUROPEANS IN THE UNITED STATES
Rosen, L. The Kortelisy escape

EASTERN RELIGIONS
Robinson, K. The years of rice and salt

EASTERN SHORE, MARYLAND
Roberts, N. Chesapeake blue

Easy prey Sandford, J.

Easy Rawlins mysteries [series] Mosley, W.

EATING DISORDERS
Thomas, S. Oligarchy

Weiner, J. Mrs. Everything

EAVESDROPPING

Berg, G. The operator

Ullman, E. By blood

The **ebb** tide Lewis, B.

ECCENTRIC BOYS

Porter, M. Lanny

ECCENTRIC FAMILIES

Atkinson, K. Human croquet

Ashford, J. Lord Sebastian's secret

Jackson, S. We have always lived in the castle

Jones, S. The uninvited guests

Lutz, L. Curse of the Spellmans

Lutz, L. The last word

Lutz, L. The Spellman files

Proulx, A. Postcards

Smith, D. I capture the castle

Wharton, E. The children

ECCENTRIC GIRLS

Scott, J. Tourmaline

ECCENTRIC MEN

Beagle, P. A fine and private place

Cervantes Saavedra, M. Don Quixote

Cheever, J. Bullet Park

Gilbert, D. & sons

Munro, A. Lives of girls and women

Pyper, A. The homecoming

Shteyngart, G. Super sad true love story

Stout, R. The doorbell rang

Stout, R. Gambit

ECCENTRIC MEN -- AUSTRIA

Bernhard, T. Frost

ECCENTRIC MOTHERS

Butler, K. Pretty ugly

ECCENTRIC PARENTS

Bourdeaut, O. Waiting for Bojangles

ECCENTRIC WOMEN

Childress, M. Crazy in Alabama

Drabble, M. The witch of Exmoor

Gaitskill, M. Veronica

MacLean, S. One good earl deserves a lover

McQuiston, J. The spinster's guide to scandalous behavior

Simpson, M. Anywhere but here

Steinke, R. Holy skirts

Winslow, D. In West Mills

ECCENTRICS AND ECCENTRICITIES

Arnett, K. Mostly dead things

Auster, P. The Brooklyn follies

Backman, F. My grandmother asked me to tell you she's sorry

Baker, T. The little giant of Aberdeen County

Barker, N. Darkmans

Bellow, S. The adventures of Augie March

Boyle, T. The relive box

Boyne, J. The heart's invisible furies

Brown, R. Six of one

Calvino, I. The baron in the trees

Carter, A. Nights at the circus

Cheng, B. Southern cross the dog

Colfer, E. Plugged

Cotterill, C. Killed at the whim of a hat

Coupland, D. Microserfs

Crummey, M. Sweetland

Cusset, C. Life of David Hockney

DeLillo, D. White noise

Diaz, J. The brief wondrous life of Oscar Wao

Dickens, C. Nicholas Nickleby

Dicks, M. Unexpectedly, Milo

Doctorow, E. Homer and Langley

Dodd, C. Because I'm watching

Doyle, A. The complete Sherlock Holmes

Drury, T. The driftless area

Dufresne, J. Deep in the shade of paradise

Echenoz, J. Lightning

Ellis, M. Keeping bedlam at bay in the Prague Cafe

Enger, L. Virgil Wander

Evison, J. All about Lulu

Evison, J. West of here

Fowler, C. Bryant & May

Gaige, A. Schroder

Gallagher, S. The bedlam detective

Gander, F. As a friend

Gray, J. A lady never lies

Hoeg, P. The history of Danish dreams

Hosking, J. Three years with the rat

Irving, J. The world according to Garp

Kane, J. Rules for visiting

Kidd, J. Things in jars

Kroese, R. The last iota

Kunzru, H. Gods without men

Lourey, J. January thaw

Luiselli, V. The story of my teeth

Makkai, R. The hundred-year house

McCall Smith, A. The Department of Sensitive Crimes

McCracken, E. Bowlaway

McMurtry, L. Sin killer

McMurtry, L. Terms of endearment

Mortimer, J. Quite honestly

Mukherjee, B. Miss new India

Murakami, H. Kafka on the shore

Niffenegger, A. The time traveler's wife

O'Connor, F. Wise blood

Ondaatje, M. Warlight

Osondu, E. This house is not for sale

Palmer, D. Mary Toft; or, the rabbit queen

Perec, G. Life

Perez, R. Jim Henson's tale of sand

Pessl, M. Special topics in calamity physics

Pietroni, A. Ruby's spoon

Pistalo, V. Tesla

Racculia, K. Bellweather rhapsody

Ridgway, K. Hawthorn & Child

Robbins, T. Fierce invalids home from hot climates

Robbins, T. Jitterbug perfume

Robbins, T. Skinny legs and all
Robbins, T. Still life with Woodpecker
Rock, P. The shelter cycle
Ruiz Zafon, C. The prisoner of heaven
Ruiz Zafon, C. The shadow of the wind
Saums, M. Thistle & Twigg
Sayers, D. Whose body?
Sherrill, S. The minotaur takes his own sweet time
Spark, M. A far cry from Kensington
Stephens, A. Famous adopted people
Stibbe, N. Reasons to be cheerful
Tokarczuk, O. Flights
Trigiani, A. Big Cherry Holler
Trigiani, A. Big Stone Gap
Tyler, A. A patchwork planet
Varley, J. Dark lightning
Varley, J. Red lightning
Wallace, C. The blind contessa's new machine
Wallace, D. Big fish
Wallace, D. The watermelon king
White, B. Quite a year for plums
Wright, A. Carpentaria
Echo burning Child, L.
An **echo** in the bone Gabaldon, D.
The **echo** killing Daugherty, C.
The **echo** maker Powers, R.
Echo Park Connelly, M.
ECHO PARK, LOS ANGELES, CALIFORNIA
Skyhorse, B. Madonnas of Echo Park
Echoes of the dead Spencer, S.
Eclipse Banville, J.
Eclipse Patterson, R.
ECO-TERRORISM
Glass, J. The widower's tale
See, C. There will never be another you
ECO-TERRORISTS
Box, C. Savage run
Cussler, C. Blue gold
ECOLOGICAL DISTURBANCES
Modesitt, L. The one-eyed man
ECOLOGISTS
Gordimer, N. Get a life
Modesitt, L. The one-eyed man
ECOLOGY
Atwood, M. Oryx and Crake
Fowler, T. A good neighborhood
Kingsolver, B. Flight behavior
Robinson, K. Antarctica
ECONOMIC ASSISTANCE, AMERICAN
Wibberley, L. The mouse that roared
ECONOMIC DEVELOPMENT
Binchy, M. Whitethorn Woods
Lispector, C. The besieged city
ECONOMISTS
Balasubramanyam, R. Professor Chandra follows his bliss
ECSTASY (CHRISTIANITY)
Hansen, R. Mariette in ecstasy

Ed Eagle novels [series] Woods, S.
Ed King Guterson, D.
Edda of burdens [series] Bear, E.
Eddie Flynn novels [series] Cavanagh, S.
Eden Lem, S.
Eden Close Shreve, A.
Eden mine Hulse, S.
Edgar Allan Poe and the jewel of Peru Street, K.
Edgar and Lucy Lodato, V.
Edge Deaver, J.
Edge of danger Higgins, J.
Edge of dark water Lansdale, J.
Edge of eternity Follett, K.
The **edge** of impropriety Rosenthal, P.
The **edge** of the Earth Schwarz, C.
EDINBURGH, SCOTLAND
Atkinson, K. One good turn
Atkinson, K. When will there be good news?
McCall Smith, A. The forgotten affairs of youth
McCall Smith, A. The lost art of gratitude
Parry, A. The way of all flesh
Rankin, I. Black and blue
Rankin, I. The black book
Rankin, I. The beat goes on
Rankin, I. The complaints
Rankin, I. Dead souls
Rankin, I. Exit music
Rankin, I. The falls
Rankin, I. The hanging garden
Rankin, I. The impossible dead
Rankin, I. The naming of the dead
Rankin, I. A question of blood
Rankin, I. Rather be the devil
Rankin, I. Resurrection men
Rankin, I. Set in darkness
Spark, M. The prime of Miss Jean Brodie
Townsend, S. Number 10
Welsh, I. Dead men's trousers
Welsh, I. Porno
Welsh, I. Skagboys
Welsh, I. Trainspotting
Welsh, K. The unquiet heart
Welsh, K. The wages of sin
Wojtas, O. Miss Blaine's prefect and the golden samovar
EDINBURGH, SCOTLAND -- HISTORY -- 19TH CEN-TURY
Perry, A. The sins of the wolf
Pirie, D. The patient's eyes
The **Edison** effect Pajer, B.
EDISON, THOMAS A (THOMAS ALVA), 1847-1931
Dos Passos, J. 1919
Moore, G. The last days of night
Pajer, B. The Edison effect
Edisto Powell, P.
EDITORS
Chabon, M. Wonder boys
Eco, U. Numero zero

Leithauser, B. The art student's war
Morgan, S. One summer in Paris

EIGHTEEN-YEAR-OLDS

Bird, S. The Yokota Officers Club

The **eighth** girl Chung, M.

The **eighth** sister Dugoni, R.

Eileen Moshfegh, O.

Einstein's dreams Lightman, A.

EINSTEIN, ALBERT, 1879-1955

Lightman, A. Einstein's dreams

EISENHOWER, DWIGHT D (DWIGHT DAVID), 1890-1969 ATTEMPTED ASSASSINATION

Higgins, J. Flight of eagles

EISENHOWER, DWIGHT D (DWIGHT DAVID), 1890-1969 MILITARY LEADERSHIP

Shaara, J. The rising tide
Shaara, J. The steel wave

El Paso Groom, W.

EL PASO, TEXAS

Gaspar de Alba, A. Desert blood

EL SALVADOR

Didion, J. A book of common prayer

ELBA, ITALY

Scott, J. Tourmaline

ELBE, LILI, DIED 1931

Ebershoff, D. The Danish girl

Elder races [series] Harrison, T.

Eleanor Rigby Coupland, D.

Eleanor Roosevelt mysteries [series] Roosevelt, E.

ELEANOR,, OF AQUITAINE, QUEEN, CONSORT OF HENRY II, KING OF ENGLAND, 1122?-1204

Franklin, A. The serpent's tale
Penman, S. Cruel as the grave
Penman, S. Devil's brood
Penman, S. Dragon's lair
Penman, S. The Queen's man

ELEANOR,, OF PROVENCE, QUEEN, CONSORT OF HENRY III, KING OF ENGLAND, 1223 OR 1224-1291

Jones, S. Four sisters, all queens

ELECTIONS

Atkins, A. The shameless
Black, L. Let justice descend
Coonts, S. Liberty's last stand
Hill, N. The nix
Houellebecq, M. Submission
Liss, D. A spectacle of corruption
Older, M. Infomocracy
Perry, A. Southampton Row
Rowling, J. The casual vacancy
Ryan, H. The other woman
Stewart, A. Miss Kopp just won't quit
Vidal, G. 1876

ELECTIONS -- NORTH CAROLINA

Karon, J. Out to Canaan
Maron, M. Bootlegger's daughter

ELECTIONS -- UNITED STATES

Patterson, R. No safe place

ELECTIVE MUTISM

McBain, E. Alice in jeopardy

ELECTRA (GREEK MYTHOLOGY)

Toibin, C. House of names

ELECTRIC ALARMS

Amidon, S. Security

The **electric** hotel Smith, D.

ELECTRIC LIGHTING

Moore, G. The last days of night

ELECTRIC SHOCK

Pajer, B. Capacity for murder

ELECTRIC SHOCK THERAPY

Greer, A. The impossible lives of Greta Wells
Garey, J. Too bright to hear too loud to see

ELECTRICAL ENGINEERING

Echenoz, J. Lightning
Pistalo, V. Tesla

ELECTRICAL ENGINEERS

Echenoz, J. Lightning
Hunt, S. The invention of everything else
Lahiri, J. The namesake
Pajer, B. Capacity for murder
Pajer, B. The Edison effect
Pistalo, V. Tesla

ELECTRICIANS -- DEATH

Pajer, B. The Edison effect

ELECTRICITY

Barr, M. Watershed
Williams, N. This is happiness

ELECTRICITY -- HISTORY

Pajer, B. Fatal induction
Pajer, B. A spark of death

ELECTRONIC BULLETIN BOARDS

Smith, J. New Orleans beat

ELECTRONIC GAMES INDUSTRY AND TRADE

Robb, J. Fantasy in death

ELECTRONIC SURVEILLANCE

Beckett, L. Gamechanger
Hurwitz, G. They're watching

The **elegance** of the hedgehog Barbery, M.

Elegies for the brokenhearted Hodgen, C.

Elemental logic [series] Marks, L.

ELEMENTARY SCHOOL TEACHERS

Messud, C. The woman upstairs

ELEMENTARY SCHOOLS

Gelman, L. Class mom
Gelman, L. You've been volunteered

Elena Standish [series] Perry, A.

The **elephant** keeper Nicholson, C.

The **Elephant's** journey Saramago, J.

The **Elephanta** suite Theroux, P.

ELEPHANTS

Everett, P. Suder
Gruen, S. Water for elephants
Khan, V. The perplexing theft of the jewel in the crown
Nicholson, C. The elephant keeper
Picoult, J. Leaving time

Clements, R. Revenger
Follett, K. A column of fire
George, M. Elizabeth I
Harper, K. The poyson garden
Marston, E. The bawdy basket
Marston, E. The devil's apprentice
Marston, E. The roaring boy
Marston, E. The vagabond clown
Marston, E. The wanton angel
Maxwell, R. The queen's bastard
Maxwell, R. The wild Irish
Morgan, J. The secret life of William Shakespeare
Phillips, A. The king at the edge of the world
Plaidy, J. The captive Queen of Scots
Rutherfurd, E. London
Wolfe, S. The course of all treasons

Elizabethan spy novels [series] Wolfe, S.
Ella Minnow Pea Dunn, M.
Ellen Foster Gibbons, K.
Ellen Foster duology [series] Gibbons, K.

ELLIS, BRET EASTON
Ellis, B. Lunar Park

Elmer Gantry Lewis, S.
Elmet Mozley, F.

ELOPEMENT
Burns, O. Cold Sassy tree
Cather, W. My Antonia
Fielding, H. The history of Tom Jones, a foundling
Willig, L. The deception of the emerald ring

Elroy Nights Barthelme, F.
Elsewhere, home Aboulela, L.
The **elvenbane** Norton, A.
Elvenblood Norton, A.

ELVES
Kay, G. The summer tree
McGuire, S. Rosemary and rue
Norton, A. Elvenblood
Norton, A. The elvenbane
Novik, N. Spinning silver
Pratchett, T. Lords and ladies
Tolkien, J. Beren and Luthien
Tolkien, J. The children of Hurin
Tolkien, J. The fall of Gondolin
Tolkien, J. The fellowship of the ring
Tolkien, J. The lord of the rings
Tolkien, J. The return of the king
Tolkien, J. The Silmarillion
Tolkien, J. The two towers
Warrington, F. Elfland
Warrington, F. Grail of the summer stars
Warrington, F. Midsummer night

Elvis Cole/Joe Pike novels [series] Crais, R.

ELVIS PRESLEY IMPERSONATORS
Abani, C. GraceLand

Elza's kitchen Fitten, M.

EMAIL
Batuman, E. The idiot

EMAIL CORRESPONDENCE
Gelman, L. Class mom
Gelman, L. You've been volunteered
Marks, J. Fangland

EMANCIPATION OF MINORS
Robotham, M. Good girl, bad girl

EMBASSY BUILDINGS
Patchett, A. Bel canto

Embassytown Mieville, C.
Embers of war Powell, G.
Embers of war [series] Powell, G.

EMBEZZLEMENT
Pavone, C. The expats
Pronzini, B. The crimes of Jordan Wise

EMBEZZLERS
Eugenides, J. Fresh complaint

Embla Nystrom investigations [series] Tursten, H.

EMBROIDERY
Chevalier, T. A single thread

EMBRYO FREEZING
Picoult, J. Sing you home

EMBRYO TRANSFER -- MORAL AND ETHICAL AS-PECTS
Picoult, J. Sing you home

EMERALDS
Westlake, D. The hot rock

EMERSON, RALPH WALDO, 1803-1882
Lock, N. A fugitive in Walden Woods
Pearl, M. The Dante Club

EMEZI, AKWAEKE
Emezi, A. Freshwater

The **emigrants** ;, W. G. Sebald ; translated by Michael Hulse.
Sebald, W.

Emile Cinq-Mars mysteries [series] Farrow, J.
Emily, alone O'Nan, S.

EMINENT DOMAIN
Crummey, M. Sweetland
Hulse, S. Eden mine

Emissary Locke, T.
The **emissary** Tawada, Y.
Emma Austen, J.
Emma Bronte, C.
Emma Djan novels [series] Quartey, K.
Emma in the night Walker, W.

EMOTIONAL ABUSE
Erdrich, L. Shadow tag
O'Leary, B. The flatshare
Price, N. Sleeping with the enemy
Rooney, S. Normal people
Whitehead, C. The Nickel boys

EMOTIONAL MATURITY
Roth, P. The professor of desire
Tyler, A. A patchwork planet

EMOTIONAL PROBLEMS
Grant, H. The glass demon

EMOTIONALLY ABUSED CHILDREN
Watson, J. Asta in the wings

Pratchett, T. The last hero
Pratchett, T. Thief of time
Pressfield, S. 36 righteous men
Robbins, T. Skinny legs and all
This way to the end times
Tremblay, P. The cabin at the end of the world
Vonnegut, K. Cat's cradle
Vonnegut, K. Galapagos
Vonnegut, K. Slapstick
Whitehead, C. Zone one
Winters, B. Countdown City
Winters, B. The last policeman
Winters, B. World of trouble

END OF THE WORLD (ASTRONOMY)

Wilson, R. Spin

End of watch King, S.

Endangered Cush, J.

Ender Wiggin [series] Card, O.

Ender's game Card, O.

The **endless** beach Colgan, J.

Endless love Spencer, S.

Endless night Christie, A.

Endurance Lake, J.

Endymion Simmons, D.

ENEMIES

Asaro, C. Primary inversion
Beauman, N. Madness is better than defeat
Bouchet, A. Nightchaser
Bourne, J. The spymaster's lady
Bradley, A. A wicked way to win an earl
Burke, J. House of the rising sun
Child, L. Persuader
Corey, J. Persepolis rising
Cornwell, B. Sword of kings
Cornwell, B. War of the wolf
Cussler, C. Final option
Cussler, C. Shadow tyrants
Daly, P. Open your eyes
Dickey, E. Finding Gideon
Dodd, C. What doesn't kill her
El-Mohtar, A. This is how you lose the time war
Flyte, M. City of lost dreams
French, J. The true Bastards
Gaiman, N. Anansi boys
Galbraith, R. Career of evil
Goss, T. The sinister mystery of the mesmerizing girl
Grippando, J. The girl in the glass box
Hansen, R. The assassination of Jesse James by the coward Robert Ford
Higashino, K. Malice
Horowitz, A. Moriarty
Huston, C. Every last drop
K'wan Animal II
K'wan Revelations
Lake, J. Endurance
Lake, J. Green
Lee, Y. Raven stratagem

Leonard, E. The Hot Kid
Marshall, A. A crown for cold silver
Matthiessen, P. Killing Mister Watson
O'Brien, E. Girl
Parker, R. Rough weather
Parker, S. Coldwater
Pattison, E. Blood of the oak
Piccirilli, T. The last whisper in the dark
Rai, A. Hate to want you
Robertson, M. Moriarty returns a letter
Rollins, J. The demon crown
Ruiz Zafon, C. The prisoner of heaven
Schwab, V. A conjuring of light
Schwab, V. A darker shade of magic
Schwab, V. A gathering of shadows
Schwab, V. Vengeful
Schwab, V. Vicious
Scottoline, L. Feared
Shannon, S. The bone season
Silva, D. The new girl
Weber, D. Shadow of freedom
Woods, S. Stealth

Enemies, a love story Singer, I.

The **enemy** Child, L.

Enemy of God Cornwell, B.

ENERGY RESOURCES

Hamilton, P. Great North Road
Stout, D. Titanshade

ENFORCERS (CRIMINALS)

Dickey, E. Bad men and wicked women
Dickey, E. Before we were wicked
Pelecanos, G. Drama city

ENG, 1811-1874

Slouka, M. God's fool

ENGAGED PERSONS

Abdul-Jabbar, K. Mycroft Holmes
Alexander, T. With this pledge
Ashe, K. The earl
Ashford, J. Lord Sebastian's secret
Ashley Antoinette, 1. Butterfly
Barry, D. Insane city
Bowen, R. The victory garden
Burns, O. Leaving Cold Sassy
Cameron, W. Repo madness
Carpenter, E. Every single secret
Center, K. How to walk away
Cole, A. A princess in theory
Cook, R. Cell
Dare, T. Say yes to the marquess
Dean, A. Bellfield Hall
Divakaruni, C. Oleander girl
Eason, K. How Rory Thorne destroyed the multiverse
Ferraris, Z. Finding Nouf
Gaiman, N. Anansi boys
Haigh, J. Mrs. Kimble
Hodges, C. Rumor has it
James, E. Kiss me, Annabel

Jenoff, P. The ambassador's daughter
Kwan, K. China rich girlfriend
Kwan, K. Crazy rich Asians
Lethem, J. Chronic city
Maron, M. High country fall
McCall Smith, A. Blue shoes and happiness
McCall Smith, A. The Kalahari typing school for men
McGuire, S. Night and silence
McInerny, R. Irish coffee
McKenzie, E. The portable Veblen
McPherson, C. A step so grave
Mina, D. Field of blood
Murray, V. Lust
O'Donohue, C. The lover's knot
Orenstein, H. Love at first like
Packer, A. The dive from Clausen's pier
Palmer, L. Otherwise engaged
Paris, B. Bring me back
Pears, I. Death and restoration
Phillips, S. Call me irresistible
Rabb, J. Among the living
Ramsay, F. Scone Island
Ryan, K. Long shot
Sayers, D. Clouds of witness
Sebastian, C. It takes two to tumble
Siger, J. Target Tinos
Simpson, R. What the dead leave behind
Sparks, N. The Notebook
Starr, J. Lights out
Swift, G. Here we are
Vreeland, S. Luncheon of the boating party
Welsh, K. The unquiet heart

ENGAGEMENT

Alexander, V. What happens at Christmas
Ervin, K. Mina's joint
Haigh, J. Mrs. Kimble
Helprin, M. In sunlight and in shadow
Heyer, G. The grand Sophy
Kamali, M. The stationery shop
Link, C. The other child
MacLean, S. One good earl deserves a lover
McCall Smith, A. The forgotten affairs of youth
McCall Smith, A. The full cupboard of life
Palmer, L. Otherwise engaged
Scott, A. The low road

ENGAGEMENT RINGS

Orenstein, H. Love at first like

ENGELHARDT, AUGUST, 1877-1919

Kracht, C. Imperium

ENGELS, FRIEDRICH, 1820-1895 FAMILY

McCrea, G. Mrs. Engels

The **engineer's** wife Wood, T.

ENGINEERS

Anders, C. All the birds in the sky
Barr, M. Watershed
Bohjalian, C. The sandcastle girls
Furst, A. The spies of Warsaw

Grenville, K. The idea of perfection
Harris, R. Pompeii
Howrey, M. The wanderers
Miller, A. Pure
Oz, A. Don't call it night
Percy, W. The last gentleman
Pontoppidan, H. Lucky Per
Rosen, L. The tenth witness
Vonnegut, K. Player piano
Watts, P. Blindsight
Wood, T. The engineer's wife

The **engines** of God McDevitt, J.

ENGLAND

Adichie, C. Americanah
Alexander, V. The Lady Travelers Guide to larceny with a dashing stranger
Alexander, V. The Lady Travelers Guide to scoundrels and other gentlemen
Archer, J. Best kept secret
Archer, J. Only time will tell
Archer, J. This was a man
Ashford, J. Heir to the duke
Ashford, J. Lord Sebastian's secret
Ashford, J. What the duke doesn't know
Aslam, N. Maps for lost lovers
Atkinson, K. Big sky
Atkinson, K. Case histories
Atkinson, K. Human croquet
Bagshawe, T. Adored
Baker, J. The body lies
Balasubramanyam, R. Professor Chandra follows his bliss
Balogh, M. Simply love
Balogh, M. Someone to hold
Balogh, M. Someone to love
Balogh, M. Someone to remember
Balogh, M. Someone to trust
Balogh, M. Someone to wed
Banville, J. The sea
Barber, L. A girl named Anna
Barker, P. Another world
Barnes, J. The only story
Barnes, J. The sense of an ending
Barnes, J. The somnambulist
Bartlett, N. The disappearance boy
Bauer, B. Snap
Beaton, M. Agatha Raisin and the quiche of death
Beaton, M. Agatha Raisin and the witch of Wyckhadden
Beaton, M. Pushing up daisies
Berne, L. You may kiss the bride
Berry, C. A legacy of murder
Billingham, M. Their little secret
Bolton, S. The craftsman
Bowen, K. Between the devil and the duke
Bowen, K. I've got my duke to keep me warm
Bowen, K. A rogue by night
Bradley, C. The golden tresses of the dead
Bradley, C. The grave's a fine and private place

Bradley, C. I am half-sick of shadows
Bradley, C. A red herring without mustard
Bradley, C. Speaking from among the bones
Bradley, C. The sweetness at the bottom of the pie
Bradley, C. Thrice the brinded cat hath mew'd
Bradley, C. The weed that strings the hangman's bag
Bragg, M. A son of war
Brett, S. Mrs Pargeter's principle
Brett, S. Murder unprompted
Brett, S. The torso in the town
Burrowes, G. The trouble with dukes
Butland, S. The lost for words bookshop
Buxbaum, J. After you
Byatt, A. Babel Tower
Cannon, J. Three things about Elsie
Carlyle, C. A duke changes everything
Carver, T. The surrogate
Chevalier, T. A single thread
Christie, A. And then there were none
Christie, A. The body in the library
Christie, A. Curtain
Christie, A. Endless night
Christie, A. The murder at the vicarage
Christie, A. A murder is announced
Christie, A. The pale horse
Ciotta, B. Her sky cowboy
Ciotta, B. His clockwork canary
Cleeves, A. The long call
Cocks, H. The royal we
Coe, J. The rain before it falls
Cohen, T. They all fall down
Cole, D. Ragdoll
Coleridge, N. A much married man
Collins, M. Ready set rogue
Croft, P. The second time I saw you
Crombie, D. A bitter feast
Crombie, D. Mourn not your dead
Cumming, C. The Trinity Six
Cusset, C. Life of David Hockney
Daly, P. Open your eyes
Daniels, N. Too close
Deighton, L. London match
Delaney, J. The girl before
Dexter, C. The daughters of Cain
Dexter, C. The remorseful day
Dexter, C. The way through the woods
Dickens, C. Martin Chuzzlewit
Dickinson, P. The yellow room conspiracy
Drabble, M. The dark flood rises
Drabble, M. The witch of Exmoor
Dunmore, E. Bringing down the duke
Dunmore, H. Exposure
Edwards, R. Darling
Evans, H. A place for us
Evans, J. The white devil
Evaristo, B. Girl, woman, other
Faulks, S. Charlotte Gray

Faulks, S. Jeeves and the wedding bells
Faye, L. The whole art of detection
Fforde, J. The Eyre affair
Fforde, J. Lost in a good book
Fforde, J. Shades of grey
Finch, C. The last passenger
Forbes, C. A tall history of sugar
Fowler, C. Bryant & May
Frayn, M. Headlong
Frear, C. Stone cold heart
Frear, C. Sweet little lies
French, N. The lying room
Fuller, C. Bitter orange
Fuller, C. Our endless numbered days
Gaiman, N. Anansi boys
Gaiman, N. The ocean at the end of the lane
Gardam, J. Last friends
Gardam, J. The man in the wooden hat
Gash, J. The rich and the profane
Gaskell, E. North and South
George, E. A banquet of consequences
George, E. Believing the lie
George, E. Careless in red
George, E. Just one evil act
George, E. The punishment she deserves
George, E. This body of death
George, E. What came before he shot her
Goddard, R. Beyond recall
Goddard, R. Into the blue
Goddard, R. Long time coming
Golding, M. Little darlings
Grant, L. We had it so good
Greene, G. Brighton Rock
Greene, G. The captain and the enemy
Griffith, N. Hild
Griffiths, E. A dying fall
Griffiths, E. The stone circle
Griffiths, E. The stranger diaries
Grimes, M. The Old Wine Shades
Grimes, M. The winds of change
Gruber, M. The book of air and shadows
Guhrke, L. Governess gone rogue
Guhrke, L. The truth about love and dukes
Guillory, J. Royal holiday
Haddon, M. The curious incident of the dog in the night-time
Hadley, T. Clever girl
Hale, S. Austenland
Hamer, K. The girl in the red coat
Hannah, S. Perfect little children
Hannah, S. The wrong mother
Harris, R. Enigma
Harris, R. The ghost
Harris, R. The second sleep
Harris, S. The color of Bee Larkham's murder
Harrod-Eagles, C. Old bones
Hart, J. Damage
Harvey, J. A darker shade of blue

Mozley, F. Elmet
Murdoch, I. An accidental man
Murdoch, I. The bell
Murdoch, I. The book and the brotherhood
Murdoch, I. A fairly honourable defeat
Murdoch, I. The good apprentice
Murdoch, I. The philosopher's pupil
Murdoch, I. The sea, the sea
Naipaul, V. Magic seeds
Nevill, A. The house of small shadows
Nicholls, D. Us
Nicholls, O. Love, unscripted
North, A. The Whisper Man
Novik, N. His majesty's dragon
O'Connor, J. Star of the Sea
O'Flynn, C. The news where you are
O'Leary, B. The flatshare
Palliser, C. The unburied
Parker, L. The Austen playbook
Peet, M. The Murdstone trilogy
Perry, A. A Christmas return
Perry, A. Shoulder the sky
Peters, E. Fallen into the pit
Peters, E. Guardian of the horizon
Phillips, A. The king at the edge of the world
Phillips, C. A distant shore
Phillips, C. Foreigners
Porter, H. The bell ringers
Porter, M. Lanny
Putney, M. No longer a gentleman
Quick, A. I thee wed
Raichev, R. Assassins at Ospreys
Rayne, S. Property of a lady
Rendell, R. The babes in the wood
Rendell, R. End in tears
Rendell, R. Harm done
Rendell, R. Heartstones
Rendell, R. Kissing the gunner's daughter
Rendell, R. Not in the flesh
Rendell, R. Road rage
Rendell, R. Simisola
Rendell, R. A sleeping life
Rendell, R. The tree of hands
Ripley, M. Mr Campion's fault
Ripley, M. Mr. Campion's war
Robertson, M. The Baker Street translation
Robertson, M. The brothers of Baker Street
Robinson, P. Children of the revolution
Robinson, P. Close to home
Robinson, P. Cold is the grave
Robinson, P. The first cut
Robinson, P. Friend of the devil
Robinson, P. Innocent graves
Robinson, P. Piece of my heart
Robinson, P. Playing with fire
Robinson, P. Strange affair
Robotham, M. The night ferry

Rodale, M. Lady Bridget's diary
Rowson, P. Death lies beneath
Rowson, P. Undercurrent
Rushdie, S. The ground beneath her feet
Ryan, J. The spies of Shilling Lane
Sahota, S. The year of the runaways
Sarginson, S. The wonderful
Sayers, D. Busman's honeymoon
Sayers, D. Gaudy night
Sayers, D. Have his carcase
Sayers, D. Murder must advertise
Sayers, D. The nine tailors
Sayers, D. Thrones, dominations
Sayers, D. Whose body?
Shannon, S. The bone season
Shannon, S. The mime order
Shaw, V. Strange Practice
Shaw, W. Salt lane
Sillitoe, A. Saturday night and Sunday morning
Simonson, H. Major Pettigrew's last stand
Simpson, D. Dead and gone
Smith, A. There but for the
Spark, M. Aiding & abetting
Spark, M. A far cry from Kensington
Spark, M. Memento mori
Spencer, M. Barbarous
Spencer, M. Dangerous
Spencer, S. Backlash
Spencer, S. Best served cold
Spencer, S. Dead end
Spencer, S. The dead hand of history
Spencer, S. Death's dark shadow
Spencer, S. A dying fall
Spencer, S. Echoes of the dead
Spencer, S. The hidden
Spencer, S. Lambs to the slaughter
Spencer, S. The ring of death
Spencer, S. Thicker than water
Spencer, S. A walk with the dead
St. James, S. The haunting of Maddy Clare
Steadman, C. Mr. Nobody
Steiner, S. Missing, presumed
Steiner, S. Persons unknown
Stibbe, N. Reasons to be cheerful
Stott, R. Ghostwalk
Stratford, S. Red letter days
Swift, G. Last orders
Swift, G. Wish you were here
Thomas, R. Firewatching
Toibin, C. The master
Trollope, J. The best of friends
Trollope, J. The men and the girls
Trollope, J. Next of kin
Trollope, J. Other people's children
Truss, L. The man that got away
Tudor, C. The chalk man
Turansky, C. No ocean too wide

Nickson, C. Gods of gold
Nickson, C. On Copper Street
Palliser, C. The quincunx
Penrose, A. Murder at half moon gate
Penrose, A. Murder at Kensington Palace
Penrose, A. Murder on Black Swan Lane
Pulley, N. The Bedlam stacks
Pulley, N. The lost future of Pepperharrow
Pulley, N. The watchmaker of Filigree Street
Putney, M. The marriage spell
Quinn, J. An offer from a gentleman
Smith, M. Rose
Thomas, S. The luckiest lady in London
Willis, C. To say nothing of the dog

ENGLAND -- HISTORY -- 20TH CENTURY

Airth, R. The decent inn of death
Bowen, R. The victory garden
Byatt, A. The children's book
Byatt, A. Ragnarok
Connolly, J. The book of lost things
Dunmore, H. The lie
Gallagher, S. The bedlam detective
Gardam, J. God on the rocks
Guttridge, P. The thing itself
Jio, S. The last camellia
King, L. The beekeeper's apprentice
Liardet, F. We must be brave
MacNeal, S. The king's justice
McEwan, I. Atonement
Nicholson, W. Motherland
Perry, A. Death in focus
Runcie, J. The road to Grantchester
Runcie, J. Sidney Chambers and the forgiveness of sins
Runcie, J. Sidney Chambers and the perils of the night
Runcie, J. Sidney Chambers and the persistence of love
Runcie, J. Sidney Chambers and the problem of evil
Runcie, J. Sidney Chambers and the shadow of death
Sackville-West, V. The Edwardians
Shaffer, M. The Guernsey Literary and Potato Peel Pie Society
Simonson, H. The summer before the war
Waters, S. The night watch
White, R. A lady unrivaled
Willig, L. The Ashford affair
Willis, C. To say nothing of the dog

ENGLAND -- HISTORY -- MEDIEVAL PERIOD, 1066-1485

Crace, J. Harvest
Franklin, A. Mistress of the art of death
Penman, S. Falls the shadow
Walters, M. The last hours

ENGLAND -- HISTORY -- VICTORIA, 1837-1901

Bradford, B. Master of his fate
Perry, S. The Essex serpent
Raybourn, D. A curious beginning
Raybourn, D. A dangerous collaboration
Raybourn, D. A murderous relation

Raybourn, D. A perilous undertaking
Raybourn, D. A treacherous curse

ENGLAND -- IMMIGRATION AND EMIGRATION

Levy, A. Small island

ENGLAND -- RACE RELATIONS

Levy, A. Small island

ENGLAND -- RULERS

Penman, S. When Christ and his saints slept

ENGLAND -- SOCIAL CONDITIONS -- 19TH CENTURY

Cho, Z. Sorcerer to the crown
Dickens, C. Bleak House
Dickens, C. Little Dorrit
Dickens, C. Nicholas Nickleby
Dickens, C. The Pickwick papers
Hardy, T. Jude the obscure

ENGLAND -- SOCIAL CONDITIONS -- 20TH CENTURY

Levy, A. Small island
Pietroni, A. Ruby's spoon
Speller, E. The return of Captain John Emmett
Speller, E. The strange fate of Kitty Easton

ENGLAND -- SOCIAL LIFE AND CUSTOMS

Amis, M. Lionel Asbo
Gardam, J. The people on Privilege Hill and other stories
Ridgway, K. Hawthorn & Child
Trollope, J. The other family

ENGLAND -- SOCIAL LIFE AND CUSTOMS -- 16TH CENTURY

Campisi, M. Sin eater
Morgan, J. The secret life of William Shakespeare
Newman, S. The heavens

ENGLAND -- SOCIAL LIFE AND CUSTOMS -- 17TH CENTURY

Gregory, P. Tidelands

ENGLAND -- SOCIAL LIFE AND CUSTOMS -- 18TH CENTURY

Austen, J. Northanger Abbey
Austen, J. Persuasion
Bailey, M. An appetite for violets
Freeman, A. The fair fight
Fielding, H. The history of Tom Jones, a foundling
Gowar, I. The mermaid and Mrs. Hancock
James, E. Desperate duchesses
James, E. Three weeks with Lady X
Kleypas, L. Secrets of a summer night
Koen, K. Through a glass darkly
Nicholson, C. The elephant keeper
Richardson, S. Clarissa, or, The history of a young lady
Richardson, S. Pamela

ENGLAND -- SOCIAL LIFE AND CUSTOMS -- 1910-1936

Forster, E. Howards End
Forster, E. A room with a view
Smith, D. I capture the castle
Waugh, E. Vile bodies

ENGLAND -- SOCIAL LIFE AND CUSTOMS -- 1945-

Drabble, M. The sea lady

ENGLAND -- SOCIAL LIFE AND CUSTOMS -- 19TH CENTURY

Trollope, A. Doctor Thorne
Trollope, A. The Eustace diamonds
Trollope, A. Framley parsonage
Trollope, A. The last chronicle of Barset
Trollope, A. The Prime Minister
Trollope, A. The warden
Waite, O. The lady's guide to celestial mechanics
Waters, S. Fingersmith
Waters, S. Tipping the velvet

ENGLAND -- SOCIAL LIFE AND CUSTOMS -- 20TH CENTURY

Benson, E. Make way for Lucia
Byatt, A. A whistling woman
Gardam, J. The flight of the maidens
Hilton, J. Good-bye, Mr. Chips
Horowitz, A. Magpie murders
Jones, S. The uninvited guests
Joyce, G. The limits of enchantment
Kelly, S. The wages of desire
Lawrence, D. Lady Chatterley's lover
Lawrence, D. The rainbow
Lawrence, D. Sons and lovers
Lawrence, D. Women in love
Macdonald, M. Tamsin Harte
Mitchell, D. Black Swan Green
Mitford, N. The pursuit of love ;
Parmar, P. Vanessa and her sister
Penney, S. The invisible ones
Pym, B. Excellent women
Runcie, J. Canvey Island
Sackville-West, V. All passion spent
Sackville-West, V. The Edwardians
Snow, C. Strangers and brothers
Solomons, N. House of Gold
Waugh, E. Brideshead revisited
Waugh, E. The complete stories of Evelyn Waugh
Waugh, E. Decline and fall
Woolf, V. The years

ENGLAND -- SOCIAL LIFE AND CUSTOMS -- 21ST CENTURY

Rowling, J. The casual vacancy

ENGLAND -- SOCIAL LIFE AND CUSTOMS -- 6TH CENTURY

Twain, M. A Connecticut Yankee in King Arthur's Court
England, England Barnes, J.

ENGLAND, SOUTHERN

Lelic, S. The child who

ENGLISH AS A SECOND LANGUAGE -- STUDY AND TEACHING

Shepard, K. The Celestials

ENGLISH CIVIL WAR, 1642-1649

Gregory, P. Tidelands
Norfolk, L. John Saturnall's feast
English history novels [series] Maxwell, R.

ENGLISH IN SCOTLAND

London, J. Wild wicked Scot

ENGLISH LANGUAGE

Graedon, A. The word exchange
Schine, C. The Grammarians

ENGLISH LANGUAGE -- STUDY AND TEACHING

Byatt, A. Babel Tower

ENGLISH LANGUAGE TEACHERS

Cusk, R. Outline
Cusk, R. Transit
English passengers Kneale, M.
The **English** patient Ondaatje, M.
English, August Chatterjee, U.
Engraved on the heart Johnson, T.

ENGRAVERS

Dean, M. I, Hogarth
Enigma Harris, R.

ENIGMA MACHINE

Harris, R. Enigma
Enigma of China Qiu, X.
Enigma variations Aciman, A.

ENJOYMENT

Williams, L. Supper club

ENLIGHTENMENT (BUDDHISM)

Hesse, H. Siddhartha

ENLIGHTENMENT (EUROPEAN INTELLECTUAL MOVEMENT)

Gilbert, E. The signature of all things
The **enlightenment** of bees Linden, R.
The **ensemble** Gabel, A.

ENTERTAINERS

Kehlmann, D. Tyll
McMurtry, L. Buffalo girls
Phillips, C. Dancing in the dark
Randisi, R. Hey there (you with the gun in your hand)
Roberts, N. Honest illusions
Skarmeta, A. The dancer and the thief

ENTERTAINMENT INDUSTRY AND TRADE

Cline, R. My liar
Davis, F. The Chelsea girls
Smith, A. Spring

ENTERTAINMENT INDUSTRY AND TRADE -- HOLLYWOOD, CALIFORNIA

Leonard, E. Be cool

ENTHUSIASM IN SENIOR MEN -- CRETE

Kazantzakis, N. Zorba the Greek

ENTITLEMENT ATTITUDES

Gunesekera, R. Suncatcher
Lutz, L. The swallows
Oates, J. Evil eye
Entity novels [series] Devon, C.
Entombed Fairstein, L.

ENTOMOLOGISTS

Abe, K. The woman in the dunes

ENTREPRENEURS

Gilman, S. The ice cream queen of Orchard Street
Hill, R. The woodcutter
Matthiessen, P. Bone by bone
McDevitt, J. The Cassandra Project
Millhauser, S. Martin Dressler

Tolkien, J. The return of the king
Tolkien, J. The two towers
White, E. Dragonshadow
White, E. Heartstone

EPIC FICTION

Coleridge, N. Godchildren
Follett, K. Edge of eternity
Follett, K. Fall of giants
Follett, K. Winter of the world
Gilbert, E. The signature of all things
Lee, C. The surrendered
Malouf, D. Ransom
McMurtry, L. Comanche moon
McMurtry, L. Dead man's walk
McMurtry, L. Lonesome Dove
McMurtry, L. Streets of Laredo
Meyer, P. The son
Mitchell, M. Gone with the wind
Rutherfurd, E. The forest
Rutherfurd, E. London
Rutherfurd, E. Paris
Rutherfurd, E. The princes of Ireland
Rutherfurd, E. The rebels of Ireland
Rutherfurd, E. Russka
Rutherfurd, E. Sarum
Sayles, J. A moment in the sun
Saylor, S. Roma
Scott, W. Ivanhoe
Serpell, N. The old drift
Vargas Llosa, M. The war of the end of the world
Walker, A. The temple of my familiar

EPIDEMIC ENCEPHALITIS

Self, W. Umbrella

EPIDEMICS

Barclay, L. The twenty-three
Barnes, S. Domino Falls
Brockmeier, K. The brief history of the dead
Brooks, M. World War Z
Bunn, T. Outbreak
Cameron, M. Oath of office
Camus, A. The plague
Cook, R. Pandemic
Foster, A. Relic
Groff, L. Arcadia
Heller, P. The dog stars
Hill, J. The Fireman
King, S. Sleeping beauties
King, S. The stand
Koepp, D. Cold storage
Kress, N. If tomorrow comes
Lai, L. The tiger flu
Ma, L. Severance
Makkai, R. The great believers
Mandel, E. Station Eleven
Marcus, B. The flame alphabet
Newman, S. The country of Ice Cream Star
Nunez, S. Salvation city

Pinsker, S. A song for a new day
Reed, I. Mumbo jumbo
Roiphe, A. An imperfect lens
Rollins, J. The demon crown
Roth, P. Nemesis
Saramago, J. Blindness
Scalzi, J. Lock in
Shepherd, P. The book of M
Slaughter, K. The last widow
Stewart, G. Earth abides
Toro, G. The strain
Walker, K. The dreamers
Wendig, C. Wanderers
Wilson, D. The Andromeda evolution
Yan, L. Dream of Ding Village

EPIDEMICS -- 14TH CENTURY

Willis, C. Doomsday book

EPIDEMIOLOGISTS

Wendig, C. Wanderers

EPILEPSY

Enright, A. The forgotten waltz
Harding, P. Tinkers
Lukas, M. The Oracle of Stamboul

EPISCOPAL CHURCH.

Spencer-Fleming, J. All mortal flesh
Spencer-Fleming, J. In the bleak midwinter

EPISCOPAL CHURCH CLERGY

Karon, J. At home in Mitford
Karon, J. In this mountain
Karon, J. A new song
Karon, J. Out to Canaan

EPISCOPALIANS

Karon, J. In this mountain
Price, R. The good priest's son
Spencer-Fleming, J. Hid from our eyes
Spencer-Fleming, J. Through the evil days

EPISTOLARY NOVELS

Adiga, A. The white tiger
Adkins, M. When you read this
Banks, R. Cloudsplitter
Bauer, C. Frances and Bernard
Bivald, K. The readers of Broken Wheel recommend
Coetzee, J. Age of Iron
Cooley, M. The archivist
Crowley, J. Lord Byron's novel
Doyle, R. Threshold
Dunn, M. Ella Minnow Pea
El-Mohtar, A. This is how you lose the time war
Foer, J. Everything is illuminated
Grass, G. Dog years
Hall, L. Speak
Hijuelos, O. Twain & Stanley enter paradise
Hosseini, K. Sea prayer
Ivey, E. To the bright edge of the world
Lupton, R. Sister
Miyamoto, T. Kinshu
Norman, H. What is left the daughter

Dallas, S. Westering women
Davys, T. Amberville
DeLillo, D. Falling man
Deighton, L. Berlin game
Dumas, A. The count of Monte Cristo
Evaristo, B. Blonde roots
Ewan, C. Long time lost
Feehan, C. Shadow rider
Furnivall, K. The red scarf
Gabaldon, D. Outlander
Goldin, M. The escape room
Gottlieb, E. Best boy
Hage, R. De Niro's game
Hayder, M. Poppet
Hunter, S. Dirty white boys
Ignatius, D. The increment
JaQuavis The dopeman's wife
Johnson, C. Hell is empty
Johnson, D. Nobody move
Jonasson, J. The accidental further adventures of the hundred-year-old man
Kane, B. Spartacus
Kelton, E. Texas vendetta
Keneally, T. Shame and the captives
Kidd, S. The book of longings
Krall, H. Chasing the king of hearts
L'Amour, L. The last of the breed
Lalami, L. The Moor's account
Lee, P. Runner
Lee, P. Signal
Liss, D. A spectacle of corruption
Mabanckou, A. Black Moses
Marillier, J. Daughter of the forest
McCann, C. Zoli
Naslund, S. Abundance
Nesbo, J. Headhunters
Nesbo, J. Midnight sun
Norton, C. What doesn't kill her
O'Brian, P. The wine-dark sea
O'Brien, E. Girl
Perkins-Valdez, D. Wench
Quick, A. The other lady vanishes
Rajaniemi, H. The fractal prince
Rajaniemi, H. The quantum thief
Reed, I. Flight to Canada
Rubenfeld, J. The interpretation of murder
Simon, M. The last Jew standing
Sofer, D. The Septembers of Shiraz
Souljah,. A deeper love inside
Spufford, F. Golden hill
Stark, R. Ask the parrot
Stark, R. Breakout
Tatlock, A. Promises to keep
Ulinich, A. Petropolis
Verne, J. The mysterious island
Vestal, S. Daredevils
Westheimer, D. Von Ryan's express

White, S. Dry ice
Whitehead, C. The underground railroad

ESCAPES -- TIBET
L'Amour, L. May there be a road

ESCORT SERVICES (PROSTITUTION)
Bryant, N. Madam, may I
Hoang, H. The kiss quotient
Perry, T. The boyfriend

ESPERANTO -- HISTORY
Skibell, J. A curable romantic

ESPIONAGE
Atkinson, K. Transcription
Bell, T. Overkill
Bennett, R. City of blades
Bennett, R. City of stairs
Berenson, A. The prisoner
Brandreth, B. The assassin of Verona
Brandreth, B. The spy of Venice
Butler, R. The hot country
Chiaverini, J. Resistance women
Cole, A. An extraordinary union
Cumming, C. A colder war
Cumming, C. A divided spy
Cumming, C. The Moroccan girl
Cumming, C. The Trinity Six
Downing, D. Diary of a dead man on leave
Duenas, M. The time in between
Dugoni, R. The eighth sister
Dunmore, H. Exposure
Follett, K. Edge of eternity
Forsyth, F. The fox
Gleason, C. Murder at the capitol
Harris, O. A shadow intelligence
Harris, R. An officer and a spy
Jin, H. A map of betrayal
Joinson, S. The photographer's wife
Kanon, J. Los Alamos
Kennedy, D. The moment
Khoury, R. Empire of lies
Lamb, A. Roboteer
Lawton, J. Hammer to fall
Lawton, J. Then we take Berlin
Ledgard, J. Submergence
London, J. Wild wicked Scot
Matthews, J. The Kremlin's candidate
McCarry, C. The mulberry bush
Meacham, L. Dragonfly
Perez-Reverte, A. What we become
Priest, C. Clementine
Reich, C. The take
Ripley, M. Mr. Campion's war
Ryan, A. The waking fire
Seymour, G. Vagabond
Shacochis, B. The woman who lost her soul
Steinhauer, O. The Cairo affair
Steinhauer, O. The last tourist
Stross, C. Empire Games

Mengestu, D. How to read the air

ETHNIC GROUPS

Bledsoe, A. The hum and the shiver

Bledsoe, A. Gather her round

Bledsoe, A. Long black curl

Bledsoe, A. Wisp of a thing

Deb, S. The point of return

ETHNIC IDENTITY

Brinkley, J. A lucky man

Fajardo-Anstine, K. Sabrina & Corina

Gay, R. Ayiti

Hulme, K. The bone people

Larsen, R. I am Radar

Lee, D. Country of origin

Loh, V. Breaking the tongue , by Vyvyane Loh.

Phillips, C. Dancing in the dark

Phillips, C. Foreigners

Smith, Z. On beauty

Solomon, A. Disgruntled

Stephens, A. Famous adopted people

Walker, A. The temple of my familiar

ETHNIC RESTAURANTS, SHOPS, ETC

Bates, J. Midnight at the Dragon Cafe

ETHNICITY

Chacon, D. And the shadows took him

Smith, Z. The autograph man

ETHNOLOGICAL MUSEUMS

Smith, D. Bright and distant shores

ETHNOLOGISTS

Le Guin, U. The left hand of darkness

Etta and Otto and Russell and James Hooper, E.

EUCALYPTUS

Bail, M. Eucalyptus

Eucalyptus Bail, M.

EUGENE, OREGON

Diehl, H. Lifelines

Eugenia Potter mysteries [series] Rich, V.

EUGENICS

Butler, O. Adulthood rites

Butler, O. Dawn

Butler, O. Imago

Kramer, L. Search for my heart

Lehane, D. Shutter Island

Eugenie Grandet Balzac, H.

EULOGIES

Burton, J. The eulogist

The **eulogist** Burton, J.

EUNUCHS

Amirrezvani, A. Equal of the sun

Renault, M. The Persian boy

Euphoria King, L.

EUROPA (SATELLITE)

Varley, J. Rolling thunder

EUROPE

Auel, J. The clan of the cave bear

Boyden, J. Three day road

Brown, D. The Da Vinci code

Cole, A. A prince on paper

Cramer, W. Levi's will

Cusk, R. Kudos

Ewan, C. Long time lost

Fleming, I. From Russia with love

Ignatius, D. Body of lies

Ishiguro, K. The unconsoled

James, H. Daisy Miller

Khoury, R. Empire of lies

Levi, P. If not now, when?

Lunde, M. The end of the ocean

Mackall, D. With love, wherever you are

Mina, D. Conviction

Murakami, H. Colorless Tsukuru Tazaki and his years of pilgrimage

Nicholls, D. Us

Porter, H. Firefly

Putney, M. Once a soldier

Rachman, T. The Italian teacher

Saylor, S. The seven wonders

Saylor, S. The triumph of Caesar

Sebald, W. Austerlitz

Soderberg, A. The other son

Steinke, R. Holy skirts

Turow, S. Ordinary heroes

Wilson, D. The clockwork dynasty

EUROPE -- 19TH CENTURY

Dinesen, I. Seven Gothic tales

EUROPE -- FOREIGN RELATIONS -- RUSSIA

Bell, T. Overkill

EUROPE -- HISTORY -- 1492-1648

Walton, J. Lent

EUROPE -- HISTORY -- 15TH CENTURY

Dunnett, D. Niccolo rising

EUROPE -- HISTORY -- 17TH CENTURY

Eco, U. The island of the day before

Kehlmann, D. Tyll

Maalouf, A. Balthasar's odyssey

EUROPE -- HISTORY -- 1871-1918

Ford, F. Parade's end

Pears, I. Stone's fall

EUROPE -- HISTORY -- 18TH CENTURY

King, R. Domino

EUROPE -- HISTORY -- 1918-1945

Furst, A. The foreign correspondent

Shaara, J. The rising tide

Shaara, J. The steel wave

EUROPE -- HISTORY -- 1939-1945

Bailey, P. Uncle Rudolf

EUROPE -- HISTORY -- 20TH CENTURY

Apelfeld, A. The man who never stopped sleeping

McCann, C. Zoli

McFadden, B. The Book of Harlan

Orringer, J. The invisible bridge

EUROPE -- HISTORY -- 476-1492

Eco, U. Baudolino

Jones, S. Four sisters, all queens

Willis, C. Doomsday book

EUROPE -- SOCIAL LIFE AND CUSTOMS
James, H. Complete stories, 1898-1910

EUROPE -- SOCIAL LIFE AND CUSTOMS -- 1918-1945
Lewis, S. Dodsworth

EUROPE -- SOCIAL LIFE AND CUSTOMS -- 19TH CEN-TURY
James, H. Complete stories, 1864-1874
James, H. Complete stories, 1874-1884
James, H. Complete stories, 1884-1891
James, H. Complete stories, 1892-1898

EUROPE -- SOCIAL LIFE AND CUSTOMS -- 20TH CEN-TURY
Hemingway, E. The sun also rises
Horan, N. Loving Frank

Europe central Vollmann, W.

EUROPEAN AFRICANS
Coetzee, J. Summertime
Gordimer, N. The conservationist
Lessing, D. The grass is singing
Naipaul, V. Guerrillas

EUROPEAN AMERICAN MEN
Mosley, W. The man in my basement
Vernon, O. A killing in this town

EUROPEAN AMERICAN WOMEN
Alam, R. That kind of mother
Mengestu, D. The beautiful things that heaven bears

EUROPEAN AMERICANS
Gurganus, A. White people

EUROPEAN AMERICANS -- RELATIONS WITH INDI-ANS
Berger, T. Little Big Man
McMurtry, L. Zeke and Ned

EUROPEAN RENAISSANCE
Dunant, S. Blood and beauty
Follett, K. A column of fire
Follett, K. World without end
Maalouf, A. Leo Africanus
Poole, S. The Borgia mistress
Rice, A. The vampire Armand
Walton, J. Lent

EUROPEAN RENAISSANCE -- ITALY
Dunant, S. In the company of the courtesan
Eco, U. The name of the rose
Stone, I. The agony and the ecstasy

EUROPEAN UNION
McDonald, I. The Dervish House

EUROPEAN UNION COUNTRIES
McDonald, I. The Dervish House

EUROPEANS IN DEVELOPING COUNTRIES
Conrad, J. Lord Jim

EUROPEANS IN INDIA
Jhabvala, R. At the end of the century

EUROPEANS IN INDONESIA
Conrad, J. Victory

EUROPEANS IN THE UNITED STATES
Gordon, M. The liar's wife

The **Eustace** diamonds Trollope, A.

EUTHANASIA
Sem-Sandberg, S. The chosen ones
White, S. Kill me
Wolfe, G. The shadow of the torturer

EUTHANASIA -- AMSTERDAM, NETHERLANDS
McEwan, I. Amsterdam

Eva Luna Allende, I.

Eva's eye Fossum, K.

EVACUATION OF CIVILIANS
Link, C. The other child
Morton, K. The distant hours

Evan Smoak thrillers [series] Hurwitz, G.

EVANGELICALISM
Oates, J. A book of American martyrs
Weir, M. The book of Essie

EVANGELISTS
Cleeves, A. The long call
Robbins, T. Skinny legs and all
Smith, J. Mean woman blues
Stark, R. Comeback

EVANGELISTS -- UNITED STATES
Lewis, S. Elmer Gantry

Eve Rossi novels [series] Pintoff, S.

Even the dogs McGregor, J.

Evening Minot, S.

Evening in paradise Berlin, L.

Evening primrose Matlwa, K.

The **evening** road Hunt, L.

The **evening** star McMurtry, L.

Eventide Haruf, K.

Ever faithful Barnett, K.

The **ever-running** man Muller, M.

EVERGLADES, FLORIDA
Hiaasen, C. Nature girl
Hiaasen, C. Skinny dip
MacDonald, J. The long lavender look
Matthiessen, P. Bone by bone
Matthiessen, P. Killing Mister Watson
Russell, K. Swamplandia!

EVERGLADES, FLORIDA -- HISTORY -- 19TH CEN-TURY
Matthiessen, P. Shadow country

Every breath Sparks, N.

Every broken trust Rodriguez, L.

Every day is for the thief Cole, T.

Every fifteen minutes Scottoline, L.

Every heart a doorway McGuire, S.

Every hidden fear Rodriguez, L.

Every last breath Rushdan, J.

Every last drop Huston, C.

Every last one Quindlen, A.

Every last secret Rodriguez, L.

Every man dies alone Fallada, H.

Every man for himself Bainbridge, B.

Every note played Genova, L.

Every single secret Carpenter, E.

Everybody's fool Russo, R.

Everybody's son Umrigar, T.

EVERYDAY LIFE

Offill, J. Weather

Everyday people

Everyman Roth, P.

Everyone dies McGarrity, M.

Everything Asian Woo, S.

Everything belongs to us Wuertz, Y.

Everything I left unsaid O'Keefe, M.

Everything I never told you Ng, C.

Everything inside Danticat, E.

Everything is illuminated Foer, J.

Everything matters! Currie, R.

Everything under Johnson, D.

Everything you have is mine Scoppettone, S.

Everywhere you don't belong Bump, G.

EVICTION

Nunez, S. The friend

Ryan, H. Truth be told

Westlake, D. Brothers keepers

EVIDENCE (LAW)

Koryta, M. How it happened

Smith, B. Crow's landing

Evidence of things unseen Wiggins, M.

Evidence trilogy [series] Banville, J.

Evil eye Oates, J.

EVOLUTION

Clarke, A. Childhood's end

Crichton, M. Prey

Wilson, D. The Andromeda evolution

EVOLUTION -- PHILOSOPHY

Stott, R. The coral thief

EVOLUTION -- RESEARCH

McDonald, R. Mr. Darwin's shooter

EVOLUTION AND RELIGION

McDonald, R. Mr. Darwin's shooter

The evolution of Bruno Littlemore Hale, B.

Evvie Drake starts over Holmes, L.

Ewert Grens thrillers [series] Roslund, A.

EXAGGERATION

Setterfield, D. The thirteenth tale

Excalibur Cornwell, B.

EXCAVATION

Cotterill, C. Slash and burn

EXCAVATIONS (ARCHAEOLOGY)

Brown, R. Murder at Monticello, or, Old sins

Child, L. Deep storm

Faber, M. The courage consort

Fortier, A. The lost sisterhood

Goodman, C. The night villa

Hart, E. Lake of sorrows

Kelly, J. The moon tunnel

Peters, E. The hippopotamus pool

Peters, E. Seeing a large cat

Reichs, K. Bones to ashes

Reichs, K. Break no bones

Smith, S. The ruins

Stabenow, D. So sure of death

EXCAVATIONS (ARCHAEOLOGY) -- EGYPT

Peters, E. Children of the storm

Peters, E. The deeds of the disturber

Peters, E. The golden one

Peters, E. Guardian of the horizon

Peters, E. He shall thunder in the sky

Peters, E. Lion in the valley

EXCAVATIONS (ARCHAEOLOGY) -- MESOPOTAMIA

Unsworth, B. Land of marvels

EXCAVATIONS (PALEONTOLOGY)

Phillips, H. The need

Excellent women Pym, B.

EXCHANGE STUDENTS

Fitzpatrick, L. Lights all night long

Meyers, K. The work of wolves

The execution Wolf, D.

The execution of Noa P. Singleton Silver, E.

The executioner's song Mailer, N.

EXECUTIONS AND EXECUTIONERS

Block, L. All the flowers are dying

Butcher, J. Proven guilty

Camus, A. The stranger

Dickens, C. A tale of two cities

Draven, G. Phoenix unbound

Estleman, L. The master executioner

Gregory, P. The last Tudor

Karnezis, P. The maze

Li, Y. The vagrants

Morrow, J. The last witchfinder

Plaidy, J. Murder most royal

Potzsch, O. The beggar king

Potzsch, O. The dark monk

Potzsch, O. The hangman's daughter

Potzsch, O. The play of death

Wiesel, E. The judges

Winthrop, E. The mercy seat

Wolfe, G. The claw of the conciliator

Zhou, H. Death notice

EXECUTIONS AND EXECUTIONERS -- FRANCE -- HISTORY

Naslund, S. Abundance

EXECUTIONS AND EXECUTIONERS -- GREAT BRITAIN -- HISTORY

Maxwell, R. The secret diary of Anne Boleyn

EXECUTIONS AND EXECUTIONERS -- PALESTINE

Wiesel, E. Dawn

EXECUTIVE SEARCH SERVICES

Nesbo, J. Headhunters

EXECUTIVES

Bing, S. You look nice today

Garey, J. Too bright to hear too loud to see

Landon, S. Wishing for us

Lightman, A. The diagnosis

Robotham, M. The wreckage

EXECUTIVES -- UNITED STATES

EXPATRIATE AUTHORS -- FRANCE
McLain, P. The Paris wife
EXPATRIATES
Baldwin, J. Giovanni's room
Bernhard, E. The books of the dead
Camus, A. The fall
Chiaverini, J. Resistance women
DeLillo, D. The names
Ellis, M. Keeping bedlam at bay in the Prague Cafe
Garcia Marquez, G. Strange pilgrims
Hallinan, T. Fools' river
James, H. Daisy Miller
Jin, H. The boat rocker
Lasdun, J. Afternoon of a faun
Leavitt, D. The two Hotel Francforts
Loh, V. Breaking the tongue , by Vyvyane Loh.
Mangan, C. Tangerine
Maugham, W. The razor's edge
Miller, H. Tropic of Cancer
Mina, D. Slip of the knife
Portis, C. Gringos
Russo, R. Bridge of sighs
Scott, J. Tourmaline
Shteyngart, G. The Russian debutante's handbook
Unsworth, B. After Hannibal
Vargas Llosa, M. The bad girl
EXPATRIATES -- BUDAPEST, HUNGARY
Phillips, A. Prague
EXPATRIATES -- HOLLYWOOD, CALIFORNIA
Waugh, E. The loved one
EXPATRIATES -- PARIS, FRANCE
Furst, A. The foreign correspondent
EXPATRIATES -- SPAIN
Hemingway, E. The sun also rises
The **expats** Pavone, C.
EXPECTATION (PSYCHOLOGY)
Crace, J. Quarantine
Esquivel, L. Like water for chocolate
Flaubert, G. Madame Bovary
Fu, K. For today I am a boy
Ishiguro, K. The unconsoled
Jalaluddin, U. Ayesha at last
Lalli, S. The matchmaker's list
Lipsyte, S. The ask
Murata, S. Convenience store woman
Ng, C. Everything I never told you
Oates, J. Blonde
Roth, P. Portnoy's complaint
Shteyngart, G. The Russian debutante's handbook
Wiseman, B. Listening to love
EXPEDITIONS
Lem, S. Fiasco
Preston, D. Old bones
Pulley, N. The Bedlam stacks
Sargent, C. Museum of human beings
VanderMeer, J. Acceptance
Vandermeer, J. Annihilation

VanderMeer, J. Authority
Watts, P. Blindsight
EXPERIMENTAL DRUGS
Glynn, A. Receptor
EXPERIMENTAL FICTION
Barth, J. Chimera
Barth, J. The floating opera
Barth, J. Giles Goat-Boy ;
Barth, J. The last voyage of somebody the sailor
Barth, J. The sot-weed factor
Barthelme, D. Sixty stories
Calvino, I. If on a winter's night a traveler
Coover, R. Going for a beer
Danielewski, M. The familiar.
Danielewski, M. House of leaves
Danielewski, M. Only revolutions
Dos Passos, J. Manhattan transfer
Ellis, M. Keeping bedlam at bay in the Prague Cafe
Ellmann, L. Ducks, Newburyport
Joyce, J. Finnegans wake
Lim, E. Dear cyborgs
Marcus, B. The flame alphabet
Mitchell, D. Cloud atlas
Pava, S. A naked singularity
Pava, S. Personae
Pynchon, T. Inherent vice
Rawle, G. Woman's world
Roussel, R. Locus solus
Stridsberg, S. Valerie
Woolf, V. Jacob's room
Woolf, V. The waves
EXPERIMENTAL MEDICINE
Freeman, B. The night bird
EXPERIMENTAL PSYCHOLOGY
Hoeg, P. Borderliners
EXPERIMENTS
Boyle, T. The Terranauts
Foster, A. Relic
Peikoff, K. Mother knows best
Stross, C. Glasshouse
Vidich, P. The coldest warrior
Wilson, C. Dead girl in 2A
Yang, J. The descent of monsters
EXPLOITATION
Brown, P. Morning star
Erdrich, L. The night watchman
Lessing, D. The fifth child
Mitchell, D. Cloud atlas
Robinson, K. Red Mars
Rucker, R. Hylozoic
Wood, S. The Quintland sisters
EXPLORATION
Chiang, T. Exhalation
Gappah, P. Out of darkness, shining light
Starling, C. The luminous dead
VanderMeer, J. Acceptance
Verne, J. Journey to the centre of the Earth

EXPLORERS
Gappah, P. Out of darkness, shining light
Gilman, C. Herland
Golden, C. Ararat
Hijuelos, O. Twain & Stanley enter paradise
Ivey, E. To the bright edge of the world
Lalami, L. The Moor's account
Michener, J. Caribbean
Michener, J. Centennial
Penney, S. Under a pole star
Sackville-West, V. The Edwardians
Simmons, D. The Terror

EXPLORERS -- GREAT BRITAIN
Wheeler, R. The canyon of bones

EXPLOSIONS
Box, C. Savage run
Clegg, B. Did you ever have a family
Grippando, J. Black horizon
Reichs, K. Deadly decisions
Woodrell, D. The Maid's Version

EXPLOSIVES
Munier, P. A borrowing of bones

Exposure Dunmore, H.

EXTENDED FAMILIES
Andrews, D. Owl be home for Christmas
Araghi, A. The immortals of Tehran
Artson, B. Odessa, Odessa
Butler, N. Little faith
Castellani, C. All this talk of love
Castillo, E. America is not the heart
Coleridge, N. A much married man
Erdrich, L. Love medicine
Ghaffari, R. To keep the sun alive
Goldbloom, G. On division
Lessing, D. The sweetest dream
Moniz, T. Big familia
Murphy, T. Correspondents
Rozan, S. Paper son
Seth, V. A suitable boy
Sexton, M. The revisioners
Trollope, J. The other family
Vuong, O. On Earth we're briefly gorgeous
Ward, J. Sing, unburied, sing
Woodson, J. Red at the bone

EXTINCT ANIMALS
Flores, F. Tears of the trufflepig

EXTINCT CITIES
Golden, C. The pandora room
Preston, D. Thunderhead

EXTINCT CITIES -- GERMANY
Flynn, M. Eifelheim

EXTINCT CITIES -- UNITED STATES
Delany, S. Dhalgren

EXTINCTION (BIOLOGY)
Beagle, P. The last unicorn
Foster, A. Relic
Millet, L. How the dead dream

Saramago, J. The cave

EXTORTION
Bennett, A. First earl I see tonight
Berry, S. The Warsaw protocol
Bourne, J. Rogue spy
Brooks, B. Blood storm
Buwalda, P. Bonita Avenue
Byrne, K. How to love a duke in ten days
Chandler, R. The big sleep
Christie, A. The murder of Roger Ackroyd
Chandler, R. The annotated Big sleep
Clinch, J. Marley
Cobbs Hoffman, E. The Hamilton affair
Coben, H. The stranger
Connolly, J. The burning soul
Crompton, R. Hell's gate
Dare, T. When a Scot ties the knot
Dickey, E. Bad men and wicked women
Eco, U. Numero zero
Ellis, D. In the company of liars
Fowler, C. Bryant & May
Goddard, R. Into the blue
Grafton, S. Y is for yesterday
Gruber, M. The forgery of Venus
Gundar-Goshen, A. Waking lions
Hallinan, T. Crashed
Harris, E. Basketball Jones
Harrison, T. Dragon bound
Jackson, J. Never have I ever
James, E. Four nights with the duke
Jio, S. The last camellia
Krentz, J. Copper Beach
Lansdale, J. Honky tonk samurai
Laukkanen, O. Deception Cove
Leon, D. The golden egg
Leonard, E. Freaky deaky
Leonard, E. The Hot Kid
Lovesey, P. Waxwork
Lutz, L. Revenge of the Spellmans
Marlette, D. Magic time
Martin, W. Cape Cod
Mathews, B. The world of tomorrow
Meltzer, B. The tenth justice
Moore, K. To seduce an angel
Morgan Jones, C. The jackal's share
Mosley, W. Six Easy pieces
Muller, M. The broken promise land
Murdoch, I. The green knight
Murdoch, I. The nice and the good
Neel, J. To die for
Nugent, L. Lying in wait
O'Connell, C. The chalk girl
Page, K. The body in the big apple
Paretsky, S. Total recall
Parker, R. Hush money
Parker, R. Potshot
Parks, B. Say nothing

Perry, A. Bedford Square
Perry, A. Belgrave Square
Perry, A. Blind justice
Perry, T. Fidelity
Pronzini, B. Nemesis
Quick, A. The mystery woman
Quick, A. Slightly shady
Quincy, D. Murder in Mayfair
Randisi, R. Hey there (you with the gun in your hand)
Rankin, I. Rather be the devil
Rigosi, G. Night bus
Roberts, N. Chesapeake blue
Rose, M. Cartier's hope
Rosenthal, P. The edge of impropriety
Ryan, H. What you see
Sakey, M. The blade itself
Sanders, L. McNally's dilemma
Sanders, L. McNally's secret
Sandford, J. Silken prey
Shepard, S. The one inside
Smith, S. A simple plan
Spark, M. Aiding & abetting
Spark, M. A far cry from Kensington
Spark, M. Memento mori
Spencer, M. Scandalous
Spiegelman, P. Black maps
Steinhauer, O. The Bridge of Sighs
Stewart, A. Girl waits with gun
Sullivan, M. Theft of swords
Tran, V. Dragonfish
Vargas Llosa, M. The discreet hero
Wambaugh, J. Floaters
Warren, R. All the king's men
White, R. A lady unrivaled
Winslow, D. The kings of cool
Winslow, D. Savages
Woods, S. The money shot
Woods, T. True to the game

EXTORTION -- CALIFORNIA
Macdonald, R. Sleeping beauty
EXTORTION -- FLORIDA
Hiaasen, C. Strip tease
EXTORTION -- MASSACHUSETTS
Page, K. The body in the bog
EXTORTION -- SOUTH CAROLINA
Hart, C. White elephant dead
EXTRAMARITAL AFFAIRS
Abbott, M. Bury me deep
Abbott, S. The future of love
Alcott, K. A touch of stardust
Amidon, S. Human capital
Amis, M. The zone of interest
Atkinson, K. One good turn
Atwood, M. Life before man
Ausubel, R. Sons and daughters of ease and plenty
Banks, R. Continental drift
Banville, J. The blue guitar

Barnes, D. Nightwood
Barth, J. The end of the road
Bates, J. Midnight at the Dragon Cafe
Beagin, J. Vacuum in the dark
Benchley, P. Jaws
Bhuvaneswar, C. White dancing elephants
Bijan, D. The last days of Cafe Leila
Bilal, P. The ghost runner
Bloom, A. White houses
Bohjalian, C. The buffalo soldier
Brockmeier, K. The truth about Celia
Brownrigg, S. Morality tale
Bryant, N. Message from a mistress
Bussi, M. Black water lilies
Byatt, A. Possession
Chase, L. Your scandalous ways
Cheek, C. Cape May
Cheever, J. The Wapshot chronicle
Cheever, J. The Wapshot scandal
Clark, M. The Jezebel remedy
Clark, W. Payback is a mutha
Cobbs Hoffman, E. The Hamilton affair
Conroy, P. The prince of tides
Cook, T. The Chatham School affair
Cook, T. Sandrine's case
Cookson, C. The year of the virgins
Coomer, J. One vacant chair
D'Souza, T. The Konkans
Davies, R. Murther and walking spirits
De Bernieres, L. Birds without wings
De Kretser, M. The life to come
Dean, L. The idea of love
Dickinson, P. The yellow room conspiracy
Dolan, H. Bad things happen
Dreiser, T. Sister Carrie
Dubus, A. Dirty love
Dufresne, J. Deep in the shade of paradise
Dufresne, J. Requiem, Mass.
Durrell, L. Balthazar
Durrell, L. Justine
Enright, A. The forgotten waltz
Erdrich, L. The painted drum
Essbaum, J. Hausfrau
Evans, D. Ordinary people
Evans, N. The horse whisperer
Faulks, S. Birdsong
Faulks, S. On Green Dolphin Street
Feeney, A. Sometimes I lie
Ferraris, Z. Kingdom of strangers
Finder, J. Judgment
Flaubert, G. Madame Bovary
Follett, K. Eye of the needle
Ford, F. The good soldier
Ford, F. Parade's end
Ford, R. A multitude of sins
Francis, D. Wedding Bush Road
French, N. The lying room

Richardson, S. Pamela
Riley, J. The serpent garden
Rooney, S. Conversations with friends
Roth, P. The ghost writer
Rushdie, S. Shalimar the Clown
Ryan, H. The other woman
Sanders, L. The fourth deadly sin
Sanders, L. The sixth commandment
Seton, A. Katherine
Shreve, A. Fortune's rocks
Shreve, A. The last time they met
Shriver, L. The post-birthday world
Sillitoe, A. Saturday night and Sunday morning
Simenon, G. Maigret and the black sheep
Simenon, G. Maigret and the Saturday caller
Singer, I. Enemies, a love story
Singer, I. The magician of Lublin
Smith, D. The constable's tale
Smith, J. If she were dead
Smith, Z. On beauty
Sontag, S. The volcano lover
Souljah,. The coldest winter ever
Spark, M. Memento mori
Spencer, S. The dead hand of history
Spencer-Fleming, J. All mortal flesh
Stachniak, E. The Winter Palace
Steel, D. First sight
Stegner, W. Angle of repose
Steinhauer, O. The Cairo affair
Strout, E. Amy and Isabelle
Swinson, K. A gangster and a gentleman
Swinson, K. Who's wife extraordinaire now
Thomas, S. Private arrangements
Tolstoy, L. Anna Karenina
Trollope, J. The best of friends
Trollope, J. Marrying the mistress
Trollope, J. A Spanish lover
Trueblood, V. Seven loves
Turow, S. Presumed innocent
Tursten, H. Winter grave
Tyler, A. Morgan's passing
Upadhyay, S. The guru of love
Updike, J. Gertrude and Claudius
Updike, J. Licks of love
Updike, J. Memories of the Ford administration
Updike, J. Rabbit, run
Urquhart, J. The night stages
Wallace, C. The blind contessa's new machine
Waller, R. The bridges of Madison County
Waters, S. The night watch
Weir, A. Anna of Kleve
Weiss, L. If the creek don't rise
Weldon, F. The life and loves of a she-devil
Weldon, F. Worst fears
Westlake, D. Memory
Williams, T. The Roman spring of Mrs. Stone
Winspear, J. Maisie Dobbs

Wolfe, P. The lost diary of M
Wolitzer, M. The wife
Woodrell, D. The Maid's Version
Yap, F. Yesterday
Zane, 1. Addicted
Zevin, G. The hole we're in
Extraordinary adventures of the Athena Club [series] Goss, T.
The **extraordinary** life of Sam Hell Dugoni, R.
An **extraordinary** union Cole, A.
EXTRASENSORY PERCEPTION
Hoeg, P. The quiet girl
EXTREME ENVIRONMENTS
Anders, C. The city in the middle of the night
Weir, A. The Martian
Extremely loud and incredibly close Foer, J.
EXTREMISM
Ahmad, J. The wandering falcon
Gunaratne, G. In our mad and furious city
Hayes, T. I am Pilgrim
Mankell, H. Before the frost
McCarry, C. Old boys
Richler, M. Barney's version
Rushdie, S. Shalimar the Clown
EXTREMISM -- UNITED STATES
Lewis, S. It can't happen here
EXTREMISTS
Hamill, P. Tabloid city
Henderson, S. Fourth of July Creek
Hunter, S. Game of snipers
Lutz, J. Lightning
McBride, J. The good lord bird
Solomon, R. An unkindness of ghosts
Williams, D. The stars now unclaimed
EYAK INDIANS
Ivey, E. To the bright edge of the world
EYE
Cleave, P. A killer harvest
Morrison, T. The bluest eye
The **eye** in the door Barker, P.
The **eye** of God Rollins, J.
Eye of the needle Follett, K.
Eye of the storm Higgins, J.
Eyes wide open Gross, A.
The **Eyre** affair Fforde, J.

F

FABERGE EGGS
Sanders, L. McNally's gamble
The **face** of a stranger Perry, A.
The **face** of trespass Rendell, R.
FACE PERCEPTION
Harris, S. The color of Bee Larkham's murder
FACTORIES
Bolano, R. 2666
Brown, S. White hot

Dekker, T. Red
Dekker, T. White
Donoghue, E. The wonder
Douglas, L. Magnificent obsession
Endo, S. Silence
Faber, M. The book of strange new things
Fabry, C. War room
Ganshert, K. Life after
Goodwin, B. Revelation
Greene, G. The power and the glory
Hatcher, R. Cross my heart
Hatcher, R. Who I am with you
Hauck, R. Once upon a prince
Henry, P. Becoming Mrs. Lewis
Irvin, K. Tell her no lies
Isaac, K. Then there was you
Johnson, T. Engraved on the heart
Kate, J. Love and other mistakes
Kingsbury, K. A Baxter family Christmas
Kingsbury, K. When we were young
Kirkpatrick, J. One more river to cross
Kirkpatrick, J. This road we traveled
Lewis, B. The brethren
Lewis, B. The preacher's daughter
Linden, R. The enlightenment of bees
MacLaverty, B. Midwinter break
Martin, C. Send down the rain
McDermott, A. Someone
Morris, M. Man in the blue moon
Nelson, C. If we make it home
Pearson, R. A long time comin'
Percy, W. Lancelot
Peterson, T. What comes my way
Phoenix, M. The space between words
Pittman, A. The seamstress
Rawlings, D. The baggage handler
Rivers, F. The masterpiece
Robinson, M. Gilead
Robinson, M. Home
Robinson, M. Lila
Rubart, J. The long journey to Jake Palmer
Russell, M. The sparrow
Spencer, S. Man in the woods
Stewart, A. Stars in the grass
Tatlock, A. Promises to keep
Toibin, C. The testament of Mary
Turansky, C. No ocean too wide
Turner, B. The secret life of Sarah Hollenbeck
Turner, B. Wooing Cadie McCaffrey
Tyers, K. Shivering world
Wall, C. The dearly beloved
Warren, T. The replacement wife
White, R. A lady unrivaled
Whitlow, R. A time to stand
Wiseman, B. Listening to love
Wright, J. The house on Foster Hill

FAITH (JUDAISM)

Andrews, M. Of fire and lions
Chabon, M. The Yiddish Policemen's Union
Goldbloom, G. On division
Hoffman, A. The world that we knew
Markovits, A. I am forbidden

FAITH -- PSYCHOLOGY
Waugh, E. Brideshead revisited

FAITH AND REASON
Goldstein, R. 36 arguments for the existence of God

Faith Fairchild mysteries [series] Page, K.

FAITH HEALERS
Bambara, T. The salt eaters
Howatch, S. The heartbreaker

FAITH HEALING
Bambara, T. The salt eaters
Bergstrom, H. Steal the north
Howatch, S. The heartbreaker

FAITH IN MEN
Bohjalian, C. Secrets of Eden
Greene, G. The power and the glory
Reimringer, J. Vestments

FAITH IN WOMEN
Gregory, P. The constant princess

Faithful place French, T.

The **faithful** spy Berenson, A.

Fake like me Bourland, B.

FAKE NEWS
Goldberg, L. Fake truth

Fake truth Goldberg, L.

Falconer Cheever, J.

FALCONERS
Box, C. The disappeared

The **fall** Camus, A.

The **fall** Mawer, S.

The **fall** guy Lasdun, J.

Fall of giants Follett, K.

The **fall** of Gondolin Tolkien, J.

The **fall** of Hyperion Simmons, D.

Fall or, Dodge in hell Stephenson, N.

The **fallen** Parker, T.

Fallen Slaughter, K.

The **fallen** Atkins, A.

The **fallen** Baldacci, D.

Fallen empire [series] Draven, G.

Fallen into the pit Peters, E.

Fallen land Brown, T.

Fallen women [series] Chase, L.

Falling for you Wade, B.

Falling in love Leon, D.

Falling into bed with a duke Heath, L.

Falling man DeLillo, D.

Falling out of time Grossman, D.

Fallout Paretsky, S.

The **falls** Oates, J.

The **falls** Rankin, I.

FALLS (ACCIDENTS)
Hill Gumbao, T. The summer of dead toys

Adichie, C. Half of a yellow sun

Adler-Olsen, J. Victim 2117

Agee, J. The bones of paradise

Ahava, S. Things that fall from the sky

Akunin, B. Sister Pelagia and the white bulldog

Alarcon, D. The king is always above the people

Alexander, V. What happens at Christmas

Alharthi, J. Celestial bodies

Ali, M. Brick Lane

Allende, I. A long petal of the sea

Allio, K. Buddhism for Western children

Alther, L. Kinflicks

Alvar, M. In the country

Alyan, H. Salt houses

Apostol, G. Gun dealers' daughter

Archer, J. The prodigal daughter

Atkinson, K. Human croquet

Attenberg, J. The Middlesteins

Austen, J. Mansfield Park

Austen, J. Pride and prejudice

Ausubel, R. Sons and daughters of ease and plenty

Baker, J. Longbourn

Balogh, M. Simply love

Banks, I. The crow road

Banks, R. Cloudsplitter

Banner, C. The house at the edge of night

Barber, L. A girl named Anna

Barclay, L. Elevator pitch

Barclay, L. No safe house

Barker, N. Darkmans

Barnes, J. The only story

Bartels, E. We hope for better things

Beagle, P. Summerlong

The best American mystery stories 2019

Beauvoir, S. The Mandarins

Beckerman, H. If only I could tell you

Benjamin, C. The immortalists

Bennett, A. First earl I see tonight

Berry, W. That distant land

Betts, D. Souls raised from the dead

Biguenet, J. Oyster

Bijan, D. The last days of Cafe Leila

Bird, S. Daughter of a daughter of a queen

Birmingham, S. Carriage trade

Blackwell, J. Letters from Paris

Blume, J. In the unlikely event

Bohjalian, C. The night strangers

Bordas, C. How to behave in a crowd

Boswell, R. Century's son

Bourdeaut, O. Waiting for Bojangles

Box, C. Blue heaven

Box, C. Open season

Box, C. Trophy hunt

Box, C. Winterkill

Bradbury, J. The wild inside

Bradbury, R. Dandelion wine

Bradley, C. The golden tresses of the dead

Breslin, J. I don't want to go to jail

Brookner, A. Family and friends

Brown, R. Before and after

Buck, P. The good Earth

Bulawayo, N. We need new names

Burns, A. Little constructions

Butler, M. Pickle's progress

Butler, S. Ten things I've learnt about love

Bybee, C. Staying for good

Byrne, T. Ghosts and lightning

Cander, C. The weight of a piano

Card, M. These ghosts are family

Cash, W. This dark road to mercy

Cash, W. The last ballad

Castellani, C. All this talk of love

Chanter, C. The well

Charlton, B. Spellbreaker

Chen, D. Brothers

Chen, M. Here and now and then

Choi, A. Kay's lucky coin variety

Christie, M. Greenwood

Cleeves, A. Wild fire

Clegg, B. Did you ever have a family

Clemmons, Z. What we lose

Coake, C. You came back

Coetzee, J. The childhood of Jesus

Colgan, J. The endless beach

Coplin, A. The orchardist

Cramer, W. Levi's will

Crane, S. Maggie

Crouch, B. Dark matter

Cruz, A. Dominicana

D'Souza, T. The Konkans

Daniel, S. Stiltsville

Danielewski, M. The familiar.

Danielewski, M. House of leaves

Davies, P. The fortunes

Davis, K. Duplex

Davis, L. A body in the bathhouse

De Robertis, C. Cantoras

DeBoard, P. The fragile world

Deb, S. The point of return

Dee, J. The privileges

Diamant, A. The red tent

Dibdin, M. Ratking

Dodd, C. Strangers she knows

Donati, S. Where the light enters

Dorris, M. A yellow raft in blue water

Drabble, M. The witch of Exmoor

Dufresne, J. Deep in the shade of paradise

Dupont, E. The American fiancee

Ebershoff, D. The 19th wife

Eggers, D. A hologram for the king

Eisenberg, D. The twilight of the superheroes

Elkins, A. Dying on the vine

Ellis, B. The vanished bride

Ellison, J. A small indiscretion

Luiselli, V. Lost children archive
Lukas, M. The last watchman of Old Cairo
MacDonald, A. When we were Vikings
Mackintosh, C. After the end
Makumbi, J. Kintu
Malamud, B. The assistant
Manning, K. My notorious life
Marillier, J. Daughter of the forest
Marra, A. The tsar of love and techno
Martin, C. Long way gone
McCracken, E. Bowlaway
McCullough, C. The first man in Rome
McDermott, A. After this
McHugh, L. The wolf wants in
McPhee, M. Gorgeous lies
McPherson, C. A step so grave
Mda, Z. The Madonna of Excelsior
Mehta, R. No other world
Meloy, M. Do not become alarmed
Meloy, M. Liars and saints
Montimore, M. Oona out of order
Moreno-Garcia, S. Gods of jade and shadow
Morgan, C. The sport of kings
Morgan, S. The Christmas sisters
Moriarty, L. Truly madly guilty
Morrow, J. The last witchfinder
Morton, B. Florence Gordon
Munro, A. The view from Castle Rock
Murphy, Y. The call
Napolitano, A. Dear Edward
Nelson, C. More than we remember
Nguyen, P. The mountains sing
Nguyen, V. The refugees
Nicholls, D. Us
Novak, B. This heart of mine
Novic, S. Girl at war
Nugent, L. Lying in wait
Nunez, E. Grace
Oates, J. Because it is bitter, and because it is my heart
Offill, J. Dept. of speculation
Offill, J. Weather
Ogawa, Y. The housekeeper and the professor
Orner, P. Love and shame and love
Palwick, S. The necessary beggar
Pamuk, O. Silent house
Patchett, A. Run
Perry, A. Death in focus
Piccirilli, T. The last kind words
Picoult, J. Lone wolf
Pilcher, R. The shell seekers
Pobi, R. City of windows
Porter, M. Lanny
Potzsch, O. The poisoned pilgrim
Potzsch, O. The werewolf of Bamberg
Poyer, D. Overthrow
Price, R. The good priest's son
Pronzini, B. Nightcrawlers

Proulx, A. Barkskins
Puzo, M. The last don
Quade, K. Night at the fiestas
Quindlen, A. Every last one
Quindlen, A. Miller's Valley
Quinn, J. An offer from a gentleman
Quinn, K. The huntress
Reddi, R. Passage west
Rhys, R. Fatal inheritance
Richardson, S. Pamela
Ripley, M. Mr Campion's fault
Robinson, M. Home
Robinson, R. Cost
Rodale, M. Lady Bridget's diary
Rojas Contreras, I. Fruit of the drunken tree
Roth, P. Everyman
Rowell, R. Landline
Roy, A. An atlas of impossible longing
Roy, A. The god of small things
Rushdie, S. The moor's last sigh
Rutherfurd, E. The forest
Rutherfurd, E. London
Rutherfurd, E. The princes of Ireland
Rutherfurd, E. The rebels of Ireland
Rutherfurd, E. Russka
Rutherfurd, E. Sarum
Sakey, M. A better world
Sakey, M. Brilliance
Saylor, S. Roma
Scott, J. Tourmaline
Sebastian, C. It takes two to tumble
See, L. The tea girl of Hummingbird Lane
Serpell, N. The old drift
Shalev, M. Two she-bears
Shamsie, K. Home fire
Shanbhag, V. Ghachar ghochar
Shannon, D. The Manson curse
Shaw, I. Beggarman, thief
Shields, C. The stone diaries
Shimotakahara, L. After the bloom
Shipman, V. The heirloom garden
Shupe, J. The prince of Broadway
Simpson, D. Dead and gone
Simpson, M. Anywhere but here
Singer, I. Collected stories
Sittenfeld, C. Eligible
Smiley, J. Early warning
Smiley, J. Golden age
Smiley, J. Some luck
Smith, A. The accidental
Smith, Z. White teeth
Snow, C. Strangers and brothers
Stewart, A. Girl waits with gun
Stewart, A. Stars in the grass
Stoker, D. Dracul
Strout, E. Anything is possible
Stuart, D. Shuggie Bain

Soniah Kamal Unmarriageable

FAMILIES -- SOUTH AFRICA

Gordimer, N. July's people

FAMILIES -- SOUTHERN STATES

Adams, A. A southern exposure

O'Connor, F. The violent bear it away

FAMILIES -- TEXAS

Meyer, P. The son

FAMILIES -- UNITED STATES

Bauman, B. Broken sleep

Sedaris, D. Holidays on ice

FAMILIES -- UPPER MIDWEST

Hoover, M. The quickening

FAMILIES -- VERMONT

Morris, M. Songs in ordinary time

FAMILIES -- VIRGINIA

Smith, L. Family linen

FAMILIES -- WALES

Llewellyn, R. How green was my valley

FAMILIES OF AIRPLANE ACCIDENT VICTIMS

Auster, P. The book of illusions

FAMILIES OF KIDNAPPING VICTIMS

Meloy, M. Do not become alarmed

Parks, B. Say nothing

FAMILIES OF MILITARY PERSONNEL

Benedict, H. Wolf season

Fallon, S. You know when the men are gone

Hannah, K. Home front

Hannah, K. The nightingale

Powers, K. The yellow birds

Sarginson, S. The wonderful

FAMILIES OF MISSING PERSONS

Hart, E. Haunted ground

Heller, P. Celine

Mitchard, J. No time to wave goodbye

Reisman, N. The first desire

Robinson, P. Strange affair

FAMILIES OF MURDER VICTIMS

Aslam, N. Maps for lost lovers

Baldacci, D. Long road to mercy

Baldacci, D. A minute to midnight

Blackmore, R. Lorna Doone

Bobotis, A. The last list of Miss Judith Kratt

Buxbaum, J. After you

Clark, M. I've got my eyes on you

Constantine, L. The last time I saw you

Cook, T. Sandrine's case

Daugherty, C. The echo killing

French, T. Broken harbor

Gaylin, A. Never look back

Hart, J. The king of lies

Isaacs, S. As husbands go

K'wan Hoodlum

Koryta, M. The prophet

O'Connell, C. Find me

O'Connell, C. Mallory's oracle

Oates, J. A book of American martyrs

Parker, R. Sea change

Patterson, R. Balance of power

Pickard, N. The scent of rain and lightning

Rankin, I. Blood hunt

Redfern, E. The music of the spheres

Salvalaggio, K. Bone dust white

Schaitkin, A. Saint X

Sebold, A. The lovely bones

Stabenow, D. A taint in the blood

The **family** Puzo, M.

FAMILY AND ADDICTION

Holmes, S. B-more careful

FAMILY AND ALCOHOLISM

Breslin, J. Table money

Bronte, A. The tenant of Wildfell Hall

FAMILY AND DEATH

Agee, J. A death in the family

Alarcon, D. The king is always above the people

Greenfeld, K. True

Toibin, C. Nora Webster

Urrea, L. The house of broken angels

Yoshimoto, B. Moshi-moshi

Family and friends Brookner, A.

FAMILY AND MENTAL ILLNESS

Bourdeaut, O. Waiting for Bojangles

Haslett, A. Imagine me gone

Reisman, N. The first desire

FAMILY AND SUICIDE

Arnett, K. Mostly dead things

Boswell, R. Century's son

Kamal, S. It all falls down

Lodato, V. Edgar and Lucy

McDermott, A. The ninth hour

Oates, J. The falls

Straub, P. Lost boy lost girl

Winthrop, E. The why of things

FAMILY AND WAR

Aramburu, F. Homeland

Baker, J. The undertow

Benedict, H. Wolf season

Donoghue, E. Akin

Hosseini, K. Sea prayer

Leithauser, B. The art student's war

Loigman, L. The wartime sisters

Moyes, J. The girl you left behind

FAMILY AND WORK

Brownrigg, S. The delivery room

FAMILY BUSINESSES

Arnett, K. Mostly dead things

Banner, C. The house at the edge of night

Bijan, D. The last days of Cafe Leila

Bradford, B. Just rewards

Bradford, B. A woman of substance

Christie, M. Greenwood

Crombie, D. Kissed a sad goodbye

Dickens, C. Dombey and Son

Evanovich, J. One for the money

Frame, R. Havisham
Heger, A. Crazy cupid love
Higgins, K. The best man
Higgins, K. The perfect match
Hunting, H. Handle with care
Johnson, R. No one in the world
Joyce, G. The limits of enchantment
Kate, J. A girl's guide to the Outback
Krentz, J. White lies
Lewis, K. Half of what you hear
Lutz, L. Curse of the Spellmans
Lutz, L. The last word
Lutz, L. Revenge of the Spellmans
Malamud, B. The assistant
Martin, K. Beyond reason
Merbeth, K. Fortuna
Paretsky, S. Fire sale
Perrotta, T. Joe College
Phillips, S. First star I see tonight
Pineiro, C. One summer night
Putney, M. The burning point
Robards, K. The ultimatum
Roberts, N. Come sundown
Russo, R. Empire Falls
Stradal, J. The lager queen of Minnesota
Taneja, P. We that are young

FAMILY CELEBRATIONS
Woodson, J. Red at the bone

Family chronicles [series] Singer, I.

FAMILY CURSES
Diaz, J. The brief wondrous life of Oscar Wao
Fine, J. What should be wild
Makumbi, J. Kintu
Serpell, N. The old drift
Shannon, D. The Manson curse

FAMILY ESTATES
Austen, J. Northanger Abbey
Baker, J. Longbourn
Balogh, M. Simply love
Bennett, A. First earl I see tonight
Blake, S. The guest book
Bradley, C. The golden tresses of the dead
Burrowes, G. The soldier
Cleage, P. Some things I never thought I'd do
Crombie, D. A bitter feast
Du Maurier, D. Rebecca
Eco, U. The mysterious flame of Queen Loana
Fielding, J. The bad daughter
Fine, J. What should be wild
Forster, E. Howards End
French, T. The witch elm
Ghaffari, R. To keep the sun alive
Hart, E. Haunted ground
Hoffman, A. The marriage of opposites
Hollinghurst, A. The stranger's child
Jackson, S. We have always lived in the castle
Klassen, J. The painter's daughter

Kleypas, L. Cold-hearted rake
Macmillan, G. The nanny
McHugh, L. Arrowood
McPherson, C. A step so grave
Morton, K. The house at Riverton
Pyper, A. The homecoming
Robertson, I. Island of bones
Seton, A. Dragonwyck
Vine, B. The minotaur
The **family** Fang Wilson, K.

FAMILY FARMS
FitzGerald, G. Redemption Mountain
McGahan, A. The white earth
Smiley, J. A thousand acres

FAMILY FEUDS
Aramburu, F. Homeland
Archer, J. Best kept secret
Archer, J. The prodigal daughter
Beverley, J. Tempting fortune
Biguenet, J. Oyster
Boyle, T. World's end
Bradley, A. A wicked way to win an earl
Doig, I. Mountain time
Eliot, G. The mill on the Floss
Fortier, A. Juliet
Kelton, E. Texas vendetta
Lackberg, C. The stonecutter
Long, J. The legend of Lyon Redmond
Martin, W. Cape Cod
O'Brien, E. Wild Decembers
Pineiro, C. One summer night
Rai, A. Hate to want you
Ryan, J. Restless rancher
Saberhagen, F. Farslayer's story

FAMILY FORTUNES
Souljah,. Midnight and the meaning of love
Family furnishings Munro, A.

FAMILY HISTORY
Bartels, E. We hope for better things
Cander, C. The weight of a piano
Card, M. These ghosts are family
Chung, C. The tenth muse
Ghosh, A. Gun Island
Gyasi, Y. Homegoing
Halfon, E. Mourning
Hamill, S. A cosmology of monsters
Olson, N. Before the devil fell
Oyeyemi, H. Gingerbread
Patchett, A. Commonwealth
Sexton, M. The revisioners
Shalev, M. Two she-bears
Smith, M. Blackwood
Staples, D. This town sleeps
Williams, B. All the ways we said goodbye
Family honor Parker, R.

FAMILY KILLING
Mina, D. The long drop

Robards, K. The last victim
Silvis, R. Two days gone
A **family** lexicon Ginzburg, N.
Family linen Smith, L.

FAMILY LORE

McCracken, E. Bowlaway
The **family** man Lipman, E.
Family money Bawden, N.
The **family** Moskat Singer, I.

FAMILY PROBLEMS

Abraham, T. Black Sunday
Abu-Jaber, D. Birds of paradise
Austin, L. All she ever wanted
Beattie, A. A wonderful stroke of luck
Berg, E. Once upon a time, there was you
Blundell, J. The high season
Booth, C. Bronxwood
Booth, C. Kendra
Child, L. Echo burning
Chu, W. The lives of tao
Conroy, P. The prince of tides
Dee, J. A thousand pardons
Dickens, C. Dombey and Son
Francis, D. Wedding Bush Road
Fuqua, J. Gone and back again
George, E. What came before he shot her
Goodwin, B. Revelation
Gordimer, N. None to accompany me
Greenfeld, K. True
Hamill, S. A cosmology of monsters
Harper, J. The lost man
Higgins, K. Now that you mention it
Hilderbrand, E. Winter in paradise
Holmes, S. B-more careful
Just, W. An unfinished season
Kenney, J. Talk to me
Kimmel, F. No good asking
Kincaid, J. Annie John
Lessing, D. The fifth child
Lundrigan, N. Glass boys
Mitchell, D. Black Swan Green
Morrison, T. The bluest eye
Oates, J. Because it is bitter, and because it is my heart
Oates, J. Broke heart blues
Oates, J. The falls
Oates, J. The gravedigger's daughter
Oates, J. Little bird of heaven
Oates, J. Marya
Oates, J. We were the Mulvaneys
Osondu, E. This house is not for sale
Petterson, P. I refuse
Shields, C. Unless
Sittenfeld, C. Eligible
Smiley, J. A thousand acres
Smith, A. The accidental
Sosa, M. The worst best man
Tan, L. What we were promised

Theroux, P. The Mosquito Coast
Toews, M. A complicated kindness
Tsao, T. The majesties
Walker, K. The age of miracles
Wuertz, Y. Everything belongs to us

FAMILY RECIPES

Oyeyemi, H. Gingerbread

FAMILY RELATIONSHIPS

Abbott, M. The fever
Acker, J. The limits of the world
Adam, C. Golden child
Adebayo, A. Stay with me
Adelman, M. Piece of mind
Adiga, A. Selection day
Akunin, B. Sister Pelagia and the white bulldog
Albert, E. The book of Dahlia
Alenyikov, M. Ivan and Misha
Alexie, S. Flight
Alharthi, J. Celestial bodies
Aliu, X. Brass
Allen, S. First frost
Allende, I. The house of the spirits
Alther, L. Kinflicks
Alyan, H. Salt houses
Amidon, S. Human capital
Amis, M. Lionel Asbo
Anam, T. The bones of grace
Antoinette, A. The Cartel
Antoinette, A. The Cartel 2
Antoinette, A. The Cartel 3
Antopol, M. The UnAmericans
Archer, J. Nothing ventured
Arimah, L. What it means when a man falls from the sky
Arnett, K. Mostly dead things
Arnoult, D. Sufficient grace
Artson, B. Odessa, Odessa
Ashley, J. The madness of Lord Ian Mackenzie
Atkinson, K. Case histories
Atkinson, K. A god in ruins
Atkinson, K. Human croquet
Attenberg, J. All this could be yours
Attenberg, J. The Middlesteins
Atwood, M. The blind assassin
Atwood, M. Bluebeard's egg and other stories
Atwood, M. Moral disorder
Auster, P. 4 3 2 1
Austin, L. All she ever wanted
Awad, M. 13 ways of looking at a fat girl
Azzopardi, T. Winterton blue
Baca, J. The importance of a piece of paper
Bagshawe, T. Adored
Baker, E. Keeping the house
Baker, T. The little giant of Aberdeen County
Balasubramanyam, R. Professor Chandra follows his bliss
Baldacci, D. One summer
Baldwin, J. Going to meet the man
Bambara, T. Gorilla, my love

Dickens, C. Dombey and Son

Dickey, E. The business of lovers

Diehl, H. Lifelines

Dillard, A. The Maytrees

Doctorow, E. The book of Daniel

Doctorow, E. Homer and Langley

Doctorow, E. Ragtime

Doctorow, E. World's Fair

Doerr, A. All the light we cannot see

Donati, S. Where the light enters

Donoghue, E. Akin

Dorris, M. Cloud chamber

Dorris, M. A yellow raft in blue water

Downing, S. He started it

Doyle, R. Paddy Clarke, ha-ha-ha

Drabble, M. The dark flood rises

Drabble, M. The witch of Exmoor

Duffy, B. House of echoes

Dufresne, J. Requiem, Mass.

Dunant, S. The birth of Venus

Dykes, A. Whose waves these are

Edgarian, C. Three stages of amazement

Edvardsson, M. A nearly normal family

Eggers, D. How we are hungry

Eliot, G. The mill on the Floss

Ellis, B. Lunar Park

Ellmann, L. Ducks, Newburyport

Enger, L. The high divide

Englander, N. The ministry of Special Cases

Enright, A. Actress

Enright, A. The Green Road

Epstein, J. The love song of A. Jerome Minkoff, and other stories

Erdrich, L. The beet queen

Erdrich, L. The painted drum

Erdrich, L. The plague of doves

Erdrich, L. The round house

Erdrich, L. Shadow tag

Evans, H. A place for us

Everett, P. Suder

Evison, J. This is your life, Harriet Chance!

Fabry, C. War room

Fajardo-Anstine, K. Sabrina & Corina

Faulkner, W. The hamlet

Faulkner, W. Uncollected stories of William Faulkner

Fay, J. The shortest way home

Ferber, E. So big

Ferris, J. The unnamed

Fielding, J. The bad daughter

Fisher, K. The silent wife

Fitzgerald, P. The blue flower

Flagg, F. Standing in the rainbow

Foer, J. Here I am

Forman, G. Leave me

Foster, L. Sisters of summer's end

Fowler, K. We are all completely beside ourselves

Francis, D. Wedding Bush Road

Frank, D. Folly Beach

Franzen, J. The corrections

Franzen, J. Freedom

Frear, C. Sweet little lies

French, N. Tuesday's gone

French, T. Faithful place

Freudenberger, N. The dissident

Fuller, C. Our endless numbered days

Fuller, J. Abbeville

Gage, E. The ladies of Managua

Gaige, A. Schroder

Gailey, S. Magic for liars

Galsworthy, J. The Forsyte saga

Gardam, J. God on the rocks

Gaskell, E. North and South

Genova, L. Every note played

Genova, L. Left neglected

Gessen, K. A terrible country

Gestern, H. The people in the photo

Ghaffari, R. To keep the sun alive

Ghosh, A. The glass palace

Gibbons, K. Charms for the easy life

Gideon, M. Wife 22

Gifford, B. Wyoming

Gilbert, D. & sons

Ginzburg, N. A family lexicon

Giordano, P. Like family

Glass, J. Three Junes

Glass, J. The widower's tale

Goldbloom, G. On division

Goodwin, B. Revelation

Greene, A. Long Man

Greer, A. The impossible lives of Greta Wells

Gregory, P. Tidelands

Grodstein, L. A friend of the family

Grossman, D. To the end of the land

Gustine, A. You should pity us instead

Hadley, T. Bad dreams and other stories

Hadley, T. Clever girl

Hadley, T. The past

Hamill, S. A cosmology of monsters

Hannah, K. The nightingale

Haruf, K. Benediction

Hashemzadeh Bonde, G. What we owe

Hazzard, S. The great fire

Hegi, U. The vision of Emma Blau

Heller, J. Good as Gold

Helprin, M. Paris in the present tense

Hempel, A. Sing to it

Henderson, S. Fourth of July Creek

Hepworth, S. The secrets of midwives

Heyer, G. The grand Sophy

Higgins, K. Life and other inconveniences

Higgins, K. Now that you mention it

Hilderbrand, E. The perfect couple

Hilderbrand, E. What happens in paradise

Hoeg, P. The history of Danish dreams

Moore, L. A gate at the stairs
Moore, L. The unseen world
Mootoo, S. Moving forward sideways, like a crab
Morgan, R. The road from Gap Creek
Moriarty, L. Big little lies
Moriarty, L. The husband's secret
Morris, M. Songs in ordinary time
Mortimer, J. Quite honestly
Morton, B. Florence Gordon
Mosley, W. And sometimes I wonder about you
Mott, J. The returned
Moyes, J. The peacock emporium
Mozley, F. Elmet
Mukherjee, N. A life apart
Mukherjee, N. The lives of others
Muller, M. The broken promise land
Muller, M. The cavalier in white
Munoz Molina, A. A manuscript of ashes
Munro, A. Runaway
Murdoch, I. The philosopher's pupil
Murphy, T. Correspondents
Murray, P. Skippy dies
NDiaye, M. Ladivine
Nahai, G. The luminous heart of Jonah S.
Naipaul, V. A house for Mr. Biswas
Naslund, S. The fountain of St. James Court
Nemirovsky, I. Fire in the blood
Ng, C. Everything I never told you
Nguyen, P. The mountains sing
Nichols, L. Vessel
Nickson, C. Cold cruel winter
Nickson, C. The constant lovers
Norman, H. What is left the daughter
Nunez, E. Anna in-between
O'Farrell, M. This must be the place
O'Flynn, C. The news where you are
O'Nan, S. Emily, alone
O'Nan, S. Henry, himself
O'Neill, J. At swim, two boys
Oates, J. Carthage
Oates, J. Evil eye
Oates, J. Little bird of heaven
Oates, J. We were the Mulvaneys
Obioma, C. The fishermen
Oliveras, P. Their perfect melody
Osondu, E. This house is not for sale
Otsuka, J. When the emperor was divine
Overholser, W. Death of a cattle king
Oyeyemi, H. Boy, Snow, Bird
Oyeyemi, H. Gingerbread
Oyeyemi, H. The opposite house
Oz, A. The same sea
Ozick, C. Heir to the glimmering world
Packer, A. The children's crusade
Palmer, D. The new husband
Palwick, S. The necessary beggar
Pamuk, O. A strangeness in my mind

Panowich, B. Bull Mountain
Panowich, B. Like lions
Paretsky, S. Fire sale
Parmar, P. Vanessa and her sister
Patchett, A. Commonwealth
Patchett, A. The Dutch house
Paul, G. The lost daughter
Pearson, R. A long time comin'
Penman, S. Devil's brood
Penman, S. A king's ransom
Percy, B. The wilding
Percy, W. The moviegoer
Petterson, P. I curse the river of time
Petterson, P. I refuse
Phillips, A. The tragedy of Arthur
Phillips, C. Dancing in the dark
Picoult, J. My sister's keeper
Phillips, J. Lark and Termite
Picoult, J. Lone wolf
Pilcher, R. The shell seekers
Price, R. Roxanna Slade
Proulx, A. Bad dirt
Proulx, A. Fine just the way it is
Pyper, A. The homecoming
Pywell, S. What happened to Henry
Quindlen, A. Miller's Valley
Quindlen, A. Object lessons
Rachman, T. The Italian teacher
Ramsay, F. Stranger room
Ray, K. No country
Redhill, M. Consolation
Reiken, F. Day for night
Reisman, N. The first desire
Rendell, R. Kissing the gunner's daughter
Rice, L. Little night
Richmond, M. No one you know
Rimmer, K. Truths I never told you
Robb, C. A twisted vengeance
Roberts, N. Come sundown
Robinson, K. Aurora
Robinson, M. Gilead
Robinson, R. Cost
Rodrigues Fowler, Y. Stubborn archivist
Rosnay, T. Sarah's key
Roth, H. Call it sleep
Roth, P. The anatomy lesson
Roth, P. Letting go
Roth, P. Portnoy's complaint
Roth, P. When she was good
Roth, P. Zuckerman unbound
Roy, A. An atlas of impossible longing
Russell, K. Swamplandia!
Russo, R. Bridge of sighs
Rutherfurd, E. The princes of Ireland
Rutherfurd, E. The rebels of Ireland
Salinger, J. Franny and Zooey
Sankaran, L. The hope factory

Woolf, V. The years
Wouk, H. War and remembrance
Wouk, H. The winds of war
Wyld, E. After the fire, a still small voice
Yoshimoto, B. Goodbye Tsugumi
Young, W. The shack
Zailckas, K. Mother, mother
Zevin, G. The hole we're in
Zevin, G. Young Jane Young

FAMILY RELATIONSHIPS -- GREAT BRITAIN
Baker, J. The undertow

FAMILY RELATIONSHIPS -- THE WEST (UNITED STATES)
McMurtry, L. Boone's Lick

FAMILY RELATIONSHIPS -- VERMONT
Proulx, A. Postcards

FAMILY REUNIONS
Berg, E. The art of mending
Evans, H. A place for us
Lipman, E. The family man
MacDonald, J. The lonely silver rain
McEwan, I. Saturday
Mitchard, J. The deep end of the ocean
Orange, T. There there
Peters, E. Children of the storm
Rice, L. Little night
Schwartz, J. Northwest corner
Strout, E. My name is Lucy Barton
Varley, J. Rolling thunder
Welty, E. Losing battles
Welty, E. Stories, essays & memoir

FAMILY SAGAS
Abulhawa, S. The blue between sky and water
Acker, J. The limits of the world
Alharthi, J. Celestial bodies
Allen, S. The girl who chased the moon
Allende, I. The house of the spirits
Allende, I. Portrait in sepia
Alyan, H. Salt houses
Anstruther, E. A perfect explanation
Araghi, A. The immortals of Tehran
Archer, J. Best kept secret
Archer, J. Only time will tell
Archer, J. The prodigal daughter
Archer, J. This was a man
Artson, B. Odessa, Odessa
Atkinson, K. Human croquet
Baker, E. Keeping the house
Baker, J. The undertow
Banner, C. The house at the edge of night
Bauman, B. Broken sleep
Benjamin, C. The immortalists
Birmingham, S. The Auerbach will
Blake, S. The guest book
Blume, J. In the unlikely event
Bohjalian, C. The sandcastle girls
Boyle, T. World's end

Bradford, B. A woman of substance
Bradford, B. Just rewards
Bradford, B. Master of his fate
Brennert, A. Daughter of Moloka'i
Brkic, C. The first rule of swimming
Brown, D. Creek Mary's blood
Brown, R. Six of one
Buck, P. The good Earth
Card, M. These ghosts are family
Castellani, C. All this talk of love
Castillo, E. America is not the heart
Cheever, J. The Wapshot chronicle
Cheever, J. The Wapshot scandal
Chen, D. Brothers
Christie, M. Greenwood
Colvin, J. Africaville
Coster, N. Halsey Street
Cramer, W. Levi's will
Crummey, M. Galore
Cunningham, M. Flesh and blood
Davies, R. Murther and walking spirits
De la Roche, M. Jalna
Deb, S. The point of return
Deon, N. Grace
Djavadi, N. Disoriental
Dorris, M. Cloud chamber
Dorris, M. A yellow raft in blue water
Dunnett, D. Niccolo rising
Dupont, E. The American fiancee
Enright, A. Actress
Enright, A. The Green Road
Faulkner, W. Absalom, Absalom!
Faulkner, W. The hamlet
Follett, K. Edge of eternity
Follett, K. Fall of giants
Follett, K. Winter of the world
Fuller, J. Abbeville
Gage, E. The ladies of Managua
Gaines, E. The autobiography of Miss Jane Pittman
Galsworthy, J. The Forsyte saga
Garcia Marquez, G. One hundred years of solitude
Garcia, C. The Aguero sisters
Ghaffari, R. To keep the sun alive
Ghosh, A. The glass palace
Gibbons, K. Charms for the easy life
Gilbert, E. The signature of all things
Ginzburg, N. A family lexicon
Gregory, P. Tidelands
Gyasi, Y. Homegoing
Haigh, J. Baker Towers
Hawthorne, N. The house of the seven gables
Hegi, U. The vision of Emma Blau
Hill, R. Hanta Yo
Hoeg, P. The history of Danish dreams
Hollinghurst, A. The stranger's child
Howatch, S. Cashelmara
Jakes, J. Love and war

Atwood, M. The blind assassin
Austin, L. All she ever wanted
Babson, M. The company of cats
Baker, J. The undertow
Balogh, M. Someone to love
Barclay, L. Broken promise
Barclay, L. Far from true
Barker, P. Another world
Barr, N. What Rose forgot
Barry, B. The map of true places
Bartels, E. We hope for better things
Bates, J. Midnight at the Dragon Cafe
Bauermeister, E. The scent keeper
Bauman, B. Broken sleep
Beattie, A. The doctor's house
Beckerman, H. If only I could tell you
Belfer, L. And after the fire
Bender, A. The particular sadness of lemon cake
Bennett, R. American elsewhere
Berg, E. The art of mending
Beverley, J. Devilish
Beverley, J. My lady notorious
Bird, S. The flamenco academy
Birmingham, S. Carriage trade
Black, B. Christine Falls
Blackwell, J. Letters from Paris
Blake, S. The guest book
Bobotis, A. The last list of Miss Judith Kratt
Bohjalian, C. The double bind
Bohjalian, C. The sandcastle girls
Bradford, B. Just rewards
Bradford, B. Power of a woman
Brkic, C. The first rule of swimming
Bronte, C. Jane Eyre
Brouwer, S. Thief of glory
Brown, T. Gods of Howl Mountain
Burdick, S. The girls with no names
Burke, A. The better sister
Buwalda, P. Bonita Avenue
Byatt, A. The children's book
Callanan, L. Paris by the book
Caputo, P. Crossers
Card, M. These ghosts are family
Carter, S. New England white
Cartwright, J. To heaven by water
Castellani, C. All this talk of love
Castillo, L. Shamed
Center, K. How to walk away
Cha, S. Your house will pay
Chabon, M. Moonglow
Chakraborty, S. The kingdom of copper
Chavez, H. No bad deed
Chen, D. Brothers
Child, L. The enemy
Child, L. Past tense
Christie, M. Greenwood
Clark, M. The melody lingers on

Clarke, L. A single breath
Cleeton, C. Next year in Havana
Cocco, G. Shadows on the lake
Coe, J. The rain before it falls
Coleridge, N. Godchildren
Cunningham, M. Flesh and blood
De Robertis, C. Perla
De los Santos, M. The precious one
DeCarlo, M. The art of crash landing
Deane, S. Reading in the dark
Dev, S. The Bollywood bride
Dimechkie, K. Lifted by the great nothing
Divakaruni, C. Oleander girl
Doan, A. The summer list
Donoghue, E. Akin
Dorris, M. A yellow raft in blue water
Downing, S. He started it
Dufresne, J. Deep in the shade of paradise
Dykes, A. Whose waves these are
Edwards, K. The memory keeper's daughter
Elliott, L. The missing years
Ellison, J. Tear me apart
Enger, L. Undiscovered country
Enright, A. Actress
Enright, A. The gathering
Epstein, J. Wunderland
Erdrich, L. Love medicine
Evans, H. A place for us
Fabry, C. The promise of Jesse Woods
Fielding, J. The bad daughter
Finch, C. The vanishing man
Finder, J. The fixer
Fisher, K. The silent wife
Flagg, F. Fried green tomatoes at the Whistle Stop Cafe
Fortier, A. Juliet
Fowler, E. The road to Cardinal Valley
Frankel, L. This is how it always is
French, T. The witch elm
Friedland, E. The floating Feldmans
Fuller, C. Our endless numbered days
Gabaldon, D. Written in my own heart's blood
Gage, E. The ladies of Managua
Gardam, J. God on the rocks
Gardner, L. Love you more
Gardner, L. The neighbor
Gaylin, A. Never look back
George, E. Believing the lie
Gerritsen, T. Playing with fire
Gestern, H. The people in the photo
Gilbert, D. & sons
Glass, J. The whole world over
Godwin, G. Flora
Goodwin, B. Revelation
Goonan, K. This shared dream
Grau, S. The keepers of the house
Gray, A. The care and feeding of ravenously hungry girls
Green, N. The angel of Montague Street

Power, S. The grass dancer
Pronzini, B. Hardcase
Putney, M. The marriage spell
Pyper, A. The homecoming
Ragan, T. Buried deep
Ramsay, F. Stranger room
Rawle, G. Woman's world
Rendell, R. The babes in the wood
Restrepo, L. Delirium
Rhodes, J. Voodoo dreams
Rhys, R. Fatal inheritance
Rice, L. Last day
Riley, L. The girl on the cliff
Rimmer, K. Truths I never told you
Robb, C. A twisted vengeance
Roberts, N. Dark witch
Roberts, N. The obsession
Robertson, I. Instruments of darkness
Robertson, I. Island of bones
Robinson, M. Home
Robotham, M. The other wife
Rosnay, T. Sarah's key
Roy, L. Gone too long
Ruiz Zafon, C. The labyrinth of the spirits
Rushdie, S. The golden house
Ryan, J. Restless rancher
Ryan, J. The spies of Shilling Lane
Santopolo, J. More than words
Sarvas, M. Memento Park
Schwartz, J. Northwest corner
Schwarz, C. Drowning Ruth
Scott, J. Follow me
Scottoline, L. Don't go
Searles, J. Help for the haunted
See, L. Dreams of joy
See, L. The island of sea women
See, L. Shanghai girls
Setterfield, D. The thirteenth tale
Shafak, E. The bastard of Istanbul
Shepherd, L. A fatal likeness
Shimotakahara, L. After the bloom
Slaughter, K. Pieces of her
Smiley, J. Early warning
Smiley, J. Golden age
Smiley, J. A thousand acres
Smith, L. Fair and tender ladies
St. Aubyn, E. At last
Stabenow, D. Restless in the grave
Stabenow, D. Though not dead
Stewart, M. The wicked day
Strout, E. Amy and Isabelle
Strout, E. My name is Lucy Barton
Styles, T. A hustler's son
Styles, T. Raunchy
Sundstol, V. The land of dreams
Swyler, E. Light from other stars
Tan, A. The kitchen god's wife

Tan, A. The Valley of Amazement
Thomas, R. Firewatching
Tie, N. The bathing women
Tremblay, P. A head full of ghosts
Trigiani, A. Big Stone Gap
Tsao, T. The majesties
Turow, S. Ordinary heroes
Udall, B. The lonely polygamist
Vann, D. Aquarium
Veletzos, R. The girl they left behind
Vida, V. Let the Northern Lights erase your name
Vine, B. Anna's book
Walls, J. The silver star
Ware, R. The death of Mrs. Westaway
Weir, M. The book of Essie
White, S. Dry ice
Wiggs, S. The beekeeper's ball
Wiggs, S. The ocean between us
Wilhelm, K. The good children
Williams, B. All the ways we said goodbye
Williams, B. The golden hour
Willig, L. The Ashford affair
Willig, L. The summer country
Wright, J. The house on Foster Hill
Wyld, E. After the fire, a still small voice
Yarbrough, S. Safe from the neighbors
Zander, J. The swimmer

FAMILY SECRETS -- CUBA
Garcia, C. The Aguero sisters
FAMILY STORYTELLING
L'Engle, M. Certain women
Wallace, D. Big fish
FAMILY TRADITIONS
Esquivel, L. Like water for chocolate
McDermott, A. After this
Singer, I. The family Moskat
Tyler, A. Digging to America
Family trust Wang, K.
The **family** upstairs Jewell, L.
FAMILY VACATIONS
Friedland, E. The floating Feldmans
Levy, D. Swimming home
Nicholls, D. Us
Straub, E. The vacationers
FAMILY VIOLENCE
Burns, A. Little constructions
Byatt, A. Babel Tower
Carey, M. Someone like me
Cunningham, M. Flesh and blood
DuPree, K. Shattered
Edwardson, A. Sail of stone
Enriquez, M. Things we lost in the fire
Erdrich, L. The night watchman
Gardner, L. Love you more
Hoover, C. It ends with us
King, S. Dolores Claiborne
LaValle, V. The changeling

Fforde, J. Shades of grey

Ford, J. The empire of ice cream

Gaiman, N. Anansi boys

Gaiman, N. Fragile things

Gaiman, N. Good omens

Gaiman, N. The ocean at the end of the lane

Gaiman, N. Trigger warning

Gilman, L. Flesh and fire

Goldman, W. The princess bride

Hackwith, A. The library of the unwritten

Hawkins, S. The library at Mount Char

Jemisin, N. How long 'til black future month?

Jemisin, N. The killing moon

Johnson, K. The dream-quest of Vellitt Boe

Johnson, M. Pym

Kay, G. Children of earth and sky

Kiernan, C. The very best of Caitlin R. Kiernan

Krueger, P. Steel crow saga

Lake, J. Endurance

Lake, J. Green

Lanagan, M. The brides of Rollrock Island

Larkwood, A. The unspoken name

Latin@ rising

Lavery, D. The merry spinster

Le Guin, U. The beginning place

Le Guin, U. The other wind

Lewis, C. Till we have faces

Link, K. Magic for beginners

Maaren, K. Weave a circle round

Maguire, G. Son of a witch

Maguire, G. Wicked

Marillier, J. Daughter of the forest

Marks, L. Fire logic

McGuire, S. Beneath the sugar sky

McGuire, S. Down among the sticks and bones

McGuire, S. Every heart a doorway

McGuire, S. In an absent dream

McGuire, S. Middlegame

McKillip, P. Alphabet of thorn

McKillip, P. Ombria in shadow

Moore, A. Jerusalem

Morgenstern, E. The starless sea

Naslund, B. Blood of an exile

Nebula Awards showcase 2017

The new voices of fantasy

New suns

Norton, A. Golden trillium

Novik, N. His majesty's dragon

Novik, N. Spinning silver

Novik, N. Uprooted

Palwick, S. The necessary beggar

Parry, H. The unlikely escape of Uriah Heep

Peet, M. The Murdstone trilogy

Penelope, L. Song of blood and stone

Penelope, L. Whispers of shadow & flame

Polk, C. Witchmark

Poore, M. Reincarnation blues

Pratchett, T. The color of magic

Pratchett, T. Equal rites

Pratchett, T. The fifth elephant

Pratchett, T. Going postal

Pratchett, T. Guards! Guards!

Pratchett, T. The last hero

Pratchett, T. Lords and ladies

Pratchett, T. Men at arms

Pratchett, T. Monstrous regiment

Pratchett, T. Pyramids

Pratchett, T. Reaper man

Pratchett, T. Small gods

Pratchett, T. Thief of time

Pratchett, T. Thud!

Pratchett, T. The truth

Pratchett, T. Witches abroad

Pratchett, T. Wyrd sisters

Roanhorse, R. Trail of lightning

Rogues

Rushdie, S. East, West

Rushdie, S. Two years eight months and twenty-eight nights

Ryan, A. The waking fire

Saberhagen, F. Coinspinner's story

Saberhagen, F. Farslayer's story

Saberhagen, F. Mindsword's story

Saberhagen, F. Shieldbreaker's story

Saberhagen, F. Sightblinder's story

Saberhagen, F. Stonecutter's story

Saberhagen, F. Wayfinder's story

Saberhagen, F. Woundhealer's story

Savage, S. Firmin

Schwab, V. A conjuring of light

Schwab, V. A darker shade of magic

Schwab, V. A gathering of shadows

Siegel, J. Prospero's children

Sisters of the revolution

Solomon, R. The deep

Stephenson, N. The rise and fall of D.O.D.O.

Stories

Sullivan, M. Theft of swords

Suri, T. Empire of sand

Suri, T. Realm of ash

Swift, J. Gulliver's travels

Tesh, E. Silver in the wood

Tolkien, J. The Silmarillion

Turtledove, H. Into the darkness

Turtledove, H. Rulers of the darkness

Vandermeer, J. Finch

Vandermeer, J. The third bear

Vollmann, W. Last stories and other stories

Vonnegut, K. Slapstick

Walton, J. Among others

Warrington, F. Elfland

Warrington, F. Grail of the summer stars

Warrington, F. Midsummer night

Wilkins, K. Veil of gold

Wolfe, G. The best of Gene Wolfe

Munro, A. Dear life
Murakami, H. Kafka on the shore
Newman, S. The heavens
Niffenegger, A. The time traveler's wife
O'Connor, F. The violent bear it away
Oakley, C. You were there too
Obioma, C. The fishermen
Obioma, C. An orchestra of minorities
Pava, S. Personae
Pontoppidan, H. Lucky Per
Putney, M. A kiss of fate
Roberts, N. Dance upon the air
Rothfuss, P. The name of the wind
Rothfuss, P. The wise man's fear
Savage, S. Firmin
Serle, R. In five years
Stewart, M. The hollow hills
Stewart, M. The wicked day
Towles, A. Rules of civility
Vonnegut, K. Breakfast of champions
Vonnegut, K. Cat's cradle
Vonnegut, K. Galapagos
Vonnegut, K. Hocus pocus
Vonnegut, K. The sirens of Titan
Vonnegut, K. Slaughterhouse-five

FATE AND FATALISM -- RELIGIOUS ASPECTS
Andrews, M. Isaiah's daughter
The **fate** of Katherine Carr Cook, T.
The **fated** sky Kowal, M.
Fates and furies Groff, L.

FATHER AND ADULT CHILD
Glass, J. The widower's tale
Mosley, W. All I did was shoot my man
Murphy, D. Tiny Americans
Sanders, L. McNally's puzzle

FATHER AND ADULT DAUGHTER
Andrews, M. Sunset Beach
Barry, B. The map of true places
Begley, L. About Schmidt
Berger, T. Reinhart's women
Brown, S. White hot
Burke, J. The New Iberia blues
Coben, H. Run away
Coetzee, J. Disgrace
Dickey, E. Bad men and wicked women
Dodd, C. Virtue Falls
Doig, I. Ride with me, Mariah Montana
James, H. The golden bowl
Kitt, S. Celluloid memories
Lipman, E. Good riddance
MacDonald, J. The lonely silver rain
Mankell, H. Before the frost
Millet, L. Ghost lights
Rendell, R. Harm done
Rendell, R. Kissing the gunner's daughter
Vidal, G. 1876
Wiggins, M. The shadow catcher

FATHER AND ADULT SON
Ball, J. Census
Bellow, S. Seize the day
Box, C. The highway
Boyle, T. The harder they come
Cramer, W. Levi's will
Everett, P. Percival Everett by Virgil Russell
Haruf, K. Benediction
Hawley, N. The good father
Iles, G. The bone tree
Iles, G. Mississippi blood
Iles, G. Natchez burning
K'wan Animal II
Kenney, J. Truth in advertising
Nadel, B. The Ottoman cage
O'Nan, S. The names of the dead
Russo, R. Bridge of sighs
Savage, S. The way of the dog
Stabenow, D. So sure of death
Wallace, D. Big fish

FATHER AND CHILD
Dowlatabadi, M. The colonel
Grass, G. The box
Johnson, A. The first part last
Kadare, I. The successor
Kaminsky, S. Murder on the Trans-Siberian Express
Khalfah, K. Death is hard work
McPhee, M. Gorgeous lies
Mozley, F. Elmet
Reisman, N. The first desire
Stead, C. The man who loved children
Updike, J. Rabbit is rich

FATHER AND TEENAGER
Finder, J. Suspicion
Father Dowling mysteries [series] McInerny, R.

FATHER FIGURES
Brown, J. Addie Pray
Downing, D. Diary of a dead man on leave
Father Koesler mysteries [series] Kienzle, W.
Father of the rain King, L.

FATHER-DESERTED CHILDREN
Andrews, M. Sunset Beach
Bauer, B. Snap
Boyle, T. World's end
Garey, J. Too bright to hear too loud to see
Haigh, J. Mrs. Kimble
Lopez Barrio, C. The house of the impossible loves
Murphy, D. Tiny Americans

FATHER-DESERTED FAMILIES
Doyle, R. Paddy Clarke, ha-ha-ha
Enger, L. The high divide
Gregory, P. Tidelands
Kneale, M. When we were Romans
Morris, M. Man in the blue moon
Rachman, T. The Italian teacher
Sexton, M. A kind of freedom
Shafak, E. Honor

Turner, N. Natural born hustler
Tyler, A. Dinner at the Homesick Restaurant

FATHER-DESERTED FAMILIES -- THE WEST (UNITED STATES)

McMurtry, L. Boone's Lick

FATHER-SEPARATED BOYS

Eggers, D. What is the what
Gifford, B. Wyoming
Greene, G. The captain and the enemy
Wayne, T. The love song of Jonny Valentine

FATHER-SEPARATED BOYS -- NORTH CAROLINA

Earley, T. Jim the boy

FATHER-SEPARATED CHILDREN

Bennett, R. The troupe
Kennedy, D. The big picture
Marra, A. A constellation of vital phenomena
Straub, P. Mr. X
Tyler, A. Dinner at the Homesick Restaurant

FATHER-SEPARATED FAMILIES

Attenberg, J. The Middlesteins
Benedetti, M. Springtime in a broken mirror
De los Santos, M. The precious one
Grames, J. The seven or eight deaths of Stella Fortuna
K'wan Section 8
Kwan, K. China rich girlfriend
McGahan, A. The white earth
Monroe, M. God don't like ugly
Weiner, J. Good in bed

FATHER-SEPARATED GIRLS

Braffet, K. Last seen leaving

FATHER-SEPARATED TEENAGE BOYS

Restrepo, L. No place for heroes

FATHER-SEPARATED TEENAGE GIRLS

Ulinich, A. Petropolis

FATHERHOOD

Atkinson, K. A god in ruins
Balasubramanyam, R. Professor Chandra follows his bliss
Ballard, J. The kindness of women
LaValle, V. The changeling
Simsion, G. The Rosie effect
Simsion, G. The Rosie result

Fatherland Harris, R.

FATHERS

Abbott, S. The future of love
Baker, K. The house of the stag
Blackstock, T. Smoke screen
Boswell, R. Century's son
Bradley, C. Thrice the brinded cat hath mew'd
Cramer, W. Levi's will
Cunningham, M. Flesh and blood
Edwards, K. The memory keeper's daughter
Elliott, L. The missing years
Findley, T. The piano man's daughter
Fox, C. Redemption point
Gurganus, A. The practical heart
Haslett, A. Imagine me gone
Houellebecq, M. The map and the territory

Hugo, V. Les miserables
Jewell, L. The making of us
Penny, L. A better man
Perrotta, T. The abstinence teacher
Perrotta, T. Little children
Scott, J. Tourmaline
Seiffert, R. A boy in winter
Smith, S. A simple plan
Stewart, D. The Babe Ruth deception
Tudor, C. The other people

FATHERS -- DEATH

Adelman, M. Piece of mind
Amirrezvani, A. The blood of flowers
Archer, J. Only time will tell
Arnett, K. Mostly dead things
Attenberg, J. All this could be yours
Bacon, C. There is room for you
Benaron, N. Running the rift
Benz, C. The gone dead
Bialosky, J. House under snow
Bird, S. The flamenco academy
Butler, R. Perfume River
Campbell, B. Once upon a river
Cather, W. My Antonia
Cather, W. O pioneers!
Cheever, J. The Wapshot chronicle
Ciotta, B. Her sky cowboy
Ciotta, B. His clockwork canary
Cleeves, A. The long call
Crowley, J. Lord Byron's novel
Currie, R. Flimsy little plastic miracles
Deb, S. The point of return
Doig, I. Mountain time
Dostoyevsky, F. The brothers Karamazov
Ephron, H. Night night, sleep tight
Foer, J. Extremely loud and incredibly close
Forsyth, F. The kill list
Gaiman, N. Anansi boys
Hart, J. The king of lies
Hunter, J. Forbidden to love the duke
Hunter, S. Black light
Hunting, H. Handle with care
Jin, Y. A hero born
Jones, T. The better liar
K'wan Hoodlum
Khalfah, K. Death is hard work
Krivak, A. The bear
Lalami, L. The other Americans
Mengestu, D. The beautiful things that heaven bears
Mina, D. The end of the wasp season
Moniz, T. Big familia
Mosley, W. Gone fishin'
Nesbo, J. The son
Oe, K. Death by water
Olmstead, R. Coal black horse
Phillips, S. It had to be you
Portis, C. True grit

Pyper, A. The homecoming
Quinn, J. An offer from a gentleman
Ramsay, F. Countdown
Redhill, M. Consolation
Rose, M. Cartier's hope
Santopolo, J. More than words
Savas, A. Walking on the ceiling
Scego, I. Adua
Smith, W. Birds of prey
Strout, E. The Burgess boys
Taylor, B. Real life
Turow, S. Ordinary heroes
Van der Vliet Oloomi, A. Call me Zebra
Vida, V. Let the Northern Lights erase your name
Wallace, D. Big fish
Welty, E. The optimist's daughter
Wroblewski, D. The story of Edgar Sawtelle
Yoshimoto, B. Moshi-moshi
Zimmer, M. Wild side of the river

FATHERS -- SUICIDE

Wallace, D. Infinite jest

FATHERS AND DAUGHTERS

Afshar, T. Thief of Corinth
Allen, S. First frost
Amidon, S. Human capital
Anton, M. Apprentice
Antopol, M. The UnAmericans
Araghi, A. The immortals of Tehran
Atkinson, K. Case histories
Atwood, M. Cat's eye
Austen, J. Emma
Banks, R. Affliction
Banville, J. Eclipse
Bauermeister, E. The scent keeper
Beams, C. The illness lesson
Berger, T. Neighbors
Betts, D. Souls raised from the dead
Beverley, J. My lady notorious
Birmingham, S. Carriage trade
Bloom, A. Lucky us
Bourne, J. My lord and spymaster
Box, C. Open season
Box, C. Vicious circle
Box, C. Winterkill
Bradley, C. Speaking from among the bones
Bradley, C. The sweetness at the bottom of the pie
Brockmeier, K. The truth about Celia
Burns, R. Body slam
Butler, S. Ten things I've learnt about love
Cameron, W. Repo madness
Cash, W. This dark road to mercy
Cather, W. My Antonia
Chen, M. Here and now and then
Cook, T. Sandrine's case
Crowley, J. Lord Byron's novel
Danticat, E. Claire of the sea light
Davies, C. West

De Robertis, C. Perla
De los Santos, M. The precious one
Dickens, C. Dombey and Son
Dickens, C. Little Dorrit
Dickens, C. A tale of two cities
Divakaruni, C. Oleander girl
Dixon, S. Interstate
Doerr, A. All the light we cannot see
Eliot, G. Silas Marner
Enright, A. The forgotten waltz
Ephron, H. Night night, sleep tight
Ferber, E. So big
Fforde, J. The Eyre affair
Frame, R. Havisham
Frear, C. Sweet little lies
Fuller, C. Our endless numbered days
Gaddis, W. Agape agape
Gaige, A. Schroder
Gardiner, M. Unsub
Garey, J. Too bright to hear too loud to see
Gertler, S. Drifting
Gibson, W. Pattern recognition
Gordimer, N. No time like the present
Goss, T. The strange case of the alchemist's daughter
Graedon, A. The word exchange
Grant, H. The glass demon
Greene, G. Our man in Havana
Grunberg, A. Tirza
Hart, C. Resort to murder
Hoffman, A. The Museum of Extraordinary Things
Hurwitz, G. You're next
Ishiguro, K. An artist of the floating world
Jackson, N. The star side of Bird Hill
James, H. The portrait of a lady
Jenkins, B. Tempest
Jenoff, P. The ambassador's daughter
Joinson, S. The photographer's wife
Jones, T. Silver sparrow
Kamal, S. It all falls down
Kellerman, J. The genius
King, L. Father of the rain
Kittredge, W. The willow field
Kostova, E. The historian
Krivak, A. The bear
L'Engle, M. Certain women
Larsson, S. The girl with the dragon tattoo
Lee, C. A gesture life
Lee, H. Go set a watchman
Lee, H. To kill a mockingbird
Lehane, D. Sacred
Lipman, E. The family man
Lyon, A. The sweet girl
Majmudar, A. Partitions
Marillier, J. Daughter of the forest
McCann, C. Apeirogon
McGuire, S. Down among the sticks and bones
McKinlay, J. The good ones

Dickens, C. Dombey and Son
Dimechkie, K. Lifted by the great nothing
Doig, I. Mountain time
Doig, I. The whistling season
Doiron, P. The poacher's son
Dostoyevsky, F. The brothers Karamazov
Doyle, R. The guts
Dugoni, R. The conviction
Dunn, K. The Dragonfly
Ellis, B. Lunar Park
Enger, L. Undiscovered country
Englander, N. The ministry of Special Cases
Finder, J. The fixer
Ford, R. Independence Day
Ford, R. The lay of the land
Fu, K. For today I am a boy
Gaiman, N. Anansi boys
George, N. The book of dreams
Gilbert, D. & sons
Glass, J. Three Junes
Grant, L. We had it so good
Grass, G. Crabwalk
Grodstein, L. A friend of the family
Hage, R. Beirut Hellfire Society
Harding, P. Tinkers
Harkaway, N. Angelmaker
Hart, J. Damage
Hart, J. Down river
Hart, J. The king of lies
Haruf, K. Plainsong
Heller, J. Good as Gold
Holdstock, P. Here I am!
Holt, A. Odd numbers
Hosseini, K. Sea prayer
Jones, S. The outcast
Kay, G. Under heaven
Keating, H. The soft detective
Keilson, H. Life goes on
Kennedy, W. Ironweed
Kittredge, W. The willow field
Klein, M. Con ed
Lam, V. The headmaster's wager
Larsen, R. The selected works of T. S. Spivet
Lehane, D. Live by night
Lehane, D. World gone by
Leonard, E. The Hot Kid
Little, T. Where there's smoke
Lodge, D. Paradise news
Lourie, R. A hatred for tulips
Luiselli, V. The story of my teeth
Machart, B. The wake of forgiveness
Mailer, N. The castle in the forest
Malik, T. Three bargains
Marias, J. A heart so white
Marlette, D. Magic time
Martin, C. Long way gone
Matar, H. Anatomy of a disappearance

Maxwell, R. The queen's bastard
McCarthy, C. The road
Miller, R. Jacob's folly
Morante, E. Arturo's island
Mosley, W. Known to evil
Mosley, W. The long fall
Mosley, W. When the thrill is gone
Mukherjee, N. A state of freedom
North, A. The Whisper Man
Oates, J. Little bird of heaven
Oz, A. The same sea
Paton, A. Cry, the beloved country
Pattison, E. Beautiful ghosts
Pelecanos, G. The way home
Penman, S. Devil's brood
Percy, B. The wilding
Percy, W. The last gentleman
Peters, E. Brother Cadfael's penance
Peters, E. Fallen into the pit
Petterson, P. Out stealing horses
Phillips, A. The tragedy of Arthur
Picoult, J. Lone wolf
Porter, M. Grief is the thing with feathers
Preston, D. The codex
Puzo, M. The godfather
Puzo, M. The Sicilian
Rachman, T. The Italian teacher
Ragan, T. Deranged
Recacoechea S., J. American visa
Rees, M. The fourth assassin
Robinson, M. Gilead
Robinson, M. Home
Robinson, P. Piece of my heart
Rothmann, R. To die in spring
Rowland, L. The snow empress
Rucker, R. Postsingular
Ruiz Zafon, C. The prisoner of heaven
Ruiz Zafon, C. The shadow of the wind
Runcie, J. Canvey Island
Rushdie, S. Haroun and the sea of stories
Rushdie, S. Quichotte
Sarvas, M. Memento Park
Sayers, D. The documents in the case
Schwartz, J. Northwest corner
Scibona, S. The volunteer
Self, W. The book of Dave
Shteyngart, G. Lake Success
Simon, M. The last Jew standing
Smith, M. Stalin's ghost
Smith, W. Birds of prey
Smith, W. Monsoon
Stabenow, D. Though not dead
Stegner, W. The Big Rock Candy Mountain
Taseer, A. The way things were
Theroux, P. The Mosquito Coast
Trumbo, D. Johnny got his gun
Turow, S. Ordinary heroes

Moore, J. The night market
O'Connell, C. Dead famous
Pavone, C. The expats
Perkins, S. Murder once removed
Pobi, R. City of windows
Preston, D. City of endless night
Preston, D. Crooked river
Preston, D. Verses for the dead
Robards, K. The last victim
Scalzi, J. Head on
Scalzi, J. Lock in
Smith, M. Gorky Park
Smith, M. Tatiana
Souljah,. The coldest winter ever
Steinhauer, O. The middleman
Stout, R. The doorbell rang
Sundstol, V. The land of dreams
Yocum, R. A welcome murder

FBI INFORMANTS
Grisham, J. The firm

FBI OFFICIALS AND EMPLOYEES
Coulter, C. Paradox
Harris, T. Red dragon
Harris, T. The silence of the lambs
James, J. Something about you

FBI OFFICIALS AND EMPLOYEES, WOMEN
Harris, T. Hannibal

FBI suspense thriller series [series] Coulter, C.
FBI/US Attorney novels [series] James, J.

FEAR
Barclay, L. Elevator pitch
D'Eramo, L. Deviation
Garcia Marquez, G. Strange pilgrims
Greene, G. The human factor
Hoffman, A. The ice queen
Huston, C. Skinner
 The living dead
Lovestam, S. The truth behind the lie
McFarlane, F. The night guest
Meuleman, S. Find me gone
Nabb, M. Some bitter taste
O'Brien, E. In the forest
Pratchett, T. Thud!
Racculia, K. Bellweather rhapsody
Seiffert, R. A boy in winter
Wendig, C. Wanderers
Wong, D. John dies at the end

FEAR IN CHILDREN
King, S. It

FEAR IN MEN
Amdahl, G. I am death
Barnes, J. The noise of time
Box, C. Blue heaven
Bragi Olafsson, 1. The pets
Celine, L. Journey to the end of the night
King, S. Misery
Moore, C. A dirty job

Roth, P. Indignation

FEAR IN TEENAGE BOYS
Hunter, E. The blackboard jungle

FEAR IN WOMEN
Bohjalian, C. The double bind
Hegi, U. Children and fire
Kellerman, J. Private eyes
Lippman, L. I'd know you anywhere
MacDonald, J. The turquoise lament
Mackintosh, C. I see you
Mangan, C. Tangerine
Phillips, G. Fierce kingdom
Phillips, H. The need
Rivers, F. Redeeming love
Seton, A. Green darkness
Swanson, P. Her every fear
Zan, K. The never list

Fear nothing Gardner, L.

FEAR OF FLYING
 Flight or fright

Fear of flying Jong, E.

FEAR OF INTIMACY
Bandele, A. Daughter
Cole, A. A prince on paper

Feared Scottoline, L.

Fearless in Texas Dell, K.

Fearless Jones Mosley, W.

Fearless Jones novels [series] Mosley, W.

A **feast** for crows Martin, G.

The **feast** of love Baxter, C.

A **feast** of snakes Crews, H.

The **feast** of the Goat Vargas Llosa, M.

Feast your eyes Goldberg, M.

Feathered serpent, dark heart of sky Bowles, D.

FEDERAL WITNESS PROTECTION PROGRAM
Epperson, T. Sailor
Faust, C. Choke hold
Leonard, E. Killshot
Muller, M. Both ends of the night
Walter, J. Citizen Vince

Feed Grant, M.

Feedback Grant, M.

Felix in the underworld Mortimer, J.

Fellow travelers Mallon, T.

The **fellowship** of the ring Tolkien, J.

FEMALE FRIENDSHIP
Acampora, L. The paper wasp
Adams, E. The secret, book & scone society
Alameddine, R. An unnecessary woman
Albert, E. After birth
Alcott, K. A touch of stardust
Arnoult, D. Sufficient grace
Arsenault, E. In search of the Rose notes
Atwood, M. Cat's eye
Awad, M. 13 ways of looking at a fat girl
Awad, M. Bunny
Bahr, H. The Judas Field

Umrigar, T. The secrets between us
Umrigar, T. The space between us
Updike, J. The widows of Eastwick
Updike, J. The witches of Eastwick
Vine, B. The House of Stairs
Walbert, K. She was like that
Ware, R. In a dark, dark wood
Ware, R. The lying game
Waters, S. The night watch
Weiner, J. Good in bed
Weiss, L. If the creek don't rise
Whitaker, K. The animators
Wiggs, S. The Oysterville sewing circle
Williams, L. Supper club
Williams, T. The Roman spring of Mrs. Stone
Winfrey, K. Waiting for Tom Hanks
Woodson, J. Another Brooklyn
Yoshimoto, B. Goodbye Tsugumi
Zan, K. The never list

FEMALE FRIENDSHIP -- CALIFORNIA
Mapson, J. Bad Girl Creek

FEMALE FRIENDSHIP -- GREAT BRITAIN
Cleave, C. Gold

FEMALE FRIENDSHIP -- MIDDLE WEST
Hoover, M. The quickening

FEMALE GANG LEADERS
De Leon, A. Side chick nation

FEMALE GANGS
Diamond, D. Boss divas
Diamond, D. Gangsta divas
Diamond, D. King divas
Diamond, D. Street divas
Oates, J. Foxfire

FEMALE IMPERSONATORS
McBride, J. The good lord bird
The **female** persuasion Wolitzer, M.

FEMININE BEAUTY (AESTHETICS)
Berg, E. Never change
Gaitskill, M. Veronica
James, E. The ugly duchess
Layton, E. To wed a stranger

FEMININITY
Ellis, H. American housewife
Rawle, G. Woman's world
Walker, S. Dietland

FEMINISM
Ahern, C. Roar
Armfield, J. Salt slow
Diamant, A. The Boston girl
Hustvedt, S. The blazing world
Irving, J. The world according to Garp
James, H. Daisy Miller
Lavery, D. The merry spinster
Newitz, A. The future of another timeline
Otto, W. Eight girls taking pictures
Shields, C. Unless
  Sisters of the revolution

Updike, J. The witches of Eastwick
Woolf, V. Mrs. Dalloway

FEMINISM -- SOMALIA
Farah, N. Knots

FEMINISTS
Darznik, J. Song of a captive bird
Drabble, M. The sea lady
French, M. The women's room
Horan, N. Loving Frank
Kidd, S. The invention of wings
Lessing, D. The golden not(ebk.)
Lessing, D. A ripple from the storm
McCall Smith, A. Blue shoes and happiness
Newman, J. Mary
Paretsky, S. Bitter medicine
Paretsky, S. Blacklist
Paretsky, S. Blood shot
Paretsky, S. Breakdown
Paretsky, S. Brush back
Paretsky, S. Burn marks
Paretsky, S. Critical mass
Paretsky, S. Fallout
Paretsky, S. Fire sale
Paretsky, S. Guardian angel
Paretsky, S. Hardball
Paretsky, S. Hard time
Paretsky, S. Indemnity only
Paretsky, S. Total recall
Paretsky, S. Tunnel vision
Paretsky, S. Windy city blues
Scoppettone, S. Everything you have is mine
Scoppettone, S. Gonna take a homicidal journey
Scoppettone, S. My sweet untraceable you
Stridsberg, S. Valerie
Vargas Llosa, M. The way to paradise
Walker, S. Dietland
Wolitzer, M. The female persuasion
Woolf, V. The voyage out

FEMMES FATALES
  Dangerous women
Hammett, D. The Maltese falcon
Hemingway, E. The sun also rises
Hilton, L. Maestra
Lippman, L. Sunburn
Minh, D. Neon empire
Moore, C. Noir
Pynchon, T. V

FENCERS -- SPAIN
Perez-Reverte, A. The fencing master

FENCING
Craig, P. A vineyard killing
Perez-Reverte, A. The fencing master
The **fencing** master Perez-Reverte, A.
Fenwick Sisters affairs [series] Hunter, J.
The **feral** detective Lethem, J.

FERDINAND V,, KING OF SPAIN, 1452-1516
Gregory, P. The constant princess

The **fifth** vial Palmer, M.

The **fifth** witness Connelly, M.

FIFTIES (AGE)
Ford, R. The lay of the land
Lemaitre, P. Inhuman resources
Mosley, W. Known to evil
Mosley, W. The long fall
Ozick, C. Foreign bodies
Porter, C. The seep

Fight Club Palahniuk, C.

The **fighter** Smith, M.

FIGHTER PILOTS
Asaro, C. Primary inversion
Deutermann, P. The nugget
Groot, T. Flame of resistance
Torday, D. The last flight of Poxl West

FIGHTER PILOTS -- UNITED STATES
Michener, J. The bridges at Toko-Ri

FIGHTER PLANES
Brown, D. The Kremlin strike

Fighting for the dead Oldham, N.

FIGURINES -- COLLECTORS AND COLLECTING
Chatwin, B. Utz

FILIPINO AMERICAN WOMEN
Ramos, J. The farm

FILIPINOS
Alvar, M. In the country

FILM
Puig, M. Kiss of the spider woman

FILM -- PRESERVATION
Estleman, L. Frames

FILM ACTORS AND ACTRESSES
Alcott, K. A touch of stardust
Auster, P. The book of illusions
Bagshawe, T. Adored
Cameron, C. Just a summer fling
Dee, J. A thousand pardons
Furst, A. Mission to Paris
Gaynor, H. Meet me in Monaco
Harvey, J. Gone to ground
Hurwitz, G. They're watching
Kaminsky, S. To catch a spy
Kaminsky, S. Dancing in the dark
Kaminsky, S. A fatal glass of beer
Kaminsky, S. Tomorrow is another day
Leonard, E. LaBrava
Letts, E. Finding Dorothy
Oates, J. Blonde
Randisi, R. Hey there (you with the gun in your hand)
Vidal, G. Hollywood
Walter, J. Beautiful ruins

FILM COMEDIANS
Kaminsky, S. A fatal glass of beer

FILM FESTIVALS
Davies, R. Murther and walking spirits
Gaynor, H. Meet me in Monaco

FILM INDUSTRY AND TRADE

Allen, J. I lost my girlish laughter
Bagshawe, T. Adored
Beauman, N. Madness is better than defeat
Bradley, C. I am half-sick of shadows
Burke, J. The New Iberia blues
Butcher, J. Proven guilty
Cline, R. My liar
Dev, S. A Bollywood affair
Dev, S. The Bollywood bride
Letts, E. Finding Dorothy
Phillips, S. What I did for love
Puzo, M. The last don
Quick, A. The girl who knew too much
Smith, D. The electric hotel
Sosa, M. Acting on impulse
Updike, J. In the beauty of the lilies
West, N. Novels and other writings
Winfrey, K. Waiting for Tom Hanks

FILM INDUSTRY AND TRADE -- CORRUPT PRACTIC-ES -- HOLLYWOOD, CALIFORNIA
Leonard, E. Get Shorty

FILM INDUSTRY AND TRADE -- HISTORY
Estleman, L. Frames

FILM INDUSTRY AND TRADE -- HOLLYWOOD, CALI-FORNIA
Didion, J. Play it as it lays
Fitzgerald, F. The last tycoon
Leonard, E. Be cool
Waugh, E. The loved one

FILM INDUSTRY AND TRADE -- HOLLYWOOD, CALI-FORNIA -- HISTORY
Vidal, G. Hollywood

FILM INDUSTRY AND TRADE EXECUTIVES
Fitzgerald, F. The last tycoon
Kroese, R. The last iota

FILM INDUSTRY AND TRADE EXECUTIVES -- HOL-LYWOOD, CALIFORNIA
Garey, J. Too bright to hear too loud to see

FILM LOCATIONS
Craig, P. A shoot on Martha's Vineyard

FILM PRODUCERS AND DIRECTORS
Allen, J. I lost my girlish laughter
Bagshawe, T. Adored
Dev, S. A Bollywood affair
Koryta, M. So cold the river
Rice, L. Last kiss

FILM PRODUCERS AND DIRECTORS -- HOLLYWOOD, CALIFORNIA
Leonard, E. Be cool

FILM PRODUCERS AND DIRECTORS -- UNITED STATES
Woods, S. Santa Fe rules

FILM PROJECTIONISTS
Nicholls, O. Love, unscripted

FILM STUDIOS
Allen, J. I lost my girlish laughter

FILM THEATER MANAGERS

Fire and ice [series] Ridpath, M.
The **fire** baby Kelly, J.
Fire down below Golding, W.
FIRE FIGHTERS
  Blackstock, T. Smoke screen
  Buchman, M. Pure heat
  Center, K. Things you save in a fire
  Jimenez, A. The friend zone
Fire in the blood Nemirovsky, I.
Fire logic Marks, L.
Fire on the mountain Desai, A.
Fire on the waters Poyer, D.
Fire sale Paretsky, S.
The **fire** sermon Haig, F.
Fire sermon [series] Haig, F.
A **fire** upon the deep Vinge, V.
The **firebird** Kearsley, S.
Firebird Powell, M.
Firefly Porter, H.
Firefly summer Binchy, M.
Firehawks [series] Buchman, M.
Firelight Callihan, K.
The **Fireman** Hill, J.
FIRES
  Bradbury, R. Fahrenheit 451
  Canty, K. The underworld
  Castillo, L. A gathering of secrets
  Currie, R. Flimsy little plastic miracles
  Draper, S. Forged by fire
  Francis, F. Crisis
  Hill, J. The Fireman
  Hoffman, A. The Museum of Extraordinary Things
  King, S. Firestarter
  Macdonald, R. The underground man
  Spencer-Fleming, J. Through the evil days
FIRES -- MONTREAL, QUEBEC
  Reichs, K. Death du jour
Firestarter King, S.
Firewall Mankell, H.
Firewatching Thomas, R.
FIREWORKS
  McPherson, C. Scot free
A **firing** offense Ignatius, D.
The **firm** Grisham, J.
Firmin Savage, S.
FIRST CONTACT (ANTHROPOLOGY)
  Lalami, L. The Moor's account
FIRST CONTACT OF INDIGENOUS PEOPLES WITH EUROPEANS
  Osborne, D. The coming
The **first** cut Robinson, P.
The **first** deadly sin Sanders, L.
The **first** desire Reisman, N.
First earl I see tonight Bennett, A.
FIRST EDITIONS
  Block, L. The burglar in the library
First frost Allen, S.

FIRST IMPRESSIONS
  Ohlsson, K. Unwanted
First Lady Phillips, S.
The **first** law Lescroart, J.
First love, and other stories Turgenev, I.
FIRST LOVES
  Aciman, A. Call me by your name
  Aciman, A. Enigma variations
  Aciman, A. Find me
  Banville, J. Ancient light
  Blume, J. In the unlikely event
  Bond, C. Ruby
  Buchman, M. The night is mine
  Calvi, M. Dear George, Dear Mary
  Carlino, R. Swear on this life
  Creech, S. The whole way home
  Dev, S. The Bollywood bride
  Echlin, K. The disappeared
  Eco, U. The mysterious flame of Queen Loana
  Fitch, J. Paint it black
  Francis, P. The orphans of Race Point
  French, T. Faithful place
  Golden, A. Memoirs of a geisha
  Hijuelos, O. Beautiful Maria of my soul
  Hijuelos, O. The mambo kings play songs of love
  Horn, D. Eternal life
  Kawakami, M. Ms. Ice Sandwich
  Linden, R. Ascension of larks
  Long, J. The legend of Lyon Redmond
  McFarlane, M. Don't you forget about me
  Mishima, Y. The sound of waves
  Murakami, H. South of the border, west of the sun
  O'Connor, J. Ghost light
  O'Neill, H. The Lonely Hearts Hotel
  Rai, A. Wrong to need you
  Rooney, S. Normal people
  Roth, P. Indignation
  Schami, R. Sophia
  Sparks, N. A walk to remember
  Stone, I. Lust for life
  Walsh, M. My sunshine away
The **first** man in Rome McCullough, C.
FIRST NATIONS (CANADA)
  Kamal, S. It all falls down
  Proulx, A. Barkskins
  Rice, W. Moon of the crusted snow
First North Americans [series] Gear, K.
First of state Greer, R.
The **first** part last Johnson, A.
First position Brayden, M.
The **first** rule Crais, R.
The **first** rule of swimming Brkic, C.
FIRST SEXUAL EXPERIENCE
  McEwan, I. On Chesil Beach
First sight Steel, D.
First star I see tonight Phillips, S.
FIRST WORLD WAR ERA (1914-1918)

FLAPPERS
Rosen, R. Dollface

FLASHBACKS
Ackerman, E. Waiting for Eden
Bala, S. The boat people
Bardugo, L. Ninth house
Black, S. Anything for you
Clegg, B. Did you ever have a family
Crombie, D. A bitter feast
Daoud, K. The Meursault investigation
Deon, N. Grace
Eco, U. The island of the day before
Foley, L. The hunting party
Kelly, E. The poison tree
Letts, E. Finding Dorothy
Mangan, C. Tangerine
Meltzer, B. The escape artist
Moore, L. Long bright river
Pinborough, S. Behind her eyes
Robotham, M. Life or death
Rotert, R. Last night at the blue angel
Rushdie, S. Shalimar the Clown
Shacochis, B. The woman who lost her soul
Swift, G. Mothering Sunday
Tran, V. Dragonfish
Tudor, C. The chalk man
Vargas Llosa, M. The discreet hero

Flashed Castile, Z.

Flashmob Farnsworth, C.

The **flatshare** O'Leary, B.

Flaubert's parrot Barnes, J.

FLAUBERT, GUSTAVE, 1821-1880 CRITICISM AND IN-TERPRETATION
Flaubert, G. Sentimental education

FLAUBERT, GUSTAVE, 1821-1880 STUDY AND TEACH-ING
Barnes, J. Flaubert's parrot

Flavia Albia mysteries [series] Davis, L.

Flavia De Luce mysteries [series] Bradley, C.

Fleishman is in trouble Brodesser-Akner, T.

Flesh and blood Cunningham, M.

Flesh and fire Gilman, L.

Flesh house MacBride, S.

Fletch Mcdonald, G.

Fletch mysteries [series] Mcdonald, G.

The **flicker** of old dreams Henderson, S.

FLIGHT
Benjamin, M. The aviator's wife
Flight or fright
Mieville, C. Perdido Street Station
Saint-Exupery, A. Night flight

Flight Alexie, S.

The **flight** attendant Bohjalian, C.

FLIGHT ATTENDANTS
Bohjalian, C. The flight attendant
Leonard, E. Rum punch

Flight behavior Kingsolver, B.

Flight of eagles Higgins, J.

Flight of the Intruder Coonts, S.

The **flight** of the maidens Gardam, J.

Flight of the Old Dog Brown, D.

Flight or fright

The **flight** portfolio Orringer, J.

Flight to Canada Reed, I.

FLIGHTS
Flight or fright
Wilson, C. Dead girl in 2A

Flights Tokarczuk, O.

Flimsy little plastic miracles Currie, R.

FLINT, MICHIGAN
Ashley Antoinette, 1. Butterfly
JaQuavis The dopeman's wife

FLIRTATION
DeLuca, J. Well met

Floaters Wambaugh, J.

The **floating** Feldmans Friedland, E.

The **floating** opera Barth, J.

Flood of fire Ghosh, A.

FLOODPLAINS
Quindlen, A. Miller's Valley

FLOODS
Cheng, B. Southern cross the dog
D'Agostino, K. The antiques
Eliot, G. The mill on the Floss
Keller, J. Last ragged breath
Montag, K. After the flood
Runcie, J. Canvey Island

FLOODS -- NETHERLANDS
Moor, M. The storm

FLOOR TRADERS (FINANCE)
Campbell, A. On the floor
Gross, A. Reckless

Flora Godwin, G.

Florence Gordon Morton, B.

FLORENCE, ITALY
Elkins, A. Dying on the vine
Grindle, L. Villa Triste
Nabb, M. Some bitter taste
Stone, I. The agony and the ecstasy

FLORENCE, ITALY -- HISTORY -- 1421-1737
Dunant, S. The birth of Venus

FLORENCE, ITALY -- HISTORY -- 15TH CENTURY
Walton, J. Lent

FLORENCE, ITALY -- SOCIAL CONDITIONS
Rushdie, S. The enchantress of Florence

FLORIDA
Arnett, K. Mostly dead things
Banks, R. Continental drift
Barber, L. A girl named Anna
Butler, R. Perfume River
Clement, J. Gun love
Cramer, W. Levi's will
Daniel, S. Stiltsville
DePoy, P. Sidewalk saint

FOOTBALL COACHES
Majors, I. Love's winning plays
FOOTBALL FANS
Leonard, E. Mr. Paradise
FOOTBALL PLAYERS
Phillips, S. Natural born charmer
FOOTBALL TEAM OWNERS
Pava, S. Lost empress
FOOTBALL TEAMS
Pava, S. Lost empress
The **footprints** of God Iles, G.
For his pleasure Bell, S.
For love Miller, S.
For real Hall, A.
For the duke's eyes only Bell, L.
For the love of money Tyree, O.
For today I am a boy Fu, K.
For whom the bell tolls Hemingway, E.
Forbidden Jenkins, B.
FORBIDDEN CITY, BEIJING, CHINA.
Min, A. Empress Orchid
Forbidden hearts [series] Rai, A.
FORBIDDEN LOVE
Bledsoe, A. Long black curl
Dunant, S. Sacred hearts
Malik, T. Three bargains
Rose, M. Tiffany blues
Forbidden lovers novels [series] Bell, S.
Forbidden promises Williams, S.
The **forbidden** rose Bourne, J.
Forbidden to love the duke Hunter, J.
FORCED LABOR
Alexander, V. The Magdalen girls
Boulle, P. The bridge over the River Kwai
Flanagan, R. The narrow road to the deep north
Furnivall, K. The red scarf
Furst, A. Under occupation
Lee, C. On such a full sea
Muller, H. The hunger angel
Pattison, E. The skull mantra
Pulley, N. The lost future of Pepperharrow
FORCED LABOR -- SOVIET UNION
Solzhenitsyn, A. One day in the life of Ivan Denisovich
FORCED MARRIAGE
Amirrezvani, A. The blood of flowers
Anam, T. The bones of grace
Dare, A. The girl with the louding voice
Gregory, P. The taming of the queen
James, E. Four nights with the duke
MacGregor, J. The bride who got lucky
Nemirovsky, I. Fire in the blood
Rhys, J. Wide Sargasso Sea
Willig, L. The betrayal of the blood lily
FORCED RELOCATIONS
De Bernieres, L. Birds without wings
Ellroy, J. Perfidia
Pitts, L. Freeman

Ford County Grisham, J.
FORD, GERALD R, 1913-2006
Updike, J. Memories of the Ford administration
FORD, ROBERT, 1862-1892
Hansen, R. The assassination of Jesse James by the coward Robert Ford
FORECASTING
Clark, G. The bucket list
FORECLOSURE
Connelly, M. The fifth witness
Ryan, H. Truth be told
Foreign affairs Lurie, A.
Foreign bodies Ozick, C.
The **foreign** correspondent Furst, A.
FOREIGN CORRESPONDENTS
Cartwright, J. To heaven by water
A **foreign** country Cumming, C.
Foreign soil Clarke, M.
FOREIGN STUDENTS
Palahniuk, C. Pygmy
Foreigner Cherryh, C.
Foreigner universe. First foreigner sequence [series] Cherryh, C.
Foreigners Phillips, C.
FORENSIC ANTHROPOLOGISTS
Elkins, A. Dying on the vine
Elkins, A. Unnatural selection
FORENSIC ANTHROPOLOGY
Elkins, A. Dying on the vine
Elkins, A. Unnatural selection
Lovesey, P. Skeleton Hill
Reichs, K. Bones to ashes
FORENSIC MEDICINE
Cornwell, P. Chaos
Cornwell, P. Postmortem
Reichs, K. Bones to ashes
FORENSIC PATHOLOGISTS
Deaver, J. The empty chair
FORENSIC PSYCHOLOGISTS
Robotham, M. Good girl, bad girl
FORENSIC PSYCHOLOGY
Carr, C. The alienist
Carr, C. The angel of darkness
White, S. Dry ice
White, S. Kill me
White, S. The siege
FORENSIC SCIENCE
Rankin, I. A question of blood
FORENSIC SCIENCES
Abu-Jaber, D. Origin
Connelly, M. Echo Park
Gardiner, M. The Dirty Secrets Club
Gerritsen, T. The bone garden
Griffiths, E. The dark angel
Griffiths, E. A dying fall
Griffiths, E. The house at sea's end
Griffiths, E. The stone circle

Shalev, M. Two she-bears
Shreve, A. The last time they met
Starnone, D. Ties
Strout, E. My name is Lucy Barton
Thomas, S. My beautiful enemy
Toole, F. Pound for pound
Ward, A. Forgive me
Wells, R. Divine secrets of the Ya-Ya Sisterhood
Williams, N. This is happiness

FORGIVENESS (CHRISTIANITY)
Austin, L. All she ever wanted
Martin, C. Send down the rain

FORGIVENESS IN WOMEN
Berg, E. The art of mending
The **forgotten** Kellerman, F.
The **forgotten** affairs of youth McCall Smith, A.
Forgotten journey Ocampo, S.
The **forgotten** waltz Enright, A.

FORMER ACTORS AND ACTRESSES
O'Farrell, M. This must be the place

FORMER AMISH
Castillo, L. A gathering of secrets
Castillo, L. Shamed
Cramer, W. Levi's will

FORMER ASSASSINS
Hart, J. Iron house
Hurwitz, G. Hellbent
Hurwitz, G. Into the fire
Hurwitz, G. The Nowhere Man
Hurwitz, G. Orphan X
Hurwitz, G. Out of the dark
Meyer, D. Heart of the hunter
Rice, A. Of love and evil
Shrier, H. Boston cream
Woods, S. The money shot
Woods, S. Skin game
Woods, S. Smooth operator

FORMER ATHLETES
Fields, H. Last Chance Llama Ranch

FORMER BASEBALL PLAYERS
Huston, C. Caught stealing
Kennedy, W. Ironweed
Parker, R. Death in paradise
Stewart, D. The Babe Ruth deception
Updike, J. Rabbit, run
Yocum, R. A welcome murder

FORMER BOXERS
Liss, D. A spectacle of corruption

FORMER BOYFRIENDS
Cabot, M. No judgments
French, N. Friday on my mind
Greer, A. Less
Hoover, C. It ends with us
Rader-Day, L. The black hour
Stringer, V. Still dirty
Swanson, P. Her every fear

FORMER CAPTIVES

Carey, M. Someone like me
O'Brien, E. Girl
Roy, L. Gone too long
Spencer, M. Dangerous
Walker, W. Emma in the night

FORMER CHILD ACTORS AND ACTRESSES
Hallinan, T. Crashed

FORMER CIA AGENTS
DeLillo, D. Libra
Hagberg, D. Abyss
Jin, H. A map of betrayal
Ludlum, R. The Prometheus deception
Pavone, C. The expats
Pavone, C. The Paris diversion
Ramsay, F. Scone Island
Ramsay, F. Stranger room
Robbins, T. Fierce invalids home from hot climates
Steinhauer, O. The last tourist
Woods, S. Skin game
Woods, S. Smooth operator
Zander, J. The swimmer

FORMER CIRCUS PERFORMERS
Brown, D. The way to Bright Star

FORMER CLERGYMEN
Gaskell, E. North and South
Haigh, J. Mrs. Kimble

FORMER COLLEGE FOOTBALL PLAYERS
Lohmann, J. Winning Ruby Heart

FORMER COLLEGE TEACHERS
Erpenbeck, J. Go, went, gone
Powers, R. Orfeo

FORMER CONVICTS
Armstrong, R. The don con
Atkins, A. The broken places
Atkins, A. The sinners
Atkinson, K. When will there be good news?
Auster, P. The Brooklyn follies
Baldacci, D. One good deed
Baldacci, D. Redemption
Bell, S. For his pleasure
Block, L. A ticket to the boneyard
Burrowes, G. My one and only duke
Cameron, W. Repo madness
Ca$h Trust no man
Ca$h Trust no man 2
Ca$h Trust no man 3
Chabon, M. Moonglow
Clarke, B. An arsonist's guide to writers' homes in New
  England
Coleman, R. Where it hurts
Connolly, J. The burning soul
Dickens, C. Great expectations
Gaiman, N. American gods
Gamboa, S. Necropolis
Gardner, L. Alone
Goddard, R. Long time coming
Greaves, C. Hard twisted

FORMER FOSTER CHILDREN
London, S. The Aussie next door
Meader, K. Playing with fire

FORMER FRIENDS
Berger, T. Vital parts
Brodesser-Akner, T. Fleishman is in trouble
Constantine, L. The last time I saw you
Dicks, M. The perfect comeback of Caroline Jacobs
Doyle, R. Smile
French, N. Thursday's children
Hannah, S. Perfect little children
Higgins, K. The perfect match
Jenkins, B. Breathless
McPherson, C. The child garden
Murdoch, I. Nuns and soldiers
Perry, A. A Christmas return
Rock, P. The shelter cycle
Schwab, V. Vengeful
Schwab, V. Vicious
Stone, N. The verdict

FORMER GIRLFRIENDS
James, L. I want you back
McCarthy, R. A handful of ashes
Palmer, L. Otherwise engaged
Pynchon, T. Inherent vice
Ruff, M. 88 names
Shteyngart, G. Lake Success
Turner, B. Wooing Cadie McCaffrey

FORMER HOCKEY PLAYERS
James, L. I want you back

FORMER HUSBANDS
Beaton, M. Death of a macho man
Bird, S. The gap year
Corry, J. The dead ex
Diehl, H. Lifelines
Dodd, C. Virtue Falls
Ellis, D. In the company of liars
Hall, P. Lights! Camera! Puzzles!
Hiaasen, C. Nature girl
Higashino, K. The devotion of suspect X
Martin, S. The pleasure of my company
Miller, S. The good mother
Miyamoto, T. Kinshu
North, A. The life and death of Sophie Stark
Ozick, C. Foreign bodies
Parker, R. Melancholy baby
Parker, R. Shrink rap
Portis, C. The dog of the South
Reichs, K. Break no bones
Simon, M. Cremains of the day

FORMER HUSBANDS -- DEATH
Scottoline, L. Come home
Sisco, A. A deadly habit

FORMER HUSBANDS -- NORTH CAROLINA
Maron, M. Up jumps the Devil

FORMER INTELLIGENCE OFFICERS
Ripley, M. Mr. Campion's war

FORMER JOURNALISTS
Lehane, D. Since we fell
Portis, C. The dog of the South

FORMER LAWYERS
Keller, J. Bone on bone
Leonard, E. Mr. Paradise
Picoult, J. My sister's keeper
Schlink, B. Self's deception
Schlink, B. Self's punishment
Schlink, B. Self's murder
Stabenow, D. A deeper sleep
Stabenow, D. A fine and bitter snow
Stabenow, D. A grave denied
Stabenow, D. Hunter's moon
Stabenow, D. Killing grounds
Stabenow, D. A night too dark
Stabenow, D. Restless in the grave
Stabenow, D. The singing of the dead
Stabenow, D. A taint in the blood
Stabenow, D. Though not dead
Stabenow, D. Whisper to the blood

FORMER LIBRARIANS
Glass, J. The widower's tale
Hart, E. City of ink

FORMER LOVERS
Atkins, A. The redeemers
Balogh, M. Only enchanting
Balogh, M. Someone to remember
Bell, L. For the duke's eyes only
Bell, M. The color of night
Blackstock, T. Smoke screen
Bledsoe, A. The hum and the shiver
Bybee, C. Staying for good
Carter, S. New England white
Carver, T. The surrogate
Castille, S. In your corner
Coben, H. Don't let go
Coben, H. Long lost
Cohen, T. The summer we lost her
Cole, K. Dreams of a dark warrior
Cook, T. A dancer in the dust
Creech, S. The whole way home
Dahl, K. The courier
Dane, L. The best kind of trouble
DeLillo, D. Underworld
Dickey, E. Finding Gideon
Dimon, H. Mercy
Dodd, C. The woman who couldn't scream
Ervin, K. Mina's joint
George, N. The book of dreams
Gillham, D. City of women
Greene, G. The end of the affair
Hand, E. Available dark
Hand, E. Hard light
Harrod-Eagles, C. Headlong
Hauck, R. How to catch a prince
Hewson, D. A season for the dead

Box, C. The bitterroots
Box, C. Blue heaven
Box, C. The highway
Brown, S. Fat Tuesday
Bruen, K. Cross
Bruen, K. Galway girl
Bruen, K. The guards
Coleman, R. What you break
Coleman, R. Where it hurts
Collins, M. Ask not
Connolly, J. The burning soul
Connelly, M. Dark sacred night
Connelly, M. The wrong side of goodbye
Constantine, K. Blood mud
Coyle, M. Yesterday's echo
Craig, P. A shoot on Martha's Vineyard
Craig, P. Third strike
Craig, P. A vineyard killing
Crais, R. The first rule
DeMille, N. Wild fire
Disher, G. Under the cold bright lights
Dobyns, S. Saratoga payback
Dunning, J. Booked to die
Dunning, J. The bookman's wake
Faust, C. Money shot
Fox, C. Crimson Lake
Fox, C. Redemption point
Friedman, D. Don't ever get old
Friedman, D. Running out of road
Garcia-Roza, L. December heat
Gardiner, M. Phantom instinct
Harvey, J. A darker shade of blue
Harvey, M. We all fall down
Hiaasen, C. Skinny dip
Hillerman, T. The shape shifter
Hillerman, T. The sinister pig
Hillerman, T. The wailing wind
Horowitz, A. The sentence is death
Horowitz, A. The word is murder
Kellerman, J. The genius
Kerr, P. March violets
Khan, V. The perplexing theft of the jewel in the crown
Kimmel, F. No good asking
King, S. End of watch
King, S. Mr. Mercedes
Koryta, M. Tonight I said goodbye
Krentz, J. Running hot
Krueger, W. Vermilion drift
Lansdale, J. A fine dark line
Lescroart, J. The first law
Lescroart, J. The hearing
Lescroart, J. Nothing but the truth
Lescroart, J. The oath
Levien, D. City of the sun
Lovesey, P. Diamond solitaire
Lovesey, P. Upon a dark night
Lutz, J. Burn

Lutz, J. Final seconds
Lutz, J. Lightning
Mankell, H. The return of the dancing master
Nesbo, J. The bat
Nesbo, J. Phantom
Nesbo, J. Police
Nesbo, J. The thirst
O'Malley, T. We were kings
O'Mara, T. Crooked numbers
Ohlsson, K. Hostage
Parker, T. The blue hour
Parker, T. Pacific beat
Parker, T. Storm runners
Pattison, E. Beautiful ghosts
Pattison, E. The lord of death
Pattison, E. Mandarin gate
Pattison, E. Prayer of the dragon
Pattison, E. The skull mantra
Pattison, E. Water touching stone
Perrotta, T. Little children
Perry, T. The bomb maker
Perry, T. The boyfriend
Perry, T. Pursuit
Persson, L. The dying detective
Picoult, J. Leaving time
Pronzini, B. Nightcrawlers
Robotham, M. The wreckage
Rodriguez, L. Every broken trust
Sanders, L. The fourth deadly sin
Sanders, L. The second deadly sin
Sanders, L. The third deadly sin
Sandford, J. Winter prey
Shepherd, L. A fatal likeness
Shepherd, L. The Solitary House
Slaughter, K. The kept woman
Solares, M. Don't send flowers
Spiegelman, P. Black maps
Stabenow, D. No fixed line
Winslow, D. The dawn patrol
Woods, S. Below the belt
Woods, S. Fast & loose

FORMER POLICE -- BATH, ENGLAND
Lovesey, P. The vault
FORMER POLICE -- NEW YORK (STATE)
Bayard, L. The pale blue eye
FORMER POLICE -- SOVIET UNION
Smith, M. Polar Star
FORMER POLICE -- WASHINGTON, D.C.
Pelecanos, G. Hell to pay
Pelecanos, G. Soul circus
FORMER POLICE CHIEFS
Guttridge, P. The thing itself
FORMER POLICEWOMEN
Follett, K. Whiteout
Holt, A. Odd numbers
McDermid, V. How the dead speak
Parker, R. Family honor

Parker, R. Melancholy baby
Parker, R. Shrink rap
Spencer, S. The shivering turn

FORMER PRESIDENTS
Clark, M. My gal Sunday

FORMER PRIESTS
Levack, S. Demon of the air

FORMER PRIME MINISTERS
Harris, R. The ghost

FORMER PRISONERS OF WAR
Friedman, D. Don't ever get old
Silko, L. Ceremony
Tan, T. The garden of evening mists

FORMER PRIVATE INVESTIGATORS
Dobyns, S. Saratoga payback

FORMER PROFESSIONAL ATHLETES
Bailey, T. Fix her up
Karunatilaka, S. The legend of Pradeep Mathew

FORMER PROFESSIONAL TENNIS PLAYERS
Woo, S. Love love

FORMER PROSTITUTES
Gaitskill, M. Don't cry
Lake, J. Endurance
McKinney-Whetstone, D. Leaving Cecil Street
Rendell, R. A judgement in stone

FORMER PSYCHIATRIC HOSPITAL PATIENTS
White, S. Dry ice

FORMER PUPPETEERS
Roth, P. Sabbath's theater

FORMER ROCK MUSICIANS
Gilman, S. Donna has left the building
Kunzru, H. Gods without men
Tropper, J. One last thing before I go

FORMER RODEO PERFORMERS
Weatherspoon, R. A cowboy to remember

FORMER SHERIFFS
Atkins, A. The redeemers
Harrison, J. The great leader
Keller, J. Bone on bone
Krueger, W. Vermilion drift
Sallis, J. Sarah Jane

FORMER SOCCER PLAYERS
Castile, Z. Flashed

FORMER SPECIAL FORCES MEMBERS
Coben, H. Fool me once
Finder, J. Buried secrets
Finder, J. Guilty minds
Finder, J. Vanished
Lee, P. Dark site
Quirk, M. Cold barrel zero
Quirk, M. Dead man switch
Rankin, I. Blood hunt
Sharp, Z. Fox hunter
Sharp, Z. Second shot

FORMER SPECIAL FORCES OFFICERS
McCarthy, C. No country for old men

FORMER SPIES

Cumming, C. A colder war
Cumming, C. A divided spy
Hayes, T. I am Pilgrim
Lawton, J. Then we take Berlin
Malliet, G. A demon summer
Malliet, G. Pagan spring
McCarry, C. Old boys
Montclair, A. The right sort of man
Smith, T. Agent 6

FORMER SPIES -- GREAT BRITAIN
Cumming, C. A colder war
Cumming, C. A foreign country
Malliet, G. A fatal winter
Malliet, G. Wicked autumn
Porter, H. White hot silence
Putney, M. No longer a gentleman

FORMER TEACHERS
Beattie, A. A wonderful stroke of luck
Rowland, R. Cold country
Strout, E. Olive, again
Wilder, T. Theophilus North

FORMER TEXAS RANGERS
Kelton, E. The way of the coyote

FORMER THIEVES
Thompson, T. Rosewater
Thompson, T. The Rosewater insurrection
Thompson, T. The Rosewater redemption

FORMER WIVES
Berkowitz, I. Old flame
Brodesser-Akner, T. Fleishman is in trouble
Burke, A. The better sister
Geagley, B. Year of the hyenas
Genova, L. Every note played
Harrod-Eagles, C. Headlong
Jin, H. The boat rocker
Lipman, E. The family man
Lowry, M. Under the volcano
Miyamoto, T. Kinshu
Parker, R. Sea change
Parker, R. Stone cold
Robinson, P. Playing with fire
Tropper, J. One last thing before I go
Truong, M. The sweetest fruits

The **forsaken** Atkins, A.

The **Forsyte** saga Galsworthy, J.

Forsyte saga [series] Galsworthy, J.

FORT LAUDERDALE, FLORIDA
MacDonald, J. Cinnamon skin
MacDonald, J. The green ripper
MacDonald, J. The lonely silver rain
MacDonald, J. The long lavender look
MacDonald, J. A purple place for dying
MacDonald, J. The scarlet ruse
MacDonald, J. The turquoise lament

FORT SUMTER (CHARLESTON, SC : FORT) -- SIEGE, 1861
Poyer, D. A country of our own

Poyer, D. Fire on the waters
FORT WORTH, TEXAS
Coomer, J. One vacant chair
FORTIES (AGE)
Bradford, B. Power of a woman
Brandt, H. The Whites
Dyer, G. Jeff in Venice, death in Varanasi
Elkins, A. A long time coming
Haywood, S. The cactus
Kirshenbaum, B. Rabbits for food
McMillan, T. How Stella got her groove back
Miller, K. An angry-ass black woman
Fortuna Merbeth, K.
Fortunate son Mosley, W.
Fortune favors the wicked Romain, T.
FORTUNE HUNTERS
Collins, W. The moonstone
Heyer, G. Black sheep
James, H. The wings of the dove
Warren, T. The replacement wife
Fortune smiles Johnson, A.
The **fortune** teller's daughter Wilson, S.
FORTUNE TELLING
Engelmann, K. The Stockholm octavo
Merimee, P. Carmen
Fortune's rocks Shreve, A.
FORTUNE-TELLERS
Benjamin, C. The immortalists
Frost, K. The reluctant fortune-teller
O'Connell, C. Mallory's oracle
Simenon, G. Maigret and the fortuneteller
Tyler, A. Searching for Caleb
The **fortunes** Davies, P.
The **forty** days of Musa Dagh Werfel, F.
FOSSILS
Davies, C. West
FOSTER BROTHERS
McLayne, A. Highland promise
FOSTER CARE
Clement, J. Gun love
Diffenbaugh, V. The language of flowers
Fagan, J. The Panopticon
Gardner, L. Look for me
Hurwitz, G. You're next
Parks, B. Closer than you know
FOSTER CHILD ABUSE
Hulme, K. The bone people
FOSTER CHILDREN
Bronte, E. Wuthering Heights
Corry, J. The dead ex
DuPree, K. Shattered
Fitch, J. White oleander
Gibbons, K. Ellen Foster
Gibbons, K. The life all around me by Ellen Foster
Ludwig, B. Ginny Moon
Smith, M. The fighter
Umrigar, T. Everybody's son

FOSTER DAUGHTERS
Ludwig, B. Ginny Moon
FOSTER FAMILY
Stabenow, D. Whisper to the blood
FOSTER FATHERS
Coplin, A. The orchardist
Greene, G. The captain and the enemy
Hulme, K. The bone people
FOSTER HOME CARE
Gibbons, K. The life all around me by Ellen Foster
FOSTER MOTHERS
Gibbons, K. The life all around me by Ellen Foster
Overton, H. The runaway
Sekaran, S. Lucky boy
Smith, M. The fighter
FOSTER PARENTS
Bohjalian, C. The buffalo soldier
Box, C. Winterkill
Leckie, A. Provenance
FOSTER SONS
Nelscott, K. Days of rage
FOSTER TEENAGERS
Carr, B. Opioid, Indiana
Ferencik, E. Into the jungle
Foucault's pendulum Eco, U.
Foundation Asimov, I.
Foundation and empire Asimov, I.
Foundation series [series] Asimov, I.
FOUNDRY WORKERS
Brown, S. White hot
Foundryside Bennett, R.
The **fountain** of St. James Court Naslund, S.
The **fountainhead** Rand, A.
Four nights with the duke James, E.
Four sisters, all queens Jones, S.
Four souls Erdrich, L.
Four spirits Naslund, S.
Four ways to forgiveness Le Guin, U.
The **four-gated** city Lessing, D.
FOUR-YEAR-OLD BOYS
Audur A. Olafsdottir, 1. Butterflies in November
Hawley, N. Before the fall
McLaughlin, E. The nanny diaries
Starnone, D. Trick
FOUR-YEAR-OLD GIRLS
Nunez, E. Grace
FOURTEEN-YEAR-OLD BOYS
Bauer, B. Snap
Blau, J. The summer of naked swim parties
Stabenow, D. A grave denied
FOURTEEN-YEAR-OLD BOYS -- ORANGE COUNTY, CALIFORNIA
Rosenberg, N. Interest of justice
FOURTEEN-YEAR-OLD GIRLS
Booth, C. Kendra
Brunt, C. Tell the wolves I'm home
Fridlund, E. History of wolves

Harris, T. Hannibal rising
Helprin, M. Paris in the present tense
Hertmans, S. The convert
Hoffman, A. The marriage of opposites
Holdstock, P. Here I am!
Houellebecq, M. The map and the territory
Houellebecq, M. Submission
Kerangal, M. The cook
Kerangal, M. The heart
Kerr, P. Prussian blue
Longworth, M. Murder on the Ile Sordou
Louis, E. The end of Eddy
Maugham, W. Of human bondage
Meyer, N. The adventure of the peculiar protocols
Miller, H. Tropic of Cancer
Murdoch, I. Nuns and soldiers
Murphy, Y. Signed, Mata Hari
NDiaye, M. Three strong women
Olafur Johann Olafsson The sacrament
Orringer, J. The flight portfolio
Phoenix, M. The space between words
Portis, C. Masters of Atlantis
Rademacher, C. Deadly Camargue
Rhys, R. Fatal inheritance
Roussel, R. Locus solus
Sand, G. Marianne
Scott, C. The poppy wife
Shaw, V. Dreadful company
Simenon, G. Maigret and the black sheep
Simenon, G. Maigret and the fortuneteller
Simenon, G. Maigret and the killer
Simenon, G. Maigret and the madwoman
Simenon, G. Maigret and the Saturday caller
Simenon, G. Maigret and the toy village
Simenon, G. Maigret and the wine merchant
Simenon, G. Maigret bides his time
Simenon, G. Maigret goes home
Simenon, G. Maigret's memoirs
Simenon, G. My friend Maigret
Spark, M. Aiding & abetting
Tregillis, I. The mechanical
Trevanian The summer of Katya
Vargas Llosa, M. The bad girl
Vargas Llosa, M. The way to paradise
Winspear, J. Maisie Dobbs

FRANCE -- HISTORY
Bourne, J. The forbidden rose
Roberts, M. Ignorance
Rutherfurd, E. Paris
Sebald, W. Vertigo

FRANCE -- HISTORY -- 14TH CENTURY
Cornwell, B. 1356
Cornwell, B. The archer's tale
Druon, M. The iron king
Riley, J. In pursuit of the green lion

FRANCE -- HISTORY -- 17TH CENTURY
Dumas, A. Twenty years after

FRANCE -- HISTORY -- 18TH CENTURY
Gabaldon, D. Dragonfly in amber
Kearsley, S. A desperate fortune
Pittman, A. The seamstress
Rosenthal, P. The bookseller's daughter
Suskind, P. Perfume

FRANCE -- HISTORY -- 1914-1940
Sartre, J. The age of reason

FRANCE -- HISTORY -- 19TH CENTURY
Bayard, L. The black tower
Bourne, J. The spymaster's lady
Chee, A. The queen of the night
Sedgwick, M. Mister Memory
Welch, J. The heartsong of Charging Elk

FRANCE -- HISTORY -- 20TH CENTURY
Del Amo, J. Animalia
Dunmore, H. The lie
Furst, A. Mission to Paris
Hoffman, A. The world that we knew
Keneally, T. The daughters of Mars
Lopez Barrio, C. The house of the impossible loves
Moyes, J. The girl you left behind
Nicholson, W. Motherland
Proust, M. Time regained
Schwarz-Bart, A. The last of the just
Van Booy, S. The illusion of separateness

FRANCE -- HISTORY -- BOURBONS, 1589-1790
Dumas, A. The three musketeers

FRANCE -- HISTORY -- CAPETIANS, 987-1328
Druon, M. The iron king

FRANCE -- HISTORY -- CHARLES VII, 1422-1461
Twain, M. Personal recollections of Joan of Arc

FRANCE -- HISTORY -- CONSULATE AND FIRST EMPIRE, 1799-1815
Putney, M. No longer a gentleman
Willig, L. The deception of the emerald ring
Willig, L. The garden intrigue
Willig, L. The masque of the Black Tulip
Willig, L. The secret history of the Pink Carnation
Willig, L. The seduction of the Crimson Rose

FRANCE -- HISTORY -- FEBRUARY REVOLUTION, 1848
Flaubert, G. Sentimental education

FRANCE -- HISTORY -- GERMAN OCCUPATION, 1914-1918
Faulks, S. Birdsong

FRANCE -- HISTORY -- GERMAN OCCUPATION, 1940-1945
Bates, H. Fair stood the wind for France
Belfoure, C. The Paris architect
Black, C. Three hours in Paris
Doerr, A. All the light we cannot see
Faulks, S. Charlotte Gray
Faulks, S. Paris echo
Follett, K. Jackdaws
Furst, A. A hero of France
Furst, A. Under occupation

Slouka, M. God's fool

FREAKS (ENTERTAINERS)

Hoffman, A. The Museum of Extraordinary Things

Freaky deaky Leonard, E.

Fred Carver mysteries [series] Lutz, J.

Frederica Potter series [series] Byatt, A.

FREDERICKSBURG, BATTLE OF, 1862

Shaara, J. Gods and generals

Fredrika Bergman mysteries [series] Ohlsson, K.

FREE AFRICAN AMERICANS

Faye, L. Seven for a secret

FREE ENTERPRISE

Gaddis, W. J R

Free falling, as if in a dream Persson, L.

A **free** life Jin, H.

FREE WILL AND DETERMINISM

Butler, R. Hell

Ellory, R. Bad signs

Guterson, D. Ed King

Jacobs, N. The last equation of Isaac Severy

Lopez Barrio, C. The house of the impossible loves

Obioma, C. An orchestra of minorities

Tregillis, I. The mechanical

Vonnegut, K. Timequake

FREED SLAVES

Atakora, A. Conjure women

Bird, S. Daughter of a daughter of a queen

Chiaverini, J. Mrs. Lincoln's dressmaker

Cho, Z. Sorcerer to the crown

Cobbs Hoffman, E. The Tubman command

Cole, A. An extraordinary union

Cole, A. An unconditional freedom

Colvin, J. Africaville

Deon, N. Grace

Doctorow, E. The march

Hambly, B. Lady of perdition

Jenkins, B. Rebel

Jones, E. The known world

Kelton, E. The way of the coyote

Leveen, L. The secrets of Mary Bowser

Levy, A. The long song

McCann, C. Transatlantic

Michener, J. Chesapeake

Morrison, T. Beloved

Sexton, M. The revisioners

Truong, M. The sweetest fruits

Willig, L. The summer country

FREED SLAVES -- NEW ORLEANS, LOUISIANA

Johnson, C. Middle Passage

FREED SLAVES -- TEXAS

Jiles, P. The color of lightning

FREEDOM

Adams, R. Watership Down

Clarke, A. Childhood's end

Conklin, T. The house girl

Cusk, R. Kudos

Danielewski, M. Only revolutions

Evaristo, B. Blonde roots

Fowles, J. The magus

Furnivall, K. The red scarf

It occurs to me that I am America

Jiles, P. The color of lightning

Kelly, M. Lilac girls

Le Guin, U. Orsinian tales

Leveen, L. The secrets of Mary Bowser

Levy, A. The long song

Lock, N. A fugitive in Walden Woods

Ma, J. Beijing coma

McDermott, A. After this

Mda, Z. The Madonna of Excelsior

Mukherjee, N. A state of freedom

Noire G-Spot

Rand, A. We the living

Sackville-West, V. The Edwardians

Sartre, J. The age of reason

Solomon, R. The deep

Swinson, K. I'm New York's finest

Thom, J. Panther in the sky

Vestal, S. Daredevils

Warren, R. Band of angels

Wecker, H. The golem and the jinni

Wells, H. The invisible man

Whitehead, C. The underground railroad

Woods, R. Remembrance

Zamyatin, Y. We

Freedom Franzen, J.

FREEDOM OF RELIGION

Brooks, G. People of the book

Freedomland Price, R.

Freeman Pitts, L.

FREEMASONRY

Brown, D. The lost symbol

FREIGHT AND FREIGHTAGE

Zimmer, M. The long hitch

FREIGHTERS

Furst, A. Dark voyage

FREIGHTERS -- BRAZIL

L'Amour, L. May there be a road

FRENCH AMERICANS

Donoghue, E. Akin

FRENCH CANADIANS

Wood, S. The Quintland sisters

FRENCH IN EGYPT

Roiphe, A. An imperfect lens

FRENCH IN ENGLAND

Dickens, C. A tale of two cities

Jakeman, J. In the kingdom of mists

FRENCH IN NORTH AMERICA

Smith, D. The constable's tale

FRENCH IN RUSSIA

Makine, A. Dreams of my Russian summers

FRENCH IN THE UNITED STATES

Carey, P. Parrot and Olivier in America

Pearl, M. The Poe shadow

Bognanni, P. The house of tomorrow
Bohjalian, C. The buffalo soldier
Bohjalian, C. The double bind
Booth, C. Kendra
Bouchet, A. Nightchaser
Bradbury, R. Dandelion wine
Bram, C. Lives of the circus animals
Brandt, H. The Whites
Bronte, C. Jane Eyre
Brookner, A. Brief lives
Brookner, A. Hotel Du Lac
Brooks, G. Caleb's crossing
Bruen, K. The guards
Brunt, C. Tell the wolves I'm home
Bryant, N. Message from a mistress
Cameron, M. Code of honor
Cannon, J. Three things about Elsie
Capote, T. Breakfast at Tiffany's
Carey, P. Parrot and Olivier in America
Cervantes Saavedra, M. Don Quixote
Chabon, M. Telegraph Avenue
Chevalier, T. A single thread
Childs, L. Lavender blue murder
Cisneros, S. The house on Mango Street
Cleave, C. Gold
Cocks, H. The royal we
Collins, C. The gamal
Colwin, L. Happy all the time
Conlon, E. Red on red
Conroy, P. South of Broad
Cotterill, C. Don't eat me
D'Souza, T. Whiteman
Daniel, S. Stiltsville
Danler, S. Sweetbitter
Danticat, E. Everything inside
Dicks, M. Memoirs of an imaginary friend
Doiron, P. Almost midnight
Donoghue, E. Frog music
Dunant, S. In the company of the courtesan
Durrell, L. Balthazar
Edgerton, C. Walking across Egypt
Eggers, D. How we are hungry
Ehirim, N. Prince of monkeys
Eisenberg, D. The twilight of the superheroes
Ellis, B. Imperial bedrooms
Ellison, J. Good girls lie
Ephron, H. Night night, sleep tight
Fabry, C. The promise of Jesse Woods
Fay, J. The shortest way home
Fitzpatrick, L. Lights all night long
Foley, L. The hunting party
Ford, F. The good soldier
Ford, J. Songs of Willow Frost
Forman, G. Leave me
Forna, A. Happiness
Fowler, K. The Jane Austen book club
Frayn, M. Spies

Fuentes, C. Destiny and desire
Fuller, C. Bitter orange
Furnivall, K. The red scarf
Gabel, A. The ensemble
Gander, F. As a friend
Gaynor, H. Meet me in Monaco
Ghosh, A. The glass palace
Gilman, S. Donna has left the building
Ginzburg, N. A family lexicon
Godwin, G. Unfinished desires
Goenawan, C. The perfect world of Miwako Sumida
Grant, L. We had it so good
Grenville, K. The lieutenant
Groen, H. On the bright side
Grushin, O. The line
Guillory, J. The proposal
Guillory, J. The wedding party
Gunesekera, R. Suncatcher
Guterson, D. The other
Hallberg, G. City on fire
Hamilton, J. A map of the world
Hannah, K. The great alone
Harkaway, N. The gone-away world
Haruf, K. Our souls at night
Haywood, G. Cemetery Road
Heller, P. The river
Henderson, S. The flicker of old dreams
Horlock, M. The book of lies
Iles, G. Cemetery road
Ishiguro, K. Never let me go
Jacobson, H. The Finkler question
Jaswal, B. Erotic stories for Punjabi widows
Jiles, P. News of the world
Jimenez, A. The friend zone
Joinson, S. A lady cyclist's guide to Kashgar
Joseph, F. Niya
Just, W. Rodin's debutante
K'wan Gangsta
Kantaria, A. I know you
Karunatilaka, S. The legend of Pradeep Mathew
Kawakami, M. Ms. Ice Sandwich
Kelly, M. Lost roses
Kerangal, M. The cook
Kerouac, J. On the road
Khadivi, L. A good country
Kibler, J. Home for erring and outcast girls
Kiefer, C. The infinite tides
King, S. It
Kingsolver, B. The bean trees
Kline, C. Orphan train
Knowles, J. A separate peace
Lee, J. The starlet and the spy
Lewis, B. The preacher's daughter
Lewis, S. Main street
Li, Y. The vagrants
Liardet, F. We must be brave
Lim, E. Dear cyborgs

Wilson, R. Spin
Winman, S. Tin man
Winslow, D. The kings of cool
Winton, T. The shepherd's hut
Wolitzer, M. The Interestings
Wong, D. John dies at the end
Woolf, V. The waves
Wuertz, Y. Everything belongs to us
Yates, C. Black chalk
Yoon, P. Run me to earth
Yoshimoto, B. The lake
Youngson, A. Meet me at the museum
Zan, K. The never list

Frog music Donoghue, E.

A **frolic** of his own Gaddis, W.

The **frolic** of the beasts Mishima, Y.

From bondage Roth, H.

From here to eternity Jones, J.

From Manhattan with love [series] Morgan, S.

From Russia with love Fleming, I.

FRONTIER AND PIONEER LIFE

American West

Barry, S. Days without end
Bittner, R. Logan's lady
Bradbury, R. The Martian chronicles
Brand, M. Max Brand's best western stories
Brooks, B. Blood storm
Card, O. Saints
Cather, W. A lost lady
Cooper, J. The last of the Mohicans
Czerneda, J. A turn of light
Dallas, S. The last midwife
Dallas, S. Westering women
Davies, C. West
Diaz, H. In the distance
Doig, I. Dancing at the Rascal Fair
Doig, I. The whistling season
Enger, L. The high divide
Estleman, L. The master executioner
Everett, P. God's country
Gilman, L. The cold eye
Goodman, J. In want of a wife
Goodman, J. A touch of forever
Grey, Z. Woman of the frontier
Groom, W. El Paso
Guthrie, A. The big sky
Haldane, S. The devil's making
Harte, B. The best short stories of Bret Harte
Howarth, P. Only killers and thieves
Jenkins, B. Breathless
Jenkins, B. Forbidden
Kelton, E. Hard ride
Kent, K. The outcasts
Kirkpatrick, J. One more river to cross
Kirkpatrick, J. This road we traveled
Larison, J. Whiskey when we're dry
Leonard, E. The complete Western stories of Elmore Leon-

ard.

Levine, D. Arabella of Mars
Matthiessen, P. Killing Mister Watson
Matthiessen, P. Shadow country
McMurtry, L. Zeke and Ned
Meyer, P. The son
Michener, J. Centennial
Munro, A. The view from Castle Rock
Overholser, W. Death of a cattle king
Putnam, J. These honored dead
Raymond, J. The half-life
Richards, D. The mustanger and the lady
Rolvaag, O. Giants in the Earth
Russell, M. Doc
Russell, M. Epitaph
Schanbacher, G. Crossing Purgatory
Silko, L. Gardens in the dunes
Soli, T. The removes
Sontag, S. In America
Urrea, L. Queen of America
Vanderhaeghe, G. The last crossing
Warren, R. World enough and time
Wascom, K. The blood of heaven
Welty, E. The robber bridegroom
Wheeler, R. The canyon of bones
Wheeler, R. North star
deWitt, P. The Sisters brothers

FRONTIER AND PIONEER LIFE -- ALASKA

Ivey, E. The snow child

FRONTIER AND PIONEER LIFE -- CANADA

Penney, S. The tenderness of wolves

FRONTIER AND PIONEER LIFE -- EVERGLADES, FLORIDA

Matthiessen, P. Bone by bone

FRONTIER AND PIONEER LIFE -- GREAT PLAINS (UNITED STATES)

Coldsmith, D. Tallgrass

FRONTIER AND PIONEER LIFE -- MARYLAND

Pynchon, T. Mason & Dixon

FRONTIER AND PIONEER LIFE -- NEBRASKA

Cather, W. My Antonia
Cather, W. O pioneers!

FRONTIER AND PIONEER LIFE -- NEW MEXICO

Richter, C. The sea of grass

FRONTIER AND PIONEER LIFE -- NEW ZEALAND

Tremain, R. The colour

FRONTIER AND PIONEER LIFE -- NORTHWEST, CA-NADIAN

Freedman, B. Mrs. Mike

FRONTIER AND PIONEER LIFE -- OHIO

Richter, C. The awakening land

FRONTIER AND PIONEER LIFE -- OREGON

Keesey, A. Little century

FRONTIER AND PIONEER LIFE -- PACIFIC NORTH-WEST

Fowler, K. Sarah Canary

FRONTIER AND PIONEER LIFE -- PENNSYLVANIA

Petrie, N. The wild one
Pollock, D. The devil all the time
Proulx, A. Postcards
Rajaniemi, H. The fractal prince
Rajaniemi, H. The quantum thief
Reiken, F. Day for night
Richards, D. The mustanger and the lady
Robotham, M. Life or death
Robotham, M. Suspect
Sallis, J. Drive
Sallis, J. Driven
Saramago, J. Cain
Spark, M. Aiding & abetting
Suarez, D. Change agent
Swinson, K. The safe house
Thelen, A. The island of second sight
Watkins, J. Secrets of a side bitch
Weber, C. Man on the run
Wilson, G. The bird king
Winslow, D. Satori
Woodrell, D. Winter's bone

FUGITIVES -- TRENTON, NEW JERSEY
Evanovich, J. One for the money
The **full** cupboard of life McCall Smith, A.
Full throttle Hill, J.
Full wolf moon Child, L.

FULLER, R BUCKMINSTER, 1895-1983
  INFLUENCE
Bognanni, P. The house of tomorrow
Fumbled Martin, A.

FUNDAMENTALISM
Anam, T. The bones of grace
Aslam, N. Maps for lost lovers
Cussler, C. Sacred stone
Forsyth, F. The kill list
Hamid, M. Exit west
Harris, E. I say a little prayer
Littell, R. Vicious circle
Mirvis, T. The outside world
Pamuk, O. Snow
Rushdie, S. Two years eight months and
  twenty-eight nights

FUNDAMENTALISTS
Baldwin, J. Go tell it on the mountain
Berenson, A. The faithful spy
Bergstrom, H. Steal the north
Butler, O. Parable of the talents
Ebershoff, D. The 19th wife
Gardam, J. God on the rocks
Higgins, J. Rough justice
Khadra, Y. The swallows of Kabul
Ledgard, J. Submergence
Littell, R. Vicious circle
Nunez, S. Salvation city
Oates, J. A book of American martyrs
Perrotta, T. The abstinence teacher
Picoult, J. Sing you home

Tyler, A. Saint Maybe
Weir, M. The book of Essie
Zevin, G. The hole we're in
Funeral games Renault, M.
FUNERAL HOMES
Henderson, S. The flicker of old dreams
Ross, A. Miss Julia takes the wheel
Sanders, L. McNally's trial
Simon, M. Cremains of the day
Waugh, E. The loved one
Funeral in blue Perry, A.
FUNERALS
Banks, I. The crow road
Diehl, H. Lifelines
Downing, S. He started it
Gage, E. The ladies of Managua
Gaiman, N. The ocean at the end of the lane
Hage, R. Beirut Hellfire Society
Harris, R. The second sleep
Jeffries, S. Project Duchess
Kay, G. Under heaven
Lipman, E. The dearly departed, Elinor Lipman.
Ma, J. Stick out your tongue
Pronzini, B. Mourners
St. Aubyn, E. At last
Swift, G. Wish you were here
Welty, E. The optimist's daughter
FUNGI
Vandermeer, J. Finch
FUR INDUSTRY AND TRADE
Aalborg, G. River of porcupines
FUR TRADERS
Michener, J. Centennial
The **furies** Lowe, K.
FURNITURE INDUSTRY AND TRADE
Mason, R. Who killed Piet Barol?
Watts, S. No one is coming to save us
FURNITURE SALES PERSONNEL
McCall Smith, A. In the company of cheerful ladies
Further out than you thought Carter, M.
FUTILITY (PSYCHOLOGY)
Abe, K. The woman in the dunes
Kafka, F. The castle
Future home of the living god Erdrich, L.
The **future** of another timeline Newitz, A.
The **future** of love Abbott, S.
FUTURE PUNISHMENT
Butler, R. Hell
FUTURISM (LITERARY MOVEMENT) -- SOVIET UNION
Littell, R. The Mayakovsky tapes
FUTURISTIC ROMANCES
Bouchet, A. Nightchaser
Castle, J. Illusion Town
Futuristic violence and fancy suits Wong, D.
FUTURISTS
Sterling, B. Pirate Utopia

Box, C. Open season
Box, C. Savage run
Box, C. Trophy hunt
Box, C. Vicious circle
Box, C. Winterkill
Box, C. Wolf pack
Doiron, P. Almost midnight
Doiron, P. Bad Little Falls
Doiron, P. The poacher's son
Doiron, P. The precipice
Doiron, P. Stay hidden
Munier, P. A borrowing of bones

Gamechanger Beckett, L.

GAMEKEEPERS

Lawrence, D. Lady Chatterley's lover

GAMES

James, E. Kiss me, Annabel
Morgenstern, E. The night circus
Tudor, C. The chalk man
Yates, C. Black chalk

The **games** Kosmatka, T.

GANG LEADERS

Barry, K. City of Bohane

GANG MEMBERS

Beverly, W. Dodgers
Gran, S. Claire DeWitt and the city of the dead
K'wan Gangsta
K'wan Gutter
Paretsky, S. Hardball

GANG RAPE

Hunter, E. The blackboard jungle
Noire G-Spot

GANG RAPE -- AFGHANISTAN

Hosseini, K. The kite runner

GANGES RIVER

Endo, S. Deep river

GANGS

Atkins, A. The lost ones
Barry, K. City of Bohane
Beverly, W. Dodgers
Blake, J. The house of Wolfe
Box, C. Badlands
Brookmyre, C. When the devil drives
Brookmyre, C. Where the bodies are buried
Bump, G. Everywhere you don't belong
Burke, M. Team seven
Ca$h Thugs cry
Ca$h Trust no man
Ca$h Trust no man 2
Ca$h Trust no man 3
Chacon, D. And the shadows took him
Child, L. Blue moon
Clement, J. Prayers for the stolen
Conlon, E. Red on red
Diamond, D. Boss divas
Diamond, D. Gangsta divas
Diamond, D. King divas

French, J. The true Bastards
Green, N. The angel of Montague Street
Harvey, M. We all fall down
Hunter, E. The blackboard jungle
K'wan Gangsta
K'wan Gutter
Lee, F. Jade City
Lessing, D. The fifth child
Mabanckou, A. Black Moses
MacBride, S. Blind eye
MacBride, S. Close to the bone
Mark, D. Original skin
Mosley, W. The right mistake
Nelscott, K. Stone cribs
Newton, C. Start shooting
O'Mara, T. Crooked numbers
Parker, R. Double deuce
Parker, R. Potshot
Parker, R. Walking shadow
Parker, R. Stranger in paradise
Parker, T. L.A. outlaws
Pelecanos, G. Drama city
Ridgway, K. Hawthorn & Child
Sandford, J. Golden prey
Scott, A. The low road
Vachss, A. Two trains running
Vollmann, W. The rainbow stories
Williams, K. Harlem on lock

GANGS -- MONTEREY, CALIFORNIA

Steinbeck, J. Tortilla Flat

Gangsta K'wan
Gangsta divas Diamond, D.
Gangsta novels [series] K'wan
A **gangster** and a gentleman Swinson, K.
Gangsterland Goldberg, T.

GANGSTERS

Abbott, M. Queenpin
Amdahl, G. I am death
Berkowitz, I. Old flame
Chandler, R. The long goodbye
Clark, W. Thugs and the women who love them
Colfer, E. Plugged
Doctorow, E. Billy Bathgate
Ellroy, J. Blood's a rover
Goldberg, T. Gangsterland
Goodis, D. Nightfall
Gray, E. Love & a gangsta
Green, N. The angel of Montague Street
Greene, G. Brighton Rock
Gross, A. Button man
Guttridge, P. The thing itself
Hallinan, T. Fields where they lay
Hunter, S. Hot springs
Kaminsky, S. Dancing in the dark
Kasasian, M. Dark dawn over Steep House
Kaufmann, N. Dying is my business
Lehane, D. Live by night

Leonard, E. Charlie Martz and other stories
Leonard, E. The Hot Kid
Mark, D. Cruel mercy
McBride, J. Deacon King Kong
McDonald, I. River of gods
Mosley, W. Devil in a blue dress
Nesbo, J. Midnight sun
Parker, R. Cold service
Parker, R. Double play
Pelecanos, G. The big blowdown
Puzo, M. The godfather
Puzo, M. The Sicilian
Rabe, P. Anatomy of a killer ;
Randisi, R. Hey there (you with the gun in your hand)
Reich, C. The take
Rosen, R. Dollface
Twardoch, S. The king of Warsaw
Weir, A. Artemis
Woods, T. Dutch

GANGSTERS -- EDINBURGH, SCOTLAND
Rankin, I. The hanging garden
Ganymede Priest, C.
The **gap** year Bird, S.

GARBAGE COLLECTION -- CORRUPT PRACTICES
Leon, D. About face

GARBAGE COLLECTORS
Boswell, R. Century's son
The **garden** intrigue Willig, L.
Garden of beasts Deaver, J.
A **garden** of earthly delights Oates, J.
The **garden** of evening mists Tan, T.
The **garden** of evil Hewson, D.
Garden of lies Quick, A.
The **garden** of the Finzi-Continis Bassani, G.
Garden spells Allen, S.

GARDENERS
Coetzee, J. Life & times of Michael K
Hale, S. Austenland
Koontz, D. The husband
Quindlen, A. Every last one

GARDENING
Allen, S. Garden spells
Tan, T. The garden of evening mists

GARDENING -- SOCIETIES, ETC
Albert, S. The Darling Dahlias and the cucumber tree

GARDENS
Allen, S. Garden spells
Bowen, R. The victory garden
Bussi, M. Black water lilies
Shipman, V. The heirloom garden
Tan, T. The garden of evening mists
Gardens in the dunes Silko, L.
The **gargoyle** Davidson, A.

GARGOYLES
Pandian, G. The accidental alchemist

GARLAND, JUDY
Letts, E. Finding Dorothy

GARUDA (MYTHICAL BIRD)
Mieville, C. Perdido Street Station
Gas City Estleman, L.
A **gate** at the stairs Moore, L.
The **gate** to Women's Country Tepper, S.

GATED COMMUNITIES
Headley, M. The mere wife
Rojas Contreras, I. Fruit of the drunken tree
Rouda, K. The favorite daughter
Gateway Pohl, F.

GATEWAY FANTASY
Beagle, P. The unicorn sonata
Connolly, J. The book of lost things
Dekker, T. Black
Dekker, T. Red
Dekker, T. White
Gaiman, N. Stardust
Grossman, L. The magician king
Kay, G. The summer tree
Maaren, K. Weave a circle round
McGuire, S. Every heart a doorway
McGuire, S. Beneath the sugar sky
McGuire, S. Down among the sticks and bones
McGuire, S. In an absent dream
Schwab, V. A conjuring of light
Schwab, V. A darker shade of magic
Schwab, V. A gathering of shadows
Warrington, F. Elfland
Warrington, F. Grail of the summer stars
Warrington, F. Midsummer night
Wilkins, K. Veil of gold
Gather her round Bledsoe, A.
Gather the daughters Melamed, J.
Gather the fortunes Camp, B.
The **gathering** Enright, A.
A **gathering** of old men Gaines, E.
A **gathering** of secrets Castillo, L.
A **gathering** of shadows Schwab, V.
Gathering of waters McFadden, B.

GAUCHOS
Borges, J. Collected fictions
Gaudy night Sayers, D.

GAUGUIN, PAUL, 1848-1903
Maugham, W. The moon and sixpence
Vargas Llosa, M. The way to paradise

GAUTAMA BUDDHA
Hesse, H. Siddhartha

GAY ACTORS
Bram, C. Lives of the circus animals

GAY BOYS
Washington, B. Lot

GAY COMMUNITIES
Maupin, A. Tales of the city

GAY COUPLES
Castellani, C. Leading men
Cruse, H. The complete Wendel
Moniz, T. Big familia

Ramadan, A. The clothesline swing

GAY CULTURE

Cassara, J. The house of impossible beauties

Cruse, H. The complete Wendel

Kramer, L. Search for my heart

Maupin, A. Tales of the city

GAY CULTURE -- TURKEY

Somer, M. The serenity murders

GAY FATHERS

Millet, L. How the dead dream

GAY HUSBANDS

Cleeves, A. The long call

Evaristo, B. Mr. Loverman

GAY LAWYERS

Lipman, E. The family man

GAY MEN

Aciman, A. Find me

Auster, P. The Brooklyn follies

Baldwin, J. Another country

Baldwin, J. Early novels and stories

Baldwin, J. Giovanni's room

Baldwin, J. Just above my head

Baldwin, J. Tell me how long the train's been gone

Barry, S. Days without end

Bartlett, N. The disappearance boy

Boyne, J. The heart's invisible furies

Burroughs, W. Naked lunch

Cameron, P. The city of your final destination

Chabon, M. The amazing adventures of Kavalier & Clay

Charles, K. Wanted, a gentleman

Cruse, H. The complete Wendel

Cullin, M. Undersurface

Cusset, C. Life of David Hockney

Ebershoff, D. The 19th wife

Evaristo, B. Mr. Loverman

Festing, I. The bird keeper

Forster, E. Maurice

Freeman, A. The fair fight

Glass, J. Three Junes

Glass, J. The whole world over

Greene, G. Collected stories

Greenwell, G. What belongs to you

Greer, A. Less

Hall, A. For real

Harvey, J. Gone to ground

Hensher, P. King of the badgers

Henson, P. Into the blue

Hollinghurst, A. The Sparsholt affair

Kanon, J. Los Alamos

Koen, K. Through a glass darkly

Kramer, L. Search for my heart

Leavitt, D. The two Hotel Francforts

Leon, D. Unto us a son is given

Lessing, D. The good terrorist

Louis, E. The end of Eddy

Mallon, T. Fellow travelers

Maupin, A. Tales of the city

McQuiston, C. Red, white & royal blue

Mehta, R. No other world

Mehta, R. Quarantine

Muller, M. While other people sleep

Murdoch, I. The bell

Murdoch, I. A fairly honourable defeat

Nava, M. Carved in bone

Owen, L. The quick

Parker, R. Melancholy baby

Puig, M. Kiss of the spider woman

Renault, M. The Persian boy

Ridgway, K. Hawthorn & Child

Rowland, L. The hangman's secret

Rush, N. Mortals

Sanders, J. Speakers of the dead

Sebastian, C. It takes two to tumble

Sebastian, C. The Lawrence Browne affair

Smith, C. Silent city

Staples, D. This town sleeps

Sundstol, V. The land of dreams

Taylor, B. Real life

Tesh, E. Silver in the wood

Thomas, R. Firewatching

Toibin, C. The blackwater lightship

Truong, M. The book of salt, Monique Truong.

Unsworth, B. After Hannibal

White, E. The beautiful room is empty

Winman, S. Tin man

Wolitzer, M. The Interestings

Wolitzer, M. Surrender, Dorothy

GAY MEN -- ANCIENT GREECE

Renault, M. The last of the wine

GAY MEN -- BERLIN, GERMANY

Isherwood, C. The Berlin stories

GAY MEN -- GREAT BRITAIN

Barker, P. The eye in the door

GAY MEN -- IDENTITY

Alenyikov, M. Ivan and Misha

GAY MEN -- MANHATTAN, NEW YORK CITY

D'Erasmo, S. The sky below

GAY MEN -- OUTING

Parker, R. Hush money

GAY MEN -- PSYCHOLOGY

O'Hagan, A. Be near me

GAY MEN -- PSYCHOTHERAPY

White, E. The beautiful room is empty

GAY MEN -- RELATIONS WITH WOMEN

Gide, A. The immoralist

Knight, D. Butterfly tattoo

Lipman, E. The family man

GAY MEN -- RELIGIOUS LIFE

Harris, E. I say a little prayer

GAY MEN -- SEXUALITY

Bram, C. Lives of the circus animals

Gide, A. The immoralist

Greenwell, G. Cleanness

White, E. The beautiful room is empty

Rindell, S. The other typist
Schwartz, J. The commoner
See, L. Peony in love
Smith, Z. White teeth
Soli, T. The removes
Solomon, A. Leaving Lucy Pear
Solomon, R. An unkindness of ghosts
Spencer, S. The dead hand of history
Stewart, A. Kopp sisters on the march
Stewart, A. Miss Kopp just won't quit
Stibbe, N. Reasons to be cheerful
Tepper, S. Singer from the sea
Thomas, S. Not quite a husband
Thomas, S. Oligarchy
Tyler, A. Vinegar girl
Urrea, L. Into the beautiful North
Vreeland, S. Clara and Mr. Tiffany
Watson, B. Miss Jane
Woolf, V. Orlando

GENDER ROLE -- POLITICAL ASPECTS
McEwan, I. Sweet tooth

GENDER ROLE AND CHILDREN
Winter, K. Annabel

GENEALOGY
Mosley, W. Trouble is what I do
Silver, M. Mary Coin
Wade, B. True to you
The **general** in his labyrinth Garcia Marquez, G.
The **general** of the dead army Kadare, I.

GENERAL RELATIVITY (PHYSICS)
Lightman, A. Einstein's dreams

GENERALS
Bolano, R. By night in Chile
Dekker, T. Black
Dekker, T. Red
Dekker, T. White
Gingrich, N. Grant comes east
Jakes, J. Savannah, or, A gift for Mr. Lincoln
Renault, M. Funeral games
Shaara, J. Gods and generals
Shaara, J. Gone for soldiers
Shaara, J. The last full measure
Vollmann, W. Europe central

GENERALS -- CENTRAL AFRICA
Ballard, J. The day of creation

GENERALS -- ITALY
Kadare, I. The general of the dead army

GENERATION GAP
Alharthi, J. Celestial bodies
Alther, L. Kinflicks
Alyan, H. Salt houses
Bagshawe, T. Adored
Castillo, E. America is not the heart
Cramer, W. Levi's will
Deb, S. The point of return
Gage, E. The ladies of Managua
Meloy, M. Liars and saints

Mirvis, T. The outside world
Mukherjee, N. The lives of others
Robinson, M. Home
Roth, P. American pastoral
Sackville-West, V. The Edwardians
Sankaran, L. The hope factory
Smith, Z. On beauty
Tan, A. The bonesetter's daughter
Tan, A. The Joy Luck Club
Tan, A. The kitchen god's wife
Trollope, J. The men and the girls
Winslow, D. The kings of cool
Woodson, J. Red at the bone

GENERATION GAP -- RUSSIA
Turgenev, I. Fathers and sons
Generation loss Hand, E.

GENERATION X
Ellis, B. Imperial bedrooms

GENERATIONS
Dupont, E. The American fiancee
Saylor, S. Roma

GENERATIONS -- UNITED STATES
Fuller, J. Abbeville

GENEROSITY
Adimi, K. Our riches
Generosity Powers, R.
Genesis Cook, R.

GENETIC CODE
Powers, R. The Gold Bug Variations

GENETIC ENGINEERING
Butler, O. Adulthood rites
Butler, O. Dawn
Butler, O. Imago
Crichton, M. Next
Gonzales, L. Lucy
Grant, M. Parasite
Hamilton, P. The dreaming void
Herbert, F. Dune
Huxley, A. Brave new world
Kosmatka, T. The games
Kress, N. Beggars in Spain
Lamb, A. Roboteer
McDonald, I. River of gods
Mieville, C. Embassytown
Morgan, R. Thirteen
Suarez, D. Change agent
Wilhelm, K. Where late the sweet birds sang

GENETIC GENEALOGY
Cook, R. Genesis

GENETIC RESEARCH
Grimes, L. Quick fix
Powers, R. Generosity

GENETICALLY ENGINEERED ANIMALS
Atwood, M. Maddaddam
Atwood, M. The year of the flood

GENETICALLY ENGINEERED MEN
Lamb, A. Roboteer

Faulks, S. Jeeves and the wedding bells
Flagg, F. Standing in the rainbow
Frank, D. Folly Beach
Frank, D. Queen bee
Gibbons, K. Charms for the easy life
Gloss, M. The hearts of horses
Goudge, E. Green Dolphin Street
Hart, C. Death walked in
Hart, C. Murder walks the plank
Hart, C. Resort to murder
Hart, C. White elephant dead
Hart, C. Yankee Doodle dead
Heyer, G. The grand Sophy
Hollis, L. Poppy Harmon investigates
Karon, J. At home in Mitford
Karon, J. In this mountain
Karon, J. A new song
Karon, J. Out to Canaan
Kingsbury, K. A Baxter family Christmas
Kingsbury, K. When we were young
Landvik, L. Chronicles of a radical hag
Lathen, E. Brewing up a storm
Lathen, E. East is east
Lathen, E. Something in the air
Malliet, G. A demon summer
Malliet, G. A fatal winter
Malliet, G. Pagan spring
Malliet, G. Wicked autumn
McCall Smith, A. Blue shoes and happiness
McCall Smith, A. The comforts of a muddy Saturday
McCall Smith, A. The Department of Sensitive Crimes
McCall Smith, A. The Double Comfort Safari Club
McCall Smith, A. The forgotten affairs of youth
McCall Smith, A. The full cupboard of life
McCall Smith, A. The good husband of Zebra Drive
McCall Smith, A. In the company of cheerful ladies
McCall Smith, A. The Kalahari typing school for men
McCall Smith, A. The Limpopo Academy of Private Detection
McCall Smith, A. The lost art of gratitude
McCall Smith, A. The No. 1 Ladies' Detective Agency
McCall Smith, A. The Saturday big tent wedding party
McKevett, G. Murder in her stocking
McKevett, G. Murder in the corn maze
Meier, L. Silver anniversary murder
O'Donohue, C. The lover's knot
Page, K. The body in the big apple
Page, K. The body in the bog
Page, K. The body in the casket
Page, K. The body in the vestibule
Page, K. The body in the wake
Perkins, S. Murder once removed
Peters, E. Children of the storm
Peters, E. The deeds of the disturber
Peters, E. The golden one
Peters, E. Guardian of the horizon
Peters, E. He shall thunder in the sky

Peters, E. The hippopotamus pool
Peters, E. The last camel died at noon
Peters, E. Lion in the valley
Peters, E. The mummy case
Peters, E. Seeing a large cat
Peters, E. The snake, the crocodile, and the dog
Pilcher, R. Coming home
Pilcher, R. The shell seekers
Plain, B. Crescent City
Plain, B. The golden cup
Plain, B. Harvest
Plain, B. Tapestry
Pym, B. An academic question
Pym, B. Excellent women
Raichev, R. Assassins at Ospreys
Roberts, G. Adam and evil
Roberts, G. The bluest blood
Robinson, M. Gilead
Robinson, M. Home
Robinson, M. Lila
Roosevelt, E. The Hyde Park murder
Roosevelt, E. Murder and the First Lady
Roosevelt, E. Murder at midnight
Roosevelt, E. Murder in the Blue Room
Roosevelt, E. Murder in the map room
Roosevelt, E. Murder in the Oval Office
Roosevelt, E. Murder at the palace
Roosevelt, E. Murder in the Rose Garden
Roosevelt, E. The White House pantry murder
Ross, A. Miss Julia delivers the goods
Ross, A. Miss Julia takes the wheel
Ross, A. Miss Julia throws a wedding
Saums, M. Thistle & Twigg
Scoppettone, S. Too darn hot
Shaffer, M. The Guernsey Literary and Potato Peel Pie Society
Simon, C. Grey dawn
Simon, C. Stages of Grey
Simonson, H. Major Pettigrew's last stand
Tatlock, A. Promises to keep
Trigiani, A. Big Cherry Holler
Trigiani, A. Big Stone Gap
Tyler, A. The accidental tourist
Tyler, A. The amateur marriage
Tyler, A. Back when we were grownups
Tyler, A. The beginner's goodbye
Tyler, A. Breathing lessons
Tyler, A. Celestial navigation
Tyler, A. Clock dance
Tyler, A. The clock winder
Tyler, A. Digging to America
Tyler, A. Dinner at the Homesick Restaurant
Tyler, A. Earthly possessions
Tyler, A. Ladder of years
Tyler, A. Morgan's passing
Tyler, A. Noah's compass
Tyler, A. A patchwork planet

James, E. Three weeks with Lady X
James, E. Too Wilde to wed
James, E. Wilde in love
Jeffries, S. The art of sinning
Liss, D. A spectacle of corruption
London, J. The year of living scandalously
Nickson, C. The hocus girl
Putney, M. Once a soldier
Redfern, E. The music of the spheres
Robertson, I. Anatomy of murder
Robertson, I. Circle of shadows
Robertson, I. Instruments of darkness
Robertson, I. Island of bones
Rutherfurd, E. London
Willig, L. The betrayal of the blood lily
Willig, L. The deception of the emerald ring
Willig, L. The garden intrigue
Willig, L. The lure of the moonflower
Willig, L. The masque of the Black Tulip
Willig, L. The orchid affair
Willig, L. The secret history of the Pink Carnation
Willig, L. The seduction of the Crimson Rose
Willig, L. The temptation of the night jasmine

GEORGIAN ROMANCES

Ashe, K. The duke
Ashe, K. The prince
Beverley, J. Devilish
Beverley, J. My lady notorious
Beverley, J. Something wicked
Beverley, J. Tempting fortune
Chase, L. A duke in shining armor
Chase, L. Silk is for seduction
Heyer, G. These old shades
Hoyt, E. Wicked intentions
Hunter, M. The conquest of Lady Cassandra
Hunter, M. The surrender of Miss Fairbourne
James, E. Desperate duchesses
James, E. Four nights with the duke
James, E. Seven minutes in heaven
James, E. Three weeks with Lady X
James, E. Too Wilde to wed
James, E. Wilde in love
London, J. The year of living scandalously
Putney, M. Once a soldier
Willig, L. The betrayal of the blood lily
Willig, L. The deception of the emerald ring
Willig, L. The garden intrigue
Willig, L. The lure of the moonflower
Willig, L. The masque of the Black Tulip
Willig, L. The orchid affair
Willig, L. The secret history of the Pink Carnation
Willig, L. The seduction of the Crimson Rose
Willig, L. The temptation of the night jasmine

GEOTHERMAL ENERGY

Watts, P. Starfish

Gerhard Self mysteries [series] Schlink, B.

GERMAN AMERICANS

Deaver, J. Garden of beasts
Epstein, J. Wunderland
Erdrich, L. The Master Butchers Singing Club
Fleischmann, R. How quickly she disappears
Hegi, U. The vision of Emma Blau
Millhauser, S. Martin Dressler

GERMAN REUNIFICATION

Grass, G. Too far afield

GERMANS

Kerr, P. Field gray
Kerr, P. March violets
Schlink, B. Self's deception
Schlink, B. Self's murder
Schlink, B. Self's punishment

GERMANS IN CANADA

Norman, H. What is left the daughter

GERMANS IN FRANCE

Doerr, A. All the light we cannot see
Higgins, J. Night of the fox
Remarque, E. All quiet on the western front

GERMANS IN GREAT BRITAIN

Airth, R. The decent inn of death
Buchan, J. The thirty-nine steps
Follett, K. Eye of the needle
Weir, A. Anna of Kleve

GERMANS IN GREECE

Cussler, C. The Mediterranean caper
Serafim, L. When the devil's idle

GERMANS IN GUERNSEY (CHANNEL ISLANDS)

Horlock, M. The book of lies

GERMANS IN ITALY

Unsworth, B. After Hannibal

GERMANS IN NEW YORK STATE

Steinke, R. Holy skirts

GERMANS IN RUSSIA

Stachniak, E. The Winter Palace

GERMANS IN SPAIN

Bolano, R. The Third Reich

GERMANS IN THE SOVIET UNION

Remarque, E. A time to love and a time to die

GERMANS IN THE UNITED STATES

Stewart, A. Lady cop makes trouble

GERMANTOWN (PHILADELPHIA, PA)

Tyree, O. Flyy girl

GERMANY

Amis, M. The zone of interest
Belfer, L. And after the fire
Bernhard, T. Wittgenstein's nephew
Boll, H. The lost honor of Katharina Blum
Diehl, H. Lifelines
Downing, D. Diary of a dead man on leave
Ford, F. The good soldier
Fuller, C. Our endless numbered days
Grant, H. The glass demon
Grant, H. The vanishing of Katharina Linden
Grass, G. The call of the toad
Harris, R. Fatherland

Ghachar ghochar Shanbhag, V.

GHANA

Quartey, K. Children of the street

Quartey, K. Gold of our fathers

Quartey, K. The missing American

Quartey, K. Murder at Cape Three Points

Quartey, K. Wife of the gods

GHANA -- HISTORY

Gyasi, Y. Homegoing

GHETTOES

Beukes, L. Zoo city

GHETTOES -- LAGOS, NIGERIA

Abani, C. GraceLand

GHETTOES, AFRICAN AMERICAN

Wright, R. Native son

GHETTOES, AFRICAN AMERICAN -- HARLEM, NEW YORK CITY

K'wan Hoodlum

K'wan Street dreams

Petry, A. The street

GHETTOES, HISPANIC AMERICAN

Diaz, J. The brief wondrous life of Oscar Wao

GHETTOES, JEWISH

Uris, L. Mila 18

GHETTOES, JEWISH -- EASTERN EUROPE

Schwarz-Bart, A. The last of the just

GHETTOES, JEWISH -- KRAKOW, POLAND

Keneally, T. Schindler's list

GHETTOES, JEWISH -- WARSAW, POLAND

Krall, H. Chasing the king of hearts

Shepard, J. The book of Aron

The **ghost** Harris, R.

The **ghost** bride Choo, Y.

Ghost gone wild Hart, C.

Ghost light O'Connor, J.

Ghost lights Millet, L.

Ghost moon Robards, K.

The **ghost** road Barker, P.

The **ghost** runner Bilal, P.

Ghost ship Cussler, C.

GHOST STORIES

Bohjalian, C. The night strangers

Evans, J. The white devil

Hill, J. Heart-shaped box

James, H. The turn of the screw

Koryta, M. The ridge

McMahon, J. The invited

More deadly than the male

Murdoch, I. The sea, the sea

Nevill, A. The house of small shadows

Poe's children

St. James, S. The broken girls

St. James, S. The haunting of Maddy Clare

Straub, P. Ghost story

Tan, A. The hundred secret senses

Waters, S. The little stranger

Ghost story Straub, P.

Ghost summer Due, T.

Ghost train to New Orleans Lafferty, M.

Ghost wall Moss, S.

The **ghost** writer Roth, P.

GHOSTS

Aaronovitch, B. Midnight riot

Anderson, K. Death warmed over

Bardugo, L. Ninth house

Barzak, C. One for sorrow

Beagle, P. A fine and private place

Bennett, J. Bitter spirits

Bohjalian, C. The night strangers

Brink, A. The rights of desire

Bronte, E. Wuthering Heights

Brown, K. The clairvoyants

Cameron, W. Repo madness

Camp, B. Gather the fortunes

Cantero, E. Meddling kids

Card, M. These ghosts are family

Choo, Y. The ghost bride

Cotterill, C. The coroner's lunch

Davies, R. Murther and walking spirits

Dean, P. Tam Lin

Deon, N. Grace

Deveraux, J. Someone to love

Diamond, E. An accidental light

Dickens, C. A Christmas carol

Evans, J. The white devil

Freudenberger, N. Lost and wanted

Gaiman, N. Trigger warning

Garcia Marquez, G. One hundred years of solitude

Gerritsen, T. The shape of night

Godwin, G. Grief cottage

Hanson, H. The driver

Hart, C. Ghost gone wild

Hill, J. Heart-shaped box

Hoffman, A. The third angel

Irwin, S. The broken ones

Irwin, S. The dead path

Jackson, S. The haunting of Hill House

James, H. The turn of the screw

Johnson, D. Train dreams

Jones, D. Second grave on the left

Jones, S. The uninvited guests

Koryta, M. The ridge

Le Carre, J. The tailor of Panama

Lippman, L. Lady in the lake

McCormack, M. Solar bones

McCrumb, S. She walks these hills

McFadden, B. Gathering of waters

McHugh, L. Arrowood

McMahon, J. The invited

More deadly than the male

Murdoch, I. The sea, the sea

Nevill, A. The house of small shadows

Neville, S. The ghosts of Belfast

Obreht, T. Inland

Giovanni's room Baldwin, J.

Girl O'Brien, E.

GIRL AMATEUR DETECTIVES

Lourey, J. Unspeakable things

Girl at war Novic, S.

GIRL BASEBALL PLAYERS

Jen, G. The resisters

The **girl** before Delaney, J.

The **girl** behind the red rope Dekker, T.

GIRL BOARDING SCHOOL STUDENTS

French, T. The secret place

GIRL DETECTIVES

Bradley, C. As chimney sweepers come to dust

Bradley, C. The golden tresses of the dead

Bradley, C. The grave's a fine and private place

Bradley, C. I am half-sick of shadows

Bradley, C. A red herring without mustard

Bradley, C. Speaking from among the bones

Bradley, C. The sweetness at the bottom of the pie

Bradley, C. Thrice the brinded cat hath mew'd

Bradley, C. The weed that strings the hangman's bag

GIRL DROWNING VICTIMS

Lackberg, C. The stonecutter

GIRL HEROES

Stephenson, N. The diamond age,

GIRL HIKERS -- APPALACHIAN TRAIL

King, S. The girl who loved Tom Gordon

GIRL HITCHHIKERS

Brown, L. Fay

GIRL IMMIGRANTS

Bulawayo, N. We need new names

The **girl** in green Miller, D.

Girl in hyacinth blue Vreeland, S.

The **girl** in the garden Wallace, M.

The **girl** in the glass box Grippando, J.

Girl in the rearview mirror Dimberg, K.

The **girl** in the red coat Hamer, K.

The **girl** in the spider's web Lagercrantz, D.

The **girl** in the tower Arden, K.

A **girl** is a half-formed thing McBride, E.

GIRL KIDNAPPING VICTIMS

Child, L. The hard way

Gardner, L. Alone

Greenwood, T. Rust & stardust

Kennedy, R. Presidio

Lippman, L. What the dead know

O'Brien, E. Girl

Phillips, J. Disappearing earth

Picoult, J. Vanishing acts

Ragan, T. Deadly recall

A **girl** like her Hibbert, T.

Girl meets duke [series] Dare, T.

GIRL MURDER VICTIMS

Flynn, G. Sharp objects

French, T. In the woods

Lackberg, C. The stonecutter

Mizushima, M. Killing trail

Persson, L. The dying detective

Sandford, J. Deep freeze

GIRL MURDER WITNESSES

O'Connell, C. The chalk girl

Pajer, B. Fatal induction

A **girl** named Anna Barber, L.

The **girl** next door Parks, B.

The **girl** of his dreams Leon, D.

The **girl** on the cliff Riley, L.

The **girl** on the train Hawkins, P.

GIRL ORPHANS

Atkinson, K. Started early, took my dog

Dickens, C. The old curiosity shop

GIRL PRODIGIES

Moore, L. The unseen world

Rosner, J. The yellow bird sings

GIRL PSYCHICS

Lee, P. Runner

GIRL REBELS

Kincaid, J. Annie John

GIRL SCIENTISTS

Bradley, C. As chimney sweepers come to dust

Bradley, C. The golden tresses of the dead

Bradley, C. The grave's a fine and private place

Bradley, C. A red herring without mustard

Bradley, C. Speaking from among the bones

Bradley, C. The sweetness at the bottom of the pie

Bradley, C. Thrice the brinded cat hath mew'd

GIRL SLAVES

Hill, L. Someone knows my name

Johnson, K. Little black girl lost

The **girl** they left behind Veletzos, R.

Girl waits with gun Stewart, A.

The **girl** who chased the moon Allen, S.

The **girl** who fell from the sky Durrow, H.

The **girl** who kicked the hornet's nest Larsson, S.

The **girl** who knew too much Quick, A.

The **girl** who lived twice Lagercrantz, D.

The **girl** who loved Tom Gordon King, S.

The **girl** who played Go Shan, S.

The **girl** who played with fire Larsson, S.

The **girl** who takes an eye for an eye Lagercrantz, D.

Girl with a pearl earring Chevalier, T.

The **girl** with the dragon tattoo Larsson, S.

The **girl** with the louding voice Dare, A.

The **girl** you left behind Moyes, J.

A **girl's** guide to the Outback Kate, J.

Girl, woman, other Evaristo, B.

GIRLS

Al Rawi, S. The Baghdad clock

Backman, F. My grandmother asked me to tell you she's sorry

Balaskovits, A. Magic for unlucky girls

Berg, E. We are all welcome here

Brown, J. Addie Pray

Byatt, A. Ragnarok

Choi, A. Kay's lucky coin variety

GLEN CANYON
  Barr, N. The rope
Glitz Leonard, E.
GLITZ AND GLAMOUR NOVELS
  Bagshawe, T. Adored
  Bradford, B. Power of a woman
  Burton, T. Social creature
  Marren, S. A Palm Beach wife
GLOBAL ENVIRONMENTAL CHANGE
  Egan, G. Perihelion summer
GLOBAL FINANCIAL CRISIS, 2008-2009
  Dee, J. The locals
GLOBAL WARMING
  Kingsolver, B. Flight behavior
  Reynolds, A. Permafrost
  Robinson, K. New York 2140
GLOBAL WARMING -- PREVENTION
  McEwan, I. Solar
GLOBALIZATION
  Kowal, M. The calculating stars
GLOBALIZATION (ECONOMICS)
  Eggers, D. What is the what
The **glorious** heresies McInerney, L.
Glorious heresies [series] McInerney, L.
Glorious victorious Darcys [series] Ciotta, B.
GLOVE INDUSTRY AND TRADE
  Roth, P. American pastoral
Gnomon Harkaway, N.
GO (GAME)
  Shan, S. The girl who played Go
Go down, Moses Faulkner, W.
Go set a watchman Lee, H.
Go tell it on the mountain Baldwin, J.
Go to my grave McPherson, C.
Go, went, gone Erpenbeck, J.
GOALS AND OBJECTIVES
  Aliu, X. Brass
  Baldwin, J. The Wilshire sun
  Serle, R. In five years
  Wang, K. Family trust
Goat Mountain Vann, D.
GOATS
  Barth, J. Giles Goat-Boy ;
GOBLINS
  Donohue, K. The stolen child
  French, J. The Grey Bastards
  Griffin, K. The glass god
  Griffin, K. Stray souls
  Harrison, T. Dragon bound
  McGuire, S. In an absent dream
GOD
  Saramago, J. Cain
  Updike, J. In the beauty of the lilies
  Williams, J. Ninety-nine stories of God
GOD (CHRISTIANITY)
  Walton, J. Lent
  Young, W. The shack

GOD (CHRISTIANITY) -- WILL
  Hauck, R. Once upon a prince
GOD (JUDAISM)
  Wiesel, E. Night, Dawn, The accident
God bless you, Mr. Rosewater Vonnegut, K.
God don't like ugly Monroe, M.
God don't novels [series] Monroe, M.
God help the child Morrison, T.
A **god** in ruins Atkinson, K.
The **god** of small things Roy, A.
God on the rocks Gardam, J.
God still don't like ugly Monroe, M.
God's country Everett, P.
The **god's** eye view Eisler, B.
God's fool Slouka, M.
Godchildren Coleridge, N.
GODDESS WORSHIP
  Golding, W. The inheritors
The **godfather** Puzo, M.
Godfather series (Mario Puzo) [series] Puzo, M.
GODFATHERS
  Coleridge, N. Godchildren
  Maguire, G. Hiddensee
GODMOTHERS
  Laurens, S. A rake's vow
Gods and beasts Mina, D.
Gods and generals Shaara, J.
GODS AND GODDESSES
  Banville, J. The infinities
  Barker, P. The silence of the girls
  Bear, E. All the windwracked stars
  Bennett, R. City of blades
  Bennett, R. City of miracles
  Bennett, R. City of stairs
  Camp, B. The city of lost fortunes
  Camp, B. Gather the fortunes
  Carey, J. Starless
  Emezi, A. Freshwater
  Gaiman, N. American gods
  Gruber, M. Night of the jaguar
  Hawkins, S. The library at Mount Char
  Jemisin, N. The hundred thousand kingdoms
  Jemisin, N. The killing moon
  Johnson, K. The dream-quest of Vellitt Boe
  Kay, G. The summer tree
  Kuang, R. The dragon republic
  Kuang, R. The poppy war
  Lafferty, M. Ghost train to New Orleans
  Lafferty, M. The shambling guide to New York City
  Lake, J. Endurance
  Lake, J. Green
  Larkwood, A. The unspoken name
  Leckie, A. The Raven tower
  Liu, K. The grace of kings
  Lyons, J. The name of all things
  Orullian, P. The unremembered
  Pratchett, T. Small gods

The **golden** bowl James, H.

Golden Buddha Cussler, C.

Golden child Adam, C.

The **golden** cup Plain, B.

The **golden** egg Leon, D.

Golden hill Spufford, F.

The **golden** hour Williams, B.

The **golden** house Rushdie, S.

The **golden** legend Aslam, N.

The **golden** leopard Kerstan, L.

The **golden** not(ebk.) Lessing, D.

The **golden** ocean O'Brian, P.

The **golden** one Peters, E.

Golden prey Sandford, J.

GOLDEN RETRIEVERS

Koontz, D. The darkest evening of the year

The **golden** season Brockway, C.

Golden son Brown, P.

The **golden** tresses of the dead Bradley, C.

Golden trillium Norton, A.

Goldengrove Prose, F.

The **goldfinch** Tartt, D.

Goldfinger Fleming, I.

GOLDSMITHS

Penman, S. The Queen's man

Goldy Bear mysteries [series] Davidson, D.

GOLEM

Hoffman, A. The world that we knew

Ozick, C. The Puttermesser papers

Pratchett, T. Going postal

Pratchett, T. Thud!

Sherwood, F. The book of splendor

Wecker, H. The golem and the jinni

The **golem** and the jinni Wecker, H.

GOLF

Coyne, J. The caddie who played with hickory

GOLFERS

Coyne, J. The caddie who played with hickory

Shefchik, R. Amen corner

The **Goliath** bone Spillane, M.

GOLIATH, (BIBLICAL GIANT) RELICS

Spillane, M. The Goliath bone

Gone Kellerman, J.

Gone Hayder, M.

Gone and back again Fuqua, J.

Gone by midnight Fox, C.

Gone cold Corleone, D.

The **gone** dead Benz, C.

Gone fishin' Mosley, W.

Gone for soldiers Shaara, J.

Gone girl Flynn, G.

Gone to ground Harvey, J.

Gone to soldiers Piercy, M.

Gone too long Roy, L.

Gone with the wind Mitchell, M.

GONE WITH THE WIND (MOTION PICTURE)

Alcott, K. A touch of stardust

Kaminsky, S. Tomorrow is another day

The **gone-away** world Harkaway, N.

Gonna take a homicidal journey Scoppettone, S.

GOOD AND EVIL

Albahari, D. Gotz and Meyer

Arden, K. The bear and the nightingale

Arden, K. The winter of the witch

Baker, K. The house of the stag

Banks, I. Consider Phlebas

Banks, I. The player of games

Banks, I. Use of weapons

Banks, R. Continental drift

Banks, R. Lost memory of skin

Banville, J. The book of evidence

Barker, C. Weaveworld

Barth, J. The sot-weed factor

Bear, G. Anvil of stars

Bear, G. The forge of God

Bennett, R. The troupe

Blatty, W. The exorcist

Bradbury, R. Something wicked this way comes

Brown, L. Joe

Bulgakov, M. The master and Margarita

Bunyan, J. The pilgrim's progress

Burgess, A. A clockwork orange

Burke, J. Wayfaring stranger

Butler, R. Hell

Callihan, K. Firelight

Card, O. Ender's game

Carey, M. Someone like me

Castle, J. The lost night

Cheever, J. Bullet Park

Cornell, P. London falling

Cronin, J. The city of mirrors

Cronin, J. The passage

Cronin, J. The twelve

Czerneda, J. A turn of light

Davidson, A. The boatman's daughter

Davys, T. Amberville

Dekker, T. The girl behind the red rope

Draven, G. Phoenix unbound

Feehan, C. Dark illusion

Gaiman, N. The ocean at the end of the lane

Garcia Marquez, G. In evil hour

Garcia Marquez, G. One hundred years of solitude

Gilman, L. Flesh and fire

Golden, C. Ararat

Golding, W. The inheritors

Golding, W. Lord of the flies

Greene, G. The tenth man

Gregory, D. We are all completely fine

Griffin, K. The glass god

Griffin, K. Stray souls

Grossman, L. The magician king

Grossman, L. The magician's land

Grossman, L. The magicians

Hair, D. Mage's blood

Good girl, bad girl Robotham, M.
Good girls lie Ellison, J.
The good husband of Zebra Drive McCall Smith, A.
Good in bed Weiner, J.
Good Indian girls Sidhu, R.
Good kings, bad kings Nussbaum, S.
The good lord bird McBride, J.

GOOD LUCK
Johnson, D. Nobody move

GOOD LUCK CHARMS
Westlake, D. What's the worst that could happen?
The good mother Miller, S.
A good neighborhood Fowler, T.
Good omens Gaiman, N.
The good ones McKinlay, J.
The good priest's son Price, R.
A good rake is hard to find Collins, M.
Good riddance Lipman, E.
A good scent from a strange mountain Butler, R.
The good soldier Ford, F.
The good suicides Hill Gumbao, T.
The good terrorist Lessing, D.
Good time coming Harris, C.
Good-bye, Mr. Chips Hilton, J.

GOOD-BYES
Tyler, A. The beginner's goodbye
Goodbye for now Frankel, L.
The goodbye look, Ross Macdonald. Macdonald, R.
Goodbye to the dead Freeman, B.
Goodbye Tsugumi Yoshimoto, B.
Goodbye without leaving Colwin, L.
Goodbye, Columbus, and five short stories Roth, P.

GOOGLE (FIRM)
Sloan, R. Mr. Penumbra's 24-hour bookstore
Gorgeous lies McPhee, M.
Gorilla, my love Bambara, T.
Gorky Park Smith, M.

GOSPEL SINGERS
Baldwin, J. Just above my head
Flagg, F. Standing in the rainbow

GOSSIP COLUMNISTS
Leigh, E. Forever your earl

GOSSIPING AND GOSSIPS
Babson, M. The company of cats
Benson, E. Make way for Lucia
Berg, G. The operator
Bradley, A. A season of ruin
Burns, A. Milkman
Dunne, D. People like us
Dunne, D. Too much money
Eco, U. Numero zero
Galen, S. When you give a duke a diamond
Garcia Marquez, G. In evil hour
Gogol, N. Dead souls
Hibbert, T. A girl like her
Leigh, E. Forever your earl
Lewis, S. Main street

McKevett, G. Murder in her stocking
Mishima, Y. The sound of waves
Quick, A. The girl who knew too much
Quick, A. The other lady vanishes
Shaw, M. Murder at the mill
Spencer-Fleming, J. All mortal flesh
West, K. Minor dramas & other catastrophes
Wilder, T. Theophilus North

GOTH CULTURE (SUBCULTURE)
Galloway, G. As simple as snow
Prose, F. Blue angel
Sandford, J. Phantom prey

GOTHIC FICTION
Bolton, S. The craftsman
Bronte, C. Emma
Bronte, C. Jane Eyre
Bronte, E. Wuthering Heights
Brown, K. The clairvoyants
Collins, W. The woman in white
Crowley, J. Lord Byron's novel
Dinesen, I. Seven Gothic tales
Du Maurier, D. Rebecca
Duffy, B. House of echoes
Egan, J. The keep
Elliott, L. The missing years
Evans, J. The white devil
Faye, L. Jane Steele
Fine, J. What should be wild
Fuller, C. Bitter orange
Gerritsen, T. The shape of night
Griffiths, E. The stranger diaries
Harrison, R. The return
Hawthorne, N. The house of the seven gables
Hunt, S. Mr. Splitfoot
Hurley, A. Devil's Day
Jackson, S. The haunting of Hill House
Jackson, S. We have always lived in the castle
James, H. The turn of the screw
Jewell, L. I found you
Kiernan, C. The drowning girl
Kostova, E. The historian
Lea, C. The glass woman
Lewis, M. The monk
Maturin, C. Melmoth the wanderer
McHugh, L. Arrowood
McPherson, C. Go to my grave
Morton, K. The distant hours
Oates, J. The accursed
Oates, J. Evil eye
Owen, L. The quick
Palliser, C. Rustication
Perry, S. Melmoth
Poe, E. Complete stories and poems of Edgar Allan Poe
Poe, E. The narrative of Arthur Gordon Pym of Nantucket
Purcell, L. The silent companions
Radcliffe, A. The mysteries of Udolpho
Rice, A. Blackwood farm

Sakey, M. Brilliance
Sandford, J. Shock wave
Slaughter, K. The kept woman
Slaughter, K. The last widow
Smith, M. Love her madly
Smith, M. She smiled sweetly
Smith, M. She's not there
Thompson, T. Rosewater
Thompson, T. The Rosewater insurrection

GOVERNMENT INVESTIGATORS -- MINNESOTA
Sandford, J. Deadline
Sandford, J. Mad River
Sandford, J. Storm Front

GOVERNMENT MISSIONS
Forsyth, F. The kill list
Willig, L. The lure of the moonflower

GOVERNMENT OWNERSHIP OF INDUSTRY AND TRADE
Rand, A. We the living

GOVERNMENT RELATIONS WITH INDIGENOUS PEOPLES
Brown, D. Creek Mary's blood
Cook, D. Reservation nation
Osborne, D. The coming

GOVERNMENT RESEARCH
Morgan, R. Thirteen

GOVERNMENTAL INVESTIGATIONS
Shteyngart, G. Lake Success
The **governor's** wife Harvey, M.

GOVERNORS
DeSilva, B. A scourge of vipers
Glass, J. The whole world over
Percy, B. Red moon
Ryan, H. The other woman
Williams, B. The golden hour

GOVERNORS' SPOUSES
Seton, A. The Winthrop woman
Gower Street detectives [series] Kasasian, M.
Grace Deon, N.
Grace Nunez, E.

GRACE (CHRISTIAN THEOLOGY)
Parrish, C. Still life

GRACE (THEOLOGY)
O'Connor, F. Wise blood
Grace Chu and John Knox novels [series] Pearson, R.
The **grace** of kings Liu, K.

GRACE,, PRINCESS OF MONACO, 1929-1982
Gaynor, H. Meet me in Monaco
GraceLand Abani, C.

GRADUATE STUDENTS
Aciman, A. Call me by your name
Aciman, A. Harvard square
Boyle, T. Outside looking in
Cameron, P. The city of your final destination
Choi, S. My education
Crichton, M. Micro
French, T. The likeness

Hosking, J. Three years with the rat
Jin, H. The crazed
McCrumb, S. She walks these hills
Morgenstern, E. The starless sea
Naam, R. Nexus
Rader-Day, L. The black hour
Simon, C. Grey dawn
Simon, C. Stages of Grey
Taylor, B. Real life
Wayne, T. Apartment

GRAFFITI ARTISTS
Rivers, F. The masterpiece

GRAIL
Brown, D. The Da Vinci code
Burke, J. House of the rising sun
Cornwell, B. The archer's tale
Lovett, C. The lost book of the Grail
White, T. The once and future king
Grail of the summer stars Warrington, F.
Grail Quest (Bernard Cornwell) [series] Cornwell, B.
The **Grammarians** Schine, C.

GRAND CANYON
Baldacci, D. Long road to mercy
Ford, R. A multitude of sins
The **grand** dark Kadrey, R.

GRAND FENWICK
Wibberley, L. The mouse that roared

GRAND JURY
Lescroart, J. Nothing but the truth
The **grand** Sophy Heyer, G.
Grand union Smith, Z.
Grandad, there's a head on the beach Cotterill, C.

GRANDCHILDREN
McKevett, G. Murder in her stocking
McKevett, G. Murder in the corn maze

GRANDDAUGHTERS
Barr, N. What Rose forgot
Beckerman, H. If only I could tell you
Hepworth, S. The secrets of midwives
Macdonald, M. The Trevarton inheritance

GRANDFATHER AND CHILD
Foer, J. Everything is illuminated

GRANDFATHER AND GRANDDAUGHTER
Desai, K. The inheritance of loss
Dunn, K. The Dragonfly
Erdrich, L. The plague of doves
McCann, C. Zoli
Miller, D. Norwegian by night
Rosen, L. The Kortelisy escape
Vonnegut, K. Slapstick

GRANDFATHER AND GRANDSON
Butler, N. Little faith
Chabon, M. Moonglow
Heacox, K. Jimmy Bluefeather
Meno, J. Marvel and a wonder
Starnone, D. Trick
Tawada, Y. The emissary

Beverley, J. Devilish
Beverley, J. My lady notorious
Beverley, J. Something wicked
Beverley, J. Tempting fortune
Dean, A. Bellfield Hall
Dean, A. A place of confinement
Dean, A. A woman of consequence
Donoghue, E. Slammerkin
Hunter, M. The conquest of Lady Cassandra
Hunter, M. The surrender of Miss Fairbourne
James, E. Four nights with the duke
James, E. Seven minutes in heaven
James, E. Three weeks with Lady X
London, J. The year of living scandalously
Putney, M. No longer a gentleman
Robertson, I. Anatomy of murder
Robertson, I. Circle of shadows
Robertson, I. Instruments of darkness
Robertson, I. Island of bones

GREAT BRITAIN -- HISTORY -- GEORGE IV, 1820-1830
Nickson, C. The hocus girl

GREAT BRITAIN -- HISTORY -- GEORGE V, 1910-1936
Morton, K. The house at Riverton
Perry, A. No graves as yet
Perry, A. Shoulder the sky

GREAT BRITAIN -- HISTORY -- GEORGE VI, 1936-1952
Mawer, S. The fall
Winspear, J. The American agent

GREAT BRITAIN -- HISTORY -- HENRY II, 1154-1189
Franklin, A. The serpent's tale
Penman, S. Devil's brood
Penman, S. Time and chance

GREAT BRITAIN -- HISTORY -- HENRY III, 1216-1272
Penman, S. Falls the shadow

GREAT BRITAIN -- HISTORY -- HENRY IV, 1399-1413
Robb, C. A murdered peace

GREAT BRITAIN -- HISTORY -- HENRY VI, 1422-1461
Gregory, P. The lady of the rivers

GREAT BRITAIN -- HISTORY -- HENRY VII, 1485-1509
Gregory, P. The constant princess

GREAT BRITAIN -- HISTORY -- HENRY VIII, 1509-1547
Andersen, L. The Boleyn king
Gregory, P. The Boleyn inheritance
Gregory, P. The constant princess
Gregory, P. The other Boleyn girl
Gregory, P. The taming of the queen
Mantel, H. Bring up the bodies
Mantel, H. Wolf Hall
Maxwell, R. The secret diary of Anne Boleyn
Plaidy, J. Murder most royal
Riley, J. The serpent garden
Sansom, C. Revelation
Sansom, C. Lamentation
Sansom, C. Sovereign
Weir, A. Anna of Kleve

GREAT BRITAIN -- HISTORY -- HOUSE OF YORK, 1461-1485

Gregory, P. The red queen

GREAT BRITAIN -- HISTORY -- JAMES I, 1603-1625
Norfolk, L. John Saturnall's feast
Winterson, J. The daylight gate

GREAT BRITAIN -- HISTORY -- JAMES II, 1685-1688
Blackmore, R. Lorna Doone

GREAT BRITAIN -- HISTORY -- MARY I, 1553-1558
Gregory, P. The last Tudor
Weir, A. Innocent traitor
Weir, A. The Lady Elizabeth

GREAT BRITAIN -- HISTORY -- MEDIEVAL PERIOD, 1066-1485
Follett, K. World without end
Penman, S. The reckoning
Penman, S. Time and chance
Peters, E. Brother Cadfael's penance
Peters, E. Dead man's ransom
Peters, E. The hermit of Eyton Forest
Peters, E. The holy thief
Peters, E. Monk's hood
Peters, E. The pilgrim of hate
Peters, E. The potter's field
Peters, E. A rare Benedictine
Peters, E. The rose rent
Peters, E. St. Peter's fair
Peters, E. The sanctuary sparrow
Peters, E. The virgin in the ice
Royal, P. Covenant with hell
Royal, P. Sanctity of hate
Royal, P. Satan's lullaby

GREAT BRITAIN -- HISTORY -- NORMAN PERIOD, 1066-1154
Penman, S. When Christ and his saints slept

GREAT BRITAIN -- HISTORY -- PLANTAGENETS, 1154-1399
Penman, S. Here be dragons
Penman, S. The reckoning
Seton, A. Katherine

GREAT BRITAIN -- HISTORY -- REGENCY, 1811-1820
Baker, J. Longbourn
Balogh, M. Someone to remember
Balogh, M. Someone to trust
Balogh, M. Someone to wed
Bell, L. How the duke was won
Bowen, K. A rogue by night
Bradley, A. A season of ruin
Bradley, A. A wicked way to win an earl
Burrowes, G. Tremaine's true love
Chase, L. Miss Wonderful
Collins, M. A good rake is hard to find
Crowley, J. Lord Byron's novel
Greeley, M. The clergyman's wife
Harrington, A. An inconvenient duke
Heyer, G. The grand Sophy
Kinsale, L. Lessons in French
Leigh, E. Forever your earl
Leigh, E. Scandal takes the stage

Leigh, E. Temptations of a wallflower
Lloyd, C. Death comes to the nursery
MacKenzie, S. Bedding Lord Ned
MacLean, S. The rogue not taken
Moore, K. To seduce an angel
Quick, A. I thee wed
Romain, T. Fortune favors the wicked
Waite, O. The lady's guide to celestial mechanics

GREAT BRITAIN -- HISTORY -- RESTORATION, 1660-1688

Du Maurier, D. Frenchman's creek
Morrow, J. The last witchfinder
Pears, I. An instance of the fingerpost
Phillips, C. The Devlin diary

GREAT BRITAIN -- HISTORY -- RICHARD I, 1189-1199

Penman, S. Dragon's lair
Penman, S. A king's ransom
Penman, S. Lionheart
Scott, W. Ivanhoe

GREAT BRITAIN -- HISTORY -- RICHARD III, 1483-1485

Gregory, P. The red queen
Penman, S. The sunne in splendour

GREAT BRITAIN -- HISTORY -- ROMAN PERIOD, 55 BC-449 AD

Davis, L. A body in the bathhouse
Downie, R. Caveat emptor
Downie, R. Medicus
Downie, R. Semper Fidelis
Downie, R. Tabula rasa
Downie, R. Terra incognita

GREAT BRITAIN -- HISTORY -- STEPHEN, 1135-1154

Follett, K. The pillars of the earth
Franklin, A. The siege winter
Peters, E. Brother Cadfael's penance
Peters, E. Dead man's ransom
Peters, E. The summer of the Danes

GREAT BRITAIN -- HISTORY -- STUARTS, 1603-1714

Barth, J. The sot-weed factor

GREAT BRITAIN -- HISTORY -- TUDORS, 1485-1603

Andersen, L. The Boleyn king
Gregory, P. The last Tudor
Mantel, H. Bring up the bodies
Mantel, H. Wolf Hall
Maxwell, R. The secret diary of Anne Boleyn
Plaidy, J. Murder most royal
Sansom, C. Tombland
Seton, A. Green darkness
Weir, A. Anna of Kleve
Weir, A. Innocent traitor
Weir, A. The Lady Elizabeth

GREAT BRITAIN -- HISTORY -- VICTORIA, 1837-1901

Birch, C. Jamrach's menagerie
Burrowes, G. The bridegroom wore plaid
Byrne, K. The duke with the dragon tattoo
Byrne, K. The hunter
Callihan, K. Firelight
Fowles, J. The French lieutenant's woman

Frampton, M. Put up your duke
Goss, T. The sinister mystery of the mesmerizing girl
Goss, T. The strange case of the alchemist's daughter
Gray, J. How to tame your duke
Heath, L. Falling into bed with a duke
Humphreys, H. Afterimage
Kleypas, L. Cold-hearted rake
Kleypas, L. Devil in spring
Kleypas, L. Marrying Winterborne
Kleypas, L. Secrets of a summer night
Mason, T. The Darwin affair
Maugham, W. Cakes and ale
McCrea, G. Mrs. Engels
Milan, C. The duchess war
Quick, A. 'Til death do us part
Rowland, L. Bedlam
Rowland, L. The secret adventures of Charlotte Bronte
Saintcrow, L. The Iron Wyrm Affair
Saintcrow, L. The ripper affair
Shepherd, L. A fatal likeness
Shepherd, L. The Solitary House
Welsh, K. The unquiet heart
Welsh, K. The wages of sin
Wilde, O. The picture of Dorian Gray

GREAT BRITAIN -- HISTORY -- WARS OF THE ROSES, 1455-1485

Gregory, P. The lady of the rivers
Gregory, P. The red queen
Penman, S. The sunne in splendour

GREAT BRITAIN -- HISTORY -- WILLIAM AND MARY, 1689-1702

Plaidy, J. William's wife

GREAT BRITAIN -- HISTORY, MILITARY -- 19TH CENTURY

Mallinson, A. A close run thing

GREAT BRITAIN -- HISTORY, NAVAL -- 18TH CENTURY

Lambdin, D. Hostile shores
Lambdin, D. King's captain
O'Brian, P. The golden ocean
O'Brian, P. The unknown shore

GREAT BRITAIN -- HISTORY, NAVAL -- 19TH CENTURY

Forester, C. Admiral Hornblower in the West Indies
Forester, C. Beat to quarters
Forester, C. Commodore Hornblower
Forester, C. Flying colours
Forester, C. Hornblower and the Atropos
Forester, C. Hornblower and the Hotspur
Forester, C. Lieutenant Hornblower
Forester, C. Lord Hornblower
Forester, C. Mr. Midshipman Hornblower
Forester, C. Ship of the line
O'Brian, P. Blue at the mizzen
O'Brian, P. The commodore
O'Brian, P. The hundred days
O'Brian, P. Master and commander

O'Brian, P. The wine-dark sea
O'Brian, P. The yellow admiral

GREAT BRITAIN -- POLITICS AND GOVERNMENT -- 16TH CENTURY

Mantel, H. Bring up the bodies
Mantel, H. Wolf Hall

GREAT BRITAIN -- POLITICS AND GOVERNMENT -- 1979-1997

Welsh, I. Skagboys
Welsh, I. Trainspotting

GREAT BRITAIN -- POLITICS AND GOVERNMENT -- 19TH CENTURY

Perry, A. Buckingham Palace gardens
Perry, A. Death on Blackheath
Perry, A. Midnight at Marble Arch
Perry, A. Seven Dials
Perry, A. Southampton Row
Trollope, A. The Eustace diamonds
Trollope, A. The Prime Minister

GREAT BRITAIN -- POLITICS AND GOVERNMENT -- 21ST CENTURY

Shamsie, K. Home fire

GREAT BRITAIN -- POPULAR CULTURE -- HISTORY -- 19TH CENTURY

Jarvis, S. Death and Mr. Pickwick

GREAT BRITAIN -- RULERS

Penman, S. The reckoning
Penman, S. Time and chance

GREAT BRITAIN -- RULERS -- FAMILY RELATION-SHIPS

Penman, S. Devil's brood

GREAT BRITAIN -- SOCIAL CONDITIONS -- 1945-

Smith, Z. White teeth

GREAT BRITAIN -- SOCIAL CONDITIONS -- 19TH CENTURY

Hodder, M. The strange affair of Spring Heeled Jack

GREAT BRITAIN -- SOCIAL CONDITIONS -- VICTORIA, 1837-1901

Llewellyn, R. How green was my valley

GREAT BRITAIN -- SOCIAL LIFE AND CUSTOMS -- 17TH CENTURY

Dean, M. I, Hogarth
Defoe, D. Moll Flanders

GREAT BRITAIN -- SOCIAL LIFE AND CUSTOMS -- 1945-

Amis, K. Lucky Jim

GREAT BRITAIN -- SOCIAL LIFE AND CUSTOMS -- 19TH CENTURY

Baker, J. Longbourn
Bell, L. For the duke's eyes only
Bell, L. One fine duke
Bell, L. What a difference a duke makes
Bennett, A. First earl I see tonight
Carlyle, C. A duke changes everything
Frame, R. Havisham

GREAT BRITAIN -- SOCIAL LIFE AND CUSTOMS -- 20TH CENTURY

Atkinson, K. Transcription
Baker, J. The undertow
Ballard, J. The complete stories of J.G. Ballard.
Coe, J. Number 11
Greene, G. Collected stories
Greene, G. The last word and other stories
Hollinghurst, A. The Sparsholt affair
Hollinghurst, A. The stranger's child
Morton, K. The house at Riverton
Waugh, E. Brideshead revisited

GREAT BRITAIN -- SOCIAL LIFE AND CUSTOMS -- 21ST CENTURY

Coe, J. Number 11
Smith, A. Spring
Smith, A. Winter

GREAT BRITAIN -- SOCIAL LIFE AND CUSTOMS -- GEORGE III, 1760-1820

Bronte, A. The tenant of Wildfell Hall

GREAT BRITAIN -- SOCIAL LIFE AND CUSTOMS -- GEORGE IV, 1820-1830

Bronte, A. The tenant of Wildfell Hall

GREAT BRITAIN -- SOCIAL LIFE AND CUSTOMS -- VICTORIA, 1837-1901

Bradford, B. Master of his fate
Bronte, A. The tenant of Wildfell Hall
Faber, M. The crimson petal and the white
Galsworthy, J. The Forsyte saga
Goodwin, D. The American heiress
Palliser, C. Rustication
Thomas, S. Beguiling the beauty
Thomas, S. My beautiful enemy
Thomas, S. Ravishing the heiress
Thomas, S. Tempting the bride

GREAT BRITAIN SPECIAL OPERATIONS EXECUTIVE

Follett, K. Jackdaws

GREAT BRITAIN. ARMY EAST INDIAN TROOPS.

Ondaatje, M. The English patient

GREAT BRITAIN. ARMY OFFICERS

Mason, D. The piano tuner

GREAT BRITAIN. ARMY OFFICERS FRANCE

Faulks, S. Birdsong

GREAT BRITAIN. ARMY. CAVALRY OFFICERS

Mallinson, A. A close run thing

GREAT BRITAIN. METROPOLITAN POLICE OFFICE. CRIMINAL INVESTIGATION DEPARTMENT

Coulter, C. The devil's triangle
Coulter, C. The end game
Coulter, C. The final cut
Coulter, C. The lost key

GREAT BRITAIN. ROYAL AIR FORCE

Higgins, J. Flight of eagles

GREAT BRITAIN. ROYAL AIR FORCE AIRMEN

Atkinson, K. A god in ruins

GREAT BRITAIN. ROYAL AIR FORCE VETERANS

Goddard, R. Never go back

GREAT BRITAIN. ROYAL NAVY

Forester, C. Mr. Midshipman Hornblower

Hart, J. Down river
Hunter, S. The 47th samurai
Knox, T. Kockroach
Lashner, W. A killer's kiss
Le Carre, J. The constant gardener
Le Carre, J. The tailor of Panama
Lewis, S. Main street
Lunde, M. The end of the ocean
MacKenzie, S. Bedding Lord Ned
Mandel, E. The glass hotel
Mason, R. Who killed Piet Barol?
McDonald, I. New moon
McKillip, P. Ombria in shadow
Moore, C. The serpent of Venice
Muller, M. City of whispers
Nahai, G. The luminous heart of Jonah S.
Nemirovsky, I. Suite Francaise
Nickson, C. The constant lovers
Norris, F. McTeague
Overholser, W. Death of a cattle king
Paretsky, S. Shell game
Patterson, R. Dark lady
Pickard, N. The scent of rain and lightning
Pilcher, R. The shell seekers
Preston, D. Old bones
Priest, C. The inexplicables
Pronzini, B. The crimes of Jordan Wise
Puzo, M. The family
Rash, R. Serena
Reichs, K. Grave secrets
Robinson, K. Antarctica
Robotham, M. Life or death
Russell, M. Epitaph
Sanders, L. McNally's gamble
Sanders, L. McNally's luck
Sanders, L. The second deadly sin
Santora, N. Fifteen digits
Schwarz, C. All is vanity
Smith, M. Baked
Steadman, C. Something in the water
Steinbeck, J. The pearl
Strange, M. Follow me down
Stringer, V. Still dirty
Tremain, R. The colour
Turner, N. A hustler's wife
Unsworth, B. Land of marvels
Unsworth, B. Sacred hunger
Unsworth, B. The songs of the kings
Vargas Llosa, M. The discreet hero
Vinge, V. The children of the sky
Vonnegut, K. God bless you, Mr. Rosewater
Weir, A. Innocent traitor
Weir, A. The Lady Elizabeth
Westlake, D. Brothers keepers

GREED (MOTION PICTURE)
Estleman, L. Frames

GREED IN MEN

Anderson, K. The last days of Krypton
Aswani, A. Chicago
Collins, W. The moonstone
deWitt, P. The Sisters brothers
Dickens, C. A Christmas carol
Frazier, C. Nightwoods
Goddard, R. Beyond recall
Hawthorne, N. The house of the seven gables
Kellerman, J. Devil's waltz
Levin, I. A kiss before dying
Smith, S. A simple plan
Stone, I. The agony and the ecstasy

GREED IN WOMEN
Stringer, V. Dirty Red
Trollope, A. The Eustace diamonds

GREEK AMERICAN MEN
Pelecanos, G. Shame the devil
Pelecanos, G. The sweet forever

GREEK AMERICANS
Eugenides, J. Middlesex

Greek Islands mysteries [series] Serafim, L.
Greek mysteries (Jeffrey Siger) [series] Siger, J.
Greeks bearing gifts Kerr, P.

GREEKS IN TURKEY
George, M. Helen of Troy
Karnezis, P. The maze

Green Lake, J.
Green Bone saga [series] Lee, F.
Green darkness Seton, A.
Green Dolphin Street Goudge, E.
Green house Vargas Llosa, M.
The **green** knight Murdoch, I.
Green Mars Robinson, K.

GREEN MOVEMENT
Rendell, R. Road rage
The **green** ripper MacDonald, J.
The **Green** Road Enright, A.
Green sun Anderson, K.
Green Universe [series] Lake, J.

GREENBERG, JOANNE, 1932-
Greenberg, J. I never promised you a rose garden
The **greengage** summer Godden, R.
Greenhollow duology [series] Tesh, E.

GREENLAND
Cussler, C. Sacred stone
Hoeg, P. Smilla's sense of snow
Leithauser, B. The promise of elsewhere
Penney, S. Under a pole star

GREENLAND -- HISTORY -- 18TH CENTURY
Leine, K. The prophets of Eternal Fjord

GREENWICH VILLAGE, NEW YORK CITY
Brownmiller, S. Waverly Place
Scoppettone, S. Everything you have is mine
Scoppettone, S. My sweet untraceable you
Wall, C. The dearly beloved

**GREENWICH VILLAGE, NEW YORK CITY -- SOCIAL
LIFE AND CUSTOMS -- 20TH CENTURY**

Saunders, G. Lincoln in the bardo
Sebold, A. The lovely bones
Swyler, E. Light from other stars
Tartt, D. The goldfinch
Trollope, J. Next of kin
Trollope, J. The other family
Tyler, A. The beginner's goodbye
Tyler, A. The tin can tree
Van der Vliet Oloomi, A. Call me Zebra
Watson, M. The dream peddler
Weiner, J. Little earthquakes
Wells, B. The end of loneliness
White, C. The wife and the widow
Wolitzer, M. Surrender, Dorothy
Wroblewski, D. The story of Edgar Sawtelle
Yoshimoto, B. Moshi-moshi

GRIEF -- PSYCHOLOGICAL ASPECTS

Umrigar, T. The weight of heaven

Grief cottage Godwin, G.

GRIEF COUNSELING PROGRAMS

Lehane, D. Sacred

GRIEF IN ANIMALS

Nunez, S. The friend

GRIEF IN BOYS

Lodato, V. Edgar and Lucy

GRIEF IN CHILDREN

Brinkman, K. Up high in the trees
Connolly, J. The book of lost things

GRIEF IN FAMILIES

Bird, S. The flamenco academy
Diamond, E. An accidental light
Edwards, K. The memory keeper's daughter
Larsen, R. The selected works of T. S. Spivet
Lodato, V. Mathilda Savitch
Stewart, A. Stars in the grass
Winthrop, E. The why of things

GRIEF IN GIRLS

Godwin, G. Flora

GRIEF IN MEN

Auster, P. The book of illusions
Baldwin, J. Just above my head
Banville, J. The sea
Begley, L. About Schmidt
Bergen, D. See the child
Block, L. A drop of the hard stuff
Blum, J. The lost family
Bohjalian, C. The sandcastle girls
Burke, J. Black cherry blues
Carlson, R. Five skies
Coleman, R. Where it hurts
Currie, R. Flimsy little plastic miracles
Daisley, S. Coming rain
Deveraux, J. Someone to love
Dickens, C. Dombey and Son
Dunmore, H. The lie
Fleming, I. You only live twice
Flores, F. Tears of the trufflepig

George, E. Careless in red
Harper, J. The lost man
Heathcock, A. Volt
Hill, J. Horns
Hill, S. The risk of darkness
Johnson, D. Train dreams
Kiefer, C. The infinite tides
Lawrence, D. Sons and lovers
Le Carre, J. The constant gardener
Le Guin, U. The other wind
Lehane, D. Mystic river
Lovesey, P. The house sitter
Lovett, C. The bookman's tale
Malouf, D. Ransom
Martel, Y. The high mountains of Portugal
May, P. The blackhouse
McEwan, I. The child in time
Miller, D. Norwegian by night
Mosley, W. Six Easy pieces
Nickson, C. Cold cruel winter
Norman, H. Next life might be kinder
Oe, K. The changeling
Panowich, B. Like lions
Perry, A. No graves as yet
Reich, C. Rules of deception
Row, J. Your face in mine
Scottoline, L. Don't go
Shelley, M. Frankenstein
Smith, T. Agent 6
Styron, W. Lie down in darkness
Swift, G. Wish you were here
Toole, F. Pound for pound
Walton, J. Necessity

GRIEF IN MOTHERS

Peikoff, K. Mother knows best

GRIEF IN TEENAGE GIRLS

Russell, K. Swamplandia!

GRIEF IN TEENAGERS

Searles, J. Help for the haunted

GRIEF IN WOMEN

Adamson, G. The outlander
Arnoult, D. Sufficient grace
Barry, B. The map of true places
Bird, S. The flamenco academy
Bynum, S. Ms. Hempel chronicles
Carpenter, E. Until the day I die
Clegg, B. Did you ever have a family
Clemmons, Z. What we lose
Coben, H. Hold tight
Edwards, Y. The mother
Fitch, J. Paint it black
Fox, L. Days of awe
Isaacs, S. As husbands go
Keneally, T. Woman of the inner sea
Lennon, J. Familiar
Mackintosh, C. I let you go
Makine, A. The woman who waited

Morante, E. Arturo's island
Naslund, S. Abundance
Ondaatje, M. The cat's table
Ondaatje, M. Warlight
Pamuk, O. A strangeness in my mind
Petterson, P. Out stealing horses
Pilcher, R. Coming home
Preston, C. The scrapbook of Frankie Pratt
Prose, F. Goldengrove
Proust, M. Swann's way
Proust, M. Within a budding grove
Quade, K. Night at the fiestas
Quindlen, A. Miller's Valley
Rachman, T. The Italian teacher
Remarque, E. All quiet on the western front
Roth, P. Indignation
Shields, C. The stone diaries
Smiley, J. Early warning
Smiley, J. Golden age
Smith, B. A tree grows in Brooklyn
Souljah,. A deeper love inside
Steinbeck, J. The long valley
Stibbe, N. Reasons to be cheerful
Straub, E. Modern lovers
Torres, J. We the animals
Tremain, R. The Gustav sonata
Vann, D. Aquarium
Vuong, O. On Earth we're briefly gorgeous
Walls, J. Half broke horses
Wells, B. The end of loneliness
White, E. A boy's own story
Wilson, K. The family Fang
Winman, S. Tin man
Woodson, J. Another Brooklyn
Woodson, J. Red at the bone
Woolf, V. Jacob's room
Woolf, V. The waves
Yoshimoto, B. The lake

GROWING UP -- AFRICA
Lessing, D. Martha Quest

GROWING UP -- KANSAS
Hughes, L. Not without laughter

GROWTH (PSYCHOLOGY)
Bognanni, P. The house of tomorrow
Butler, H. The new me
Just, W. Rodin's debutante
Murakami, H. Blind willow, sleeping woman
Parks, G. The learning tree

GUADALCANAL, BATTLE OF, 1942-1943
Jones, J. The thin red line

GUADALUPE MOUNTAINS NATIONAL PARK
Barr, N. Track of the cat

GUANO
Fleming, I. Doctor No
The **guardian** Sparks, N.
Guardian (Karen Robards) [series] Robards, K.
GUARDIAN AND WARD

Amis, M. Lionel Asbo
Bailey, P. Uncle Rudolf
Burrowes, G. The soldier
Carcaterra, L. Tin badges
Coetzee, J. The childhood of Jesus
Dare, T. The governess game
Donoghue, E. Akin
Godwin, G. Flora
Heyer, G. These old shades
James, E. Seven minutes in heaven
Kasasian, M. Dark dawn over Steep House
Kleypas, L. Christmas Eve at Friday Harbor
MacDonald, A. When we were Vikings
Massey, S. The widows of Malabar Hill
Ondaatje, M. Warlight
Phillips, S. First Lady
Radcliffe, A. The mysteries of Udolpho
Roberts, N. Sea swept
Sjon, 1. The blue fox
Stabenow, D. A grave denied
Tyler, A. The amateur marriage
Wiggs, S. The Oysterville sewing circle
Guardian angel Paretsky, S.
Guardian of the horizon Peters, E.
Guardian series (Mary Jo Putney) [series] Putney, M.
The **guardians** Grisham, J.

GUARDS
Aridjis, C. Asunder
Erdrich, L. The night watchman
Lovesey, P. Diamond solitaire
The **guards** Bruen, K.
Guards! Guards! Pratchett, T.

GUATEMALA
Allende, I. In the midst of winter
Reichs, K. Grave secrets

GUERNSEY (CHANNEL ISLANDS)
Horlock, M. The book of lies
Shaffer, M. The Guernsey Literary and Potato Peel Pie Society
The **Guernsey** Literary and Potato Peel Pie Society Shaffer, M.

GUERRILLA WARFARE
Hamid, M. Exit west
Hemingway, E. For whom the bell tolls
Huston, C. Skinner
Marks, L. Fire logic
Tan, T. The garden of evening mists

GUERRILLAS
Apelfeld, A. To the edge of sorrow
Banks, R. Cloudsplitter
Binet, L. HHhH
Dahl, K. The courier
Hemingway, E. For whom the bell tolls
Levi, P. If not now, when?
Guerrillas Naipaul, V.

GUERRILLAS -- CENTRAL AFRICA
Ballard, J. The day of creation

Piccirilli, T. The last kind words
Picoult, J. The storyteller
Prcic, I. Shards
The road ahead
Roth, H. Requiem for Harlem
Runcie, J. Canvey Island
Schlink, B. Self's punishment
Schwartz, J. Northwest corner
Shelley, M. Frankenstein
Singer, I. Enemies, a love story
Spencer, S. Man in the woods
Strout, E. The Burgess boys
Tartt, D. The secret history
Winslow, D. The dawn patrol
Wroblewski, D. The story of Edgar Sawtelle

GUILT IN MEN -- JAPAN
Okuizumi, H. The stones cry out

GUILT IN TEENAGE BOYS
Tyler, A. Saint Maybe

GUILT IN WOMEN
Cameron, P. The city of your final destination
Dicks, M. Unexpectedly, Milo
Ephron, H. You'll never know, dear
Gander, F. As a friend
Hamilton, J. A map of the world
Hardy, T. Tess of the d'Urbervilles
Jerkins, G. The ninth step
Joss, M. The night following
Lippman, L. I'd know you anywhere
McEwan, I. Atonement
McHugh, L. Arrowood
Murphy, Y. Signed, Mata Hari
Perry, A. Bedford Square
Savas, A. Walking on the ceiling
Scott, J. The kept
Silver, E. The execution of Noa P. Singleton
Spencer, S. A walk with the dead
Styron, W. Sophie's choice
Toibin, C. The testament of Mary
Ward, A. Forgive me

Guilty Elliot, L.
Guilty minds Finder, J.
Guilty not guilty Francis, F.

GUITARISTS
Bird, S. The flamenco academy

GULF COAST (UNITED STATES) -- HISTORY -- 19TH CENTURY
Kent, K. The outcasts

GULF COAST, FLORIDA
Koryta, M. The Cypress House
White, R. Salt river

GULF COAST, MISSISSIPPI
Barthelme, F. Elroy Nights
Ward, J. Salvage the bones
Ward, J. Sing, unburied, sing

GULF OF MEXICO
Cussler, C. Sea of greed

Gulliver's travels Swift, J.

GUN ACCIDENTS
Reichs, K. Deadly decisions
Treuer, D. Prudence

GUN CONTROL
Patterson, R. Balance of power
Gun dealers' daughter Apostol, G.

GUN INDUSTRY AND TRADE
Patterson, R. Balance of power
Whittle, T. The dangerous edge of things
Gun Island Ghosh, A.
Gun love Clement, J.

GUN SMUGGLERS
Greene, G. The captain and the enemy
Leonard, E. Rum punch

GUN THEFTS
Constantine, K. Blood mud

GUNFIGHTERS
Brand, M. Max Brand's best western stories
Brooks, B. Blood storm
deWitt, P. The Sisters brothers
Dexter, P. Deadwood
Grey, Z. Riders of the purple sage
Kent, K. The outcasts
Knott, R. Robert B. Parker's Buckskin
Lansdale, J. Paradise sky
Parker, R. Appaloosa
Parker, R. Blue-eyed devil
Parker, R. Gunman's rhapsody
Russell, M. Epitaph
Schaefer, J. Shane
Swarthout, G. The shootist

GUNFIGHTS
Estleman, L. The adventures of Johnny Vermillion
Kelton, E. Hard ride
Knott, R. Robert B. Parker's Buckskin
Parker, R. Appaloosa
Parker, R. Blue-eyed devil
Parker, R. Brimstone
Russell, M. Epitaph
Swinson, K. A gangster and a gentleman
Gunman's rhapsody Parker, R.

GUNS
Burns, A. Little constructions
Clement, J. Gun love
Hunter, S. Game of snipers
McAllister, T. How to be safe

GUNSHOT VICTIMS
Ballard, J. Kingdom come
Box, C. Long range
Brown, S. Ricochet
Bruen, K. Cross
Christie, A. The murder at the vicarage
Christie, A. A murder is announced
Crumley, J. Bordersnakes
Faye, L. The Paragon Hotel
Lovesey, P. Diamond dust

Trollope, J. The other family

Vidal, G. Empire

HALF-BROTHERS AND SISTERS

Jewell, L. The making of us

Plaidy, J. The captive Queen of Scots

HALF-HUMAN HYBRIDS

French, J. The Grey Bastards

French, J. The true Bastards

McGuire, S. Chimes at midnight

McGuire, S. Night and silence

McGuire, S. Once broken faith

McGuire, S. Rosemary and rue

Norton, A. The elvenbane

Rushdie, S. Two years eight months and twenty-eight nights

Stout, D. Titanshade

The **half-life** Raymond, J.

The **half-made** world Gilman, F.

Half-made world novels [series] Gilman, F.

Half-past dawn Doetsch, R.

HALF-SISTERS

Balogh, M. Someone to hold

Bell, L. How the duke was won

Bloom, A. Lucky us

Elliott, L. The missing years

Flynn, G. Sharp objects

Gyasi, Y. Homegoing

Harper, K. The poyson garden

Jones, T. Silver sparrow

Krentz, J. White lies

Tan, A. The hundred secret senses

Halfblood chronicles [series] Norton, A.

HALFWAY HOUSES (FOR ALCOHOLICS, DRUG ADDICTS, RUNAWAYS, ETC)

Meno, J. The boy detective fails

Wallace, D. Infinite jest

HALIFAX, NOVA SCOTIA

Norman, H. The museum guard

Norman, H. Next life might be kinder

The **hall** of singing caryatids Pelevin, V.

HALLOWEEN

Bradbury, R. Something wicked this way comes

Ewan, C. Dark tides

McKevett, G. Murder in the corn maze

O'Nan, S. The night country

HALLUCINATIONS AND ILLUSIONS

Arnoult, D. Sufficient grace

Bolano, R. Amulet

Burns, C. Black hole

Burroughs, W. Naked lunch

Ellis, B. Lunar Park

Fowles, J. The magus

Gruber, M. The forgery of Venus

Harrison, M. Light

Jackson, C. The lost weekend

Koryta, M. So cold the river

Mieville, C. The city & the city

Norman, H. Next life might be kinder

St. James, S. The haunting of Maddy Clare

HALLUCINOGENIC DRUG USE

Lupton, R. Sister

HALLUCINOGENIC DRUGS

Boyle, T. Outside looking in

Wolfe, P. The lost diary of M

Halsey Street Coster, N.

The **Hamilton** affair Cobbs Hoffman, E.

HAMILTON, ALEXANDER, 1757-1804

Cobbs Hoffman, E. The Hamilton affair

HAMILTON, ELIZABETH SCHUYLER, 1757-1854

Cobbs Hoffman, E. The Hamilton affair

HAMILTON, EMMA, 1761?-1815

Sontag, S. The volcano lover

HAMILTON, WILLIAM, 1730-1803

Sontag, S. The volcano lover

Hamish Macbeth mysteries [series] Beaton, M.

The **hamlet** Faulkner, W.

Hammer to fall Lawton, J.

HAMPEL, ELISE, 1903-1943

Fallada, H. Every man dies alone

HAMPEL, OTTO HERMANN, 1897-1943

Fallada, H. Every man dies alone

HAMPTONS, NEW YORK

Knopf, C. The last refuge

Moore, L. Making waves

HAMPTONS, NEW YORK -- SOCIAL LIFE AND CUSTOMS

Ganek, D. The summer we read Gatsby

HAN, KANG, 1970- FAMILY

Han, K. The white book

HANCOCK, WINFIELD SCOTT, 1824-1886

Shaara, J. Gods and generals

The **hand** that first held mine O'Farrell, M.

A **handful** of ashes McCarthy, R.

HANDICRAFT SHOPS

Malpas, J. Leave me breathless

Handle with care Hunting, H.

The **handmaid's** tale Atwood, M.

Handmaid's tale [series] Atwood, M.

The **handyman** See, C.

The **hanged** man Inbinder, G.

HANGING

Melville, H. Billy Budd, foretopman

Roberts, G. The bluest blood

The **hanging** garden Rankin, I.

The **hanging** girl Adler-Olsen, J.

Hanging hill Hayder, M.

Hangman Cole, D.

The **hangman's** daughter Potzsch, O.

Hangman's daughter tales [series] Potzsch, O.

Hangman's holiday Sayers, D.

The **hangman's** secret Rowland, L.

Hanley & Rivka mysteries [series] Pirrone, D.

Hannah Trevor novels [series] Lawrence, M.

Hanne Wilhelmsen novels [series] Holt, A.

Hannibal Harris, T.

Vinge, V. A deepness in the sky
Vinge, V. A fire upon the deep
Vinge, V. Rainbows end
Watts, P. Blindsight
Weir, A. Artemis
Weir, A. The Martian
Hard time Paretsky, S.
Hard twisted Greaves, C.
The **hard** way Child, L.
Hardball Paretsky, S.
HARDBOILED FICTION
Berkowitz, I. Old flame
  The best American noir of the century
Block, L. All the flowers are dying
Block, L. A drop of the hard stuff
Block, L. Eight million ways to die
Block, L. The sins of the fathers
Block, L. A ticket to the boneyard
Block, L. When the sacred ginmill closes
Brandt, H. The Whites
Brookmyre, C. Black widow
Bruen, K. Cross
Bruen, K. Galway girl
Bruen, K. The guards
Burke, J. Black cherry blues
Burke, J. Heaven's prisoners
Burke, J. The New Iberia blues
Burke, J. Robicheaux
Burns, R. Body slam
Butcher, J. Proven guilty
Chabon, M. The Yiddish Policemen's Union
Chandler, R. The annotated Big sleep
Chandler, R. The big sleep
Chandler, R. The lady in the lake
Chandler, R. The long goodbye
Coben, H. Long lost
Coleman, R. What you break
Coleman, R. Where it hurts
Collins, M. Ask not
Collins, M. The wrong Quarry
Coyle, M. Yesterday's echo
Crais, R. Chasing darkness
Crais, R. A dangerous man
Crais, R. The first rule
Crumley, J. Bordersnakes
Crumley, J. The final country
Crumley, J. The last good kiss
Crumley, J. The wrong case
Davys, T. Amberville
De Giovanni, M. The crocodile
Estleman, L. Amos Walker
Estleman, L. Infernal angels
Estleman, L. A smile on the face of the tiger
Finlay, M. The murder pit
Garcia-Roza, L. Alone in the crowd
Garcia-Roza, L. December heat
Goldman, M. The shallows

Gran, S. Claire DeWitt and the city of the dead
Gran, S. The infinite blacktop
Hammett, D. The glass key
Hammett, D. The Maltese falcon
Hanson, H. The driver
Harvey, M. The Chicago way
Harvey, M. The fifth floor
Harvey, M. The governor's wife
Harvey, M. We all fall down
Himes, C. Cotton comes to Harlem
Kaminsky, S. Dancing in the dark
Kaminsky, S. A fatal glass of beer
Kaminsky, S. Murder on the Trans-Siberian Express
Kaminsky, S. To catch a spy
Kaminsky, S. Tomorrow is another day
Kerr, P. Field gray
Kerr, P. Greeks bearing gifts
Kerr, P. The lady from Zagreb
Kerr, P. A man without breath
Kerr, P. March violets
Kerr, P. Metropolis
Kerr, P. Prussian blue
Knopf, C. The last refuge
Lehane, D. Prayers for rain
Lehane, D. Sacred
Lemaitre, P. Irene
Lethem, J. Motherless Brooklyn
Mieville, C. The city & the city
Morgan, R. Altered carbon
Morgan, R. Broken angels
Mosley, W. Fearless Jones
Mosley, W. Trouble is what I do
Muller, M. Both ends of the night
Muller, M. The broken promise land
Muller, M. Burn out
Muller, M. City of whispers
Muller, M. The dangerous hour
Muller, M. Dead midnight
Muller, M. The ever-running man
Muller, M. There's something in a Sunday
Muller, M. A walk through the fire
Muller, M. Vanishing point
Muller, M. Where echoes live
Muller, M. While other people sleep
Muller, M. A wild and lonely place
Muller, M. Wolf in the shadows
O'Malley, T. Serpents in the cold
O'Malley, T. We were kings
Osborne, L. Only to sleep
Parker, R. Back story
Parker, R. Chance
Parker, R. Cold service
Parker, R. Death in paradise
Parker, R. Double deuce
Parker, R. Double play
Parker, R. Hugger Mugger
Parker, R. Hush money

Segal, E. Love story
Simon, C. Grey dawn
Simon, C. Stages of Grey
Harvest Plain, B.
Harvest Crace, J.

HASIDIM -- BROOKLYN, NEW YORK CITY
Potok, C. The gift of Asher Lev
Potok, C. My name is Asher Lev

HASIDISM
Dahl, J. Conviction
Goldbloom, G. On division
Markovits, A. I am forbidden

HATE
Barry, D. Lunatics
Candlish, L. Those people
Hegi, U. Stones from the river
Moody, D. Hater
Pratchett, T. Thud!
Vernon, O. A killing in this town

HATE CRIMES
Atkins, A. The forsaken
Campbell, B. Your blues ain't like mine
Harvey, J. Gone to ground
Iles, G. Mississippi blood
Locke, A. Bluebird, bluebird
Mullen, T. Lightning men
Phillips, C. A distant shore
Phillips, C. Foreigners
Pronzini, B. Nightcrawlers
Shames, T. An unsettling crime for Samuel Craddock
Siger, J. Target Tinos
Winer, J. Her kind of case

HATE GROUPS
Brown, S. The witness
Iles, G. Mississippi blood
Mullen, T. Lightning men
Roy, L. Gone too long

HATE IN MEN
K'wan Gutter

HATE IN WOMEN
Martin, V. Property

HATE MAIL
Page, K. The body in the bog
Hate to want you Rai, A.
Hater Moody, D.
Hater novels [series] Moody, D.
Hateship, friendship, courtship, loveship, marriage Munro, A.

HATHAWAY, ANNE, 1556?-1623
Morgan, J. The secret life of William Shakespeare
A **hatred** for tulips Lourie, R.
Haunted ground Hart, E.

HAUNTED HOTELS
King, S. The shining
St. James, S. The Sun Down motel

HAUNTED HOUSES
Danielewski, M. House of leaves
Deveraux, J. Someone to love

Gerritsen, T. The shape of night
Godwin, G. Flora
Hamill, S. A cosmology of monsters
Hawthorne, N. The house of the seven gables
Jackson, S. The haunting of Hill House
Link, K. Magic for beginners
More deadly than the male
Nevill, A. The house of small shadows
Purcell, L. The silent companions
Rayne, S. Property of a lady
Rendell, R. Heartstones
Straub, P. Lost boy lost girl
Waters, S. The little stranger

HAUNTED HOUSES -- NEW ORLEANS, LOUISIANA
Roberts, N. Midnight Bayou

HAUNTED PLACES
Brundage, E. All things cease to appear
Dean, A. A place of confinement
Dean, A. A woman of consequence
More deadly than the male
St. James, S. The haunting of Maddy Clare

HAUNTED SCHOOLS
Evans, J. The white devil
The **haunting** of Hill House Jackson, S.
The **haunting** of L. Norman, H.
The **haunting** of Maddy Clare St. James, S.
Hausfrau Essbaum, J.
Havana Hunter, S.
Havana Bay Smith, M.
Havana storm Cussler, C.
The **Havana** World Series Latour, J.

HAVANA, CUBA
Cleeton, C. Next year in Havana
Garcia, C. Dreaming in Cuban
Garcia, C. King of Cuba
Greene, G. Our man in Havana
Hemingway, E. To have and have not
Latour, J. The Havana World Series
Montero, M. Dancing to "Almendra"
Sanchez, T. King Bongo
Smith, M. Havana Bay
Have his carcase Sayers, D.
Haven Weatherspoon, R.
Havisham Frame, R.

HAWAII
Crichton, M. Micro
Henson, P. Into the blue
Lodge, D. Paradise news
MacDonald, J. The turquoise lament
Muller, M. A walk through the fire
Rizzuto, R. Shadow child
Hawaii Michener, J.

HAWAII -- HISTORY
Michener, J. Hawaii

HAWAIIANS
Michener, J. Hawaii
Hawk quest Lyndon, R.

Heartbreak hotel Landis, J.

Heartbreak of a hustler's wife Turner, N.

The **heartbreaker** Howatch, S.

Heartbreaker Bay novels [series] Shalvis, J.

Hearts Wolitzer, H.

Hearts and bones Lawrence, M.

The **hearts** of horses Gloss, M.

The **hearts** of men Butler, N.

Hearts of the missing Potenza, C.

The **heartsong** of Charging Elk Welch, J.

Heartstone White, E.

Heartstone [series] White, E.

Heartstones Rendell, R.

Heat and dust Jhabvala, R.

Heat lightning Sandford, J.

The **heat** of the day Bowen, E.

HEAT WAVES (METEOROLOGY)

  Shannon, D. Chaos of crime

The **heather** blazing Toibin, C.

HEAVEN

  Albom, M. The five people you meet in heaven

  Albom, M. The next person you meet in Heaven

  Sebold, A. The lovely bones

Heaven trilogy [series] Johnson, A.

Heaven, my home Locke, A.

Heaven's prisoners Burke, J.

The **heavens** Newman, S.

The **heavens** may fall Eskens, A.

HEBRIDES

  May, P. The blackhouse

HEDGE FUNDS

  Amidon, S. Human capital

  Finder, J. Buried secrets

HEDONISM

  Baker, N. House of holes

  Kadrey, R. The grand dark

  Kerouac, J. The dharma bums

  Percy, W. The moviegoer

  Walsh, H. Brass

  Weinberg, K. The truants

Heechee saga [series] Pohl, F.

The **heir** Burrowes, G.

Heir to the duke Ashford, J.

Heir to the empire Zahn, T.

Heir to the glimmering world Ozick, C.

The **heirloom** garden Shipman, V.

HEIRLOOMS

  Alexander, V. The Lady Travelers Guide to larceny with a dashing stranger

  Avon, J. In peppermint peril

  Bobotis, A. The last list of Miss Judith Kratt

HEIRS AND HEIRESSES

  Akunin, B. Sister Pelagia and the white bulldog

  Alexander, V. The Lady Travelers Guide to scoundrels and other gentlemen

  Andersen, L. The Boleyn deceit

  Andersen, L. The Boleyn king

  Andersen, L. The Boleyn reckoning

  Archer, J. Best kept secret

  Asaro, C. Primary inversion

  Balogh, M. Someone to love

  Balogh, M. Someone to wed

  Bateman, K. This earl of mine

  Bear, E. Shattered pillars

  Beverley, J. Devilish

  Boyle, E. Along came a duke

  Burrowes, G. The bridegroom wore plaid

  Burrowes, G. The heir

  Burrowes, G. My one and only duke

  Calvi, M. Dear George, Dear Mary

  Castle, J. Illusion Town

  Chandler, R. The annotated Big sleep

  Chandler, R. The big sleep

  Christie, A. Endless night

  Cole, A. A duke by default

  Collins, M. Ready set rogue

  Connelly, M. The wrong side of goodbye

  Cornwell, B. Excalibur

  Cornwell, B. The winter king

  Dare, T. The duchess deal

  Dare, T. When a Scot ties the knot

  Dean, A. A place of confinement

  Dunnett, D. Niccolo rising

  Goodwin, D. The American heiress

  Guhrke, L. How to lose a duke in ten days

  Guhrke, L. When the marquess met his match

  Hallberg, G. City on fire

  Hammett, D. The glass key

  Hauck, R. How to catch a prince

  Heath, L. Falling into bed with a duke

  Helprin, M. In sunlight and in shadow

  Helprin, M. Winter's tale

  Jackson, B. Forged in desire

  James, H. The portrait of a lady

  James, H. The wings of the dove

  Jeffries, S. The art of sinning

  Jemisin, N. The hundred thousand kingdoms

  Johnson, S. Blaze

  Kellerman, J. Private eyes

  Kwan, K. China rich girlfriend

  Maum, C. Costalegre

  McDonald, I. New moon

  Michels, E. The rebel heir

  Mishima, Y. The sound of waves

  Muller, M. City of whispers

  Phillips, A. The king at the edge of the world

  Phillips, S. It had to be you

  Pineiro, C. One summer night

  Pirie, D. The patient's eyes

  Plaidy, J. The captive Queen of Scots

  Plaidy, J. Murder most royal

  Pope, J. One warm winter

  Putney, M. Once a soldier

  Ragan, T. Buried deep

Gregory, P. The other Boleyn girl
Gregory, P. The taming of the queen
Mantel, H. Bring up the bodies
Riley, J. The serpent garden
Sansom, C. Sovereign
Weir, A. Anna of Kleve

HENRY VIII, KING OF ENGLAND, 1491-1547 WIVES
Maxwell, R. The secret diary of Anne Boleyn
Plaidy, J. Murder most royal

Henry and Rachel Saville, L.
Henry and Sunday mysteries [series] Clark, M.
Henry Christie mysteries [series] Oldham, N.
Henry Farrell novels [series] Bouman, T.
Henry Rios mysteries [series] Nava, M.
Henry Thompson novels [series] Huston, C.
Henry, himself O'Nan, S.

HEPHAESTION
Renault, M. The Persian boy

Her body and other parties Machado, C.
Her every fear Swanson, P.
Her kind of case Winer, J.
Her last day Ragan, T.
Her other secret Dimon, H.
Her secret life Warren, T.
Her sky cowboy Ciotta, B.

HERB GARDENING
Bowen, R. The victory garden

HERBAL MEDICINE
Joyce, G. The limits of enchantment
Preston, D. The codex

HERBALISTS
Bohjalian, C. The night strangers
Bowen, R. The victory garden
Joyce, G. The limits of enchantment
Peters, E. Brother Cadfael's penance
Peters, E. Dead man's ransom
Peters, E. The hermit of Eyton Forest
Peters, E. The holy thief
Peters, E. Monk's hood
Peters, E. The pilgrim of hate
Peters, E. The potter's field
Peters, E. A rare Benedictine
Peters, E. The rose rent
Peters, E. St. Peter's fair
Peters, E. The sanctuary sparrow
Peters, E. The summer of the Danes
Peters, E. The virgin in the ice

HERCULANEUM (EXTINCT CITY)
Goodman, C. The night villa

Hercule Poirot mysteries [series] Christie, A.
The **herd** Bartz, A.
Here and gone Beck, H.
Here and now and then Chen, M.
Here be dragons Penman, S.
Here comes the sun Dennis-Benn, N.
Here I am Foer, J.
Here I am! Holdstock, P.

Here I go again Lancaster, J.
Here we are Swift, G.

HEREDITY
Crichton, M. Next
Makumbi, J. Kintu
O'Connell, C. Stone angel

HERESY
Self, W. The book of Dave
Walton, J. Lent

The **heretic's** daughter Kent, K.

HERETICS
Harris, R. The second sleep

Herland Gilman, C.

HERMES (GREEK DEITY)
Alexis, A. Fifteen dogs

The **hermit** of Eyton Forest Peters, E.

HERMITAGE MUSEUM, ST. PETERSBURG, RUSSIA
Dean, D. The madonnas of Leningrad

HERMITS
Owens, D. Where the crawdads sing
Parker, S. Purgatory road
Peters, E. The hermit of Eyton Forest
Winton, T. The shepherd's hut

A **hero** born Jin, Y.
A **hero** of France Furst, A.

HEROES AND HEROINES
Auel, J. The clan of the cave bear
Blackmore, R. Lorna Doone
Conrad, J. Nostromo
Cussler, C. Pacific vortex!
Fountain, B. Billy Lynn's long halftime walk
Hair, D. Mage's blood
Hair, D. Scarlet tides
Jin, Y. A hero born
Lake, J. Endurance
Lake, J. Green
Locke, T. Enclave
MacLaughlin, N. Wake, siren
McDevitt, J. A talent for war
Orullian, P. The unremembered
Oyeyemi, H. Mr. Fox
Pratchett, T. The color of magic
Pratchett, T. The last hero
Rothfuss, P. The name of the wind
Rothfuss, P. The wise man's fear
Tolkien, J. Beren and Luthien
Tolkien, J. The hobbit, or, there and back again
Tolkien, J. The fellowship of the ring
Tolkien, J. The return of the king
Tolkien, J. The two towers

HEROES AND HEROINES IN MASS MEDIA
Chabon, M. The amazing adventures of Kavalier & Clay

HEROES AND HEROINES, ENGLISH
Orczy, E. The Scarlet Pimpernel

HEROES AND HEROINES, GREEK
Renault, M. The bull from the sea
Renault, M. The king must die

Shriver, L. We need to talk about Kevin

Sparks, N. A walk to remember

Straub, P. A dark matter

Weir, M. The book of Essie

HIGH SCHOOL TEACHERS

Baxter, C. Saul and Patsy

Founds, K. When mystical creatures attack!

Haruf, K. Plainsong

Johnson, L. The most dangerous place on earth

Kaufman, B. Up the down staircase

King, S. 11

McAllister, T. How to be safe

Perrotta, T. The abstinence teacher

Russell, K. My dark Vanessa

Strout, E. Amy and Isabelle

HIGH SCHOOL TEACHERS -- INNER CITY

Hunter, E. The blackboard jungle

HIGH SCHOOLS

Bump, G. Everywhere you don't belong

Johnson, L. The most dangerous place on earth

Kaufman, B. Up the down staircase

King, S. Carrie

Rader-Day, L. Little pretty things

Sandford, J. Deep freeze

Shriver, L. We need to talk about Kevin

West, K. Minor dramas & other catastrophes

The **high** season Blundell, J.

HIGH TECHNOLOGY

Brown, D. The Moscow offensive

Chiang, T. Exhalation

Crouch, B. Recursion

Cussler, C. The rising sea

El-Mohtar, A. This is how you lose the time war

Gibson, W. Agency

Hart, R. The warehouse

Kress, N. If tomorrow comes

Kress, N. Tomorrow's kin

Nguyen, K. New waves

Pynchon, T. Bleeding edge

Quirk, M. Cold barrel zero

Quirk, M. Dead man switch

Robinson, K. 2312

Robinson, K. Aurora

Soule, C. Anyone

Stephenson, N. Fall or, Dodge in hell

Weinstein, A. Children of the new world

Wells, M. All systems red

HIGH TECHNOLOGY INDUSTRY AND TRADE

Chang, A. Days of distraction

Cohen, J. Book of numbers

Crichton, M. Prey

HIGH TECHNOLOGY WEAPONS

Bell, T. Overkill

Poyer, D. Overthrow

Westlake, D. Forever and a death

Highgate Rise Perry, A.

Highland grooms [series] London, J.

Highland pleasures [series] Ashley, J.

Highland promise McLayne, A.

HIGHLAND ROMANCES

Ashley, J. Lady Isabella's scandalous marriage

Ashley, J. The madness of Lord Ian Mackenzie

Banks, M. Never seduce a Scot

Burrowes, G. The trouble with dukes

Garwood, J. The bride

London, J. Wild wicked Scot

McLayne, A. Highland promise

Ranney, K. The Scottish duke

HIGHLANDS, SCOTLAND

Ashe, K. The earl

Elliott, L. The missing years

Foley, L. The hunting party

McLayne, A. Highland promise

Morgan, S. The Christmas sisters

Ranney, K. The Scottish duke

Scott, A. Beneath the abbey wall

Scott, A. A double death on the Black Isle

Scott, A. A kind of grief

Scott, A. The low road

Ware, R. The turn of the key

HIGHLANDS, SCOTLAND -- HISTORY -- 13TH CENTURY

Banks, M. Never seduce a Scot

HIGHLANDS, SCOTLAND -- HISTORY -- 18TH CENTURY

London, J. Wild wicked Scot

HIGHLANDS, SCOTLAND -- HISTORY -- 19TH CENTURY

Burnet, G. His bloody project

HIGHLANDS, SCOTLAND -- SOCIAL LIFE AND CUSTOMS -- 19TH CENTURY

Burrowes, G. The bridegroom wore plaid

The **Highsmith** reader Highsmith, P.

The **highway** Box, C.

Highway 59 [series] Locke, A.

HIJACKING OF AIRCRAFT

Ohlsson, K. Hostage

HIJACKING OF SHIPS

Wolfe, G. Home fires

HIKERS

Carr, R. What we find

Child, L. Full wolf moon

Doiron, P. The precipice

HIKING

Grossman, D. To the end of the land

Nelson, C. If we make it home

Nevill, A. The ritual

Hild Griffith, N.

HILDA,, OF WHITBY, SAINT, 614-680

Griffith, N. Hild

HILDEGARD VON BINGEN,, SAINT, 1098-1179

Sharratt, M. Illuminations

HIMALAYA MOUNTAINS REGION

Desai, K. The inheritance of loss

Gilman, L. The cold eye
Gilman, L. Silver on the road
Goss, T. The sinister mystery of the mesmerizing girl
Goss, T. The strange case of the alchemist's daughter
Gowar, I. The mermaid and Mrs. Hancock
Hand, E. Mortal love
Harkness, D. Shadow of night
Harkness, D. Time's convert
Ishiguro, K. The buried giant
Jin, Y. A hero born
Kay, G. Children of earth and sky
Kay, G. The last light of the sun
Kay, G. River of stars
Kay, G. Under heaven
Kidd, J. Things in jars
Kuang, R. The dragon republic
Kuang, R. The poppy war
Maguire, G. After Alice
Maguire, G. Hiddensee
Miller, M. Circe
Moreno-Garcia, S. Gods of jade and shadow
Morgenstern, E. The night circus
Nicholas, D. Something red
Nicholas, D. Throne of darkness
Nicholas, D. The wicked
North, C. The pursuit of William Abbey
Novik, N. His majesty's dragon
Pike, S. The lost queen
Pulley, N. The Bedlam stacks
Pulley, N. The lost future of Pepperharrow
Pulley, N. The watchmaker of Filigree Street
Saintcrow, L. The Iron Wyrm Affair
Saintcrow, L. The ripper affair
Schwab, V. A conjuring of light
Schwab, V. A darker shade of magic
Schwab, V. A gathering of shadows
Sherwood, F. The book of splendor
Stewart, M. The crystal cave
Stewart, M. The hollow hills
Stewart, M. The last enchantment
Stewart, M. The wicked day
Sutcliff, R. Sword at sunset
Urquhart, J. Away
Vyleta, D. Smoke
Walton, J. Lent
Wecker, H. The golem and the jinni
White, T. The once and future king
Wilson, G. The bird king
Woods, R. Remembrance

HISTORICAL FICTION

Aalborg, G. River of porcupines
Abbott, M. Bury me deep
Achebe, C. Things fall apart
Adamson, G. The outlander
Adichie, C. Half of a yellow sun
Adimi, K. Our riches
Agee, J. The bones of paradise

Alcott, K. A touch of stardust
Alexander, V. The Magdalen girls
Allende, I. Daughter of fortune
Allende, I. A long petal of the sea
Allende, I. Portrait in sepia
Amirrezvani, A. The blood of flowers
Amirrezvani, A. Equal of the sun
Amis, M. The zone of interest
Anderson, A. The summer guest
Anstruther, E. A perfect explanation
Anton, M. Apprentice
Apelfeld, A. Blooms of darkness
Apelfeld, A. The man who never stopped sleeping
Apelfeld, A. To the edge of sorrow
Araghi, A. The immortals of Tehran
Archer, J. Best kept secret
Archer, J. Only time will tell
Archer, J. This was a man
Arnow, H. The dollmaker
Atakora, A. Conjure women
Atkinson, K. A god in ruins
Atkinson, K. Transcription
Auel, J. The clan of the cave bear
Avery, E. The last nude
Bahr, H. The Judas Field
Bainbridge, B. Every man for himself
Baker, J. Longbourn
Ballard, J. Empire of the sun
Banner, C. The house at the edge of night
Barker, P. The eye in the door
Barker, P. The ghost road
Barker, P. Regeneration
Barker, S. The incarnations
Barnes, J. The noise of time
Barnett, L. Jam on the Vine
Barr, M. Watershed
Barry, S. Days without end
Bassani, G. The garden of the Finzi-Continis
Bates, H. Fair stood the wind for France
Bausch, R. Peace
Beach, E. Run silent, run deep
Beams, C. The illness lesson
Beauman, N. Madness is better than defeat
Belfer, L. And after the fire
Belfoure, C. The Paris architect
Benedict, M. Lady Clementine
Benedict, M. The only woman in the room
Benioff, D. City of thieves
Benjamin, M. Alice I have been
Benjamin, M. The aviator's wife
Benton, J. Lilli de Jong
Berg, G. The operator
Binet, L. HHhH
Birch, C. Jamrach's menagerie
Bird, S. Daughter of a daughter of a queen
Black, C. Three hours in Paris
Blackmore, R. Lorna Doone

Duenas, M. The time in between
Dumas, A. The man in the iron mask
Dumas, A. The three musketeers
Dumas, A. Twenty years after
Dunant, S. The birth of Venus
Dumas, A. The three musketeers
Dunant, S. In the company of the courtesan
Dunant, S. Sacred hearts
Dunant, S. Blood and beauty
Dunmore, H. The lie
Dunnett, D. Niccolo rising
Dybek, N. The Verdun affair
Earley, T. Jim the boy
Ebershoff, D. The 19th wife
Ebershoff, D. The Danish girl
Eco, U. Baudolino
Edugyan, E. Half-blood blues
Edugyan, E. Washington Black
Egan, J. Manhattan Beach
Engelmann, K. The Stockholm octavo
Epstein, J. Wunderland
Erdrich, L. The Master Butchers Singing Club
Erdrich, L. The night watchman
Faber, M. The crimson petal and the white
Falcones de Sierra, I. Cathedral of the sea
Fallada, H. Every man dies alone
Faulkner, W. Absalom, Absalom!
Faulks, S. Charlotte Gray
Faulks, S. Birdsong
Fay, K. The map of lost memories
Findley, T. The piano man's daughter
Fitzgerald, P. The blue flower
Flanagan, R. Gould's book of fish
Flanagan, R. The narrow road to the deep north
Flanagan, T. The tenants of time
Flanagan, T. The year of the French
Follett, K. A column of fire
Follett, K. Edge of eternity
Follett, K. Fall of giants
Follett, K. The pillars of the earth
Follett, K. Winter of the world
Follett, K. World without end
Ford, F. Parade's end
Ford, J. Songs of Willow Frost
Forester, C. Admiral Hornblower in the West Indies
Forester, C. The African Queen
Forester, C. Beat to quarters
Forester, C. Flying colours
Forester, C. Hornblower and the Atropos
Forester, C. Hornblower and the Hotspur
Forester, C. Lieutenant Hornblower
Forester, C. Lord Hornblower
Forester, C. Mr. Midshipman Hornblower
Forester, C. Ship of the line
Forester, C. Commodore Hornblower
Fowler, T. Z
Fowler, T. A well-behaved woman

Fowles, J. The French lieutenant's woman
Frame, R. Havisham
Franck, J. Blindness of the heart
Franklin, A. The siege winter
Frazier, C. Cold Mountain
Frazier, C. Thirteen moons
Frazier, C. Varina
Freedman, B. Mrs. Mike
Freeman, A. The fair fight
French, A. Billy
Fuentes, C. The death of Artemio Cruz
Gabaldon, D. A breath of snow and ashes
Gabaldon, D. Dragonfly in amber
Gabaldon, D. Drums of autumn
Gabaldon, D. An echo in the bone
Gabaldon, D. The fiery cross
Gabaldon, D. Outlander
Gabaldon, D. Voyager
Gabaldon, D. Written in my own heart's blood
Gaines, E. The autobiography of Miss Jane Pittman
Gappah, P. Out of darkness, shining light
Gass, W. Middle C
Gaynor, H. The lighthouse keeper's daughter
Gaynor, H. Meet me in Monaco
Gear, K. People of the masks
Gear, K. People of the mist
George, M. The confessions of young Nero
George, M. Elizabeth I
George, M. Helen of Troy
George, M. The splendor before the dark
Ghosh, A. The glass palace
Ghosh, A. Sea of poppies
Ghosh, A. River of smoke
Ghosh, A. Flood of fire
Gilbert, E. The signature of all things
Gilbert, E. City of girls
Gillham, D. City of women
Gloss, M. The hearts of horses
Godwin, G. Flora
Golden, A. Memoirs of a geisha
Golding, W. Close quarters
Golding, W. Fire down below
Golding, W. Rites of passage
Golding, W. The inheritors
Goodwin, D. The American heiress
Goudge, E. Green Dolphin Street
Grames, J. The seven or eight deaths of Stella Fortuna
Grass, G. The tin drum
Graves, R. Claudius the god and his wife Messalina
Graves, R. I, Claudius
Greaves, C. Hard twisted
Greeley, M. The clergyman's wife
Greene, A. Long Man
Greene, G. The quiet American
Greenwood, T. Rust & stardust
Gregory, P. The Boleyn inheritance
Gregory, P. The constant princess

Kelly, J. The light over London
Kelly, M. Lilac girls
Kelly, M. Lost roses
Kelton, E. Badger boy
Keneally, T. The daughters of Mars
Keneally, T. Schindler's list
Keneally, T. Shame and the captives
Kennedy, W. Chango's beads and two-tone shoes
Kennedy, W. Ironweed
Kent, H. Burial rites
Kent, K. The heretic's daughter
Kibler, J. Home for erring and outcast girls
Kidd, S. The book of longings
Kidd, S. The invention of wings
Kim, C. If you leave me
Kim, E. The kinship of secrets
Kimani, P. Dance of the Jakaranda
King, L. Euphoria
Kingsolver, B. The Poisonwood Bible
Kirk, D. Sword of honor
Klein, R. The moth diaries
Kneale, M. English passengers
Koen, K. Before Versailles
Koen, K. Through a glass darkly
Koestler, A. Darkness at noon
Konar, A. Mischling
Krall, H. Chasing the king of hearts
Kramer, L. Search for my heart
Krivak, A. The signal flame
Krivak, A. The sojourn
Krueger, W. This tender land
Kunzru, H. The impressionist
Kutsukake, L. The translation of love
Kuznetsov, A. Babi Yar
Laker, R. To dance with kings
Lalami, L. The Moor's account
Lam, V. The headmaster's wager
Lambdin, D. Hostile shores
Lambdin, D. King's captain
Lanchester, J. Fragrant Harbor
Lansdale, J. Edge of dark water
Lawton, J. Then we take Berlin
Le Guin, U. Orsinian tales
Lea, C. The glass woman
Leavitt, D. The two Hotel Francforts
Lebrecht, N. The song of names
Lee, J. The starlet and the spy
Lee, M. Pachinko
Lehane, D. The given day
Lehane, D. Live by night
Leimbach, M. The man from Saigon
Leine, K. The prophets of Eternal Fjord
Leithauser, B. The art student's war
Lent, J. Lost nation
Lent, J. A slant of light
Letts, E. Finding Dorothy
Leveen, L. The secrets of Mary Bowser

Levi, P. If not now, when?
Levitt, P. Come with me to Babylon
Levy, A. The long song
Levy, A. Small island
Li, Y. The vagrants
Liardet, F. We must be brave
Littell, R. The Mayakovsky tapes
Littell, R. The Stalin epigram
Llewellyn, R. How green was my valley
Llywelyn, M. 1916
Llywelyn, M. 1921
Llywelyn, M. 1949
Llywelyn, M. After Rome
Lock, N. American meteor
Lock, N. A fugitive in Walden Woods
Loh, V. Breaking the tongue , by Vyvyane Loh.
Loigman, L. The two-family house
Loigman, L. The wartime sisters
London, J. The golden age
Lourie, R. A hatred for tulips
Lowenthal, M. Charity girl
Lyndon, R. Hawk quest
Lyon, A. The sweet girl
Ma, J. Beijing coma
Maalouf, A. Balthasar's odyssey
Maalouf, A. Leo Africanus
Macdonald, M. Tamsin Harte
Macdonald, M. The Trevarton inheritance
Machart, B. The wake of forgiveness
Macneal, E. The doll factory
Mahfuz, N. Palace walk
Mailer, N. Ancient evenings
Mailer, N. The castle in the forest
Majmudar, A. Partitions
Makine, A. Music of a life
Mallinson, A. A close run thing
Mallon, T. Bandbox
Mallon, T. Fellow travelers
Mallon, T. Watergate
Malouf, D. Ransom
Malouf, D. Remembering Babylon
Mamet, D. Chicago
Mangan, C. Tangerine
Manicka, R. The rice mother
Manning, K. My notorious life
Mantel, H. Bring up the bodies
Mantel, H. Wolf Hall
Marlantes, K. Deep river
Marlantes, K. Matterhorn
Martin, V. Property
Martin, W. Cape Cod
Mason, D. The piano tuner
Mason, R. Who killed Piet Barol?
Mathews, B. The world of tomorrow
Mathis, A. The twelve tribes of Hattie
Matthiessen, P. Bone by bone
Matthiessen, P. Killing Mister Watson

Otsuka, J. The Buddha in the attic

Oz, A. Don't call it night

Oz, A. Panther in the basement

Ozick, C. Heir to the glimmering world

Palmer, D. Mary Toft; or, the rabbit queen

Parini, J. The passages of H.M.

Parks, S. Getting mother's body

Parmar, P. Vanessa and her sister

Paton, A. Ah, but your land is beautiful

Patterson, M. Rebellion

Paul, G. The lost daughter

Paulits, J. Kemosabe

Pears, I. The dream of Scipio

Peebles, F. The seamstress

Peebles, F. The air you breathe

Penman, S. Devil's brood

Penman, S. Falls the shadow

Penman, S. Here be dragons

Penman, S. A king's ransom

Penman, S. Lionheart

Penman, S. The reckoning

Penman, S. The sunne in splendour

Penman, S. Time and chance

Penman, S. When Christ and his saints slept

Penney, S. Under a pole star

Perez-Reverte, A. What we become

Perkins-Valdez, D. Wench

Perry, A. No graves as yet

Perry, A. Shoulder the sky

Perry, S. The Essex serpent

Pesci, D. Amistad

Peters, R. Hell or Richmond

Phillips, A. Prague

Phillips, C. Dancing in the dark

Phillips, C. Foreigners

Phillips, C. A view of the empire at sunset

Phillips, J. Lark and Termite

Phillips, J. Quiet dell

Piatote, B. The beadworkers

Piercy, M. Gone to soldiers

Piercy, M. Sex wars

Pietroni, A. Ruby's spoon

Pilcher, R. Coming home

Pipkin, J. Woodsburner

Pistalo, V. Tesla

Pitts, L. Freeman

Plaidy, J. The captive Queen of Scots

Plaidy, J. Murder most royal

Plaidy, J. The pleasures of love

Plaidy, J. William's wife

Plain, B. Crescent City

Plain, B. The golden cup

Plain, B. Harvest

Plain, B. Tapestry

Powning, B. The sea captain's wife

Poyer, D. A country of our own

Poyer, D. Fire on the waters

Prescott, L. The secrets we kept

Preston, C. The scrapbook of Frankie Pratt

Proulx, A. Accordion crimes

Proulx, A. Barkskins

Purcell, L. The silent companions

Puzo, M. The family

Pynchon, T. Against the day

Pynchon, T. Mason & Dixon

Pywell, S. What happened to Henry

Quinn, K. Ribbons of scarlet

Rabb, J. Among the living

Rachman, T. The Italian teacher

Ramzipoor, E. The ventriloquists

Randel, W. The empress of bright moon

Rash, R. The cove

Rash, R. Serena

Rawles, N. My Jim

Ray, K. No country

Raymond, J. The half-life

Read, P. Alice in exile

Reddi, R. Passage west

Redhill, M. Consolation

Reed, I. Mumbo jumbo

Reisman, N. The first desire

Remarque, E. A time to love and a time to die

Renault, M. The bull from the sea

Renault, M. Funeral games

Renault, M. The king must die

Renault, M. The last of the wine

Renault, M. The Persian boy

Reuss, F. Mohr

Rhodes, J. Voodoo dreams

Rhys, J. Wide Sargasso Sea

Richler, N. Your mouth is lovely

Riley, J. In pursuit of the green lion

Riley, J. The serpent garden

Riley, J. A vision of light

Rizzuto, R. Shadow child

Robbins, D. Last citadel

Robbins, D. War of the rats

Roberts, M. Ignorance

Robertson, I. The Paris winter

Robinson, M. Gilead

Rogan, C. The lifeboat

Roiphe, A. An imperfect lens

Rolvaag, O. Giants in the Earth

Romano-Lax, A. The Spanish bow

Rooney, K. Lillian Boxfish takes a walk

Rose, M. Cartier's hope

Rose, M. Tiffany blues

Rosen, R. Dollface

Rosenberg, J. Confessions of the fox

Rosnay, T. Sarah's key

Rosner, J. The yellow bird sings

Rotert, R. Last night at the blue angel

Roth, P. Nemesis

Rothmann, R. To die in spring

Stott, R. The coral thief
Straight, S. A million nightingales
Stratford, S. Red letter days
Styron, W. The confessions of Nat Turner
Styron, W. Sophie's choice
Sundaresan, I. The splendor of silence
Suri, M. The age of Shiva
Swift, G. Mothering Sunday
Szabo, M. Abigail
Tademy, L. Cane River
Tan, A. The Joy Luck Club
Tan, A. The Valley of Amazement
Tan, T. The garden of evening mists
Taseer, A. The way things were
Thelen, A. The island of second sight
Thomas, D. The white hotel
Toibin, C. The master
Toibin, C. The testament of Mary
Tolstoy, L. War and peace
Towles, A. A gentleman in Moscow
Towles, A. Rules of civility
Tremain, R. The colour
Tremain, R. Music & silence
Treuer, D. Prudence
Trevanian The summer of Katya
Truong, M. The book of salt, Monique Truong.
Tsukiyama, G. The street of a thousand blossoms
Tsypkin, L. Summer in Baden-Baden
Turner, N. My name is Resolute
Twain, M. Personal recollections of Joan of Arc
Unsworth, B. Land of marvels
Unsworth, B. The quality of mercy
Unsworth, B. Sacred hunger
Unsworth, B. The songs of the kings
Updike, J. Gertrude and Claudius
Uris, L. Armageddon
Uris, L. Exodus
Uris, L. Mila 18
Uris, L. Redemption
Uris, L. Trinity
Urquhart, J. The night stages
Urquhart, R. The visionist
Urrea, L. The hummingbird's daughter
Urrea, L. Queen of America
Van Booy, S. The illusion of separateness
Vanderbes, J. Easter Island
Vargas Llosa, M. The dream of the Celt
Vargas Llosa, M. The war of the end of the world
Vargas Llosa, M. The way to paradise
Veletzos, R. The girl they left behind
Verble, M. Cherokee America
Vidal, G. 1876
Vidal, G. Burr
Vidal, G. Empire
Vidal, G. The golden age
Vidal, G. Hollywood
Vidal, G. Lincoln

Vidal, G. Washington, D. C.
Vollmann, W. Europe central
Vreeland, S. Clara and Mr. Tiffany
Vreeland, S. Luncheon of the boating party
Vreeland, S. The passion of Artemisia
Wall, C. The dearly beloved
Wallace, L. Ben-Hur
Walters, M. The last hours
Warren, R. Band of angels
Warren, R. World enough and time
Wascom, K. The blood of heaven
Waters, S. Fingersmith
Waters, S. The little stranger
Waters, S. The night watch
Waters, S. The paying guests
Waters, S. Tipping the velvet
Watson, B. Miss Jane
Watson, L. Let him go
Weiner, J. Mrs. Everything
Weir, A. Anna of Kleve
Weir, A. A dangerous inheritance
Weir, A. Innocent traitor
Weir, A. The Lady Elizabeth
Welch, J. The heartsong of Charging Elk
Welty, E. The robber bridegroom
Werfel, F. The forty days of Musa Dagh
West, J. The friendly persuasion
Whitehead, C. The Nickel boys
Whitehead, C. The underground railroad
Wieland, L. Paris, 7 a.m.
Wiggins, M. Evidence of things unseen
Williams, B. All the ways we said goodbye
Williams, B. The golden hour
Williams, B. The summer wives
Willig, L. The summer country
Willocks, T. The religion
Winawer, M. The scribe of Siena
Wingate, L. Before we were yours
Winslow, D. In West Mills
Winterson, J. The passion
Winthrop, E. The mercy seat
Wolfe, P. The lost diary of M
Wood, S. The Quintland sisters
Wood, T. The engineer's wife
Woodrell, D. The Maid's Version
Wouk, H. The Caine mutiny
Wouk, H. War and remembrance
Wouk, H. The winds of war
Wuertz, Y. Everything belongs to us
Yanique, T. Land of love and drowning
Yoon, P. Run me to earth
Yourcenar, M. Memoirs of Hadrian
Zola, E. Nana

HISTORICAL HORROR
Katsu, A. The deep
Katsu, A. The hunger
Owen, L. The quick

King, L. The beekeeper's apprentice
King, L. The game
Lansdale, J. A fine dark line
Lansdale, J. Sunset and sawdust
Lansdale, J. The thicket
Lawrence, M. Hearts and bones
Levack, S. Demon of the air
Liss, D. A spectacle of corruption
Lloyd, C. Death comes to the nursery
Lovesey, P. Waxwork
MacNeal, S. The king's justice
Marston, E. The bawdy basket
Marston, E. The devil's apprentice
Marston, E. The roaring boy
Marston, E. The vagabond clown
Marston, E. The wanton angel
Mason, T. The Darwin affair
Massey, S. The Satapur moonstone
Massey, S. The widows of Malabar Hill
McCrumb, S. The ballad of Frankie Silver
McCrumb, S. The ballad of Tom Dooley
McCrumb, S. She walks these hills
McPherson, C. A step so grave
Meyer, N. The adventure of the peculiar protocols
Meyer, N. The seven-per-cent solution
Montclair, A. The right sort of man
Montero, M. Dancing to "Almendra"
Moore, G. The Sherlockian
Morrell, D. Murder as a fine art
Morrell, D. Ruler of the night
Morton, C. Stealing Mona Lisa
Mosley, W. Bad boy Brawly Brown
Mosley, W. Black Betty
Mosley, W. Blonde faith
Mosley, W. Charcoal Joe
Mosley, W. Cinnamon kiss
Mosley, W. Devil in a blue dress
Mosley, W. Fearless Jones
Mosley, W. Little green
Mosley, W. Little Scarlet
Mosley, W. A little yellow dog
Mosley, W. A red death
Mosley, W. Rose gold
Mosley, W. Six Easy pieces
Mosley, W. White butterfly
Mukherjee, A. A necessary evil
Mukherjee, A. Smoke and ashes
Mukherjee, A. A rising man
Mullen, T. Darktown
Mullen, T. Lightning men
Natt och Dag, N. The wolf and the watchman
Nelscott, K. Days of rage
Nelscott, K. Stone cribs
Neubauer, E. Murder at the Mena House
Nickson, C. At the dying of the year
Nickson, C. Cold cruel winter
Nickson, C. Come the fear

Nickson, C. The constant lovers
Nickson, C. Gods of gold
Nickson, C. The hocus girl
Nickson, C. On Copper Street
O'Connor, J. Star of the Sea
O'Malley, T. Serpents in the cold
O'Malley, T. We were kings
Pajer, B. Capacity for murder
Pajer, B. The Edison effect
Pajer, B. Fatal induction
Pajer, B. A spark of death
Palliser, C. The quincunx
Palliser, C. Rustication
Palliser, C. The unburied
Pamuk, O. My name is Red
Parker, R. Double play
Parris, S. Sacrilege
Parris, S. Treachery
Parry, A. The way of all flesh
Pattison, E. Blood of the oak
Pawel, R. Death of a nationalist
Pearce, M. A dead man in Barcelona
Pearl, M. The Dante chamber
Pearl, M. The Dante Club
Pearl, M. The last Dickens
Pearl, M. The Poe shadow
Pearl, M. The technologists
Pears, I. An instance of the fingerpost
Pears, I. Stone's fall
Penman, S. Cruel as the grave
Penman, S. Dragon's lair
Penman, S. The Queen's man
Penney, S. The tenderness of wolves
Penrose, A. Murder at half moon gate
Penrose, A. Murder at Kensington Palace
Perez-Reverte, A. The siege
Penrose, A. Murder on Black Swan Lane
Perry, A. Bluegate Fields
Perry, A. Blood on the water
Perry, A. A breach of promise
Perry, A. Buckingham Palace gardens
Perry, A. Cain his brother
Perry, A. Cardington Crescent
Perry, A. A Christmas message
Perry, A. A Christmas return
Perry, A. A dangerous mourning
Perry, A. Dark tide rising
Perry, A. Death in focus
Perry, A. Death of a stranger
Perry, A. Death on Blackheath
Perry, A. Defend and betray
Perry, A. The face of a stranger
Perry, A. Farriers' Lane
Perry, A. Funeral in blue
Perry, A. Half Moon Street
Perry, A. Highgate Rise
Perry, A. The Hyde Park headsman

Saylor, S. Rubicon

Saylor, S. The seven wonders

Saylor, S. The triumph of Caesar

Saylor, S. Wrath of the furies

Scoppettone, S. Too darn hot

Sedgwick, M. Mister Memory

Sedley, K. The Tintern treasure

Sepetys, R. Out of the Easy

Shaw, W. A song for the brokenhearted

Shepherd, L. A fatal likeness

Shepherd, L. The Solitary House

Shields, K. A study in revenge

Shields, K. The truth of all things

Simmons, D. Drood

Simmons, D. The fifth heart

Simpson, R. Let the dead keep their secrets

Simpson, R. What the dead leave behind

Smith, D. The constable's tale

Smith, M. Stallion Gate

Solomon, B. The attempted murder of Teddy Roosevelt

Solomon, B. The murder of Willie Lincoln

Spann, S. Claws of the cat

Spann, S. Blade of the Samurai

Spann, S. Trial on Mount Koya

Speller, E. The return of Captain John Emmett

Speller, E. The strange fate of Kitty Easton

Starr, M. Unhallowed ground

Stewart, A. Kopp sisters on the march

Stewart, A. Lady cop makes trouble

Stewart, A. Miss Kopp just won't quit

Stewart, A. Miss Kopp's midnight confessions

Stewart, D. The Babe Ruth deception

Straley, J. The big both ways

Street, K. Edgar Allan Poe and the jewel of Peru

Tallis, F. Vienna blood

Thomson, E. Beloved poison

Thomson, E. The blood

Truss, L. The man that got away

Welsh, K. The unquiet heart

Welsh, K. The wages of sin

Winspear, J. The American agent

Winspear, J. Birds of a feather

Winspear, J. Maisie Dobbs

Wojtas, O. Miss Blaine's prefect and the golden samovar

Wolfe, S. The course of all treasons

Yi, C. The investigation

Zimler, R. The last Kabbalist of Lisbon

Zimler, R. The seventh gate

Zimmerman, J. The orphanmaster

HISTORICAL REENACTMENTS

Moss, S. Ghost wall

Palahniuk, C. Choke

Sherrill, S. The minotaur takes his own sweet time

HISTORICAL RESEARCH

Phoenix, M. The space between words

HISTORICAL ROMANCES

Alexander, V. The Lady Travelers Guide to larceny with a
dashing stranger

Alexander, V. The Lady Travelers Guide to scoundrels and
other gentlemen

Alexander, V. What happens at Christmas

Archer, Z. Dangerous seduction

Ashe, K. The duke

Ashe, K. The earl

Ashe, K. The prince

Ashford, J. Heir to the duke

Ashford, J. Lord Sebastian's secret

Ashford, J. What the duke doesn't know

Ashley, J. Lady Isabella's scandalous marriage

Ashley, J. The madness of Lord Ian Mackenzie

Balogh, M. The arrangement

Balogh, M. The escape

Balogh, M. More than a mistress

Balogh, M. Only enchanting

Balogh, M. The secret mistress

Balogh, M. Simply love

Balogh, M. Someone to hold

Balogh, M. Someone to love

Balogh, M. Someone to remember

Balogh, M. Someone to trust

Balogh, M. Someone to wed

Banks, M. Never seduce a Scot

Bateman, K. This earl of mine

Bell, L. For the duke's eyes only

Bell, L. How the duke was won

Bell, L. One fine duke

Bell, L. What a difference a duke makes

Bennett, A. First earl I see tonight

Berne, L. You may kiss the bride

Beverley, J. Devilish

Beverley, J. My lady notorious

Beverley, J. Something wicked

Beverley, J. Tempting fortune

Bittner, R. Logan's lady

Bonner, C. Lily

Bourne, J. The black hawk

Bourne, J. The forbidden rose

Bourne, J. My lord and spymaster

Bourne, J. Rogue spy

Bourne, J. The spymaster's lady

Bowen, K. Between the devil and the duke

Bowen, K. I've got my duke to keep me warm

Bowen, K. A rogue by night

Bowman, V. The accidental countess

Bowman, V. Secrets of a wedding night

Bowman, V. The unexpected duchess

Boyle, E. Along came a duke

Boyle, E. And the miss ran away with the rake

Bradley, A. A season of ruin

Bradley, A. A wicked way to win an earl

Brockway, C. The golden season

Brockway, C. No place for a dame

Brockway, C. So enchanting

Burrowes, G. The bridegroom wore plaid

McLayne, A. Highland promise
McQuiston, J. The spinster's guide to scandalous behavior
Michels, E. The rebel heir
Milan, C. The duchess war
Moore, K. To seduce an angel
Nash, S. Between the Duke and the deep blue sea
Noble, K. The game and the governess
Putney, M. A kiss of fate
Putney, M. Loving a lost lord
Putney, M. The marriage spell
Putney, M. No longer a gentleman
Putney, M. Not quite a wife
Putney, M. Nowhere near respectable
Putney, M. Once a soldier
Quick, A. The girl who knew too much
Quick, A. I thee wed
Quick, A. The other lady vanishes
Quick, A. Slightly shady
Quick, A. 'Til death do us part
Quinn, J. The lady most willing
Quinn, J. An offer from a gentleman
Quinn, J. The secrets of Sir Richard Kenworthy
Ranney, K. The Scottish duke
Raybourn, D. Silent in the grave
Rodale, M. Lady Bridget's diary
Romain, T. Fortune favors the wicked
Rosenthal, P. The bookseller's daughter
Rosenthal, P. The edge of impropriety
Sebastian, C. It takes two to tumble
Sebastian, C. The Lawrence Browne affair
Shupe, J. The courtesan duchess
Shupe, J. The prince of Broadway
Shupe, J. The rogue of Fifth Avenue
Spencer, M. Barbarous
Spencer, M. Dangerous
Spencer, M. Scandalous
Thomas, S. Beguiling the beauty
Thomas, S. The luckiest lady in London
Thomas, S. My beautiful enemy
Thomas, S. Not quite a husband
Thomas, S. Private arrangements
Thomas, S. Ravishing the heiress
Thomas, S. Tempting the bride
Waite, O. The lady's guide to celestial mechanics
Wallace, C. The blind contessa's new machine
Willig, L. The betrayal of the blood lily
Willig, L. The deception of the emerald ring
Willig, L. The garden intrigue
Willig, L. The lure of the moonflower
Willig, L. The masque of the Black Tulip
Willig, L. The orchid affair
Willig, L. The secret history of the Pink Carnation
Willig, L. The seduction of the Crimson Rose
Willig, L. The temptation of the night jasmine

HISTORICAL SOCIETIES
McLarty, R. Art in America

HISTORICAL THRILLERS

Black, B. The secret guests
Black, C. Three hours in Paris
Burke, J. House of the rising sun
Burnet, G. His bloody project
Butler, R. The hot country
Butler, R. Paris in the dark
Cussler, C. The chase
Cussler, C. The cutthroat
Cussler, C. The Titanic secret
Cussler, C. The wrecker
Deutermann, P. The Iceman
Deutermann, P. The nugget
Downing, D. Diary of a dead man on leave
Dunmore, H. Exposure
Fleischmann, R. How quickly she disappears
Follett, K. Eye of the needle
Follett, K. Jackdaws
Furnivall, K. The red scarf
Furst, A. Blood of victory
Furst, A. Dark voyage
Furst, A. The foreign correspondent
Furst, A. A hero of France
Furst, A. Mission to Paris
Furst, A. Under occupation
Furst, A. Spies of the Balkans
Furst, A. The spies of Warsaw
Goldstone, L. Assassin of shadows
Gross, A. The one man
Harris, R. Enigma
Harris, R. An officer and a spy
Higgins, J. The eagle has flown
Higgins, J. The eagle has landed
Higgins, J. Flight of eagles
Higgins, J. Luciano's luck
Higgins, J. Night of the fox
Horn, D. All other nights
King, R. Domino
Koryta, M. The Cypress House
Latour, J. The Havana World Series
Lehane, D. World gone by
Lippman, L. Lady in the lake
McGuire, I. The North water
Moore, G. The last days of night
Murphy, Y. Signed, Mata Hari
Neville, S. Ratlines
O'Brien, T. The Lincoln conspiracy
Perez-Reverte, A. Captain Alatriste
Phillips, A. The king at the edge of the world
Quinn, K. The huntress
Rindell, S. The other typist
Schutt, B. The Darwin strain
Scott, J. Tourmaline
Smith, T. Agent 6
Smith, T. Child 44
Smith, M. December 6
Smith, T. The secret speech
Steinhauer, O. The Bridge of Sighs

HOLIDAY MYSTERIES

Andrews, D. Owl be home for Christmas
Avon, J. In peppermint peril
Berry, C. A legacy of murder
Hart, C. Yankee Doodle dead
McKevett, G. Murder in her stocking
Shaw, M. Murder at the mill

HOLIDAY ROMANCES

Alexander, V. What happens at Christmas
Balogh, M. Someone to trust
Blackstock, T. Catching Christmas
Bryant, N. Christmas with the billionaire
Burrowes, G. Lady Sophie's Christmas wish
Guillory, J. Royal holiday
Kleypas, L. Christmas Eve at Friday Harbor
Laurens, S. By winter's light
Morgan, S. Miracle on 5th Avenue
Snow, J. An Alaskan Christmas

HOLIDAYS -- UNITED STATES

Sedaris, D. Holidays on ice
Holidays on ice Sedaris, D.
Holland family saga [series] Burke, J.

HOLLIDAY, JOHN H, 1851-1887

Parker, R. Gunman's rhapsody
Russell, M. Doc
Russell, M. Epitaph
The **hollow** Christie, A.
The **hollow** hills Stewart, M.
Hollow kingdom Buxton, K.
Hollow man Pryor, M.
Hollow man [series] Pryor, M.
The **hollow** men McCarthy, R.
Hollows novels (Lisa Unger) [series] Unger, L.
Holly Barker novels [series] Woods, S.
Hollywood Vidal, G.

HOLLYWOOD BLACKLIST

Stratford, S. Red letter days
Hollywood homicide Garrett, K.

HOLLYWOOD, CALIFORNIA

Alcott, K. A touch of stardust
Allen, J. I lost my girlish laughter
Bagshawe, T. Adored
Benedict, M. The only woman in the room
Brunkhorst, A. The gilded Life of Matilda Duplaine
Childress, M. Crazy in Alabama
Connelly, M. Dark sacred night
Connelly, M. The late show
Ephron, H. Night night, sleep tight
Estleman, L. Frames
Fitzgerald, F. The last tycoon
Garrett, K. Hollywood homicide
Hallinan, T. Fields where they lay
Jhabvala, R. My nine lives
Kaminsky, S. A fatal glass of beer
Kaminsky, S. Tomorrow is another day
Kaminsky, S. To catch a spy
Kaminsky, S. Dancing in the dark

Lauren, C. Dating you
Leonard, E. Be cool
Leonard, E. Get Shorty
Oates, J. Blonde
Phillips, S. What I did for love
Puzo, M. The last don
Quick, A. The girl who knew too much
Quick, A. The other lady vanishes
Rivers, F. Bridge to haven
Sarvas, M. Memento Park
Schulberg, B. What makes Sammy run?
Stratford, S. Red letter days
Vidal, G. Hollywood
Woods, S. The money shot

HOLLYWOOD, CALIFORNIA -- HISTORY -- 20TH CENTURY

Bloom, A. Lucky us
Pynchon, T. Against the day
Smith, D. The electric hotel

HOLLYWOOD, CALIFORNIA -- SOCIAL LIFE AND CUSTOMS

Waugh, E. The loved one
Holmes on the range Hockensmith, S.
Holmes on the range mysteries [series] Hockensmith, S.

HOLMES, OLIVER WENDELL, 1809-1894

Pearl, M. The Dante Club

HOLOCAUST (1933-1945)

Albahari, D. Gotz and Meyer
Amis, M. Time's arrow, or The nature of the offense
Amis, M. The zone of interest
Apelfeld, A. To the edge of sorrow
Auslander, S. Hope
Bassani, G. The garden of the Finzi-Continis
Clayton, M. The last train to London
D'Eramo, L. Deviation
Englander, N. What we talk about when we talk about Anne Frank
Erpenbeck, J. Visitation
Foer, J. Everything is illuminated
Gross, A. The one man
Harris, R. Fatherland
Hoffman, A. The world that we knew
Iles, G. Black cross
Kosinski, J. The painted bird
Krall, H. Chasing the king of hearts
Matthiessen, P. In paradise
McCann, C. Zoli
Orringer, J. The flight portfolio
Picoult, J. The storyteller
Plain, B. Tapestry
Roberts, M. Ignorance
Rosner, J. The yellow bird sings
Russell, M. A thread of grace
Sebald, W. Austerlitz
Sebald, W. The emigrants ;, W. G. Sebald ; translated by Michael Hulse.
Seiffert, R. A boy in winter

Mina, D. Still midnight
Phillips, H. The need
Slaughter, K. The good daughter
Tremblay, P. The cabin at the end of the world

HOME NURSING

Berg, E. Never change

HOME OWNERSHIP

Hoffman, A. Blackbird house
Mosley, W. The man in my basement
Roberts, N. Midnight Bayou

Home sweet homicide Rice, C.

The **homecoming** Pyper, A.

HOMECOMING (SCHOOL)

Sparks, N. A walk to remember

HOMECOMINGS

Banks, I. The crow road
Bijan, D. The last days of Cafe Leila
Blackstock, T. Smoke screen
Bond, C. Ruby
Boyne, J. The house of special purpose
Bradley, C. Thrice the brinded cat hath mew'd
Brown, S. White hot
Butler, S. Ten things I've learnt about love
Bybee, C. Staying for good
Byrne, T. Ghosts and lightning
Cleage, P. What looks like crazy on an ordinary day
Cole, T. Every day is for the thief
Coster, N. Halsey Street
D'Agostino, K. The antiques
Dicks, M. The perfect comeback of Caroline Jacobs
Dundas, C. The blaze
Fielding, J. The bad daughter
Fowler, E. The road to Cardinal Valley
Francis, D. Wedding Bush Road
Frank, D. Folly Beach
Fuller, C. Our endless numbered days
Gottlieb, E. Best boy
Groff, L. Arcadia
Guhrke, L. How to lose a duke in ten days
Hart, E. City of ink
Hauck, R. The wedding chapel
Higgins, K. The best man
Higgins, K. Now that you mention it
Hill, R. The woodcutter
Jones, S. The outcast
Kennedy, W. Ironweed
King, S. It
Kneale, M. When we were Romans
Lasser, S. Say nice things about Detroit
Lee, H. Go set a watchman
Lennon, J. Castle
Lim, R. Natalie Tan's book of luck and fortune
London, J. The charmer in chaps
Majors, I. Penelope Lemon
Markley, S. Ohio
Marlette, D. Magic time
Martin, C. Long way gone

McCall Smith, A. The Double Comfort Safari Club
McFadden, B. Gathering of waters
McHugh, L. Arrowood
McLaren, K. The road to enchantment
Morgan, S. The Christmas sisters
Mukherjee, N. A state of freedom
Nichols, L. Vessel
Okorafor, N. Binti
Phillips, C. Perfect fit
Phillips, S. Heroes are my weakness
Price, R. The good priest's son
Ratner, V. Music of the ghosts
Redondo, D. The invisible guardian
  The road ahead
Robinson, M. Home
Shalvis, J. Second chance summer
Singh, N. A madness of sunshine
Smith, M. Blackwood
Starr, J. Lights out
Strout, E. The Burgess boys
Trollope, J. Second honeymoon
Tyree, O. For the love of money
Weiner, J. Little earthquakes
Wiggs, S. The Oysterville sewing circle

HOMECOMINGS -- NEW YORK (STATE)

Potok, C. The gift of Asher Lev

Homegoing Gyasi, Y.

Homeland Aramburu, F.

HOMELESS FAMILIES

Clement, J. Gun love

HOMELESS MEN

Arnaldur Indridason, 1. Reykjavik nights
Butler, S. Ten things I've learnt about love
Coetzee, J. Age of Iron
Cullin, M. Undersurface
Haddam, J. Hardscrabble road
Pronzini, B. Spook

HOMELESS MEN -- NEW ORLEANS, LOUISIANA

Cotter, B. Fever chart

HOMELESS PEOPLE WITH MENTAL ILLNESSES

Pronzini, B. Spook

HOMELESS PERSONS

Banks, R. Lost memory of skin
Butler, R. Perfume River
Kubica, M. Pretty baby
Manfredi, V. A winter's night
McGregor, J. Even the dogs
Muller, M. There's something in a Sunday
Palmer, M. The last surgeon
Paretsky, S. Tunnel vision
Steinbeck, J. Cannery Row
Vollmann, W. The rainbow stories

HOMELESS TEENAGERS

Burns, C. Black hole
Guterson, D. Our Lady of the Forest
Haruf, K. Plainsong
Lippman, L. No good deeds

Camus, A. The stranger
Deb, S. The point of return
Hoffman, A. The story sisters
Meloy, M. Liars and saints
Pinborough, S. Cross her heart
Smith, A. The accidental

Honeydew Pearlman, E.

Honeymooners Kinder, C.

HONEYMOONS

Cheek, C. Cape May
Estleman, L. Something borrowed, something black
Greene, G. Collected stories
Grippando, J. Black horizon
McEwan, I. Black dogs
O'Nan, S. The odds
Sayers, D. Busman's honeymoon
Steadman, C. Something in the water

HONG KONG

Gardam, J. The man in the wooden hat
Gardam, J. Old Filth
Hazzard, S. The great fire
Lanchester, J. Fragrant Harbor
Nesbo, J. The leopard

HONG KONG -- HISTORY -- 1997-

Westlake, D. Forever and a death

Honky tonk samurai Lansdale, J.

HONOR

Alexis, A. The hidden keys
Clavell, J. Shogun
Kay, G. Under heaven
Kerstan, L. Heart of the tiger
Kirk, D. Sword of honor
Richardson, S. Pamela
Shafak, E. Honor

Honor Crownover, J.

Honor Shafak, E.

Honor Harrington novels. Main series [series] Weber, D.

Honor Harrington novels. Saganami Island [series] Weber, D.

HONOR IN MEN

Conrad, J. Lord Jim
Higgins, J. Edge of danger
Parker, R. Appaloosa
Parker, R. Blue-eyed devil

HONOR KILLINGS

Aslam, N. Maps for lost lovers
Bilal, P. The ghost runner
Shafak, E. Honor

The **honor** of the queen Weber, D.

Honor thy thug Clark, W.

The **honorary** consul Greene, G.

The **honourable** schoolboy Le Carre, J.

Hood rat novels [series] K'wan

Hoodlum K'wan

HOODOO

Reed, I. Mumbo jumbo

Hook Runyon mysteries [series] Russell, S.

Hoops (Kennedy Ryan) [series] Ryan, K.

HOOVER, J EDGAR, 1895-1972

Berry, S. The bishop's pawn
Ellroy, J. The cold six thousand

Hop-Ciki-Yaya mysteries [series] Somer, M.

HOPE

Afshar, T. Thief of Corinth
Bauermeister, E. The school of essential ingredients
Couto, M. Rain
Danticat, E. The dew breaker
Desai, K. The inheritance of loss
Fowler, E. The road to Cardinal Valley
Gilman, F. The half-made world
Grushin, O. The line
Levitt, P. Come with me to Babylon
Lopez Barrio, C. The house of the impossible loves
Lynn, A. Now you see it
McCann, C. Let the great world spin
Meyer, P. American rust
Quindlen, A. Every last one
Simpson, M. Anywhere but here
Singer, I. Collected stories

Hope Auslander, S.

HOPE (CHRISTIANITY)

White, R. A lady unrivaled

HOPE DIAMOND

Rose, M. Cartier's hope

A **hope** divided Cole, A.

The **hope** factory Sankaran, L.

HOPE IN BOYS

Vlautin, W. Lean on Pete

Hope River novels [series] Harman, P.

HOPI INDIANS -- SPIRITUAL LIFE

Picoult, J. Vanishing acts

Hopscotch Cortazar, J.

Horace Winter says goodbye Bowman, C.

Horatio Hornblower saga [series] Forester, C.

Hornblower and the Atropos Forester, C.

Hornblower and the Hotspur Forester, C.

HORNER, SALLY

Greenwood, T. Rust & stardust

Hornet flight Follett, K.

Horns Hill, J.

HORROR

Ahlborn, A. The devil crept in
American fantastic tales
Ajvide Lindqvist, J. Let the right one in
Barnes, S. Domino Falls
Benchley, P. Jaws
Bennett, R. American elsewhere
Bennett, R. The troupe
The best of the best horror of the year
Blatty, W. The exorcist
Bohjalian, C. The night strangers
Bradbury, R. The illustrated man
Bradbury, R. Something wicked this way comes
Brooks, M. World War Z

St. James, S. The Sun Down motel
Stevenson, R. The strange case of Dr. Jekyll and Mr. Hyde
Stoker, B. Dracula
Stoker, B. The new annotated Dracula
Stoker, D. Dracul
Straub, P. Ghost story
Straub, P. Mr. X
Straub, P. Lost boy lost girl
Straub, P. A dark matter
Suskind, P. Perfume
Toro, G. The strain
Tremblay, P. The cabin at the end of the world
Tremblay, P. Disappearance at Devil's Rock
Tremblay, P. Growing things and other stories
Tremblay, P. A head full of ghosts
Vandelly, T. Theme music
Waters, S. The little stranger
Wellington, D. Positive
Wells, H. The island of Dr. Moreau
Whitehead, C. Zone one
Wolfe, G. The land across
Wong, D. John dies at the end
Wong, D. This book is full of spiders

HORROR FILM PRODUCERS AND DIRECTORS --
HOLLYWOOD, CALIFORNIA
Leonard, E. Get Shorty

HORROR FILMS
Gerritsen, T. I know a secret

HORROR STORIES
Grant, H. The glass demon

HORROR STORY AUTHORS
King, S. Misery
Phillips, S. Heroes are my weakness

HORSE BREEDERS
Machart, B. The wake of forgiveness
McLain, P. Circling the sun

HORSE BREEDING
Morgan, C. The sport of kings

HORSE FARMS
Hatcher, R. Cross my heart
Smith, B. Shoot the dog
Horse heaven Smiley, J.

HORSE RACE BETTING
Pufahl, S. On swift horses

HORSE RACING
Francis, D. Smokescreen
Francis, F. Crisis
Francis, F. Guilty not guilty
Francis, F. Pulse
Gordon, J. Lord of misrule
Machart, B. The wake of forgiveness
Morgan, C. The sport of kings
Parker, R. Hugger Mugger
Smiley, J. Horse heaven

HORSE RACING INDUSTRY AND TRADE
Gordon, J. Lord of misrule

HORSE STEALING

McMurtry, L. Lonesome Dove
HORSE STEALING -- TEXAS
McMurtry, L. Comanche moon
HORSE THEFTS
Dobyns, S. Saratoga payback
HORSE TRAINERS
Gloss, M. The hearts of horses
Gordon, J. Lord of misrule
McLain, P. Circling the sun
Meyers, K. The work of wolves
Stansel, I. The last cowboys of San Geronimo
HORSE TRAINING -- NORTHERN MEXICO
McCarthy, C. All the pretty horses
A **horse** walks into a bar Grossman, D.
The **horse** whisperer Evans, N.
HORSE WHISPERERS
Evans, N. The horse whisperer
The **horse's** mouth Cary, J.
HORSES
Evans, N. The horse whisperer
Gaitskill, M. The mare
Gloss, M. The hearts of horses
Greaves, C. Hush money
Kay, G. Under heaven
McCarthy, C. All the pretty horses
Meno, J. Marvel and a wonder
Meyers, K. The work of wolves
Smith, B. Shoot the dog
HORTICULTURE
White, B. Quite a year for plums
HOSPITAL ADMINISTRATORS
Kellerman, J. Devil's waltz
HOSPITAL CARE
Strout, E. My name is Lucy Barton
HOSPITAL PATIENTS
Bailey, P. Chapman's odyssey
Cook, R. Coma
Coupland, D. Eleanor Rigby
London, J. The golden age
Miller, R. Jacob's folly
Persson, L. The dying detective
Tey, J. The daughter of time
Ware, R. In a dark, dark wood
HOSPITAL PATIENTS -- MORTALITY
Lescroart, J. The oath
HOSPITAL WARDS
Davidson, A. The gargoyle
HOSPITALITY
Waters, S. The paying guests
HOSPITALS
Alexander, T. With this pledge
Bock, C. Alice & Oliver
Cook, R. Coma
Cook, R. Host
Forna, A. The memory of love
George, N. The book of dreams
Lawler, L. Don't wake up

Towles, A. A gentleman in Moscow
Walter, J. Beautiful ruins
Williams, B. All the ways we said goodbye

HOTELS -- SWITZERLAND

Brookner, A. Hotel Du Lac

HOTELS -- VERMONT

Lipman, E. The inn at Lake Devine
The **hottest** dishes of the Tartar cuisine Bronsky, A.
Hotwire Kava, A.
Hour of the red god Crompton, R.
The **hours** Cunningham, M.
The **house** at Riverton Morton, K.
The **house** at sea's end Griffiths, E.
The **house** at the edge of night Banner, C.

HOUSE CLEANERS

Patric, A. Black rock white city

HOUSE CLEANING

Ephron, H. Careful what you wish for

HOUSE CONSTRUCTION

Haslett, A. Union Atlantic

HOUSE DEMOLITION

Robertson, R. The long take
A **house** for Mr. Biswas Naipaul, V.
The **house** girl Conklin, T.
House made of dawn Momaday, N.
House of blues Smith, J.
The **house** of broken angels Urrea, L.
House of Earth trilogy [series] Buck, P.
House of echoes Duffy, B.
House of Falconer [series] Bradford, B.
House of Gold Solomons, N.
House of holes Baker, N.
The **house** of impossible beauties Cassara, J.
House of leaves Danielewski, M.
House of names Toibin, C.
House of Niccolo [series] Dunnett, D.
The **House** of Silk Horowitz, A.
The **house** of small shadows Nevill, A.
The **house** of special purpose Boyne, J.
House of splendid isolation O'Brien, E.
The **House** of Stairs Vine, B.
The **house** of the impossible loves Lopez Barrio, C.
House of the rising sun Burke, J.
The **house** of the seven gables Hawthorne, N.
The **house** of the spirits Allende, I.
The **house** of the stag Baker, K.
The **house** of the Vestals Saylor, S.
The **house** of tomorrow Bognanni, P.
The **house** of Wolfe Blake, J.
House on fire Finder, J.
The **house** on Foster Hill Wright, J.
The **house** on Mango Street Cisneros, S.

HOUSE PAINTERS

Starr, J. Lights out
House rules Picoult, J.

HOUSE SELLING

Hadley, T. The past

The **house** sitter Lovesey, P.
House under snow Bialosky, J.

HOUSEBOATS

Bolton, S. A dark and twisted tide
Johnson, D. Everything under

HOUSEGUESTS

Jones, S. The uninvited guests
Kane, J. Rules for visiting
Morgan, S. The Christmas sisters
Smith, A. The accidental
Smith, A. There but for the
Walker, C. Man of the year

HOUSEHOLD ACTIVITIES

Boll, H. Billiards at half-past nine
Pearson, A. How hard can it be?

HOUSEHOLD EMPLOYEES

Adiga, A. Amnesty
Atwood, M. Alias Grace
Baker, J. Longbourn
Brooks, G. Caleb's crossing
Burrowes, G. The heir
Cary, J. The horse's mouth
Cather, W. My Antonia
Christie, A. Mrs. McGinty's dead
Collins, S. The confessions of Frannie Langton
deWitt, P. Undermajordomo Minor
Dexter, C. The daughters of Cain
Doig, I. The whistling season
Du Maurier, D. Rebecca
Faulkner, W. Requiem for a nun
Fredericks, M. Death of a new American
Gaitskill, M. Veronica
Gordimer, N. July's people
Hosseini, K. The kite runner
Humphreys, H. Afterimage
Ishiguro, K. The remains of the day
King, S. Dolores Claiborne
Lambert, C. The children's home
Lessing, D. The grass is singing
Lloyd, C. Death comes to the nursery
McBain, E. Alice in jeopardy
McCaffrey, A. Dragonflight
McCall Smith, A. The comforts of a muddy Saturday
McCall Smith, A. The forgotten affairs of youth
McCullers, C. The member of the wedding
Mengiste, M. The shadow king
Morton, K. The house at Riverton
Neely, B. Blanche cleans up
O'Connor, J. Star of the Sea
Ogawa, Y. The housekeeper and the professor
Okparanta, C. Under the udala trees
Pamuk, O. Silent house
Pears, I. An instance of the fingerpost
Quinn, J. An offer from a gentleman
Ranney, K. The Scottish duke
Rendell, R. A judgement in stone
Richardson, S. Pamela

Houston series [series] McMurtry, L.
HOUSTON, TEXAS
  Burke, J. The jealous kind
  Daughters, A. You cannot mess this up
  Dow, D. Confessions of an innocent man
  McMurtry, L. Terms of endearment
  Washington, B. Lot
How are you going to save yourself Holmes, J.
How green was my valley Llewellyn, R.
How hard can it be? Pearson, A.
How it all began Lively, P.
How it happened Koryta, M.
How late it was, how late Kelman, J.
How long 'til black future month? Jemisin, N.
How quickly she disappears Fleischmann, R.
How Rory Thorne destroyed the multiverse Eason, K.
How Stella got her groove back McMillan, T.
How the dead dream Millet, L.
How the dead speak McDermid, V.
How the duke was won Bell, L.
How the Garcia girls lost their accents Alvarez, J.
How the light gets in Penny, L.
How to be both Smith, A.
How to be safe McAllister, T.
How to behave in a crowd Bordas, C.
How to catch a prince Hauck, R.
How to forget a duke Lorret, V.
How to hack a heartbreak Rockaway, K.
How to live safely in a science fictional universe Yu, C.
How to lose a duke in ten days Guhrke, L.
How to love a duke in ten days Byrne, K.
How to make an American quilt Otto, W.
How to read the air Mengestu, D.
How to tame your duke Gray, J.
How to walk away Center, K.
How we are hungry Eggers, D.
Howards End Forster, E.
Huck out west Coover, R.
HUDSON RIVER
  Seton, A. Dragonwyck
HUDSON VALLEY
  Boyle, T. World's end
  Prose, F. Primitive people
HUDSON'S BAY COMPANY.
  Aalborg, G. River of porcupines
Hugger Mugger Parker, R.
HUGHES, TED, 1930-1998
  Moses, K. Wintering
HUGUENOTS
  Laker, R. To dance with kings
  Phoenix, M. The space between words
HULL, ENGLAND
  Mark, D. The dark winter
  Mark, D. Original skin
  Mark, D. Sorrow bound
The **hum** and the shiver Bledsoe, A.
Human acts Han, K.

HUMAN BEHAVIOR
  Barnhill, K. Dreadful young ladies and other stories
  Birch, C. Jamrach's menagerie
  Boyle, T. The Terranauts
  Chiang, T. Exhalation
  Diaz, J. This is how you lose her
  Duncan, G. The last werewolf
  Enriquez, M. Things we lost in the fire
  Hendricks, G. An anonymous girl
  Mishima, Y. The frolic of the beasts
  Murakami, H. Blind willow, sleeping woman
  Murakami, H. Men without women
  Nemirovsky, I. Suite Francaise
   Not one of us
  Pynchon, T. Against the day
  Schweblin, S. Mouthful of birds
  Thompson-Spires, N. Heads of the colored people
  Woolf, V. To the lighthouse
HUMAN BODY
  Giordano, P. The human body
  Soule, C. Anyone
The **human** body Giordano, P.
HUMAN BODY PARTS INDUSTRY AND TRADE
  Kellerman, J. The clinic
  Leonard, E. Raylan
  Li, Y. The vagrants
  Palmer, M. The fifth vial
  Welsh, I. Dead men's trousers
Human capital Amidon, S.
The **human** comedy Saroyan, W.
Human croquet Atkinson, K.
HUMAN ECOLOGY
  Boyle, T. The Terranauts
HUMAN EMBRYO
  Picoult, J. Sing you home
HUMAN EVOLUTION
  Butler, O. Adulthood rites
  Butler, O. Dawn
  Butler, O. Imago
  Erdrich, L. Future home of the living god
  Golding, W. The inheritors
  Gregory, D. The devil's alphabet
  Michener, J. The covenant
  Naam, R. Nexus
  Rutherfurd, E. Sarum
  Stross, C. Glasshouse
  Suarez, D. Change agent
  Van Vogt, A. Slan
  Vonnegut, K. Galapagos
HUMAN EXPERIMENTATION IN MEDICINE
  Browne, S. Less than hero
  Cook, R. Nano
  Cronin, J. The city of mirrors
  Cronin, J. The passage
  Cronin, J. The twelve
  de Beauvoir, J. Asylum
  Goddard, R. Never go back

Johnson, C. Another man's moccasins
Levien, D. City of the sun
Luna, L. The Janes
Rao, S. Girls burn brighter
Reichs, K. Bones of the lost
Rodriguez, L. Every broken trust
Rosen, L. The Kortelisy escape
Suarez, D. Change agent
Wingate, L. Before we were yours

HUMAN TRAFFICKING VICTIMS

Cussler, C. Ghost ship
Greenwood, K. Unnatural habits
Harvey, J. Cold in hand
Hill Gumbao, T. The summer of dead toys
Hobbs, A. Stealing candy
Johnson, C. Another man's moccasins
Levien, D. City of the sun

HUMAN-ALIEN ENCOUNTERS

Lansdale, J. The complete Drive-in
Varley, J. Demon
Varley, J. Titan
Varley, J. Wizard

HUMAN-ALIEN HYBRIDS

Butler, O. Adulthood rites
Butler, O. Dawn
Butler, O. Imago
Mieville, C. Perdido Street Station

HUMAN-ANIMAL COMMUNICATION

Greenidge, K. We love you, Charlie Freeman

HUMAN-ANIMAL RELATIONSHIPS

Baume, S. Spill simmer falter wither
Greenidge, K. We love you, Charlie Freeman

HUMAN/ALIEN ENCOUNTERS

Anders, C. The city in the middle of the night
Box, C. Trophy hunt
Bradbury, R. The Martian chronicles
Brin, D. Existence
Burke, S. Semiosis
Butler, O. Dawn
Butler, O. Imago
Cambias, J. A darkling sea
Cherryh, C. Foreigner
Cunningham, M. Specimen days
Emshwiller, C. The secret city
Flynn, M. Eifelheim
Gilman, C. Dark orbit
Haig, M. The humans
Hamilton, P. Great North Road
Harrison, M. Nova swing
Heinlein, R. Starship troopers
Kress, N. If tomorrow comes
Kress, N. Tomorrow's kin
Kunzru, H. Gods without men
Lamb, A. Roboteer
Le Guin, U. The birthday of the world
Le Guin, U. The left hand of darkness
Lem, S. Eden

Lem, S. Fiasco
Lem, S. His master's voice
Lem, S. Solaris
Mieville, C. Embassytown
Not one of us
Okorafor, N. Binti
Sagan, C. Contact
Scalzi, J. Old man's war
Scalzi, J. Redshirts
Tepper, S. Grass
Thompson, T. Rosewater
Thompson, T. The Rosewater insurrection
Thompson, T. The Rosewater redemption
Turnbull, C. The lesson
Valente, C. Space opera
Vinge, V. The children of the sky
Vinge, V. A fire upon the deep
Wells, H. The war of the worlds
Wilson, D. The Andromeda evolution
Wilson, R. Blind Lake
Wilson, R. Spin
Wolfe, G. Home fires

HUMAN/ANIMAL COMMUNICATION

Danielewski, M. The familiar.
Evans, N. The horse whisperer
Gruen, S. The ape house
Gruen, S. Water for elephants
Hale, B. The evolution of Bruno Littlemore
Martineau, M. Kingdom of exiles
Nicholas, D. Something red
Nicholas, D. The wicked
Novik, N. His majesty's dragon
Parkhurst, C. The dogs of Babel
Simon, C. Dogs don't lie
Simon, C. Panthers play for keeps
Wroblewski, D. The story of Edgar Sawtelle

HUMAN/ANIMAL RELATIONSHIPS

Adelman, M. Piece of mind
Akunin, B. Sister Pelagia and the white bulldog
Arikawa, H. The travelling cat chronicles
Auster, P. Timbuktu
Bear, E. Steles of the sky
Buxton, K. Hollow kingdom
Cameron, W. A dog's promise
Cameron, W. The dogs of Christmas
Celello, E. Leaning to stay
Crais, R. Suspect
Crichton, M. Next
Danielewski, M. The familiar.
Fowler, K. We are all completely beside ourselves
Gruen, S. The ape house
Gruen, S. Water for elephants
Hale, B. The evolution of Bruno Littlemore
Jiang, R. Wolf totem
Koontz, D. The darkest evening of the year
Krivak, A. The bear
London, J. White Fang

Hiaasen, C. Lucky you
Hiaasen, C. Nature girl
Hiaasen, C. Star Island
Hiaasen, C. Strip tease
Hughes, L. Simple speaks his mind
Jonasson, J. The accidental further adventures of the hundred-year-old man
Kohnstamm, T. Lake City
Landvik, L. Chronicles of a radical hag
Lansdale, J. Vanilla Ride
Leithauser, B. The promise of elsewhere
Lodge, D. Paradise news
Lutz, L. Curse of the Spellmans
Lutz, L. The last word
Lutz, L. Revenge of the Spellmans
Lutz, L. The Spellman files
Majors, I. Penelope Lemon
Mallon, T. Bandbox
Martin, S. The pleasure of my company
McCall Smith, A. The Department of Sensitive Crimes
Moore, C. Sacre bleu
Moore, C. The serpent of Venice
Perrotta, T. Joe College
Portis, C. The dog of the South
Portis, C. Gringos
Portis, C. Masters of Atlantis
Pratchett, T. The color of magic
Pratchett, T. Equal rites
Pratchett, T. The fifth elephant
Pratchett, T. Going postal
Pratchett, T. Guards! Guards!
Pratchett, T. The last hero
Pratchett, T. Lords and ladies
Pratchett, T. Men at arms
Pratchett, T. Monstrous regiment
Pratchett, T. Pyramids
Pratchett, T. Reaper man
Pratchett, T. Small gods
Pratchett, T. Thief of time
Pratchett, T. Thud!
Pratchett, T. The truth
Pratchett, T. Witches abroad
Pratchett, T. Wyrd sisters
Rawle, G. Woman's world
Robbins, T. Fierce invalids home from hot climates
Robbins, T. Jitterbug perfume
Robbins, T. Skinny legs and all
Robbins, T. Still life with Woodpecker
Rojstaczer, S. The mathematician's shiva
Roth, P. The anatomy lesson
Roth, P. The ghost writer
Roth, P. The great American novel
Roth, P. The professor of desire
Roth, P. Sabbath's theater
Roth, P. Zuckerman bound
Roth, P. Zuckerman unbound
Rucker, R. Hylozoic

Russo, R. Straight man
Scalzi, J. Redshirts
Semple, M. Where'd you go, Bernadette
Sinha, I. Animal's people
Sisco, A. A deadly habit
Sthers, A. Holy lands
Tanen, S. There's a word for that
Townsend, S. The Adrian Mole diaries
Valente, C. Space opera
Wibberley, L. The mouse that roared
Williams, C. Stairway to hell
Willis, C. To say nothing of the dog
Wilson, K. Nothing to see here
Winkler, A. Dog war
Wodehouse, P. The best of Wodehouse
Wodehouse, P. My man Jeeves
Wojtas, O. Miss Blaine's prefect and the golden samovar
Wong, D. This book is full of spiders
Yu, C. How to live safely in a science fictional universe
The **hunchback** of Notre Dame Hugo, V.
The **hundred** days O'Brian, P.
The **hundred** secret senses Tan, A.
The **hundred** thousand kingdoms Jemisin, N.
HUNDRED YEARS' WAR, 1339-1453
　　Cornwell, B. 1356
　　Cornwell, B. The archer's tale
　　Riley, J. In pursuit of the green lion
　　Rutherfurd, E. Paris
The **hundred-year** house Makkai, R.
HUNGARIAN AMERICANS
　　Sarvas, M. Memento Park
HUNGARIANS IN FRANCE
　　Miller, A. Oxygen
HUNGARY
　　Fitten, M. Elza's kitchen
　　Linden, R. The enlightenment of bees
　　Szabo, M. Abigail
HUNGARY -- HISTORY -- 1939-1945
　　Sarvas, M. Memento Park
HUNGARY -- POLITICS AND GOVERNMENT
　　Musil, R. The man without qualities
HUNGER
　　Benioff, D. City of thieves
　　McCarthy, C. The road
　　Muller, H. The hunger angel
　　Williams, L. Supper club
The **hunger** Katsu, A.
The **hunger** angel Muller, H.
HUNGER STRIKES
　　Erpenbeck, J. Go, went, gone
The **hungry** tide Ghosh, A.
The **hunt** for Red October Clancy, T.
Hunted past reason Matheson, R.
The **hunter** Byrne, K.
The **hunter** Stark, R.
Hunter's moon Stabenow, D.
HUNTER, DAVID, 1802-1886

Coben, H. The stranger
Cohen, T. The summer we lost her
Coleridge, N. A much married man
Cook, T. Sandrine's case
Cookson, C. The year of the virgins
Cooley, M. The archivist
Coomer, J. One vacant chair
Coover, R. Huck out west
Corry, J. My husband's wife
Crace, J. Quarantine
Craig, C. Miss Burma
Cronin, A. Citadel
Cumyn, A. Losing it
D'Souza, T. The Konkans
Daniel, S. Stiltsville
Davies, R. The rebel angels
DeLillo, D. White noise
DeMille, N. Wild fire
Dee, J. The privileges
Deighton, L. Berlin game
Diehl, H. Lifelines
Dillard, A. The Maytrees
Doerr, H. Stones for Ibarra
Downing, S. My lovely wife
Elkins, A. Unnatural selection
Erdrich, L. Shadow tag
Estleman, L. Gas City
Evans, D. Ordinary people
Evison, J. This is your life, Harriet Chance!
Faber, M. The book of strange new things
Fallada, H. Every man dies alone
Faulkner, W. Pylon
Faulkner, W. Requiem for a nun
Ferris, J. The unnamed
Fforde, J. Lost in a good book
Flaubert, G. Madame Bovary
Florio, G. Silent hearts
Flynn, G. Gone girl
Fox, L. Days of awe
Frampton, M. Put up your duke
Franzen, J. Freedom
Frayn, M. Headlong
Friedland, E. The intermission
Gabaldon, D. A breath of snow and ashes
Gabaldon, D. Dragonfly in amber
Gabaldon, D. Drums of autumn
Gabaldon, D. An echo in the bone
Gabaldon, D. The fiery cross
Gabaldon, D. Outlander
Gabaldon, D. Voyager
Gabaldon, D. Written in my own heart's blood
Gaige, A. Sea wife
Galsworthy, J. The Forsyte saga
Gardam, J. The man in the wooden hat
Gardner, L. The neighbor
Genova, L. Left neglected
Gertler, S. Drifting

Gideon, M. Wife 22
Gifford, B. Wyoming
Glass, J. The whole world over
Goodman, J. In want of a wife
Goodwin, D. The American heiress
Gordimer, N. Get a life
Gordimer, N. The pickup
Greene, G. The quiet American
Gregory, P. The Boleyn inheritance
Gregory, P. The constant princess
Grey, Z. Woman of the frontier
Groff, L. Fates and furies
Guhrke, L. How to lose a duke in ten days
Gurganus, A. Oldest living Confederate widow tells all
Hallberg, G. City on fire
Hannah, K. Home front
Hardy, T. Jude the obscure
Hassib, R. A pure heart
Hauck, R. The wedding chapel
Hawthorne, N. The scarlet letter
Heller, J. Good as Gold
Heller, P. Celine
Higgins, J. Day of reckoning
Hill, S. The various haunts of men
Hillerman, T. The shape shifter
Hodgkinson, A. 22 Britannia Road
Hoffman, A. Skylight confessions
Hollingshead, G. Bedlam
Hoover, C. All your perfects
Hunter, E. The blackboard jungle
Hurston, Z. Their eyes were watching God
Hurwitz, G. They're watching
Hurwitz, G. You're next
Ishiguro, K. The buried giant
Itani, F. Tell
Ivey, E. The snow child
James, E. Four nights with the duke
Jewell, L. I found you
Jhabvala, R. My nine lives
Joinson, S. The photographer's wife
Jones, E. The known world
Jones, T. An American marriage
Kaufman, S. Diary of a mad housewife
Kelly, C. Secrets of a happy marriage
Kelly, J. The fire baby
Kelly, J. The moon tunnel
Kennedy, D. The big picture
King, L. Euphoria
Kingsbury, K. When we were young
Klassen, J. The painter's daughter
Koontz, D. The husband
Kunzru, H. Gods without men
LaValle, V. The changeling
Lahiri, J. The lowland
Langton, J. The deserter
Larsen, N. Passing
Lawrence, D. The rainbow

Rush, N. Subtle bodies
Ruskovich, E. Idaho
Russo, R. Bridge of sighs
Saint-Exupery, A. Night flight
Sayers, D. Busman's honeymoon
Sayers, D. Thrones, dominations
Saylor, S. The judgment of Caesar
Schwarz, C. The edge of the Earth
Scott, P. Staying on
Scott, W. The bride of Lammermoor
See, L. Shanghai girls
Seo, M. The only child
Seton, A. Green darkness
Shepherd, P. The book of M
Shreve, A. Sea glass
Shriver, L. So much for that
Shriver, L. We need to talk about Kevin
Simsion, G. The Rosie effect
Simsion, G. The Rosie result
Smith, Z. On beauty
Solomons, N. House of Gold
Sontag, S. The volcano lover
Spencer-Fleming, J. Hid from our eyes
Stabenow, D. A deeper sleep
Stapley, M. The last resort
Steinhauer, O. The Cairo affair
Stoker, B. Dracula
Stoker, B. The new annotated Dracula
Stringer, V. Let that be the reason
Suri, M. The age of Shiva
Swift, G. Wish you were here
Swinson, K. Wifey
Tan, A. The hundred secret senses
Thelen, A. The island of second sight
Theroux, P. The Elephanta suite
Thomas, M. We are not ourselves
Thomas, S. Not quite a husband
Thomas, S. Tempting the bride
Tremain, R. The colour
Trigiani, A. Big Cherry Holler
Trollope, J. Second honeymoon
Trueblood, V. Seven loves
Tsypkin, L. Summer in Baden-Baden
Turner, N. Heartbreak of a hustler's wife
Tyler, A. The amateur marriage
Tyler, A. Breathing lessons
Tyler, A. Vinegar girl
Vann, D. Caribou Island
Vonnegut, K. Slaughterhouse-five
Walker, A. The color purple
Wall, C. The dearly beloved
Walter, J. The financial lives of the poets
Weiner, J. Little earthquakes
Weisgall, D. The world before her
Weldon, F. The life and loves of a she-devil
Weldon, F. Worst fears
Wiggs, S. The ocean between us

Wolitzer, M. The wife
Wood, T. The engineer's wife
Woods, S. Santa Fe rules
Woolf, V. Between the acts
Woolf, V. To the lighthouse
Yarbrough, S. Safe from the neighbors
Zane Addicted

HUSBAND AND WIFE -- BILOXI, MISSISSIPPI
Barthelme, F. Bob the gambler
HUSBAND AND WIFE -- BOTSWANA
McCall Smith, A. The Double Comfort Safari Club
HUSBAND AND WIFE -- BRAZIL
Amado, J. Dona Flor and her two husbands
HUSBAND AND WIFE -- CALIFORNIA
Rivers, F. And the shofar blew
HUSBAND AND WIFE -- CUBA
Garcia, C. The Aguero sisters
HUSBAND AND WIFE -- ILLINOIS
McInerny, R. Requiem for a realtor
HUSBAND AND WIFE -- MASSACHUSETTS
Wharton, E. Ethan Frome
HUSBAND AND WIFE -- MEXICO
Steinbeck, J. The pearl
HUSBAND AND WIFE -- NETHERLANDS
Chevalier, T. Girl with a pearl earring
HUSBAND AND WIFE -- NEW HAMPSHIRE
Shreve, A. The weight of water
HUSBAND AND WIFE -- SAN FRANCISCO, CALIFOR-NIA
Pronzini, B. Fever
Pronzini, B. Savages
HUSBAND AND WIFE -- SOUTHERN STATES
Welty, E. The ponder heart
HUSBAND AND WIFE -- SPAIN
Munoz Molina, A. In her absence
HUSBAND AND WIFE -- VENICE, ITALY
Leon, D. Uniform justice
HUSBAND KILLING
Sanders, L. McNally's dilemma
The **husband's** secret Moriarty, L.
HUSBAND-AND-WIFE DETECTIVES
Clark, M. My gal Sunday
Crombie, D. A bitter feast
DeMille, N. Wild fire
Hammett, D. The thin man
Hart, C. White elephant dead
Kellerman, F. The forgotten
Kellerman, F. Jupiter's bones
Kellerman, F. Prayers for the dead
Kellerman, F. Serpent's tooth
King, L. The game
Muller, M. Burn out
Muller, M. The ever-running man
Neel, J. To die for
Pears, I. The immaculate deception
Perry, A. Bedford Square
Perry, A. Belgrave Square

I am half-sick of shadows Bradley, C.
I am legend Matheson, R.
I am Not Sidney Poitier Everett, P.
I am Pilgrim Hayes, T.
I am Radar Larsen, R.
I am the brother of XX Jaeggy, F.
I capture the castle Smith, D.
I curse the river of time Petterson, P.
I don't want to go to jail Breslin, J.
I found you Jewell, L.
I know a secret Gerritsen, T.
I know who you are Feeney, A.
I know you Kantaria, A.
I let you go Mackintosh, C.
I lock my door upon myself Oates, J.
I lost my girlish laughter Allen, J.
I married a Communist Roth, P.
I never promised you a rose garden Greenberg, J.
I refuse Petterson, P.
I sailed with Magellan Dybek, S.
I say a little prayer Harris, E.
I see you Mackintosh, C.
I shall be near to you McCabe, E.
I shall not want Spencer-Fleming, J.
I thee wed Quick, A.
I want you back James, L.
I will send rain Meadows, R.
I'd know you anywhere Lippman, L.
I'm New York's finest Swinson, K.
I'm not scared Ammaniti, N.
I'm thinking of ending things Reid, I.
I've got my duke to keep me warm Bowen, K.
I've got my eyes on you Clark, M.
I, Claudius Graves, R.
I, Hogarth Dean, M.
I, robot Asimov, I.
I, sniper Hunter, S.
I, Tituba, Black witch of Salem Conde, M.
Ian Ludlow novels [series] Goldberg, L.
Ibis trilogy [series] Ghosh, A.
Icarus Meyer, D.
ICE
Vonnegut, K. Cat's cradle
ICE AGE (GEOLOGY)
Robinson, K. Blue Mars
ICE AGE (GEOLOGY) -- EUROPE
Auel, J. The clan of the cave bear
The **ice** beneath her Grebe, C.
Ice cold heart Tracy, P.
The **ice** cream queen of Orchard Street Gilman, S.
ICE CREAM TRUCKS
Gilman, S. The ice cream queen of Orchard Street
The **ice** princess Lackberg, C.
The **ice** queen Hoffman, A.
The **ice** queen Neuhaus, N.
ICE-SKATING
Drury, T. The driftless area

ICELAND
Hand, E. Available dark
Indriðason, A. Outrage
Indriðason, A. Reykjavik nights
Indriðason, A. The shadow district
Indriðason, A. Strange shores
Jónasson, R. The island
Mallon, T. Finale
Ólafsdóttir, A. Butterflies in November
Olafsson, O. The sacrament
Petrie, N. The wild one
Ridpath, M. Far north
Verne, J. Journey to the centre of the Earth
ICELAND -- HISTORY -- 17TH CENTURY
Lea, C. The glass woman
ICELAND -- HISTORY -- 19TH CENTURY
Kent, H. Burial rites
The **Iceman** Deutermann, P.
IDAHO
Box, C. Blue heaven
Carlson, R. Five skies
Dodd, C. Obsession Falls
Hatcher, R. Cross my heart
Hatcher, R. Who I am with you
Hunter, S. Game of snipers
Hunter, S. Time to hunt
Johnson, D. Train dreams
Ruskovich, E. Idaho
Stirling, S. Dies the fire
Vestal, S. Daredevils
Idaho Ruskovich, E.
The **idea** of love Dean, L.
The **idea** of perfection Grenville, K.
IDEALISM
Ackerman, E. Dark at the crossing
Cervantes Saavedra, M. Don Quixote
Dolan-Leach, C. We went to the woods
Flaubert, G. Sentimental education
Grant, L. We had it so good
Greene, G. The quiet American
Kunzru, H. My revolutions
Littell, R. The Mayakovsky tapes
Lock, N. A fugitive in Walden Woods
Naipaul, V. Magic seeds
Richardson, S. Clarissa, or, The history of a young lady
Warren, R. World enough and time
IDEALISM IN MEN
Pasternak, B. Doctor Zhivago
Stead, C. The man who loved children
Theroux, P. The Lower River
IDEALISM IN WOMEN
Hale, S. Austenland
Nunez, S. The last of her kind
IDEAS (PHILOSOPHY)
Lawrence, D. Women in love
Pava, S. Personae
IDENTICAL TWIN BROTHERS

Gran, S. The infinite blacktop
Greengrass, J. Sight
Greer, A. The impossible lives of Greta Wells
Harris, E. Basketball Jones
Harris, E. I say a little prayer
Harris, E. Invisible life
Hassib, R. A pure heart
Hoeg, P. The quiet girl
Hoffman, A. The dovekeepers
Hoffman, A. Skylight confessions
Holmes, J. How are you going to save yourself
Hubbard, L. The talented Ribkins
Hustvedt, S. The blazing world
Irving, J. In one person
Jacobson, H. The Finkler question
James, M. The book of night women
Jaswal, B. Erotic stories for Punjabi widows
Jen, G. World and town
Jewell, L. The family upstairs
Jewell, L. The making of us
Jin, H. A good fall
Jin, M. Little gods
Johnson, D. Everything under
Jones, S. Mongrels
Joss, M. Among the missing
Kafka, F. Collected stories
Kamal, S. It all falls down
Kaufman, S. Diary of a mad housewife
Kiernan, C. The drowning girl
Knausgaard, K. My struggle.
Krauss, N. Forest Dark
Kundera, M. Immortality
Kunzru, H. The impressionist
Kunzru, H. My revolutions
Kwok, J. Searching for Sylvie Lee
Lahiri, J. The namesake
Larison, J. Whiskey when we're dry
Larsen, N. Passing
Larsen, R. I am Radar
Lee, D. Country of origin
Lee, M. Pachinko
Lerner, B. Leaving the Atocha Station
Lerner, B. The Topeka school
Lessing, D. The four-gated city
Lessing, D. The golden not(ebk.)
Lewis, C. Till we have faces
Lightman, A. The diagnosis
Locke, A. Bluebird, bluebird
Loh, V. Breaking the tongue , by Vyvyane Loh.
Martine, A. A memory called empire
Mda, Z. The Madonna of Excelsior
Mehta, R. No other world
Mengestu, D. All our names
Merey, I. A + e 4ever
Mieville, C. Perdido Street Station
Miles, J. Anatomy of a miracle
Millet, L. How the dead dream

Millet, L. Magnificence
Moore, L. The unseen world
Morgan, R. Thirteen
Mosley, W. John Woman
Mosley, W. The man in my basement
Mukherjee, B. Miss new India
Murakami, H. Blind willow, sleeping woman
Murakami, H. Colorless Tsukuru Tazaki and his years of
  pilgrimage
Naipaul, V. A house for Mr. Biswas
Naipaul, V. Magic seeds
Naslund, S. The fountain of St. James Court
Naylor, G. Linden Hills
Naylor, G. The men of Brewster Place
Nguyen, V. The refugees
Nguyen, V. The sympathizer
Oates, J. Blonde
Oates, J. The gravedigger's daughter
Oates, J. Little bird of heaven
Oates, J. Marya
Oates, J. Middle age
Oates, J. My life as a rat
Okorafor, N. Binti
Orwell, G. 1984
Otsuka, J. The Buddha in the attic
Oyeyemi, H. Boy, Snow, Bird
Oyeyemi, H. The opposite house
Ozick, C. Heir to the glimmering world
Palliser, C. The quincunx
Patchett, A. State of wonder
Pearlman, E. Honeydew
Pessl, M. Special topics in calamity physics
Phillips, C. Dancing in the dark
Phillips, C. Foreigners
Phillips, C. A view of the empire at sunset
Phillips, H. The need
Picoult, J. Vanishing acts
Pomerantz, S. Rich boy
Porter, C. The seep
Potok, C. My name is Asher Lev
Price, R. Clockers
Pronzini, B. Spook
Qashu, S. Second person singular
Reid, I. I'm thinking of ending things
Rice, A. Christ the Lord
Robinson, P. Friend of the devil
Rodrigues Fowler, Y. Stubborn archivist
Roth, H. A star shines over Mt. Morris Park
Roth, P. Goodbye, Columbus, and five short stories
Row, J. Your face in mine
Roy, A. All the lives we never lived
Roy, A. The ministry of utmost happiness
Satyal, R. No one can pronounce my name
Savage, S. Firmin
Savas, A. Walking on the ceiling
Seay, M. The mirror thief
See, L. The tea girl of Hummingbird Lane

Holt, V. The black opal
James, E. Seven minutes in heaven
James, E. Three weeks with Lady X
Kunzru, H. The impressionist
Shreve, A. Fortune's rocks
Stewart, M. The wicked day

ILLEGITIMATE CHILDREN OF ROYALTY
London, J. The trouble with honor
Maxwell, R. The queen's bastard
Plaidy, J. The captive Queen of Scots
Rushdie, S. The enchantress of Florence
Stewart, M. The crystal cave
Suri, T. Realm of ash

ILLINOIS
Armstrong, K. Wherever she goes
Aswani, A. Chicago
Boswell, R. Century's son
Bradbury, R. Dandelion wine
Bradbury, R. Something wicked this way comes
Cisneros, S. The house on Mango Street
Coyne, J. The caddie who played with hickory
Fuller, J. Abbeville
Just, W. An unfinished season
Lombardo, C. The most fun we ever had
McInerny, R. Requiem for a realtor
Newton, C. Calumet City
Newton, C. Start shooting
Phillips, J. Quiet dell
Pinter, J. Hide away
Straub, P. Lost boy lost girl
Strout, E. Anything is possible
Tatlock, A. Promises to keep
Wallace, D. The pale king

ILLINOIS -- HISTORY -- 19TH CENTURY
Putnam, J. These honored dead

ILLINOIS -- HISTORY -- 20TH CENTURY
Horan, N. Loving Frank

ILLITERATE MEN
Ashford, J. Lord Sebastian's secret
Barnett, K. Ever faithful

ILLITERATE WOMEN
Sapphire Push
The **illness** lesson Beams, C.
The **illumination** Brockmeier, K.
Illumination night Hoffman, A.

ILLUMINATION OF BOOKS AND MANUSCRIPTS
Pamuk, O. My name is Red
Illuminations Sharratt, M.
The **illusion** of separateness Van Booy, S.
Illusion Town Castle, J.
Illusion Town novels [series] Castle, J.
Illusions Pronzini, B.

ILLUSTRATED BOOKS
Brennan, M. A natural history of dragons
Foer, J. Extremely loud and incredibly close
Hosseini, K. Sea prayer
Larsen, R. The selected works of T. S. Spivet

Pessl, M. Night film
Preston, C. The scrapbook of Frankie Pratt
Saint-Exupery, A. The little prince
The **illustrated** man Bradbury, R.

ILLUSTRATORS
Starnone, D. Trick

IMAGE
Marren, S. A Palm Beach wife

IMAGE -- SOCIAL ASPECTS
Harris, E. Basketball Jones

IMAGE CONSULTANTS
Evanovich, S. Under the table

IMAGINARY CREATURES
Bear, E. Stone mad
Camp, B. The city of lost fortunes
Camp, B. Gather the fortunes
Flores, F. Tears of the trufflepig
Golding, M. Little darlings
James, M. Black leopard, red wolf
Johnson, D. Everything under
Johnson, K. The dream-quest of Vellitt Boe
Lyons, J. The ruin of kings
Marshall, A. A crown for cold silver
Mitchell, D. Slade House
The new voices of fantasy
Shaw, V. Dreadful company
Shaw, V. Strange Practice
Stories
Stout, D. Titanshade
Wilson, G. The bird king

IMAGINARY EMPIRES
Asaro, C. Primary inversion
Banks, I. Consider Phlebas
Banks, I. The player of games
Corey, J. Tiamat's wrath
Craddock, C. An alchemy of masques and mirrors
Craddock, C. A labyrinth of scions and sorcery
Draven, G. Phoenix unbound
Hair, D. Mage's blood
Hair, D. Scarlet tides
Jemisin, N. The fifth season
Jemisin, N. The obelisk gate
Jemisin, N. The stone sky
Khoury, R. Empire of lies
Krueger, P. Steel crow saga
Lee, Y. Ninefox gambit
Lee, Y. Raven stratagem
Lee, Y. Revenant gun
Liu, K. The grace of kings
Liu, K. The wall of storms
Martine, A. A memory called empire
Ryan, A. The waking fire
Scalzi, J. The collapsing empire
Simmons, D. The fall of Hyperion
Simmons, D. Hyperion
Suri, T. Realm of ash
Wagers, K. There before the chaos

Tepper, S. The gate to Women's Country
Tolkien, J. The children of Hurin
Tregillis, I. The mechanical
Turtledove, H. Into the darkness
Turtledove, H. Rulers of the darkness
Valentine, G. Mechanique
Vonnegut, K. Slapstick
Wagers, K. There before the chaos
Weber, D. Shadow of freedom
Weber, D. The short victorious war
Wibberley, L. The mouse that roared
Wilson, D. The clockwork dynasty
Winter, E. The rage of dragons
Wolfe, G. The citadel of the Autarch
Wolfe, G. The claw of the conciliator
Wolfe, G. Home fires
Wolfe, G. The sword of the Lictor
Wolfe, G. The urth of the new sun
Zahn, T. Dark force rising
Zahn, T. Heir to the empire
Zahn, T. The last command

IMAGINATION
Moshfegh, O. Death in her hands
Oyeyemi, H. Mr. Fox
Stories

IMAGINATION IN BOYS
Coelho, P. The alchemist
Connolly, J. The book of lost things

IMAGINATION IN GIRLS
King, S. The girl who loved Tom Gordon

IMAGINATION IN MEN
Cauwelaert, D. One-way
Cervantes Saavedra, M. Don Quixote
Saramago, J. The history of the siege of Lisbon
Tidhar, L. A man lies dreaming

IMAGINATION IN TEENAGE GIRLS
Austen, J. Northanger Abbey
Greenberg, J. I never promised you a rose garden

IMAGINATION IN WOMEN
Hoffman, A. The story sisters

Imagine me gone Haslett, A.

Imago Butler, O.

IMITATION
Gerritsen, T. The apprentice
Sandford, J. Broken prey

The **immaculate** deception Pears, I.

IMMIGRANT FAMILIES
Abu-Jaber, D. Crescent
Acker, J. The limits of the world
Alvarez, J. How the Garcia girls lost their accents
Artson, B. Odessa, Odessa
Birmingham, S. The Auerbach will
Dev, S. Pride, prejudice, and other flavors
Erpenbeck, J. The book of words
Gross, A. Button man
Halfon, E. Mourning
Kim, E. The kinship of secrets

Lahiri, J. The namesake
Lalami, L. The other Americans
Lalli, S. The matchmaker's list
Lee, M. Pachinko
Mehta, R. No other world
Richman, A. The secret of clouds
Rivero, M. The affairs of the Falcons
Roth, H. A diving rock on the Hudson
Roth, H. From bondage
Roth, H. Requiem for Harlem
Roth, H. A star shines over Mt. Morris Park
Satyal, R. No one can pronounce my name
Shaw, I. Rich man, poor man
Sinclair, U. The jungle
Woo, S. Everything Asian
Zhang, J. Sour heart

IMMIGRANT WORKERS
Ondaatje, M. In the skin of a lion
Potzsch, O. The play of death

IMMIGRANTS
Aciman, A. Harvard square
Adichie, C. Americanah
Adichie, C. The thing around your neck
Alenyikov, M. Ivan and Misha
Ali, M. Brick Lane
Aliu, X. Brass
Allende, I. In the midst of winter
Alvarez, J. How the Garcia girls lost their accents
Antoinette, A. Murderville
Aslam, N. Maps for lost lovers
Aswani, A. Chicago
Castellani, C. All this talk of love
Castillo, E. America is not the heart
Chabon, M. The amazing adventures of Kavalier & Clay
Cole, T. Open city
Crucet, J. Make your home among strangers
Danticat, E. The dew breaker
Davies, P. The fortunes
Diaz, H. In the distance
Dimechkie, K. Lifted by the great nothing
Doctorow, E. Ragtime
Doig, I. Dancing at the Rascal Fair
Dos Passos, J. Manhattan transfer
Erdrich, L. The Master Butchers Singing Club
Erpenbeck, J. Go, went, gone
Everyday people
Faulks, S. Paris echo
Gaige, A. Schroder
Gay, R. Ayiti
Gibb, C. Sweetness in the belly
Gilman, S. The ice cream queen of Orchard Street
Golding, W. Fire down below
Golding, W. Rites of passage
Goudge, E. Green Dolphin Street
Gunaratne, G. In our mad and furious city
Hashemzadeh Bonde, G. What we owe
Hegi, U. The vision of Emma Blau

Piercy, M. Sex wars
Richler, M. Barney's version
Roth, H. Call it sleep
Wiesel, E. A mad desire to dance

IMMIGRANTS, KOREAN

Kim, A. Miracle Creek

IMMIGRANTS, POLISH

Krauss, N. The history of love

IMMIGRANTS, RUSSIAN

Piercy, M. Sex wars
Shteyngart, G. The Russian debutante's handbook
Ulinich, A. Petropolis

IMMIGRANTS, TURKISH

Gunday, H. The few

IMMIGRATION AND EMIGRATION

Acker, J. The limits of the world
Adiga, A. Amnesty
Alvar, M. In the country
Alvarez, J. How the Garcia girls lost their accents
Bulawayo, N. We need new names
Card, O. Saints
Cauwelaert, D. One-way
Cleave, C. Little Bee
Coetzee, J. The childhood of Jesus
Cruz, A. Dominicana
Erpenbeck, J. Go, went, gone
Grames, J. The seven or eight deaths of Stella Fortuna
Hamid, M. Exit west
Lalami, L. The other Americans
Levy, A. Small island
Mengestu, D. The beautiful things that heaven bears
Mengestu, D. How to read the air
Michener, J. Centennial
Michener, J. Chesapeake
Michener, J. The covenant
Michener, J. Hawaii
Murphy, T. Correspondents
Recacoechea S., J. American visa
Robinson, K. Blue Mars
Rutherfurd, E. The rebels of Ireland
Sahota, S. The year of the runaways
Smith, A. Spring
Toibin, C. Brooklyn
Turansky, C. No ocean too wide
Vuong, O. On Earth we're briefly gorgeous
Wolfe, T. Back to blood

IMMIGRATION PRISONS

Clarke, M. Foreign soil
The **immoralist** Gide, A.

IMMORTALISM

Arden, K. The bear and the nightingale
Borges, J. Collected fictions
Coulter, C. The last second
Kaufmann, N. Dying is my business
King, S. Doctor Sleep
Leckie, A. Ancillary justice
Leckie, A. Ancillary mercy

Leckie, A. Ancillary sword
Maaren, K. Weave a circle round
Morgan, R. Altered carbon
Morgan, R. Broken angels
Robbins, T. Jitterbug perfume
Tolkien, J. Beren and Luthien
Tyers, K. Shivering world
Westerfeld, S. The killing of worlds
Westerfeld, S. The risen empire
Wilson, D. The clockwork dynasty
Woolf, V. Orlando
The **immortalists** Benjamin, C.

IMMORTALITY

Araghi, A. The immortals of Tehran
Baker, K. In the garden of Iden
Cole, K. Dreams of a dark warrior
Cronin, J. The city of mirrors
Cronin, J. The passage
Cronin, J. The twelve
Grass, G. The flounder
Haig, M. The humans
Hamill, P. Forever
Horn, D. Eternal life
Kundera, M. Immortality
Maturin, C. Melmoth the wanderer
Poore, M. Reincarnation blues
Rice, A. Blackwood farm
Rice, A. Blood and gold
Rice, A. Blood canticle
Rice, A. Interview with the vampire
Rice, A. Memnoch the devil
Rice, A. Merrick
Rice, A. Prince Lestat
Rice, A. The queen of the damned
Rice, A. The tale of the body thief
Rice, A. The vampire Armand
Rice, A. The vampire Lestat
Saramago, J. Death with interruptions
Sherwood, F. The book of splendor
Shteyngart, G. Super sad true love story
Sloan, R. Mr. Penumbra's 24-hour bookstore
Westerfeld, S. The killing of worlds
Wilde, O. The picture of Dorian Gray
Wright, J. The golden age
Zelazny, R. Lord of light
Immortality Kundera, M.
Immortals after dark series [series] Cole, K.
The **immortals** of Tehran Araghi, A.

IMMUNITY

Grant, M. Parasite

IMPATIENCE

Dee, J. The privileges
An **imperfect** lens Roiphe, A.
The **imperfectionists** Rachman, T.
Imperial bedrooms Ellis, B.
Imperial Radch [series] Leckie, A.

IMPERIALISM

In **search of lost time** [series] Proust, M.

In search of the Rose notes Arsenault, E.

In sunlight and in shadow Helprin, M.

In the beauty of the lilies Updike, J.

In the bleak midwinter Spencer-Fleming, J.

In the company of cheerful ladies McCall Smith, A.

In the company of liars Ellis, D.

In the company of the courtesan Dunant, S.

In the country Alvar, M.

In the country of last things Auster, P.

In the country of men Matar, H.

In the crosshairs Coughlin, J.

In the dark places Robinson, P.

In the distance Diaz, H.

In the first circle Solzhenitsyn, A.

In the forest O'Brien, E.

In the full light of the sun Clark, C.

In the garden of Iden Baker, K.

In the heat of the night Ball, J.

In the kingdom of men Barnes, K.

In the kingdom of mists Jakeman, J.

In the Lake of the Woods O'Brien, T.

In the midst of winter Allende, I.

In the miso soup , Ryu Murakami ; translated by Ralph McCarthy. Murakami, R.

In the morning I'll be gone McKinty, A.

In the shadow of Gotham Pintoff, S.

In the skin of a lion Ondaatje, M.

In the teeth of the evidence Sayers, D.

In the unlikely event Blume, J.

In the woods French, T.

In this mountain Karon, J.

In twenty years Scotch, A.

In want of a wife Goodman, J.

In war times Goonan, K.

In West Mills Winslow, D.

In your corner Castille, S.

INCA SHAMANS

Robbins, T. Fierce invalids home from hot climates

INCANTATIONS

Palahniuk, C. Lullaby

The **incarnations** Barker, S.

The **incense** game Rowland, L.

INCEST

Amis, M. Lionel Asbo

Faulkner, W. The sound and the fury

King, S. Dolores Claiborne

Mailer, N. Ancient evenings

Mailer, N. The castle in the forest

Meloy, M. Liars and saints

Morrison, T. The bluest eye

Nabokov, V. Ada

Perry, A. Cardington Crescent

Pronzini, B. Blue lonesome

Roth, H. A diving rock on the Hudson

Roth, H. Requiem for Harlem

Sapphire Push

Shacochis, B. The woman who lost her soul

Stewart, M. The wicked day

INCEST VICTIMS

Draper, S. Forged by fire

Nussbaum, S. Good kings, bad kings

Incident at Twenty-mile Trevanian

Incognegro Johnson, M.

INCOME DISTRIBUTION

Ganshert, K. No one ever asked

Wong, D. Futuristic violence and fancy suits

INCOMPETENCE

Golding, W. Close quarters

Golding, W. Fire down below

Lem, S. His master's voice

An **inconvenient** duke Harrington, A.

The **increment** Ignatius, D.

INCUBI

Lafferty, M. Ghost train to New Orleans

Lafferty, M. The shambling guide to New York City

INDECENT ASSAULT

Amidon, S. Security

An **indecent** obsession McCullough, C.

INDECISION IN MEN

Barth, J. The end of the road

Indemnity only Paretsky, S.

INDENTURED SERVANTS

Amirrezvani, A. The blood of flowers

Dare, A. The girl with the louding voice

Urquhart, R. The visionist

INDEPENDENCE (PERSONAL QUALITY)

Archer, J. Nothing ventured

Beagle, P. Summerlong

Coetzee, J. Slow man

Coupland, D. Microserfs

Gibbons, K. The life all around me by Ellen Foster

Vargas Llosa, M. The way to paradise

Independence Day Ford, R.

INDEPENDENCE IN AFRICAN AMERICAN WOMEN

Hurston, Z. Their eyes were watching God

Rhodes, J. Voodoo dreams

INDEPENDENCE IN BOYS

Mosley, W. Fortunate son

INDEPENDENCE IN MEN

Parker, R. Cold service

Pontoppidan, H. Lucky Per

INDEPENDENCE IN ROMANI GIRLS

McCann, C. Zoli

INDEPENDENCE IN SINGLE WOMEN

Balogh, M. Someone to remember

Bell, L. One fine duke

Berg, E. Never change

INDEPENDENCE IN TEENAGE GIRLS

Amirrezvani, A. The blood of flowers

Dare, A. The girl with the louding voice

Franklin, M. My brilliant career

Gibbons, K. The life all around me by Ellen Foster

Lessing, D. The grass is singing

INDEPENDENCE IN YOUNG WOMEN
Franklin, M. My brilliant career

INDIA
Acker, J. The limits of the world
Adiga, A. Selection day
Anappara, D. Djinn patrol on the purple line
Carter, M. The strangler vine
Chatterjee, U. English, August
Colombani, L. The braid
D'Souza, T. The Konkans
Desai, A. Clear light of day
Desai, A. Fire on the mountain
Dev, S. A Bollywood affair
Dev, S. The Bollywood bride
Dev, S. A distant heart
Divakaruni, C. Oleander girl
Dyer, G. Jeff in Venice, death in Varanasi
Endo, S. Deep river
Festing, I. The bird keeper
Freudenberger, N. The newlyweds
Ghosh, A. The hungry tide
Hall, T. The case of the deadly butter chicken
Hall, T. The case of the love commandos
Hesse, H. Siddhartha
Jhabvala, R. At the end of the century
Joshi, A. The henna artist
Khan, V. The perplexing theft of the jewel in the crown
King, L. The game
Kunzru, H. The impressionist
Lahiri, J. The lowland
Malik, T. Three bargains
Markandaya, K. Nectar in a sieve
Massey, S. The Satapur moonstone
Massey, S. The widows of Malabar Hill
Mehta, R. No other world
Mukherjee, N. A state of freedom
Naipaul, V. Magic seeds
Narayan, R. Malgudi days
Narayan, R. Under the banyan tree and other stories
Oleksiw, S. The wrath of Shiva
Peters, E. Death to the landlords!
Raheem, Z. The marriage clock
Rao, S. Girls burn brighter
Roy, A. The god of small things
Roy, A. The ministry of utmost happiness
Rushdie, S. The ground beneath her feet
Rushdie, S. The moor's last sigh
Sahota, S. The year of the runaways
Sankaran, L. The hope factory
Sundaresan, I. The splendor of silence
Suri, M. The age of Shiva
Taneja, P. We that are young
Theroux, P. The Elephanta suite
Umrigar, T. The secrets between us
Umrigar, T. The space between us
Umrigar, T. The weight of heaven
Willig, L. The betrayal of the blood lily

Willig, L. The orchid affair

INDIA -- HISTORY
Ghosh, A. The glass palace

INDIA -- HISTORY -- 1947
Seth, V. A suitable boy

INDIA -- HISTORY -- 1947-1971
Deb, S. The point of return
Mistry, R. A fine balance
Rushdie, S. Midnight's children

INDIA -- HISTORY -- 19TH CENTURY
Ghosh, A. Flood of fire
Ghosh, A. River of smoke
Ghosh, A. Sea of poppies
Moran, M. Rebel queen
Thomas, S. Not quite a husband

INDIA -- HISTORY -- 20TH CENTURY
Deb, S. The point of return
Mehta, G. Raj
Mukherjee, N. The lives of others
Nicholson, W. Motherland
Roy, A. All the lives we never lived
Scott, P. Staying on
Taseer, A. The way things were

INDIA -- HISTORY -- 21ST CENTURY
McDonald, I. River of gods

INDIA -- HISTORY -- BRITISH OCCUPATION, 1765-1947
Moran, M. Rebel queen
Mukherjee, A. A necessary evil
Mukherjee, A. A rising man
Mukherjee, A. Smoke and ashes

INDIA -- HISTORY -- PARTITION, 1947
Majmudar, A. Partitions
Roy, A. An atlas of impossible longing

INDIA -- INTERFAITH RELATIONS
Rushdie, S. The moor's last sigh

INDIA -- POLITICS AND GOVERNMENT -- 1947-1971
Deb, S. The point of return
Mistry, R. A fine balance
Rushdie, S. Midnight's children

INDIA -- POLITICS AND GOVERNMENT -- 20TH CENTURY
Deb, S. The point of return

INDIA -- RACE RELATIONS
Jhabvala, R. Heat and dust

INDIA -- RULERS
Jhabvala, R. Heat and dust

INDIA -- SOCIAL CONDITIONS
Kandasamy, M. When I hit you, or, A portrait of the writer as a young wife
Shanbhag, V. Ghachar ghochar

INDIA -- SOCIAL CONDITIONS -- 20TH CENTURY
Mukherjee, N. The lives of others
Sinha, I. Animal's people
Taseer, A. The way things were

INDIA -- SOCIAL LIFE AND CUSTOMS
Adiga, A. Last man in tower
Adiga, A. The white tiger

Cook, D. Reservation nation

INDIANS OF NORTH AMERICA -- RELATIONS WITH EUROPEAN-AMERICANS

Berger, T. Little Big Man
Coldsmith, D. Tallgrass
Erdrich, L. Tracks
McMurtry, L. Zeke and Ned

INDIANS OF NORTH AMERICA -- RELATIONS WITH MISSIONARIES, TRADERS, ETC

Guthrie, A. The big sky
Michener, J. Centennial
Osborne, D. The coming
Silko, L. Almanac of the dead
Silko, L. Gardens in the dunes

INDIANS OF NORTH AMERICA -- RITES AND CERE-MONIES

Erdrich, L. LaRose

INDIANS OF NORTH AMERICA -- SOCIAL LIFE AND CUSTOMS

Osborne, D. The coming
Piatote, B. The beadworkers

INDIANS OF NORTH AMERICA -- SOUTHWEST (UNITED STATES)

Leonard, E. The complete Western stories of Elmore Leonard.

INDIANS OF NORTH AMERICA -- URBAN RESIDENCE

Orange, T. There there

INDIANS OF NORTH AMERICA -- WARS

Barry, S. Days without end
Bird, S. Daughter of a daughter of a queen
O'Brien, D. The contract surgeon
Osborne, D. The coming

INDIANS OF NORTH AMERICA -- WARS -- 1866-1895

O'Brien, D. The contract surgeon
Soli, T. The removes

INDIANS OF NORTH AMERICA -- WASHINGTON (STATE)

Alexie, S. Reservation blues

INDIANS OF SOUTH AMERICA

Ferencik, E. Into the jungle

INDIFFERENCE (PERSONAL QUALITY)

Wallant, E. The pawnbroker

INDIGENOUS PEOPLES

Piatote, B. The beadworkers
Stanley, M. Dying to live

INDIGENOUS PEOPLES -- LAND RIGHTS

Grenville, K. The secret river

INDIGENOUS PEOPLES -- RELATIONS WITH MISSIONARIES, TRADERS, ETC

Grenville, K. The lieutenant
Grenville, K. The secret river

INDIGENOUS PEOPLES' RIGHTS

Grenville, K. The lieutenant
Grenville, K. The secret river

Indignation Roth, P.

INDIVIDUAL DIFFERENCES

Wall, C. The dearly beloved

Wells, R. Divine secrets of the Ya-Ya Sisterhood

INDIVIDUALISM

Rand, A. The fountainhead

INDIVIDUALISM IN LITERATURE

Balzac, H. Cousin Bette

INDIVIDUALISM IN MEN

London, J. Martin Eden

INDIVIDUALITY

Asimov, I. Foundation and empire
Asimov, I. I, robot
Backman, F. My grandmother asked me to tell you she's sorry
Dostoyevsky, F. Notes from underground
Hesse, H. The fairy tales of Hermann Hesse
Lombardo, C. The most fun we ever had
O'Brien, E. In the forest
Rand, A. The fountainhead
Vonnegut, K. Galapagos
Wilhelm, K. Where late the sweet birds sang

INDOCHINA -- HISTORY -- WAR FOR NATIONAL LIBERATION, 1946-1954

Greene, G. The quiet American

INDONESIA

Conrad, J. Victory
Murphy, Y. Signed, Mata Hari
Tsao, T. The majesties

INDONESIA -- HISTORY -- JAPANESE OCCUPATION, 1942-1945

Brouwer, S. Thief of glory

Indranan war [series] Wagers, K.

INDUSTRIAL ACCIDENTS

DeLillo, D. White noise

INDUSTRIAL REVOLUTION

Cunningham, M. Specimen days
Gilbert, E. The signature of all things
Lambdin, D. King's captain
Rutherfurd, E. Sarum

INDUSTRIAL REVOLUTION

Lawrence, D. The rainbow
Lawrence, D. Women in love
Zola, E. Germinal

INDUSTRIALISTS

Beauman, N. Madness is better than defeat
Force, M. Deceived by desire
Gaskell, E. North and South
Gordimer, N. The conservationist
Sankaran, L. The hope factory
Shepard, K. The Celestials
Sjowall, M. Murder at the Savoy
Unsworth, B. The quality of mercy

INDUSTRIALIZATION

Card, O. Saints
Gaskell, E. North and South
Lawrence, D. Women in love

INDUSTRIES

Gilman, F. The half-made world

INEQUALITY

Anstruther, E. A perfect explanation
Archer, J. Best kept secret
Ashley, J. The madness of Lord Ian Mackenzie
Austen, J. Sense and sensibility
Babson, M. The company of cats
Baca, J. The importance of a piece of paper
Balogh, M. Someone to love
Bawden, N. Family money
Bennett, R. American elsewhere
Benz, C. The gone dead
Beverley, J. Devilish
Birmingham, S. The Auerbach will
Birmingham, S. Carriage trade
Bobotis, A. The last list of Miss Judith Kratt
Boyle, E. Along came a duke
Brenner, J. Drawing home
Bronte, E. Wuthering Heights
Burrowes, G. The heir
Callender, K. Queen of the conquered
Carey, L. The stolen child
Carlyle, C. A duke changes everything
Carlyle, L. Never lie to a lady
Carr, R. The wanderer
Christie, M. Greenwood
Cline, E. Ready player one
Collins, M. Ready set rogue
Collins, W. The woman in white
Cornwell, B. The last kingdom
Cornwell, B. Sword of kings
Cornwell, B. War of the wolf
Cramer, W. Levi's will
Crumley, J. Bordersnakes
Dahlie, M. The best of youth
Dare, T. Romancing the duke
Dare, T. Say yes to the marquess
Dare, T. When a Scot ties the knot
DeCarlo, M. The art of crash landing
Dickens, C. Little Dorrit
Dickens, C. Our mutual friend
Doig, I. Mountain time
Downing, S. He started it
Drabble, M. The witch of Exmoor
Eason, K. How Rory Thorne destroyed the multiverse
Eliot, G. Middlemarch
Faye, L. Jane Steele
Fitzgerald, F. The beautiful and damned
Fortier, A. Juliet
Frampton, M. Put up your duke
Gaddis, W. Agape agape
Ganek, D. The summer we read Gatsby
George, M. The confessions of young Nero
Goddard, R. Beyond recall
Gratton, T. The queens of Innis Lear
Gregory, P. The lady of the rivers
Gregory, P. The last Tudor
Gregory, P. The red queen
James, H. The portrait of a lady

Jewell, L. The family upstairs
Johnson, R. No one in the world
Keller, J. Last ragged breath
Kleypas, L. Cold-hearted rake
Kostova, E. The historian
Kubica, M. The other Mrs.
Kwan, K. Rich people problems
Lansdale, J. Devil red
Leon, D. Unto us a son is given
London, J. The trouble with honor
Long, J. Angel in a devil's arms
MacLean, S. A rogue by any other name
Massey, S. The widows of Malabar Hill
Maxwell, R. The secret diary of Anne Boleyn
McCullough, C. The first man in Rome
McGahan, A. The white earth
McInerny, R. Requiem for a realtor
McKillip, P. Ombria in shadow
McQuiston, J. The spinster's guide to scandalous behavior
Merbeth, K. Fortuna
Miller, M. Biloxi
Millet, L. Magnificence
Mishima, Y. The sound of waves
Mosley, W. And sometimes I wonder about you
Nahai, G. The luminous heart of Jonah S.
Ozick, C. Heir to the glimmering world
Palliser, C. The quincunx
Paretsky, S. Fire sale
Parker, T. Cold pursuit
Patchett, A. The Dutch house
Pava, S. Lost empress
Penman, S. Devil's brood
Penman, S. The sunne in splendour
Penman, S. When Christ and his saints slept
Phillips, A. The king at the edge of the world
Phillips, S. It had to be you
Phillips, S. Match me if you can
Plaidy, J. The captive Queen of Scots
Plaidy, J. Murder most royal
Plaidy, J. The pleasures of love
Porter, H. The bell ringers
Pratchett, T. The fifth elephant
Pratchett, T. Pyramids
Preston, D. The codex
Putney, M. Loving a lost lord
Quinn, J. The lady most willing
Raichev, R. Assassins at Ospreys
Randel, W. The empress of bright moon
Rhys, R. Fatal inheritance
Riley, J. In pursuit of the green lion
Robertson, M. The Baker Street translation
Russell, M. Dreamers of the day
Ryan, J. Restless rancher
Sansom, C. Lamentation
Sansom, C. Tombland
Sayers, D. The unpleasantness at the Bellona Club
Scego, I. Adua

Corry, J. The dead ex
Dahl, J. Conviction
Dallas, S. The last midwife
Daly, P. Clear my name
Deaver, J. The empty chair
Dow, D. Confessions of an innocent man
Fox, C. Crimson Lake
Fox, C. Redemption point
Freeman, B. Goodbye to the dead
French, N. Waiting for Wednesday
Goddard, R. Beyond recall
Gorman, E. Bad moon rising
Grippando, J. Money to burn
Grisham, J. The guardians
Hanson, H. The driver
Hill, R. The woodcutter
Hodgson, A. The last confession of Thomas Hawkins
Iles, G. Mortal fear
Isaacs, S. After all these years
Katzenbach, J. Just cause
Lashner, W. A killer's kiss
Lescroart, J. The first law
Limon, M. The line
Mayor, A. Tag man
McCrumb, S. The ballad of Tom Dooley
McPherson, C. Scot free
Meyer, P. American rust
Morrell, D. Murder as a fine art
Neuhaus, N. Snow White must die
Ohlsson, K. The disappeared
Owen, H. Oregon Hill
Owen, H. Parker Field
Paretsky, S. Brush back
Potzsch, O. The beggar king
Pronzini, B. Fever
Quirk, M. Cold barrel zero
Quirk, M. Dead man switch
Raimondo, L. Dante's poison
Robertson, M. The Baker Street translation
Robertson, M. The brothers of Baker Street
Rosenfelt, D. Don't tell a soul
Rozan, S. Paper son
Sayers, D. Strong poison
Saylor, S. The judgment of Caesar
Scott, A. Beneath the abbey wall
Simon, C. Grey dawn
Sisco, A. A deadly habit
Smith, B. The return of Kid Cooper
Smith, M. Love her madly
Smith, T. Child 44
Spencer-Fleming, J. All mortal flesh
Stanley, M. Death of the mantis
Steinhauer, O. The tourist
Turner, N. Forever a hustler's wife
Turow, S. Presumed innocent
Winer, J. Her kind of case
Woods, S. Santa Fe rules

INNOCENCE (PERSONAL QUALITY)
Ammaniti, N. I'm not scared
Barth, J. The sot-weed factor
Bassani, G. The garden of the Finzi-Continis
Heinlein, R. Stranger in a strange land
Williams, K. Sweet Giselle
Wolfe, T. I am Charlotte Simmons
INNOCENCE (PSYCHOLOGY)
Koen, K. Through a glass darkly
Wiesel, E. The judges
Innocent blood James, P.
Innocent graves Robinson, P.
Innocent in death Robb, J.
Innocent traitor Weir, A.
The **innocents** Atkins, A.
The **innocents** Crummey, M.
INNS
Andrews, D. Owl be home for Christmas
Lewis, K. Half of what you hear
Wade, B. Falling for you
INQUISITION
Michener, J. Mexico
Rollins, J. Crucible
Zimler, R. The last Kabbalist of Lisbon
INQUISITION -- FRANCE
Berry, S. The Templar legacy
INQUISITION -- SPAIN
Baker, K. In the garden of Iden
Falcones de Sierra, I. Cathedral of the sea
Perez-Reverte, A. Captain Alatriste
Wilson, G. The bird king
Insane city Barry, D.
The **insane** train Russell, S.
INSANITY (LAW)
Burnet, G. His bloody project
INSCRIPTIONS
Ruiz Zafon, C. The prisoner of heaven
INSECTS
Kafka, F. The metamorphosis
INSECURITY (PSYCHOLOGY)
Abbott, M. The fever
Mosley, W. Six Easy pieces
Oates, J. The falls
Wayne, T. Apartment
INSIDE PASSAGE (PACIFIC NORTHWEST)
Straley, J. The big both ways
Inside the O'Briens Genova, L.
INSOMNIA
Enard, M. Compass
Garcia Marquez, G. The general in his labyrinth
Palahniuk, C. Fight Club
INSOMNIACS
Dekker, T. Black
Dekker, T. Red
Dekker, T. White
Inspector Alan Banks mysteries [series] Robinson, P.
Inspector Armand Gamache mysteries [series] Penny, L.

Chiaverini, J. Resistance women
Chung, C. The tenth muse
Hesse, H. Steppenwolf
McEwan, I. Sweet tooth
Mosley, W. John Woman
Muller, H. The fox was ever the hunter
Orringer, J. The flight portfolio
Smith, Z. On beauty
Stephenson, N. Anathem
Tartt, D. The secret history

INTELLECTUALS -- ALGERIA

Wideman, J. Fanon

INTELLIGENCE

Bradley, C. As chimney sweepers come to dust
Bradley, C. A red herring without mustard
Bradley, C. Speaking from among the bones
Bradley, C. The sweetness at the bottom of the pie
Bradley, C. Thrice the brinded cat hath mew'd
Lyon, A. The sweet girl
Stephenson, N. Anathem
Van Vogt, A. Slan
Vinge, V. The children of the sky
Vinge, V. A deepness in the sky
Vinge, V. A fire upon the deep

INTELLIGENCE OFFICERS

Bell, T. Overkill
Berenson, A. The faithful spy
Cameron, M. Oath of office
Cameron, M. Power and empire
Church, J. A drop of Chinese blood
Clements, R. Revenger
Cussler, C. Golden Buddha
Dare, T. Do you want to start a scandal
De la Motte, A. MemoRandom
De la Motte, A. Ultimatum
Fleming, I. From Russia with love
Freed, D. Hot start
Hall, A. The quiller memorandum
Higgins, J. Bad company
Higgins, J. Midnight runner
Higgins, J. Rough justice
Huston, C. Skinner
Ignatius, D. The increment
Johnson, D. Tree of smoke
Kadare, I. The successor
King, L. The game
Le Carre, J. A most wanted man
Le Carre, J. The spy who came in from the cold
Littell, R. The company
Ludlum, R. The Prometheus deception
McCarry, C. Old boys
McEwan, I. Sweet tooth
O'Brian, P. Blue at the mizzen
O'Brian, P. The commodore
O'Brian, P. The hundred days
O'Brian, P. The wine-dark sea
O'Brian, P. The yellow admiral

Older, M. Infomocracy
Parnell, S. Man of war
Perez-Reverte, A. What we become
Perry, A. Shoulder the sky
Porter, H. Firefly
Powell, G. Embers of war
Redfern, E. The music of the spheres
Silva, D. The black widow
Silva, D. The kill artist
Silva, D. The new girl
Silva, D. The other woman
Stephenson, N. The rise and fall of D.O.D.O.
Wilkinson, L. American spy
Willig, L. The garden intrigue
Willig, L. The lure of the moonflower
Woods, S. The money shot
Woods, S. Skin game

INTELLIGENCE OFFICERS -- UNITED STATES

Ignatius, D. The increment
Woods, S. Smooth operator

INTELLIGENCE SERVICE

Baldacci, D. Hell's Corner
Bell, T. Overkill
Berenson, A. The deceivers
Berenson, A. The prisoner
Berry, S. The bishop's pawn
Berry, S. The lost order
Berry, S. The Malta exchange
Berry, S. The Warsaw protocol
Black, B. The secret guests
Butler, R. Paris in the dark
Cameron, M. Code of honor
Cameron, M. Power and empire
Carter, S. Back channel
Clancy, T. Clear and present danger
Coes, B. Bloody Sunday
Cole, D. Hangman
Coonts, S. The armageddon file
Coonts, S. The art of war
Cumming, C. A colder war
Cumming, C. A divided spy
Cumming, C. The Trinity Six
Cussler, C. Final option
Cussler, C. Shadow tyrants
Cussler, C. Typhoon fury
De la Motte, A. MemoRandom
De la Motte, A. Ultimatum
Dugoni, R. The eighth sister
Eisler, B. The god's eye view
Eisler, B. The killer collective
Eisler, B. The night trade
Fesperman, D. Safe houses
Finder, J. The switch
Gross, A. The one man
Hagberg, D. Abyss
Harris, O. A shadow intelligence
Higgins, J. Confessional

Interdependency novels [series] Scalzi, J.
INTERDIMENSIONAL TRAVEL
Beagle, P. The unicorn sonata
Cogman, G. The burning page
Cogman, G. The invisible library
Cogman, G. The masked city
Cogman, G. The mortal word
Czerneda, J. A turn of light
Davis, K. Duplex
Larkwood, A. The unspoken name
McGuire, S. Beneath the sugar sky
McGuire, S. Down among the sticks and bones
McGuire, S. Every heart a doorway
McGuire, S. In an absent dream
Warrington, F. Elfland
Warrington, F. Grail of the summer stars
Warrington, F. Midsummer night
Zelazny, R. Donnerjack

Interest of justice Rosenberg, N.
The **Interestings** Wolitzer, M.
INTERETHNIC CONFLICT
Craig, C. Miss Burma
Deb, S. The point of return
Okorafor, N. Who fears death
Spark, M. The Mandelbaum gate
INTERETHNIC FAMILIES
Tyler, A. Digging to America
INTERETHNIC FRIENDSHIP
Faulks, S. Paris echo
Iweala, U. Speak no evil
Tyler, A. Digging to America
INTERETHNIC MARRIAGE
Craig, C. Miss Burma
Erdrich, L. The plague of doves
Freudenberger, N. The newlyweds
Michener, J. Hawaii
INTERETHNIC RELATIONS
Desai, K. The inheritance of loss
Frazier, C. Thirteen moons
Gaitskill, M. The mare
Gordimer, N. The pickup
Kimani, P. Dance of the Jakaranda
Michener, J. Tales of the South Pacific
Miller, D. Norwegian by night
Ondaatje, M. Anil's ghost
Shafak, E. Honor
Tyler, A. Digging to America
Yanagihara, H. The people in the trees
INTERETHNIC ROMANCE
Aalborg, G. River of porcupines
Acker, J. The limits of the world
Echlin, K. The disappeared
Freudenberger, N. The newlyweds
McMillan, T. How Stella got her groove back
Michener, J. Tales of the South Pacific
Okparanta, C. Under the udala trees
INTERFAITH COUPLES

Pontoppidan, H. Lucky Per
INTERFAITH FAMILIES
Lukas, M. The last watchman of Old Cairo
INTERFAITH FRIENDSHIP
Epstein, J. Wunderland
INTERFAITH MARRIAGE
Roth, P. American pastoral
Walton, J. Farthing
INTERFAITH RELATIONS
Faulkner, C. Finding Georgina
Littell, R. Vicious circle
INTERFAITH ROMANCE
Baxter, C. Saul and Patsy
Blake, S. The guest book
De Bernieres, L. Birds without wings
Falcones de Sierra, I. Cathedral of the sea
Schami, R. Sophia
Wiseman, B. Listening to love
INTERFAITH ROMANCE -- BROOKLYN, NEW YORK CITY
Malamud, B. The assistant
INTERFAITH ROMANCE -- VERMONT
Lipman, E. The inn at Lake Devine
INTERGENERATIONAL COMMUNICATION
Acker, J. The limits of the world
Alther, L. Kinflicks
Kimani, P. Dance of the Jakaranda
Scego, I. Adua
Wang, K. Family trust
Watts, S. No one is coming to save us
INTERGENERATIONAL FRIENDSHIP
Barthelme, F. Elroy Nights
Berg, E. Night of miracles
Berg, E. The story of Arthur Truluv
Bohjalian, C. The buffalo soldier
Brunt, C. Tell the wolves I'm home
Extence, G. The universe versus Alex Woods
Gaitskill, M. Veronica
Grant, H. The vanishing of Katharina Linden
Hunter, E. The blackboard jungle
Makkai, R. The borrower
Morgan, S. One summer in Paris
O'Hagan, A. Be near me
Pamuk, O. The red-haired woman
Picoult, J. The storyteller
Reid, T. Forever, interrupted
Shipman, V. The heirloom garden
Smith, A. Autumn
Toole, F. Pound for pound
INTERGENERATIONAL FRIENDSHIP -- PALESTINE
Oz, A. Panther in the basement
INTERGENERATIONAL RELATIONS
Akhtar, A. American dervish
Auster, P. Sunset Park
Blume, J. In the unlikely event
Bradford, B. Just rewards
Butler, N. The hearts of men

Kerr, P. Field gray
Kerr, P. Greeks bearing gifts
Kerr, P. Prussian blue
Khoury, R. Empire of lies
Lawton, J. Hammer to fall
Le Carre, J. Smiley's people
Le Carre, J. The spy who came in from the cold
Littell, R. The company
Ludlum, R. The Bourne identity
Ludlum, R. The Bourne supremacy
Ludlum, R. The Bourne ultimatum
Ludlum, R. The Prometheus deception
Ludlum, R. The Sigma protocol
MacInnes, H. Ride a pale horse
MacInnes, H. The Venetian affair
Mankell, H. The troubled man
Matthews, J. The Kremlin's candidate
McCarry, C. Old boys
Morgan Jones, C. The silent oligarch
Paretsky, S. Shell game
Parker, R. Cold service
Pearl, M. The Poe shadow
Pearson, R. Choke point
Pearson, R. The red room
Perry, A. Blood on the water
Perry, A. Death in focus
Perry, A. Midnight at Marble Arch
Perry, A. Shoulder the sky
Porter, H. Firefly
Porter, H. White hot silence
Prescott, L. The secrets we kept
Reich, C. The take
Robbins, T. Fierce invalids home from hot climates
Robotham, M. The wreckage
Rozan, S. The Shanghai Moon
Ruff, M. 88 names
Runcie, J. Sidney Chambers and the perils of the night
Schutt, B. The Darwin strain
Sebastian, T. Fatal ally
Siger, J. Target Tinos
Silva, D. The black widow
Silva, D. The kill artist
Silva, D. The new girl
Silva, D. The other woman
Smith, M. Havana Bay
Smith, M. Polar Star
Smith, M. Red Square
Steinhauer, O. All the old knives
Steinhauer, O. The tourist
Stross, C. Empire Games
Tata, A. Dark winter
Watt, H. To the lions
Winslow, D. Satori
Wolf, D. The execution
Wolf, D. The intercept
Wolf, D. The ultimatum
Wouk, H. A hole in Texas

Zander, J. The swimmer

INTERNATIONAL INTRIGUE -- CHINA
Pearson, R. The risk agent

INTERNATIONAL INTRIGUE -- EGYPT
Peters, E. The golden one

INTERNATIONAL RELATIONS
Bennett, R. City of blades
Bennett, R. City of stairs
Carter, S. Back channel
Child, L. Bad luck and trouble
Child, L. Nothing to lose
Cumming, C. A colder war
Cussler, C. Golden Buddha
Lee, F. Jade war
Littell, R. The company
Liu, K. The wall of storms
McQuiston, C. Red, white & royal blue
Ohlsson, K. Hostage
Palahniuk, C. Pygmy
Poyer, D. Overthrow
Ricciardi, D. Warning light
Saylor, S. Wrath of the furies
Schwab, V. A gathering of shadows
Taylor, B. Daughter of war
Wibberley, L. The mouse that roared
Wilkinson, L. American spy

INTERNATIONAL RELIEF
Linden, R. The enlightenment of bees

INTERNATIONAL RELIEF -- AFRICA
D'Souza, T. Whiteman

INTERNET
Cohen, J. Book of numbers
Farnsworth, C. Flashmob
Ferris, J. To rise again at a decent hour
Franzen, J. Purity
Iles, G. Mortal fear
Katzenbach, J. What comes next
Majors, I. Penelope Lemon

INTERNET -- SOCIAL ASPECTS
Meyer, D. Icarus

INTERNET GAMES
Allende, I. Ripper
Rankin, I. The falls

INTERNET INDUSTRY AND TRADE
Eggers, D. The circle

INTERNET PORNOGRAPHY
Buwalda, P. Bonita Avenue
Iles, G. Mortal fear

INTERNET PREDATORS
Laukkanen, O. The watcher in the wall

INTERNS
Zevin, G. Young Jane Young

INTERNS (MEDICINE)
Grodstein, L. A friend of the family

INTERPERSONAL ATTRACTION
Aalborg, G. River of porcupines
Alexander, T. A note yet unsung

Harkness, D. A discovery of witches
Harkness, D. Shadow of night
Harrington, A. An inconvenient duke
Harrison, N. Montauk
Hatcher, R. Cross my heart
Helprin, M. Paris in the present tense
Higgins, K. The best man
Higgins, K. The perfect match
Hilderbrand, E. What happens in paradise
Hoang, H. The bride test
Hoang, H. The kiss quotient
Hodges, C. Rumor has it
Hoffman, A. The third angel
Hoyt, E. Wicked intentions
Hunt, S. The invention of everything else
Hunter, J. Forbidden to love the duke
Isaac, K. Then there was you
Jackson, B. Forged in desire
Jalaluddin, U. Ayesha at last
James, E. Desperate duchesses
James, E. Four nights with the duke
James, E. Seven minutes in heaven
James, E. Three weeks with Lady X
James, J. Something about you
Jenkins, B. Breathless
Jenkins, B. Forbidden
Jenkins, B. Tempest
Jenoff, P. The ambassador's daughter
Jimenez, A. The friend zone
Johnson, L. A sparkle of silver
Johnson, S. Blaze
Joinson, S. The photographer's wife
Kate, J. A girl's guide to the Outback
Kate, J. Love and other mistakes
Kerangal, M. The cook
Kitt, S. Celluloid memories
Kleypas, L. Christmas Eve at Friday Harbor
Knight, D. Butterfly tattoo
Koontz, D. Innocence
Krentz, J. Copper Beach
Landon, S. Wishing for us
Laureano, C. The Saturday Night Supper Club
Lauren, C. Roomies
Laurens, S. By winter's light
Laurens, S. The pursuits of Lord Kit Cavanaugh
Lawrence, D. Sons and lovers
Layne, L. Passion on Park Avenue
Lewis, B. The ebb tide
Lin, J. The dragon and the pearl
Lohmann, J. Winning Ruby Heart
Loren, R. The one for you
Loren, R. The one you can't forget
Lorret, V. How to forget a duke
MacGregor, J. The bride who got lucky
MacKenzie, S. Bedding Lord Ned
MacLean, S. Brazen and the Beast
MacLean, S. Never judge a lady by her cover

MacLean, S. A rogue by any other name
MacLean, S. The rogue not taken
MacLean, S. Wicked and the wallflower
Macomber, D. If not for you
Mallery, S. Best of my love
Mallery, S. The summer of Sunshine and Margot
Martin, A. Blitzed
Martin, A. Fumbled
Martin, C. Send down the rain
Matthews, J. The Kremlin's candidate
Matthews, J. Red sparrow
McEwan, I. Sweet tooth
McKinlay, J. The good ones
McMurtry, L. Rhino ranch
McQuiston, J. The spinster's guide to scandalous behavior
Milan, C. The duchess war
Moggach, D. Tulip fever
Moore, K. To seduce an angel
Morgan, S. The Christmas sisters
Morgan, S. Miracle on 5th Avenue
Morgenstern, E. The starless sea
Murray, V. Lust
Nash, S. Between the Duke and the deep blue sea
Nissenson, H. The pilgrim
Noble, K. The game and the governess
O'Keefe, M. Crazy thing called love
Parker, L. The Austen playbook
Pearlman, E. Honeydew
Penrose, A. Murder at Kensington Palace
Perry, A. Death in focus
Perry, S. The Essex serpent
Phillips, C. Perfect fit
Phillips, S. The great escape
Putney, M. Loving a lost lord
Putney, M. No longer a gentleman
Quick, A. The girl who knew too much
Quick, A. The other lady vanishes
Quick, A. Otherwise engaged
Quick, A. 'Til death do us part
Quincy, D. Murder at the opera
Quinn, J. The secrets of Sir Richard Kenworthy
Rai, A. Hate to want you
Rai, A. The right swipe
Rai, A. Wrong to need you
Ramsay, H. Summer on Moonlight Bay
Ranney, K. The Scottish duke
Renault, M. The bull from the sea
Renault, M. The last of the wine
Rice, L. The lemon orchard
Richards, D. The mustanger and the lady
Rivers, F. The masterpiece
Roberts, N. Come sundown
Roberts, N. Dark witch
Roberts, N. Honest illusions
Roberts, N. Midnight Bayou
Roberts, N. Sea swept
Rodale, M. Lady Bridget's diary

Banville, J. The infinities

Bauermeister, E. The school of essential ingredients

Baxter, C. The feast of love

Beagin, J. Vacuum in the dark

Beattie, A. A wonderful stroke of luck

The best American mystery stories 2019

Beauman, N. Madness is better than defeat

Beauvoir, S. The Mandarins

Benjamin, C. The immortalists

Berg, E. The story of Arthur Truluv

Berlin, L. Evening in paradise

Berlin, L. A manual for cleaning women

Bhuvaneswar, C. White dancing elephants

Bird, S. The flamenco academy

Blau, J. The Wonder Bread summer

Block, S. Oliver Loving

Blume, J. In the unlikely event

Boianjiu, S. The people of forever are not afraid

Bond, C. Ruby

Boyle, T. The harder they come

Boyle, T. The relive box

Boyle, T. The Terranauts

Brinkley, J. A lucky man

Brownrigg, S. The delivery room

Bruen, K. Cross

Buckman, D. Because the rain

Butland, S. The lost for words bookshop

Butler, M. Pickle's progress

Cander, C. The weight of a piano

Carey, L. The stolen child

Carter, S. New England white

Castellani, C. Leading men

Catton, E. The luminaries

Chambers, B. A closed and common orbit

Chambers, B. The long way to a small, angry planet

Chen, D. Brothers

Christie, M. Greenwood

Clark, C. In the full light of the sun

Clegg, B. Did you ever have a family

Clemmons, Z. What we lose

Cline, E. The girls

Coe, J. Number 11

Coe, J. The terrible privacy of Maxwell Sim

Collins, C. The gamal

Cortazar, J. Hopscotch

Crummey, M. Galore

Cruse, H. The complete Wendel

Danticat, E. Claire of the sea light

Danticat, E. Everything inside

De Giovanni, M. The crocodile

De Kretser, M. The life to come

Diaz, H. In the distance

Diaz, J. The brief wondrous life of Oscar Wao

Diaz, J. This is how you lose her

Diffenbaugh, V. The language of flowers

Doctorow, E. Andrew's brain

Doctorow, E. Homer and Langley

Dolan-Leach, C. We went to the woods

Dorris, M. A yellow raft in blue water

Doyle, B. The plover

Drabble, M. A day in the life of a smiling woman

Dunant, S. In the company of the courtesan

Dunn, K. The Dragonfly

Earley, T. Mr. Tall

Eggers, D. How we are hungry

Enard, M. Compass

Everyday people

Evison, J. Lawn boy

Fay, J. The shortest way home

Fernandez, M. The museum of eterna's novel

Ferris, J. To rise again at a decent hour

Fitzgerald, P. The means of escape

Follett, K. Edge of eternity

Follett, K. Winter of the world

Ford, R. Let me be Frank with you

Ford, R. A multitude of sins

Forna, A. Happiness

Francis, D. Wedding Bush Road

Franklin, A. The serpent's tale

Franzen, J. Freedom

Franzen, J. Purity

Freudenberger, N. The dissident

Freudenberger, N. The newlyweds

Gabel, A. The ensemble

Gainza, M. The optic nerve

Gaitskill, M. Don't cry

Galbraith, R. Career of evil

Galbraith, R. Lethal white

Galbraith, R. The silkworm

Garcia, C. The Lady Matador's hotel

Gay, R. Ayiti

Gelman, L. Class mom

Gelman, L. You've been volunteered

Geni, A. The lightkeepers

George, N. The book of dreams

George, N. The little Paris bookshop

Gestern, H. The people in the photo

Gibson, C. Beyond the point

Gilb, D. The Flowers

Giordano, P. Like family

Gordon, M. The liar's wife

Graley, L. The current that carries

Greene, A. Long Man

Gregory, D. We are all completely fine

Groot, T. The sentinels of Andersonville

Gross, A. The one man

Grushin, O. The line

Gurganus, A. Local souls

Gustine, A. You should pity us instead

Hadley, T. Bad dreams and other stories

Hallberg, G. City on fire

Halliday, L. Asymmetry

Han, K. Human acts

Handke, P. Crossing the Sierra de Gredos

Richman, A. The secret of clouds
Ridgway, K. Hawthorn & Child
Robinson, K. Aurora
Rooney, S. Conversations with friends
Roth, P. Exit ghost
Rowling, J. The casual vacancy
Roy, A. The ministry of utmost happiness
Russo, R. Bridge of sighs
Russo, R. Everybody's fool
Ryan, A. The waking fire
Salinger, J. Nine stories
Salter, J. Last night
Satyal, R. No one can pronounce my name
Schami, R. Sophia
Schanbacher, G. Crossing Purgatory
Schwartz, J. The red daughter
Schweblin, S. Fever dream
Schweblin, S. Mouthful of birds
Scibona, S. The volunteer
See, C. The handyman
Shaffer, M. The Guernsey Literary and Potato Peel Pie Society
Shanbhag, V. Ghachar ghochar
Shaykh, H. One thousand and one nights
Shepard, J. The world to come
Sherrill, S. The minotaur takes his own sweet time
Sidhu, R. Good Indian girls
Silber, J. Improvement
Sinha, I. Animal's people
Smiley, J. A thousand acres
Smith, A. The accidental
Smith, A. Autumn
Smith, G. The maze at Windermere
Smith, L. Oral history
Smith, Z. Grand union
Spark, M. The girls of slender means
Spark, M. Memento mori
Spencer, S. A dying fall
Starnone, D. Trick
Steinbeck, J. The long valley
Stridsberg, S. Valerie
Stringer, V. Dirty Red
Strout, E. Anything is possible
Strout, E. Olive Kitteridge
Strout, E. Olive, again
Thompson-Spires, N. Heads of the colored people
Tie, N. The bathing women
Toibin, C. The empty family
Tolstaya, T. Aetherial worlds
Towles, A. A gentleman in Moscow
Treuer, D. Prudence
Trevor, W. Last stories
Trueblood, V. Seven loves
Turner, B. Wooing Cadie McCaffrey
Tyler, A. Clock dance
Unsworth, B. After Hannibal
Uris, L. Redemption

Valdes, A. Dirty Girls on top
Vandelly, T. Theme music
Walker, K. The dreamers
Wallace, D. Oblivion
Wallace, D. The pale king
Wallace, M. The girl in the garden
Walser, R. The assistant
Waters, S. The paying guests
Watson, B. Miss Jane
Watts, S. No one is coming to save us
Wendig, C. Wanderers
White, B. Quite a year for plums
Whitehead, C. Sag Harbor
Whittall, Z. Holding still for as long as possible
Wickersham, J. The news from Spain
Wideman, J. American histories
Willis, C. Crosstalk
Wilson, C. Dead girl in 2A
Winman, S. Tin man
Wolitzer, H. Hearts
Wolitzer, M. Surrender, Dorothy
Yates, C. Grist Mill Road
Youngson, A. Meet me at the museum
Zaman, N. Up in the main house & other stories

INTERPLANETARY RELATIONS
Banks, I. Consider Phlebas
Banks, I. The player of games
Banks, I. Use of weapons
Brown, P. Morning star
Cambias, J. A darkling sea
Chambers, B. A closed and common orbit
Chambers, B. The long way to a small, angry planet
Corey, J. Persepolis rising
Corey, J. Tiamat's wrath
Doctorow, C. Rapture of the nerds
Harrison, M. Nova swing
Merbeth, K. Fortuna
New suns
Okorafor, N. Binti
Okorafor, N. Binti : home
Okorafor, N. Binti : the night masquerade
Scalzi, J. The collapsing empire
Scalzi, J. Redshirts
Tepper, S. Grass
Valente, C. Space opera
Wagers, K. There before the chaos
Weber, D. The honor of the queen
Williams, D. The stars now unclaimed

INTERPOL
O'Donohue, C. Beyond the pale
Suarez, D. Change agent

INTERPOL AGENTS
Suarez, D. Change agent
The **interpretation** of murder Rubenfeld, J.

INTERPRETERS
Ghosh, A. The hungry tide
Kolpan, G. Magic words

Lee, J. The starlet and the spy
Marias, J. Your face tomorrow, vol.1
Marias, J. Your face tomorrow, vol.2
Marias, J. Your face tomorrow, vol. 3
Qiu, X. Death of a red heroine

INTERRACIAL ADOPTION

Alam, R. That kind of mother
Morrison, T. A mercy
Ng, C. Little fires everywhere
Tyler, A. Digging to America

INTERRACIAL COMMUNICATION

Grenville, K. The lieutenant

INTERRACIAL COUPLES

Baldwin, J. Another country
Butler, O. Kindred
Hunt, L. The evening road
Martin, A. Blitzed
Martin, A. Fumbled
Nelscott, K. Stone cribs
Porter, R. The travelers
Sosa, M. The worst best man
Stewart, D. The Babe Ruth deception

INTERRACIAL DATING

Baldwin, J. Tell me how long the train's been gone
Christopher, A. Not the girl you marry
Dev, S. Pride, prejudice, and other flavors

INTERRACIAL FAMILIES

Alam, R. That kind of mother
Bohjalian, C. The buffalo soldier
Chung, C. The tenth muse
Dorris, M. Cloud chamber
Faye, G. Small country
Gordimer, N. My son's story
Grau, S. The keepers of the house
Murphy, T. Correspondents
Ng, C. Everything I never told you
Proulx, A. Barkskins
Smith, Z. On beauty
Tyler, A. Digging to America

INTERRACIAL FRIENDSHIP

Abdul-Jabbar, K. The empty birdcage
Abdul-Jabbar, K. Mycroft and Sherlock
Abdul-Jabbar, K. Mycroft Holmes
Arnoult, D. Sufficient grace
Baldwin, J. Tell me how long the train's been gone
Campbell, B. Brothers and sisters
Chiaverini, J. Mrs. Lincoln's dressmaker
Cooper, J. The last of the Mohicans
Crandall, S. Whistling past the graveyard
Edugyan, E. Washington Black
Eggers, D. A hologram for the king
Hunter, E. The blackboard jungle
Kidd, S. The secret life of bees
Lansdale, J. Honky tonk samurai
Lansdale, J. Vanilla Ride
Levy, A. Small island
Mosley, W. Fortunate son

Naslund, S. Four spirits
O'Brien, D. The contract surgeon
Parker, R. Double play
Pelecanos, G. Hell to pay
Pelecanos, G. Soul circus
Sexton, M. The revisioners
Simonson, H. Major Pettigrew's last stand
Smith, Z. White teeth
Stockett, K. The help
Toole, F. Pound for pound

INTERRACIAL MARRIAGE

Daly, P. Open your eyes
Gilb, D. The Flowers
Gordimer, N. No time like the present
Grau, S. The keepers of the house
Greene, G. The human factor
House, S. A parchment of leaves
Kunzru, H. Gods without men
Larsen, N. Passing
See, L. Dragon bones
Tan, A. The kitchen god's wife
West, D. The wedding

INTERRACIAL PARENTING

Sanders, D. Clover

INTERRACIAL ROMANCE

Allende, I. The Japanese lover
Brink, A. Philida
Carty-Williams, C. Queenie
Chang, A. Days of distraction
Charles, K. Wanted, a gentleman
Cole, A. A duke by default
Cole, A. An extraordinary union
Cole, A. A prince on paper
Cole, A. An unconditional freedom
Dane, L. Broken open
Fowler, T. A good neighborhood
Frazier, C. Thirteen moons
Gordimer, N. My son's story
Guillory, J. The proposal
Guillory, J. The wedding date
Guterson, D. Snow falling on cedars
Hibbert, T. Get a life, Chloe Brown
Jance, J. Skeleton Canyon
Johnson, S. Blaze
King, L. Father of the rain
Lessing, D. The grass is singing
Lethem, J. Dissident gardens
Levy, A. The long song
Loren, R. The one you fight for
Naipaul, V. Half a life
Oates, J. Because it is bitter, and because it is my heart
Oates, J. I lock my door upon myself
Reid, K. Such a fun age
Rice, L. The lemon orchard
Serpell, N. The old drift
Smith, M. Stallion Gate
Sundaresan, I. The splendor of silence

Updike, J. Brazil
Weatherspoon, R. Rafe
Weatherspoon, R. Xeni
Willig, L. The summer country

INTERRACIAL SEX
Jhabvala, R. Heat and dust
Mda, Z. The Madonna of Excelsior

INTERSPECIES ROMANCE
Broder, M. The pisces
Feehan, C. Dark illusion

Interstate Dixon, S.

INTERSTELLAR COMMUNICATION
Lem, S. His master's voice
Sagan, C. Contact

INTERSTELLAR RELATIONS
Bujold, L. Shards of honor
Bujold, L. The warrior's apprentice
Harrison, M. Nova swing
Lem, S. Fiasco
Martine, A. A memory called empire
Scalzi, J. The collapsing empire
Scalzi, J. Redshirts
Vinge, J. The snow queen
Watts, P. Blindsight

Interview with the vampire Rice, A.

INTERVIEWING
McGregor, J. The reservoir tapes
Ullmann, L. Unquiet
Updike, J. Seek my face

INTERVIEWS
Hand, E. Generation loss
Reid, T. Daisy Jones & the Six

INTIMACY (PSYCHOLOGY)
Berne, L. You may kiss the bride
Daniel, S. Stiltsville
Diaz, J. This is how you lose her
Ford, R. A multitude of sins
Ginzburg, N. A family lexicon
Greenwell, G. Cleanness
Greenwell, G. What belongs to you
Grossman, D. Be my knife
Itani, F. Deafening
McEwan, I. On Chesil Beach

Into the beautiful North Urrea, L.
Into the black nowhere Gardiner, M.
Into the blue Goddard, R.
Into the blue Henson, P.
Into the darkness Turtledove, H.
Into the drowning deep Grant, M.
Into the drowning deep [series] Grant, M.
Into the fire Hurwitz, G.
Into the jungle Ferencik, E.

INTRIGUE
Atkinson, K. Transcription
Bailey, M. An appetite for violets
Baker, J. Longbourn
Barclay, L. Parting shot

Barclay, L. The twenty-three
Beauman, N. Madness is better than defeat
Bell, L. For the duke's eyes only
Benedict, M. The only woman in the room
Black, B. The secret guests
Brandreth, B. The assassin of Verona
Brandreth, B. The spy of Venice
Carter, M. The strangler vine
Chee, A. The queen of the night
Corey, J. Tiamat's wrath
Dimberg, K. Girl in the rearview mirror
Eisler, B. The god's eye view
Finder, J. Guilty minds
Finder, J. House on fire
Galen, S. Third son's a charm
Gibson, W. The peripheral
Hart, E. City of ink
Haydon, E. The Merchant Emperor
Hurley, K. The stars are legion
Kay, G. Children of earth and sky
Lewis, T. GBH
Mason, T. The Darwin affair
Mina, D. Conviction
Morrell, D. Ruler of the night
Neubauer, E. Murder at the Mena House
Nickson, C. The hocus girl
Orringer, J. The flight portfolio
Orullian, P. The unremembered
Paretsky, S. Dead land
Phillips, A. The king at the edge of the world
Pohl, F. The space merchants
Quirk, M. Cold barrel zero
Quirk, M. Dead man switch
Ricciardi, D. Warning light
Rose, M. Cartier's hope
Rothschild, H. The improbability of love
Schwab, V. A darker shade of magic
Shannon, S. The mime order
Shaw, M. Murder at the mill
Solomon, B. The attempted murder of Teddy Roosevelt
Steinhauer, O. The last tourist
Stephenson, N. Fall or, Dodge in hell
Stoker, D. Dracul
Thomson, E. Beloved poison
Walters, M. The last hours
Weir, A. Anna of Kleve
White, R. A lady unrivaled
Whitehead, C. The intuitionist
Woods, S. Below the belt
Woods, S. Fast & loose
Woods, S. Smooth operator

INTROSPECTION
Groff, L. Arcadia
Howrey, M. The wanderers
McCormack, M. Solar bones
Proust, M. Remembrance of things past
Proust, M. Time regained

Iles, G. Cemetery road
Lagercrantz, D. The girl in the spider's web
Lagercrantz, D. The girl who lived twice
Lagercrantz, D. The girl who takes an eye for an eye
Larsson, S. The girl who kicked the hornet's nest
Larsson, S. The girl who played with fire
Larsson, S. The girl with the dragon tattoo
Mcdonald, G. Fletch
Pessl, M. Night film
Shaw, L. The network

INVESTMENT ADVISERS
Pearson, A. How hard can it be?

INVESTMENT BANKERS
Campbell, A. On the floor
Goldin, M. The escape room
Ludlum, R. The Sigma protocol
McCall Smith, A. The lost art of gratitude

INVESTMENT CLUBS
Krentz, J. When all the girls have gone

INVESTMENTS
Amidon, S. Human capital
Finder, J. Buried secrets
Pavone, C. The Paris diversion

INVINSKAYA, OLGA
Prescott, L. The secrets we kept

INVISIBILITY
Berger, T. Being invisible
Wells, H. The invisible man

Invisible Auster, P.
Invisible boy Read, C.
The **invisible** bridge Orringer, J.
Invisible cities Calvino, I.
The **invisible** guardian Redondo, D.
The **invisible** library Cogman, G.
Invisible library [series] Cogman, G.
Invisible life Harris, E.
Invisible life trilogy [series] Harris, E.
Invisible man Ellison, R.
The **invisible** man Wells, H.
The **invisible** ones Penney, S.
Invisible planets Liu, K.
Invisible prey Sandford, J.
The **invited** McMahon, J.

IOWA
Bivald, K. The readers of Broken Wheel recommend
Bruni, S. The night Gwen Stacy died
Canty, K. The underworld
Darnielle, J. Universal harvester
Drury, T. The driftless area
Drury, T. Pacific
Lee, P. Dark site
McHugh, L. Arrowood
Price, N. Sleeping with the enemy
Rich, V. The cooking school murders
Robinson, M. Gilead
Robinson, M. Home
Robinson, M. Lila

Smiley, J. Early warning
Smiley, J. Golden age
Smiley, J. Some luck
Smiley, J. A thousand acres
Waller, R. The bridges of Madison County

IOWA -- SOCIAL LIFE AND CUSTOMS -- 20TH CENTURY
Gorman, E. Bad moon rising
Gorman, E. Riders on the storm

IOWA CITY, IOWA
Roth, P. Letting go

IPHIGENIA (MYTHOLOGICAL CHARACTER)
Unsworth, B. The songs of the kings

IQ novels [series] Ide, J.

IRAN
Ahmad, J. The wandering falcon
Khan, A. Among the ruins
Mandanipour, S. Moon brow

IRAN -- FOREIGN RELATIONS -- UNITED STATES
Cameron, M. Oath of office

IRAN -- HISTORY
Amirrezvani, A. Equal of the sun
Djavadi, N. Disoriental

IRAN -- HISTORY -- 20TH CENTURY
Araghi, A. The immortals of Tehran
Bijan, D. The last days of Cafe Leila
Darznik, J. Song of a captive bird

IRAN -- HISTORY -- COUP D'ETAT, 1953
Kamali, M. The stationery shop

IRAN -- HISTORY -- ISLAMIC REVOLUTION, 1979-1997
Dowlatabadi, M. The colonel
Ghaffari, R. To keep the sun alive
Hashemzadeh Bonde, G. What we owe
Sofer, D. The Septembers of Shiraz

IRAN -- HISTORY -- TO 640 A D
Renault, M. The Persian boy

IRAN -- SOCIAL CONDITIONS -- 20TH CENTURY
Sofer, D. The Septembers of Shiraz

IRAN -- SOCIAL LIFE AND CUSTOMS
Bijan, D. The last days of Cafe Leila

IRAN -- SOCIAL LIFE AND CUSTOMS -- 17TH CENTURY
Amirrezvani, A. The blood of flowers

IRAN-IRAQ WAR, 1980-1988
Mandanipour, S. Moon brow

IRANIAN AMERICAN WOMEN
Bijan, D. The last days of Cafe Leila

IRANIAN AMERICANS
Cameron, P. The city of your final destination
Khadivi, L. A good country

IRAQ
Abrams, D. Fobbit
Miller, D. The girl in green
Murphy, T. Correspondents
Sharp, Z. Fox hunter
Swift, G. Wish you were here
Zimmerman, D. The sandbox

Carey, L. The stolen child
Doyle, R. A star called Henry
Harrison, C. Beyond absolution
Neville, S. Ratlines
Toibin, C. Brooklyn

IRELAND -- HISTORY -- CIVIL WAR, 1922-1923
Llywelyn, M. 1921
Llywelyn, M. 1949

IRELAND -- HISTORY -- EASTER RISING, 1916
Llywelyn, M. 1916
O'Neill, J. At swim, two boys
Uris, L. Trinity

IRELAND -- HISTORY -- FRENCH INVASION, 1798
Flanagan, T. The year of the French

IRELAND -- HISTORY -- REBELLION OF 1798
Flanagan, T. The year of the French

IRELAND -- POLITICS AND GOVERNMENT -- 20TH CENTURY
Higgins, J. Touch the devil
Llywelyn, M. 1921
Llywelyn, M. 1949

IRELAND -- SOCIAL CONDITIONS
McInerney, L. The glorious heresies
Rutherfurd, E. The rebels of Ireland
Uris, L. Redemption

IRELAND -- SOCIAL CONDITIONS -- 1837-1901
Uris, L. Trinity

IRELAND -- SOCIAL CONDITIONS -- 20TH CENTURY
Barry, S. The secret scripture
Boyne, J. The heart's invisible furies
Joyce, J. Finnegans wake
Joyce, J. A portrait of the artist as a young man
Joyce, J. Ulysses

IRELAND -- SOCIAL CONDITIONS -- 21ST CENTURY
Enright, A. Yesterday's weather

IRELAND -- SOCIAL LIFE AND CUSTOMS -- 20TH CENTURY
Black, B. The secret guests
Joyce, J. Dubliners
Toibin, C. The heather blazing

IRELAND -- SOCIAL LIFE AND CUSTOMS -- VICTORIA, 1837-1901
Archer, Z. Dangerous seduction

Irene Lemaitre, P.
Irene Chavez novels [series] Jenkins, V.
The **iris** fan Rowland, L.
Iris Grey novels [series] Shaw, M.

IRISH
Barry, K. Night boat to Tangier

IRISH AMERICAN FAMILIES
McDermott, A. Charming Billy
McDermott, A. At weddings and wakes

IRISH AMERICAN FAMILIES -- WESTCHESTER COUNTY, NEW YORK
Quindlen, A. Object lessons

IRISH AMERICAN MEN
Guterson, D. The other

House, S. A parchment of leaves
McDermott, A. Charming Billy

IRISH AMERICAN WOMEN
Freedman, B. Mrs. Mike
Llywelyn, M. 1916
Smith, M. She smiled sweetly

IRISH AMERICANS
Black, B. Christine Falls
Dorris, M. Cloud chamber
Harvey, M. Brighton
Helprin, M. Winter's tale
Kennedy, W. Chango's beads and two-tone shoes
Manning, K. My notorious life
McDermott, A. Charming Billy
McDermott, A. The ninth hour
McDermott, A. Someone
Pirrone, D. Shall we not revenge
Sakey, M. The blade itself
Thomas, M. We are not ourselves
Willis, C. Crosstalk

IRISH AMERICANS -- DISCRIMINATION
Faye, L. The gods of Gotham

IRISH CANADIANS
Atwood, M. Alias Grace
Urquhart, J. Away

IRISH CIVIL WAR, 1922-1923
Llywelyn, M. 1921
Irish coffee McInerny, R.

IRISH IN EUROPE
MacLaverty, B. Midwinter break

IRISH IN NEW YORK CITY
McCann, C. Let the great world spin
Robb, J. Naked in death

IRISH IN THE UNITED STATES
Hamill, P. Forever
Lauren, C. Roomies
Lordan, B. But come ye back , Beth Lordan
Mathews, B. The world of tomorrow
O'Connor, J. Star of the Sea
O'Malley, T. We were kings
Toibin, C. Brooklyn

Irish independence series [series] Llywelyn, M.

IRISH POTATO FAMINE (1845-1852)
O'Connor, J. Star of the Sea
Uris, L. Trinity

IRISH REPUBLICAN ARMY
Clancy, T. Patriot games
Doyle, R. A star called Henry
Higgins, J. Confessional
Higgins, J. The eagle has flown
Higgins, J. The eagle has landed
Higgins, J. Eye of the storm
Higgins, J. Touch the devil

IRISH REPUBLICAN ARMY.
McKinty, A. The cold, cold ground
McKinty, A. In the morning I'll be gone
Mina, D. Slip of the knife

Michener, J. Tales of the South Pacific

Island of bones Robertson, I.

The **island** of Dr. Moreau Wells, H.

Island of Mure novels [series] Colgan, J.

The **island** of sea women See, L.

The **island** of second sight Thelen, A.

The **island** of the day before Eco, U.

The **islanders** Moore, M.

ISLANDS

Adler-Olsen, J. The hanging girl

Bannalec, J. The killing tide

Blake, S. The guest book

Butler, S. Cygnet

Callender, K. Queen of the conquered

Carpenter, E. The weight of lies

Christie, A. And then there were none

Cleeves, A. Raven black

Cleeves, A. Thin air

Coetzee, J. Foe

Coleridge, N. Godchildren

Crichton, M. Pirate latitudes

Crummey, M. The innocents

Currie, R. Flimsy little plastic miracles

Daugherty, C. Revolver road

Dodd, C. Strangers she knows

Doiron, P. Stay hidden

Dunn, M. Ella Minnow Pea

Follett, K. Eye of the needle

Geni, A. The lightkeepers

Golding, W. Lord of the flies

Hand, E. Generation loss

Harkaway, N. Tigerman

Harrison, N. Montauk

Hauck, R. Once upon a prince

James, P. The lighthouse

James, P. The skull beneath the skin

Johnson, L. A sparkle of silver

Kincaid, J. Annie John

Kracht, C. Imperium

Lanagan, M. The brides of Rollrock Island

Marsh, N. Dead water

Melville, H. Omoo

Mitchell, D. The thousand autumns of Jacob De Zoet

Moore, M. The islanders

Nichols, P. The rocks

Ogawa, Y. The memory police

Parker, R. Rough weather

Pope, J. One warm winter

Ragnar Jonasson, 1. The island

Ramsay, F. Scone Island

Roberts, N. Dance upon the air

Schutt, B. The Darwin strain

Scott, J. Tourmaline

See, L. The island of sea women

Tamirat, N. The parking lot attendant

Verne, J. The mysterious island

Vonnegut, K. Cat's cradle

Vonnegut, K. Galapagos

Wells, H. The island of Dr. Moreau

Westlake, D. Watch your back!

Yanique, T. Land of love and drowning

ISLANDS -- GREECE

Fowles, J. The magus

ISLANDS -- IRELAND

Carey, L. The stolen child

ISLANDS -- MASSACHUSETTS

Lehane, D. Shutter Island

Parker, R. Trouble in Paradise

ISLANDS -- NORTH CAROLINA

Karon, J. A new song

ISLANDS -- SCOTLAND

May, P. The blackhouse

ISLANDS -- SOUTH CAROLINA

Naylor, G. Mama Day

ISLANDS -- TROPICS

Buffett, J. A salty piece of land

Islands of blood and storm [series] Callender, K.

ISLANDS OF THE AEGEAN

Fowles, J. The magus

Michaels, A. Fugitive pieces

Serafim, L. The devil takes half

Serafim, L. When the devil's idle

ISLANDS OF THE PACIFIC

Kracht, C. Imperium

Mailer, N. The naked and the dead

Verne, J. The mysterious island

ISLE OF MAN

Ewan, C. Dark tides

Ewan, C. Long time lost

Isle of Palms novels [series] Monroe, M.

ISLE OF PALMS, SOUTH CAROLINA

Monroe, M. Beach house reunion

ISLE OF WIGHT (ENGLAND)

Barnes, J. England, England

ISOLATIONISM

Anderson, K. The last days of Krypton

Kress, N. Tomorrow's kin

Merullo, R. The talk-funny girl

Roth, P. The plot against America

Zamyatin, Y. We

ISRAEL

Abulhawa, S. The blue between sky and water

Artson, B. Odessa, Odessa

Bezmozgis, D. The betrayers

Castel-Bloom, O. Textile

Foer, J. Here I am

Gamboa, S. Necropolis

Grossman, D. A horse walks into a bar

Grossman, D. To the end of the land

Gundar-Goshen, A. Waking lions

Kemelman, H. Monday the rabbi took off

Krauss, N. Forest Dark

Oz, A. Don't call it night

Rice, A. Christ the Lord

Ferrante, E. Those who leave and those who stay
George, E. Just one evil act
Ginzburg, N. A family lexicon
Giordano, M. Auntie Poldi and the Vineyards of Etna
Giordano, P. The solitude of prime numbers
Godden, R. Battle of the Villa Fiorita
Goodman, C. The night villa
Grames, J. The seven or eight deaths of Stella Fortuna
Griffiths, E. The dark angel
Harris, T. Hannibal
Heller, J. Catch-22
Hewson, D. The garden of evil
James, H. The portrait of a lady
Langton, J. The thief of Venice
Leon, D. About face
Leon, D. Beastly things
Leon, D. Blood from a stone
Leon, D. Drawing conclusions
Leon, D. Falling in love
Leon, D. The girl of his dreams
Leon, D. The golden egg
Leon, D. A question of belief
Leon, D. Trace elements
Leon, D. Uniform justice
Leon, D. Unto us a son is given
Nabb, M. Some bitter taste
Pears, I. The immaculate deception
Perry, A. Death in focus
Porter, H. White hot silence
Rachman, T. The imperfectionists
Rigosi, G. Night bus
Rushdie, S. The enchantress of Florence
Spark, M. The driver's seat
Starnone, D. Ties
Stone, I. The agony and the ecstasy
Svevo, I. Zeno's conscience
Unsworth, B. After Hannibal
Walter, J. Beautiful ruins
Weisgall, D. The world before her
Westheimer, D. Von Ryan's express
Williams, T. The Roman spring of Mrs. Stone

ITALY -- ANTIQUITIES
Harris, R. Pompeii

ITALY -- COURTS AND COURTIERS
Dunant, S. In the company of the courtesan

ITALY -- FOREIGN RELATIONS -- SPAIN
Phillips, C. The Rossetti letter

ITALY -- HISTORY
Dunant, S. Sacred hearts

ITALY -- HISTORY -- 1492-1559
Dunant, S. Blood and beauty
Dunant, S. In the company of the courtesan
Puzo, M. The family

ITALY -- HISTORY -- 14TH CENTURY
Eco, U. The name of the rose

ITALY -- HISTORY -- 15TH CENTURY
Poole, S. The Borgia mistress

Walton, J. Lent

ITALY -- HISTORY -- 17TH CENTURY
Vreeland, S. The passion of Artemisia

ITALY -- HISTORY -- 1914-1922
Hemingway, E. A farewell to arms

ITALY -- HISTORY -- 1914-1945
Manfredi, V. A winter's night

ITALY -- HISTORY -- 1922-1945
Silone, I. Bread and wine

ITALY -- HISTORY -- 19TH CENTURY
Rosenthal, P. The edge of impropriety
Wallace, C. The blind contessa's new machine

ITALY -- HISTORY -- 20TH CENTURY
Eco, U. Numero zero
Ondaatje, M. The English patient

ITALY -- HISTORY -- GERMAN OCCUPATION, 1943-1945
Grindle, L. Villa Triste
Russell, M. A thread of grace

ITALY -- HISTORY -- HISTORY -- 20TH CENTURY
Perez-Reverte, A. What we become

ITALY -- SOCIAL LIFE AND CUSTOMS
Spencer, E. The southern woman

ITALY -- SOCIAL LIFE AND CUSTOMS -- 16TH CENTURY
Dunant, S. In the company of the courtesan

ITALY -- SOCIAL LIFE AND CUSTOMS -- 18TH CENTURY
Bailey, M. An appetite for violets
Calvino, I. The baron in the trees

ITALY -- SOCIAL LIFE AND CUSTOMS -- 19TH CENTURY
Gray, J. A duke never yields
Gray, J. A lady never lies

ITALY -- SOCIAL LIFE AND CUSTOMS -- 20TH CENTURY
Morante, E. Arturo's island

ITHACA, NEW YORK
Chang, A. Days of distraction

ITINERANT PREACHERS
Lewis, S. Elmer Gantry

IVAN IV, THE TERRIBLE, CZAR OF RUSSIA, 1530-1584
Rutherfurd, E. Russka

Ivan and Misha Alenyikov, M.

Ivanhoe Scott, W.

IVORY
Perry, A. The shifting tide

J

J. P. Beaumont mysteries [series] Jance, J.

J R Gaddis, W.

Jack Aubrey and Stephen Maturin novels [series] O'Brian, P.

Jack Holmes and his friend White, E.

Jack Lennon investigations [series] Neville, S.

Jack Logan novels [series] Shaw, L.

Plaidy, J. Murder most royal

Jane Steele Faye, L.

Jane Whitefield novels [series] Perry, T.

Jane Wunderly novels [series] Neubauer, E.

The **Janes** Luna, L.

Janet Watson chronicles [series] O'Dell, C.

JANITORS -- ILLINOIS

Bradbury, R. Something wicked this way comes

JANUARY

Lourey, J. January thaw

The **January** dancer Flynn, M.

January dancer [series] Flynn, M.

January thaw Lourey, J.

The **Janus** stone Griffiths, E.

JAPAN

Arikawa, H. The travelling cat chronicles

Ayatsuji, Y. The Decagon House murders

Bird, S. The Yokota Officers Club

Fleming, I. You only live twice

Goenawan, C. The perfect world of Miwako Sumida

Goenawan, C. Rainbirds

Hazzard, S. The great fire

Higashino, K. The devotion of suspect X

Higashino, K. The miracles of the Namiya General Store

Hunter, S. The 47th samurai

Kawabata, Y. The sound of the mountain

Lathen, E. East is east

Minato, K. Confessions

Mishima, Y. The decay of the angel

Mishima, Y. The frolic of the beasts

Mishima, Y. Spring snow

Murakami, H. After dark

Murakami, H. After the quake

Murakami, H. Colorless Tsukuru Tazaki and his years of pilgrimage

Murakami, H. Kafka on the shore

Murakami, H. Killing commendatore

Murakami, H. South of the border, west of the sun

Murakami, H. The wind-up bird chronicle

Murata, S. Convenience store woman

Obregon, N. Blue light Yokohama

Oe, K. Death by water

Oe, K. Nip the buds, shoot the kids

Oe, K. A quiet life

Okuizumi, H. The stones cry out

Peace, D. Occupied city

Rizzuto, R. Shadow child

Tawada, Y. The emissary

Yoshimoto, B. Goodbye Tsugumi

Yoshimoto, B. The lake

JAPAN -- HISTORY -- 16TH CENTURY

Spann, S. Blade of the Samurai

Spann, S. Claws of the cat

Spann, S. Trial on Mount Koya

JAPAN -- HISTORY -- 1787-1868

Mitchell, D. The thousand autumns of Jacob De Zoet

JAPAN -- HISTORY -- 17TH CENTURY

Endo, S. Silence

Kirk, D. Sword of honor

JAPAN -- HISTORY -- 1926-1945

Lee, C. A gesture life

JAPAN -- HISTORY -- 1945-

Schwartz, J. The commoner

JAPAN -- HISTORY -- 20TH CENTURY

Kutsukake, L. The translation of love

Yi, C. The investigation

JAPAN -- HISTORY -- ALLIED OCCUPATION, 1945-1952

Hazzard, S. The great fire

Ishiguro, K. An artist of the floating world

Peace, D. Occupied city

Peace, D. Tokyo year zero

JAPAN -- HISTORY -- GENROKU PERIOD, 1688-1704

Rowland, L. The incense game

Rowland, L. The iris fan

Rowland, L. The Shogun's daughter

Rowland, L. The snow empress

JAPAN -- HISTORY -- PERIOD OF CIVIL WARS, 1480-1603

Clavell, J. Shogun

JAPAN -- POLITICS AND GOVERNMENT -- 1912-1945

Mishima, Y. Runaway horses

JAPAN -- SOCIAL LIFE AND CUSTOMS

Murata, S. Convenience store woman

JAPAN -- SOCIAL LIFE AND CUSTOMS -- 20TH CENTURY

Higashino, K. Malice

Higashino, K. Newcomer

Lee, M. Pachinko

Mishima, Y. The sound of waves

Tsukiyama, G. The street of a thousand blossoms

JAPAN -- SOCIAL LIFE AND CUSTOMS -- 21ST CENTURY

Murakami, R. In the miso soup , Ryu Murakami ; translated by Ralph McCarthy.

JAPANESE AMERICAN FAMILIES

Otsuka, J. When the emperor was divine

JAPANESE AMERICANS

Guterson, D. Snow falling on cedars

Lee, C. A gesture life

JAPANESE AMERICANS -- FORCED REMOVAL AND INCARCERATION, 1942-1945

Dallas, S. Tallgrass

Ellroy, J. Perfidia

Ellroy, J. This storm

Otsuka, J. The Buddha in the attic

Otsuka, J. When the emperor was divine

Rizzuto, R. Shadow child

JAPANESE CANADIANS

Kutsukake, L. The translation of love

Shimotakahara, L. After the bloom

JAPANESE IN FRANCE

Barbery, M. The elegance of the hedgehog

JAPANESE IN INDIA

Endo, S. Deep river

JERUSALEM, ISRAEL -- SOCIAL CONDITIONS -- 20TH CENTURY

Spark, M. The Mandelbaum gate

Jesse Stone mysteries [series] Parker, R.

Jesse Sutherlin mysteries [series] Ramsay, F.

Jessie Cole novels [series] Ragan, T.

JESUIT MISSIONARIES

Russell, M. The sparrow

JESUITS

Eco, U. The island of the day before

Russell, M. Children of God

Russell, M. The sparrow

JESUS CHRIST

Asch, S. The Nazarene

Crace, J. Quarantine

Kazantzakis, N. The last temptation of Christ

Kidd, S. The book of longings

Percy, W. Lancelot

Percy, W. The second coming

Rice, A. Christ the Lord

Toibin, C. The testament of Mary

Wallace, L. Ben-Hur

JESUS CHRIST CHILDHOOD AND YOUTH

Rice, A. Christ the Lord

JESUS CHRIST CRUCIFIXION

Bulgakov, M. The master and Margarita

JESUS CHRIST FAMILY

Rice, A. Christ the Lord

JESUS CHRIST FRIENDS AND ASSOCIATES

Williams, N. John

JEWEL THIEVES

Collins, W. The moonstone

Coulter, C. The final cut

Greenwood, K. Death by water

Roberts, N. Honest illusions

Westlake, D. The hot rock

JEWELERS

Orenstein, H. Love at first like

Reisman, N. The first desire

Rose, M. Cartier's hope

JEWELRY

Chevalier, T. Girl with a pearl earring

Hunter, M. The conquest of Lady Cassandra

Parks, S. Getting mother's body

Trollope, A. The Eustace diamonds

JEWELRY THEFT

Ashford, J. What the duke doesn't know

Block, L. The burglar in the closet

Collins, W. The moonstone

Coulter, C. The final cut

Greenwood, K. Death by water

Hollis, L. Poppy Harmon investigates

Khan, V. The perplexing theft of the jewel in the crown

Lindsay, J. Just watch me

London, J. The year of living scandalously

Lowell, E. Pearl Cove

Rozan, S. The Shanghai Moon

Runcie, J. Sidney Chambers and the shadow of death

Sayers, D. The nine tailors

Simenon, G. Maigret bides his time

Tan, L. What we were promised

Westlake, D. The hot rock

Jewels of the Ton [series] Galen, S.

JEWISH AMERICAN AUTHORS

Roth, P. The anatomy lesson

Roth, P. Exit ghost

Roth, P. The ghost writer

Roth, P. My life as a man

Roth, P. Zuckerman bound

Roth, P. Zuckerman unbound

JEWISH AMERICAN BOYS

Doctorow, E. World's Fair

Roth, H. Call it sleep

Roth, H. A star shines over Mt. Morris Park

JEWISH AMERICAN FAMILIES

Birmingham, S. Carriage trade

Doctorow, E. Ragtime

Heller, J. Good as Gold

Oates, J. The gravedigger's daughter

Plain, B. Crescent City

Plain, B. Harvest

Plain, B. Tapestry

Rojstaczer, S. The mathematician's shiva

Roth, P. American pastoral

Roth, P. The plot against America

Roth, H. Requiem for Harlem

JEWISH AMERICAN MEN

Allende, I. In the midst of winter

Bellow, S. Herzog

Bellow, S. Mr. Sammler's planet

Bellow, S. Novels, 1944-1953

Bellow, S. Seize the day

Chabon, M. The Yiddish Policemen's Union

Epstein, J. The love song of A. Jerome Minkoff, and other stories

Horn, D. The world to come

Plain, B. Tapestry

Pomerantz, S. Rich boy

Potok, C. The gift of Asher Lev

Roth, H. From bondage

Roth, H. Requiem for Harlem

Roth, P. Everyman

Roth, P. My life as a man

Roth, P. Portnoy's complaint

JEWISH AMERICAN MEN -- IDENTITY

Roth, P. American pastoral

Roth, P. The anatomy lesson

Roth, P. Exit ghost

Roth, P. The ghost writer

Roth, P. Goodbye, Columbus, and five short stories

Roth, P. The human stain

Roth, P. I married a Communist

Roth, P. Letting go

Roth, P. Zuckerman bound

JEWISH MEN

Aciman, A. Harvard square
Amis, M. The zone of interest
Auster, P. 4 3 2 1
Bailey, P. Uncle Rudolf
Baxter, C. Saul and Patsy
Begley, L. About Schmidt
Bezmozgis, D. The betrayers
Brodesser-Akner, T. Fleishman is in trouble
Chabon, M. The amazing adventures of Kavalier & Clay
Cohen, J. Book of numbers
Craig, C. Miss Burma
Friedman, D. Running out of road
Gross, A. The one man
Heller, J. Good as Gold
Helprin, M. Paris in the present tense
Hertmans, S. The convert
Jacobson, H. The Finkler question
Keilson, H. Life goes on
Le Carre, J. The tailor of Panama
Liss, D. A spectacle of corruption
Michaels, A. Fugitive pieces
Neugeboren, J. 1940
Parini, J. The Damascus road
Roth, P. Letting go
Simon, M. The last Jew standing
Skibell, J. A curable romantic
Stern, S. The Pinch
Sthers, A. Holy lands
Styron, W. Sophie's choice
Torday, D. The last flight of Poxl West
Wallant, E. The pawnbroker
Walton, J. Farthing
Wiesel, E. Dawn
Wiesel, E. Hostage
Wiesel, E. Night, Dawn, The accident

JEWISH MEN -- IDENTITY

Smith, Z. The autograph man

JEWISH MOURNING CUSTOMS

Rojstaczer, S. The mathematician's shiva

JEWISH RESISTANCE AND REVOLTS

Levi, P. If not now, when?

JEWISH TEENAGE GIRLS

Bank, M. The wonder spot
Greenberg, J. I never promised you a rose garden

JEWISH TEENAGERS

Clayton, M. The last train to London

JEWISH WAY OF LIFE

Englander, N. What we talk about when we talk about Anne
 Frank
Jacobson, H. The Finkler question
Singer, I. Collected stories
Singer, I. The family Moskat
Singer, I. The magician of Lublin
Zimler, R. The last Kabbalist of Lisbon

JEWISH WAY OF LIFE -- LOWER EAST SIDE, NEW YORK CITY

Roth, H. Call it sleep

JEWISH WOMEN

Albert, E. The book of Dahlia
Anton, M. Apprentice
Benedict, M. The only woman in the room
Black, C. Murder in the Marais
Bohjalian, C. Skeletons at the feast
Burke, J. Wayfaring stranger
Dahl, K. The courier
Diamant, A. The Boston girl
Drndic, D. Trieste
Durrell, L. Justine
Falcones de Sierra, I. Cathedral of the sea
Franck, J. Blindness of the heart
Horn, D. Eternal life
Isaacs, S. As husbands go
King, L. The game
Kowal, M. The calculating stars
Kowal, M. The fated sky
Leavitt, D. The two Hotel Francforts
Lethem, J. Dissident gardens
Lippman, L. Lady in the lake
Matthiessen, P. In paradise
Norman, H. The museum guard
Novik, N. Spinning silver
Ozick, C. The Puttermesser papers
Piercy, M. Gone to soldiers
Pontoppidan, H. Lucky Per
Richler, N. Your mouth is lovely
Roberts, M. Ignorance
Russell, M. Epitaph
Shapiro, B. The muralist
Sherwood, F. The book of splendor
Smith, J. Star of Persia
Solomon, A. Leaving Lucy Pear
Spark, M. The Mandelbaum gate

JEWS

Aciman, A. Call me by your name
Aciman, A. Find me
Albahari, D. Gotz and Meyer
Antopol, M. The UnAmericans
Apelfeld, A. The man who never stopped sleeping
Apelfeld, A. To the edge of sorrow
Artson, B. Odessa, Odessa
Black, C. Murder in the Marais
Bohjalian, C. Skeletons at the feast
Cossette, C. Shelter of the most high
Dahl, J. Conviction
Englander, N. The ministry of Special Cases
Englander, N. What we talk about when we talk about Anne
 Frank
Faulkner, C. Finding Georgina
Franklin, A. Mistress of the art of death
Halfon, E. Mourning
Helprin, M. In sunlight and in shadow
Krauss, N. Forest Dark
Lebrecht, N. The song of names

JILTED WOMEN
Duenas, M. The time in between
Frame, R. Havisham
Frantz, L. The lacemaker
Higgins, K. The best man
Higgins, K. The perfect match
Kamali, M. The stationery shop
Kinsale, L. Lessons in French
Krentz, J. When all the girls have gone
Lopez Barrio, C. The house of the impossible loves
Mallery, S. California girls
Malone, M. Bad blood
Sosa, M. The worst best man
Williams, N. This is happiness
Jim Henson's tale of sand Perez, R.
Jim the boy Earley, T.
Jimm Juree mysteries [series] Cotterill, C.
Jimmy Bluefeather Heacox, K.
Jimmy Paz series [series] Gruber, M.
Jitterbug perfume Robbins, T.
Jo Beckett series [series] Gardiner, M.
JOAN OF ARC,, SAINT, 1412-1431
Gregory, P. The lady of the rivers
Twain, M. Personal recollections of Joan of Arc
Joanna Brady mysteries [series] Jance, J.
Joanna Stark mysteries [series] Muller, M.
Joanne Ross novels [series] Scott, A.
JOB HUNTING
Hynes, J. Next
JOB SATISFACTION
Wilson, S. The man in the gray flannel suit
JOB STRESS
Amdahl, G. I am death
JOCKEYS
Francis, F. Pulse
Francis, D. Smokescreen
Joe Brown, L.
Joe College Perrotta, T.
Joe Grey mysteries [series] Murphy, S.
Joe Gunther mysteries [series] Mayor, A.
Joe Leaphorn and Jim Chee mysteries [series] Hillerman, T.
Joe Pickett novels [series] Box, C.
Joe Pitt casebook [series] Huston, C.
Joe Victim Cleave, P.
Joe Wilderness novels [series] Lawton, J.
JOHANNESBURG, SOUTH AFRICA
Beukes, L. Slipping
Beukes, L. Zoo city
Clemmons, Z. What we lose
Paton, A. Cry, the beloved country
John Williams, N.
John Coffin mysteries [series] Butler, G.
John Corey novels [series] DeMille, N.
John dies at the end Wong, D.
John dies at the end [series] Wong, D.
JOHN FRANKLIN ARCTIC EXPEDITION, (1845-1851?)
Simmons, D. The Terror

John Hayes novels [series] Quirk, M.
JOHN HENRY
Whitehead, C. John Henry Days
John Henry Cole novels [series] Brooks, B.
John Henry Days Whitehead, C.
John Keller novels [series] Block, L.
John Madden novels [series] Airth, R.
John March novels [series] Spiegelman, P.
JOHN PAUL II,, POPE, 1920-2005
Higgins, J. Confessional
John Putnam Thatcher mysteries [series] Lathen, E.
John Rain novels [series] Eisler, B.
John Saturnall's feast Norfolk, L.
John Shakespeare series [series] Clements, R.
John Smith (Christopher Farnsworth) [series] Farnsworth, C.
John Wells novels [series] Berenson, A.
John Woman Mosley, W.
JOHN, KING OF ENGLAND, 1167-1216
Penman, S. Cruel as the grave
Penman, S. Dragon's lair
Penman, S. Here be dragons
Penman, S. The Queen's man
Scott, W. Ivanhoe
JOHN, OF GAUNT, DUKE OF LANCASTER, 1340-1399
Seton, A. Katherine
JOHN, THE APOSTLE, SAINT
Williams, N. John
Johnny got his gun Trumbo, D.
JOHNSON, ROBERT, 1911-1938
Alexie, S. Reservation blues
Mosley, W. RL's dream
JOHNSON, SAMUEL, 1709-1784
Theroux, M. Strange bodies
JOKES
Grossman, D. A horse walks into a bar
JOKING RELATIONSHIPS
Wallace, D. Big fish
Jonah Geller novels [series] Shrier, H.
Jonathan Argyll and Flavia DiStefano mysteries [series] Pears, I.
Jonathan Ransom novels [series] Reich, C.
Jonathan Strange & Mr. Norrell Clarke, S.
Jonathan Stride novels [series] Freeman, B.
JONES,, MOTHER, 1837-1930
Montgomery, J. The widows
Joseph O'Loughlin and Vincent Ruiz novels [series] Robotham, M.
JOSEPH, HUSBAND OF MARY
Rice, A. Christ the Lord
JOURNALISM
Delinsky, B. Lake news
Eco, U. Numero zero
Watt, H. To the lions
JOURNALISM -- POLITICAL ASPECTS
Allende, I. Of love and shadows
JOURNALISTIC ETHICS

DeSilva, B. Providence rag

JOURNALISTS

Allende, I. Of love and shadows
Asimov, I. I, robot
Baldacci, D. The fallen
Beukes, L. Broken monsters
Bolano, R. Nazi literature in the Americas
Boll, H. The lost honor of Katharina Blum
Braun, L. The cat who ate Danish modern
Braun, L. The cat who went underground
Brookmyre, C. Black widow
Brown, D. Creek Mary's blood
Brunkhorst, A. The gilded Life of Matilda Duplaine
Carr, C. The alienist
Carr, C. The angel of darkness
Christopher, A. Not the girl you marry
Connelly, M. The scarecrow
De Leon, A. Side chick nation
Delinsky, B. Lake news
Dexter, P. Spooner
Doig, I. Ride with me, Mariah Montana
Dunne, D. People like us
Dunne, D. Too much money
Dyer, G. Jeff in Venice, death in Varanasi
Eco, U. Numero zero
Farah, N. Crossbones
Faulkner, W. Pylon
Finder, J. The fixer
Flint, E. Little deaths
Furst, A. Blood of victory
Garcia Marquez, G. Memories of my melancholy whores
Grant, M. Feed
Grant, M. Feedback
Grant, M. Deadline
Grass, G. Crabwalk
Greene, G. Brighton Rock
Grisham, J. The pelican brief
Gruen, S. The ape house
Guterson, D. Snow falling on cedars
Hamill, P. Tabloid city
Harris, T. Red dragon
Harrod-Eagles, C. Game over
Hiaasen, C. Lucky you
Hijuelos, O. Twain & Stanley enter paradise
Ignatius, D. A firing offense
James, M. A brief history of seven killings
Jin, H. The boat rocker
Jones, J. The silence
Karnezis, P. The maze
Katzenbach, J. Just cause
Kelly, J. The fire baby
Kelly, J. The moon tunnel
Kennedy, W. Chango's beads and two-tone shoes
Landvik, L. Chronicles of a radical hag
Lasdun, J. Afternoon of a faun
Laureano, C. The Saturday Night Supper Club
Lemaitre, P. Irene

Leonard, E. The Hot Kid
Lippman, L. Lady in the lake
Lohmann, J. Winning Ruby Heart
Lynn, A. Now you see it
Mallon, T. Bandbox
Mallon, T. Watergate
Mamet, D. Chicago
Marlette, D. Magic time
Martinson, T. The reign of the Kingfisher
McDonald, I. River of gods
Mcdonald, G. Fletch
Miller, D. The girl in green
Moehringer, J. Sutton
Montero, M. Dancing to "Almendra"
Muller, M. Point Deception
O'Donovan, G. The priest
Owen, H. The bottom
Owen, H. The devil's triangle
Owen, H. Oregon Hill
Owen, H. Parker Field
Palahniuk, C. Lullaby
Parker, T. California girl
Parks, B. The girl next door
Patterson, R. No safe place
Petrie, N. Burning bright
Phillips, S. First Lady
Pratchett, T. The truth
Price, R. Freedomland
Rachman, T. The imperfectionists
Rademacher, C. Deadly Camargue
Ragan, T. Buried deep
Ragan, T. Deadly recall
Ragan, T. Her last day
Raimondo, L. Dante's poison
Ramzipoor, E. The ventriloquists
Restrepo, L. No place for heroes
Robertson, R. The long take
Robinson, P. Piece of my heart
Ruiz Zafon, C. The angel's game
Sa'dawi, A. Frankenstein in Baghdad
Sanders, J. Speakers of the dead
Sandford, J. Deadline
Shannon, D. The Manson curse
Sidor, S. The mirror's edge
Stroby, W. Some die nameless
Title, S. The undateable
Vidal, G. 1876
Vidal, G. Washington, D. C.
Ware, R. The woman in cabin ten
Warren, R. All the king's men
Wiggs, S. The beekeeper's ball
Wolfe, T. Back to blood

JOURNALISTS -- IRELAND
Llywelyn, M. 1921
JOURNALISTS -- NEW HAMPSHIRE
Delinsky, B. Lake news
JOURNALISTS -- NEWFOUNDLAND AND LABRADOR

Proulx, A. The shipping news

JOURNALISTS -- PARIS, FRANCE

Furst, A. The foreign correspondent

JOURNALISTS -- SCOTLAND

Scott, A. Beneath the abbey wall

Scott, A. A double death on the Black Isle

Scott, A. A kind of grief

Scott, A. The low road

JOURNALISTS -- UNITED STATES

Mcdonald, G. Fletch

Michener, J. Mexico

Orringer, J. The flight portfolio

Journey to the centre of the Earth Verne, J.

Journey to the end of the night Celine, L.

JOY AND SORROW

Krauss, N. Great house

Smiley, J. Early warning

Smiley, J. Golden age

Smiley, J. Some luck

JOY AND SORROW IN WOMEN

Cunningham, M. The hours

Joy in the morning Smith, B.

The **Joy** Luck Club Tan, A.

JOYCE, JAMES, 1882-1941

Joyce, J. A portrait of the artist as a young man

JUAN DE FUCA RIDGE

Watts, P. Starfish

Jubilee Walker, M.

JUDAEA (REGION)

Wallace, L. Ben-Hur

JUDAH LOEW BEN BEZALEL, CA 1525-1609

Sherwood, F. The book of splendor

JUDAISM

Brooks, G. People of the book

Goldberg, T. Gangsterland

Miller, R. Jacob's folly

Wiesel, E. A mad desire to dance

Zimler, R. The last Kabbalist of Lisbon

Judas Oz, A.

Judas child O'Connell, C.

The **Judas** Field Bahr, H.

Jude the obscure Hardy, T.

A **judgement** in stone Rendell, R.

JUDGES

Box, C. Long range

Buckley, C. Supreme Courtship

Finder, J. Guilty minds

Grossman, D. A horse walks into a bar

Longworth, M. Death at the Chateau Bremont

Longworth, M. Murder in the Rue Dumas

Marlette, D. Magic time

Nugent, L. Lying in wait

Parks, B. Say nothing

Perry, A. Farriers' Lane

Pope, B. The missing Italian girl

Toibin, C. The heather blazing

Trollope, J. Marrying the mistress

The **judges** Wiesel, E.

JUDGES -- DEATH

Roosevelt, E. Murder at midnight

JUDGES -- RETIREMENT

Desai, K. The inheritance of loss

JUDGES -- SAVANNAH, GEORGIA

Brown, S. Ricochet

JUDGMENT

Wiesel, E. The judges

Judgment Finder, J.

The **judgment** of Caesar Saylor, S.

JUDICIAL CORRUPTION

Brown, S. Ricochet

Dugoni, R. The conviction

Marston, E. The bawdy basket

JUDICIAL ERROR

Arvin, R. Blood of angels

Baldacci, D. Redemption

Bell, S. For his pleasure

Buchanan, E. You only die twice

Daly, P. Clear my name

Dow, D. Confessions of an innocent man

Grisham, J. The guardians

King, C. Stiletto justice

Lepionka, K. The last place you look

Liss, D. A spectacle of corruption

McCrumb, S. The ballad of Frankie Silver

Mina, D. Conviction

Neuhaus, N. Snow White must die

Parker, R. Small vices

Persson Giolito, M. Beyond all reasonable doubt

Smith, M. Love her madly

Weber, C. Man on the run

Williams, B. The summer wives

Winthrop, E. The mercy seat

JUDICIAL SYSTEM

Kushner, R. The Mars room

Pava, S. A naked singularity

JUDICIAL SYSTEM -- GREAT BRITAIN

Dickens, C. Bleak House

The **jugger** Stark, R.

Jules Maigret mysteries [series] Simenon, G.

Julia and Louise novels [series] Brown, R.

Julian Comstock Wilson, R.

Julie Kalas novels [series] Koenig, M.

Juliet Fortier, A.

July's people Gordimer, N.

JUNG, C G (CARL GUSTAV), 1875-1961

Rubenfeld, J. The interpretation of murder

The **jungle** Sinclair, U.

JUNGLE ANIMALS

Ferencik, E. Into the jungle

JUNGLE SURVIVAL

Ferencik, E. Into the jungle

Smith, S. The ruins

JUNGLES

Ferencik, E. Into the jungle

KANSAS

Cameron, P. The city of your final destination
Durham, D. Gabriel's story
Grecian, A. The saint of wolves and butchers
Hughes, L. Not without laughter
Lerner, B. The Topeka school
McHugh, L. The wolf wants in
Paretsky, S. Dead land
Paretsky, S. Fallout
Parks, G. The learning tree
Roy, L. Bent Road

KANSAS -- HISTORY

Coldsmith, D. Tallgrass

KANSAS -- HISTORY -- 20TH CENTURY

Peterson, J. Early's fall

KANSAS -- HISTORY -- CIVIL WAR, 1861-1865

Robinson, M. Gilead

KANSAS CITY, MISSOURI

Barnett, L. Jam on the Vine
Connell, E. Mrs. Bridge
Flynn, G. Dark places
Gelman, L. Class mom
Gelman, L. You've been volunteered

KAREN (SOUTHEAST ASIAN PEOPLE)

Craig, C. Miss Burma

Karen Pirie novels [series] McDermid, V.

KARMA

Lancaster, J. Here I go again
Poore, M. Reincarnation blues

KASHI, CHINA

Joinson, S. A lady cyclist's guide to Kashgar

Kat Campbell mysteries [series] Ritter, T.

Kate Burkholder thrillers [series] Castillo, L.

Kate Clifford novels [series] Robb, C.

Kate Hamilton mystery [series] Berry, C.

Kate Moore novels [series] Pavone, C.

Kate Reddy novels [series] Pearson, A.

Kate Shugak mysteries [series] Stabenow, D.

Kate Waters novels (Fiona Barton) [series] Barton, F.

KATHARINE, DUCHESS OF LANCASTER, 1350-1403

Seton, A. Katherine

Katherine Seton, A.

Kathleen Mallory mysteries [series] O'Connell, C.

Katya Hijazi novels [series] Ferraris, Z.

Kay Scarpetta mysteries [series] Cornwell, P.

Kay's lucky coin variety Choi, A.

KAZAKHSTAN

Harris, O. A shadow intelligence

KECKLEY, ELIZABETH, CA 1818-1907

Chiaverini, J. Mrs. Lincoln's dressmaker

The **keep** Egan, J.

Keep her safe Hannah, S.

Keep you close Cleveland, K.

The **keeper** Moor, J.

The **keeper** of lost causes Adler-Olsen, J.

The **keepers** of the house Grau, S.

Keeping bedlam at bay in the Prague Cafe Ellis, M.

Keeping faith Picoult, J.

Keeping the house Baker, E.

Keeping up with the Cavendishes [series] Rodale, M.

Keeping watch King, L.

KEILSON, HANS, 1909-2011

Keilson, H. Life goes on

Kemosabe Paulits, J.

Ken Swift novels [series] Dickey, E.

Kendra Booth, C.

KENNEDY, JOHN F (JOHN FITZGERALD), 1917-1963

Buckley, W. Mongoose, R.I.P.
Ellroy, J. American tabloid
Wolfe, P. The lost diary of M

KENNEDY, JOHN F (JOHN FITZGERALD), 1917-1963 ASSASSINATION

DeLillo, D. Libra
Ellroy, J. The cold six thousand
Goonan, K. This shared dream
King, S. 11

KENNEDY, ROBERT FRANCIS, 1925-1968

Buckley, W. Mongoose, R.I.P.

KENT, ENGLAND

Bradley, A. A wicked way to win an earl
Marston, E. The vagabond clown
Morton, K. The distant hours
Shaw, W. The birdwatcher
Simpson, D. Dead by morning
Simpson, D. Last seen alive
Simpson, D. No laughing matter
Simpson, D. Once too often

KENTUCKY

Berry, W. Jayber Crow
Bisson, T. Any day now
Dorris, M. Cloud chamber
Fleming, I. Goldfinger
House, S. A parchment of leaves
Jensen, N. The sisters
Koryta, M. The ridge
Leonard, E. Raylan
Mason, B. Patchwork
Mason, B. Shiloh and other stories
Moyes, J. The giver of stars
Offutt, C. Country dark
Warren, R. Band of angels
Warren, R. World enough and time

KENTUCKY -- HISTORY -- 20TH CENTURY

Morgan, C. The sport of kings

KENTUCKY -- SOCIAL LIFE AND CUSTOMS

Berry, W. That distant land

KENYA

Acker, J. The limits of the world
Crompton, R. Hell's gate
Crompton, R. Hour of the red god
Drayson, N. A guide to the birds of East Africa
Le Carre, J. The constant gardener
Levine, J. Bingo's run
McLain, P. Circling the sun

Fortier, A. The lost sisterhood
Fowler, C. Bryant & May
Fox, C. Gone by midnight
Fox, C. Redemption point
Galen, S. Third son's a charm
Gardner, L. Find her
Gay, R. An untamed state
Gear, K. People of the masks
Golding, W. Darkness visible
Goldman, W. The princess bride
Gowdy, B. Helpless
Grimes, L. In a fix
Groom, W. El Paso
Hamer, K. The girl in the red coat
Hayder, M. Gone
Hiaasen, C. Star Island
Higgins, J. Touch the devil
Hill, J. NOS4A2
Hill, S. The pure in heart
Hobbs, A. Stealing candy
Hurwitz, G. The Nowhere Man
Hurwitz, G. The survivor
Jeffries, S. What the duke desires
Johnson, A. The orphan master's son
Jones, D. A bad day for sunshine
Kaminsky, S. Murder on the Trans-Siberian Express
Kellerman, J. Gone
Kelton, E. The way of the coyote
Kidd, J. Things in jars
King, L. Keeping watch
King, S. The Institute
Koontz, D. The husband
Lansdale, J. The thicket
Laukkanen, O. The professionals
Leonard, E. The Hot Kid
Lippman, L. What the dead know
MacBride, S. Shatter the bones
Mallon, T. Bandbox
Marillier, J. Daughter of the forest
McBain, E. Alice in jeopardy
McBain, E. The frumious bandersnatch
McCall Smith, A. The No. 1 Ladies' Detective Agency
McEwan, I. The child in time
McHugh, L. Arrowood
McKinty, A. The chain
Meloy, M. Do not become alarmed
Meyer, D. Heart of the hunter
Mina, D. Still midnight
Mitchard, J. The deep end of the ocean
Mitchard, J. No time to wave goodbye
Muller, M. Where echoes live
Muller, M. Wolf in the shadows
Murphy, S. Cat pay the devil
Norton, C. What doesn't kill her
O'Brien, E. In the forest
O'Connell, C. Judas child
Oe, K. Somersault

Ohlsson, K. Unwanted
Palmer, M. The fifth vial
Paretsky, S. Hardball
Parker, R. Rough weather
Parker, R. Stranger in paradise
Parker, R. Thin air
Patterson, J. Along came a spider
Penman, S. Dragon's lair
Peters, E. Children of the storm
Peters, E. The hippopotamus pool
Peters, E. The summer of the Danes
Petrie, N. The wild one
Picoult, J. Vanishing acts
Preston, D. The Obsidian chamber
Price, R. Freedomland
Pronzini, B. Nightcrawlers
Pynchon, T. Inherent vice
Quinn, J. The lady most willing
Raybourn, D. A curious beginning
Rendell, R. The tree of hands
Rowland, L. The secret adventures of Charlotte Bronte
Rowland, L. The snow empress
Rushdie, S. The enchantress of Florence
Sakey, M. The blade itself
Sanders, L. McNally's puzzle
Saunders, G. Tenth of December
Saylor, S. Raiders of the Nile
Scerbanenco, G. A private Venus
Scott, J. The kept
Slaughter, K. Undone
Smith, B. Shoot the dog
Smith, M. Three stations
Smith, W. Monsoon
Soderberg, A. The other son
Souljah, Midnight and the meaning of love
Spencer-Fleming, J. Through the evil days
Steinhauer, O. An American spy
Stephens, A. Famous adopted people
Stirling, S. A meeting at Corvallis
Sullivan, M. Theft of swords
Tan, A. The Valley of Amazement
Tudor, C. The other people
Turner, N. My name is Resolute
Tyler, A. Earthly possessions
Umrigar, T. Everybody's son
Unger, L. The stranger inside
Vine, B. Grasshopper
Westlake, D. The road to ruin
Williams, K. Sweet Giselle
Wolfe, G. The land across

KIDNAPPING -- CALIFORNIA
Winslow, D. The kings of cool
Winslow, D. Savages

KIDNAPPING -- ITALY
Faletti, G. A pimp's notes

KIDNAPPING -- MANHATTAN, NEW YORK CITY
Westlake, D. Good behavior

Kindred spirits Bannister, J.

Kinflicks Alther, L.

The **king** at the edge of the world Phillips, A.

King Bongo Sanchez, T.

King divas Diamond, D.

The **king** is always above the people Alarcon, D.

The **king** must die Renault, M.

King of Cuba Garcia, C.

The **king** of lies Hart, J.

King of the badgers Hensher, P.

The **king** of Warsaw Twardoch, S.

KING, MARTIN LUTHER, JR, 1929-1968 ASSASSINA-TION

Berry, S. The bishop's pawn

Ellroy, J. The cold six thousand

Pelecanos, G. Hard revolution

KING, MARTIN LUTHER,, JR, 1929-1968 INFLUENCE

Whitehead, C. The Nickel boys

King, queen, knave Nabokov, V.

King's captain Lambdin, D.

The **king's** justice MacNeal, S.

A **king's** ransom Penman, S.

Kingdom come Ballard, J.

The **kingdom** of bones Gallagher, S.

The **kingdom** of copper Chakraborty, S.

Kingdom of exiles Martineau, M.

Kingdom of strangers Ferraris, Z.

Kingdom of the blind Penny, L.

Kingkiller chronicles [series] Rothfuss, P.

Kingmaker chronicles [series] Bouchet, A.

The **kingmaker's** daughter Gregory, P.

The **kings** of cool Winslow, D.

Kings of infinite space Hynes, J.

KINGSLEY, MARY HENRIETTA, 1862-1900

Bausch, R. Hello to the cannibals

KINGSMARKHAM, ENGLAND

Rendell, R. Simisola

Kingston cycle series [series] Polk, C.

Kinsey Millhone mysteries [series] Grafton, S.

Kinship novels [series] Montgomery, J.

The **kinship** of secrets Kim, E.

KINSHIP-BASED SOCIETY

Ahmad, J. The wandering falcon

Golding, W. The inheritors

King, L. Euphoria

Patchett, A. State of wonder

Wright, A. Carpentaria

Kinshu Miyamoto, T.

Kintu Makumbi, J.

KIOWA INDIANS

Jiles, P. News of the world

KIOWA INDIANS -- RELIGION

Momaday, N. The ancient child

KIOWA INDIANS -- WARS

Jiles, P. The color of lightning

KIOWA WOMEN SHAMANS

Momaday, N. The ancient child

Kirk McGarvey adventures [series] Hagberg, D.

Kirk Stevens and Carla Windermere novels [series] Laukkanen, O.

KIRUNA, SWEDEN

Larsson, A. Until thy wrath be past

A **kiss** before dying Levin, I.

Kiss me, Annabel James, E.

A **kiss** of fate Putney, M.

Kiss of the spider woman Puig, M.

The **kiss** quotient Hoang, H.

Kiss the girls Patterson, J.

Kiss the girls and make them cry Clark, M.

Kissed a sad goodbye Crombie, D.

KISSING

James, E. Kiss me, Annabel

Kissing the gunner's daughter Rendell, R.

The **kitchen** god's wife Tan, A.

The **kite** runner Hosseini, K.

Kitty Pangborn novels [series] Richards, L.

Klara Walldeen novels [series] Zander, J.

KLEPTOMANIA

Egan, J. A visit from the Goon Squad

KLONDIKE GOLD FIELDS

London, J. The call of the wild

KLONDIKE RIVER VALLEY, YUKON TERRITORY

London, J. White Fang

KNIGHTS AND KNIGHTHOOD

Cervantes Saavedra, M. Don Quixote

Cornwell, B. Enemy of God

Cornwell, B. Excalibur

Cornwell, B. The winter king

Follett, K. A column of fire

Follett, K. World without end

Holland, C. Jerusalem

Martin, G. A clash of kings

Martin, G. A feast for crows

Martin, G. A game of thrones

Martin, G. A storm of swords

Robb, C. A twisted vengeance

Scott, W. Ivanhoe

Seton, A. Katherine

Twain, M. A Connecticut Yankee in King Arthur's Court

KNIGHTS AND KNIGHTHOOD -- FRANCE

Cornwell, B. The archer's tale

KNIGHTS AND KNIGHTHOOD -- GREAT BRITAIN

White, T. The once and future king

KNIGHTS OF MALTA.

Berry, S. The Malta exchange

Willocks, T. The religion

KNIGHTS TEMPLAR (MASONIC ORDER)

Berry, S. The Templar legacy

Druon, M. The iron king

Potzsch, O. The dark monk

Knockemstiff Pollock, D.

Knots Farah, N.

KNOWLEDGE

Alexis, A. Fifteen dogs

Robbins, D. Last citadel

KURSK, RUSSIA

Robbins, D. Last citadel

Kurt Wallander mysteries [series] Mankell, H.

KWAZULU-NATAL, SOUTH AFRICA

Nunn, M. Blessed are the dead

Nunn, M. Present darkness

Kyoichiro Kaga mysteries [series] Higashino, K.

KYOTO, JAPAN

Mishima, Y. The temple of the golden pavilion

KYOTO, JAPAN -- HISTORY -- 16TH CENTURY

Spann, S. Blade of the Samurai

Spann, S. Claws of the cat

Spann, S. Trial on Mount Koya

KYOTO, JAPAN -- HISTORY -- 20TH CENTURY

Golden, A. Memoirs of a geisha

KYOTO, JAPAN -- SOCIAL LIFE AND CUSTOMS

Golden, A. Memoirs of a geisha

KYRGYZSTAN

DeLillo, D. Zero K

L

L S D

Boyle, T. Outside looking in

L S D USE

Boyle, T. Outside looking in

L. A. quartet [series] Ellroy, J.

L.A. confidential Ellroy, J.

L.A. outlaws Parker, T.

LA JOLLA, CALIFORNIA

Coyle, M. Yesterday's echo

LA PAZ, BOLIVIA

Recacoechea S., J. American visa

LABOR CAMPS -- CALIFORNIA

Steinbeck, J. The grapes of wrath

LABOR DISPUTES

Brown, S. White hot

Zola, E. Germinal

LABOR DISPUTES -- HISTORY -- 20TH CENTURY

Pynchon, T. Against the day

LABOR EXPLOITATION

Emshwiller, C. The secret city

Sinclair, U. The jungle

LABOR LEADERS

Aguilar Camin, H. Death in Veracruz

Cash, W. The last ballad

LABOR MOVEMENT

Cash, W. The last ballad

Russell, M. The women of the copper country

Straley, J. The big both ways

LABOR MOVEMENT -- UNITED STATES -- HISTORY -- 20TH CENTURY

Shreve, A. Sea glass

LABOR ORGANIZERS

Johnston, W. The colony of unrequited dreams

LABOR ORGANIZING

Russell, M. The women of the copper country

LABOR UNIONS

Brown, S. White hot

Cash, W. The last ballad

Just, W. An unfinished season

Lehane, D. The given day

Marlantes, K. Deep river

Ondaatje, M. In the skin of a lion

Shepard, K. The Celestials

Westlake, D. The road to ruin

Whitehead, C. The intuitionist

LABOR UNIONS -- CORRUPT PRACTICES

Paretsky, S. Indemnity only

Schulberg, B. Waterfront

LABOR UNIONS -- ELECTIONS

Whitehead, C. The intuitionist

LABOR UNIONS -- STEVEDORES

Schulberg, B. Waterfront

LABOR UNIONS -- UNITED STATES

Ellroy, J. American tabloid

LaBrava Leonard, E.

Labyrinth Coulter, C.

A **labyrinth** of scions and sorcery Craddock, C.

The **labyrinth** of the spirits Ruiz Zafon, C.

LABYRINTHS

Borges, J. Collected fictions

Borges, J. Ficciones

Labyrinths of Echo [series] Frei, M.

The **lacemaker** Frantz, L.

Lacey Flint novels [series] Bolton, S.

Ladder of years Tyler, A.

A **ladder** to the sky Boyne, J.

Ladies and gentlemen Ross, A.

Ladies of Lantern Street [series] Quick, A.

The **ladies** of Managua Gage, E.

Ladies of the manor [series] White, R.

LADIES-IN-WAITING

Buckley, F. The doublet affair

Gregory, P. The Boleyn inheritance

Ladivine NDiaye, M.

Lady astronaut novels [series] Kowal, M.

Lady Bridget's diary Rodale, M.

Lady Chatterley's lover Lawrence, D.

Lady Clementine Benedict, M.

Lady cop makes trouble Stewart, A.

A **lady** cyclist's guide to Kashgar Joinson, S.

Lady Derring takes a lover Long, J.

The **Lady** Elizabeth Weir, A.

The **lady** from Zagreb Kerr, P.

The **lady** in the lake Chandler, R.

Lady in the lake Lippman, L.

Lady Isabella's scandalous marriage Ashley, J.

Lady Julia Grey novels [series] Raybourn, D.

The **Lady** Matador's hotel Garcia, C.

The **lady** most willing Quinn, J.

A **lady** never lies Gray, J.

Lady of perdition Hambly, B.

McGahan, A. The white earth
McLarty, R. Art in America
LAND USE
Paretsky, S. Dead land
Landfall Mallon, T.
LANDFILLS
Oates, J. The falls
Wright, A. Carpentaria
Landline Rowell, R.
Landlocked Lessing, D.
LANDLORD AND TENANT
Blundell, J. The high season
Danticat, E. The dew breaker
Delaney, J. The girl before
Levy, A. Small island
Marwood, A. The killer next door
Mosley, W. The man in my basement
Ng, C. Little fires everywhere
LANDLORDS
Coster, N. Halsey Street
Marston, E. The wanton angel
LANDOWNERS
Bryant, N. Christmas with the billionaire
Gogol, N. Dead souls
Hart, E. Haunted ground
Machart, B. The wake of forgiveness
Martin, W. Cape Cod
O'Brien, E. Wild Decembers
Peters, E. Death to the landlords!
Putney, M. A kiss of fate
LANDOWNERS -- AUSTRALIA
McGahan, A. The white earth
LANDSCAPE GARDENING
Evison, J. Lawn boy
LANDSLIDES
Adamson, G. The outlander
LANGUAGE AND LANGUAGES
DeLillo, D. The names
Itani, F. Deafening
Knausgaard, K. My struggle.
Lanchester, J. Fragrant Harbor
Loh, V. Breaking the tongue , by Vyvyane Loh.
Marcus, B. The flame alphabet
McGuire, S. Middlegame
Stephenson, N. The rise and fall of D.O.D.O.
LANGUAGE AND LANGUAGES -- GRAMMARS
Schine, C. The Grammarians
LANGUAGE AND TECHNOLOGY
Graedon, A. The word exchange
The **language** of flowers Diffenbaugh, V.
Lanny Porter, M.
LANSKY, MEYER, 1902-1983
Latour, J. The Havana World Series
LAOS
Cotterill, C. Don't eat me
Cotterill, C. The second biggest nothing
Cotterill, C. Slash and burn

Yoon, P. Run me to earth
LAOS -- HISTORY -- 1975-
Cotterill, C. The coroner's lunch
Cotterill, C. Disco for the departed
LAPLAND
Vida, V. Let the Northern Lights erase your name
LAPTOP COMPUTERS
Finder, J. The switch
LARGE FAMILIES
Lessing, D. The fifth child
Osondu, E. This house is not for sale
Urrea, L. The house of broken angels
**LARGE FAMILIES -- WESTCHESTER COUNTY, NEW
    YORK**
Quindlen, A. Object lessons
The **largesse** of the sea maiden Johnson, D.
Lark and Termite Phillips, J.
LaRose Erdrich, L.
LAS VEGAS, NEVADA
Abani, C. The secret history of Las Vegas
Bell, M. The color of night
Bock, C. Beautiful children
Goldberg, T. Gangsterland
Parker, R. Chance
Pufahl, S. On swift horses
Puzo, M. The last don
Randisi, R. Hey there (you with the gun in your hand)
Seay, M. The mirror thief
Tartt, D. The goldfinch
Tran, V. Dragonfish
Vlautin, W. Don't skip out on me
The **last** ballad Cash, W.
Last bus to wisdom Doig, I.
The **last** camel died at noon Peters, E.
The **last** camellia Jio, S.
Last Chance Llama Ranch Fields, H.
The **last** child Hart, J.
The **last** chronicle of Barset Trollope, A.
Last citadel Robbins, D.
The **last** command Zahn, T.
The **last** confession of Thomas Hawkins Hodgson, A.
The **last** cowboys of San Geronimo Stansel, I.
The **last** crossing Vanderhaeghe, G.
The **last** dance McBain, E.
Last day Rice, L.
LAST DAYS
Coetzee, J. Age of Iron
D'Agostino, K. The antiques
Oates, J. Wild nights
Ramadan, A. The clothesline swing
Schweblin, S. Fever dream
The **last** days of Cafe Leila Bijan, D.
The **last** days of Krypton Anderson, K.
The **last** days of night Moore, G.
The **last** days of Ptolemy Grey Mosley, W.
The **last** detective Lovesey, P.
The **last** Dickens Pearl, M.

Laurence Bartram novels [series] Speller, E.
LAVEAU, MARIE, 1794-1881
  Rhodes, J. Voodoo dreams
Lavender blue murder Childs, L.
Lavinia Lake and Tobias March series [series] Quick, A.
LAW
  Clark, M. The substitution order
Law at Angel's Landing Overholser, W.
LAW CLERKS
  Meltzer, B. The tenth justice
  Stone, N. The verdict
LAW ENFORCEMENT
  Cole, D. Hangman
  Doiron, P. Almost midnight
  Hunter, S. Game of snipers
  Johnson, C. Land of wolves
  Kelton, E. Badger boy
  Kelton, E. Texas vendetta
  Leonard, E. Charlie Martz and other stories
  Leonard, E. When the women come out to dance
  Overholser, W. Law at Angel's Landing
  Reichs, K. A conspiracy of bones
LAW FIRMS
  Andrews, M. Sunset Beach
  Goldman, M. The shallows
  Grisham, J. The firm
  Paretsky, S. Shell game
  Sanders, L. The tenth commandment
  Santora, N. Fifteen digits
  Scottoline, L. Feared
  Stone, N. The verdict
  Woods, S. Below the belt
  Woods, S. A delicate touch
  Woods, S. Fast & loose
LAW STUDENTS
  Parshall, S. Bleeding through
  Schlink, B. The reader
Lawless K'wan
Lawn boy Evison, J.
The **Lawrence** Browne affair Sebastian, C.
LAWRENCE, T E (THOMAS EDWARD), 1888-1935
  Russell, M. Dreamers of the day
The **laws** of invisible things Huyler, F.
LAWYERS
  Abramowitz, A. Thank you, goodnight
  Arvin, R. Blood of angels
  Atkins, A. Wicked city
  Atkinson, K. Case histories
  Bala, S. The boat people
  Barth, J. The floating opera
  Begley, L. About Schmidt
  Blake, R. A dark anatomy
  Brown, S. White hot
  Camus, A. The fall
  Cary, J. The horse's mouth
  Clark, M. The Jezebel remedy
  Connelly, M. The brass verdict

Connelly, M. The fifth witness
Connelly, M. The gods of guilt
Connelly, M. The Lincoln lawyer
Craig, P. Third strike
Crichton, M. Next
Dickens, C. Bleak House
Dugoni, R. The conviction
Dugoni, R. My sister's grave
Dugoni, R. Murder one
Ellis, D. In the company of liars
Eskens, A. The heavens may fall
Ferris, J. The unnamed
Francis, D. Wedding Bush Road
Gaddis, W. A frolic of his own
Galsworthy, J. The Forsyte saga
Gardam, J. Last friends
Gardam, J. The man in the wooden hat
Gardam, J. Old Filth
Gorman, E. Riders on the storm
Greaves, C. Hush money
Greene, G. The tenth man
Grippando, J. The girl in the glass box
Grisham, J. The firm
Grisham, J. The guardians
Grisham, J. The last juror
Hart, J. The king of lies
Iles, G. Turning angel
Irvin, K. Tell her no lies
James, P. A certain justice
Jones, J. The silence
K'wan Lawless
Kennedy, D. The big picture
King, C. Stiletto justice
Kitt, S. Celluloid memories
Lashner, W. A killer's kiss
Lauren, C. Sweet filthy boy
Lee, H. To kill a mockingbird
Lelic, S. The child who
Lescroart, J. The first law
Lescroart, J. Guilt
Lescroart, J. The hearing
Lescroart, J. The oath
Mankell, H. The man who smiled
Maron, M. Shooting at loons
Martini, S. Compelling evidence
McDermid, V. How the dead speak
McPherson, C. Strangers at the gate
Mina, D. The red road
Moore, G. The last days of night
Morgan Jones, C. The silent oligarch
Morgan Jones, C. The jackal's share
Mortimer, J. Rumpole's return
Mosley, W. Cinnamon kiss
Nava, M. Carved in bone
Oates, J. The falls
Patterson, R. No safe place
Pava, S. A naked singularity

Atkinson, K. Started early, took my dog
Nickson, C. At the dying of the year
Nickson, C. Cold cruel winter
Nickson, C. Come the fear
Nickson, C. The constant lovers
Nickson, C. The hocus girl

LEEDS, ENGLAND -- HISTORY -- 19TH CENTURY
Nickson, C. Gods of gold
Nickson, C. On Copper Street
Left at the altar [series] Malone, M.
The **left** hand of darkness Le Guin, U.
Left neglected Genova, L.

LEFT-WING EXTREMISTS
Cumming, C. The Moroccan girl
Steinhauer, O. The middleman
The **leftovers** Perrotta, T.

LEGACIES
Smith, Z. Grand union
Legacy of faith novels [series] Hatcher, R.
A **legacy** of murder Berry, C.

LEGAL ASSISTANCE TO POOR PEOPLE
Grippando, J. The girl in the glass box

LEGAL DOCUMENTS
Santora, N. Fifteen digits

LEGAL SERVICES
Grisham, J. The guardians

LEGAL STORIES
Bing, S. You look nice today
Kim, A. Miracle Creek
Mortimer, J. Rumpole's return
Murray, V. Stand your ground
Nava, M. Carved in bone
Pirro, J. Sly fox
Whitlow, R. A time to stand
Winer, J. Her kind of case
Legal tender Scottoline, L.

LEGAL THRILLERS
Arvin, R. Blood of angels
Burnet, G. His bloody project
Cavanagh, S. Thirteen
Clark, M. Blood defense
Clark, M. Final judgment
Clark, M. The Jezebel remedy
Clark, M. The substitution order
Connelly, M. The brass verdict
Connelly, M. The fifth witness
Connelly, M. The gods of guilt
Connelly, M. The Lincoln lawyer
Cook, T. Sandrine's case
Dow, D. Confessions of an innocent man
Dugoni, R. The conviction
Dugoni, R. Murder one
Edvardsson, M. A nearly normal family
Fairstein, L. Blood oath
Fairstein, L. Entombed
Finder, J. Judgment
Grippando, J. Black horizon

Grippando, J. The girl in the glass box
Grisham, J. The client
Grisham, J. The firm
Grisham, J. The guardians
Grisham, J. The pelican brief
Grisham, J. A time to kill
Hart, J. The king of lies
Iles, G. The bone tree
Iles, G. The devil's punchbowl
Iles, G. Mississippi blood
Iles, G. Natchez burning
Iles, G. Turning angel
Landay, W. Defending Jacob
Lashner, W. A killer's kiss
Lelic, S. The child who
Lescroart, J. The first law
Lescroart, J. Guilt
Lescroart, J. The hearing
Lescroart, J. Nothing but the truth
Lescroart, J. The oath
Marlette, D. Magic time
Martini, S. Compelling evidence
Meltzer, B. The tenth justice
Meltzer, B. The zero game
Moore, G. The holdout
Moore, G. The last days of night
Parks, B. Say nothing
Patterson, R. Balance of power
Patterson, R. Dark lady
Patterson, R. Eclipse
Persson Giolito, M. Beyond all reasonable doubt
Scottoline, L. Feared
Scottoline, L. Legal tender
Silver, E. The execution of Noa P. Singleton
Stone, N. The verdict
Turow, S. Presumed innocent
Turow, S. Testimony
Twain, M. Pudd'nhead Wilson ;
Vaughan, S. Anatomy of a scandal
Walker, W. Crime of privilege
The **legend** of Lyon Redmond Long, J.
The **legend** of Pradeep Mathew Karunatilaka, S.

LEGENDS
Jance, J. Queen of the night
McDonald, I. The Dervish House
Redondo, D. The invisible guardian
Legends of the condor heroes [series] Jin, Y.
Legends of the realm [series] Locke, T.

LEGENDS, NATIVE AMERICAN
Roanhorse, R. Trail of lightning

LEGISLATION
Meltzer, B. The zero game
Sanders, J. Speakers of the dead

LEGISLATORS -- UNITED STATES
Patterson, R. No safe place

LEICESTER, ROBERT DUDLEY,, EARL OF, 1532?-1588
Maxwell, R. The queen's bastard

Bellow, S. Herzog
Bowman, C. Horace Winter says goodbye
Boyle, E. And the miss ran away with the rake
Byatt, A. Possession
Cantor, M. Death and other happy endings
Christie, A. The A B C murders
El-Mohtar, A. This is how you lose the time war
Epstein, J. Wunderland
Faber, M. The book of strange new things
Gestern, H. The people in the photo
Higashino, K. The miracles of the Namiya General Store
Jones, T. An American marriage
Kamali, M. The stationery shop
King, S. Mr. Mercedes
Kutsukake, L. The translation of love
MacLean, S. A rogue by any other name
O'Leary, B. The flatshare
Pearson, R. A long time comin'
Preston, D. Verses for the dead
Richardson, S. Pamela
Robertson, M. The Baker Street letters
Robertson, M. The Baker Street translation
Robertson, M. The brothers of Baker Street
Robertson, M. Moriarty returns a letter
Shaffer, M. The Guernsey Literary and Potato Peel Pie Society
Simenon, G. Maigret and the black sheep
Sthers, A. Holy lands
Stoker, D. Dracul
Vuong, O. On Earth we're briefly gorgeous
Youngson, A. Meet me at the museum
Yourcenar, M. Memoirs of Hadrian

LETTERING
Clayborn, K. Love lettering
LETTERS
Backman, F. My grandmother asked me to tell you she's sorry
Bear, E. The stone in the skull
Berry, S. The Malta exchange
Fuentes, C. The eagle's throne
Griffiths, E. The stone circle
Hart, C. Letter from home
McBain, E. Hark!
Miyamoto, T. Kinshu
Moriarty, L. The husband's secret
O'Connor, F. Collected works
Phillips, C. The Rossetti letter
Reich, C. The take
Robinson, M. Gilead
Schumacher, J. Dear committee members
Shaffer, M. The Guernsey Literary and Potato Peel Pie Society
Turow, S. Ordinary heroes
Ware, R. The turn of the key
West, N. Novels and other writings
Letters from Paris Blackwell, J.
Letting go Roth, P.

LETTING GO (PSYCHOLOGY)
Bird, S. The gap year
LEUKEMIA
Cleave, C. Gold
Levi's will Cramer, W.
Leviathan Auster, P.
Leviathan wakes Corey, J.
Lew Archer novels [series] Macdonald, R.
LEWIS AND CLARK EXPEDITION, (1804-1806)
Sargent, C. Museum of human beings
Lewis trilogy [series] May, P.
LEWIS, C S (CLIVE STAPLES), 1898-1963
Henry, P. Becoming Mrs. Lewis
LEXICOGRAPHERS
Arsenault, E. The broken teaglass
Johnson, D. Everything under
Lexicon Barry, M.
LEXINGTON, KENTUCKY
Edwards, K. The memory keeper's daughter
LGBTQIA COMICS
Cruse, H. The complete Wendel
Merey, I. A + e 4ever
LGBTQIA FICTION
Aciman, A. Call me by your name
Aciman, A. Enigma variations
Aciman, A. Find me
Afrika, T. Bitter Eden
Baldwin, J. Another country
Baldwin, J. Early novels and stories
Baldwin, J. Giovanni's room
Barnett, L. Jam on the Vine
Barry, S. Days without end
Bartlett, N. The disappearance boy
Bledsoe, L. The big bang symphony
Bloom, A. White houses
Brayden, M. First position
Brown, R. Rubyfruit jungle
Cassara, J. The house of impossible beauties
Castellani, C. Leading men
Charles, K. Wanted, a gentleman
Cheever, J. Falconer
Choi, S. My education
Cusset, C. Life of David Hockney
De Robertis, C. Cantoras
De Robertis, C. The gods of tango
Dennis-Benn, N. Here comes the sun
Eugenides, J. Middlesex
Evaristo, B. Mr. Loverman
Festing, I. The bird keeper
Forster, E. Maurice
Fu, K. For today I am a boy
Gaspar de Alba, A. Desert blood
Greenwell, G. Cleanness
Greenwell, G. What belongs to you
Greer, A. Less
Hall, A. For real
Harris, E. Basketball Jones

Palliser, C. The unburied

Sayers, D. The unpleasantness at the Bellona Club

LIBRARIES -- ITALY

Eco, U. The name of the rose

The **library** at Mount Char Hawkins, S.

The **library** of the unwritten Hackwith, A.

LIBRARY TRUSTEES -- SOUTH CAROLINA

Hart, C. Yankee Doodle dead

LIBYA -- POLITICS AND GOVERNMENT -- 1969-

Matar, H. In the country of men

Licks of love Updike, J.

The **lie** Dunmore, H.

Lie down in darkness Styron, W.

Liebermann papers [series] Tallis, F.

The **lieutenant** Grenville, K.

Lieutenant Hornblower Forester, C.

LIFE

Bradbury, R. Dandelion wine

Brown, K. The life Lucy knew

Hadley, T. Bad dreams and other stories

Perec, G. Life

Life Perec, G.

Life & times of Michael K Coetzee, J.

Life after Ganshert, K.

LIFE AFTER DEATH

Abulhawa, S. The blue between sky and water

Albom, M. The five people you meet in heaven

Albom, M. The next person you meet in Heaven

Beagle, P. A fine and private place

Bonnaffons, A. The regrets

Brockmeier, K. The brief history of the dead

Choo, Y. The ghost bride

Davies, R. Murther and walking spirits

Flynn, M. The January dancer

Hill, J. Heart-shaped box

Irwin, S. The broken ones

Lee, Y. Ninefox gambit

Lee, Y. Revenant gun

Majmudar, A. Partitions

Pyper, A. The damned

Richardson, K. Greywalker

Sebold, A. The lovely bones

Stephenson, N. Fall or, Dodge in hell

Tyler, A. The beginner's goodbye

Vollmann, W. Last stories and other stories

Westerfeld, S. The killing of worlds

Westerfeld, S. The risen empire

Life after life Atkinson, K.

The **life** all around me by Ellen Foster Gibbons, K.

Life among giants Roorbach, B.

The **life** and death of Sophie Stark North, A.

The **life** and loves of a she-devil Weldon, F.

Life and other inconveniences Higgins, K.

A **life** apart Mukherjee, N.

Life before man Atwood, M.

LIFE CHANGE EVENTS

Kingsbury, K. When we were young

LIFE CHANGE EVENTS

Acker, J. The limits of the world

Adelman, M. Piece of mind

Ahava, S. Things that fall from the sky

Alarcon, D. At night we walk in circles

Aliu, X. Brass

Allende, I. In the midst of winter

Allende, I. A long petal of the sea

Allio, K. Buddhism for Western children

Anshaw, C. Carry the one

Antoinette, A. Butterfly

Arnoult, D. Sufficient grace

Artson, B. Odessa, Odessa

Atkinson, K. Started early, took my dog

Atkinson, K. Transcription

Attenberg, J. The Middlesteins

Auster, P. 4 3 2 1

Ausubel, R. Sons and daughters of ease and plenty

Backman, F. My grandmother asked me to tell you she's sorry

Baldacci, D. One summer

Balogh, M. Someone to hold

Balogh, M. Someone to love

Bandele, A. Daughter

Barnes, J. The only story

Bauermeister, E. The scent keeper

Beagle, P. In Calabria

Beyda, E. The body double

Bijan, D. The last days of Cafe Leila

Bivald, K. The readers of Broken Wheel recommend

Block, S. Oliver Loving

Blumenfeld, A. The cast

Boianjiu, S. The people of forever are not afraid

Bradford, B. Master of his fate

Buntin, J. Marlena

Butland, S. The lost for words bookshop

Butler, M. Pickle's progress

Buxbaum, J. After you

Cameron, P. The city of your final destination

Cander, C. The weight of a piano

Cantor, M. Death and other happy endings

Card, M. These ghosts are family

Carr, R. Virgin river

Carr, R. What we find

Cash, W. This dark road to mercy

Center, K. How to walk away

Clark, M. The substitution order

Colgan, J. The endless beach

Colin, E. The memory thief

Corman, A. Prized possessions

Coupland, D. Eleanor Rigby

Crouch, B. Dark matter

D'Eramo, L. Deviation

D'Erasmo, S. The sky below

Daniels, N. Too close

Dark, A. Think of England

Dastgir, R. A small fortune

O'Nan, S. The night country
Oates, J. The doll-master
Oates, J. Wild nights
Obioma, C. The fishermen
Offutt, C. Country dark
Ólafsdóttir, A. Butterflies in November
Olafsson, O. The sacrament
Ozick, C. The Puttermesser papers
Parini, J. The Damascus road
Parrish, C. Still life
Perrotta, T. The leftovers
Petterson, P. I curse the river of time
Phillips, G. Fierce kingdom
Pochoda, I. Visitation Street
Ramqvist, K. The white city
Read, C. Valley of ashes
Remarque, E. All quiet on the western front
Remarque, E. The road back
Ricciardi, D. Warning light
Robinson, M. Lila
Rooney, S. Normal people
Rothmann, R. To die in spring
Rubart, J. The long journey to Jake Palmer
Ruskovich, E. Idaho
Sahota, S. The year of the runaways
Scibona, S. The volunteer
Serpell, N. The old drift
Shafak, E. Honor
Shepard, S. The one inside
Shields, C. The stone diaries
Shreve, A. Testimony
Shriver, L. So much for that
Shteyngart, G. Lake Success
Simonson, H. The summer before the war
Smith, Z. NW
Solomon, A. Leaving Lucy Pear
Sparks, N. Every breath
Stevens, C. Never let you go
Stockett, K. The help
Stroud, C. The shimmer
Swinson, K. Lifestyles of the rich and shameless
Theroux, P. The Lower River
Treuer, D. Prudence
Trollope, J. A Spanish lover
Tropper, J. One last thing before I go
Truong, M. The sweetest fruits
Turner, B. The secret life of Sarah Hollenbeck
VanderMeer, J. Borne
Vyleta, D. Smoke
Ware, R. The lying game
Watson, S. Before I go to sleep
Waxman, A. The bookish life of Nina Hill
Wells, B. The end of loneliness
Westlake, D. Memory
Whitaker, K. The animators
Whitehead, C. The Nickel boys
Wiggs, S. The Oysterville sewing circle

Wilhelm, K. The good children
Winman, S. Tin man
Wong, D. Futuristic violence and fancy suits
Wood, T. The engineer's wife
Wrobel, S. Darling Rose Gold
Yates, C. Grist Mill Road
Yoon, P. Run me to earth
Young, W. The shack
Zevin, G. The storied life of A. J. Fikry
Zevin, G. Young Jane Young

LIFE CHANGE EVENTS -- PSYCHOLOGICAL AS-PECTS
Giordano, P. The solitude of prime numbers

LIFE CHANGE EVENTS IN CHILDREN
Petterson, P. Out stealing horses

LIFE CHANGE EVENTS IN TEENAGERS
Toews, M. A complicated kindness
Life goes on Keilson, H.

LIFE IMPRISONMENT
Kushner, R. The Mars room

LIFE INSURANCE
McBain, E. Alice in jeopardy
The **life** Lucy knew Brown, K.
The **life** of an unknown man Makine, A.
Life of David Hockney Cusset, C.
The **life** of objects Moore, S.
Life of Pi Martel, Y.

LIFE ON OTHER PLANETS
Anders, C. The city in the middle of the night
Adams, D. The hitchhiker's guide to the galaxy
Adams, D. The restaurant at the end of the universe
Anderson, K. The last days of Krypton
Asimov, I. Foundation
Asimov, I. Foundation and empire
Asimov, I. Second foundation
Banks, I. The hydrogen sonata
Beukes, L. Slipping
Bradbury, R. The Martian chronicles
Brown, P. Golden son
Brown, P. Red rising
Burke, S. Semiosis
Cambias, J. A darkling sea
Card, O. Ender's game
Chambers, B. Record of a spaceborn few
Corey, J. Abaddon's gate
Corey, J. Babylon's ashes
Corey, J. Caliban's war
Corey, J. Cibola burn
Corey, J. Nemesis games
Corey, J. Persepolis rising
Corey, J. Tiamat's wrath
Delany, S. Aye, and Gomorrah
Egan, G. Schild's ladder
Faber, M. The book of strange new things
Flynn, M. The January dancer
Gilman, C. Dark orbit
Hamilton, P. The dreaming void

Lights all night long Fitzpatrick, L.

Lights out Starr, J.

Lights! Camera! Puzzles! Hall, P.

Like death Maupassant, G.

Like family Giordano, P.

Like lions Panowich, B.

Like water for chocolate Esquivel, L.

The **likeness** French, T.

Lila Robinson, M.

Lilac girls Kelly, M.

Lilli de Jong Benton, J.

Lillian Boxfish takes a walk Rooney, K.

Lily Bonner, C.

LIMA, PERU

Alarcon, D. Lost City Radio

Vargas Llosa, M. Aunt Julia and the scriptwriter

Limitless novels [series] Glynn, A.

The **limits** of enchantment Joyce, G.

The **limits** of the world Acker, J.

The **Limpopo** Academy of Private Detection McCall Smith, A.

Lincoln Vidal, G.

Lincoln and Speed novels [series] Putnam, J.

LINCOLN COLLEGE (UNIVERSITY OF OXFORD)

Finch, C. The September Society

The **Lincoln** conspiracy O'Brien, T.

Lincoln in the bardo Saunders, G.

The **Lincoln** lawyer Connelly, M.

Lincoln Perry mysteries [series] Koryta, M.

Lincoln Rhyme mysteries [series] Deaver, J.

LINCOLN, ABRAHAM, 1809-1865

Gleason, C. Murder at the capitol

Putnam, J. These honored dead

Saunders, G. Lincoln in the bardo

Solomon, B. The murder of Willie Lincoln

Vidal, G. Lincoln

LINCOLN, ABRAHAM, 1809-1865 ASSASSINATION

O'Brien, T. The Lincoln conspiracy

LINCOLN, MARY TODD, 1818-1882

Chiaverini, J. Mrs. Lincoln's dressmaker

Newman, J. Mary

O'Brien, T. The Lincoln conspiracy

LINCOLN, WILLIAM WALLACE, 1850-1862

Solomon, B. The murder of Willie Lincoln

Lincoln's White House mysteries [series] Gleason, C.

Linda Wallander mysteries [series] Mankell, H.

Linda Wallheim mysteries [series] Harrison, M.

LINDBERGH, ANNE MORROW, 1906-2001

Benjamin, M. The aviator's wife

LINDBERGH, CHARLES A (CHARLES AUGUSTUS), 1902-1974

Benjamin, M. The aviator's wife

Roth, P. The plot against America

Linden Hills Naylor, G.

The **line** Grushin, O.

The **line** Limon, M.

Line of fire White, S.

LINGUISTS

Barry, M. Lexicon

Locke, T. Emissary

Parkhurst, C. The dogs of Babel

Russell, M. Children of God

Russell, M. The sparrow

Stephenson, N. The rise and fall of D.O.D.O.

Watts, P. Blindsight

Links Farah, N.

Links trilogy [series] Farah, N.

LION

Andrews, M. Of fire and lions

Lion in the valley Peters, E.

Lionel Asbo Amis, M.

Lionheart Penman, S.

LIPOGRAMS

Dunn, M. Ella Minnow Pea

LIQUOR SMUGGLING

Stegner, W. The Big Rock Candy Mountain

LISBON, PORTUGAL

Antunes, A. The return of the caravels

Leavitt, D. The two Hotel Francforts

Saramago, J. All the names

LISBON, PORTUGAL -- HISTORY

Saramago, J. The history of the siege of Lisbon

LISBON, PORTUGAL -- HISTORY -- 16TH CENTURY

Zimler, R. The last Kabbalist of Lisbon

The **list** of Adrian Messenger MacDonald, P.

Listening to love Wiseman, B.

LISTS

Clark, G. The bucket list

Hibbert, T. Get a life, Chloe Brown

MacDonald, P. The list of Adrian Messenger

LISZT, FRANZ, 1811-1886

Rayne, S. Music macabre

LITERACY

Moyes, J. The giver of stars

LITERARY AGENTS

Harrod-Eagles, C. Headlong

Peet, M. The Murdstone trilogy

LITERARY FICTION

Aboulela, L. Elsewhere, home

Abraham, T. Black Sunday

Abu-Jaber, D. Crescent

Abu-Jaber, D. Origin

Acampora, L. The paper wasp

Acampora, L. The wonder garden

Achebe, C. Things fall apart

Aciman, A. Call me by your name

Aciman, A. Enigma variations

Aciman, A. Find me

Aciman, A. Harvard square

Ackerman, E. Dark at the crossing

Ackerman, E. Waiting for Eden

Adam, C. Golden child

Adams, A. A southern exposure

Adebayo, A. Stay with me

Banks, R. Affliction
Banks, R. Cloudsplitter
Banks, R. Continental drift
Banks, R. Lost memory of skin
Banks, R. The sweet hereafter
Banville, J. Ancient light
Banville, J. The blue guitar
Banville, J. The book of evidence
Banville, J. Eclipse
Banville, J. The infinities
Banville, J. The sea
Barbery, M. The elegance of the hedgehog
Barker, N. Darkmans
Barker, P. The eye in the door
Barker, P. The ghost road
Barker, S. The incarnations
Barnes, J. England, England
Barnes, J. Flaubert's parrot
Barnes, J. A history of the world in 10 1
Barnes, J. The noise of time
Barnes, J. The only story
Barnes, J. The sense of an ending
Barry, K. City of Bohane
Barry, K. Night boat to Tangier
Barry, S. Days without end
Barry, S. The secret scripture
Barth, J. Chimera
Barth, J. The end of the road
Barth, J. The floating opera
Barth, J. Giles Goat-Boy ;
Barth, J. The last voyage of somebody the sailor
Barth, J. The sot-weed factor
Batuman, E. The idiot
Bauermeister, E. The scent keeper
Baume, S. Spill simmer falter wither
Beagin, J. Vacuum in the dark
Beah, I. Radiance of tomorrow
Beams, C. The illness lesson
Beattie, A. A wonderful stroke of luck
Beatty, P. The sellout
Beauvoir, S. The woman destroyed
Beckett, S. Murphy
Begley, L. About Schmidt
Bellow, S. The adventures of Augie March
Bellow, S. The Bellarosa connection
Bellow, S. Dangling man
Bellow, S. The dean's December
Bellow, S. Henderson the rain king
Bellow, S. Herzog
Bellow, S. Humboldt's gift
Bellow, S. More die of heartbreak
Bellow, S. Mr. Sammler's planet
Bellow, S. Novels, 1944-1953
Bellow, S. Ravelstein
Bellow, S. Seize the day
Bender, A. The particular sadness of lemon cake
Benedetti, M. Springtime in a broken mirror

Benjamin, C. The immortalists
Benjamin, M. Alice I have been
Benjamin, M. The aviator's wife
Bennett, B. The mothers
Benz, C. The gone dead
Berry, W. Jayber Crow
Berry, W. That distant land
Beukes, L. Slipping
Bezmozgis, D. The betrayers
Bijan, D. The last days of Cafe Leila
Bloom, A. Lucky us
Blum, J. The lost family
Bock, C. Alice & Oliver
Bolano, R. 2666
Bolano, R. Amulet
Bolano, R. By night in Chile
Bolano, R. Distant star
Bolano, R. Last evenings on Earth
Bolano, R. Monsieur Pain
Bolano, R. The savage detectives
Bolano, R. The Third Reich
Boll, H. Billiards at half-past nine
Boll, H. The clown
Boll, H. The silent angel
Bond, C. Ruby
Bonnaffons, A. The regrets
Bonnaffons, A. The wrong heaven
Bordas, C. How to behave in a crowd
Borges, J. Collected fictions
Borges, J. Ficciones
Bourdeaut, O. Waiting for Bojangles
Bowles, D. Feathered serpent, dark heart of sky
Bowles, P. The sheltering sky
Bowman, D. Big bang
Boyden, J. Three day road
Boyden, J. Through black spruce
Boyle, T. The harder they come
Boyle, T. Outside looking in
Boyle, T. The tortilla curtain
Boyle, T. The women
Boyne, J. The absolutist
Boyne, J. The heart's invisible furies
Boyne, J. A ladder to the sky
Brinkley, J. A lucky man
Brockmeier, K. The brief history of the dead
Brodesser-Akner, T. Fleishman is in trouble
Bronsky, A. The hottest dishes of the Tartar cuisine
Brookner, A. Brief lives
Brookner, A. Family and friends
Brookner, A. Hotel Du Lac
Brooks, G. Caleb's crossing
Brooks, G. People of the book
Broun, B. Night of the animals
Brown, L. Fay
Brown, L. Joe
Brown, T. Gods of Howl Mountain
Brown, L. Tiny love

Cunningham, M. The snow queen
Cusk, R. Kudos
Cusk, R. Outline
Cusk, R. Transit
Dalton, T. Boy swallows universe
Danielewski, M. The familiar.
Danielewski, M. House of leaves
Danticat, E. Claire of the sea light
Danticat, E. Everything inside
Daoud, K. The Meursault investigation
Dare, A. The girl with the louding voice
Darnielle, J. Universal harvester
Davidson, A. The boatman's daughter
Davies, C. West
Davies, P. The fortunes
Davies, R. The cunning man
Davies, R. Fifth business
Davies, R. Murther and walking spirits
Davies, R. The rebel angels
Davis, K. Duplex
De Bernieres, L. Birds without wings
De Kretser, M. The life to come
De Robertis, C. Cantoras
DeLillo, D. Falling man
DeLillo, D. Libra
DeLillo, D. The names
DeLillo, D. Underworld
DeLillo, D. White noise
Deane, S. Reading in the dark
Dektar, M. The Ash family
Delany, S. Dhalgren
Dennis-Benn, N. Patsy
Deon, N. Grace
Depestre, R. Hadriana in all my dreams
Desai, A. Clear light of day
Desai, A. Fire on the mountain
Desai, K. The inheritance of loss
deWitt, P. The Sisters brothers
Dexter, P. Paris Trout
Diaz, J. The brief wondrous life of Oscar Wao
Diaz, J. This is how you lose her
Dickens, C. Dombey and Son
Dickens, C. Great expectations
Didion, J. A book of common prayer
Didion, J. Play it as it lays
Dimitri, F. The book of hidden things
Djavadi, N. Disoriental
Doctorow, E. All the time in the world
Doctorow, E. Andrew's brain
Doctorow, E. Billy Bathgate
Doctorow, E. The book of Daniel
Doctorow, E. Doctorow
Doctorow, E. Homer and Langley
Doctorow, E. The march
Doctorow, E. Ragtime
Doctorow, E. World's Fair
Doctorow, E. The march

Doerr, A. All the light we cannot see
Dolan-Leach, C. We went to the woods
Donoghue, E. Akin
Donoghue, E. Frog music
Donoghue, E. Room
Donoghue, E. Slammerkin
Donoghue, E. The wonder
Dos Passos, J. 1919
Dos Passos, J. The 42nd parallel
Dos Passos, J. Manhattan transfer
Dovlatov, S. Pushkin Hills
Doyle, R. Paddy Clarke, ha-ha-ha
Doyle, R. Threshold
Drabble, M. The pure gold baby
Drabble, M. The dark flood rises
Drabble, M. The sea lady
Dreiser, T. An American tragedy
Drndic, D. Trieste
Duncan, G. By blood we live
Duncan, G. The last werewolf
Duncan, G. Talulla rising
Dupont, E. The American fiancee
Durrell, L. Balthazar
Durrell, L. Clea
Durrell, L. Justine
Durrell, L. Mountolive
Durrow, H. The girl who fell from the sky
Dyer, G. Jeff in Venice, death in Varanasi
Earley, T. Mr. Tall
Echenoz, J. Lightning
Echlin, K. The disappeared
Eco, U. Baudolino
Eco, U. Foucault's pendulum
Eco, U. The island of the day before
Eco, U. The mysterious flame of Queen Loana
Eco, U. The name of the rose
Eco, U. Numero zero
Edugyan, E. Half-blood blues
Egan, J. A visit from the Goon Squad
Egan, J. Manhattan Beach
Ehirim, N. Prince of monkeys
Eisenberg, D. The twilight of the superheroes
El-Mohtar, A. This is how you lose the time war
Eliot, G. Adam Bede
Ellison, J. A small indiscretion
Ellison, R. Invisible man
Ellison, R. Three days before the shooting . . .
Ellmann, L. Ducks, Newburyport
Emezi, A. Freshwater
Enard, M. Compass
Enger, L. The high divide
Englander, N. The ministry of Special Cases
Englander, N. What we talk about when we talk about Anne Frank
Enright, A. Actress
Enright, A. The forgotten waltz
Enright, A. The gathering

Galchen, R. American innovations
Gamboa, S. Necropolis
Gao, X. Soul mountain
Garcia Marquez, G. The autumn of the patriarch
Garcia Marquez, G. Chronicle of a death foretold
Garcia Marquez, G. Collected novellas
Garcia Marquez, G. In evil hour
Garcia Marquez, G. The general in his labyrinth
Garcia Marquez, G. Leaf storm, and other stories
Garcia Marquez, G. Love in the time of cholera
Garcia Marquez, G. Memories of my melancholy whores
Garcia Marquez, G. One hundred years of solitude
Garcia Marquez, G. Strange pilgrims
Gardam, J. The man in the wooden hat
Gardam, J. Last friends
Gardam, J. Old Filth
Garner, H. The spare room
Gaskell, E. Cranford
Gaskell, E. North and South
Gay, R. Difficult women
Gay, R. Ayiti
Gay, R. An untamed state
Geni, A. The wildlands
Gessen, K. A terrible country
Gestern, H. The people in the photo
Ghosh, A. Flood of fire
Ghosh, A. The glass palace
Ghosh, A. Gun Island
Ghosh, A. The hungry tide
Ghosh, A. River of smoke
Ghosh, A. Sea of poppies
Gide, A. The immoralist
Gilbert, D. & sons
Ginzburg, N. A family lexicon
Giordano, P. The human body
Giordano, P. Like family
Giordano, P. The solitude of prime numbers
Glass, J. Three Junes
Glass, J. The whole world over
Glass, J. The widower's tale
Godden, R. Battle of the Villa Fiorita
Godden, R. The greengage summer
Godden, R. Pippa passes
Godwin, G. Flora
Godwin, G. Grief cottage
Godwin, G. Unfinished desires
Goenawan, C. Rainbirds
Goldberg, M. Feast your eyes
Goldbloom, G. On division
Golding, W. Close quarters
Golding, W. Darkness visible
Golding, W. The inheritors
Golding, W. Lord of the flies
Golding, W. Rites of passage
Goldstein, R. 36 arguments for the existence of God
Gordimer, N. The conservationist
Gordimer, N. Get a life

Gordimer, N. July's people
Gordimer, N. My son's story
Gordimer, N. No time like the present
Gordimer, N. None to accompany me
Gordimer, N. The pickup
Gordon, J. Lord of misrule
Gordon, M. The liar's wife
Gowar, I. The mermaid and Mrs. Hancock
Graedon, A. The word exchange
Graley, L. The current that carries
Grant, L. We had it so good
Grass, G. The box
Grass, G. Crabwalk
Grass, G. The flounder
Grau, S. The keepers of the house
Gray, A. The care and feeding of ravenously hungry girls
Greene, A. Bloodroot
Greene, A. Long Man
Greene, G. Brighton Rock
Greene, G. The captain and the enemy
Greene, G. Collected stories
Greene, G. The end of the affair
Greene, G. The heart of the matter
Greene, G. The honorary consul
Greene, G. The human factor
Greene, G. The last word and other stories
Greene, G. The power and the glory
Greene, G. The quiet American
Greene, G. The tenth man
Greengrass, J. Sight
Greenidge, K. We love you, Charlie Freeman
Greenwell, G. Cleanness
Greenwell, G. What belongs to you
Greer, A. The impossible lives of Greta Wells
Greer, A. Less
Grenville, K. The idea of perfection
Grenville, K. The secret river
Grodstein, L. A friend of the family
Grodstein, L. Our short history
Groff, L. Arcadia
Groff, L. Fates and furies
Groff, L. Florida
Grossman, D. Be my knife
Grossman, D. Falling out of time
Grossman, D. A horse walks into a bar
Grossman, D. To the end of the land
Gruen, S. The ape house
Gruen, S. Water for elephants
Grushin, O. The line
Gunaratne, G. In our mad and furious city
Gunday, H. The few
Gunesekera, R. Suncatcher
Guskin, S. The forgetting time
Gustine, A. You should pity us instead
Guterson, D. Ed King
Guterson, D. Our Lady of the Forest
Guterson, D. The other

James, M. A brief history of seven killings
Jarvis, S. Death and Mr. Pickwick
Jaswal, B. Erotic stories for Punjabi widows
Jen, G. World and town
Jhabvala, R. At the end of the century
Jhabvala, R. Heat and dust
Jhabvala, R. My nine lives
Jiang, R. Wolf totem
Jin, H. The boat rocker
Jin, H. The crazed
Jin, H. A free life
Jin, H. A good fall
Jin, H. A map of betrayal
Jin, H. Nanjing requiem
Jin, H. Waiting
Jin, H. War trash
Jin, M. Little gods
John, E. Born on a Tuesday
Johnson, A. Fortune smiles
Johnson, A. The orphan master's son
Johnson, C. Middle Passage
Johnson, D. Everything under
Johnson, D. The largesse of the sea maiden
Johnson, D. Train dreams
Johnson, D. Tree of smoke
Johnson, L. The most dangerous place on earth
Johnston, W. The colony of unrequited dreams
Jones, E. The known world
Jones, J. From here to eternity
Jones, T. An American marriage
Jones, T. Silver sparrow
Jordan, H. When she woke
Joss, M. Half broken things
Joss, M. The night following
Joyce, J. Dubliners
Joyce, J. Finnegans wake
Joyce, J. A portrait of the artist as a young man
Joyce, J. Ulysses
Kadare, I. Agamemnon's daughter
Kadare, I. The general of the dead army
Kadare, I. The successor
Kadare, I. The three-arched bridge
Kafka, F. The castle
Kafka, F. The metamorphosis
Kafka, F. The trial
Kandasamy, M. When I hit you, or, A portrait of the writer as a young wife
Kane, J. Rules for visiting
Kantor, M. Andersonville
Karlsson, J. The room
Karunatilaka, S. The legend of Pradeep Mathew
Kawabata, Y. The sound of the mountain
Kawakami, M. Ms. Ice Sandwich
Kehlmann, D. Tyll
Kelman, J. How late it was, how late
Keneally, T. The daughters of Mars
Keneally, T. Schindler's list

Keneally, T. Shame and the captives
Kennedy, D. The moment
Kennedy, W. Chango's beads and two-tone shoes
Kennedy, W. Ironweed
Kerangal, M. The cook
Kerangal, M. The heart
Kerouac, J. The dharma bums
Kerouac, J. On the road
Kerouac, J. Road novels 1957-1960
Kesey, K. One flew over the cuckoo's nest
Kesey, K. Sometimes a great notion
Khadivi, L. A good country
Khadra, Y. The swallows of Kabul
Khalfah, K. Death is hard work
Kilalea, K. Ok, Mr. Field
Kim, Y. Diary of a murderer
Kimani, P. Dance of the Jakaranda
Kincaid, J. Annie John
Kincaid, J. The autobiography of my mother
Kincaid, J. Lucy
Kincaid, J. See now then
Kinder, C. Honeymooners
King, L. Father of the rain
King, L. Writers & lovers
Kingsolver, B. Flight behavior
Kingsolver, B. The Poisonwood Bible
Kingsolver, B. Unsheltered
Kirshenbaum, B. Rabbits for food
Kline, C. Orphan train
Knausgaard, K. My struggle.
Kneale, M. English passengers
Knowles, J. A separate peace
Ko, L. The leavers
Konar, A. Mischling
Kostova, E. The historian
Kostova, E. The shadow land
Kracht, C. Imperium
Krauss, N. Great house
Krauss, N. Forest Dark
Krauss, N. The history of love
Kundera, M. Immortality
Kundera, M. The unbearable lightness of being
Kunzru, H. Gods without men
Kunzru, H. The impressionist
Kunzru, H. My revolutions
Kunzru, H. White tears
Kushner, R. The Mars room
Kwok, J. Searching for Sylvie Lee
LaValle, V. The changeling
Lahiri, J. The lowland
Lahiri, J. The namesake
Lalami, L. The other Americans
Lanchester, J. Fragrant Harbor
Larison, J. Whiskey when we're dry
Larsen, N. Passing
Larsen, R. I am Radar
Lasdun, J. Afternoon of a faun

Mawer, S. The fall

Mayer, M. Aerialists

McAllister, T. How to be safe

McAllister, T. The young widower's handbook

McBride, E. A girl is a half-formed thing

McBride, J. The good lord bird

McBride, J. Five-carat soul

McCann, C. Apeirogon

McCann, C. Let the great world spin

McCann, C. Transatlantic

McCarthy, C. All the pretty horses

McCarthy, C. Blood meridian, or, The evening redness in the West

McCarthy, C. Cities of the plain

McCarthy, C. The crossing

McCarthy, C. No country for old men

McCarthy, C. The road

McCarthy, T. Satin Island

McCormack, M. Solar bones

McCrea, G. Mrs. Engels

McCullers, C. The heart is a lonely hunter

McCullers, C. The member of the wedding

McCullers, C. Reflections in a golden eye

McDermott, A. After this

McDermott, A. At weddings and wakes

McDermott, A. Charming Billy

McDermott, A. Child of my heart

McDermott, A. The ninth hour

McDermott, A. Someone

McDermott, A. That night

McEwan, I. Amsterdam

McEwan, I. Atonement

McEwan, I. Black dogs

McEwan, I. The child in time

McEwan, I. Nutshell

McEwan, I. On Chesil Beach

McEwan, I. Saturday

McEwan, I. Solar

McFadden, B. Gathering of waters

McGhee, A. The opposite of fate

McGregor, J. Even the dogs

McGregor, J. The reservoir tapes

McGuane, T. Cloudbursts

McGuane, T. Gallatin Canyon

McHugh, L. Arrowood

McInerney, L. The glorious heresies

McKenzie, E. The portable Veblen

McLean, F. The Van Apfel girls are gone

McMurtry, L. Buffalo girls

McMurtry, L. Comanche moon

McMurtry, L. Dead man's walk

McMurtry, L. The evening star

McMurtry, L. Lonesome Dove

McMurtry, L. Streets of Laredo

McMurtry, L. Terms of endearment

McMurtry, L. Rhino ranch

Mda, Z. The Madonna of Excelsior

Means, D. Instructions for a funeral

Meek, J. The heart broke in

Mehta, R. No other world

Mengestu, D. How to read the air

Mengiste, M. The shadow king

Meno, J. Marvel and a wonder

Messud, C. The woman upstairs

Meyer, P. American rust

Michaels, A. Fugitive pieces

Michener, J. Tales of the South Pacific

Miller, A. Pure

Miller, H. Tropic of Cancer

Miller, H. Tropic of Capricorn

Miller, K. Augustown

Miller, M. Circe

Miller, M. Biloxi

Miller, M. The song of Achilles

Miller, R. Jacob's folly

Millet, L. Ghost lights

Millet, L. How the dead dream

Millet, L. Magnificence

Millhauser, S. Martin Dressler

Minot, S. Evening

Mistry, R. A fine balance

Mitchell, D. Black Swan Green

Mitchell, D. The bone clocks

Mitchell, D. Cloud atlas

Mitchell, D. Slade House

Mitchell, D. The thousand autumns of Jacob De Zoet

Momaday, N. The ancient child

Momaday, N. House made of dawn

Moody, R. Right livelihoods

Moore, A. Jerusalem

Moore, A. The lighthouse

Moore, B. The lonely passion of Judith Hearne

Moore, L. A gate at the stairs

Moore, L. The unseen world

Mootoo, S. Moving forward sideways, like a crab

Morgan, C. The sport of kings

Morgan, J. The secret life of William Shakespeare

Morrison, T. Paradise

Morrison, T. Beloved

Morrison, T. The bluest eye

Morrison, T. Jazz

Morrison, T. Song of Solomon

Morrison, T. Sula

Morrison, T. Tar baby

Morrison, T. Love

Morrison, T. A mercy

Morrison, T. Home

Morrison, T. God help the child

Morton, B. Florence Gordon

Moshfegh, O. Eileen

Moshfegh, O. Death in her hands

Moshfegh, O. My year of rest and relaxation

Mosley, W. John Woman

Moss, S. Ghost wall

Oates, J. We were the Mulvaneys

Oates, J. Wild nights

Obioma, C. The fishermen

Obioma, C. An orchestra of minorities

Obreht, T. Inland

Obreht, T. The tiger's wife

Oe, K. The changeling

Oe, K. Death by water

Oe, K. A quiet life

Oe, K. Somersault

Offill, J. Dept. of speculation

Offill, J. Weather

Offutt, C. Country dark

Okparanta, C. Under the udala trees

Olafur Johann Olafsson The sacrament

Olmstead, R. Far bright star

Olmstead, R. The coldest night

Olsen, T. Tell me a riddle

Ómarsdóttir, K. Children in Reindeer Woods

Ondaatje, M. Anil's ghost

Ondaatje, M. The cat's table

Ondaatje, M. The English patient

Ondaatje, M. In the skin of a lion

Ondaatje, M. Warlight

Onyebuchi, T. Riot baby

Orange, T. There there

Orner, P. Love and shame and love

Orringer, J. The invisible bridge

Osborne, L. The forgiven

Osondu, E. This house is not for sale

Otsuka, J. The Buddha in the attic

Otto, W. Eight girls taking pictures

Owen, L. The quick

Owens, D. Where the crawdads sing

Oyeyemi, H. Boy, Snow, Bird

Oyeyemi, H. Gingerbread

Oyeyemi, H. What is not yours is not yours

Oz, A. Judas

Oz, A. The same sea

Ozeki, R. A tale for the time being

Ozick, C. Foreign bodies

Ozick, C. The Puttermesser papers

Packer, A. The children's crusade

Paley, G. The collected stories

Palliser, C. The quincunx

Palliser, C. The unburied

Pamuk, O. The museum of innocence

Pamuk, O. My name is Red

Pamuk, O. The red-haired woman

Pamuk, O. Silent house

Pamuk, O. Snow

Pamuk, O. A strangeness in my mind

Panowich, B. Bull Mountain

Panowich, B. Like lions

Parkhurst, C. The dogs of Babel

Patchett, A. Bel canto

Patchett, A. The Dutch house

Paton, A. Cry, the beloved country

Patric, A. Black rock white city

Pava, S. Lost empress

Pava, S. Personae

Peace, D. Occupied city

Peace, D. Tokyo year zero

Pearlman, E. Binocular vision

Pearlman, E. Honeydew

Pears, I. An instance of the fingerpost

Penney, S. The tenderness of wolves

Percy, B. Red moon

Percy, B. The wilding

Percy, W. The last gentleman

Percy, W. The moviegoer

Perec, G. Life

Perez-Reverte, A. The Club Dumas

Perez-Reverte, A. The fencing master

Perez-Reverte, A. The painter of battles

Perez-Reverte, A. The siege

Perry, S. Melmoth

Pessl, M. Night film

Pessl, M. Special topics in calamity physics

Petry, A. The street

Petterson, P. I curse the river of time

Petterson, P. I refuse

Petterson, P. Out stealing horses

Phillips, C. A distant shore

Phillips, H. The beautiful bureaucrat

Phillips, H. The need

Phillips, J. Disappearing earth

Piatote, B. The beadworkers

Piercy, M. Gone to soldiers

Piercy, M. Sex wars

Plath, S. The bell jar

Pochoda, I. These women

Pollock, D. The devil all the time

Pollock, D. Knockemstiff

Porter, M. Grief is the thing with feathers

Porter, M. Lanny

Porter, R. The travelers

Powers, R. The echo maker

Powers, R. Generosity

Powers, R. The Gold Bug Variations

Powers, R. The overstory

Powers, K. The yellow birds

Powning, B. The sea captain's wife

Prcic, I. Shards

Price, R. The good priest's son

Price, R. Roxanna Slade

Prose, F. Blue angel

Prose, F. Goldengrove

Prose, F. Household saints

Prose, F. Primitive people

Proulx, A. Accordion crimes

Proulx, A. Bad dirt

Proulx, A. Barkskins

Proulx, A. Fine just the way it is

Sahota, S. The year of the runaways

Salter, J. All that is

Saramago, J. All the names

Saramago, J. Blindness

Saramago, J. Cain

Saramago, J. The cave

Saramago, J. Death with interruptions

Saramago, J. The history of the siege of Lisbon

Saramago, J. The manual of painting and calligraphy

Sarton, M. A reckoning

Sarvas, M. Memento Park

Satyal, R. No one can pronounce my name

Saunders, G. In persuasion nation

Saunders, G. Lincoln in the bardo

Saunders, G. Tenth of December

Savage, S. Glass

Savage, S. The way of the dog

Savas, A. Walking on the ceiling

Scego, I. Adua

Schami, R. Sophia

Schine, C. The Grammarians

Schlink, B. The reader

Schulberg, B. Waterfront

Schulman, H. Come with me

Schwartz, J. The red daughter

Schweblin, S. Fever dream

Schweblin, S. Mouthful of birds

Scibona, S. The volunteer

Scott, P. Staying on

Scott, R. The world doesn't require you

Seay, M. The mirror thief

Sebald, W. Austerlitz

Sebald, W. The emigrants ;, W. G. Sebald ; translated by
  Michael Hulse.

Sebald, W. Vertigo

Sebold, A. The lovely bones

See, L. The tea girl of Hummingbird Lane

Sekaran, S. Lucky boy

Self, W. Shark

Self, W. Umbrella

Sem-Sandberg, S. The chosen ones

Senna, D. New people

Serpell, N. The old drift

Sexton, M. A kind of freedom

Sexton, M. The revisioners

Shacochis, B. The woman who lost her soul

Shafak, E. 10 minutes 38 seconds in this strange world

Shafak, E. Honor

Shakar, A. Luminarium

Shalev, M. Two she-bears

Shamsie, K. Home fire

Shepard, J. The world to come

Shepard, S. The one inside

Shepherd, P. The book of M

Shields, C. The stone diaries

Shields, C. Unless

Sholokhov, M. The Don flows home to the sea

Shreve, A. Testimony

Shreve, A. The weight of water

Sidhu, R. Good Indian girls

Silber, J. Improvement

Silko, L. Almanac of the dead

Silko, L. Ceremony

Silko, L. Gardens in the dunes

Sillitoe, A. Saturday night and Sunday morning

Singer, I. The brothers Ashkenazi

Singer, I. Enemies, a love story

Singer, I. The family Moskat

Singer, I. The magician of Lublin

Sittenfeld, C. You think it, I'll say it

Sloan, R. Mr. Penumbra's 24-hour bookstore

Sloin, H. Art on fire

Smiley, J. A thousand acres

Smith, A. Autumn

Smith, A. How to be both

Smith, A. Spring

Smith, A. There but for the

Smith, A. Winter

Smith, B. A tree grows in Brooklyn

Smith, D. Bright and distant shores

Smith, G. The maze at Windermere

Smith, M. The fighter

Smith, Z. Grand union

Smith, Z. NW

Smith, Z. On beauty

Smith, Z. Swing time

Smith, Z. White teeth

Solares, M. Don't send flowers

Soli, T. The lotus eaters

Soli, T. The removes

Solomon, R. An unkindness of ghosts

Solzhenitsyn, A. One day in the life of Ivan Denisovich

Sontag, S. In America

Sontag, S. The volcano lover

Spark, M. Aiding & abetting

Spark, M. The girls of slender means

Spark, M. The Mandelbaum gate

Spark, M. Memento mori

Spark, M. The prime of Miss Jean Brodie

Staples, D. This town sleeps

Stedman, M. The light between oceans

Stegner, W. Angle of repose

Stegner, W. Crossing to safety

Stein, G. The art of racing in the rain

Steinbeck, J. Cannery Row

Steinbeck, J. East of Eden

Steinbeck, J. The grapes of wrath

Steinbeck, J. The long valley

Steinbeck, J. Of mice and men

Steinbeck, J. The pearl

Steinbeck, J. Tortilla Flat

Straight, S. A million nightingales

Strout, E. Amy and Isabelle

Strout, E. Anything is possible

Wallace, D. Brief interviews with hideous men
Wallace, D. The pale king
Walsh, M. My sunshine away
Ward, J. Salvage the bones
Ward, J. Sing, unburied, sing
Warren, R. All the king's men
Warren, R. World enough and time
Washington, B. Lot
Waters, S. Fingersmith
Waters, S. The little stranger
Waters, S. The night watch
Waters, S. The paying guests
Waters, S. Tipping the velvet
Watkins, C. Gold fame citrus
Watson, L. Let him go
Watts, S. No one is coming to save us
Waugh, E. Brideshead revisited
Waugh, E. The complete stories of Evelyn Waugh
Wayne, T. Apartment
Weldon, F. The life and loves of a she-devil
Wells, B. The end of loneliness
West, K. Minor dramas & other catastrophes
Wharton, E. Ethan Frome
Whitehead, C. The intuitionist
Whitehead, C. The underground railroad
Wideman, J. American histories
Wideman, J. Fanon
Wiesel, E. A mad desire to dance
Wiggins, M. Evidence of things unseen
Wilkinson, L. American spy
Williams, L. A selfie as big as the Ritz
Williams, L. Supper club
Williams, N. This is happiness
Williams, T. The Roman spring of Mrs. Stone
Wilson, G. The bird king
Wilson, K. The family Fang
Winman, S. Tin man
Winslow, D. In West Mills
Winter, K. Annabel
Winterson, J. Frankissstein
Winthrop, E. The mercy seat
Winton, T. The shepherd's hut
Wolfe, P. The lost diary of M
Wolfe, T. The web and the rock
Wolff, T. Old school
Woodrell, D. The Maid's Version
Woodrell, D. Winter's bone
Woods, C. Things to do when you're goth in the country
Woods, R. Remembrance
Woodson, J. Another Brooklyn
Woodson, J. Red at the bone
Woolf, V. The waves
Wright, A. Carpentaria
Wright, R. Eight men
Wright, R. Native son
Wright, R. Uncle Tom's children
Wroblewski, D. The story of Edgar Sawtelle

Yanagihara, H. A little life
Yanagihara, H. The people in the trees
Yanique, T. Land of love and drowning
Yates, C. Grist Mill Road
Yi, C. The investigation
Yoon, P. The mountain
Yoon, P. Run me to earth
Yoshimoto, B. The lake
Youngson, A. Meet me at the museum
Yu, C. Interior Chinatown
Zaman, N. Up in the main house & other stories
Zapata, M. The lost book of Adana Moreau
Zhang, J. Sour heart
Zumas, L. Red clocks

LITERARY FORGERIES AND HOAXES
Carey, P. My life as a fake

LITERARY HISTORIANS
Barnes, J. Flaubert's parrot
Byatt, A. Possession
Crowley, J. Lord Byron's novel
Fforde, J. The Eyre affair
Fforde, J. Lost in a good book
Moore, G. The Sherlockian

LITERARY MOVEMENTS
Bolano, R. The savage detectives

LITERARY RESEARCH
Byatt, A. Possession

LITERARY SOCIETIES
Fairstein, L. Entombed

LITERATURE
Henry, P. Becoming Mrs. Lewis
Ugresic, D. Fox

LITERATURE AND SOCIETY
Van der Vliet Oloomi, A. Call me Zebra

LITERATURE TEACHERS
Griffiths, E. The stranger diaries

LITHUANIAN AMERICANS
Sinclair, U. The jungle
The **litter** of the law Brown, R.
Little Carey, E.
Little Bee Cleave, C.

LITTLE BIG HORN, BATTLE OF THE, 1876
Berger, T. Little Big Man
Jones, D. The court-martial of George Armstrong Custer
Lock, N. American meteor
Little Big Man Berger, T.
Little bird of heaven Oates, J.
Little black girl lost Johnson, K.
Little black girl lost [series] Johnson, K.
Little black girl lost 2 Johnson, K.
Little century Keesey, A.
Little children Perrotta, T.
Little comfort Hill, E.
Little constructions Burns, A.
Little darlings Golding, M.
Little deaths Flint, E.
Little Dorrit Dickens, C.

London celebrities [series] Parker, L.
London falling Cornell, P.
London falling novels [series] Cornell, P.
London fields Amis, M.
London match Deighton, L.
London novels (Sherry Thomas) [series] Thomas, S.
LONDON TERRORIST BOMBINGS, LONDON, ENG-
   LAND, 2005
   Rankin, I. The naming of the dead
LONDON, ENGLAND
   Aaronovitch, B. Broken homes
   Aaronovitch, B. Midnight riot
   Aaronovitch, B. Moon over Soho
   Ali, M. Brick Lane
   Amis, M. London fields
   Amis, M. The pregnant widow
   Archer, J. Nothing ventured
   Archer, J. This was a man
   Aridjis, C. Asunder
   Ashley Antoinette, 1. Butterfly
   Babson, M. The company of cats
   Bailey, P. Uncle Rudolf
   Ballard, J. Kingdom come
   Balogh, M. Someone to hold
   Balogh, M. Someone to love
   Balogh, M. Someone to wed
   Barnes, J. The only story
   Barnes, J. The somnambulist
   Bauer, B. The beautiful dead
   Beckett, S. Murphy
   Benn, J. Billy Boyle
   Beverley, J. Devilish
   Beverley, J. My lady notorious
   Beverley, J. Something wicked
   Beverley, J. Tempting fortune
   The big book of Sherlock Holmes stories
   Bolton, S. A dark and twisted tide
   Bolton, S. Now you see me
   Bourne, J. Rogue spy
   Bowen, E. The heat of the day
   Bradford, B. Just rewards
   Bradley, A. A season of ruin
   Brookner, A. Brief lives
   Brookner, A. Family and friends
   Broun, B. Night of the animals
   Brown, D. The Da Vinci code
   Brownrigg, S. The delivery room
   Burrowes, G. Lady Sophie's Christmas wish
   Burrowes, G. My one and only duke
   Burrowes, G. The trouble with dukes
   Butler, S. Ten things I've learnt about love
   Buxbaum, J. After you
   Byatt, A. Possession
   Byrne, K. The hunter
   Campbell, A. On the floor
   Candlish, L. Our house
   Carty-Williams, C. Queenie

   Cary, J. The horse's mouth
   Chung, M. The eighth girl
   Clarke, S. Jonathan Strange & Mr. Norrell
   Cleave, C. Little Bee
   Clinch, J. Marley
   Cogman, G. The burning page
   Cogman, G. The invisible library
   Cogman, G. The masked city
   Cogman, G. The mortal word
   Cohen, T. They all fall down
   Cole, D. Ragdoll
   Cornell, P. London falling
   Corry, J. My husband's wife
   Crombie, D. Kissed a sad goodbye
   Crombie, D. Mourn not your dead
   Cronin, A. Citadel
   Cross, N. Luther. The calling
   Crowell, J. Etched on me
   Cusk, R. Transit
   Dastgir, R. A small fortune
   Deighton, L. Berlin game
   Delaney, J. The girl before
   Drabble, M. The pure gold baby
   Duncan, G. By blood we live
   Duncan, G. The last werewolf
   Duncan, G. Talulla rising
   Ellison, J. A small indiscretion
   Evaristo, B. Mr. Loverman
   Faulks, S. A week in December
   Feeney, A. Sometimes I lie
   Fielding, H. Bridget Jones's diary
   Finch, C. The last passenger
   Finch, C. The vanishing man
   Finlay, M. The murder pit
   Forna, A. Happiness
   Fowler, C. Bryant & May
   Frayn, M. Spies
   Frear, C. Stone cold heart
   Frear, C. Sweet little lies
   Freeman, D. A lady's guide to etiquette and murder
   French, N. Blue Monday
   French, N. Tuesday's gone
   French, N. Waiting for Wednesday
   George, E. A banquet of consequences
   George, E. Believing the lie
   George, E. Just one evil act
   George, E. The punishment she deserves
   George, E. This body of death
   George, E. What came before he shot her
   Gibb, C. Sweetness in the belly
   Gibson, W. Pattern recognition
   Gowar, I. The mermaid and Mrs. Hancock
   Greene, G. The end of the affair
   Griffin, K. The glass god
   Griffin, K. Stray souls
   Grimes, M. The Old Wine Shades
   Gunaratne, G. In our mad and furious city

Robertson, M. The Baker Street letters
Robertson, M. The Baker Street translation
Robertson, M. The brothers of Baker Street
Robertson, M. Moriarty returns a letter
Robinson, P. All the colors of darkness
Robotham, M. Close your eyes
Robotham, M. The other wife
Robotham, M. The night ferry
Robotham, M. Say you're sorry
Robotham, M. Suspect
Rodale, M. Lady Bridget's diary
Rodrigues Fowler, Y. Stubborn archivist
Rosenberg, J. Confessions of the fox
Roth, P. The professor of desire
Rourke, L. The canal
Rushdie, S. The satanic verses
Sayers, D. The documents in the case
Schwab, V. A conjuring of light
Schwab, V. A darker shade of magic
Schwab, V. A gathering of shadows
Self, W. The book of Dave
Shafak, E. Honor
Shamsie, K. Home fire
Shannon, S. The bone season
Shannon, S. The mime order
Shaw, V. Strange Practice
Shreve, A. The pilot's wife
Shriver, L. The post-birthday world
Smith, Z. The autograph man
Smith, Z. NW
Smith, Z. Swing time
Smith, Z. White teeth
Spark, M. A far cry from Kensington
Spark, M. The girls of slender means
Spark, M. Memento mori
St. Aubyn, E. At last
Stachniak, E. The chosen maiden
Stevenson, R. The strange case of Dr. Jekyll and Mr. Hyde
Stone, N. The verdict
Stratford, S. Red letter days
Swanson, P. Her every fear
Thomas, B. A good enough mother
Tidhar, L. A man lies dreaming
Townsend, S. Number 10
Trollope, J. Second honeymoon
Vine, B. Anna's book
Vine, B. Grasshopper
Walton, J. Farthing
Weir, A. A dangerous inheritance
Wilde, O. The picture of Dorian Gray
Winspear, J. Birds of a feather
Winspear, J. Maisie Dobbs

LONDON, ENGLAND -- HISTORY

Purcell, L. The silent companions
Rutherfurd, E. London

LONDON, ENGLAND -- HISTORY -- 12TH CENTURY

Penman, S. Cruel as the grave

LONDON, ENGLAND -- HISTORY -- 15TH CENTURY

Sedley, K. The Tintern treasure

LONDON, ENGLAND -- HISTORY -- 16TH CENTURY

Brandreth, B. The assassin of Verona
Brandreth, B. The spy of Venice

LONDON, ENGLAND -- HISTORY -- 1800-1950

Orczy, E. The old man in the corner
Perry, A. Blind justice
Perry, A. Blood on the water
Perry, A. Dark tide rising
Perry, A. A sunless sea

LONDON, ENGLAND -- HISTORY -- 18TH CENTURY

Dickens, C. A tale of two cities
Donoghue, E. Slammerkin
Hodgson, A. The last confession of Thomas Hawkins
Hollingshead, G. Bedlam
Hoyt, E. Wicked intentions
Hunter, M. The conquest of Lady Cassandra
Hunter, M. The surrender of Miss Fairbourne
King, R. Domino
Liss, D. A spectacle of corruption
Redfern, E. The music of the spheres
Robertson, I. Anatomy of murder

LONDON, ENGLAND -- HISTORY -- 1960-1969

Shaw, W. A song for the brokenhearted

LONDON, ENGLAND -- HISTORY -- 19TH CENTURY

Abdul-Jabbar, K. The empty birdcage
Abdul-Jabbar, K. Mycroft and Sherlock
Abdul-Jabbar, K. Mycroft Holmes
Bourne, J. The black hawk
Bourne, J. My lord and spymaster
Bowman, V. Secrets of a wedding night
Bowman, V. The unexpected duchess
Charles, K. Wanted, a gentleman
Dickens, C. David Copperfield
Dickens, C. Great expectations
Dickens, C. Little Dorrit
Faye, L. Jane Steele
Faye, L. The whole art of detection
Galen, S. When you give a duke a diamond
Horowitz, A. The House of Silk
Horowitz, A. Moriarty
Kidd, J. Things in jars
Layton, E. To wed a stranger
Lovesey, P. Waxwork
MacKenzie, S. Bedding Lord Ned
Penrose, A. Murder at half moon gate
Penrose, A. Murder at Kensington Palace
Penrose, A. Murder on Black Swan Lane
Perry, A. Bedford Square
Perry, A. Belgrave Square
Perry, A. Bethlehem Road
Perry, A. Bluegate Fields
Perry, A. A breach of promise
Perry, A. Buckingham Palace gardens
Perry, A. Cain his brother
Perry, A. Cardington Crescent

Saunders, K. The secrets of Wishtide
Stoker, B. Dracula
Stoker, B. The new annotated Dracula
Thomas, S. Private arrangements
Waters, S. Tipping the velvet

LONDON, ENGLAND -- SOCIAL LIFE AND CUSTOMS -- 20TH CENTURY

Joinson, S. A lady cyclist's guide to Kashgar

LONDON, ENGLAND -- SOCIAL LIFE AND CUSTOMS -- 21ST CENTURY

Carey, P. The chemistry of tears

LONDON, ENGLAND -- SOCIAL LIFE AND CUSTOMS -- VICTORIA, 1837-1901

Goss, T. The sinister mystery of the mesmerizing girl
Goss, T. The strange case of the alchemist's daughter

LONDON, JACK, 1876-1916

London, J. Martin Eden

Lone wolf Picoult, J.

LONELINESS

Acampora, L. The paper wasp
Atilgan, Y. Motherland hotel
Awad, M. Bunny
Baker, T. The little giant of Aberdeen County
Beagle, P. A fine and private place
Benedetti, M. Springtime in a broken mirror
Berg, E. The story of Arthur Truluv
Bledsoe, L. The big bang symphony
Bradbury, R. The Martian chronicles
Brinkman, K. Up high in the trees
Bryant, N. Madam, may I
Cole, T. Open city
Coupland, D. Eleanor Rigby
De Kretser, M. The life to come
Erdrich, L. The beet queen
Fowler, C. Bryant & May
Golding, W. Darkness visible
Haigh, J. Mrs. Kimble
Haruf, K. Our souls at night
Heller, Z. What was she thinking?
Herlihy, J. Midnight cowboy
Hunt, S. The dark dark
Johnson, D. Tree of smoke
Kantaria, A. I know you
Kawabata, Y. The sound of the mountain
Krauss, N. The history of love
Loren, R. The one you fight for
McCracken, E. The giant's house
McCullers, C. The heart is a lonely hunter
McCullers, C. The member of the wedding
Mukherjee, N. A life apart
Murakami, H. Blind willow, sleeping woman
Murakami, H. Men without women
O'Brien, E. House of splendid isolation
O'Donnell, L. The death of bees
Ozeki, R. A tale for the time being
Rash, R. The cove
Reisman, N. The first desire

The road ahead
Saramago, J. All the names
Satyal, R. No one can pronounce my name
Savage, S. Firmin
Seton, A. Katherine
Steinbeck, J. Cannery Row
Taylor, B. Real life
Vonnegut, K. Slapstick
Wiesel, E. A mad desire to dance
Winman, S. Tin man
Yoon, P. The mountain

LONELINESS IN GIRLS

McCullers, C. The member of the wedding

LONELINESS IN MEN

Daoud, K. The Meursault investigation
De Giovanni, M. The crocodile
Forster, E. Maurice
Foster, A. Relic
Greene, G. The human factor
Jin, H. War trash
Kafka, F. The metamorphosis
Karon, J. At home in Mitford
Malamud, B. The fixer
Matheson, R. I am legend
Nadzam, B. Lamb
O'Neill, J. Netherland
Powers, R. Orfeo
Wayne, T. Apartment
Whitehead, C. Zone one

LONELINESS IN WOMEN

Berg, E. Never change
Brookner, A. Brief lives
Cather, W. A lost lady
Chase, L. Your scandalous ways
Coupland, D. Eleanor Rigby
Flagg, F. Fried green tomatoes at the Whistle Stop Cafe
Larsen, N. Passing
Lutz, L. The passenger
Moore, B. The lonely passion of Judith Hearne
Moore, L. Long bright river
Moshfegh, O. Eileen
Orstavik, H. Love
Strout, E. Olive Kitteridge
Strout, E. Olive, again
Watson, B. Miss Jane

The **loneliness** of the long-distance runner Sillitoe, A.
The **Lonely** Hearts Hotel O'Neill, H.
The **lonely** passion of Judith Hearne Moore, B.
The **lonely** polygamist Udall, B.
The **lonely** silver rain MacDonald, J.
The **lonely** witness Boyle, W.

Loner Wayne, T.

LONERS

Burnet, G. The disappearance of Adele Bedeau
Byrne, K. The hunter
Cleeves, A. Raven black
Dostoyevsky, F. Notes from underground

Lords of the Armory [series] Harrington, A.
Lorna Doone Blackmore, R.
Los Alamos Kanon, J.
LOS ALAMOS, NEW MEXICO
Kanon, J. Los Alamos
Nesbit, T. The wives of Los Alamos
Smith, M. Stallion Gate
LOS ANGELES COUNTY, CALIFORNIA -- RACE RELATIONS
Boyle, T. The tortilla curtain
LOS ANGELES REBELLION, APRIL 29-MAY 2, 1992
Carter, M. Further out than you thought
LOS ANGELES, CALIFORNIA
Abu-Jaber, D. Crescent
Acampora, L. The paper wasp
Antoinette, A. Murderville
Baldwin, J. The Wilshire sun
Beatty, P. The sellout
Beyda, E. The body double
Boyle, T. The tortilla curtain
Broder, M. The pisces
Campbell, B. Brothers and sisters
Carter, M. Further out than you thought
Cha, S. Your house will pay
Chandler, R. The annotated Big sleep
Chandler, R. The big sleep
Chandler, R. The lady in the lake
Chandler, R. The long goodbye
Clark, M. Blood defense
Clark, M. Final judgment
Collins, M. Ask not
Connelly, M. The black ice
Connelly, M. The brass verdict
Connelly, M. The burning room
Connelly, M. The crossing
Connelly, M. Dark sacred night
Connelly, M. Echo Park
Connelly, M. The fifth witness
Connelly, M. The gods of guilt
Connelly, M. The late show
Connelly, M. The night fire
Connelly, M. The scarecrow
Connelly, M. The wrong side of goodbye
Crais, R. Chasing darkness
Crais, R. A dangerous man
Crais, R. Demolition angel
Crais, R. The first rule
Crais, R. Suspect
Dick, P. Do androids dream of electric sheep?
Dickey, E. Bad men and wicked women
Dickey, E. The business of lovers
Drury, T. Pacific
Ellis, B. Imperial bedrooms
Ellroy, J. L.A. confidential
Ephron, H. Night night, sleep tight
Epperson, T. Sailor
Estleman, L. Something borrowed, something black

Evison, J. All about Lulu
Fitch, J. Paint it black
Fitch, J. White oleander
Freudenberger, N. The dissident
Friedland, E. The intermission
Gardiner, M. The dark corners of the night
Gardiner, M. Phantom instinct
Gifford, B. The stars above Veracruz
Greenfeld, K. True
Guillory, J. The proposal
Hallinan, T. Crashed
Hanson, H. The driver
Haywood, G. Cemetery Road
Hurwitz, G. The crime writer
Hurwitz, G. The survivor
Ide, J. Hi five
Jacobs, N. The last equation of Isaac Severy
Kellerman, F. The forgotten
Kellerman, F. Jupiter's bones
Kellerman, F. Milk and honey
Kellerman, F. Prayers for the dead
Kellerman, F. Serpent's tooth
Kellerman, J. Time bomb
Kitt, S. Celluloid memories
Kroese, R. The last iota
Millet, L. How the dead dream
Mosley, W. Blonde faith
Mosley, W. Charcoal Joe
Mosley, W. Cinnamon kiss
Mosley, W. The last days of Ptolemy Grey
Mosley, W. Little green
Mosley, W. Little Scarlet
Mosley, W. A little yellow dog
Mosley, W. A red death
Mosley, W. The right mistake
Mosley, W. Rose gold
Mosley, W. Six Easy pieces
Mosley, W. White butterfly
Nahai, G. The luminous heart of Jonah S.
Nava, M. Carved in bone
Noire Candy licker
Noire G-Spot
Overton, H. The runaway
Parker, T. L.A. outlaws
Perry, T. The bomb maker
Pochoda, I. These women
Pyne, D. Catalina eddy
Raheem, Z. The marriage clock
Richards, L. Death was in the blood
Rivers, F. The masterpiece
Robertson, M. The Baker Street letters
Robertson, M. Moriarty returns a letter
Rowell, R. Landline
Rushdie, S. Shalimar the Clown
Sallis, J. Drive
Sallis, J. Driven
Santiago, D. Famous all over town

Cohen, L. The grief of others
Collins, C. The gamal
Cooper, E. Caged
Coster, N. Halsey Street
Couto, M. Rain
Cross-Smith, L. Whiskey & ribbons
Crouch, B. Recursion
Cumming, C. A divided spy
Daniel, S. Stiltsville
Danticat, E. Claire of the sea light
Darnielle, J. Universal harvester
De Kretser, M. The life to come
DeBoard, P. The fragile world
Deane, S. Reading in the dark
Delaney, J. The girl before
Deveraux, J. Someone to love
Diaz, J. The brief wondrous life of Oscar Wao
Diaz, J. This is how you lose her
Dickens, C. Dombey and Son
Dimon, H. Her other secret
Doctorow, E. Andrew's brain
Doig, I. Mountain time
Donati, S. Where the light enters
Donoghue, E. Akin
Donohue, K. The stolen child
Drake, L. The sweet spot
Dunmore, H. The lie
Dybek, N. The Verdun affair
Dybek, S. I sailed with Magellan
Dykes, A. Whose waves these are
Echlin, K. The disappeared
Edwards, K. The memory keeper's daughter
Edwards, Y. The mother
Eggers, D. What is the what
Emezi, A. Freshwater
Enger, L. Virgil Wander
Englander, N. The ministry of Special Cases
Ephron, H. You'll never know, dear
Erdrich, L. The round house
Everyday people
Evison, J. The revised fundamentals of caregiving
Evison, J. This is your life, Harriet Chance!
Fabry, C. The promise of Jesse Woods
Faulks, S. Birdsong
Flanagan, R. The narrow road to the deep north
Flournoy, A. The Turner house
Foer, J. Extremely loud and incredibly close
Force, M. Five years gone
Forna, A. Happiness
Fowler, K. We are all completely beside ourselves
Fox, L. Days of awe
Frank, D. Folly Beach
Frankel, L. Goodbye for now
Frazier, C. Nightwoods
Frazier, C. Thirteen moons
French, M. The women's room
Freudenberger, N. Lost and wanted

Gage, E. The ladies of Managua
Gaige, A. Schroder
Garcia Marquez, G. Strange pilgrims
George, E. Careless in red
George, N. The book of dreams
Gertler, S. Drifting
Gibb, C. Sweetness in the belly
Gifford, B. Wyoming
Giordano, P. The solitude of prime numbers
Glass, J. Three Junes
Godwin, G. Flora
Godwin, G. Grief cottage
Gohlke, C. Promise me this
Graley, L. The current that carries
Greene, G. The end of the affair
Greengrass, J. Sight
Greer, A. The impossible lives of Greta Wells
Griffin, A. When all is said
Grossman, D. A horse walks into a bar
Hage, R. Beirut Hellfire Society
Halfon, E. Mourning
Hamill, S. A cosmology of monsters
Han, K. Human acts
Han, K. The white book
Hannah, K. The nightingale
Hart, C. Letter from home
Haruf, K. Benediction
Hatcher, R. Who I am with you
Haywood, S. The cactus
Helprin, M. Paris in the present tense
Henderson, S. The flicker of old dreams
Henry, P. Becoming Mrs. Lewis
Hill, N. The nix
Hill, S. The risk of darkness
Hoffman, A. The ice queen
Hoffman, A. The story sisters
Hoffman, A. The world that we knew
Hood, A. The obituary writer
Horn, D. The world to come
Horrocks, C. The vexations
Hulse, S. Black River
Hynes, J. Kings of infinite space
Indriðason, A. Strange shores
Ishiguro, K. The buried giant
Itani, F. Tell
Jewell, L. Then she was gone
Jimenez, S. The vanished birds
Jin, H. The crazed
Jin, M. Little gods
Johnston, T. The current
Jones, T. An American marriage
Joss, M. Among the missing
Joss, M. Half broken things
Just, W. An unfinished season
Kadare, I. The general of the dead army
Kamali, M. The stationery shop
Katsu, A. The deep

Roslund, A. Pen 33
Rothfuss, P. The name of the wind
Rothfuss, P. The wise man's fear
Rubart, J. The long journey to Jake Palmer
Runcie, J. Canvey Island
Runcie, J. The road to Grantchester
Ruskovich, E. Idaho
Russo, R. Everybody's fool
Sainz Borgo, K. It would be night in Caracas
Sala, S. Forever my hero
Salinger, J. Nine stories
Santopolo, J. More than words
Saramago, J. Blindness
Sarginson, S. The wonderful
Saunders, G. Lincoln in the bardo
Saville, L. Henry and Rachel
Schaitkin, A. Saint X
Schanbacher, G. Crossing Purgatory
Scotch, A. In twenty years
Scott, C. The poppy wife
Scott, J. The kept
Sebold, A. The lovely bones
Shakar, A. Luminarium
Shalev, M. Two she-bears
Sherrill, S. The minotaur takes his own sweet time
Shipman, V. The heirloom garden
Smith, Z. The autograph man
Stedman, M. The light between oceans
Stewart, A. Stars in the grass
Stroud, C. The shimmer
Strout, E. Olive Kitteridge
Strout, E. Olive, again
Styron, W. Lie down in darkness
Swift, G. Wish you were here
Swyler, E. Light from other stars
T. I. Power & Beauty
Tan, T. The garden of evening mists
Tartt, D. The goldfinch
Thomas, B. A good enough mother
Toibin, C. The empty family
Toole, F. Pound for pound
Torday, D. The last flight of Poxl West
Tran, V. Dragonfish
Trigiani, A. Big Cherry Holler
Trueblood, V. Seven loves
Turner, N. Black widow
Tyler, A. The beginner's goodbye
Umrigar, T. The space between us
Unger, L. The red hunter
Unger, L. Under my skin
Uris, L. Redemption
Van der Vliet Oloomi, A. Call me Zebra
Vuong, O. On Earth we're briefly gorgeous
Wallace, D. Mr. Sebastian and the Negro magician
Wallace, M. The girl in the garden
Wallant, E. The pawnbroker
Ward, A. Forgive me

Warrington, F. Midsummer night
Watson, M. The dream peddler
Weiner, J. Little earthquakes
Weiner, J. Mrs. Everything
Wells, B. The end of loneliness
Wharton, E. The children
Wickersham, J. The news from Spain
Wideman, J. American histories
Wieland, L. Paris, 7 a.m.
Wiesel, E. Night, Dawn, The accident
Wiggs, S. The Oysterville sewing circle
Williams, N. This is happiness
Wilson, C. Dead girl in 2A
Winawer, M. The scribe of Siena
Winter, E. The rage of dragons
Winthrop, E. The why of things
Wolitzer, M. Surrender, Dorothy
Woo, S. Love love
Woodson, J. Another Brooklyn
Yang, J. The ascent to godhood
Yang, J. The red threads of fortune
Yoshimoto, B. Moshi-moshi
Young, W. The shack
Zailckas, K. Mother, mother

LOSS OF CONSCIOUSNESS
Bartz, A. The lost night
Moshfegh, O. My year of rest and relaxation
Nichols, L. Vessel
Unger, L. Under my skin
Lost and wanted Freudenberger, N.

LOST ANIMALS
Adams, D. Dirk Gently's holistic detective agency
The **lost** art of gratitude McCall Smith, A.

LOST ARTICLES
Barry, D. Insane city
Castle, J. The lost night
Child, L. The midnight line
Follett, K. Whiteout
Goodis, D. Nightfall
Kroese, R. The last iota
Ogawa, Y. The memory police
Sansom, C. Lamentation
The **lost** book of Adana Moreau Zapata, M.
The **lost** book of the Grail Lovett, C.

LOST BOOKS
Anderson, A. The summer guest
Gruber, M. The book of air and shadows
Zapata, M. The lost book of Adana Moreau
The **lost** boy Lackberg, C.
Lost boy lost girl Straub, P.

LOST CHILDREN
Liardet, F. We must be brave
Luiselli, V. Lost children archive
Lost children archive Luiselli, V.
Lost City Radio Alarcon, D.
The **lost** daughter Ferrante, E.
The **lost** daughter Paul, G.

Baldwin, J. Another country
Baldwin, J. Giovanni's room
Banks, I. The crow road
Bates, J. Midnight at the Dragon Cafe
Beagle, P. Summerlong
Bender, A. The particular sadness of lemon cake
Bhuvaneswar, C. White dancing elephants
Bonnaffons, A. The regrets
Canin, E. America America
Chen, D. Brothers
Coetzee, J. Slow man
Cook, T. Sandrine's case
Danielewski, M. Only revolutions
Davis, K. Duplex
Diaz, J. This is how you lose her
Dunant, S. The birth of Venus
Duncan, G. The last werewolf
Dupont, E. The American fiancee
Dybek, S. I sailed with Magellan
Ebershoff, D. The Danish girl
Falcones de Sierra, I. Cathedral of the sea
Ford, R. A multitude of sins
Frazier, C. Thirteen moons
Gabaldon, D. A breath of snow and ashes
Gabaldon, D. Dragonfly in amber
Gabaldon, D. Drums of autumn
Gabaldon, D. An echo in the bone
Gabaldon, D. The fiery cross
Gabaldon, D. Outlander
Gabaldon, D. Voyager
Gabaldon, D. Written in my own heart's blood
Gaitskill, M. Veronica
Garcia Marquez, G. Memories of my melancholy whores
Gertler, S. Drifting
Gessen, K. All the sad young literary men
Groff, L. Fates and furies
Hazzard, S. The great fire
Heller, Z. What was she thinking?
Helprin, M. Winter's tale
Henry, P. Becoming Mrs. Lewis
Hoffman, A. The probable future
Hoffman, A. The world that we knew
Hugo, V. The hunchback of Notre Dame
Hunt, S. The invention of everything else
Itani, F. Deafening
Itani, F. Tell
Jimenez, S. The vanished birds
July, M. No one belongs here more than you
Kundera, M. Immortality
Le Guin, U. The beginning place
Lewis, C. Till we have faces
Makine, A. The woman who waited
Manicka, R. The rice mother
Martin, S. The pleasure of my company
McCracken, E. Bowlaway
McEwan, I. On Chesil Beach
McKillip, P. Alphabet of thorn

Meyers, K. The work of wolves
Monroe, M. God still don't like ugly
Morrison, T. God help the child
Munoz Molina, A. In her absence
Nemirovsky, I. Fire in the blood
Nunez, E. Grace
O'Brien, E. Wild Decembers
Perez-Reverte, A. The painter of battles
Poore, M. Reincarnation blues
Powning, B. The sea captain's wife
Proust, M. Time regained
Proust, M. Within a budding grove
Pywell, S. What happened to Henry
Reisman, N. The first desire
Russell, M. Dreamers of the day
Rutherfurd, E. The princes of Ireland
Saramago, J. Death with interruptions
See, L. Peony in love
Shan, S. The girl who played Go
Shields, C. The republic of love
Skarmeta, A. The dancer and the thief
Sparks, N. A walk to remember
Stibbe, N. Reasons to be cheerful
Stringer, V. Let that be the reason
Suri, M. The age of Shiva
Tolkien, J. Beren and Luthien
Tolstaya, T. Aetherial worlds
Torday, D. The last flight of Poxl West
Trueblood, V. Seven loves
Vargas Llosa, M. The bad girl
Vollmann, W. Last stories and other stories
Vreeland, S. Luncheon of the boating party
Ward, A. Forgive me
Whitaker, K. The animators
Wickersham, J. The news from Spain
Wiggins, M. The shadow catcher
Wolfe, G. The shadow of the torturer
Woods, T. True to the game

Love Morrison, T.
Love Orstavik, H.
Love & a gangsta Gray, E.
Love and other mistakes Kate, J.
Love and ruin McLain, P.
Love and shame and love Orner, P.
Love and war Jakes, J.
Love at first like Orenstein, H.
Love at the resort [series] Foster, L.
**LOVE CANAL CHEMICAL WASTE LANDFILL, NIAGA-
  RA FALLS, NEW YORK**
  Oates, J. The falls
Love her madly Smith, M.
LOVE IN FILMS
  Nicholls, O. Love, unscripted
Love in the ruins Percy, W.
Love in the time of cholera Garcia Marquez, G.
LOVE LETTER WRITING
  Brockmeier, K. The illumination

O'Neill, H. The Lonely Hearts Hotel
Oakley, C. You were there too
Olmstead, R. The coldest night
Orringer, J. The invisible bridge
Oyeyemi, H. Mr. Fox
Oz, A. Don't call it night
Pasternak, B. Doctor Zhivago
Pears, I. The dream of Scipio
Perez-Reverte, A. What we become
Pitts, L. Freeman
Plain, B. The golden cup
Plain, B. Harvest
Powers, R. The Gold Bug Variations
Read, P. Alice in exile
Reay, K. The Bronte plot
Reid, T. Forever, interrupted
Remarque, E. A time to love and a time to die
Roy, A. An atlas of impossible longing
Sada, D. Almost never
Salter, J. All that is
Sand, G. Marianne
Saville, L. Henry and Rachel
See, L. Peony in love
Segal, E. Love story
Serle, R. In five years
Seth, V. A suitable boy
Seton, A. Katherine
Shields, C. The republic of love
Shreve, A. Eden Close
Shreve, A. The last time they met
Skarmeta, A. The dancer and the thief
Smith, B. Joy in the morning
Soli, T. The lotus eaters
Sontag, S. The volcano lover
Souljah,. Midnight and the meaning of love
Sparks, N. Every breath
Sparks, N. The
Sparks, N. A walk to remember
Spencer, S. Endless love
Sundaresan, I. The splendor of silence
Trevanian The summer of Katya
Trollope, J. Next of kin
Trollope, J. A Spanish lover
Tyler, A. The accidental tourist
Tyler, A. Celestial navigation
Updike, J. Brazil
Veletzos, R. The girl they left behind
Vreeland, S. Luncheon of the boating party
Wallace, C. The blind contessa's new machine
Waller, R. The bridges of Madison County
Wickersham, J. The news from Spain
Williams, B. The summer wives
Wilson, S. The fortune teller's daughter
Love story Segal, E.
LOVE TRIANGLES
Amis, M. London fields
Amis, M. The pregnant widow

Andersen, L. The Boleyn king
Atwood, M. Life before man
Austen, J. Northanger Abbey
Auster, P. Invisible
Auster, P. Leviathan
Barth, J. The end of the road
Barth, J. The floating opera
Bates, J. Midnight at the Dragon Cafe
Bird, S. The flamenco academy
Bonnaffons, A. The regrets
Bonner, C. Lily
Bowman, V. The accidental countess
Bowman, V. The unexpected duchess
Boyle, E. Along came a duke
Braithwaite, O. My sister, the serial killer
Brownrigg, S. Morality tale
Burrowes, G. The bridegroom wore plaid
Byatt, A. The biographer's tale
Cameron, P. The city of your final destination
Cary, J. The horse's mouth
Ca$h Trust no man 2
Ca$h Trust no man 3
Chen, D. Brothers
Choi, S. My education
Clark, W. Payback ain't enough
Clark, W. Payback with ya life
Colin, E. The memory thief
Collins, W. The woman in white
Dare, T. Say yes to the marquess
Davies, R. The rebel angels
De Bernieres, L. Birds without wings
De la Roche, M. Jalna
Dean, P. Tam Lin
Deaver, J. The coffin dancer
Dermansky, M. Very nice
Deutermann, P. Pacific glory
Drayson, N. A guide to the birds of East Africa
Dufresne, J. Deep in the shade of paradise
Eliot, G. Adam Bede
Ellison, J. A small indiscretion
Erdrich, L. The Master Butchers Singing Club
Ervin, K. Mina's joint
Esquivel, L. Like water for chocolate
Eugenides, J. The marriage plot
Evanovich, J. Turbo twenty-three
Evanovich, S. Under the table
Faulks, S. Birdsong
Fielding, H. Bridget Jones's diary
FitzGerald, G. Redemption Mountain
Force, M. Five years gone
Fowles, J. The French lieutenant's woman
Franzen, J. Freedom
Furnivall, K. The red scarf
Gaiman, N. Anansi boys
Garcia Marquez, G. Love in the time of cholera
Gardam, J. Last friends
Gardam, J. The man in the wooden hat

Warren, R. World enough and time
Warren, S. Rescue me
Warren, T. The replacement wife
Warrington, F. Elfland
Watkins, J. Secrets of a side bitch
Watkins, J. Secrets of a side bitch 2
Weinberg, K. The truants
Wharton, E. Ethan Frome
White, E. Jack Holmes and his friend
Williams, K. Harlem on lock
Williams, K. Sweet Giselle
Willig, L. The deception of the emerald ring
Winman, S. Tin man
Woods, S. Santa Fe rules
Yu, H. Brothers

LOVE TRIANGLES -- HOLLYWOOD, CALIFORNIA

Waugh, E. The loved one

Love undercover [series] Foster, L.

Love you more Gardner, L.

Love's winning plays Majors, I.

Love, again Lessing, D.

LOVE, NAT, 1854-1921

Lansdale, J. Paradise sky

Love, unscripted Nicholls, O.

LOVE-HATE RELATIONSHIPS

Blackstock, T. Shadow in Serenity
Kincaid, J. Annie John
Lauren, C. Dating you
Thomas, S. Tempting the bride

The **loved** one Waugh, E.

Lovejoy mysteries [series] Gash, J.

LOVELACE, ADA KING, COUNTESS OF, 1815-1852

Crowley, J. Lord Byron's novel

The **lovely** bones Sebold, A.

Lovemurder Black, S.

The **lover's** knot O'Donohue, C.

LOVER'S REUNIONS

O'Keefe, M. Crazy thing called love

LOVERS

Aciman, A. Enigma variations
Alison, J. The marriage of the sea
Anderton, J. Debris
Bauer, A. The forever marriage
Baxter, C. The feast of love
Bulgakov, M. The master and Margarita
Chee, A. The queen of the night
Cheek, C. Cape May
Cleeves, A. Wild fire
Coetzee, J. Elizabeth Costello
Collins, C. The gamal
Danler, S. Sweetbitter
Dickey, E. The blackbirds
Dumas, A. Camille
Dunant, S. In the company of the courtesan
Ellison, J. A small indiscretion
Flanagan, R. The narrow road to the deep north
Force, M. Five years gone

Freeman, B. Goodbye to the dead
Gregory, P. The white princess
Guillory, J. The proposal
Hardy, T. The return of the native
Harris, E. I say a little prayer
Harris, O. A shadow intelligence
Heath, L. Falling into bed with a duke
Kent, K. The outcasts
Koontz, D. The darkest evening of the year
Lackberg, C. The lost boy
Lansdale, J. A fine dark line
Ledgard, J. Submergence
Lippman, L. Sunburn
Locascio, L. Open me
Mallon, T. Landfall
Maxwell, R. The queen's bastard
McPhee, M. Gorgeous lies
Mengestu, D. All our names
Muller, H. The fox was ever the hunter
Murakami, H. Killing commendatore
Nabokov, V. King, queen, knave
Oates, J. Evil eye
Pelecanos, G. The double
Penney, S. Under a pole star
Poole, S. The Borgia mistress
Pulley, N. The lost future of Pepperharrow
Randel, W. The empress of bright moon
Renault, M. The Persian boy
Richmond, M. No one you know
Robinson, P. Strange affair
Rooney, S. Normal people
Rosenberg, J. Confessions of the fox
Ross, A. Ladies and gentlemen
Schami, R. Sophia
Scharer, W. The age of light
Shamsie, K. Home fire
Sharp, Z. Fox hunter
Smith, M. She's not there
Soli, T. The lotus eaters
Sontag, S. In America
Spencer, S. Endless love
Swift, G. Mothering Sunday
Tolkien, J. Beren and Luthien
Trueblood, V. Seven loves
Vargas Llosa, M. The bad girl
Waller, R. The bridges of Madison County
Waters, S. The night watch
Wiggins, M. Evidence of things unseen
Woods, S. Below the belt
Woods, S. Fast & loose

LOVERS -- DEATH

Atwood, M. Life before man
Bledsoe, A. Wisp of a thing
Carey, P. The chemistry of tears
Gardiner, M. Phantom instinct
Hill, J. Horns

LOVERS' REUNIONS

LUDDITES
   Brin, D. Existence
   Egan, J. The keep
LUGGAGE
   Rawlings, D. The baggage handler
Luis Mendoza mysteries [series] Shannon, D.
LUKE,, SAINT
   Parini, J. The Damascus road
Lullaby Palahniuk, C.
LUMBEE INDIANS
   Humphreys, J. Nowhere else on earth
LUMBER INDUSTRY AND TRADE
   Christie, M. Greenwood
   Goudge, E. Green Dolphin Street
   Kesey, K. Sometimes a great notion
   Proulx, A. Barkskins
   Rash, R. Serena
LUMBER WORKERS
   Guterson, D. Our Lady of the Forest
   Hill, R. The woodcutter
   Straley, J. The big both ways
LUMBER WORKERS -- OREGON
   Kesey, K. Sometimes a great notion
The **luminaries** Catton, E.
Luminarium Shakar, A.
The **luminous** dead Starling, C.
The **luminous** heart of Jonah S. Nahai, G.
Luna novels (Ian McDonald) [series] McDonald, I.
LUNAR BASES
   Weir, A. Artemis
Lunar Park Ellis, B.
Lunatics Barry, D.
Luncheon of the boating party Vreeland, S.
The **lure** of the moonflower Willig, L.
Lush life Price, R.
LUST
   Brink, A. Philida
   Cheek, C. Cape May
   Choi, S. My education
   Dane, L. Broken open
   Dickey, E. Bad men and wicked women
   Dickey, E. Before we were wicked
   Dickey, E. The business of lovers
   Dimon, H. Mercy
   Gamboa, S. Necropolis
   Garcia Marquez, G. Memories of my melancholy whores
   Gide, A. The immoralist
   Hammett, D. The glass key
   Hart, J. Damage
   Hunt, S. The dark dark
   Lewis, M. The monk
   Moore, C. The serpent of Venice
   Murray, V. Lust
   Sada, D. Almost never
   Sanders, L. McNally's gamble
   Sanders, L. McNally's luck
   Singh, N. Silver silence

   Stewart, M. The last enchantment
Lust Murray, V.
Lust for life Stone, I.
LUST IN MEN
   Dean, M. I, Hogarth
Luther. The calling Cross, N.
LUXEMBOURG
   Pavone, C. The expats
LUXOR, EGYPT
   Peters, E. The golden one
Lydia Chin and Bill Smith mysteries [series] Rozan, S.
The **lying** game Ware, R.
Lying in wait Nugent, L.
The **lying** room French, N.
Lying with strangers Grippando, J.
LYNCHING
   Atkins, A. The forsaken
   Clark, W. The ox-bow incident
   Erdrich, L. The plague of doves
   Faulkner, W. Intruder in the dust
   Hunt, L. The evening road
   North, C. The pursuit of William Abbey
   Sandford, J. Naked prey
   Vernon, O. A killing in this town
LYNCHING -- MISSISSIPPI
   Nordan, L. Wolf whistle
**LYNCHING -- SOUTHERN STATES -- HISTORY -- 20TH
   CENTURY**
   Johnson, M. Incognegro
LYON, FRANCE
   Page, K. The body in the vestibule

M

M I 5
   Atkinson, K. Transcription
   McEwan, I. Sweet tooth
   McKinty, A. In the morning I'll be gone
   Seymour, G. Vagabond
M I 6
   Bell, T. Overkill
   Cumming, C. A colder war
   Cumming, C. A divided spy
   Cumming, C. A foreign country
   Follett, K. Eye of the needle
   Harris, O. A shadow intelligence
   Lawton, J. Hammer to fall
   Porter, H. Firefly
   Sebastian, T. Fatal ally
MacAlister family [series] Garwood, J.
Macbeth Nesbo, J.
MACEDONIA, GREECE
   Lyon, A. The sweet girl
MacGregor novels [series] Burrowes, G.
The **MacGuffin** Elkin, S.
Machineries of empire [series] Lee, Y.
MACHINERY

Maggie Gardiner and Jack Renner novels [series] Black, L.
Maggie Hope mysteries [series] MacNeal, S.
Maggie O'Dell novels [series] Kava, A.
Maggody and the moonbeams Hess, J.

MAGGODY, ARKANSAS

Hess, J. Maggody and the moonbeams

MAGIC

Aaronovitch, B. Midnight riot
Aaronovitch, B. Moon over Soho
Allen, S. First frost
Allen, S. Garden spells
Allen, S. The girl who chased the moon
Anders, C. All the birds in the sky
Arden, K. The girl in the tower
Arden, K. The winter of the witch
Baker, K. The house of the stag
Bardugo, L. Ninth house
Barker, C. Weaveworld
Barnhill, K. Dreadful young ladies and other stories
Beagle, P. The last unicorn
Beagle, P. Summerlong
Bear, E. All the windwracked stars
Bear, E. Range of ghosts
Bear, E. The red-stained wings
Bear, E. Shattered pillars
Bear, E. The stone in the skull
Bender, A. The particular sadness of lemon cake
Bennett, R. Foundryside
Bledsoe, A. Gather her round
Bledsoe, A. The hum and the shiver
Bledsoe, A. Long black curl
Bledsoe, A. Wisp of a thing
Bolano, R. Monsieur Pain
Bouchet, A. Breath of fire
Bouchet, A. A promise of fire
Bradbury, R. The illustrated man
Butcher, J. Proven guilty
Callender, K. Queen of the conquered
Callihan, K. Firelight
Camp, B. The city of lost fortunes
Camp, B. Gather the fortunes
Carter, A. Nights at the circus
Castle, J. Illusion Town
Chakraborty, S. The city of brass
Chakraborty, S. The empire of gold
Chakraborty, S. The kingdom of copper
Charlton, B. Spellwright
Cho, Z. Sorcerer to the crown
Clarke, S. Jonathan Strange & Mr. Norrell
Cogman, G. The burning page
Cogman, G. The invisible library
Cogman, G. The masked city
Cogman, G. The mortal word
Craddock, C. An alchemy of masques and mirrors
Craddock, C. A labyrinth of scions and sorcery
Czerneda, J. A turn of light
Dean, P. Tam Lin

Diachenko, S. Vita nostra
Donohue, K. The stolen child
Draven, G. Phoenix unbound
Durst, S. The queen of blood
Eason, K. How Rory Thorne destroyed the multiverse
Engelmann, K. The Stockholm octavo
Erdrich, L. Tracks
Flyte, M. City of dark magic
Flyte, M. City of lost dreams
Frei, M. The stranger's magic
Gailey, S. Magic for liars
Gaiman, N. Anansi boys
Gaiman, N. Stardust
Gaiman, N. Trigger warning
Gilman, F. The half-made world
Gilman, L. The cold eye
Gilman, L. Hard magic
Glass, J. The women's war
Gratton, T. The queens of Innis Lear
Griffin, K. The glass god
Griffin, K. Stray souls
Grossman, L. The magician king
Grossman, L. The magician's land
Hackwith, A. The library of the unwritten
Hair, D. Mage's blood
Hair, D. Scarlet tides
Harkness, D. The book of life
Harkness, D. A discovery of witches
Harkness, D. Shadow of night
Hawkins, S. The library at Mount Char
Haydon, E. Destiny
Haydon, E. The Merchant Emperor
Haydon, E. Prophecy
Hill, J. Horns
Hoffman, A. Skylight confessions
Hunt, S. The dark dark
Ishiguro, K. The buried giant
Jemisin, N. How long 'til black future month?
Jemisin, N. The killing moon
Jones, D. A sudden wild magic
Kay, G. The last light of the sun
Kay, G. The summer tree
Kay, G. Tigana
Krueger, P. Steel crow saga
Kurland, L. Star of the morning
Lackey, M. The fairy godmother
Lake, J. Endurance
Lake, J. Green
Lanagan, M. The brides of Rollrock Island
Le Guin, U. The beginning place
Le Guin, U. The other wind
Leckie, A. The Raven tower
Lee, F. Jade City
Lee, F. Jade war
Locke, T. Emissary
Lyons, J. The name of all things
Lyons, J. The ruin of kings

MAGIC BOXES

Kaufmann, N. Dying is my business

Magic for beginners Link, K.

Magic for liars Gailey, S.

Magic for unlucky girls Balaskovits, A.

MAGIC GUITARS

Alexie, S. Reservation blues

The **Magic** Mountain Mann, T.

MAGIC POTIONS

Gilman, L. Flesh and fire

MAGIC RINGS

Tolkien, J. The fellowship of the ring

Tolkien, J. The lord of the rings

Tolkien, J. The return of the king

Tolkien, J. The two towers

MAGIC ROCKS

Gaiman, N. Stardust

Lyons, J. The name of all things

Walton, J. Lent

Magic seeds Naipaul, V.

MAGIC SWORDS

Hamill, P. Forever

Kurland, L. Star of the morning

Saberhagen, F. Coinspinner's story

Saberhagen, F. Farslayer's story

Saberhagen, F. Mindsword's story

Saberhagen, F. Shieldbreaker's story

Saberhagen, F. Sightblinder's story

Saberhagen, F. Stonecutter's story

Saberhagen, F. Wayfinder's story

Saberhagen, F. Woundhealer's story

MAGIC TELEPHONES

Rowell, R. Landline

Magic time Marlette, D.

MAGIC TRICKS

Rosen, L. The Kortelisy escape

Magic words Kolpan, G.

MAGICAL BOOKS

Cogman, G. The burning page

Cogman, G. The invisible library

Cogman, G. The masked city

Cogman, G. The mortal word

Hackwith, A. The library of the unwritten

MAGICAL REALISM

Allende, I. Daughter of fortune

Allende, I. Eva Luna

Allende, I. The house of the spirits

Allende, I. Of love and shadows

Allende, I. Portrait in sepia

Allende, I. The stories of Eva Luna

Amado, J. Dona Flor and her two husbands

Araghi, A. The immortals of Tehran

Armfield, J. Salt slow

Atkinson, K. Human croquet

Bail, M. Eucalyptus

Bender, A. The particular sadness of lemon cake

Borges, J. Ficciones

Calvino, I. The baron in the trees

Calvino, I. If on a winter's night a traveler

Calvino, I. Invisible cities

Carey, L. The stolen child

Carter, A. Nights at the circus

Coates, T. The water dancer

Couto, M. Sleepwalking land

Depestre, R. Hadriana in all my dreams

Erdrich, L. LaRose

Esquivel, L. Like water for chocolate

Flores, F. Tears of the trufflepig

Foer, J. Everything is illuminated

Forbes, C. A tall history of sugar

Fuentes, C. Destiny and desire

Garcia Marquez, G. The autumn of the patriarch

Garcia Marquez, G. Chronicle of a death foretold

Garcia Marquez, G. Collected novellas

Garcia Marquez, G. The general in his labyrinth

Garcia Marquez, G. Leaf storm, and other stories

Garcia Marquez, G. Love in the time of cholera

Garcia Marquez, G. Memories of my melancholy whores

Garcia Marquez, G. One hundred years of solitude

Garcia Marquez, G. Strange pilgrims

Helprin, M. Winter's tale

Higashino, K. The miracles of the Namiya General Store

Hoeg, P. The history of Danish dreams

Hoffman, A. The marriage of opposites

Hoffman, A. Practical magic

Hoffman, A. The probable future

Hoffman, A. The river king

Hoffman, A. The rules of magic

Hoffman, A. Skylight confessions

Hoffman, A. The story sisters

Hoffman, A. Turtle moon

Hoffman, A. The world that we knew

Hubbard, L. The talented Ribkins

Hulme, K. The bone people

Hunt, S. The dark dark

Ivey, E. The snow child

Johnson, D. Train dreams

Kehlmann, D. Tyll

Knox, T. Kockroach

Lopez Barrio, C. The house of the impossible loves

Mandanipour, S. Moon brow

Mandel, E. The glass hotel

McFadden, B. Gathering of waters

Morrison, T. Beloved

Nahai, G. The luminous heart of Jonah S.

Oyeyemi, H. Boy, Snow, Bird

Oyeyemi, H. Gingerbread

Oyeyemi, H. What is not yours is not yours

Prose, F. Household saints

Rock, P. The shelter cycle

Ruiz Zafon, C. The angel's game

Ruiz Zafon, C. The prisoner of heaven

Ruiz Zafon, C. The labyrinth of the spirits

Ruiz Zafon, C. The shadow of the wind

Koryta, M. How it happened
Kotzwinkle, W. The bear went over the mountain
Kubica, M. The other Mrs.
Meier, L. Silver anniversary murder
Millet, L. Sweet lamb of heaven
Miranda, M. The last house guest
Ogilvie, E. When the music stopped
Page, K. The body in the wake
Phillips, S. Heroes are my weakness
Ramsay, F. Scone Island
Rich, V. The baked bean supper murders
Rickards, J. Winter's end
Roberts, N. Shelter in place
Robinson, R. Cost
Russell, K. My dark Vanessa
Russo, R. Empire Falls
Shields, K. The truth of all things
Strout, E. The Burgess boys
Strout, E. Olive Kitteridge
Strout, E. Olive, again
Watson, J. Asta in the wings
Zevin, G. Young Jane Young

MAINE -- HISTORY -- 18TH CENTURY
Lawrence, M. Hearts and bones

MAINSTREAM FICTION
Abramowitz, A. Thank you, goodnight
Adelman, M. Piece of mind
Adkins, M. When you read this
Ahava, S. Things that fall from the sky
Albert, E. The book of Dahlia
Alenyikov, M. Ivan and Misha
Allen, S. Garden spells
Allen, S. The girl who chased the moon
Allen, S. First frost
Amidon, S. Human capital
Arnoult, D. Sufficient grace
Attenberg, J. The Middlesteins
Audur A. Olafsdottir, 1. Butterflies in November
Backman, F. Britt-Marie was here
Backman, F. Beartown
Backman, F. A man called Ove
Backman, F. My grandmother asked me to tell you she's
  sorry
Backman, F. Us against you
Baker, T. The little giant of Aberdeen County
Bala, S. The boat people
Balasubramanyam, R. Professor Chandra follows his bliss
Baldacci, D. One summer
Barnes, K. In the kingdom of men
Barthelme, F. Bob the gambler
Barthelme, F. Elroy Nights
Barthelme, F. Painted desert
Bauermeister, E. The school of essential ingredients
Bawden, N. Family money
Beattie, A. Chilly scenes of winter
Beckerman, H. If only I could tell you
Bender, K. Refund

Benedict, H. Wolf season
Berg, E. The art of mending
Berg, E. The confession club
Berg, E. The last time I saw you
Berg, E. Never change
Berg, E. Night of miracles
Berg, E. Once upon a time, there was you
Berg, E. The story of Arthur Truluv
Berg, E. We are all welcome here
Bergen, D. See the child
Bergstrom, H. Steal the north
Bhuvaneswar, C. White dancing elephants
Binchy, M. Firefly summer
Binchy, M. Whitethorn Woods
Bivald, K. The readers of Broken Wheel recommend
Blackwell, J. Letters from Paris
Block, S. Oliver Loving
Blumenfeld, A. The cast
Bohjalian, C. The buffalo soldier
Bowman, C. Horace Winter says goodbye
Boyle, T. The tortilla curtain
Boyle, T. When the killing's done
Brown, E. The weird sisters
Brown, K. The life Lucy knew
Brown, R. Before and after
Brown, R. Half a heart
Brown, R. Tender mercies
Brownmiller, S. Waverly Place
Bruni, S. The night Gwen Stacy died
Brunkhorst, A. The gilded Life of Matilda Duplaine
Brunt, C. Tell the wolves I'm home
Butler, S. Ten things I've learnt about love
Callanan, L. Paris by the book
Cameron, W. The dogs of Christmas
Campbell, A. On the floor
Cantor, M. Death and other happy endings
Caputo, P. Crossers
Carlson, S. Almost Graceland
Carter, M. Further out than you thought
Cartwright, J. To heaven by water
Carty-Williams, C. Queenie
Celello, E. Leaning to stay
Chung, C. The tenth muse
Clarke, L. A single breath
Cleage, P. What looks like crazy on an ordinary day
Cleave, C. Little Bee
Cogburn, E. Ava's place
Colgan, J. The endless beach
Colin, E. The memory thief
Colombani, L. The braid
Colwin, L. Happy all the time
Cooney, E. The mountaintop school for dogs and other sec-
  ond chances
Cosse, L. A novel bookstore
Creech, S. The whole way home
Cronin, A. Citadel
Crosbie, L. Where did you sleep last night?

Perrotta, T. The abstinence teacher
Perrotta, T. Joe College
Perrotta, T. Little children
Picoult, J. Change of heart
Picoult, J. House rules
Picoult, J. Keeping faith
Picoult, J. Leaving time
Picoult, J. Lone wolf
Picoult, J. My sister's keeper
Picoult, J. Nineteen minutes
Picoult, J. Sing you home
Picoult, J. A spark of light
Picoult, J. The storyteller
Picoult, J. Vanishing acts
Powell, P. Edisto
Quindlen, A. Object lessons
Racculia, K. Tuesday Mooney talks to ghosts
Ramos, J. The farm
Rice, L. The lemon orchard
Richman, A. The secret of clouds
Robinson, R. Cost
Rooney, S. Conversations with friends
Rossner, J. Looking for Mr. Goodbar
Rowell, R. Landline
Rowling, J. The casual vacancy
Sanders, D. Clover
Santopolo, J. More than words
Scotch, A. In twenty years
Semple, M. Where'd you go, Bernadette
Serle, R. In five years
Shreve, A. The last time they met
Shreve, A. The pilot's wife
Shriver, L. The post-birthday world
Shriver, L. So much for that
Shteyngart, G. Lake Success
Simonson, H. Major Pettigrew's last stand
Simsion, G. The Rosie effect
Simsion, G. The Rosie project
Simsion, G. The Rosie result
Sittenfeld, C. Eligible
Sittenfeld, C. Sisterland
Smiley, J. Horse heaven
Sparks, N. The
Sparks, N. A walk to remember
Stephens, A. Famous adopted people
Stern, S. The Pinch
Stradal, J. The lager queen of Minnesota
Straub, E. The vacationers
Trigiani, A. Big Cherry Holler
Trigiani, A. Big Stone Gap
Trollope, J. The best of friends
Trollope, J. Brother and sister
Trollope, J. Marrying the mistress
Trollope, J. The men and the girls
Trollope, J. Next of kin
Trollope, J. The other family
Trollope, J. Other people's children

Trollope, J. Second honeymoon
Trollope, J. A Spanish lover
Tropper, J. One last thing before I go
Tyler, A. The accidental tourist
Tyler, A. The amateur marriage
Tyler, A. The beginner's goodbye
Tyler, A. Breathing lessons
Tyler, A. Celestial navigation
Tyler, A. The clock winder
Tyler, A. Digging to America
Tyler, A. Dinner at the Homesick Restaurant
Tyler, A. Earthly possessions
Tyler, A. Ladder of years
Tyler, A. Morgan's passing
Tyler, A. Noah's compass
Tyler, A. A patchwork planet
Tyler, A. Saint Maybe
Tyler, A. Searching for Caleb
Tyler, A. A slipping-down life
Tyler, A. The tin can tree
Urrea, L. Into the beautiful North
Vatner, J. Carnegie Hill
Wallace, M. The girl in the garden
Waller, R. The bridges of Madison County
Walls, J. The silver star
Walter, J. Beautiful ruins
Walter, J. The financial lives of the poets
Warren, T. The replacement wife
Weir, M. The book of Essie
Whitaker, K. The animators
White, B. Quite a year for plums
Williams, K. Tell the machine goodnight
Wilson, K. Nothing to see here
Winthrop, E. The why of things
Wolitzer, M. The Interestings
Wolitzer, M. Surrender, Dorothy
Wolitzer, M. The wife
Woo, S. Love love
Yoshimoto, B. Moshi-moshi
Zevin, G. The storied life of A. J. Fikry
Zevin, G. Young Jane Young

Maisie Dobbs Winspear, J.

Maisie Dobbs novels [series] Winspear, J.

The **majesties** Tsao, T.

Major Pettigrew's last stand Simonson, H.

MAJOR, JOHN, 1943- ATTEMPTED ASSASSINATION
Higgins, J. Eye of the storm

MAJORCA, SPAIN
Nichols, P. The rocks
Straub, E. The vacationers
Thelen, A. The island of second sight

Makana mysteries [series] Bilal, P.

Make me Child, L.

Make way for Lucia Benson, E.

Make your home among strangers Crucet, J.

MAKEOVERS (BEAUTY CARE)
Evanovich, S. Under the table

MALE FRIENDSHIP -- CALIFORNIA
Kinder, C. Honeymooners
MALE FRIENDSHIP -- NEW MEXICO
McCarthy, C. Cities of the plain
MALE FRIENDSHIP -- TEXAS
McMurtry, L. Comanche moon
MALE FRIENDSHIP -- UNITED STATES -- HISTORY
Parini, J. The passages of H.M.
MALE IMPERSONATORS
Allende, I. Daughter of fortune
Ashe, K. The prince
Bird, S. Daughter of a daughter of a queen
De Robertis, C. The gods of tango
Elison, M. The book of the unnamed midwife
Erdrich, L. The last report on the miracles at Little No Horse
Guhrke, L. Governess gone rogue
Hand, E. Curious toys
Larison, J. Whiskey when we're dry
Levine, D. Arabella of Mars
McCabe, E. I shall be near to you
Scott, J. The kept
Thomson, E. Beloved poison
Thomson, E. The blood
MALE PROSTITUTES
Herlihy, J. Midnight cowboy
Howatch, S. The heartbreaker
MALE RAPE
Perry, A. The silent cry
MALE RAPE -- AFGHANISTAN
Hosseini, K. The kite runner
MALE RAPE VICTIMS
O'Connor, F. The violent bear it away
MALE RAPE VICTIMS -- AFGHANISTAN
Hosseini, K. The kite runner
MALE STRIPTEASERS
Castile, Z. Flashed
Malgudi days Narayan, R.
Malice Higashino, K.
MALICIOUS ACCUSATION
Anthony, M. Diary of a young girl
Ashley, J. The madness of Lord Ian Mackenzie
Beck, H. Here and gone
Bourne, J. My lord and spymaster
Buchan, J. The thirty-nine steps
Callaghan, M. Billy, come home
Callihan, K. Firelight
Cameron, M. Code of honor
Cook, T. Sandrine's case
Crace, J. Harvest
Craddock, C. A labyrinth of scions and sorcery
Cussler, C. The Gray Ghost
Dallas, S. The last midwife
Davis, F. The Chelsea girls
De Giovanni, M. The crocodile
Delinsky, B. Lake news
Dumas, A. The count of Monte Cristo
Edugyan, E. Washington Black

Elias, G. Danse macabre
Eliot, G. Silas Marner
Elliot, L. Guilty
Faust, C. Money shot
Flanagan, R. The unknown terrorist
Flint, E. Little deaths
Francis, P. The orphans of Race Point
Franklin, A. Mistress of the art of death
Frantz, L. The lacemaker
Freed, D. Hot start
French, N. Friday on my mind
Gallagher, S. The kingdom of bones
Hannah, S. The mystery of three quarters
Hawthorne, N. The house of the seven gables
Iles, G. The bone tree
Iles, G. Natchez burning
Irvin, K. Tell her no lies
Johnson, M. Incognegro
Katsu, A. The hunger
Kellerman, F. Serpent's tooth
Kent, C. The loving husband
Kent, H. Burial rites
MacDonald, J. The long lavender look
Malamud, B. The fixer
McAllister, T. How to be safe
McGuire, S. Night and silence
Moore, K. To seduce an angel
Mortimer, J. Felix in the underworld
Mosley, W. Down the river unto the sea
Muller, M. Cyanide Wells
Muller, M. The dangerous hour
Neubauer, E. Murder at the Mena House
Nickson, C. The hocus girl
Nugent, A. Soul murder
Parks, B. Closer than you know
Perry, T. Vanishing act
Pronzini, B. Nemesis
Quirk, M. Cold barrel zero
Quirk, M. Dead man switch
Rai, A. Wrong to need you
Rankin, I. Black and blue
Raybourn, D. A perilous undertaking
Reid, K. Such a fun age
Schami, R. Sophia
Scottoline, L. Feared
Smith, L. On Agate Hill
Walton, J. Farthing
Wilson, G. The bird king
Malloren chronicles [series] Beverley, J.
Mallory's oracle O'Connell, C.
MALMO, SWEDEN
McCall Smith, A. The Department of Sensitive Crimes
MALTA
Berry, S. The Malta exchange
MALTA -- HISTORY -- 1530-1798
Willocks, T. The religion
The **Malta** exchange Berry, S.

Fleischmann, R. How quickly she disappears
Fowles, J. The magus
George, M. The confessions of young Nero
Gilman, L. Silver on the road
Guterson, D. Our Lady of the Forest
Hamilton, S. The second life of Nick Mason
Hendricks, G. An anonymous girl
Hurley, K. The stars are legion
Iggulden, C. The abbot's tale
James, H. The wings of the dove
King, S. The Institute
Lyons, J. The name of all things
MacLean, S. Wicked and the wallflower
Massey, S. The Satapur moonstone
Massey, S. The widows of Malabar Hill
McKinty, A. The chain
Mosley, W. The man in my basement
Nadzam, B. Lamb
Nesbo, J. Macbeth
Pinborough, S. Behind her eyes
Puzo, M. The family
Russell, K. My dark Vanessa
Smith, G. The maze at Windermere
Stage, Z. Baby teeth
Starling, C. The luminous dead
Thomas, R. Firewatching
Vinge, V. Rainbows end

MANIPULATION BY MEN
Barry, S. The secret scripture
Boyne, J. A ladder to the sky
Delaney, J. The perfect wife
Grippando, J. Lying with strangers
Haigh, J. Mrs. Kimble
Kandasamy, M. When I hit you, or, A portrait of the writer as a young wife
Lutz, L. The passenger
Murdoch, I. A fairly honourable defeat
Noire G-Spot
Sakey, M. The blade itself
Simmons, D. The fifth heart
Unsworth, B. After Hannibal
Unsworth, B. The songs of the kings
Wilson, K. The family Fang

MANIPULATION BY PARENTS
Weir, A. Innocent traitor
Weir, A. The Lady Elizabeth

MANIPULATION BY TEENAGE GIRLS
Scottoline, L. After Anna

MANIPULATION BY WOMEN
Amis, M. London fields
Constantine, L. The last Mrs. Parrish
Crane, S. Maggie
Gardner, L. Alone
Jones, S. The other woman
King, S. Misery
Mangan, C. Tangerine
Merimee, P. Carmen

North, A. The life and death of Sophie Stark
Overton, H. The runaway
Parker, R. Appaloosa
Rendell, R. The face of trespass
Rogan, C. The lifeboat
Rouda, K. The favorite daughter
Spark, M. The driver's seat
Stringer, V. Dirty Red
Stringer, V. Still dirty
Thackeray, W. Vanity fair
Turow, S. Presumed innocent
Warren, T. The replacement wife
Wrobel, S. Darling Rose Gold
Zailckas, K. Mother, mother

MANITOBA
Bergen, D. See the child
Norman, H. The haunting of L.
Toews, M. A complicated kindness

MANNERS AND CUSTOMS
Alharthi, J. Celestial bodies
Burrowes, G. The trouble with dukes
Colette, 1. The complete Claudine
Colwin, L. Happy all the time
Dos Passos, J. 1919
Fitzgerald, F. Novels and stories, 1920-1922
Fitzgerald, F. The short stories of F. Scott Fitzgerald
Fitzgerald, F. Six tales of the jazz age and other stories
Gardam, J. The people on Privilege Hill and other stories
Gaskell, E. North and South
Hemingway, E. The short stories
Jackson, S. The lottery
James, H. Complete stories, 1864-1874
Joyce, G. The limits of enchantment
Kipling, R. Collected stories
Lawrence, D. The rainbow
Mitford, N. The pursuit of love ;
Sackville-West, V. The Edwardians
Thomas, D. The collected stories
Waugh, E. The complete stories of Evelyn Waugh
Waugh, E. Decline and fall
Wharton, E. Collected stories, 1891-1910
Wharton, E. Collected stories, 1911-1937
Williams, T. Collected stories

MANORS
Airth, R. The decent inn of death
Elliott, L. The missing years
Fuller, C. Bitter orange
Galbraith, R. Lethal white
James, H. The portrait of a lady
Jio, S. The last camellia
Jones, S. The uninvited guests
Joss, M. Half broken things
Norfolk, L. John Saturnall's feast
Roussel, R. Locus solus
Sebastian, C. The Lawrence Browne affair
White, R. A lady unrivaled
Woolf, V. Between the acts

MARGATE, ENGLAND
Deveraux, J. Someone to love

MARGUERITE,, QUEEN, CONSORT OF LOUIS IX, KING OF FRANCE, 1221-1295
Jones, S. Four sisters, all queens

MARIA NIKOLAEVNA,, GRAND DUCHESS, DAUGHTER OF NICHOLAS II, EMPEROR OF RUSSIA, 1899-1918
Paul, G. The lost daughter

MARIANA TRENCH
Grant, M. Into the drowning deep

Marianne Sand, G.

MARIE ANTOINETTE,, QUEEN OF FRANCE, 1755-1793
Naslund, S. Abundance

Mariette in ecstasy Hansen, R.

MARIJUANA
Smith, M. Baked

MARIJUANA GROWING
Sexton, M. A kind of freedom

MARIJUANA SMUGGLING
Winslow, D. The kings of cool
Winslow, D. Savages

MARIJUANA USE
Chabon, M. Wonder boys
Quartey, K. Children of the street
Quartey, K. Wife of the gods

MARINA, CA 1505-CA 1530
Sherwood, F. Night of sorrows

MARINE ANIMALS
Watts, P. Starfish

MARINE ANIMALS IN ART
Flanagan, R. Gould's book of fish

MARINE ANIMALS IN MEDICINE
Hall, J. Red sky at night

MARINE BIOLOGISTS
Benchley, P. Jaws
Drabble, M. The sea lady
Hiaasen, C. Skinny dip
White, R. Salt river

MARINE BIOLOGISTS -- MONTEREY, CALIFORNIA
Steinbeck, J. Cannery Row

MARINE BIOLOGY
Matthiessen, P. Far Tortuga

MARINE ENGINEERS
Cussler, C. Odessa Sea
Watts, P. Starfish

Marine mystery crime novels [series] Rowson, P.

MARINE SCIENTISTS
Hiaasen, C. Skinny dip

MARINES
Burdett, J. Bangkok 8
Marlantes, K. Matterhorn
Olmstead, R. The coldest night
Uris, L. Battle cry

MARINES -- UNITED STATES -- HISTORY -- WORLD WAR II
Kittredge, W. The willow field

MARITAL CONFLICT
Ackerman, E. Waiting for Eden
Adams, L. The bromance book club
Adler-Olsen, J. A conspiracy of faith
Anshaw, C. Carry the one
Anstruther, E. A perfect explanation
Armstrong, R. The don con
Audur A. Olafsdottir, 1. Butterflies in November
Bellow, S. Herzog
Bellow, S. More die of heartbreak
Bialosky, J. The prize
Bijan, D. The last days of Cafe Leila
Bock, C. Beautiful children
Brodesser-Akner, T. Fleishman is in trouble
Brundage, E. All things cease to appear
Butler, R. Perfume River
Castel-Bloom, O. Textile
Celello, E. Leaning to stay
Choi, S. My education
Clark, M. The Jezebel remedy
Clark, W. Honor thy thug
Clark, W. Justify my thug
Clarke, B. The price of the haircut
Coben, H. The stranger
Cohen, L. The grief of others
Cohen, T. The summer we lost her
Crombie, D. Water like a stone
Crosbie, L. Where did you sleep last night?
De Giovanni, M. The crocodile
Dean, M. The time it takes to fall
Dicks, M. Unexpectedly, Milo
Doyle, R. Smile
Edgarian, C. Three stages of amazement
Edwards, Y. The mother
Ephron, H. Careful what you wish for
Essbaum, J. Hausfrau
Evans, D. Ordinary people
Fabry, C. War room
Flynn, G. Gone girl
Ford, R. The lay of the land
Fowler, T. Z
Fox, L. Days of awe
Frear, C. Stone cold heart
Friedland, E. The intermission
Gaige, A. Sea wife
Gideon, M. Wife 22
Gilmore, J. The mothers
Glass, J. The whole world over
Grunberg, A. Tirza
Hadley, T. The past
Hannah, K. Home front
Hansen, R. A wild surge of guilty passion
Harvey, J. Gone to ground
Hauck, R. The wedding chapel
Hood, A. The obituary writer
Hoover, C. All your perfects
Hurwitz, G. They're watching

Chandler, R. The long goodbye
Osborne, L. Only to sleep

MARQUIS AND MARCHIONESSES

Beverley, J. Devilish
Bowman, V. Secrets of a wedding night
Carlyle, L. Never lie to a lady
Collins, M. Ready set rogue
Dare, T. Do you want to start a scandal
Dare, T. Say yes to the marquess
Guhrke, L. When the marquess met his match
MacLean, S. The rogue not taken
McQuiston, J. The spinster's guide to scandalous behavior

Marquitta Skeet Bannion mysteries [series] Rodriguez, L.

MARRIAGE

Abbott, S. The future of love
Adebayo, A. Stay with me
Albert, E. After birth
Alexie, S. Blasphemy
Allende, I. A long petal of the sea
Allende, I. Portrait in sepia
Antopol, M. The UnAmericans
Atwood, M. Moral disorder
Austen, J. Pride and prejudice
Baker, E. Keeping the house
Ballard, J. The kindness of women
Bateman, K. This earl of mine
Bauer, A. The forever marriage
Berg, E. Once upon a time, there was you
Blum, J. The lost family
Boyle, T. Outside looking in
Brownrigg, S. Morality tale
Bryant, N. Message from a mistress
Burrowes, G. Tremaine's true love
Byatt, A. The children's book
Capote, T. Breakfast at Tiffany's
Carver, R. What we talk about when we talk about love
Castle, J. Illusion Town
Celello, E. Leaning to stay
Cheek, C. Cape May
Choo, Y. The ghost bride
Coben, H. The stranger
Coleridge, N. A much married man
Collins, W. The moonstone
Colwin, L. Goodbye without leaving
Daniel, S. Stiltsville
Delaney, J. The perfect wife
Dillard, A. The Maytrees
Ebershoff, D. The Danish girl
Edgarian, C. Three stages of amazement
Erdrich, L. Shadow tag
Esquivel, L. Like water for chocolate
Everett, P. Suder
Fabry, C. War room
Ferrante, E. The story of a new name
Flaubert, G. Madame Bovary
Ford, F. Parade's end
Freudenberger, N. The newlyweds

Gardam, J. Last friends
Gardam, J. The man in the wooden hat
Garey, J. Too bright to hear too loud to see
Giordano, P. Like family
Gordimer, N. None to accompany me
Gowar, I. The mermaid and Mrs. Hancock
Gregory, P. The lady of the rivers
Gregory, P. The kingmaker's daughter
Gregory, P. The red queen
Gregory, P. The white princess
Groff, L. Fates and furies
Haigh, J. Mrs. Kimble
Hardy, T. Jude the obscure
Harrod-Eagles, C. Game over
Henry, P. Becoming Mrs. Lewis
Hoover, C. All your perfects
House, S. A parchment of leaves
Hurston, Z. Their eyes were watching God
Isaacs, S. As husbands go
James, E. Desperate duchesses
James, E. Four nights with the duke
James, H. The golden bowl
James, H. The portrait of a lady
Jones, T. An American marriage
Kidd, S. The book of longings
Kim, C. If you leave me
Kincaid, J. See now then
Kittredge, W. The willow field
Lackey, M. The fairy godmother
Laurens, S. A rake's vow
Lawrence, D. The rainbow
Lawrence, D. Sons and lovers
Lazarin, D. Back talk
Leroy, M. Postcards from Berlin
Lessing, D. The grass is singing
Lessing, D. A proper marriage
Lipsyte, S. The ask
MacAlister, K. The truth about Leo
MacLaverty, B. Midwinter break
Mahmoud, L. Amreekiya
Maxwell, R. The secret diary of Anne Boleyn
McCall Smith, A. The Double Comfort Safari Club
McCall Smith, A. The full cupboard of life
McCall Smith, A. In the company of cheerful ladies
McDermott, A. Someone
McMurtry, L. Terms of endearment
Meloy, M. Liars and saints
Miller, S. The senator's wife
Miyamoto, T. Kinshu
Moore, E. The Supremes at Earl's All-You-Can-Eat
Murphy, Y. The call
Naslund, S. Ahab's wife, or, the star gazer
Nicholls, D. Us
Niffenegger, A. The time traveler's wife
O'Brien, E. The country girls trilogy and epilogue
Oakley, C. You were there too
Offill, J. Dept. of speculation

Solomon, B. The attempted murder of Teddy Roosevelt
Steel, D. First sight
Swanson, P. The kind worth killing
Toibin, C. The heather blazing
Tyler, A. Morgan's passing
Updike, J. Licks of love
Updike, J. Rabbit is rich
Updike, J. Rabbit, run
Wharton, E. Ethan Frome
White, E. Jack Holmes and his friend
Wouk, H. A hole in Texas

MARRIED MEN -- DEATH
Bloom, A. White houses
Bussi, M. Black water lilies
Carpenter, E. Until the day I die
Gregory, P. The constant princess
Higgins, J. The White House connection
Hilderbrand, E. What happens in paradise
Hilderbrand, E. Winter in paradise
Isaacs, S. After all these years
Macmillan, G. The nanny
Martin, C. Send down the rain
Mosley, W. Debbie doesn't do it anymore
Riley, J. The serpent garden
Unger, L. Under my skin
White, C. The wife and the widow

MARRIED MEN -- ITALY
Svevo, I. Zeno's conscience

**MARRIED MEN -- RELATIONS WITH SINGLE WOM-
EN**
Faber, M. The crimson petal and the white
Smith, A. The accidental

MARRIED MEN -- SEXUALITY
Ebershoff, D. The Danish girl

MARRIED PEOPLE
Alison, J. The marriage of the sea
Amado, J. Dona Flor and her two husbands
Amis, M. The zone of interest
Andrews, M. Of fire and lions
Archer, J. This was a man
Arudpragasam, A. The story of a brief marriage
Atwood, M. Life before man
Barth, J. The end of the road
Baxter, C. Saul and Patsy
Billingsley, R. The secret she kept
Brekke, J. The fifth element
Brennan, M. A natural history of dragons
Brennan, M. The tropic of serpents
Brennan, M. Within the sanctuary of wings
Brown, S. Mean streak
Brownrigg, S. The delivery room
Colwin, L. Happy all the time
Cunningham, M. By nightfall
Daly, P. Open your eyes
Dexter, P. Paris Trout
Doerr, H. Stones for Ibarra
Edgarian, C. Three stages of amazement

Edwards, K. The memory keeper's daughter
Enger, L. Undiscovered country
Erdrich, L. Four souls
Erdrich, L. The Master Butchers Singing Club
Fitzgerald, F. The beautiful and damned
Flynn, G. Gone girl
Ford, F. Parade's end
Friedland, E. The intermission
Gaitskill, M. The mare
Goodman, C. The sea of lost girls
Hadley, T. The past
Hammett, D. The thin man
Hannah, K. Home front
Haslett, A. Imagine me gone
Hauck, R. How to catch a prince
Hegi, U. The vision of Emma Blau
Hemingway, E. To have and have not
Hiaasen, C. Skinny dip
Hijuelos, O. Twain & Stanley enter paradise
Hoffman, A. Skylight confessions
Hurwitz, G. They're watching
Iles, G. Third degree
Jemc, J. The grip of it
Joyce, J. Ulysses
Khadra, Y. The swallows of Kabul
Kingsolver, B. Flight behavior
Kubica, M. The other Mrs.
Lombardo, C. The most fun we ever had
Lordan, B. But come ye back , Beth Lordan
Marias, J. Thus bad begins
Miller, S. The senator's wife
Mishima, Y. The frolic of the beasts
Mitchell, M. Gone with the wind
Moriarty, L. Truly madly guilty
Murdoch, I. The nice and the good
Naylor, G. Mama Day
Neel, J. To die for
Netzer, L. Shine shine shine
Nicholson, W. Motherland
Niffenegger, A. The time traveler's wife
Nunez, E. Grace
O'Brien, T. In the Lake of the Woods
O'Donohue, C. Beyond the pale
O'Nan, S. The odds
Osborne, L. The forgiven
Packer, A. The children's crusade
Palmer, D. Version control
Paris, B. Behind closed doors
Parker, S. Purgatory road
Pavone, C. The expats
Pavone, C. The Paris diversion
Perrotta, T. Little children
Perry, S. The Essex serpent
Putney, M. Not quite a wife
Rhys, J. Quartet
Rhys, J. Wide Sargasso Sea
Robotham, M. Suspect

Joss, M. The night following
Kandasamy, M. When I hit you, or, A portrait of the writer as a young wife
King, C. Stiletto justice
Kirshenbaum, B. Rabbits for food
Klein, M. Con ed
Kubica, M. Pretty baby
LaPlante, A. A circle of wives
Larsen, N. Passing
Lawrence, D. Lady Chatterley's lover
Lea, C. The glass woman
Lehane, D. Since we fell
Leroy, M. Postcards from Berlin
Lessing, D. The grass is singing
Lessing, D. A proper marriage
Liardet, F. We must be brave
Lippman, L. After I'm gone
Lippman, L. Sunburn
Lispector, C. The besieged city
MacDonald, J. A purple place for dying
Malerman, J. Unbury Carol
Mangan, C. Tangerine
McCrumb, S. If I'd killed him when I met him
McEwan, I. Nutshell
Min, A. Becoming Madame Mao
Morgan, R. The road from Gap Creek
Moyes, J. The girl you left behind
Moyes, J. The peacock emporium
Munro, A. Runaway
Nesbit, T. The wives of Los Alamos
O'Brien, E. The country girls trilogy and epilogue
Oakley, C. You were there too
Oates, J. I lock my door upon myself
Pamuk, O. Snow
Parks, B. Closer than you know
Parrish, C. Still life
Patterson, M. Rebellion
Perez-Reverte, A. What we become
Phillips, H. The beautiful bureaucrat
Powning, B. The sea captain's wife
Randel, W. The empress of bright moon
Restrepo, L. Delirium
Rhys, R. Fatal inheritance
Riley, J. A vision of light
Rock, P. The shelter cycle
Roth, P. When she was good
Rowell, R. Landline
Satyal, R. No one can pronounce my name
Scego, I. Adua
Scott, C. The poppy wife
Shefchik, R. Amen corner
Smith, J. If she were dead
Steinhauer, O. All the old knives
Swinson, K. Who's wife extraordinaire now
Trigiani, A. Big Cherry Holler
Turner, N. Forever a hustler's wife
Tyler, A. Back when we were grownups

Tyler, A. Clock dance
Vaughan, S. Anatomy of a scandal
White, C. The wife and the widow
Winterson, J. The passion
Wolitzer, M. The wife
Zane Addicted

MARRIED WOMEN -- DEATH
Baldacci, D. One summer
Francis, F. Guilty not guilty
Gardam, J. Old Filth
Grippando, J. Money to burn
McAllister, T. The young widower's handbook
Moore, C. A dirty job
North, A. The Whisper Man
Scottoline, L. Don't go
Smith, T. Agent 6
Tyler, A. The beginner's goodbye
Woods, S. Santa Fe rules

MARRIED WOMEN -- FRANCE
Flaubert, G. Madame Bovary

MARRIED WOMEN -- IDENTITY
Colwin, L. Goodbye without leaving
Tyler, A. Ladder of years
Wood, T. The engineer's wife

MARRIED WOMEN -- KANSAS CITY, MISSOURI
Connell, E. Mrs. Bridge

MARRIED WOMEN -- PSYCHOLOGY
Stead, C. The man who loved children

Marrying the mistress Trollope, J.
Marrying Winterborne Kleypas, L.

MARS (PLANET)
Bradbury, R. Bradbury stories
Bradbury, R. The illustrated man
Bradbury, R. The Martian chronicles
Brown, P. Golden son
Brown, P. Morning star
Brown, P. Red rising
Hurley, K. The light brigade
Levine, D. Arabella of Mars
Rajaniemi, H. The fractal prince
Rajaniemi, H. The quantum thief
Varley, J. Red lightning
Varley, J. Rolling thunder

MARS (PLANET) -- COLONIZATION
Hurley, K. The light brigade
Robinson, K. Blue Mars
Robinson, K. Green Mars
Robinson, K. The Martians
Robinson, K. Red Mars
Wilson, R. Spin

MARS (PLANET) -- EXPLORATION
Heinlein, R. Stranger in a strange land
Michener, J. Space
Varley, J. Red thunder
Weir, A. The Martian
The **Mars** room Kushner, R.
Mars trilogy [series] Robinson, K.

Crompton, R. Hour of the red god

MASCULINITY
Miller, H. Tropic of Capricorn
Sapphire. The kid

The **masked** city Cogman, G.

MASKS
Bradley, C. Speaking from among the bones

Mason & Dixon Pynchon, T.

Mason novels [series] Berg, E.

MASON, CHARLES, 1728-1786
Pynchon, T. Mason & Dixon

MASON-DIXON LINE
Pynchon, T. Mason & Dixon

The **masque** of the Black Tulip Willig, L.

MASQUERADES
Ranney, K. The Scottish duke

MASS BURIALS
Kerr, P. The lady from Zagreb
Kerr, P. A man without breath

MASS MEDIA
Abrams, D. Fobbit
Beagle, P. In Calabria
Benjamin, M. The aviator's wife
Bradbury, R. Fahrenheit 451
Clark, M. Blood defense
Finley, J. The dark above
Handke, P. Crossing the Sierra de Gredos
Hensher, P. King of the badgers
Marrs, J. The passengers
Meek, J. The heart broke in
Palahniuk, C. Lullaby
Porter, M. Lanny
Saunders, G. In persuasion nation
Stephenson, N. The diamond age,
Wayne, T. The love song of Jonny Valentine
Wouk, H. A hole in Texas

MASS MEDIA -- SOCIAL ASPECTS
Flanagan, R. The unknown terrorist

MASS MEDIA AND CULTURE
Altschul, A. Deus ex machina

MASS MEDIA AND PUBLIC OPINION -- UNITED STATES
Pohl, F. The space merchants

MASS MURDER
Albahari, D. Gotz and Meyer
Berenson, A. The faithful spy
Bohjalian, C. The sandcastle girls
Dazieri, S. Kill the angel
Ellroy, J. L.A. confidential
Hayes, T. I am Pilgrim
Holt, A. Odd numbers
Kellerman, F. Serpent's tooth
King, S. Mr. Mercedes
Koontz, D. Intensity
Muller, M. Point Deception
Perry, T. Pursuit
Persson Giolito, M. Quicksand

Phillips, C. Unthinkable
Rendell, R. A judgement in stone
Sandford, J. Mad River
Shriver, L. We need to talk about Kevin
Sjowall, M. The laughing policeman
Tsao, T. The majesties

MASS MURDER INVESTIGATION
Peace, D. Occupied city

MASS MURDERERS
King, S. End of watch
King, S. Mr. Mercedes
Perry, T. Pursuit

MASS SHOOTINGS
Block, S. Oliver Loving
Kellerman, J. Time bomb
McAllister, T. How to be safe
Parker, R. School days
Persson Giolito, M. Quicksand
Picoult, J. Nineteen minutes
Rankin, I. A question of blood
Roberts, N. Shelter in place
Shriver, L. We need to talk about Kevin
Slaughter, K. The good daughter

MASS SUICIDE
Hoffman, A. The dovekeepers

MASSACHUSETTS
Amidon, S. Security
Arsenault, E. The broken teaglass
Batuman, E. The idiot
Beams, C. The illness lesson
Berne, S. The dogs of Littlefield
Burke, M. Team seven
Cheever, J. The Wapshot chronicle
Cheever, J. The Wapshot scandal
Dillard, A. The Maytrees
Dubus, A. Dirty love
Dufresne, J. Requiem, Mass.
Fay, J. The shortest way home
Finder, J. The fixer
Genova, L. Inside the O'Briens
Genova, L. Left neglected
Greenidge, K. We love you, Charlie Freeman
Grossman, L. The magician king
Grossman, L. The magician's land
Haddam, J. Cheating at solitaire
Haslett, A. Union Atlantic
Hawley, N. Before the fall
Higgins, G. The friends of Eddie Coyle
Hilderbrand, E. The perfect couple
Hilderbrand, E. Summer of '69
Hoffman, A. Blackbird house
Hoffman, A. The probable future
Hoffman, A. The red garden
Hoffman, A. The river king
King, L. Writers & lovers
Lahiri, J. The namesake
Landay, W. Defending Jacob

Guhrke, L. When the marquess met his match
Lalli, S. The matchmaker's list
Lorret, V. How to forget a duke
Montclair, A. The right sort of man
Phillips, S. Match me if you can
Quick, A. 'Til death do us part
Sand, G. Marianne

MATCHMAKING

Balogh, M. The arrangement
Balogh, M. Simply love
Grimes, L. In a fix
Heger, A. Crazy cupid love
Kerr, L. Wild on my mind
Lalli, S. The matchmaker's list
MacKenzie, S. Bedding Lord Ned
Phillips, S. Match me if you can
Title, S. The undateable

MatchUp

MATE SELECTION

Amirrezvani, A. The blood of flowers
Ashford, J. What the duke doesn't know
Austen, J. Sense and sensibility
Balogh, M. The escape
Balogh, M. Only enchanting
Bell, L. How the duke was won
Bell, L. One fine duke
Berne, L. You may kiss the bride
Boyle, E. And the miss ran away with the rake
Bradley, A. A season of ruin
Burrowes, G. The trouble with dukes
Byrne, K. The duke with the dragon tattoo
Byrne, K. How to love a duke in ten days
Choi, A. Kay's lucky coin variety
Curran, K. My lady's choosing
Dare, T. The duchess deal
Dare, T. The governess game
Feehan, C. Dark illusion
Garriott, L. Promised
Guhrke, L. When the marquess met his match
Heath, L. Falling into bed with a duke
Heyer, G. Black sheep
James, E. Three weeks with Lady X
James, E. Seven minutes in heaven
James, E. Wilde in love
James, E. Too Wilde to wed
Kleypas, L. Secrets of a summer night
Kleypas, L. Devil in spring
Lewis, B. The ebb tide
Lin, J. The lotus palace
Long, J. The legend of Lyon Redmond
Lorret, V. How to forget a duke
MacLean, S. Wicked and the wallflower
McCall Smith, A. The full cupboard of life
McLayne, A. Highland promise
Michels, E. The rebel heir
Monroe, M. Bad blood
Phillips, S. Match me if you can

Quinn, J. The secrets of Sir Richard Kenworthy
Rodale, M. Lady Bridget's diary
Showalter, G. Shadow and ice
Simsion, G. The Rosie project
Sittenfeld, C. Eligible
Soniah Kamal Unmarriageable
Spear, T. A billionaire wolf for Christmas
Thomas, S. The luckiest lady in London
Tyler, A. The amateur marriage
Wade, B. Falling for you
Wade, B. True to you
Warren, T. The replacement wife
White, R. A lady unrivaled

MATE SELECTION FOR MEN

Burrowes, G. The heir
Engelmann, K. The Stockholm octavo
James, E. Desperate duchesses
Phillips, S. Match me if you can

MATE SELECTION FOR WOMEN

Austen, J. Emma
Austen, J. Northanger Abbey
Balogh, M. The secret mistress
Boyle, E. Along came a duke
Hardy, T. Far from the madding crowd
James, E. Seven minutes in heaven
James, E. Three weeks with Lady X
James, E. Too Wilde to wed
James, E. Wilde in love
Mitford, N. The pursuit of love ;

MATERIAL CULTURE

Brin, D. Existence
Lamberson, G. The frenzy way
Leckie, A. Provenance
Martel, Y. The high mountains of Portugal
McBride, J. Five-carat soul
Morgan, R. Broken angels
Pattison, E. Blood of the oak
Schwab, V. A darker shade of magic
Stabenow, D. Though not dead
Stephenson, N. Anathem
Wilkins, K. Veil of gold
Willis, C. To say nothing of the dog

MATERIALISM

Banks, R. Continental drift
Norris, F. McTeague
Saunders, G. In persuasion nation

MATERNAL DEPRIVATION

Gertler, S. Drifting
Wallace, D. The watermelon king

MATERNAL LOVE

Phillips, H. The need
Walbert, K. She was like that

MATERNAL LOVE -- FICTION

Suri, M. The age of Shiva

MATERNITY HOMES

Kibler, J. Home for erring and outcast girls

MATERNITY LEAVE

Sandford, J. Holy ghost
Thompson, T. The Rosewater redemption
Wolfe, T. Back to blood
Wright, A. Carpentaria

MAYORS -- NORTH CAROLINA

Karon, J. Out to Canaan

The **Maytrees** Dillard, A.

The **maze** Karnezis, P.

The **maze** at Windermere Smith, G.

McAlister family novels [series] Turansky, C.

MCCARTHY, JOSEPH, 1908-1957

Stratford, S. Red letter days

MCCARTHYISM

Davis, F. The Chelsea girls
Kramer, L. Search for my heart
Mallon, T. Fellow travelers
Roth, P. I married a Communist
Stratford, S. Red letter days

McDade cycle [series] Bonner, C.

MCGAVOCK CONFEDERATE CEMETERY (FRANK-LIN, TENN.)

Hicks, R. The widow of the South

MCGAVOCK, CAROLINE E WINDER, 1829-1905

Hicks, R. The widow of the South

McGuire brothers [series] Humphreys, S.

MCKINLEY, WILLIAM, 1843-1901 ASSASSINATION

Goldstone, L. Assassin of shadows

McNally's dilemma Sanders, L.

McNally's gamble Sanders, L.

McNally's luck Sanders, L.

McNally's puzzle Sanders, L.

McNally's secret Sanders, L.

McNally's trial Sanders, L.

McTeague Norris, F.

Me before you Moyes, J.

Me before you [series] Moyes, J.

ME TOO MOVEMENT

Baker, C. Whisper network

Meadowlark Abrams, M.

Mean streak Brown, S.

Mean woman blues Smith, J.

MEANING (PSYCHOLOGY)

Adams, D. The hitchhiker's guide to the galaxy
Albom, M. The five people you meet in heaven
Barth, J. The floating opera
Bellow, S. Humboldt's gift
Camus, A. The plague
Camus, A. The stranger
Dick, P. The man in the high castle
Hesse, H. Narcissus and Goldmund
Hesse, H. Siddhartha
Ishiguro, K. The buried giant
Kafka, F. The castle
McCormack, M. Solar bones
Musil, R. The man without qualities
Wallace, D. The pale king
Yourcenar, M. Memoirs of Hadrian

The **means** of escape Fitzgerald, P.

MEAT INDUSTRY AND TRADE -- CORRUPT PRACTICES

Sinclair, U. The jungle

MEAT WORKERS -- HEALTH AND SAFETY

Sinclair, U. The jungle

The **mechanical** Tregillis, I.

MECHANICAL TOYS

Carey, P. The chemistry of tears

MECHANICS

Bender, T. The last ghost dancer
Bouchet, A. Nightchaser
Bybee, C. Staying for good
Macomber, D. If not for you

Mechanique Valentine, G.

Meddling kids Cantero, E.

MEDIATORS

Vaughn, C. Bannerless

MEDICAL CARE

Bock, C. Alice & Oliver
Browne, S. Less than hero
McEwan, I. The children act
Nunez, E. Anna in-between

MEDICAL CARE -- ACCESSIBILITY

Matlwa, K. Evening primrose

MEDICAL CARE -- CORRUPT PRACTICES

Lescroart, J. The oath

MEDICAL CARE -- CORRUPT PRACTICES -- SOVIET UNION

Solzhenitsyn, A. Cancer ward

MEDICAL CARE -- COSTS

Shriver, L. So much for that

MEDICAL CARE REFORM

Eliot, G. Middlemarch

MEDICAL ETHICS

Iles, G. The footprints of God
Lescroart, J. The oath
Peikoff, K. Mother knows best
Picoult, J. Change of heart

MEDICAL GENETICS

Genova, L. Inside the O'Briens
Peikoff, K. Mother knows best
Tyers, K. Shivering world

MEDICAL INNOVATIONS

Peikoff, K. Mother knows best

MEDICAL MALPRACTICE

Cook, R. Charlatans
Cook, R. Host
Lescroart, J. The oath
McCall Smith, A. The comforts of a muddy Saturday
Paretsky, S. Bitter medicine

MEDICAL RESEARCH

Lupton, R. Sister
Palmer, M. The fifth vial
Patchett, A. State of wonder
Willis, C. Passage

MEDICAL RESEARCH FRAUD

Penman, S. Lionheart
Penman, S. The Queen's man
Penman, S. The reckoning
Penman, S. The sunne in splendour
Penman, S. Time and chance
Penman, S. When Christ and his saints slept
Peters, E. Brother Cadfael's penance
Peters, E. Dead man's ransom
Peters, E. The hermit of Eyton Forest
Peters, E. The holy thief
Peters, E. Monk's hood
Peters, E. The pilgrim of hate
Peters, E. The potter's field
Peters, E. A rare Benedictine
Peters, E. The rose rent
Peters, E. St. Peter's fair
Peters, E. The sanctuary sparrow
Peters, E. The summer of the Danes
Peters, E. The virgin in the ice
Pike, S. The lost queen
Plaidy, J. The captive Queen of Scots
Rice, A. Angel time
Riley, J. In pursuit of the green lion
Robb, C. The cross-legged knight
Robb, C. A gift of Sanctuary
Robb, C. A murdered peace
Robb, C. The riddle of St. Leonard's
Royal, P. Covenant with hell
Royal, P. Sanctity of hate
Royal, P. Satan's lullaby
Scott, W. Ivanhoe
Sedley, K. The Tintern treasure
Sharratt, M. Illuminations
Starr, M. Unhallowed ground
Walters, M. The last hours
Willis, C. Doomsday book
Winawer, M. The scribe of Siena

MEDIEVAL ROMANCES
Banks, M. Never seduce a Scot
Garwood, J. The bride
McLayne, A. Highland promise

MEDIEVAL SCIENCE
Weber, D. Off Armageddon reef

MEDIOCRITY
Gass, W. Middle C

MEDITATION
Winspear, J. Birds of a feather
The **Mediterranean** caper Cussler, C.

MEDITERRANEAN ISLANDS
Willocks, T. The religion

MEDITERRANEAN REGION
Scott, J. Tourmaline
Willocks, T. The religion

MEDITERRANEAN REGION -- HISTORY
Sontag, S. The volcano lover

MEDITERRANEAN REGION -- HISTORY -- 16TH CENTURY

Maalouf, A. Leo Africanus

MEDITERRANEAN SEA
Cussler, C. Sea of greed

MEDIUMS
Bennett, J. Bitter spirits
Murphy, S. The possessions
Medlar mysteries [series] Deveraux, J.

MEDUSE (SHIP)
Barnes, J. A history of the world in 10 1
Meet me at the museum Youngson, A.
Meet me in Monaco Gaynor, H.
A **meeting** at Corvallis Stirling, S.

MEETINGS
Mosley, W. The right mistake
Meg and Jo Kantra, V.
Meg Langslow mysteries [series] Andrews, D.

MEHNDI (BODY PAINTING)
Joshi, A. The henna artist
Melancholy baby Parker, R.

MELBOURNE, VICTORIA
Clarke, M. Foreign soil
Garner, H. The spare room
Greenwood, K. Death by water
Melmoth Perry, S.
Melmoth the wanderer Maturin, C.
The **melody** lingers on Clark, M.

MELVILLE, HERMAN, 1819-1891
Melville, H. Omoo
Parini, J. The passages of H.M.
The **member** of the wedding McCullers, C.
Memento mori Spark, M.
Memento Park Sarvas, M.
Memnoch the devil Rice, A.
Memo from Turner Willocks, T.
Memoir trilogy [series] Coetzee, J.
Memoirs of a geisha Golden, A.
Memoirs of an imaginary friend Dicks, M.
Memoirs of Hadrian Yourcenar, M.
Memoirs of John Watson [series] Meyer, N.
Memoirs of Lady Trent [series] Brennan, M.
MemoRandom De la Motte, A.
MemoRandom [series] De la Motte, A.

MEMORIALS
Tan, T. The garden of evening mists

MEMORIES
Abrams, M. Meadowlark
Abu-Jaber, D. Origin
Aciman, A. Enigma variations
Adler-Olsen, J. Victim 2117
Albom, M. The five people you meet in heaven
Allende, I. Portrait in sepia
Antoinette, A. Murderville
Apelfeld, A. The man who never stopped sleeping
Apostol, G. Gun dealers' daughter
Artson, B. Odessa, Odessa
Attenberg, J. All this could be yours
Atwood, M. Cat's eye

McGregor, J. The reservoir tapes
McKevett, G. Murder in her stocking
Means, D. Hystopia
Meno, J. The boy detective fails
Meuleman, S. Find me gone
Montimore, M. Oona out of order
Morrison, T. Jazz
Morrison, T. Love
Newman, J. Mary
Nicholls, O. Love, unscripted
Nunez, S. The last of her kind
O'Leary, B. The flatshare
O'Nan, S. Snow angels
Oates, J. Pursuit
Ocampo, S. The promise
Oe, K. The changeling
Ogawa, Y. The memory police
Pamuk, O. Silent house
Parker, R. Double play
Pelecanos, G. The turnaround
Petterson, P. Out stealing horses
Picoult, J. Vanishing acts
Powers, R. The echo maker
Proust, M. Remembrance of things past
Proust, M. Swann's way
Proust, M. Time regained
Proust, M. Within a budding grove
Ramadan, A. The clothesline swing
Ramqvist, K. The white city
Ratner, V. Music of the ghosts
Rayfiel, T. In pinelight
Richardson, C. The end of the alphabet
Richman, A. The secret of clouds
Robinson, P. The first cut
Rock, P. The shelter cycle
Rooney, K. Lillian Boxfish takes a walk
Ruskovich, E. Idaho
Russell, K. My dark Vanessa
Russo, R. Chances are...
Saer, J. The sixty-five years of Washington
Sainz Borgo, K. It would be night in Caracas
Sallis, J. Sarah Jane
Savas, A. Walking on the ceiling
Schweblin, S. Fever dream
Scott, J. Follow me
Shafak, E. 10 minutes 38 seconds in this strange world
Shaffer, M. The Guernsey Literary and Potato Peel Pie Society
Shaw, W. The birdwatcher
Shepard, S. The one inside
Simenon, G. Maigret's memoirs
Sittenfeld, C. Prep
Solomon, R. The deep
Sparks, N. A walk to remember
Steadman, C. Mr. Nobody
Stegner, W. Crossing to safety
Sternbergh, A. The blinds

Stoker, D. Dracul
Swift, G. Here we are
Ullmann, L. Unquiet
Van Meter, C. Creatures
Vasquez, J. The shape of the ruins
Vreeland, S. Girl in hyacinth blue
Walton, J. My real children
Weinstein, A. Children of the new world
Wells, B. The end of loneliness
Wiesel, E. The judges
Wiesel, E. Night, Dawn, The accident
Woodson, J. Another Brooklyn
Yates, C. Grist Mill Road

MEMORIES -- PSYCHOLOGICAL ASPECTS

Barnes, J. The sense of an ending
Binet, L. HHhH
Carpenter, E. Every single secret
Miller, A. Oxygen
Moore, A. The lighthouse
O'Brien, T. In the Lake of the Woods
Prcic, I. Shards

Memories of my melancholy whores Garcia Marquez, G.
Memories of the Ford administration Updike, J.

MEMORY

Acevedo, C. The distant marvels
Alarcon, D. At night we walk in circles
Amis, M. The pregnant widow
Auster, P. Invisible
Baldacci, D. Redemption
Banasky, C. The suicide of Claire Bishop
Banville, J. Ancient light
Boudjedra, R. The Barbary figs
Brown, K. The life Lucy knew
Chanter, C. The well
Cleave, P. Trust no one
Colin, E. The memory thief
Corry, J. The dead ex
Crouch, B. Recursion
Doctorow, E. Andrew's brain
Doyle, R. Smile
Echlin, K. The disappeared
Eco, U. The mysterious flame of Queen Loana
Eggers, D. The circle
Enger, L. Virgil Wander
Ephron, H. Night night, sleep tight
Freeman, B. The night bird
Gardner, L. Fear nothing
Guskin, S. The forgetting time
Hadley, T. Clever girl
Healey, E. Elizabeth is missing
Irving, J. Avenue of mysteries
Ishiguro, K. The buried giant
Ishiguro, K. The unconsoled
Joyce, G. Some kind of fairy tale
Kawabata, Y. The sound of the mountain
Knausgaard, K. My struggle.
LaPlante, A. Turn of mind

Tan, T. The garden of evening mists

MEN -- MORTALITY
D'Erasmo, S. The sky below

MEN -- NEW HAMPSHIRE
Banks, R. Affliction

Lent, J. Lost nation

MEN -- PERSONAL CONDUCT
Harkness, D. Time's convert

Joyce, J. Ulysses

MEN -- PSYCHOLOGY
Aciman, A. Enigma variations

Afrika, T. Bitter Eden

Amdahl, G. I am death

Auster, P. 4 3 2 1

Beattie, A. A wonderful stroke of luck

Bragi Olafsson, 1. The pets

Doyle, R. Smile

Ford, F. Parade's end

Grossman, D. A horse walks into a bar

Ishiguro, K. The remains of the day

Jacobson, H. The Finkler question

Joyce, J. Finnegans wake

Kennedy, D. The moment

Lehane, D. Mystic river

Leithauser, B. The promise of elsewhere

Munoz Molina, A. In her absence

Murakami, H. Men without women

Pamuk, O. A strangeness in my mind

Roth, H. From bondage

Toibin, C. The heather blazing

Tropper, J. One last thing before I go

Vargas Llosa, M. The discreet hero

MEN -- RELATIONS WITH MARRIED WOMEN
Meyers, K. The work of wolves

MEN -- RELIGIOUS LIFE
Goldstein, R. 36 arguments for the existence of God

MEN -- SEXUALITY
Beattie, A. The doctor's house

Herlihy, J. Midnight cowboy

Maugham, W. Of human bondage

McCullers, C. Reflections in a golden eye

Nabokov, V. Lolita

Toibin, C. The master

Vine, B. The chimney sweeper's boy

Wallace, D. Brief interviews with hideous men

MEN -- SHEPPERTON, LONDON, ENGLAND
Ballard, J. The kindness of women

MEN -- SOUTH AFRICA
Cartwright, J. To heaven by water

MEN -- SPAIN
Pawel, R. Death of a nationalist

MEN -- SPIRITUAL LIFE
Berenson, A. The faithful spy

Momaday, N. The ancient child

Rubart, J. The man he never was

MEN -- TURKEY
Pamuk, O. The museum of innocence

Men against the sea Nordhoff, C.

MEN AND CATS
Arikawa, H. The travelling cat chronicles

Huston, C. Caught stealing

MEN AND DOGS
Auster, P. Timbuktu

Cameron, W. Repo madness

London, J. The call of the wild

London, J. White Fang

Miller, M. Biloxi

Pelecanos, G. Drama city

Rosenfelt, D. Bark of night

Russell, S. The insane train

MEN AND HORSES
Meyers, K. The work of wolves

MEN AND NATURE
Cather, W. Death comes for the archbishop

Coplin, A. The orchardist

Evison, J. West of here

Guterson, D. The other

Heller, P. The river

Powers, R. The overstory

Rash, R. Something rich and strange

MEN AND SUCCESS
Bradford, B. Master of his fate

Kerangal, M. The cook

Price, R. Samaritan

Stone, I. The agony and the ecstasy

Welsh, I. Dead men's trousers

The men and the girls Trollope, J.

Men at arms Pratchett, T.

MEN COLLEGE TEACHERS
Roth, P. The human stain

MEN CRIMINALS
Leonard, E. Killshot

MEN DANCERS
Perez-Reverte, A. What we become

MEN NURSES
Beckett, S. Murphy

Butler, K. Pretty ugly

Dicks, M. Unexpectedly, Milo

Fay, J. The shortest way home

O'Leary, B. The flatshare

The men of Brewster Place Naylor, G.

MEN OPERA SINGERS
Bailey, P. Uncle Rudolf

MEN PSYCHICS
Cotterill, C. The coroner's lunch

Heinlein, R. Stranger in a strange land

Tepper, S. The gate to Women's Country

MEN RECLUSES
Castile, Z. Flashed

Clarke, S. Jonathan Strange & Mr. Norrell

Finley, J. The dark above

Phillips, S. Heroes are my weakness

Quick, A. 'Til death do us part

Robertson, I. Island of bones

Thompson, J. The killer inside me
Vonnegut, K. Breakfast of champions
Wells, H. The invisible man
White, S. Dry ice
Woods, S. Palindrome

MEN WITH PARANOIA
Amdahl, G. I am death
Robinson, P. All the colors of darkness
Walker, C. Man of the year

MEN WITH PROSTATE CANCER
Ford, R. The lay of the land

MEN WITH SCHIZOPHRENIA
Barclay, L. Trust your eyes
Callaghan, M. Billy, come home

MEN WITH TERMINAL ILLNESSES
Bailey, P. Chapman's odyssey
Baldacci, D. One summer
Berg, E. Never change
Card, M. These ghosts are family
Gaddis, W. Agape agape
Garcia Marquez, G. The general in his labyrinth
Greene, G. The end of the affair
Guskin, S. The forgetting time
Jewell, L. The making of us
L'Engle, M. Certain women
Nabokov, V. Look at the harlequins!
Ramadan, A. The clothesline swing
Richardson, C. The end of the alphabet
Toibin, C. The blackwater lightship
Wallace, D. Big fish
White, S. Kill me

MEN WITH TERMINAL ILLNESSES -- FAMILY RELATIONSHIPS
Haruf, K. Benediction
Men without women Murakami, H.

MEN'S DREAMS
Cather, W. O pioneers!
Dekker, T. Black
Dekker, T. Red
Dekker, T. White
Joyce, J. Finnegans wake
Tidhar, L. A man lies dreaming

MEN'S FANTASIES
Amis, K. Lucky Jim
Gruber, M. The forgery of Venus
Harrison, M. Light
Roth, P. Exit ghost

MEN'S ORGANIZATIONS
Collins, M. A good rake is hard to find
Dickens, C. The Pickwick papers
Levin, I. The Stepford wives
Palahniuk, C. Fight Club

MEN-HEADED FAMILIES
Porter, M. Grief is the thing with feathers
Puzo, M. The godfather
Puzo, M. The Sicilian

MEN/MEN RELATIONS
Aciman, A. Call me by your name
Aciman, A. Enigma variations
Aciman, A. Find me
Barry, S. Days without end
Castellani, C. Leading men
Cleeves, A. The long call
Cruse, H. The complete Wendel
Cusset, C. Life of David Hockney
Drabble, M. The dark flood rises
Evaristo, B. Mr. Loverman
Festing, I. The bird keeper
Forster, E. Maurice
Greenwell, G. Cleanness
Greenwell, G. What belongs to you
Hall, A. For real
Harris, E. Basketball Jones
Harris, E. I say a little prayer
Henson, P. Into the blue
Knight, D. Butterfly tattoo
Leon, S. Wanderer
Mehta, R. Quarantine
Moniz, T. Big familia
Morgenstern, E. The starless sea
Nava, M. Carved in bone
Orringer, J. The flight portfolio
Owen, L. The quick
Polk, C. Witchmark
Pufahl, S. On swift horses
Pulley, N. The lost future of Pepperharrow
Pulley, N. The watchmaker of Filigree Street
Renault, M. The last of the wine
Renault, M. The Persian boy
Sebastian, C. It takes two to tumble
Sebastian, C. The Lawrence Browne affair
Staples, D. This town sleeps
Taylor, B. Real life
Tesh, E. Silver in the wood
Winman, S. Tin man
Yourcenar, M. Memoirs of Hadrian

MEN/WOMEN RELATIONS
50 Cent Blow
Aalborg, G. River of porcupines
Abbott, S. The future of love
Abu-Jaber, D. Crescent
Aciman, A. Enigma variations
Aciman, A. Harvard square
Ackerman, E. Dark at the crossing
Adams, L. The bromance book club
Adichie, C. Americanah
Adichie, C. The thing around your neck
Aguilar Camin, H. Death in Veracruz
Akunin, B. Sister Pelagia and the white bulldog
Alarcon, D. At night we walk in circles
Alexander, T. A note yet unsung
Alexander, T. With this pledge
Alexander, V. The Lady Travelers Guide to larceny with a
  dashing stranger

Bird, S. Daughter of a daughter of a queen

Bird, S. The flamenco academy

Bishop, A. Written in red

Bittner, R. Logan's lady

Black, C. Murder in the rue de Paradis

Blackstock, T. Catching Christmas

Blackstock, T. Smoke screen

Blackwell, J. Letters from Paris

Blau, J. The Wonder Bread summer

Bloom, A. White houses

Bohjalian, C. The sandcastle girls

Bohjalian, C. The sleepwalker

Boianjiu, S. The people of forever are not afraid

Bolano, R. Last evenings on Earth

Bond, C. Ruby

Bonnaffons, A. The regrets

Bonner, C. Lily

Bouchet, A. Breath of fire

Bouchet, A. Nightchaser

Bouchet, A. A promise of fire

Bourland, B. Fake like me

Bourne, J. The black hawk

Bourne, J. The forbidden rose

Bourne, J. My lord and spymaster

Bourne, J. Rogue spy

Bourne, J. The spymaster's lady

Bowen, K. Between the devil and the duke

Bowen, K. I've got my duke to keep me warm

Bowen, K. A rogue by night

Bowman, V. The accidental countess

Bowman, V. Secrets of a wedding night

Bowman, V. The unexpected duchess

Boyle, E. Along came a duke

Boyle, E. And the miss ran away with the rake

Boyle, T. The women

Boyne, J. Crippen

Bradford, B. Just rewards

Bradley, A. A season of ruin

Bradley, A. A wicked way to win an earl

Braithwaite, O. My sister, the serial killer

Brashares, A. My name is memory

Brekke, J. The fifth element

Brink, A. The rights of desire

Brockway, C. The golden season

Brockway, C. No place for a dame

Brockway, C. So enchanting

Broder, M. The pisces

Bronte, A. The tenant of Wildfell Hall

Bronte, C. Jane Eyre

Bronte, E. Wuthering Heights

Brown, K. The clairvoyants

Brown, K. The life Lucy knew

Brown, S. Fat Tuesday

Brown, S. Mean streak

Brown, S. Outfox

Brown, S. White hot

Brown, S. The witness

Brown, T. Gods of Howl Mountain

Bruen, K. The guards

Brunkhorst, A. The gilded Life of Matilda Duplaine

Bryant, N. Christmas with the billionaire

Bryant, N. Madam, may I

Buchman, M. Pure heat

Buck, P. The good Earth

Buckley, C. Supreme Courtship

Bujold, L. Shards of honor

Bujold, L. The warrior's apprentice

Burke, J. House of the rising sun

Burke, J. The New Iberia blues

Burke, J. Wayfaring stranger

Burrowes, G. The bridegroom wore plaid

Burrowes, G. The captive

Burrowes, G. The heir

Burrowes, G. My one and only duke

Burrowes, G. The soldier

Burrowes, G. Tremaine's true love

Burrowes, G. The trouble with dukes

Butcher, J. Proven guilty

Butler, M. Pickle's progress

Byatt, A. The biographer's tale

Byatt, A. Possession

Byatt, A. A whistling woman

Bybee, C. Staying for good

Byrne, K. The duke with the dragon tattoo

Byrne, K. The hunter

Ca$h Thugs cry

Cabot, M. No judgments

Callanan, L. Paris by the book

Callihan, K. Firelight

Calvi, M. Dear George, Dear Mary

Calvino, I. If on a winter's night a traveler

Cameron, C. Just a summer fling

Cameron, P. The city of your final destination

Cameron, W. The dogs of Christmas

Cameron, W. Repo madness

Campbell, B. Brothers and sisters

Canin, E. America America

Caputo, P. Acts of faith

Carlino, R. Swear on this life

Carlson, M. A Christmas by the sea

Carlyle, C. A duke changes everything

Carlyle, L. Never lie to a lady

Carpenter, E. Every single secret

Carr, R. Virgin river

Carr, R. The wanderer

Carr, R. What we find

Carroll, J. Fault lines

Carver, R. What we talk about when we talk about love

Castile, Z. Flashed

Castille, S. In your corner

Castle, J. Illusion Town

Castle, J. The lost night

Cather, W. The song of the lark

Center, K. Things you save in a fire

Drury, T. The driftless area
Du Maurier, D. Frenchman's creek
Du Maurier, D. Jamaica Inn
Du Maurier, D. Rebecca
Dubus, A. Dirty love
Dufresne, J. Deep in the shade of paradise
Dunant, S. The birth of Venus
Dunant, S. In the company of the courtesan
Dunmore, E. Bringing down the duke
Durrell, L. Balthazar
Durrell, L. Clea
Durrell, L. Justine
Durrell, L. Mountolive
Dybek, S. I sailed with Magellan
Dybek, N. The Verdun affair
Dyer, G. Jeff in Venice, death in Varanasi
Ebershoff, D. The Danish girl
Eco, U. Numero zero
Eggers, D. How we are hungry
Eisenberg, D. The twilight of the superheroes
Eisler, B. The god's eye view
Eliot, G. Middlemarch
Ellroy, J. Perfidia
Emshwiller, C. The secret city
Epstein, J. The love song of A. Jerome Minkoff, and other stories
Erdrich, L. Love medicine
Erdrich, L. Tracks
Esquivel, L. Like water for chocolate
Estleman, L. Frames
Estleman, L. Gas City
Eugenides, J. The marriage plot
Evanovich, J. One for the money
Evanovich, J. Turbo twenty-three
Evanovich, S. Under the table
Faber, M. The crimson petal and the white
Falcones de Sierra, I. Cathedral of the sea
Faulks, S. Birdsong
Faulks, S. Charlotte Gray
Faulks, S. Jeeves and the wedding bells
Fay, J. The shortest way home
Feehan, C. Dark illusion
Feehan, C. Shadow rider
Fforde, J. Shades of grey
Fielding, H. Bridget Jones's diary
Fielding, H. The history of Tom Jones, a foundling
Fielding, J. All the wrong places
Fields, H. Last Chance Llama Ranch
Fisher, S. The absinthe earl
FitzGerald, G. Redemption Mountain
Fitzgerald, F. The beautiful and damned
Fitzgerald, F. The last tycoon
Fitzgerald, P. The blue flower
Flagg, F. Fried green tomatoes at the Whistle Stop Cafe
Flanagan, R. The narrow road to the deep north
Fleming, I. From Russia with love
Fleming, I. On Her Majesty's secret service

Flynn, G. Sharp objects
Flynn, M. The January dancer
Flyte, M. City of dark magic
Flyte, M. City of lost dreams
Foley, L. The hunting party
Follett, K. A column of fire
Follett, K. Eye of the needle
Forbes, C. A tall history of sugar
Force, M. Deceived by desire
Force, M. Five years gone
Ford, R. Independence Day
Ford, R. The lay of the land
Ford, R. A multitude of sins
Forester, C. The African Queen
Forna, A. The memory of love
Fortier, A. Juliet
Fortier, A. The lost sisterhood
Foster, L. Run the risk
Foster, L. Sisters of summer's end
Foster, L. Under pressure
Fowles, J. The French lieutenant's woman
Frampton, M. The duke's guide to correct behavior
Frampton, M. Put up your duke
Francis, D. Smokescreen
Frank, D. Queen bee
Franklin, A. The serpent's tale
Frantz, L. The lacemaker
Franzen, J. Purity
Frazier, C. Thirteen moons
Frazier, C. Varina
Freedman, B. Mrs. Mike
Freeman, B. Goodbye to the dead
French, M. The women's room
Freudenberger, N. The dissident
Fuentes, C. The death of Artemio Cruz
Furnivall, K. The red scarf
Furst, A. Spies of the Balkans
Furst, A. The spies of Warsaw
Gabaldon, D. A breath of snow and ashes
Gabaldon, D. Dragonfly in amber
Gabaldon, D. Drums of autumn
Gabaldon, D. An echo in the bone
Gabaldon, D. The fiery cross
Gabaldon, D. Outlander
Gabaldon, D. Voyager
Gabaldon, D. Written in my own heart's blood
Gage, E. The ladies of Managua
Galbraith, R. Career of evil
Galbraith, R. Lethal white
Galen, S. Third son's a charm
Galen, S. When you give a duke a diamond
Gallagher, S. The kingdom of bones
Galsworthy, J. The Forsyte saga
Gander, F. As a friend
Ganek, D. The summer we read Gatsby
Ganshert, K. Life after
Garcia Marquez, G. Love in the time of cholera

Hijuelos, O. Beautiful Maria of my soul
Hijuelos, O. The mambo kings play songs of love
Hilderbrand, E. The perfect couple
Hilderbrand, E. What happens in paradise
Hill, J. Heart-shaped box
Hill, S. The various haunts of men
Hoang, H. The bride test
Hoang, H. The kiss quotient
Hodges, C. Rumor has it
Hoffman, A. The dovekeepers
Hoffman, A. Illumination night
Hoffman, A. The Museum of Extraordinary Things
Hoffman, A. The third angel
Hoffman, A. Turtle moon
Hoffman, A. The world that we knew
Holmes, J. How are you going to save yourself
Holmes, L. Evvie Drake starts over
Holmes, S. B-more careful
Holt, V. The black opal
Hooper, K. Stealing shadows
Hoover, C. All your perfects
Hoover, C. It ends with us
Horan, N. Loving Frank
Horn, D. All other nights
Howatch, S. The heartbreaker
Hoyt, E. Wicked intentions
Hughes, L. Short stories
Humphreys, S. Trouble walks in
Hunt, S. The dark dark
Hunter, J. Forbidden to love the duke
Hunter, M. The conquest of Lady Cassandra
Hunter, M. The surrender of Miss Fairbourne
Hunting, H. Handle with care
Hurwitz, G. Into the fire
Hynes, J. Kings of infinite space
Hynes, J. Next
Ibrahim, A. Season of crimson blossoms
Ide, J. Hi five
Ignatius, D. The sun king
Isaac, K. Then there was you
Jackson, B. Forged in desire
Jacobson, H. The mighty walzer
Jakes, J. On secret service
Jakes, J. Savannah, or, A gift for Mr. Lincoln
Jalaluddin, U. Ayesha at last
James, E. Desperate duchesses
James, E. Four nights with the duke
James, E. Kiss me, Annabel
James, E. Seven minutes in heaven
James, E. Three weeks with Lady X
James, E. Too Wilde to wed
James, E. The ugly duchess
James, E. When Beauty tamed the Beast
James, E. Wilde in love
James, H. Daisy Miller
James, H. The portrait of a lady
James, H. The turn of the screw

James, J. Something about you
James, L. I want you back
James, P. The lighthouse
Jeffries, S. The art of sinning
Jeffries, S. Project Duchess
Jeffries, S. 'Twas the night after Christmas
Jeffries, S. What the duke desires
Jenkins, B. Breathless
Jenkins, B. Forbidden
Jenkins, B. Tempest
Jenoff, P. The ambassador's daughter
Jewell, L. Then she was gone
Jhabvala, R. At the end of the century
Jimenez, A. The friend zone
Jin, H. A free life
Jin, H. Waiting
John, E. Born on a Tuesday
Johnson, K. Little black girl lost 2
Johnson, K. Little black girl lost
Johnson, L. A sparkle of silver
Johnson, M. Smitten by the Brit
Johnson, S. Blaze
Johnson, T. Engraved on the heart
Johnston, W. The colony of unrequited dreams
Joinson, S. The photographer's wife
Jones, D. A bad day for sunshine
Jones, D. Second grave on the left
Jones, D. A sudden wild magic
Jones, S. The other woman
Jones, T. An American marriage
Jong, E. Fear of flying
Jungstedt, M. The inner circle
K'wan The fix
K'wan The Diamond empire
K'wan Diamonds and Pearl
K'wan Section 8
Kadare, I. Agamemnon's daughter
Kamali, M. The stationery shop
Kanon, J. Los Alamos
Kantra, V. Meg and Jo
Karon, J. At home in Mitford
Kate, J. A girl's guide to the Outback
Kate, J. Love and other mistakes
Kazantzakis, N. Zorba the Greek
Kellerman, J. Therapy
Kelly, J. The light over London
Kelton, E. Hard ride
Kennedy, D. The moment
Kennedy, W. Chango's beads and two-tone shoes
Kent, K. The outcasts
Kerouac, J. On the road
Kerr, L. Wild on my mind
Kim, C. If you leave me
King, L. Writers & lovers
King, S. 11
Kinsale, L. Lessons in French
Kirkpatrick, J. This road we traveled

MacLean, S. Never judge a lady by her cover
MacLean, S. No good duke goes unpunished
MacLean, S. One good earl deserves a lover
MacLean, S. The rogue not taken
MacLean, S. Wicked and the wallflower
Macomber, D. If not for you
Mailer, N. The executioner's song
Majors, I. Love's winning plays
Makine, A. Music of a life
Makine, A. The woman who waited
Makkai, R. The hundred-year house
Mallery, S. Best of my love
Mallery, S. The summer of Sunshine and Margot
Malone, M. Bad blood
Malpas, J. Leave me breathless
Manchette, J. Fatale
Marias, J. The infatuations
Marias, J. Thus bad begins
Marillier, J. Daughter of the forest
Marlette, D. Magic time
Martin, A. Blitzed
Martin, A. Fumbled
Martin, C. Long way gone
Martin, C. Send down the rain
Martin, K. Beyond reason
Martin, S. Shopgirl
Martineau, M. Kingdom of exiles
Mason, R. Who killed Piet Barol?
Matthews, J. The Kremlin's candidate
Matthews, J. Palace of treason
Matthews, J. Red sparrow
Maugham, W. Cakes and ale
Maugham, W. The moon and sixpence
Maugham, W. Of human bondage
Maugham, W. The razor's edge
Maupin, A. Tales of the city
Maxwell, R. The queen's bastard
McAllister, T. The young widower's handbook
McCall Smith, A. The comforts of a muddy Saturday
McCall Smith, A. The forgotten affairs of youth
McCall Smith, A. The full cupboard of life
McCall Smith, A. The Kalahari typing school for men
McCall Smith, A. In the company of cheerful ladies
McCall Smith, A. The lost art of gratitude
McCarry, C. The mulberry bush
McCullough, C. An indecent obsession
McDermott, A. That night
McEwan, I. On Chesil Beach
McEwan, I. Sweet tooth
McFarlane, M. Don't you forget about me
McKenzie, E. The portable Veblen
McKinlay, J. The good ones
McLain, P. Love and ruin
McLayne, A. Highland promise
McMurtry, L. Terms of endearment
McQuiston, J. The spinster's guide to scandalous behavior
Mda, Z. The whale caller

Meader, K. Playing with fire
Meadows, R. I will send rain
Meek, J. The heart broke in
Meloy, M. Liars and saints
Meltzer, B. The inner circle
Mengestu, D. All our names
Merimee, P. Carmen
Michels, E. The rebel heir
Michener, J. Tales of the South Pacific
Mieville, C. Perdido Street Station
Milan, C. The duchess war
Millay, K. The sea of tranquility
Miller, H. Tropic of Cancer
Miller, H. Tropic of Capricorn
Miller, R. Jacob's folly
Miller, S. For love
Miller, S. The senator's wife
Millet, L. How the dead dream
Min, A. Empress Orchid
Mishima, Y. The frolic of the beasts
Mitchell, D. The bone clocks
Mitchell, D. The thousand autumns of Jacob De Zoet
Mizushima, M. Burning ridge
Moehringer, J. Sutton
Moggach, D. Tulip fever
Monroe, M. Bad blood
Montero, M. Dancing to "Almendra"
Moore, C. You suck
Moore, K. To seduce an angel
Moore, L. Making waves
Moore, M. The islanders
Morgan, S. The Christmas sisters
Morgan, S. Miracle on 5th Avenue
Moriarty, L. The husband's secret
Morris, H. Cilka's journey
Morris, M. Man in the blue moon
Morrow, J. The last witchfinder
Morton, K. The house at Riverton
Mosher, H. On Kingdom Mountain
Moyes, J. The peacock emporium
Muller, H. The fox was ever the hunter
Munier, P. A borrowing of bones
Munro, A. Hateship, friendship, courtship, loveship, marriage
Munro, A. Selected stories
Munro, A. The view from Castle Rock
Murakami, H. After the quake
Murakami, H. Colorless Tsukuru Tazaki and his years of pilgrimage
Murata, S. Convenience store woman
Murdoch, I. A fairly honourable defeat
Murdoch, I. The good apprentice
Murdoch, I. The nice and the good
Murdoch, I. Nuns and soldiers
Murphy, Y. Signed, Mata Hari
Murray, V. Lust
Mychea He loves me, he loves you not

Putney, M. Not quite a wife
Putney, M. Once a soldier
Quick, A. Crystal gardens
Quick, A. Garden of lies
Quick, A. The girl who knew too much
Quick, A. I thee wed
Quick, A. The mystery woman
Quick, A. The other lady vanishes
Quick, A. Otherwise engaged
Quick, A. Slightly shady
Quick, A. 'Til death do us part
Quincy, D. Murder at the opera
Quindlen, A. Miller's Valley
Quinn, J. The lady most willing
Quinn, J. An offer from a gentleman
Quinn, J. The secrets of Sir Richard Kenworthy
Rabb, J. Among the living
Rabe, P. Anatomy of a killer ;
Racculia, K. Tuesday Mooney talks to ghosts
Raheem, Z. The marriage clock
Rai, A. Hate to want you
Rai, A. The right swipe
Rai, A. Wrong to need you
Raichev, R. Assassins at Ospreys
Ramqvist, K. The white city
Ramsay, H. Summer on Moonlight Bay
Rand, A. We the living
Ranney, K. The Scottish duke
Rash, R. Above the waterfall
Rash, R. The cove
Rash, R. Something rich and strange
Raybourn, D. A murderous relation
Raybourn, D. Silent in the grave
Reay, K. The Bronte plot
Recacoechea S., J. American visa
Reichs, K. A conspiracy of bones
Rendell, R. The bridesmaid
Renault, M. The bull from the sea
Rendell, R. The face of trespass
Renault, M. The king must die
Rhys, J. Quartet
Rhys, J. Wide Sargasso Sea
Rice, A. The witching hour
Rice, L. The lemon orchard
Richards, D. The mustanger and the lady
Richardson, C. The end of the alphabet
Richardson, K. Greywalker
Richman, A. The secret of clouds
Richmond, M. No one you know
Rigosi, G. Night bus
Riley, J. The serpent garden
Rivers, F. The masterpiece
Rivers, F. Redeeming love
Robards, K. Ghost moon
Robards, K. The ultimatum
Robb, C. The cross-legged knight
Robbins, T. Fierce invalids home from hot climates

Robbins, T. Jitterbug perfume
Robbins, T. Skinny legs and all
Robbins, T. Still life with Woodpecker
Roberts, N. Chesapeake blue
Roberts, N. Come sundown
Roberts, N. Dance upon the air
Roberts, N. Dark witch
Roberts, N. Honest illusions
Roberts, N. Midnight Bayou
Roberts, N. The obsession
Roberts, N. Sea swept
Robinson, K. The Martians
Robinson, M. Lila
Robotham, M. Life or death
Rockaway, K. How to hack a heartbreak
Rodale, M. Lady Bridget's diary
Roiphe, A. An imperfect lens
Romain, T. Fortune favors the wicked
Romano-Lax, A. The Spanish bow
Rooney, S. Normal people
Rose, M. Cartier's hope
Rose, M. Tiffany blues
Rosen, R. Dollface
Rosenthal, P. The edge of impropriety
Rossner, J. Looking for Mr. Goodbar
Rotert, R. Last night at the blue angel
Roth, H. From bondage
Roth, P. Exit ghost
Roth, P. Indignation
Roth, P. My life as a man
Roth, P. Portnoy's complaint
Roth, P. The professor of desire
Roth, P. Sabbath's theater
Rothschild, H. The improbability of love
Rowell, R. Landline
Rowland, L. The secret adventures of Charlotte Bronte
Ruiz Zafon, C. The angel's game
Ruiz Zafon, C. The shadow of the wind
Runcie, J. Canvey Island
Runcie, J. Sidney Chambers and the perils of the night
Runcie, J. Sidney Chambers and the problem of evil
Rush, N. Mating
Rushdan, J. Every last breath
Russell, M. Epitaph
Rutherfurd, E. The forest
Rutherfurd, E. Sarum
Ryan, J. Restless rancher
Ryan, K. Long shot
Sada, D. Almost never
Sala, S. Forever my hero
Salter, J. All that is
Salter, J. Last night
Sand, G. Marianne
Sanders, L. McNally's secret
Santopolo, J. More than words
Saramago, J. The history of the siege of Lisbon
Sayers, D. Gaudy night

Thomas, S. Tempting the bride
Title, S. The undateable
Tolstoy, L. Anna Karenina
Tremain, R. The colour
Tremain, R. Music & silence
Trigiani, A. Big Cherry Holler
Trigiani, A. Big Stone Gap
Trollope, J. The best of friends
Trueblood, V. Seven loves
Truong, M. The sweetest fruits
Turansky, C. No ocean too wide
Turner, B. The secret life of Sarah Hollenbeck
Turner, B. Wooing Cadie McCaffrey
Turner, N. Black widow
Turner, N. Natural born hustler
Tyers, K. Shivering world
Tyler, A. The accidental tourist
Tyler, A. Celestial navigation
Tyler, A. Noah's compass
Tyler, A. A patchwork planet
Tyler, A. Vinegar girl
Unger, L. Crazy love you
Updike, J. Gertrude and Claudius
Updike, J. Licks of love
Updike, J. Memories of the Ford administration
Updike, J. Rabbit is rich
Uris, L. Armageddon
Urquhart, J. Away
Urquhart, J. The night stages
Vachss, A. Two trains running
Valdes, A. Dirty Girls on top
Van der Vliet Oloomi, A. Call me Zebra
Vandelly, T. Theme music
Vargas Llosa, M. Aunt Julia and the scriptwriter
Vargas Llosa, M. The bad girl
Vargas Llosa, M. The discreet hero
Veletzos, R. The girl they left behind
Vonnegut, K. The sirens of Titan
Vreeland, S. Girl in hyacinth blue
Vreeland, S. Luncheon of the boating party
Wade, B. Falling for you
Wade, B. True to you
Walker, A. The temple of my familiar
Wallace, D. Brief interviews with hideous men
Waller, R. The bridges of Madison County
Walser, R. The assistant
Walsh, H. Brass
Walter, J. Citizen Vince
Walton, J. Farthing
Warren, S. Rescue me
Warren, T. Her secret life
Warrington, F. Elfland
Warrington, F. Grail of the summer stars
Waters, S. The night watch
Watkins, C. Gold fame citrus
Watkins, J. Secrets of a side bitch
Watkins, J. Secrets of a side bitch 2

Waugh, E. Brideshead revisited
Waugh, E. Vile bodies
Wayne, T. Loner
Weatherspoon, R. Rafe
Weatherspoon, R. Xeni
Weiner, J. Good in bed
Weiner, J. In her shoes
Weiner, J. Little earthquakes
Weir, A. A dangerous inheritance
Weir, A. Innocent traitor
Weir, A. The Lady Elizabeth
Welsh, K. The unquiet heart
Whelan, J. My Oxford year
White, B. Quite a year for plums
White, E. Dragonshadow
White, E. Heartstone
White, R. A lady unrivaled
White, S. Dry ice
White, S. Tears of a hustler
White, S. Tears of a hustler 2
Whittall, Z. Holding still for as long as possible
Wickersham, J. The news from Spain
Wiggins, M. Evidence of things unseen
Wiggins, M. The shadow catcher
Wiggs, S. The beekeeper's ball
Wiggs, S. The ocean between us
Williams, B. All the ways we said goodbye
Williams, B. The golden hour
Williams, K. Harlem on lock
Williams, N. This is happiness
Williams, S. Forbidden promises
Williams, T. The Roman spring of Mrs. Stone
Willig, L. The betrayal of the blood lily
Willig, L. The deception of the emerald ring
Willig, L. The garden intrigue
Willig, L. The secret history of the Pink Carnation
Willig, L. The lure of the moonflower
Willig, L. The masque of the Black Tulip
Willig, L. The orchid affair
Willig, L. The seduction of the Crimson Rose
Willig, L. The temptation of the night jasmine
Willis, C. To say nothing of the dog
Willis, C. Crosstalk
Winawer, M. The scribe of Siena
Winfrey, K. Waiting for Tom Hanks
Winkler, A. Dog war
Winman, S. Tin man
Winslow, D. The dawn patrol
Winter, E. The rage of dragons
Winterson, J. The passion
Wiseman, B. Listening to love
Wolfe, P. The lost diary of M
Wolfe, T. I am Charlotte Simmons
Wolitzer, M. The female persuasion
Woo, S. Love love
Wood, T. The engineer's wife
Woods, S. A delicate touch

Minato, K. Confessions
Strout, E. Olive Kitteridge

MIDDLE WEST

Attenberg, J. The Middlesteins
Bellow, S. Ravelstein
Bender, T. The last ghost dancer
Braun, L. The cat who ate Danish modern
Braun, L. The cat who went underground
Child, L. One shot
DeLillo, D. White noise
Dean, P. Tam Lin
Drury, T. The driftless area
Drury, T. Pacific
Franzen, J. The corrections
Gass, W. Middle C
Gifford, B. Wyoming
Hamilton, J. A map of the world
Kasischke, L. The raising
King, S. End of watch
King, S. Finders keepers
King, S. Mr. Mercedes
Lerner, B. The Topeka school
Markley, S. Ohio
O'Connell, C. Find me
Patterson, R. Dark lady
Roth, P. When she was good
Sidor, S. The mirror's edge
Smith, B. Joy in the morning
Stradal, J. The lager queen of Minnesota
Taylor, B. Real life
Turow, S. Presumed innocent
Wong, D. John dies at the end

MIDDLE WEST -- SOCIAL LIFE AND CUSTOMS

Palahniuk, C. Pygmy

MIDDLE-AGE

Oates, J. Middle age
Rush, N. Subtle bodies
Tyler, A. Breathing lessons

MIDDLE-AGED COUPLES

Guillory, J. Royal holiday
O'Nan, S. The odds

MIDDLE-AGED MEN

Arnaldur Indridason, 1. Outrage
Azzopardi, T. Winterton blue
Banville, J. The sea
Barnes, J. The sense of an ending
Barthelme, F. Elroy Nights
Bellow, S. Henderson the rain king
Bellow, S. Humboldt's gift
Bellow, S. Seize the day
Berger, T. Reinhart's women
Berger, T. Vital parts
Brodesser-Akner, T. Fleishman is in trouble
Brown, L. Joe
Coe, J. The terrible privacy of Maxwell Sim
Coetzee, J. Disgrace
Dean, L. The idea of love

Doig, I. Mountain time
Dostoyevsky, F. Notes from underground
Doyle, R. The guts
Elkin, S. The MacGuffin
Ellis, B. Imperial bedrooms
Freeman, C. All that I have
Gordimer, N. The conservationist
Greer, A. Less
Grenville, K. The idea of perfection
Grossman, D. Be my knife
Grunberg, A. Tirza
Heller, J. Good as Gold
Hesse, H. Steppenwolf
Houellebecq, M. Submission
Jackson, C. The lost weekend
Jewell, L. Watching you
Kenney, J. Truth in advertising
Klein, M. Con ed
Kunzru, H. My revolutions
Lewis, S. Dodsworth
Lodge, D. Paradise news
MacDonald, J. The lonely silver rain
Mankell, H. Firewall
Mankell, H. The troubled man
Maugham, W. The moon and sixpence
McEwan, I. Saturday
McEwan, I. Solar
Mda, Z. The whale caller
Moore, A. The lighthouse
Mortimer, J. Felix in the underworld
Nadzam, B. Lamb
Naipaul, V. A house for Mr. Biswas
Naipaul, V. Magic seeds
Nicholls, D. Us
Noire G-Spot
Pamuk, O. The red-haired woman
Potok, C. The gift of Asher Lev
Price, R. The good priest's son
Robotham, M. Suspect
Roth, P. The anatomy lesson
Russo, R. Empire Falls
Russo, R. Straight man
Smith, A. There but for the
Smith, M. The fighter
Sparks, N. A walk to remember
Toibin, C. The heather blazing
Trollope, J. Marrying the mistress
Trollope, J. Second honeymoon
Turow, S. Presumed innocent
Tyler, A. The beginner's goodbye
Udall, B. The lonely polygamist
Updike, J. Rabbit is rich
Wharton, E. The children

MIDDLE-AGED MEN -- BOLIVIA

Recacoechea S., J. American visa

MIDDLE-AGED MEN -- FAMILY RELATIONSHIPS

Auster, P. The Brooklyn follies

Powell, G. Embers of war
Scalzi, J. Old man's war
Weber, D. By schism rent asunder
Weber, D. Off Armageddon reef
Westerfeld, S. The killing of worlds
Westerfeld, S. The risen empire

MILITARY SECRETS

Benedict, M. The only woman in the room
L'Amour, L. The last of the breed
Lee, P. Dark site
Marias, J. Your face tomorrow, vol.1
Marias, J. Your face tomorrow, vol.2
Marias, J. Your face tomorrow, vol. 3
Shields, S. The Cassandra

MILITARY SERVICE

De Robertis, C. Perla
Stewart, A. Kopp sisters on the march

MILITARY SPOUSES

Fallon, S. You know when the men are gone
Gillham, D. City of women
Jones, S. Small wars

MILITARY STRATEGY

Brooks, M. World War Z
Cornwell, B. 1356
Gingrich, N. Gettysburg
Gingrich, N. Grant comes east
Gleason, C. Murder at the capitol
Lee, Y. Raven stratagem
Liu, K. The wall of storms

**MILITARY STRATEGY -- UNITED STATES -- HISTORY
-- WORLD WAR II**

Shaara, J. The rising tide
Shaara, J. The steel wave

MILITARY SURGEONS

O'Dell, C. A study in honor

MILITARY TACTICS

Clancy, T. Patriot games
Novik, N. His majesty's dragon

MILITARY TRAINING CAMPS

Dees, C. Beyond the limit
Stewart, A. Kopp sisters on the march

MILITIA MOVEMENT

Hiaasen, C. Lucky you
Parker, R. Night passage

MILITIA MOVEMENT -- MAINE

Parker, R. Hush money

MILITIAS AND IRREGULAR ARMIES

Gabaldon, D. The fiery cross
Hage, R. De Niro's game
Wendig, C. Wanderers

Milk and honey Kellerman, F.

Milkman Burns, A.

The **mill** on the Floss Eliot, G.

MILL TOWNS

Cash, W. The last ballad
Strout, E. Amy and Isabelle

MILL WORKERS

Shreve, A. Fortune's rocks
Shreve, A. Sea glass

MILLENNIALISM -- UNITED STATES

Palahniuk, C. Fight Club

Millennium novels (Stieg Larsson) [series] Lagercrantz, D.

Millennium novels (Stieg Larsson) [series] Larsson, S.

Millennium people Ballard, J.

Miller's Valley Quindlen, A.

MILLER, HENRY, 1891-1980

Miller, H. Tropic of Cancer
Miller, H. Tropic of Capricorn

MILLER, KAREN E QUINONES

Miller, K. An angry-ass black woman

MILLER, LEE, 1907-1977

Scharer, W. The age of light

A **million** nightingales Straight, S.

MILLIONAIRES

Atkinson, K. One good turn
Bellow, S. Henderson the rain king
Christie, A. And then there were none
Evanovich, S. Under the table
Fowles, J. The magus
Guterson, D. Ed King
Hawley, N. Before the fall
Isaacs, S. After all these years
Kress, N. Beggars in Spain
Leonard, E. The Hot Kid
Ondaatje, M. In the skin of a lion
Perry, T. Dead aim
Sanders, L. The tenth commandment
Spiegelman, P. Black maps
Stone, N. The verdict

MILLS AND MILLWORK

Shreve, A. Fortune's rocks

Millworth Manor [series] Alexander, V.

Milo Milodragovitch mysteries [series] Crumley, J.

Milo Weaver trilogy [series] Steinhauer, O.

MILWAUKEE, WISCONSIN

Petrie, N. The drifter

The **mime** order Shannon, S.

Mina's joint Ervin, K.

Mina's joint [series] Ervin, K.

MIND AND REALITY

McCarthy, T. Satin Island

MIND CONTROL

Asimov, I. Foundation and empire
Asimov, I. Second foundation
Barry, M. Lexicon
Callender, K. Queen of the conquered
Glynn, A. Receptor
Grant, M. Feed
Grant, M. Feedback
Harrison, M. Light
Huang, S. Zero sum game
Lehane, D. Prayers for rain
Lehane, D. Shutter Island

Mind games Mehl, N.

Sandford, J. Storm Front
Sandford, J. Storm prey
Sandford, J. Sudden prey
Stanley, M. Dying to live
Staples, D. This town sleeps
Stradal, J. The lager queen of Minnesota
Sundstol, V. The land of dreams
Tracy, P. Ice cold heart
Treuer, D. Prudence
West, K. Minor dramas & other catastrophes
Wilson, R. Blind Lake

Minnesota trilogy [series] Sundstol, V.
Minor dramas & other catastrophes West, K.

MINOR LEAGUE BASEBALL

Owen, H. Parker Field

MINORITIES

Craig, C. Miss Burma
Pochoda, I. These women
Price, R. Freedomland

The **minority** report Dick, P.

MINORITY RIGHTS

Percy, B. Red moon

The **minotaur** Vine, B.

MINOTAUR (GREEK MYTHOLOGY)

Renault, M. The bull from the sea
Renault, M. The king must die
Sherrill, S. The minotaur takes his own sweet time

Minotaur novels (Steven Sherrill) [series] Sherrill, S.
The **minotaur** takes his own sweet time Sherrill, S.

MINSTREL SHOWS

Phillips, C. Dancing in the dark

MINSTRELS

Phillips, C. Dancing in the dark

A **minute** to midnight Baldacci, D.
Minutes of glory, and other stories Ngugi wa Thiong'o, 1.
Miracle Creek Kim, A.
Miracle on 34th Street Davies, V.
Miracle on 5th Avenue Morgan, S.

MIRACLES

Binchy, M. Whitethorn Woods
Carey, L. The stolen child
Donoghue, E. The wonder
Miles, J. Anatomy of a miracle
Picoult, J. Keeping faith
Schutt, B. The Darwin strain

MIRACLES (CHRISTIANITY)

Erdrich, L. The beet queen

The **miracles** of the Namiya General Store Higashino, K.
The **mirror** thief Seay, M.
The **mirror's** edge Sidor, S.

MIRRORS

Oyeyemi, H. Boy, Snow, Bird
Seay, M. The mirror thief

MISADVENTURES

Adams, D. Dirk Gently's holistic detective agency
Adams, D. The hitchhiker's guide to the galaxy
Adams, D. Life, the universe, and everything

Adams, D. The restaurant at the end of the universe
Aira, C. The seamstress and the wind
Barry, D. Lunatics
Barry, D. Insane city
Berger, T. Being invisible
Bragi Olafsson, 1. The pets
Cooper, T. The marauders
Coover, R. Huck out west
Cotter, B. Fever chart
Dickens, C. The Pickwick papers
Doyle, B. The plover
Faulks, S. Jeeves and the wedding bells
Fielding, H. The history of Tom Jones, a foundling
Fowler, K. Sarah Canary
Golding, W. Close quarters
Jonasson, J. The accidental further adventures of the hundred-year-old man
Karunatilaka, S. The legend of Pradeep Mathew
MacLean, S. The rogue not taken
Moore, C. You suck
Pynchon, T. Gravity's rainbow
Pynchon, T. V
Rodale, M. Lady Bridget's diary
Russo, R. Everybody's fool
Russo, R. The risk pool
Sansom, I. The case of the missing books
Smith, Z. The autograph man
Spufford, F. Golden hill
Steinbeck, J. Tortilla Flat
Ulinich, A. Petropolis
Warren, R. World enough and time
Waters, S. The little stranger
Waters, S. Tipping the velvet
Waugh, E. Decline and fall
Williams, C. Stairway to hell
Wodehouse, P. The inimitable Jeeves
Wodehouse, P. My man Jeeves

Misadventures in matchmaking [series] Lorret, V.

MISBEHAVIOR

Freeman, C. All that I have

MISCARRIAGE

Mahmoud, L. Amreekiya
Riley, L. The girl on the cliff

MISCHIEF

Dexter, P. Spooner
Groen, H. On the bright side
Rogues

MISCHIEF IN BOYS

Porter, M. Lanny

Mischling Konar, A.

MISCONCEPTIONS

Chaon, D. Ill will

MISERLINESS

Dickens, C. A Christmas carol
Norris, F. McTeague

Misery King, S.

MISFITS (PERSONS)

MISFITS (PERSONS) -- SOUTHERN STATES

MISOGYNY

MISSILES

MISSING BOYS

Ahlborn, A. The devil crept in
Box, C. Paradise Valley
Buehlman, C. The Suicide Motor Club
Ellis, B. Lunar Park
Faye, L. The Paragon Hotel
Grimes, M. The Old Wine Shades
James, M. Black leopard, red wolf
Levien, D. City of the sun
Locke, A. Heaven, my home
Lourey, J. Unspeakable things
North, A. The Whisper Man
O'Connell, C. Blind sight
Penny, L. The nature of the beast
Peters, E. The hermit of Eyton Forest
Porter, M. Lanny
Rader-Day, L. The day I died
Seiffert, R. A boy in winter

MISSING CHILDREN
Anappara, D. Djinn patrol on the purple line
Bambara, T. Those bones are not my child
Beck, H. Here and gone
Bock, C. Beautiful children
Bolton, S. The craftsman
Box, C. Blue heaven
Bradley, C. A red herring without mustard
Brockmeier, K. The truth about Celia
Candlish, L. Our house
Child, L. Worth dying for
Corby, G. The Marathon conspiracy
Corleone, D. Gone cold
Corleone, D. Good as gone
Corleone, D. Payoff
Danticat, E. Claire of the sea light
Dazieri, S. Kill the father
DePoy, P. Sidewalk saint
Englander, N. The ministry of Special Cases
Ephron, H. You'll never know, dear
Faulkner, C. Finding Georgina
Forna, A. Happiness
Fox, C. Gone by midnight
French, N. Blue Monday
Greene, A. Long Man
Grimes, M. The Old Wine Shades
Hart, J. The last child
Hoffman, A. Turtle moon
Irwin, S. The dead path
Kidd, J. Things in jars
Kunzru, H. Gods without men
Lovestam, S. The truth behind the lie
Luiselli, V. Lost children archive
Macdonald, R. The underground man
McCall Smith, A. The No. 1 Ladies' Detective Agency
McDermid, V. A place of execution
McEwan, I. The child in time
McGhee, A. The opposite of fate
Meloy, M. Do not become alarmed
Meyer, D. Devil's peak

Mitchard, J. The deep end of the ocean
O'Connell, C. Find me
Ohlsson, K. Unwanted
Petrie, N. The wild one
Potzsch, O. The hangman's daughter
Quinn, S. The right side
Read, C. Invisible boy
Reichs, K. A conspiracy of bones
Rendell, R. The tree of hands
Roy, L. Gone too long
Ryan, H. The wrong girl
Sidor, S. The mirror's edge
Tudor, C. The other people
Tursten, H. Winter grave
Vine, B. Anna's book
Watson, M. The dream peddler
Young, W. The shack
Zimmerman, J. The orphanmaster

MISSING GIRLS
Ackerman, E. Dark at the crossing
Atkinson, K. Case histories
Brockmeier, K. The truth about Celia
Burdick, S. The girls with no names
Castillo, L. Shamed
Cohen, T. The summer we lost her
Corey, J. Caliban's war
Corey, J. Leviathan wakes
Eisler, B. All the devils
Franklin, T. Crooked letter, crooked letter
Gardner, L. Love you more
Griffiths, E. The crossing places
Hamer, K. The girl in the red coat
Hayder, M. Gone
Hensher, P. King of the badgers
Jones, D. A bad day for sunshine
Lackberg, C. The preacher
McHugh, L. Arrowood
McHugh, L. The wolf wants in
Moore, G. The holdout
Muller, M. A wild and lonely place
Nickson, C. Gods of gold
Phillips, J. Disappearing earth
Rankin, I. The falls
Reichs, K. Bones to ashes
Reichs, K. Grave secrets
Robotham, M. Say you're sorry
Rock, P. The shelter cycle
Sager, R. The last time I lied
Speller, E. The strange fate of Kitty Easton
St. James, S. The broken girls
White, E. Dragonshadow

MISSING IN ACTION
Cotterill, C. Slash and burn
Dybek, N. The Verdun affair
Faulks, S. Charlotte Gray
Palaia, M. The given world
Scott, C. The poppy wife

Guskin, S. The forgetting time
Hall, T. The case of the love commandos
Hammett, D. The thin man
Harris, S. The color of Bee Larkham's murder
Harrison, M. The bishop's wife
Harvey, J. Far cry
Hayder, M. Skin
Hayder, M. The treatment
Healey, E. Elizabeth is missing
Henderson, S. Fourth of July Creek
Hill, S. The various haunts of men
Hillerman, T. The shape shifter
Hosking, J. Three years with the rat
Hunter, E. The moment she was gone
Hunter, S. Pale horse coming
Jewell, L. I found you
Joss, M. Among the missing
Joyce, G. Some kind of fairy tale
Kelman, J. How late it was, how late
King, L. The game
Konar, A. Mischling
Koryta, M. Tonight I said goodbye
Kostova, E. The historian
Krentz, J. River road
Kwok, J. Searching for Sylvie Lee
Langton, J. The thief of Venice
Larsson, S. The girl with the dragon tattoo
Lee, C. On such a full sea
Lee, D. Country of origin
Les Becquets, D. Breaking wild
Limon, M. The line
Lippman, L. What the dead know
Lutz, L. The Spellman files
Lynn, A. Now you see it
MacBride, S. Close to the bone
Mankell, H. The troubled man
Mason, J. Three graves full
Matar, H. Anatomy of a disappearance
McCarry, C. Old boys
McGuire, S. Night and silence
McKay, A. The witches of New York
McLean, F. The Van Apfel girls are gone
Meuleman, S. Find me gone
Meyer, D. Trackers
Mieville, C. The city & the city
Millet, L. Ghost lights
Mitchard, J. No time to wave goodbye
Mitchell, D. Slade House
Moriarty, J. Gravity is the thing
Mosley, W. Blonde faith
Mosley, W. Cinnamon kiss
Mosley, W. Little green
Muller, M. Both ends of the night
Muller, M. City of whispers
Muller, M. Wolf in the shadows
Murakami, H. South of the border, west of the sun
Novey, I. Ways to disappear

Nunn, M. Blessed are the dead
O'Brien, T. In the Lake of the Woods
O'Donovan, G. Dublin dead
Oates, J. The accursed
Oates, J. Carthage
Ogawa, Y. The memory police
Oleksiw, S. The wrath of Shiva
Ondaatje, M. In the skin of a lion
Palaia, M. The given world
Paretsky, S. Blacklist
Paretsky, S. Hardball
Paretsky, S. Indemnity only
Parker, R. Valediction
Patchett, A. State of wonder
Patterson, M. Rebellion
Paul, B. Under Tower Peak
Penney, S. The tenderness of wolves
Penny, L. A better man
Penny, L. How the light gets in
Penny, L. The long way home
Perry, A. Cain his brother
Perry, A. Death on Blackheath
Perry, A. The twisted root
Peters, E. The last camel died at noon
Peters, E. The snake, the crocodile, and the dog
Pope, B. The missing Italian girl
Potenza, C. Hearts of the missing
Potzsch, O. The poisoned pilgrim
Powell, G. Embers of war
Preston, D. The codex
Preston, D. The Obsidian chamber
Pronzini, B. Fever
Pyne, D. Twentynine Palms
Quartey, K. The missing American
Quartey, K. Wife of the gods
Racculia, K. Bellweather rhapsody
Raichev, R. Assassins at Ospreys
Rankin, I. The black book
Ratner, V. Music of the ghosts
Reichs, K. Bones to ashes
Reichs, K. Break no bones
Reisman, N. The first desire
Rendell, R. The babes in the wood
Rendell, R. Harm done
Rendell, R. Simisola
Richardson, K. Greywalker
Riley, J. In pursuit of the green lion
Ripley, N. Find you in the dark
Roanhorse, R. Trail of lightning
Roberts, N. Come sundown
Robertson, M. The Baker Street letters
Robinson, P. Close to home
Robinson, P. In the dark places
Robinson, P. Strange affair
Robotham, M. The wreckage
Rowland, L. Bedlam
Ryan, W. The twelfth department

Gran, S. Claire DeWitt and the city of the dead
Gran, S. The infinite blacktop
Green, N. The angel of Montague Street
Griffin, K. The glass god
Grimes, M. The Old Wine Shades
Hall, T. The case of the love commandos
Hallinan, T. Fools' river
Harris, S. The color of Bee Larkham's murder
Harvey, J. Far cry
Harvey, M. The governor's wife
Hayder, M. Ritual
Hayder, M. Skin
Heller, P. Celine
Hensher, P. King of the badgers
Hill, S. The shadows in the street
Hosking, J. Three years with the rat
James, M. Black leopard, red wolf
Jones, J. The silence
Katzenbach, J. What comes next
Kerr, P. March violets
Khan, A. Among the ruins
Kidd, J. Things in jars
King, L. The game
Lansdale, J. Honky tonk samurai
Lee, D. Country of origin
Lehane, D. Sacred
Lepionka, K. The last place you look
Limon, M. The line
Littlejohn, E. Lost Lake
Locke, A. Heaven, my home
Luesse, V. Missing Isaac
Lynn, A. Now you see it
Macdonald, R. The underground man
Mankell, H. Before the frost
McGuire, S. Night and silence
Miller, D. American by day
Mosley, W. And sometimes I wonder about you
Mosley, W. Blonde faith
Mosley, W. Cinnamon kiss
Mosley, W. Devil in a blue dress
Mosley, W. Fearless Jones
Mosley, W. Little green
Mosley, W. A red death
Mosley, W. Rose gold
Muller, M. Vanishing point
Muller, M. Where echoes live
Neuhaus, N. Snow White must die
Nickson, C. Gods of gold
O'Connell, C. Blind sight
Oates, J. Carthage
Olshan, J. Black diamond fall
Parker, R. Rough weather
Parker, R. Thin air
Pattison, E. Water touching stone
Penney, S. The invisible ones
Penny, L. A better man
Penny, L. How the light gets in

Penny, L. The long way home
Penny, L. The nature of the beast
Peters, E. The rose rent
Peters, E. The virgin in the ice
Picoult, J. Leaving time
Pochoda, I. Visitation Street
Porter, M. Lanny
Powell, G. Embers of war
Preston, D. The Obsidian chamber
Pronzini, B. Hellbox
Quartey, K. The missing American
Quinn, S. Dog on it
Quinn, S. The right side
Rader-Day, L. The day I died
Ragan, T. Buried deep
Rankin, I. Dead souls
Rankin, I. The falls
Raybourn, D. A dangerous collaboration
Rendell, R. Not in the flesh
Robertson, M. The Baker Street letters
Robinson, P. Close to home
Sager, R. The last time I lied
Sandford, J. Phantom prey
Saunders, K. The case of the wandering scholar
Scott, A. The low road
Semple, M. Where'd you go, Bernadette
Shames, T. A risky undertaking for Loretta Singletary
Sharfeddin, H. Mineral spirits
Shrier, H. Boston cream
Singh, N. A madness of sunshine
Smith, J. 82 Desire
Smith, M. The Siberian dilemma
Solares, M. Don't send flowers
Speller, E. The strange fate of Kitty Easton
Spencer, S. Backlash
Spencer, S. The shivering turn
Stanley, M. Deadly harvest
Steiner, S. Missing, presumed
Swinson, K. The safe house
Wade, B. Falling for you
Walker, W. Emma in the night
White, S. The siege

MISSING PERSONS INVESTIGATION -- CALIFORNIA
Pronzini, B. Illusions

MISSING PERSONS INVESTIGATION -- GERMANY
Schlink, B. Self's deception

MISSING PERSONS INVESTIGATION -- LAS VEGAS, NEVADA
Parker, R. Chance

MISSING PERSONS INVESTIGATION -- NEW ORLEANS, LOUISIANA
Castro, J. Hell or high water

MISSING TEENAGE BOYS
Adam, C. Golden child
Robinson, P. Close to home
Tremblay, P. Disappearance at Devil's Rock

MISSING TEENAGE GIRLS

Barton, F. The suspect
Chancellor, B. Sycamore
Gardner, L. Look for me
Harrod-Eagles, C. Old bones
Hobbs, A. Stealing candy
Lepionka, K. The last place you look
Lethem, J. The feral detective
McGregor, J. The reservoir tapes
Meyers, K. Twisted tree
Overton, H. The runaway
Patterson, J. Kiss the girls
Pochoda, I. Visitation Street
Racculia, K. Bellweather rhapsody
Russell, K. Swamplandia!
Solares, M. Don't send flowers
Spencer, S. The shivering turn
Walker, W. Emma in the night

MISSING TEENAGERS

Barclay, L. A tap on the window
Coben, H. The boy from the woods
Collins, M. The wrong Quarry
Jewell, L. Then she was gone
Quinn, S. Dog on it
Robards, K. The last victim
Roberts, G. Adam and evil

MISSING WOMEN

Abbott, J. The three Beths
Adler-Olsen, J. The hanging girl
Adler-Olsen, J. The keeper of lost causes
Adler-Olsen, J. The scarred woman
Alexander, V. The Lady Travelers Guide to scoundrels and
    other gentlemen
Atkinson, K. When will there be good news?
Auster, P. The Brooklyn follies
Belle, K. Dear wife
Bohjalian, C. The sleepwalker
Box, C. The disappeared
Box, C. The highway
Boyden, J. Through black spruce
Braffet, K. Last seen leaving
Brekke, J. The fifth element
Brown, K. The clairvoyants
Brown, S. Outfox
Brown, S. Ricochet
Burnet, G. The disappearance of Adele Bedeau
Child, L. Never go back
Cleeves, A. The long call
Cortazar, J. Hopscotch
Cussler, C. The cutthroat
Deaver, J. The never game
Dugoni, R. My sister's grave
Ellis, B. The vanished bride
Eskens, A. Nothing more dangerous
Finlay, M. The murder pit
Fleischmann, R. How quickly she disappears
Flynn, G. Gone girl
Frost, K. The reluctant fortune-teller

Grimes, M. The Old Wine Shades
Hall, J. Buzz cut
Harris, O. A shadow intelligence
Harrison, R. The return
Hart, E. Haunted ground
Harvey, J. Darkness, darkness
Hill, S. The shadows in the street
Hoffman, A. The Museum of Extraordinary Things
Jeffries, S. The art of sinning
Kasischke, L. The raising
Krentz, J. When all the girls have gone
Kroese, R. The last iota
Lehane, D. Sacred
Les Becquets, D. Breaking wild
Lewis, B. The missing
Littlejohn, E. Lost Lake
Lutz, L. Curse of the Spellmans
Lynn, A. Now you see it
MacLean, S. No good duke goes unpunished
Mandel, E. The glass hotel
Mankell, H. Before the frost
Marks, J. Fangland
McMahon, J. The one I left behind
Mieville, C. Perdido Street Station
Minh, D. Neon empire
Montgomery, J. The widows
Moore, L. Long bright river
Mosley, W. Black Betty
Mosley, W. Devil in a blue dress
Muller, M. Cyanide Wells
Muller, M. Vanishing point
Murakami, H. The wind-up bird chronicle
Ocampo, S. The promise
Paris, B. Bring me back
Parker, R. Thin air
Penney, S. The invisible ones
Perry, T. Death benefits
Peters, E. The rose rent
Picoult, J. Leaving time
Pronzini, B. Hellbox
Ragan, T. Buried deep
Ragan, T. Her last day
Raybourn, D. A dangerous collaboration
Robb, C. A twisted vengeance
Rose, J. The blackest bird
Russo, R. Chances are...
Ryan, H. The other woman
Ryan, J. The spies of Shilling Lane
Sager, R. Lock every door
Schlink, B. Self's deception
Shames, T. A risky undertaking for Loretta Singletary
Sharfeddin, H. Mineral spirits
Singh, N. A madness of sunshine
Smith, M. The Siberian dilemma
Spencer, S. Backlash
Tran, V. Dragonfish
The **missing** world Livesey, M.

Calvino, I. The baron in the trees
Calvino, I. If on a winter's night a traveler
Calvino, I. Invisible cities
Camus, A. The plague
Camus, A. The stranger
Capote, T. Breakfast at Tiffany's
Celine, L. Journey to the end of the night
Chandler, R. The annotated Big sleep
Chandler, R. The big sleep
Chandler, R. The long goodbye
Cheever, J. The Wapshot chronicle
Doctorow, E. Ragtime
Dos Passos, J. 1919
Dos Passos, J. The 42nd parallel
Du Maurier, D. Rebecca
Durrell, L. Balthazar
Durrell, L. Clea
Durrell, L. Justine
Durrell, L. Mountolive
Eco, U. The name of the rose
Ellison, R. Invisible man
Faulkner, W. Absalom, Absalom!
Faulkner, W. As I lay dying
Faulkner, W. Go down, Moses
Faulkner, W. The hamlet
Faulkner, W. Intruder in the dust
Faulkner, W. Light in August
Faulkner, W. Pylon
Faulkner, W. The reivers
Faulkner, W. Requiem for a nun
Faulkner, W. Sanctuary
Faulkner, W. The sound and the fury
Faulkner, W. Uncollected stories of William Faulkner
Ferber, E. So big
Fitzgerald, F. The beautiful and damned
Fitzgerald, F. The last tycoon
Fitzgerald, F. Novels and stories, 1920-1922
Fitzgerald, F. The short stories of F. Scott Fitzgerald
Fitzgerald, F. This side of paradise
Fitzgerald, F. Six tales of the jazz age and other stories
Ford, F. Parade's end
Forster, E. Howards End
Forster, E. Maurice
Forster, E. A passage to India
Forster, E. A room with a view
Fowles, J. The French lieutenant's woman
Fowles, J. The magus
Gaddis, W. The recognitions
Galsworthy, J. The Forsyte saga
Garcia Marquez, G. The autumn of the patriarch
Garcia Marquez, G. Chronicle of a death foretold
Garcia Marquez, G. Collected novellas
Garcia Marquez, G. The general in his labyrinth
Garcia Marquez, G. In evil hour
Garcia Marquez, G. Leaf storm, and other stories
Garcia Marquez, G. Love in the time of cholera
Garcia Marquez, G. Memories of my melancholy whores

Garcia Marquez, G. One hundred years of solitude
Garcia Marquez, G. Strange pilgrims
Gide, A. The immoralist
Golding, W. Lord of the flies
Grass, G. The tin drum
Graves, R. I, Claudius
Greene, G. Brighton Rock
Greene, G. The end of the affair
Greene, G. The heart of the matter
Greene, G. The honorary consul
Greene, G. The power and the glory
Greene, G. The quiet American
Hammett, D. The Maltese falcon
Heller, J. Catch-22
Hemingway, E. A farewell to arms
Hemingway, E. For whom the bell tolls
Hemingway, E. The Nick Adams stories
Hemingway, E. The old man and the sea
Hemingway, E. The snows of Kilimanjaro and other stories
Hemingway, E. The sun also rises
Hemingway, E. To have and have not
Hesse, H. Siddhartha
Hesse, H. Steppenwolf
Hughes, L. Not without laughter
Hurston, Z. Their eyes were watching God
Huxley, A. Brave new world
Irving, J. The Cider House rules
Irving, J. A prayer for Owen Meany
Irving, J. The world according to Garp
Isherwood, C. The Berlin stories
Joyce, J. Dubliners
Joyce, J. Finnegans wake
Jones, J. From here to eternity
Joyce, J. A portrait of the artist as a young man
Joyce, J. Ulysses
Kafka, F. The castle
Kafka, F. The metamorphosis
Kafka, F. The trial
Kazantzakis, N. Zorba the Greek
Kerouac, J. The dharma bums
Kerouac, J. On the road
Kerouac, J. Road novels 1957-1960
Kesey, K. One flew over the cuckoo's nest
Kesey, K. Sometimes a great notion
Knowles, J. A separate peace
Koestler, A. Darkness at noon
Larsen, N. Passing
Lawrence, D. Lady Chatterley's lover
Lawrence, D. The rainbow
Lawrence, D. Sons and lovers
Lawrence, D. Women in love
Lee, H. To kill a mockingbird
Lessing, D. The golden not(ebk.)
Lewis, S. Babbitt
Lewis, S. Elmer Gantry
Lewis, S. Main street
Lockridge, R. Raintree County

Welty, E. The ponder heart
Welty, E. The robber bridegroom
Welty, E. Stories, essays & memoir
West, N. Novels and other writings
Wharton, E. The children
Wharton, E. Collected stories, 1891-1910
Wharton, E. Collected stories, 1911-1937
Wharton, E. Ethan Frome
White, T. The once and future king
Wilson, S. The man in the gray flannel suit
Wolfe, T. The bonfire of the vanities
Wolfe, T. Look homeward, angel
Wolfe, T. You can't go home again
Woolf, V. Jacob's room
Woolf, V. Between the acts
Woolf, V. Mrs. Dalloway
Woolf, V. Orlando
Woolf, V. To the lighthouse
Woolf, V. The voyage out
Woolf, V. The waves
Woolf, V. The years
Wouk, H. The Caine mutiny
Wright, R. Eight men
Wright, R. Native son
Wright, R. Uncle Tom's children
Yourcenar, M. Memoirs of Hadrian
Zamyatin, Y. We
Modern love [series] Rai, A.
Modern lovers Straub, E.
MODERN WESTERNS
Doig, I. The bartender's tale
Henderson, S. The flicker of old dreams
Johnson, C. Another man's moccasins
Johnson, C. Dark horse
Johnson, C. Death without company
Johnson, C. Hell is empty
Johnson, C. Land of wolves
Johnson, C. Spirit of steamboat
Kennedy, R. Presidio
Kittredge, W. The willow field
McCarthy, C. All the pretty horses
McCarthy, C. No country for old men
McMurtry, L. Rhino ranch
Myers, A. Continental divide
Paul, B. Under Tower Peak
Rowland, R. Cold country
Stansel, I. The last cowboys of San Geronimo
Sternbergh, A. The blinds
MODERNIZATION (SOCIAL SCIENCES)
Burns, O. Leaving Cold Sassy
Cather, W. A lost lady
Desai, K. The inheritance of loss
Dos Passos, J. Manhattan transfer
Mukherjee, B. Miss new India
Pontoppidan, H. Lucky Per
Rourke, L. The canal
MOGADISHU, SOMALIA

Farah, N. Crossbones
Farah, N. Knots
Farah, N. Links
MOHEGAN INDIANS
Cooper, J. The last of the Mohicans
Mohr Reuss, F.
MOHR, MAX, B 1891
Reuss, F. Mohr
MOJAVE DESERT
Kunzru, H. Gods without men
Lalami, L. The other Americans
Parker, S. Purgatory road
MOLAY, JACQUES DE, CA 1243-1314
Druon, M. The iron king
MOLECULAR BIOLOGISTS
Crichton, M. Prey
Powers, R. The Gold Bug Variations
MOLECULAR EVOLUTION
Wilson, D. The Andromeda evolution
MOLES (SPIES)
Berenson, A. The prisoner
Cumming, C. A colder war
Deighton, L. Berlin game
Deighton, L. London match
Hunter, S. Time to hunt
Jin, H. A map of betrayal
Matthews, J. The Kremlin's candidate
Matthews, J. Red sparrow
Nguyen, V. The sympathizer
Woods, S. Smooth operator
Moll Flanders Defoe, D.
Mollisan Town quartet [series] Davys, T.
The **moment** Kennedy, D.
A **moment** in the sun Sayles, J.
The **moment** she was gone Hunter, E.
MONACO
Gaynor, H. Meet me in Monaco
MONARCHY
Quinn, K. Ribbons of scarlet
Twain, M. A Connecticut Yankee in King Arthur's Court
MONASTERIES
Pears, I. Death and restoration
Penny, L. The beautiful mystery
Potzsch, O. The poisoned pilgrim
Reichs, K. Deja dead
Stephenson, N. Anathem
MONASTIC LIBRARIES -- ITALY
Eco, U. The name of the rose
MONASTICISM AND RELIGIOUS ORDERS
Royal, P. Sanctity of hate
MONASTICISM AND RELIGIOUS ORDERS (BUD-DHIST)
Mishima, Y. The temple of the golden pavilion
MONASTICISM AND RELIGIOUS ORDERS -- ROME
Davis, L. One virgin too many
MONASTICISM AND RELIGIOUS ORDERS FOR MEN
Berry, S. The Templar legacy

Shaw, V. Strange Practice
Sullivan, M. Theft of swords
Willocks, T. The religion
MONKS -- ALBANIA -- 14TH CENTURY
Kadare, I. The three-arched bridge
MONKS -- GERMANY
Hesse, H. Narcissus and Goldmund
MONMOUTH'S REBELLION, 1685
Blackmore, R. Lorna Doone
MONMOUTH, WALES
Donoghue, E. Slammerkin
MONOGAMY
Shriver, L. The post-birthday world
MONROE, MARILYN, 1926-1962
Lee, J. The starlet and the spy
Oates, J. Blonde
Monsieur Pain Bolano, R.
Monsoon Smith, W.
Monster Kellerman, J.
MONSTERS
Armfield, J. Salt slow
Asimov, I. Second foundation
Butcher, J. Proven guilty
Cantero, E. Meddling kids
Gallagher, S. The bedlam detective
Goss, T. The strange case of the alchemist's daughter
Hamill, S. A cosmology of monsters
Hill, J. Horns
Hill, J. NOS4A2
Johnson, M. Pym
Kosmatka, T. The games
LaValle, V. The devil in silver
Lovesey, P. The vault
Malerman, J. Bird box
Mieville, C. Perdido Street Station
Nevill, A. The ritual
  New suns
Nicholas, D. Something red
Pratchett, T. The color of magic
Priest, C. The inexplicables
Roanhorse, R. Trail of lightning
Sa'dawi, A. Frankenstein in Baghdad
Shelley, M. Frankenstein
Sullivan, M. Theft of swords
Watts, P. Starfish
White, E. Dragonshadow
Wolfe, G. The claw of the conciliator
Wolfe, G. The sword of the Lictor
Wong, D. John dies at the end
Yang, J. The descent of monsters
Yang, J. The red threads of fortune
Monstrous regiment Pratchett, T.
MONTANA
Box, C. The bitterroots
Box, C. The highway
Box, C. Paradise Valley
Burke, J. Black cherry blues

Castile, Z. Flashed
Child, L. Die trying
Crumley, J. The last good kiss
Doig, I. The bartender's tale
Doig, I. Mountain time
Doig, I. The whistling season
Dorris, M. A yellow raft in blue water
Dundas, C. The blaze
Evans, N. The horse whisperer
Henderson, S. The flicker of old dreams
Henderson, S. Fourth of July Creek
Hulse, S. Black River
Hulse, S. Eden mine
Kennedy, D. The big picture
Kittredge, W. The willow field
Koryta, M. Those who wish me dead
Larsen, R. The selected works of T. S. Spivet
McGuane, T. Crow fair
Peterson, T. What comes my way
Roberts, N. Come sundown
Rowland, R. Cold country
Ryan, J. Restless rancher
Salvalaggio, K. Bone dust white
Sharfeddin, H. Mineral spirits
Warren, S. Rescue me
Watson, L. As good as gone
Watson, L. Let him go
MONTANA -- DESCRIPTION AND TRAVEL
Doig, I. Ride with me, Mariah Montana
MONTANA -- HISTORY
Smith, B. The return of Kid Cooper
MONTANA -- HISTORY -- 19TH CENTURY
Doig, I. Dancing at the Rascal Fair
Hockensmith, S. Holmes on the range
Hockensmith, S. On the wrong track
MONTANA -- HISTORY -- 20TH CENTURY
Doig, I. Dancing at the Rascal Fair
MONTANA -- SOCIAL LIFE AND CUSTOMS -- 20TH CENTURY
Bowen, P. Badlands
Montana rescue [series] Warren, S.
Montana trilogy (Ivan Doig) [series] Doig, I.
Montauk Harrison, N.
MONTAUK, NEW YORK
Harrison, N. Montauk
Monte Walsh Schaefer, J.
MONTEREY, CALIFORNIA
Steinbeck, J. Cannery Row
Steinbeck, J. Tortilla Flat
MONTEZUMA II,, EMPEROR OF MEXICO, CA 1480-1520
Levack, S. Demon of the air
MONTFORT, SIMON DE, EARL OF LEICESTER, 1208?-1265
Penman, S. Falls the shadow
Montgomery and Taggert clans series [series] Deveraux, J.
MONTGOMERY, ALABAMA -- RACE RELATIONS

Johnson, D. The largesse of the sea maiden
Mitchell, D. The bone clocks
Moore, A. Jerusalem
O'Brien, T. Going after Cacciato
Rice, A. Interview with the vampire
Rice, A. Blackwood farm
Rice, A. Blood and gold
Rice, A. Blood canticle
Rice, A. Memnoch the devil
Rice, A. Merrick
Rice, A. Prince Lestat
Rice, A. The queen of the damned
Rice, A. The tale of the body thief
Rice, A. The vampire Lestat
Roth, P. Everyman
Roth, P. Letting go
Spark, M. Memento mori
Tolkien, J. Beren and Luthien
Updike, J. The afterlife and other stories
White, S. Kill me
Yanagihara, H. The people in the trees
Mortals Rush, N.

MOSAICS
Forna, A. The hired man
The **Moscow** offensive Brown, D.

MOSCOW, RUSSIA
Bulgakov, M. The master and Margarita
Gessen, K. A terrible country
Gibson, W. Pattern recognition
Higgins, J. Rough justice
Kaminsky, S. Murder on the Trans-Siberian Express
Matthews, J. Palace of treason
Morgan Jones, C. The silent oligarch
Smith, M. Gorky Park
Smith, M. Red Square
Smith, M. The Siberian dilemma
Smith, M. Stalin's ghost
Smith, M. Tatiana
Smith, M. Three stations
Smith, M. Wolves eat dogs
Tolstaya, T. The slynx
Towles, A. A gentleman in Moscow
Winterson, J. The passion

MOSCOW, RUSSIA -- POLITICS AND GOVERNMENT
Ryan, W. The darkening field
Ryan, W. The twelfth department

MOSCOW, RUSSIA -- SOCIAL LIFE AND CUSTOMS
Grushin, O. The line

MOSCOW, RUSSIA, TRIALS, 1936-1937
Koestler, A. Darkness at noon
Moshi-moshi Yoshimoto, B.

MOSQUES
John, E. Born on a Tuesday
The **Mosquito** Coast Theroux, P.

MOSSAD
Hunter, S. Game of snipers

MOSSAD AGENTS

Silva, D. The kill artist
The **most** dangerous place on earth Johnson, L.
The **most** dangerous thing Lippman, L.
The **most** fun we ever had Lombardo, C.
Most likely to [series] Bybee, C.
A **most** wanted man Le Carre, J.
Mostly dead things Arnett, K.

MOTELS
McPherson, C. Scot & soda
St. James, S. The Sun Down motel
Wallace, M. The girl in the garden
The **moth** diaries Klein, R.
The **mother** Edwards, Y.

MOTHER AND ADULT CHILD
Bawden, N. Family money
Brookner, A. Family and friends
Enright, A. The Green Road
Rawle, G. Woman's world
Smith, L. Family linen

MOTHER AND ADULT DAUGHTER
Alther, L. Kinflicks
Arnett, K. Mostly dead things
Arnoult, D. Sufficient grace
Azzopardi, T. Winterton blue
Beckerman, H. If only I could tell you
Coster, N. Halsey Street
Cumyn, A. Losing it
Didion, J. A book of common prayer
Ephron, H. You'll never know, dear
Evison, J. This is your life, Harriet Chance!
Flynn, G. Sharp objects
Frank, D. Queen bee
Gaylin, A. Never look back
Gelman, L. You've been volunteered
Gibbons, K. Charms for the easy life
Macmillan, G. The nanny
Mallery, S. California girls
Mann, T. The black swan
McGuire, S. Night and silence
Nunez, E. Anna in-between
Roth, P. I married a Communist
Sebold, A. The almost moon
Slaughter, K. Fallen
Vann, D. Caribou Island
Wells, R. Divine secrets of the Ya-Ya Sisterhood

MOTHER AND ADULT SON
Auslander, S. Hope
Castel-Bloom, O. Textile
Coetzee, J. Life & times of Michael K
Coupland, D. Eleanor Rigby
Drndic, D. Trieste
Horn, D. Eternal life
Jones, S. The other woman
Lennon, J. Familiar
Palahniuk, C. Choke
See, C. There will never be another you
St. Aubyn, E. At last

Plain, B. Harvest
Priest, C. Boneshaker
Ramqvist, K. The white city
Scottoline, L. Come home
Sekaran, S. Lucky boy
Solomon, A. Leaving Lucy Pear
Strout, E. My name is Lucy Barton
Thomas, B. A good enough mother
Truong, M. The sweetest fruits
Walbert, K. She was like that
Ward, A. Forgive me
Weiner, J. Little earthquakes

MOTHERHOOD -- PSYCHOLOGICAL ASPECTS

Stage, Z. Baby teeth
Mothering Sunday Swift, G.
Motherland Nicholson, W.
Motherland hotel Atilgan, Y.
Motherless Brooklyn Lethem, J.

MOTHERS

Arnow, H. The dollmaker
Barclay, L. Broken promise
Bock, C. Alice & Oliver
Cash, W. The last ballad
Coates, T. The water dancer
Coben, H. Hold tight
Coetzee, J. Elizabeth Costello
Cunningham, M. The hours
Donoghue, E. Frog music
Edwards, K. The memory keeper's daughter
Edwards, Y. The mother
Ellmann, L. Ducks, Newburyport
Enright, A. The Green Road
Fisher, K. The silent wife
Fox, C. Gone by midnight
Freudenberger, N. Lost and wanted
Gardner, L. Love you more
Gelman, L. Class mom
Gilman, S. Donna has left the building
Hamilton, J. A map of the world
Hannah, S. Perfect little children
Jemisin, N. The fifth season
Jemisin, N. The obelisk gate
Jemisin, N. The stone sky
Kingsolver, B. Flight behavior
Lazarin, D. Back talk
Lovestam, S. The truth behind the lie
Mda, Z. The Madonna of Excelsior
Miller, S. The good mother
Miyamoto, T. Kinshu
Moriarty, L. The husband's secret
Murray, V. Stand your ground
Perrotta, T. Little children
Pope, B. The missing Italian girl
Quartey, K. Wife of the gods
Quindlen, A. Every last one
Schweblin, S. Fever dream
Scott, J. Tourmaline

Silver, M. Mary Coin
Stuart, D. Shuggie Bain
Van Meter, C. Creatures
Wolitzer, M. Surrender, Dorothy
Woolf, V. To the lighthouse
The **mothers** Gilmore, J.
The **mothers** Bennett, B.

MOTHERS -- DEATH

Ahava, S. Things that fall from the sky
Allen, S. The girl who chased the moon
Baker, K. The bird of the river
Barker, N. Darkmans
Brinkman, K. Up high in the trees
Byrne, T. Ghosts and lightning
Coetzee, J. Life & times of Michael K
Constantine, L. The last time I saw you
Evison, J. All about Lulu
Farah, N. Links
Greenfeld, K. True
Greengrass, J. Sight
Haywood, S. The cactus
Higgins, J. Edge of danger
Holdstock, P. Here I am!
Jin, M. Little gods
Kelly, E. The burning air
Kent, K. The heretic's daughter
King, L. Writers & lovers
Lansdale, J. Edge of dark water
Lipman, E. The dearly departed, Elinor Lipman.
Lipman, E. Good riddance
Macmillan, G. The perfect girl
Maguire, G. Son of a witch
Netzer, L. Shine shine shine
Porter, M. Grief is the thing with feathers
Rizzuto, R. Shadow child
Runcie, J. Canvey Island
Russell, K. Swamplandia!
Sainz Borgo, K. It would be night in Caracas
Sapphire The kid
Sargent, C. Museum of human beings
Sebold, A. The almost moon
Shafak, E. Honor
Souljah S. The coldest winter ever
St. Aubyn, E. At last
Straub, P. Lost boy lost girl
Tartt, D. The goldfinch
Tinti, H. The twelve lives of Samuel Hawley
Tyler, A. Celestial navigation
Van Vogt, A. Slan
Yoshimoto, B. The lake

MOTHERS -- PSYCHOLOGY

McKinty, A. The chain

MOTHERS AND DAUGHTERS

Abbott, J. The three Beths
Abbott, P. Concrete angel
Aliu, X. Brass
Allen, S. Garden spells

Oates, J. Blonde
Oyeyemi, H. Boy, Snow, Bird
Oyeyemi, H. Gingerbread
Packer, A. Songs without words
Picoult, J. Keeping faith
Picoult, J. Leaving time
Pinborough, S. Cross her heart
Pronzini, B. Crazybone
Quindlen, A. Object lessons
Quinn, S. The right side
Ragan, T. Buried deep
Rayne, S. Property of a lady
Redhill, M. Consolation
Reichs, K. Deja dead
Riley, L. The girl on the cliff
Robards, K. Ghost moon
Robb, C. A twisted vengeance
Robinson, K. Aurora
Rosner, J. The yellow bird sings
Rotert, R. Last night at the blue angel
Rouda, K. The favorite daughter
Ryan, J. The spies of Shilling Lane
Sandford, J. Mind prey
Sarton, M. A reckoning
Schwarz, C. Drowning Ruth
Scottoline, L. After Anna
Sebold, A. The almost moon
See, L. Dreams of joy
See, L. The tea girl of Hummingbird Lane
Semple, M. Where'd you go, Bernadette
Seth, V. A suitable boy
Shafak, E. The bastard of Istanbul
Shaw, W. Salt lane
Shields, C. Unless
Shimotakahara, L. After the bloom
Shipman, V. The heirloom garden
Shreve, A. The pilot's wife
Silver, E. The execution of Noa P. Singleton
Simpson, M. Anywhere but here
Slaughter, K. Pieces of her
Smith, A. How to be both
Smith, L. Fair and tender ladies
Solomon, A. Leaving Lucy Pear
Stage, Z. Baby teeth
Straight, S. A million nightingales
Strout, E. Amy and Isabelle
Strout, E. Anything is possible
Strout, E. My name is Lucy Barton
Styles, T. Raunchy
Styles, T. Raunchy 2
Tan, A. The bonesetter's daughter
Tan, A. The Valley of Amazement
Tatlock, A. Promises to keep
Tepper, S. Singer from the sea
Trueblood, V. Seven loves
Tsukiyama, G. Dreaming water
Tudor, C. The other people

Tyers, K. Shivering world
Tyler, A. Dinner at the Homesick Restaurant
Unger, L. The red hunter
Vann, D. Aquarium
Vida, V. Let the Northern Lights erase your name
Vine, B. Anna's book
Vine, B. The minotaur
Walls, J. The silver star
Walton, J. Among others
Watson, J. Asta in the wings
Weiner, J. Little earthquakes
Wieland, L. Paris, 7 a.m.
Wolitzer, H. Hearts
Woodson, J. Red at the bone
Wrobel, S. Darling Rose Gold
Zailckas, K. Mother, mother
Zevin, G. Young Jane Young

MOTHERS AND DAUGHTERS -- IRAN
Amirrezvani, A. The blood of flowers

MOTHERS AND DAUGHTERS -- LOS ANGELES, CALIFORNIA
Tan, A. The kitchen god's wife

MOTHERS AND DAUGHTERS -- MEXICO
Esquivel, L. Like water for chocolate

MOTHERS AND DAUGHTERS -- NETHERLANDS
Chevalier, T. Girl with a pearl earring

MOTHERS AND DAUGHTERS -- OHIO
Bialosky, J. House under snow

MOTHERS AND DAUGHTERS -- SAN FRANCISCO, CALIFORNIA
Tan, A. The Joy Luck Club

MOTHERS AND SONS
Barton, F. The suspect
Bear, E. Blood and iron
Beck, H. Lost you
Bourdeaut, O. Waiting for Bojangles
Box, C. Badlands
Boyne, J. The heart's invisible furies
Brinkman, K. Up high in the trees
Brouwer, S. Thief of glory
Brown, T. Gods of Howl Mountain
Buehlman, C. The Suicide Motor Club
Carey, L. The stolen child
Carey, P. His illegal self
Carlson, M. A Christmas by the sea
Child, L. The enemy
Cleveland, K. Keep you close
Colin, E. The memory thief
Colvin, J. Africaville
Cunningham, M. The hours
Cush, J. Endangered
Cusk, R. Transit
Daoud, K. The Meursault investigation
Drury, T. Pacific
Epperson, T. Sailor
Everett, P. Erasure
Everett, P. Suder

Cole, A. A duke by default
Cole, A. An extraordinary union
Cole, A. A hope divided
Cole, A. A prince on paper
Cole, A. A princess in theory
Cole, A. An unconditional freedom
Dev, S. A Bollywood affair
Dev, S. The Bollywood bride
Dev, S. A distant heart
Dev, S. Pride, prejudice, and other flavors
Guillory, J. The proposal
Guillory, J. Royal holiday
Guillory, J. The wedding date
Guillory, J. The wedding party
Hibbert, T. Get a life, Chloe Brown
Hibbert, T. A girl like her
Hoang, H. The bride test
Hodges, C. Rumor has it
Jackson, B. Forged in desire
Jenkins, B. Breathless
Jenkins, B. Forbidden
Jenkins, B. Rebel
Jenkins, B. Tempest
Kitt, S. Celluloid memories
Lalli, S. The matchmaker's list
Loren, R. The one you fight for
Martin, A. Blitzed
Martin, A. Fumbled
Oliveras, P. Their perfect melody
Pope, J. One warm winter
Rai, A. The right swipe
Ryan, K. Long shot
Weatherspoon, R. A cowboy to remember
Weatherspoon, R. Rafe
Weatherspoon, R. Xeni
Williams, S. Forbidden promises

MULTICULTURALISM
Conde, M. The story of the cannibal woman
  Everyday people
Jaswal, B. Erotic stories for Punjabi widows

MULTINATIONAL CORPORATIONS
Fforde, J. Lost in a good book

MULTIPLE SCLEROSIS
Price, R. The good priest's son

MULTIRACIAL BOYS
Fowler, T. A good neighborhood
Grey, Z. Woman of the frontier
Murr, N. The perfect man
Washington, B. Lot

MULTIRACIAL CHILDREN
Durrow, H. The girl who fell from the sky
Faye, L. The Paragon Hotel
George, E. What came before he shot her
Jackson, J. The almost sisters
Mda, Z. The Madonna of Excelsior
Ward, J. Sing, unburied, sing
Wiggs, S. The Oysterville sewing circle

MULTIRACIAL GIRLS
Brennert, A. Daughter of Moloka'i
Jen, G. The resisters
Mda, Z. The Madonna of Excelsior
Mengestu, D. The beautiful things that heaven bears
Oyeyemi, H. Boy, Snow, Bird

MULTIRACIAL MEN
Aaronovitch, B. Midnight riot
Amis, M. Lionel Asbo
Burdett, J. Bangkok 8
Dev, S. Pride, prejudice, and other flavors
Edugyan, E. Half-blood blues
Faulkner, W. Light in August
Furst, A. The foreign correspondent
Holmes, J. How are you going to save yourself
Jenkins, B. Forbidden
Krueger, W. Vermilion drift
Michener, J. Mexico
Mosley, W. John Woman
Nunn, M. Present darkness
Owen, H. The bottom
Owen, H. Oregon Hill
Owen, H. Parker Field
Penney, S. The invisible ones
Shields, K. A study in revenge
Vanderhaeghe, G. The last crossing

MULTIRACIAL PERSONS
Brown, R. Half a heart
Divakaruni, C. Oleander girl
Franck, J. Blindness of the heart
Grenville, K. Sarah Thornhill
Humphreys, J. Nowhere else on earth
Kincaid, J. The autobiography of my mother
Kunzru, H. The impressionist
Lee, D. Country of origin
McQuiston, C. Red, white & royal blue
Mda, Z. The Madonna of Excelsior
Muller, M. Cyanide Wells
Newman, S. The heavens
Orange, T. There there
Rodriguez, L. Every last secret
Ryan, K. Long shot
Senna, D. New people
Styles, T. Redbone
Tademy, L. Cane River

MULTIRACIAL PERSONS -- IDENTITY
Warren, R. Band of angels

MULTIRACIAL TEENAGERS
Straight, S. A million nightingales

MULTIRACIAL WOMEN
Ashford, J. What the duke doesn't know
Christopher, A. Not the girl you marry
Clemmons, Z. What we lose
Cole, A. A hope divided
Collins, S. The confessions of Frannie Langton
Donati, S. Where the light enters
Erdrich, L. The painted drum

Brown, R. Murder at Monticello, or, Old sins
Brown, R. Wish you were here
Brown, S. Fat Tuesday
Brownmiller, S. Waverly Place
Bruen, K. Galway girl
Buchan, J. The thirty-nine steps
Buckman, D. Because the rain
Buehlman, C. The Suicide Motor Club
Bulgakov, M. The master and Margarita
Burke, A. The better sister
Burke, J. The New Iberia blues
Burnet, G. His bloody project
Burns, R. Body slam
Bussi, M. Black water lilies
Byrne, K. How to love a duke in ten days
Camp, B. The city of lost fortunes
Campisi, M. Sin eater
Carter, S. New England white
Castillo, L. Shamed
Catton, E. The luminaries
Chabon, M. The Yiddish Policemen's Union
Chandler, R. The lady in the lake
Chandler, R. The long goodbye
Chanter, C. The well
Charlton, B. Spellwright
Cheever, J. Bullet Park
Child, L. Bad luck and trouble
Child, L. Echo burning
Child, L. Make me
Child, L. Never go back
Child, L. Night school
Child, L. No middle name
Child, L. Personal
Child, L. A wanted man
Childs, L. Lavender blue murder
Christie, A. Endless night
Christie, A. The pale horse
Clark, M. Blood defense
Clark, M. Death wears a beauty mask and other stories
Clark, M. Final judgment
Clark, M. I've got my eyes on you
Clark, M. The Jezebel remedy
Clark, M. The melody lingers on
Clark, M. My gal Sunday
Cleave, P. Trust no one
Cleeves, A. Raven black
Cleeves, A. The long call
Clements, R. Martyr
Clinch, J. Finn
Coben, H. Don't let go
Cogman, G. The mortal word
Collins, M. The wrong Quarry
Conde, M. The story of the cannibal woman
Connelly, M. The black ice
Connolly, S. The lost traveller
Cook, R. Coma
Cook, R. Genesis

Cook, T. The fate of Katherine Carr
Cook, T. Instruments of night
Corey, J. Abaddon's gate
Corey, J. Caliban's war
Cornwell, B. The last kingdom
Cornwell, P. Chaos
Cotterill, C. The coroner's lunch
Cotterill, C. Disco for the departed
Cotterill, C. Grandad, there's a head on the beach
Cotterill, C. Killed at the whim of a hat
Cotterill, C. Slash and burn
Coulter, C. Labyrinth
Coyle, M. Yesterday's echo
Crais, R. Chasing darkness
Crais, R. Demolition angel
Crais, R. A dangerous man
Crombie, D. A bitter feast
Crombie, D. Mourn not your dead
Crombie, D. Water like a stone
Cross, N. Luther. The calling
Cumming, C. The Trinity Six
Cussler, C. Celtic empire
Dahl, J. Conviction
Dallas, S. Tallgrass
Davis, L. The ides of April
Davis, L. One virgin too many
Dazieri, S. Kill the king
De Giovanni, M. The bastards of Pizzofalcone
DeLillo, D. The names
DeMille, N. Wild fire
DeSilva, B. Providence rag
DeSilva, B. Rogue Island
DeSilva, B. A scourge of vipers
Deane, S. Reading in the dark
Dexter, P. Paris Trout
Dickens, C. Oliver Twist, or The parish boy's progress
Dickens, C. Our mutual friend
Dickinson, P. The yellow room conspiracy
Didion, J. A book of common prayer
Dimon, H. Her other secret
Disher, G. Under the cold bright lights
Doiron, P. The precipice
Donoghue, E. The wonder
Dostoyevsky, F. Crime and punishment
Downie, R. Terra incognita
Dreiser, T. An American tragedy
Du Maurier, D. Jamaica Inn
Dunne, D. Too much money
Ebershoff, D. The 19th wife
Eco, U. The name of the rose
Eco, U. Numero zero
Elias, G. Danse macabre
Elkins, A. A long time coming
Elkins, A. Unnatural selection
Ellis, B. Lunar Park
Ellison, J. Good girls lie
Ellory, R. Saints of New York

Horowitz, A. Moriarty	King, S. It
Horowitz, A. The sentence is death	Knopf, C. The last refuge
Horowitz, A. The word is murder	Knopf, C. You're dead
Howarth, P. Only killers and thieves	Koontz, D. The husband
Hunter, S. The 47th samurai	Koontz, D. Innocence
Hunter, S. I, sniper	Koryta, M. The prophet
Hunter, S. Time to hunt	Koryta, M. The ridge
Hurwitz, G. Into the fire	Krentz, J. Running hot
Huston, C. Half the blood of Brooklyn	Krentz, J. White lies
Indriðason, A. Reykjavik nights	Kristin Omarsdottir, 1. Children in Reindeer Woods
Indriðason, A. The shadow district	Krueger, W. Ordinary grace
Iles, G. Cemetery road	Krueger, W. Vermilion drift
Iles, G. The devil's punchbowl	LaPlante, A. A circle of wives
Iles, G. The footprints of God	LaPlante, A. Turn of mind
Iles, G. Turning angel	Lackberg, C. The hidden child
Irwin, S. The dead path	Lackberg, C. The ice princess
Isaacs, S. As husbands go	Lackberg, C. The lost boy
JaQuavis The dopeman's wife	Lackberg, C. The preacher
Jackson, S. The lottery	Lackberg, C. The stonecutter
Jacobs, N. The last equation of Isaac Severy	Lange, R. Angel baby
James, J. Something about you	Langton, J. The deserter
James, P. Innocent blood	Langton, J. The thief of Venice
James, P. The lighthouse	Larsson, A. Until thy wrath be past
Jemisin, N. The fifth season	Larsson, S. The girl who played with fire
Jemisin, N. The killing moon	Lashner, W. A killer's kiss
Jemisin, N. The obelisk gate	Lathen, E. Brewing up a storm
Jemisin, N. The stone sky	Lathen, E. East is east
Jewell, L. Watching you	Lathen, E. Something in the air
Johnson, C. Death without company	Laurens, S. Devil's bride
Johnson, K. Little black girl lost 2	Lawrence, M. Hearts and bones
Jungstedt, M. The inner circle	Le Carre, J. The spy who came in from the cold
K'wan Diamonds and Pearl	Lehane, D. Mystic river
K'wan Hoodlum	Lehane, D. Since we fell
K'wan Lawless	Lent, J. A slant of light
Kaminsky, S. Murder on the Trans-Siberian Express	Leon, D. The girl of his dreams
Katsu, A. The hunger	Lescroart, J. The hearing
Keller, J. Bone on bone	Lescroart, J. Nothing but the truth
Keller, J. Fast falls the night	Lescroart, J. The oath
Keller, J. A killing in the hills	Levin, I. A kiss before dying
Kellerman, F. Milk and honey	Link, C. The other child
Kellerman, J. Bones	Link, C. The watcher
Kellerman, J. Gone	Lippman, L. Hardly knew her
Kelly, E. Broadchurch	Lippman, L. No good deeds
Kelly, S. The wages of desire	Lippman, L. Sunburna
Kelton, E. Texas vendetta	Lippman, L. What the dead know
Kemelman, H. Monday the rabbi took off	Littlejohn, E. Lost Lake
Kemelman, H. One fine day the rabbi bought a cross	Lloyd, C. Death comes to the nursery
Kemelman, H. Thursday the Rabbi walked out	Locke, A. The cutting season
Kennedy, D. The big picture	Longworth, M. Murder on the Ile Sordou
Kennedy, W. Ironweed	Lovesey, P. Bertie and the seven bodies
Kerr, P. Field gray	Lovesey, P. Skeleton Hill
Kerr, P. The lady from Zagreb	Lovesey, P. Waxwork
Kerr, P. A man without breath	Lovett, C. The bookman's tale
Kerstan, L. Heart of the tiger	Lowe, K. The furies
Kim, Y. Diary of a murderer	Lundrigan, N. Glass boys
King, D. Bitch	MacBride, S. Dying light
King, S. End of watch	MacDonald, J. Cinnamon skin

Paretsky, S. Blood shot
Paretsky, S. Burn marks
Paretsky, S. Dead land
Paretsky, S. Guardian angel
Paretsky, S. Fire sale
Paretsky, S. Hard time
Paretsky, S. Indemnity only
Paretsky, S. Total recall
Paretsky, S. Tunnel vision
Paretsky, S. Windy city blues
Paris, B. The breakdown
Parker, R. Brimstone
Parker, R. Now and then
Parker, T. Cold pursuit
Parker, R. Sea change
Parker, T. The fallen
Parshall, S. Bleeding through
Parshall, S. Poisoned ground
Parsons, K. Doing harm
Patterson, R. Dark lady
Pattison, E. Beautiful ghosts
Pattison, E. Blood of the oak
Pattison, E. Bones of the earth
Pattison, E. Prayer of the dragon
Pearl, M. The Poe shadow
Pears, I. An instance of the fingerpost
Pelecanos, G. Shame the devil
Pelevin, V. The hall of singing caryatids
Peloquin, L. Dark rooms
Penney, S. The tenderness of wolves
Penny, L. A better man
Penny, L. Bury your dead
Penny, L. Glass houses
Penny, L. A great reckoning
Penny, L. Kingdom of the blind
Penny, L. Still life
Penny, L. A trick of the light
Penrose, A. Murder at Kensington Palace
Perez-Reverte, A. The siege
Perkins, S. Murder once removed
Perry, A. Buckingham Palace gardens
Perry, A. A Christmas message
Perry, A. Death on Blackheath
Perry, A. Midnight at Marble Arch
Perry, T. Dead aim
Persson, L. Another time, another life
Persson, L. Free falling, as if in a dream
Pessl, M. Night film
Pessl, M. Special topics in calamity physics
Petrie, N. Burning bright
Piccirilli, T. The last kind words
Picoult, J. Change of heart
Pope, B. The missing Italian girl
Porter, H. The bell ringers
Price, R. Lush life
Pronzini, B. The violated
Pryor, M. Hollow man

Pynchon, T. Bleeding edge
Pyne, D. Twentynine Palms
Quartey, K. Gold of our fathers
Quartey, K. Wife of the gods
Quick, A. 'Til death do us part
Quincy, D. Murder at the opera
Quincy, D. Murder in Mayfair
Quirk, M. Dead man switch
Racculia, K. Bellweather rhapsody
Ragan, T. Buried deep
Raimondo, L. Dante's dilemma
Ramsay, F. Stranger room
Randisi, R. Hey there (you with the gun in your hand)
Rankin, I. Blood hunt
Rankin, I. Exit music
Rankin, I. The naming of the dead
Rankin, I. Rather be the devil
Rankin, I. Set in darkness
Raybourn, D. A murderous relation
Read, C. The crazy school
Redfern, E. The music of the spheres
Redondo, D. The invisible guardian
Reichs, K. Bare bones
Reichs, K. Bones of the lost
Reichs, K. Bones to ashes
Reichs, K. Break no bones
Reichs, K. Deadly decisions
Reichs, K. Grave secrets
Reichs, K. Monday mourning
Rendell, R. The bridesmaid
Rendell, R. Collected stories
Rendell, R. Live flesh
Rendell, R. The tree of hands
Reynolds, A. The prefect
Richards, L. Death was in the blood
Richmond, M. No one you know
Rigosi, G. Night bus
Rinehart, M. The circular staircase
Rinehart, M. Miss Pinkerton
Robb, C. The cross-legged knight
Robb, J. Innocent in death
Robb, J. Naked in death
Roberts, N. Come sundown
Roberts, N. The obsession
Robinson, L. Murder at the feast of rejoicing
Robinson, L. Murder at the god's gate
Robinson, P. All the colors of darkness
Robinson, P. Close to home
Robinson, P. Friend of the devil
Robinson, P. Piece of my heart
Robinson, P. Playing with fire
Robinson, P. Strange affair
Robotham, M. The night ferry
Rodriguez, L. Every broken trust
Rodriguez, L. Every hidden fear
Rollins, J. The eye of God
Rollins, J. The sixth extinction

Smith, M. The Siberian dilemma
Smith, M. Stalin's ghost
Smith, M. Three stations
Smith, M. Tatiana
Smith, S. A simple plan
Smith, T. Agent 6
Smith, T. The secret speech
Soderberg, A. The other son
Solomon, B. The attempted murder of Teddy Roosevelt
Somer, M. The serenity murders
Soule, M. The crows
Spain, J. With our blessing
Spann, S. Blade of the Samurai
Spann, S. Claws of the cat
Spark, M. The driver's seat
Spencer, S. Best served cold
Spencer, S. Death's dark shadow
Spencer, S. A dying fall
Spencer, S. The hidden
Spencer, S. Man in the woods
Spencer, S. Thicker than water
Spencer-Fleming, J. Through the evil days
Spillane, M. Kill me, darling
Stabenow, D. A fine and bitter snow
Stabenow, D. A night too dark
Stanley, M. A carrion death
Stark, R. The jugger
Steiner, S. Persons unknown
Stott, R. Ghostwalk
Strange, M. Follow me down
Straub, P. A dark matter
Straub, P. Mystery
Stroby, W. Some die nameless
Styles, T. A hustler's son
Sundstol, V. The land of dreams
Swanson, P. Her every fear
Swanson, P. The kind worth killing
Tartt, D. The secret history
Tey, J. The daughter of time
Thomas, S. Oligarchy
Thompson, J. The killer inside me
Transgressions
Tudor, C. The chalk man
Turnbull, C. The lesson
Turner, N. Forever a hustler's wife
Tursten, H. Hunting game
Turton, S. The 7 1
Umrigar, T. The weight of heaven
Unger, L. The stranger inside
Unger, L. Under my skin
Vandermeer, J. Finch
Vasquez, J. The sound of things falling
Vaughn, C. Bannerless
Verble, M. Cherokee America
Vine, B. Anna's book
Vine, B. The chimney sweeper's boy
Vine, B. The House of Stairs

Vine, B. The minotaur
Walker, W. Crime of privilege
Walton, J. Farthing
Wambaugh, J. Floaters
Ward, A. Forgive me
Ware, R. In a dark, dark wood
Ware, R. The woman in cabin ten
Warren, R. World enough and time
Waters, S. The paying guests
Watkins, J. Secrets of a side bitch
Watkins, J. Secrets of a side bitch 2
Wellington, D. Positive
Wells, H. The invisible man
Wiesel, E. Dawn
Williams, B. The golden hour
Williams, K. Dirty to the grave
Winspear, J. Maisie Dobbs
Wolfe, P. The lost diary of M
Woods, S. Chiefs
Woods, S. New York dead
Woods, S. Orchid beach
Woods, S. Palindrome
Woods, S. Santa Fe rules
Woods, T. Alibi
Woods, T. Dutch
Yi, C. The investigation
Zan, K. The never list
Zane Addicted
Zimler, R. The last Kabbalist of Lisbon
Zimmer, M. Wild side of the river
deWitt, P. Undermajordomo Minor

MURDER -- ALABAMA
McCammon, R. Boy's life
MURDER -- ALASKA
Stabenow, D. A deeper sleep
MURDER -- CALIFORNIA
Macdonald, R. Sleeping beauty
MURDER -- CHINA
Qiu, X. Don't cry Tai Lake
Qiu, X. Enigma of China
MURDER -- COTSWOLD, ENGLAND
Dexter, C. The remorseful day
MURDER -- FLORIDA
Matthiessen, P. Killing Mister Watson
MURDER -- HISTORY
Robertson, I. Anatomy of murder
MURDER -- ICELAND
Ridpath, M. Far north
MURDER -- ILLINOIS
McInerny, R. Requiem for a realtor
MURDER -- IRELAND
Nugent, A. Soul murder
MURDER -- JAPAN
Rowland, L. The incense game
MURDER -- KENYA
Le Carre, J. The constant gardener
MURDER -- LOS ANGELES, CALIFORNIA

Armstrong, K. Watcher in the woods
Arsenault, E. The broken teaglass
Arvin, R. Blood of angels
Atkins, A. The innocents
Atkins, A. The ranger
Atkins, A. Wicked city
Avon, J. In peppermint peril
Ayatsuji, Y. The Decagon House murders
Bailey, M. An appetite for violets
Baldacci, D. The fallen
Baldacci, D. Long road to mercy
Baldacci, D. One good deed
Baldacci, D. Redemption
Bannalec, J. Death in Brittany
Bannalec, J. The killing tide
Bannister, J. Silent footsteps
Barclay, L. Broken promise
Barclay, L. Far from true
Barclay, L. No safe house
Barclay, L. A noise downstairs
Barclay, L. Parting shot
Barclay, L. Trust your eyes
Barclay, L. The twenty-three
Barnard, R. Death of a literary widow
Bartz, A. The lost night
Bauer, B. Snap
Bayard, L. The black tower
Bayard, L. The pale blue eye
Beaton, M. Agatha Raisin and the quiche of death
Beaton, M. Agatha Raisin and the witch of Wyckhadden
Beaton, M. Death of a macho man
Beaton, M. Pushing up daisies
Benn, J. Billy Boyle
Bennett, R. City of miracles
Bennett, R. City of stairs
Berne, S. The dogs of Littlefield
Bernhard, E. The books of the dead
Berry, C. A legacy of murder
  The best American mystery stories 2018
  The best American mystery stories 2019
Beukes, L. Broken monsters
Billingham, M. Their little secret
Black, B. Christine Falls
Black, B. Wolf on a string
Black, C. Murder in the Bastille
Black, C. Murder in the Marais
Black, C. Murder in the rue de Paradis
Black, L. That darkness
Black, L. Let justice descend
Black, L. Suffer the children
Black, S. Anything for you
Blake, R. A dark anatomy
Block, L. The burglar in the library
Block, L. A drop of the hard stuff
Block, L. Eight million ways to die
Block, L. The sins of the fathers
Bolton, S. The craftsman

Bolton, S. A dark and twisted tide
Borjlind, C. Spring tide
Bouman, T. Dry bones in the valley
Box, C. Badlands
Box, C. Open season
Box, C. Trophy hunt
Box, C. Winterkill
Boyle, W. The lonely witness
Bradley, C. The grave's a fine and private place
Bradley, C. I am half-sick of shadows
Bradley, C. A red herring without mustard
Bradley, C. Speaking from among the bones
Bradley, C. The sweetness at the bottom of the pie
Bradley, C. The weed that strings the hangman's bag
Brandt, H. The Whites
Braun, L. The cat who ate Danish modern
Braun, L. The cat who went underground
Brett, S. Murder unprompted
Brett, S. The torso in the town
Brookmyre, C. When the devil drives
Brookmyre, C. Where the bodies are buried
Brooks, B. Blood storm
Brooks, B. Frontier justice
Brown, D. The Da Vinci code
Brown, R. The litter of the law
Brown, R. Murder at Monticello, or, Old sins
Brown, R. Wish you were here
Bruen, K. Cross
Bruen, K. Galway girl
Bruen, K. The guards
Buchanan, E. You only die twice
Burdett, J. Bangkok 8
Burke, A. The better sister
Burke, J. Black cherry blues
Burke, J. The New Iberia blues
Burke, J. Robicheaux
Burns, R. Body slam
Bussi, M. Black water lilies
Carpenter, E. The weight of lies
Carter, S. New England white
Castillo, L. A gathering of secrets
Castillo, L. Shamed
Child, L. The affair
Child, L. The enemy
Child, L. Full wolf moon
Child, L. Killing floor
Child, L. Make me
Child, L. Never go back
Child, L. Night school
Child, L. Personal
Child, L. A wanted man
Christie, A. The A B C murders
Christie, A. The body in the library
Christie, A. Curtain
Christie, A. The hollow
Christie, A. Mrs. McGinty's dead
Christie, A. The murder at the vicarage

Fesperman, D. Safe houses
Fielding, J. All the wrong places
Finch, C. A beautiful blue death
Finch, C. The last passenger
Finlay, M. The murder pit
Flynn, G. Sharp objects
Flyte, M. City of dark magic
Fossum, K. Bad intentions
Fossum, K. Eva's eye
Fowler, C. Bryant & May
Fox, C. Redemption point
Francis, F. Crisis
Francis, F. Guilty not guilty
Francis, F. Pulse
Frear, C. Stone cold heart
Frear, C. Sweet little lies
Fredericks, M. Death of a new American
Freeman, B. The night bird
Freeman, D. A lady's guide to etiquette and murder
French, N. Dark Saturday
French, N. The day of the dead
French, N. Friday on my mind
French, N. Sunday silence
French, N. Thursday's children
French, N. Tuesday's gone
French, N. Waiting for Wednesday
French, T. Broken harbor
French, T. In the woods
French, T. The likeness
French, T. The secret place
Friedman, D. Riot most uncouth
Gailey, S. Magic for liars
Galbraith, R. Career of evil
Galbraith, R. Lethal white
Galbraith, R. The silkworm
Gallagher, S. The bedlam detective
Garcia-Roza, L. Alone in the crowd
Gardiner, M. The Dirty Secrets Club
Gardner, L. Fear nothing
Gardner, L. Find her
Gardner, L. Look for me
Gardner, L. Love you more
Gardner, L. The neighbor
Gardner, L. Never tell
Garrett, K. Hollywood homicide
Gaylin, A. Never look back
Geagley, B. Year of the hyenas
George, E. Believing the lie
George, E. This body of death
George, E. Careless in red
George, E. The punishment she deserves
Gerritsen, T. The bone garden
Gilman, L. Hard magic
Giordano, M. Auntie Poldi and the Vineyards of Etna
Gleason, C. Murder at the capitol
Goddard, R. Never go back
Goenawan, C. Rainbirds

Goldman, M. The shallows
Goodman, C. The sea of lost girls
Gorman, E. Bad moon rising
Gorman, E. Riders on the storm
Grafton, S. "A" is for alibi
Grafton, S. X
Grafton, S. Y is for yesterday
Gran, S. Claire DeWitt and the city of the dead
Gran, S. The infinite blacktop
Greaves, C. Hush money
Grebe, C. After she's gone
Grebe, C. The ice beneath her
Greer, R. First of state
Griffiths, E. The dark angel
Griffiths, E. A dying fall
Griffiths, E. The stone circle
Griffiths, E. The stranger diaries
Grimes, M. The Old Wine Shades
Grindle, L. Villa Triste
Grisham, J. The guardians
Gross, A. Eyes wide open
Gross, A. Reckless
Gruber, M. Valley of bones
Guttridge, P. The thing itself
Haldane, S. The devil's making
Hall, P. Lights! Camera! Puzzles!
Hall, T. The case of the deadly butter chicken
Hambly, B. Lady of perdition
Hamill, P. Tabloid city
Hammett, D. The Maltese falcon
Hand, E. Curious toys
Hannah, S. The mystery of three quarters
Hanson, H. The driver
Harkaway, N. Gnomon
Harrington, A. An inconvenient duke
Harris, S. The color of Bee Larkham's murder
Harrison, C. Beyond absolution
Harrod-Eagles, C. Game over
Harrod-Eagles, C. Headlong
Harrod-Eagles, C. Old bones
Hart, C. Ghost gone wild
Hart, C. Resort to murder
Hart, C. White elephant dead
Hart, C. Yankee Doodle dead
Hart, E. The book of Killowen
Hart, E. City of ink
Harvey, J. Darkness, darkness
Harvey, M. The Chicago way
Hayder, M. Hanging hill
Harvey, M. Pulse
Hayder, M. Skin
Haywood, G. Cemetery Road
Hess, J. Maggody and the moonbeams
Hewson, D. The garden of evil
Hiaasen, C. Bad monkey
Higashino, K. Malice
Higashino, K. Newcomer

Lescroart, J. The oath
Lethem, J. Motherless Brooklyn
Levin, I. A kiss before dying
Limon, M. The line
Limon, M. Mr. Kill
Lin, J. The lotus palace
Link, C. The other child
Link, C. The watcher
Lippman, L. Hush hush
Lippman, L. Lady in the lake
Lippman, L. No good deeds
Lippman, L. What the dead know
Littlejohn, E. Inherit the bones
Lloyd, C. Death comes to the nursery
Locke, A. Bluebird, bluebird
Locke, A. The cutting season
Lodato, V. Mathilda Savitch
Longworth, M. Death at the Chateau Bremont
Longworth, M. Murder in the Rue Dumas
Longworth, M. Murder on the Ile Sordou
Lourey, J. January thaw
Lovesey, P. Beau death
Lovesey, P. Bertie and the seven bodies
Lovesey, P. Diamond dust
Lovesey, P. The house sitter
Lovesey, P. The last detective
Lovesey, P. Skeleton Hill
Lovesey, P. The tooth tattoo
Lovesey, P. The vault
Lovesey, P. Waxwork
Luna, L. The Janes
Lupton, R. Sister
MacBride, S. Dying light
MacDonald, J. Cinnamon skin
MacDonald, J. The green ripper
MacDonald, J. The lonely silver rain
MacDonald, J. The long lavender look
MacDonald, J. A purple place for dying
MacDonald, P. The list of Adrian Messenger
MacGregor, J. The bride who got lucky
Mackintosh, C. I let you go
Malliet, G. A fatal winter
Malliet, G. Pagan spring
Malliet, G. Wicked autumn
Mankell, H. The dogs of Riga
Mankell, H. Firewall
Mankell, H. The man who smiled
Mankell, H. One step behind
Mankell, H. The return of the dancing master
Mark, D. Cruel mercy
Mark, D. The dark winter
Mark, D. Original skin
Mark, D. Sorrow bound
Maron, M. Bootlegger's daughter
Maron, M. Shooting at loons
Maron, M. Storm track
Maron, M. Uncommon clay

Maron, M. Up jumps the Devil
Marsh, N. False scent
Marsh, N. Grave mistake
Marsh, N. Last ditch
Marsh, N. Light thickens
Marsh, N. When in Rome
Marston, E. The roaring boy
Marston, E. The vagabond clown
Massey, S. The Satapur moonstone
Massey, S. The widows of Malabar Hill
Mayor, A. Red herring
Mayor, A. The sniper's wife
Mayor, A. Tag man
McBain, E. The big bad city
McBain, E. Fat Ollie's book
McBain, E. The last dance
McBain, E. Nocturne
McCall Smith, A. The Double Comfort Safari Club
McCarthy, R. The hollow men
McClure, J. The steam pig
McCrumb, S. If ever I return, pretty Peggy-O
McDermid, V. The distant echo
McDermid, V. How the dead speak
McGuire, S. Chimes at midnight
McGuire, S. Every heart a doorway
McGuire, S. Once broken faith
McGuire, S. Rosemary and rue
McHugh, L. The wolf wants in
McInerny, R. Celt and pepper
McKevett, G. Murder in her stocking
McKevett, G. Murder in the corn maze
McKinty, A. The cold, cold ground
McKinty, A. In the morning I'll be gone
McPherson, C. The child garden
McPherson, C. Scot free
McPherson, C. Scot & soda
McPherson, C. A step so grave
McPherson, C. Strangers at the gate
Mcdonald, G. Fletch
Meier, L. Silver anniversary murder
Meyer, D. Devil's peak
Meyer, D. Icarus
Mieville, C. The city & the city
Mina, D. Conviction
Mina, D. The dead hour
Mina, D. The end of the wasp season
Mina, D. Gods and beasts
Mina, D. Slip of the knife
Miranda, M. The last house guest
Mizushima, M. Burning ridge
Mizushima, M. Killing trail
Mizushima, M. Stalking ground
Montclair, A. The right sort of man
Montero, M. Dancing to "Almendra"
Moor, J. The keeper
Moore, G. The Sherlockian
Moore, J. The night market

Parshall, S. Poisoned ground
Patterson, J. Along came a spider
Patterson, J. Private
Pattison, E. Blood of the oak
Pattison, E. Bones of the earth
Pattison, E. The lord of death
Pattison, E. Mandarin gate
Pattison, E. Prayer of the dragon
Pattison, E. The skull mantra
Pattison, E. Water touching stone
Pawel, R. Death of a nationalist
Pearce, M. A dead man in Barcelona
Pears, I. The immaculate deception
Pears, I. The last judgement
Pelecanos, G. The double
Peloquin, L. Dark rooms
Penman, S. Cruel as the grave
Penman, S. The Queen's man
Penny, L. A better man
Penny, L. Bury your dead
Penny, L. The cruelest month
Penny, L. Glass houses
Penny, L. A great reckoning
Penny, L. Kingdom of the blind
Penny, L. The nature of the beast
Penny, L. Still life
Penny, L. A trick of the light
Penrose, A. Murder at half moon gate
Penrose, A. Murder at Kensington Palace
Perez-Reverte, A. The siege
Perkins, S. Murder once removed
Perry, A. Bedford Square
Perry, A. Belgrave Square
Perry, A. Bethlehem Road
Perry, A. Bluegate Fields
Perry, A. A breach of promise
Perry, A. Buckingham Palace gardens
Perry, A. Cain his brother
Perry, A. Cardington Crescent
Perry, A. A Christmas return
Perry, A. A dangerous mourning
Perry, A. Death of a stranger
Perry, A. Death on Blackheath
Perry, A. Defend and betray
Perry, A. The face of a stranger
Perry, A. Farriers' Lane
Perry, A. Funeral in blue
Perry, A. Half Moon Street
Perry, A. Highgate Rise
Perry, A. The Hyde Park headsman
Perry, A. Midnight at Marble Arch
Perry, A. Paragon Walk
Perry, A. Pentecost Alley
Perry, A. Resurrection Row
Perry, A. Seven Dials
Perry, A. The shifting tide
Perry, A. The silent cry

Perry, A. The sins of the wolf
Perry, A. Slaves of obsession
Perry, A. Southampton Row
Perry, A. A sunless sea
Perry, A. Traitors Gate
Perry, A. The twisted root
Perry, A. Weighed in the balance
Perry, A. The Whitechapel conspiracy
Perry, T. Fidelity
Persson, L. Free falling, as if in a dream
Pessl, M. Special topics in calamity physics
Peters, E. The deeds of the disturber
Peters, E. Fallen into the pit
Peters, E. The golden one
Peters, E. Lion in the valley
Peters, E. The mummy case
Peterson, J. Early's fall
Phillips, C. Unthinkable
Phillips, J. Quiet dell
Piccirilli, T. The last kind words
Picoult, J. House rules
Pinter, J. Hide away
Pintoff, S. In the shadow of Gotham
Pirrone, D. Shall we not revenge
Pobi, R. City of windows
Polansky, D. Low town
Pope, B. The missing Italian girl
Potenza, C. Hearts of the missing
Potzsch, O. The beggar king
Potzsch, O. The dark monk
Potzsch, O. The hangman's daughter
Potzsch, O. The play of death
Potzsch, O. The poisoned pilgrim
Potzsch, O. The werewolf of Bamberg
Pratchett, T. Thud!
Preston, D. City of endless night
Price, R. Lush life
Price, S. By gaslight
Pronzini, B. Spook
Pronzini, B. The violated
Putnam, J. These honored dead
Quartey, K. Gold of our fathers
Quartey, K. Murder at Cape Three Points
Quick, A. Garden of lies
Quick, A. The girl who knew too much
Quick, A. The other lady vanishes
Quincy, D. Murder at the opera
Quincy, D. Murder in Mayfair
Rader-Day, L. Little pretty things
Ragan, T. Deranged
Raichev, R. Assassins at Ospreys
Raimondo, L. Dante's dilemma
Raimondo, L. Dante's poison
Raimondo, L. Dante's wood
Ramsay, F. Countdown
Ramsay, F. Scone Island
Rankin, I. The black book

Sandford, J. Mortal prey
Sandford, J. Naked prey
Sandford, J. Night prey
Sandford, J. Phantom prey
Sandford, J. Rules of prey
Sandford, J. Silken prey
Sansom, C. Sovereign
Sansom, C. Tombland
Saums, M. Thistle & Twigg
Saunders, K. The secrets of Wishtide
Sayers, D. Busman's honeymoon
Sayers, D. Clouds of witness
Sayers, D. The documents in the case
Sayers, D. The five red herrings
Sayers, D. Gaudy night
Sayers, D. Hangman's holiday
Sayers, D. Have his carcase
Sayers, D. In the teeth of the evidence
Sayers, D. Lord Peter
Sayers, D. Murder must advertise
Sayers, D. The nine tailors
Sayers, D. Strong poison
Sayers, D. Thrones, dominations
Sayers, D. The unpleasantness at the Bellona Club
Sayers, D. Whose body?
Saylor, S. A mist of prophecies
Saylor, S. Rubicon
Scalzi, J. Head on
Scalzi, J. Lock in
Scerbanenco, G. A private Venus
Schmidt, S. See what I have done
Schofield, D. Time of departure
Scoppettone, S. Everything you have is mine
Scoppettone, S. Gonna take a homicidal journey
Scoppettone, S. My sweet untraceable you
Scoppettone, S. Too darn hot
Scott, A. Beneath the abbey wall
Scott, A. A double death on the Black Isle
Scott, A. The low road
Scott, A. A kind of grief
Scott, J. Mausoleum
Scottoline, L. Come home
Scottoline, L. Don't go
Sedgwick, M. Mister Memory
Sedley, K. The Tintern treasure
See, L. Dragon bones
Sepetys, R. Out of the Easy
Serafim, L. The devil takes half
Serafim, L. When the devil's idle
Shames, T. An unsettling crime for Samuel Craddock
Shannon, D. Chaos of crime
Shannon, D. The Manson curse
Sharfeddin, H. Mineral spirits
Shaw, W. The birdwatcher
Shaw, W. Salt lane
Shaw, W. A song for the brokenhearted
Shelton, P. Thin ice

Shepherd, L. A fatal likeness
Shoham, L. Asylum city
Siger, J. Mykonos after midnight
Siger, J. Target Tinos
Silver, E. The execution of Noa P. Singleton
Silvis, R. Two days gone
Simenon, G. Maigret and the black sheep
Simenon, G. Maigret and the fortuneteller
Simenon, G. Maigret and the killer
Simenon, G. Maigret and the madwoman
Simenon, G. Maigret and the Saturday caller
Simenon, G. Maigret and the toy village
Simenon, G. Maigret and the wine merchant
Simenon, G. Maigret bides his time
Simenon, G. Maigret goes home
Simenon, G. Maigret in Holland
Simenon, G. My friend Maigret
Simmons, D. The fifth heart
Simon, C. Dogs don't lie
Simon, C. Grey dawn
Simon, C. Panthers play for keeps
Simon, C. Stages of Grey
Simon, M. Cremains of the day
Simpson, D. Dead and gone
Simpson, D. Dead by morning
Simpson, D. Doomed to die
Simpson, D. Last seen alive
Simpson, D. No laughing matter
Simpson, R. Let the dead keep their secrets
Sjowall, M. Cop killer
Sjowall, M. The locked room
Slaughter, K. Fallen
Slaughter, K. Criminal
Slaughter, K. The kept woman
Smith, B. Crow's landing
Smith, B. Shoot the dog
Smith, C. Silent city
Smith, D. The constable's tale
Smith, F. Night fall
Smith, J. Crescent City kill
Smith, J. House of blues
Smith, J. Jazz funeral
Smith, J. New Orleans beat
Smith, M. Havana Bay
Smith, M. Polar Star
Smith, M. Red Square
Smith, M. She smiled sweetly
Smith, M. She's not there
Smith, M. Stalin's ghost
Smith, M. Three stations
Smith, M. Wolves eat dogs
Solomon, B. The murder of Willie Lincoln
Somer, M. The serenity murders
Soule, M. The crows
Spain, J. With our blessing
Spann, S. Blade of the Samurai
Spencer, S. Best served cold

MURDER INVESTIGATION -- NOTTINGHAM, ENG-LAND

Harvey, J. Cold in hand

MURDER INVESTIGATION -- ORANGE COUNTY, CALIFORNIA

Rosenberg, N. Interest of justice

MURDER INVESTIGATION -- QUEBEC (PROVINCE)

Penny, L. The beautiful mystery

MURDER INVESTIGATION -- ROME

Davis, L. One virgin too many

MURDER INVESTIGATION -- SAN FRANCISCO, CALIFORNIA

Pronzini, B. Savages

MURDER INVESTIGATION -- SAUDI ARABIA

Ferraris, Z. Kingdom of strangers

MURDER INVESTIGATION -- SCOTLAND

May, P. The blackhouse

MURDER INVESTIGATION -- SHANGHAI, CHINA

Qiu, X. Death of a red heroine
Qiu, X. When red is black

MURDER INVESTIGATION -- SUSSEX, ENGLAND

Robertson, I. Instruments of darkness

MURDER INVESTIGATION -- SWEDEN

Kepler, L. The hypnotist
Mankell, H. Before the frost
Mankell, H. The man from Beijing

MURDER INVESTIGATION -- TEXAS

Child, L. Echo burning

MURDER INVESTIGATION -- UTAH

Zimmer, M. The long hitch

MURDER INVESTIGATION -- VIRGINIA

McCrumb, S. If I'd killed him when I met him

MURDER INVESTIGATION -- WALES

Robb, C. A gift of Sanctuary

MURDER INVESTIGATION -- WASHINGTON, D.C.

Ellory, R. A simple act of violence

MURDER INVESTIGATION -- WISCONSIN

Tracy, P. Monkeewrench

MURDER INVESTIGATION -- YORKSHIRE, ENGLAND

Robinson, P. Cold is the grave
Robinson, P. Innocent graves

A **murder** is announced Christie, A.

Murder most royal Plaidy, J.

Murder must advertise Sayers, D.

The **murder** of Roger Ackroyd Christie, A.

The **murder** of Willie Lincoln Solomon, B.

Murder on Black Swan Lane Penrose, A.

Murder on the Ile Sordou Longworth, M.

Murder on the Orient Express Christie, A.

Murder on the Trans-Siberian Express Kaminsky, S.

Murder once removed Perkins, S.

Murder one Dugoni, R.

MURDER PARTIES

Hart, C. Murder walks the plank

The **murder** pit Finlay, M.

MURDER SUSPECTS

Abbott, J. Blame

Adams, E. The secret, book & scone society
Andrew, S. Recipes for love and murder
Baldacci, D. One good deed
Barnes, J. The somnambulist
Bayard, L. The black tower
Beaton, M. Agatha Raisin and the quiche of death
Beaton, M. Death of a macho man
Beaton, M. Pushing up daisies
Black, C. Murder in the rue de Paradis
Box, C. Vicious circle
Boylan, J. Long black veil
Brown, R. Before and after
Buchanan, C. The painted girls
Burke, A. The better sister
Burke, J. Robicheaux
Burnet, G. The disappearance of Adele Bedeau
Callaghan, M. Billy, come home
Cavanagh, S. Thirteen
Chaon, D. Ill will
Child, L. Full wolf moon
Child, L. Killing floor
Christie, A. Curtain
Christie, A. The hollow
Christie, A. Mrs. McGinty's dead
Christie, A. The murder at the vicarage
Christie, A. A murder is announced
Christie, A. The murder of Roger Ackroyd
Christie, A. The pale horse
Clark, M. Final judgment
Clark, M. I've got my eyes on you
Coben, H. Don't let go
Coben, H. Run away
Collins, S. The confessions of Frannie Langton
Cook, R. Charlatans
Corleone, D. Gone cold
Cotterill, C. Killed at the whim of a hat
Coyle, M. Yesterday's echo
Cush, J. Endangered
Davis, L. The ides of April
Doiron, P. The poacher's son
Dolan, H. Bad things happen
Downie, R. Semper Fidelis
Dunn, K. The Dragonfly
Elias, G. Danse macabre
Fitzpatrick, L. Lights all night long
Flynn, G. Gone girl
Francis, F. Guilty not guilty
Franklin, A. The serpent's tale
Freed, D. Hot start
French, N. Dark Saturday
French, N. The day of the dead
French, N. Friday on my mind
French, N. Sunday silence
Garcia-Roza, L. Alone in the crowd
Gardiner, M. Into the black nowhere
Gardner, L. The neighbor
George, E. Believing the lie

Royal, P. Sanctity of hate
Rozan, S. Paper son
Sanders, J. Speakers of the dead
Sanders, L. The fourth deadly sin
Saums, M. Thistle & Twigg
Schaitkin, A. Saint X
Scott, J. Mausoleum
Scottoline, L. After Anna
Scottoline, L. Every fifteen minutes
Sedgwick, M. Mister Memory
Serafim, L. When the devil's idle
Silvis, R. Two days gone
Simon, C. Grey dawn
Spencer, S. The dead hand of history
Spencer, S. The hidden
Spencer, S. Thicker than water
Stout, R. Gambit
Swanson, P. Eight perfect murders
Thomas, R. Firewatching
Tyree, O. Leslie
Walton, J. Farthing
Welsh, K. The unquiet heart
White, S. Compound fractures
Whittle, T. The dangerous edge of things
Williams, B. The summer wives
Wroblewski, D. The story of Edgar Sawtelle
Yap, F. Yesterday
Yocum, R. A welcome murder

MURDER SUSPECTS -- GREAT BRITAIN
Peters, E. The pilgrim of hate

MURDER SUSPECTS -- SAN FRANCISCO, CALIFORNIA
Pronzini, B. Savages
Murder unprompted Brett, S.

MURDER VICTIMS
Anderson, K. Death warmed over
Barclay, L. Elevator pitch
Black, S. Anything for you
Bohjalian, C. Secrets of Eden
Brandt, H. The Whites
Brown, S. Ricochet
Brundage, E. All things cease to appear
Cash, W. The last ballad
Christie, A. And then there were none
Cole, D. Ragdoll
Cook, T. A dancer in the dust
Coulter, C. Paradox
Cross-Smith, L. Whiskey & ribbons
Daugherty, C. Revolver road
Davies, R. Murther and walking spirits
Erpenbeck, J. Visitation
French, N. The lying room
Goldman, M. The shallows
Grebe, C. After she's gone
Hannah, S. The mystery of three quarters
Harrison, C. Beyond absolution
Hawkins, P. The girl on the train

Hill, J. Horns
Hurwitz, G. Into the fire
Kasasian, M. Dark dawn over Steep House
Kellerman, J. The genius
Kepler, L. The hypnotist
Khan, A. The unquiet dead
Kubica, M. The other Mrs.
Lafferty, M. Six wakes
Lansdale, J. Edge of dark water
Matthiessen, P. Shadow country
Meyer, D. Icarus
Mina, D. The long drop
Montgomery, J. The widows
Moody, D. Hater
Neuhaus, N. The ice queen
O'Brien, E. In the forest
Palwick, S. Mending the moon
Phillips, C. A distant shore
Pronzini, B. Spook
Pronzini, B. The violated
Reichs, K. A conspiracy of bones
Rosenfelt, D. Bark of night
Sebold, A. The lovely bones
Shepard, S. Reputation
Simpson, R. What the dead leave behind
Smith, F. Night fall
Sveistrup, S. The chestnut man
Swanson, P. Eight perfect murders
Tey, J. The daughter of time
Murder walks the plank Hart, C.

MURDER WITNESSES
Barclay, L. A noise downstairs
Barclay, L. Trust your eyes
Boyle, W. The lonely witness
Dodd, C. Virtue Falls
Freeman, B. Goodbye to the dead
Hawkins, P. The girl on the train
James, J. Something about you
Kaminsky, S. Tomorrow is another day
Keller, J. A killing in the hills
Koontz, D. The husband
Koryta, M. Those who wish me dead
Leonard, E. Tishomingo blues
Levine, J. Bingo's run
McCammon, R. Boy's life
Miller, D. Norwegian by night
Newitz, A. The future of another timeline
O'Connell, C. The man who cast two shadows
Oates, J. My life as a rat
Paris, B. The breakdown
Parks, G. The learning tree
Phillips, C. Unthinkable
Salvalaggio, K. Bone dust white
Simon, C. Panthers play for keeps
Sjowall, M. The man on the balcony
Skyhorse, B. Madonnas of Echo Park
Smith, J. New Orleans beat

Harrod-Eagles, C. Headlong
Hayder, M. Birdman
Hayder, M. Skin
Jakeman, J. In the kingdom of mists
O'Connell, C. Find me
Price, S. By gaslight
Spencer, S. Backlash
Tallis, F. Vienna blood

MUTINY

Johnson, C. Middle Passage
Lambdin, D. King's captain
Nordhoff, C. Men against the sea
Nordhoff, C. Pitcairn's Island
O'Brian, P. The unknown shore
Poe, E. The narrative of Arthur Gordon Pym of Nantucket
Simmons, D. The Terror
Unsworth, B. Sacred hunger
Varley, J. Dark lightning
Wouk, H. The Caine mutiny

Mutiny on the Bounty [series] Nordhoff, C.

MUTISM

Davidson, A. The boatman's daughter
My Antonia Cather, W.
My beautiful enemy Thomas, S.
My best friend's exorcism Hendrix, G.
My boyfriend's wife Mychea
My brilliant career Franklin, M.
My brilliant friend Ferrante, E.
My dark Vanessa Russell, K.
My education Choi, S.
My father's tears and other stories Updike, J.
My friend Maigret Simenon, G.
My gal Sunday Clark, M.
My grandmother asked me to tell you she's sorry Backman, F.
My husband's wife Corry, J.
My Jim Rawles, N.
My lady notorious Beverley, J.
My lady's choosing Curran, K.
My liar Cline, R.
My life as a fake Carey, P.
My life as a man Roth, P.
My life as a rat Oates, J.
My lord and spymaster Bourne, J.
My lovely wife Downing, S.
My man Jeeves Wodehouse, P.
My name is Asher Lev Potok, C.
My name is Lucy Barton Strout, E.
My name is memory Brashares, A.
My name is Red Pamuk, O.
My name is Resolute Turner, N.
My nine lives Jhabvala, R.
My notorious life Manning, K.
My one and only duke Burrowes, G.
My Oxford year Whelan, J.
My real children Walton, J.
My revolutions Kunzru, H.
My sister, the serial killer Braithwaite, O.

My sister's grave Dugoni, R.
My sister's keeper Picoult, J.
My son's story Gordimer, N.
My struggle [series] Knausgaard, K.
My struggle. Knausgaard, K.
My sunshine away Walsh, M.
My sweet untraceable you Scoppettone, S.
My year of rest and relaxation Moshfegh, O.

MYCENAE (EXTINCT CITY)

George, M. Helen of Troy
Toibin, C. House of names

MYCOTOXICOSES

Sayers, D. The documents in the case
Mycroft and Sherlock Abdul-Jabbar, K.
Mycroft Holmes Abdul-Jabbar, K.
Mycroft Holmes novels (Kareem Abdul-Jabbar) [series]
Abdul-Jabbar, K.

MYKONOS (ISLAND) -- SOCIAL LIFE AND CUSTOMS

Siger, J. Mykonos after midnight
Mykonos after midnight Siger, J.
Myron Bolitar mysteries [series] Coben, H.

MYRTLE BEACH, SOUTH CAROLINA

Koryta, M. Tonight I said goodbye

MYSTERIES

Abani, C. The secret history of Las Vegas
Abdul-Jabbar, K. Mycroft and Sherlock
Abdul-Jabbar, K. Mycroft Holmes
Abdul-Jabbar, K. The empty birdcage
Abu-Jaber, D. Origin
Akunin, B. The coronation
Akunin, B. Sister Pelagia and the white bulldog
Albert, S. Bittersweet
Allende, I. Ripper
Amis, M. London fields
Anappara, D. Djinn patrol on the purple line
Anderson, K. Death warmed over
Andrews, M. Sunset Beach
Armstrong, K. Alone in the wild
Armstrong, K. Watcher in the woods
Arsenault, E. The broken teaglass
Arsenault, E. In search of the Rose notes
Atkinson, K. Big sky
Atkinson, K. Case histories
Atkinson, K. One good turn
Atkinson, K. Started early, took my dog
Atkinson, K. When will there be good news?
Ayatsuji, Y. The Decagon House murders
Ball, J. In the heat of the night
Bannalec, J. Death in Brittany
Bannister, J. Kindred spirits
Bannister, J. Silent footsteps
Barclay, L. Broken promise
Barclay, L. Far from true
Barclay, L. Parting shot
Barclay, L. A tap on the window
Barclay, L. The twenty-three
Barnard, R. Death of a literary widow

Cook, T. The crime of Julian Wells
Cook, T. A dancer in the dust
Cook, T. The fate of Katherine Carr
Cook, T. Instruments of night
Corby, G. The Marathon conspiracy
Corby, G. The Pericles Commission
Cornwell, P. Chaos
Cornwell, P. Postmortem
Cotterill, C. The coroner's lunch
Cotterill, C. Disco for the departed
Cotterill, C. Don't eat me
Cotterill, C. Grandad, there's a head on the beach
Cotterill, C. Killed at the whim of a hat
Cotterill, C. The second biggest nothing
Cotterill, C. Slash and burn
Coyle, M. Yesterday's echo
Craig, P. A shoot on Martha's Vineyard
Craig, P. Third strike
Craig, P. A vineyard killing
Crais, R. Chasing darkness
Crais, R. A dangerous man
Crais, R. The first rule
Crombie, D. A bitter feast
Crombie, D. Kissed a sad goodbye
Crombie, D. Mourn not your dead
Crombie, D. Water like a stone
Crompton, R. Hell's gate
Crompton, R. Hour of the red god
Cross, A. The collected stories
Cross, N. Luther. The calling
Crumley, J. The final country
Crumley, J. The last good kiss
Crumley, J. The wrong case
Dahl, A. Bad Blood
Dahl, A. Misterioso
Dahl, J. Conviction
Dahl, K. The courier
Davis, L. A body in the bathhouse
Davis, L. The ides of April
Davis, L. One virgin too many
Davys, T. Amberville
De Giovanni, M. The bastards of Pizzofalcone
DePoy, P. Sidewalk saint
DeSilva, B. Providence rag
DeSilva, B. Rogue Island
DeSilva, B. A scourge of vipers
Deaver, J. The coffin dancer
Deaver, J. The empty chair
Deaver, J. Garden of beasts
Deaver, J. The stone monkey
Deveraux, J. A willing murder
Dexter, C. The daughters of Cain
Dexter, C. The remorseful day
Dexter, C. The way through the woods
Dibdin, M. Ratking
Dickinson, P. The yellow room conspiracy
Disher, G. Under the cold bright lights

Dobyns, S. Saratoga payback
Doiron, P. Almost midnight
Doiron, P. Stay hidden
Dolan, H. Bad things happen
Dolan, H. Very bad men
Downie, R. Caveat emptor
Downie, R. Medicus
Downie, R. Semper Fidelis
Downie, R. Tabula rasa
Downie, R. Terra incognita
Doyle, A. The complete Sherlock Holmes
Dugoni, R. My sister's grave
Dunning, J. Booked to die
Dunning, J. The bookman's wake
Edwardson, A. Sail of stone
Elias, G. Danse macabre
Elias, G. Death and transfiguration
Elkins, A. Dying on the vine
Elkins, A. A long time coming
Elkins, A. Unnatural selection
Ellory, R. Saints of New York
Ellory, R. A simple act of violence
Eriksson, K. The princess of Burundi
Eskens, A. The heavens may fall
Eskens, A. Nothing more dangerous
Estleman, L. Amos Walker
Estleman, L. Infernal angels
Estleman, L. A smile on the face of the tiger
Evanovich, J. Look alive twenty-five
Evanovich, J. One for the money
Evanovich, J. Turbo twenty-three
Farrow, J. The storm murders
Faye, L. The gods of Gotham
Faye, L. Seven for a secret
Ferraris, Z. Finding Nouf
Ferraris, Z. Kingdom of strangers
Finch, C. A beautiful blue death
Finch, C. The September Society
Ford, J. The shadow year
Fossum, K. Bad intentions
Fossum, K. Eva's eye
Fowler, C. Bryant & May
Fox, C. Gone by midnight
Franklin, A. Mistress of the art of death
Franklin, A. The serpent's tale
Freed, D. Hot start
Friedman, D. Don't ever get old
Friedman, D. Running out of road
Gailey, S. Magic for liars
Galbraith, R. Career of evil
Galbraith, R. The cuckoo's calling
Galbraith, R. Lethal white
Galbraith, R. The silkworm
Garcia-Roza, L. Alone in the crowd
Garcia-Roza, L. December heat
Gardiner, M. The Dirty Secrets Club
Garrett, K. Hollywood homicide

Isaacs, S. After all these years

Isaacs, S. As husbands go

Ishiguro, K. When we were orphans

Jacobs, N. The last equation of Isaac Severy

Jakeman, J. In the kingdom of mists

James, P. The black tower

James, P. A certain justice

James, P. Death in holy orders

James, P. Death of an expert witness

James, P. Devices and desires

James, P. The lighthouse

James, P. Original sin

James, P. The private patient

James, P. The skull beneath the skin

James, P. A taste for death

James, P. An unsuitable job for a woman

Jance, J. Birds of prey

Jance, J. Queen of the night

Jance, J. Skeleton Canyon

Jenkins, V. An unattended death

Jio, S. The last camellia

Johnson, C. Another man's moccasins

Johnson, C. Dark horse

Johnson, C. Death without company

Johnson, D. Detroit shuffle

Johnson, C. Hell is empty

Johnson, C. Land of wolves

Johnson, C. Spirit of steamboat

Jones, J. The silence

Jungstedt, M. The inner circle

Kaminsky, S. Dancing in the dark

Kaminsky, S. A fatal glass of beer

Kaminsky, S. Murder on the Trans-Siberian Express

Kaminsky, S. To catch a spy

Kaminsky, S. Tomorrow is another day

Katzenbach, J. Just cause

Keating, H. The soft detective

Keller, J. Bone on bone

Keller, J. Fast falls the night

Keller, J. A killing in the hills

Keller, J. Last ragged breath

Kellerman, F. The forgotten

Kellerman, F. Jupiter's bones

Kellerman, F. Milk and honey

Kellerman, F. Prayers for the dead

Kellerman, F. Serpent's tooth

Kellerman, J. Bones

Kellerman, J. The clinic

Kellerman, J. Devil's waltz

Kellerman, J. The genius

Kellerman, J. Gone

Kellerman, J. Monster

Kellerman, J. Private eyes

Kellerman, J. Self-defense

Kellerman, J. Therapy

Kellerman, J. Time bomb

Kelly, E. Broadchurch

Kelly, J. The fire baby

Kelly, J. The moon tunnel

Kemelman, H. Monday the rabbi took off

Kemelman, H. One fine day the rabbi bought a cross

Kemelman, H. Thursday the Rabbi walked out

Kepler, L. The hypnotist

Kepler, L. The rabbit hunter

Kepler, L. The sandman

Kerley, J. The death collectors

Kerr, P. Field gray

Kerr, P. The lady from Zagreb

Kerr, P. A man without breath

Kerr, P. March violets

Khan, V. The perplexing theft of the jewel in the crown

Kienzle, W. The rosary murders

King, L. The beekeeper's apprentice

King, L. The game

Knopf, C. Dead anyway

Knopf, C. The last refuge

Knopf, C. You're dead

Koenig, M. Nine days

Koryta, M. How it happened

Koryta, M. Tonight I said goodbye

Krentz, J. River road

Krueger, W. Ordinary grace

Krueger, W. Vermilion drift

LaPlante, A. A circle of wives

LaPlante, A. Turn of mind

Lackberg, C. The ice princess

Lackberg, C. The hidden child

Lackberg, C. The lost boy

Lackberg, C. The preacher

Lackberg, C. The stonecutter

Lagercrantz, D. The girl in the spider's web

Lagercrantz, D. The girl who lived twice

Lagercrantz, D. The girl who takes an eye for an eye

Lalami, L. The other Americans

Lamberson, G. The frenzy way

Langton, J. The deserter

Langton, J. Murder at Monticello

Langton, J. The thief of Venice

Lansdale, J. The bottoms

Lansdale, J. Devil red

Lansdale, J. Honky tonk samurai

Lansdale, J. Sunset and sawdust

Lansdale, J. Vanilla Ride

Larsson, A. Until thy wrath be past

Larsson, S. The girl who kicked the hornet's nest

Larsson, S. The girl who played with fire

Larsson, S. The girl with the dragon tattoo

Lawrence, D. The dead sit round in a ring

Lee, D. Country of origin

Lehane, D. Prayers for rain

Lehane, D. Sacred

Leon, D. About face

Leon, D. Beastly things

Leon, D. Blood from a stone

McCall Smith, A. The forgotten affairs of youth
McCall Smith, A. The lost art of gratitude
McCammon, R. Boy's life
McCarthy, R. A handful of ashes
McCarthy, R. The hollow men
McClure, J. The steam pig
McCrumb, S. If ever I return, pretty Peggy-O
McCrumb, S. If I'd killed him when I met him
McDermid, V. The distant echo
McDermid, V. How the dead speak
McDermid, V. A place of execution
McGarrity, M. Everyone dies
McGown, J. Murder at the old vicarage
McGown, J. Verdict unsafe
McInerny, R. Celt and pepper
McInerny, R. Irish coffee
McInerny, R. Requiem for a realtor
McMahon, J. The one I left behind
McPherson, C. The child garden
McPherson, C. Quiet neighbors
McPherson, C. Scot & soda
McPherson, C. Scot free
Mcdonald, G. Fletch
Meno, J. The boy detective fails
Meyer, N. The adventure of the peculiar protocols
Meyer, N. The seven-per-cent solution
Miller, D. American by day
Mina, D. The dead hour
Mina, D. The end of the wasp season
Mina, D. Field of blood
Mina, D. Gods and beasts
Mina, D. The red road
Mina, D. Slip of the knife
Mina, D. Still midnight
Mizushima, M. Burning ridge
Mizushima, M. Killing trail
Mizushima, M. Stalking ground
Moor, J. The keeper
Moore, C. Sacre bleu
Mortimer, J. Felix in the underworld
Mortimer, J. Quite honestly
Mortimer, J. Rumpole's return
Morton, C. Stealing Mona Lisa
Moshfegh, O. Death in her hands
Mosley, W. All I did was shoot my man
Mosley, W. And sometimes I wonder about you
Mosley, W. Bad boy Brawly Brown
Mosley, W. Black Betty
Mosley, W. Blonde faith
Mosley, W. Charcoal Joe
Mosley, W. Cinnamon kiss
Mosley, W. Devil in a blue dress
Mosley, W. Down the river unto the sea
Mosley, W. Gone fishin'
Mosley, W. Known to evil
Mosley, W. Little green
Mosley, W. Little Scarlet

Mosley, W. A little yellow dog
Mosley, W. The long fall
Mosley, W. A red death
Mosley, W. Rose gold
Mosley, W. Six Easy pieces
Mosley, W. Trouble is what I do
Mosley, W. When the thrill is gone
Mosley, W. White butterfly
Muller, M. Both ends of the night
Muller, M. The broken promise land
Muller, M. Burn out
Muller, M. The cavalier in white
Muller, M. City of whispers
Muller, M. Cyanide Wells
Muller, M. The dangerous hour
Muller, M. Dead midnight
Muller, M. The ever-running man
Muller, M. There's something in a Sunday
Muller, M. Point Deception
Muller, M. Vanishing point
Muller, M. A walk through the fire
Muller, M. Where echoes live
Muller, M. While other people sleep
Muller, M. A wild and lonely place
Muller, M. Wolf in the shadows
Munier, P. A borrowing of bones
Nabb, M. Some bitter taste
Nadel, B. The Ottoman cage
Nava, M. Carved in bone
Neel, J. To die for
Neely, B. Blanche cleans up
Nelscott, K. Stone cribs
Nesbo, J. The bat
Nesbo, J. Cockroaches
Nesbo, J. The devil's star
Nesbo, J. The leopard
Nesbo, J. Nemesis
Nesbo, J. Phantom
Nesbo, J. Police
Nesbo, J. The redbreast
Nesbo, J. The redeemer
Nesbo, J. The snowman
Nesbo, J. The thirst
Neuhaus, N. The ice queen
Neuhaus, N. Snow White must die
Nickson, C. At the dying of the year
Nickson, C. Cold cruel winter
Nickson, C. Come the fear
Nickson, C. The constant lovers
Nugent, A. Soul murder
Nunn, M. A beautiful place to die
Nunn, M. Blessed are the dead
Nunn, M. Present darkness
Nykanen, H. Nights of awe
O'Connell, C. Blind sight
O'Connell, C. The chalk girl
O'Connell, C. Crime school

Penman, S. Dragon's lair

Penney, S. The invisible ones

Penman, S. The Queen's man

Penney, S. The tenderness of wolves

Penny, L. The beautiful mystery

Penny, L. A better man

Penny, L. Bury your dead

Penny, L. The cruelest month

Penny, L. Glass houses

Penny, L. A great reckoning

Penny, L. How the light gets in

Penny, L. Kingdom of the blind

Penny, L. The long way home

Penny, L. The nature of the beast

Penny, L. Still life

Penny, L. A trick of the light

Perez-Reverte, A. The Club Dumas

Perez-Reverte, A. The fencing master

Perry, A. Bedford Square

Perry, A. Belgrave Square

Perry, A. Bethlehem Road

Perry, A. Blind justice

Perry, A. Bluegate Fields

Perry, A. A breach of promise

Perry, A. Buckingham Palace gardens

Perry, A. Cain his brother

Perry, A. Cardington Crescent

Perry, A. A dangerous mourning

Perry, A. Death of a stranger

Perry, A. Death on Blackheath

Perry, A. Defend and betray

Perry, A. The face of a stranger

Perry, A. Farriers' Lane

Perry, A. Funeral in blue

Perry, A. Half Moon Street

Perry, A. Highgate Rise

Perry, A. The Hyde Park headsman

Perry, A. Midnight at Marble Arch

Perry, A. Paragon Walk

Perry, A. Pentecost Alley

Perry, A. Resurrection Row

Perry, A. Seven Dials

Perry, A. The shifting tide

Perry, A. The silent cry

Perry, A. The sins of the wolf

Perry, A. Slaves of obsession

Perry, A. Southampton Row

Perry, A. A sunless sea

Perry, A. Traitors Gate

Perry, A. The twisted root

Perry, A. Weighed in the balance

Perry, A. The Whitechapel conspiracy

Perry, T. Dead aim

Perry, T. Death benefits

Perry, T. Fidelity

Perry, T. Pursuit

Persson, L. The dying detective

Pessl, M. Special topics in calamity physics

Peters, E. Brother Cadfael's penance

Peters, E. Children of the storm

Peters, E. Dead man's ransom

Peters, E. Death to the landlords!

Peters, E. The deeds of the disturber

Peters, E. Fallen into the pit

Peters, E. The golden one

Peters, E. Guardian of the horizon

Peters, E. He shall thunder in the sky

Peters, E. The hermit of Eyton Forest

Peters, E. The hippopotamus pool

Peters, E. The holy thief

Peters, E. The last camel died at noon

Peters, E. Lion in the valley

Peters, E. Monk's hood

Peters, E. The mummy case

Peters, E. Night train to Memphis

Peters, E. The pilgrim of hate

Peters, E. The potter's field

Peters, E. Seeing a large cat

Peters, E. A rare Benedictine

Peters, E. The rose rent

Peters, E. St. Peter's fair

Peters, E. The sanctuary sparrow

Peters, E. The snake, the crocodile, and the dog

Peters, E. The summer of the Danes

Peters, E. Trojan gold

Peters, E. The virgin in the ice

Peterson, J. Early's fall

Phillips, C. The Devlin diary

Phillips, C. The Rossetti letter

Phillips, C. Unthinkable

Pickard, N. The scent of rain and lightning

Pintoff, S. In the shadow of Gotham

Pirie, D. The patient's eyes

Pirro, J. Sly fox

The plot thickens

Pobi, R. City of windows

Pochoda, I. Visitation Street

Poe, E. Complete stories and poems of Edgar Allan Poe

Poole, S. The Borgia mistress

Pope, B. The missing Italian girl

Potenza, C. Hearts of the missing

Potzsch, O. The beggar king

Potzsch, O. The dark monk

Potzsch, O. The hangman's daughter

Potzsch, O. The poisoned pilgrim

Potzsch, O. The werewolf of Bamberg

Price, R. Clockers

Pronzini, B. Blue lonesome

Pronzini, B. Bones

Pronzini, B. Crazybone

Pronzini, B. Fever

Pronzini, B. Hardcase

Pronzini, B. Hellbox

Pronzini, B. Illusions

Rodriguez, L. Every broken trust
Rodriguez, L. Every hidden fear
Rodriguez, L. Every last secret
Roorbach, B. Life among giants
Rose, J. The blackest bird
Rosen, L. The tenth witness
Rosenberg, N. Interest of justice
Rosenfelt, D. Bark of night
Roslund, A. Pen 33
Ross, A. Mr. Peanut
Rowland, L. Bedlam
Rowland, L. The incense game
Rowland, L. The iris fan
Rowland, L. The secret adventures of Charlotte Bronte
Rowland, L. The Shogun's daughter
Rowland, L. The snow empress
Rowland, R. Cold country
Rowson, P. Death lies beneath
Rowson, P. Undercurrent
Royal, P. Sanctity of hate
Rozan, S. Paper son
Rozan, S. The Shanghai Moon
Rozan, S. Winter and night
Rubenfeld, J. The interpretation of murder
Runcie, J. Sidney Chambers and the forgiveness of sins
Runcie, J. Sidney Chambers and the perils of the night
Runcie, J. Sidney Chambers and the persistence of love
Runcie, J. Sidney Chambers and the problem of evil
Runcie, J. Sidney Chambers and the shadow of death
Russell, S. The insane train
Ryan, H. The other woman
Ryan, H. Say no more
Ryan, H. Truth be told
Ryan, H. What you see
Ryan, H. The wrong girl
Ryan, W. The darkening field
Ryan, W. The twelfth department
Sallis, J. The killer is dying
Salvalaggio, K. Bone dust white
Sanders, L. The first deadly sin
Sanders, L. The fourth deadly sin
Sanders, L. McNally's dilemma
Sanders, L. McNally's gamble
Sanders, L. McNally's luck
Sanders, L. McNally's puzzle
Sanders, L. McNally's secret
Sanders, L. McNally's trial
Sanders, L. The second deadly sin
Sanders, L. The sixth commandment
Sanders, L. The tenth commandment
Sanders, L. The third deadly sin
Sanders, L. The Timothy files
Sanders, L. Timothy's game
Sansom, C. Lamentation
Sansom, C. Revelation
Sansom, C. Sovereign
Sansom, C. Tombland

Sansom, I. The case of the missing books
Sayers, D. Thrones, dominations
Sayers, D. Busman's honeymoon
Sayers, D. Clouds of witness
Sayers, D. The documents in the case
Sayers, D. The five red herrings
Sayers, D. Gaudy night
Sayers, D. Hangman's holiday
Sayers, D. Have his carcase
Sayers, D. In the teeth of the evidence
Sayers, D. Lord Peter
Sayers, D. Murder must advertise
Sayers, D. The nine tailors
Sayers, D. Strong poison
Sayers, D. The unpleasantness at the Bellona Club
Sayers, D. Whose body?
Saylor, S. The house of the Vestals
Saylor, S. The judgment of Caesar
Saylor, S. A mist of prophecies
Saylor, S. Raiders of the Nile
Saylor, S. Rubicon
Saylor, S. The seven wonders
Saylor, S. The triumph of Caesar
Saylor, S. Wrath of the furies
Scerbanenco, G. A private Venus
Scerbanenco, G. Traitors to all
Schlink, B. Self's deception
Schlink, B. Self's murder
Schlink, B. Self's punishment
Schofield, D. Time of departure
Scoppettone, S. Everything you have is mine
Scoppettone, S. Gonna take a homicidal journey
Scoppettone, S. My sweet untraceable you
Scott, A. Beneath the abbey wall
Scott, A. A double death on the Black Isle
Scott, A. The low road
Scott, A. A kind of grief
Scott, J. Mausoleum
See, L. Dragon bones
Sepetys, R. Out of the Easy
Serafim, L. The devil takes half
Serafim, L. When the devil's idle
Shames, T. An unsettling crime for Samuel Craddock
Shames, T. A risky undertaking for Loretta Singletary
Shannon, D. Chaos of crime
Sharfeddin, H. Mineral spirits
Sharp, Z. Second shot
Shaw, W. The birdwatcher
Shefchik, R. Amen corner
Shelton, P. Thin ice
Shields, K. A study in revenge
Shields, K. The truth of all things
Shoham, L. Asylum city
Shrier, H. Boston cream
Sidor, S. The mirror's edge
Sidor, S. Skin River
Siger, J. Mykonos after midnight

Tey, J. The daughter of time
Thomas, R. Firewatching
Tokarczuk, O. Drive your plow over the bones of the dead
Transgressions
Turner, N. Heartbreak of a hustler's wife
Turton, S. The 7 1
Walton, J. Farthing
Wambaugh, J. Finnegan's week
Wambaugh, J. Floaters
Whittle, T. The dangerous edge of things
Winslow, D. The dawn patrol
Winspear, J. The American agent
Winspear, J. Birds of a feather
Winspear, J. Maisie Dobbs
Yocum, R. A welcome murder
Zimler, R. The seventh gate
Zimmerman, J. The orphanmaster
de Beauvoir, J. Asylum
The **mysteries** of Udolpho Radcliffe, A.
The **mysterious** flame of Queen Loana Eco, U.
The **mysterious** island Verne, J.
Mystery Straub, P.

MYSTERY AND DETECTIVE STORIES
Grant, H. The glass demon

MYSTERY BOOKSTORE OWNERS
Hart, C. Murder walks the plank

MYSTERY BOOKSTORE OWNERS -- SOUTH CAROLINA
Hart, C. Death walked in
Hart, C. White elephant dead
Hart, C. Yankee Doodle dead
The **mystery** of three quarters Hannah, S.

MYSTERY STORY WRITERS
Cook, T. Instruments of night
Hart, C. Murder walks the plank
Horowitz, A. The sentence is death
Horowitz, A. The word is murder
Morgan, S. Miracle on 5th Avenue
Quick, A. 'Til death do us part
Sayers, D. Have his carcase

MYSTERY STORY WRITING
Estleman, L. A smile on the face of the tiger
Mystery with recipes [series] Crawford, I.
The **mystery** woman Quick, A.
Mystic Creek novels [series] Anderson, C.
Mystic river Lehane, D.

MYSTICISM
Bennett, R. The troupe
Cotterill, C. Disco for the departed
Koontz, D. Innocence
Shafak, E. The bastard of Istanbul
Zimler, R. The last Kabbalist of Lisbon

MYSTICISM -- CHRISTIANITY
Rock, P. The shelter cycle

MYSTICS
Mitchell, D. The bone clocks
Murakami, H. The wind-up bird chronicle

MYTHICAL CREATURES
Beagle, P. The last unicorn
Beagle, P. The unicorn sonata
Gaiman, N. Norse mythology
Martineau, M. Kingdom of exiles
Porter, M. Lanny
Sherrill, S. The minotaur takes his own sweet time
Wecker, H. The golem and the jinni

MYTHOLOGICAL FICTION
Arden, K. The bear and the nightingale
Arden, K. The girl in the tower
Arden, K. The winter of the witch
Barker, P. The silence of the girls
Barth, J. Chimera
Bear, E. All the windwracked stars
Bear, E. Blood and iron
Bear, E. Ink and steel
Byatt, A. Ragnarok
Gaiman, N. American gods
Gaiman, N. Anansi boys
Gaiman, N. Norse mythology
Hand, E. Mortal love
Kazinski, A. The last good man
Lewis, C. Till we have faces
Marillier, J. Daughter of the forest
McDonald, I. River of gods
Miller, M. Circe
Momaday, N. The ancient child
Moreno-Garcia, S. Gods of jade and shadow
Oyeyemi, H. The opposite house
Power, S. The grass dancer
Sherrill, S. The minotaur takes his own sweet time
Tesh, E. Silver in the wood
Toibin, C. House of names
Unsworth, B. The songs of the kings
Walton, J. Necessity
Zelazny, R. Lord of light

MYTHOLOGY
Tepper, S. The visitor

MYTHOLOGY, AZTEC
Bowles, D. Feathered serpent, dark heart of sky

MYTHOLOGY, CELTIC
Hamill, P. Forever
Marillier, J. Daughter of the forest

MYTHOLOGY, CLASSICAL
MacLaughlin, N. Wake, siren

MYTHOLOGY, FOLKLORE, AND LEGENDS
Gaiman, N. Norse mythology

MYTHOLOGY, GREEK
Barth, J. Chimera
George, M. Helen of Troy
Miller, M. Circe
Toibin, C. House of names

MYTHOLOGY, JUDAIC
Kazinski, A. The last good man

MYTHOLOGY, NORSE
Byatt, A. Ragnarok

Tolstoy, L. War and peace
Willig, L. The deception of the emerald ring
Willig, L. The garden intrigue
Willig, L. The lure of the moonflower
Willig, L. The masque of the Black Tulip
Willig, L. The secret history of the Pink Carnation
Willig, L. The seduction of the Crimson Rose
Winterson, J. The passion

NAPOLEONIC WARS, 1800-1815 -- NAVAL OPERATIONS

O'Brian, P. Master and commander

NAPOLEONIC WARS, 1800-1815 -- NAVAL OPERATIONS, BRITISH

Forester, C. Beat to quarters
Forester, C. Flying colours
Forester, C. Hornblower and the Atropos
Forester, C. Hornblower and the Hotspur
Forester, C. Lieutenant Hornblower
Forester, C. Lord Hornblower
Forester, C. Mr. Midshipman Hornblower
Forester, C. Ship of the line
O'Brian, P. The commodore
O'Brian, P. The hundred days

NARCISSISM

Seton, A. Dragonwyck
Walker, W. Emma in the night
Zailckas, K. Mother, mother

NARCISSISM IN WOMEN

Weldon, F. Worst fears

Narcissus and Goldmund Hesse, H.

NARCOTICS INVESTIGATION

Kent, K. The burn
Kent, K. The dime

The **narrative** of Arthur Gordon Pym of Nantucket Poe, E.

The **narrow** road to the deep north Flanagan, R.

NARVAEZ, PANFILO DE, -1528

Lalami, L. The Moor's account

NASH, RICHARD, 1674-1761

Lovesey, P. Beau death

NASHVILLE, TENNESSEE

Adams, L. The bromance book club
Alexander, T. A note yet unsung
Arvin, R. Blood of angels
Creech, S. The whole way home
Martin, C. Long way gone

NASSAU, BAHAMAS

Williams, B. The golden hour

Natalie Tan's book of luck and fortune Lim, R.

Natchez burning Iles, G.

NATCHEZ, MISSISSIPPI

Iles, G. The bone tree
Iles, G. The devil's punchbowl
Iles, G. Mississippi blood
Iles, G. Natchez burning
Iles, G. Turning angel

Nathan Heller novels [series] Collins, M.

NATIONAL CHARACTERISTICS

Makumbi, J. Kintu

NATIONAL CHARACTERISTICS, AMERICAN

Gaiman, N. American gods

NATIONAL CHARACTERISTICS, ENGLISH

Barnes, J. England, England
Mitford, N. The pursuit of love ;

NATIONAL GALLERY (GREAT BRITAIN)

Aridjis, C. Asunder

NATIONAL LIBERATION MOVEMENTS

Furst, A. A hero of France
Hammad, I. The Parisian, or, Al-Barisi

NATIONAL PARKS AND RESERVES -- WEST TEXAS

Barr, N. Track of the cat

NATIONAL SECURITY

Baldacci, D. Hell's Corner
Bell, T. Overkill
Brown, D. The Kremlin strike
Brown, D. The Moscow offensive
Cameron, M. Code of honor
Cameron, M. Oath of office
Cameron, M. Power and empire
Church, J. Bamboo and blood
Church, J. A corpse in the Koryo
Coes, B. Bloody Sunday
Coonts, S. The armageddon file
Coonts, S. The Russia account
Eisler, B. The god's eye view
Finder, J. The switch
Ohlsson, K. Hostage
Parnell, S. Man of war
Porter, H. Firefly
Rollins, J. The devil colony
Rollins, J. The eye of God
Rollins, J. The sixth extinction
Simmons, D. The fifth heart
Slaughter, K. The last widow
Stross, C. Empire Games
Tata, A. Dark winter
Wouk, H. A hole in Texas

NATIONAL SECURITY -- UNITED STATES

Child, L. Bad luck and trouble

NATIONAL TRANSPORTATION SAFETY BOARD.

Haynes, D. Crashers

NATIONAL UNDERWATER AND MARINE AGENCY

Cussler, C. Blue gold
Cussler, C. Celtic empire
Cussler, C. Ghost ship
Cussler, C. Havana storm
Cussler, C. Nighthawk
Cussler, C. Odessa Sea
Cussler, C. The Pharaoh's secret
Cussler, C. The rising sea
Cussler, C. Sea of greed
Cussler, C. Serpent

NATIONALISM

Craig, C. Miss Burma
Desai, K. The inheritance of loss

Grant, M. Parasite
Gregory, D. Afterparty
Harkaway, N. Gnomon
Hart, R. The warehouse
Houellebecq, M. Submission
Jen, G. The resisters
King, S. Sleeping beauties
Kroese, R. The last iota
Lai, L. The tiger flu
Le Guin, U. The lathe of heaven
Lem, S. His master's voice
Lim, E. Dear cyborgs
Mackintosh, C. I see you
Marrs, J. The passengers
McCarthy, C. The road
McDevitt, J. The Cassandra Project
McDonald, I. New moon
McDonald, I. River of gods
Melamed, J. Gather the daughters
Minh, D. Neon empire
Moore, J. The night market
Naam, R. Nexus
Nemett, A. We can save us all
O'Dell, C. A study in honor
Orwell, G. 1984
Palmer, D. Version control
Palwick, S. The necessary beggar
A people's future of the United States
Pinsker, S. A song for a new day
Pressfield, S. 36 righteous men
Rich, N. Odds against tomorrow
Robinson, K. New York 2140
Russell, M. The sparrow
Sallis, J. Others of my kind
Scalzi, J. Head on
Scalzi, J. Lock in
Scalzi, J. Redshirts
Self, W. The book of Dave
Shannon, S. The bone season
Shannon, S. The mime order
Shepherd, P. The book of M
Soule, C. Anyone
Starling, C. The luminous dead
Stephenson, N. Fall or, Dodge in hell
Stross, C. Accelerando
Stross, C. Empire Games
Suarez, D. Change agent
Tawada, Y. The emissary
Thompson, T. Rosewater
Thompson, T. The Rosewater insurrection
Thompson, T. The Rosewater redemption
VanderMeer, J. Borne
VanderMeer, J. Dead astronauts
Vaughn, C. Bannerless
Vinge, V. Rainbows end
Vonnegut, K. Slapstick
Vonnegut, K. Welcome to the monkey house

Walker, K. The age of miracles
Walton, J. My real children
Watkins, C. Gold fame citrus
Weir, A. Artemis
Williams, K. Tell the machine goodnight
Willis, C. Crosstalk
Wong, D. Futuristic violence and fancy suits
Zumas, L. Red clocks

NEAR-DEATH EXPERIENCE
Auster, P. Oracle night
Douglas, L. Magnificent obsession
Grames, J. The seven or eight deaths of Stella Fortuna
Higgins, K. Now that you mention it
Hoffman, A. The ice queen
Pyper, A. The damned
Schwab, V. Vicious
Urrea, L. The hummingbird's daughter
Willis, C. Passage

NEAR-DEATH EXPERIENCE -- RESEARCH
Willis, C. Passage
The **nearest** exit Steinhauer, O.
A **nearly** normal family Edvardsson, M.

NEBRASKA
Cather, W. A lost lady
Cather, W. O pioneers!
Child, L. Worth dying for
Powers, R. The echo maker
Rowell, R. Landline
Stark, R. The jugger

NEBRASKA -- HISTORY
Agee, J. The bones of paradise

NEBRASKA -- HISTORY -- 19TH CENTURY
Cather, W. My Antonia
Kolpan, G. Magic words
Nebula Awards showcase 2017
The **necessary** beggar Palwick, S.
A **necessary** evil Mukherjee, A.
Necessary people Pitoniak, A.
Necessity Walton, J.

NECROPHILIA
Moore, C. You suck
Necropolis Gamboa, S.
Nectar in a sieve Markandaya, K.
The **need** Phillips, H.

NEED (PSYCHOLOGY)
Dubus, A. Dirty love
Need you series [series] James, L.

NEEDLEWORK
Chevalier, T. A single thread

NEFERTITI,, QUEEN OF EGYPT, 14TH CENT BC
Greenwood, K. Out of the Black Land

NEGEV
Oz, A. Don't call it night

NEGOTIATION
Cameron, M. Power and empire
Kerr, P. Hitler's peace
Singh, N. Silver silence

Rozan, S. Winter and night
Verne, J. Journey to the centre of the Earth
Neptune's brood Stross, C.
Nero novels [series] George, M.
Nero Wolfe mysteries [series] Stout, R.
NERO,, EMPEROR OF ROME, 37-68
George, M. The confessions of young Nero
George, M. The splendor before the dark
Sienkiewicz, H. Quo vadis
NERUDA, PABLO, 1904-1973
Allende, I. A long petal of the sea
NERVOUS BREAKDOWN
Beyda, E. The body double
Founds, K. When mystical creatures attack!
Kirshenbaum, B. Rabbits for food
Lessing, D. The golden not(ebk.)
Marlette, D. Magic time
Momaday, N. The ancient child
Plath, S. The bell jar
Rooney, K. Lillian Boxfish takes a walk
NERVOUS SYSTEM -- DEGENERATION
Genova, L. Every note played
Netherland O'Neill, J.
NETHERLANDS
Burton, J. The miniaturist
Buwalda, P. Bonita Avenue
Groen, H. On the bright side
Koch, H. The dinner
Kostova, E. The historian
Kwok, J. Searching for Sylvie Lee
Moor, M. The storm
Pearson, R. Choke point
Robotham, M. The night ferry
Rosen, L. The tenth witness
Simenon, G. Maigret in Holland
Tregillis, I. The mechanical
NETHERLANDS -- HISTORY -- 17TH CENTURY
Chevalier, T. Girl with a pearl earring
Plaidy, J. William's wife
Smith, D. The last painting of Sara De Vos
NETHERLANDS -- HISTORY -- 19TH CENTURY
Stone, I. Lust for life
**NETHERLANDS -- HISTORY -- WARS OF INDEPEN-
DENCE, 1556-1648**
Moggach, D. Tulip fever
**NETHERLANDS -- SOCIAL CONDITIONS -- 20TH CEN-
TURY**
Boyne, J. The heart's invisible furies
NETHERLANDS -- SOCIAL LIFE AND CUSTOMS
Vreeland, S. Girl in hyacinth blue
**NETHERLANDS -- SOCIAL LIFE AND CUSTOMS --
17TH CENTURY**
Chevalier, T. Girl with a pearl earring
The **network** Shaw, L.
NEUROLOGISTS
Powers, R. The echo maker
Watson, S. Before I go to sleep

Willis, C. Passage
Neuromancer Gibson, W.
NEUROSCIENTISTS
Crouch, B. Recursion
McKenzie, E. The portable Veblen
NEUROSES IN MEN
Martin, S. The pleasure of my company
Moore, A. The lighthouse
NEUROSURGEONS
Douglas, L. Magnificent obsession
McEwan, I. Saturday
NEUTRALITY
Tolkien, J. The fall of Gondolin
NEVADA
Bock, C. Beautiful children
Clark, W. The ox-bow incident
Crichton, M. Prey
Jenkins, B. Forbidden
MacDonald, J. A purple place for dying
Parker, S. Purgatory road
Pronzini, B. Blue lonesome
Never change Berg, E.
The **never** game Deaver, J.
Never go back Child, L.
Never go back Goddard, R.
Never have I ever Jackson, J.
Never judge a lady by her cover MacLean, S.
Never let me go Ishiguro, K.
Never let you go Stevens, C.
Never lie to a lady Carlyle, L.
The **never** list Zan, K.
Never look back Gaylin, A.
Never seduce a Scot Banks, M.
Never tell Gardner, L.
Neverhome Hunt, L.
Neville family trilogy [series] Carlyle, L.
NEVILLE, RICHARD,, EARL OF WARWICK, 1428-1471
Gregory, P. The kingmaker's daughter
NEW ADULT FICTION
Croft, P. The second time I saw you
Crownover, J. Honor
Henson, P. Into the blue
Hoover, C. All your perfects
Hoover, C. It ends with us
Lauren, C. Sweet filthy boy
Millay, K. The sea of tranquility
NEW AGE
Portis, C. Gringos
Redfield, J. The celestine prophecy
NEW AGERS
Barnes, S. Domino Falls
NEW AMSTERDAM -- HISTORY
Zimmerman, J. The orphanmaster
The **new** annotated Dracula Stoker, B.
NEW BUSINESSES
Coupland, D. Microserfs
Nguyen, K. New waves

Lahiri, J. The namesake
Perrotta, T. Joe College
White, S. The siege
New Hercule Poirot mysteries [series] Hannah, S.
The **new** husband Palmer, D.
The **New** Iberia blues Burke, J.
NEW IBERIA, LOUISIANA
Burke, J. Black cherry blues
Burke, J. Heaven's prisoners
Burke, J. The New Iberia blues
NEW IDENTITIES
Belle, K. Dear wife
Card, M. These ghosts are family
Cramer, W. Levi's will
Dimon, H. Her other secret
Ewan, C. Long time lost
Joss, M. Among the missing
Kennedy, D. The big picture
Knopf, C. Dead anyway
Loren, R. The one you fight for
Moore, K. Sexy Lexy
Perry, T. Vanishing act
Ragan, T. Buried deep
Steadman, C. Mr. Nobody
Vine, B. The chimney sweeper's boy
NEW JERSEY
Auster, P. 4 3 2 1
Cheek, C. Cape May
Coben, H. Don't let go
Colfer, E. Plugged
Diaz, J. The brief wondrous life of Oscar Wao
Evanovich, J. Look alive twenty-five
Evanovich, J. Turbo twenty-three
Fitzgerald, F. Novels and stories, 1920-1922
Ford, R. Independence Day
Ford, R. The lay of the land
Ford, R. Let me be Frank with you
Grodstein, L. A friend of the family
Kingsolver, B. Unsheltered
Levitt, P. Come with me to Babylon
Lodato, V. Edgar and Lucy
McPhee, M. Gorgeous lies
Mirvis, T. The outside world
Oates, J. The accursed
Parks, B. The girl next door
Parks, B. The player
Perrotta, T. Joe College
Perrotta, T. The leftovers
Pineiro, C. One summer night
Price, R. Clockers
Price, R. Freedomland
Rosenfelt, D. Bark of night
Rosenfelt, D. Black and blue
Rosenfelt, D. Blackout
Rosenfelt, D. Don't tell a soul
Roth, P. Indignation
Roth, P. Nemesis

Rozan, S. Winter and night
Stewart, A. Miss Kopp just won't quit
Swinson, K. Wifey's next sticky situation
Unger, L. The red hunter
Wolitzer, H. Hearts
Woo, S. Everything Asian
Woods, T. Dutch
NEW JERSEY -- HISTORY -- 20TH CENTURY
Stewart, A. Girl waits with gun
NEW JERSEY -- SOCIAL LIFE AND CUSTOMS -- 20TH CENTURY
Blume, J. In the unlikely event
Larsen, R. I am Radar
The **new** me Butler, H.
NEW MEXICO
Allio, K. Buddhism for Western children
Barry, J. Don't turn around
Beagin, J. Vacuum in the dark
Bennett, R. American elsewhere
Bird, S. The flamenco academy
Glass, J. The whole world over
Hillerman, T. The shape shifter
Hillerman, T. The sinister pig
Hillerman, T. The wailing wind
Jones, D. A bad day for sunshine
Leonard, E. Charlie Martz and other stories
McCarthy, C. Cities of the plain
McCarthy, C. The crossing
McEwan, I. Solar
McLaren, K. The road to enchantment
Nesbit, T. The wives of Los Alamos
Nichols, J. The Milagro Beanfield War
Potenza, C. Hearts of the missing
Quade, K. Night at the fiestas
Richter, C. The sea of grass
Smith, M. Stallion Gate
Valdes, A. Dirty Girls on top
Winslow, D. The border
Winslow, D. The cartel
NEW MEXICO -- HISTORY -- 19TH CENTURY
Cather, W. Death comes for the archbishop
New Mexico trilogy [series] Nichols, J.
New moon McDonald, I.
NEW MOTHERS
Alam, R. That kind of mother
Albert, E. After birth
Eriksson, K. The princess of Burundi
Evans, D. Ordinary people
Golding, M. Little darlings
Griffiths, E. A dying fall
Griffiths, E. The house at sea's end
Lackberg, C. The hidden child
Molloy, A. The perfect mother
Ramqvist, K. The white city
Rimmer, K. Truths I never told you
Spencer, S. Thicker than water
NEW NEIGHBORS

D'Agostino, K. The antiques
Dobyns, S. Saratoga payback
Dolan-Leach, C. We went to the woods
Fowler, T. A well-behaved woman
Freudenberger, N. The newlyweds
Gaitskill, M. The mare
Groff, L. Arcadia
Grossman, L. The magicians
Hansen, R. Mariette in ecstasy
Higgins, K. The best man
Higgins, K. The perfect match
Hunt, S. Mr. Splitfoot
Isaacs, S. After all these years
Lasdun, J. The fall guy
Lee, C. A gesture life
Lennon, J. Castle
McDermott, A. Child of my heart
McGhee, A. The opposite of fate
Miller, D. American by day
Murphy, D. Tiny Americans
Nabokov, V. Pnin
O'Donohue, C. The lover's knot
O'Nan, S. The names of the dead
Oates, J. Broke heart blues
Oates, J. Carthage
Oates, J. The falls
Oates, J. Foxfire
Oates, J. The gravedigger's daughter
Oates, J. Little bird of heaven
Oates, J. Middle age
Oates, J. We were the Mulvaneys
Perry, T. Vanishing act
Phillips, C. Perfect fit
Pitoniak, A. Necessary people
Puzo, M. The godfather
Ramos, J. The farm
Russo, R. Bridge of sighs
Russo, R. Everybody's fool
Russo, R. The risk pool
Shreve, A. Eden Close
Shriver, L. We need to talk about Kevin
Smith, B. Shoot the dog
Spencer, S. Man in the woods
Spencer-Fleming, J. Hid from our eyes
Spiegelman, P. Black maps
St. James, S. The Sun Down motel
Straub, P. Ghost story
Torres, J. We the animals
Unger, L. Crazy love you
Walker, C. Man of the year
Westlake, D. Bad news
Westlake, D. Drowned hopes
Wood, J. Upstate
Yates, C. Grist Mill Road

NEW YORK (STATE) -- HISTORY -- 19TH CENTURY
Bayard, L. The pale blue eye
Donati, S. Where the light enters

NEW YORK (STATE) -- HISTORY -- 20TH CENTURY
Hoffman, A. The Museum of Extraordinary Things
**NEW YORK (STATE) -- HISTORY -- FRENCH AND IN-
DIAN WAR, 1754-1763**
Cooper, J. The last of the Mohicans
NEW YORK (STATE) -- POLITICS AND GOVERNMENT
Canin, E. America America
NEW YORK (STATE) -- RACE RELATIONS
Oates, J. Because it is bitter, and because it is my heart
Oates, J. I lock my door upon myself
**NEW YORK (STATE) -- RACE RELATIONS -- HISTORY
-- 20TH CENTURY**
Doctorow, E. Ragtime
**NEW YORK (STATE) -- SOCIAL CONDITIONS -- 17TH
CENTURY**
Boyle, T. World's end
**NEW YORK (STATE) -- SOCIAL CONDITIONS -- 20TH
CENTURY**
Boyle, T. World's end
**NEW YORK (STATE) -- SOCIAL LIFE AND CUSTOMS
-- 20TH CENTURY**
Rayfiel, T. In pinelight
New York 2140 Robinson, K.
NEW YORK CITY
50 Cent Blow
Abbott, S. The future of love
Aciman, A. Enigma variations
Adelman, M. Piece of mind
Alenyikov, M. Ivan and Misha
Alison, J. The marriage of the sea
Allende, I. In the midst of winter
Alvarez, J. How the Garcia girls lost their accents
Apostol, G. Gun dealers' daughter
Archer, J. Best kept secret
Archer, J. Only time will tell
Auster, P. The Brooklyn follies
Auster, P. Invisible
Bacon, C. There is room for you
Baldwin, J. Another country
Baldwin, J. Go tell it on the mountain
Baldwin, J. If Beale Street could talk
Baldwin, J. Just above my head
Baldwin, J. Tell me how long the train's been gone
Banasky, C. The suicide of Claire Bishop
Bandele, A. Daughter
Bank, M. The wonder spot
Barclay, L. Elevator pitch
Barclay, L. Trust your eyes
Bartz, A. The lost night
Beagle, P. A fine and private place
Begley, L. About Schmidt
Bellow, S. Mr. Sammler's planet
Bellow, S. Seize the day
Berkowitz, I. Old flame
Birmingham, S. The Auerbach will
Birmingham, S. Carriage trade
Bisson, T. Any day now

Gruber, M. The book of air and shadows

Hale, S. Austenland

Hall, P. Lights! Camera! Puzzles!

Hallberg, G. City on fire

Hamill, P. Tabloid city

Hammett, D. The thin man

Hand, E. Generation loss

Hand, E. Mortal love

Hart, J. Iron house

Hassib, R. A pure heart

Hauck, R. The wedding chapel

Hayes, T. I am Pilgrim

Heller, P. Celine

Helprin, M. In sunlight and in shadow

Helprin, M. Winter's tale

Hendricks, G. An anonymous girl

Herlihy, J. Midnight cowboy

Higgins, J. The White House connection

Hijuelos, O. Beautiful Maria of my soul

Hijuelos, O. The mambo kings play songs of love

Himes, C. Cotton comes to Harlem

Hoffman, A. The rules of magic

Horn, D. Eternal life

Horn, D. The world to come

Hughes, L. Simple speaks his mind

Humphreys, S. Trouble walks in

Hunt, S. The invention of everything else

Hunter, E. The moment she was gone

Johnson, A. The first part last

K'wan Animal

K'wan Animal II

K'wan The Diamond empire

K'wan Diamonds and Pearl

K'wan Gangsta

K'wan The fix

K'wan Revelations

K'wan Section 8

K'wan Welfare wifeys

Kaufman, B. Up the down staircase

Kaufman, S. Diary of a mad housewife

Kellerman, J. The genius

Kennedy, D. The big picture

Kenney, J. Talk to me

Kenney, J. Truth in advertising

Kirshenbaum, B. Rabbits for food

Knox, T. Kockroach

Ko, L. The leavers

Kotzwinkle, W. The bear went over the mountain

Krauss, N. The history of love

Kress, N. Tomorrow's kin

Kunzru, H. White tears

Kwok, J. Searching for Sylvie Lee

LaValle, V. The changeling

LaValle, V. The devil in silver

Lafferty, M. The shambling guide to New York City

Lahiri, J. The namesake

Lamberson, G. The frenzy way

Larsen, N. Passing

Lasdun, J. Afternoon of a faun

Lathen, E. Brewing up a storm

Lauren, C. Roomies

Layne, L. Passion on Park Avenue

Levitt, P. Come with me to Babylon

Lipman, E. Good riddance

Loigman, L. The wartime sisters

Lutz, J. Final seconds

Ma, L. Severance

Mallon, T. Bandbox

Mandel, E. The glass hotel

Mark, D. Cruel mercy

Markovits, A. I am forbidden

Marks, J. Fangland

Mayor, A. The sniper's wife

McBain, E. The big bad city

McBain, E. Fat Ollie's book

McBain, E. The frumious bandersnatch

McBain, E. Hark!

McBain, E. The last dance

McBain, E. Nocturne

McCann, C. Let the great world spin

McDermott, A. Charming Billy

McDermott, A. The ninth hour

McKay, A. The witches of New York

McLaughlin, E. The nanny diaries

Meno, J. The boy detective fails

Meuleman, S. Find me gone

Miller, H. Tropic of Capricorn

Miller, K. An angry-ass black woman

Millhauser, S. Martin Dressler

Molloy, A. The perfect mother

Moody, R. Right livelihoods

Morgan, S. Miracle on 5th Avenue

Morrison, T. Jazz

Morton, B. Florence Gordon

Moshfegh, O. My year of rest and relaxation

Mosley, W. All I did was shoot my man

Mosley, W. And sometimes I wonder about you

Mosley, W. Down the river unto the sea

Mosley, W. Known to evil

Mosley, W. The long fall

Mosley, W. RL's dream

Mosley, W. Trouble is what I do

Mosley, W. When the thrill is gone

Mychea He loves me, he loves you not

Naylor, G. Mama Day

Noire G-Spot

Novic, S. Girl at war

Nunez, E. Anna in-between

Nunez, S. The last of her kind

O'Connell, C. Blind sight

O'Connell, C. The chalk girl

O'Connell, C. Crime school

O'Connell, C. Dead famous

O'Connell, C. Find me

White, S. Tears of a hustler
Whitehead, C. Zone one
Willig, L. The Ashford affair
Wolf, D. The execution
Wolf, D. The intercept
Wolf, D. The ultimatum
Wolfe, T. The bonfire of the vanities
Wolitzer, M. The wife
Woods, S. A delicate touch
Woods, S. New York dead
Woodson, J. Another Brooklyn
Woodson, J. Red at the bone
Wouk, H. Marjorie Morningstar
Yanagihara, H. A little life
Yates, C. Grist Mill Road
Zailckas, K. Mother, mother
Zhang, J. Sour heart

NEW YORK CITY -- HISTORY -- 1775-1865
Rose, J. The blackest bird

NEW YORK CITY -- HISTORY -- 1898-1951
Doctorow, E. World's Fair
Llywelyn, M. 1916

NEW YORK CITY -- HISTORY -- 1900-1945
Dos Passos, J. 1919

NEW YORK CITY -- HISTORY -- 19TH CENTURY
Manning, K. My notorious life
Moore, G. The last days of night
Sanders, J. Speakers of the dead
Simpson, R. Let the dead keep their secrets
Simpson, R. What the dead leave behind
Wecker, H. The golem and the jinni

NEW YORK CITY -- HISTORY -- 20TH CENTURY
Chabon, M. The amazing adventures of Kavalier & Clay
Doctorow, E. Homer and Langley
Dos Passos, J. 1919
Egan, J. Manhattan Beach
Hoffman, A. The Museum of Extraordinary Things
James, M. A brief history of seven killings
Keane, M. Fever
Pintoff, S. In the shadow of Gotham
Rubenfeld, J. The interpretation of murder
Stewart, A. Lady cop makes trouble
Stewart, A. Miss Kopp's midnight confessions

NEW YORK CITY -- HISTORY -- 21ST CENTURY
Conklin, T. The house girl

NEW YORK CITY -- HISTORY -- COLONIAL PERIOD, 1600-1775
Spufford, F. Golden hill
Zimmerman, J. The orphanmaster

NEW YORK CITY -- SOCIAL LIFE AND CUSTOMS
Bambara, T. Gorilla, my love
Bram, C. Lives of the circus animals
Dunne, D. People like us
Dunne, D. Too much money
Eisenberg, D. The twilight of the superheroes
Hughes, L. Short stories
Lethem, J. Dissident gardens

Martin, S. An object of beauty

NEW YORK CITY -- SOCIAL LIFE AND CUSTOMS -- 19TH CENTURY
Shupe, J. The prince of Broadway
Shupe, J. The rogue of Fifth Avenue
Wood, T. The engineer's wife

NEW YORK CITY -- SOCIAL LIFE AND CUSTOMS -- 20TH CENTURY
Bauer, C. Frances and Bernard
Davis, F. The Chelsea girls
Desai, K. The inheritance of loss
Flint, E. Little deaths
Gross, A. Button man
Loigman, L. The two-family house
Mathews, B. The world of tomorrow
Rose, M. Cartier's hope
Roth, H. Call it sleep
Rubenfeld, J. The interpretation of murder
Shapiro, B. The muralist
Steinke, R. Holy skirts

NEW YORK CITY -- SOCIAL LIFE AND CUSTOMS -- 21ST CENTURY
Jin, H. The boat rocker
Newman, S. The heavens

NEW YORK CITY. GRAND CENTRAL TERMINAL.
Davis, F. The masterpiece

NEW YORK CITY. POLICE DEPARTMENT
Deaver, J. The coffin dancer
Deaver, J. The stone monkey

New York dead Woods, S.

New York Review Books classics [series] Ginzburg, N.

NEW YORK STATE
Albert, E. After birth
Bailey, T. Fix her up
Duffy, B. House of echoes
Mehta, R. No other world
Unger, L. The stranger inside

NEW YORK WORLD'S FAIR, (1939-1940)
Doctorow, E. World's Fair

NEW YORK, CITY
Gruber, M. The return

NEW ZEALAND
Cleave, P. The cleaner
Cleave, P. Joe Victim
Cleave, P. Trust no one
Gifford, B. The stars above Veracruz
Goudge, E. Green Dolphin Street
Hulme, K. The bone people
Singh, N. A madness of sunshine
Uris, L. Redemption

NEW ZEALAND -- HISTORY -- 19TH CENTURY
Catton, E. The luminaries
Grenville, K. Sarah Thornhill
Tremain, R. The colour

NEWARK, NEW JERSEY
Ca$h Thugs cry
Parks, B. The girl next door

Stott, R. Ghostwalk

Next Crichton, M.

Next Hynes, J.

Next life might be kinder Norman, H.

Next of kin Trollope, J.

The **next** person you meet in Heaven Albom, M.

Next year in Havana Cleeton, C.

Nexus Naam, R.

Nexus novels (Ramez Naam) [series] Naam, R.

NEZ PERCE INDIANS

Osborne, D. The coming

NIAGARA FALLS

O'Nan, S. The odds

Oates, J. The falls

Nic Costa mysteries [series] Hewson, D.

NICARAGUA

Gage, E. The ladies of Managua

Niccolo rising Dunnett, D.

The **nice** and the good Murdoch, I.

NICE, FRANCE

Donoghue, E. Akin

Levy, D. Swimming home

NICHOLAS II,, EMPEROR OF RUSSIA, 1868-1918

Akunin, B. The coronation

Nicholas Bracewell mysteries [series] Marston, E.

Nicholas Nickleby Dickens, C.

The **Nick** Adams stories Hemingway, E.

Nick Heller novels [series] Finder, J.

Nick Mason novels [series] Hamilton, S.

Nick Reid novels [series] Gavin, R.

The **Nickel** boys Whitehead, C.

NIECES

Ragan, T. Her last day

Rice, L. Little night

Schwarz, C. Drowning Ruth

NIECES -- DEATH

MacDonald, J. Cinnamon skin

NIECES -- SOUTHERN STATES

Welty, E. The ponder heart

NIECES AND NEPHEWS

Vine, B. The House of Stairs

NIECES AND NEPHEWS -- 19TH CENTURY

Trollope, A. Doctor Thorne

NIGERIA

Abraham, T. Black Sunday

Adebayo, A. Stay with me

Adichie, C. Americanah

Adichie, C. The thing around your neck

Braithwaite, O. My sister, the serial killer

Cole, T. Every day is for the thief

Cussler, C. The oracle

Dare, A. The girl with the louding voice

Ehirim, N. Prince of monkeys

Emezi, A. Freshwater

Iweala, U. Speak no evil

John, E. Born on a Tuesday

O'Brien, E. Girl

Obioma, C. The fishermen

Obioma, C. An orchestra of minorities

Okparanta, C. Under the udala trees

Osondu, E. Voice of America

Thompson, T. Rosewater

Thompson, T. The Rosewater insurrection

Thompson, T. The Rosewater redemption

NIGERIA -- COLONIZATION

Achebe, C. Things fall apart

NIGERIA -- HISTORY

Achebe, C. Things fall apart

NIGERIA -- HISTORY -- CIVIL WAR, 1967-1970

Adichie, C. Half of a yellow sun

NIGERIA -- SOCIAL CONDITIONS

Ibrahim, A. Season of crimson blossoms

NIGERIA -- SOCIAL LIFE AND CUSTOMS

Abani, C. GraceLand

NIGERIAN AMERICANS

Iweala, U. Speak no evil

NIGERIANS IN ENGLAND

Adichie, C. Americanah

Cleave, C. Little Bee

Rendell, R. Simisola

NIGERIANS IN THE UNITED STATES

Adichie, C. Americanah

Adichie, C. The thing around your neck

Cole, T. Open city

Emezi, A. Freshwater

NIGHT

Fowler, C. Bryant & May

Murakami, H. After dark

Night and silence McGuire, S.

Night at the fiestas Quade, K.

The **night** bird Freeman, B.

Night boat to Tangier Barry, K.

Night bus Rigosi, G.

The **night** circus Morgenstern, E.

The **night** country O'Nan, S.

Night fall Smith, F.

The **night** ferry Robotham, M.

Night film Pessl, M.

The **night** fire Connelly, M.

Night flight Saint-Exupery, A.

NIGHT FLYING

Saint-Exupery, A. Night flight

The **night** following Joss, M.

The **night** gardener Pelecanos, G.

The **night** guest McFarlane, F.

The **night** Gwen Stacy died Bruni, S.

The **night** is mine Buchman, M.

The **night** market Moore, J.

Night night, sleep tight Ephron, H.

Night of miracles Berg, E.

Night of sorrows Sherwood, F.

Night of the animals Broun, B.

Night of the fox Higgins, J.

Night of the jaguar Gruber, M.

Ninety-nine stories of God Williams, J.

NINJA

Souljah, S. Midnight and the meaning of love

Spann, S. Blade of the Samurai

Spann, S. Claws of the cat

Spann, S. Trial on Mount Koya

The **ninth** hour McDermott, A.

Ninth house Bardugo, L.

The **ninth** step Jerkins, G.

Nip the buds, shoot the kids Oe, K.

The **nix** Hill, N.

Niya Joseph, F.

NO (THE WORD)

NDiaye, M. Three strong women

NO 1 LADIES' DETECTIVE AGENCY (IMAGINARY ORGANIZATION)

McCall Smith, A. Blue shoes and happiness

McCall Smith, A. The Double Comfort Safari Club

McCall Smith, A. The full cupboard of life

McCall Smith, A. The good husband of Zebra Drive

McCall Smith, A. In the company of cheerful ladies

McCall Smith, A. The Kalahari typing school for men

McCall Smith, A. The Limpopo Academy of Private Detection

McCall Smith, A. The No. 1 Ladies' Detective Agency

McCall Smith, A. The Saturday big tent wedding party

No bad deed Chavez, H.

No country Ray, K.

No country for old men McCarthy, C.

No crystal stair Rutland, E.

No fixed line Stabenow, D.

No good asking Kimmel, F.

No good deeds Lippman, L.

No good duke goes unpunished MacLean, S.

No graves as yet Perry, A.

No judgments Cabot, M.

No laughing matter Simpson, D.

No longer a gentleman Putney, M.

No middle name Child, L.

No ocean too wide Turansky, C.

No one belongs here more than you July, M.

No one can pronounce my name Satyal, R.

No one ever asked Ganshert, K.

No one in the world Johnson, R.

No one is coming to save us Watts, S.

No one you know Richmond, M.

No other world Mehta, R.

No place for a dame Brockway, C.

No place for heroes Restrepo, L.

No safe house Barclay, L.

No safe place Patterson, R.

No time like the present Gordimer, N.

No time to wave goodbye Mitchard, J.

The **No.** 1 Ladies' Detective Agency McCall Smith, A.

No. 1 Ladies' Detective Agency [series] McCall Smith, A.

NOAH'S ARK

Barnes, J. A history of the world in 10 1

Golden, C. Ararat

Noah's compass Tyler, A.

NOBEL PRIZE WINNERS

Keating, H. The soft detective

McEwan, I. Solar

Yanagihara, H. The people in the trees

NOBILITY

Ashe, K. The earl

Ashford, J. Heir to the duke

Ashford, J. Lord Sebastian's secret

Ashford, J. What the duke doesn't know

Balogh, M. The secret mistress

Balogh, M. Simply love

Balogh, M. Someone to love

Bennett, A. The uncommon reader

Bowen, K. I've got my duke to keep me warm

Boyle, E. Along came a duke

Boyle, E. And the miss ran away with the rake

Brockway, C. The golden season

Bujold, L. Shards of honor

Bujold, L. The warrior's apprentice

Burrowes, G. The bridegroom wore plaid

Burrowes, G. The captive

Burrowes, G. The soldier

Burrowes, G. Tremaine's true love

Burrowes, G. The trouble with dukes

Byrne, K. How to love a duke in ten days

Callihan, K. Firelight

Chase, L. A duke in shining armor

Chase, L. Your scandalous ways

Ciotta, B. Her sky cowboy

Ciotta, B. His clockwork canary

Cocks, H. The royal we

Collins, W. The woman in white

Craddock, C. A labyrinth of scions and sorcery

Crowley, J. Lord Byron's novel

Dumas, A. Camille

Dunnett, D. Niccolo rising

Egan, J. The keep

Frampton, M. The duke's guide to correct behavior

Frampton, M. Put up your duke

Galen, S. When you give a duke a diamond

Garriott, L. Promised

Garwood, J. The bride

Golding, W. Close quarters

Golding, W. Fire down below

Golding, W. Rites of passage

Gregory, P. The constant princess

Gregory, P. The Boleyn inheritance

Gregory, P. The last Tudor

Gregory, P. The other Boleyn girl

Guhrke, L. The truth about love and dukes

Guhrke, L. When the marquess met his match

Heyer, G. These old shades

Hoyt, E. Wicked intentions

Hunter, J. Forbidden to love the duke

Hunter, M. The conquest of Lady Cassandra

Abbott, M. Bury me deep
Abbott, M. Queenpin
Aguilar Camin, H. Death in Veracruz
Atkins, A. Wicked city
Auster, P. Oracle night
Boyle, W. City of margins
The best American noir of the century
Cooper, T. The marauders
Ellroy, J. American tabloid
Ellroy, J. Blood's a rover
Ellroy, J. The cold six thousand
Estleman, L. Gas City
Faletti, G. A pimp's notes
Gavin, R. Beluga
Gifford, B. The stars above Veracruz
Green, N. The angel of Montague Street
Hammett, D. The thin man
Harrison, J. The great leader
Johnson, D. Nobody move
Kennedy, W. Ironweed
Knox, T. Kockroach
Lange, R. Angel baby
Lehane, D. Mystic river
Levin, I. A kiss before dying
Lewis, T. GBH
Lippman, L. Hardly knew her
Lippman, L. Sunburn
Manchette, J. Fatale
Mandel, E. The singer's gun
Moore, C. Noir
Moore, J. The night market
Neville, S. The ghosts of Belfast
Neville, S. Ratlines
Newton, C. Calumet City
Newton, C. Start shooting
Nicholson, G. The city under the skin
Peace, D. Occupied city
Peace, D. Tokyo year zero
Pelecanos, G. Drama city
Pelecanos, G. The man who came uptown
Pelecanos, G. Shame the devil
Pelecanos, G. The sweet forever
Pelecanos, G. The turnaround
Polansky, D. Low town
Pronzini, B. Step to the graveyard easy
Pryor, M. Hollow man
Pynchon, T. Inherent vice
Pyne, D. Catalina eddy
Pyne, D. Twentynine Palms
Rabe, P. Anatomy of a killer ;
Recacoechea S., J. American visa
Sallis, J. Drive
Sallis, J. Driven
Solares, M. Don't send flowers
Solomita, S. A good day to die
Stark, R. Dirty money
Starr, J. Lights out

Tidhar, L. A man lies dreaming
Tran, V. Dragonfish
Walter, J. Citizen Vince
Wolfe, G. The land across
NOISE
McPherson, C. Strangers at the gate
A **noise** downstairs Barclay, L.
The **noise** of time Barnes, J.
Nola Cespedes novels [series] Castro, J.
NOMADS
Ahmad, J. The wandering falcon
Jiang, R. Wolf totem
NON-GOVERNMENTAL ORGANIZATIONS
Florio, G. Silent hearts
NONAGENARIAN MEN
Mosley, W. The last days of Ptolemy Grey
NONAGENARIANS
Garcia Marquez, G. Memories of my melancholy whores
Gurganus, A. Oldest living Confederate widow tells all
NONALCOHOLIC BEER
Lathen, E. Brewing up a storm
NONCONFORMISTS
Barry, S. Days without end
Kracht, C. Imperium
McGuire, S. In an absent dream
Mozley, F. Elmet
Spark, M. The prime of Miss Jean Brodie
Truong, M. The sweetest fruits
Walker, S. Dietland
NONCONFORMITY
Murata, S. Convenience store woman
None to accompany me Gordimer, N.
NONPROFIT ORGANIZATIONS
Cook, T. A dancer in the dust
Hobbs, A. Stealing candy
NONTRADITIONAL FAMILIES
Coetzee, J. The childhood of Jesus
Joss, M. Half broken things
Nora Gavin and Cormac Maguire series [series] Hart, E.
Nora Kelly novels (Preston & Child) [series] Preston, D.
Nora Watts novels [series] Kamal, S.
Nora Webster Toibin, C.
NORFOLK, ENGLAND
Azzopardi, T. Winterton blue
Griffiths, E. The crossing places
Griffiths, E. A dying fall
Griffiths, E. The house at sea's end
Griffiths, E. The Janus stone
Higgins, J. The eagle has flown
Higgins, J. The eagle has landed
James, P. Devices and desires
Smith, A. The accidental
Normal people Rooney, S.
NORMALITY (PSYCHOLOGY)
Hesse, H. The fairy tales of Hermann Hesse
NORMAN PERIOD (1066-1154)
Follett, K. The pillars of the earth

Franklin, A. The siege winter
Penman, S. When Christ and his saints slept
Peters, E. Brother Cadfael's penance
Peters, E. Dead man's ransom
Peters, E. The hermit of Eyton Forest
Peters, E. The holy thief
Peters, E. Monk's hood
Peters, E. The pilgrim of hate
Peters, E. The potter's field
Peters, E. A rare Benedictine
Peters, E. The rose rent
Peters, E. St. Peter's fair
Peters, E. The sanctuary sparrow
Peters, E. The summer of the Danes
Peters, E. The virgin in the ice
Rutherfurd, E. London

NORMANDY
Groot, T. Flame of resistance
Wieland, L. Paris, 7 a.m.

NORMANDY INVASION, JUNE 6, 1944
Higgins, J. Night of the fox
Shaara, J. The steel wave

NORMANS IN ENGLAND
Rutherfurd, E. London

Norse mythology Gaiman, N.

NORTH AFRICA
Cussler, C. The oracle
Watt, H. To the lions

NORTH AFRICA -- HISTORY, MILITARY -- 20TH CENTURY
Shaara, J. The rising tide

NORTH AMERICA
Atwood, M. The handmaid's tale
Atwood, M. The testaments
Graedon, A. The word exchange
Tregillis, I. The mechanical

NORTH AMERICA -- EXPLORATION
Lalami, L. The Moor's account

North and South Gaskell, E.

North and South Jakes, J.

North and South trilogy [series] Jakes, J.

NORTH ATLANTIC OCEAN
Monsarrat, N. The cruel sea

NORTH CAROLINA
Adams, A. A southern exposure
Adams, E. The secret, book & scone society
Allen, S. First frost
Allen, S. Garden spells
Allen, S. The girl who chased the moon
Ball, J. In the heat of the night
Bambara, T. Gorilla, my love
Barr, N. What Rose forgot
Brown, S. Mean streak
Brown, T. Gods of Howl Mountain
Cash, W. This dark road to mercy
Child, L. The enemy
Cook, D. Reservation nation

Deaver, J. The empty chair
Dektar, M. The Ash family
Earley, T. Jim the boy
Edgerton, C. Walking across Egypt
Fowler, T. A good neighborhood
Gibbons, K. Charms for the easy life
Gibbons, K. Ellen Foster
Gibbons, K. The life all around me by Ellen Foster
Godwin, G. Flora
Godwin, G. Unfinished desires
Gurganus, A. Local souls
Hart, J. Down river
Hart, J. Iron house
Hart, J. The king of lies
Hart, J. The last child
Hodges, C. Rumor has it
Hooper, K. Stealing shadows
Huyler, F. The laws of invisible things
Iles, G. The footprints of God
Kantra, V. Meg and Jo
Karon, J. At home in Mitford
Karon, J. In this mountain
Karon, J. Out to Canaan
Maron, M. High country fall
Maron, M. Bootlegger's daughter
Maron, M. Shooting at loons
Maron, M. Uncommon clay
Maron, M. Up jumps the Devil
McCrumb, S. The ballad of Tom Dooley
McKinlay, J. The good ones
O'Keefe, M. Everything I left unsaid
Owens, D. Where the crawdads sing
Patterson, J. Kiss the girls
Pearson, R. A long time comin'
Pessl, M. Special topics in calamity physics
Price, R. The good priest's son
Rash, R. Above the waterfall
Rash, R. Nothing gold can stay
Reichs, K. A conspiracy of bones
Reichs, K. Deadly decisions
Reichs, K. Death du jour
Ross, A. Miss Julia delivers the goods
Ross, A. Miss Julia takes the wheel
Ross, A. Miss Julia throws a wedding
Sparks, N. Every breath
Sparks, N. The guardian
Sparks, N. The notebook
Sparks, N. A walk to remember
Walker, A. The temple of my familiar
Watts, S. No one is coming to save us
Weiss, L. If the creek don't rise
Winslow, D. In West Mills
Wolfe, T. Look homeward, angel

NORTH CAROLINA -- HISTORY -- 1865-1918
Smith, L. On Agate Hill

NORTH CAROLINA -- HISTORY -- 18TH CENTURY
Smith, D. The constable's tale

NORTH CAROLINA -- HISTORY -- 19TH CENTURY
McCrumb, S. The ballad of Frankie Silver
NORTH CAROLINA -- HISTORY -- 20TH CENTURY
Cash, W. The last ballad
Frazier, C. Nightwoods
Rash, R. The cove
Rash, R. Serena
NORTH CAROLINA -- HISTORY -- CIVIL WAR, 1861-1865
Frazier, C. Cold Mountain
Humphreys, J. Nowhere else on earth
Slouka, M. God's fool
NORTH CAROLINA -- HISTORY -- COLONIAL PERIOD, 1600-1775
Gabaldon, D. The fiery cross
NORTH CAROLINA -- HISTORY -- REVOLUTION, 1775-1783
Gabaldon, D. A breath of snow and ashes
Gabaldon, D. An echo in the bone
NORTH CAROLINA -- RACE RELATIONS
Maron, M. Storm track
NORTH DAKOTA
Box, C. Badlands
Box, C. Paradise Valley
Erdrich, L. The beet queen
Erdrich, L. Four souls
Erdrich, L. LaRose
Erdrich, L. The last report on the miracles at Little No Horse
Erdrich, L. Love medicine
Erdrich, L. The Master Butchers Singing Club
Erdrich, L. The night watchman
Erdrich, L. The painted drum
Erdrich, L. The plague of doves
Erdrich, L. The round house
Erdrich, L. Tracks
Power, S. The grass dancer
Sandford, J. Golden prey
Watson, L. Let him go
NORTH DAKOTA -- HISTORY -- 1889-1918
O'Brien, D. The contract surgeon
NORTH KOREA
Church, J. Bamboo and blood
Church, J. A corpse in the Koryo
Church, J. A drop of Chinese blood
Church, J. Hidden moon
Johnson, A. The orphan master's son
Stephens, A. Famous adopted people
NORTH KOREA -- POLITICS AND GOVERNMENT
Bandi, 1. The accusation
Coes, B. Bloody Sunday
NORTH MACEDONIA
Porter, H. Firefly
NORTH POLE EXPEDITIONS
Penney, S. Under a pole star
NORTH SEA
Ware, R. The woman in cabin ten
North star Wheeler, R.

The **North** water McGuire, I.
NORTH WEST COMPANY.
Aalborg, G. River of porcupines
NORTHAMPTONSHIRE, ENGLAND
Moore, A. Jerusalem
Northanger Abbey Austen, J.
NORTHEAST INDIA -- INTERETHNIC RELATIONS
Deb, S. The point of return
NORTHEAST INDIA -- SOCIAL CONDITIONS
Deb, S. The point of return
NORTHEASTERN STATES
Harris, R. The ghost
NORTHERN CALIFORNIA
Carr, R. Virgin river
Gardiner, M. Unsub
Lelchuk, S. Save me from dangerous men
Muller, M. Cyanide Wells
Muller, M. Point Deception
Pronzini, B. A wasteland of strangers
Pynchon, T. Vineland
Rivers, F. Bridge to haven
Sharpe, T. Barbed wire heart
NORTHERN ENGLAND
Moss, S. Ghost wall
Nickson, C. The hocus girl
NORTHERN EUROPE
Kay, G. The last light of the sun
NORTHERN IRELAND
Deane, S. Reading in the dark
McKinty, A. The cold, cold ground
McKinty, A. In the morning I'll be gone
Moore, B. The lonely passion of Judith Hearne
Sansom, I. The case of the missing books
Seymour, G. Vagabond
Shaw, W. The birdwatcher
NORTHERN IRELAND -- HISTORY -- 1969-1994
Burns, A. Milkman
O'Brien, E. House of splendid isolation
NORTHERN IRELAND -- POLITICS AND GOVERNMENT
Neville, S. The ghosts of Belfast
NORTHERN MEXICO
McCarthy, C. All the pretty horses
NORTHERN STATES
Coates, T. The water dancer
NORTHMEN AND NORTHWOMEN
Kay, G. The last light of the sun
NORTHUMBERLAND, ENGLAND
Cleeves, A. The crow trap
Gaynor, H. The lighthouse keeper's daughter
NORTHUMBRIA (KINGDOM) -- HISTORY
Cornwell, B. Sword of kings
Cornwell, B. War of the wolf
NORTHUMBRIA (KINGDOM) -- HISTORY -- 9TH CENTURY
Cornwell, B. The last kingdom
Northwest corner Schwartz, J.

NOVELS IN VERSE
Cisneros, S. The house on Mango Street
Robertson, R. The long take
Novels, 1944-1953 Bellow, S.
NOVELS-WITHIN-NOVELS
Atwood, M. The blind assassin
Auster, P. Oracle night
Bulgakov, M. The master and Margarita
Carlino, R. Swear on this life
Chabon, M. Wonder boys
Crowley, J. Lord Byron's novel
Egan, J. The keep
Everett, P. Erasure
Foer, J. Everything is illuminated
Krauss, N. The history of love
Livesey, M. Criminals
Means, D. Hystopia
Naslund, S. The fountain of St. James Court
Wiggins, M. The shadow catcher
Willig, L. The betrayal of the blood lily
Willig, L. The deception of the emerald ring
Willig, L. The masque of the Black Tulip
Willig, L. The orchid affair
Willig, L. The secret history of the Pink Carnation
Willig, L. The seduction of the Crimson Rose
Willig, L. The temptation of the night jasmine
Now and then Parker, R.
Now that you mention it Higgins, K.
Now you see it Lynn, A.
Now you see me Bolton, S.
Nowhere else on earth Humphreys, J.
The **Nowhere** Man Hurwitz, G.
Nowhere near respectable Putney, M.
NUCLEAR ACCIDENTS
Smith, M. Wolves eat dogs
NUCLEAR HOLOCAUST SURVIVORS
Butler, O. Adulthood rites
Butler, O. Dawn
NUCLEAR PHYSICISTS -- IRAN
Ignatius, D. The increment
NUCLEAR POWER PLANTS
James, P. Devices and desires
NUCLEAR SUBMARINES
Clancy, T. The hunt for Red October
Cussler, C. Pacific vortex!
NUCLEAR TERRORISM
DeMille, N. Wild fire
NUCLEAR WARFARE
King, S. 11
Miller, W. A canticle for Leibowitz
Varley, J. Demon
Walton, J. My real children
NUCLEAR WEAPONS
Burdick, E. Fail-safe
Campbell, R. Treason
Carter, S. Back channel
Coes, B. Bloody Sunday

Coonts, S. The art of war
Coulter, C. The last second
Cussler, C. Odessa Sea
Parnell, S. Man of war
Poyer, D. Overthrow
Ricciardi, D. Warning light
Shields, S. The Cassandra
Stross, C. Empire Games
Tata, A. Dark winter
Wibberley, L. The mouse that roared
NUCLEAR WEAPONS -- IRAN
Ignatius, D. The increment
NUCLEAR WEAPONS THEFTS
Parnell, S. Man of war
NUDISM
Blau, J. The summer of naked swim parties
NUDISTS
Kracht, C. Imperium
The **nugget** Deutermann, P.
NUMA files [series] Cussler, C.
Number 10 Townsend, S.
Number 11 Coe, J.
Numero zero Eco, U.
NUNEZ CABEZA DE VACA, ALVAR, ACTIVE 16TH CENTURY
Lalami, L. The Moor's account
NUNS
Akunin, B. Sister Pelagia and the white bulldog
Buehlman, C. The Suicide Motor Club
Follett, K. A column of fire
Follett, K. World without end
Godwin, G. Unfinished desires
Goudge, E. Green Dolphin Street
Gruber, M. Valley of bones
Haddam, J. Hardscrabble road
Hansen, R. Mariette in ecstasy
Harrison, C. Beyond absolution
Higgins, J. Luciano's luck
Hoeg, P. The quiet girl
Lanchester, J. Fragrant Harbor
McBain, E. The big bad city
McDermott, A. The ninth hour
Murdoch, I. The bell
Olafur Johann Olafsson The sacrament
Royal, P. Covenant with hell
Royal, P. Sanctity of hate
Royal, P. Satan's lullaby
Sharratt, M. Illuminations
Sisco, A. A deadly habit
Smith, D. The darkest heart
Vargas Llosa, M. Green house
NUNS -- FRANCE
Neville, K. The eight
NUNS -- HISTORY -- MEDIEVAL PERIOD, 1066-1485
Peters, E. The virgin in the ice
NUNS -- ITALY
Dunant, S. Sacred hearts

Kellerman, J. The clinic
Mann, T. Death in Venice and seven other stories
Maugham, W. The moon and sixpence
Melville, H. Moby-Dick; or, The whale
Millhauser, S. Martin Dressler
Murdoch, I. The sea, the sea
Nabokov, V. Lolita
Nabokov, V. Pale fire
Pamuk, O. The museum of innocence
Pronzini, B. Blue lonesome
Pynchon, T. Vineland
Quick, A. 'Til death do us part
Rendell, R. The bridesmaid
Rendell, R. The face of trespass
Rendell, R. Live flesh
Ripley, N. Find you in the dark
Ruiz Zafon, C. The angel's game
Ruiz Zafon, C. The shadow of the wind
Saramago, J. All the names
Smith, Z. The autograph man
Straub, P. Mystery
Tyler, A. Morgan's passing
Ullman, E. By blood
Walker, W. All is not forgotten

OBSESSION IN WOMEN
Cain, C. One Kick
Frame, R. Havisham
Heller, Z. What was she thinking?
Joss, M. The night following
King, S. Misery
Mann, T. The black swan
Messud, C. The woman upstairs
Rindell, S. The other typist
Robinson, P. The first cut
St. James, S. The haunting of Maddy Clare
Styles, T. Redbone

OBSESSIVE-COMPULSIVE DISORDER
Byatt, A. The children's book
Echenoz, J. Lightning
Hill, S. The risk of darkness
Lackberg, C. The ice princess
Martin, S. The pleasure of my company
Pistalo, V. Tesla
Scottoline, L. Every fifteen minutes

OBSESSIVE-COMPULSIVE DISORDER IN MEN
Dicks, M. Unexpectedly, Milo
LaValle, V. The devil in silver
The **Obsidian** chamber Preston, D.

OBSTETRICIANS -- MAINE
Irving, J. The Cider House rules

OCCULT CENTERS, GROUPS, ETC
Portis, C. Masters of Atlantis

OCCULT CRIME
Cantero, E. Meddling kids
Cornell, P. London falling
Jungstedt, M. The inner circle

OCCULT CRIME VICTIMS

Jungstedt, M. The inner circle
OCCULTISM
Bardugo, L. Ninth house
Fowler, C. Bryant & May
Merimee, P. Carmen
OCCUPATIONAL HEALTH AND SAFETY
Brown, S. White hot
OCCUPATIONS
Apelfeld, A. Blooms of darkness
Moore, C. A dirty job
Mysliwski, W. Stone upon stone
Wallace, D. The pale king
Occupied city Peace, D.
The **ocean** at the end of the lane Gaiman, N.
The **ocean** between us Wiggs, S.
OCEAN BOTTLES
Adler-Olsen, J. A conspiracy of faith
OCEAN CURRENTS
Bunn, T. Outbreak
OCEAN LINERS
Katsu, A. The deep
Porter, K. Ship of fools
Rogan, C. The lifeboat
OCEAN TRAVEL
Birch, C. Jamrach's menagerie
Cussler, C. Typhoon fury
DeMille, N. The Cuban affair
Doyle, B. The plover
Gabaldon, D. An echo in the bone
Gaige, A. Sea wife
Golding, W. Close quarters
Golding, W. Fire down below
Golding, W. Rites of passage
Grant, M. Into the drowning deep
Holdstock, P. Here I am!
Katsu, A. The deep
King, L. The game
Laukkanen, O. Gale force
Lunde, M. The end of the ocean
Martel, Y. Life of Pi
Montag, K. After the flood
O'Connor, J. Star of the Sea
Ondaatje, M. The cat's table
Powning, B. The sea captain's wife
Woolf, V. The voyage out
OCEAN TRAVEL -- ATLANTIC OCEAN
Porter, K. Ship of fools
OCEANIA
Michener, J. Tales of the South Pacific
Smith, D. Bright and distant shores
Vargas Llosa, M. The way to paradise
OCEANS
Ledgard, J. Submergence
Lem, S. Solaris
Matthiessen, P. Far Tortuga
Preston, D. Crooked river
Wright, A. Carpentaria

October Daye novels [series] McGuire, S.

The **October** list Deaver, J.

OCTOGENARIAN MEN

Wilder, T. Theophilus North

OCTOGENARIAN WOMEN

Crawford, I. A catered Christmas cookie exchange

Marsh, N. Dead water

Weldon, F. Chalcot Crescent

OCTOGENARIANS

Albom, M. The five people you meet in heaven

Diamant, A. The Boston girl

Fowler, C. Bryant & May

Griffin, A. When all is said

Groen, H. On the bright side

Hooper, E. Etta and Otto and Russell and James

Leonard, E. Mr. Paradise

Miller, D. Norwegian by night

Parker, T. Cold pursuit

Rooney, K. Lillian Boxfish takes a walk

Sparks, N. The not(ebk.)

Wilder, T. Theophilus North

Odd numbers Holt, A.

Odd Singsaker [series] Brekke, J.

The **odds** O'Nan, S.

Odds against tomorrow Rich, N.

Odessa Sea Cussler, C.

Odessa, Odessa Artson, B.

ODIN (NORSE DEITY)

Gaiman, N. Norse mythology

ODORS

Bauermeister, E. The scent keeper

ODYSSEUS (GREEK MYTHOLOGY)

Miller, M. Circe

Unsworth, B. The songs of the kings

Of fire and lions Andrews, M.

Of human bondage Maugham, W.

Of love and evil Rice, A.

Of love and shadows Allende, I.

Of mice and men Steinbeck, J.

Of time and the river Wolfe, T.

Off Armageddon reef Weber, D.

An **offer** from a gentleman Quinn, J.

OFFICE ENVIRONMENT

Karlsson, J. The room

OFFICE POLITICS

Goldin, M. The escape room

Mina, D. Still midnight

Phillips, H. The beautiful bureaucrat

Schumacher, J. Dear committee members

OFFICE ROMANCE

Fielding, H. Bridget Jones's diary

Hynes, J. Kings of infinite space

Kellerman, F. Milk and honey

Rockaway, K. How to hack a heartbreak

OFFICE WORKERS

Coupland, D. Microserfs

Hynes, J. Kings of infinite space

Karlsson, J. The room

Pulley, N. The watchmaker of Filigree Street

Saramago, J. All the names

An **officer** and a spy Harris, R.

OFFICES

Robertson, M. The Baker Street letters

OFFSHORE OIL

Cussler, C. Sea of greed

OFFSHORE OIL WELL DRILLING RIGS

Grippando, J. Black horizon

OGLALA INDIANS

O'Brien, D. The contract surgeon

OGLALA INDIANS -- MARSEILLE

Welch, J. The heartsong of Charging Elk

OGLALA INDIANS -- WARS

O'Brien, D. The contract surgeon

OGLALA INDIANS IN FRANCE

Welch, J. The heartsong of Charging Elk

OHIO

Baldacci, D. One summer

Baldacci, D. Redemption

Berg, G. The operator

Bialosky, J. House under snow

Black, L. Let justice descend

Black, L. Suffer the children

Brown, E. The weird sisters

Castillo, L. A gathering of secrets

Castillo, L. Shamed

Cole, A. An unconditional freedom

Cramer, W. Levi's will

Ellmann, L. Ducks, Newburyport

Fftch, M. Stay and fight

Lepionka, K. The last place you look

Markley, S. Ohio

Monroe, M. God don't like ugly

Monroe, M. God still don't like ugly

Montgomery, J. The widows

Morrison, T. The bluest eye

Morrison, T. Sula

Ng, C. Everything I never told you

Ng, C. Little fires everywhere

Oates, J. A book of American martyrs

Roslund, A. Cell 8

Roth, P. Indignation

Rouda, K. Best day ever

Satyal, R. No one can pronounce my name

Smith, S. A simple plan

Walker, N. Cherry

Winfrey, K. Waiting for Tom Hanks

Woods, R. Remembrance

Yocum, R. A welcome murder

Ohio Markley, S.

OHIO -- HISTORY

Chevalier, T. The last runaway

OHIO -- HISTORY -- 18TH CENTURY

Richter, C. The awakening land

OHIO -- HISTORY -- 19TH CENTURY

OLMECS -- RELIGION
Bowles, D. Feathered serpent, dark heart of sky
OLUWALE, DAVID, 1930-1969
Phillips, C. Foreigners
OLYMPIC ATHLETES
Lohmann, J. Winning Ruby Heart
Richards, L. Death was in the blood
OLYMPIC GAMES
Cleave, C. Gold
Coldsmith, D. The long journey home
Jen, G. The resisters
Kosmatka, T. The games
OLYMPIC GAMES (11TH :, 1936 :, BERLIN, GERMANY)
Deaver, J. Garden of beasts
OLYMPIC MEDAL WINNERS
Lohmann, J. Winning Ruby Heart
OMAN
Alharthi, J. Celestial bodies
OMAN -- SOCIAL LIFE AND CUSTOMS
Alharthi, J. Celestial bodies
Omar Yussef mysteries [series] Rees, M.
Ombria in shadow McKillip, P.
OMENS
Bledsoe, A. The hum and the shiver
Omoo Melville, H.
On Agate Hill Smith, L.
On Basilisk Station Weber, D.
On beauty Smith, Z.
On Chesil Beach McEwan, I.
On Copper Street Nickson, C.
On division Goldbloom, G.
On Earth we're briefly gorgeous Vuong, O.
On Green Dolphin Street Faulks, S.
On Her Majesty's secret service Fleming, I.
On Kingdom Mountain Mosher, H.
On secret service Jakes, J.
On such a full sea Lee, C.
On swift horses Pufahl, S.
On the black hill Chatwin, B.
On the bright side Groen, H.
On the floor Campbell, A.
On the road Kerouac, J.
On the wrong track Hockensmith, S.
Once a soldier Putney, M.
The **once** and future king White, T.
Once and future king [series] White, T.
Once broken faith McGuire, S.
Once too often Simpson, D.
Once upon a prince Hauck, R.
Once upon a river Campbell, B.
Once upon a time, there was you Berg, E.
One day in the life of Ivan Denisovich Solzhenitsyn, A.
One fine day the rabbi bought a cross Kemelman, H.
One fine duke Bell, L.
One flew over the cuckoo's nest Kesey, K.
One for sorrow Barzak, C.
One for the money Evanovich, J.

The **one** for you Loren, R.
One good deed Baldacci, D.
One good earl deserves a lover MacLean, S.
One good turn Atkinson, K.
One hundred years of solitude Garcia Marquez, G.
The **one** I left behind McMahon, J.
The **one** inside Shepard, S.
One Kick Cain, C.
One last thing before I go Tropper, J.
The **one** man Gross, A.
One Mississippi Childress, M.
One more river to cross Kirkpatrick, J.
One perfect lie Scottoline, L.
One shot Child, L.
One step behind Mankell, H.
One summer Baldacci, D.
One summer in Paris Morgan, S.
One summer night Pineiro, C.
One thousand and one nights Shaykh, H.
One vacant chair Coomer, J.
One virgin too many Davis, L.
One warm winter Pope, J.
The **one** you can't forget Loren, R.
The **one** you fight for Loren, R.
The **one-eyed** man Modesitt, L.
ONE-NIGHT STANDS (INTERPERSONAL RELATIONS)
Finder, J. Judgment
Gaitskill, M. Don't cry
Guillory, J. The wedding party
Jackson, J. The almost sisters
Lauren, C. Sweet filthy boy
Lowenthal, M. Charity girl
Rai, A. Hate to want you
Ranney, K. The Scottish duke
Thomas, R. Firewatching
One-way Cauwelaert, D.
Ones who got away [series] Loren, R.
ONLINE DATING
Brodesser-Akner, T. Fleishman is in trouble
Fielding, J. All the wrong places
Frankel, L. Goodbye for now
Majors, I. Penelope Lemon
Nesbo, J. The thirst
Palmer, D. Version control
Rai, A. The right swipe
Shames, T. A risky undertaking for Loretta Singletary
Steiner, S. Missing, presumed
ONLINE IDENTITY THEFT
Ferris, J. To rise again at a decent hour
ONLINE ROMANCE
Block, L. All the flowers are dying
ONLINE SHOPPING
Hart, R. The warehouse
ONLY CHILD
Fitch, J. Paint it black
The **only** child Seo, M.
Only enchanting Balogh, M.

Cossette, C. Shelter of the most high
Croft, P. The second time I saw you
Cumming, C. A divided spy
Cumming, C. The Moroccan girl
Currie, R. Everything matters!
Danielewski, M. The familiar.
Danticat, E. Claire of the sea light
Dekker, T. Black
Dekker, T. Red
Dekker, T. White
Dickey, E. Before we were wicked
Dunant, S. The birth of Venus
Ehirim, N. Prince of monkeys
Emshwiller, C. The secret city
Englander, N. The ministry of Special Cases
Finder, J. Suspicion
Flournoy, A. The Turner house
Force, M. Five years gone
Fridlund, E. History of wolves
Gabaldon, D. A breath of snow and ashes
Greeley, M. The clergyman's wife
Greenwell, G. Cleanness
Greer, A. The impossible lives of Greta Wells
Griffin, A. When all is said
Harrison, M. Light
Hempel, A. Sing to it
Jiles, P. News of the world
Jimenez, S. The vanished birds
Kienzle, W. The rosary murders
Koontz, D. Velocity
Lancaster, J. Here I go again
Lessing, D. A proper marriage
Lethem, J. The feral detective
Linden, R. Ascension of larks
Lombardo, C. The most fun we ever had
London, S. The Aussie next door
Lourie, R. A hatred for tulips
Mackintosh, C. After the end
Mailer, N. The castle in the forest
Manning, M. The victim
Mastai, E. All our wrong todays
McGhee, A. The opposite of fate
McPherson, C. Strangers at the gate
Miller, M. Biloxi
Morris, H. Cilka's journey
Oates, J. My life as a rat
Packer, A. Songs without words
Palmer, D. The new husband
Pelecanos, G. The way home
Perry, T. The old man
Picoult, J. Lone wolf
Ramsay, H. Summer on Moonlight Bay
Rushdie, S. East, West
Sahota, S. The year of the runaways
Sainz Borgo, K. It would be night in Caracas
Sakey, M. The blade itself
Scego, I. Adua

Schulman, H. Come with me
Scott, A. The low road
Sebastian, C. It takes two to tumble
Shepard, S. Reputation
Simon, M. The last Jew standing
Smith, Z. NW
Solomons, N. House of Gold
Steadman, C. Something in the water
Turow, S. Ordinary heroes
Veletzos, R. The girl they left behind
Waldman, A. A door in the earth
Walton, J. My real children
Watt, H. To the lions
Wiesel, E. Dawn
Winawer, M. The scribe of Siena
Winter, E. The rage of dragons
Wiseman, B. Listening to love
Ca$h Trust no man

OPUS DEI.
  Bolano, R. By night in Chile
  Brown, D. The Da Vinci code
The **oracle** Cussler, C.
Oracle night Auster, P.
The **Oracle** of Stamboul Lukas, M.
ORACLES
  Lukas, M. The Oracle of Stamboul
  Vinge, J. The snow queen
ORAL HISTORIANS
  Brooks, M. World War Z
ORAL HISTORIES
  Brooks, M. World War Z
  Smith, L. Oral history
Oral history Smith, L.
ORANGE COUNTY, CALIFORNIA
  Parker, T. Black water
  Rosenberg, N. Interest of justice
  Rouda, K. The favorite daughter
Orange world and other stories Russell, K.
ORANGUTAN
  Grimes, L. Quick fix
The **orchard** of lost souls Mohamed, N.
The **orchardist** Coplin, A.
ORCHARDS
  Coplin, A. The orchardist
  Ghaffari, R. To keep the sun alive
  Johnson, C. Treeborne
An **orchestra** of minorities Obioma, C.
ORCHESTRAS
  Alexander, T. A note yet unsung
  Tremain, R. Music & silence
The **orchid** affair Willig, L.
Orchid beach Woods, S.
ORCHID GROWERS
  Stout, R. The doorbell rang
  Stout, R. Gambit
ORCS
  French, J. The Grey Bastards

Knox, T. Kockroach
Lagercrantz, D. The girl who lived twice
Lagercrantz, D. The girl who takes an eye for an eye
Latour, J. The Havana World Series
Laukkanen, O. Gale force
Laukkanen, O. The professionals
Lee, F. Jade City
Lee, F. Jade war
Lehane, D. Live by night
Lehane, D. World gone by
Lewis, T. GBH
Longworth, M. Death at the Chateau Bremont
MacBride, S. Blind eye
MacBride, S. Dying light
MacDonald, J. The lonely silver rain
MacDonald, J. The scarlet ruse
Mallon, T. Bandbox
Mamet, D. Chicago
Mark, D. Cruel mercy
Mark, D. Sorrow bound
Marks, J. Fangland
Martin, K. Beyond reason
McInerney, L. The glorious heresies
Mieville, C. Perdido Street Station
Montero, M. Dancing to "Almendra"
Mortimer, J. Quite honestly
Mosley, W. Debbie doesn't do it anymore
Mosley, W. Devil in a blue dress
Mosley, W. Known to evil
Mosley, W. The long fall
Nesbo, J. Blood on snow
O'Neill, H. The Lonely Hearts Hotel
Panowich, B. Like lions
Paretsky, S. Shell game
Parker, R. Night passage
Parker, R. Stranger in paradise
Parker, T. The fallen
Parker, T. Storm runners
Parks, B. The player
Pearson, R. Choke point
Perry, T. The informant
Pirrone, D. Shall we not revenge
Polansky, D. Low town
Puzo, M. The godfather
Puzo, M. The Sicilian
Qiu, X. Red mandarin dress
Quartey, K. The missing American
Quinn, S. Dog on it
Rabe, P. Anatomy of a killer ;
Ramqvist, K. The white city
Rankin, I. The hanging garden
Rankin, I. The naming of the dead
Rankin, I. Rather be the devil
Rankin, I. Resurrection men
Rosen, L. The Kortelisy escape
Rosen, R. Dollface
Scerbanenco, G. A private Venus

Sharpe, T. Barbed wire heart
Shrier, H. Boston cream
Shteyngart, G. The Russian debutante's handbook
Siger, J. Target Tinos
Simon, M. The last Jew standing
Smith, D. The darkest heart
Smith, M. Tatiana
Soderberg, A. The other son
Spillane, M. Kill me, darling
Stewart, A. Girl waits with gun
Straley, J. The big both ways
Swinson, K. A gangster and a gentleman
Tinti, H. The twelve lives of Samuel Hawley
Turner, N. A hustler's wife
Turow, S. Testimony
Watkins, J. Secrets of a side bitch
Watkins, J. Secrets of a side bitch 2
Weir, A. Artemis
Westlake, D. Get real
Westlake, D. Watch your back!
Westlake, D. What's so funny?
White, S. Tears of a hustler 2
Winslow, D. The border
Winslow, D. The cartel
Winspear, J. The American agent
Woods, T. True to the game
Woods, T. True to the game II
Woods, T. True to the game III
Woods, T. Dutch

ORGANIZED CRIME -- ITALY
Faletti, G. A pimp's notes
ORGANIZED CRIME -- RUSSIA
Smith, M. Red Square
ORGANIZED CRIME -- WASHINGTON, D.C.
Pelecanos, G. The cut
ORGANIZED CRIME AND GAMBLING
Latour, J. The Havana World Series
Pronzini, B. Fever
Puzo, M. The last don
ORGANIZED CRIME AND HEROIN TRAFFIC
K'wan Hoodlum
ORGANIZED CRIME INVESTIGATION
Perry, T. The informant
ORGASM
Adams, L. The bromance book club
ORIENT EXPRESS (TRAIN)
Christie, A. Murder on the Orient Express
Meyer, N. The adventure of the peculiar protocols
Origin Abu-Jaber, D.
The **origin** of the Brunists Coover, R.
Original sin James, P.
Original skin Mark, D.
Orlando Woolf, V.
ORNITHOLOGISTS
Drayson, N. A guide to the birds of East Africa
Festing, I. The bird keeper
Street, K. Edgar Allan Poe and the jewel of Peru

Roy, A. An atlas of impossible longing
Sapphire The kid
Shepard, J. The book of Aron
Sinha, I. Animal's people
Smith, D. Bright and distant shores
Stedman, M. The light between oceans
Swift, G. Mothering Sunday
Tsukiyama, G. The street of a thousand blossoms
Vlautin, W. Don't skip out on me
Warrington, F. Grail of the summer stars
Waters, S. Fingersmith
Wells, B. The end of loneliness
Welty, E. Delta wedding
Wiesel, E. A mad desire to dance
Wiggs, S. The Oysterville sewing circle
Wilhelm, K. The good children
Yoon, P. Run me to earth
Zimmerman, J. The orphanmaster

ORPHANS -- CHINA
Ishiguro, K. When we were orphans

ORPHANS -- EUROPE
Sebald, W. Austerlitz

ORPHANS -- KOREA
Lee, C. The surrendered

ORPHANS -- MAINE
Irving, J. The Cider House rules

ORPHANS -- NORTH CAROLINA
Smith, L. On Agate Hill

The **orphans** of Race Point Francis, P.

Orsinian tales Le Guin, U.

ORTHODOX JEWS
Kellerman, F. The forgotten
Kellerman, F. Jupiter's bones
Kellerman, F. Milk and honey
Kellerman, F. Prayers for the dead
Kellerman, F. Serpent's tooth
Mirvis, T. The outside world
Pirrone, D. Shall we not revenge

ORTHODOX JUDAISM
Mirvis, T. The outside world

Orwell Brennan mysteries [series] Strange, M.

Oryx and Crake Atwood, M.

OSGOOD, JAMES R (JAMES RIPLEY), 1836-1892
Pearl, M. The last Dickens

OSLO, NORWAY
Dahl, K. The courier
Holt, A. Odd numbers
Miller, D. Norwegian by night
Nesbo, J. The bat
Nesbo, J. Blood on snow
Nesbo, J. The devil's star
Nesbo, J. Nemesis
Nesbo, J. The leopard
Nesbo, J. Phantom
Nesbo, J. Police
Nesbo, J. The redeemer
Nesbo, J. The snowman

Nesbo, J. The son
Nesbo, J. The thirst

OSTRACISM
Faulkner, W. Light in August
Harris, C. Good time coming
Hawthorne, N. The scarlet letter
Hibbert, T. A girl like her
Hoffman, A. Practical magic
Keane, M. Fever
Kress, N. Beggars in Spain
O'Brien, E. Girl
Searles, J. Help for the haunted
Winslow, D. In West Mills

OSWALD, LEE HARVEY, 1939-1963
DeLillo, D. Libra

The **other** Guterson, D.
The **other** Americans Lalami, L.
The **other** Boleyn girl Gregory, P.
The **other** child Link, C.
The **other** family Trollope, J.
The **other** lady vanishes Quick, A.
The **other** Mrs. Kubica, M.
The **other** people Tudor, C.
Other people's children Trollope, J.
The **other** son Soderberg, A.
The **other** typist Rindell, S.
The **other** wife Robotham, M.
The **other** wind Le Guin, U.
The **other** woman Jones, S.
The **other** woman Ryan, H.
The **other** woman Silva, D.
Others of my kind Sallis, J.
Otherwise engaged Palmer, L.
Otherwise engaged Quick, A.

OTTAWA, ONTARIO
Cumyn, A. Losing it
Shields, C. The stone diaries

The **Ottoman** cage Nadel, B.

OTTOMAN EMPIRE (1299-1922)
Hammad, I. The Parisian, or, Al-Barisi

Our endless numbered days Fuller, C.
Our house Candlish, L.
Our kind of traitor Le Carre, J.
Our Lady of the Forest Guterson, D.
Our man in Havana Greene, G.
Our mutual friend Dickens, C.
Our riches Adimi, K.
Our short history Grodstein, L.
Our souls at night Haruf, K.
Our story begins Wolff, T.
Out of darkness, shining light Gappah, P.
Out of the Black Land Greenwood, K.
Out of the dark Hurwitz, G.
Out of the Easy Sepetys, R.
Out stealing horses Petterson, P.
Out to Canaan Karon, J.
Outbreak Bunn, T.

The **Oxford** book of science fiction stories
Oxford time travel novels [series] Willis, C.
OXFORD, ENGLAND
  Benjamin, M. Alice I have been
  Butler, G. Death lives next door
  Cartwright, J. To heaven by water
  Dexter, C. The daughters of Cain
  Dexter, C. The remorseful day
  Dexter, C. The way through the woods
  Dunmore, E. Bringing down the duke
  Sayers, D. Gaudy night
  Shannon, S. The bone season
  Shannon, S. The mime order
  Spencer, S. The shivering turn
  Vanderhaeghe, G. The last crossing
  Whelan, J. My Oxford year
  Willis, C. Blackout
  Yates, C. Black chalk
OXFORD, ENGLAND -- HISTORY
  Willis, C. To say nothing of the dog
OXFORD, ENGLAND -- HISTORY -- 17TH CENTURY
  Pears, I. An instance of the fingerpost
OXFORDSHIRE, ENGLAND
  Johnson, D. Everything under
OXFORDSHIRE, ENGLAND -- HISTORY -- 14TH CEN-TURY
  Starr, M. Unhallowed ground
Oxygen Miller, A.
Oyster Biguenet, J.
The **Oysterville** sewing circle Wiggs, S.
OZARK MOUNTAIN REGION
  Eskens, A. Nothing more dangerous
  Hess, J. Maggody and the moonbeams
  Woodrell, D. Winter's bone
OZARK MOUNTAIN REGION
  McMurtry, L. Zeke and Ned

P

P. J. Benson mysteries [series] Soule, M.
P. T. A.
  Ganshert, K. No one ever asked
  Gelman, L. Class mom
  Gelman, L. You've been volunteered
Pachinko Lee, M.
Pacific Drury, T.
PACIFIC AREA
  Deutermann, P. The Iceman
  McCullough, C. An indecent obsession
Pacific beat Parker, T.
PACIFIC COAST (UNITED STATES)
  Gardiner, M. The Dirty Secrets Club
Pacific glory Deutermann, P.
PACIFIC NORTHWEST
  Alexie, S. Blasphemy
  Bauermeister, E. The scent keeper
  Bauermeister, E. The school of essential ingredients

Coplin, A. The orchardist
Crumley, J. The wrong case
Dodd, C. Dead girl running
Dodd, C. What doesn't kill her
Dorris, M. Cloud chamber
Dorris, M. A yellow raft in blue water
Piatote, B. The beadworkers
Priest, C. Boneshaker
Pyper, A. The homecoming
Raymond, J. The half-life
Stirling, S. Dies the fire
Stirling, S. A meeting at Corvallis
PACIFIC NORTHWEST -- HISTORY -- 19TH CENTURY
  Overholser, W. Death of a cattle king
PACIFIC NORTHWEST FICTION
  Alexie, S. Blasphemy
  Alexie, S. Flight
  Alexie, S. Reservation blues
  Bauermeister, E. The school of essential ingredients
  Bowen, P. Badlands
  Brautigan, R. An unfortunate woman
  Burke, J. Black cherry blues
  Burns, C. Black hole
  Coplin, A. The orchardist
  Dean, D. The madonnas of Leningrad
  Dexter, P. Spooner
  Doig, I. Dancing at the Rascal Fair
  Doig, I. Mountain time
  Doig, I. Ride with me, Mariah Montana
  Doig, I. The whistling season
  Doyle, B. The plover
  Evison, J. The revised fundamentals of caregiving
  Evison, J. West of here
  Ford, J. Songs of Willow Frost
  Fowler, K. Sarah Canary
  Gloss, M. The hearts of horses
  Guterson, D. The other
  Guterson, D. Our Lady of the Forest
  Guterson, D. Snow falling on cedars
  Haynes, D. Crashers
  Jance, J. Birds of prey
  Johnson, D. Train dreams
  Kesey, K. One flew over the cuckoo's nest
  Kesey, K. Sometimes a great notion
  Kirkpatrick, J. This road we traveled
  Kittredge, W. The willow field
  Krentz, J. Copper Beach
  Le Guin, U. The lathe of heaven
  Margolin, P. Wild justice
  McGuane, T. Gallatin Canyon
  Pajer, B. Capacity for murder
  Pajer, B. The Edison effect
  Pajer, B. Fatal induction
  Pajer, B. A spark of death
  Priest, C. Boneshaker
  Priest, C. The inexplicables
  Raymond, J. The half-life

Kellerman, J. The genius
Murakami, H. Killing commendatore
Nesbo, J. Headhunters
Perec, G. Life
Perez-Reverte, A. The painter of battles
Pilcher, R. The shell seekers
Pratchett, T. Thud!
Sarvas, M. Memento Park
Sayers, D. The five red herrings
Warrington, F. Grail of the summer stars

PAINTING -- COLLECTORS AND COLLECTING
Rothschild, H. The improbability of love

PAINTING -- PRIVATE COLLECTIONS
Frayn, M. Headlong

PAINTING, DUTCH
Mason, J. The hidden things

PAINTING, DUTCH -- 17TH CENTURY
Smith, D. The last painting of Sara De Vos

PAINTING, FLEMISH -- FORGERIES
Gaddis, W. The recognitions

PAINTING, FRENCH
Bussi, M. Black water lilies

PAKISTAN
Ahmad, J. The wandering falcon
Aslam, N. The blind man's garden
Aslam, N. The golden legend
Church, J. Bamboo and blood
Hall, T. The case of the deadly butter chicken
Hall, T. The case of the love commandos
Soniah Kamal Unmarriageable

PAKISTAN -- BOUNDARIES
Hunter, S. Dead zero

PAKISTAN -- HISTORY -- 20TH CENTURY
Majmudar, A. Partitions

PAKISTAN -- SOCIAL CONDITIONS
Mueenuddin, D. In other rooms, other wonders

PAKISTANI AMERICANS
Akhtar, A. American dervish

PAKISTANIS IN AFGHANISTAN
Aslam, N. The blind man's garden

PAKISTANIS IN ENGLAND
Aslam, N. Maps for lost lovers

PAKISTANIS IN GREAT BRITAIN
Dastgir, R. A small fortune
Simonson, H. Major Pettigrew's last stand

PAKISTANIS IN THE UNITED STATES
Dermansky, M. Very nice
Palace of rogues [series] Long, J.
Palace of treason Matthews, J.
Palace walk Mahfuz, N.

PALACES
Davis, L. A body in the bathhouse
Stephens, A. Famous adopted people
The **pale** blue eye Bayard, L.
Pale fire Nabokov, V.
The **pale** horse Christie, A.
Pale horse coming Hunter, S.

Pale horse, pale rider Porter, K.
The **pale** king Wallace, D.

PALEONTOLOGISTS
Swanwick, M. Bones of the Earth

PALEONTOLOGY
Michener, J. Centennial

PALEONTOLOGY -- CRETACEOUS
Bakker, R. Raptor red

PALEONTOLOGY -- MESOZOIC
Bakker, R. Raptor red

PALESTINE
Agnon, S. Only yesterday
Oz, A. Panther in the basement

PALESTINE -- HISTORY
Hammad, I. The Parisian, or, Al-Barisi

PALESTINE -- HISTORY -- 1917-1948
Joinson, S. The photographer's wife
Shalev, M. Two she-bears

PALESTINE -- HISTORY -- 1929-1948
Oz, A. Panther in the basement
Uris, L. Exodus

PALESTINE -- HISTORY -- 20TH CENTURY
Alyan, H. Salt houses

PALESTINE -- HISTORY -- TO 70 AD
Wallace, L. Ben-Hur

PALESTINIAN AMERICAN WOMEN
Mahmoud, L. Amreekiya

PALESTINIAN MEN
Littell, R. Vicious circle
Rees, M. The fourth assassin

PALESTINIAN WOMEN
Rees, M. The fourth assassin

PALESTINIANS
Abulhawa, S. The blue between sky and water
Littell, R. Vicious circle
McCann, C. Apeirogon
Qashu, S. Second person singular
Silva, D. The kill artist

PALESTINIANS -- DIASPORA
Alyan, H. Salt houses

PALESTINIANS -- IDENTITY
Hammad, I. The Parisian, or, Al-Barisi

PALESTINIANS IN NEW YORK CITY
Rees, M. The fourth assassin
Palindrome Woods, S.
A **Palm** Beach wife Marren, S.

PALM BEACH, FLORIDA
Marren, S. A Palm Beach wife
Sanders, L. McNally's dilemma
Sanders, L. McNally's gamble
Sanders, L. McNally's luck
Sanders, L. McNally's puzzle
Sanders, L. McNally's secret
Sanders, L. McNally's trial
Walker, W. Crime of privilege

PALM SPRINGS, CALIFORNIA
Hollis, L. Poppy Harmon investigates

Kelly, J. The light over London
Kibler, J. Home for erring and outcast girls
Kingsolver, B. Unsheltered
Kline, C. Orphan train
Kostova, E. The shadow land
L'Engle, M. Certain women
Les Becquets, D. Breaking wild
Lewis, T. GBH
Lim, E. Dear cyborgs
Link, C. The other child
Lovett, C. The bookman's tale
Makkai, R. The great believers
Makkai, R. The hundred-year house
McCann, C. Transatlantic
McCann, C. Zoli
McCrumb, S. The ballad of Frankie Silver
Miller, A. Oxygen
Miller, K. Augustown
Moore, G. The Sherlockian
Morton, K. The distant hours
Moyes, J. The girl you left behind
Mukherjee, N. A life apart
Murakami, H. Kafka on the shore
Naslund, S. The fountain of St. James Court
Neville, K. The eight
Obreht, T. The tiger's wife
Oksanen, S. When the doves disappeared
Paul, G. The lost daughter
Pears, I. The dream of Scipio
Phillips, C. The Rossetti letter
Phoenix, M. The space between words
Picoult, J. The storyteller
Purcell, L. The silent companions
Rayne, S. Music macabre
Redhill, M. Consolation
Restrepo, L. No place for heroes
Rosnay, T. Sarah's key
Roy, A. All the lives we never lived
Russell, K. My dark Vanessa
Scottoline, L. One perfect lie
Seay, M. The mirror thief
Sexton, M. The revisioners
Shreve, A. The weight of water
Shriver, L. The post-birthday world
Silver, M. Mary Coin
Slaughter, K. Pieces of her
Smith, A. How to be both
Smith, D. The electric hotel
Smith, D. The last painting of Sara De Vos
Smith, G. The maze at Windermere
Soule, C. Anyone
St. James, S. The broken girls
St. James, S. The Sun Down motel
Stern, S. The Pinch
Swyler, E. Light from other stars
Tidhar, L. A man lies dreaming
Torday, D. The last flight of Poxl West

Turow, S. Ordinary heroes
Vargas Llosa, M. Aunt Julia and the scriptwriter
Vargas Llosa, M. The way to paradise
Walter, J. Beautiful ruins
Wiggins, M. The shadow catcher
Williams, B. All the ways we said goodbye
Williams, B. The golden hour
Willig, L. The Ashford affair
Willig, L. The betrayal of the blood lily
Willig, L. The deception of the emerald ring
Willig, L. The garden intrigue
Willig, L. The lure of the moonflower
Willig, L. The masque of the Black Tulip
Willig, L. The orchid affair
Willig, L. The secret history of the Pink Carnation
Willig, L. The seduction of the Crimson Rose
Willig, L. The summer country
Willig, L. The temptation of the night jasmine
Willis, C. Blackout
Wilson, D. The clockwork dynasty
Wingate, L. Before we were yours
Wright, J. The house on Foster Hill
Wyld, E. After the fire, a still small voice

PARALLEL UNIVERSES
Barker, C. Weaveworld
Chiang, T. Exhalation
Cogman, G. The burning page
Cogman, G. The mortal word
Crouch, B. Dark matter
Dekker, T. Black
Dekker, T. Red
Dekker, T. White
Frei, M. The stranger's magic
Goonan, K. This shared dream
Greer, A. The impossible lives of Greta Wells
Hosking, J. Three years with the rat
Kay, G. The summer tree
Lancaster, J. Here I go again
Lennon, J. Familiar
McGuire, S. Beneath the sugar sky
McGuire, S. Down among the sticks and bones
McGuire, S. Every heart a doorway
McGuire, S. In an absent dream
McGuire, S. Middlegame
Mieville, C. The city & the city
Murakami, H. 1Q84
Nabokov, V. Ada
Newitz, A. The future of another timeline
Rucker, R. Postsingular
Schwab, V. A conjuring of light
Schwab, V. A darker shade of magic
Schwab, V. A gathering of shadows
Stross, C. Empire Games
Walton, J. My real children
Warrington, F. Elfland
Warrington, F. Grail of the summer stars
Warrington, F. Midsummer night

PARASITES

Grant, M. Parasite

Parasitology [series] Grant, M.

A **parchment** of leaves House, S.

PARENT AND ADULT CHILD

Albert, E. The book of Dahlia

Brockmeier, K. The brief history of the dead

Flournoy, A. The Turner house

Francis, D. Wedding Bush Road

Franzen, J. The corrections

Genova, L. Inside the O'Briens

Gordimer, N. Get a life

Lessing, D. The good terrorist

Levy, D. Hot milk

Macomber, D. If not for you

McPhee, M. Gorgeous lies

Meloy, M. Liars and saints

Meyer, P. American rust

Mootoo, S. Moving forward sideways, like a crab

Novey, I. Ways to disappear

O'Nan, S. Emily, alone

Picoult, J. Lone wolf

Price, R. The good priest's son

Raheem, Z. The marriage clock

Robinson, R. Cost

Stross, C. Accelerando

Tanen, S. There's a word for that

Woo, S. Love love

PARENT AND CHILD

Bates, J. Midnight at the Dragon Cafe

Berg, E. Once upon a time, there was you

Blum, J. The lost family

Brockmeier, K. The truth about Celia

Butler, N. Little faith

Buwalda, P. Bonita Avenue

Byatt, A. The children's book

Cheever, J. The Wapshot scandal

Coake, C. You came back

Coben, H. Hold tight

Dean, L. The idea of love

Doctorow, E. The book of Daniel

Edvardsson, M. A nearly normal family

Edwards, K. The memory keeper's daughter

Ferrante, E. The lost daughter

Foer, J. Here I am

Grant, L. We had it so good

Grey, Z. Woman of the frontier

Griffin, A. When all is said

Grossman, D. Falling out of time

Haslett, A. Imagine me gone

Hodgkinson, A. 22 Britannia Road

Holsinger, B. The gifted school

Iweala, U. Speak no evil

Jhabvala, R. My nine lives

Just, W. An unfinished season

Kellerman, F. Jupiter's bones

Koch, H. The dinner

Larsen, R. I am Radar

Lippman, L. Hush hush

Lordan, B. But come ye back , Beth Lordan

Majors, I. Penelope Lemon

Marcus, B. The flame alphabet

McCall Smith, A. The good husband of Zebra Drive

McDermott, A. After this

McKinty, A. The chain

Meloy, M. Liars and saints

Mirvis, T. The outside world

Munro, A. Selected stories

Osondu, E. This house is not for sale

Perrotta, T. Little children

Picoult, J. My sister's keeper

Quade, K. Night at the fiestas

Sebold, A. The almost moon

Shriver, L. We need to talk about Kevin

Swyler, E. Light from other stars

Tyler, A. Dinner at the Homesick Restaurant

Ullmann, L. Unquiet

Wiggs, S. The ocean between us

Wilson, K. The family Fang

PARENT AND CHILD -- VENICE, ITALY

Leon, D. Uniform justice

PARENT AND TEENAGER

Abu-Jaber, D. Birds of paradise

Cleveland, K. Keep you close

Edvardsson, M. A nearly normal family

Landvik, L. Chronicles of a radical hag

Marcus, B. The flame alphabet

Parker, R. School days

Pearson, A. How hard can it be?

PARENT-SEPARATED BOYS

Bailey, P. Uncle Rudolf

Ballard, J. Empire of the sun

Ishiguro, K. When we were orphans

Ko, L. The leavers

PARENT-SEPARATED CHILDREN

Ausubel, R. Sons and daughters of ease and plenty

PARENTAL KIDNAPPING

Beck, H. Here and gone

Cash, W. This dark road to mercy

Fuller, C. Our endless numbered days

Gaige, A. Schroder

Gertler, S. Drifting

Picoult, J. Vanishing acts

Rader-Day, L. The day I died

Ryan, H. What you see

PARENTAL LOVE

Ball, J. Census

Johnson, A. The first part last

PARENTHOOD

Cross-Smith, L. Whiskey & ribbons

Grodstein, L. Our short history

Hemmings, K. The possibilities

Johnson, A. The first part last

LaValle, V. The changeling

Beauvoir, S. The Mandarins
Bellow, S. Ravelstein
Bernhard, E. The books of the dead
Black, C. Murder in the Marais
Black, C. Murder in the rue de Paradis
Black, C. Three hours in Paris
Blackwell, J. Letters from Paris
Bolano, R. Monsieur Pain
Bourdeaut, O. Waiting for Bojangles
Brown, D. The Da Vinci code
Buchanan, C. The painted girls
Callanan, L. Paris by the book
Camus, A. The fall
Chee, A. The queen of the night
Coben, H. Long lost
Corleone, D. Good as gone
Cortazar, J. Hopscotch
Djavadi, N. Disoriental
Edugyan, E. Half-blood blues
Gaitskill, M. Veronica
George, N. The little Paris bookshop
Gestern, H. The people in the photo
Harkness, D. Time's convert
Helprin, M. Paris in the present tense
Hoffman, A. The story sisters
Kearsley, S. A desperate fortune
Khoury, R. Empire of lies
Lauren, C. Sweet filthy boy
Lemaitre, P. Irene
Makkai, R. The great believers
Maugham, W. The moon and sixpence
Maugham, W. Of human bondage
McLain, P. The Paris wife
Miller, A. Oxygen
Miller, H. Tropic of Cancer
Morgan, S. One summer in Paris
Orringer, J. The invisible bridge
Ozick, C. Foreign bodies
Pavone, C. The Paris diversion
Pears, I. The last judgement
Perec, G. Life
Perez-Reverte, A. The Club Dumas
Pope, B. The missing Italian girl
Proust, M. Within a budding grove
Reich, C. The take
Rhys, J. Quartet
Rice, A. The vampire Armand
Rosnay, T. Sarah's key
Roussel, R. Locus solus
Savas, A. Walking on the ceiling
Shaw, V. Dreadful company
Simenon, G. Maigret and the black sheep
Simenon, G. Maigret and the fortuneteller
Simenon, G. Maigret and the killer
Simenon, G. Maigret and the madwoman
Simenon, G. Maigret and the Saturday caller
Simenon, G. Maigret and the wine merchant

Simenon, G. Maigret bides his time
Simenon, G. Maigret goes home
Simenon, G. Maigret's memoirs
Spark, M. Aiding & abetting
Stachniak, E. The chosen maiden
Stewart, M. Nine coaches waiting
Stott, R. The coral thief
Truong, M. The book of salt, Monique Truong.
Tsao, T. The majesties
Wieland, L. Paris, 7 a.m.
Woods, S. Skin game

PARIS, FRANCE -- HISTORY
Hammad, I. The Parisian, or, Al-Barisi
Rutherfurd, E. Paris

PARIS, FRANCE -- HISTORY -- 1715-1789
Miller, A. Pure

PARIS, FRANCE -- HISTORY -- 1789-1799
Dickens, C. A tale of two cities

PARIS, FRANCE -- HISTORY -- 17TH CENTURY
Dumas, A. Twenty years after

PARIS, FRANCE -- HISTORY -- 1870-1940
Robertson, I. The Paris winter

PARIS, FRANCE -- HISTORY -- 1919-1939
Pynchon, T. Against the day

PARIS, FRANCE -- HISTORY -- 19TH CENTURY
Sedgwick, M. Mister Memory

PARIS, FRANCE -- HISTORY -- 20TH CENTURY
Jenoff, P. The ambassador's daughter
Morton, C. Stealing Mona Lisa
Williams, B. All the ways we said goodbye

PARIS, FRANCE -- HISTORY -- GERMAN OCCUPA-TION, 1940-1944
Belfoure, C. The Paris architect
Faulks, S. Paris echo
Furst, A. Under occupation
Harmel, K. The room on Rue Amelie
Kelly, M. Lilac girls
Meacham, L. Dragonfly

PARIS, FRANCE -- HISTORY -- REVOLUTION, 1789-1799
Carey, E. Little
Quinn, K. Ribbons of scarlet

PARIS, FRANCE -- HISTORY -- TO 1515
Hugo, V. The hunchback of Notre Dame

PARIS, FRANCE -- SOCIAL CONDITIONS
Balzac, H. Cousin Bette

PARIS, FRANCE -- SOCIAL LIFE AND CUSTOMS -- 18TH CENTURY
Heyer, G. These old shades
Miller, A. Pure

PARIS, FRANCE -- SOCIAL LIFE AND CUSTOMS -- 19TH CENTURY
Dumas, A. Camille
Flaubert, G. Sentimental education
Horrocks, C. The vexations
Jeffries, S. What the duke desires
Zola, E. Nana

PASTEUR, LOUIS, 1822-1895
Roiphe, A. An imperfect lens

The **pastor's** husband Warren, T.

PATAGONIA (ARGENTINA AND CHILE)
Aira, C. The seamstress and the wind

Patchwork Mason, B.

A **patchwork** planet Tyler, A.

PATENTS
Moore, G. The last days of night

Newitz, A. Autonomous

PATERNITY
Archer, J. Only time will tell

Cleage, P. Some things I never thought I'd do

Clinch, J. Finn

Doig, I. The bartender's tale

Raimondo, L. Dante's wood

Rushdie, S. Shalimar the Clown

Urrea, L. The hummingbird's daughter

Weiner, J. Little earthquakes

PATHOGENIC MICROORGANISMS
Wilson, D. The Andromeda evolution

PATHOLOGISTS
Black, B. Christine Falls

The **patient's** eyes Pirie, D.

PATIENTS
Cohen, T. They all fall down

PATRIARCHS
Araghi, A. The immortals of Tehran

Cohen, T. The summer we lost her

Dastgir, R. A small fortune

Garcia Marquez, G. The autumn of the patriarch

Garcia Marquez, G. One hundred years of solitude

PATRIARCHY
Glass, J. The women's war

Lutz, L. The swallows

Toews, M. Women talking

PATRIARCHY -- JAPAN
Mishima, Y. The sound of waves

Patrick Kenzie and Angela Gennaro novels [series] Lehane, D.

Patrick McLanahan novels [series] Brown, D.

Patrick Melrose novels [series] St. Aubyn, E.

Patrik Hedstrom mysteries [series] Lackberg, C.

Patriot games Clancy, T.

PATRIOTISM
Fountain, B. Billy Lynn's long halftime walk

Michener, J. Tales of the South Pacific

Pratchett, T. Monstrous regiment

Rash, R. The cove

PATROCLUS (GREEK MYTHOLOGY)
Barker, P. The silence of the girls

Miller, M. The song of Achilles

Patsy Dennis-Benn, N.

PATTERN PERCEPTION
Clayborn, K. Love lettering

Gibson, W. Pattern recognition

Kazinski, A. The last good man

Powers, R. The Gold Bug Variations

Pattern recognition Gibson, W.

PATTON, GEORGE S, 1885-1945 MILITARY LEADERSHIP
Shaara, J. The rising tide

Shaara, J. The steel wave

Paul Christopher novels [series] McCarry, C.

Paul Madriani novels [series] Martini, S.

Paul Samson novels [series] Porter, H.

PAUL,, THE APOSTLE, SAINT
Afshar, T. Thief of Corinth

Parini, J. The Damascus road

Paula Spencer novels [series] Doyle, R.

The **pawnbroker** Wallant, E.

PAWNBROKERS
Wallant, E. The pawnbroker

Payback ain't enough Clark, W.

Payback is a mutha Clark, W.

Payback novels [series] Clark, W.

Payback with ya life Clark, W.

The **paying** guests Waters, S.

Payoff Corleone, D.

PEACE
Adams, R. Watership Down

Clarke, A. Childhood's end

Littell, R. Vicious circle

Liu, C. Death's end

Vonnegut, K. Armageddon in retrospect

Peace Bausch, R.

PEACE -- SOMALIA
Farah, N. Knots

PEACE ACTIVISTS
Barker, P. Regeneration

Farah, N. Knots

Gorman, E. Riders on the storm

Hunter, S. I, sniper

McCann, C. Apeirogon

Sayers, V. The powers

Shaw, W. Salt lane

PEACE CONFERENCES
Cogman, G. The mortal word

PEACE OFFICERS
Russell, M. Doc

PEACE-BUILDING
McCann, C. Apeirogon

The **peacock** emporium Moyes, J.

The **pearl** Steinbeck, J.

Pearl Cove Lowell, E.

PEARL DIVERS
Steinbeck, J. The pearl

PEARL HARBOR, ATTACK ON, 1941
Deutermann, P. The nugget

Smith, M. December 6

PEARL HARBOR, HAWAII -- HISTORY -- 20TH CENTURY
Smith, M. December 6

PEARL INDUSTRY AND TRADE

PENNSYLVANIA -- SOCIAL LIFE AND CUSTOMS -- 20TH CENTURY

Updike, J. Rabbit is rich
Updike, J. Rabbit, run

Pennyroyal Green [series] Long, J.

PENOBSCOT INDIANS

Kline, C. Orphan train

Pentecost Alley Perry, A.

PENZANCE, ENGLAND

Ware, R. The death of Mrs. Westaway

Peony in love See, L.

PEOPLE IN COMAS

Block, S. Oliver Loving
Boyden, J. Through black spruce
Brown, K. The life Lucy knew
Cook, R. Coma
Dykes, A. Whose waves these are
George, N. The book of dreams
Koontz, D. Velocity
Landvik, L. Chronicles of a radical hag
Ma, J. Beijing coma
Maguire, G. Son of a witch
Mark, D. Cruel mercy
McGhee, A. The opposite of fate
Miller, K. An angry-ass black woman
Powers, R. The echo maker
Rankin, I. The hanging garden
Reiken, F. Day for night
Self, W. Umbrella
Shakar, A. Luminarium
Soderberg, A. The other son
Tsao, T. The majesties

PEOPLE IN COMAS -- FAMILY RELATIONSHIPS

Kelly, J. The fire baby
Kelly, J. The moon tunnel

The **people** in the photo Gestern, H.
The **people** in the trees Yanagihara, H.
People like us Dunne, D.
The **people** of forever are not afraid Boianjiu, S.
People of the book Brooks, G.
People of the masks Gear, K.
People of the mist Gear, K.
The **people** on Privilege Hill and other stories Gardam, J.

PEOPLE WHO ARE BLIND

Doerr, A. All the light we cannot see
Flagg, F. Standing in the rainbow
Mitchell, D. Cloud atlas
Raimondo, L. Dante's dilemma
Raimondo, L. Dante's poison
Saramago, J. Blindness

PEOPLE WHO ARE DEAF

Maaren, K. Weave a circle round

PEOPLE WHO ARE INTERSEX

Eugenides, J. Middlesex
Roy, A. The ministry of utmost happiness
Winter, K. Annabel

PEOPLE WHO ARE MUTE

Stage, Z. Baby teeth

PEOPLE WHO HAVE HAD AMPUTATIONS

Coetzee, J. Slow man
Guterson, D. Snow falling on cedars
Kaminsky, S. Murder on the Trans-Siberian Express
Mandanipour, S. Moon brow
Pobi, R. City of windows
Russell, S. The insane train

PEOPLE WHO HAVE HAD HEART ATTACKS

De los Santos, M. The precious one
Forman, G. Leave me

PEOPLE WHO HAVE HAD STROKES

Deb, S. The point of return
Jin, H. The crazed
Persson, L. The dying detective

PEOPLE WHO HAVE HAD STROKES -- FAMILY RELATIONSHIPS

Finder, J. The fixer

PEOPLE WITH AIDS

Bellow, S. Ravelstein
Cunningham, M. The hours
Gaitskill, M. Veronica
Huston, C. Half the blood of Brooklyn
Kramer, L. Search for my heart
Makkai, R. The great believers
Toibin, C. The blackwater lightship

PEOPLE WITH ALZHEIMER'S DISEASE

Cleave, P. Trust no one
Cumyn, A. Losing it
Dean, D. The madonnas of Leningrad
Dufresne, J. Deep in the shade of paradise
Everett, P. Erasure
LaPlante, A. Turn of mind
Palahniuk, C. Choke
Robinson, R. Cost
Vinge, V. Rainbows end

PEOPLE WITH AMNESIA

Apostol, G. Gun dealers' daughter
Auster, P. Travels in the scriptorium
Brown, S. The witness
Dybek, N. The Verdun affair
Eco, U. The mysterious flame of Queen Loana
Greene, G. The last word and other stories
Ishiguro, K. The buried giant
Lightman, A. The diagnosis
Livesey, M. The missing world
Perry, A. Defend and betray
Perry, A. The face of a stranger
Putney, M. Loving a lost lord

PEOPLE WITH AMYOTROPHIC LATERAL SCLEROSIS

Rosenberg, N. Interest of justice

PEOPLE WITH ANOREXIA

Pearlman, E. Honeydew

PEOPLE WITH ASPERGER'S SYNDROME

Hoang, H. The kiss quotient

PEOPLE WITH AUTISM

PEOPLE WITH MENTAL ILLNESSES -- CARE AND TREATMENT
Kesey, K. One flew over the cuckoo's nest

PEOPLE WITH MENTAL ILLNESSES -- FAMILY RELATIONSHIPS
Fuqua, J. Gone and back again

PEOPLE WITH MULTIPLE SCLEROSIS
Coupland, D. Eleanor Rigby

PEOPLE WITH MUSCULAR DYSTROPHY
Evison, J. The revised fundamentals of caregiving

PEOPLE WITH PARAPLEGIA
Keller, J. Bone on bone
Lohmann, J. Winning Ruby Heart
Miles, J. Anatomy of a miracle
Rendell, R. Live flesh
Wilson, D. The Andromeda evolution

PEOPLE WITH PARKINSON'S DISEASE
Barry, B. The map of true places
Franzen, J. The corrections
Robotham, M. Suspect

PEOPLE WITH POLIOMYELITIS
Berg, E. We are all welcome here
London, J. The golden age

PEOPLE WITH POST-TRAUMATIC STRESS DISORDER
Dazieri, S. Kill the father
Laukkanen, O. Deception Cove
Mandanipour, S. Moon brow
Mukherjee, A. Smoke and ashes
Powell, G. Embers of war
Robertson, R. The long take

PEOPLE WITH QUADRIPLEGIA
Deaver, J. The coffin dancer
Deaver, J. The empty chair
Deaver, J. The stone monkey

PEOPLE WITH SCHIZOPHRENIA
Banasky, C. The suicide of Claire Bishop
Boyle, T. The harder they come
Hunter, E. The moment she was gone
Kiernan, C. The drowning girl
LaValle, V. The devil in silver
Vine, B. The minotaur

PEOPLE WITH SCHIZOPHRENIA -- FAMILY RELATIONSHIPS
Callaghan, M. Billy, come home

PEOPLE WITH TERMINAL ILLNESSES
Beckerman, H. If only I could tell you
Bock, C. Alice & Oliver
Giordano, P. Like family
James, H. The wings of the dove
Lewis, B. The missing
Saramago, J. Death with interruptions

PEOPLE WITH TERMINAL ILLNESSES -- FAMILY RELATIONSHIPS
Banville, J. The infinities
DeLillo, D. Zero K
Genova, L. Inside the O'Briens

The **people's** act of love Meek, J.
A **people's** future of the United States

PERCEPTION
Candlish, L. Those people
Fowler, K. Sarah Canary
Harris, S. The color of Bee Larkham's murder
Kent, H. Burial rites
Munoz Molina, A. In her absence
Richardson, C. The end of the alphabet

Percival Everett by Virgil Russell Everett, P.

Perdido Street Station Mieville, C.

The **perfect** comeback of Caroline Jacobs Dicks, M.

The **perfect** couple Hilderbrand, E.

A **perfect** explanation Anstruther, E.

Perfect fit Phillips, C.

The **perfect** girl Macmillan, G.

Perfect little children Hannah, S.

The **perfect** man Murr, N.

The **perfect** match Higgins, K.

The **perfect** mother Molloy, A.

The **perfect** wife Delaney, J.

The **perfect** world of Miwako Sumida Goenawan, C.

PERFECTION
Groff, L. Arcadia
Haig, F. The fire sermon
Monroe, M. Bad blood
Poore, M. Reincarnation blues

PERFECTIONISM
Thomas, S. Oligarchy

PERFECTIONISM IN CHILDREN
Kress, N. Beggars in Spain

PERFECTIONISM IN WOMEN
Netzer, L. Shine shine shine

Perfidia Ellroy, J.

PERFORMANCE ART
Larsen, R. I am Radar

PERFORMANCE ARTISTS
Freudenberger, N. The dissident
Wilson, K. The family Fang

PERFORMING ARTS
Alarcon, D. At night we walk in circles
Bram, C. Lives of the circus animals

PERFORMING ARTS SCHOOLS
Choi, S. Trust exercise

Perfume Suskind, P.

Perfume River Butler, R.

PERFUMES
Marsh, N. False scent
Robbins, T. Jitterbug perfume
Suskind, P. Perfume

PERFUMES INDUSTRY AND TRADE
Faber, M. The crimson petal and the white
Gaynor, H. Meet me in Monaco

The **Pericles** Commission Corby, G.

Perihelion summer Egan, G.

A **perilous** undertaking Raybourn, D.

PERIODICAL EDITORS

Mann, T. Doctor Faustus
Martin, S. An object of beauty
McCall Smith, A. The Kalahari typing school for men
McCarthy, C. The road
Meek, J. The heart broke in
Mosley, W. Fortunate son
Murdoch, I. The bell
Orringer, J. The flight portfolio
Pryor, M. Hollow man
Rawle, G. Woman's world
Rawlings, D. The baggage handler
Reay, K. The Bronte plot
Rose, H. The museum of modern love
Sakey, M. The blade itself
Shreve, A. Testimony
Smith, B. The return of Kid Cooper
Smith, G. The maze at Windermere
Stevenson, R. The strange case of Dr. Jekyll and Mr. Hyde
Stone, N. The verdict
Twain, M. Adventures of Huckleberry Finn
Vargas Llosa, M. The discreet hero
Vonnegut, K. The sirens of Titan
Walker, C. Man of the year
Warren, R. All the king's men
Watt, H. To the lions
Wayne, T. Loner
Wilde, O. The picture of Dorian Gray
Yourcenar, M. Memoirs of Hadrian
Zevin, G. The hole we're in

PERSONAL FINANCE
Ryan, J. Restless rancher
Walter, J. The financial lives of the poets

PERSONAL PROPERTY
Galsworthy, J. The Forsyte saga
Personal recollections of Joan of Arc Twain, M.

PERSONAL SPACE
Smith, A. There but for the

PERSONAL TRAINERS
Sosa, M. Acting on impulse

PERSONALITY
Simsion, G. The Rosie project

PERSONALITY ASSESSMENT
Knopf, C. You're dead

PERSONALITY CHANGE
Backman, F. Britt-Marie was here
Restrepo, L. Delirium
Persons unknown Steiner, S.

PERSPECTIVE, PERSONAL
Tyler, A. Dinner at the Homesick Restaurant
Persuader Child, L.
Persuasion Austen, J.

PERSUASION (PSYCHOLOGY)
Barry, M. Lexicon

PERTH, WESTERN AUSTRALIA
London, J. The golden age

PERU
Pulley, N. The Bedlam stacks

Redfield, J. The celestine prophecy
Rivero, M. The affairs of the Falcons
Robbins, T. Fierce invalids home from hot climates
Vargas Llosa, M. The bad girl
Vargas Llosa, M. The discreet hero
Vargas Llosa, M. Green house
Vargas Llosa, M. The time of the hero

PERU -- SOCIAL LIFE AND CUSTOMS
Alarcon, D. Lost City Radio

PERUGIA, ITALY
Dibdin, M. Ratking

PERUVIAN AMERICANS
Rivero, M. The affairs of the Falcons
Perveen Mistry novels [series] Massey, S.

PESSIMISM
Barbery, M. The elegance of the hedgehog
Pet sematary King, S.

PET SHOP OWNERS
Sanders, L. McNally's puzzle

PET SHOPS
Barry, D. Lunatics

PETER I, THE GREAT, EMPEROR OF RUSSIA, 1672-1725
Rutherfurd, E. Russka
Peter Ash novels [series] Petrie, N.
Peter Decker and Rina Lazarus mysteries [series] Kellerman, F.
Peter Diamond mysteries [series] Lovesey, P.
Peter Macklin novels [series] Estleman, L.

PETIT, PHILIPPE, 1949-
McCann, C. Let the great world spin

PETRONIUS ARBITER
Sienkiewicz, H. Quo vadis
Petropolis Ulinich, A.

PETS
Cabot, M. No judgments
King, S. Pet sematary
Miller, M. Biloxi
The pets Bragi Olafsson, 1.

PETS -- DEATH
Akunin, B. Sister Pelagia and the white bulldog

PETS -- TRAVEL
Arikawa, H. The travelling cat chronicles
Phantom Nesbo, J.
Phantom instinct Gardiner, M.
Phantom prey Sandford, J.
The Pharaoh's secret Cussler, C.

PHARMACEUTICAL RESEARCH
Newitz, A. Autonomous
Patchett, A. State of wonder
Raimondo, L. Dante's poison

PHARMACEUTICAL RESEARCH -- CORRUPT PRACTICES
Glynn, A. Receptor
Le Carre, J. The constant gardener

PHARMACISTS
Flagg, F. Standing in the rainbow

Echenoz, J. Lightning
Gibson, W. Pattern recognition
Semple, M. Where'd you go, Bernadette
Phoenix unbound Draven, G.

PHOENIX, ARIZONA
Abbott, M. Bury me deep
Bacigalupi, P. The water knife
Dimberg, K. Girl in the rearview mirror
McMillan, T. Waiting to exhale
Sallis, J. The killer is dying

Phoresis Egan, G.

The **photographer's** wife Joinson, S.

PHOTOGRAPHERS
Bohjalian, C. The double bind
Coetzee, J. Slow man
Heller, P. Celine
Hoffman, A. The Museum of Extraordinary Things
Joinson, S. The photographer's wife
Kennedy, D. The big picture
Leonard, E. LaBrava
Mallon, T. Bandbox
Norman, H. The haunting of L.
Parrish, C. Still life
Redhill, M. Consolation
Rushdie, S. The ground beneath her feet
Sayers, V. The powers
Silver, M. Mary Coin
Smith, F. Night fall
Waller, R. The bridges of Madison County
Wiggins, M. The shadow catcher

PHOTOGRAPHERS' MODELS
Humphreys, H. Afterimage

PHOTOGRAPHIC MEMORY
Coates, T. The water dancer
Sedgwick, M. Mister Memory
Self, W. Umbrella

PHOTOGRAPHS
Auster, P. Travels in the scriptorium
Brown, K. The clairvoyants
Ellison, J. A small indiscretion
Gestern, H. The people in the photo
Goldberg, M. Feast your eyes
Hand, E. Available dark
Hand, E. Hard light
Jenoff, P. The lost girls of Paris
Lock, N. American meteor
Majors, I. Penelope Lemon
Parrish, C. Still life
Pearson, R. The red room
Redhill, M. Consolation
Scott, C. The poppy wife
Wiggins, M. The shadow catcher

PHOTOGRAPHY
Allende, I. Portrait in sepia
Grass, G. The box
Otto, W. Eight girls taking pictures
Perry, A. Half Moon Street

PHOTOGRAPHY OF THE NUDE
Heath, L. Falling into bed with a duke

PHOTOJOURNALISM -- UNITED STATES -- HISTORY -- 20TH CENTURY
Silver, M. Mary Coin

PHOTOJOURNALISTS
Danielewski, M. House of leaves
Leimbach, M. The man from Saigon
Rushdie, S. The ground beneath her feet

Phryne Fisher mysteries [series] Greenwood, K.

PHYSICAL THERAPISTS
Pelecanos, G. The turnaround

PHYSICIAN AND PATIENT
Barry, S. The secret scripture
Cook, R. Cell
Hollingshead, G. Bedlam
Huyler, F. The laws of invisible things
McDonald, R. Mr. Darwin's shooter
Self, W. Umbrella
Steadman, C. Mr. Nobody

PHYSICIAN DRUG ABUSERS
Irving, J. The Cider House rules

PHYSICIANS
Allende, I. A long petal of the sea
Amis, M. Time's arrow, or The nature of the offense
Aslam, N. The wasted vigil
Atkinson, K. When will there be good news?
Balzac, H. The country doctor
Barry, S. The secret scripture
Black, C. Murder in the Bastille
Bowen, K. A rogue by night
Boyne, J. Crippen
Brodesser-Akner, T. Fleishman is in trouble
Camus, A. The plague
Celine, L. Journey to the end of the night
Child, L. Deep storm
Christie, A. The murder of Roger Ackroyd
Cook, R. Cell
Cook, R. Coma
Cotterill, C. The coroner's lunch
Cronin, A. Citadel
Davies, R. The cunning man
Downie, R. Semper Fidelis
Downie, R. Tabula rasa
Dugoni, R. The extraordinary life of Sam Hell
Edwards, K. The memory keeper's daughter
Eliot, G. Middlemarch
Forster, E. A passage to India
Francis, F. Pulse
Greene, G. The honorary consul
Guillory, J. The proposal
Guillory, J. The wedding date
Hawley, N. The good father
Hawthorne, N. The scarlet letter
Huyler, F. The laws of invisible things
Iles, G. Black cross
Iles, G. Third degree

Millay, K. The sea of tranquility

The **piano** man's daughter Findley, T.

PIANO TEACHERS

Bragg, M. A son of war

The **piano** tuner Mason, D.

PIANO TUNERS

Mason, D. The piano tuner

PIANOS

Cander, C. The weight of a piano

PICARESQUE FICTION

Allende, I. Eva Luna

Auster, P. Timbuktu

Barth, J. The sot-weed factor

Beatty, P. Slumberland

Bellow, S. The adventures of Augie March

Boyne, J. The heart's invisible furies

Byrne, T. Ghosts and lightning

Carey, P. Parrot and Olivier in America

Cauwelaert, D. One-way

Celine, L. Journey to the end of the night

Cervantes Saavedra, M. Don Quixote

Coe, J. The terrible privacy of Maxwell Sim

Defoe, D. Moll Flanders

Dickens, C. Nicholas Nickleby

Dickens, C. The Pickwick papers

Doyle, R. A star called Henry

Dunn, K. Geek love

Fielding, H. The history of Tom Jones, a foundling

Grass, G. The tin drum

Jonasson, J. The accidental further adventures of the hundred-year-old man

Kehlmann, D. Tyll

King, R. Domino

Larsen, R. The selected works of T. S. Spivet

Maalouf, A. Balthasar's odyssey

Ozick, C. The Puttermesser papers

Percy, W. The last gentleman

Portis, C. The dog of the South

Roth, P. The great American novel

Roth, P. Portnoy's complaint

Smith, Z. The autograph man

Twain, M. Adventures of Huckleberry Finn

Van der Vliet Oloomi, A. Call me Zebra

Wallace, D. Big fish

Pickle's progress Butler, M.

PICKPOCKETS

Dickens, C. Oliver Twist, or The parish boy's progress

The **pickup** Gordimer, N.

The **Pickwick** papers Dickens, C.

The **picture** of Dorian Gray Wilde, O.

Picturing Will Beattie, A.

Piece of mind Adelman, M.

Piece of my heart Robinson, P.

Pieces of her Slaughter, K.

PIEGAN INDIANS

Guthrie, A. The big sky

PIG FARMING

Del Amo, J. Animalia

Sthers, A. Holy lands

PIGEONS

Echenoz, J. Lightning

PIGS

Del Amo, J. Animalia

PIGS -- BREEDING -- ENVIRONMENTAL ASPECTS

Proulx, A. That old ace in the hole

Pigs in heaven Kingsolver, B.

Pike Logan thrillers [series] Taylor, B.

PILATE, PONTIUS, 1ST CENT

Bulgakov, M. The master and Margarita

The **pilgrim** Nissenson, H.

The **pilgrim** of hate Peters, E.

The **pilgrim's** progress Bunyan, J.

PILGRIMS (NEW ENGLAND SETTLERS)

Nissenson, H. The pilgrim

PILGRIMS AND PILGRIMAGES

Crace, J. Quarantine

Endo, S. Deep river

Gunn, J. Transcendental

Potzsch, O. The poisoned pilgrim

Royal, P. Covenant with hell

Simmons, D. The fall of Hyperion

Simmons, D. Hyperion

PILGRIMS AND PILGRIMAGES, CHRISTIAN

Bunyan, J. The pilgrim's progress

Peters, E. The pilgrim of hate

Spark, M. The Mandelbaum gate

PILLAGE

Doctorow, E. The march

Sainz Borgo, K. It would be night in Caracas

The **pillars** of the earth Follett, K.

Pillars of the Earth [series] Follett, K.

The **pilot's** wife Shreve, A.

PILOTS

Benjamin, M. The aviator's wife

Bohjalian, C. The night strangers

Bolano, R. Distant star

Buchman, M. Pure heat

Caputo, P. Acts of faith

Deutermann, P. Pacific glory

Heller, P. The dog stars

Higgins, J. Flight of eagles

Joinson, S. The photographer's wife

Lathen, E. Something in the air

Priest, C. Ganymede

Saint-Exupery, A. The little prince

Saint-Exupery, A. Night flight

PILOTS -- GREAT BRITAIN

Bates, H. Fair stood the wind for France

Llywelyn, M. 1949

PILOTS -- JAPAN

Clavell, J. Shogun

A **pimp's** notes Faletti, G.

PIMPS

Hobbs, A. Stealing candy

Willis, C. Doomsday book

PLAGUE -- GERMANY -- HISTORY -- 14TH CENTURY

Flynn, M. Eifelheim

PLAGUE -- JAPAN

Oe, K. Nip the buds, shoot the kids

PLAGUE -- TREATMENT

Newman, S. The country of Ice Cream Star

The **plague** of doves Erdrich, L.

Plainsong Haruf, K.

PLANETS

Chambers, B. To be taught, if fortunate

Egan, G. Phoresis

Harrison, M. Nova swing

Starling, C. The luminous dead

Stephenson, N. Anathem

PLANETS -- COLONIZATION

Corey, J. Babylon's ashes

Corey, J. Cibola burn

Corey, J. Nemesis games

Robinson, K. Blue Mars

Robinson, K. Green Mars

Robinson, K. Red Mars

PLANETS -- EXPLORATION

Cambias, J. A darkling sea

Weir, A. The Martian

PLANNED COMMUNITIES

Smith, Z. NW

PLANNERS

Christopher, A. Not the girl you marry

PLANT CLOSINGS

Russo, R. Empire Falls

PLANT PATHOLOGISTS

White, B. Quite a year for plums

PLANTAGENET PERIOD (1154-1485)

Cornwell, B. 1356

Cornwell, B. The archer's tale

Follett, K. World without end

Franklin, A. Mistress of the art of death

Franklin, A. The serpent's tale

Gregory, P. The kingmaker's daughter

Gregory, P. The red queen

Gregory, P. The white princess

Penman, S. Cruel as the grave

Penman, S. Devil's brood

Penman, S. Dragon's lair

Penman, S. Falls the shadow

Penman, S. Here be dragons

Penman, S. A king's ransom

Penman, S. Lionheart

Penman, S. The Queen's man

Penman, S. The reckoning

Penman, S. The sunne in splendour

Penman, S. Time and chance

Robb, C. The cross-legged knight

Robb, C. A gift of Sanctuary

Robb, C. A murdered peace

Robb, C. The riddle of St. Leonard's

Robb, C. A twisted vengeance

Royal, P. Covenant with hell

Royal, P. Sanctity of hate

Royal, P. Satan's lullaby

Rutherfurd, E. London

Scott, W. Ivanhoe

Sedley, K. The Tintern treasure

Seton, A. Katherine

Starr, M. Unhallowed ground

PLANTATION HOUSES

Dufresne, J. Deep in the shade of paradise

Sparks, N. The not(ebk.)

PLANTATION LIFE

Atakora, A. Conjure women

Dufresne, J. Deep in the shade of paradise

Faulkner, W. Absalom, Absalom!

Faulkner, W. Go down, Moses

Hicks, R. The widow of the South

Jones, E. The known world

Levy, A. The long song

Locke, A. The cutting season

Martin, V. Property

Michener, J. Chesapeake

Santiago, E. Conquistadora

Stowe, H. Uncle Tom's cabin

Straight, S. A million nightingales

Walker, M. Jubilee

Willig, L. The summer country

PLANTATION LIFE -- NORTH CAROLINA

Smith, L. On Agate Hill

PLANTATION LIFE -- SOUTHERN STATES

Rawles, N. My Jim

PLANTATION OWNERS

Coates, T. The water dancer

Hicks, R. The widow of the South

PLANTATION OWNERS' SPOUSES

Hicks, R. The widow of the South

Martin, V. Property

PLANTATIONS

Hicks, R. The widow of the South

James, M. The book of night women

Mitchell, M. Gone with the wind

Tademy, L. Cane River

Warren, R. Band of angels

Welty, E. Delta wedding

PLANTATIONS -- LOUISIANA

Gaines, E. A gathering of old men

Locke, A. The cutting season

Straight, S. A million nightingales

PLANTATIONS -- MALAYSIA

Tan, T. The garden of evening mists

PLANTATIONS -- MISSISSIPPI

Odell, J. The healing

PLANTATIONS -- NORTH CAROLINA

Crafts, H. The bondwoman's narrative

Smith, L. On Agate Hill

PLANTATIONS -- VIRGINIA

Martine, A. A memory called empire
POETS
Araghi, A. The immortals of Tehran
Auster, P. Invisible
Auster, P. Timbuktu
Barth, J. The sot-weed factor
Beagle, P. In Calabria
Benz, C. The gone dead
Bolano, R. Distant star
Bolano, R. Nazi literature in the Americas
Byatt, A. Possession
Carey, P. My life as a fake
Chang, L. All is forgotten, nothing is lost
Cooley, M. The archivist
Crowley, J. Lord Byron's novel
Cunningham, M. Specimen days
Darznik, J. Song of a captive bird
Delany, S. Dhalgren
Dillard, A. The Maytrees
Fitzgerald, P. The blue flower
Hollinghurst, A. The stranger's child
Jin, H. A free life
Kostova, E. The shadow land
Lerner, B. Leaving the Atocha Station
Levy, D. Swimming home
Littell, R. The Mayakovsky tapes
Littell, R. The Stalin epigram
Makkai, R. The hundred-year house
McInerny, R. Celt and pepper
Michaels, A. Fugitive pieces
Morton, K. The house at Riverton
Moses, K. Wintering
Munoz Molina, A. A manuscript of ashes
Owen, L. The quick
Qiu, X. Death of a red heroine
Rooney, S. Conversations with friends
Sanders, J. Speakers of the dead
Senna, D. New people
Shreve, A. The last time they met
Simmons, D. The fall of Hyperion
Simmons, D. Hyperion
Vinge, V. Rainbows end
Vollmann, W. Europe central
Vuong, O. On Earth we're briefly gorgeous
Yi, C. The investigation
POETS -- PROVENCE, FRANCE
Pears, I. The dream of Scipio
POETS, AFRICAN
Coetzee, J. Elizabeth Costello
POETS, AMERICAN
Bellow, S. Humboldt's gift
Dos Passos, J. 1919
POETS, ENGLISH
Friedman, D. Riot most uncouth
Waugh, E. The loved one
POETS, ENGLISH -- 19TH CENTURY
Byatt, A. Possession

Pearl, M. The Dante chamber
Shepherd, L. A fatal likeness
POETS, ENGLISH -- 20TH CENTURY
Barker, P. The eye in the door
Barker, P. The ghost road
Barker, P. Regeneration
POETS, ISRAELI
Oz, A. Fima
POETS, MEXICAN
Bolano, R. Amulet
Bolano, R. The savage detectives
POETS, RUSSIAN -- 20TH CENTURY
Pasternak, B. Doctor Zhivago
POETS, TURKISH
Pamuk, O. Snow
Point Deception Muller, M.
The **point** of return Deb, S.
The **poison** tree Kelly, E.
Poisoned ground Parshall, S.
The **poisoned** pilgrim Potzsch, O.
Poisoner mysteries [series] Poole, S.
POISONING
Barclay, L. The twenty-three
Beaton, M. Agatha Raisin and the quiche of death
Berne, S. The dogs of Littlefield
Christie, A. The hollow
Flynn, G. Sharp objects
Franklin, A. The serpent's tale
Haddam, J. Hardscrabble road
Haddam, J. True believers
Hall, T. The case of the deadly butter chicken
Harper, K. The poyson garden
Higgins, J. Midnight runner
Jackson, S. We have always lived in the castle
McCall Smith, A. The Saturday big tent wedding party
McCrumb, S. If I'd killed him when I met him
McGuire, S. Chimes at midnight
Murdoch, I. The good apprentice
Pandian, G. The accidental alchemist
Peters, E. Monk's hood
Potzsch, O. The beggar king
Potzsch, O. The dark monk
Rash, R. Above the waterfall
Rice, A. Of love and evil
Robb, J. Innocent in death
Robertson, I. Circle of shadows
Roosevelt, E. Murder and the First Lady
Sayers, D. The unpleasantness at the Bellona Club
Saylor, S. The judgment of Caesar
Stout, R. Gambit
Tsao, T. The majesties
POISONOUS GASES
DeLillo, D. White noise
Murakami, H. After the quake
POISONOUS MUSHROOMS
Sayers, D. The documents in the case
POISONOUS PLANTS

Eriksson, K. The princess of Burundi
Estleman, L. Gas City
Evanovich, J. One for the money
Ewan, C. Dark tides
Faye, L. The gods of Gotham
Faye, L. Seven for a secret
Finch, C. A beautiful blue death
Fossum, K. Bad intentions
Fossum, K. Eva's eye
Fowler, C. Bryant & May
Freedman, B. Mrs. Mike
French, N. Blue Monday
French, N. Friday on my mind
French, N. Thursday's children
French, N. Tuesday's gone
French, N. Waiting for Wednesday
French, T. Broken harbor
French, T. Faithful place
French, T. In the woods
French, T. The secret place
Furst, A. Spies of the Balkans
Garcia-Roza, L. December heat
Genova, L. Inside the O'Briens
George, E. A banquet of consequences
George, E. Believing the lie
George, E. Careless in red
George, E. Just one evil act
George, E. The punishment she deserves
George, E. This body of death
Gerritsen, T. The apprentice
Gerritsen, T. I know a secret
Gerritsen, T. The surgeon
Gilman, D. Kaleidoscope
Goodis, D. Nightfall
Goodman, C. The sea of lost girls
Greene, G. The human factor
Griffiths, E. The stranger diaries
Grimes, M. The Old Wine Shades
Grimes, M. The winds of change
Grindle, L. Villa Triste
Guinn, M. The scribe
Hamilton, P. The dreaming void
Hammett, D. The Maltese falcon
Hannah, S. The cradle in the grave
Hannah, S. The wrong mother
Harris, R. Fatherland
Harrison, M. Nova swing
Harrod-Eagles, C. Game over
Harrod-Eagles, C. Headlong
Harvey, J. Darkness, darkness
Harvey, J. Far cry
Harvey, M. The Chicago way
Harvey, M. The fifth floor
Harvey, M. Pulse
Hayder, M. Birdman
Hayder, M. Gone
Hayder, M. Poppet

Hayder, M. Ritual
Hayder, M. Skin
Hayder, M. The treatment
Hewson, D. The garden of evil
Hewson, D. A season for the dead
Hiaasen, C. Bad monkey
Higashino, K. Malice
Higashino, K. Newcomer
Hill Gumbao, T. The summer of dead toys
Hill, S. The pure in heart
Hill, S. The risk of darkness
Hill, S. The shadows in the street
Hill, S. The various haunts of men
Houellebecq, M. The map and the territory
Humphreys, S. Trouble walks in
Hunt, A. City of saints
James, P. The black tower
James, P. A certain justice
James, P. Death of an expert witness
James, P. Devices and desires
James, P. The lighthouse
James, P. The private patient
James, P. Original sin
James, P. A taste for death
Kellerman, F. The forgotten
Kellerman, F. Jupiter's bones
Kellerman, F. Milk and honey
Kellerman, F. Prayers for the dead
Kellerman, F. Serpent's tooth
Kellerman, J. Gone
Kellerman, J. Therapy
Kent, C. The loving husband
Kent, K. The burn
Kent, K. The dime
Kent, K. The outcasts
Kepler, L. The hypnotist
Kepler, L. The sandman
Kerr, P. Metropolis
Koontz, D. The husband
Koontz, D. Velocity
Lackberg, C. The ice princess
Lackberg, C. The hidden child
Lackberg, C. The preacher
Lackberg, C. The stonecutter
Lamberson, G. The frenzy way
Larsson, A. Until thy wrath be past
Laukkanen, O. Criminal enterprise
Laukkanen, O. The professionals
Lawrence, D. The dead sit round in a ring
Lehane, D. The given day
Leonard, E. Freaky deaky
Lescroart, J. The first law
Lescroart, J. The hearing
Lovesey, P. The house sitter
Lovesey, P. The last detective
Lovesey, P. The tooth tattoo
Lovesey, P. Waxwork

Price, R. Lush life

Pronzini, B. The violated

Pyne, D. Catalina eddy

Qiu, X. Shanghai redemption

Quartey, K. Gold of our fathers

Rankin, I. The beat goes on

Rankin, I. The complaints

Rankin, I. Exit music

Rankin, I. The impossible dead

Rendell, R. The babes in the wood

Rendell, R. End in tears

Rendell, R. Harm done

Rendell, R. Kissing the gunner's daughter

Rendell, R. Road rage

Rendell, R. A sleeping life

Rendell, R. Simisola

Rendell, R. Speaker of Mandarin

Reynolds, A. The prefect

Rigosi, G. Night bus

Rindell, S. The other typist

Robinson, P. Careless love

Robinson, P. Children of the revolution

Robinson, P. Close to home

Robinson, P. In the dark places

Robotham, M. The night ferry

Rose, J. The blackest bird

Rosenfelt, D. Black and blue

Rosenfelt, D. Blackout

Rosenfelt, D. Don't tell a soul

Rowland, L. The Ripper's shadow

Rowland, R. Cold country

Rowson, P. Death lies beneath

Rowson, P. Undercurrent

Ryan, H. The other woman

Ryan, H. Truth be told

Ryan, H. What you see

Sanders, L. The first deadly sin

Sanders, L. The tenth commandment

Sandford, J. Buried prey

Sandford, J. Naked prey

Sandford, J. Night prey

Sandford, J. Silken prey

Sandford, J. Storm prey

Sedgwick, M. Mister Memory

Serafim, L. The devil takes half

Serafim, L. When the devil's idle

Shames, T. An unsettling crime for Samuel Craddock

Shannon, D. Chaos of crime

Shaw, W. The birdwatcher

Shaw, W. A song for the brokenhearted

Silvis, R. Two days gone

Simpson, D. Dead and gone

Simpson, D. Dead by morning

Smith, F. Night fall

Smith, M. Red Square

Smith, M. The Siberian dilemma

Smith, M. Tatiana

Smith, T. Child 44

Solomita, S. A good day to die

Spencer, S. Backlash

Spencer, S. Best served cold

Spencer, S. Death's dark shadow

Spencer, S. Echoes of the dead

Spencer, S. Lambs to the slaughter

Spencer, S. The ring of death

Spencer, S. A walk with the dead

Stanley, M. Death of the mantis

Stark, R. Ask the parrot

Steinhauer, O. The Bridge of Sighs

Straley, J. The big both ways

Strange, M. Follow me down

Swinson, K. Lifestyles of the rich and shameless

Tallis, F. Vienna blood

Tracy, P. Monkeewrench

Tran, V. Dragonfish

Transgressions

Wambaugh, J. The blue knight

Wambaugh, J. Finnegan's week

Wambaugh, J. Floaters

Wambaugh, J. The new centurions

Watkins, J. Secrets of a side bitch

Westlake, D. Bank shot

White, S. Tears of a hustler 2

Winters, B. Countdown City

Winters, B. The last policeman

Winters, B. World of trouble

Wolf, D. The execution

Woods, S. New York dead

Wright, A. Carpentaria

Yocum, R. A welcome murder

Zhou, H. Death notice

Police Nesbo, J.

POLICE -- ALASKA

Chabon, M. The Yiddish Policemen's Union

POLICE -- ARKANSAS

Hess, J. Maggody and the moonbeams

POLICE -- AUSTIN, TEXAS

Simon, M. The last Jew standing

POLICE -- BALTIMORE, MARYLAND

Lippman, L. What the dead know

POLICE -- BANGKOK, THAILAND

Burdett, J. Bangkok 8

POLICE -- BATH, ENGLAND

Lovesey, P. Diamond dust

Lovesey, P. Skeleton Hill

Lovesey, P. Upon a dark night

Lovesey, P. The vault

POLICE -- BERLIN, GERMANY

Deaver, J. Garden of beasts

POLICE -- BLACKPOOL, ENGLAND

Oldham, N. Fighting for the dead

POLICE -- BRIGHTON, ENGLAND

Guttridge, P. The thing itself

POLICE -- CALIFORNIA

POLICE -- REYKJAVIK, ICELAND
Arnaldur Indridason, 1. Outrage

POLICE -- SAN DIEGO, CALIFORNIA
Parker, T. Cold pursuit
Parker, T. The fallen

POLICE -- SCOTLAND
Beaton, M. Death of a macho man
MacBride, S. Blind eye
MacBride, S. Close to the bone
MacBride, S. Shatter the bones
McDermid, V. The distant echo
Rankin, I. Black and blue

POLICE -- SEATTLE, WASHINGTON
Jance, J. Birds of prey

POLICE -- SHANGHAI, CHINA
Qiu, X. Death of a red heroine
Qiu, X. Don't cry Tai Lake
Qiu, X. Enigma of China
Qiu, X. Red mandarin dress
Qiu, X. When red is black

POLICE -- SOUTH AFRICA
Nunn, M. A beautiful place to die
Nunn, M. Blessed are the dead
Nunn, M. Present darkness
Paton, A. Too late the phalarope

POLICE -- SOVIET UNION
Smith, M. Gorky Park
Smith, M. The Siberian dilemma
Smith, M. Tatiana

POLICE -- SPAIN
Pawel, R. Death of a nationalist

POLICE -- SPECIAL WEAPONS AND TACTICS UNITS
Gardner, L. Alone

POLICE -- SPOKANE, WASHINGTON
Walter, J. Citizen Vince

POLICE -- STOCKHOLM, SWEDEN
Sjowall, M. Cop killer
Sjowall, M. The laughing policeman
Sjowall, M. The locked room
Sjowall, M. The man on the balcony
Sjowall, M. Murder at the Savoy

POLICE -- SUSSEX, ENGLAND
Rendell, R. Not in the flesh

POLICE -- SWEDEN
Mankell, H. Before the frost
Mankell, H. The dogs of Riga
Mankell, H. Firewall
Mankell, H. The man who smiled
Mankell, H. One step behind
Mankell, H. The return of the dancing master
Mankell, H. The troubled man
Roslund, A. Cell 8

POLICE -- TOKYO, JAPAN
Lee, D. Country of origin
Peace, D. Tokyo year zero

POLICE -- VENICE, ITALY
Leon, D. About face

Leon, D. Beastly things
Leon, D. Blood from a stone
Leon, D. Drawing conclusions
Leon, D. Falling in love
Leon, D. The girl of his dreams
Leon, D. The golden egg
Leon, D. A question of belief
Leon, D. Uniform justice

POLICE -- VERMONT
Mayor, A. Red herring
Mayor, A. Tag man

POLICE -- VICTORIA, BRITISH COLUMBIA
Haldane, S. The devil's making

POLICE -- WASHINGTON, D.C.
Patterson, J. Kiss the girls
Pelecanos, G. Hard revolution
Pelecanos, G. The night gardener

POLICE -- WEST AFRICA
Greene, G. The heart of the matter

POLICE -- YORKSHIRE, ENGLAND
Robinson, P. All the colors of darkness
Robinson, P. Cold is the grave
Robinson, P. Friend of the devil
Robinson, P. Innocent graves
Robinson, P. Piece of my heart
Robinson, P. Playing with fire
Robinson, P. Strange affair

POLICE BRUTALITY
Bandele, A. Daughter
Bump, G. Everywhere you don't belong
Burke, J. The jealous kind
MacDonald, J. The long lavender look
Mosley, W. Down the river unto the sea
Onyebuchi, T. Riot baby
Whitlow, R. A time to stand

POLICE CHIEFS
Ball, J. In the heat of the night
Benchley, P. Jaws
Constantine, K. The man who liked to look at himself
Estleman, L. Gas City
Higgins, K. The best man
Hilderbrand, E. The perfect couple
Koenig, M. Nine days
McGarrity, M. Everyone dies
Nesbo, J. Macbeth
Parker, R. Blue-eyed devil
Parker, R. Death in paradise
Parker, R. Sea change
Parker, R. Stone cold
Parker, R. Stranger in paradise
Parker, R. Trouble in Paradise
Phillips, C. Perfect fit
Pronzini, B. The violated
Russo, R. Everybody's fool
Shames, T. A risky undertaking for Loretta Singletary
Shames, T. An unsettling crime for Samuel Craddock
Siger, J. Target Tinos

Parker, T. Black water
Parker, T. The fallen
Parker, T. The renegades
Slaughter, K. Cop Town
POLICE PATROL
Anderson, K. Green sun
POLICE PROCEDURALS
Anderson, K. Green sun
Bannalec, J. Death in Brittany
Bannalec, J. The killing tide
Bannister, J. Silent footsteps
Brookmyre, C. When the devil drives
Brookmyre, C. Where the bodies are buried
Burke, J. Black cherry blues
Burke, J. Heaven's prisoners
Burke, J. The New Iberia blues
Burke, J. Robicheaux
Church, J. Bamboo and blood
Church, J. A corpse in the Koryo
Church, J. A drop of Chinese blood
Church, J. Hidden moon
Cleeves, A. The crow trap
Cleeves, A. Raven black
Cleeves, A. Thin air
Cleeves, A. Wild fire
Cocco, G. Shadows on the lake
Connelly, M. The black ice
Connelly, M. The burning room
Connelly, M. The crossing
Connelly, M. Echo Park
Connelly, M. Dark sacred night
Connelly, M. The wrong side of goodbye
Cornell, P. London falling
Crais, R. Demolition angel
Crombie, D. A bitter feast
Crombie, D. Kissed a sad goodbye
Crombie, D. Mourn not your dead
Crombie, D. Water like a stone
Cross, N. Luther. The calling
Dahl, A. Bad Blood
Dahl, A. Misterioso
De Giovanni, M. The bastards of Pizzofalcone
De Giovanni, M. The crocodile
Dexter, C. The daughters of Cain
Dexter, C. The remorseful day
Dexter, C. The way through the woods
Dibdin, M. Ratking
Dugoni, R. My sister's grave
Edwardson, A. Sail of stone
Ellroy, J. Perfidia
Ellroy, J. This storm
Frear, C. Stone cold heart
Frear, C. Sweet little lies
French, T. Broken harbor
French, T. Faithful place
French, T. In the woods
French, T. The likeness

French, T. The secret place
George, E. A banquet of consequences
George, E. Believing the lie
George, E. Careless in red
George, E. Just one evil act
George, E. The punishment she deserves
George, E. This body of death
George, E. What came before he shot her
Griffiths, E. The stone circle
Hannah, S. The cradle in the grave
Hannah, S. The wrong mother
Harrod-Eagles, C. Headlong
Harrod-Eagles, C. Game over
Harrod-Eagles, C. Old bones
Harvey, J. Cold in hand
Harvey, J. Darkness, darkness
Harvey, M. Pulse
Hayder, M. Birdman
Hayder, M. Gone
Hayder, M. Poppet
Hayder, M. Ritual
Hayder, M. Skin
Hayder, M. The treatment
Hill, S. The pure in heart
Hill, S. The risk of darkness
Hill, S. The shadows in the street
Hill, S. The various haunts of men
Hillerman, T. The shape shifter
Hillerman, T. The sinister pig
Hillerman, T. The wailing wind
James, P. The black tower
James, P. A certain justice
James, P. Death in holy orders
James, P. Death of an expert witness
James, P. Devices and desires
James, P. Original sin
James, P. The lighthouse
James, P. The private patient
James, P. A taste for death
Jenkins, V. An unattended death
Jones, D. A bad day for sunshine
Jungstedt, M. The inner circle
Kelly, E. Broadchurch
Kent, K. The burn
Kent, K. The dime
Khan, A. Among the ruins
Khan, A. The unquiet dead
Lackberg, C. The hidden child
Lackberg, C. The ice princess
Lackberg, C. The preacher
Lackberg, C. The stonecutter
Lemaitre, P. Irene
Leon, D. About face
Leon, D. Beastly things
Leon, D. Blood from a stone
Leon, D. Drawing conclusions
Leon, D. Falling in love

Rankin, I. The impossible dead
Rankin, I. The naming of the dead
Rankin, I. A question of blood
Rankin, I. Rather be the devil
Rankin, I. Resurrection men
Rankin, I. Set in darkness
Redondo, D. The invisible guardian
Rendell, R. The babes in the wood
Rendell, R. End in tears
Rendell, R. Harm done
Rendell, R. Kissing the gunner's daughter
Rendell, R. Not in the flesh
Rendell, R. Road rage
Rendell, R. A sleeping life
Rendell, R. Simisola
Rendell, R. Speaker of Mandarin
Ridpath, M. Far north
Robb, J. Fantasy in death
Robb, J. Innocent in death
Robb, J. Naked in death
Robinson, P. All the colors of darkness
Robinson, P. Careless love
Robinson, P. Children of the revolution
Robinson, P. Close to home
Robinson, P. Cold is the grave
Robinson, P. Friend of the devil
Robinson, P. In the dark places
Robinson, P. Innocent graves
Robinson, P. Piece of my heart
Robinson, P. Playing with fire
Robinson, P. Strange affair
Rowson, P. Death lies beneath
Rowson, P. Undercurrent
Salvalaggio, K. Bone dust white
Sandford, J. Certain prey
Sandford, J. Chosen prey
Sandford, J. Bloody genius
Sandford, J. Broken prey
Sandford, J. Buried prey
Sandford, J. Deadline
Sandford, J. Deep freeze
Sandford, J. Easy prey
Sandford, J. Field of prey
Sandford, J. Golden prey
Sandford, J. Heat lightning
Sandford, J. Hidden prey
Sandford, J. Holy ghost
Sandford, J. Invisible prey
Sandford, J. Mad River
Sandford, J. Mind prey
Sandford, J. Mortal prey
Sandford, J. Naked prey
Sandford, J. Phantom prey
Sandford, J. Night prey
Sandford, J. Rules of prey
Sandford, J. Shock wave
Sandford, J. Silent prey

Sandford, J. Silken prey
Sandford, J. Storm Front
Sandford, J. Storm prey
Sandford, J. Sudden prey
Sandford, J. Winter prey
Serafim, L. The devil takes half
Serafim, L. When the devil's idle
Shaw, W. The birdwatcher
Shaw, W. Salt lane
Shaw, W. A song for the brokenhearted
Silvis, R. Two days gone
Simenon, G. Maigret and the black sheep
Simenon, G. Maigret and the fortuneteller
Simenon, G. Maigret and the killer
Simenon, G. Maigret and the madwoman
Simenon, G. Maigret and the Saturday caller
Simenon, G. Maigret and the toy village
Simenon, G. Maigret and the wine merchant
Simenon, G. Maigret bides his time
Simenon, G. Maigret goes home
Simenon, G. Maigret in Holland
Simenon, G. Maigret's memoirs
Simenon, G. My friend Maigret
Sjowall, M. Cop killer
Sjowall, M. The laughing policeman
Sjowall, M. The locked room
Sjowall, M. The man on the balcony
Sjowall, M. Murder at the Savoy
Slaughter, K. Fallen
Slaughter, K. Undone
Smith, C. Silent city
Smith, M. Gorky Park
Smith, M. Havana Bay
Smith, M. Polar Star
Smith, M. Red Square
Smith, M. The Siberian dilemma
Smith, M. Stalin's ghost
Smith, M. Tatiana
Smith, M. Three stations
Smith, M. Wolves eat dogs
Spain, J. With our blessing
Spencer, S. Best served cold
Spencer, S. Dead end
Spencer, S. The hidden
Spencer, S. Thicker than water
Sveistrup, S. The chestnut man
Thomas, R. Firewatching
Tursten, H. Hunting game
Tursten, H. Winter grave
Wambaugh, J. The blue knight
Wambaugh, J. Finnegan's week
Wambaugh, J. Floaters
Wambaugh, J. The new centurions

POLICE PSYCHOLOGISTS

Patterson, J. Along came a spider
Patterson, J. Kiss the girls

POLICE QUESTIONING

Mankell, H. Before the frost

POLICEWOMEN -- YORKSHIRE, ENGLAND

Robinson, P. Playing with fire
Robinson, P. Strange affair

POLIOMYELITIS

Godwin, G. Flora
Roth, P. Nemesis

POLISH AMERICAN BOYS

Dybek, S. I sailed with Magellan

POLISH AMERICAN FAMILIES

Dybek, S. I sailed with Magellan

POLISH AMERICAN MEN

Dybek, S. I sailed with Magellan

POLISH AMERICAN WOMEN

Archer, J. The prodigal daughter

POLISH AMERICANS

Dybek, S. I sailed with Magellan
Sontag, S. In America

Polish boxer novels [series] Halfon, E.

POLISH PEOPLE IN ENGLAND

Hodgkinson, A. 22 Britannia Road

POLITICAL ACTIVISTS

Ballard, J. Millennium people
Forbes, C. A tall history of sugar
Gessen, K. A terrible country
Kostova, E. The shadow land
Ma, J. Beijing coma
Piercy, M. Vida
Shoham, L. Asylum city

POLITICAL CAMPAIGNS

Meader, K. Playing with fire
Millet, L. Sweet lamb of heaven
Rowling, J. The casual vacancy
Sandford, J. Silken prey
Smith, J. The kindness of strangers
Vidal, G. 1876

POLITICAL CARTOONS

Penrose, A. Murder at half moon gate
Penrose, A. Murder at Kensington Palace
Penrose, A. Murder on Black Swan Lane

POLITICAL CONSULTANTS

Amirrezvani, A. Equal of the sun

POLITICAL CORRUPTION

Adichie, C. Half of a yellow sun
Adiga, A. The white tiger
Asimov, I. Second foundation
Atwood, M. The blind assassin
Brett, S. Mrs Pargeter's principle
Church, J. Bamboo and blood
Church, J. A corpse in the Koryo
Church, J. Hidden moon
Coel, M. Blood memory
Cornwell, B. Enemy of God
Cornwell, B. Excalibur
Cornwell, B. The winter king
Crompton, R. Hour of the red god
Crumley, J. The final country

Cumming, C. A foreign country
DeSilva, B. Providence rag
DeSilva, B. A scourge of vipers
Deb, S. The point of return
Dee, J. A thousand pardons
Dibdin, M. Ratking
Dowlatabadi, M. The colonel
Dumas, A. The man in the iron mask
Dumas, A. Twenty years after
Dunant, S. Blood and beauty
Dunnett, D. Niccolo rising
Eisler, B. The killer collective
Ellis, D. In the company of liars
Ellroy, J. American tabloid
Ellroy, J. Blood's a rover
Ellroy, J. The cold six thousand
Faye, L. The gods of Gotham
Faye, L. Seven for a secret
Fuentes, C. The eagle's throne
Garcia Marquez, G. The general in his labyrinth
Garcia Marquez, G. In evil hour
Gogol, N. Dead souls
Gordimer, N. No time like the present
Grant, M. Blackout
Grant, M. Deadline
Grant, M. Feed
Grant, M. Feedback
Gregory, P. The last Tudor
Hammett, D. The glass key
Harris, R. The ghost
Harvey, M. The fifth floor
Harvey, M. The governor's wife
Hiaasen, C. Skin tight
Hunt, A. City of saints
James, M. A brief history of seven killings
Jemisin, N. The killing moon
Johnson, A. The orphan master's son
Jones, J. The silence
Kadare, I. Agamemnon's daughter
Keilson, H. Life goes on
Kelton, E. The way of the coyote
Kennedy, W. Chango's beads and two-tone shoes
Kerr, P. March violets
King, S. Firestarter
Koryta, M. The Cypress House
Kostova, E. The shadow land
Lam, V. The headmaster's wager
Le Carre, J. A delicate truth
Le Carre, J. The tailor of Panama
Le Guin, U. The dispossessed
Leon, D. Blood from a stone
Leon, D. A question of belief
Leon, D. Uniform justice
Lescroart, J. The hearing
Lin, J. The dragon and the pearl
Littell, R. The Stalin epigram
Mankell, H. The dogs of Riga

Ellroy, J. Blood's a rover
Ellroy, J. The cold six thousand
Englander, N. The ministry of Special Cases
Erpenbeck, J. The book of words
Farah, N. Crossbones
Farah, N. Knots
Farah, N. Links
Fftch, M. Stay and fight
Flanagan, R. The unknown terrorist
Florio, G. Silent hearts
Fuentes, C. The eagle's throne
Fuentes, C. The years with Laura Diaz
Garcia, C. King of Cuba
Garcia, C. The Lady Matador's hotel
Ghaffari, R. To keep the sun alive
Gibb, C. Sweetness in the belly
Grass, G. Too far afield
Greene, G. The quiet American
Gunaratne, G. In our mad and furious city
Hage, R. De Niro's game
Hamid, M. Exit west
Han, K. Human acts
Heller, J. Good as Gold
Jiang, R. Wolf totem
Jin, H. The boat rocker
Jin, H. The crazed
John, E. Born on a Tuesday
Johnson, A. The orphan master's son
Jordan, H. When she woke
Kadare, I. Agamemnon's daughter
Kadare, I. The general of the dead army
Kadare, I. The successor
Kingsolver, B. Unsheltered
Koestler, A. Darkness at noon
Lalami, L. The Moor's account
Lessing, D. The good terrorist
Lethem, J. Dissident gardens
Lewis, S. It can't happen here
Limon, M. The line
Limon, M. Mr. Kill
Lopez, J. A beautiful young woman
Ma, J. China dream
Mabanckou, A. Black Moses
Mahfuz, N. Palace walk
Majmudar, A. Partitions
Mallon, T. Finale
Mallon, T. Landfall
Mallon, T. Watergate
Malraux, A. Man's hope
Matar, H. Anatomy of a disappearance
Matar, H. In the country of men
McCann, C. Apeirogon
Mengestu, D. All our names
Mengestu, D. How to read the air
Mistry, R. A fine balance
Mohamed, N. The orchard of lost souls
Mosley, W. RL's dream

Mosley, W. The right mistake
Mueenuddin, D. In other rooms, other wonders
Mukherjee, N. A life apart
Muller, H. The fox was ever the hunter
Muller, H. The hunger angel
Naipaul, V. A bend in the river
Naipaul, V. Guerrillas
Naipaul, V. Magic seeds
O'Connor, R. Buffalo soldiers
Obioma, C. The fishermen
Okparanta, C. Under the udala trees
Onyebuchi, T. Riot baby
Orwell, G. Animal farm
Pamuk, O. Snow
Pamuk, O. A strangeness in my mind
Paton, A. Ah, but your land is beautiful
Paton, A. Cry, the beloved country
Paton, A. Too late the phalarope
A people's future of the United States
Quinn, K. Ribbons of scarlet
Rand, A. We the living
Restrepo, L. Delirium
Restrepo, L. No place for heroes
Roth, P. The plot against America
Rush, N. Mortals
Rushdie, S. The golden house
Russell, M. Dreamers of the day
Sahota, S. The year of the runaways
Sainz Borgo, K. It would be night in Caracas
Sankaran, L. The hope factory
Saramago, J. The manual of painting and calligraphy
Schami, R. Sophia
Shamsie, K. Home fire
Silone, I. Bread and wine
Sinclair, U. The jungle
Solzhenitsyn, A. Cancer ward
Solzhenitsyn, A. In the first circle
Steele, A. Coyote
Suri, M. The age of Shiva
Theroux, P. The Lower River
Tie, N. The bathing women
Townsend, S. Number 10
Trollope, A. The Prime Minister
Updike, J. Memories of the Ford administration
Vargas Llosa, M. The feast of the Goat
Vasquez, J. The shape of the ruins
Vidal, G. 1876
Vidal, G. Burr
Vidal, G. Empire
Vidal, G. The golden age
Vidal, G. Lincoln
Vidal, G. Washington, D. C.
Waldman, A. A door in the earth
Warren, R. All the king's men
Wibberley, L. The mouse that roared
Zola, E. Germinal
POLITICAL INTRIGUE

POLITICAL LEADERSHIP

POLITICAL LETTER-WRITING

POLITICAL ORATORY

POLITICAL PARTICIPATION

POLITICAL PARTIES -- SOUTH AFRICA -- HISTORY -- 20TH CENTURY

POLITICAL PERSECUTION

POLITICAL PERSECUTION -- SOVIET UNION

POLITICAL PRISONERS

Archer, J. This was a man
Benedetti, M. Springtime in a broken mirror
Khan, A. Among the ruins
Koestler, A. Darkness at noon
Matar, H. In the country of men
Pattison, E. The skull mantra
Pattison, E. Water touching stone
Peters, E. The summer of the Danes
Puig, M. Kiss of the spider woman
Saramago, J. The manual of painting and calligraphy
Weir, A. A dangerous inheritance

POLITICAL PRISONERS -- IRAN
Sofer, D. The Septembers of Shiraz

POLITICAL PRISONERS -- PERU
Alarcon, D. Lost City Radio

POLITICAL PRISONERS -- SIBERIA
Richler, N. Your mouth is lovely

POLITICAL PRISONERS -- SOVIET UNION
Holland, T. The archivist's story
Solzhenitsyn, A. In the first circle
Solzhenitsyn, A. One day in the life of Ivan Denisovich

POLITICAL PRISONS -- SIBERIA
Richler, N. Your mouth is lovely

POLITICAL REFUGEES
Allende, I. Of love and shadows
Farah, N. Crossbones
Farah, N. Links
Majmudar, A. Partitions

POLITICAL RISK INSURANCE
DeLillo, D. The names

POLITICAL SCIENCE
Benedict, M. Lady Clementine
Clarke, S. Jonathan Strange & Mr. Norrell
Dunant, S. The birth of Venus
Fuentes, C. The years with Laura Diaz
Garcia, C. The Lady Matador's hotel
Greene, G. The honorary consul
Houellebecq, M. Submission
Kadare, I. The successor
Kerr, P. Hitler's peace
Lethem, J. The feral detective
Liss, D. A spectacle of corruption
Locascio, L. Open me
Mallon, T. Finale
Mallon, T. Landfall
Min, A. Empress Orchid
Palmer, A. Too like the lightning
Pamuk, O. Snow
Piercy, M. Sex wars
Pratchett, T. Thud!
Wouk, H. A hole in Texas
Wright, A. Carpentaria

POLITICAL SCIENCE -- PHILOSOPHY
McCrea, G. Mrs. Engels

POLITICAL SURVEILLANCE
Boll, H. The lost honor of Katharina Blum
Khan, A. Among the ruins

POLITICAL THRILLERS
Baldacci, D. Hell's Corner
Berry, S. The bishop's pawn
Berry, S. The lost order
Berry, S. The Malta exchange
Berry, S. The Warsaw protocol
Cameron, M. Code of honor
Cameron, M. Power and empire
Cameron, M. Oath of office
Cleveland, K. Keep you close
Coes, B. Bloody Sunday
Coes, B. The Russian
Coonts, S. The Russia account
Dimberg, K. Girl in the rearview mirror
Eisler, B. The god's eye view
Finder, J. Guilty minds
Finder, J. The switch
Higgins, J. Bad company
Higgins, J. Day of reckoning
Higgins, J. Edge of danger
Higgins, J. Eye of the storm
Higgins, J. Midnight runner
Higgins, J. Rough justice
Higgins, J. The White House connection
Ignatius, D. The sun king
Le Carre, J. The constant gardener
Littell, R. Vicious circle
Meltzer, B. The inner circle
Meltzer, B. The tenth justice
Meltzer, B. The zero game
Patterson, R. Balance of power
Patterson, R. No safe place
Patterson, R. Protect and defend
Persson, L. Another time, another life
Persson, L. Free falling, as if in a dream
Porter, H. The bell ringers
Powell, M. Firebird
Reich, C. The take
Sakey, M. A better world
Sakey, M. Brilliance
Shaw, L. The network
Steinhauer, O. The Bridge of Sighs
Stross, C. Empire Games
Tata, A. Dark winter
Vachss, A. Two trains running
Wiesel, E. Hostage

POLITICAL VALUES
Smith, A. Spring

POLITICAL VIOLENCE
Alarcon, D. Lost City Radio
Ballard, J. Millennium people
Djavadi, N. Disoriental
Erpenbeck, J. The book of words
Garcia, C. The Lady Matador's hotel
Gordimer, N. None to accompany me
Hamid, M. Exit west
Han, K. Human acts

Perry, A. Southampton Row
Townsend, S. Number 10
Woolf, V. Mrs. Dalloway

POLITICS AND CULTURE

Card, O. Ender's game
Koen, K. Through a glass darkly
Lessing, D. The good terrorist
McCullough, C. The first man in Rome
Suri, M. The age of Shiva
Vidal, G. Lincoln
Vonnegut, K. Cat's cradle

POLITICS AND CULTURE -- CHINA

Thien, M. Do not say we have nothing

POLITICS AND CULTURE -- SOUTH AFRICA

Gordimer, N. Life times

POLITICS AND LITERATURE

McEwan, I. Sweet tooth

POLLUTION

Chen, Q. Waste tide
Harkaway, N. Tigerman
Leon, D. About face
Qiu, X. Don't cry Tai Lake

POLO, MARCO, 1254-1323?

Calvino, I. Invisible cities

POLTERGEISTS

Jackson, S. The haunting of Hill House

POLYAMORY

Faulkner, W. Pylon

POLYGAMY

Adebayo, A. Stay with me
Card, O. Saints
Ebershoff, D. The 19th wife
Fisher, T. The wives
Grey, Z. Riders of the purple sage
Jones, T. Silver sparrow
Udall, B. The lonely polygamist
Vestal, S. Daredevils

POLYNESIA

Melville, H. Omoo

POLYNESIANS

Michener, J. Hawaii

Pompeii Harris, R.

POMPEII (EXTINCT CITY)

Harris, R. Pompeii

POMPEY, THE GREAT, 106-48 BC

Saylor, S. The judgment of Caesar
Saylor, S. Rubicon

PONCA INDIANS

Kolpan, G. Magic words
The **ponder** heart Welty, E.

PONY EXPRESS

Coover, R. Huck out west

PONZI SCHEMES

Mandel, E. The glass hotel

POOR AFRICAN AMERICAN FAMILIES

Tyree, O. Leslie

POOR BOYS

Birch, C. Jamrach's menagerie

POOR BOYS -- EMPLOYMENT

Dickens, C. David Copperfield

POOR CHILDREN

Dickens, C. Great expectations
Dreiser, T. An American tragedy
Rushdie, S. Midnight's children
Wingate, L. Before we were yours

POOR FAMILIES

Adam, C. Golden child
Allison, D. Bastard out of Carolina
Arnow, H. The dollmaker
Caldwell, E. Tobacco Road
Dickens, C. Our mutual friend
Lake, J. Green
Markandaya, K. Nectar in a sieve
Naylor, G. The women of Brewster Place
Parks, S. Getting mother's body
Patchett, A. Run
Proulx, A. Postcards
Roberts, N. Chesapeake blue
Rutherfurd, E. The forest
Smith, B. A tree grows in Brooklyn
Smith, D. I capture the castle
Stegner, W. The Big Rock Candy Mountain
Strout, E. Anything is possible
Turansky, C. No ocean too wide

POOR GIRLS

Crane, S. Maggie

POOR MEN

Celine, L. Journey to the end of the night
Maugham, W. Of human bondage
Miller, H. Tropic of Cancer
Obioma, C. An orchestra of minorities
Starr, J. Lights out

POOR PEOPLE

Armstrong, R. The don con
Baca, J. The importance of a piece of paper
Backman, F. Britt-Marie was here
Brown, R. Rubyfruit jungle
Buck, P. The good Earth
Dickens, C. Oliver Twist, or The parish boy's progress
Dos Passos, J. Manhattan transfer
Faulkner, W. Absalom, Absalom!
Forster, E. Howards End
Gardam, J. Last friends
Kerstan, L. Heart of the tiger
Macneal, E. The doll factory
Mistry, R. A fine balance
Mosley, W. RL's dream
Mozley, F. Elmet
Mukherjee, N. A state of freedom
Oates, J. Them
Shanbhag, V. Ghachar ghochar
Silver, M. Mary Coin
Steinbeck, J. Tortilla Flat

POOR PEOPLE -- CALIFORNIA

Leithauser, B. The art student's war
Moggach, D. Tulip fever
Portrait in sepia Allende, I.
The **portrait** of a lady James, H.
A **portrait** of the artist as a young man Joyce, J.
PORTRAIT PAINTERS
Ashe, K. The prince
Saramago, J. The manual of painting and calligraphy
PORTRAIT PAINTING
Shaw, M. Murder at the mill
PORTRAITS
Ashe, K. The prince
Banasky, C. The suicide of Claire Bishop
Gaynor, H. The lighthouse keeper's daughter
Kawakami, M. Ms. Ice Sandwich
Lovett, C. The bookman's tale
Maturin, C. Melmoth the wanderer
Moggach, D. Tulip fever
Moyes, J. The girl you left behind
Tey, J. The daughter of time
Wilde, O. The picture of Dorian Gray
PORTSMOUTH, ENGLAND
Rowson, P. Death lies beneath
Rowson, P. Undercurrent
PORTUGAL
Leavitt, D. The two Hotel Francforts
Martel, Y. The high mountains of Portugal
Perez-Reverte, A. The Club Dumas
Saramago, J. All the names
Saramago, J. The manual of painting and calligraphy
PORTUGAL -- COLONIES -- AFRICA
Naipaul, V. Half a life
PORTUGAL -- HISTORY -- 16TH CENTURY
Zimler, R. The last Kabbalist of Lisbon
PORTUGAL -- HISTORY -- MARIA I, 1777-1816
Willig, L. The lure of the moonflower
PORTUGAL -- POLITICS AND GOVERNMENT -- 20TH CENTURY
Antunes, A. The return of the caravels
PORTUGAL -- SOCIAL LIFE AND CUSTOMS -- 20TH CENTURY
Antunes, A. The return of the caravels
PORTUGUESE IN JAPAN
Endo, S. Silence
Spann, S. Trial on Mount Koya
Positive Wellington, D.
Possessing the secret of joy Walker, A.
Possession Byatt, A.
The **possessions** Murphy, S.
POSSESSIVENESS
Galsworthy, J. The Forsyte saga
Jones, S. The other woman
Sparks, N. The guardian
The **possibilities** Hemmings, K.
POST TRAUMATIC STRESS DISORDER
Martin, C. Send down the rain
Walker, N. Cherry

POST-APARTHEID ERA
Brink, A. The rights of desire
Conde, M. The story of the cannibal woman
Gordimer, N. No time like the present
Gordimer, N. The pickup
POST-APARTHEID ERA -- SOUTH AFRICA
Mda, Z. The Madonna of Excelsior
Mda, Z. The whale caller
POST-APOCALYPSE
Bacigalupi, P. The windup girl
Brooks, M. World War Z
Butler, O. Parable of the sower
Buxton, K. Hollow kingdom
Delany, S. Dhalgren
Dick, P. Do androids dream of electric sheep?
Elison, M. The book of Etta
Elison, M. The book of Flora
Elison, M. The book of the unnamed midwife
Erdrich, L. Future home of the living god
Fforde, J. Shades of grey
Haig, F. The fire sermon
Harkaway, N. The gone-away world
Harris, R. The second sleep
King, S. The stand
Kress, N. After the fall, before the fall, during the fall
Krivak, A. The bear
Lee, C. On such a full sea
Mandel, E. Station Eleven
Marcus, B. The flame alphabet
Matheson, R. I am legend
McCarthy, C. The road
Miller, W. A canticle for Leibowitz
Montag, K. After the flood
Newman, S. The country of Ice Cream Star
Okorafor, N. Who fears death
Pinsker, S. A song for a new day
Roanhorse, R. Trail of lightning
Stewart, G. Earth abides
Stirling, S. Dies the fire
Stirling, S. A meeting at Corvallis
Stirling, S. The protector's war
Tawada, Y. The emissary
Theroux, M. Far north
This way to the end times
VanderMeer, J. Borne
VanderMeer, J. Dead astronauts
Vaughn, C. Bannerless
Wellington, D. Positive
The **post-birthday** world Shriver, L.
POST-COMMUNISM
Kostova, E. The shadow land
POST-CONVICTION REMEDIES
Grisham, J. The guardians
POST-INDUSTRIAL SOCIETY
Mieville, C. Perdido Street Station
POST-TRAUMATIC STRESS DISORDER
Barclay, L. A noise downstairs

Smiley, J. Golden age
Steinhauer, O. The Bridge of Sighs
Swift, G. Here we are
Tremain, R. The Gustav sonata
Veletzos, R. The girl they left behind
Wuertz, Y. Everything belongs to us

POSTWAR RECONSTRUCTION

Jenoff, P. The ambassador's daughter

Potshot Parker, R.

The **potter's** field Peters, E.

POTTERS

Arsenault, E. In search of the Rose notes
Doctorow, C. Rapture of the nerds
Saramago, J. The cave

POTTERS -- NORTH CAROLINA

Maron, M. Uncommon clay

Pound for pound Toole, F.

POVERTY

Abraham, T. Black Sunday
Adiga, A. The white tiger
Arnow, H. The dollmaker
Booth, C. Bronxwood
Brown, J. Addie Pray
Burnet, G. His bloody project
Camus, A. The plague
Camus, A. The stranger
Chariandy, D. Brother
Chen, Q. Waste tide
Cisneros, S. The house on Mango Street
Colombani, L. The braid
Coover, R. The origin of the Brunists
Del Amo, J. Animalia
Dennis-Benn, N. Here comes the sun
Dickens, C. Little Dorrit
Doctorow, E. Ragtime
Dostoyevsky, F. Crime and punishment
Eggers, D. What is the what
Enriquez, M. Things we lost in the fire
Erdrich, L. Love medicine
Fajardo-Anstine, K. Sabrina & Corina
Ferrante, E. My brilliant friend
Finlay, M. The murder pit
Fowler, T. A well-behaved woman
Gala, M. The Black Cathedral
George, E. What came before he shot her
Greene, A. Bloodroot
Harman, P. The midwife of Hope River
Hughes, L. Short stories
King, S. Sleeping beauties
Kingsolver, B. Flight behavior
Levine, J. Bingo's run
Levitt, P. Come with me to Babylon
Malik, T. Three bargains
Manfredi, V. A winter's night
Markandaya, K. Nectar in a sieve
Maugham, W. The moon and sixpence
Meno, J. Marvel and a wonder

Miller, K. An angry-ass black woman
Miller, K. Augustown
Mukherjee, N. A state of freedom
Patchett, A. The Dutch house
Pelecanos, G. The turnaround
Pittman, A. The seamstress
Pochoda, I. These women
Rash, R. Burning bright
Roberts, M. Ignorance
Robertson, I. The Paris winter
Shanbhag, V. Ghachar ghochar
Sherwood, F. The book of splendor
Sinclair, U. The jungle
Singh, N. A madness of sunshine
Smith, M. The fighter
Strout, E. My name is Lucy Barton
Tsypkin, L. Summer in Baden-Baden
Umrigar, T. Everybody's son
Umrigar, T. The secrets between us
Vann, D. Aquarium
Ward, J. Sing, unburied, sing
Wright, R. Native son
Zhang, J. Sour heart

POVERTY -- HARLEM, NEW YORK CITY

Petry, A. The street

The **power** Alderman, N.

Power & Beauty T. I., (.

POWER (SOCIAL SCIENCES)

Abbott, M. Queenpin
Alderman, N. The power
Allio, K. Buddhism for Western children
Amirrezvani, A. Equal of the sun
Anderson, K. The last days of Krypton
Asimov, I. I, robot
Bacigalupi, P. The water knife
Barry, K. City of Bohane
Barry, M. Lexicon
Bennett, R. Foundryside
Berry, S. The Malta exchange
Berry, S. The Warsaw protocol
Black, B. Wolf on a string
Bouchet, A. Breath of fire
Bouchet, A. A promise of fire
Bradford, B. A woman of substance
Burnet, G. His bloody project
Callender, K. Queen of the conquered
Chen, Q. Waste tide
Cline, R. My liar
Coben, H. The boy from the woods
Coben, H. Fool me once
Cooper, E. Buried
Cornwell, B. Sword of kings
Cornwell, B. War of the wolf
Coulter, C. Labyrinth
Cussler, C. The rising sea
Dimberg, K. Girl in the rearview mirror
Dunant, S. Blood and beauty

Ellis, M. Keeping bedlam at bay in the Prague Cafe
Flyte, M. City of dark magic
Flyte, M. City of lost dreams
Lawton, J. Hammer to fall
Perry, S. Melmoth
Seymour, G. Vagabond

PRAGUE, CZECH REPUBLIC -- HISTORY

Sherwood, F. The book of splendor

PRAGUE, CZECH REPUBLIC -- HISTORY -- 16TH CENTURY

Black, B. Wolf on a string

PRAGUE, CZECH REPUBLIC -- HISTORY -- 20TH CENTURY

Kerr, P. The lady from Zagreb
Kerr, P. A man without breath

PRAIRIE LIFE

Coldsmith, D. Tallgrass
Rolvaag, O. Giants in the Earth

PRAYER

Fabry, C. War room
Mitchard, J. The deep end of the ocean
Salinger, J. Franny and Zooey
A **prayer** for Owen Meany Irving, J.
Prayer of the dragon Pattison, E.
Prayers for rain Lehane, D.
Prayers for the dead Kellerman, F.
Prayers for the stolen Clement, J.

PRAYING MANTIS

Pelevin, V. The hall of singing caryatids
The **preacher** Lackberg, C.
The **preacher's** daughter Lewis, B.

PREACHING

Atwood, M. Maddaddam
O'Connor, F. Wise blood
Precious Cummings novels [series] King, D.
The **precious** one De los Santos, M.

PRECIOUS STONES

Gaiman, N. Stardust
The **precipice** Doiron, P.

PRECOGNITION

Amis, M. London fields
Auster, P. Oracle night
Dick, P. The minority report
Irving, J. A prayer for Owen Meany
Kellerman, J. Monster
Koryta, M. The Cypress House
Pickard, N. The scent of rain and lightning
Pulley, N. The lost future of Pepperharrow
Pulley, N. The watchmaker of Filigree Street

PREDATION (BIOLOGY)

Koepp, D. Cold storage
The **prefect** Reynolds, A.

PREGNANCY

Billingsley, R. The secret she kept
Kantaria, A. I know you
Klassen, J. The painter's daughter
McGhee, A. The opposite of fate

Nawaz, S. Bone and bread
Ramos, J. The farm
Sada, D. Almost never
Stringer, V. Dirty Red
Thomas, S. Private arrangements

PREGNANT TEENAGERS

Bronsky, A. The hottest dishes of the Tartar cuisine
Coplin, A. The orchardist
Haruf, K. Plainsong
Joss, M. Half broken things
The **pregnant** widow Amis, M.

PREGNANT WOMEN

Albert, E. After birth
Borjlind, C. Spring tide
Brown, T. Fallen land
Burrowes, G. My one and only duke
Butler, K. Pretty ugly
Clark, W. Payback with ya life
DeCarlo, M. The art of crash landing
Dickey, E. Bad men and wicked women
Erdrich, L. Future home of the living god
Faulkner, W. Light in August
Goldbloom, G. On division
Griffiths, E. The Janus stone
Hashemzadeh Bonde, G. What we owe
Hatcher, R. Who I am with you
Haywood, S. The cactus
Hemmings, K. The possibilities
Hepworth, S. The secrets of midwives
Hill, J. The Fireman
Hunt, S. Mr. Splitfoot
Hunter, E. The blackboard jungle
Iles, G. Third degree
Joss, M. Among the missing
K'wan Gutter
Kittredge, W. The willow field
Lansdale, J. Sunset and sawdust
Lemaitre, P. Irene
Littlejohn, E. Inherit the bones
Lloyd, C. Death comes to the nursery
Lupton, R. Sister
Marrs, J. The passengers
McEwan, I. Nutshell
McGarrity, M. Everyone dies
McLaren, K. The road to enchantment
McPherson, C. Quiet neighbors
Michener, J. Tales of the South Pacific
Miller, S. The senator's wife
Mina, D. The end of the wasp season
Napolitano, A. Dear Edward
Ohlsson, K. Silenced
Oyeyemi, H. The opposite house
Parks, S. Getting mother's body
Pearson, R. A long time comin'
Peterson, J. Early's fall
Phillips, C. Unthinkable
Picoult, J. A spark of light

Block, L. A drop of the hard stuf

Block, L. Eight million ways to die

Block, L. The sins of the fathers

Block, L. A ticket to the boneyard

Block, L. When the sacred ginmill closes

Bradley, C. The golden tresses of the dead

Brookmyre, C. When the devil drives

Brookmyre, C. Where the bodies are buried

Bruen, K. Cross

Bruen, K. Galway girl

Bruen, K. The guards

Burns, R. Body slam

Butcher, J. Proven guilty

Chandler, R. The annotated Big sleep

Chandler, R. The big sleep

Chandler, R. The lady in the lake

Chandler, R. The long goodbye

Child, L. Full wolf moon

Christie, A. The A B C murders

Christie, A. Curtain

Christie, A. The hollow

Christie, A. Mrs. McGinty's dead

Christie, A. The murder of Roger Ackroyd

Christie, A. Murder on the Orient Express

Clare, A. The woman who spoke to spirits

Coben, H. The boy from the woods

Collins, M. Ask not

Connelly, M. Dark sacred night

Connelly, M. The wrong side of goodbye

Connolly, J. A book of bones

Connolly, J. The burning soul

Connolly, J. The woman in the woods

Constantine, K. Blood mud

Corby, G. The Marathon conspiracy

Corby, G. The Pericles Commission

Corleone, D. Good as gone

Corleone, D. Gone cold

Corleone, D. Payoff

Crais, R. Chasing darkness

Crais, R. A dangerous man

Crais, R. The first rule

Crumley, J. Bordersnakes

Crumley, J. The final country

Crumley, J. The wrong case

Cussler, C. The Gray Ghost

Cussler, C. The Titanic secret

Davis, L. A body in the bathhouse

Davis, L. The ides of April

Davis, L. One virgin too many

Dazieri, S. Kill the angel

Dobyns, S. Saratoga payback

Doyle, A. The complete Sherlock Holmes

Drury, T. Pacific

Estleman, L. Amos Walker

Estleman, L. Infernal angels

Estleman, L. A smile on the face of the tiger

Faye, L. The whole art of detection

Finch, C. The last passenger

Finch, C. The vanishing man

Finder, J. House on fire

Finlay, M. The murder pit

Fox, C. Crimson Lake

Fox, C. Gone by midnight

Fox, C. Redemption point

Friedman, D. Don't ever get old

Galbraith, R. Career of evil

Galbraith, R. The cuckoo's calling

Galbraith, R. Lethal white

Galbraith, R. The silkworm

Gleason, C. Murder at the capitol

Goldman, M. The shallows

Haddam, J. Cheating at solitaire

Haddam, J. Hardscrabble road

Haddam, J. True believers

Hall, T. The case of the deadly butter chicken

Hall, T. The case of the love commandos

Hallinan, T. Crashed

Hammett, D. The Maltese falcon

Hammett, D. The thin man

Hannah, S. The mystery of three quarters

Harvey, J. Cold in hand

Harvey, J. A darker shade of blue

Harvey, M. The Chicago way

Harvey, M. The fifth floor

Harvey, M. The governor's wife

Harvey, M. We all fall down

Huston, C. Every last drop

Huston, C. Half the blood of Brooklyn

Ide, J. Hi five

James, M. Black leopard, red wolf

Jeffries, S. What the duke desires

Kamal, S. It all falls down

Kaminsky, S. Dancing in the dark

Kaminsky, S. A fatal glass of beer

Kaminsky, S. To catch a spy

Kaminsky, S. Tomorrow is another day

Kasasian, M. Dark dawn over Steep House

Kellerman, J. Bones

Kerr, P. Field gray

Kerr, P. A man without breath

Kerr, P. March violets

King, S. End of watch

Koryta, M. Tonight I said goodbye

Krentz, J. When all the girls have gone

Kroese, R. The last iota

Krueger, W. Vermilion drift

Lawton, J. Then we take Berlin

Lehane, D. Prayers for rain

Lehane, D. Sacred

Lepionka, K. The last place you look

Lethem, J. The feral detective

Lethem, J. Motherless Brooklyn

Lovestam, S. The truth behind the lie

Luna, L. The Janes

Saylor, S. The judgment of Caesar
Saylor, S. A mist of prophecies
Saylor, S. Rubicon
Saylor, S. The triumph of Caesar
Schlink, B. Self's deception
Schlink, B. Self's murder
Schlink, B. Self's punishment
Shepherd, L. A fatal likeness
Shepherd, L. The Solitary House
Shrier, H. Boston cream
Simmons, D. The fifth heart
Spiegelman, P. Black maps
Spillane, M. The Goliath bone
Spillane, M. Kill me, darling
Spillane, M. A long time dead
Stout, R. The doorbell rang
Stout, R. Gambit
Street, K. Edgar Allan Poe and the jewel of Peru
Tidhar, L. A man lies dreaming
Urquhart, R. The visionist
Winslow, D. The dawn patrol
Woods, S. A delicate touch
Woods, S. New York dead
Woods, S. Stealth

PRIVATE INVESTIGATORSNAPOLIS, INDIANA
Levien, D. City of the sun
The **private** patient James, P.

PRIVATE POLICE
Amidon, S. Security
Shields, K. A study in revenge
Shields, K. The truth of all things

PRIVATE SCHOOLS
Cook, T. The Chatham School affair
Hoeg, P. Borderliners
Hoffman, A. The river king
Iles, G. Turning angel
Ishiguro, K. Never let me go
Lutz, L. The swallows
Murray, P. Skippy dies
O'Connell, C. Judas child
Sittenfeld, C. Prep

PRIVATE SECURITY SERVICES
Amidon, S. Security
Cussler, C. Sacred stone
Foster, L. Under pressure
Johnson, L. A sparkle of silver
Muller, M. The ever-running man
O'Malley, T. Serpents in the cold
Perry, T. The bomb maker
Sharp, Z. Fox hunter
A **private** Venus Scerbanenco, G.

PRIVATEERS
Lambdin, D. Hostile shores
O'Brian, P. The wine-dark sea
Spencer, M. Scandalous
The **privileges** Dee, J.
The **prize** Bialosky, J.

Prized possessions Corman, A.
Prizes Frame, J.

PRO-LIFE MOVEMENT
Patterson, R. No safe place
Patterson, R. Protect and defend
The **probable** future Hoffman, A.

PROBATION
Clark, M. The substitution order

PROBATION OFFICERS
Sisco, A. A deadly habit

PROBLEM YOUTH
Adam, C. Golden child
Black, L. Suffer the children
Fagan, J. The Panopticon
O'Hagan, A. Be near me
Pelecanos, G. The way home
Read, C. The crazy school
Souljah,. A deeper love inside

PROCEDURE (LAW)
Guttridge, P. The thing itself

PROCTOR, EZEKIAL, 1831-1907
McMurtry, L. Zeke and Ned

PRODEMOCRACY MOVEMENT (CHINA)
Ma, J. Beijing coma
The **prodigal** daughter Archer, J.

PRODIGAL SON (PARABLE)
Martin, C. Long way gone

PROFESSIONAL ATHLETES
Henson, P. Into the blue
Rai, A. The right swipe
Scalzi, J. Head on

PROFESSIONAL BASEBALL PLAYERS
Adams, L. The bromance book club
Malamud, B. The natural
Parker, R. Double play

PROFESSIONAL BASEBALL PLAYERS -- BOSTON, MASSACHUSETTS
King, S. The girl who loved Tom Gordon

PROFESSIONAL BASEBALL TEAMS
DeLillo, D. Underworld

PROFESSIONAL BASKETBALL PLAYERS
Harris, E. Basketball Jones
Slaughter, K. The kept woman

PROFESSIONAL CONFERENCES
Andrews, D. Owl be home for Christmas
Gamboa, S. Necropolis

PROFESSIONAL ETHICS
Parker, R. Cold service

PROFESSIONAL FOOTBALL
Martin, A. Blitzed
Martin, A. Fumbled

PROFESSIONAL FOOTBALL COACHES
Phillips, S. It had to be you

PROFESSIONAL FOOTBALL PLAYERS
Martin, A. Fumbled

PROFESSIONAL FOOTBALL TEAMS
Phillips, S. It had to be you

Ibrahim, A. Season of crimson blossoms

PROSELYTIZING

Atwood, M. Maddaddam

PROSPECTORS

London, J. The call of the wild

Prospero's children Siegel, J.

PROSTITUTES

Algren, N. A walk on the wild side

Apelfeld, A. Blooms of darkness

Block, L. Eight million ways to die

Block, L. The sins of the fathers

Brooks, B. Blood storm

Brooks, B. Frontier justice

Bryant, N. Madam, may I

Buckman, D. Because the rain

Catton, E. The luminaries

Crane, S. Maggie

Crumley, J. The last good kiss

Dennis-Benn, N. Here comes the sun

Dexter, C. The daughters of Cain

Dexter, P. Deadwood

Donoghue, E. Frog music

Dumas, A. Camille

Ellis, M. Keeping bedlam at bay in the Prague Cafe

Faber, M. The crimson petal and the white

Galen, S. When you give a duke a diamond

Garcia-Roza, L. December heat

Gifford, B. The stars above Veracruz

Groot, T. Flame of resistance

Hobbs, A. Stealing candy

Isaacs, S. As husbands go

Karnezis, P. The maze

Kellerman, J. Bones

Lansdale, J. Honky tonk samurai

Lawrence, D. The dead sit round in a ring

Leonard, E. Mr. Paradise

McBain, E. Hark!

McCann, C. Let the great world spin

McInerney, L. The glorious heresies

Meyer, D. Devil's peak

Natt och Dag, N. The wolf and the watchman

O'Connell, C. Crime school

Pelecanos, G. The big blowdown

Perry, A. Buckingham Palace gardens

Perry, A. Pentecost Alley

Perry, A. The silent cry

Rivers, F. Redeeming love

Rosenberg, J. Confessions of the fox

Rowland, L. The Ripper's shadow

Russell, M. Doc

Sada, D. Almost never

Simon, M. The last Jew standing

Tallis, F. Vienna blood

Vargas Llosa, M. Green house

Vollmann, W. The rainbow stories

Welsh, K. The wages of sin

Zola, E. Nana

PROSTITUTES -- CHINA

Murakami, H. After dark

PROSTITUTES -- CIUDAD JUAREZ, MEXICO

McCarthy, C. Cities of the plain

PROSTITUTES -- GREAT BRITAIN

Defoe, D. Moll Flanders

Downie, R. Medicus

PROSTITUTES -- LA PAZ, BOLIVIA

Recacoechea S., J. American visa

PROSTITUTES -- MARSEILLE

Welch, J. The heartsong of Charging Elk

PROSTITUTES -- ORANGE COUNTY, CALIFORNIA

Rosenberg, N. Interest of justice

PROSTITUTES -- TEXAS

McMurtry, L. Comanche moon

PROSTITUTION

Alexander, V. The Magdalen girls

Bond, C. Ruby

Capote, T. Breakfast at Tiffany's

DuPree, K. Shattered

Faber, M. The crimson petal and the white

Holmes, S. B-more careful

Johnson, K. Little black girl lost

Johnson, K. Little black girl lost 2

Nabb, M. Some bitter taste

Parker, T. The fallen

Perry, T. The boyfriend

Scerbanenco, G. A private Venus

Stringer, V. Let that be the reason

Styles, T. Black and ugly

Tan, A. The Valley of Amazement

Turner, N. A hustler's wife

Vargas Llosa, M. Green house

Walsh, H. Brass

PROSTITUTION -- KYOTO, JAPAN

Golden, A. Memoirs of a geisha

Protect and defend Patterson, R.

PROTECTION RACKET

Parker, R. Blue-eyed devil

PROTECTIVENESS

Apelfeld, A. To the edge of sorrow

Hoffman, A. Practical magic

Hoffman, A. The world that we knew

Kellerman, J. Private eyes

Koch, H. The dinner

Koryta, M. Those who wish me dead

Martin, S. The pleasure of my company

Perry, T. Vanishing act

Singh, N. Silver silence

Woods, R. Remembrance

PROTECTIVENESS IN CHILDREN

George, E. What came before he shot her

PROTECTIVENESS IN MEN

Barclay, L. No safe house

Barry, S. Days without end

Bell, L. One fine duke

Box, C. Blue heaven

PSYCHE (GREEK DEITY)
Lewis, C. Till we have faces

PSYCHIATRIC CLINICS
Bulgakov, M. The master and Margarita

PSYCHIATRIC HOSPITAL CARE
Kesey, K. One flew over the cuckoo's nest

PSYCHIATRIC HOSPITAL PATIENTS
Barry, S. The secret scripture
Bulgakov, M. The master and Margarita
Collins, W. The woman in white
Greenberg, J. I never promised you a rose garden
Hayder, M. Poppet
Kepler, L. The sandman
Kepler, L. Stalker
Kesey, K. One flew over the cuckoo's nest
LaValle, V. The devil in silver
Lehane, D. Shutter Island
Norton, C. What doesn't kill her
Percy, W. Lancelot
Sanders, L. The fourth deadly sin

PSYCHIATRIC HOSPITAL PATIENTS -- ITALY
Svevo, I. Zeno's conscience

PSYCHIATRIC HOSPITALS
Barry, S. The secret scripture
Burdick, S. The girls with no names
Cohen, T. They all fall down
Crowell, J. Etched on me
Daniels, N. Too close
de Beauvoir, J. Asylum
Hand, E. Mortal love
Hayder, M. Poppet
Hollingshead, G. Bedlam
Kesey, K. One flew over the cuckoo's nest
Kirshenbaum, B. Rabbits for food
LaValle, V. The devil in silver
Lehane, D. Shutter Island
Mandanipour, S. Moon brow
Meno, J. The boy detective fails
Newman, J. Mary
Rowland, L. Bedlam
Schlink, B. Self's deception
Sedgwick, M. Mister Memory
Self, W. Umbrella
Stewart, A. Miss Kopp just won't quit
Waters, S. Fingersmith

PSYCHIATRIC RESEARCH
Hollingshead, G. Bedlam

PSYCHIATRIST AND PATIENT
Barker, P. Regeneration
Cohen, T. They all fall down
Daniels, N. Too close
Le Guin, U. The lathe of heaven

PSYCHIATRISTS
Abani, C. The secret history of Las Vegas
Barker, P. The eye in the door
Barker, P. Regeneration
Barth, J. The end of the road

Chung, M. The eighth girl
Cohen, T. They all fall down
Cole, T. Open city
Forna, A. Happiness
Forna, A. The memory of love
Freeman, B. The night bird
Freudenberger, N. The dissident
Glass, J. The whole world over
Hand, E. Mortal love
Harris, T. The silence of the lambs
Hill, R. The woodcutter
Miller, S. The good mother
Moshfegh, O. My year of rest and relaxation
Murdoch, I. The good apprentice
Raimondo, L. Dante's dilemma
Raimondo, L. Dante's poison
Robotham, M. Suspect
Sanders, L. The fourth deadly sin
Self, W. Shark
Self, W. Umbrella
Walker, W. All is not forgotten
Walker, W. Emma in the night
Wolfe, T. Back to blood

PSYCHIATRISTS -- ALGERIA
Wideman, J. Fanon

PSYCHIATRISTS -- GREAT BRITAIN
Barker, P. The ghost road

PSYCHIATRISTS WITH MENTAL ILLNESSES
Harris, T. Hannibal

PSYCHIATRY
Lightman, A. The diagnosis

PSYCHIC ABILITY
Bardugo, L. Ninth house
Bennett, J. Bitter spirits
Camp, B. The city of lost fortunes
Camp, B. Gather the fortunes
Castle, J. Illusion Town
Farnsworth, C. Flashmob
Farnsworth, C. Killfile
Feehan, C. Shadow rider
Harvey, M. Pulse
Herbert, F. Dune
James, M. The book of night women
King, S. Doctor Sleep
King, S. End of watch
King, S. Firestarter
Krentz, J. Running hot
Le Guin, U. The lathe of heaven
Onyebuchi, T. Riot baby
Quick, A. Crystal gardens
Quick, A. The mystery woman
Rice, A. The witching hour
Searles, J. Help for the haunted
Simon, C. Dogs don't lie
Simon, C. Panthers play for keeps
Singh, N. Silver silence
Sittenfeld, C. Sisterland

Alison, J. The marriage of the sea

Amdahl, G. I am death

Amidon, S. Human capital

Amis, M. The zone of interest

Ammaniti, N. I'm not scared

Aridjis, C. Asunder

Arnett, K. Mostly dead things

Aslam, N. The golden legend

Aslam, N. Maps for lost lovers

Aslam, N. The wasted vigil

Aswani, A. Chicago

Atilgan, Y. Motherland hotel

Atwood, M. Alias Grace

Atwood, M. Cat's eye

Auster, P. The book of illusions

Auster, P. The Brooklyn follies

Auster, P. Invisible

Auster, P. Oracle night

Bacon, C. There is room for you

Bailey, P. Chapman's odyssey

Bailey, P. Uncle Rudolf

Baker, D. Young man with a horn

Baldwin, J. Giovanni's room

Baldwin, J. The Wilshire sun

Ball, J. The way through doors

Ballard, J. The day of creation

Banasky, C. The suicide of Claire Bishop

Bandele, A. Daughter

Banks, R. Lost memory of skin

Banville, J. Ancient light

Banville, J. The blue guitar

Banville, J. Eclipse

Banville, J. The infinitie

Banville, J. The sea

Barbash, T. The last good chance

Barker, P. Another world

Barnes, D. Nightwood

Barnes, J. The only story

Barnes, J. The sense of an ending

Barry, B. The map of true places

Barry, S. The secret scripture

Barzak, C. One for sorrow

Bauer, A. The forever marriage

Bausch, R. Hello to the cannibals

Baxter, C. The feast of love

Baxter, C. Saul and Patsy

Beattie, A. The doctor's house

Beattie, A. A wonderful stroke of luck

Beauvoir, S. The Mandarins

Begley, L. About Schmidt

Bell, M. The color of night

Bellow, S. Herzog

Bellow, S. Mr. Sammler's planet

Bellow, S. Novels, 1944-1953

Bellow, S. Ravelstein

Bellow, S. Seize the day

Bennett, B. The mothers

Berger, T. Neighbors

Berger, T. Reinhart's women

Berger, T. Vital parts

Bialosky, J. House under snow

Bialosky, J. The prize

Bilenchi, R. The chill

Bing, S. You look nice today

Bird, S. The Yokota Officers Club

Black, B. Christine Falls

Bock, C. Beautiful children

Bohjalian, C. The buffalo soldier

Bohjalian, C. The double bind

Bolano, R. The savage detectives

Boswell, R. Century's son

Boudjedra, R. The Barbary figs

Bowen, E. The heat of the day

Bowles, P. The sheltering sky

Boyle, T. The harder they come

Boyle, T. The Terranauts

Boyne, J. A history of loneliness

Braffet, K. Last seen leaving

Bram, C. Lives of the circus animals

Brautigan, R. An unfortunate woman

Breslin, J. Table money

Brinkman, K. Up high in the trees

Brkic, C. The first rule of swimming

Brockmeier, K. The illumination

Brockmeier, K. The truth about Celia

Brown, R. Before and after

Brownrigg, S. The delivery room

Buckman, D. Because the rain

Buntin, J. Marlena

Butler, M. Pickle's progress

Butler, N. The hearts of men

Buxbaum, J. After you

Byatt, A. Babel Tower

Byatt, A. The biographer's tale

Byatt, A. A whistling woman

Bynum, S. Ms. Hempel chronicles

Campbell, B. Brothers and sisters

Camus, A. The fall

Camus, A. The stranger

Cannon, J. Three things about Elsie

Carlson, R. Five skies

Cary, J. The horse's mouth

Castel-Bloom, O. Textile

Cather, W. A lost lady

Chabon, M. Moonglow

Chang, L. All is forgotten, nothing is lost

Cheever, J. Bullet Park

Cheever, J. Falconer

Choi, S. My education

Cleage, P. What looks like crazy on an ordinary day

Cleave, C. Gold

Clement, J. Prayers for the stolen

Cline, E. The girls

Coake, C. You came back

Freudenberger, N. Lost and wanted
Fridlund, E. History of wolves
Fuqua, J. Gone and back again
Gaddis, W. Agape agape
Gaige, A. Schroder
Gaige, A. Sea wife
Gainza, M. The optic nerve
Gaitskill, M. Don't cry
Gaitskill, M. Veronica
Galloway, G. As simple as snow
Gardam, J. Last friends
Gardam, J. The man in the wooden hat
Gardam, J. Old Filth
Garey, J. Too bright to hear too loud to see
Gertler, S. Drifting
Ghosh, A. The hungry tide
Gibb, C. Sweetness in the belly
Gifford, B. Wyoming
Giordano, P. The human body
Giordano, P. The solitude of prime numbers
Glass, J. Three Junes
Glass, J. The whole world over
Goenawan, C. The perfect world of Miwako Sumida
Goenawan, C. Rainbirds
Golding, W. Darkness visible
Golding, W. Lord of the flies
Gordimer, N. Get a life
Gordimer, N. No time like the present
Gottlieb, E. Best boy
Greenberg, J. I never promised you a rose garden
Greene, G. The captain and the enemy
Greene, G. The end of the affair
Greene, G. The heart of the matter
Greene, G. The quiet American
Greene, G. The tenth man
Greenwell, G. Cleanness
Greenwell, G. What belongs to you
Griffin, A. When all is said
Grodstein, L. A friend of the family
Grossman, D. A horse walks into a bar
Grossman, D. To the end of the land
Guterson, D. The other
Guterson, D. Our Lady of the Forest
Haddon, M. The curious incident of the dog in the night-time
Hannaham, J. Delicious foods
Hansen, R. Mariette in ecstasy
Harding, P. Tinkers
Hardy, T. Far from the madding crowd
Hardy, T. The return of the native
Hardy, T. Tess of the d'Urbervilles
Haruf, K. Benediction
Haruf, K. Eventide
Haruf, K. Plainsong
Haslett, A. Imagine me gone
Heller, P. The painter
Heller, P. The river
Heller, Z. What was she thinking?

Herlihy, J. Midnight cowboy
Hesse, H. Narcissus and Goldmund
Hesse, H. Siddhartha
Hesse, H. Steppenwolf
Hill, N. The nix
Hodgkinson, A. 22 Britannia Road
Hoeg, P. Borderliners
Hoffman, A. The ice queen
Hoffman, A. Skylight confessions
Hoffman, A. The third angel
Howatch, S. The heartbreaker
Howrey, M. The wanderers
Hulse, S. Black River
Hunter, E. The blackboard jungle
Hurston, Z. Their eyes were watching God
Hustvedt, S. The blazing world
Irving, J. Avenue of mysteries
Irving, J. In one person
Irving, J. A prayer for Owen Meany
Ishiguro, K. An artist of the floating world
Ishiguro, K. The remains of the day
Ishiguro, K. When we were orphans
Jackson, C. The lost weekend
Jacobson, H. The Finkler question
James, H. Complete stories, 1874-1884
James, H. Complete stories, 1884-1891
James, H. Complete stories, 1892-1898
James, H. Complete stories, 1898-1910
James, H. Daisy Miller
James, H. The golden bowl
James, H. The portrait of a lady
James, H. The turn of the screw
James, H. The wings of the dove
Jin, H. The crazed
Johnson, D. Tree of smoke
Johnson, L. The most dangerous place on earth
Jong, E. Fear of flying
Joyce, J. Finnegans wake
Joyce, J. Ulysses
Kazantzakis, N. Zorba the Greek
Kellerman, J. The genius
Keneally, T. Woman of the inner sea
Kerangal, M. The cook
Kerangal, M. The heart
Kiernan, C. The drowning girl
King, L. Father of the rain
Kosinski, J. Being there
Kostova, E. The shadow land
Krauss, N. The history of love
Krueger, W. Ordinary grace
Kunzru, H. The impressionist
Kunzru, H. My revolutions
Lahiri, J. The lowland
Larsen, N. Passing
Lasdun, J. Afternoon of a faun
Lasser, S. Say nice things about Detroit
Lawson, M. Crow Lake

O'Farrell, M. The hand that first held mine

O'Hagan, A. Be near me

O'Nan, S. Emily, alone

O'Nan, S. Henry, himself

O'Nan, S. Snow angels

O'Neill, J. Netherland

Oates, J. Because it is bitter, and because it is my heart

Oates, J. A book of American martyrs

Oates, J. Broke heart blues

Oates, J. The falls

Oates, J. Foxfir

Oates, J. A garden of earthly delights

Oates, J. The gravedigger's daughter

Oates, J. I lock my door upon myself

Oates, J. Little bird of heaven

Oates, J. Marya

Oates, J. Middle age

Oates, J. My life as a rat

Oates, J. Them

Oates, J. We were the Mulvaneys

Odell, J. The healing

Ogawa, Y. The housekeeper and the professor

Okuizumi, H. The stones cry out

Olafsson, O. The sacrament

Ondaatje, M. Anil's ghost

Orstavik, H. Love

Oyeyemi, H. The opposite house

Oz, A. Fima

Ozick, C. Foreign bodies

Palahniuk, C. Choke

Palaia, M. The given world

Palmer, D. Mary Toft; or, the rabbit queen

Palwick, S. Mending the moon

Parkhurst, C. The dogs of Babel

Patchett, A. Bel canto

Patchett, A. Run

Patchett, A. State of wonder

Pelecanos, G. The turnaround

Percy, W. Lancelot

Percy, W. The moviegoer

Percy, W. The second coming

Perez-Reverte, A. The painter of battles

Perrotta, T. Little children

Persson Giolito, M. Quicksand

Petterson, P. I curse the river of time

Petterson, P. I refuse

Phillips, C. A distant shore

Phillips, C. Foreigners

Picoult, J. House rules

Picoult, J. Sing you home

Picoult, J. The storyteller

Piercy, M. Vida

Plath, S. The bell jar

Pomerantz, S. Rich boy

Powers, R. The echo maker

Powers, R. The Gold Bug Variations

Prcic, I. Shards

Price, R. Freedomland

Price, R. The good priest's son

Price, R. Roxanna Slade

Prose, F. Goldengrove

Puig, M. Kiss of the spider woman

Pywell, S. What happened to Henry

Quindlen, A. Every last one

Rachman, T. The imperfectionists

Rand, A. The fountainhead

Rayfiel, T. In pinelight

Raymond, J. The half-life

Restrepo, L. Delirium

Rodrigues Fowler, Y. Stubborn archivist

Rooney, K. Lillian Boxfish takes a walk

Rooney, S. Conversations with friends

Rosnay, T. Sarah's key

Rotert, R. Last night at the blue angel

Roth, P. The anatomy lesson

Roth, P. The dying animal

Roth, P. Everyman

Roth, P. Exit ghost

Roth, P. The human stain

Roth, P. Letting go

Roth, P. My life as a man

Roth, P. Zuckerman bound

Rush, N. Subtle bodies

Rushdie, S. Shalimar the Clown

Russell, K. My dark Vanessa

Sackville-West, V. All passion spent

Salinger, J. The catcher in the rye

Salinger, J. Franny and Zooey

Salinger, J. Raise high the roof beam, carpenters,

Sallis, J. Sarah Jane

Sanders, L. The first deadly sin

Sanders, L. The fourth deadly sin

Sanders, L. The second deadly sin

Sanders, L. The third deadly sin

Saramago, J. Death with interruptions

Sartre, J. Nausea

Savage, S. The way of the dog

Schwartz, J. Northwest corner

Schwarz, C. All is vanity

Schwarz, C. Drowning Ruth

Sebald, W. The emigrants

Sebold, A. The almost moon

Sebold, A. The lovely bones

See, C. The handyman

See, C. There will never be another you

Shafak, E. 10 minutes 38 seconds in this strange world

Sharratt, M. Illuminations

Shriver, L. We need to talk about Kevin

Skyhorse, B. Madonnas of Echo Park

Slaughter, K. Undone

Smith, A. The accidental

Smith, A. Autumn

Smith, A. Spring

Smith, A. Winter

Psychological profiler novels (Camilla Grebe) [series]

PSYCHOLOGICAL RESEARCH

PSYCHOLOGICAL SUSPENSE

Daniels, N. Too close

Delaney, J. Believe me

Delaney, J. The girl before

Delaney, J. The perfect wife

Downing, S. My lovely wife

Du Maurier, D. Rebecca

Edvardsson, M. A nearly normal family

Edwards, R. Darling

Ellison, J. Good girls lie

Ellison, J. Tear me apart

Ephron, H. You'll never know, dear

Eriksson, K. The princess of Burundi

Feeney, A. I know who you are

Feeney, A. Sometimes I lie

Finn, A. The woman in the window

Fisher, T. The wives

Flint, E. Little deaths

Flynn, G. Dark places

Flynn, G. Gone girl

Flynn, G. Sharp objects

Foley, L. The hunting party

Fossum, K. Bad intentions

Fossum, K. Eva's eye

Franklin, T. Crooked letter, crooked letter

Freeman, B. Thief River Falls

French, N. Blue Monday

French, N. Dark Saturday

French, N. The day of the dead

French, N. Friday on my mind

French, N. The lying room

French, N. Sunday silence

French, N. Thursday's children

French, N. Tuesday's gone

French, N. Waiting for Wednesday

French, T. Broken harbor

French, T. Faithful place

French, T. In the woods

French, T. The likeness

French, T. The secret place

Gardner, L. Alone

Gaylin, A. Never look back

Goddard, R. Into the blue

Goddard, R. Never go back

Golding, M. Little darlings

Goodman, C. The night villa

Goodman, C. The sea of lost girls

Greaves, C. Hard twisted

Green, G. Ravens

Greene, G. Brighton Rock

Greer, A. The impossible lives of Greta Wells

Grippando, J. Lying with strangers

Grunberg, A. Tirza

Gundar-Goshen, A. Waking lions

Guterson, D. Snow falling on cedars

Hamer, K. The girl in the red coat

Hannah, S. The cradle in the grave

Hannah, S. Perfect little children

Hannah, S. The wrong mother

Harris, T. Hannibal

Harris, T. Hannibal rising

Harris, T. Red dragon

Harris, T. The silence of the lambs

Hart, J. Damage

Hart, J. The king of lies

Hart, J. The last child

Hawkins, P. The girl on the train

Hawley, N. The good father

Healey, E. Elizabeth is missing

Hendricks, G. An anonymous girl

Higashino, K. The devotion of suspect X

Highsmith, P. The Highsmith reader

Hill, R. The stranger house

Hill, R. The woodcutter

Hill, S. The shadows in the street

Hunter, E. The moment she was gone

Hurwitz, G. The survivor

Hurwitz, G. You're next

James, P. Innocent blood

Jemc, J. The grip of it

Jerkins, G. The ninth step

Jewell, L. I found you

Jewell, L. Then she was gone

Jones, S. The other woman

Jones, T. The better liar

Joss, M. Among the missing

Joss, M. Half broken things

Joss, M. The night following

Kantaria, A. I know you

Kasischke, L. The raising

Katzenbach, J. The analyst

Katzenbach, J. Just cause

Katzenbach, J. What comes next

Kellerman, J. Bones

Kellerman, J. The clinic

Kellerman, J. Devil's waltz

Kellerman, J. Gone

Kellerman, J. Monster

Kellerman, J. Private eyes

Kellerman, J. Self-defense

Kellerman, J. Therapy

Kellerman, J. Time bomb

Kelly, E. The burning air

Kelly, E. The poison tree

Kennedy, D. The big picture

Kennedy, D. The moment

Kent, C. The loving husband

King, S. Dolores Claiborne

King, S. Misery

Klein, R. The moth diaries

Knight, R. The secretary

Koch, H. The dinner

Kubica, M. The other Mrs.

Kubica, M. Pretty baby

LaPlante, A. Turn of mind

Unger, L. Under my skin
Vandelly, T. Theme music
Vine, B. Anna's book
Vine, B. The chimney sweeper's boy
Vine, B. The House of Stairs
Vine, B. Grasshopper
Vine, B. The minotaur
Walker, C. Man of the year
Walker, W. All is not forgotten
Walker, W. Emma in the night
Ware, R. In a dark, dark wood
Ware, R. The death of Mrs. Westaway
Ware, R. The lying game
Ware, R. The turn of the key
Ware, R. The woman in cabin ten
Watson, S. Before I go to sleep
Weinberg, K. The truants
Williams, A. The stranger you seek
Wilson, C. Dead girl in 2A
Wrobel, S. Darling Rose Gold
Yap, F. Yesterday
Yates, C. Black chalk
Yates, C. Grist Mill Road
Zailckas, K. Mother, mother

PSYCHOLOGICAL WARFARE
Harris, O. A shadow intelligence
Kay, G. Tigana

PSYCHOLOGIST AND PATIENT
Carpenter, E. Every single secret

PSYCHOLOGISTS
Ballard, J. Millennium people
Block, L. All the flowers are dying
Boyle, T. Outside looking in
Carr, C. The alienist
Carr, C. The angel of darkness
Chaon, D. Ill will
Gilman, F. The half-made world
Kellerman, J. Bones
Kellerman, J. The clinic
Kellerman, J. Devil's waltz
Kellerman, J. Gone
Kellerman, J. Monster
Kellerman, J. Private eyes
Kellerman, J. Self-defense
Kellerman, J. Time bomb
Kellerman, J. Therapy
Knopf, C. You're dead
Lem, S. Solaris
Lerner, B. The Topeka school
Nabokov, V. Ada
Overton, H. The runaway
Pinborough, S. Behind her eyes
Raimondo, L. Dante's wood
Seo, M. The only child
Ullman, E. By blood
White, S. Compound fractures
White, S. Dry ice

White, S. Kill me
White, S. Line of fir
White, S. The siege

PSYCHOLOGY
Oates, J. The doll-master
Schweblin, S. Mouthful of birds

PSYCHOLOGY -- EXPERIMENTS
Hendricks, G. An anonymous girl

PSYCHOLOGY TEACHERS
Goldstein, R. 36 arguments for the existence of God
Hendricks, G. An anonymous girl

PSYCHOMETRY
Gilman, D. Kaleidoscope

PSYCHOPATHS
Abani, C. The secret history of Las Vegas
Alexis, A. The hidden keys
Beukes, L. Broken monsters
Black, S. The killing lessons
Black, S. Lovemurder
Bruen, K. Galway girl
Cain, C. One Kick
Clark, M. Blood defense
Cooper, E. Buried
Coulter, C. Paradox
Dexter, P. Paris Trout
Ellory, R. Bad signs
French, N. The day of the dead
French, N. Sunday silence
Gardner, L. Alone
Grafton, S. X
Grafton, S. Y is for yesterday
Greaves, C. Hard twisted
Greene, G. Brighton Rock
Harris, T. Hannibal
Harris, T. Red dragon
Harris, T. The silence of the lambs
Kerley, J. The death collectors
King, S. End of watch
King, S. Finders keepers
King, S. Mr. Mercedes
Koontz, D. The darkest evening of the year
Koontz, D. The husband
Koontz, D. Intensity
Koontz, D. Velocity
Lehane, D. Prayers for rain
Levin, I. A kiss before dying
Manning, M. The victim
Margolin, P. Wild justice
Mason, T. The Darwin affair
Means, D. Hystopia
Murakami, R. In the miso soup
O'Brien, E. In the forest
Palmer, M. The last surgeon
Paris, B. Behind closed doors
Parsons, K. Doing harm
Perry, A. Paragon Walk
Perry, T. Pursuit

Pryor, M. Hollow man
Pyper, A. The damned
Rickards, J. Winter's end
Sanders, L. The third deadly sin
Sandford, J. Mind prey
Sandford, J. Winter prey
Scottoline, L. Every fifteen minutes
Stage, Z. Baby teeth
Suskind, P. Perfume
Thompson, J. The killer inside me
White, S. Dry ice

PSYCHOPATHS -- THE WEST (UNITED STATES)
McMurtry, L. Streets of Laredo

PSYCHOSES
Cotter, B. Fever chart
Freeman, B. The night bird
Harrison, M. Light
Jemc, J. The grip of it

PSYCHOTHERAPIST AND PATIENT
Barry, B. The map of true places
Brownrigg, S. The delivery room
French, N. Blue Monday
Greenberg, J. I never promised you a rose garden
Kellerman, J. Therapy
Robotham, M. Suspect
Spark, M. Aiding & abetting
Thomas, B. A good enough mother
White, S. Compound fractures
White, S. Line of fire

PSYCHOTHERAPISTS
French, N. Blue Monday
Gregory, D. We are all completely fine
McPhee, M. Gorgeous lies
Palumbo, D. Night terrors
Parker, R. Shrink rap

PSYCHOTHERAPY
Chung, M. The eighth girl
Lutz, L. Revenge of the Spellmans
Ullman, E. By blood
Walker, W. All is not forgotten

PSYCHOTHERAPY MALPRACTICE
Lehane, D. Prayers for rain

PSYCHOTHERAPY PATIENTS
Collins, C. The gamal
Kellerman, J. Therapy
Theroux, M. Strange bodies

PSYCHOTROPIC DRUGS
Moody, R. Right livelihoods

PUBLIC DEFENDERS
Nava, M. Carved in bone
Pava, S. A naked singularity
Winer, J. Her kind of case

PUBLIC HEALTH
Donati, S. Where the light enters
Leon, D. Trace elements
Miller, A. Pure

PUBLIC HOSPITALS

Welsh, K. The wages of sin

PUBLIC HOUSING
Chariandy, D. Brother
Gunaratne, G. In our mad and furious city
K'wan Section 8
McBride, J. Deacon King Kong
Moore, A. Jerusalem
Naylor, G. The men of Brewster Place
Naylor, G. The women of Brewster Place
Parker, R. Double deuce
Price, R. Freedomland
Price, R. Samaritan
Smith, Z. NW

PUBLIC OFFICIALS
Deb, S. The point of return
Pratchett, T. The fifth elephant
Stanley, M. A death in the family

PUBLIC OPINION
Flint, E. Little deaths
Ibrahim, A. Season of crimson blossoms
Townsend, S. Number 10

PUBLIC PROSECUTORS
Arvin, R. Blood of angels
Gran, S. Claire DeWitt and the city of the dead
Hunter, S. Hot springs
James, J. Something about you
Keller, J. Last ragged breath
Landay, W. Defending Jacob
Lippman, L. No good deeds
Pirro, J. Sly fox
Turow, S. Presumed innocent

PUBLIC RELATIONS
Dee, J. A thousand pardons
George, E. This body of death

PUBLIC RELATIONS CONSULTANTS
Adkins, M. When you read this
Manning, M. The victim

PUBLIC SAFETY
Bala, S. The boat people

PUBLIC SCHOOLS
Hunter, E. The blackboard jungle
Smith, C. Silent city

PUBLICITY AGENTS
McDevitt, J. The Cassandra Project

PUBLISHERS AND PUBLISHING
Abbott, S. The future of love
Adimi, K. Our riches
Boyne, J. A ladder to the sky
Cosse, L. A novel bookstore
Cusk, R. Kudos
Dahlie, M. The best of youth
Fielding, H. Bridget Jones's diary
Ignatius, D. The sun king
James, P. Original sin
Jarvis, S. Death and Mr. Pickwick
Kotzwinkle, W. The bear went over the mountain
Lafferty, M. Ghost train to New Orleans

Lafferty, M. The shambling guide to New York City
McBain, E. Fat Ollie's book
Muller, M. Dead midnight
Pearl, M. The last Dickens
Peet, M. The Murdstone trilogy
Spark, M. A far cry from Kensington
Pudd'nhead Wilson ; Twain, M.

PUEBLO INDIANS
Potenza, C. Hearts of the missing

PUEBLO INDIANS -- NEW MEXICO
Silko, L. Ceremony
Smith, M. Stallion Gate

PUERTO RICANS
Quinonez, E. Bodega dreams

PUERTO RICO
De Leon, A. Side chick nation

PUERTO RICO -- HISTORY -- 19TH CENTURY
Santiago, E. Conquistadora

PUGET SOUND
Beagle, P. Summerlong
Jenkins, V. An unattended death

PULP FICTION
Collins, M. The wrong Quarry
Faust, C. Choke hold
Faust, C. Money shot
Moore, C. Noir
Tidhar, L. A man lies dreaming
Van Vogt, A. Slan
Westlake, D. Forever and a death
Pulse Francis, F.
Pulse Harvey, M.

PUMA -- WEST TEXAS
Barr, N. Track of the cat

PUNISHMENT
Campisi, M. Sin eater
Crace, J. Harvest
Naslund, B. Blood of an exile
Palwick, S. The necessary beggar
Zhou, H. Death notice
The **punishment** she deserves George, E.

PUNK CULTURE
Hallberg, G. City on fire
Vollmann, W. The rainbow stories

PUNK ROCK MUSIC
Coe, J. The rotters' club
Fitch, J. Paint it black
Gilman, S. Donna has left the building

PUNK ROCK MUSICIANS
Bognanni, P. The house of tomorrow
Egan, J. A visit from the Goon Squad

PUPPETEERS
Bradley, C. The weed that strings the hangman's bag
Phillips, S. Heroes are my weakness

PUPPETRY
Larsen, R. I am Radar

PUPPETS
Carr, B. Opioid, Indiana

Coover, R. Pinocchio in Venice
Nevill, A. The house of small shadows

PUPPIES
Cameron, W. The dogs of Christmas

PURDAH
Massey, S. The widows of Malabar Hill
Pure Miller, A.
The **pure** gold baby Drabble, M.
A **pure** heart Hassib, R.
Pure heat Buchman, M.
The **pure** in heart Hill, S.

PURGATORY
Rice, A. Memnoch the devil
Saunders, G. Lincoln in the bardo
Purgatory road Parker, S.

PURITAN WOMEN -- MASSACHUSETTS
Seton, A. The Winthrop woman

PURITANS
Gregory, P. Tidelands
Hawthorne, N. The scarlet letter
Marston, E. The devil's apprentice
Nissenson, H. The pilgrim
Purity Franzen, J.
The **purity** of vengeance Adler-Olsen, J.
A **purple** place for dying MacDonald, J.

PURPOSE IN LIFE
Atkinson, K. Life after life
Bellow, S. The adventures of Augie March
Bellow, S. Henderson the rain king
Beverly, W. Dodgers
Butler, H. The new me
Cameron, W. A dog's promise
Cartwright, J. To heaven by water
Currie, R. Everything matters!
Erpenbeck, J. Go, went, gone
George, N. The book of dreams
Gideon, M. Wife 22
Gran, S. The infinite blacktop
Johnson, D. The largesse of the sea maiden
Kafka, F. Collected stories
Levy, D. Hot milk
Lim, E. Dear cyborgs
Malamud, B. The natural
Maugham, W. The razor's edge
McCormack, M. Solar bones
Moyes, J. The giver of stars
Newman, S. The heavens
Oates, J. My life as a rat
Percy, W. The moviegoer
Reid, I. I'm thinking of ending things
Saint-Exupery, A. The little prince
Shakar, A. Luminarium
Shreve, A. Sea glass
Sosin, D. The long-shining waters
Stone, I. Lust for life
Van der Vliet Oloomi, A. Call me Zebra
Vlautin, W. Don't skip out on me

The **queen** of blood Durst, S.

Queen of the conquered Callender, K.

The **queen** of the damned Rice, A.

The **queen** of the night Chee, A.

Queen of the night Jance, J.

The **queen's** bastard Maxwell, R.

The **Queen's** man Penman, S.

Queenie Carty-Williams, C.

Queenmaker Edghill, I.

Queenpin Abbott, M.

Queens of England [series] Plaidy, J.

The **queens** of Innis Lear Gratton, T.

Queens of Innis Lear [series] Gratton, T.

Queens of Renthia [series] Durst, S.

QUEENS, NEW YORK CITY

Breslin, J. Table money

Flint, E. Little deaths

Gray, E. Love & a gangsta

Hansen, R. A wild surge of guilty passion

Jin, H. A good fall

LaValle, V. The changeling

LaValle, V. The devil in silver

Thomas, M. We are not ourselves

QUEENSLAND

Carey, P. His illegal self

Harper, J. The lost man

McGahan, A. The white earth

Wright, A. Carpentaria

QUEENSLAND -- HISTORY -- 19TH CENTURY

Malouf, D. Remembering Babylon

A **question** of belief Leon, D.

A **question** of blood Rankin, I.

QUESTIONING

Dekker, T. The girl behind the red rope

Koestler, A. Darkness at noon

Varley, J. Red lightning

QUESTIONS AND ANSWERS

Cook, T. The crime of Julian Wells

Rice, A. Christ the Lord

QUESTS

Alexis, A. The hidden keys

Asher, N. The skinner

Azzopardi, T. Winterton blue

Baker, K. The bird of the river

Beagle, P. The last unicorn

Bear, E. Blood and iron

Bear, E. The red-stained wings

Bear, E. The stone in the skull

Bell, L. For the duke's eyes only

Benioff, D. City of thieves

Bolano, R. The savage detectives

Burke, J. House of the rising sun

Butler, O. Parable of the sower

Carey, J. Starless

Cervantes Saavedra, M. Don Quixote

Ciotta, B. Her sky cowboy

Ciotta, B. His clockwork canary

Clarke, B. An arsonist's guide to writers' homes in New England

Cline, E. Ready player one

Connolly, J. The book of lost things

Couto, M. Sleepwalking land

Davies, C. West

Durst, S. The queen of blood

Fay, K. The map of lost memories

Foer, J. Extremely loud and incredibly close

Fortier, A. Juliet

Foster, A. Relic

French, J. The Grey Bastards

Gabaldon, D. Drums of autumn

Gaiman, N. Stardust

Haydon, E. Prophecy

Ishiguro, K. The buried giant

James, M. Black leopard, red wolf

Johnson, K. The dream-quest of Vellitt Boe

Kurland, L. Star of the morning

Lackey, M. The fairy godmother

Lai, L. The tiger flu

Le Guin, U. The beginning place

Leckie, A. Ancillary justice

Leckie, A. Ancillary mercy

Leckie, A. Ancillary sword

Lee, C. On such a full sea

Locke, T. Emissary

Locke, T. Enclave

Lyndon, R. Hawk quest

Lyons, J. The ruin of kings

Maalouf, A. Balthasar's odyssey

Martel, Y. The high mountains of Portugal

Martin, G. A dance with dragons

Martineau, M. Kingdom of exiles

Mason, D. The piano tuner

Montag, K. After the flood

Moreno-Garcia, S. Gods of jade and shadow

Morgenstern, E. The starless sea

Novik, N. Uprooted

Olmstead, R. Coal black horse

Orullian, P. The unremembered

Peet, M. The Murdstone trilogy

Poore, M. Reincarnation blues

Porter, C. The seep

Preston, D. The codex

Preston, D. Thunderhead

Pulley, N. The Bedlam stacks

Recacoechea S., J. American visa

Rothfuss, P. The name of the wind

Rothfuss, P. The wise man's fear

Roy, A. All the lives we never lived

Rushdie, S. Quichotte

Russell, K. Swamplandia!

Saberhagen, F. Coinspinner's story

Saberhagen, F. Farslayer's story

Saberhagen, F. Mindsword's story

Saberhagen, F. Shieldbreaker's story

Baldwin, J. Another country

Baldwin, J. Going to meet the man

Baldwin, J. If Beale Street could talk

Baldwin, J. Just above my head

Baldwin, J. Tell me how long the train's been gone

Ball, J. In the heat of the night

Bambara, T. Gorilla, my love

Bambara, T. Those bones are not my child

Banks, R. Cloudsplitter

Barnett, L. Jam on the Vine

Beatty, P. The sellout

Beatty, P. Slumberland

Benz, C. The gone dead

Berg, E. We are all welcome here

Blake, S. The guest book

Bobotis, A. The last list of Miss Judith Kratt

Boyle, T. The tortilla curtain

Brown, R. Half a heart

Brown, R. Murder at Monticello, or, Old sins

Campbell, B. Brothers and sisters

Campbell, B. Your blues ain't like mine

Carey, P. A long way from home

Carter, S. New England white

Carty-Williams, C. Queenie

Cha, S. Your house will pay

Chang, A. Days of distraction

Childress, M. One Mississippi

Clarke, B. The price of the haircut

Clarke, M. Foreign soil

Clemmons, Z. What we lose

Clinch, J. Finn

Coetzee, J. Age of Iron

Coetzee, J. Disgrace

Coetzee, J. Foe

Cole, T. Open city

Collins, K. Whatever happened to interracial love?

Colwin, L. Goodbye without leaving

Conroy, P. South of Broad

Cush, J. Endangered

Dennis-Benn, N. Here comes the sun

Depestre, R. Hadriana in all my dreams

Dexter, P. Paris Trout

Edwards, R. Darling

Ellison, R. Invisible man

Ellison, R. Three days before the shooting . . .

Eskens, A. Nothing more dangerous

Everett, P. God's country

Everett, P. I am Not Sidney Poitier

Faulkner, W. Go down, Moses

Faulkner, W. Intruder in the dust

Faye, L. The Paragon Hotel

Flagg, F. Fried green tomatoes at the Whistle Stop Cafe

Forbes, C. A tall history of sugar

Gaines, E. The autobiography of Miss Jane Pittman

Gaines, E. A gathering of old men

Gala, M. The Black Cathedral

Ganshert, K. No one ever asked

Gilbert, E. City of girls

Gordimer, N. July's people

Gordimer, N. No time like the present

Grau, S. The keepers of the house

Greenidge, K. We love you, Charlie Freeman

Grisham, J. A time to kill

Gyasi, Y. Homegoing

Haldane, S. The devil's making

Himes, C. Cotton comes to Harlem

Holsinger, B. The gifted school

Hubbard, L. The talented Ribkins

Hughes, L. Short stories

Hughes, L. Simple speaks his mind

Hulme, K. The bone people

Hunt, L. The evening road

Hurston, Z. Hitting a straight lick with a crooked stick

Iles, G. The bone tree

Iles, G. Natchez burning

Jackson, J. The almost sisters

Jhabvala, R. Heat and dust

Johnson, K. Little black girl lost

Johnson, K. Little black girl lost 2

Johnson, M. Incognegro

Johnson, M. Pym

Kennedy, W. Chango's beads and two-tone shoes

Kunzru, H. The impressionist

Lalami, L. The other Americans

Lansdale, J. A fine dark line

Lansdale, J. Paradise sky

Lansdale, J. Sunset and sawdust

Lansdale, J. The thicket

Larsen, N. Passing

Lee, H. Go set a watchman

Lee, H. To kill a mockingbird

Lehane, D. The given day

Lepionka, K. The last place you look

Lessing, D. Landlocked

Lessing, D. Martha Quest

Leveen, L. The secrets of Mary Bowser

Levy, A. The long song

Levy, A. Small island

Lippman, L. Lady in the lake

Locke, A. Bluebird, bluebird

Locke, A. Heaven, my home

Luesse, V. Missing Isaac

Malamud, B. The fixer

Mason, R. Who killed Piet Barol?

Mathis, A. The twelve tribes of Hattie

McBride, J. Five-carat soul

McClure, J. The steam pig

Meloy, M. Do not become alarmed

Mengestu, D. The beautiful things that heaven bears

Meno, J. Marvel and a wonder

Michener, J. Chesapeake

Michener, J. The covenant

Miller, K. An angry-ass black woman

Miller, K. Augustown

Baldwin, J. Another country
Baldwin, J. Go tell it on the mountain
Baldwin, J. Going to meet the man
Baldwin, J. If Beale Street could talk
Baldwin, J. Just above my head
Baldwin, J. Tell me how long the train's been gone
Ball, J. In the heat of the night
Bambara, T. Those bones are not my child
Banks, R. Cloudsplitter
Banks, R. Continental drift
Barnett, L. Jam on the Vine
Bartels, E. We hope for better things
Beatty, P. The sellout
Benz, C. The gone dead
Blake, S. The guest book
Bohjalian, C. Skeletons at the feast
Bond, C. Ruby
Campbell, B. Brothers and sisters
Card, M. These ghosts are family
Carr, B. Opioid, Indiana
Cather, W. A lost lady
Cha, S. Your house will pay
Charles, K. Wanted, a gentleman
Chiaverini, J. Mrs. Lincoln's dressmaker
Childress, M. Crazy in Alabama
Cho, Z. Sorcerer to the crown
Coates, T. The water dancer
Coldsmith, D. The long journey home
Collins, K. Notes from a black woman's diary
Colvin, J. Africaville
Cush, J. Endangered
Dev, S. Pride, prejudice, and other flavors
Dexter, P. Paris Trout
Edwards, R. Darling
Ellison, R. Three days before the shooting . . .
Ellroy, J. Blood's a rover
Eskens, A. Nothing more dangerous
Everett, P. God's country
Fajardo-Anstine, K. Sabrina & Corina
Faulkner, W. Light in August
Faye, L. The Paragon Hotel
Fowler, K. Sarah Canary
Fowler, T. A good neighborhood
French, A. Billy
Gaines, E. The autobiography of Miss Jane Pittman
Grunberg, A. Tirza
Guinn, M. The scribe
Guterson, D. Snow falling on cedars
Gyasi, Y. Homegoing
Himes, C. Cotton comes to Harlem
Holmes, J. How are you going to save yourself
Howard, R. Driving the king
Howarth, P. Only killers and thieves
Hughes, L. Short stories
Hunt, L. The evening road
Hunter, S. Pale horse coming
Hurston, Z. Hitting a straight lick with a crooked stick

Iles, G. The devil's punchbowl
Iles, G. Mississippi blood
Jen, G. The resisters
Jenkins, B. Rebel
Johnson, M. Incognegro
Jones, T. An American marriage
Jordan, H. Mudbound
Kellerman, J. Time bomb
Kelton, E. Badger boy
Kelton, E. The way of the coyote
Kimani, P. Dance of the Jakaranda
Kowal, M. The calculating stars
Kowal, M. The fated sky
Kuang, R. The dragon republic
Kuang, R. The poppy war
Kunzru, H. White tears
Kwok, J. Searching for Sylvie Lee
Lansdale, J. Edge of dark water
Lansdale, J. Paradise sky
Lee, D. Country of origin
Lee, H. Go set a watchman
Lee, H. To kill a mockingbird
Leon, D. Blood from a stone
Lessing, D. Martha Quest
Lessing, D. A ripple from the storm
Leveen, L. The secrets of Mary Bowser
Levin, I. The boys from Brazil
Levy, A. Small island
Limon, M. The line
Lippman, L. Lady in the lake
Lock, N. A fugitive in Walden Woods
Locke, A. Bluebird, bluebird
Locke, A. Heaven, my home
Loh, V. Breaking the tongue , by Vyvyane Loh.
Luesse, V. Missing Isaac
MacBride, S. Close to the bone
Malouf, D. Remembering Babylon
Marlette, D. Magic time
Matthiessen, P. Bone by bone
Mda, Z. The Madonna of Excelsior
Mengestu, D. The beautiful things that heaven bears
Michener, J. Chesapeake
Michener, J. The covenant
Michener, J. Tales of the South Pacific
Mitchell, D. Cloud atlas
Moody, R. Right livelihoods
Moore, L. A gate at the stairs
Morgan, C. The sport of kings
Morrison, T. Home
Morrison, T. A mercy
Morrison, T. Song of Solomon
Mosley, W. Fortunate son
Mosley, W. Trouble is what I do
Moss, S. Ghost wall
Mullen, T. Darktown
Mullen, T. Lightning men
Naylor, G. Linden Hills

Wendig, C. Wanderers

RADIO PLAYWRITING

Vargas Llosa, M. Aunt Julia and the scriptwriter

RADIO PROGRAMS

Alarcon, D. Lost City Radio

Atkinson, K. Transcription

RADIO STATIONS

Alarcon, D. Lost City Radio

Hay, E. Late nights on air

RADIO TALK SHOW HOSTS AND GUESTS

Haddam, J. Hardscrabble road

Shields, C. The republic of love

RADIO WAVES

Larsen, R. I am Radar

RADIOACTIVE POLLUTION

Smith, M. Wolves eat dogs

RADIOACTIVITY

Cussler, C. Sacred stone

Rafe Weatherspoon, R.

Ragdoll Cole, D.

The **rage** of dragons Winter, E.

Ragnarok Byatt, A.

Ragtime Doctorow, E.

Raiders of the Nile Saylor, S.

RAIDS (MILITARY SCIENCE)

Cobbs Hoffman, E. The Tubman command

Crichton, M. Pirate latitudes

RAILROAD ACCIDENTS

Cussler, C. The wrecker

Jones, S. The uninvited guests

RAILROAD ACCIDENTS -- PSYCHOLOGICAL AS-PECTS

Simmons, D. Drood

RAILROAD CONSTRUCTION WORKERS

Kimani, P. Dance of the Jakaranda

RAILROAD ENGINEERS

Goodman, J. A touch of forever

RAILROAD OWNERS

Perry, A. Death of a stranger

RAILROAD POLICE

Russell, S. The insane train

RAILROAD STATIONS

Davis, F. The masterpiece

Murakami, H. Colorless Tsukuru Tazaki and his years of pilgrimage

RAILROAD TRAVEL

Christie, A. Murder on the Orient Express

Hawkins, P. The girl on the train

Kaminsky, S. Murder on the Trans-Siberian Express

Koryta, M. The Cypress House

Larsen, R. The selected works of T. S. Spivet

Priest, C. Dreadnought

Simmons, D. Drood

RAILROAD WORKERS

Goodman, J. A touch of forever

Johnson, D. Train dreams

RAILROADS

Cussler, C. The wrecker

Groom, W. El Paso

Kimani, P. Dance of the Jakaranda

Russell, S. The insane train

RAILROADS -- NEBRASKA

Cather, W. A lost lady

Rain Couto, M.

The **rain** before it falls Coe, J.

RAIN FORESTS

Crichton, M. Micro

Wilson, D. The Andromeda evolution

RAIN MAKERS

Bellow, S. Henderson the rain king

Rainbirds Goenawan, C.

The **rainbow** Lawrence, D.

The **rainbow** stories Vollmann, W.

Rainbows end Vinge, V.

Rainshadow novels [series] Castle, J.

Raintree County Lockridge, R.

Raise high the roof beam, carpenters, Salinger, J.

The **raising** Kasischke, L.

Raj Mehta, G.

A **rake's** vow Laurens, S.

RAMA (IMAGINARY SPACE VEHICLE)

Clarke, A. Rendezvous with Rama

Rama series [series] Clarke, A.

RAMSES III,, KING OF EGYPT

Geagley, B. Year of the hyenas

RANCH LIFE

Drake, L. The sweet spot

Hockensmith, S. Holmes on the range

Hockensmith, S. On the wrong track

Larsen, R. The selected works of T. S. Spivet

Meyers, K. The work of wolves

Proulx, A. Fine just the way it is

RANCH LIFE -- CALIFORNIA

Steinbeck, J. Of mice and men

RANCH LIFE -- MONTANA

Doig, I. Dancing at the Rascal Fair

RANCH LIFE -- NEVADA

Kittredge, W. The willow field

RANCH LIFE -- WYOMING

Proulx, A. Bad dirt

RANCHERS

Anderson, C. Mulberry moon

Box, C. Blue heaven

Carlson, R. Five skies

Daisley, S. Coming rain

Dane, L. Broken open

Evans, N. The horse whisperer

Harper, J. The lost man

Haruf, K. Eventide

Haruf, K. Plainsong

Kelton, E. Hard ride

Kelton, E. The way of the coyote

Meyer, P. The son

Meyers, K. The work of wolves

Michener, J. Centennial
Myers, A. Continental divide
Overholser, W. Death of a cattle king
Parker, R. Appaloosa
Proulx, A. That old ace in the hole
Richter, C. The sea of grass
Roberts, N. Come sundown
Rowland, R. Cold country
Schaefer, J. Shane
Smith, B. Crow's landing
Urrea, L. The hummingbird's daughter
Watson, L. As good as gone
Zimmer, M. Wild side of the river

RANCHERS' SPOUSES
Meyers, K. The work of wolves

RANCHES
Albert, S. Bittersweet
Box, C. The bitterroots
Box, C. The disappeared
Box, C. Wolf pack
Fields, H. Last Chance Llama Ranch
Goodman, J. In want of a wife
Groom, W. El Paso
Harper, J. The lost man
Hockensmith, S. Holmes on the range
Hockensmith, S. On the wrong track
March, E. Jackson
McLaren, K. The road to enchantment
Myers, A. Continental divide
Proulx, A. That old ace in the hole
Roberts, N. Come sundown
Ryan, J. Restless rancher
Schaefer, J. Shane
Vlautin, W. Don't skip out on me
Walls, J. Half broke horses

RANCHES -- CALIFORNIA
Fowler, E. The road to Cardinal Valley
L'Amour, L. The Californios

RANCHES -- CALIFORNIA -- 19TH CENTURY
Sontag, S. In America

RANCHES -- NEW MEXICO
McCarthy, C. Cities of the plain

RANCHING
Hockensmith, S. Holmes on the range
Hockensmith, S. On the wrong track
Random harvest Hilton, J.
Range of ghosts Bear, E.

RANGE WARS
Keesey, A. Little century

RANGELANDS
Keesey, A. Little century
The **ranger** Atkins, A.

RANSOM
Akunin, B. The coronation
Blake, J. The house of Wolfe
Child, L. The hard way
Deaver, J. The October list

Gay, R. An untamed state
Gowdy, B. Helpless
Koontz, D. The husband
Laukkanen, O. The professionals
Lyndon, R. Hawk quest
MacBride, S. Shatter the bones
McBain, E. Alice in jeopardy
McBain, E. The frumious bandersnatch
Mina, D. Still midnight
Mosley, W. Charcoal Joe
Mosley, W. Rose gold
Muller, M. Wolf in the shadows
Parker, R. Painted ladies
Penman, S. Dragon's lair
Perry, A. Dark tide rising
Rader-Day, L. The day I died
Ransom Malouf, D.

RAP MUSIC
K'wan Welfare wifeys

RAP MUSIC INDUSTRY AND TRADE
K'wan Section 8
Noire Candy licker

RAP MUSICIANS
K'wan Welfare wifeys
Souljah S. The coldest winter ever

RAPE
Anthony, M. Diary of a young girl
Box, C. The bitterroots
Campbell, B. Once upon a river
Cornell, P. London falling
DuPree, K. Shattered
Faulkner, W. Sanctuary
Faust, C. Money shot
Gabaldon, D. A breath of snow and ashes
Gabaldon, D. Dragonfly in amber
Gabaldon, D. Drums of autumn
Gabaldon, D. Outlander
Gay, R. An untamed state
Grisham, J. The last juror
Harris, C. Good time coming
Lasdun, J. Afternoon of a faun
Levin, I. Rosemary's baby
Lowe, K. The furies
Mukherjee, B. Miss new India
O'Donovan, G. The priest
Oates, J. Them
Ohlsson, K. Silenced
Parker, R. Stone cold
Perry, A. Midnight at Marble Arch
Perry, A. The silent cry
Richardson, S. Clarissa, or, The history of a young lady
Ryan, H. Say no more
Scoppettone, S. Everything you have is mine
Smith, J. Louisiana hotshot
Vreeland, S. The passion of Artemisia
Walker, W. All is not forgotten
Walker, W. Crime of privilege

Walsh, M. My sunshine away
Wolfe, T. A man in full

RAPE INVESTIGATION
Box, C. The bitterroots
Conlon, E. Red on red
Connelly, M. The wrong side of goodbye
French, N. Thursday's children
Limon, M. Mr. Kill
McGown, J. Verdict unsafe
Oldham, N. Fighting for the dead
Scoppettone, S. Everything you have is mine

RAPE SUSPECTS
Lasdun, J. Afternoon of a faun

RAPE VICTIMS
Brink, A. Philida
Byrne, K. How to love a duke in ten days
Corman, A. Prized possessions
Davis, A. Wonder when you'll miss me
Erdrich, L. The round house
Faulkner, W. Requiem for a nun
Faulkner, W. Sanctuary
Gardner, L. Find her
Gerritsen, T. The surgeon
Grey, Z. Woman of the frontier
Hardy, T. Tess of the d'Urbervilles
Kasasian, M. Dark dawn over Steep House
Lawler, L. Don't wake up
Lawrence, M. Hearts and bones
McGhee, A. The opposite of fate
Mda, Z. The Madonna of Excelsior
Nelscott, K. Stone cribs
Newton, C. Start shooting
O'Brien, E. Girl
Parks, B. Closer than you know
Pronzini, B. The violated
Richardson, S. Clarissa, or, The history of a young lady
Sebold, A. The lovely bones
Sharp, Z. Fox hunter
Shreve, A. Eden Close
Tademy, L. Cane River
Toews, M. Women talking
Turow, S. Presumed innocent
Umrigar, T. Everybody's son
Unger, L. The red hunter
Vaughan, S. Anatomy of a scandal
Walsh, M. My sunshine away
Welsh, K. The wages of sin
Wolfe, T. A man in full

RAPISTS
Grafton, S. Y is for yesterday
Pronzini, B. The violated
Rendell, R. Live flesh
Sharp, Z. Fox hunter
Raptor red Bakker, R.

RAPTURE (CHRISTIAN ESCHATOLOGY)
Nunez, S. Salvation city
Rapture of the nerds Doctorow, C.

RARE AND ENDANGERED ANIMALS
Box, C. Open season
Meyer, D. Trackers
Millet, L. How the dead dream
Reichs, K. Bare bones
Woods, S. Skin game

RARE AND ENDANGERED PLANTS
Baker, K. In the garden of Iden
Jio, S. The last camellia
A **rare** Benedictine Peters, E.

RARE BOOK LIBRARIES
Ruiz Zafon, C. The shadow of the wind

RARE BOOKS
Bernhard, E. The books of the dead
Block, L. The burglar in the library
Dunning, J. Booked to die
Dunning, J. The bookman's wake
Goodman, A. The cookbook collector
Gruber, M. The book of air and shadows
Krentz, J. Copper Beach
Maalouf, A. Balthasar's odyssey
Perez-Reverte, A. The Club Dumas
Reay, K. The Bronte plot
Rollins, J. Crucible
Ruiz Zafon, C. The labyrinth of the spirits
Ruiz Zafon, C. The prisoner of heaven
Ruiz Zafon, C. The shadow of the wind
Runcie, J. Sidney Chambers and the persistence of love

RARE BOOKS -- COLLECTORS AND COLLECTING
Grossman, D. Be my knife

RASTAFARI MOVEMENT
Miller, K. Augustown

RASTAFARIANS
James, M. A brief history of seven killings
Michener, J. Caribbean

RAT PACK
Randisi, R. Hey there (you with the gun in your hand)
Rat pack mysteries [series] Randisi, R.
Rather be the devil Rankin, I.

RATIONALISM
Voltaire, 1. Candide and other stories

RATIONING
Weldon, F. Chalcot Crescent
Ratking Dibdin, M.
Ratlines Neville, S.

RATS
Hosking, J. Three years with the rat
O'Connell, C. The chalk girl
Savage, S. Firmin

RATTLESNAKES
Crews, H. A feast of snakes
Raunchy Styles, T.
Raunchy 2 Styles, T.
Rav Hisda's daughter [series] Anton, M.
Ravelstein Bellow, S.
Raven black Cleeves, A.
Raven stratagem Lee, Y.

Reamde Stephenson, N.
Reaper man Pratchett, T.
REASON
Maguire, G. After Alice
Reasons to be cheerful Stibbe, N.
Rebecca Du Maurier, D.
Rebecka Martinsson mysteries [series] Larsson, A.
Rebekah Roberts novels [series] Dahl, J.
Rebel Jenkins, B.
The **rebel** angels Davies, R.
The **rebel** heir Michels, E.
Rebel powers Bausch, R.
Rebel queen Moran, M.
Rebellion Patterson, M.
REBELLIONS -- IRELAND -- 16TH CENTURY
Maxwell, R. The wild Irish
REBELS
Acevedo, C. The distant marvels
Apostol, G. Gun dealers' daughter
Baker, K. The house of the stag
Banks, R. Cloudsplitter
Beckett, L. Gamechanger
Caputo, P. Acts of faith
Kay, G. A brightness long ago
Le Guin, U. The dispossessed
Liu, K. The grace of kings
Moran, M. Rebel queen
Mukherjee, N. The lives of others
O'Neill, J. At swim, two boys
Penelope, L. Whispers of shadow & flame
Scott, W. Rob Roy
Vandermeer, J. Finch
Vonnegut, K. Player piano
REBELS -- IRELAND -- HISTORY -- 20TH CENTURY
Doyle, R. A star called Henry
Llywelyn, M. 1949
The **rebels** of Ireland Rutherfurd, E.
Receptor Glynn, A.
RECESSION (ECONOMICS)
Eggers, D. A hologram for the king
Flournoy, A. The Turner house
Markley, S. Ohio
Shteyngart, G. Super sad true love story
RECIPES
Andrew, S. Recipes for love and murder
Andrew, S. The Satanic mechanic
Bailey, M. An appetite for violets
Colgan, J. The endless beach
Recipes for love and murder Andrew, S.
Reckless Gross, A.
Reckless in Texas Dell, K.
The **reckoning** Penman, S.
A **reckoning** Sarton, M.
The **reckoning,** Jeff Long. Long, J.
RECLUSES
Allen, S. The girl who chased the moon
Aridjis, C. Asunder

Ashe, K. The duke
Barclay, L. Trust your eyes
Beagle, P. A fine and private place
Brunkhorst, A. The gilded Life of Matilda Duplaine
Clarke, S. Jonathan Strange & Mr. Norrell
Darnielle, J. Universal harvester
Doctorow, E. Homer and Langley
Eliot, G. Silas Marner
Fleming, I. You only live twice
Gilbert, D. & sons
Godwin, G. Grief cottage
Guterson, D. The other
Keller, J. Last ragged breath
Kellerman, J. The genius
King, S. Finders keepers
Krauss, N. Great house
Lambert, C. The children's home
Murdoch, I. The sea, the sea
Shipman, V. The heirloom garden
Ware, R. In a dark, dark wood
The **recognitions** Gaddis, W.
RECONCILIATION
Atkinson, K. Case histories
Cantor, M. Death and other happy endings
Cole, T. Every day is for the thief
Cramer, W. Levi's will
Flanery, P. Absolution
Genova, L. Every note played
Higgins, K. Life and other inconveniences
Higgins, K. Now that you mention it
Jeffries, S. 'Twas the night after Christmas
Kamali, M. The stationery shop
Mahmoud, L. Amreekiya
Mda, Z. The Madonna of Excelsior
Murphy, D. Tiny Americans
Pelecanos, G. The turnaround
Perry, A. A Christmas return
See, L. Dreams of joy
Vernon, O. A killing in this town
RECONCILIATION IN MARRIAGE
DeLillo, D. Falling man
Guhrke, L. How to lose a duke in ten days
Lowry, M. Under the volcano
Shupe, J. The courtesan duchess
RECONCILIATION IN MEN
Franklin, T. Crooked letter, crooked letter
RECONSTRUCTION (1939-1951)
Hazzard, S. The great fire
RECONSTRUCTION (UNITED STATES HISTORY)
Gaines, E. The autobiography of Miss Jane Pittman
Mitchell, M. Gone with the wind
Smith, L. On Agate Hill
Tademy, L. Cane River
RECORD COLLECTING
Kunzru, H. White tears
RECORD INDUSTRY AND TRADE -- HOLLYWOOD, CALIFORNIA

Groot, T. The sentinels of Andersonville
Hand, E. Generation loss
Hatcher, R. Cross my heart
Hodgen, C. Elegies for the brokenhearted
Howatch, S. The heartbreaker
Hulme, K. The bone people
Hulse, S. Black River
Hulse, S. Eden mine
Kearsley, S. The firebird
Kennedy, D. The big picture
Kerstan, L. Heart of the tiger
King, L. Keeping watch
Krueger, W. Ordinary grace
Lent, J. A slant of light
Lewis, B. The missing
Lohmann, J. Winning Ruby Heart
Lowry, M. Under the volcano
MacLean, S. No good duke goes unpunished
Machart, B. The wake of forgiveness
Malamud, B. The natural
Malik, T. Three bargains
Martin, C. Long way gone
McCann, C. Let the great world spin
McEwan, I. Atonement
McGregor, J. Even the dogs
McInerney, L. The glorious heresies
Minot, S. Evening
Morrison, T. Home
Mosley, W. All I did was shoot my man
Mosley, W. Debbie doesn't do it anymore
Mosley, W. Fortunate son
Mott, J. The returned
Nissenson, H. The pilgrim
Norman, H. Next life might be kinder
O'Connor, F. The violent bear it away
Olafur Johann Olafsson The sacrament
Parker, R. Brimstone
Pelecanos, G. The way home
Percy, W. The moviegoer
Piccirilli, T. The last kind words
Pickard, N. The scent of rain and lightning
Picoult, J. Change of heart
Pronzini, B. Step to the graveyard easy
Proulx, A. The shipping news
Putney, M. The burning point
Rice, A. Blood canticle
Rice, A. Interview with the vampire
Rice, A. Prince Lestat
Rivers, F. The masterpiece
Rivers, F. Redeeming love
Sapphire Push
Schwartz, J. Northwest corner
Seton, A. Katherine
Smith, T. Child 44
Theroux, M. Far north
Toole, F. Pound for pound
Updike, J. The widows of Eastwick

Walter, J. Citizen Vince
Walton, J. Lent
Ward, A. Forgive me
Warrington, F. Midsummer night
Wiggins, M. The shadow catcher
Williams, B. The summer wives
Winslow, D. The border
Winslow, D. The cartel
Winslow, D. The dawn patrol
Redemption Uris, L.
Redemption Baldacci, D.
REDEMPTION (CHRISTIANITY)
　　Rivers, F. Bridge to haven
Redemption Mountain FitzGerald, G.
Redemption novels (Sarah Castille) [series] Castille, S.
Redemption point Fox, C.
Redemption road Hart, J.
REDEX RELIABILITY CAR TRIALS (RACE)
　　Carey, P. A long way from home
REDHEADS
　　Burrowes, G. The trouble with dukes
　　Callihan, K. Firelight
　　Lippman, L. Sunburn
Redshirts Scalzi, J.
Reeve LeClaire novels [series] Norton, C.
Reflections in a golden eye McCullers, C.
REFORM JUDAISM
　　Rabb, J. Among the living
REFORMATION
　　Seton, A. Green darkness
REFUGEE CAMPS
　　Abulhawa, S. The blue between sky and water
　　Arudpragasam, A. The story of a brief marriage
　　El Akkad, O. American war
　　Palwick, S. The necessary beggar
　　Turow, S. Testimony
REFUGEES
　　Abulhawa, S. The blue between sky and water
　　Ackerman, E. Dark at the crossing
　　Adichie, C. Americanah
　　Adler-Olsen, J. Victim 2117
　　Ahmad, J. The wandering falcon
　　Allende, I. A long petal of the sea
　　Alyan, H. Salt houses
　　Apelfeld, A. The man who never stopped sleeping
　　Aswani, A. Chicago
　　Bala, S. The boat people
　　Bohjalian, C. Skeletons at the feast
　　Clarke, M. Foreign soil
　　Coetzee, J. The childhood of Jesus
　　Colombani, L. The braid
　　Couto, M. Sleepwalking land
　　Cunningham, M. Specimen days
　　Doctorow, E. The march
　　Egan, G. Schild's ladder
　　Fowler, C. Bryant & May
　　Furst, A. Blood of victory

Burrowes, G. My one and only duke
Burrowes, G. The soldier
Burrowes, G. Tremaine's true love
Chase, L. Don't tempt me
Chase, L. Miss Wonderful
Chase, L. Your scandalous ways
Collins, M. A good rake is hard to find
Collins, M. Ready set rogue
Crowley, J. Lord Byron's novel
Curran, K. My lady's choosing
Dare, T. A night to surrender
Dare, T. A week to be wicked
Dare, T. Romancing the duke
Dare, T. Say yes to the marquess
Dare, T. When a Scot ties the knot
Dare, T. Do you want to start a scandal
Dare, T. The duchess deal
Dare, T. The governess game
Force, M. Deceived by desire
Galen, S. Third son's a charm
Galen, S. When you give a duke a diamond
Garriott, L. Promised
Greeley, M. The clergyman's wife
Harrington, A. An inconvenient duke
Heyer, G. Black sheep
Heyer, G. The grand Sophy
Hunter, J. Forbidden to love the duke
James, E. Kiss me, Annabel
James, E. The ugly duchess
Jeffries, S. 'Twas the night after Christmas
Kerstan, L. The golden leopard
Kerstan, L. Heart of the tiger
Kinsale, L. Lessons in French
Klassen, J. The painter's daughter
Laurens, S. Devil's bride
Laurens, S. A rake's vow
Layton, E. To wed a stranger
Leigh, E. Forever your earl
Leigh, E. Scandal takes the stage
Leigh, E. Temptations of a wallflower
Lloyd, C. Death comes to the nursery
London, J. The trouble with honor
Long, J. Angel in a devil's arms
Long, J. Lady Derring takes a lover
Long, J. The legend of Lyon Redmond
Lorret, V. How to forget a duke
MacAlister, K. The truth about Leo
MacGregor, J. The bride who got lucky
MacKenzie, S. Bedding Lord Ned
MacLean, S. A rogue by any other name
MacLean, S. One good earl deserves a lover
MacLean, S. No good duke goes unpunished
MacLean, S. Never judge a lady by her cover
MacLean, S. The rogue not taken
Michels, E. The rebel heir
Moore, K. To seduce an angel
Nash, S. Between the Duke and the deep blue sea

Noble, K. The game and the governess
Penrose, A. Murder at Kensington Palace
Penrose, A. Murder on Black Swan Lane
Putney, M. Loving a lost lord
Putney, M. No longer a gentleman
Putney, M. Not quite a wife
Quick, A. I thee wed
Quick, A. Slightly shady
Quincy, D. Murder at the opera
Quincy, D. Murder in Mayfair
Quinn, J. An offer from a gentleman
Quinn, J. The lady most willing
Quinn, J. The secrets of Sir Richard Kenworthy
Rodale, M. Lady Bridget's diary
Romain, T. Fortune favors the wicked
Rosenthal, P. The edge of impropriety
Sebastian, C. It takes two to tumble
Sebastian, C. The Lawrence Browne affair
Thomas, S. Private arrangements
Waite, O. The lady's guide to celestial mechanics
Willig, L. The summer country

REGENCY ROMANCES

Ashe, K. The earl
Ashford, J. Heir to the duke
Ashford, J. Lord Sebastian's secret
Ashford, J. What the duke doesn't know
Balogh, M. The arrangement
Balogh, M. The escape
Balogh, M. More than a mistress
Balogh, M. Only enchanting
Balogh, M. The secret mistress
Balogh, M. Simply love
Balogh, M. Someone to hold
Balogh, M. Someone to love
Balogh, M. Someone to remember
Balogh, M. Someone to trust
Balogh, M. Someone to wed
Bateman, K. This earl of mine
Bell, L. For the duke's eyes only
Bell, L. How the duke was won
Bell, L. One fine duke
Bell, L. What a difference a duke makes
Bennett, A. First earl I see tonight
Berne, L. You may kiss the bride
Bourne, J. The black hawk
Bourne, J. The spymaster's lady
Bowen, K. Between the devil and the duke
Bowen, K. I've got my duke to keep me warm
Bowen, K. A rogue by night
Bowman, V. The accidental countess
Bowman, V. Secrets of a wedding night
Bowman, V. The unexpected duchess
Boyle, E. Along came a duke
Boyle, E. And the miss ran away with the rake
Bradley, A. A season of ruin
Bradley, A. A wicked way to win an earl
Brockway, C. The golden season

Regeneration Barker, P.
REGENERATION (BIOLOGY)
Regeneration trilogy (Pat Barker) [series] Barker, P.
REGENSBERG, IZOLD
REGGAE MUSICIANS
REGIME CHANGE
REGRESSION (CIVILIZATION)
REGRESSION (PSYCHOLOGY)
REGRET

Turner, B. Wooing Cadie McCaffrey
Updike, J. Licks of love
Van Booy, S. The illusion of separateness
Ward, A. Forgive me

REGRET IN MEN
Barnes, J. The sense of an ending
Savage, S. The way of the dog

REGRET IN SENIOR MEN
Nemirovsky, I. Fire in the blood
Roth, P. Everyman

REGRET IN SENIOR WOMEN
Minot, S. Evening

REGRET IN WOMEN
Didion, J. Play it as it lays
Lee, J. The starlet and the spy
The **regrets** Bonnaffons, A.

REHABILITATION
Shefchik, R. Amen corner
Tanen, S. There's a word for that

REHABILITATION CENTERS
Tanen, S. There's a word for that

REHABILITATION COUNSELING
Sallis, J. Others of my kind
The **reign** of the Kingfisher Martinson, T.

REINCARNATION
Atkinson, K. Life after life
Barker, S. The incarnations
Brashares, A. My name is memory
Cameron, W. A dog's promise
Cleage, P. Some things I never thought I'd do
Cole, K. Dreams of a dark warrior
Davidson, A. The gargoyle
Greer, A. The impossible lives of Greta Wells
Guskin, S. The forgetting time
Helprin, M. Winter's tale
Horn, D. Eternal life
Mailer, N. Ancient evenings
Miller, R. Jacob's folly
Mishima, Y. The temple of dawn
Mitchell, D. Cloud atlas
Poore, M. Reincarnation blues
Seton, A. Green darkness
Tan, A. The hundred secret senses
Turton, S. The 7 1
Williams, C. Stairway to hell
Zelazny, R. Lord of light
Reincarnation blues Poore, M.
Reinhart saga [series] Berger, T.
Reinhart's women Berger, T.
The **reivers** Faulkner, W.

REJECTION (PSYCHOLOGY)
Hart, J. Down river
Hendrix, G. My best friend's exorcism
Kafka, F. The metamorphosis
Lessing, D. The fifth child
Myers, A. Continental divide
Rivers, F. Bridge to haven

Sloin, H. Art on fire
Swarthout, G. Bless the beasts and children
Williams, K. Tell the machine goodnight

REJECTION (PSYCHOLOGY) IN MEN
Fitzgerald, F. This side of paradise

RELATIVITY (PHYSICS)
Haldeman, J. The forever war
Relic Foster, A.

RELIC THEFTS
Westlake, D. Don't ask

RELICS
Brown, D. The Da Vinci code
Cornwell, B. 1356
Cussler, C. Sacred stone
Grant, H. The glass demon
Sandford, J. Storm Front
Shields, K. A study in revenge
Spillane, M. The Goliath bone

RELIGION
Akhtar, A. American dervish
Burton, J. The miniaturist
Butler, O. Parable of the sower
Cather, W. Death comes for the archbishop
Coover, R. The origin of the Brunists
Cornwell, B. The last kingdom
Dick, P. The man in the high castle
Dostoyevsky, F. The brothers Karamazov
Dunant, S. The birth of Venus
Goldstein, R. 36 arguments for the existence of God
Hage, R. Beirut Hellfire Society
Hamer, K. The girl in the red coat
Heinlein, R. Stranger in a strange land
Lamb, A. Roboteer
Lansdale, J. A fine dark line
Mann, T. The Magic Mountain
Miller, K. Augustown
Miller, W. A canticle for Leibowitz
Oe, K. Somersault
Phillips, A. The king at the edge of the world
Pywell, S. What happened to Henry
Rush, N. Mortals
Rushdie, S. Two years eight months and twenty-eight nights
Russell, M. Children of God
Russell, M. The sparrow
Scott, W. Rob Roy
Simmons, D. The rise of Endymion
Smith, Z. On beauty
Tepper, S. Grass
Vonnegut, K. Cat's cradle
Vonnegut, K. The sirens of Titan
Vonnegut, K. Welcome to the monkey house
Zelazny, R. Lord of light
The **religion** Willocks, T.

RELIGION -- SOCIAL ASPECTS
Waugh, E. Brideshead revisited

RELIGION AND CULTURE
Achebe, C. Things fall apart

Remembrance of things past Proust, M.

REMINISCING IN OLD AGE

Alameddine, R. An unnecessary woman
Bailey, P. Uncle Rudolf
Banville, J. Ancient light
Barnes, J. The only story
Barry, K. Night boat to Tangier
Bolano, R. By night in Chile
Boudjedra, R. The Barbary figs
Boyne, J. The house of special purpose
Cannon, J. Three things about Elsie
Cartwright, J. To heaven by water
Chung, C. The tenth muse
Coe, J. The rain before it falls
Davies, R. The cunning man
Dean, D. The madonnas of Leningrad
Diamant, A. The Boston girl
Dickinson, P. The yellow room conspiracy
Drndic, D. Trieste
Flagg, F. Fried green tomatoes at the Whistle Stop Cafe
Forna, A. The memory of love
Garcia Marquez, G. Memories of my melancholy whores
Gardam, J. Last friends
Gardam, J. Old Filth
Gilbert, E. City of girls
Griffin, A. When all is said
Gruen, S. Water for elephants
Hannah, K. The nightingale
Harding, P. Tinkers
Hijuelos, O. Beautiful Maria of my soul
Hijuelos, O. The mambo kings play songs of love
Makine, A. Dreams of my Russian summers
Makine, A. The life of an unknown man
Moehringer, J. Sutton
Morton, K. The house at Riverton
Moshfegh, O. Eileen
Murdoch, I. The sea, the sea
Nabokov, V. Ada
Nabokov, V. Look at the harlequins!
Nemirovsky, I. Fire in the blood
O'Nan, S. Henry, himself
Portis, C. True grit
Rawles, N. My Jim
Rayfiel, T. In pinelight
Robinson, M. Gilead
Robinson, M. Home
Roth, H. A diving rock on the Hudson
Roth, H. From bondage
Roth, H. Requiem for Harlem
Roth, H. A star shines over Mt. Morris Park
Roth, P. The plot against America
Roth, P. Sabbath's theater
Roy, A. All the lives we never lived
Smith, D. The electric hotel
Spark, M. A far cry from Kensington
Tyler, A. A spool of blue thread
Ullmann, L. Unquiet

Updike, J. Seek my face
Welty, E. The optimist's daughter
Williams, N. This is happiness

REMORSE

Danticat, E. The dew breaker
Grenville, K. The secret river

The **remorseful** day Dexter, C.

The **removes** Soli, T.

REMUS (ROMAN MYTHOLOGY)

Saylor, S. Roma

RENAISSANCE (1300-1600)

Brandreth, B. The assassin of Verona
Brandreth, B. The spy of Venice
Dunant, S. Blood and beauty
Dunant, S. In the company of the courtesan
Dunnett, D. Niccolo rising
Follett, K. A column of fire
Gregory, P. The constant princess
Maalouf, A. Leo Africanus
Mantel, H. Bring up the bodies
Poole, S. The Borgia mistress
Stone, I. The agony and the ecstasy
Tremain, R. Music & silence
Walton, J. Lent

RENAISSANCE FAIRS

DeLuca, J. Well met

Rendezvous with Rama Clarke, A.

Renee Ballard novels [series] Connelly, M.

The **renegades** Parker, T.

RENNES-LE-CHATEAU, FRANCE

Berry, S. The Templar legacy

RENO, NEVADA

Kittredge, W. The willow field
Palwick, S. The necessary beggar

RENOIR, AUGUSTE, 1841-1919

Vreeland, S. Luncheon of the boating party

RENOIR, AUGUSTE, 1841-1919 LUNCHEON OF THE BOATING PARTY

Vreeland, S. Luncheon of the boating party

RENOVATION (ARCHITECTURE)

Carlson, M. A Christmas by the sea
Deveraux, J. A willing murder
Lennon, J. Castle
McKinlay, J. The good ones

RENT AND RENTING

Styles, T. Redbone

RENTAL HOUSING

Quick, A. Crystal gardens

REPAIRERS

Albom, M. The five people you meet in heaven
Cameron, C. Just a summer fling
Dimon, H. Her other secret
Haywood, G. Cemetery Road
Hibbert, T. Get a life, Chloe Brown
See, C. The handyman
Stabenow, D. A grave denied

REPARATIONS

Simmons, D. The Terror
Sorenson, J. Aftershock
Spencer, M. Scandalous
Spillane, M. The Consummata
Stirling, S. A meeting at Corvallis
Sullivan, M. Theft of swords
Varley, J. Red lightning
Warren, S. Rescue me
Willig, L. The lure of the moonflower

RESEARCH
Abbott, M. Give me your hand
Brennan, M. A natural history of dragons
Brennan, M. The tropic of serpents
Brennan, M. Within the sanctuary of wings
Egan, G. Schild's ladder
Flynn, M. Eifelheim
Gappah, P. Out of darkness, shining light
Liu, C. The dark forest
Liu, C. The three-body problem
Nesbit, T. The wives of Los Alamos
Phillips, C. The Rossetti letter
Racculia, K. Tuesday Mooney talks to ghosts
Rayne, S. Music macabre
Turnbull, C. The lesson
Willis, C. Blackout

RESEARCH INSTITUTES
Child, L. Deep storm

RESEARCH INSTITUTES -- ANATARCTIC REGIONS
Brockmeier, K. The brief history of the dead

RESENTFULNESS
Bates, J. Midnight at the Dragon Cafe
Black, B. The secret guests
Chang, L. All is forgotten, nothing is lost
Cleeves, A. Wild fire
Dorris, M. A yellow raft in blue water
Edwards, R. Darling
Enright, A. The gathering
Goldin, M. The escape room
Holsinger, B. The gifted school
Kelly, C. Secrets of a happy marriage
Reisman, N. The first desire
Runcie, J. Canvey Island
Williams, T. The Roman spring of Mrs. Stone

RESENTFULNESS IN MEN
Baker, K. The house of the stag
Moyes, J. Me before you
Pelecanos, G. The way home
Reservation blues Alexie, S.
Reservation nation Cook, D.
Reservoir novels [series] McGregor, J.
The **reservoir** tapes McGregor, J.

RESERVOIRS -- NEW YORK (STATE)
Westlake, D. Drowned hopes

RESILIENCE (PERSONAL QUALITY)
Boyden, J. Through black spruce
Cleave, C. Little Bee
Kimmel, F. No good asking

Morris, H. Cilka's journey
Oates, J. The gravedigger's daughter

RESILIENCE IN BOYS
Mosley, W. Fortunate son

RESILIENCE IN WOMEN
Krall, H. Chasing the king of hearts
Landis, J. Heartbreak hotel

RESISTANCE (PSYCHOLOGY)
Orwell, G. 1984
Williams, L. Supper club

RESISTANCE (PSYCHOLOGY) IN CHILDREN
Ellmann, L. Ducks, Newburyport
Hoeg, P. Borderliners

RESISTANCE (PSYCHOLOGY) IN TEENAGE BOYS
Whitehead, C. The Nickel boys

RESISTANCE (PSYCHOLOGY) IN TEENAGE GIRLS
Dunant, S. Sacred hearts
Szabo, M. Abigail

RESISTANCE TO GOVERNMENT
Aslam, N. The golden legend
Atwood, M. The testaments
Bandi, 1. The accusation
Binet, L. HHhH
Brown, P. Golden son
Brown, P. Red rising
Buckley, F. The siren queen
Chiaverini, J. Resistance women
Deane, S. Reading in the dark
Fallada, H. Every man dies alone
Furst, A. Blood of victory
Furst, A. A hero of France
Jen, G. The resisters
Older, M. Infomocracy
Percy, B. Red moon
Puig, M. Kiss of the spider woman
Restrepo, L. No place for heroes
Robb, C. A murdered peace
Rushdie, S. Shalimar the Clown
Stross, C. Glasshouse
Yang, J. The ascent to godhood
Yang, J. The black tides of heaven
Zahn, T. Dark force rising
Zahn, T. Heir to the empire
Zahn, T. The last command
Zimler, R. The seventh gate

RESISTANCE TO LAND DEVELOPMENT
Box, C. Blue heaven
FitzGerald, G. Redemption Mountain

RESISTANCE TO MILITARY OCCUPATION
Belfoure, C. The Paris architect
Benn, J. Billy Boyle
Binet, L. HHhH
Faulks, S. Charlotte Gray
Furst, A. Blood of victory
Furst, A. Spies of the Balkans
Grindle, L. Villa Triste
Groot, T. Flame of resistance

Lee, P. Dark site
Lee, P. Runner
Lee, P. Signal

RETIRED MILITARY PERSONNEL -- SOUTH CAROLINA

Hart, C. Yankee Doodle dead

RETIRED TEACHERS

Lively, P. How it all began
Penny, L. Still life
Phillips, C. A distant shore
Picoult, J. The storyteller

RETIREES

Bear, E. Stone mad
Deb, S. The point of return
Disher, G. Under the cold bright lights
Donoghue, E. Akin
Erpenbeck, J. Go, went, gone
Friedman, D. Running out of road
Hauck, R. The wedding chapel
Hiaasen, C. Skin tight
Indriðason, A. The shadow district
Khan, V. The perplexing theft of the jewel in the crown
Kilalea, K. Ok, Mr. Field
King, S. Mr. Mercedes
Krauss, N. Forest Dark
Leonard, E. Mr. Paradise
McCarry, C. Old boys
Miller, M. Biloxi
Osborne, L. Only to sleep
Penny, L. The long way home
Persson, L. The dying detective
Powers, R. Orfeo
Simonson, H. Major Pettigrew's last stand
Tyler, A. Noah's compass
Unsworth, B. After Hannibal

RETIREES -- IRELAND

Lordan, B. But come ye back , Beth Lordan

RETIREMENT

Bowman, C. Horace Winter says goodbye
Dobyns, S. Saratoga payback
Harrison, J. The great leader
Harvey, J. Darkness, darkness
Hunter, S. Game of snipers
Rankin, I. Exit music
Rash, R. Above the waterfall
Shriver, L. So much for that
Smiley, J. A thousand acres
Wambaugh, J. The blue knight

RETIREMENT COMMUNITIES

Groen, H. On the bright side
Hollis, L. Poppy Harmon investigates
Weiner, J. In her shoes

RETROVIRUSES

Gregory, D. The devil's alphabet
The **return** Gruber, M.
The **return** Harrison, R.

RETURN MIGRATION -- MEXICO

Urrea, L. Into the beautiful North
The **return** of Captain John Emmett Speller, E.
The **return** of Kid Cooper Smith, B.
The **return** of the caravels Antunes, A.
The **return** of the dancing master Mankell, H.
The **return** of the king Tolkien, J.
The **return** of the native Hardy, T.
The **returned** Mott, J.

REUNIONS

Abrams, M. Meadowlark
Albom, M. The next person you meet in Heaven
Anders, C. All the birds in the sky
Bezmozgis, D. The betrayers
Blumenfeld, A. The cast
Cantero, E. Meddling kids
Choi, S. Trust exercise
Doan, A. The summer list
Dodd, C. Virtue Falls
Doyle, R. Smile
Drabble, M. The sea lady
Fabry, C. The promise of Jesse Woods
French, N. Thursday's children
Harrison, R. The return
Johnson, C. Spirit of steamboat
Leon, S. Wanderer
McFarlane, M. Don't you forget about me
Monroe, M. Beach house reunion
Morrison, T. Sula
Mosley, W. Fortunate son
Nichols, L. Vessel
O'Farrell, M. The vanishing act of Esme Lennox
Rader-Day, L. Little pretty things
Ragnar Jonasson, 1. The island
Rai, A. Wrong to need you
Rice, A. The vampire Armand
Rock, P. The shelter cycle
Rush, N. Subtle bodies
Scotch, A. In twenty years
Singer, I. Enemies, a love story
Thomas, S. My beautiful enemy
Tyler, A. Digging to America
Welty, E. The optimist's daughter

REUNIONS -- SCOTLAND

Goddard, R. Never go back
Revelation Sansom, C.
Revelation Goodwin, B.
Revelation space Reynolds, A.
Revelation space universe [series] Reynolds, A.
Revelations K'wan
Revenant gun Lee, Y.

REVENGE

Adiga, A. The white tiger
Ajvide Lindqvist, J. Let the right one in
Amis, M. The zone of interest
Archer, Z. Dangerous seduction
Armstrong, R. The don con
Asher, N. The skinner

Higgins, J. Edge of danger
Higgins, J. Midnight runner
Higgins, J. Rough justice
Higgins, J. The White House connection
Hill, J. Horns
Hill, R. The woodcutter
Hodges, C. Rumor has it
Holmes, S. B-more careful
Howarth, P. Only killers and thieves
Hunter, S. The 47th samurai
Hurley, K. The stars are legion
JaQuavis The dopefiend
Jakes, J. Love and war
Jakes, J. North and South
James, E. Four nights with the duke
James, P. Innocent blood
James, P. Original sin
Jenkins, B. Rebel
Johnson, C. Dark horse
K'wan Animal
K'wan Animal II
K'wan Gutter
K'wan Hoodlum
K'wan Welfare wifeys
Kasischke, L. The raising
Kay, G. Children of earth and sky
Kay, G. Tigana
Kellerman, J. The clinic
Kelly, E. The burning air
Kelton, E. Texas vendetta
Kerstan, L. Heart of the tiger
King, C. Stiletto justice
King, D. Bitch
Knopf, C. Dead anyway
Koontz, D. The darkest evening of the year
Krentz, J. Secret sisters
Kuang, R. The dragon republic
Kuang, R. The poppy war
Lansdale, J. Paradise sky
Larsson, S. The girl who kicked the hornet's nest
Lasdun, J. The fall guy
Layne, L. Passion on Park Avenue
Leckie, A. Ancillary justice
Leckie, A. Ancillary mercy
Leckie, A. Ancillary sword
Leckie, A. The Raven tower
Lehane, D. Mystic river
Leonard, E. Glitz
Lippman, L. Sunburn
Littell, R. Vicious circle
Long, J. Angel in a devil's arms
Lowe, K. The furies
Lutz, J. Burn
Lutz, J. Lightning
Lutz, L. The swallows
MacDonald, J. The green ripper
MacDonald, J. The lonely silver rain

MacDonald, J. The long lavender look
MacLean, S. A rogue by any other name
MacLean, S. Wicked and the wallflower
Malouf, D. Ransom
Mamet, D. Chicago
Marshall, A. A crown for cold silver
Marston, E. The bawdy basket
Marston, E. The wanton angel
Martini, S. Compelling evidence
Mayor, A. Tag man
Mayor, A. The sniper's wife
McBain, E. Hark!
McCarry, C. The mulberry bush
McCarthy, C. No country for old men
McDermid, V. The distant echo
McKinty, A. In the morning I'll be gone
McPherson, C. Go to my grave
Meek, J. The heart broke in
Meyer, D. Devil's peak
Michels, E. The rebel heir
Min, A. Becoming Madame Mao
Minato, K. Confessions
Monroe, M. Bad blood
Moore, K. To seduce an angel
Muller, M. The broken promise land
Muller, M. While other people sleep
Nahai, G. The luminous heart of Jonah S.
Nash, S. Between the Duke and the deep blue sea
Nelscott, K. Stone cribs
Neuhaus, N. The ice queen
Neuhaus, N. Snow White must die
Neville, S. The ghosts of Belfast
Newton, C. Calumet City
Nickson, C. Cold cruel winter
North, C. The pursuit of William Abbey
Novik, N. Uprooted
Oates, J. Evil eye
Oates, J. Foxfire
Ohlsson, K. Silenced
Ohlsson, K. Unwanted
Palliser, C. The quincunx
Palumbo, D. Night terrors
Parker, R. Cold service
Parker, S. Coldwater
Parker, T. Black water
Parker, T. Cold pursuit
Parker, T. Pacific beat
Parker, T. Storm runners
Patterson, J. Private
Pawel, R. Death of a nationalist
Peikoff, K. Mother knows best
Pelecanos, G. Drama city
Pelecanos, G. Shame the devil
Peloquin, L. Dark rooms
Persson, L. Free falling, as if in a dream
Pessl, M. Night film
Pinborough, S. Dead to her

Revenger novels [series] Reynolds, A.

REVENUE AGENTS

Downie, R. Caveat emptor

Franklin, A. Mistress of the art of death

Reverend Clare Fergusson mysteries [series] Spencer-Fleming, J.

Reverend Mother mysteries [series] Harrison, C.

The **revised** fundamentals of caregiving Evison, J.

The **revisioners** Sexton, M.

REVIVALS

Harris, E. I say a little prayer

Lewis, S. Elmer Gantry

Stark, R. Comeback

REVOLUTIONARIES

Anders, C. The city in the middle of the night

Brown, P. Morning star

Cleeton, C. Next year in Havana

Cumming, C. The Moroccan girl

Frantz, L. The lacemaker

Fuentes, C. The old gringo

Gage, E. The ladies of Managua

Ghosh, A. The hungry tide

Hugo, V. Les miserables

Hunter, S. Havana

Koestler, A. Darkness at noon

Lessing, D. The good terrorist

Lessing, D. Landlocked

Littell, R. The Mayakovsky tapes

Malraux, A. Man's hope

McCrea, G. Mrs. Engels

Meek, J. The people's act of love

Mengestu, D. All our names

Naipaul, V. Guerrillas

Naipaul, V. Magic seeds

Parker, R. Back story

Pittman, A. The seamstress

Restrepo, L. No place for heroes

Robbins, T. Still life with Woodpecker

Robinson, K. Green Mars

Robinson, K. Red Mars

Rush, N. Mortals

Sainz Borgo, K. It would be night in Caracas

Scott, W. Rob Roy

Shaara, J. Gone for soldiers

Steinhauer, O. The middleman

Sterling, B. Pirate Utopia

Thompson, T. Rosewater

Thompson, T. The Rosewater insurrection

Thompson, T. The Rosewater redemption

Vargas Llosa, M. The war of the end of the world

Wascom, K. The blood of heaven

Weldon, F. Chalcot Crescent

Zola, E. Germinal

REVOLUTIONARIES -- ALGERIA

Wideman, J. Fanon

REVOLUTIONARIES -- CUBA

Garcia, C. Dreaming in Cuban

REVOLUTIONARIES -- DUBLIN, IRELAND

Llywelyn, M. 1916

REVOLUTIONARIES -- FRANCE -- HISTORY -- 18TH CENTURY

Naslund, S. Abundance

REVOLUTIONARIES -- IRELAND

Llywelyn, M. 1949

REVOLUTIONARIES -- LATIN AMERICA

Bolano, R. Amulet

REVOLUTIONARIES -- MEXICO

Olmstead, R. Far bright star

REVOLUTIONARIES -- RUSSIA

Richler, N. Your mouth is lovely

REVOLUTIONARY AMERICA (1775-1783)

Frantz, L. The lacemaker

Gabaldon, D. A breath of snow and ashes

Gabaldon, D. An echo in the bone

Gabaldon, D. Written in my own heart's blood

Harkness, D. Time's convert

Hill, L. Someone knows my name

Turner, N. My name is Resolute

REVOLUTIONARY FRANCE (1789-1799)

Carey, E. Little

Dickens, C. A tale of two cities

Orczy, E. The Scarlet Pimpernel

Quinn, K. Ribbons of scarlet

Sabatini, R. Scaramouche

REVOLUTIONS

Araghi, A. The immortals of Tehran

Boudjedra, R. The Barbary figs

Carey, E. Little

Didion, J. A book of common prayer

Engelmann, K. The Stockholm octavo

Flanagan, T. The year of the French

Fuentes, C. The old gringo

Garcia, C. King of Cuba

Ghaffari, R. To keep the sun alive

Glass, J. The women's war

Hashemzadeh Bonde, G. What we owe

Herbert, F. Dune

Hugo, V. Les miserables

Koestler, A. Darkness at noon

Le Guin, U. The dispossessed

Malraux, A. Man's hope

Meek, J. The people's act of love

Quinn, K. Ribbons of scarlet

Robinson, K. The Martians

Russell, M. Children of God

Rutherfurd, E. Paris

Shaara, J. Gone for soldiers

Silko, L. Almanac of the dead

Wilson, D. Robogenesis

Wilson, D. Robopocalypse

REVOLUTIONS -- CHINA

Chen, D. Brothers

Gao, X. Soul mountain

Liu, C. The three-body problem

Perry, A. Pentecost Alley
Prose, F. Primitive people
Rendell, R. A judgement in stone
Richards, L. Death was in the blood
Riley, L. The girl on the cliff
Robards, K. Ghost moon
Rushdie, S. The golden house
Sanders, L. McNally's gamble
Sanders, L. McNally's trial
Seth, V. A suitable boy
Shupe, J. The rogue of Fifth Avenue
Solomons, N. House of Gold
Stout, D. Titanshade
Tan, L. What we were promised
Taneja, P. We that are young
Tarkington, B. The magnificent Ambersons
Tsao, T. The majesties
Tyler, A. A patchwork planet
Veletzos, R. The girl they left behind
Vine, B. The minotaur
Walker, W. All is not forgotten
Walker, W. Crime of privilege
Wang, K. Family trust
Ware, R. The death of Mrs. Westaway
Ware, R. The turn of the key
Williams, B. The summer wives
Willocks, T. Memo from Turner
Woolf, V. The years

RICH FAMILIES -- HOUSTON, TEXAS
Brown, R. Half a heart

RICH GIRLS
Thomas, S. Oligarchy

Rich man, poor man Shaw, I.

RICH MEN
Amis, M. London fields
Ashley Antoinette, 1. Butterfly
Babson, M. The company of cats
Berne, L. You may kiss the bride
Binchy, M. Firefly summer
Birmingham, S. Carriage trade
Brockway, C. No place for a dame
Bronte, C. Jane Eyre
Burrowes, G. Tremaine's true love
Burton, J. The miniaturist
Byrne, K. How to love a duke in ten days
Christie, A. Murder on the Orient Express
Clark, M. Kiss the girls and make them cry
Cohen, J. Book of numbers
Coleridge, N. Godchildren
Dare, T. The wallflower wager
De Leon, A. Side chick nation
Dunmore, E. Bringing down the duke
Egan, J. The keep
Eliot, G. Adam Bede
Everett, P. I am Not Sidney Poitier
Faber, M. The crimson petal and the white
Finder, J. Suspicion

Force, M. Deceived by desire
Fuentes, C. The death of Artemio Cruz
Glynn, A. Paradime
Goenawan, C. Rainbirds
Guterson, D. Ed King
Heinlein, R. Stranger in a strange land
Hill, J. Horns
Hoang, H. The bride test
Hugo, V. Les miserables
James, E. Three weeks with Lady X
Jenkins, B. Forbidden
Kleypas, L. Marrying Winterborne
Koryta, M. So cold the river
Layne, L. Passion on Park Avenue
London, J. The charmer in chaps
Martin, K. Beyond reason
Mosley, W. The man in my basement
Nickson, C. Come the fear
Paretsky, S. Breakdown
Parker, T. Cold pursuit
Percy, W. The second coming
Perry, T. Dead aim
Poyer, D. Fire on the waters
Pynchon, T. Bleeding edge
Pynchon, T. Inherent vice
Robb, J. Fantasy in death
Shaw, W. A song for the brokenhearted
Shteyngart, G. Lake Success
Starr, J. Lights out
Stephenson, N. Fall or, Dodge in hell
Vonnegut, K. God bless you, Mr. Rosewater
Vonnegut, K. The sirens of Titan
Warren, T. The replacement wife
Watt, H. To the lions
Westlake, D. Get real
Westlake, D. Watch your back!
Westlake, D. What's so funny?

RICH MEN -- FRANCE
Greene, G. The tenth man

RICH MEN -- SOUTHERN STATES
Welty, E. The ponder heart

RICH MEN -- UNITED STATES
Lewis, S. Dodsworth

Rich novels (Kevin Kwan) [series] Kwan, K.

RICH PEOPLE
Faulks, S. Jeeves and the wedding bells

RICH PEOPLE
Amidon, S. Human capital
Bainbridge, B. Every man for himself
Birmingham, S. Carriage trade
Blundell, J. The high season
Boyle, T. The tortilla curtain
Brookner, A. Family and friends
Brunkhorst, A. The gilded Life of Matilda Duplaine
Canin, E. America America
Chandler, R. The annotated Big sleep
Chandler, R. The big sleep

RICHARD III, KING OF ENGLAND, 1452-1485
Penman, S. The sunne in splendour
Tey, J. The daughter of time
Richard Hannay adventures [series] Buchan, J.
RICHARD I,, KING OF ENGLAND, 1157-1199
Penman, S. Cruel as the grave
Penman, S. Dragon's lair
Penman, S. Lionheart
Penman, S. A king's ransom
Penman, S. The Queen's man
Scott, W. Ivanhoe
Richard Jury mysteries [series] Grimes, M.
Richard Nottingham mysteries [series] Nickson, C.
RICHELIEU, ARMAND JEAN DU PLESSIS, CARDINAL, DUC DE, 1585-1642
Dumas, A. The three musketeers
RICHMOND, VIRGINIA
Cornwell, P. Postmortem
Owen, H. The bottom
Owen, H. The devil's triangle
Owen, H. Oregon Hill
Owen, H. Parker Field
Turner, N. A hustler's wife
Rick Cahill crime novels [series] Coyle, M.
Ricochet Brown, S.
The **riddle** of St. Leonard's Robb, C.
RIDDLES
Bear, E. The red-stained wings
Mosher, H. On Kingdom Mountain
Murakami, H. Kafka on the shore
Ride a pale horse MacInnes, H.
Ride with me, Mariah Montana Doig, I.
Riders of the purple sage Grey, Z.
Riders on the storm Gorman, E.
The **ridge** Koryta, M.
Rifter series (Peter Watts) [series] Watts, P.
RIGHT AND WRONG
Caputo, P. Crossers
Cervantes Saavedra, M. Don Quixote
Wendig, C. Wanderers
Wiesel, E. The judges
Right livelihoods Moody, R.
The **right** mistake Mosley, W.
The **right** side Quinn, S.
The **right** sort of man Montclair, A.
The **right** swipe Rai, A.
RIGHT TO EDUCATION
Dare, A. The girl with the louding voice
RIGHT WHALES
Mda, Z. The whale caller
RIGHT-WING EXTREMISTS
Bolano, R. Nazi literature in the Americas
Griffiths, E. A dying fall
Haddam, J. Hardscrabble road
Spillane, M. The Goliath bone
RIGHTEOUS GENTILES IN THE HOLOCAUST
Bellow, S. The Bellarosa connection

Grindle, L. Villa Triste
Orringer, J. The flight portfolio
Russell, M. A thread of grace
RIGHTEOUS GENTILES IN THE HOLOCAUST -- FRANCE
Wieland, L. Paris, 7 a.m.
RIGHTEOUS GENTILES IN THE HOLOCAUST -- GERMANY
Keneally, T. Schindler's list
The **rights** of desire Brink, A.
Riley Wolfe novels [series] Lindsay, J.
The **ring** of death Spencer, S.
Ring of fire Taylor, B.
RINGS
Child, L. The midnight line
Westlake, D. What's the worst that could happen?
RIO DE JANEIRO, BRAZIL
Garcia-Roza, L. Alone in the crowd
Garcia-Roza, L. December heat
Novey, I. Ways to disappear
RIO GRANDE
Fuentes, C. The crystal frontier
RIO GRANDE VALLEY
MacDonald, J. Cinnamon skin
Riot baby Onyebuchi, T.
RIOT GRRRL MOVEMENT
Newitz, A. The future of another timeline
Riot most uncouth Friedman, D.
RIOTS
Barthelme, F. Painted desert
Bump, G. Everywhere you don't belong
Gunaratne, G. In our mad and furious city
Marston, E. The roaring boy
Rice, A. Christ the Lord
RIOTS -- LOS ANGELES, CALIFORNIA
Mosley, W. Little Scarlet
RIOTS -- WASHINGTON, D.C.
Pelecanos, G. Hard revolution
Ripper Allende, I.
The **ripper** affair Saintcrow, L.
The **Ripper's** shadow Rowland, L.
A **ripple** from the storm Lessing, D.
The **rise** and fall of D.O.D.O. Stephenson, N.
The **rise** of Endymion Simmons, D.
The **risen** empire Westerfeld, S.
Risen kingdoms [series] Craddock, C.
A **rising** man Mukherjee, A.
The **rising** sea Cussler, C.
The **rising** tide Shaara, J.
RISK
Deutermann, P. The Iceman
Egan, G. Phoresis
Heller, P. The dog stars
The **risk** agent Pearson, R.
The **risk** of darkness Hill, S.
The **risk** pool Russo, R.
RISK-TAKING (PSYCHOLOGY)

Sanders, L. McNally's secret
Sandford, J. Golden prey
Sedley, K. The Tintern treasure
Shannon, D. Chaos of crime
Stabenow, D. Whisper to the blood
Stark, R. Breakout
Stark, R. Comeback
Strange, M. Follow me down
Westlake, D. Watch your back!
Westlake, D. What's so funny?
Woods, T. Alibi

ROBBERY -- MINNESOTA

Sandford, J. Storm prey

ROBBERY INVESTIGATION

Kerr, P. March violets
Laukkanen, O. Criminal enterprise
Mosley, W. All I did was shoot my man
Sanders, L. McNally's secret
Sandford, J. Golden prey
Sandford, J. Storm prey
Sedley, K. The Tintern treasure

ROBBERY SUSPECTS

Brown, S. Outfox
Robert B. Parker's Buckskin Knott, R.
Robert Langdon novels [series] Brown, D.

ROBESON COUNTY, NORTH CAROLINA

Humphreys, J. Nowhere else on earth

ROBESON, PAUL, 1898-1976

Truong, M. The book of salt, Monique Truong.
Robicheaux Burke, J.

ROBIN HOOD (LEGENDARY CHARACTER)

Scott, W. Ivanhoe
Robinson Crusoe Defoe, D.

ROBINSON, JACKIE, 1919-1972

Parker, R. Double play
Robogenesis Wilson, D.
Robopocalypse Wilson, D.
Robopocalypse novels [series] Wilson, D.
Roboteer Lamb, A.
Roboteer novels [series] Lamb, A.

ROBOTICS

Asimov, I. I, robot
Delaney, J. The perfect wife
Huston, C. Skinner
Lamb, A. Roboteer
Wells, M. All systems red

ROBOTS

Asimov, I. I, robot
Banks, I. Use of weapons
Bear, G. Anvil of stars
Bear, G. The forge of God
Carey, P. The chemistry of tears
Crichton, M. Micro
Davis, K. Duplex
Green, H. An absolutely remarkable thing
Hall, L. Speak
Hodder, M. The strange affair of Spring Heeled Jack

Lamb, A. Roboteer
Levin, I. The Stepford wives
Newitz, A. Autonomous
Pohl, F. Gateway
Stross, C. Neptune's brood
Stross, C. Saturn's children
Tidhar, L. Central Station
Tregillis, I. The mechanical
Weinstein, A. Children of the new world
Wells, M. All systems red
Wilson, D. The clockwork dynasty
Wilson, D. Robogenesis
Wilson, D. Robopocalypse

ROBOTS -- BEHAVIOR

Asimov, I. I, robot

ROCHESTER, NEW YORK

Freudenberger, N. The newlyweds

ROCK CONCERTS

Robinson, P. Piece of my heart

ROCK GROUPS

Abramowitz, A. Thank you, goodnight
Bauman, B. Broken sleep
Reid, T. Daisy Jones & the Six
Rock Manning goes for broke Anders, C.

ROCK MUSIC

Bauman, B. Broken sleep
Reid, T. Daisy Jones & the Six
Rushdie, S. The ground beneath her feet
Williams, C. Stairway to hell

ROCK MUSICIANS

Carlson, S. Almost Graceland
Crosbie, L. Where did you sleep last night?
Dane, L. The best kind of trouble
Echlin, K. The disappeared
Hill, J. Heart-shaped box
Reid, T. Daisy Jones & the Six
Reiken, F. Day for night
Tyler, A. A slipping-down life
Wendig, C. Wanderers

ROCK MUSICIANS -- DEATH

Hiaasen, C. Basket case

ROCKETRY -- HISTORY

Michener, J. Space

ROCKETS (AVIATION)

McDevitt, J. The Cassandra Project

ROCKETS (ORDNANCE)

Pynchon, T. Gravity's rainbow
The rocks Nichols, P.
Rocksburg, Pennsylvania novels [series] Constantine, K.

ROCKY MOUNTAIN REGION

Carr, R. What we find

ROCKY MOUNTAINS

Carlson, R. Five skies

RODEO PERFORMERS

Box, C. Vicious circle
Kittredge, W. The willow field

RODEOS

Adler-Olsen, J. The Marco effect
Davies, R. The rebel angels
Merimee, P. Carmen
Pajer, B. Fatal induction
Penney, S. The invisible ones
Siger, J. Target Tinos

ROMANIES -- EUROPE

McCann, C. Zoli

ROMANOV DYNASTY (1613-1917)

Akunin, B. The coronation
Akunin, B. Sister Pelagia and the white bulldog
Boyne, J. The house of special purpose
Dostoyevsky, F. The brothers Karamazov
Dostoyevsky, F. Notes from underground
Gogol, N. Dead souls
Richler, N. Your mouth is lovely
Stachniak, E. The Winter Palace
Tolstoy, L. Anna Karenina
Tolstoy, L. War and peace
Turgenev, I. Fathers and sons
The **Romanov** ransom Cussler, C.

ROMANOV, HOUSE OF

Boyne, J. The house of special purpose
Paul, G. The lost daughter

ROMANS

Downie, R. Caveat emptor
Downie, R. Medicus
Downie, R. Semper Fidelis
Downie, R. Tabula rasa
Downie, R. Terra incognita
Saylor, S. Raiders of the Nile
Saylor, S. Roma
Saylor, S. Wrath of the furies

ROMANS -- PROVENCE, FRANCE

Kay, G. Ysabel

ROMANS IN EGYPT

Saylor, S. The judgment of Caesar

ROMANS IN GREAT BRITAIN

Davis, L. A body in the bathhouse

ROMANS IN PROVENCE

Kay, G. Ysabel

ROMANTIC COMEDIES

Adams, L. The bromance book club
Bailey, T. Fix her up
Christopher, A. Not the girl you marry
Clayborn, K. Love lettering
Criswell, M. What to do about Annie?
DeLuca, J. Well met
Fields, H. Last Chance Llama Ranch
Greer, A. Less
Harris, E. Not a day goes by
Heger, A. Crazy cupid love
Hibbert, T. Get a life, Chloe Brown
Isaac, K. Then there was you
Jalaluddin, U. Ayesha at last
Jimenez, A. The friend zone
Lalli, S. The matchmaker's list

Lauren, C. Dating you
Lipman, E. Good riddance
McFarlane, M. Don't you forget about me
McQuiston, C. Red, white & royal blue
Mda, Z. The whale caller
Moore, C. You suck
O'Leary, B. The flatshare
Orenstein, H. Love at first like
Parker, L. The Austen playbook
Rodale, M. Lady Bridget's diary
Simsion, G. The Rosie effect
Simsion, G. The Rosie project
Simsion, G. The Rosie result
Sittenfeld, C. Eligible
Soniah Kamal Unmarriageable
Sosa, M. The worst best man
Trigiani, A. Big Stone Gap
Winfrey, K. Waiting for Tom Hanks

ROMANTIC COMEDY FILMS

Turner, B. Wooing Cadie McCaffrey

ROMANTIC LOVE

Adams, L. The bromance book club
Austen, J. Pride and prejudice
Beagle, P. A fine and private place
Benedict, M. Lady Clementine
Bloom, A. White houses
Brashares, A. My name is memory
Brockway, C. So enchanting
Byatt, A. Possession
Chase, L. Don't tempt me
Dare, T. Romancing the duke
Dev, S. A distant heart
Dyer, G. Jeff in Venice, death in Varanasi
El-Mohtar, A. This is how you lose the time war
Faulks, S. Birdsong
Fitzgerald, P. The blue flower
Garcia Marquez, G. Love in the time of cholera
George, N. The book of dreams
Greeley, M. The clergyman's wife
Hale, S. Austenland
Hall, T. The case of the love commandos
Hazzard, S. The transit of Venus
Hoang, H. The bride test
James, E. The ugly duchess
Kincaid, J. See now then
Krauss, N. The history of love
London, J. The golden age
Loren, R. The one you fight for
Makine, A. The woman who waited
McCabe, E. I shall be near to you
Miller, S. For love
Nicholls, O. Love, unscripted
Obioma, C. An orchestra of minorities
Perez-Reverte, A. What we become
Rashan, N. You make me wanna
Richardson, C. The end of the alphabet
Runcie, J. The road to Grantchester

Rushdie, S. The ground beneath her feet
Saramago, J. Death with interruptions
Saville, L. Henry and Rachel
Scott, W. Ivanhoe
Serpell, N. The old drift
Shreve, A. The last time they met
Smith, A. How to be both
Sundaresan, I. The splendor of silence
Thomas, S. Tempting the bride
Tremain, R. Music & silence
Treuer, D. Prudence
Turner, B. Wooing Cadie McCaffrey
Wall, C. The dearly beloved
Waller, R. The bridges of Madison County
Wells, B. The end of loneliness
Williams, B. All the ways we said goodbye
Williams, N. This is happiness

ROMANTIC SUSPENSE
Antoinette, A. The Cartel
Antoinette, A. The Cartel 2
Antoinette, A. The Cartel 3
Azzopardi, T. Winterton blue
Bell, S. At his mercy
Bell, S. For his pleasure
Bradford, B. Power of a woman
Brown, S. Fat Tuesday
Brown, S. Mean streak
Brown, S. Outfox
Brown, S. Ricochet
Brown, S. White hot
Brown, S. The witness
Buchman, M. The night is mine
Buchman, M. Pure heat
Castle, J. The lost night
Crownover, J. Honor
Dees, C. Beyond the limit
Dimon, H. Her other secret
Dodd, C. Because I'm watching
Dodd, C. Obsession Falls
Dodd, C. The woman who couldn't scream
Du Maurier, D. Jamaica Inn
Foster, L. Run the risk
Foster, L. Under pressure
Garwood, J. Wired
Holt, V. The black opal
Hooper, K. Stealing shadows
Jackson, B. Forged in desire
Kanon, J. Los Alamos
Kearsley, S. A desperate fortune
Kerstan, L. Heart of the tiger
Krentz, J. Copper Beach
Krentz, J. River road
Krentz, J. Running hot
Krentz, J. Secret sisters
Krentz, J. When all the girls have gone
Krentz, J. White lies
Landis, J. Heartbreak hotel

Laurens, S. Devil's bride
Lowell, E. Pearl Cove
Malpas, J. Leave me breathless
Marlette, D. Magic time
Martin, K. Beyond reason
Quick, A. The girl who knew too much
Quick, A. I thee wed
Quick, A. The other lady vanishes
Quick, A. Otherwise engaged
Quick, A. 'Til death do us part
Raybourn, D. Silent in the grave
Robards, K. Ghost moon
Robards, K. The last victim
Robards, K. The ultimatum
Robb, J. Fantasy in death
Robb, J. Innocent in death
Robb, J. Naked in death
Roberts, N. Come sundown
Roberts, N. Dark witch
Roberts, N. Honest illusions
Roberts, N. Midnight Bayou
Roberts, N. The obsession
Rushdan, J. Every last breath
Sorenson, J. Aftershock
Sparks, N. The guardian

ROMANTICISM -- FRANCE
Hugo, V. The hunchback of Notre Dame

ROME -- HISTORY
Saylor, S. Roma

ROME -- HISTORY -- CIVIL WAR, 49-45 BC
Saylor, S. The judgment of Caesar
Saylor, S. A mist of prophecies

ROME -- HISTORY -- EMPIRE, 30 BC-284 AD
Graves, R. Claudius the god and his wife Messalina
Graves, R. I, Claudius

ROME -- HISTORY -- EMPIRE, 30 BC-476 AD
Davis, L. A body in the bathhouse
Davis, L. The ides of April
Davis, L. One virgin too many
Downie, R. Medicus
Downie, R. Terra incognita
Pears, I. The dream of Scipio

ROME -- HISTORY -- EMPIRE, 30 BC-96 AD
Bulgakov, M. The master and Margarita

ROME -- HISTORY -- HADRIAN, 117-138
Downie, R. Terra incognita
Yourcenar, M. Memoirs of Hadrian

ROME -- HISTORY -- NERO, 54-68
George, M. The confessions of young Nero
George, M. The splendor before the dark
Sienkiewicz, H. Quo vadis

ROME -- HISTORY -- REPUBLIC, 265-30 BC
McCullough, C. The first man in Rome
Saylor, S. The house of the Vestals
Saylor, S. A mist of prophecies
Saylor, S. Raiders of the Nile
Saylor, S. Rubicon

Saylor, S. The seven wonders
Saylor, S. The triumph of Caesar
Saylor, S. Wrath of the furies

ROME -- HISTORY -- TIBERIUS, 14-37
Wallace, L. Ben-Hur

ROME -- HISTORY -- VESPASIAN, 69-79
Davis, L. A body in the bathhouse
Davis, L. The ides of April
Davis, L. One virgin too many
Kane, B. Spartacus

ROME -- RULERS
Sienkiewicz, H. Quo vadis

ROME, ITALY
Dazieri, S. Kill the angel
Dazieri, S. Kill the father
Dazieri, S. Kill the king
Harris, R. Pompeii
Hewson, D. The garden of evil
Hewson, D. A season for the dead
Kneale, M. When we were Romans
Leithauser, B. The promise of elsewhere
Marsh, N. When in Rome
Pears, I. Death and restoration
Pears, I. The immaculate deception
Pears, I. The last judgement
Rice, A. Of love and evil
Scego, I. Adua
Schami, R. Sophia
Williams, T. The Roman spring of Mrs. Stone

ROME, ITALY -- HISTORY -- 1420-1798
Dunant, S. In the company of the courtesan

ROME, ITALY -- HISTORY -- 15TH CENTURY
Poole, S. The Borgia mistress

ROME, ITALY -- SOCIAL LIFE AND CUSTOMS -- 16TH CENTURY
Dunant, S. In the company of the courtesan

ROMMEL, ERWIN, 1891-1944
Shaara, J. The steel wave

ROMMEL, ERWIN, 1891-1944 MILITARY LEADERSHIP
Shaara, J. The rising tide

ROMULUS (ROMAN MYTHOLOGY)
Saylor, S. Roma

ROOFS
Vine, B. Grasshopper

ROOKIE POLICE
Gruber, M. Valley of bones
Mankell, H. Before the frost
Palmer, M. The society
Pelecanos, G. Hard revolution
Steinhauer, O. The Bridge of Sighs

Room Donoghue, E.
The **room** Karlsson, J.
The **room** on Rue Amelie Harmel, K.
A **room** with a view Forster, E.

Roomies Lauren, C.

ROOMMATES
Aridjis, C. Asunder

Dean, P. Tam Lin
Gottlieb, E. Best boy
Henson, P. Into the blue
Leonard, E. Mr. Paradise
Miller, S. While I was gone
Millet, L. Magnificence
Murray, P. Skippy dies
O'Leary, B. The flatshare
Styles, T. Redbone

ROOMS
Karlsson, J. The room

ROOSEVELT, ELEANOR, 1884-1962
Bloom, A. White houses
Roosevelt, E. The Hyde Park murder
Roosevelt, E. Murder and the First Lady
Roosevelt, E. Murder at midnight
Roosevelt, E. Murder at the palace
Roosevelt, E. Murder in the Blue Room
Roosevelt, E. Murder in the map room
Roosevelt, E. Murder in the Oval Offi
Roosevelt, E. Murder in the Rose Garden
Roosevelt, E. The White House pantry murder

ROOSEVELT, FRANKLIN D (FRANKLIN DELANO), 1882-1945
Kerr, P. Hitler's peace
Roosevelt, E. Murder in the Oval Office
Roosevelt, E. The White House pantry murder
Wouk, H. War and remembrance
Wouk, H. The winds of war

ROOSEVELT, THEODORE, 1858-1919
Carr, C. The alienist
Solomon, B. The attempted murder of Teddy Roosevelt
Vidal, G. Empire

The **rope** Barr, N.

The **rosary** murders Kienzle, W.

ROSATO & ASSOCIATES (IMAGINARY ORGANIZATION)
Scottoline, L. Legal tender

Rosato and Associates novels [series] Scottoline, L.

Rose Smith, M.

Rose gold Mosley, W.

The **rose** rent Peters, E.

ROSE, BILLY, 1899-1966
Bellow, S. The Bellarosa connection

Rosemary and rue McGuire, S.

Rosemary's baby Levin, I.

ROSENBERG, ETHEL, 1915-1953
Doctorow, E. The book of Daniel

ROSENBERG, JULIUS, 1918-1953
Doctorow, E. The book of Daniel

Rosewater Thompson, T.

The **Rosewater** insurrection Thompson, T.

The **Rosewater** redemption Thompson, T.

The **Rosie** effect Simsion, G.

Rosie novels (Graeme Simsion) [series] Simsion, G.

The **Rosie** project Simsion, G.

The **Rosie** result Simsion, G.

Trollope, J. Next of kin
Watson, J. Asta in the wings
Woodrell, D. Winter's bone

RURAL FAMILIES -- CANADA
Lawson, M. Crow Lake

RURAL FAMILIES -- ICELAND
Kent, H. Burial rites

RURAL FAMILIES -- OKLAHOMA
Steinbeck, J. The grapes of wrath

RURAL LIFE
Adam, C. Golden child
Airth, R. The decent inn of death
Armstrong, K. Alone in the wild
Baker, J. The body lies
Baker, J. Longbourn
Balogh, M. The arrangement
Balogh, M. The escape
Beagle, P. In Calabria
Berry, W. That distant land
Black, B. The secret guests
Bledsoe, A. Gather her round
Bourdeaut, O. Waiting for Bojangles
Burns, O. Cold Sassy tree
Burns, O. Leaving Cold Sassy
Butler, N. Little faith
Caldwell, E. Tobacco Road
Campbell, B. American salvage
Canty, K. The underworld
Chatwin, B. On the black hill
Christie, A. Endless night
Clark, M. The substitution order
Connolly, S. The lost traveller
Del Amo, J. Animalia
Dolan-Leach, C. We went to the woods
Eliot, G. Adam Bede
Eliot, G. Middlemarch
Eliot, G. Silas Marner
Faulkner, W. Uncollected stories of William Faulkner
Francis, D. Wedding Bush Road
Freeman, B. Thief River Falls
Gavin, R. Beluga
Graley, L. The current that carries
Hardy, T. Far from the madding crowd
Hardy, T. The return of the native
Harper, J. The lost man
Joyce, G. The limits of enchantment
Kim, A. Miracle Creek
Link, C. The other child
Locascio, L. Open me
Lourey, J. Unspeakable things
Manfredi, V. A winter's night
McCormack, M. Solar bones
McEwan, I. Atonement
McMahon, J. The invited
Mehta, R. No other world
Mishima, Y. The frolic of the beasts
Mitford, N. The pursuit of love ;

Morgan, R. The road from Gap Creek
Moyes, J. The giver of stars
Mozley, F. Elmet
O'Farrell, M. This must be the place
Oates, J. We were the Mulvaneys
Rademacher, C. Deadly Camargue
Rowland, R. Cold country
Sallis, J. Sarah Jane
Saunders, K. The case of the wandering scholar
Schweblin, S. Fever dream
Shalev, M. Two she-bears
Shaw, W. Salt lane
Simonson, H. Major Pettigrew's last stand
Simonson, H. The summer before the war
Smith, L. Oral history
Smith, M. Blackwood
Steadman, C. Mr. Nobody
Sternbergh, A. The blinds
Tokarczuk, O. Drive your plow over the bones of the dead
Tremblay, P. The cabin at the end of the world
Waldman, A. A door in the earth
Watson, M. The dream peddler
Weiss, L. If the creek don't rise
Wilson, S. The fortune teller's daughter
Wood, S. The Quintland sisters

RURAL LIFE -- 19TH CENTURY
Gaskell, E. Cranford
Trollope, A. Barchester Towers
Trollope, A. Doctor Thorne
Trollope, A. Framley parsonage
Trollope, A. The last chronicle of Barset

RURAL LIFE -- AUSTRALIA
Daisley, S. Coming rain

RURAL LIFE -- CANADA
Winter, K. Annabel

RURAL LIFE -- KANSAS
Roy, L. Bent Road

RURAL LIFE -- KENTUCKY
Mason, B. Shiloh and other stories

RURAL LIFE -- MAINE
Irving, J. The Cider House rules
Jewett, S. The country of the pointed firs and other stories
Rich, N. Odds against tomorrow

RURAL LIFE -- MISSISSIPPI
Welty, E. Losing battles

RURAL LIFE -- PENNSYLVANIA
Bouman, T. Dry bones in the valley

RURAL LIFE -- VIRGINIA
Trigiani, A. Big Cherry Holler
Trigiani, A. Big Stone Gap

RURAL LIFENA
Lockridge, R. Raintree County
Reynolds, M. The Starlite Drive-in

RURAL NOIR
Brown, L. Gods of Howl Mountain
Brown, T. Joe
Campbell, B. American salvage

Campbell, B. Once upon a river
Darnielle, J. Universal harvester
Faulkner, W. Sanctuary
Frazier, C. Nightwoods
Greaves, C. Hard twisted
Heathcock, A. Volt
Meyer, P. American rust
Panowich, B. Bull Mountain
Panowich, B. Like lions
Pollock, D. The devil all the time
Pollock, D. Knockemstiff
Rash, R. Above the waterfall
Rash, R. Burning bright
Rash, R. The cove
Rash, R. Nothing gold can stay
Rash, R. Something rich and strange
Sallis, J. Sarah Jane
Sharpe, T. Barbed wire heart
Watson, L. Let him go
Woodrell, D. Winter's bone

RURAL PHYSICIANS -- 19TH CENTURY
Trollope, A. Doctor Thorne

RURAL POOR -- MISSISSIPPI
Ward, J. Salvage the bones

RURAL POOR PEOPLE
Caldwell, E. Tobacco Road
Silver, M. Mary Coin
Ward, J. Sing, unburied, sing
Wharton, E. Ethan Frome

RURAL WOMEN
Frazier, C. Nightwoods
Long, J. Hot in Hellcat Canyon
Owens, D. Where the crawdads sing

Ruso mysteries [series] Downie, R.

RUSSIA
Arden, K. The bear and the nightingale
Arden, K. The girl in the tower
Arden, K. The winter of the witch
Campbell, R. Treason
Dostoyevsky, F. Crime and punishment
Fitzpatrick, L. Lights all night long
Gessen, K. A terrible country
Gogol, N. The collected tales of Nikolai Gogol
Harris, R. Archangel
Makine, A. Dreams of my Russian summers
Malamud, B. The fixer
Marra, A. The tsar of love and techno
Meyer, N. The adventure of the peculiar protocols
Pelevin, V. The hall of singing caryatids
Phillips, J. Disappearing earth
Read, P. Alice in exile
Sebastian, T. Fatal ally
Smith, M. Red Square
Wilkins, K. Veil of gold
Wilson, D. The clockwork dynasty

RUSSIA -- FOREIGN RELATIONS -- EUROPE
Bell, T. Overkill

RUSSIA -- FOREIGN RELATIONS -- UNITED STATES
Brown, D. The Kremlin strike
Coughlin, J. Long shot
Dugoni, R. The eighth sister
Matthews, J. The Kremlin's candidate
Matthews, J. Palace of treason
Matthews, J. Red sparrow

RUSSIA -- HISTORY
Rutherfurd, E. Russka

RUSSIA -- HISTORY -- 1801-1917
Akunin, B. The coronation
Dostoyevsky, F. Notes from underground

RUSSIA -- HISTORY -- 18TH CENTURY
Kearsley, S. The firebird

RUSSIA -- HISTORY -- 1904-1914
Richler, N. Your mouth is lovely

RUSSIA -- HISTORY -- 1914-1917
Boyne, J. The house of special purpose

RUSSIA -- HISTORY -- 1991-
Marra, A. A constellation of vital phenomena

RUSSIA -- HISTORY -- 19TH CENTURY
Akunin, B. Sister Pelagia and the white bulldog
Dostoyevsky, F. The best short stories of Dostoevsky
Dostoyevsky, F. The brothers Karamazov
Gogol, N. Dead souls
Richler, N. Your mouth is lovely
Wojtas, O. Miss Blaine's prefect and the golden samovar

RUSSIA -- HISTORY -- 20TH CENTURY
Kelly, M. Lost roses
Pasternak, B. Doctor Zhivago
Richler, N. Your mouth is lovely
Towles, A. A gentleman in Moscow

RUSSIA -- HISTORY -- ALEXANDER I, 1801-1825
Tolstoy, L. War and peace

RUSSIA -- HISTORY -- CATHERINE II, 1762-1796
Stachniak, E. The Winter Palace

RUSSIA -- HISTORY -- NICHOLAS II, 1894-1917
Boyne, J. The house of special purpose

RUSSIA -- POLITICS AND GOVERNMENT -- 1991-
Harris, R. Archangel

RUSSIA -- SOCIAL CONDITIONS -- 19TH CENTURY
Turgenev, I. Fathers and sons

RUSSIA -- SOCIAL LIFE AND CUSTOMS -- 19TH CENTURY
Tolstoy, L. Anna Karenina
Turgenev, I. Fathers and sons

The **Russia** account Coonts, S.

The **Russian** Coes, B.

RUSSIAN AMERICAN CRIMINALS
Koryta, M. Tonight I said goodbye

RUSSIAN AMERICAN FAMILIES
Alenyikov, M. Ivan and Misha

RUSSIAN AMERICAN WOMEN
Dean, D. The madonnas of Leningrad

RUSSIAN AMERICANS
Birmingham, S. The Auerbach will
Boswell, R. Century's son

Dean, D. The madonnas of Leningrad
Gessen, K. A terrible country
Nabokov, V. Novels and memoirs, 1941-51
Nabokov, V. Pnin
Shteyngart, G. The Russian debutante's handbook
The **Russian** debutante's handbook Shteyngart, G.

RUSSIAN ORTHODOX CHURCH.
Akunin, B. Sister Pelagia and the white bulldog

RUSSIAN REVOLUTION AND CIVIL WAR (1917-1921)
Kelly, M. Lost roses
Meek, J. The people's act of love
Pasternak, B. Doctor Zhivago
Sholokhov, M. The Don flows home to the sea
Stachniak, E. The chosen maiden

RUSSIANS IN CUBA
Smith, M. Havana Bay

RUSSIANS IN ENGLAND
Boyne, J. The house of special purpose

RUSSIANS IN FRANCE
Furst, A. Blood of victory
Houellebecq, M. The map and the territory

RUSSIANS IN ROMANIA
Furst, A. Blood of victory

RUSSIANS IN THE UNITED STATES
Alenyikov, M. Ivan and Misha
Coes, B. The Russian
Fitzpatrick, L. Lights all night long
Hoffman, A. The Museum of Extraordinary Things
Sandford, J. Hidden prey
Ulinich, A. Petropolis

RUSSIANS IN UKRAINE
Smith, M. Wolves eat dogs

Russka Rutherfurd, E.

Rust & stardust Greenwood, T.

Rustication Palliser, C.

Ruth Galloway mysteries [series] Griffiths, E.

RUTH, BABE, 1895-1948
Stewart, D. The Babe Ruth deception

RUTHLESSNESS IN MEN
Stegner, W. The Big Rock Candy Mountain

RUTHLESSNESS IN WOMEN
Patterson, R. Dark lady

RWANDA
Benaron, N. Running the rift
Leonard, E. Pagan babies

RWANDA -- HISTORY -- CIVIL WAR, 1994
Faye, G. Small country

Ryan DeMarco novels [series] Silvis, R.

S

S. S.
Schlink, B. The reader
Seiffert, R. A boy in winter

S. S. OFFICERS
Mailer, N. The castle in the forest
Robbins, D. Last citadel

Sabbath's theater Roth, P.

SABOTAGE
Anderton, J. Debris
Barclay, L. Elevator pitch
Coonts, S. The armageddon file
Cumming, C. A colder war
Cussler, C. The wrecker
Deaver, J. The stone monkey
French, N. Waiting for Wednesday
Hallinan, T. Crashed
Herbert, F. Dune
Higgins, C. Lightless
Lauren, C. Dating you
Laurens, S. The pursuits of Lord Kit Cavanaugh
Michener, J. The bridges at Toko-Ri
Muller, M. A walk through the fire
Peters, E. Children of the storm
Reichs, K. 206 Bones
Robinson, K. Antarctica
Stabenow, D. Restless in the grave
Sundin, S. Through waters deep
Turtledove, H. Into the darkness
Turtledove, H. Rulers of the darkness
Woods, S. Stealth

SABOTAGE -- GREECE
Cussler, C. The Mediterranean caper

SABOTAGE -- NORWAY -- HISTORY -- GERMAN OC-CUPATION, 1940-1945
Benn, J. Billy Boyle

Sabrina & Corina Fajardo-Anstine, K.

SACAGAWEA
Sargent, C. Museum of human beings

The **sacrament** Olafur Johann Olafsson

SACRAMENTO, CALIFORNIA
Ragan, T. Buried deep
Ragan, T. Deadly recall
Ragan, T. Deranged
Ragan, T. Her last day

Sacre bleu Moore, C.

Sacred Lehane, D.

SACRED BOOKS
Brooks, G. People of the book
Self, W. The book of Dave

Sacred hearts Dunant, S.

Sacred hunger Unsworth, B.

SACRED SPACE
Binchy, M. Whitethorn Woods
Mason, R. Who killed Piet Barol?
Spann, S. Trial on Mount Koya

Sacred stone Cussler, C.

Sacrilege Parris, S.

SADISM
Gallagher, S. The kingdom of bones
Katzenbach, J. What comes next
Roosevelt, E. Murder at midnight
Zan, K. The never list

SADISTS

Coupland, D. Eleanor Rigby
Fabry, C. War room
Flagg, F. Standing in the rainbow
Wallace, D. Big fish
Watson, M. The dream peddler
SALINAS RIVER VALLEY (CALIF)
Steinbeck, J. Of mice and men
SALINAS VALLEY, CALIFORNIA
Steinbeck, J. East of Eden
Steinbeck, J. The long valley
SALISBURY PLAIN, ENGLAND
Rutherfurd, E. Sarum
SALISBURY, ROBERT CECIL, EARL OF, 1563-1612
Clements, R. Revenger
The **salt** eaters Bambara, T.
Salt houses Alyan, H.
SALT LAKE CITY, UTAH
Hunt, A. City of saints
Salt lane Shaw, W.
Salt river White, R.
Salt slow Armfield, J.
A **salty** piece of land Buffett, J.
SALVAGE
Forester, C. Hornblower and the Atropos
Laukkanen, O. Gale force
Redhill, M. Consolation
Rosen, L. The tenth witness
Salvage the bones Ward, J.
SALVATION
Nunez, S. Salvation city
SALVATION (CHRISTIANITY)
Rice, A. Of love and evil
SALVATION ARMY.
Nesbo, J. The redeemer
Salvation city Nunez, S.
Sam Acquillo mysteries [series] Knopf, C.
Sam Briscoe novels [series] Hamill, P.
Sam Dryden novels [series] Lee, P.
Sam McCain mysteries [series] Gorman, E.
Sam Skarda mysteries [series] Shefchik, R.
Sam Wyndham novels [series] Mukherjee, A.
Samantha Brinkman novels [series] Clark, M.
Samaritan Price, R.
SAMBA MUSIC
Peebles, F. The air you breathe
The **same** sea Oz, A.
SAMI (EUROPEAN PEOPLE)
Vida, V. Let the Northern Lights erase your name
Samuel Craddock mysteries [series] Shames, T.
SAMURAI
Clavell, J. Shogun
Hunter, S. The 47th samurai
Kirk, D. Sword of honor
Rowland, L. The snow empress
Rowland, L. The incense game
Rowland, L. The iris fan
Rowland, L. The Shogun's daughter

Spann, S. Blade of the Samurai
Spann, S. Claws of the cat
Spann, S. Trial on Mount Koya
SAN (AFRICAN PEOPLE)
Andrew, S. The Satanic mechanic
Michener, J. The covenant
Stanley, M. Death of the mantis
Stanley, M. Dying to live
SAN ANTONIO, TEXAS
Estleman, L. Something borrowed, something black
Irvin, K. Tell her no lies
Toole, F. Pound for pound
SAN ANTONIO, TEXAS -- HISTORY -- 19TH CENTURY
Jiles, P. News of the world
SAN DIEGO, CALIFORNIA
Luna, L. The Janes
Martini, S. Compelling evidence
Parker, T. Cold pursuit
Parker, T. The fallen
Pufahl, S. On swift horses
Pyne, D. Catalina eddy
Rankin, I. Blood hunt
Sorenson, J. Aftershock
Urrea, L. The house of broken angels
Vinge, V. Rainbows end
Wambaugh, J. Finnegan's week
Wambaugh, J. Floaters
SAN FRANCISCO BAY AREA
Gardiner, M. Unsub
Johnson, L. The most dangerous place on earth
Lelchuk, S. Save me from dangerous men
Packer, A. The children's crusade
San Francisco novels (Jonathan Moore) [series] Moore, J.
SAN FRANCISCO, CALIFORNIA
Allende, I. Ripper
Anders, C. All the birds in the sky
Bennett, J. Bitter spirits
Black, S. Anything for you
Black, S. The killing lessons
Black, S. Lovemurder
Chen, M. Here and now and then
Conroy, P. South of Broad
Crumley, J. The last good kiss
Dev, S. Pride, prejudice, and other flavors
Diffenbaugh, V. The language of flowers
Dunne, J. The red, white, and blue
Ellison, J. A small indiscretion
Freeman, B. The night bird
Gabel, A. The ensemble
Gardiner, M. The Dirty Secrets Club
Goodwin, B. Revelation
Greer, A. The impossible lives of Greta Wells
Kerouac, J. The dharma bums
Kushner, R. The Mars room
Lescroart, J. Guilt
Lescroart, J. The hearing
Lescroart, J. Nothing but the truth

Lescroart, J. The oath
Lim, R. Natalie Tan's book of luck and fortune
Lutz, L. Curse of the Spellmans
Lutz, L. The last word
Lutz, L. Revenge of the Spellmans
Lutz, L. The Spellman file
Maupin, A. Tales of the city
McGuire, S. Chimes at midnight
McGuire, S. Night and silence
McGuire, S. Once broken faith
McGuire, S. Rosemary and rue
Moore, C. A dirty job
Moore, C. Noir
Moore, C. You suck
Moore, J. The night market
Morgan, R. Altered carbon
Mosley, W. Cinnamon kiss
Muller, M. Both ends of the night
Muller, M. The broken promise land
Muller, M. Burn out
Muller, M. The cavalier in white
Muller, M. City of whispers
Muller, M. The dangerous hour
Muller, M. Dead midnight
Muller, M. The ever-running man
Muller, M. There's something in a Sunday
Muller, M. Vanishing point
Muller, M. A walk through the fir
Muller, M. Where echoes live
Muller, M. While other people sleep
Muller, M. A wild and lonely place
Muller, M. Wolf in the shadows
Ng, F. Bone
Norris, F. McTeague
Patterson, J. 1st to die
Patterson, R. Eclipse
Perry, T. Death benefits
Phillips, C. Unthinkable
Pronzini, B. Bones
Pronzini, B. Crazybone
Pronzini, B. Fever
Pronzini, B. Hardcase
Pronzini, B. Hellbox
Pronzini, B. Illusions
Pronzini, B. In an evil time
Pronzini, B. Mourners
Pronzini, B. Nightcrawlers
Pronzini, B. Quarry
Pronzini, B. Savages
Pronzini, B. Spook
Pronzini, B. Step to the graveyard easy
Pronzini, B. The stolen gold affair
Richmond, M. No one you know
Rivers, F. Redeeming love
Shafak, E. The bastard of Istanbul
Shalvis, J. Sweet little lies
Sloan, R. Mr. Penumbra's 24-hour bookstore

Tan, A. The bonesetter's daughter
Tan, A. The Joy Luck Club
Tan, A. The Valley of Amazement
Title, S. The undateable
Tyler, A. The amateur marriage
Ullman, E. By blood
Walker, A. The temple of my familiar

SAN FRANCISCO, CALIFORNIA -- HISTORY -- 19TH CENTURY
Donoghue, E. Frog music

SAN FRANCISCO, CALIFORNIA -- HISTORY -- 20TH CENTURY
Hammett, D. The Maltese falcon
Otsuka, J. The Buddha in the attic

SAN FRANCISCO, CALIFORNIA -- SOCIAL LIFE AND CUSTOMS
Allende, I. The Japanese lover

SAN JUAN ISLANDS
Kleypas, L. Christmas Eve at Friday Harbor

SANATORIUMS
Mann, T. The Magic Mountain
Pajer, B. Capacity for murder

SANCHA, OF PROVENCE, QUEEN, CONSORT OF RICHARD, KING OF THE ROMANS, 1225-1261
Jones, S. Four sisters, all queens

Sanctity of hate Royal, P.

Sanctuary Faulkner, W.

The **sanctuary** sparrow Peters, E.

SAND
Abe, K. The woman in the dunes

The **sandbox** Zimmerman, D.

The **sandcastle** girls Bohjalian, C.

The **sandman** Kepler, L.

Sandrine's case Cook, T.

SANDWICH GENERATION
Robinson, R. Cost

SANKARA, THOMAS, 1949-1987
Wilkinson, L. American spy

Sano Ichiro mysteries [series] Rowland, L.

SANTA ANNA, ANTONIO LOPEZ DE, 1794-1876
Shaara, J. Gone for soldiers

SANTA BARBARA, CALIFORNIA
Perry, T. Dead aim

SANTA CRUZ ISLAND, CALIFORNIA
Boyle, T. When the killing's done

Santa Fe rules Woods, S.

SANTA FE, NEW MEXICO
Cather, W. Death comes for the archbishop
Coldsmith, D. Tallgrass
McGarrity, M. Everyone dies
Woods, S. Below the belt
Woods, S. Santa Fe rules

SANTA MONICA, CALIFORNIA
Martin, S. The pleasure of my company

SANTA TERESA (CALIF : IMAGINARY PLACE)
Grafton, S. "A" is for alibi

SANTERIA

Oyeyemi, H. The opposite house
Sarah Canary Fowler, K.
Sarah Gilchrist series [series] Welsh, K.
Sarah Jane Sallis, J.
Sarah Thornhill Grenville, K.
Sarah's key Rosnay, T.

SARAJEVO (BOSNIA AND HERCEGOVINA) -- HISTO-RY -- SIEGE, 1992-1996
Patric, A. Black rock white city
Saratoga payback Dobyns, S.

SARATOGA SPRINGS, NEW YORK
Dobyns, S. Saratoga payback
Wood, J. Upstate
Sarum Rutherfurd, E.

SASKATCHEWAN
Ford, R. Canada

SASSOON, SIEGFRIED, 1886-1967
Barker, P. The eye in the door
Barker, P. Regeneration
Satan's lullaby Royal, P.
The **Satanic** mechanic Andrew, S.
The **satanic** verses Rushdie, S.

SATANISM
Flynn, G. Dark places
Levin, I. Rosemary's baby
Lewis, M. The monk
Perez-Reverte, A. The Club Dumas
The **Satapur** moonstone Massey, S.

SATIE, ERIK, 1866-1925
Horrocks, C. The vexations
Satin Island McCarthy, T.

SATIRICAL FICTION
Abrams, D. Fobbit
Adiga, A. The white tiger
Adjei-Brenyah, N. Friday black
Allen, J. I lost my girlish laughter
Altschul, A. Deus ex machina
Amidon, S. Security
Amis, K. Lucky Jim
Amis, M. Lionel Asbo
Auslander, S. Hope
Austen, J. Northanger Abbey
Ballard, J. Kingdom come
Ballard, J. Millennium people
Barnes, J. England, England
Barry, M. Lexicon
Barth, J. Giles Goat-Boy ;
Barth, J. The sot-weed factor
Beatty, P. The sellout
Bellow, S. Henderson the rain king
Berger, T. Being invisible
Bernhard, T. Woodcutters
Bourland, B. Fake like me
Braithwaite, O. My sister, the serial killer
Brooks, M. World War Z
Brown, R. Rubyfruit jungle
Browne, S. Less than hero

Buckley, C. Supreme Courtship
Butler, H. The new me
Butler, K. Pretty ugly
Butler, R. Hell
Chatwin, B. Utz
Clarke, B. The price of the haircut
Coe, J. Number 11
Currie, R. Flimsy little plastic miracles
DeLillo, D. White noise
Dee, J. A thousand pardons
Dickens, C. Bleak House
Dickens, C. Little Dorrit
Dickens, C. Martin Chuzzlewit
Dickens, C. Our mutual friend
Dickens, C. The Pickwick papers
Dovlatov, S. Pushkin Hills
Drabble, M. The witch of Exmoor
Dunne, D. People like us
Dunne, D. Too much money
Eco, U. Numero zero
Eggers, D. The circle
Ellis, H. American housewife
Everett, P. Erasure
Everett, P. God's country
Everett, P. I am Not Sidney Poitier
Ferris, J. To rise again at a decent hour
Fielding, H. The history of Tom Jones, a foundling
Fitzgerald, F. The beautiful and damned
Fountain, B. Billy Lynn's long halftime walk
Frankel, L. Goodbye for now
Fuentes, C. The eagle's throne
Gaddis, W. A frolic of his own
Gaddis, W. J R
Gessen, K. A terrible country
Greene, G. Our man in Havana
Guterson, D. Ed King
Hale, B. The evolution of Bruno Littlemore
Heller, J. Catch-22
Heller, J. Good as Gold
Heller, Z. What was she thinking?
Hiaasen, C. Skinny dip
Houellebecq, M. Submission
Hynes, J. Kings of infinite space
Hynes, J. Next
Johnson, M. Pym
Jones, S. The uninvited guests
Kesey, K. One flew over the cuckoo's nest
Koch, H. The dinner
Kotzwinkle, W. The bear went over the mountain
Kramer, L. Search for my heart
Lethem, J. Dissident gardens
Lewis, S. Babbitt
Lewis, S. Dodsworth
Lewis, S. Elmer Gantry
Lewis, S. Main street
Lipsyte, S. The ask
Ma, J. China dream

Michener, J. Space

Saturn's children Stross, C.

SAUDI ARABIA

Barnes, K. In the kingdom of men

Eggers, D. A hologram for the king

Ferraris, Z. Finding Nouf

Ferraris, Z. Kingdom of strangers

Saul and Patsy Baxter, C.

SAUNDERS, MARY, DIED 1764

Donoghue, E. Slammerkin

The **savage** detectives Bolano, R.

Savage news Yellin, J.

Savage run Box, C.

Savages Pronzini, B.

Savages Winslow, D.

SAVANNAH, GEORGIA

Brown, S. Ricochet

Daugherty, C. A beautiful corpse

Daugherty, C. The echo killing

Jakes, J. Savannah, or, A gift for Mr. Lincoln

Johnson, T. Engraved on the heart

Page, K. The body in the casket

Pinborough, S. Dead to her

Rabb, J. Among the living

Savannah, or, A gift for Mr. Lincoln Jakes, J.

SAVANT SYNDROME

Haddon, M. The curious incident of the dog in the night-time

Lukas, M. The Oracle of Stamboul

Netzer, L. Shine shine shine

Oe, K. A quiet life

Save me from dangerous men Lelchuk, S.

SAVO ISLAND, BATTLE OF, 1942

Deutermann, P. Pacific glory

SAVONAROLA, GIROLAMO, 1452-1498

Dunant, S. The birth of Venus

Walton, J. Lent

SAVOY HOTEL, LONDON, ENGLAND

Jakeman, J. In the kingdom of mists

SAWMILL WORKERS

House, S. A parchment of leaves

Saxon stories (Bernard Cornwell) [series] Cornwell, B.

SAXONS

Cornwell, B. Sword of kings

Cornwell, B. War of the wolf

Pike, S. The lost queen

SAXOPHONISTS

Goonan, K. In war times

Say nice things about Detroit Lasser, S.

Say no more Ryan, H.

Say nothing Parks, B.

Say yes to the marquess Dare, T.

Say you're one of them Akpan, U.

Say you're sorry Robotham, M.

Scandal & scoundrel [series] MacLean, S.

Scandal takes the stage Leigh, E.

Scandalous Spencer, M.

SCANDALS

Alcott, K. A touch of stardust

Ashley, J. Lady Isabella's scandalous marriage

Backman, F. Beartown

Balogh, M. More than a mistress

Balogh, M. Someone to hold

Balogh, M. Someone to love

Benton, J. Lilli de Jong

Bowen, K. Between the devil and the duke

Bowman, V. Secrets of a wedding night

Bradley, A. A season of ruin

Bradley, A. A wicked way to win an earl

Carter, S. New England white

Chase, L. Don't tempt me

Chase, L. Your scandalous ways

Creech, S. The whole way home

Dare, T. Do you want to start a scandal

DeWoskin, R. Big girl small

Dickinson, P. The yellow room conspiracy

Dimberg, K. Girl in the rearview mirror

Dunne, D. People like us

Engelmann, K. The Stockholm octavo

Finch, C. The vanishing man

Fowler, T. A well-behaved woman

Galen, S. When you give a duke a diamond

Gilbert, E. City of girls

Godwin, G. Unfinished desires

Gray, J. A lady never lies

Guhrke, L. The truth about love and dukes

Harris, E. I say a little prayer

Harris, R. An officer and a spy

Harrod-Eagles, C. Headlong

Hatcher, R. Who I am with you

Hoffman, A. The marriage of opposites

Holt, V. The black opal

Horan, N. Loving Frank

Hunter, M. The conquest of Lady Cassandra

Hunting, H. Handle with care

Hurston, Z. Their eyes were watching God

Hustvedt, S. The blazing world

James, E. When Beauty tamed the Beast

James, H. Daisy Miller

Jeffries, S. The art of sinning

Kleypas, L. Devil in spring

Koen, K. Before Versailles

Leon, D. The golden egg

Lewis, K. Half of what you hear

Lohmann, J. Winning Ruby Heart

London, J. The trouble with honor

MacLean, S. Never judge a lady by her cover

MacLean, S. No good duke goes unpunished

MacLean, S. The rogue not taken

Marren, S. A Palm Beach wife

Maxwell, R. The queen's bastard

McCullough, C. An indecent obsession

Meek, J. The heart broke in

Neely, B. Blanche cleans up

O'Hagan, A. Be near me

Sjowall, M. The locked room
Sjowall, M. The man on the balcony
Sjowall, M. Murder at the Savoy
Soderberg, A. The other son
Sundstol, V. The land of dreams
Sveistrup, S. The chestnut man
Tursten, H. Hunting game
Tursten, H. Winter grave

SCAPEGOATS (PERSONS)
Barker, P. The eye in the door
Hamilton, J. A map of the world
Limon, M. The line
Scaramouche Sabatini, R.

SCARBOROUGH, ONTARIO
Chariandy, D. Brother

SCARCITY -- SOCIAL ASPECTS
Pohl, F. The space merchants
The **scarecrow** Connelly, M.
The **scarlet** letter Hawthorne, N.
The **Scarlet** Pimpernel Orczy, E.
Scarlet Pimpernel series [series] Orczy, E.
The **scarlet** ruse MacDonald, J.
Scarlet tides Hair, D.
The **scarred** woman Adler-Olsen, J.

SCARS
Freeman, A. The fair fight
Pressfield, S. 36 righteous men
Quinn, S. The right side

SCAVENGER HUNTS
Doan, A. The summer list
Racculia, K. Tuesday Mooney talks to ghosts

SCAVENGING
VanderMeer, J. Borne
Scenes from early life Hensher, P.
The **scent** keeper Bauermeister, E.
The **scent** of rain and lightning Pickard, N.

SCHEHERAZADE
Barth, J. Chimera
Schild's ladder Egan, G.
Schindler's list Keneally, T.

SCHINDLER, OSKAR, 1908-1974
Keneally, T. Schindler's list

SCHIZOPHRENIA
Billingsley, R. The secret she kept
Kiernan, C. The drowning girl

SCHOLARS AND ACADEMICS
Anton, M. Apprentice
Barnes, J. Flaubert's parrot
Black, B. Wolf on a string
Bolano, R. 2666
Brown, E. The weird sisters
Eliot, G. Middlemarch
Oz, A. Judas
Pearl, M. The technologists
Rader-Day, L. The black hour
Rosenberg, J. Confessions of the fox
Runcie, J. Sidney Chambers and the forgiveness of sins

Runcie, J. Sidney Chambers and the perils of the night
Runcie, J. Sidney Chambers and the problem of evil
Sandford, J. Bloody genius
Simmons, D. The fall of Hyperion
Simmons, D. Hyperion
Taseer, A. The way things were
Theroux, M. Strange bodies
Turtledove, H. Rulers of the darkness
Wilder, T. Theophilus North

SCHOLARSHIPS AND FELLOWSHIPS
Lerner, B. Leaving the Atocha Station

SCHOOL BUS ACCIDENTS
Banks, R. The sweet hereafter

SCHOOL CHILDREN
Hegi, U. Children and fire
School days Parker, R.

SCHOOL DISTRICTS
Ganshert, K. No one ever asked
School for dukes [series] Bell, L.

SCHOOL NURSES
Hamilton, J. A map of the world
The **school** of essential ingredients Bauermeister, E.

SCHOOL PRINCIPALS
Lam, V. The headmaster's wager
Smith, C. Silent city

SCHOOL SHOOTINGS
Block, S. Oliver Loving
Kellerman, J. Time bomb
Loren, R. The one for you
Loren, R. The one you fight for
McAllister, T. How to be safe
Parker, R. School days
Persson Giolito, M. Quicksand
Picoult, J. Nineteen minutes
Rankin, I. A question of blood
Shriver, L. We need to talk about Kevin
Slaughter, K. The good daughter

SCHOOL YEARBOOKS
Lipman, E. Good riddance

SCHOOLS
Corby, G. The Marathon conspiracy
Cussler, C. The oracle
Diachenko, S. Vita nostra
Doig, I. The whistling season
Doyle, R. Smile
Gailey, S. Magic for liars
Ganshert, K. No one ever asked
Grossman, L. The magician king
Grossman, L. The magician's land
Grossman, L. The magicians
Holsinger, B. The gifted school
Krueger, W. This tender land
Laurens, S. The pursuits of Lord Kit Cavanaugh
March, W. The bad seed
McCall Smith, A. The Limpopo Academy of Private Detection
Moriarty, L. Big little lies

Chiang, T. Stories of your life and others

Chu, W. The lives of tao

Clarke, A. 2001

Clarke, A. Childhood's end

Clarke, A. The collected stories of Arthur C. Clarke

Clarke, A. Rendezvous with Rama

Cline, E. Ready player one

Corey, J. Abaddon's gate

Corey, J. Babylon's ashes

Corey, J. Caliban's war

Corey, J. Cibola burn

Corey, J. Leviathan wakes

Corey, J. Nemesis games

Corey, J. Persepolis rising

Corey, J. Tiamat's wrath

Crouch, B. Dark matter

Crouch, B. Recursion

Davis, K. Duplex

Delany, S. Aye, and Gomorrah

Delaney, J. The perfect wife

Delany, S. Dhalgren

Delany, S. Stars in my pocket like grains of sand

Dick, P. Do androids dream of electric sheep?

Dick, P. The man in the high castle

Dick, P. The minority report

Doctorow, C. Radicalized

Doctorow, C. Rapture of the nerds

Doctorow, C. Walkaway

Due, T. Ghost summer

Eason, K. How Rory Thorne destroyed the multiverse

Egan, G. Perihelion summer

Egan, G. Schild's ladder

Eggers, D. A hologram for the king

El-Mohtar, A. This is how you lose the time war

Elison, M. The book of Etta

Elison, M. The book of Flora

Elison, M. The book of the unnamed midwife

Emshwiller, C. The secret city

Faber, M. The book of strange new things

Finley, J. The dark above

Flynn, M. The January dancer

Flynn, M. Eifelheim

Foster, A. Relic

Fowler, K. Sarah Canary

Gibson, W. Neuromancer

Gibson, W. Pattern recognition

Gibson, W. The peripheral

Gilman, C. Dark orbit

Gilman, C. Herland

Gladstone, M. Empress of forever

Goonan, K. In war times

Goonan, K. This shared dream

Graedon, A. The word exchange

Grant, M. Parasite

Green, H. An absolutely remarkable thing

Gregory, D. Afterparty

Gunn, J. Transcendental

Haig, F. The fire sermon

Haig, M. The humans

Haldeman, J. The forever war

Hall, L. Speak

Hamilton, P. The dreaming void

Hamilton, P. Great North Road

Hamilton, P. Pandora's star

Harkaway, N. Angelmaker

Harkaway, N. Gnomon

Harkaway, N. The gone-away world

Harrison, M. Light

Harrison, M. Nova swing

Heinlein, R. The moon is a harsh mistress

Heinlein, R. Starship troopers

Heinlein, R. Stranger in a strange land

Herbert, F. Dune

Higgins, C. Lightless

Hosking, J. Three years with the rat

Huang, S. Zero sum game

Hurley, K. The light brigade

Hurley, K. The stars are legion

Huxley, A. Brave new world

Ishiguro, K. Never let me go

Jemisin, N. How long 'til black future month?

Jen, G. The resisters

Jimenez, S. The vanished birds

Kadrey, R. The grand dark

Khoury, R. Empire of lies

Kosmatka, T. The games

Kowal, M. The calculating stars

Kowal, M. The fated sky

Kress, N. After the fall, before the fall, during the fall

Kress, N. Beggars in Spain

Kress, N. If tomorrow comes

Kress, N. Tomorrow's kin

Lafferty, M. Six wakes

Lai, L. The tiger flu

Lansdale, J. The complete Drive-in

Latin@ rising

Le Guin, U. The birthday of the world

Le Guin, U. The dispossessed

Le Guin, U. Four ways to forgiveness

Le Guin, U. The lathe of heaven

Le Guin, U. The left hand of darkness

Le Guin, U. The telling

Leckie, A. Ancillary justice

Leckie, A. Ancillary mercy

Leckie, A. Ancillary sword

Leckie, A. Provenance

Lee, Y. Ninefox gambit

Lee, Y. Raven stratagem

Lee, Y. Revenant gun

Lem, S. Eden

Lem, S. Fiasco

Lem, S. His master's voice

Lem, S. Solaris

Levine, D. Arabella of Mars

Suarez, D. Change agent
Swanwick, M. Bones of the Earth
Swyler, E. Light from other stars
Tepper, S. The gate to Women's Country
Tepper, S. Grass
Tepper, S. Singer from the sea
Tepper, S. The visitor
Thompson, T. Rosewater
Thompson, T. The Rosewater insurrection
Thompson, T. The Rosewater redemption
Tidhar, L. Central Station
Turnbull, C. The lesson
Valente, C. Radiance
Valente, C. Space opera
Van Vogt, A. Slan
VanderMeer, J. Annihilation
VanderMeer, J. Acceptance
VanderMeer, J. Authority
VanderMeer, J. Borne
VanderMeer, J. Dead astronauts
Varley, J. Dark lightning
Varley, J. Demon
Varley, J. Red lightning
Varley, J. Red thunder
Varley, J. Rolling thunder
Varley, J. Titan
Varley, J. Wizard
Verne, J. Journey to the centre of the Earth
The very best of the best
Vinge, J. The snow queen
Vinge, J. The summer queen
Vinge, J. World's end
Vinge, V. The children of the sky
Vinge, V. A deepness in the sky
Vinge, V. A fire upon the deep
Vinge, V. Rainbows end
Vonnegut, K. Galapagos
Vonnegut, K. Player piano
Vonnegut, K. The sirens of Titan
Vonnegut, K. Slaughterhouse-five
Vonnegut, K. Timequake
Vonnegut, K. Welcome to the monkey house
Wagers, K. After the crown
Wagers, K. There before the chaos
Walker, K. The age of miracles
Walton, J. My real children
Walton, J. Necessity
Watts, P. Blindsight
Watts, P. Starfish
This way to the end times
Weber, D. By schism rent asunder
Weber, D. The honor of the queen
Weber, D. Off Armageddon reef
Weber, D. On Basilisk Station
Weber, D. Shadow of freedom
Weber, D. The short victorious war
Weinstein, A. Children of the new world

Weir, A. Artemis
Weir, A. The Martian
Wells, H. The complete short stories of H. G. Wells
Wells, H. The invisible man
Wells, H. The island of Dr. Moreau
Wells, H. The time machine
Wells, H. The war of the worlds
Wells, M. All systems red
Wendig, C. Wanderers
Westerfeld, S. The killing of worlds
Westerfeld, S. The risen empire
Wilhelm, K. Where late the sweet birds sang
Williams, D. The stars now unclaimed
Willis, C. Blackout
Willis, C. Crosstalk
Willis, C. Doomsday book
Willis, C. Passage
Willis, C. To say nothing of the dog
Wilson, D. The Andromeda evolution
Wilson, D. The clockwork dynasty
Wilson, D. Robogenesis
Wilson, D. Robopocalypse
Wilson, R. Blind Lake
Wilson, R. Julian Comstock
Wilson, R. Spin
Winters, B. Countdown City
Winters, B. The last policeman
Winters, B. World of trouble
Winterson, J. Frankissstein
Wolfe, G. The best of Gene Wolfe
Wolfe, G. The citadel of the Autarch
Wolfe, G. The claw of the conciliator
Wolfe, G. Home fire
Wolfe, G. The shadow of the torturer
Wolfe, G. The sword of the Lictor
Wolfe, G. The urth of the new
Wright, J. The golden age
Yap, F. Yesterday
The year's best science fiction
Yu, C. How to live safely in a science fictional universe
Zahn, T. Dark force rising
Zahn, T. Heir to the empire
Zahn, T. The last command
Zamyatin, Y. We
Zelazny, R. Donnerjack
Zelazny, R. Lord of light

SCIENCE FICTION AUTHORS
Savage, S. Firmin
SCIENCE FICTION GAMES
Banks, I. The player of games
SCIENCE FICTION MYSTERIES
Adams, D. Dirk Gently's holistic detective agency
Gibson, W. Pattern recognition
Hamilton, P. Great North Road
Harkaway, N. Angelmaker
Hodder, M. The strange affair of Spring Heeled Jack
Kroese, R. The last iota

Edwardson, A. Sail of stone
Elliott, L. The missing years
Fagan, J. The Panopticon
Foley, L. The hunting party
Follett, K. Eye of the needle
Follett, K. Whiteout
Glass, J. Three Junes
Goddard, R. Never go back
Higgins, J. Edge of danger
Higgins, J. Midnight runner
Hill, S. The shadows in the street
Joss, M. Among the missing
Livesey, M. Criminals
MacBride, S. Blind eye
MacBride, S. Close to the bone
MacBride, S. Cold granite
MacBride, S. Flesh house
MacBride, S. Shatter the bones
May, P. The blackhouse
McCall Smith, A. The comforts of a muddy Saturday
McCall Smith, A. The forgotten affairs of youth
McCall Smith, A. The lost art of gratitude
McDermid, V. The distant echo
McPherson, C. The child garden
McPherson, C. Go to my grave
McPherson, C. Quiet neighbors
McPherson, C. Strangers at the gate
Mina, D. Conviction
Mina, D. The dead hour
Mina, D. Field of blood
Mina, D. Slip of the knife
Morgan, S. The Christmas sisters
O'Farrell, M. The vanishing act of Esme Lennox
O'Hagan, A. Be near me
Pirie, D. The patient's eyes
Rankin, I. Black and blue
Rankin, I. Blood hunt
Rankin, I. Exit music
Rankin, I. The naming of the dead
Rankin, I. Rather be the devil
Rankin, I. Set in darkness
Ranney, K. The Scottish duke
Sayers, D. The five red herrings
Sayers, D. Strong poison
Scott, A. Beneath the abbey wall
Scott, A. A double death on the Black Isle
Scott, A. A kind of grief
Scott, A. The low road
Ware, R. The turn of the key
Welsh, K. The wages of sin
Woods, S. Stealth

SCOTLAND -- HISTORY -- 13TH CENTURY
Banks, M. Never seduce a Scot
SCOTLAND -- HISTORY -- 15TH CENTURY
McLayne, A. Highland promise
SCOTLAND -- HISTORY -- 1689-1745
Kearsley, S. The firebird

SCOTLAND -- HISTORY -- 18TH CENTURY
Gabaldon, D. Dragonfly in amber
Gabaldon, D. Outlander
Gabaldon, D. Voyager
Putney, M. A kiss of fate
Scott, W. The bride of Lammermoor
SCOTLAND -- HISTORY -- 6TH CENTURY
Pike, S. The lost queen
SCOTLAND -- HISTORY -- MARY STUART, 1542-1567
Plaidy, J. The captive Queen of Scots
SCOTLAND -- HISTORY -- TO 1057
Pike, S. The lost queen
SCOTLAND -- SOCIAL CONDITIONS -- 18TH CENTURY
Scott, W. Rob Roy
SCOTLAND -- SOCIAL LIFE AND CUSTOMS
Cleeves, A. Raven black
Cleeves, A. Thin air
Cleeves, A. Wild fire
SCOTLAND -- SOCIAL LIFE AND CUSTOMS -- 18TH CENTURY
London, J. Wild wicked Scot
SCOTLAND -- SOCIAL LIFE AND CUSTOMS -- 19TH CENTURY
Ashe, K. The earl
Ashe, K. The duke
Ashe, K. The prince
James, E. Kiss me, Annabel
Laurens, S. By winter's light
Parry, A. The way of all flesh
Welsh, K. The unquiet heart
SCOTLAND -- SOCIAL LIFE AND CUSTOMS -- 20TH CENTURY
McPherson, C. A step so grave
Spark, M. The prime of Miss Jean Brodie
SCOTLAND YARD
Christie, A. Towards zero
Crombie, D. Kissed a sad goodbye
Crombie, D. Mourn not your dead
Finch, C. A beautiful blue death
Finch, C. The September Society
Grimes, M. The winds of change
James, P. The black tower
James, P. A certain justice
James, P. Death in holy orders
James, P. Death of an expert witness
James, P. Devices and desires
James, P. The lighthouse
James, P. Original sin
James, P. A taste for death
MacDonald, P. The list of Adrian Messenger
Neel, J. To die for
Pearce, M. A dead man in Barcelona
Price, S. By gaslight
SCOTLAND YARD.
Crombie, D. A bitter feast
Crombie, D. Water like a stone

George, E. A banquet of consequences
George, E. Believing the lie
George, E. This body of death
George, E. Careless in red
George, E. Just one evil act
Grimes, M. The Old Wine Shades
James, P. The private patient
Lovesey, P. Waxwork
Marsh, N. Dead water
Marsh, N. False scent
Marsh, N. Grave mistake
Marsh, N. Last ditch
Marsh, N. Light thickens
Marsh, N. When in Rome
Tey, J. The daughter of time

SCOTS
Burrowes, G. The trouble with dukes
Wojtas, O. Miss Blaine's prefect and the golden samovar

SCOTS IN AMERICA
Gabaldon, D. A breath of snow and ashes
Gabaldon, D. Drums of autumn
Gabaldon, D. An echo in the bone
Gabaldon, D. The fiery cross
Gabaldon, D. Written in my own heart's blood

SCOTS IN LONG ISLAND, NEW YORK
Glass, J. Three Junes

SCOTS IN MONTANA
Doig, I. Dancing at the Rascal Fair

SCOTS IN THE UNITED STATES
Glass, J. Three Junes
Mark, D. Cruel mercy
McPherson, C. Scot & soda
McPherson, C. Scot free
Pattison, E. Blood of the oak
Weatherspoon, R. Xeni

SCOTT, WINFIELD, 1786-1866
Shaara, J. Gone for soldiers
The **Scottish** duke Ranney, K.

SCOTTISH RESISTANCE AND REVOLTS
Scott, W. Rob Roy

SCOTTISH STEWART PERIOD (1371-1603)
McLayne, A. Highland promise
Plaidy, J. The captive Queen of Scots
A **scourge** of vipers DeSilva, B.

SCOUTING (RECONNAISSANCE)
Cobbs Hoffman, E. The Tubman command
Coover, R. Huck out west
The **scrapbook** of Frankie Pratt Preston, C.

SCRAPBOOKS
Preston, C. The scrapbook of Frankie Pratt

SCREENPLAY WRITING
Winfrey, K. Waiting for Tom Hanks

SCREENWRITERS
Baldwin, J. The Wilshire sun
Hurwitz, G. They're watching
Walter, J. Beautiful ruins
The **scribe** Guinn, M.

The **scribe** of Siena Winawer, M.
SCRIBES
Greenwood, K. Out of the Black Land

SCROLLS
Cussler, C. The oracle
Fay, K. The map of lost memories
McCarry, C. Old boys

SCRUPLES
O'Nan, S. Henry, himself

SCUBA DIVING
Steadman, C. Something in the water

SCULPTORS
Blackwell, J. Letters from Paris
Brown, R. Before and after
Carey, E. Little
Robbins, T. Skinny legs and all

SCULPTORS -- UNITED STATES
Just, W. Rodin's debutante

SCULPTURE
Blackwell, J. Letters from Paris
Brown, D. Angels & demons
Just, W. Rodin's debutante
O'Connell, C. Killing critics
The **sea** Banville, J.
The **sea** captain's wife Powning, B.
Sea change Parker, R.
Sea glass Shreve, A.
The **sea** lady Drabble, M.

SEA LEVEL
Cussler, C. The rising sea
Egan, G. Perihelion summer
Robinson, K. New York 2140

SEA MONSTERS
Grant, M. Into the drowning deep
Moore, C. The serpent of Venice
Simmons, D. The Terror
Sea of fertility [series] Mishima, Y.
The **sea** of grass Richter, C.
Sea of greed Cussler, C.
The **sea** of lost girls Goodman, C.
Sea of poppies Ghosh, A.
The **sea** of tranquility Millay, K.
Sea prayer Hosseini, K.

SEA STORIES
Beach, E. Run silent, run deep
Clancy, T. The hunt for Red October
Conrad, J. Lord Jim
Cussler, C. Golden Buddha
Cussler, C. Pacific vortex!
Cussler, C. Sacred stone
Doyle, B. The plover
Forester, C. Admiral Hornblower in the West Indies
Forester, C. Beat to quarters
Forester, C. Commodore Hornblower
Forester, C. Flying colours
Forester, C. Hornblower and the Atropos
Forester, C. Hornblower and the Hotspur

Forester, C. Lieutenant Hornblower
Forester, C. Lord Hornblower
Forester, C. Mr. Midshipman Hornblower
Forester, C. Ship of the line
Furst, A. Dark voyage
Golding, W. Close quarters
Golding, W. Fire down below
Golding, W. Rites of passage
Heggen, T. Mister Roberts
Johnson, C. Middle Passage
Lambdin, D. King's captain
Lambdin, D. Hostile shores
London, J. The sea-wolf
Matthiessen, P. Far Tortuga
McGuire, I. The North water
Melville, H. Billy Budd, foretopman
Melville, H. Moby-Dick; or, The whale
Monsarrat, N. The cruel sea
Nordhoff, C. Men against the sea
Nordhoff, C. Pitcairn's Island
O'Brian, P. Blue at the mizzen
O'Brian, P. The commodore
O'Brian, P. The golden ocean
O'Brian, P. The hundred days
O'Brian, P. Master and commander
O'Brian, P. The unknown shore
O'Brian, P. The wine-dark sea
O'Brian, P. The yellow admiral
Poe, E. The narrative of Arthur Gordon Pym of Nantucket
Poyer, D. A country of our own
Poyer, D. Fire on the waters
Poyer, D. Overthrow
Sabatini, R. Captain Blood
Simmons, D. The Terror
Smith, W. Birds of prey
Smith, W. Monsoon
Verne, J. The mysterious island
Wolfe, G. Pirate freedom
Wouk, H. The Caine mutiny
Sea swept Roberts, N.
Sea trilogy [series] Golding, W.
SEA TURTLES
Hoffman, A. Turtle moon
Sea wife Gaige, A.
The **sea,** the sea Murdoch, I.
The **sea-wolf** London, J.
SEAFARING LIFE
Birch, C. Jamrach's menagerie
Conrad, J. Complete short fiction of Joseph Conrad
Gaige, A. Sea wife
Ghosh, A. Flood of fire
Ghosh, A. River of smoke
Heggen, T. Mister Roberts
Lambdin, D. King's captain
McGuire, I. The North water
O'Brian, P. Blue at the mizzen
O'Brian, P. The hundred days

O'Brian, P. Master and commander
Powning, B. The sea captain's wife
Poyer, D. The whiteness of the whale
Sabatini, R. Captain Blood
Wolfe, G. Pirate freedom
SEAFOOD INDUSTRY AND TRADE
Cooper, T. The marauders
SEALING
Grenville, K. Sarah Thornhill
London, J. The sea-wolf
The **seamstress** Peebles, F.
The **seamstress** Pittman, A.
The **seamstress** and the wind Aira, C.
SEAMSTRESSES
Aira, C. The seamstress and the wind
Dare, T. The duchess deal
Duenas, M. The time in between
Peebles, F. The seamstress
Pittman, A. The seamstress
Sherwood, F. The book of splendor
Sean Dillon thrillers [series] Higgins, J.
Sean Duffy novels [series] McKinty, A.
SEANCES
Clare, A. The woman who spoke to spirits
SEARCH AND RESCUE OPERATIONS
Deutermann, P. The nugget
Gaynor, H. The lighthouse keeper's daughter
Higgins, J. The eagle has flown
Higgins, J. Night of the fox
Kadare, I. The general of the dead army
Les Becquets, D. Breaking wild
Shalvis, J. Second chance summer
Snow, J. An Alaskan Christmas
Sundaresan, I. The splendor of silence
Warren, S. Rescue me
SEARCH DOGS
Picoult, J. Vanishing acts
Search for my heart Kramer, L.
SEARCHING
Brekke, J. The fifth element
Brkic, C. The first rule of swimming
Forbes, C. A tall history of sugar
Grunberg, A. Tirza
Hill, R. The stranger house
Jemisin, N. The fifth season
Jemisin, N. The obelisk gate
Jemisin, N. The stone sky
Konar, A. Mischling
Lovett, C. The bookman's tale
Lovett, C. The lost book of the Grail
Luesse, V. Missing Isaac
Perry, S. The Essex serpent
Pitts, L. Freeman
Preston, D. Old bones
Pufahl, S. On swift horses
Redhill, M. Bellevue square
Sjon, 1. The blue fox

SECOND PERSON NARRATIVES

Acampora, L. The paper wasp
Auster, P. Invisible
Barnes, J. The only story
Calvino, I. If on a winter's night a traveler
Gao, X. Soul mountain
Hendricks, G. An anonymous girl
Leckie, A. The Raven tower
McAllister, T. The young widower's handbook
Second person singular Qashu, S.
Second shot Sharp, Z.
The **second** sleep Harris, R.
The **second** time I saw you Croft, P.

SECOND WIVES

Blum, J. The lost family
Brownrigg, S. Morality tale
Fisher, K. The silent wife
Lea, C. The glass woman
Welty, E. The optimist's daughter

SECOND WORLD WAR ERA (1939-1945)

Adimi, K. Our riches
Afrika, T. Bitter Eden
Amis, M. The zone of interest
Apelfeld, A. Blooms of darkness
Apelfeld, A. To the edge of sorrow
Arnaldur Indridason, 1. The shadow district
Ballard, J. Empire of the sun
Bausch, R. Peace
Beach, E. Run silent, run deep
Belfoure, C. The Paris architect
Benioff, D. City of thieves
Benn, J. Billy Boyle
Binet, L. HHhH
Black, B. The secret guests
Black, C. Three hours in Paris
Blake, S. The postmistress
Bohjalian, C. Skeletons at the feast
Boulle, P. The bridge over the River Kwai
Bowen, E. The heat of the day
Byatt, A. Ragnarok
Chiaverini, J. Resistance women
Clayton, M. The last train to London
Connolly, J. The book of lost things
Dallas, S. Tallgrass
Deutermann, P. The Iceman
Deutermann, P. The nugget
Deutermann, P. Pacific glory
Doerr, A. All the light we cannot see
Downing, D. Diary of a dead man on leave
Egan, J. Manhattan Beach
Ellroy, J. Perfidia
Ellroy, J. This storm
Faulks, S. Charlotte Gray
Fleischmann, R. How quickly she disappears
Follett, K. Eye of the needle
Follett, K. Hornet flight
Follett, K. Jackdaws

Furst, A. Blood of victory
Furst, A. A hero of France
Furst, A. Under occupation
Gillham, D. City of women
Gross, A. The one man
Hannah, K. The nightingale
Harmel, K. The room on Rue Amelie
Hoffman, A. The world that we knew
Kelly, J. The light over London
Kelly, M. Lilac girls
Kelly, S. The wages of desire
Kerr, P. Greeks bearing gifts
Kerr, P. Prussian blue
Knowles, J. A separate peace
Konar, A. Mischling
Krall, H. Chasing the king of hearts
Lehane, D. World gone by
Leithauser, B. The art student's war
Loh, V. Breaking the tongue , by Vyvyane Loh.
Loigman, L. The wartime sisters
MacNeal, S. The king's justice
Mackall, D. With love, wherever you are
Mailer, N. The naked and the dead
Maum, C. Costalegre
Mawer, S. The glass room
McFadden, B. The Book of Harlan
Meacham, L. Dragonfly
Mengiste, M. The shadow king
Michener, J. Tales of the South Pacific
Monsarrat, N. The cruel sea
Moore, C. Noir
Nemirovsky, I. Suite Francaise
Nesbit, T. The wives of Los Alamos
Nicholson, W. Motherland
Norman, H. What is left the daughter
Oksanen, S. When the doves disappeared
Ondaatje, M. The English patient
Orringer, J. The flight portfolio
Orringer, J. The invisible bridge
Otsuka, J. The Buddha in the attic
Otsuka, J. When the emperor was divine
Pears, I. The dream of Scipio
Piercy, M. Gone to soldiers
Pilcher, R. Coming home
Plain, B. Tapestry
Pynchon, T. Gravity's rainbow
Ramzipoor, E. The ventriloquists
Remarque, E. A time to love and a time to die
Ripley, M. Mr. Campion's war
Rizzuto, R. Shadow child
Robbins, D. Last citadel
Robbins, D. War of the rats
Roberts, M. Ignorance
Roosevelt, E. Murder in the map room
Rosner, J. The yellow bird sings
Russell, M. A thread of grace
Ryan, J. The spies of Shilling Lane

Le Carre, J. The tailor of Panama
Leigh, E. Temptations of a wallflower
Lelchuk, S. Save me from dangerous men
Leonard, E. Mr. Paradise
Liss, D. A spectacle of corruption
Littlejohn, E. Inherit the bones
MacDonald, J. The green ripper
MacLean, S. Never judge a lady by her cover
Makine, A. Music of a life
Malpas, J. Leave me breathless
Maxwell, R. The queen's bastard
Michels, E. The rebel heir
Moor, J. The keeper
Moore, K. Sexy Lexy
Muller, M. Burn out
Muller, M. Cyanide Wells
Noble, K. The game and the governess
Orczy, E. The Scarlet Pimpernel
Parker, T. L.A. outlaws
Penrose, A. Murder at Kensington Palace
Perry, A. Shoulder the sky
Phillips, C. A distant shore
Phillips, S. First Lady
Pratchett, T. Monstrous regiment
Quick, A. The other lady vanishes
Raichev, R. Assassins at Ospreys
Ranney, K. The Scottish duke
Rendell, R. A sleeping life
Robinson, P. Friend of the devil
Robotham, M. Good girl, bad girl
Row, J. Your face in mine
Ruff, M. 88 names
Scottoline, L. One perfect lie
Shupe, J. The courtesan duchess
Silone, I. Bread and wine
Slaughter, K. Pieces of her
Stevenson, R. The strange case of Dr. Jekyll and Mr. Hyde
Stewart, A. Kopp sisters on the march
Thomas, S. Beguiling the beauty
Thomson, E. The blood
Willig, L. The deception of the emerald ring
Willig, L. The masque of the Black Tulip
Willig, L. The secret history of the Pink Carnation
Willig, L. The seduction of the Crimson Rose
Willig, L. The temptation of the night jasmine
The **secret** life of bees Kidd, S.
The **secret** life of Sarah Hollenbeck Turner, B.
The **secret** life of William Shakespeare Morgan, J.
The **secret** mistress Balogh, M.
The **secret** of clouds Richman, A.
The **secret** place French, T.

SECRET PLACES

Hill, J. NOS4A2

The **secret** river Grenville, K.
The **secret** scripture Barry, S.

SECRET SERVICE

Child, L. Without fail

Clements, R. Martyr
Follett, K. Eye of the needle
Follett, K. Jackdaws
Furst, A. Blood of victory
Furst, A. Dark voyage
Goldstone, L. Assassin of shadows
Harris, R. Enigma
Higgins, J. Bad company
Higgins, J. Day of reckoning
Higgins, J. The eagle has flow
Higgins, J. The eagle has landed
Higgins, J. Edge of danger
Higgins, J. Eye of the storm
Higgins, J. Midnight runner
Higgins, J. Night of the fox
Higgins, J. Touch the devil
Higgins, J. The White House connection
Iles, G. Black cross
Marias, J. Your face tomorrow, vol.1
Marias, J. Your face tomorrow, vol.2
Marias, J. Your face tomorrow, vol. 3
Persson, L. Another time, another life
Sundaresan, I. The splendor of silence

SECRET SERVICE -- GREAT BRITAIN

Deighton, L. Berlin game
Fleming, I. Casino royale
Fleming, I. Doctor No
Fleming, I. Goldfinger
Fleming, I. The man with the golden gun

SECRET SERVICE -- ISRAEL

Silva, D. The kill artist

SECRET SERVICE -- ITALY

Rigosi, G. Night bus

SECRET SERVICE -- SOVIET UNION

Smith, T. Agent 6
Smith, T. Child 44
Smith, T. The secret speech

SECRET SERVICE -- UNITED STATES

Phillips, S. First Lady

SECRET SERVICE -- UNITED STATES

Roosevelt, E. Murder in the map room

SECRET SERVICE -- UNITED STATES -- HISTORY --
CIVIL WAR, 1861-1865

Jakes, J. On secret service

The **secret** she kept Billingsley, R.

Secret sisters Krentz, J.

SECRET SOCIETIES

Adams, E. The secret, book & scone society
Adams, L. The bromance book club
Archer, Z. Dangerous seduction
Ashe, K. The earl
Baldacci, D. Hell's Corner
Bardugo, L. Ninth house
Barry, M. Lexicon
Bayard, L. The pale blue eye
Bear, E. Ink and steel
Berry, S. The bishop's pawn

Bennett, B. The mothers
Bennett, R. American elsewhere
Bennett, R. City of stairs
Bennett, R. City of miracles
Bennett, R. Foundryside
Benz, C. The gone dead
Berg, E. The confession club
Berg, G. The operator
Berry, C. A legacy of murder
Berry, S. The Templar legacy
Beyda, E. The body double
Bialosky, J. The prize
Bird, S. The Yokota Officers Club
Birmingham, S. Carriage trade
Black, L. Let justice descend
Black, L. Suffer the children
Black, S. Anything for you
Blackwell, J. Letters from Paris
Blake, R. A dark anatomy
Blake, S. The postmistress
Bledsoe, A. Gather her round
Block, S. Oliver Loving
Bohjalian, C. Secrets of Eden
Bohjalian, C. The sleepwalker
Bolano, R. By night in Chile
Bond, C. Ruby
Boswell, R. Century's son
Bouchet, A. Nightchaser
Bourland, B. Fake like me
Bourne, J. My lord and spymaster
Bourne, J. The spymaster's lady
Box, C. The bitterroots
Boyden, J. Through black spruce
Boylan, J. Long black veil
Boyne, J. The absolutist
Boyne, J. A history of loneliness
Boyne, J. A ladder to the sky
Bradbury, J. The wild inside
Bradbury, R. The Martian chronicles
Bradbury, R. Something wicked this way comes
Brenner, J. Drawing home
Brookmyre, C. Black widow
Brown, K. The clairvoyants
Brunkhorst, A. The gilded Life of Matilda Duplaine
Bryant, N. Christmas with the billionaire
Bryant, N. Message from a mistress
Buchan, J. The thirty-nine steps
Burrowes, G. The heir
Burrowes, G. Lady Sophie's Christmas wish
Burton, J. The miniaturist
Bussi, M. Black water lilies
Butler, M. Pickle's progress
Butler, R. Perfume River
Byrne, K. The hunter
Byrne, K. How to love a duke in ten days
Camp, B. The city of lost fortunes
Camp, B. Gather the fortunes

Candlish, L. Our house
Cannon, J. Three things about Elsie
Carlson, R. Five skies
Carpenter, E. Every single secret
Carpenter, E. The weight of lies
Castillo, E. America is not the heart
Castillo, L. A gathering of secrets
Chambers, B. A closed and common orbit
Chambers, B. The long way to a small, angry planet
Charles, K. Wanted, a gentleman
Chee, A. The queen of the night
Child, L. Deep storm
Child, L. The hard way
Child, L. Nothing to lose
Child, L. Worth dying for
Childress, M. One Mississippi
Chizmar, R. A long December
Christie, A. And then there were none
Chung, C. The tenth muse
Chung, M. The eighth girl
Clark, M. Blood defense
Clark, M. Final judgment
Clark, M. I've got my eyes on you
Clark, M. The Jezebel remedy
Cleave, P. A killer harvest
Cleeves, A. The crow trap
Cleeves, A. The long call
Cleeves, A. Raven black
Cleeves, A. Thin air
Clegg, B. Did you ever have a family
Coben, H. The boy from the woods
Coben, H. Don't let go
Coben, H. Fool me once
Coben, H. The stranger
Coe, J. Number 11
Coel, M. Blood memory
Cogman, G. The invisible library
Cogman, G. The masked city
Cohen, L. The grief of others
Cole, A. An unconditional freedom
Cole, D. Hangman
Cole, K. Dreams of a dark warrior
Coleman, R. What you break
Coleman, R. Where it hurts
Collins, C. The gamal
Connelly, M. The night fire
Connolly, J. The burning soul
Connolly, S. The lost traveller
Constantine, L. The last Mrs. Parrish
Cook, R. Genesis
Cook, R. Nano
Cook, T. A dancer in the dust
Cook, T. Sandrine's case
Coomer, J. One vacant chair
Corey, J. Abaddon's gate
Corey, J. Babylon's ashes
Corey, J. Caliban's war

Goenawan, C. The perfect world of Miwako Sumida

Goldbloom, G. On division

Goldin, M. The escape room

Gonzales, L. Lucy

Goodman, C. The sea of lost girls

Goodman, J. In want of a wife

Goodman, J. A touch of forever

Grant, H. The vanishing of Katharina Linden

Grebe, C. After she's gone

Greene, G. Brighton Rock

Gregory, D. The devil's alphabet

Griffin, A. When all is said

Grippando, J. The girl in the glass box

Grisham, J. The client

Groff, L. Fates and furies

Gruber, M. The book of air and shadows

Guterson, D. The other

Hall, T. The case of the deadly butter chicken

Hamilton, P. Great North Road

Hamilton, S. The lock artist

Hand, E. Generation loss

Hannah, K. The nightingale

Hannah, S. Perfect little children

Harman, P. The midwife of Hope River

Harper, J. The dry

Harper, J. The lost man

Harris, E. Not a day goes by

Harris, R. The ghost

Harrison, M. The bishop's wife

Harrison, R. The return

Harrod-Eagles, C. Headlong

Hart, C. Murder walks the plank

Hart, E. The book of Killowen

Hart, E. City of ink

Hart, J. Iron house

Hart, J. Redemption road

Harvey, M. Brighton

Harvey, M. The fifth floor

Harvey, M. The governor's wife

Hassib, R. A pure heart

Hatcher, R. Who I am with you

Hauck, R. How to catch a prince

Hawkins, P. The girl on the train

Hawkins, S. The library at Mount Char

Hawley, N. Before the fall

Hawthorne, N. The scarlet letter

Hayder, M. Hanging hill

Haywood, G. Cemetery Road

Hegi, U. Stones from the river

Heller, P. Celine

Hemmings, K. The possibilities

Hibbert, T. A girl like her

Higashino, K. Newcomer

Higgins, J. Bad company

Hilderbrand, E. What happens in paradise

Hilderbrand, E. Winter in paradise

Hill, E. Little comfort

Hill, J. The Fireman

Hill, J. Heart-shaped box

Hill, R. The stranger house

Hillerman, T. The shape shifter

Hoang, H. The bride test

Hoeg, P. The quiet girl

Hoffman, A. The ice queen

Hoover, C. All your perfects

Hoover, M. The quickening

Horowitz, A. The sentence is death

Horowitz, A. The word is murder

Hoyt, E. Wicked intentions

Hunter, M. The surrender of Miss Fairbourne

Hurwitz, G. Into the fire

Huston, C. The shotgun rule

Iles, G. Cemetery road

Iles, G. Third degree

Ishiguro, K. Never let me go

Itani, F. Tell

JaQuavis The dopeman's wife

Jackson, J. Never have I ever

James, M. The book of night women

James, P. Death in holy orders

Jemisin, N. The fifth season

Jemisin, N. The obelisk gate

Jemisin, N. The stone sky

Jenkins, V. An unattended death

Jerkins, G. The ninth step

Jewell, L. Watching you

Jimenez, A. The friend zone

Jin, M. Little gods

Jio, S. The last camellia

Johnson, C. Spirit of steamboat

Johnson, D. Everything under

Johnson, K. The dream-quest of Vellitt Boe

Johnson, R. No one in the world

Joinson, S. The photographer's wife

Jones, S. The outcast

Jones, T. The better liar

Joshi, A. The henna artist

Joss, M. Among the missing

Joyce, G. The limits of enchantment

Just, W. An unfinished season

K'wan Animal

K'wan Animal II

K'wan Lawless

K'wan Revelations

Kamali, M. The stationery shop

Kantaria, A. I know you

Karlsson, J. The room

Kasischke, L. The raising

Katsu, A. The deep

Keller, J. Fast falls the night

Keller, J. Last ragged breath

Kellerman, J. Therapy

Kelly, E. Broadchurch

Kelly, E. The poison tree

Meyers, K. Twisted tree
Milan, C. The duchess war
Miles, J. Anatomy of a miracle
Mina, D. Conviction
Mina, D. The long drop
Miranda, M. The last house guest
Mitchell, D. The bone clocks
Mizushima, M. Killing trail
Mizushima, M. Stalking ground
Modesitt, L. The one-eyed man
Molloy, A. The perfect mother
Montgomery, J. The widows
Moore, J. The night market
Moore, M. The islanders
Moriarty, L. The husband's secret
Moriarty, L. Nine perfect strangers
Morrell, D. Ruler of the night
Mortimer, J. Quite honestly
Morton, K. The house at Riverton
Muller, M. The cavalier in white
Murakami, H. After dark
Murakami, H. Killing commendatore
Murphy, S. The possessions
Murphy, Y. Signed, Mata Hari
Murr, N. The perfect man
Nemirovsky, I. Fire in the blood
Nesbit, T. The wives of Los Alamos
Neubauer, E. Murder at the Mena House
Neuhaus, N. The ice queen
Ng, C. Little fires everywhere
Nguyen, K. New waves
Nickson, C. The constant lovers
Nickson, C. The hocus girl
Novic, S. Girl at war
O'Brien, T. In the Lake of the Woods
Oates, J. Evil eye
Oates, J. Jack of spades
Oates, J. Pursuit
Oksanen, S. When the doves disappeared
Olson, N. Before the devil fell
Ozick, C. Heir to the glimmering world
Page, K. The body in the big apple
Palliser, C. Rustication
Paretsky, S. Blacklist
Paretsky, S. Critical mass
Paretsky, S. Total recall
Parker, R. Now and then
Parker, R. Painted ladies
Parker, R. Thin air
Parker, T. The fallen
Parker, T. L.A. outlaws
Parks, B. Say nothing
Parrish, C. Still life
Parshall, S. Poisoned ground
Patterson, R. Protect and defend
Pavone, C. The expats
Pavone, C. The Paris diversion

Pearl, M. The Dante Club
Penman, S. The Queen's man
Penny, L. A better man
Penny, L. Bury your dead
Penny, L. Glass houses
Penny, L. A great reckoning
Penny, L. Kingdom of the blind
Perry, A. Dark tide rising
Perry, A. Death in focus
Perry, A. No graves as yet
Perry, A. Shoulder the sky
Perry, S. Melmoth
Perry, T. Fidelity
Persson, L. Another time, another life
Peters, E. Fallen into the pit
Peters, E. The snake, the crocodile, and the dog
Peterson, T. What comes my way
Phillips, H. The beautiful bureaucrat
Phillips, J. Quiet dell
Pinborough, S. Behind her eyes
Pinborough, S. Cross her heart
Pinborough, S. Dead to her
Pochoda, I. Visitation Street
Polk, C. Witchmark
Poole, S. The Borgia mistress
Powers, R. The echo maker
Poyer, D. Overthrow
Pratchett, T. Thud!
Preston, D. Old bones
Pronzini, B. The stolen gold affair
Pulley, N. The Bedlam stacks
Purcell, L. The silent companions
Putney, M. Nowhere near respectable
Pyper, A. The homecoming
Quincy, D. Murder in Mayfair
Rader-Day, L. Little pretty things
Rash, R. The cove
Raybourn, D. A curious beginning
Raybourn, D. A dangerous collaboration
Raybourn, D. A perilous undertaking
Raybourn, D. Silent in the grave
Raybourn, D. A treacherous curse
Rayne, S. Music macabre
Rayne, S. Property of a lady
Redhill, M. Consolation
Redondo, D. The invisible guardian
Reich, C. Rules of deception
Reich, C. The take
Reichs, K. A conspiracy of bones
Rice, A. The witching hour
Richmond, M. No one you know
Ripley, M. Mr Campion's fault
Rivers, F. The masterpiece
Robards, K. The ultimatum
Robb, C. A murdered peace
Roberts, N. Midnight Bayou
Robertson, I. The Paris winter

Cusk, R. Outline
Faulks, S. A week in December
Ishiguro, K. The remains of the day
O'Hagan, A. Be near me
Yap, F. Yesterday

SELF-DECEPTION IN WOMEN

Richardson, S. Clarissa, or, The history of a young lady

SELF-DEFENSE

Mason, J. The hidden things
Perry, T. Dead aim
Sharfeddin, H. Mineral spirits
Self-defense Kellerman, J.

SELF-DEFENSE (LAW)

Murdoch, I. The green knight

SELF-DESTRUCTIVE BEHAVIOR

Baker, D. Young man with a horn
Bennett, B. The mothers
Broder, M. The pisces
Butler, H. The new me
Byrne, T. Ghosts and lightning
Chaon, D. Ill will
Flynn, G. Sharp objects
Greenwell, G. What belongs to you
Hoffman, A. Skylight confessions
Jackson, C. The lost weekend
Johnson, L. The most dangerous place on earth
Moses, K. Wintering
O'Hara, J. Appointment in Samarra
Sittenfeld, C. Prep
Spark, M. The driver's seat
Tsypkin, L. Summer in Baden-Baden
Unger, L. Crazy love you
Walker, C. Man of the year
Yanagihara, H. A little life

SELF-DESTRUCTIVE BEHAVIOR IN MEN

Chabon, M. Wonder boys
Duncan, G. The last werewolf
St. Aubyn, E. At last
Stevenson, R. The strange case of Dr. Jekyll and Mr. Hyde

SELF-DESTRUCTIVE BEHAVIOR IN TEENAGERS

Giordano, P. The solitude of prime numbers

SELF-DESTRUCTIVE BEHAVIOR IN WOMEN

Hand, E. Generation loss
Roth, P. My life as a man
Stephens, A. Famous adopted people
Walsh, H. Brass

SELF-DISCLOSURE

Cusk, R. Outline

SELF-DISCOVERY

Ahern, C. Roar
Bauermeister, E. The scent keeper
Beagin, J. Vacuum in the dark
Beatty, P. Slumberland
Beverly, W. Dodgers
Bialosky, J. The prize
Brown, E. The weird sisters
Chang, A. Days of distraction

Chung, C. The tenth muse
Coelho, P. The alchemist
Doyle, B. The plover
Dugoni, R. The extraordinary life of Sam Hell
Edugyan, E. Washington Black
Eggers, D. How we are hungry
Erdrich, L. Shadow tag
Eugenides, J. Fresh complaint
Evanovich, S. Under the table
  Everyday people
Franzen, J. Freedom
Gao, X. Soul mountain
Ghosh, A. Gun Island
Green, H. An absolutely remarkable thing
Jones, S. Mongrels
Joseph, F. Niya
Krauss, N. Forest Dark
Lauren, C. Sweet filthy boy
Lebrecht, N. The song of names
Lethem, J. Dissident gardens
Lipman, E. The dearly departed, Elinor Lipman.
Lipman, E. The pursuit of Alice Thrift
Locascio, L. Open me
London, J. The charmer in chaps
Mabanckou, A. Black Moses
Malamud, B. The fixer
McLaren, K. The road to enchantment
Monroe, M. God still don't like ugly
Murakami, H. 1Q84
Packer, A. The dive from Clausen's pier
Rose, H. The museum of modern love
Rubart, J. The man he never was
Tolkien, J. The hobbit, or, there and back again
Walker, A. The temple of my familiar

SELF-DISCOVERY IN BOYS

Bradbury, R. Dandelion wine
Bradbury, R. Something wicked this way comes
Fuqua, J. Gone and back again

SELF-DISCOVERY IN GIRLS

Hazzard, S. The great fire

SELF-DISCOVERY IN MEN

Aciman, A. Find me
Auster, P. Leviathan
Bellow, S. Henderson the rain king
Bellow, S. Seize the day
Davies, R. Murther and walking spirits
Eugenides, J. The marriage plot
Foer, J. Here I am
Fountain, B. Billy Lynn's long halftime walk
Garcia Marquez, G. Memories of my melancholy whores
Garey, J. Too bright to hear too loud to see
Garey, J. Too bright to hear too loud to see
Gide, A. The immoralist
Golding, W. Close quarters
Golding, W. Fire down below
Golding, W. Rites of passage
Hawley, N. The good father

Hesse, H. Steppenwolf
Hynes, J. Next
Kenney, J. Truth in advertising
Kerouac, J. The dharma bums
Kiefer, C. The infinite tides
Lerner, B. Leaving the Atocha Station
Maugham, W. The razor's edge
Michener, J. The bridges at Toko-Ri
Morrison, T. Song of Solomon
Murakami, H. Colorless Tsukuru Tazaki and his years of pilgrimage
Murakami, H. The wind-up bird chronicle
Naslund, B. Blood of an exile
O'Neill, J. Netherland
Oe, K. The changeling
Olmstead, R. Far bright star
Percy, W. The moviegoer
Roth, P. The anatomy lesson
Roth, P. The ghost writer
Roth, P. Goodbye, Columbus, and five short stories
Roth, P. The professor of desire
Roth, P. Zuckerman bound
Roth, P. Zuckerman unbound
Saramago, J. The manual of painting and calligraphy
Shields, C. The republic of love
Shteyngart, G. Lake Success
Skibell, J. A curable romantic
Smith, D. The constable's tale
Theroux, P. The Lower River
Toole, F. Pound for pound
Wiesel, E. The judges
Wilson, S. The man in the gray flannel suit
Yu, H. Brothers

SELF-DISCOVERY IN TEENAGE BOYS
Aciman, A. Call me by your name
Myers, A. Continental divide
Toole, F. Pound for pound

SELF-DISCOVERY IN TEENAGE GIRLS
Cruz, A. Dominicana
Fagan, J. The Panopticon
Kincaid, J. Annie John
Lessing, D. Martha Quest
Vestal, S. Daredevils

SELF-DISCOVERY IN TEENAGERS
Walls, J. The silver star

SELF-DISCOVERY IN WOMEN
Abraham, T. Black Sunday
Ali, M. Brick Lane
Arnoult, D. Sufficient grace
Atwood, M. Cat's eye
Backman, F. Britt-Marie was here
Bank, M. The wonder spot
Batuman, E. The idiot
Benjamin, M. The aviator's wife
Bishop, A. Written in red
Brownrigg, S. Morality tale
Bruni, S. The night Gwen Stacy died

Campbell, A. On the floor
Carty-Williams, C. Queenie
Cather, W. The song of the lark
Chevalier, T. A single thread
Cusk, R. Transit
DeCarlo, M. The art of crash landing
Farah, N. Knots
Ferrante, E. The story of a new name
Ferrante, E. Those who leave and those who stay
Flagg, F. Fried green tomatoes at the Whistle Stop Cafe
Frank, D. Folly Beach
Gideon, M. Wife 22
Goldbloom, G. On division
Hale, S. Austenland
Haywood, S. The cactus
James, P. Innocent blood
Jordan, H. When she woke
Joshi, A. The henna artist
Kearsley, S. A desperate fortune
King, L. Father of the rain
Lancaster, J. Here I go again
Lennon, J. Familiar
Lessing, D. Love, again
Linden, R. Ascension of larks
McCann, C. Zoli
McDermott, A. Someone
McMillan, T. Waiting to exhale
Morgan, S. One summer in Paris
Munro, A. Lives of girls and women
Nin, A. Cities of the interior
Oates, J. The gravedigger's daughter
Oates, J. Marya
Phillips, H. The need
Phillips, S. It had to be you
Quindlen, A. Object lessons
Rhodes, J. Voodoo dreams
Russell, M. Dreamers of the day
Schwarz, C. The edge of the Earth
Shumway, C. Ten girls to watch
Strout, E. My name is Lucy Barton
Swift, G. Mothering Sunday
Tie, N. The bathing women
Van der Vliet Oloomi, A. Call me Zebra
Vida, V. Let the Northern Lights erase your name
Warren, R. Band of angels
Williams, L. Supper club
Willig, L. The Ashford affair
Woolf, V. The voyage out

SELF-DOUBT
Adelman, M. Piece of mind
Gibson, C. Beyond the point
Leine, K. The prophets of Eternal Fjord
Lombardo, C. The most fun we ever had
Muller, M. Vanishing point
O'Nan, S. Henry, himself
Reid, K. Such a fun age

SELF-DOUBT IN MEN

Mankell, H. The dogs of Riga

SELF-DOUBT IN WOMEN
Ervin, K. Mina's joint

SELF-ESTEEM
Bellow, S. Seize the day
Bender, K. Refund
Bryant, N. Madam, may I
Cline, E. The girls
Naylor, G. The men of Brewster Place

SELF-ESTEEM IN BOYS
Fuqua, J. Gone and back again
Mailer, N. The castle in the forest

SELF-ESTEEM IN GIRLS
Morrison, T. The bluest eye

SELF-ESTEEM IN WOMEN
Awad, M. 13 ways of looking at a fat girl
Butler, H. The new me
Oates, J. Blonde
Styles, T. Black and ugly
Valdes, A. Dirty Girls on top
Walker, S. Dietland
Weiner, J. Mrs. Everything

SELF-EVALUATION
Kelton, E. Badger boy

SELF-EVALUATION IN MEN
Auster, P. The Brooklyn follies

SELF-FULFILLMENT
Cocks, H. The royal we
Coe, J. The terrible privacy of Maxwell Sim
Coupland, D. Eleanor Rigby
Currie, R. Everything matters!
De Kretser, M. The life to come
Dyer, G. Jeff in Venice, death in Varanasi
Forna, A. Happiness
Franzen, J. Freedom
Freeman, A. The fair fight
Hesse, H. Siddhartha
Hill, N. The nix
Hooper, E. Etta and Otto and Russell and James
Kenney, J. Talk to me
Kerangal, M. The cook
Kosinski, J. The devil tree
Lawrence, D. The rainbow
Lipman, E. The pursuit of Alice Thrift
Macomber, D. If not for you
Moore, E. The Supremes sing the happy heartache blues
Moore, M. The islanders
Moriarty, J. Gravity is the thing
Moyes, J. The peacock emporium
Nadzam, B. Lamb
Nguyen, V. The refugees
Nicholls, O. Love, unscripted
Nissenson, H. The pilgrim
Packer, A. The dive from Clausen's pier
Phillips, S. Call me irresistible
Pomerantz, S. Rich boy
Quindlen, A. Miller's Valley

Rachman, T. The Italian teacher
Roy, A. The ministry of utmost happiness
Rubart, J. The long journey to Jake Palmer
Schwarz, C. All is vanity
Sears, M. Black Fridays
Smith, G. The maze at Windermere
Tyler, A. Breathing lessons
Wouk, H. Marjorie Morningstar

SELF-FULFILLMENT -- RELIGIOUS ASPECTS
Reimringer, J. Vestments

SELF-FULFILLMENT IN AFRICAN AMERICAN WOMEN
Hurston, Z. Their eyes were watching God

SELF-FULFILLMENT IN MEN
Bolano, R. The savage detectives
Conrad, J. Lord Jim
Evison, J. Lawn boy
George, N. The little Paris bookshop
Joyce, J. A portrait of the artist as a young man
Kerouac, J. On the road
McGuane, T. Gallatin Canyon
Pamuk, O. A strangeness in my mind
Potok, C. My name is Asher Lev
Roth, P. Exit ghost
Roth, P. Indignation
Toole, J. A confederacy of dunces

SELF-FULFILLMENT IN MIDDLE-AGED WOMEN
Trollope, J. Second honeymoon

SELF-FULFILLMENT IN TEENAGE BOYS
Ford, R. Canada

SELF-FULFILLMENT IN TEENAGE GIRLS
Gibbons, K. The life all around me by Ellen Foster

SELF-FULFILLMENT IN WOMEN
Adelman, M. Piece of mind
Audur A. Olafsdottir, 1. Butterflies in November
Backman, F. Britt-Marie was here
Bandele, A. Daughter
Bauer, A. The forever marriage
Benton, J. Lilli de Jong
Berg, E. The confession club
Buntin, J. Marlena
Butland, S. The lost for words bookshop
Bynum, S. Ms. Hempel chronicles
Castro, J. Hell or high water
Clark, G. The bucket list
Colin, E. The memory thief
Colombani, L. The braid
Colwin, L. Goodbye without leaving
Danler, S. Sweetbitter
Dennis-Benn, N. Here comes the sun
Dicks, M. The perfect comeback of Caroline Jacobs
Eliot, G. The mill on the Floss
Ervin, K. Mina's joint
Essbaum, J. Hausfrau
Evanovich, S. Under the table
Ferrante, E. Those who leave and those who stay
Fitten, M. Elza's kitchen

Lanagan, M. The brides of Rollrock Island

The **sellout** Beatty, P.

SEMANTICS (PHILOSOPHY)

Gao, X. Soul mountain

SEMERKET

Geagley, B. Year of the hyenas

Semerket mysteries [series] Geagley, B.

Semiosis Burke, S.

Semiosis duology [series] Burke, S.

SEMIOTICS

Eugenides, J. The marriage plot

Semper Fidelis Downie, R.

The **senator's** wife Miller, S.

SENATORIAL CANDIDATES

Stabenow, D. The singing of the dead

Send down the rain Martin, C.

SENECA INDIANS

Perry, T. Vanishing act

SENECA WOMEN

Perry, T. Vanishing act

SENEGALESE WOMEN IN FRANCE

NDiaye, M. Three strong women

SENIOR AUTHORS

Krauss, N. The history of love

SENIOR COUPLES

Hooper, E. Etta and Otto and Russell and James

MacLaverty, B. Midwinter break

Scott, P. Staying on

SENIOR MEN

Albom, M. The five people you meet in heaven

Albom, M. The next person you meet in Heaven

Auster, P. The book of illusions

Auster, P. Travels in the scriptorium

Backman, F. A man called Ove

Bailey, P. Uncle Rudolf

Balasubramanyam, R. Professor Chandra follows his bliss

Banville, J. Ancient light

Barker, P. Another world

Begley, L. About Schmidt

Bellow, S. Mr. Sammler's planet

Berg, E. The story of Arthur Truluv

Bowman, C. Horace Winter says goodbye

Burns, O. Cold Sassy tree

Cartwright, J. To heaven by water

Christie, A. The A B C murders

Christie, A. Curtain

Christie, A. The hollow

Christie, A. Mrs. McGinty's dead

Christie, A. The murder of Roger Ackroyd

Christie, A. Murder on the Orient Express

Cleave, P. Trust no one

Coetzee, J. Slow man

Coover, R. Pinocchio in Venice

Cotterill, C. The coroner's lunch

Cotterill, C. Disco for the departed

Couto, M. Sleepwalking land

Cunningham, M. Specimen days

Donoghue, E. Akin

Drury, T. The driftless area

Dunne, D. Too much money

Egan, J. A visit from the Goon Squad

Foer, J. Extremely loud and incredibly close

Friedman, D. Don't ever get old

Friedman, D. Running out of road

Frost, K. The reluctant fortune-teller

Fuentes, C. The death of Artemio Cruz

Gaines, E. A gathering of old men

Garcia Marquez, G. The autumn of the patriarch

Garcia, C. King of Cuba

Gilbert, D. & sons

Glass, J. The widower's tale

Goddard, R. Never go back

Grant, H. The vanishing of Katharina Linden

Greene, G. The last word and other stories

Griffin, A. When all is said

Groen, H. On the bright side

Hubbard, L. The talented Ribkins

Ishiguro, K. An artist of the floating world

Jonasson, J. The accidental further adventures of the hundred-year-old man

Kawabata, Y. The sound of the mountain

Koryta, M. So cold the river

Krauss, N. Forest Dark

Lansdale, J. A fine dark line

Leonard, E. Mr. Paradise

Ludlum, R. The Sigma protocol

MacDonald, J. The scarlet ruse

Makine, A. The life of an unknown man

Mann, T. Death in Venice and seven other stories

McCarry, C. Old boys

McDermott, A. Child of my heart

McGuane, T. Gallatin Canyon

McMurtry, L. Rhino ranch

Mosley, W. The last days of Ptolemy Grey

Murakami, H. Kafka on the shore

Murdoch, I. The sea, the sea

O'Nan, S. Henry, himself

Oe, K. Death by water

Osborne, L. Only to sleep

Oz, A. Judas

Petterson, P. Out stealing horses

Picoult, J. Vanishing acts

Rayfiel, T. In pinelight

Ripley, M. Mr. Campion's war

Robinson, M. Gilead

Roth, H. A diving rock on the Hudson

Roth, H. From bondage

Roth, H. Requiem for Harlem

Roth, H. A star shines over Mt. Morris Park

Roth, P. Everyman

Russo, R. Bridge of sighs

Saramago, J. The cave

Savage, S. The way of the dog

Scalzi, J. Old man's war

Schlink, B. Self's deception
Schlink, B. Self's murder
Schlink, B. Self's punishment
Smith, A. Autumn
Trollope, J. The men and the girls
Tyler, A. Noah's compass
Updike, J. My father's tears and other stories
Vann, D. Aquarium
Vargas Llosa, M. The discreet hero
Wheeler, R. North star
Wiesel, E. A mad desire to dance
Wolfe, T. A man in full

SENIOR MEN -- AUSTRIA
Bernhard, T. Frost

SENIOR MEN -- BERLIN, GERMANY
Grass, G. Too far afield

SENIOR MEN -- CRETE
Kazantzakis, N. Zorba the Greek

SENIOR MEN -- CUBA
Hemingway, E. The old man and the sea

SENIOR MEN -- DEATH
Michaels, A. Fugitive pieces

SENIOR MEN -- FAMILY RELATIONSHIPS
Doig, I. Mountain time
Harding, P. Tinkers

SENIOR MEN -- FRIENDSHIP
Swift, G. Last orders

SENIOR MEN -- IRELAND
Joyce, J. Finnegans wake

SENIOR MEN -- ISRAEL
Oz, A. The same sea

SENIOR MEN -- JAPAN
Mishima, Y. The decay of the angel
Mishima, Y. The temple of dawn

SENIOR MEN -- SEXUALITY
Garcia Marquez, G. Memories of my melancholy whores
Roth, P. The dying animal
Roth, P. Exit ghost
Roth, P. Sabbath's theater

SENIOR MEN -- SOUTHERN STATES
Welty, E. The ponder heart

SENIOR MURDER VICTIMS
Sandford, J. Invisible prey
Stanley, M. Dying to live

SENIOR NUNS
DeLillo, D. Underworld

SENIOR ROMANCE
Sparks, N. The notebook

SENIOR WOMEN
Alameddine, R. An unnecessary woman
Allende, I. The Japanese lover
Backman, F. Britt-Marie was here
Barry, S. The secret scripture
Berg, E. Night of miracles
Brett, S. Mrs Pargeter's principle
Brown, R. Six of one
Cannon, J. Three things about Elsie

Christie, A. The body in the library
Christie, A. The murder at the vicarage
Christie, A. A murder is announced
Christie, A. Three blind mice, and other stories
Coetzee, J. Age of Iron
Dean, D. The madonnas of Leningrad
Deveraux, J. A willing murder
Dickens, C. Great expectations
Drabble, M. The dark flood rises
Drndic, D. Trieste
Evans, H. A place for us
Evison, J. This is your life, Harriet Chance!
Flagg, F. Fried green tomatoes at the Whistle Stop Cafe
Friedland, E. The floating Feldmans
Frost, K. The reluctant fortune-teller
Gaiman, N. The ocean at the end of the lane
Garcia-Roza, L. Alone in the crowd
Gessen, K. A terrible country
Giordano, M. Auntie Poldi and the Vineyards of Etna
Gurganus, A. Oldest living Confederate widow tells all
Harkaway, N. Angelmaker
Hart, C. Resort to murder
Haslett, A. Union Atlantic
Healey, E. Elizabeth is missing
Heller, P. Celine
Heller, Z. What was she thinking?
Hollis, L. Poppy Harmon investigates
Horn, D. Eternal life
Jewett, S. The country of the pointed firs and other stories
Joss, M. Half broken things
Kline, C. Orphan train
LaPlante, A. Turn of mind
Lively, P. How it all began
McFarlane, F. The night guest
McKevett, G. Murder in the corn maze
McMillan, T. It's not all downhill from here
McMurtry, L. The evening star
Minot, S. Evening
Morton, B. Florence Gordon
Morton, K. The distant hours
Moshfegh, O. Death in her hands
Munro, A. Runaway
Nabb, M. Some bitter taste
O'Farrell, M. The vanishing act of Esme Lennox
O'Nan, S. Emily, alone
Penny, L. How the light gets in
Phillips, C. A distant shore
Rawles, N. My Jim
Rinehart, M. Miss Pinkerton
Rooney, K. Lillian Boxfish takes a walk
Ross, A. Miss Julia delivers the goods
Ross, A. Miss Julia throws a wedding
Sackville-West, V. All passion spent
Sandford, J. Invisible prey
Sarton, M. A reckoning
Sebold, A. The almost moon
Shipman, V. The heirloom garden

Stradal, J. The lager queen of Minnesota
Strout, E. Olive, again
Tyler, A. Clock dance
Umrigar, T. The secrets between us
Updike, J. Seek my face
Walton, J. My real children
Willig, L. The Ashford affair
Winer, J. Her kind of case

SENIOR WOMEN -- FRIENDSHIP

Gurganus, A. Oldest living Confederate widow tells all
Tatlock, A. Promises to keep

SENIOR WOMEN -- NORTH CAROLINA

Edgerton, C. Walking across Egypt

SENIOR WOMEN -- PSYCHOLOGY

Lessing, D. Love, again

SENIOR WOMEN -- SEXUALITY

Lessing, D. Love, again

SENIOR WOMEN AUTHORS

Lively, P. Moon tiger

SENIORS

Atwood, M. Stone mattress
Backman, F. A man called Ove
Bannalec, J. Death in Brittany
Butler, R. Perfume River
Butler, S. Cygnet
Cotterill, C. Don't eat me
Cotterill, C. Slash and burn
Drabble, M. The dark flood rises
Evison, J. This is your life, Harriet Chance!
Gardam, J. Old Filth
Groen, H. On the bright side
Helprin, M. Paris in the present tense
Indriðason, A. Strange shores
Jance, J. Birds of prey
Jonasson, J. The accidental further adventures of the hundred-year-old man
King, S. Doctor Sleep
LaPlante, A. Turn of mind
Moore, E. The Supremes sing the happy heartache blues
Mosley, W. The last days of Ptolemy Grey
Neuhaus, N. The ice queen
Parker, R. Potshot
Perry, T. The old man
Pronzini, B. Nightcrawlers
Shames, T. A risky undertaking for Loretta Singletary
Simonson, H. Major Pettigrew's last stand
Spark, M. Memento mori
Straub, P. Ghost story
Tanen, S. There's a word for that
Tyler, A. A spool of blue thread
Youngson, A. Meet me at the museum

SENIORS -- CARE

Gessen, K. A terrible country

SENIORS -- IDENTITY

Harding, P. Tinkers

SENIORS -- SEXUALITY

McMurtry, L. The evening star

SENSATIONALISM IN JOURNALISM

Rose, J. The blackest bird

Sense and sensibility Austen, J.

The **sense** of an ending Barnes, J.

SENSES AND SENSATION

Bauermeister, E. The scent keeper
Harris, S. The color of Bee Larkham's murder
Tan, A. The hundred secret senses
Tokarczuk, O. Flights

SENSITIVITY (PERSONAL QUALITY)

Barker, N. Darkmans

SENSITIVITY IN MEN

Barker, N. Darkmans

SENSITIVITY IN TEENAGERS

Salinger, J. The catcher in the rye

SENSORY DEPRIVATION

Malerman, J. Bird box

The **sentence** is death Horowitz, A.

Sentimental education Flaubert, G.

The **sentinels** of Andersonville Groot, T.

SEOUL, KOREA

Lee, J. The starlet and the spy
Limon, M. Mr. Kill
Wuertz, Y. Everything belongs to us

A **separate** peace Knowles, J.

SEPARATED BROTHERS

Vanderhaeghe, G. The last crossing

SEPARATED COUPLES

Benedetti, M. Springtime in a broken mirror
DeLillo, D. Falling man
Guhrke, L. How to lose a duke in ten days
James, E. The ugly duchess
Keane, M. Fever
Mackall, D. With love, wherever you are
McPherson, C. Quiet neighbors
Moses, K. Wintering
O'Neill, H. The Lonely Hearts Hotel
Pitts, L. Freeman
Shupe, J. The courtesan duchess
Spencer-Fleming, J. I shall not want

SEPARATED FRIENDS, RELATIVES, ETC

Abraham, T. Black Sunday
Barton, F. The suspect
Booth, C. Bronxwood
Bulgakov, M. The master and Margarita
Carey, P. The chemistry of tears
Coover, R. Huck out west
Fowler, E. The road to Cardinal Valley
Gyasi, Y. Homegoing
Hage, R. De Niro's game
Hamilton, J. A map of the world
Jensen, N. The sisters
Jin, H. War trash
Krueger, W. This tender land
Morrison, T. Sula
Nichols, P. The rocks
O'Brien, E. Time and tide

Daugherty, C. The echo killing

Deaver, J. The coffin dancer

Deaver, J. The never game

Deaver, J. The stone monkey

Donati, S. Where the light enters

Ellory, R. The anniversary man

Fowler, C. Bryant & May

Franklin, A. Mistress of the art of death

Freeman, B. The night bird

Gardiner, M. The dark corners of the night

Gardiner, M. Into the black nowhere

Gardiner, M. Unsub

Gerritsen, T. I know a secret

Gerritsen, T. The surgeon

Grossman, P. Children of wrath

Guinn, M. The scribe

Hamilton, P. Great North Road

Hayder, M. Birdman

Hooper, K. Stealing shadows

Irwin, S. The broken ones

James, P. Devices and desires

Kava, A. Hotwire

Kellerman, J. Monster

Kepler, L. The rabbit hunter

Kepler, L. The sandman

Kepler, L. Stalker

Kerley, J. The death collectors

Kerr, P. Metropolis

Kienzle, W. The rosary murders

Lamberson, G. The frenzy way

Lemaitre, P. Irene

Lovesey, P. The house sitter

MacBride, S. Close to the bone

MacBride, S. Cold granite

MacBride, S. Flesh house

MacNeal, S. The king's justice

Mayor, A. Red herring

Mehl, N. Mind games

Mukherjee, A. Smoke and ashes

Murphy, S. Cat pay the devil

Nesbo, J. The bat

Nesbo, J. The leopard

Nesbo, J. The snowman

Nesbo, J. The thirst

O'Connell, C. Find me

O'Malley, T. Serpents in the cold

Obregon, N. Blue light Yokohama

Parker, R. Stone cold

Pearl, M. The Dante chamber

Pearl, M. The Dante Club

Pelecanos, G. The night gardener

Perry, T. Pursuit

Perry, T. The boyfriend

Pressfield, S. 36 righteous men

Preston, D. Verses for the dead

Preston, D. City of endless night

Quartey, K. Children of the street

Rankin, I. Black and blue

Redondo, D. The invisible guardian

Reichs, K. Deja dead

Ripley, N. Find you in the dark

Rowland, L. The Ripper's shadow

Ryan, H. The other woman

Sanders, L. The first deadly sin

Sandford, J. Broken prey

Sandford, J. Buried prey

Sandford, J. Field of prey

Sandford, J. Rules of prey

Sandford, J. Silent prey

Sandford, J. Winter prey

Shields, K. The truth of all things

Sjowall, M. The man on the balcony

Slaughter, K. Cop Town

Smith, T. Child 44

Spann, S. Trial on Mount Koya

Spencer, S. The ring of death

Stanley, M. Deadly harvest

Stroud, C. The shimmer

Sveistrup, S. The chestnut man

Swanson, P. Eight perfect murders

Williams, A. The stranger you seek

Zimmerman, J. The orphanmaster

SERIAL MURDER INVESTIGATION -- TOKYO, JAPAN

Peace, D. Tokyo year zero

SERIAL MURDERERS

Abu-Jaber, D. Origin

Bauer, B. The beautiful dead

Black, S. The killing lessons

Black, S. Lovemurder

Box, C. Paradise Valley

Brown, S. Outfox

Carr, C. The alienist

Chizmar, R. A long December

Cleave, P. The cleaner

Cleave, P. Joe Victim

Cole, D. Ragdoll

Connelly, M. Echo Park

Cooper, E. Buried

Craddock, C. A labyrinth of scions and sorcery

DeSilva, B. Providence rag

Deaver, J. The coffin dancer

Deaver, J. The never game

Deaver, J. The stone monkey

Dodd, C. Strangers she knows

Donati, S. Where the light enters

Downing, S. My lovely wife

Ellison, J. Good girls lie

Ellory, R. The anniversary man

Faye, L. The gods of Gotham

Fielding, J. All the wrong places

Franklin, A. Mistress of the art of death

Gallagher, S. The kingdom of bones

Gardiner, M. The dark corners of the night

Gardiner, M. Into the black nowhere

SERIAL MURDERERS -- GREAT BRITAIN
SERIAL MURDERERS -- MONTREAL, QUEBEC
SERIAL MURDERERS -- SAN FRANCISCO, CALIFOR-NIA
SERIAL MURDERERS -- SCOTLAND
SERIAL MURDERERS -- TWIN CITIES METROPOLI-TAN AREA
SERIAL MURDERERS -- WISCONSIN
SERIAL MURDERS

Braun, L. The cat who went underground
Callihan, K. Firelight
Carver, T. The surrogate
Chaon, D. Ill will
Child, L. One shot
Christie, A. The A B C murders
Cleave, P. The cleaner
Cohen, T. They all fall down
Connolly, J. A book of bones
Cooper, E. Caged
Cornwell, P. Postmortem
Cussler, C. The cutthroat
Dahl, A. Bad Blood
Dahl, A. Misterioso
de Beauvoir, J. Asylum
De Giovanni, M. The crocodile
Dodd, C. The woman who couldn't scream
Estleman, L. Gas City
Faye, L. Jane Steele
Fowler, C. Bryant & May
Franklin, A. Mistress of the art of death
Freeman, B. The night bird
Gardner, L. Alone
Gerritsen, T. The apprentice
Gerritsen, T. The bone garden
Gerritsen, T. The surgeon
Greaves, C. Hard twisted
Gruber, M. Night of the jaguar
Hand, E. Available dark
Harris, T. Red dragon
Harris, T. The silence of the lambs
Hart, E. Lake of sorrows
Hayder, M. Birdman
Hewson, D. A season for the dead
Iles, G. Mortal fear
Jakeman, J. In the kingdom of mists
Katzenbach, J. Just cause
Kellerman, J. Monster
Kellerman, J. Therapy
Kelly, J. The fire baby
Kepler, L. The sandman
Kepler, L. Stalker
Kerley, J. The death collectors
Kienzle, W. The rosary murders
Koontz, D. Velocity
Lamberson, G. The frenzy way
Lansdale, J. The bottoms
Lansdale, J. Devil red
Lemaitre, P. Irene
Lovesey, P. The house sitter
Ludlum, R. The Sigma protocol
MacBride, S. Cold granite
MacBride, S. Flesh house
MacNeal, S. The king's justice
Mankell, H. One step behind
Margolin, P. Wild justice
Mark, D. The dark winter

Mark, D. Sorrow bound
Mayor, A. Red herring
McGarrity, M. Everyone dies
McMahon, J. The one I left behind
Mina, D. The long drop
Mosley, W. White butterfly
Muller, M. Point Deception
Murakami, R. In the miso soup , Ryu Murakami ; translated by Ralph McCarthy.
Nesbo, J. The snowman
Nesbo, J. The leopard
Nickson, C. At the dying of the year
Obregon, N. Blue light Yokohama
Owen, H. The bottom
Palmer, M. The last surgeon
Palmer, M. The society
Patterson, J. 1st to die
Pelecanos, G. The night gardener
Phillips, C. The Devlin diary
Preston, D. Verses for the dead
Rendell, R. Simisola
Rinehart, M. Miss Pinkerton
Robards, K. The last victim
Roberts, N. Shelter in place
Robinson, P. The first cut
Robotham, M. Close your eyes
Ryan, H. The other woman
Saintcrow, L. The Iron Wyrm Affair
Sanders, L. The first deadly sin
Sandford, J. Broken prey
Sandford, J. Buried prey
Sandford, J. Field of prey
Sandford, J. Heat lightning
Smith, M. She's not there
Solomita, S. A good day to die
St. James, S. The Sun Down motel
Stanley, M. Deadly harvest
Straub, P. Lost boy lost girl
Suskind, P. Perfume
Tallis, F. Vienna blood

SERIAL MURDERS -- MEXICO
Gaspar de Alba, A. Desert blood
SERIAL MURDERS -- MINNEAPOLIS, MINNESOTA
Sandford, J. Certain prey
Sandford, J. Chosen prey
SERIAL MURDERS -- MINNESOTA
Tracy, P. Monkeewrench
SERIAL MURDERS -- SAUDI ARABIA
Ferraris, Z. Kingdom of strangers
SERIAL MURDERS -- TOKYO, JAPAN
Peace, D. Tokyo year zero
SERIAL MURDERS -- WASHINGTON, D.C.
Ellory, R. A simple act of violence
SERIAL MURDERS -- WISCONSIN
Sidor, S. Skin River
SERIAL RAPE
Fairstein, L. Entombed

Whitehead, C. The Nickel boys

SEX CUSTOMS
Greenwell, G. Cleanness
MacLean, S. One good earl deserves a lover
Maugham, W. Cakes and ale
Maupin, A. Tales of the city
Miller, H. Tropic of Cancer
Miller, H. Tropic of Capricorn

SEX DISCRIMINATION
Atwood, M. The handmaid's tale
Atwood, M. The testaments
Brown, R. Rubyfruit jungle
Elison, M. The book of Etta
Elison, M. The book of Flora
Elison, M. The book of the unnamed midwife

SEX EDUCATION FOR TEENAGERS
Perrotta, T. The abstinence teacher

SEX GAMES
O'Keefe, M. Everything I left unsaid

SEX IN ART
Dean, M. I, Hogarth

SEX INDUSTRY AND TRADE
Borjlind, C. Spring tide
Faust, C. Choke hold
Faust, C. Money shot
Holmes, S. Bad girlz
Larsson, S. The girl who played with fire
Lewis, T. GBH
Murakami, R. In the miso soup , Ryu Murakami ; translated
  by Ralph McCarthy.

SEX OFFENDERS
Banks, R. Lost memory of skin
Byatt, A. The children's book
Harrison, J. The great leader
Pronzini, B. The violated
Sandford, J. Broken prey

SEX SCANDALS
Heller, Z. What was she thinking?
Jhabvala, R. Heat and dust
McEwan, I. Amsterdam

SEX SCANDALS -- HISTORY
Shreve, A. Fortune's rocks

SEX TOURISM
Murakami, R. In the miso soup , Ryu Murakami ; translated
  by Ralph McCarthy.
Sex wars Piercy, M.

SEX WORKERS
Greenwell, G. What belongs to you
Nadel, B. The Ottoman cage
Shafak, E. 10 minutes 38 seconds in this strange world

SEX-ORIENTED BUSINESSES
Lee, D. Country of origin

SEXAGENARIANS
Roth, P. Sabbath's theater

SEXAGENARIANS -- TEXAS
McMurtry, L. Rhino ranch

SEXISM
Alexander, T. A note yet unsung
Ashe, K. The prince
Atwood, M. The handmaid's tale
Barnett, L. Jam on the Vine
Brown, R. Rubyfruit jungle
Cho, Z. Sorcerer to the crown
Collins, K. Notes from a black woman's diary
Darznik, J. Song of a captive bird
Davis, F. The masterpiece
Ellis, B. The vanished bride
Fowler, K. Sarah Canary
French, M. The women's room
Gibson, C. Beyond the point
Gilman, C. Herland
Grass, G. The flounder
Hunt, L. The evening road
Hurston, Z. Hitting a straight lick with a crooked stick
Jakeman, J. In the kingdom of mists
Kowal, M. The calculating stars
Kowal, M. The fated sky
Le Guin, U. Four ways to forgiveness
Lippman, L. Lady in the lake
Lutz, L. The swallows
McCall Smith, A. The Kalahari typing school for men
Melamed, J. Gather the daughters
Okorafor, N. Who fears death
Pochoda, I. These women
Shields, S. The Cassandra
Stewart, A. Lady cop makes trouble
Stewart, A. Miss Kopp's midnight confessions
Stratford, S. Red letter days
Wood, T. The engineer's wife
Yellin, J. Savage news
Zumas, L. Red clocks

SEXISM IN EMPLOYMENT
Baker, C. Whisper network
Center, K. Things you save in a fire
Gentry, A. Last woman standing
Rockaway, K. How to hack a heartbreak
Schofield, D. Time of departure

SEXISM IN POLITICS AND GOVERNMENT
Weber, D. The honor of the queen

SEXISM IN THE CATHOLIC CHURCH
Alexander, V. The Magdalen girls

SEXISM IN UNIVERSITIES AND COLLEGES
French, M. The women's room

SEXPLOITATION
Pelevin, V. The hall of singing caryatids

SEXUAL ATTRACTION
Afrika, T. Bitter Eden
Archer, Z. Dangerous seduction
Ashe, K. The duke
Ashe, K. The prince
Bailey, T. Fix her up
Bell, L. For the duke's eyes only
Bell, L. How the duke was won
Bell, L. One fine duke

Spencer, M. Barbarous
Spencer, M. Dangerous
Spencer, M. Scandalous
Weatherspoon, R. Haven
Weatherspoon, R. Rafe
Weatherspoon, R. Xeni
Whelan, J. My Oxford year
Williams, S. Forbidden promises
Winfrey, K. Waiting for Tom Hanks
Woods, S. Stealth

SEXUAL CONSENT
Russell, K. My dark Vanessa

SEXUAL DOMINANCE AND SUBMISSION
Bell, S. At his mercy
Bell, S. For his pleasure
Hall, A. For real
Weatherspoon, R. Haven

SEXUAL ETHICS
Garcia Marquez, G. Memories of my melancholy whores
Lawrence, D. Lady Chatterley's lover

SEXUAL ETHICS FOR TEENAGERS
Choi, S. Trust exercise

SEXUAL EXCITEMENT
Murray, V. Lust

SEXUAL FANTASIES
Baker, N. House of holes
Thomas, D. The white hotel

SEXUAL FREEDOM
Aslam, N. Maps for lost lovers
Heinlein, R. Stranger in a strange land
See, L. Peony in love

SEXUAL HARASSMENT
Baker, C. Whisper network
Bing, S. You look nice today
Campbell, B. Brothers and sisters
Connelly, M. The late show
Gentry, A. Last woman standing
Scottoline, L. Every fifteen minutes

SEXUAL HARASSMENT VICTIMS
Lutz, L. The swallows

SEXUAL MINORITY TEENAGERS
McGuire, S. Every heart a doorway

SEXUAL ORIENTATION
Baldwin, J. Giovanni's room

SEXUAL REVOLUTION
Amis, M. The pregnant widow

SEXUAL SLAVERY
Akpan, U. Say you're one of them
Hill Gumbao, T. The summer of dead toys
Larsson, S. The girl who played with fire
Min, A. Empress Orchid
Rao, S. Girls burn brighter

SEXUAL VIOLENCE
Abraham, T. Black Sunday
Beams, C. The illness lesson
Bond, C. Ruby
Dare, A. The girl with the louding voice

Deon, N. Grace
DuPree, K. Shattered
Hegi, U. Stones from the river
Rendell, R. Simisola
Woodson, J. Another Brooklyn

SEXUAL VIOLENCE VICTIMS
Clark, M. Kiss the girls and make them cry
Eisler, B. All the devils
Eisler, B. Livia Lone
Eisler, B. The night trade
Shafak, E. 10 minutes 38 seconds in this strange world
Thomas, B. A good enough mother

SEXUALITY
Abbott, S. The future of love
Aciman, A. Find me
Adams, L. The bromance book club
Adichie, C. Half of a yellow sun
Amis, M. Lionel Asbo
Aswani, A. Chicago
Bagshawe, T. Adored
Baker, N. House of holes
Baldwin, J. Another country
Baldwin, J. Giovanni's room
Ballard, J. The kindness of women
Barth, J. The floating opera
Barth, J. The sot-weed factor
Bear, E. Steles of the sky
Bell, M. The color of night
Bellow, S. More die of heartbreak
Bhuvaneswar, C. White dancing elephants
Blau, J. The Wonder Bread summer
Bond, C. Ruby
Bram, C. Lives of the circus animals
Broder, M. The pisces
Burton, J. The miniaturist
Canin, E. A doubter's almanac
Capri, N. The pussy trap
Carlyle, L. Never lie to a lady
Carter, A. Burning your boats
Chase, L. Your scandalous ways
Cheever, J. Falconer
Cheever, J. The Wapshot chronicle
Choi, S. My education
Choi, S. Trust exercise
Clark, W. Justify my thug
Clark, W. Honor thy thug
Clark, W. Payback is a mutha
Clark, W. Thugs and the women who love them
Coetzee, J. Disgrace
Dean, M. I, Hogarth
Dermansky, M. Very nice
Dickey, E. The blackbirds
Dickey, E. The business of lovers
Didion, J. Play it as it lays
Doctorow, E. Ragtime
Dolan-Leach, C. We went to the woods
Doyle, R. Threshold

Waters, S. The paying guests
Waters, S. Tipping the velvet
Watkins, J. Secrets of a side bitch
Watkins, J. Secrets of a side bitch 2
Wayne, T. Loner
Weatherspoon, R. Haven
Welsh, I. Dead men's trousers
Welsh, I. Porno
Welsh, I. Skagboys
Welsh, I. Trainspotting
White, E. Jack Holmes and his friend
Williams, K. Dirty to the grave
Winterson, J. Frankissstein
Wolfe, T. I am Charlotte Simmons
Woods, S. New York dead
Zamyatin, Y. We
Zane, 1. Addicted

SEXUALITY -- SPIRITUAL ASPECTS
Momaday, N. The ancient child

SEXUALITY AND POWER (SOCIAL SCIENCES)
Gardner, L. Alone

SEXUALLY ABUSED BOYS
Sapphire, 1. The kid
Sargent, C. Museum of human beings

SEXUALLY ABUSED CHILDREN
Allison, D. Bastard out of Carolina
Draper, S. Forged by fire
Rosen, L. The Kortelisy escape

SEXUALLY ABUSED TEENAGERS
K'wan Street dreams
Oates, J. Foxfire

SEXUALLY ABUSED WOMEN
DuPree, K. Shattered
Fairstein, L. Blood oath
Perkins-Valdez, D. Wench
Pronzini, B. Blue lonesome

SEXUALLY TRANSMITTED DISEASES
Burns, C. Black hole

SEXUALLY TRANSMITTED DISEASES -- GOVERN- MENT POLICY
Lowenthal, M. Charity girl

Sexy Lexy Moore, K.
Seymour of Special Branch [series] Pearce, M.

SEYMOUR, ROBERT, 1798-1836
Jarvis, S. Death and Mr. Pickwick

The **shack** Young, W.
Shades of grey Fforde, J.
Shadow and ice Showalter, G.
The **shadow** catcher Wiggins, M.
Shadow child Rizzuto, R.
Shadow country Matthiessen, P.
The **shadow** district Arnaldur Indridason, 1.
Shadow in Serenity Blackstock, T.
A **shadow** intelligence Harris, O.
The **shadow** king Mengiste, M.
The **shadow** land Kostova, E.
Shadow of freedom Weber, D.

Shadow of night Harkness, D.
The **shadow** of the torturer Wolfe, G.
The **shadow** of the wind Ruiz Zafon, C.
Shadow rider Feehan, C.
Shadow riders novels [series] Feehan, C.
Shadow tag Erdrich, L.
Shadow tyrants Cussler, C.
The **shadow** year Ford, J.

SHADOWS
North, C. The pursuit of William Abbey
Shepherd, P. The book of M
The **shadows** in the street Hill, S.
Shadows on the lake Cocco, G.

SHAKERS
Urquhart, R. The visionist

SHAKESPEARE, JOHN, DIED 1601
Clements, R. Martyr
Clements, R. Revenger

SHAKESPEARE, WILLIAM, 1564-1616
Bear, E. Ink and steel
Brandreth, B. The assassin of Verona
Brandreth, B. The spy of Venice
Gruber, M. The book of air and shadows
Morgan, J. The secret life of William Shakespeare
Rutherfurd, E. London

SHAKESPEARE, WILLIAM, 1564-1616 AUTHORSHIP
Lovett, C. The bookman's tale
Phillips, A. The tragedy of Arthur

Shalimar the Clown Rushdie, S.
Shall we not revenge Pirrone, D.
The **shallows** Goldman, M.

SHAMANISM
Gruber, M. Night of the jaguar

SHAMANS
Brooks, G. Caleb's crossing
Gear, K. People of the mist
Gruber, M. Night of the jaguar
Kuang, R. The dragon republic
Kuang, R. The poppy war
McCall Smith, A. The No. 1 Ladies' Detective Agency
Meek, J. The people's act of love
Norton, A. The elvenbane
Roanhorse, R. Trail of lightning
Stanley, M. Dying to live

Shamble & Die Investigations [series] Anderson, K.
The **shambling** guide to New York City Lafferty, M.
Shambling Guides [series] Lafferty, M.

SHAME
Bear, E. All the windwracked stars
Dubus, A. Dirty love
Giordano, P. The solitude of prime numbers
Goenawan, C. The perfect world of Miwako Sumida
Goldbloom, G. On division
Keneally, T. Shame and the captives
McEwan, I. Atonement
Orner, P. Love and shame and love
Putney, M. The marriage spell

Winterson, J. Frankissstein

SHELLEY, PERCY BYSSHE, 1792-1822

Shepherd, L. A fatal likeness

The **shelter** cycle Rock, P.

Shelter in place Roberts, N.

Shelter of the most high Cossette, C.

The **sheltering** sky Bowles, P.

SHELTERS FOR THE HOMELESS

Bohjalian, C. The double bind

The **shepherd's** hut Winton, T.

SHEPHERDS

Ahmad, J. The wandering falcon

Hardy, T. Far from the madding crowd

Hurley, A. Devil's Day

Jiang, R. Wolf totem

Johnson, C. Land of wolves

SHEPPARD, JACK, 1702-1724

Rosenberg, J. Confessions of the fox

SHEPPERTON, LONDON, ENGLAND

Ballard, J. The kindness of women

SHERIFFS

Armstrong, K. Alone in the wild

Armstrong, K. Watcher in the woods

Atkins, A. The broken places

Atkins, A. The fallen

Atkins, A. The innocents

Atkins, A. The forsaken

Atkins, A. The lost ones

Atkins, A. The shameless

Atkins, A. The sinners

Benchley, P. Jaws

Bowen, P. Badlands

Dodd, C. The woman who couldn't scream

Freeman, C. All that I have

Hulse, S. Eden mine

Johnson, C. Another man's moccasins

Johnson, C. Dark horse

Johnson, C. Death without company

Johnson, C. Hell is empty

Johnson, C. Land of wolves

Johnson, C. Spirit of steamboat

Johnston, T. The current

Jones, E. The known world

Koryta, M. The ridge

Laukkanen, O. Deception Cove

Long, J. Wild at Whiskey Creek

McCarthy, C. No country for old men

McCrumb, S. She walks these hills

Muller, M. Point Deception

Overholser, W. Law at Angel's Landing

Panowich, B. Bull Mountain

Panowich, B. Like lions

Parshall, S. Bleeding through

Parshall, S. Poisoned ground

Peterson, J. Early's fall

Ramsay, F. Countdown

Ramsay, F. Stranger room

Rash, R. Above the waterfall

Rickards, J. Winter's end

Ross, A. Miss Julia throws a wedding

Sharfeddin, H. Mineral spirits

Sternbergh, A. The blinds

Stewart, A. Girl waits with gun

Stewart, A. Lady cop makes trouble

Stewart, A. Miss Kopp's midnight confessions

SHERIFFS -- APPALACHIAN REGION

McCrumb, S. If ever I return, pretty Peggy-O

SHERIFFS -- TENNESSEE

McCrumb, S. The ballad of Frankie Silver

SHERIFFS -- TEXAS

Thompson, J. The killer inside me

SHERIFFS -- VIRGINIA

Ramsay, F. Scone Island

Sherlock Holmes mysteries [series] Doyle, A.

Sherlock Holmes novels (Anthony Horowitz) [series]

Horowitz, A.

The **Sherlockian** Moore, G.

SHERMAN'S MARCH THROUGH THE CAROLINAS

Doctorow, E. The march

SHERMAN'S MARCH TO THE SEA

Brown, T. Fallen land

Doctorow, E. The march

Jakes, J. Savannah, or, A gift for Mr. Lincoln

SHERMAN, WILLIAM TECUMSEH, 1820-1891

Doctorow, E. The march

Jakes, J. Savannah, or, A gift for Mr. Lincoln

SHETLAND ISLANDS

Cleeves, A. Thin air

Cleeves, A. Wild fire

SHETLAND ISLANDS -- SOCIAL LIFE AND CUSTOMS

Cleeves, A. Raven black

Shetland mysteries [series] Cleeves, A.

SHIAH ISLAM

Black, C. Murder in the rue de Paradis

Shieldbreaker's story Saberhagen, F.

The **shifting** tide Perry, A.

Shiloh and other stories Mason, B.

The **shimmer** Stroud, C.

Shine shine shine Netzer, L.

The **shining** King, S.

Shinobi mysteries [series] Spann, S.

SHIP CAPTAINS

Ashford, J. What the duke doesn't know

Bourne, J. My lord and spymaster

Bujold, L. Shards of honor

Bujold, L. The warrior's apprentice

Conrad, J. Heart of darkness

Cussler, C. Golden Buddha

Cussler, C. Sacred stone

Doyle, B. The plover

Forester, C. Admiral Hornblower in the West Indies

Forester, C. Commodore Hornblower

Forester, C. Hornblower and the Atropos

Forester, C. Hornblower and the Hotspur

Shooting at loons Maron, M.

The **shootist** Swarthout, G.

Shootist [series] Swarthout, G.

Shopgirl Martin, S.

SHOPKEEPERS

Higashino, K. The miracles of the Namiya General Store

Simonson, H. Major Pettigrew's last stand

SHOPLIFTING

Hallinan, T. Fields where they lay

SHOPPING MALLS

Ballard, J. Kingdom come

Hallinan, T. Fields where they lay

SHORT BOYS

Hoffman, A. Illumination night

Levine, J. Bingo's run

SHORT MEN

Bujold, L. The warrior's apprentice

SHORT PEOPLE

Lemaitre, P. Irene

SHORT STORIES

Aboulela, L. Elsewhere, home

Acampora, L. The wonder garden

Adams, A. The stories of Alice Adams

Adichie, C. The thing around your neck

Adjei-Brenyah, N. Friday black

Ahern, C. Roar

Akpan, U. Say you're one of them

Alarcon, D. The king is always above the people

Aleichem, S. Tevye the dairyman and the railroad stories

Alenyikov, M. Ivan and Misha

Alexie, S. Blasphemy

Allende, I. The stories of Eva Luna

Alomar, O. The teeth of the comb & other stories

Alvar, M. In the country

American fantastic tales

American West

Anaya, R. The man who could fly and other stories

Antopol, M. The UnAmericans

Archer, J. And thereby hangs a tale

Arimah, L. What it means when a man falls from the sky

Armfield, J. Salt slow

Asimov, I. I, robot

Atwood, M. Bluebeard's egg and other stories

Atwood, M. Moral disorder

Atwood, M. Stone mattress

Baca, J. The importance of a piece of paper

Balaskovits, A. Magic for unlucky girls

Baldwin, J. Going to meet the man

Ballard, J. The complete stories of J.G. Ballard.

Bambara, T. Gorilla, my love

Bandi, 1. The accusation

Barnhill, K. Dreadful young ladies and other stories

Barthelme, D. Sixty stories

Bausch, R. The stories of Richard Bausch

Baxter, C. There's something I want you to do

Bear, G. The collected stories of Greg Bear

Beattie, A. The state we're in

Beauvoir, S. The woman destroyed

Bender, K. Refund

Bergman, M. Almost famous women

Berlin, L. Evening in paradise

Berlin, L. A manual for cleaning women

Berry, W. That distant land

The best American mystery stories 2017

The best American mystery stories 2018

The best American mystery stories 2019

The best American mystery stories of the century

The best American noir of the century

The best American science fiction and fantasy 2019

The best American short stories 2019

The best of the best horror of the year

Beukes, L. Slipping

Bhuvaneswar, C. White dancing elephants

The big book of Sherlock Holmes stories

The big book of science fiction

Bolano, R. Last evenings on Earth

Bonnaffons, A. The wrong heaven

Borges, J. Collected fictions

Borges, J. Ficciones

Boyle, T. The relive box

Bradbury, R. Bradbury stories

Bradbury, R. The illustrated man

Bradbury, R. The Martian chronicles

Brand, M. The collected stories of Max Brand

Brand, M. Max Brand's best western stories

Brinkley, J. A lucky man

Broken stars

Brown, L. Tiny love

Buffett, J. A salty piece of land

Butler, O. Bloodchild

Butler, R. A good scent from a strange mountain

Campbell, B. American salvage

Capote, T. Breakfast at Tiffany's

Capote, T. The complete stories of Truman Capote

Capote, T. The grass harp

Carter, A. Burning your boats

Carver, R. What we talk about when we talk about love

A century of great Western stories

Chai, M. Useful phrases for immigrants

Chekhov, A. Early short stories, 1883-1888

Chekhov, A. Later short stories, 1888-1903

Chiang, T. Exhalation

Chiang, T. Stories of your life and others

Child, L. No middle name

Chizmar, R. A long December

Christie, A. Three blind mice, and other stories

Clark, M. Death wears a beauty mask and other stories

Clark, M. My gal Sunday

Clarke, A. The collected stories of Arthur C. Clarke

Clarke, B. The price of the haircut

Clarke, M. Foreign soil

Colette, 1. The collected stories of Colette

Collins, K. Notes from a black woman's diary

Collins, K. Whatever happened to interracial love?

Kipling, R. Collected stories
L'Amour, L. May there be a road
Latin@ rising
Lavery, D. The merry spinster
Lazarin, D. Back talk
Le Guin, U. The birthday of the world
Le Guin, U. Orsinian tales
Leonard, E. Charlie Martz and other stories
Leonard, E. The complete Western stories of Elmore Leonard.
Leonard, E. When the women come out to dance
Link, K. Magic for beginners
Lippman, L. Hardly knew her
The living dead
Lovecraft, H. Tales
Ma, J. Stick out your tongue
MacLaughlin, N. Wake, siren
Machado, C. Her body and other parties
Malamud, B. The complete stories
The mammoth book of steampunk
Mann, T. Death in Venice and seven other stories
Marra, A. The tsar of love and techno
Mason, B. Shiloh and other stories
Mason, B. Patchwork
MatchUp
Mayer, M. Aerialists
McBride, J. Five-carat soul
McCrumb, S. Foggy Mountain breakdown and other stories
McGuane, T. Gallatin Canyon
McGuane, T. Crow fair
McGuane, T. Cloudbursts
McHugh, M. After the apocalypse
Means, D. Instructions for a funeral
Mehta, R. Quarantine
Melville, H. The complete shorter fiction
More deadly than the male
Mosley, W. Six Easy pieces
Mueenuddin, D. In other rooms, other wonders
Munro, A. Open secrets
Munro, A. Selected stories
Munro, A. Hateship, friendship, courtship, loveship, marriage
Munro, A. Runaway
Munro, A. The view from Castle Rock
Munro, A. Too much happiness
Munro, A. Dear life
Munro, A. Family furnishings
Murakami, H. After the quake
Murakami, H. Blind willow, sleeping woman
Murakami, H. Men without women
Nabokov, V. The stories of Vladimir Nabokov
Narayan, R. Malgudi days
Narayan, R. Under the banyan tree and other stories
Nebula Awards showcase 2017
New Cthulhu
The new space opera
New suns

The new voices of fantasy
Ngugi wa Thiong'o Minutes of glory, and other stories
Nguyen, V. The refugees
Nightmares
The Norton book of science fiction
Not one of us
O'Brien, T. The things they carried
O'Connor, F. Collected works
O'Connor, F. The complete stories
O'Connor, F. Collected stories
The O. Henry prize stories 2019
Oates, J. Wild nights
Oates, J. Evil eye
Oates, J. The doll-master
Ocampo, S. Forgotten journey
Olsen, T. Tell me a riddle
Orczy, E. The old man in the corner
Osondu, E. Voice of America
Oyeyemi, H. What is not yours is not yours
Paley, G. The collected stories
Paretsky, S. Windy city blues
Pearlman, E. Binocular vision
Pearlman, E. Honeydew
A people's future of the United States
Piatote, B. The beadworkers
The plot thickens
Poe, E. Complete stories and poems of Edgar Allan Poe
Poe's children
Pollock, D. Knockemstiff
Porter, K. The collected stories of Katherine Anne Porter
Porter, K. Pale horse, pale rider
Proulx, A. Bad dirt
Proulx, A. Fine just the way it is
Proust, M. The complete short stories of Marcel Proust
The Pushcart Prize 2020 XLIV
Quade, K. Night at the fiestas
Queen, E. The best of Ellery Queen
Rankin, I. The beat goes on
Rash, R. Burning bright
Rash, R. Nothing gold can stay
Rash, R. Something rich and strange
Rendell, R. Blood lines
Rendell, R. Collected stories
The road ahead
Robinson, K. The Martians
Rogues
Ross, A. Ladies and gentlemen
Roth, J. The collected stories of Joseph Roth
Roth, P. Goodbye, Columbus, and five short stories
Runcie, J. Sidney Chambers and the perils of the night
Runcie, J. Sidney Chambers and the problem of evil
Rushdie, S. East, West
Russell, K. Orange world and other stories
Russell, K. Vampires in the lemon grove
Salinger, J. Nine stories
Salter, J. Last night
Saunders, G. In persuasion nation

Cooper, T. The marauders

SHRINES

Peters, E. The pilgrim of hate

Sandford, J. Holy ghost

Shrink rap Parker, R.

SHROPSHIRE, ENGLAND

Peters, E. Fallen into the pit

Rayne, S. Property of a lady

Smith, F. Night fall

SHROUD OF TURIN

McCarthy, T. Satin Island

SHTETL

Aleichem, S. Tevye's daughters

Aleichem, S. Tevye the dairyman and the railroad stories

Singer, I. The family Moskat

Singer, I. The magician of Lublin

Shuggie Bain Stuart, D.

Shutter Island Lehane, D.

SHYNESS IN MEN

Frost, K. The reluctant fortune-teller

Jacobson, H. The mighty walzer

SHYNESS IN TEENAGE GIRLS

Strout, E. Amy and Isabelle

SHYNESS IN WOMEN

Dare, T. When a Scot ties the knot

Hay, E. Late nights on air

Milan, C. The duchess war

SIAMESE CAT

Braun, L. The cat who ate Danish modern

Braun, L. The cat who went underground

SIBERIA

Kaminsky, S. Murder on the Trans-Siberian Express

L'Amour, L. The last of the breed

Morris, H. Cilka's journey

Richler, N. Your mouth is lovely

Theroux, M. Far north

Ulinich, A. Petropolis

SIBERIA -- HISTORY -- 20TH CENTURY

Furnivall, K. The red scarf

SIBERIA -- HISTORY -- REVOLUTION, 1917-1921

Meek, J. The people's act of love

The **Siberian** dilemma Smith, M.

SIBLING RIVALRY

Atwood, M. The blind assassin

De los Santos, M. The precious one

Dostoyevsky, F. The brothers Karamazov

Farrell, H. What ever happened to Baby Jane?

Frank, D. Queen bee

Friedland, E. The floating Feldmans

Gregory, P. The other Boleyn girl

Hassib, R. A pure heart

Lombardo, C. The most fun we ever had

Schine, C. The Grammarians

Smith, W. Monsoon

Stachniak, E. The chosen maiden

Stansel, I. The last cowboys of San Geronimo

Steinbeck, J. East of Eden

Tie, N. The bathing women

Weiner, J. In her shoes

The **Sicilian** Puzo, M.

SICILY, ITALY

Colombani, L. The braid

Elkins, A. Unnatural selection

Giordano, M. Auntie Poldi and the Vineyards of Etna

Higgins, J. Luciano's luck

Puzo, M. The Sicilian

SICILY, ITALY -- HISTORY

Hersey, J. A bell for Adano

SICILY, ITALY -- HISTORY -- 1870-1945

Shaara, J. The rising tide

SICK CHILDREN

Helprin, M. Paris in the present tense

Kellerman, J. Devil's waltz

Leroy, M. Postcards from Berlin

Mackintosh, C. After the end

Mosley, W. Cinnamon kiss

Richman, A. The secret of clouds

Tawada, Y. The emissary

Tsukiyama, G. Dreaming water

SICK FATHERS

Ball, J. Census

Coster, N. Halsey Street

Gifford, B. Wyoming

Kate, J. Love and other mistakes

Kerstan, L. Heart of the tiger

Sparks, N. Every breath

Woo, S. Love love

SICK GIRLS

Mosley, W. Cinnamon kiss

SICK MEN

Maguire, G. Son of a witch

Wang, K. Family trust

SICK MOTHERS

Flournoy, A. The Turner house

Turansky, C. No ocean too wide

SICK PERSONS

Burns, C. Black hole

Child, L. Deep storm

Colombani, L. The braid

Dev, S. A distant heart

French, J. The true Bastards

Huyler, F. The laws of invisible things

Lispector, C. The besieged city

Maguire, G. Son of a witch

Pajer, B. Capacity for murder

Price, R. The good priest's son

Rose, H. The museum of modern love

SICK WOMEN

Gaitskill, M. Veronica

Helprin, M. Winter's tale

Keane, M. Fever

Layton, E. To wed a stranger

Saylor, S. The judgment of Caesar

Siddhartha Hesse, H.

Simon Westow novels [series] Nickson, C.
Simon Ziele mysteries [series] Pintoff, S.
A **simple** act of violence Ellory, R.
A **simple** plan Smith, S.
Simple speaks his mind Hughes, L.
Simply irresistible Shalvis, J.
Simply love Balogh, M.
Simply quartet (Mary Balogh) [series] Balogh, M.

SIN
Campisi, M. Sin eater
Hawthorne, N. The scarlet letter
Lewis, M. The monk

Sin eater Campisi, M.
Sin killer McMurtry, L.

SINATRA, FRANK, 1915-1998
Randisi, R. Hey there (you with the gun in your hand)

Since we fell Lehane, D.

SINCLAIR, UPTON, 1878-1968
Oates, J. The accursed

SINDBAD THE SAILOR (LEGENDARY CHARACTER)
Barth, J. The last voyage of somebody the sailor

Sinful suitors [series] Jeffries, S.
Sing to it Hempel, A.
Sing you home Picoult, J.
Sing, unburied, sing Ward, J.

SINGAPORE
Kwan, K. Crazy rich Asians
Kwan, K. Rich people problems
Suarez, D. Change agent

SINGAPORE -- HISTORY -- JAPANESE OCCUPATION, 1942-1945
Loh, V. Breaking the tongue , by Vyvyane Loh.

Singer from the sea Tepper, S.
The **singer's** gun Mandel, E.

SINGERS
Abramowitz, A. Thank you, goodnight
Bailey, P. Uncle Rudolf
Colwin, L. Goodbye without leaving
Creech, S. The whole way home
Erdrich, L. The Master Butchers Singing Club
Faber, M. The courage consort
Kay, G. Tigana
Kimani, P. Dance of the Jakaranda
King, R. Domino
Penelope, L. Song of blood and stone
Penelope, L. Whispers of shadow & flame
Varley, J. Rolling thunder
Whittall, Z. Holding still for as long as possible
Williams, C. Stairway to hell

SINGING
Harris, E. I say a little prayer
Patchett, A. Bel canto
Toibin, C. Nora Webster

SINGING CONTESTS
Valente, C. Space opera

The **singing** of the dead Stabenow, D.
A **single** breath Clarke, L.

SINGLE FATHERS
Baldacci, D. One summer
Barclay, L. Broken promise
Bell, L. How the duke was won
Bell, L. What a difference a duke makes
Burrowes, G. The captive
Finder, J. Suspicion
Frank, D. Queen bee
Gertler, S. Drifting
Greene, G. Our man in Havana
Hallinan, T. Crashed
Hegi, U. The vision of Emma Blau
Hunter, J. Forbidden to love the duke
Jenkins, B. Tempest
Jewell, L. Then she was gone
Kate, J. Love and other mistakes
Kerr, L. Wild on my mind
Landon, S. Wishing for us
Lehane, D. World gone by
McKinlay, J. The good ones
Mizushima, M. Burning ridge
Mizushima, M. Killing trail
Mizushima, M. Stalking ground
Moore, C. A dirty job
North, A. The Whisper Man
Novak, B. This heart of mine
Pajer, B. Fatal induction
Pajer, B. A spark of death
Robards, K. Ghost moon
Scottoline, L. Every fifteen minutes
Sebastian, C. It takes two to tumble
Tyler, A. Saint Maybe
Vlautin, W. Lean on Pete
Warren, T. The replacement wife

SINGLE MEN
Barth, J. The end of the road
Berger, T. Being invisible
Berry, W. Jayber Crow
Cameron, W. The dogs of Christmas
Capote, T. Breakfast at Tiffany's
Chase, L. Miss Wonderful
Davies, R. Fifth business
Gray, J. A duke never yields
Haruf, K. Eventide
Haruf, K. Plainsong
Lurie, A. Foreign affairs
Mallery, S. Best of my love
Murdoch, I. The sea, the sea
Packer, A. The children's crusade
Phillips, S. Match me if you can
Phillips, S. Natural born charmer
Rowland, R. Cold country
Runcie, J. Sidney Chambers and the shadow of death
Saramago, J. The history of the siege of Lisbon
Sparks, N. The notebook
Tyler, A. Celestial navigation
White, R. Salt river

Wodehouse, P. The inimitable Jeeves
Wodehouse, P. My man Jeeves

SINGLE MEN AND CHILDREN

Wharton, E. The children

SINGLE MOTHERS

Aliu, X. Brass
Armstrong, K. Wherever she goes
Balogh, M. Simply love
Bandele, A. Daughter
Beck, H. Lost you
Benton, J. Lilli de Jong
Berg, E. We are all welcome here
Bowen, R. The victory garden
Box, C. The bitterroots
Box, C. Blue heaven
Boyne, J. The heart's invisible furies
Brookner, A. Family and friends
Brown, R. Half a heart
Butler, N. Little faith
Byatt, A. Babel Tower
Byatt, A. A whistling woman
Carey, M. Someone like me
Carlson, M. A Christmas by the sea
Cash, W. The last ballad
Cleveland, K. Keep you close
Cocco, G. Shadows on the lake
Cogburn, E. Ava's place
Connelly, M. The fifth witness
Cush, J. Endangered
Dark, A. Think of England
Dell, K. Reckless in Texas
Dolan, H. Bad things happen
Drabble, M. The pure gold baby
Duncan, G. Talulla rising
Ferrante, E. Those who leave and those who stay
Fitch, J. White oleander
Flint, E. Little deaths
Foster, L. Sisters of summer's end
Goldberg, M. Feast your eyes
Gowdy, B. Helpless
Guskin, S. The forgetting time
Hadley, T. Clever girl
Haigh, J. Baker Towers
Haigh, J. Mrs. Kimble
Hamer, K. The girl in the red coat
Harris, J. Chocolat
Haruf, K. Eventide
Higgins, K. Life and other inconveniences
Hoang, H. The bride test
James, L. I want you back
Jenkins, V. An unattended death
Jewell, L. I found you
K'wan Revelations
Kibler, J. Home for erring and outcast girls
Kingsolver, B. The bean trees
Kingsolver, B. Pigs in heaven
Kushner, R. The Mars room

Landis, J. Heartbreak hotel
Lawrence, M. Hearts and bones
Little, T. Where there's smoke
Lundrigan, N. Glass boys
MacLean, S. Never judge a lady by her cover
Majors, I. Penelope Lemon
Martin, A. Fumbled
Martin, S. The pleasure of my company
McBain, E. Alice in jeopardy
McCall Smith, A. The lost art of gratitude
McMillan, T. How Stella got her groove back
Minato, K. Confessions
Molloy, A. The perfect mother
Monroe, M. God don't like ugly
Moore, L. Long bright river
Moore, M. The islanders
Moriarty, J. Gravity is the thing
Morris, M. Man in the blue moon
Naylor, G. The women of Brewster Place
Ng, C. Little fires everywhere
Orstavik, H. Love
Palmer, D. The new husband
Patchett, A. Run
Perry, S. The Essex serpent
Picoult, J. Keeping faith
Pinborough, S. Behind her eyes
Pinborough, S. Cross her heart
Pinter, J. Hide away
Price, R. Freedomland
Rader-Day, L. The day I died
Rai, A. Wrong to need you
Reiken, F. Day for night
Richler, N. Your mouth is lovely
Rivers, F. The masterpiece
Robards, K. Ghost moon
Rotert, R. Last night at the blue angel
Scott, A. Beneath the abbey wall
Scottoline, L. One perfect lie
Sekaran, S. Lucky boy
Sexton, M. A kind of freedom
Sexton, M. The revisioners
Shafak, E. The bastard of Istanbul
Shaw, W. Salt lane
Silber, J. Improvement
Soderberg, A. The other son
Spencer, S. The dead hand of history
Stevens, C. Never let you go
Strout, E. Amy and Isabelle
Styles, T. Raunchy
Toibin, C. Nora Webster
Tyler, A. Clock dance
Unger, L. The red hunter
Vuong, O. On Earth we're briefly gorgeous
Walbert, K. She was like that
Wallace, M. The girl in the garden
Waxman, A. The bookish life of Nina Hill
Weatherspoon, R. Rafe

Wrobel, S. Darling Rose Gold

SINGLE MOTHERS -- IRELAND

Llywelyn, M. 1949

SINGLE PARENT FAMILIES

Bandele, A. Daughter

SINGLE PARENTS

Rendell, R. The tree of hands

SINGLE PEOPLE

Fielding, H. Bridget Jones's diary

SINGLE TEENAGE FATHERS

Johnson, A. The first part last

A **single** thread Chevalier, T.

SINGLE WOMEN

Bambara, T. Those bones are not my child

Barnett, K. Ever faithful

Berg, E. Never change

Beverley, J. Devilish

Beverley, J. Something wicked

Beverley, J. Tempting fortune

Boyle, E. Along came a duke

Boyle, E. And the miss ran away with the rake

Capote, T. Breakfast at Tiffany's

Carty-Williams, C. Queenie

Chase, L. Miss Wonderful

Cohen, T. The summer we lost her

Coupland, D. Eleanor Rigby

Dare, T. A night to surrender

Dare, T. Romancing the duke

Dare, T. The wallflower wager

Dean, A. Bellfield Hall

Dean, A. A woman of consequence

Fielding, H. Bridget Jones's diary

Gerritsen, T. The shape of night

Gray, J. A duke never yields

Hale, S. Austenland

Heyer, G. Black sheep

Heyer, G. The grand Sophy

Hibbert, T. A girl like her

Hoang, H. The kiss quotient

Jackson, S. The haunting of Hill House

Laurens, S. A rake's vow

Landon, S. Wishing for us

London, S. The Aussie next door

Loren, R. The one for you

MacKenzie, S. Bedding Lord Ned

MacLean, S. Brazen and the Beast

MacLean, S. Wicked and the wallflower

Mapson, J. Bad Girl Creek

Milan, C. The duchess war

Moore, B. The lonely passion of Judith Hearne

Phillips, S. Match me if you can

Phillips, S. Natural born charmer

Pym, B. Excellent women

Quick, A. I thee wed

Rinehart, M. The circular staircase

Rossner, J. Looking for Mr. Goodbar

Rothschild, H. The improbability of love

Ryan, J. Restless rancher

Schmidt, S. See what I have done

Shumway, C. Ten girls to watch

Sittenfeld, C. Eligible

Spark, M. The girls of slender means

Title, S. The undateable

Trigiani, A. Big Stone Gap

Wade, B. Falling for you

Wade, B. True to you

Waters, S. The paying guests

Winfrey, K. Waiting for Tom Hanks

Winterson, J. The daylight gate

SINGLE WOMEN -- INTERPERSONAL RELATIONS

Weiner, J. In her shoes

SINGLE WOMEN -- MASSACHUSETTS

Wharton, E. Ethan Frome

SINGLE-PARENT FAMILIES

Baldacci, D. One summer

Beattie, A. Picturing Will

Bergstrom, H. Steal the north

Hoffman, A. Turtle moon

Lee, H. To kill a mockingbird

O'Neill, J. Netherland

Tatlock, A. Promises to keep

Wolitzer, H. Hearts

SINGLE-PARENT FAMILIES -- HARLEM, NEW YORK CITY

Petry, A. The street

The **sinister** mystery of the mesmerizing girl Goss, T.

The **sinister** pig Hillerman, T.

The **sinners** Atkins, A.

SINO-JAPANESE CONFLICT, 1937-1945

Jin, H. Nanjing requiem

The **sins** of the fathers Block, L.

The **sins** of the wolf Perry, A.

The **siren** queen Buckley, F.

The **sirens** of Titan Vonnegut, K.

Sister Lupton, R.

Sister Carrie Dreiser, T.

Sister Pelagia and the white bulldog Akunin, B.

Sister Pelagia mysteries [series] Akunin, B.

SISTERHOOD

Braithwaite, O. My sister, the serial killer

Sisterland Sittenfeld, C.

SISTERS

Adkins, M. When you read this

Alharthi, J. Celestial bodies

Allen, S. First frost

Allen, S. Garden spells

Alvarez, J. How the Garcia girls lost their accents

Austen, J. Mansfield Park

Austen, J. Persuasion

Austen, J. Pride and prejudice

Austen, J. Sense and sensibility

Baker, T. The little giant of Aberdeen County

Barber, L. A girl named Anna

Barr, N. What Rose forgot

Rice, L. Little night
Rimmer, K. Before I let you go
Rojas Contreras, I. Fruit of the drunken tree
Schine, C. The Grammarians
Schmidt, S. See what I have done
Schwarz, C. Drowning Ruth
Searles, J. Help for the haunted
See, L. Shanghai girls
Shalvis, J. Simply irresistible
Shalvis, J. The sweetest thing
Shepard, S. Reputation
Simpson, D. Dead by morning
Sittenfeld, C. Eligible
Sittenfeld, C. Sisterland
Slaughter, K. The good daughter
Slaughter, K. Pretty girls
Smiley, J. A thousand acres
Smith, A. Winter
Smith, L. Fair and tender ladies
Soniah Kamal Unmarriageable
St. James, S. The broken girls
Stewart, A. Girl waits with gun
Stewart, A. Kopp sisters on the march
Stewart, A. Lady cop makes trouble
Stewart, A. Miss Kopp just won't quit
Stewart, A. Miss Kopp's midnight confessions
Stradal, J. The lager queen of Minnesota
Stross, C. Neptune's brood
Thomas, S. Not quite a husband
Tie, N. The bathing women
Tremblay, P. A head full of ghosts
Trollope, J. A Spanish lover
Tsao, T. The majesties
Turner, N. The Banks sisters
Wade, B. True to you
Walker, W. Emma in the night
Walls, J. The silver star
Warren, S. Rescue me
Weiner, J. In her shoes
Weiner, J. Mrs. Everything
Wood, J. Upstate
Woods, S. Santa Fe rules
Zailckas, K. Mother, mother
The **sisters** Jensen, N.
SISTERS -- 19TH CENTURY
Gaskell, E. Cranford
SISTERS -- CUBA
Garcia, C. The Aguero sisters
SISTERS -- DEATH
Atwood, M. The blind assassin
Erdrich, L. The painted drum
Frazier, C. Nightwoods
Goenawan, C. Rainbirds
Harrington, A. An inconvenient duke
Harris, T. Hannibal rising
Hassib, R. A pure heart
Hill, S. The pure in heart

Kubica, M. The other Mrs.
Lodato, V. Mathilda Savitch
Lupton, R. Sister
Meno, J. The boy detective fails
Potzsch, O. The beggar king
Prose, F. Goldengrove
Quincy, D. Murder at the opera
Richmond, M. No one you know
Rosenberg, N. Interest of justice
Schaitkin, A. Saint X
Shaw, W. A song for the brokenhearted
Wilkinson, L. American spy
SISTERS -- EUROPE
Jones, S. Four sisters, all queens
SISTERS -- FAMILY RELATIONSHIPS
O'Farrell, M. The vanishing act of Esme Lennox
SISTERS -- FLORIDA
Garcia, C. The Aguero sisters
SISTERS -- KYOTO, JAPAN
Golden, A. Memoirs of a geisha
SISTERS -- MAINE
Ogilvie, E. When the music stopped
SISTERS -- NETHERLANDS
Moor, M. The storm
SISTERS -- OHIO
Bialosky, J. House under snow
SISTERS -- SOUTH CAROLINA
Kidd, S. The secret life of bees
SISTERS -- SOUTHERN STATES
Walker, A. The color purple
SISTERS -- UNITED STATES
Tan, A. The hundred secret senses
The **Sisters** brothers deWitt, P.
SISTERS OF MURDER VICTIMS
Pronzini, B. Mourners
Sisters of summer's end Foster, L.
Sisters of the revolution
SISTERS-IN-LAW
Link, C. The watcher
Six Easy pieces Mosley, W.
Six of one Brown, R.
Six tales of the jazz age and other stories Fitzgerald, F.
Six Tudor queens [series] Weir, A.
Six wakes Lafferty, M.
SIX-YEAR-OLD BOYS
Grodstein, L. Our short history
SIX-YEAR-OLD GIRLS
Kingsolver, B. Pigs in heaven
Sixkill Parker, R.
SIXTEEN-YEAR-OLD BOYS
Booth, C. Bronxwood
Childress, M. One Mississippi
Coben, H. Hold tight
Connelly, M. The scarecrow
Danielewski, M. Only revolutions
Johnson, A. The first part last
Pratchett, T. Thief of time

Warren, R. Band of angels

SLAVE-TRADE -- GULF OF GUINEA
O'Brian, P. The commodore

SLAVEHOLDERS
Butler, O. Kindred
Doctorow, E. The march
Odell, J. The healing

SLAVEHOLDERS -- LOUISIANA
Straight, S. A million nightingales

SLAVERY
Atakora, A. Conjure women
Beatty, P. The sellout
Bishop, A. Written in red
Brink, A. Philida
Callender, K. Queen of the conquered
Caputo, P. Acts of faith
Card, M. These ghosts are family
Cho, Z. Sorcerer to the crown
Coates, T. The water dancer
Cobbs Hoffman, E. The Tubman command
Deon, N. Grace
Draven, G. Phoenix unbound
Evaristo, B. Blonde roots
Faulkner, W. Go down, Moses
Gappah, P. Out of darkness, shining light
Gyasi, Y. Homegoing
Hambly, B. Lady of perdition
Hill, L. Someone knows my name
Jakes, J. Love and war
Jakes, J. North and South
Jakes, J. On secret service
Jones, E. The known world
Kidd, S. The invention of wings
Lalami, L. The Moor's account
Le Guin, U. Four ways to forgiveness
Leveen, L. The secrets of Mary Bowser
Lock, N. A fugitive in Walden Woods
Locke, A. The cutting season
Martin, G. A dance with dragons
Martin, V. Property
McBride, J. Song yet sung
Morrison, T. Beloved
Morrison, T. A mercy
Odell, J. The healing
Pearson, R. Choke point
Perkins-Valdez, D. Wench
Pitts, L. Freeman
Putnam, J. These honored dead
Rawles, N. My Jim
Reed, I. Flight to Canada
Rhodes, J. Voodoo dreams
Robinson, M. Gilead
Santiago, E. Conquistadora
Solomon, R. The deep
Solomon, R. An unkindness of ghosts
Tidhar, L. A man lies dreaming
Tregillis, I. The mechanical

Turner, N. My name is Resolute
Twain, M. Adventures of Huckleberry Finn
Unsworth, B. Sacred hunger
Vidal, G. Lincoln
Vinge, V. A deepness in the sky
Warren, R. Band of angels
Wascom, K. The blood of heaven
Whitehead, C. The underground railroad
Woods, R. Remembrance

SLAVERY -- CONNECTICUT
Pesci, D. Amistad

SLAVERY -- JAMAICA
Levy, A. The long song

SLAVERY -- LOUISIANA
Gaines, E. The autobiography of Miss Jane Pittman
Straight, S. A million nightingales
Tademy, L. Cane River

SLAVERY -- MARYLAND
Butler, O. Kindred

SLAVERY -- MISSOURI
Twain, M. Pudd'nhead Wilson ;

SLAVERY -- UNITED STATES
Stowe, H. Uncle Tom's cabin

SLAVERY -- VIRGINIA
Styron, W. The confessions of Nat Turner

SLAVES
Conklin, T. The house girl
Deon, N. Grace
Edugyan, E. Washington Black
Evaristo, B. Blonde roots
Gabaldon, D. Voyager
James, M. The book of night women
Jemisin, N. The hundred thousand kingdoms
Jones, E. The known world
Lalami, L. The Moor's account
Le Guin, U. Four ways to forgiveness
Levack, S. Demon of the air
Michener, J. Caribbean
Peters, E. The last camel died at noon
Phillips, C. Foreigners
Rawles, N. My Jim
Reed, I. Flight to Canada
Saylor, S. The house of the Vestals
Saylor, S. A mist of prophecies
Saylor, S. Raiders of the Nile
Saylor, S. Roma
Stowe, H. Uncle Tom's cabin
Straight, S. A million nightingales
Willig, L. The summer country

SLAVES -- EMANCIPATION
Brink, A. Philida
Downie, R. Medicus

SLAVES -- ROME
Wallace, L. Ben-Hur

SLAVES -- UNITED STATES
Pesci, D. Amistad

SLAVES -- UNITED STATES -- SOCIAL CONDITIONS

Coates, T. The water dancer
Slaves of obsession Perry, A.
SLED DOGS
Bradbury, J. The wild inside
SLED DOGS -- ALASKA
Brand, M. Chinook
London, J. The call of the wild
SLEEP
Apelfeld, A. The man who never stopped sleeping
Fforde, J. Early riser
Walker, K. The dreamers
SLEEP DISORDERS
King, S. Sleeping beauties
Walker, K. The dreamers
SLEEP WALKERS
Barnes, J. The somnambulist
Wendig, C. Wanderers
SLEEP-WALKING
Barnes, J. The somnambulist
Bohjalian, C. The sleepwalker
Sleeping beauties King, S.
Sleeping beauty Macdonald, R.
A **sleeping** life Rendell, R.
Sleeping with the enemy Price, N.
Sleeping with the entity Devon, C.
The **sleepwalker** Bohjalian, C.
Sleepwalking land Couto, M.
Slightly shady Quick, A.
SLIGO, IRELAND
Barry, S. The secret scripture
Slip of the knife Mina, D.
Slipping Beukes, L.
A **slipping-down** life Tyler, A.
Slow man Coetzee, J.
Slumberland Beatty, P.
SLUMLORDS
Neely, B. Blanche cleans up
SLUMS
Anappara, D. Djinn patrol on the purple line
Beukes, L. Zoo city
Crane, S. Maggie
Hoyt, E. Wicked intentions
Levine, J. Bingo's run
Moore, A. Jerusalem
Perry, A. Highgate Rise
Perry, A. The silent cry
Roth, H. Call it sleep
Shanbhag, V. Ghachar ghochar
Sinha, I. Animal's people
Solomon, R. An unkindness of ghosts
Umrigar, T. The secrets between us
Sly fox Pirro, J.
The **slynx** Tolstaya, T.
SMALL BUSINESS
Frankel, L. Goodbye for now
Small change [series] Walton, J.
SMALL COUNTRIES

Wibberley, L. The mouse that roared
Small country Faye, G.
A **small** fortune Dastgir, R.
Small gods Pratchett, T.
A **small** indiscretion Ellison, J.
Small island Levy, A.
SMALL TOWN ECONOMIC DEVELOPMENT
Guterson, D. Our Lady of the Forest
SMALL TOWN FAMILIES
Wolfe, T. Look homeward, angel
SMALL TOWN LIFE
Adams, E. The secret, book & scone society
Anderson, C. Mulberry moon
Avon, J. In peppermint peril
Backman, F. Beartown
Backman, F. Britt-Marie was here
Backman, F. Us against you
Baker, T. The little giant of Aberdeen County
Bambara, T. Gorilla, my love
Baume, S. Spill simmer falter wither
Benson, E. Make way for Lucia
Berg, E. Night of miracles
Berg, G. The operator
Berne, S. The dogs of Littlefield
Berry, W. That distant land
Berry, W. Jayber Crow
Binchy, M. Circle of friends
Binchy, M. Whitethorn Woods
Blackstock, T. Shadow in Serenity
Blake, S. The postmistress
Block, S. Oliver Loving
Bohjalian, C. The buffalo soldier
Bond, C. Ruby
Bradbury, R. The Martian chronicles
Braun, L. The cat who went underground
Brockmeier, K. The truth about Celia
Brown, R. Before and after
Bruni, S. The night Gwen Stacy died
Burns, O. Cold Sassy tree
Burns, O. Leaving Cold Sassy
Bussi, M. Black water lilies
Bybee, C. Staying for good
Canty, K. The underworld
Carlson, M. A Christmas by the sea
Carr, B. Opioid, Indiana
Carr, R. Virgin river
Cather, W. The song of the lark
Chancellor, B. Sycamore
Chatterjee, U. English, August
Cheever, J. The Wapshot chronicle
Cheever, J. The Wapshot scandal
Child, L. Killing floor
Childress, M. One Mississippi
Cleeves, A. Raven black
Cleeves, A. Thin air
Cleeves, A. Wild fire
Coleridge, N. A much married man

Colgan, J. The endless beach
Collins, C. The gamal
Connolly, J. The burning soul
Crummey, M. Galore
Darnielle, J. Universal harvester
Deb, S. The point of return
Deveraux, J. A willing murder
Dimitri, F. The book of hidden things
Drury, T. Pacific
Duffy, B. House of echoes
Dufresne, J. Deep in the shade of paradise
Dugoni, R. The extraordinary life of Sam Hell
Edgerton, C. Walking across Egypt
Eskens, A. Nothing more dangerous
Forna, A. The hired man
French, A. Billy
Gerritsen, T. The shape of night
Grau, S. The keepers of the house
Gray, A. The care and feeding of ravenously hungry girls
Greene, A. Long Man
Grisham, J. Ford County
Gurganus, A. Local souls
Haigh, J. Baker Towers
Haruf, K. Eventide
Haruf, K. Plainsong
Haruf, K. Our souls at night
Hegi, U. Stones from the river
Henderson, S. The flicker of old dreams
Higgins, K. Now that you mention it
Hill, R. The stranger house
Hoffman, A. The ice queen
Hoffman, A. The red garden
Hoffman, A. The river king
Hooper, K. Stealing shadows
Hunt, L. The evening road
Iles, G. Cemetery road
Jackson, S. The lottery
Jemc, J. The grip of it
Keller, J. Bone on bone
Keller, J. Last ragged breath
Kelly, E. Broadchurch
Kesey, K. Sometimes a great notion
King, S. Carrie
King, S. Elevation
Krentz, J. River road
Krueger, W. Vermilion drift
L'Amour, L. May there be a road
Landvik, L. Chronicles of a radical hag
Lee, H. Go set a watchman
Lelic, S. The child who
Lennon, J. Castle
Lewis, K. Half of what you hear
Lewis, S. Main street
Liardet, F. We must be brave
Lispector, C. The besieged city
Majors, I. Penelope Lemon
Mallery, S. Best of my love

Mann, T. Buddenbrooks
McAllister, T. How to be safe
McBride, E. A girl is a half-formed thing
McCracken, E. Bowlaway
McCrumb, S. If ever I return, pretty Peggy-O
McDermid, V. A place of execution
McGown, J. Murder at the old vicarage
McGregor, J. The reservoir tapes
McKevett, G. Murder in her stocking
McKevett, G. Murder in the corn maze
McKinlay, J. The good ones
McPherson, C. Quiet neighbors
Michaels, F. Deep harbor
Miranda, M. The last house guest
Mitchell, D. Black Swan Green
Mizushima, M. Killing trail
Mizushima, M. Stalking ground
Moore, E. The Supremes sing the happy heartache blues
Morrison, T. Sula
Munro, A. Open secrets
Munro, A. Selected stories
Murphy, Y. The call
Norman, H. The bird artist
Novak, B. This heart of mine
O'Connell, C. Stone angel
Oates, J. Carthage
Oates, J. I lock my door upon myself
Obioma, C. The fishermen
Otto, W. How to make an American quilt
Oz, A. Don't call it night
Packer, A. The dive from Clausen's pier
Parshall, S. Poisoned ground
Penny, L. A better man
Penny, L. The cruelest month
Penny, L. Kingdom of the blind
Penny, L. Still life
Penny, L. A trick of the light
Perrotta, T. The abstinence teacher
Phillips, S. Call me irresistible
Price, R. Freedomland
Price, R. Roxanna Slade
Pronzini, B. A wasteland of strangers
Quincy, D. Murder in Mayfair
Rayfiel, T. In pinelight
Rendell, R. Harm done
Rendell, R. The babes in the wood
Ripley, M. Mr Campion's fault
Ross, A. Miss Julia takes the wheel
Ross, A. Miss Julia throws a wedding
Rowland, R. Cold country
Rowling, J. The casual vacancy
Rozan, S. Winter and night
Russo, R. Bridge of sighs
Russo, R. Empire Falls
Russo, R. Everybody's fool
Russo, R. Nobody's fool
Sala, S. Forever my hero

Nordan, L. Wolf whistle

SMALL TOWN LIFE -- MISSOURI

Flagg, F. Standing in the rainbow

Murr, N. The perfect man

Twain, M. Pudd'nhead Wilson ;

SMALL TOWN LIFE -- MONTANA

Doig, I. The bartender's tale

SMALL TOWN LIFE -- NEBRASKA

Cather, W. A lost lady

SMALL TOWN LIFE -- NEW HAMPSHIRE

Banks, R. Affliction

Delinsky, B. Lake news

SMALL TOWN LIFE -- NEW SOUTH WALES

Grenville, K. The idea of perfection

SMALL TOWN LIFE -- NEW YORK (STATE)

Banks, R. The sweet hereafter

Barbash, T. The last good chance

O'Donohue, C. The lover's knot

Russo, R. The risk pool

Straub, P. Ghost story

**SMALL TOWN LIFE -- NEWFOUNDLAND AND LAB-
RADOR**

Proulx, A. The shipping news

SMALL TOWN LIFE -- NORTH CAROLINA

Earley, T. Jim the boy

Gibbons, K. The life all around me by Ellen Foster

Godwin, G. Unfinished desires

Hart, J. Down river

Hart, J. The last child

Karon, J. At home in Mitford

Karon, J. In this mountain

Karon, J. A new song

Karon, J. Out to Canaan

Maron, M. Bootlegger's daughter

Maron, M. High country fall

Maron, M. Shooting at loons

Maron, M. Storm track

Maron, M. Uncommon clay

Maron, M. Up jumps the Devil

Rash, R. Above the waterfall

SMALL TOWN LIFE -- NORTH DAKOTA

Erdrich, L. The plague of doves

SMALL TOWN LIFE -- OHIO

Pollock, D. Knockemstiff

SMALL TOWN LIFE -- OKLAHOMA

DeCarlo, M. The art of crash landing

Hart, C. Letter from home

SMALL TOWN LIFE -- ONTARIO

Munro, A. Lives of girls and women

SMALL TOWN LIFE -- OREGON

Carr, R. The wanderer

Chacon, D. And the shadows took him

SMALL TOWN LIFE -- OZARK MOUNTAIN REGION

Woodrell, D. Winter's bone

SMALL TOWN LIFE -- PENNSYLVANIA

Meyer, P. American rust

O'Nan, S. Snow angels

Ritter, T. Devil's night

Russo, R. Straight man

SMALL TOWN LIFE -- SCOTLAND

O'Hagan, A. Be near me

Scott, A. A kind of grief

Scott, A. The low road

SMALL TOWN LIFE -- SOUTH CAROLINA

Kidd, S. The secret life of bees

SMALL TOWN LIFE -- SOUTH DAKOTA

Meyers, K. Twisted tree

SMALL TOWN LIFE -- SOUTHERN STATES

Capote, T. The grass harp

Welty, E. The ponder heart

SMALL TOWN LIFE -- SOVIET UNION

Rutherfurd, E. Russka

SMALL TOWN LIFE -- SWEDEN

Eriksson, K. The princess of Burundi

SMALL TOWN LIFE -- TENNESSEE

Gregory, D. The devil's alphabet

SMALL TOWN LIFE -- TEXAS

Albert, S. Bittersweet

McMurtry, L. Rhino ranch

Shames, T. An unsettling crime for Samuel Craddock

SMALL TOWN LIFE -- THE WEST (UNITED STATES)

Parker, R. Appaloosa

Parker, R. Blue-eyed devil

Parker, R. Brimstone

SMALL TOWN LIFE -- TURKEY

Karnezis, P. The maze

SMALL TOWN LIFE -- VIRGINIA

Brown, R. Murder at Monticello, or, Old sins

Brown, R. Wish you were here

Smith, L. Family linen

SMALL TOWN LIFE -- WASHINGTON (STATE)

Evison, J. West of here

SMALL TOWN LIFE -- WEST VIRGINIA

Fabry, C. The promise of Jesse Woods

FitzGerald, G. Redemption Mountain

Keller, J. A killing in the hills

SMALL TOWN LIFE -- WISCONSIN

Sidor, S. Skin River

SMALL TOWN LIFE -- WYOMING

Johnson, C. Another man's moccasins

Johnson, C. Dark horse

Johnson, C. Death without company

Johnson, C. Hell is empty

Proulx, A. Bad dirt

Trevanian Incident at Twenty-mile

SMALL TOWNS

Adams, E. The secret, book & scone society

Ahlborn, A. The devil crept in

Albert, S. The Darling Dahlias and the cucumber tree

Anders, A. Under her skin

Andrews, D. Owl be home for Christmas

Andric, I. The bridge on the Drina

Atkins, A. The shameless

Avon, J. In peppermint peril

Meno, J. Marvel and a wonder
Morrison, T. Home
Mott, J. The returned
Murdoch, I. The philosopher's pupil
O'Hara, J. Appointment in Samarra
Oakley, C. You were there too
Oates, J. A book of American martyrs
Oates, J. Broke heart blues
Oates, J. Little bird of heaven
Orstavik, H. Love
Paretsky, S. Fallout
Pinter, J. Hide away
Pronzini, B. The violated
Rader-Day, L. The day I died
Ramsay, H. Summer on Moonlight Bay
Roberts, N. The obsession
Russo, R. Bridge of sighs
Sala, S. Forever my hero
Sallis, J. Sarah Jane
Sanders, L. The sixth commandment
Sandford, J. Winter prey
Saroyan, W. The human comedy
Shames, T. A risky undertaking for Loretta Singletary
Sidor, S. The mirror's edge
Slaughter, K. Pretty girls
Smith, M. Blackwood
Spain, J. With our blessing
Spencer, S. Lambs to the slaughter
Spencer-Fleming, J. Hid from our eyes
St. James, S. The broken girls
St. James, S. The Sun Down motel
Steadman, C. Mr. Nobody
Stevens, C. Never let you go
Tursten, H. Winter grave
Urrea, L. The water museum
Warren, S. Rescue me
Watson, M. The dream peddler
Whitehead, C. Apex hides the hurt
Whitlow, R. A time to stand
Wiggs, S. The beekeeper's ball
Woodrell, D. The Maid's Version
Woods, S. Chiefs
Wright, J. The house on Foster Hill
Yocum, R. A welcome murder
Zumas, L. Red clocks

SMALL TOWNS -- CALIFORNIA
Novak, B. This heart of mine
SMALL TOWNS -- CANADA
Bates, J. Midnight at the Dragon Cafe
SMALL TOWNS -- FRANCE
Nemirovsky, I. Fire in the blood
Roberts, M. Ignorance
SMALL TOWNS -- MAINE
King, S. Salem's lot
SMALL TOWNS -- MONTANA
Salvalaggio, K. Bone dust white
SMALL TOWNS -- NEW YORK (STATE)

Phillips, C. Perfect fit
SMALL TOWNS -- NORTH CAROLINA
Allen, S. First frost
Allen, S. Garden spells
Frazier, C. Nightwoods
Karon, J. At home in Mitford
SMALL TOWNS -- ONTARIO
Strange, M. Follow me down
SMALL TOWNS -- PERU
Vargas Llosa, M. Green house
SMALL TOWNS -- SPAIN
Romano-Lax, A. The Spanish bow
SMALL TOWNS -- SWEDEN
Mankell, H. Firewall
Mankell, H. The man who smiled
SMALL TOWNS -- VERMONT
Morris, M. Songs in ordinary time
SMALL TOWNS -- VIRGINIA
Ramsay, F. Scone Island
Ramsay, F. Stranger room
Trigiani, A. Big Cherry Holler
Trigiani, A. Big Stone Gap
Walls, J. The silver star
SMALL TOWNS -- WISCONSIN
Sidor, S. Skin River
Small vices Parker, R.
Small wars Jones, S.
SMALL, AMBROSE, 1866-1919
Ondaatje, M. In the skin of a lion
SMALL-TOWN LIFE
Bohjalian, C. Secrets of Eden
Freeman, C. All that I have
SMALL-TOWN LIFE -- NEW HAMPSHIRE
Picoult, J. Nineteen minutes
SMALLPOX
Kent, K. The heretic's daughter
Rowland, L. The Shogun's daughter
SMALLWOOD, JOSEPH R, 1900-1991
Johnston, W. The colony of unrequited dreams
SMELL
Bauermeister, E. The scent keeper
Suskind, P. Perfume
Smile Doyle, R.
A **smile** on the face of the tiger Estleman, L.
Smiley's people Le Carre, J.
Smilla's sense of snow Hoeg, P.
SMITH, LILY CASEY, 1901-1968
Walls, J. Half broke horses
Smitten by the Brit Johnson, M.
Smoke Vyleta, D.
Smoke [series] Vyleta, D.
Smoke and ashes Mukherjee, A.
Smoke screen Blackstock, T.
SMOKEJUMPERS
Buchman, M. Pure heat
Smokescreen Francis, D.
Smokey Dalton novels [series] Nelscott, K.

Craddock, C. An alchemy of masques and mirrors
DeWoskin, R. Big girl small
Diaz, J. The brief wondrous life of Oscar Wao
Drabble, M. The sea lady
Eggers, D. How we are hungry
Frankel, L. This is how it always is
Fridlund, E. History of wolves
Giordano, P. The solitude of prime numbers
Harris, E. I say a little prayer
Hesse, H. The fairy tales of Hermann Hesse
James, H. Daisy Miller
Jen, G. World and town
July, M. No one belongs here more than you
Kleypas, L. Secrets of a summer night
Maguire, G. Wicked
Morrison, T. The bluest eye
Morrison, T. Sula
Murray, P. Skippy dies
Oates, J. Blonde
Phillips, S. It had to be you
Shelley, M. Frankenstein
Stone, I. The agony and the ecstasy
Wells, H. The invisible man
Wolfe, T. I am Charlotte Simmons

SOCIAL ACCEPTANCE IN CHILDREN
Winter, K. Annabel

SOCIAL ACTION
Mortimer, J. Quite honestly

SOCIAL ADVOCACY
Russell, M. The women of the copper country
Shields, C. Unless

SOCIAL ADVOCATES
Mosley, W. The right mistake
Nickson, C. On Copper Street

SOCIAL BEHAVIOR
Diaz, J. This is how you lose her
Smith, Z. NW

SOCIAL CHANGE
Alderman, N. The power
Alharthi, J. Celestial bodies
Anam, T. The bones of grace
Aw, T. We, the survivors
Bowman, D. Big bang
Coe, J. The rotters' club
Coster, N. Halsey Street
Del Amo, J. Animalia
Desai, K. The inheritance of loss
Dos Passos, J. Manhattan transfer
Ferrante, E. The story of the lost child
Festing, I. The bird keeper
Follett, K. Edge of eternity
Follett, K. Winter of the world
Ford, F. Parade's end
Ghaffari, R. To keep the sun alive
Glass, J. The women's war
Hammad, I. The Parisian, or, Al-Barisi
Hilderbrand, E. Summer of '69

Hoeg, P. The history of Danish dreams
Hollinghurst, A. The Sparsholt affair
Houellebecq, M. Submission
Jin, H. A free life
Joyce, G. The limits of enchantment
Kimani, P. Dance of the Jakaranda
Kingsolver, B. Unsheltered
Kostova, E. The shadow land
Lee, H. Go set a watchman
Ma, J. Beijing coma
Ma, J. China dream
Moreno-Garcia, S. Gods of jade and shadow
Onyebuchi, T. Riot baby
Pinsker, S. A song for a new day
Pittman, A. The seamstress
Pontoppidan, H. Lucky Per
Robertson, R. The long take
Robinson, K. New York 2140
Rooney, K. Lillian Boxfish takes a walk
Schami, R. Sophia
Serpell, N. The old drift
Sholokhov, M. The Don flows home to the sea
Smith, A. Autumn
Smith, A. Spring
Smith, A. Winter
Smith, B. The return of Kid Cooper
Unsworth, B. The quality of mercy
Wall, C. The dearly beloved
Zumas, L. Red clocks

SOCIAL CHANGE -- CHINA
Chen, D. Brothers
Thien, M. Do not say we have nothing

SOCIAL CHANGE -- PSYCHOLOGICAL ASPECTS
Sofer, D. The Septembers of Shiraz

SOCIAL CLASSES
Adiga, A. Selection day
Adiga, A. The white tiger
Aliu, X. Brass
Anderton, J. Debris
Austen, J. Mansfield Park
Austen, J. Pride and prejudice
Aw, T. We, the survivors
Bacigalupi, P. The water knife
Bainbridge, B. Every man for himself
Baker, J. Longbourn
Balogh, M. The arrangement
Bambara, T. Gorilla, my love
Bambara, T. The salt eaters
Barbery, M. The elegance of the hedgehog
Benson, E. Make way for Lucia
Bhuvaneswar, C. White dancing elephants
Brockway, C. No place for a dame
Buck, P. The good Earth
Burnet, G. His bloody project
Burrowes, G. The heir
Burrowes, G. The soldier
Burton, J. The miniaturist

Unsworth, B. The quality of mercy
Vanderbes, J. Strangers at the feast
Vyleta, D. Smoke
Wascom, K. The blood of heaven
Wells, H. The invisible man
Welty, E. Delta wedding
White, E. Heartstone
Williams, B. The golden hour
Winter, E. The rage of dragons
Wolfe, T. The bonfire of the vanities
Wolff, T. Old school
Woodson, J. Red at the bone
Woolf, V. Jacob's room
Woolf, V. Mrs. Dalloway
Yap, F. Yesterday
Zaman, N. Up in the main house & other stories

SOCIAL CLASSES -- 19TH CENTURY
Dickens, C. Our mutual friend
Putney, M. Nowhere near respectable

SOCIAL CLASSES -- AFGHANISTAN
Hosseini, K. The kite runner

SOCIAL CLASSES -- PAKISTAN
Mueenuddin, D. In other rooms, other wonders

SOCIAL CLASSES -- PARIS, FRANCE
Balzac, H. Cousin Bette

SOCIAL CLASSES -- ROME
McCullough, C. The first man in Rome

SOCIAL CLASSES AND FAMILY
Umrigar, T. The space between us
Wright, A. Carpentaria

SOCIAL CONFLICT
Adiga, A. Last man in tower
Arden, K. The bear and the nightingale
Beauvoir, S. The Mandarins
Bouman, T. Dry bones in the valley
Boyle, T. When the killing's done
Boyle, T. World's end
Frazier, C. Varina
Ganshert, K. No one ever asked
Hair, D. Mage's blood
Hammad, I. The Parisian, or, Al-Barisi
Hensher, P. Scenes from early life
Holsinger, B. The gifted school
Jenkins, B. Forbidden
Kadrey, R. The grand dark
Kress, N. Tomorrow's kin
Kwan, K. Crazy rich Asians
Lafferty, M. Ghost train to New Orleans
Lafferty, M. The shambling guide to New York City
Lutz, L. The swallows
Matlwa, K. Evening primrose
McKinty, A. The cold, cold ground
McKinty, A. In the morning I'll be gone
Mozley, F. Elmet
Mukherjee, N. The lives of others
Natt och Dag, N. The wolf and the watchman
Porter, M. Lanny

Read, C. Invisible boy
Rice, A. Blood communion
Stirling, S. A meeting at Corvallis
Street, K. Edgar Allan Poe and the jewel of Peru
Thien, M. Do not say we have nothing
Twardoch, S. The king of Warsaw
Walton, J. Necessity
Woolf, V. Mrs. Dalloway

SOCIAL CONTROL
Beckett, L. Gamechanger
Burgess, A. A clockwork orange
Stephenson, N. The diamond age,
Watkins, C. Gold fame citrus
Social creature Burton, T.

SOCIAL CRITICISM
Lethem, J. Chronic city

SOCIAL ETHICS
Camus, A. The fall

SOCIAL EVOLUTION
Beckett, L. Gamechanger

SOCIAL FORECASTING
Asimov, I. Foundation

SOCIAL GROUPS
Dektar, M. The Ash family

SOCIAL HISTORY
Akpan, U. Say you're one of them

SOCIAL INTERACTION
Smith, A. There but for the

SOCIAL ISOLATION
Albert, E. After birth
Armstrong, K. Watcher in the woods
Bates, J. Midnight at the Dragon Cafe
Beagle, P. In Calabria
Beauman, N. Madness is better than defeat
Beckett, S. Murphy
Bell, M. The color of night
Bognanni, P. The house of tomorrow
Bradbury, R. The Martian chronicles
Butler, S. Cygnet
Campisi, M. Sin eater
Camus, A. The plague
Carpenter, E. Every single secret
Conrad, J. Victory
Crummey, M. The innocents
Darnielle, J. Wolf in white van
Dev, S. A distant heart
Diaz, J. This is how you lose her
Dolan-Leach, C. We went to the woods
Dostoyevsky, F. Notes from underground
Fine, J. What should be wild
Fowler, C. Bryant & May
Freudenberger, N. The dissident
Gardam, J. Old Filth
Geni, A. The lightkeepers
Gerritsen, T. The shape of night
Green, G. Ravens
Hill, S. The risk of darkness

Butler, O. Dawn
Butler, O. Imago
Butler, O. Kindred
Butler, O. Parable of the sower
Butler, O. Parable of the talents
Cambias, J. A darkling sea
DeLillo, D. Zero K
Doctorow, C. Radicalized
Eggers, D. A hologram for the king
Elison, M. The book of Etta
Elison, M. The book of Flora
Elison, M. The book of the unnamed midwife
Emshwiller, C. The secret city
Gilman, C. Herland
Haig, M. The humans
Hall, L. Speak
Heinlein, R. The moon is a harsh mistress
Heinlein, R. Stranger in a strange land
Jemisin, N. The fifth season
Jemisin, N. The obelisk gate
Jemisin, N. The stone sky
King, S. Sleeping beauties
Kowal, M. The calculating stars
Kowal, M. The fated sky
Le Guin, U. The birthday of the world
Le Guin, U. The dispossessed
Le Guin, U. Four ways to forgiveness
Le Guin, U. The left hand of darkness
Le Guin, U. The telling
Liu, K. Invisible planets
Mieville, C. Embassytown
Miller, W. A canticle for Leibowitz
Newitz, A. The future of another timeline
O'Dell, C. A study in honor
Pinsker, S. A song for a new day
Russell, M. Children of God
Russell, M. The sparrow
Sisters of the revolution
Solomon, R. An unkindness of ghosts
Stross, C. Glasshouse
Tepper, S. The gate to Women's Country
Tepper, S. Grass
Tepper, S. Singer from the sea
Tepper, S. The visitor
Walton, J. My real children
Wells, H. The time machine
Wilson, R. Julian Comstock
Zamyatin, Y. We

SOCIAL SCIENCE RESEARCH
MacLean, S. One good earl deserves a lover

SOCIAL STATUS
Balogh, M. Someone to hold
Burton, T. Social creature
Colombani, L. The braid
Fitzgerald, F. This side of paradise
James, E. Three weeks with Lady X
London, J. Martin Eden

Marren, S. A Palm Beach wife
Thackeray, W. Vanity fair
Wolfe, T. I am Charlotte Simmons

SOCIAL STATUS -- GREAT BRITAIN
Faber, M. The crimson petal and the white

SOCIAL STRUCTURE
Achebe, C. Things fall apart
Doctorow, C. Radicalized
Doctorow, C. Walkaway
Kincaid, J. Annie John
Winter, K. Annabel

SOCIAL VALUES
Smith, A. Spring

SOCIAL WORKERS
DePoy, P. Sidewalk saint
Faye, L. The gods of Gotham
Goodwin, B. Revelation
Henderson, S. Fourth of July Creek
Offutt, C. Country dark
Qashu, S. Second person singular
Roberts, N. Sea swept

SOCIALISM
Chatwin, B. Utz
Nickson, C. On Copper Street
Sinclair, U. The jungle
Waters, S. Tipping the velvet

SOCIALISM -- SOVIET UNION
Solzhenitsyn, A. Cancer ward

SOCIALITES
Bergman, M. Almost famous women
Capote, T. Breakfast at Tiffany's
Constantine, L. The last Mrs. Parrish
Dunne, D. Too much money
Fitzgerald, F. The beautiful and damned
Fowler, T. A well-behaved woman
Fowler, T. Z
Hamill, P. Tabloid city
Hart, C. White elephant dead
Heller, P. Celine
Hunt, A. City of saints
Jakes, J. On secret service
Lethem, J. Chronic city
Marren, S. A Palm Beach wife
Moyes, J. The peacock emporium
Read, C. Invisible boy
Waugh, E. Vile bodies
Willig, L. The garden intrigue
The **society** Palmer, M.

SOCIETY OF FRIENDS INDIANA
West, J. The friendly persuasion

SOCIOLOGISTS
Banks, R. Lost memory of skin
Berne, S. The dogs of Littlefield

SOCIOLOGY
Berne, S. The dogs of Littlefield
Rader-Day, L. The black hour
Socrates Fortlow novels [series] Mosley, W.

Wiesel, E. Dawn
Winterson, J. The passion
Woolf, V. Jacob's room
Zahn, T. Dark force rising
Zahn, T. Heir to the empire
Zahn, T. The last command
Zimmerman, D. The sandbox

SOLDIERS -- AUSTRALIA
Bowen, R. The victory garden
Keneally, T. The daughters of Mars

SOLDIERS -- AUSTRIA
Krivak, A. The sojourn

SOLDIERS -- DRUG USE
O'Connor, R. Buffalo soldiers

SOLDIERS -- FRANCE
Dumas, A. The three musketeers
Dumas, A. Twenty years after

SOLDIERS -- FRANCE -- HISTORY -- 18TH CENTURY
Flanagan, T. The year of the French

SOLDIERS -- GERMANY
Boll, H. The silent angel
Jenoff, P. The ambassador's daughter
Nemirovsky, I. Suite Francaise
Remarque, E. A time to love and a time to die

SOLDIERS -- GREAT BRITAIN
Barker, P. Regeneration
Jakeman, J. In the kingdom of mists
Jones, S. Small wars
Ondaatje, M. The English patient

SOLDIERS -- GREAT BRITAIN -- 20TH CENTURY
Barker, P. The ghost road

SOLDIERS -- GREAT BRITAIN -- HISTORY -- 20TH CENTURY
Faulks, S. Birdsong

SOLDIERS -- IRELAND -- HISTORY -- 18TH CENTURY
Flanagan, T. The year of the French

SOLDIERS -- ITALY
Giordano, P. The human body
Mengiste, M. The shadow king

SOLDIERS -- JAPAN
Lee, C. A gesture life

SOLDIERS -- UNITED STATES
Heller, J. Catch-22
Hersey, J. A bell for Adano
Higgins, J. Night of the fox
Olmstead, R. Far bright star
Powers, K. The yellow birds
Pynchon, T. Gravity's rainbow
The road ahead
Shaara, J. Gone for soldiers
Trumbo, D. Johnny got his gun
Turow, S. Ordinary heroes

SOLDIERS -- UNITED STATES -- HISTORY -- WORLD WAR I
Lowenthal, M. Charity girl

SOLDIERS -- UNITED STATES -- PSYCHOLOGY
O'Brien, T. The things they carried

Soledad County novels [series] Muller, M.
SOLID WASTE DISPOSAL
Chen, Q. Waste tide
Leon, D. About face
The **Solitary** House Shepherd, L.
SOLITUDE
Burrowes, G. Lady Sophie's Christmas wish
Coetzee, J. Foe
Defoe, D. Robinson Crusoe
Frazier, C. Nightwoods
Freudenberger, N. The dissident
Garcia Marquez, G. One hundred years of solitude
Giordano, P. The solitude of prime numbers
Johnson, D. Train dreams
Koontz, D. Innocence
Krivak, A. The bear
Morante, E. Arturo's island
Reid, I. I'm thinking of ending things
Starnone, D. Trick
Winton, T. The shepherd's hut
Woods, S. Palindrome
Wyld, E. After the fire, a still small voice
Yoshimoto, B. The lake
The **solitude** of prime numbers Giordano, P.
Solomon Gursky was here Richler, M.
SOMALI AMERICANS
Farah, N. Crossbones
Farah, N. Links
SOMALIA
Farah, N. Crossbones
Farah, N. Links
Ledgard, J. Submergence
Mohamed, N. The orchard of lost souls
Scego, I. Adua
Some bitter taste Nabb, M.
Some die nameless Stroby, W.
Some kind of fairy tale Joyce, G.
Some luck Smiley, J.
Some things I never thought I'd do Cleage, P.
Someday Quilts mysteries [series] O'Donohue, C.
Someone McDermott, A.
Someone knows my name Hill, L.
Someone like me Carey, M.
Someone to hold Balogh, M.
Someone to love Balogh, M.
Someone to love Deveraux, J.
Someone to remember Balogh, M.
Someone to trust Balogh, M.
Someone to wed Balogh, M.
Somersault Oe, K.
Something about you James, J.
Something borrowed, something black Estleman, L.
Something in the air Lathen, E.
Something in the water Steadman, C.
Something red Nicholas, D.
Something red [series] Nicholas, D.
Something rich and strange Rash, R.

Mda, Z. The whale caller
Meyer, D. Icarus
Meyer, D. Heart of the hunter
Meyer, D. Trackers
Paton, A. Cry, the beloved country
Ward, A. Forgive me
Willocks, T. Memo from Turner

SOUTH AFRICA -- HISTORY
Michener, J. The covenant

SOUTH AFRICA -- HISTORY -- 1909-1961
Nunn, M. A beautiful place to die
Nunn, M. Blessed are the dead
Nunn, M. Present darkness

SOUTH AFRICA -- HISTORY -- 1989-
Gordimer, N. No time like the present

SOUTH AFRICA -- HISTORY -- 19TH CENTURY
Brink, A. Philida

SOUTH AFRICA -- HISTORY -- 20TH CENTURY
Mda, Z. The Madonna of Excelsior

SOUTH AFRICA -- POLITICS AND GOVERNMENT -- 1994-
Matlwa, K. Evening primrose

SOUTH AFRICA -- RACE RELATIONS
Coetzee, J. Age of Iron
Gordimer, N. July's people
Gordimer, N. My son's story
Gordimer, N. None to accompany me
Lessing, D. The grass is singing
McClure, J. The steam pig
Mda, Z. The Madonna of Excelsior
Paton, A. Ah, but your land is beautiful
Paton, A. Cry, the beloved country
Paton, A. Too late the phalarope

SOUTH AFRICA -- SOCIAL CONDITIONS -- 1981-
Coetzee, J. Disgrace

SOUTH AFRICA -- SOCIAL CONDITIONS -- 20TH CENTURY
McClure, J. The steam pig

SOUTH AFRICA -- SOCIAL LIFE AND CUSTOMS
Coetzee, J. Summertime
Gordimer, N. No time like the present

SOUTH AFRICA -- SOCIAL LIFE AND CUSTOMS -- 20TH CENTURY
Mason, R. Who killed Piet Barol?

SOUTH AFRICANS
McClure, J. The steam pig
Paton, A. Cry, the beloved country

SOUTH AFRICANS IN ENGLAND
Greene, G. The human factor

SOUTH AMERICA
Alarcon, D. At night we walk in circles
Alarcon, D. Lost City Radio
Allende, I. Eva Luna
Allende, I. The stories of Eva Luna
Cussler, C. Blue gold
Garcia Marquez, G. The autumn of the patriarch
Gifford, B. The stars above Veracruz

O'Brian, P. The wine-dark sea
Patchett, A. Bel canto
Skarmeta, A. The dancer and the thief
Stroby, W. Some die nameless
Toews, M. Women talking
Vargas Llosa, M. The bad girl

SOUTH AMERICA -- HISTORY
Allende, I. The house of the spirits

SOUTH AMERICA -- HISTORY -- 19TH CENTURY
Conrad, J. Nostromo
Garcia Marquez, G. The general in his labyrinth

SOUTH ASIANS
Bhuvaneswar, C. White dancing elephants

SOUTH AUSTRALIA
Francis, D. Wedding Bush Road

SOUTH BEND, INDIANA
McInerny, R. Celt and pepper
McInerny, R. Irish coffee

SOUTH CAROLINA
Allison, D. Bastard out of Carolina
Baldacci, D. One summer
Bobotis, A. The last list of Miss Judith Kratt
Brown, S. Outfox
Brown, S. The witness
Childs, L. Lavender blue murder
Conroy, P. The prince of tides
Dunn, M. Ella Minnow Pea
Ephron, H. You'll never know, dear
Frank, D. Folly Beach
Godwin, G. Grief cottage
Hart, C. Death walked in
Hart, C. Murder walks the plank
Hart, C. White elephant dead
Hart, C. Yankee Doodle dead
Hendrix, G. My best friend's exorcism
Matthiessen, P. Bone by bone
Monroe, M. Beach house reunion
Naylor, G. Mama Day
Ramsay, H. Summer on Moonlight Bay
Sanders, D. Clover

SOUTH CAROLINA -- HISTORY -- 19TH CENTURY
Kidd, S. The invention of wings

SOUTH CAROLINA -- HISTORY -- CIVIL WAR, 1861-1865
Cobbs Hoffman, E. The Tubman command
Doctorow, E. The march

SOUTH CAROLINA -- RACE RELATIONS
Kidd, S. The secret life of bees
Sanders, D. Clover

SOUTH CENTRAL LOS ANGELES, CALIFORNIA
Mosley, W. The last days of Ptolemy Grey

SOUTH DAKOTA
Child, L. 61 hours
Meyers, K. Twisted tree
Meyers, K. The work of wolves

SOUTH DAKOTA -- HISTORY -- 19TH CENTURY
Lansdale, J. Paradise sky

Gaines, E. A gathering of old men
Gibbons, K. Charms for the easy life
Gibbons, K. Ellen Foster
Gibbons, K. The life all around me by Ellen Foster
Godwin, G. Flora
Godwin, G. Unfinished desires
Graley, L. The current that carries
Grau, S. The keepers of the house
Greene, A. Bloodroot
Greene, A. Long Man
Gurganus, A. Oldest living Confederate widow tells all
Hart, J. Down river
Hicks, R. The widow of the South
House, S. A parchment of leaves
Hurston, Z. Their eyes were watching God
Jackson, J. The almost sisters
Jackson, J. Never have I ever
Johnson, C. Treeborne
Jones, T. An American marriage
Jones, T. Silver sparrow
Jordan, H. Mudbound
Keller, J. Fast falls the night
Keller, J. A killing in the hills
Keller, J. Last ragged breath
Keller, J. Bone on bone
Kidd, S. The invention of wings
Kidd, S. The secret life of bees
Lansdale, J. The bottoms
Lansdale, J. A fine dark line
Lee, H. Go set a watchman
Lee, H. To kill a mockingbird
Maron, M. Bootlegger's daughter
Maron, M. High country fall
Maron, M. Shooting at loons
Maron, M. Storm track
Maron, M. Uncommon clay
Maron, M. Up jumps the Devil
McCarthy, C. Blood meridian, or, The evening redness in the West
McCrumb, S. The ballad of Frankie Silver
McCrumb, S. The ballad of Tom Dooley
McCrumb, S. If ever I return, pretty Peggy-O
McCrumb, S. She walks these hills
McCullers, C. The heart is a lonely hunter
McCullers, C. The member of the wedding
McCullers, C. Reflections in a golden eye
Miller, M. Biloxi
Mitchell, M. Gone with the wind
Monroe, M. Beach house reunion
Morgan, R. The road from Gap Creek
Morris, W. Taps
Morrison, T. Beloved
Nordan, L. Wolf whistle
O'Connor, F. Collected works
O'Connor, F. The complete stories
O'Connor, F. The violent bear it away
O'Connor, F. Wise blood

Owen, H. The bottom
Owen, H. The devil's triangle
Owen, H. Oregon Hill
Owen, H. Parker Field
Panowich, B. Bull Mountain
Panowich, B. Like lions
Pearson, R. A long time comin'
Percy, W. The last gentleman
Percy, W. The moviegoer
Percy, W. The second coming
Price, R. The good priest's son
Rash, R. Above the waterfall
Rash, R. Burning bright
Rash, R. The cove
Rash, R. Nothing gold can stay
Rash, R. Serena
Rash, R. Something rich and strange
Smith, J. New Orleans beat
Smith, J. 82 Desire
Smith, J. Crescent City kill
Smith, J. House of blues
Smith, J. Jazz funeral
Smith, J. The kindness of strangers
Smith, J. Louisiana hotshot
Smith, J. Mean woman blues
Smith, J. New Orleans beat
Smith, L. Fair and tender ladies
Smith, L. Family linen
Smith, L. On Agate Hill
Smith, L. Oral history
Smith, M. Blackwood
Smith, M. The fighter
Stockett, K. The help
Styron, W. Lie down in darkness
Tademy, L. Cane River
Toole, J. A confederacy of dunces
Trigiani, A. Big Cherry Holler
Trigiani, A. Big Stone Gap
Twain, M. Adventures of Huckleberry Finn
Vernon, O. A killing in this town
Walker, A. The color purple
Walker, A. The third life of Grange Copeland
Walker, M. Jubilee
Walsh, M. My sunshine away
Ward, J. Salvage the bones
Ward, J. Sing, unburied, sing
Warren, R. All the king's men
Warren, R. Band of angels
Warren, R. World enough and time
Wascom, K. The blood of heaven
Watson, B. Miss Jane
Watts, S. No one is coming to save us
Weiss, L. If the creek don't rise
Wells, R. Divine secrets of the Ya-Ya Sisterhood
Welty, E. The collected stories of Eudora Welty
Welty, E. Delta wedding
Welty, E. Losing battles

SOUTHERN STATES -- RACE RELATIONS -- HISTORY -- 19TH CENTURY
Coates, T. The water dancer
Whitehead, C. The underground railroad

SOUTHERN STATES -- RACE RELATIONS -- HISTORY -- 20TH CENTURY
Naslund, S. Four spirits
Whitehead, C. The Nickel boys

SOUTHERN STATES -- SOCIAL LIFE AND CUSTOMS
Gilchrist, E. Collected stories
Johnson, C. Treeborne
O'Connor, F. The complete stories
Spencer, E. The southern woman

SOUTHERN STATES -- SOCIAL LIFE AND CUSTOMS -- 19TH CENTURY
Atakora, A. Conjure women

SOUTHERN STATES -- SOCIAL LIFE AND CUSTOMS -- 20TH CENTURY
McCullers, C. The member of the wedding
McCullers, C. Reflections in a golden eye
Welty, E. The collected stories of Eudora Welty
Welty, E. Delta wedding
Welty, E. Stories, essays & memoir
The **southern** woman Spencer, E.

SOUTHWEST (UNITED STATES)
Anaya, R. The man who could fly and other stories
Baca, J. The importance of a piece of paper
Bacigalupi, P. The water knife
Berlin, L. A manual for cleaning women
Leonard, E. The complete Western stories of Elmore Leonard.
Obreht, T. Inland
Parks, S. Getting mother's body
Perez, R. Jim Henson's tale of sand
Richter, C. The sea of grass
Sallis, J. Sarah Jane
Silko, L. Gardens in the dunes
Swarthout, G. Bless the beasts and children

SOUTHWEST (UNITED STATES) -- HISTORY -- 20TH CENTURY
Groom, W. El Paso

SOUTHWEST (UNITED STATES) -- RACE RELATIONS
Silko, L. Almanac of the dead

SOUVENIRS (KEEPSAKES)
Eco, U. The mysterious flame of Queen Loana
Reay, K. The Bronte plot
Sovereign Sansom, C.

SOVIET UNION
Barnes, J. The noise of time
Bezmozgis, D. The betrayers
Bronsky, A. The hottest dishes of the Tartar cuisine
Cander, C. The weight of a piano
Clancy, T. The cardinal of the Kremlin
Dean, D. The madonnas of Leningrad
Fleming, I. From Russia with love
Harris, R. Archangel
Horn, D. The world to come

Littell, R. The Stalin epigram
Makine, A. The woman who waited
Muller, H. The hunger angel
Prescott, L. The secrets we kept
Remarque, E. A time to love and a time to die
Sholokhov, M. And quiet flows the Don
Smith, M. Polar Star
Solzhenitsyn, A. Cancer ward
Solzhenitsyn, A. One day in the life of Ivan Denisovich

SOVIET UNION -- FOREIGN RELATIONS -- UNITED STATES
Brown, D. Flight of the Old Dog
Burdick, E. Fail-safe
Schwartz, J. The red daughter

SOVIET UNION -- HISTORY
Furnivall, K. The red scarf
Rutherfurd, E. Russka

SOVIET UNION -- HISTORY -- 1925-1953
Holland, T. The archivist's story
Koestler, A. Darkness at noon
Smith, T. Agent 6
Smith, T. Child 44
Smith, T. The secret speech

SOVIET UNION -- HISTORY -- 1985-1991
Mankell, H. The dogs of Riga

SOVIET UNION -- HISTORY -- 20TH CENTURY
Makine, A. Music of a life
Paul, G. The lost daughter

SOVIET UNION -- HISTORY -- GERMAN OCCUPATION, 1941-1944
Kuznetsov, A. Babi Yar
Robbins, D. Last citadel
Robbins, D. War of the rats

SOVIET UNION -- HISTORY -- REVOLUTION, 1917-1921
Meek, J. The people's act of love
Pasternak, B. Doctor Zhivago
Paul, G. The lost daughter
Sholokhov, M. And quiet flows the Don

SOVIET UNION -- POLITICS AND GOVERNMENT
Littell, R. The Mayakovsky tapes

SOVIET UNION -- POLITICS AND GOVERNMENT -- 1917-1936
Rand, A. We the living

SOVIET UNION -- POLITICS AND GOVERNMENT -- 1936-1953
Holland, T. The archivist's story
Ryan, W. The darkening field
Ryan, W. The twelfth department
Solzhenitsyn, A. In the first circle

SOVIET UNION -- SOCIAL CONDITIONS -- 1917-1936
Rand, A. We the living

SOVIET UNION -- SOCIAL CONDITIONS -- 1917-1945
Bulgakov, M. The master and Margarita

SOVIET UNION -- SOCIAL LIFE AND CUSTOMS
Vollmann, W. Europe central

SOVIET UNION. AIR FORCE. NIGHT WITCHES REGIMENT

Kowal, M. The fated sky
Lostetter, M. Noumenon
Michener, J. Space
Scalzi, J. The collapsing empire
Steele, A. Coyote
Stephenson, N. Seveneves

SPACE FLIGHT

Adams, D. The hitchhiker's guide to the galaxy
Adams, D. The restaurant at the end of the universe
Anderson, K. The last days of Krypton
Asaro, C. Primary inversion
Asher, N. The skinner
Asimov, I. Foundation
Asimov, I. Foundation and empire
Banks, I. The hydrogen sonata
Banks, I. Matter
Bear, G. Anvil of stars
Bouchet, A. Nightchaser
Bradbury, R. Bradbury stories
Bradbury, R. The illustrated man
Bradbury, R. The Martian chronicles
Bujold, L. Shards of honor
Bujold, L. The warrior's apprentice
Butler, O. Dawn
Cambias, J. A darkling sea
Chambers, B. A closed and common orbit
Chambers, B. The long way to a small, angry planet
Chambers, B. Record of a spaceborn few
Chu, W. The lives of tao
Clarke, A. 2001
Corey, J. Abaddon's gate
Corey, J. Babylon's ashes
Corey, J. Caliban's war
Corey, J. Cibola burn
Corey, J. Leviathan wakes
Corey, J. Nemesis games
Egan, G. Schild's ladder
Flynn, M. The January dancer
Gunn, J. Transcendental
Haldeman, J. The forever war
Hamilton, P. Pandora's star
Harrison, M. Light
Harrison, M. Nova swing
Herbert, F. Dune
Jimenez, S. The vanished birds
Kress, N. If tomorrow comes
Lafferty, M. Six wakes
Leckie, A. Ancillary justice
Leckie, A. Ancillary mercy
Leckie, A. Ancillary sword
Lem, S. Solaris
Levine, D. Arabella of Mars
Liu, C. Death's end
Lostetter, M. Noumenon
McDevitt, J. The engines of God
Michener, J. Space
Morgan, R. Broken angels

Morgan, R. Thirteen
New suns
O'Keefe, M. Velocity weapon
Okorafor, N. Binti
Pohl, F. Gateway
Robinson, K. Aurora
Robinson, K. The Martians
Russell, M. Children of God
Russell, M. The sparrow
Sagan, C. Contact
Scalzi, J. The collapsing empire
Simmons, D. Endymion
Simmons, D. The rise of Endymion
Steele, A. Coyote
Stross, C. Neptune's brood
Stross, C. Saturn's children
Swyler, E. Light from other stars
Tepper, S. Grass
Valente, C. Radiance
Varley, J. Titan
Varley, J. Dark lightning
Varley, J. Red lightning
Varley, J. Red thunder
Varley, J. Rolling thunder
Vinge, V. A fire upon the deep
Vonnegut, K. Slaughterhouse-five
Zelazny, R. Lord of light

SPACE FLIGHT TO MARS

Howrey, M. The wanderers
Vonnegut, K. The sirens of Titan
Weir, A. The Martian

SPACE FLIGHT TO THE MOON

McDevitt, J. The Cassandra Project
Netzer, L. Shine shine shine
The **space** merchants Pohl, F.
Space Odyssey series [series] Clarke, A.

SPACE OPERA

Asaro, C. Primary inversion
Asimov, I. Foundation
Asimov, I. Foundation and empire
Asimov, I. Second foundation
Banks, I. Consider Phlebas
Banks, I. The hydrogen sonata
Banks, I. Matter
Banks, I. The player of games
Banks, I. Use of weapons
Bujold, L. Shards of honor
Bujold, L. The warrior's apprentice
Chambers, B. A closed and common orbit
Chambers, B. The long way to a small, angry planet
Chambers, B. Record of a spaceborn few
Cherryh, C. Foreigner
Corey, J. Leviathan wakes
Corey, J. Caliban's war
Corey, J. Cibola burn
Corey, J. Abaddon's gate
Corey, J. Nemesis games

Vonnegut, K. The sirens of Titan
Wagers, K. After the crown
Weber, D. On Basilisk Station
Wells, H. The war of the worlds
Zamyatin, Y. We
Zelazny, R. Lord of light

SPACE WARFARE

Asaro, C. Primary inversion
Banks, I. Consider Phlebas
Banks, I. Matter
Banks, I. The player of games
Banks, I. Use of weapons
Bear, G. Anvil of stars
Bear, G. The forge of God
Bujold, L. Shards of honor
Bujold, L. The warrior's apprentice
Card, O. Ender's game
Card, O. Speaker for the dead
Corey, J. Leviathan wakes
Corey, J. Caliban's war
Corey, J. Cibola burn
Corey, J. Abaddon's gate
Corey, J. Nemesis games
Corey, J. Babylon's ashes
Corey, J. Persepolis rising
Corey, J. Tiamat's wrath
Haldeman, J. The forever war
Heinlein, R. The moon is a harsh mistress
Heinlein, R. Starship troopers
Jones, D. A sudden wild magic
Lamb, A. Roboteer
Lee, Y. Ninefox gambit
Lee, Y. Raven stratagem
Lee, Y. Revenant gun
McDevitt, J. A talent for war
Mieville, C. Embassytown
O'Keefe, M. Velocity weapon
Okorafor, N. Binti
Okorafor, N. Binti
Scalzi, J. Old man's war
Scalzi, J. Redshirts
Simmons, D. The fall of Hyperion
Simmons, D. Hyperion
Tepper, S. Grass
Vinge, V. The children of the sky
Vinge, V. A deepness in the sky
Vinge, V. A fire upon the deep
Vonnegut, K. The sirens of Titan
Weber, D. The honor of the queen
Weber, D. On Basilisk Station
Weber, D. Shadow of freedom
Weber, D. The short victorious war
Westerfeld, S. The killing of worlds
Westerfeld, S. The risen empire
Williams, D. The stars now unclaimed
Wolfe, G. Home fires
Zahn, T. Dark force rising

Zahn, T. Heir to the empire
Zahn, T. The last command

SPACE WEAPONS

Brown, D. Flight of the Old Dog

SPACE-BASED MISSILE DEFENSES -- SOVIET UNION

Brown, D. Flight of the Old Dog

SPACESHIP CAPTAINS

Reynolds, A. Revenger
Scalzi, J. The collapsing empire
Simmons, D. The fall of Hyperion
Simmons, D. Hyperion

SPAIN

Barry, K. Night boat to Tangier
Bourdeaut, O. Waiting for Bojangles
Forester, C. Commodore Hornblower
Handke, P. Crossing the Sierra de Gredos
Hill Gumbao, T. The good suicides
Hill Gumbao, T. The summer of dead toys
Lerner, B. Leaving the Atocha Station
Levy, D. Hot milk
Marias, J. The infatuations
Munoz Molina, A. In her absence
Nichols, P. The rocks
Redondo, D. The invisible guardian
Romano-Lax, A. The Spanish bow
Ruiz Zafon, C. The angel's game
Straub, E. The vacationers
Trollope, J. A Spanish lover
Van der Vliet Oloomi, A. Call me Zebra

SPAIN -- HISTORY -- 14TH CENTURY

Falcones de Sierra, I. Cathedral of the sea

SPAIN -- HISTORY -- 15TH CENTURY

Gregory, P. The constant princess
Wilson, G. The bird king

SPAIN -- HISTORY -- 16TH CENTURY

Cervantes Saavedra, M. Don Quixote

SPAIN -- HISTORY -- 17TH CENTURY

Perez-Reverte, A. Captain Alatriste

SPAIN -- HISTORY -- 1939-1975

Munoz Molina, A. A manuscript of ashes
Ruiz Zafon, C. The labyrinth of the spirits

SPAIN -- HISTORY -- 19TH CENTURY

Merimee, P. Carmen
Perez-Reverte, A. The siege

SPAIN -- HISTORY -- 20TH CENTURY

Lopez Barrio, C. The house of the impossible loves

SPAIN -- HISTORY -- ARAB PERIOD, 711-1492

Gregory, P. The constant princess

SPAIN -- HISTORY -- CIVIL WAR, 1936-1939

Allende, I. A long petal of the sea
Duenas, M. The time in between
Follett, K. Winter of the world
Hemingway, E. For whom the bell tolls
Malraux, A. Man's hope
McLain, P. Love and ruin
Ruiz Zafon, C. The labyrinth of the spirits
Thelen, A. The island of second sight

Banks, I. Use of weapons
Bateman, K. This earl of mine
Benn, J. Billy Boyle
Bennett, R. City of blades
Black, C. Three hours in Paris
Bourne, J. The black hawk
Bourne, J. The forbidden rose
Brandreth, B. The assassin of Verona
Brandreth, B. The spy of Venice
Cameron, M. Power and empire
Carey, P. Parrot and Olivier in America
Carlyle, L. Never lie to a lady
Chase, L. Your scandalous ways
Chen, M. Here and now and then
Church, J. A corpse in the Koryo
Clancy, T. The hunt for Red October
Clements, R. Martyr
Clements, R. Revenger
Cole, A. An extraordinary union
Cole, A. A hope divided
Cole, A. An unconditional freedom
Cumming, C. A colder war
Cumming, C. A divided spy
Cussler, C. Sacred stone
Deighton, L. London match
Dick, P. The man in the high castle
Doctorow, E. The book of Daniel
Dugoni, R. The eighth sister
Dunmore, H. Exposure
Eisler, B. The god's eye view
Follett, K. Hornet flight
Forsyth, F. The fox
Furst, A. Blood of victory
Furst, A. Mission to Paris
Furst, A. Spies of the Balkans
Furst, A. Under occupation
Greene, G. The last word and other stories
Harris, O. A shadow intelligence
Harris, R. Archangel
Harris, R. The ghost
Harris, R. An officer and a spy
Haynes, D. Crashers
Higgins, J. Confessional
Higgins, J. Luciano's luck
Higgins, J. Rough justice
Higgins, J. Touch the devil
Horn, D. All other nights
Ignatius, D. Body of lies
Ignatius, D. The increment
Inbinder, G. The hanged man
Jakes, J. On secret service
Johnson, A. The orphan master's son
Johnson, D. Tree of smoke
Kay, G. Children of earth and sky
Kerr, P. Hitler's peace
Kerr, P. Prussian blue
King, L. The game

Le Carre, J. Agent running in the field
Le Carre, J. A most wanted man
Le Carre, J. Our kind of traitor
Lehane, D. World gone by
Loh, V. Breaking the tongue , by Vyvyane Loh.
Ludlum, R. The Bourne identity
Ludlum, R. The Bourne ultimatum
MacAlister, K. The truth about Leo
Mankell, H. The troubled man
Marias, J. Your face tomorrow, vol.1
Marias, J. Your face tomorrow, vol.2
Marias, J. Your face tomorrow, vol. 3
McCarry, C. The mulberry bush
McCarry, C. Old boys
Meacham, L. Dragonfly
Meyer, N. The adventure of the peculiar protocols
Muller, H. The fox was ever the hunter
Murdoch, I. The nice and the good
Nguyen, V. The sympathizer
Nickson, C. The hocus girl
O'Donohue, C. Beyond the pale
Ondaatje, M. The English patient
Parris, S. Treachery
Penelope, L. Song of blood and stone
Penman, S. Cruel as the grave
Perry, A. Death in focus
Peters, E. He shall thunder in the sky
Phillips, A. The king at the edge of the world
Poyer, D. A country of our own
Prescott, L. The secrets we kept
Quick, A. The mystery woman
Quick, A. Otherwise engaged
Quick, A. Slightly shady
Reich, C. The take
Robinson, P. All the colors of darkness
   Rogues
Ruff, M. 88 names
Seymour, G. Vagabond
Shacochis, B. The woman who lost her soul
Silva, D. The black widow
Silva, D. The new girl
Silva, D. The other woman
Steinhauer, O. The Cairo affair
Steinhauer, O. The tourist
Stross, C. Empire Games
Sundaresan, I. The splendor of silence
Wilkinson, L. American spy
Wolfe, G. The land across
Wolfe, S. The course of all treasons
Spies Frayn, M.

SPIES -- CONFEDERATE STATES OF AMERICA
Jakes, J. On secret service

SPIES -- FRANCE
Bourne, J. Rogue spy
Bourne, J. The spymaster's lady
Furst, A. The spies of Warsaw
Groot, T. Flame of resistance

Coelho, P. The alchemist
Redfield, J. The celestine prophecy
SPIRITUAL JOURNEYS
Bunyan, J. The pilgrim's progress
Gao, X. Soul mountain
Goudge, E. Green Dolphin Street
Heacox, K. Jimmy Bluefeather
Jhabvala, R. My nine lives
Maugham, W. The razor's edge
Rawlings, D. The baggage handler
Saunders, G. Lincoln in the bardo
SPIRITUAL LIFE
Martel, Y. The high mountains of Portugal
Redfield, J. The celestine prophecy
Yourcenar, M. Memoirs of Hadrian
SPIRITUAL LIFE -- BUDDHISM
Hesse, H. Siddhartha
SPIRITUAL RETREATS
Matthiessen, P. In paradise
SPIRITUAL WARFARE
Gaiman, N. American gods
SPIRITUALISM
Murdoch, I. The good apprentice
Murphy, S. The possessions
Penny, L. The cruelest month
SPIRITUALISTS
Bear, E. Stone mad
SPIRITUALITY
Allio, K. Buddhism for Western children
Bender, T. The last ghost dancer
Brooks, G. Caleb's crossing
Carlson, R. Five skies
Cather, W. Death comes for the archbishop
Cunningham, M. The snow queen
Doyle, R. Threshold
Oe, K. Somersault
Okorafor, N. Who fears death
Palmer, A. Too like the lightning
Potenza, C. Hearts of the missing
Shakar, A. Luminarium
Walton, J. Lent
Williams, J. Ninety-nine stories of God
The **splendor** before the dark George, M.
The **splendor** of silence Sundaresan, I.
SPOILED CHILDREN
Szabo, M. Abigail
SPOKANE INDIAN RESERVATION
Alexie, S. Reservation blues
SPOKANE INDIANS -- WASHINGTON (STATE)
Alexie, S. Reservation blues
SPOKANE, WASHINGTON
Walter, J. Citizen Vince
SPONTANEOUS COMBUSTION
Hill, J. The Fireman
SPONTANEOUS HUMAN COMBUSTION
Wilson, K. Nothing to see here
Spook Pronzini, B.

A **spool** of blue thread Tyler, A.
Spooner Dexter, P.
SPORES
Hill, J. The Fireman
The **sport** of kings Morgan, C.
SPORTS
Adiga, A. Selection day
Backman, F. Beartown
Backman, F. Us against you
McInerny, R. Irish coffee
SPORTS AGENTS
Phillips, S. Match me if you can
SPORTS BETTING
Hall, T. The case of the deadly butter chicken
Latour, J. The Havana World Series
SPORTS BETTING -- CORRUPT PRACTICES
DeSilva, B. A scourge of vipers
SPORTS INJURIES
Warrington, F. Midsummer night
SPORTS RIVALRY
Backman, F. Us against you
SPORTS ROMANCES
Adams, L. The bromance book club
Castille, S. In your corner
James, L. I want you back
Lohmann, J. Winning Ruby Heart
Martin, A. Blitzed
Martin, A. Fumbled
Phillips, S. First star I see tonight
Phillips, S. It had to be you
Phillips, S. Natural born charmer
Ryan, K. Long shot
SPORTS TEAMS
Backman, F. Beartown
Backman, F. Us against you
SPORTS-AGENTS
Coben, H. Long lost
SPORTSWRITERS
Karunatilaka, S. The legend of Pradeep Mathe   w
SPOUSES OF CLERGY
Greeley, M. The clergyman's wife
Miller, S. While I was gone
Page, K. The body in the bog
Page, K. The body in the vestibule
Rivers, F. And the shofar blew
SPOUSES OF MURDER VICTIMS
Buckman, D. Because the rain
Coben, H. Long lost
Pronzini, B. The violated
SPOUSES OF PREGNANT WOMEN
Cross-Smith, L. Whiskey & ribbons
Harrod-Eagles, C. Game over
Sprawl trilogy [series] Gibson, W.
SPRING
Smith, A. Spring
Williams, N. This is happiness
Spring Smith, A.

SPRING BREAK
Perrotta, T. Joe College
Spring snow Mishima, Y.
Spring tide Borjlind, C.
SPRING-HEELED JACK (LEGENDARY CHARACTER)
Hodder, M. The strange affair of Spring Heeled Jack
SPRINGS
Schutt, B. The Darwin strain
Springtime in a broken mirror Benedetti, M.
SPY FICTION
Bell, T. Overkill
Berenson, A. The deceivers
Berenson, A. The faithful spy
Berenson, A. The prisoner
Black, C. Three hours in Paris
Buchan, J. The thirty-nine steps
Buckley, W. Mongoose, R.I.P.
Clancy, T. The cardinal of the Kremlin
Clancy, T. Clear and present danger
Coonts, S. The armageddon file
Coonts, S. The art of war
Coonts, S. Liberty's last stand
Coonts, S. The Russia account
Cumming, C. A colder war
Cumming, C. A divided spy
Cumming, C. A foreign country
Cumming, C. The Moroccan girl
Cumming, C. The Trinity Six
Cussler, C. Golden Buddha
Cussler, C. Sacred stone
Deighton, L. Berlin game
Deighton, L. London match
Downing, D. Diary of a dead man on leave
Dugoni, R. The eighth sister
Dunmore, H. Exposure
Eisler, B. The god's eye view
Eisler, B. The killer collective
Fesperman, D. Safe houses
Fleming, I. Casino royale
Fleming, I. Doctor No
Fleming, I. From Russia with love
Fleming, I. Goldfinger
Fleming, I. The man with the golden gun
Fleming, I. On Her Majesty's secret service
Fleming, I. You only live twice
Follett, K. Eye of the needle
Follett, K. Hornet flight
Follett, K. Jackdaws
Forsyth, F. The kill list
Furst, A. Blood of victory
Furst, A. Dark voyage
Furst, A. The foreign correspondent
Furst, A. A hero of France
Furst, A. Mission to Paris
Furst, A. Spies of the Balkans
Furst, A. The spies of Warsaw
Furst, A. Under occupation

Goldberg, L. Fake truth
Greene, G. The human factor
Greene, G. Our man in Havana
Hagberg, D. Abyss
Hall, A. The quiller memorandum
Harkaway, N. Angelmaker
Harris, O. A shadow intelligence
Harris, R. Enigma
Hayes, T. I am Pilgrim
Higgins, J. Bad company
Higgins, J. Confessional
Higgins, J. Day of reckoning
Higgins, J. Edge of danger
Higgins, J. Eye of the storm
Higgins, J. Midnight runner
Higgins, J. Night of the fox
Higgins, J. Rough justice
Higgins, J. Touch the devil
Higgins, J. The White House connection
Horn, D. All other nights
Ignatius, D. Body of lies
Ignatius, D. A firing offense
Ignatius, D. The increment
Jin, H. A map of betrayal
Kanon, J. Los Alamos
Kerr, P. Hitler's peace
Lawton, J. Hammer to fall
Le Carre, J. Agent running in the fiel
Le Carre, J. A delicate truth
Le Carre, J. The honourable schoolboy
Le Carre, J. A most wanted man
Le Carre, J. Our kind of traitor
Le Carre, J. Smiley's people
Le Carre, J. The spy who came in from the cold
Le Carre, J. The tailor of Panama
Le Carre, J. Tinker, tailor, soldier, spy
Littell, R. The company
Ludlum, R. The Prometheus deception
MacInnes, H. The Venetian affair
Matthews, J. The Kremlin's candidate
Matthews, J. Palace of treason
Matthews, J. Red sparrow
McCarry, C. The mulberry bush
McCarry, C. Old boys
McEwan, I. Sweet tooth
Murphy, Y. Signed, Mata Hari
O'Donohue, C. Beyond the pale
Pavone, C. The expats
Pavone, C. The Paris diversion
Pearson, R. Choke point
Pearson, R. The red room
Pearson, R. The risk agent
Phillips, A. The king at the edge of the world
Porter, H. The bell ringers
Porter, H. Firefly
Porter, H. White hot silence
Priest, C. Clementine

Quick, A. Otherwise engaged
Redfern, E. The music of the spheres
Reich, C. Rules of deception
Reich, C. The take
Sebastian, T. Fatal ally
Seymour, G. Vagabond
Silva, D. The black widow
Silva, D. The kill artist
Silva, D. The new girl
Silva, D. The other woman
Steinhauer, O. All the old knives
Steinhauer, O. An American spy
Steinhauer, O. The Cairo affair
Steinhauer, O. The last tourist
Steinhauer, O. The nearest exit
Steinhauer, O. The tourist
Stross, C. Empire Games
Wilkinson, L. American spy
Zander, J. The swimmer
The **spy** of Venice Brandreth, B.

SPY SHIPS
Cussler, C. Golden Buddha
Cussler, C. Sacred stone
The **spy** who came in from the cold Le Carre, J.
Spymaster series [series] Bourne, J.
The **spymaster's** lady Bourne, J.

SQUATTER SETTLEMENTS
Grenville, K. The secret river

SQUATTERS
Auster, P. Sunset Park
Lessing, D. The good terrorist
Watkins, C. Gold fame citrus

SQUIRES -- SPAIN
Cervantes Saavedra, M. Don Quixote

SRI LANKA
Arudpragasam, A. The story of a brief marriage
Bala, S. The boat people
Gunesekera, R. Suncatcher
Karunatilaka, S. The legend of Pradeep Mathew

SRI LANKA -- HISTORY -- 20TH CENTURY
Ondaatje, M. Anil's ghost

SRI LANKA -- HISTORY -- CIVIL WAR, 1983-2009
Arudpragasam, A. The story of a brief marriage

SRI LANKANS
Adiga, A. Amnesty

ST ANDREWS, SCOTLAND
McDermid, V. The distant echo

ST LOUIS, MISSOURI
Ervin, K. Gunz and roses
Ervin, K. Mina's joint
Mehl, N. Mind games

ST PAUL, MINNESOTA
Franzen, J. Freedom
Sandford, J. Buried prey
Sandford, J. Field of prey
Sandford, J. Silken prey
Sandford, J. Storm prey

ST PETERSBURG, RUSSIA
Dostoyevsky, F. Crime and punishment
Gogol, N. The collected tales of Nikolai Gogol
Makine, A. The life of an unknown man
Stachniak, E. The chosen maiden
Wilkins, K. Veil of gold

ST PETERSBURG, RUSSIA -- HISTORY -- TO 1917
Boyne, J. The house of special purpose

ST PETERSBURG, RUSSIA -- SIEGE, 1941-1944
Benioff, D. City of thieves
Dean, D. The madonnas of Leningrad

ST SIMON'S ISLAND, GEORGIA
Hauck, R. Once upon a prince

ST VALENTINE'S DAY MASSACRE, CHICAGO, ILLI-NOIS, 1929
Rosen, R. Dollface

St. Benet's trilogy [series] Howatch, S.
St. Peter's fair Peters, E.

STABBING VICTIMS
Bolton, S. Now you see me
Child, L. A wanted man
Marston, E. The vagabond clown
Ryan, H. What you see
Scott, W. The bride of Lammermoor

STABLE HANDS
Nicholson, C. The elephant keeper
Vlautin, W. Lean on Pete

STABLES
Francis, F. Crisis
Roberts, N. Dark witch

STAGE MANAGERS
Marston, E. The bawdy basket
Marston, E. The devil's apprentice
Marston, E. The roaring boy
Marston, E. The vagabond clown
Marston, E. The wanton angel

STAGECOACH DRIVERS
Zimmer, M. The long hitch

STAGED DEATHS
Bennett, R. City of stairs
Boylan, J. Long black veil
Clark, M. The melody lingers on
Currie, R. Flimsy little plastic miracles
Hannah, S. Keep her safe
Knopf, C. Dead anyway
Martinson, T. The reign of the Kingfisher
Osborne, L. Only to sleep
Polk, C. Witchmark
Price, N. Sleeping with the enemy

Stages of Grey Simon, C.

STAINED GLASS
Grant, H. The glass demon

STAINED GLASS WINDOWS
Grant, H. The glass demon

Stairway to hell Williams, C.
The **Stalin** epigram Littell, R.
Stalin's ghost Smith, M.

Muller, M. While other people sleep
O'Nan, S. The names of the dead
Owen, H. The devil's triangle
Paris, B. The breakdown
Parker, R. Shrink rap
Parker, R. Walking shadow
Parker, T. Storm runners
Parshall, S. Bleeding through
Pinborough, S. Cross her heart
Pirie, D. The patient's eyes
Preston, D. Thunderhead
Pronzini, B. In an evil time
Quick, A. 'Til death do us part
Rankin, I. Set in darkness
Reichs, K. Deja dead
Rendell, R. End in tears
Roberts, N. The obsession
Schaitkin, A. Saint X
Slaughter, K. Pretty girls
Stevens, C. Never let you go
Theroux, P. The Elephanta suite
Wayne, T. Loner
Whittle, T. The dangerous edge of things
Woods, T. True to the game III
Wright, J. The house on Foster Hill
Zane, 1. Addicted
Stalking ground Mizushima, M.
STALKING VICTIMS
Grippando, J. Lying with strangers
Handke, P. Crossing the Sierra de Gredos
Sparks, N. The guardian
Stallion Gate Smith, M.
STAMFORD, CONNECTICUT
Knopf, C. Dead anyway
STAMP COLLECTING
Block, L. Hit me
Block, L. Hit me
Bradley, C. The sweetness at the bottom of the pie
Erdrich, L. The plague of doves
MacDonald, J. The scarlet ruse
STAMP THEFTS
MacDonald, J. The scarlet ruse
Sanders, L. McNally's secret
The **stand** King, S.
Stand your ground Murray, V.
STAND-UP COMEDIANS
McDonald, I. River of gods
STAND-UP COMEDY
Grossman, D. A horse walks into a bar
Standing in the rainbow Flagg, F.
STANLEY, HENRY M (HENRY MORTON), 1841-1904
Hijuelos, O. Twain & Stanley enter paradise
STANTON, ELIZABETH CADY, 1815-1902
Carr, C. The angel of darkness
Piercy, M. Sex wars
A **star** called Henry Doyle, R.
Star Island Hiaasen, C.

Star of Persia Smith, J.
Star of the morning Kurland, L.
Star of the Sea O'Connor, J.
A **star** shines over Mt. Morris Park Roth, H.
The **star** side of Bird Hill Jackson, N.
STAR WARS FICTION
Zahn, T. Dark force rising
Zahn, T. Heir to the empire
Zahn, T. The last command
Star Wars novels. Thrawn trilogy [series] Zahn, T.
Stardust Gaiman, N.
Starfish Watts, P.
Starless Carey, J.
The **starless** sea Morgenstern, E.
The **starlet** and the spy Lee, J.
The **Starlite** Drive-in Reynolds, M.
STARS
Wolfe, G. The urth of the new sun
The **stars** above Veracruz Gifford, B.
The **stars** are legion Hurley, K.
Stars in my pocket like grains of sand Delany, S.
Stars in the grass Stewart, A.
The **stars** now unclaimed Williams, D.
Starship troopers Heinlein, R.
Start shooting Newton, C.
Started early, took my dog Atkinson, K.
Starting over Wakefield, D.
STARVATION
Cooper, E. Caged
STATE GOVERNMENTS -- FINANCE
DeSilva, B. A scourge of vipers
A **state** of freedom Mukherjee, N.
State of wonder Patchett, A.
STATE PARKS -- ALASKA
Stabenow, D. A night too dark
STATE POLICE
Hunter, S. Dirty white boys
Stabenow, D. A fine and bitter snow
Stabenow, D. Restless in the grave
Stabenow, D. So sure of death
Stabenow, D. A grave denied
STATE POLICE -- ALASKA
Stabenow, D. A deeper sleep
Stabenow, D. A taint in the blood
STATE POLICE -- MASSACHUSETTS
Gardner, L. Alone
Gardner, L. Fear nothing
Gardner, L. Find her
Gardner, L. Love you more
The **state** we're in Beattie, A.
STATE-SPONSORED TERRORISM
Boll, H. The lost honor of Katharina Blum
Erpenbeck, J. The book of words
Garcia, C. King of Cuba
Hugo, V. Les miserables
Le Guin, U. Orsinian tales
Lewis, S. It can't happen here

Brownmiller, S. Waverly Place

STEINBERG, LISA, 1981-1987

Brownmiller, S. Waverly Place

Steles of the sky Bear, E.

Stella Mooney mysteries [series] Lawrence, D.

STEM CELLS

Reichs, K. Grave secrets

A **step** so grave McPherson, C.

Step to the graveyard easy Pronzini, B.

STEPBROTHERS

Cole, A. A prince on paper

Yu, H. Brothers

STEPBROTHERS AND STEPSISTERS

Chen, D. Brothers

London, J. The trouble with honor

Mosley, W. Fortunate son

Murdoch, I. The good apprentice

Patchett, A. Commonwealth

Roberts, N. Chesapeake blue

Wharton, E. The children

STEPCHILDREN

Barker, P. Another world

Brownrigg, S. Morality tale

Burke, A. The better sister

Seo, M. The only child

Trollope, J. Other people's children

Wolitzer, H. Hearts

STEPCHILDREN -- FAMILY RELATIONSHIPS

Trollope, J. Marrying the mistress

Trollope, J. Other people's children

STEPDAUGHTERS

Edwards, R. Darling

Kelly, C. Secrets of a happy marriage

Knight, D. Butterfly tattoo

Lipman, E. The family man

Oyeyemi, H. Boy, Snow, Bird

Scottoline, L. Come home

Tepper, S. The visitor

STEPFATHERS

Allison, D. Bastard out of Carolina

Beattie, A. Picturing Will

Dexter, P. Spooner

Dickens, C. David Copperfield

Gilb, D. The Flowers

Lundrigan, N. Glass boys

Mason, J. The hidden things

Ryan, H. What you see

Trollope, J. Other people's children

STEPFATHERS -- FAMILY RELATIONSHIPS

Trollope, J. Other people's children

STEPFATHERS -- TEXAS

Mosley, W. Gone fishin'

The **Stepford** wives Levin, I.

Stephanie Plum mysteries [series] Evanovich, J.

STEPHEN, KING OF ENGLAND, 1097?-1154

Franklin, A. The siege winter

STEPMOTHERS

DeLillo, D. Zero K

Edwards, R. Darling

Lackey, M. The fairy godmother

Marillier, J. Daughter of the forest

Matar, H. Anatomy of a disappearance

Morante, E. Arturo's island

Oyeyemi, H. Boy, Snow, Bird

Patchett, A. The Dutch house

Quinn, J. An offer from a gentleman

Seo, M. The only child

Trollope, J. Marrying the mistress

Trollope, J. Other people's children

Tyler, A. Back when we were grownups

Welty, E. The optimist's daughter

STEPMOTHERS -- FAMILY RELATIONSHIPS

Trollope, J. Other people's children

STEPMOTHERS -- SOUTH CAROLINA

Sanders, D. Clover

Steppenwolf Hesse, H.

STEPSISTERS

Evison, J. All about Lulu

Jackson, J. The almost sisters

Krentz, J. When all the girls have gone

Lackey, M. The fairy godmother

STEPSONS

Higgins, K. The perfect match

STEREOTYPES (SOCIAL PSYCHOLOGY)

Aboulela, L. Elsewhere, home

Tsao, T. The majesties

Yu, C. Interior Chinatown

STEVEDORES

Schulberg, B. Waterfront

Vann, D. Aquarium

STEWARTS

Carlyle, C. A duke changes everything

Stick out your tongue Ma, J.

STIGMATIZATION

Hansen, R. Mariette in ecstasy

Jordan, H. When she woke

Picoult, J. Keeping faith

Spark, M. Aiding & abetting

Stiletto justice King, C.

Still dirty Stringer, V.

Still life Parrish, C.

Still life Penny, L.

Still life with Woodpecker Robbins, T.

Still midnight Mina, D.

Still missing Stevens, C.

STILLBIRTH

Smith, L. On Agate Hill

Stiltsville Daniel, S.

The **Stingaree** Brand, M.

STOCK MARKET

Lathen, E. Something in the air

Sanders, L. The Timothy files

Sanders, L. Timothy's game

STOCK MARKET -- CORRUPT PRACTICES

Sala, S. Forever my hero

The **story** of a brief marriage Arudpragasam, A.

Story of a crime trilogy [series] Persson, L.

The **story** of a new name Ferrante, E.

The **story** of Arthur Truluv Berg, E.

The **story** of Edgar Sawtelle Wroblewski, D.

The **story** of my teeth Luiselli, V.

The **story** of the cannibal woman Conde, M.

The **story** of the lost child Ferrante, E.

The **story** sisters Hoffman, A.

The **storyteller** Picoult, J.

STORYTELLERS

Crace, J. The gift of stones

Ramadan, A. The clothesline swing

Rushdie, S. Haroun and the sea of stories

Rushdie, S. The enchantress of Florence

Setterfield, D. The thirteenth tale

STORYTELLERS -- AUSTRALIA

Bail, M. Eucalyptus

STORYTELLING

Acevedo, C. The distant marvels

Allende, I. Eva Luna

Apostol, G. Insurrecto

Backman, F. My grandmother asked me to tell you she's sorry

Barth, J. Chimera

Barth, J. The last voyage of somebody the sailor

Bradbury, R. The illustrated man

Calvino, I. Invisible cities

Catton, E. The luminaries

Coetzee, J. Elizabeth Costello

Couto, M. Sleepwalking land

Crummey, M. Galore

Eco, U. Baudolino

Gaiman, N. Anansi boys

Ghosh, A. Gun Island

Gifford, B. The stars above Veracruz

Grossman, D. A horse walks into a bar

Gunn, J. Transcendental

Krivak, A. The bear

Lavery, D. The merry spinster

Lim, E. Dear cyborgs

Luiselli, V. The story of my teeth

Makine, A. Dreams of my Russian summers

Manfredi, V. A winter's night

Martel, Y. Life of Pi

Morgenstern, E. The starless sea

Oyeyemi, H. Gingerbread

Palmer, D. The dream of perpetual motion

Ramadan, A. The clothesline swing

Rosner, J. The yellow bird sings

Rothfuss, P. The name of the wind

Rushdie, S. Haroun and the sea of stories

Shalev, M. Two she-bears

Shaykh, H. One thousand and one nights

Straub, P. Ghost story

Tolkien, J. The fall of Gondolin

Ugresic, D. Fox

Wallace, D. Mr. Sebastian and the Negro magician

Wiesel, E. Hostage

Wright, A. Carpentaria

STOWAWAYS

Holdstock, P. Here I am!

MacLean, S. The rogue not taken

Pearlman, E. Honeydew

Phillips, C. Foreigners

Poe, E. The narrative of Arthur Gordon Pym of Nantucket

Straight man Russo, R.

The **strain** Toro, G.

Strain trilogy [series] Toro, G.

Strange affair Robinson, P.

The **strange** affair of Spring Heeled Jack Hodder, M.

Strange bodies Theroux, M.

The **strange** case of Dr. Jekyll and Mr. Hyde Stevenson, R.

The **strange** case of the alchemist's daughter Goss, T.

The **strange** fate of Kitty Easton Speller, E.

Strange pilgrims Garcia Marquez, G.

Strange Practice Shaw, V.

Strange shores Arnaldur Indridason, 1.

Strange weather Hill, J.

A **strangeness** in my mind Pamuk, O.

The **stranger** Camus, A.

The **stranger** Coben, H.

The **stranger** diaries Griffiths, E.

The **stranger** house Hill, R.

Stranger in a strange land Heinlein, R.

Stranger in paradise Parker, R.

The **stranger** inside Unger, L.

Stranger room Ramsay, F.

The **stranger** you seek Williams, A.

The **stranger's** child Hollinghurst, A.

The **stranger's** magic Frei, M.

STRANGERS

Arudpragasam, A. The story of a brief marriage

Barry, J. Don't turn around

Bradbury, J. The wild inside

Braffet, K. Last seen leaving

Burrowes, G. Lady Sophie's Christmas wish

Camus, A. The fall

Christie, A. And then there were none

Coben, H. The stranger

Cossette, C. Shelter of the most high

Crace, J. Harvest

Dekker, T. The girl behind the red rope

Finder, J. Judgment

Fleischmann, R. How quickly she disappears

Hannah, S. The mystery of three quarters

Hawkins, P. The girl on the train

Hill, R. The stranger house

Jewell, L. I found you

Kawakami, M. Ms. Ice Sandwich

Kubica, M. Pretty baby

Kurland, L. Star of the morning

Lake, J. Green

T. I. Trouble & triumph
Turner, N. Black widow
Turner, N. Forever a hustler's wife
Turner, N. Heartbreak of a hustler's wife
Turner, N. A hustler's wife
Turner, N. Natural born hustler
Tyree, O. Flyy girl
Tyree, O. For the love of money
Tyree, O. Leslie
Walsh, H. Brass
White, S. Tears of a hustler
White, S. Tears of a hustler 2
Williams, K. Dirty to the grave
Williams, K. Harlem on lock
Woods, T. Dutch
Woods, T. True to the game
Woods, T. True to the game II
Woods, T. True to the game III

STREET LIFE -- PHILADELPHIA, PENNSYLVANIA
Holmes, S. Bad girlz

STREET MUSICIANS
Petrie, N. Tear it down
Smith, J. Jazz funeral
The **street** of a thousand blossoms Tsukiyama, G.

STREET VENDORS
Gilman, S. The ice cream queen of Orchard Street
Pamuk, O. A strangeness in my mind
The **streets** have no king JaQuavis
Streets of Laredo McMurtry, L.

STRENGTH AND WEAKNESS
Haigh, J. Mrs. Kimble

STRESS
MacBride, S. Flesh house

STRESS IN MEN
Powers, K. The yellow birds

STRIKEBREAKERS
Kesey, K. Sometimes a great notion

STRIKES
Cash, W. The last ballad
Gaskell, E. North and South
Harvey, J. Darkness, darkness
Just, W. An unfinished season
Kesey, K. Sometimes a great notion
Lehane, D. The given day
Nickson, C. Gods of gold
Russell, M. The women of the copper country
Spencer, S. Lambs to the slaughter
Stewart, A. Girl waits with gun

STRIKES -- COAL MINERS
Zola, E. Germinal

STRIKES -- TRANSPORT WORKERS
Craig, P. Third strike

STRING QUARTETS (GROUPS)
Gabel, A. The ensemble

STRINGED INSTRUMENTS
Gabel, A. The ensemble

STRIP CLUB COMPETITION -- FLORIDA

Hiaasen, C. Strip tease
STRIP CLUBS
Noire G-Spot
Strip tease Hiaasen, C.
STRIPTEASERS
Barry, D. Insane city
Carter, M. Further out than you thought
Chung, M. The eighth girl
Crownover, J. Honor
Flanagan, R. The unknown terrorist
Holmes, S. Bad girlz
Kushner, R. The Mars room
Mosley, W. White butterfly
STRIPTEASERS -- FLORIDA
Hiaasen, C. Strip tease
STROKES
Albert, E. The book of Dahlia
Strong poison Sayers, D.
STUART PERIOD (1603-1714)
Blackmore, R. Lorna Doone
Du Maurier, D. Frenchman's creek
Gregory, P. Tidelands
London, J. Wild wicked Scot
Morrow, J. The last witchfinder
Norfolk, L. John Saturnall's feast
Pears, I. An instance of the fingerpost
Phillips, C. The Devlin diary
Plaidy, J. The pleasures of love
Plaidy, J. William's wife
Rutherfurd, E. London
Winterson, J. The daylight gate
Stubborn archivist Rodrigues Fowler, Y.
STUDENT EXPULSION
Ware, R. The lying game
STUDENT FILMS
Collins, K. Notes from a black woman's diary
STUDENT MOVEMENTS
Han, K. Human acts
STUDENT MOVEMENTS -- MEXICO
Bolano, R. Amulet
STUDENT ORGANIZATIONS
Ayatsuji, Y. The Decagon House murders
STUDENT SECRET SOCIETIES
Lowe, K. The furies
Lutz, L. The swallows
STUDENT SUSPENSION
Carr, B. Opioid, Indiana
STUDENT TEACHERS
Rader-Day, L. The black hour
STUDENTS
Albahari, D. Gotz and Meyer
Blau, J. The Wonder Bread summer
Eugenides, J. Fresh complaint
John, E. Born on a Tuesday
Leon, S. Wanderer
Mengestu, D. All our names
Mistry, R. A fine balance

Eugenides, J. The virgin suicides
SUBURBAN WOMEN
Jackson, J. Never have I ever
SUBURBS
Cheever, J. The Wapshot scandal
Fowler, T. A good neighborhood
Hoffman, A. Local girls
Huston, C. The shotgun rule
McLean, F. The Van Apfel girls are gone
Moriarty, L. Big little lies
Paretsky, S. Blacklist
Perrotta, T. The abstinence teacher
Quindlen, A. Object lessons
SUBVERSIVE ACTIVITIES
Harkaway, N. Gnomon
SUBWAYS
Smith, M. Stalin's ghost
SUCCESS (CONCEPT)
Balasubramanyam, R. Professor Chandra follows his bliss
Baldwin, J. The Wilshire sun
Bloom, A. Lucky us
Chang, L. All is forgotten, nothing is lost
Cusset, C. Life of David Hockney
De Kretser, M. The life to come
Dee, J. The privileges
Dreiser, T. An American tragedy
Dreiser, T. Sister Carrie
Ferber, E. So big
Gregory, P. The red queen
Monroe, M. Bad blood
Shanbhag, V. Ghachar ghochar
Shteyngart, G. Lake Success
Vonnegut, K. Breakfast of champions
Wolitzer, M. The Interestings
Succession [series] Westerfeld, S.
The **successor** Kadare, I.
Such a fun age Reid, K.
SUDAN
Caputo, P. Acts of faith
Peters, E. The last camel died at noon
SUDAN -- HISTORY -- CIVIL WAR, 1955-1972
Eggers, D. What is the what
SUDANESE IN EGYPT
Bilal, P. The ghost runner
SUDANESE IN THE UNITED STATES
Arvin, R. Blood of angels
SUDDEN DEATH
Oates, J. Middle age
SUDDEN INFANT DEATH SYNDROME
Hannah, S. The cradle in the grave
Palahniuk, C. Lullaby
Sudden prey Sandford, J.
A **sudden** wild magic Jones, D.
Suder Everett, P.
Suffer the children Black, L.
SUFFERING
Baldwin, J. Going to meet the man

Brockmeier, K. The illumination
Eliot, G. Middlemarch
Gordimer, N. The conservationist
Krall, H. Chasing the king of hearts
Parker, S. Purgatory road
Perry, S. Melmoth
Rothmann, R. To die in spring
Ward, J. Sing, unburied, sing
SUFFERING -- RELIGIOUS ASPECTS -- CHRISTIANITY
Young, W. The shack
SUFFERING IN MEN
Dostoyevsky, F. Notes from underground
Sufficient grace Arnoult, D.
SUFFOLK, ENGLAND
French, N. Friday on my mind
French, N. Thursday's children
SUFFRAGE
Follett, K. Fall of giants
Perry, A. Bethlehem Road
SUFFRAGIST MOVEMENT
Dunmore, E. Bringing down the duke
Fowler, T. A well-behaved woman
SUFFRAGISTS
Ford, F. Parade's end
Johnson, D. Detroit shuffle
Newman, J. Mary
Nickson, C. On Copper Street
Piercy, M. Sex wars
Plain, B. The golden cup
SUFFRAGISTS -- WASHINGTON (STATE)
Fowler, K. Sarah Canary
SUGAR INDUSTRY AND TRADE
Hiaasen, C. Strip tease
SUGAR INDUSTRY AND TRADE -- CORRUPT PRACTICES
Hiaasen, C. Strip tease
SUGAR PLANTATION OWNERS
Willig, L. The summer country
SUGAR PLANTATIONS
Santiago, E. Conquistadora
Straight, S. A million nightingales
Willig, L. The summer country
SUGAR PLANTATIONS -- HAWAII
Michener, J. Hawaii
SUGAR PLANTATIONS -- JAMAICA
Levy, A. The long song
Sugar Street Mahfuz, N.
SUGAR WORKERS -- HAITI
Danticat, E. The farming of bones
SUGARCANE
Matthiessen, P. Bone by bone
SUICIDAL BEHAVIOR
Backman, F. A man called Ove
Conroy, P. The prince of tides
Darnielle, J. Wolf in white van
Goddard, R. Beyond recall

Rankin, I. Dead souls
Robinson, P. Careless love
Roosevelt, E. The Hyde Park murder
Scott, A. A kind of grief
Speller, E. The return of Captain John Emmett
Starr, M. Unhallowed ground
White, S. Line of fire

SUICIDE INVESTIGATION -- CHINA

Qiu, X. Enigma of China

The **Suicide** Motor Club Buehlman, C.

SUICIDE NOTES

Abbott, J. Blame

The **suicide** of Claire Bishop Banasky, C.

SUICIDE PACTS

McEwan, I. Amsterdam
Styron, W. Sophie's choice
Yoshimoto, B. Moshi-moshi

SUICIDE VICTIMS

Bartz, A. The lost night
Bourland, B. Fake like me
Brundage, E. All things cease to appear
Goenawan, C. The perfect world of Miwako Sumida
Gross, A. Eyes wide open
Hill Gumbao, T. The good suicides
Littell, R. The Mayakovsky tapes
Mina, D. The end of the wasp season
Moses, K. Wintering
Muller, M. Dead midnight
Palwick, S. Mending the moon
Palwick, S. The necessary beggar
St. James, S. The haunting of Maddy Clare
Straub, P. Lost boy lost girl

SUING (LAW)

Bing, S. You look nice today
Carey, P. My life as a fake
Moore, G. The last days of night
Oates, J. The falls
Patterson, R. Balance of power
Picoult, J. My sister's keeper
Richler, M. Solomon Gursky was here
Scottoline, L. Feared

A **suitable** boy Seth, V.

Suite Francaise Nemirovsky, I.

SUL TAEHAKKYO

Wuertz, Y. Everything belongs to us

Sula Morrison, T.

SULLA, LUCIUS CORNELIUS, 138-78 BC

McCullough, C. The first man in Rome

Sullivan Lake romances [series] Cameron, C.

Sullivan's Crossing [series] Carr, R.

SULTANS

Khoury, R. Empire of lies

SUMMER

Aciman, A. Call me by your name
Atkins, A. The redeemers
Balogh, M. Simply love
Bender, T. The last ghost dancer

Bernhard, E. The books of the dead
Blau, J. The summer of naked swim parties
Bradbury, R. Dandelion wine
Doan, A. The summer list
Fabry, C. The promise of Jesse Woods
Glass, J. Three Junes
Hand, E. Curious toys
Hay, E. Late nights on air
Hilderbrand, E. The perfect couple
Lippman, L. Sunburn
Mallery, S. The summer of Sunshine and Margot
McLarty, R. Art in America
Molloy, A. The perfect mother
O'Malley, T. We were kings
Whitehead, C. Sag Harbor
Yoshimoto, B. Goodbye Tsugumi

The **summer** before the war Simonson, H.

SUMMER CAMPS

Butler, N. The hearts of men
Sager, R. The last time I lied
Swarthout, G. Bless the beasts and children

The **summer** country Willig, L.

The **summer** guest Anderson, A.

Summer in Baden-Baden Tsypkin, L.

The **summer** list Doan, A.

Summer of '69 Hilderbrand, E.

The **summer** of dead toys Hill Gumbao, T.

The **summer** of Katya Trevanian

The **summer** of naked swim parties Blau, J.

The **summer** of Sunshine and Margot Mallery, S.

The **summer** of the Danes Peters, E.

Summer on Moonlight Bay Ramsay, H.

The **summer** queen Vinge, J.

SUMMER RESORTS

Maron, M. High country fall
Smith, A. The accidental

SUMMER RESORTS -- NEW YORK (STATE)

Benchley, P. Jaws

The **summer** tree Kay, G.

The **summer** we lost her Cohen, T.

The **summer** we read Gatsby Ganek, D.

The **summer** wives Williams, B.

Summerlong Beagle, P.

Summertime Coetzee, J.

SUMMIT MEETINGS -- SCOTLAND

Rankin, I. The naming of the dead

SUMO WRESTLERS

Lovesey, P. Diamond solitaire

SUMO WRESTLING

Tsukiyama, G. The street of a thousand blossoms

SUN

Wilson, R. Spin

The **sun** also rises Hemingway, E.

The **Sun** Down motel St. James, S.

The **sun** king Ignatius, D.

Sunburn Lippman, L.

Suncatcher Gunesekera, R.

James, M. The book of night women
Jones, S. The uninvited guests
Katsu, A. The deep
Katsu, A. The hunger
Kaufmann, N. Dying is my business
Kay, G. Ysabel
Kenyon, S. Dark bites
Kidd, J. Things in jars
King, S. Carrie
King, S. Doctor Sleep
King, S. Elevation
King, S. Firestarter
King, S. It
King, S. Night shift
King, S. Pet sematary
King, S. Salem's lot
King, S. The shining
King, S. Sleeping beauties
King, S. The stand
Koryta, M. The ridge
Koryta, M. So cold the river
Lafferty, M. Ghost train to New Orleans
Lafferty, M. The shambling guide to New York City
Lamberson, G. The frenzy way
McBride, J. Song yet sung
McGuire, S. Chimes at midnight
McGuire, S. Rosemary and rue
Miller, M. Circe
Mitchell, D. Slade House
More deadly than the male
Murakami, H. After dark
Murakami, H. Blind willow, sleeping woman
Nevill, A. The house of small shadows
North, C. The pursuit of William Abbey
O'Connell, C. Mallory's oracle
O'Connell, C. The man who cast two shadows
Oates, J. The accursed
Percy, B. Red moon
Porter, M. Lanny
Rayne, S. Property of a lady
Rhodes, J. Voodoo dreams
Rice, A. Blood communion
Richardson, K. Greywalker
Ruiz Zafon, C. The angel's game
Rushdie, S. Midnight's children
Schwab, V. Vicious
Setterfield, D. The thirteenth tale
Shannon, D. The Manson curse
Shannon, S. The bone season
Shannon, S. The mime order
Shaw, V. Dreadful company
Shaw, V. Strange Practice
Shaykh, H. One thousand and one nights
Stories
Stott, R. Ghostwalk
Straub, P. A dark matter
Tremblay, P. Disappearance at Devil's Rock

Updike, J. The widows of Eastwick
Urquhart, J. Away
Waters, S. The little stranger
Wolfe, G. The land across
Woods, R. Remembrance

SUPERNATURAL MYSTERIES
Cameron, W. Repo madness
Cantero, E. Meddling kids
Connolly, J. A book of bones
Connolly, J. The burning soul
Connolly, J. The woman in the woods
Frei, M. The stranger's magic
Gallagher, S. The bedlam detective
Gallagher, S. The kingdom of bones
Hart, C. Ghost gone wild
Harvey, M. Pulse
Irwin, S. The broken ones
Olson, N. Before the devil fell
Pandian, G. The accidental alchemist
Racculia, K. Bellweather rhapsody
Rayne, S. Property of a lady
Rhodes, J. Yellow moon
Shannon, D. The Manson curse
Shaw, V. Dreadful company
Shaw, V. Strange Practice
Simon, C. Dogs don't lie
Simon, C. Grey dawn
Simon, C. Panthers play for keeps
Simon, C. Stages of Grey

SUPERSTITION
Atakora, A. Conjure women
Blake, R. A dark anatomy
Campisi, M. Sin eater
Carey, L. The stolen child
Choo, Y. The night tiger
Colgan, J. The endless beach
Gregory, P. Tidelands
Hoffman, A. The river king
Hurley, A. Devil's Day
Jackson, S. We have always lived in the castle
Kent, K. The heretic's daughter
Lea, C. The glass woman
McPherson, C. A step so grave
Michener, J. Caribbean
Perry, S. Melmoth
Potzsch, O. The werewolf of Bamberg
Pratchett, T. Thud!
Rash, R. The cove
Redondo, D. The invisible guardian
Scott, A. A kind of grief
Tepper, S. The visitor
Unsworth, B. The songs of the kings
Winterson, J. The daylight gate
Zimmerman, J. The orphanmaster

SUPERVILLAINS
Wong, D. Futuristic violence and fancy suits

SUPERVISORS

Pynchon, T. Mason & Dixon

SURVIVAL

Adams, R. Watership Down
Al Rawi, S. The Baghdad clock
Anders, C. The city in the middle of the night
Asimov, I. Foundation and empire
Auster, P. In the country of last things
Bakker, R. Raptor red
Baldwin, J. Going to meet the man
Barclay, L. No safe house
Bear, E. All the windwracked stars
Bear, G. Anvil of stars
Benioff, D. City of thieves
Boyne, J. The heart's invisible furies
Brown, P. Golden son
Brown, P. Red rising
Brown, T. Fallen land
Calvino, I. Invisible cities
Christie, M. Greenwood
Conde, M. The story of the cannibal woman
Couto, M. Sleepwalking land
Cronin, J. The city of mirrors
Cronin, J. The passage
Cronin, J. The twelve
Crummey, M. The innocents
Darnielle, J. Wolf in white van
Doctorow, C. Walkaway
Dreiser, T. Sister Carrie
Durrow, H. The girl who fell from the sky
Egan, G. Perihelion summer
Egan, G. Phoresis
Eggers, D. What is the what
Erpenbeck, J. Go, went, gone
Faye, G. Small country
Ferencik, E. Into the jungle
Finder, J. The fixer
Flynn, G. Dark places
Foer, J. Extremely loud and incredibly close
Goldin, M. The escape room
Golding, W. The inheritors
Gregory, D. We are all completely fine
Hannaham, J. Delicious foods
Harmel, K. The room on Rue Amelie
Hawley, N. Before the fall
Heller, J. Catch-22
Heller, P. The dog stars
Heller, P. The river
Hill, J. The Fireman
Holmes, S. Bad girlz
Hughes, L. Short stories
K'wan Diamonds and Pearl
Kirkpatrick, J. One more river to cross
Lai, L. The tiger flu
Lake, J. Endurance
Lake, J. Green
Lalami, L. The Moor's account
Lamb, A. Roboteer

Lansdale, J. Paradise sky
Lutz, L. The passenger
Mabanckou, A. Black Moses
Makine, A. The life of an unknown man
Malerman, J. Bird box
Mark, D. The dark winter
Matheson, R. I am legend
McCaffrey, A. Dragonflight
McDonald, I. New moon
McHugh, M. After the apocalypse
Mitchell, M. Gone with the wind
Moody, D. Hater
Newman, S. The country of Ice Cream Star
O'Keefe, M. Velocity weapon
Oksanen, S. When the doves disappeared
Pelecanos, G. The turnaround
Phillips, G. Fierce kingdom
Proulx, A. Barkskins
Pyper, A. The homecoming
Rice, W. Moon of the crusted snow
Roy, L. Gone too long
Sainz Borgo, K. It would be night in Caracas
Saramago, J. Blindness
Schwab, V. Vengeful
Seiffert, R. A boy in winter
Self, W. Shark
Snipes, W. Talon of God
Stabenow, D. Less than a treason
Stephenson, N. Seveneves
Stevens, C. Still missing
Straley, J. The big both ways
Stroby, W. Some die nameless
Theroux, M. Far north
Turow, S. Testimony
VanderMeer, J. Annihilation
VanderMeer, J. Borne
Verne, J. The mysterious island
Walls, J. Half broke horses
Watts, P. Starfish
Weir, A. The Martian
Wellington, D. Positive
Winton, T. The shepherd's hut
Wong, D. Futuristic violence and fancy suits

SURVIVAL (AFTER AIRPLANE ACCIDENTS, SHIP-WRECKS, ETC)

Barnes, J. A history of the world in 10 1
Coetzee, J. Foe
Defoe, D. Robinson Crusoe
Golding, W. Lord of the flies
Grass, G. Crabwalk
Hilton, J. Lost horizon
Martel, Y. Life of Pi
Matthiessen, P. Far Tortuga
Napolitano, A. Dear Edward
Ondaatje, M. The English patient
Poe, E. The narrative of Arthur Gordon Pym of Nantucket
Rogan, C. The lifeboat

SUSPENSE STORY WRITING

Daly, P. Open your eyes

SUSPICION

Abbott, J. The three Beths
Abbott, M. You will know me
Bannister, J. Kindred spirits
Barnett, K. Ever faithful
Barton, F. The suspect
Baume, S. Spill simmer falter wither
Black, B. The secret guests
Bolton, S. The craftsman
Brundage, E. All things cease to appear
Chanter, C. The well
Chizmar, R. A long December
Clark, M. Death wears a beauty mask and other stories
Clark, M. The melody lingers on
Cleeves, A. Raven black
Cleveland, K. Keep you close
Cohen, T. They all fall down
Constantine, L. The last time I saw you
Cook, T. The crime of Julian Wells
Cook, T. Sandrine's case
Dallas, S. Tallgrass
Davis, L. The ides of April
Deighton, L. London match
Dickinson, P. The yellow room conspiracy
Ellis, B. Lunar Park
French, N. Blue Monday
French, N. Dark Saturday
French, N. The day of the dead
French, N. Friday on my mind
French, N. Sunday silence
Garwood, J. The bride
Goddard, R. Never go back
Goldman, M. The shallows
Griffiths, E. The stranger diaries
Grunberg, A. Tirza
Hayder, M. Birdman
Jemc, J. The grip of it
Jewell, L. Then she was gone
Johnson, C. Dark horse
Kelly, E. Broadchurch
Kerr, P. Field gray
Kubica, M. The other Mrs.
Lackberg, C. The hidden child
Lasdun, J. Afternoon of a faun
Leon, D. The girl of his dreams
Leon, D. Unto us a son is given
Leroy, M. Postcards from Berlin
MacDonald, J. The turquoise lament
Marlette, D. Magic time
Marwood, A. The killer next door
Miranda, M. The last house guest
Mosley, W. Blonde faith
Mosley, W. Charcoal Joe
Mosley, W. Little green
Mosley, W. Rose gold

Muller, H. The fox was ever the hunter
Murphy, S. The possessions
O'Donnell, L. The death of bees
Oates, J. The doll-master
Oates, J. Little bird of heaven
Olshan, J. Black diamond fall
Owens, D. Where the crawdads sing
Palliser, C. Rustication
Palmer, L. Otherwise engaged
Parker, T. L.A. outlaws
Parks, B. Say nothing
Parsons, K. Doing harm
Perry, A. Cardington Crescent
Perry, A. Dark tide rising
Powers, R. Orfeo
Pronzini, B. Savages
Pulley, N. The watchmaker of Filigree Street
Robb, C. A twisted vengeance
Rosenfelt, D. Don't tell a soul
Rowland, R. Cold country
Schaitkin, A. Saint X
Simpson, D. Dead by morning
Sisco, A. A deadly habit
Smith, D. The constable's tale
Steinhauer, O. The Bridge of Sighs
Swanson, P. Her every fear
Swinson, K. I'm New York's finest
Tursten, H. Winter grave
Urquhart, R. The visionist
Walker, C. Man of the year
Walsh, M. My sunshine away
Woodrell, D. The Maid's Version
Wroblewski, D. The story of Edgar Sawtelle

Suspicion Finder, J.

SUSSEX, ENGLAND

Gaiman, N. The ocean at the end of the lane
Long, J. The legend of Lyon Redmond
Lovesey, P. The house sitter

SUSSEX, ENGLAND -- HISTORY -- 18TH CENTURY

Robertson, I. Instruments of darkness

SUSTAINABILITY

Vaughn, C. Bannerless

SUSTAINABLE COMMUNITIES

Boyle, T. The Terranauts

SUSTAINABLE LIVING

Fftch, M. Stay and fight

Sutherland scandals [series] Bradley, A.

Sutton Moehringer, J.

SUTTON, WILLIE

Moehringer, J. Sutton

The **swallows** Lutz, L.

The **swallows** of Kabul Khadra, Y.

Swamplandia! Russell, K.

SWAMPS

Davidson, A. The boatman's daughter
Russell, K. Swamplandia!

SWAMPS -- FLORIDA

Blackstock, T. Shadow in Serenity
Brown, J. Addie Pray
Brown, S. Outfox
Camp, B. The city of lost fortunes
Clark, M. The substitution order
Clark, W. Payback is a mutha
Drury, T. Pacific
Estleman, L. The adventures of Johnny Vermillion
Fowler, C. Bryant & May
French, N. Tuesday's gone
Gavin, R. Beluga
Gogol, N. Dead souls
Greaves, C. Hard twisted
Haigh, J. Mrs. Kimble
Herlihy, J. Midnight cowboy
Higgins, G. The friends of Eddie Coyle
Hill, E. Little comfort
Hilton, L. Maestra
Himes, C. Cotton comes to Harlem
Hunt, S. Mr. Splitfoot
Johnson, D. Nobody move
Jones, T. The better liar
Kaminsky, S. A fatal glass of beer
Klein, M. Con ed
Lawton, J. Then we take Berlin
Leonard, E. Pagan babies
Levine, J. Bingo's run
Lipman, E. The pursuit of Alice Thrift
London, J. The trouble with honor
MacLean, S. Brazen and the Beast
MacLean, S. Wicked and the wallflower
Mandel, E. The singer's gun
Mason, R. Who killed Piet Barol?
Michels, E. The rebel heir
Michener, J. Space
Mosley, W. When the thrill is gone
Nesbo, J. Headhunters
Palahniuk, C. Choke
Parker, R. Potshot
Phillips, J. Quiet dell
Piccirilli, T. The last whisper in the dark
Portis, C. Gringos
Pratchett, T. Going postal
Pronzini, B. Step to the graveyard easy
Quartey, K. The missing American
Quick, A. The other lady vanishes
Rigosi, G. Night bus
Robards, K. The ultimatum
Robotham, M. The wreckage
Sanders, L. The tenth commandment
Seay, M. The mirror thief
Sebastian, C. The Lawrence Browne affair
Smith, B. All hat
Smith, M. December 6
Spufford, F. Golden hill
Stewart, A. Lady cop makes trouble
Stringer, V. Dirty Red

Stringer, V. Still dirty
Tamirat, N. The parking lot attendant
Turner, N. Forever a hustler's wife
Waters, S. Fingersmith
Westlake, D. Bad news
Westlake, D. Bank shot
Westlake, D. The road to ruin

SWINDLERS AND SWINDLING -- ARGENTINA
Morton, C. Stealing Mona Lisa

SWINDLERS AND SWINDLING -- MISSISSIPPI RIVER
Melville, H. The confidence-man

SWINDLERS AND SWINDLING -- NEW ORLEANS, LOUISIANA
Smith, J. Crescent City kill

SWINDLERS AND SWINDLING -- VERMONT
Morris, M. Songs in ordinary time
Swing time Smith, Z.
The **switch** Finder, J.

SWITZERLAND
Abramowitz, A. Thank you, goodnight
Brookner, A. Hotel Du Lac
Essbaum, J. Hausfrau
Ludlum, R. The Sigma protocol
Reich, C. Rules of deception

SWITZERLAND -- HISTORY -- 20TH CENTURY
Tremain, R. The Gustav sonata

SWORD AND SORCERY
French, J. The Grey Bastards
French, J. The true Bastards
Norton, A. Golden trillium
Saberhagen, F. Coinspinner's story
Saberhagen, F. Farslayer's story
Saberhagen, F. Mindsword's story
Saberhagen, F. Shieldbreaker's story
Saberhagen, F. Sightblinder's story
Saberhagen, F. Stonecutter's story
Saberhagen, F. Wayfinder's story
Saberhagen, F. Woundhealer's story
Sullivan, M. Theft of swords
Winter, E. The rage of dragons
Sword at sunset Sutcliff, R.
Sword of honor Kirk, D.
Sword of kings Cornwell, B.
The **sword** of the Lictor Wolfe, G.

SWORDFIGHTERS
Dumas, A. The three musketeers
Goldman, W. The princess bride
Kirk, D. Sword of honor
Perez-Reverte, A. Captain Alatriste
Sabatini, R. Scaramouche

SWORDMAKING
Cole, A. A duke by default

SWORDPLAY
Dumas, A. The three musketeers
Dumas, A. Twenty years after

McCracken, E. The giant's house

TALL WOMEN

Baker, T. The little giant of Aberdeen County

Tallgrass Coldsmith, D.

Tallgrass Dallas, S.

Tallie Graver mysteries [series] Simon, M.

TALLNESS AND SHORTNESS

Irving, J. A prayer for Owen Meany

Weldon, F. The life and loves of a she-devil

TALMUD

Anton, M. Apprentice

Talon of God Snipes, W.

Talulla rising Duncan, G.

Tam Lin Dean, P.

The **taming** of the queen Gregory, P.

TAMPA, FLORIDA

Lehane, D. World gone by

Tamsin Harte Macdonald, M.

Tang Dynasty [series] Lin, J.

TANG DYNASTY (618-907)

Kay, G. Under heaven

Lin, J. The dragon and the pearl

Lin, J. The lotus palace

Tangerine Mangan, C.

TANGO (DANCE)

Perez-Reverte, A. What we become

TANGO MUSIC

De Robertis, C. The gods of tango

TANKS (MILITARY SCIENCE)

Robbins, D. Last citadel

Shaara, J. The rising tide

TANN, GEORGIA, 1891-1950

Wingate, L. Before we were yours

Tannhauser trilogy [series] Willocks, T.

Tannie Maria novels [series] Andrew, S.

TANNING

Markandaya, K. Nectar in a sieve

A **tap** on the window Barclay, L.

Tapestry Plain, B.

TAPEWORMS

Grant, M. Parasite

Taps Morris, W.

Tar baby Morrison, T.

Target Tinos Siger, J.

TAROT

Burke, J. The New Iberia blues

Ware, R. The death of Mrs. Westaway

TASMANIA

Clarke, L. A single breath

TASMANIA -- HISTORY -- 1803-1900

Kneale, M. English passengers

TASTE

Bender, A. The particular sadness of lemon cake

A **taste** for death James, P.

Tatiana Smith, M.

TATTOO ARTISTS

Danielewski, M. House of leaves

TATTOOING

Anders, A. Under her skin

Bradbury, R. The illustrated man

Byrne, K. The duke with the dragon tattoo

Nicholson, G. The city under the skin

Owen, H. The bottom

Shafak, E. The bastard of Istanbul

TAX EVASION

Hoeg, P. The quiet girl

TAX EVASION INVESTIGATION

Iles, G. Third degree

TAXICAB DRIVERS

Aciman, A. Harvard square

Blackstock, T. Catching Christmas

Kostova, E. The shadow land

Rivero, M. The affairs of the Falcons

Schaitkin, A. Saint X

Self, W. The book of Dave

TAXIDERMISTS

Martel, Y. Beatrice and Virgil

TAXIDERMY

Arnett, K. Mostly dead things

Millet, L. Magnificence

Nevill, A. The house of small shadows

TEA

Avon, J. In peppermint peril

See, L. The tea girl of Hummingbird Lane

The **tea** girl of Hummingbird Lane See, L.

TEA INDUSTRY AND TRADE

Crombie, D. Kissed a sad goodbye

TEA PLANTATIONS -- MALAYSIA

Tan, T. The garden of evening mists

Tea Shop mysteries (Laura Childs) [series] Childs, L.

TEACHER-STUDENT COMMUNICATION

Cusk, R. Outline

TEACHER-STUDENT RELATIONSHIPS

Auster, P. Timbuktu

Beattie, A. A wonderful stroke of luck

Bell, S. At his mercy

Chang, L. All is forgotten, nothing is lost

Choi, S. Trust exercise

Clarke, S. Jonathan Strange & Mr. Norrell

Coetzee, J. Disgrace

Cumyn, A. Losing it

Dermansky, M. Very nice

Founds, K. When mystical creatures attack!

Hardy, T. Jude the obscure

Heller, Z. What was she thinking?

Jin, H. The crazed

Messud, C. The woman upstairs

Moore, G. The holdout

Murdoch, I. The philosopher's pupil

Murray, P. Skippy dies

Prose, F. Blue angel

Richman, A. The secret of clouds

Roberts, G. Adam and evil

Roth, P. The dying animal

Moore, G. The last days of night
Pohl, F. Gateway
Shakar, A. Luminarium
Stephenson, N. Anathem
Stephenson, N. Reamde
Stephenson, N. Snow crash
Sterling, B. Pirate Utopia
Twain, M. A Connecticut Yankee in King Arthur's Court
Vinge, V. Rainbows end
Vonnegut, K. While mortals sleep
Ware, R. The turn of the key
Weber, D. By schism rent asunder
Zelazny, R. Lord of light

TECHNOLOGY -- SOCIAL ASPECTS
Anderton, J. Debris
Fforde, J. Shades of grey
Gaddis, W. Agape agape
Graedon, A. The word exchange
Guterson, D. Ed King
Lightman, A. The diagnosis
Liu, K. Invisible planets
Naam, R. Nexus
Robinson, K. Green Mars
Schulman, H. Come with me
Williams, K. Tell the machine goodnight

TECHNOLOGY AND CIVILIZATION
Bradbury, R. The illustrated man
Cather, W. A lost lady
Chen, Q. Waste tide
Chiang, T. Exhalation
Crichton, M. Prey
Cunningham, M. Specimen days
Goonan, K. In war times
Hall, L. Speak
Mastai, E. All our wrong todays
McDonald, I. River of gods
Michener, J. Space
Rutherfurd, E. Sarum
Stirling, S. Dies the fire
Stirling, S. A meeting at Corvallis
Stirling, S. The protector's war
Stross, C. Accelerando
Wilson, D. Robogenesis
Wilson, D. Robopocalypse
Zamyatin, Y. We

TECUMSEH, SHAWNEE CHIEF, 1768-1813
Thom, J. Panther in the sky
Teddy Fay novels [series] Woods, S.

TEENAGE ABORTION
McKinney-Whetstone, D. Leaving Cecil Street

TEENAGE ABUSE VICTIMS
Abani, C. GraceLand
Guterson, D. Our Lady of the Forest
Whitehead, C. The Nickel boys

TEENAGE ARSONISTS
Clarke, B. An arsonist's guide to writers' homes in New
  England

TEENAGE ATHLETES
Abbott, M. You will know me

TEENAGE BALLET DANCERS
Godden, R. Pippa passes

TEENAGE BASKETBALL PLAYERS
Burke, M. Team seven

TEENAGE BOY PRODIGIES
Racculia, K. Bellweather rhapsody

TEENAGE BOY/BOY RELATIONS
O'Neill, J. At swim, two boys
Vuong, O. On Earth we're briefly gorgeous

TEENAGE BOY/GIRL RELATIONS
Bergstrom, H. Steal the north
Blau, J. The summer of naked swim parties
Booth, C. Bronxwood
Booth, C. Kendra
Brashares, A. My name is memory
Burke, J. The jealous kind
Choi, S. Trust exercise
Galloway, G. As simple as snow
Greene, G. Brighton Rock
Jones, T. Silver sparrow
Just, W. An unfinished season
Kittredge, W. The willow field
McHugh, L. The wolf wants in
Merey, I. A + e 4ever
Mishima, Y. The sound of waves
Olmstead, R. The coldest night
Sittenfeld, C. Prep
Sparks, N. A walk to remember
Toews, M. A complicated kindness
Ulinich, A. Petropolis
Varley, J. Red lightning
Walker, K. The age of miracles

TEENAGE BOYS
Abani, C. GraceLand
Adam, C. Golden child
Adler-Olsen, J. The Marco effect
Alexie, S. Flight
Amis, M. Lionel Asbo
Apelfeld, A. The man who never stopped sleeping
Atkinson, K. Big sky
Barzak, C. One for sorrow
Bennett, R. The troupe
Beverly, W. Dodgers
Bilenchi, R. The chill
Burns, O. Cold Sassy tree
Cheever, J. The Wapshot chronicle
Cleave, P. A killer harvest
Cline, E. Ready player one
Coben, H. Hold tight
Coe, J. The rotters' club
Coover, R. Huck out west
Cush, J. Endangered
Dau, S. The book of Jonas
Dazieri, S. Kill the king
Deb, S. The point of return

McInerney, L. The glorious heresies

TEENAGE DRUG USERS

Iles, G. Turning angel

TEENAGE EMPLOYEES

Carr, B. Opioid, Indiana

TEENAGE FATHERS

Johnson, A. The first part last

Tyler, A. Saint Maybe

TEENAGE GIRL ABUSE VICTIMS

Merullo, R. The talk-funny girl

TEENAGE GIRL DRUG ABUSERS

Buntin, J. Marlena

TEENAGE GIRL JOURNALISTS

Hart, C. Letter from home

TEENAGE GIRL KIDNAPPING VICTIMS

Silva, D. The new girl

TEENAGE GIRL MURDER VICTIMS

Atkins, A. The innocents

Cook, T. Instruments of night

Cooper, E. Caged

Elliot, L. Guilty

Ferraris, Z. Finding Nouf

French, N. Thursday's children

Goodman, C. The sea of lost girls

Hannah, S. Keep her safe

Luna, L. The Janes

Meyers, K. Twisted tree

Parker, R. Death in paradise

Persson Giolito, M. Beyond all reasonable doubt

Reichs, K. Monday mourning

Sebold, A. The lovely bones

TEENAGE GIRLS

Abbott, J. Blame

Abbott, J. The three Beths

Abu-Jaber, D. Birds of paradise

Alderman, N. The power

Alexander, V. The Magdalen girls

Aliu, X. Brass

Atkinson, K. When will there be good news?

Austen, J. Northanger Abbey

Barber, L. A girl named Anna

Barclay, L. No safe house

Beagle, P. The unicorn sonata

Berg, E. The story of Arthur Truluv

Blau, J. The summer of naked swim parties

Bonner, C. Lily

Brunt, C. Tell the wolves I'm home

Burdick, S. The girls with no names

Burns, A. Milkman

Butler, S. Cygnet

Campbell, B. Once upon a river

Campisi, M. Sin eater

Clement, J. Gun love

Cline, E. The girls

Crosbie, L. Where did you sleep last night?

Cruz, A. Dominicana

D'Eramo, L. Deviation

Dare, A. The girl with the louding voice

Davis, A. Wonder when you'll miss me

Diachenko, S. Vita nostra

Doan, A. The summer list

Dunant, S. The birth of Venus

Dunant, S. Sacred hearts

Edwards, R. Darling

Ellison, J. Good girls lie

Ellison, J. Tear me apart

Erpenbeck, J. The book of words

Eugenides, J. Middlesex

Eugenides, J. The virgin suicides

Fagan, J. The Panopticon

Faulkner, C. Finding Georgina

Ferencik, E. Into the jungle

Finder, J. Suspicion

Fitzgerald, P. The blue flower

Fowler, T. A good neighborhood

French, T. The secret place

Fridlund, E. History of wolves

Galloway, G. As simple as snow

Gaynor, H. The lighthouse keeper's daughter

Gibbons, K. The life all around me by Ellen Foster

Grames, J. The seven or eight deaths of Stella Fortuna

Grant, H. The glass demon

Greenfeld, K. True

Greenidge, K. We love you, Charlie Freeman

Guterson, D. Our Lady of the Forest

Hand, E. Curious toys

Hart, C. Letter from home

Hayder, M. Hanging hill

Hoffman, A. The river king

Horlock, M. The book of lies

Humphreys, J. Nowhere else on earth

Iweala, U. Speak no evil

Joyce, G. The limits of enchantment

Keller, J. A killing in the hills

Kelly, M. Lilac girls

Kincaid, J. Annie John

King, S. Carrie

Klein, R. The moth diaries

Kostova, E. The historian

Krauss, N. The history of love

Larison, J. Whiskey when we're dry

Lent, J. Lost nation

Lessing, D. Martha Quest

Lodato, V. Mathilda Savitch

Lowe, K. The furies

Ludwig, B. Ginny Moon

Lyon, A. The sweet girl

Maaren, K. Weave a circle round

Macmillan, G. The perfect girl

Marcus, B. The flame alphabet

Maum, C. Costalegre

McDermott, A. Child of my heart

McGuire, S. Down among the sticks and bones

McHugh, L. The wolf wants in

Greene, G. Brighton Rock
Mankell, H. Firewall
Oates, J. Broke heart blues
Sandford, J. Mad River
Shriver, L. We need to talk about Kevin

TEENAGE MUSICIANS
Macmillan, G. The perfect girl

TEENAGE NONCONFORMISTS
Franklin, M. My brilliant career

TEENAGE NUNS
Hansen, R. Mariette in ecstasy

TEENAGE ORPHANS
Carcaterra, L. Tin badges
Edgerton, C. Walking across Egypt
Hunt, S. Mr. Splitfoot

TEENAGE PARENTS
Johnson, A. The first part last

TEENAGE PREGNANCY
Aliu, X. Brass
Baldwin, J. If Beale Street could talk
Bennett, B. The mothers
Bronsky, A. The hottest dishes of the Tartar cuisine
Gaynor, H. The lighthouse keeper's daughter
Greenwood, K. Unnatural habits
Martin, A. Fumbled
McKinney-Whetstone, D. Leaving Cecil Street
Meloy, M. Liars and saints
Moniz, T. Big familia
Ward, J. Salvage the bones
Weir, M. The book of Essie

TEENAGE PRISONERS
Persson Giolito, M. Quicksand

TEENAGE PRISONERS -- SHANGHAI, CHINA
Ballard, J. Empire of the sun

TEENAGE PROSTITUTES
Donoghue, E. Slammerkin
Garcia Marquez, G. Memories of my melancholy whores
Pelecanos, G. Hell to pay

TEENAGE PROSTITUTION
Hobbs, A. Stealing candy
Parker, R. Family honor
Pelecanos, G. Hell to pay
Williams, K. Harlem on lock

TEENAGE PSYCHICS
King, S. Carrie

TEENAGE RAPE VICTIMS
Parker, R. Stone cold

TEENAGE REFUGEES
Porter, H. Firefly

TEENAGE ROMANCE
Bonner, C. Lily
Choi, S. Trust exercise
Desai, K. The inheritance of loss
Fowler, T. A good neighborhood
Kamali, M. The stationery shop
Sagan, F. Bonjour tristesse
Sepetys, R. Out of the Easy

Shreve, A. The last time they met

TEENAGE ROMANCE -- JAPAN
Mishima, Y. The sound of waves

TEENAGE SERIAL MURDERERS
DeSilva, B. Providence rag

TEENAGE SLAVES
Straight, S. A million nightingales

TEENAGE WIZARDS
Grossman, L. The magicians

TEENAGERS
Allende, I. Ripper
Backman, F. Beartown
Backman, F. Us against you
Baker, K. The bird of the river
Barnes, S. Domino Falls
Baxter, C. Saul and Patsy
Brashares, A. My name is memory
Bruen, K. The guards
Burke, J. The jealous kind
Coben, H. Hold tight
Dallas, S. Tallgrass
Danielewski, M. Only revolutions
Davis, A. Wonder when you'll miss me
Drury, T. Pacific
Edwards, Y. The mother
Fabry, C. The promise of Jesse Woods
Fitzpatrick, L. Lights all night long
Freudenberger, N. The dissident
Galloway, G. As simple as snow
Hallberg, G. City on fire
Johnson, L. The most dangerous place on earth
Khadivi, L. A good country
Link, K. Magic for beginners
McDermott, A. That night
McGuire, S. Every heart a doorway
Meltzer, B. The zero game
Moore, C. You suck
O'Nan, S. The night country
Parker, R. School days
Phillips, A. Prague
Price, R. Lush life
Quindlen, A. Every last one
Read, C. The crazy school
Rucker, R. Hylozoic
Sparks, N. A walk to remember
Stabenow, D. A grave denied
Straub, P. A dark matter
Varley, J. Red lightning
Vinge, V. The children of the sky
Walsh, M. My sunshine away
Whitehead, C. Sag Harbor
Wiggs, S. The ocean between us
Yoshimoto, B. Goodbye Tsugumi
Yu, H. Brothers

TEENAGERS -- ALCOHOL USE
Amidon, S. Human capital
Lathen, E. Brewing up a storm

Trollope, J. The men and the girls

Westlake, D. Get real

TELEVISION CELEBRITIES

Fowler, T. A good neighborhood

TELEVISION FOOD PROGRAMS

Berger, T. Reinhart's women

TELEVISION INDUSTRY AND TRADE

Pitoniak, A. Necessary people

Yellin, J. Savage news

TELEVISION JOURNALISM

Pitoniak, A. Necessary people

TELEVISION JOURNALISTS

Butler, R. Hell

Flanagan, R. The unknown terrorist

Follett, K. Whiteout

TELEVISION NEWS

Barthelme, F. Painted desert

Kenney, J. Talk to me

Marks, J. Fangland

Pitoniak, A. Necessary people

TELEVISION NEWSCASTERS AND COMMENTATORS

Kenney, J. Talk to me

O'Flynn, C. The news where you are

TELEVISION PERSONALITIES

Buckley, C. Supreme Courtship

Byatt, A. A whistling woman

Cleave, P. Joe Victim

Hart, E. The book of Killowen

TELEVISION PRODUCERS AND DIRECTORS

Altschul, A. Deus ex machina

Richler, M. Barney's version

TELEVISION PROGRAMS

Byatt, A. A whistling woman

Crawford, I. A catered Christmas cookie exchange

Rushdie, S. Quichotte

Somer, M. The serenity murders

TELEVISION TALK SHOW HOSTS AND GUESTS

Smith, J. Mean woman blues

Tell Itani, F.

Tell her no lies Irvin, K.

Tell me a riddle Olsen, T.

Tell me how long the train's been gone Baldwin, J.

Tell the machine goodnight Williams, K.

Tell the wolves I'm home Brunt, C.

The **telling** Le Guin, U.

Temeraire [series] Novik, N.

Temperance Brennan mysteries [series] Reichs, K.

Tempest Jenkins, B.

The **Templar** legacy Berry, S.

The **temple** of dawn Mishima, Y.

The **temple** of my familiar Walker, A.

The **temple** of the golden pavilion Mishima, Y.

TEMPLES

Beauman, N. Madness is better than defeat

TEMPORARY EMPLOYEES

Butler, H. The new me

Cleary, J. The sundowners

Hynes, J. Kings of infinite space

TEMPORARY EMPLOYMENT

Barr, N. The rope

TEMPTATION

Bradbury, R. Something wicked this way comes

Clark, W. Thug lovin'

Maturin, C. Melmoth the wanderer

Nissenson, H. The pilgrim

Oates, J. The accursed

Reimringer, J. Vestments

Rice, A. Christ the Lord

Shriver, L. The post-birthday world

Warren, T. The pastor's husband

Wouk, H. A hole in Texas

TEMPTATION (CHRISTIANITY)

Lewis, M. The monk

The **temptation** of the night jasmine Willig, L.

Temptations of a wallflower Leigh, E.

Tempting fortune Beverley, J.

Tempting the bride Thomas, S.

Ten girls to watch Shumway, C.

Ten things I've learnt about love Butler, S.

TEN THOUSAND ISLANDS, FLORIDA

Russell, K. Swamplandia!

TEN-YEAR-OLD BOYS

Bohjalian, C. The buffalo soldier

Doyle, R. Paddy Clarke, ha-ha-ha

French, A. Billy

Haruf, K. Plainsong

Sharfeddin, H. Mineral spirits

TEN-YEAR-OLD BOYS -- NORTH CAROLINA

Earley, T. Jim the boy

TEN-YEAR-OLD GIRLS

Grant, H. The vanishing of Katharina Linden

Jackson, N. The star side of Bird Hill

Pronzini, B. Crazybone

Rotert, R. Last night at the blue angel

TEN-YEAR-OLD GIRLS -- SOUTH CAROLINA

Sanders, D. Clover

The **tenant** of Wildfell Hall Bronte, A.

The **tenants** of time Flanagan, T.

Tender mercies Brown, R.

TENDERNESS (PERSONAL QUALITY)

Anders, A. Under her skin

The **tenderness** of wolves Penney, S.

TENNESSEE

Alther, L. Kinflicks

Barr, M. Watershed

Bledsoe, A. Gather her round

Bledsoe, A. The hum and the shiver

Bledsoe, A. Long black curl

Bledsoe, A. Wisp of a thing

Dekker, T. The girl behind the red rope

Greene, A. Bloodroot

Greene, A. Long Man

Gregory, D. The devil's alphabet

Grisham, J. The firm

Sakey, M. Brilliance
See, C. There will never be another you
Seymour, G. Vagabond
Silva, D. The kill artist
Silva, D. The other woman
Winslow, D. Satori
Wolf, D. The intercept

TERRORISM -- GERMANY
Schlink, B. Self's deception

TERRORISM -- JAPAN
Mishima, Y. Runaway horses
Murakami, H. After the quake

TERRORISM -- JERUSALEM, ISRAEL
Robbins, T. Skinny legs and all

TERRORISM -- PREVENTION
Adler-Olsen, J. Victim 2117
Berenson, A. The deceivers
Brown, D. The Moscow offensive
Cameron, M. Power and empire
Cleveland, K. Keep you close
Coughlin, J. Long shot
Cussler, C. Sacred stone
DeMille, N. Wild fire
Ellis, D. In the company of liars
Forsyth, F. The kill list
Hagberg, D. Abyss
Harvey, M. We all fall down
Higgins, J. Midnight runner
Holt, A. Odd numbers
Hunter, S. Soft target
Le Carre, J. A delicate truth
Ohlsson, K. Hostage
Rosenfelt, D. Blackout
Rushdan, J. Every last breath
Tata, A. Dark winter
Taylor, B. Ring of fire
Westlake, D. Forever and a death

TERRORISM -- PSYCHOLOGICAL ASPECTS
DeLillo, D. Falling man

TERRORISM INVESTIGATION
Holt, A. Odd numbers
Peters, E. Death to the landlords!

TERRORISM VICTIMS' FAMILIES
Aramburu, F. Homeland

TERRORISTS
Adler-Olsen, J. Victim 2117
Bala, S. The boat people
Bilal, P. The ghost runner
Butler, R. Paris in the dark
Child, L. Bad luck and trouble
Coulter, C. The devil's triangle
Coulter, C. The end game
Crais, R. Demolition angel
Cunningham, M. Specimen days
Cussler, C. Sacred stone
Dees, C. Beyond the limit
Ellis, D. In the company of liars

Faletti, G. A pimp's notes
Flanagan, R. The unknown terrorist
Hayes, T. I am Pilgrim
Higgins, C. Lightless
Higgins, C. Lightless
Higgins, J. Rough justice
Hulse, S. Eden mine
Huston, C. Skinner
Ignatius, D. Body of lies
Khadivi, L. A good country
Kunzru, H. My revolutions
Littell, R. Vicious circle
MacDonald, J. Cinnamon skin
MacDonald, J. The green ripper
Marlette, D. Magic time
McCarry, C. The mulberry bush
O'Brien, E. House of splendid isolation
Ohlsson, K. Hostage
Palahniuk, C. Pygmy
Parker, R. Now and then
Peters, E. Death to the landlords!
Porter, H. Firefly
Rosenfelt, D. Blackout
Spillane, M. The Goliath bone
Steinhauer, O. All the old knives
Steinhauer, O. The last tourist
Steinhauer, O. The middleman
Yang, J. The descent of monsters

TERRORISTS -- ARAB COUNTRIES
DeLillo, D. Falling man

TERRORISTS -- IRELAND
Higgins, J. Edge of danger
Higgins, J. Eye of the storm
Higgins, J. The White House connection

TERRORISTS -- PSYCHOLOGY
DeLillo, D. Falling man

Tesla Pistalo, V.

TESLA, NIKOLA, 1856-1943
Echenoz, J. Lightning
Hunt, S. The invention of everything else
Pistalo, V. Tesla

Tess Monaghan mysteries [series] Lippman, L.

Tess of the d'Urbervilles Hardy, T.

TEST PILOTS
L'Amour, L. The last of the breed

The **testament** of Mary Toibin, C.

The **testaments** Atwood, M.

Testimony Shreve, A.

Testimony Turow, S.

Tevye the dairyman and the railroad stories Aleichem, S.

Tevye's daughters Sholem Aleichem, 1.

TEXAS
Abbott, J. Blame
Albert, S. Bittersweet
Barnett, L. Jam on the Vine
Barr, N. Track of the cat
Berlin, L. Evening in paradise

TEXTILE MILLS
Cash, W. The last ballad
THAI AMERICANS
Burdett, J. Bangkok 8
Eisler, B. All the devils
Eisler, B. Livia Lone
Eisler, B. The night trade
THAI-AMERICANS
Slouka, M. God's fool
THAILAND
Barton, F. The suspect
Boulle, P. The bridge over the River Kwai
Burdett, J. Bangkok 8
Cotterill, C. Grandad, there's a head on the beach
Cotterill, C. Killed at the whim of a hat
Eisler, B. The night trade
Hallinan, T. Fools' river
THAILAND -- HISTORY -- 20TH CENTURY
Flanagan, R. The narrow road to the deep north
THAMES RIVER
Bolton, S. A dark and twisted tide
Jakeman, J. In the kingdom of mists
James, P. Original sin
Perry, A. Blood on the water
Thank you, goodnight Abramowitz, A.
THANKSGIVING DAY
Albert, S. Bittersweet
Ford, R. The lay of the land
Penny, L. Still life
Vanderbes, J. Strangers at the feast
That darkness Black, L.
That deadman dance Scott, K.
That distant land Berry, W.
That kind of mother Alam, R.
That night McDermott, A.
That old ace in the hole Proulx, A.
The Breaking Point [series] Crownover, J.
The Brothers Sinister [series] Milan, C.
The Brown sisters [series] Hibbert, T.
The burning [series] Winter, E.
The Company [series] Baker, K.
The Duke's men [series] Jeffries, S.
THE FENS, ENGLAND
Kelly, J. The fire baby
Kelly, J. The moon tunnel
The founders [series] Bennett, R.
The Human Comedy [series] Balzac, H.
The last roundup (Roddy Doyle) [series] Doyle, R.
The last werewolf trilogy [series] Duncan, G.
The Lords of Worth [series] Bowen, K.
The Loyal League [series] Cole, A.
The Montgomerys and Armstrongs [series] Banks, M.
The Palliser novels [series] Trollope, A.
The Protectorate [series] O'Keefe, M.
The Protectors (Brenda Jackson) [series] Jackson, B.
The Rajes [series] Dev, S.
The Ravenels [series] Kleypas, L.

The Sacketts [series] L'Amour, L.
THE SIXTIES GENERATION
Nunez, S. The last of her kind
Pynchon, T. Vineland
The Smythe-Smith quartet [series] Quinn, J.
The Spare Heirs [series] Michels, E.
THE TROUBLES, 1968-1998
Burns, A. Milkman
McKinty, A. The cold, cold ground
McKinty, A. In the morning I'll be gone
THE WEST (CANADA)
Brand, M. The Stingaree
Vanderhaeghe, G. The last crossing
THE WEST (UNITED STATES -- SOCIAL LIFE AND CUSTOMS -- 19TH CENTURY
Lansdale, J. Paradise sky
THE WEST (UNITED STATES)
Bear, E. Stone mad
Berger, T. Little Big Man
Cheever, J. The Wapshot scandal
Dallas, S. Tallgrass
Diaz, H. In the distance
Doig, I. The whistling season
Enger, L. The high divide
Erdrich, L. The Master Butchers Singing Club
Erdrich, L. The painted drum
Estleman, L. The master executioner
Fajardo-Anstine, K. Sabrina & Corina
Goodman, J. A touch of forever
Guthrie, A. The big sky
Holbert, B. Whiskey
Johnson, C. Another man's moccasins
Johnson, C. Dark horse
Johnson, C. Death without company
Johnson, C. Hell is emptyKelton, E. Hard ride
Leonard, E. The complete Western stories of Elmore Leonard.
Lock, N. American meteor
Meyer, P. The son
Paul, B. Under Tower Peak
Peterson, T. What comes my way
Portis, C. True grit
Proulx, A. That old ace in the hole
Scapellato, J. Big lonesome
Schanbacher, G. Crossing Purgatory
Stegner, W. Angle of repose
Stegner, W. The Big Rock Candy Mountain
Swarthout, G. The shootist
Vanderhaeghe, G. The last crossing
Walls, J. Half broke horses
Watson, L. Let him go
Westward
THE WEST (UNITED STATES) -- EXPLORATION
Michener, J. Centennial
THE WEST (UNITED STATES) -- HISTORY
Osborne, D. The coming
THE WEST (UNITED STATES) -- HISTORY -- 1848-1950

Their perfect melody Oliveras, P.

Them Oates, J.

Theme music Vandelly, T.

Then she was gone Jewell, L.

Then there was you Isaac, K.

Then we take Berlin Lawton, J.

THEOCRACY

Atwood, M. The handmaid's tale

Atwood, M. The testaments

Seton, A. The Winthrop woman

THEODICY

Young, W. The shack

THEOLOGICAL SEMINARIES -- EAST ANGLIA, ENGLAND

James, P. Death in holy orders

THEOLOGY

Atwood, M. Maddaddam

Theophilus North Wilder, T.

THEORIES

Tokarczuk, O. Drive your plow over the bones of the dead

THERA (ISLANDS)

Walton, J. Necessity

Therapy Kellerman, J.

There before the chaos Wagers, K.

There but for the Smith, A.

There is room for you Bacon, C.

There there Orange, T.

There will never be another you See, C.

There's a word for that Tanen, S.

There's something I want you to do Baxter, C.

There's something in a Sunday Muller, M.

These ghosts are family Card, M.

These honored dead Putnam, J.

These old shades Heyer, G.

These women Pochoda, I.

THESEUS (GREEK MYTHOLOGY)

Renault, M. The bull from the sea

Renault, M. The king must die

THESSALONIKE, GREECE

Furst, A. Spies of the Balkans

They all fall down Cohen, T.

They're watching Hurwitz, G.

Thicker than water Spencer, S.

The **thicket** Lansdale, J.

Thief of Corinth Afshar, T.

Thief of glory Brouwer, S.

Thief of time Pratchett, T.

The **thief** of Venice Langton, J.

Thief River Falls Freeman, B.

THIEVES

Adler-Olsen, J. The Marco effect

Afshar, T. Thief of Corinth

Alexis, A. The hidden keys

Atkins, A. The redeemers

Banville, J. The book of evidence

Banville, J. The blue guitar

Berry, C. A legacy of murder

Block, L. The burglar in the closet

Block, L. The burglar in the library

Brown, T. Fallen land

Cash, W. This dark road to mercy

deWitt, P. Undermajordomo Minor

Drury, T. The driftless area

Faulkner, W. The reivers

Hallinan, T. Crashed

Hallinan, T. Fields where they lay

Hallinan, T. Fools' river

Hamilton, S. The second life of Nick Mason

Harrison, T. Dragon bound

Helprin, M. Winter's tale

Higashino, K. The miracles of the Namiya General Store

Kaufmann, N. Dying is my business

Kennedy, R. Presidio

Krueger, P. Steel crow saga

Laurens, S. A rake's vow

Leckie, A. Provenance

Lindsay, J. Just watch me

Mabanckou, A. Black Moses

Mathews, B. The world of tomorrow

Mayor, A. Tag man

McBain, E. The big bad city

McMurtry, L. Streets of Laredo

Meno, J. Marvel and a wonder

Muller, M. The cavalier in white

Nickson, C. The hocus girl

Ondaatje, M. The English patient

Parker, T. L.A. outlaws

Perez-Reverte, A. What we become

Peters, E. The hippopotamus pool

Peters, E. Night train to Memphis

Petrie, N. Tear it down

Potzsch, O. The dark monk

Pratchett, T. Thief of time

Price, R. Lush life

Quick, A. Slightly shady

Rajaniemi, H. The fractal prince

Rajaniemi, H. The quantum thief

Robards, K. The ultimatum

Rosenberg, J. Confessions of the fox

Ryan, A. The waking fire

Sallis, J. Drive

Sallis, J. Driven

Sandford, J. Storm Front

Schwab, V. A conjuring of light

Schwab, V. A darker shade of magic

Skarmeta, A. The dancer and the thief

Spillane, M. The Goliath bone

Stark, R. Ask the parrot

Stark, R. Breakout

Stark, R. Comeback

Stark, R. The hunter

Stott, R. The coral thief

Sullivan, M. Theft of swords

Tyler, A. Earthly possessions

Thorne chronicles [series] Eason, K.

THOROUGHBRED HORSE FARMS
Parker, R. Hugger Mugger

THOROUGHBRED HORSES
Morgan, C. The sport of kings

THORPE, JIM, 1887-1953
Coldsmith, D. The long journey home

Those bones are not my child Bambara, T.

Those people Candlish, L.

Those who leave and those who stay Ferrante, E.

Those who wish me dead Koryta, M.

Though not dead Stabenow, D.

THOUGHT AND THINKING
Brodesser-Akner, T. Fleishman is in trouble
Brookner, A. Hotel Du Lac
Henry, P. Becoming Mrs. Lewis
Lyon, A. The sweet girl
Moore, A. The lighthouse
Oates, J. Wild nights
Savage, S. Glass

A **thousand** acres Smiley, J.

The **thousand** autumns of Jacob De Zoet Mitchell, D.

A **thousand** pardons Dee, J.

A **thread** of grace Russell, M.

THREAT (PSYCHOLOGY)
Barr, N. What Rose forgot
Beah, I. Radiance of tomorrow
Burns, A. Milkman
Clare, A. The woman who spoke to spirits
Clark, M. Death wears a beauty mask and other stories
Clark, M. Kiss the girls and make them cry
Cleeves, A. Wild fire
Constantine, L. The last time I saw you
Cornwell, P. Chaos
Cussler, C. Nighthawk
Cussler, C. The Pharaoh's secret
Daniel, R. Hacked
Daugherty, C. Revolver road
Feeney, A. I know who you are
Foster, L. Under pressure
Gaylin, A. Never look back
Hampton, B. Stalker
Hand, E. Hard light
Humphreys, S. Trouble walks in
Hurwitz, G. You're next
Iles, G. Third degree
Jackson, B. Forged in desire
Koontz, D. Velocity
Krentz, J. When all the girls have gone
Marwood, A. The killer next door
Millet, L. Sweet lamb of heaven
Owen, H. The bottom
Quick, A. 'Til death do us part
Reid, I. I'm thinking of ending things
Rice, W. Moon of the crusted snow
Roberts, N. The obsession
Roberts, N. Shelter in place

Ryan, H. Say no more
Tudor, C. The other people
VanderMeer, J. Annihilation
VanderMeer, J. Acceptance
VanderMeer, J. Authority
Wright, J. The house on Foster Hill

Three bargains Malik, T.

The **three** Beths Abbott, J.

Three blind mice, and other stories Christie, A.

Three day road Boyden, J.

Three days before the shooting . . . Ellison, R.

THREE GORGES PROJECT, CHINA
See, L. Dragon bones

Three graves full Mason, J.

Three hours in Paris Black, C.

Three Junes Glass, J.

Three lives Stein, G.

The **three** musketeers Dumas, A.

Three musketeers series [series] Dumas, A.

Three Sisters Island trilogy [series] Roberts, N.

Three stages of amazement Edgarian, C.

Three stations Smith, M.

Three strong women NDiaye, M.

Three things about Elsie Cannon, J.

Three weeks with Lady X James, E.

Three years with the rat Hosking, J.

The **three-arched** bridge Kadare, I.

The **three-body** problem Liu, C.

THREE-YEAR-OLD GIRLS
Miller, S. The good mother

Threshold Doyle, R.

Thrice the brinded cat hath mew'd Bradley, C.

THRILLERS AND SUSPENSE
Abbott, J. Blame
Abbott, M. The fever
Abbott, M. You will know me
Abrams, M. Meadowlark
Adler-Olsen, J. The absent one
Adler-Olsen, J. A conspiracy of faith
Adler-Olsen, J. The hanging girl
Adler-Olsen, J. The keeper of lost causes
Adler-Olsen, J. The Marco effec
Adler-Olsen, J. The purity of vengeance
Adler-Olsen, J. The scarred woman
Adler-Olsen, J. Victim 2117
Atkins, A. The broken places
Atkins, A. The fallen
Atkins, A. The forsaken
Atkins, A. The innocents
Atkins, A. The lost ones
Atkins, A. The ranger
Atkins, A. The redeemers
Atkins, A. The shameless
Atkins, A. The sinners
Atkins, A. Wicked city
Baker, C. Whisper network
Baldacci, D. The fallen

Coughlin, J. In the crosshairs
Coughlin, J. Long shot
Coulter, C. The devil's triangle
Coulter, C. The end game
Coulter, C. The final cut
Coulter, C. Labyrinth
Coulter, C. The last second
Coulter, C. The lost key
Coulter, C. Paradox
Coulter, C. The sixth day
Crais, R. Demolition angel
Crais, R. Suspect
Crichton, M. Pirate latitudes
Crichton, M. Micro
Cumming, C. A colder war
Cumming, C. A divided spy
Cumming, C. A foreign country
Cussler, C. Blue gold
Cussler, C. Celtic empire
Cussler, C. Final option
Cussler, C. Ghost ship
Cussler, C. Pacific vortex!
Cussler, C. Golden Buddha
Cussler, C. The Gray Ghost
Cussler, C. Havana storm
Cussler, C. Nighthawk
Cussler, C. Odessa Sea
Cussler, C. The oracle
Cussler, C. The Pharaoh's secret
Cussler, C. The rising sea
Cussler, C. The Romanov ransom
Cussler, C. Sacred stone
Cussler, C. Sea of greed
Cussler, C. Serpent
Cussler, C. Shadow tyrants
Cussler, C. Typhoon fury
Daly, P. Clear my name
Daly, P. Open your eyes
Daniel, R. Hacked
Daugherty, C. A beautiful corpse
Daugherty, C. The echo killing
Daugherty, C. Revolver road
Dazieri, S. Kill the angel
Dazieri, S. Kill the father
Dazieri, S. Kill the king
De la Motte, A. MemoRandom
De la Motte, A. Ultimatum
DeMille, N. The deserter
DeMille, N. Wild fire
Deaver, J. Edge
Deaver, J. The never game
Deaver, J. The October list
Dickey, E. Finding Gideon
Dimberg, K. Girl in the rearview mirror
Dodd, C. Dead girl running
Dodd, C. Strangers she knows
Dodd, C. What doesn't kill her

Dodd, C. Virtue Falls
Doetsch, R. Half-past dawn
Doiron, P. Bad Little Falls
Doiron, P. The poacher's son
Doiron, P. The precipice
Dow, D. Confessions of an innocent man
Downing, S. He started it
Dugoni, R. The conviction
Dugoni, R. The eighth sister
Dugoni, R. Murder one
Dundas, C. The blaze
Edvardsson, M. A nearly normal family
Egan, J. The keep
Eisler, B. All the devils
Eisler, B. The god's eye view
Eisler, B. The killer collective
Eisler, B. Livia Lone
Eisler, B. The night trade
Elliot, L. Guilty
Ellis, D. In the company of liars
Ellory, R. The anniversary man
Ellory, R. Bad signs
Ephron, H. Careful what you wish for
Ephron, H. Night night, sleep tight
Epperson, T. Sailor
Estleman, L. Something borrowed, something black
Ewan, C. Dark tides
Ewan, C. Long time lost
Fairstein, L. Blood oath
Fairstein, L. Entombed
Ferencik, E. Into the jungle
Fesperman, D. Safe houses
Fielding, J. All the wrong places
Fielding, J. The bad daughter
Finder, J. Guilty minds
Finder, J. House on fire
Finder, J. Judgment
Finder, J. The switch
Flyte, M. City of dark magic
Flyte, M. City of lost dreams
Follett, K. Hornet flight
Follett, K. Whiteout
Forsyth, F. The fox
Forsyth, F. The kill list
Fox, C. Crimson Lake
Fox, C. Gone by midnight
Fox, C. Redemption point
Francis, D. Smokescreen
Francis, F. Crisis
Francis, F. Guilty not guilty
Francis, F. Pulse
Frayn, M. Spies
Frear, C. Stone cold heart
Frear, C. Sweet little lies
Freeman, B. Goodbye to the dead
Freeman, B. Marathon
Freeman, B. The night bird

Kamal, S. It all falls down
Kava, A. Hotwire
Kazinski, A. The last good man
Kerr, P. Hitler's peace
King, C. Stiletto justice
King, L. Keeping watch
King, S. 11/22/63
King, S. End of watch
King, S. Finders keepers
King, S. The girl who loved Tom Gordon
King, S. The Institute
King, S. Mr. Mercedes
Klaussmann, L. Tigers in red weather
Klein, M. Con ed
Koepp, D. Cold storage
Koontz, D. The darkest evening of the year
Koontz, D. The husband
Koontz, D. Innocence
Koontz, D. Intensity
Koontz, D. Velocity
Koryta, M. If she wakes
Koryta, M. The prophet
Koryta, M. Those who wish me dead
Lashner, W. A killer's kiss
Laukkanen, O. Criminal enterprise
Laukkanen, O. Deception Cove
Laukkanen, O. Gale force
Laukkanen, O. The professionals
Laukkanen, O. The watcher in the wall
Lawton, J. Hammer to fall
Le Carre, J. The constant gardener
Le Carre, J. A most wanted man
Le Carre, J. Our kind of traitor
Lee, P. Dark site
Lee, P. Runner
Lee, P. Signal
Lehane, D. Mystic river
Lehane, D. Since we fell
Lelchuk, S. Save me from dangerous men
Lelic, S. The child who
Leonard, E. Charlie Martz and other stories
Leonard, E. LaBrava
Leonard, E. Rum punch
Les Becquets, D. Breaking wild
Lescroart, J. Guilt
Levien, D. City of the sun
Levin, I. The boys from Brazil
Levin, I. A kiss before dying
Lippman, L. And when she was good
Lippman, L. The most dangerous thing
Littell, R. Vicious circle
Livesey, M. The missing world
Long, J. The reckoning, Jeff Long.
Lourey, J. Unspeakable things
Lowe, K. The furies
Ludlum, R. The Bourne identity
Ludlum, R. The Bourne supremacy

Ludlum, R. The Bourne ultimatum
Ludlum, R. The Prometheus deception
Ludlum, R. The Sigma protocol
Luna, L. The Janes
Lutz, J. Final seconds
Lutz, L. The swallows
Lynn, A. Now you see it
MacInnes, H. Prelude to terror
MacInnes, H. Ride a pale horse
Malik, T. Three bargains
Mankell, H. The troubled man
March, W. The bad seed
Mason, J. The hidden things
MatchUp
Matheson, R. Hunted past reason
Matthews, J. The Kremlin's candidate
Matthews, J. Red sparrow
Matthews, J. Palace of treason
McBain, E. Alice in jeopardy
McCarry, C. The mulberry bush
McCarry, C. Old boys
McCrumb, S. Foggy Mountain breakdown and other stories
McHugh, L. The wolf wants in
McKinty, A. The chain
McLarty, R. Art in America
McLaughlin, J. Bearskin
McMahon, J. The invited
Meltzer, B. The escape artist
Meltzer, B. The inner circle
Meltzer, B. The tenth justice
Meltzer, B. The zero game
Meuleman, S. Find me gone
Meyer, D. Devil's peak
Meyer, D. Heart of the hunter
Meyer, D. Icarus
Meyer, D. Trackers
Miller, D. Norwegian by night
Mina, D. Conviction
Miranda, M. The last house guest
Mitchard, J. The deep end of the ocean
Mitchard, J. No time to wave goodbye
Morgan Jones, C. The jackal's share
Morgan Jones, C. The silent oligarch
Mosby, S. You can run
Murakami, R. In the miso soup , Ryu Murakami ; translated
  by Ralph McCarthy.
Nesbo, J. Blood on snow
Nesbo, J. Headhunters
Nesbo, J. Midnight sun
Nesbo, J. The son
Neville, S. The ghosts of Belfast
Newton, C. Calumet City
Newton, C. Start shooting
Nichols, L. Vessel
Nicholson, G. The city under the skin
Noire Candy licker
Noire G-Spot

Sandford, J. Silent prey
Sandford, J. Silken prey
Sandford, J. Storm prey
Sandford, J. Sudden prey
Sandford, J. Winter prey
Saul, J. Midnight voices
Scottoline, L. Legal tender
Scottoline, L. Come home
Scottoline, L. Don't go
Scottoline, L. Every fifteen minutes
Scottoline, L. Feared
Scottoline, L. One perfect lie
Sebastian, T. Fatal ally
Seo, M. The only child
Seymour, G. Vagabond
Sharp, Z. Fox hunter
Silva, D. The kill artist
Silva, D. The black widow
Silva, D. The new girl
Silva, D. The other woman
Singh, N. A madness of sunshine
Slaughter, K. Criminal
Slaughter, K. Fallen
Slaughter, K. The kept woman
Slaughter, K. The last widow
Slaughter, K. Pieces of her
Slaughter, K. Pretty girls
Slaughter, K. Undone
Smith, M. Gorky Park
Smith, M. Havana Bay
Smith, M. Polar Star
Smith, M. Red Square
Smith, M. The Siberian dilemma
Smith, M. Stalin's ghost
Smith, M. Tatiana
Smith, M. Three stations
Smith, M. Wolves eat dogs
Smith, S. A simple plan
Solomita, S. A good day to die
Steinhauer, O. An American spy
Steinhauer, O. The Cairo affair
Steinhauer, O. The last tourist
Steinhauer, O. The middleman
Steinhauer, O. The nearest exit
Steinhauer, O. The tourist
Stroby, W. Some die nameless
Stroud, C. The shimmer
Tata, A. Dark winter
Taylor, B. Daughter of war
Taylor, B. Ring of fire
Tracy, P. Ice cold heart
Tracy, P. Monkeewrench
Tudor, C. The chalk man
Tudor, C. The other people
Tyree, O. Leslie
Vasquez, J. The sound of things falling
Vidich, P. The coldest warrior

Walker, W. Crime of privilege
Wambaugh, J. The blue knight
Wambaugh, J. The new centurions
Watt, H. To the lions
Weber, C. Man on the run
Westlake, D. Forever and a death
White, C. The wife and the widow
White, R. Salt river
White, S. Kill me
White, S. Dry ice
White, S. The siege
White, S. Line of fire
White, S. Compound fractures
Wiesel, E. Hostage
Willocks, T. Memo from Turner
Winslow, D. The kings of cool
Winslow, D. Satori
Winslow, D. Savages
Wolf, D. The execution
Wolf, D. The intercept
Wolf, D. The ultimatum
Woods, S. Below the belt
Woods, S. Chiefs
Woods, S. A delicate touch
Woods, S. Fast & loose
Woods, S. The money shot
Woods, S. New York dead
Woods, S. Orchid beach
Woods, S. Palindrome
Woods, S. Santa Fe rules
Woods, S. Skin game
Woods, S. Smooth operator
Woods, S. Stealth
Woods, T. Alibi
Zan, K. The never list
Zander, J. The swimmer
Zhou, H. Death notice
Throne of darkness Nicholas, D.
Thrones, dominations Sayers, D.
Through a glass darkly Koen, K.
Through black spruce Boyden, J.
Through the evil days Spencer-Fleming, J.
Through waters deep Sundin, S.
Thud! Pratchett, T.
Thug lovin' Clark, W.
Thug matrimony Clark, W.
Thug novels [series] Clark, W.
Thugs and the women who love them Clark, W.
Thugs cry Ca$h
Thugs cry novels (Ca$h) [series] Ca$h
Thunder and lightning (John Varley) [series] Varley, J.
Thunder Point novels [series] Carr, R.
Thunderhead Preston, D.
Thursday Next novels [series] Fforde, J.
Thursday the Rabbi walked out Kemelman, H.
Thursday's children French, N.
Thus bad begins Marias, J.

TIME TRAVEL (FUTURE)

Gladstone, M. Empress of forever
Goonan, K. In war times
Kress, N. After the fall, before the fall, during the fall
Robinson, K. Galileo's dream
Serle, R. In five years
Simmons, D. Endymion
Stevens, F. The heads of Cerberus

TIME TRAVEL (PAST)

Adams, D. Life, the universe, and everything
Alexie, S. Flight
Baker, K. In the garden of Iden
Barth, J. The last voyage of somebody the sailor
Butler, O. Kindred
Daughters, A. You cannot mess this up
Gabaldon, D. Dragonfly in amber
Gabaldon, D. Drums of autumn
Gabaldon, D. An echo in the bone
Gabaldon, D. Outlander
Gabaldon, D. Voyager
Gabaldon, D. Written in my own heart's blood
Greer, A. The impossible lives of Greta Wells
Gruber, M. The forgery of Venus
Harkness, D. Shadow of night
King, S. 11
Maaren, K. Weave a circle round
Newman, S. The heavens
Reynolds, A. Permafrost
Rice, A. Angel time
Seton, A. Green darkness
Simmons, D. The rise of Endymion
Stephenson, N. The rise and fall of D.O.D.O.
Twain, M. A Connecticut Yankee in King Arthur's Court
Willis, C. Blackout
Willis, C. Doomsday book
Willis, C. To say nothing of the dog
Winawer, M. The scribe of Siena
Wojtas, O. Miss Blaine's prefect and the golden samovar
Wolfe, G. Pirate freedom

TIME TRAVEL ROMANCES

Gabaldon, D. A breath of snow and ashes
Gabaldon, D. Dragonfly in amber
Gabaldon, D. Drums of autumn
Gabaldon, D. An echo in the bone
Gabaldon, D. The fiery cross
Gabaldon, D. Outlander
Gabaldon, D. Voyager
The **time** traveler's wife Niffenegger, A.
Time's arrow, or The nature of the offense Amis, M.
Time's convert Harkness, D.
Timequake Vonnegut, K.
Timothy Cone mysteries [series] Sanders, L.
The **Timothy** files Sanders, L.
Timothy's game Sanders, L.
Tin badges Carcaterra, L.
The **tin** can tree Tyler, A.
The **tin** drum Grass, G.

Tin man Winman, S.
Tinker, tailor, soldier, spy Le Carre, J.
Tinkers Harding, P.
The **Tintern** treasure Sedley, K.
Tiny Americans Murphy, D.
Tiny love Brown, L.
Tipping the velvet Waters, S.
Tirza Grunberg, A.
Tishomingo blues Leonard, E.
Titan Varley, J.

TITANIC (STEAMSHIP)

Bainbridge, B. Every man for himself
Cussler, C. The Titanic secret
Gohlke, C. Promise me this
Katsu, A. The deep
The **Titanic** secret Cussler, C.

TITANS (MYTHOLOGY)

Miller, M. Circe
Titanshade Stout, D.

TITLES OF HONOR AND NOBILITY

Rodale, M. Lady Bridget's diary

TITUBA

Conde, M. I, Tituba, Black witch of Salem
To be taught, if fortunate Chambers, B.
To catch a spy Kaminsky, S.
To dance with kings Laker, R.
To die for Neel, J.
To die in spring Rothmann, R.
To have and have not Hemingway, E.
To heaven by water Cartwright, J.
To keep the sun alive Ghaffari, R.
To kill a mockingbird Lee, H.
To kill a mockingbird [series] Lee, H.
To rise again at a decent hour Ferris, J.
To say nothing of the dog Willis, C.
To seduce an angel Moore, K.
To the bright edge of the world Ivey, E.
To the edge of sorrow Apelfeld, A.
To the end of the land Grossman, D.
To the far blue mountains L'Amour, L.
To the lighthouse Woolf, V.
To the lions Watt, H.
To wed a stranger Layton, E.

TOASTS

Griffin, A. When all is said
Tobacco Road Caldwell, E.
Toby Peters mysteries [series] Kaminsky, S.

TODDLERS

Martin, S. The pleasure of my company

TOHOKU EARTHQUAKE AND TSUNAMI, JAPAN, 2011

Ozeki, R. A tale for the time being

TOHONO O'ODHAM INDIANS -- ARIZONA

Jance, J. Queen of the night

TOKLAS, ALICE B, 1877-1967

Truong, M. The book of salt, Monique Truong.
Tokyo trilogy [series] Peace, D.
Tokyo year zero Peace, D.

TORTURE VICTIMS
Danticat, E. The dew breaker
Wolfe, G. The shadow of the torturer

TORTURERS
Danticat, E. The dew breaker
Potzsch, O. The hangman's daughter
Wolfe, G. The citadel of the Autarch
Wolfe, G. The claw of the conciliator
Wolfe, G. The shadow of the torturer
Wolfe, G. The sword of the Lictor
Wolfe, G. The urth of the new sun

Total recall Paretsky, S.

TOTALITARIANISM
Bandi, 1. The accusation
Bennett, R. City of blades
Bennett, R. City of stairs
Bradbury, R. Fahrenheit 451
Church, J. A corpse in the Koryo
Church, J. Hidden moon
Erpenbeck, J. The book of words
Huxley, A. Brave new world
Jen, G. The resisters
Kafka, F. The trial
Koestler, A. Darkness at noon
Liu, K. Invisible planets
Ma, J. China dream
Muller, H. The fox was ever the hunter
Muller, H. The hunger angel
Nabokov, V. Novels and memoirs, 1941-51
Oksanen, S. When the doves disappeared
Orwell, G. 1984
Orwell, G. Animal farm
Rand, A. We the living
Weldon, F. Chalcot Crescent
Zamyatin, Y. We

TOTALITARIANISM -- CZECHOSLOVAKIA
Kundera, M. The unbearable lightness of being

TOTALITARIANISM -- GERMANY
Harris, R. Fatherland

TOTALITARIANISM -- PSYCHOLOGICAL ASPECTS
Saramago, J. The manual of painting and calligraphy

TOTALITARIANISM -- SOVIET UNION
Koestler, A. Darkness at noon

TOTALITARIANISM -- UNITED STATES
Lewis, S. It can't happen here

A **touch** of forever Goodman, J.
A **touch** of stardust Alcott, K.
Touch the devil Higgins, J.
Touchstone agency novels [series] Burns, R.

TOULOUSE-LAUTREC, HENRI DE, 1864-1901
Moore, C. Sacre bleu

TOUR GROUPS
Marsh, N. When in Rome

TOUR GUIDES (PERSONS)
Dovlatov, S. Pushkin Hills
Hiaasen, C. Nature girl
Marsh, N. When in Rome

TOURETTE SYNDROME
Lethem, J. Motherless Brooklyn

TOURISM
Harrison, M. Nova swing
Miranda, M. The last house guest
New suns
The **tourist** Steinhauer, O.

TOURISTS
Mda, Z. The whale caller
Sandford, J. Holy ghost
Serafim, L. When the devil's idle
Smith, S. The ruins
Sundstol, V. The land of dreams
Wood, S. The Quintland sisters

TOURMALINE
Scott, J. Tourmaline
Tourmaline Scott, J.

TOURNAMENTS
Bouchet, A. Breath of fire
Towards zero Christie, A.

TOWER OF LONDON (LONDON, ENGLAND)
Higgins, J. The eagle has flown
Weir, A. A dangerous inheritance

TOXINS
Chen, Q. Waste tide
Sayers, D. The documents in the case

TOYMAKERS
Maguire, G. Hiddensee

TOYS
Davys, T. Amberville
Trace elements Leon, D.
Track of the cat Barr, N.

TRACKERS
Deaver, J. The never game
Everett, P. God's country
Meyer, D. Trackers
Trackers Meyer, D.

TRACKERS -- TEXAS
McMurtry, L. Comanche moon

TRACKING AND TRAILING
Box, C. Paradise Valley
Grecian, A. The saint of wolves and butchers
Hunter, S. Game of snipers
Meyer, D. Trackers
Penney, S. The tenderness of wolves
Tracks Erdrich, L.
Tracy Crosswhite novels [series] Dugoni, R.
Tracy Ellison novels [series] Tyree, O.

TRADERS
Locke, T. Enclave

TRADING AND SWAPPING
Swanson, P. Her every fear
Vinge, V. A deepness in the sky

TRADING POSTS
Mitchell, D. The thousand autumns of Jacob De Zoet

TRADITION (PHILOSOPHY)
Abe, K. The woman in the dunes

Transcendental novels [series] Gunn, J.

TRANSCENDENTALISTS (NEW ENGLAND)
Lock, N. A fugitive in Walden Woods

TRANSCONTINENTAL JOURNEYS
Shteyngart, G. Lake Success

TRANSCONTINENTAL RAILROAD (UNITED STATES)
Lock, N. American meteor

Transcription Atkinson, K.

TRANSFER STUDENTS
Ellison, J. Good girls lie

TRANSFORMATIONS (MAGIC)
Armfield, J. Salt slow
Czerneda, J. A turn of light
Diachenko, S. Vita nostra
Gaiman, N. Stardust
Harkness, D. Time's convert
Hill, J. Horns
Hill, J. NOS4A2
Ivey, E. The snow child
Kafka, F. The metamorphosis
Knox, T. Kockroach
Woolf, V. Orlando

TRANSFORMATIONS, PERSONAL
Ashford, J. Heir to the duke
Auster, P. Timbuktu
Bailey, T. Fix her up
Balogh, M. Someone to love
Berg, E. Never change
Cusk, R. Transit
Danielewski, M. House of leaves
Dickens, C. A Christmas carol
Gilman, S. Donna has left the building
Kleypas, L. Cold-hearted rake
Krauss, N. Forest Dark
Lancaster, J. Here I go again
Linden, R. The enlightenment of bees
Mallery, S. Best of my love
Miller, R. Jacob's folly
Moriarty, L. Nine perfect strangers
Patchett, A. State of wonder
Rodale, M. Lady Bridget's diary
Rubart, J. The man he never was
Shalvis, J. Simply irresistible
Shanbhag, V. Ghachar ghochar
Shteyngart, G. Super sad true love story
Smith, A. The accidental
Tropper, J. One last thing before I go

TRANSGENDER CHILDREN
Frankel, L. This is how it always is
Johnson, D. Everything under

TRANSGENDER PERSONS
Boylan, J. Long black veil
Cassara, J. The house of impossible beauties
Elison, M. The book of Etta
Elison, M. The book of Flora
Fu, K. For today I am a boy
Mehta, R. No other world

Moore, E. The Supremes sing the happy heartache blues
Mootoo, S. Moving forward sideways, like a crab
Rosenberg, J. Confessions of the fox
Woolf, V. Orlando

TRANSGENDER TEENAGE GIRLS
Cassara, J. The house of impossible beauties

TRANSGENDER TEENAGERS
Myers, A. Continental divide

Transgressions

TRANSGRESSIVE FICTION
Burgess, A. A clockwork orange
Burroughs, W. Naked lunch
Dunn, K. Geek love
Kramer, L. Search for my heart
Miller, H. Tropic of Cancer
Miller, H. Tropic of Capricorn
Murakami, R. In the miso soup , Ryu Murakami ; translated by Ralph McCarthy.
Palahniuk, C. Fight Club
Palahniuk, C. Lullaby

Transit Cusk, R.

The **transit** of Venus Hazzard, S.

TRANSITIONING (GENDER IDENTITY)
Ebershoff, D. The Danish girl

TRANSLATING AND INTERPRETING
Kutsukake, L. The translation of love
Phoenix, M. The space between words
Qiu, X. When red is black

The **translation** of love Kutsukake, L.

TRANSLATIONS -- AFRIKAANS TO ENGLISH
Meyer, D. Devil's peak
Meyer, D. Icarus
Meyer, D. Trackers

TRANSLATIONS -- ALBANIAN TO ENGLISH
Kadare, I. The three-arched bridge

TRANSLATIONS -- ARABIC TO ENGLISH
Al Rawi, S. The Baghdad clock
Al-Ramli, M. The president's gardens
Alharthi, J. Celestial bodies
Alomar, O. The teeth of the comb & other stories
Aswani, A. Chicago
Khalfah, K. Death is hard work
Mahfuz, N. Palace walk
Mahfuz, N. Sugar Street
Sa'dawi, A. Frankenstein in Baghdad

TRANSLATIONS -- CHINESE TO ENGLISH
Broken stars
Chen, Q. Waste tide
Gao, X. Soul mountain
Jiang, R. Wolf totem
Jin, Y. A hero born
Liu, C. Ball lightning
Liu, C. The dark forest
Liu, C. Death's end
Liu, C. The three-body problem
Liu, K. Invisible planets
Ma, J. Beijing coma

Proust, M. Within a budding grove
Rademacher, C. Deadly Camargue
Roussel, R. Locus solus
Sagan, F. Bonjour tristesse
Saint-Exupery, A. The little prince
Saint-Exupery, A. Night flight
Sand, G. Marianne
Sartre, J. The age of reason
Sartre, J. Nausea
Sartre, J. Reprieve
Sartre, J. Troubled sleep
Schwarz-Bart, A. The last of the just
Shan, S. The girl who played Go
Simenon, G. Maigret and the black sheep
Simenon, G. Maigret and the fortuneteller
Simenon, G. Maigret and the killer
Simenon, G. Maigret and the madwoman
Simenon, G. Maigret and the Saturday caller
Simenon, G. Maigret and the toy village
Simenon, G. Maigret and the wine merchant
Simenon, G. Maigret bides his time
Simenon, G. Maigret goes home
Simenon, G. Maigret in Holland
Simenon, G. Maigret's memoirs
Simenon, G. My friend Maigret
Sthers, A. Holy lands
Verne, J. Around the world in eighty days
Verne, J. Journey to the centre of the Earth
Verne, J. The mysterious island
Voltaire Candide and other stories
Wiesel, E. Dawn
Wiesel, E. Hostage
Wiesel, E. The judges
Wiesel, E. A mad desire to dance
Wiesel, E. Night, Dawn, The accident
Yourcenar, M. Memoirs of Hadrian
Zola, E. Germinal
Zola, E. Nana

TRANSLATIONS -- GERMAN TO ENGLISH

Bannalec, J. Death in Brittany
Bannalec, J. The killing tide
Bernhard, T. Frost
Bernhard, T. The loser
Bernhard, T. Woodcutters
Boll, H. Billiards at half-past nine
Boll, H. The clown
Boll, H. The lost honor of Katharina Blum
Boll, H. The silent angel
Bronsky, A. The hottest dishes of the Tartar cuisine
Erpenbeck, J. The book of words
Erpenbeck, J. Go, went, gone
Erpenbeck, J. Visitation
Fallada, H. Every man dies alone
Franck, J. Blindness of the heart
George, N. The book of dreams
George, N. The little Paris bookshop
Giordano, M. Auntie Poldi and the Vineyards of Etna

Grass, G. The call of the toad
Grass, G. Cat and mouse
Grass, G. Crabwalk
Grass, G. Dog years
Grass, G. The flounder
Grass, G. The tin drum
Grass, G. Too far afield
Handke, P. Crossing the Sierra de Gredos
Hesse, H. The fairy tales of Hermann
Hesse, H. Narcissus and Goldmund
Hesse, H. Siddhartha
Hesse, H. Steppenwolf
Kafka, F. The castle
Kafka, F. The metamorphosis
Kafka, F. The trial
Kehlmann, D. Tyll
Keilson, H. Life goes on
Kracht, C. Imperium
Link, C. The other child
Link, C. The watcher
Mann, T. The black swan
Mann, T. Buddenbrooks
Mann, T. Death in Venice and seven other stories
Mann, T. Doctor Faustus
Mann, T. The Magic Mountain
Muller, H. The fox was ever the hunter
Muller, H. The hunger angel
Musil, R. The man without qualities
Neuhaus, N. The ice queen
Neuhaus, N. Snow White must die
Potzsch, O. The beggar king
Potzsch, O. The dark monk
Potzsch, O. The hangman's daughter
Potzsch, O. The play of death
Potzsch, O. The poisoned pilgrim
Potzsch, O. The werewolf of Bamberg
Remarque, E. All quiet on the western front
Remarque, E. The road back
Remarque, E. A time to love and a time to die
Roth, J. The collected stories of Joseph Roth
Rothmann, R. To die in spring
Schami, R. Sophia
Schlink, B. The reader
Schlink, B. Self's deception
Schlink, B. Self's murder
Schlink, B. Self's punishment
Sebald, W. Austerlitz
Sebald, W. The emigrants ;, W. G. Sebald ; translated by
  Michael Hulse.
Sebald, W. Vertigo
Suskind, P. Perfume
Thelen, A. The island of second sight
Traven, B. The treasure of the Sierra Madre
Walser, R. The assistant
Wells, B. The end of loneliness
Werfel, F. The forty days of Musa Dagh

TRANSLATIONS -- GREEK TO ENGLISH

Ogawa, Y. The housekeeper and the professor
Ogawa, Y. The memory police
Okuizumi, H. The stones cry out
Tawada, Y. The emissary
Yoshimoto, B. Goodbye Tsugumi
Yoshimoto, B. The lake
Yoshimoto, B. Moshi-moshi

TRANSLATIONS -- KANNADA TO ENGLISH

Shanbhag, V. Ghachar ghochar

TRANSLATIONS -- KOREAN TO ENGLISH

Bandi The accusation
Han, K. Human acts
Kim, Y. Diary of a murderer
Lee, J. The starlet and the spy
Yi, C. The investigation

TRANSLATIONS -- NORWEGIAN TO ENGLISH

Brekke, J. The fifth element
Dahl, K. The courier
Fossum, K. Bad intentions
Fossum, K. Eva's eye
Holt, A. Odd numbers
Knausgaard, K. My struggle.
Lunde, M. The end of the ocean
Nesbo, J. The bat
Nesbo, J. Blood on snow
Nesbo, J. Cockroaches
Nesbo, J. The devil's star
Nesbo, J. Headhunters
Nesbo, J. The leopard
Nesbo, J. Midnight sun
Nesbo, J. Nemesis
Nesbo, J. Phantom
Nesbo, J. Police
Nesbo, J. The redbreast
Nesbo, J. The redeemer
Nesbo, J. The snowman
Nesbo, J. The son
Nesbo, J. The thirst
Orstavik, H. Love
Petterson, P. I curse the river of time
Petterson, P. I refuse
Petterson, P. Out stealing horses
Rolvaag, O. Giants in the Earth
Ullmann, L. Unquiet

TRANSLATIONS -- PERSIAN TO ENGLISH

Dowlatabadi, M. The colonel
Mandanipour, S. Moon brow

TRANSLATIONS -- POLISH TO ENGLISH

Lem, S. Eden
Lem, S. Fiasco
Lem, S. His master's voice
Lem, S. Solaris
Sienkiewicz, H. Quo vadis
, Tokarczuk, O. Drive your plow over the bones of the dead
Tokarczuk, O. Flights
Twardoch, S. The king of Warsaw

TRANSLATIONS -- PORTUGUESE TO ENGLISH

Amado, J. Dona Flor and her two husbands
Amado, J. Gabriela, clove and cinnamon
Antunes, A. The return of the caravels
Coelho, P. The alchemist
Couto, M. Rain
Couto, M. Sleepwalking land
Garcia-Roza, L. Alone in the crowd
Garcia-Roza, L. December heat
Lispector, C. The besieged city
Saramago, J. All the names
Saramago, J. Blindness
Saramago, J. Cain
Saramago, J. The cave
Saramago, J. Death with interruptions
Saramago, J. The Elephant's journey
Saramago, J. The history of the siege of Lisbon
Saramago, J. The manual of painting and calligraphy

TRANSLATIONS -- RUSSIAN TO ENGLISH

Akunin, B. The coronation
Akunin, B. Sister Pelagia and the white bulldog
Bulgakov, M. The master and Margarita
Chekhov, A. Early short stories, 1883-1888
Chekhov, A. Later short stories, 1888-1903
Diachenko, S. Vita nostra
Dostoyevsky, F. The best short stories of Dostoevsky
Dostoyevsky, F. The brothers Karamazov
Dostoyevsky, F. Crime and punishment
Dostoyevsky, F. Notes from underground
Dovlatov, S. Pushkin Hills
Frei, M. The stranger's magic
Gogol, N. The collected tales of Nikolai Gogol
Gogol, N. Dead souls
Kuznetsov, A. Babi Yar
Nabokov, V. King, queen, knave
Nabokov, V. The stories of Vladimir Nabokov
Pasternak, B. Doctor Zhivago
Pelevin, V. The hall of singing caryatids
Sholokhov, M. And quiet flows the Don
Solzhenitsyn, A. Cancer ward
Solzhenitsyn, A. In the first circle
Solzhenitsyn, A. One day in the life of Ivan Denisovich
Tolstaya, T. Aetherial worlds
Tolstaya, T. The slynx
Tolstoy, L. Anna Karenina
Tolstoy, L. Divine and human and other stories
Tolstoy, L. War and peace
Tsypkin, L. Summer in Baden-Baden
Turgenev, I. Fathers and sons
Turgenev, I. First love, and other stories
Zamyatin, Y. We

TRANSLATIONS -- SERBIAN TO ENGLISH

Albahari, D. Gotz and Meyer
Pistalo, V. Tesla

TRANSLATIONS -- SERBO-CROATIAN TO ENGLISH

Andric, I. The bridge on the Drina

TRANSLATIONS -- SPANISH TO ENGLISH

Aguilar Camin, H. Death in Veracruz

TRANSLATIONS -- SWEDISH TO ENGLISH

Grebe, C. The ice beneath her

Hashemzadeh Bonde, G. What we owe

Jonasson, J. The accidental further adventures of the hundred-year-old man

Jungstedt, M. The inner circle

Karlsson, J. The room

Kepler, L. The hypnotist

Kepler, L. The rabbit hunter

Kepler, L. The sandman

Kepler, L. Stalker

Lackberg, C. The hidden child

Lackberg, C. The ice princess

Lackberg, C. The lost boy

Lackberg, C. The preacher

Lackberg, C. The stonecutter

Lagercrantz, D. The girl who lived twice

Lagercrantz, D. The girl in the spider's web

Lagercrantz, D. The girl who takes an eye for an eye

Larsson, A. Until thy wrath be past

Larsson, S. The girl who kicked the hornet's nest

Larsson, S. The girl who played with fire

Larsson, S. The girl with the dragon tattoo

Lovestam, S. The truth behind the lie

Mankell, H. Before the frost

Mankell, H. The dogs of Riga

Mankell, H. Firewall

Mankell, H. The man from Beijing

Mankell, H. The man who smiled

Mankell, H. One step behind

Mankell, H. The return of the dancing master

Mankell, H. The troubled man

Natt och Dag, N. The wolf and the watchman

Ohlsson, K. The disappeared

Ohlsson, K. Hostage

Ohlsson, K. Silenced

Ohlsson, K. Unwanted

Persson Giolito, M. Beyond all reasonable doubt

Persson Giolito, M. Quicksand

Persson, L. Another time, another life

Persson, L. The dying detective

Persson, L. Free falling, as if in a dream

Ramqvist, K. The white city

Roslund, A. Cell 8

Roslund, A. Pen 33

Sem-Sandberg, S. The chosen ones

Sjowall, M. Cop killer

Sjowall, M. The laughing policeman

Sjowall, M. The locked room

Sjowall, M. The man on the balcony

Sjowall, M. Murder at the Savoy

Soderberg, A. The other son

Stridsberg, S. Valerie

Tursten, H. Hunting game

Tursten, H. Winter grave

Zander, J. The swimmer

TRANSLATIONS -- TURKISH TO ENGLISH

Atilgan, Y. Motherland hotel

Demirtas, S. Dawn

Gunday, H. The few

Pamuk, O. My name is Red

Pamuk, O. The museum of innocence

Pamuk, O. The red-haired woman

Pamuk, O. Silent house

Pamuk, O. Snow

Pamuk, O. A strangeness in my mind

Somer, M. The serenity murders

TRANSLATIONS -- VIETNAMESE TO ENGLISH

Bao, N. The sorrow of war

Nguyen, P. The mountains sing

TRANSLATIONS -- YIDDISH TO ENGLISH

Aleichem, S. Tevye the dairyman and the railroad stories

Aleichem, S. Tevye's daughters

Singer, I. The brothers Ashkenazi

Singer, I. Collected stories

Singer, I. Enemies, a love story

Singer, I. The family Moskat

Singer, I. The magician of Lublin

TRANSLATORS

Ackerman, E. Dark at the crossing

Apostol, G. Insurrecto

Foer, J. Everything is illuminated

Marias, J. A heart so white

McKillip, P. Alphabet of thorn

Miller, A. Oxygen

Novey, I. Ways to disappear

Qiu, X. Death of a red heroine

Qiu, X. When red is black

Sherwood, F. Night of sorrows

TRANSPHOBIA

Myers, A. Continental divide

TRANSPLANTATION OF ORGANS, TISSUES, ETC

Cook, R. Coma

Cook, R. Pandemic

Kerangal, M. The heart

Palmer, M. The fifth vial

Picoult, J. Change of heart

TRANSPORTATION

Hurley, K. The light brigade

Sagan, C. Contact

TRANSYLVANIA, ROMANIA

Marks, J. Fangland

Stoker, B. Dracula

Stoker, B. The new annotated Dracula

TRAPPERS

Raymond, J. The half-life

Wurlitzer, R. The drop edge of yonder

TRAUMATIC BRAIN INJURY

French, T. The witch elm

TRAVEL WRITERS

Cook, T. The fate of Katherine Carr

Hallinan, T. Fools' river

Kennedy, D. The moment

Wolfe, G. The land across

TRAVEL WRITERS -- BALTIMORE, MARYLAND

TREE CLIMBING

Calvino, I. The baron in the trees

A **tree** grows in Brooklyn Smith, B.

TREE HOUSES

Calvino, I. The baron in the trees

The **tree** of hands Rendell, R.

Tree of smoke Johnson, D.

Treeborne Johnson, C.

TREES

Christie, M. Greenwood

Fowler, T. A good neighborhood

Powers, R. The overstory

Tremaine's true love Burrowes, G.

TRENCH WARFARE

Boyden, J. Three day road

Boyne, J. The absolutist

Faulks, S. Birdsong

Itani, F. Deafening

Krivak, A. The sojourn

Remarque, E. All quiet on the western front

TRENTON, NEW JERSEY

Evanovich, J. Look alive twenty-five

Evanovich, J. One for the money

Evanovich, J. Turbo twenty-three

The **Trevarton** inheritance Macdonald, M.

The **trial** Kafka, F.

The **trial** of Elizabeth Cree Ackroyd, P.

Trial on Mount Koya Spann, S.

TRIALS

Bing, S. You look nice today

Finder, J. Judgment

Gardam, J. Last friends

Kafka, F. The trial

Koestler, A. Darkness at noon

Marlette, D. Magic time

McEwan, I. The children act

McLarty, R. Art in America

Mina, D. The red road

Mortimer, J. Rumpole's return

O'Connell, C. Dead famous

Parks, B. Say nothing

Perry, A. Blind justice

Phillips, J. Quiet dell

Pirro, J. Sly fox

Rand, A. The fountainhead

Vreeland, S. The passion of Artemisia

Zumas, L. Red clocks

TRIALS (ASSAULT AND BATTERY)

Connelly, M. The Lincoln lawyer

TRIALS (CHILD CUSTODY)

Byatt, A. Babel Tower

Miller, S. The good mother

Shreve, A. Fortune's rocks

TRIALS (DIVORCE)

Byatt, A. Babel Tower

TRIALS (ESPIONAGE)

Doctorow, E. The book of Daniel

TRIALS (MURDER)

Ackroyd, P. The trial of Elizabeth Cree

Arvin, R. Blood of angels

Atwood, M. Alias Grace

Burnet, G. His bloody project

Camus, A. The stranger

Cavanagh, S. Thirteen

Clark, M. Blood defense

Collins, S. The confessions of Frannie Langton

Connelly, M. The brass verdict

Connelly, M. The fifth witness

Connelly, M. The gods of guilt

Cook, T. Sandrine's case

Cush, J. Endangered

Daly, P. Clear my name

Edvardsson, M. A nearly normal family

Edwards, Y. The mother

Faulkner, W. Intruder in the dust

Faulkner, W. Sanctuary

Grisham, J. The last juror

Guterson, D. Snow falling on cedars

Hansen, R. A wild surge of guilty passion

Holt, V. The black opal

Iles, G. Mississippi blood

Iles, G. Turning angel

Kelton, E. Texas vendetta

Kim, A. Miracle Creek

Lelic, S. The child who

Lescroart, J. Guilt

Lescroart, J. The oath

Lippman, L. Wilde Lake

Martini, S. Compelling evidence

Mina, D. The long drop

Moore, G. The holdout

Murray, V. Stand your ground

Penny, L. Glass houses

Perry, A. The sins of the wolf

Persson Giolito, M. Quicksand

Picoult, J. Nineteen minutes

Sayers, D. Clouds of witness

Scottoline, L. After Anna

Stabenow, D. A deeper sleep

Stone, N. The verdict

Turow, S. Presumed innocent

Twain, M. Pudd'nhead Wilson ;

Whitlow, R. A time to stand

Winer, J. Her kind of case

Wolfe, T. The bonfire of the vanities

Wright, R. Native son

TRIALS (MURDER) -- MISSISSIPPI

Grisham, J. A time to kill

Nordan, L. Wolf whistle

TRIALS (MURDER) -- NEW ORLEANS, LOUISIANA

Grisham, J. The client

TRIALS (MURDER) -- SOUTHERN STATES

Welty, E. The ponder heart

TRIALS (MUTINY)

Malouf, D. Ransom
Miller, M. The song of Achilles
The **truants** Weinberg, K.

TRUCK DRIVERS

Aira, C. The seamstress and the wind
Albahari, D. Gotz and Meyer
Carlson, S. Almost Graceland
Martin, K. Beyond reason

TRUCK FARMING -- ILLINOIS

Ferber, E. So big

TRUCKING INDUSTRY AND TRADE

Martin, K. Beyond reason
True Greenfeld, K.
The **true** Bastards French, J.
True believers Haddam, J.

TRUE CRIME WRITERS

Cook, T. The crime of Julian Wells
True gentlemen novels [series] Burrowes, G.
True grit Portis, C.
True to the game Woods, T.
True to the game [series] Woods, T.
True to the game II Woods, T.
True to the game III Woods, T.
True to you Wade, B.

TRUE-CRIME TELEVISION PROGRAMS

Moore, G. The holdout

TRUJILLO MOLINA, RAFAEL LEONIDAS, 1891-1961 ASSASSINATION

Vargas Llosa, M. The feast of the Goat
Truly madly guilty Moriarty, L.

TRUMPETERS

Baker, D. Young man with a horn
Morris, W. Taps

TRUST

Anders, C. All the birds in the sky
Azzopardi, T. Winterton blue
Barnett, K. Ever faithful
Barry, J. Don't turn around
Bishop, A. Written in red
Brown, K. The life Lucy knew
Butland, S. The lost for words bookshop
Ca$h Trust no man
Ca$h Trust no man 2
Ca$h Trust no man 3
Center, K. Things you save in a fire
Chase, L. Your scandalous ways
Cohen, T. They all fall down
Cole, A. A princess in theory
Cook, T. Instruments of night
Dallas, S. The last midwife
De la Motte, A. MemoRandom
De la Motte, A. Ultimatum
Frear, C. Sweet little lies
Goodman, A. The cookbook collector
Grippando, J. Lying with strangers
Harris, C. Good time coming
Hatcher, R. Cross my heart

Irvin, K. Tell her no lies
James, L. I want you back
Kearsley, S. A desperate fortune
Krentz, J. Secret sisters
Laurens, S. By winter's light
Lee, Y. Ninefox gambit
Leon, D. The girl of his dreams
Meltzer, B. The tenth justice
Monroe, M. Bad blood
Moore, J. The night market
Mosley, W. Fortunate son
Nunez, E. Grace
O'Keefe, M. Everything I left unsaid
Palmer, D. The new husband
Parker, R. Double play
Penelope, L. Whispers of shadow & flame
Santora, N. Fifteen digits
Steinhauer, O. The tourist
Thomas, S. My beautiful enemy
Wagers, K. After the crown
Walker, C. Man of the year
Weber, C. Man on the run
Winton, T. The shepherd's hut
Trust exercise Choi, S.

TRUST IN CHILDREN

Box, C. Blue heaven

TRUST IN GOD

Andrews, M. Isaiah's daughter

TRUST IN MEN

Cameron, C. Just a summer fling
Inbinder, G. The hanged man
Meyer, P. American rust
Ranney, K. The Scottish duke

TRUST IN WOMEN

Anderson, C. Mulberry moon
Blackstock, T. Shadow in Serenity
Foster, L. Run the risk
Hoover, C. It ends with us
Mallery, S. Best of my love
Morris, M. Man in the blue moon
Picoult, J. Change of heart
Roberts, N. The obsession
Shalvis, J. Simply irresistible
Sosa, M. Acting on impulse
Trust no man Ca$h
Trust no man 2 Ca$h
Trust no man 3 Ca$h
Trust no man novels [series] Ca$h
Trust no one Cleave, P.
Trust your eyes Barclay, L.

TRUSTS AND TRUSTEES

MacDonald, J. The lonely silver rain
MacDonald, J. A purple place for dying

TRUTH

Ashley, J. The madness of Lord Ian Mackenzie
Cantor, M. Death and other happy endings
Carey, P. My life as a fake

Castro, J. Hell or high water

Cusk, R. Outline

Eason, K. How Rory Thorne destroyed the multiverse

Flanery, P. Absolution

Hilderbrand, E. What happens in paradise

Hill, R. The woodcutter

Lasdun, J. Afternoon of a faun

Lethem, J. Chronic city

Macmillan, G. The perfect girl

Marias, J. The infatuations

McDevitt, J. A talent for war

Nesbo, J. The son

North, C. The pursuit of William Abbey

Olshan, J. Black diamond fall

Pattison, E. Beautiful ghosts

Phillips, C. The Rossetti letter

Picoult, J. Change of heart

Rice, A. Christ the Lord

Rosenfelt, D. Don't tell a soul

Scott, J. Follow me

Seay, M. The mirror thief

Wolfe, T. You can't go home again

The **truth** Pratchett, T.

TRUTH -- RELIGIOUS ASPECTS -- BUDDHISM

Kerouac, J. The dharma bums

The **truth** about Celia Brockmeier, K.

The **truth** about Leo MacAlister, K.

The **truth** about love and dukes Guhrke, L.

Truth be told Ryan, H.

The **truth** behind the lie Lovestam, S.

Truth in advertising Kenney, J.

The **truth** of all things Shields, K.

TRUTHFULNESS AND FALSEHOOD

Eliot, G. Silas Marner

Horlock, M. The book of lies

Rothfuss, P. The name of the wind

Smith, A. The accidental

TRUTHFULNESS AND FALSEHOOD IN CHILDREN

Wilhelm, K. The good children

Truths I never told you Rimmer, K.

The **tsar** of love and techno Marra, A.

TSUNAMIS

Ozeki, R. A tale for the time being

Varley, J. Red lightning

TUBERCULOSIS

Evans, J. The white devil

Garcia Marquez, G. The general in his labyrinth

The **Tubman** command Cobbs Hoffman, E.

TUBMAN, HARRIET, 1820?-1913

Cobbs Hoffman, E. The Tubman command

Tucker mysteries [series] Daniel, R.

TUCSON, ARIZONA

Kingsolver, B. The bean trees

Silko, L. Almanac of the dead

Tudor novels (Philippa Gregory) [series] Gregory, P.

TUDOR PERIOD (1485-1603)

Andersen, L. The Boleyn king

Bear, E. Ink and steel

Buckley, F. The doublet affair

Buckley, F. The siren queen

Clements, R. Martyr

Clements, R. Revenger

Follett, K. A column of fire

George, M. Elizabeth I

Gregory, P. The Boleyn inheritance

Gregory, P. The constant princess

Gregory, P. The last Tudor

Gregory, P. The other Boleyn girl

Gregory, P. The taming of the queen

Harper, K. The poyson garden

Mantel, H. Bring up the bodies

Mantel, H. Wolf Hall

Marston, E. The bawdy basket

Marston, E. The devil's apprentice

Marston, E. The roaring boy

Marston, E. The vagabond clown

Marston, E. The wanton angel

Maxwell, R. The queen's bastard

Maxwell, R. The secret diary of Anne Boleyn

Maxwell, R. The wild Irish

Morgan, J. The secret life of William Shakespeare

Phillips, A. The king at the edge of the world

Plaidy, J. The captive Queen of Scots

Plaidy, J. Murder most royal

Rutherfurd, E. London

Sansom, C. Lamentation

Sansom, C. Revelation

Sansom, C. Sovereign

Sansom, C. Tombland

Weir, A. Anna of Kleve

Weir, A. Innocent traitor

Weir, A. The Lady Elizabeth

Wolfe, S. The course of all treasons

Tudor series (Jean Plaidy) [series] Plaidy, J.

Tuesday Mooney talks to ghosts Racculia, K.

Tuesday's gone French, N.

Tufa novels [series] Bledsoe, A.

Tulip fever Moggach, D.

TULIPS

Moggach, D. Tulip fever

TUNGUSKA EXPLOSION, 1908

Pynchon, T. Against the day

TUNISIA

Cumming, C. A foreign country

Tunnel vision Paretsky, S.

TUNNELS

Cocco, G. Shadows on the lake

Kelly, J. The moon tunnel

TUPELO, MISSISSIPPI

Berg, E. We are all welcome here

Turbo twenty-three Evanovich, J.

TURIN, ITALY

McCarthy, T. Satin Island

TURKEY

Ackerman, E. Dark at the crossing
Cumming, C. A colder war
Demirtas, S. Dawn
Golden, C. Ararat
Gunday, H. The few
Hayes, T. I am Pilgrim
Karnezis, P. The maze
Lukas, M. The Oracle of Stamboul
Pamuk, O. Silent house
Pamuk, O. A strangeness in my mind
Shafak, E. 10 minutes 38 seconds in this strange world
Somer, M. The serenity murders

TURKEY -- HISTORY -- 1918-1960
Werfel, F. The forty days of Musa Dagh

TURKEY -- HISTORY -- 20TH CENTURY
De Bernieres, L. Birds without wings

TURKEY -- HISTORY -- OTTOMAN EMPIRE, 1288-1918
Willocks, T. The religion

TURKEY -- SOCIAL LIFE AND CUSTOMS
Pamuk, O. Snow

TURKEY -- SOCIAL LIFE AND CUSTOMS -- 20TH CENTURY
Nadel, B. The Ottoman cage

TURKISH AMERICANS
Batuman, E. The idiot

A **turn** of light Czerneda, J.
Turn of mind LaPlante, A.
The **turn** of the key Ware, R.
The **turn** of the screw James, H.
The **turnaround** Pelecanos, G.
The **Turner** house Flournoy, A.
Turner series (Cat Sebastian) [series] Sebastian, C.

TURNER'S SLAVE REVOLT, SOUTHAMPTON, VIRGINIA, 1831
Styron, W. The confessions of Nat Turner

TURNER, NAT, 1800?-1831
Styron, W. The confessions of Nat Turner
Wideman, J. American histories

Turning angel Iles, G.

TURPIN, RANDOLPH
Phillips, C. Foreigners

The **turquoise** lament MacDonald, J.
Turtle moon Hoffman, A.

TURTLES
Matthiessen, P. Far Tortuga

TUSCANY, ITALY
Bourne, J. Rogue spy
Elkins, A. Dying on the vine
Gray, J. A duke never yields
Gray, J. A lady never lies

TUSCANY, ITALY -- SOCIAL LIFE AND CUSTOMS
Bilenchi, R. The chill

TUSSAUD, MARIE, 1761-1850
Carey, E. Little

TUTANKHAMEN, KING OF EGYPT
Robinson, L. Murder at the god's gate

TUTORING

Richman, A. The secret of clouds

TUTORS
Bryant, N. Madam, may I
Guhrke, L. Governess gone rogue
Laurens, S. By winter's light
Saylor, S. The seven wonders
Sebastian, C. It takes two to tumble
Upadhyay, S. The guru of love
Wilder, T. Theophilus North

TV TIE-INS
Carr, C. The alienist
Cleeves, A. Wild fire
Cross, N. Luther. The calling
Johnson, C. Land of wolves
Kelly, E. Broadchurch
Runcie, J. The road to Grantchester

Twain & Stanley enter paradise Hijuelos, O.

TWAIN, MARK, 1835-1910
Hijuelos, O. Twain & Stanley enter paradise
Oates, J. Wild nights

TWAIN, MARK, 1835-1910 ADVENTURES OF HUCKLEBERRY FINN CRITICISM AND INTERPRETATION
Twain, M. Adventures of Huckleberry Finn

The **twelfth** department Ryan, W.
The **twelve** Cronin, J.
The **twelve** lives of Samuel Hawley Tinti, H.
The **twelve** tribes of Hattie Mathis, A.

TWELVE-STEP PROGRAMS
Wallace, D. Infinite jest

TWELVE-YEAR-OLD BOYS
Ajvide Lindqvist, J. Let the right one in
Bock, C. Beautiful children
Childress, M. Crazy in Alabama
Connolly, J. The book of lost things
Frazier, C. Thirteen moons
Hiaasen, C. Nature girl
McCammon, R. Boy's life
Woo, S. Everything Asian

TWELVE-YEAR-OLD BOYS -- ILLINOIS
Bradbury, R. Dandelion wine

TWELVE-YEAR-OLD BOYS -- PALESTINE
Oz, A. Panther in the basement

TWELVE-YEAR-OLD GIRLS
Allison, D. Bastard out of Carolina
Barbery, M. The elegance of the hedgehog
Jakes, J. Savannah, or, A gift for Mr. Lincoln
McCullers, C. The member of the wedding
Smith, A. The accidental
Tinti, H. The twelve lives of Samuel Hawley
Vann, D. Aquarium

TWELVE-YEAR-OLD GIRLS -- FLORIDA
Dean, M. The time it takes to fall

TWELVE-YEAR-OLDS
Doig, I. The bartender's tale
Hair, D. Mage's blood
McBride, J. The good lord bird

TWELVE-YEAR-OLDS -- CENTRAL AFRICA

Prescott, L. The secrets we kept
Rindell, S. The other typist

U

U.S.A. series [series] Dos Passos, J.
UFO ABDUCTIONS
Evanovich, J. Look alive twenty-five
Finley, J. The dark above
Vonnegut, K. Slaughterhouse-five
UFOS
Moore, C. Noir
UGANDA
Makumbi, J. Kintu
The **ugly** duchess James, E.
UKRAINE
Apelfeld, A. Blooms of darkness
Apelfeld, A. To the edge of sorrow
Artson, B. Odessa, Odessa
Campbell, R. Treason
Higgins, J. Confessional
Powell, M. Firebird
Smith, M. Wolves eat dogs
UKRAINE -- HISTORY -- 19TH CENTURY
Anderson, A. The summer guest
UKRAINE -- HISTORY -- GERMAN OCCUPATION, 1941-1944
Foer, J. Everything is illuminated
Seiffert, R. A boy in winter
UKRAINIANS IN THE UNITED STATES
Kiefer, C. The infinite tides
Parker, R. Cold service
ULSTER VOLUNTEER FORCE
McKinty, A. The cold, cold ground
McKinty, A. In the morning I'll be gone
Ultimatum De la Motte, A.
The **ultimatum** Robards, K.
The **ultimatum** Wolf, D.
ULTIMATUMS
Long, J. The legend of Lyon Redmond
Ulysses Joyce, J.
Umbrella Self, W.
UMBRIA, ITALY
Unsworth, B. After Hannibal
The **UnAmericans** Antopol, M.
An **unattended** death Jenkins, V.
The **unbearable** lightness of being Kundera, M.
The **unburied** Palliser, C.
Unbury Carol Malerman, J.
UNCERTAINTY
Levy, D. Hot milk
Pynchon, T. Against the day
Walton, J. My real children
UNCLE AND NEPHEW
Bailey, P. Uncle Rudolf
Bellow, S. More die of heartbreak
Carcaterra, L. Tin badges

Carr, B. Opioid, Indiana
Church, J. A drop of Chinese blood
Dickens, C. Nicholas Nickleby
Dybek, S. I sailed with Magellan
Harris, T. Hannibal rising
Nabokov, V. King, queen, knave
O'Connor, F. The violent bear it away
Quinn, J. The lady most willing
Scott, W. Rob Roy
UNCLE AND NIECE
Belfer, L. And after the fire
Boyden, J. Through black spruce
Elliot, L. Guilty
Goddard, R. Long time coming
Hubbard, L. The talented Ribkins
Lively, P. How it all began
Walls, J. The silver star
Uncle Rudolf Bailey, P.
Uncle Tom's cabin Stowe, H.
Uncle Tom's children Wright, R.
UNCLES
Bailey, P. Uncle Rudolf
Cornwell, B. The last kingdom
Doig, I. Last bus to wisdom
Edgarian, C. Three stages of amazement
Erdrich, L. The night watchman
French, T. The witch elm
Maturin, C. Melmoth the wanderer
McGahan, A. The white earth
Rozan, S. Winter and night
Smith, L. On Agate Hill
Torday, D. The last flight of Poxl West
Verne, J. Journey to the centre of the Earth
Wroblewski, D. The story of Edgar Sawtelle
Zimler, R. The last Kabbalist of Lisbon
UNCLES -- DEATH
Atkins, A. The ranger
Brunt, C. Tell the wolves I'm home
Irvin, K. Tell her no lies
UNCLES -- FRANCE
Stewart, M. Nine coaches waiting
UNCLES -- NORTH CAROLINA
Earley, T. Jim the boy
UNCLES -- SOUTHERN STATES
Welty, E. The ponder heart
Uncollected stories of William Faulkner Faulkner, W.
Uncommon clay Maron, M.
The **uncommon** reader Bennett, A.
An **unconditional** freedom Cole, A.
UNCONDITIONAL LOVE
Cameron, W. The dogs of Christmas
UNCONSCIOUS BIAS
Umrigar, T. Everybody's son
The **unconsoled** Ishiguro, K.
The **undateable** Title, S.
UNDEAD
Anderson, K. Death warmed over

UNDERGROUND RAILROAD

Chevalier, T. The last runaway
Coates, T. The water dancer
Cole, A. A hope divided
Faye, L. Seven for a secret
Johnson, T. Engraved on the heart
Lock, N. A fugitive in Walden Woods
Michener, J. Chesapeake
Whitehead, C. The underground railroad
Woods, R. Remembrance

The **underground** railroad Whitehead, C.
Undermajordomo Minor deWitt, P.

UNDERSEA COLONIES

Cambias, J. A darkling sea

UNDERSTANDING (PERSONAL QUALITY)

Perrotta, T. The abstinence teacher

Undersurface Cullin, M.

UNDERTAKERS

Hage, R. Beirut Hellfire Society
Henderson, S. The flicker of old dreams
Meltzer, B. The escape artist
Nelscott, K. Days of rage
Waugh, E. The loved one

The **undertow** Baker, J.

UNDERWATER ARCHAEOLOGY

Child, L. Deep storm

UNDERWATER ARCHAEOLOGY -- NORTH ATLANTIC
OCEAN

Cussler, C. Serpent

UNDERWATER CITIES

Cambias, J. A darkling sea
Solomon, R. The deep

UNDERWATER EXPLORATION

Cambias, J. A darkling sea
Watts, P. Starfish

UNDERWATER RESCUE OPERATIONS

Cussler, C. Pacific vortex!

UNDERWATER WARFARE

Cussler, C. Havana storm

The **underworld** Canty, K.
Underworld DeLillo, D.
Underworld U.S.A. trilogy [series] Ellroy, J.
Undiscovered country Enger, L.

UNDOCUMENTED IMMIGRANTS

Adiga, A. Amnesty
Allende, I. In the midst of winter
Boyle, T. The tortilla curtain
Caputo, P. Crossers
Deaver, J. The stone monkey
Dennis-Benn, N. Patsy
Gordimer, N. The pickup
Grippando, J. The girl in the glass box
Ko, L. The leavers
Lalami, L. The other Americans
Leon, D. Blood from a stone
Lovestam, S. The truth behind the lie
Luiselli, V. Lost children archive

Phillips, C. A distant shore
Prose, F. Primitive people
Rivero, M. The affairs of the Falcons
Sahota, S. The year of the runaways
Sekaran, S. Lucky boy
Skyhorse, B. Madonnas of Echo Park
Urrea, L. Into the beautiful North
Wiggs, S. The Oysterville sewing circle

UNDOCUMENTED WORKERS

Boyle, T. The tortilla curtain
Leon, D. Blood from a stone
Phillips, C. A distant shore
Prose, F. Primitive people
Sekaran, S. Lucky boy
Skyhorse, B. Madonnas of Echo Park

Undone Slaughter, K.

UNEMPLOYED PERSONS

Ballard, J. Kingdom come
Bellow, S. Seize the day
Erpenbeck, J. Go, went, gone
Laukkanen, O. The professionals
Marston, E. The devil's apprentice
Mosley, W. The man in my basement
Stockett, K. The help
Zola, E. Germinal

UNEMPLOYED PERSONS -- FAMILY RELATIONSHIPS

Dean, M. The time it takes to fall

UNEMPLOYED PERSONS -- NEW YORK (STATE)

Russo, R. Nobody's fool

UNEMPLOYED WOMEN

Box, C. Paradise Valley

UNEMPLOYMENT

Finder, J. The fixer
Glynn, A. Paradime
Lemaitre, P. Inhuman resources
Whitlow, R. A time to stand

The **unexpected** duchess Bowman, V.
Unexpectedly, Milo Dicks, M.
Unfinished desires Godwin, G.
An **unfinished** season Just, W.
An **unfortunate** woman Brautigan, R.
Unhallowed ground Starr, M.

UNHAPPINESS

Barnes, J. The only story
Garcia, C. The Lady Matador's hotel
Lessing, D. Landlocked
Lessing, D. A proper marriage
Miller, M. Biloxi
Updike, J. Rabbit, run

UNHAPPINESS IN MEN

Berger, T. Being invisible
Garcia Marquez, G. The general in his labyrinth
Gide, A. The immoralist
O'Connor, F. Wise blood

UNHAPPINESS IN WOMEN

Ashley, A. Butterfly
Crane, S. Maggie

UNITED STATES -- FOREIGN RELATIONS -- SOVIET UNION

Brown, D. Flight of the Old Dog
Burdick, E. Fail-safe
Schwartz, J. The red daughter

UNITED STATES -- HISTORY

Kramer, L. Search for my heart

UNITED STATES -- HISTORY -- 1783-1815

Thom, J. Panther in the sky

UNITED STATES -- HISTORY -- 1783-1865

Vidal, G. Burr

UNITED STATES -- HISTORY -- 1815-1861

McBride, J. Song yet sung
Vidal, G. Lincoln

UNITED STATES -- HISTORY -- 1815-1865

Shaara, J. Gone for soldiers

UNITED STATES -- HISTORY -- 1865-1898

Pitts, L. Freeman
Priest, C. Dreadnought
Vidal, G. 1876

UNITED STATES -- HISTORY -- 1865-1921

Pynchon, T. Against the day
Urrea, L. Queen of America

UNITED STATES -- HISTORY -- 1900-1945

Dos Passos, J. 1919

UNITED STATES -- HISTORY -- 1901-1909

Vidal, G. Empire

UNITED STATES -- HISTORY -- 1913-1921

Dos Passos, J. 1919
Dos Passos, J. The 42nd parallel
Lowenthal, M. Charity girl

UNITED STATES -- HISTORY -- 1919-1933

Baker, D. Young man with a horn
Fowler, T. Z
Lehane, D. Live by night
Maugham, W. The razor's edge

UNITED STATES -- HISTORY -- 1933-1945

Shaara, J. The rising tide
Shaara, J. The steel wave

UNITED STATES -- HISTORY -- 1945-

Berger, T. Vital parts

UNITED STATES -- HISTORY -- 1961-1969

DeLillo, D. Libra

UNITED STATES -- HISTORY -- 19TH CENTURY

Banks, R. Cloudsplitter
Bird, S. Daughter of a daughter of a queen
Chiaverini, J. Mrs. Lincoln's dressmaker
Davies, P. The fortunes
Gyasi, Y. Homegoing
Hijuelos, O. Twain & Stanley enter paradise
Jakes, J. North and South
Jenkins, B. Tempest
Jiles, P. News of the world
Newman, J. Mary
O'Brien, T. The Lincoln conspiracy
Parini, J. The passages of H.M.
Patterson, M. Rebellion

Rawles, N. My Jim
Robinson, M. Gilead
Sayles, J. A moment in the sun
Schmidt, S. See what I have done
Whitehead, C. The underground railroad

UNITED STATES -- HISTORY -- 20TH CENTURY

Benjamin, M. The aviator's wife
Davies, P. The fortunes
Dos Passos, J. 1919
Gross, A. The one man
Kelly, M. Lost roses
Mallon, T. Finale
Means, D. Hystopia
Pywell, S. What happened to Henry
Russell, M. The women of the copper country
Shimotakahara, L. After the bloom
Smiley, J. Early warning
Smiley, J. Golden age
Smiley, J. Some luck
Vidal, G. The golden age

UNITED STATES -- HISTORY -- 21ST CENTURY

El Akkad, O. American war
Luiselli, V. Lost children archive
Mallon, T. Landfall

UNITED STATES -- HISTORY -- CIVIL WAR, 1861-1865

Bahr, H. The Judas Field
Brown, D. The way to Bright Star
Brown, T. Fallen land
Crane, S. The red badge of courage
Frazier, C. Varina
Gingrich, N. Gettysburg
Gingrich, N. Grant comes east
Hicks, R. The widow of the South
Horn, D. All other nights
Hunt, L. Neverhome
Jakes, J. Love and war
Jakes, J. Savannah, or, A gift for Mr. Lincoln
Kelton, E. Badger boy
Langton, J. The deserter
Lent, J. A slant of light
Lockridge, R. Raintree County
McCabe, E. I shall be near to you
Mitchell, M. Gone with the wind
Newman, J. Mary
Olmstead, R. Coal black horse
Peters, R. Hell or Richmond
Plain, B. Crescent City
Reed, I. Flight to Canada
Shaara, J. Gods and generals
Shaara, J. The last full measure
Shaara, M. The killer angels
Walker, M. Jubilee
Warren, R. Band of angels
West, J. The friendly persuasion

UNITED STATES -- HISTORY -- CIVIL WAR, 1861-1865 -- AFRICAN AMERICAN TROOPS

Cobbs Hoffman, E. The Tubman command

Reed, I. Mumbo jumbo

UNITED STATES -- RELATIONS -- RUSSIA

Goldberg, L. Fake truth

UNITED STATES -- RELIGION -- COLONIAL PERIOD, 1600-1775

Calvi, M. Dear George, Dear Mary

UNITED STATES -- RURAL CONDITIONS

Proulx, A. Postcards

UNITED STATES -- SOCIAL CONDITIONS

Kosinski, J. Being there

Newitz, A. The future of another timeline

UNITED STATES -- SOCIAL CONDITIONS -- 1918-1932

Larsen, N. Passing

UNITED STATES -- SOCIAL CONDITIONS -- 1997-

Roth, P. The human stain

UNITED STATES -- SOCIAL CONDITIONS -- 20TH CENTURY

Boyne, J. The heart's invisible furies

Michener, J. Space

Sinclair, U. The jungle

UNITED STATES -- SOCIAL LIFE AND CUSTOMS

Angelo, M. Followers

Bausch, R. The stories of Richard Bausch

Campbell, B. American salvage

Hood, A. The obituary writer

Yates, R. The collected stories of Richard Yates

UNITED STATES -- SOCIAL LIFE AND CUSTOMS -- 1865-1918

Fowler, T. A well-behaved woman

Stewart, A. Miss Kopp just won't quit

Stewart, A. Miss Kopp's midnight confessions

Wharton, E. Collected stories, 1891-1910

UNITED STATES -- SOCIAL LIFE AND CUSTOMS -- 18TH CENTURY

Cobbs Hoffman, E. The Hamilton affair

UNITED STATES -- SOCIAL LIFE AND CUSTOMS -- 1910-1919

Stewart, A. Kopp sisters on the march

UNITED STATES -- SOCIAL LIFE AND CUSTOMS -- 1918-1945

Lewis, S. Dodsworth

UNITED STATES -- SOCIAL LIFE AND CUSTOMS -- 1919-1933

Fitzgerald, F. Novels and stories, 1920-1922

UNITED STATES -- SOCIAL LIFE AND CUSTOMS -- 19TH CENTURY

Barry, S. Days without end

Carey, P. Parrot and Olivier in America

Crafts, H. The bondwoman's narrative

James, H. Complete stories, 1864-1874

Wharton, E. Collected stories, 1891-1910

UNITED STATES -- SOCIAL LIFE AND CUSTOMS -- 20TH CENTURY

Adams, A. The stories of Alice Adams

Baldwin, J. Go tell it on the mountain

Baldwin, J. Going to meet the man

Barth, J. Giles Goat-Boy ;

Carver, R. What we talk about when we talk about love

Cruse, H. The complete Wendel

Doctorow, E. The book of Daniel

Doctorow, E. Ragtime

Evison, J. All about Lulu

Fitzgerald, F. The short stories of F. Scott Fitzgerald

Fitzgerald, F. Six tales of the jazz age and other stories

Gaitskill, M. Don't cry

Gurganus, A. The practical heart

Klaussmann, L. Tigers in red weather

McDermott, A. After this

Roth, P. Goodbye, Columbus, and five short stories

See, L. Shanghai girls

Stridsberg, S. Valerie

Updike, J. In the beauty of the lilies

Updike, J. Licks of love

Vonnegut, K. Armageddon in retrospect

Vonnegut, K. Bagombo snuff box

Wharton, E. Collected stories, 1891-1910

Wharton, E. Collected stories, 1911-1937

UNITED STATES -- SOCIAL LIFE AND CUSTOMS -- 21ST CENTURY

The best American mystery stories 2017

The best American mystery stories 2018

Diaz, J. This is how you lose her

Gaitskill, M. Don't cry

Wayne, T. The love song of Jonny Valentine

Woods, C. Things to do when you're goth in the country

UNITED STATES -- TERRITORIAL EXPANSION

Osborne, D. The coming

UNITED STATES ARMY GERMANY

O'Connor, R. Buffalo soldiers

UNITED STATES CIVIL WAR, 1861-1865

Bahr, H. The Judas Field

Barry, S. Days without end

Brown, D. The way to Bright Star

Brown, T. Fallen land

Cobbs Hoffman, E. The Tubman command

Coover, R. Huck out west

Crane, S. The red badge of courage

Doctorow, E. The march

Frazier, C. Cold Mountain

Gingrich, N. Gettysburg

Gingrich, N. Grant comes east

Gurganus, A. Oldest living Confederate widow tells all

Hicks, R. The widow of the South

Horn, D. All other nights

Humphreys, J. Nowhere else on earth

Hunt, L. Neverhome

Jakes, J. Love and war

Jakes, J. On secret service

Jakes, J. Savannah, or, A gift for Mr. Lincoln

Johnson, T. Engraved on the heart

Kantor, M. Andersonville

Kelton, E. Badger boy

Langton, J. The deserter

Lent, J. A slant of light

UNITED STATES. INTERNAL REVENUE SERVICE OFFICIALS AND EMPLOYEES

Millet, L. Ghost lights
Wallace, D. The pale king

UNITED STATES. NATIONAL AERONAUTICS AND SPACE ADMINISTRATION

Dean, M. The time it takes to fall
McDevitt, J. The Cassandra Project
Michener, J. Space

UNITED STATES. NATIONAL ARCHIVES AND RECORDS ADMINISTRATION

Meltzer, B. The inner circle

UNITED STATES. NATIONAL PARK SERVICE OFFICIALS AND EMPLOYEES.

Barr, N. Destroyer angel
Barr, N. Track of the cat

UNITED STATES. NATIONAL SECURITY AGENCY.

Iles, G. The footprints of God

UNITED STATES. NAVY

Clancy, T. The hunt for Red October
Poyer, D. Fire on the waters
Wouk, H. War and remembrance
Wouk, H. The winds of war

UNITED STATES. NAVY AVIATION

Michener, J. The bridges at Toko-Ri

UNITED STATES. NAVY HISTORY

Poyer, D. A country of our own

UNITED STATES. NAVY OFFICERS

Heggen, T. Mister Roberts
Sundin, S. Through waters deep
Wiggs, S. The ocean between us

UNITED STATES. NAVY. SEALS.

Campbell, R. Treason

UNITED STATES. OFFICE OF STRATEGIC SERVICES

Kerr, P. Hitler's peace

UNITED STATES. SECRET SERVICE

Goldstone, L. Assassin of shadows
Leonard, E. LaBrava

UNITED STATES. SECRET SERVICE OFFICIALS AND EMPLOYEES

Costello, M. Big if

UNITED STATES. SECRET SERVICE OFFICIALS AND EMPLOYEES, WOMEN

Patterson, J. Along came a spider

UNITED STATES. SECRETARY OF STATE.

Solomon, B. The attempted murder of Teddy Roosevelt

UNITED STATES. SUPREME COURT

Buckley, C. Supreme Courtship
Meltzer, B. The tenth justice

Universal harvester Darnielle, J.
Universe after [series] Williams, D.
The **universe** versus Alex Woods Extence, G.

UNIVERSITIES AND COLLEGES

Aciman, A. Harvard square
Amis, K. Lucky Jim
Awad, M. Bunny
Baker, J. The body lies

Bardugo, L. Ninth house
Barth, J. Giles Goat-Boy ;
Bolano, R. Distant star
Byatt, A. Babel Tower
Byatt, A. Possession
Cho, Z. Sorcerer to the crown
Croft, P. The second time I saw you
Davies, R. The rebel angels
DeLillo, D. White noise
Dunmore, E. Bringing down the duke
Eugenides, J. The marriage plot
Griffiths, E. A dying fall
Johnson, K. The dream-quest of Vellitt Boe
Longworth, M. Murder in the Rue Dumas
Mosley, W. John Woman
Murdoch, I. The book and the brotherhood
Okorafor, N. Binti
Pajer, B. The Edison effect
Pajer, B. Fatal induction
Pajer, B. A spark of death
Paretsky, S. Fallout
Parker, R. Hush money
Prose, F. Blue angel
Pym, B. An academic question
Rodriguez, L. Every broken trust
Rodriguez, L. Every last secret
Rodriguez, L. Every hidden fear
Rooney, S. Normal people
Ryan, H. Say no more
Sandford, J. Bloody genius
Sayers, D. Gaudy night
Shepard, S. Reputation
Smith, Z. On beauty
Stegner, W. Crossing to safety
Tartt, D. The secret history
Walker, K. The dreamers
Wayne, T. Loner
Weinberg, K. The truants
Whelan, J. My Oxford year
Wolfe, T. I am Charlotte Simmons

UNIVERSITIES AND COLLEGES -- ADMINISTRATION

Lipsyte, S. The ask

UNIVERSITIES AND COLLEGES -- FACULTY

Russo, R. Straight man

UNIVERSITIES AND COLLEGES -- MIDDLE WEST

Dean, P. Tam Lin
Smith, B. Joy in the morning

UNIVERSITY OF CAMBRIDGE STUDENTS

James, P. An unsuitable job for a woman

UNIVERSITY OF NOTRE DAME

McInerny, R. Celt and pepper
McInerny, R. Irish coffee

UNIVERSITY OF OXFORD

Cartwright, J. To heaven by water
Murdoch, I. The book and the brotherhood
Waugh, E. Brideshead revisited
Willis, C. To say nothing of the dog

McLaughlin, E. The nanny diaries
Mitford, N. The pursuit of love ;
Moore, L. Making waves
Morgan Jones, C. The jackal's share
Morgan Jones, C. The silent oligarch
Neely, B. Blanche cleans up
Oates, J. The accursed
Osborne, L. The forgiven
Pelevin, V. The hall of singing caryatids
Perez-Reverte, A. What we become
Pinborough, S. Dead to her
Raybourn, D. A dangerous collaboration
Raybourn, D. A perilous undertaking
Raybourn, D. A treacherous curse
Read, C. The crazy school
Read, C. Invisible boy
Sackville-West, V. The Edwardians
Sanders, L. The first deadly sin
Sayers, D. Whose body?
Seth, V. A suitable boy
Shupe, J. The prince of Broadway
Spark, M. Aiding & abetting
Spark, M. Memento mori
Spencer, S. The shivering turn
St. Aubyn, E. At last
Straub, P. Mystery
Towles, A. Rules of civility
Vatner, J. Carnegie Hill
Vaughan, S. Anatomy of a scandal
Vreeland, S. Luncheon of the boating party
Waugh, E. Decline and fall
Williams, B. The summer wives
Wodehouse, P. The inimitable Jeeves
Woods, S. A delicate touch

UPPER CLASS -- HISTORY
Zola, E. Nana

UPPER CLASS -- IRELAND
Black, B. Christine Falls

UPPER CLASS -- JAPAN
Mishima, Y. Spring snow

UPPER CLASS -- PHILADELPHIA, PENNSYLVANIA
Roberts, G. The bluest blood

UPPER CLASS -- TENNESSEE
Alexander, T. A note yet unsung

UPPER CLASS WOMEN
Canin, E. America America

UPPER EAST SIDE, NEW YORK CITY
Fairstein, L. Entombed
Gilbert, D. & sons
Layne, L. Passion on Park Avenue
Moshfegh, O. My year of rest and relaxation
Vatner, J. Carnegie Hill

UPPER MIDWEST
Hoover, M. The quickening

UPPER WEST SIDE, NEW YORK CITY
Helprin, M. Winter's tale
Lipman, E. The family man

Morton, B. Florence Gordon
Uprooted Novik, N.
Upstate Wood, J.
Uptown girls [series] Shupe, J.

UPWARD MOBILITY
Thackeray, W. Vanity fair
Towles, A. Rules of civility

URBAN EROTICA
Hobbs, A. Stealing candy
Noire Candy licker
Noire G-Spot
Rashan, N. You make me wanna
Swinson, K. Lifestyles of the rich and shameless
Zane Addicted

URBAN FAMILIES
Palahniuk, C. Lullaby

URBAN FANTASY
Aaronovitch, B. Broken homes
Aaronovitch, B. Midnight riot
Aaronovitch, B. Moon over Soho
Aaronovitch, B. Whispers under ground
Bardugo, L. Ninth house
Beukes, L. Zoo city
Bishop, A. Written in red
Bledsoe, A. Long black curl
Bledsoe, A. Gather her round
Bledsoe, A. The hum and the shiver
Bledsoe, A. Wisp of a thing
Butcher, J. Proven guilty
Camp, B. The city of lost fortunes
Camp, B. Gather the fortunes
Cornell, P. London falling
Flyte, M. City of dark magic
Flyte, M. City of lost dreams
Gailey, S. Magic for liars
Gilman, L. Hard magic
Griffin, K. The glass god
Griffin, K. Stray souls
Grimes, L. In a fix
Grimes, L. Quick fix
Hamill, P. Forever
Jones, D. Second grave on the left
Joyce, G. Some kind of fairy tale
Kaufmann, N. Dying is my business
Lafferty, M. Ghost train to New Orleans
Lafferty, M. The shambling guide to New York City
McGuire, S. Chimes at midnight
McGuire, S. Night and silence
McGuire, S. Once broken faith
McGuire, S. Rosemary and rue
Polansky, D. Low town
Richardson, K. Greywalker
Saintcrow, L. Trailer park fae
Shaw, V. Dreadful company
Shaw, V. Strange Practice
Snipes, W. Talon of God
Stout, D. Titanshade

UTAH

Ebershoff, D. The 19th wife
Grey, Z. Riders of the purple sage
Harrison, M. The bishop's wife
Howrey, M. The wanderers
Hunt, A. City of saints
Mailer, N. The executioner's song
Miller, W. A canticle for Leibowitz
Udall, B. The lonely polygamist

UTAH -- HISTORY -- 19TH CENTURY

Zimmer, M. The long hitch

UTAHRAPTOR

Bakker, R. Raptor red

UTE BOYS

Borland, H. When the legends die

UTE INDIANS

Borland, H. When the legends die

UTERINE FIBROIDS

Jimenez, A. The friend zone

UTOPIANS

Theroux, P. The Mosquito Coast

UTOPIAS

Banks, I. Matter
Gilman, C. Herland
Hilton, J. Lost horizon
Kingsolver, B. Unsheltered
Le Guin, U. The dispossessed
Mastai, E. All our wrong todays
Palmer, A. Too like the lightning
Porter, C. The seep
Sontag, S. In America
Unsworth, B. Sacred hunger
Vargas Llosa, M. The war of the end of the world
Wells, H. The time machine

Utz Chatwin, B.

UZBEKISTAN

Solzhenitsyn, A. Cancer ward

V

V Pynchon, T.
V. I. Warshawski mysteries [series] Paretsky, S.
VACATION HOMES

Cohen, T. The summer we lost her
Force, M. Deceived by desire
Hilderbrand, E. The perfect couple
Monroe, M. Beach house reunion
Page, K. The body in the wake
Pineiro, C. One summer night
Rinehart, M. The circular staircase
Rubart, J. The long journey to Jake Palmer
Williams, B. The summer wives

The **vacationers** Straub, E.

VACATIONS

Amis, M. The pregnant widow
Beck, H. Lost you
Cameron, C. Just a summer fling

Carpenter, E. Until the day I die
Cognetti, P. The eight mountains
Dexter, C. The way through the woods
Ferrante, E. The lost daughter
Force, M. Deceived by desire
Guillory, J. Royal holiday
Hale, S. Austenland
Hill, S. The shadows in the street
Inbinder, G. The hanged man
Jónasson, R. The island
Kane, J. Rules for visiting
Kemelman, H. One fine day the rabbi bought a cross
Kunzru, H. Gods without men
Le Carre, J. Our kind of traitor
Longworth, M. Murder on the Ile Sordou
MacLaverty, B. Midwinter break
Moore, A. The lighthouse
Morgan, S. One summer in Paris
Mortimer, J. Rumpole's return
Naylor, G. Mama Day
Potzsch, O. The werewolf of Bamberg
Ramsay, F. Scone Island
Reichs, K. Bare bones
Reiken, F. Day for night
Rouda, K. Best day ever
Russo, R. Chances are...
Scoppettone, S. Gonna take a homicidal journey
Snow, J. An Alaskan Christmas
Sosa, M. Acting on impulse
Theroux, P. The Elephanta suite
Tursten, H. Hunting game
Wieland, L. Paris, 7 a.m.
Woolf, V. To the lighthouse

VACCINES

Bunn, T. Outbreak
Dekker, T. Black
Dekker, T. Red
Dekker, T. White
Follett, K. Whiteout
Meek, J. The heart broke in

VACUUM

Egan, G. Schild's ladder

VACUUM CLEANER SALES PERSONNEL

Greene, G. Our man in Havana

Vacuum in the dark Beagin, J.
Vagabond Seymour, G.
The **vagabond** clown Marston, E.
The **vagrants** Li, Y.
Valediction Parker, R.
Valentino mysteries [series] Estleman, L.
Valerie Stridsberg, S.
Valerie Hart novels [series] Black, S.
VALETS

Sayers, D. The nine tailors
Sayers, D. Whose body?
Wodehouse, P. My man Jeeves

Valkyrie Ops [series] Dees, C.

VATICAN CITY
Berry, S. The Malta exchange
Brown, D. Angels & demons
Hewson, D. A season for the dead

VAUDEVILLE
Bennett, R. The troupe

VAUDEVILLE PERFORMERS
Swift, G. Here we are
The **vault** Lovesey, P.
Vault of heaven [series] Orullian, P.

VEGANS
Pandian, G. The accidental alchemist

VEGETARIANS
Evison, J. All about Lulu
Kracht, C. Imperium
Veil of gold Wilkins, K.
Veiled worlds trilogy [series] Anderton, J.

VEILS
Balogh, M. Someone to wed
Farah, N. Knots
Velocity Koontz, D.
Velocity weapon O'Keefe, M.
The **Venetian** affair MacInnes, H.

VENEZUELA
Cussler, C. Blue gold
Sainz Borgo, K. It would be night in Caracas
Vengeful Schwab, V.

VENICE (ITALY)
James, H. The wings of the dove

VENICE BEACH, FLORIDA
Seay, M. The mirror thief

VENICE, ITALY
Alexander, V. The Lady Travelers Guide to larceny with a
    dashing stranger
Alison, J. The marriage of the sea
Coover, R. Pinocchio in Venice
Dyer, G. Jeff in Venice, death in Varanasi
Langton, J. The thief of Venice
Leon, D. About face
Leon, D. Beastly things
Leon, D. Blood from a stone
Leon, D. Drawing conclusions
Leon, D. Falling in love
Leon, D. The girl of his dreams
Leon, D. The golden egg
Leon, D. A question of belief
Leon, D. Trace elements
Leon, D. Uniform justice
Leon, D. Unto us a son is given
MacInnes, H. The Venetian affair
Mann, T. Death in Venice and seven other stories
Rice, A. The vampire Armand
Shupe, J. The courtesan duchess
Weisgall, D. The world before her
Winterson, J. The passion

VENICE, ITALY -- HISTORY
Moore, C. The serpent of Venice

Sebald, W. Vertigo

VENICE, ITALY -- HISTORY -- 1508-1797
Brandreth, B. The assassin of Verona
Brandreth, B. The spy of Venice
Dunant, S. In the company of the courtesan

VENICE, ITALY -- HISTORY -- 16TH CENTURY
Seay, M. The mirror thief

VENICE, ITALY -- HISTORY -- 17TH CENTURY
Phillips, C. The Rossetti letter

VENICE, ITALY -- SOCIAL LIFE AND CUSTOMS -- 16TH CENTURY
Dunant, S. In the company of the courtesan

VENICE, ITALY -- SOCIAL LIFE AND CUSTOMS -- 19TH CENTURY
Chase, L. Your scandalous ways
The **ventriloquists** Ramzipoor, E.

VENTURE CAPITALISTS
Barnes, J. England, England
Crichton, M. Next
Deaver, J. The October list
Westlake, D. The road to ruin

VENUS (PLANET)
Valente, C. Radiance

VENUS (PLANET) -- EXPLORATION
Pohl, F. The space merchants
Vera Stanhope novels [series] Cleeves, A.

VERACRUZ, MEXICO
Fuentes, C. The years with Laura Diaz
The **verdict** Stone, N.
Verdict unsafe McGown, J.
The **Verdun** affair Dybek, N.

VERDUN, FRANCE
Dybek, N. The Verdun affair
Verlaque and Bonnet mysteries [series] Longworth, M.

VERMEER, JOHANNES, 1632-1675
Chevalier, T. Girl with a pearl earring
Vreeland, S. Girl in hyacinth blue
Vermilion drift Krueger, W.

VERMONT
Alther, L. Kinflicks
Auster, P. The book of illusions
Bohjalian, C. The buffalo soldier
Bohjalian, C. The double bind
Bohjalian, C. Secrets of Eden
Bohjalian, C. The sleepwalker
Freeman, C. All that I have
Irving, J. In one person
Lipman, E. The inn at Lake Devine
Mayor, A. Red herring
Mayor, A. Tag man
McMahon, J. The invited
Morris, M. Songs in ordinary time
Mosher, H. On Kingdom Mountain
Munier, P. A borrowing of bones
Olshan, J. Black diamond fall
Perry, T. The old man
St. James, S. The broken girls

VICARS

Malliet, G. A demon summer
Malliet, G. A fatal winter
Malliet, G. Pagan spring
Malliet, G. Wicked autumn
McGown, J. Murder at the old vicarage
Ohlsson, K. Silenced
Runcie, J. Sidney Chambers and the shadow of death

VICE-PRESIDENTS -- UNITED STATES

Costello, M. Big if
Vidal, G. Burr

VICES

Baxter, C. There's something I want you to do
Stevenson, R. The strange case of Dr. Jekyll and Mr. Hyde

VICHY (FRANCE)

Orringer, J. The flight portfolio

Vicious Schwab, V.

Vicious circle Box, C.

Vicious circle Littell, R.

Vicky Bliss mysteries [series] Peters, E.

The **victim** Manning, M.

Victim 2117 Adler-Olsen, J.

VICTIM SERVICES

Oliveras, P. Their perfect melody

VICTIMS

Gregory, D. We are all completely fine
Pava, S. Personae

VICTIMS -- PSYCHOLOGY

Wiesel, E. Dawn

VICTIMS OF CRIMES

Crumley, J. Bordersnakes
Crumley, J. The final country
Pelecanos, G. The turnaround
Price, R. Samaritan

VICTIMS OF TERRORISM

DeLillo, D. Falling man
Patchett, A. Bel canto
Phoenix, M. The space between words

VICTIMS OF VIOLENT CRIMES

Baker, J. The body lies
Bell, S. At his mercy
Bell, S. For his pleasure
Daly, P. Open your eyes
Mason, J. The hidden things
Penny, L. Still life
Price, R. Samaritan
Robinson, P. The first cut
Sager, R. Final girls

Victor Carl novels [series] Lashner, W.

VICTORIA, BRITISH COLUMBIA

Haldane, S. The devil's making

VICTORIA, QUEEN OF GREAT BRITAIN, 1819-1901 ASSASSINATION ATTEMPTS

Hodder, M. The strange affair of Spring Heeled Jack

VICTORIAN ERA (1837-1901)

Ackroyd, P. The trial of Elizabeth Cree
Alexander, V. The Lady Travelers Guide to larceny with a dashing stranger
Alexander, V. The Lady Travelers Guide to scoundrels and other gentlemen
Alexander, V. What happens at Christmas
Archer, Z. Dangerous seduction
Ashley, J. Lady Isabella's scandalous marriage
Ashley, J. The madness of Lord Ian Mackenzie
Birch, C. Jamrach's menagerie
Bradford, B. Master of his fate
Bronte, A. The tenant of Wildfell Hall
Burrowes, G. The bridegroom wore plaid
Byrne, K. The duke with the dragon tattoo
Byrne, K. How to love a duke in ten days
Byrne, K. The hunter
Callihan, K. Firelight
Carlyle, C. A duke changes everything
Clare, A. The woman who spoke to spirits
Collins, W. The moonstone
Collins, W. The woman in white
Dunmore, E. Bringing down the duke
Ellis, B. The vanished bride
Faber, M. The crimson petal and the white
Faye, L. The whole art of detection
Finch, C. A beautiful blue death
Finch, C. The September Society
Finlay, M. The murder pit
Fowles, J. The French lieutenant's woman
Frampton, M. Put up your duke
Freeman, D. A lady's guide to etiquette and murder
Gaiman, N. Stardust
Gallagher, S. The kingdom of bones
Galsworthy, J. The Forsyte saga
Goss, T. The sinister mystery of the mesmerizing girl
Goss, T. The strange case of the alchemist's daughter
Gray, J. How to tame your duke
Guhrke, L. Governess gone rogue
Guhrke, L. The truth about love and dukes
Hardy, T. Far from the madding crowd
Heath, L. Falling into bed with a duke
Humphreys, H. Afterimage
Kasasian, M. Dark dawn over Steep House
Kidd, J. Things in jars
Kleypas, L. Cold-hearted rake
Kleypas, L. Devil in spring
Kleypas, L. Marrying Winterborne
Kleypas, L. Secrets of a summer night
Laurens, S. By winter's light
Laurens, S. The pursuits of Lord Kit Cavanaugh
Lovesey, P. Waxwork
Macneal, E. The doll factory
Mason, T. The Darwin affair
McCrea, G. Mrs. Engels
McGuire, I. The North water
McQuiston, J. The spinster's guide to scandalous behavior
Meyer, N. The seven-per-cent solution
Milan, C. The duchess war
Morrell, D. Ruler of the night

VICTORIAN HOUSES

VICTORIAN MYSTERIES

Perry, A. Cardington Crescent
Perry, A. A dangerous mourning
Perry, A. Dark tide rising
Perry, A. Death on Blackheath
Perry, A. Defend and betray
Perry, A. Death of a stranger
Perry, A. The face of a stranger
Perry, A. Farriers' Lane
Perry, A. Funeral in blue
Perry, A. Half Moon Street
Perry, A. Highgate Rise
Perry, A. The Hyde Park headsman
Perry, A. Midnight at Marble Arch
Perry, A. Paragon Walk
Perry, A. Pentecost Alley
Perry, A. Resurrection Row
Perry, A. Seven Dials
Perry, A. The shifting tide
Perry, A. The silent cry
Perry, A. The sins of the wolf
Perry, A. Slaves of obsession
Perry, A. Southampton Row
Perry, A. A sunless sea
Perry, A. Traitors Gate
Perry, A. The twisted root
Perry, A. Weighed in the balance
Perry, A. The Whitechapel conspiracy
Price, S. By gaslight
Quick, A. Garden of lies
Rowland, L. The hangman's secret
Rowland, L. The Ripper's shadow
Saunders, K. The case of the wandering scholar
Saunders, K. The secrets of Wishtide
Shepherd, L. A fatal likeness
Shepherd, L. The Solitary House
Thomson, E. Beloved poison
Thomson, E. The blood

Victorian mysteries (Laura Joh Rowland) [series] Rowland, L.

Victorian rebels [series] Byrne, K.

VICTORIAN ROMANCES
  Alexander, V. The Lady Travelers Guide to larceny with a
    dashing stranger
  Alexander, V. The Lady Travelers Guide to scoundrels and
    other gentlemen
  Alexander, V. What happens at Christmas
  Archer, Z. Dangerous seduction
  Ashley, J. Lady Isabella's scandalous marriage
  Ashley, J. The madness of Lord Ian Mackenzie
  Burrowes, G. The bridegroom wore plaid
  Byrne, K. The duke with the dragon tattoo
  Byrne, K. How to love a duke in ten days
  Byrne, K. The hunter
  Callihan, K. Firelight
  Carlyle, C. A duke changes everything
  Dunmore, E. Bringing down the duke
  Frampton, M. Put up your duke

Gray, J. How to tame your duke
Guhrke, L. Governess gone rogue
Guhrke, L. The truth about love and dukes
Heath, L. Falling into bed with a duke
Kleypas, L. Cold-hearted rake
Kleypas, L. Devil in spring
Kleypas, L. Secrets of a summer night
Kleypas, L. Marrying Winterborne
Laurens, S. By winter's light
Laurens, S. The pursuits of Lord Kit Cavanaugh
McQuiston, J. The spinster's guide to scandalous behavior
Milan, C. The duchess war
Quick, A. 'Til death do us part
Ranney, K. The Scottish duke
Thomas, S. Beguiling the beauty
Thomas, S. The luckiest lady in London
Thomas, S. My beautiful enemy
Thomas, S. Ravishing the heiress
Thomas, S. Tempting the bride

VICTORIANA
  Dickens, C. Great expectations
  Dickens, C. Oliver Twist, or The parish boy's progress
  Lovesey, P. Bertie and the seven bodies
  Trollope, A. Barchester Towers
  Trollope, A. The Eustace diamonds
  Trollope, A. Framley parsonage
  Trollope, A. The Prime Minister
  Willis, C. To say nothing of the dog

Victory Conrad, J.

The **victory** garden Bowen, R.

VICTORY GARDENS
  Bowen, R. The victory garden

Vida Piercy, M.

VIDEO GAMES
  Deaver, J. The never game
  Gibson, W. The peripheral

VIDEO GAMES INDUSTRY AND TRADE
  Deaver, J. The never game

VIDEO STORES
  Darnielle, J. Universal harvester

VIDEOS
  Blumenfeld, A. The cast
  Danielewski, M. The familiar.
  Darnielle, J. Universal harvester
  Finder, J. Judgment

VIDOCQ, FRANCOIS EUGENE, 1775-1857
  Bayard, L. The black tower

Vienna blood Tallis, F.

VIENNA, AUSTRIA
  Benedict, M. The only woman in the room
  Bernhard, T. Woodcutters
  Clayton, M. The last train to London
  Meyer, N. The seven-per-cent solution
  Musil, R. The man without qualities
  Skibell, J. A curable romantic

VIENNA, AUSTRIA -- HISTORY -- 19TH CENTURY
  Perry, A. Funeral in blue

VIETNAMESE AMERICANS
Butler, R. A good scent from a strange mountain
Hoang, H. The bride test
Nguyen, V. The refugees
Tran, V. Dragonfish
Vuong, O. On Earth we're briefly gorgeous

VIETNAMESE IN FRANCE
Truong, M. The book of salt, Monique Truong.

VIETNAMESE IN THE UNITED STATES
Hoang, H. The bride test
Johnson, C. Another man's moccasins
Nguyen, V. The sympathizer

The **view** from Castle Rock Munro, A.

A **view** of the empire at sunset Phillips, C.

VIGILANTES
Black, L. Let justice descend
Black, L. Suffer the children
Browne, S. Less than hero
Gardner, L. Fear nothing
Gardner, L. Find her
Harkaway, N. Tigerman
Hurwitz, G. Orphan X
King, L. Keeping watch
Lovesey, P. Skeleton Hill
Martinson, T. The reign of the Kingfisher
Meyer, D. Devil's peak
Parker, S. Coldwater
Roslund, A. Pen 33
Sandford, J. Silent prey
Solomon, A. Disgruntled
Unger, L. The stranger inside
Woods, T. Dutch
Zhou, H. Death notice

VIGILANTES -- NEW ORLEANS, LOUISIANA
Smith, J. Crescent City kill

VIGILANTES -- TEXAS
Bonner, C. Lily

VIKINGS
Cornwell, B. The last kingdom
Cornwell, B. Sword of kings
Cornwell, B. War of the wolf
Grimes, L. In a fix
Kay, G. The last light of the sun
MacDonald, A. When we were Vikings

Vile bodies Waugh, E.

Villa Triste Grindle, L.

VILLA, PANCHO, 1878-1923
Groom, W. El Paso
Olmstead, R. Far bright star

VILLAGE COMMUNITIES -- FRANCE
Nemirovsky, I. Fire in the blood

VILLAGES
Abe, K. The woman in the dunes
Al-Ramli, M. The president's gardens
Alharthi, J. Celestial bodies
Arden, K. The bear and the nightingale
Austen, J. Emma

Beaton, M. Death of a macho man
Beaton, M. Pushing up daisies
Brennan, M. A natural history of dragons
Brennan, M. The tropic of serpents
Bussi, M. Black water lilies
Christie, A. The murder at the vicarage
Coleridge, N. A much married man
Connolly, S. The lost traveller
Crace, J. Harvest
Crombie, D. A bitter feast
Crombie, D. Mourn not your dead
Dev, S. A Bollywood affair
Deb, S. The point of return
Donoghue, E. The wonder
Dunmore, H. The lie
Eliot, G. Adam Bede
Erdrich, L. The painted drum
Garcia Marquez, G. In evil hour
Garcia Marquez, G. One hundred years of solitude
Goenawan, C. The perfect world of Miwako Sumida
Gurganus, A. The practical heart
Harris, R. The second sleep
Hawthorne, N. The scarlet letter
Heacox, K. Jimmy Bluefeather
Hegi, U. Children and fire
Hibbert, T. A girl like her
Hill, R. The stranger house
Jackson, S. The lottery
Joyce, G. The limits of enchantment
Kelly, S. The wages of desire
Lai, L. The tiger flu
Lea, C. The glass woman
Liardet, F. We must be brave
Louis, E. The end of Eddy
Malliet, G. A fatal winter
Malliet, G. A demon summer
Malliet, G. Pagan spring
Malliet, G. Wicked autumn
McGregor, J. The reservoir tapes
Mda, Z. The whale caller
Mitchell, D. Black Swan Green
Mysliwski, W. Stone upon stone
Nicholson, C. The elephant keeper
O'Brien, E. In the forest
Peebles, F. The seamstress
Penny, L. A better man
Penny, L. Kingdom of the blind
Porter, M. Lanny
Potzsch, O. The beggar king
Potzsch, O. The dark monk
Potzsch, O. The hangman's daughter
Potzsch, O. The play of death
Quartey, K. Wife of the gods
Sayers, D. Busman's honeymoon
Sayers, D. The nine tailors
Scott, P. Staying on
See, L. The island of sea women

Burgess, A. A clockwork orange
Burnet, G. His bloody project
Butler, O. Parable of the sower
Butler, O. Parable of the talents
Byrne, T. Ghosts and lightning
Caputo, P. Acts of faith
Caputo, P. Crossers
Card, O. Ender's game
Carver, R. What we talk about when we talk about love
Cleage, P. Some things I never thought I'd do
Clement, J. Prayers for the stolen
Coady, L. The antagonist
Coetzee, J. Life & times of Michael K
Conrad, J. Heart of darkness
Coover, R. Noir
Corey, J. Abaddon's gate
Corey, J. Babylon's ashes
Corey, J. Caliban's war
Corey, J. Cibola burn
Corey, J. Nemesis games
Crichton, M. Pirate latitudes
Cronin, J. The city of mirrors
Cronin, J. The passage
Cronin, J. The twelve
Crumley, J. Bordersnakes
Crumley, J. The final country
D'Eramo, L. Deviation
Dalton, T. Boy swallows universe
Danticat, E. The dew breaker
Deaver, J. The coffin dancer
Deb, S. The point of return
Del Amo, J. Animalia
Didion, J. A book of common prayer
Doctorow, E. Ragtime
Ellory, R. The anniversary man
Enriquez, M. Things we lost in the fire
Erpenbeck, J. Visitation
Estleman, L. Gas City
Farah, N. Crossbones
Farah, N. Links
Faust, C. Choke hold
Faust, C. Money shot
Ferrante, E. My brilliant friend
Flanagan, R. The narrow road to the deep north
Gerritsen, T. Playing with fire
Gray, E. Love & a gangsta
Greene, G. Collected stories
Hage, R. De Niro's game
Hand, E. Available dark
Hand, E. Hard light
Hansen, R. A wild surge of guilty passion
Harris, T. Hannibal rising
Harvey, M. Brighton
Hayder, M. Ritual
Heinlein, R. Starship troopers
House, S. A parchment of leaves
Hunter, S. Havana

Hunter, S. Hot springs
Huston, C. Caught stealing
Huston, C. Every last drop
Iles, G. The devil's punchbowl
Irwin, S. The dead path
James, M. The book of night women
James, M. A brief history of seven killings
Jen, G. World and town
Johnson, A. The orphan master's son
Johnson, D. Nobody move
Katsu, A. The hunger
Katzenbach, J. The analyst
Katzenbach, J. Just cause
Kepler, L. The rabbit hunter
Khadra, Y. The swallows of Kabul
King, S. It
King, S. Sleeping beauties
Knox, T. Kockroach
Laukkanen, O. The professionals
Ledgard, J. Submergence
Lehane, D. Live by night
Lennon, J. Castle
Leon, D. A question of belief
Lewis, T. GBH
Li, Y. The vagrants
MacBride, S. Blind eye
MacBride, S. Flesh house
MacDonald, J. The long lavender look
Majmudar, A. Partitions
Malerman, J. Bird box
Martin, G. A clash of kings
Martin, G. A dance with dragons
Martin, G. A feast for crows
Martin, G. A game of thrones
Martin, G. A storm of swords
Mayor, A. Red herring
McCann, C. Apeirogon
McCarthy, C. No country for old men
McCullough, C. An indecent obsession
McDermott, A. That night
Mohamed, N. The orchard of lost souls
Montag, K. After the flood
Montero, M. Dancing to "Almendra"
Moody, D. Hater
Morgan, R. Thirteen
Mosley, W. Fearless Jones
Mosley, W. The right mistake
Moss, S. Ghost wall
Mott, J. The returned
Mukherjee, B. Miss new India
Murr, N. The perfect man
Nesbo, J. Nemesis
Neville, S. The ghosts of Belfast
Newton, C. Start shooting
Nicholson, C. The elephant keeper
Nickson, C. At the dying of the year
Noire G-Spot

Marlette, D. Magic time

VIOLENCE AGAINST NATIVE AMERICANS

Sundstol, V. The land of dreams

VIOLENCE AGAINST PROSTITUTES

Fossum, K. Eva's eye

Hewson, D. The garden of evil

VIOLENCE AGAINST RADICALS

Gorman, E. Riders on the storm

VIOLENCE AGAINST TEENAGE GIRLS

Yates, C. Grist Mill Road

VIOLENCE AGAINST WOMEN

Adler-Olsen, J. The scarred woman

Baker, J. The body lies

Bolano, R. 2666

Bond, C. Ruby

Bradbury, J. The wild inside

Burns, A. Little constructions

Carver, T. The surrogate

Castillo, E. America is not the heart

Castillo, L. A gathering of secrets

Connelly, M. The late show

Cornwell, P. Postmortem

De Robertis, C. Cantoras

Deon, N. Grace

Dodd, C. The woman who couldn't scream

Donati, S. Where the light enters

Eisler, B. All the devils

Grippando, J. The girl in the glass box

Hambly, B. Lady of perdition

Harris, T. Hannibal

Harris, T. The silence of the lambs

Hayder, M. Birdman

King, S. Sleeping beauties

Lagercrantz, D. The girl in the spider's web

Lagercrantz, D. The girl who lived twice

Lagercrantz, D. The girl who takes an eye for an eye

Larsson, S. The girl who kicked the hornet's nest

Larsson, S. The girl who played with fire

Larsson, S. The girl with the dragon tattoo

Lawler, L. Don't wake up

Lelchuk, S. Save me from dangerous men

Lemaitre, P. Irene

Limon, M. Mr. Kill

MacBride, S. Dying light

Mina, D. The end of the wasp season

Mina, D. The red road

Moore, L. Long bright river

Murakami, H. After dark

O'Brien, E. Girl

O'Donovan, G. The priest

O'Malley, T. Serpents in the cold

Perez-Reverte, A. The siege

Perry, A. A sunless sea

Perry, T. Vanishing act

Petrie, N. Tear it down

Petrie, N. The wild one

Pochoda, I. These women

Rao, S. Girls burn brighter

Rendell, R. Harm done

Roberts, N. Dance upon the air

Rollins, J. Crucible

Rowland, L. The Ripper's shadow

Ryan, H. Say no more

Sager, R. Final girls

Sanders, L. McNally's luck

Shields, S. The Cassandra

Shoham, L. Asylum city

Shreve, A. Eden Close

Slaughter, K. Undone

Spillane, M. The Consummata

Toews, M. Women talking

Tracy, P. Ice cold heart

VIOLENCE IN AFRICAN AMERICAN MEN

Noire Candy licker

VIOLENCE IN BOYS

Lessing, D. The fifth child

VIOLENCE IN CHILDREN

Seo, M. The only child

Stage, Z. Baby teeth

VIOLENCE IN GANGS

Barry, K. City of Bohane

Child, L. Blue moon

K'wan Gangsta

O'Mara, T. Crooked numbers

Winer, J. Her kind of case

VIOLENCE IN MASS MEDIA

Elliot, L. Guilty

VIOLENCE IN MEN

Barker, P. The silence of the girls

Bolano, R. The Third Reich

Burke, J. The jealous kind

Burns, A. Milkman

Child, L. Blue moon

Clark, M. Kiss the girls and make them cry

Coes, B. The Russian

Crace, J. Quarantine

Dimitri, F. The book of hidden things

Donati, S. Where the light enters

Flagg, F. Fried green tomatoes at the Whistle Stop Cafe

Ford, R. Canada

Garcia Marquez, G. Chronicle of a death foretold

Geni, A. The wildlands

Gifford, B. The stars above Veracruz

Greene, A. Bloodroot

Gruber, M. The return

Hand, E. Curious toys

Hannah, K. The great alone

Harrison, M. Light

Harvey, M. The fifth floor

Heller, P. The painter

Hunter, S. Dirty white boys

Johnson, C. Death without company

K'wan Gutter

Kandasamy, M. When I hit you, or, A portrait of the writer as

Parshall, S. Bleeding through
Parshall, S. Poisoned ground
Patchett, A. Commonwealth
Ramsay, F. Countdown
Ramsay, F. Scone Island
Ramsay, F. Stranger room
Robards, K. The last victim
Smith, L. Fair and tender ladies
Smith, L. Family linen
Smith, L. Oral history
Swinson, K. The safe house
Trigiani, A. Big Cherry Holler
Trigiani, A. Big Stone Gap
Turner, N. Black widow
Turner, N. A hustler's wife
Vandelly, T. Theme music
Walls, J. The silver star
Wilhelm, K. Where late the sweet birds sang

VIRGINIA -- HISTORY
Coates, T. The water dancer

VIRGINIA -- HISTORY -- 1775-1865
Leveen, L. The secrets of Mary Bowser
Peters, R. Hell or Richmond

VIRGINIA -- HISTORY -- 19TH CENTURY
Conklin, T. The house girl
Michener, J. Mexico
Pearl, M. The Poe shadow

VIRGINIA -- HISTORY -- CIVIL WAR, 1861-1865
Crane, S. The red badge of courage
Perry, A. Slaves of obsession

VIRGINIA -- HISTORY -- COLONIAL PERIOD, 1600-1775
L'Amour, L. To the far blue mountains
Settle, M. O Beulah land

VIRGINIA -- SOCIAL CONDITIONS -- 19TH CENTURY
Jones, E. The known world

VIRGINIA BEACH, VIRGINIA
Robards, K. The last victim

VIRGINITY
Blau, J. The summer of naked swim parties

VIRGINITY -- SOCIAL ASPECTS
Pamuk, O. The museum of innocence

VIRGINS
Spencer, M. Scandalous

VIRTUAL COMMUNITY
West, K. Minor dramas & other catastrophes

VIRTUAL REALITY
Beckett, L. Gamechanger
Bradbury, R. The illustrated man
Cline, E. Ready player one
Harrison, M. Light
Palmer, D. The dream of perpetual motion
Pinsker, S. A song for a new day
Robb, J. Fantasy in death
Ruff, M. 88 names
Scalzi, J. Lock in
Shakar, A. Luminarium

Stephenson, N. Reamde
Stephenson, N. Snow crash
Tidhar, L. Central Station
Weinstein, A. Children of the new world
Zelazny, R. Donnerjack

VIRTUAL REALITY GAMES
Chiang, T. The lifecycle of software objects

VIRTUAL SEX
Iles, G. Mortal fear

Virtue Falls Dodd, C.

Virtue Falls [series] Dodd, C.

VIRTUES
Baxter, C. There's something I want you to do
Stevenson, R. The strange case of Dr. Jekyll and Mr. Hyde
Stoker, B. Dracula
Stoker, B. The new annotated Dracula

VIRUS DISEASES
Asher, N. The skinner
Dekker, T. Black
Dekker, T. Red
Dekker, T. White
Scalzi, J. Head on
Scalzi, J. Lock in
Stewart, G. Earth abides
Toro, G. The strain
Whitehead, C. Zone one

VIRUSES
Chen, Q. Waste tide
Cronin, J. The city of mirrors
Cronin, J. The passage
Cronin, J. The twelve
Follett, K. Whiteout
Grant, M. Blackout
Grant, M. Deadline
Grant, M. Feed
Grant, M. Feedback
Mandel, E. Station Eleven
Tidhar, L. Central Station
Vinge, V. Rainbows end
Wilson, D. The Andromeda evolution

VISAS
Lauren, C. Roomies
Recacoechea S., J. American visa

VISCOUNTS AND VISCOUNTESSES
Ashford, J. Heir to the duke
Balogh, M. Someone to remember
Layton, E. To wed a stranger
Leigh, E. Scandal takes the stage
Thomas, S. Tempting the bride

VISEGRAD (BOSNIA AND HERCEGOVINA : EAST)
Andric, I. The bridge on the Drina

Vish Puri mysteries [series] Hall, T.

The **vision** of Emma Blau Hegi, U.

A **vision** of light Riley, J.

VISION QUESTS
Momaday, N. The ancient child

The **visionist** Urquhart, R.

Coetzee, J. Life & times of Michael K
Cohen, J. Book of numbers
Conrad, J. Heart of darkness
Coomer, J. One vacant chair
Coover, R. Huck out west
Crandall, S. Whistling past the graveyard
Cumming, C. A divided spy
Cussler, C. Odessa Sea
Danielewski, M. Only revolutions
Dare, T. A week to be wicked
Diaz, H. In the distance
Dickens, C. Martin Chuzzlewit
Dickens, C. The old curiosity shop
Dickens, C. The Pickwick papers
Doig, I. Ride with me, Mariah Montana
Doyle, B. The plover
Doyle, R. Threshold
Eggers, D. What is the what
Elison, M. The book of the unnamed midwife
Enard, M. Compass
Enger, L. The high divide
Enright, A. The Green Road
Fielding, H. The history of Tom Jones, a foundling
Ford, R. Let me be Frank with you
Fortier, A. Juliet
Fowler, K. Sarah Canary
Frazier, C. Cold Mountain
Frazier, C. Thirteen moons
Gabaldon, D. Voyager
Gaige, A. Schroder
Gappah, P. Out of darkness, shining light
Garey, J. Too bright to hear too loud to see
George, N. The little Paris bookshop
Ghosh, A. Flood of fire
Ghosh, A. Gun Island
Ghosh, A. River of smoke
Ghosh, A. Sea of poppies
Gifford, B. The stars above Veracruz
Gilman, L. The cold eye
Gilman, L. Silver on the road
Golding, W. Close quarters
Golding, W. Fire down below
Golding, W. Rites of passage
Green, J. The mark of the king
Greer, A. Less
Grossman, L. The magician king
Grossman, L. The magician's land
Gruber, M. The return
Halfon, E. Mourning
Hamid, M. Exit west
Handke, P. Crossing the Sierra de Gredos
Hertmans, S. The convert
Hijuelos, O. Twain & Stanley enter paradise
Hill, L. Someone knows my name
Hooper, E. Etta and Otto and Russell and James
Hunt, S. Mr. Splitfoot
Hunter, S. The 47th samurai

Irving, J. Avenue of mysteries
James, H. Daisy Miller
Jiles, P. News of the world
Johnson, M. Pym
Joinson, S. A lady cyclist's guide to Kashgar
Jonasson, J. The accidental further adventures of the hundred-year-old man
Kane, J. Rules for visiting
Kay, G. Children of earth and sky
Kay, G. Under heaven
Kehlmann, D. Tyll
Kelly, M. Lost roses
Kerouac, J. On the road
Khalfah, K. Death is hard work
King, S. Firestarter
Kittredge, W. The willow field
Krivak, A. The bear
Krueger, W. This tender land
Lalami, L. The Moor's account
Lanchester, J. Fragrant Harbor
Larison, J. Whiskey when we're dry
Larsen, R. The selected works of T. S. Spivet
Le Guin, U. The dispossessed
Le Guin, U. The left hand of darkness
Lefteri, C. The beekeeper of Aleppo
Leithauser, B. The promise of elsewhere
Livesey, M. Criminals
Lodge, D. Paradise news
Lyndon, R. Hawk quest
Ma, J. Stick out your tongue
Maalouf, A. Balthasar's odyssey
MacAlister, K. The truth about Leo
McAllister, T. The young widower's handbook
Mitchell, D. The bone clocks
Murakami, H. Colorless Tsukuru Tazaki and his years of pilgrimage
NDiaye, M. Ladivine
Nesbo, J. The bat
Nesbo, J. The redbreast
Newman, S. The country of Ice Cream Star
Nordhoff, C. Men against the sea
Nordhoff, C. Pitcairn's Island
O'Farrell, M. This must be the place
Obioma, C. An orchestra of minorities
Parini, J. The Damascus road
Parks, S. Getting mother's body
Pattison, E. Blood of the oak
Pattison, E. Water touching stone
Peebles, F. The air you breathe
Penney, S. The tenderness of wolves
Perry, A. A Christmas message
Perry, A. A Christmas return
Phillips, S. The great escape
Pitts, L. Freeman
Pohl, F. Gateway
Porter, K. Ship of fools
Potzsch, O. The werewolf of Bamberg

Lock, N. A fugitive in Walden Woods

WALES

Balogh, M. Simply love

Chatwin, B. On the black hill

Cronin, A. Citadel

Fforde, J. Early riser

Fforde, J. The Eyre affair

Mackintosh, C. I let you go

Mawer, S. The fall

Penman, S. Dragon's lair

WALES -- HISTORY -- 1063-1284

Penman, S. Here be dragons

Penman, S. The reckoning

WALES -- HISTORY -- 12TH CENTURY

Peters, E. The summer of the Danes

WALES -- HISTORY -- 14TH CENTURY

Robb, C. A gift of Sanctuary

WALES -- HISTORY -- TO 1536

Penman, S. Here be dragons

WALES -- SOCIAL LIFE AND CUSTOMS

Llewellyn, R. How green was my valley

Thomas, D. The collected stories

WALES -- SOCIAL LIFE AND CUSTOMS -- 19TH CENTURY

James, E. When Beauty tamed the Beast

A **walk** on the wild side Algren, N.

A **walk** through the fire Muller, M.

A **walk** to remember Sparks, N.

A **walk** with the dead Spencer, S.

Walkaway Doctorow, C.

Walker family [series] Jance, J.

WALKER, GEORGE, 1873-1911

Phillips, C. Dancing in the dark

WALKING

Hooper, E. Etta and Otto and Russell and James

Saer, J. The sixty-five years of Washington

Walking across Egypt Edgerton, C.

Walking on the ceiling Savas, A.

Walking shadow Parker, R.

The **wall** of storms Liu, K.

WALL STREET, NEW YORK CITY

Goldin, M. The escape room

Lathen, E. Brewing up a storm

Lathen, E. East is east

Lathen, E. Something in the air

Sanders, L. The Timothy files

Sanders, L. Timothy's game

Sears, M. Black Fridays

Towles, A. Rules of civility

Wallflower series [series] Kleypas, L.

The **wallflower** wager Dare, T.

WALLS

Gaiman, N. Stardust

Walt Longmire mysteries [series] Johnson, C.

WAMPANOAG INDIANS

Brooks, G. Caleb's crossing

The **wanderer** Carr, R.

Wanderer Leon, S.

The **wanderers** Howrey, M.

Wanderers Wendig, C.

WANDERERS AND WANDERING

Ahmad, J. The wandering falcon

Child, L. No middle name

Conrad, J. Lord Jim

French, J. The true Bastards

Gao, X. Soul mountain

Jones, S. Mongrels

Kerouac, J. Road novels 1957-1960

Lippman, L. Sunburn

Lock, N. American meteor

Maturin, C. Melmoth the wanderer

Parker, R. Appaloosa

Proulx, A. Postcards

Richler, M. Solomon Gursky was here

Wendig, C. Wanderers

The **wandering** falcon Ahmad, J.

A **wanted** man Child, L.

Wanted, a gentleman Charles, K.

The **wanton** angel Marston, E.

The **Wapshot** chronicle Cheever, J.

The **Wapshot** scandal Cheever, J.

Wapshot series [series] Cheever, J.

WAR

Adimi, K. Our riches

Apelfeld, A. Blooms of darkness

Blake, S. The postmistress

Bourne, J. The spymaster's lady

Brooks, M. World War Z

Celine, L. Journey to the end of the night

Dupont, E. The American fiancee

El Akkad, O. American war

Florio, G. Silent hearts

Follett, K. Edge of eternity

Follett, K. Winter of the world

Frazier, C. Varina

Furst, A. Spies of the Balkans

Gabaldon, D. An echo in the bone

Gabaldon, D. Written in my own heart's blood

George, M. Helen of Troy

Hage, R. Beirut Hellfire Society

Harmel, K. The room on Rue Amelie

Heller, J. Catch-22

Hurley, K. The light brigade

Jakes, J. Love and war

Jones, J. From here to eternity

Kay, G. A brightness long ago

Kay, G. River of stars

Khoury, R. Empire of lies

Kristin Omarsdottir, 1. Children in Reindeer Woods

Kuang, R. The poppy war

Mailer, N. The naked and the dead

Malraux, A. Man's hope

Mandanipour, S. Moon brow

Manfredi, V. A winter's night

O'Brien, T. Going after Cacciato
Palaia, M. The given world
Perez-Reverte, A. The siege
Polk, C. Witchmark
Remarque, E. All quiet on the western front
Roy, A. All the lives we never lived
Ryan, J. The spies of Shilling Lane
Sayles, J. A moment in the sun
Shepard, J. The book of Aron
Shields, S. The Cassandra
Simonson, H. The summer before the war
Solomons, N. House of Gold
Spark, M. The girls of slender means
Speller, E. The return of Captain John Emmett
Speller, E. The strange fate of Kitty Easton
Waldman, A. A door in the earth

WAR CASUALTIES
Doctorow, E. The march
Dybek, N. The Verdun affair
Mackall, D. With love, wherever you are
Sa'dawi, A. Frankenstein in Baghdad
Scott, C. The poppy wife

WAR CORRESPONDENTS
Abrams, D. Fobbit
Butler, R. Paris in the dark
McLain, P. Love and ruin
Murphy, T. Correspondents
Perry, A. Shoulder the sky
Quinn, K. The huntress

WAR CORRESPONDENTS -- GREAT BRITAIN
Greene, G. The quiet American

WAR CORRESPONDENTS -- UNITED STATES
Butler, R. The hot country

WAR CRIME TRIALS
Schlink, B. The reader

WAR CRIMES
Hazzard, S. The great fire
Khan, A. The unquiet dead
Lee, Y. Revenant gun
Turow, S. Testimony

WAR CRIMES -- HISTORY -- VIETNAM WAR, 1961-1975
O'Brien, T. In the Lake of the Woods

WAR CRIMES -- HISTORY -- WORLD WAR II
Goddard, R. Long time coming

WAR CRIMINALS
Bilal, P. The burning gates
Grecian, A. The saint of wolves and butchers
Khan, A. The unquiet dead
Rankin, I. The hanging garden

WAR CRIMINALS -- GERMAN
Cussler, C. The Mediterranean caper

WAR GAMES
Bolano, R. The Third Reich

WAR MEMORIALS
Dykes, A. Whose waves these are

WAR NEUROSES

Ford, F. Parade's end
Powers, K. The yellow birds
The war of the end of the world Vargas Llosa, M.
War of the rats Robbins, D.
War of the wolf Cornwell, B.
The war of the worlds Wells, H.

WAR ON TERRORISM, 2001-2009
Harris, R. The ghost
Le Carre, J. A most wanted man
The road ahead

WAR PHOTOGRAPHERS
Perez-Reverte, A. The painter of battles
War room Fabry, C.

WAR STORIES
Abrams, D. Fobbit
Afrika, T. Bitter Eden
Albahari, D. Gotz and Meyer
Aramburu, F. Homeland
Arudpragasam, A. The story of a brief marriage
Bahr, H. The Judas Field
Ballard, J. Empire of the sun
Bao, N. The sorrow of war
Barker, P. The eye in the door
Barker, P. The ghost road
Barker, P. Regeneration
Barker, P. The silence of the girls
Bates, H. Fair stood the wind for France
Bausch, R. Peace
Bausch, R. Rebel powers
Beach, E. Run silent, run deep
Beah, I. Radiance of tomorrow
Benaron, N. Running the rift
Bird, S. Daughter of a daughter of a queen
Bohjalian, C. Skeletons at the feast
Boianjiu, S. The people of forever are not afraid
Boulle, P. The bridge over the River Kwai
Boyden, J. Three day road
Boyne, J. The absolutist
Brouwer, S. Thief of glory
Cobbs Hoffman, E. The Tubman command
Cooper, J. The last of the Mohicans
Cornwell, B. 1356
Cornwell, B. The archer's tale
Couto, M. Sleepwalking land
Crane, S. The red badge of courage
De Bernieres, L. Birds without wings
Dean, D. The madonnas of Leningrad
Del Vecchio, J. The 13th valley
Deutermann, P. Pacific glory
Doctorow, E. The march
El Akkad, O. American war
Faulks, S. Birdsong
Faulks, S. Charlotte Gray
Follett, K. Hornet flight
Follett, K. Jackdaws
Ford, F. Parade's end
Forester, C. Commodore Hornblower

WAR VICTIMS

WAR WOUNDS

Van Booy, S. The illusion of separateness

The **warden** Trollope, A.

The **warehouse** Hart, R.

Warlight Ondaatje, M.

Warlord chronicles [series] Cornwell, B.

WARLORDS

Bouchet, A. Breath of fire

Bouchet, A. A promise of fire

Caputo, P. Acts of faith

Farah, N. Crossbones

Farah, N. Knots

Kay, G. A brightness long ago

Rowland, L. The snow empress

WARLORDS -- JAPAN

Clavell, J. Shogun

WARLORDS -- MOGADISHU, SOMALIA

Farah, N. Links

Warning light Ricciardi, D.

The **warrior's** apprentice Bujold, L.

WARRIORS

Banks, M. Never seduce a Scot

Barker, P. The silence of the girls

Bear, E. All the windwracked stars

Bear, E. Steles of the sky

Bennett, R. City of blades

Carey, J. Starless

Chakraborty, S. The city of brass

Chakraborty, S. The empire of gold

Chakraborty, S. The kingdom of copper

Cole, K. Dreams of a dark warrior

Cornwell, B. The last kingdom

Cornwell, B. Sword of kings

Cornwell, B. War of the wolf

Couto, M. Sleepwalking land

Durst, S. The queen of blood

Feehan, C. Dark illusion

Hair, D. Scarlet tides

Ishiguro, K. The buried giant

Jin, Y. A hero born

Kirk, D. Sword of honor

Leckie, A. The Raven tower

Lin, J. The dragon and the pearl

Lyndon, R. Hawk quest

Malouf, D. Ransom

McDonald, L. The battle sylph

McLayne, A. Highland promise

Miller, M. The song of Achilles

Nicholas, D. Throne of darkness

Nicholas, D. The wicked

Showalter, G. Shadow and ice

Snipes, W. Talon of God

Tepper, S. The gate to Women's Country

Thom, J. Panther in the sky

Winter, E. The rage of dragons

WARS OF THE ROSES, 1455-1485

Gregory, P. The lady of the rivers

Gregory, P. The red queen

Penman, S. The sunne in splendour

WARSAW GHETTO UPRISING, 1943

Uris, L. Mila 18

The **Warsaw** protocol Berry, S.

WARSAW, POLAND

Berry, S. The Warsaw protocol

Skibell, J. A curable romantic

Twardoch, S. The king of Warsaw

Uris, L. Mila 18

WARSAW, POLAND -- HISTORY

Furst, A. The spies of Warsaw

The **wartime** sisters Loigman, L.

WARWICKSHIRE, ENGLAND

Waters, S. The little stranger

WASHINGTON (DC)

Meltzer, B. The inner circle

O'Brien, T. The Lincoln conspiracy

WASHINGTON (STATE)

Alexie, S. Reservation blues

Beagle, P. Summerlong

Crosbie, L. Where did you sleep last night?

Dexter, P. Spooner

Dimon, H. Her other secret

Dodd, C. Dead girl running

Dodd, C. Obsession Falls

Dodd, C. Virtue Falls

Dodd, C. What doesn't kill her

Dugoni, R. Murder one

Dugoni, R. My sister's grave

Dugoni, R. The conviction

Evison, J. Lawn boy

Evison, J. The revised fundamentals of caregiving

Fisher, T. The wives

Fowler, K. Sarah Canary

Grodstein, L. Our short history

Guterson, D. The other

Guterson, D. Our Lady of the Forest

Guterson, D. Snow falling on cedars

Hannah, K. Home front

Holbert, B. Whiskey

Jenkins, V. An unattended death

Kleypas, L. Christmas Eve at Friday Harbor

Krentz, J. Copper Beach

Marlantes, K. Deep river

Pajer, B. Capacity for murder

Pajer, B. The Edison effect

Robbins, T. Jitterbug perfume

Roberts, N. The obsession

Shalvis, J. Simply irresistible

Shalvis, J. The sweetest thing

Shields, S. The Cassandra

Stein, G. The art of racing in the rain

Straley, J. The big both ways

Trueblood, V. Seven loves

Wiggs, S. The ocean between us

Wiggs, S. The Oysterville sewing circle

Wilson, D. The Andromeda evolution

Oates, J. The falls
Waterfront Schulberg, B.
Watergate Mallon, T.
WATERGATE SCANDAL
　Mallon, T. Watergate
　Vonnegut, K. Jailbird
WATERLOO, BATTLE OF, 1815
　Mallinson, A. A close run thing
The **watermelon** king Wallace, D.
WATERMELONS -- ALABAMA
　Wallace, D. The watermelon king
Watershed Barr, M.
Watership Down Adams, R.
Watson trilogy [series] Matthiessen, P.
WATSON, EDGAR J, 1855-1910
　Matthiessen, P. Shadow country
WATTS RIOT, LOS ANGELES, CALIFORNIA, 1965
　Mosley, W. Little Scarlet
WATTS, LOS ANGELES, CALIFORNIA
　Mosley, W. Bad boy Brawly Brown
　Mosley, W. Devil in a blue dress
　Mosley, W. Fearless Jones
　Mosley, W. A red death
　Mosley, W. Six Easy pieces
WATTS, LOS ANGELES, CALIFORNIA -- HISTORY
　Mosley, W. Little Scarlet
Waverley family novels [series] Allen, S.
Waverley novels [series] Scott, W.
Waverly Place Brownmiller, S.
The **waves** Woolf, V.
Waves of freedom [series] Sundin, S.
WAX MODELLERS
　Carey, E. Little
Waxwork Lovesey, P.
WAXWORKS
　Carey, E. Little
　Truss, L. The man that got away
The **way** home Pelecanos, G.
A **way** in the world Naipaul, V.
The **way** of all flesh Parry, A.
The **way** of the coyote Kelton, E.
The **way** of the dog Savage, S.
The **way** things were Taseer, A.
The **way** through doors Ball, J.
The **way** through the woods Dexter, C.
The **way** to Bright Star Brown, D.
The **way** to paradise Vargas Llosa, M.
Wayfarers (Becky Chambers) [series] Chambers, B.
Wayfaring stranger Burke, J.
Wayfinder's story Saberhagen, F.
Ways to disappear Novey, I.
Wayward children [series] McGuire, S.
We Zamyatin, Y.
We all fall down Harvey, M.
We are all completely beside ourselves Fowler, K.
We are all completely fine Gregory, D.
We are all welcome here Berg, E.

We are not ourselves Thomas, M.
We can save us all Nemett, A.
We had it so good Grant, L.
We have always lived in the castle Jackson, S.
We hope for better things Bartels, E.
We love you, Charlie Freeman Greenidge, K.
We must be brave Liardet, F.
We need new names Bulawayo, N.
We need to talk about Kevin Shriver, L.
We that are young Taneja, P.
We the animals Torres, J.
We the living Rand, A.
We went to the woods Dolan-Leach, C.
We were kings O'Malley, T.
We were the Mulvaneys Oates, J.
We, the survivors Aw, T.
WEALTH
　Begley, L. About Schmidt
　Bender, K. Refund
　Blake, S. The guest book
　Brockway, C. The golden season
　Fowler, T. A well-behaved woman
　Gaddis, W. J R
　MacAlister, K. The truth about Leo
　Shanbhag, V. Ghachar ghochar
　Swinson, K. Lifestyles of the rich and shameless
WEAPONS
　Brown, D. The Moscow offensive
　Clark, P. The black god's drums
　Cussler, C. Final option
　Cussler, C. Nighthawk
　Cussler, C. The Pharaoh's secret
　Cussler, C. The rising sea
　Cussler, C. Shadow tyrants
　Haydon, E. The Merchant Emperor
　Higgins, J. Day of reckoning
　Kuang, R. The poppy war
　Leckie, A. Ancillary justice
　Leckie, A. Ancillary mercy
　Leckie, A. Ancillary sword
　Liu, C. Ball lightning
　Nesbit, T. The wives of Los Alamos
　Saintcrow, L. Trailer park fae
WEAPONS OF MASS DESTRUCTION
　Harkaway, N. Angelmaker
　Taylor, B. Daughter of war
WEATHER
　Butler, S. Cygnet
　Coulter, C. The devil's triangle
　Farrow, J. The storm murders
Weather Offill, J.
WEATHER CONTROL
　Putney, M. A kiss of fate
WEATHER FORECASTERS
　Parker, T. Storm runners
Weave a circle round Maaren, K.
WEAVERS

Welty, E. Stories, essays & memoir
Wench Perkins-Valdez, D.
The **werewolf** of Bamberg Potzsch, O.
WEREWOLVES
  Child, L. Full wolf moon
  Duncan, G. By blood we live
  Duncan, G. The last werewolf
  Duncan, G. Talulla rising
  Hodder, M. The strange affair of Spring Heeled Jack
  Jones, S. Mongrels
  Lamberson, G. The frenzy way
  Percy, B. Red moon
  Potzsch, O. The werewolf of Bamberg
  Pratchett, T. The fifth elephant
  Pratchett, T. Thud!
  Spear, T. A billionaire wolf for Christmas
Werner family saga [series] Plain, B.
WERNER'S SYNDROME
  Tsukiyama, G. Dreaming water
WESSEX, ENGLAND
  Hardy, T. Jude the obscure
  Hardy, T. Tess of the d'Urbervilles
West Davies, C.
WEST AFRICA
  D'Souza, T. Whiteman
  Greene, G. The heart of the matter
  Patterson, R. Eclipse
  Smith, Z. Swing time
  Thompson, T. Rosewater
  Thompson, T. The Rosewater insurrection
  Thompson, T. The Rosewater redemption
WEST AFRICANS IN FRANCE
  NDiaye, M. Three strong women
WEST BANK (JORDAN RIVER)
  Spark, M. The Mandelbaum gate
WEST BERLIN, GERMANY
  Boyne, J. A ladder to the sky
  Kennedy, D. The moment
WEST GERMANY
  Fesperman, D. Safe houses
  Hegi, U. Stones from the river
WEST HAM UNITED (SOCCER TEAM)
  Cornell, P. London falling
WEST INDIAN AMERICAN FAMILIES
  Jackson, N. The star side of Bird Hill
WEST INDIAN AMERICANS
  De Leon, A. Side chick nation
  Jackson, N. The star side of Bird Hill
  O'Neill, J. Netherland
WEST INDIAN WOMEN
  Kincaid, J. Lucy
WEST INDIANS
  Kincaid, J. Annie John
  Nunez, E. Anna in-between
WEST INDIANS IN ENGLAND
  Evaristo, B. Mr. Loverman
WEST INDIANS IN GREAT BRITAIN

Abdul-Jabbar, K. Mycroft and Sherlock
WEST INDIES
  Hilderbrand, E. What happens in paradise
  Hilderbrand, E. Winter in paradise
  Hoffman, A. The marriage of opposites
  Naipaul, V. Guerrillas
  Phillips, C. A view of the empire at sunset
  Saville, L. Henry and Rachel
  Willig, L. The summer country
WEST INDIES -- HISTORY -- 18TH CENTURY
  Gabaldon, D. Voyager
WEST INDIES -- HISTORY -- 19TH CENTURY
  Rhys, J. Wide Sargasso Sea
West of here Evison, J.
West of the Pecos Grey, Z.
WEST POINT, NEW YORK
  Bayard, L. The pale blue eye
  Jakes, J. North and South
WEST SUSSEX, ENGLAND
  Griffiths, E. The stranger diaries
  London, J. The year of living scandalously
WEST TEXAS
  Crumley, J. Bordersnakes
  McCarthy, C. All the pretty horses
WEST VIRGINIA
  Fabry, C. The promise of Jesse Woods
  FitzGerald, G. Redemption Mountain
  Gordon, J. Lord of misrule
  Keller, J. Bone on bone
  Keller, J. Fast falls the night
  Keller, J. A killing in the hills
  Keller, J. Last ragged breath
  Olmstead, R. The coldest night
  Phillips, J. Lark and Termite
  Settle, M. O Beulah land
  Whitehead, C. John Henry Days
WEST VIRGINIA -- HISTORY -- 20TH CENTURY
  Harman, P. The midwife of Hope River
WEST VIRGINIA -- RURAL CONDITIONS
  Pollock, D. The devil all the time
WEST-INDIAN WOMEN
  Kincaid, J. The autobiography of my mother
WESTCHESTER COUNTY, NEW YORK
  Pintoff, S. In the shadow of Gotham
  Pirro, J. Sly fox
Westcott novels [series] Balogh, M.
Westering women Dallas, S.
WESTERN AUSTRALIA
  Winton, T. The shepherd's hut
WESTERN AUSTRALIA -- RACE RELATIONS
  Scott, K. That deadman dance
WESTERN FRONT (WORLD WAR I)
  Boyne, J. The absolutist
  Scott, C. The poppy wife
WESTERN ROMANCES
  Bittner, R. Logan's lady
  Bonner, C. Lily

Dell, K. Fearless in Texas
Dell, K. Mistletoe in Texas
Dell, K. Reckless in Texas
Drake, L. The sweet spot
Goodman, J. In want of a wife
Goodman, J. A touch of forever
Jenkins, B. Breathless
Jenkins, B. Forbidden
Jenkins, B. Tempest
London, J. The charmer in chaps
Long, J. Hot in Hellcat Canyon
Long, J. Wild at Whiskey Creek
Phillips, S. First Lady
Phillips, S. Call me irresistible
Phillips, S. What I did for love
Ryan, J. Restless rancher
Weatherspoon, R. A cowboy to remember
Western saga (A.B. Guthrie, Jr.) [series] Guthrie, A.
Western trilogy [series] Vanderhaeghe, G.
WESTERNS
  American West
  Berger, T. Little Big Man
  Brand, M. Beyond the outposts
  Brand, M. Chinook
  Brand, M. The collected stories of Max Brand
  Brand, M. Max Brand's best western stories
  Brand, M. The Stingaree
  Brooks, B. Blood storm
  Brooks, B. Frontier justice
  Brooks, B. Winter kill
  A century of great Western stories
    Westward
  Clark, W. The ox-bow incident
  Coldsmith, D. The long journey home
  Coldsmith, D. Tallgrass
  deWitt, P. The Sisters brothers
  Dexter, P. Deadwood
  Diaz, H. In the distance
  Durham, D. Gabriel's story
  Enger, L. The high divide
  Estleman, L. The adventures of Johnny Vermillion
  Estleman, L. The master executioner
  Everett, P. God's country
  Grey, Z. Riders of the purple sage
  Grey, Z. West of the Pecos
  Grey, Z. Woman of the frontier
  Groom, W. El Paso
  Guthrie, A. The big sky
  Hansen, R. The assassination of Jesse James by the coward Robert Ford
  Harte, B. The best short stories of Bret Harte
  Hockensmith, S. Holmes on the range
  Hockensmith, S. On the wrong track
  Hulse, S. Eden mine
  Jones, D. The court-martial of George Armstrong Custer
  Keesey, A. Little century
  Kelton, E. Hard ride

Kelton, E. Texas vendetta
Kelton, E. The way of the coyote
Kent, K. The outcasts
Knott, R. Robert B. Parker's Buckskin
Kolpan, G. Magic words
L'Amour, L. Bendigo Shafter
L'Amour, L. The Californios
L'Amour, L. End of the drive
L'Amour, L. May there be a road
L'Amour, L. To the far blue mountains
Lansdale, J. Paradise sky
Leonard, E. Charlie Martz and other stories
Leonard, E. The complete Western stories of Elmore Leonard.
Leonard, E. The Hot Kid
Leonard, E. When the women come out to dance
McCarthy, C. Blood meridian, or, The evening redness in the West
McMurtry, L. Boone's Lick
McMurtry, L. Buffalo girls
McMurtry, L. Comanche moon
McMurtry, L. Dead man's walk
McMurtry, L. Lonesome Dove
McMurtry, L. Sin killer
McMurtry, L. Streets of Laredo
McMurtry, L. Zeke and Ned
Meyer, P. The son
Michener, J. Centennial
O'Brien, D. The contract surgeon
Overholser, W. Death of a cattle king
Overholser, W. Law at Angel's Landing
Parker, R. Appaloosa
Parker, R. Brimstone
Parker, R. Blue-eyed devil
Parker, R. Gunman's rhapsody
Paulits, J. Kemosabe
Portis, C. True grit
Proulx, A. Bad dirt
Proulx, A. Fine just the way it is
Richards, D. The mustanger and the lady
Richter, C. The sea of grass
Russell, M. Doc
Russell, M. Epitaph
Scapellato, J. Big lonesome
Schaefer, J. The collected stories of Jack Schaefer
Schaefer, J. Monte Walsh
Schaefer, J. Shane
Schanbacher, G. Crossing Purgatory
Smith, B. The return of Kid Cooper
Soli, T. The removes
Swarthout, G. The shootist
Thom, J. Panther in the sky
Traven, B. The treasure of the Sierra Madre
Trevanian Incident at Twenty-mile
Vanderhaeghe, G. The last crossing
Wheeler, R. The canyon of bones
Wheeler, R. North star

Wurlitzer, R. The drop edge of yonder
Zimmer, M. The long hitch
Zimmer, M. Wild side of the river

WESTINGHOUSE, GEORGE, 1846-1914
Moore, G. The last days of night

WESTMINSTER ABBEY.
Rutherfurd, E. London

Westward

WETLAND CONSERVATION
Page, K. The body in the bog

WEXFORD COUNTY, IRELAND
Toibin, C. The blackwater lightship
Toibin, C. The heather blazing

WEXFORD, IRELAND
Toibin, C. Nora Webster

The **whale** caller Mda, Z.

WHALE WATCHING
Mda, Z. The whale caller

WHALERS
Naslund, S. Ahab's wife, or, the star gazer

WHALES
Crummey, M. Galore
Mda, Z. The whale caller
Poyer, D. The whiteness of the whale
Van Meter, C. Creatures

WHALING
McGuire, I. The North water
Melville, H. Moby-Dick; or, The whale
Melville, H. Omoo
Poyer, D. The whiteness of the whale

WHALING SHIPS
Melville, H. Omoo
Poe, E. The narrative of Arthur Gordon Pym of Nantucket

What a difference a duke makes Bell, L.
What belongs to you Greenwell, G.
What belongs to you [series] Greenwell, G.
What came before he shot her George, E.
What comes my way Peterson, T.
What comes next Katzenbach, J.
What doesn't kill her Dodd, C.
What doesn't kill her Norton, C.
What ever happened to Baby Jane? Farrell, H.
What happened to Henry Pywell, S.
What happens at Christmas Alexander, V.
What happens in paradise Hilderbrand, E.
What I did for love Phillips, S.
What is left the daughter Norman, H.
What is not yours is not yours Oyeyemi, H.
What is the what Eggers, D.
What it means when a man falls from the sky Arimah, L.
What looks like crazy on an ordinary day Cleage, P.
What makes Sammy run? Schulberg, B.
What Rose forgot Barr, N.
What should be wild Fine, J.
What the dead know Lippman, L.
What the dead leave behind Simpson, R.
What the duke desires Jeffries, S.

What the duke doesn't know Ashford, J.
What to do about Annie? Criswell, M.
What was she thinking? Heller, Z.
What we become Perez-Reverte, A.
What we find Carr, R.
What we lose Clemmons, Z.
What we owe Hashemzadeh Bonde, G.
What we talk about when we talk about Anne Frank Englander, N.
What we talk about when we talk about love Carver, R.
What we were promised Tan, L.
What you break Coleman, R.
What you see Ryan, H.
What's so funny? Westlake, D.
What's the worst that could happen? Westlake, D.
Whatever happened to interracial love? Collins, K.

WHEELCHAIR USERS
Moyes, J. Me before you
Nussbaum, S. Good kings, bad kings
Robbins, T. Fierce invalids home from hot climates
Vachss, A. Two trains running

When a Scot ties the knot Dare, T.
When all is said Griffin, A.
When all the girls have gone Krentz, J.
When Beauty tamed the Beast James, E.
When Christ and his saints slept Penman, S.
When I hit you, or, A portrait of the writer as a young wife Kandasamy, M.
When in Rome Marsh, N.
When mystical creatures attack! Founds, K.
When red is black Qiu, X.
When she was good Roth, P.
When she woke Jordan, H.
When the devil drives Brookmyre, C.
When the devil's idle Serafim, L.
When the doves disappeared Oksanen, S.
When the elephants dance Holthe, T.
When the emperor was divine Otsuka, J.
When the killing's done Boyle, T.
When the legends die Borland, H.
When the marquess met his match Guhrke, L.
When the music stopped Ogilvie, E.
When the sacred ginmill closes Block, L.
When the thrill is gone Mosley, W.
When the women come out to dance Leonard, E.
When we were orphans Ishiguro, K.
When we were Romans Kneale, M.
When we were Vikings MacDonald, A.
When we were young Kingsbury, K.
When will there be good news? Atkinson, K.
When you give a duke a diamond Galen, S.
When you read this Adkins, M.
When you see me Gardner, L.
Where did you sleep last night? Crosbie, L.
Where echoes live Muller, M.
Where it hurts Coleman, R.
Where late the sweet birds sang Wilhelm, K.

Wicked Maguire, G.

The **wicked** Nicholas, D.

Wicked and the wallflower MacLean, S.

Wicked autumn Malliet, G.

Wicked city Atkins, A.

The **wicked** day Stewart, M.

Wicked deceptions [series] Shupe, J.

Wicked intentions Hoyt, E.

Wicked quills of London [series] Leigh, E.

A **wicked** way to win an earl Bradley, A.

Wicked years [series] Maguire, G.

WICKEDNESS

Maguire, G. Son of a witch

Maguire, G. Wicked

Wide Sargasso Sea Rhys, J.

The **widow** of the South Hicks, R.

Widow's walk Parker, R.

The **widower's** tale Glass, J.

WIDOWERS

Alexander, T. With this pledge

Auster, P. The book of illusions

Backman, F. A man called Ove

Baldacci, D. One summer

Baldacci, D. Redemption

Ball, J. Census

Banville, J. The sea

Barclay, L. Broken promise

Bayard, L. The pale blue eye

Begley, L. About Schmidt

Bell, S. For his pleasure

Berg, E. The story of Arthur Truluv

Blum, J. The lost family

Bradley, C. The sweetness at the bottom of the pie

Brink, A. The rights of desire

Brockmeier, K. The illumination

Burke, J. Robicheaux

Burns, O. Cold Sassy tree

Chaon, D. Ill will

Coyle, M. Yesterday's echo

Daisley, S. Coming rain

Daniel, R. Hacked

Davies, C. West

Delaney, J. The girl before

Doig, I. Ride with me, Mariah Montana

Donoghue, E. Akin

Drayson, N. A guide to the birds of East Africa

Du Maurier, D. Rebecca

Dugoni, R. The conviction

Dugoni, R. Murder one

Dunn, K. The Dragonfly

Erdrich, L. Tracks

Eskens, A. The heavens may fall

Extence, G. The universe versus Alex Woods

Flores, F. Tears of the trufflepig

Fossum, K. Bad intentions

Fossum, K. Eva's eye

Freeman, B. Goodbye to the dead

Gaiman, N. American gods

Ganshert, K. Life after

Garwood, J. The bride

Glass, J. The widower's tale

Gruber, M. The return

Haddam, J. True believers

Haruf, K. Our souls at night

Hegi, U. The vision of Emma Blau

Helprin, M. Paris in the present tense

Hill, S. The risk of darkness

Hulse, S. Black River

Iles, G. Turning angel

Irwin, S. The dead path

Jenkins, B. Tempest

Jiles, P. News of the world

Johnson, D. Train dreams

Karnezis, P. The maze

Kostova, E. The historian

Le Guin, U. The other wind

Lehane, D. Sacred

Lovesey, P. Diamond dust

Lovesey, P. The house sitter

Lovett, C. The bookman's tale

MacKenzie, S. Bedding Lord Ned

Machart, B. The wake of forgiveness

Mason, J. Three graves full

McAllister, T. The young widower's handbook

Miller, D. Norwegian by night

Moore, C. A dirty job

Morgan, S. Miracle on 5th Avenue

Murphy, S. The possessions

Norman, H. Next life might be kinder

North, A. The Whisper Man

O'Malley, T. We were kings

Ohlsson, K. The disappeared

Overholser, W. Death of a cattle king

Oz, A. The same sea

Palahniuk, C. Lullaby

Palmer, D. The new husband

Parker, T. Storm runners

Parkhurst, C. The dogs of Babel

Percy, W. The second coming

Perry, T. The old man

Plaidy, J. Murder most royal

Porter, M. Grief is the thing with feathers

Price, R. The good priest's son

Proulx, A. The shipping news

Quartey, K. The missing American

Reid, T. Forever, interrupted

Reisman, N. The first desire

Rosenfelt, D. Don't tell a soul

Ross, A. Mr. Peanut

Saintcrow, L. Trailer park fae

Sala, S. Forever my hero

Saville, L. Henry and Rachel

Scalzi, J. Old man's war

Schanbacher, G. Crossing Purgatory

L'Amour, L. Bendigo Shafter
L'Amour, L. The Californios
Lahiri, J. The lowland
Lalami, L. The other Americans
Landis, J. Heartbreak hotel
Lansdale, J. Sunset and sawdust
Lashner, W. A killer's kiss
Laukkanen, O. Deception Cove
Laurens, S. By winter's light
Lawrence, D. The rainbow
Leon, D. Drawing conclusions
Lessing, D. The sweetest dream
Letts, E. Finding Dorothy
Linden, R. Ascension of larks
Long, J. Hot in Hellcat Canyon
Long, J. Lady Derring takes a lover
Lutz, L. The passenger
Marias, J. The infatuations
McBain, E. Alice in jeopardy
McFarlane, F. The night guest
McMurtry, L. Terms of endearment
Meek, J. The people's act of love
Millet, L. Magnificence
Mistry, R. A fine balance
Mohamed, N. The orchard of lost souls
Montgomery, J. The widows
Moshfegh, O. Death in her hands
Moyes, J. The girl you left behind
Muller, M. The cavalier in white
Murdoch, I. Nuns and soldiers
Newman, J. Mary
O'Brien, E. House of splendid isolation
O'Nan, S. Emily, alone
Oates, J. The falls
Osborne, L. Only to sleep
Oz, A. Judas
Parker, R. Widow's walk
Parrish, C. Still life
Patterson, M. Rebellion
Perez-Reverte, A. The Club Dumas
Perry, S. The Essex serpent
Perry, T. Fidelity
Petrie, N. The drifter
Phillips, J. Quiet dell
Phillips, S. First Lady
Piercy, M. Sex wars
Pinter, J. Hide away
Priest, C. Dreadnought
Putney, M. A kiss of fate
Quick, A. Garden of lies
Rabb, J. Among the living
Rai, A. Wrong to need you
Raybourn, D. Silent in the grave
Rayne, S. Property of a lady
Redhill, M. Consolation
Renault, M. Funeral games
Riley, J. In pursuit of the green lion

Riley, J. The serpent garden
Robb, C. A twisted vengeance
Robertson, I. Circle of shadows
Rosenthal, P. The edge of impropriety
Ross, A. Miss Julia throws a wedding
Sala, S. Forever my hero
Sanders, L. McNally's gamble
Sanders, L. The tenth commandment
Saul, J. Midnight voices
Saums, M. Thistle & Twigg
Saunders, K. The case of the wandering scholar
Saunders, K. The secrets of Wishtide
Savage, S. Glass
Scott, J. The kept
See, C. There will never be another you
Sharfeddin, H. Mineral spirits
Sharratt, M. Daughters of the Witching Hill
Shaw, L. The network
Shipman, V. The heirloom garden
Shreve, A. The last time they met
Shreve, A. The pilot's wife
Silver, M. Mary Coin
Simenon, G. Maigret goes home
Simonson, H. Major Pettigrew's last stand
Slaughter, K. Cop Town
Smith, L. On Agate Hill
Spark, M. A far cry from Kensington
Sparks, N. The guardian
Spencer, M. Barbarous
Stabenow, D. Whisper to the blood
Stansel, I. The last cowboys of San Geronimo
Strout, E. Olive, again
Tan, A. The bonesetter's daughter
Thomas, S. Beguiling the beauty
Toibin, C. Nora Webster
Trollope, A. The Eustace diamonds
Tyler, A. Back when we were grownups
Umrigar, T. The space between us
Unger, L. Under my skin
Updike, J. The widows of Eastwick
Vanderbes, J. Easter Island
Vine, B. The minotaur
Vreeland, S. Clara and Mr. Tiffany
Waite, O. The lady's guide to celestial mechanics
Waters, S. The paying guests
Weldon, F. Worst fears
White, C. The wife and the widow
Wilder, T. Theophilus North
Winkler, A. Dog war
Wolitzer, H. Hearts
Wright, J. The house on Foster Hill
The **widows** Montgomery, J.

WIDOWS -- AUSTRALIA
Lowell, E. Pearl Cove
WIDOWS -- BALTIMORE, MARYLAND
Tyler, A. The clock winder
WIDOWS -- NORTH CAROLINA

WILDERNESS SURVIVAL

Aalborg, G. River of porcupines
Boyle, T. The Terranauts
Coben, H. The boy from the woods
Crace, J. Quarantine
Crichton, M. Micro
Dodd, C. What doesn't kill her
Fuller, C. Our endless numbered days
Golden, C. Ararat
Golding, W. Lord of the flies
Hannah, K. The great alone
Heller, P. The river
Katsu, A. The hunger
King, S. The girl who loved Tom Gordon
Koryta, M. Those who wish me dead
Krivak, A. The bear
Les Becquets, D. Breaking wild
Matheson, R. Hunted past reason
McCrumb, S. She walks these hills
Nelson, C. If we make it home
Nicholas, D. Something red
Owens, D. Where the crawdads sing
Paul, B. Under Tower Peak
Simmons, D. The Terror
Stabenow, D. Less than a treason
Stabenow, D. No fixed line
Stirling, S. Dies the fire
Vann, D. Caribou Island
Wheeler, R. The canyon of bones

WILDERNESS SURVIVAL -- ANATARCTIC REGIONS

Brockmeier, K. The brief history of the dead

WILDERNESS SURVIVAL -- SIBERIA

L'Amour, L. The last of the breed

Wildes of Lindow Castle [series] James, E.

WILDFIRE FIGHTERS

Buchman, M. Pure heat
Shalvis, J. Second chance summer

WILDFIRES

Blackstock, T. Smoke screen
Buchman, M. Pure heat
Koryta, M. Those who wish me dead

The **wilding** Percy, B.
The **wildlands** Geni, A.

WILDLIFE

Geni, A. The lightkeepers
White, B. Quite a year for plums

WILDLIFE CONSERVATION

Ghosh, A. The hungry tide

WILDLIFE REFUGES

Geni, A. The lightkeepers

WILDLIFE REFUGES -- FLORIDA

Hiaasen, C. Nature girl

WILDLIFE REFUGES -- KENYA

Drayson, N. A guide to the birds of East Africa

WILDLIFE WATCHING

Drayson, N. A guide to the birds of East Africa

Will Anderson novels [series] Johnson, D.

Will Trent series [series] Slaughter, K.
Willi Kraus novels [series] Grossman, P.

WILLIAM III, KING OF GREAT BRITAIN, 1650-1702

Plaidy, J. William's wife

William Chance [series] Finley, J.
William Monk and Hester Latterly mysteries [series] Perry, A.
William Shakespeare novels (Benet Brandreth) [series] Brandreth, B.
William Warwick novels [series] Archer, J.
William's wife Plaidy, J.

WILLIAM, OF WYKEHAM, BISHOP OF WINCHESTER, 1324-1404

Robb, C. The cross-legged knight

WILLIAM, PRINCE, DUKE OF CAMBRIDGE, 1982- AT-TEMPTED ASSASSINATION

Clancy, T. Patriot games

WILLIAMS SYNDROME

O'Connell, C. The chalk girl

WILLIAMS, BERT, 1874-1922

Phillips, C. Dancing in the dark

WILLIAMS, CATHY, B 1844

Bird, S. Daughter of a daughter of a queen

WILLIAMS, TENNESSEE, 1911-1983

Castellani, C. Leading men

WILLIAMSBURG, VIRGINIA

Frantz, L. The lacemaker

WILLIAMSON COUNTY (TENN)

Hicks, R. The widow of the South

Willie Black mysteries [series] Owen, H.
A **willing** murder Deveraux, J.
The **willow** field Kittredge, W.

WILLS

Avon, J. In peppermint peril
D'Agostino, K. The antiques
Jones, T. The better liar
Massey, S. The widows of Malabar Hill
Penny, L. Kingdom of the blind
Pyper, A. The homecoming
Rhys, R. Fatal inheritance
Robertson, M. The Baker Street translation
Sayers, D. The unpleasantness at the Bellona Club
Stabenow, D. Though not dead
Ware, R. The death of Mrs. Westaway

The **Wilshire** sun Baldwin, J.

WILSON, WOODROW, 1856-1924

Oates, J. The accursed
Vidal, G. Hollywood

WILTSHIRE, ENGLAND

Joss, M. The night following
Speller, E. The strange fate of Kitty Easton

The **wind-up** bird chronicle Murakami, H.
Windham brides [series] Burrowes, G.
Windham novels [series] Burrowes, G.
The **winds** of change Grimes, M.
The **winds** of war Wouk, H.

WINDSOR, EDWARD, DUKE OF, 1894-1972

Stein, G. The art of racing in the rain
Watts, S. No one is coming to save us
Wishing for us Landon, S.
Wisp of a thing Bledsoe, A.
The **witch** elm French, T.
WITCH HUNTING
Hawthorne, N. The house of the seven gables
Morrow, J. The last witchfinder
WITCH HUNTING -- SALEM, MASSACHUSETTS
Conde, M. I, Tituba, Black witch of Salem
The **witch** of Exmoor Drabble, M.
WITCHCRAFT
Franklin, A. Mistress of the art of death
Hayder, M. Ritual
Hayder, M. Skin
Hoffman, A. Practical magic
Hoffman, A. The rules of magic
Lowe, K. The furies
MacBride, S. Close to the bone
McCall Smith, A. Blue shoes and happiness
McKay, A. The witches of New York
Morrow, J. The last witchfinder
Olson, N. Before the devil fell
Pietroni, A. Ruby's spoon
Potzsch, O. The hangman's daughter
Scott, A. A kind of grief
Shields, K. The truth of all things
Updike, J. The witches of Eastwick
Winterson, J. The daylight gate
WITCHCRAFT -- HISTORY -- 17TH CENTURY
Sharratt, M. Daughters of the Witching Hill
WITCHCRAFT -- LANCASHIRE, ENGLAND
Sharratt, M. Daughters of the Witching Hill
WITCHCRAFT -- NEW ORLEANS, LOUISIANA
Rice, A. Merrick
Rice, A. The witching hour
WITCHCRAFT -- RITES AND CEREMONIES
Olson, N. Before the devil fell
WITCHCRAFT -- SALEM, MASSACHUSETTS
Kent, K. The heretic's daughter
WITCHCRAFT -- SALEM, MASSACHUSETTS -- HISTORY -- 17TH CENTURY
Conde, M. I, Tituba, Black witch of Salem
WITCHES
Barnhill, K. Dreadful young ladies and other stories
Beaton, M. Agatha Raisin and the witch of Wyckhadden
Brockway, C. So enchanting
Cole, K. Dreams of a dark warrior
Cornell, P. London falling
Davidson, A. The boatman's daughter
Gaiman, N. Stardust
Harkness, D. The book of life
Harkness, D. A discovery of witches
Harkness, D. Shadow of night
Hoffman, A. Practical magic
Hoffman, A. The rules of magic
Jones, D. A sudden wild magic

Joyce, G. The limits of enchantment
Lanagan, M. The brides of Rollrock Island
Maguire, G. Son of a witch
Maguire, G. Wicked
Marillier, J. Daughter of the forest
McKay, A. The witches of New York
McKillip, P. Alphabet of thorn
Miller, M. Circe
Novik, N. Uprooted
Palahniuk, C. Lullaby
Power, S. The grass dancer
Pratchett, T. Lords and ladies
Pratchett, T. Witches abroad
Pratchett, T. Wyrd sisters
Rice, A. Blood canticle
Rice, A. Merrick
Rice, A. The witching hour
Richardson, K. Greywalker
Stewart, M. The last enchantment
Stirling, S. The protector's war
WITCHES -- MASSACHUSETTS
Roberts, N. Dance upon the air
WITCHES -- RHODE ISLAND
Updike, J. The widows of Eastwick
Witches abroad Pratchett, T.
The **witches** of Eastwick Updike, J.
The **witches** of New York McKay, A.
WITCHES' APPRENTICES
McKay, A. The witches of New York
The **witching** hour Rice, A.
Witchmark Polk, C.
With love, wherever you are Mackall, D.
With our blessing Spain, J.
With this pledge Alexander, T.
Within a budding grove Proust, M.
Within the sanctuary of wings Brennan, M.
Without fail Child, L.
The **witness** Brown, S.
WITNESSES
Aaronovitch, B. Midnight riot
Adiga, A. Amnesty
Atkinson, K. One good turn
Beverly, W. Dodgers
Box, C. Wolf pack
Boylan, J. Long black veil
Collins, M. Ask not
Connelly, M. The fifth witness
Cullin, M. Undersurface
Daly, P. Clear my name
Durrow, H. The girl who fell from the sky
Flynn, G. Dark places
Grisham, J. The client
Grisham, J. The pelican brief
Hannah, S. Keep her safe
Hill Gumbao, T. The summer of dead toys
Kasischke, L. The raising
Leonard, E. Killshot

London, J. The call of the wild

Wolves eat dogs Smith, M.

The **woman** destroyed Beauvoir, S.

The **woman** in cabin ten Ware, R.

The **woman** in the dunes Abe, K.

The **woman** in the window Finn, A.

The **woman** in the woods Connolly, J.

The **woman** in white Collins, W.

A **woman** of consequence Dean, A.

A **woman** of substance Bradford, B.

Woman of the frontier Grey, Z.

Woman of the inner sea Keneally, T.

The **woman** upstairs Messud, C.

The **woman** who couldn't scream Dodd, C.

The **woman** who lost her soul Shacochis, B.

The **woman** who spoke to spirits Clare, A.

The **woman** who waited Makine, A.

The **woman** who walked into doors Doyle, R.

Woman's world Rawle, G.

WOMANIZERS

Alexander, V. The Lady Travelers Guide to scoundrels and other gentlemen

Armstrong, R. The don con

Bateman, K. This earl of mine

Bell, L. One fine duke

Boyle, E. And the miss ran away with the rake

Bradley, A. A season of ruin

Bradley, A. A wicked way to win an earl

Cabot, M. No judgments

Cole, A. A prince on paper

Dare, T. The governess game

Dare, T. Say yes to the marquess

Dare, T. The wallflower wager

Dupont, E. The American fiancee

Garriott, L. Promised

Gray, J. A duke never yields

Guhrke, L. When the marquess met his match

Jeffries, S. 'Twas the night after Christmas

Kleypas, L. Cold-hearted rake

Kleypas, L. Devil in spring

Lambdin, D. King's captain

Leigh, E. Forever your earl

London, J. The charmer in chaps

MacLean, S. One good earl deserves a lover

MacLean, S. The rogue not taken

Mishima, Y. The frolic of the beasts

Moore, E. The Supremes sing the happy heartache blues

WOMEN

Ahern, C. Roar

Balaskovits, A. Magic for unlucky girls

Beattie, A. The state we're in

Benson, E. Make way for Lucia

Bergman, M. Almost famous women

Bhuvaneswar, C. White dancing elephants

Binchy, M. Circle of friends

Bronte, A. The tenant of Wildfell Hall

Butler, O. Bloodchild

Collins, K. Notes from a black woman's diary

Conklin, T. The house girl

Conroy, P. The prince of tides

Dallas, S. The Persian Pickle Club

Dangerous women

Desai, A. Clear light of day

Desai, A. Fire on the mountain

Egan, G. Phoresis

Ellis, H. American housewife

Fine, J. What should be wild

Forster, E. Howards End

Fowles, J. The French lieutenant's woman

Fuentes, C. The years with Laura Diaz

Gainza, M. The optic nerve

Garcia, C. Dreaming in Cuban

Gaskell, E. Cranford

Gibb, C. Sweetness in the belly

Gilchrist, E. Collected stories

Gordimer, N. The pickup

Griffiths, E. The stranger diaries

Grindle, L. Villa Triste

Hardy, T. The return of the native

Hegi, U. The vision of Emma Blau

Hoffman, A. The dovekeepers

Hoffman, A. The third angel

Howland, B. Calm sea and prosperous voyage

Ishiguro, K. Never let me go

Jhabvala, R. My nine lives

Kearsley, S. A desperate fortune

Kelly, M. Lilac girls

Kerstan, L. Heart of the tiger

Kleypas, L. Secrets of a summer night

Lippman, L. Hardly knew her

Machado, C. Her body and other parties

Marren, S. A Palm Beach wife

Mehta, G. Raj

Millet, L. How the dead dream

Mitchell, M. Gone with the wind

Montimore, M. Oona out of order

Moore, C. You suck

Munro, A. Open secrets

Munro, A. Runaway

Munro, A. Selected stories

Nin, A. Cities of the interior

O'Hara, J. Butterfield 8

Ocampo, S. Forgotten journey

Otto, W. How to make an American quilt

Phillips, J. Disappearing earth

Plath, S. The bell jar

Price, R. Roxanna Slade

Rhys, J. Quartet

Richardson, C. The end of the alphabet

Roth, P. When she was good

Sexton, M. The revisioners

Shepard, S. Reputation

Shields, C. The stone diaries

Stein, G. Three lives

Maxwell, R. The wild Irish
Nicholas, D. Something red
Nicholas, D. Throne of darkness
Nicholas, D. The wicked

WOMEN -- ISTANBUL, TURKEY
Shafak, E. The bastard of Istanbul

WOMEN -- ITALY
D'Eramo, L. Deviation
Spencer, E. The southern woman

WOMEN -- ITALY -- SOCIAL CONDITIONS -- 16TH CENTURY
Dunant, S. In the company of the courtesan
Dunant, S. Sacred hearts

WOMEN -- JAMAICA
Miller, K. Augustown

WOMEN -- JAPAN
Schwartz, J. The commoner

WOMEN -- KENTUCKY
Arnow, H. The dollmaker

WOMEN -- LOUISIANA
Wells, R. Divine secrets of the Ya-Ya Sisterhood

WOMEN -- MALAYSIA
Manicka, R. The rice mother
Tan, T. The garden of evening mists

WOMEN -- MISSISSIPPI
Welty, E. The optimist's daughter

WOMEN -- MUGHAL EMPIRE
Rushdie, S. The enchantress of Florence

WOMEN -- MYTHOLOGY
MacLaughlin, N. Wake, siren

WOMEN -- NORTH CAROLINA
Gibbons, K. Charms for the easy life

WOMEN -- NORTH DAKOTA
Erdrich, L. The beet queen

WOMEN -- PERSONAL CONDUCT
Carey, M. Someone like me
McKinty, A. The chain

WOMEN -- PHILADELPHIA, PENNSYLVANIA
Holmes, S. Bad girlz

WOMEN -- POLITICAL ACTIVITY
Lessing, D. A ripple from the storm

WOMEN -- PSYCHOLOGY
Acevedo, C. The distant marvels
Bauer, A. The forever marriage
Blundell, J. The high season
Butland, S. The lost for words bookshop
Center, K. Things you save in a fire
Chanter, C. The well
De Robertis, C. Cantoras
Emezi, A. Freshwater
Frame, R. Havisham
Gage, E. The ladies of Managua
Gay, R. Difficult women
Hendricks, G. An anonymous girl
Jackson, J. Never have I ever
Levy, D. Swimming home
McKenzie, E. The portable Veblen

Pochoda, I. These women
Schwartz, J. The red daughter
Spark, M. The driver's seat
Stridsberg, S. Valerie
Weldon, F. The life and loves of a she-devil

WOMEN -- PUERTO RICO
Price, R. Freedomland

WOMEN -- RELIGIOUS LIFE
Turner, B. The secret life of Sarah Hollenbeck

WOMEN -- SAUDI ARABIA
Ferraris, Z. Finding Nouf

WOMEN -- SEXUALITY
Alther, L. Kinflicks
Amado, J. Dona Flor and her two husbands
Broder, M. The pisces
Lawrence, D. Women in love
Murdoch, I. The bell
Rashan, N. You make me wanna
Thomas, D. The white hotel
Walsh, H. Brass

WOMEN -- SOCIAL CONDITIONS
Alderman, N. The power
Alexander, V. The Magdalen girls
Bronte, A. The tenant of Wildfell Hall
Donati, S. Where the light enters
Goss, T. The sinister mystery of the mesmerizing girl
Kibler, J. Home for erring and outcast girls
Shafak, E. 10 minutes 38 seconds in this strange world
Zevin, G. Young Jane Young

WOMEN -- SOCIAL CONDITIONS -- 19TH CENTURY
Franklin, M. My brilliant career
Galsworthy, J. The Forsyte saga
Zola, E. Nana

WOMEN -- SOCIAL CONDITIONS -- 20TH CENTURY
Joinson, S. A lady cyclist's guide to Kashgar

WOMEN -- SOCIAL LIFE AND CUSTOMS
Evaristo, B. Girl, woman, other

WOMEN -- SOMALIA
Mohamed, N. The orchard of lost souls

WOMEN -- SOUTH AMERICA
Allende, I. Eva Luna

WOMEN -- SOUTHERN STATES
Hauck, R. Once upon a prince
Johnson, C. Treeborne
Spencer, E. The southern woman

WOMEN -- SOVIET UNION
Fleming, I. From Russia with love

WOMEN -- SPAIN
Merimee, P. Carmen

WOMEN -- SPIRITUAL LIFE
Arnoult, D. Sufficient grace
Gilbert, E. The signature of all things
Twain, M. Personal recollections of Joan of Arc

WOMEN -- TEXAS
Dos Passos, J. 1919

WOMEN -- VIRGINIA
Smith, L. Fair and tender ladies

Page, K. The body in the wake
Perkins, S. Murder once removed
Perry, A. Death in focus
Persson, L. The dying detective
Peters, E. Children of the storm
Peters, E. The golden one
Peters, E. Guardian of the horizon
Peters, E. He shall thunder in the sky
Peters, E. The hippopotamus pool
Peters, E. The last camel died at noon
Peters, E. Night train to Memphis
Peters, E. Seeing a large cat
Peters, E. The snake, the crocodile, and the dog
Peters, E. Trojan gold
Quick, A. Crystal gardens
Quick, A. The mystery woman
Racculia, K. Tuesday Mooney talks to ghosts
Rader-Day, L. Little pretty things
Raichev, R. Assassins at Ospreys
Raybourn, D. A dangerous collaboration
Raybourn, D. A murderous relation
Raybourn, D. A perilous undertaking
Raybourn, D. A treacherous
Read, C. The crazy school
Read, C. Invisible boy
Read, C. Valley of ashes
Rich, V. The baked bean supper murders
Rich, V. The cooking school murders
Rich, V. The Nantucket diet murders
Robb, C. A murdered peace
Robb, C. A twisted vengeance
Roberts, G. Adam and evil
Roberts, G. The bluest blood
Robertson, I. Anatomy of murder
Robertson, I. Circle of shadows
Robertson, I. Instruments of darkness
Robertson, I. Island of bones
Ross, A. Miss Julia delivers the goods
Ross, A. Miss Julia takes the wheel
Ross, A. Miss Julia throws a wedding
Royal, P. Covenant with hell
Royal, P. Sanctity of hate
Royal, P. Satan's lullaby
Ryan, H. The other woman
Ryan, H. Truth be told
Ryan, H. The wrong girl
Saums, M. Thistle & Twigg
Shaw, M. Murder at the mill
Shelton, P. Thin ice
Simon, C. Dogs don't lie
Simon, C. Panthers play for keeps
Simon, M. Cremains of the day
Simpson, R. Let the dead keep their secrets
Simpson, R. What the dead leave behind
Spencer-Fleming, J. All mortal flesh
Spencer-Fleming, J. I shall not want
Spencer-Fleming, J. In the bleak midwinter

Tokarczuk, O. Drive your plow over the bones of the dead

WOMEN AMATEUR DETECTIVES -- SOUTH CAROLINA
Hart, C. Death walked in
WOMEN AMBULANCE DRIVERS
Nicholson, W. Motherland
Waters, S. The night watch
WOMEN AND ART
Munoz Molina, A. In her absence
WOMEN AND BIRDS
Simon, C. Panthers play for keeps
WOMEN AND CATS
Barbery, M. The elegance of the hedgehog
Simon, C. Dogs don't lie
Simon, C. Grey dawn
Simon, C. Panthers play for keeps
Simon, C. Stages of Grey
WOMEN AND DOGS
Koontz, D. The darkest evening of the year
Mizushima, M. Burning ridge
Mizushima, M. Killing trail
Mizushima, M. Stalking ground
Nunez, S. The friend
Parker, R. Melancholy baby
Stabenow, D. Less than a treason
Winkler, A. Dog war
Woods, S. Orchid beach
WOMEN AND HORSES
Roberts, N. Dark witch
WOMEN AND NATURE
Griffith, N. Hild
Harman, P. The midwife of Hope River
Powers, R. The overstory
Watson, B. Miss Jane
WOMEN AND POLITICS
Didion, J. A book of common prayer
Quinn, K. Ribbons of scarlet
WOMEN AND SUCCESS
Avery, E. The last nude
Loigman, L. The wartime sisters
WOMEN AND THE MILITARY
Dees, C. Beyond the limit
WOMEN AND THE SEA
Powning, B. The sea captain's wife
WOMEN AND WAR
Barker, P. The silence of the girls
Benedict, H. Wolf season
Bowen, R. The victory garden
Dees, C. Beyond the limit
Demirtas, S. Dawn
Epstein, J. Wunderland
Faulks, S. Paris echo
Harris, C. Good time coming
Hicks, R. The widow of the South
Jenoff, P. The lost girls of Paris
Kelly, J. The light over London
Lee, J. The starlet and the spy

Sandford, J. Certain prey

WOMEN ASSISTANT DISTRICT ATTORNEYS

Fairstein, L. Blood oath

Kellerman, J. The genius

Patterson, J. 1st to die

Pirro, J. Sly fox

WOMEN ASTRONAUTS

Chambers, B. To be taught, if fortunate

Kowal, M. The calculating stars

Kowal, M. The fated sky

Lethem, J. Chronic city

Nichols, L. Vessel

Swyler, E. Light from other stars

WOMEN ASTRONOMERS

Sagan, C. Contact

WOMEN ATHLETES

Lohmann, J. Winning Ruby Heart

WOMEN AUTHORS

Atwood, M. The blind assassin

Awad, M. Bunny

Baker, J. The body lies

Bergman, M. Almost famous women

Bohjalian, C. Secrets of Eden

Bowman, V. Secrets of a wedding night

Brookner, A. Hotel Du Lac

Byatt, A. The children's book

Carpenter, E. The weight of lies

Coetzee, J. Elizabeth Costello

Coetzee, J. Slow man

Cusk, R. Kudos

Deveraux, J. A willing murder

Dodd, C. Because I'm watching

Doiron, P. Stay hidden

Drabble, M. The witch of Exmoor

Ellis, D. In the company of liars

Ferrante, E. The story of a new name

Ferrante, E. The story of the lost child

Ferrante, E. Those who leave and those who stay

Flanery, P. Absolution

Freeman, B. Thief River Falls

Godwin, G. Flora

Guillory, J. The proposal

James, E. Four nights with the duke

Jewett, S. The country of the pointed firs and other stories

Jin, H. The boat rocker

Kandasamy, M. When I hit you, or, A portrait of the writer as a young wife

Kellerman, J. The clinic

Kennedy, D. The big picture

Kidd, S. The book of longings

King, L. Writers & lovers

Kirshenbaum, B. Rabbits for food

Krauss, N. Forest Dark

Lackberg, C. The hidden child

Lackberg, C. The ice princess

Lauren, C. Roomies

Lessing, D. The golden notebook

Moore, K. Sexy Lexy

Moriarty, L. Nine perfect strangers

Morrow, J. The last witchfinder

Naslund, S. The fountain of St. James Court

Ocampo, S. The promise

Ozeki, R. A tale for the time being

Parker, R. Shrink rap

Phillips, C. A view of the empire at sunset

Preston, C. The scrapbook of Frankie Pratt

Raichev, R. Assassins at Ospreys

Robinson, P. The first cut

Rosenthal, P. The edge of impropriety

Rowland, L. Bedlam

Rowland, L. The secret adventures of Charlotte Bronte

Setterfield, D. The thirteenth tale

Shaffer, M. The Guernsey Literary and Potato Peel Pie Society

Shelton, P. Thin ice

Shields, C. Unless

Shumway, C. Ten girls to watch

Smith, J. If she were dead

Spencer, S. Man in the woods

Strout, E. My name is Lucy Barton

Truong, M. The book of salt, Monique Truong.

Turner, B. The secret life of Sarah Hollenbeck

Vine, B. The House of Stairs

Ware, R. In a dark, dark wood

Watson, S. Before I go to sleep

Weldon, F. Chalcot Crescent

Zapata, M. The lost book of Adana Moreau

WOMEN AUTHORS -- 19TH CENTURY

Michaels, B. Houses of stone

WOMEN AUTHORS -- MAINE

Ogilvie, E. When the music stopped

WOMEN AUTHORS, AMERICAN

Plath, S. The bell jar

WOMEN AUTHORS, ENGLISH

Ellis, B. The vanished bride

WOMEN AUTHORS, ENGLISH -- 14TH CENTURY

Riley, J. A vision of light

WOMEN AUTHORS, ENGLISH -- 20TH CENTURY

Cunningham, M. The hours

WOMEN BAIL BOND AGENTS

Evanovich, J. Look alive twenty-five

Evanovich, J. One for the money

Evanovich, J. Turbo twenty-three

WOMEN BAKERS

Devon, C. Sleeping with the entity

Glass, J. The whole world over

Mallery, S. Best of my love

Stradal, J. The lager queen of Minnesota

WOMEN BALLET DANCERS

Roorbach, B. Life among giants

WOMEN BANKERS

Campbell, A. On the floor

Campbell, B. Brothers and sisters

Handke, P. Crossing the Sierra de Gredos

Lauren, C. Sweet filthy boy
Pintoff, S. In the shadow of Gotham
Robinson, P. The first cut
Shumway, C. Ten girls to watch
Waldman, A. A door in the earth

WOMEN COLLEGE STUDENTS
Alther, L. Kinflicks
Amidon, S. Security
Bardugo, L. Ninth house
Batuman, E. The idiot
Bell, S. At his mercy
Bohjalian, C. The double bind
Bolano, R. Amulet
Braffet, K. Last seen leaving
Brown, K. The clairvoyants
Carpenter, E. Until the day I die
Castile, Z. Flashed
Dean, P. Tam Lin
Dunmore, E. Bringing down the duke
Kellerman, J. Private eyes
Kelly, E. The poison tree
McLaughlin, E. The nanny diaries
Norton, C. What doesn't kill her
Nunez, S. The last of her kind
Parker, R. Melancholy baby
Plath, S. The bell jar
Rooney, S. Conversations with friends
Roth, P. The dying animal
Steiner, S. Missing, presumed
Umrigar, T. The space between us
Walsh, H. Brass
Weinberg, K. The truants
Willis, C. Doomsday book
Wolfe, T. I am Charlotte Simmons
Yoshimoto, B. Goodbye Tsugumi

WOMEN COLLEGE STUDENTS -- JAPAN
Murakami, H. After dark

WOMEN COLLEGE TEACHERS
Allende, I. In the midst of winter
Bear, E. Blood and iron
Boswell, R. Century's son
Byatt, A. Possession
Fortier, A. The lost sisterhood
Gaspar de Alba, A. Desert blood
Hewson, D. A season for the dead
Johnson, K. The dream-quest of Vellitt Boe
Johnson, M. Smitten by the Brit
Loren, R. The one you fight for
McKinlay, J. The good ones
Oates, J. Marya
Rader-Day, L. The black hour
Robinson, R. Cost
Sayers, D. Gaudy night
Weinberg, K. The truants

WOMEN COLUMNISTS
Guhrke, L. The truth about love and dukes
Johnston, W. The colony of unrequited dreams

WOMEN COMPOSERS
Bledsoe, L. The big bang symphony

WOMEN COMPUTER PROGRAMMERS
Rockaway, K. How to hack a heartbreak
Tracy, P. Monkeewrench

WOMEN COMPUTER SCIENTISTS
Gladstone, M. Empress of forever

WOMEN CONCENTRATION CAMP SURVIVORS
Turow, S. Ordinary heroes

WOMEN COOKS
Abu-Jaber, D. Crescent
Amado, J. Gabriela, clove and cinnamon
Bauermeister, E. The school of essential ingredients
Bledsoe, L. The big bang symphony
Buchman, M. The night is mine
Bybee, C. Staying for good
Davidson, D. Killer pancake
Davidson, D. The last suppers
Glass, J. The whole world over
Jenkins, B. Forbidden
Keane, M. Fever
Laureano, C. The Saturday Night Supper Club
Lim, R. Natalie Tan's book of luck and fortune
Lipman, E. The inn at Lake Devine
McCall Smith, A. Blue shoes and happiness
Rich, V. The baked bean supper murders
Rich, V. The cooking school murders
Rich, V. The Nantucket diet murders
Weatherspoon, R. A cowboy to remember
Wiggs, S. The beekeeper's ball

WOMEN COOKS -- MEXICO
Esquivel, L. Like water for chocolate

WOMEN CORONERS
Cornwell, P. Chaos
Cornwell, P. Postmortem
Patterson, J. 1st to die
Slaughter, K. Fallen
Slaughter, K. The last widow

WOMEN COUSINS
Wharton, E. Ethan Frome

WOMEN CRIME VICTIMS
Bohjalian, C. The double bind
Lippman, L. I'd know you anywhere

WOMEN CRIMINALS
Abbott, M. Queenpin
Burns, A. Little constructions
Davidson, A. The boatman's daughter
Hill, N. The nix
Speight, S. The pleasure of pain
Watkins, J. Secrets of a side bitch 2

WOMEN CRYPTOGRAPHERS
Brown, D. The Da Vinci code

WOMEN CULT LEADERS -- TEXAS
Reichs, K. Death du jour

WOMEN DANCERS
Brayden, M. First position

WOMEN DEATH ROW PRISONERS

Ohlsson, K. Silenced
Ohlsson, K. Unwanted
Palmer, M. The society
Parker, T. Black water
Parker, T. The blue hour
Patterson, J. 1st to die
Pava, S. Personae
Pears, I. The immaculate deception
Pears, I. The last judgement
Perry, A. Belgrave Square
Perry, A. Bethlehem Road
Perry, A. Bluegate Fields
Perry, A. Buckingham Palace gardens
Perry, A. Cardington Crescent
Perry, A. Death on Blackheath
Perry, A. Half Moon Street
Perry, A. Highgate Rise
Perry, A. The Hyde Park headsman
Perry, A. Midnight at Marble Arch
Perry, A. Paragon Walk
Perry, A. Pentecost Alley
Perry, A. Resurrection Row
Perry, A. Seven Dials
Perry, A. Southampton Row
Perry, A. Traitors Gate
Perry, A. The Whitechapel conspiracy
Perry, T. Dead aim
Peters, E. The deeds of the disturber
Peters, E. The mummy case
Phillips, C. Unthinkable
Potenza, C. Hearts of the missing
Redondo, D. The invisible guardian
Rich, V. The baked bean supper murders
Rich, V. The cooking school murders
Rich, V. The Nantucket diet murders
Ripley, N. Find you in the dark
Ritter, T. Devil's night
Robb, J. Fantasy in death
Robb, J. Innocent in death
Robb, J. Naked in death
Rodriguez, L. Every broken trust
Rodriguez, L. Every hidden fear
Roosevelt, E. The Hyde Park murder
Roosevelt, E. Murder and the First Lady
Roosevelt, E. Murder at midnight
Roosevelt, E. Murder at the palace
Ruiz Zafon, C. The labyrinth of the spirits
Salvalaggio, K. Bone dust white
Scoppettone, S. Too darn hot
Smith, J. 82 Desire
Smith, J. Mean woman blues
Spencer, S. A dying fall
Steiner, S. Missing, presumed
Steiner, S. Persons unknown
Tursten, H. Hunting game
Tursten, H. Winter grave
Wambaugh, J. Finnegan's week

Whittle, T. The dangerous edge of things
Williams, A. The stranger you seek
WOMEN DETECTIVES -- ARKANSAS
Hess, J. Maggody and the moonbeams
WOMEN DETECTIVES -- GREAT BRITAIN
Fforde, J. Lost in a good book
WOMEN DETECTIVES -- MICHIGAN
Dolan, H. Bad things happen
WOMEN DETECTIVES -- NEW ORLEANS, LOUISIANA
Smith, J. Crescent City kill
Smith, J. House of blues
Smith, J. Jazz funeral
Smith, J. The kindness of strangers
Smith, J. New Orleans beat
WOMEN DETECTIVES -- SAUDI ARABIA
Ferraris, Z. Kingdom of strangers
WOMEN DETECTIVES -- WASHINGTON, D.C.
Roosevelt, E. Murder in the Blue Room
Roosevelt, E. Murder in the map room
Roosevelt, E. Murder in the Oval Office
Roosevelt, E. Murder in the Rose Garden
Roosevelt, E. The White House pantry murder
WOMEN DETECTIVES -- YORKSHIRE, ENGLAND
Robinson, P. Playing with fire
Robinson, P. Strange affair
WOMEN DIPLOMATS
Martine, A. A memory called empire
WOMEN DISTRICT ATTORNEYS
Lippman, L. Wilde Lake
WOMEN DIVERS
Hayder, M. Ritual
See, L. The island of sea women
WOMEN DOCUMENTARY FILMMAKERS
Muller, M. A walk through the fire
WOMEN DOG TRAINERS -- BALTIMORE, MARYLAND
Tyler, A. The accidental tourist
WOMEN DOMESTICS -- NETHERLANDS
Chevalier, T. Girl with a pearl earring
WOMEN DRAMATISTS
Bausch, R. Hello to the cannibals
Leigh, E. Scandal takes the stage
Lessing, D. Love, again
Woolf, V. Between the acts
WOMEN DRIFTERS
Braffet, K. Last seen leaving
WOMEN DRUG ABUSERS
Coben, H. Run away
Moore, L. Long bright river
Ward, J. Sing, unburied, sing
WOMEN DRUG DEALERS
Stringer, V. Let that be the reason
Turner, N. A hustler's wife
WOMEN DRUG ENFORCEMENT AGENTS
Child, L. Persuader
WOMEN EDITORS
Anderson, A. The summer guest
Carey, P. My life as a fake

McCrumb, S. If ever I return, pretty Peggy-O

WOMEN FOLKLORISTS

Shields, C. The republic of love

Stern, S. The Pinch

WOMEN FOREIGN CORRESPONDENTS

Ward, A. Forgive me

WOMEN FORENSIC ANTHROPOLOGISTS

Ondaatje, M. Anil's ghost

Reichs, K. 206 Bones

Reichs, K. Bones of the lost

Reichs, K. Bones to ashes

Reichs, K. Break no bones

Reichs, K. A conspiracy of bones

Reichs, K. Deadly decisions

Reichs, K. Death du jour

Reichs, K. Deja dead

Reichs, K. Grave secrets

Reichs, K. Monday mourning

WOMEN FORENSIC ANTHROPOLOGISTS -- NORTH CAROLINA

Reichs, K. Bare bones

WOMEN FORENSIC ANTHROPOLOGISTS -- VIRGINIA

McCrumb, S. If I'd killed him when I met him

WOMEN FORENSIC PATHOLOGISTS

Cornwell, P. Chaos

Cornwell, P. Postmortem

Franklin, A. The serpent's tale

Gerritsen, T. The bone garden

WOMEN FORENSIC PSYCHIATRISTS

Daniels, N. Too close

Gardiner, M. The Dirty Secrets Club

WOMEN FORENSIC PSYCHOLOGISTS

Black, L. Let justice descend

Black, L. Suffer the children

O'Connell, C. Judas child

WOMEN FORENSIC SCIENTISTS

Abu-Jaber, D. Origin

Black, L. That darkness

Estleman, L. Frames

Gerritsen, T. The bone garden

Reichs, K. Bones to ashes

WOMEN FORMER CONVICTS

Jordan, H. When she woke

Novak, B. This heart of mine

Sandlin, L. The bird boys

WOMEN FREED SLAVES

Hill, L. Someone knows my name

WOMEN FUGITIVES

Faye, L. The Paragon Hotel

Flanagan, R. The unknown terrorist

Frazier, C. Varina

Isaacs, S. After all these years

Lutz, L. The passenger

Roth, P. American pastoral

Shannon, S. The mime order

WOMEN GAMBLERS

Bowen, K. Between the devil and the duke

WOMEN GARDENERS

Albert, S. The Darling Dahlias and the cucumber tree

Kane, J. Rules for visiting

WOMEN GARDENERS -- CALIFORNIA

Mapson, J. Bad Girl Creek

WOMEN GENEALOGISTS

Perkins, S. Murder once removed

WOMEN GENERALS

Marshall, A. A crown for cold silver

WOMEN GEOLOGISTS

Bledsoe, L. The big bang symphony

Dodd, C. Virtue Falls

WOMEN GHOSTWRITERS

Tan, A. The bonesetter's daughter

WOMEN GLASS ARTISTS

Vreeland, S. Clara and Mr. Tiffany

WOMEN GOLFERS

Lipman, E. The dearly departed, Elinor Lipman.

WOMEN GRADUATE STUDENTS

Awad, M. Bunny

Carlino, R. Swear on this life

Cole, A. A princess in theory

Davies, R. The rebel angels

French, M. The women's room

Hill, R. The stranger house

Lee, D. Country of origin

Shamsie, K. Home fire

Simon, C. Grey dawn

Simon, C. Stages of Grey

Whelan, J. My Oxford year

Willig, L. The betrayal of the blood lily

Willig, L. The deception of the emerald ring

Willig, L. The masque of the Black Tulip

Willig, L. The secret history of the Pink Carnation

Willig, L. The seduction of the Crimson Rose

Willig, L. The temptation of the night jasmine

WOMEN HACKERS

Doctorow, C. Radicalized

WOMEN HEALERS

Atakora, A. Conjure women

Brown, T. Gods of Howl Mountain

Gibbons, K. Charms for the easy life

Gregory, P. Tidelands

Nicholas, D. Something red

Nicholas, D. The wicked

Odell, J. The healing

Putney, M. The marriage spell

Riley, J. A vision of light

Urrea, L. The hummingbird's daughter

Urrea, L. Queen of America

WOMEN HEART SURGEONS

Gerritsen, T. The surgeon

WOMEN HERBALISTS

Joyce, G. The limits of enchantment

WOMEN HEROIN ADDICTS

Robinson, P. Playing with fire

Fields, H. Last Chance Llama Ranch
Flynn, G. Sharp objects
Greenwood, K. Unnatural habits
Hart, C. Letter from home
Hart, C. Resort to murder
Harvey, J. Gone to ground
Hauck, R. How to catch a prince
Hood, A. The obituary writer
Ignatius, D. The sun king
Irvin, K. Tell her no lies
James, P. The private patient
Lessing, D. The sweetest dream
Lourey, J. January thaw
McDermid, V. A place of execution
McLain, P. Love and ruin
Meuleman, S. Find me gone
Mina, D. The dead hour
Mina, D. Field of blood
Mina, D. Slip of the knife
Murphy, T. Correspondents
O'Donovan, G. Dublin dead
Patterson, J. 1st to die
Patterson, R. Balance of power
Phillips, J. Quiet dell
Price, R. Freedomland
Quick, A. The girl who knew too much
Read, C. The crazy school
Read, C. Invisible boy
Read, C. Valley of ashes
Rooney, S. Conversations with friends
Rose, M. Cartier's hope
Rosnay, T. Sarah's key
Ryan, H. The other woman
Ryan, H. Say no more
Ryan, H. Truth be told
Ryan, H. What you see
Ryan, H. The wrong girl
Schine, C. The Grammarians
Smith, M. The Siberian dilemma
Smith, M. Tatiana
Solomon, B. The attempted murder of Teddy Roosevelt
Spencer, S. A dying fall
St. James, S. The broken girls
Unger, L. The stranger inside
Ward, A. Forgive me
Weiner, J. Good in bed
Williams, B. The golden hour
Winspear, J. The American agent
Yellin, J. Savage news

WOMEN JOURNALISTS -- NEW ORLEANS, LOUISIANA
Castro, J. Hell or high water

WOMEN JUDGES
Finder, J. Judgment
Mankell, H. The man from Beijing
Maron, M. Bootlegger's daughter
Maron, M. High country fall

Maron, M. Shooting at loons
McEwan, I. The children act
Picoult, J. Nineteen minutes

WOMEN JUDGES -- NORTH CAROLINA
Maron, M. Storm track
Maron, M. Uncommon clay
Maron, M. Up jumps the Devil

WOMEN JUDGES -- ORANGE COUNTY, CALIFORNIA
Rosenberg, N. Interest of justice

WOMEN JURORS
Jackson, B. Forged in desire

WOMEN KIDNAPPING VICTIMS
Brown, S. Fat Tuesday
Chase, L. Don't tempt me
Child, L. The hard way
Coulter, C. Labyrinth
Cumming, C. A foreign country
Everett, P. God's country
Gay, R. An untamed state
Gerritsen, T. The apprentice
Katzenbach, J. What comes next
Koontz, D. The husband
Naslund, B. Blood of an exile
Nicholson, G. The city under the skin
Norton, C. What doesn't kill her
O'Brien, E. Girl
Palmer, M. The fifth vial
Pronzini, B. Nightcrawlers
Rollins, J. Crucible
Sandford, J. Mind prey
Shelton, P. Thin ice
Street, K. Edgar Allan Poe and the jewel of Peru

WOMEN LABOR LEADERS
Russell, M. The women of the copper country

WOMEN LABOR ORGANIZERS
Straley, J. The big both ways
Vargas Llosa, M. The way to paradise

WOMEN LACE MAKERS
Moore, S. The life of objects

WOMEN LANDOWNERS
Mosher, H. On Kingdom Mountain

WOMEN LAW STUDENTS
Estleman, L. Frames
Grisham, J. The pelican brief

WOMEN LAW TEACHERS
Longworth, M. Death at the Chateau Bremont
Longworth, M. Murder in the Rue Dumas

WOMEN LAWYERS
Baker, C. Whisper network
Barry, D. Insane city
Blackstock, T. Catching Christmas
Brown, S. The witness
Castille, S. In your corner
Celello, E. Leaning to stay
Clark, M. Blood defense
Clark, M. Final judgment
Coben, H. The boy from the woods

WOMEN MURDER SUSPECTS

Berry, C. A legacy of murder
Brookmyre, C. Black widow
Brooks, B. Winter kill
Brown, S. Ricochet
Coben, H. Long lost
Ellis, D. In the company of liars
Force, M. Deceived by desire
Freeman, B. Goodbye to the dead
Gardner, L. Never tell
Gruber, M. Valley of bones
Hambly, B. Lady of perdition
Hurston, Z. Their eyes were watching God
Ide, J. Hi five
Kerstan, L. Heart of the tiger
Lippman, L. Hardly knew her
Miranda, M. The last house guest
Moore, K. To seduce an angel
Neubauer, E. Murder at the Mena House
Parker, R. Widow's walk
Putnam, J. These honored dead
Robb, J. Innocent in death
Sayers, D. Strong poison
Scottoline, L. Legal tender
Soule, M. The crows
Spann, S. Claws of the cat
Stewart, A. Kopp sisters on the march
Ware, R. The turn of the key

WOMEN MURDER VICTIMS

Albert, S. The Darling Dahlias and the cucumber tree
Atkinson, K. Started early, took my dog
Barnes, K. In the kingdom of men
Bauer, B. The beautiful dead
Block, L. The burglar in the closet
Block, L. Eight million ways to die
Black, L. That darkness
Block, L. When the sacred ginmill closes
Bolton, S. Now you see me
Braun, L. The cat who ate Danish modern
Brundage, E. All things cease to appear
Burke, J. The New Iberia blues
Cameron, W. Repo madness
Child, L. The affair
Clark, M. The Jezebel remedy
Cleeves, A. The crow trap
Connolly, J. A book of bones
Connolly, J. The woman in the woods
Cornwell, P. Postmortem
Cussler, C. The cutthroat
Daugherty, C. A beautiful corpse
Dean, A. Bellfield Hall
Delaney, J. Believe me
Deon, N. Grace
Dexter, C. The remorseful day
Dodd, C. Dead girl running
Doiron, P. Stay hidden
Dow, D. Confessions of an innocent man

Downie, R. Medicus
Fleming, I. Goldfinger
Frear, C. Stone cold heart
Fredericks, M. Death of a new American
French, T. The likeness
Gardiner, M. Into the black nowhere
Gerritsen, T. The bone garden
Gerritsen, T. The shape of night
Hamill, P. Tabloid city
Harris, T. Hannibal
Harris, T. The silence of the lambs
Higgins, J. Day of reckoning
Hilderbrand, E. The perfect couple
Hill, S. The shadows in the street
Horan, N. Loving Frank
Kaminsky, S. Dancing in the dark
Kepler, L. Stalker
Khan, A. Among the ruins
Kroese, R. The last iota
LaPlante, A. Turn of mind
Lackberg, C. The ice princess
Lackberg, C. The preacher
Larsson, A. Until thy wrath be past
Lippman, L. After I'm gone
Lovesey, P. Skeleton Hill
MacDonald, J. The green ripper
Malliet, G. A fatal winter
Malliet, G. Wicked autumn
Mamet, D. Chicago
McMahon, J. The one I left behind
McPherson, C. A step so grave
Mizushima, M. Stalking ground
Moor, J. The keeper
Mosby, S. You can run
Moshfegh, O. Death in her hands
Mosley, W. White butterfly
Muller, M. Point Deception
Neubauer, E. Murder at the Mena House
Nickson, C. Come the fear
Parker, R. Chance
Parker, R. Paper doll
Parker, R. Sixkill
Parker, R. Small vices
Parker, T. California girl
Parry, A. The way of all flesh
Peters, E. The potter's field
Peterson, J. Early's fall
Pintoff, S. In the shadow of Gotham
Pronzini, B. A wasteland of strangers
Putnam, J. These honored dead
Ragnar Jonasson, 1. The island
Raimondo, L. Dante's wood
Rankin, I. Rather be the devil
Reichs, K. Deja dead
Reichs, K. Grave secrets
Rice, L. Last day
Robb, J. Naked in death

Robinson, P. Friend of the devil
Robotham, M. Good girl, bad girl
Roosevelt, E. Murder in the Blue Room
Rose, J. The blackest bird
Rossner, J. Looking for Mr. Goodbar
Rowland, L. The incense game
Rowland, L. The Ripper's shadow
Rowland, L. The secret adventures of Charlotte Bronte
Rubenfeld, J. The interpretation of murder
Scerbanenco, G. A private Venus
Sharfeddin, H. Mineral spirits
Shreve, A. The weight of water
Sjowall, M. The man on the balcony
Smith, M. Three stations
Spain, J. With our blessing
Spencer, S. Backlash
Spencer-Fleming, J. Hid from our eyes
Spencer-Fleming, J. In the bleak midwinter
Stabenow, D. A deeper sleep
Suskind, P. Perfume
Tracy, P. Ice cold heart
Turton, S. The 7 1
Whittle, T. The dangerous edge of things
Wright, J. The house on Foster Hill
Yap, F. Yesterday

WOMEN MURDER VICTIMS -- CHESAPEAKE BAY RE-GION
Gear, K. People of the mist
WOMEN MURDER WITNESSES
Foster, L. Run the risk
Koontz, D. Intensity
Leonard, E. Mr. Paradise
WOMEN MURDERERS
Adler-Olsen, J. The scarred woman
Atkinson, K. Case histories
Atwood, M. Alias Grace
Donoghue, E. Slammerkin
Faye, L. Jane Steele
Fitch, J. White oleander
Fox, C. Gone by midnight
Hansen, R. A wild surge of guilty passion
Kent, H. Burial rites
King, S. Dolores Claiborne
Kushner, R. The Mars room
Nunez, S. The last of her kind
Purcell, L. The silent companions
Raimondo, L. Dante's dilemma
Richler, N. Your mouth is lovely
Ruskovich, E. Idaho
Sanders, L. The third deadly sin
Scott, W. The bride of Lammermoor
Styles, T. A hustler's son
Swanson, P. The kind worth killing
Toibin, C. House of names
WOMEN MURDERERS -- NORTH CAROLINA
McCrumb, S. The ballad of Frankie Silver
WOMEN MUSEUM CURATORS

Grenville, K. The idea of perfection
Peters, E. Night train to Memphis
WOMEN MUSICIANS
Alexander, T. A note yet unsung
Bergman, M. Almost famous women
Creech, S. The whole way home
Jewell, L. The family upstairs
McBain, E. The frumious bandersnatch
McEwan, I. On Chesil Beach
McLaren, K. The road to enchantment
Pinsker, S. A song for a new day
Quinn, J. The secrets of Sir Richard Kenworthy
WOMEN MYSTERY STORY WRITERS
Hart, C. Resort to murder
Raichev, R. Assassins at Ospreys
Rice, C. Home sweet homicide
Sayers, D. Strong poison
Sayers, D. Thrones, dominations
WOMEN MYSTICS
Riley, J. A vision of light
WOMEN NEUROSCIENTISTS
Cooper, E. Buried
Cooper, E. Caged
WOMEN NEUROSURGEONS
Dev, S. Pride, prejudice, and other flavors
WOMEN NEWSPAPER EDITORS
Hiaasen, C. Basket case
WOMEN NEWSPAPER EMPLOYEES
Vidal, G. The golden age
WOMEN NONCONFORMISTS
Jhabvala, R. Heat and dust
WOMEN OCEANOGRAPHERS
Cussler, C. Odessa Sea
The **women** of Brewster Place Naylor, G.
The **women** of the copper country Russell, M.
WOMEN OPERA SINGERS
Cather, W. The song of the lark
Patchett, A. Bel canto
WOMEN PAINTERS
Alison, J. The marriage of the sea
Avery, E. The last nude
Dunant, S. The birth of Venus
O'Farrell, M. The hand that first held mine
Penny, L. A trick of the light
Robertson, I. The Paris winter
Rose, M. Tiffany blues
Sloin, H. Art on fire
Updike, J. Seek my face
Vreeland, S. The passion of Artemisia
WOMEN PAINTERS -- 16TH CENTURY
Riley, J. The serpent garden
WOMEN PAINTERS -- CANADA
Atwood, M. Cat's eye
WOMEN PARK RANGERS
Barr, N. Destroyer angel
Barr, N. The rope
Barr, N. Track of the cat

WOMEN PAROLE OFFICERS
Bell, S. For his pleasure
Pelecanos, G. Drama city

WOMEN PATHOLOGISTS
Hart, E. The book of Killowen
Hart, E. Haunted ground
Hart, E. Lake of sorrows

WOMEN PEDIATRICIANS
Brown, R. Before and after
Slaughter, K. Fallen

WOMEN PERFORMANCE ARTISTS
Steinke, R. Holy skirts

WOMEN PHARMACISTS
Trigiani, A. Big Cherry Holler
Trigiani, A. Big Stone Gap

WOMEN PHILOSOPHERS
McCall Smith, A. The forgotten affairs of youth
McCall Smith, A. The lost art of gratitude

WOMEN PHOTOGRAPHERS
Allende, I. Portrait in sepia
Beattie, A. Picturing Will
Geni, A. The lightkeepers
Goldberg, M. Feast your eyes
Hand, E. Available dark
Hand, E. Generation loss
Hand, E. Hard light
Hauck, R. The wedding chapel
Humphreys, H. Afterimage
Linden, R. Ascension of larks
Long, J. The reckoning, Jeff Long.
Meek, J. The people's act of love
Otto, W. Eight girls taking pictures
Perry, A. Death in focus
Roberts, N. The obsession
Rowland, L. The hangman's secret
Rowland, L. The Ripper's shadow
Scharer, W. The age of light
Silver, M. Mary Coin
Trollope, J. Next of kin
Woods, S. Palindrome

WOMEN PHOTOGRAPHERS -- NEW HAMPSHIRE
Shreve, A. The weight of water

WOMEN PHOTOJOURNALISTS
Chung, M. The eighth girl
Doig, I. Ride with me, Mariah Montana
Long, J. The reckoning, Jeff Long.
Petrie, N. Tear it down
Shacochis, B. The woman who lost her soul
Soli, T. The lotus eaters

WOMEN PHYSICAL THERAPISTS
Clark, W. Thugs and the women who love them

WOMEN PHYSICIANS
Anderson, A. The summer guest
Bohjalian, C. The red lotus
Cornwell, P. Chaos
Donati, S. Where the light enters
Franklin, A. Mistress of the art of death

Franklin, A. The serpent's tale
Gabaldon, D. A breath of snow and ashes
Gabaldon, D. Drums of autumn
Gabaldon, D. An echo in the bone
Gabaldon, D. The fiery cross
Gabaldon, D. Voyager
Gabaldon, D. Written in my own heart's blood
Grippando, J. Lying with strangers
Higgins, K. Now that you mention it
Kelly, M. Lilac girls
Lai, L. The tiger flu
Lawler, L. Don't wake up
Lipman, E. The pursuit of Alice Thrift
Mackintosh, C. After the end
Marra, A. A constellation of vital phenomena
Matlwa, K. Evening primrose
Obreht, T. The tiger's wife
Phillips, C. The Devlin diary
Rhodes, J. Yellow moon
Shaw, V. Dreadful company
Shaw, V. Strange Practice
Slaughter, K. Undone
Snipes, W. Talon of God
Tepper, S. The gate to Women's Country
Thomas, S. Not quite a husband
Weatherspoon, R. Rafe
Winawer, M. The scribe of Siena
Woods, S. Stealth

WOMEN PHYSICISTS
Flynn, M. Eifelheim
Goonan, K. In war times
Jin, M. Little gods

WOMEN PHYSICISTS -- CHINA
Wouk, H. A hole in Texas

WOMEN PIANISTS
Singh, N. A madness of sunshine

WOMEN PILOTS
Asaro, C. Primary inversion
Carr, R. The wanderer
Hannah, K. Home front
Kowal, M. The calculating stars
McLain, P. Circling the sun
Muller, M. Both ends of the night
Piercy, M. Gone to soldiers
Quinn, K. The huntress
Rice, L. Last day
Urquhart, J. The night stages

WOMEN PIRATES -- IRELAND
Maxwell, R. The wild Irish

WOMEN PLANTATION OWNERS
Santiago, E. Conquistadora
Willig, L. The summer country

WOMEN PLANTATION OWNERS -- SAVANNAH, GEORGIA
Jakes, J. Savannah, or, A gift for Mr. Lincoln

WOMEN POETS
Albert, E. After birth

tion

McCall Smith, A. The No. 1 Ladies' Detective Agency
McCall Smith, A. The Saturday big tent wedding party
McGuire, S. Night and silence
McGuire, S. Once broken faith
McPherson, C. A step so grave
Muller, M. Both ends of the night
Muller, M. The broken promise land
Muller, M. Burn out
Muller, M. City of whispers
Muller, M. The dangerous hour
Muller, M. Dead midnight
Muller, M. The ever-running man
Muller, M. There's something in a Sunday
Muller, M. Vanishing point
Muller, M. A walk through the fir
Muller, M. Where echoes live
Muller, M. While other people sleep
Muller, M. A wild and lonely place
Muller, M. Wolf in the shadows
Nickson, C. The hocus girl
Paretsky, S. Bitter medicine
Paretsky, S. Blacklist
Paretsky, S. Blood shot
Paretsky, S. Breakdown
Paretsky, S. Brush back
Paretsky, S. Burn marks
Paretsky, S. Critical mass
Paretsky, S. Dead land
Paretsky, S. Fallout
Paretsky, S. Fire sale
Paretsky, S. Guardian angel
Paretsky, S. Hard time
Paretsky, S. Hardball
Paretsky, S. Indemnity only
Paretsky, S. Shell game
Paretsky, S. Total recall
Paretsky, S. Tunnel vision
Paretsky, S. Windy city blues
Parker, R. Family honor
Parker, R. Melancholy baby
Parker, R. Shrink rap
Phillips, S. First star I see tonight
Pronzini, B. The stolen gold affair
Pynchon, T. Bleeding edge
Quartey, K. The missing American
Ragan, T. Buried deep
Ragan, T. Deadly recall
Ragan, T. Deranged
Ragan, T. Her last day
Richards, L. Death was in the blood
Richardson, K. Greywalker
Rowland, L. The hangman's secret
Rozan, S. Paper son
Rozan, S. The Shanghai Moon
Rozan, S. Winter and night
Saunders, K. The case of the wandering scholar

Saunders, K. The secrets of Wishtide
Scoppettone, S. Everything you have is mine
Scoppettone, S. Gonna take a homicidal journey
Scoppettone, S. My sweet untraceable you
Smith, J. Louisiana hotshot
Spencer, S. The shivering turn
Stabenow, D. A deeper sleep
Stabenow, D. A fine and bitter snow
Stabenow, D. A grave denied
Stabenow, D. Hunter's moon
Stabenow, D. Killing grounds
Stabenow, D. Less than a treason
Stabenow, D. A night too dark
Stabenow, D. No fixed line
Stabenow, D. Restless in the grave
Stabenow, D. The singing of the dead
Stabenow, D. A taint in the blood
Stabenow, D. Though not dead
Stabenow, D. Whisper to the blood
Winspear, J. The American agent
Winspear, J. Birds of a feather
Winspear, J. Maisie Dobbs

WOMEN PROFESSIONAL EMPLOYEES
Bartz, A. The herd
Williams, K. Tell the machine goodnight
WOMEN PROOFREADERS
Gaitskill, M. Veronica
WOMEN PROPHETS
Saylor, S. A mist of prophecies
WOMEN PSYCHIATRIC HOSPITAL PATIENTS
Chabon, M. Moonglow
Gruber, M. Valley of bones
Kirshenbaum, B. Rabbits for food
O'Farrell, M. The vanishing act of Esme Lennox
WOMEN PSYCHIATRISTS
Gardiner, M. The Dirty Secrets Club
Iles, G. The footprints of God
Jenkins, V. An unattended death
Parker, R. Melancholy baby
Sandford, J. Mind prey
Spark, M. Aiding & abetting
Steadman, C. Mr. Nobody
WOMEN PSYCHICS
Amis, M. London fields
Asaro, C. Primary inversion
Bouchet, A. Breath of fire
Bouchet, A. A promise of fire
Brown, K. The clairvoyants
Butler, O. Parable of the sower
Butler, O. Parable of the talents
Castle, J. Illusion Town
Clare, A. The woman who spoke to spirits
Conde, M. The story of the cannibal woman
Gilman, D. Kaleidoscope
Gran, S. Claire DeWitt and the city of the dead
Greene, A. Bloodroot
Gregory, P. The lady of the rivers

Gregory, P. The last Tudor
Gregory, P. The taming of the queen
Harper, K. The poyson garden
Haydon, E. The Merchant Emperor
Lin, J. The dragon and the pearl
Martin, G. A dance with dragons
Maxwell, R. The wild Irish
McCaffrey, A. Dragonflight
McGuire, S. Chimes at midnight
McKillip, P. Alphabet of thorn
Min, A. Empress Orchid
Moran, M. Rebel queen
Nicholas, D. Throne of darkness
Nicholas, D. The wicked
Penman, S. Time and chance
Phillips, A. The king at the edge of the world
Pike, S. The lost queen
Plaidy, J. The captive Queen of Scots
Plaidy, J. Murder most royal
Plaidy, J. The pleasures of love
Plaidy, J. William's wife
Randel, W. The empress of bright moon
Rushdie, S. The enchantress of Florence
Rutherfurd, E. Sarum
Saintcrow, L. The Iron Wyrm Affair
Saintcrow, L. The ripper affair
Scalzi, J. The collapsing empire
Shannon, S. The priory of the orange tree
Smith, J. Star of Persia
Stachniak, E. The Winter Palace
Stevens, F. The heads of Cerberus
Updike, J. Gertrude and Claudius
Vinge, J. The snow queen
Wagers, K. After the crown
Wagers, K. There before the chaos
Walters, M. The last hours
Willig, L. The lure of the moonflower
Willig, L. The temptation of the night jasmine
Wolfe, S. The course of all treasons
Yang, J. The ascent to godhood

WOMEN RULERS -- EUROPE
Jones, S. Four sisters, all queens

WOMEN RULERS -- FRANCE
Naslund, S. Abundance

WOMEN RULERS -- GREAT BRITAIN
George, M. Elizabeth I
Maxwell, R. The secret diary of Anne Boleyn

WOMEN RULERS -- JAPAN
Schwartz, J. The commoner

WOMEN RUNNERS
Lohmann, J. Winning Ruby Heart

WOMEN SAINTS
Griffith, N. Hild
Twain, M. Personal recollections of Joan of Arc
Urrea, L. The hummingbird's daughter
Urrea, L. Queen of America

WOMEN SALES PERSONNEL

Rose, J. The blackest bird
Turner, N. Natural born hustler

WOMEN SCHOLARS AND ACADEMICS
Collins, M. Ready set rogue
Drabble, M. The sea lady
Harkness, D. A discovery of witches
Harkness, D. The book of life
Harkness, D. Shadow of night
Michaels, B. Houses of stone
Phillips, C. The Rossetti letter

WOMEN SCIENTISTS
Asimov, I. I, robot
Benedict, M. The only woman in the room
Brennan, M. A natural history of dragons
Brennan, M. The tropic of serpents
Brennan, M. Within the sanctuary of wings
Brockmeier, K. The brief history of the dead
Cole, A. A princess in theory
Cussler, C. Blue gold
Dare, T. A week to be wicked
Freudenberger, N. Lost and wanted
Gilman, C. Dark orbit
Hagberg, D. Abyss
Kazinski, A. The last good man
Newitz, A. Autonomous
Peikoff, K. Mother knows best
Phillips, H. The need
Pulley, N. The watchmaker of Filigree Street
Sagan, C. Contact
Soule, C. Anyone
Tepper, S. The visitor
Tyers, K. Shivering world
Vandermeer, J. Annihilation
Waite, O. The lady's guide to celestial mechanics
Wilson, D. The clockwork dynasty

WOMEN SCREENWRITERS
Davis, F. The Chelsea girls
Stratford, S. Red letter days

WOMEN SCULPTORS
Weisgall, D. The world before her*

WOMEN SERIAL MURDERERS
Braithwaite, O. My sister, the serial killer
Patterson, J. 1st to die
Rowland, L. The hangman's secret

WOMEN SERIAL MURDERERS -- MINNEAPOLIS, MINNESOTA
Sandford, J. Certain prey

WOMEN SEXAGENARIANS
Higgins, J. The White House connection
Minot, S. Evening

WOMEN SHAMANS
Griffin, K. The glass god
Griffin, K. Stray souls
Okorafor, N. Who fears death

WOMEN SHARPSHOOTERS
Larison, J. Whiskey when we're dry
McMurtry, L. Buffalo girls

WOMEN SHERIFFS
Child, L. The affair
Heathcock, A. Volt
Hooper, K. Stealing shadows
Jance, J. Skeleton Canyon
Jones, D. A bad day for sunshine
Lansdale, J. Sunset and sawdust
Montgomery, J. The widows
Sallis, J. Sarah Jane
Stewart, A. Miss Kopp just won't quit

WOMEN SHERIFFS -- ARKANSAS
Hess, J. Maggody and the moonbeams

WOMEN SHIP CAPTAINS
Laukkanen, O. Gale force
Shalvis, J. Sweet little lies

WOMEN SHOPKEEPERS
Childs, L. Lavender blue murder
Whittle, T. The dangerous edge of things

WOMEN SINGERS
Faye, L. The Paragon Hotel
Hiaasen, C. Star Island
Letts, E. Finding Dorothy
Long, J. Wild at Whiskey Creek
McBain, E. The frumious bandersnatch
Noire Candy licker
Penelope, L. Song of blood and stone
Penelope, L. Whispers of shadow & flame
Reid, T. Daisy Jones & the Six
Rotert, R. Last night at the blue angel
Rushdie, S. The ground beneath her feet

WOMEN SINGERS -- ILLINOIS
McInerny, R. Requiem for a realtor

WOMEN SINGERS -- NEW HAMPSHIRE
Delinsky, B. Lake news

WOMEN SLAVES
Barker, P. The silence of the girls
Brink, A. Philida
Clinch, J. Finn
Crafts, H. The bondwoman's narrative
Le Guin, U. Four ways to forgiveness
Leveen, L. The secrets of Mary Bowser
Levy, A. The long song
Martin, V. Property
Odell, J. The healing
Perkins-Valdez, D. Wench
Sherwood, F. Night of sorrows
Straight, S. A million nightingales
Tademy, L. Cane River

WOMEN SLAVES -- HISTORY -- 17TH CENTURY
Conde, M. I, Tituba, Black witch of Salem

WOMEN SLAVES -- LOUISIANA
Gaines, E. The autobiography of Miss Jane Pittman

WOMEN SOCIAL ADVOCATES
Arvin, R. Blood of angels
Ashe, K. The earl
Marlantes, K. Deep river

WOMEN SOCIAL WORKERS

Mengestu, D. All our names
Rendell, R. Harm done

WOMEN SOLDIERS
Bird, S. Daughter of a daughter of a queen
Dees, C. Beyond the limit
Gibson, C. Beyond the point
Hunt, L. Neverhome
Hurley, K. The light brigade
Krueger, P. Steel crow saga
Lee, Y. Ninefox gambit
Meltzer, B. The escape artist
Mohamed, N. The orchard of lost souls
Moran, M. Rebel queen
O'Keefe, M. Velocity weapon
Pratchett, T. Monstrous regiment
Weber, D. Shadow of freedom

WOMEN SOLDIERS -- ISRAEL
Boianjiu, S. The people of forever are not afraid

WOMEN SONGWRITERS
Dufresne, J. Deep in the shade of paradise

WOMEN SPACESHIP CAPTAINS
Bouchet, A. Nightchaser
McDevitt, J. The engines of God
Weber, D. The honor of the queen
Weber, D. On Basilisk Station
Weber, D. Shadow of freedom
Weber, D. The short victorious war

WOMEN SPIES
Bennett, R. City of stairs
Bourne, J. The black hawk
Bourne, J. Rogue spy
Bourne, J. The spymaster's lady
Buckley, F. The doublet affair
Buckley, F. The siren queen
Chiaverini, J. Resistance women
Harkaway, N. Angelmaker
Higgins, J. Night of the fox
Jenoff, P. The lost girls of Paris
Leveen, L. The secrets of Mary Bowser
Matthews, J. The Kremlin's candidate
Matthews, J. Palace of treason
Matthews, J. Red sparrow
McEwan, I. Sweet tooth
Meacham, L. Dragonfly
Murphy, Y. Signed, Mata Hari
Priest, C. Clementine
Putney, M. No longer a gentleman
Ryan, A. The waking fire
Sebastian, T. Fatal ally
Soule, C. Anyone
Stachniak, E. The Winter Palace
Tregillis, I. The mechanical
Willig, L. The betrayal of the blood lily
Willig, L. The deception of the emerald ring
Willig, L. The lure of the moonflowe
Willig, L. The masque of the Black Tulip
Willig, L. The orchid affai

Willig, L. The secret history of the Pink Carnation
Willig, L. The seduction of the Crimson Rose
Willig, L. The temptation of the night jasmine

WOMEN SPIES -- GERMANY
Frayn, M. Spies

WOMEN SPIES -- GREAT BRITAIN
Follett, K. Jackdaws

WOMEN SPIES -- SOVIET UNION
Fleming, I. From Russia with love

WOMEN SPIRITUALISTS
Perry, A. Southampton Row

WOMEN STALKERS
Parker, R. Hush money

WOMEN STALKING VICTIMS
Bannister, J. Silent footsteps
Grippando, J. Lying with strangers
Pirie, D. The patient's eyes
Quick, A. 'Til death do us part

WOMEN STAND-UP COMEDIANS
Leonard, E. Pagan babies

WOMEN STUDENTS
Durst, S. The queen of blood
Johnson, K. The dream-quest of Vellitt Boe
Martin, S. The pleasure of my company

WOMEN SUPREME COURT JUSTICES
Patterson, R. Protect and defend

WOMEN SURFERS
Moore, L. Making waves

WOMEN SURGEONS
Ashe, K. The prince
Brookmyre, C. Black widow
Carr, R. What we find
Snow, J. An Alaskan Christmas

WOMEN SWINDLERS
Chakraborty, S. The city of brass
Chakraborty, S. The empire of gold
Chakraborty, S. The kingdom of copper
Hilton, L. Maestra
K'wan Section 8
Robards, K. The ultimatum
Spark, M. Aiding & abetting
Women talking Toews, M.

WOMEN TEA INDUSTRY AND TRADE EXECUTIVES
Crombie, D. Kissed a sad goodbye

WOMEN TEACHERS
Abe, K. The woman in the dunes
Balogh, M. Simply love
Beams, C. The illness lesson
Bynum, S. Ms. Hempel chronicles
Foster, L. Under pressure
Goodman, C. The sea of lost girls
Hegi, U. Children and fire
Heller, Z. What was she thinking?
Jalaluddin, U. Ayesha at last
Kostova, E. The shadow land
Lynn, A. Now you see it
Marshall, C. Christy

Minato, K. Confessions
Ozick, C. Foreign bodies
Read, C. The crazy school
Reynolds, A. Permafrost
Richman, A. The secret of clouds
Roberts, G. Adam and evil
Roberts, G. The bluest blood
Russell, M. Dreamers of the day
Simonson, H. The summer before the war
Spark, M. The prime of Miss Jean Brodie
West, K. Minor dramas & other catastrophes
Winslow, D. In West Mills

WOMEN TELEVISION JOURNALISTS
Bauer, B. The beautiful dead
Coyle, M. Yesterday's echo
Kerley, J. The death collectors
Marks, J. Fangland

WOMEN TELEVISION NEWSCASTERS AND COMMENTATORS
Pitoniak, A. Necessary people
Woods, S. New York dead

WOMEN TELEVISION PERSONALITIES
Byatt, A. A whistling woman
O'Keefe, M. Crazy thing called love

WOMEN TELEVISION PRODUCERS AND DIRECTORS
Elliott, L. The missing years
Hannah, S. The cradle in the grave
Stratford, S. Red letter days

WOMEN TELEVISION WRITERS
Rowell, R. Landline

WOMEN TERRORISTS
Higgins, J. Midnight runner
Lessing, D. The good terrorist

WOMEN TEXTILE WORKERS
Cash, W. The last ballad

WOMEN THEATRICAL PRODUCERS AND DIRECTORS
Wells, R. Divine secrets of the Ya-Ya Sisterhood

WOMEN THIEVES
Bennett, R. Foundryside
Beverley, J. My lady notorious
Bouchet, A. Nightchaser
De Leon, A. Side chick nation
McCall Smith, A. Blue shoes and happiness
Merimee, P. Carmen
Pears, I. Death and restoration
Robards, K. The ultimatum

WOMEN TRACKERS
Bradbury, J. The wild inside

WOMEN TRANSLATORS
Alameddine, R. An unnecessary woman
Anderson, A. The summer guest
Audur A. Olafsdottir, 1. Butterflies in November
McKillip, P. Alphabet of thorn
Meyer, N. The adventure of the peculiar protocols
Perry, S. Melmoth

WOMEN TRAPEZE AND HIGH-WIRE PERFORMERS
Carter, A. Nights at the circus

WOMEN WITH BRAIN INJURIES
Adelman, M. Piece of mind
Genova, L. Left neglected

WOMEN WITH CANCER
Albert, E. The book of Dahlia
Bock, C. Alice & Oliver
Coetzee, J. Age of Iron
Colombani, L. The braid
Garner, H. The spare room
Hashemzadeh Bonde, G. What we owe
McMurtry, L. Terms of endearment
Shriver, L. So much for that
Stabenow, D. A taint in the blood

WOMEN WITH DEPRESSION
Bambara, T. The salt eaters
Bird, S. The Yokota Officers Club
Cunningham, M. The hours
Gaige, A. Sea wife
Haigh, J. Mrs. Kimble
Hustvedt, S. The blazing world
Kimmel, F. No good asking
Kirshenbaum, B. Rabbits for food
Knausgaard, K. My struggle.
Lessing, D. The golden notebook
Lessing, D. The grass is singing
Plath, S. The bell jar
Price, R. Roxanna Slade
Wood, J. Upstate

WOMEN WITH DIABETES
McMillan, T. It's not all downhill from here

WOMEN WITH DISABILITIES
Adelman, M. Piece of mind
Binchy, M. Firefly summer
Jones, E. The known world
Millet, L. Ghost lights
Murakami, H. South of the border, west of the sun
Robinson, P. Friend of the devil

WOMEN WITH DISABILITIES -- CALIFORNIA
Mapson, J. Bad Girl Creek

WOMEN WITH DISFIGUREMENTS
Glass, J. The whole world over
O'Connell, C. Dead famous

WOMEN WITH EMOTIONAL ILLNESSES
McCullers, C. Reflections in a golden eye

WOMEN WITH EPILEPSY
Johnson, T. Engraved on the heart

WOMEN WITH HIV
Styles, T. Black and ugly

WOMEN WITH MEMORY DISORDERS
LaPlante, A. Turn of mind

WOMEN WITH MENTAL ILLNESSES
Abbott, P. Concrete angel
Arnoult, D. Sufficient grace
Billingsley, R. The secret she kept
Bing, S. You look nice today
Cookson, C. The year of the virgins
Cooley, M. The archivist

Cunningham, M. The hours
Emezi, A. Freshwater
Everett, P. Suder
Faber, M. The crimson petal and the white
Findley, T. The piano man's daughter
Founds, K. When mystical creatures attack!
Fowler, T. Z
Kaminsky, S. Murder on the Trans-Siberian Express
Kellerman, J. Time bomb
Kirshenbaum, B. Rabbits for food
Lessing, D. The four-gated city
Lessing, D. The golden notebook
Livesey, M. Criminals
MacDonald, J. The turquoise lament
Moses, K. Wintering
Muller, M. While other people sleep
Newman, J. Mary
Plath, S. The bell jar
Prose, F. Household saints
Purcell, L. The silent companions
Rendell, R. The bridesmaid
Rhys, J. Wide Sargasso Sea
Roth, P. My life as a man
Roy, A. An atlas of impossible longing
Schwarz, C. Drowning Ruth
Sebold, A. The almost moon
Smith, L. Fair and tender ladies
Stridsberg, S. Valerie

WOMEN WITH MENTAL ILLNESSES -- TEXAS
Reichs, K. Death du jour

WOMEN WITH MULTIPLE SCLEROSIS
Tan, A. The kitchen god's wife

WOMEN WITH POLIOMYELITIS
Berg, E. We are all welcome here
Stegner, W. Crossing to safety

WOMEN WITH QUADRIPLEGIA
Berg, E. We are all welcome here

WOMEN WITH SCHIZOPHRENIA
Arnoult, D. Sufficient grace
Butler, G. Death lives next door

WOMEN WITH TERMINAL ILLNESSES
Adkins, M. When you read this
Albert, E. The book of Dahlia
Antoinette, A. Murderville
Cantor, M. Death and other happy endings
Coetzee, J. Age of Iron
Didion, J. A book of common prayer
Garner, H. The spare room
Kelly, J. The fire baby
Lively, P. Moon tiger
McMahon, J. The one I left behind
Minot, S. Evening
Pearson, R. A long time comin'
Sallis, J. The killer is dying
Schweblin, S. Fever dream
Segal, E. Love story
Tsukiyama, G. Dreaming water

Shipman, V. The heirloom garden
Silver, M. Mary Coin
Stockett, K. The help
Stradal, J. The lager queen of Minnesota
Tan, A. The bonesetter's daughter
Tan, A. The Joy Luck Club
Tan, A. The kitchen god's wife
Tie, N. The bathing women
Tsukiyama, G. Dreaming water
Tyler, A. Back when we were grownups
Tyler, A. Ladder of years
Valdes, A. Dirty Girls on top
Warren, T. Her secret life
Weiner, J. In her shoes
Weiner, J. Little earthquakes
Weiner, J. Mrs. Everything
Weiss, L. If the creek don't rise
Wells, R. Divine secrets of the Ya-Ya Sisterhood
Wiggs, S. The Oysterville sewing circle
Zevin, G. Young Jane Young

Women's Murder Club [series] Patterson, J.

WOMEN'S MURDER CLUB (IMAGINARY ORGANIZA-TION)

Patterson, J. 1st to die

WOMEN'S ORGANIZATIONS

Dallas, S. The Persian Pickle Club
Williams, L. Supper club

WOMEN'S PERIODICALS

Rawle, G. Woman's world

WOMEN'S RESISTANCE AND REVOLTS

Le Guin, U. Four ways to forgiveness

WOMEN'S RIGHTS

Dare, A. The girl with the louding voice
Elison, M. The book of Etta
Elison, M. The book of Flora
Kidd, S. The invention of wings
MacGregor, J. The bride who got lucky
Manning, K. My notorious life
Massey, S. The widows of Malabar Hill
Pamuk, O. Snow
Piercy, M. Sex wars

WOMEN'S RIGHTS -- HISTORY

Newitz, A. The future of another timeline

WOMEN'S ROLE

Ahern, C. Roar
Alameddine, R. An unnecessary woman
Ali, M. Brick Lane
Anam, T. The bones of grace
Anstruther, E. A perfect explanation
Atwood, M. The handmaid's tale
Atwood, M. Moral disorder
Beams, C. The illness lesson
Benton, J. Lilli de Jong
Brennan, M. A natural history of dragons
Brennan, M. The tropic of serpents
Brennan, M. Within the sanctuary of wings
Carlyle, L. Never lie to a lady

Cather, W. A lost lady
Chung, C. The tenth muse
Colombani, L. The braid
Conde, M. The story of the cannibal woman
Darznik, J. Song of a captive bird
Eliot, G. Middlemarch
Eliot, G. The mill on the Floss
Elison, M. The book of Etta
Elison, M. The book of Flora
Farah, N. Knots
Flaubert, G. Madame Bovary
Fowler, T. A well-behaved woman
Gibson, C. Beyond the point
Gilman, C. Herland
Greene, A. Bloodroot
James, H. The portrait of a lady
Kay, G. River of stars
Kowal, M. The calculating stars
Le Guin, U. The birthday of the world
Le Guin, U. The dispossessed
Le Guin, U. The left hand of darkness
Macneal, E. The doll factory
Mahmoud, L. Amreekiya
The mammoth book of steampunk
Manning, K. My notorious life
Maxwell, R. The secret diary of Anne Boleyn
Melamed, J. Gather the daughters
Mukherjee, B. Miss new India
Oates, J. A garden of earthly delights
Otto, W. Eight girls taking pictures
Perry, A. A dangerous mourning
Riley, J. The serpent garden
Riley, J. A vision of light
Rindell, S. The other typist
Rose, M. Cartier's hope
Shafak, E. The bastard of Istanbul
Tepper, S. Singer from the sea
Tyler, A. Vinegar girl
Weiner, J. Mrs. Everything
Zumas, L. Red clocks

WOMEN'S ROLE -- IRAN

Amirrezvani, A. The blood of flowers

WOMEN'S ROLE -- UNITED STATES -- HISTORY -- 20TH CENTURY

Horan, N. Loving Frank

WOMEN'S ROMANTIC FICTION

Hoffman, A. The third angel
Mallery, S. The summer of Sunshine and Margot
The **women's** room French, M.

WOMEN'S SHELTERS

Alexander, V. The Magdalen girls
Harrington, A. An inconvenient duke
Kibler, J. Home for erring and outcast girls
Moor, J. The keeper
Morrison, T. Paradise
Neel, J. To die for
Warren, T. Her secret life

Canty, K. The underworld
Dee, J. The locals
Doyle, R. Paddy Clarke, ha-ha-ha
Haigh, J. Baker Towers
Lawrence, D. Sons and lovers
Louis, E. The end of Eddy
McDermott, A. Child of my heart
Oates, J. Them
Stuart, D. Shuggie Bain

WORKING CLASS MEN
Canin, E. America America
Hardy, T. Jude the obscure
Kelman, J. How late it was, how late
London, J. Martin Eden

WORKING CLASS MEN -- GREAT BRITAIN
Barker, P. The ghost road

WORKING CLASS NEIGHBORHOODS
Lehane, D. Mystic river

WORKING CLASS TEENAGERS
Huston, C. The shotgun rule

WORKING CLASS WOMEN
Breslin, J. Table money
Doyle, R. The woman who walked into doors
Nunez, S. The last of her kind

WORKING DOGS
Munier, P. A borrowing of bones

WORKING MOTHERS
Fabry, C. War room
Forman, G. Leave me
Pearson, A. How hard can it be?
Phillips, H. The need

WORKING POOR PEOPLE
Louis, E. The end of Eddy

WORKING-CLASS
Boyle, W. City of margins
Flint, E. Little deaths

WORKING-CLASS FAMILIES
Moss, S. Ghost wall
The **world** according to Garp Irving, J.
World and town Jen, G.
The **world** before her Weisgall, D.
The **world** doesn't require you Scott, R.
World enough and time Warren, R.
World gone by Lehane, D.

WORLD HEALTH ORGANIZATION
Reynolds, A. Permafrost

**WORLD HEALTH ORGANIZATION CENTRAL AFRI-
CAN OPERATIONS**
Ballard, J. The day of creation
World of spies [series] O'Donohue, C.
The **world** of tomorrow Mathews, B.
World of trouble Winters, B.

WORLD POLITICS
Carter, S. Back channel
Follett, K. Edge of eternity
Follett, K. Fall of giants
Follett, K. Winter of the world

Higgins, J. Bad company
McEwan, I. Saturday

WORLD POLITICS -- 20TH CENTURY
Kerr, P. Hitler's peace

WORLD SERIES (BASEBALL)
Latour, J. The Havana World Series
The **world** that we knew Hoffman, A.
The **world** to come Horn, D.
The **world** to come Shepard, J.

WORLD WAR I
Barker, P. Regeneration
Boyden, J. Three day road
Boyne, J. The absolutist
Burke, J. House of the rising sun
Butler, R. Paris in the dark
Byatt, A. The children's book
Celine, L. Journey to the end of the night
Dos Passos, J. 1919
Dunmore, H. The lie
Faulks, S. Birdsong
Follett, K. Fall of giants
Gohlke, C. Promise me this
Itani, F. Deafening
Keneally, T. The daughters of Mars
King, L. The beekeeper's apprentice
Krivak, A. The signal flame
Krivak, A. The sojourn
Lowenthal, M. Charity girl
Mann, T. The Magic Mountain
Morris, M. Man in the blue moon
Moyes, J. The girl you left behind
Perry, A. No graves as yet
Perry, A. Shoulder the sky
Rash, R. The cove
Remarque, E. All quiet on the western front
Remarque, E. The road back
Riley, L. The girl on the cliff
Russell, M. Dreamers of the day
Scott, C. The poppy wife
Self, W. Umbrella
Simonson, H. The summer before the war
Solomons, N. House of Gold
Steinbeck, J. East of Eden
Trumbo, D. Johnny got his gun
Uris, L. Redemption
Willig, L. The Ashford affair
Winspear, J. Birds of a feather
Winspear, J. Maisie Dobbs
Woolf, V. Jacob's room

WORLD WAR I -- AFRICA
Forester, C. The African Queen

WORLD WAR I -- CAUSES
Buchan, J. The thirty-nine steps
Pynchon, T. Against the day

WORLD WAR I -- EGYPT
Peters, E. The golden one

WORLD WAR I -- FRANCE

Harris, T. Hannibal rising
Hegi, U. Stones from the river
Hegi, U. The vision of Emma Blau
Heller, J. Catch-22
Higgins, J. Bad company
Higgins, J. The eagle has flown
Higgins, J. The eagle has landed
Higgins, J. Flight of eagles
Higgins, J. Luciano's luck
Higgins, J. Night of the fox
Iles, G. Black cross
Indriðason, A. The shadow district
Jenoff, P. The lost girls of Paris
Jones, J. From here to eternity
Jones, J. The thin red line
Kaminsky, S. Dancing in the dark
Kaminsky, S. A fatal glass of beer
Kaminsky, S. To catch a spy
Kaminsky, S. Tomorrow is another day
Kelly, J. The light over London
Kelly, M. Lilac girls
Kelly, S. The wages of desire
Keneally, T. Shame and the captives
Kerr, P. Field gray
Knowles, J. A separate peace
Krivak, A. The signal flame
L'Amour, L. May there be a road
Lanchester, J. Fragrant Harbor
Lessing, D. Landlocked
Leithauser, B. The art student's war
Lessing, D. A ripple from the storm
Levi, P. If not now, when?
Link, C. The other child
Lourie, R. A hatred for tulips
Mackall, D. With love, wherever you are
Mailer, N. The naked and the dead
Manicka, R. The rice mother
Mawer, S. The fall
McCullough, C. An indecent obsession
McEwan, I. Black dogs
Meacham, L. Dragonfly
Michener, J. Space
Michener, J. Tales of the South Pacific
Monsarrat, N. The cruel sea
Moore, S. The life of objects
Morton, K. The distant hours
Nemirovsky, I. Fire in the blood
Nesbit, T. The wives of Los Alamos
Nesbo, J. The redbreast
Nicholson, W. Motherland
Oksanen, S. When the doves disappeared
Otsuka, J. The Buddha in the attic
Pears, I. The last judgement
Pelecanos, G. The big blowdown
Plain, B. Tapestry
Pynchon, T. Gravity's rainbow
Ramzipoor, E. The ventriloquists

Reisman, N. The first desire
Remarque, E. A time to love and a time to die
Robbins, D. Last citadel
Robbins, D. War of the rats
Rosner, J. The yellow bird sings
Rothmann, R. To die in spring
Roy, A. All the lives we never lived
Runcie, J. The road to Grantchester
Sarvas, M. Memento Park
Sayers, V. The powers
Scoppettone, S. Too darn hot
Sebald, W. Austerlitz
Sebald, W. The emigrants ;, W. G. Sebald ; translated by
    Michael Hulse.
Self, W. Shark
Shaara, J. The rising tide
Shaara, J. The steel wave
Shaffer, M. The Guernsey Literary and Potato Peel Pie So-
    ciety
Shapiro, B. The muralist
Shimotakahara, L. After the bloom
Spark, M. The girls of slender means
Stephenson, N. Cryptonomicon
Sundaresan, I. The splendor of silence
Szabo, M. Abigail
Tan, T. The garden of evening mists
Tremain, R. The Gustav sonata
Treuer, D. Prudence
Turow, S. Ordinary heroes
Uris, L. Battle cry
Van Booy, S. The illusion of separateness
Vollmann, W. Europe central
Vonnegut, K. Armageddon in retrospect
Vonnegut, K. Slaughterhouse-five
Walton, J. Farthing
Westheimer, D. Von Ryan's express
Wiggins, M. Evidence of things unseen
Willis, C. Blackout
Willis, C. To say nothing of the dog
Winspear, J. The American agent
Wouk, H. War and remembrance
Wouk, H. The winds of war

World War II (David L. Robbins) [series] Robbins, D.
Bragg, M. A son of war
Hazzard, S. The great fire

WORLD WAR II -- AERIAL OPERATIONS, AMERICAN
Shaara, J. The steel wave

WORLD WAR II -- ART AND THE WAR
Ishiguro, K. An artist of the floating world
Rothschild, H. The improbability of love

WORLD WAR II -- AUSTRIA
Clayton, M. The last train to London

WORLD WAR II -- CALIFORNIA
Otsuka, J. When the emperor was divine

WORLD WAR II -- CANADA
Norman, H. What is left the daughter

WORLD WAR II -- CANADIAN PARTICIPATION

Clayton, M. The last train to London
Dahl, K. The courier
WORLD WAR II -- UNITED STATES
Egan, J. Manhattan Beach
Ellroy, J. Perfidia
Saroyan, W. The human comedy
WORLD WAR II -- WASHINGTON, D.C.
Roosevelt, E. Murder in the map room
WORLD WAR II -- WOMEN
Clayton, M. The last train to London
Hart, C. Letter from home
Loigman, L. The wartime sisters
Mengiste, M. The shadow king
Waters, S. The night watch
WORLD WAR II -- WOMEN'S PARTICIPATION
Follett, K. Jackdaws
Piercy, M. Gone to soldiers
WORLD WAR II -- YUGOSLAVIA
Albahari, D. Gotz and Meyer
WORLD WAR II HOME FRONT
Blake, S. The postmistress
Bowen, E. The heat of the day
Byatt, A. Ragnarok
Leithauser, B. The art student's war
MacNeal, S. The king's justice
Nesbit, T. The wives of Los Alamos
Otsuka, J. The Buddha in the attic
Otsuka, J. When the emperor was divine
Roosevelt, E. Murder in the map room
Ryan, J. The spies of Shilling Lane
Sayers, V. The powers
Scoppettone, S. Too darn hot
Shields, S. The Cassandra
World War II novels [series] Shaara, J.
WORLD WAR II VETERANS
Baldacci, D. One good deed
Belfer, L. And after the fire
Bragg, M. A son of war
Chabon, M. Moonglow
Dillard, A. The Maytrees
Edwardson, A. Sail of stone
Guterson, D. Snow falling on cedars
Hazzard, S. The great fire
Hunter, S. Hot springs
Hunter, S. Havana
Hunter, S. Pale horse coming
Johnson, C. Spirit of steamboat
Jordan, H. Mudbound
Levy, A. Small island
McCarthy, C. No country for old men
Mosley, W. Fearless Jones
O'Malley, T. Serpents in the cold
O'Malley, T. We were kings
Parker, R. Double play
Peters, E. Fallen into the pit
Robertson, R. The long take
Runcie, J. The road to Grantchester

Salter, J. All that is
Silko, L. Ceremony
Sparks, N. The notebook
Swift, G. Last orders
Torday, D. The last flight of Poxl West
Turow, S. Ordinary heroes
Waters, S. The little stranger
Wilson, S. The man in the gray flannel suit
WORLD WAR II VETERANS -- JAPAN
Okuizumi, H. The stones cry out
World War Z Brooks, M.
WORLD WAR, 1939-1945 -- UNITED STATES
Sayers, V. The powers
WORLD WIDE WEB
Zelazny, R. Donnerjack
World without end Follett, K.
World's end Boyle, T.
World's end Vinge, J.
World's End Bureau [series] Clare, A.
World's Fair Doctorow, E.
WORMHOLES (ASTROPHYSICS)
Hamilton, P. Pandora's star
Wormwood trilogy [series] Thompson, T.
WORRY
Offill, J. Weather
WORRY IN GIRLS
Lodato, V. Mathilda Savitch
The **worst** best man Sosa, M.
Worst fears Weldon, F.
Worth dying for Child, L.
WOUND HEALING
Apelfeld, A. The man who never stopped sleeping
WOUNDED KNEE, SOUTH DAKOTA
Brown, D. Creek Mary's blood
Woundhealer's story Saberhagen, F.
WOUNDS AND INJURIES
Brown, S. Mean streak
Castile, Z. Flashed
Dell, K. Mistletoe in Texas
Kilalea, K. Ok, Mr. Field
O'Keefe, M. Velocity weapon
The **wrath** of Shiva Oleksiw, S.
Wrath of the furies Saylor, S.
The **wreckage** Robotham, M.
The **wrecker** Cussler, C.
WRECKERS (PLUNDERERS OF SHIPS)
Du Maurier, D. Jamaica Inn
WRECKING
Putney, M. The burning point
Savage, S. Firmin
WRESTLERS
Burns, R. Body slam
WRESTLING
Burns, R. Body slam
Wrexford and Sloane historical mysteries [series] Penrose, A.
WRIGHT, FRANK LLOYD, 1867-1959
Horan, N. Loving Frank

X

Okorafor, N. Binti : home
Okorafor, N. Binti : the night masquerade
Owens, D. Where the crawdads sing
 A people's future of the United States
Pulley, N. The lost future of Pepperharrow
Pulley, N. The watchmaker of Filigree Street
Reddi, R. Passage west
Smith, A. Autumn

XERXES I, KING OF PERSIA, 519-465 OR 4 BC

Smith, J. Star of Persia

XHOSA (AFRICAN PEOPLE)

Meyer, D. Heart of the hunter

Y

Y is for yesterday Grafton, S.
Ya-Yas [series] Wells, R.

YACHT RACING

Wambaugh, J. Floaters

YACHTS

Laurens, S. The pursuits of Lord Kit Cavanaugh
MacDonald, J. The lonely silver rain
McBain, E. The frumious bandersnatch
Mina, D. Conviction
Parker, R. Sea change

YALE UNIVERSITY

Bardugo, L. Ninth house
Perrotta, T. Joe College
White, S. The siege

YANGTZE RIVER

See, L. Dragon bones

YANGTZE RIVER GORGES (CHINA)

See, L. Dragon bones

YANGTZE RIVER VALLEY, CHINA

See, L. Dragon bones
Yankee Doodle dead Hart, C.
The **year** of living scandalously London, J.
The **year** of the flood Atwood, M.
The **year** of the French Flanagan, T.
Year of the hyenas Geagley, B.
The **year** of the runaways Sahota, S.
The **year** of the virgins Cookson, C.
The **year's** best science fiction
Year's best science fiction (Gardner Dozois) [series]
The **years** Woolf, V.
The **years** of rice and salt Robinson, K.
The **years** with Laura Diaz Fuentes, C.
The **yellow** admiral O'Brian, P.
The **yellow** bird sings Rosner, J.
The **yellow** birds Powers, K.
Yellow moon Rhodes, J.
A **yellow** raft in blue water Dorris, M.
The **yellow** room conspiracy Dickinson, P.

YELLOWFACE

Davies, P. The fortunes

YELLOWKNIFE, NORTHWEST TERRITORIES

Hay, E. Late nights on air

YELLOWSTONE NATIONAL PARK

Barnett, K. Ever faithful
Heller, P. Celine
Yesterday Yap, F.
Yesterday's echo Coyle, M.
Yesterday's kin [series] Kress, N.
Yesterday's weather Enright, A.
The **Yiddish** Policemen's Union Chabon, M.
The **Yokota** Officers Club Bird, S.

YORK, ENGLAND

Butland, S. The lost for words bookshop
Clarke, S. Jonathan Strange & Mr. Norrell
Robb, C. The cross-legged knight
Robb, C. A murdered peace
Robb, C. A twisted vengeance

YORKSHIRE, ENGLAND

Atkinson, K. Big sky
Ellis, B. The vanished bride
Gardam, J. The flight of the maidens
Jewell, L. I found you
Link, C. The other child
Mozley, F. Elmet
Ripley, M. Mr Campion's fault
Robinson, P. All the colors of darkness
Robinson, P. Children of the revolution
Robinson, P. Close to home
Robinson, P. Cold is the grave
Robinson, P. The first cut
Robinson, P. Friend of the devil
Robinson, P. Innocent graves
Robinson, P. Piece of my heart
Robinson, P. Playing with fire
Robinson, P. Strange affair

YORUBA (AFRICAN PEOPLE) -- RELIGION

Oyeyemi, H. The opposite house
You came back Coake, C.
You can run Mosby, S.
You can't go home again Wolfe, T.
You can't keep a good woman down Walker, A.
You cannot mess this up Daughters, A.
You know when the men are gone Fallon, S.
You look nice today Bing, S.
You make me wanna Rashan, N.
You may kiss the bride Berne, L.
You only die twice Buchanan, E.
You only live twice Fleming, I.
You should pity us instead Gustine, A.
You suck Moore, C.
You think it, I'll say it Sittenfeld, C.
You were there too Oakley, C.
You will know me Abbott, M.
You'll never know, dear Ephron, H.
You're dead Knopf, C.
You're next Hurwitz, G.
You've been volunteered Gelman, L.

YOUNG ADULTS

Auster, P. Sunset Park

Cauwelaert, D. One-way
McMurtry, L. Dead man's walk
Meyer, P. American rust
Raymond, J. The half-life

YOUNG MEN -- HONG KONG
Lanchester, J. Fragrant Harbor

YOUNG MEN -- IDENTITY
Conrad, J. Lord Jim
Donohue, K. The stolen child

YOUNG MEN -- INTERPERSONAL RELATIONS
Miller, M. The song of Achilles

YOUNG MEN -- PERSONAL CONDUCT
Fountain, B. Billy Lynn's long halftime walk
Roth, P. Nemesis

YOUNG MEN -- PSYCHOLOGY
Lehane, D. Live by night
Powers, K. The yellow birds

YOUNG MEN -- RELATIONS WITH OLDER MEN
Aciman, A. Find me
Mallon, T. Fellow travelers

YOUNG MEN -- RELATIONS WITH OLDER WOMEN
Balogh, M. Someone to trust
Barnes, J. The only story
Durrell, L. Mountolive
Grodstein, L. A friend of the family
Guterson, D. Ed King
McMillan, T. How Stella got her groove back
Oz, A. Judas
Roth, H. Requiem for Harlem
Sackville-West, V. The Edwardians
Scego, I. Adua
Schlink, B. The reader
Williams, T. The Roman spring of Mrs. Stone

YOUNG MEN -- UNITED STATES
Palahniuk, C. Fight Club
The **young** widower's handbook McAllister, T.

YOUNG WIDOWS
Allende, I. A long petal of the sea
Bateman, K. This earl of mine
Black, C. Three hours in Paris
Goodman, J. A touch of forever
March, E. Jackson
Neubauer, E. Murder at the Mena House
Rogan, C. The lifeboat
Suri, T. Realm of ash

YOUNG WOMEN
Abbott, M. Queenpin
Albert, E. The book of Dahlia
Arden, K. The bear and the nightingale
Arden, K. The girl in the tower
Arden, K. The winter of the witch
Atwood, M. The handmaid's tale
Atwood, M. The year of the flood
Austen, J. Emma
Austen, J. Pride and prejudice
Austen, J. Sense and sensibility
Avery, E. The last nude

Ball, J. The way through doors
Banasky, C. The suicide of Claire Bishop
Bank, M. The wonder spot
Barry, J. Don't turn around
Batuman, E. The idiot
Bausch, R. Hello to the cannibals
Beams, C. The illness lesson
Bennett, B. The mothers
Bergstrom, H. Steal the north
Bird, S. The flamenco academy
Blau, J. The Wonder Bread summer
Boianjiu, S. The people of forever are not afraid
Boyle, E. Along came a duke
Boyle, E. And the miss ran away with the rake
Boyle, W. The lonely witness
Brontë, C. Jane Eyre
Bruni, S. The night Gwen Stacy died
Brunkhorst, A. The gilded Life of Matilda Duplaine
Burton, J. The miniaturist
Burton, T. Social creature
Butler, H. The new me
Bynum, S. Ms. Hempel chronicles
Cabot, M. No judgments
Capote, T. Breakfast at Tiffany's
Carlino, R. Swear on this life
Carpenter, E. The weight of lies
Cather, W. The song of the lark
Chase, L. Don't tempt me
Chevalier, T. A single thread
Clark, G. The bucket list
Cleave, C. Little Bee
Clemmons, Z. What we lose
Colette, 1. The complete Claudine
Croft, P. The second time I saw you
Crucet, J. Make your home among strangers
Cunningham, M. Specimen days
Czerneda, J. A turn of light
Danler, S. Sweetbitter
Dare, T. A week to be wicked
Dektar, M. The Ash family
Delaney, J. The girl before
Dickens, C. Little Dorrit
Dimberg, K. Girl in the rearview mirror
Divakaruni, C. Oleander girl
Donoghue, E. Slammerkin
Echlin, K. The disappeared
Egan, J. Manhattan Beach
Egan, J. A visit from the Goon Squad
Evaristo, B. Blonde roots
Faber, M. The crimson petal and the white
Faulkner, W. Sanctuary
Fitch, J. Paint it black
Forster, E. Howards End
Forster, E. A room with a view
Franklin, A. The siege winter
Franzen, J. Purity
Frost, K. The reluctant fortune-teller

Turner, N. My name is Resolute
Tyree, O. Leslie
Urrea, L. The hummingbird's daughter
Urrea, L. Queen of America
Valdes, A. Dirty Girls on top
Van der Vliet Oloomi, A. Call me Zebra
Varley, J. Rolling thunder
Vida, V. Let the Northern Lights erase your name
Vine, B. Grasshopper
Walker, W. All is not forgotten
Walton, J. Among others
Ware, R. The death of Mrs. Westaway
White, E. Heartstone
Williams, L. Supper club
Willis, C. Crosstalk
Wilson, G. The bird king
Wong, D. Futuristic violence and fancy suits
Woolf, V. The voyage out
Wuertz, Y. Everything belongs to us
Zevin, G. Young Jane Young
YOUNG WOMEN -- 18TH CENTURY
Richardson, S. Clarissa, or, The history of a young lady
YOUNG WOMEN -- CALIFORNIA
Tyree, O. For the love of money
YOUNG WOMEN -- DEATH
Oates, J. Little bird of heaven
YOUNG WOMEN -- EDINBURGH, SCOTLAND
Welsh, I. Porno
Welsh, I. Skagboys
Welsh, I. Trainspotting
YOUNG WOMEN -- EUROPE
James, H. Daisy Miller
YOUNG WOMEN -- FRIENDSHIP
Kleypas, L. Secrets of a summer night
YOUNG WOMEN -- IDENTITY
Ball, J. The way through doors
Hodgen, C. Elegies for the brokenhearted
YOUNG WOMEN -- JAPAN
Oe, K. A quiet life
Schwartz, J. The commoner
YOUNG WOMEN -- MEXICO
Urrea, L. Into the beautiful North
YOUNG WOMEN -- MISSISSIPPI
Welty, E. The optimist's daughter
YOUNG WOMEN -- PSYCHOLOGY
Center, K. How to walk away
Linden, R. The enlightenment of bees
YOUNG WOMEN -- RELATIONS WITH OLDER MEN
Aciman, A. Find me
Amidon, S. Security
Bronte, C. Jane Eyre
Brown, L. Fay
Castel-Bloom, O. Textile
Cruz, A. Dominicana
Eliot, G. Middlemarch
Greene, G. The heart of the matter
Hardy, T. Tess of the d'Urbervilles

Leonard, E. Mr. Paradise
Mallon, T. Fellow travelers
Marston, E. The wanton angel
McDermott, A. Child of my heart
Sand, G. Marianne
Shreve, A. Fortune's rocks
Trollope, J. The men and the girls
YOUNG WOMEN -- SAN FRANCISCO, CALIFORNIA
Diffenbaugh, V. The language of flowers
YOUNG WOMEN -- SEXUALITY
Lawrence, D. The rainbow
Shreve, A. Fortune's rocks
YOUNG WOMEN -- SYDNEY, NEW SOUTH WALES
Flanagan, R. The unknown terrorist
YOUNG, ANN ELIZA, B 1844
Ebershoff, D. The 19th wife
YOUNGER BROTHERS AND SISTERS
Hilderbrand, E. Summer of '69
YOUNGEST CHILD
Esquivel, L. Like water for chocolate
Scott, J. Tourmaline
Your blues ain't like mine Campbell, B.
Your face in mine Row, J.
Your face tomorrow, vol.1 Marias, J.
Your face tomorrow, vol.2 Marias, J.
Your face tomorrow, vol. 3 Marias, J.
Your house will pay Cha, S.
Your mouth is lovely Richler, N.
Your scandalous ways Chase, L.
Ysabel Kay, G.
YUCATAN PENINSULA
Buffett, J. A salty piece of land
Portis, C. Gringos
YUGOSLAV WAR, 1991-1995
Novic, S. Girl at war
YUGOSLAV WAR, 1991-1995 -- PSYCHOLOGICAL ASPECTS
Brownrigg, S. The delivery room
YUGOSLAVIA -- HISTORY -- 1918-1945
Albahari, D. Gotz and Meyer
YUGOSLAVIA -- HISTORY -- AXIS OCCUPATION, 1941-1945
Albahari, D. Gotz and Meyer
Yugoslavian trilogy [series] Andric, I.
YUKON TERRITORY
Armstrong, K. Alone in the wild
Armstrong, K. Watcher in the woods
London, J. White Fang
YUPPIES
Wolfe, T. The bonfire of the vanities

Z

Z Fowler, T.
ZAMBIA
Meyer, D. Heart of the hunter
Serpell, N. The old drift